The Editor's Page

This edition includes a new chapter ranking barristers who specialise in sanctions law (see page 501). The implementation of sanctions in recent years has led to a significant demand for legal advice from companies trading with countries affected.

Our coverage of Northern Ireland has continued to expand with the inclusion of two new specialist sections – real estate litigation and personal injury (see page 547).

Our research into the market continues to deepen as we talk to an ever-increasing number of clients who instruct members of the Bar. We thank all those who have generously given us their time.

James Cowdell

Published by Chambers & Partners Publishing
39 Parker Street, London WC2B 5PQ
Tel 0207 606 8844
Fax 0207 831 5662
Email info@chambersandpartners.co.uk

Publisher Michael Chambers
Editor-in-Chief Rieta Ghosh

Bar Editor James Cowdell
Deputy Bar Editors Alistair Faiers, Madeleine Allen

Solicitors Editor Michael Perkin
Solicitors Deputies Editors Steven Preston, Indy Tsang, Francois Gill, Mandeep Sran, Eleanor Burt

Business Development Director Brad Sirott
A-Z Co-ordinator Saskia Van Emden
Production Jasper John, David Nobakht, Paul Cummings

Orders to Chambers & Partners Publishing
39 Parker Street, London WC2B 5PQ

ISBN 978-0-85514-126-4

Surveys and commentary

England & Wales

Northern Ireland

Scotland

LEADERS AT THE BAR

INDEXES

Our Editorial Team

Here you can see our editors, deputy editors and researchers. They are all currently (October 2016) working full-time at our head office in central London. More biographical information can be found on the 'About Us' page of our website.

The Editors

The Editors are responsible for the overall content of their guides and for managing the research team.

Rieta Ghosh
Publishing Director. Graduated in Ancient History at Durham University. Former Client Information Manager with a European market research agency. Previously worked at a leading business advisory company.

Michael Perkin
UK Editor. Graduated in English Language and Linguistics from the University of Sheffield. Worked as a journalist for Hayters Press Agency and has had copy printed in a number of national newspapers, including The Daily Telegraph and the Mail on Sunday.

James Cowdell
UK Bar Editor. Barrister. Read Modern History at The Queen's College, Oxford. Practised at the Criminal Bar for five years and was a fee earner in the family department of a leading London law firm.

Alex Marsh
Editor, Chambers Unpublished. Graduated with a First in English Literature from Manchester University. Also has an MA with Distinction in Contemporary Literature and Novel Writing. Has previously worked as a researcher with a City headhunting firm and at a business knowledge centre.

Alice Gormley
Global Industries Editor. Graduated in 2013 with a First in History from Cambridge University where she edited The Cambridge Student. Has previously worked in communications and literary roles, and writes music in her spare time.

Antony Cooke
Student Editor. Graduated from Durham University in Russian & French. Taught English at St Petersburg State University. Previously worked at Michelin, and PricewaterhouseCoopers as an audit associate in Investment Management. Fluent in Russian and French.

Ben Nickson
Global Industries Editor. Graduated with a BA in English Literature from Cambridge University in 2007, and has recently completed a GDL with BPP College in Bristol. Has also worked in the civil service as a freelance copy-editor and writer.

Chris Kay
Seminar Manager. Graduated from Keele University with an LLB in Law and Philosophy. Went on to complete the LPC with distinction and has practised as a solicitor.

Claire Oxborrow
Editor, Global Practice Guides. Graduated with a First in Modern History from the University of St Andrews in 2005. During postgraduate studies at the LSE she worked as a visiting lecturer at the University of Roehampton. After completing the GDL and the LPC she spent time as a volunteer at the Brunel Museum.

Edward Shum
Editor for Africa, the Middle East, Caribbean and Global-wide sections. Studied Law at Magdalene College, Cambridge. Previously worked at a South London law firm.

Joanna Lane
Editor, Chambers Canada. Graduated in Public Affairs and Management and International Development from Carleton University in Canada and holds a Postgraduate Diploma in Journalism from the London School of Journalism. Speaks French.

Laura Mills
USA Editor. Graduated with a BA in History and Middle Eastern Studies from the University of Pittsburgh and an MA in Middle Eastern Studies from the School of Oriental and African Studies, University of London. Has studied French, Arabic, Spanish and Turkish.

Marlene Hermann
Europe Editor. Graduated from the University of Nottingham with a BA in English and History before completing an MA in Politics and Contemporary History. Speaks fluent German.

Rhodri Holtham
Latin America Editor. Graduated from the University of Nottingham with a 2:1 in History and Hispanic Studies, before completing an MSc in Latin America Politics from the Institute for the Study of the Americas, University of London. Passionate about Cuba having lived, studied and worked in Havana. Speaks Spanish and a bit of Portuguese.

Rocío Suárez
Seminars Manager: Women in Law. Graduated from the University of Seville with a degree in European Affairs. Completed an LLM in International Relations from La Rioja International University after completing a BA in Law at the University of Huelva in Spain. She has travelled extensively through Europe and South America and speaks Spanish, English and Italian.

Sarah Kogan
Asia-Pacific Editor. Graduated from Oxford University in 2004 with a degree in English Language & Literature. Worked in the television industry for several years as a researcher and associate producer. Subsequently completed the GDL in 2011 at the College of Law.

Simon Christian
High Net Worth Editor. Studied Law at University College London and has been called to the Bar at the Middle Temple.

The Deputy Editors

The Deputy Editors work with the Researchers and the Editor to ensure the rankings and commentary are a true reflection of the market.

Alistair Faiers
UK Bar Deputy Editor. Graduated in 2012 from the University of Warwick with a BA in English and Latin Literature. Writes and directs plays for his theatre company in his spare time.

Chris Nicholson
High Net Worth Deputy Editor. Completed BA and MA degrees in History at UCL, where he also submitted his PhD in History. Has co-edited two books on Central and Eastern Europe, and served on the editorial boards of two academic journals.

Christopher Teevan
USA Deputy Editor. Graduated from the University of Warwick in 2006 with Honours in English Literature. Also holds an MA in Creative Writing from Royal Holloway, University of London.

Dennis Li
Asia-Pacific Deputy Editor. Graduated with an MA (Merit) in Publishing from University College London. Considerable editing and project management experience in publishing. Native Mandarin speaker and also speaks German.

Eleanor Burt
UK Deputy Editor. Graduated with a BA (Hons) in History from University College London in 2011, specialising in London history. Went on to complete the GDL and LPC, finishing in 2013.

Francesca Lean
Europe Deputy Editor. Graduated from Newcastle University in 2008 with a BA in French and German, with Spanish. Has previously worked in multilingual financial recruitment. Speaks French and German.

Francois Gill
UK Deputy Editor. Graduated with a First in History from University College London in 2006. Went on to complete a Masters in the subject at UCL. Speaks French.

François Le Grand
Latin America Deputy Editor. Graduated from Royal Holloway with a BA in Human Geography. Studied International Relations in Brazil for two years before becoming a full-time translator working in English, Spanish, French and Portuguese.

Frida Sjöstedt
Europe Deputy Editor. Completed the GDL at BPP Law School in London in 2014. Also holds a First-class degree in Hospitality Management from University of Brighton, and a distinction HE Certificate in Mathematics from Birkbeck College. Speaks German and Swedish.

Hannah Taylor
Latin America Deputy Editor. Graduated from King's College London with a bachelor of Art (Hons) in Hispanic Studies and Portuguese and Brazilian Studies. Has previously lived and studied in Spain, Portugal, Brazil and Peru.

Harry Dalton
USA Deputy Editor. Graduated from the University of Nottingham in 2012 with a BA in Politics. Received his NCTJ training qualification from the Press Association.

Indy Tsang
UK Deputy Editor. Graduated from Regent's Park College, Oxford, with a degree in English Literature. Was active in student drama and writes fiction in her spare time.

Jane Pasquali
USA Deputy Editor. Graduated with a First in Spanish and Italian from Exeter University in 2007. Has lived and taught in Madrid and Barcelona, and worked for three years in a financial spread-betting company in London. Awarded a PGCE with Distinction in Primary Education and Spanish in 2011.

Jessica Bird
Unpublished Deputy Editor. Graduated from the University of York in 2013 with a BA (First) in English and Related Literature. Has taught English in Kerala, India, is involved with a number of charity organisations and writes for several online publications in her spare time.

Jurgita Meskauškaitė
Europe Deputy Editor. Graduated with an MA in Development Management from the University of Westminster in 2007. Fluent in Russian and Lithuanian.

Lana Neil
Unpublished Deputy Editor. Graduated in 2014 with an LLB in Law from the University of Bristol. Previous work experience includes interning at corporate law firms and volunteering for numerous charities and NGOs, specifically in research for the Open Society Justice Initiative.

Madeleine Allen
UK Bar Deputy Editor. Graduated with a BA (Hons) in English from Queen Mary University of London (2013). Went on to complete an MA in Eighteenth-Century Studies (Distinction) at King's College London (2014).

Mandeep Sran
UK Deputy Editor. Graduated in Law from the School of Oriental and African Studies (SOAS) at the University of London, and completed the Legal Practice Course at the Nottingham Law School. Qualified as a solicitor specialising in litigation in 2009.

Matthew Lewis
Europe Deputy Editor. Graduated from King's College London in 2010 with a BA in Hispanic Studies with English and from University College London in 2012 with an MA in English Literature. Works as a book and film critic in his free time.

Monty Collyer
Graduted in 2014 from the University of St Andrews with an MA (Hons) French and Spanish (with integrated year abroad). Has previously worked in intellectual property law in Costa Rica.

Natalia Davies
Asia-Pacific Deputy Editor. Graduated from Queen Mary University of London in 2012 with a BA (Hons) in English. Has spent six months working in Australia, and has experience in freelance copywriting.

Nick Fogarty
Asia-Pacific Deputy Editor. Graduated with a BA in Asian Studies and Creative Writing from the University of Melbourne in 2010 and has since worked as a radio and multimedia journalist for the Australian Broadcasting Corporation. Speaks basic Chinese and enjoys playing guitar.

The Deputy Editors *continued*

Oliver Dimsdale
Global Deputy Editor. Holds an MA in English Literature from the University of Warwick and an MLitt in Creative Writing from the University of St Andrews. Previously worked within the UK Ministry of Justice and as a journalist in Honduras.

Paul Rance
Student Deputy Editor. Graduated from Exeter University with a First in English Literature, and also spent a year abroad at the University of Toronto to read Canadian Literature. Completed an MA in English at UCL in 2010.

Peter Whitfield
USA Deputy Editor. Gained an MA with Distinction in Philosophy at Birkbeck College, University of London, and is currently working towards a research degree in the subject at the same institution. Previously earned a BA in English Literature from the University of Newcastle-upon-Tyne.

Phil Roe
Chambers Associate Deputy Editor. Joined Chambers & Partners in 2007 from a global executive search firm, where he advised private equity clients. Graduated with an MA in English from Oxford University, and is a theatre critic for London-based newspapers in his free time.

Rachel Annandale
Global Deputy Editor. Graduated from UCL in 2014 with a degree in Linguistics. Speaks Spanish and is currently learning Arabic.

Rick Jakubowski
Europe Deputy Editor. Graduated from Oxford University with a BA in Law. Has previously practised as a pensions solicitor in London and travelled extensively through North America. Has also run his own live music events project in addition to writing and performing his own original songs.

Rosie Johnson
Latin America Deputy Editor. Graduated from the University of Birmingham in 2014 with a first in Spanish and Japanese, having spent a year living in Seville and Tokyo.

Sam Morris
Student Deputy Editor. Graduated from the University of Leiden, the Netherlands, with a First in Political Science in 2008 and from the London School of Economics with an MSc in Comparative Politics in 2009. Has worked for the Dutch Ministry of Foreign Affairs. Speaks Dutch and German.

Steven Preston
UK Deputy Editor. Graduated from University College London with an LLB.

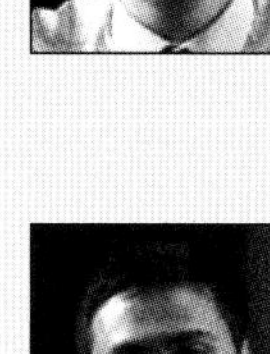

Toby Eccleshall
USA Deputy Editor. Graduated from the University of Birmingham with a BA in German and Russian Studies and subsequently completed the GDL at Brunel University. Has previously worked as an English teacher in Moscow.

Vian Chowdhury
UK/USA Deputy Editor. Graduated in 2011 with an MSc in Development Economics. Previously lived in Indonesia.

Yvonne Berman
Asia-Pacific Deputy Editor. Having completed a law degree (at the University of North London), became a member of the Bar of England and Wales (non-practising) and spent several years in industry and private practice in IP, specialising in trade marks and copyright.

The Assistant Editors and Senior Researchers

The Assistant Editors and Senior Researchers are responsible for interviewing clients and lawyers, and for assisting with the rankings and commentary.

Alex Bartlett
UK/USA Assistant Editor. Graduated from King's College London with a First-class Honours degree in Classics. Went on to complete a Graduate Diploma in Law with commendation at the University of Law. Particular interests include Alternative Dispute Resolution and Family Law.

Alex McFadyen
Unpublished Senior Researcher. Completed an MA in Creative Writing at the University of Manchester in 2014, where he was taught by Jeanette Winterson. In his spare time he writes about contemporary music and campaigns on environmental issues.

Anna Winter
Student/Associate Senior Researcher. Graduated with a BA in English Literature from Balliol College, Oxford. Took journalism qualifications following internships at The Observer and New Statesman magazine.

Anna-Marie Linnell
HNW Senior Researcher. Recently finished a PhD studentship with the Stuart Successions Project and is preparing her thesis for submission. Has published academic work and research pieces for blogs with non-academic audiences. Is also qualified to teach English as a second language and has taught in Lesotho, Kenya and the UK.

Anthony Leech
Unpublished Senior Researcher. Graduated from Cambridge in Politics, Psychology and Sociology in 2014 and continued his studies there with an MPhil in International Relations and Politics (2015), specialising in contemporary political philosophy.

Carlota Garcia-Patel
Latin America Senior Researcher. Graduated from Queen Mary, University of London, with a BA in Hispanic Studies and Portuguese. Studied abroad in both Spain and Portugal.

The Assistant Editors and Senior Researchers *continued*

Daniel Arthur
Asia-Pacific Assistant Editor. Graduated from the University of Southampton with a BA in History before completing an MA in World History & Cultures at King's College London. Previously lived in Brazil and the Netherlands working as a Portuguese-English translator.

Daniel Fisher
UK/USA Assistant Editor. Graduated from Queen Mary University of London with a degree in Film (BA) in 2012. Previously worked in video production.

David Brooks
Student/Associate Senior Researcher. Graduated from the University of Leicester in 2013 with a 2:1 in French & English Literature. Spent a year teaching English as a foreign language in Québec and is fluent in French.

David Watson
Asia-Pacific Assistant Editor. Has a BA in Modern History from Keble College, Oxford, an MA in War Studies from King's College, London, and over 20 years' experience researching military historical matters for a Ministry of Defence agency.

Douglas Clarke-Williams
UK/USA Senior Researcher. Graduated from the University of Sussex with a First in English Literature and American Studies, having spent a year studying abroad at the University of California, Berkeley.

Eleanor Veryard
Student Assistant Editor. Graduated in 2011 with a BA in History before completing an MA in Early Modern History from the University of Sheffield. While at University worked as head of research and then editor-in-chief for a monthly student magazine.

Ellena Herman
Asia-Pacific Assistant Editor. Graduated from Durham University with a BA in Modern Languages. Previously worked in publishing in Bordeaux and speaks French and Spanish.

Emma Hart
UK/USA Senior Researcher. Graduated in 2014 with a BA (Hons) in English Literature from the University of Manchester and went on to take the GDL at BPP University. Has previously worked as a teacher in both the UK and Malaysia.

Estella McCusker
Europe Senior Researcher. Completed an MA in Writing for Stage and Broadcast Media from the Royal Central School of Speech and Drama in 2014. Has lived and worked as an English teacher in Spain.

Fiona Wong
Unpublished Assistant Editor. Holds a BA (First) and an MPhil in English from the Chinese University of Hong Kong, and a PhD in English and Comparative Literary Studies from the University of Warwick. Has been writing for publishing companies and an online magazine. Speaks Cantonese and Mandarin.

Ilan Fertig
Unpublished Senior Researcher. Graduated from the University of Leeds in 2013, gaining a BA (Hons) in History and English.

Inês Cortesão
Europe Assistant Editor. Graduated from Nova University of Lisbon with a degree in English and Literature, and studied abroad at the University of Southampton for one semester. Portuguese is her first language.

James Ager
UK/USA Senior Researcher. Holds a BA in Modern Languages & Cultures from the University of Durham, which included placements abroad in Ceuta and Morocco. Speaks Spanish and Arabic with basic French, Farsi and Italian, and is a casual film critic.

Jamie Horne
Unpublished Assistant Editor. Graduated in 2008 from Emmanuel College, Cambridge, with an Honours degree in History.

Jessica Jacobsen
UK/USA Senior Researcher. Graduated in English Law and French Law from the University of Manchester in 2012. This included spending a year studying French Law and Language in Lyon, France. Previously worked in legal administration. Speaks French and Spanish.

John Lawson
Unpublished Senior Researcher. Studied French Literature to Masters level at King's College, Cambridge. Interested in contemporary literature, photography and philosophy.

John White
Europe Assistant Editor. Studied History and Anthropology at the University of Sussex, graduating with a 2:1 BA in 2009. Completed the GDL with Distinction at the University of Law – Bloomsbury in 2013. In between university and law school worked as a chef in seafood restaurants in both Brighton and New Zealand and for the last two years volunteered at a human rights charity.

Jonathan Block
Latin America Assistant Editor. Graduated from the University of Nottingham with a First in Politics. Has completed work experience in the real estate and legal sectors.

Joseph Chapman
High Net Worth Senior Researcher. Graduated from the University of Leicester in 2013 with a 2:1 in French & English Literature. Spent a year teaching English as a foreign language in Québec and is fluent in French.

Karl Read
Europe Assistant Editor. Graduated in 2012 from Durham University with an LLB.

Kathrin Ecke
Latin America Senior Researcher. Graduated in Law from Torcuato Di Tella University in 2011. Completed an MA in Journalism at La Nación newspaper in 2014. Has previously worked for law firms in Argentina. Speaks Spanish and German.

Louis Bacon
Senior Researcher Europe. Graduated from the University of Warwick in 2013 with a degree in French and German Studies. Fluent in German, having worked in roles requiring proficiency in the language since graduating, and has also done some freelance proof-reading and editing work.

Lydia Burt
UK/USA Assistant Editor. Graduated from UCL in 2012 with a Masters in Film Studies. Previously studied American & English Literature at the University of East Anglia and spent a year abroad at Roanoke College, Virginia.

Magdalena Parkitna
Global Senior Researcher. Graduated in 2014 from City University London where she completed an MA in Investigative Journalism. Has lived in the United States where she did a double major in journalism and political science. Speaks Polish.

María Amo González
Latin America Senior Researcher. Graduated from the Universidad de Sevilla with a degree in Journalism. Worked at several radio stations as a culture journalist before moving to London, where she worked as an events journalist for a Spanish media company. Native Spanish speaker and also speaks intermediate French.

Michael Foulkes
Europe Senior Researcher. Currently completing a PhD in 17th Century French theatre, having studied French and German at Durham University. Keen rower and cricketer who has self-published a history of his college boat club.

Nisha Sawon
Canada Assistant Editor. Graduated from the University of Southampton in 2013 with an LLB in law. Volunteers as a copywriter for a local charity in her spare time.

Robert Li
UK/USA Senior Researcher. Graduated in Modern Chinese Studies from Leeds University, later completing the CPE at Westminster University. Speaks Mandarin Chinese.

Sanjana Kapila
Europe Senior Researcher. Graduated with a BA (Hons) in English from University College London in 2013. Went on to complete the GDL.

Thomas Green
Europe Senior Researcher. Graduated from the University of Leeds with a First-class Honours BA in English Language and Literature and an MA in Romantic Literature and Culture.

Tobias Waters
Asia-Pacific Assistant Editor. Graduated from the University of Kent with a BA in English and American Literature, and also holds an MA in English Literary Studies from the University of Durham.

Tola Onasanya
UK/USA Senior Researcher. Studied Chemistry at the University of St Andrews, graduating in 2014. He was previously an intern at a publishing house in Dubai and speaks French.

Zahra Damji
UK/USA Senior Researcher. Graduated in Law from the University of Birmingham in 2014. Previous work experience at a national newspaper and as news editor for a student newspaper.

The Researchers

The Researchers are responsible for interviewing clients and lawyers, and for assembling the data needed for the rankings and commentary.

Alastair Gold
Graduated in 2014 with a BA in English Literature from the University of Warwick. Speaks basic French and Russian.

Alexis Self
Graduated from the University of Sussex in 2012 with a BA in Modern History. Prior to joining Chambers he worked as a copywriter and freelance journalist.

Andre Armenian
Graduated in 2013 from the University of Kent with a First-class degree in Law. Obtained an LLM at University College London in 2015. Called to the Bar in 2016, having completed the Bar Professional Training Course with an Exhibition scholarship from Inner Temple.

Amalia Neenan
Graduated in 2014 with a degree in Law from the University of Kent. Studied the Bar Professional Training Course at City University London and is also an ADR Group Accredited Civil & Commercial Mediator.

Amy Barnicoat-Hood
Graduated from King's College London with a 2:1 in English Language & Communication. Before joining Chambers, spent a number of years working as a teacher and translator in Madrid.

Andrew Dobson
Studied Philosophy and Literature at Warwick, and later studied at the Centre for Research in Modern European Philosophy. Is a sometime speaker of German.

Anne-Marie McCluskey
Graduated with a First in Celtic from the University of Edinburgh in 2015. Speaks some Scottish Gaelic and Japanese.

Anthony Perkins
Graduated from Lancaster University with a BA (Hons) and MA in History, with a research specialty in 20th Century Colonial African History.

Assallah Tahir
Graduated from the University of Cambridge with a First in English, before completing a Masters in Victorian Literature at the University of Oxford. Fluent in Arabic.

Beatrice Chan
Holds an LLB in Law from the University of Bristol. Speaks Cantonese and Mandarin, and active in voluntary services.

Callum Adams
Graduated with First-class Honours in Philosophy and Politics from the University of York. Worked as a journalist for The National Student and has had work featured in The Times and Lonely Planet.

Callum Bland
Graduated from Northumbria University with a masters in Law. Has also completed a Legal Practice Course (LPC).

The Researchers *continued*

Cameron Marsh
Completed a BA in Ancient History from UCL in 2014, going on to do an MA in Ancient History, also at UCL, with a focus on the Late Roman Republic.

Catrin Wallace
Graduated in 2014 with an LLB from Aberystwyth University and completed an LLM in International Development Law and Human Rights from the University of Warwick. Speaks fluent Welsh.

Cecile Guerin
Completed a Masters in History and International Relations at LSE. Previously worked in journalism and for the French Embassy in London. Speaks fluent French and Spanish.

Christopher Coldicott
Graduated in 2014 with a degree in English and Theatre from the University of Sheffield. A frequent performer in everything from musicals to stand up – though will refuse to tell jokes or do a dance.

Chris McNally
Graduated from Queen's University Belfast (QUB) with a BA Joint Hons in English & Linguistics. Also has an MA in Law from QUB and completed the Legal Practice Course at City Law School London in 2012. Before joining Chambers & Partners, worked at a legal headhunting firm in the City.

Ciara Corrigan
Graduated in 2015 from the University of Bristol where she studied Law. Writes broadly in her spare time with a particular interest in comedy writing and recently performed at the Edinburgh Fringe Festival.

Cindy Capo-Chichi
Graduated from the University of Paris with an LLB and from ISIT with a degree in Lawyer-Linguist. Went on to complete a Masters specialising in International Law and European Activates followed by a Masters in International Trade and Commercial Law.

Daniel Shamaun
Graduated in 2012 with a Masters in the History of Science, Medicine, Environment and Technology from Kent University. Has worked as a writer, journalist and proof-reader in London and Antwerp.

Daniel Sultan
Graduated from London's King's College in 2010 (Geography BA). Recently completed a Masters degree in Globalisation at University College London. Interests include sports and travel.

Eleanor Crundwell
Graduated from King's College London in 2015 with a degree in Hispanic Studies with English, including a year abroad studying in Barcelona.

Eleri Luff
Graduated from King's College London with a degree in Philosophy & German. Worked abroad in Berlin and Lisbon before returning to London to complete a Masters in Translation at UCL.

Eloise Hanes
Graduated with a BA (Hons) in English from the University of Southampton (2014). Went on to complete an MA in Eighteenth-Century Studies at King's College London taught in conjunction with The British Museum (2015).

Flora Arduini
Graduated Cum Laude LL.M. Globalisation and Law specialisation Human Rights at Maastricht University. Has legal research experience in Italy, the Netherlands and Brazil.

Genevieve Armstrong
Graduated from the University of Oxford in 2015 with a degree in Classics. Previously worked for English Heritage.

George Murray
Graduated in 2015 with an LLB (Hons) in Law from the University of Sussex.

Georgia Traher
With a BA (Hons) in English Literature and Creative Writing from Bath Spa University she previously ran a website for a start-up company aimed at teen writers. Has an interest in literature and is a competitive dancer.

Geraint Thomas
Graduated from Durham University with a BA (Hons) in English Literature and History in 2014, before completing a Masters in Modern History with a directed focus on Native American rights. Interests include travel and 20th century American novels.

Helen Rowland
Graduated from King's College London in 2015 with a degree in Hispanic Studies with English, including a year abroad studying in Barcelona.

Henry Asson
Read English at Oxford. Graduated 2015.

Ian Buerger
Graduated from the University of Edinburgh with an MA in History & Politics in 2011, a Bachelor of Law in 2013 and a Postgraduate Diploma in Professional Legal Practice in 2014. Has working experience in the legal sector in both Canada and Scotland.

Ilaria Iovieno
Graduated in 2014 with a BA in International Affairs and Economics, and concluded an LLM in International Development Law and Human Rights at the University of Warwick in 2015. Has lived and worked in India in international development and women's empowerment. Native Italian speaker, fluent in English, intermediate French and Spanish and basic Hindi.

Isaac Martin
Holds a BA (Hons) in Russian Studies from the University of Leeds, including a year abroad at Moscow State University. Speaks Russian.

Isabel Mee
Graduated from Girton College, University of Cambridge in 2015 with a 2:1 in Law. Fluent in Spanish.

Isabelle Higgins
Graduated from Trinity College, Dublin, in 2016 with first class honours BA in English Literature, including a year abroad at The University of Chicago.

James Coffey
Graduated from Exeter University in 2015 with an LLB Law Degree. Has previously worked within legal roles.

The Researchers *continued*

James Haggerty
Spent two years living abroad in the Nordic countries for a Masters in Viking and Medieval Norse Studies. Graduated with an MPhil/MA from the universities of Iceland and Oslo in 2014. Previously studied History at the University of Birmingham.

James Roberts
Graduated from the University of Warwick in 2015 with a 2:1 LLB (Hons) Law degree. Has previously worked as a Legal Project Assistant in Germany and Czech Republic, and continues to publish articles on topical legal developments for online publications.

James Watts
Graduated from the University of Exeter in 2015 with a BA (Hons) in History and Economics, with a research specialism in the 19th Century British Radical movement.

Jessica King
Graduated from the University of Birmingham in 2015 with a BA in Modern Languages (French with Chinese). Spent a year studying in Montpellier and Beijing. Also speaks some German, plays the piano and enjoys choral singing.

Joe Jackson
Graduated from the University of Manchester in Politics and Modern History in 2015. Previously worked for a recruitment firm in Manchester.

John Hodgson
Graduated from Exeter University in 2014 with a BA (Hons) in English. Wrote for the university newspaper as a sports writer. He previously spent a year teaching English and coaching sport at a school in Hampshire.

Joshua Collier
Graduated from the University of Newcastle in 2014 with a degree in Politics, having spent a semester at the University of Copenhagen. Previously worked in Communications for a specialist healthcare agency.

Kate Nevin
Graduated from Queen Mary University of London with a First-class BA in Comparative Literature, before completing an MA in History at UCL. Grew up in Italy and is bilingual in English and Italian. Previous professional experience includes teaching English and working for charities.

Katie Beere
Graduated from the University of Cambridge in 2014 with a degree in Modern and Medieval Languages (French and Latin literature & Philosophy). Spent a year at the École normale supérieure in Paris. Previous experience includes editing, working in charities and on civil society policy.

Katya Gorska
Holds a BA in French and Russian from Oxford, and completed a MSc in political science from SOAS with distinction. Speaks French, Russian and Polish.

Kit Gilchrist
Completed an MA in History and French at the University of Aberdeen and an MSc in Ancient Philosophy at the University of Edinburgh.

Kushraj Cheema
Graduated with a BA in English Language and Literature from King's College London, having also studied abroad at the University of North Carolina at Chapel Hill. Has worked previously in communications and fashion, and is a keen writer and blogger.

Laura Barber
Graduated in 2015 with a BA (Hons) in History from Cardiff University. She enjoys music and literature.

Liv Klingert
Graduated with an MA in English Literature and Philosophy from the University of Glasgow (2013) and an MSc in Film Studies from the University of Edinburgh (2014). Has worked in a start-up environment and completed an internship at a publishing company in Denmark. Speaks Danish.

Lottie Chesterman
Graduated from the University of Edinburgh in 2015 with an MA (Hons) degree in Spanish and Italian. She has also spent time living and studying in both Granada and Milan.

Luke Redstone
Graduated from King's College London in 2014 with a BA (Hons) in Philosophy. Went on to study the GDL at BPP Waterloo.

Luke Vincett
Graduated from Loughborough University with a BA (Hons) in English.

Maia Foulis
Graduated from Stendhal University in Grenoble (France) with a Masters degree in English literature. Has previously worked as a French lectrice for St Edmund Hall and Trinity College (University of Oxford). Fluent in French.

Maria Sol Rubio
Graduated in Law in 2013 from the University of Buenos Aires (UBA) and is a qualified Argentinian lawyer. Has worked in both the public and private sector. Speaks Spanish, English, Italian and French.

Matthew Court
Graduated from the University of Nottingham in 2014 with a degree in American Literature, History and Politics, having spent a year studying abroad at the University of Illinois at Urbana-Champaign.

Matthew Cripsey
Graduated with a First in French from the University of Warwick before studying for an MA in Translation at the University of Leeds. Has lived and worked in Paris and the Ardèche and remains active as a freelance translator and editor.

Mauricio Bisol
Graduated in Geography and in Cinema & TV in Brazil and holds a Master's Degree in International Cooperation - Development & Emergencies from Milan. Lived in Italy for 6 years working with communication and journalism. Fluent in Portuguese, English and Italian.

Mellisha Mallikage
Holds a BSc in Economics from the University of Leeds. Speaks fluent Japanese with a JLPT N1 qualification, and maintains a strong passion for Japanese culture. Also speaks basic Singhalese.

Michael Bird
Graduated from Royal Holloway, University of London with a BA in History. Prior to Chambers, Michael worked for US-based entertainment websites, and continues to review music in his spare time.

The Researchers *continued*

Monica Tantalean
LLM in Law and Development from the University of Manchester and a graduate in Law from the Pontificia Universidad Catolica del Peru. Fluent in Spanish and Portuguese. Previous professional experience includes working at law firms and not-for-profit organisations.

Natalie Bertram
Graduated in 2016 from the University of Exeter with a BA Hons in English Literature. Freelances as a proofreader in her free time.

Olivia Mackay
Graduated with 2.1 MA(Hons) in Classical Studies from the University of St Andrews in 2013. Previously worked in the art world at Dulwich Picture Gallery and Colnaghi.

Orsolya Kerek
Graduated from the University of St Andrews, with a B.Sc. (Honours) Economics with French. Has lived and worked in Luxembourg. Speaks English, Hungarian, Italian and French.

Patrick Owen Smith
Patrick graduated with a First in Ancient History from Royal Holloway in 2011. Prior to working at Chambers, he was a literacy teacher in South London.

Phil Robinson
Graduated from Queen Mary, University of London with a BA in English.

Phoebe Eccles
Studied Philosophy and Literature at the University of Warwick. Afterwards completed a Master's in Cultural Analysis at the University of Amsterdam, where she also edited the student literary journal.

Rachel Lambert
Graduated from King's College London in 2014 with a 2:1 in Law LLB. Practised her legal research skills when volunteering at Citizens Advice and for Lawyers Without Borders

Rita Martins
Holds a masters degree in Civil and Criminal Litigation from the Faculty of Law, Catholic University of Lisbon and a postgraduate degree in European, International and Economic Criminal Law, from the Faculty of Law, University of Coimbra. Worked as a dispute resolution and litigation lawyer in Lisbon and is a member of the Portuguese Bar Association. Native Portuguese speaker and also speaks basic Spanish.

Robert Baldwin
Studied English Literature at the University of Birmingham. Interested in Modernism and music.

Robinson Redmond
Graduating with an LLB from the University of Aberdeen in 2012, Robinson interned with the Legal Resources Centre, a human rights NGO based in South Africa. Before joining Chambers he worked in the energy industry, liaising between suppliers and brokers.

Roisin McLaughlin-Dowd
Graduated from the University of Exeter with a degree in Classical Studies with Proficiency in Italian, including a year abroad in Ontario studying Classics with French.

Rosheen Iyer
Graduated in 2013 with a 2:1 in English Literature from the University of Exeter, before completing the Graduate Diploma in Law at the University of Law in 2014. Completed the Bar Professional Training Course and was called to the Bar in 2015 having received an Exhibition Award and the Philip Teichman Award from The Honourable Society of the Inner Temple.

Ruaidhri McLaughlin Dowd
Studied Philosophy at Lancaster University and graduated in 2016. Intersted in music, politics and philosophy.

Ruta Zubaite
Graduated from University of Manchester with a degree in LLB English Law with French Law. Has previously worked in legal roles. Speaks Lithuanian and French.

Sam Grant
Graduated in 2014 with a BA in History before going on to complete an MA in Human Rights from University College London.

Sam Lindsay
Graduated from the University of York with a degree in History. Has since worked in both research and heritage.

Tina Lally
Graduated from the School of Oriental and African Studies (SOAS) with a BA (Hons) Chinese (Modern and Classical). Previously interned at a law firm specialising in intellectual property in Guangdong province. Has travelled extensively through China.

Tom Lewis
Graduated in 2015 with a BA in History from the University of Sheffield.

Vanessa Wireko-Brobbe
Graduated with a 2:1 in Law from the University of Kent in 2014. Vanessa has since been employed within the insurance sector whilst educating herself on socio-political and economic development in the UK and its impact on international relations.

Vicky Bates
Graduated from Robinson College, Cambridge with a BA Hons in English Literature. Has spent time working in France.

Victoria Hamblen
Graduated from SOAS with a degree in Chinese and Politics. Has worked in Madrid as an EFL teacher and in the UK as a legal clerk. Speaks fluent Spanish.

Xerxes Tengra
Studied History and Law at Nottingham University and has worked at international law firms in both Brussels and London.

Yasarah Qureshi
Graduated from the School of Oriental and African Studies (SOAS) in 2015 with a BA (Hons) in Middle Eastern Studies. Extensive experience working in criminal defence and the geo-politics, current affairs and policy research/analysis of the MENA region.

Leading Sets by number of rankings

Sets by number of rankings

Ranked in 19 practice areas
39 Essex Street
Blackstone Chambers

Ranked in 18 practice areas
Kings Chambers

Ranked in 15 practice areas
Matrix Chambers
No5 Chambers

Ranked in 13 practice areas
Brick Court Chambers
Doughty Street Chambers

Ranked in 12 practice areas
Maitland Chambers

Ranked in 11 practice areas
Fountain Court Chambers
Guildhall Chambers
St Philips Chambers
Wilberforce Chambers
Crown Office Chambers
Essex Court Chambers
Monckton Chambers
Serle Court

Ranked in 19 practice areas

39 Essex Chambers

39 Essex Chambers is a formidable force at the Bar with a broad sweep of specialisms. The set continues to justify its market-leading reputation for matters of community care and mental capacity, with "the King and Queen of Court of Protection work" Alexander Ruck Keene and Victoria Butler-Cole each appearing this year in landmark cases concerning the jurisdiction of the court. This practice forms a significant part of the set's wider expertise in administrative and public law, which sees its members instructed in human rights and civil liberties cases concerning detention, assisted suicide and hospitalisation, amongst others. Members also represent a long list of local authorities in judicial reviews and disputes, including in the areas of education, planning and environmental law. The set's expertise in built and natural environment matters is well known, and among the many factors recommending it to instructing parties is the presence of the outstanding Stephen Tromans QC, whom market sources consider "the leader in a field of his own, crossing both planning and environmental law." For clients managing major construction and infrastructure projects at a late stage of development, 39 Essex represents a fine choice as it fields an impressive group of silks and juniors with expertise in international disputes, adjudication and arbitration. Among them is the "devastating advocate" Stuart Catchpole QC, whose expertise sees him consistently rated as one of the leading silks for energy and projects disputes, as well as professional negligence claims against engineers, architects and builders. The set's expertise in professional liability is not limited to the construction sector, however, with members handling disciplinary cases for regulators and defendants in the legal, financial services, medical and veterinary fields as well. Here the set can offer leading counsel at all levels, including the stellar David Bradly and excellent fellow junior Andrew Tabachnik, as well as highly regarded silks Hodge Malek QC and Gregory Treverton-Jones QC. Joint head of chambers Neil Block QC specialises in medical negligence and personal injury cases, and is recognised — alongside the set's hugely impressive bench of personal injury counsel — for handling cases of the highest value and complexity in this field.

Blackstone Chambers

Many of the hundred plus members of Blackstone Chambers are considered by market commentators to be some of "the finest legal minds in the country." They share an extraordinary 216 Chambers rankings between them, with a significant portion of these having been awarded — predictably enough — within the set's core disciplines of administrative and public law, civil liberties and human rights. In these areas, instructing parties are spoilt for choice: Blackstone's extensive bench of respected seniors includes the "astonishing" James Eadie QC, the "awesome" Dinah Rose QC, the "extraordinary" Lord Pannick QC and "one of the brightest barristers at the bar" in Michael Fordham QC. At the junior level, the set plays host to the "undoubtedly talented" Ben Jaffey, considered by many to be a silk in waiting, and "standout junior" Tom Hickman, who is "a first choice for sensitive cases involving the state security services." Members are also recognised for their work in public international law matters where human rights and public law overlap, in cases involving immigration, diplomatic immunity and sanctions regimes. Among the long list of high profile cases members have handled over the past year are Rahmatullah v Secretary of State for the Home Department, a case concerning allegations of unlawful rendition and torture, and Nouazli v Secretary of State before the Supreme Court, which concerned the legality of detention of EU nationals pending deportation. Regularly appearing before the ECHR, members are also considered "top for European law" more generally; the set can field specialists in competition, IP, data protection, immigration and environmental law. Blackstone has long been a leading name in civil fraud and is well-stocked with excellent seniors and juniors handling international fraud cases, asset tracing and injunctive relief. The stellar Charles Flint QC and Javan Herberg QC top the bill for financial services regulatory work, advising both regulators and leading institutions, and also form part of the set's excellent line-up of professional discipline practitioners through their work advising financial sector clients on disciplinary proceedings. The practice also benefits from members' expertise in professional discipline matters arising in the medical, education and sport sectors. Blackstone is named "the best known set in the sports law market" with commentators stating that "no other set comes close for depth of experience" in ethics and regulatory issues, employment contract disputes and broadcasting matters. Adam Lewis QC is "in a league of his own" and remains the stand out sports law silk at the set — and, indeed, in the country. At the junior level, sources are full of praise for "true sports specialist" Nick de Marco, who this year was elevated to star ranking in our listings. The set's media and entertainment practice is highlighted for copyright, commercial and regulatory cases in broadcast and print media; in the music industry, "outstanding advocate" Ian Mill QC "remains top of the class." Finally, a group of "supremely good barristers" make up the set's employment practice, including the "ferociously clever" Paul Goulding QC and the very popular Diya Sen Gupta, a junior highlighted for her effective advocacy and user-friendliness.

Ranked in 18 practice areas:

Kings Chambers

Kings Chambers remains a go-to set on the North and North-Eastern Circuits, and is known to many instructing solicitors as a place to find "London quality in the regions." The set is home to market-leading counsel for financial, company, partnership, chancery and insolvency disputes, especially in its Manchester and Leeds offices. "Terrifying cross-examiner" Lesley Anderson QC is considered one of the best in the North for her work in commercial, chancery, and insolvency cases, among others, and "excellent orator" Paul Chaisty QC chalks up top-tier rankings in chancery, commercial, professional negligence and company law. In Birmingham, Kings is building on the leading practices of Richard Clayton QC in human rights, civil liberties, public and administrative law, Sarah Clover and Ben Williams in licensing, and Satinder Hunjan QC in clinical negligence and personal injury cases. The set continues to be considered a standout chambers for planning, acting for local authorities, major developers and house builders on a wide range of matters, including appeals, inquiries, hearings and judicial reviews. Kings' bench in this area features the "consistently pragmatic and commercial" Paul Tucker QC, "accomplished advocate" David Manley QC, "tenacious cross-examiner" Vincent Fraser QC and the "innovative and strategic" Anthony Crean QC. Kings remains the only set highlighted in this guide for real estate litigation in the Northern Circuit, fielding specialists to handle dilapidations, insolvencies, and landlord and tenant disputes. With nearly seventy individuals achieving Chambers rankings this year, the set retains its title as the undisputed king in the North.

Ranked in 15 practice areas:

Matrix Chambers

Matrix Chambers maintains its reputation as "a forward thinking" set which "brings a modern and contemporary dynamic to cases." The set fields a number of "incredibly bright people doing incredible human rights work" such as Ben Emmerson QC, a top-class silk with a broad practice encompassing all manner of public law and criminal cases. Many highly regarded criminal law experts are among the set's members, including "doyenne of the Criminal Bar" Clare Montgomery QC. Matrix also brings its "co-operative approach to problem solving" to an array of complex community care cases. Defamation and privacy matters often feature in the set's case load and Matrix tenants have recently acted in various cases arising from the high-profile phone hacking scandals. In addition, barristers such as the star-rated Phillippa Kaufmann QC regularly advocate on behalf of claimants in actions against a range of public authorities. The set is also home to "such giants in the education field" as Helen Mountfield QC and David Wolfe QC. Mountfield recently handled the well-publicised student loan eligibility case R (Tigere) v Secretary of State for Business, Innovation & Skills, while a successful challenge to the legality of the new GCSE Religious Studies syllabus on behalf of the British Humanist Association is among Wolfe's recent case list. Matrix also undertakes a wide variety of high-stakes employment cases, as well as complex environment work. Those in the clerks' room at the set are also praised, with one source saying: "The clerks are really responsive and you know they will help you out. They manage to achieve things others can't and are enthusiastic and keen."

No5 Chambers

One of the country's best-known sets, with a particularly strong reputation for its work on the Midlands Circuit, No5 Chambers is a chambers with enviable size and strength. It operates "like a well-oiled machine" and is admired for its "good team players who are highly commercial in their approach." No5 is also praised for its effective and friendly clerks who "work with you and stay in touch to keep you updated" and "go out of their way to assist in whatever way they can." The set's tenants attract all manner of complex instructions, from notable built and natural environment actions, to family matters and criminal cases. Members are regularly called on to appear in the Court of Protection. Many barristers at the set also exhibit substantial expertise in clinical negligence, personal injury and health and safety matters. In terms of standout individuals at this broad set, planning expert Martin Kingston QC remains "at the top of his game," while "persuasive, articulate advocate" Nageena Khalique QC maintains a quality public law and human rights practice. Head of chambers Mark Anderson QC is one of the set's "formidably intelligent" commercial barristers.

Ranked in 13 practice areas:

Brick Court Chambers

Widely regarded as one of London's top commercial sets where "the quality of the work is very high," Brick Court continues to provide an exceptional service to its loyal following of instructing solicitors. "It is my first choice for heavyweight or difficult cases," says one source, with another adding: "It's a very bright and talented group of lawyers who work very hard." Barristers at the set handle complex cases within the core disciplines of public, European and competition law, as well as a huge raft of commercial disputes of high value and importance. Members such as Helen Davies QC, who "a number of clients would always regard as their number one choice," are often called upon to handle energy disputes. The set's tenants regularly appear in overseas courts, including in the BVI and Singapore. In addition, members here are able to offer strong representation in arbitrations. Brick Court has a reputation for quality counsel ranging from highly experienced silks, such as the legendary and "absolutely fantastic" arbitrator Lord Hoffmann, to rising star juniors. Among the set's roster of top-notch silks is Mark Howard QC who is "incisive and highly intelligent with, most notably, exceptional authority as an advocate." The set is also home to public law expert Martin Chamberlain QC, a relatively new silk who has nonetheless made an impression on his peers. One interviewee goes so far as to say: "Chamberlain is one of the best advocates I have ever seen." David Anderson QC is one of the set's European law experts and is highly praised. "He is perfect," enthuses one source, continuing: "His thinking and his actions are always on point." The set also has an enviable stable of notable junior barristers, including Fionn Pilbrow and Sarah Ford, who attract extensive praise for their excellent practices. The Brick Court barristers are ably supported by a widely praised clerking team which includes two senior clerks, the "terrific" Julian Hawes and the "easy to deal with" Ian Moyer, as well as two deputy senior clerks, the "brilliant" Paul Dennison and the "really responsive" Tony Burgess.

Doughty Street

A superb set well known for its "exceptionally good" and "dedicated, large team of specialists." Doughty Street's accomplished members are also well-equipped to handle cases in the areas of civil liberties and human rights law, crime, immigration and product liability. Impressed commentators say that they are "always phenomenal," "highly knowledgeable," and people with a "huge breadth of experience." The set is recognised for its strength and depth in the senior ranks, and also boasts "a very good set of juniors, who are committed and bright." Leading silks include Heather Williams QC, "the leading authority on police law," who has an "astonishing ability to produce excellence every time," as well as "the leading claimant silk for product liability," Robin Oppenheim QC. Doughty Street is also home to "top-end," "tremendous" immigration law junior, Laura Dubinsky, and the justly trumpeted Edward Fitgzgerald QC, one of the leading human rights and extradition lawyers of his generation, The set also earns plaudits for its "always extremely effective" clerking team, led by Mark Dembovsky. Instructing solicitors report that the clerks are "always keen to help and go out of their way to assist us."

Ranked in 12 practice areas:

Maitland Chambers

A noted commercial chancery set which is regularly instructed in high-profile, complex cases such as Gorbunova v Berezovsky and Goldtrail v Aydin. The set has considerable expertise in handling the largest matters, many of which take place in overseas jurisdictions. Its excellent line-up of silks and juniors, described by their peers as "impressive players," "do lots of great work" and are particularly strong in civil fraud cases. The "exceptionally talented QCs" here include Paul Girolami, who is "at the top of his game and must be one of the best chancery silks available," and the "excellent and highly experienced" Catherine Addy. The set also fields some of the strongest charity law barristers, including Christopher McCall QC, who is widely acknowledged as being "at the forefront," as well as leading junior Matthew Smith, who "has been involved in many of the leading cases in the area." Senior clerk John Wiggs and his team receive high praise for their dedication to the provision of excellent client service: "The clerks are fantastic and just so helpful. They go above and beyond and nothing is too much trouble."

Ranked in 11 practice areas:

Fountain Court Chambers

Fountain Court Chambers is known for its depth of expertise across a broad range of areas. It is variously referred to as "the pre-eminent banking and financial services set," "a first-rate commercial set," and "the chambers you go to for aviation." It offers additional strength in the areas of travel and civil fraud. The set is commended for its strength in depth, and is said to offer "top silks and juniors in every major practice area." Silks include the "outstandingly clever" Michael Crane QC, acknowledged as "the number one silk for aviation matters," the "really smart and charming" banking supremo Bankim Thanki QC, and the "absolutely phenomenal" commercial practitioner David Railton QC. The set also offers high-calibre juniors, including the "extremely bright" and "technically excellent" James Cutress as well as the "very impressive" Robin Barclay who is praised for being "absolutely on top of his area." Barclay is but one of a number of new arrivals at the set this year, as it looks to expand. One of the most eye-catching of these is Richard Lissack QC, recently of Outer Temple Chambers, who is noted for his regulatory and financial expertise. The clerking team, led by the "absolutely excellent" Paul Martesyn, and "brilliant" Alex Taylor, is also very highly thought of. According to commentators, "the clerking at Fountain Court is exceptional — they're very professional and proactive and understand the needs of the clients.

Guildhall Chambers

A dominant force on the Western Circuit and one of the leading chambers outside London. The set houses highly rated barristers with a heterogeneous collection of expertise resulting in it being ranked in eleven sections of our guide, and enjoying top-tier bandings in banking and finance, crime and employment. The set houses seven heavyweight silks, as well as dozens of leading juniors. Lawyers of particular note include Hugh Sims QC who is described as "a highly accomplished advocate who wins the trust of judges, is easy to work with, massively commercial, creative with solutions and highly practical," and the "technically outstanding and user-friendly" senior junior Jermey Bamford. The clerking team, led by Justin Emmett and Lucy Northeast, are described as "very impressive," with one interviewee stating: "You couldn't get a better clerking team."

St Philips Chambers

The pre-eminent set in the Midlands as demonstrated by its top-tier rankings across the board in our guide, but also one that is active on the North Eastern Circuit and one with a burgeoning presence in London as illustrated by its recent merger with leading shipping set Stone Chambers. Its areas of expertise are sundry and its barristers regularly work on marquee cases in fields as disparate as company law, health & safety and real estate. There are 14 silks at St Philips including the inimitable Edward Pepperall QC who is described as "a pragmatic and clinical advocate who is user friendly and fantastic in front of clients," and the "hugely intelligent" John Randall QC. Its junior ranks are similarly strong, containing excellent lawyers such as John Brennan, who is described as "brilliant, very thorough and methodical with his work." The quality of its barristers is matched by its practice management team. Joe Wilson is the chief clerk and leads "an absolutely fantastic clerking team. The clerks are very responsive and bend over backwards to help."

Wilberforce Chambers

A dominant force for all types of chancery work, noted for housing an outstanding team of client-focused lawyers. The set is considered "one of the standout names for offshore work" and is widely regarded as a first port of call for private client tax matters. It also excels at general commercial litigation and has a noted specialism in pensions law. The set has quality from top to bottom and is known for having a "list of outstanding juniors that just goes on and on." Its bench of leading silks includes the venerable Robert Ham QC who is described as "a doyen of the contentious trusts world" and Brian Green QC who is described as "one of the big superstar names at the Chancery Bar." They have recently been joined by a number of new members as Wilberforce scooped up members from both 3 Stone Buildings and the now defunct 11 Stone Buildings, amongst others. The clerking team is led by practice director Nicholas Luckman who is said to run "a very efficient and professional ship," and head clerk Mark Rushton who "gives great service." Ranked in 10 practice areas:

Crown Office Chambers

Crown Office Chambers has long operated at the summit of fields such as health and safety, personal injury and property damage, and has one of the highest concentrations of expertise in insurance liability, regulatory and tort law in the country. It is further noted for its skill in the areas of product liability and clinical and professional negligence, and is a leading destination for those faced with high-value construction disputes. One instructing solicitor of long-standing says: "They have a strength in depth that is difficult to match — if there is a complex issue they tend to be at the top of my list, and there is always someone who can assist." Interviewees are similarly impressed by the service culture at the set, rigorously upheld by senior managing clerk Andy Flanagan and a team of senior clerks dedicated to specific practice areas at which members excel. One source says it is "absolutely superb - benchmark-level service," while another says: "The clerks are efficient and friendly and good at turning requests around in a short period of time." Among the set's leading barristers are the "exceptional" Simon Antrobus, a star-rated health and safety specialist who is also highly recommended for inquests, public inquiries and consumer law matters; the "brilliant" Charlotte Jones, one of the country's leading clinical negligence barristers; and the "outstanding" Daniel Shapiro, a master of an impressive range of disciplines, including insurance, professional negligence and property damage.

Essex Court Chambers

Universally acknowledged as one of the Bar's magic circle sets, Essex Court Chambers is "one of only a few chambers able to provide a string of top-quality advocates for significant High Court commercial disputes." The set has been keenly involved in international arbitration since its development and remains at the summit of this practice area. It is also highly rated in civil fraud, public international law and, of course, commercial dispute resolution. Chambers is a leading destination for complex and high-value banking and finance, insurance and indirect tax matters, and members are also highly sought-after for advice and advocacy relating to employment law, shipping and energy and natural resources. The "superb" clerks, led by Joe Ferrigno and David Grief, "run a very commercial and practical set of chambers," are "extremely responsive" and "obey the golden rule of not double-booking barristers." They facilitate interactions with busy barristers at the very top of their chosen fields, such as VV Veeder, "one of the most sought-after arbitrators in the world;" "stunning employment law advocate" Andrew Hochhauser QC; indirect tax expert Roderick Cordara QC, described by one source as "the go-to for the most intricate VAT matters;" the "truly exceptional" Vaughan Lowe QC, recommended as much for his advocacy as his magisterial command of public and international law; and the "phenomenally smart" Toby Landau QC, an international arbitration and public law expert. They are but a few of the immensely accomplished counsel who together make up this venerable stable.

Monckton Chambers

One of the very best sets for competition, European and public law, Monckton Chambers is now ranked in ten practice areas. It tops the tables in an impressive six practice areas (community care, competition, European law, public procurement, indirect tax and telecommunications) and is also acknowledged as a destination of choice for administrative and public law, data protection, environment and sports law. Further, members of chambers are recognised as leaders in the fields of civil liberties and human rights, education and police law. Senior clerk David Hockney and his team are commended for the "top-notch" service provided to instructing parties, with one saying: "The clerks are helpful, proactive, ring back when they say they will and are as co-operative as possible when it comes to juggling schedules." They support luminaries such as leading competition silk Daniel Beard QC, a "first-rate, extraordinary lawyer" and a "great strategist;" Michael Bowsher QC, a public procurement specialist who "identifies the key issues and answers the difficult questions with unmatched authority;" competition, European and telecommunications law expert Josh Holmes, who is "a tremendous asset to any team;" and Valentina Sloane, a leading indirect tax and public procurement barrister described as "incredibly intelligent and always impeccably prepared." This is just a snapshot of the expertise and experience on offer at Monckton, a chambers of "very erudite, cogent people" who "strike the right balance between intellectual rigour and commercial reality." On the whole, the set is characterised by "commitment to the best interests of the client."

Serle Court

Serle Court has a long-standing reputation in commercial and chancery work, with market commentators highlighting the set as "one of the very best commercial chancery sets, and one of the few that genuinely competes in both traditional chancery and commercial litigation." Its senior bench features "true grandee of the Chancery Bar" Alan Boyle QC and the "very learned" Frank Hinks QC. At a junior level, charity and trusts expert William Henderson draws praise for his "encyclopaedic knowledge of charity law," and the "articulate and charming" Dakis Hagen is tipped as a "rising star at the Bar." 2016 saw Richard Wilson QC and Daniel Lightman QC take on postnominals, further swelling Serle Court's already considerable ranks of chancery and company silks. The set's excellent reputation in offshore matters sees it appearing in cases arising in the Channel Islands, Hong Kong, the BVI and other Caribbean jurisdictions, and members are recognised for a host of related areas of work, including company law, restructuring and insolvency, and civil fraud. John Machell QC's work in partnership and LLP matters earns him a star ranking for the fourth year since his accession to Queen's Counsel. Instructing solicitors are also full of praise for the clerks room, headed by Steve Whitaker, saying: "The clerking is first-class. The senior clerks are unfailingly helpful and give reliable advice about alternative counsel when the first choice is not available."

Sets with the most barrister rankings

The table shows the 50 sets that have achieved the highest number of barrister rankings in this edition. The number of rankings includes barristers ranked more than once. Where two or more sets gained the same number of rankings, the smaller one appears first in the table.

Position	Position Last Year	Set	Number of Rankings	Number of Barristers
1	1	Blackstone Chambers	216	103
2	2	39 Essex Chambers	180	128
3=	3	Brick Court Chambers	177	85
3=	5	Fountain Court	177	79
5	4	Matrix Chambers	159	88
6	6	Essex Court Chambers	135	85
7	7	Doughty Street Chambers	133	137
8	8	Kings Chambers	130	115
9	9	No5	128	256
10	23	Wilberforce Chambers	124	54
11=	12=	One Essex Court	121	94
11=	12=	Maitland Chambers	121	71
13	16	Landmark Chambers	117	84
14	11	11KBW	115	61
15	10	3 Verulam Buildings	111	67
16	12=	4 New Square	110	81
17	15	Serle Court	108	60
18	24=	St Philips Chambers	99	170
19	19=	3 Raymond Buildings Barristers	95	50
20=	18	Monckton Chambers	93	60
20=	17	4 Pump Court	93	63
20=	21	Guildhall Chambers	93	83
23=	19=	1 Crown Office Row	89	71
23=	26	Garden Court Chambers	89	182
23=	24=	Keating Chambers	89	58
26	22	Crown Office Chambers	84	103
27	31	7 King's Bench Walk	82	60
28=	30	Serjeants' Inn Chambers	81	60
28=	27	Outer Temple Chambers	81	84
28=	28	XXIV Old Buildings	81	42
31	29	Atkin Chambers	79	44
32=	36=	Exchange Chambers	70	161
32=	32	South Square	70	42
34	33=	Quadrant Chambers	67	64
35	35	20 Essex Street	66	66
36=	36=	4 Stone Buildings	65	33
36=	39	Radcliffe Chambers	65	53
38	33=	St John's Chambers	64	85
39	41=	2 Bedford Row	56	75
40=	43=	Old Square Chambers	51	75
40=	41=	2 Hare Court	51	58
40=	46=	5 Stone Buildings	51	32
43=	43=	Francis Taylor Building	50	61
43=	46=	Enterprise Chambers	50	42
45=	40	Cornerstone Barristers	49	51
45=	38	Devereux	49	50
47=	50	2TG – 2 Temple Gardens	48	59
47=	–	New Square Chambers	48	47
49	45	Littleton Chambers	47	56
50=	–	Erskine Chambers	46	30
50=	46=	6KBW College Hill	46	43

Sets with the highest proportion of barrister rankings

This table measures the total number of barrister rankings as a proportion of the size of the set. The number of rankings includes barristers ranked more than once.

Position	Position Last Year	Set	Number of Rankings	Number of Barristers	Rankings as a % of size
1	1	Cloth Fair Chambers	19	7	271
2	17	Wilberforce	124	54	229
3	3	Fountain Court	178	79	225
4=	2	Blackstone Chambers	216	103	209
4=	4	Brick Court Chambers	178	85	209
6	5	4 Stone Buildings	65	33	196
7	9	XXIV Old Buildings	81	42	192
8	6	3 Raymond Buildings Barristers	95	50	190
9	7=	11KBW	115	61	188
10	10	Matrix Chambers	159	88	180
11	11	Atkin Chambers	79	44	179
12	7=	Serle Court	106	60	176
13	14	Maitland Chambers	121	71	170
14	13	South Square	70	42	166
15	12	3 Verulam Buildings	111	67	165
16	16	Essex Court Chambers	135	85	158
17	18	Monckton Chambers	93	60	155
18	27=	Erskine Chambers	46	30	153
19	15	5 Stone Buildings	48	32	150
20	20	Keating Chambers	86	58	148
21	19	4 Pump Court	93	63	147
22	22	39 Essex Chambers	180	128	140
23	30=	Landmark Chambers	117	84	139
24	24	7 King's Bench Walk	82	60	136
25=	23	4 New Square	110	81	135
25=	35	Serjeants' Inn Chambers	81	60	135
25=	27=	One Brick Court	23	17	135
28	32=	One Essex Court	121	94	128
29=	29	1 Crown Office Row	89	71	125
29=	21	Byrom Street Chambers	20	16	125
31	25	Radcliffe Chambers	65	53	122
32=	30=	8 New Square	36	30	120
32=	32=	Field Court Tax	6	5	120
34	34	Enterprise Chambers	49	42	116
35=	38=	Kings Chambers	130	115	113
35=	36	Pump Court Tax	41	36	113
37=	38=	Guildhall Chambers	93	83	112
37=	26	11 South Square	18	16	112
39	49=	11 New Square	10	9	111
40	37	Falcon Chambers	44	40	110
41	48	6KBW College Hill	46	43	106
42=	49=	Hogarth Chambers	21	20	105
42=	49=	The Chambers of Andrew Mitchell QC	20	19	105
44	40	Quadrant Chambers	67	64	104
45	41	New Square Chambers	48	47	102
46	49=	Partnership Counsel	2	2	100
47=	42=	Outer Temple Chambers	83	84	98
47=	45	Cornerstone Barristers	50	51	98
47=	44	Devereux	49	50	98
50	42=	Doughty Street Chambers	133	137	97

Stars at the Bar

The Stars at the Bar have proved their excellence across a range of practice areas.

Jonathan Crow QC: 4 Stone Buildings

Jonathan Crow QC is well summed-up by a source who says: "He is as good as you will find in London, and his background as 'Treasury Devil' gives him an astonishingly versatile repertoire." His is an admirably broad-ranging commercial practice, and he is star-rated in our guide in some of the most competitive fields of the Bar. Market sources remark on his masterful advocacy, saying: "He has a great style, his thoughts are well marshalled and he gets to the point quickly." Another source says he is "a great wordsmith" in the service of his "forensic" intellect. His written work comes in for similar praise: "His opinions are just superb, they're clear, incisive and well-reasoned," according to one of his peers. "No one is more respected by the court than he" in matters before the Chancery division and proceedings concerning complex questions of company law. He is also top-rated with regard to financial services, public law and insolvency, and is highly sought after for civil fraud and offshore cases. Recent instructions have seen him appear before the Supreme Court in the dispute between JSC BTA Bank and Mukhtar Ablyazov, which concerned the interpretation and application of the standard form freezing order. He also played a leading role in Ecclestone v HMRC, in which the Revenue sought to unwind a £1 billion tax settlement. His talents are neatly encapsulated by an interviewee who said: "He's intellectually brilliant and manages to make complicated issues seem unbelievably simple and straightforward."

Bankim Thanki QC: Fountain Court Chambers

Bankim Thanki QC is, in the words of one source: "The doyen of banking and regulatory litigation" and is sought after by solicitors for his "calm, analytical advice and impeccable judgement." He has a practice of impressive breadth, and is top-rated in five practice areas as defined by this guide, and highly rated in a further five. His particular appeal derives from his marriage of striking intellectual acuity with a reassuring and personable manner. "He's a lovely man with a huge brain and tremendous encyclopaedic knowledge of banking law - clients love him," says one instructing solicitor. His advocacy style is light on aggression – sources point to his "understated" court performances – but is no less tough for it. One source says: "He is bulletproof – his arguments are amazing and his instincts are second to none." As for his written work, he is "able to transform the most complex of arguments into straightforward and eloquent submissions." He is considered to be at the top of the field in banking and finance, commercial litigation and civil fraud, and is one of the finest aviation lawyers in the country. He is also highly recommended for cases concerned with insurance, the travel industry and professional negligence, and is an experienced arbitrator. He recently appeared in the first trial in the Financial List for Barclays in a test case addressing the construction of LMA standard terms. One market source speaks for many in saying Thanki is "an outstanding legal asset on big cases who is just an exceptionally nice person and really good to work with. It's that combination which sets him apart."

Alan Steinfeld QC: XXIV Old Buildings

Alan Steinfeld QC is, by universal consensus, "an intellectual giant — his memory is extraordinary and his knowledge of the law is second to none." Instructing parties find this celebrated chancery silk "incredibly supportive" and remark on his "outstanding judgement." One says: "I use him when I want someone tough, versatile and clever." A leitmotif in references for him is his remarkable facility for concision. "He's very clear in his thinking and great at drawing the strings of a case together; he'll distil what we've spent hours talking about on half a sheet of paper." His advocacy also places him among the very best — "he is a master in the courtroom, who has a fantastic rapport with judges and explains matters in a lucid and relaxed manner." He is "truly outstanding on appeal," and it is often noted that "judges defer to him on points of law." Steinfeld is ranked in the first tier for commercial and traditional chancery, offshore, partnership and trusts, and he is also highly recommended for complex disputes concerning company law and insolvency. Many years of success in civil fraud and professional negligence cases makes him a first port of call for solicitors with practices in those areas too. His recent work includes shareholder litigation arising from Lloyds' 2008 takeover of HBOS and the defence of a USD1 billion claim following the failure of a US hedge fund incorporated in Guernsey. This "fantastically intelligent and charming" silk remains one of the most sought-after and respected figures at the Bar.

Mark Howard QC: Brick Court Chambers

Mark Howard QC is "one of a handful of of real superstar performers in the courtroom," admired for his "exceptional analytical and strategic skills coupled with his expertise as an advocate." His consummate mastery of the art of court advocacy is the most common and compelling theme brought up by his peers when discussing him. He "is very good at getting to the key points and identifying the winning and losing arguments, and he also reads the court and judges very well." He further enjoys notoriety for being a "ferocious cross-examiner who can tear apart the most confident and well-prepared witnesses." Opposing counsel salute him as "a force of nature," and admire his "unflappability" and "clinical" analysis of the problem put before the court. Sources also stress the importance of his "clear and effective submissions on points of law" in determining his team's fortunes in any given matter. Another market commentator says: "In addition to his well-known qualities, I would like to add that his client management skills are excellent." Howard is star-rated by this guide for banking and finance and commercial disputes, and is also at the top of the tables for civil fraud, energy and natural resources and professional negligence. He is also highly recommended for competition, insurance and offshore cases, and for international arbitration. His recent work includes acting for Ukrainian businessman Gennadiy Bogolyubov in Pinchuk v Kolomoisky & Bogolyubov, concerning the ownership of a commodities business. As summarised by one solicitor: "He is really strong in court and a very strong analyst and examiner — one of the first you would look to if you need a heavy hitter."

David Pannick QC: Blackstone Chambers

Lord Pannick QC is "one of the most brilliant minds at the Bar" and a leading light in adminstrative and public law, civil liberties and humans rights. His reputation in these areas is second to none, and his expertise is considered to be "unparalleled." Instructing solicitors say that "he lives up to his considerable reputation by demonstrating legal and client relation skills of the very highest order" and add that he is "knowledgeable, focused, practical, immensely experienced and clear in his views." He is known for his versatility and can turn his hand to a wide range of matters, including European law, immigration, professional discipline, media and entertainment, sports and telecoms cases. Sources are consequently broad in their praise, with one simply saying he is "excellent at everything and one of the cleverest guys around." He is known for his ability on his feet, and is praised as a "stellar advocate who is extremely authoritative in court" and someone who "captivates people." Recent work includes acting for MGN in a Court of Appeal case to determine the amount of damages to be awarded to victims of phone hacking. Pannick by name but not by nature, he is praised by instructing solicitors as "very assured" and able to remain "incredibly unflustered in difficult circumstances."

Hugh Sims QC: Guildhall Chambers
Hugh Sims QC is one of the foremost advocates on the Western Circuit, and is considered by market commentators to be "an absolutely brilliant advocate with an exceptional brain" who "lives for the court." Sources agree that he "wins the trust of judges" and "has a style of presentation that judges like very much, " whilst maintaining "an excellent mixture of being both academic and user-friendly." He is popular among instructing solicitors, who appreciate that he "works very, very hard to make sure that the service levels are always up to standard" and praise his "ability to easily present his advice to the client" and "talk at a level clients understand." His facility for reading an audience is highlighted by one source, who comments that he is "very good at speaking directly to people and adapting the way he addresses different parties in order to get the best for the client." Sources are also quick to highlight his commercial and tactical awareness. He has made his transition to silk "seamlessly," according to peers, and is considered by instructing parties to be "one of the best commercial silks on the regional circuit, despite only having been appointed QC in 2014." His typical work load is a blend of commercial chancery, partnership, company, insolvency and professional negligence cases. He recently acted for a lender in its professional negligence claim against an accountancy firm, arising out of the due diligence report for the purchase of a US medical homecare company. An exceptional all-round performer, Sims is "great on paper, great on his feet and very good to put in front of clients."

James Eadie QC: Blackstone Chambers
It is no surprise that James Eadie QC remains the UK government's go-to counsel for the defence of controversial legislation and policy, given that some consider him "the best advocate at the Bar." He has advised the government on a catalogue of landmark civil liberties, human rights and immigration cases in the Supreme Court and ECHR, and has also appeared in several of the major public inquests and inquiries of recent years. His work as Treasury Devil also sees him advising on data protection matters, as evidenced by his appearance in a Court of Appeal case brought by a number of MPs concerning the compatibility of DRIPA with EU law. Market commentators are full of praise for his courtroom advocacy, saying: "He has good judgement and doesn't take bad points, which is why judges know they can rely on what he says." Sources report that "everything he does is done with real flair and ability," and that "he makes things sound reasonable that others couldn't." He commands universal respect among his peers, with one commenting: "There is no one to beat him – the court wants to hear what he has to say. It makes you want to scream sometimes because, even if you disagree, you can't argue with the quality of the argument and the beauty of how it is expressed. You have to be at the very top of your game with James."

David Perry QC: 6KBW College Hill
"Wonderful to work with and incredibly hard-working," David Perry QC is universally admired for his high-level criminal law practice. Not only is he an exceptional adviser on POCA matters, he also maintains a broad general and financial crime practice and advises on a wide variety of high-profile cases. A "phenomenal advocate," he attracts a wealth of praise for his appellate work and regularly appears in criminal courts in various overseas jurisdictions, with recent experience of complex matters in both the Cayman Islands and Hong Kong. Sources describe Perry as "the smartest guy in the country" and joke: "He has three brains!" Despite his reputation as a formidable intellect and "one of the best barristers at the Bar," he is also known to be "very down-to-earth and very easy to deal with."

Nigel Giffin QC: 11KBW
Nigel Giffin QC is a hugely respected silk with an enviable and wide-reaching reputation. Described as "undoubtedly outstanding" by his peers and "a master tactician with excellent advocacy skills" by an instructing solicitor, Giffin retains his position as a leading public procurement silk. According to sources, his "encyclopaedic knowledge of procurement" is just a part of his broad knowledge of public law more generally. He regularly handles high-profile cases regarding the decisions of local government bodies, including those concerning education and social services. Though he consistently works on complex and high-level cases, Giffin is still able to "simplify things for the client," say sources. In fact, this talented silk has such a breadth of knowledge and skills that one source goes so far as to say: "He is my favourite barrister. He is a really good all-rounder, who is very user-friendly, and very easy and pleasant to deal with. He has a very lean but precise style so everything he writes is absolutely perfect and no longer than it needs to be." His recent work includes successfully acting for the London Borough of Tower Hamlets in its dispute with the London Borough of Bromley concerning the ownership of Henry Moore's Draped Seated Woman sculpture.

Paul Chaisty QC: Kings Chambers
Paul Chaisty QC has an impressive seven rankings in this year's Chambers guide and remains one of the top barristers active on the Northern Circuit. An accomplished commercial litigator, he handles an array of complex business disputes, including partnership cases. This celebrated polymath is also an expert in property litigation, professional negligence cases and insolvency matters. One interviewee described him as "world-class" whilst another said: "He is the most formidable advocate and most creative lawyer I have come across." Not only is Chaisty admired for his advocacy skills, he is also considered "very good at written work and keeping things quite simple." His recent work has included several multimillion-pound cases and he is regularly called upon to appear in the BVI and the Bahamas. "He gets straight to the point," says an appreciative source, who continues: "At QC level there is a very expensive hourly rate but he is really good value because he will get to grips with something very quickly and give a very quick opinion."

Michael Brindle QC: Fountain Court Chambers
The "outstanding" Michael Brindle QC is a highly distinguished practitioner who is widely viewed as one of the top commercial barristers in the country. The breadth of his expertise in banking and finance disputes is impressive and he has recent experience of substantial professional negligence claims in the financial services sector. He is noted for his extensive work for the FCA and his substantial international practice. Brindle is particularly commended for his "formidable" advocacy, with one source noting that "he is fantastic on his feet" while another says: "He has a very, very charming and persuasive style of advocacy." Also of note is Brindle's sheer level of experience at the London Bar, which causes one source to comment: "He's been there, seen it, done it and won it — there's nothing he hasn't seen."

Antony Zacaroli QC: South Square
An exceptional silk highlighted for his mastery of a variety of areas. He is "a superb insolvency lawyer," who is "fantastic on the chancery side," and "one of the brightest silks at the Banking and Finance Bar." He is also highly adept at handling company law and financial services matters. Sources marvel at his outstanding technical ability, his "very clear and impressive written work," and his brilliant" advocacy, which renders him "the first choice of many." He is also noted for being "unsurpassed in terms of his responsiveness and his ability to work seamlessly with the other counsel and solicitors on the team." Sources are quick to highlight his involvement in some of the most complex and high-profile cases of recent years, which include the Waterfall II proceedings and the litigation arising out of the collapse of the Icelandic bank Landsbanki. In the words of one source: "He is excellent — I don't think I've worked with anyone who is any better.

John Howell QC: Blackstone Chambers
The "absolutely superb" and "incredibly clever" John Howell QC is lauded for his "deeply impressive grasp of very complex legal points," and, as such, is someone instructing solicitors "would involve in anything complex — any-

thing going to the Supreme Court or of huge importance otherwise." Sources marvel at his "fantastic command of the facts and the law," which leaves him "always thoroughly prepared for anything which may be thrown at him." He is a leading light in the field of public law, with a particular emphasis on local government matters. In the words of one source: "He is superb at anything to do with local government— there is no point going anywhere else." He is also said to have a "fantastic reputation for environmental law work." Renowned as a "great advocate," he is routinely sought out to advise on very high-profile work, recent examples of which include appearing in the public inquiry into the 2010 Great Yarmouth Harbour Revision Order application. Sources universally agree that "he is extremely intelligent and has an immense ability to carry the court. His general air of authority is unlike anyone else: he is on a plane above others."

Philip Jones QC: Serle Court

Philip Jones is a highly respected silk who is "at the top of his game." He is commended for his "wide range of ability — he handles a real cross-section of work and does it all brilliantly." He is considered a "complete heavyweight in the commercial chancery area," and also offers strong expertise in the areas of company law and partnership. He is appreciated by instructing solicitors for his "calm and confident manner. He puts the lay client at ease and is very good at drawing out the most significant points of an argument and commanding the attention of the court." They also draw attention to his "excellent grasp of the commercial realities of each possible outcome." Peers are also highly complimentary, and agree that "he is really solid as an opponent. He's absolutely delightful and a very safe pair of hands." Jones is regularly sought out to act in international matters including proceedings in the British Virgin Islands High Court and Court of Appeal, and he recently defended Monaco-based accountants and service providers against a negligence claim following the collapse of an investment fund in the Cayman Islands. "He has encyclopaedic knowledge and a great intellect, but he treats everybody in the room as his equal," enthuses one source.

Paul Girolami QC: Maitland Chambers

"Time and time again people are impressed by Paul Girolami." He is a "big name" among solicitors and peers alike, and those that instruct him declare that he is "at the top of our list," and "one of the best company law silks at the Bar. He is very good at presenting technical matters to the higher courts, and also has a good understanding of offshore trusts — that makes him a terrific choice." "Someone who must be one of the best chancery silks available," he "is ideally suited for complex fraud claims," because "he is possibly the cleverest silk at the London Bar." Commentators describe him as a "particular favourite," because of the strong mix of skills he brings to the table: "He is exceptionally gifted. Very engaging, committed and inclusive, he's a brilliant orator and one of the most able and nicest silks one could ever work with." Girolami is acknowledged for his strong ability to handle cases with international elements, and was recently instructed to act for one of the defendants in the Libyan Investment Authority's USD1.5 billion action against Société Générale concerning alleged bribery.

Dinah Rose QC: Blackstone Chambers

A celebrated public law and human rights barrister who is widely viewed as the first port of call for difficult, high-profile cases. She is renowned for the breadth of her expertise with one peer labelling her "a star who is fantastically brilliant at everything that she does." She has a reputation as a leading court performer with one instructing solicitor saying: "I can't speak highly enough of her ability in terms of presentation to the court; she's formidable in an approachable way and she really gets the trust of the clients." One peer says of her: "She is a very forceful advocate who is quite phenomenal." Outside of the civil liberties and human rights field, Dinah also excels as an advocate in areas as disperate as employment, telecommunications and professional discipline. Her recent work includes advising journalists from The Guardian on challenging the Attorney General's refusal to publish letters from Prince Charles to government ministers.

Pushpinder Saini QC: Blackstone Chambers

A multi-talented silk who is able to provide high quality advice to clients on a diverse range of matters. His areas of expertise are manifold and include public law, media, telecommunications, civil liberties, financial services and sanctions. He is lauded by peers, instructing solicitors and clients alike and is described as "an exceptionally talented counsel" who is "excellent with clients and clear in his advice." Also "extremely experienced and someone who demonstrates excellent judgement" he is "strategically brilliant and has all the details at his fingertips." He is well known for his formidable intellect with one interviewee saying: "He is quick to understand the facts and issues in a complex case and adept at identifying points which others miss." His recent work includes advising the appellant in Nouazli v Secretary of State before the Supreme Court. The case concerned the rights of EU nationals facing deportation and whether they could be detained prior to their removal.

Robert Miles QC: 4 Stone Buildings

A pre-eminent company and commercial-focused barrister who is described as being at the "top of his game" and "a class apart." He is "very highly regarded as a banking and insolvency silk," and is also noted for his "detailed knowledge of complex financial products." His excellence is best summed up by one instructing solicitor who explained that "Robert is exceptional. He has incredible judgement, he is excellent on his feet, is very measured and is willing to call a spade a spade." That same source continued: "He's very good with clients, inspires confidence, and he excites them by being enthusiastic about their case. He's very willing to give an opinion and he's happy to stick his neck out." "Good to work with, he takes responsibility for things, and the buck stops with him." He regularly works on high-profile and high-value cases, as exemplified by his recent representation of the Icelandic bank Kaupthing as it sought to defend claims of conspiracy and malicious prosecution launched by Vincent and Robert Tchenguiz.

Clare Montgomery QC: Matrix Chambers

An undisputed leader in her field who is described as "the doyenne of the Criminal Bar." Her expertise extends to a range of areas and she is lauded for her multifaceted practice and skill set. She is called the "standout unbeatable superstar of the extradition world" and a "top player in the field" of financial crime. Montgomery is famed for her incredible intellect and is variously described as being "overwhelmingly clever" and "the biggest brain at the Bar." Her evident intelligence is matched by her superlative client focus and she is recommended for her ability to give "easy to digest, no-nonsense advice." She returned to the UK in 2015 after spending significant time in Hong Kong representing property magnate Thomas Kwok in his appeal against corruption charges.

Client Service at the Bar

The following sets are particularly commended for their provision of quality client service.

1 Chancery Lane

Sources characterise 1 Chancery Lane as "a brilliant chambers offering some of the best clerking in the country, without a shadow of a doubt." The "absolutely fantastic" Clark Chessis is "exactly what you want in a senior clerk," according to market commentators. He "runs the team extremely well" and is lauded for his "great market knowledge, which enables him to always select just the right barrister for any given case." Commentators also heap praise upon the broader clerking team, describing them as "experts who absolutely know what they're doing," and "just a great group of people to deal with." They are "very organised, responsive and efficient, and never promise what they can't deliver." Impressed instructing solicitors cite their "very good relationships with the clerks" as a major reason for the frequent repeat instructions received by the set, as well as the clerks' provision of a "highly personal service." Overall, commentators "cannot fault the set, from the clerks through to the barristers. Nothing is too much trouble, they never have to be asked twice, and they deliver a service above and beyond what you would expect."

1 Crown Office Row

1 Crown Office Row "recognises how important service is and provides fantastic clerking which is second to none." The "well-organised" chambers receives particular praise for its extensive seminar programme, which spans areas as diverse as London, Manchester, Newcastle and Leeds, and is noted for its superior meeting facilities following the refurbishment of its conference rooms. Instructing solicitors report that the "amazing team of clerks" housed in the set make 1 Crown Office Row a "go-to chambers." In the words of one source, "the clerks are just great and are one of the biggest selling points of the set." The clerking team is led by the highly regarded Matthew Phipps, whom sources describe as "fantastic, experienced and very approachable." His team is also well respected, with sources commenting on the clerks' "brilliance and their ability to build strong relationships with instructing solicitors." They are further praised for their deft management of matters and for their ability to resolve issues with ease, including those relating to fees and costs. Sources report a very high level of satisfaction with the service overall, and agree that "the very accommodating and very organised clerking team make it easy to use 1 Crown Office Row." In addition to its celebrated clerking team, the set also distributes an annual newsletter and is responsible for running the 'Human Rights Blog', a respected, award-winning resource that provides both insightful commentary and a platform for discussion and debate.

9 Gough Square

Commentators report that they are "very satisfied" with the service provided by the staff at 9 Gough Square. "From the receptionists and clerks through to the head of chambers, they are reliably friendly, polite, professional, well presented and welcoming." Many solicitors cite the "highly organised clerking team" as a key motivation for instructing the set, adding that "they really do go above and beyond the call of duty and are always happy to help, which makes instructing solicitors' lives very easy." Head clerk, Michael Goodridge, "runs the show," and is characterised as an "exceptional, extremely helpful" member of the team. Commentators enthuse that "there is no senior clerk more committed or enthusiastic than Michael – he has a knack for making things happen and is instrumental to the success of this chambers." He is also considered to be "commercially astute and able to resolve issues quickly given his excellent grasp of the market." Goodridge is lauded for the way in which he "runs a well-organised ship," consisting of "excellent clerks who are really on the ball and highly effective." The "helpful and attentive" clerking team receive further praise for their "very commercially minded and realistic approach."

Fountain Court Chambers

Fountain Court Chambers is highlighted for its "excellent, all-round service." According to impressed sources, "the clerking team provides impeccable assistance and advice; you can't ask for much more." Alex Taylor leads the clerking team, while Paul Martenstyn continues to act in the capacity of deputy senior clerk. They are singled out as "a class above the rest" given their "responsiveness, approachability and true understanding of the value of commercial relationships. They will always match the right counsel to the right cases, and they're not salesmen; they want to offer quality at the right price." According to market commentators, the wider clerking team consists of "incredibly responsive, helpful, organised, commercially minded and customer-focused" individuals. The set is praised for its transparent billing and willingness to engage in "sensible discussions on fees," while the clerks are also lauded for the way in which they are "enormously accommodating when advice is needed at short notice." Instructing solicitors particularly appreciate that the chambers "never oversells or over-promises." Overall, "the staff here are just brilliant – they always go above and beyond the call of duty, and nothing is too much hassle. The service is exceptional."

One Essex Court

Given the extensive range of cases handled by the tenants at One Essex Court, instructing solicitors appreciate that the set has "great depth in the clerking team." The chambers boasts "universally excellent clerking," and commentators note that "whichever clerk you deal with, they are always responsive and responsible." Solicitors are confident that "if you say that a case involves certain aspects, and a client has certain needs, the clerks will always come up with a fair and accurate account of each barrister they suggest." Sources also consider those in the clerks' room to be helpful when assistance is required at short notice, with one source saying: "Knowing you have someone on hand to help makes you really feel that One Essex are part of the team." Darren Burrows is the senior clerk at the set and attracts a wealth of praise for his extensive experience and knowledge. "Burrows is an absolute legend," says one source. "His responsiveness is incredible and he knows the chambers inside and out." Sources summarise that "the thing that really sets One Essex Court apart is the clerking and the whole mentality of how they do their job. They're wonderful."

Serjeants' Inn

The quality clerking team at Serjeants' Inn Chambers is known to be "very friendly, well organised and always happy to assist with finding a barrister at the last minute." This "co-operative, helpful and responsive" team is noted for being particularly easy to deal with and highly approachable. Commentators direct praise at the set's "absolutely brilliant" Lee Johnson, a "lovely and down-to-earth" senior clerk with a "solution-orientated" approach. In addition, the group is commended for its ability to put on excellent training sessions, and the director of client care, Catherine Calder, is singled out for praise: "She is seriously impressive and stunningly well organised. She is one of those people you want to hire for any job and is just worth her weight in gold." She is ably assisted by Jon Comlay, whose "high-brow approach to the job" is much appreciated by commentators. Interviewees also comment on the set's impressive premises at 85 Fleet Street, particularly highlighting the integration of technology into the fabric of the building. One source acknowledges that this use of technology "sounds like a small thing, but is really important and makes a big difference to a lay client."

2 Hare Court

Sources attest that the clerks at 2 Hare Court are "very approachable, organised, contactable even late into the night, and always clear about what they can achieve and offer." They are highly knowledgeable about the various practice areas covered by the set's barristers, and are particularly praised for their ability to swiftly match up the most appropriate member of counsel to each case. One impressed source enthuses: "The clerks are outstanding. They bend over backwards to help and have an incisive understanding of specialist areas of law which enables them to tailor their assistance accordingly." This "well-oiled machine" is led by director of clerking Julian Campbell, who is "incredibly supportive, highly efficient and someone who applies commerciality to his clerking." Ben Heaviside, the set's "fantastic" senior practice clerk, is also highly praised by instructing solicitors. In addition, practice clerk Tara Johnson is regarded as "the queen of clerks" by one impressed source, who says: "Tara is keen to learn about each case to ensure that it is carefully allocated. She always goes above and beyond and attends to requests instantaneously. She is incredibly personable and holds exceptional knowledge about members of chambers' practice and development."

5 Paper Buildings

The clerks' room at 5 Paper Buildings receives widespread praise from instructing solicitors. One source describes the "exceptional service" provided by the clerks, who are known to be "extremely accommodating and extremely communicative." Another interviewee commends the way in which solicitors can "reliably deal with one point of contact who is always absolutely up-to-date with the cases, which is a very sensible way of managing things." Crucially, sources find that the set "takes a really reasonable approach to fees which makes it very easy to have frank conversations" regarding costs and clients' budgets. The seven-strong clerking and administrative team is led by the "smart and charming" Dale Jones, who has held the senior clerk role since 2004. Jones is characterised as a "very responsive and no-nonsense" individual who offers a true wealth of experience.

4 New Square

Senior clerk Lizzy Stewart heads the clerking team, which is described as "very helpful, friendly and accommodating." Instructing solicitors are impressed by the responsiveness, commitment and turnaround time of the team, with one commenting that "the clerks are spot-on; they are always available and always willing to try to help with things at short notice," and another adding that "they will go the extra mile to get things done within 24 hours, if needs be." Solicitors appreciate the clerks' in-depth knowledge of the counsel's strengths and specialisms, saying: "The clerks are always able to deliver someone at the right level and with the right expertise, regardless of the issue or how unusual it might be. They have a good understanding of the barristers' particular strengths, and they always make recommendations with plenty of explanation as to why." Lizzy Stewart epitomises the set's attitude to client service given her "approachability and willingness to have open discussions." Two deputy senior clerks are also highlighted by commentators: Dennis Peck "repeatedly goes above and beyond what is asked of him," and Alex Dolby is "very quick and very helpful." Overall, the impression is of "a modern, outward-looking chambers" housing "very personable clerks and barristers."

11KBW

Senior clerks Lucy Barbett and Mark Dann manage a clerks room that provides an "absolutely first-class service," and is staffed by a team who are "very helpful and attentive, from the most senior through to the juniors." Solicitors comment that "Lucy Barbett is wonderful. She's highly attuned to client needs and is just so good at picking the right barrister for a case. If Lucy promises she will do something, you know she will. There's no question that she won't deliver." Sources are similarly appreciative of Mark Dann, who is characterised as "very helpful and responsive." Instructing parties report "a more modern feel" to 11KBW's clerking: user-friendly, responsive, dedicated and supportive are common epithets for the team, who "could not be nicer or more accommodating" and who " will readily go the extra mile to assist." They are particularly praised for their sensitivity to solicitors' requirements, with sources saying that "they are mindful of your needs, and understand the pressures of being a solicitor and the need to give a quick response. They really take the trouble to understand the work we are doing." Candour and flexibility characterise the set's fee arrangements, with one solicitor reporting that "billing is always clear and transparent, and I always feel like I can talk to clerks about it." Sources also appreciate that clerks are "good at suggesting which barrister will be appropriate for a case, and can usually find someone at very short notice." One of the set's distinguishing attributes is its willingness to provide extra services. Sources "really value that additional support given to practitioners," and report that regional conferences are "an invaluable service that we wouldn't normally get access to locally." Solicitors also appreciate the set's "useful and regularly updated FOIA blog." With an "extremely knowledgeable group of barristers who deliver a top-quality and cost-effective service" and an administrative team who are "among the best clerks in London," counsel and clerks alike share the credit for 11KBW's reputation as "a very well-run and organised chambers." Instructing solicitors continue to find that "the set is very keen on maintaining client relationships," and state that "the mentality of their barristers is what attracts us and our clients to them."

Monckton Chambers

Senior clerk David Hockney is a "charming guy and a pleasure to deal with." He has a reputation for being "very responsive and easy to talk to with regard to fees." He runs an excellent and user-friendly team, which is known for its responsiveness, approachability and commercial awareness. First junior clerk John Keegan is "great, very responsive and good at getting listings." The senior clerking team beneath him is made up of: the "brilliant" Sam Fullilove; Gemma Goodwin, who is "always at the end of the phone" and "very good at getting back to you"; and Steven Duffet, who is "very effective, very kind, and always has all the details about the case." Solicitors also praise clerks "at the junior end who go out of their way to get what you need." This dedication is typical of the team, which is "singled out for being exceptionally helpful and going the extra mile when you have difficult cases." As well as being open to discussions on fees, the clerking team is "keen to sort out any issues," and one source would have "no hesitation in picking up the phone and speaking to them candidly." The set's client service is summed up by one solicitor, who says: "The clerking has been absolutely perfect; head clerk David Hockney runs a very sharp operation there. They like to find a way to facilitate all pockets and be pragmatic, and they're willing to accommodate you which means, in turn, you keep going back for more." Another satisfied customer commented: "The chambers as a whole is fantastic. The commitment to the best interests of the client is exemplary and the barristers are very ably supported by everyone from the receptionist to the clerks. Monckton is a class act."

Matrix Chambers

Matrix Chambers takes a relatively unusual but highly successful approach to case administration, dividing practice areas among dedicated clerking teams. Jason Housden is the senior practice manager and leads Practice Team X, which handles the administration of telecoms, commercial, corporate compliance, competition, EU law, human rights, immigration, public law, community care, health and mental health, education and environmental law cases. Sources find him "particularly impressive and very quick to respond." Cliff Holland is head of Practice Team M, which handles clerking for employment, media, information and sports law cases, while Paul Venables heads Practice Team T, which looks after arbitration, public international law, crime, extradition, regulatory, inquests and inquiries, and police law. Both these two are known for their geniality and in-depth knowledge of the practice areas they handle. Solicitors find the practice team model "very forward-thinking" and consider Matrix to be "one of the best sets in terms of how it is run." Sources report that one of the many selling points for instructing parties is that the clerks "truly take the time to understand what solicitor clients want and readily accommodate all the requests we make, whilst being extremely personable." Counsel are routinely described as user-friendly, easy to work with and good with clients. This modern and dynamic chambers is considered to be "the gold standard of clerking" and, from clerks to counsel, "has an ethos that is very supportive."

Atkin Chambers

Led by senior clerk Justin Wilson, the team at Atkin is described as "absolutely top of the range and in a league of its own." It is highlighted as a modern and innovative set, and one that "doesn't rely on past reputation or rest on its laurels." The group's approach is captured by sources who note that "their clerks go above and beyond for you and are always thinking of new ways to help." The set's service focus came up again and again during our research and is epitomised by Justin who receives particular praise for "taking the time to get to know you so he knows exactly what you want and who you would work well with." The wider team is also highly praised and includes "committed, service-focused clerks, all of whom are pleasant to work with and can't do enough to help." The team is also consistently praised for its fairness on fees, with sources noting that "the clerks place an impetus on giving you the best bang for your buck." "They are very good at doing deals on fees," and "they assist you with costs and budgets."

Brick Court Chambers

A set that is singled out for its "first-rate" clerking and "client service-oriented, commercial approach." Instructing solicitors describe a clerks room that is "extremely efficient and keen to assist and respond immediately to queries or requests," as well as one that is "organised, helpful and a flawless operation overall." The team is led by Julian Hawes and Ian Moyler, who "run a good shop," alongside deputy senior clerk Paul Dennison, who is praised for his "extreme efficiency." The group is applauded for its understanding of the firms it works with. "They get to know you as a client and recommend people who will be a good fit," reports one source, whilst another notes that they are "transparent about availability and strike the right balance between making people available and not over selling people who are too busy." The clerks are noted for being forward-thinking, as exemplified by one source who says "they've adapted to the post-Jackson world and they have a good understanding of cost and client demands."

Francis Taylor Building

Sources are unequivocal when they describe the clerking at Francis Taylor as "absolutely top-rate." Instructing solicitors run out of superlatives when detailing the team's excellence, with one saying: "The clerking is exemplary. The best. I can't fault it to be honest, the client care ticks all of the boxes." The group is said to manage its barristers very well, with sources noting that "they know all the availability and have sensible discussions on fees, which makes the whole process tremendously easy." The team's commercial acumen is second to none, as demonstrated by the clerks' "commercial mindedness and understanding of the different requirements of its clients" and its "ability to match the style of barrister to the differing needs of commercial and private clients." Francis Taylor Building is best summed up, as it was by one interviewee, as "a very efficient and friendly set where the clerks are unerringly helpful and accommodating."

Henderson Chambers

A set conspicuous for the high-quality client service dispensed by its "top-class" clerking team. Interviewees speak of a "very sophisticated, top-notch operation" led by chief clerk John White. Instructing solicitors reveal that "John and the clerks at Henderson have always been excellent and without doubt go beyond expectations." Users of the set talk of the relaxed yet effective work style of the "highly personable team." Numerous sources echoed the sentiment that "the fact the clerks and barristers are very nice people to deal with is really valued by the client." A recurring theme of the commentary from our interviews was the reliability of the clerking team. One solicitor noted that "you don't get bumped from the diary for potentially sexier work," whilst another notes that "they will find the right-level person for the piece of work and, if it's urgent, they'll really work to find someone in the time you need." They are further praised along these lines for being "very helpful in terms of recommending people and giving price and fee estimates." One impressed source said: "They are just reliable. You never feel let down by them and they set out to deliver a high level of service."

7KBW

Instructing solicitors flock to 7KBW because of its winning "combination of excellent barristers and a first-rate clerking team." Senior clerk Bernie Hyatt is highlighted for his "very engaging" manner and facility for forging and maintaining strong relationships, which are underpinned by his organisational ability: "Bernie's the man to make a plan," says one solicitor. Also charged with running the team, senior clerk Greg Leyden is, according to one source, "one of the primary reasons I go to the set: he's very good at putting you with the right people." The culture of service they oversee is "always extremely friendly and commercially minded," as witnessed by reports that "the clerks are very responsive, very accommodating and adept at arranging listings and counsels' diaries." Another source adds: "I have never seen more supportive clerks in my life — whether it be responding to questions, requests for numbers or just queries about availability, they really seem to care." The combined impressions of the support offered by the team are perhaps best summarised by a client who said: "The clerks at 7KBW make such a difference: they provide a committed and excellent service and are a credit to the chambers." The set is further blessed in having practice development and marketing director Brian Lee on board. Lee is a man of great experience who is noted for his great market contacts and in-depth knowledge of the commercial law scene both domestically and overseas.

Old Square Chambers

Long-standing clients of the set remark on the "Rolls-Royce service" they have enjoyed seamlessly over the years. William Meade oversees the "top-notch clerking" here, and is "a proactive, forward-looking senior clerk who instils that approach in the rest of the team." Another source adds: "He is absolutely brilliant: if I have a certain type of case and client, I know whoever he recommends will be an excellent fit." A number of solicitors are grateful for the lengths the clerks will go to on their behalf, with one recalling: "We instructed them at the last minute a couple of times and they were efficient and swift in getting us a barrister." Another sums up the prevailing sentiment that "they can't do enough for you – they are very receptive and very supportive." As well as a tireless work ethic, sources also report that "the value for money is outstanding," and that the set is "very competitive and accommodating on rates." The overall impression revealed by an impressive array of positive references is one of a set which is joined-up and dedicated to client service at all levels, from barristers who "go the extra mile to ensure cases are properly prepared" to clerks who "organise the diaries effectively. If we need to shoehorn a conference in ASAP, you can be sure that it will be pencilled in."

4 Pump Court

Interviewees find the set "takes a modern approach to dealing with clients and providing the ever-evolving services which barristers these days are called upon to produce." The task of marshalling the set's powerful resources falls to chief executive Carolyn McCombe and senior clerks Stewart Gibbs and Carl Wall. Sources say "the clerking has always been good there: they return calls quickly, they make you feel very welcome and are very attentive." Instructing solicitors appreciate that "they never try and foist people on you; rather, they listen to what you're looking for on each case and try and match you to the appropriate counsel." Another source adds: "They have a great knack for finding absolutely the right person at the right price, and they understand the need to invest in long-term relationships with instructing solicitors." A common theme in interviews is that, given the talent housed by the set, "they're one of the most competitively priced chambers," and "are open to discussions about fees - they understand the world we live in." Another hallmark of the chambers is its "very collegiate" spirit; the barristers "operate as a very close-knit set and the silks often recommend juniors to us." One source neatly sums up: "The whole team is efficient in their communication, clear in their fee estimates and understand the need to act in unison with instructing solicitors to provide a seamless client service."

Ropewalk Chambers
Interviewees find the operation at Ropewalk "pleasingly modern and easy to deal with," while the clerks are praised for their "deep understanding of the market." The clerking team is led by Tony Hill, a man of great good cheer, who, according to one long-standing user of the set, "will always find a means by which he can get something sorted out, even if I'm asking for instructions at the last minute." He presides over a service culture that encourages "friendly and co-operative" interactions with solicitors and clients. Sources describe the clerks as "courteous, accommodating, absolutely lovely and anxious to please." "They ensure that if you can't get your counsel of choice, there is always someone there as a back-up who is as good as your first choice." Another source says: "They will always find out exactly what the case is about before recommending someone, and will always find someone that they know will do the job well." The set's fees, for a stable of extremely talented and accomplished barristers, are deemed to be very reasonable, and sources find the clerks are prepared to be flexible in budget discussions, leaving interviewees "satisfied with the value for money" on offer. The overwhelming impression is of a set where "the clerking is superb: they're always happy to help and will go the extra mile to do so."

Direct Access to the Bar

Since 2004, significant changes to the law have ensured that there is greater direct access to the Bar. This comes in two forms.

(A) Licensed Access
Individuals or organisations with expertise in specialist areas of the law are able to apply to the Bar Standards Board to be licensed to instruct barristers directly via the licensed access scheme. If successful, the licence holder is permitted to instruct any member of the Bar for advice, and in certain circumstances representation, in areas relating to the licence holder's field of expertise. Potential licence holders must go before the Access to the Bar Committee in order to satisfy certain criteria. Matters which will be looked at include the type of work the body wishes to refer directly to a barrister, its expertise or experience, its familiarity with any relevant area of the law and its ability to obtain and prepare information for the barrister.

(B) Public Access
Public access enables members of the public to directly instruct a barrister without having to first seek out a solicitor or other intermediary. Prior to the implementation of public access, clients were required to involve a solicitor or a recognised third party who would then instruct the barrister on the client's behalf.

The key benefits of public access for clients are financial; having removed the need to engage a solicitor, clients have public access to the Bar without the added legal expenditure of engaging a law firm.

Clients are able to make use of this new system across the full scope of work undertaken by barristers. Public access is designed principally for cases which are relatively straightforward in their nature, and clients are advised to carefully consider the differences between the services offered by barristers and solicitors before seeking to instruct a barrister through the scheme.

Barristers are expert advisers and advocates, and as such clients may use the scheme to garner specialist legal advice, to instruct a barrister to appear on their behalf in court, or to draft legal documents. A barrister is not permitted to issue legal proceedings upon a client's behalf, or to instruct an expert witness on a client's behalf.

Not all barristers are able to receive instructions through the public access scheme; in order to qualify they must have attended a public access training course which has been approved by the Bar Standards Board, except for in special instances where training might be waived.

Clients are also advised that even barristers who are fully qualified for the scheme are not obliged to accept public access instructions.

For clients seeking assistance from the Bar who cannot afford to pay, there are certain circumstances where financial support can be obtained from the Bar Pro Bono Unit, a registered charity which helps to find free legal assistance from volunteer barristers. The Bar Pro Bono Unit is able to assist clients in receiving both advice and representation.

In this year's publication, those barristers who are authorised to accept instructions under the public access scheme appear in our tables and under their set profiles with an 'A' appended to their names.

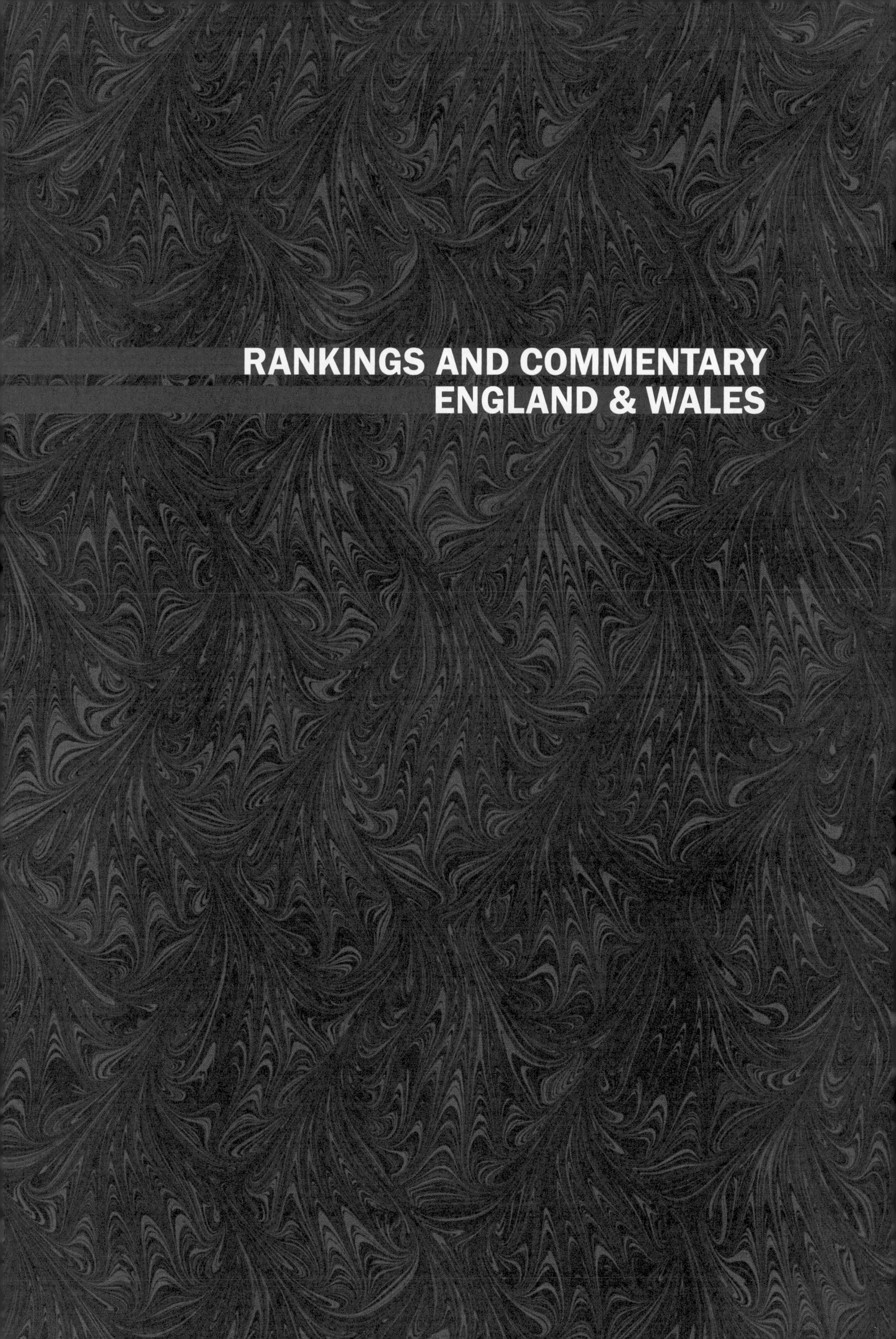
RANKINGS AND COMMENTARY
ENGLAND & WALES

Administrative & Public Law

Contents:

LONDON

Administrative & Public Law
Leading Sets
Band 1
Blackstone Chambers *
Band 2
Brick Court Chambers *
Doughty Street Chambers *
11KBW *
Matrix Chambers *
Monckton Chambers *
Band 3
1 Crown Office Row *
39 Essex Chambers *
Landmark Chambers *
* *Indicates set / individual with profile.*
[A] *direct access (see p.24).*
◊ *(ORL) = Other Ranked Lawyer.*
Alphabetical order within each band. Band 1 is highest.

Administrative & Public Law	
Senior Statesmen	
Senior Statesmen: distinguished older partners	**Lester of Herne Hill** Anthony *Blackstone Chambers*
Beloff Michael *Blackstone Chambers*	
Leading Silks	
Star individuals	**Maclean** Alan *Blackstone Chambers*
Chamberlain Martin *Brick Court Chambers* *	**Montgomery** Clare *Matrix Chambers* *
Eadie James *Blackstone Chambers*	**Morris** Fenella *39 Essex Chambers*
Fordham Michael *Blackstone Chambers*	**Phillips** Rory *3 Verulam Buildings (ORL)* ◊
Pannick David *Blackstone Chambers*	**Sheldon** Clive *11KBW* *
Rose Dinah *Blackstone Chambers*	**Steyn** Karen *11KBW* *
Band 1	**Stilitz** Daniel *11KBW* *
Anderson David *Brick Court Chambers*	**Wolfe** David *Matrix Chambers*
Carss-Frisk Monica *Blackstone Chambers*	**Band 4**
Crow Jonathan *4 Stone Buildings (ORL)* ◊ *	**Beer** Jason *5 Essex Court (ORL)* ◊ *
Drabble Richard *Landmark Chambers*	**Bourne** Charles *11KBW* [A] *
Emmerson Ben *Matrix Chambers*	**Bowen** Paul *Brick Court Chambers* *
Fitzgerald Edward *Doughty Street Chambers*	**Clayton** Richard *4-5 Gray's Inn Square (ORL)* ◊
Giffin Nigel *11KBW* *	**Coppel** Philip *Cornerstone Barristers (ORL)* ◊ [A]
Gordon Richard *Brick Court Chambers*	**Cory-Wright** Charles *39 Essex Chambers*
Havers Philip *1 Crown Office Row*	**Cragg** Stephen *Monckton Chambers*
Howell John *Blackstone Chambers*	**Foster** Alison *39 Essex Chambers* *
Kaufmann Phillippa *Matrix Chambers*	**Friedman** Danny *Matrix Chambers*
Lieven Nathalie *Landmark Chambers*	**Gallafent** Kate *Blackstone Chambers*
Perry David *6KBW College Hill (ORL)* ◊	**Giovannetti** Lisa *39 Essex Chambers*
Pleming Nigel *39 Essex Chambers*	**Guthrie** James *3 Hare Court (ORL)* ◊
Saini Pushpinder *Blackstone Chambers*	**Hall** Jonathan *6KBW College Hill (ORL)* ◊
Swift Jonathan *11KBW* *	**Harrison** Stephanie *Garden Court Chambers (ORL)* ◊
Band 2	**Knox** Peter *3 Hare Court (ORL)* ◊
Bailin Alex *Matrix Chambers* *	**Kovats** Steven *39 Essex Chambers*
Béar Charles *Fountain Court Chambers (ORL)* ◊ *	**Lock** David *Landmark Chambers* [A]
de la Mare Thomas *Blackstone Chambers*	**Monaghan** Karon *Matrix Chambers*
Goudie James *11KBW* *	**O'Connor** Andrew *Temple Garden Chambers (ORL)* ◊
Grodzinski Sam *Blackstone Chambers*	**O'Neill** Aidan *Matrix Chambers*
Herberg Javan *Blackstone Chambers*	**Pitt-Payne** Timothy *11KBW* *
Husain Raza *Matrix Chambers*	**Shaw** Mark *Blackstone Chambers*
Keith Hugo *3 Raymond Buildings Barristers (ORL)* ◊ *	**Simor** Jessica *Matrix Chambers*
Maurici James *Landmark Chambers*	**Smith** Kassie *Monckton Chambers*
McCullough Angus *1 Crown Office Row*	**Southey** Hugh *Matrix Chambers* *
Mountfield Helen *Matrix Chambers*	**Strachan** James *39 Essex Chambers*
Owen Tim *Matrix Chambers*	**Stratford** Jemima *Brick Court Chambers*
Richards Jenni *39 Essex Chambers* *	**Turner** Jon *Monckton Chambers*
Tam Robin *Temple Garden Chambers (ORL)* ◊	**Wise** Ian *Monckton Chambers* [A]
Ward Tim *Monckton Chambers* [A] *	**New Silks**
Westgate Martin *Doughty Street Chambers*	**Bretherton** Kerry *Tanfield Chambers (ORL)* ◊ [A] *
Band 3	**Busch** Lisa *Landmark Chambers*
Beard Daniel *Monckton Chambers*	**Facenna** Gerry *Monckton Chambers* [A] *
Coppel Jason *11KBW* *	**Fatima** Shaheed *Blackstone Chambers*
Demetriou Marie *Brick Court Chambers*	**Hyam** Jeremy *1 Crown Office Row*
Dutton Timothy *Fountain Court Chambers (ORL)* ◊ *	**Kennelly** Brian *Blackstone Chambers*
Elvin David *Landmark Chambers*	**Lester** Maya *Brick Court Chambers* *
Hermer Richard *Matrix Chambers*	**Proops** Anya *11KBW* *
Hoskins Mark *Brick Court Chambers* *	**Squires** Daniel *Matrix Chambers*
Johnson Jeremy *5 Essex Court (ORL)* ◊ *	**Wheeler** Marina *1 Crown Office Row*
Knafler Stephen *Landmark Chambers*	

Band 1

Blackstone Chambers

See profile on p.813

THE SET

Blackstone Chambers is widely recognised as a market leader in the field of administrative and public law. Clients highlight the "outstanding selection of advocates" on offer, explaining that there is "an incredible range of talent at all levels" and "unrivalled strength and depth." The team offers expertise in all facets of public and administrative law, with related strengths in commercial, human rights and EU law. Members receive instructions from the UK and foreign governments, local authorities, regulators and other public bodies subject to challenge, as well individual, NGO and commercial claimants seeking to overturn public body decision-making. Many of the highest-profile administrative and public law cases involve barristers from Blackstone Chambers. Recent highlights include Secretary of State for Work and Pensions v Hewstone, Bevan & Jeffrey, involving challenges to retrospective validation of sanctions imposed on individuals claiming jobseeker's allowance; and Transport for London v Uber London Limited, which determined the scope of the restriction on taximeters under the Private Hire (Vehicles) London Act 1998.

Client service: "The service is excellent. They always answer enquiries quickly and efficiently." "The clerking team is very helpful. No matter who picks up the phone, they are very good at answering your questions and putting you in touch with the right person." Senior clerk Gary Oliver leads the team.

SILKS

Michael Beloff QC Continues to be instructed in highly complex domestic and international public law challenges. He is particularly notable for his expertise in commercial and regulatory judicial reviews. **Strengths:** "Produces insightful analysis and compelling arguments." "Has a brilliant mind and is very good on his feet. Hugely respected and knowledgeable." **Recent work:** Advised London Metal Exchange on a change to regulatory rules and, in particular, consultation obligations with potential public law ramifications.

Anthony Lester of Herne Hill QC Distinguished advocate who has operated at the forefront of constitutional law and human rights for many decades. He continues to utilise public and administrative law proceedings to encourage legal reform on topics such as press freedom and abortion. **Strengths:** "An incredibly impressive practitioner."

James Eadie QC Continues to be the UK government's top choice to defend controversial legislation

Administrative & Public Law

Leading Juniors

Star individuals

- **Hickman** Tom *Blackstone Chambers*
- **Jaffey** Ben *Blackstone Chambers*

Band 1

- **Buley** Tim *Landmark Chambers*
- **Buttler** Chris *Matrix Chambers* [A]
- **Gallagher** Caoilfhionn *Doughty Street Chambers* [A] *
- **Straw** Adam *Doughty Street Chambers*

Band 2

- **Armstrong** Nicholas *Matrix Chambers*
- **Blundell** David *Landmark Chambers*
- **Callaghan** Catherine *Blackstone Chambers*
- **Dobbin** Clair *3 Raymond Buildings Barristers (ORL)* ◊ *
- **Grange** Kate *39 Essex Chambers*
- **Macdonald** Alison *Matrix Chambers* *
- **Moffett** Jonathan *11KBW* [A] *
- **Palmer** Robert *Monckton Chambers* [A]
- **Rogers** Amy *11KBW* *

Band 3

- **Auburn** Jonathan *11KBW* [A] *
- **Blake** Julian *11KBW* *
- **Broach** Steve *Monckton Chambers*
- **Bunting** Jude *Doughty Street Chambers*
- **Clement** Joanne *11KBW* *
- **Collier** Jane *Blackstone Chambers*
- **Grubeck** Nikolaus *Monckton Chambers*
- **Hannett** Sarah *Matrix Chambers* [A]
- **McClelland** James *Fountain Court Chambers (ORL)* ◊ *
- **Patel** Naina *Blackstone Chambers*
- **Patel** Parishil *39 Essex Chambers*
- **Ruck Keene** Alexander *39 Essex Chambers* *
- **Sharland** Andrew *11KBW* [A] *
- **Steele** Iain *Blackstone Chambers*
- **Suterwalla** Azeem *Monckton Chambers* *
- **Wakefield** Victoria *Brick Court Chambers*
- **Watson** Ben *3 Raymond Buildings Barristers (ORL)* ◊ [A] *

Band 4

- **Apps** Katherine *Littleton Chambers (ORL)* ◊ *
- **Banner** Charles *Landmark Chambers*
- **Birdling** Malcolm *Brick Court Chambers*
- **Boyd** Jessica *Blackstone Chambers*
- **Broadfoot** Samantha *Landmark Chambers*
- **Burton** Jamie *Doughty Street Chambers*
- **Butler-Cole** Victoria *39 Essex Chambers*
- **Davidson** Rosemary *6KBW College Hill (ORL)* ◊
- **Dixon** Emma *Blackstone Chambers*
- **Emmerson** Heather *11KBW* *
- **Harrop-Griffiths** Hilton *Field Court Chambers (ORL)* ◊
- **Jones** Oliver *Brick Court Chambers* *
- **Jones** Tristan *Blackstone Chambers*
- **Knight** Christopher *11KBW* *
- **Leventhal** Zoe *Landmark Chambers*
- **Love** Sarah *Brick Court Chambers*
- **Luh** Shu Shin *Garden Court Chambers (ORL)* ◊
- **McGurk** Brendan *Monckton Chambers*
- **Mussa** Hanif *Blackstone Chambers*
- **Rahman** Shaheen *1 Crown Office Row*
- **Richards** Tom *Blackstone Chambers*
- **Street** Amy *Serjeants' Inn Chambers (ORL)* ◊ *
- **Yeginsu** Can *4 New Square (ORL)* ◊ *

Up-and-coming individuals

- **Campbell** Fraser *Blackstone Chambers*
- **Morrison** Julianne *Monckton Chambers*

** Indicates individual with profile.*

[A] direct access (see p.24).

◊ (ORL) = Other Ranked Lawyer.

Alphabetical order within each band. Band 1 is highest.

and policy. His expertise extends across all aspects of administrative and public law, including national security, human rights and immigration. **Strengths:** "Phenomenal work rate and ability." "He absorbs facts at lightning speed. He is always strategic and forward-thinking." "He has good judgement and doesn't take bad points, which is why judges know they can rely on what he says." **Recent work:** Appeared for the UK government in Rahmatullah v Secretary of State for the Home Department, a case concerning alleged unlawful rendition and torture.

Michael Fordham QC Especially strong on administrative and public law cases which invoke novel points of law. He maintains a varied practice, acting in cases with a strong crossover with human rights, commercial and EU law. **Strengths:** "One of the most committed silks around. He immerses himself in the case and every detail of it. Incredibly compelling written and oral advocacy. He wins cases no one else would stand a chance at, and it makes a phenomenal difference to have him on public law cases." **Recent work:** Represented the Public Law Project in a judicial review challenging the lawfulness of the proposed residence test for civil legal aid on the grounds that it was ultra vires, disproportionate and discriminatory.

David Pannick QC Seasoned silk who handles high-level administrative and public law cases at both domestic and international levels. His broad experience includes constitutional, human rights, EU and commercial law. **Strengths:** "He is just the most impressive advocate. He has an ability to distil cases down to their core elements and present them in a way that almost writes the judge's judgment for them." "His expertise in public law is unparalleled and his advice is always clear, succinct and to the point." **Recent work:** Instructed by a claimant who challenged the fairness of his conviction for murder before the ECHR on the basis that his defence case was heard in camera.

Dinah Rose QC Champions difficult public law arguments on behalf of individual and commercial claimants. She is regularly instructed in significant challenges to legislation and government policy on the grounds of human rights and EU law. **Strengths:** "Exceptionally robust and forceful advocate. She exudes a real command of the materials and is exceptional at holding the court's attention." "A dauntless advocate who shows total commitment to a client's cause. She has exceptional public law expertise and provides clear, strategic advice." **Recent work:** Represented a journalist from the Guardian in a judicial review of the Attorney General's decision to override a ruling of the Upper Tribunal that required the publication of letters written by Prince Charles to government ministers.

Monica Carss-Frisk QC Typically advocates on behalf of commercial clients seeking to challenge regulatory decisions including those relating to competition and financial services law. Her expertise in immigration and human rights law complements her robust practice. **Strengths:** "Outstanding judgement and ability to think on her feet, with an excellent grasp of detail." "She's been very impressive all around, as you would expect from such an experienced QC. She is very good at drafting submissions and her style of advocacy is on point and persuasive without being aggressive or flowery. She gets to the heart of key issues." **Recent work:** Represented Uber in a claim for declaratory relief to determine whether private hire vehicles registered with Uber were equipped with a 'taximeter' for the purposes of Section 11 of the Private Hire (Vehicles) London Act 1998.

John Howell QC Highly regarded for his depth of knowledge and wealth of experience. His enviable practice involves a notable focus on claims involving local government, procurement and environmental law. **Strengths:** "He is extremely intelligent and has an immense ability to carry the court. His general air of authority is unlike anyone else: he is on a plane above others." "He is bright, intellectual, thorough and turns things around very quickly." **Recent work:** Successfully represented EnergySolutions in an appeal against the Nuclear Decommissioning Authority. The matter considered whether or not an unsuccessful bidder to a public contract retains the right to damages if no proceedings are issued during the standstill period.

Pushpinder Saini QC Noted for his extensive knowledge of commercial and regulatory judicial review. He represents claimants and defendants in public law cases before the administrative, appellate and European courts. **Strengths:** "An exceptionally talented counsel. He is extremely bright, decisive and gets to the heart of issues quickly. He is also enjoyable to work with." **Recent work:** Acted for the SFO in a £300 million claim brought by the Tchenguiz brothers for misfeasance in respect of false allegations of financial misconduct and fraud alongside breach of the Human Rights Act 1998.

Thomas de la Mare QC Frequently involved in high-profile challenges to primary and secondary legislation. His notably broad expertise includes public law cases which overlap with commercial, human rights and EU law. **Strengths:** "Combines a comprehensive grasp of the law with an easy, friendly manner." "Mind-blowing performance which is impressive to watch. He wows the court and comes up with clever ways of putting his arguments across." "Incredibly bright and creative. He is your man for tricky cases where you want to explore novel possibilities." **Recent work:** Acted for a group of claimants and the Criminal Bar Association in a challenge against the legality of the Quality Assurance Scheme for Advocates. The matter turned on the proper approach to intensity of review under the EU proportionality test.

Sam Grodzinski QC His impressively broad administrative and public law expertise includes commercial judicial reviews and human rights claims. Recent mandates include challenges against decisions of HMRC and the police. **Strengths:** "He's succinct, clear in arguments, intellectually fierce and very charming with clients and judges." "Exceptional in his ability to deal with questions from the Bench." **Recent work:** Acted for Bernie Ecclestone in his judicial review claim against HMRC's decision to assess him for over £1 billion tax. The matter concerned his alleged control over offshore trusts.

Javan Herberg QC Particularly well placed to handle administrative and public law cases that involve financial services regulation. He represents commercial clients, regulators and other public bodies in complex judicial reviews. **Strengths:** "Very knowledgeable and switched on, particularly financial services judicial review-related work. Very easy to work with and respected by clients." "His advocacy is excellent and compelling." **Recent work:** Acted for NATS on the judicial review of the alleged failure of CAA to comply with consultation obligations in respect of airspace changes.

Alan Maclean QC Notable emphasis on judicial reviews that arise in the context of professional discipline. He regularly represents claimants and defendants in administrative and public law proceedings. **Strengths:** "Razor sharp and gets to grips with legislative or procedural matters extremely quickly." "He is intellectually impressive, inquisitive, knowledgeable, client-focused and clear in his advice. He is also very easy to deal with, pragmatic and personable." **Recent work:** Acted for the Royal Institute of Chartered Surveyors in successfully resisting a judicial review claim based on alleged apparent bias.

Kate Gallafent QC Represents government departments, regulators and other public bodies in judicial review proceedings. Her notably broad expertise includes a particular emphasis on data protection and the right to privacy under Article 8 of the ECHR. **Strengths:** "Her teamwork and supportive nature really stand out. She is very user-friendly and comes up with pragmatic solutions." "Not afraid to stand up to senior judges and excellent on her research." **Recent work:** Appeared for Sport England in a challenge to its adoption of a policy requiring a sport to consist of a physical activity. The matter centred on the eligibility of so-called "mind sports" such as bridge and chess.

Mark Shaw QC Predominantly defends important challenges to regulatory policies and disciplinary decisions in the healthcare sector. He also advises public bodies on regulatory reform and potential grounds for challenge. **Strengths:** "Down-to-earth, professional advice. He is user-friendly, bright and able to analyse complex situations with ease." **Recent work:** Instructed by the GMC to resist a judicial review challenge to the disclosure of expert reports to complainants in medical disciplinary cases under domestic statute, common law and Article 8 of ECHR.

Shaheed Fatima QC Possesses remarkable expertise in administrative and public law, including claims pursued under human rights and international law. She also advises public bodies on the validity and implications of legislative reform. **Strengths:** "She really knows her stuff and is an outstanding advocate. She is one of the most impressive barristers of her call anywhere. An absolute star." "Her poise and clarity of submission really stand out." **Recent work:** Instructed by a group of Afghan nationals detained at Camp Bastion in Afghanistan in a challenge against the lawfulness of their detention on the grounds of international human rights and humanitarian law.

Brian Kennelly QC Acclaimed advocate who focuses on administrative and public law cases arising in the context of telecommunications, competition and other spheres of EU regulation. He is also experienced in litigation involving sanctions imposed by the EU. **Strengths:** "He has a creative approach as well as breadth of analysis." "A wonderfully technical lawyer." **Recent work:** Defended Telecommunications Regulatory Commission BVI against a challenge to a finding of an anti-competitive margin squeeze.

JUNIORS

Tom Hickman Immensely knowledgeable in administrative and public law. He acts in significant challenges to legislation and regulatory decisions, appearing on behalf of claimants, defendants and interveners. **Strengths:** "A brilliant mind, academically and strategically. He is very good to bounce ideas off and is second to none for public law." "His advice is excellent and commercially focused. He is also very user-friendly." **Recent work:** Successfully obtained a declaration of incompatibility of the Jobseekers Act 2013 which retrospectively overruled a Court of Appeal decision holding that benefits sanctions had been unlawfully imposed on benefits claimants.

Ben Jaffey Superb advocate who frequently appears unled at first instance and appellate proceedings. His broad public and administrative law expertise includes human rights, national security and data protection cases. **Strengths:** "An incredibly smart and wonderful advocate with whom it is always a total joy to work." **Recent work:** Successfully acted for ClientEarth in the Supreme Court on an EU law challenge to the UK's failure to meet air quality standards in London and other major urban areas.

Catherine Callaghan Defends central government departments and regulators in a wide range of judicial reviews including challenges to legislation and policy. She receives particular praise for her strategic approach to litigation. **Strengths:** "An excellent balance of legal rigour with pragmatism and client-accessible advice." "Very thoughtful and good at explaining issues to clients who are unfamiliar with the law." **Recent work:** Acted for the Human Fertilisation and Embryology Authority in defence of a high-profile judicial review challenge. The case centred on the regulator's refusal to authorise export of the claimant's deceased daughter's frozen eggs for fertility treatment in the USA.

Jane Collier Involved in significant administrative and public law cases on behalf of clients in the public sector, including regulators and local authorities. She defends challenges to procurement, competition, freedom of information and environmental decisions. **Strengths:** "A real team player who gets right into the detail. A valuable asset to any team and a pleasure to work with." "Absolutely fantastic. She never leaves any stone unturned. She is thorough, diligent and a real pleasure to work with." **Recent work:** Acted as junior counsel for the London Borough of Enfield in a judicial review challenge to a decision concerning procurement of a rail franchise.

Naina Patel Maintains a varied administrative and public law practice which involves significant challenges to primary and secondary legislation as well as regulatory appeals. She has vast experience of representing applicants, defendants and interveners in judicial reviews. **Strengths:** "Great written work, she is incredibly responsive and imaginative in her approach." "Very diligent and bright." **Recent work:** Acted for the Public Law Project in a challenge to the proposed residence test for civil legal aid on the grounds that the test was ultra vires and discriminatory.

Iain Steele His wide-ranging law practice encompasses claims pursued under EU, human rights and constitutional law. He represents claimants and defendants before the administrative and appellate courts. **Strengths:** "He has a very deep knowledge of public law. He really understands the area very well." "His drafting is extremely clear and persuasive and he is excellent with clients." "Iain gets to grips with the issues quickly. He works very hard and is superb under pressure." **Recent work:** Represented two prominent MPs in a judicial review challenge to controversial new powers requiring retention of communications data by telecommunications operators under the Data Retention and Investigatory Powers Act 2014.

Jessica Boyd Advocates on behalf of clients in the private, public and charities sectors. She has particular expertise in commercial and regulatory judicial reviews including claims involving EU and competition law. **Strengths:** "Very user-friendly and gets to grips with the detail incredibly quickly." **Recent work:** Acted as sole counsel for the claimant in a judicial review of the Liverpool CCG's decision to continue to commission homeopathy.

Emma Dixon Considerable expertise in public and administrative law challenges involving charities, human rights and environmental law. She receives instructions from NGOs, regulators and individuals. **Strengths:** "Extremely bright, has good clarity of thought, is robust when she needs to be and is a good team player." "Her advice is always clear and she rapidly gets up to speed in new scenarios." **Recent work:** Appeared in the Supreme Court and in the ECJ in a landmark air pollution case. Successfully argued for a declaration that the UK is in breach of EU air quality limits for nitrogen dioxide.

Tristan Jones Represents claimants and respondents in judicial review proceedings challenging primary and secondary legislation. He is also adept in claims against decisions of regulators and other public bodies. **Strengths:** "Very impressive. Sharp, clever and a clear advocacy style." "Excellent legal analysis and written work." "A real eye for detail in very complex cases." "His advice is progressive and always focuses on advancing the client's case." **Recent work:** Represented Blue Bio Pharmaceuticals in a challenge to an MHRA decision on whether products are medicinal.

Hanif Mussa Represents private corporations and public bodies, including government departments, in novel administrative law challenges. He has notable experience of appearing before the first instance, appellate and EU courts. **Strengths:** "Scarily intelligent, and produces fantastic thinking and drafting." "Very available, useful and personable with great technical ability." **Recent work:** Acted for the Secretary of State for Justice in successfully defending a judicial review brought by a group of prisoners arguing that the lack of rehabilitative assistance was a breach of their rights under Article 5(1) ECHR.

Tom Richards Handles public and administrative law claims on behalf of clients in the UK and abroad. His wide-ranging practice includes fairness, ultra vires and proportionality challenges to public body decisions. **Strengths:** "Very good drafting and legal analysis." **Recent work:** Appeared before the Supreme Court on behalf of members of the Criminal Bar in a challenge to the legality of the Legal Services Board's adoption of the Quality Assurance Scheme for Advocates.

Fraser Campbell Regularly instructed in significant judicial reviews affecting the energy sector. He also handles judicial reviews challenging regulatory decisions involving pharmaceutical and healthcare professionals. **Strengths:** "Extremely thorough, easy to work with, very good at drafting and extremely economic, which clients appreciate." "Thinks outside the box and comes up with ideas that aren't immediately obvious." **Recent work:** Represented Scottish and Southern Energy in a judicial review challenging the Gas and Electricity Markets Authority's reforms to electricity transmission charging. It was posited that the reforms were discriminatory towards conventional electricity generators in favour of renewable generators.

Band 2

Brick Court Chambers

See profile on p.816

THE SET

Brick Court Chambers is a strong choice for public and administrative law cases involving an overlap with EU and commercial law. Recently, several members were involved in challenges against the UK's regulations requiring plain packaging for cigarettes. Other highlights include Uber v Transport for London, Holmcroft v KPMG and Bank Mellat v HM Treasury. Members act on behalf of claimants and defendants in challenges to regulatory and legislative provisions. The set is also increasingly receiving instructions in public law cases concerning social justice and human rights. Clients comment that "they've got an impressively deep bench and a broad range of good players, so they are a good port of call for big disputes."

Client service: "Very organised, efficient and helpful. A flawless operation overall." "Clerking service is very friendly, very hands-on and very good." The team is led by senior clerks Julian Hawes and Ian Moyler.

SILKS

Martin Chamberlain QC (see p.614) Hugely respected silk who receives particular praise for his expansive knowledge and formidable intellect. He is regularly instructed by claimants, defendants and interveners to handle cases of significant importance in the context of national security and human rights law. **Strengths:** "Very able intellectually but also strategically. He knows how to pull the rug out from the other side's feet." "An impressive and persuasive advocate. Great assurance, intelligence and the ability to persuade very effectively in both oral and written submissions." **Recent work:** Represented the Lord Chancellor in the Divisional Court and Court of Appeal, successfully defending a challenge to the Lord Chancellor's decision to significantly reduce the number of criminal legal aid contracts.

David Anderson QC Exceedingly strong on public law challenges pursued under EU law. In his role as Independent Reviewer of Terrorism Legislation, he has been producing influential reports on the efficacy of anti-terrorism acts. **Strengths:** "Hugely assured. Having him as your advocate is like being driven in a Rolls-Royce Silver Shadow." "He is a very clear advocate. Judges will adopt what he says into their judgments." "Combines adept client-handling skills with an exceptionally strong strategic instinct. A delight to work with." **Recent work:** Represented Japan Tobacco International in a very high-profile challenge to the legality of plain packaging for cigarettes, which the group of claimants argued was a deprivation of their intellectual property rights, for which they should be compensated under the ECHR, the EU Charter of Fundamental Rights and the common law.

Richard Gordon QC Accomplished silk who operates at the forefront of administrative and constitutional law. He is particularly proficient at public law claims which overlap with EU law. **Strengths:** "Extremely wide knowledge in this field. Provides innovative and flexible advice on complex legal issues at very short notice. Very easy to work with." "Hugely experienced, great manner and also very commercially astute." **Recent work:** Acting for 23 local authorities in Wales in a major judicial review challenge brought against Welsh Local Health Boards over health and social care financing of registered nurses.

Marie Demetriou QC Commands great respect for her expertise in public law cases involving provisions of EU law. She also handles cases concerning human rights, data protection, immigration and asylum and public international law, **Strengths:** "Really strong on her feet. She has real weight and presence in court. She can hold her own against unpleasant and aggressive opponents and is also really good with the client. A pleasure to deal with." "A deep understanding and analytically bright. She is utterly charming and quickly establishes a rapport with both judges and clients." **Recent work:** Leading counsel for Philip Morris in a high-profile challenge to the UK's plain packaging regulations which will mandate uniform packaging for all cigarettes and preclude tobacco companies from using any trade marks.

Mark Hoskins QC (see p.675) Handles judicial reviews in the commercial and regulatory spheres. He is frequently instructed to defend legislative and regulatory provisions in litigation up to the Supreme Court. **Strengths:** "Extremely user-friendly and easily reachable for consultations. He is extremely sharp, instantly sees the key arguments and has an admirably clear and crisp style of drafting." **Recent work:** Represented the Hong Kong Communications Authority in a judicial review brought by Television Broadcasts Limited challenging a censure concerning its employment contract practices.

Paul Bowen QC (see p.600) Handles judicial reviews that involve the application of human rights law to the criminal justice system. He increasingly handles public law claims in the commercial and financial services spheres. **Strengths:** "A phenomenal grasp of his area of law. In court, his submissions are carefully organised and intelligently presented with an eye to the tribunal and the difficult subject matter he is often dealing with." "A really creative lawyer and a great advocate. He is dynamic and pioneering." **Recent work:** Acted for the Cayman Islands Health Services Authority in considering the constitutionality of a statutory defence against clinical negligence proceedings following the coming into force of the new Cayman Islands Constitution.

Jemima Stratford QC Counsels clients in public and administrative law challenges pursued under EU law. She has particular expertise in claims involving the pharmaceutical and energy sectors. **Strengths:** "She is extremely hard-working and never misses deadlines. She is always well prepared for any case and her advice is very measured and thorough." **Recent work:** Advised Ofgem on a claim concerning funding of a renewable energy plant, which raised issues of statutory construction and EU state aid law.

Maya Lester QC (see p.700) Brings a deep expertise in EU and human rights law to domestic and international public law proceedings. She receives instructions from individuals, NGOs and public bodies. **Strengths:** "Able to turn out high-quality work in a limited time. Her brain works at a different speed. She is delightfully modest and easy to work with and has a total grasp of the law." "She is really good with clients, gives measured, considered advice, and comes across as the voice of reason in court." **Recent work:** Represented a group of Chagossians in a judicial review of the Foreign and Commonwealth Office's (FCO) decision to impose a Marine Protection Zone around the Chagos Islands, which involved a novel argument under EU law considering the meaning of the provisions of the EC Treaty on overseas territories.

JUNIORS

Victoria Wakefield Represents corporations, NGOs and individuals challenging legislation and regulatory decisions. She is particularly adept at public law cases with a significant EU law overlap. **Strengths:** "Combines common sense, intellectual rigour and a real willingness to roll up her sleeves." "A really good written style. Clear, communicative and enthusiastic. Very approachable and easy to work with." **Recent work:** Represented Japan Tobacco International in a challenge to the legality of the plain packaging requirement for cigarettes, alleging deprivation of the claimants' intellectual property rights.

Malcolm Birdling Handles a broad range of public and administrative law challenges arising in the context of commercial and human rights law. He advocates for claimants and defendants in judicial reviews. **Strengths:** "Has a very good legal mind and is extremely easy to get along with. He is also particularly well informed. He is always easy to reach and prompt with his responses." **Recent work:** Instructed as junior counsel for the defendants in six joined cases concerning the circumstances in which legal aid must be made available in the UK. The areas considered included immigration cases, matters involving victims of trafficking and the issues surrounding applications for refugee family reunion.

Oliver Jones (see p.686) Instructed by regulators, government departments and other public bodies to defend significant public law challenges, often involving EU law. He has recently handled cases concerning taxation, competition, transportation and local government law. **Strengths:** "Very bright and hands-on. Good at getting up to speed with complex facts quickly, and then being able to give sensible advice on complicated issues. Also approachable and calm in a crisis." "A very thorough junior, absolutely up to speed on EU and public law issues, who has excellent judgement as to what will work with a court. He is reliable, dependable, drafts very nicely and gets the job done." **Recent work:** Represented the CMA in an appeal to the Supreme Court relating to the scope of the CMA's powers to regulate mergers following Eurotunnel's acquisition of SeaFrance's assets.

Sarah Love Her broad public and administrative law expertise ranges from commercial to regulatory issues. She represents claimants and defendants in important challenges to legislation and public body decisions. **Recent work:** Acted for the Department of Health in a challenge to its power to share information with the Home Office regarding unpaid NHS debts.

Doughty Street Chambers

See profile on p.828

THE SET

Doughty Street Chambers remains dedicated to representing marginalised claimants in public and administrative law proceedings. Members also receive instructions from NGOs seeking to intervene in judicial reviews. The set is especially noted for its expertise in public law claims which invoke human rights law, particularly in the context of welfare reform and criminal justice. Its commitment to social justice has earned its members the reputation of being "leading defenders of human rights." Recently, its highly skilled advocates have

been leading high-profile challenges against the government's imposition of a bedroom tax and cap on welfare benefits. Clients enthuse that the set "offers a range of skills, expertise and high-calibre counsel across the board."
Client service: Led by chief executive Mark Dembovsky, the clerks are "always extremely effective. They are always keen to help and go out of their way to assist us." "The clerks are very friendly and approachable."

SILKS
Edward Fitzgerald QC Pre-eminent silk with vast experience in domestic and international public law. He is recommended particularly for cases involving human rights, criminal and constitutional law. **Strengths:** "He has a great command of the subject matter and is a very creative lawyer. He not only has a mastery of the law and facts, but is also able to bring novel ideas to the table." "His advocacy in public law matters commands the attention of the court. He demonstrates a real commitment to the work he does." **Recent work:** Represented Louis Oliver Bancoult in a claim to reopen the case against his removal from the Chagos Islands following a decision by the FCO to impose a Marine Protection Zone around the islands.

Martin Westgate QC Typically acts for individual claimants and NGOs seeking to challenge legislation and public body decisions. He is particularly strong in cases involving welfare cuts and social justice. **Strengths:** "A tenacious advocate who is intelligent and prepared to stand up to the court." "Great attention to detail and thorough in his analysis. Inspires a lot of confidence." **Recent work:** Successfully challenged a decision of the Lord Chancellor to remove guaranteed legal aid funding in judicial review cases where the court has not granted permission.

JUNIORS
Caoilfhionn Gallagher (see p.649) Has an established reputation as one of the top juniors at the Public Law Bar. She is instructed to represent claimants in England and Northern Ireland on high-profile challenges to legislation and government policy. **Strengths:** "Absolutely superb and incredibly fluent. She was completely on top of the brief, knew all of the right buttons to press with the judge and showed real tenacity." "A good combination of being passionate about what she is doing but also hard-working and knowledgeable. She is the full house." "Incredibly bright, intelligent and very good at tactics. Her writing is superb. She is on the ball, organised and detailed. Just totally easy to work with." **Recent work:** Represented the claimants in a test case which considered whether the Secretary of State for Work and Pensions had unlawfully discriminated against disabled people by failing to exempt their unpaid full-time carers from the benefit cap.

Adam Straw Popular choice for claimants and interveners in public law challenges arising in the context of national security, criminal law and immigration detention proceedings. He has particular expertise in public law cases that overlap with human rights law. **Strengths:** "A very impressive junior lawyer who is great with clients. He comes up with extremely original and creative legal arguments." "Outstanding intellect and work ethic." "Very good at the tactical side of a case. He will figure out all the directions a case can take." **Recent work:** Represented the interveners, The Pat Finucane Centre and Rights Watch UK, in a claim considering the government's duties to investigate historic deaths and those taking place abroad, under Article 2 ECHR and under domestic public law.

Jude Bunting Excellent track record of successfully challenging legislation, policy and decisions of public bodies. His expertise encompasses human rights, data protection and prison law. **Strengths:** "Very intelligent and exceptionally hard-working. He takes on novel cases which push at the boundaries of the law." "One of the most approachable counsel to work with. Extremely diligent and effective." "Manages to combine determination with consideration." **Recent work:** Acted for two Green Party politicians in a public law challenge to the policy of the Security Services regarding the surveillance of correspondence sent and received by members of the Houses of Parliament.

Jamie Burton Involved in significant challenges to local authority decisions on the provision of public services and welfare benefits. He has particular expertise in claims involving social housing and community care. **Strengths:** "A phenomenal advocate who is exceptionally bright and very practical." "He has an almost encyclopaedic knowledge, not only of domestic law but also of the EHRC governing this area. He is extremely thorough in his research and is adept at advancing and deflecting highly technical arguments." "Very knowledgeable, exceptionally hard-working and determined, with excellent judgement." **Recent work:** Represented the appellant in a challenge against the Royal Borough of Kensington and Chelsea in regard to the intensity of review to be applied by the court when considering decisions regarding welfare benefits.

11KBW
See profile on p.867

THE SET
11KBW is renowned for its public sector offering, and represents local authorities, government departments and other public bodies in significant public and administrative law cases before the administrative and appellate courts. Members also act for individuals, corporates and NGOs seeking to challenge public body decisions. The set's broad public law expertise includes notable strength in claims involving education, community care, procurement and human rights law. Recently, individuals from the set have been involved in a series of high-profile challenges to the Lord Chancellor's changes to legal aid. Clients comment that 11KBW offers "a very good range of expertise" and "a guarantee of high quality."
Client service: Led by senior clerks Lucy Barbet and Mark Dann, the clerking team is "amazing and makes clients' lives easier." "The clerks are very helpful and attentive, from the most senior to junior clerks. They remember you as a client, are mindful of your needs, and are very good at communicating with you."

SILKS
Nigel Giffin QC (see p.653) Instructed by local authorities and other public bodies in a wide range of contentious and non-contentious public law matters. He is an expert in education, human rights and public procurement cases. **Strengths:** "Very impressive. He gets right to the heart of an issue straight away. Very clear advice. Very intelligent." "Offers sage advice and is someone who is very willing to bring new ideas." **Recent work:** Represented the Broads Authority in a judicial review challenging the legality of describing the Norfolk and Suffolk Broads as a 'national park' for the purposes of encouraging tourism.

Jonathan Swift QC (see p.777) Revered for his depth of knowledge in administrative and public law. He has extensive experience of advocating for government departments and other public bodies in judicial reviews, and has a notable emphasis on claims involving national security, sanctions, human rights and constitutional law. **Strengths:** "High quality of advocacy and a real presence in court." "A consummate barrister. Exceedingly good on the law and very able in his submissions." "Really good at getting through an awful lot of detail and translating it into something cogent and easy to follow." **Recent work:** Acted in Youssef v Secretary of State for Foreign and Commonwealth Affairs in defence of the Foreign Secretary's decision to ask the UN Security Council and the European Council to recognise the claimant as a terrorist and to apply financial sanctions to him. The claimant contended that the decision was made based on information obtained by torture.

James Goudie QC (see p.657) Regularly represents local authorities in judicial review proceedings involving housing, social welfare and state aid. He is also adept at public law claims pursued under human rights law. **Strengths:** "He is very brief, concise, very authoritative and very clear. When you deal with him, you listen more than you talk because he knows his stuff so well. If you want clarity and authority, he is the man to go to." "Courts love him. He has everything at his fingertips." **Recent work:** Acted for Warwickshire County Council in rolled-up judicial review proceedings in which the council was accused of failure to consult properly, or at all, on proposed cuts to funding for social care services for disabled children.

Jason Coppel QC (see p.624) Particularly strong in challenges involving public procurement, human rights and data protection. He is instructed by central and local government, NGOs and individual claimants. **Strengths:** "Laser-like precision and clear, commercial legal advice. Inspires real confidence." "His advocacy is extremely clear and powerful." "Very robust in his position, which is reassuring to clients." **Recent work:** Appeared on behalf of the claimant NGO in R (Gulf Centre for Human Rights) v Prime Minister, a judicial review challenging amendments to the Ministerial Code removing ministers' obligations to comply with international law and uphold the administration of justice.

Clive Sheldon QC (see p.763) Instructed by central and local government clients in public and administrative law proceedings. His expertise is wide-ranging and includes welfare, licensing, procurement and education. He is especially well versed in arguments based on discrimination. **Strengths:** "Robust and persuasive in both oral and written submissions. Very collegiate approach and good with the client." "An easy guy to work with. He is adaptable, quick and flexible. He makes himself available and gives pragmatic advice." **Recent work:** Represented the Secretary of State for Transport in a challenge to rail franchise arrangements for East Anglia. The London Borough of Enfield had sought to unlock a multibillion-pound development by introducing a more frequent service to Angel Road Station.

Karen Steyn QC (see p.773) Has notable strength in administrative and public law claims involving national security and international relations. She is frequently instructed by government departments to defend important challenges. **Strengths:** "A phenomenally hard-working, astonishingly strong lawyer who writes exceptionally well. She's a fantastic team player who is well liked by clients and solicitors alike." "She can cover academic matters in a practical way." **Recent work:** Appeared on behalf of the UK government in Al-Waheed v Ministry of Defence, a case in which the claimant contended that his detention during the armed conflict in Iraq was in breach of Article 5 of the ECHR.

Daniel Stilitz QC (see p.773) Established silk adept at managing a broad range of administrative and public law cases on behalf of claimants and defendants. Recent mandates include challenges to decisions on housing, healthcare, agriculture and insurance. **Strengths:** "Very responsive, pragmatic and quick to identify key issues." "Calm under pressure and very comprehensive." **Recent work:** Acted for NHS England in Whythenshawe Special Ltd v NHS CCGs & Others, intervening as an interested party in the judicial review challenge to hospital reorganisation in Greater Manchester.

Charles Bourne QC (see p.600) Acts in complex judicial reviews on behalf of central and local government. Also advises public bodies on the lawfulness of changes to service delivery models and consultation requirements. **Strengths:** "He is a very good advocate and he is very clear and measured." **Recent work:** Resisted a judicial review challenge brought by a transgender claimant to the Department of Work and Pensions' system of holding pension and benefits history, including personal details.

Timothy Pitt-Payne QC (see p.739) Focuses his public law prowess on cases that involve information law. He frequently appears in judicial reviews considering the disclosure of data under the Freedom of Information (FOI) Act 2000 and the Environmental Information Regulations 2004. **Strengths:** "Phenomenally clever." "Excellent client service." **Recent work:** Represented the Information Commissioner in a widely publicised case about whether letters between the Prince of Wales and government departments should be disclosed under FOI legislation.

Anya Proops QC (see p.744) Focuses her administrative and public law practice on cases involving information law. She acts for claimants, defendants and the Information Commissioner in judicial review challenges to the scope and application of data protection legislation. **Strengths:** "A determined, strong advocate." **Recent work:** Represented the Commissioner of Police for the Metropolis in a challenge to a decision made by the president of the Family Court Division. The ruling had ordered disclosure of certain DNA profiles held by the Met Police for use in establishing paternity in family law proceedings.

JUNIORS

Jonathan Moffett (see p.720) Frequently entrusted with administrative and public law instructions by the UK and Welsh governments as well as other public bodies. His substantive expertise encompasses environmental, human rights, education and local government law. **Strengths:** "Continues to impress with his encyclopaedic knowledge of the law and his ability to set out complex legal matters with real clarity and authority. His commitment to his client's cause is sensational and his work ethic second to none." **Recent work:** Acted for the Welsh government in a challenge brought by a consortium of environmental organisations against proposals to build a new motorway to the south of Newport in order to relieve congestion problems on the M4.

Amy Rogers (see p.754) Brings her significant administrative and public law expertise to large commercial disputes. She is also proficient at handling procurement and legislative challenges on behalf of claimants and respondents. **Strengths:** "Very, very bright and very commercial." "Incredibly hard-working, tremendous judgement. She knows the law inside out and is great to work with." **Recent work:** Continues to represent the Iranian commercial bank Bank Mellat in a long-running challenge to the sanctions imposed against it by HM Treasury. The matter involves a multibillion-pound human rights damages claim.

Jonathan Auburn (see p.586) Undertakes important test cases challenging legislation, government policy and public body decision-making. He is instructed by central government departments and local authorities as well as claimants. **Strengths:** "He has a fantastic knowledge of public law." "Offers pragmatic, client-friendly advice." "Very approachable and flexible in the way that he works and has a very good understanding of clients' needs." **Recent work:** Represented the UK government in a judicial review challenging the compatibility of UK laws on detention of foreign criminals with EU law on freedom of movement.

Julian Blake (see p.597) Represents the UK government in judicial reviews contesting controversial acts of the state in the context of national security. He is also involved in significant public international law cases including challenges against the imposition of financial sanctions. **Strengths:** "Really personable, really intelligent. Clear, user-friendly advice. He makes himself part of the team." "Clients just love him. He works hard for them and understands their concerns and business. Lay clients also appreciate him because he is able to explain complex areas of law in an accessible manner." **Recent work:** Appeared for the Secretary of State for the Home Department in a judicial review pursued by David Miranda challenging his detention at Heathrow Airport, concerning Article 10 ECHR and whether a person carrying journalistic material can fall within the definition of a terrorist as defined in the Terrorism Act 2000.

Joanne Clement (see p.619) Handles a broad range of administrative and public law disputes before the Administrative, Appeal and Supreme Courts. Recent mandates include bringing and defending challenges to decisions about access to healthcare, access to justice, allocation of public funds and the provision of public services. **Strengths:** "She is very experienced in judicial review, which comes across in the strategic advice she provides." "Combines sound advice with first-rate advocacy skills." "Bright, proactive, organised and a pleasure to work with." **Recent work:** Acted for the Welsh government in a challenge considering the duties of NHS bodies to assess the needs of individuals in their area and to provide treatment locally.

Andrew Sharland (see p.762) Acts in complex judicial reviews challenging the legislation and decisions of local and central government. He is an expert in human rights and equality cases. **Strengths:** "Has an excellent legal brain and excellent knowledge of the area. He is tactically very good and punchy in court when he needs to be." "Pragmatic approach and great understanding of the issues." **Recent work:** Acted for Leicester City Council in a challenge to the decision-making process concerning where Richard III should be buried. The claimants, distant relatives of Richard III, argued that the lack of consultation as to the burial site infringed their Article 8 ECHR rights.

Heather Emmerson (see p.641) Predominantly instructed by central and local government as well as NHS bodies to defend controversial decisions and legislation. She appears in judicial reviews and human rights claims before the domestic courts and the ECHR. **Strengths:** "She is incredibly bright and combines that with being practical and user-friendly." **Recent work:** Served as counsel to the FCO in a series of claims brought before the ECHR challenging the current legislative scheme for police retaining DNA information, photographs of suspects in custody and criminal records.

Christopher Knight (see p.692) Appears in administrative and public law cases on behalf of claimants, defendants and interveners. Recent mandates encompass procurement, housing, human rights, public misconduct and local government law. **Strengths:** "Phenomenally clever but also able to articulate it well." "Very approachable and very thorough. He is always very responsive, and turns around instructions quickly but thoroughly. He is willing to help at a moment's notice." **Recent work:** Instructed by the London Criminal Courts Solicitors' Association and the Criminal Law Solicitors' Association to challenge a decision of the Lord Chancellor's which would reduce the number of criminal legal aid duty solicitor contracts being tendered.

Matrix Chambers

See profile on p.876

THE SET

Matrix Chambers houses "an impressive array of barristers" specialising in public and administrative law. Clients report that "in terms of the quality of counsel, you know that anyone they give you will be exceptional." Its broad offering includes a notable emphasis on public international law and claims which derive from criminal law proceedings. Other significant areas of expertise include commercial, EU and human rights law. Members have recently been involved in high-profile challenges to the Lord Chancellor's reforms, looking at whether those reforms were compatible with human rights. The set habitually receives instructions from individual claimants, NGOs and public bodies.

Client service: "One of the best-run sets. Very professional and forward-thinking." "The gold standard of clerking. They take the time to understand what solicitor clients want." "The Matrix practice team are the best I deal with. They are exceptionally helpful and supportive, especially in times of crisis." At the helm is chief executive Lindsay Scott.

SILKS

Ben Emmerson QC Outstanding reputation for his expertise in the overlap between public and human rights law. His recent practice involves a notable emphasis on public inquiries as well as related judicial reviews. **Strengths:** "Huge gravitas and a wealth of public law experience. He provides extremely sound advice." "Impressive knowledge of domestic and EU public law principles. He is a forceful and effective advocate." **Recent work:** Served as counsel to the historic abuse inquiry headed by Justice Lowell Goddard.

Phillippa Kaufmann QC Predominantly acts in public law challenges which arise in the context of the criminal justice system. Recent mandates include significant challenges to the Lord Chancellor's legal aid reforms. **Strengths:** "Has a phenomenal intellect and takes a really incisive approach to cases." "Amazing command of the facts and law." **Recent work:** Acted for the Public Law Project in a challenge to the operation of the Exceptional Case Funding scheme established to grant legal aid in cases no longer in scope to ensure compliance with Convention rights.

Alex Bailin QC (see p.587) Adept at the application of public and administrative law in the criminal justice and commercial spheres. He routinely appears in domestic and international public law and human rights proceedings. **Strengths:** "Smart, easy to work with and very responsive. Good with clients and user-friendly." "Able to go to the Supreme Court and get those mega-brainy judges to listen closely to him." **Recent work:** Appeared for the Equality and Human Rights Commission in a Supreme Court case concerning the legality of the collection and retention of information on political protesters by the police.

Raza Husain QC Pre-eminent silk whose administrative and public law experience is predominantly in the area of immigration and asylum. He represents claimants seeking to challenge decisions of the Home Secretary and other public bodies. **Strengths:** "Has encyclopaedic knowledge of the subject and is a real presence in court." "Extraordinary legal mind. He worked incredibly hard to make sure he presented the best case for the client. An exceptional advocate. He brings lots of ideas and always questions points in order to generate better pleadings." **Recent work:** Represented the appellant seeking to challenge the Home Secretary's interpretation of public interest in criminal deportation and its compatibility with Article 8 of the ECHR.

Helen Mountfield QC Brings her considerable expertise in equality law to public and administrative law cases. She predominantly represents claimants in judicial reviews where public policy is under scrutiny for being discriminatory. **Strengths:** "She is excellent: clever, committed to the work, thorough, collaborative, hard-working and just an absolute pleasure to work with." "She is very pragmatic and takes a soft approach to hard issues. She comes up with practical solutions to legal problems and thinks through all of the practical implications of decisions." "Her drafting, deep understanding of issues and creative shaping of arguments were most helpful." **Recent work:** Represented a claimant who was considered ineligible for a student loan because she lacked settled immigration status. The matter challenged the regulations for eligibility for a student loan, alleging unlawful discrimination in relation to access to education.

Tim Owen QC Habitually appears in domestic and international public law proceedings. His expertise encompasses judicial reviews challenging police practice and other claims in the criminal context. **Strengths:** "A forceful presence in the field." "Pragmatic and full of insight on public law matters." **Recent work:** Represented protester John Catt in his challenge against the actions of the police after details of his peaceful political activities had been recorded over a ten-year period on the secret National Domestic Extremism Database.

Richard Hermer QC Predominantly acts for individuals and groups of claimants seeking to challenge legislation and public body decision-making. He has considerable experience of public international law and human rights claims. **Strengths:** "He has a brilliant strategic brain. When you bring him in on an issue, he is quick to see all the different angles and give you direction going forward." "An uncanny knack for arguing difficult cases." "He is a very good leader of large teams of lawyers. He is hard-working and also effective in his advocacy." **Recent work:** Represented the Public Law Project in a judicial review of the government's changes to the Exceptional Case Funding scheme for publicly funded cases, which was deemed by the High Court to be unlawful and has led to a radical overhaul of the scheme.

Clare Montgomery QC (see p.720) Renowned advocate whose public law work spans a number of areas, including challenges to the scope and legality of criminal and regulatory law. She has a particular emphasis on administrative and public law claims which rely on human rights grounds. **Strengths:** "An impressive range of work and a good advocate." "Extremely nice to work with and extremely to the point: she doesn't mince words but she never offends." **Recent work:** Represented the Secretary of State for Justice in a judicial review challenging the compliance of the 'householder defence' law with Article 2 of the ECHR.

David Wolfe QC Represents individual claimants and NGOs seeking to challenge decisions of local authorities, government departments and other public bodies. Recent mandates include claims involving housing, welfare, education and data protection law. **Strengths:** "A wonderful mixture of skills. An extremely impressive advocate who provides incredibly clear drafting and is fantastic with clients. A real pleasure to work with." **Recent work:** Represented Shelter in its intervention in a Supreme Court case which established that local housing authorities could not properly discharge their duties under the Housing Act 1996 by offering "out-of-borough" accommodation without having properly considered the needs of affected children and families.

Danny Friedman QC Frequently appears in domestic and international public law proceedings, especially where there is an overlap with human rights and criminal law. Of particular note is his expertise in cases that consider the UK government's duties in the context of international conflict. **Strengths:** "Imaginative and strategic." "He is just a powerhouse of ideas and energy. A great lawyer and advocate. He is phenomenally hard-working. He eats, drinks and sleeps a case." "Extremely forensic in dissecting huge cases." **Recent work:** Represented the appellants seeking a public inquiry into the massacre of 25 people in 1948 by the Scots Guards in colonial Malaya. The case examined the duties to conduct investigations under both the common law and the ECHR, and whether proportionality should now be considered a common law ground of judicial review.

Karon Monaghan QC Noted for her expertise in public and administrative law cases pursued on the grounds of equality and human rights law. She has considerable experience of challenging welfare reform on behalf of marginalised claimants. **Strengths:** "Her ability to digest cases, work out the main arguments quickly and draft strong skeleton arguments is deeply impressive." "She is fearless, utterly user-friendly and down-to-earth but immensely clever." "Good at demystifying the law for clients and very good at getting to the heart of issues. She is good on her feet, eloquent and really impresses clients." **Recent work:** Intervened on behalf of Liberty in a challenge to amendments to immigration law which would introduce pre-entry language requirements.

Aidan O'Neill QC Extensive experience in administrative and public law claims involving EU and human rights law. He is regularly instructed by claimants in England and Scotland to appear in judicial review proceedings up to the Supreme Court. **Strengths:** "Very knowledgeable and practical in relation to proceedings with a Scottish dimension, and an expert on EU law." "His written advocacy is very strong. He is both comprehensive and knowledgeable about the subject, and his oral advocacy is sound. Virtually unrivalled experience of appearing in the higher courts." **Recent work:** Acted in Sandiford v Foreign and Commonwealth Office, a case considering whether the FCO had duties under European law to provide funding for legal representation of British nationals facing the death penalty abroad.

Jessica Simor QC Enjoys a busy administrative and public law practice which includes experience in commercial judicial reviews and human rights claims. Her experience in challenges to the scope and application of taxation laws is of particular note. **Strengths:** "Bright, hard-working and very knowledgeable." "She is a passionate and committed advocate." **Recent work:** Represented HMRC in a judicial review challenge brought by Telefónica challenging the requirement for telecoms companies to change the method by which they calculate VAT deduction for customers when they are abroad.

Hugh Southey QC (see p.770) Leads significant challenges to legislation and policy, particularly in the areas of crime, extradition and immigration. He is especially proficient at challenging police conduct through judicial reviews. **Strengths:** "Thorough and comprehensive. He responds quickly and provides extremely detailed analysis of issues. Unflappable in court and extremely impressive on his feet. He is always extremely well prepared." **Recent work:** Represented the claimant before the Court of Appeal in a challenge to the power of stop and search without reasonable suspicion, which was argued to be incompatible with the ECHR on the basis of statistics which suggested racial discrimination.

Daniel Squires QC Acts in domestic and international public law proceedings, often where there is a significant human rights overlap. He is particularly strong on cases arising in the context of national security and criminal justice. **Strengths:** "A great strategic thinker." "An incredibly effective advocate. He is good at picking out the best points and presenting them well." "Very bright, focused and strategically minded. He produces high-quality submissions and is succinct, approachable and easy to work with." **Recent work:** Represented the Equality and Human Rights Commission in a claim before the Supreme Court regarding the legality of Schedule 7 of the Terrorism Act 2000, which allows the police to stop and question anyone passing through an airport without any requirement for reasonable suspicion.

JUNIORS

Chris Buttler Considerable experience challenging government departments' and other public bodies' decisions. He is particularly proficient at claims which rely on human rights law. **Strengths:** "Exceptionally bright barrister who is decisive and clear in his advice and arguments. He instils confidence." "Strategic and effective." "So succinct in his written work that he can say in five pages what others would use 50 for. A logical style which makes it difficult to disagree with him." **Recent work:** Acted for the Equality and Human Rights Commission, which was successful in establishing that the Secretary of State for Communities and Local Government's practice of 'recovering' planning appeals in Traveller cases constituted unlawful race discrimination.

Nicholas Armstrong Routinely handles significant challenges involving data protection and the right to privacy. His broad administrative and public law practice also includes a notable emphasis on immigration and social welfare. **Strengths:** "Highly committed and creative barrister." "A very able and effective advocate." "It's amazing how well he distils things into understandable points for the court. He's very tenacious." **Recent work:** Represented a group of claimants in a challenge regarding the lawfulness of requiring the NHS to disclose patient information to the Home Office so that immigration sanctions might be imposed.

Alison Macdonald (see p.705) Handles a wide array of administrative and public law claims arising in the context of criminal and civil litigation. She has particular experience in challenges against the scope and exercise of police powers. **Strengths:** "She demonstrates real maturity and produces highly imaginative written advocacy. Her arguments are always interesting to read as she is extremely bright." **Recent work:** Acting for the National Union of Journalists in a challenge to the retention of large amounts of information about journalists on the National Domestic Extremism Database.

Sarah Hannett Instructed in judicial reviews by claimants, interveners and defendants. She is particularly proficient at public law claims which involve human rights law. **Strengths:** "Very approachable and gives sound advice that is balanced, reasonable and practical." "Very collaborative in her approach and excellent in her written work." "She is very sharp and tenacious." **Recent work:** Represented Just for Kids, interveners in a Supreme Court appeal which considered the lawfulness of the regulations governing eligibility for student support, which excluded students who did not have indefinite leave to remain in the UK.

Moncton Chambers

See profile on p.877

THE SET

Monckton Chambers continues to develop its administrative and public law offering, attracting an increasing number of cases in respect of human rights, community care and data protection. The set also maintains its strength in regulatory public law, with a particular emphasis on the interaction between domestic and EU law. Clients are quick to praise the barristers here for their "strength across the board in judicial review and public law work." Members receive instructions from individual and commercial claimants as well as defendants. Their notable recent engagements include the high-profile challenges to the Data Retention and Investigatory Powers Act 2014 and the Welfare Reform Act 2012.

Client service: "The clerking is very strong. They are efficient, very straightforward and flexible in terms of fee negotiations." "The clerks are very approachable, they respond swiftly to enquiries and will go out of their way to find alternative counsel for you if necessary." The team is led by senior clerk David Hockney.

SILKS

Tim Ward QC (see p.789) Brings his considerable EU law expertise to bear on public and administrative law disputes. He typically acts for corporate clients in challenges to regulatory decisions. **Strengths:** "A genuinely talented advocate with the intellectual firepower to deal with complex cases. He delivers attractive and easily understood submissions. Even when arguments are technical or dull, he brings them to life." "Excellent judgement and a great team player." **Recent work:** Acted for a group of companies engaged in oil drilling in the North Sea in a challenge to the new, adverse tax regime affecting their activities which was brought in under EU and human rights law.

Daniel Beard QC Focuses his administrative and public law practice on commercial and regulatory judicial reviews. He is particularly renowned for his expertise in claims that involve EU law. **Strengths:** "An extremely smart lawyer." "He is imaginative and presents academically." "Punchy and to the point." **Recent work:** Represented the government in a judicial review brought by David Davis MP and Tom Watson MP challenging controversial emergency data retention legislation.

Stephen Cragg QC Predominantly appears in public law claims connected with the criminal justice system, including judicial review challenges to police conduct. He is also noted for his experience in public law cases that involve community care. **Strengths:** "Depth of knowledge and experience. He knows the system inside out." "A really nice guy, easy to work with, committed and knowledgeable." "Excellent experience, and able to pick up points very quickly and run with them." **Recent work:** Acted for the Law Society in a challenge to the president of the Court of Protection's findings that incapacitated persons deprived of their liberty in care settings do not have the right to be party to proceedings or to have an oral hearing of their case.

Kassie Smith QC A noted authority on judicial review, particularly in the commercial and regulatory spheres. She also advises regulators and corporations on non-contentious administrative and public law matters. **Strengths:** "A consummate professional, she knows everything there is to know about judicial review and has a real clarity and focus about her." She brings simplicity to complexity." **Recent work:** Represented the Secretary of State for the Department for Environment, Food and Rural Affairs in a judicial review challenge to the government's failure to comply with EU emission limits for nitrogen dioxide in London.

Jon Turner QC Frequently appears in administrative and public law cases in the commercial and regulatory spheres. His practice also encompasses cases concerning environmental protection. **Strengths:** "Brilliant on his feet." "An extremely dedicated QC who is always helpful, gets to the nub of issues and is willing to go the extra mile to make sure you get the best advice." **Recent work:** Successfully acted for BT in an appeal against a Competition Appeal Tribunal judgment which had overturned Ofcom's decision to force Sky to offer its core premium sports channels to other Pay TV businesses. BT, supported by the regulator, argued that the tribunal had failed to deal with important economic issues regarding the affordability of Sky's prices.

Ian Wise QC Typically represents claimants in challenges against legislation and decisions of public bodies up to the higher courts. He is particularly active in the areas of welfare reform and social justice. **Strengths:** "A pragmatic and approachable silk with a wealth of public law experience. Very determined and knowledgeable. Down-to-earth and good with clients." "Tenacious and regularly exposes new ground in cases. He is clearly very experienced and a real heavyweight." **Recent work:** Represented a group of claimants in a challenge to the government's benefit cap regime, which was argued to be discriminatory against single parents and their children contrary to ECHR rights and the United Nations Convention on the Rights of the Child.

Gerry Facenna QC (see p.643) Broad depth of administrative and public law expertise, with a particular emphasis on EU law and regulatory matters. He is also adept at judicial reviews involving human rights law. **Strengths:** "Always calm and collected in difficult cases." "Very clear presentation: he doesn't take unnecessary points and is highly convincing to the other side." **Recent work:** Represented the Ministry of Defence in a judicial review challenge concerning the failure to hold an inquiry into the death of a Royal Military Policeman killed in Iraq in 2003 under Article 2 ECHR.

JUNIORS

Robert Palmer Capable of handling a wide range of administrative and public law matters including commercial, regulatory and human rights claims. He represents claimants and defendants in judicial reviews challenging decisions of central government, local authorities and regulators. **Strengths:** "An excellent public law junior whose written and oral advocacy often has the elegance and clarity of a QC." "Very impressive, with great clarity and a deep understanding of the application of law. His presentation is always clear and concise." **Recent work:** Represented Jewish Human Rights Watch in a challenge with regard to various local authorities' decision to boycott produce from the West Bank and Gaza.

Steve Broach Has considerable experience of bringing challenges against local and central government decisions. He is particularly committed to handling cases involving disabled claimants. **Strengths:** "Knows the law inside out; he offers swift, practical advice in complex areas of law which are constantly evolving. He is both dynamic and precise, working well with professionals and clients alike." **Recent work:** Successfully acted for the claimant in R (HA) v London Borough of Ealing, a case which challenged Ealing's policy of requiring a certain period of residence before allowing applicants to go on its housing register.

Nikolaus Grubeck Highly knowledgeable on the overlap between public and human rights law. His expertise in cases concerning national security and foreign affairs is of particular note. He receives instructions from both claimants and defendants. **Strengths:** "Brilliant, writes beautifully, is hard-working and totally unflappable. He is really good with clients." "A wonderfully creative litigator." "Technically one of the most gifted barristers that I have come across, he's absolutely meticulous." **Recent work:** Instructed by the Secretary of State for Health to defend a major challenge by four of the world's largest tobacco companies against the UK government's Standardised Packaging of Tobacco Products Regulation 2015.

Azeem Suterwalla (see p.776) Committed to representing marginalised claimants in a wide range of public law matters including challenges to immigration detention and cuts to public services. He is also knowledgeable about information law and data protection. **Strengths:** "Approachable and quick to turn around work. A sensible, pragmatic and no-nonsense approach. A very good trial lawyer. Easy to work with." "He's a very effective and engaging advocate." **Recent work:** Represented the claimants in a challenge to the Data Retention and Investigatory Powers Act 2014. The case considered whether the act breaches the EU Charter of Fundamental Rights and the ECHR.

Brendan McGurk Predominantly defends public bodies, including government departments, in judicial reviews. His broad substantive expertise includes human rights, competition and taxation. **Strengths:** "Very bright, fantastically responsive." "Highly diligent and intelligent junior." **Recent work:** Acted for the defendant Secretary of State for Defence in a judicial review concerning the deaths of six Royal Military Policemen in Iraq in 2003. The matter raised questions surrounding the scope of the defendant's obligations under Article 2 to hold a full and independent investigation.

Julianne Morrison Involved in significant public and administrative law challenges on behalf of both claimants and defendants. She regularly handles significant information and EU law claims. **Strengths:** "She's remarkably clever and quick, and she writes beautifully." **Recent work:** Appeared for the government in a claim brought by major tobacco companies alleging that the introduction of standardised packaging breached their rights to property under the ECHR and the EU Charter.

Band 3

1 Crown Office Row

See profile on p.826

THE SET

1 Crown Office Row accepts instructions from claimants, respondents and interveners in public and administrative law proceedings. The set is particularly strong in judicial reviews that arise in the field of healthcare and mental health. Other areas of note include national security, human rights, professional discipline and inquests. Members have recently appeared in R (Black) v Secretary of State for Justice, which considered the lawfulness of a ban on smoking in prisons.

Client service: "The chambers is well clerked and offers good resources to solicitors." "Really helpful. They made every effort to make sure that I had someone available and that papers were delivered to the right counsel. They were really on the ball." Senior clerk Matthew Phipps is "very experienced" and "very approachable."

SILKS

Philip Havers QC Instructed by claimants and defendants in contentious and non-contentious public law matters. He is particularly adept at defending NHS bodies in challenges against changes to service provision. **Strengths:** "He has the ear of the court, is canny and knows which are the good points to make. A very succinct advocate." **Recent work:** Acted for the Healthcare Together Committees in a challenge to the reconfiguration of hospital services in Manchester.

Angus McCullough QC Skilled advocate who focuses on the overlap between administrative, human rights and immigration law. In his role as special advocate, he handles sensitive litigation involving questions of national security. **Strengths:** "He is a really imaginative lawyer. He spots very difficult points others would miss and then argues them effectively." "Exceptionally bright and adept at identifying issues immediately. He has an air of authority while remaining completely down-to-earth and is a pleasure to instruct."

Jeremy Hyam QC Particularly proficient at public and administrative law cases arising in the context of healthcare and community care. He handles judicial reviews that consider decisions of NHS Trusts, professional regulators and other public bodies. **Strengths:** "Superb written work. He makes complex law easy to understand. Also superb on his feet. Judges hang on his every word." "He is very thorough and knowledgeable."

Marina Wheeler QC Notable emphasis on public law cases involving issues of national security and armed conflict. She represents the NHS as well as central and local government in judicial review proceedings considering the provision of public services and the duties of public bodies. **Strengths:** "Bright and incisive." "Very precise and clear advice that clients can readily understand."

JUNIORS

Shaheen Rahman Particular emphasis on healthcare regulation, including judicial reviews challenging government policy and decisions of professional regulators. She also appears in national security cases as a special advocate. **Strengths:** "Dogged and tenacious." "Very thorough and clear about the client's responsibilities and liabilities. Informative and clear advice." **Recent work:** Acted for the claimant in a landmark challenge to the government's stance that the Health Act 2006, with regard to the ban on smoking in communal areas, does not apply to prisons on the grounds of Crown Immunity and is, therefore, unenforceable.

39 Essex Chambers

See profile on p.840

THE SET

39 Essex Chambers is home to a large number of public law specialists who represent claimants and defendants. The set is especially strong in the areas of healthcare, mental capacity, regulatory and disciplinary law. It also offers expertise in local government, environment and education law. "The set has great range and depth, so you can be confident there will nearly always be an expert in the field available to assist, even at short notice," clients enthuse. Members are often involved in cases of significance before the higher courts, such as M v Bury CCG, a landmark case where a person in a minimally conscious state was allowed to have life-sustaining treatment withdrawn. Another highlight has been the Kenyan Emergency Group Litigation, a challenge brought by 40,000 Kenyans seeking damages for alleged human rights abuses committed during British colonial rule.

Client service: "Brilliant. They really go the extra mile, which makes all the difference, particularly on urgent or high-profile cases." "They are problem solvers. They put themselves out to find representation even at short notice. They are approachable, helpful and all very client-focused." Michael Kaplan leads the clerking team.

SILKS

Nigel Pleming QC Established public and administrative law silk capable across a wide range of subjects. Recent mandates involve human rights, public, international and local government law. **Strengths:** "A wonderful advocate with the wisdom of experience." "Always thoroughly prepared and someone with a fantastic court manner. Able to take difficult matters and pare them down to the essential issues, even with really technical subject matter. Very warm and very good client skills. Excellent legal analysis." "An excellent oral advocate and very tactically astute." **Recent work:** Instructed on behalf of BAT in a challenge to the government's proposals to introduce standardised packaging of tobacco products.

Jenni Richards QC (see p.751) Wide-ranging public and administrative law practice which includes significant challenges arising in the context of healthcare and inquests. She is instructed by individuals, regulators, local authorities and other public bodies on contentious and non-contentious matters. **Strengths:** "Extremely impressive. She is focused and very bright and gets to the point. She is also a brilliant advocate who can get to the heart of the matter." "Good all-round knowledge of many areas. She can turn her hand to anything. She is extremely well liked by clients. She comes up with novel and interesting arguments." **Recent work:** Represented two GPs in a judicial review challenge to the investigative and decision-making processes of the Health Service Ombudsman, who had produced a report holding the GPs responsible for a patient's death.

Fenella Morris QC Typically handles administrative and public law cases which arise in the healthcare setting. She acts for claimants, NGOs, NHS bodies and local authorities. **Strengths:** "Approachable, proactive and a problem solver." "She has an excellent analytical mind and is able to convey the heart of a case clearly and succinctly." **Recent work:** Represented the campaign group Keep Wythenshawe Special in a challenge to the reconfiguration of hospitals across Greater Manchester.

Charles Cory-Wright QC Renowned for his work as a special advocate. He is often involved in sensitive cases regarding terrorism and national security. **Strengths:** "Really great to work with, thoughtful and meticulous." **Recent work:** Defended the government against a challenge brought by a terrorist suspect countering a decision made by the Home Secretary that the suspect be required to live outside London.

Alison Foster QC (see p.647) Focuses her public and administrative law practice on regulatory matters, and is a noted expert on taxation. She is experienced in representing claimants and defendants before administrative tribunals and appellate courts. **Strengths:** "She's great to work with. A very, very charming advocate. Clients love her. She gets on top of things quickly and has got a really good manner in court." **Recent work:** Appeared on behalf of Cheryl James's family at the inquest into her death, allegedly through suicide, at the Deepcut army barracks in 1995.

Lisa Giovannetti QC Acts for claimants and defendants in significant judicial review proceedings which involve human rights law. Recent cases have involved welfare reform, immigration, national security and international relations. **Strengths:** "She's a very engaging advocate and has an attractive courtroom style. Judges listen when she speaks." **Recent work:** Represented the claimants in a judicial review of the Department of Work and Pensions' administration of Personal Independence Payments, which involved lengthy delays that were found to be unlawful by the High Court.

Steven Kovats QC Predominantly defends controversial decisions of the UK government. His wide-ranging experience in public and administrative law involves cases about criminal justice, foreign affairs, national security, immigration and human rights. **Strengths:** "He has all bases covered. He is all over the detail, from the high level to the minutiae. He has great presence in court. Clients love him." "Concise and to the point. Judges like him because he doesn't take points without merit." **Recent work:** Acting for the FCO in a Supreme Court appeal against the government's decision to establish a Marine Protected Area around the Chagos Islands. In particular, the case considered the legality of relying on a WikiLeaks cable as evidence of an improper purpose.

James Strachan QC Handles administrative and public law cases on behalf of claimants and defendants. He is experienced in claims arising in the criminal justice and financial spheres. **Strengths:** "A barrister of very high capability, who has a very broad base of expertise and produces creative arguments." "Very thoughtful and client-focused. His advice is authoritative." **Recent work:** Appeared for the Ministry of Justice in R (Nicklinson and Lamb) v Secretary of State for Justice, a highly important case in the Supreme Court concerning the right to die.

JUNIORS

Kate Grange Frequently instructed by the UK government in significant judicial review challenges. Her public law practice includes a notable emphasis on human rights and national security. **Strengths:** "She is very knowledgeable and very bright." "Totally dedicated. She fights her corner very strongly and is an absolute delight to work with." **Recent work:** Instructed to defend a judicial review of the Secretary of State's decision to exclude two controversial speakers from the UK on the basis that they had expressed views that fostered hatred and might lead to inter-community violence in the UK.

Parishil Patel Notable focus on administrative and public law matters involving healthcare. He is also experienced in judicial review proceedings involving public procurement and local government. **Strengths:** "Excellent with clients, giving them clear and practical advice." "A very succinct advocate. A very good cross-examiner." "Pragmatic and sensible." **Recent work:** Acted for the defendant in a challenge to the Health Research Authority's policy to promote transparency in human research and to require registration of all clinical trials in the UK.

Alexander Ruck Keene (see p.756) Focuses his administrative and public law practice on the scope and application of mental capacity law. He regularly acts for applicants in novel legal challenges. **Strengths:** "An encyclopaedic knowledge of the subject area." "An extremely industrious barrister." **Recent work:** Appeared in a Court of Appeal case considering the limits of the Court of Protection's jurisdiction and, in particular, whether the Court of Protection is limited to choosing between available options or whether it can require other options to be put on the table.

Victoria Butler-Cole Commands great respect among clients and peers for her vast expertise and impressive advocacy. Her broad health and social care practice includes a substantial number of administrative and public law cases. **Strengths:** "She is very accessible and flexible in the way she provides advice and is able to cut through the issues very quickly. She is very good with clients." "Very knowledgeable, very approachable and very friendly. She produces wonderful arguments" **Recent work:** Represented the claimant in a judicial review challenging the decision of a Coroner that the deceased, a woman with Down's Syndrome who died in intensive care, was not in state detention and therefore a jury was not required for the inquest.

Landmark Chambers

See profile on p.873

THE SET

Landmark Chambers offers "very good strength and depth" in administrative and public law. It is particularly prominent in judicial reviews concerning planning and regulatory decisions, often where EU law is invoked. The set is also very strong in the areas of social justice, human rights and immigration. Recently, members have successfully challenged Northern Ireland's prohibition on abortion in cases of rape, incest and serious foetal abnormality. Members receive instructions from central and local government, regulators, corporations, NGOs and individual claimants. "They have delivered for us so consistently," comment clients.

Client service: Jay Fullilove leads the "immensely helpful" team of clerks. "They are always willing to answer the phone and help. Very reliable. You don't think twice about instructing Landmark because the service is of such a high standard." "The clerks are efficient and respond quickly."

SILKS

Richard Drabble QC Renowned advocate noted for his expertise in administrative and public law cases concerning social justice and human rights. He is also experienced in handling EU, regulatory and planning challenges on behalf of claimants, defendants and interveners. **Strengths:** "A barrister with formidable intellect, who has great expertise across a wide range of subject areas and vast experience to draw from. He is a persuasive advocate with an absolute command of his subject matter." "Good at finding innovative points even in unpromising cases." **Recent work:** Instructed by then Mayor of London, Boris Johnson, to resist a judicial review challenging his direction to the Fire Authority to substantially cut the number of London fire stations.

Nathalie Lieven QC Brings successful challenges to legislation, government policy and public body decision-making, appearing on behalf of individual claimants and NGOs. She is especially capable in cases involving human rights law, immigration and principles of public international law. **Strengths:** "Outstanding advocate who is extremely clear and convincing. A pleasure to work with and great with clients." "Impeccable judgement, highly experienced and can present difficult cases highly attractively." **Recent work:** Acted for the Northern Ireland Human Rights Commission in seeking a declaration of incompatibility against the criminalisation of abortion in cases of rape, incest and fatal foetal abnormality, which was argued to be in breach of Articles 3, 8 and 14 ECHR.

James Maurici QC Often seen on complex judicial reviews in the planning, environment and regulatory spheres. He is also experienced in local government, EU and human rights law. He advises public bodies and private clients in non-contentious public law matters. **Strengths:** "Combines intelligence, insight and ease of use." "Measured in his approach, incredibly meticulous and thorough. He has a mind like a razor. Can enter a situation and give you the answer immediately. Just outstanding." **Recent work:** Successfully resisted a judicial review on the scope of the powers, duties and responsibilities of the Parliamentary and Health Service Ombudsman when investigating complaints against GPs.

David Elvin QC Specialises in judicial reviews involving planning, infrastructure and property. He represents public bodies and private clients in contentious and non-contentious administrative law matters. **Strengths:** "A very clever, smart advocate." **Recent work:** Represented HS2 Action Alliance in a series of judicial reviews challenging the government's policy and safeguarding directions concerning the proposed high-speed rail network.

Stephen Knafler QC Well equipped to provide representation in a broad range of public and administrative law cases. He is particularly strong in immigration, human rights and social care. **Strengths:** "Brings a sense of authority and clarity to a case. A willingness to take into account different views. A great public law lawyer." "Great work ethic, intellect and affability." "Very good on his feet, produces excellent paperwork and is very imaginative." **Recent work:** Represented the claimant in a judicial review against the Home Secretary, appraising a different approach for case management in the High Court and Court of Appeal in public law cases and private law cases, particularly in relation to time extensions and relief from sanctions.

David Lock QC Brings his deep expertise in healthcare to his public and administrative law practice. He is also experienced in judicial reviews relating to local government and police law. **Strengths:** "Good political as well as legal and commercial insight." "He's always got a practical solution and very much thinks outside the box." "Manages to make something incredibly complex into something very clear, succinct and easy to explain. He is quite persuasive and very committed to the area of work." **Recent work:** Represented Cornwall Council in a Supreme Court case defining the meaning of 'ordinary residence' for a person with learning difficulties who lacked the decision-making capacity of where to live, impacting on local authority support.

Lisa Busch QC Popular choice for the defence of controversial government decisions in administrative and public law proceedings. Her broad expertise encompasses human rights, immigration and planning law. **Strengths:** "A skilled advocate who is lovely to listen to." "Calm, clear, measured, reliable and first-rate judgement." "She is a good advocate for difficult, sensitive cases because she is so thoughtful and can present cases in a tactful and humane way." **Recent work:** Represented the defendant, the Home Secretary, in a claim by the appellant that removing his six-year-old daughter, who was severely disabled and had complex needs, from the UK would involve a violation of her rights under Articles 3 and 8 of the ECHR.

JUNIORS

Tim Buley Masterful representation of claimants and defendants in high-profile judicial review challenges to legislation and important public body decisions. His broad practice encompasses commercial, regulatory and human rights claims. **Strengths:** "A robust advocate." "Very good in court. Very experienced and a wonderful, forward-thinking strategist." **Recent work:** Served as junior counsel for the Child Poverty Action Group in a high-profile challenge to the government's imposition of a £500 per household limit on benefits. The 'benefit cap' was argued to be unjustifiably discriminatory against women and lone parents.

David Blundell Instructed in significant challenges to government legislation on behalf of claimants, defendants and interveners. He is particularly proficient at claims involving human rights and EU law. **Strengths:** "He is highly impressive. Thorough, knowledgeable, has excellent judgement and is very good with clients." "His ability to identify and exploit unique arguments is excellent." **Recent work:** Represented the Northern Ireland Human Rights Commission in a successful challenge to the legality of prohibition on abortion in Northern Ireland in cases of rape, incest and serious foetal abnormality.

Charles Banner Handles a diverse array of public and administrative law matters with a particular emphasis on EU and regulatory law. Recent cases have involved community care, criminal, broadcasting, immigration and planning law. **Strengths:** "A pleasure to deal with. He is responsive, clear and concise in the advice he provides. He is also affable, approachable and client-friendly." **Recent work:** Represented Cornwall Council in a judicial review concerning the correct approach to a person's 'ordinary residence' for the purposes of assessing which local authority is liable to pay for their care under the National Assistance Act 1948.

Samantha Broadfoot Adept at managing public law proceedings invoking human rights law and claims challenging the interpretation of legislation. She regularly receives instructions from central government departments, local authorities and individual claimants. **Strengths:** "A delightful advocate, very hard-working, and she produces clear, thorough and well-reasoned arguments. Her analysis is always thoughtful and accurate, and she is a real team player as well. Completely reliable, hard-working and very nice." **Recent work:** Represented the government in three linked cases concerning the proper interpretation of Section 3C of the Immigration Act 1971, which automatically extends a person's existing leave until their application for further leave to remain is decided.

Zoe Leventhal Involved in substantial public law challenges in welfare reform and social justice. She is capable of representing claimants, interveners and defendants in judicial review. **Strengths:** "Total dedication to the cases she is involved in. Her attention to detail and grasp of the issues is hugely impressive." "Extremely clear, concise and accurate on paper and in oral advocacy. A very warm and engaging advocate." "A very good lawyer but she also understands the social policy, which is very important." **Recent work:** Instructed by the Public Law Project in a high-profile judicial review challenging cuts to the availability of legal aid and its effect on victims of domestic violence. It was argued that the evidential requirements in the regulations make it impossible for large numbers of genuine victims to obtain legal aid.

Other Ranked Lawyers

Philip Coppel QC (Cornerstone Barristers) Has extensive experience of acting for claimants and defendants in public and regulatory challenges. He is recommended especially for matters within the housing sphere. **Strengths:** "He is very sharp and can quickly get his head around a complex factual timeline. He's a convincing performer in court, and it's impressive to see him fire off new ideas. He's a creative thinker." **Recent work:** Represented the claimant in a judicial review challenging the Parliamentary and Health Service Ombudsman's refusal to investigate St Thomas's Hospital's loss of the claimant's recently deceased daughter's medical records.

Jeremy Johnson QC (see p.684) (5 Essex Court) Handles administrative and public law proceedings with significant police law elements. He represents police forces and other state agents across the country in sensitive judicial reviews, inquests and public inquiries. His mandates often involve an overlap with human rights law. **Strengths:** "His understanding of the subject matter is immense." "Has a huge appetite for work and a practical insight that is appreciated by clients."

Jason Beer QC (see p.593) (5 Essex Court) Adept at managing administrative and public law proceedings relating to police conduct and data retention. He is also active in the field of public inquiries and acts in judicial reviews challenging coronial decisions. **Strengths:** "Very impressed by his client care. He involves himself deeply in cases and stays on top of everything." "His technical abilities truly stand out. Easy to have confidence in him." "Understated and takes a reasonable line. He gains the confidence of courts by being agreeable." **Recent work:** Counselled the Commissioner for the Police of the Metropolis in a judicial review challenging the detention of David Miranda at Heathrow Airport under Schedule 7 of the Terrorism Act 2000.

Hilton Harrop-Griffiths (Field Court Chambers) An authority on judicial reviews involving local authorities. He is immensely knowledgeable about the powers and duties of local authorities, particularly in relation to social care. **Strengths:** "He very quickly gets to grips with a case." "Very knowledgeable about the area of law." **Recent work:** Represented Wiltshire Council in a dispute between four local authorities and the Secretary of State for Health about the test for ordinary residence for the purposes of the National Assistance Act 1948 in the case of a person who lacks the mental capacity to decide where to live.

Charles Béar QC (see p.593) (Fountain Court Chambers) Accepts administrative and public law instructions from claimants and defendants within the regulatory and commercial spheres. He also receives non-contentious public law instructions, advising on governance, compliance and possible grounds of review. **Strengths:** "A clever and authoritative silk." "His advice was beautifully clear and robust because he had gone the extra mile to consider conflicting views. Really helpful." **Recent work:** Represented the claimant, an insurance broker, in a successful challenge against a decision of the Financial Ombudsman Service to assume jurisdiction over a complaint concerning the broking of directors' and officers' liability insurance.

Timothy Dutton QC (see p.638) (Fountain Court Chambers) Standout advocate who manages public law proceedings in the regulatory and disciplinary spheres. He advises regulators on their powers and duties, and also acts on behalf of claimants and defendants in judicial reviews and public inquiries. **Strengths:** "He is extremely authoritative in court and extremely good with clients. He provides clear advice and gets to the heart of issues. He tends to win cases, too, which is important at the end of the day." **Recent work:** Instructed by the Bar Standards Board in a challenge to the QASA Advocacy Assurance Scheme brought by a group of criminal barristers with the support of the Criminal Bar Association and the Law Society. The claim alleged that the scheme breached constitutional law principles, as well as the independence of both the judiciary and barristers.

James McClelland (see p.711) (Fountain Court Chambers) Focuses his considerable public law prowess on commercial and regulatory cases, particularly in the financial services sector. He is capable of counselling claimants and defendants on judicial review and regulatory proceedings. **Strengths:** "A very useful combination of commercial and public law experience, and an unswerving eye for detail. Extremely diligent." "Extremely bright, utterly dedicated and very meticulous. He chases down every point to completion, making sure you don't miss anything." **Recent work:** Acted for the claimant seeking declarations as to which of two factions in the Libyan civil war should, as a matter of English public law, be recognised as the legitimate government of Libya. The dispute will determine who is entitled to control the USD67 billion assets held by the Libyan Investment Authority.

Stephanie Harrison QC (Garden Court Chambers) Strong choice for public law challenges involving immigration and asylum. She has been at the forefront of challenges on behalf of vulnerable claimants to the Home Secretary's policies on immigration detention. She is also frequently instructed in judicial reviews against the Special Immigration Appeals Commission's decisions. **Strengths:** "Amazing energy, amazing analytical skills and tactically brilliant. A fantastic advocate who can turn a difficult case and hostile court into a positive outcome for the client. A phenomenon – she's incredibly hard-working and has a great grasp of the facts and details." "She is an outstanding advocate, who reads the court incredibly well, and a shrewd negotiator who is always focused on her client's objectives. Simply excellent." **Recent work:** Represented the Equality and Human Rights Commission in a challenge against the Home Secretary's policy of detaining asylum seekers while their claims and appeals were determined under the Detained Fast Track system.

Shu Shin Luh (Garden Court Chambers) Pursues significant public law challenges on behalf of marginalised claimants and interveners. She is particularly committed to enforcing the rights of children. Her substantive expertise includes immigration, human rights, social welfare and education. **Strengths:** "An exceptionally clever barrister who is incredibly quick, and has excellent judgement and instincts. A totally safe pair of hands. She is always about five steps ahead of you, which can be disconcerting but helpful." "Passionate, committed and a real fighter." "Exemplary work ethic. Due to her expertise in a number of areas, she is able to advise on complex cases arising from the interrelationship between numerous areas of law." **Recent work:** Acted in an intervention on behalf of Shelter Children's Legal Service in a test case considering the correct approach for a housing authority to take when arranging provision of temporary accommodation for a homeless family with five children.

Richard Clayton QC (4-5 Gray's Inn Square) Notable for his expertise in public law matters involving an overlap with human rights. He is also recognised for his vast knowledge of constitutional law.

Strengths: "He is very academic but also very sharp when it comes to tactics. He is very good at guiding you on what the judge is likely to be thinking." "Outstandingly clever." **Recent work:** Represented Watch Tower in a challenge to the Charity Commission's statutory inquiry into the Jehovah's Witness safeguarding policy following convictions for historic sex abuse against three of its members.

James Guthrie QC (3 Hare Court) Appears in complex public law matters, with a notable emphasis on proceedings before the Privy Council. His experience includes cases of constitutional importance involving Commonwealth jurisdictions. **Strengths:** "He has a huge background in this area and great confidence. A brave counsel. He is not afraid of making difficult arguments. Someone with steel." "Amazingly prompt, responsive and timely. Fantastic attentiveness." **Recent work:** Represented one of the claimants in a high-profile dispute regarding competing rights of entry to the Official Roll of the Baronetage. The matter was heard before a special sitting of seven Supreme Court Justices.

Peter Knox QC (3 Hare Court) Particularly adept at managing public law proceedings before the Privy Council. His broad practice involves important constitutional cases as well as commercial work involving public bodies. **Strengths:** "He is superb at stepping into a complicated, very fast-paced situation." "Incredibly bright and capable. He can turn his hand to any area of law." **Recent work:** Represented 153 of the Republic of Trinidad and Tobago's municipal police officers in a constitutional motion brought against the state in relation to its failure to introduce regulations regarding the governance of municipal police.

David Perry QC (6KBW College Hill) Specialises in judicial review proceedings arising in criminal justice. He is particularly adept at managing claims invoking human rights law. He is also instructed in contentious and non-contentious regulatory public law. **Strengths:** "He is utterly calm and has the best judgement. He is understated but has this enormous intelligence and assuredness." **Recent work:** Instructed by the Crown Solicitor's Office to appear in a judicial review challenging the jury's verdict in an inquest into the deaths of two IRA members killed by British forces in 1990.

Jonathan Hall QC (6KBW College Hill) Specialises in administrative and public law cases overlapping with human rights and criminal law. He is particularly strong in the context of national security and regularly defends the use of "no suspicion" powers under Schedule 7 of the Terrorism Act 2000. **Strengths:** "A powerful advocate who can see both sides of an argument and really fine-tune his approach." "Effective as an advocate and good at explaining ideas to the court." "He has a real eye for detail, and is incredibly approachable and friendly as well." **Recent work:** Represented the UK government in a claim brought by the wife of a convicted terrorist. She contended that her rights were violated when she was questioned by police under anti-terrorism legislation while at East Midlands Airport.

Rosemary Davidson (6KBW College Hill) Frequently instructed by central government departments to act in significant domestic and international public law proceedings. She is particularly knowledgeable about sanctions, national security and criminal justice. **Strengths:** "She is incredibly bright, amazingly thorough, has a really good eye for detail and amazing judgement." "So rigorous and detailed. She never gives up and doesn't let any tiny loose ends go. Everything gets pulled together and tidied up." **Recent work:** Acted for the Secretary of State in a high-profile judicial review brought by NAPO, a probation union, against the proposed privatisation of the probation service.

Katherine Apps (see p.584) (Littleton Chambers) Excels when representing claimants and defendants in complex judicial reviews. She is particularly proficient at public law claims invoking equality and human rights law. She typically acts for central government in challenges to public policy and decisions. **Strengths:** "Really skilled and effective. She comes up with excellent ideas." "She's efficient, clever and nice to deal with." "An excellent lawyer and very thorough." **Recent work:** Appeared on behalf of the Secretary of State for Work and Pensions in a judicial review challenging the Department for Work and Pensions' process for assessing Employment and Support Allowance eligibility on the basis that it allegedly failed to make reasonable adjustments for people with mental health problems.

Can Yeginsu (see p.801) (4 New Square) Acts in a wide array of public law proceedings arising in the commercial and media spheres. He is also experienced in judicial reviews concerning coronial decisions. **Strengths:** "He has an excellent brain." "A very eloquent and articulate speaker about public law and human rights." **Recent work:** Instructed by Media Legal Defence Initiative, Article 19 and English PEN in the Court of Appeal proceedings relating to the detention of David Miranda under Schedule 7 to the Terrorism Act 2000. The case considered the purpose and scope of Schedule 7 and the protection of journalistic sources and material under human rights law.

Hugo Keith QC (see p.689) (3 Raymond Buildings Barristers) Combines significant strength in criminal and public law. He acts for claimants and defendants in cases concerning criminal justice, extradition, sanctions, national security and terrorism. **Strengths:** "A versatile, clever lawyer who is very easy to work with. Super bright." "Organised, pleasant to work with and a very thorough knowledge of the developing law in this area." **Recent work:** Represented the Metropolitan Police Service in a judicial review challenging the verdict of lawful killing returned by the jury in the inquest into the death of Mark Duggan.

Clair Dobbin (see p.634) (3 Raymond Buildings Barristers) Typically acts for central government departments and other public bodies in complex judicial reviews involving the criminal justice system. She is also proficient at public law proceedings invoking human rights law. **Strengths:** "A delightful opponent. She is hard-working, an attractive advocate and knows the law very well. Fantastic." **Recent work:** Served as counsel for the Home Secretary in important proceedings relating to the UK's ability to extradite an individual facing a whole-life tariff in the USA for the most serious of offences.

Ben Watson (see p.790) (3 Raymond Buildings Barristers) Represents defendants in sensitive judicial reviews involving human rights and criminal law. He is particularly experienced in public law claims relating to the UK government's actions in armed conflicts. **Strengths:** "Fantastic, very responsive and very good at strategy." "Energetic, enthusiastic, bright and effective. Reassuring to have him on your team." **Recent work:** Successfully defended a challenge to the Ministry of Defence's ongoing assistance to the Sudanese military.

Amy Street (see p.775) (Serjeants' Inn Chambers) Instructed in contentious and non-contentious public law matters, especially where there is a significant human rights overlap. She is particularly experienced in cases considering deprivation of liberty and mental capacity. **Strengths:** "A great analytical mind. Very committed to this work." "Excellent. She is a formidable junior and perhaps the most thorough of all the advocates I have led." **Recent work:** Instructed by the Welsh Ministers in a Court of Appeal case considering whether or not the Mental Health Review Tribunal can discharge a patient it decides has been unlawfully deprived of liberty under community treatment orders.

Jonathan Crow QC (see p.627) (4 Stone Buildings) Operates at the forefront of commercial and regulatory public law. He handles cases of importance before the highest domestic courts as well as the ECJ and the ECHR. **Strengths:** "He is hugely impressive, on top of the detail, very easy to work with, user-friendly and good with clients. A truly excellent silk. He is able to deal with questioning that comes his way while sticking to his train of argument. A persuasive and pleasant advocate who is a real joy to watch." **Recent work:** Successfully represented the government in the Supreme Court in a judicial review regarding an incident in December 1948 when British troops shot and killed 24 civilians in what was then the Federation of Malaya.

Kerry Bretherton QC (see p.602) (Tanfield Chambers) Specialises in public law challenges involving an overlap with property law. She has considerable experience in challenges against local authority decisions on social housing. **Strengths:** "Very impressive and very measured. Excellent drafting skills. Very persuasive and good with clients." "She will find a point no one else would see and then successfully appeal." "Her drafting is excellent; she has a wonderful tone." **Recent work:** Represented the appellants in McDonald v McDonald, which considered whether Article 8 is engaged when possession is sought by a private landlord.

Robin Tam QC (Temple Garden Chambers) Handles significant public and administrative law challenges relating to immigration and asylum. He is frequently instructed to defend the Home Secretary in judicial review proceedings. **Strengths:** "A safe, steady pair of hands. Calm and impartial." "A gentle style which belies a sharp advocate. The way he presents points is brilliant. He never gets rattled under pressure." **Recent work:** Represented the Home Secretary in two joint cases concerning the requirements for lawful immigration detention of children and the relationship between the Home Office's decision making and the local authority's age assessment processes.

Andrew O'Connor QC (Temple Garden Chambers) Recommended for complex cases in national security, terrorism and foreign affairs. He is particularly favoured by central government clients to defend controversial decisions in judicial reviews. **Strengths:** "He's very good at getting to the nub of a case and identifying the issues that will be of concern to judges. A very realistic advocate and also very thorough." "A class act. He puts arguments across very smoothly. It is very difficult for judges not to believe and like him. A very, very nice manner in court." "Bright and sharp. His submissions are so clearly written and effective." **Recent work:** Represents the UK government in proceedings before the Investigatory Powers Tribunal concerning the legality of the acquisition and use of bulk personal datasets by the intelligence and security agencies.

Rory Phillips QC (3 Verulam Buildings) Predominantly represents government departments and intelligence agencies in significant public law challenges. He is especially experienced in cases regarding national security and foreign affairs. **Strengths:** "An effective, brilliant advocate. Manages cases amazingly." "Very impressive in court. A natural authority. Exceptionally well prepared." "Friendly when he needs to be but also tough when he needs to be. He can adapt to any situation." "He is very hands-on, strategically wise, a great advocate and a real team player." **Recent work:** Represented the UK government in Belhaj v Straw and others, a claim for damages in regard to alleged extraordinary rendition and complicity in torture. The case considered the applicability of sovereign immunity.

MIDLANDS

Administrative & Public Law
Leading Silks
Band 1
Clayton Richard *Kings Chambers* *
Khalique Nageena *No5 Chambers* [A]
Leading Juniors
Band 1
Ahmad Mirza *St Philips Chambers* *
Mandalia Vinesh *No5 Chambers* [A]

Ranked Lawyers

Richard Clayton QC (see p.618) (Kings Chambers) Extensive experience of appearing in judicial review proceedings on behalf of applicants and respondents. His deep knowledge of administrative and public law covers area such as local government, welfare cuts, human rights and constitutional law. **Strengths:** "He has a very broad understanding of public law." "He is very academic but also very sharp when it comes to tactics. He is very good at guiding you on what the judge is likely to be thinking." **Recent work:** Acted for the English Bridge Union, the applicant in a judicial review challenging the English Sports Council's definition of sport as an activity involving a physical element, therefore excluding "mind sports" such as bridge and chess.

Nageena Khalique QC (No5 Chambers) Predominantly represents NHS Trusts, local authorities, coroners and other public bodies in judicial review proceedings. She has particular focus on claims arising in healthcare, Court of Protection and community care. **Strengths:** "She is very user-friendly and personable, and her written pleadings are extremely clear, concise and well argued. She tries to look at any angle that will get an advantage for the client. On her feet, she has a knack for picking up on what judges want to hear and targets submissions accordingly." **Recent work:** Successfully represented West Midlands Ambulance Service NHS Foundation Trust in a challenge against the Trust's adoption of the NHS Pathways Triage System following the death of an individual with learning difficulties.

Vinesh Mandalia (No5 Chambers) Frequently acts in judicial review proceedings involving immigration and asylum decisions, often on behalf of the Home Secretary. He's also adept at representing HMRC in public law claims. **Strengths:** "Helpful and approachable." "His advocacy is fantastic. He doesn't get flustered, even in the most challenging cases." **Recent work:** Represented HMRC in an application for appeal brought by scrap metal company GB Housley. The subject of the challenge was HMRC's refusal to exercise its discretion under VAT regulations and the jurisdiction of the First-tier and Upper Tribunals to consider this exercise of discretion.

Mirza Ahmad (see p.580) (St Philips Chambers) Represents claimants and defendants in administrative and public law challenges to decisions made by local authorities, regulators and other public bodies. His background working in-house in local government adds depth to his public law expertise. **Strengths:** "Excellent client skills." "Pragmatic advice." "A great deal of public law experience."

NORTHERN/NORTH EASTERN

Administrative & Public Law
Leading Sets
Band 1
Garden Court North
Kings Chambers *
Leading Silks
Band 1
Weatherby Pete *Garden Court North*
* Indicates set / individual with profile.
[A] direct access (see p.24).
◊ (ORL) = Other Ranked Lawyer.
Alphabetical order within each band. Band 1 is highest.

Administrative & Public Law
Leading Juniors
Band 1
Fullwood Adam *39 Essex Chambers (ORL)* ◊
Band 2
Burrows Simon *Kings Chambers* *
Cartwright Sophie *Deans Court Chambers (ORL)* ◊ *
Hussain Tasaddat *Broadway House (ORL)* ◊ *
Jagadesham Vijay *Garden Court North*
Karim Sam *Kings Chambers* *
Stanbury Matthew *Garden Court North*
Stone Kate *Garden Court North*
Band 3
Draycott Paul *Doughty Street Chambers (ORL)* ◊
Hunter John *Kings Chambers* *
McCormack Ben *Garden Court North*

Band 1

Garden Court North

THE SET

Garden Court North is a hugely respected set specialising in representing claimants in a wide range of administrative and public law challenges. Sources commend the set's "very able practitioners." The team has particular expertise in public law matters involving human rights, immigration, housing, community care, prison law and welfare. Additional notable strengths include inquests and public inquiries. Recently, the set was involved in the judicial review G and H v Upper Tribunal and the Secretary of State for the Home Department, a notable challenge against the Upper Tribunal's decision to refuse permission for an appeal from the First-tier Tribunal.

Client service: Sarah Wright leads the clerking team.

SILKS

Pete Weatherby QC Particularly adept at utilising human rights arguments as grounds for challenging public body decision-making and policy. He is notably active in judicial reviews and inquests involving the criminal justice system. **Strengths:** "He's very clear and focused in arguments. He has an ability to work across a range of areas such as crime, damages and human rights, all of which require different styles of advocacy. He puts a lot of research and work into cases, which brings value."

JUNIORS

Vijay Jagadesham Has considerable experience of acting in administrative and public law matters involving immigration and prison law decisions. He has notable experience representing children and other vulnerable claimants. **Strengths:** "He is good at running legal points and isn't frightened of innovative legal arguments. A capable barrister."

Matthew Stanbury Specialises in public and administrative law cases with civil liberties and human rights crossover. He has considerable experience of cases which arise in the context of prison and criminal law. **Strengths:** "An excellent advocate."

Kate Stone Instructed to represent claimants in a broad range of administrative and public law cases. She is particularly adept at judicial reviews and inquests which concern prison and human rights law. **Strengths:** "Her skeleton arguments are excellent. As an advocate, she's on the ball and gets right to the point. She's an economical advocate, which makes her effective."

Ben McCormack Predominantly acts in claims against local authorities' and other public bodies' housing and community care decisions. He is also proficient at inquests and regularly appears before the Court of Protection. **Strengths:** "Undoubtedly works hard for clients." "He is very friendly and easy for judges and opponents to interact with. A pleasure to work with and always open to new suggestions."

Kings Chambers

See profile on p.968

THE SET

Kings Chambers is notable for its broad administrative and public law practice catering to both claimants and respondents. In particular, it is a popular choice for local authorities, central government departments and other public bodies being challenged by judicial review. Sources describe Kings Chambers as "the lead set for advising defendants." The team also receives praise for offering "London quality in the regions." It also offers notable expertise across the areas of healthcare, community care, social welfare and immigration.

Client service: "They are always very professional and helpful." The clerking team is led by William Brown.

JUNIORS

Simon Burrows (see p.607) Predominantly handles public law challenges surrounding mental health treatment including mental capacity and deprivation of liberty matters. Also experienced in cases concerning the withdrawal of treatment and inquests investigating deaths in psychiatric institutions. **Strengths:** "He is very good at putting parties at ease. He has a nice manner, he's approachable and his drafting is faultless." **Recent work:** Acted on behalf of the appellant in AMA v Greater Manchester West Mental Health Trust and Others, concerning the circumstances in which a welfare deputy can apply to withdraw an appeal against a patient's detention under the Mental Health Act.

Sam Karim (see p.688) Handles commercial judicial reviews on behalf of public bodies and private clients. He maintains a strong focus on public law challenges in the areas of healthcare, community care and mental capacity. **Strengths:** "He's extremely professional and also extremely practical and sensible." "A very good advocate in the courts." "He is very good at negotiating with other parties and bringing them round to his way of thinking." **Recent work:** Represented the Secretary of State for Business, Innovation and Skills in judicial review proceedings brought by 1st Choice Engines, challenging an unusual notice issued under Sections 447 and 452A of the Companies Act 1985.

John Hunter (see p.678) Extensive expertise acting for commercial claimants and public bodies in claims against planning decisions. He is also experienced in the areas of immigration, education, housing and prison law. **Strengths:** "Very good advocate." "He is very, very straightforward. In terms of working with him, he is very reassuring. You know that he will support you." "Incredibly good memory and a genuine interest and enthusiasm about the law and its detail." **Recent work:** Served as counsel to East Sussex County Council in judicial review proceedings brought by Newhaven Port and Properties contesting the applicability of village green status to a beach and, consequently, the rights of local residents to access the beach.

Other Ranked Lawyers

Tasaddat Hussain (see p.679) (Broadway House) Acclaimed for his expertise in administrative and public law cases concerning immigration and asylum. He is also adept at judicial reviews challenging public body decisions in healthcare, social care and prison law. **Strengths:** "A very good advocate who is particularly thorough."

Sophie Cartwright (see p.612) (Deans Court Chambers) Renowned for her expertise in inquests. She is frequently engaged in judicial review proceedings challenging the scope of inquests and the conduct of coroners. She routinely acts for local authorities and healthcare trusts in challenges against policy and decisions. **Strengths:** "Hard-working, well informed and well prepared." "A lawyer with a very good grasp of the law, she is a persuasive advocate who is strong in negotiations." "Really good with clients and witnesses." **Recent work:** Represented Mersey Care NHS Foundation Trust in an appeal against a judicial review decision regarding Ashworth Hospital's introduction of a Night Time Confinement Policy, which was being challenged by a patient on the grounds that it breached Articles 5 and 8 of the ECHR.

Paul Draycott (Doughty Street Chambers) Predominantly acts in challenges against decisions made by the Administrative Court, government departments and other public bodies in immigration and asylum claims. He is particularly adept at deploying human rights law as the basis of public law litigation. **Strengths:** "Extremely knowledgeable and experienced. He is thorough and precise in all that he does and is a great legal mind to have on board." "His style of advocacy is effective and efficient." **Recent work:** Advised the claimant in a decision about the appropriate costs order which should be issued in the wake of a successful judicial review.

Adam Fullwood (39 Essex Chambers) An expert at dealing with public law decisions relating to healthcare, education, mental capacity and social housing, among others. He routinely acts on behalf of both claimants and defendants, and is appointed to the Attorney General's Regional Panel. **Strengths:** "Very knowledgeable in public law." "Great breadth. He is equally at home acting for families and public authorities. He brings great authority to cases and has the ear of the court. Great experience." **Recent work:** Represented Lancashire CC in an appeal against a First-tier Tribunal decision dismissing arguments brought by parents concerning the provision of special education needs and the right approach towards comparative school costs.

WALES & CHESTER

Administrative & Public Law
Leading Silks
Band 1
Williams Rhodri *30 Park Place* [A]
Senior Statesmen
Senior Statesmen: distinguished older partners
Walters Graham *Civitas Law*
Leading Juniors
Band 1
Hillier Victoria *Civitas Law* *
Up-and-coming individuals
Rhys James Owain *Civitas Law* *
* *Indicates individual with profile.*
[A] *direct access (see p.24).*
Alphabetical order within each band. Band 1 is highest.

Ranked Lawyers

Graham Walters (Civitas Law) Extensive experience appearing in public inquiries on a wide range of regulatory issues including food safety, public transportation, licensing and state aid. He receives particular praise for his knowledge of Welsh planning law.

Victoria Hillier (see p.672) (Civitas Law) Frequently entrusted with controversial administrative public law claims relating to the criminal justice system. Her expertise also covers housing law, human rights and equality law. She routinely appears on behalf of state agents in inquests. **Strengths:** "She is excellent, very bright and user-friendly." "Very thorough preparation. She gets to know the papers very well. She is a very persuasive advocate. I enjoy watching her cross-examine because she does it so softly that witnesses don't realise that they are being grilled." **Recent work:** Instructed by the Welsh government to secure a possession order and an injunction for the recovery of land where a group of travellers was encamped.

Owain Rhys James (see p.750) (Civitas Law) Appears in a wide array of administrative and public law cases on behalf of claimants and respondents. He has particular experience of claims involving immigration and asylum. **Strengths:** "Has the ability to take a lot of documents and extract the most important issues." "He is unflappable, which is really nice because he can keep a calm head when everyone else is losing theirs. His drafting is nice and clear." **Recent work:** Represented an individual claimant challenging the Secretary of State for Work and Pensions' refusal to pay the claimant's Disability Living Allowance amid allegations of fraud, which were contested at the hearing.

Rhodri Williams QC (30 Park Place) Acts for applicants and respondents in administrative and public law proceedings including judicial reviews. He has particular experience of handling challenges against cuts to public services. His additional areas of expertise include EU and public procurement law. **Strengths:** "Always very well prepared and a thorough researcher." **Recent work:** Successfully represented the defendant, Neath Port Talbot CBC, in a judicial review concerning its decision to close two primary schools.

Contents:

LONDON

Agriculture & Rural Affairs
Leading Sets
Band 1
Falcon Chambers *
Band 2
Francis Taylor Building *
Landmark Chambers *
Maitland Chambers *
New Square Chambers *
9 Stone Buildings *
Leading Silks
Band 1
Chapman Vivian R *9 Stone Buildings* *
Jourdan Stephen *Falcon Chambers*
Laurence George *New Square Chambers* *
Massey William *Pump Court Tax Chambers (ORL)* ◊ *
Mercer Hugh *Essex Court Chambers (ORL)* ◊
Band 2
Edwards Douglas *Francis Taylor Building* *
Karas Jonathan *Falcon Chambers* *
Band 3
Ellis Morag *Francis Taylor Building*
Elvin David *Landmark Chambers*
Fancourt Timothy *Falcon Chambers* *
Gaunt Jonathan *Falcon Chambers* *
Morshead Timothy *Landmark Chambers*
Wonnacott Mark *Maitland Chambers*
New Silks
Shea Caroline *Falcon Chambers*
Leading Juniors
Band 1
Crail Ross *New Square Chambers*
Hutton Caroline *Enterprise Chambers (ORL)* ◊
Moss Joanne *Falcon Chambers*
Thomas Nigel *Maitland Chambers* *
Windsor Emily *Falcon Chambers* *
Band 2
Healey Greville *Falcon Chambers* *
Petchey Philip *Francis Taylor Building*
Taskis Catherine *Falcon Chambers* *
Band 3
Honey Richard *Francis Taylor Building* [A] *
Jones Karen *Tanfield Chambers (ORL)* ◊
Ollech Joseph *Falcon Chambers* *
Peters Edward *Falcon Chambers* *
Radley-Gardner Oliver *Falcon Chambers*
Simpson Edwin *New Square Chambers* *
Westaway Ned *Francis Taylor Building*
Wilmshurst Paul *9 Stone Buildings* *
** Indicates set / individual with profile.*
[A] direct access (see p.24).
◊ (ORL) = Other Ranked Lawyer.
Alphabetical order within each band. Band 1 is highest.

Band 1

Falcon Chambers
See profile on p.842

THE SET

This set continues to stand well above any other in the agricultural sphere due, in part, to the sheer number of members it can devote to the area. Its members have a wide range of specialist knowledge across niche areas of agricultural law and are "the people you go to for top-rate technical expertise" and "the mustard on leading edge cases." One market commentator states: "I have every now and again strayed outside Falcon Chambers, but invariably regret it. For property matters, or property-related matters such as farming partnership disputes, Falcon Chambers is the place to go."

Client service: Steven Francis leads the clerking team. "He's really good and always very, very helpful, as is the whole support team there."

SILKS

Stephen Jourdan QC Garners praise from all corners, and is a known leader in rural property matters. He's renowned for his expertise in landlord and tenant disputes and those concerning farming partnerships. **Strengths:** "What you get is forensic attention to detail and complete mastery of the documents. He's an absolute rock you can rely on; you know you're in the best possible hands." **Recent work:** Represented a farmer in defending a right of way over neighbouring land. The court found in favour of Mr Jourdan's client, as his use of the land for food production was a correct interpretation of the right of way agreement from 1991.

Jonathan Karas QC (see p.687) Has an active practice handling cases concerning agricultural tenancies, development and property relief. Peers praise him for his detail-oriented approach and the sheer breadth of issues upon which he is able to give in-depth advice. **Strengths:** "He's an outstanding advocate, particularly for High Court or Supreme Court cases. He is outstanding on village greens and commons." **Recent work:** Successfully represented Lt Col David Wood in proving that he and those riding to and from his commercial stables had a right of way over a track on adjoining land.

Timothy Fancourt QC (see p.643) Handles agricultural and rural affairs cases as part of his highly successful general property practice. "A class act," who is known for his technical approach; he is especially active in cases concerning tenancies, agricultural holdings and shooting rights. **Strengths:** "Excellent in cross-examination, and hugely experienced in all aspects of property law." "You go to him when you want to bring someone in with reputation." **Recent work:** Acted for an agricultural landowner in Elveden Farms v Usher, a case concerning the right to terminate a lease on shooting premises.

Jonathan Gaunt QC (see p.651) Highly regarded silk with a well-developed real property practice covering issues such as restrictive covenants and easements. He also regularly acts in disputes between landlords and tenants, and tackles rural property cases more generally. **Strengths:** "He is a true heavyweight." "He has an absolutely fantastic grasp of the law, and is particularly good on rights of way and covenant issues." **Recent work:** Acted for the defendants in the high-profile proprietary estoppel case of Davies v Davies.

Caroline Shea QC A relatively new silk who has a well-developed rural property practice. She is noted for her particular strength in agricultural landlord and tenant work as well as for her knowledge of proprietary estoppel. **Strengths:** "She is absolutely outstanding. She is not only a great lawyer but she has excellent client skills." **Recent work:** Represented the widow of a tenant seeking succession pursuant to the Agricultural Holdings Act 1986. Succession was accepted by the Agricultural Lands Tribunal.

JUNIORS

Joanne Moss Widely recognised as an expert on agricultural tenancies. Her practice also includes cases concerning greenfield site acquisition, vacant possession and notices to quit. **Strengths:** "She provides robust and practical advice. When it comes to agricultural tenancies, she's top of the tree."

Emily Windsor (see p.798) Highly regarded junior with an active property litigation practice. On the rural side, she offers expertise in such areas as proprietary estoppel and agricultural holdings. **Strengths:** "Emily is a delightful person to deal with." "She's superb, very thorough and very bright." **Recent work:** Acted in Harefold v Gower, representing a party who was claiming for benefit of an agricultural tenancy over a Devon estate worth £10 million.

Greville Healey (see p.668) Advises on a range of agricultural landlord and tenant matters, and also regularly acts for institutional lenders on matters concerning secured lending on agricultural property. **Strengths:** "Demonstrates a broad and thorough understanding of the legal issues at hand. He has a very keen mind and a great ability to get to the nub of any matter very quickly." **Recent work:** Represented Chargrove Parish Council in its successful resistance to a claim that an agricultural right of way had been acquired over a village green.

Catherine Taskis (see p.778) Well-regarded junior whose residential and commercial property practice has a distinct agricultural focus. She advises on real property, and landlord and tenant law. **Strengths:** "She's extremely good and particularly adept at forensic cross-examination." "Very good for agricultural holdings advice and succession claims." **Recent work:** Acted in an arbitration for a tenant appealing a notice to quit not served under the Agricultural Holdings Act 1986.

Joseph Ollech (see p.730) An impressive junior who specialises in real estate litigation. His areas of expertise include restrictive covenants, easements and land registration. **Strengths:** "In a set of chambers where everyone is clever, one always senses that Joe would rank amongst the very cleverest. His advisory work is outstanding." **Recent work:** Acted on a dispute between two fisheries concerning rights to a shared water table.

Edward Peters (see p.736) Strong when it comes to agricultural tenancy disputes and those concerning farming partnerships. **Strengths:** "He's incredibly thorough, very bright and highly approachable. In court he's superb at cross-examination." **Recent work:** Acted in the long-running case of Collins v Collins, a five-party dispute over the dissolution of a family farming partnership that owned 645 acres of farmland.

Oliver Radley-Gardner Up-and-coming advocate with a strong rural practice. He works on cases concerning rights of way, boundary disputes and farming succession claims. **Strengths:** "Of the crop of outstanding youngsters at Falcon Chambers, Oliver is one of the very best. He has a first-class intellect and very good client skills." **Recent work:** Acted in Crown Estate v Wakley, a case concerning a breached lease and the resulting failure of a farm business.

Band 2

Francis Taylor Building
See profile on p.849

THE SET
A planning and local government law set that is well placed to advise on rural public law matters. It boasts strength in depth in town and village green cases and further handles matters concerning covenants, easements and rights of way. Members offer additional expertise in the planning and development issues relevant to many public access claims. Individuals also act as inspectors and contribute to renowned publications.
Client service: "The clerks, led by Paul Coveney, are very, very good."

SILKS
Douglas Edwards QC (see p.639) Well regarded for his work on town and village greens applications, he is regularly instructed by local authorities and private landowners in these cases and matters concerning common land. **Strengths:** "He's an authority on town and village greens. He's incredibly good to work with, incredibly efficient and he really knows his stuff. He's very good with clients and can wipe the floor with the other side." **Recent work:** Challenged the town green registration of land in Essex which functions as an operational port.

Morag Ellis QC Acts in a wide range of planning matters and has a strong town and village green practice. She also advises on the implications of development applications on rural land. **Strengths:** "A very good cross-examiner with a very good command of all of issues." **Recent work:** Successfully resisted a TVG application for land now held privately but formerly owned by the MoD.

JUNIORS
Philip Petchey Has a significant planning practice with a focus on town and village greens work. He also counts footpath and common land law cases amongst his areas of expertise. **Strengths:** "A very senior junior who is academically excellent in his subject as well as being a fine lawyer."

Richard Honey (see p.674) Public access specialist who also sits as a village green inspector. He is additionally adept at handling cases concerning protected species and habitats. **Strengths:** "He has a very measured, never over-the-top, advocacy style and can unpick any legal problem however knotty." **Recent work:** Acted as an inspector, advising on an application to register Herne Downs as a village green.

Ned Westaway Handles cases relating to commons, village greens and rights of way. He is regularly instructed by rights of way authorities and groups such as The Ramblers' Association. **Strengths:** "He is extremely thorough and very good at picking out case law. His method of questioning and cross-examining is impressive, he's firm but fair." **Recent work:** Acted in B D Harris Farm Trust v South Downs National Park Authority, appearing for the appellant to the Authority's decision not to allow a permanent residential dwelling to support beef suckler herd, grazing by sheep and conservation management.

Landmark Chambers
See profile on p.873

THE SET
A set noted for its strength in planning, property and environmental law, Landmark Chambers has a strong reputation for tackling agricultural cases. Members offer expertise in cases concerning rights of way and public access. They are also expert at handling disputes between landlord and tenant.
Client service: The set's clerking team is led by Jay Fullilove.

SILKS
David Elvin QC A planning and environmental law specialist of some renown who acts for landowners and local authorities in cases concerning development of agricultural land. **Strengths:** "He's clear, concise, to the point and someone you can have ultimate faith and confidence in as an advocate."

Timothy Morshead QC Maintains a real property practice with an agricultural bent. He handles cases covering such matters as town and village greens, highways and tenancies. **Strengths:** "He's extremely intelligent and rounded in his understanding of all property law issues. He's a particular expert when it comes to cases concerning registration and proprietary estoppel." **Recent work:** Acted successfully in Beech v Kennerley, a Court of Appeal case concerning the distinction between a personal right and an easement.

Maitland Chambers
See profile on p.875

THE SET
Maitland Chambers is particularly prominent in real estate litigation; a number of members also have specialist knowledge of agricultural matters. Barristers regularly handle landlord and tenant disputes relating to agricultural holdings and farm businesses. Chambers also houses individuals with expertise in farming partnership disputes.
Client service: Chambers' senior clerk is the much respected John Wiggs.

SILKS
Mark Wonnacott QC Has a broad property litigation practice and is particularly praised for his strength in cases relating to manorial rights, minerals and land registry. **Strengths:** "He does this work properly; he's impressive all round."

JUNIORS
Nigel Thomas (see p.780) Handles agriculture-related cases as part of his broad chancery practice law and has a caseload that takes in matters concerning farm tenancies, partnerships and water law. He presides as Chair of the Midlands Area Agricultural Land Tribunal. **Strengths:** "He's a very specialised agriculture lawyer," who is "completely unflappable and always takes the weight off the instructing solicitor's shoulders."

New Square Chambers
See profile on p.882

THE SET
New Square Chambers has noted strength when it comes to public access and highways law, with its members being expert in cases concerning rights of way and village greens. Barristers in the set contribute to leading publications and act as inspectors in public inquiries into town or village green applications. The frequency with which New Square members appear in Supreme Court cases is noteworthy.
Client service: Phil Reeves is head of clerking in chambers.

SILKS
George Laurence QC (see p.696) A true heavyweight in matters of public access law who is widely lauded for the significance of his contribution to this field. He also deals more generally with rural property disputes. **Strengths:** "He's immensely impressive, intellectually rounded and someone with a huge depth of knowledge in village green matters and property law more generally." "He combines a great legal mind with great advocacy skills." **Recent work:** Acted for Newhaven Town Council, ensuring that a decision to register the town's west beach as a village green was upheld in the Court of Appeal.

JUNIORS
Ross Crail A real property specialist with a significant practice in the area of highways, common land and other public access law. She regularly acts for local authorities, landowners and developers. **Strengths:** "She has a formidable intellect." **Recent work:** Appointed by Kent County Council to conduct an inquiry regarding the existence of a public right to recreational use of a beach.

Edwin Simpson (see p.765) Rural property practitioner who regularly acts in both public and private rights of way cases. He is noted for his academic credentials and is, additional to his legal practice, a member of Oxford University's law faculty. **Strengths:** "He's a part-time academic who brings a rigorous academic approach to all his cases." **Recent work:** Acted for a landowner in resisting an application to change a map of minor highways affecting a right of way over their land. Deals with the issue of the existence of a right of way following the destruction of the corresponding land or structure.

9 Stone Buildings
See profile on p.915

THE SET
9 Stone Buildings houses individuals with experience in matters of agricultural and property law generally, but is particularly noted for its work on town and village greens and public access cases. One source proclaims that "it has the best barristers who are at the forefront of thinking on town and village green applications."
Client service: Alan Austin is the senior clerk in chambers.

SILKS
Vivian Chapman QC (see p.615) Experienced silk from a chancery background who maintains a strong real property practice. He is widely regarded as a leading authority on town and village greens. **Strengths:** "He has an extremely deep knowledge and understanding of his subject and is highly regarded by the judiciary. His opinions are always a model of

concision, and extremely thorough." **Recent work:** Acted for a landowner in a public inquiry, resisting registration of Cae Prior as a new village green.

JUNIORS

Paul Wilmshurst (see p.797) Advises on land and property law including matters relating to village greens, commons and rights of way. He often represents local authorities and acts as an inspector in public inquiries. **Strengths:** "He's a rising star of that chambers, who is fully in command of all the legal issues and has a broad grasp of the subject." **Recent work:** Acted in Christopher Benham v Brookland Investments Limited, appearing for a Guernsey-based landowner of some 60 acres of agricultural land who was opposing an application to register the land as a new village green under the Commons Act 2006.

Other Ranked Lawyers

Hugh Mercer QC (Essex Court Chambers) An expert on European law who is highly regarded for his work on farming subsidies and the Common Agricultural Policy. He has, of late, handled a number of matters concerning food and the Basic Payment Scheme. Mercer regularly acts for the NFU and has also represented French and Belgian farming unions on EU law issues. **Strengths:** "He gives erudite, comprehensive and accurate advice." **Recent work:** Instructed by Welsh lowland farmers to consider a possible challenge to a revised regime for implementing Basic Payment Scheme. The new regime arose from a decision by Welsh Ministers to split Welsh land into lowland, SDA and moorland and to pay EU aids in a ratio of 12:10:1.

Caroline Hutton (Enterprise Chambers) Property litigation expert with experience in agricultural disputes such as those concerning tenancies and conveyancing. She is additionally adept at boundary disputes and cases involving mineral and sporting rights. **Strengths:** "She is extremely able, and expresses herself to the clients in a simple, comprehensible way. She's also very good on tactics and advocacy."

William Massey QC (see p.709) (Pump Court Tax Chambers) Widely regarded as the leading light for cases concerning tax issues relating to landed estates. Heritage property, agricultural property relief and estate tax planning are all areas of expertise for him. **Strengths:** "William is at the very top of his tree and is very clear with clients." "Without doubt, the leading tax QC for heritage matters."

Karen Jones (Tanfield Chambers) Public law specialist and former adviser to the Country Land and Business Association. She is regularly instructed in cases involving issues of town or village greens and rights of way. **Strengths:** "Karen's expertise on public rights of way is there for all to see. She provides clear and incisive advice and is very easy to work with."

SOUTH EASTERN

Agriculture & Rural Affairs
Leading Juniors
Band 1
Monnington Bruce *Fenners Chambers*

Ranked Lawyers

Bruce Monnington (Fenners Chambers) Deals with a range of property and public law cases in the rural field, including matters of land law, rights of way and tenancy disputes. He is also active in trusts, wills and estates work. **Strengths:** "He is extremely responsive and proactive."

WESTERN

Agriculture & Rural Affairs
Leading Silks
Band 1
Blohm Leslie *St John's Chambers*
Leading Juniors
Band 1
Batstone William *Guildhall Chambers*
Band 2
Newsom George *Guildhall Chambers*
Troup Alex *St John's Chambers* [A]
[A] *direct access (see p.24).*
Alphabetical order within each band. Band 1 is highest.

Ranked Lawyers

William Batstone (Guildhall Chambers) A highly regarded barrister with a broad agricultural and rural property practice. He is noted for his expertise in agricultural tenancy disputes. **Strengths:** "He really is an expert in the field of agricultural tenancies – his knowledge and experience are unrivalled. His advice is always produced promptly and it is clear and easy to follow. He is also very easy to work with and approachable."

George Newsom (Guildhall Chambers Chambers) Acts in disputes of land, partnerships and estates, with experience in matters of freeholds, tenancies and rights of way. He is recognised as an expert in matters of restrictive covenants. **Strengths:** "Very precise, technically knowledgeable barrister." "Great attention to detail and encyclopaedic knowledge of the law in this area."

Leslie Blohm QC (St John's Chambers) Maintains a formidable reputation in rural property law on the Western circuit. He is widely praised for his strength in village greens and proprietary estoppel cases concerning farms. **Strengths:** "He wows clients and has an amazing gift to explain the most complicated issues in an easy and understandable manner. Very decent guy to get on with." "He's a good man – he's able, he's pleasant, and he's a quintessentially good barrister." **Recent work:** Represented Bristol City Council in an application to register a playing field as a town or village green to prevent future development.

Alex Troup (St John's Chambers) His practice takes in disputes between farming landlords and tenants, and he is an expert in proprietary estoppel claims. **Strengths:** "He's really formidable in the area. He's client-friendly, very impressive on paper and a fantastic performer in court." **Recent work:** Successfully acted for the claimant in Hamilton v Barkhuysen, a dispute over rights of grazing and access to a Cornish moor. The claimant's costs were paid in full by the defendant.

ART AND CULTURAL PROPERTY LAW: An Introduction

Contributed by 5 Stone Buildings

While it is still very much an emerging practice area, the field of art and cultural property continues to grow at the English Bar. This has largely been driven by the development of specialist art law teams at a small number of solicitors' firms and the increasing focus on sector-based specialisms across the legal marketplace.

The landscape in this area continues to be altered by the changing nature of the commercial art market. The international increase in the saleability of the very best art has led to a corresponding increase in the volume of transactions in this area, while ever-increasing values have seen a rise in the value and complexity of the work in this field (both non-contentious and contentious). The practice area remains notably small and extremely specialised, with relatively few practitioners offering deep experience and expertise in the sphere.

The wealth of knowledge brought to the field by these practitioners is one of the key factors underpinning the development of the practice area, at both the junior and senior ends of the Bar.

Overview of 2015-16

Despite the relatively small size of the art and cultural property law field, the volume of work, both contentious and non-contentious, has continued to increase steadily over the past twelve months. Although the boundaries of the practice area are often difficult to define, the common thread of all the work in this area is that it centres around art, the art market or cultural property.

Disputes as to ownership title and agency continue to form a significant part of the workload in this area. In common with other legal fields involving international transactions, the art and cultural property sphere often raises difficult conflicts of laws arguments. Claims concerning possession (rather than ownership) and involving bailment and consignment continue to play a significant role. The continued growth of domestic and international regulation in this area has ensured a significant increase in transactional advisory work. Counsel is regularly being provided on the drafting of consignment and loan agreements, as well as on the effect of various consumer protection measures.

The taxation of art is also an important and valuable source of work. While the majority of this is non-contentious, disputes of a contentious nature do inevitably arise. The acceptance in lieu and related schemes have continued to provide a significant source of work (though this is often less prominent at the Bar than among solicitors' firms). Issues involving the export and import (temporary or permanent) of artwork are a similarly significant feature.

Restitutionary claims have continued to increase and expand in complexity. These fall into a number of categories, including civil claims based on common law principles of restitution and claims brought in reliance on foreign statutory regimes. Looted and stolen art (which, in common with much of the work in this practice area, invariably has a cross-border element) has continued to be a feature of the contentious landscape. Claims before the Spoliation Advisory Panel involving the 1970 UNESCO Convention have continued to be fewer in number, but nonetheless remain an important feature of work in this field.

The year ahead and beyond

The majority of indicators would suggest that the next twelve months will continue to see greater recognition of this emerging specialism. The acknowledgement of art and cultural property as a distinct, sector-based practice area will likely continue to lead to a steady increase in work of this type. Over recent years, cases which are in the public sphere have evidenced an increasing willingness of the court to engage with the international art market on its own terms (in particular in considering the manner in which attribution and valuation are arrived at). It is to be expected that this trend will continue as the court becomes more used to such claims and as the sophistication of the legal analysis applied continues to increase.

In general terms, the factors that have led to the increase in art and cultural property work mean that it is likely that the complexity and volume of such work will continue over the coming year and beyond. The rise in values, which has driven much of this increase in activity, shows no sign of reversing. This, together with the increasing sophistication of consumers and institutions operating in the field, points to the further cementation of art and cultural property as an established specialism at the English Bar in the immediate future.

Contents:

LONDON

Art and Cultural Property Law	
Leading Silks	
Band 1	
Legge Henry	*5 Stone Buildings* *
Palmer Norman E	*5 Stone Buildings* *
Band 2	
Aldridge James	*Maitland Chambers* *
Cooper Gilead	*Wilberforce Chambers* *
Harwood Richard	*39 Essex Chambers* *
Onslow Andrew	*3 Verulam Buildings*
Smouha Joe	*Essex Court Chambers*
New Silks	
Edwards Richard	*3 Verulam Buildings*
Mumford David	*Maitland Chambers* *
Leading Juniors	
Band 1	
Harris Luke	*5 Stone Buildings* *
Band 2	
Bruce Andrew	*Serle Court* *
Franses Jessica	*The 36 Group*
Holland Jordan	*5 Stone Buildings* *

** Indicates individual with profile.*

Alphabetical order within each band. Band 1 is highest.

Ranked Lawyers

Joe Smouha QC (Essex Court Chambers) Enjoys a superb reputation amongst solicitors for his ability to handle complex commercial disputes across a wide range areas. He has represented clients in a number of art and cultural property disputes. **Strengths:** "He is ferociously intelligent, very client-friendly and someone who communicates complex issues in a very comprehensible way." **Recent work:** Represented Leslie Wexner and Copley Motorcars in a case against Bonhams concerning the ownership of a 1954 Ferrari 375-Plus.

Richard Harwood QC (see p.666) (39 Essex Chambers) Renowned for his expertise in cases relating to the removal of artworks from listed buildings. He also advises major clients on export controls relating to culturally significant artefacts. **Strengths:** "He's an absolute expert in heritage matters." "A highly intelligent individual who has an immediate grasp of the issues in a case."

David Mumford QC (see p.724) (Maitland Chambers) A highly sought-after silk noted for his ability to handle heavyweight commercial disputes. He has significant experience of representing auction houses in cases concerning the authenticity and provenance of artworks. **Strengths:** "He is a first-rate advocate and his written work is turned around with amazing speed."

Andrew Bruce (see p.605) (Serle Court) Handles a substantial real estate litigation practice alongside his impressive art and cultural property work. He is especially adept at representing clients in attribution disputes. **Strengths:** "He's always to the point, and doesn't dodge any of the issues. He definitely takes a view."

Henry Legge QC (see p.699) (5 Stone Buildings) A leading chancery barrister who is well known for his ability to handle major cases concerning works of art. He has notable expertise in a wide range of matters and he regularly handles title disputes, attribution matters and spoliation advisory panel claims. **Strengths:** "He is very good. He is an expert on the artworks market, and has a real in-depth knowledge of the subject."

Norman Palmer QC (Hon) (see p.733) (5 Stone Buildings) A long-standing figure in this field who is regularly involved in the most significant art and cultural property matters. He works with a wide range of clients including dealers, collectors, institutions and governments, and is an acknowledged authority on the recovery of historically important objects. **Strengths:** "He is the oracle. Everybody goes to him for advice on the most complicated things as he is the pre-eminent silk in the field of art and cultural property law." He's incredibly meticulous."

James Aldridge QC (see p.581) (Maitland Chambers) An experienced commercial chancery practitioner who acts for clients in a variety of art and cultural property matters. He handles forgery claims, attribution disputes and cases concerning looted artwork. **Strengths:** "He's commerical and very user-friendly." "He's absolutely brilliant."

Luke Harris (see p.665) (5 Stone Buildings) A first-class junior who works with high-profile clients including governments, auction houses and private clients. He handles an impressively varied range of art and cultural property matters, and is frequently involved in title, insurance, partnership and contractual disputes. **Strengths:** "He is the go-to junior for art cases. Very good with clients and excellent at delivering quality advice, he's well versed in the area of bailment and the more esoteric aspects of art and cultural property law." "He's very personable, very nice and very thorough. He thinks around the issues and comes back with instructive comments."

Jordan Holland (see p.674) (5 Stone Buildings) Has a strong practice handling significant contentious and non-contentious art law matters. He has considerable experience in authenticity disputes and auction house claims, and works with noteworthy clients including collectors, dealers, institutions and governments. **Strengths:** "Very hands on and knowledgeable in the area, he's alert to all the issues and a pleasure to work with." "He is great and very commercially minded."

Jessica Franses (The 36 Group) Extremely well known throughout the art world for her dedication to art law matters, including those concerning sales negotiations and contracts, exhibition loan agreements, provenance and title. She works with a wide variety of clients including galleries, dealers, collectors, museums and artists. **Strengths:** "She is passionate about art law."

Andrew Onslow QC (3 Verulam Buildings) A highly respected advocate with particular expertise in professional negligence, fraud and banking and finance disputes. His art and cultural property practice is focused on advising and representing auction houses. **Strengths:** "He's an expert in defending auction houses." "A smart, hard-working and accessible QC who gets on top of the details in a case right from the off."

Richard Edwards QC (3 Verulam Buildings) A well-regarded banking and finance silk who is noteworthy for having previously worked as an art dealer. His art and cultural property work sees him advising and representing clients involved in title and attribution disputes. **Strengths:** "He loves works of art cases and is fascinated by art history, so he really gets into the detail." "I think he is a very strong barrister who is knowledgeable and has a good understanding of how the art market works."

Gilead Cooper QC (see p.623) (Wilberforce Chambers) An accomplished and admired traditional chancery silk who also handles disputes concerning important art and cultural property. His work takes in proceedings before the Spoliation Advisory Panel. **Strengths:** "He's very good at handling intricate points about what museums can and cannot do."

Contents:

LONDON

Aviation
Leading Sets
Band 1
Fountain Court Chambers *
Quadrant Chambers *
Band 2
XXIV Old Buildings *
Leading Silks
Star individuals
Crane Michael *Fountain Court Chambers* *
Band 1
Kealey Gavin *7 King's Bench Walk (ORL)* ◊
Lawson Robert *Quadrant Chambers* *
Shah Akhil *Fountain Court Chambers* *
Shepherd Philip *XXIV Old Buildings*
Thanki Bankim *Fountain Court Chambers* *
Band 2
Calver Neil *Brick Court Chambers (ORL)* ◊
McLaren Michael *Fountain Court Chambers* *
Moriarty Stephen *Fountain Court Chambers* *
Band 3
Béar Charles *Fountain Court Chambers* *
Kimbell John *Quadrant Chambers* *
Steel John *39 Essex Chambers (ORL)* ◊ Ⓐ *
Taylor John *Fountain Court Chambers* *
New Silks
Phelps Rosalind *Fountain Court Chambers* *
Leading Juniors
Band 1
Marland Timothy *Quadrant Chambers*
Reeve Matthew *Quadrant Chambers* *
Shah Bajul *XXIV Old Buildings*
Band 2
Chambers Jonathan *Quadrant Chambers*
Cutress James *Fountain Court Chambers* *
Deal Katherine *3 Hare Court (ORL)* ◊
Milner Alexander *Fountain Court Chambers* *
Band 3
Barrett Stephanie *Quadrant Chambers* *
Cumming Edward *XXIV Old Buildings*
Duffy James *Fountain Court Chambers* *
Howard Anneli *Monckton Chambers (ORL)* ◊ Ⓐ *
Up-and-coming individuals
Bird Tom *Quadrant Chambers*
** Indicates set / individual with profile.*
Ⓐ direct access (see p.24).
◊ (ORL) = Other Ranked Lawyer.
Alphabetical order within each band. Band 1 is highest.

Band 1

Fountain Court Chambers

See profile on p.847

THE SET

Robust aviation-specialist chambers with an unparalleled depth of top-quality barristers. Fountain Court Chambers offers clients an all-encompassing service across the entirety of aviation law, and its members are frequently instructed in cases arising from commerical, insurance, regulatory and personal injury-related claims. One solicitor attests that "if it's intellect you want to throw at a problem, then this is the chambers you go to." Recent cases that members have handled include Virgin Atlantic v Koito & Mitsubishi, a significant defect claim involving the allegation of manipulated product safety test results, and Alpstream & Ors v PK Finance, a leading case with regard to issues pertaining to enforcement action by a mortgage.

Client service: "The staff here are just brilliant, nothing is too much. They go above and beyond the call of duty and provide exceptional service." "They are very commercial and very responsive." Alex Taylor leads the clerking team.

SILKS

Michael Crane QC (see p.625) The pre-eminent specialist aviation silk, whose outstanding practice takes in the market's more sophisticated and visible disputes. Clients value his depth of experience, courtroom gravitas and approachable manner, and continue to instruct him in a diverse scope of cases concerning insurance, regulatory, commercial and insolvency matters, to name but a few. **Strengths:** "He's absolutely one of a kind – outstandingly clever and nice. He's superb." "Our go-to silk for something important." **Recent work:** Successfully represented Virgin Atlantic in a product liability claim against Koito & Mitsubishi regarding the allegation of the defendants having misrepresented equipment test results and implemented unapproved modifications.

Akhil Shah QC (see p.762) An in-demand silk who enjoys a reputation for providing clients with well-considered, first-rate legal counsel. Clients appreciate his cerebral and professional demeanor, which he applies to a multitude of aviation cases including those related to regulatory, financial and commercial disputes. **Strengths:** "Akhil couples an unrivalled eye for forensic detail with a pragmatic commercial approach. He is a reliable sounding board and a pleasure to work with." **Recent work:** Represented the insurers of the operator of the helicopter that fatally crashed at the St. George building construction in Vauxhall in 2013.

Bankim Thanki QC (see p.780) A "formidable and heavily in-demand" barrister who is also the deputy head of chambers. He is regularly instructed in considerable transactional, commercial and regulatory matters in domestic and international jurisdictions. **Strengths:** "Extremely astute and personable QC, who is able to transform the most complex of arguments into straightforward and eloquent submissions." **Recent work:** Successfully defended China Southern Airlines against claims of conspiracy and breach of contract brought by Tigris, the purchaser, following a USD124 million sale of six Airbus aircraft.

Michael McLaren QC (see p.713) Held in high regard by clients and peers alike for his effective advocacy and zealous work ethic. His practice has a noteworthy commercial edge but is not limited in scope in the aviation market as he regularly acts in matters regarding regulatory and contractual issues. **Strengths:** "Michael is a tireless worker who masters every angle of his brief and is, in particular, a truly formidable cross-examiner." **Recent work:** Acted on Dubai Financial Group v National Air Services, an appeal against the refusal to set aside a USD10.3 million default judgment.

Stephen Moriarty QC (see p.721) Widely respected for his erudite and scrupulous practice, he applies his impressive commercial pedigree to financially concerned aviation cases. He is regularly involved in complex and law defining cases. **Strengths:** "A well-established practitioner." **Recent work:** Acted for the defendant in Alpstream & Ors v PK Airfinance regarding an allegation of unnecessary maintenance works done to a repossessed aircraft, a major case in terms of aircraft finance and mortgage issues.

Charles Béar QC (see p.593) A commended advocate and trusted legal adviser, widely recognised for his cross-examination prowess. He is frequently involved in heavyweight aviation cases where his commercial tact is well appreciated. **Strengths:** "I think he's one of the best commercial barristers in terms of his paperwork. I'm constantly impressed with the quality of his advice to clients and his courtroom performance." **Recent work:** Acted for Alpstream AG in a considerable case concerning an aircraft procured at an allegedly unlawfully low price, which raised numerous mortgage-related issues pertinent beyond aviation.

John Taylor QC (see p.778) Operates a broad practice of which aviation represents a substantial part. He applies his vast commercial expertise to matters concerning aircraft leasing, sales, insurance, regulation and product liability. **Strengths:** "A very practical thinker who makes difficult concepts very accessible. I found him to be overall very effective." "John helped us energetically at short notice and against a very tight timeframe." **Recent work:** Represented the defendant in Virgin Atlantic v Mitsubishi, a major product liability dispute regarding the contractual specification and regulatory compliance of aircraft seats supplied to the claimant.

Rosalind Phelps QC (see p.736) A new silk with a burgeoning aviation practice. She is well regarded for her proficiency in matters of particular technical complexity, especially utilised in the financial and insurance sectors for airline and airport clients. **Strengths:** "She has developed a good reputation for certainly complex aviation commercial disputes." **Recent work:** Was lead in the Alpstream & Ors v PK Airfinance case where she defended the defendant against accusations of unnecessary maintenance work and unlawful sale.

JUNIORS

James Cutress (see p.628) An in-demand junior whose diverse caseload often includes appearances in intricate cases relating to leasing and financing disputes and insurance matters. **Strengths:** "He's very good at cutting to the chase, paring things back and focusing on the main issues." **Recent work:** Appeared as sole counsel in Bharat v Embraer, a USD10 million claim against a manufacturer for supposedly refusing the sale agreement of an aircraft.

Alexander Milner (see p.718) Experienced junior barrister with renowned intellect and clarity of vision. In his multifaceted aviation practice he acts as litigator and arbitrator in claims arising from leasing, financing and insurance disputes. **Strengths:** "He has a fine eye for forensic detail and a skill for calmly testing the robustness of an argument." "He's really exceptional." **Recent work:** Acted as sole counsel on behalf of a wealthy Saudi Arabian businessman in a

USD5 million claim relating to the breach of a sales agreement.

James Duffy (see p.637) A regular in substantial commercial aviation disputes, who acts for a client base comprised of airlines and airports in sophisticated and high-profile cases. **Strengths:** "Very responsive and collaborative – a great team player. He provides high-quality advocacy, both written and oral – in particular, he's good on his feet in the face of a challenging tribunal." **Recent work:** Instructed by Rolls-Royce with regards to perspective disputes brought about by irregular financial reporting of the client's Norwegian engine subsidiary.

Quadrant Chambers

See profile on p.901

THE SET

A widely respected set in the aviation market, composed of a collection of highly regarded and sought after specialist barristers. Members are consummate practitioners across a range of industry work, and handle everything from regulatory and insurance matters to commercial disputes and acquisitions. One client reports of the barristers that "all of them are very personable, attentive, good on their feet, and give an all-round very solid performance." Notable cases recently handled by the set include Rogers v Hoyle, a pivotal case in terms of the admissibility of Air Accident Investigation Reports in civil proceedings.

Client service: The clerking is jointly led by Gary Ventura and Simon Slattery. "The clerks are very attentive and very approachable." "The clerks always turn things around, are very user-friendly and give good pricing. They're very much value for money."

SILKS

Robert Lawson QC (see p.697) Hugely experienced senior silk, prolific across a multitude of high-value, large-scale aviation cases. Praised for his approachable disposition and extensive technical knowledge by clients and peers alike, he represents top-tier solicitors, insurers and household-name airlines in matters as varied as product liability, regulatory and jurisdictional disputes. **Strengths:** "One of his strongest points is his advocacy; on his feet he is very convincing." "Really knowledgeable and user-friendly." **Recent work:** Acted for Cathay Pacific, successfully objecting to Jetstar Hong Kong's operating licence request, a move which will have had a profound impact on the growth of low-fare air travel in the region.

John Kimbell QC (see p.691) Well-regarded silk, known in the market for his intellect and ability to crystallise disparate points of information. Active particularly on matters pertaining to aircraft finance, air accidents, personal injury and insurance. **Strengths:** "Smart and pragmatic. Eloquently identifies the risks for each party in difficult complex litigation. He is completely fearless." "He was very good and had a down to earth approach which was refreshing." **Recent work:** Acted in Rogers v Hoyle, an innovative case which, in the wake of a fatal helicopter crash, established the admissibility of air accident reports in civil proceedings.

JUNIORS

Timothy Marland Employs his insurance industry background when representing clients in cases connected with aircraft finance, disaster liability and loss-related matters. Regarded by peers and clients as having an intimate and market-leading knowledge of the insurance landscape. **Strengths:** "Tim is responsive and user-friendly, with excellent experience of aircraft lease disputes." "Very good technical knowledge and understanding of the aviation industry. Very easy to work with." **Recent work:** Appeared in Air Namibia v BCI Leasing, a significant action in the commercial court brought about by the attempted redelivery of an aircraft following the termination of a lease agreement.

Matthew Reeve (see p.750) Widely acclaimed junior barrister with a tremendous degree of experience at the Aviation Bar, particularly with respect to personal injury and fatality claims, and cases involving executive aircraft. He is also sought after for his liability, insurance and reinsurance practice. **Strengths:** "He can handle pretty much any aviation-related dispute." "A specialist in all areas of aviation. Very detailed and thorough. Shows great compassion for, and understanding of, clients." **Recent work:** Acted in Cassley v GMP Securities & Sundance, a case which, in the wake of a fatal air accident in the Democratic Republic of the Congo, scrutinised the travel agency function of employers and delivered important opinions on their duty of care.

Jonathan Chambers A tenacious advocate with an admired intellectual capacity. He operates an all-encompassing aviation practice that spans personal injury and fatality, insurance, and contractual matters. **Strengths:** "Jonathan is a very approachable senior junior. He is easy to work with, responsive and quickly identifies the key issues." **Recent work:** Appeared in a widely publicised coroner's inquest, and civil proceedings, on behalf of the deceased pilot following a fatal helicopter crash in Northern Ireland.

Stephanie Barrett (see p.590) A flourishing junior practitioner whose advocacy skills are applauded by clients and peers alike. She provides her client base of airports and airlines with advisory and drafting counsel in matters ranging from personal injury to baggage delay claims. **Strengths:** "Excellent advocate, who is extremely hard working and easy to work with." "Very strong and very responsive." **Recent work:** Successfully acted for the defendant in a case involving issues of the responsibility of airlines to make provisions for disabled passengers unable to fly in economy, but unable to afford an upgrade.

Tom Bird An ascending junior barrister with a growing portfolio of aviation cases. Admired for his approachable manner and intelligence, he approaches aviation with commercial tact and panoramic scope. **Strengths:** "A lawyer with a tremendous knowledge of the aviation sector, who is user friendly and exceptionally bright." "I think Tom is a rising star. He's responsive, accessible, bright, tenacious, and user-friendly." **Recent work:** Acted as sole counsel for Sylmar Aviation in a dispute arising from defective maintenance work, which raised sophisticated airworthiness requirement and international regulation issues.

Band 2

XXIV Old Buildings

See profile on p.884

THE SET

Solid set housing a number of market-leading barristers and covering a spectrum of aviation-related matters. Members are frequently embroiled in cases varying from finance and purchasing disputes, to product liability and negligence claims, and regulatory and insurance matters. One satisfied interviewee reports that "they have good strength in depth. They are good all the way, from younger juniors right up to senior barristers. I've not come across anybody I wouldn't use." Recent work undertaken by the set includes acting in Ethiopian Airlines 787 Dreamliner v Honeywell Instrumar & Ultralife, a high-profile product liability claim.

Client service: As joint senior practice managers, Dan Wilson and Paul Matthews lead the clerking team, which is admired by clients for its friendliness and flexibility. "I find the clerks very helpful. I really thought nothing was too much trouble for them." "The clerks are very keen to be proactive."

SILKS

Philip Shepherd QC A market-leading expert known for his commerciality and excellent courtroom demeanour. He is regularly instructed by premier aviation firms in high-profile cases related to leasing and product liability disputes, with a noted military niche. **Strengths:** "He offers very pragmatic advice which is incredibly commercial. He thinks outside the box and comes up with alternative solutions." "He doesn't just know law, he knows aviation." **Recent work:** Appeared in the widely publicised Jet2.com v Blackpool dispute, a foremost case in terms of the use of best endeavours clauses in commercial contracts, with applications beyond the remit of aviation.

JUNIORS

Bajul Shah An enormously capable and experienced junior whose strong market profile is built out of his usability and firm technical grasp. He is regularly instructed to handle cases related to leasing and insolvency disputes as well as regulatory matters. **Strengths:** "He's very easy to work with – commerical and very solid." "Bajul is very bright and very hard working. He's a really reliable pair of hands, and a pleasure to work with." **Recent work:** Represented Monarch Airlines in a dispute against Travelworld Vacations regarding compensation claims brought about following the termination of their commercial relationship.

Edward Cumming A blossoming presence at the aviation bar, he is particularly adept in technically sophisticated matters relating to regulatory and financing matters. **Strengths:** "He shows maturity beyond his years, and is very user-friendly." "He's really a fantastic all-rounder – he has that combination of efficiency and intelligence." **Recent work:** Acted as sole counsel for the defendant in Boulevard Two Aircraft v Air Italy, a high-value dispute regarding the supposedly late re-delivery of a leased aircraft.

Other Ranked Lawyers

Neil Calver QC (Brick Court Chambers) A popular barrister held in high esteem by clients and peers for his versatility and quality advocacy. Frequently instructed as an arbitrator and litigator, he has an acknowledged insurance specialisation. **Strengths:** "He is a great mind, and very personable. On paper, and with clients, he's really good." "A quality all-rounder." **Recent work:** Continues to act in numerous arbitrations as both an advocate and an arbitrator.

John Steel QC (see p.772) (39 Essex Chambers) A qualified pilot, clients appreciate his immense experience and technical comprehension. This industry enthusiasm complements his significant planning law expertise, and positions him as an excellent barrister to act in aviation cases regarding airport development and local government law. **Strengths:** "His charm and knowledge of flying and aviation is quite intense – regulations which would confuse anyone else to death he understands. He is also very enthusiastic for the subject." **Recent work:** Advised the London Borough of Newham in regards to the £200 million expansion of London City Airport, a multifaceted case requiring varying overlapping legal disciplines.

Katherine Deal (3 Hare Court) An excellent claimant barrister whose intellect and determined advocacy has earned her a solid market profile. She specialises in cases regarding personal injury claims and fatal aviation accidents. **Strengths:** "She's very accessible and a phenomenal advocate." "She demonstrated excellent skills in a complicated international air accident litigation." **Recent work:** Acted in Morris & Maher v Ravenair, a sensitive dispute regarding issues as to whether the defendant was responsible for the cost of relocating the claimants who had suffered acute PTSD following an aircraft crashing into their gardens.

Gavin Kealey QC (7 King's Bench Walk) A significant figure at the Aviation Bar who applies his immense commercial experience to a great many high-profile aviation-related cases, a number of which have an insurance slant to them. **Strengths:** "Gavin is intellectually powerful, rigorous and fearless. He rapidly absorbs new context and circumstances for cases." "He's a silk who can turn his hand to anything. He's exceptional." "A colourful, tenacious advocate." **Recent work:** Continues to act in numerous substantial arbitrations concerning aviation insurance.

Anneli Howard (see p.675) (Monckton Chambers) Her proficiency in regulatory and competition law is reflected by her appointment as standing counsel for the CAA. She is also capable when handling aviation matters with European and public law overlap. **Strengths:** "Very user-friendly – she knows how to handle clients." "She's particularly outstanding. She's a very measured and calm barrister who's very pragmatic and practical in her advice." **Recent work:** Advised the CAA as to the economic regulation of airport operation services in terms of the proposed new runway as part of the widely publicised expansion of Heathrow Airport.

Contents:

LONDON

Banking & Finance
Leading Sets
Band 1
Fountain Court Chambers *
Band 2
Brick Court Chambers *
One Essex Court *
3 Verulam Buildings *
Band 3
Essex Court Chambers *
South Square *
Band 4
20 Essex Street *
4 Stone Buildings *
* Indicates set / individual with profile.
[A] direct access (see p.24).
◊ (ORL) = Other Ranked Lawyer.
Alphabetical order within each band. Band 1 is highest.

Banking & Finance	
Leading Silks	
Star individuals	**Hill** Richard G *4 Stone Buildings* *
Brindle Michael *Fountain Court Chambers* *	**Kitchener** Neil *One Essex Court*
Dicker Robin *South Square* *	**Millett** Richard *Essex Court Chambers*
Grabiner Anthony *One Essex Court*	**Odgers** John *3 Verulam Buildings*
Hapgood Mark *Brick Court Chambers*	**Orr** Craig *One Essex Court* *
Howard Mark *Brick Court Chambers*	**Quest** David *3 Verulam Buildings*
Rabinowitz Laurence *One Essex Court*	**Taylor** John *Fountain Court Chambers* *
Railton David *Fountain Court Chambers*	**Trower** William *South Square* *
Zacaroli Antony *South Square* *	**Waters** Malcolm *Radcliffe Chambers (ORL)* ◊ *
Band 1	**Band 4**
Auld Stephen *One Essex Court*	**Birt** Simon *Brick Court Chambers*
Beltrami Adrian *3 Verulam Buildings*	**Calver** Neil *Brick Court Chambers*
Foxton David *Essex Court Chambers*	**Coleman** Richard *Fountain Court Chambers* *
Handyside Richard *Fountain Court Chambers* *	**Cousins** Jeremy *Radcliffe Chambers (ORL)* ◊
Lord Tim *Brick Court Chambers*	**Dale** Derrick *Fountain Court Chambers* *
Malek Ali *3 Verulam Buildings*	**Davies** Helen *Brick Court Chambers*
McQuater Ewan *3 Verulam Buildings*	**Davies-Jones** Jonathan *3 Verulam Buildings*
Miles Robert *4 Stone Buildings*	**Dhillon** Jasbir *Brick Court Chambers*
Mitchell Andrew *Fountain Court Chambers* *	**Gibaud** Catherine *3 Verulam Buildings*
Salter Richard *3 Verulam Buildings*	**Goodall** Patrick *Fountain Court Chambers* *
Thanki Bankim *Fountain Court Chambers* *	**Gruder** Jeffrey *Essex Court Chambers* *
Tolaney Sonia *One Essex Court*	**Hardwick** Matthew *3 Verulam Buildings*
Toledano Daniel *One Essex Court*	**Kimmins** Charles *20 Essex Street*
Wolfson David *One Essex Court*	**Lavender** Nicholas *Serle Court (ORL)* ◊
Band 2	**Malek** Hodge M *39 Essex Chambers (ORL)* ◊
Choo Choy Alain *One Essex Court*	**Marshall** Philip *Serle Court (ORL)* ◊ *
Cox Raymond *Fountain Court Chambers* *	**Pilling** Benjamin *4 Pump Court (ORL)* ◊ *
Davies Rhodri *One Essex Court*	**Robertson** Patricia *Fountain Court Chambers* *
Howe Timothy *Fountain Court Chambers* *	**Saini** Pushpinder *Blackstone Chambers (ORL)* ◊
Nash Jonathan *3 Verulam Buildings*	**Salzedo** Simon *Brick Court Chambers* *
Onslow Andrew *3 Verulam Buildings*	**Smith** Tom *South Square* *
Smouha Joe *Essex Court Chambers*	**Strong** Benjamin *One Essex Court*
Sutcliffe Andrew *3 Verulam Buildings*	**Tozzi** Nigel *4 Pump Court (ORL)* ◊ *
Band 3	**Trace** Anthony *Maitland Chambers (ORL)* ◊ *
Allison David *South Square* *	**Twigger** Andrew M *Maitland Chambers (ORL)* ◊ *
Baker Andrew *20 Essex Street*	**New Silks**
Blayney David *Serle Court (ORL)* ◊ *	**Bayfield** Daniel *South Square* *
Chapman Jeffrey *Fountain Court Chambers* *	**Edwards** Richard *3 Verulam Buildings*
Crow Jonathan *4 Stone Buildings* *	**Kenny** Julian *20 Essex Street*
de Garr Robinson Anthony *One Essex Court* *	**Mumford** David *Maitland Chambers (ORL)* ◊ *
Downes Paul *2TG - 2 Temple Gardens (ORL)* ◊ [A] *	**Phelps** Rosalind *Fountain Court Chambers* *
Goldring Jeremy *South Square* *	**Valentin** Ben *Fountain Court Chambers* *

Band 1

Fountain Court Chambers
See profile on p.847

THE SET

Fountain Court Chambers holds a position as the pre-eminent set in banking and finance matters, and features a host of top-class silks and juniors at all levels of seniority capable of acting both for and against banks and financial institutions in the most complex and significant of cases. Additionally, members are noted for their expertise in related areas such as professional negligence and insurance. Both silks and juniors have been intimately involved in recent leading cases in relation to Libor manipulation and to those stemming from regulatory or judicial findings of product mis-selling.

Client service: "Fountain Court has very, very good clerks who are excellent at putting real thought into who else might be suitable for a case if someone is not available." Alex Taylor leads the clerking team.

SILKS

Michael Brindle QC (see p.603) An immensely capable silk with a top-class practice in a wide range of areas, including financial services, professional negligence and commercial dispute resolution. His practice in banking and finance matters includes the expert representation of oligarch, domestic and international clients. **Strengths:** "He has as much gravitas in court as anybody at the Bar. He is absolutely at the top of his game." "Because he has been to the Supreme Court so many times, he backs himself. He is quite happy to take brave decisions and is an all-round advocate." **Recent work:** Represented Russian investment bank Renaissance Capital in a dispute with African Minerals concerning success fees under engagement letters relating to an iron ore mine in Sierra Leone.

David Railton QC Vastly experienced advocate with a practice spanning the full range of disputes in banking and finance. He has particularly deep recent expertise in issues arising from the financial crash of 2008. He is also a highly adept practitioner in insurance and general commercial cases. **Strengths:** "He is terrific. A fine advocate with meticulous attention to detail, he is very steady and robust under pressure." "Absolutely phenomenal. Quietly spoken but fantastically bright, a very clear thinker and a real delight to work with." **Recent work:** Acted for RBS and four of its directors in the extremely high-profile case of the £12 billion issue of rights in 2008, in which the claimants alleged that the prospectus for the issue did not contain sufficient information to adequately determine its true value.

Richard Handyside QC (see p.663) Enjoys an outstanding reputation for the quality of his representation in big-ticket banking and finance disputes, most often acting on behalf of investment banks and financial institutions. He is particularly noted for his market-leading expertise in issues facing banks arising from the Libor manipulation scandal. **Strengths:** "An expert on Libor manipulation claims and highly sought after by a number of bank clients, he brings genuine insight to one of the most complex issues presently before the courts." "His judgement is very good since he reads the court very well. Incredibly diligent, bright and effective." **Recent work:** Represented Dexia Crediop SpA in its dispute with Prato, an Italian local authority, relating to a number of interest rate swaps. Dexia sought a declaration that the swaps were valid and binding, while Prato contended that they were invalid under various provisions of Italian law.

Andrew Mitchell QC (see p.719) Has quickly established himself as a silk of choice for complex finance litigation, with an especially strong standing in interest rate swaps disputes. He is also a noted practitioner in commercial dispute resolution and insurance cases. **Strengths:** "The go-to silk for most banks facing derivatives mis-selling claims. He is a smooth and persuasive advocate with a real appreciation of the craft of persuading a judge." "He is very

Banking & Finance	
Leading Juniors	
Band 1	
Atrill Simon	*Fountain Court Chambers* *
John Laura	*Fountain Court Chambers* *
Zellick Adam	*Fountain Court Chambers* *
Band 2	
Brent Richard	*3 Verulam Buildings*
Hattan Simon	*Serle Court (ORL)* ◊ *
King Edmund	*Essex Court Chambers*
King Henry	*Fountain Court Chambers* *
Kramer Adam	*3 Verulam Buildings* *
MacDonald James	*One Essex Court* *
McClelland James	*Fountain Court Chambers* *
Patton Conall	*One Essex Court* *
Polley Alexander	*One Essex Court* *
Sher Adam	*Fountain Court Chambers* *
Shivji Sharif	*4 Stone Buildings* *
Band 3	
Cutress James	*Fountain Court Chambers* *
Duffy James	*Fountain Court Chambers* *
Khan Farhaz	*Outer Temple Chambers (ORL)* ◊
Lazarus Michael	*3 Verulam Buildings* *
Midwinter Stephen	*Brick Court Chambers*
Morrison Craig	*Brick Court Chambers* *
Murray David	*Fountain Court Chambers* *
Oppenheimer Tamara	*Fountain Court Chambers* *
Parker Matthew	*3 Verulam Buildings* *
Pilbrow Fionn	*Brick Court Chambers*
Wilson Ian	*3 Verulam Buildings*
Band 4	
Brown Hannah	*One Essex Court*
Edwards William	*3 Verulam Buildings*
Forbes Smith Henry	*One Essex Court*
Hobson Fred	*Brick Court Chambers* *
Isaac Sebastian	*One Essex Court*
McIlroy David	*Forum Chambers (ORL)* ◊
Milner Alexander	*Fountain Court Chambers* *
Mott Richard	*One Essex Court* *
Robins Stephen	*South Square* *
Simpson David	*3 Verulam Buildings*
Singla Tony	*Brick Court Chambers* *
Wheeler Giles	*Fountain Court Chambers* *
Willan James	*Essex Court Chambers*
Yeo Nik	*Fountain Court Chambers* *
Up-and-coming individuals	
Eschwege Richard	*Brick Court Chambers* *
Shah Nehali	*One Essex Court*

** Indicates individual with profile.*

◊ (ORL) = Other Ranked Lawyer.

Alphabetical order within each band. Band 1 is highest.

bright, very commercial, strategic and creative in terms of solutions." **Recent work:** Defended Barclays in a swaps case that was the first action in the retail banking context for contractual estoppel.

Bankim Thanki QC (see p.780) Extraordinarily versatile silk with a superb reputation in an array of practice areas including civil fraud, financial services, offshore and international arbitration, among others. He has acted for a variety of clients in the realm of banking disputes including retail, investment and central banks, often where there is an overlap between contentious regulatory and banking issues. **Strengths:** "Clients love him. He has a huge brain and a tremendous, encyclopaedic knowledge of banking law." "The doyen of banking and regulatory litigation. Offers calm, analytical advice and impeccable judgement." **Recent work:** Acted for Barclays in the first case on the Financial List as it was the leading test case on the construction of LMA terms.

Raymond Cox QC (see p.625) Highly experienced banking and financial services silk with a great deal of expertise in derivatives, securities and insolvency matters. His recent work has seen him handling disputes addressing issues of mortgage interest rate alteration in tracker products and cases concerning secured loan facilities. **Strengths:** "Outstanding. He is incredibly smart, has a good eye for detail, thinks of all the angles and his written advice is excellent." "He is extremely knowledgeable, clear and user-friendly." **Recent work:** Acted for West Bromwich Mortgage Company in a dispute concerning the proper construction of a contractual document for a buy-to-let mortgage.

Timothy Howe QC (see p.676) Exceptionally capable advocate with an enormous amount of experience in handling disputes arising in a large number of areas beyond banking including insurance, international arbitration and professional negligence. Within banking and finance, he is especially visible handling cases stemming from allegations of Libor and Euribor manipulation and from the collapse of Lehman Brothers. **Strengths:** "Combines huge intellect with impressive strategic nous and client skills. At the top of his game in banking matters." "Absolutely excellent – extremely responsive, very bright, hard-working and accommodating." **Recent work:** Acted for a group of banks in a case addressing the legal consequences of the alleged Euribor manipulation by RBS and its effect on a EUR1 billion syndicated loan facility.

Jeffrey Chapman QC (see p.614) Highly capable and respected advocate whose practice in banking and finance commonly overlaps with his wider expertise in commercial fraud matters. He has additional noted ability in connection to international disputes, financial regulatory and arbitration proceedings. **Strengths:** "Exceptionally user-friendly." **Recent work:** Acted for a businesswoman in bringing a claim against HSBC Private Bank in London and Monaco in connection to her forex dealings, which she had previously complained a number of times were being wrongly executed.

John Taylor QC (see p.778) Experienced silk with a strong track record of representing banks both in the English courts and overseas. He has particular experience in cases addressing the operation of standard terms and the mis-selling of interest rate swaps. **Strengths:** "He is very understated but has a razor-sharp mind and quickly gets to the nub of complex legal issues. He is able to see the dénouement of a case from a long way out." "John is a very strong advocate who prepares extremely well and is always on top of every point." **Recent work:** Defended RBS in an action brought by Morris Group, a leading house builder, contending that interest rate swaps it had entered into with the bank ought to be rescinded due to being misrepresented as a result of alleged Libor manipulation.

Richard Coleman QC (see p.620) Enjoys a reputation as an intelligent and commercial silk equally adept at bringing claims against the banks as defending them. He is especially well versed in handling cases dealing with allegations of the mis-selling of interest rate swaps and has wider expertise in professional discipline matters. **Strengths:** "He is excellent. A silk not afraid to get into the detail, very commercial, responsive, clever and personable." "He has a mastery of the issues, clarity of thought and explanation, and a calm demeanour when handling interest rate hedging disputes." **Recent work:** Acted for VIP Engineering and Marketing as one of a number of defendants in a case brought by Standard Chartered Bank for the recovery of a disputed debt of USD140 million relating to the construction of a power plant.

Derrick Dale QC (see p.628) Offers a great deal of expertise in handling financial disputes dealing with a range of issues, typically in the defence of banks. His practice in this area often overlaps with his wider experience in handling professional negligence and civil fraud matters. **Strengths:** "Derrick Dale has a fantastic eye for detail, and is good at seeing things as the court would." **Recent work:** Defended IBRC against four claims by high net worth individuals, who contended that negligent advice and mis-statements amounted to mis-selling with respect to the Somerston Investment.

Patrick Goodall QC (see p.656) Rapidly establishing himself in silk as an advocate of choice for complex financial disputes turning on intricate questions of technical law and matters with a potentially wide significance. He is experienced in acting both for and against banks and financial institutions. **Strengths:** "He is extremely user-friendly, technically excellent, is all over the facts and legal issues and is very available." "He offers a potent mix of commerciality and sensible, digestible legal advice." **Recent work:** Acted for HM Treasury in a high-profile damages claim for USD4 billion brought by Iranian Bank Mellat. The action stemmed from a previous Supreme Court decision finding that the sanctions imposed on the bank by the UK relating to the wider sanctions regime against Iran were unlawful.

Patricia Robertson QC (see p.753) An experienced and versatile practitioner with a strong track record of representing clients in litigation in the banking sector, especially in cases addressing allegations of regulatory breaches. In addition to her expertise in financial disputes, she is also a noted advocate with respect to professional discipline and negligence matters. **Strengths:** "She is meticulous, incredibly bright and really gets into the detail of cases." "Wonderful to work with – she is calm, measured and makes herself available." **Recent work:** Defended Ulster Bank in a claim brought by a number of investors alleging financial mis-selling and breach of fiduciary duty in relation to a property investment in Canary Wharf that suffered a total loss in 2008.

Rosalind Phelps QC (see p.736) Takes silk this year on the back of a highly successful career at the junior Bar in a diverse range of areas. Further to being a highly respected banking practitioner, she enjoys a strong reputation in civil fraud disputes. **Strengths:** "Incredibly bright and super efficient. She is very good on her feet in court, very practical, commercial and strategically minded." "She is extremely bright and enjoyable to work with. Her promotion to QC this year was well deserved." **Recent work:** Represented Lloyds Bank in a number of cases relating to the alleged mis-selling of derivatives products and to the manipulation of the Libor index.

Ben Valentin QC (see p.786) Has taken silk this year after enjoying a rapid rise up the rankings in a number of related practice areas, including civil fraud, international commercial arbitration and commercial dispute resolution besides undoubted expertise in banking cases. He has appeared in a number of leading cases for the defence of major banks and financial institutions. **Strengths:** "Superb. His preparation was very strong and his advocacy is very forceful and straight." "Not only is he extremely clever, his work rate is phenomenal, his manner is easy, and he is a real team player and very practical." **Recent work:** Acted for Goldman Sachs in two related claims brought by Singaporean investors in connection to loan defaults.

JUNIORS

Simon Atrill (see p.586) Exceptionally able senior junior with a very strong track record in appearing in an array of banking matters for a range of clients including central, investment and retail banks. He has additional expertise in the impact of Shari'a on derivatives sold in the Middle East. **Strengths:** "His impressive analytical skills are combined with a true depth of knowledge in the financial services sector. A delight to work with." "He is able to take complex issues and transform them into accessible advice with a clear steer as to the best course of action." **Recent work:** Acted for Credit Suisse in a case against Titan Europe concerning EUR1 billion of loan notes, and whether certain notes should be closed out and the income payable to different classes of noteholders.

Laura John (see p.683) Rises to the top rank of juniors amid strong praise from peers, clients and instructing solicitors for her highly accomplished and versatile advocacy in complex banking matters. She is regularly instructed on behalf of sophisticated international clients in contractual disputes and cases concerning derivatives, especially where there are issues surrounding the manipulation of Libor and Euribor. **Strengths:** "She is very good on her feet: clear, direct, persuasive and likeable, as well as being pragmatic and analytically very strong." "She is very detailed, writes well, gives good advice and is a very good advocate." **Recent work:** Defended RBS against a highly significant claim brought by Marme Inversiones for misrepresentation on the basis of the alleged rigging of Euribor.

Adam Zellick (see p.802) Rises to the first group of banking juniors this year amid growing appreciation among peers and clients alike for his accomplished advocacy in a wide range of financial disputes. He has acted successfully in cases addressing diverse issues such as derivatives and swaps to the manipulation of Libor. **Strengths:** "Hard-working and has excellent advocacy and drafting skills." "A very bright guy and has very good tactical thinking." **Recent work:** Acted for ten claimants in a highly significant test case concerning a syndicated lending and credit contingent swap valued at USD150 million. An issue of dispute is whether Libor manipulation means this and other such transactions are unenforceable and should be set aside.

James McClelland (see p.711) Enjoys a reputation as a highly intelligent junior practitioner with a wide-ranging practice spanning a variety of areas. Besides his expertise in commercial and banking disputes, he has noted ability and experience in handling cases arising in administrative and public law and professional discipline. **Strengths:** "Absolutely outstanding. He has such intellectual rigour and tenacity that he won't let a point drop – he shakes it and shakes it until he's got a better answer." "Supremely bright and a star for the future." **Recent work:** Acted on behalf of RBS and its former directors in the RBS rights issue litigation as part of a team led by David Railton QC and Sonia Tolaney QC.

Adam Sher (see p.763) A well-regarded junior with substantial experience in a wide range of commercial and banking matters. Many of his cases have an international dimension and he has benefited from having been led by a large number of the luminaries in the financial disputes field. **Strengths:** "Extremely clever and very imaginative, he is determined, confident and offers very powerful analysis." "Relentlessly enthusiastic and has a brilliant grasp of detail." **Recent work:** Defended RBS against Property Alliance Group in a leading Libor case before the English courts.

Henry King (see p.691) A highly able and experienced junior whose practice in banking and financial regulatory disputes is informed, in part, by his accountant's qualification. He is well versed in handling claims on behalf of central and investment banks, and has very visible experience in relation to derivatives cases. **Strengths:** "Henry is very bright, collaborative, extremely personable and user-friendly." "He has great energy, enthusiasm and is a brilliant team player whilst not being afraid to form his own view on an issue." **Recent work:** Represented PwC in high-profile litigation arising in connection to the Tomlinson Report, alleging that certain banks and professional advisers knowingly pushed troubled businesses into default in order to generate revenue.

James Cutress (see p.628) Well-respected junior whose practice in banking and finance accompanies a wider expertise in insurance and general commercial dispute resolution. His recent cases in banking include matters dealing with sanctions, fraud and mortgaging issues. **Strengths:** "Technically excellent and great at focusing on the true issues. James gives clients real confidence." "Excellent, well-rounded individual who provides first-class service." **Recent work:** Acted for Alpstream AG in a successful claim against PK Airfinance alleging conspiracy to acquire an aircraft it had repossessed as a mortgagee by unlawful means.

James Duffy (see p.637) is a smart up-and-coming junior at Fountain Court who is tactically astute. **Recent work:** Successfully represented UBS in its defence against an action brought by Decura claiming to be entitled to terminate an introduction and outsourcing agreement between the parties valued at USD200 million on the grounds that a public announcement by UBS had activated a material adverse change clause.

David Murray (see p.724) Enjoys a growing reputation as a versatile junior experienced in appearing before the English courts and the Dubai International Finance Centre on behalf of a range of banking clients. He is particularly adept at handling cases relating to the mis-selling of financial products. **Strengths:** "He was superb – unflappable and so eloquent on his feet." "He is a good, solid junior. Very clever and sensible." **Recent work:** Represented Deutsche Bank in an action against Petromena concerning allegedly negligent advice and breach of duty relating to the issuance of a USD300 million bond by Petromena.

Tamara Oppenheimer (see p.730) Highly respected banking junior with a reputation as an intelligent and skilled advocate. Her practice spans banking, commercial and professional negligence matters. She also has experience of representing the government in her capacity as a member of the Treasury B Panel of Counsel. **Strengths:** "She is very clever, and such a clear advocate." "She is very bright and good with clients." **Recent work:** Acted for Nomura in a case against Banca Monte dei Paschi dei Siena concerning derivative transactions with a nominal value in excess of £3 billion.

Alexander Milner (see p.718) Accomplished junior who shows capability acting both for and against banks. He is experienced in cases connected with interest rate hedging products. He speaks fluent Russian and a number of his recent cases in the banking sphere have come from the CIS region as a result. **Strengths:** "He is very hard-working and very bright." **Recent work:** Acted for Vitaly Arkhangelsky in his high-profile dispute with Bank St Petersburg concerning allegations of conspiracy to defraud him of assets worth around USD100 million. The Court of Appeal granted a very rare anti-enforcement injunction in favour of Mr Arkhangelsky in relation to a determination of the Russian courts.

Nik Yeo (see p.802) Enjoys a solid standing among instructing solicitors and his peers for his practice in structured finance litigation matters. He has additional noted proficiency in handling professional negligence and commercial international arbitration proceedings. **Strengths:** "He is very committed and hard-working and is articulate and quick thinking on his feet." "Nik is very detail-oriented and thorough in his preparation." **Recent work:** Acted for Gemini in a highly complex valuation dispute in which securities were issued in relation to commercial property purportedly worth £1.2 billion that was subsequently valued at around a third of that amount.

Giles Wheeler (see p.793) Joins the listings this year amid growing praise for his adept representation in a range of banking disputes. He is especially well versed in handling derivatives litigation. **Strengths:** "He's top-notch. His drafting skills are excellent, he's great on his feet, is very user-friendly and his advice is sound." "He is a senior junior who is basically at the same level as a silk." **Recent work:** Advised Barclays on a dispute with UniCredit as to whether the latter was entitled to terminate three credit guarantees.

Band 2

Brick Court Chambers

See profile on p.816

THE SET

A highly respected set with a significant roster of leading commercial and banking silks and juniors of all levels of seniority, many of whom appear regularly in cases affecting the industry as a whole. Brick Court's barristers are widely seen as foremost experts in the areas of Libor manipulation, large-scale insolvency and its impact on related contractual arrangements, and multi-jurisdictional bank restructuring. Its deep bench of counsel is well versed in acting both for and against banks and other financial institutions.

Client service: "The clerks and support staff are extremely efficient. They are keen to assist and respond immediately to queries and requests." Julian Hawes and Ian Moyler run the team.

SILKS

Mark Hapgood QC An undisputed titan of the Banking Bar with a string of successes in headline cases under his belt. He is widely respected for his expertise in commercial finance disputes, most recently involving issues relating to trusts and other debt securities. **Strengths:** "Mark is particularly adept at cutting to the heart of complicated issues and presenting them simply and clearly. He provides practical commercial and strategic advice and is a very persuasive advocate." "Absolutely in the category of super silks. He is one of the pre-eminent banking silks around." **Recent work:** Led a team of three silks and a junior in the Supreme Court for a bank sued as transferee of Saudi Arabian shares valued at around USD300 million, in a case addressing whether a trust can create property rights in foreign assets not recognised by the local law.

Mark Howard QC One of the very finest silks of his generation, with a stellar practice spanning a large number of areas. Besides his exceptional ability in banking and finance disputes, he has further expertise in energy, civil fraud, professional negligence and international arbitration proceedings. **Strengths:** "He gives clever, shrewd and realistic advice and, above all, excels in cross-examination. He also obviously has the respect of the court." "A strong cross-examiner and a good advocate." **Recent work:** Successfully represented Citibank in a high-profile case brought by Terra Firma for £1.5 billion in relation to the acquisition of EMI prior to the financial crash of 2008. The claim for fraud was withdrawn during trial.

Tim Lord QC Highly experienced banking silk known for his forthright and robust advocacy, often on behalf of clients challenging banking practices. He is also noted for his wider expertise in professional negligence and civil fraud cases. **Strengths:** "A formidable opponent. He is fantastically good at dealing with difficult factual cases and at working out which buttons he needs to press to get the judge on his side." "He is a fighter who is extremely good in court and is very tenacious." **Recent work:** Acted for Bank St Petersburg in its dispute with Vitaly Arkhangelsky.

Simon Birt QC Has established himself in silk as a skilled advocate in banking and general commercial disputes. His work in financial matters often concerns cases arising from the financial crash and credit crisis. **Strengths:** "Simon's great strength is that nothing ever fazes him. Throughout twists and turns in proceedings, he is calm, collected and analytical." "He is brilliant: incredibly hard-working, approachable, responsive, fantastic on paper and very good with difficult clients." **Recent work:** Acted as junior silk to Tim Lord QC on behalf of Bank of St Petersburg in its dispute with Vitaly Arkhangelsky.

Helen Davies QC Joint head of chambers and an advocate of some renown in relation to commercial, energy and competition law disputes. She has appeared in a number of leading banking cases including those addressing issues of fraud, mis-selling and the interpretation of the ISDA Master Agreement. **Strengths:** "She is exceptional, has a phenomenally impressive grasp of cases, is clear-thinking and learned, and is a very good advocate." "She is absolutely at the top of her game." **Recent work:** Represented Lloyds Banking Group defending a claim for over £250 million brought by shareholders in Lloyds alleging it negligently failed to reveal and misrepresented the true financial position of HBOS prior to its acquisition by Lloyds in 2008.

Neil Calver QC Maintains a diverse practice not only as an advocate in insurance and banking cases, but also in the capacity of arbitrator in international proceedings. He often represents oligarch clients in financial disputes. **Strengths:** "He is amazing with clients, spots killer points early on and is a great strategist." "He is an attractive advocate." **Recent work:** Acted for Alexander Kotton in the Supreme Court of Gibraltar in relation to the discharge of a freezing injunction.

Jasbir Dhillon QC Enjoys a solid reputation as a banking silk with a number of appearances in leading cases to his name. Besides his expertise in securitisation and derivatives cases, he has additional experience in handling contentious regulatory proceedings. **Strengths:** "He is very good on the technical details of banking disputes." "First-rate commercial counsel who is impressive in the more complex disputes." **Recent work:** Appeared on behalf of Enasarco in a successful claim for USD61.5 million against Lehman Brothers in a complex structured derivative product. The dispute is now a leading case on the calculation and determination of loss under the 1992 ISDA Master Agreement.

Simon Salzedo QC (see p.758) Enters the listings as a banking and finance silk this year amid growing appreciation of his accomplished advocacy in a number of discrete areas within the field, including in tax indemnity and duties of care in relation to bankers' references. He is also a noted advocate in the fields of professional negligence and insurance. **Strengths:** "He is very, very precise, is strong in cross-examination and has a huge brain." "Very bright and good to deal with." **Recent work:** Acted as co-lead counsel for Kommunale Wasserwerke Leipzig (KWL) in its high-profile dispute with UBS.

JUNIORS

Stephen Midwinter Highly regarded as a junior with respect to a number of related practice areas including insurance, energy and civil fraud matters. He is also often instructed as sole counsel in banking cases. **Strengths:** "He has a high speed of delivery without compromising on quality. He just produces excellent pieces of work in a very short space of time. He's incredibly good value to use as a result." "Midwinter is absolute class as a senior junior. You do not want him on the other side. He is very lean, very strong and very direct, very effective." **Recent work:** Represented KWL as senior junior in its high-profile dispute with UBS.

Craig Morrison (see p.722) Rises up the listings this year on the back of appearances in a number of headline cases in the banking field and praise from peers and instructing solicitors alike. Many of the cases on which he is instructed turn on fundamental issues of fraud. **Strengths:** "Incredibly hard-working, utterly cheerful and a delight throughout." "His is a lively and versatile intellect." **Recent work:** Represented Goldman Sachs in proceedings stemming from the administration of Lehman Brothers International regarding the correct interpretation of the ISDA Master Agreement.

Fionn Pilbrow Enjoys an excellent reputation as an accomplished junior sought after by eminent silks and instructing solicitors in a number of practice areas. He is considered a leading commercial and civil fraud practitioner and offers additional expertise in relation to energy, insurance and banking cases. **Strengths:** "His analysis and drafting are excellent, and he is hugely popular with solicitors since he is easy to work with." "Very flexible and amazingly able to turn around work quickly." **Recent work:** Acted for Bayerische Landesbank in its claim for damages against Bernie Ecclestone and others in relation to the sale of its stake in Formula One.

Tony Singla (see p.766) Leading competition law junior with excellent standing with regard to commercial, media and fraud cases. In banking and finance he has noted experience in relation to matters addressing issues of fraud and shareholder disputes. **Strengths:** "He gives the confidence that he absolutely believes in his case. He knows his own mind, fights his corner and is a good, strong advocate." "Very impressive. He is hard-working, intelligent and has a bright future ahead of him." **Recent work:** Represented Lloyds Banking Group in the litigation stemming from the acquisition of HBOS.

Fred Hobson (see p.673) Enters the listings this year as a banking and finance junior, having already been recognised for his work in general commercial dispute resolution. His experience in this area includes issues stemming from private equity acquisitions. **Strengths:** "He is very good, particularly in terms of his cross-examination." **Recent work:** Acted as junior counsel, led by Mark Howard QC, for Citibank in the high-profile dispute with Terra Firma.

Richard Eschwege (see p.641) Enjoys a rapidly growing reputation for his accomplished junior representation in banking disputes as well as in commercial litigation. His practice in banking and finance focuses on issues surrounding the enforcement of guarantees and breaches of confidence. **Strengths:** "An extraordinarily clever chap. The level of his analysis and drafting is years beyond what you would expect for someone of his call." "Incredibly able and one of the best juniors around at the moment." **Recent work:** Represented Bank St Petersburg as junior counsel on its claim against Vitaly Arkhangelsky.

One Essex Court

See profile on p.833

THE SET

One Essex Court offers a large number of exceptionally able silks and juniors, including some among the select few regarded as pre-eminent in the field of banking and finance. Its members are regularly instructed by magic and silver circle firms in the most significant and hard-fought matters in the industry including, in recent times, the RBS rights issue litigation and Terra Firma v Citibank. They are also noted for their deep expertise in related practice areas including civil fraud, international commercial arbitration, energy and professional negligence.

Client service: "They treat their clients with respect and don't overbook diaries. They are so responsible, so professional and see things as long-term relationships. They essentially run their clerking as a firm." Darren Burrows leads the clerking team.

SILKS

Stephen Auld QC Maintains a highly respected practice across a number of areas, including civil fraud, with a focus on cases addressing complicated contractual arrangements. Of late, he has been acting in a swathe of financial cases linked to manipulation of benchmark rates. **Strengths:** "A very smooth and persuasive advocate who is good at cutting through knotty issues to get to the heart of things." "A no-nonsense, charming and confident advocate who is great with clients." Recent work: Instructed on behalf of Wingate, a subsidiary of Guardian Care Homes, in a case seeking damages for consequential losses stemming from the alleged manipulation of Libor.

Anthony Grabiner QC A doyen of the Commercial Bar with several decades of experience of appearing in the leading cases of the day, including a significant number in the House of Lords and the Supreme Court. **Strengths:** "His sense of the lie of the land is incredible. He is so approachable, open and unbelievably intuitive." "A huge name at the Bar.

He is very user-friendly, has a great manner with clients and has real gravitas and precision." **Recent work:** Acted as lead silk for Terra Firma in its high-profile dispute with Citi.

Laurence Rabinowitz QC Widely considered one of the pre-eminent silks of the London Bar with an outstanding reputation as a brilliant advocate capable of handling the most complex and intricate disputes with aplomb. Besides his expertise in banking and commercial cases, he is also highly accomplished with regard to civil fraud and international arbitration proceedings. **Strengths:** "He is fantastic. He has a sort of intellectual courage, a willingness to confront difficulties in his own case." "He can cover in a day issues that would normally take a leader a month. Judges have deferred to him." **Recent work:** Acted for Banco Santander Totta in the five related cases against Portuguese public transport companies.

Sonia Tolaney QC A major recent addition to the One Essex Court bench having arrived from 3 Verulam Buildings, Tolaney enjoys a standing as an exceptionally talented advocate with regard to banking and finance disputes. She offers clients additional expertise in commercial, civil fraud and insolvency cases. **Strengths:** "She has the ear of the court and can make submissions that go down like sweetmeats." "An incredibly persuasive advocate with an excellent courtroom manner in terms of presenting a reasonable face to the court. She knows what points to concede and what to pursue." **Recent work:** Instructed as part of the team representing RBS and its former directors in the RBS rights issue litigation.

Daniel Toledano QC Outstanding silk of choice for many leading banks and hedge funds in complex disputes, with particular recent experience in cases concerning the provision of investment advice. He is also a highly rated advocate for civil fraud and general commercial matters. **Strengths:** "A first-rate legal mind with great judgement. He is surely one of the best trial advocates of his generation." "Clients adore him because he is so calm and measured. He is a great team player and a phenomenal cross-examiner." **Recent work:** Acted for European investors in a claim against ratings agency McGraw-Hill International in its AAA rating for CPDO notes created by a major bank.

David Wolfson QC Has established himself as a silk of great repute capable of arguing forcefully and persuasively in the most complex of banking and finance disputes. **Strengths:** "Very impressive. He is super smart and brilliant at dealing with clients and experts. He doesn't waffle – he jumps straight to the strongest points." "David is very charismatic. A hugely engaging speaker and convincing advocate." **Recent work:** Represented Morgan Stanley in the Supreme Court in an appeal by Tael One Partners that turned on the proper meaning of the LMA standard terms for the sale of debt in the secondary market.

Alain Choo Choy QC An advocate with broad-ranging expertise across a number of practice areas central to One Essex Court, including banking and civil fraud. He has a particularly strong reputation in points of conflict of law and jurisdiction cases. **Strengths:** "He is utterly charming and clearly knows the detail. Judges trust and react very well to him." "Extremely bright, he is a very powerful advocate." **Recent work:** Acted for UniCredit handling an indemnity claim against Barclays Bank in respect of an Italian tax exemption on payments made under a structured investment product created by Barclays for the bank.

Rhodri Davies QC Especially accomplished in regard to cases stemming from the credit crunch, and has a particular interest in financial disputes involving issues of bondholder rights, credit facility and share sale agreements. He has further experience of handling professional negligence cases, most often those addressing alleged accountants' negligence. **Strengths:** "He is extremely persuasive on his feet, smooth and confident with clients, no-nonsense and to the point." "He is very experienced and reliable, with a deep perspective and the ability to create confidence in clients with ease." **Recent work:** Represented Stichting Vestia in a case against Credit Suisse for a termination sum under ISDA transactions following a closeout.

Anthony de Garr Robinson QC (see p.631) Enjoys a growing reputation for his capable representation of sophisticated domestic and international clients in a range of disputes including those relating to company law and civil fraud as well as banking and finance. He is also registered to practise in the British Virgin Islands, Bahamas and DIFC. **Strengths:** "Anthony delivers advice that is tangible and practical and is incredibly user-friendly." "He is very technically gifted and very hard-working." **Recent work:** Defended Canada Life against a claim by 84 investors who made investments in certain investment funds through a Canada Life offshore insurance wrapper. The claimants allege breaches of duty in respect of both the management of the funds and the investment advice which caused them to invest in the funds.

Neil Kitchener QC Maintains a wide-ranging and well-respected practice encompassing civil fraud, insolvency, arbitration, company law and energy disputes. His recent representations in banking cases have included those addressing allegations of negligence and breaches of fiduciary duty. **Strengths:** "He is excellent. All over the factual detail and can come up with extremely complex analysis off the top of his head." **Recent work:** Acted for Sabre Oil and Gas on a claim against Standard Bank over the amount of fees, interest and transaction expenses charged by the defendant.

Craig Orr QC (see p.731) Has a markedly international practice, often appearing in the courts of both Europe and the Far East on behalf of banks and claimants against them. His practice in financial disputes focuses on matters involving complex investment arrangements and derivatives. **Strengths:** "A hugely impressive individual, he is incredibly conscientious and incredibly intelligent. A safer pair of hands couldn't be at the wheel." "He is very bright, very painstaking and leaves no stone unturned." **Recent work:** Defended Kroll Associates against a claim for USD500 million alleging conspiracy in connection to their engagement with the former chairman of Bank Alkair, a Bahraini investment bank.

Benjamin Strong QC Recent silk with a good reputation as an accomplished advocate in commercial disputes, especially those arising in the banking industry. His career as a barrister is built on several years as a solicitor at leading firm Slaughter and May. **Strengths:** "He is great with clients, very responsive and quick to grasp and identify solutions to complex issues." "Outstanding. His ability to consume and assimilate a vast amount of material and provide very cogent advice and oral advocacy is very impressive." **Recent work:** Acted for Stichting Vestia in its dispute with Credit Suisse International.

JUNIORS

James MacDonald (see p.705) Joins the set this year from 3 Verulam Buildings, bringing highly respected expertise in handling complex banking and finance disputes. His practice in this area is diverse, spanning multi-jurisdictional cases and enforcement proceedings. **Strengths:** "A fantastic all-rounder. His written work is excellent and he is a very strong trial advocate who is also great with clients." "He is as happy handling a short trial on his own in a defended recoveries case as he is being led in a derivatives mis-selling matter." **Recent work:** Appeared as junior for ratings agencies Standard & Poor's and Moody's in a case addressing the duties owed by such agencies when providing ratings for financial products.

Conall Patton (see p.734) Enjoys a fast-growing standing among peers and instructing solicitors for his outstanding written advocacy across a range of areas including banking, competition law and energy. Such is the regard in which he is held that he often acts unled in major cases. **Strengths:** "He produces beautifully written advocacy – he has an incredible way of expressing himself that is very effective." "A highly intelligent advocate with an excellent understanding of complex financial products. His expertise in derivatives and structured notes is particularly impressive." **Recent work:** Represented Odeon Capital Group as sole counsel in a Commercial Court trial brought by Molton Street Capital in respect of bond trading.

Alexander Polley (see p.739) Leading junior of choice for a range of major solicitors and eminent silks, with a reputation as an exemplary technician. His practice in banking and finance matters often overlaps with his wider expertise in civil fraud and professional negligence. **Strengths:** "He is phenomenally good at producing high-quality work under time pressure. He can synthesise a lot of complex material quickly and work out the best approach and points to develop." "He knows the law exceptionally well, is incredibly hard-working and clever. A very good lawyer." **Recent work:** Defended Société Générale against the Libyan Investment Authority's high-profile suit valued at USD1.6 billion, regarding certain structured investments procured, allegedly, by bribery.

Henry Forbes Smith Solid junior with a banking practice informed, in part, by his former career as a capital markets lawyer in New York at US firm Davis Polk. He has a particular interest in cases dealing with securities, options trading and derivatives. **Strengths:** "He is a great cross-examiner and a very clever guy." **Recent work:** Acted for Lehman Brothers in an appeal against a judgment concerning the timing of valuation of closeout under the ISDA Master Agreement.

Hannah Brown Solid junior with a banking practice that often overlaps with her wider expertise in fraud and negligence. She has further interest in insurance cases. **Strengths:** "She is simply perfect in all respects – very smart and wonderful at handling complex ideas." **Recent work:** Represented Open Joint Stock Company Alfa-Bank in enforcement proceedings in relation to a Russian judgment for £8.8 million, in which the defendant raised allegations of fraud and that the Russian proceedings were conducted in violation of natural justice.

Sebastian Isaac Has a growing reputation as a capable junior whose commercial disputes practice is not limited to banking and finance disputes. In this field, he has particular experience in securities cases and those turning on allegations of fraud. **Strengths:** "He is really clever, very able, very competent and totally reliable as a junior." "Very user-friendly, commercial, responsive and technically brilliant."

Richard Mott (see p.723) Established junior with a practice encompassing arbitration, energy, and banking and finance disputes. He has an additional interest in cases addressing issues of civil fraud. **Strengths:** "An incredibly bright junior who is a pleasure to work with, gets stuck in and always fights the client's corner." "Very intellectual but also commercial at the same time. He really rolls up his sleeves and gets into the detail." **Recent work:** Acted for Citibank in resisting a claim for declamatory relief, and counterclaiming for around USD270 million under a series of obligated repo transactions in relation to an alleged metals fraud in China.

Nehali Shah A young, up-and-coming junior who has forged a growing reputation across a number of related fields for being a highly intelligent and hard-working practitioner. She has particularly pronounced experience with regard to noteholder, private equity and restructuring cases. **Strengths:** "She is brilliant – both technically very strong and someone with the ability to master complex issues and materials quickly. She also has the most elegant manner when working with us." "Nehali is a highly capable junior. She is very bright, has an eye for detail and is a strong team player." **Recent work:** Acted for Terra Firma in the high-profile dispute with Citibank in relation to the acquisition of EMI.

3 Verulam Buildings

See profile on p.924

THE SET

A lauded collection of barristers well versed in the intricacies of banking and finance litigation, with members at all levels experienced in appearing in leading and often precedent-setting cases. Market sources are forthcoming in their praise of the set's silks' and juniors' abilities, and instructing solicitors are especially appreciative of the fact that "they understand the importance of the counsel/barrister relationship and invest a lot of time in making sure it works." Its members garner praise in related areas of expertise including financial professional negligence, contentious regulatory proceedings and civil fraud.

Client service: "Stephen Penson's clerking team is excellent. The clerks are commercial, proactive and extremely helpful, which can transform an instructing solicitor's day."

SILKS

Adrian Beltrami QC Enjoys an excellent reputation for his highly adept advocacy in a wide range of practice areas, proving effective in civil fraud, insolvency and general commercial disputes as well as those relating to banking and finance. His current caseload includes a number of matters dealing with allegations of Libor and Euribor manipulation. **Strengths:** "He is very good at reading the courtroom and can adapt his strategy if need be. He has a dry wit that comes across well in court." "A superstar who totally has the ear of the court, he is never flustered by anything." **Recent work:** Acted for Barclays in a high-profile dispute with Rhino Enterprises that eventually settled concerning the alleged mis-selling of certain swaps in relation to the alleged manipulation of Libor.

Ali Malek QC Highly skilled advocate with an enviable track record of appearing in leading financial cases. He has a great depth of experience across a large number of related legal spheres including financial services, commercial arbitration and civil fraud. He is particularly adept at derivatives cases. **Strengths:** "An excellent choice for matters requiring a high degree of product knowledge coupled with a high degree of expertise in regulatory matters." "He is very good on strategy and has a very commanding presence in court." **Recent work:** Represented four Portuguese public transport companies in a high-profile case brought by Banco Santander Totta alleging EUR1.4 billion was owed on derivative transactions.

Ewan McQuater QC Joint head of chambers Ewan McQuater QC has an outstanding reputation as a highly versatile commercial silk with a well-established practice in banking and finance disputes. His caseload in the field is diverse, ranging from insolvency to national bonds. **Strengths:** "He is very, very good, both technically and in terms of his advocacy." "Very nice to work with, very smart and terrific in cross-examination." **Recent work:** Acted for DZ Bank AG in its dispute with the administrators of Lehman Brothers International concerning a number of claims and counterclaims in respect of the valuation and eligibility of certain counterparty repo positions.

Richard Salter QC Enormously experienced banking silk with a recent focus on cases dealing with insolvency and the limits of tracing and restitution. He has additional noted expertise in commercial disputes and arbitration proceedings. **Strengths:** "He is impressively erudite, fiercely analytical and strategically astute." "He knows banking law inside out and commands respect because of that wealth of experience." **Recent work:** Represented Novo Banco in a significant dispute with Goldman Sachs concerning the extent to which the English courts should recognise actions taken by the central bank of Portugal under an EU Directive relating to a structured finance facility valued at USD835 million.

Jonathan Nash QC Enjoys an outstanding reputation for his accomplished advocacy in a range of banking disputes, with a special focus on cases addressing issues arising from complex derivative transactions. He has frequently been instructed in valuation cases stemming from the collapse of Lehman Brothers. **Strengths:** "Clients like him since he gives them a judge-led view and because he is also able to strategise beyond the scope of a single decision." "He can argue the inarguable because he is exceptionally eloquent." **Recent work:** Acted on behalf of the largest claimant group in the RBS rights issue litigation bringing a claim of £1.8 billion.

Andrew Onslow QC Highly accomplished commercial and banking silk with a very well-respected practice taking in a number of related areas. He has additional expertise in relation to art and cultural property law, as well as civil fraud and professional negligence. **Strengths:** "Outstanding. He has no airs and graces and absolutely gets stuck in." "He is a very accomplished practitioner and advocate." **Recent work:** Represented a £1.3 billion claimant group in the renowned RBS rights issue class action.

Andrew Sutcliffe QC Versatile banking and finance advocate whose practice in the area often overlaps with his wider expertise in civil fraud matters. He has additional prowess in relation to media and entertainment cases. **Strengths:** "An extremely good, all-round insolvency and banking lawyer." **Recent work:** Acted for Andrew Charalambous in a complex £10 million property dispute with Barclays and Healys LLP. The case addressed allegations of undue influence and misrepresentation on the part of the bank and the solicitor.

John Odgers QC Has established a solid reputation in silk as a banking and commercial disputes practitioner, aided, in part, by being the editor of a leading textbook in the field. He has additional noted expertise in regulatory financial services and civil fraud matters. **Strengths:** "He is a very solid junior silk who knows his banking law extremely well and is a really valuable part of a counsel team." "He is very enjoyable to work with and has a very thorough and detailed approach to everything." **Recent work:** Acted for the claimant Dutch institutional pension fund Vervoer in a dispute with its fiduciary investment manager, Goldman Sachs, concerning investment management decisions made during and after the subprime mortgage crisis.

David Quest QC Offers accomplished advocacy in a number of discrete areas in banking and finance including early termination of agreements and exchange bonds. He is also a noted practitioner in offshore and civil fraud disputes. **Strengths:** "He is exceptionally bright and strategic, with a particular gift for financial products disputes." "He provides concise, pragmatic advice and skilful advocacy." **Recent work:** Represented HSBC in the successful defence against a claim brought by a businessperson for foreign exchange trading losses in excess of £20 million.

Jonathan Davies-Jones QC Highly experienced banking practitioner whose knowledge and understanding of the area is due, in part, to his previous career as an investment banker specialising in M&A. He has wider expertise in commercial dispute resolution and civil fraud. **Strengths:** "Absolutely exceptional. He is extraordinarily clever, he is brilliant on his feet and can argue the most complex cases in court." "He is fantastic – incredibly precise and never gives up." **Recent work:** Acted successfully on behalf of Comune di Prato in a complex interest rate swaps dispute with a value of around EUR60 million. It is the first case in which the English courts have directly applied a foreign system of law under the Rome Convention.

Catherine Gibaud QC Offers wide-ranging expertise across a number of issues in the field, including the mis-selling of derivatives, swaps and the interpretation of the ISDA Master Agreement. She also has experience in handling financial negligence claims. **Strengths:** "She is very client-friendly and is very good at getting to the detail." "She is a good advocate and a very hard worker who gives her all for her clients." **Recent work:** Acted for the liquidators of Carlyle Capital Corporation on bringing a claim against its former directors and managers for breaches of fiduciary duty and of contract, wrongful trading, misfeasance and negligence. The claim is valued at over USD1 billion.

Matthew Hardwick QC Maintains a diverse and well-respected practice taking in restructuring and insolvency disputes as well as general commercial and banking litigation. His extensive experience in the latter includes derivatives, swaps, trade finance and securities cases. **Strengths:** "His work ethic and attention to detail are outstanding. He is able to dissect and understand a large volume of documents within a short period of time, as demonstrated by his comprehensive written submissions and clear, concise advocacy." "Incredibly sharp with excellent drafting skills." **Recent work:** Instructed at a late stage to represent Wani LLP in its swaps mis-selling claim against RBS, leading to a settlement on favourable terms. The case is now a leading reference for late amendments to a claim.

Richard Edwards QC Takes silk this year after a junior career that saw him establish himself as a leading figure in the arts and cultural property world. His work in banking and finance matters centres on swaps cases, with further experience in enforcement of guarantees and security cases. **Strengths:** "He is calm, authoritative and a good tactician, as well as being excellent to work with." "A delightful guy to work with and has very strong knowledge of the banking sector." **Recent work:** Acted while a junior for Crestsign in its high-profile case against NatWest for the alleged mis-selling of an interest rate swap. The matter is an important case in respect to the distinction between advised and non-advised sales.

JUNIORS

Richard Brent Accomplished banking junior whose practice includes wider expertise in matters concerning the regulation of financial services. His work in the banking sphere focuses on swaps mis-selling cases on behalf of domestic and international institutions. **Strengths:** "He is strong on the details – when he is reviewing witness statements, he'll pick up on details that are absolutely crucial." "Very clever. He has sound judgement and expresses himself very clearly." **Recent work:** Acted as senior junior for the defendant Portuguese public transport companies in the case brought by Banco Santander Totta.

Adam Kramer (see p.693) Unusually versatile junior with a diverse practice taking in a number of areas including energy, insurance and civil fraud as well as banking and finance. He has appeared in a number of the most significant cases of recent years, including the landmark Bank Charges Litigation. **Strengths:** "He is very, very good on his feet and is able to hit the right note, whoever he is in front of, whether in the Court of Appeal or the Supreme Court." "Absolutely brilliant. He is fantastically bright and very effective." **Recent work:** Acted as a senior junior for one of the claimant groups in the RBS rights issue litigation.

Michael Lazarus (see p.697) Enjoys an excellent reputation as a highly experienced and accomplished senior junior whose representation of banking and finance clients accompanies a wider and much lauded practice. He is in addition considered the leading junior in contentious information technology matters. **Strengths:** "He is an exceptionally clever man who could be a silk." "Very good. He is user-friendly, helpful, good tactically and cool under pressure." **Recent work:** Represented Threadneedle Asset Management in the defence of a claim brought by Otkritie Capital for USD100 million on the basis of an allegation that the defendant is vicariously liable for a conspiracy conducted by a former employee.

Matthew Parker (see p.733) Well-regarded junior with a solid reputation in relation to banking and finance cases. He has further expertise in handling civil fraud and professional negligence matters, as well as those dealing with offshore issues. **Strengths:** "A fighter. He is responsive, charming, very intelligent and has a wonderful rapport with clients." "He can outperform QCs and can perform both the disciplines of oral and written advocacy in a fantastic way." **Recent work:** Acted for the second defendant in a claim for over £100 million arising from investments in a commercial property in Canary Wharf. The claim was with regard to allegations of misrepresentation in an information memorandum and breaches of fiduciary duty. The case was struck out after a three-day hearing.

Ian Wilson Enjoys a good reputation with regard to his representation in banking matters which commonly turn on issues of securities, swaps, options and structured financial products. He also has noted expertise in relation to the Consumer Credit Act. **Strengths:** "His written advice is excellent – extremely thorough, yet concise. He is also very approachable and user-friendly." "He is very quick-thinking, skilful in cross-examination and incredibly good with the client in terms of allaying any concerns they might have." **Recent work:** Successfully represented Clydesdale Bank in a complex claim for £17 million relating to the unauthorised release of a security and unauthorised lending. At issue were allegations of fraud, conspiracy and negligence.

William Edwards Well-established junior whose practice includes arbitration, insolvency, fraud and negligence matters alongside his central expertise in banking and finance. **Strengths:** "He has a compendious knowledge of the law, is incredibly bright and a pleasure to work with." "Phenomenally bright and offers formidable, in-depth analysis." **Recent work:** Acted for Loreley Financing in a claim valued at USD72 million against the estate of Lehman Brothers arising from the sale of CDO notes.

David Simpson A banking and finance specialist who is regularly instructed by major investment and retail banks in high-value matters. He has additional noted expertise in technical and contentious regulatory proceedings, often on behalf of the FCA. **Strengths:** "Terrific. He is incredibly efficient, organised, incisive, thoughtful and a wizard with technology." "He is bright, capable, very flexible and asks the right questions." **Recent work:** Represented the private banking arm of Credit Suisse in a claim for around £30 million brought by a high net worth client in relation to the liquidation of a USD60 million investment portfolio.

Band 3

Essex Court Chambers

See profile on p.836

THE SET

A collection of highly capable barristers whose regular involvement in banking litigation often overlaps with the set's wider expertise in shipping, commodities and arbitration proceedings. Members of Essex Court Chambers are noted for their capability in handling complex matters spanning borders and jurisdictions, and are highly experienced in appearing in forums around the world. Additional areas of expertise in which counsel are regularly instructed include fraud and insurance.

Client service: "Joe Ferrigno's clerking is very good and responsive."

SILKS

David Foxton QC Enjoys a reputation as an outstandingly intelligent and experienced advocate well versed in the full range of disputes in the banking and finance arena. He has appeared in a number of the most significant banking cases of recent times, and has further extensive expertise in commercial arbitration proceedings under all major arbitral rules. **Strengths:** "A tremendously creative and pleasant advocate who judges listen to." "He is fantastic. A thoroughly likeable guy to work with, thoughtful and clever." **Recent work:** Acted for Goldman Sachs in Waterfall III, the third hearing in relation to the funding costs under the ISDA Master Agreement in connection to the collapse of Lehman Brothers.

Joe Smouha QC Exceptionally able silk with a diverse practice encompassing the adept handling of complex proceedings in civil fraud, and banking and finance. He is additionally an accomplished advocate in international arbitrations, as well as sitting as an arbitrator. **Strengths:** "A fantastic silk with a great ability to cut through very complex scenarios to get to the key issues to move the matter forward." "He oozes class. A pleasure to deal with, and a smooth, persuasive and effective advocate." **Recent work:** Acted for Barclays on the dispute with UniCredit concerning the indemnification of Italian tax liabilities pursuant to payments arising under a structured investment product supplied by Barclays.

Richard Millett QC Versatile advocate with a practice beyond banking and finance that includes offshore, commercial chancery and international arbitration proceedings. He is also noted for his representation in media and insurance disputes. **Strengths:** "A great advocate. He is passionate, very detailed and very innovative." "He doesn't sit on the fence but gives you a view of how things will pan out and can grapple well with complex issues."

Jeffrey Gruder QC (see p.661) Leading arbitrator with wider expertise in relation to general commercial and shipping disputes. His practice in banking and finance focuses primarily on securities and derivatives cases. **Strengths:** "A very strong advocate capable of delivering a carefully crafted argument." "A characterful but effective advocate."

JUNIORS

Edmund King Established junior with a highly respected practice spanning a diverse array of related areas including commercial chancery, arbitration, civil fraud, shipping and commodities. He has further noted expertise in handling indirect tax issues. **Strengths:** "He doesn't advise in a vacuum but has the ability to marry technically strong analysis with the commercial context of a case." "He is very bright and very sure-footed. When you get a piece of work from him, you know you can rely on it."

James Willan Has enjoyed a rapid rise up the rankings with respect to a wide range of practice areas based, in part, on his reputation as an extremely capable and intelligent junior with the ability to handle the most complex and intricate of issues. Besides banking disputes, he is accomplished in representing clients in civil fraud, offshore and arbitration proceedings. **Strengths:** "A superstar on all fronts. His intellect, analytical skills, ability to master documents, advocacy and his confident and assertive advice are all superb." "Ridiculously impressive. A junior who performs way, way beyond his years." **Recent work:** Acted for Dexia Crediop in a dispute with Provincia di Crotone concerning interest rate swaps valued in excess of EUR50 million.

South Square

See profile on p.910

THE SET

South Square is the leading restructuring and insolvency set whose members' work in the banking and finance industry often arises in this context. Its enviable roster of counsel is often instructed by leading solicitors in highly intricate disputes, many of which address issues relating to securitisation and derivatives transactions. Recent headline cases in which both silks and juniors have appeared include Landsbanki v Rabobank, a dispute concerning closeouts and the application of the 1992 ISDA Master Agreement, and the Waterfall applications stemming from the collapse of Lehman Brothers.

Client service: "Practice manager Jim Costa is excellent – very responsive and helpful. In arranging consultations and sorting out billing, he always gets it right first time." Mike Killick and Dylan Playfoot are the joint senior clerks.

SILKS

Robin Dicker QC (see p.633) Outstanding advocate with a particularly strong reputation for handling the most significant and high-value restructuring and insolvency disputes, including those arising in the banking industry. He is also widely regarded as one of the leading silks in company law and offshore matters. **Strengths:** "He is a brilliant, incredibly articulate, intellectually rigorous barrister." "He is very clever and very able. Clients love him and judges respect him." **Recent work:** Acted for the first three respondents in the highly significant Waterfall II application stemming from the collapse of Lehman Brothers.

Antony Zacaroli QC (see p.802) Exceptionally talented and respected silk with a practice in banking and finance disputes primarily centred on restructuring and insolvency matters in the industry. His technical facility in a number of areas, including in company law and financial regulatory cases, receives praise from a range of sources. **Strengths:** "His legal knowledge and application is exceptionally good, but he is also very good at appreciating the client's commercial position and thinking about how to present his knowledge to that end." "He is incredibly bright and very technical, as well as being user-friendly and very personable." **Recent work:** Appeared on behalf of Wentworth Sons Sub-Debt Sàrl in the Waterfall II proceedings.

David Allison QC (see p.583) Recent silk who enjoys a growing reputation in a number of related fields both in terms of the strength of his advocacy and for his willingness to tackle the detail of complex cases. Beyond banking and finance, he has additional expertise in company law, offshore and insolvency matters, among others. **Strengths:** "He gets into the detail rather than simply relying on technical knowledge of the law and he is really responsive and user-friendly." "His advocacy is really good, assertive – he works well on his feet." **Recent work:** Represented Rabobank in its defence of a claim brought by Landsbanki in connection to the closeout of an ISDA Master Agreement. The case dealt with issues of valuation and foreign currency pricing.

Jeremy Goldring QC (see p.656) Accomplished advocate with a strong reputation in a number of fields including company law, insolvency, and banking and finance. His practice in the latter focuses primarily on issues in connection to securitisation and derivatives. **Strengths:** "He is extremely clever, very sensible and practical." "He obviously makes the effort to read the papers to understand the background to the situation and tries to help you find a solution that is both practical and solves the problem." **Recent work:** Acted for BNY Mellon Corporate Trustee in a case determining Lloyds Banking Group's right to redeem capital notes issued during the financial crisis in advance of their maturity dates.

William Trower QC (see p.784) An exceptional restructuring and insolvency silk whose practice in finance often concerns such matters arising in the banking industry. He is also noted for further expertise in relation to company law and corporate fraud in the civil context. **Strengths:** "He is very articulate and very smooth in terms of putting points across persuasively." **Recent work:** Represented Landsbanki in a closeout and set-off dispute with UBS.

Tom Smith QC (see p.769) Quickly establishing himself in silk as an advocate of choice for leading instructing solicitors in an array of fields. Besides his strong reputation in banking disputes, he has additional aptitude in marshalling proceedings in company law and insolvency. **Strengths:** "Enormously committed and responsive. A great intellect and advocate." "Extremely talented and a pleasure to work with. A go-to junior QC for banking insolvency matters." **Recent work:** Acted on behalf of GSO Capital Partners in a case against Barclays Bank in relation to debt trades undertaken in respect of Spanish gaming company Codere. The case was one of the first substantive judgments on the new Financial List.

Daniel Bayfield QC (see p.592) Takes silk this year on the back of a highly successful junior career that saw him gain an excellent reputation in commercial chancery and insolvency disputes as well as banking cases. He is also an advocate of some repute in regard to sports law matters. **Strengths:** "Daniel is very bright and able. He combines a sound legal approach with pragmatic advice and is user-friendly and responsive." "He is very bright and has good judgement – a very strong junior silk." **Recent work:** Represented UBS in its defence of an action brought by Landsbanki concerning issues of closeout and set-off.

JUNIORS

Stephen Robins (see p.753) Leading restructuring and insolvency junior whose practice in banking matters very often overlaps with that field. He is also noted for his expertise in civil fraud. **Strengths:** "He is very bright, very capable and an excellent draftsman." "A precise thinker and energetic." **Recent work:** Acted in the Court of Appeal for The Bank of New York Mellon in the dispute with Lloyds Banking Group concerning its right to redeem capital notes that had been issued during the financial crisis.

Band 4

20 Essex Street

See profile on p.838

THE SET

20 Essex Street offers a number of well-respected silks who are highly experienced in handling complex financial disputes, most often those relating to derivatives, interest rate swaps, structured products and mis-selling. Its members are additionally very well versed in appearing in international commercial arbitration proceedings under all major rules, with further noted capability in shipping, EU and public international law.

Client service: "Their clerks are comparable to the top end of the marketplace in every respect." Senior clerk Neil Palmer leads the team.

SILKS

Andrew Baker QC Enjoys a strong reputation for his banking and finance practice, which focuses primarily on cases of insolvency, derivatives and structured financial products. **Strengths:** "He is terribly bright, very nice and really good at banking and finance work." **Recent work:** Represented Lehman Brothers in one of its final remaining administration proceedings, valued at around EUR65 million, to recover sums payable from DZ Bank.

Charles Kimmins QC Highly accomplished shipping and international arbitration silk with a well-respected banking and commercial litigation practice. His financial disputes work centres on derivatives, civil fraud and cases examining the application of the 1992 ISDA Master Agreement. **Strengths:** "Fantastic. He is completely on top of the detail at all times, extremely well prepared and wears his intelligence lightly." "He is really constructive, fabulous. He has perfect recall of the relevant cases and is extremely adept at understanding the issues." **Recent work:** Acted for financiers Technomar in seeking declaratory relief and damages relating to rights arising under a number of financing documents.

Julian Kenny QC Took silk this year off the back of his strong reputation in contentious proceedings in the banking and shipping arenas. He is especially interested in ISDA issues and the determination of closeouts. **Strengths:** "He is intellectually very able, calm, measured and has a good sense of humour." "He is bright, analytical and thorough."

4 Stone Buildings

See profile on p.913

THE SET

4 Stone Buildings houses highly respected silks and juniors who handle banking litigation as part of their superior commercial chancery practice. Counsel at 4 Stone Buildings also offer additional expertise in relation to public law proceedings and contentious financial regulatory cases.

Client service: "One can get spectacular client service from the clerks room. They foster deep, long-standing relationships, are attentive and can be contacted at any time of day or night. When one needs them to step up, they always deliver." David Goddard is the set's senior clerk.

SILKS

Robert Miles QC Exceptionally well regarded in a diverse range of practice areas, being widely seen as one of a select leading few in company and banking law. He has appeared as an advocate in a large number of the most significant finance cases of recent years, and has had a recent focus on cases concerning the redemption of capital notes. **Strengths:** "He combines fantastic technical ability, strategic judgement and user-friendliness with powerful and incisive advocacy. He is full of ideas, inspires huge confidence in clients and is willing to give clear views and to be bold." "A reassuringly clear thinker." **Recent work:** Defended Goldman Sachs in its case against the Libyan Investment Authority, valued at USD1 billion, relating to investments made in 2008.

Jonathan Crow QC (see p.627) One of the leading silks of his generation, Jonathan Crow QC maintains an outstanding level of representation across an unusually diverse range of practice areas. His presence at the forefront of company law and other chancery matters is accompanied by leading expertise in public law, financial services, offshore and insolvency disputes. **Strengths:** "An exceptional advocate. He is very user-friendly and has a very sharp mind." "A grandee who is down-to-earth. He has great charm, great authority and manages to have a magisterial quality without being stuffy." **Recent work:** Acted as Advocate to the Supreme Court in the high-profile dispute between JSC BTA Bank and Mukhtar Ablyazov that addressed the interpretation and application of the standard form freezing order.

Richard Hill QC (see p.671) Occupies a position among the finest company law advocates in the London Bar, as well as highly respected expertise in commercial and civil fraud disputes. His practice in banking matters often involves the representation of oligarchs and high net worth individuals in claims against financial institutions. **Strengths:** "He is very bright and someone to call on for knotty problems." **Recent work:** Represented Al-Khorafi in a quantum hearing gaining USD73 million in damages from Bank Sarasin in relation to the mis-selling of structured investment products.

JUNIORS

Sharif Shivji (see p.764) Has a fast-growing reputation as a highly accomplished banking junior, whose practice in the area is partly informed by his background as a derivatives trader. He is also often called upon by instructing solicitors for representation in company law and offshore disputes. **Strengths:** "He is really good on his feet, is very commercial, technically brilliant and can understand complex financial products." "A proper banking junior well capable of a mature presentation of the issues." **Recent work:** Appeared in the case between Standard & Poor's and Deutsche Bank concerning the liability of ratings agencies for the ratings they grant financial products.

Other Ranked Lawyers

Pushpinder Saini QC (Blackstone Chambers) An extraordinarily versatile advocate whose interaction with the banking and finance realm is primarily through his deep expertise in public law and contentious regulatory proceedings. He has additional experience in handling civil fraud claims and cases heard in the British Virgin Islands. **Strengths:** "He is an excellent advocate who has a talent for strategy and achieving commercial outcomes." "Very calm and offers very good client service." **Recent work:** Defended the SFO against a claim brought by the Tchenguiz brothers for misfeasance in relation to false allegations made of fraud and financial misconduct.

Hodge Malek QC (39 Essex Chambers) A silk with an excellent standing in the wider Financial Bar, with an especially good reputation in relation to regulatory and financial crime matters. His practice in banking litigation has seen him acting in a number of leading cases affecting the industry, most notably in connection to the mis-selling of PPI and to the manipulation of Libor. **Strengths:** "Hodge is concise, impressive and pithy. He will achieve something in a very direct way." "He's extremely personable and is very good at explaining strategy and in giving his views." **Recent work:** Defended NatWest against an action brought by both Pakistan and India in connection with funds, now valued at over £34 million, that had been transferred from the Nizam in 1948 during the annexation of Hyderabad by India.

David McIlroy (Forum Chambers) Enters the rankings this year on the back of a strong track record of appearances in cases in the banking field, most commonly in alleged mis-selling of interest rate hedging products. He has further expertise in advising on the regulatory framework for the financial industry. **Strengths:** "He is at the forefront of banking law in England." "A man of obvious assets, his advice is phenomenal." **Recent work:** Acted for the claimant, Wainford Holdings, in a dispute with RBS in which Wainford claimed rescission on the basis of manipulation of Libor.

Anthony Trace QC (see p.783) (Maitland Chambers) Joins the banking and finance listings this year in addition to already being featured in a large number of related areas including commercial dispute resolution, company law, offshore and civil fraud. Among the many leading cases of recent years in which he has been involved is the dispute between Mukhtar Ablyazov and JSC BTA Bank. **Strengths:** "A tenacious and experienced advocate, with excellent judgement and an easy-going, charming manner." "He is a first-rate advocate and leader." **Recent work:** Acted for Lloyds Bank in a case valued at £75 million concerning the alleged mis-selling of swaps.

Andrew Twigger QC (see p.785) (Maitland Chambers) Moves this year to Maitland from Three Stone Buildings, where he was formerly joint head of chambers. His respected banking and finance practice is accompanied by a broader commercial disputes and commercial chancery expertise. **Strengths:** "He is very thorough and his drafting is impeccable since he really gets his head around all the issues." "He is technically brilliant and has great attention to detail." **Recent work:** Represented Natixis in a claim against NRAM that addressed whether NRAM, as issuer of bonds, was liable directly to Natixis for interest on the collateral it had deposited pursuant to the ISDA Credit Support Annex.

David Mumford QC (see p.724) (Maitland Chambers) New silk this year following an outstanding junior career in which he established himself as a junior of choice for many leading solicitors in a number of areas including commercial chancery, banking and civil fraud. His financial disputes practice has recently focused on issues of fraud and insolvency in the industry. **Strengths:** "He has an amazing breadth of knowledge, is extremely clever and is an excellent advocate." "David is extremely bright, client-friendly and approachable." **Recent work:** Acted for Canary Wharf Finance in a case against Deutsche Trustee Company, the securitisation of the Canary Wharf estate and whether certain notes could be redeemed without paying a premium being at issue.

Farhaz Khan (Outer Temple Chambers) A highly respected junior with especially deep expertise in regulatory proceedings. In the realm of banking litigation, he has a good recent track record in Libor and securitisation cases. **Strengths:** "An extremely bright and analytical barrister who demonstrates judgement well beyond his years." "An expert on interest rate protection products and mis-selling." **Recent work:** Acted for the junior noteholders in a dispute concerning the correct allocation of funds received by way of sales and premiums in an approximately USD1 billion commercial mortgage-backed securitisation.

Benjamin Pilling QC (see p.738) (4 Pump Court) Recent silk who has had little trouble establishing himself as a leader in a wide variety of practice areas including information technology, construction and professional negligence. His banking and finance practice commonly sees him acting in high-value mis-selling matters for investment and retail banks. **Strengths:** "Delightful. He has beautiful judgement in what will work in court. An absolute delight to work with and very clever." "Clients love him – he is very bright, switched on and really makes an effort." **Recent work:** Acted for Landsbanki in a case against UBS concerning the closeout of complex derivatives transactions following insolvency.

Nigel Tozzi QC (see p.783) (4 Pump Court) A long-standing figure at the London Bar, with highly respected practices in a wide range of areas. He is especially adept in professional negligence, information technology and energy proceedings, while his banking litigation work most commonly arises in the context of derivatives disputes, both for and against banks and financial institutions. **Strengths:** "Very quick witted. He is really clever and penetrating." "He is extremely bright, practical and quick." **Recent work:** Acted for Alpha Development in a dispute with Barclays Wealth in its capacity of provider of fiduciary and administration services, and against several former directors for failing to ensure that Alpha complied with various covenants of a loan on a property development in Chelsea, such that the project collapsed.

Malcolm Waters QC (see p.790) (Radcliffe Chambers) A long-standing member of the Banking and Finance Bar, with an excellent reputation as the foremost authority on the Consumer Credit Act. He maintains both an advisory and contentious practice, often acting for banks, building societies and other mutual financial institutions. **Strengths:** "The guru on the Consumer Credit Act, who gets his technical points across extremely well." "His analysis of consumer protection legislation is really amazing." **Recent work:** Acted for NRAM in a test case to determine the status of unregulated loan agreements processed and documented as though they were regulated by the Consumer Credit Act.

Jeremy Cousins QC (Radcliffe Chambers) Widely praised for his intuitive and experienced approach to litigation concerning the banking and finance industry, with a particular recent focus on the law around loan notes. He also regularly sits as a deputy High Court judge. **Strengths:** "His encyclopaedic knowledge of the law combined with his thorough preparation makes him unbeatable." **Recent work:** Represented Rosserlane in its dispute with Credit Suisse concerning the sale of an oilfield, allegedly undervalued by several hundreds of millions of dollars.

David Blayney QC (see p.597) (Serle Court) Has a growing reputation in silk as a highly technically capable banking lawyer who is involved at the centre of some of the most significant cases in the field. He is also noted for his expertise in relation to commercial chancery, company law and partnership disputes. **Strengths:** "He is an unusually intelligent lawyer, excellent in terms of pulling out knotty, intricate problems." "He has the very unusual combination of being fantastic on detail while also being able to see the bigger picture. He has brilliant tactical judgement." **Recent work:** Acted as a key figure in the team of silks and juniors defending RBS and its former directors in the rights issue litigation.

Nicholas Lavender QC (Serle Court) Respected advocate with a commercial disputes practice centred on the banking sector. He has been involved in a number of leading cases heard not only in the English courts but also in arbitral proceedings and in the ECHR. **Strengths:** "Level-headed and efficient, he displays great knowledge and judgement." "He is terrifically good. Very assured, sound and calming." **Recent work:** Represented RBS in a dispute with Dongbu Insurance in which it sought a declaration that it had a binding settlement with respect to structured notes or, alternatively, that it had validly terminated the option for payment of premium, valued at around £20 million.

Philip Marshall QC (see p.708) (Serle Court) Highly experienced silk with a wide-ranging practice centred on commercial matters heard in the Chancery Division. He focuses on complex disputes turning on issues of company law, civil fraud and insolvency as well as banking and finance. **Strengths:** "Philip is a superb advocate who balances aggression with excellent judgement. A first choice if the case requires a barrister to get across the detail." "A real fighter who is very tenacious." **Recent work:** Appeared in the dispute between BTA Bank and Mukhtar Ablyazov.

Simon Hattan (see p.667) (Serle Court) Enjoys a growing reputation as an accomplished banking junior with a practice that has seen him appear in a number of headline cases of recent years. He has further noted expertise in contentious financial regulatory matters. **Strengths:** "An excellent choice for regulated matters or those involving fraud. Offers robust advice and has the ability to identify the issues that must be resolved." "One of the best banking juniors around, he is very down-to-earth, pragmatic and sensible." **Recent work:** Acted as part of the defence team representing RBS and four of its former directors in the rights issue litigation.

Paul Downes QC (see p.636) (2TG – 2 Temple Gardens) Highly capable commercial silk with a solidly established following in the realm of banking and finance. His recent work in the area includes matters in connection to swaps and derivatives and the application of ISDA Master Agreements. **Strengths:** "An excellent silk, who is very tactically astute and communicates in a no-nonsense, clear way." "He is very practical and client-friendly." **Recent work:** Acted in a dispute between a regulated payments service provider and a major UK bank with respect to the granting of injunctive relief on an account that had been frozen pursuant to the Proceeds of Crime Act.

NORTHERN

Banking & Finance
Leading Sets
Band 1
Kings Chambers *
Leading Silks
New Silks
Harper Mark *Kings Chambers* *
Leading Juniors
Band 1
Temple Eleanor *Kings Chambers* *

Band 1

Kings Chambers

See profile on p.968

THE SET

Kings Chambers maintains its dominant position as the leading set for banking and finance on the Northern Circuit. Its members provide a broad range of financial expertise and act for a diverse array of clients including primary and secondary lenders and borrowers, trade and asset finance companies, banks and customers. Particular areas of expertise include breach of mandate claims, the enforcement of domestic and commercial security and asset security, negligence, misrepresentation and mis-selling claims, as well as a wide range of securities matters.

Client service: "The clerks at Kings are the best. They have a lot of contacts in the courts and are very good at getting stuff listed and getting the papers sorted. They are very efficient, friendly and helpful." "The clerking is the best of any chambers we deal with." Colin Griffin is the chief clerk for commercial matters.

SILKS

Mark Harper QC (see p.664) An excellent recent silk with an impressively broad financial practice. His areas of expertise include banking and finance, shareholder and company disputes, professional negligence and sports. Highlighted by sources for his litigation expertise. **Strengths:** "The speed at which he can turn things round is incredible. He is a great advocate who is quick at thinking on his feet, and his way with the judiciary is great." "He is fantastic." **Recent work:** Acted in Co-op Bank v Philips, defending a counterclaim brought against a bank alleging the provision of negligent advice.

JUNIORS

Eleanor Temple (see p.779) A highly regarded junior with a broad commercial practice that takes in director disqualification and company law, in addition to her banking expertise. She has a wealth of experience in the area of international banking and finance litigation work, and particular expertise in cases involving the Channel Islands. **Strengths:** "She is an excellent advocate and nothing seems to faze her. You know she'll always do a good job for you." "She is a wonderful advocate who is great on her feet and gets to the bottom of problems immediately. She's great in conference and is very impressive in court." **Recent work:** Acted in Nasir v Verma, a large finance case regarding property transactions in India.

WESTERN

Banking & Finance
Leading Sets
Band 1
Guildhall Chambers *
Leading Silks
Band 1
Davies Stephen *Guildhall Chambers*
Sims Hugh *Guildhall Chambers*
Leading Juniors
Band 1
Fentem Ross *Guildhall Chambers*
Levy Neil *Guildhall Chambers*
McMeel Gerard *Guildhall Chambers*
Virgo John *Guildhall Chambers*
Band 2
Ramel Stefan *Guildhall Chambers*
* *Indicates set / individual with profile.*
Alphabetical order within each band. Band 1 is highest.

Band 1

Guildhall Chambers
See profile on p.938
THE SET
The undisputed pre-eminent banking and finance set on the Western Circuit, Guildhall Chambers offers clients counsel of all levels of seniority and is well versed in handling the full range of disputes in the area. Members are called on to handle claims all the way up to the Supreme Court and have been involved in a significant number of the leading banking cases of recent years, including a number arising from the Libor scandal.
Client service: "An extremely professional but approachable chambers. The clerks always respond to e-mails promptly and if your chosen counsel is not available, they will always suggest a suitable alternative." Mike Norton is the set's commercial clerk.

SILKS
Stephen Davies QC A highly regarded QC whose banking practice is often informed by his specialism in restructuring and insolvency. He has additional expertise in relation to allegations of the manipulation of financial benchmarks. **Strengths:** "A fearless advocate, who is a very passionate, remarkably hard-working, diligent, creative and client-friendly counsel." "Very helpful, very thorough, and very confident in the stances he takes." **Recent work:** Acted for the claimant in a case brought against Barclays Bank to rescind interest rate swaps on the basis of manipulation of the Libor benchmark.

Hugh Sims QC Has a highly respected, broad-ranging commercial practice that includes deep expertise in an array of areas, including chancery, company law, professional negligence and insolvency-related disputes. His work in the area of banking and finance includes acting both for and against banks and other financial institutions. **Strengths:** "He is extremely clever and very quick. He considers all matters in great detail and is really thoughtful. A pleasure to work with." "He is very commercial, very good with clients and has a style of presentation that judges like very much." **Recent work:** Acted for the claimant lender against a firm of accountants in a claim of professional negligence in relation to a due diligence report concerning the purchase of a US medical homecare company. The matter is on appeal to the Supreme Court.

JUNIORS
Ross Fentem Maintains a diverse banking litigation practice, and has particularly pronounced expertise in cases concerning consumer credit, guarantees and securities disputes. He is well versed in acting both for and against major banks, and has often appeared as sole counsel. **Strengths:** "He is unflappable. He's fantastically persuasive and very easy to get on with." "Exceptionally bright, very user-friendly and punches well above his weight for his year of call." **Recent work:** Acted in General Asset Management v Halligan, a security dispute involving a claim under a mortgage securing various asset finance obligations.

Neil Levy A widely respected banking and finance specialist with three decades of experience of acting successfully for a wide range of clients in the industry. He is additionally interested in financial disputes in connection to professional negligence and insolvency. **Strengths:** "He is very astute, extremely detailed, focused, pragmatic and easy to work with." "Technically very able indeed. He makes the extremely complex seem rather more straightforward than it actually is." **Recent work:** Acted for the claimants in bringing a claim against Lloyds Bank to rescind interest rate swaps on the basis of the manipulation of Libor.

Gerard McMeel Highly experienced junior counsel whose banking and finance practice centres on the representation of banks, insurance companies and financial intermediaries. He is especially expert in handling claims arising out of unsuccessful investments, Ponzi schemes and interest rate swap mis-selling. **Strengths:** "A first-class financial services specialist." **Recent work:** Represented 452 investors in bringing a Commercial Court claim against a US foreign exchange company which had allegedly solicited hundreds of millions of dollars from investors by way of an unauthorised UK representative.

John Virgo Enjoys an outstanding reputation as a highly capable junior who handles disputes for a strong client base. He has additional wider expertise in relation to professional negligence matters, particularly as they apply to the banking industry. **Strengths:** "He is exceptional. Very flexible, very client-facing and very adept at finding solutions." "Superb. He has a high-level view but also gets into the detail to get a real understanding of a case." **Recent work:** Appeared in a group action brought against Equitable Life on behalf of 400 trapped annuitants who alleged mis-selling of with-profits annuities. A multiparty settlement was reached.

Stefan Ramel Solid junior with a wide-ranging commercial practice encompassing company law and insolvency matters in addition to a core of banking and finance disputes. He regularly acts on behalf of major banks and other lending institutions in a number of forums. **Strengths:** "He's a very technically able barrister who is very, very good on paper. He's particularly good on the insolvency side of banking work." **Recent work:** Acted for Bank of Scotland in a claim against litigants in person seeking a money judgment following default on a loan.

Contents:

LONDON Commercial

Chancery: Commercial
Leading Sets
Band 1
Maitland Chambers *
Serle Court *
4 Stone Buildings *
Band 2
XXIV Old Buildings *
South Square *
Wilberforce Chambers *
Band 3
Enterprise Chambers *
Erskine Chambers *
New Square Chambers *
3 Verulam Buildings *
* Indicates set / individual with profile.
◊ (ORL) = Other Ranked Lawyer.
Alphabetical order within each band. Band 1 is highest.

Chancery: Commercial
Leading Silks
Star individuals
Crow Jonathan *4 Stone Buildings* *
Girolami Paul *Maitland Chambers* *
Miles Robert *4 Stone Buildings*
Band 1
Beltrami Adrian *3 Verulam Buildings*
Bompas George *4 Stone Buildings* *
Boyle Alan *Serle Court* *
Dicker Robin *South Square* *
Gourgey Alan *Wilberforce Chambers*
Jones Elizabeth *Serle Court* *
Jones Philip *Serle Court* *
Marshall Philip *Serle Court* *
McQuater Ewan *3 Verulam Buildings*
Mowschenson Terence *Wilberforce Chambers*
Newman Catherine *Maitland Chambers* *
Smith Stephen *Erskine Chambers* *
Steinfeld Alan *XXIV Old Buildings*
Trace Anthony *Maitland Chambers* *
Zacaroli Antony *South Square* *
Band 2
Arden Peter *Erskine Chambers* *
Ayliffe James *Wilberforce Chambers*
Bhaloo Zia *Enterprise Chambers*
Brisby John *4 Stone Buildings* *
Brownbill David *XXIV Old Buildings*
Cohen Lawrence *Wilberforce Chambers*
Collings Matthew *Maitland Chambers* *
Cousins Jeremy *Radcliffe Chambers (ORL)* ◊
Croxford Ian *Wilberforce Chambers*
de Garr Robinson Anthony *One Essex Court (ORL)* ◊ *
Grant Thomas *Maitland Chambers*
Hill Richard G *4 Stone Buildings* *
Millett Richard *Essex Court Chambers (ORL)* ◊
Moss Gabriel *South Square*
Nicholls John *Maitland Chambers* *
Norbury Hugh *Serle Court* *
Pymont Christopher *Maitland Chambers* *
Rowley Keith *Radcliffe Chambers (ORL)* ◊ *
Smith Joanna *Wilberforce Chambers*
Tager Romie *Selborne Chambers (ORL)* ◊ *
Tolaney Sonia *One Essex Court (ORL)* ◊
Twigger Andrew M *Maitland Chambers* *
Wardell John *Wilberforce Chambers*
Band 3
Adkin Jonathan *Fountain Court Chambers (ORL)* ◊ *
Ashworth Lance *Serle Court* *
Blayney David *Serle Court* *
Chivers David *Erskine Chambers* *
Cullen Edmund *Maitland Chambers* *
Davis-White Malcolm *XXIV Old Buildings*
Dowley Dominic *Serle Court* *
Gibbon Michael *Maitland Chambers* *
Goldring Jeremy *South Square* *
Hilliard Lexa *Wilberforce Chambers*
Machell John *Serle Court* *
Malek Ali *3 Verulam Buildings*
McGrath Paul *Essex Court Chambers (ORL)* ◊
Moeran Fenner *Wilberforce Chambers*
Moverley Smith Stephen *XXIV Old Buildings*
Smith Tom *South Square* *
Talbot Rice Elspeth *XXIV Old Buildings*
Tipples Amanda *Maitland Chambers* *
Weatherill Bernard *Enterprise Chambers*
Band 4
Aldridge James *Maitland Chambers* *
Allison David *South Square* *
Ayres Andrew *Maitland Chambers*
Caddick Nicholas *Hogarth Chambers (ORL)* ◊
Clutterbuck Andrew *4 Stone Buildings* *
Cunningham Mark *Maitland Chambers* *
Levy Robert *XXIV Old Buildings*
Lowe Thomas *Wilberforce Chambers*
Phillips Mark *South Square* *
Potts James *Erskine Chambers* *
Reed Rupert *Wilberforce Chambers*
Shekerdemian Marcia *Wilberforce Chambers*
Stallworthy Nicolas *Outer Temple Chambers (ORL)* ◊
Toube Felicity *South Square* *
Tregear Francis *XXIV Old Buildings*
Levy Juliette *Cerulean Chambers (ORL)* ◊
New Silks
Bayfield Daniel *South Square* *
Lightman Daniel *Serle Court* *
Mumford David *Maitland Chambers* *
Penny Tim *Wilberforce Chambers*

Band 1

Maitland Chambers

See profile on p.875

THE SET

Maitland Chambers has long been a market leader for commercial chancery work, and enjoys a formidable reputation. Its cadre of QCs and juniors consistently attracts matters of the highest value and quality. A small sample of recent cases for the set includes ongoing litigation from the high-profile Lehman Brothers collapse and new instructions from leading FTSE companies. Sources say: "Whenever I see anybody from Maitland, whether it be in writing or on their feet, it is always very impressive." **Client service:** The clerking team, headed by John Wiggs, is widely described as efficient. "The clerking there is very good; it is a really professional outfit."

SILKS

Paul Girolami QC (see p.653) A highly regarded silk whose thriving commercial chancery practice benefits from his experience in a wide range of legal areas, including company law and civil fraud. He attracts some of the most complicated work at the Chancery Bar, including numerous cases with an international component. **Strengths:** "He's at the top of his game and must be one of the best chancery silks available. He's an extremely powerful advocate and very easy to work with." "Paul Girolami is excellent and very nice indeed."

Catherine Newman QC (see p.727) A senior barrister praised for her "consummate skill." She has experience of representing clients in a spectrum of commercial chancery matters, and is particularly strong on company law, fraud and trusts cases. **Strengths:** "Catherine is incredibly sharp. She's very good with clients and can make complicated principles understandable to a lay party. She's also extremely impressive in terms of the volume that she can get on top of in a short space of time – in a document-heavy case, she's able to understand and absorb information very quickly." "I always think that for a difficult case she's very good." **Recent work:** Appeared in a breach of warranty claim arising out of a £17.5 million commercial acquisition by a private equity fund.

Anthony Trace QC (see p.783) Renowned for his spirited handling of heavy litigation in the commercial and chancery courts. He regularly advises clients on cases arising from insolvency, banking and finance disputes. **Strengths:** "He's excellent as he's very tenacious in court and he fights points very hard. Clients like the fact that he has some spine to him." "He is very bright and can make a bad case look good." **Recent work:** Acted in Gorbunova v Berezovsky, a high-profile case involving alleged propriety estoppels and trusts.

Thomas Grant QC A "hard-working and talented advocate" who has a thriving reputation for commercial chancery work. While he has the capacity to handle a range of chancery disputes, his main area of interest is civil fraud, and he is also a noted expert on freezing orders. **Strengths:** "He is first-class – he's massively intelligent and has broad knowledge. He is a real perfectionist when it comes to his written opinions, and he's also good on his feet." "He treats everyone respectfully and he is superbly thorough. He gets good results in difficult cases." **Recent work:** Appeared in Metropolitan Housing Trust v Taylor

Chancery: Commercial

Leading Juniors

Band 1	
Addy Catherine	*Maitland Chambers* *
Akkouh Tim	*Erskine Chambers* *
de Mestre Andrew	*4 Stone Buildings* *
Denton-Cox Gregory	*4 Stone Buildings* *
Hagen Dakis	*Serle Court* *
Hutton Louise	*Maitland Chambers* *
Pringle Watson	*Maitland Chambers* *
Band 2	
Bailey James	*New Square Chambers*
Barker James	*Enterprise Chambers*
Drake David	*Serle Court* *
Eaton Turner David	*New Square Chambers* *
Gillett Emily	*Erskine Chambers* *
Greenwood Paul	*4 Stone Buildings* *
Halkerston Graeme	*Wilberforce Chambers*
Harrison Christopher	*4 Stone Buildings* *
Higgo Justin	*Serle Court* *
King Edmund	*Essex Court Chambers (ORL)* ◊
Mallin Max	*Wilberforce Chambers*
Mold Andrew	*Wilberforce Chambers*
Pickering James	*Enterprise Chambers*
Richardson Giles	*Serle Court* *
Shivji Sharif	*4 Stone Buildings* *
Singla Nikki	*Wilberforce Chambers*
Band 3	
Adamyk Simon	*New Square Chambers*
Boardman Christopher	*Radcliffe Chambers (ORL)* ◊
Boeddinghaus Hermann	*4 Stone Buildings* *
Calland Timothy	*Maitland Chambers*
Cloherty Adam	*XXIV Old Buildings*
Cohen Edward	*Enterprise Chambers*
Fisher Richard	*South Square* *
Francis Edward	*Enterprise Chambers*
Gentleman Tom	*4 Stone Buildings* *
Gunaratna Kavan	*Enterprise Chambers*
Hall Taylor Alex	*4 New Square (ORL)* ◊ *
Hattan Simon	*Serle Court* *
Hood Nigel	*New Square Chambers*
Ife Linden	*Enterprise Chambers*
John Benjamin	*Maitland Chambers* *
Kalfon Olivier	*Maitland Chambers* *
Keller Ciaran	*Maitland Chambers* *
Khan Farhaz	*Outer Temple Chambers (ORL)* ◊
Kynoch Duncan	*Selborne Chambers (ORL)* ◊ *
Ohrenstein Dov	*Radcliffe Chambers (ORL)* ◊ *
Ovey Elizabeth	*Radcliffe Chambers (ORL)* ◊ *
Pester Iain	*Wilberforce Chambers*
Riley Jamie	*Littleton Chambers (ORL)* ◊
Sawyer Edward	*Wilberforce Chambers*
Scott Tiffany	*Wilberforce Chambers*
Sheehan James	*Maitland Chambers* *
Staff Marcus	*XXIV Old Buildings*
Trompeter Nicholas	*Selborne Chambers (ORL)* ◊ [A] *
Walton Alastair	*Maitland Chambers*
Weale James	*Serle Court* *
Band 4	
Allcock Jonathan	*Maitland Chambers* *
Bor Harris	*Wilberforce Chambers* *
Collingwood Timothy	*Serle Court* *
de Verneuil Smith Peter	*3 Verulam Buildings* *
den Besten Ruth	*Serle Court* *
Foskett Rosanna	*Maitland Chambers* *
Gavaghan Jonathan	*Ten Old Square (ORL)* ◊
Graham Thomas	*New Square Chambers*
Harrison Nicholas	*Serle Court* *
Hayman George	*Maitland Chambers* *
Head Peter	*Blackstone Chambers (ORL)* ◊
Hughes Jessica	*XXIV Old Buildings*
Jeavons Anne	*3 Verulam Buildings*
Majumdar Shantanu	*Radcliffe Chambers (ORL)* ◊
McCluskey Alec	*Maitland Chambers* *
McCreath James	*Wilberforce Chambers*
Munby Thomas	*Maitland Chambers* *
Pay Adrian	*New Square Chambers* *
Peters David	*Essex Court Chambers (ORL)* ◊
Shaw Benjamin	*Erskine Chambers* *
Staunton Ulick	*Radcliffe Chambers (ORL)* ◊
Up-and-coming individuals	
Murphy Emer	*Wilberforce Chambers*
Newton Laura	*Brick Court Chambers (ORL)* ◊ *
Wigley Joseph	*4 Stone Buildings* *

** Indicates individual with profile.*
[A] direct access (see p.24).
◊ (ORL) = Other Ranked Lawyer.
Alphabetical order within each band. Band 1 is highest.

and Others, a case involving serious allegations of conspiracy and fraud.

Matthew Collings QC (see p.620) An experienced QC with a diverse commercial chancery practice, who is particularly good at company law and insolvency. He has represented clients in major fraud and asset-tracing cases, both in the UK and offshore. **Strengths:** "He is very approachable, makes the law fun and is extremely good on his feet." "He is known as someone whom people can approach with difficult cases, and he's not afraid to run points." **Recent work:** Appeared in NGM Developments v Wallis, a complex fraudulent misrepresentation case.

John Nicholls QC (see p.727) Well-established silk who handles a range of commercial chancery matters, but who has a particular focus on banking and financial services cases. He counts major banks and investment funds among his clients. **Strengths:** "He's superb and his written work is very good indeed." "He's a terrific lawyer but he's also genuinely user-friendly and a pleasure to work with; a proactive individual who's good with clients." **Recent work:** Acted in major litigation arising out of Tate & Lyle's sale of its European sugar business.

Christopher Pymont QC (see p.745) Head of chambers at Maitland and a hugely experienced commercial chancery practitioner, particularly on commercial and property law matters. He has a reputation as an unflappable, statesmanlike advocate. **Strengths:** "Christopher is calm, serene, and never gets flustered. He can understand what the client's objectives are, and has an uncanny ability to spot the points that would be of interest to the court." "He's a really smooth, calm presence, and brilliant with clients." **Recent work:** Represented the claimant in a ground-breaking case regarding breach of trust by a fiduciary agent, which was heard in the Supreme Court.

Andrew Twigger QC (see p.785) Broad-based commercial chancery practitioner at home in both the Chancery Division and the Commercial Court. He has experience of dealing with an array of cases including those concerning complicated asset-tracing, insolvency and shareholder disputes. **Strengths:** "He's very thorough and his drafting's impeccable. He really gets his head round all the issues and gets stuck in." **Recent work:** Acted in Wood v Sureterm Direct Ltd, a claim arising out of the sale of an insurance business.

Edmund Cullen QC (see p.628) An adaptable practitioner who often acts for clients in high-stakes chancery litigation involving alleged fraud and shareholder disputes. He also has expertise in media and entertainment law. **Strengths:** "He is a pleasure to deal with and gives first-rate advice." "He has a very nice manner and people trust him – both the court and his opponents." **Recent work:** Appeared for the tax adviser of a property investment company in a major case involving allegations of fraud.

Michael Gibbon QC (see p.652) Frequently instructed in large commercial chancery disputes with complicated financial and tax issues. He benefits from his experience working as an investment banker before coming to the Bar, and is further acknowledged for his expertise in company law, as well as restructuring and insolvency work. **Strengths:** "Clever, focused and able to pick up complex issues very quickly." **Recent work:** Represented the defendant in Goldtrail v Aydin, a major case involving alleged dishonest assistance in a breach of directors' duty.

Amanda Tipples QC (see p.781) A versatile chancery and commercial practitioner who handles complicated arbitrations, property disputes and insolvency cases. She also sits as a Deputy High Court Judge in the Chancery Division. **Strengths:** "She is reasonable and trustworthy. She takes the right points and really is phenomenal at organisation." **Recent work:** Acted for CL Projects and Lord Avebury in a long-running partnership dispute that raised complex valuation issues.

James Aldridge QC (see p.581) The "very robust" James Aldridge is well regarded for his diverse chancery practice. He is particularly noted for expertise in sensitive cases with allegations of fraud attached to them. **Strengths:** "A superb advocate who is a nice, clever man. When handling cases he deals with moving goal posts well." **Recent work:** Acted in Shearer & Dawes v Spring, a case concerning the law of tender before action.

Mark Cunningham QC (see p.628) Well-regarded silk who has specialist knowledge in company law and tax. He is experienced in complex cross-border disputes, and has appeared for clients in overseas courts such as the Court of Appeal in Grand Cayman. **Strengths:** "He is a very effective advocate and an aggressive cross-examiner. He's very practical."

Andrew Ayres QC A recent silk with wide-ranging experience in commercial chancery work. His practice encompasses civil fraud, tax matters, insolvency issues and cases concerning fiduciary obligations. **Strengths:** "He is a real team player. He understands the dynamics of a case and has the emotional intelligence to comprehend the different pressures the client is under. He does a fantastic job in terms of drafting, analysis and advocacy." **Recent work:** Represented two defendants in a complex missing trader fraud claim brought by the liquidator of an energy trading company.

David Mumford QC (see p.724) Recent silk with an excellent reputation for commercial chancery work. His varied caseload often takes in matters with an international scope, and his clients range from major banks to FTSE-listed businesses. **Strengths:** "He is just superb and it is unsurprising that he has taken silk – he is going to be a fantastic QC." "Extraordinary." **Recent work:** Appeared in BAT v Sequana, a global indemnity case involving sensitive points of principle on issues such as the declaration of dividends.

JUNIORS

Catherine Addy (see p.579) A "very efficient" junior who attracts some of the most complicated work at the Chancery Bar. She handles a range of commercial chancery matters, and has particular expertise in insolvency law. **Strengths:** "She is excellent and highly experienced. A barrister with a broad practice, she keeps plates spinning and speaks in a straightforward manner which clients can understand." **Recent work:** Acted in a major multiparty litigation initiated by UBS which concerned allegations of fraud and breach of directors' duties.

Louise Hutton (see p.679) An experienced junior with a strong commercial chancery practice. She advises clients on a range of matters including those relating to shareholder disputes, breach of directors' duties and litigation arising from major insolvencies. **Strengths:** "She is very impressive, has a good mind and is a good team player as well." "She is very thorough and good at keeping her eye on the bigger picture." **Recent work:** Represented the administrators of an LBIE shareholder in an application for directions as to how recoveries made by the administrators should be applied.

Watson Pringle (see p.743) A popular junior with a strong commercial chancery practice, who is often instructed as sole counsel when not being led by silks. His caseload is multi-jurisdictional, and covers a spectrum of chancery-related matters. He is an expert on conflicts of law. **Strengths:** "Charming, down-to-earth and very user-friendly. He gets the judge's ear from the get-go and really presents well." **Recent work:** Appeared as sole counsel for the applicant in Goncharova v Zolotova, a case which involved application of the Evidence (Proceedings in Foreign Jurisdictions) Act. This was a multi-jurisdictional inheritance dispute.

Alastair Walton A "beguiling advocate with a very nice manner in court." His practice takes in a range of commercial chancery matters, including litigation arising out of shareholder acquisitions and property disputes. **Strengths:** "He is one of the brightest barristers that you can get, and someone who is truly brilliant at analysing contracts. His analytical skills are second to none." "The best draftsman there is. His writing is so precise and so concise."

James Sheehan (see p.763) A talented junior building an impressive commercial chancery practice. He handles both UK-based cases and those with a multi-jurisdictional scope. **Strengths:** "He is very good – young, bright, easy to work with and energetic." **Recent work:** Represented a large Middle East property developer and a Bahraini bank in a conspiracy claim in the Commercial Court.

Timothy Calland Has a versatile commercial chancery practice and particular expertise in representing clients in property insolvency matters. He also handles a range of company and financial services cases. **Strengths:** "He is really easy to deal with and extremely good with difficult clients – he's extremely down-to-earth and really understands the commercial side of things." **Recent work:** Acted for the defendant in Loose v Lynn Shellfish, a case raising complicated land law issues regarding trespass on a private fishery.

Benjamin John (see p.683) His commercial chancery practice takes in cases in the UK and offshore. He represents clients with sophisticated trust and estate structures, and also handles cases involving partnership issues and professional negligence. **Strengths:** "He is phenomenally clever, a supreme tactician and someone much loved by clients." **Recent work:** Acted in Sibir Energy v Slocom Trading, a Court of Appeal case concerning various loan and security agreements relating to French assets.

Olivier Kalfon (see p.687) A former merchant banker who has a well-respected commercial chancery practice both onshore and offshore, and is admitted to the Bar in the Cayman Islands. His practice is heavily freighted with banking and finance and company law cases. **Strengths:** "He is personable, commercial and fully understands the business and commercial context within which banks work. He is very popular with clients and highly respected in his area."

Ciaran Keller (see p.689) Has a growing and diverse commercial chancery practice, and handles cases both in the UK and internationally. His clients include the international super-wealthy and leading multinationals. **Strengths:** "Ciaran was excellent to work with – he was unflappable, very unpretentious, very bright and really on top of it." **Recent work:** Acted for British American Tobacco in BAT Industries v Sequana, a case relating to the recovery of unlawful dividends.

Rosanna Foskett (see p.647) An "absolute star" with a rising reputation in commercial chancery work. She has acted in some of the most high-profile commercial chancery disputes of recent months. **Strengths:** "She is very competent in court, has a lovely manner and is a pleasure to be around." **Recent work:** Represented the claimants in Dar Al Arkan v Al Refai, a breach of confidence and defamation case.

Thomas Munby (see p.724) Known for his "intellectual firepower," he acts either with a leader or as sole counsel in high-stakes banking, finance and civil fraud disputes, among others. **Strengths:** "Absolutely fantastic, great to deal with and seriously clever." "He has phenomenal intellectual capability."

George Hayman (see p.667) An experienced commercial chancery practitioner who also handles civil fraud and media and entertainment work. He appears in major litigation in the Chancery Court, and is also called to the Bar of the Eastern Caribbean Supreme Court (BVI). **Strengths:** "He is fantastic and very commercial, and he really looks for ways to achieve the desired result for the client." "He's been absolutely brilliant – we always get very solid and dependable advice." **Recent work:** Acted for the claimant, a Latvian bank, in the major fraud case of SA Latvijas Krajbanka v Vladimir Antonov.

Jonathan Allcock (see p.582) He is both led by silks and also appears as a sole counsel in a range of commercial chancery matters, including contests over beneficial ownership, arbitrations and professional negligence matters. **Strengths:** "His advocacy is excellent and his pleadings are very good as well." **Recent work:** Appeared in Rawlinson & Hunters Trustees SA and Robert Tchenguiz, a complex, high-stakes case in which he made several applications as sole counsel.

Alec McCluskey (see p.712) Generalist commercial chancery junior with particular experience in banking and finance disputes, professional negligence cases and property litigation. He also handles general business litigation and insolvency work. **Strengths:** "Incredibly intelligent, incredibly user-friendly and liked by clients." "He's very hard-working, proactive, a team player, and a good bloke to have on your side."

Serle Court

See profile on p.908

THE SET

Serle Court regularly handles innovative commercial chancery work both at home and abroad. Its impressive silks and juniors are praised for their strength in depth, and handle complicated chancery litigation across the board. Recent matters include cases arising out of the Madoff fraud and those concerning major international trusts and company law. Commentators say of the set: "Serle Court has a very strong intellectual base. Its members are highly intelligent, user-friendly, approachable and supportive." "This is the most commercial of the chancery sets. It offers a variety of skill sets that others can't provide, and houses some of the biggest names at the Bar."

Client service: Sources say that the clerks are "responsive, always easy to talk to and easy to get on with." Head clerk Steve Whitaker is singled out for special praise – "Steve Whitaker is always helpful. The service you get from him is ahead of any other chambers."

SILKS

Elizabeth Jones QC (see p.685) Heralded for her varied commercial chancery practice, she has experience in contentious trusts, civil fraud and property work. She is also an expert in banking and financial services. Much of her work is cross-border, and she has vast experience of handling cases in the Channel Islands and has further been called to the Bar in the British Virgin Islands. **Strengths:** "She works well in a teams and is fabulously clever, yet has the ability to wear her cleverness lightly." "She gets to grips with intricate detail in a short space of time. She's also very impressive on her feet." **Recent work:** Acted in a major case regarding alleged breach of fiduciary duty and the recovery of company loans. She appeared on behalf of an international businessman and philanthropist.

Alan Boyle QC (see p.601) An outstanding silk who handles some of the most complicated cases of onshore and offshore litigation at the Chancery Bar. He attracts work from a number of leading financial institutions. **Strengths:** "Alan Boyle is a very important figure at the Chancery Bar. He has trenchant views and fights tooth and nail. It is very nice for the client to know they have someone who is utterly on their side." "He's a true grandee of the Chancery Bar and an absolute pleasure to work with." **Recent work:** Acted in Kingate Global Fund v Kingate Management, a major unjust enrichment and contract case arising out of the Madoff fraud.

Philip Jones QC (see p.686) A leading QC who counts major banks and institutions among his clients. His global practice spans commercial chancery cases heard both in the UK and offshore jurisdictions including the British Virgin Islands. **Strengths:** "He is charming and a complete heavyweight in this area." "He has encyclopaedic knowledge and a great intellect, but he treats everybody in the room as his equal. His advice is pragmatic."

Philip Marshall QC (see p.708) A "very robust and highly experienced individual" with a formidable reputation. His broad-based practice sees him handling civil fraud, professional negligence and banking and finance litigation. **Strengths:** "He's fierce and incredibly good. His handle on the law is incredible and he is just an amazing advocate."

Hugh Norbury QC (see p.728) A "very charming" silk with a wealth of experience. He has the skills to handle a variety of matters at the Chancery Bar, but is especially well known for complex civil fraud cases. **Strengths:** "Tactically he is right on the money." "He is really quite exceptional and a pleasure to deal with. His arguments are excellent and well judged." **Recent work:** Appeared for Coca-Cola Enterprises in a case involving misappropriated assets that required additional proceedings in Jersey.

Lance Ashworth QC (see p.585) Established silk who handles a variety of commercial chancery matters, particularly major shareholder disputes including unfair prejudice petitions. **Strengths:** "An all-rounder who is very good with clients and a pleasure to work with. He is very good in court, extremely hard-working, and he does everything thoroughly and well."

David Blayney QC (see p.597) Has a broad-based commercial chancery practice and acts on behalf of a range of high-profile clients including banking groups. His cases range from major shareholder disputes and trust litigation to fraud and bribery claims, and he has further noteworthy experience in banking and finance matters. **Strengths:** "He is incredibly lateral and creative in his thinking, and also has a mastery of detail. He is very calm, circumspect and wise."

Dominic Dowley QC (see p.636) Experienced silk whose practice incorporates an array of commercial matters, but has notable strength in civil fraud and asset-tracing cases. Recently, he has handled a number of international trust disputes and fraud claims. **Strengths:** "He understands and explains difficult legal concepts and manages to use the tools of the law in such a way as to get an outstanding result for his client."

John Machell QC (see p.705) Has a strong commercial chancery practice and is particularly renowned for his work in partnership law. He is also an expert in major litigation arising from company or trust disputes, and international fraud claims. **Strengths:** "He tells it as it is and will give you a very fair view of the chances of success. He is also very authoritative and great on his feet." **Recent work:** Represented the defendant in Salem v Salem, a high-stakes trust and commercial partnership case.

Daniel Lightman QC (see p.701) "Very talented" recently appointed silk with a broad commercial chancery practice, who is well regarded by his peers. His practice is heavy on cases concerning company law, alleged breach of fiduciary duty and fraud. **Strengths:** "He has very good attention to detail and is good at understanding an unusual brief."

JUNIORS

Dakis Hagen (see p.661) A leading junior in both traditional and commercial chancery, who has considerable experience of representing clients in offshore cases. **Strengths:** "He's articulate, charming, and someone with an absolutely brilliant brain. He's a man of boundless energy – he keeps going when everybody else is flagging and he is always on the money." **Recent work:** Acted in Hayward v Striker, a dispute over the control and ownership of a substantial trust and corporate structure in the Bahamas.

David Drake (see p.636) A junior with impressive experience who has noteworthy expertise in civil fraud and company work. He counts major public sector bodies and corporate leaders among his clients. **Strengths:** "His written work is the best I've seen. It's just so clear, easy to follow and polished. He's got a real economy in the way he writes, and he says exactly what he needs to, no more or less. He's a cut above the rest." **Recent work:** Appeared for the NHS in England in Secretary of State for Health v Servier Laboratories, a claim against the largest private pharmaceutical company in France.

Justin Higgo (see p.671) Well regarded for his work on behalf of clients facing UK and international commercial chancery disputes. He has substantial experience in civil fraud cases. **Strengths:** "He is confident and can pick out points that are going to win cases." **Recent work:** Instructed in Glenn v Watson, proceedings to set aside a shareholders' agreement relating to the establishment and operation of an investment business on the grounds of deceit.

Giles Richardson (see p.751) Popular junior whose work covers the spectrum of commercial chancery matters, and who has particular experience of handling offshore disputes and trust litigation. He is often instructed by leading solicitors to work on complicated multi-jurisdictional cases. **Strengths:** "He is charming to deal with, and is a very skilled and effective communicator." "He is a senior junior who is very highly regarded in the contentious trusts world."

Simon Hattan (see p.667) Senior junior with a well-regarded commercial chancery practice, who has expertise in banking and finance litigation. His work further includes major cases concerning breach of fiduciary duty and multi-jurisdictional fraud claims. **Strengths:** "He had a career in banking before he came to the Bar, and it really shows in the work he does; his knowledge of banking concepts is impressive. He is incredibly knowledgeable, highly committed and someone with a great sense of humour."

James Weale (see p.791) Well-regarded junior with a good profile in the commercial chancery world. His varied practice takes in professional negligence matters, major trust litigation and insolvency disputes. **Strengths:** "Very committed, intelligent and personable." "He stands his ground well and tackles the issues in an exemplary fashion." **Recent work:** Acted in Tseitline v Mikhelson, a multi-jurisdictional contract dispute regarding a major property development.

Timothy Collingwood (see p.620) A respected practitioner whose practice spans shareholder disputes and breach of duty cases as well as commercial contract litigation. He is called to the Bar in the Cayman Islands is often seen handling cases there. **Strengths:** "He is a great team player and has a full handle on the detail." "He's very client-friendly and he explains things well." **Recent work:** Acted in Brett v Migration Solutions Holdings, a shareholder dispute regarding a data centre operating company.

Ruth den Besten (see p.632) Has a wide-ranging practice that encompasses cases concerning civil fraud, trusts, insolvency and company law. She often represents major banking clients. **Strengths:** "She is always a pleasure to deal with while at the same time being reassuringly robust in her views. She drafts impressively and concisely and is great in court." "Ruth is bright and a great team player."

Nicholas Harrison (see p.666) Has worked on high-stakes commercial litigation for over two decades, and has acted for a wide range of clients including senior politicians and banking groups. In addition to handling commercial chancery cases in England, he has experience of representing clients in offshore jurisdictions including the Bahamas and the British Virgin Islands. **Strengths:** "Brilliant and very bright." "He is wonderful to work alongside and his written work is exemplary."

4 Stone Buildings

See profile on p.913

THE SET

The "top-drawer" 4 Stone Buildings has an excellent reputation for handling complex commercial chancery work. Its highly specialised team containing some of the leading silks at the Chancery Bar, including Jonathan Crow QC and Robert Miles QC, and an impressive group of talented juniors. As one source explains:"The hallmark of 4 Stone Buildings is the responsiveness and sometimes hyper-responsiveness of barristers. They are willing to approach problems from a very hands-on standpoint, and they are willing to roll up their sleeves and dig into a case." All areas of commercial chancery work are handled, with both trusts and company law being particular specialisms.

Client service: The clerking team is headed by senior clerk David Goddard. "The clerksroom is incredibly helpful and diligent." "David Goddard is a shrewd clerk of the old school. He understands the offshore litigation market, and we respect his candour and skill in managing both his administrative team and his barristers."

SILKS

Robert Miles QC An acclaimed advocate who marries sophisticated technical knowledge with a nuanced and highly praised approach in court. His enviable caseload consists of some of the biggest and most sophisticated cases at the Chancery Bar, many of which are international in scope. **Strengths:** "Robert is exceptional. He has incredible judgement, is excellent on his feet, and is very measured in his approach. He has the ear of the court and inspires confidence in clients – he excites them by being enthusiastic about their case." "He is a tremendous barrister who is very good at turning technical advice into something that makes sense from the client's point of view. He's clear so there's never any woolliness or messing around." **Recent work:** Represented the Icelandic bank Kaupthing in defending claims brought by the Tchenguiz brothers for conspiracy and malicious prosecution. The claims were alleged to be worth more than £2 billion.

Jonathan Crow QC (see p.627) An outstanding leader in commercial chancery work, with a formidable reputation in the market. He is heralded for his wide and varied practice, and has considerable experience in company and commercial litigation as well as public law. **Strengths:** "He has got great judgement when it comes to the wider commercial issues in legal disputes, he thinks outside the box and he has a very measured approach in court." "He is just a joy to listen to; he speaks sense and is incredibly elegant." **Recent work:** Acted in Ecclestone v HMRC, a trial brought by Bernie Ecclestone's ex-wife in which a tax settlement in the region of £1 billion is at stake.

George Bompas QC (see p.598) A "charming" QC with an impressive reputation for his work on a spectrum of commercial chancery matters, particularly those with a financial services flavour. Much of his work involves an offshore component, and he is a Judge of the Courts of Appeal of Guernsey and Jersey, as well as a Deputy High Court Judge in the UK. **Strengths:** "George Bompas is unbelievably strong in financial services work. He was brought in on a case and gave extraordinarily clear and helpful advice." **Recent work:** Acted for Richard Desmond in a major case raising issues of breach of duty and the Financial Services Act.

John Brisby QC (see p.603) Well-regarded silk with a thriving commercial chancery practice, with particular strength in company law cases. He has substantial experience of working on UK-based and international litigation, and has appeared before the courts of the Isle of Man, the Bahamas and the Cayman Islands among others. **Strengths:** "He is bright, hard-working and creative and he never backs down. His form of defence is attack and he's very effective at it." "He has got enormous experience and a very strong strategic overview." **Recent work:** Acted for the claimant in a major shareholder dispute concerning control of a group of ultra-luxury hotels.

Richard Hill QC (see p.671) Handles a variety of complicated work at the Chancery Bar, from banking and fraud cases to insolvency work. He has particular expertise in advising clients on capital market issues, and counts groups of bondholders and bond trustees among those who instruct him. **Strengths:** "You can ask a question and get an answer in three minutes. He is very clear and to the point." **Recent work:** Acted for the defendant in a case involving alleged breach of fiduciary duty during the multibillion-pound acquisition of a major FTSE 100 company.

Andrew Clutterbuck QC (see p.619) A recent silk with a strong reputation for commercial chancery work. Much of his work involves a cross-border component, and he is called to the Cayman Islands Bar as well as, for certain issues, the Bar of the Turks and Caicos Islands. **Strengths:** "He is excellent: really good, quick and very insightful. He can make sense of what could be a real quagmire." **Recent work:** Advised a corporate bond trustee on matters connected with the Bell Group litigation in Western Australia. The case involved the liquidation of the insolvent Bell Group and distribution of shares.

JUNIORS

Andrew de Mestre (see p.631) A popular senior junior who has an increasingly strong reputation in commercial chancery work and counts major banks and companies among his clients. His practice covers a range of matters, and he has noteworthy experience in company and insolvency law as well as cases involving bond issues and securitisation transactions. **Strengths:** "Andrew de Mestre is very good indeed and he has a lovely manner about him." "He's a real standout person." **Recent work:** Acted for Global Energy Horizons Corporation in a major claim involving alleged breach of fiduciary duty.

Gregory Denton-Cox (see p.632) A junior who has cut his teeth on some of the most complicated cases at the Chancery Bar. His diverse commercial chancery practice incorporates shareholder disputes, fraud and asset recovery and insolvency claims. **Strengths:** "He's very good at breaking ideas down into quite simple language, and when he produces a skeleton it's always a very clever piece of work." "He is very good and has excellent presentation skills." **Recent work:** Acted for Goldman Sachs in a claim brought by the Libyan Investment Authority.

Paul Greenwood (see p.660) Has an established commercial chancery practice which takes in such areas as fraud and insolvency work, among others. He often represents clients on matters with a cross-border component, and has particular expertise in Gibraltar, where he is called to the Bar for specific cases. **Strengths:** "He has a seriously impressive ability to quickly grasp a complex case and clearly distil the legal principles." "He's very polished, very good and always well prepared." **Recent work:** Appeared in a high-stakes unfair prejudice petition in the Chancery Court.

Christopher Harrison (see p.665) Senior junior with considerable experience of commercial chancery work in the UK and overseas. He has a history of handling a range of commercial chancery matters, including those concerning shareholder disputes and liquidity, and has appeared on behalf of clients including major banks and the spouse of an international oligarch. **Strengths:** "He is very, very sensible and good at giving strategic advice about how to structure a case." **Recent work:** Represented the owner of Weston-super-Mare pier after a calamitous and highly publicised fire. This was a £40 million claim to recover damages.

Sharif Shivji (see p.764) Has a broad-based commercial chancery practice. As befits someone who has years of experience of working in the financial services industry, many of his cases have a complicated banking or financial services component. **Strengths:** "Sharif is incredibly hard-working and very willing to roll his sleeves up and get stuck in to the analysis of a financially complex project." "A client-friendly, thoughtful strategist who is a pleasure to work with." **Recent work:** Represented the defendant in Autonomy Corporation v Dr Michael Lynch, a major case involving alleged breach of fiduciary duty and fraud.

Tom Gentleman (see p.651) At home in both the Commercial Court and Chancery Court, he has a varied practice and experience of high-stakes shareholder disputes and insolvency cases. He acts on behalf of UK-based and international clients, and is called to the Bar in the Cayman Islands as well as the UK. **Strengths:** "He absorbed a complicated brief very quickly and well, and instilled confidence in the client." "A rising star." **Recent work:** Appeared for the defendant in a High Court trial raising complicated issues in relation to the validity of a corporate reconstruction in the asset management industry.

Hermann Boeddinghaus (see p.598) Experienced barrister comfortable with corporate litigation and commercial disputes in the Chancery Division. He has notable experience of handling cases that relate to financial fraud and asset recovery, but his broad-based practice also includes commercial arbitrations and shareholder disputes. **Strengths:** "He is smart, writes well, and is both tenacious and systematic in his analysis." "Hermann is very calm and focused, and has an impressive ability to process information and impose a coherent structure upon voluminous evidence within a short space of time. His manner with clients is both reassuring and authoritative, and he inspires them with confidence." **Recent work:** Acted for Glenn Maud, the UK property investor, in major, complex litigation regarding the contested acquisition of the Santander Group headquarters in Madrid.

Joseph Wigley (see p.795) Promising junior with experience of handling insolvency and general commercial litigation in the Chancery Division. He represents clients in UK-based and international cases. **Strengths:** "He has an excellent grasp of the issues and is a pleasure to work with." **Recent work:** Acted for the defendant in Global Energy Horizons Corp v Gray, a complex chancery dispute regarding alleged breach of fiduciary duties.

Band 2

XXIV Old Buildings

See profile on p.884

THE SET

One of the major commercial chancery sets, XXIV Old Buildings is praised by peers for being a "trailblazer in offshore work." Its experienced group of silks and juniors have expertise across different jurisdictions, and handle high-profile cases in the Middle East and the Caribbean among others. They have a rich diet of chancery work and are instructed in insolvency, fraud, trusts, professional negligence and partnership cases among many others. Major recent matters undertaken include Libyan Investment Authority v Goldman Sachs and Beresovsky v Harsin.

Client service: "The clerks are all responsive, very user-friendly and pleasant to work with. They chase on fees but do so politely and are understanding of the pressures and constraints that instructing solicitors labour under." The chambers director is Sue Medder, a former partner at Withers.

SILKS

Alan Steinfeld QC "A true force to be reckoned with," who has impressive experience of handling the most complex, high-value and heavyweight pieces of commercial chancery litigation in the market. **Strengths:** "He's a doyen of this world and can turn his hand to anything. He is lovely, but also a tenacious thinker and he won't let go of a point." "He has a remarkable facility for distilling a lot of information down to the most important points in a very short time. You can have lots of ideas, show him masses of documents and talk to him for hours. At the end of the day he'll have the answer written down on half a piece of paper." **Recent work:** Acted in shareholder litigation arising from Lloyds' 2008 takeover of HBOS.

David Brownbill QC Highly regarded silk commended for his work in high-value and complex commercial chancery disputes, in particular those with a complicated trust component. His practice spans numerous jurisdictions, and he has substantive experience of advising clients on offshore matters. **Strengths:** "He has a really good view of trusts law which most other barristers don't have. A lawyer who understands offshore trust structures and how they work, he is afforded a lot of respect by judges. It's obvious that he really knows what he's talking about." **Recent work:** Acted in Akers v Samba, a major case arising from the insolvency of a Cayman Islands company.

Malcolm Davis-White QC Established silk with an excellent reputation in company law and a strong record in commercial chancery work generally. Much of his work relates to complicated tax matters, trustee duties and insolvency. **Strengths:** "He is a really good advocate who is very clever and has good judgement." "He can cheer up a hearing because he has such an effervescent personality." **Recent work:** Handled an appeal by a taxpayer against VAT assessments for VAT carousel fraud.

Stephen Moverley Smith QC Has a broad-based commercial chancery practice and considerable expertise in working in offshore jurisdictions. He frequently acts in multi-jurisdictional fraud cases and breach of duty claims. **Strengths:** "He is one of the most creative QCs you can find. He has got a very nice touch when drafting, has very good cross-examination skills and is exceptionally thorough as well as user-friendly." **Recent work:** Represented the successful defendants in a civil fraud action brought by a major Russian bank.

Elspeth Talbot Rice QC Has a wide-ranging practice, part of which involves representing major trusts and business owners in fiduciary duty cases and shareholder disputes. **Strengths:** "What I like about her is her attention to detail and her conviction – she will stand up in court and say what she thinks. Clients certainly like that." "She is extremely fluent and good at getting on top of a case." **Recent work:** Advised the beneficiaries and trustee of a Jersey-based trust in Walker v Egerton Vernon, a major breach of trust case.

Robert Levy QC Well known and highly regarded for his complicated commercial chancery work in the UK and numerous offshore jurisdictions. He handles a range of matters and has notable expertise in civil fraud cases. **Strengths:** "Brilliant for aggressive high-value offshore disputes." "A lawyer with sufficient gravitas to control the courtroom, he explains how things work in a simple way, while at the same time building a good rapport with his clients." **Recent work:** Appeared before the Court of Appeal of the Eastern Caribbean Supreme Court in a case regarding the insolvency of a Caribbean hotel. The matter involved conflict of laws questions about cross-jurisdictional insolvency.

Francis Tregear QC Has a broad commercial chancery practice which sees him handle important matters both in the UK courts and in offshore jurisdictions. He is particularly strong on company law and banking and finance cases. **Strengths:** "He has a wonderfully relaxed court manner and an extremely effective and persuasive style." **Recent work:** Acted in Chancery Division and Court of Appeal proceedings concerning an application for a worldwide freezing order in support of multibillion-dollar litigation in Moscow.

JUNIORS

Adam Cloherty A "hard-hitting" junior with a wide commercial chancery practice. Many of his cases are international, and he has an extensive knowledge of international tax law. **Strengths:** "He is very calm and gives sensible, pragmatic advice." **Recent work:** Junior counsel for claimant in Property Alliance Group v The Royal Bank of Scotland, a case concerning claims arising from the Libor scandal.

Marcus Staff Well-established junior, many of whose cases involve a cross-border element. He has noteworthy expertise in civil fraud claims and insolvency work. **Strengths:** "Very clever and easy to deal with." "He will pursue a case tenaciously."

Jessica Hughes A well-recognised expert in high-value domestic and international trusts cases who represents businesses and private clients in both litigation and arbitration. **Strengths:** "She's very bright, very quick and very thorough." **Recent work:** Retained to act in Sana Hassib Sabbagh v Wael Khoury, representing two brothers in the Commercial Court in response to their sister's claim for a share of their father's estate.

South Square

See profile on p.910

THE SET

South Square is highly commended for its strength in insolvency work, and has an influential team of silks and juniors who have the capacity to handle a range of commercial chancery work. Sources are quick to highlight the talented barristers at the set, who frequently represent clients in shareholder disputes, banking cases and commercial litigation involving trusts. "They are super-smart, super-clever, and you know that you can go to them for very technical issues," explains one interviewee.

Client service: The clerks are led by Mike Killick and Dylan Playfoot. "They are really good, very responsive, helpful and timely. They are very reasonable and realistic."

SILKS

Robin Dicker QC (see p.633) A leading insolvency barrister held in high regard for his general commercial chancery work. He advises clients on a broad range of issues, and has had experience in some of the major banking and finance cases of recent years. **Strengths:** "He has this calm and relentlessly logical approach to everything, and you get the impression that nothing is ever going to faze him. He is very good at dealing with emotional clients and stressful situations, and you never feel that anything is ever going to catch him out." "A very elegant advocate and a very clever man."

Antony Zacaroli QC (see p.802) Handles the most important pieces of commercial chancery litigation and is known for his superior advocacy skills. He represents clients in a range of matters, and has particular experience in insolvency and financial services disputes. **Strengths:** "Antony's advice as lead counsel is always considered and spot-on, and he explains things in phenomenally clear terms." "He's got a very methodical and attractive style of advocacy. Judges don't interrupt unless it's absolutely necessary." **Recent work:** Has been acting in litigation arising out of the collapse of the Icelandic bank Landsbanki.

Gabriel Moss QC Esteemed insolvency practitioner with a truly global practice, who advises clients on complex multi-jurisdictional disputes. **Strengths:** "He's absolutely brilliant and a very good example of someone who can keep cases simple. He's a lovely advocate who has a very elegant and simple way of doing things."

Tom Smith QC (see p.769) Represents clients in a range of commercial matters, and has particular specialism in cases with a financial element. **Strengths:** "Absolutely superb." "He's very highly regarded and he has good client skills." **Recent work:** Acted for the claimant in a major claim against HSBC involving questions about the duties of custodians and administrators of investment funds. The case was heard before the Grand Court of the Cayman Islands.

Jeremy Goldring QC (see p.656) An "ideal silk" with a broad commercial chancery practice, who has particular experience of representing clients in restructuring and insolvency cases, both in the UK and in offshore jurisdictions. **Strengths:** "He is very much a hands-on person who likes to spend time talking things through. He delivers work to deadline and does a good job on his feet." **Recent work:** Acted for the trustee in BNY Mellon Corporate Trustee Services v LBG Capital, a dispute over the redemption of capital notes.

Mark Phillips QC (see p.737) No stranger to big-ticket commercial litigation, he has appeared in a number of large commercial chancery cases over recent years. His practice further includes banking and finance disputes. **Strengths:** "He's extremely direct, has good tactical judgement and is a tenacious advocate."

David Allison QC (see p.583) Has experience of handling complicated trust, asset-tracing and shareholder disputes. Many of his cases have a cross-border component. **Strengths:** "He inspires a great deal of confidence, carries a remarkable deal of authority and is really assured for someone who has not been in silk for all that long." "He is extremely user-friendly, and very good at adapting to the client's commercial situation and giving advice that is tailored accordingly. He is also very accessible and will make room for your urgent needs." **Recent work:** Acted for a respondent to the Waterfall II application arising out of the administration of Lehman Brothers.

Felicity Toube QC (see p.783) The "incredibly bright" Felicity Toube has a strong handle on insolvency and company law cases. Her practice sees her handling matters both in the UK and abroad, and she has particular expertise in the Cayman Islands. **Strengths:** "She is user-friendly, commercial and responsive. She had some really tricky applications and she was so persuasive; it was the true art of advocacy in action."

Daniel Bayfield QC (see p.592) New silk who is particularly well regarded for his expertise in insolvency litigation, and has additional experience of handling a wide range of chancery matters for clients. **Strengths:** "A charming individual" who is "very impressive on the insolvency side." **Recent work:** Acted in litigation arising from the Lehman Brothers International (Europe) insolvency.

JUNIORS

Richard Fisher (see p.645) Experienced junior with an impressive commercial chancery practice, who often represents clients in matters relating to corporate disputes and commercial fraud. He has further noteworthy expertise in restructuring and insolvency work. **Strengths:** "His written work is superb and he's super-responsive." "Incredibly bright and diligent." **Recent work:** Acted in a major case relating to the ownership of a Cayman Islands incorporated holding company.

Wilberforce Chambers

See profile on p.925

THE SET

Renowned across the legal market for traditional chancery work, Wilberforce also has a strong and growing reputation for commercial matters at the Chancery Bar. The team consists of a number of leading silks and high-quality juniors, who have expertise in fraud, company law disputes and major trust litigation in the UK and other jurisdictions. Sources say: "Everybody there is at the top of their game. They reply and deal with matters in a way that appeases clients."

Client service: Wilberforce's clerking team, led by senior clerk Mark Rushton, is seen to be highly efficient. "The clerks are responsive, commercial and they will phone you from wherever they are. It's just a great set." Practice director Nicholas Luckman is also praised for running "a very efficient and professional ship."

SILKS

Alan Gourgey QC Popular advocate with clients and other professionals, who has an excellent track record at the Chancery Bar. He advises clients on a spectrum of commercial chancery issues, and regularly handles UK and international litigation and arbitration work. **Strengths:** "He is simply superb. He gets through papers at lightning speed and spots killer points. He is also exceptionally user-friendly and advises with humour as well as incision."

Terence Mowschenson QC Has accumulated a wealth of experience over a long career. While he can handle a range of commercial chancery matters, both in the UK and offshore, his practice concentrates in particular on cases with a complicated business element. **Strengths:** "He is very approachable and really good on the detail. He went through a huge bundle of documents in really good time and marked everything up. He's also a nice guy to be around." **Recent work:** Represented the claimant in a dispute over shareholder ownership of one of Russia's largest airlines. The case was heard in the Commercial Court of the British Virgin Islands.

James Ayliffe QC A veteran of the Commercial Chancery Bar whose substantial caseload includes company, property, financial services and pensions law cases, to name but a few. **Strengths:** "He has an excellent legal brain and is good in a team. He really assists in the formulation of how to take a matter forward, and is the epitome of the modern QC." **Recent work:** Represented the defendant in Royal Mail Estates v Maples Teesdale, a high-value dispute concerning the sale of a major West London property.

Lawrence Cohen QC A successful and highly regarded silk whose practice focuses on high-value and complicated cases. He has experience in a range of matters, and particular expertise in dealing with financial services litigation. **Strengths:** "He is one of the best chancery silks around – clients love him and he is great at working in a team with both them and the solicitors. He's a great strategist who is considered in his advice and helpful." **Recent work:** Acted for a leading law firm in a major professional negligence claim involving English and Mexican tax law.

Ian Croxford QC Experienced silk with a rich history of work at the Chancery Bar. He is particularly adept at civil fraud and major professional negligence claims. **Strengths:** "He's a very engaging and attractive advocate." "An old-school gentleman lawyer but also a bit of a street fighter."

John Wardell QC Respected commercial chancery practitioner whose work spans a range of matters at the Chancery Bar, but who has a growing focus on major civil fraud claims. He also has expertise in professional negligence. **Strengths:** "He's quick, good on his feet and someone who can see the wood for the trees." **Recent work:** Acted in Actial v De Simone, a case involving allegations of fraud and conspiracy concerning the control of a probiotic medical product sold in the UK, Europe and the USA.

Joanna Smith QC Rising silk with an impressive portfolio of recent cases, ranging from professional negligence and insolvency matters to regulatory work. She represents clients in both the Chancery Division and the Commercial Court. **Strengths:** "She is very user-friendly, very bright and definitely a star of the future." "She is charming, works hard and can always be relied upon to come to the table with fresh ideas. She has not only got the legal attributes but she also gets on with the judges." **Recent work:** Represented the successful appellant in Cavendish Square Holdings BV v Makdessi, a ground-breaking case relating to the law of penalty clauses.

Lexa Hilliard QC Has experience in a range of commercial chancery matters including company and insolvency cases. She is active both domestically and internationally. **Strengths:** "Her ability to get up to speed very quickly is very, very impressive. To take on board the amount of information she does is an impressive skill." **Recent work:** Advised on a construction dispute between Pioneer Point and London & Regent Construction.

Rupert Reed QC A popular choice for Middle Eastern clients, who has carved out a distinctive reputation in the commercial chancery market. His work spans property development and investment disputes, as well as cases that relate to commercial transactions or trust arrangements. He handles work across multiple jurisdictions. **Strengths:** "Rupert's special skill set is anything to do with the Middle East, and he is also very good on work with a fraud element." "He's very bright." **Recent work:** Acted for a widow of the late King Fahd of Saudi Arabia in the case of Asturion Foundation v Aljawharah bint Ibrahim Abdulaziz Alibrahim. The matter involved issues surrounding the validity of gifts under Liechtenstein, Saudi and Islamic law.

Marcia Shekerdemian QC Particularly good on insolvency and partnership cases, she is widely praised for the approach she takes with both clients and opponents. **Strengths:** "She is highly thought of and has an excellent reputation." "She has an extensive knowledge of insolvency points and is able to adeptly deal with some pretty strange and unique circumstances." **Recent work:** Represented a group of 4,000 bondholders in a case arising from the collapse of a Luxembourg investment company. The matter raised complex questions of trusts law.

Thomas Lowe QC Handles a variety of cases including those relating to high-stakes insolvency restructuring and complex cross-border fraud. He has a strong offshore bent to his practice. **Strengths:** "He has got a very fine intellect. Fiendishly clever, he has great clarity of thought, and is able to discern the correct points very quickly." "He is a fabulous advocate who is very calm even when dealing with hard-fought cases."

Fenner Moeran QC A large proportion of his chancery work pertains to sophisticated pensions litigation, although he also acts for clients in a range of other matters. **Strengths:** "He is a confident and attractive advocate who is a fast worker." **Recent work:** Appeared before the Court of Appeal in Ballinger v Mercer, a multimillion-pound professional negligence case.

Tim Penny QC Recent silk whose varied practice encompasses cross-border fraud claims and freezing orders, shareholder disputes and cases concerning media and entertainment law. **Strengths:** "Very effective at dealing with the competing interests of parties involved in litigation." **Recent work:** Represented the claimant in Avrahami v Biran, a commercial fraud case which raised points of law on fiduciary duties and necessitated a worldwide freezing order.

JUNIORS

Graeme Halkerston A "fantastically able commercial chancery junior" who brings an interesting perspective due to his experience of working at an offshore law firm. The majority of his cases are international in nature, and include cross-border insolvency and trusts matters. **Strengths:** "He has an encyclopaedic knowledge of all things relating to insolvency and company disputes. His depth and breadth of offshore knowledge makes him a standout." **Recent work:** Intervened on behalf of Barclays Bank in Cayman Islands liquidation proceedings to reverse permission of the Grand Court to bring claims in excess of USD80 million against the bank. The claims arose out of the collapse of the ICP fund group following a major fraud.

Max Mallin An experienced junior who before coming to the Bar worked in banking. He handles a range a commercial chancery matters, and has particular experience in contract cases and those concerning breach of directors' duties and professional negligence. **Strengths:** "He is extremely focused and business-minded. He's an ideal barrister because he is very sensible, intelligent, excellent at cross-examination and very good with clients. He has it down to an art."

Andrew Mold A skilled junior whose diverse practice combines complex commercial chancery work with expertise in more traditional chancery matters. His commercial work sees him handling cases relating to breaches of fiduciary duties, civil fraud and trusts, and he is active both in the UK and offshore. **Strengths:** "He is an excellent chap who is highly clever and practical." "His pleadings are clear and concise." **Recent work:** Acted in a high-profile dispute in relation to One Hyde Park, the ultra high-value Knightsbridge residential property development.

Nikki Singla An "extremely personable and commercial" junior with substantial experience of a variety of commercial chancery matters. He acts for clients in UK-based and international litigation, and regularly appears in the Cayman Islands and Bermuda. **Strengths:** "He did a fine job of leading us through the quagmire of a case where everything went wrong. He is a great advocate and has just been a steady pair of hands who is calm in the face of a storm. His advocacy, both oral and written, is top-notch." **Recent work:** Represented ReachLocal in a conspiracy claim against a rival business.

Edward Sawyer An "incredibly industrious" junior with a growing multi-jurisdictional chancery practice. His work takes in fraud and asset tracing, financial services cases, pensions litigation and company disputes. **Strengths:** "He has a fantastic eye for detail and a Trojan work ethic." "He is an exceedingly good draftsman who is very thoughtful and has a keen eye for detail. He's brilliant at memorising facts which he can then pull out of a hat when he needs them." **Recent work:** Acted in IBM v Dalgleish, a case concerning a breach of 4,000 employment contracts by IBM.

Iain Pester Has a broad commercial chancery practice which encompasses company litigation, partnership disputes and civil fraud work. He often undertakes multi-jurisdictional cases and, being a Russian speaker, regularly acts on behalf of international clients based in the CIS. **Strengths:** "He does a lot of Russian work and is excellent." "He is very, very bright and an outstanding advocate."

Tiffany Scott An established junior with a versatile skill set, whose practice includes UK-based and international work. She routinely handles cases involving breach of fiduciary duty as well as funds and partnership disputes. **Strengths:** "She is extremely good at handling appeals and is a good draftswoman." **Recent work:** Acted for the bank in Investec Bank (Channel Islands) v Kamyab, a case regarding the authenticity of certain trust deeds.

James McCreath A young junior with a thriving practice, who has acted in some major commercial chancery cases in recent months. He works both as sole counsel and alongside leaders on matters including large shareholder disputes and insolvency cases. **Strengths:** "He is an outstanding junior who has really good attention to detail, and is incredibly responsive, helpful and hard-working. He's exactly the type of person you would want on your case." **Recent work:** Acted as junior counsel in the Supreme Court case of Cavendish Square v Talel El Makdessi, a precedent-setting case concerning the law of contractual penalties.

Harris Bor (see p.599) Regularly appears as junior counsel alongside heavyweight silks in big-ticket litigation. He also leads his own cases, many of which have a contract or company law flavour, and he further handles professional negligence and banking litigation. **Strengths:** "He has very good drafting skills and clients really like him." **Recent work:** Junior counsel for Vincent Tchenguiz in his £2.2 billion case against Grant Thornton and the collapsed Icelandic bank Kaupthing.

Emer Murphy Has noteworthy experience in property and pensions work, and has appeared in major recent cases relating to fraud and professional negligence. **Strengths:** "A thinker and a doer." "She adds real value and makes good contributions." **Recent work:** Acted in the high-profile matter of Clutterbuck and Paton v Al Amoudi, a four-week trial in the Chancery Division of the High Court.

Band 3

Enterprise Chambers

See profile on p.950

THE SET

A solid set that handles the full spread of commercial chancery work, but proves particularly strong in property and insolvency matters. It has full national reach, boasting as it does branch offices in Newcastle and Leeds, and is involved in cases on a global scale. Its team includes the well-respected head of chambers Zia Bhaloo, who can count on the support of a strong cadre of juniors. One solicitor comments: "This is a chambers with a strong history that has long had involvement in major pieces of litigation."

Client service: Michael Couling is the chambers director, and the senior clerk in London is Antony Armstrong. Sources say: "The clerks are very good. They are organised and responsive."

SILKS

Zia Bhaloo QC Renowned for her work in property litigation, but also handles a wider range of chancery work. She handles an array of matters including professional negligence claims, and a number of her cases have a multi-jurisdictional angle. **Strengths:** "She is clever, tough and really uncompromising in the way she deals with her work."

Bernard Weatherill QC Has four decades of experience of the Chancery Bar to bring to his corporate and individual clients. He has substantial experience of representing them in company law matters and is also an expert in professional negligence cases. **Strengths:** "A sophisticated fighter who is technically thorough, user-friendly and not afraid to get stuck in to big, difficult cases." **Recent work:** Acted for the claimant in a company law dispute concerning a number of large family companies.

JUNIORS

James Barker Experienced junior well versed in complex litigation at the Chancery Bar. He handles a range of commercial chancery matters, and has a particular focus on trusts, claims for equity remedies and fiduciary duty cases. **Strengths:** "He is impressive on his feet, robust, well prepared and very professional." **Recent work:** Acted for the Bank of Scotland in litigation to recover loans provided to four individuals to fund a large-scale development project.

James Pickering Very well-regarded junior with considerable experience in commercial chancery work. He is frequently instructed to appear in insolvency matters. **Strengths:** "He is utterly charming, and clients are generally enthralled by him. He's a very effective cross-examiner who has a patient but very effective style which is true to his personality. Calm, measured and in control, he's always on top of his brief." **Recent work:** Acted for the creditors in a case concerning the liquidation of Mintpal. This raised unusual questions about fraud claims involving cryptocurrencies such as Bitcoin.

Edward Francis Broad-based commercial chancery practitioner who represents clients in partnership, professional negligence and property-related insolvency cases. He has particular experience in property disputes. **Strengths:** "He has very extensive knowledge and will know the name of a case and the section of the statute just like that. He spots what other people don't spot." **Recent work:** Acted for the leaseholders of a student accommodation development in Liverpool in a dispute concerning the management of the property. The case raised questions about the application of the Commonhold and Leasehold Reform Act 2002 to student accommodation.

Edward Cohen Has a long-established commercial chancery practice and considerable experience of representing clients in multi-jurisdictional matters. **Strengths:** "Offers excellent legal analysis combined with shrewd commercial judgement." **Recent work:** Acted for the claimants in Rosserlane Consultants v Credit Suisse International, a complex breach of contract case.

Kavan Gunaratna Attracts regular work from major institutions, local authorities and landowners. He handles a range of matters at the Chancery Bar, but is especially involved in insolvency and property law cases. **Strengths:** "With Kavan you'll always get someone who has gone through all the papers with a fine-tooth comb, so his advice is very strong." "He's very sensible, very persuasive and very good with clients." **Recent work:** Acted in Carlin Music Corporation v Japp, Re: Kismet Film Productions Ltd, appearing for a worldwide music publisher in a fraud claim brought against its former UK Chief Operating Officer.

Linden Ife Handles a diverse set of commercial chancery matters ranging from breach of fiduciary duty and directors' misfeasance claims to complex shareholder disputes and insolvency cases. Her clients include major businesses and leading banks. **Strengths:** "She is very forthright and has a knack for presenting an argument in a way that the judges find convincing. She has all the casework at her fingertips and is technically very sound." **Recent work:** Acted for a bank in a claim arising from a major loan, which concerned the construction of a subordination agreement and deeds of priority.

Erskine Chambers

See profile on p.832

THE SET

Erksine Chambers is noted for the "serious quality" of the commercial chancery work it undertakes. It handles insolvency, banking and finance, civil fraud and other general commercial disputes, and is the undoubted market leader for company law work. Barristers at the set have worked on some of the most high-profile commercial chancery litigation to reach the courts in recent years, including cases arising from the insolvencies of Lehman Brothers and the Icelandic bank Kaupthing. Their recent major instructions have included BTA Bank v Ablyazov and the RBS rights issue litigation.

Client service: Sources say: "The clerks at Erskine Chambers are good. They divide things up between themselves well, and they are all very pleasant to deal with." Chris Reade and Mark Swallow are the senior clerks.

SILKS

Stephen Smith QC (see p.769) Acclaimed silk with an excellent reputation for civil fraud litigation. He attracts work from institutional and high-profile individual clients, and is particularly good on heavy disclosure applications and freezing orders. **Strengths:** "Stephen is a fabulous advocate and incredible at knowing how to put a case, as he's extremely experienced and has been in some of the biggest and most high-profile cases around. He is also fantastic to work with as he's great at leading a team and provides that confident assurance you need in a QC." "He has great respect from the court." **Recent work:** Acted in Mezhprombank v Pugachev, a complex international case involving landmark judgments about disclosure of interest in a discretionary trust.

Peter Arden QC (see p.584) A leader for restructuring and insolvency work who also undertakes wider commercial chancery work. He is frequently instructed in matters related to the financial services industry, as well as fraud claims in the context of large liquidations. **Strengths:** "He is extremely responsive and very user-friendly, as well as sensible and measured in his approach and his advice." **Recent work:** Acted in Edgeworth Capital v Maud, a complicated insolvency case arising from the Marme group litigation.

David Chivers QC (see p.616) Highly respected QC with an excellent company law practice. He further handles complex insolvency and banking disputes, many of which have an international or offshore element. **Strengths:** "He is a very clever and understated man." **Recent work:** Acted in a major dispute between shareholders of the private equity firm Charterhouse Capital.

James Potts QC (see p.741) Has experience of handling major cases both in the UK and offshore. Over the years he has been a regular feature in the higher courts including the Supreme Court and the Privy Council. Company, insolvency, banking and financial services cases all form part of his practice. **Strengths:** "He has encyclopaedic knowledge of corporate law, and is spot-on in his judgement calls." **Recent work:** Acted for the claimant in Autonomy

Corporation Ltd v Lynch & Hussain, a case involving major fraud and deceit claims.

JUNIORS

Tim Akkouh (see p.580) A popular junior with an excellent reputation for handling a broad range of commercial chancery work. He is particularly well known for tackling complicated insolvency, company and trusts work. **Strengths:** "A go-to man for heavyweight chancery work. He's always got time for you, is very good with clients, and just has a lovely way about him. He's also fiercely intelligent and can cut through issues quickly." "His drafting is very good, he knows the law inside out and he's very easy to get on with. He has a great future ahead of him." **Recent work:** Principal junior for the bank in BTA Bank v Ablyazov, a ground-breaking fraud case before the Supreme Court.

Emily Gillett (see p.653) Well-regarded commercial chancery practitioner with expertise in fraud cases and asset recovery. He represents clients both in litigation and arbitration in the UK and overseas. **Strengths:** "She is very prepared, very thorough and she has a very nice court manner." **Recent work:** Junior counsel in BTA Bank v Ablyazov, which raised innovative points concerning estoppel and abuse of process.

Benjamin Shaw (see p.763) Has a growing commercial chancery litigation practice built up from his established expertise in company law and insolvency. He has a niche practice advising clients on the corporate and commercial implications of high-value divorces where one or both parties have substantial business interests. **Strengths:** "He is a good technical lawyer with good drafting skills, who works well in a team." **Recent work:** Acted in litigation arising from the Lehman Brothers insolvency.

New Square Chambers

See profile on p.882

THE SET

New Square Chambers is a set with a truly international reach that is very active not just in the UK but in a number of overseas jurisdictions, including those in the Caribbean. Its members handle high-value, complex cases and are particularly strong on company law, insolvency matters and major cross-border trust disputes. Those instructing say: "This is a set that is strong at all levels and has people who can tackle cases however large or complex they may be. The individuals here are very good at finding solutions to problems, however intractable those problems may seem."

Client service: Head of clerking Phil Reeves and his team win praise for their agile approach. "The clerks are ace and are very good at finding a solution to the many problems I present them with." "They are always there and approachable and have a good rapport with the courts. If you have an issue they seem to be able to get you the information."

JUNIORS

James Bailey Respected junior who acts for clients in complex commercial chancery cases, many of which have a company law or insolvency angle. He is a member of the Chancery Bar Association and COMBAR, a specialist Bar Association for those representing the business community. **Strengths:** "He is extremely bright. Although he is a senior junior and is used to working independently, he also works very well as part of a team. He is very personable and knows the law very well." **Recent work:** Acted in Thevarajah v Riordan and Others, a case arising from a share sale agreement which reached the Supreme Court.

David Eaton Turner (see p.639) Has a strong commercial chancery practice which stems from his expertise in company and insolvency law. He is comfortable handling offshore and multi-jurisdictional cases, and has been called to the Bar of the British Virgin Islands. **Strengths:** "He is the most charming and gentlemanly opponent, and is very clever and respectful." **Recent work:** Acted for the defendant in Goldtrail Travel v Black Pearl Investments, a major claim concerning alleged breach of a director's duties and dishonest assistance.

Nigel Hood Established junior with considerable commercial chancery experience, who often handles multi-jurisdictional fraud claims. He is particularly well regarded for his work on cases involving the CIS. **Strengths:** "He does difficult freezing injunction work and has vast experience of the area." **Recent work:** Acted for a defendant in a major trial brought by Russia's largest privately owned bank. The case involved complicated deceit and money laundering claims.

Simon Adamyk Broad-based commercial chancery practitioner who has notable expertise in international commercial arbitrations and high-value banking disputes. He is called to the Bar of the Eastern Caribbean Supreme Court, and frequently handles international cases raising complex cross-border issues. **Strengths:** "He is technically superb and the quality of his written work is excellent." **Recent work:** Represented the former chairman of the board of directors of two Jersey-based investment funds in a case raising issues of alleged breach of duty.

Adrian Pay (see p.734) A senior junior with a wealth of experience in major commercial chancery matters. He is often instructed to handle complicated shareholder disputes, as well as company and insolvency matters. **Strengths:** "Technically very skilful. He's able to swiftly answer complex problems on a wide range of topics." **Recent work:** Acted for the minority shareholder in Caldero Trading v Beppler & Jacobson, a petition for just and equitable winding-up.

Thomas Graham A long-standing practitioner with a strong reputation for commercial chancery work. He is particularly noted for his experience with regard to shareholder disputes and insolvency matters. **Strengths:** "Tom's advocacy skills are second to none. He gets the job done in court." **Recent work:** Acted in Musion Events v Maass, a challenge under Section 68 of the Arbitration Act 1996 raising questions about the validity of an arbitrator's appointment.

3 Verulam Buildings

See profile on p.924

THE SET

A set of chambers of great pedigree whose barristers are highly commended for their work on big-ticket litigation. One instructing solicitor says: "3VB is a go-to set for major commercial matters. It is an obvious choice if you have a complex banking and finance, fraud or contractual case." Recent matters handled by the members include Tchenguiz v Grant Thornton and a major piece of litigation arising from the Phones 4u insolvency.

Client service: The chambers director is Robin Jackson and the "personable" clerking team is led by practice manager Stephen Penson. "Administratively, the way the clerks work and the service they provide is really excellent."

SILKS

Ewan McQuater QC Leading commercial silk who has a wealth of experience acting on behalf of institutional clients and high-profile individuals. **Strengths:** "Ewan is calm, measured and incredibly knowledgeable, especially on offshore commercial matters. When you're acting for insolvency practitioners, he's brilliant in that context." **Recent work:** Defended property developers Nick and Christian Candy in a high-profile case brought by their former business associate.

Adrian Beltrami QC An experienced silk whose commercial chancery practice covers a range of areas, although he tends to specialise in banking and financial services disputes. He advises his considerable client base on UK-based and international matters. **Strengths:** "He is a fine advocate who is efficient and a good opponent. If he gives you his word on something then that is it. You can spend a lifetime building a reputation as good as he's got."

Ali Malek QC Although renowned in the Commercial Court, Malek also has an excellent reputation for his work in the Chancery Division. He handles a range of cases, many of which have an international flavour. **Strengths:** "He is a very persuasive and charming advocate who can turn his hand to most things." "An exceptional lawyer." **Recent work:** Acted for a Ukrainian billionaire in a dispute over high-value London property.

JUNIORS

Peter de Verneuil Smith (see p.631) A well-regarded and well-liked junior who specialises in banking, fraud and professional negligence cases, among others. He has experience of working in the Channel Islands and of handling sophisticated trust litigation across different jurisdictions. **Strengths:** "No matter when you need him he is always available, and he produces good-quality work quickly. He's very intelligent and comes up with creative solutions, but it's his responsiveness that really stands out." "Extremely dedicated and fully on top of all the materials in a case." **Recent work:** Junior counsel for one group of claimants in the RBS rights group litigation, a £7 billion shareholder dispute.

Anne Jeavons A regular in the Chancery courts and the Commercial Court who has had involvement in more big cases than most barristers of her call. Equally at home being led or acting as sole counsel, she is a veteran of the long-running Berezovsky litigation. **Strengths:** "Incredibly thorough." **Recent work:** Acted in RDK International v Huckshott Ltd & Others; Khan v Asif & Others, conjoined proceedings involving a dispute between two businessmen.

Other Ranked Lawyers

Peter Head (Blackstone Chambers) He has a busy practice, and regularly handles fraud, insolvency and banking disputes. **Strengths:** "Combines excellent drafting skills together with very calm, confident and articulate advocacy."

Laura Newton (see p.727) (Brick Court Chambers) A junior carving out an excellent reputation for commercial chancery work. Her caseload covers a broad range of matters, but she is particularly known for her work on fraud matters. **Strengths:** "She is extremely able and disarmingly bright."

Juliette Levy (Cerulean Chambers) Handles a range of commercial chancery matters, and has particular experience in fraud cases and telecoms-related disputes. **Strengths:** "User-friendly and pragmatic, she is unbelievably dedicated and able to really focus on your case." **Recent work:** Acted in Plantation Holdings (FZ) v Dubai Islamic Bank PJSC, a major breach of contract case.

Anthony de Garr Robinson QC (see p.631) (One Essex Court) A "quite exceptional" silk who handles complex commercial chancery litigation in the UK and offshore. He has a diverse practice which takes in both litigation and international arbitration work. **Strengths:** "He is phenomenally intelligent and can see the issues that need to be dealt with. He also gets involved in the case – he rolls his sleeves up and is a team member who engages and discusses." **Recent work:** Appeared for a major media organisation in 2 The Door v The Financial Times, a major conspiracy claim.

Sonia Tolaney QC (One Essex Court) A talented silk frequently instructed in the most important cases. She counts major banks and institutions among her clients, and handles matters in numerous jurisdictions. **Strengths:** "She is very articulate when on her feet, and has a good rapport with the judge. She is someone who is obviously enormously bright, talented and creative, and her written work is always very clear." **Recent work:** Appeared for RBS in a massive group shareholder litigation. The group claimants allege that statements made in the bank's rights issue prospectus regarding its financial health were misleading.

Richard Millett QC (Essex Court Chambers) A heavy hitter in the Chancery Division with experience of handling large shareholder and investor disputes. Much of his work is international and he has represented clients in fraud and asset-tracing cases across major offshore jurisdictions. **Strengths:** "He's prepared to do hard grunt work and get his hands dirty by doing the actual drafting. Because he began as a chancery practitioner and is now at a predominantly commercial set, he has good knowledge and an academic love of law as well as sound commercial instincts. There is a depth of knowledge, and it shows."

Paul McGrath QC (Essex Court Chambers) A distinguished civil fraud barrister who acts for clients in a range of high-stakes cross-border matters. He is an expert when it comes to the validity of offshore trust structures, insolvency cases and international asset tracing. **Strengths:** "He is a very solid QC who literally wrote the book on injunctions. He has a very good temperament and explains things well to the offshore courts." "He's an academic by background, who's an extremely good lawyer and a great authority on cases." **Recent work:** Acted in a case involving an alleged fraud in relation to a Cayman Islands fund. The matter raised landmark questions about the application of the 2006 Cross-Border Insolvency Regulations.

Edmund King (Essex Court Chambers) Respected junior who has experience of handling major litigation and arbitrations. Much of his work contains an international element. **Strengths:** "Very bright and hard-working." "He is confident, fearless and tenacious."

David Peters (Essex Court Chambers) Established practitioner with a broad commercial chancery practice who is particularly good at civil fraud cases. **Strengths:** "He is very clear in his thinking, very authoritative and very articulate." **Recent work:** Leading counsel in a multimillion-pound fraud dispute involving complicated family company interests.

Jonathan Adkin QC (see p.579) (Fountain Court Chambers) Recent silk with a growing reputation. His diverse commercial chancery practice encompasses major fraud and trusts litigation, both in the UK and offshore. **Strengths:** "Highly confident and very able, he can turn his hand to just about anything." "He has a good, robust court manner and takes no prisoners." **Recent work:** Acted in a major case in the Chancery Division involving the alleged misappropriation of funds from a Russian bank.

Nicholas Caddick QC (Hogarth Chambers) An experienced QC with a broad-based commercial chancery practice. He advises clients on matters that incorporate elements of company, trusts and intellectual property law. **Strengths:** "He is incredibly knowledgeable and has a lot of gravitas before the court." **Recent work:** Acted for Eco-Farming Ltd in a misfeasance claim against a liquidator.

Jamie Riley (Littleton Chambers) Has experience in both UK-based matters and complex cross-border disputes. He is particularly good at insolvency and complex banking and finance litigation. **Strengths:** "He's got a good insolvency background and is excellent with clients. If you've got a case that involves difficult clients, he's your man as he's unflappable." "He's a really solid, dependable and relaxed advocate who has a really nice court manner." **Recent work:** Acted for the defendant in an application for a worldwide freezing injunction in support of proceedings in Israel.

Alex Hall Taylor (see p.662) (4 New Square) His varied commercial chancery practice encompasses cases with a property, insolvency, partnership or sophisticated trust element. He has notable expertise in professional negligence. **Strengths:** "He's top-drawer. A good trial lawyer and a nice guy." **Recent work:** Acted for a holding company in a multi-jurisdictional case involving allegations of fraud.

Jonathan Gavaghan (Ten Old Square) Esteemed junior who handles shareholder disputes and fraud work in the UK and abroad. He is also well regarded for his expertise in partnership litigation. **Strengths:** "Clients love him – he hits the button, gives them value for money, and they have faith in his analysis." "He is extremely technically competent, a pleasant character and someone who is very bright." **Recent work:** Acted in Patley Wood Farm v Brake, a commercial international arbitration arising from a partnership dispute.

Nicolas Stallworthy QC (Outer Temple Chambers) "Tenacious beyond belief," Nicolas Stallworthy handles a range of commercial chancery matters including trusts cases and high-stakes professional negligence claims. He is also esteemed for his expertise in pensions litigation. **Strengths:** "He is a very creative lawyer who is quite dogged and an intimidating opponent. He will think of every angle to a case." **Recent work:** Acted in the major pensions case of IBM v Dalgleish, which concerned breach of duties to employees.

Farhaz Khan (Outer Temple Chambers) Has a sophisticated commercial chancery practice spanning banking disputes, regulatory matters and pensions work. He is particularly well regarded for chancery work in the financial services sector. **Strengths:** "His judgement is impeccable. He's very adaptable and will provide proper imaginative solutions." **Recent work:** Acted for the administrator of an insolvent company in a case that involved complicated questions about contractual obligations and the payment of Section 75 debts.

Jeremy Cousins QC (Radcliffe Chambers) Experienced silk with an impressive record who acts for clients in a range of commercial chancery cases. He handles anything from major shareholder disputes to large professional negligence cases. **Strengths:** "He's very calm and assured, and you know he's carefully considered things. His clients have a lot of faith in his advice." **Recent work:** Represented Rosserlane Consultants in a case involving the alleged undervaluation of an oilfield.

Keith Rowley QC (see p.756) (Radcliffe Chambers) An experienced QC with a substantial portfolio of work spanning a variety of matters in the Chancery Division. He is particularly strong in pensions and professional negligence cases. **Strengths:** "He is very good at seeing how the facts fit together in large cases and he quickly identifies what you need from witnesses."

Christopher Boardman (Radcliffe Chambers) Experienced advocate who has notable expertise in insolvency matters and multi-jurisdictional banking and finance disputes. As a former international derivatives trader, he has particular insight into the financial services industry. **Strengths:** "He's really excellent – a proper advocate who knows his way around the courtroom and is great at trial." **Recent work:** Acted for the liquidator of a failed litigation finance fund with regard to claims against solicitors who received financing from the fund.

Dov Ohrenstein (see p.729) (Radcliffe Chambers) Focuses on business disputes including those relating to breach of fiduciary duty, company law, contractual claims, professional negligence and insolvency. He often handles financial services cases both for and against banks. **Strengths:** "An experienced barrister with an approachable manner." **Recent work:** Acted in a case involving a dispute over the ownership of a multimillion-pound company.

Elizabeth Ovey (see p.732) (Radcliffe Chambers) Handles matters relating to building societies and financial institutions, as well as pensions and professional negligence claims. **Strengths:** "She is a very surefooted advocate who is very bright and covers all the angles in her written advice. She's a really capable adviser to have on your team if you have a complex case." **Recent work:** Represented a receiver in a claim for possession of a number of buy-to-let properties.

Shantanu Majumdar (Radcliffe Chambers) Junior with an impressively varied commercial chancery practice, who regularly handles litigation and arbitrations both in the UK and abroad. **Strengths:** "He has got a really nice courtroom manner, and always comes across as unruffled." **Recent work:** Acted in a multimillion-pound case relating to alleged fraud and breach of fiduciary duty relating to a number of offshore companies.

Ulick Staunton (Radcliffe Chambers) Has a broad-based commercial chancery practice and considerable experience in company and partnership work. Staunton also regularly handles substantial trusts and probate cases. **Strengths:** "Ulick Staunton is particularly good in conference and he provides excellent commercial advice to the clients."

Romie Tager QC (see p.777) (Selborne Chambers) Well-established silk with a solid reputation at the Chancery Bar. He represents clients in a full range of matters and is an expert in cross-border fraud and breach of duty claims. **Strengths:** "He's really the best QC I know in terms of cross-examination. He thinks on his feet very quickly and doesn't miss a thing. He's also very tenacious." **Recent work:** Acted for the defendant in a matter involving alleged fraudulent misrepresentation. The case raised complicated issues in relation to Maltese law.

Duncan Kynoch (see p.693) (Selborne Chambers) Comfortable in the High Court and Court of Appeal, his work incorporates a variety of commercial chancery matters. Many of his recent cases have involved property law and related insolvency work. **Recent work:** Acted for the former partner of failed law firm Halliwells, in a case involving loan repayments and partnership obligations.

Nicholas Trompeter (see p.784) (Selborne Chambers) Adaptable commercial chancery practitioner who counts banks and large institutional lenders among his clients. His practice takes in civil fraud and asset recovery, property disputes and contractual claims. **Strengths:** "Nick's very quick at dealing with things. He's client-friendly, solicitor-friendly, bright and hard-working." **Recent work:** Acted for a government-backed investment fund in restitution proceedings which raised complex issues over the definition of conspiracy.

LONDON Traditional

Chancery: Traditional
Leading Sets
Band 1
XXIV Old Buildings *
Ten Old Square *
5 Stone Buildings *
Wilberforce Chambers *
Band 2
New Square Chambers *
Radcliffe Chambers *
Serle Court *
Band 3
Maitland Chambers *
* *Indicates set / individual with profile.*
Alphabetical order within each band. Band 1 is highest.

Chancery: Traditional	
Leading Silks	
Star individuals	
Green Brian	*Wilberforce Chambers*
Taube Simon	*Ten Old Square* *
Band 1	
Angus Tracey	*5 Stone Buildings* *
Barlow Francis	*Ten Old Square* *
Boyle Alan	*Serle Court* *
Brownbill David	*XXIV Old Buildings*
Cooper Gilead	*Wilberforce Chambers* *
Furness Michael	*Wilberforce Chambers*
Ham Robert	*Wilberforce Chambers*
Hinks Frank	*Serle Court* *
Le Poidevin Nicholas	*New Square Chambers*
Legge Henry	*5 Stone Buildings* *
McCall Christopher	*Maitland Chambers* *
Rajah Eason	*Ten Old Square* *
Reed Penelope	*5 Stone Buildings* *
Steinfeld Alan	*XXIV Old Buildings*
Talbot Rice Elspeth	*XXIV Old Buildings*
Warnock-Smith Shân	*5 Stone Buildings* *
Band 2	
Laurence George	*New Square Chambers* *
Tidmarsh Christopher	*5 Stone Buildings* *
Band 3	
Crampin Peter	*Radcliffe Chambers*
Driscoll Michael	*Maitland Chambers* *
Jones Elizabeth	*Serle Court* *
Martin John	*Wilberforce Chambers*
Moeran Fenner	*Wilberforce Chambers*
Newman Catherine	*Maitland Chambers* *
Pearce Robert	*Radcliffe Chambers* *
Rowley Keith	*Radcliffe Chambers* *
Russen Jonathan	*Maitland Chambers* *
Tregear Francis	*XXIV Old Buildings*
New Silks	
Hilliard Jonathan	*Wilberforce Chambers*
Wilson Richard	*Serle Court* *

Band 1

XXIV Old Buildings

See profile on p.884

THE SET

XXIV Old Buildings is a venerable member of the traditional Chancery Bar, but one that has not hesitated to modernise in recent times. Its areas of particular expertise include trusts, professional negligence, probate and charities. Sources say that the set is "very good and it has gone to a higher level" under the management of chambers director Sue Medder, formerly a partner at Withers. "It is forward-thinking in terms of fee structures and business development, and has a very progressive attitude to building up the business." "Solicitors are encouraged to build individual relationships with the barristers and this makes instructing counsel all the more pleasant an experience."

Client service: "The clerks are always very affable, efficient and easy to deal with." Sue Medder is chambers director, and Dan Wilson and Paul Matthews are the senior practice managers.

SILKS

David Brownbill QC A well-established figure at the Chancery Bar, whose areas of expertise include trusts and offshore work. He is a sought-after silk for complex, high-end litigation of significant value. **Strengths:** "His legal knowledge, particularly in relation to offshore trusts, is second to none, and he is excellent both in conference and in terms of handling the client." "He was completely on top of the brief and gently persuasive." **Recent work:** Acted in a shareholder dispute concerning a high-value listed Guernsey company operating in Moscow. The matter involved proceedings in multiple jurisdictions.

Alan Steinfeld QC Steinfeld has a superlative reputation as a traditional chancery silk, and is regarded as one of the Chancery Bar's best advocates. He is widely praised for his concision and clarity of thought. **Strengths:** "What is impressive about Alan is that he gets the case so quickly, and he writes clearly and succinctly. He has all these years of experience behind him and he knows the right buttons to press." "He's an intellectual giant with an extraordinary memory." **Recent work:** Acted for the defendants in a USD1 billion claim relating to the failure of a US hedge fund incorporated in Guernsey.

Elspeth Talbot Rice QC A hugely admired chancery barrister who is universally praised for her skilful and tenacious advocacy in tough cases. She handles offshore litigation and domestic matters, and is a first-choice silk for heavily contested disputes. **Strengths:** "She's an incredibly bright individual. She cuts through all of the background to find the issues straight away, and is very incisive and very commercial." "A formidable opponent who is thoroughly respected by her professional clients and idolised by her lay clients. Just absolutely superb. If you don't agree with Elspeth you have to have a very, very good reason." **Recent work:** Acted for the beneficiaries and new trustee of a large Jersey trust in a £100 million claim for grossly negligent breach of trust. Trust funds had been poured into speculative trading companies leading to huge losses.

Francis Tregear QC Experienced chancery barrister who has been involved in several high-value, complex matters recently. He is particularly expert in offshore trusts and company law matters. **Strengths:** "He's a very thoughtful lawyer, and also is very accessible and easy to work with. He's very careful and meticulous." **Recent work:** Instructed on behalf of the joint official liquidators with regard to the liquidation of a private equity fund in the Cayman Islands.

JUNIORS

Michael King King is one of the Chancery Bar's leading senior juniors, with particular expertise in trusts and inheritance matters. He also has considerable experience as a mediator. **Strengths:** "He's good value for money. He has the right amount of gravitas and knowledge of the subject area, and is a good people reader." **Recent work:** Acted in a dispute over a departing fund manager's entitlement to a sum from an asset management business.

Andrew Holden Holden has a strong offshore trusts practice and is widely regarded as a leading expert in the niche area of trust protectors. As well as trusts litigation matters, he also handles matters relating to the structuring and drafting of trusts documentation. **Strengths:** "He is an outstanding trusts specialist. Andrew, despite his relatively young age, has written the main textbook on trust protectors and he gets a lot of work off the back of that. He is very intelligent and really gets on top of the evi-

Chancery: Traditional
Leading Juniors
Star individuals
Henderson William *Serle Court* *
Tucker Lynton *New Square Chambers*
Band 1
Child Andrew J *Wilberforce Chambers*
Dew Richard *Ten Old Square* *
Dumont Thomas *Radcliffe Chambers* *
Hagen Dakis *Serle Court* *
King Michael *XXIV Old Buildings*
McDonnell Constance *Serle Court* *
Meadway Susannah *Ten Old Square* *
Rees David *5 Stone Buildings* *
Rich Barbara *5 Stone Buildings* *
Sartin Leon *5 Stone Buildings* *
Whitehouse Christopher *5 Stone Buildings* *
Band 2
Bedworth Georgia *Ten Old Square* *
Brightwell James *New Square Chambers*
Bryant Judith *Wilberforce Chambers*
Campbell Emily *Wilberforce Chambers*
Cumming Edward *XXIV Old Buildings*
Feltham Piers *Radcliffe Chambers* *
Goldsmith Joseph *5 Stone Buildings* *
Holden Andrew *XXIV Old Buildings*
Hubbard Mark *New Square Chambers*
Learmonth Alexander *New Square Chambers* *
Richardson Giles *Serle Court* *
Shah Bajul *XXIV Old Buildings*
Studer Mark *Wilberforce Chambers*
Weaver Elizabeth *XXIV Old Buildings*
West Mark *Radcliffe Chambers* *
Band 3
Arnfield Robert *Ten Old Square* *
Cloherty Adam *XXIV Old Buildings*
Holmes Justin *Radcliffe Chambers* *
McQuail Katherine *Radcliffe Chambers* *
Moffett William *Radcliffe Chambers* *
Mold Andrew *Wilberforce Chambers*
Mullis Roger *Radcliffe Chambers* *
O'Sullivan Michael *5 Stone Buildings* *
Quint Francesca *Radcliffe Chambers* *
Scott Tiffany *Wilberforce Chambers*
Staunton Ulick *Radcliffe Chambers*
Band 4
Allardice Miranda *5 Stone Buildings* *
Arkush Jonathan *Enterprise Chambers (ORL)* ◊
Baxter Mark *5 Stone Buildings* *
Beasley Tom *Radcliffe Chambers* *
Edge Charlotte *5 Stone Buildings* *
Ford Charlotte *New Square Chambers* *
Haren Sarah *5 Stone Buildings* *
Hill-Smith Alexander *New Square Chambers* *
Holbech Charles *New Square Chambers* *
Hughes Jessica *XXIV Old Buildings*
Nurse Gordon *Radcliffe Chambers*
Ovey Elizabeth *Radcliffe Chambers* *
Rowell David *9 Stone Buildings (ORL)* ◊
Selway Kate *Radcliffe Chambers* *
Stewart Smith Rodney *New Square Chambers*
Thomas Nigel *Maitland Chambers* *
Wells Nathan *Radcliffe Chambers* *
Up-and-coming individuals
Fletcher Thomas *New Square Chambers*
Holland Jordan *5 Stone Buildings* *
Pickering Leon *Ten Old Square* *
* *Indicates individual with profile.*
◊ *(ORL) = Other Ranked Lawyer.*
Alphabetical order within each band. Band 1 is highest.

dence." "He is hugely talented and impressive with a masterful command of both the facts and the law."

Bajul Shah Maintains a strong domestic and offshore trusts and probate litigation practice. He also advises on complex charities matters. **Strengths:** "He's a very commercial barrister and an extremely good team player." **Recent work:** Advised the liquidators of the Herald Fund, one of the biggest Madoff feeder funds, in respect of claims against the Madoff estate in excess of USD2 billion.

Elizabeth Weaver Senior junior with extensive experience of trusts and probate disputes. She also takes instructions in restructuring and insolvency, company law and real estate litigation matters. **Strengths:** "She's very forthright and quite tenacious. You want her on your side, not on the other side. She is very clear on her advice and in conferences." **Recent work:** Advised the trustees in a complex dispute involving challenges to the validity of Guernsey trusts in Italian proceedings.

Adam Cloherty A rising star at the Chancery Bar with a rapidly growing international trusts, funds and charities litigation practice. He often appears in the courts of a range of offshore jurisdictions. **Strengths:** "He is a no-fuss barrister. He gets on and deals with the points and gives short shrift to irrelevancies and time-wasting." **Recent work:** Acted for the claimant remainder beneficiary in a dispute with former trustees over the administration of a trust fund worth over £100 million.

Edward Cumming Takes instructions in the full range of traditional chancery matters. Cumming has a substantial offshore and company law practice, and has appeared unled in major Court of Appeal cases. **Strengths:** "Very proactive. He can take huge volumes of information and turn them round into something comprehensible very quickly." "He can explain complex and detailed trust law in an easy manner. and is very sharp and detailed in his advice." **Recent work:** Has been acting in Crociani v Crociani, a heavyweight, high-value international trusts dispute with proceedings in a number of jurisdictions around the world.

Jessica Hughes Trusts and estates litigation specialist with a substantial practice offshore. She often handles high-value and sensitive estates disputes. **Strengths:** "She's very bright, very quick and very thorough, and has a high level of intelligence." **Recent work:** Acted for two brothers in relation to a will dispute whereby a sister is claiming a USD600 million share of the deceased father's estate.

Ten Old Square

See profile on p.885

THE SET

Ten Old Square has a deep bench of expert traditional chancery practitioners, including a number of strong juniors who support three hugely well-regarded silks in Simon Taube, Francis Barlow and Eason Rajah. Its members excel in private client work, including matters relating to wills and probate, trusts, private client income and inheritance taxation. Those instructing say Ten Old Square has "a very specialist and a really friendly team with lots of really good barristers." "The barristers are efficient and charming, and they generally bend over backwards to accommodate my work," enthuses another solicitor.

Client service: "The clerking led by Keith Plowman is very good. The clerks are sensible, pragmatic and a good team. They are very accommodating and understanding."

SILKS

Simon Taube QC (see p.778) Star individual instructed to handle high-value litigation and top-quality advisory matters. Taube is experienced in tax planning, offshore and domestic trusts and estates, charities, professional negligence and family provision matters. **Strengths:** "He's top of the tree. He is very good at strategic masterminding. If you want an opinion that's likely to squash your opponent and stop something in its tracks, Simon Taube is go-to." **Recent work:** Involved in a seven-week trial of a breach of trust case, involving English trust law, Swiss fiduciary law and Liechtenstein law on establishments.

Francis Barlow QC (see p.589) Head of chambers with a strong practice in offshore matters and before England and Wales courts. He has particular experience in drafting and advising on trusts. **Strengths:** "The king of the trust variation world. He really is very good at it and he knows how to read the court."

Eason Rajah QC (see p.747) Rajah is instructed in major cases including those in offshore jurisdictions. He has a strong advisory practice and handles heavyweight trials and appeals. **Strengths:** "He is an excellent advocate and one of the best around. He's able to press a point, persuade a judge and keep them focused on the issues." **Recent work:** Acted for His Exalted Highness the 8th Nizam of Hyderabad in a claim brought by Pakistan against NatWest, for payment of funds which have been held in a bank account since 1947.

JUNIORS

Richard Dew (see p.633) Well-known junior with expertise in wills, trusts and probate. He also handles professional negligence and private client taxation. **Strengths:** "He is incredibly commercial, effective and efficient. When you have a problem that is complicated he is very good at untying the Gordian knot." **Recent work:** Acted for the director of a trust company on disclosure issues relating to Mezhprombank v Pugachev, a USD1 billion civil fraud case.

Susannah Meadway (see p.715) Specialist in matters concerning landed estates. Meadway has particular expertise in applications to the court under the Variation of Trust Act and is an expert in trusts rectification cases. **Strengths:** "She's superb. She's technically excellent, very thorough, very clear and highly practical. She has superb drafting skills and is highly efficient." "Perceptive, helpful and thorough, she's easy to discuss issues with."

Georgia Bedworth (see p.593) Has a strong traditional chancery practice with a focus on contentious and non-contentious trusts and estates matters. Bedworth acts for landed estates, and is regularly instructed in applications under the Variation of Trusts Act. **Strengths:** "She is extremely fastidious and insightful when it comes to drafting trusts." "She is extremely approachable, very good with clients, very empathetic and someone who inspires confidence from the beginning." **Recent work:** Successfully claimed for recognition of a trust created in Oregon. The Recognition of Trusts Act case went to a six-day trial and stemmed from divorce proceedings involving a London property.

Robert Arnfield (see p.585) Has notable experience in both contentious and non-contentious traditional chancery. Arnfield has key expertise in trusts, wills and estate administration. **Strengths:** "He provides clear opinions, and does not adopt the approach of sitting on the fence. This is hugely helpful when you're advising clients and making decisions. Obviously a balanced answer is provided, but a route forward is always known."

Leon Pickering (see p.737) Up-and-coming junior with a varied chancery practice. Pickering has experience of being instructed in high-value matters with an international element. **Strengths:** "He's very clever, academic and good fun." "Although he's junior, that masks the experience he brings. His drafting is great, he's hands-on and his response times are very quick." **Recent work:** Acted as junior counsel for His Exalted Highness the 8th Nizam of Hyderabad in the long-running Pakistan v NatWest case. He specifically advised on the matter's succession elements.

5 Stone Buildings

See profile on p.914

THE SET

5 Stone Buildings is a go-to traditional chancery set with a depth and breadth of talent and experience among both its silks and its junior counsel. Its members specialise in the full range of trusts, estates, charities, pensions and private client tax work, and are particularly sought out for their expertise in Court of Protection matters. Instructing solicitors say 5 Stone is "a really superb, rounded set. In terms of volume and specialism they are right up there."

Client service: "The clerking is really good. Senior clerk Paul Jennings is someone you can ring and have an upfront chat with. He says 'leave it with me' and comes back with precisely what you've asked for. He understands exactly how this game works." "5 Stone Buildings is one of our go-to sets. Their rates are relatively reasonable and the clerking is great."

SILKS

Tracey Angus QC (see p.584) Has a broad traditional chancery practice with particular experience in probate, trusts, family provision and Court of Protection issues. Those instructing him say he is a skilled tactician and an impressive operator. **Strengths:** "A very forceful advocate who clearly has the ear of the court. She's got the sort of gravitas that you look for in a silk. Completely unruffled, always." **Recent work:** Recently appeared in Dellal v Dellal, a high-value contentious estate matter.

Henry Legge QC (see p.699) Highly regarded traditional chancery practitioner with niche expertise in art law. He is particularly well known for tackling substantial pensions work and complex trusts law matters. **Strengths:** "He is just great fun and always a joy to work with. Clever and practical." "He is a chancery heavyweight who is never anything other than impressive."

Penelope Reed QC (see p.749) Her areas of focus include trusts, wills, contentious probate and family provision claims. She is especially highly regarded for 1975 Act cases and related inheritance work, complex trusts law and Court of Protection matters. **Strengths:** "Penny is faultless. Her advice is delivered succinctly and without hesitation, inspiring the greatest of confidence in both her instructing solicitors and her clients." "She had a good grasp of complex trust issues, provided practical advice and was helpful in guiding the client to a pragmatic solution."

Shân Warnock-Smith QC (see p.790) Widely regarded as one of the leading names at the Chancery Bar, Warnock-Smith is described as a joy to work with and a highly client-conscious lawyer. She has considerable experience in offshore trusts litigation, and also handles trusts, estates and charities cases before the England and Wales courts. **Strengths:** "She commands the floor and judges follow her and listen to her. They have a great deal of respect for her. She is a really, really important member of the English Bar." "She's highly responsive and willing to jump in at a moment's notice. She's very good on her feet, very well known to the judges offshore and very well respected."

Christopher Tidmarsh QC (see p.781) A sought-after expert for offshore trusts and taxation matters. He also regularly handles trust administration cases before the English courts, as well as professional negligence and pensions work. **Strengths:** "He gets the job done in a quick and clean fashion without any unnecessary grandstanding."

JUNIORS

David Rees (see p.750) Senior junior who advises on a range of contentious and non-contentious work. Rees is widely thought of as an expert in trust administration. **Strengths:** "He's outstanding especially on Court of Protection cases." "He delivers very detailed, accurate advice which is understandable to clients."

Barbara Rich (see p.750) An expert in contentious succession and trusts litigation, as well as property and affairs work in the Court of Protection. She is also an experienced mediator. **Strengths:** "She is academically very good and also steely and pragmatic in her approach." "Excellent on paper: her drafting is clear and concise."

Leon Sartin (see p.759) A senior junior with a broad-ranging traditional chancery practice. He wins praise for his work on trusts, estates and taxation cases, and has particular experience in drafting trusts documentation and capital taxation issues. **Strengths:** "One of the outstanding juniors. He makes the most difficult problems very clear. He's very clear on the steps that need to be taken to achieve an objective."

Christopher Whitehouse (see p.794) Advises on all elements of private client taxation, wills and trusts. He is highlighted for his work on inheritance tax cases, including agricultural and business property relief matters. **Strengths:** "He is legendary. He is encyclopaedic, and he is one of those people who is tremendously user-friendly. He is very solid and really knows his stuff."

Joseph Goldsmith (see p.656) Has a broad chancery practice that takes in trusts, wills and probate, private client tax and Court of Protection matters. He also handles ecclesiastical law matters. **Strengths:** "He is a hard-working junior counsel" who provides "excellent technical advice."

Charlotte Edge (see p.639) A rising star among juniors at the Chancery Bar, with particular expertise in contentious work including will contests and claims involving executors and trustees. She appears in cases with a leader and also leads her own 1975 Act cases. **Strengths:** "Good at fee structuring and working in the interests of the client, she is fast on her feet, very clear and concise, and very good in the courtroom." **Recent work:** Handled a case concerning a contested will where the deceased owned a number of investment properties, the disposition of which was affected by a deed of variation signed just before her death.

Michael O'Sullivan (see p.731) Handles a wide-ranging chancery practice including Court of Protection work and trust litigation. He also has experience in pensions cases and Court of Protection work. **Strengths:** "Experienced and takes a pragmatic approach." "Produces quality opinions and drafting with speed and efficiency."

Mark Baxter (see p.592) Expert in contentious probate and Inheritance Act claims. He also handles professional negligence and Court of Protection cases. **Strengths:** "He's got a very straightforward way of speaking. He is always very diplomatic and polite but he is direct. Clients in difficult situations benefit from a bit of rational talking and he's very reassuring in that way." **Recent work:** Acted on a residuary estate beneficiaries' application to remove independent executors for misconduct. Baxter succeeded in defending two of the three executors and obtained an order for costs against the beneficiaries.

Miranda Allardice (see p.582) Has strong expertise in Court of Protection, matrimonial finance and trusts and estates cases including 1975 Act claims. She also has a mediation practice. **Strengths:** "She's very nice in conference, puts the client at ease, and doesn't make things complicated. She gives realistic expectations." "She is good on the more fraught matters – as a mediator she is very firm, practical and realistic, and clients like her."

Sarah Haren (see p.664) Has a broad traditional chancery practice and principal expertise in probate, estate administration, Court of Protection matters and trusts. She is instructed in both contentious and non-contentious matters. **Strengths:** "She is phenomenally clever. She really cuts through things, but is very practical and sensible in trying to resolve matters for her clients." **Recent work:** Instructed in a probate dispute in which a will supposedly made by the deceased cohabiting partner is alleged to be a forgery.

Jordan Holland (see p.674) Widely regarded as one of the standout up-and-coming juniors at the Chancery Bar. He appears in major offshore and domestic traditional chancery matters including will contests, trusts litigation and Court of Protection. **Strengths:** "His style of advocacy is relaxed but punchy. He's sensible and he gets to the nub of the matter quickly." **Recent work:** Acted as sole counsel for the claimant in a four-day High Court contested will case.

Wilberforce Chambers

See profile on p.925

THE SET

Wilberforce is a leading set with a stellar reputation in traditional chancery, whose members' expertise spans all aspects of the area. "The chambers is exceptional in terms of the quality of its silks and juniors," says one instructing solicitor. It is particularly strong on private client trusts, tax and estates work, including offshore trusts cases. Another source reports: "Wilberforce is the set that probably has the widest and deepest talent for private client work. The barristers are a tremendous bunch."

Client service: "Mark Rushton, their head clerk, is great, and those under him are all incredibly responsive and super polite on the phone. They are good at looking after their clients – both solicitor clients and their lay clients."

SILKS

Brian Green QC An "exceptional" chancery silk who is widely praised for his work on high-value offshore trusts litigation and pensions work. He is an "extremely astute" practitioner and the top choice of many leading firms for big-ticket disputes involving knotty trusts law problems. **Strengths:** "If I was a client I would want Brian Green every single time. He is brilliant and a very good advocate. The way in which he presents arguments to the court is very attractive and persuasive, and he is very human and good at dealing with clients. He is a star." "Brian Green is one of the big superstar names at the Chancery Bar. You get a pretty unerring sense of what will and won't work from him, and he's a great advocate." **Recent work:** Acted for a charitable foundation in a USD16 billion dispute before the Court of Final Appeal in Hong Kong.

Gilead Cooper QC (see p.623) A trusts specialist who often appears in significant offshore cases, particularly in the British Virgin Islands. He also acts in high-value domestic trusts litigation in the Chancery Division and the Court of Appeal. **Strengths:** "He's a trial barrister. He is a supergun you bring out for the cases where you really want to get on with matters." **Recent work:** Represented one of the parties in a Lebanese family dispute concerning complex trust arrangements in the UK, Guernsey and Lebanon.

Michael Furness QC Expert in onshore and offshore trusts and tax litigation, who has additional experience in professional negligence matters. His cases often involve complex, multi-jurisdictional trusts and taxation issues. **Strengths:** "He has one of the biggest brains on the planet, and is really thoughtful and really wise. You get clarity of thought with him and he can distil technical problems in ways not many other people can." **Recent work:** Successfully acted for the executors in a dispute regarding the construction of Lucian Freud's will.

Robert Ham QC A hugely experienced practitioner who specialises in trusts and taxation matters, handling both contentious and non-contentious work. He also has expertise in pensions and professional negligence matters. **Strengths:** "A doyen of the contentious trusts world, who is one of the strongest on the paperwork." "He's very commercial for someone who is so knowledgeable. From the outside you might think he's rather old-school, but actually he's massively commercial and very good at cutting through all the rubbish and getting to the point. Clients like him because he doesn't take awkward technical points which are academically interesting but take you nowhere."

John Martin QC Head of chambers with a broad-ranging chancery practice. He is often instructed in contentious trust matters, and has a huge amount of experience of offshore litigation. **Strengths:** "Really very good senior man. One is glad to have him on one's side."

Fenner Moeran QC A specialist in complex family disputes who frequently receives instructions to handle delicate trusts matters of significant value. Moeran has also developed a substantial offshore disputes practice. **Strengths:** "His ability to work with offshore lawyers, onshore lawyers and a large team is second to none." **Recent work:** Leading counsel for a number of offshore fiduciaries in a family trusts dispute between ultra high net worth brothers. The case involves high-value trust assets in Guernsey and spans multiple jurisdictions.

Jonathan Hilliard QC Hilliard recently took silk and is widely seen as one of the Chancery Bar's future stars. He is frequently involved in matters relating to complex offshore structures, and has a wide-ranging practice that sees him acting in matters in Gibraltar, the Isle of Man and Bermuda. **Strengths:** "He's exceptionally bright and clearly destined for great things. He's very easy to use; you can just pick up the phone and have a chat and resolve issues." "He has got to be one of the youngest silks ever. He's exceptionally bright and very good with clients."

JUNIORS

Andrew Child Leading traditional chancery junior who regularly advises on breach of trust claims with international legal dimensions. He often handles major cases, appearing unled against silks. **Strengths:** "He is technically excellent in contentious trust and probate matters, particularly those with a foreign element." "He is exceptionally good on his feet, and highly rated for his trusts and pensions work."

Judith Bryant Senior junior with an extensive trusts litigation and advisory practice. She often advises on trusts variation matters, trustees' applications and disputes over the interpretation of complex trusts documentation. **Strengths:** "It's the way she cuts through the technical stuff and doesn't show off by quoting statute. She's very easy with the clients as she's approachable, empathetic and down-to-earth." "Very nice to work with, very calm and someone who gives very clear advice."

Emily Campbell Campbell advises on complex wealth planning matters, and has considerable experience in contentious and non-contentious private client work. She handles trusts and estates issues, including offshore trusts, and is also an expert in private client tax matters. **Strengths:** "Clear and to the point. She will not only clearly analyse all the problems, but will always look to provide creative ways of solving them." **Recent work:** Acted for Swiss resident trustees in a breach of trust claim concerning a will trust and a related Liechtenstein foundation.

Mark Studer Wide-ranging chancery practitioner with key expertise in trusts drafting, who regularly advises on the construction and interpretation of trusts documentation. Studer has a significant charities law practice, and also undertakes instructions in professional negligence and property litigation matters. **Strengths:** "Mark Studer has a really very precise and intellectual approach to trusts law and is extremely knowledgeable on case law and drafting." "He has a good grasp of complex issues and provides practical advice."

Andrew Mold Junior with a broad chancery practice who regularly appears against silks in court. Mold has particular expertise in breach of trust matters, and is excellent at handling the trust elements of high-value divorce proceedings. **Strengths:** "Andrew Mold is a silk in waiting. He's very practical and won't get wrapped up in the law; he understands the underlying commercial requirements of the client." **Recent work:** Advised on a divorce case in which the majority of the USD12 billion assets in dispute were held in a Cypriot trust structure. The case featured parallel proceedings in England, Switzerland, Cyprus, the British Virgin Islands, Singapore and Florida.

Tiffany Scott Has a wealth of experience in the full range of traditional chancery work, representing clients including charities and high net worth individuals. Scott receives praise for the insight and concision she shows in her "very good written work." **Strengths:** "She continues to impress people and she's thoroughly lovely." **Recent work:** Junior counsel for the Marquesa Soledad Cabeza de Vaca in a case brought by her son regarding a £160 million trust fund.

Band 2

New Square Chambers

See profile on p.882

THE SET

An "ambitious set" with a strong presence in traditional chancery work, New Square Chambers has a large team working in this practice area, with well-regarded practitioners at both silk and junior level. Clients and instructing solicitors frequently choose New Square Chambers barristers for high-value litigation relating to offshore trusts, in addition to other unusual and complicated trust arrangements. The set is highly valued for its highly pragmatic approach to cases, with one source reporting: "Clients don't like it when you are over-legalistic, but this doesn't happen at New Square Chambers, where the barristers are open to more commercial approaches."

Client service: "The clerks are very responsive with regard to conference calls, fee quotes and estimated timetables for work requested." Phil Reeves is head of clerking.

SILKS

Nicholas Le Poidevin QC Top-level traditional chancery silk who regularly appears in precedent-setting wills and trusts cases, and co-edits the authoritative 'Lewin on Trusts'. He wins praise for the eloquence and elegance of his drafts and opinions. **Strengths:** "His mastery of the subject is nothing short of breathtaking. He has a really delightful manner and is an effective advocate in court. He's a delightful person to work with." **Recent work:** Represented the trustees in a protracted family dispute over trust assets valued at around £117 million.

George Laurence QC (see p.696) Has a varied traditional chancery caseload and noted expertise in village greens and public right of way matters. He is highlighted for his careful and rigorous approach to esoteric, intellectually challenging issues. **Strengths:** "He is so charming and self-effacing in the way he deals with matters. He goes through authorities with great care." **Recent work:** Represented Newhaven Town Council in seeking to uphold a decision relating to the registration of a beach as a village green.

JUNIORS

Lynton Tucker Exceptionally experienced senior junior with huge experience in domestic and offshore trusts work, particularly breach of trust, conflict of interest and Beddoe applications. Tucker is also the senior editor of 'Lewin on Trusts'. **Strengths:** "Lynton Tucker is the oracle on technical trust law." "Everyone looks up to him for the ultimate answer."

James Brightwell Has a strong traditional chancery practice involving trusts and estates litigation, as well as non-contentious work. Brightwell is frequently involved in matters with an international dimension. **Strengths:** "James is always excellent on paper, and with clients he explains clearly, calmly and succinctly what needs to be done. He is right on his prediction of outcomes." **Recent work:** Acted as trusts specialist for the President of India in a matter relating to funds settled by the Nizam of Hyderabad in 1948.

Mark Hubbard Has a wide-ranging practice in traditional chancery which includes Inheritance Act claims and estate administration. He has particular experience in onshore and offshore trust matters. **Strengths:** "Mark provides advice which is not only of the highest quality, dealing with the legal technicalities of a matter, but which is also of sound practical application. He is excellent in conference and is well liked by clients." **Recent work:** Advised on a complicated international estates case involving US, Jersey and England and Wales legal issues.

Alexander Learmonth (see p.698) Noted expert on wills and succession, who has additional expertise in property litigation. **Strengths:** "He is crackingly good. He is top-level bright, and very smooth and articulate in how he does things." **Recent work:** Appeared in the Manchester High Court with regard to a will construction, successfully arguing that unusual wording in the will did not give priority to pecuniary legacies over the gift of the deceased's business to his son.

Charlotte Ford (see p.646) A rising star at the junior end who "punches well above her call," according to instructing solicitors. Ford is frequently instructed in estates and trusts matters, and handles both litigation and advisory work. **Strengths:** "She has outstanding legal knowledge, and a real commitment to the case. She is a pleasure to work with and really helpful." **Recent work:** Advised the beneficiaries of an estate on an application to remove the executor.

Alexander Hill-Smith (see p.672) Strong on real property cases, and an expert in landlord and tenant related matters. Hill-Smith also advises on professional negligence cases. **Strengths:** "Alex puts the client at ease and deals with all legal and practical issues competently." **Recent work:** Successfully defended an individual who was being sued by Aldermore Bank for in excess of £1 million in a matter relating to a remortgage transaction.

Charles Holbech (see p.673) Has a strong private client practice with key specialism in tax, trusts, wills and succession cases. He often acts in contentious probate matters. **Strengths:** "He is superb at detail. He advises on some esoteric points of law, and drills right into the detail." **Recent work:** Appeared in a three-day trial in a contested will case.

Rodney Stewart Smith Has a wealth of experience in trusts administration, estates and probate. He also has a strong practice in property law matters including village green cases. **Strengths:** "An elder statesman who is very good on property and trusts and very clear on paper." "Provides thorough, thoughtful advice, and is quick to establish the issues."

Thomas Fletcher A widely praised up-and-coming junior who is rapidly developing a reputation for his impressive advice on complex offshore trusts cases. **Strengths:** "He's very keen and eager, and had a great interest in the matter and gave some very good opinions. He knows how to hold his own, he's very diligent and it doesn't take you long to trust in his view on things." **Recent work:** Successfully acted for former trustees with regard to an offshore matter involving personal liability for a breach of trust.

Radcliffe Chambers

See profile on p.903

THE SET

Radcliffe Chambers' members provide experienced advice and advocacy on trusts, wills and estates, property, tax and Court of Protection matters, and win praise for their expertise and user-friendliness at all levels. One source explains: "They are very reliable generally as a set. If I needed a last-minute person, I would ring this chambers and say 'who have you got?' because the people there are all good. They are reliable, sound and solid." "I've used an awful lot of chambers in my time but they stand out to me," reports another instructing solicitor. "They're just so easy to deal with that it makes our job easy."

Client service: Keith Nagle and John Clark are Radcliffe's joint senior clerks. "The clerks are amazing. They make every effort to assist wherever possible. They go out of their way to make sure that when I phone up any queries have been dealt with."

SILKS

Peter Crampin QC Operates a broad traditional chancery practice. He specialises in trusts, charities and property law. **Strengths:** "Very able in a range of technical issues."

Robert Pearce QC (see p.735) A strong traditional chancery lawyer who is an expert in trust drafting and probate disputes, and a market leader in charity law. **Strengths:** "He's very clear, confident and articulate. He is able to break instructions down into various segments and make them much more understandable." **Recent work:** Advised a farmer on the availability of agricultural property relief from inheritance tax in relation to his agricultural tenancy.

Keith Rowley QC (see p.756) Represents a wide variety of clients in trusts litigation and business disputes. He is particularly noted for his pensions work. **Strengths:** "He's very knowledgeable. He's quite understated in court, but has a quiet authority." **Recent work:** Represented survivors of sexual abuse in claims against the estate of Jimmy Savile. The case raised issues about the evidence required to sanction a trustee or executor of a charitable trust and the executor's duty towards the claimants.

JUNIORS

Thomas Dumont (see p.637) Sought-after senior junior with extensive traditional chancery experience. Dumont is widely praised for his client-handling skills. **Strengths:** "He is absolutely expert and he's very good with clients. He builds a good relationship with them. We are often dealing with stressed situations and he is very good at empathising with clients without letting them stray off track." **Recent work:** Acted in an application to remove and replace the executors of a multimillion-pound estate.

Piers Feltham (see p.643) Traditional chancery specialist with particular knowledge of the law of estoppel. Feltham appears both in the UK and overseas, drafting and advising on trusts and property matters. **Strengths:** "He is outstanding, just outstanding. He is at the top of his game and very clever. He provides sound, strategic advice in a timely manner."

Mark West (see p.792) Tackles a chancery practice with a real property and trusts focus. West is treasurer of the Chancery Bar Association and a Deputy Judge of the Upper Tribunal (Administrative Appeals Chamber). **Strengths:** "He is incredibly bright, and has so much experience and knowledge that he's always someone that you would turn to if you were faced with a tricky problem and needed clear and concise advice. He has that gravitas that works well with clients." **Recent work:** Acted for a mother and daughter on the succession to an agricultural tenancy upon the death of the father. The succession was initially agreed by the landlord but subsequently denied, and the case raised issues of proprietary estoppel.

Justin Holmes (see p.674) Private client specialist with strong experience in Court of Protection matters, contentious probate cases and trust disputes. He is highlighted for his excellent client manner in conference and for his skilful advocacy. **Strengths:** "Clients always warm to Justin as he is very friendly and takes time to get to know them. He explains matters to clients well and is always prepared to listen to their questions. He is a delight to work with."

Katherine McQuail (see p.714) Has a practice centred on probate, inheritance, trusts and Court of Protection matters. She also advises on professional negligence cases. **Strengths:** "She's just very easy to deal with, very straightforward, and in touch all the time." **Recent work:** Successfully handled a 1975 Act financial provision claim for the deceased's long-term partner against the estranged wife of the deceased. The case raised issues about tenancy in common and the definition of a cohabitant in provision claims.

William Moffett (see p.720) Acts for trustees and beneficiaries in wills and trusts disputes. Moffett is particularly knowledgeable in Inheritance Act 1975 claims and will contests. **Strengths:** "He's a very good all-rounder. His drafting's very good and in mediation he is great at winning the confidence of the mediator and pressing home an advantage."

Roger Mullis (see p.724) Experienced in contentious probate, estate administration and family provision. Mullis is instructed by a variety of high-profile clients. **Strengths:** "He's a real detailer, who is very bright and conscientious. His written work is very thorough. There was one case where I thought we were doomed, and he came up with ideas we hadn't thought of. It saved the day." **Recent work:** Acted for the claimant landlord in a dispute with a tenant over a break clause, concerning whether certain conditions of the contract had been waived or varied, or if the landlord was estopped by convention from relying on them.

Francesca Quint (see p.746) Has a strong focus on cases concerning wills, trusts and charities. Quint is also an accredited mediator. **Strengths:** "She is clear, practical and pragmatic and is willing to take a view on matters."

Ulick Staunton Has a broad traditional chancery practice, and handles both contentious and non-contentious matters. Staunton has expertise in Court of Protection, trusts, wills, probate, property and professional negligence. **Strengths:** "He's an extremely effective advocate, and he is exceptional at cross-examination, which is a skill that is crucial to a barrister." **Recent work:** Appeared in Fowlds v Fowlds, a case concerning beneficial ownership of shares in a property investment company.

Tom Beasley (see p.593) Has a core practice relating to property, wills and trusts, and is also instructed in civil fraud matters, including forgery cases and claims of conversion. **Strengths:** "He is excellent on trust-related disputes and his written work is very good." "He was on top of everything, sensible and very good with the client. His paperwork was always done on time and he was good on his feet." **Recent**

work: Acted for the defendant, an Egyptian charity, in a matter concerning the defrauding of the charity by one of its trustees.

Gordon Nurse Widely experienced chancery barrister with a long-standing reputation. Nurse also sits as a Deputy Master in the Chancery Division.

Elizabeth Ovey (see p.732) Broad-ranging chancery practitioner specialising in building society and pensions matters, as well as professional negligence work. She also edits a number of well-regarded works on trusts and mortgages law. **Strengths:** "She is very thorough and very conscientious, and a lot of people respect her." **Recent work:** Acted in an application under the Trustee Act 1925 for the appointment of a new trustee.

Kate Selway (see p.761) Experienced litigator with a caseload focused on trusts, wills, probate and estate administration, charities and Court of Protection. She is praised for her concise and clear advice, her effective and versatile advocacy style and her approachable manner with lay clients. **Strengths:** "Her paperwork is excellent, and she is extremely clear and very thorough. She's great with clients and they have a lot of confidence in her." **Recent work:** Advised on the construction of a will with regard to trustee obligations and charitable gifts.

Nathan Wells (see p.792) Private client, land law and professional negligence expert. His caseload includes trusts, wills, probate, administration of estates and family provision matters. **Strengths:** "The quality of his written work is excellent. He is invariably well prepared and always appears calm and unruffled, even in circumstances where others might become flustered." **Recent work:** Represented two of the respondents in a High Court application made as a consequence of earlier trust litigation. The applicant sought to set off monies she was due from one of the respondents against an earlier costs order made against her (and in favour of the respondents). The application was successfully resisted.

Serle Court
See profile on p.908

THE SET

Although best known as a commercial chancery set, Serle Court also has a strong presence in traditional chancery, and has members who are instructed in the full range of matters in this field. Sources say Serle Court is one of the sets with the "greatest breadth and depth" in offshore and contentious trusts work. It handles matters of the greatest worth and complexity and has "some seriously capable people there." The set's traditional chancery offering has recently been bolstered by the arrival of Richard Wilson QC and Constance McDonnell from a rival set.

Client service: "The clerking is first-class. The senior clerks are unfailingly helpful and give reliable advice about alternative counsel if the first choice is not available." Steve Whitaker is Serle Court's head clerk.

SILKS

Alan Boyle QC (see p.601) Senior silk and head of chambers, whose practice takes in trusts and probate litigation of the greatest value and importance. **Strengths:** "He never ceases to impress and when he gets his teeth into a case he is unstoppable. He really throws his all into his clients' cases. He is hugely hard-working, and meticulous in his preparation, and one of the barristers whom you can see judges really sit up and listen to." **Recent work:** Handled a heavyweight case concerning one of the largest feeder funds into the Madoff Ponzi scheme.

Frank Hinks QC (see p.672) Traditional chancery specialist with decades of experience in trust and probate matters. He provides advice and handles litigation both domestically and offshore. **Strengths:** "He keeps a low profile but he is effective. His advice is full of clarity and he leaves no stone unturned. Hinks is a wonderful source of knowledge and modesty itself considering his standing at the Bar."

Elizabeth Jones QC (see p.685) Established trusts and probate silk who has a wealth of international experience, having appeared in cases in Jersey, Guernsey, the Cayman Islands, Panama, Switzerland and Liechtenstein. **Strengths:** "When we have something extremely difficult she is who we talk to. She is never fazed. Her written is work is as impressive as her oral advocacy." **Recent work:** Advised on a significant English trust dispute concerning assets of over £100 million, with complicated issues regarding the division of assets as well as the duties and removal of trustees.

Richard Wilson QC (see p.798) Negotiates a traditional chancery practice involving a substantial amount of international work, and frequently advises landed estates and institutional trustees. **Strengths:** "He is a very good advocate who is very considered and measured." **Recent work:** Acted for a charity in a high-profile contested will case.

JUNIORS

William Henderson (see p.669) Star individual who is praised for his work with private clients, trustees and trust companies. Henderson's practice typically involves trusts, probate, estate administration, charities and professional negligence matters. **Strengths:** "Will produces written work of an extremely high standard, that is technically very sound but easy to understand. He's both very good with lay clients, and friendly and approachable." "He's very knowledgeable and trusted by the court and clients alike."

Dakis Hagen (see p.661) Focus his practice on cases concerning trust disputes, wills and estates. He also acts in divorce matters which feature property or trust law. **Strengths:** "Dakis is a go-to barrister for trusts disputes and is particularly strong on complex, technical points. He has proved himself time and again to be exceptionally hard-working and accessible. I consider him at least as capable as many QCs I have worked with." **Recent work:** Appeared unled against a silk in a high-value Inheritance Act claim.

Constance McDonnell (see p.712) Has a practice centred on contentious trusts and probate cases, as well as Inheritance Act 1975 claims. McDonnell also appears in Court of Protection matters. **Strengths:** "She is very clear and very authoritative in the area of trusts and probates. Very clear, she is brilliant with clients and understands how to do deals in cases. She's a fighter."

Giles Richardson (see p.751) Has a vibrant practice and proves particularly strong in restructuring and insolvency matters and company law. He often appears in international cases. **Strengths:** "You can call him up and have a frank and candid conversation with him. He's a man with a supreme intellect who understands the dynamics of the offshore world and fulfils his mandates admirably." **Recent work:** Instructed in proceedings brought against a former trustee for alleged breaches of trust causing significant loss.

Band 3

Maitland Chambers
See profile on p.875

THE SET

A number of barristers at Maitland have busy traditional chancery practices, and regularly accept instructions in wills and trusts disputes, offshore cases and charities law matters. The set is also well known for handling property litigation and company law cases.

Client service: "The clerks are approachable, helpful, friendly and happy to suggest alternatives where needed." John Wiggs is the senior clerk.

SILKS

Christopher McCall QC (see p.711) Hugely respected and experienced barrister with decades of experience in traditional chancery. McCall's areas of specialism include trusts, tax and charity law. **Strengths:** "A colossus in this field, he's right at the pinnacle." "Hugely experienced and learned."

Michael Driscoll QC (see p.637) Has a broad traditional chancery practice, and is instructed both offshore and in domestic matters that involve trusts, fraud and property disputes. **Strengths:** "He's got a real knack of creating great pressure on the other side by being reasonable at all times." "He's exceptionally thorough and clear in his opinions."

Catherine Newman QC (see p.727) A hugely experienced barrister whose practice takes in a wide range of domestic and international work. Her busy caseload includes contract, equity and trusts matters along with company and partnership disputes. **Strengths:** "Catherine is incredibly sharp-witted and very good with clients. She can make complicated principles understandable to a lay party, and is extremely impressive in terms of the volume of information that she can get on top of in a short space of time. She's able to understand and absorb documents very quickly."

Jonathan Russen QC (see p.757) Highly experienced in matters involving offshore trusts and breach of fiduciary duty. He is often instructed in financial services matters and general commercial litigation. **Strengths:** "His opinions were excellent, he was clearly very well prepared and he was good with the clients." **Recent work:** Acted for the current trustees of a will trust under which rival beneficiaries have competing claims regarding the scope of power of appointment and the validity of its exercise by previous trustees.

JUNIORS

Nigel Thomas (see p.780) Experienced chancery barrister who has been instructed in matters relating to forfeiture proceedings under a will, and claims against the estate of a deceased. He also sits as a Chancery Recorder. **Strengths:** "A senior junior, who is a good man for sensitive cases." **Recent work:** Advised on how to deal with claims on an estate brought by survivors of childhood sexual abuse perpetrated by the deceased.

Other Ranked Lawyers

Jonathan Arkush (Enterprise Chambers) Regularly handles trusts, wills and family provision cases, and is also an experienced mediator. **Strengths:** "He's so experienced he can turn his hand to pretty much anything in the mediation world." **Recent work:**

Acted on a dispute between siblings which centred on the administration of the mother's estate.

David Rowell (9 Stone Buildings) Has a broad chancery practice with a specialism in private client work. He is often instructed in trusts litigation, land law matters and charities cases. **Strengths:** "He is fantastic, and has a rare ability to produce written work that comes out like a first-class essay. He's very qualified in his field, which is contentious probate and chancery work, and his knowledge is outstanding. His advice is always spot-on." **Recent work:** Acted in a dispute as to whether or not the rights expressed in the Human Rights Act 1998 alter the interpretation of pre-1970 wills that discriminated against illegitimate and adopted children.

MIDLANDS

Chancery
Leading Sets
Band 1
St Philips Chambers *
Band 2
No5 Chambers *
Leading Silks
Band 1
Randall John *St Philips Chambers* *
Band 2
Anderson Mark *No5 Chambers* [A]
Leading Juniors
Band 1
Brennan John *St Philips Chambers* *
Burden Angus *St Philips Chambers* [A] *
Mitchell David *No5 Chambers* [A]
Morgan James *St Philips Chambers* *
Taylor David *No5 Chambers* [A]
Band 2
Charman Andrew *St Philips Chambers* [A] *
Maguire Andrew *St Philips Chambers* [A]
Preston Nicola *No5 Chambers*
Up-and-coming individuals
Corfield Louise *No5 Chambers* *
* *Indicates set / individual with profile.*
[A] *direct access (see p.24).*
Alphabetical order within each band. Band 1 is highest.

Band 1

St Philips Chambers

See profile on p.934

THE SET

This well-established Birmingham set benefits from a national platform and a strong reputation for high-quality chancery work on the Midland Circuit. Its members are experienced in commercial and traditional chancery, including insolvency, trusts and inheritance claims. One interviewee describes St Philips as "a very good chambers," adding that "their administration is excellent and they're quite flexible." Another source explains: "They are very user-friendly, they're accessible, and all the barristers I've used have all been very approachable and down-to-earth."

Client service: Those instructing say: "They're efficient, and they've always got somebody who can do the job at whatever level." Joe Wilson leads the clerking team.

SILKS

John Randall QC (see p.748) A leading silk on the Midland Circuit with a very strong commercial chancery practice. Handles a wide range of commercial disputes and property matters. **Strengths:** "Hugely intelligent and good with clients, John manages to combine an encyclopaedic knowledge of the law with a first-rate appreciation of strategy and excellent eye for detail." **Recent work:** Instructed in Regency Villas v Diamond Resorts, which concerned easements over a golf course purportedly granted to the owners of a timeshare.

JUNIORS

John Brennan (see p.602) Widely regarded as an excellent chancery practitioner. He maintains a chancery practice with key expertise in shareholder litigation and property disputes. **Strengths:** "John is excellent; his tenacity is unrivalled." "He is brilliant, very thorough and methodical with his work." **Recent work:** Advised on a dispute between farming partners over the division of the profits received by the partnership.

Angus Burden (see p.607) Well-established junior advising on a range of traditional chancery matters. He largely focuses on contentious probate issues and trusts. **Strengths:** "He's very able and practical in the mediation setting." "He has a very relaxed approach: he's firm and pursues the right line properly but his manner isn't aggressive, he talks in a very low-key, calm sort of way." **Recent work:** Acted in a dispute over whether or not valid prior notice had been given for the transfer of a mosque from an unincorporated charitable association to a charitable trust.

James Morgan (see p.721) An experienced commercial chancery practitioner, particularly adept on civil fraud and insolvency matters. He also handles company law matters. **Strengths:** "His advice is always spot-on, he's always across the brief. He's very good with clients, dispensing the right advice in the right way." **Recent work:** Represented the claimant and third parties in a directors' misfeasance claim after liquidation.

Andrew Charman (see p.615) Established commercial litigation practitioner with experience in trusts and property disputes. He has also written on the subject of shareholder litigation and maintains a mediation practice. **Recent work:** Advised the claimant in a case concerning deferred consideration on the sale of a business and involving a counterclaim for breach of warranty.

Andrew Maguire Acts on a broad range of commercial chancery disputes, offering expertise in unfair prejudice petitions and other shareholder litigation matters as well as contract law. He also advises on professional negligence cases. **Strengths:** "He's got an exceptionally good way with lay clients. He's quite fearless and commercially very realistic." **Recent work:** Acted in a breach of contract and fiduciary duty case, which concerned a design engineer's diversion of business away from a joint venture where relations between the partners had broken down.

Band 2

No5 Chambers

See profile on p.931

THE SET

No5 Chambers is a key set on the Midland Circuit, notable for its deep bench in chancery work. Its barristers handle probate, property and commercial disputes around the country. One source says: "I have huge confidence in their ability to provide an excellent service." Another comments: "They give good advice, I've never gone to court and lost with them. Any preparation from any of the barristers is always very good."

Client service: "The clerks are very, very accommodating. They will go out of their way to assist in whatever they can." James Parks is the senior clerk.

SILKS

Mark Anderson QC Well reputed for his wide-ranging knowledge of commercial and banking matters. He regularly advises on partnership disputes and breach of duty cases. **Strengths:** "His written work is excellent. It's always, pithy, concise and entirely accurate. Up on his feet is where he excels; he's a formidable advocate. He's always very well prepared, he's several steps ahead of his opponent and I don't think he's ever lost anything for me."

JUNIORS

David Mitchell A lauded junior with extensive experience of traditional chancery matters. He has an impressive practice in contentious probate and property litigation. **Strengths:** "He's very good up on his feet. He's helpful to judges, he's not a man that postures, he's very civil to witnesses but extremely sharp on cross-examination. He never misses anything, he's very quick-witted." "Clients like him, he's very personable, down-to-earth and nice to them, and his paperwork is always very good." **Recent work:** Handled an Inheritance Act claim which turned on questions as to the claimant's country of domicile and whether she and the deceased had in fact been divorced at the time of death.

David Taylor A well-established property specialist with a developed chancery practice, including expertise in landlord and tenant and proprietary estoppel matters. He also sits as a judge of the First-tier Tribunal (Property Chamber). **Strengths:** "He's a very calming influence in the court, never appears to be aggressive at all but gets what he needs." **Recent work:** Represented the son of a farming family in a proprietary estoppel claim, achieving a settlement at mediation.

Nicola Preston Widely praised by both instructing solicitors and opponents for her skilful advocacy. She counts a broad range of chancery matters within her remit. **Strengths:** "She's always very thorough; she's a very pleasant lady and she can be forceful when necessary. Her advocacy is very good and her written work is too." **Recent work:** Acting successfully for a tenant in an adverse possession claim involving novel questions as to the meaning of encroachment.

Louise Corfield (see p.624) A rising star of the Midland Circuit in traditional chancery work. She regularly acts in contested probate and Inheritance Act claims, and also advises on real property matters. **Strengths:** "Louise has a really good manner: she can extract information from the clients and get through to them." **Recent work:** Handled a mediation concerning a probate dispute over a beneficial interest in a property.

NORTH EASTERN

Chancery
Leading Sets
Band 1
Enterprise Chambers *
St Philips Chambers *
Leading Silks
Band 1
Jory Hugh *Enterprise Chambers*
Leading Juniors
Band 1
Harrison Sarah *St Philips Chambers* *
Klein Jonathan *Enterprise Chambers*
Band 2
Groves Hugo *Enterprise Chambers*
Kelly Sean *St Philips Chambers* *
Roberts Stuart *St Philips Chambers* *
Band 3
Crossley Dominic *St Philips Chambers* *
Goldberg Simon *Trinity Chambers (ORL)* ◊
Griffin Margaret *Enterprise Chambers*
Rodger Jonathan *Enterprise Chambers*
Walker Bruce *Exchange Chambers (ORL)* ◊
Up-and-coming individuals
Heath Duncan *Enterprise Chambers*
** Indicates set / individual with profile.*
◊ (ORL) = Other Ranked Lawyer.
Alphabetical order within each band. Band 1 is highest.

Band 1

Enterprise Chambers

See profile on p.950

THE SET

With bases in Newcastle and Leeds, Enterprise Chambers offers a strong North Eastern presence in chancery work. The set is viewed as a first-choice destination for equitable commercial matters by many solicitors, who value its members' experience in insolvency and contract disputes. One source in particular calls them "the outstanding set for contentious chancery commercial work." Another praises Enterprise's strength in traditional chancery matters: "They are my go-to chambers for property, wills and trusts."

Client service: A source says the clerking team is "very good, very nice to talk to and very quick to deal with queries." London-based senior clerk Antony Armstrong receives support from Joanne Caunt and Ellen Cockcroft in Leeds and from Bethany Thompson in Newcastle.

SILKS

Hugh Jory QC The region's standout commercial chancery practitioner, with a fine reputation for shareholder disputes and insolvency work. As part of his broader practice, he is regularly instructed by shareholders in sporting organisations. **Strengths:** "His banking background, easy manner and authoritative advice makes heavyweight corporate insolvency and banking work a breeze." "He's very, very good, and certainly very well regarded in the North Eastern Circuit."

JUNIORS

Jonathan Klein A traditional chancery specialist who also advises on commercial disputes. He is particularly noted for his technical strength in the area of property law. **Strengths:** "Opponents know that he will know the case and the law inside out before he steps into the court." "Jonathan's advice was brilliant in terms of presenting what was a very complicated matter in a way that could be understandable to clients. Extremely impressive." **Recent work:** Representing the claimant in Greig v Lauchlan, seeking to recover an interest in a group of companies and a portfolio of residential properties. The case turns on constructive and resulting trusts issues.

Hugo Groves Commercial litigator who regularly acts on shareholder disputes in the Chancery Division. Widely lauded for his expertise in the area of insolvency law. **Strengths:** "An accomplished and knowledgeable barrister who always seems to get the right result, and great with clients." "Extremely pleasant to deal with and nothing is too much trouble. His practical knowledge is peerless."

Margaret Griffin Experienced chancery practitioner with experience in both personal and commercial matters. She is instructed in a range of trusts, probate and family business disputes. **Strengths:** "I've seen her in court and she's something to be reckoned with. She has a very direct and no-nonsense style, and I think clients really like that."

Jonathan Rodger Commercial chancery practitioner who acts on insolvency matters and shareholder agreements. Also instructed in property cases, with particular expertise in boundary disputes. **Strengths:** "He is very approachable, clients understand exactly what he's saying and his pleadings are clear and succinct." **Recent work:** Acting on a boundary dispute revolving around the difference between a deed plan and the completed property.

Duncan Heath A rising star of the North Eastern Circuit for commercial and traditional chancery work. Praised widely for his capabilities in insolvency and probate matters. **Strengths:** "Duncan has a well-deserved excellent reputation in the Leeds market. He gives solid and well thought out advice, is refreshingly approachable and easily builds a rapport with clients." **Recent work:** Acting in Pritchard v Lebtron-Trowell for the residuary beneficiary of an estate seeking removal of an executor.

St Philips Chambers

See profile on p.934

THE SET

This is a long-standing group of chancery practitioners with a solid reputation in Leeds and a key part of the ever-growing national practice at St Philips. The set houses some of the region's leading traditional chancery juniors, who advise on tax and trusts matters and also handle litigation. Members are also noted for their capabilities in commercial chancery matters.

Client service: The clerking team, led by Colin Hedley, is described as "really easy to get on with" and is praised for its "very quick turnaround."

JUNIORS

Sarah Harrison (see p.666) Very well known on the circuit for both advisory and contentious traditional chancery work, she maintains an active practice in capital taxation, trusts and probate matters. **Strengths:** "A formidable and extremely knowledgeable counsel who we regularly instruct to fight our clients' corner." **Recent work:** Acted in the case of Caro v Patel regarding the construction of a will governing a £7 million estate.

Sean Kelly (see p.689) Well-regarded junior with a broad commercial practice. His chancery work includes acting in partnership cases and shareholder disputes including unfair prejudice petitions. **Strengths:** "He is robust and gets to grips with a case quickly while not losing sight of overall commercial objectives." **Recent work:** Advised on a petition to wind up a farming partnership which held assets of approximately £18 million.

Stuart Roberts (see p.753) Established junior maintaining a mixed traditional and commercial chancery practice. Probate work is his particular area of focus, especially claims under the Inheritance Act 1975. **Strengths:** "He is extremely thorough and builds a strong rapport with clients from the outset."

Dominic Crossley (see p.627) His broad chancery practice continues to develop in strength, and has an emphasis on real property, tenancies and probate work. Crossley also acts on general commercial matters. **Strengths:** "His client manner is where he excels: he explains things in a clear way and understands the underlying issues really well."

Other Ranked Lawyers

Bruce Walker (Exchange Chambers) An experienced chancery practitioner with a particular focus on real property and tenancy disputes. Also acts in both commercial and traditional chancery matters including partnerships, trusts and probate. **Strengths:** "He has a very calm, measured approach and is very knowledgeable, with a good client care manner. He is my number one port of call." **Recent work:** Acted in Willow Design (in liquidation) v London Ebor, resisting claims by the liquidators to beneficial ownership of land.

Simon Goldberg (Trinity Chambers) Commercial litigation specialist praised for his technical knowledge and client manner. Maintains an active practice in shareholder disputes, including allegations of unfair prejudice. **Strengths:** "Top quality, pragmatic and easy to work with." **Recent work:** Acted for the defendants in a right of way dispute concerning land in Northumberland, succeeding in having the claim dismissed.

NORTHERN

Chancery	
Leading Sets	
Band 1	
Kings Chambers *	
Band 2	
Exchange Chambers *	
9 St John Street *	
Leading Silks	
Band 1	
Anderson Lesley	*Kings Chambers* *
Bartley Jones Edward	*Exchange Chambers*
Casement David	*Kings Chambers* *
Cawson Mark	*Exchange Chambers* *
Chaisty Paul	*Kings Chambers* *
Band 2	
Berkley David	*1 Gray's Inn Chambers (ORL)* ◊
New Silks	
Harper Mark	*Kings Chambers* *
Mohyuddin David	*Exchange Chambers*
Leading Juniors	
Band 1	
Berragan Neil	*Kings Chambers* *
Doyle Louis	*Kings Chambers* *
Latimer Andrew	*Kings Chambers* *
Band 2	
Fryer-Spedding James	*9 St John Street* *
Grantham Andrew	*Kings Chambers* *
Halliwell Mark	*Kings Chambers* *
Maynard-Connor Giles	*Exchange Chambers*
Temple Eleanor	*Kings Chambers* *
Terry Jeffrey	*Kings Chambers* *
Vinson Andrew	*Exchange Chambers*
Band 3	
Cadwallader Neil	*Exchange Chambers*
Chapman Richard	*18 St John Street (ORL)* ◊
Clegg Sebastian	*Deans Court Chambers (ORL)* ◊
d'Arcy Eleanor	*Kings Chambers* *
Gilchrist David	*9 St John Street*
Green David	*Atlantic Chambers (ORL)* ◊
Price Richard	*9 St John Street*
Vicary Joanna	*9 St John Street*

** Indicates set / individual with profile.*
◊ (ORL) = Other Ranked Lawyer.
Alphabetical order within each band. Band 1 is highest.

Band 1

Kings Chambers

See profile on p.968

THE SET

Kings Chambers is a leading set on the Northern Circuit, with a strong team of chancery specialists handling the full range of work in this area. "They have huge strength and depth that no other chambers round here could match," says one fellow barrister. Kings Chambers' members act for clients ranging from private individuals to local authorities and central government in both traditional and commercial chancery cases. The set has particular experience in dealing with disputes concerning land and property as well as in trust and probate matters. "I rate them very highly," says an instructing solicitor, adding: "They tend to deal with fairly complex work and have a wide variety of people available from junior to senior. They've always got plenty of choice if your first choice isn't available, and I've never had a problem finding someone suitable for my cases."

Client service: "The clerks are always excellent to deal with and very pragmatic; they always sort out everything you need." Colin Griffin is the practice manager and a key contact at the set.

SILKS

Lesley Anderson QC (see p.583) Highly esteemed practitioner who deals with all aspects of chancery and commercial litigation. She also regularly acts as a mediator and has particular expertise in corporate and company law, commercial property disputes and personal insolvency matters. **Strengths:** "She is fantastic. A very formidable advocate and she instils a sense of confidence in you when advocating on your behalf. Really top-drawer." **Recent work:** Acted in a challenge to the validity of a deathbed will on the basis that the testator lacked capacity.

David Casement QC (see p.612) A well-renowned barrister whose practice covers the full range of commercial disputes. He has expertise in banking, finance and securities law, and also practises extensively in corporate and personal insolvency matters. **Strengths:** "He is very good on tactics and really understands the psychology of negotiation." "He is absolutely excellent. Very highly regarded and a very good all-round lawyer." **Recent work:** Represented New Order in a derivative action brought by former bassist Peter Hook alleging breaches of fiduciary duty.

Paul Chaisty QC (see p.614) A well-established chancery and commercial litigation silk with specialist expertise in fraud cases and partnership disputes. He is also called to the Bar in the Bahamas and British Virgin Islands. **Strengths:** "He is very good in court and is an excellent orator." "He is fantastic – very thorough, and his written work is also excellent." **Recent work:** Acted in a multimillion-pound damages claim for alleged misrepresentation and breach of fiduciary duty in connection with a sale of shares.

Mark Harper QC (see p.664) Highly regarded recent silk praised for his work on heavyweight litigation. He is highlighted for company law and shareholder litigation, professional negligence, sports-related disputes and general commercial work. **Strengths:** "His reputation is excellent and he gives a first-rate service to clients." "He is very pragmatic, very user-friendly and very good on his feet." **Recent work:** Acted in a common law derivative action in relation to an LLP.

JUNIORS

Neil Berragan (see p.595) He frequently acts in civil fraud, partnership disputes and shareholder litigation. He is also an experienced arbitrator in both domestic and international disputes. **Strengths:** "He is a fantastic advocate: he is someone who will take a case and grab it by the neck." "A highly regarded barrister who is always very well prepared." **Recent work:** Defended a company which was sued by former directors following a compulsory acquisition. The directors claim that they were required to sell shares, which they said were worth several million pounds, for a nominal price.

Andrew Latimer (see p.696) He has extensive experience in company law, including unfair prejudice petitions, breaches of fiduciary duty and actions against directors. He also has experience in insolvency litigation. **Strengths:** "He is very good on his feet and great with clients. He can bring a very tranquil attitude to quite fraught matters." "A great all-round lawyer, and I know many people adore him."

Louis Doyle (see p.636) An established practitioner in commercial chancery work with extensive experience of complex and high-value claims. He has specialist expertise in insolvency matters and company law, especially shareholder and director disputes. **Strengths:** "I rate his advocacy skills and technical knowledge very highly." "Both clients and judges seem to absolutely love him." **Recent work:** Acting for a defendant in a substantial claim by a bank for possession of commercial property and financial instruments.

Andrew Grantham (see p.658) Experienced senior junior in commercial chancery litigation, representing public companies, professional firms and financial institutions. He focuses particularly on civil fraud, business partnerships and professional negligence cases. **Strengths:** "A very brainy lawyer who always fights very hard for his client." "His written work and advice is always to a very high standard." **Recent work:** Acted for the defendant in a derivative action brought by a minority shareholder in relation to an alleged misappropriation of company assets.

Mark Halliwell (see p.662) A respected barrister who acts for clients including banks, development companies and public authorities. His practice focuses on property, trusts, succession and insolvency matters. **Strengths:** "I've been very impressed by his depth of knowledge and his ability to cut through the complexities and focus on the core issues." "He has great presence in court." **Recent work:** Acted for the claimants in a private nuisance claim arising from the operation of a poultry slaughterhouse.

Eleanor Temple (see p.779) Handles a range of commercial litigation matters, especially insolvency, partnerships, international trusts disputes and asset tracing. Her clients include insolvency practitioners, banks, multinationals and private equity houses. **Strengths:** "She is excellent. She is tremendously clear and eloquent in court and has a very persuasive style." "Her written work is very good and innovative." **Recent work:** Acted for the claimant in a dispute with Google Ireland over payments received after the presentation of a winding-up petition.

Jeffrey Terry (see p.779) Extensive experience before the Mercantile Court and the Technology and Construction Court, as well as the Chancery Division. He is also an experienced arbitrator and mediator. **Strengths:** "He possesses major experience and knowledge." "He is really good to work with. He really understood the issues and concerns we had."

Eleanor d'Arcy (see p.628) Has developed a strong practice in commercial and chancery law, specialising in restructuring and insolvency. She also acts on residential and commercial property matters and trust litigation. **Strengths:** "She is tremendously hard-working and always gives her all for clients. A safe pair of hands." **Recent work:** Acted for a claimant in a successful action against the landlords for unlawful eviction, and made a further successful claim before the Court of Appeal for substantial damages.

Band 2

Exchange Chambers

See profile on p.956

THE SET

Exchange has a prominent presence on the Northern Circuit with chambers in Liverpool, Manchester and Leeds. The set has considerable experience of dealing with a wide range of commercial and traditional chancery cases and is known for acting in a number of high-value and complex disputes. One instructing solicitor says they provide "a very high level of service – I'm very pleased with them. They are very competent and practical."

Client service: "The clerks are really efficient and approachable and they always turn things round quickly. They even recommend to us who they think the work is best placed with." Jonathan I'Anson is the practice manager and a key contact at the set.

SILKS

Edward Bartley Jones QC Highly experienced silk whose practice covers all areas of commercial chancery. He is particularly renowned for professional negligence claims, FCA regulatory work, judicial reviews and human rights. **Strengths:** "He is very well thought of and is considered to be a very determined and ferocious advocate."

Mark Cawson QC (see p.613) Regularly represents financial institutions, governmental organisations, public companies and private clients in commercial disputes. His practice focuses on insolvency, company and partnership disputes, property litigation and civil fraud. **Strengths:** "He is very calm and collected in court and he always knows what he is doing." "I rate him very highly and he has a particularly strong reputation for insolvency work." **Recent work:** Acted for a daughter in claim to recover shares said to have been misappropriated by her father through the use of fraudulent share transfer forms.

David Mohyuddin QC Specialises in insolvency, professional negligence and sports-related disputes. He also deals with commercial fraud matters, shareholder disputes and asset recovery. **Strengths:** "He is very forensic and analytical in his approach and his arguments are very well put together." "A very personable type and he is good on his feet." **Recent work:** Defending NatWest against allegations by a former company director that the bank had conspired with the rest of the board to ensure a director's loan was not repaid.

JUNIORS

Giles Maynard-Connor Known for his expertise in corporate fraud, insolvency and professional negligence claims. He also advises the Secretary of State on public interest winding-up petitions and directors' disqualification proceedings. **Strengths:** "He is technically brilliant, aggressive when he needs be, and very commercially minded." "Time and time again, he achieves results beyond the clients' expectations." **Recent work:** Acted for the lender in its claim against a firm of solicitors for breach of undertaking and breach of trust as a result of fraudulent behaviour by the firm's client.

Andrew Vinson Regularly represents large companies, directors, multinationals and high net worth individuals in commercial disputes. He focuses particularly on property matters, insolvency law, professional negligence and contractual disputes. **Strengths:** "He is very switched-on and I would recommend him in the future." "He can get his head round complex cases quite quickly."

Neil Cadwallader His practice encompasses a broad range of commercial chancery work. He has particular experience in property disputes and landlord and tenant matters, partnership law and professional negligence. **Strengths:** "He is a pleasure to deal with; a very good orator who charms his audience into submission." "He is extremely clever and has immense gravitas."

9 St John Street

See profile on p.973

THE SET

A well-renowned set with a significant reputation on the Northern Circuit for commercial and traditional chancery work. The set's members are involved in a range of high-profile matters and regularly deal with property disputes, company and commercial law, wills, trusts and contentious probate. It also offers a high-quality mediation service having a team of experienced mediators. "I rate them very highly and they have a set of very knowledgeable barristers," says one interviewee. "They're always very helpful, quick to come back, and they're good with clients, managing expectations well."

Client service: "A good clerking team which is very efficient and responsive – always quick to come back and usually very helpful." Tony Morrissey is the practice manager and a key contact at the set.

JUNIORS

James Fryer-Spedding (see p.649) His areas of expertise include professional negligence, commercial contracts, corporate insolvency and partnership disputes. He is also expert in traditional chancery areas such as property and contentious probate. **Strengths:** "A very good and persuasive advocate; he always does an excellent job." "His advice is always clear and he is very good on his feet at trial." **Recent work:** Successfully defended a proprietary estoppel claim in the High Court over part of a property development site.

David Gilchrist Experienced commercial chancery litigation practitioner who acts on property law, including landlord and tenant matters. He also deals with company law and professional negligence, and is an accredited mediator. **Strengths:** "A very knowledgeable and tenacious advocate." "He is able to advise on matters of considerable complexity."

Richard Price Well-respected advocate with specialist expertise in charities and property disputes. He regularly acts for clients in insolvency disputes, wills and trusts cases and professional negligence matters. **Strengths:** "His advice is almost always spot-on and he is very responsive to clients' needs." "He has the requisite experience and gravitas behind him to be successful."

Joanna Vicary Extensive experience in traditional chancery matters, with particular expertise in contentious probate and breach of trust claims. Also handles real estate litigation, insolvency and tax matters. **Strengths:** "She has got us some excellent results and our clients are very impressed by her." "She is very good with clients and very responsive to their needs and our requests. I have no doubt that she is able to manage our clients very well." **Recent work:** Acted for the defendant in a case which turned on whether monies had been given to the defendant as a gift or in return for a half-share in her home.

Other Ranked Lawyers

David Berkley QC (1 Gray's Inn Chambers) Has more than 20 years' experience in chancery work. He is known for commercial property disputes, employment, professional negligence and regulatory law. **Strengths:** "A very nice chap; he is a very eloquent speaker with good advocacy skills."

David Green (Atlantic Chambers) Deals with all aspects of general commercial chancery. He acts for clients in property litigation, wills, trusts and contentious probate matters. **Strengths:** "Tremendously pleasant to deal with. His style and manner is very refined and he is popular with clients and instructing solicitors."

Sebastian Clegg (Deans Court Chambers) His work mainly encompasses property matters and company and partnership disputes. He also deals with trust and probate litigation, civil fraud and insolvency work. **Strengths:** "He was really very excellent. He has the ability to get to the point and has the courage to give clients advice they don't want to hear when needed." **Recent work:** Acted for the defendant in a fraudulent misrepresentation case in relation to a EUR100 million transfer from the claimant company.

Richard Chapman (18 St John Street) Experienced practitioner on a range of disputes in a variety of commercial and chancery courts. He is adept at handling property disputes, company law, insolvency and trusts. **Strengths:** "He is very good and has lots of strengths. He has an incredible set of skills." "I rate him very highly and he does some very sophisticated and complex work."

WALES & CHESTER

Chancery
Senior Statesmen
Senior Statesmen: distinguished older partners
Walters Graham *Civitas Law (ORL)* ◊
Leading Juniors
Band 1
Hughes Gwydion *9 Park Place (ORL)* ◊
Band 2
Davies Angharad *30 Park Place (ORL)* ◊
Jones Emyr *9 Park Place (ORL)* ◊
Kember Richard *9 Park Place (ORL)* ◊

Ranked Lawyers

Graham Walters (Civitas Law) His chancery practice focuses on wills, trusts and probate issues and property or land disputes. He also handles public law matters. **Strengths:** "He's a favourite choice. He is highly regarded."

Angharad Davies (30 Park Place) Has a wide-ranging chancery practice and particular expertise in disputes over the construction and interpretation of wills. She also handles Court of Protection, insolvency and land law cases. **Strengths:** "She is dedicated, proactive and an expert in this field."

Gwydion Hughes (9 Park Place) Has experience acting in property, trusts and probate chancery work. Also handles general commercial litigation matters. **Strengths:** "Super, he is a very balanced and coherent advocate who takes good points." **Recent work:** Represented a client in a judicial review of a decision granting planning permission to erect a wind turbine.

Emyr Jones (9 Park Place) Has a practice that encompasses estate administration, contested probate and general Inheritance Act claims. He also represents clients in land law and landlord and tenant work. **Strengths:** "He is very talented and has a great future ahead of him. He is good on his feet and an effective advocate."

Richard Kember (9 Park Place) Focuses on wills, trust and probate work and land disputes. His caseload includes TOLATA claims and Court of Protection and inheritance matters. **Strengths:** "He is excellent. He provides a first-class service and is easy to use. He is willing to go the extra mile."

WESTERN

Chancery
Leading Sets
Band 1
Guildhall Chambers *
St John's Chambers *
Leading Silks
Band 1
Blohm Leslie *St John's Chambers*
Sims Hugh *Guildhall Chambers*
Leading Juniors
Star individuals
Troup Alex *St John's Chambers* Ⓐ
Band 1
Bamford Jeremy *Guildhall Chambers*
Sharples John *St John's Chambers* Ⓐ
Wales Matthew *Guildhall Chambers*
Band 2
Auld Charles *St John's Chambers*
Dickinson John FH *St John's Chambers* Ⓐ *
Jones Christopher *St John's Chambers*
Paton Ewan *Guildhall Chambers*
Band 3
Berkley Michael *Magdalen Chambers (ORL)* ◊
Leslie Marie *Colleton Chambers (ORL)* ◊
Marsden Andrew *Commercial Chambers (ORL)* ◊ Ⓐ
Sahonte Rajinder *Guildhall Chambers*
Walsh Tim *Guildhall Chambers*
* *Indicates set / individual with profile.*
Ⓐ *direct access (see p.24).*
◊ *(ORL) = Other Ranked Lawyer.*
Alphabetical order within each band. Band 1 is highest.

Band 1

Guildhall Chambers

See profile on p.938

THE SET

Guildhall Chambers is a pre-eminent set in Bristol whose members are described as "excellent in their field." They handle chancery work that takes in contentious trusts, wills and probate disputes, as well as pensions, agriculture and charity law cases. Members also have experience in insolvency, company law and shareholder disputes. "They're an excellent chambers, no doubt about that," says a source.

Client service: Justin Emmett is principal civil clerk and Charlie Ellis handles property and estates instructions. Those instructing say: "Their clerking is superb, Charlie Ellis is lovely, very good service."

SILKS

Hugh Sims QC Has a broad chancery practice which includes company disputes, real property and partnership matters. He also has experience in commercial and insolvency litigation. **Strengths:** "He is very strong and good on his feet." **Recent work:** Appeared before the Chancery Division in London in a case concerning the Sherlock Holmes Museum.

JUNIORS

Matthew Wales Instructed in a range of real estate litigation including property-related insolvency and professional negligence matters. He also acts for clients in property and affairs cases in the Court of Protection. **Strengths:** "He is excellent in giving sound practical advice and not afraid to warn clients off risky ventures, helping clients get to a sensible position. His written work is always extremely lucid." **Recent work:** Advised a director of a catering company on how to respond to a demand for repayment of what is alleged to be a director's loan account.

Jeremy Bamford Chancery litigator with a specific focus on insolvency disputes for both individuals and companies. He also handles related matters such as directors' disqualification proceedings and actions against insolvency practitioners, as well as shareholder disputes and breach of warranty claims. **Recent work:** Represented HMRC in an administration application against Lotus Formula 1 Racing Team regarding unpaid PAYE/NIC.

Ewan Paton An experienced traditional chancery practitioner who acts for clients in landlord and tenant, real property and estate matters. His particular focus is on real property litigation and inheritance disputes. **Strengths:** "A go-to barrister for anything tricky in probate. He is comfortable with procedure and tends to see solutions very clearly." **Recent work:** Acted for client in an adverse possession case concerning a courtyard.

Tim Walsh Focuses his practice on probate and property law. He has experience with contentious probate, inheritance claims and real property disputes. **Strengths:** "He is very thorough on facts and law, able to go from the detail to the bigger picture with ease." **Recent work:** Acted in a will contest involving issues of proprietary estoppel.

Rajinder Sahonte His chancery practice covers probate, real estate and Court of Protection work. He also has a niche in town and village greens and public rights of way. **Strengths:** "He is extremely approachable, very user-friendly. Nothing is too much trouble and he always fights your corner and will argue everything with the other side. He has a great deal of knowledge particularly in connection with contested probate and property litigation." **Recent work:** Acted for the defendant in a professional negligence claim relating to the misidentifying of one of the two applicants for a remortgage of jointly-owned land.

St John's Chambers

See profile on p.941

THE SET

St John's is one of the leading chancery chambers on the Western Circuit, and is described as a "very good set with contentious probate barristers who have very good knowledge of this area." It has a particular strength in traditional chancery, particularly complex property litigation, contentious trusts and inheritance disputes. Its members also take instructions in commercial chancery matters.

Client service: Rob Bocock is the practice manager. Sources say that the "clerking is very good. Rob Bocock is a really good guy, really accessible."

SILKS

Leslie Blohm QC Experienced chancery practitioner with experience appearing in front of the highest courts. His practice encompasses property and commercial litigation, as well as probate, Inheritance Act disputes and village green work. **Strengths:** "He is a cut above – a brilliant advocate and an exceptionally clever man. He is easy to get along with, supportive and practical." **Recent work:** Appeared in a high-profile proprietary estoppel case, where the owners of a valuable dairy farm were alleged to have cut their daughter out of their will despite repeated assurances that she would be rewarded for her years of hard work on the farm. The dispute was dubbed the 'Cowshed Cinderella' case.

JUNIORS

Alex Troup Standout junior with a busy traditional chancery practice. Very strong on contentious trusts and probate work and complex property litigation. **Strengths:** "A rising star of the Chancery Bar specialising in contentious probate litigation who is helpful, robust and clear in his advice." **Recent work:** Acted in a contentious probate claim where one party seeks to have her late mother's will set aside for undue influence.

John Sharples Advises on real property, and is often instructed by public authorities, developers and landowners. He has expertise representing clients in real estate litigation matters. **Strengths:** "Powerful intellect with a human touch. He is very down-to-earth, approachable and personable." **Recent work:** Successfully represented the claimant in a boundary dispute and adverse possession case.

Charles Auld Acts for clients in property disputes and contentious probate. He also takes instructions in professional negligence and partnership matters. **Strengths:** "Certainly very impressive, he's been around so long he knows his stuff." **Recent work:** Appeared in an estate dispute between a brother and sister over their parents' farm.

John Dickinson (see p.633) Has a broad chancery practice, dealing with company law and shareholder litigation, restructuring and insolvency cases and contentious trusts and probate work. **Strengths:** "He is very good on the detail and also quite dogged. Once he analyses a case he knows what the answer is and pursues it. Excellent."

Christopher Jones Particularly adept on trusts issues. His practice includes probate matters both contentious and non-contentious, landlord and tenant disputes and property litigation. **Strengths:** "Excellent knowledge of all matters relating to trusts." **Recent work:** Represented the claimant in a successful application to rectify the jurisdiction clause of a trust instrument. The original instrument also incorrectly put the settlors among the class of beneficiaries.

Other Ranked Lawyers

Marie Leslie (Colleton Chambers) Her chancery practice covers wills, probate and real property. She also represents clients in Court of Protection matters and financial relief from family issues. **Recent work:** Instructed on an Inheritance Act claim made against the deceased's estate.

Andrew Marsden (Commercial Chambers) Founder of the set, he is a barrister whose chancery practice covers company and partnership law. He regularly deals with contractual and agency disputes. **Strengths:** "Very good with clients and solicitors, he tends to go the extra mile." **Recent work:** Advised on an unfair prejudice petition relating to a care home operator.

Michael Berkley (Magdalen Chambers) Exeter-based practitioner with significant experience. His chancery practice includes probate and wills work, property disputes and contentious trusts. **Strengths:** "If someone said: 'I have a chancery problem and need an Exeter barrister,' I would give Michael's name."

Charities

Contents:

LONDON

Charities	
Leading Sets	
Band 1	
Radcliffe Chambers *	
Band 2	
Maitland Chambers *	
Band 3	
Wilberforce Chambers *	
Senior Statesmen	
Senior Statesmen: distinguished older partners	
Picarda Hubert	*Chambers of Hubert Picarda QC (ORL)* ◊
Leading Silks	
Star individuals	
McCall Christopher	*Maitland Chambers* *
Pearce Robert	*Radcliffe Chambers* *
Band 1	
Crampin Peter	*Radcliffe Chambers*
Taube Simon	*Ten Old Square (ORL)* ◊ *
Band 2	
Furness Michael	*Wilberforce Chambers*
Kessler James	*Old Square Tax Chambers (ORL)* ◊ *
Tipples Amanda	*Maitland Chambers* *
Band 3	
Warnock-Smith Shân	*5 Stone Buildings (ORL)* ◊ *
Leading Juniors	
Star individuals	
Quint Francesca	*Radcliffe Chambers* *
Smith Matthew	*Maitland Chambers* *
Band 1	
Dumont Thomas	*Radcliffe Chambers* *
Henderson William	*Serle Court (ORL)* ◊ *
Band 2	
King Michael	*XXIV Old Buildings (ORL)* ◊
Mullen Mark	*Radcliffe Chambers* *
Studer Mark	*Wilberforce Chambers*
Winfield Joshua	*Radcliffe Chambers* *
Band 3	
Lewison Josh	*Radcliffe Chambers* *
Westwood Andrew	*Maitland Chambers* *

** Indicates set / individual with profile.*
◊ (ORL) = Other Ranked Lawyer.
Alphabetical order within each band. Band 1 is highest.

Band 1

Radcliffe Chambers

See profile on p.903

THE SET

Radcliffe Chambers has long been regarded as the leading set for charity-related matters. It houses a strong bench of silks and juniors who advise on all aspects of charity law and represent parties in several of the sector's most high-profile disputes. The barristers here handle everything from charity formation and governance, to cases concerning charity land and assets, and education law. Members also offer advice on ancillary issues such as tax, insolvency and succession law.

Client service: Keith Nagle and John Clark are the senior clerks of the set. "The clerks are excellent. They are extremely helpful and efficient, and get back to you straight away."

SILKS

Robert Pearce QC (see p.735) Widely regarded as a leading silk for charity disputes as well as advisory work. Recent clients include housing associations, faith-based charities and independent schools. **Strengths:** "He is incisive and at the forefront of his profession." "He is absolutely brilliant in court. He is extremely clever and very good at succinctly describing a legal case." **Recent work:** Acted as the charities specialist on an appeal to the Charity Tribunal regarding the charitable status of the Human Dignity Trust.

Peter Crampin QC Has had much success in charity law cases, and also has a practice with additional focus on trust and property law. He is active both domestically and in overseas jurisdictions. **Strengths:** "He takes an incisive approach to his work, and has a very powerful intellect." "He is very able on a range of technical issues."

JUNIORS

Francesca Quint (see p.746) Highly praised for her advisory work in particular, she does a lot of work relating to education and faith-based charities. She is also an accredited mediator and a former deputy commissioner at the Charity Commission. **Strengths:** "She is outstanding and enormously experienced – there is no one better to turn to." "She is excellent; responsive, informed and incisive."

Thomas Dumont (see p.637) Has a number of top charities as clients, and is a sought-after litigator for contentious disputes regarding trust analysis and tax exemption. **Strengths:** "His advice is always intelligent and clear, and he has excellent judgement." "He is prompt and clear, and gives practical advice."

Mark Mullen (see p.724) Particularly noted for his strength in cases concerning charity governance, mergers and property disposal. He frequently represents charities in litigation, but has also acted for the Attorney General on several occasions. **Strengths:** "He is user-friendly and has strong analytical skills combined with pragmatism." "He is excellent, and his advice is helpful and practical." **Recent work:** Represented the appellant charities in King v Chiltern Dog Rescue in the Court of Appeal. This case concerned the extent of the doctrine of donatio mortis causa.

Joshua Winfield (see p.798) Strongly focused on litigation but also conducts drafting and advisory work. He has particular experience of working with religious charities and unincorporated associations. Strengths: "He gives good technical advice, and is clearly a rising star in this area." Recent work: Acted in Sheikh v Hussain, representing members of a group elected to the management committee of a mosque charity. The case concerned a claim against the previous committee, who had refused to leave office.

Josh Lewison (see p.701) Generally assists charities with dispute resolution. He has also advised several foreign charities looking to establish themselves in England. **Strengths:** "He is always happy to help, and his advice and manner are both excellent. He is also quite robust; you don't get 'I'm not sure' answers with him." **Recent work:** Continues to represent the trustees of a temple in the doctrinal dispute of Rai v Ahir.

Band 2

Maitland Chambers

See profile on p.875

THE SET

Members here are particularly strong on contentious charity disputes, and act for charities, educational institutions and local authorities. Recent cases have concerned issues such as the public benefit of religious charities, VAT liability and charity constitutions. The set also frequently hosts seminars for solicitors, providing them with industry updates, and has individuals who deliver talks at external events.

Client service: John Wiggs is the senior clerk of a team that is described as "approachable and pragmatic."

SILKS

Christopher McCall QC (see p.711) A leading charity silk praised for his work on constitutional issues facing many notable non-profit organisations. He is particularly known for advising on trust and tax matters. **Strengths:** "He is a highly experienced charity silk, who is well respected. He is very good at seeing new angles in cases and presenting them convincingly." "He has unrivalled expertise and experience."

Amanda Tipples QC (see p.781) Held in high esteem for her handling of complex charity law cases. She is particularly known for advising on trust issues. **Strengths:** "She is very commercial and user-friendly. She answers the clients' questions about what to do for the best practically." "A barrister of great intellectual rigour, she is adaptable and gives commercial advice."

JUNIORS

Matthew Smith (see p.769) Celebrated junior who has appeared in several leading charity cases in England, Wales and Northern Ireland. He advises on all issues relating to charities including questions of trustee duties and land ownership. He is also an expert on the law relating to charities and politics. **Strengths:** "His opinions, ability with clients and court performance are all excellent." "He is pragmatic, commercially minded, and easy to talk to. He understands what the client wants." **Recent work:** Represented the trustees of Independent Press Regulation Trust in an appeal against the Charity Commission following that body's decision to refuse registration of a trust designed to promote high ethical standards amongst journalists.

Andrew Westwood (see p.793) Has long experience of representing charities as well as the Attorney General and the Charity Commission. **Strengths:** "His quality of advice and commitment to service are outstanding and they engender absolute confidence in the client and those instructing him." **Recent work:** Acted for JUSTICE and REDRESS as interested parties in connection with an appeal by Human Dignity Trust against the Charity Commission's decision to refuse to register it as a charity.

Band 3

Wilberforce Chambers

See profile on p.925

THE SET

A leading chancery set whose members frequently represent parties in notable charity cases, both domestically and offshore. Recent reported disputes have concerned gift construction and trust issues. Several of the set's members specialise in cases concerning charities and tax avoidance.

Client service: Mark Rushton heads a clerking team that is "excellent and very well organised."

SILKS

Michael Furness QC An accomplished silk with long experience, most notably in trust-related matters. He is particularly active in onshore and offshore tax litigation. **Strengths:** "He has an excellent mind and is very thoughtful. His analysis is spot-on and he is highly responsive." **Recent work:** Advised the Cup Trust on its approach to tax avoidance schemes entered into by previous trustees.

JUNIORS

Mark Studer Advises on trusts, estates, property and conveyancing law, and has a number of major charities as clients. He is best known for private client litigation in the UK and other jurisdictions including Hong Kong, The Bahamas, Bermuda and Guernsey. **Strengths:** "He is an excellent draftsman who goes about his business in a very straightforward fashion and gives clear advice." **Recent work:** Assisted the appellants in a Hong Kong Final Court of Appeal case concerning the will of Nina Wang, formerly Asia's richest woman.

Other Ranked Lawyers

Hubert Picarda QC (Chambers of Hubert Picarda QC) Greatly experienced silk who has committed the majority of his long-standing career to charity law. He has advised all types of charities including educational, religious and medical ones. His knowledge covers every aspect of charity law, but he is particularly adept at government and Charity Commission policies and compliance issues.

Michael King (XXIV Old Buildings) A robust adviser to charity organisations, many of whose cases involve probate disputes. He is increasingly active in mediation involving charities. **Strengths:** "He is very wise and charming and delivers clear and sensible advice every time."

Simon Taube QC (see p.778) (Ten Old Square) Leading silk who frequently represents parties in some of the most prominent charity litigation in the UK and other common law jurisdictions. His expertise covers related chancery areas such as trusts, estates and professional negligence. **Strengths:** "He is extremely knowledgeable and provides comprehensive and clear advice."

William Henderson (see p.669) (Serle Court) Held in high regard for his charity work, he handles a broad range of contentious issues, but has a particular focus on tax-related disputes. **Strengths:** "He has encyclopaedic knowledge of charity law, and applies it in a common-sense way."

James Kessler QC (see p.690) (Tax Chambers 15 Old Square) Widely recognised as a leading silk for tax issues relating to charities. **Strengths:** "He has deep technical knowledge, and he is very good with clients." "He is experienced, measured and authoritative."

Contents:

LONDON

Civil Liberties & Human Rights
Leading Sets
Band 1
Blackstone Chambers *
Matrix Chambers *
Band 2
Doughty Street Chambers *
Garden Court Chambers *
Band 3
Brick Court Chambers *
1 Crown Office Row *
39 Essex Chambers *
11KBW *
Landmark Chambers *
* *Indicates set / individual with profile.*
Ⓐ *direct access (see p.24).*
◊ *(ORL) = Other Ranked Lawyer.*
Alphabetical order within each band. Band 1 is highest.

Civil Liberties & Human Rights
Senior Statesmen
Senior Statesmen: distinguished older partners
Lester of Herne Hill Anthony *Blackstone Chambers*

Leading Silks	
Star individuals	**Southey** Hugh *Matrix Chambers* *
Eadie James *Blackstone Chambers*	**Swift** Jonathan *11KBW* *
Emmerson Ben *Matrix Chambers*	**Band 3**
Fordham Michael *Blackstone Chambers*	**Clayton** Richard *4-5 Gray's Inn Square (ORL)* ◊
Lieven Nathalie *Landmark Chambers*	**de la Mare** Thomas *Blackstone Chambers*
Pannick David *Blackstone Chambers*	**Demetriou** Marie *Brick Court Chambers*
Rose Dinah *Blackstone Chambers*	**Farbey** Judith *Doughty Street Chambers* Ⓐ
Band 1	**Giffin** Nigel *11KBW* *
Chamberlain Martin *Brick Court Chambers* *	**Gordon** Richard *Brick Court Chambers*
Fitzgerald Edward *Doughty Street Chambers*	**Harrison** Stephanie *Garden Court Chambers*
Hermer Richard *Matrix Chambers*	**Knafler** Stephen *Landmark Chambers*
Howell John *Blackstone Chambers*	**Maurici** James *Landmark Chambers*
Husain Raza *Matrix Chambers*	**O'Neill** Aidan *Matrix Chambers*
Kaufmann Phillippa *Matrix Chambers*	**Ryder** Matthew *Matrix Chambers* *
McCullough Angus *1 Crown Office Row*	**Simor** Jessica *Matrix Chambers*
Owen Tim *Matrix Chambers*	**Steyn** Karen *11KBW* *
Pleming Nigel *39 Essex Chambers*	**Westgate** Martin *Doughty Street Chambers*
Williams Heather *Doughty Street Chambers*	**Wolfe** David *Matrix Chambers*
Band 2	**Band 4**
Bailin Alex *Matrix Chambers* *	**Coppel** Jason *11KBW* *
Bowen Paul *Brick Court Chambers* *	**Cragg** Stephen *Monckton Chambers (ORL)* ◊
Carss-Frisk Monica *Blackstone Chambers*	**Giovannetti** Lisa *39 Essex Chambers*
Drabble Richard *Landmark Chambers*	**Hill** Mark *Francis Taylor Building (ORL)* ◊ *
Friedman Danny *Matrix Chambers*	**Morris** Fenella *39 Essex Chambers*
Grodzinski Sam *Blackstone Chambers*	**Strachan** James *39 Essex Chambers*
Havers Philip *1 Crown Office Row*	**Stratford** Jemima *Brick Court Chambers*
Monaghan Karon *Matrix Chambers*	**New Silks**
Montgomery Clare *Matrix Chambers* *	**Fatima** Shaheed *Blackstone Chambers*
Mountfield Helen *Matrix Chambers*	**Hyam** Jeremy *1 Crown Office Row*
Otty Timothy *Blackstone Chambers*	**Lester** Maya *Brick Court Chambers* *
Richards Jenni *39 Essex Chambers* *	**Squires** Daniel *Matrix Chambers*
Saini Pushpinder *Blackstone Chambers*	

Band 1

Blackstone Chambers

See profile on p.813

THE SET

Blackstone Chambers is a market-leading set housing a formidable roster of highly esteemed advocates. Its members are recognised for their adroit handling of an array of major, high-profile civil liberties and human rights cases such as Beghal v Director of Public Prosecutions which investigated the power of state agents to detain, question and search individuals at borders and ports under the Terrorism Act 2000. Its varied client base includes both respondents and applicants, while solicitors particularly highlight the chambers' "standout silks and spectacular breadth of juniors; it's like having Messi, Neymar and Suarez on your side when you instruct Blackstone."

Client service: "The clerks are utterly polite and always accessible." "There is a whole number of players involved in the clerking, and every one of them is efficient and responsive." Gary Oliver leads the clerking team.

SILKS

James Eadie QC Treasury devil with a stellar reputation in the field of civil liberties and human rights, he is regularly instructed in high-profile judicial review proceedings. He is a familiar face in the ECHR and a recognised authority on HRA challenges. **Strengths:** "He's extremely able, always well informed and incredibly fair and balanced." "Very cool and calm, with a brain the size of a planet." "The star individual for government work, a fantastic barrister. He's absolutely worthy of his reputation." **Recent work:** Represented the government in Hutchison v UK, a case investigating the compatibility of the UK's life sentencing system with Article 3 of the ECHR.

Michael Fordham QC Famed practitioner with vast experience, he is a regular fixture in complex human rights cases heard before the Supreme Court. His broad practice sees him routinely acting on behalf of a varied clientele, including claimants, defendants and third parties. **Strengths:** "With incredibly compelling written and oral advocacy, he succeeds in cases that no one would normally have a chance at." "Provides authoritative and comprehensive advice, and is a highly focused, clear and concise advocate." **Recent work:** Acted for the claimants in R (Keyu) v Secretary of State for Foreign and Commonwealth Affairs, investigating whether there was a human rights obligation to investigate a British military massacre of Malaysian villagers in 1948.

David Pannick QC An undisputed leader at the Bar, he has extensive experience of handling the most significant, high-profile human rights cases before domestic, European and international courts. He is a popular choice amongst both claimants and defendants given his broad-based expertise and formidable reputation. **Strengths:** "Without question he's superb. He's a man of great intellect who can turn his hand to almost anything." "An absolute mega-star with a very humble approach and impeccable judgement." **Recent work:** Acted for the claimants in Khodorkovsky and Lebedev v Russia, an ECHR case involving a series of human rights claims brought against the Russian government.

Dinah Rose QC Renowned for her superlative advocacy, she has a standout reputation for handling the most significant civil liberties and human rights cases. Her distinguished practice sees her regularly appearing in the CJEU, Supreme Court and Court of Appeal. **Strengths:** "Utterly charming and a true professional, she's a great strategist who knows when to fight and when to concede." "She is incredible, at the absolute top of her game. A superb advocate." "Deservedly extremely popular with the judiciary as a result of her concise and compelling arguments." **Recent work:** Appeared in R (Davis and Watson) v Secretary of State for the Home Department, a judicial review challenge to new statutory powers requiring the retention of communications data by telecommunications operators.

John Howell QC Formidable advocate who receives accolades for his well-established public law and human rights practice. A highly respected figure amongst his peers, who is noted for his vast intellect. **Strengths:** "John is absolutely incredible in terms of having all the information at his fingertips; he's a good thinker with wonderful skills of analysis." "An undoubtedly brilliant advocate."

Monica Carss-Frisk QC Joint head of Blackstone Chambers, she is an esteemed practitioner offering top-quality advice and advocacy to a diverse client base, including high-profile individual claimants and various public authorities. Her notably broad-based expertise encompasses areas such as freedom of in-

Civil Liberties & Human Rights
Leading Juniors
Star individuals
Hickman Tom *Blackstone Chambers*
Jaffey Ben *Blackstone Chambers*
Band 1
Buley Tim *Landmark Chambers*
Gallagher Caoilfhionn *Doughty Street Chambers* 🄰 *
Macdonald Alison *Matrix Chambers* *
Band 2
Brander Ruth *Doughty Street Chambers*
Bunting Jude *Doughty Street Chambers*
Straw Adam *Doughty Street Chambers*
Band 3
Armstrong Nicholas *Matrix Chambers*
Buttler Chris *Matrix Chambers* 🄰
Clement Joanne *11KBW* *
Dubinsky Laura *Doughty Street Chambers*
Gerry Alison *Doughty Street Chambers*
Kilroy Charlotte *Doughty Street Chambers*
Knights Samantha *Matrix Chambers*
Patel Naina *Blackstone Chambers*
Rahman Shaheen *1 Crown Office Row*
Simblet Stephen *Garden Court Chambers*
Steele Iain *Blackstone Chambers*
Wagner Adam *1 Crown Office Row*
Weston Amanda *Garden Court Chambers*
Band 4
Birdling Malcolm *Brick Court Chambers*
Butler-Cole Victoria *39 Essex Chambers*
Cross Tom *11KBW* *
Denholm Graham *Landmark Chambers*
Gardner Piers *Monckton Chambers (ORL)* ◊ 🄰
Gask Alex *Doughty Street Chambers*
Hemingway Sarah *Garden Court Chambers*
Hirst Leonie *Garden Court Chambers*
Law Helen *Matrix Chambers*
Leventhal Zoe *Landmark Chambers*
Metcalfe Eric *Monckton Chambers (ORL)* ◊
Morris Anna *Garden Court Chambers*
O'Callaghan Declan *Landmark Chambers*
Pievsky David *Blackstone Chambers*
Poole Tom *3 Hare Court (ORL)* ◊
Prochaska Elizabeth *Matrix Chambers* *
Sandell Adam *Matrix Chambers*
Suterwalla Azeem *Monckton Chambers (ORL)* ◊ *
Up-and-coming individuals
Clooney Amal *Doughty Street Chambers* *
Nicholls Jesse *Doughty Street Chambers*
* Indicates individual with profile.
🄰 direct access (see p.24).
◊ (ORL) = Other Ranked Lawyer.
Alphabetical order within each band. Band 1 is highest.

formation, immigration and disability discrimination. **Strengths:** "She is always totally focused on the best interests of her client and shows great strategic thinking." "Her submissions are very smooth, and she is a calming influence for both the client and the court." **Recent work:** Appeared in Akerman-Livingstone v Aster, a test case considering the approach to disability discrimination raised as a defence in possession proceedings brought by a social landlord.

Sam Grodzinski QC Highly thought of barrister who wins particular praise for his advocacy style and intellectual prowess. He routinely tackles complex matters on behalf of both claimants and defendants, including central and local government bodies. **Strengths:** "He's succinct, clear in his arguments and judges really like him." "He's very nice to deal with, thorough and very clear; a high-class barrister." **Recent work:** Appeared in R (Rotsztein) v Inner London Coroner, a test case for the Jewish and Muslim communities about what approach a coroner should take with regard to invasive autopsies.

Timothy Otty QC Particularly noted for his adroit handling of cases concerning state immunity and economic sanctions. He is regularly called on to tackle high-profile, complex matters before domestic, European and international courts. **Strengths:** "An extraordinarily experienced QC whose impressive skill shows through in his in-depth analysis. He's a genuinely warm and wonderful barrister." "Relaxed and easy to work with." **Recent work:** Appeared in Bank Mellat v HM Treasury, a £4 billion damages claim arising from unlawful imposition of sanctions.

Pushpinder Saini QC Accomplished representative of the Crown, government departments and regulators in complex judicial review proceedings, domestically and in Europe. He is regularly called upon by international businesses, given his notably in-depth knowledge of EU sanctions. **Strengths:** "He's superb: his advocacy is very strong, and he's excellent with clients and clear in his advice." "Extremely experienced, he demonstrates excellent judgement." **Recent work:** Acted for the appellant in Nouazli v Secretary of State, a Supreme Court appeal concerning the civil rights of EU nationals pending deportation.

Thomas de la Mare QC Esteemed practitioner whose broad-based expertise runs the full gamut of civil liberties and human rights law. He is a regular feature in cases concerning terrorism, torture and free speech. **Strengths:** "He is an excellent lateral thinker who reliably produces good written advice." "He's able to come up with novel ideas and to implement them effectively; an extremely innovative advocate." **Recent work:** Acted for the respondent in NA (Pakistan) v SSHD, a case concerning the immigration rights of a Pakistani wife who had suffered serious domestic abuse at the hands of her husband, an EU national.

Shaheed Fatima QC Routinely provides expert representation to NGOs, governments and private individuals, domestically and in Europe. Her broad expertise covers areas such as immigration, sanctions and unlawful detention. **Strengths:** "She's an excellent lawyer, very talented." "She has a wonderfully logical mind." **Recent work:** Acted for the claimant in Djakishev v Kazakhstan, a complaint alleging a range of extensive human rights violations, including breach of fair trial rights and arbitrary detention.

Anthony Lester of Herne Hill QC A hugely respected and much sought-after authority in the field of civil liberties and human rights, he has been involved in a number of major, landmark cases over the course of his distinguished career at the Bar. **Strengths:** "He has an immense reputation in the field."

JUNIORS

Tom Hickman Highly capable junior who is well known for his notable experience in appellate cases. He regularly appears before all levels of court, including the Supreme Court and the ECHR, litigating both for and against regulatory, government and public bodies. **Strengths:** "He's got a good brain and a wonderful drafting style. He is a real asset when it comes to bigger, more complex legal questions." "Combines tenacity and great expertise; he is a formidable junior." **Recent work:** Appeared in R (Reilly (No. 2)) v Secretary of State for Work and Pensions, successfully obtaining a declaration of incompatibility of the Jobseekers Act 2013 with a previous Court of Appeal ruling regarding benefit sanctions.

Ben Jaffey Has a diverse client base comprising individuals, companies, central and local government, regulators and public interest groups. He is held in high esteem for his expertise in areas such as detention, data retention and the environment. **Strengths:** "He's a great advocate and a true leader of cases." "He is a brilliant barrister and a delight to work with." **Recent work:** Successfully acted for the claimant in R (ClientEarth) v SSEFRA, a Supreme Court EU law challenge regarding the UK's failure to meet air quality standards in London and other major urban areas.

Naina Patel Offers expert advice across the full spectrum of human rights and public law matters, demonstrating particular skill in complex judicial review proceedings. She is regularly called upon to handle significant cases concerning defence and foreign policy. **Strengths:** "She produces great written work, is incredibly responsive and is a wonderfully imaginative advocate." "Her oral advocacy is always impressive." **Recent work:** Acted for the respondent in R (A and P) v Secretary of State for Justice. The case involved multiple Article 8 ECHR challenges regarding amendments to CRB checks.

Iain Steele Commands considerable respect in the field and is a regular feature in specialist tribunals and the Administrative Court. He is an adroit representative of both claimants and respondents, offering expertise in areas such as social security, community care and prisoners' rights. **Strengths:** "A really great drafter, he is very engaging and wonderful with clients." "Always a pleasure to work with, he's friendly, reliable and produces excellent written work." **Recent work:** Assisted Liberty with its high-profile intervention in the Supreme Court case of R (Roberts) v Commissioner of Police of the Metropolis. This case concerned statutory powers to stop and search individuals under the Criminal Justice and Public Order Act 1994.

David Pievsky Highly regarded junior with a wealth of experience in the field, he regularly handles cases concerning property rights, the right to privacy and freedom of expression. He is particularly noted for his aptitude in matters concerning the right to protest and religious expression. **Strengths:** "He's obviously very bright. He runs a wonderful practice and enjoys a sterling reputation." **Recent work:** Advised the Secretary of State in Morgan v Ministry of Justice, a case concerning the prison categorisation of a convicted murderer who denies the offence.

Matrix Chambers

See profile on p.876

THE SET

Matrix Chambers is a distinguished set which remains absolutely dedicated to its work in the field of civil liberties and human rights. The standout team of silks and juniors housed in chambers are held in high esteem for their expert representation of both claimants and defendants, including private individuals, NGOs, charities, large-scale businesses and trade unions. Its accomplished members offer specialist expertise in a vast array of areas, including unlawful detention, miscarriages of justice, immigration, public law and complex issues concerning the ECHR. Given its stellar reputation, Matrix regularly attracts instructions in the most high-profile matters, with a recent highlight being its representation of Alexander Litvinenko's widow at the inquiry into his death.

Client service: "The clerks are always clear and helpful. They accommodate all the requests we make and they're extremely personable. A pleasure to work with." "The clerks organise things very well and keep everything moving in good humour, even when they're under significant time pressure." Jason Housden leads the clerking team.

SILKS

Ben Emmerson QC Founding member of the set with an esteemed international practice encompassing public, criminal and human rights law. A highly sought-after advocate, he makes regular appearances before all levels of the domestic courts, the ECJ and the International Criminal Court. **Strengths:** "He's got an outstanding command of civil liberties and human rights, and is an absolutely dedicated, hard-working practitioner." "A real force to be reckoned with, he's a doyen of human rights law." **Recent work:** Served as counsel in Justice Lowell Goddard's high-profile Historic Child Abuse Inquiry investigating institutional failures to protect children.

Richard Hermer QC Renowned practitioner in the field of public law, who is regularly called upon to handle the most significant, high-profile human rights and civil liberties cases in the UK. His practice has a particularly strong international focus. **Strengths:** "His strategic vision gets big teams working in sync, and he gets to the root of complex cases extremely quickly." "An effective advocate who makes the complicated easily digestible." **Recent work:** Acted in SXH v Crown Prosecution Service, a challenge concerning a young Somali woman who was trafficked into the UK and then arrested and detained for failing to have a passport.

Raza Husain QC Renowned public law barrister who specialises in immigration and civil liberties work. He has extensive experience of appearing before the Supreme Court and is routinely called upon by publicly funded claimant clients. **Strengths:** "He's a creative thinker who approaches cases with a lot of energy." "He has an encyclopaedic knowledge of refugee case law and an extraordinary legal mind." **Recent work:** Acted in HA (Iraq) v SSHD, an Article 8 challenge to a criminal deportation.

Phillippa Kaufmann QC Highly regarded human rights specialist who regularly attracts instructions in high-profile, significant judicial review proceedings. She demonstrates notably deep knowledge in prisoners' rights matters and human rights cases arising out of the Iraq war. **Strengths:** "She's excellent in cross-examination and has a wonderful advocacy style which helps to get juries on side." "She brings incisive intellect to every case she considers." **Recent work:** Acted on behalf of two victims of serious sexual attack in DSD and NBV v Commissioner of Police of the Metropolis. This high-profile, significant matter concerned serial offender John Worboys, a taxi driver who committed more than 105 attacks on women, and centred on allegations that the police failed to conduct an effective investigation into the reported crimes.

Tim Owen QC Hugely respected advocate with a wide-ranging practice running the full gamut of human rights issues. He is particularly recognised for his aptitude in complex judicial review proceedings and for his expert grasp of criminal and police law. **Strengths:** "Highly respected by all tribunals." "He's got sufficient experience to tell how the court is minded and to adapt his style accordingly, and he's an excellent cross-examiner of witnesses." **Recent work:** Acted for the claimant in R (John Catt) v Metropolitan Police Commissioner. This was a Supreme Court case challenging the actions of the police, who recorded details of Catt's peaceful political activities over a 10-year period on the secret National Domestic Extremism Database.

Alex Bailin QC (see p.587) Hugely respected for his civil liberties and human rights work, his highly active practice has a strong criminal law slant. He routinely receives instructions in significant matters concerning police power, data retention and torture issues, and is a familiar face in the Supreme Court, Administrative Court and ECHR. **Strengths:** "He's very strategic, which is helpful in interventions, and tends to be three or four steps ahead of everyone else." "Has a very easy-going style of advocacy that really wins the court over." **Recent work:** Instructed by a number of major news outlets, including the BBC, The Times and the Daily Telegraph, in the Litvinenko Inquiry.

Danny Friedman QC Respected barrister with a broad-based practice spanning public, human rights and criminal law. He has a particular focus on matters concerning terrorism, national security and armed conflicts, and has recently been highly active in legacy cases involving human rights abuse in Northern Ireland. **Strengths:** "He's a powerhouse of ideas and energy, a great lawyer and advocate and phenomenally hard working." "He is an amazing strategist who really sees the big picture without losing sight of the detail." **Recent work:** Acted in McConville v PSNI, a case concerning the disappearance of Jean McConville in Belfast in 1972. The matter centred on a claim under Article 2 and the common law to gain access to a report by the PSNI Historical Enquiries Team.

Karon Monaghan QC Skilled practitioner with far-reaching expertise in human rights, discrimination and equality, employment and EU law. She regularly attracts instructions in high-profile, significant matters from a diverse range of clients, including charities, trade unions and private claimants. **Strengths:** "She's good at demystifying the law for clients, and very good at getting to the heart of complex issues." "Her deep understanding of equality and discrimination is almost unrivalled." **Recent work:** Assisted Liberty with its high-profile intervention in the Supreme Court case R (Ali and Bibi) v SSHD. This was a challenge to amendments to the Immigration Rules to introduce pre-entry language requirements.

Clare Montgomery QC (see p.720) Particularly highly regarded for her adroit handling of public law and due process matters. She regularly acts both for and against the government in significant, high-profile cases. **Strengths:** "Extremely pleasant to work with and always on point. She doesn't mince her words but she never offends." "A great draftsman, she is very quick and has a strong, logical mind." **Recent work:** Acted for the government in R (on the application of Denby Collins) v Secretary of State for Justice, a case investigating whether the so-called householder's defence complied with Article 2 of the ECHR.

Helen Mountfield QC High-profile advocate in the field of civil liberties and human rights, she serves as a deputy High Court judge in the Administrative Court. She remains a popular choice for major public law cases and is a recognised specialist in complex EU law issues. **Strengths:** "Cutting-edge work, especially around equality and public service cuts." "A barrister of incredible intellect, she is hugely committed to her cases and to her clients." **Recent work:** Acted as a special advocate for the appellant in DD v Secretary of State for Justice. She successfully quashed conditions of a Terrorism Prevention and Investigation Measure which contradicted Articles 3 and 9 of the ECHR.

Hugh Southey QC (see p.770) Recognised expert in the fields of immigration, human rights and prison law, who demonstrates notable skill in cases concerning mental health, extradition and sexual offences. He is a regular fixture in the Supreme Court and is widely respected by peers. **Strengths:** "A true strategist, he's approachable, anticipates obstacles early on and doesn't put on unnecessary airs and graces in court." "Efficient, organised and on top of his papers despite his incredible workload." **Recent work:** Acted in R (Roberts) v Commissioner of Police for Metropolis, a case considering whether police stop and search powers are compatible with the ECHR.

Aidan O'Neill QC Dual-qualified in both Scotland and England, he concentrates his practice on constitutional, EU and human rights law. He offers particular insight into the domestic effects of the EU Charter, and is noted for his deft handling of matters involving complex elements of criminal and employment law. **Strengths:** "His written advocacy is excellent. He's an utterly comprehensive and knowledgeable advocate with virtually unrivalled experience in the higher courts." **Recent work:** Appeared in R (Sandiford) v Foreign and Commonwealth Office. This case considered whether the FCO had duties under the ECHR and EU Charter of Fundamental Rights to provide legal funding to British nationals facing the death penalty abroad.

Matthew Ryder QC (see p.757) Has developed a respected niche in human rights matters concerning media, police, surveillance and privacy elements. He is frequently instructed in significant police misconduct, state surveillance and journalists' rights work, and has handled several major undercover policing cases. **Strengths:** "He's fantastic on private law discrimination claims against the police, and his pleadings are always succinct and compelling." **Recent work:** Appeared in R (Miranda) v Commissioner of Police for the Metropolis, a high-profile public law challenge regarding misuse of public law powers and breaches of Articles 5, 8 and 10 of the ECHR.

Jessica Simor QC Established silk with a diverse client base comprised of individuals, large corporations, NGOs, government departments and regulatory bodies. She regularly tackles significant cases before the Supreme Court and the ECHR. **Strengths:** "She's extremely knowledgeable, and is a skilful advocate with enviable clarity and focus." **Recent work:** Acted in R (Patrick McKenna and Ingenious Media) v HMRC, a matter centring on the HMRC's alleged breach of confidentiality duties.

David Wolfe QC Esteemed civil liberties and human rights silk, who is widely respected for his adroit handling of complex judicial review proceedings on behalf of a diverse range of clients. He receives praise for his polished oral advocacy and notable breadth of knowledge. **Strengths:** "He has a very succinct style, so his delivery is very sharp and to the point."

"Unassuming and generous with his time, he speedily gets to the crux of the issue." **Recent work:** Acted for a group of parents in Fox v Secretary of State for Education, successfully challenging the legality of the content of new GCSE Religious Studies subject on the basis that it prioritised the teaching of religious views.

Daniel Squires QC Newly minted silk who is hugely popular with both claimants and the government. His fine reputation attracts instructions in high-profile cases in the field, and regularly sees him appearing before the Supreme Court as lead counsel. **Strengths:** "Strong in almost every area, he is highly intelligent, insightful and conscientious. He's wonderful on the detail, great at keeping to deadlines and just a thoroughly pleasant individual to work with." **Recent work:** Acted on behalf of two prisoners in R (Bourgass & Hussain) v Secretary of State for Justice. Succeeded in a landmark appeal establishing that prisoners are entitled to a fair hearing before they can be subject to prolonged segregation, and cannot be segregated for more than 72 hours without external review.

JUNIORS

Alison Macdonald (see p.705) Sought-after junior for complex civil liberties matters, including significant judicial review proceedings concerning human rights and criminal law. She often handles major multi-jurisdictional investigations as part of her flourishing public law practice. **Strengths:** "She's first rate, incredibly bright and capable of dealing with complex issues by turning them into understandable concepts." "Communicative, reliable and very enthusiastic." **Recent work:** Acted for the claimant in National Union of Journalists v Metropolitan Police, a case challenging the retention of large amounts of information about journalists on the Met's Domestic Extremism Database.

Nicholas Armstrong Skilled junior with a respected civil liberties practice. He regularly handles public law disputes, inquests and private law actions. **Strengths:** "Brings novel arguments to the table which are compelling and successful." "It's amazing how well he distils things into understandable points for the court." **Recent work:** Appeared in a 10-week inquest representing the family of a private security contractor who had, along with a colleague, been murdered by a contractor in Iraq.

Chris Buttler Frequently handles judicial reviews concerning fundamental rights and claims for damages under the HRA. He regularly assists claimant clients with challenges against government bodies, demonstrating particular skill in matters concerning human trafficking. **Strengths:** "He's very clear, focused and insightful in terms of legal analysis, and he produces excellent written work." "He is tactically shrewd and well liked by the court." **Recent work:** Acted for the claimant in R (Letts) v Lord Chancellor, successfully establishing that the Lord Chancellor's Guidance on granting legal aid to bereaved families for representation at inquests was misleading and inaccurate.

Samantha Knights Respected junior with a high-profile practice, who has recently been instructed in several major national security cases before the High Court and Court of Appeal. She is a recognised expert on the ECHR, and regularly tackles cases against the MoD concerning British action in armed conflicts. **Strengths:** "She is very measured in her advice and takes pains to see the other side's point of view so that she can better demolish it." "She's very incisive and reliably provides top-quality support and assistance." **Recent work:** Assisted the British Red Cross with its intervention in the Court of Appeal test case, R (Gudanaviciene & Ors) v Director of Legal Aid Agency & Anor. The case considered whether family reunion cases in the refugee context are eligible for legal aid.

Adam Sandell Practising doctor as well as a junior barrister, who draws upon his extensive medical knowledge to better represent vulnerable, marginalised or disadvantaged people. He is esteemed for his adroit handling of complex judicial reviews and demonstrates notable expertise in prison law and health-related matters. **Recent work:** Appeared in AM v GMC acting on behalf of an individual suffering from locked-in syndrome who wished to end his life. This was a call for judicial review of the GMC's policy on assisted suicide.

Helen Law Fine junior with a varied caseload consisting of public, civil and criminal law. Her flourishing human rights practice sees her regularly handling claims against the government concerning failures of the criminal justice system. **Strengths:** "She works with medical experts very well and is very highly respected. A real asset to any team." "An extremely thorough advocate and a brilliant tactician." **Recent work:** Appeared in a number of test cases investigating the civil liability of the MoD for the detention and mistreatment of detainees held by the UK during the Iraq war.

Elizabeth Prochaska (see p.744) Held in high regard for her active civil liberties and human rights practice. She is often called upon by large corporations, NGOs and statutory bodies for her expert counsel regarding their legal responsibilities under the HRA. She is particularly well equipped to handle cases concerning the rights of women and children. **Strengths:** "Her advocacy is excellent, she really holds her own amongst the silks." **Recent work:** Acted as First Junior Counsel in the Goddard Inquiry into Child Sexual Abuse.

Band 2

Doughty Street Chambers

See profile on p.828

THE SET

With human rights and civil liberties at the heart of its practice, Doughty Street Chambers is well equipped to represent a diverse range of clients before both domestic and international courts. The set houses a number of distinguished advocates in the field, from juniors through to silks. Its esteemed members have vast experience across the board, and offer specialist expertise in areas such as international crime, abuse of police powers, immigration, discrimination and children's rights. Several of its key practitioners have recently been involved in the high-profile Hillsborough Inquest, predominantly acting on behalf of bereaved families. Market commentators value the chambers' "huge breadth of experience and high-quality work."

Client service: "The clerks are very helpful, easy to deal with and well able to sort out practical problems." "They are always keen to help, and they go out of their way to assist." Mark Dembovsky leads the clerking team.

SILKS

Edward Fitzgerald QC Highly acclaimed, he offers vast experience across the field of public, criminal and international human rights law. He is regularly called upon to handle the most significant, highly publicised cases, routinely appearing before the Court of Appeal, the Supreme Court and the ECHR. **Strengths:** "His intellectual ability is almost unmatched; he is passionate about his work." "He has the knowledge of every case at his fingertips, and in court he really fights for his clients." **Recent work:** Appeared before the ECHR in Aswat v UK, a case considering the extradition of terror suspect Haroon Aswat.

Heather Williams QC Esteemed civil liberties and human rights barrister displaying key strengths in discrimination and abuse of police powers claims. She offers broader expertise in employment matters and is an experienced advocate in major, high-profile inquests. **Strengths:** "She is possibly the leading authority on police law, and is an excellent trial advocate." "She has outstanding knowledge of the law and a wonderful advocate on her feet." **Recent work:** Represented a bereaved family at the Hillsborough Inquest.

Judith Farbey QC Established silk with a respected administrative and public law practice. She has a particular focus on complex immigration matters and is often called upon to advise on judicial review proceedings concerning unlawful detention and the criminal justice system. **Strengths:** "She's fantastic: very responsive, easy to work with and always able to explain things clearly." "She's always fair and very hard working, and she has impeccable judgement."

Martin Westgate QC Distinguished human rights practitioner with a broad practice, who demonstrates great strength in complex public law matters. His complementary expertise in the areas of social housing and welfare only serve to strengthen his work in the field of civil liberties and human rights. **Strengths:** "He takes on board others' ideas and works well in a team." "He is a cerebral and versatile human rights silk." **Recent work:** Appeared in R (Ben Hoare Bell and others) v Lord Chancellor, a matter concerning the decision to remove guaranteed legal aid funding in judicial review cases where the court has not granted permission.

JUNIORS

Caoilfhionn Gallagher (see p.649) Commands great respect in the field of human rights and civil liberties. Her broad areas of expertise include media law, children's rights, community care and national security, and she is particularly noted for her adroit handling of matters concerning the failure of state bodies. **Strengths:** "She's exceptionally thorough, innovative and highly conscientious." "A very committed advocate who knows the law back to front." **Recent work:** Assisted charity Just for Kids Law with their campaign for greater protection for 17-year-olds held in police custody.

Ruth Brander Demonstrates great skill in an array of matters, including police actions, prisoners' rights claims and criminal appeals. She is recognised for her specialist knowledge of international sodomy laws and regularly handles cases concerning the use of stop and search measures in the UK. **Strengths:** "She's able to work in a pragmatic and practical way and is especially good at assisting vulnerable clients." "She's sensible, precise and efficient." **Recent work:** Acted in Pitman and Hernandez v The State of Trinidad and Tobago. This was a constitutional challenge to the imposition of the mandatory death penalty in the cases of two appellants with diminished mental capacity.

Jude Bunting Enjoys a strong track record of appearing in major human rights cases on behalf of a range of clients, including NGOs, the media and vulnerable individuals. He has recently acted in a high-impact matter which changed the law regarding surveillance of parliamentarians. **Strengths:** "He's attentive, he has excellent attention to detail and he's a really innovative thinker." "He's completely on top of new developments in this field." **Recent work:** Assisted the Family Planning Association with its high-profile intervention in a case concerning abortion law in Northern Ireland.

Adam Straw Experienced junior offering broad expertise across the fields of public law and human rights, he routinely appears before all levels of court in the UK and is a regular feature in the ECHR. **Strengths:** "He thinks outside the box and has an innovative legal mind." "A junior of choice in this field, he's an amazing human rights thinker who knows the law inside out." **Recent work:** Appeared in R (Hallam) v Secretary of State for Justice, a case concerning a man who was wrongly convicted of murder at 17 years of age. The case centred on the contention that UK laws limiting compensation for miscarriages of justice contravene ECHR Article 6.

Alison Gerry Respected human rights junior who routinely provides expert advice on complex mental health-related matters. She is also recognised for her aptitude in the areas of police and prison law. **Strengths:** "She is confident, approachable and shows great empathy towards her clients." "She has a fantastic ability to grasp complex cases quickly."

Laura Dubinsky Regularly handles false imprisonment claims and prison law challenges, typically on behalf of claimants and intervening parties. She is also an extremely highly regarded immigration expert who routinely appears before the Supreme Court. **Strengths:** "A hugely committed barrister who gives everything to a case, she has an impressive grasp on the law and is incredibly tenacious." "She is very confident in court." **Recent work:** Represented the appellant in R (Nouzali) v Secretary of State for the Home Department. This was a Supreme Court appeal considering whether the power to detain EEA nationals without a set time limit prior to deportation is compatible with EU law.

Charlotte Kilroy Dynamic human rights junior with a respected practice, who demonstrates broad skill in the field. She is noted for her strength in complex immigration cases and matters involving undercover police investigations. **Strengths:** "She comes up with innovative arguments, she's confident, assured, and works extremely hard." "She has a very strategic approach, and makes ambitious arguments which pay off."

Alex Gask Handles challenges brought against public authorities, and is an expert in police law, prison law and children's rights. His practice benefits from his prior experience as an in-house solicitor at Liberty, the human rights NGO. **Strengths:** "He is pragmatic, dynamic and a brilliant all-rounder." "He is very good with clients, has good attention to detail, and is very efficient." **Recent work:** Served as junior counsel to the family of Private Gavin Williams in the inquest into his death, which was caused by the unlawful use of physical training as punishment.

Amal Clooney (see p.619) A key operator in the field of international human rights, she has recently assisted the UN Special Envoy and Special Rapporteur in high-profile cases regarding the Syria crisis and drone use regulations. **Strengths:** "She is very approachable and provides extremely good attention to detail." **Recent work:** Acted in Tymoshenko v Ukraine, an ECHR case regarding criminal proceedings brought against the ex-Prime Minister of Ukraine in 2011.

Jesse Nicholls Enjoys a sterling reputation in the civil liberties and human rights sphere given his deft handling of complex inquests and deep knowledge of police law. He has recently acted on behalf of 77 bereaved families in the Hillsborough Inquest. **Strengths:** "He relates well to his clients and has a proven record of challenging decisions made by state bodies." "He goes out of his way to help with technical points and is available at short notice." **Recent work:** Acted in Ibrahim Djelal v Commissioner of Police of the Metropolis, a case concerning significant assault committed by a police officer. He successfully secured £50,000 on behalf of the claimant.

Garden Court Chambers

See profile on p.851

THE SET

Garden Court Chambers houses a committed team of highly skilled advocates whose reputation in the field of civil liberties and human rights is well deserved. It remains a go-to set for domestic, European and international clients, and regularly wins instructions in the highest-profile, landmark disputes in the field. The breadth of its members' knowledge and expertise is notable, encompassing areas such as community care, crime, immigration, inquests and prison law. The chambers is particularly highly regarded for its commitment to publicly-funded work and adroit representation of vulnerable clients and NGOs. Many of its eminent barristers have recently been engaged in a number of highly-publicised, complex cases, including Lord Pitchford's Undercover Policing Inquiry and the Hillsborough Inquests.

Client service: "They're well organised, helpful and always prompt." "The clerks are excellent, they're quick to respond and very flexible." Phil Bampfylde leads the clerking team.

SILKS

Stephanie Harrison QC Dynamic silk with a varied practice, who demonstrates prowess in official misconduct, discrimination, minority rights and unlawful detention matters. In particular, she is highly regarded for her deft handling of complex judicial review challenges and is noted for the sensitive approach she takes when working with vulnerable individuals and families. **Strengths:** "A wonderfully strategic thinker, who's very smart and always one step ahead of the opponent." "She's a visionary and a highly effective advocate." **Recent work:** Appeared before the Court of Appeal in B v SSHD, a case considering the legality of intrusive bail conditions imposed on grounds of national security.

JUNIORS

Stephen Simblet Regularly called upon to provide expert assistance in claims brought against the police. He is also singled out for his adept representation of bereaved families in matters concerning psychiatric detention and custody deaths. **Strengths:** "He is extremely bright and handles complex legal points with ease." "He's great with clients and good at putting people at ease." **Recent work:** Acted in Vian v Commissioner of Police, a case concerning allegations of malicious prosecution and false imprisonment arising out of an unsolved gangland murder.

Amanda Weston Distinguished junior who is regularly called on to handle complex judicial review proceedings and significant immigration cases. She is an established presence in the sphere, regularly appearing before domestic and European courts, including the Special Immigration Appeals Commission. **Strengths:** "She has vast experience and a huge amount of knowledge." "She is extremely bright, tactically excellent, tenacious and determined." **Recent work:** Acted in R (ota) ZX v National Probation Service, a case considering whether the National Probation Service had breached the HRA by preventing an offender from seeing his three young children.

Sarah Hemingway Frequently instructed by claimants in multi-claim and multi-handed civil jury trials. She is particularly well versed in matters concerning malicious prosecution, assault and false imprisonment. **Strengths:** "She is very approachable, motivated and reliably provides quality advice." **Recent work:** Acted for the claimants in Ramsden, Dutton, Martin & Martin v Commissioner of Police. This high-profile, four-hand civil claim centred on allegations of false imprisonment, assault and malicious prosecution.

Leonie Hirst Respected junior whose diverse civil liberties practice has a notable emphasis on deprivation of liberty matters, whether in the context of mental health, prison or immigration. She is a skilful representative of highly vulnerable clients, including those who are disabled or incapacitated. **Strengths:** "She is a committed advocate and highly client-focused; she works extremely hard and brings home the results." "She's unflappable in complex and trying situations." **Recent work:** Acted in R (JM and others) v SSHD, a case considering the government's Detained Fast Track policy.

Anna Morris Demonstrates notable proficiency in significant, protest-related claims brought against the police. She has particularly deep knowledge of UK-sanctioned torture in foreign jurisdictions and the human rights of prisoners transferring into the EU. **Strengths:** "She's one of the few people who can combine huge intellectual prowess with very practical skills." **Recent work:** Acted in Ellen Yianni v Chief Constable of Police for Essex. She successfully obtained a significant settlement for a young woman who was assaulted and arrested whilst acting as a medic's assistant during the Dale Farm evictions.

Band 3

Brick Court Chambers

See profile on p.816

THE SET

Brick Court Chambers is a well-respected set offering key strengths across the areas of European law, commercial law, civil liberties and human rights. Its formidable team of barristers are regularly sought-after to assist with major cases concerning data protection, economic sanctions and significant damages claims for torture. Liberty v GCHQ, a recent case questioning whether the monitoring of communications in the UK is compatible with human rights law, is a fine example of the high-profile work undertaken

by the set. Instructing solicitors report that "Brick Court has an impressively deep bench and a broad range of experienced advocates."
Client service: "The clerking team is very responsive, and they will be very straight with you when it comes to timing and cost." Julian Hawes and Ian Moyler lead the clerking team.

SILKS
Martin Chamberlain QC (see p.614) Regularly acts for both defendants and claimants in high-profile civil liberties and human rights cases. He offers vast experience to a diverse range of clients, including political NGOs, international financial institutions and the Lord Chancellor. **Strengths:** "He shows great assurance, intelligence and the ability to persuade very effectively in both oral and written submissions." "He inspires great confidence in court." **Recent work:** Represented the Investigatory Powers Tribunal in Liberty v GCHQ, a case considering whether state policy on the interception of communications was compatible with human rights law.

Paul Bowen QC (see p.600) Distinguished practitioner who regularly handles both domestic and international human rights and public law claims. His broad-based expertise covers areas such as data protection, mental health and disability rights, and his highly active practice sees him making regular appearances before the Supreme Court and the Privy Council. **Strengths:** "A creative lawyer and a great advocate, he is dynamic and pioneering." "His ability to retain information really stands out; he is effective, informative, personable and good fun to work with." **Recent work:** Represented a victim of a serious householder assault in R (Denby Collins) v Ministry of Justice. This case considered the compatibility of Article 2 with UK householder defence laws.

Marie Demetriou QC Esteemed silk demonstrating core strength in areas such as political protest, asylum, immigration and torture. She is typically seen assisting claimants and interveners. **Strengths:** "She's gently persuasive and one of the most charming advocates on the stage." "She has a wonderfully conversational advocacy style which anyone can follow." **Recent work:** Acted for multiple claimants in Sophocleus and others v Secretary of State for Foreign Affairs. This case concerned historical torture carried out by British colonial authorities in Cyprus in the 1950s.

Richard Gordon QC Offers vast experience across the field of civil liberties and human rights, with a particular specialism in cases concerning terrorism. He is well known for his work on behalf of the Special Immigration Appeals Commission and for his significant contribution to leading literature in the sphere. **Strengths:** "He's really excellent on human rights law." "He is a top-notch public lawyer." **Recent work:** Acted in Dwyer v Welsh Ministers, a major judicial review in Wales concerning fundamental rights and access to services under the NHS.

Jemima Stratford QC Has cultivated a highly-respected practice in the field of civil liberties and human rights. She regularly handles an array of high-profile, significant cases, covering areas such as the rights of pregnant workers, state immunity rules and torture allegations. **Strengths:** "She is able to cut through a lot of dry and academic material with ease and is extremely user-friendly." **Recent work:** Counselled the All Party Parliamentary Group on Drones on the public law and human rights consequences of the Edward Snowden leaks.

Maya Lester QC (see p.700) Routinely acts for both private and public respondents and applicants in human rights cases. She has vast experience of appearing before domestic and EU courts, and is particularly knowledgeable on the subject of EU sanctions. **Strengths:** "Her brain works at a different speed, and she's delightfully modest and easy to work with." "She's one of the leading lights for sanctions." **Recent work:** Acted as sole counsel in Gill and others v SoS for the Home Department, an appeal against the proscription of the International Silk Youth Federation under the Terrorism Act 2000.

JUNIORS
Malcolm Birdling Respected junior who is regularly called upon to appear before all levels of court in complex human rights cases. He serves on the Attorney General's C Panel and is recognised for his in-depth knowledge of EU law. **Strengths:** "He can hit the ground running and really get his head around a case at top speed." "He's always a pleasure to deal with and judges are highly receptive to his advocacy style." **Recent work:** Acted in R (Letts) v Lord Chancellor, a high-profile case considering the obligation of the state to provide legal aid at inquests.

1 Crown Office Row
See profile on p.826
THE SET
1 Crown Office Row exhibits considerable strength in the field of civil liberties and human rights, stemming from its notable proficiency in key areas such as medical, environmental and immigration law. Its esteemed members are regularly called upon to act for government departments in major human rights disputes concerning freedom of information, national security and terrorism. Recently, a number of its barristers acted for the government in Begraj and Begraj v Ministry of Justice, an Article 6 claim for significant damages on the grounds of 'caste discrimination.'
Client service: "Their clerks are fantastic in terms of fees and costs issues." "The clerking team is wonderfully accommodating." Matthew Phipps is the senior clerk.

SILKS
Angus McCullough QC Esteemed human rights lawyer, who centres much of his work around environment and health-related matters and demonstrates considerable expertise in major inquests. He is noted for his deft handling of cases concerning deportation, forced marriage and clinical negligence. **Strengths:** "He has an air of authority whilst remaining completely down to earth, and is a pleasure to work with." "He's really clued up on terrorism and fair trial questions."

Philip Havers QC Esteemed silk with a diverse and wide-ranging portfolio of human rights and civil liberties work. He is highly respected for his approach to sensitive cases concerning matters such as mental health, assisted suicide and complex aspects of clinical negligence. **Strengths:** "He speaks with huge authority in court and has a wonderful style." "He's very thorough." **Recent work:** Represented the trust in the case of Bostridge v Oxleas Foundation Trust, considering whether a mental patient could claim damages for an ECHR Article 5 infraction.

Jeremy Hyam QC Newly minted silk offering a wealth of experience in the civil liberties and human rights sphere. His broad-based expertise encompasses areas such as health, environment and professional discipline, while he has a particularly well-established reputation in the field of administrative and public law. **Strengths:** "He pushes the boundaries with great success; Jeremy knows his areas of law inside-out and is always happy to go the extra mile on behalf of his clients."

JUNIORS
Shaheen Rahman Noted junior with a strong track record in the realm of civil liberties and human rights. She is particularly highly regarded for her deep knowledge of prison law, advising recently on the proposed smoking ban, and is frequently instructed in matters concerning disability, religious freedom and EU law. **Strengths:** "She was really impressive on her feet." **Recent work:** Served as Special Advocate in CF v SSHD, a long-running terrorism-related activity case.

Adam Wagner Versatile junior who regularly appears in high-profile human rights cases, both for and against public authorities. He is well regarded for his aptitude in the fields of immigration and prison law, and is also known for his work in public inquiries. He further serves on the Attorney General's C Panel of Counsel and runs the acclaimed UK Human Rights Blog. **Strengths:** "He's very enthusiastic about the case, good on the law and gives clear advice." **Recent work:** Represented the State in Begraj and Begraj v Ministry of Justice, striking out an Article 6 damages claim, which resulted from an unprecedented 'caste discrimination' claim.

39 Essex Chambers
See profile on p.840
THE SET
39 Essex Chambers has a long-standing reputation in the field given its impressive bench of quality advocates, all of whom are well equipped to handle cutting-edge civil liberties and human rights matters. A strong base of experience in public law enables the barristers housed in the set to assist clients with human rights issues across a number of disciplines. The chambers also continues to attract instructions in major judicial review proceedings and high-value HRA damages claims. Significant matters recently handled by the set include R (Nicklinson and Lamb) v Secretary of State for Justice, a case challenging the criminalisation of assisted suicide.
Client service: "The clerking is brilliant, there's nothing they won't do for you." David Barnes is the chief executive and director of clerking.

SILKS
Nigel Pleming QC Draws on vast experience of handling administrative and public law matters, including individual human rights-related matters and commercial regulations. He is known for his frequent appearances in landmark civil liberties cases, which he handles in Hong Kong and the Caribbean, as well as domestically. **Strengths:** "He is a very charming individual and good with the court." "He's pragmatic and has a strong understanding of local and central government." **Recent work:** Acted for the appellant in the Supreme Court case R (Bancoult) v Secretary of State for Foreign and Commonwealth Affairs. This was a case concerning the government's decision to ban fishing around the Chagos Islands and to establish a Marine Protected Area.

Jenni Richards QC (see p.751) Respected human rights silk who routinely acts for both claimants and defendants. She demonstrates great skill across a number of areas, including local government, prison law and community care. **Strengths:** "From the first meeting it was clear that she was switched on, direct, confident and always has everything under control." "A brilliant advocate who can get to the heart of the matter." **Recent work:** Acted for mental health patient Dale Lee-Hirons against the Secretary of State for Justice, on the requirement to justify a patient's recall to hospital under ECHR Article 5.

Lisa Giovannetti QC Esteemed practitioner offering expert advice on asylum, immigration and national security. She is regularly sought out by public authorities, government bodies and individual claimants, often appearing on their behalf before the Supreme Court and the ECHR. **Strengths:** "She's pleasant to deal with and intellectually very strong." "She is measured and clear in her advice, and her advocacy goes down very well with the court." **Recent work:** Successfully defended the Home Secretary against a challenge to the decision to summarily remove foreign students whose fraudulent English language test results were no longer valid.

Fenella Morris QC Dynamic silk with a highly varied practice and a wealth of experience in civil liberties and human rights. She has a strong track record of handling complex matters within commercial, health and social care contexts, often tackling significant cases at the ECHR and before all levels of domestic court. **Strengths:** "She's good on mental health stuff." **Recent work:** Acted in R (YZ) v Oxleas NHS Foundation Trust and others, a claim for damages for false imprisonment and breaches of the ECHR. The claimant was a transsexual psychiatric patient who had been moved into a maximum security environment against his will.

James Strachan QC Well versed in the arena of civil liberties and human rights, he regularly contributes to high-profile cases centring on complex issues such as miscarriages of justice and the classification of Scientology as a religion. **Strengths:** "He's smooth in a way that judges like, and he makes complicated propositions seem simple." **Recent work:** Appeared for the State in R (Nicklinson and Lamb) v Secretary of State for Justice, a case considering the legality of assisted suicide and the 'right to die' of a man suffering from locked-in syndrome.

JUNIORS

Victoria Butler-Cole Focuses her practice on health and social care-related violations of human rights. She regularly handles significant damages claims and is highly regarded for her skilful handling of complex judicial review proceedings. **Strengths:** "She cuts to the chase and she's very precise and clear in her presentation." "An impressive junior, she is clear, focused, hard working and diligent." **Recent work:** Acted in The Queen (on the application of LF) v HM Senior Coroner for Inner South London. This case helped to define what constitutes deprivation of liberty (Article 5) in hospital intensive care settings, and the meaning of state detention under the Coroners and Justice Act 2009.

Tom Cross (see p.627) Often appears unled in key civil liberties and human rights cases. His broad practice encompasses prison law, complex judicial reviews and significant claims for damages. He displays particular strength in the area of religious rights, a topic on which he has recently co-authored an acclaimed book. **Strengths:** "He has a deep understanding of the law and is always pleasant to deal with." "He's very personable and very well informed on equality issues." **Recent work:** Instructed by the government in Smith v Carillion, a case which queried whether the limitation of detriment claims arising from union membership was compatible with ECHR Article 11.

11KBW

See profile on p.867

THE SET

Members of 11KBW are adept at tackling a diverse range of civil liberties and human rights matters, displaying capability across areas such as immigration, mental health, sanctions and information law. Its broad client base mainly comprises defendants, although the set is also well regarded for its adept representation of claimants. It has a track record of undertaking pro bono and publicly funded work. Its skilled members are regularly called upon by individuals, government departments, local authorities, regulatory bodies and NGOs in significant cases. A recent highlight for the set has been its instruction in R(Barda) v Mayor of London, a challenge to a decision to fence off part of Parliament Square Gardens to prevent its occupation by demonstrators. The matter centred on Articles 10 and 11 of the ECHR, the issues of right to assembly and free speech.

Client service: "The clerks are accommodating, helpful and always polite and courteous." Lucy Barbet and Mark Dann are the joint senior clerks leading the team.

SILKS

Jonathan Swift QC (see p.777) Demonstrates a thorough command of civil liberties and human rights cases, and is also an expert in constitutional law, data protection and planning law. He shows particular proficiency in major cases concerning international sanctions and national security. **Strengths:** "Within seconds of speaking to him, you can tell he's an expert." "He's a very effective advocate." **Recent work:** Defended the Foreign Secretary against a challenge regarding the legality of a decision which placed the claimants, Ahmed Sarkandi and others, on a list of sanctioned individuals.

Nigel Giffin QC (see p.653) Public law specialist with particularly deep knowledge of local government and environment law. He offers a wealth of experience in complex judicial review proceedings. **Strengths:** "He is approachable, bright and very knowledgeable about public law and procurement." "He is incisive, hard working, on top of the law and a great advocate on his feet."

Karen Steyn QC (see p.773) Given her extensive experience in the field of civil liberties and human rights, she often appears before both British courts and the ECHR. She is frequently instructed on behalf of local authorities, regulatory bodies and claimant individuals. **Strengths:** "She's phenomenally hard working, she writes exceptionally well and is a fantastic team player who's liked by clients and solicitors alike." "She's very analytical and thorough in her work." **Recent work:** Acted for the government in R (Evans) v Attorney General, a challenge brought against the decision to veto disclosure of letters written to ministers by Prince Charles.

Jason Coppel QC (see p.624) Tackles a broad array of cutting-edge human rights work, both in the British courts and in the ECHR. Operating as a member of the Attorney General's 'A' Panel, he is regularly called upon to represent various departments of the central UK government. **Strengths:** "He's a slick operator, a good advocate and good on paper too." "He is wonderfully clear and persuasive in court." **Recent work:** Defended the government against a number of claims, brought domestically and in EU courts, regarding the right of UK prisoners to vote in General and European Parliament elections.

JUNIORS

Joanne Clement (see p.619) Highly regarded for her adept representation of both claimant and defendant clients, often in landmark human rights cases. Her comprehensive offering covers areas such as privacy rights, religious freedoms and deaths in detention. **Strengths:** "Her written advocacy is wonderful, she's a very impressive advocate." **Recent work:** Acted for the defence in R (Dyer) v the Welsh Ministers and Abertawe Bro Morgannwg University Health Board and others. This matter involved a claim that NHS entities had illegally failed to provide regional accommodation for a mental health patient, therefore breaching ECHR Article 8 and the UN Convention on the Rights of Persons with Disabilities.

Landmark Chambers

See profile on p.873

THE SET

This well-regarded chambers routinely attracts instructions from NGOs, commercial entities and the government. The set houses a deep bench of highly skilled juniors and silks, who offer specialist expertise in areas such as immigration, healthcare, environment, social welfare and planning, and are particularly well thought of for their deft handling of complex judicial review proceedings. Recent work carried out by this chambers includes Idira v SSHD, a case considering the legality of detaining immigrants in prison rather than specific Immigration Removal Centres.

Client service: "Their clerks are highly competent, they provide very fast responses and always give us options." "They're always willing to help and very reliable." Jay Fullilove leads the clerking team.

SILKS

Nathalie Lieven QC Standout silk with an almost unrivalled reputation for handling civil liberties and human rights-related cases. Her diverse client base consists of both private and corporate claimants, NGOs and central and local government. Well known for her depth of expertise, she is particularly praised for her work in the fields of immigration, environment and planning law. **Strengths:** "She's got impeccable judgement, she's highly experienced and she can present a difficult case highly attractively." "She's great on her feet, robust and likeable as an advocate." **Recent work:** Acted in Northern Irish Human Rights Commission v Northern Ireland Minister for Justice, a landmark case regarding abortion and the scope of the HRA.

Richard Drabble QC Highly experienced practitioner with vast experience of appearing before all levels of UK courts and European judicial authorities. He is particularly well known for his appellate work and deep knowledge of international law and local government issues, such as planning and public law. **Strengths:** "He will find a way to make something complex easy to understand." "A very effective advocate who chooses points carefully." **Recent work:** Appeared in Al-Sirri v Secretary of State DD (Afghanistan) v Secretary of State, a case considering whether the Geneva Convention protects people who have acted contrary to the principles of the UN.

Stephen Knafler QC A recent addition from Garden Court Chambers, he brings a wealth of expertise in areas such as community care, immigration, mental health and detention. He is able to draw upon his previous experience as a solicitor to inform his civil liberties and human rights work. **Strengths:** "He's a real asset with a huge amount of confidence. He brings clarity, simplicity and calmness to any case." "He is an authority in the field and has great courtroom presence." **Recent work:** Acted R (JM and others) v SSHD, a judicial review challenge to the lawfulness of the Fast Track Detention System.

James Maurici QC A highly experienced civil liberties and human rights silk who is regularly called on to appear in ground-breaking, high-profile cases. His highly active practice sees him regularly appearing before domestic, European and international courts. **Strengths:** "Given his encyclopaedic knowledge he is able to present and respond to anything thrown at him, and he's a pleasure to work with." "He is very intelligent and dedicated." **Recent work:** Represented Iraqi civilians in R (Ali Zaki Mousa) v Secretary of State for the Home Department. This case concerned nearly 200 unlawful killings of Iraqi civilians by the British Armed Forces, and up to 800 cases of torture and degrading treatment.

JUNIORS

Tim Buley Operates at every level of domestic court, frequently appearing on behalf of central and local government, individuals and pressure groups. His portfolio encompasses diverse matters, covering areas such as planning, environmental, social welfare and immigration. **Strengths:** "He's very good at focusing on the main issues and is highly impressive in court." "Judges have a lot of respect for him, he knows how to run the court." **Recent work:** Intervened on behalf of the Child Poverty Action Group in R (JS) v SSWP. This case investigated whether the state's £500 benefits cap discriminates against single parents and women.

Graham Denholm Particularly well known for his sterling work in the field of immigration, he routinely undertakes complex deportation and asylum cases. He frequently brings civil actions and judicial reviews against the Home Office with regard to immigration detention, and offers further expertise in the fields of social security and planning. **Strengths:** "He's reliable, knowledgeable and intuitive, and his written work is very strong." "He is very clued up on the judicial review process, is very persuasive and is good on his feet." **Recent work:** Acted in Idira v SSHD, a case considering the legality of holding detained immigrants in prison grounds instead of specific Immigration Removal Centres.

Zoe Leventhal Routinely instructed in high-profile matters in the human rights field, she displays a particular flair for environmental, planning, immigration and social security law. She has experience of appearing before the Supreme Court and regularly acts for both claimants and the government. **Strengths:** "She always sees both sides of the argument, and has a really strong knowledge of the legislation." "She shows total dedication to her cases and clients." **Recent work:** Acted in Mirga v Secretary of State for Work and Pensions. This case considered the lawfulness of the UK benefit system for EU migrant workers and, in particular, the compatibility of the 'right to reside' test with EU law.

Declan O'Callaghan Highly experienced senior junior offering a wealth of expertise across diverse areas such as mental health, asylum, unlawful detention, prisoners' rights and the death penalty. His renowned practice is international in scope, involving in situ pro bono work as far afield as India and Sri Lanka. **Strengths:** "He continues to lead the pack on cases relating to immigration." "He's affable and works wonderfully in a team by keeping things dynamic and organised." **Recent work:** Served as Amicus Curiae to the Ugandan High Court in the Kigula Beneficiaries Appeals. He assisted with the resentencing of over 600 death penalty cases following the declaration that the imposition of the mandatory death penalty was unconstitutional.

Other Ranked Lawyers

Mark Hill QC (see p.671) (Francis Taylor Building) Well versed in complex human rights matters pertaining to faith and religious liberty. He is particularly highly regarded for this niche specialism, and is a regular feature in domestic, European and US courts. **Strengths:** "He is a particularly sharp drafter." **Recent work:** Acted in Khaira v Shergill, a dispute regarding the ownership and management of two Sikh Gurdwaras.

Richard Clayton QC (4-5 Gray's Inn Square) Routinely instructed in major constitutional and human rights matters which see him making regular appearances in the Privy Council and Supreme Court. He has co-authored an essential textbook on human rights and serves as the UK representative to the Venice Commission. **Strengths:** "His command of the subject is almost second to none. He's thoughtful, approachable, and very client-focused." **Recent work:** Acted in Magyar Helsinki v Hungary, a case considering whether freedom of expression under Article 10 includes a right of access to information.

Tom Poole (3 Hare Court) Highly regarded junior in the field of civil liberties and human rights. He habitually handles significant matters concerning unlawful detention, discrimination and immigration, and demonstrates key strength in appellate matters, especially before the Privy Council. **Strengths:** "Very fair and very knowledgeable, he tends to handle the state's work and he's excellent at that." "He has a fantastic intellect, and he is absolutely thorough and reliable." **Recent work:** Appeared in The Queen (on the application of MD Haider Ali) v SSHD, a claim involving the detention by the Home Secretary of a foreign national suffering from a mental illness.

Stephen Cragg QC (Monckton Chambers) Renowned human rights silk with a particular focus on social welfare, criminal justice and community care cases. He habitually represents claimants at inquests and in police law matters. Additionally, he serves on the Executive of the Bar Human Rights Committee. **Strengths:** "He's easy to work with, committed and knowledgeable." "He is highly respected for the breadth of his experience and for his innovative litigation." **Recent work:** Acted in R (T, JB) v SSJ and SSHD, successfully challenging the compatibility of the Rehabilitation of Offenders Act and Criminal Records disclosure policy with ECHR Article 8.

Piers Gardner (Monckton Chambers) Highly regarded for his in-depth knowledge of EU law, particularly the ECHR. He advises throughout the UK and Europe on data and property protection, jurisdictional issues and extradition matters. **Strengths:** "He's completely transparent, easy to talk to, and his research and writing are fantastic." "He has a great understanding of people and complex legal situations." **Recent work:** Represented the claimant refugee in Trushin v National Crime Agency, a challenge to the NCA's processing of his personal data without purpose or justification.

Eric Metcalfe (Monckton Chambers) Esteemed human rights practitioner who is a familiar face in the Supreme Court. He regularly handles high-profile, sensitive cases on behalf of a diverse clientele, and offers specialist insight into matters concerning the EU Charter of Fundamental Rights. **Strengths:** "He has a very nice manner in court and is clearly very competent." "Eric Metcalfe is very good, a sound young junior." **Recent work:** Acted in Liberty and others v GCHQ and others. This was a challenge brought by Liberty concerning the UK intelligence services' disproportionate use of blanket surveillance of mobile phones and emails.

Azeem Suterwalla (see p.776) (Monckton Chambers) Respected practitioner with a broad human rights practice. He demonstrates particular insight into the rights of children, social housing law and matters concerning state retention of information. He is regularly instructed in major human rights cases at all levels of UK court. **Strengths:** "He's a very good trial lawyer with a sensible, pragmatic, no-nonsense approach." "Azeem Suterwalla is efficient and always ready to help with queries." **Recent work:** Acted for the claimants in SSHD v Davis, a case considering whether certain state data retention powers breach the EU Charter and Convention.

MIDLANDS

Civil Liberties & Human Rights
Leading Silks
Band 1
Clayton Richard *Kings Chambers* *
Khalique Nageena *No5 Chambers* [A]

Ranked Lawyers

Richard Clayton QC (see p.618) (Kings Chambers) Habitually appears before the Supreme Court and Privy Council in a diverse range of matters pertaining to constitutional and human rights. He makes regular and valued contributions to textbooks on the HRA, and serves as the UK's representative in the Venice Commission. **Strengths:** "Very academic and a superb advocate." **Recent work:** Acted for the government of the UK as a third party in Magyar Helsinki v Hungary, a case which reached the Grand Chamber of the ECHR.

Nageena Khalique QC (No5 Chambers) Head of No5 Chambers' public law group, she routinely handles matters focused on human rights issues such as disability rights, freedom from arbitrary detention and the right to life. Her diverse client base includes individuals and public bodies, while her busy practice sees her making regular appearances before the Court of Appeal. **Strengths:** "She's user-friendly, concise in her advocacy and good with clients." "Her written work is outstanding; her skeletons appear in judgements without any amendment." **Recent work:** Represented the deceased's son in the inquest into the death of Iris Chapman, an individual who had been a resident in a care home. The matter investigated the deceased's deprivation of liberty under the Mental Capacity Act and involved considerations of systemic neglect and corporate manslaughter.

NORTHERN

Civil Liberties & Human Rights
Leading Sets
Band 1
Doughty Street Chambers *
Garden Court North
Kings Chambers *
Leading Silks
Band 1
Weatherby Pete *Garden Court North*
Leading Juniors
Band 1
Stanage Nick *Doughty Street Chambers* [A]
Band 2
Fullwood Adam *39 Essex Chambers (ORL)* ◊
Jagadesham Vijay *Garden Court North*
Karim Sam *Kings Chambers* *
Nicholson John *Kenworthy's Chambers (ORL)* ◊
Stanbury Matthew *Garden Court North*
* *Indicates set / individual with profile.*
[A] *direct access (see p.24).*
◊ *(ORL) = Other Ranked Lawyer.*
Alphabetical order within each band. Band 1 is highest.

Band 1

Doughty Street Chambers

See profile on p.828

THE SET

Doughty Street Chambers demonstrates strong capabilities in the area of civil liberties and human rights. Its members offer deep knowledge of the HRA and ECHR, and are well versed in all aspects of international human rights law. The set is regularly called upon by a range of clients, including trade union members, vulnerable individuals and non-governmental organisations, given its comprehensive insight into areas such as immigration, deprivation of liberty and freedom of expression. Instructing solicitors describe Doughty Street as "an extremely dynamic and energising set to work with."

Client service: "The clerking is always extremely effective. They are always keen to help and go out of their way to assist." Mark Dembovsky is the set's chief executive.

JUNIORS

Nick Stanage Highly regarded junior offering a broad range of expertise, encompassing areas such as immigration, actions against the police and significant judicial reviews. His human rights practice also extends to handling detainees' rights in several foreign jurisdictions such as Jordan, Tunisia and Turkey. **Strengths:** "He is an astute and quick-witted advocate with excellent analytical skills." "He has the ability to empathise with clients and to explain legal issues clearly."

Garden Court North

THE SET

Garden Court North houses an established team of barristers who are committed to the field of civil liberties and human rights. Its strong track record in areas such as immigration, asylum, prison law and miscarriages of justice distinguishes the chambers as a go-to human rights set outside of London. Alongside its stellar reputation domestically, Garden Court offers a practice which is international in scope, with members frequently tackling major human rights matters as far afield as Bahrain, Colombia and the USA.

Client service: Sarah Wright is the senior clerk.

SILKS

Pete Weatherby QC Accomplished human rights silk who routinely handles matters concerning protests, miscarriages of justice and complex elements of prison law. He is well versed in EU and international human rights issues, and regularly attracts instructions in high-profile, significant judicial reviews. **Strengths:** "He is thorough, efficient and effective." "His approach is very inclusive, which makes him a pleasure to work with. He's a wonderful team player."

JUNIORS

Vijay Jagadesham Respected junior offering broad-based expertise in areas such as immigration, prison law and data protection. He is particularly well known for his deft handling of matters involving vulnerable adults.

Matthew Stanbury Highly regarded for his wide-ranging civil liberties practice, encompassing areas such as Court of Protection cases, miscarriages of justice, prisoner-related judicial reviews and significant Crown Court matters. His diverse client base includes prisoners, bereaved families and various individuals facing criminal charges.

Kings Chambers

See profile on p.968

THE SET

Kings Chambers continues to stand out in the field of civil liberties and human rights, regularly attracting instructions in high-profile matters concerning asylum law, planning and mental health issues. The set is recognised for its adroit handling of complex matters on behalf of both claimants and defendants, with a recent highlight being its involvement in Magyar Helsinki v Hungary. This was a case considering whether freedom of expression under Article 10 includes a right of access to information.

Client service: "The clerks keep everything up to date and keep us well informed." William Brown is the chief clerk for planning, environmental, administrative and public law and local government.

JUNIORS

Sam Karim (see p.688) Accomplished junior with a flourishing civil liberties and human rights practice. He regularly undertakes pro bono work on behalf of a range of clients, and offers vast expertise in areas such as prison, education, immigration and healthcare law. **Strengths:** "He's a very skilful advocate who is always remarkably calm and in control, he never gets fazed by the complexities of a case." "He puts his points across succinctly and never wavers." **Recent work:** Acted for the Secretary of State for Business, Innovation and Skills in a commercial judicial review. The investigated a decision made by the Secretary to investigate a company and seek information without outlining specific concerns in light of Sections 447 and 452A of the Companies Act 1985.

Other Ranked Lawyers

Adam Fullwood (39 Essex Chambers) Focuses his respected civil liberties and human rights practice on the representation of care providers and care home proprietors. He is noted for his expert knowledge of local government and education law, and offers particular insight into cases concerning complex mental health issues. **Strengths:** "He is very subtle, very accessible to clients and a very effective, straightforward advocate." "He's very good in complex cases."

John Nicholson (Kenworthy's Chambers) Respected senior junior whose practice has a particular emphasis on immigration issues, such as detention and deportation. He regularly undertakes work on behalf of individuals seeking asylum or fleeing persecution, and is particularly noted for his deft handling of significant judicial review proceedings. **Strengths:** "For immigration, he's one of the best claimant barristers on the Northern Circuit. He fights every point for his clients and is absolutely dedicated."

Contents:

LONDON

Clinical Negligence
Leading Sets
Band 1
1 Crown Office Row *
Band 2
Serjeants' Inn Chambers *
Band 3
Hailsham Chambers *
Band 4
7BR *
Outer Temple Chambers *
2TG - 2 Temple Gardens *
Band 5
1 Chancery Lane
Cloisters *
Crown Office Chambers *
9 Gough Square *
Band 6
Devereux *
Doughty Street Chambers *
39 Essex Chambers *
* Indicates set / individual with profile.
🄰 direct access (see p.24).
◊ (ORL) = Other Ranked Lawyer.
Alphabetical order within each band. Band 1 is highest.

Clinical Negligence	
Senior Statesmen	
Senior Statesmen: distinguished older partners	
Badenoch James *1 Crown Office Row*	
Leading Silks	
Star individuals	**Burton** Frank *12 King's Bench Walk (ORL)* ◊ *
Maskrey Simeon *7BR*	**Donovan** Joel *Cloisters* *
Band 1	**Evans** David *1 Crown Office Row*
Bishop Edward *1 Chancery Lane*	**Forde** Martin *1 Crown Office Row*
Block Neil *39 Essex Chambers* *	**Harrison** Caroline *2TG - 2 Temple Gardens* 🄰 *
Bowron Margaret *1 Crown Office Row*	**Hitchcock** Patricia *Cloisters* *
Browne Benjamin *2TG - 2 Temple Gardens* *	**Mylonas** Michael *Serjeants' Inn Chambers* *
de Navarro Michael *2TG - 2 Temple Gardens* 🄰 *	**Nolan** Dominic *Hailsham Chambers* *
Francis Robert *Serjeants' Inn Chambers* *	**Pittaway** David *Hailsham Chambers* *
Gibson Christopher *Outer Temple Chambers*	**Porter** Martin *2TG - 2 Temple Gardens* 🄰 *
Glancy Robert *Devereux* *	**Readhead** Simon *1 Chancery Lane*
Gumbel Elizabeth-Anne *1 Crown Office Row*	**Ritchie** Andrew *9 Gough Square* *
Havers Philip *1 Crown Office Row*	**Rodway** Susan *39 Essex Chambers*
Hopkins Adrian *Serjeants' Inn Chambers* *	**Watson** James *Serjeants' Inn Chambers* *
Hutton Alexander *Hailsham Chambers* *	**Band 3**
Johnston Christopher *Serjeants' Inn Chambers* *	**Bebb** Gordon *Outer Temple Chambers*
Lambert Christina *1 Crown Office Row*	**Coonan** Kieran *1 Crown Office Row*
McCullough Angus *1 Crown Office Row*	**de Bono** John *Serjeants' Inn Chambers* *
Miller Stephen *1 Crown Office Row*	**Edis** William *1 Crown Office Row*
Moon Angus *Serjeants' Inn Chambers* *	**Hugh-Jones** George *Serjeants' Inn Chambers* *
Oppenheim Robin *Doughty Street Chambers*	**Levy** Jacob *9 Gough Square* *
Post Andrew *Hailsham Chambers* *	**O'Rourke** Mary *Old Square Chambers (ORL)* ◊
Rees Paul *1 Crown Office Row*	**Preston** Hugh *7BR* 🄰
Spencer Martin *Hailsham Chambers* 🄰 *	**New Silks**
Sweeting Derek *7BR* 🄰	**Bradley** Clodagh *1 Crown Office Row*
Taylor Simon W *Cloisters*	**Dolan** Bridget *Serjeants' Inn Chambers* *
Vaughan Jones Sarah *2TG - 2 Temple Gardens* *	**Gollop** Katharine *Serjeants' Inn Chambers* *
Weir Robert *Devereux* *	**Horne** Michael *Serjeants' Inn Chambers* *
Westcott David *Outer Temple Chambers*	**Hyam** Jeremy *1 Crown Office Row*
Whitting John *1 Crown Office Row*	**Latimer-Sayer** William *Cloisters* *
Wilson-Smith Christopher *Outer Temple Chambers* *	**Skelton** Peter *1 Crown Office Row*
Band 2	**Thomas** Owain *1 Crown Office Row*
Aldous Grahame *9 Gough Square* *	**Weitzman** Adam *7BR*
Antelme Alexander *Crown Office Chambers*	**Witcomb** Henry *1 Crown Office Row*
Booth Richard *1 Crown Office Row*	

Band 1

1 Crown Office Row

See profile on p.826

THE SET

1 Crown Office Row warrants its current position as London's leading set in the clinical negligence market as it houses a fine array of highly capable silks and juniors whose depth of knowledge and expertise is well acknowledged. The set's already impressive roster of silks was boosted this year when six new silks were appointed, a number of whom have expertise in clinical negligence. Members bring to bear a breadth of experience in all areas of the sector, and handle cases of the utmost severity and of the highest value. They continue to be instructed in very high-profile cases both within the UK and in various other jurisdictions including the Caribbean and Hong Kong.

Client service: The clerking team is led by the highly regarded Matthew Phipps. "Their clerking is second to none. No other chambers compares to them and the benefit is that when you ring up you immediately go to a clerk and they're very good at getting back to you. The team is just great and is one of the biggest selling points of the chambers."

SILKS

James Badenoch QC A highly skilled barrister with expert knowledge and experience of clinical negligence amassed over a lengthy career. He is noted for his unrivalled understanding of the medical field. **Strengths:** "An absolutely first-rate advocate." "He's in a league of his own." "A brilliant cross-examiner who is completely in command of things."

Margaret Bowron QC Highly regarded barrister, representing both claimants and defendants in high-value clinical negligence claims. Widely recognised within the clinical negligence community for her specialist expertise, she devotes a substantial part of her practice to claims of the utmost complexity and severity. **Strengths:** "She's very concise in her advice and she's exceedingly good in the way she manages a case." "She's excellent, experienced, knows what she's doing and you just know there's going to be no nonsense." **Recent work:** Acted on behalf of a claimant who had suffered cerebral palsy along with a brachial plexus injury.

Elizabeth-Anne Gumbel QC Highly revered amongst peers for her wealth of knowledge and her significant expertise which she brings to bear when handling clinical negligence and personal injury claims. She is particularly good at cases pertaining to brain damage and birth injury claims. **Strengths:** "She is a powerhouse with a phenomenal work ethic and a huge heart." "She's just quality from start to finish." **Recent work:** Acted on behalf of various claimants who had undergone breast surgery which was alleged to have been inappropriate.

Philip Havers QC Highly esteemed barrister noted for his far-reaching expertise in multiple areas of clinical negligence. He also devotes much of his practice to an array of other disciplines including personal injury, human rights and environmental. **Strengths:** "He's incredibly knowledgeable, vastly experienced and somebody you always feel completely safe with. " **Recent work:** Acted on behalf of the defendant, Hull NHS Trust, in a claim which alleged failure to deliver steroids to a pregnant woman during labour.

Christina Lambert QC A silk with a wealth of experience of acting on behalf of both claimants and defendants in an array of clinical negligence matters. Regularly handles major cases in the Court of Appeal and the Supreme Court, and has particular expertise

Clinical Negligence
Leading Juniors
Star individuals
Jackson Matthew *Hailsham Chambers* *
Band 1
Boyle Gerard *Serjeants' Inn Chambers* *
Cartwright Richard *Devereux* *
Davidson Ranald *Serjeants' Inn Chambers* *
Dyer Simon *Cloisters*
Ellis Peter *7BR* [A] *
Furniss Richard *42 Bedford Row (ORL)* ◇
Guthrie Cara *Outer Temple Chambers*
Hallissey Caroline *Serjeants' Inn Chambers* *
Jones Charlotte *Crown Office Chambers*
Korn Adam *7BR*
Mangat Tejina *Hailsham Chambers*
Matthews Julian D *7BR*
Mishcon Jane *Hailsham Chambers* *
Neale Fiona *Hailsham Chambers* *
Partridge Richard *Serjeants' Inn Chambers* *
Pendlebury Jeremy *7BR*
Tracy Forster Jane *Hailsham Chambers* *
Woolf Eliot *Outer Temple Chambers*
Band 2
Aldridge James *Outer Temple Chambers*
Baker Richard *7BR* *
Davy Neil *Serjeants' Inn Chambers* *
Formby Emily *39 Essex Chambers* *
Holl-Allen Jonathan *Serjeants' Inn Chambers* *
Hough Christopher *Doughty Street Chambers*
Kennedy Andrew *1 Crown Office Row*
Lambert Sarah *1 Crown Office Row*
Martin Bradley *2TG - 2 Temple Gardens* [A] *
Mauladad Farrah *Crown Office Chambers*
Price Clare *Hailsham Chambers* *
Samuel Gerwyn *Doughty Street Chambers*
Sullivan Lisa *Cloisters* *
Toogood Claire *Crown Office Chambers* *
Trusted Harry *Outer Temple Chambers*
Vickers Rachel *Outer Temple Chambers*
Walker Adam *7BR* *
Band 3
Barnes Matthew *1 Crown Office Row*
Begley Laura *9 Gough Square* *
Bradley Ben *Outer Temple Chambers*
Carpenter Jamie *Hailsham Chambers* *
Charles Henry *12 King's Bench Walk (ORL)* ◇ *
Cridland Simon *Serjeants' Inn Chambers* *
Ewins Catherine *Hailsham Chambers* *
Foster Charles *Serjeants' Inn Chambers* *
Godfrey Hannah *Cloisters* *
Goodwin Deirdre *7BR* *
Greaney Nicola *39 Essex Chambers* *
Hand Jonathan *Outer Temple Chambers* *
Harris Roger *2TG - 2 Temple Gardens* [A] *
Hockton Andrew *Serjeants' Inn Chambers* *
Johnson Laura *1 Chancery Lane* [A]
Keegan Leslie *7BR*
Kemp Christopher *Outer Temple Chambers*
King Simon *7BR*
Matthewson Scott *42 Bedford Row (ORL)* ◇
Meakin Timothy *7BR* [A]
Peacock Nicholas *Hailsham Chambers* *
Powell Debra *Serjeants' Inn Chambers* *
Rahman Shaheen *1 Crown Office Row*
Rogerson Judith *1 Crown Office Row*
Sheldon Neil *1 Crown Office Row*
Stephenson Christopher *9 Gough Square* *
Tavares Nathan *Outer Temple Chambers*
Band 4
Bertram Jonathan *7BR* *
Bloom Margaret *Hardwicke (ORL)* ◇
Catford Gordon *Crown Office Chambers*
Colin Giles *1 Crown Office Row*
Hill Matthew *1 Crown Office Row*
Jacobs Linda *Cloisters* *
Knight Heidi *Serjeants' Inn Chambers* *
McKechnie Stuart *9 Gough Square* *
McLeish Martyn *Cloisters*
Mortimer Sophie *1 Chancery Lane*
Myhill David *Crown Office Chambers* *
Naughton Sebastian *Serjeants' Inn Chambers* *
Power Eloise *Serjeants' Inn Chambers* *
Stagg Paul *1 Chancery Lane* [A]
Thomson David *1 Chancery Lane*
Wheatley Simon *7BR*
Wraight William *2TG - 2 Temple Gardens* *
Up-and-coming individuals
Hughes Anna *2TG - 2 Temple Gardens* *
Juckes David *Hailsham Chambers* *
Rathod Pritesh *1 Crown Office Row*
* *Indicates individual with profile.*
[A] *direct access (see p.24).*
◇ *(ORL) = Other Ranked Lawyer.*
Alphabetical order within each band. Band 1 is highest.

in wrongful birth claims and complex medical matters. **Strengths:** "There are very few people who are better on their feet than her." "A star of her generation. She has a wonderful grasp of the detail of a case but can also see the bigger picture and is an excellent strategist."

Angus McCullough QC An experienced advocate who commands great respect amongst his peers for his evident skills. His expertise stretches beyond just clinical negligence matters, encompassing such areas as health, environmental law and human rights. **Strengths:** "He's brilliant with the clients and highly incisive and intelligent." "He is incredibly clever, very astute and a fine advocate." **Recent work:** Served as leading silk representing the defendant in a claim relating to negligent spinal cord surgery.

Stephen Miller QC Has a stellar reputation as one of the doyens of the clinical negligence world, having amassed a wealth of specialist knowledge over a lengthy career. He focuses his practice on high-profile, high-value cases including inquiries and multi-party actions. **Strengths:** "He is an extremely smooth advocate and someone with vast experience who has profound knowledge." "If you need a power hitter then Stephen is the guy to go to as he has gravitas and experience."

Paul Rees QC Highly revered by his peers, he is widely recognised for his involvement in some of the most significant cases tried in the High Court and the Court of Appeal. **Strengths:** "Exceptionally skilled negotiator." "He is incredibly forensic and you get 100% with him." "Works fantastically hard and has great attention to detail."

John Whitting QC An experienced advocate sought after by both claimants and defendants for his skill and expertise in a wide array of clinical negligence matters of various degrees of complexity and value. His particular area of interest lies in spinal cord injury claims and brain damage cases. **Strengths:** "He's one of the fiercest and brightest cross-examiners I've ever seen. He's a real destroyer in cross-examination." "He's razor sharp." **Recent work:** Defended East Kent University NHS Foundation Trust in a case where it was alleged by the claimant that she had not been informed that her unborn child faced a 3% risk of suffering a chromosomal abnormality.

Richard Booth QC Has a broad practice encompassing multiple areas of medical law. He also specialises in various other disciplines such as personal injury, veterinary law and sports law. **Strengths:** "Robust and excellent advocate." "He is a very effective cross-examiner who has a very impressive grasp of the intricacies of the papers." **Recent work:** Successfully defended Medway NHS Foundation Trust against a claim which alleged failure to treat the claimant's stroke.

David Evans QC Recognised for his skill in handling clinical negligence matters of the highest value and utmost severity. He represents both claimants and defendants in an array of claims, primarily focusing his practice on spinal cord injury claims and brain damage cases. **Strengths:** "He is superb and a master of detail." "Exceptional with clients and a great strategist in high-value complex claims."

Martin Forde QC Has extensive expertise on the full gamut of health law, an area to which he devotes a substantial portion of his practice. Acting for both claimants and defendants, he undertakes clinical negligence claims of the greatest severity. **Strengths:** "He leaves no stone unturned in pursuit of the best outcome for his clients."

Kieran Coonan QC Has amassed a great wealth of knowledge and experience over his lengthy career spanning almost 50 years. He devotes much of his practice to the defence of medical professionals such as doctors and dentists and also lends his expertise to personal injury matters, inquests and public inquiries. **Strengths:** "He is very smooth and has a lovely manner. Clients love him."

William Edis QC Has a broad practice incorporating various aspects of clinical negligence law. He is known for his comprehensive knowledge of healthcare and medical law. **Strengths:** "A brilliant analytical mind." "Erudite and eloquent, and has a real charm about him."

Clodagh Bradley QC Has amassed over 20 years' experience practising in the field of medical law, gaining expertise in the most complicated areas of this field. She continues to handle an impressive caseload including obstetric, infant brain injury and GP negligence claims. **Strengths:** "A first-class barrister who fights to the end and provides sound advice." **Recent work:** Acted for a claimant who suffered cerebral palsy resulting from cardiac arrest.

Jeremy Hyam QC A specialist barrister, well versed in the field of clinical negligence law and highly experienced in all areas of medical law. He continues to develop his expertise in these areas as he builds his career as a new silk. **Strengths:** "He is thoughtful, calm under pressure and a good strategist."

Peter Skelton QC A prominent practitioner in the clinical negligence market who acts on behalf of both claimants and defendants in an array of medical matters. He is highly expert in the areas of inquests and inquiries and is currently leading the investigation regarding the Goddard Inquiry. **Strengths:** "Very assiduous and very practical." **Recent work:** Successfully represented the claimant in a claim against Hillingdon Hospital NHS Trust concerning its failure to advise the claimant of possible signs and symptoms of DVT after surgery.

Owain Thomas QC Represents both claimants and defendants in an array of clinical negligence matters, specifically focusing on high-value catastrophic injury cases including birth injury claims. He is also regularly sought out by various medical bodies for his capabilities in inquest work. **Strengths:** "He is super-bright and his attention to detail is incredible." "His ability to distil the key issues in a claim from a variety of complicated sources at lightning speed never fails to impress."

Henry Witcomb QC A distinguished practitioner widely recognised for his insightful knowledge and expertise on quantum. His practice encompasses all aspects of clinical negligence including wrongful death cases, brain injury matters and catastrophic spinal injury claims. **Strengths:** "Very knowledgeable when it comes to complex medical negligence cases." "Excellent on the quantification of complicated cases and fantastic with clients." **Recent work:** Currently representing numerous Kenyan women and girls who claim that British Airways pilot Simon Wood, who later committed suicide, sexually abused them.

JUNIORS

Andrew Kennedy Acts for claimants and defendants, tackling the most complex claims both in terms of value and difficulty. He has an extensive practice which branches out into professional discipline and other regulatory law. **Strengths:** "Hugely experienced and adopts a very thorough approach to a case." **Recent work:** Represented the defendant in a claim concerning the delayed diagnosis of a spinal tumour that ultimately resulted in the claimant suffering multiple injuries including psychiatric and mobility ones.

Sarah Lambert A widely respected junior with a wealth of knowledge and experience of operating in the clinical negligence and healthcare fields. She is highly adept at handling all manner of medical claims including those of the greatest difficulty. **Strengths:** "Particularly robust when dealing with high-value, complex clinical negligence matters." "She gets to the root of the case very quickly and is excellent on her feet." **Recent work:** Represented a claimant regarding the delayed diagnosis of what was found to be a spinal tumour which led to the claimant also suffering multiple bowel, psychiatric and bladder injuries.

Matthew Barnes Principally focuses his practice on all aspects of medical law including areas of public law, inquest work and clinical negligence. He devotes much of his practice to representing both claimants and defendants in catastrophic injury claims ranging in both value and complexity. **Strengths:** "An excellent practitioner and a very, very good advocate." "He has an exceptionally bright mind blended with great pragmatism and tactical thinking." **Recent work:** Currently acting on behalf of a claimant in a case concerning a catastrophic brain injury which the claimant sustained at birth.

Shaheen Rahman Frequently instructed by both claimants and defendants in cases of the highest value and greatest sensitivity, including claims arising from obstetric injuries and matters concerning delayed cancer diagnosis. **Strengths:** "She's bold and tenacious and she stands her ground." **Recent work:** Successfully represented the family of a deceased man who died as a result of intestinal obstruction, having been sent home on two occasions by A&E.

Judith Rogerson Has experience and knowledge in many areas of medical law, and handles various claims in relation to plastic surgery, GPs and gynaecology. She is also well versed in handling complex brain injury matters and undertakes inquest work. **Strengths:** "She's ambitious and realistic and makes sure she gets the best outcome for the client."

Neil Sheldon Frequently sought out by medical professionals for his extensive knowledge and expertise in the clinical negligence field. His experience representing both claimants and defendants before the GDC and GMC has earned praise from peers. **Strengths:** "Very bright and on the ball." "He's outstandingly good." "A highly persuasive advocate who achieves excellent results at trial."

Giles Colin Highly experienced barrister, who applies over 20 years of knowledge and expertise to his broad practice. His practice encompasses many areas of the law, including regulatory work, inquests and personal injury matters. **Strengths:** "He is a practical man who is personable and realistic."

Matthew Hill Experienced in clinical negligence law as well as other areas such as professional discipline. He is also an inquests and inquiries expert and he has recently returned from acting as first junior to the Hillsborough inquest. **Strengths:** "His written and oral advice is clear, concise and well thought out." **Recent work:** Acted on behalf of a defendant facing allegations of negligent spinal surgery.

Pritesh Rathod Distinguished legal practitioner, renowned for his specialist skills in the areas of clinical negligence and personal injury. He advises both claimants and defendants, acting in matters ranging in value and complexity. **Strengths:** "His advocacy is something that is strongly in his favour." **Recent work:** Acted on behalf of a claimant who had suffered severe brain damage as a result of the defendant's failure to identify a herpes virus contracted from the mother.

Band 2

Serjeants' Inn Chambers

See profile on p.907

THE SET

Serjeants' Inn receives praise for the excellence of its members and for the in-depth knowledge they bring to bear. Individuals here are greatly experienced in all areas of clinical negligence law and tackle cases of maximum value and complexity. Matters handled include claims relating to cerebral palsy, brain damage and spinal cord injury, amongst others. The set's talented silks and juniors are also regularly instructed in judicial reviews and multiparty actions, and further undertake medical disciplinary cases. Over the years, they have been involved in a number of law-changing cases including Sidaway and Chester v Afshar.

Client service: The clerks receive praise for their responsiveness and for their immediate resolution of any issues that arise. One interviewee stated: "The clerks are amazing. They go above and beyond and they strive to assist as much as they can."

SILKS

Robert Francis QC (see p.648) Applauded by peers and clients within the clinical negligence field for his outstanding wealth of knowledge and experience amassed over 30 years. He is regularly instructed in high-profile, complex cases. **Strengths:** "He is a formidable advocate and a tremendous negotiator." **Recent work:** Represented NHSLA in a case where it had been alleged that the claimant suffered a second stroke, resulting in him suffering 'locked-in syndrome', as a result of a hospital and ambulance failing to detect the stroke and thus delaying treatment.

Adrian Hopkins QC (see p.674) An esteemed silk who impresses peers and clients with his prowess. He represents both claimants and defendants and is highly sought after by leading firms seeking to benefit from his experience of handling high-value, complex cases. **Strengths:** "He is very impressive on all fronts." "His forensic analysis in really complicated, medical and factual cases is unsurpassed."

Christopher Johnston QC (see p.684) Standout practitioner who is revered for his analytical prowess and who has extensive experience of handling clinical negligence claims of great value and complexity. **Strengths:** "He is ferociously bright and a formidable opponent." "He's always meticulously prepared and gets fantastic results." **Recent work:** Successfully obtained a settlement on behalf of a claimant who suffered brain damage at birth.

Angus Moon QC (see p.720) Widely acknowledged for his expertise in the clinical negligence arena and for his involvement in high-profile, complex cases. He continues to represent both claimants and defendants in cases of the utmost severity. **Strengths:** "He has an impressive ability to absorb the complexities of a case and cut through them to the main issues, expressing his views in a concise and easy-to-understand way." **Recent work:** Acted in Reaney v North Staff Trust, a case regarding the test of causation in the Court of Appeal.

Michael Mylonas QC (see p.725) Applauded for the breadth of his practice, he is regularly sought after to lead high-profile, high-value cases. **Strengths:** "His preparation is meticulous and he gets fantastic results for clients." "He is a powerful and formidable court advocate." **Recent work:** Successfully recovered up to 93% of damages along with education costs for a claimant who was born prematurely and underweight, and who suffered brain damage as a result of being discharged without the defendant hospital checking his blood sugar levels.

James Watson QC (see p.791) Impresses with his knowledge and experience of handling high-value cases, specifically those involving claims of brain damage or obstetric injury. He represents both claimants and defendants. **Strengths:** "He has an eye for detail and his meticulous preparation and focus really distinguish him from the rest of the crowd." "He is very experienced and absolutely knows the ins and outs of clinical negligence." **Recent work:** Led in a claim brought against a GP who had allegedly failed to diagnose the claimant's arm ischaemia, resulting in the amputation of the limb.

John de Bono QC (see p.631) Admired in the clinical negligence world for his legal prowess and involvement in high-profile claims. He acts on behalf of defendants and claimants, and is frequently instructed in the most difficult cases. **Strengths:** "A highly intelligent, considerate and astute barrister. His knowledge, experience and ability to tackle and explain complex issues with ease is invaluable."

Recent work: Served as counsel to child claimants petitioning for damages following their sexual abuse by Addenbrooke's Hospital paediatrician Dr Myles Bradbury.

George Hugh-Jones QC (see p.677) Experienced practitioner with a far-reaching medical law practice that incorporates many areas including inquest work. **Strengths:** "An excellent advocate with first-class drafting and client care skills." "He is so thorough and very trustworthy." **Recent work:** Acted as claimant counsel in an appeal where the defendant had failed to notice spots on the claimant's body and as a result failed to diagnose meningitis.

Bridget Dolan QC (see p.635) A distinguished practitioner who has many years of experience. Having been a former forensic psychologist, she has particular expertise in cases surrounding psychiatric healthcare, and handles both matters arising out of negligence by psychiatric healthcare professionals and claims for damages for psychiatric injury following negligently inflicted physical injury. **Strengths:** "She has an excellent command of complex issues."

Katharine Gollop QC (see p.656) Well-regarded barrister who is well versed in undertaking complex matters on behalf of both claimant and defendant parties. She continues to broaden and develop her practice, and has undertaken a number of cosmetic, stillbirth and psychiatric cases. **Strengths:** "She has a strong work ethic and immerses herself in a case, using her keen analytical skills to good effect, and responding quickly to queries and instructions when needed." "She's a tough negotiator and has very sound judgement." **Recent work:** Involved in a case alleging the delayed diagnosis of subarachnoid haemorrhage.

Michael Horne QC (see p.675) Has amassed a great wealth of experience having practised in this area of law since his call in 1992. He possesses significant expertise in handling cases involving severe neurological injuries or complex birth injuries. **Strengths:** "His attention to detail is such as I have never known and he's more on top of the medicine than some of the doctors." "He has a particularly sensitive, empathetic and gentle manner with clients, yet combines this with a razor-sharp intellect and judgement." "He is exceptionally thorough and he leaves no stone unturned." **Recent work:** Instructed on behalf of a claimant who sustained a severe brain injury and later died after suffering cardiac arrest 12 days subsequent to cardiac bypass surgery.

JUNIORS

Gerard Boyle (see p.601) Frequently instructed by leading medical bodies including the MPS and MDDUS to undertake highly complex cases. **Strengths:** "He has a really sharp mind and gets to the root of the problem quickly." "An excellent advocate with first-class drafting skills." **Recent work:** Acted on behalf of a GP successfully defending claims alleging a delayed diagnosis of a subarachnoid haemorrhage.

Ranald Davidson (see p.629) Greatly admired for his extensive medical knowledge and expertise in the clinical negligence field. He handles cases across the full range of value and severity. **Strengths:** "He's medically qualified so he has the wonderful advantage of understanding both the medicine and the law." **Recent work:** Instructed on behalf of Oxford University Hospital in a case where the claimant had developed an infection following heart surgery.

Caroline Hallissey (see p.662) Handles an array of complex clinical negligence cases, acting predominantly on behalf of claimants. Her areas of focus include claims arising from spinal and obstetric injuries. **Strengths:** "Her advocacy skills are impressive in court and make you pleased to have her on your side." **Recent work:** Successfully represented a claimant who suffered urological problems as a result of the delayed diagnosis of cauda equine syndrome and spinal decompression.

Richard Partridge (see p.734) A qualified doctor who brings extensive knowledge gained from his years as a medical practitioner. He serves as counsel to both claimants and defendants in complex clinical negligence matters. **Strengths:** "Always excellently prepared, and his advocacy style is brilliant." "He's captivating and engaging in the courtroom." **Recent work:** Acted as counsel for the claimant in a case concerning allegations of failure to assess a bowel anastomosis after surgery.

Neil Davy (see p.630) Handles the full array of clinical negligence cases, and has a particular specialism in complex dental cases. He is regularly sought out to undertake matters of the highest value, such as spinal cord injury claims or catastrophic brain injury cases. **Strengths:** "He is a powerful advocate and court performer." "He is well prepared, always impressive in conference and an extremely good negotiator." **Recent work:** Instructed on behalf of the defendant in a quantum claim in relation to the death of a patient whilst in surgery.

Jonathan Holl-Allen (see p.674) A high-ranking barrister with a wealth of experience and knowledge. He represents both claimants and defendants in cases ranging from the relatively straightforward to those of the greatest difficulty. **Strengths:** "He is a very experienced clinical negligence practitioner who has an excellent grasp of detail." **Recent work:** Successfully represented a claimant in obtaining significant damages following the failure of Milton Keynes General Hospital to treat a streptococcus infection. This failure resulted in the claimant sustaining brain damage.

Simon Cridland (see p.626) Admired for his far-reaching practice which encompasses cases concerning, amongst other things, wrongful birth, cerebral palsy and claims under the Fatal Accident Act. He regularly acts for both claimant and defendants in high-value cases. **Strengths:** "He is gentle with clients but he is also to the point." **Recent work:** Acted on behalf of a claimant regarding a case concerning a failure to diagnose spinal lesions by both a GP and an NHS trust.

Charles Foster (see p.647) Specialist practitioner frequently sought out by leading firms to handle complex claims. He is well versed in handling a range of matters pertaining to the medical field, including cases of withdrawal of treatment and clinical confidentiality. **Strengths:** "His grasp of the medical facts and his forensic questioning of experts is second to none." **Recent work:** Acted for a defendant in successfully contesting allegations that throat surgery had been performed without sufficient justification.

Andrew Hockton (see p.673) Has a far-reaching practice, but devotes much of his time to undertaking complex cases pertaining to cerebral palsy and other catastrophic injuries. **Strengths:** "He has a very impressive knowledge of the procedure." **Recent work:** Acted on behalf of a GP employed at the Countess of Chester Hospital in relation to a claim concerning delayed diagnosis of cancer.

Debra Powell (see p.741) Devotes much of her practice to the representation of families, doctors and hospitals in an array of clinical negligence cases, handling matters of great severity and sensitivity. **Strengths:** "She's great on paper, great in conference and great in court." "Her written advice is detailed, comprehensive and always accurate." **Recent work:** Obtained a settlement for a claimant who suffered meningitis as a child, resulting in brain damage and loss of hearing. The defendant was alleged to have failed to diagnose the condition.

Heidi Knight (see p.692) A junior with an impressive portfolio of successful cases to her name, who is regularly sought out to undertake complex clinical negligence matters, including those pertaining to cosmetic surgery, psychiatric issues and obstetrics claims. **Strengths:** "She is technically astute and very able." "She is exceptionally clear and forward-thinking." **Recent work:** Represented the claimant in a Fatal Accidents Act claim where it had been alleged that the death of a 15-year-old asthmatic was the result of the hospital's failure to take a medication assessment or make provisions to ensure the long-term treatment and consultation of the deceased.

Sebastian Naughton (see p.725) Represents both claimants and defendants in clinical negligence cases ranging in both complexity and value. He has particular expertise in claims concerning birth injuries, GP negligence and plastic surgery. **Strengths:** "He has a very personable manner with clients and he is so down-to-earth." **Recent work:** Represented the claimant in a Fatal Accidents Act claim where a paramedic had failed to diagnose the claimant's cardiac symptoms. He was instructed instead to go to his GP surgery, where he later collapsed and died.

Eloise Power (see p.741) A formidable junior highly regarded for her vast experience and enviable catalogue of high-profile, high-value cases. Her clinical negligence practice continues to develop, and she has recently undertaken a number of surgical negligence and gynaecological cases. **Strengths:** "She's very thorough and incredibly supportive to clients." **Recent work:** Currently representing a claimant in relation to a metal-on-metal hip prosthesis implant, partially designed by the operating surgeon, which failed, leaving the claimant disabled.

Band 3

Hailsham Chambers

See profile on p.857

THE SET

Hailsham Chambers boasts a list of barristers who are highly expert in all manner of clinical negligence cases, and who act on behalf of both claimants and defendants. Members are routinely sought out to undertake high-value claims, often involving complex matters of fact and legal questioning. They act in matters funded privately, by Legal Aid or CFA. One interviewee described them as being "excellent in every department."

Client service: "The clerks, led by Stephen Smith, are astonishingly good and very, very efficient. They are good at getting back to you and they are also very accommodating. They don't make empty recommendations and they really do think about whether a barrister is suitable to work with a particular solicitor. They run a very tight ship."

SILKS

Alexander Hutton QC (see p.679) Highly sought-after silk with over 20 years' experience of practising within the field of medical law. He is applauded by peers for his ability to handle cases of the highest value and greatest complexity, and is recognised for his excellence on quantum. **Strengths:** "He is extremely thorough, user-friendly, responsive and excellent on his feet." "Quite simply excellent on every level." **Recent work:** Instructed by Bedford Hospitals NHS Trust regarding quantum only in relation to a case where a baby had suffered severe brain damage.

Andrew Post QC (see p.741) Demonstrates far-reaching expertise in the field and handles high-value matters, ranging in sensitivity and severity, for both claimants and defendants. He has a particular interest in cases arising from birth injury claims and those pertaining to neurosurgery. **Strengths:** "Andrew has an exceptional ability to dissect and analyse complex legal issues. He is very professional, compassionate with the clients and a tough, determined negotiator." "An excellent advocate with a forensic approach to investigation." **Recent work:** Acted on behalf of the St George's Healthcare NHS Trust regarding a claim surrounding a haematoma contracted post spinal surgery, which the surgeons had failed to diagnose and treat. The claimant later discontinued the claim.

Martin Spencer QC (see p.770) Head of chambers and a barrister with a diverse clinical negligence practice who represents both claimants and defendants. He regularly handles high-quantum claims. **Strengths:** "He's exceptionally impressive and knowledgeable." "Offers superb client skills and technical excellence." "Martin is a silk of the highest order; his outstanding advocacy skills and willingness to fight make him a formidable force." **Recent work:** Instructed in the case of Heather Poile v Maidstone & Tunbridge Wells NHS Trust, where the claimant developed spinal cord compression as a result of the defendant's failure to perform spinal decompression surgery.

Dominic Nolan QC (see p.728) Has amassed a wealth of knowledge over his lengthy career. His particular area of expertise lies in matters involving breach of duty and causation, specifically in relation to severe brain and spinal injury claims. **Strengths:** "He's super-bright and very at home tackling medical and legal issues. He really makes it his business to understand the science behind the medicine."

David Pittaway QC (see p.738) Lauded by market sources for his wealth of experience and extensive expertise. He acts on behalf of both claimants and defendants in high-profile matters, undertaking cases arising from catastrophic injuries. He regularly handles matters involving cauda equina and birth injury. **Strengths:** "He's got huge gravitas, which is recognised by clients, his opponents and judges." "A shrewd operator with a true mastery of tactics." **Recent work:** Acted on behalf of Spire Healthcare, defending against 750 claims of negligent breast surgery.

JUNIORS

Matthew Jackson (see p.681) Hailed for having a brilliant legal mind which he applies to a wide range of cases including those concerning neurosurgery, cardiology and plastic surgery. He almost exclusively acts on behalf of defendants such as the MPS and NHSLA. **Strengths:** "He works doggedly to get the answer, which means that he will pay huge attention to the evidence and scrutinise matters without losing sight of the bigger picture." "He is incredibly absorbed by what he does and he is a brilliant communicator with clients, experts and judges." **Recent work:** Instructed in the case of Howard v Mayday Healthcare NHS Trust where claims of delayed diagnosis of spinal cord surgery and negligently performed surgery were brought against the hospital.

Tejina Mangat Praised by market sources for her medical expertise, she represents claimants in highly complex cases spanning the full range of clinical negligence matters. **Strengths:** "She's incredibly diligent and her work rate is quite astonishing." "Outstanding in terms of her technical detail, she is meticulous and knowledgeable. She's medically qualified and it shows as she's always error-free." "Her attention to detail and sheer capacity for hard work is unrivalled."

Jane Mishcon (see p.718) Highly regarded and praised by market sources for her intellect and charming manner. Her practice encompasses a wide range of clinical negligence areas and she is also sought after to chair independent inquiries. **Strengths:** "She's incredibly sharp and has a fantastic grasp of medicine." **Recent work:** Successfully defended South Tees NHS Foundation Trust in an MRSA acquisition case where the claimant asserted that the COSHH Regulations 2002 were only applicable to inpatients who had acquired MRSA in hospital.

Fiona Neale (see p.726) Hailed by commentators for her depth of knowledge and extensive practice, she is routinely instructed on matters involving spinal surgery, neurosurgery and cardiology. **Strengths:** "Instructing her is like getting a silk for your money. She's exceptional on her feet." **Recent work:** Instructed in a claim concerning aspergillosis.

Jane Tracy Forster (see p.783) Handles all manner of clinical negligence matters ranging from relatively straightforward claims concerning anaesthesia to highly complex cases involving vascular surgery. She continues to devote much of her practice to birth-related injury claims, and also regularly handles cerebral palsy and obstetric matters. **Strengths:** "She is fantastic and wipes the floor with the other side." **Recent work:** Represented the claimant in a case brought against North Cumbria Hospitals NHS Trust, alleging harm caused by an obstetrician who had knowingly allowed a broken tip of a needle to remain in the abdomen of the claimant after a caesarean section.

Clare Price (see p.743) A prominent practitioner in the clinical negligence market who acts for both claimants and defendants in a variety of cases ranging in value and complexity. Of late, she has devoted her practice to handling cases arising from obstetric, amputation and cancer-related claims. **Strengths:** "Very meticulous and thorough in her approach." "She's brilliant and incisive, and knows the medicine really well."

Jamie Carpenter (see p.611) A well-regarded junior regularly instructed in high-value cases by both claimants and defendants. He also appears at inquests acting on behalf of health professionals and bereaved families. **Strengths:** "He is extremely bright and clear in his advice." "A terrier in court but with such a charming manner. He almost always wins."

Catherine Ewins (see p.642) Has a diverse caseload and regularly tackles complex, high-value claims. Recently, she has focused her practice on matters pertaining to delayed diagnosis and failure to diagnose. **Strengths:** "She is extremely intelligent and has an incredible in-depth understanding of the law whilst remaining attuned to the sensitivities of the client." "She's very clever and her attention to detail is outstanding."

Nicholas Peacock (see p.735) Highly praised by market sources for his meticulous analysis of cases. He is routinely instructed by both patients and medical organisations to undertake clinical negligence matters at all levels. **Strengths:** "His best strength is his razor-sharp eye for detail." "He is extremely experienced and extremely clever." **Recent work:** Represented the claimant in a case brought against a GP who failed to refer the claimant after they had presented with chest pains.

David Juckes (see p.687) Well regarded by market sources for the breadth of his clinical negligence practice. He is regularly instructed by healthcare organisations and hospital trusts. **Strengths:** "He is very bright, has an excellent manner with clients and is very quick at turning around advice to a consistently high standard." "His strengths lie in having an eye for detail and the ability to forensically analyse medical reports." **Recent work:** Acted on behalf of a claimant who alleged that clinicians at Abertawe Bro Morgannwg University Local Health Board had failed to notice signs of limb ischaemia and vascular insufficiency.

Band 4

7BR

See profile on p.814

THE SET

7 Bedford Row is a strong set which handles an extensive range of clinical negligence cases, and acts on behalf of both claimants and defendant medical and healthcare organisations. The set is applauded for its members' high quality, and secures instructions in cases of the highest calibre. It is in demand to handle the most complex and severe cases, and has enjoyed a number of high-profile wins in recent times. Of late, members have appeared in the Supreme Court case of Woodland v Essex County Council, as well as Manna v Central Manchester NHS Trust, a multimillion-pound birth injury claim.

Client service: The clerking team is led by Paul Eeles and Rod McGurk. "The clerks are always receptive to us in terms of our needs and the necessity for quick turnaround."

SILKS

Simeon Maskrey QC Renowned for his outstanding knowledge and expertise in the clinical negligence field, and his prowess in medical jurisprudence generally. He has a particular interest in catastrophic injury cases. **Strengths:** "The best of the best and the biggest brain of any silk." "He is a legend in the world of claimant clinical negligence, and is a fearless advocate who always fights for his clients." "A force to be reckoned with. His analytical skills are second to none." **Recent work:** Represented a claimant who had sustained a serious brain injury as a result of hypoxia.

Derek Sweeting QC Highly esteemed silk applauded for his ability to undertake clinical negligence cases of the utmost severity and greatest difficulty. He predominantly acts on behalf of claimants. **Strengths:** "He is outstanding and has very persuasive advocacy skills." "He has a very calm manner, is clear-headed and gives excellent advice." **Recent work:** Acted on behalf of a claimant who sustained a brain injury at birth, resulting in cerebral palsy.

Hugh Preston QC A well-respected barrister with significant experience of handling cases of the highest value and complexity on behalf of claimants. He has a broad practice encompassing many areas such as cancer and dental cases, but has a particular interest in severe birth injury claims. **Strengths:** "Brilliant – knows his stuff and is extremely approachable." **Recent work:** Currently representing the claimant, a high achiever with a First Class degree and a PhD, who suffered cerebral palsy from birth.

Adam Weitzman QC Handles a wide range of clinical negligence cases including claims arising from wrongful birth, vascular surgery and failure to diagnose cancer. His practice is predominantly focused on representing claimants against the NHSLA in maximum severity claims. **Strengths:** "He's really astute and fearless." "He's hard-working and genuinely cares about the client's cause." **Recent work:** Acted on behalf of an infant claimant who suffered cerebral palsy at birth as a result of a negligent delivery.

JUNIORS

Peter Ellis (see p.640) A leading barrister who handles complex matters such as those pertaining to spinal cord and brain injuries. He is regularly instructed by leading UK firms to undertake the most severe cases. **Strengths:** "He's got a very large breadth of knowledge." **Recent work:** Currently involved in an inquest regarding the death of a teenage girl who left a psychiatric ward only to commit suicide later on a railway.

Adam Korn An experienced barrister with a specialist practice focused on all aspects of clinical negligence. He has particular expertise in handling obstetric and cardiology-related issues and is regularly instructed in cases where severe neurological injuries have been sustained. **Strengths:** "Tactically impressive and good with clients." "He is very thorough and knows his law."

Julian D Matthews Has over 30 years' experience of handling the most complex cases of the highest value. He is instructed by both claimants and defendants, and has spearheaded landmark cases such as Gregg v Scott. **Strengths:** "He is very impressive and very sensible." "He's got the confidence and gravitas to take on any case." "A very senior junior who operates beyond the level of most QCs." **Recent work:** Acted on behalf of a claimant who was left disabled after undergoing negligently performed total knee surgery.

Jeremy Pendlebury Has expertise in obstetric and brain injury cases, and mainly acts for claimants. **Strengths:** "He has a vast knowledge of clinical negligence and has an excellent understanding of medicine." "Exceptionally bright and thorough, and always aims to get the very best result for the client." **Recent work:** Represented a claimant who suffered a stroke leading to brain damage and above-the-knee amputation. It was alleged that the claimant's GP had been negligent in not referring his patient to a cardiologist three weeks prior to the stroke.

Richard Baker (see p.588) A highly skilled barrister specialising almost exclusively in clinical negligence matters. He also handles fatal accident cases and inquest matters. **Strengths:** "An outstanding junior whose advocacy is superb. The quality of his work is exceptional." "Determined and dogged in his approach." **Recent work:** Involved in a quantum trial in relation to a cerebral palsy case where damages of £9.5 million were recovered on a periodical payment basis.

Adam Walker (see p.788) Receives instructions from both claimants and defendants on a wide range of clinical negligence issues, and also appears regularly at coroners' inquests. **Strengths:** "His paperwork is outstanding and he never makes any mistakes." "Clients just love him. He is really accessible, quick with paperwork and his attention to detail is second to none." **Recent work:** Acted for a claimant who experienced respiratory arrest and later suffered brain injury as a result of the defendant hospital's failure to observe the claimant after he had been administered morphine.

Deirdre Goodwin (see p.656) A highly adept barrister who has vast experience of handling catastrophic injury claims. She undertakes the most complex of cases, predominantly focusing on matters concerning severe brain injury and delayed diagnosis. **Strengths:** "Her legal expertise and level of technical knowledge is tremendous."

Leslie Keegan Undertakes a varied caseload of complex matters, and is expert in all areas of medical law. He has a particular interest in cases arising from severe brain injury claims. **Strengths:** "Clients like him and he's very approachable."

Simon King Highly experienced senior junior noted for expertise in clinical negligence, personal injury and regulatory work. He is instructed by both claimants and defendants in an array of cases ranging in value and complexity. **Strengths:** "An immensely tough and capable advocate." "He is extremely knowledgeable, sharp and great in conference." **Recent work:** Instructed in a case where it was alleged that the claimant's wife had died as a result of medics' negligence in failing to notice indicators of lung cancer.

Timothy Meakin Demonstrates vast knowledge and expertise when handling clinical negligence cases of the utmost severity. He predominantly focuses his practice on the representation of claimants and medical organisations, appearing in cases of the highest value. **Strengths:** "A very approachable barrister, who shows meticulous attention to detail and has an excellent rapport with clients." "He's just brilliant at thinking of stuff that you've never even dreamt of and getting you moving forward." **Recent work:** Acted for a claimant left significantly disabled as a result of the late diagnosis of lower spine paralysis.

Jonathan Bertram (see p.595) An experienced clinical negligence barrister with a practice predominantly focused on the representation of claimants. He handles a wide range of cases and has appeared in a number of inquests. **Strengths:** "He is very good on the detail; his enthusiasm for the work and subject matter shines out." "He is very incisive in his ability to get to grips with things, and he knows the law." **Recent work:** Acted on behalf of a claimant in a wrongful birth claim, where it was asserted that had the claimant been made aware that her baby was likely to have Down's Syndrome, she would have terminated the pregnancy.

Simon Wheatley Well-regarded senior junior who specialises in all areas of clinical negligence including cases concerning plastic surgery and catastrophic birth injury. He has recently been instructed in numerous cases relating to breast damage resulting from plastic surgery and missed diagnosis of cancer. **Strengths:** "He's a very good advocate who is very experienced and has a good manner and style about him."

Outer Temple Chambers

See profile on p.887

THE SET

An accomplished set that boasts a quality group of barristers experienced at representing both claimants and defendants. Members are instructed by leading firms to handle thoroughly complex cases of the highest value, particularly those relating to severe birth and neurological injuries. They continue to develop their profile in this area of law, and defence organisations such as the MPS and MDU increasingly turn to them to take on their more difficult cases.

Client service: "The efficiency and helpfulness of the clerks is second to none." "They're all very helpful and friendly and they're very approachable." The head of the clinical negligence clerking team is Graham Woods.

SILKS

Christopher Gibson QC An expert on the full spectrum of clinical negligence law, who is recognised for his superior intellect and experience. His additional areas of focus also include personal injury and professional negligence. **Strengths:** "Highly experienced and has the ability to cut through complex issues." "A highly intelligent and thoughtful barrister who listens, assimilates the information and then gets to the point promptly." **Recent work:** Instructed by the wife of a deceased man who suffered brain damage whilst undergoing a surgical biopsy.

David Westcott QC Held in high regard by peers for his specialist expertise, particularly in catastrophic injury claims. He acts on behalf of both claimants and defendants in high-value, highly complex cases. **Strengths:** "Highly intelligent and always well prepared," he "finds practical ways of achieving the best outcomes for clients." **Recent work:** Acted on behalf of a cardiologist in a claim where it had been alleged that he had failed to properly screen a professional footballer who later collapsed as a result of a heart attack.

Christopher Wilson-Smith QC (see p.798) Widely praised for his expertise amassed over 30 years. He is frequently instructed by both claimants and defendants in high-profile cases, a number of which concern birth injury claims. **Strengths:** "He is simply phenomenal. His ability to grasp the facts within seconds and cross-examine astutely is a prized skill." **Recent work:** Instructed in Simon Barnett v Medway NHS Trust Kent, a claim brought against the hospital alleging a misdiagnosis and failure to detect a spinal abscess that later led to paralysis.

Gordon Bebb QC Has a notable clinical negligence practice, predominantly handling claims arising from cerebral palsy and wrongful birth. He is also an expert in spinal injury cases. **Strengths:** "He is so experienced and has exceptional client skills." **Recent work:** Instructed in Joan Pickup v York Hospitals NHS Foundation Trust, a case alleging failure to detect neurological deterioration of the claimant following an operation.

JUNIORS

Cara Guthrie Handles various claims including those relating to spinal injury, cerebral palsy and brain injury. She acts on behalf of claimants in cases ranging in value and sensitivity. **Strengths:** "She is incredibly intelligent, and quickly grasps and offers solutions to complex issues. Her analysis of cases is excellent." **Recent work:** Instructed in Sarah Marquis v Homerton University Hospital, a claim for loss of earnings resulting from a delayed diagnosis of appendicitis.

Eliot Woolf Has an enviable caseload and handles a wide range of high-value claims both for claimants and defendants, including those arising from spinal injuries and orthopaedic surgery. **Strengths:** "He's a very clever operator." "He is absolutely brilliant intellectually." **Recent work:** Acted on behalf of a claimant in a case concerning negligently performed hip surgery.

James Aldridge A significant player in the market who has over 25 years' experience. He tackles a wide range of cases including those arising from cerebral palsy, wrongful birth and surgical negligence. **Strengths:** "Hard-working and extremely thorough, he is excellent at managing experts and clients alike." "Pragmatic and approachable, he has particular expertise in fatal claims." **Recent work:** Instructed in King v Basildon & Thurrock University Hospitals NHS Foundation Trust. This was a claim of surgical negligence against the hospital concerning an internal carotid endarterectomy.

Harry Trusted Handles catastrophic injury cases including those involving brain damage and birth injury. His impressive client roster includes patients, NHS hospital trusts and clinicians. **Strengths:** "An insightful and very approachable barrister who has a commanding presence." **Recent work:** Acted on behalf of a claimant who had a fall in a West Hertfordshire Hospital Trust hospital and suffered a neurological injury.

Rachel Vickers Acts for both claimants and defendant medical bodies such as the NHSLA, MDU and the MPS, and is particularly noted for her work on claims involving high-value neonatal or spinal injuries. In the last year she has undertaken a number of cerebral palsy cases. **Strengths:** "Very thorough and shows a high level of attention to detail." "She is forensic, intelligent and approachable." **Recent work:** Represented a claimant in a case against Medway Hospitals NHS Foundation Trust. The claimant had become tetraplegic as a result of a delayed analysis of her congenital spinal condition.

Ben Bradley Instructed by both claimants and defendant practitioners in complex clinical negligence cases, particularly those arising from catastrophic injuries. He has substantial experience of handling cases pertaining to glaucoma, spinal cord injury and neonatal deaths. **Strengths:** "He is an extremely able barrister who performs well above his call." **Recent work:** Acted in a case against Specsavers where the claimant lost their sight as a result of a missed diagnosis of glaucoma.

Jonathan Hand (see p.663) A well-regarded junior who receives instructions from both claimants and defendants, particularly on cases involving severe neurological injuries. **Strengths:** "He is careful, diligent, well prepared and a good negotiator." "He's a smart thinker who is willing to go outside the box on difficult cases."

Christopher Kemp Well-regarded practitioner who is regularly instructed in high-value cases. He has particular expertise in cerebral palsy and Erb's palsy. **Strengths:** "He is a dogged and tenacious advocate." "Provides an excellent service and is a particularly strong negotiator." **Recent work:** Represented the claimant in a case brought against St George's Healthcare NHS Trust alleging failure to identify and diagnose a spinal fracture.

Nathan Tavares A specialist in the field who has particular expertise in cases involving spinal cord injuries, psychiatric negligence and birth injuries. **Strengths:** "He has a lightning-fast grasp of issues and is always ready to assist." **Recent work:** Acted for a claimant in a case regarding a delay in the diagnosis of a spinal abscess.

2TG – 2 Temple Gardens

See profile on p.920

THE SET

A standout set undertaking cases for both claimants and defendants. Its members are proficient in all areas of clinical negligence, and handle an array of cases including those pertaining to birth injury, spinal cord injury and severe brain injury. They continue to be instructed to handle multimillion-pound cases on a national scale, and are well regarded for their "polished and very professional" approach both to their work and their clients.

Client service: Sources continue to be impressed by the clerking service, with senior clerk, Lee Tyler receiving praise from one interviewee who comments that "he stands out and always does his best to accommodate." His team is described as being "on the ball, courteous and efficient."

SILKS

Benjamin Browne QC (see p.605) He is noted for his mastery in cases involving catastrophic birth injury claims and negligent diagnosis. Browne acts on behalf of both claimants and defendants, employing his many years of experience to champion the interests of his clients. **Strengths:** "He brings great authority and great gravitas to his cases." "He has a great presence and is an excellent advocate." **Recent work:** Recently handled an appeal to the Privy Council from the Bermudian Court of Appeal. The case concerned the proper approach to causation in a clinical negligence context with particular reference to the material contribution test and the judgment in Bailey v MOD.

Michael de Navarro QC (see p.631) Highly praised by peers and other market sources for his clinical negligence expertise, particularly when it comes to catastrophic injury cases such as brain and spinal cord injury claims. He handles everything from small injury claims to those of the highest value and severity. **Strengths:** "He has gravitas and a great legal brain." **Recent work:** Acted as counsel for a specialist cardiologist and Tottenham Hostpur FC doctors, in a claim where an academy player had allegedly suffered a heart attack and brain damage through the negligence of the defendants.

Sarah Vaughan Jones QC (see p.786) A leading silk admired by peers and clients alike for her expansive medical knowledge and years of professional experience. She undertakes highly complex and sensitive cases for both claimants and defendants. **Strengths:** "She's very bright, incredibly thorough and good company." "She's got a really good manner with clients and witnesses, and does an incredibly thorough job." **Recent work:** Represented a defendant hospital in a claim where cerebral palsy had been sustained by the claimant at birth.

Caroline Harrison QC (see p.665) A high-ranking silk specialising in clinical negligence, with a particular focus on cases arising from adult brain damage, as well as neonatal and spinal injuries. She is also an expert in niche areas of medical law such as Wegener's Granulomatosis and microbiological causation in septic arthritis. **Strengths:** "She is excellent on her feet and not afraid to stand her ground and take a risk based on her impeccable judgement." "She's extremely good at getting the best out of everybody, particularly in conference." **Recent work:** Acted as counsel for the claimants in relation to the suicide of their teenage daughter. The deceased had developed an eating disorder and had been prematurely discharged from out-patient treatment.

Martin Porter QC (see p.740) An experienced barrister, highly proficient at handling complex clinical negligence matters including those arising from psychiatric and brain injury. His practice is primarily defendant-focused. **Strengths:** "He has a really high level of advocacy." "He is very thorough and at the same time highly pragmatic." **Recent work:** Represented a GP in a claim alleging that there had been a failure to diagnose a young child with meningitis.

JUNIORS

Bradley Martin (see p.708) Handles a broad range of cases, and has particular interest in claims arising from catastrophic injuries to the spine and brain. **Strengths:** "He's a superb advocate." "He's got a very natural and persuasive delivery and he makes his arguments well and effectively. He's what you would call a winner."

Roger Harris (see p.665) Well-regarded junior noted for his particular expertise handling cases arising from catastrophic injuries. He is an expert on cases relating to birth injuries, plastic surgery and mental health. **Strengths:** "He's shrewd and prepared to roll his sleeves up." **Recent work:** Currently representing the claimant, a patient at the Barking Havering and Redbridge Hospitals NHS Trust, who jumped out of a first-floor window at the hospital soon after being admitted.

William Wraight (see p.800) A barrister with a depth of knowledge and expertise drawn from his years as a surgeon and medical professor at Cambridge University. He has been instructed in an array of cases including those arising from missed diagnosis of scoliosis. **Strengths:** "He has an excellent understanding of medicine and the law." "His experience and knowledge is well beyond his call."

Anna Hughes (see p.677) An experienced barrister, regularly sought after to undertake high-value, complex cases in the fields of both clinical negligence and personal injury. Her particular expertise in quantum makes her an asset in multimillion-pound cases. **Strengths:** "She's personable, good to deal with, professional, well organised and generally very impressive." "She's pragmatic and very, very bright." **Recent work:** Instructed by the defendant, University Hospitals of Morecambe Bay NHS Trust, in relation to a claim that the claimant had developed cerebral palsy as a result of staff negligence.

Band 5

1 Chancery Lane

THE SET

A well-respected set whose members represent both claimants and defendants in a wide array of cases concerning such issues as fatal accidents, spinal injuries and cerebral palsy. On the defendant side they act for a number of defence organisations such as the MDU, health authorities and doctors. Its members have far-reaching expertise covering the full gamut of clinical negligence matters, are able to undertake individual cases ranging in value and complexity as well as large multiparty actions.

Client service: "The clerks at 1 Chancery lane, led by the inimitable Clark Chessis, are friendly, helpful and reliable. They are a real asset to the chambers."

SILKS

Edward Bishop QC A high-ranking silk with over 30 years' experience in the field of clinical negligence, who is admired for his depth of knowledge. He is regularly instructed by both claimants and defendants, and has handled important cases such as Smith v Chief Constable of Sussex Police. **Strengths:** "Edward is excellent with clients and able to deal with the most complex of cases, cutting straight to the heart of the matter." "He takes a pragmatic approach to cases, is popular with claimants, and offers excellent analysis of the strengths and weaknesses of a case." **Recent work:** Successfully defended East Kent Hospitals NHS Foundation Trust against a claim alleging that the hospital had failed to diagnose and treat an infection. This failure resulted in a spinal abscess, infarction and paralysis.

Simon Readhead QC Impresses both with his knowledge of complex medical negligence matters and his meticulous approach to his work. He has a very broad practice and is recognised for his work on claims involving catastrophic and neurological injuries. **Strengths:** "He is absolutely excellent and incredibly thorough. He is superb with clients and an incredible advocate." **Recent work:** Instructed by the defendant trust, Colchester Hospital University NHS Trust, in a case where a child was born with serious mental and physical disabilities.

JUNIORS

Laura Johnson Applauded for the versatility of her practice, she is experienced in an array of clinical negligence cases varying in complexity from obstetric claims to cancer-related matters. She acts for both claimants and defendant organisations. **Strengths:** "Laura is tenacious, has an eye for detail and is a tough negotiator." "She's incisive and gives very helpful advice."

Sophie Mortimer A lawyer with substantial experience of handling clinical negligence cases on behalf of claimants and defendants. She is also highly experienced in inquests, and is regularly instructed to undertake personal injury claims. **Strengths:** "She pays attention to detail, and you feel confident that nothing will slip through the net when she is dealing with your case." "She's personable, pragmatic, bullish and very good with clients."

Paul Stagg A junior who handles matters for both claimants and defendants. Commentators commend him for his meticulousness and the rapport he builds with clients. **Strengths:** "He shows fantastic attention to detail." "He's incredibly knowledgeable and it feels like having a heavyweight on your team when he's involved." **Recent work:** Acted for the NHSLA in a matter where the deceased had committed suicide as a result of failures regarding treatment.

David Thomson A barrister renowned for his medical knowledge and expertise gained from previously practising as a junior surgeon and GP. He has particular expertise in complex cases involving catastrophic and neurological injury. **Strengths:** "Very good for complicated medical cases." "He has the knowledge and skills, and always inspires confidence." **Recent work:** Acted for Nottingham University NHS Trust in a case where the claimant had his leg amputated as a result of vascular disease.

Cloisters

See profile on p.821

THE SET

A set with a highly acclaimed claimant-focused team that undertakes a broad spectrum of cases encompassing all areas of medical law. Members handle high-value, complex cases concerning the likes of catastrophic brain and spinal cord injuries, as well as obstetrics-related claims. Sources say of Cloisters that it is "an excellent set with some excellent members who are committed to good service and good values."

Client service: The "always very helpful and accommodating" senior clerk Glenn Hudson was described by one interviewee as "the tops." He runs a "perfectly efficient" team where "all involved work smoothly."

SILKS

Simon W Taylor QC A dual-qualified medical doctor and barrister. He is well versed in all manner of clinical negligence cases and has particular expertise in those involving incredibly complex legal issues. **Strengths:** "He is very impressive and produces masterful advocacy." "Excellent with clients, he understands complex medical issues and is very accessible." **Recent work:** Acted in a case where the claimant had to undergo multiple amputations as a result of delayed diagnosis of an infection.

Joel Donovan QC (see p.635) Highly sought after for cases of the greatest complexity and highest value. Much of his practice is devoted to handling brain injury claims and cases arising from severe spinal injuries. **Strengths:** "Very thorough and conscientious, he takes a very methodical approach to cases and is reassuringly cautious and thoughtful."

Patricia Hitchcock QC (see p.673) Particularly admired for her work on spinal and brain injury cases, she is known for her extensive knowledge of her subject. **Strengths:** "She's just a fountain of all knowledge, and brilliant with clients." "She's empathetic and intuitive with clients, and she provides thorough advice quickly."

William Latimer-Sayer QC (see p.696) Applauded by market sources for his expertise in quantum, an area in which he is deemed to be unrivalled. He has a vast intellect and skill set, and is as happy handling clinical negligence and personal injury cases. **Strengths:** "His advice and guidance stood out like a light in a long, dark street." "He is one of the brightest stars at the Personal Injury and Clinical Negligence Bar." "His superb attention to detail and analytical skills, especially in relation to quantum, are unrivalled." **Recent work:** Instructed in a quantum trial regarding a 12-year-old boy who had suffered cerebral palsy as a result of medical negligence at birth. An award of £14.5 million was secured.

JUNIORS

Simon Dyer A leading junior who is highly skilled on the full range of medical law, and has a particular focus on cases involving complex cerebral palsy and spinal injuries. **Strengths:** "Hugely experienced barrister who is excellent with clients." "He's particularly competent at identifying key medical issues and gets to the nub of the issues very quickly." **Recent work:** Successfully represented the claimant in an action brought against Royal Cornwall Hospital concerning a surgeon's failure to diagnose scoliosis.

Lisa Sullivan (see p.776) Highly skilled barrister, who routinely tackles high-value delayed diagnosis of cancer cases as well as highly complex abdominal surgery and spinal injury claims. **Strengths:** "She's a very skilful junior and is a good advocate." "She is very bright, approachable and clear."

Hannah Godfrey (see p.655) Regularly instructed by leading firms to handle maximum severity cases. She has handled a number of matters concerning cerebral palsy, spinal injury and breast enlargement surgery. **Strengths:** "She is very able, very intelligent, very thorough and good at thrashing out the issues and coming to the best conclusion." "Whether in a cross-examination or a negotiation, she'll be someone you know will achieve results due to her absolute focus and determination."

Linda Jacobs (see p.681) New entrant to the table whose work includes cases relating to delayed diagnosis of cancer, failure to obtain consent and dental negligence. **Strengths:** "She is really good at advocacy." "She was a nurse before, so her medical knowledge is fantastic." **Recent work:** Instructed on behalf of the claimant, a widow, whose husband died as a result of a pulmonary embolism after he was not treated with Herparin by the defendant hospital.

Martyn McLeish Established clinical negligence barrister, widely known for handling high-value cases involving a wide range of medical issues. He tackles a diverse caseload, and is frequently instructed on claims concerning cerebral palsy and psychiatric injuries. **Strengths:** "He is clear, concise and always approachable. He handles clients and experts well."

Crown Office Chambers

See profile on p.824

THE SET

A strong set boasting an enviable list of highly adept barristers. Its members act on behalf of both claimants and defendants, including private individuals, healthcare providers and the NHSLA. Barristers routinely tackle highly complex cases and resolve difficult matters of quantum. One enthused interviewee praised the set for being "extremely skilled, professional and well organised."

Client service: "It is a first-class, professional yet friendly service." "The clerking at Crown Office is very efficient and the clerks respond promptly to emails and telephone calls. They are also flexible when it comes to facilities and fees." The senior managing clerk is Andy Flanagan.

SILKS

Alexander Antelme QC A barrister of great intellect, who has a large caseload of complex high-value matters. He receives instructions from both claimants and defendant organisations including the MDU and the NHSLA. **Strengths:** "He is a good advocate who is calm and impressive in court." "He's impressive, very bright and always on top of the case." **Recent work:** Instructed by the defendant in a claim where allegations were brought against North West London Hospital NHS Trust for failure to appropriately diagnose a spinal abscess.

JUNIORS

Charlotte Jones A leading junior barrister devoted to the field of clinical negligence. She is instructed on behalf of both claimants, defendant health organisations, the NHSLA amongst them. **Strengths:** "She is very experienced and brilliant at everything." "She's fantastic with clients and has a very calm, controlled and prepared manner."

Farrah Mauladad Has extensive experience of handling a wide range of matters on behalf of both claimants and defendants. Her caseload includes matters involving psychiatry, osteopathy and general surgery. **Strengths:** "Farrah is an impressive advocate" who "displays really good attention to detail."

Claire Toogood (see p.783) Praised for her medical knowledge and experience of handling an array of clinical negligence matters varying in complexity. She is highly sought after by leading firms and defence organisations including the MPS and the NHSLA. **Strengths:** "She is excellent on her feet and fantastic at cross-examination." "Her analytical, compassionate approach to cases is appreciated by instructing solicitors and clients alike." **Recent work:** Instructed by a claimant who brought a claim of delayed diagnosis of testicular cancer against his doctor.

Gordon Catford Has particular expertise in the fields of clinical negligence and personal injury, and regularly receives instructions from leading firms to undertake high-value cases. **Strengths:** "Very positive and a good communicator. He makes things clear to the client."

David Myhill (see p.725) Applauded by commentators for his extensive medical knowledge, which he applies to cases on behalf of both claimants and defence organisations. He is also very experienced in appearing at inquests. **Strengths:** "He is an absolute super-brain, but he is also extremely approachable and friendly." **Recent work:** Instructed by two defendant trusts and the NHS Commissioning Board in a claim where it was alleged that there had been a failure on the part of the defendants to diagnose septic arthritis following knee replacement surgery.

9 Gough Square

See profile on p.854

THE SET

9 Gough Square is an accomplished set whose members are highly adept at dealing with the full range of clinical negligence cases, and particularly good at high-value birth injury matters and claims arising out of spinal surgery. Its individuals receive instructions from both claimants and defendants, and are noted for their professionalism. Commentators praise them for their "willingness to please and their constant striving for perfection in court." As well as handling clinical negligence matters, they are well-versed in related areas such as inquests and personal injury.

Client service: "The clerks are very efficient, communicative, upbeat and happy to help. They always seem to enjoy their roles and this shows in their eagerness to assist wherever possible and to do so expeditiously." The clerking team is led by the well-regarded Michael Goodridge, who is described by sources as being "exceptional."

SILKS

Grahame Aldous QC (see p.581) Routinely instructed by claimants and defendants to undertake complex, high-value cases. **Strengths:** "He has excellent advocacy skills and is a good all-round barrister." "He is a very good performer and has a lot of gravitas." **Recent work:** Instructed in a case where the claimant was left severely handicapped having suffered a stroke as a result of the defendant's failure to diagnose and treat a cranial aneurysm.

Andrew Ritchie QC (see p.752) A standout silk noted for his great expertise and formidable intellect. He has recently been handling failure to diagnose cases, as well as cardiology and urology-related claims. **Strengths:** "Offers excellent analysis of the key issues and the evidence required for a claim to succeed." "He is excellent with clients, very knowledgeable and a good advocate." **Recent work:** Instructed in Smith v Heart of England, a case concerning the defendant's failure to diagnose cancer, resulting in the amputation of the claimant's foot.

Jacob Levy QC (see p.700) A well respected silk with over 30 years' experience. He devotes much of his practice to claimant-focused work, and is regularly instructed in all manner of cases ranging from the relatively modest to those of the greatest complexity. **Strengths:** "He is phenomenally wise and personable, and offers exceptional client care, attention to detail and excellent judgement." "He has an excellent grip of the facts and is extremely tenacious."

JUNIORS

Laura Begley (see p.594) A rising star in the clinical negligence sector, who undertakes a growing caseload of complex cases. She impresses with her pragmatic approach when handling matters on behalf of both claimants and defendants. **Strengths:** "She adopts a tenacious yet pragmatic approach to cases." "She's very approachable and very attuned to the commercial realities of the case."

Christopher Stephenson (see p.772) A specialist clinical negligence barrister whose practice is exclusively claimant-based. His caseload includes cases concerning plastic surgery, failure to diagnose and wrongful birth claims. **Strengths:** "He's very friendly to deal with and good at looking at things from every angle." "He's absolutely fantastic with clients and excellent at explaining the legal complexities of a case." **Recent work:** Represented the claimant in a case brought against the NHS Commissioning Board. The claimant had undergone unnecessary knee surgery and later developed a debilitating pain condition which rendered her housebound.

Stuart McKechnie (see p.713) New entrant to this year's table, whose expertise lies in handling catastrophic claims involving complex matters of law. **Strengths:** "He's incredibly hard-working and extraordinarily bright." **Recent work:** Instructed in Field v Barts Health NHS Trust. The claimant alleged that the negligent treatment she received during pregnancy led to the death of her baby.

Band 6

Devereux

See profile on p.827

THE SET

Devereux has a well-regarded team of specialist clinical negligence barristers that is commended for its handling of an array of complex matters for both claimants and defendants. Its members regularly handle cases involving damages that run into millions of pounds and are acknowledged for their work in the personal injury field as well as the clinical negligence sector.

Client service: The clerks are "excellent, accommodating , knowledgeable and responsive." Vince Plant leads the team.

SILKS

Robert Glancy QC (see p.653) Has amassed a wealth of knowledge over a lengthy career spanning over 40 years. He generally acts for claimants in cases relating to catastrophic spinal and brain injury. **Strengths:** "He's really brilliant and always wants to get the best for the client." **Recent work:** Represented a claimant against Royal Free Hampstead NHS Trust. The case concerned a barrister whose career was reduced by ten years following negligent medical treatment received when undergoing appendix surgery.

Robert Weir QC (see p.792) An accomplished silk with noted handling of catastrophic injuries claims including those relating to cerebral palsy and brain injury. **Strengths:** "He is very forensic on the detail and he cares about the issues and the clients." "He is so sharp, so bright and so intelligent." **Recent work:** Acted in JXMX v Dartford and Gravesham NHS Trust, representing PIBA in the Court. He successfully promoted an entirely new legal test to be applied to the issue of anonymity on approval hearings.

JUNIORS

Richard Cartwright (see p.612) An experienced junior who is a former chartered accountant and highly skilled on quantum. **Strengths:** "Passionate about getting the best result every time, he leaves no stone unturned." "He is very approachable, never gives up on a case and will go the extra mile." "He can take on a case which looks hopeless and turn it around."

Doughty Street Chambers

See profile on p.828

THE SET

Members act solely on the claimant side and are no strangers to high-profile and extremely sensitive cases. They regular handle claims relating to severe brain injuries, cerebral palsy and fatal accidents, and possess expertise in overlapping areas such as product liability.

Client service: "The clerks are very friendly and very nice." Kevin Kelly handles the clinical negligence side of the clerking at the set.

SILKS

Robin Oppenheim QC Has considerable experience and a wide-ranging practice that takes in complex obstetric and brain injury cases and neonatal claims, among others. **Strengths:** "He is outstanding in his intellect and has a speedy grasp of the legal principles and medical and factual issues in a case." "He is just a total intellectual heavyweight." "Compassionate and astute, he is almost unsurpassed in his analysis of difficult causation arguments."

JUNIORS

Christopher Hough High-ranking junior who focuses his practice predominantly on claimant work, and is instructed in an array of matters varying in both value and complexity. **Strengths:** "He is extremely approachable and has a very good bedside manner with the clients." "He is ingenious and able to formulate novel solutions to complex problems." **Recent work:** Instructed in a claim brought against Buckinghamshire Hospitals NHS Trust regarding undetected and untreated jaundice which resulted in the claimant suffering kernicterus.

Gerwyn Samuel A standout barrister, praised by commentators for his fearless and highly tactical approach to complex clinical negligence matters. He devotes much of his practice to cases involving catastrophic brain injuries and spinal damage. **Strengths:** "He has excellent negotiation skills, is innovative in finding practical solutions to litigation problems and is an excellent advocate." "He is very knowledgeable, through and tenacious, and has an excellent client manner." **Recent work:** Acted on behalf of the claimant, a mother who suffered severe brain damage as a result of being dismissed by the defendant GP when she complained of feeling faint 12 days after giving birth.

39 Essex Chambers

See profile on p.840

THE SET

An acclaimed set noted for representing both claimants and defendants in a broad range of matters. Members receive instructions from leading firms to undertake all manner of cases, many of them very serious in nature, involving such issues as delayed diagnosis of cancer and catastrophic birth injury. One commentator said "39 Essex is a very forward-thinking and commercially minded set that is alert to issues in the market."

Client service: "The team is very efficient and always return calls and emails promptly." Alastair Davidson is the senior clerk.

SILKS

Neil Block QC (see p.598) A silk with a comprehensive understanding of the full spectrum of clinical negligence law, who is admired for the depth of his intellect and experience. He has an exclusively defendant practice, handling a range of cases for health authorities, the NHSLA and professional insurers. **Strengths:** "He has a wonderful ability to focus on the key issues and see the wood for the trees." "He is excellent and calm and has experience coming out of his ears." **Recent work:** Recently instructed on a birth trauma case of great value.

Susan Rodway QC Widely admired by peers and commentators for her active involvement in landmark decisions within the field of clinical negligence. She focuses her practice predominantly on claimant work undertaking serious cases, some of which involve international claimants. **Strengths:** "She has great depth of knowledge and an incredible court presence."

JUNIORS

Emily Formby (see p.646) Handles a diverse caseload on behalf of both claimants and defendants, including matters relating to birth trauma injuries, failed diagnosis and wrongful treatment. **Strengths:** "She is excellent with clients and is obviously extremely bright and thorough."

Nicola Greaney (see p.659) Regularly instructed by healthcare providers as well as the NHSLA and claimants. Her areas of experience includes claims concerning delay in the diagnosis of cancer, cerebral palsy and catastrophic birth injury. **Strengths:** "She is a really effective advocate and a really good negotiator." "She is an excellent junior who is extremely bright and very good at understanding complex arguments." **Recent work:** Instructed in a case where a doctor allegedly inserted an arterial catheter into a 24-week-old baby.

Other Ranked Lawyers

Richard Furniss (42 Bedford Row) Widely known for his extensive experience acting on behalf of both claimants and defendants. He routinely handles cases concerning cerebral palsy, as well as a range of catastrophic injury claims. **Strengths:** "He is an astute and experienced negotiator." "His ability to get straight to the heart of the matter endears him to solicitors and clients alike." **Recent work:** Acted in a case against Medway NHS Trust concerning the severing of a nerve during knee surgery which resulted in the claimant developing compartment syndrome.

Scott Matthewson (42 Bedford Row) Head of the firm's clinical negligence and personal injury department, and no stranger to handling clinical negligence cases of the greatest value and complexity. **Strengths:** "A very knowledgeable and charming advocate who has a lovely manner and is good in negotiation." **Recent work:** Represented the claimant, an 11-week-old baby, in a matter regarding the failure of a defendant hospital to detect a congenital diaphragmatic hernia which resulted in the claimant suffering a gut strangulation.

Margaret Bloom (Hardwicke) A dually qualified practitioner who employs extensive medical knowledge gained as a former GP to handle highly complex clinical negligence cases. She has particular expertise in severe brain injury claims. **Strengths:** "She was a GP, so she has got a massive amount of medical and legal knowledge."

Frank Burton QC (see p.608) (12 King's Bench Walk) Admired by peers and commentators for his vast knowledge and experience within the clinical negligence and personal injury fields. **Strengths:** "He is a fair, honest, hugely knowledgeable and very attractive advocate who has great integrity." "He is utterly brilliant in a quiet manner."

Henry Charles (see p.615) (12 King's Bench Walk) Well regarded for his expertise in cases involving obstetrics and brain and spinal injuries. He also has considerable expertise in the personal injury arena. **Strengths:** "An experienced all-rounder" who is "very thorough and prepared to put in the work on difficult cases." **Recent work:** Instructed in Millward v Brighton & Sussex University Hospitals NHS Trust. The claimant had been left in a persistent vegetative state as a result of a brain injury suffered during surgery.

Mary O'Rourke QC (Old Square Chambers) An accomplished clinical negligence and personal injury barrister whose practice is mainly defendant-based. She regularly represents NHS trusts and medical practitioners. **Strengths:** "She is very experienced and her knowledge of medicine and the issues is very impressive." "An outstanding advocate." **Recent work:** Represented the defendant in a matter where the claimant died during routine gynaecological surgery to remove fibroids.

MIDLANDS

Clinical Negligence
Leading Sets
Band 1
No5 Chambers *
Leading Silks
Band 1
Hunjan Satinder *Kings Chambers (ORL)* ◊ *
Band 2
Bright Christopher *No5 Chambers* *
Jones Jonathan *No5 Chambers* *
Khalique Nageena *No5 Chambers* 🄰
New Silks
Fox Simon *No5 Chambers*
* *Indicates set / individual with profile.*
🄰 *direct access (see p.24).*
◊ *(ORL) = Other Ranked Lawyer.*
Alphabetical order within each band. Band 1 is highest.

Clinical Negligence
Leading Juniors
Band 1
Punt Jonathan *No5 Chambers*
Rochford Thomas *St Philips Chambers (ORL)* ◊ *
Band 2
Coughlan John *No5 Chambers*
Cox Jason *Ropewalk Chambers (ORL)* ◊
Evans Andrew *St Philips Chambers (ORL)* ◊ *
Gamble Jamie *No5 Chambers* *
Gupta Mamta *No5 Chambers*
Herbert Douglas *Ropewalk Chambers (ORL)* ◊
Hirst Karl *No5 Chambers*
Pitchers Henry *No5 Chambers*
Tyack David *No5 Chambers*
Gamble Jamie *No5 Chambers* *
Up-and-coming individuals
Grimshaw Richard *No5 Chambers*

Band 1

No5 Chambers

See profile on p.931

THE SET

A standout set in the Midlands for clinical negligence cases of varying complexity and value. Its members act on behalf of both claimants and defendants including NHS hospital and clinical commissioning groups, healthcare professionals and private individuals. Sources regard the set as being of a high-calibre and containing several top-notch silks and juniors. Its members are known for their depth of knowledge and their experience of handling instructions nationwide.

Client service: "The clerks are friendly, fast and efficient and will do anything they can to help." "The clerks know what they're doing, they know the marketplace and the local solicitors. They will go out of their way." Martin Hulbert and Zoe Tinnion are the senior practice managers.

SILKS

Christopher Bright QC (see p.603) Possesses an impressive case history particularly when it comes to cases involving issues of funding and causation in extreme cerebral palsy and neonatal brain injury claims. Interviewees appreciate his thorough and balanced approach. **Strengths:** "Very knowledgeable, communicative and client-facing." "He really drills into every case to make sure we've got every detail." **Recent work:** Acted on behalf of the claimant in a cerebral palsy matter of the utmost severity which settled for several millions of pounds, covering damages and future care.

Jonathan Jones QC (see p.685) He acts on behalf of both claimants and defendants in clinical negligence cases with particularly complicated or unique legal aspects. Sources praise his eye for detail and ability to grasp cases quickly. **Strengths:** "His attention to detail is second to none. For academic detail, you go to him." "He's just got a lovely, methodical way of dealing with a case." **Recent work:** Instructed in an obstetrics negligence claim against the Cayman Island Health Authority which involved complex issues surrounding purported immunity of the state-run hospital from legal action.

Nageena Khalique QC She draws on a wide range of clinical expertise spanning medical, dental and surgical negligence to represent both claimants and public bodies. Claims related to the Human Rights Act are a particular area of expertise. **Strengths:** "Fantastic on her feet." "She has a good understanding of public and mental health law, which is useful." **Recent work:** Instructed in an alleged psychiatric negligence claim resulting in the suicide of a prisoner.

Simon Fox QC Qualified in both medicine and law, he brings expertise from his earlier career to his practice. Of late, he has been instructed to handle cases concerning negligent neurosurgery, cerebral palsy and delay of diagnosis of a brain tumour. **Strengths:** "A good all-rounder." "Always a safe pair of hands and good with clients."

JUNIORS

Jonathan Punt As a former surgeon, he brings a wealth of medical knowledge to his practice, and is a particular expert in paediatric neurosurgery. Highly regarded for his work in brain injury claims. **Strengths:** "He has lots of gravitas and brings real authority to cases that he is involved in." "Meticulous on complex medical claims." **Recent work:** Worked on an inquest involving the death of a baby boy after medical professionals failed to identify his rare heart condition.

John Coughlan He possesses a substantial amount of expertise in severe and complex claimant work but is also busy on the defendant side. Market sources praise his calm and measured manner. **Strengths:** "No one can beat him when it comes to detail." "He doesn't get flustered at court, even when surprising things happen." **Recent work:** Acted in a case concerning failure to investigate a cerebral aneurysm that stretched over five years, eventually settling for £1.3 million.

David Tyack A highly praised junior who regularly acts in complex and uncommon clinical negligence cases. He is particularly knowledgeable on failure to diagnose, spinal injury and fatal claims. **Strengths:** "Very intelligent and can absorb a huge amount of detail very quickly." "Very little escapes his eye." **Recent work:** Instructed in a matter alleging negligence of an army GP resulting in faecal incontinence for the claimant.

Mamta Gupta A widely respected junior, she is noted for her outstanding client skills and dedication. She is frequently instructed in cases involving obstetrics and gynaecology. **Strengths:** "She's empathetic and you feel that she will go the extra mile for the clients." "Always delivers what she promises." **Recent work:** Represented a woman at a five-day inquest whose son committed suicide whilst in hospital care.

Karl Hirst Wins unanimous praise from peers, who highlight his engaging manner as a key strength. Has seen a recent uptick in clinical negligence cases involving brain and spinal injuries. **Strengths:** "His ability to put clients at ease is very useful." "He gives pragmatic, sensible advice and he does it very well." **Recent work:** Instructed in a case where the client continued to suffer from medical issues after abdominal surgery.

Henry Pitchers Well regarded for his client skills and particularly knowledgeable in cases involving amputations as well as brain and spinal injuries. **Strengths:** "He has great empathy and understanding for clients. If you have someone who is very vulnerable he's just the sort of person to have." "Written work is excellent, he doesn't skip any details." **Recent work:** Acted in a matter involving alleged negligence in abdominal surgery.

Jamie Gamble (see p.650) He is frequently instructed in high-value matters of extreme severity and particularly knowledgeable in spinal injury. **Strengths:** "Very thorough in dealing with experts." "Very approachable, nice style." **Recent work:** Engaged in a case concerning failure to diagnose chlamydia resulting in an ectopic pregnancy.

Richard Grimshaw Well versed in representing both claimants and defendants in clinical negligence cases. Peers are quick to note his growing reputation in this field. **Strengths:** "Easy to get hold of and goes above and beyond what is required of him." "Tactically insightful with impressive attention to detail."

Other Ranked Lawyers

Satinder Hunjan QC (see p.678) (Kings Chambers) An extremely knowledgeable silk with experience of the full gamut of clinical negligence matters, particularly high-value and complex cases involving cerebral palsy and sports-related injuries. Commentators highlight his sensitivity towards client needs. **Strengths:** "His tactical awareness is excellent." "The closer we get to the court door, the more his capabilities shine through."

Jason Cox (Ropewalk Chambers) He is recognised by peers for his ability to handle both high and low-value claims and is regularly instructed in catastrophic matters. **Strengths:** "Very thorough and great attention to detail." "Somebody who can get to the heart of the case quickly."

Douglas Herbert (Ropewalk Chambers) A specialist in professional negligence whose practice has an emphasis on clinical negligence claims. Frequently handles highly complex matters including those relating to brain damage or spinal injury. **Strengths:** "He's fantastic – strong in negotiations, has an eye for detail and is very good with the clients." "Very experienced and good on his feet. Clients are confident in what he says." **Recent work:** Acted in a multimillion-pound claim involving a road traffic incident.

Thomas Rochford (see p.754) (St Philips Chambers) Well known for handling a range of cases including fatalities and those relating to failure to diagnose. Much of his practice is claimant-based, and he is applauded for his experience and methodical approach. **Strengths:** "Very experienced, calm and methodical. A barrister that the clients always respond well to." "He's very quick at coming back to you."

Andrew Evans (see p.641) (St Philips Chambers) A junior with a developing practice in cases involving negligence in dentistry and cosmetic surgery. Peers acknowledge his ability to handle complex and sensitive claims. **Strengths:** "Pragmatic but compassionate at the same time." "Fantastic with clients." **Recent work:** Acted on behalf of a claimant who suffered due to negligent anti-ageing cosmetic surgery.

NORTH EASTERN

Clinical Negligence
Leading Sets
Band 1
Parklane Plowden
Leading Silks
Band 1
Lewis Andrew *Park Square Barristers (ORL)* ◊
Leading Juniors
Band 1
Axon Andrew *Parklane Plowden*
Pritchard Sarah *Kings Chambers (ORL)* ◊ *
Band 2
Copnall Richard *Parklane Plowden* *
Elgot Howard *Parklane Plowden*
Friday Stephen *Parklane Plowden*
Hill Michael *Trinity Chambers (ORL)* ◊

Band 1

Parklane Plowden

THE SET

Boasts outstanding capabilities in diverse clinical negligence claims in the North East. Its widely renowned senior juniors often act for either claimants or defendants on claims that attract huge damages, including those relating to cerebral palsy, acquired brain injury and paraplegia. The set houses a broader team of junior barristers who advise on delayed diagnosis, orthopaedic surgery and psychiatric harm cases. Its members also handle fatal claims at inquest stages and beyond.

Client service: "Head clerk Andy Gray in particular is very approachable and a phone call to him will resolve any issue." "If for some reason someone isn't available they can always find a good alternative. They know their cases and they know their barristers so will recommend the most suitable person."

JUNIORS

Andrew Axon Acts on either the claimant or defendant side of heavyweight serious injury claims including those arising from surgical negligence, delayed diagnosis of diseases and a failure to supervise those at risk of suicide. He is head of chambers and is widely renowned for his handling of cerebral palsy and acquired brain injury claims. **Strengths:** "He is carrying out very senior work and I would consider him for cases where I might otherwise instruct a QC." "He has a keen eye for medical detail, is easy to get on with and is very approachable." **Recent work:** Achieved a settlement for the claimant in Duke Burns v North Cumbria University Hospital, in which a patient suffered severe spinal cord damage and paraplegia following the delayed diagnosis of a spinal infection.

Howard Elgot Assists with long-running and typically high-value claims on behalf of claimants and defendants. Has recent experience in child brain injury and failed orthopaedic surgery cases. **Strengths:** "He is excellent at dealing with liability in difficult clinical negligence claims. He has a thorough knowledge of both medicine and the law." "He is a safe pair of hands and is reliable and academic." **Recent work:** Represented the claimant in Carrick v NHS Commissioning Board. The claim related to negligence after the claimant suffered a stroke in prison.

Stephen Friday Continues to build a strong reputation for his handling of lower-value but complex cases including adult fatal and stillbirth claims resulting from the delayed diagnosis of medical conditions. Also advises on surgical negligence cases. **Strengths:** "In conference, he is good at getting experts to answer questions in a way that is easy to understand." "He is a good team leader when dealing with multiple experts and witnesses who are distressed or upset." **Recent work:** Advised the claimant in Matthew Taylor v MOD, which settled following the MOD's admission on causation in the failure to diagnose a scaphoid fracture. The case raised various issues relating to non-medically qualified persons conducting GP clinics for the MOD.

Richard Copnall (see p.623) Earns considerable praise for his work on clinical negligence inquests that lead to civil claims. **Strengths:** "He is analytical, very sharp and really gets to the bottom of cases. He won't leave an issue alone until he can understand it and everyone else understands it." "He is a tough cross-examiner and a good person to get in when you have a difficult client."

Other Ranked Lawyers

Sarah Pritchard (see p.744) (Kings Chambers) Stands out for her work on the defence side of high-value and highly complex claims. Handles difficult issues relating to consent, the care of patients at risk of suicide and calculations of quantum in fatal or severe disability cases. Sarah Pritchard operates from both the Leeds and the Manchester addresses of Kings Chambers. **Strengths:** "She's able to really get to the nub of the issues and identify where everyone's weaknesses are in order to effectively negotiate." "She is clever and tough; a doughty opponent who can demolish her opponents."

Andrew Lewis QC (Park Square Barristers) Queen's Counsel and head of chambers with deep experience in complex clinical negligence. He is frequently sought out to handle major birth injury claims that typically involve cerebral palsy and other brain damage to babies. **Strengths:** "Clients like him. He has a grasp of what is required in these cases, is not out of touch and clients take to him immediately." "He is quick to grasp things and will raise questions ahead of any meeting if he needs to, so everything runs much more smoothly."

Michael Hill (Trinity Chambers) Has a well-established reputation as a key clinical negligence barrister with a particular focus on dental claims. He represents both claimants and defendants. **Strengths:** "He has a good rapport with clients and is excellent with expert witnesses. He is thorough, has a good understanding of the law and, with his dental background, has strong medical knowledge also." "He always makes himself available and sticks to deadlines."

NORTHERN

Clinical Negligence
Leading Sets
Band 1
Byrom Street Chambers *
Band 2
Kings Chambers *
** Indicates set / individual with profile.*
◊ (ORL) = Other Ranked Lawyer.
Alphabetical order within each band. Band 1 is highest.

Clinical Negligence
Leading Silks
Band 1
Braslavsky Nicholas *Kings Chambers* *
Grime Stephen *Deans Court Chambers (ORL)* ◊
Hatfield Sally *Byrom Street Chambers* *
Heaton David *Byrom Street Chambers* *
Melton Christopher *Byrom Street Chambers* *
Poole Nigel *Kings Chambers* *
Rowley James *Byrom Street Chambers* *
Band 2
Allen Darryl *Byrom Street Chambers* *
Braithwaite Bill *Exchange Chambers (ORL)* ◊
Hunter Winston *Byrom Street Chambers* *
Machell Raymond *Byrom Street Chambers*
Martin Gerard *Exchange Chambers (ORL)* ◊
Redfern Michael *St Johns Buildings (ORL)* ◊
Yip Amanda *Exchange Chambers (ORL)* ◊

Band 1

Byrom Street Chambers

See profile on p.960

THE SET

Stands out for its superb offering, particularly at QC level, and a correspondingly excellent track record in complex and high-value catastrophic injury claims. Its members regularly handle birth injury cases in which baby and mother have suffered physical or psychiatric harm as a result of negligent obstetric care. The set's experienced juniors are tremendously popular due to their ability to take on both high-value and lower-value cases including orthopaedic surgery, spinal and fatal delayed diagnosis claims.

Client service: "At Byrom they make the effort to know you and to understand the kind of service you want from a barrister." "Senior clerk Steve Price will move mountains to help. Particularly on tough cases where each side has multiple experts the clerks do everything they can to massage the diary to make things happen."

SILKS

Sally Hatfield QC (see p.667) Among the most popular silks for child brain injury and fatal cases that require sensitive handling of clients. Has a broad practice that includes highly complex secondary psychiatric harm cases and claims arising from the delayed diagnosis of spinal injuries or cancers.

Clinical Negligence
Leading Juniors
Band 1
Feeny Charles *Complete Counsel (ORL)* ◊
Pritchard Sarah *Kings Chambers* *
Ruck Mary *Byrom Street Chambers* *
Band 2
Bridgman Andrew *St Johns Buildings (ORL)* ◊
Eccles David *Deans Court Chambers (ORL)* ◊
Forrest Alastair *18 St John Street (ORL)* ◊
Limb Christopher *18 St John Street (ORL)* ◊ *
Mulholland Helen *Kings Chambers* *
Norton Richard *St Johns Buildings (ORL)* ◊
Owen Wendy *St Johns Buildings (ORL)* ◊
Roussak Jeremy *Kings Chambers* *
Smith Michael *Deans Court Chambers (ORL)* ◊
Steward Claire *Kings Chambers* *
Wright Alastair *St Johns Buildings (ORL)* ◊
Band 3
Galloway Rachel *Kings Chambers* *
Grundy Philip *St Johns Buildings (ORL)* ◊
Law Charlotte *Kings Chambers* *
Maguire Stephen *Kings Chambers*
Mazzag Anthony *Cobden House Chambers (ORL)* ◊ *
McNamara Stephen *Kings Chambers* *
Naylor Kevin *Exchange Chambers (ORL)* ◊ *
Ryder Timothy *Deans Court Chambers (ORL)* ◊
Wells Jason *Byrom Street Chambers* *
* *Indicates individual with profile.*
◊ *(ORL) = Other Ranked Lawyer.*
Alphabetical order within each band. Band 1 is highest.

Strengths: "Her pleadings are fantastic; extremely clear, logical and concise." "She gets to the heart of the issues and can think outside the box."

David Heaton QC (see p.668) Regularly advises on the claimant side of cerebral palsy and other brain injury cases affecting babies as a result of negligent midwifery care. Handles cases in which mismanaged childbirth leads to gynaecological and psychiatric injuries to the mother. Also advises on complex spinal claims. **Strengths:** "He has a fabulous demeanour with clients, they warm to him and feel comfortable with him." "He knows the papers inside-out, knows the issues that can arise and takes those on in conference in a way that clients can understand."

Christopher Melton QC (see p.715) Receives superb feedback from instructing solicitors and from lay clients for his excellent communication skills. Often handles major cerebral palsy cases alongside wrongful birth and spinal claims. Has earned an impressive reputation for his experience in high-profile inquiries or cases that test novel points of law before the Supreme Court. **Strengths:** "His style puts both clients and experts at ease so that he is able to then get the most out of them." "He wouldn't think twice about deciding to just go and see the client, rather than having a conference in chambers. He has a great manner with people, is reassuring and understands what their aims are."

James Rowley QC (see p.756) Particularly well known as a leading expert on quantum issues in high-value brain injury cases. Frequently represents child claimants at all stages of complex clinical negligence cases arising from negligence at birth. Has further proven strength on the defendant side of delayed diagnosis of meningitis cases in adults and children. **Strengths:** "He is very detailed and technical, with an amazing knowledge of all quantum cases that he can just pluck from his memory." "His attention to detail and his forensic analysis is second to none."

Darryl Allen QC (see p.582) Continues to build a reputation for his ability to lead high-value clinical negligence cases at trial. Recent key court cases have examined the reliability of conflicting expert and lay witness reports in negligence claims. **Strengths:** "He is an incredible advocate; he doesn't miss a single point. He is a real fighter and is quickly able to assimilate the evidence and present it succinctly for the judge." "He is calm and clients respond very well to him. They have lots of faith and confidence in him and are happy to be guided by him." **Recent work:** Represented the claimant at appeal in Synclair v East Lancashire Hospitals NHS Trust, in which a man was wrongfully discharged from hospital following abdominal surgery.

Winston Hunter QC (see p.678) Has experience on both the defendant and claimant side of complex cases, including crossover personal injury cases in which doctors fail to spot early signs of more serious injuries. Also advises on wrongful birth, obstetrics and adult-acquired brain injury cases. **Strengths:** "Has the most massive brain in Manchester and is very switched-on." "He is a good communicator; he says so much with so few words."

Raymond Machell QC Has a broad personal injury practice that often crosses over into the clinical negligence sphere. Has acted in several large cerebral palsy cases with large periodical payment orders. **Strengths:** "He has meticulous preparation."

JUNIORS

Mary Ruck (see p.756) Hugely popular choice for highly complex fatal delayed diagnosis, spinal injury and gynaecology cases. Has further experience in child brain injury cases and niche claims relating to the negligent transmission of viruses. Mary Ruck attracts particular attention for her recent work on high-profile group litigation that raises major human rights issues. **Strengths:** "She's bright and thorough but brings some warmth to everything she does." "She is very approachable from a solicitor point of view; we can very often have conversations about a case off the cuff."

Jason Wells (see p.792) Sources often highlight his background as an NHS surgeon as a major advantage when dealing with medically complex clinical negligence cases. **Strengths:** "I was really impressed with the depth and thoroughness with which he went into the case, really taking it apart line by line." "He has a direct approach; he's sympathetic and kind, but is clinical and cuts to the chase."

Band 2

Kings Chambers

See profile on p.968

THE SET

Benefits from a sizeable group of highly regarded junior barristers and silks who offer comprehensive coverage of all types of clinical negligence cases. Leading QCs take on heavyweight litigation that often involves child brain injuries or the delayed diagnosis of serious conditions. Juniors assist predominantly on the claimant side of cases that range from high-value orthopaedics cases to more modest-value dental, prescription error, psychiatric and fatal claims. Key individuals also focus on complex defendant claims.

Client service: "Steve Loxton is the head clerk and is incredibly helpful; he is prompt at responding, easy to work with and makes dealing with the barristers there very smooth." "It is a very effective chambers and the clerking team deals with queries promptly."

SILKS

Nicholas Braslavsky QC (see p.602) Is most active on the claimant side of a wide range of clinical negligence claims including complex birth injury and delayed diagnosis cases. Has additional experience in well-publicised claims that cross over into the field of product liability and raise issues of doctors' liability for misleading marketing of products. **Strengths:** "He makes the client feel central to everything so they don't feel like they are sidelined at all. He ensures that everything is explained to them in a way they understand and is very respectful." "What stands out, really, is his technical ability; he can go beyond what we usually find in cases and is not fazed by dealing with difficult issues."

Nigel Poole QC (see p.740) Widely regarded as a hugely important clinical negligence expert with tremendous client handling and advocacy skills. Attracts instructions in major cases that test novel points of law or are medically and factually complex. Earns further praise for his academic contributions to the field. **Strengths:** "He's one of the best silks in clinical negligence nationally. He has excellent client care skills and goes above and beyond to fight issues." "He is extremely down-to-earth with no airs and graces and is very bright. He manages cases sensitively but firmly, which is a real gift, and is very quick with returning papers." **Recent work:** Represented the claimant in P v NHS Commissioning Board, in which it was held that a nurse's failure to diagnose swine flu was negligent and that the defendant was liable for her resulting care needs.

JUNIORS

Sarah Pritchard (see p.744) An important point of call for defendant solicitors spread across the North and North East who rely on her expertise in diverse clinical negligence cases. Has notable experience in spinal injuries, fatal delays in diagnosis and cases raising issues of informed consent. **Strengths:** "She is robust in negotiations with the opposite side." "She is feisty, thorough and on top of the evidence, so she knows all the caveats we could use to put pressure on the other side."

Helen Mulholland (see p.723) Receives significant praise for her flexibility to take on mid-range to larger delayed diagnosis and orthopaedics cases. Also has recent experience in high-profile surgical negligence group actions and cases that have a crucial criminal law component. **Strengths:** "She is always happy to pick up the phone and discuss things." "She is good with experts in terms of getting the information out of them, and is good with clients in terms of making sure they understand what is going on with their case."

Jeremy Roussak (see p.755) Benefits from previous experience as a surgeon, which often assists with the cross-examination of experts. Instructing solicitors recognise his ability to manage tough cases that require a robust approach. **Strengths:** "He provides a very detailed analysis" and is "very robust and straight to the point." **Recent work:** Acted for the claimant in Royal Wolverhampton Hospitals NHS Trust v Evans. The Court of Appeal upheld the decision that the doctor had been negligent in leaving a blob of cement in contact with the patient's sciatic nerve during hip surgery.

Claire Steward (see p.773) Has a broad claimant-side practice that includes cases relating to secondary psychiatric harm, ophthalmology and the delayed diagnosis of cancer. She also handles surgical negligence and criminal cases that raise complex issues as to the calculation of quantum. **Strengths:** "She can explain complicated medical matters to clients and is warm and friendly." "She manages expectations well and in meetings sets out what she's going to do, gets on with it and summarises at the end. She has an analytical and thorough approach and is good on the medical detail."

Charlotte Law (see p.696) Frequently takes on inquests in fatal cases and civil claims for psychiatric and other injuries arising from surgical negligence or failed dental treatment. **Strengths:** "When talking about the most intimate symptoms she shows really good client care skills." "Her style enables the client to understand where the case is going and if it can't proceed she can explain the reasons why. Clients feel that they can speak to her as she is very approachable."

Stephen Maguire Seen as an important personal injury lawyer with notable experience in clinical negligence cases including the delayed diagnosis and treatment of orthopaedic conditions. **Strengths:** "He's very aware of what the client has been through" and "is able to explain complex matters in a succinct and clear way that the client understands."

Stephen McNamara (see p.713) Continues to impress interviewees with his capabilities in increasingly complex cases. He has particular expertise in psychiatric harm cases and claims brought under the Human Rights Act 1998, alongside a broader practice that includes neonatal death and delayed diagnosis cases. **Strengths:** "Has a great understanding of clinical negligence and the issues that we face in cases. He has good tactical awareness." "He is obviously highly intelligent and he is well informed and bold."

Rachel Galloway (see p.650) Stands out for her work on inquests into fatal cases arising under diverse circumstances, including sensitive cases in which mentally ill patients have not received adequate care. She also advises on the delayed diagnosis of cancers or other conditions in adults and children. **Strengths:** "She is confident and always available on the other end of the phone." "She offers very fast turnaround of documents and is excellent with clients."

Other Ranked Lawyers

Charles Feeny (Complete Counsel) Widely recognised as a leading clinical negligence specialist who has significant exposure to recent key court cases. Popular choice for defendant firms looking to fight intricate cases on causation and quantum. Also acts on the claimant side of high-value claims. **Strengths:** "He deals with an equal amount of claimant and defendant work, which is useful as he is always thinking about a case from both sides' perspective." "He is excellent on his feet, always well prepared and a natural speaker who gets to the point." **Recent work:** Acted for the appellant trust in Reaney v University Hospital of North Staffordshire NHS Trust & Anr, a high-profile case in which a patient who was already paralysed developed pressure sores as a result of negligent care.

Stephen Grime QC (Deans Court Chambers) A well-respected silk with terrific experience in a huge variety of civil claims including major clinical negligence cases. He is skilled on both the claimant and defendant side of cerebral palsy claims. **Strengths:** "He has a calm demeanour. He's unflappable." "He is vastly experienced and this shows in everything he does. He is clever and able to assimilate large quantities of information quickly."

David Eccles (Deans Court Chambers) Known for recent work on the defendant side of diverse clinical negligence, personal injury and police law cases. Also receives praise for his work with claimants. **Strengths:** "He is perceptive in terms of his analysis of the issues as to quantum."

Michael Smith (Deans Court Chambers) Typically advises defendants on personal injury and clinical negligence claims that include birth injury and other catastrophic cases.

Timothy Ryder (Deans Court Chambers) Experienced practitioner with an exclusive focus on claimant cases. He regularly works on infant brain injury cases and also handles spinal injury and misdiagnosis of cancer cases.

Gerard Martin QC (Exchange Chambers) Key catastrophic injury silk with an important clinical negligence practice. Specialises in high-value acquired brain injury cases on behalf of children and adults. Has further standout expertise in amputation cases including those that result from clinical negligence. **Strengths:** "His knowledge of prosthetics and amputee injuries is phenomenal. He has taken it upon himself to know everything there is to know about prosthetics." "He commands the respect of the court and his preparation is first-rate."

Amanda Yip QC (Exchange Chambers) Impresses due to her role in crucial court cases that have refined the scope of clinical negligence law. Often assists child claimants with cerebral palsy and other acquired brain injury cases. Has additional recent exposure to adult spinal and brain injury claims. **Strengths:** "She is fantastic to just pick up the phone and call. She has I don't know how many cases but she switches on, remembers everything about your case and gives quick advice with a view to formal papers later on." "She presents the case really succinctly and gets the points across." **Recent work:** Instructed on the claimant side of leading Court of Appeal case Liverpool Women's Hospital NHS Foundation v Ronayne. The case examined the hurdles to a claimant establishing liability for secondary psychiatric harm in a hospital setting.

Bill Braithwaite QC (Exchange Chambers) Focuses on brain injury cases arising either from straight personal injury situations or from cases of clinical negligence. Interviewees praise his respectful and sensitive way of working with children and adults who have suffered catastrophic brain injuries. **Strengths:** "He predominantly specialises in brain injury, so from his knowledge and experience we're happy to instruct him with very vulnerable clients." "In conference, if the client has any questions, he is just a constant reassurance to them."

Kevin Naylor (see p.725) (Exchange Chambers) Often highlighted as a strong choice for smaller cases arising from negligent dental or cosmetic surgery. He has further proven capabilities in fatal cases and those relating to psychiatric harm. **Strengths:** "He was formerly a GP, which gives him some really good insight into clinical negligence cases." "He's very accommodating via email and always gets back to me quickly."

Michael Redfern QC (St Johns Buildings) Has a strong focus on brain injury cases including cerebral palsy claims resulting from obstetric negligence. **Strengths:** "He provides reassurance to clients where it is obviously technically very complicated and a stressful time for them." "He brings a lot of experience to the table."

Andrew Bridgman (St Johns Buildings) Remains a popular choice for dental cases owing, in part, to his experience gained working in the dental profession. Andrew Bridgman also advises on orthopaedics and failure to diagnose cases. **Strengths:** "He has a good grasp of the medical issues, is able to deal with issues in conference very succinctly and is liked by clients." "He has a particular understanding of dental issues."

Richard Norton (St Johns Buildings) Handles a huge range of clinical negligence cases including wrongful birth, delay in diagnosis and surgical negligence claims. Interviewees note his suitability for cases that require a strict approach to the management of client expectations. **Strengths:** "He identifies all the issues to the extent that the client fully appreciates what the main points are in their case and the difficulties that we may encounter." "He's very down-to-earth with the client and has a sensible and practical approach." **Recent work:** Advised on wrongful birth case H v University Hospitals of Morecambe Bay NHS FT, in which the mother was able to recover the costs of bringing up a disabled child.

Wendy Owen (St Johns Buildings) Particularly active on the claimant side of cases in which the delayed diagnosis or delayed treatment of various conditions leads to disability, amputation, brain damage or death. Draws on her previous experience as a defendant solicitor and a deputy district judge. **Strengths:** "She is tactically astute and brings a lot of experience from her previous roles into what she does with us." "She understands the solicitor's perspective, is excellent with clients and has a good working knowledge of this area of law."

Alastair Wright (St Johns Buildings) Advises on fatal cases and claims with an important psychiatric health angle as part of his broader personal injury and industrial disease practice. Recent standout mandates include an inquest into the suicide of a soldier who was released from police custody. **Strengths:** "He doesn't sit on the fence; he gives a proper opinion on what he thinks and fights hard for the client." "A good brain; he is shrewd, considers things carefully and is sensible." **Recent work:** Represented the claimant in Shaw v Dr Kovac and University of Leicester Hospital NHS Trust. The High Court judge held that an elderly patient who died in surgery had not given informed consent to experimental heart surgery.

Philip Grundy (St Johns Buildings) Experienced catastrophic injury specialist who is increasingly noted for activity on high-value cases in the clinical negligence sphere. Handles delayed diagnosis of spinal injuries, cancers or other conditions. Also well known for work on amputation cases. **Strengths:** "His attention to detail is absolutely second to none." "He is focused, determined and has all of the underlying attributes you would expect, but he delivers them in a genial and affable way."

Alastair Forrest (18 St John Street) Long-standing presence with vast experience in complex clinical negligence cases. He works closely with key healthcare bodies on regulatory matters. **Strengths:** "He is excellent; definitely a favoured barrister."

Christopher Limb (see p.701) (18 St John Street) Stands out for his exclusive focus on clinical negligence work and his correspondingly strong capabilities in technically and medically complex cases. Regularly handles cerebral palsy and other high-value claims. **Strengths:** "He is thorough, is great with complex and high-value cases and is nice with people." "He pays great attention to detail and gets straight to the real issues."

Anthony Mazzag (see p.711) (Cobden House Chambers) Earns considerable praise for his claimant-side practice that often sees him working on delayed diagnosis of cancer, surgical or orthopaedic negligence cases. **Strengths:** "He's very approachable; the kind of barrister who is quite happy if you send him an email between formal instructions or give him a ring, which really helps to move cases along." "He is really understanding of the client's needs and makes sensible and practical decisions."

WALES & CHESTER

Clinical Negligence
Leading Juniors
Band 1
Jones Nicholas David *Civitas Law* *
Thomas Bryan *Civitas Law* *

Ranked Lawyers

Nicholas Jones (see p.686) (Civitas Law) A junior with almost three decades of experience in cases of clinical negligence. He is routinely instructed in matters related to catastrophic injury such as brain and spinal injuries as well as limb amputations. **Strengths:** "He's very knowledgeable about the law and thoughtful about the advice he gives. Very good with clients, approachable, hard-working and accessible." "He's very good at analysing the medical evidence and directing the medical experts to the crucial details." **Recent work:** Acted on behalf of a claimant who suffered serious orthopaedic injuries following a motorcycle accident that greatly impacted his earning capacity.

Bryan Thomas (see p.780) (Civitas Law) A highly respected junior with extensive experience in a broad range of high-value matters relating to clinical negligence. Representative work includes complex cerebral palsy, failure to diagnose cancer and brain injury matters. **Strengths:** "He's excellent with clients, very approachable and always accessible." "He is very solid, very tenacious as a barrister and isn't afraid to put matters in front of a judge."

WESTERN

Clinical Negligence
Leading Sets
Band 1
Guildhall Chambers *
St John's Chambers *
Band 2
3PB Barristers *
Leading Silks
New Silks
Fox Simon *No5 Chambers (ORL)* ◊
Leading Juniors
Star individuals
Plowden Selena *Guildhall Chambers*
Band 1
Dunlop Hamish *3PB Barristers*
Grice Timothy *St John's Chambers*
Leeper Tom *St John's Chambers* [A]
Snell John *Guildhall Chambers*
Townsend James *Guildhall Chambers*
Band 2
Bennett Daniel *Doughty Street Chambers (ORL)* ◊
Lomas Mark *3PB Barristers*
McKinlay Vanessa *St John's Chambers*
Regan David *St John's Chambers* [A]
Sowersby Robert *Guildhall Chambers*
Stamp Abigail *Guildhall Chambers*
Weston Louis *3PB Barristers*
Zeb Emma *St John's Chambers* [A]
Up-and-coming individuals
Holme Sophie *Guildhall Chambers*
* *Indicates set / individual with profile.*
[A] *direct access (see p.24).*
◊ *(ORL) = Other Ranked Lawyer.*
Alphabetical order within each band. Band 1 is highest.

Band 1

Guildhall Chambers
See profile on p.938

THE SET
One of the leading sets for clinical negligence on the Western Circuit, noted for its presence on the most challenging and prominent claims. Its members act for claimants, medical defence organisations and commercial care providers. The set's expertise ranges from catastrophic brain and spinal injuries to fatal claims. The set is well versed in related matters, including inquests and professional indemnity proceedings.

Client service: "The clerks are always organised and really amenable to client circumstances, turning things around quickly to do what they can to help." "The chambers have good support staff who always respond promptly and run training days which are useful." Wendy Shaw and Heather Bidwell are the clerks for the personal injury and clinical negligence teams.

JUNIORS

Selena Plowden Has built up an impressive reputation representing both claimants and defendants in an array of complex claims in her clinical negligence and personal injury practice. Acts in a wide range of maximum severity cases including those relating to catastrophic neurological injuries, birth injuries, and missed diagnoses of cancer. **Strengths:** "She has an excellent client manner and a very thorough understanding of the details." "She is absolutely fantastic; no stone is left unturned, she's very organised, competent on her feet and is brilliant with medical experts." **Recent work:** Acted for a claimant who suffered an above-knee amputation following knee replacement surgery by a private surgeon.

John Snell Demonstrates particular expertise in clinical negligence, personal injury and equine litigation. He acts in high-value claims often concerning cerebral palsy, spinal injuries and obstetric damage. **Strengths:** "Helpful, thoughtful and insightful." "He's very experienced and very thorough. He has good medical knowledge." "He tends to be on particularly complicated cases on liability. He can process information very quickly and distil it into advice." **Recent work:** Defended an NHS Trust in connection with a claim of delayed diagnosis and treatment of raised intracranial pressure causing total blindness of the claimant.

James Townsend Experienced and well versed in medical law, his practice encompasses clinical negligence and disciplinary hearings. He acts primarily for claimants on such matters as those involving serious post-vasectomy pain and delays in diagnosis. He continues to provide his expertise in matters arising from negligent storage of gametes. **Strengths:** "Provides sound advice coupled with subtle advocacy skills capable of winning over the most formidable tribunal." "He's very efficient, knowledgeable and effective." **Recent work:** Acted for a claimant whose sperm was destroyed through negligent storage.

Robert Sowersby Praised by sources for his ability on technically complex claims. He handles a wide-ranging clinical negligence caseload, often tackling matters concerning surgical negligence and substandard care. **Strengths:** "He's very efficient, helpful and friendly. He is one of those people that can take something complex and simplify it for everyone to understand and get to the heart of the matter. He is also excellent at dealing with sensitive cases. You want him in your corner."

Abigail Stamp Receives great acclaim for her ability to handle complicated matters. She acts on a wide range of high-value cases, often concerning surgical negligence, delayed diagnosis as well as inquests arising from psychiatric injuries and negligent care. **Strengths:** "She's able to grasp the intricacies of medical negligence cases quickly and hold her own in detailed expert discussions." "A very stable and secure pair of hands."

Sophie Holme Acts for claimants and defendants, gaining significant recognition for her clinical negligence practice. In addition, she also offers expertise in personal injury and serves as counsel at inquests. **Strengths:** "She's very precise and thorough. She takes time to understand complex issues and is good with clients and experts alike." "A safe pair of hands and detail-oriented." "Incredibly meticulous and very good in a fight." **Recent work:** Successfully defended a nurse accused of inappropriate practice.

St John's Chambers

See profile on p.941

THE SET

Acts for both claimants and an increasing number of defendants in complex and high-profile claims. The set has an impressive reach in the South West and is praised by solicitors for its established team and "undoubtedly good reputation" on the Western Circuit. Its members handle a diverse range of challenging cases including catastrophic injury, surgical error and dental negligence. It is committed to training, often housing events and contributing to conferences.

Client service: "The clerking is extremely helpful and it is well resourced." Sources praise clerk Adam Marston and practice manager Annette Bushell as "warm, friendly and very organised." "The clerks are excellent. They are extremely approachable, practical and will accommodate your needs." Derek Jenkins acts as chief executive.

JUNIORS

Timothy Grice Has a great deal of experience of representing claimants in high-value cases concerning catastrophic injury. His substantial clinical negligence practice encompasses brain and spinal injury, fatal claims and surgical negligence. **Strengths:** "He's very confident on his feet and has a logical approach. He's very methodical and pays attention to detail." "He's meticulous on paper, and provides helpful and thorough advice. He gets to the nub of the issue in a concise way."

Tom Leeper A specialist in clinical negligence claims, he is sought after by solicitors for his detailed approach to cases. He covers a range of cases, often concerning birth injury and surgical negligence. He is also an expert in psychiatric claims and inquests. He was appointed as Junior Counsel to the Crown, part of the Attorney General's Civil List. **Strengths:** "An experienced clinical negligence barrister and a real safe pair of hands." "He turns up with detailed notes of the issues and his pleadings are spectacular. His attention to detail is phenomenal."

Vanessa McKinlay Draws on experience as a former senior physiotherapist in the NHS when addressing technical and complex claims, and is recognised for expertise in medical law. Head of the practice group, she represents claimant and defendant clients. **Strengths:** "She has the ability to dilute information down and cut to the chase." "Her background as a former physiotherapist stands her in good stead for grasping medical issues; she gets experts onboard quite easily."

David Regan Represents claimants and defendants as part of his comprehensive clinical negligence practice, and is also active in professional negligence, personal injury and employment law. He frequently handles fatal accidents and failures in general practice. **Strengths:** "Very thorough and good on quantum." "He's very good on fatal cases and on tricky medical issues. He's very nice with clients and expresses difficult issues to the client in understandable terms."

Emma Zeb Undertakes an array of clinical negligence claims for claimants and defendants, including those concerning complex issues of breach of duty and causation. In addition, she is skilled in dental claims and has an ample caseload of personal injury and inquest work. **Strengths:** "A formidable and impressive advocate. She has a detailed approach to evidence in conference and a realistic approach to strategy in difficult cases." "She's very thorough and good on her feet; very in control." **Recent work:** Acted for a claimant with pre-existing spina bifida who developed severe pressure sores.

Band 2

3PB Barristers

See profile on p.892

THE SET

This London set offers a network across England, and has a sizeable group operating on the Western Circuit. Its members undertake complex clinical negligence claims, and are experienced in both NHS and private healthcare matters. They are routinely instructed on behalf a range of clients including those who lack capacity, children and families of the deceased.

Client service: "An excellent service; we can always talk to them." "They have a really good set of clerks who are very user-friendly." Mark Heath acts as chambers director.

JUNIORS

Hamish Dunlop Recognised for his approach to complex cases, he demonstrates particular expertise in handling cauda equina matters. He provides additional support on care and housing requirements, as well as on dependency claims. **Strengths:** "He is very thorough and approachable." "His real strength is in the testing of evidence. He can focus on factual evidence and chronology very well."

Mark Lomas Focuses on representing claimants in a wide range of maximum severity cases including those relating to catastrophic injury. His practice covers the London Bar and Western Circuit. He routinely acts in surgical negligence matters and delay in diagnoses. In addition, he is adept at dental claims. **Strengths:** "Excellent with clients and experts." "He's exceptional at what he does due to his experience over the years. He instils a great deal of confidence in the clients." **Recent work:** Successfully acted for a claimant in connection with a claim for negligent shoulder surgery leading to four revision procedures and permanent restriction of function.

Louis Weston A highly experienced barrister practising across the London Bar and Western Circuit. He handles a range of clinical negligence claims including those relating to delayed diagnoses and cosmetic surgery. He also acts in cases concerning negligent veterinary treatment and veterinary products. **Recent work:** Acted for a claimant in a matter concerning the mismanagement of delivery.

Other Ranked Lawyers

Daniel Bennett (Doughty Street Chambers) A well-regarded practitioner with a wide-ranging caseload involving clinical negligence, personal injury and product liability claims. He acts predominantly for claimants and often acts in cases concerning psychiatric injury or substandard care. He also regularly handles claims relating to surgical negligence and fatal incidents. **Strengths:** "He is so committed to the claimant's cause and is very passionate about ensuring that people are appropriately presented. He has a real passion for justice."

Simon Fox (No5 Chambers) Receives great acclaim for his extensive experience in the field and for his ability to tackle complex medical cases due to his background as a doctor. He is highly sought after for his expertise in high-value cases, and acts for both claimants and defendants. He often handles matters involving catastrophic brain or spinal injuries. In particular, he demonstrates further expertise in neurosurgical and neuroendocrine negligence. **Strengths:** "He has a wealth of experience in high-value cases and can be relied upon for a sensible, thorough approach." "An extremely talented and experienced counsel, able to get the very best from medical experts."

Contents:

LONDON

Commercial Dispute Resolution
Leading Sets
Band 1
Brick Court Chambers *
One Essex Court *
Essex Court Chambers *
Fountain Court Chambers *
Band 2
Blackstone Chambers *
20 Essex Street *
7 King's Bench Walk *
3 Verulam Buildings *
Band 3
Maitland Chambers *
Quadrant Chambers *
Serle Court *
Band 4
4 New Square *
4 Pump Court *
4 Stone Buildings *
Wilberforce Chambers *
** Indicates set with profile.*
Alphabetical order within each band. Band 1 is highest.

Band 1

Brick Court Chambers
See profile on p.816

THE SET

An undisputed heavyweight that handles the most complex, high-stakes litigation heard in the London courts and globally. It possesses enormous strength in depth and has some of the very finest names at the Bar within its ranks. Uniform excellence is a given and such is the standard of entry into the set that solicitors say: "The set has an extraordinarily deep pool of people to draw on. If you throw a stone there you are bound to hit someone brilliant." In recent years the barristers have been heavily involved in Russian oligarch work, having been instructed in matters such as the Pinchuk litigation and the Bank of St Petersburg v Arkhangelsky case.

Client service: "The clerks have very good relationships with the commercial courts." Solicitors say: "They understand our business and client pressures, and always deliver by being responsive and flexible when it comes to fee arrangements and resourcing needs." The clerking team is lead by Ian Moyler and Julian Hawes.

SILKS

Mark Howard QC One of the very top commercial litigators, who takes the lead role in some of the most significant cases currently being heard. His calmness under pressure and ability to manage huge multi-jurisdictional cases are much admired. **Strengths:** "Formidable in terms of his exceptional analytical and strategic skills, and an advocate with ferocious cross-examination skills." "His legal ability is just flawless, and he masters the case at hand every time." **Recent work:** Represented Ukrainian businessman Gennadiy Bogolyubov in Pinchuk v Kolomoisky & Bogolyubov. The case was one of the largest disputes in the London courts and focused on the ownership of a commodities business.

Helen Davies QC A very well thought-of barrister who is hugely experienced across a wide range of commercial work. She is highly respected for her work representing banks in leading cases, and also wins plaudits for her work in the energy sector. **Strengths:** "She has strong strategic intuition, is great on her feet and is always extremely persuasive." "She is incredibly calm under pressure." **Recent work:** Acted for Lloyds Banking Group in a claim brought against the directors of the group by 5% of Lloyds shareholders. The claim centred on alleged misrepresentation of HBOS's financial position prior to its acquisition by Lloyds in 2008.

Mark Hapgood QC An immensely skilled silk with long experience of leading big-ticket cases in a number of commercial law areas. He is widely respected by solicitors and the Bar alike, and particularly celebrated for his handling of major banking disputes. **Strengths:** "He is bright, hard-working, great with clients, very commercial and devastating on his feet." "He is one of the best all-rounders at the Bar, and a person to trust with bet-the-company cases."

Charles Hollander QC Acknowledged for his incisive thinking and breadth of commercial experience, and someone whose work on major interlocutory matters garners particular praise. He is known for his hugely impressive intellect and client-friendly attitude. **Strengths:** "A sound, methodical thinker who is good at getting the court to listen to what he has to say." "He is good to work with, an excellent advocate and an acknowledged expert on documentary evidence." **Recent work:** Represented the chair of the Libyan Investment Authority (LIA), Mr Breish, in a case against Goldman Sachs and Société Générale. The litigation concerned a dispute over who has the authority to act for the LIA following the civil war in Libya.

Tim Lord QC A go-to barrister for complex banking disputes who is in demand from banks and investors alike. Commentators laud him for his ability to identify the key issues in a case, present well to a court and keep his strategic aims in mind at all times. **Strengths:** "A fantastic technician and superb cross-examiner who is very client-friendly." "Good, clear, logical and thorough, he gets on well with clients and solicitors without exception. He's always a pleasure to work with." **Recent work:** Retained by the Bank of St Petersburg to defend it against allegations made by former customer Arkhangelsky. Arkhangelsky alleges that the bank colluded with Russian establishment figures to steal its business empire.

Neil Calver QC Highly proficient at work originating from Russia and the Commonwealth of Independent States (CIS), he is particularly known for handling big-ticket insurance matters. His analysis of legal matters and the ease with which he works in a team are particular attributes of his. **Strengths:** "Very commercial and client-friendly." "He's a robust performer and a good advocate who is really good fun as well, which is important if you're working on something stressful." **Recent work:** Acted for Adrilla and Zamin in a dispute involving iron ore mine licences in Brazil. The other party, the Kazakh government-owned ENRC, alleged that the licences were obtained through corruption and so payment was not due.

Simon Salzedo QC (see p.758) A "master of detail" who is regularly instructed in large disputes in the Commercial Court. His strength on his feet and his superior cross-examination skills win praise from the market. He is particularly well regarded for his expertise in conflicts of law cases and accountancy-related disputes. **Strengths:** "Understated, collected and incredibly impressive on his feet." "A barrister with outstanding legal knowledge and a detail-focused and analytical mind who is perfect for complex financial disputes." **Recent work:** Defended the former CFO of Autonomy, Sushovan Hussain, against claims of alleged false accounting linked to a USD12 billion write-down following Autonomy's acquisition by Hewlett-Packard.

Tom Adam QC The architect of a thriving commercial law practice, who is particularly noted for handling professional negligence cases on behalf of solicitors, accountants and insurance brokers. He is also an expert in banking, shipping and energy cases. **Strengths:** "A superb analyst who is excellent to work with." "He is very clever, incisive and effective." **Recent work:** Represented Arcadia Petroleum in a claim against executives of a privately owned oil trading group. Arcadia alleges the group diverted money and profits away from the company into their own vehicles.

Michael Bools QC Possesses a wide-ranging and impressive commercial law practice, and is active in major instances of litigation both at home and abroad. He is a particular expert on freezing orders. **Strengths:** "An intellectual heavyweight who is always thorough and detailed in his preparation." "He's got exactly the right touch for the big cases" and is "excellent on his feet." **Recent work:** Represented Bambino Holdings, the Ecclestone family trust, in litigation following the sale by BayernLB of its stake in CVC Partners. The litigation centred on claims that the shares were undervalued.

Jonathan Hirst QC A highly experienced silk with decades of commercial law experience behind him, he has appeared in countless appeal cases. He is particularly knowledgeable on international trade, insurance, shipping and energy matters. **Strengths:** "An excellent strategist who always sees the bigger picture." **Recent work:** Leading counsel for Mrs Swaters, now proved to be the owner of a Ferrari sold for £10 million at the Bonhams Goodwood Festival of Speed auction in 2014. There were multiple claimants to the proceeds of sale.

Daniel Jowell QC (see p.687) Regularly instructed by leading solicitors in complex litigation covering a range of commercial law areas. His work on fraud and shareholder disputes concerning oligarchs and high net worth individuals has been of particular note in recent years. **Strengths:** "He adopts a calm and considered approach." "He is a good advocate and a very very bright lawyer." **Recent work:** Acted as lead counsel for Angela and Alexandra Shamoon,

Commercial Dispute Resolution London

Commercial Dispute Resolution

Leading Silks

Star individuals

Brindle Michael *Fountain Court Chambers* *
Gaisman Jonathan *7 King's Bench Walk*
Grabiner Anthony *One Essex Court*
Howard Mark *Brick Court Chambers*
Rabinowitz Laurence *One Essex Court*

Band 1

Butcher Christopher *7 King's Bench Walk*
Crane Michael *Fountain Court Chambers* *
Crow Jonathan *4 Stone Buildings* *
Davies Helen *Brick Court Chambers*
Foxton David *Essex Court Chambers*
Girolami Paul *Maitland Chambers* *
Hapgood Mark *Brick Court Chambers*
Hollander Charles *Brick Court Chambers*
Lord Tim *Brick Court Chambers*
Malek Ali *3 Verulam Buildings*
McCaughran John *One Essex Court*
Miles Robert *4 Stone Buildings*
Onslow Andrew *3 Verulam Buildings*
Railton David *Fountain Court Chambers*
Smith Stephen *Erskine Chambers (ORL)* ◊ *
Smouha Joe *Essex Court Chambers*
Thanki Bankim *Fountain Court Chambers* *
Toledano Daniel *One Essex Court*
Wolfson David *One Essex Court*

Band 2

Anderson Robert *Blackstone Chambers*
Auld Stephen *One Essex Court*
Beltrami Adrian *3 Verulam Buildings*
Berry Steven *Essex Court Chambers*
Boyle Alan *Serle Court* *
Brisby John *4 Stone Buildings* *
Calver Neil *Brick Court Chambers*
Cavender David *One Essex Court* *
Choo Choy Alain *One Essex Court*
de Garr Robinson Anthony *One Essex Court* *
Downes Paul *2TG - 2 Temple Gardens (ORL)* ◊ [A] *
Dunning Graham *Essex Court Chambers* *
Edey Philip *20 Essex Street*
Fenwick Justin *4 New Square* *
Flynn Vernon *Essex Court Chambers*
Freedman Clive *7 King's Bench Walk* *
Goodall Patrick *Fountain Court Chambers* *
Gourgey Alan *Wilberforce Chambers*
Green Andrew *Blackstone Chambers*
Handyside Richard *Fountain Court Chambers* *
Hill Richard G *4 Stone Buildings* *
Hunter Andrew *Blackstone Chambers*
Jones Philip *Serle Court* *
Kitchener Neil *One Essex Court*
MacLean Kenneth *One Essex Court*
Matthews Duncan *20 Essex Street*
McGrath Paul *Essex Court Chambers*
McQuater Ewan *3 Verulam Buildings*
Mill Ian *Blackstone Chambers*
Nash Jonathan *3 Verulam Buildings*
Onions Jeffery *One Essex Court*
Orr Craig *One Essex Court* *
Philipps Guy *Fountain Court Chambers* *
Ritchie Stuart *Fountain Court Chambers* *
Saini Pushpinder *Blackstone Chambers*
Salzedo Simon *Brick Court Chambers* *
Steinfeld Alan *XXIV Old Buildings (ORL)* ◊
Tolaney Sonia *One Essex Court*
Tozzi Nigel *4 Pump Court* *
Trace Anthony *Maitland Chambers* *
Zacaroli Antony *South Square (ORL)* ◊ *

Band 3

Adam Tom *Brick Court Chambers*
Adkin Jonathan *Fountain Court Chambers* *
Ashworth Lance *Serle Court* *
Baker Andrew *20 Essex Street*
Bools Michael *Brick Court Chambers*
Boulton Richard *One Essex Court*
Croxford Ian *Wilberforce Chambers*
Dale Derrick *Fountain Court Chambers* *
Day Anneliese *4 New Square* *
Dicker Robin *South Square (ORL)* ◊ *
Dohmann Barbara *Blackstone Chambers*
Graham Charles *One Essex Court*
Hirst Jonathan *Brick Court Chambers*
Hochhauser Andrew *Essex Court Chambers*
Hossain Sa'ad *One Essex Court*
Howe Robert *Blackstone Chambers*
Howe Timothy *Fountain Court Chambers* *
Jacobs Richard *Essex Court Chambers*
Jones Elizabeth *Serle Court* *
Jowell Daniel *Brick Court Chambers* *
Kealey Gavin *7 King's Bench Walk*
Lowenstein Paul *3 Verulam Buildings*
Machell John *Serle Court* *
Maclean Alan *Blackstone Chambers*
Malek Hodge M *39 Essex Chambers (ORL)* ◊
Marshall Philip *Serle Court* *
Matovu Harry *Brick Court Chambers* *
Millett Richard *Essex Court Chambers*
Mitchell Andrew *Fountain Court Chambers* *
Mowschenson Terence *Wilberforce Chambers*
Odgers John *3 Verulam Buildings*
Pollock Gordon *Essex Court Chambers*
Rainey Simon *Quadrant Chambers* *
Rubin Stephen *Fountain Court Chambers* *
Russen Jonathan *Maitland Chambers* *
Sabben-Clare Rebecca *7 King's Bench Walk*
Salter Richard *3 Verulam Buildings*
Stanley Paul *Essex Court Chambers*
Sutcliffe Andrew *3 Verulam Buildings*
Tager Romie *Selborne Chambers (ORL)* ◊ *
Waller Richard *7 King's Bench Walk*
Wardell John *Wilberforce Chambers*
Weisselberg Tom *Blackstone Chambers*

Band 4

Allison David *South Square (ORL)* ◊ *
Béar Charles *Fountain Court Chambers* *
Bingham Camilla *One Essex Court*
Birt Simon *Brick Court Chambers*
Blayney David *Serle Court* *
Bompas George *4 Stone Buildings* *
Chapman Jeffrey *Fountain Court Chambers* *
Chivers David *Erskine Chambers (ORL)* ◊ *
Cogley Stephen *XXIV Old Buildings (ORL)* ◊
Collings Matthew *Maitland Chambers* *
Dougherty Charles *2TG - 2 Temple Gardens (ORL)* ◊ *
Douglas Michael *4 Pump Court* *
Elkington Ben *4 New Square* *
Gunning Alexander *4 Pump Court* *
Kimmins Charles *20 Essex Street*
Levy Robert *XXIV Old Buildings (ORL)* ◊
Lockey John *Essex Court Chambers* *
Masefield Roger *Brick Court Chambers* *
Moriarty Stephen *Fountain Court Chambers* *
Norbury Hugh *Serle Court* *
Oudkerk Daniel *Essex Court Chambers*
Pillow Nathan *Essex Court Chambers*
Potts James *Erskine Chambers (ORL)* ◊ *
Quest David *3 Verulam Buildings*
Robertson Patricia *Fountain Court Chambers* *
Samek Charles *Littleton Chambers (ORL)* ◊
Smith Tom *South Square (ORL)* ◊ *
Talbot Rice Elspeth *XXIV Old Buildings (ORL)* ◊
Twigger Andrew M *Maitland Chambers* *
White Antony *Matrix Chambers (ORL)* ◊ *

Band 5

Blanchard Claire *Essex Court Chambers*
Cordara Roderick *Essex Court Chambers* *
Davenport Simon *3 Hare Court (ORL)* ◊
Davies Huw *Essex Court Chambers* *
Davies Rhodri *One Essex Court*
Davies-Jones Jonathan *3 Verulam Buildings*
de la Mare Thomas *Blackstone Chambers*
Dhillon Jasbir *Brick Court Chambers*
Doctor Brian *Fountain Court Chambers* *
Fealy Michael *One Essex Court* *
Fletcher Andrew *3 Verulam Buildings*
George Andrew *Blackstone Chambers*
Gillis Richard *One Essex Court*
Goldring Jeremy *South Square (ORL)* ◊ *
Gruder Jeffrey *Essex Court Chambers* *
Hardwick Matthew *3 Verulam Buildings*
Houseman Stephen *Essex Court Chambers*
Jarvis John *3 Verulam Buildings*
Jones Nigel *Hardwicke (ORL)* ◊ [A]
Kirby PJ *Hardwicke (ORL)* ◊ [A]
Lavender Nicholas *Serle Court*
Lewis David *20 Essex Street*
McLaren Michael *Fountain Court Chambers* *
Mitchell Gregory *3 Verulam Buildings*
Morgan Richard *Maitland Chambers* *
Slade Richard *Brick Court Chambers*
Strong Benjamin *One Essex Court*
Swainston Michael *Brick Court Chambers*
Taylor John *Fountain Court Chambers* *
ter Haar Roger *Crown Office Chambers (ORL)* ◊

New Silks

Cohen Jonathan *Littleton Chambers (ORL)* ◊
Fatima Shaheed *Blackstone Chambers*
Head David *3 Verulam Buildings*
Lightman Daniel *Serle Court* *
Mumford David *Maitland Chambers* *
Phelps Rosalind *Fountain Court Chambers* *
Plewman SC Thomas *Brick Court Chambers*
Ramsden James *39 Essex Chambers (ORL)* ◊ [A] *
Valentin Ben *Fountain Court Chambers* *

** Indicates individual with profile.*
[A] direct access (see p.24).
◊ (ORL) = Other Ranked Lawyer.
Alphabetical order within each band. Band 1 is highest.

Commercial Dispute Resolution	
Leading Juniors	
Band 1	**Band 4**
Brocklebank James *7 King's Bench Walk* *	**Allen** Rupert *Fountain Court Chambers* *
Goldsmith Jamie *One Essex Court*	**Barker** James *Enterprise Chambers (ORL)* ◊
Lazarus Michael *3 Verulam Buildings* *	**Blakeley** Richard *Brick Court Chambers* *
Patton Conall *One Essex Court* *	**Brier** Jeremy *Essex Court Chambers*
Pilbrow Fionn *Brick Court Chambers*	**Brown** Edward *Essex Court Chambers*
Polley Alexander *One Essex Court* *	**Cook** Matthew *One Essex Court*
Willan James *Essex Court Chambers*	**Craig** Nicholas *3 Verulam Buildings*
Band 2	**de Verneuil Smith** Peter *3 Verulam Buildings* *
Akkouh Tim *Erskine Chambers (ORL)* ◊ *	**den Besten** Ruth *Serle Court* *
Boase Anna *One Essex Court*	**Elliott** Steven *One Essex Court*
Gledhill Orlando *One Essex Court* *	**Hobson** Fred *Brick Court Chambers* *
Haydon Alec *Brick Court Chambers*	**Kulkarni** Yash *Quadrant Chambers* *
Isaac Sebastian *One Essex Court*	**Lascelles** David *Littleton Chambers (ORL)* ◊ *
John Laura *Fountain Court Chambers* *	**Lynch** Ben *Fountain Court Chambers* *
King Edmund *Essex Court Chambers*	**Mallin** Max *Wilberforce Chambers*
Kramer Adam *3 Verulam Buildings* *	**Murray** David *Fountain Court Chambers* *
MacDonald James *One Essex Court* *	**Phipps** Sandy *One Essex Court* *
McClelland James *Fountain Court Chambers* *	**Power** Richard *Fountain Court Chambers* *
Midwinter Stephen *Brick Court Chambers*	**Riches** Philip *20 Essex Street*
Milner Alexander *Fountain Court Chambers* *	**Rogers** Amy *11KBW (ORL)* ◊ *
Oppenheimer Tamara *Fountain Court Chambers* *	**Spalton** George *4 New Square* *
Ratcliffe Peter *3 Verulam Buildings*	**Staunton** Ulick *Radcliffe Chambers (ORL)* ◊
Singla Tony *Brick Court Chambers* *	**Wood** Emily *Essex Court Chambers*
Zellick Adam *Fountain Court Chambers* *	**Band 5**
Band 3	**Abram** Sarah *Brick Court Chambers*
Adamyk Simon *New Square Chambers (ORL)* ◊	**Emmett** Laurence *One Essex Court*
Atrill Simon *Fountain Court Chambers* *	**Eschwege** Richard *Brick Court Chambers* *
Colton Simon *One Essex Court*	**Fulton** Andrew *20 Essex Street*
Cumming Edward *XXIV Old Buildings (ORL)* ◊	**Hubbard** Daniel *One Essex Court*
Cutress James *Fountain Court Chambers* *	**Ife** Linden *Enterprise Chambers (ORL)* ◊
Davies David *Essex Court Chambers*	**Jackson** Hugh *Selborne Chambers (ORL)* ◊ *
Dilnot Anna *Essex Court Chambers*	**Jeavons** Anne *3 Verulam Buildings*
Harris Christopher *3 Verulam Buildings*	**Jones** Emma *One Essex Court* *
Higgo Justin *Serle Court* *	**Lewis** David *Hardwicke (ORL)* ◊ [A]
John Benjamin *Maitland Chambers* *	**Lidington** Gary *Radcliffe Chambers (ORL)* ◊ *
Jones Oliver *Brick Court Chambers* *	**Majumdar** Shantanu *Radcliffe Chambers (ORL)* ◊
Keller Ciaran *Maitland Chambers* *	**Marshall** Paul *No5 Chambers (ORL)* ◊
Levey Edward *Fountain Court Chambers* *	**Mills** Simon *Five Paper (ORL)* ◊ [A]
Mott Richard *One Essex Court* *	**Ohrenstein** Dov *Radcliffe Chambers (ORL)* ◊ *
Nambisan Deepak *Fountain Court Chambers* *	**Parker** Benjamin *7 King's Bench Walk*
Parker Matthew *3 Verulam Buildings* *	**Richmond** Jeremy *Quadrant Chambers* *
Pillai Rajesh *3 Verulam Buildings*	**Rothschild** Gerard *Brick Court Chambers*
Reffin Clare *One Essex Court* [A]	**Saoul** Daniel *4 New Square* *
Sinclair Paul *Fountain Court Chambers* *	**Sloboda** Nicholas *One Essex Court* *
Vinall Mark *Blackstone Chambers*	**Tan** Charlotte *20 Essex Street*
Weekes Robert *Blackstone Chambers*	**Temmink** Robert-Jan *Quadrant Chambers* *
West Colin *Brick Court Chambers*	**Up-and-coming individuals**
	Shah Nehali *One Essex Court*

** Indicates individual with profile.*
[A] direct access (see p.24).
◊ (ORL) = Other Ranked Lawyer.
Alphabetical order within each band. Band 1 is highest.

the widow and daughter of the late Israeli billionaire Sami Shamoon, in defending a High Court claim concerning a significant shareholding in a company worth approximately USD500 million.

Harry Matovu QC (see p.709) Frequently instructed in high-value domestic and international disputes. The breadth of his practice is a real strength, and he can typically be seen handling anything from post-M&A disputes to fraud and professional negligence disputes. **Strengths:** "He is a really classy performer." "A punchy advocate who is good at fraud and asset-tracing cases." **Recent work:** Represented engineering group Wärtsilä with regard to a USD500 million fraud and conspiracy claim surrounding the construction and operation of a power plant in Dar es Salaam, in Tanzania.

Simon Birt QC Possesses particular expertise in Russian and CIS disputes, and is often seen in cases with fraud, conspiracy, breach of duty or offshore elements to them. He is also active in insurance, professional negligence and banking matters. **Strengths:** "He is a great example of the new generation of top silks – he's not as bombastic as the old breed while still producing a brilliant work product." "He is extremely intelligent, highly user-friendly and always has a full grasp of the complex details in any given case." **Recent work:** Acted for the Bank of St Petersburg in a case against a former client who claimed his signature was forged on contracts of guarantee.

Roger Masefield QC (see p.708) He is actively involved in cases across a broad range of sectors including insurance, energy and finance. The strength of his reasoning and his sharpness are particularly lauded. **Strengths:** "Cerebral and very good on paper." "He has an extremely flexible approach and thoroughly committed to the case." **Recent work:** Acting for the Libyan Investment Authority against Goldman Sachs in a claim to rescind nine complex derivative transactions worth in excess of USD1.2 billion.

Jasbir Dhillon QC Maintains a diverse and varied commercial practice that is heavy on banking and finance and shareholder disputes, many of which are international in nature. **Strengths:** "Commercially minded and user-friendly." "He thinks around a subject very well." **Recent work:** Represented Enasarco in its successful claim for USD61.5 million from Lehman Brothers. The claim concerned a complex structured derivative product marketed by the bank.

Richard Slade QC Well regarded for his work on international disputes arising out of the failure of joint venture agreements. He is also frequently instructed in fraud, bribery, banking and insurance litigation. **Strengths:** "Excellent at cutting to the heart of the matter and very user-friendly." "Very bright and always able to find a new angle." **Recent work:** Acted in GBM MEC v GBMH, a claim for payment for mining engineering services.

Michael Swainston QC Offers clients superior advocacy skills that have been tested at the highest level in both the English courts and abroad. He has experience of assisting a wide range of international clients including Russian, South American and Indian entities. **Strengths:** "Tough and to the point, he inspires great confidence." "He is phenomenally hard-working and very busy but always manages to make you feel like you are at the top of his list." **Recent work:** Acted for Eclairs, a company owned by a Ukrainian oligarch, in a dispute concerning voting rights and ownership of oil company JKX.

Thomas Plewman SC QC Took silk this year having proved himself over many years to be an incisive and powerful junior. He has experience of handling high-stakes professional negligence and financial services litigation, among other matters, and is also noted as an expert in post-M&A disputes. **Strengths:** "Highly commercial and very authoritative in court." "Thomas is a very hard-working, tenacious barrister who is incisive and clear-thinking in his advice, both orally and on paper. He is a robust cross-examiner who offers clear and pragmatic advice to clients." **Recent work:** Acted as junior counsel for International Oil & Gas Technology Fund in claims relating to the termination of an investment fund management agreement.

JUNIORS

Fionn Pilbrow One of the most prominent general commercial juniors at the Bar. He is highly respected for the quality of his oral advocacy and has good experience of leading cases on his own. **Strengths:** "He is really excellent as his advice is clear and logical, and his advocacy is persuasive." "He is a quite brilliant advocate who judges absolutely love." **Recent work:** Represented the Arcadia group in a claim against a number of oil trading companies owned by shipping billionaire John Fredriksen. Arcadia claims to have been defrauded of nearly USD400 million.

Alec Haydon Works closely with leading silks on big-ticket commercial disputes, and has experience of large-scale fraud and insurance claims and professional negligence matters. **Strengths:** "A very commercially minded and clear advocate." "He has extremely good analytical skills and is quick at grasping complex factual situations and industry concepts." **Recent work:** Acted for Ukrainian oligarch Victor Pinchuk in his claim alleging entitlement to shares in Ukrainian steel plant KZhRK. The plant is worth in excess of USD1 billion.

Stephen Midwinter A successful junior who is highly regarded for his versatility and breadth of practice. He is regularly led on big-ticket matters, but also handles major cases as sole counsel. **Strengths:** "He's very cerebral and very commercial. You just know that he's going to turn over every stone." "Extremely impressive and extremely bright." **Recent work:** Acted for Bigtincan in a claim concerning alleged breach of IP rights relating to productivity apps.

Tony Singla (see p.766) Has been involved in a number of highly significant cases over the last year both for and against financial institutions. He is also active in director disputes and regularly appears in cases concerning large group actions. **Strengths:** "Industrious and clever, he is a team player." "He has very good analytical skills and is a pragmatic adviser." **Recent work:** Acted for Lloyds Banking Group in group litigation brought against it by thousands of shareholders. The case arose out of Lloyds' £12 billion acquisition of HBOS in 2008.

Oliver Jones (see p.686) An in-demand junior with a broad commercial practice, who is active in cases concerning fraud, asset freezing, insurance, banking and post-M&A dispute resolution. He also possesses significant expertise in public law matters. **Strengths:** "Extremely bright, inventive and user-friendly junior" who is "very approachable, and considered in his approach." **Recent work:** Represented Sushovan Hussain, the former CFO of Autonomy, in a £3 billion claim brought by Hewlett-Packard against Mr Hussain and former CEO Michael Lynch. HP contended that its USD11 billion purchase price for Autonomy was artificially inflated by USD5 billion as a result of an accounting fraud perpetrated by Mr Lynch and Mr Hussain.

Colin West Has a broad commercial practice that covers a wide range of areas. These include contractual disputes in the shipping, insurance and civil fraud arenas. **Strengths:** "Incredibly hard-working and insightful." "He is bright and no-nonsense in his approach."

Richard Blakeley (see p.597) Has experience of working on a wide range of international matters including oligarch disputes, banking and international corruption cases and conspiracy matters. **Strengths:** "He advances his case in a very persuasive way, and has a great understated style which is really attractive, particularly in difficult cases." "He has a very, very strong work ethic and will turn papers round late at night." **Recent work:** Represented the Libyan Investment Authority as it tried to recover more than USD2 billion. The fund alleged that it was the victim of a fraudulent and corrupt scheme between Société Générale and other parties.

Fred Hobson (see p.673) Highly able commercial junior who is often brought in to handle some of the toughest cases currently being heard. He regularly represents Russian and CIS clients. **Recent work:** Acted for Citibank in defending a £2.3 billion fraud claim brought by Terra Firma. The claim arose from Guy Hands' ill-fated acquisition of EMI in 2007. Terra Firma alleged that Citibank, which advised EMI, made fraudulent misrepresentations about the status of other bidders in the auction.

Sarah Abram "A good advocate" who has very strong litigation and arbitration practices. She is particularly skilled at handling commercial cases with a European law element to them. **Strengths:** "She's really willing to get stuck into a case and gets to the nub of very complicated cases in a ridiculously quick time." **Recent work:** Instructed by Thames Water Utilities in a Part 8 claim in the Commercial Court. The claim related to whether Thames Water must make payments to the Canal & River Trust in respect of Thames Water's abstraction of water from the River Lee.

Richard Eschwege (see p.641) A well-known and widely lauded up-and-coming junior with a burgeoning commercial practice. He is noted for his attention to detail in document-heavy cases. **Strengths:** "A fast-rising star and someone with an absolutely brilliant legal mind." "Incredibly bright and hard-working, he delivers work to such a high standard." **Recent work:** Successfully acted for BP in a case concerning the consequences of a failure to supply natural gas from the North Sea under long-term gas sales agreements.

Gerard Rothschild A capable commercial junior who represents a wide range of commercial clients in significant litigation. He is further esteemed for his EU and public law practices. **Strengths:** "A very clever and cerebral lawyer." "He adopts a good, intelligent approach on pleadings and offers very clear advice which helps the clients." **Recent work:** Acted in Hinduja Automotive Ltd v BMW (UK) Investments Ltd, a case looking at BMW's liability for industrial injuries dating back to the operations of Leyland Motors in the 1960s.

One Essex Court

See profile on p.833

THE SET

One Essex Court has long been a magnet for commercial cases of the greatest magnitude, value and importance. Stuffed to the gunwales with leading barristers, it handles all manner of commercial litigation, proving particularly strong in banking and finance, fraud and energy-related cases. Matters of interest members have handled recently include the RBS rights issue litigation, Libyan Investment Authority v Goldman Sachs, the Pinchuk litigation and the Marathon Asset Management case. In a boon to the set they have recently been joined by three members from rival chambers 3 Verulam Buildings, one of whom is the much-respected Sonya Tolaney QC, a key player in the commercial litigation market. **Client service:** "The clerks are really on the ball. They don't push the wrong sort of person on you and don't push on fees. They are absolutely spot-on and very modern in their outlook." Darren Burrows leads the clerking team.

SILKS

Anthony Grabiner QC Over the last 40 years he has been involved with and led many of the highest-profile matters to reach the London courts. He is a man for the big occasion who is also noted for the strength of his arbitration practice. **Strengths:** "When it comes to client management and strategic discussions he can be trusted implicitly." "He has massive gravitas, which he deploys effectively both in and out of court." **Recent work:** Acted on appeal for HRH Prince Abdul Aziz bin Fahd, who it is claimed entered into an oral agreement in June 2003 with Ms Janan George Harb, whereby he agreed to pay her £12 million and sign over two Chelsea properties.

Laurence Rabinowitz QC A stellar barrister who is renowned for being one of the very best that the Bar in London has to offer. He takes the lead in many of the highest-profile banking and finance, company law, energy, civil fraud, competition and professional liability cases. **Strengths:** "He is very approachable, gives sound and practical advice and commands a lot of respect among his peers." "He wears his phenomenal intellect lightly and has huge charm." **Recent work:** Represented Mr Igor Kolomoisky in a USD2 billion case brought against him by fellow Ukrainian oligarch Victor Pinchuk. The matter involved the ownership of an iron ore mine in Ukraine.

John McCaughran QC A phenomenal advocate who is a go-to silk for many magic circle firms. He is perhaps best known for his work in the energy sector but can handle all manner of general commercial matters. He is regularly called upon to represent clients in offshore litigation in the British Virgin Islands (BVI) and the Cayman Islands. **Strengths:** "He's fabulous to work with, as he's bright, hard-working and extremely good company." "A top-tier oil and gas silk." **Recent work:** Acted for Providence Resources in a dispute with Transocean Drilling UK. Providence sought damages after hiring a drilling rig from Transocean which proved to be defective.

Daniel Toledano QC An "absolutely outstanding advocate" and a truly brilliant silk who possesses an incredibly varied and vibrant practice. He is frequently seen handling matters relating to energy and utilities, civil fraud, international commercial arbitration and sport. The strategic thinking he brings to case wins him plaudits. **Strengths:** "He possesses a great intellect and is a smart reader of the court." "Exceptionally bright and always on top of the detail, he works very efficiently with teams of solicitors." **Recent work:** Defended Ernst & Young against professional negligence proceedings worth £25 million. The claim arose out of financial due diligence carried out by EY in connection with the 2007 acquisition of the Esporta Leisure Group from private equity firm Duke Street Capital.

David Wolfson QC A brilliant lawyer who focuses his practice on energy and finance cases among others. He also handles high-stakes arbitration both as counsel and as an arbitrator. Wolfson draws praise for his down-to-earth manner and willingness to fight for his client. **Strengths:** "He does not sit on the fence but instead reaches considered views and sticks to his guns." "He is very impressive in court and very authoritative." **Recent work:** Acted for EE in connection with claims initiated by various parties that arose out of the administration of Phones 4u.

Stephen Auld QC Represents a diverse range of clients in cases concerning complex contractual arrangements, civil fraud and banking and finance. His ability to both command the authority of a courtroom and remain user-friendly draws particular praise from the market. **Strengths:** "He is tactically brilliant and is an extremely good advocate." "A charming and confident advocate, who is great with clients." **Recent work:** Acted in Wingate v Lloyds Bank. This was a claim that a settlement between the parties was void because the bank had failed to tell Wingate of its involvement in Libor manipulation.

David Cavender QC (see p.613) A fine barrister who has a practice coving a broad spectrum of commercial matters. He regularly handles cases involving tax, banking and finance and civil fraud. **Strengths:** "Extremely capable commercial silk" who is both "insightful and robust." **Recent work:** Acted on behalf of a number of UK construction companies in the Construction Industry Vetting Information Group Litigation. The case arose out of the alleged creation of a blacklist of construction workers said to have been used by major construction companies when choosing staff.

Alain Choo Choy QC A hugely respected silk who is adept at a staggering variety of high-value work. His particular areas of focus include banking, civil fraud, energy and conflict of laws disputes. He is frequently instructed in international matters. **Strengths:** "He is incredibly hard-working and has a very nice manner with solicitors and judges." "An excellent trial advocate whom judges really listen to." **Recent work:** Instructed in a dispute between Russian businessmen regarding the financing of a real estate development in Russia. Jurisdictional issues were involved concerning the attempted service of proceedings in England.

Anthony de Garr Robinson QC (see p.631) Frequently seen in High Court and appellate proceedings, offshore litigation and international arbitration, he is active in company, fraud and banking work. **Strengths:** "He has shown great skill in getting to grips with complex accounting issues and is a good team player." "He's extremely bright and good on his feet." **Recent work:** Acted for the Financial Times in a conspiracy claim brought against it, the Guardian and others. The claim was brought by the former delivery agent for the FT and the Guardian, which alleged that the two papers had conspired with others to effectively steal its business.

Neil Kitchener QC Banking and finance, civil fraud, company and insolvency, energy and professional negligence matters all form part of his busy practice. The quality of his analysis and advocacy were remarked upon by numerous interviewees. **Strengths:** "He's brilliantly intelligent, quite aggressive in his approach without being reckless, and just great to deal with." "He's incredibly responsive." **Recent work:** Represented more than 600 construction workers in group litigation against numerous major construction companies. The case related to historic alleged blacklisting by employers.

Kenneth MacLean QC Has experience of representing clients both at home and in offshore proceedings in both Anguilla and the BVI. His is an incredibly varied practice, as illustrated by the fact that he is brought into high-profile commercial matters yet also acts as a member of the Premier League Disciplinary Panel. **Strengths:** "He gives sensible, no-nonsense, commercial advice." "He's a fierce advocate and a good cross-examiner." **Recent work:** Assisted Çukurova in its long-running dispute with the Alfa group of Russia over control of Turkcell, the leading mobile phone operator in Turkey.

Jeffery Onions QC An experienced and insightful barrister who is brilliant whether in court or in an advisory role. He possesses deep experience across a whole range of sectors, and regularly handles banking, insolvency, insurance, oil and gas, and sport and media-related cases. **Strengths:** "He has formidable technical knowledge and is a demon cross-examiner." "He's fantastically hands-on for such a senior leading counsel." **Recent work:** Acted for IBM in its dispute with the National Trust. The Trust alleged that IBM failed to deliver IT services in accordance with its obligations and misrepresented its capabilities under the master services agreement.

Craig Orr QC (see p.731) Frequently instructed by major international law firms to handle tough commercial litigation, he is well regarded for his work in the banking, fraud and insurance sectors. He is an expert in cases involving conspiracy and breach of duty. **Strengths:** "He is a fantastic leader who gives strong strategic direction and is calm under pressure." "An insightful and diligent counsel who is always very responsive." **Recent work:** Acted for Kroll UK in defending a USD500 million claim for conspiracy and breach of confidence arising out of its engagement by the former chair of Bank Alkhair, a Bahrain investment bank. The case raises complex issues of fraud and corruption.

Sonia Tolaney QC Recently moved to One Essex Court from 3 Verulam Buildings, she is the architect of a brilliant banking and finance practice that sees her leading some of the highest-profile matters around. She is also adept at dealing with fraud and insolvency cases. **Strengths:** "A serious presence in the market and a great strategist." "She is clear, concise and authoritative, as well as very user-friendly." **Recent work:** Acted for RBS and its former directors in a case where thousands of claimants were seeking to recover £4 billion in respect of the 2008 RBS rights issue.

Richard Boulton QC Possesses a broad commercial practice that straddles a wide range of related areas. Matters handled include civil fraud cases, financial disputes and complex damages claims. His numerical and accounting ability play a useful role in his practice. **Strengths:** "Recommended for his tenacity, hard work, unflagging good humour and willingness to roll up his sleeves." **Recent work:** Instructed by Re3 waste management company in a dispute with Bracknell Forest, Reading and Wokingham borough councils. The matter concerned a long-term PFI contract for waste management and recycling.

Charles Graham QC Has a varied practice and possesses particularly strong knowledge and expertise in oil and gas disputes. He is also adept at professional negligence and civil fraud cases. **Strengths:** "Extremely hard-working and personable." "He's the kind of silk you want for very difficult cases when the client is in real trouble." **Recent work:** Acting for second defendant Kroll Associates in Dar Al Arkan Real Estate Development & Others v Al Refai & Others. The case looked at whether the court had jurisdiction to commit a director of the claimant companies for contempt, even though that director was resident out of the jurisdiction.

Sa'ad Hossain QC Active in energy and shareholder disputes and financial instrument litigation as well as numerous other commercial areas. **Strengths:** "A clear leader in the new generation of silks, he's quick, efficient and a real team player." "A very thoughtful barrister with very strong drafting skills." **Recent work:** Retained by two divisions of Talisman Sinopec Energy in a dispute with BG. The case concerned neighbouring North Sea oilfields and alleged overcharging under an agreement for the provision of transportation, processing and operating services.

Camilla Bingham QC Active both at home and abroad, she appears in the highest courts in England and has also been called to the Bars of the Cayman Islands and the BVI. She has a broad commercial practice and is an expert in jurisdiction and conflict of laws. **Strengths:** "Smart and savvy, she really gets to the heart of the problem and comes up with solutions very quickly." "She is very bright and creative in her thinking." **Recent work:** Represented a subsidiary of Centrica in Commercial Court proceedings centring on the construction and rectification of a suite of agreements concerning the extraction and processing of gas in the East Irish Sea.

Rhodri Davies QC A widely respected commercial silk with strong and varied business law practice. His work routinely involves cases concerning banking and finance, and accountants' negligence. He is an expert in actions involving interest rate swaps and other derivatives. **Strengths:** "Highly commercial and completely unflappable." "Extremely persuasive on his feet and smooth and confident with clients." **Recent work:** Acted in a complex dispute concerning alleged auditors' negligence. The case concerned an investment fund and raised a number of significant legal issues including the recoverability of trading and market losses from auditors.

Michael Fealy QC (see p.643) Has a busy commercial practice and is often engaged in energy, fraud and insolvency cases. **Strengths:** "Extremely diligent, he offers first-class legal analysis." "Utterly tenacious and a joy to work with, particularly on cross-border disputes." **Recent work:** Represented Dentsu Aegis Networks in a claim for damages of £200 million for breach of warranty and fraud following the acquisition of a market research business.

Richard Gillis QC Possesses a broad commercial practice, and offers clients particular insight into cases where company law and insolvency collide. He is also frequently seen in professional negligence matters. **Strengths:** "Razor-sharp in his analysis." "Incredibly diligent, hard-working and effective." **Recent work:** Acted for Dr Ambrosie Bryant Chukwueloka Orjiako in defending a claim brought by a number of banks.

Benjamin Strong QC A well-regarded commercial practitioner who focuses much of his practice on servicing the financial sector. He is also active in professional negligence matters. **Strengths:** "He is great with clients and quick to grasp and identify solutions to complex issues." "A bright, tenacious and hungry new silk." **Recent work:** Defended law firm Hammonds in a solicitors' negligence claim launched by investment firm Sun Capital Partners.

JUNIORS

Jamie Goldsmith One of the most capable junior barristers currently at the Bar, he draws praise for his eye for detail, industry and pure brainpower. Banking and civil fraud continue to be mainstays of his practice, and he is also strong on professional negligence matters. **Strengths:** "Intellectually out of the top drawer and very user-friendly." "He's extremely bright, incredibly responsive and he comes back with very strong analysis of the case quite quickly." **Recent work:** Acting for 14 investors in a large and complex dispute arising out of alleged negligence by Standard & Poor's and RBS. The damages claimed exceed EUR130 million.

Conall Patton (see p.734) One of the top juniors at the Commercial Bar, he has a deep understanding of energy, competition, banking and finance matters. He is widely praised for his written work and his incisive analysis of legal issues. **Strengths:** "He is unquestionably brilliant intellectually and is completely dedicated." "He is unbelievably clever and quick at getting to the heart of an issue." **Recent work:** Retained by Igor Kolomoisky in his USD2 billion case against fellow Ukrainian oligarch Victor Pinchuk concerning the ownership of a Ukrainian iron ore mine.

Alexander Polley (see p.739) Possesses a far-reaching international commercial practice that encompasses a wide range of business law matters. He is particularly well versed in professional negligence, banking and civil fraud matters. **Strengths:** "Extremely good at quickly getting to the heart of huge volumes of information, he promptly identifies practical solutions." "He's really efficient and good at managing the big cases." **Recent work:** Acted for property developers the Candy brothers and their company CPC in dealing with claims for conspiracy arising out of CPC's enforcement of a loan agreement against a borrower.

Anna Boase Frequently led by top silks but has also developed a strong practice acting as sole counsel. Her eye for detail, analytical ability and capacity for hard work were all praised by top law firms. Boase is strong on banking, contract and company law issues. **Strengths:** "Very bright, hard-working and approachable." "She has excellent legal skills and is very user-friendly." **Recent work:** Acted for Indian company Jaiprakash Associates, which has staged and promoted the first ever Formula One motor races in India, defending a claim for USD51 million brought by Bernie Ecclestone's company.

Orlando Gledhill (see p.654) Strong junior who gains praise for his intellectual rigour and commercial-mindedness. He is particularly active in banking, energy, pharmaceutical and IT disputes. **Strengths:** "An outstanding draftsman who is always fully committed to the cause and is very strong on quantum issues." "Impressively intelligent and extremely hard-working, he stands his ground against QCs and judges and gets results." **Recent work:** Acted for British Gas in a £9 million claim against A.L. Challis arising from a contract for the distribution of shower regulators.

Sebastian Isaac Focuses his practice on high-stakes international disputes often with a Russian or CIS angle. He is active in energy, professional discipline and banking disputes among others. **Strengths:** "An intelligent advocate who is delightful to work with." "He is a hard-working, bright and confident advocate." **Recent work:** Acted on behalf of Alliance Bernstein, a leading fund manager, with regard to claims brought by the trustees of the pension fund of Philips. The claims concern the construction and management of a portfolio of MBS in 2007.

James MacDonald (see p.705) A recent recruit to the set and a very strong junior who appears in market-leading cases being led by some of the best silks in the business. He is particularly adept at financial and banking disputes. **Strengths:** "He produces excellent work." "He is responsive and understands what the client is trying to achieve." **Recent work:** Retained as lead junior for the ratings agencies in McGraw-Hill v Deutsche Apotheker, RBS & Others. The case concerns the duties owed by ratings agencies when rating financial products.

Simon Colton Has experience of acting as lead junior in a number of high-profile fraud and banking matters, some of which concern oligarchs. His work in Russian litigation draws particular praise. **Strengths:** "Exceptionally intelligent, incisive, versatile and a talented communicator." "He's a real expert in the law of restitution and is very user-friendly." **Recent work:** Represented Banco Santander Totta in five related Commercial Court actions against Portuguese transport companies, arising out of swaps concluded between 2005 and 2007.

Richard Mott (see p.723) Experienced at handling a wide range of commercial matters, and particularly active in civil fraud, banking and finance, energy and general commercial disputes. **Strengths:** "A smooth advocate with a very compelling style." "He is very collaborative and fiercely bright." **Recent work:** Acted for Citibank against Mercuria Energy Trading in a USD270 million claim. The case arises out of a substantial metals fraud alleged to have taken place in China.

Clare Reffin Exceptionally able junior who is frequently seen in top-level domestic and international disputes. Peers laud her for the depth of her legal knowledge and her quick comprehension of tangled cases. **Strengths:** "A very effective advocate whose trial preparation is second to none." "She is meticulous, intelligent and a great team player." **Recent work:** Acted for the government of India in a case concerning £35 million of funds deposited by the late Nizam of Hyderabad frozen at NatWest since 1948 due to Pakistan's invocation of state immunity.

Matthew Cook He wins plaudits from the market for his knowledge of competition and regulatory matters in particular, but is also active in other areas such as banking and fraud. **Strengths:** "He is extremely bright and exceptionally numerate. In one recent case he had a better grasp of the quantum arguments than anyone at trial, and that includes the experts." **Recent work:** Acted for Roskilde Bank in proceedings relating to allegations of fraudulent or negligent misrepresentation during its issue of subordinated notes.

Steven Elliott "A great choice for any commercial dispute," according to sources. His work focuses on the fraud and banking areas, and he is a noted expert on jurisdictional matters. **Strengths:** "He has a remarkable ability to digest and process large volumes of complex information and then present his case compellingly." "A very good tactician." **Recent work:** Acted for investment fund Hirco in a £350 million dispute with its promoter and joint venture partner concerning development projects in India. The case involved allegations of fraud and breach of directors' fiduciary duties.

Sandy Phipps (see p.737) Joins the chambers this year from 3 Verulam Buildings, and brings with him a broad commercial practice that takes in cases involving professional negligence and fraud. **Strengths:** "Clients appreciate his very commercial approach." "He is decisive, shows excellent attention to detail, and offers sound commercial advice." **Recent work:** Defended Société Générale against a USD1.5 billion claim for damages from the Libyan Investment Authority (LIA). The claim related to investments totalling around USD2.1 billion made by the LIA with Société Générale during the Gaddafi era.

Laurence Emmett Active across a wide range of sectors, he has particular knowledge of energy, financial services and art and antiques disputes. **Strengths:** "He is a very clever draftsman who is creative in his analysis of difficult legal problems." "He really thinks deeply about the issues, and is not afraid to come up with novel arguments in difficult cases." **Recent work:** Acted for Hascol Petroleum in a dispute relating to a series of deals for the sale and purchase of fuel oil and diesel between a UAE trading house and a Pakistani distributor.

Daniel Hubbard As much at home handling commercial litigation as he is tackling arbitration, he is well known for the expertise he brings to civil fraud and contractual disputes. He also handles work in the oil and gas sector. **Strengths:** "He is assured and quick to grasp the issues." **Recent work:** Acted for Jean-Claude and Jane Andre in their claim against Clydesdale Bank for breach of bailment.

Emma Jones (see p.685) A promising and hard-working young junior who regularly handles high-value company and energy disputes involving both domestic and overseas clients. **Strengths:** "Her ability to turn out a 150-page submission in a short period of time to a ridiculously high standard was very impressive." "She is very methodical, diligent and hard-working." **Recent work:** Acted for two divisions of Talisman Sinopec Energy in a dispute with BG. The matter concerned alleged overcharging under an agreement for the provision of transportation, processing and operating services in North Sea gas fields.

Nicholas Sloboda (see p.767) Enters the rankings this year on the back of widespread praise from lawyers and clients alike. His intelligence and sensible manner when under pressure are particularly commented upon. **Strengths:** "He has a lightness of touch that is the envy of many." "A forceful and persuasive advocate who outshines opponents who are far more senior." **Recent work:** Defended Kroll Associates against USD800 million of claims brought in the Commercial Court. The case raised allegations of breaches of banking practice and regulations in the Middle East.

Nehali Shah Provides adept counsel on a wide range of commercial issues, but is most noted for handling cases relating to banking and finance, insolvency, oil and gas, civil fraud and professional liability. **Strengths:** "Really hands-on and committed to all aspects of the case." "She is phenomenally bright and has a very good manner with clients." **Recent work:** Retained by private equity firm Terra Firma in its USD2 billion fraud claim against Citibank arising out of its acquisition of EMI in 2007.

Essex Court Chambers
See profile on p.836

THE SET

A gold-standard commercial set that provides top counsel for cases involving a wide range of complex business issues. Its silks and juniors are frequently called upon to handle bet-the-company cases involving banking, energy, civil fraud, insurance, shareholder, partnership and ownership disputes. They have tremendous commercial and legal experience right across their ranks and together represent "a real powerhouse of a team." Important matters they have handled in recent times include Yukos v Russian Federation, a case concerning the enforcement of a USD50 billion arbitration award. Solicitors say of them: "The barristers at Essex Court are exceptional. They work exceedingly well as a team, they clearly engage with each other, and their opinions are very well thought out."

Client service: "David Grief is an expert clerk who understands case requirements, and the internal mechanism of each barrister. He maintains a friendly relationship with instructing solicitors." "Co-senior clerk Joe Ferrigno is great at managing barristers and the relationship with solicitors."

SILKS

David Foxton QC Hugely esteemed by solicitors and peers alike due to the strength of his intellect, his depth of experience and his breadth of practice. He has recently handled cases involving derivative trading, Libor manipulation and fraud. **Strengths:** "A charming, exceptionally intelligent advocate who gets on top of materials quickly and instils confidence in clients and judges alike." "He has a brain the size of a planet and charm to go with it." **Recent work:** Acted in PAG v RBS, a case concerning alleged Libor manipulation and the mis-selling of financial products. This was the Libor test case.

Joe Smouha QC Has a broad commercial practice and frequently represents clients in the highest courts both at home and abroad. He receives plaudits for both his litigation and arbitration work. **Strengths:** "Top-flight advocate who offers impeccable client service." "He has an easy style and is both quick to turn round papers and humorous in his approach. He has always read his papers, is thorough in his preparation, and can be relied upon." **Recent work:** Represented Barclays in its dispute with Italian investment bank UniCredit. The case concerned a Profit Participating Securities Programme between the two banks.

Steven Berry QC A forceful and persuasive advocate who has experience of leading big-ticket disputes. He "continues to perform at the highest level, despite being such a busy silk." His experience in insurance, shipping and commodities disputes draws particular praise. **Strengths:** "User-friendly and a fearsome cross-examiner." "He's a brilliant trial lawyer and a superb strategist."

Graham Dunning QC (see p.637) Described by the market as "an incredible strategist and someone with a brilliant legal mind," he has experience across a broad range of commercial matters. He is particularly active in offshore disputes and international litigation and arbitration. **Strengths:** "He has an innate sense of justice and wants to do the best that he possibly can for his clients." "Graham is extremely commercial in his approach and able to get into the depth of the case very quickly." **Recent work:** Handled a Court of Appeal hearing concerning state immunity and enforcement of an arbitration award payable to the Central Bank of Iraq.

Vernon Flynn QC A "superb advocate" who has long experience of handling big-ticket, multi-jurisdictional disputes. His ability to work in a team and the dynamism he displays when handling cases come in for particular praise from the market. **Strengths:** "He is very client-friendly and has charm and charisma that work wonders with the judges." "A lawyer with a brilliant courtroom manner who is hugely impressive when it comes to predicting judicial instincts." **Recent work:** Instructed in USD100 million Dubai-based litigation involving a property deal and allegations of breach of trust.

Paul McGrath QC Hugely respected for his work on big-ticket fraud and asset-tracing and freezing actions. His depth of understanding really makes him stand out in the area. **Strengths:** "A real heavyweight on fraud cases. He is not one of these silks with airs and graces but is a real member of the team." "He easily explains the most complex ideas in the type of simple terms that both clients and the court really appreciate." **Recent work:** Advised the shareholders of oil company Yukos on the enforcement of a USD50 billion arbitration award against the Russian state.

Andrew Hochhauser QC Has very impressive commercial and employment practices and is particularly at home on cases where these two areas intersect. He regularly handles cases concerning professional negligence, dishonesty and restrictive covenants. **Strengths:** "A leader with real gravitas." "He is quick with his paperwork and shows excellent judgement." **Recent work:** Acted for Stena Drilling in a claim against Grizzly Business for a USD2.5 million success fee follow the awarding of a USD1 billion contract with Shell.

Richard Jacobs QC Possesses a fine commercial practice and is especially highly regarded for his work on Bermuda Form arbitration proceedings in the insurance sector. He is described by peers as being "responsive and effective." **Strengths:** "A lawyer with a truly great intellect who is very good on the detail." "He is a first-class advocate and knows how to get the legal high ground in a dispute." **Recent work:** Defended insurance broker Aon with regard to a multimillion-dollar claim made against it by ORLEN Lietuva. The claim alleged negligence in the placement of business interruption insurance.

Richard Millett QC A very well-respected barrister with significant commercial disputes experience. He receives particular plaudits for his forceful advocacy and his ability to think laterally when handling cases. **Strengths:** "Gets on top of complex issues and is not shy to give uncaveated opinions." "He is commercially incisive and user-friendly." **Recent work:** Acted for the defendant in Egiazaryan v City of Moscow, a case concerning a Russian oligarch and a hotel-building project in Russia.

Gordon Pollock QC Has decades of experience of leading top-level commercial litigation across a range of sectors. He is particularly highly regarded for his fraud, banking and energy-related work. **Strengths:** "He offers clear and effective advice and is a brilliant courtroom operator." "Forceful and effective, he's a great choice for a difficult case."

Paul Stanley QC An "excellent advocate and strategist" who caters to a diverse client base. He is active in complex civil fraud and insurance matters as well as more general commercial work. **Strengths:** "One of the brightest lawyers that you could hope to meet." "So clever and a really smooth advocate as well."

John Lockey QC (see p.703) Held in high regard for his work for insurers, brokers and financial institutions. He is equally at home in either litigation or arbitration settings, and is often seen handling international work. **Strengths:** "He provides clear and timely advice and is user-friendly." **Recent work:** Represented SBM in seeking to recover USD1.3 billion from insurers for alleged losses on the construction of the YME drilling platform.

Daniel Oudkerk QC Lauded for the breadth of his commercial expertise, he is frequently called upon by financial institutions, brokers and insurers to handle tough litigation. He is adept at shareholder dispute, partnership and fraud matters. **Strengths:** "He inspires confidence in the client and has a very clear vision of how a case should be run." "The confidence that he oozed held us together." **Recent work:** Acted in the high-profile construction industry blacklisting case.

Nathan Pillow QC A relatively new silk who impresses barristers and solicitors alike with his "impeccable oral advocacy" and "lovely command of a courtroom." **Strengths:** "One of the brightest lawyers that you could hope to meet." "He's thorough, measured and has the ear of the court." **Recent work:** Acted for Russian financial group Otkritie Securities in a USD180 million conspiracy claim against 19 defendants.

Claire Blanchard QC A highly capable silk who is regularly instructed in a wide range of commercial disputes. These have included matters relating to the sports, employment, energy and entertainment sectors. **Strengths:** "Very easy to work with. She's just very conscientious and likes working on the details."

Roderick Cordara QC (see p.624) Has an enviable international practice and is frequently instructed in large pieces of litigation and arbitration. Her particular areas of strength include shipping and energy. **Strengths:** "Brilliant in terms of his command of the law and case strategy." "He is engaged, informed and very well liked by clients." **Recent work:** He has been advising on multiple shipbuilding and rig-building claims against a variety of Chinese shipyards.

Huw Davies QC (see p.629) A "strong commercial practitioner" who offers clients a wide range of expertise across a range of matters. He is often seen in aviation, fraud and insurance disputes. **Strengths:** "A very bright QC who is easy to work with, has great commercial acumen and possesses excellent advocacy skills." "A cool and calm advocate who is nevertheless tough and likes a challenge."

Jeffrey Gruder QC (see p.661) A highly committed barrister who has recently been involved in key cases looking at subrogation and professional privilege. He is regularly instructed in major fraud and banking litigation. **Strengths:** "He's very good on the law and has a lot of common sense." **Recent work:** Involved in the litigation between BTA Bank and Kazakh businessman Mukhtar Ablyazov. He was asked to advise on the extent of privilege attached to communications between Mr Ablyazov and his counsel.

Stephen Houseman QC "A responsive, concise and clear" barrister who makes his clients feel comfortable in tough litigation settings. He has strong experience of handling disputes with multi-jurisdictional issues. **Strengths:** "User-friendly, commercial and collaborative, he represents a very good, all-round package." "Robust and punchy in his advice, he has great analytical skills and is a hard-working team player whom it is a pleasure to work with." **Recent work:** Defended a subsidiary of Chinese state-owned bank ICBC against a claim launched by Odyssey Aviation. The claim concerned payment of a success fee for advisory services.

JUNIORS

James Willan A leading junior with experience in top-level commercial disputes including civil fraud and banking cases. He is widely held to be a "really effective advocate" and is particularly good at handling cases involving reams of documents. **Strengths:** "He's a very strong advocate who gets to the point and produces very succinct written work." "He is fantastic at dealing with complex forensic issues." **Recent work:** Acted for Italian investment bank Dexia Crediop in its Commercial Court claims against the Province of Crotone. The case concerned complex interest rate swaps worth more than EUR50 million.

Edmund King A junior with experience of a wide range of commercial work, whose written submissions draw plaudits from peers. Banking disputes are a particular forte of his. **Strengths:** "He is very personable, very dedicated and very passionate about the cases that he handles." "He's super-bright and an absolute delight to work with."

David Davies A highly respected senior junior who has handled a number of significant commercial cases. He is often to be seen handling complex, multi-jurisdictional oligarch-related work. **Strengths:** "Fabulously user-friendly and very clever, he turns things around extraordinarily quickly." "Shows fine judgement and provides excellent legal analysis." **Recent work:** Acted as senior junior for the former majority shareholders of Yukos in seeking to enforce a USD50 billion arbitral award against the Russian Federation.

Anna Dilnot Having previously qualified as a solicitor and then moved to the Bar, she has a deep understanding of the needs of both clients and those that instruct her. She receives praise for her "fantastic attention to detail" and responsiveness, and is particularly noted for her expertise in fraud. **Strengths:** "Very intelligent and quick to get to the issues, she's a real fighter who you can trust with serious cases." **Recent work:** Represented the French and Spanish states in an appeal against the London Steam Ship Owners Mutual Insurance Association. The dispute arose out of the sinking of the vessel 'Prestige' off the coast of France and Spain in 2002, which caused severe environmental damage.

Jeremy Brier Well regarded for his multi-jurisdictional practice and particularly good on shipping matters. His ability to manage client expectations and deliver results has won him many fans in the market. **Strengths:** "Bright and knowledgeable, he has a good eye for detail and is a clear and decisive thinker." "He's highly efficient, very responsive and just very good with clients." **Recent work:** Acted as sole junior for Russian oligarch Ashot Egiazaryan in three major multimillion-dollar claims in the Commercial Court. The case concerned a hotel-building project in Russia.

Edward Brown Frequently instructed in company, insolvency, fraud and banking disputes, he regularly tackles cases with an international angle. **Strengths:** A "tenacious junior" who is "clever and thorough." "His advice is clear and his approach direct." **Recent work:** Represented Indian manufacturer Castex Technologies in USD200 million litigation against a number of hedge funds. The claim concerned convertible bonds and allegations of share price manipulation.

Emily Wood Negotiates an active litigation and international arbitration practice acting for blue-chip clients. Wood receives plaudits for both the strength of her advocacy and her written work. **Strengths:** "Just incredibly eloquent and utterly had her head around an incredibly complex matter." "She is brilliant and incredibly personable." **Recent work:** Defended Barclays against a £300 million claim brought against it by UniCredit. The case concerned an indemnity relating to a transaction between the banks.

Fountain Court Chambers

See profile on p.847

THE SET

One of the finest commercial sets around, Fountain Court is home to expert silks and juniors who are au fait with all manner of commercial litigation and are regularly involved in matters of the highest value and complexity. Its ranks have recently been swelled with the lateral hire of a number of highly reputed barristers from other chambers, and the set has shown its ongoing commitment to its clients by introducing a new commercial crime team. Members here handle the full gamut of commercial cases and are expert in aviation, insurance, professional negligence and commercial contract cases. Banking and finance is a particular forte of the set and its barristers have been involved in the full range of credit crunch disputes, as well as matters arising from allegations of market rigging in the forex and Libor markets. Recent cases of note that the set has handled include Deutsche Bank v Unitech, the MasterCard litigation, Property Alliance Group Ltd v Royal Bank of Scotland, and the Construction Industry Vetting Information Group Litigation. Solicitors say: "Fountain Court is a progressive and commercially minded set that is full of talented barristers who are approachable and there to help."

Client service: "The clerks are all approachable, down-to-earth and very responsive. They provide a quick turnaround on work." Alex Taylor leads the team, ably assisted by Paul Martenstyn. Both are applauded for their accessibility, promptness of response and "willingness to really get to know all of the people concerned with the many cases they are dealing with."

SILKS

Michael Brindle QC (see p.603) A leading light at the London Bar who is instructed in a wide range of big-ticket litigation. He is particularly adept at matters concerning banking and finance, company law, professional negligence, insurance and international trade. **Strengths:** "He's extremely bright, he's client-friendly and he provides good leadership." "He adds gravitas to any team." **Recent work:** Represented Russian state-owned companies Sovcomflot and Novoship in the Fiona Trust litigation in the Court of Appeal.

Michael Crane QC (see p.625) A fantastic advocate who argues precedent-setting cases in front of the highest courts. His work in the aviation field is particularly lauded, but he is also an expert in insurance, energy and media work. Solicitors regularly turn to him for important arbitration matters. **Strengths:** "He is absolutely superb, a charming individual, and someone who is in tremendous demand." "He is one of the smoothest advocates that you will ever meet." **Recent work:** Acted in the Supreme Court in a case looking at the scope of the 1886 Riot (Damages) Act following the destruction of property during the 2011 London riots. The court considered whether consequential loss is recoverable in claims for damage to commercial property.

David Railton QC A highly respected silk with a fine commercial practice, who has handled a number of high-value and very important cases arising out of the 2008 financial crisis. He has also been active in a number of matters relating to Libor manipulation. **Strengths:** "He is a fine advocate who shows meticulous attention to detail." "He's extremely clever, exceptionally user-friendly and highly reliable." **Recent work:** Acted for RBS and four former RBS directors in connection with claims brought against them by shareholders. The case arose out of the £12 billion rights issue by the bank in 2008.

Bankim Thanki QC (see p.780) A highly adept advocate who has a vibrant commercial practice. His offshore work continues to flourish and he is frequently seen representing clients in the BVI and the Isle of Man. He currently serves as deputy head of chambers. **Strengths:** "A really smart lawyer with a charming manner who is tough underneath." **Recent work:** Acted for Teva and its subsidiary Cephalon in a £100 million claim in the Commercial Court. The case, which concerned a leukaemia drug manufacturing contract, alleged economic duress and bad faith against Wockhardt India and its UK subsidiaries.

Patrick Goodall QC (see p.656) Well versed in fraud, sanctions, financial instrument and shareholder cases, among others, and often retained for cases with international elements. **Strengths:** "Knowledgeable and produces tidy advocacy." "His written work is especially impressive." **Recent work:** Acted for Mr Kolomoisky in proceedings with Mr Bogolyubov against fellow oligarch Mr Pinchuk. The case was valued at USD2 billion.

Richard Handyside QC (see p.663) A firm favourite with magic circle firms, he handles the toughest litigation, much of it banking and finance-related. He has recently handled a number of claims relating to alleged rigging of the Libor market. **Strengths:** "He is very, very impressive in the courtroom and has real gravitas." "He will give a considered view and always weighs up the options carefully." **Recent work:** Instructed by UBS in a dispute with Decura following the termination of an introduction and outsourcing agreement between the two parties.

Guy Philipps QC (see p.736) A hugely respected commercial litigator with a broad business practice. He is frequently seen in matters involving the banking, financial services, insurance and reinsurance, and professional negligence sectors. **Strengths:** "A good advocate, he can cut through all the detail and just get to the point very efficiently." "An extremely accomplished financial services practitioner." **Recent work:** Represented Barclays in seeking to recover USD56 million in outstanding loans from 220 former Dewey & LeBoeuf partners. The firm had borrowed the money to fund its capital contributions, but filed for bankruptcy in 2012.

Stuart Ritchie QC (see p.752) Regularly acts for directors and senior executives facing breach of fiduciary duty claims and other legal issues. He is also highly adept at handling commercial contracts disputes both in court and at arbitration. **Strengths:** "A real genius who is both commercially minded and user-friendly." "Very good forensically, he can really dig down into the details of a case." **Recent work:** Acted for the National Housing Trust of Jamaica in an appeal to the Privy Council against an award of JMD214 million in compound interest made in arbitral proceedings in Jamaica. The case concerned a disputed housing project in St Thomas.

Jonathan Adkin QC (see p.579) A very highly regarded young silk with a vibrant commercial practice, who has been particularly active in recent years handling work for Russian and CIS clients. His hands-on approach to complex litigation draws particular praise from the market. **Strengths:** "Unflappable and commendably pragmatic when dealing with issues requiring great urgency." "A very fine draftsman and a powerful advocate." **Recent work:** Instructed in a USD1.3 billion claim brought in the Chancery Division by Russian state agencies against a former oligarch accused of removing substantial funds from a major Russian bank.

Derrick Dale QC (see p.628) A versatile and commercially astute barrister who is involved in major disputes on a regular basis. Solicitors appreciate his wide skill set and ability to get complex legal arguments down on paper in a usable fashion. **Strengths:** "A persuasive advocate and an excellent team player." "He is equally as good with difficult judges as he is difficult clients." **Recent work:** Acted for DHL defending a £74 million claim for breach of confidence in relation to the transition of services between Bibby and DHL at Nisa's Scunthorpe division.

Timothy Howe QC (see p.676) Has long experience of representing financial institutions, banks and corporates in hard-fought litigation. Sources describe him as "one of the hardest-working silks at the Bar and a real asset to any team." **Strengths:** "He is very effective and commercial in his approach." "He is very measured in his advice and is very client-friendly and responsive." **Recent work:** Successfully acted for Credit Suisse in an EUR85 million claim against leading Dutch housing corporation Vestia. The case concerned interest rate derivatives.

Andrew Mitchell QC (see p.719) Has a strong reputation for representing banks in claims involving interest rate and credit swaps and Libor manipulation. He has also been called upon to appear in profit-sharing disputes, and is active in insurance matters. **Strengths:** "He is a fantastic advocate with presence and gravitas in court." "He is extremely good on his feet and is both charming and charismatic." **Recent work:** Acted for Barclays both with regard to its PPI litigation and in Thornbridge v Barclays, the only swaps case the bank took to trial.

Stephen Rubin QC (see p.756) Respected silk with experience of handling a wide range of commercial matters. He is highly regarded for his work representing high net worth individuals from Russia and the CIS in disputes heard in London. His commitment to his clients and formidable advocacy were particularly remarked upon by sources. **Strengths:** "Experienced and commercial." "He has a really, really sharp mind when it comes to analysing problems and coming up with strategy." **Recent work:** Represented a trio of oligarchs, Chodiev, Machkevitch and Ibragimov, in a complex fraud claim against Kirill Stein.

Charles Béar QC (see p.593) An impressive advocate with a strong administrative and public law practice, who also handles a good deal of financial services and banking work. He is frequently to be seen representing clients in mis-selling matters and advising them on regulatory issues. **Strengths:** "Stunningly brilliant" and "really clever." **Recent work:** Acted for Danish bank Roskilde in a high-profile mis-selling matter concerning the secondary market purchase of USD30 million of loan notes six months before the bank's collapse.

Jeffrey Chapman QC (see p.614) Talented silk with an expansive commercial practice. Solicitors laud him for his ability to provide "robust, commercial and pragmatic advice" that they can then take to their clients. **Strengths:** "Intensely bright and highly commercial." "He is meticulous and has an effective and persuasive style of advocacy." **Recent work:** Acted for investment banker Jeffrey Blue in suing the owner of Sports Direct and Newcastle United FC, Mike Ashley, in the Commercial Court. Mr Blue was seeking £14 million promised to him if he helped get the Sports Direct share price above £8 per share.

Stephen Moriarty QC (see p.721) A commercial silk who is particularly highly regarded for his work in insurance, aviation and professional negligence matters. His ability to understand where the judges want to go in a case was remarked upon by interviewees. **Strengths:** "A fantastic mix of the cerebral and the user-friendly." "He is super-intelligent even by the high standards of the Commercial Bar." **Recent work:** Acted for aviation finance company Airfinance in a six-week Commercial Court action brought against it by companies controlled by Alexander Lebedev.

Patricia Robertson QC (see p.753) Frequently instructed in big-ticket commercial disputes, she is highly regarded for her work in financial services, banking and professional negligence matters. **Strengths:** "Extremely thorough and impressive in front of clients." **Recent work:** Successfully extricated construction firm Cleveland Bridge from a large-scale group action being taken against it by a number of major construction companies.

Brian Doctor QC (see p.634) Handles significant fraud disputes both in London and in various places around the world including South Africa, Paraguay, Russia and the BVI. **Strengths:** "He's very unstuffy and rolls his sleeves up and gets stuck in. He gets a remarkable amount done in a short space of time." **Recent work:** Defended G4S against a claim made by 43 South Africans against G4S plc and G4S South Africa alleging maltreatment in a privatised prison in South Africa. The case raised new questions regarding the appropriateness of the English courts to rule on claims against privatised state organisations abroad.

Michael McLaren QC (see p.713) Has an excellent reputation among members of the Bar for the quality of his commercial practice. He is particularly active in aviation, professional discipline and large-scale infrastructure project disputes. **Strengths:** "An extremely commercial and highly pragmatic silk." "His ability to marshal very complex problems and facts is second to none." **Recent work:** Assisted a large group of English investors in an action against Cypriot banks. The group had invested in holiday properties, and lost their money when property prices plummeted in Cyprus following the financial crash.

John Taylor QC (see p.778) Has a formidable banking and finance practice, and experience of acting in complex interest rate swap and financial instrument litigation for banks. He also regularly undertakes significant aviation matters. **Strengths:** "He is brilliant on the detail and has a good court presence." "A very strong advocate who prepares extremely well and is always on top of every point." **Recent work:** Represented Barclays, NatWest, RBS and other banks in defending numerous claims that interest rate hedging products were mis-sold to business customers.

Rosalind Phelps QC (see p.736) A fine barrister who took silk this year. She acts in major aviation, pharmaceutical, banking and finance matters to name but a few. **Strengths:** "A very thorough and bright barrister" who is "effective at getting to the point." **Recent work:** Represented Lloyds Bank in a range of litigation concerning claims it had mis-sold high-value derivatives products to commercial customers. The allegations also concerned the fixing of Libor rates by banks.

Ben Valentin QC (see p.786) Took silk this year on the back of a highly successful career at the junior Bar. Major civil fraud, offshore and banking disputes are the mainstay of his practice. **Strengths:** "Smart, responsive, and someone with good judgement." "He is a very fine advocate known for the quality of his preparation." **Recent work:** Counsel for Sonera in proceedings in the BVI seeking to enforce a USD1 billion ICC arbitration award against Çukurova. The dispute related to the telecommunications sector.

JUNIORS

Laura John (see p.683) Handles a busy litigation practice and acts for both domestic and international clients. She is particularly good at advising on injunctive relief, and is an expert on freezing orders and search orders. **Strengths:** "An effortlessly capable barrister with a strong banking practice." "Practical, user-friendly and upbeat." **Recent work:** Acted for RBS in defending a claim alleging fraudulent misrepresentation in relation to an interest rate swap. The case arose out of Libor-rigging allegations.

James McClelland (see p.711) Particularly active in banking and finance matters and has had a key role in some of the largest cases currently in the London courts. Sources describe him as "supremely bright" and "a real star for the future." **Strengths:** "Diligent and one of the brightest junior barristers around." "He is engaging, very bright and very thoughtful." **Recent work:** Represented RBS and its former directors defending a multibillion-pound group action brought by institutional and private investors following the bank's collapse.

Alexander Milner (see p.718) Has experience of handling some of the highest-value litigation in London and is noted for his prowess in international arbitration. His Russian language skills make him particularly attractive for Russian and CIS disputes. **Strengths:** "Brilliant in every respect, he's thorough, attentive and responsive." "A highly intelligent lawyer who really rolls up his sleeves." **Recent work:** Represented Mr Pugachev at numerous hearings in the High Court and Court of Appeal in proceedings brought against him by Russia's Deposit Insurance Agency. The case arose out of the collapse of Mezhdunarodniy Promyshlenniy Bank.

Tamara Oppenheimer (see p.730) A highly regarded junior with a robust commercial practice. She is particularly well known for her work in the banking and finance, professional negligence and aviation sectors. **Strengths:** "She's very clear, direct in her approach and a good advocate. She is very easy to deal with and she knows how to work with solicitors and their clients." "Her attention to detail is fantastic." **Recent work:** Acted for Mitsui Sumitomo Insurance in the Court of Appeal handling a claim relating to the 2011 London riots brought under the Riot (Damages) Act 1886.

Adam Zellick (see p.802) Well regarded for his efforts in banking, aviation and civil fraud. His work as sole counsel in some hugely significant matters marks him out as a junior to watch. **Strengths:** "He is a very bright guy who brings good tactical thinking to the table." "He is very bright and a natural discussion leader." **Recent work:** Acted as sole counsel for NatWest in the Hyderabad funds case. This was a dispute between India, Pakistan and an Indian royal dynasty over the ownership of monies deposited with the bank during the Partition of India in 1948.

Simon Atrill (see p.586) Has a flourishing commercial dispute practice. He focuses his attention on big-ticket, international disputes in English courts, and also undertakes complex cases overseas. **Strengths:** "He is a clever junior who, even by the standards of the Bar, is very bright." "A delight to work with and a man with impressive analytical skills." **Recent work:** Defended claims brought against gold mining companies operating in Tanzania arising from injuries inflicted on various local people. The matter involved novel issues relating to anti-suit injunctions and vicarious liability for unlawful actions of the Tanzanian police.

James Cutress (see p.628) Aviation, banking and insurance are the mainstays of his practice. Solicitors admire him for the hard work and sheer intellect he brings to bear on tough litigation. **Strengths:** "Measured, sensible and reasonable." "He's technically excellent and great at focusing on the true issues in a case. He gives clients real confidence." **Recent work:** Acted for a fund manager with regard to a claim in the Cayman Islands for over USD500 million that arose out of the Madoff fraud.

Edward Levey (see p.700) Possesses a wide commercial practice that takes in complex financial instrument, energy and commercial fraud cases. He also has experience of acting in offshore disputes. **Strengths:** "A great team member." "He instils confidence in the clients by offering practical advice and taking a robust approach with the other side." **Recent work:** Acted in a claim brought against the Central Bank of Nigeria arising out of a fraud alleged to have taken place in 1986 involving the Nigerian State Security Service.

Deepak Nambisan (see p.725) A highly regarded counsel in a number of practice areas who is particularly accomplished in civil fraud, aviation and banking litigation. His ability to operate unled receives praise from the market. **Strengths:** "He worked incredibly hard and got through a vast amount of detail in the case." "A super junior who really operates at silk level." **Recent work:** Acted as lead counsel in a dispute arising out of the termination by ITV2 of a contract with production company MR H TV. The termination concerned a Peter Andre and Kerry Katona reality TV series.

Paul Sinclair (see p.766) He is frequently led by top silks and is often seen acting in matters concerning property and finance. He has recently been instructed in a large dispute concerning Libor manipulation. **Strengths:** "Very clever and user-friendly." "He is extremely quick, exceptionally bright and a pleasure to deal with." **Recent work:** Acted for Johan Eliasch in a bitterly contested joint venture dispute concerning the ownership of the ultra-luxury Aman Resorts hotel chain.

Rupert Allen (see p.582) Led by top silks in complex, big-ticket banking and telecommunication disputes. Sources comment on the thorough nature of his written product. **Strengths:** "He is a very bright guy who gets on top of matters impressively quickly." "He is really responsive and very thoughtful." **Recent work:** Represented ARC Capital Holdings, a Cayman-based investment fund, in relation to a claim for negligence and breach of contract against its former investment manager.

Ben Lynch (see p.704) Particularly active in insurance, professional negligence and contractual disputes. **Strengths:** "Incredibly hard-working and really gets into the detail of a case." "He can be quite radical and think outside of the box." **Recent work:** Handled an appeal in a key case for the insurance industry looking at the meaning and effect of the aggregation clause in solicitors' professional indemnity insurance.

David Murray (see p.724) Joins the rankings this year having been frequently instructed by leading firms in high-stakes litigation. Major firms appreciate the calming influence he brings to cases and his ability to see the wood for the trees. **Strengths:** "A barrister with top-drawer drafting skills." "He is unflappable despite there being a bullish barrister on the other side." **Recent work:** China Southern Airlines was being sued by Tigris for allegedly breaching a USD140 million contract for the sale of six Boeing 737 aircraft. Murray successfully had the case dismissed on appeal.

Richard Power (see p.742) Power is both led and acts as sole counsel in some impressive pieces of litigation, and is an expert on banking and financial instruments. Commentators claim that "he ticks all the boxes" one would want from a junior. **Strengths:** "Clear, concise, committed and client-friendly." "His pleadings are very well crafted." **Recent work:** Acted as sole counsel for Depfa in its dispute with UBS in the Court of Appeal. Depfa was successful at first instance in securing a judgment for USD116 million.

Band 2

Blackstone Chambers

See profile on p.813

THE SET

A premier set that is as happy handling top-level commercial work as it is leading public law cases. It attracts many of the best pieces of commercial litigation both at home and abroad, and is particularly strong in banking and finance, technology and media-related matters. Its clients include many of the best in-house solicitors and the set caters to a wide range of FTSE 100 companies. Its recent cases of note include Tchenguiz v Serious Fraud Office, Libyan Investment Authority v Société Générale and Others, matters arising out of the Madoff fraud, and Re Bonhams, a case concerning the sale of a 1954 Ferrari for over £10.5 million.

Client service: One solicitor says: "The clerks offer a premium service and are interested in creating deep, long-standing relationships. They're attentive and can be contacted at any time of day or night, and if I need them to step up they always deliver." "They match you with the appropriate barrister and are frank and honest about people's ability and availability." The clerks are led by Gary Oliver.

SILKS

Robert Anderson QC Well regarded for his civil fraud, media and entertainment work. Sources praise him as an effective advocate who has the ability to build an excellent report with a tribunal. **Strengths:** "Bright, thoughtful and unfailingly courteous. He is well prepared and succinct when on his feet." "A superb advocate who's incredibly user-friendly." **Recent work:** Acted for the Dubai Islamic Bank in a claim against it for USD1.2 billion arising out of a restructuring agreement concluded in the wake of a multimillion-dollar commercial credit fraud.

Andrew Green QC Has a fine practice representing commercial and government bodies in complex financial cases. The power of his advocacy and his ability on his feet are widely commented upon by both solicitors and his peers at the Bar. **Strengths:** "He is an excellent cross-examiner and a very commercially minded guy." **Recent work:** Acted for the claimant in Crown Bidco Ltd v Vertu Holdings, a case concerning the sale by Nokia of the Vertu luxury mobile phones business.

Andrew Hunter QC A well-regarded silk with a diverse, high-value practice. He has a strong understanding of international fraud, insurance and financial disputes. **Strengths:** "He is user-friendly and very good with clients – he just instils confidence in them." "He is ferociously intelligent. Hardly anyone grapples with difficult legal issues and distils them into effective pleadings better than him." **Recent work:** Acted as leading counsel for various companies in the AIG group with regard to a £100 million claim by multiple former bank employees. The claim was for sums under a deferred compensation scheme.

Ian Mill QC Lauded for his technical ability, he has both a wide practice and a broad range of clients. His work on media disputes is particularly highly regarded. **Strengths:** "Affable and great fun to work with." "An outstanding advocate who has first-class cross-examination skills." **Recent work:** Acted for auction house Bonhams in four interrelated actions in the Commercial Court arising from the sale in June 2014 of a 1954 Ferrari. The car had been sold for over £10.5 million.

Pushpinder Saini QC Commentators consistently praise his ability to get his teeth into matters and quickly come up with commercial solutions. He has been active in a number of high-profile energy and fraud matters over the last year. **Strengths:** "He's an exceptional advocate who prepares thoroughly, is incredibly quick-thinking and is excellent with clients." "He is able to understand facts and issues in a complex case very quickly and advise accordingly." **Recent work:** Defended the SFO in a £300 million claim by the Tchenguiz brothers claiming misfeasance in respect of false allegations of financial misconduct and fraud.

Barbara Dohmann QC Hugely experienced commercial silk with decades of litigation experience. She possesses a broad practice that covers banking, insurance, professional negligence and IP. **Strengths:** "Fantastic at bringing focus to a case." "She has a razor-sharp legal mind and superb judgement."

Robert Howe QC Has an excellent commercial practice and is instructed in a wide range of matters. He is particularly well known for his work handling media, IP, confidential information and fraud matters. **Strengths:** "He gets straight to the heart of the matter, holds the attention of the court and devastates opponents with his advocacy." "He is excellent on his feet and very bright." **Recent work:** Instructed for the defendant, Bank of America Merrill Lynch, in an USD850 million dispute with a Vincent Tchenguiz property group. The matter concerns issues arising out of termination of a loan facility.

Alan Maclean QC Highly regarded commercial counsel who handles a broad range of issues, and is noted for the power of his advocacy. His areas of expertise include banking and finance, telecoms and competition law, to name but a few. **Strengths:** "He is perceptive, authoritative, clever and an excellent cross-examiner." **Recent work:** Acted in Bilta (UK) Ltd v Nazir, an important seven-judge Supreme Court case that considered secondary liability for fraud.

Tom Weisselberg QC Tackles a wide range of sophisticated commercial matters including those involving technology, the media and IP. His ability to quickly come up with solutions for clients was widely commented upon. **Strengths:** "Supremely able and affable, he's a wonderful asset to any litigation team." "He's incredibly user-friendly, super-able and very fast." **Recent work:** Acted for HMRC in a high-profile Commercial Court action involving Bernie and Slavica Ecclestone. The case involved issues of commercial and public law relating to a settlement agreement concluded by HMRC with Mr and Mrs Ecclestone.

Thomas de la Mare QC Active in both the commercial and public law spheres, and has a deep understanding of human rights and European law. **Strengths:** "He is robust, creative and practical." "Amazingly talented and a great lateral thinker." **Recent work:** Acted for Lebara in its claim against close commercial rival Lyca concerning Lyca's actions in blocking Lyca customers from using their mobile data plans to access or use Lebara websites or services.

Andrew George QC Has handled a broad range of large-scale commercial claims for individuals, government bodies and corporates. Solicitors particularly admire his performances in court. **Strengths:** "Sees the issues that matter straight away and has a great grasp of financial services." "He is incredibly clear in his thinking and has a great mind." **Recent work:** Represented the Libyan Investment Authority in a USD2 billion claim against Société Générale. The case concerned allegations of bribery during Gaddafi's time in power in Libya.

Shaheed Fatima QC Seen as one of the brightest young silks of her generation, she is equally good at both commercial and public law cases. She is particularly active when it comes to jurisdictional issues, international claims and arbitrational enforcement. **Strengths:** "She is very, very client-friendly. I have no compunction about putting her on call with me and a general counsel when we have to give advice people don't want to hear." "Absolutely brilliant and absolutely reliable." **Recent work:** Represented the defendant in Harb v Aziz, a contractual claim worth over £12 million. The case followed the dismissal of the defendant's sovereign immunity by the Court of Appeal.

JUNIORS

Mark Vinall Possesses a broad commercial practice that encompasses sectors as diverse as media and entertainment, civil fraud and insurance. He wins plaudits for his intelligence approach in tough cases and his ability to work well with clients. **Strengths:** "Responsive, thorough and good on his feet, he is relentless in his pursuit of the good points in a case." "Fiendishly intelligent and extremely hard-working." **Recent work:** Junior counsel for the auction house Bonhams in a complex and high-profile Commercial Court dispute concerning a 1950s racing Ferrari which was sold at the Goodwood Festival of Speed auction.

Robert Weekes Frequently led by silks in big-ticket, international matters being heard in UK courts and international arbitration forums. He is active in fraud, banking and shareholder matters. **Strengths:** "He has immense gravitas in court, and is clearly going to be a total star." "A brilliant thinker who has ten solutions to every problem." **Recent work:** Junior counsel for Crown BidCo in its dispute with Nokia following its purchase of the Vertu luxury phone manufacturer.

20 Essex Street

See profile on p.838

THE SET

20 Essex Street has long been known for its work in the shipping world, a sector where it still holds sway. It has, however, many more strings to its bow and has involvement in a wide variety of commercial litigation. Members here regularly handle banking and finance, fraud, insolvency, competition and regulatory work for a broad spread of leading instructing solicitors. They are a fixture in some of the most celebrated cases of the day, examples being OMV v Petrom, Libyan Investment Authority v Goldman Sachs International, and the MasterCard litigation. Other matters they have handled include the RBS shareholder litigation and the long-running EUR4.4 billion 'Prestige' case which arose out of a large-scale ecological disaster.

Client service: "The clerking team led by Neil Palmer goes above and beyond. When there is a rush they can run down to court quickly and help us out using their relationships with the court staff. They are also very honest at talking about barristers when we are looking for people to instruct."

SILKS

Philip Edey QC Handles a broad commercial practice, but is particularly adept at complex energy, shipping, banking and structured products disputes. The strength of his advocacy and his ability to hold the court's attention wins him plaudits. **Strengths:** "He is a brilliant advocate and a wonderful leader. He ran one of the most devasting cross-examinations that I have ever seen." He's a solid advocate and certainly has the ear of the court." **Recent work:** Acted as joint leader of the team acting for the Libyan Investment Authority in its litigation against Goldman Sachs. The sovereign wealth fund was claiming more than USD1 billion.

Duncan Matthews QC A "powerful advocate" who has experience of leading huge civil fraud actions at all levels of the English court system. Much of his work involves major overseas clients, and he has lately been involved in Russian fraud and Icelandic bank matters. **Strengths:** "He has a brilliant command of the court and really marshals his materials well." "He gets total respect from judges and is someone who can give credibility to a case that doesn't necessarily deserve it." **Recent work:** Instructed by OMV Petrom in its claim against Glencore International. Petrom contends that Glencore systematically defrauded it by delivering blended cargoes of crude oil in the place of the more expensive grades of oil.

Andrew Baker QC Handles a diverse practice that sees him tackle shipping, commodities, insurance, transportation and banking cases. He is also active in international arbitration forums and is a CEDR-accredited mediator. **Strengths:** "He was really really good on the detail and quickly got up to speed on specific aspects of the case." **Recent work:** Represented Lehman Brothers International (Europe) in its EUR65 million dispute with DZ Bank and The Bank of New York Mellon. This was a significant dispute arising out of the finalisation of Lehman's UK administration.

Charles Kimmins QC A respected commercial silk who is active across a broad range of sectors. Shipping, energy and telecoms cases all form part of his practice. He is also frequently involved in international arbitration work. **Strengths:** "He's really constructive and his knowledge of cases is brilliant." "He is a class act and a lovely guy." **Recent work:** Defended Venezuelan national oil company PDVSA against a USD55 million claim brought by CVH Offshore. The claimant sought payment for the provision of offshore energy rig contracts.

David Lewis QC Has an active international arbitration and commercial litigation practice, and receives particular praise for his work in the shipping sector. Having previously lived and practised in Singapore he is well schooled in international dispute resolution in Asia. **Strengths:** "Sharp-witted, commercial and user-friendly." "He is extremely reassuring and basically knows his stuff very well." **Recent work:** Successfully acted for English Electric in a test case concerning corporate liability for historic asbestos claims.

JUNIORS

Philip Riches Recently joined the set having previously been at Stone Chambers. He regularly handles major pieces of cross-border litigation concerning the energy, mining, shipping and telecoms sectors. **Strengths:** "He is clever, he communicates well, and he has a great deal of commercial acumen." **Recent work:** Acted for IPM Energy Trading against Carillion Energy Services in a dispute concerning the UK government's carbon offset scheme. The £16 million claim related to Carillion's alleged failure to deliver carbon savings under the scheme.

Andrew Fulton Has a strong focus on banking and financial disputes, and experience of working on complex derivatives and structured product matters. He garners praise for his user-friendly approach. **Strengths:** "Hands-on, practical and someone who produces very effective written and oral advocacy." "He's quick to grasp complex issues and identify commercial solutions." **Recent work:** Retained on a breach of warranty claim arising out of a share purchase agreement. The Hut Group alleged an overstatement of profits in relation to a business it had purchased. The defendants counterclaimed for fraudulent breach of warranty.

Charlotte Tan A highly regarded junior who is trusted by top silks to handle big-ticket matters. She has experience of acting in huge fraud, insurance and shipping cases, and is viewed as someone who punches well above her level of call. **Strengths:** "She produces high-quality paperwork that is seriously well reasoned and beautifully put together." "She is the best junior that I have worked with due to the quality of her advice, her commercial approach and her responsiveness." **Recent work:** Charlotte acted as junior in the landmark 'Prestige' case. The case related to one of the largest oil spills in history, and Spain and France's subsequent attempts to recover up to EUR4.5 billion in compensation for extensive pollution damage suffered.

7 King's Bench Walk

See profile on p.871

THE SET

A hugely regarded insurance set that year on year broadens the scope of its commercial litigation work. Members are involved in a wide variety of matters relating to civil fraud, professional negligence, banking and general contract disputes, and are described as being "sensible, experienced and sophisticated practitioners." They produce a strong showing in the energy and shipping markets and increasingly attract work of great importance. Individuals here have been involved in the Excalibur case, Cattles v PwC, the Yukos litigation and the OW Bunkers bankruptcy matter.

Client service: "An excellent set with a great clerking team led by Bernie Hyatt and Greg Leyden." Brian Lee is the practice development and marketing director, and maintains very strong links with solicitors both domestically and internationally.

SILKS

Jonathan Gaisman QC One of the top silks practising in London today and a barrister with a huge breadth to his practice, he is brought in to handle the largest pieces of litigation. Big-ticket energy disputes remain a key pillar of his practice, but he is also frequently called on to handle insurance, shareholder and professional negligence matters among others. **Strengths:** "The brightest guy, who really has the brain for any complex commercial matter. He outsmarted the whole tribunal." "For bet-the-company cases he's the person." **Recent work:** Represented SBM Offshore in a claim concerning losses following the evacuation and subsequent decommissioning of a brand new oil platform located in the Norwegian North Sea. The case considered successive operational delays and the discovery of cracks in the cement of the foundations of the platform.

Christopher Butcher QC Has experience of leading top cases at all levels of the court system right up to the Supreme Court. He is frequently called upon to represent clients in international forums including Bermuda, Singapore and the Cayman Islands. Although known for the depth of his insurance experience, he is also highly respected for his work in shipping and professional negligence among other areas. **Strengths:** "A very clever and hard-working silk with exceptional cross-examination skills, who has a very incisive mind." "He is an excellent tactician." **Recent work:** Successfully defended Grant Thornton against a claim for breach of duty brought by Renewable Power & Light.

Clive Freedman QC (see p.648) A barrister with a truly international practice who has made upwards of 50 appearances in the Court of Appeal. His Russian language skills stand him in good stead when handling cases involving Russian and CIS clients and opposition. **Strengths:** "Totally thorough and a marvellous cross-examiner." "One of the most hard-working people out there. He captures the court's attention and puts his client's case really well." **Recent work:** Successfully acted for Sebry in its claim brought against Companies House concerning a mistaken entry by Companies House on its register stating that a long-established company was in liquidation.

Gavin Kealey QC Head of chambers, who is well regarded for his work across a range of commercial law, but best known for handling insurance, aviation and shipping cases. He is also often instructed as an arbitrator in high-profile matters. **Strengths:** "Offers well-reasoned and detailed advice." "Really bright and very commercial." **Recent work:** Brought in to give expert testimony on English law to the US Federal District Court in Memphis, Tennessee in a multimillion-dollar case concerning Smith & Nephew.

Rebecca Sabben-Clare QC Respected for her work in insurance and professional negligence matters. She has a reputation for providing sound, user-friendly advice. **Strengths:** "She is really extremely bright and someone who gives commercial and forthright advice." "An exceptionally good advocate and adviser who always impresses clients and the courts." **Recent work:** Acted on an auditors' negligence case in the Commercial Court concerning the collapse of subprime lender Cattles. Cattles asserted that PwC negligently audited its 2006 and 2007 financial statements, fundamentally mis-stating the financial position of the company.

Richard Waller QC Regularly appears in shipping and insurance cases, and has a number of fraud trials under his belt. His cross-examination skills and doggedness in pursuit of his goals are noted by peers. **Strengths:** "Always adopts a very sensible and practical approach. He keeps calm and is good fun to work with." "A fine barrister who does an exceptional job for clients." **Recent work:** Represented his client in a USD100 million dispute concerning the transfer of a portfolio of 37 hotels managed by the Thistle Hotel Group.

JUNIORS

James Brocklebank (see p.603) A highly regarded junior who assists on big-ticket matters. He is seen in a wide variety of commercial cases including those involving energy, insurance and international trade. **Strengths:** "He's got a very good style, he's very concise and he gets the ear of the judge." "He is incredibly thorough." **Recent work:** Acted in an insurance dispute concerning the insurance of the MY 'Galatea' superyacht. He successfully defeated the claim against his broker clients in a three-week Commercial Court trial.

Benjamin Parker "A master of the detail" and a well-regarded junior who is at ease on his feet. He has experience of appearing in front of the Court of Appeal and Supreme Court in highly contentious matters. **Strengths:** "Very good on the legal side and an absolute pleasure to deal with." "He has a calm and measured style." **Recent work:** Instructed in the Supreme Court case of British American Tobacco v Exel Europe. This is a key case concerning the international carriage of goods that raises fundamental issues to do with the interpretation of the international CMR Convention.

3 Verulam Buildings

See profile on p.924

THE SET

A very well thought-of set with great experience across a number of areas. It is held in the highest possible esteem for its work on major pieces of banking and finance litigation, but also has the talent to handle all types of commercial litigation and international arbitration. Major solicitors' firms both at home and abroad instruct it in matters of great moment. Examples include Yukos v The Russian Federation, Arcadia Group v Visa and MasterCard, Terra Firma v Citigroup, and Phones 4u Limited v Vodafone.

Client service: "The clerks are user-friendly and straight down the line." "They'll dedicate their time to helping you find the right counsel, and you know you're not going to get dumped with someone who isn't the right fit." The "exceptionally friendly and helpful" Stephen Penson leads the team.

SILKS

Ali Malek QC A silk with great depth of experience who is particularly noted for his work in international banking, energy and shareholder disputes. **Strengths:** "One of the outstanding practitioners in the banking area." "He's very good at dealing with the big points in a case, and extremely skilled when it comes to case strategy." **Recent work:** Acted in Starbev v Interbrew Central European Holdings, a case concerning an investment fund's acquisition of Anheuser-Busch's CEE drinks business.

Andrew Onslow QC Banking, financial services, fraud and professional negligence disputes all form major struts of his commercial practice. His ability on his feet and user-friendly style make him popular with both clients and solicitors. **Strengths:** "He's thoughtful, shows good judgement and is detailed in his work." "A fantastic advocate." **Recent work:** Acted for a £1.3 billion claimant group in a £4 billion class action securities claim against RBS arising out of its £12 billion rights issue.

Adrian Beltrami QC Has particular expertise in banking, financial services, fraud and asset-tracing cases. He is trusted to lead some of the most significant fraud actions currently being heard in the English courts. **Strengths:** "Bright and extremely sensible, he is able to cut through the legal technicalities and produce common-sense advice." **Recent work:** Acted for Société Générale, which was being sued for £1.5 billion by the Libyan Investment Authority in respect of investments made during the Gaddafi regime.

Ewan McQuater QC Handles banking, civil fraud and general commercial matters at the highest level. He is frequently instructed in cases that have an offshore element to them and has experience of representing clients before the Privy Council. **Strengths:** "Really good at standing up and saying what he thinks, he gives any case he's on a clear direction." "An excellent leader and a compelling advocate." **Recent work:** Defended Vodafone against a claim brought by the administrators of Phones 4u. The case centred on allegations that that Vodafone, in combination with other mobile network operators, had caused the insolvency of Phones 4u.

Jonathan Nash QC Has a truly international commercial litigation practice, and is an expert in banking and finance, insurance and professional negligence disputes. His ability to be "ice cool" under intense pressure and give unvarnished advice was praised by clients. **Strengths:** "Excellent on the detail and is hard-working and approachable." "Articulate and measured in his approach." **Recent work:** Instructed on behalf of Renault Sport SAS in connection with its acquisition of the Lotus Formula One motor racing team. He helped resist an administration petition and advised on issues arising in the course of the acquisition.

Paul Lowenstein QC Highly regarded for the breadth of his commercial work across a wide range of sectors. He possesses the ability to effectively marshal cases with large numbers of parties. His particular areas of interest include cases relating to IT, civil fraud, and the retail and entertainment sectors. **Strengths:** "A fearless advocate who's very strategic, very user-friendly and very robust." "Razor-sharp and super-responsive, he's a team player and a real fighter." **Recent work:** Represented a large group of national retailers including Arcadia Group, ASDA, House of Fraser and Next in a case against MasterCard and Visa. The claim related to the payment of credit and debit card fees and alleged anti-competitive practices by the card companies.

John Odgers QC Focuses his practice on highly contentious banking and financing disputes. His tactical nous and ability to provide a high level of strategic overview while also focusing on the detail of a case are particularly noted. **Strengths:** "He remains calm under pressure and is totally unflappable." "He is incredibly responsive and really rolls up his sleeves." **Recent work:** Acted in Akers v Samba Financial Group, a USD300 million claim by Cayman Islands liquidators under the Cross-Border Insolvency Regulations.

Richard Salter QC Enjoys an excellent reputation among his peers for his work across a wide range of commercial litigation. He is particularly esteemed for his banking, finance and insolvency advice. Salter has experience in offshore matters, and has represented clients both in the Privy Council and in foreign jurisdictions. **Strengths:** "Impressively erudite and fiercely analytical, he is strategically astute in his approach to a case." "A man for the most difficult appeals." **Recent work:** Appeared before the Privy Council representing the Central Bank of Ecuador. The case involved an allegation that a fraud was committed against an insolvent Ecuadorian bank by its owners and controllers.

Andrew Sutcliffe QC Enjoys a strong reputation among peers and solicitors for the breadth of his commercial practice. He is frequently seen on banking, civil fraud and media and entertainment matters. **Strengths:** "Shows excellent dedication and support to the cause and is a real team player." "He's sensible on fees and hugely accessible." **Recent work:** Acted for Hertz against a £10 million claim brought by Ryanair. The dispute arose from Hertz's termination of a long-term contract regarding the exclusive supply of cars to Ryanair passengers.

David Quest QC Extremely adept counsel who possesses expertise across a wide range of commercial areas, and proves particularly good at banking, insurance, fraud and industrial disputes. He is noted for his skill in handling disputes surrounding complex financial products. **Strengths:** "Very down-to-earth and very bright." "Exceptionally bright and strategic." **Recent work:** Acted for private equity fund Chamonix in defending a claim by fellow private equity fund Caledonia concerning the alleged misuse of a confidential business opportunity.

Jonathan Davies-Jones QC As a former investment banker, he is able to bring an informed view to the banking cases he undertakes. He is also well respected for the strength of his civil fraud practice. **Strengths:** "Extraordinarily clever, he takes a pragmatic approach and is very user-friendly." "Phenomenally bright and a delight to work with." **Recent work:** Defended Niranjan Hiranandani against a £350 million claim brought by Isle of Man investment company Hirco. The dispute arose out of losses sustained on investments in Indian real estate developments following the global financial crisis and slumps in the Indian IT and real estate sectors.

Andrew Fletcher QC Has experience in cases involving professional negligence, insolvency, contract and company law among other areas. He is also frequently involved in arbitration. **Strengths:** "He is very good on his feet, is very measured and has the ear of the judge." **Recent work:** Represented RZB Bank in mediation proceedings to resolve issues of double proof in respect of its claims, exceeding £20 million, due under repo contracts which were terminated by reason of the collapse of Lehman Brothers.

Matthew Hardwick QC Well regarded for his shipping, energy and civil fraud practice. He has experience of acting in overseas jurisdictions on offshore matters, and is frequently seen in cases being heard in the BVI. **Strengths:** "Quick-thinking, personable and commercially astute." "Incredibly sharp and someone with excellent drafting skills." **Recent work:** Acted for two defendants in Standard Chartered Bank (Hong Kong) Ltd v Independent Power of Tanzania Ltd & Others, a multi-jurisdictional dispute concerning the recovery of syndicated lending totalling around USD140 million.

John Jarvis QC A widely regarded silk who focuses his work on banking and finance disputes. His ability to work ferociously hard and his acuity of mind were much commented on by interviewees. He also acts as an arbitrator. **Strengths:** "John's brilliant analysis, strategic thinking and excellent advocacy combined with his user-friendly approach make him a natural choice for complex matters." "He represents a treasure chest of experience." **Recent work:** Acted in Tuvana v Barclays Bank, a £44 million damages claims against Barclays for deceit and negligence in relation to the mis-sale of a £325 million multi-callable interest rate swap.

Gregory Mitchell QC Has a long-standing commercial litigation practice and regularly represents a wide range of clients in tough domestic and international cases. **Strengths:** "Gives very straightforward advice which is easy to follow and pragmatic."

David Head QC Highly regarded counsel who offers clients broad commercial litigation expertise. He receives praise both for the forensic manner with which he approaches cases and for the strength of his advocacy. **Strengths:** "A superb advocate in terms of both written and oral work." "He's really bright, easy-going and responsive." **Recent work:** Instructed as sole advocate on behalf of BAT in resisting claims by an Iranian national that he suffered torture and personal injury at the hands of the company's distribution agents in the Middle East.

JUNIORS

Michael Lazarus (see p.697) Well regarded for his work in banking, IT and telecoms, and sale and purchase disputes. He is often brought into hard-fought international arbitrations. **Strengths:** "Extremely intelligent, very meticulous and never fazed by any situations thrown at him." "With him you get a silk's mind at junior prices." **Recent work:** Acted in Otkritie v Threadneedle, a USD120 million claim based on an allegation that Threadneedle was vicariously liable for a conspiracy conducted by its former employee together with several employees of the claimant's group.

Adam Kramer (see p.693) Well thought-of barrister with a broad commercial practice, who is frequently seen in banking, energy and insurance matters. His knowledge of contract damages in particular is noted. **Strengths:** "Very, very clever and good at handling the detail in a case." "He's very bright and fantastic on his feet." **Recent work:** Acted for a £1.3 billion claimant group in a £4 billion class action securities claim against RBS arising out of its £12 billion rights issue conducted in 2008.

Peter Ratcliffe Handles a huge variety of commercial dispute work and is a sought-after junior for big cases. He is often instructed in complex cross-border and jurisdictional matters, and regularly tackles cases relating to insurance, professional negligence and the media and entertainment industries. **Strengths:** "Very good in court" and "one of the top juniors at the Commercial Bar." **Recent work:** Acted as the leading junior for Citi in its defence of Terra Firma's high-profile £2 billion claim arising out of its acquisition of EMI in 2007.

Christopher Harris Has been led in some of the largest commercial cases pursued in the UK in recent times. His international arbitration and public international law practices also catch the eye. **Strengths:** "He is very smart, very responsive and very easy to work with." "He is incredibly bright, great with clients and very accessible." **Recent work:** Represented the Russian Federation against the former shareholders of Yukos in resisting enforcement of a USD50 billion arbitral award.

Matthew Parker (see p.733) Well regarded for his work in contentious commercial disputes across a wide range of sectors. Sources praise his charm and intelligence and salute him for the fight he shows when acting for his client. **Strengths:** "He's extremely user-friendly and great with clients." **Recent work:** Represented Johan Eliasch in commercial litigation concerning the ownership and operation of the Aman hotel group. In this case each party accused the other of dishonest conduct in conspiring to take control of the group or seize its assets.

Rajesh Pillai Equally comfortable representing clients in the London courts or in international arbitration forums. He has experience of acting in joint venture and shareholder disputes, trusts and fraud matters, as well as banking cases. **Strengths:** "Hard-working, very bright and highly accessible." **Recent work:** Acted for Indian businessman Niranjan Hiranandani, defending a £350 million claim by AIM-listed investment company Hirco. The dispute arose out of losses on investments in Indian developments and slumps in the Indian IT and real estate sectors.

Nicholas Craig A well thought-of junior who is effective in the courtroom. His conflict of law and jurisdictional knowledge is strong given his frequent instructions in international matters. Commentators also note his excellence when handling aviation cases. **Strengths:** "Thorough and tenacious, but also pragmatic." "An experienced junior with strong commercial awareness who is an effective courtroom presence." **Recent work:** Represented Alliance Bank, a Kazakh financial institution, in a claim against a number of individuals who defrauded it of approximately USD300 million.

Peter de Verneuil Smith (see p.631) Admired for his work in banking and finance, shipping and fraud matters, he is effective both domestically and offshore in such places as the Channel Islands. His ability to respond to clients quickly and with flexibility is particularly praised. **Strengths:** "Provides prompt and well-reasoned advice." "A go-to junior for finance-related and complex multi-jurisdictional commercial litigation." **Recent work:** Instructed by insurer Titan Europe in a case looking at whether an issuer of securities can suffer a loss and sue for it so as to make a recovery for the benefit of note holders. The team won EUR32 million in damages for the client.

Anne Jeavons Enjoys a good reputation as a bright commercial junior. She is frequently seen in both the Commercial Court and Chancery Division handling challenging litigation. **Strengths:** "Very robust and a person with great intellectual ability." **Recent work:** Instructed in conjoined proceedings involving a dispute between two businessmen, Mr Khagram and Mr Khan. Issues raised involved contractual construction, agency, breach of fiduciary duty and complex factual disputes.

Band 3

Maitland Chambers

See profile on p.875

THE SET

A big beast of the Chancery Bar that sinks its teeth into some of the biggest pieces of litigation both in the UK and abroad. It regularly handles major fraud, property, insolvency and partnership cases and is a major presence in offshore jurisdictions. It is also becoming increasingly becoming involved in financial product litigation. Its recent cases of interest have included Dar Al Arkan v Al Refai, a billion-dollar fraud action brought by the largest commer-

cial entities in the Middle East, and BTA Bank v Dregon Land, a case connected with the long-running Ablyazov litigation. Members have also been involved in a number of matters arising from the Madoff fraud and the collapse of Lehman Brothers.
Client service: "The team is very quick, very sensible about fees and fee structures and receptive to the kind of clients commercial solicitors deal with." John Wiggs, who leads the team, is "a man with the right client service mentality who has regular feedback meetings with solicitors."

SILKS
Paul Girolami QC (see p.653) A leading light of the Bar who possesses a broad range of commercial experience and regularly tackles top-level cases. Particular areas of expertise include trusts, company and fraud litigation. **Strengths:** "A very, very good advocate who always has a very good read on the court." "An absolute star for interlocutory matters."

Anthony Trace QC (see p.783) Regularly called upon to handle a broad range of commercial work in the English courts and abroad. His manner with clients and skill on his feet draw widespread praise from commentators. **Strengths:** "A very skilful and fearless advocate who is highly committed to the client's cause." "He's a tenacious advocate with excellent judgement who has an easy-going, charming manner." **Recent work:** Acted in Dar Al Arkan v Al Refai & Others, a billion-dollar claim brought by some of the largest commercial entities in the Middle East arising out of the publication of a website by the defendants which made serious allegations of fraud.

Jonathan Russen QC (see p.757) Has decades of experience of handling shareholder and partnership disputes, insolvency cases, trust litigation and civil fraud matters. He is also often instructed in the financial services sector. **Strengths:** "Superb knowledge of financial services litigation and very strong on civil fraud matters." "He has a lovely style about him and is firm, but never patronising, with the clients. **Recent work:** Acting for Arizona Investments in proceedings against Standard Chartered relating to an investment which was lost as a result of the Madoff fraud.

Matthew Collings QC (see p.620) Frequently instructed by a wide range of commercial clients in high-stakes trials and appeals. He has strong company law and civil fraud practices, and regularly handles cases offshore. **Strengths:** "He has great advocacy skills" and is "knowledgeable and creative." **Recent work:** Acted in the case of Hrabalek v Hrabalek, a father and son dispute over the ownership of four Lancia Stratos classic cars.

Andrew Twigger QC (see p.785) A highly respected commercial practitioner with a broad range of sector specialisms. His ability to work well with and support clients and solicitors is particularly remarked upon. **Strengths:** "Clever, persuasive and supportive." "He's practical, user-friendly, very meticulous and hard-working."

Richard Morgan QC (see p.721) Undertakes fraud, breach of duty and insolvency matters. He is particularly well known for his asset recovery work and is highly regarded for his work obtaining and resisting freezing orders. **Strengths:** "Hard-working, he fights your corner and has a great manner with lay clients." "He fights tirelessly and is prepared to tackle issues others wouldn't." **Recent work:** Acted for Russian state entity Russtech in objecting to English jurisdiction in the matter of Erste v Red October, a case concerning conspiracy to defraud.

David Mumford QC (see p.724) A highly regarded young silk equally at home in the Commercial Court or Chancery Division. He has experience of dealing with civil fraud, partnership disputes, banking and company matters. **Strengths:** "Has a strong eye for detail coupled with an excellent strategic mind." "He is extremely bright, client-friendly and approachable." **Recent work:** Represented paper manufacturer Sequana in its dispute with BAT. The claim related to legacy liabilities resulting from the contamination of the Fox River in the USA.

JUNIORS
Benjamin John (see p.683) Has experience in high-profile international disputes involving both corporate and national entities. He is highly regarded for his civil fraud practice. **Strengths:** "He is very responsive, bright and fun to work with, and he has great technical ability." "Ben has excellent judgement and a formidable intellect." **Recent work:** Acted for Nomura International against Banca Dei Monti Paschi di Siena. The dispute centred on the enforceability and consequences of a series of highly complex structured derivative transactions that the parties entered into in 2009.

Ciaran Keller (see p.689) A versatile junior with a strong commercial chancery practice. He possesses experience of acting in top-level cases, and has handled a number of large fraud claims, commercial disputes and offshore matters. **Strengths:** "Unpretentious, unflappable and very bright." "His ability to grasp technically difficult issues sets him apart from other barristers at his level." **Recent work:** Acted for BAT against Sequana in an USD800 million dispute concerning unlawful dividends.

Quadrant Chambers
See profile on p.901

THE SET
Possesses a highly capable team of commercial litigators with a fine range of sector specialisms. The members here are particularly well regarded in the shipping, insurance and aviation sectors and are also active in significant energy disputes. They are regularly instructed to obtain interim relief and are experts in anti-suit injunctions, freezing injunctions and other urgent interlocutory relief. They are often to be seen in the Supreme Court, as evidenced by their involvement in Enviroco v Farstad.
Client service: "The clerking team is a real pleasure to deal with and provides a really smooth service. They are honest when telling you which barrister would be best for which case." The team is led by Gary Ventura and Simon Slattery.

SILKS
Simon Rainey QC (see p.746) Particular areas of expertise include shipping, energy, international trade and fraud matters. The quality of his advocacy is particularly remarked upon by peers. **Strengths:** "Exceptionally bright, he has a really wonderful mind. He is commercial and upfront." "He is slick, friendly and someone who really gets to the heart of any given matter." **Recent work:** Represented oil trader Vitol in a dispute with Perenco. The case raised questions about the oil trade practice of cross-month loading.

JUNIORS
Yash Kulkarni (see p.693) Frequently instructed by top firms, he is particularly experienced in work involving freezing and search orders, asset preservation and the appointment of receivers. **Strengths:** "A very polished performer." "He is extremely user-friendly and approachable." **Recent work:** Instructed in a case concerning a commercial claim by Smart Aluminium for payment of £2.5 million in respect of aluminium alloy that was supplied to Aalco.

Jeremy Richmond (see p.751) Instructed by corporate clients to handle a range of commercial matters, he is often seen acting on applications for interim relief. His ability to quickly understand the legal and commercial pressures of a case draws plaudits from instructing solicitors. **Strengths:** "He is able to articulate complex legal issues into everyday language, and always takes a pragmatic and well-reasoned approach to his work." "Good for legally complex disputes where the client faces a real fight." **Recent work:** Instructed in a case centred on the insolvency of OW Bunker, the largest supplier of marine fuel in the world.

Robert-Jan Temmink (see p.779) Covers a broad spectrum of work for his clients. His particular areas of expertise include shipping, aviation, construction and energy matters. **Strengths:** "Rob is both thorough and pragmatic." "His cross-examinations are extremely effective." **Recent work:** Acted in a claim brought by a Saudi national against a former employee who was a UK national. The case arose out of proceedings in Saudi Arabia for breach of fiduciary duty, fraud and theft. The sums of money involved amounted to approximately USD16 billion.

Serle Court
See profile on p.908

THE SET
A broad chancery commercial set that has the breadth of talent to cover a wide range of business matters. It is most focused on disputes relating to trusts, civil fraud, real estate, and banking and finance.
Client service: "Steve Whitaker leads a very helpful and courteous team of clerks." "They are very accommodating and easy to deal with."

SILKS
Alan Boyle QC (see p.601) A highly venerated performer who has vast experience of handling the most complex and high-value cases both at home and abroad. His particular strengths include international fraud and offshore and trusts matters. **Strengths:** "A brilliant technician who provides exceptional client service. He's magisterial." "Possesses vast experience and produces clear and authoritative advocacy." **Recent work:** Instructed in a claim for damages of more than £30 million brought against the directors of a property company for breach of their duty of care in transferring an office block in London to a Jersey trust structure at an undervalue.

Philip Jones QC (see p.686) A commercial advocate of unquestionable ability who handles major international litigation across a wide range of sectors. He has experience of acting in major fraud, joint venture failure, tax and professional negligence cases. **Strengths:** "Very good at drawing out the most significant points of an argument. He puts the lay client at ease and commands the attention of the court." "He's an outstanding choice for trusts litigation." **Recent work:** Acted for BTA Bank, a Kazakh bank, with regard to its USD6 billion claim in the Commercial Court against Mukhtar Ablyazov and his associates.

Lance Ashworth QC (see p.585) A highly regarded commercial and chancery silk who is often seen acting in international disputes in the fraud and insolvency spheres. His manner with clients and his effectiveness on a case are highlighted by sources. **Strengths:** "An authoritative advocate who commands respect from the Bench." "Very bright and client-friendly, he covers a wide range of practice areas." **Recent work:** Acted in Emmott v Michael Wilson & Partners, Ltd, appearing in the Court of Appeal for the solicitor director of a company who had been found guilty of contempt of court in the Commercial Court and sentenced to eight months' imprisonment.

Elizabeth Jones QC (see p.685) A veteran of more than 30 years at the Bar who handles an extremely broad diet of commercial litigation. She regularly handles cases concerning the music industry, financial services, fraud and contentious trusts. **Strengths:** "She gets to grips with the intricate detail of a case in a very short space of time and is very impressive on her feet." "A slick operator who's great with clients." **Recent work:** Instructed in a case where Conapro is suing The Gambia over a sale contract for the supply of petroleum products. The principal defence is that the contract was procured by bribery of a senior government official.

John Machell QC (see p.705) A "superb team player" skilled at tackling contentious partnership, joint venture and company disputes. He also has experience of leading cases concerning fraud, trusts and fiduciary matters. **Strengths:** "He cuts to the chase, gives robust and practical advice, and is impressive on his feet." "Very clever, creative and decisive." **Recent work:** Acted in Salem v Salem, a major partnership/trusts case.

Philip Marshall QC (see p.708) An "absolutely top-notch" silk with a versatile Commercial Court and Chancery practice. His fraud work, both international and domestic, wins him plaudits from the market. He is very active in offshore cases. **Strengths:** "An outstanding advocate who is extremely diligent." "He is a very effective, hands-on litigator." **Recent work:** Successfully defended mining company Erdenet Mining against a claim brought by Standard Bank in respect of project finance in Mongolia.

David Blayney QC (see p.597) Frequently seen in high-profile litigation in the banking and finance sector. He is also active in cases involving claims of bribery and those with challenging quantum issues. **Strengths:** "Extremely bright and a pleasure to work with." "He throws himself into the detail of a case and works really hard." **Recent work:** Instructed in group litigation brought by more than 20,000 individual and institutional claimants concerning the £12 billion RBS rights issue that took place in 2008.

Hugh Norbury QC (see p.728) Focuses his practice on civil fraud and breach of fiduciary duty matters, and has handled a number of offshore matters. Commentators note the amount of support he offers clients faced with difficult legal and business situations. **Strengths:** "Extremely good with clients, he always manages to make even the incredibly complex seem simple." "What was impressive was his ability to mix the hard analysis with the difficult practical issues facing the client." **Recent work:** Defended Mr Zharimbetov in BTA Bank v Ablyazov & Others, a £4 billion banking fraud case.

Nicholas Lavender QC Has a deep understanding of cases concerning banking, trusts and complex financial instruments. He also regularly handles matters relating to FCA investigations. **Strengths:** "Enormously intelligent and extremely hard-working, he is someone with exquisite judgement." **Recent work:** Represented RBS in a dispute with Dongbu Insurance concerning options in connection with the issue of Lehman-sponsored structured notes.

Daniel Lightman QC (see p.701) Offers clients deep knowledge and understanding of complex company law, fraud and fiduciary duty cases. Interviewees praise him for his ability to remain unfazed when confronted with seemingly huge technical and legal difficulties. **Strengths:** "He has exceptional knowledge and skills, particularly in relation to company and shareholder disputes." "An excellent barrister with an eye for technical detail." **Recent work:** Instructed to handle an application by the current trustees of the Tchenguiz family trusts, who had brought claims against the trusts' former trustees for negligence and breach of fiduciary duty.

JUNIORS

Justin Higgo (see p.671) A well-regarded junior with a fine chancery commercial practice. He is routinely led by established silks and has been involved with major fraud and banking matters at an international level. **Strengths:** "He has an excellent client manner and provides clear and unambiguous advice." "Extremely bright, he instinctively knows when to aggressively take the fight to the other side." **Recent work:** Acted in Standard Maritime v Fiona Trust, a case arising out of the operation of the Russian state tanker fleet.

Ruth den Besten (see p.632) Frequently instructed in high-profile litigation, arbitration and mediation matters. She has experience of acting in cases concerning swap mis-selling, injunctive and interim relief, fraud and shareholder disputes. **Strengths:** "A robust counsel with precise drafting skills. She is a pleasure to work with and a good team player." "An excellent barrister who gives high-quality commercial advice that is always well thought out." **Recent work:** Acted for the defendant in Marrache v Jyske Bank, a case concerning frauds committed by a solicitors' partnership in Gibraltar.

Band 4

4 New Square

See profile on p.880

THE SET

Regularly called upon by both top international law firms and boutique litigation firms to act in high-profile contentious matters. The team has a deep understanding of fraud, professional liability, insurance and tax matters at both a domestic and international level. Recently members have acted for a Kazakh group of companies in a USD150 million fraud claim, and have handled a high-profile dispute between two Saudi princes and a Jordanian businessman.

Client service: "Lizzy Stewart is the head of the team and just brilliant. She is always very approachable and willing to have open discussions." She is ably assisted by Dennis Peck and Alex Dolby.

SILKS

Justin Fenwick QC (see p.644) A highly regarded commercial silk active across a range of areas. He is especially good at professional liability, insurance and civil fraud matters, and regularly appears in offshore jurisdictions. **Strengths:** "Calm in a crisis and a clear thinker." "A very determined fighter and an excellent strategist." **Recent work:** Instructed in a dispute concerning the fraudulent conduct of a Middle Eastern telecoms business. The case centred on allegations of fraud on both sides and included applications to the Supreme Court in relation to relief from sanctions.

Anneliese Day QC (see p.631) Frequently called upon to assist major corporate clients with cases concerning joint ventures, private finance intiatives, contract termination and other business issues. Her accessibility to clients despite her heavy workload is much remarked upon by market sources. **Strengths:** "She is quick to grasp the issues and always has an eye for the practical solution to a problem." "Knowledgeable and tactically astute." **Recent work:** Acted on behalf of Dunnes department stores in injunctive proceedings relating to a shopping centre development in Northern Ireland.

Ben Elkington QC (see p.640) Handles cases all the way up to the Supreme Court, acting for an impressive roster of clients. His areas of particular expertise include insurance, breach of contract, fraud, professional negligence and financial instrument disputes. **Strengths:** "He is very responsive and experienced." "He's able to bring together complex cases and steer them to successful conclusions." **Recent work:** Represented the Metropolitan Police in a dispute with insurer Mitsui. The proceedings related to insurance claims following the 2011 London riots and were brought under the Riot (Damages) Act 1886.

JUNIORS

George Spalton (see p.770) A well-regarded junior who has a wealth of experience of acting in professional liability and breach of confidence cases, both at home and abroad. He is lauded by sources for his ability to keep the client's commercial concerns at forefront of his thinking. **Strengths:** "He has very sound judgement and is easy to work with." "He is very good with clients and really stands out for his commercial approach." **Recent work:** Acted for a group of claimants in a case relating to a number of tax schemes run by Ingenious Entities.

Daniel Saoul (see p.758) Having previously worked as a solicitor advocate, he has a fantastic understanding of what solicitors need from a barrister. His commerciality and passionate advocacy make him stand out from the crowd. **Strengths:** "He has proved himself to be a forceful advocate who is undeterred by unusual tactics from opponents." **Recent work:** Acted for Kazakh recycling and logistics company Kazakhstan Kagazy in a fraud-related claim against its former directors and shareholders.

4 Pump Court

See profile on p.895

THE SET

A set that is home to barristers who are known for their knowledge and expertise in insurance, energy and shipping cases. Members are known for their versatility and are increasingly being brought into large banking and finance disputes, where they act both for and against banks. IT and telecoms are other areas in which they do well. Solicitors say: "The barristers here are clever and bright, and know what they're doing. None of them are pompous and all are

very personable."
Client service: "Their clerks are very good and highly approachable. They understand the commercial pressures of a case and offer good value for money." The team is jointly led by senior clerks Carl Wall and Stewart Gibbs.

SILKS
Nigel Tozzi QC (see p.783) A hugely respected, "top-quality" commercial silk with a broad practice. He is extremely well regarded for his work in the shipping and energy sectors, and is noted for his prowess in insurance and banking cases. His manner with clients and ability to provide clear advice is noted by interviewees. **Strengths:** "A brilliant, client-friendly, judge-friendly advocate who is charming and hugely intelligent." "He's a fantastic cross-examiner who knows how to speak to clients." **Recent work:** Instructed in a claim for damages relating to an oil supply contract between Conapro and the Gambian Ministry of Petroleum. The case centres on allegations of bribery.

Michael Douglas QC (see p.635) Well known for his insurance work, and also an impressive performer in fraud, professional negligence and IT cases. **Strengths:** "He is a brilliant partner if you're involved in tough litigation." "He always manages to get the judge on his side and is a really good team player." **Recent work:** Handled a claim for breach of contract against an execution broker. The case arose from the termination of an agreement for the execution of forex trades under a computerised mirror trading foreign exchange system.

Alexander Gunning QC (see p.661) A gifted barrister with experience of professional negligence and fraud disputes, who regularly appears in an offshore context. He is well thought of for his construction law expertise. **Strengths:** "A fantastic young silk" who is "very good on big construction disputes." **Recent work:** Represented VIS Trading in an enforcement action following a USD30 million judgment its favour.

4 Stone Buildings
See profile on p.913
THE SET
Highly respected set that handles top-drawer cases in both the Chancery Division and the Queen's Bench Division. Its members' expertise covers civil fraud, insolvency, company and banking matters. Barristers here are highly active in Russian and CIS litigation, and have particular expertise in oil and gas cases.
Client service: The clerking team, led by David Goddard, is attentive and can be contacted at any time of day or night. "If I need them to step up they always deliver," says one impressed solicitor.

SILKS
Jonathan Crow QC (see p.627) One of the very best barristers at the Bar today, whose ease of advocacy and rapport with judges are much commented upon. He has led in some of the largest commercial matters in the English courts, and has recently handled a number of big-ticket Russian and CIS fraud and company law disputes. **Strengths:** "He is a very, very persuasive advocate who is right at the top of the pile." **Recent work:** Acted in the USD10 billion fraud dispute between BTA Bank and Mr Ablyazov in the Commercial Court.

Robert Miles QC A truly top-end barrister who wins plaudits for his ability to take exceptionally complex legal issues and effectively explain them in simple terms. He is instructed in a broad range of high-profile company law matters, among others. **Strengths:** "He is a measured advocate who is very good at seeing the overall structure and the broad sweep of a case." "He combines fantastic technical ability and strategic judgement with user-friendliness and powerful advocacy." **Recent work:** Represented Hewlett-Packard in its litigation against the former CEO of Autonomy, Michael Lynch. HP was seeking over USD5 billion in damages.

John Brisby QC (see p.603) Has a deep understanding of company and commercial disputes. He possesses expertise in shareholder disputes, fraud, asset recovery, schemes of arrangement and directors' duties matters. **Strengths:** "Excellent for difficult matters when you're on the ropes and you need a rottweiler to let off the leash." **Recent work:** Represented claimant Peak Hotels & Resorts in a shareholder battle for control of the Aman Resorts hotel chain.

Richard Hill QC (see p.671) Continuing to flourish since recently taking silk. His work in fraud, shareholder disputes, financial product mis-selling and post-acquisition litigation is some of the best in the market. **Strengths:** "Richard is incredibly bright and commercial, and someone who gives well-reasoned, pragmatic advice." "Very bright, and easy to use, he sees the bigger picture and is straightforward in his approach." **Recent work:** Acted for Ukrainian businessman Victor Pinchuk in his highly contentious dispute with fellow Ukrainian oligarchs Gennadiy Bogolyubov and Igor Kolomoiski. The case concerned ownership of an iron ore mine in Ukraine.

George Bompas QC (see p.598) Equally capable of representing his clients in both litigation and arbitration settings, and a lawyer who sits as an arbitrator in LCIA proceedings. The creativity of his arguments and the clarity of his analysis win him many admirers. **Strengths:** "He is a brilliant guiding light who offers strategic direction and valuable expertise. He is calm and measured, and should come with a warning, 'Opposition beware.'" "He quickly gets to grips with complex factual and legal issues and has a great presence." **Recent work:** Advised MF Global Services with regard to its administration proceedings and its potential pension liabilities.

Wilberforce Chambers
See profile on p.925
THE SET
Frequently seen in leading Commercial Court and Chancery litigation across a wide range of sectors. Professional negligence and civil fraud cases remain central to the set, but its members are just as likely to be involved in real estate, pensions, insolvency or contentious M&A work. They are increasingly involved in banking and finance matters and are noted for their strong presence in foreign jurisdictions such as Hong Kong, Singapore and the Cayman Islands. Recent matters of interest include Cavendish Square Holdings BV v Makdessi, a Supreme Court case that is now the leading authority on contractual penalties, and Les Laboratoires Servier v Apotex, another Supreme Court case concerning an application for millions of pounds worth of damages arising out of an injunction. **Client service:** "The clerks are responsive and tell you what you need to know quickly." The team is led by Mark Rushton.

SILKS
Alan Gourgey QC A "fine legal brain" and a hugely respected silk who has a wealth of experience of acting in big-ticket fraud and conspiracy claims. He is also active in IT, company law and insolvency matters. **Recent work:** "Very astute and has a good sense of both the merits of a case and the strategy needed to progress it." "He gives clear advice even in the most complex of cases." **Strengths:** Instructed in a USD150 million claim between Bank of Moscow and companies which owed money to the bank.

Ian Croxford QC Highly regarded for the depth and versatility of his practice, he has experience of leading significant commercial matters. He draws praise for his ability to fight for his clients and his provision of unvarnished counsel. **Strengths:** "Hugely experienced, you go him if you want commercial, no-nonsense advice." "He has broad shoulders and can soak up the fire that judges throw at him."

Terence Mowschenson QC A fine chancery silk with a flourishing practice that takes in banking, joint venture, company and partnership disputes. Solicitors respect the way he instils confidence in a team and admire him for his tenacity. **Strengths:** "Hugely experienced and a man with an incredibly impressive mind." "He doesn't sit on the fence and he offers advice in a way that clients understand and appreciate." **Recent work:** Successfully acted in a dispute over ownership of 20% of the shareholding of Transaero Airlines, one of Russia's largest airlines. The action was heard in the Commercial Court of the BVI.

John Wardell QC Active in complex civil fraud and professional negligence cases, both domestically and in offshore jurisdictions. Sources praise him for his natural flair and his ability to put points forward in a succinct manner. **Strengths:** "Extremely clever and very approachable, he's a strategic thinker whose cross-examination technique is a pleasure to behold." "He grasps the nub of the case very quickly." **Recent work:** Acted for PCP-LLP in a claim for in excess of £300 million brought against Barclays. The case arose out of the rescue of Barclays at the time of the financial crash.

JUNIORS
Max Mallin A former banker who understands the way financial institutions operate. He is noted for his commercial and user-friendly approach, as well as for his superior analysis of legal issues. **Strengths:** "He is very commercial and he gives good advice." "Approachable and client-focused, he is ferociously intelligent." **Recent work:** Retained in the dispute between ITV2 and HTV. He successfully won £4 million in damages for the claimant.

Other Ranked Lawyers

Roger ter Haar QC (Crown Office Chambers) Highly experienced in technology, energy, construction and professional negligence matters. **Strengths:** "Fantastic on his feet and a brilliant strategist."

James Barker (Enterprise Chambers) An accomplished commercial litigation junior, who has a good knowledge of contract disputes. He is particularly adept at share and business sale matters, as well as shareholder and partnership disputes. **Strengths:** "He is excellent technically and he always gets straight to the heart of any dispute." **Recent work:** Acted for the defendants in a dispute between shareholders of a number of associated companies. The claimants were seeking to enforce the provisions of a shareholders' agreement relating to one of the companies.

Linden Ife (Enterprise Chambers) A seasoned and experienced junior who wins plaudits for the power and persuasiveness of her advocacy. She is regularly instructed by large banks and corporates to handle a range of claims, and is particularly well regarded for her work on breach of fiduciary duty and misfeasance cases. **Strengths:** "She is very forthright, and has a knack for presenting an argument in a way that judges find convincing." **Recent work:** Acted in Carroll v Poole, a case concerning Claims Direct, the former claims management company which collapsed with losses of around £200 million.

Stephen Smith QC (see p.769) (Erskine Chambers) Frequently seen in high-profile fraud litigation, often in an international context. He has won many favourable reviews for his recent work representing Russian entities in cases of the highest value. **Strengths:** "He is very easy to work with and knowledgeable." "He's very bright and user-friendly." **Recent work:** Represented Mezhprombank against Russian oligarch Sergei Pugachev. The case has involved dozens of hearings for interim relief, and applications have been made for worldwide freezing orders, search orders and orders restraining individuals from leaving the jurisdiction.

David Chivers QC (see p.616) (Erskine Chambers) A well thought-of silk with an attractive company law, insolvency and restructuring practice. He handles a good deal of offshore and overseas work in places such as Bermuda. **Strengths:** "He is outstanding and just the consummate professional." "He finds answers to problems thought too hard to solve." **Recent work:** Involved in a dispute concerning the company which runs Viking River Cruises. The claim involved multiple proceedings in Bermuda.

James Potts QC (see p.741) (Erskine Chambers) Covers a wide range of contentious business matters and has particular expertise in banking, financial services, insolvency and company law. **Strengths:** "Great advocate with a great brain." "He has a fantastic grasp of accountancy detail and is always accessible. He's an excellent team player." **Recent work:** Handled a contractual dispute involving complex breach of warranty claims. The case hinged on accountancy and valuation issues in the context of the acquisition of part of a group of companies.

Tim Akkouh (see p.580) (Erskine Chambers) Hugely respected for the role he has played in major civil fraud and asset recovery disputes. His role as first junior in the Ablyazov fraud case, the largest ever litigated in England, is illustrative of the quality of work he undertakes. **Strengths:** "Wise beyond his years and tactically astute." "He is very careful and his written work is very good." **Recent work:** Acted for BTA Bank in the Supreme Court as it sought to continue the case against its former chairman Mukhtar Ablyazov, who is accused of stealing over USD6 billion.

Hodge Malek QC (39 Essex Chambers) Brings decades of experience to bear when handling a broad range of commercial law cases. He is highly regarded for his work in the energy, banking and finance, civil and criminal fraud, and professional discipline sectors. **Strengths:** "He has very strong analytical skills and is a leading expert in the areas of disclosure and documentary evidence." "When it comes to dealing with freezing injunctions and the Middle East you don't need to look any further than Hodge." **Recent work:** Retained by KPMG to defend it against an auditors' negligence action brought by AJEC.

James Ramsden QC (see p.747) (39 Essex Chambers) Focuses his practice on high-value cross-border fraud, asset recovery and jurisdictional disputes. His "robust and fearless" approach to advocacy draws praise from solicitors. **Strengths:** "He is businesslike, commercial, and clear and direct with clients." "He's a very confident orator, and someone who can provide unequivocal and detailed advice on the merits of the case." **Recent work:** Instructed by Cornwall Council in its £4.1 million dispute with Spectrum, the UK's largest provider of autism care. Cornwall Council successfully struck out the claim on the first day of a two-week trial.

Nigel Jones QC (Hardwicke) A seasoned silk who centres his practice on a broad range of commercial issues including joint venture and corporate governance disputes. He also takes a leading role in advising the UK's largest litigation funder on which cases to invest in at a worldwide level. **Strengths:** "Charming but with a backbone of steel, he's an outstanding commercial and legal strategist." "He's very bright and easy to work with." **Recent work:** Acted in Coll v Floreat Merchant Banking Ltd, a multimillion-pound misappropriation of confidential information claim.

PJ Kirby QC (Hardwicke) Acts in complex commercial claims for a wide range of clients including utilities, banks, investment funds and high net worth individuals. His style in both the Commercial Court and arbitration is described as being "very proactive and very eloquent." **Strengths:** "Provides excellent strategic and legal advice." "Great with clients, he is a real team player." **Recent work:** Acted in a dispute between shareholders of a company that was redeveloping a restaurant and nightclub in Dubai. One of the majority shareholders sought an injunction as he believed the defendant, who managed the redevelopment, was acting fraudulently and siphoning off funds.

David Lewis (Hardwicke) A highly capable senior junior with a broad-based commercial disputes practice. He has been led on cases all the way up to the Supreme Court, and proves particularly strong when it comes to fraud, contract law and injunction matters. **Strengths:** "Down-to-earth and very commercial." "He's very user-friendly and his turnaround times are unbeatable." **Recent work:** Involved in a case that led to a landmark ruling in the Supreme Court concerning the law relating to contractual penalties.

Simon Davenport QC (3 Hare Court) Has experience advising and acting for national entities as well as corporate clients. His advocacy style is described by interviewees as being "robust and effective." **Strengths:** "Very user-friendly and energetic." "He is superb on his feet and has judges eating out of his hand." **Recent work:** Acted for Khanty-Mansiysk Recoveries in a claim in the Commercial Court brought against solicitors' firm Forsters, which had acted in the purchase of a Russian company owning oil exploration rights.

Amy Rogers (see p.754) (11KBW) Knowledgeable when it comes to matters involving breaches of directors' and fiduciary duties, as well as duties of confidence. Claims relating to conspiracy and economic torts also remain a focus of hers. **Strengths:** "Very bright and hard-working, she is able to grasp the detail while maintaining a focus on the bigger picture." **Recent work:** Acted for the Iranian commercial bank Bank Mellat in its long-running sanctions litigation.

Charles Samek QC (Littleton Chambers) Particularly well versed in offshore commercial matters, civil fraud and interim protective relief proceedings. **Strengths:** "Very clear in terms of his thinking, advice and advocacy." "A fantastically hands-on, very user-friendly and talented advocate." **Recent work:** Instructed by Trust Risk Group in a dispute it had with US insurer AmTrust Europe concerning the placing of medical malpractice insurance in Italy.

David Lascelles (see p.696) (Littleton Chambers) A capable silk who is active on contract, sale of business and shareholder and director disputes. He is also frequently seen representing clients in fraud matters. **Strengths:** "Bright, commercial and impressive in court. He has great client skills and is very attentive." **Recent work:** Retained by Samir Arab to handle a USD30 million commercial fraud claim arising out of the grant of a 15-year mobile phone licence in Iraq.

Jonathan Cohen QC (Littleton Chambers) Tackles high-level employment disputes as well as fraud, financial services and fiduciary duty matters. He is highly experienced in injunctive relief matters. **Strengths:** "He has a wonderful client manner and really knows his stuff." "He gets to grips with a case in a clinical fashion." **Recent work:** Acted in a case for Optaglio, a leading technology company that specialises in the laser holographic etching of microchips. This was a claim against two former directors of the company who were alleged to have been involved in fraud and the misappropriation of intellectual property.

Antony White QC (see p.793) (Matrix Chambers) A highly experienced and respected silk with a vibrant commercial practice. He has deep knowledge of fraud, asset-tracing, jurisdiction and conflict of law disputes. His ability to work without the support of a team of juniors is noted by sources. **Strengths:** "A very high-quality commercial silk who is extremely thorough and who always provides excellent commercial advice." "He is very easy to work with." **Recent work:** Brought in on a commercial property dispute concerning an alleged oral profit-sharing agreement relating to the development of hotels bordering Hyde Park.

Simon Adamyk (New Square Chambers) A barrister with a strong domestic caseload who further possesses a vibrant offshore practice that sees him involved in cases heard by both the Privy Council and overseas courts. His company law expertise is particularly strong. **Strengths:** "Very commercial, very good at advising on tactics and someone with a very keen analytical mind." "His attention to detail is phenomenal. He is very switched-on and very good with the client." **Recent work:** Involved in seven of the individual sets of proceedings in the BTA Bank litigation. The case involves claims worth several billion dollars.

Paul Marshall (Cornerstone Barrister) Particularly adept at financial litigation involving interest rate hedging products. His ability to act without a leader and his skill at financial dispute work were talking points in the market. **Strengths:** "Capable and good with clients." **Recent work:** Instructed in a case concerning claims brought by the Swain family for damages for misappropriation of shares.

Alan Steinfeld QC (XXIV Old Buildings) His work in offshore disputes, especially those with insolvency elements, is especially strong. He is also highly regarded for his trusts litigation work. **Strengths:** "He is vastly experienced and has a fantastic rapport with judges." "He's relentless, and judges defer to him on points of law." **Recent work:** Defended Carlyle Capital against a USD1 billion claim arising out of the failure of a US hedge fund incorporated in Guernsey. The claim is based on breach of contract and fiduciary and other duties.

Stephen Cogley QC (XXIV Old Buildings) Frequently seen in shipping, insolvency and partnership disputes. Clients say that his cross-examination of witnesses and experts is particularly effective. **Strengths:** "A superb advocate of great commerciality who is liked by clients." "Thorough, robust and approachable."

Robert Levy QC (XXIV Old Buildings) Centres his practice on complex, highly contentious offshore matters. He represents clients in court in the Cayman Islands, Bermuda and the BVI on a regular basis. **Strengths:** "Clever and extremely quick." "He's extremely hard-working, very responsive and down-to-earth." **Recent work:** Represented numerous companies in various appeals to the Eastern Caribbean Supreme Court and the Privy Council arising out of the financial collapse of one of the Caribbean's leading hotels.

Elspeth Talbot Rice QC (XXIV Old Buildings) Handles complex offshore litigation for a wide range of City firms, and impresses with her depth of knowledge in trusts, fraud and partnership matters. **Strengths:** "A smiling assassin. She is the sort of silk that makes you happy to have her on your side and apprehensive when she's against you." "Utterly fearless, very organised and extremely engaged with both clients and the technical issues in a case." **Recent work:** Retained on a case where a dentistry business was saved from insolvency by being purchased by a company owned by the father of one of the dentists. The wife of the other dentist then claimed to be entitled to half the shares of the company.

Edward Cumming (XXIV Old Buildings) Has been led by some of the top silks in high-level disputes. His particular areas of expertise include fraud, financial product and insurance-related cases. He has also acted as sole counsel in cases in the Court of Appeal. **Strengths:** "Ferociously hard-working, but always a delight to deal with, he is clever, energetic and good at quickly getting to the nub of a problem." "He is a forthright advocate unafraid to give firm opinions on the prospects of success in a case." **Recent work:** Acted for the Libyan Investment Authority with regard to its claim that, during the Gaddafi era, Goldman Sachs had enticed it to enter into derivative investments of questionable worth.

Simon Mills (Five Paper) A highly regarded junior with a finance-focused practice, who has expertise in asset-based lending, invoice discounting and factoring cases. He is renowned for the tactical nous he brings to cases and is also noted for being active in Russian litigation. **Strengths:** "He is the first point of call for highly technical contract disputes and any litigation requiring the touch of a master strategist." "A formidable yet polite practitioner, he's very down-to-earth and absolutely outstanding on his feet." **Recent work:** Successfully defended Bibby against a government-backed investment fund and a venture capital company.

Ulick Staunton (Radcliffe Chambers) Active in a broad range of commercial fields, he handles cases relating to unfair prejudice, fraud and breach of contract, among others. He is also strong on professional negligence cases and partnership disputes. **Strengths:** "He is very measured, calm and easy to talk to about strategy."

Gary Lidington (see p.701) (Radcliffe Chambers) Focuses his practice on international commercial disputes. He is adept at complex trusts and property matters, as well as oil and gas disputes. **Strengths:** "He gives pragmatic and practical advice in a sensible, client-friendly way." "He is commercial and businesslike in his outlook." **Recent work:** Acted as junior in a dispute between Bankers Albania and British Petroleum and Oil International. The case concerned a USD54 million claim for breach of an oil supply contract.

Shantanu Majumdar (Radcliffe Chambers) Brings over 20 years' experience to his cases and is led across a wide range of commercial work. His areas of expertise range from financial contracts to construction, engineering and energy matters. **Strengths:** "He's hands-on and a great tactician when handling class actions." **Recent work:** Retained on a multimillion-pound economic tort and conspiracy claim brought by an international steel manufacturer against the director of a UAE company. The matter concerned a contract for the purchase of steel billets which were to be delivered to Iran.

Dov Ohrenstein (see p.729) (Radcliffe Chambers) A well thought-of commercial chancery barrister who has particular expertise in company disputes. These often involve directors' obligations, fiduciary duties and shareholder rights issues. He is also active in insolvency matters. **Strengths:** "An experienced barrister with an approachable manner." **Recent work:** Defended Mr Turner against his former company, Exsus Travel, which was claiming millions of pounds from him for breach of duty and failure to account.

Romie Tager QC (see p.777) (Selborne Chambers) Acts for a wide range of sophisticated clients and brings a wealth of experience to every case. He is regularly seen in trusts, fraud, property and breach of fiduciary duty litigation. **Strengths:** "Magisterial and on top of what he is doing, he's strategically very strong." "He has one of the most creative minds at the Bar." **Recent work:** Acted for Mr Nekrich in a claim for over USD40 million relating to oil trading in the mid-1990s through the medium of a Gibraltar-registered company. The case involved allegations of fraud.

Hugh Jackson (see p.681) (Selborne Chambers) Has lengthy experience of tackling a wide range of commercial disputes. These range from land and property development matters to finance, trade, technology and professional negligence cases. **Strengths:** "A good advocate who shows great attention to detail." "He is an extremely intelligent guy who comes up with things that others haven't seen."

Antony Zacaroli QC (see p.802) (South Square) An esteemed commercial practitioner who splits his time evenly between general commercial disputes and insolvency litigation. He is also active in company law matters. **Strengths:** "He is very effective in cross-examination and good at getting straight to the point." "He plays it straight and is very focused, which means judges listen to him."

Robin Dicker QC (see p.633) (South Square) A highly capable barrister whose practice spans a wide range of commercial issues. Restructuring and insolvency, civil fraud, banking and finance and company law matters all form part of his caseload. **Strengths:** "Urbane and unruffled." "He's very collaborative in his approach and deals with matters effectively and efficiently."

David Allison QC (see p.583) (South Square) A successful junior silk who is active across a wide range of areas including insolvency, debt restructuring, structured finance and company law disputes. **Strengths:** "Very efficient, client-friendly and collaborative." "He's very good on schemes of arrangement work."

Tom Smith QC (see p.769) (South Square) A relatively junior QC who is making a name for himself in both banking and finance and insolvency matters. He wins praise for his ability to quickly come to commercial solutions and for his "down-to-earth manner." **Strengths:** "Incredibly responsive, hard-working and very user-friendly." "Dynamic, user-friendly and extremely bright."

Jeremy Goldring QC (see p.656) (South Square) Handles banking and finance, restructuring, insolvency and company law disputes among others. **Strengths:** "Jeremy is clever in a most understated way. He is thorough and highly impressive when on his feet."

Paul Downes QC (see p.636) (2TG – 2 Temple Gardens) Particularly well regarded for his work in banking, civil fraud and contractual disputes, he is known for his fearlessness in court. **Strengths:** "An outstanding and confident advocate." "Offers incisive advice and is a strong advocate." **Recent work:** Defended TRW Lucas Varity Electrics Steering in a claim for EUR30 million launched by Globe Motors. The case centred on a breach of an exclusive supply agreement and misrepresentation in relation to the supply of power steering systems.

Charles Dougherty QC (see p.635) (2TG – 2 Temple Gardens) A fine commercial dispute barrister often brought in to handle challenging fraud and insurance cases. He also has experience of handling matters relating to Islamic finance. **Strengths:** "Very bright and especially good on jurisdictional issues." "He is a go-to person for urgent freezing injunctions and civil fraud matters." **Recent work:** Acted for Novoship, a Russian ship operator, in a USD150 million claim against a former director and other employees alleging breach of fiduciary duty and bribery.

MIDLANDS

Commercial Dispute Resolution
Leading Sets
Band 1
St Philips Chambers *
Band 2
No5 Chambers *
Leading Silks
Star individuals
Randall John *St Philips Chambers* *
Band 1
Anderson Mark *No5 Chambers* [A]
Khangure Avtar *St Philips Chambers*
Pepperall Edward *St Philips Chambers* *
Zaman Mohammed *No5 Chambers*
Leading Juniors
Band 1
Brennan John *St Philips Chambers* *
Charman Andrew *St Philips Chambers* [A] *
Maguire Andrew *Outer Temple Chambers*
Morgan James *St Philips Chambers* *
Taylor David *No5 Chambers* [A]
Band 2
Beever Edmund *St Philips Chambers* *
Beresford Stephen *Ropewalk Chambers (ORL)* ◊ *
Brown Marc *St Philips Chambers* *
Chaffin-Laird Olivia *No5 Chambers*
Clegg Simon *St Philips Chambers* [A] *
Gupta Amit *St Philips Chambers* *
Reed Steven *No5 Chambers* *
Tabari Ali *St Philips Chambers* *
Weaver Matthew *St Philips Chambers* *
Willetts Glenn *No5 Chambers*
Up-and-coming individuals
Mundy Robert *St Philips Chambers* *
* *Indicates set / individual with profile.*
[A] *direct access (see p.24).*
◊ *(ORL) = Other Ranked Lawyer.*
Alphabetical order within each band. Band 1 is highest.

Band 1

St Philips Chambers
See profile on p.934

THE SET

This standout team of commercial barristers remains a top choice for financial institutions and corporations in the Midlands, though its reputation has led to increasing instruction from national and international law firms as well. It offers outstanding service to clients across the field of commercial litigation, covering areas such as shareholder and director disputes, insolvency, employment and commercial fraud. Impressed instructing solicitors are quick to recommend it as a high-quality set "that matches up well against other blue-chip chambers."

Client service: Chief clerk Joe Wilson and senior civil clerk Justin Luckman lead "an absolutely fantastic clerking team that's head and shoulders above anyone else. They are very responsive and bend over backwards to help." "They are good, friendly, helpful clerks who get back to you quickly."

SILKS

John Randall QC (see p.748) An accomplished commercial practitioner who "undoubtedly" retains his status as "the best senior silk in Birmingham," according to market sources. He frequently represents financial institutions and corporations in complex commercial and chancery disputes, including breach of contract, breach of director duties and disagreements arising from corporate sales and refinancings. **Strengths:** "A very good, very commercial and responsive advocate." "Hugely intelligent and good with clients. John manages to combine an encyclopaedic knowledge of the law with a first-rate appreciation of strategy and an excellent eye for detail." "He's very approachable, client-friendly, and exudes a sense of reassurance." **Recent work:** Acted in Singh and Others v Denny's Services, successfully securing the dismissal of an application made by the defendant to strike out the original claim for nuisance and negligent demolition.

Avtar Khangure QC Head of chambers and "a tactical and commercially astute barrister" who impresses clients with his far-reaching knowledge in areas such as banking, company law, insolvency and professional negligence. His diverse clientele ranges from private individuals to major corporations. **Strengths:** "The acknowledged Midlands expert in all insolvency law matters. He's exceptionally slick and knowledgeable." "Excellent – his advocacy skills are second to none."

Edward Pepperall QC (see p.736) Hugely respected practitioner who pairs his broad commercial prowess with specialist expertise in employment law. He regularly represents clients in a range of disputes relating to professional negligence, commercial fraud and restraint of trade, among other areas. **Strengths:** "A pragmatic and clinical advocate, he is user-friendly and fantastic in front of clients." "Meticulous and detailed with a very retentive memory. He's very good at dealing with clients, and an extremely good advocate and cross-examiner."

JUNIORS

John Brennan (see p.602) An exceptional senior junior who receives accolades for his sharp intellect and detailed knowledge of commercial and chancery law. He is recognised for his provision of high-quality advice and adept representation on litigation arising out of fraud, breaches of contract, property and construction disputes. **Strengths:** "Formidably hard-working and clever, he's an astonishingly able researcher of the law and has extremely reliable judgement." "Excellent, incredibly intelligent, he gets straight to the point and gives you straightforward advice." **Recent work:** Appeared before the Supreme Court in AIB Group (UK) Plc v Mark Redler & Co, a £3.3 million claim against a solicitor regarding the unauthorised release of a mortgage advance.

Andrew Charman (see p.615) Esteemed senior junior whose previous experience as a corporate solicitor informs his highly commercial practice. He provides top-quality advocacy and advice on a variety of matters ranging from company and professional negligence disputes through to contentious trust and property issues. **Strengths:** "An astute practitioner who gets on well with clients and grasps complicated issues with ease." "Probably the best shareholder dispute lawyer in town." "Methodical, tenacious and thorough in preparation and a highly intelligent advocate." **Recent work:** Acted in Marrill Ltd & Others v Fox Evans, a £4 million professional negligence matter which alleged that inaccurate auditing and financial advice caused two companies to enter administration.

James Morgan (see p.721) Hugely respected by peers and clients for his notable proficiency in commercial and chancery disputes, particularly those relating to company insolvency. He receives praise for his attention to detail, straightforward advice and strong oral advocacy. **Strengths:** "A very user-friendly barrister who is good at dealing with clients, meticulous in his preparation, and quick at responding. He is also a very good advocate who has given one of the best performances I've ever seen in court." "He is calm, bright and always on top of the detail." **Recent work:** Represented the defendant in Pooni v Nazran, a contractual interpretation dispute regarding property investment in Dubai.

Edmund Beever (see p.594) A dedicated commercial practitioner who is recognised for his insight into insolvency, insurance and director dispute cases, amongst other areas. He frequently appears before the courts to obtain injunctive relief, freezing orders and restrictive covenants for clients engaged in commercial employment disputes. **Strengths:** "He's probably the go-to barrister for restraint of trade cases in the Midlands." "He's good in front of clients, always gets great results, is super-easy to deal with and he knows the law backwards." **Recent work:** Appeared in Sports Mobile Ltd v David Taylor, a claim for breach of confidentiality and solicitation brought against a former employee in relation to high-profile celebrity mobile phone contracts.

Amit Gupta (see p.661) "An extremely impressive junior" who has established an excellent reputation in commercial litigation, demonstrating particular strength in insolvency matters. His burgeoning practice serves a wide range of clients, including both private individuals and businesses. Market commentators are quick to highlight his skilled oral presentation and personable approach. **Strengths:** "Outstandingly responsive and academically superb, as well as a persuasive advocate." "Very thorough and good with clients, he provides straightforward and frank commercial advice." **Recent work:** Acted for the defendant in De Hoop v Pekso, a dispute over defective building works and contractual validity.

Marc Brown (see p.604) A prominent junior barrister who is recommended for his meticulous approach and strength across a number of areas, including business disputes, property issues and consumer law. He has a particular focus on restructuring and insolvency matters. **Strengths:** "Very clear drafting, quick to grasp issues and a good communicator." "Marc has impressed throughout, combining detailed strategic thinking with a willingness to fight hard right to the end of a case." **Recent work:** Successfully represented the claimant in Zaryaab v Bashir, a case concerning failure to comply with the terms of a written agreement.

Simon Clegg (see p.618) A personable and experienced barrister offering broad expertise across the field of general commercial litigation. He is particularly highly regarded for his specialist knowledge of banking and finance, insolvency and property disputes. **Strengths:** "Extremely versatile and helpful, with excellent knowledge of banking law." "A very solid and unflappable performer who inspires confidence in clients." "A very steady performer who doesn't get fazed in the heat of battle." **Recent work:** Acted in Mian Latif and Shabir Mian Mohammed v

Rashid Mohammed, a partnership dispute concerning assets of more than £1 million.

Matthew Weaver (see p.791) An accomplished commercial barrister with a particular interest in insolvency law. He provides further guidance in areas such as banking and finance, commercial fraud, company law and professional liability. **Strengths:** "A user-friendly litigator who understands the client's objectives. He is a strong technical advocate who is very bright." "A very accommodating and commercial barrister who's always thinking of the bigger picture." **Recent work:** Sought a freezing injunction in Miller & Appleton v Deakin & Others, a £1 million claim relating to the unusual refinancing of a property.

Ali Tabari (see p.777) Enters the rankings this year due to strong praise for the highly practical tenor of his advice on commercial and chancery litigation matters. He regularly acts on behalf of national firms, banks, insolvency office holders and insurance companies, amongst others. **Strengths:** "He works immensely hard. A very bright and persuasive advocate with excellent knowledge." "He is absolutely fantastic, he gives such good, measured advice and has a good way of explaining things to clients in ways which they can understand." **Recent work:** Represented the defendant in Holden v Allpay, a claim arising from the allegedly unfair dismissal of a finance director which led to a subsequent counterclaim for damages.

Robert Mundy (see p.724) An up-and-coming junior who frequently appears before the courts on behalf of financial institutions and public authorities. He receives praise for his thoughtful, measured approach and impressive advocacy style. **Strengths:** "He has great intellect and is good on his feet." "He is very clever, good with clients and highly approachable."

Band 2

No5 Chambers

See profile on p.931

THE SET

An outstanding set offering excellent representation and advice to clients on a nationwide and international basis. With abiding experience in commercial and chancery litigation, this versatile chambers has specific sector expertise spanning areas such as farming, shipping and the oil industry. Its high-calibre members are able to act in a diverse capacity, handling litigation alongside various forms of ADR. Market commentators consider it "a first point of call," citing not only its responsiveness, but also because "the quality of the barristers is just very good: you get a lot of choice at many different levels." **Client service:** Practice director Tony McDaid leads an impressive and highly praised operation, with James Parks managing the commercial clerking team. "I can't speak highly enough of the clerks, they will move mountains or run to court if they have to." "The clerks are very good, they respond very quickly and are flexible on fees."

SILKS

Mark Anderson QC Head of chambers, Anderson is held in high esteem for his formidable courtroom presence and meticulous attention to detail. He regularly represents clients from the banking, automotive and construction sectors in a variety of commercial disputes, and also has considerable professional negligence expertise. **Strengths:** "He is formidably intelligent and a good analytical lawyer." "A terrific tactician, who is devastating for the opposition." "Thorough, imaginative and a formidable trial lawyer." **Recent work:** Acted in Barrett v Treatt plc, a dispute over an earn-out claim by former shareholders and directors of a multinational company.

Mohammed Zaman QC Hugely respected silk with high-level experience in Commercial Court proceedings and international arbitrations. He habitually acts for clients in shareholder and partnership disputes, along with claims of fraud, breach of contract and fiduciary duties. Interviewees are quick to describe him as a "very accomplished advocate and cross-examiner." **Strengths:** "His preparation is second to none; he is an expert in dealing with witnesses under cross-examination." "An excellent draftsman and tenacious advocate." "He knows tactics better than anyone; he always thinks outside the box to solve problems."

JUNIORS

David Taylor A distinguished junior with an outstanding commercial litigation practice, who also handles arbitration proceedings. He is well known for his focused approach to commercial contract disputes and professional negligence claims, amongst other areas. **Strengths:** "He's exceptionally bright, good on his feet and very knowledgeable." "Quick, effective, great with the clients and gives straightforward, commercial and reasoned advice." **Recent work:** Acted in Amadeus Design & Build v Brothers Inc Limited, a construction dispute regarding allegedly defective work at a high-end Procter & Gamble facility in London.

Olivia Chaffin-Laird Impresses with her performance in cases concerning contractual disputes, professional negligence, construction and finance. She is praised for her breadth of expertise and business-minded approach. **Strengths:** "She cuts to the chase and is extremely commercial." "She works extremely hard and presents her cases well." **Recent work:** Acted in Stones & Dodd v Bebbington Brumby Townend Group Limited, a contract dispute regarding remuneration for former employees of a company who had left in order to set up their own competing company.

Steven Reed (see p.750) Highly regarded litigator who focuses his commercial practice on disputes involving jurisdictional issues, consumer law, energy and litigious IP and media matters. Sources consider him to be "a modern-thinking and very user-friendly barrister." **Strengths:** "He goes above and beyond, he lives and breathes each case." "Good with clients, solutions-driven, clever and commercially minded." "Steven is a formidable advocate and one of those barristers who speaks the judge's language." **Recent work:** Acted in Coilcolor Ltd v Camtrex Ltd to respond to an application to restrain the presentation of a winding-up petition.

Glenn Willetts Proficient across a broad range of commercial areas though with a specialist focus on insolvency cases. He regularly represents and advises clients on administration applications, undervalued transactions, directors' misfeasance and asset recovery. **Strengths:** "Very able counsel, both on his feet and on paper." "He's hugely intelligent and pleasant."

Other Ranked Lawyers

Stephen Beresford (see p.594) (Ropewalk Chambers) Attracts widespread praise for his comprehensive commercial, property and chancery practice. He handles an array of matters, such as director and shareholder disputes, construction cases and litigious tax issues, amongst others. **Strengths:** "He is extraordinarily bright, a very good draftsman and a very good man to have in a complex dispute." "Very experienced, very careful and thorough. He can be a devastatingly effective advocate, and his paperwork is always precise, shrewd and tenacious." **Recent work:** Acted in Leicestershire County Council v 5m (UL) Limited (In Administration) & Concept Roofing and Cladding Limited, a high-value dispute regarding loss of business by commercial tenants on an industrial estate.

Andrew Maguire (outer Temple Chambers) Is an accomplished chancery and commercial litigator who draws on a wealth of advocacy experience in both international and domestic disputes. His areas of expertise include injunction and restitution claims, commercial theft, breaches of trust and fiduciary obligations. **Strengths:** "One of the most people-friendly and commercially aware barristers out there. His ability to communicate at any level sets him apart. Attentive and responsive with clients: he always adds value." **Recent work:** Acted in a claim for injunctive relief and damages for the alleged theft of British Gas Trading's confidential database in British Gas Trading Ltd v Energy Save UK Ltd and Another.

NORTH EASTERN

Commercial Dispute Resolution
Leading Sets
Band 1
Enterprise Chambers *
Kings Chambers *
Band 2
St Philips Chambers *
Trinity Chambers *
Leading Silks
Band 1
Jory Hugh *Enterprise Chambers*
Leading Juniors
Band 1
Buck William *St Philips Chambers* *
Groves Hugo *Enterprise Chambers*
Latimer Andrew *Kings Chambers* *
Pipe Gregory *St Philips Chambers*
Band 2
Goldberg Simon *Trinity Chambers*
Klein Jonathan *Enterprise Chambers*
Rodger Jonathan *Enterprise Chambers*
Temple Eleanor *Kings Chambers* *
Buck William *St Philips Chambers* *
Up-and-coming individuals
Heath Duncan *Enterprise Chambers*
* *Indicates set / individual with profile.*
Alphabetical order within each band. Band 1 is highest.

Band 1

Enterprise Chambers
See profile on p.950

THE SET

Particularly prominent on the North Eastern circuit, it has well-established regional offices in Leeds and Newcastle, both of which seamlessly operate in tandem with its London headquarters. Solicitors appreciate that members are "very good with clients, very pragmatic in their approach and barristers who always add value." The strong team adeptly handles all aspects of commercial litigation, including breach of warranty claims, shareholder disputes, restraint of trade cases and a range of banking issues.

Client service: The highly praised clerking system, led by Joanne Caunt in Leeds and Bethany Thompson in Newcastle, "is very efficient, friendly, pragmatic and accommodating." "The clerks are very competitive and have an extremely personal approach – they're very user-friendly."

SILKS

Hugh Jory QC A "superb silk" whose reputation on the North Eastern circuit is second to none. His broad practice covers complex company, commercial and insolvency matters, including shareholder disputes, breach of director's duties and contentious contractual issues. He also has a niche specialism handling sports-related litigation. **Strengths:** "His advocacy was exceptional and he was fantastic with the client, making difficult points seem simple." "He is good on his feet, excellent in cross-examination and very good tactically, thinking several moves ahead."

JUNIORS

Jonathan Klein Characterised as "a quietly spoken assassin," this highly regarded senior junior attracts fantastic feedback from instructing solicitors and peers alike. He is regularly instructed on commercial and chancery disputes and enjoys a particularly excellent reputation in the field of property litigation.. **Strengths:** "He is absolutely exceptional – an outstanding academic lawyer and advocate." "Very thorough, leaves no stone unturned and has a nice bedside manner." **Recent work:** Appeared on behalf of the fourth defendant in Metcalfe Farms v Aviva Insurance Ltd and Others, a complex dispute arising out of an RTA.

Duncan Heath Hailed as a "rising star" by market commentators, Duncan Heath is singled out as a pragmatic and methodical junior who is easy to work with. He has a broad commercial and chancery practice, encompassing areas such as property, insolvency and trusts disputes. **Strengths:** "He is a great all-rounder and trial advocate." "Super-bright, very thorough and well prepared." "He gives very lucid advice and is down to earth." **Recent work:** Acted for the claimant in McCleary v Allied Irish Bank, a cross-jurisdictional matter concerning a EUR5 million property portfolio belonging to the claimant.

Hugo Groves Highly respected barrister who is frequently called upon to act in high-value commercial, company and insolvency matters. His broad experience includes partnership and shareholder disputes, breach of duty cases, unfair prejudice petitions and complex sales agreements. **Strengths:** "He is very reliable and competent, inspires confidence in both solicitors and clients, and provides sound leadership." "He is very thorough and good with clients. Provides good, practical advice."

Jonathan Rodger Senior junior who receives praise for his excellent advocacy skills and breadth of knowledge. He stands out for his specialist experience in property litigation, landlord and tenant disputes and insolvency cases. **Strengths:** "He is my first port of call for complex and high-value matters: he gets the best possible result in everything he touches." "He knows his stuff, he's very good with clients and very approachable." **Recent work:** Acted in Nicholson v Bamigbade, a boundary dispute arising out of a discrepancy between a deed plan and the property as built.

Kings Chambers
See profile on p.968

THE SET

A highly distinguished set with a market-leading reputation in Leeds, complemented by additional outposts in Manchester and Birmingham. Its members frequently act for large-scale businesses and high net worth individuals on both a national and international basis. The chambers offers expertise across a wide range of corporate and commercial matters, and offers specialist knowledge of property litigation. Solicitors choose the set because of its "very high standard and broad range of barristers at all levels."

Client service: "They have excellent clerks, led by Colin Griffin, with an extremely good understanding of the commercial litigation process, which makes it very easy to deal with them." "The clerks are proactive in handling enquiries and liaising with the court and are very good at getting back to you. As a whole, an excellent team."

JUNIORS

Andrew Latimer (see p.696) An excellent practitioner who is regarded by sources as a silk in waiting. He enjoys a strong relationship with instructing solicitors and advises a broad client base on a range of commercial and contractual claims, displaying particular experience in minority shareholder disputes. **Strengths:** "He is absolutely excellent – extremely good to work with, good with clients, a strong advocate and one of the rare barristers who is very good at mediation and negotiation, but is also prepared to fight." **Recent work:** Represented two shareholder-directors in a dispute concerning directors' duties and minority shareholder prejudice.

Eleanor Temple (see p.779) Solid senior junior with a strong market reputation who is an increasingly popular choice for complex international cases. Particularly known for banking and finance litigation and insolvency work, but also advises on corporate and general commercial matters. **Strengths:** "She is a very robust advocate who knows her onions and cuts to the chase." "She is extremely experienced. She has huge knowledge of insolvency matters and provides very pragmatic advice." **Recent work:** Acted in Round v Jackson, a claim concerning breach of fiduciary duty.

Band 2

St Philips Chambers
See profile on p.934

THE SET

St Philips is an excellent commercial set with a strong presence in Leeds and Birmingham as well as London. Members here advise on the full spectrum of corporate and commercial disputes, including those concerning contracts, partnerships, shareholders, breach of confidence and franchising. The set services a broad client base ranging from small and start-up businesses to major multinational companies, representing them in cases across the UK and abroad. Instructing solicitors are full of praise for the barristers' client service, saying: "They will develop a good relationship with the client and will be able to explain things in a way they can handle."

Client service: "The clerk team, led by Colin Hedley, is very accommodating, helping me out of rough spots and always putting me in front of someone who is appropriate."

JUNIORS

Gregory Pipe Outstanding advocate whose "knowledge of contractual disputes is second to none." A top choice for heavy commercial litigation, he regularly handles litigation with respect to shareholders, joint ventures, commercial fraud, contracts and acquisitions. **Strengths:** "He is brilliant – he's very good at getting your case organised, an excellent and astute advocate, and someone who's very good tactically and strategically." "He is very smart, ruthless and fearless and as good a barrister as you are ever going to find."

William Buck (see p.606) Solid practitioner who is recommended for his expertise in high-value cases involving multiple jurisdictions, including offshore litigation. Advises prominent private businesses in a range of claims relating to contracts, financial services, property, trusts and professional negligence. **Strengths:** "He is meticulous, measured and thorough and has become incredibly successful doing multi-jurisdictional work." "If I had a complex, high-value matter I would go to William Buck." **Recent work:** Acted in A Shade Greener v Ravenheat, a £10 million dispute concerning supply and service agreements for thousands of boiler systems.

Trinity Chambers

See profile on p.975

THE SET

Based in Newcastle and Middlesbrough, it is a well-established set which has true local expertise. Sought after by SMEs, partnerships, solicitors, individuals and local authorities, the set offers a full advisory and advocacy service catering to the full spectrum of commercial dispute resolution. Members are instructed in a wide range of disputes encompassing company and contract litigation, professional negligence, insolvency and civil fraud. They are also noted for experience in the engineering, construction and IT sectors.

Client service: "The clerks, headed by Alison Dickason, are very personable and helpful; they are open and happy to discuss expertise and are not scared to tell us if there is an issue."

JUNIORS

Simon Goldberg An excellent junior who is head of the set's commercial group. He is increasingly instructed in high-value and international disputes, and has a special focus on civil fraud. He is also extremely popular with local solicitors for a range of commercial and contract disputes, professional negligence cases, contentious probate claims and property litigation. **Strengths:** "He is very sharp and succinct in his advice, a strong advocate and a good negotiator with a good client manner – the calibre you would expect of London counsel." "He's technically superb, gets all the issues, never misses the detail and comes back very quickly with good, sound advice." **Recent work:** Represented the claimant in North East Joinery v Hutchinson & Others, a civil fraud claim involving allegations of theft of monies and diversion of business opportunities.

NORTHERN

Commercial Dispute Resolution
Leading Sets
Band 1
Exchange Chambers *
Kings Chambers *
Leading Silks
Band 1
Anderson Lesley *Kings Chambers* *
Casement David *Kings Chambers* *
Cawson Mark *Exchange Chambers* *
Chaisty Paul *Kings Chambers* *
Band 2
Bartley Jones Edward *Exchange Chambers*
New Silks
Harper Mark *Kings Chambers* *
Mohyuddin David *Exchange Chambers*
Leading Juniors
Band 1
Berragan Neil *Kings Chambers* *
Band 2
Chapman Richard *18 St John Street (ORL)* ◊
Fryer-Spedding James *9 St John Street (ORL)* ◊ *
Grantham Andrew *Kings Chambers* *
Pennifer Kelly *Kings Chambers* *
Sandbach Carly *Exchange Chambers*
Vinson Andrew *Exchange Chambers*
Band 3
Budworth Martin *Kings Chambers*
Connolly Stephen *Exchange Chambers*
Cook Christopher *Exchange Chambers*
Dainty Cheryl *Kings Chambers* *
Gilchrist David *9 St John Street (ORL)* ◊
Halliwell Mark *Kings Chambers* *
Maynard-Connor Giles *Exchange Chambers*
Rañales-Cotos Tina *Kings Chambers* *
Up-and-coming individuals
Reay Aidan *Kings Chambers* *
Tucker Ian *Exchange Chambers* *
* *Indicates set / individual with profile.*
◊ *(ORL) = Other Ranked Lawyer.*
Alphabetical order within each band. Band 1 is highest.

Band 1

Exchange Chambers

See profile on p.956

THE SET

A highly acclaimed set based in Manchester, lauded for its broad selection of renowned commercial dispute barristers. Exchange Chambers is especially well versed in cases including shareholder and partnership disputes, insolvency and director disqualification, commercial fraud and professional negligence claims. Its practitioners represent a range of clientele, including private individuals and major corporate organisations, as well as government bodies. According to one solicitor, they are "absolutely top-notch, commercially sensible in their advice as well as being very hands-on and practical."

Client service: "The clerks are excellent, as helpful as can possibly be, and they return calls promptly." "The clerks are highly commercial and they turn matters around quickly." Nick Buckley is the senior clerk for the Manchester chambers.

SILKS

Mark Cawson QC (see p.613) Extremely well-reputed silk with a wealth of experience in corporate disputes, partnership and company matters, commercial fraud and insolvency litigation. He often represents government entities, as well as banks, private businesses and individual clients. **Strengths:** "He is an incredibly calm and insightful barrister." "He is forensic in his analysis, his arguments are a joy to read." **Recent work:** Represented a bridging finance company facing a claim from a borrower that it needed to overpay to redeem.

Edward Bartley Jones QC Experienced commercial silk with almost 20 years' experience at the Bar. He is involved in a wide range of commercial and chancery disputes, and is well versed in insolvency and professional negligence matters. **Strengths:** "He's technically very good, especially on urgent pre-emptive applications." "A respected silk and an excellent lawyer."

David Mohyuddin QC New silk who is involved in a range of commercial litigation, including insolvency and directors' disqualification, as well as contentious company and shareholder matters. He also handles disputes related to claims of professional negligence, fraud and deceit. **Strengths:** "He's very well prepared and his papers are immaculate – he thinks outside the box." "He's excellent, very proactive, bright, tactical and frankly very cost-effective." **Recent work:** Acted for NatWest against a claim from a former shareholder in a limited company, contending that the bank had conspired with current shareholders to prevent payment of a director's loan to him.

JUNIORS

Carly Sandbach Well-respected junior with broad-ranging commercial and chancery litigation expertise. She often acts in matters concerning solicitors or accountants, with her expertise spanning professional negligence, insolvency litigation and company-related issues. **Strengths:** "She's a real fighter, very thorough in her preparation, very hard-working and has good commercial acumen – definitely one to watch." "She's good, and quite impressive on her feet." **Recent work:** Acted for Imperial Property Company concerning a public interest winding-up petition.

Andrew Vinson Enjoys respect in the market for his solid commercial and chancery offering, which includes directors' disqualification and insolvency, professional negligence and company disputes. He often acts for domestic and international firms, trustees and governmental office holders. **Strengths:** "A very strong commercial litigator with a great level of analytical skill." "He's quick, practical and always has a good grasp of papers." "He will fight for the client and put in a robust argument, while remaining calm and cool in court."

Giles Maynard-Connor Acclaimed barrister who is highly proficient in company and fraud matters, as well as professional negligence and insolvency-related issues. He is often instructed in cases involving directors' disqualification and company winding-up petitions, and has even acted as leading counsel for the Secretary of State. **Strengths:** "Technically brilliant, aggressive when he needs to be and commercially minded." "He provides well-considered, practical advice and is good with clients." **Recent work:** Represented LSC Finance in its claim against a firm of solicitors, relating to allegations of breach of undertaking and breach of trust.

Stephen Connolly Well-regarded and highly experienced commercial junior who is particularly adept at acting in stakeholder disputes. He also offers expertise in contentious contract issues, breach of warranty and professional negligence claims. **Strengths:** "He's quite tenacious, very bold and technically very good." "Very good in court and has excellent paperwork." **Recent work:** Acted in the appeal of Raymond v Young, a dispute over the recovery of stigma damages by one landowner against their neighbour.

Christopher Cook Well-established junior whose broad expertise encompasses company and contract matters, including shareholder and joint venture disputes. He also acts on professional negligence, insolvency and IP-related matters. **Strengths:** "He's a great barrister – approachable and client-friendly, he is nonetheless very hardcore with cross-examination." "Technically excellent but this does not detract from real fighting qualities when they are required."

Ian Tucker (see p.784) Up-and-coming junior, adept in a range of commercial matters including contentious contractual issues and insolvency-related cases. He also deals with litigation revolving around professional negligence claims and contested trusts. **Strengths:** "He's very personable and has the makings of a very successful advocate." "He is able to address unusual points in a thoughtful and intellectual manner, with a keen emphasis on practical advice."

Kings Chambers

See profile on p.968

THE SET

An outstanding chambers boasting an impressive array of high-quality silks and renowned juniors. Particular areas of expertise within the set include company and shareholder matters, injunctive relief and fraud cases. Members often represent public companies, large-scale institutions, and private firms and individuals. Notable recent cases have included disputes relating to major energy projects and property development joint ventures. One solicitor lauds them as "a go-to chambers for commercial work in Manchester," saying: "They have real superstars there."

Client service: "The clerking is the best of any chambers we deal with. Chief commercial clerk Colin Griffin stands out from others I've dealt with – he's without doubt the best clerk I've worked with in my career."

SILKS

Lesley Anderson QC (see p.583) Commands broad respect as one of the leading commercial silks on the Northern Circuit. She covers a wide range of contentious commercial and chancery matters, including company, insolvency and property disputes. **Strengths:** "She has a formidable presence as an advocate and shows softer skills with clients." "A very bright individual, very focused and always on top of papers." **Recent work:** Acted for a former consultant in Peter Elliott v Stobart Group and Others, a claim relating to the individual defendant's activities whilst employed by the business.

David Casement QC (see p.612) An esteemed practitioner described by one source as "probably the best silk outside London," David Casement QC is is eminently capable at handling numerous commercial and chancery matters, including company and partnership disputes. His practice also spans restructuring and insolvency, fraud and sports law. **Strengths:** "He's absolutely excellent, first rate and very highly regarded – just a very good all-round lawyer." "An impressive silk whose advice is technically sound and also commercial. He also has a very good manner with clients." **Recent work:** Instructed in the multi-jurisdictional Laird Resources case, involving a disputed settlement agreement between former co-venturers, with significant offshore and property elements.

Paul Chaisty QC (see p.614) Pre-eminent Northern silk with an outstanding reputation in commercial matters. He deals with a broad range of cases relating to company, shareholder and joint venture disputes, as well as breaches of contract. His practice has a significant international element, and he is also qualified at the Bar in both the British Virgin Islands and the Bahamas. **Strengths:** "He's just world-class and somebody I'd like to have for every single trial. He is so tenacious and on the ball – he never leaves a stone unturned." "He's fantastic, a great advocate, very thorough and great on paper. Excellent in every respect." **Recent work:** Acted in Wayne Shillito v Dean Hewart, a case surrounding a shareholder dispute in relation to a hotel property development.

Mark Harper QC (see p.664) Highly regarded barrister who has recently taken silk. He is particularly well known for his expertise in company and shareholder disputes, as well as cases involving partnership, professional negligence and sports law. **Strengths:** "He's always a very safe pair of hands – excellent and good with clients, he is short and succinct in his advice, which goes down well." "He's a class above most and very good on his feet before a judge." **Recent work:** Represented the claimant in Michael Coatman v Coutts & Co, a £5 million dispute relating to negligent investment advice.

JUNIORS

Kelly Pennifer (see p.736) Established senior junior with an excellent courtroom reputation. She operates within contentious commercial and construction-related cases, and is especially adept at handling injunctive relief, fraud and contract matters. **Strengths:** "She is very tenacious, superb on her feet and intellectually head and shoulders above almost any other counsel I can think of in her field." "She's very strong in court, good with clients and oozes confidence – generally speaking, one of the top barristers in Manchester." **Recent work:** Represented a local authority in Preston City Council v Africa Relief Trust, a tenancy-related dispute concerning rent rate exemptions in the charity sector.

Neil Berragan (see p.595) Senior junior who is lauded for his commercial acumen, tackling cases including urgent injunctions, shareholder disputes and company issues. He regularly appears in the commercial and mercantile courts along with the High Court and Court of Appeal, and also has an active arbitration practice. **Strengths:** "His court work is just fantastic – he's really great on his feet." "He is excellent, a very solid advocate and very good with clients." "A tough litigator who is very strong on all commercial disputes." **Recent work:** Acted for Kip McGrath Global in proceedings to enforce restrictive covenants upon a former franchisee.

Andrew Grantham (see p.658) Well-respected junior handling a range of cases that concern contractual disputes, commercial fraud and the sale of businesses and shares. He often represents banks, public companies and small firms, as well as private investors. **Strengths:** "An untiring and tenacious barrister." "He is extremely bright and offers a high standard of client service as well as sound, technical and commercial advice."

Cheryl Dainty (see p.628) Has a growing reputation for her capabilities in a wide variety of commercial dispute proceedings. She also often deals with interim applications such as injunctions and security for costs. **Strengths:** "Her advice is always enlightening, in-depth and detailed, and her advocacy skills have always produced excellent results." "I've always found her to be clever, clear-thinking and good at drafting."

Martin Budworth Noted in the market for a diverse commercial offering, which includes significant work in arbitration. He acts in company, partnership and directors' disqualification cases, as well as professional negligence and sports-related matters. **Strengths:** "He's technically bright, extremely pragmatic and excellent both on paper and in court." "He gets to the point very quickly and doesn't beat about the bush." "Good on his feet and calm under pressure." **Recent work:** Represented the claimant in Spark Response v Aspire Outsourcing & Others, a £3 million breach of fiduciary duty claim arising from a team move and contractual diversion relating to a call centre operation.

Tina Rañales-Cotos (see p.748) Maintains a solid reputation for her commercial work, which includes contentious director, partnership and shareholder matters, restrictive covenants and franchising agreements. She also handles commercially focused employment issues. **Strengths:** "Her cross-examination is brilliant, plus she's incredibly bright and approachable." "She can be ferocious and scare the other side, but is very good at presenting in a measured way." **Recent work:** Acted for the claimant firm in Balfor Recruitment v Jones & 5 Others, a breach of contract and fiduciary duty case concerning former employees and their new employer.

Aidan Reay (see p.749) Reay is quickly gaining a reputation as an up-and-coming junior, and tackles a wide range of commercial and chancery work. His specific areas of focus include partnership disputes, contract matters, insolvency cases and property matters. **Strengths:** "He's very personable and you'd be comfortable giving him more weighty jobs – beyond his years of call." "Tactically astute, he is also really good on technical contractual issues, explaining them so the court can deal with the matter properly."

Mark Halliwell (see p.662) Experienced junior with a broad commercial practice. He regularly handles matters concerning company-related disputes, including partnership and joint venture cases, as well as injunctive proceedings and insolvency matters. **Strengths:** "A heavyweight on the Northern Circuit and a delight to work with." **Recent work:** Represented the claimant in Ferguson v Fothergill, a mandatory injunction case relating to whether the claimant could perform an environmental survey within a specific site.

Other Ranked Lawyers

Richard Chapman (18 St John Street) Highly respected barrister with a wealth of commercial experience. His broad practice encompasses partnership, company, contractual and insolvency litigation. **Strengths:** "He's very responsive and very thorough: always great to have alongside you when your back's against the wall." "He gives very, very sound advice, is good with clients and is talented on his feet."

James Fryer-Spedding (see p.649) (9 St John Street) Very experienced barrister who can provide expert knowledge in chancery and commercial cases. His work includes commercial contracts, partnership disputes, professional negligence and insolvency matters. **Strengths:** "He's so user-friendly, very responsive and really commercial. He doesn't just give pure technical answers but also practical solutions." "He's very approachable and communicates very well with clients." **Recent work:** Acted for a pair of GPs in Milson & Ghosh v Armstrong & Beardsell, a partnership dispute concerning usage of doctors' premises.

David Gilchrist (9 St John Street) Well-regarded and experienced junior with an expansive commercial offering. He takes on cases including several types of company dispute, as well as contentious partnership, insolvency and construction matters. **Strengths:** "He's great on detail and very knowledgeable." "He provides technical yet commercial advice."

SOUTH EASTERN

Commercial Dispute Resolution
Leading Sets
Band 1
Crown Office Row *
3PB Barristers *
Leading Juniors
Band 1
Ashwell Paul *Crown Office Row*
Clargo John *Hardwicke (ORL)* ◊
Band 2
Davies James *3PB Barristers*
Godfrey Lauren *Crown Office Row*
Redmayne Simon *East Anglian Chambers (ORL)* ◊
Sheriff Andrew *3PB Barristers*
Wright Stuart *Crown Office Row*
* *Indicates set with profile.*
◊ *(ORL) = Other Ranked Lawyer.*
Alphabetical order within each band. Band 1 is highest.

Band 1

Crown Office Row
See profile on p.826

THE SET

Crown Office Row is a distinguished set handling all facets of commercial disputes, specialising particularly in misrepresentation, contract and partnership disputes. It regularly acts for company directors, partners, shareholders and, most notably, fraud victims, in complex, multiparty cases. The set is also known for its provision of expert advice regarding bankruptcies and IVAs, routinely receiving instructions from trustees in bankruptcy or spouses with an interest in the family home. Market sources comment that "Crown Office Row is excellent. Chambers is very responsive and houses a good range of counsel, offering diverse areas of expertise."

Client service: "The clerking is very good. They are very friendly, responsive and knowledgeable." "The clerks understand the commercial realities of litigation." Senior clerk David Bingham heads the clerking team.

JUNIORS

Stuart Wright Extensively experienced in personal injury, property and general common law, with a particular focus on matters concerning professional negligence. **Strengths:** "He's excellent with clients, very clearly spoken and gives good, comprehensive advice. He's a very calm advocate who orchestrates things well in court, and has a good manner about him."

Lauren Godfrey Has a flourishing practice focusing on commercial chancery disputes which often contain complex aspects of employment law. He acts for a broad range of clients, including insurers, banks, finance companies and senior employees, on matters concerning professional negligence, breach of fiduciary duties, IP rights and data protection. **Strengths:** "He's very robust and gives very thorough advice. He's an excellent and fierce negotiator. He's extremely easy to work with and builds a real rapport with clients very quickly." **Recent work:** Acted for the claimant in Crown United Group v Greenwood, a commercial property dispute concerning issues of fraud, tax avoidance, insolvency, professional negligence and the effect of a registration of trusts.

Paul Ashwell Well-established practitioner with a comprehensive property and commercial practice encompassing areas such as real estate, trusts, probate, contracts and planning. He comes recommended for his deft handling of complex legal disputes, and for his client management. **Strengths:** "He is very thorough and commercially minded, he always keeps up-to-date with the law and is very approachable. He's well respected by courts and judges alike."

3PB Barristers
See profile on p.892

THE SET

Excellent set that provides all-encompassing commercial expertise concerning the running of businesses. It offers notably deep knowledge in the areas of business organisation, business trading, insolvency and professional risk. It predominantly acts for businesses and individuals in the commerce, accountancy and investment sectors. Its members offer further experience in IP, energy and utilities, sports and media law. The set is highly regarded by instructing solicitors: "The chambers is really excellent for its customer service. It houses extraordinarily talented individuals and is run extremely well and professionally."

Client service: "The clerks are fantastic and extremely efficient." The clerking team is headed by chambers director Russell Porter.

JUNIORS

James Davies Renowned for his commercial dispute and property work. His areas of expertise include guarantees, partnerships and franchises. He also has a dedicated insolvency practice focusing on corporate insolvency and personal bankruptcy. **Strengths:** "He is very meticulous in his advice and good at identifying key issues quickly. He's a wonderful technical advocate who has an excellent client manner, he puts people at ease and explains things very clearly." "He has a very patient, calm manner in cross-examination, and he's very methodical."

Andrew Sheriff Frequently engaged in property and commercial disputes, and also regularly handles defamation matters. He routinely acts for both professional and direct access clients. **Strengths:** "His key strength is advocacy; he is very quick off the mark and has a real presence in the courtroom. He is able to control witnesses well and produces arguments that are very comprehensive." "He is good at handling large cases and takes in vast amounts of information quickly." **Recent work:** Acted for Asbestos Business Contractors in a dispute over the price of its work for Windermere Aquatic.

Other Ranked Lawyers

Simon Redmayne (East Anglian Chambers) Tackling a wide variety of commercial and chancery disputes, he is noted for his expertise in contested probate, trusts, contract law, land disputes and professional negligence. He is also an accomplished mediator. **Strengths:** "He is absolutely fantastic and unbelievably intelligent."

John Clargo (Hardwicke) Seasoned commercial disputes practitioner, he routinely acts for commercial and residential property clients across the full range of property law. His scope of expertise also extends to property-focused professional negligence. **Strengths:** "He is approachable, user-friendly and able to see through a problem and produce a solution."

WALES & CHESTER

Commercial Dispute Resolution
Senior Statesmen
Senior Statesmen: distinguished older partners
Walters Graham *Civitas Law*
Leading Juniors
Band 1
Hughes Gwydion *9 Park Place*
Jones Emyr *9 Park Place*
Band 2
Kember Richard *9 Park Place*
Vines Anthony *Civitas Law*

Ranked Lawyers

Graham Walters (Civitas Law) A highly experienced and versatile senior practitioner with a robust knowledge of commercial litigation, particularly as it relates to property and contractual disputes. He also offers expertise in judicial review proceedings and environmental law.

Anthony Vines (see p.787) (Civitas Law) Demonstrates notable aptitude in claims relating to the construction sector, including matters concerning defective products, working conditions and planning permission. He is also sought after for his further expertise in employment and public law. **Strengths:** "He is very good intellectually in terms of analysing the case."

Gwydion Hughes (9 Park Place) Highly sought-after practitioner with wide-ranging expertise in commercial and chancery law. He regularly attracts instructions from public bodies and private corporations in an array of matters, such as complex judicial review proceedings and contractual disputes. **Strengths:** "He is very impressive, very reasonable, clever and a smooth operator." "An excellent advocate, he is very bright and gives very clear advice." **Recent work:** Defended Cardiff City Council in a matter concerning its alleged failure to set lawful tax licences for a number of years.

Emyr Jones (9 Park Place) Regularly called upon to represent local authorities and other organisations in a variety of commercial disputes. He is particularly noted for his deft handling of insolvency, real estate and probate matters. **Strengths:** "He is very easy to work with and a confident advocate."

Richard Kember (9 Park Place) Enjoys a growing reputation in the field, and is particularly noted for his skilled handling of matters concerning professional negligence, insolvency and commercial contracts. He is also well versed in property and chancery law. **Strengths:** "He is very steadfast in his approach." "He always looks for the best outcome for his client and doesn't get caught up in minutiae."

WESTERN

Commercial Dispute Resolution
Leading Sets
Band 1
Guildhall Chambers *
Band 2
St John's Chambers *
Leading Silks
Band 1
Blohm Leslie *St John's Chambers*
Sims Hugh *Guildhall Chambers*
Band 2
Davies Stephen *Guildhall Chambers*
Palmer Adrian *Guildhall Chambers*
Leading Juniors
Band 1
Adams Guy *St John's Chambers* [A]
Dickinson John FH *St John's Chambers* [A] *
Levy Neil *Guildhall Chambers*
McMeel Gerard *Guildhall Chambers*
Pearce-Smith James *St John's Chambers*
Virgo John *Guildhall Chambers*
Band 2
Ascroft Richard *Guildhall Chambers*
Bamford Jeremy *Guildhall Chambers*
Fentem Ross *Guildhall Chambers*
Maher Martha *St John's Chambers* [A]
Marsden Andrew *Commercial Chambers (ORL)* ◊ [A]
Pointon Nicholas *St John's Chambers*
Ramel Stefan *Guildhall Chambers*
Up-and-coming individuals
Wibberley James *Guildhall Chambers*

** Indicates set / individual with profile.*
[A] direct access (see p.24).
◊ (ORL) = Other Ranked Lawyer.
Alphabetical order within each band. Band 1 is highest.

Band 1

Guildhall Chambers
See profile on p.938

THE SET

Pre-eminent chambers on the Western Circuit, well versed in all manner of commercial disputes and particularly lauded for its handling of those in the realms of insolvency and financial services. Recent work highlights include acting for 84 high net worth individuals in claims brought against Pentagon and Canada Life, arising from a British hedge fund collapse. Instructing solicitors repeatedly note the quality of services on offer and comment that the standard rivals that expected of London sets, saying: "At Guildhall you get true specialists who add value," with one interviewee adding: "Guildhall are a breath of fresh air, they are more commercial and pragmatic than a lot of London sets."

Client service: "The clerks are very impressive and they're nice guys – they would go the extra mile for what you want." "They always aim to deliver a high standard at a reasonable cost. They always try to allocate any work to the barrister of your choice or someone who is suitable and has the relevant experience if your barrister is not available." "The clerks are very approachable, they always present a way forward and they are engaged with the work that we do." "You couldn't get a better clerking team." Mike Norton is the clerk in charge of the commercial practice at the chambers.

SILKS

Hugh Sims QC A formidable barrister who handles all manner of commercial contentious issues, from disagreements coming out of commercial agency relationships to construction disputes. He tends to represent claimants or appellants in cases and is acclaimed by both instructing solicitors and opposing counsel, who describe his drafting, turnaround time, court manner and way with clients as "just superb" and "absolutely fantastic." **Strengths:** "An absolutely brilliant advocate with an exceptional brain; he lives for the court." "By far the best option in Bristol for commercial litigation work." "He's exceptionally bright and he picks things up very quickly; he's good at focusing on the overall picture and seeing how it all hangs together." "A highly accomplished advocate who wins the trust of the judges, is easy to work with, massively commercial, creative with solutions and highly practical – he finds winning solutions to very difficult situations." **Recent work:** Successfully acted for the claimants and respondents in PHS v Initial (Rentokil).

Stephen Davies QC A perfect choice for banking and insolvency disputes. Sources commend his lengthy experience practising litigation and reveal his impressive reputation in the market. His expertise includes misrepresentation, breach of duty and Libor manipulation. **Strengths:** "I'm a huge fan of his, I've seen him do a lot of advocacy and he is very good. He is prepared to take a point and push it even if he doesn't personally agree. A fearless advocate of the Bar is hard to find, and he is one of them – very passionate and remarkably hard-working, diligent, creative, gets stuck in and is hands-on." "A fantastic practitioner, a bit of a rottweiler, a good litigator and a top man." **Recent work:** Appeared in multiple claims for Angel House/Angel Group, including representing the client in allegations of misfeasance.

Adrian Palmer QC An extremely experienced barrister who is renowned for his knowledge and skills in the field as well as his hands-on, no-fuss way of tackling instructions. He has represented high-profile clients in cases ranging from breaches of contract to allegations of negligent activity. **Strengths:** "He is absolutely brilliant, he will always go the extra mile and he is still very much a grassroots lawyer who doesn't mind getting his hands dirty. He is the antithesis of arrogant." "He has an astonishing ability to assimilate detailed information and identify the core issues." **Recent work:** Appeared in JP Grimes v Gubbins, a breach of contract case regarding a development which was delayed due to the financial crisis of 2008.

JUNIORS

Neil Levy A solid choice for conflicts arising from the banking sector, including mis-selling and interest rate swaps. Interviewees commend his experience and way of impressing instructing solicitors' clients with his calm and detailed approach. **Strengths:** "Neil is an exceptional star. His offering is certainly equivalent to that in London and he is priced more in the regional market." "A very experienced senior junior who is technically very able indeed and who makes the extremely complex seem rather more straightforward than it actually is." **Recent work:** Defended Lloyds Bank in a claim raised by Knowles alleging breach of mandate.

Gerard McMeel Held in very high regard for his work in the fields of banking and finance, and especially commended for his academic prowess. He regularly acts for banks, investors and high net worth individuals. **Strengths:** "He is very measured and calm, with excellent analysis." "He has been our barrister of choice for a long time. He has a nice easy manner with us and with the clients; he's an effective advocate but also very good in conference." **Recent work:** Represented 452 investors in the Commercial Court in claims that a US foreign exchange company unlawfully solicited millions of dollars' worth of investors' money using an unauthorised UK representative.

John Virgo Tremendous advocate with a focus on financial product mis-selling, including pensions, investments and interest rate swaps, as well as related regulatory work. He is lauded for his pragmatic, experienced and flexible manner of handling cases. **Strengths:** "He has an encyclopaedic knowledge of financial services disputes, and is very deeply steeped in case law and factual knowledge." "He fights his corner for the client and he's a very good guy." **Recent work:** Appeared in Green and Rowley v Royal Bank of Scotland in a case regarding interest rate swapping over the mis-selling of hedging products.

Richard Ascroft Sources cite his experience as a solicitor as beneficial. His practice encompasses breaches of agreement, restrictive covenants and insolvency law. **Strengths:** "He is imaginative in the way that he deals with issues." "He's a fighter and a great commercial specialist; you know he won't let you down." **Recent work:** Represented the tertiary claimant in University of Wales v London College of Business regarding the defence of a £25 million counterclaim concerning allegations of a breach of university course validation agreement.

Jeremy Bamford Acts on a whole host of contentious matters, and is particularly well regarded for his knowledge of company law. His practice also includes insolvency and professional negligence. **Strengths:** "He is very bright, detailed and on top of things." "He is just as smooth as silk: unflustered, equable yet persistent." **Recent work:** Successfully acted for HMRC against the Lotus F1 Team in an administration application for unpaid PAYE/NIC totalling £2.3 million.

Ross Fentem Primarily known for his work in finance and professional negligence. He is described by market sources as approachable and well respected. **Strengths:** "His drafting is fantastically persuasive, he's very easy to get on with and he is unflappable." "He's very responsive and good at identifying and dealing with the key issues; he has a good eye for detail." **Recent work:** Appeared for claimants Prom Chem, against Rohm & Haas/Dow Chemicals, alleging the breach of a data sharing agreement. This involved liaising with the European Chemicals Agency as well as a detailed examination of EU law and the regulations about the supply of biocidal products.

Stefan Ramel Praised for his skill both on paper and in court, and instructing solicitors highlight his measured approach. His practice covers directors' disputes, professional negligence and insolvency. **Strengths:** "He is easy to get on with, practical in his outlook, very good at finding solutions, and he knows how to endear himself to the court." "A bright and accurate barrister who is pleasant to deal with." **Recent work:** Appeared for the Nationwide Building Society in several professional negligence cases including matters of liability, causation and loss.

James Wibberley Handles matters including restrictive covenants and costs disputes. Sources note the quality of his written advice. **Strengths:** "He was pragmatic, gave clear advice and negotiated a good settlement." **Recent work:** Advised the claimant, Bank of Ireland, in a professional negligence dispute against Mortimer & Carey concerning valuation reports on buy-to-let flats.

Band 2

St John's Chambers

See profile on p.941

THE SET

Respected chambers with a growing commercial practice, praised for its consideration of practicalities such as costs and funding. One impressed interviewee states: "They have the feel of a heavyweight set and they are imaginative in offering solutions to help you settle a case." Frequently handles mandates on behalf of a wide range of clients, from individuals to authorities and companies of all sizes. Recent work highlights include representing Fix Training in its claim against the Welsh Government for £1.6 million worth of unpaid services as well as damages arising from a breach of contract.

Client service: "The clerking service is very good; they have a very modern approach and they run a lot of useful, to-the-point seminars." "The team has a decent, proactive relationship with the instructing solicitor." "The clerks can generally sort something out for you at the last minute, and they are friendly, keen and enthusiastic." Robert Bocock is the practice manager for Commercial & Chancery.

SILKS

Leslie Blohm QC A superb lawyer who receives glowing feedback for his work across a whole spectrum of commercial issues such as partnership disputes, as well as real estate, agricultural and chancery matters. Instructing solicitors repeatedly commend his "user-friendly" approach to cases, adding that "he brings an element of calm." **Strengths:** "One of the cleverest people I have ever come across, his knowledge of the law is vast, he can grasp complicated situations very quickly indeed, he's outstandingly good on his feet and he's the person to turn to in times of great need." "We certainly see him as one of our foremost options in Bristol; he is very good at breaking things down and creating clarity out of confusion, taking a difficult concept and boiling it down to the nuts and bolts." "There's no stiffness in working with him, he's very approachable, he tries to make it as easy as possible for the instructing solicitors. I do like working with him."

JUNIORS

Guy Adams Held in high regard by market commentators for his skilful handling of complex trust disputes and his "ability to get to the nub of a case." His areas of expertise include a broad range of contentious matters from the areas of commercial and chancery law. **Strengths:** "He's a good thinker and he just rolls up his sleeves and gets on with it." "He is clever, forceful, bright and hard-working." **Recent work:** Appeared in Monnow v Morgan in a trial that included construction law and commercial loan agreements.

John Dickinson (see p.633) A fantastic choice for contentious probate and chancery, sources praise his particular skill in cases that involve complex numbers. He regularly receives instructions involving banking or company law. **Strengths:** "He is very bright, with a very analytical mind, and he's able to break down the case into its constituent parts, then methodically explain how he formulates his view." "The most astute finance barrister on the Western Circuit."

James Pearce-Smith Previous experience as a solicitor means that "he knows all about client service" and is able to provide alternative insight into matters such as construction disputes and claims of professional negligence. Sources note his skill at "unlocking technical issues." **Strengths:** "He is very incisive and gets to the core of a case very quickly." "We trust his judgement, he understands commercial litigation and he doesn't just look at it from an academic standpoint." "He is very strong in cross-examination; as a trial advocate that's where he really stands out." **Recent work:** Represented Dyson in two separate claims against Pearson and Nagy, both of which related to confidential information being taken unlawfully by ex-members of staff.

Martha Maher Has a broad commercial disputes practice, spanning fraud, partnership and company matters as well as insolvency. She also has expertise in ADR, and she is recommended for her experience and people skills. **Strengths:** "She likes a good close working relationship with her instructing solicitors and she's a very good trial advocate." "She is commercial, proactive and good at getting on with clients." **Recent work:** Appeared in Bennett v Avalon Investment Services and three Others over allegations of unlawful and deceitful activity on the part of a former managing director during a USD50 million finance deal, as a result of which the claimant lost £2 million in profit.

Nicholas Pointon Handles matters from all angles of commercial law, including partnership and probate disputes. He is known for the clarity of his explanations, excellent client treatment and his commercial savvy. **Strengths:** "He was very well prepared, he knew the papers inside out and was very quick on his feet – he seemed to have three or four counterarguments up his sleeve." "He's a class act who is really good at the detail – he just oozes ability." **Recent work:** Successfully acted for claimants Jambo against Hackney Borough Council in a breach of contract claim.

Other Ranked Lawyers

Andrew Marsden (Commercial Chambers) Commended for his helpful manner, he regularly handles matters across the whole breadth of commercial disputes, from shareholder and partnership matters to unfair claims and commercial agency cases. **Strengths:** "He's very accessible and very commercial in terms of his advice, and a bit of a knife fighter, which I like." "He is very client-friendly, he talks English to clients and gives them pragmatic advice, and when there is advice a client may not want to hear he gives it to them in a diplomatic way." "He's very bright, knows his subject well and drives his point home forcefully in trials." **Recent work:** Appeared in Pinewood Technologies v Avalon Motor Company in a case regarding the failure to supply a computer system.

Contents:

LONDON

Community Care	
Leading Sets	
Band 1	
39 Essex Chambers *	
11KBW *	
Landmark Chambers *	
Matrix Chambers *	
Monckton Chambers *	
Leading Silks	
Band 1	
Giffin Nigel	*11KBW* *
Howell John	*Blackstone Chambers (ORL)* ◊
Knafler Stephen	*Landmark Chambers*
Richards Jenni	*39 Essex Chambers* *
Band 2	
Bowen Paul	*Brick Court Chambers (ORL)* ◊ *
Cragg Stephen	*Monckton Chambers*
Lock David	*Landmark Chambers* [A]
Morris Fenella	*39 Essex Chambers*
Mountfield Helen	*Matrix Chambers*
Rutledge Kelvin	*Cornerstone Barristers (ORL)* ◊ *
Wise Ian	*Monckton Chambers* [A]
Wolfe David	*Matrix Chambers*
Leading Juniors	
Band 1	
Armstrong Nicholas	*Matrix Chambers*
Auburn Jonathan	*11KBW* [A] *
Broach Steve	*Monckton Chambers*
Buley Tim	*Landmark Chambers*
Butler-Cole Victoria	*39 Essex Chambers*
Buttler Chris	*Matrix Chambers* [A]
Clement Joanne	*11KBW* *
Harrop-Griffiths Hilton	*Field Court Chambers (ORL)* ◊
Band 2	
Burton Jamie	*Doughty Street Chambers (ORL)* ◊
Gallagher Caoilfhionn	*Doughty Street Chambers (ORL)* ◊ [A] *
Hannett Sarah	*Matrix Chambers* [A]
Luh Shu Shin	*Garden Court Chambers (ORL)* ◊
Sharland Andrew	*11KBW* [A] *
Suterwalla Azeem	*Monckton Chambers* *
Band 3	
Blundell David	*Landmark Chambers*
Greaney Nicola	*39 Essex Chambers* *
Harris Bethan	*Garden Court Chambers (ORL)* ◊

** Indicates set / individual with profile.*
[A] direct access (see p.24).
◊ (ORL) = Other Ranked Lawyer.
Alphabetical order within each band. Band 1 is highest.

Band 1

39 Essex Chambers
See profile on p.840

THE SET

39 Essex Chambers has a fantastic community care team consisting of members who act for a broad range of clients including local authorities, families, individuals and the Official Solicitor. Its barristers are market leaders for Court of Protection work, and are able to handle a broad range of community care issues such as leaving care duties, age disputes, mental health aftercare and care home funding. One solicitor points to the set's "solid strength and depth," adding that "they have exceptionally talented juniors together with extremely good and responsive silks."

Client service: "Peter Campbell is the clerk we deal with – he's got his finger on the pulse, and knows where we stand on availability. They've got very good clerks." Michael Kaplan and Alastair Davidson are senior clerks who work under director of clerking David Barnes.

SILKS

Jenni Richards QC (see p.751) Pre-eminent silk who acts for claimants, public interest groups, and local authorities in community care matters. She is an expert across a broad range of cases, and is particularly good at cases involving regulatory processes, compliance with the Human Rights Act and budgetary decision-making. **Strengths:** "She has good all-round knowledge of many areas and can turn her hand to anything. She's extremely well liked by clients and comes up with novel and interesting arguments." **Recent work:** Represented disabled claimants in their initial challenge to the lawfulness of the system for processing Personal Independence Payments which replaced the disability living allowance.

Fenella Morris QC Deeply experienced silk who is a fine choice for a range of community care matters. She is an expert in judicial review, a regular in the Court of Protection and someone with great knowledge of the law relating to the NHS. **Strengths:** "She's very forthright and a good economic advocate. She makes her points succinctly and has a very good brain."

JUNIORS

Victoria Butler-Cole Has a broad practice but receives particular praise for her work in Court of Protection and mental capacity cases. She is also an expert in social care, and human rights matters. **Strengths:** "She's very up-to-date with the case law, and is both strategic and practical in her advice." **Recent work:** Instructed in O v Peterborough Council, which was a judicial review challenge on behalf of an eight-year-old autistic girl concerning the council's decision to place her on a Child Protection Plan.

Nicola Greaney (see p.659) A quality public law barrister who regularly represents a broad range of clients including health bodies, local authorities and private individuals. **Strengths:** "I was against her in a bitter dispute – she brought common sense and a practical and pragmatic approach to resolving the dispute."

11KBW
See profile on p.867

THE SET

11 KBW boasts a highly respected health and community care law team replete with members who advise on a wide range of issues. Cases involving housing, data protection of patients' records and cuts to health and community care services are all undertaken. The set has impressive breadth and depth of expertise, and its individuals act in many of the leading community care cases. One recent example was R (C) v Secretary of State for Work and Pensions and Zacheus 2000 Trust, which challenged delays in the administration of Personal Independence Payments.

Client service: "The clerks are very helpful and attentive, from the most senior to the juniors. They remember you are a solicitor and are mindful of your needs." Lucy Barbet and Mark Dann are joint senior clerks.

SILKS

Nigel Giffin QC (see p.653) Renowned silk with a broad public law practice that encompasses housing, social services and education. **Strengths:** "He's very impressive. He gets right to the heart of the issue straight away, gives very clear advice and is very intelligent."

JUNIORS

Jonathan Auburn (see p.586) Top-quality practitioner whose expertise in mental capacity and mental health underpins his work across the full range of community care matters. He remains a go-to for both local authorities and claimants. **Strengths:** "He has very good knowledge of community care and is a force to be reckoned with." "He covers all the bases, and if he raises a point, you need to look into it." **Recent work:** Instructed in Re X and others, a test case to determine the correct approach to determining authorisation of deprivation of liberty.

Joanne Clement (see p.619) Stands out for her expertise in the crossover between Court of Protection and community care work. She is adept at handling cases that concern both adults and children, and is experienced in challenges to community care assessments and ordinary residence disputes. **Strengths:** "An incredibly dedicated and hard-working counsel, who provides excellent client service." **Recent work:** Acted for claimant parents in R (Morris and Thomas) v Rhondda Cynon Taff CBC which was a challenge to a local authority's decision to abolish full-time nursery education for three-year-olds.

Andrew Sharland (see p.762) Has a broad practice and is often involved in cases that involve complex human rights and immigration issues. He is instructed by a broad range of clients, including central government, local authorities and claimants. **Strengths:** "He's a knowledgeable opponent who is very effective." "He's very robust but fair." **Recent work:** Instructed in R (Karia) v Leicester City Council which was a challenge brought by a 101-year-old resident who asserted that her Article 8 right to a home for life had been violated.

Landmark Chambers
See profile on p.873

THE SET

Landmark Chambers has significant community care expertise and proves particularly good at cases concerning benefits, social care, immigration and the NHS. Members act for a broad range of clients including local authorities, NHS bodies and government entities. They have been involved in many of the leading cases in the field, including R (SO (Eritrea) v LB Barking and Dagenham, an age dispute judicial review in the Court of Appeal.

Client service: "The clerks are excellent. They are responsive and easy to get hold of." Jay Fullilove is senior clerk.

SILKS

Stephen Knafler QC Fantastic public law silk who advises and acts for local authorities, individuals and commercial organisations in community care matters. He is the general editor of Community Care Law Reports. **Strengths:** "He's a nice, straightforward advocate. He's very pleasant to deal with and one of the few who genuinely does both claimant and defendant work."

David Lock QC A noted expert on all law relating to the NHS, he has been involved in many of the leading cases in this area. **Strengths:** "He's fantastic. He's highly intelligent so he can make complex law very clear and understandable. Clients love him and his approach – he understands things from their perspective." **Recent work:** Instructed in R (Cornwall Council) v Secretary of State, a Supreme Court case on the meaning of 'ordinary residence' for a person with learning difficulties.

JUNIORS

Tim Buley Standout junior who specialises in social welfare, human rights, immigration and EU law. He is experienced in every level of domestic court and acts for a variety of clients including government and other public sector bodies, pressure groups and individuals. **Strengths:** "Tim Buley is fantastic – he's a very good public lawyer who's very straightforward to deal with. He listens to what you say and is happy to make a decision on it. He's realistic and competent."

David Blundell An experienced public lawyer who acts for claimants, defendants and interested parties. He is particularly adept at handling cases challenging policies on access to benefits. **Strengths:** "David is approachable and enthusiastic. His written work is excellent and he is an expert in European law." "He is very clever, extremely nice and formidable in court." **Recent work:** Instructed in R (Project Seventeen) v Lewisham LBC, a test case challenging the policy on the provision of support to destitute families under section 17 of the Children Act 1989.

Matrix Chambers

See profile on p.876

THE SET

Matrix Chambers has a market-leading community care practice, and has expertise in domestic social welfare, discrimination, human rights and mental capacity law. Its silks and juniors are able to handle a wide range of matters, and have a successful track record acting for both claimants and defendants. Recent highlights for the set include involvement in the much reported Aspinall and others (formerly including Bracking) v Secretary of State for Work and Pensions which was a case challenging the legality of the Secretary of State's decision to close the Independent Living Fund. One solicitor described the set as the "gold standard – they organise roundtables and seminars, they're not frightened of campaigning and putting in resources – they really do get it."

Client service: "The Matrix practice team is exceptionally helpful and supportive, especially in times of crisis." Jason Housden is the senior practice manager.

SILKS

Helen Mountfield QC Fantastic barrister who is "very good at everything she does." She is particularly well known for her work representing claimants, and has been in the Supreme Court twice in community care cases over the last year. **Strengths:** "She's a very good advocate who is very bright and pleasant to be in court with." **Recent work:** Instructed in R(MA) v Secretary of State for Work & Pensions which challenged the discriminatory impact of the absence of criteria to exclude from the bedroom tax/spare room subsidy those with a disability or a domestic violence-related need for further accommodation.

David Wolfe QC Noted community care silk who is particularly active in judicial review challenges to decisions made by health bodies and local authorities. These decisions concern such issues as service delivery, care planning, equality and capacity. He acts for a range of clients including individuals, organisations and groups. **Strengths:** "He's very bright, very personable as an advocate and very pleasant to be against." "He is frighteningly clever and his brain works ten times faster than everyone else's. He's completely on top of the material and very hands-on as a leader." **Recent work:** Acted for the claimants in W, X, Y and Z v Secretary of State for Health which challenged the legality of confidential information being passed from hospitals to the Home Office via the Department for Health.

JUNIORS

Nicholas Armstrong Pre-eminent junior who has a broad public law practice, and is particularly experienced in cases with issues of migration. He is praised in the market as one of the leading juniors for claimant work. **Strengths:** "He's a very good advocate who is very passionate and good at picking up cases that need to be done." **Recent work:** Instructed in Tigere, a case which revolved around the access to student support by migrants.

Chris Buttler A top choice for claimants, well known for his work for disabled adults, children and mentally ill people. He has a broad range of experience, and is often involved in cases brought under the European Convention of Human Rights. **Strengths:** "He's a brilliant advocate, who is incredibly bright and lovely to deal with." "He's good at focusing arguments, and provides nice and succinct pleadings." **Recent work:** Successfully acted for a claimant and her six children, ensuring they were provided with financial support and accommodation close to the children's school.

Sarah Hannett Sarah has a broad community care practice and is particularly active in cases with an element of education law. Noted for her work for both claimants and local authorities. **Strengths:** "She is brilliant – she's very approachable and gives sound advice that is balanced." "She produces excellent paperwork and is very sensible and a delight to deal with." **Recent work:** Acted for the interested party in R (Cornwall County Council) v Secretary of State for Health which explored the principles to apply to ordinary residence when a person lacks capacity.

Monckton Chambers

See profile on p.877

THE SET

Monckton Chambers is praised in the market for its work in social care. Members have been involved in many significant cases, including R (HA) v London Borough of Ealing, which was an important judgment in the housing context because it successfully challenged Ealing's policy of requiring a certain period of residence before allowing applicants to go onto their housing register under Part VI of the Housing Act 1996. Members act for a range of clients, from individuals and NGOs to private companies and public authorities.

SILKS

Stephen Cragg QC An expert in social welfare and criminal justice public law, who also has a strong Court of Protection practice. He also sits as a part-time mental health tribunal judge. **Strengths:** "His paperwork is always excellent, he's very pleasant to deal with and he's very fair." "He's very committed to community care work." **Recent work:** Instructed in Re X, a challenge to the President of the Court of Protection's findings that incapacitated persons deprived of their liberty in care settings do not have to right to be party to proceedings or have an oral hearing of their case.

Ian Wise QC Praised for his work representing claimants, he is experienced across an array of issues. His community care work is complemented by strength in local government, human rights and administrative and public law generally. **Strengths:** "He's charming, easy to deal with, and a sharp-witted practitioner. He'll take the points and take them very well, charming the judge along the way." **Recent work:** Represented two families with severely disabled children in R(M&A) v Islington LBC. The principal issue was whether the local authority has (and is obliged on the facts of the case to exercise) the power to require the housing authority to provide accommodation which ameliorates risk to children.

JUNIORS

Steve Broach Particularly well known for his work concerning the rights of disabled children and adults. He is a go-to barrister for community care work and is acknowledged in the market as "a big player." **Strengths:** "He is pragmatic, sensible, realistic and bright." "The work he does is impressive and his track record speaks for itself." "He's extremely proactive and always responsive." **Recent work:** Acted for the Nationwide Association of Fostering Providers in R v Bristol CC. This case concerned a complaint that local authorities are uniformly adopting a policy of placing children 'in-house' first.

Azeem Suterwalla (see p.776) Specialist in public and human rights law. He is an expert in work that relates to vulnerable and disabled children and adults, and is very experienced in immigration matters. **Strengths:** "He takes a sensible, pragmatic and no-nonsense approach." **Recent work:** Acted in R v Salford City Council, representing two vulnerable disabled adult claimants challenging a decision to stop a transport service to take them to and from community day centres.

Other Ranked Lawyers

John Howell QC (Blackstone Chambers) Top-quality public law silk who excels across a range of areas, such as local government, social services and human rights. He is well known for his work acting for local authorities. **Strengths:** "He is someone who has a superb academically intelligent mind." "He's just amazing."

Paul Bowen QC (see p.600) (Brick Court Chambers) Acts for a broad range of clients including claimants and public authorities. He is particularly well known for his work in cases concerning persons with mental disabilities, and is also an expert in cases concerning the closure of care homes and the assessment of services. **Strengths:** "He is really impressive, and both intelligent and creative in his approach."

Kelvin Rutledge QC (see p.757) (Cornerstone Barristers) Leading silk with a broad community care practice, who is most active representing local authorities. **Strengths:** "A tactical opponent who goes in quite hard but also takes a fair and balanced view."

Jamie Burton (Doughty Street Chambers) Involved in an array of community care issues, and particularly active in cases which involve elements of housing, social security and clinical care. **Strengths:** "He has good insight into the points to bring in a case, and he cares very much for his clients."

Caoilfhionn Gallagher (see p.649) (Doughty Street Chambers) Well known for her work acting for claimants in urgent community care judicial reviews. She is particularly experienced in cases which involve street and homeless children, and vulnerable adult prisoners seeking support whilst in custody. **Recent work:** "She's very effective and a tough opponent."

Hilton Harrop-Griffiths (Field Court Chambers) An "enormously knowledgeable" barrister, who is a leading junior acting for local authorities in community care matters. He is particularly well regarded for his work in cases concerning the relationship between immigration and asylum legislation and community care. **Strengths:** "He's very sensible and very down-to-earth." "Experienced, responsive, reliable and very knowledgeable." **Recent work:** Instructed in R (Cornwall Council) v Secretary for State for Health, a dispute about the test for ordinary residence for the purposes of the National Assistance Act 1948.

Shu Shin Luh (Garden Court Chambers) Most frequently acts for vulnerable persons in individual claims and litigation challenging public policy, although she also acts for organisations. She draws praise from the market for the determined way she acts on behalf of her clients. **Strengths:** "She is very, very good." "She takes the points and is not fazed at all – she's tough."

Bethan Harris (Garden Court Chambers) Adept at a range of community care matters, but particularly strong in cases that concern the housing needs of people with disabilities. Along with others at her set, she produces the Community Care Law Reports, and delivers training and conferences related to the area. **Strengths:** "She's wonderful on the detail." "She is very good with the clients and very caring."

COMPANY: An Introduction

Contributed by Erskine Chambers

It is still too early to know what effect the Brexit vote will have in relation to UK company law. We have introduced many measures over the years to implement Company Law Directives emanating from the EU. But would UK company law really be that different in the absence of those Directives? Is it too much red tape, or would we be where we are without the EU anyway? After all, we had long had a fairly sophisticated capital maintenance regime in place before the EU was even thought about. Similarly, we had a fairly sophisticated regime in relation to public offerings before the Prospectus Directive was implemented. Similarly, transparency appears now to be the globally accepted norm.

While some EU provisions were introduced to counter the effects of perceived ills, some were clearly designed to achieve greater harmonisation so as to facilitate the free market in goods, services, labour and capital. By way of example, there can be no doubt that the harmonisation of cross-border mergers through the EU regulations has benefited UK businesses. It has also benefited the legal sector. However, it remains the case that most of those mergers are concerned with intra-group reorganisations and rationalisations, rather than mergers between independent parties.

This last year has seen an upturn, albeit slow, in M&A work, and some of that has been put on hold as a result of the Brexit vote. However, the proposed takeover by way of scheme of arrangement of SAB Miller by AB InBev for in excess of USD100 billion has kept both transactional and litigation lawyers active both last year and this year. If completed, as expected, it will be one of the top five deals in corporate history and will create a brewing empire making about one-third of the world's beer.

BAT Industries' claims against Sequana in respect of dividends, alleged to be both unlawful dividends and transactions at an undervalue, have resulted in a judgment in favour of BAT in a sum in excess of EUR135 million, on the basis that the last of the two dividends paid constituted a transaction at an undervalue within Section 423 of the Insolvency Act 1986. The liability which it was alleged was sought to be avoided was in respect of environmental liabilities in the USA for the clean-up costs necessitated by the pollution of the Fox River caused by the discharge of polychlorinated biphenyls (PCBs). We can expect to see appeals lodged from both sides of the dispute.

The long-awaited judgment of the Supreme Court in JKX v Eclairs was delivered. The court affirmed the approach of the court laid down by the Privy Council (Lord Wilberforce) in Howard Smith v Ampol Petroleum for determining the propriety, or otherwise, of the exercise by directors of their fiduciary powers.

Corporate governance issues have continued to feed the legal market, in terms of minority buyouts, more public acquisitions, and the ever-increasing number of shareholder disputes in companies of all sizes, in part resulting from greater shareholder activism, and in many cases simply from poor governance. Those issues are not confined to small private companies. Indeed, most recently corporate governance issues are said to be at the heart of the BHS saga.

Asset recovery work, both here and abroad, continues unabated. Applications in BTA Bank v Ablyazov, commenced in 2009, have continued to occupy the courts. Judgments to date have been entered in the bank's favour for in excess of USD4.5 billion. One interim application of particular note resulted in the court directing disclosure of documents, in respect of which legal professional privilege had been claimed, on the basis of the iniquity exception to privilege.

The proceedings in Mezhprombank v Pugachev seem to be following a somewhat similar course, with dozens of interim hearings over the last twelve months. In one such application, the Court of Appeal ordered disclosure of the identities of the beneficiaries of a discretionary trust.

Just as onshore litigation continues to confound those who say that litigation is too expensive, so too does offshore litigation. The claim in AHAB v SICL for USD9 billion has seen teams of lawyers descending on Seven Mile Beach in the Cayman Islands. The proceedings, due to last six months, are being heard this year before the Chief Justice.

A little closer to home, in Guernsey, Carlyle Capital Corporation, again ably supported by teams of lawyers from the UK, is pursuing its claims for a sum in excess of USD1 billion from its directors and investment managers for alleged breaches of duty. That claim also is estimated to last for six months.

Regulatory work for the UK company lawyer is also on the increase. Proceedings before the Hearings Committee of the Takeover Panel in relation to BUMI were compromised, resulting in censures against some of those involved, while against others the proposed censures were not proceeded with.

Litigation in the British Virgin Islands continues apace, notwithstanding the problems that jurisdiction has encountered in finding sufficient judges to undertake all the work now before their courts.

Generally the markets, both here and abroad, continue to look promising for the UK company lawyer.

Contents:

LONDON

Company
Leading Sets
Band 1
Erskine Chambers *
Band 2
Maitland Chambers *
4 Stone Buildings *
Band 3
XXIV Old Buildings *
Serle Court *
South Square *
Band 4
Enterprise Chambers *
One Essex Court *
New Square Chambers *
Wilberforce Chambers *
* Indicates set / individual with profile.
◊ (ORL) = Other Ranked Lawyer.
Alphabetical order within each band. Band 1 is highest.

Company	
Leading Silks	
Star individuals	
Chivers David	*Erskine Chambers* *
Crow Jonathan	*4 Stone Buildings* *
Girolami Paul	*Maitland Chambers* *
Hollington Robin	*New Square Chambers*
Miles Robert	*4 Stone Buildings*
Moore Martin	*Erskine Chambers* *
Todd Michael	*Erskine Chambers* *
Band 1	
Bompas George	*4 Stone Buildings* *
Davis-White Malcolm	*XXIV Old Buildings*
Dicker Robin	*South Square* *
Hill Richard G	*4 Stone Buildings* *
Jones Philip	*Serle Court* *
Mabb David	*Erskine Chambers*
Mowschenson Terence	*Wilberforce Chambers*
Trower William	*South Square* *
Zacaroli Antony	*South Square* *
Band 2	
Arden Peter	*Erskine Chambers* *
Brisby John	*4 Stone Buildings* *
Collings Matthew	*Maitland Chambers* *
de Garr Robinson Anthony	*One Essex Court* *
Gibbon Michael	*Maitland Chambers* *
Green Michael	*Fountain Court Chambers (ORL)* ◊ *
Hilliard Lexa	*Wilberforce Chambers*
Marshall Philip	*Serle Court* *
Newman Catherine	*Maitland Chambers* *
Potts James	*Erskine Chambers* *
Steinfeld Alan	*XXIV Old Buildings*
Thompson Andrew	*Erskine Chambers* *
Trace Anthony	*Maitland Chambers* *
Tregear Francis	*XXIV Old Buildings*
Band 3	
Allison David	*South Square* *
Blayney David	*Serle Court* *
Boyle Alan	*Serle Court* *
Bryant Ceri	*Erskine Chambers* *
Gledhill Andreas	*Blackstone Chambers (ORL)* ◊
Goldring Jeremy	*South Square* *
Isaacs Barry	*South Square* *
Moss Gabriel	*South Square*
Moverley Smith Stephen	*XXIV Old Buildings*
Nourse Edmund	*One Essex Court* *
Shekerdemian Marcia	*Wilberforce Chambers*
Smith Tom	*South Square* *
Stubbs Rebecca	*Maitland Chambers* *
Toube Felicity	*South Square* *
Weatherill Bernard	*Enterprise Chambers*
New Silks	
Lightman Daniel	*Serle Court* *
Mumford David	*Maitland Chambers* *

Company	
Leading Juniors	
Star individuals	
Thornton Andrew	*Erskine Chambers* *
Band 1	
Davies Edward	*Erskine Chambers* *
Shaw Benjamin	*Erskine Chambers* *
Band 2	
Adair Stuart	*XXIV Old Buildings*
Addy Catherine	*Maitland Chambers* *
Banner Gregory	*Maitland Chambers* *
Collingwood Timothy	*Serle Court* *
Denton-Cox Gregory	*4 Stone Buildings* *
Dougherty Nigel	*Erskine Chambers* *
Drake David	*Serle Court* *
Eaton Turner David	*New Square Chambers* *
Gillyon Philip	*Erskine Chambers* *
Greenwood Paul	*4 Stone Buildings* *
Griffiths Ben	*Erskine Chambers* *
Harrison Christopher	*4 Stone Buildings* *
Horan Stephen	*Erskine Chambers*
Knott James	*4 Stone Buildings* *
Prentis Sebastian	*New Square Chambers*
Ritchie Richard	*XXIV Old Buildings*
Shivji Sharif	*4 Stone Buildings* *
Stokes Mary	*Erskine Chambers* *
Stonefrost Hilary	*South Square* *
Band 3	
Adamyk Simon	*New Square Chambers*
Bailey James	*New Square Chambers*
Barden Alex	*Fountain Court Chambers (ORL)* ◊ *
Boeddinghaus Hermann	*4 Stone Buildings* *
Cone John	*Erskine Chambers* *
Cumming Edward	*XXIV Old Buildings*
Gentleman Tom	*4 Stone Buildings* *
Harty Patrick	*Erskine Chambers* *
Ife Linden	*Enterprise Chambers*
Kyriakides Tina	*Radcliffe Chambers (ORL)* ◊
Lascelles David	*Littleton Chambers (ORL)* ◊ *
Lucas Bridget	*Fountain Court Chambers (ORL)* ◊ *
Mallin Max	*Wilberforce Chambers*
McCulloch Niall	*Enterprise Chambers*
O'Leary Sam	*One Essex Court* *
Page Rebecca	*Maitland Chambers* *
Parfitt Matthew	*Erskine Chambers* *
Roberts Catherine	*Erskine Chambers* *
Tomson Alastair	*4 Stone Buildings* *
Up-and-coming individuals	
Adams Paul	*Serle Court* *
Cook Alexander	*4 Stone Buildings* *
Elias Thomas	*Serle Court* *

Band 1

Erskine Chambers

See profile on p.832

THE SET

Erskine Chambers is a set that "clearly knows company law better than the rest." Individuals are frequently instructed in the major directors' duties cases, such as Eclairs Group v JKX Oil & Gas, and are also regularly called upon to handle the most significant shareholder and limited liability partnership disputes. They are also market leaders in corporate transactions and continue to advise on a host of major takeovers and M&A deals. Examples include Aviva's £5.6 billion takeover of Friends Life and the £68 billion Shell/British Gas merger. Clients assert that "no one comes close to the set in terms of depth," and are quick to underline the set's status as the "pre-eminent corporate chambers in the country."

Client service: "The clerks, led by the fantastic Mark Swallow, are efficient and responsive." "The clerks make their members available at short notice and are very commercial on fees."

SILKS

David Chivers QC (see p.616) A heavyweight practitioner in company law. He is regularly instructed in high-profile, substantial disputes, both in the UK and internationally. **Strengths:** "He is our preferred QC for company law matters. He is polished, commercial, creative, and his knowledge of company law is second to none. He is absolutely first-class." **Recent work:** Acted for the respondents in the shareholder dispute Mehta v Viking River Cruises.

Martin Moore QC (see p.721) A sought-after silk who advises on transactions and disputes. He is recognised for his strengths in complex corporate transactions and restructurings, and is also regularly sought after for his expertise in schemes of arrangement and schemes for the transfer of insurance. **Strengths:** "Highly dependable, incredibly responsive and always willing to provide a route through difficult problems." **Recent work:** Advised Visa on its USD21 billion acquisition of Visa Europe.

Michael Todd QC (see p.782) A highly respected silk with a fantastic reputation in company litigation and advisory work. He is often instructed with regard to contested takeovers and restructurings. **Strengths:** "Fantastic on complex company law issues. He will always make himself available and is fantastically responsive."

David Mabb QC Experienced across the full range of company law matters and an expert in company accounting. He is the only barrister member of the Financial Reporting Review Panel, which compels listed and other larger companies to comply with the law relating to company accounts. **Strengths:** "Provides excellent advice in a clear and concise manner. He is truly client-friendly."

Peter Arden QC (see p.584) Handles company,

insolvency and restructuring cases to a very high standard. He is adept at handling scheme of arrangement, capital maintenance and corporate governance work. **Strengths:** "He is very thoughtful, highly intelligent and very user-friendly." **Recent work:** Advised a company on issues concerning historic share buybacks in a proposed takeover.

Andrew Thompson QC (see p.780) Well known for handling company, partnership and corporate insolvency disputes. He often advises on shareholder claims and breach of fiduciary duty cases. **Strengths:** "He is our first choice for M&A transactional related issues. He has a very commercial approach and, notwithstanding his busy practice, makes himself available."

James Potts QC (see p.741) An experienced silk whose practice spans corporate, insolvency, banking, financial services and commercial law. He often appears in Court of Appeal and Supreme Court cases. **Strengths:** "He is excellent – the advice he gives is very commercial and pragmatic." **Recent work:** Successfully acted for Vetswest on a reduction of capital matter.

Ceri Bryant QC (see p.605) An impressive silk with a broad practice that spans company, insolvency and financial services work. She is experienced in corporate takeovers as well as company disputes. **Strengths:** "Technically very good and always helpful, she produces in a timely manner and has the respect of the court." **Recent work:** Successfully acted for Loch Lomond Members' Golf Club in a matter concerning the implementation of a scheme of arrangement.

JUNIORS

Andrew Thornton (see p.781) A leading junior who regularly advises on high-profile and high-value M&A. His enviable client base includes numerous FTSE 100 companies, including household names in the telecommunications and automotive sectors. **Strengths:** "Go-to barrister for schemes and any tricky company law questions." "Extremely responsive and highly experienced, he's super to deal with." "Technically excellent, straightforward, practical and approachable."

Edward Davies (see p.629) An esteemed senior junior with an excellent track record in company and insolvency cases. He often appears in high-profile disputes at the High Court and Court of Appeal. **Strengths:** "Provides thorough, constructive and practical advice." **Recent work:** Acted for British American Tobacco in Windward Prospects Ltd v Sequana, a case seeking recovery of unlawful dividends, among other issues.

Benjamin Shaw (see p.763) Advises on transactions and disputes. His sought-after expertise has seen him appear in numerous matters concerning shareholder disputes, derivative claims and Section 994 unfair prejudice petitions. **Strengths:** "Very good – he's always very sensible and very knowledgeable." **Recent work:** Successfully acted as sole counsel in Judge v Bahd, an unfair prejudice petition.

Nigel Dougherty (see p.635) Regularly handles shareholder disputes, takeovers and share acquisition agreements. He acts on contentious and non-contentious matters and is routinely instructed by leading City firms. **Strengths:** "Very hands-on, practical and helpful." "Robust and straightforward in his advice." **Recent work:** Appeared in Interactive Technology Corporation v Ferster, a case concerning fraud and asset recovery claims.

Philip Gillyon (see p.653) A distinguished junior who specialises in company and corporate insolvency law. His areas of expertise include disputed takeovers and breach of directors' duty claims. **Strengths:** "He is very considered and very hard-working. He knows his stuff on company law." **Recent work:** Acted in Greenlight Credit, Hirschl v Surrey Dragons, an unfair prejudice case that raised issues such as the circumstances in which a valuation can be challenged.

Ben Griffiths (see p.660) Specialises in commercial and financial law. He is experienced in both international and domestic disputes, including matters in the High Court and Supreme Court. **Strengths:** "Impresses with the quality of his advocacy. He's tenacious, and has good judgement and a great track record." **Recent work:** Acted in MezhpromBank v Pugachev, a dispute alleging corporate wrongdoing and misappropriation of funds.

Stephen Horan An impressive senior junior who handles company and corporate finance work. His broad expertise covers cross-border mergers and capital reorganisations. **Strengths:** "Stephen is a leading expert on cross-border mergers and has proven invaluable on a number of applications, including where we have sought to do something which has not been done before. He is very responsive and highly practical."

Mary Stokes (see p.773) A notable senior junior who handles company law, corporate insolvency and financial services matters. She is called upon to advise on both disputes and non-contentious issues. **Strengths:** "She is just exceptional and an absolute pleasure to deal with." "She is very clever and really knows what she is doing." **Recent work:** Advised a high-profile shareholder of a football club on a range of company law-related issues.

John Cone (see p.621) An experienced junior who predominantly advises on non-contentious matters. His expertise covers issues such as corporate reorganisations and schemes of arrangement. **Strengths:** "Fantastic – he's so pragmatic and experienced. He gets straight to the point and doesn't waffle."

Patrick Harty (see p.666) Handles commercial chancery work, especially company, corporate insolvency and civil fraud matters. He is experienced in unfair prejudice petitions and shareholder disputes. **Strengths:** "An extremely bright and commercial junior who tackles complex legal issues with aplomb." **Recent work:** Appeared in an unfair prejudice case concerning a hotel in Bloomsbury.

Matthew Parfitt (see p.733) Appointed to the Attorney General's B Panel of Counsel and a barrister with a wide-ranging litigious and advisory practice. **Strengths:** "He is very good on the legal analysis, and at preparing witness evidence and pleadings." **Recent work:** Represented the defendant in Fortelus v Thomas Meston, a breach of duty claim worth £2 million.

Catherine Roberts (see p.753) A respected junior who is regularly instructed in shareholder disputes. She is experienced in international cases, and has handled claims in Bermuda, Hong Kong and Singapore. **Strengths:** "She is technically polished, and has a very reassuring client manner." **Recent work:** Acted in a dispute which concerned, among other issues, the allocation of several billion shares.

Band 2

Maitland Chambers

See profile on p.875

THE SET

The "brilliant" Maitland Chambers houses an impressive roster of silks and juniors who handle a range of company matters. Its barristers are often instructed on high-profile domestic and international disputes including fiduciary duty claims and valuation challenges. Away from contentious work, members also handle advisory work in relation to high-value M&A involving clients from a range of industries. The set's strong track record ensures that it is a go-to name for company work.

Client service: The clerks at Maitland Chambers are highlighted for their responsiveness and excellent service. John Wiggs is the senior clerk.

SILKS

Paul Girolami QC (see p.653) A distinguished barrister who regularly appears at the High Court, Court of Appeal and Privy Council. He has broad expertise in company law and both handles disputes and advises on technical points on non-contentious matters. **Strengths:** "Extremely good and very nice. He's very clever, very bright and has good judgement." "A wizard intellect." "A fantastic advocate and a pleasure to deal with."

Matthew Collings QC (see p.620) A solid performer in court who has been instructed in several reported cases. He is notably active on shareholder disputes. **Strengths:** "Exceptionally good, and produces ingenious arguments." **Recent work:** Acted in Apex Global v Fi Call Ltd, a shareholder dispute involving Saudi princes.

Michael Gibbon QC (see p.652) A well-known name who regularly acts in commercial and tax cases with company law elements to them. He has a strong reputation in directors' duties cases. **Strengths:** "He is very industrious; he works tirelessly on the pleadings." **Recent work:** Recently appeared in a double derivative action, which raised allegations of breach of fiduciary duty by directors.

Catherine Newman QC (see p.727) An established and highly regarded silk at the Commercial Chancery Bar. Her expertise covers cases concerning derivatives and other financial instruments. **Strengths:** "I was very impressed with her ability to get on top of the details quickly." "Totally on top of the material and very good at cross-examining." **Recent work:** Appeared in a substantial shareholder dispute concerning issues around dividend policy, among others.

Anthony Trace QC (see p.783) Particularly well thought of for his advocacy and cross-examination skills, he is often instructed by leading City law firms. **Strengths:** "Superb performer in court." **Recent work:** Represented Burberry Middle East in an arbitration resulting from a high-value shareholders' agreement.

Rebecca Stubbs QC (see p.775) A silk with a growing reputation who focuses on company, insolvency and restructuring law. She acts on domestic and international matters and has been called to the Bar of Grenada. **Strengths:** "She is amazing, she is a machine." "Practical and effective."

David Mumford QC (see p.724) A well-regarded silk who often appears in high-profile company and commercial disputes. He takes instructions from banks, high net worth individuals and well-known corporations. **Strengths:** "Very clear and efficient." "Hugely effective, he's no-nonsense and cuts through to the chase." **Recent work:** Acted in BAT v Sequana, which raised issues about capital reductions and declaration of dividends.

JUNIORS

Catherine Addy (see p.579) Sought-after junior counsel with a strong reputation in company and insolvency matters. She handles a range of work including directors' disqualification cases. **Strengths:** "She is very analytical, very strong on her feet and very focused and realistic in her advice." **Recent work:** Acted for HMRC on company and insolvency issues in the Ingenious Tax Tribunal case.

Gregory Banner (see p.589) His broad commercial chancery practice spans company and insolvency litigation. He frequently acts in high-value cross-border disputes. **Strengths:** "He is clever and understated. He knows the law, is good to work with and is a team player." **Recent work:** Appeared for the claimant in Courtwood Holdings SA v Woodley Properties Limited, David Mellor & Others, a breach of duty and knowing receipt case.

Rebecca Page (see p.732) Has a specialism in company and insolvency disputes. She has considerable experience of shareholder disputes and regularly advises on directors' duties, handling cases both at home and abroad. **Strengths:** "Provides sound commercial and technical advice. She is a confident advocate." **Recent work:** Acted in Bilta (UK) Ltd and Others v Nazir and Others, an appeal to the Supreme Court alleging breach of duty claims against a former director.

4 Stone Buildings

See profile on p.913

THE SET

4 Stone Building is "consistently strong at company and general chancery matters." The set houses "real prestige silks" who are "as good as you'll find anywhere," and also has a strong bench of juniors. Its members handle the full spectrum of company law work, from reorganisations of capital to shareholders' disputes, such that for many clients there is "no reason to look outside of them."

Client service: "The clerks have a sensible and commercial approach to any issues" and are "very responsive and helpful." David Goddard is the senior clerk.

SILKS

Jonathan Crow QC (see p.627) Widely regarded as one of the pre-eminent silks of the Chancery Bar. He is regularly instructed in company, commercial and public law cases and is a regular in the Court of Appeal and Supreme Court. **Strengths:** "He is a very effective advocate; his thoughts are very well marshalled and he is very direct and gets to the point quickly." "He is a fantastic advocate who goes down extremely well with Caribbean judges." **Recent work:** He represented the defendants in Michael Tsiattalos & Another v Andrew Charalambous & Others, a dispute alleging fraud and conspiracy.

Robert Miles QC Has an outstanding reputation at the Bar, particularly in connection with financial, commercial and corporate matters. He is regarded as one of the best litigators in the area and is regularly called upon to handle billion-pound disputes. **Strengths:** "At the top of his game." "He's quite outstanding and exceptionally clever." **Recent work:** Acted, alongside Richard Hill QC, for the former CEO of Autonomy regarding a USD5 billion claim alleging breach of fiduciary duty and fraud.

George Bompas QC (see p.598) Regularly instructed in high-profile company disputes, he is particularly active in international jurisdictions including Hong Kong, Singapore, the Cayman Islands and Trinidad. **Strengths:** "He has an amazing ability to assimilate and digest a large amount of factual information and distil this to its core issues. He anticipates the implications of the point before most people have even grasped the point." **Recent work:** Acted in Origo Partners plc v Brooks Macdonald Asset Management Limited & Another, a case relating to the constitution of a company and the balance of advantage between different classes of shares.

Richard Hill QC (see p.671) An established practitioner with an excellent reputation for large and complex disputes. He takes instructions on banking, commercial, company and insolvency disputes. **Strengths:** "He provides a really clear strategy straight from the outset." **Recent work:** Appeared with Robert Miles QC in a breach of fiduciary duty and fraud claim brought by Autonomy against its former CEO.

John Brisby QC (see p.603) Adept and respected silk who handles a range of company work. He is experienced in issues such as shareholder disputes, reductions of capital and schemes of arrangement. **Strengths:** "He is a great choice for offshore work; he's a good team leader, and a courteous and skilful advocate who is well received in the BVI Commercial Court." **Recent work:** Acted for a minority shareholder of Viking Rivers Cruises in a minority shareholders' petition alleging oppressive conduct by the majority shareholder.

JUNIORS

James Knott (see p.692) Handles a range of company-related cases. He takes instructions in non-contentious matters as well as disputes, and is experienced in Companies Court and High Court claims. **Strengths:** "The way he works with you is far beyond his years. He can ably deal with complex work in a timely fashion, and you really feel you can rely on him. His help has been invaluable." **Recent work:** Acted in Pyrrho Investments Ltd v MWB Property Limited and Others, a high-value breach of directors' duty dispute.

Sharif Shivji (see p.764) An impressive senior junior who is often instructed in shareholder disputes and financial services-related claims. He previously worked as a derivatives trader and regularly acts without a leader. **Strengths:** "He is really creative, very energetic, and so bright that he thinks up points that aren't obvious." **Recent work:** Appeared for the claimants in Stephen Akers v Deutsche Bank AG, a substantial dispute alleging, among other things, breach of fiduciary duty by directors in connection with the sale of toxic derivative financial instruments.

Christopher Harrison (see p.665) An experienced senior junior who advises on company, civil fraud, finance and insolvency matters. He is well regarded for his handling of big-ticket claims, particularly shareholder disputes. **Strengths:** "Technically very good, he's very sensible and very strategic." **Recent work:** Acted in a dispute concerning the acquisition of a car park operator, addressing questions around share purchase agreements.

Gregory Denton-Cox (see p.632) Highly respected barrister with a broad commercial chancery practice. He is particularly active in shareholder and investor disputes. **Strengths:** "A very safe pair of hands who knows his stuff. His quality of service goes beyond his years of call." **Recent work:** Appeared for the directors in a breach of fiduciary claim brought by the liquidators of Carlyle Capital Corporation.

Paul Greenwood (see p.660) Handles company cases as part of his wider commercial chancery practice. He is adept at handling disputes with cross-border and insolvency elements. **Strengths:** "Accessible, user-friendly, sensible and pragmatic," he is "excellent at making the solicitor feel comfortable and supported." **Recent work:** Acted in The Hon David Mellor PC QC and Others v John and Frank Partridge, a long-running dispute arising from the sale of a world-leading antique business.

Alastair Tomson (see p.782) Enjoys a busy commercial chancery practice and regularly handles contentious and advisory company work. Areas of expertise include acting in unfair prejudice petitions, both for respondents and petitioners. **Strengths:** "Responsive, very able and user-friendly." **Recent work:** Acted in an unfair prejudice action and just and equitable winding-up proceedings concerning a property development company.

Tom Gentleman (see p.651) Has a specialism in shareholder disputes and regularly appears in High Court disputes as well as arbitrations. Gentleman often acts unled. **Strengths:** "He provided detailed and nuanced advice on a very brief timeline." **Recent work:** Appeared as sole counsel for the claimants in a dispute concerning the ownership of shares in a car hiring business.

Hermann Boeddinghaus (see p.598) Has a focus on corporate and commercial disputes, and also acts on advisory issues. He is frequently instructed in shareholder claims. **Strengths:** "He is a sophisticated thinker and knows a lot about the ins and outs of company law." **Recent work:** Advised P2P Global Investments on a £832 million capital reduction and reorganisation.

Alexander Cook (see p.622) Has a busy general commercial chancery and company practice. His areas of expertise include shareholder disputes and unfair prejudice petitions. **Strengths:** "Offers clear guidance and clear advice. He's someone you can feel confident about." **Recent work:** Acted as sole counsel for the defendant, a former director, in a £750,000 misfeasance claim brought by the liquidators of a management training company.

Band 3

XXIV Old Buildings

See profile on p.884

THE SET

XXIV Old Buildings continues to maintain a strong reputation in company matters, and possesses a number of experienced silks and juniors well versed in the field. Members are particularly noted for their expertise in international disputes and enjoy a fine track record for their work in offshore courts in the British Virgin Islands and Cayman Islands. The set remains a popular choice for boardroom disputes, shareholder agreements and derivative claims.

Client service: "The clerks, led by Daniel Wilson and Paul Matthews, are very quick to assign a barrister, and have very good training sessions."

SILKS

Malcolm Davis-White QC A former chairman of the Chancery Bar Association and an outstanding choice for company cases. His expertise covers everything from capital reductions to shareholder disputes. **Strengths:** "Superbly intelligent and very diligent." "He simplifies complicated issues." **Recent work:** Acted for Summit Corporation on a capital reorganisation and share capital reduction.

Alan Steinfeld QC An impressive practitioner who is frequently involved in high-profile cases. He has a wealth of experience in shareholder disputes. **Strengths:** "He is superb and a great performer." "He is bright, clever and matter-of-fact." **Recent work:** Represented the shareholders of Lloyds TSB in a breach of directors' duties case brought against former directors in connection with the bank's takeover by RBS.

Francis Tregear QC Regularly instructed by well-known City and offshore firms. He has a specialism in hedge fund and structured investment vehicle-related work. **Strengths:** "Great on shareholder disputes and good with clients." **Recent work:** Acted in Jackson & Money v Gershinson & Others, a breach of directors' duties claim which brought up issues around duties owed to creditors in relation to tax planning schemes that fail.

Stephen Moverley Smith QC Regularly instructed in high-profile company matters, particularly those with an international flavour, he is considered a silk of choice for many corporations and liquidators. **Strengths:** "He has proven to be a skilled dispute resolution strategist with a multi-jurisdictional approach." "He knows the BVI courts very well." **Recent work:** Acted in a dispute in the Cayman Islands centred on the valuation of a shareholding in a semiconductor component manufacturer headquartered in China.

JUNIORS

Richard Ritchie A well-respected senior junior with a busy company practice. He handles matters such as unfair prejudice petitions and directors' disqualification proceedings. **Strengths:** "He is very good at grasping quite large and complex issues. He can get his head around things and pick his way through complex stories." **Recent work:** Successfully appeared for a director in Official Receiver v Blackwell, a directors' disqualification case.

Stuart Adair Experienced in shareholder disputes and breach of fiduciary duty claims, he often acts on international cases. **Strengths:** "He is very commercial, robust and approachable. He can cut through the groundwork and have a meeting of minds quite quickly. He is very smart, very direct and to the point." **Recent work:** Acted in a Ukrainian arbitration regarding the sale of two companies in Ukraine. The case involved breaches of warranties in share sale agreements.

Edward Cumming A barrister with a growing reputation at the Chancery Commercial Bar who is regularly instructed in high-profile disputes including breach of directors' duties cases. **Strengths:** "He is able to pick out the key points and work really well under pressure." **Recent work:** Acted as sole counsel for several property investment companies seeking to recover missing monies from a director based in Dubai.

Serle Court

See profile on p.908

THE SET

Serle Court's barristers are a solid choice for a range of company-related disputes and non-contentious matters. It has a strong bench of silks and juniors who are adept at handling issues such as minority shareholder disputes and derivative actions. The set is seen as a strong player in the company law field, and its members are applauded for their contribution to leading written work on the subject.

Client service: "The clerking, led by Steve Whitaker, is great. The clerks are always responsive, always easy to talk to and easy to get on with. They are commercial and are always very willing to work with you on issues."

SILKS

Philip Jones QC (see p.686) A sought-after silk with a fantastic reputation in company disputes. He regularly acts in international matters including British Virgin Islands High Court and Court of Appeal proceedings. **Strengths:** "Undoubtedly good, he is taken seriously by judges and lawyers." "He is a really good all-round lawyer who is very bright and very understated." **Recent work:** Appeared in a dispute involving 20 family shareholders from Saudi Arabia. The case concerned a multimullion-pound company, Nearland Inc, headquartered in the BVI.

Philip Marshall QC (see p.708) Regularly undertakes disputes concerning directors and acquisitions. He handles cases in both domestic and international courts. **Strengths:** "He is superb. Very relaxed and persuasive, he can certainly make an argument." **Recent work:** Acted in Novatrust v Kea, which brought up issues concerning derivative claims for foreign companies, among other questions.

Alan Boyle QC (see p.601) A distinguished name at the Commercial Chancery Bar, who is the first port of call for many on company disputes. He regularly leads in high-profile cases. **Strengths:** "A barrister with vast experience who produces clear and authoritative advocacy." **Recent work:** Acted in Kingate Global Fund Limited v Kingate Management Limited, a case that raised questions around unjust enrichment and contractual entitlement.

David Blayney QC (see p.597) Respected junior silk who handles company law as part of a broad commercial and chancery practice. He is often called upon to handle breach of directors' duty and unfair prejudice proceedings.

Daniel Lightman QC (see p.701) He often acts in company law cases and is an expert in minority shareholder cases. His areas of expertise also cover derivatives claims and Section 994 petition proceedings. **Strengths:** "A very intelligent barrister." "He has very good attention to detail, and can understand an unusual brief." **Recent work:** Acted in Griffith v Gourgey, an unfair prejudice petition centred on the shares of three property development companies.

JUNIORS

Timothy Collingwood (see p.620) A highly respected junior who takes instructions on domestic and international cases. He is particularly noted for his capabilities in shareholder disputes. **Strengths:** "He is very personable, clear and good at grasping complex situations. He is also very good with clients." **Recent work:** Appeared in an unfair prejudice petition involving complaints of breach of duty, wrongful exclusion and compulsory share transfer.

David Drake (see p.636) He has a broad practice which includes advising on fraud, company and insolvency matters. Drake regularly acts in breach of directors' duties claims and unfair prejudice petitions. **Strengths:** "He is what you want as he knows his law and is lovely to work with." **Recent work:** Appeared for the defendants in DAS UK Holdings Ltd v Asplin and Others, a high-value fiduciary duty, dishonest assistance and knowing receipt dispute.

Paul Adams (see p.579) Handles a range of company disputes such as breach of fiduciary and shareholder agreement cases. He often appears both in the English Court of Appeal and the BVI Court of Appeal. **Strengths:** "A very clever chap who wears his intellect lightly. He's very pleasant to work with as his advice is always very straightforward and helpful." **Recent work:** Acted for the claimants in a breach of fiduciary duty and fraud dispute.

Thomas Elias (see p.640) Frequently acts in high-profile company disputes. He is active on a range of matters including double-derivative claims. **Strengths:** "He is really good and strategically aware." **Recent work:** Acted in Prince Abdulaziz v Apex Global, an appeal at the Supreme Court concerning conjoined unfair prejudice petitions.

South Square

See profile on p.910

THE SET

South Square continues to be "unrivalled in the insolvency world" and, through its expertise there, also proves "strong on company law issues." Its deep bench of silks are particularly active in scheme of arrangement work under the Companies Act as well as restructuring mandates. Members are regularly called upon to handle major disputes, often at the Court of Appeal and Supreme Court.

Client service: "A very busy set of chambers, but the senior clerk's team is very responsive and very client-focused. The clerks are easy to deal with and down-to-earth." Mike Killick and Dylan Playfoot lead the team.

SILKS

Robin Dicker QC (see p.633) An exceptionally able silk who is experienced in company disputes at all levels, including cases at the Supreme Court and Court of Appeal. **Strengths:** "He is exceptionally smooth and a thorough advocate." "He knows his subject, no doubt about it."

William Trower QC (see p.784) A highly experienced practitioner with a strong company and insolvency practice. He is particularly adept at disputes arising from high-profile insolvencies. **Strengths:** "He has an excellent court presence and a very commanding tone of voice." **Recent work:** Advised Celsa Holdings on a scheme of arrangement that concerned the compromise of cross-border debt.

Antony Zacaroli QC (see p.802) Has a broad chancery practice which spans company matters relating to banking, financial and insolvency law. Acts on both UK and international cases including matters in the British Virgin Islands courts. **Strengths:** "Very impressive, very smooth and very clever." "He is user-friendly and easy to deal with." **Recent work:** Acted in Jinpeng v Peak Hotels, an appeal in the British Virgin Islands against the dismissal of a winding-up petition and removal of liquidators.

Jeremy Goldring QC (see p.656) A versatile silk with a broad commercial practice who handles a range of company-related disputes. He is regularly instructed in offshore cases. **Strengths:** "He is delightful and has an excellent reputation." **Recent work:** Advised Torm on a scheme of arrangement in connection with the restructuring of USD1.4 billion debt.

Barry Isaacs QC (see p.680) Has a focus on insolvency work and related company matters, and often handles high-profile claims and company restructurings. **Strengths:** "He is a great guy to work with and very bright." **Recent work:** Advised two hedge funds on a multimillion-dollar claim brought against former investment managers and valuation agents.

Gabriel Moss QC A hugely respected and experienced silk who is instructed in insolvency, company and restructuring matters. He is regularly called upon to appear in cases in the Court of Appeal and Supreme Court. **Strengths:** "He remains the doyen of the Insolvency Bar and is hugely respected by both lawyers and judges in the Caribbean."

Tom Smith QC (see p.769) Instructed in insolvency-related company work including cases concerning schemes of arrangement and company voluntary arrangements. His clients include banks and retailers. **Strengths:** "Provides clear, crisp advice that is always useful to the client." **Recent work:** Advised Ukrainian lender Privatbank on a scheme of arrangement to restructure subordinated liabilities.

Felicity Toube QC (see p.783) A respected name both at home and in the Cayman Islands courts, who handles company dispute work. She has a wealth of experience, acting for banks and corporations. **Strengths:** "She is highly personable, and has a keen intellect." "She's very straight to the point and pragmatic." **Recent work:** Acted in a multi-jurisdictional dispute that brought up questions of transfer of shares, among other issues.

David Allison QC (see p.583) Regularly advises on scheme of arrangement, reduction of capital and breach of directors' duties cases. He is particularly active in offshore proceedings, and has handled matters before the courts in the Cayman Islands, Dubai and New York. **Strengths:** "He is very clever and presents things in a very clear way to you as a client. He's also extremely down-to-earth and nice to deal with." **Recent work:** Acted for New World Resources on its restructuring of bond debt via a scheme of arrangement.

JUNIORS

Hilary Stonefrost (see p.774) Specialises in insolvency, restructuring and company law work. She is often instructed in breach of directors' duties and scheme of arrangement cases. **Strengths:** "A highly persuasive advocate who is very calm." "A solicitors' favourite."

Band 4

Enterprise Chambers

See profile on p.950

THE SET

Enterprise Chambers has solid expertise in a range of company law issues, and is an expert in insolvency and restructuring cases. Its members are often instructed in high-profile disputes, and the chambers is seen as a more than credible alternative to the larger sets. Individuals here have, over the years, acted in a number of leading and precedent-setting company law cases such as Re: Eagle Star Insurance and, more recently, ORB v Ruhan.

Client service: Clients are particularly impressed by the responsiveness of the clerks at Enterprise Chambers. Antony Armstrong is the senior clerk.

SILKS

Bernard Weatherill QC A seasoned silk who has an impressive commercial chancery practice. He often takes instructions concerning shareholder and boardroom disputes. **Strengths:** "He is really good – he's technically thorough, user-friendly and not afraid to get stuck into big difficult cases. He's a sophisticated fighter who is very commercial." **Recent work:** Acted in Dorothy Grieg v Matthew Lauchlan & Others, a case where the claimant alleges their shareholdings in companies were transferred by misrepresentations and under undue influence.

JUNIORS

Linden Ife An experienced junior who often handles shareholders' disputes. Her clients include well-known banks and she has particular expertise in the legality of dividends. **Strengths:** "A barrister who shows plenty of fight when in the courtroom." **Recent work:** She represented JD 51 in a dispute against its parent company and a former director which brought up questions around the lawfulness of dividends and breach of directors' duties.

Niall McCulloch He is regularly instructed in company restructuring matters involving entities in the insurance sector, and has appeared in a number of reported cases. **Strengths:** "He is responsive, very perceptive and his analysis of the law is very, very good." **Recent work:** Acted for Aiteal in a breach of fiduciary case concerning distributions made before and after the company went insolvent.

One Essex Court

See profile on p.833

THE SET

One Essex Court is a fine choice for disputes concerning the Companies Act. Its members, who have in-depth knowledge of the Companies Act and the Insolvency Act, are well positioned to tackle both domestic and cross-border cases. They act for a wide-ranging client base that includes shareholders, auditors, directors, liquidators and well-known corporations, among others. Of late, they have been handling a good deal of work arising from the global banking crisis, tackling cases involving failed financial institutions and funds. By way of example, they were heavily involved in the Lehman litigation. Other recent cases include the dispute between Liverpool Football Club and Hicks and Gillett.

Client service: The clerks, led by Darren Burrows, are particularly well thought of and are noted for being very proactive.

SILKS

Anthony de Garr Robinson QC (see p.631) A highly regarded silk with a broad commercial chancery practice. He appears in High Court, Appellate Court and international arbitration proceedings. **Strengths:** "An incisive advocate with a brilliant mind." **Recent work:** Appeared in Sir Owen Glenn & Kea Investment Limited v Eric Watson & Others, a shareholder dispute concerning a £130 million investment company.

Edmund Nourse QC (see p.728) A respected silk who is an experienced litigator and arbitrator. He focuses on company, insolvency and fraud disputes. **Strengths:** "He is very charming, and clear, punchy and concise in his submissions." **Recent work:** Acted for the Barclay brothers in a dispute relating to the ownership of several well-known hotels.

JUNIORS

Sam O'Leary (see p.729) A versatile junior who is experienced in company and banking law claims. He is frequently instructed in shareholder disputes. **Strengths:** "Very bright" and "very creative in his approach." **Recent work:** Successfully acted for the defendants in Arbuthnott v Bonnyman and Others, a Section 994 petition proceeding.

New Square Chambers

See profile on p.882

THE SET

New Square Chambers has a solid profile in company law and its members are often instructed in international disputes such as shareholder claims. The set houses practitioners who also handle non-contentious work including capital reductions and schemes of arrangement. Commentators say the barristers are "great to deal with" and "easily accessible." **Client service:** "The clerking, led by Phil Reeves, has always been pretty good. They are flexible and reasonably efficient."

SILKS

Robin Hollington QC A leading company and insolvency litigator with over 35 years' experience in the field. He has an excellent reputation in shareholder disputes and has written numerous books on the subject. **Strengths:** "The leading expert in shareholder disputes." "What he doesn't know about company law, you can write on the back of a stamp." **Recent work:** Acted for an Asian hedge fund in an unfair prejudice claim brought by a shareholder.

JUNIORS

David Eaton Turner (see p.639) A respected senior junior with an impressive company, insolvency and commercial law practice. He often acts in cases involving shareholder disputes and reorganisations of capital. **Strengths:** "Very conscientious, bright and pleasant to work with." **Recent work:** Represented a majority shareholder in a dispute against a minority shareholder concerning issues around entitlement to dividends, among others.

Sebastian Prentis An experienced barrister with a focus on shareholder disputes. He has appeared in a number of reported cases. **Strengths:** "He is charming, very bright and cuts through the detail." **Recent work:** Acted for the director of Selby Salads, a supplier of salads to Tesco, in an unfair prejudice claim.

Simon Adamyk Regularly instructed in high-value disputes, he is particularly active in international jurisdictions, including the British Virgin Islands and the Bahamas. **Strengths:** "He has a keen analytical mind, is commercial and is very good at advising on tactics." **Recent work:** Represented a Bahraini company in a dispute with two Saudi Arabian companies concerning a joint venture franchise of football schools in the Middle East and North Africa.

James Bailey Has a broad commercial chancery practice and often appears in company disputes. He is particularly experienced at representing hedge funds and private equity firms. **Strengths:** "His technical ability is excellent, and he is very good at complex and detailed cases involving lots of numbers." **Recent work:** Acted in Thevarajah v Riordan and

Others, a dispute in the Supreme Court arising from a share sale agreement.

Wilberforce Chambers
See profile on p.925
THE SET
Wilberforce Chambers is a highly regarded chancery set with a growing presence in the company law arena. The set is highlighted for the breadth of its members' practices, who handled a range of advisory and contentious matters, both in UK and international courts.
Client service: "The clerks, led by Mark Rushton, are always very professional and accommodating. The are willing to always go the extra mile to accommodate the client's requirements."

SILKS
Terence Mowschenson QC An esteemed silk with an outstanding reputation in company disputes. He is often instructed in cases concerning shareholder claims and agreements. **Strengths:** "A consummate gentleman who is lovely to work with and tenacious in his views. He shows incredible client loyalty."

Lexa Hilliard QC A well-regarded silk who frequently handles claims relating to company and insolvency law. She regularly acts in cross-border shareholder disputes. **Strengths:** "She is extremely practical, gets along really well with clients and is respected by the bench."

Marcia Shekerdemian QC Enjoys a busy company practice which is complemented well by her work in insolvency and restructuring cases. She regularly advises on domestic and international disputes. **Strengths:** "She is a powerhouse. She is fair, knowledgeable and very practical in terms of understanding the outcomes rather then being esoteric about the law." **Recent work:** Acted for the administrators of The Black Ant Company on a £13 million dispute which raised issues around the Land Registration Act of 2002, among others.

JUNIORS
Max Mallin An experienced senior junior with a wide-ranging commercial chancery practice. He is regularly instructed in company law matters including Section 994 petitions and breach of fiduciary duty claims. **Strengths:** "Clear and effective in court."

Other Ranked Lawyers

Andreas Gledhill QC (Blackstone Chambers) Handles disputes centred on commercial, restructuring, financial services and company law. He regularly undertakes claims arising from share sale agreements and share valuations. **Strengths:** "He is really practical, always responsive, available 24/7, and is someone who provides advice in a well thought through manner." **Recent work:** Acted in Glengary Overseas Ltd v JKX Oil Gas, a Supreme Court appeal that raised questions over the scope of directors' fiduciary powers.

Michael Green QC (see p.659) (Fountain Court Chambers) Excellent choice for commercial disputes involving company and insolvency issues. He is increasingly active in international matters, handling cases in the Cayman Islands and Uganda. **Strengths:** "Great on shareholder disputes, he appeals to judges due to his soft-spoken approach and brilliant grasp of the arguments." **Recent work:** Acted for the liquidators of CLICO Investment Bank handling several matters including claims for breach of fiduciary duty.

Alex Barden (see p.589) (Fountain Court Chambers) Regularly instructed in disputes involving financial institutions. He is experienced in claims arising from shareholders' agreements, takeovers and joint ventures. **Strengths:** "He's very good on the technical side and great at giving guidance as to what the court will or will not most likely care about." **Strengths:** Acted in Liontrust v Flanagan, a dispute raising issues concerning limited liability partnership agreements.

Bridget Lucas (see p.704) (Fountain Court Chambers) A talented junior who is particularly active in international cases. Her areas of focus include boardroom and shareholder disputes. **Strengths:** "A great team player who is approachable, commercial and very knowledgeable." **Recent work:** Acted for the defendant in Griffin v Wainwright, a Section 994 shareholders' dispute.

David Lascelles (see p.696) (Littleton Chambers) Particularly active in contentious matters, and regularly called upon to handle shareholder disputes and claims arising from share sales. **Strengths:** "He is just a really easy guy to get on with. He is extremely bright and very user-friendly." **Recent work:** Acted in Knott & Others v Watts PLC where he defended shareholders against claims of breaches of shareholders' agreement.

Tina Kyriakides (Radcliffe Chambers) Her broad practice encompasses insolvency, banking and company law. She often handles derivative claims and winding-up petitions. **Strengths:** "She has an encyclopaedic knowledge of company law procedure." **Recent work:** Advised a shareholder with regard to a Section 994 claim against a fellow shareholder alleging exclusion from management and misappropriation of monies.

MIDLANDS

Company	
Leading Sets	
Band 1	
No5 Chambers *	
St Philips Chambers *	
Leading Silks	
Band 1	
Anderson Mark	*No5 Chambers* Ⓐ
Pepperall Edward	*St Philips Chambers* *
Band 2	
Khangure Avtar	*St Philips Chambers*
Randall John	*St Philips Chambers* *
Zaman Mohammed	*No5 Chambers*
Leading Juniors	
Band 1	
Mitchell David	*No5 Chambers* Ⓐ
Morgan James	*St Philips Chambers* *
Najib Shakil	*No5 Chambers*

** Indicates set / individual with profile.*
Ⓐ direct access (see p.24).
Alphabetical order within each band. Band 1 is highest.

Band 1

No5 Chambers
See profile on p.931
THE SET
No5 Chambers has a broad company law practice and its members are instructed in all kinds of partner, director and shareholder disputes. The set has traditionally acted for local SMEs in contentious matters but has more recently expanded its portfolio to include listed companies and international corporates, and now performs a significant quantity of advisory work. One interviewee says: "We really enjoy using them."
Client service: "The clerks are very accommodating. They will go out of their way to assist in whatever way they can, from rearranging diaries to delivering papers back to my office after a conference, and they are very flexible on fees." Tony McDaid is the set's practice director.

SILKS
Mohammed Zaman QC Maintains a diverse and international practice. He is regularly instructed to advise on high-value commercial disputes, including those with an element of partnership or property law. **Strengths:** "He is a pre-eminent person in Birmingham for dealing with shareholder and company disputes. First-class."

Mark Anderson QC A heavyweight chancery and commercial silk with an established company law practice. He specialises in the resolution of complex disputes for blue-chip and multinational clients. **Strengths:** "He is very capable intellectually, tenacious and pugnacious – a courtroom performer who likes to win." **Recent work:** Appeared before the Court of Appeal in Barrett v Treatt, a claim for earn-out.

JUNIORS
David Mitchell A sought-after chancery junior who often acts in complex litigation and cases involving large corporations. **Strengths:** "He is very client-friendly and gives good, strategic advice. He is available and helpful to instructing solicitors." **Recent work:** Advised on a Section 994 petition and related matters in Carver v Carver, involving a family-owned business worth £10 million.

Shakil Najib Experienced in company, partnership and insolvency litigation with a specialism in unfair prejudice disputes. **Strengths:** "He's very clear, pragmatic, commercially astute and very driven to achieving a good result." **Recent work:** Represented the defendant company in a £1 million claim for alleged breach of a share sale agreement.

St Philips Chambers
See profile on p.934
THE SET
St Philips Chambers is a prestigious name in company law on the Midland Circuit, and its members are instructed on behalf of public and private companies, their shareholders and directors. Some accept instructions directly in relation to matters falling under the Public Access Scheme. The set is experienced in both contentious and non-contentious law,

and is able to advise and represent parties in litigation.

Client service: "Their clerking is very good. They are responsive, easy to contact and helpful." Joe Wilson is the chief clerk and acting CEO at the set.

SILKS

Edward Pepperall QC (see p.736) An experienced litigator with a formidable specialism in complex shareholder disputes. **Strengths:** "He is an exceptional advocate with unparalleled expertise in obtaining injunctive relief." "He is user-friendly and fantastic in front of clients."

Avtar Khangure QC A well-regard silk with a broad company law practice. He has considerable expertise in shareholder disputes, claims for breach of duty and corporate restructurings. **Strengths:** "He's very good on his feet; his strength is his advocacy and the manner in which he comes across in court."

John Randall QC (see p.748) An accomplished chancery and commercial silk with a reputation for excellence in company law matters. He is noted for his experience in high-value and lengthy trials. **Strengths:** "He manages to combine an encyclopaedic knowledge of the law with a first-rate appreciation of strategy and excellent eye for detail." **Recent work:** Appeared before the Court of Appeal in Hague Plant v Hague, involving claims for breach of duty by directors.

JUNIORS

James Morgan (see p.721) A formidable chancery and commercial junior with deep knowledge of company law matters. **Strengths:** "He is very clever and applies himself well to disputes." **Recent work:** Acted for the claimant and third parties in Dickinson v NAL Realisations, a liquidation case involving a £2 million counterclaim against company directors.

NORTHERN

Company
Leading Sets
Band 1
Kings Chambers *
Leading Silks
Band 1
Casement David *Kings Chambers* *
Chaisty Paul *Kings Chambers* *

Band 1

Kings Chambers

See profile on p.968

THE SET

Kings Chambers is widely recognised as the preeminent set for company law work on the Northern Circuit. Its members have experience of handling matters from shareholder disputes to unfair prejudice actions, and are often instructed in substantial litigation for large companies.

SILKS

David Casement QC (see p.612) Go-to commercial chancery silk with a substantial arbitration practice and a reputation for excellence in complex litigation. **Strengths:** "He has an affable personality, allied with a great ability to absorb complex facts and give clear advice, especially on matters involving shareholder disputes or insolvency." **Recent work:** Acted for the band New Order in a claim for breach of fiduciary duty brought by a former member.

Paul Chaisty QC (see p.614) Well-regarded commercial and chancery practitioner with particular experience of unfair prejudice actions. Called to the Bars of the British Virgin Islands and the Bahamas. **Recent work:** Acted for the appellant in Sugarman v CJS Investments, a dispute over the construction of the company articles of association.

WESTERN

Company
Leading Sets
Band 1
Guildhall Chambers *
St John's Chambers *
Leading Silks
Band 1
Sims Hugh *Guildhall Chambers*
Leading Juniors
Band 1
Ascroft Richard *Guildhall Chambers*
Marsden Andrew *Commercial Chambers (ORL)* ◊ [A]
Band 2
Bamford Jeremy *Guildhall Chambers*
Dickinson John FH *St John's Chambers* [A] *
Pearce-Smith James *St John's Chambers*
* *Indicates set / individual with profile.*
[A] *direct access (see p.24).*
◊ *(ORL) = Other Ranked Lawyer.*
Alphabetical order within each band. Band 1 is highest.

Band 1

Guildhall Chambers

See profile on p.938

THE SET

Guildhall Chambers is highly regarded for its expertise in advocacy, advisory and drafting work concerning a broad range of company matters. The Bristol-based set offers an experienced bench of barristers who have garnered market-wide respect for their handling of shareholder disputes, matters concerning breach of directors' duties and the interpretation and drafting of shareholder agreements, among others.

Client service: "They have a very varied and wide range of expertise, and a range of different levels of seniority which can be very helpful. They're very cohesive – they work very well together and get on in a business way." Mike Norton is the set's senior commercial clerk.

SILKS

Hugh Sims QC A silk with a highly reputable practice in general commercial and insolvency work. His areas of focus and recognised expertise include company disputes, breach of fiduciary duties on behalf of directors and unfair prejudice disputes. **Strengths:** "He is an extremely good advocate in court and has a very nice style about him. He is quite persuasive." "He is absolutely brilliant on his feet, he is also incredibly good at drafting and he's very good in negotiations." **Recent work:** Acted for the applicant in a case concerning the Sherlock Holmes Society. This was a dispute regarding the rights of the purported director of the company to bring an appeal against a winding-up petition.

JUNIORS

Richard Ascroft Particularly well known for his work in shareholder disputes and internal mismanagement matters. He has specialised knowledge in directors' duties-related claims, and frequently acts for a diverse range of clients from charitable foundations to governmental bodies. **Strengths:** "He's a good advocate, he fights hard for his client and he's good at legal analysis as well." "He's very commercially minded. He gives the advice your clients need to hear, not what they want to hear." **Recent work:** Acted in Holland & Watts Ltd v Fiander Tovell LLP, a case concerning financial assistance for the acquisition of shares and the availability of a 'whitewash' procedure.

Jeremy Bamford Considered an expert in both non-contentious company advisory work and litigation, frequently handling cases involving unfair prejudice and directors' disqualifications, among others. Offers further experience in insolvency law, and works with a number of collapsed companies on a variety of legal matters. **Strengths:** "He's very, very good." "He's very meticulous but he's got a quiet authority that judges find quite seductive and persuasive. He's very good in cross-examinations and he's a very good advocate." **Recent work:** Acted for HMRC in the Lotus F1 Team case, a dispute concerning the team's recent financial difficulties.

St John's Chambers

See profile on p.941

THE SET

St John's Chambers is one of Bristol's leading sets of chambers for company advisory and advocacy work, with its barristers obtaining regular instruction in shareholder disputes, directors' duties and directors' disqualification cases. The set is praised by sources for its provision of "commercially minded advice" and the "professional and incredibly flexible" attitude of its barristers.

Client service: "Their clerks and support team are definitely up there with the best in terms of their knowledge of their own members, their recommendations and their overall attitude." The clerking team is led by Robert Bocock.

JUNIORS

John Dickinson (see p.633) Recognised for his extensive background in accountancy, Dickinson is a popular choice for a number of financial services clients, who instruct him on a range of company matters. **Strengths:** "He's very thorough and conscientious." "He is extremely user-friendly."

James Pearce-Smith Maintains a strong reputation as "an exceptional talent" in professional negligence claims and partnership disputes. Gains further recognition for his expertise in real property and insolvency work, and regularly handles cases spanning multiple legal practice areas. **Strengths:** "He's got very good attention to detail, and he provides very clear and easy-to-follow advice." "He's an exceptional junior; he's very thorough, he gives really good commercial advice and has an excellent rapport with clients. He's very savvy and a really good technical lawyer." **Recent work:** Advised a charitable company and its trustees in Whitehouse v West Somerset Railway Association, a case concerning ex-members of the association seeking injunctions for claims relating to expulsion from the membership.

Other Ranked Lawyers

Andrew Marsden (Commercial Chambers) Held in high regard for his deeply specialised company and commercial practice, he is highly sought after for instruction in disputes involving shareholders and directors of SMEs from a range of sectors. Described by sources as the "go-to guy in regional litigation," Marsden garners additional praise from his peers for his position in the Bristol market as "a genuine specialist in commercial work." **Strengths:** "He's very accessible, very commercial in terms of his advice, and a bit of a knife fighter in court." "He's very experienced – he's got the advantage of his previous life as a solicitor so he knows what the clients want." **Recent work:** Advised a hotel development group in Griffith v Gourgey and Others, a case concerning alleged unfair prejudice.

Contents:

LONDON

Competition Law
Leading Sets
Band 1
Brick Court Chambers *
Monckton Chambers *
Band 2
Blackstone Chambers *
Band 3
One Essex Court *
Senior Statesmen
Senior Statesmen: distinguished older partners
Vaughan David *Brick Court Chambers*
Leading Silks
Star individuals
Beard Daniel *Monckton Chambers*
Turner Jon *Monckton Chambers*
Band 1
Brealey Mark *Brick Court Chambers*
Davies Helen *Brick Court Chambers*
de la Mare Thomas *Blackstone Chambers*
Demetriou Marie *Brick Court Chambers*
Flynn James *Brick Court Chambers*
Hoskins Mark *Brick Court Chambers* *
Jowell Daniel *Brick Court Chambers* *
Morris Stephen *20 Essex Street (ORL)* ◊
Rose Dinah *Blackstone Chambers*
Sharpe Thomas *One Essex Court*
Thompson Rhodri *Matrix Chambers (ORL)* ◊
Ward Tim *Monckton Chambers* [A] *
Band 2
Bacon Kelyn *Brick Court Chambers*
Beal Kieron *Blackstone Chambers*
Carss-Frisk Monica *Blackstone Chambers*
Harris Paul *Monckton Chambers*
Howard Mark *Brick Court Chambers*
Peretz George *Monckton Chambers*
Pickford Meredith *Monckton Chambers* [A]
Quigley Conor *Serle Court (ORL)* ◊
Randolph Fergus *Brick Court Chambers*
Robertson Aidan *Brick Court Chambers*
Saini Pushpinder *Blackstone Chambers*
Smith Kassie *Monckton Chambers*
Stratford Jemima *Brick Court Chambers*
New Silks
Kennelly Brian *Blackstone Chambers*
Lee Sarah *Brick Court Chambers*
Lester Maya *Brick Court Chambers* *
** Indicates set / individual with profile.*
[A] direct access (see p.24).
◊ (ORL) = Other Ranked Lawyer.
Alphabetical order within each band. Band 1 is highest.

Band 1

Brick Court Chambers
See profile on p.816
THE SET
Brick Court Chambers is a top-flight competition set offering strength in depth at all levels of seniority. The barristers act on all aspects of competition law, including private damages actions and investigations, and appear for claimants and defendants. Top-level solicitors regularly instruct them on behalf of market-leading corporates; they also represent

Competition Law
Leading Juniors
Star individuals
Holmes Josh *Monckton Chambers*
Band 1
Ford Sarah *Brick Court Chambers*
Kreisberger Ronit *Monckton Chambers*
O'Donoghue Robert *Brick Court Chambers*
Piccinin Daniel *Brick Court Chambers*
Singla Tony *Brick Court Chambers* *
Band 2
Bailey David *Brick Court Chambers*
Brown Christopher *Matrix Chambers (ORL)* ◊
Gregory Julian *Monckton Chambers*
Howard Anneli *Monckton Chambers* [A] *
Jones Tristan *Blackstone Chambers*
Lask Ben *Monckton Chambers* [A]
Lindsay Alistair *Monckton Chambers* [A]
Love Sarah *Brick Court Chambers*
Patton Conall *One Essex Court* *
Rayment Ben *Monckton Chambers* [A]
Segan James *Blackstone Chambers*
Williams Rob *Monckton Chambers*
Band 3
Abram Sarah *Brick Court Chambers*
Bates Alan *Monckton Chambers* [A] *
Berridge Alison *Monckton Chambers*
Blackwood Anneliese *Monckton Chambers*
Boyd Jessica *Blackstone Chambers*
Cook Matthew *One Essex Court*
Draper Owain *One Essex Court* *
Gibson Nicholas *Matrix Chambers (ORL)* ◊
John Laura Elizabeth *Monckton Chambers*
Quirk Iain *Essex Court Chambers (ORL)* ◊
Scannell David *Brick Court Chambers*
Spitz Derek *One Essex Court*
Wakefield Victoria *Brick Court Chambers*
West Colin *Brick Court Chambers*
Woolfe Philip *Monckton Chambers* *
Up-and-coming individuals
Mussa Hanif *Blackstone Chambers*
Osepciu Ligia *Monckton Chambers*

competition regulators. Members have appeared on both sides of the leading cases of Emerald Supplies v British Airways and Unwired Planet v Samsung and Huawei. Sources say: "Brick Court has an extremely strong market offering at all levels from junior to leading counsel."

Client service: "The clerking is first-rate. They have a better understanding of costs and client demands than most, and do a good job of getting the barristers on board." Senior clerks Julian Hawes and Ian Moyler head the clerking team.

SILKS

David Vaughan QC An eminent figure and well respected by instructing solicitors. He has immense experience in all aspects of competition law. **Strengths:** "He is superb – top of his field."

Mark Brealey QC Well regarded for his work on follow-on damages actions as well as cases at the IP/competition law interface. He is experienced before both UK and EU courts. **Strengths:** "Displays all-round excellence in court and in conference." **Recent work:** He acted for Sainsbury's against MasterCard and Visa pursuing damages claims based on the allegation that the interchange fees charged by MasterCard and Visa breached competition law.

Helen Davies QC Acts in front of European and UK courts on cartels, abuse of dominance and regulatory appeals, among other things. She is admired by instructing solicitors for her broad expertise. **Strengths:** "She is utterly fantastic and absolutely cuts to the chase. She is pragmatic, strategic and terrific." **Recent work:** She acted for Servier on its defence against claims in excess of £300 million alleging anti-competitive agreements and abuse of its dominant position in relation to the blockbuster drug Perindopril.

Marie Demetriou QC Has acted recently on merger-related cases and follow-on damages actions, appearing for claimants and defendants. She has been recently appointed as Standing Counsel to the CMA. **Strengths:** "She carries immense authority in the field of competition litigation and is well known and respected by competition law practitioners. It is very good to be seen having her fighting on your side." **Recent work:** She represented the CMA in SCOP v CMA before the Supreme Court regarding the scope of the CMA's merger jurisdiction.

James Flynn QC Highly respected for his work in follow-on and standalone damages claims, IP interface cases and cartel cases. **Strengths:** "He is very user-friendly, and an iron fist in a velvet glove." **Recent work:** He advised GE and Skadden Arps on an EC oral hearing related to the GE/Alstom merger.

Mark Hoskins QC (see p.675) Highly regarded advocate praised for his user-friendly style. He has acted on numerous leading cases in abuse of dominance, cartels and market investigations. **Strengths:** "Mark is very succinct and to the point in his advice and submissions to the court. He's technically excellent and a very effective advocate." **Recent work:** He represented Streetmap in a claim for damages against Google in the High Court alleging anti-competitive practices in the way Google operates its search engine.

Daniel Jowell QC (see p.687) A popular choice among leading competition law firms who use him for their most challenging cases. He is often instructed by claimants and defendants in cartel damages cases. **Strengths:** "He is a really excellent advocate. One of the things that he brings to cases is a broader commercial experience." **Recent work:** He acted as leading counsel for Scott & Scott as claimant in an action for damages arising from the foreign exchange cartel.

Kelyn Bacon QC Esteemed by peers and instructing solicitors for her state aid expertise. She is also experienced in pharmaceutical sector cases and investigations and damages claims. **Strengths:** "She is a clear and forceful drafter, and has a very sharp conceptual intellect." **Recent work:** She was appointed as Advocate to the Supreme Court for CMA v SCOP, a case concerning the scope of the CMA's merger control jurisdiction.

Mark Howard QC Receives praise for his ability on highly technical cases. Howard has recently appeared for a number of defendants in follow-on damages litigation. **Strengths:** "A cool customer who gets his point across beautifully" and "blows the opposition away."

Fergus Randolph QC Has recently represented claimants in cartel follow-on damages claims. He is also experienced in acting for clients on behavioural mandates before the EC. **Strengths:** "He is approachable, hands-on, makes himself available and is very user-friendly." **Recent work:** He acted for Arcadia and Others on Arcadia and Others v MasterCard and Arcadia and Others v Visa, a follow-on cartel damages case stemming from MasterCard's and Visa's charging of interchange fees.

Aidan Robertson QC Has long-standing expertise in innovative competition cases. He acts for claimants and defendants in damages claims. **Strengths:** "Aidan is outstanding in every way. His advice is invariably precise and on point, and his advocacy skills are second to none." **Recent work:** He acted for intervener BMA on a judicial review challenge brought by AXA PPP against the CMA's report on private healthcare.

Jemima Stratford QC Renowned for her expertise in FRAND licensing disputes and telecoms, she has notable recent experience of appearing in the leading cases in these fields. **Strengths:** "She is a very capable leader of a team and gives good direction." **Recent work:** She acted for Unwired Planet in Unwired Planet v Samsung and Huawei, a case regarding licensing fees for mobile phone technology.

Sarah Lee QC Has particular expertise in the telecoms sector. She is also experienced in state aid and damages cases. **Strengths:** "User-friendly, pleasant to deal with and someone who understands the commercial imperative behind a case." **Recent work:** She represented the UK government in Vitesse v Commission, a state aid case concerning a decision to approve UK aid for broadband.

Maya Lester QC (see p.700) Appears frequently in competition damages cases, both follow-on and standalone, covering cartels and abuse of dominance. She is particularly experienced in judicial reviews of competition decisions. **Strengths:** "She is particularly good on complex cases, and very positive and definitive on points of law." **Recent work:** She acted for Streetmap on Streetmap v Google, a high-profile standalone abuse of dominance damages claim relating to Google's behaviour with regard to its internet search and mapping services.

JUNIORS

Sarah Ford A popular choice for follow-on cartel damages litigation having appeared, at times unled, in some of the seminal cases in this field. Her advocacy is universally praised. **Strengths:** "She is extremely good on her feet and deals with difficult questions calmly and with confidence." **Recent work:** Acted in Air Canada & Others v Emerald Supplies Ltd & Others, appearing for various non-addressee airlines in an appeal to the Court of Appeal concerning disclosure of the confidential version of a Commission decision finding an infringement of EU competition law.

Robert O'Donoghue Has practised as a solicitor in both London and Brussels. He is well regarded for his expertise in abuse of dominance cases. **Strengths:** "He has an excellent intellect and analytical capabilities, as well as deep understanding of competition law and practice. He's clear when explaining things and great on his feet." **Recent work:** He represented Google in litigation brought by Foundem claiming damages for an alleged abuse of dominance by Google with respect to the online search market.

Daniel Piccinin A former solicitor who has been involved in complex cartel damages cases and investigations, as well as cases dealing with the interface of competition and IP law. He is notably strong on the economic aspects of competition law. **Strengths:** "He is a first-class advocate who is very good with clients. Daniel works well with all levels of lawyer and will rise through the ranks." **Recent work:** Alongside Stephen Morris QC, Daniel Jowell QC and Anneli Howard he is representing Visa Europe, defending against 16 separate groups of claimants who are claiming damages as a result of Visa's charging of interchange fees.

Tony Singla (see p.766) Experienced at acting for defendants and claimants in cartel damages proceedings as well as appeals against regulators' decisions. His drafting is frequently praised by instructing solicitors as being of the highest standard. **Strengths:** "He is very good at client service and is responsive – he is very effective." **Recent work:** Led by Mark Hoskins QC, he acted for Vodafone in Vodafone v Infineon, a claim for cartel damages relating to the smart chips cartel.

David Bailey Has experience of appearing before all key competition tribunals and courts. He is one of the Standing Counsel to the CMA and is a respected academic. **Strengths:** "He has a really impressive legal mind, is extremely well organised, and is someone who always keeps to deadlines, no matter what the circumstances. He has a remarkable ability to synthesise and simplify things." **Recent work:** He represented the EC unled against Ranbaxy in Ranbaxy's appeal against the EC's 'pay for delay' decision.

Sarah Love Experienced in competition appeals as well as follow-on damages litigation. She benefits from her experience as a research economist. **Strengths:** "She produces particularly good written work and has excellent client-handling skills." **Recent work:** Led by Mark Brearley QC, she represented Sainsbury's in litigation brought against MasterCard claiming damages as a result of MasterCard's charging of interchange fees.

Sarah Abram Acts for both the CMA and private parties in cartel and abuse of dominance litigation. She has noted recent experience of handling matters in the technology and life sciences sector. **Strengths:** "She has very fine analytical skills, is very responsive and has the ability to absorb and digest complex facts and issues very rapidly." **Recent work:** Led by Mark Hoskins QC, she acted for Panasonic in its appeal against an EC decision concerning the cathode ray tubes cartel.

David Scannell Has recently acted in numerous high-profile cases in the pharmaceuticals sector. He is experienced in cartel damages litigation as well as appeals of regulatory decisions. **Strengths:** "He is a very fine drafter and really gets things done." **Recent work:** Led by Helen Davies QC , he acted for Danfoss in follow-on damages litigation brought by Gorenje stemming from cartel behaviour in the refrigerator compressors market.

Victoria Wakefield Has been active of late in numerous cases before the European courts. She is also frequently instructed on advisory mandates. **Strengths:** "She is punchy – a great team player who it's great to work with. She gives as good as she gets even when confronting a silk." **Recent work:** Led by Mark Hoskins QC, she acted for Lupin on its action for annulment of the EC's Servier 'pay for delay' decision.

Colin West Has noted expertise in competition damages claims, which he handles as part of a broad commercial practice. He is experienced in both litigation and arbitration. **Strengths:** "He has got knowledge at his fingertips and adopts a good, robust style."

Monckton Chambers

See profile on p.877

THE SET

Monckton Chambers has an outstanding array of barristers who act across the full range of competition cases. Members represent both claimants and defendants in damages actions, and appear for both EU and UK competition regulators and prestigious corporations in investigations and judicial reviews. They have a loyal following of top-flight law firms and are often sought out by corporations for advisory mandates. Of late, barristers here have represented parties on both sides of Emerald Supplies v British Airways and the Visa and MasterCard litigations. One impressed source states: "They are really specialist in competition law and have a remarkable wealth of experience in this area."

Client service: "Senior clerk David Hockney is very responsive and easy to talk to regarding fees."

SILKS

Daniel Beard QC Exceptionally well regarded by instructing solicitors and peers alike, he has been acting in a wide array of the leading competition cases this year. He is expert in all aspects of competition law litigation including cartel damages, investigations and appeals. **Strengths:** "Daniel has a fantastic grip of detail and always takes a very strategic approach." **Recent work:** He acted for J.P. Morgan in the EC investigation into alleged cartel behaviour surrounding credit default swaps.

Jon Turner QC Has a wealth of experience of appearing before all competition tribunals and courts, and is an expert in arbitration. He has been active recently on numerous cartel damages cases for claimants and defendants, and has also been involved in investigations and abuse of dominance litigation. **Strengths:** "He is an extremely assured performer. Even when given an extremely testing time he does an excellent job." **Recent work:** Led Google's defence against a case brought by Streetmap claiming damages for alleged abuse of dominance in relation to Google's online search practices.

Tim Ward QC (see p.789) Acts frequently in damages cases and judicial reviews, and has recently advised on high-profile mergers. Commentators highlight his expertise in the regulated utilities space. **Strengths:** "He has lots of experience and is easy to work with. He is very flexible and brings new ideas to the party all the time." **Recent work:** He acted for Tesco in cartel damages litigation against MasterCard and Visa stemming from their charging of interchange fees.

Paul Harris QC A robust and persuasive litigator who has recently acted in merger-related litigation and cartel damages actions, as well as cases at the IP and competition law interface. He is renowned for his expertise in sports law. **Strengths:** "He is very commercial and understands the client's position. He is aggressive when he needs to be and can be very innovative as well."

George Peretz QC Represents a broad range of clients from private companies to government bodies and the EC. While known for his expertise in state aid, he has been active recently in cartel appeals. **Strengths:** "He is very attentive to detail while at the same time being able to take an overall view of the issues at stake. He manages to convey the crux of the case in a few simple words." **Recent work:** He acted for the EC in the appeals against decisions in the Lundbeck and Servier 'pay for delay' cases.

Meredith Pickford QC Receives universal praise for his grasp of complex economic evidence. He has acted in numerous high-profile cases spanning the full range of competition law. **Strengths:** "He is strong on the economics and the pure legal aspects of cases, and he is very user-friendly. He is an integral part of the team." **Recent work:** He represented Sky in Sky v Ofcom and BT, high-profile litigation surrounding access to sports rights and channels.

Kassie Smith QC Has experience of acting for defendants and claimants in competition damages cases. She has received notable instructions from competition regulators and has acted before both EU and UK courts. **Strengths:** "Very approachable and easy to get on with, she's very fast, clear and someone who cuts to the chase." **Recent work:** Led the team that acted for the Competition Commission in various appeals before the CAT and the Court of Appeal against the decision it handed down in its private healthcare market investigation.

JUNIORS

Josh Holmes Receives universal praise from instructing solicitors and peers for his work on some of the top cases in the area of competition law. He is experienced at acting before both EU and UK courts. **Strengths:** "He is very bright and personable, and fits into a team really well." **Recent work:** Led by Jon Turner QC, he defended Google against claims for damages by Streetmap alleging an abuse of dominance by Google in relation to search results.

Ronit Kreisberger Experienced in high-profile competition cases acting for both blue-chip corporate clients and regulators. She has recently advised on investigations and cartel damages claims. **Strengths:** "She is great to work with, a fantastic advocate and very, very determined." **Recent work:** She represented Merck in its appeal against the EC's Lundbeck 'pay for delay' decision.

Julian Gregory Has a broad practice covering the full range of competition law. He has noted expertise in the telecoms sector and has recently been active in damages cases and regulatory actions. **Strengths:** "He is very able and extremely good at grasping highly technical and complex legal issues."

Anneli Howard (see p.675) Advises both regulators and private companies on the full range of competition law cases. She has been active of late in cartel damages actions and regulatory investigations. **Strengths:** She is very clear, very personable and highly approachable." **Recent work:** Led by Stephen Morris QC and Daniel Jowell QC, she acted for Visa Europe on 15 sets of proceedings brought by retailers claiming damages for Visa's charging of interchange fees.

Ben Lask Expert in competition law with a focus on telecoms and broadcasting-related cases. **Strengths:** "He is personable and really heading for great things." **Recent work:** He represented BT in BT v Ofcom, an appeal in the CAT against a decision made by Ofcom concerning wholesale charges set by BT.

Alistair Lindsay A former solicitor who is lauded by peers and instructing solicitors alike for his expertise in merger control. He also acts in regulatory appeals and has a strong advisory practice. **Strengths:** "He has a very sharp intellect and fantastic technical knowledge." **Recent work:** He has been instructed by Freshfields to advise on the £12.5 billion acquisition of EE by BT.

Ben Rayment Acts in a wide range of competition cases relating to cartel damages, merger control and investigations. He is a former legal secretary to the CAT. **Strengths:** "Ben is a creative thinker and a very good strategist when it comes to planning litigation. He is exceptionally good at giving cases a more favourable angle that others have not seen." **Recent work:** He acted for the CMA on its appeal to the Supreme Court in the Groupe Eurotunnel v CMA matter concerning the scope of the CMA's merger review jurisdiction.

Rob Williams Has recently been appointed as Standing Counsel to the CMA. He has been instructed recently in major merger cases, investigations and damages litigation. **Strengths:** "He is a first-class competition law junior who is good at drafting, very user-friendly and good with clients. **Recent work:** He acted for the CMA on two challenges brought by Ryanair against a CMA decision ordering Ryanair to reduce its shareholding in Aer Lingus from 29% to 5%.

Alan Bates (see p.591) Receives praise for his work on regulatory challenges, acting for both regulators as well as private companies. He has notable expertise before EU and UK courts. He is also lauded for his state aid expertise. **Strengths:** "He gives extremely good advice and delivers it in a user-friendly way." **Recent work:** He acted unled for Whistl in proceedings challenging the Royal Mail's introduction of a new pricing system.

Alison Berridge A former magic circle solicitor who is highly esteemed for her expertise in merger control. She has been active of late in a number investigations. **Strengths:** "She is very bright and very calm, and has particular expertise in merger control." **Recent work:** Led by Daniel Beard QC, she acted for the CMA against Ryanair, defending its decision to force Ryanair to sell its stake in Aer Lingus.

Anneliese Blackwood Acts on numerous private damages actions, most frequently for claimants but also for defendants. She is often instructed by private companies and utilities regulators. **Strengths:** "She is excellent in conference and can talk on a practical as well as an intellectual level." **Recent work:** Led by Paul Harris QC, she has acted for Emerald Supplies on Emerald Supplies v British Airways, damages litigation stemming from the EC's air cargo cartel decision.

Laura Elizabeth John A highly valued junior who has notable expertise of representing claimants in competition damages claims. She receives praise from instructing solicitors for her work ethic and availability. **Strengths:** "She is exceptionally bright and hard-working, but also very practical and a really good team player. She has no ego and is lovely to work with." **Recent work:** She acted for Microsoft Mobile on its standalone claim against Sony Europe and others for damages as a result of alleged overcharging in the batteries market.

Philip Woolfe (see p.800) Acclaimed by sources for his expertise in telecoms mandates, he frequently acts on price regulation cases. He is also experienced in private damages actions. **Strengths:** "He is excellent, turns work around very quickly and is on top of all the detail." **Recent work:** He represented the Secretary of State for Health and Others v Servier in a claim for damages arising from 'pay for delay' agreements.

Ligia Osepciu Up-and-coming junior with a broad European law practice and notable expertise in competition cases. She has recently acted on damages actions and merger cases. **Strengths:** "Offers clear, easily digestible advice and makes complex issues appear straightforward." **Recent work:** Led by Daniel Beard QC, she acted for Scottish Power in Scottish Power v ABB, a multimillion-pound cartel damages claim stemming from the power cables cartel.

Band 2

Blackstone Chambers

See profile on p.813

THE SET

Blackstone Chambers is a well-regarded set with capabilities in a broad range of competition law cases. The set's recent activity has involved participation in cartel damages claims, investigations and judicial reviews. A popular choice for regulators, top-flight companies and leading law firms, the set is regularly instructed in high-profile matters. Recent cases include Hospital Corporation of America v CMA and Deutsche Bahn & Others v MasterCard & Others. Sources say the members here are "very strong technically and capable of absorbing complex economic arguments. They display an across-the-board willingness to dive into the details and offer the right mix of innovative and pragmatic advice." **Client service:** "They are well served by their clerks, who are first-rate." Senior clerk Gary Oliver heads the clerking team.

SILKS

Thomas de la Mare QC Most frequently seen advising claimants in competition damages actions, he is a barrister who is widely admired for his creativity and innovative thinking. **Strengths:** "He is a force of nature. Hugely enthusiastic, creative and hard-working, he's a very fluent and brave advocate." **Recent work:** He represented the claimants in damages proceedings against the banks that participated in the forex cartel.

Dinah Rose QC Has a broad competition, public and European law practice. She is experienced in cartel damages actions and regulatory investigations, and is widely acclaimed as a fearless advocate. **Strengths:** "She is just wonderful, as she is tenacious, utterly brilliant on her feet and focused on winning for her client." **Recent work:** She acted for Visa Europe in follow-on damages proceedings brought by multiple retailers that stemmed from Visa's charging of interchange fees.

Kieron Beal QC Experienced in follow-on and standalone competition damages claims most frequently acting for claimants. He also advises on investigations. **Strengths:** "He is calm and unflustered and provides sound and clear advice." **Recent work:** He acted for a number of claimants against Visa and MasterCard in actions claiming damages stemming from Visa and MasterCard's charging of interchange fees.

Monica Carss-Frisk QC Has a broad administrative and public law practice, and has noted expertise in the regulated utilities sector. **Strengths:** "She is very easy to work with and provides clear advice." **Recent work:** She acted for Somerfield on a judicial review seeking to recover a penalty it had paid to the OFT as part of an early resolution agreement in relation to alleged cartel activity.

Pushpinder Saini QC Active of late in damages actions, regulatory appeals and merger litigation. He has a broad European law practice and has notable expertise in telecoms. **Strengths:** "He is quick to understand the facts and issues in a complex case, adept at identifying points which others miss; he's an efficient and highly effective advocate." **Recent work:** He represented Ofcom in litigation brought by BT challenging Ofcom's determination that BT was charging for ethernet services.

Brian Kennelly QC New silk universally praised for his excellent advocacy, he draws praise for his telecoms expertise. He has a broad European law practice and is experienced in a broad range of competition law litigation. **Strengths:** "He is going to be a big star of the future. He's a very able advocate and a very brilliant barrister." **Recent work:** He represented Ranbaxy before the General Court challenging the EC's decision in relation to 'pay for delay' settlements.

JUNIORS

Tristan Jones Draws widespread praise from peers and instructing solicitors. He is best known for representing claimants in cartel damages actions but has also appeared recently in merger cases. **Strengths:** "He is brilliant to work with. He has an excellent grasp of the detail but, critically, also adopts a very sound and commercial approach." **Recent work:** Led by Kieron Beal QC, he is representing numerous claimants in litigation against MasterCard concerning claims of damages due to MasterCard's charging of interchange fees.

James Segan Has recently been instructed on cases in the telecoms, technology and sports sectors spanning a wide range of areas from the interface of competition and IP law to regulatory appeals. **Strengths:** "He is very commercial and realistic in his advice, and has no airs and graces. He never overplays his hand." **Recent work:** Led by Lord Pannick QC, he acted for Lafarge Tarmac Holding in its appeal against the Competition Commission's divestment order.

Jessica Boyd Frequently appears in regulatory appeals representing both claimants and regulators. She has recently been involved in cases in the healthcare and TMT sectors. **Strengths:** "She is extremely bright, very approachable and someone who takes the time to engage with you as part of a team. She's clear in both her thinking and her drafting." **Recent work:** She represented Ofcom before the CAT in Sky's appeal against Ofcom's 2010 Pay TV decision.

Hanif Mussa Up-and-coming junior lauded by instructing solicitors for his abilities and personability. He has been active of late in judicial reviews and cartel damages actions. **Strengths:** "He is incredibly clever and very thoughtful. He's also very easy to engage with and a pleasure to work alongside." **Recent work:** Led by Dinah Rose QC, he acted for Hospital Corporation of America International in its appeal against a CMA decision requiring it to divest itself of hospital facilities.

Band 3

One Essex Court

See profile on p.833

THE SET

A leading commercial set with a compact but highly regarded competition offering. Chambers advises a broad range of clients including defendants and claimants in damages claims, and appears for regulators and corporates in regulatory litigation. It also offers counsel on state aid matters. Members have broad commercial expertise that affords an extra angle to their competition advice that is appreciated by those who instruct them. Notable recent cases include the Visa and MasterCard interchange fee litigation and Emerald Supplies v British Airways.

Client service: "One Essex Court has clerks who are helpful and easy to get on with." Senior clerk Darren Burrows heads the clerking team.

SILKS

Thomas Sharpe QC Has a broad practice covering behavioural cases, investigations, state aid and merger proceedings. He has special expertise and much recent experience in the utilities sector. **Strengths:** "Tom has a formidable track record and is excellent at delivering what the client needs." **Recent work:** He represented Electricity North West in two appeals to the CMA in relation to price determinations made by the Gas and Electricity Markets Authority.

JUNIORS

Conall Patton (see p.734) An expert in competition law who also has a wider commercial practice. He has recently acted in high-profile cartel damages actions. **Strengths:** "Destined to be a name in shining lights, he's one of the best juniors at the Bar." **Recent work:** Led by Jon Turner QC, he acted for British Airways in its defence of follow-on cartel damages claims stemming from the EC's air cargo decision.

Matthew Cook Has a broad corporate and commercial practice and is gaining a strong reputation for competition litigation. He is notably active in follow-on damages cases. **Strengths:** "He has an excellent knowledge of the law and an impressive ability to assimilate complex information and get straight to the point. Matthew is charming and a real pleasure to work with." **Recent work:** He defended MasterCard against various retailers claiming damages as a result of MasterCard's charging of interchange fees.

Owain Draper (see p.636) Frequently acts and advises on competition issues that form part of larger commercial disputes. He has recent experience of handling damages litigation and offering merger control advice. **Strengths:** "He is an expert in competition law. A very good and able junior, he is calm, collected and easy to work with." **Recent work:** Led by Kassie Smith QC, he represented TomTom in a cartel damages claim against Samsung following on from the EC's LCD screen cartel decision.

Derek Spitz Particularly experienced in cartel damages litigation, he acts both for claimants and defendants. He has experience of acting in some of the leading cases in this field. **Strengths:** "He is very experienced and very able." **Recent work:** He acted, led by Mark Brealey QC, in a case concerning Sainsbury's claim for damages against MasterCard alleging that MasterCard's charging of interchange fees breached competition law.

Other Ranked Lawyers

Iain Quirk (Essex Court Chambers) Has a broad EU law practice of which competition law forms an important part. In addition, he is an experienced arbitrator. **Strengths:** "His pleadings are very strong and he is enjoyable to work with."

Stephen Morris QC (20 Essex Street) Experienced in follow-on cartel damages litigation, having acted in some of the seminal cases in the field. He has also appeared in cases concerning investigations and price fixing. **Strengths:** "He is excellent, incisive and client-friendly." **Recent work:** He acted for Visa Europe as lead counsel in claims for damages made by multiple retailers alleging that Visa's charging of interchange fees breached competition law.

Rhodri Thompson QC (Matrix Chambers) Has a broad competition and EU law practice, and notable expertise in cases concerning pricing abuses. He has recently been involved in telecoms and sports cases. **Strengths:** "A wise counsel who is unflappable. He sees the bigger picture and is a crucial sounding board when it comes to strategy." **Recent work:** He acted for the CMA in relation to appeals by Lafarge Tarmac Holdings and Hope Construction Materials against the CMA's decision to force the divestment of a cement plant.

Christopher Brown (Matrix Chambers) Experienced in competition damages cases as well as state aid in the sports sector. Sources highlight his experience as a referendaire to the CMA. He is also an active academic. **Strengths:** "His competition law knowledge is phenomenal." "He is flexible in that he gives up his time at very short notice and is highly pragmatic in terms of the advice he gives." **Recent work:** Represented numerous retailers against MasterCard and Visa in litigation claiming damages for the charging of interchange fees.

Nicholas Gibson (Matrix Chambers) Former solicitor acting for both corporate and public sector clients on the full gamut of competition cases including those with a criminal cartel element. **Strengths:** "He is a big asset to the case and is a veritable workhorse." **Recent work:** He acted for the owners of Coventry City FC on their appeal regarding £14.4 million alleged state aid paid by Coventry City Council.

Conor Quigley QC (Serle Court) Leading practitioner in the field of state aid. He has recently acted on cases in the industrial and oil and gas sectors. He is also an expert in tax and public procurement matters. **Strengths:** "He is the leading barrister in the area of state aid." **Recent work:** Represented Romanian aluminium producer ALRO in proceedings in the General Court. The case revolved around a decision of the EC to open an investigation into alleged state aid.

THE REGIONS

Competition Law
Leading Juniors
Band 1
Aldred Adam *Kings Chambers* *
Went David *Exchange Chambers* *
Band 2
Knibbe Jorren *Guildhall Chambers*
O'Regan Matthew *St John's Chambers*
* *Indicates individual with profile.*
Alphabetical order within each band. Band 1 is highest.

Ranked Lawyers

David Went (see p.792) (Exchange Chambers) Formerly a distinguished solicitor at Sidley Austin in London. He has experience in a broad range of competition law and is good on merger control, investigations and follow-on damages. **Strengths:** "For merger control David has a stellar background. He is a very able individual." **Recent work:** Acted for Nordfolien as Part 20 defendant in Bord na Mona v British Polythene Industries, a cartel damages claim following on from the EC's industrial bags decision.

Jorren Knibbe (Guildhall Chambers) Former solicitor at Osborne Clark, recently returned to the Bar, who advises on the full range of competition law. **Strengths:** "He has provided first-class advice and support."

Adam Aldred (see p.581) (Kings Chambers) Former solicitor advocate at Addleshaw Goddard with broad expertise in all aspects of competition law including investigations, appeals, behavioural mandates and mergers. **Strengths:** "He is a highly regarded individual, particularly for cases involving cartels." **Recent work:** He advised Clinigen on its £225 million acquisition of Idis Group Holdings.

Matthew O'Regan (St John's Chambers) Former partner at Burges Salmon who joined the Bar in 2015. He advises on a wide range of contentious and non-contentious competition law cases. **Strengths:** "He is quickly able to digest large amounts of information relating to very complex matters. His past experience as a solicitor means he is very pragmatic and proactive in his approach to advising clients." **Recent work:** He advised ALRO on an investigation by the Romanian Competition Council into contracts with Hidroelectrica.

Contents:

LONDON

Construction
Leading Sets
Band 1
Atkin Chambers *
Keating Chambers *
Band 2
4 Pump Court *
Band 3
Crown Office Chambers *
39 Essex Chambers *
4 New Square *
Band 4
Hardwicke *
* Indicates firm / individual with profile.
[A] direct access (see p.24).
◊ (ORL) = Other Ranked Lawyer.
Alphabetical order within each band. Band 1 is highest.

Construction	
Senior Statesmen	
Senior Statesmen: distinguished older partners	
Friedman David *4 Pump Court*	
Leading Silks	
Star individuals	Sears David *Crown Office Chambers*
Brannigan Sean *4 Pump Court* *	Sinclair Fiona *4 New Square* *
Catchpole Stuart *39 Essex Chambers*	Smith Joanna *Wilberforce Chambers (ORL)* ◊
McMullan Manus *Atkin Chambers*	**Band 3**
Streatfeild-James David *Atkin Chambers*	Boulding Philip *Keating Chambers* *
Taverner Marcus *Keating Chambers* *	Bowdery Martin *Atkin Chambers*
White Andrew *Atkin Chambers* *	Bowsher Michael *Monckton Chambers (ORL)* ◊ [A] *
Band 1	Cannon Mark *4 New Square* *
Baatz Nicholas *Atkin Chambers*	Cross James *4 Pump Court* *
Barwise Stephanie *Atkin Chambers* *	Fenwick Justin *4 New Square* *
Constable Adam *Keating Chambers* *	Fernyhough Richard *Keating Chambers* *
Darling Paul *Keating Chambers* *	Hannaford Sarah *Keating Chambers* *
Dennison Stephen *Atkin Chambers*	Hughes Adrian *39 Essex Chambers*
Dennys Nicholas *Atkin Chambers*	Lofthouse Simon *Atkin Chambers* *
Furst Stephen *Keating Chambers* *	Moran Vincent *Keating Chambers* *
Nissen Alexander *Keating Chambers* *	Parkin Fiona *Atkin Chambers*
Stewart Roger *4 New Square* *	Patten Ben *4 New Square* *
ter Haar Roger *Crown Office Chambers*	Speaight Anthony *4 Pump Court*
Thomas David *Keating Chambers* *	Stansfield Piers *Keating Chambers* *
Williamson Adrian *Keating Chambers* *	Walker Steven *Atkin Chambers* *
Wilmot-Smith Richard *39 Essex Chambers*	Wilken Sean *39 Essex Chambers* *
Band 2	**Band 4**
Acton Davis Jonathan *Atkin Chambers*	Black Michael *XXIV Old Buildings (ORL)* ◊
Ansell Rachel *4 Pump Court* *	Howells James *Atkin Chambers* *
Day Anneliese *4 New Square* *	Jefford Nerys *Keating Chambers*
Doerries Chantal-Aimée *Atkin Chambers* *	Jones Nigel *Hardwicke* [A]
Goddard Andrew *Atkin Chambers* *	Lemon Jane *Keating Chambers* *
Hargreaves Simon *Keating Chambers* *	McCredie Fionnuala *Keating Chambers* *
Hughes Simon *Keating Chambers* *	Mort Justin *Keating Chambers* *
Marrin John *Keating Chambers* *	Pilling Benjamin *4 Pump Court* *
McCall Duncan *4 Pump Court*	Quiney Ben *Crown Office Chambers*
Nicholson Jeremy *4 Pump Court* *	Smith Marion *39 Essex Chambers* *
O'Farrell Finola *Keating Chambers*	**New Silks**
Rawley Dominique *Atkin Chambers* *	Franklin Kim *Crown Office Chambers*
Reed Paul *Hardwicke* [A]	Hickey Alexander *4 Pump Court* *
Rigney Andrew *Crown Office Chambers*	Hussain Riaz *Atkin Chambers* *
Rowlands Marc *Keating Chambers* *	

Band 1

Atkin Chambers
See profile on p.806
THE SET
The set houses experienced barristers who offer substantial expertise across the full range of construction-related matters. Its members are ubiquitous in the sector and regularly represent prominent employers and contractors in top-end domestic and international disputes. Atkin's barristers are frequently active in large-scale ICC arbitration and TCC cases, such as Fluor v ZPMC and GUPC v Panama Canal Authority.
Client service: The clerking team is led by Justin Wilson. "Their clerks go above and beyond for you and are always thinking of new ways to help." "They've impressed me with their attentiveness and their fairness on fees."

SILKS
Nicholas Baatz QC A top-drawer barrister with significant expertise in construction cases, particularly those which involve either professional negligence or insurance elements. His intellectual prowess and attention to detail elicit significant praise from his contemporaries. **Strengths:** "He is an incisive silk who delivers robust advice and has a great manner with clients. Extremely clever." "Very friendly, personable and eager to help. He offers tactical, commercial and realistic options." **Recent work:** Represented CIP Properties in its £18 million claim against Galliford Try and other contractors. The matter concerned the allegedly defective design and construction of a shopping, leisure and residential complex in Birmingham.

Manus McMullan QC Star silk who draws praise for his advocacy skills and tactical nous. He regularly acts in high-value construction disputes and arbitrations around the world, and is particularly good at litigious infrastructure cases. **Strengths:** "A first-rate lawyer and advocate, who is very hard working and an excellent strategist." "He's just brilliant. Courteous, charming, witty and on top of it. A real star." **Recent work:** Appeared in a number of disputes arising from the Panama Canal expansion project. The claims included cost overruns and lengthy delays, and required intimate knowledge of Panamanian law."

David Streatfeild-James QC Highly lauded silk with a sector-wide reputation as a powerful and unyielding cross-examiner. He is routinely instructed on the most technically complex construction litigation and arbitration. **Strengths:** "He's a quick thinker and excellent on his feet: when he cross-examines in court, it's a joy to behold." "Gets to the heart of a matter quickly and always gives sound advice that you can rely on." **Recent work:** Represented Amey Local Government in two disputes against Cumbria County Council and Birmingham City Council. Both matters were PFI cases involving claims of defective road work.

Andrew White QC (see p.793) Considered by one interviewee to be "the God of construction law," he is a highly distinguished silk offering unparalleled advice across areas such as oil and gas and renewables. He regularly advises major clients in high-profile construction disputes at both the national and international level. **Strengths:** "He has a very commercial, pragmatic approach and gets to the heart of issues very quickly." "He's brilliant. A top advocate who always offers very high-quality advice." **Recent work:** Acted for Fluor in its USD400 million claim against Chinese contractor, ZPMC. The matter concerned faulty wind turbine parts in an offshore wind farm.

Stephanie Barwise QC (see p.591) Top-drawer silk who advises on high-value adjudications and TCC litigation. She has a diverse practice ranging across areas such as housing disputes and energy projects. **Strengths:** "Stephanie has the ability to make even the most stressed client feel at ease. When combined with her superb advocacy, this makes her a number one choice." "I've found her to have an excellent intellect and she's first class when it comes to building and maintaining client relationships." **Re-**

Construction Leading Juniors
Band 1
Ghaly Karim *39 Essex Chambers* *
Lamont Calum *Keating Chambers* *
Leabeater James *4 Pump Court* *
Lewis Christopher *Atkin Chambers* *
Livesey Kate *4 Pump Court* *
Robb Adam *39 Essex Chambers*
Selby Jonathan *Keating Chambers* *
Band 2
Bowling James *4 Pump Court* *
Buckingham Paul *Keating Chambers* *
Chennells Mark *Atkin Chambers*
Choat Rupert *Atkin Chambers* *
Collings Nicholas *Atkin Chambers* *
Coplin Richard *Keating Chambers* *
Fenn Andrew *Atkin Chambers* *
Garrett Lucy *Keating Chambers* *
Henderson Simon *4 Pump Court* *
Laney Anna *Crown Office Chambers*
McCafferty Lynne *4 Pump Court* *
Montagu-Smith Tom *XXIV Old Buildings (ORL)* ◊
Pimlott Charles *Crown Office Chambers*
Pliener David *Hardwicke* [A]
Slow Camille *Atkin Chambers* *
Stephens Jessica *4 Pump Court* *
Townend Samuel *Keating Chambers*
Webb William *Keating Chambers* *
Wheater Michael *Hardwicke*
Winser Crispin *Crown Office Chambers*
Band 3
Bodnar Alexandra *39 Essex Chambers* *
Chambers Gaynor *Keating Chambers* *
Clarke Patrick *Atkin Chambers* *
Clay Robert *Atkin Chambers*
Crangle Thomas *4 Pump Court* *
Grange Kate *39 Essex Chambers*
Jinadu Abdul *Keating Chambers* *
Jones Jennifer *Atkin Chambers* *
Lewis Jonathan *4 Pump Court* *
Medd James *Crown Office Chambers*
O'Hagan Rachael *39 Essex Chambers* *
Packman Claire *4 Pump Court* *
Piercy Catherine *Hardwicke*
Pigott Frances *Atkin Chambers* *
Scott Holland Gideon *Keating Chambers*
Sims Alice *Keating Chambers* *
Band 4
Briggs Lucie *Atkin Chambers* *
Cheng Serena *Atkin Chambers* *
Chern Cyril *Crown Office Chambers*
Connors Jess *39 Essex Chambers*
Cowan Paul J *4 New Square* *
Crawshaw Simon *Atkin Chambers* *
Davies Evans Jane *Crown Office Chambers* *
Evans Robert *Keating Chambers* *
Hanna Ronan *Atkin Chambers* *
Khayum Zulfikar *Atkin Chambers* *
Lazur Thomas *Keating Chambers* *
Lee Krista *Keating Chambers* *
Letman Paul *3 Hare Court (ORL)* ◊
Liddell Richard *4 New Square* *
McCann Sarah *Hardwicke* [A]
Neuberger Edmund *Atkin Chambers* *
Powell Katie *4 New Square* *
Shaw Annabel *4 New Square* *
Taylor Rebecca *Crown Office Chambers*
Thompson James *Keating Chambers* *
Williams Sarah *Keating Chambers* *
Wygas Luke *4 Pump Court* *
Up-and-coming individuals
Bury Paul *Keating Chambers* *
Conroy Brenna *Hardwicke*
Hennessey Patrick *39 Essex Chambers*
Johnson David *Atkin Chambers* *
Owen Tom *Keating Chambers* *
Sareen Ben *Keating Chambers* *
Sheard David *Keating Chambers* *

* Indicates individual with profile.
[A] direct access (see p.24).
◊ (ORL) = Other Ranked Lawyer.
Alphabetical order within each band. Band 1 is highest.

cent work: Defended Riversmead Housing against a termination fee claim brought by Liberty Gas, a contractor whose ten-year term had been shortened for convenience.

Stephen Dennison QC A prominent silk who is noted for his expertise in both domestic disputes and international arbitration. He is an experienced litigator who regularly acts for significant clients, particularly in the healthcare and engineering sectors. **Strengths:** "A clever strategist, a safe pair of hands and a pleasure to deal with." "He is able to grasp key issues very quickly. I enjoyed working with him, he's highly personable." **Recent work:** Defended Healthcare Services Newcastle in its multimillion-pound PFI dispute with the local NHS Trust. The matter concerned the renewal of hospitals in Newcastle, and was eventually settled through mediation.

Nicholas Dennys QC Highly regarded silk with a strong international practice. He is particularly noted for his vast experience working with government bodies and large multinational organisations. He regularly advises on major projects, covering areas such as transport infrastructure, utilities, oil and gas. **Strengths:** "He is incredibly bright. He has this knack of appearing laid back when he is actually razor sharp." "A particularly good choice of advocate for a tricky case." **Recent work:** Represented the claimant engineering consultants, GBM Mineral Engineering, in a dispute in West Africa. The case centred around a phosphate mine in Guinea Bissau and involved allegations of breach of contract and bribery.

Dominique Rawley QC (see p.748) Sought-after silk with a particular focus on domestic infrastructure matters and disputes arising from PPP and PFI arrangements. **Strengths:** "She is a superb draftsperson who explains complex contractual arguments with great clarity. She makes the hardest arguments seem easy." "She provides attention to detail which is second to none." **Recent work:** Represented Portsmouth City Council in a dispute with contractor Ensign Highways. The matter centred around a PFI agreement for the maintenance and operation of the council's highway network.

Jonathan Acton Davis QC Senior silk who regularly acts in large-scale construction disputes. He offers experience in both major international arbitration and high-value domestic litigation. He acts for a range of clients, most notably contractors and engineering firms. **Strengths:** "A very persuasive advocate. He is incredibly user-friendly for such a senior and experienced silk." "Jonathan will find the way out of a dispute quickly, efficiently and with great client understanding."

Chantal-Aimée Doerries QC (see p.635) Highly rated silk who draws particular praise for her international tribunal work in the Far East. She also counts several public bodies in the UK among her diverse clientele. She is currently serving as the 2016 Chair of the Bar Council of England and Wales. **Strengths:** "She is good with clients and her impressive multilingual skills assist her." "Her drafting is always elegant and concise."

Andrew Goddard QC (see p.655) High-quality silk who regularly appears in big-ticket construction disputes, and has particular knowledge of the housing sector. He has experience of both domestic and cross-border litigation and arbitration, and has developed a significant practice in Hong Kong. **Strengths:** "He is clear and concise in his advice and robust in his views." "He is a fantastic advocate; the go-to man if you are in a tight spot."

Martin Bowdery QC Experienced silk who advises on a range of construction disputes, including domestic PFI actions and international arbitration. Market sources extol his imaginative approach and lateral thinking. **Strengths:** "When you are faced with a difficult case and struggling to reach a desired result, he can find the way through." "He is fantastically sharp-minded and always offers effective, strategic advice. His focus is as much on the commercial needs of the client as on resolving the issue at hand." **Recent work:** Represented Cumbria County Council in its multimillion-pound PFI dispute with Amey Local Government. The matter concerned defective highway works.

Simon Lofthouse QC (see p.703) High-quality silk with a diverse practice that is increasingly oriented towards international arbitration. He acts for a range of major clients from across the globe, including governments and contractors. **Strengths:** "Responsive, calm and very commercial in his approach." "He is excellent legally, technically and commercially." **Recent work:** Advised Allseas UK in its successful High Court action against Van Oord. The matter regarded variations, loss and expenses on a pipeline project in Shetland, Scotland.

Fiona Parkin QC Noteworthy silk who acts in TCC litigation, domestic adjudications and international arbitration. She frequently represents public bodies and private contractors in disputes arising from large infrastructure projects. **Strengths:** "Zeroes in quickly on the key points and crafts ingenious and innovative arguments in the face of challenging legal issues." "She is exceptionally thorough and always provides clear advice." **Recent work:** Acted for the government of Gibraltar in a contractual dispute with Obrascon Huearte, a contractor that had been working on a tunnelling project at Gibraltar airport.

Steven Walker QC (see p.788) Talented strategist who regularly acts for contractors in a wide range of disputes, both nationally and internationally. He has a stellar reputation for his work in domestic adjudications and regularly appears before the TCC. **Strengths:** "He is technically excellent, considered in his approach and always striving to find a practical solution." "An excellent strategist whose outstanding client service is second to none." **Recent work:** Successfully defended Beltec Engineering & Associates against allegations of incompetence following the collapse of a private London residence.

James Howells QC (see p.676) Advises on claims relating to design and construction defects in domestic disputes. His well-regarded practice also includes a strong international arbitration element. **Strengths:** "Very responsive and easy to work with. He consistently provides clear, commercial advice." "He has a highly incisive mind, gives great attention to detail and is very down to earth with clients." **Recent work:** Acted for Healthcare Services Newcastle in its dispute with Newcastle Hospitals Trust concerning a PFI contract for the renewal of local hospitals.

Riaz Hussain QC (see p.679) Newly minted silk with significant experience in construction-related PFI disputes and international arbitration. His varied practice covers areas such as high-value oil and gas projects and domestic adjudications. **Strengths:** "He is very thorough in his drafting and has a wonderfully hands-on approach." "His opinions are clear, concise and straight to the point." **Recent work:** Advised Miler & Baird in a Guernsey arbitration claim for unforeseen ground conditions, variations, loss and expense. The claim was for in excess of £2 million.

JUNIORS

Christopher Lewis (see p.700) Highly acclaimed senior junior with significant experience handling cases with energy and professional negligence elements. He acts in both domestic and cross-border matters and has notable experience in adjudication enforcement and PFI disputes. **Strengths:** "He is among the best in the sector. He has the ability to process huge amounts of information at top speed and is very good on his feet." "Forensically thorough and analytical but also commercially succinct. A pleasure to work with."

Andrew Fenn (see p.644) Sought-after junior who often appears unled in domestic litigation and international arbitration. He advises on a range of matters, including infrastructure projects and final account disputes. **Strengths:** "He is a hugely compelling advocate and is particularly good at grappling with complex delay and disruption claims." "He has both great people skills and a highly analytical mind." **Recent work:** Appeared unled on behalf of QPR Football Club in a final account dispute with a building contractor. The issue centred around works carried out on the club's Loftus Road ground.

Rupert Choat (see p.616) Draws on his previous experience as a specialist construction solicitor at CMS to inform his well-rounded practice. He acts in adjudication enforcement matters and real estate redevelopment disputes, domestically and internationally. **Strengths:** "He is very proactive and has an excellent grasp of the tricky nuances of major commercial disputes." "Very quick to grasp detail and very thorough." **Recent work:** Acted for MAN Enterprise in a USD10 million dispute regarding the redevelopment of the Al Waddan Hotel in Tripoli, Libya.

Mark Chennells Experienced senior junior who is frequently led in large-scale disputes covering areas such as renewables and property development. He increasingly acts as sole counsel in domestic disputes and various forms of ADR. **Strengths:** "The standard of his written submissions is extremely high. His language is always persuasive and his mastery of detail shines through." "He has a first-class intellect and a charming approach." **Recent work:** Led by David Streatfeild-James QC, he acted for MT Højgaard A/S, the Danish claimant responsible for the design and installation of foundations for wind turbines at Robin Rigg offshore wind farm. The matter centred around liability for defects arising from inadequacies in industry standard design code.

Nicholas Collings (see p.620) Highly respected senior junior who often acts as sole counsel in high-value disputes in the UK and the Middle East. He represents clients across a range of areas such as mixed-use development issues and transport infrastructure matters. **Strengths:** "He is an excellent advocate who provides sensible, pragmatic advice and is well liked by clients." "Exceptionally hard working and a very good team player." **Recent work:** Instructed as sole counsel in the successful enforcement of a £10 million adjudication decision on behalf of the Sisk Group. The matter involved complex issues of predetermination and third-party interference.

Camille Slow (see p.767) Highly skilled advocate who acts in a range of matters for employers and contractors, with notable experience in multi-party disputes. She regularly appears unled in cases. **Strengths:** "Her technical ability, her attention to detail and her client skills are all of the highest level." "She is very thorough and leaves no stone unturned." **Recent work:** Acted as sole counsel for Newlon Housing Trust in its claim against Sir Robert McAlpine and others regarding the social housing development at the new Emirates Stadium. The sums in dispute are in excess of £19 million.

Patrick Clarke (see p.617) Noted junior with a professional engineering background whose attention to detail is widely admired by fellow practitioners. He advises on a range of matters, domestically and abroad, with a particular emphasis on residential properties and infrastructure works. **Strengths:** "His command of technical detail and his cross-examination of expert witnesses is really something." "Very detailed junior who offers clear, well-thought-out advice. A good communicator who gets on well with clients." **Recent work:** Defended a contractor, Forcia Limited, against a £1 million claim concerning defects in the design and construction of a luxury apartment.

Robert Clay Experienced senior junior who draws praise from solicitors for his written work. He is regularly called upon by a diverse client base across a number of sectors that includes major contractors. **Strengths:** "Excellent, well-thought-out written advice." "He's very thorough and very client-friendly." **Recent work:** Appeared before the High Court on behalf of major offshore pipelay company, Allseas UK. The matter concerned variations, loss and expense on pipeline works in a large energy project in Shetland, Scotland.

Jennifer Jones (see p.685) Noted junior with considerable experience in matters concerning renewables, infrastructure, energy and professional negligence. She routinely handles litigation and high-value arbitration in the UK and abroad. **Strengths:** "She is very approachable, responsive and clear in her advice. She is able to serve both private and commercial clients extremely well." "Calm, collected and unflappable: all great qualities to have in an advocate."

Frances Pigott (see p.738) Has a well-rounded practice and is regularly called upon by a varied clientele. Her areas of expertise cover areas such as energy, infrastructure and residential developments. She has significant experience appearing before both the TCC and the Court of Appeal. **Strengths:** "She is always thorough, efficient and an excellent cross-examiner in court." "She's a machine: technically excellent and absolutely diligent in her approach." **Recent work:** Appeared before the TCC on behalf of Cumbria County Council in its PFI dispute against Amey Local Government. She was led by Martin Bowdery QC in this matter, which concerned defective highway works.

Simon Crawshaw (see p.626) Has experience of working in the transport, energy and property development sectors, primarily acting on behalf of employers and purchasers. He has been instructed in both domestic and cross-border matters. **Strengths:** "He's very thorough, pragmatic and technically excellent. I am always impressed by his sound commercial sense." "He's highly intelligent, very efficient and will always go the extra mile for the client." **Recent work:** Defended London Underground against a claim brought by a contractor, Thorntask, for payment of sums for repair and maintenance services carried out on its network. Payment had previously been suspended following the discovery that Thorntask had made undisclosed payments to London Underground employees.

Edmund Neuberger (see p.726) Highly rated junior who frequently appears in adjudications and in the TCC. He is increasingly trusted as sole counsel on cases, and regularly represents a range of clients from across the construction industry. **Strengths:** "He has an impressive ability to convey complex issues succinctly and clearly." "He's very bright and very hard working, but also very down to earth and good with clients." **Recent work:** Represented the main contractor in a £7 million dispute over the defective construction of a cutting-edge "eco-school" in Devonshire.

Lucie Briggs (see p.603) Has a strong construction practice and frequently appears in cases containing a professional negligence element. She acts in both domestic and international disputes and offers expertise across a range of sectors, including energy and commercial property. **Strengths:** "She is very switched on and pragmatic, but also remarkably client-friendly. I would rate her extremely highly." "Her cross-examination is fantastic, as is her preparation. I am really impressed by her." **Recent work:** Acted for NWF Group and Boughey Distribution in a professional negligence claim valued at £6 million. The matter concerned the defective design and construction of three warehouses which have suffered severe subsidence.

Serena Cheng (see p.616) Has a robust practice acting for contractors on technically complex engineering and energy disputes, both domestically and abroad. She regularly appears as junior counsel, and increasingly acts as sole counsel against senior juniors and respected silks. **Strengths:** "A tenacious cross-examiner whose pleadings are excellent." "She is diligent, efficient and innovative in her approach to complex issues." **Recent work:** Appeared as sole counsel in the defence of a contractor, Morris & Spottiswood, against allegations that they repudiated a contract by forging claims for variations.

Ronan Hanna (see p.663) Strong junior with experience in a number of sectors, including energy, oil and gas. He has advised purchaser and contractor clients in litigation and arbitration, both in the UK and internationally. **Strengths:** "He is good with clients and is a strong advocate." "He is super responsive and completely dedicated to the matter." **Recent**

work: Engaged by BP to defend a multimillion-pound contamination and defective product claim.

Zulfikar Khayum (see p.691) Highly regarded junior with extensive experience of appearing in international arbitration across the globe. He frequently acts in domestic and cross-border disputes, and has recently been instructed in high-value matters in Africa and the Middle East. **Strengths:** "He has a really exceptional level of commitment." "He's very hands-on, forthright and keen to get stuck in." **Recent work:** Led by Manus McMullan QC in a USD250 million ICC arbitration arising from the construction of airport lounges in Qatar.

David Johnson (see p.684) Up-and-coming junior who has been led in a number of major disputes in the transport and energy sectors, among others. He has significant experience of appearing in both domestic litigation and international arbitration. **Strengths:** "He is a pleasure to work with and his drafting is always impressive." "He is proactive, practical and gets to grips with the details of complex matters extremely quickly." **Recent work:** Successfully acted as junior counsel on behalf of Redhall Engineering Solutions after Vivergo Fuels unlawfully terminated its contract on a biofuels plant.

Keating Chambers

See profile on p.868

THE SET

A market-leading construction chambers housing an experienced team of barristers whose expertise runs the full gamut of construction law. The set's members are regularly instructed in major cases ranging from domestic TCC matters to arbitration worldwide. Counsel from Keating have recently acted on behalf of clients in numerous high-profile matters, including CIP v Galliford Try and Harding v Paice and Springal.

Client service: The clerking team is led by Declan Redmond. "The clerks really make an effort to get to know you and to understand your practice." "The clerks at Keating are excellent, provide a first-rate service and are a pleasure to deal with."

SILKS

Marcus Taverner QC (see p.778) Widely admired by barristers and solicitors alike, he is regularly instructed in high-value disputes for blue-chip players throughout the construction industry. He has a formidable practice and is regularly involved in major cases at both the domestic and international level. **Strengths:** "A phenomenal trial advocate whose cross-examination is second to none." "He exercises exceptional strategic judgement which he has honed over many years of work on important cases." **Recent work:** Acted for Hyder Consulting in its £36 million claim against Amec regarding the defective design and construction of a car park in Bournemouth.

Adam Constable QC (see p.621) Top-drawer construction silk who specialises in complex and technical construction and engineering disputes. He has an enviable domestic and international litigation and arbitration practice, with particular expertise in energy and offshore construction issues. **Strengths:** "His oral submissions are very powerful and effective. He commands the respect of the tribunal and all those with whom he engages." "First-rate ability as an advocate: his ability to recall facts is unparalleled."

Paul Darling QC (see p.629) Heavyweight silk with a strong global practice that often involves tribunal work in the Far and Middle East. His domestic work sees him regularly appearing before the TCC in an array of high-value cases. **Strengths:** "He's magnificent, a superb advocate. If you have a tricky case, you'll want to go to him." "He is a very incisive advocate. There aren't many people with more experience of the construction world than him." **Recent work:** Acted for the defendant in Henia v Beck, a case concerning the effect of payment provisions in a JCT standard form contract.

Stephen Furst QC (see p.649) Highly regarded senior silk who advises an array of clients, including public sector bodies and major contractors, on technically complex matters. He also sits as a deputy judge and recorder in the TCC. **Strengths:** "Hugely experienced, he has a calm and reassuring manner combined with a vast intellect." "His technical knowledge is incredible." **Recent work:** Acted in Cambridge City Council v BAM, a claim of over £50 million regarding cost overrun during the construction of the Cambridge Gateway.

Alexander Nissen QC (see p.728) Widely praised silk who acts for prominent employers and contractors in a range of disputes spanning the breadth of the construction industry. He has vast experience in high-value, multiparty matters at both national and international level. **Strengths:** "He's an impressive advocate, opponent and High Court judge." "He has exceptional analytical skills and is strategically very sound." **Recent work:** Acted on behalf of 90 apartment holders in the multiparty TCC case, Rendlesham Estates & Others v Barr Limited. The matter concerned a £22 million claim under the Defective Premises Act.

David Thomas QC (see p.780) Top-class silk with a sterling practice in both the UK and overseas. He is acknowledged as a leading expert on NEC contracts, and has significant experience of appearing before the Court of Appeal, TCC, ICC and Dubai World Tribunal. **Strengths:** "Very good with clients and witnesses, and excellent with experts." "His written opinions are second to none in terms of clarity and user-friendliness." **Recent work:** Defended steelwork designers, URS, against a £10 million professional negligence claim made by a contractor, Costain, regarding the design of a waste-to-power plant on the banks of the Thames.

Adrian Williamson QC (see p.797) Highly regarded silk with considerable experience representing contractor clients in adjudications and appearing before the TCC. He has particular expertise in cases containing a professional negligence element. **Strengths:** "A hugely persuasive and highly skilled advocate." "Always concise and accurate, he is particularly strong on technically complex legal issues." **Recent work:** Acted in WCC v Mitie, a substantial pensions dispute arising from construction contracts.

Simon Hughes QC (see p.677) Silk with a standout reputation given his sterling work on prominent cases at both the national and international level. He has recently been instructed in high-value litigation, adjudication and international arbitration cases running the full gamut of construction issues. **Strengths:** "He is an excellent litigation silk for multiparty actions." "He excels in providing robust advice and opinions and is a very persuasive advocate." **Recent work:** Advised Shepherd Construction on a series of high-profile adjudication and contractual disputes in London and throughout the UK.

John Marrin QC (see p.708) Highly regarded senior silk with a pre-eminent reputation as an arbitrator. As counsel, he has significant experience in domestic litigation and international arbitration and is widely recognised for his appeals work. He also serves as a deputy judge in the TCC. **Strengths:** "Supremely intelligent. Has the ability to distil and explain complex issues and arguments clearly."

Finola O'Farrell QC Widely lauded QC who is regularly instructed by major contractors on power and transport infrastructure matters. She has considerable experience of working on high-profile cases in the Middle East and has a robust PFI practice domestically. **Strengths:** "She expresses herself with clarity and precision and is excellent on tactical matters." "She is bright, attentive and manages difficult clients well: completely reliable."

Simon Hargreaves QC (see p.664) Outstanding silk who is regularly instructed in high-profile cases across a range of sectors such as transport, oil and gas and energy. He frequently acts in domestic disputes, adjudications and international arbitration. **Strengths:** "He has a very astute commercial brain and is excellent on strategy. He sees angles that others wouldn't." "He's user-friendly, extremely bright and understands the importance of service." **Recent work:** Acted in Liberty Mercian Limited V Cuddy Civil Engineering Limited, a case concerning a retail development and a landslip.

Marc Rowlands QC (see p.755) Has a robust construction practice and particular expertise in the transport sector. He has significant experience both domestically and abroad, and has been called to the Bars of Bermuda and Hong Kong. **Strengths:** "He consistently provides excellent advice and always offers a very attentive service." "He is very considered and insightful, with a prodigious appetite for work." **Recent work:** Represented Transport for London in its dispute with Heathrow Airport over Track Access rights for the Heathrow Express infrastructure.

Piers Stansfield QC (see p.771) Noteworthy silk whose practice includes frequent instruction in large and complex TCC cases. He counts a number of major contractors and engineering firms among his clients. **Strengths:** "His advocacy and turnaround times are fantastic." "Very user-friendly, intellectually agile and tactically aware." **Recent work:** Defended an engineering firm, Cameron Taylor One, against a multimillion-pound claim brought by contractors Kier Build Ltd. The matter related to the construction, demolition and subsequent rebuilding of the Castlepoint Shopping Centre in Bournemouth.

Sarah Hannaford QC (see p.663) Gifted silk witha diverse practice that includes an industry-acknowledged specialism in construction procurement. She has considerable experience of acting for public sector bodies in disputes and adjudications, and has notably represented the UK government in several major cases. **Strengths:** "She is very considered and very good on her feet." "Standout knowledge of procurement challenges." **Recent work:** Advised Jackson Civil Engineering on its successful opposition of an adjudication claim brought by fellow engineering firm Qualter Hall.

Richard Fernyhough QC (see p.644) Highly experienced and widely recognised silk who advises on a range of complex national and international projects. He has a complementary practice as an arbitrator on the global stage. **Strengths:** "He's a wonderful advocate who also enjoys an enormous reputation in construction dispute resolution." "I have the very highest regard for his practice, both in construction and arbitration."

Philip Boulding QC (see p.600) Excellent silk with a formidable Far East practice based in Hong Kong. He regularly acts on behalf of an array of major clients including government bodies and multinational, blue-chip organisations. He is active on big-ticket domestic disputes and national and international tribunals.

Vincent Moran QC (see p.721) Strong practitioner with a reputation for producing high-quality trial and tribunal work. His practice includes a focus on construction-related professional negligence and he regularly acts in large-scale cases in the TCC. **Strengths:** "A deep-thinking silk who is calm under pressure and very user-friendly." "An impressive advocate with a wealth of experience who can always be relied upon to deliver." **Recent work:** Defended Francous Clin against a £2 million claim brought by his contractor, Walter Lily Ltd. The claim alleged delay losses and planning consent violation connected with a luxury residential development in Kensington.

Jane Lemon QC (see p.699) Talented silk with vast experience in high-profile domestic litigation. She is increasingly instructed in big-ticket international arbitration and offers a depth of knowledge across the full gamut of construction issues. **Strengths:** "Incredibly hard working and dedicated to her cases, she always thinks two steps ahead." "Great with clients, thorough and diligent."

Nerys Jefford QC Silk specialising in PFI disputes who has also advised on high-value projects in the Middle East and across Europe. She offers extensive knowledge of the construction and engineering sectors and is highly regarded for her work in professional negligence claims, amongother areas. **Strengths:** "She is excellent at explaining complex issues rapidly and expressing things in layman's terms." "A truly first-rate legal mind." **Recent work:** Acted for Mapeley in its successful resistance of a £6.5 million non-statutory adjudication decision against contractors Carillion, which later settled.

Fionnuala McCredie QC (see p.712) Well-regarded silk with a notable construction procurement practice who has acted in a number of valuable adjudications and TCC litigation. **Strengths:** "She provides excellent, measured advice." "She is always extremely impressive in mediations and clients really warm to her." **Recent work:** Successfully resisted a £1.7 million adjudication award on behalf of Siemens. The case concerned conflict of interest and fraudulent misrepresentation.

Justin Mort QC (see p.722) Regularly sought out by major contractors in final accounts disputes. He is noted for his extensive experience in adjudications. **Strengths:** "He is sharp, creative, and always looking to come at things from a new angle." "He is very confident, understands highly technical issues quickly and is always able to explain complex matters in a coherent way." **Recent work:** Represented Barclays Bank in a £4 million professional negligence claim arising from the design of a highly complex chiller plant for a data centre.

JUNIORS

Calum Lamont (see p.694) Highly acclaimed junior who is frequently instructed on large construction disputes both nationally and in the Middle East. He advises on infrastructure issues and professional negligence matters among other areas, and has acted unled in both litigation and arbitration proceedings. **Strengths:** "The quality of the work and the speed with which he turns things around is unsurpassable." "He's a prime example of the modern barrister who is very easy to work with and works brilliantly as part of a team." **Recent work:** Instructed in a professional negligence action against engineering consultants valued in excess of £30 million. The case concerned the design of a large commercial car park in southern England.

Jonathan Selby (see p.761) Impressive senior junior who draws praise for his top-notch work in high-value matters, particularly before the TCC but also regarding adjudications and international arbitration. He regularly acts unled and has appeared before both the Court of Appeal and Privy Council. **Strengths:** "He is superbly bright, confident and good on his feet." "A top-grade technical lawyer who is a pleasure to work with and excellent with clients." **Recent work:** Acted on behalf of Dorchester Collection in its £1.5 million claim against Kier Construction. The case concerned 'undisclosed discounts' paid by subcontractors to Kier so that Kier would award them the subcontracts for work at the Dorchester's 45 Park Lane Hotel.

Paul Buckingham (see p.606) Excellent junior whose science and engineering background informs his burgeoning practice. He regularly acts in a range of highly technical and complex construction disputes. His sterling work in the energy and renewables sectors, both in the UK and abroad, is particularly noteworthy. **Strengths:** "Very thoughtful, hard working and reliable, he displays excellent judgement." "His technical ability marries very well with his legal skill, while his client management is excellent." **Recent work:** Led by John Marrin QC in MT Hojgaard v E.On Climate, a £20 million Court of Appeal dispute regarding defective offshore wind turbines.

Lucy Garrett (see p.650) Acclaimed junior who is regularly instructed on high-value construction litigation and arbitration worldwide. Her sector expertise includes areas such as energy and shipbuilding. **Strengths:** "Very good on paper and very robust in advocacy." "Very analytical, she makes complex problems seem simple." **Recent work:** Acted for Health Services Newcastle in its high-value dispute against Newcastle Hospitals NHS Trust. The case centred on PFI arrangements related to the construction of a local hospital.

Samuel Townend Gifted junior who is increasingly entrusted to act as sole counsel on valuable disputes before the TCC and arbitration worldwide. **Strengths:** "His strong and piercing advocacy stood out for me, along with his excellent commercial approach." "He has a sound legal mind; he is a remarkable advocate." **Recent work:** Led by Nicholas Dennys QC in GMB Minerals Engineering Consultants V GB Minerals Holdings, a TCC claim relating to a phosphate deposit in West Africa. Issues included professional negligence, overpayment and claims of bribery.

Richard Coplin (see p.623) Excellent junior with a growing practice in both domestic and cross-border matters. His prior employment as an engineer allows him expert insight into professional negligence cases. **Strengths:** "He adapts brilliantly to any and every situation." "Tactically sound and client-friendly."

William Webb (see p.791) Impressive practitioner who elicits much praise for his advocacy skill and intellectual prowess. He has appeared in court as both junior and sole counsel and his practice includes high-value matters in domestic litigation and international arbitration. **Strengths:** "Precise and analytical. He grasps the issues and cuts to the chase very quickly." "Superb technical knowledge." **Recent work:** Defended a specialist grouting contractor against a professional negligence claim brought by Grosvenor. The case centred around the subsidence and demolition of a building in Belgravia when the property next door was being rebuilt.

Gideon Scott Holland Experienced junior whose practice includes frequent instruction in contractual disputes. He has been active in arbitration and litigation cases involving property development and process engineering, among other areas. **Strengths:** "Conscientious, professional, easily contactable and proactive." "He is reliably attentive, approachable and very user-friendly." **Recent work:** Appeared as junior counsel at the appeal stage of Harding V Paice and Springall, a residential property dispute concerning issues of statute, regulations and contractual terms.

Gaynor Chambers (see p.614) Has considerable experience in adjudications and domestic litigation. She is regularly instructed by major contractors in the energy, utilities and leisure sectors. **Strengths:** "Impressive at getting to the crux of the matter quickly and very user-friendly." "We were very impressed with her written advice." **Recent work:** Acted in Merlin Entertainments (Sea Life) v Brighton Seafront Regeneration, a £2.5 million claim centring around liability for substantial leaks at the aquarium in Brighton.

Abdul Jinadu (see p.683) Experienced practitioner with a strong adjudication element to his practice. He regularly appears in domestic litigation and arbitration and has advised an array of clients including public sector bodies, developers and contractors. **Strengths:** "Extremely commercial, focused and someone who cuts straight to the crux of issues." "He is a natural communicator and very quick to establish a rapport with clients." **Recent work:** Advised liquidators on a £2 million claim to recover outstanding sums owed to a contractor by QPR football club.

Alice Sims (see p.766) Quality practitioner who regularly acts in high-profile cases in the TCC and before international tribunals. Her practice spans a wide range of the construction sector, with clients in the energy, renewables and commercial development spheres, among others. **Strengths:** "She is able to pick up complex technical issues with little guidance from clients."

James Thompson (see p.781) Strong junior often instructed in high-value domestic construction cases and international arbitrations. He has recently been heavily involved in large-scale disputes in the Caribbean and the Middle East. **Strengths:** "He's exceptionally bright and excellent at streamlining arguments." "His client-management skills and ability to understand complex claim matters are excellent." **Recent work:** Led by Alexander Nissen QC in Taylor Wimpey's £10 million claim against the project architect and contractors working on a 145-unit housing development project in Milton Keynes.

Sarah Williams (see p.796) Popular junior with a strong practice that often sees her instructed in high-value TCC litigation and international arbitration. She has a niche strength in the telecommunications infrastructure market. **Strengths:** "The written work she does is excellent." "She is hard working, diligent and proactive, and has a good grasp of the finer details." **Recent work:** Appeared before the

TCC on behalf of contractor Costain in its £16 million claim against a specialist subcontractor. The case concerned the alleged failure of equipment in a waste processing facility in Manchester.

Robert Evans (see p.642) Quality junior who advises contractors and consultants in both the UK and Hong Kong. He has particularly deep knowledge of the engineering and energy sectors, while his prior experience as a civil engineer informs his burgeoning practice. **Strengths:** "Gets to the heart of the matter quickly and provides clear commercial advice." "Very hard working with good legal and technical skills." **Recent work:** Defended the UK subsidiary of Italian joinery manufacturer CNC against a £2 million adjudication claim brought against them by a bespoke UK joinery firm.

Thomas Lazur (see p.698) Robust junior with particular strength in construction disputes in the energy sector. He has recently acted for major contractors both domestically and abroad. **Strengths:** "His written advocacy was very well organised and of a good standard." "He has the capacity to handle difficult situations with aplomb." **Recent work:** Drafted the defence for architect Populous in a three-party professional negligence dispute arising from the construction of a housing development next to the Emirates Stadium in London.

Krista Lee (see p.698) Strong junior with an engineering background who has deep knowledge across a range of construction matters. She offers additional expertise in the related fields of corporate insolvency and complex IT disputes. She regularly appears unled before the TCC. **Strengths:** "She provides excellent written work and is a subtle yet effective advocate." "She's very user-friendly, excellent at drafting and is wonderfully quick." **Recent work:** Represented the successful appellants in Wilson & Sharp Investments Ltd v Harbour View Developments. The matter required in-depth knowledge of the Housing Grants Construction and Regeneration Act, 1996.

Tom Owen (see p.732) Widely acclaimed up-and-coming junior who regularly appears as sole counsel before the TCC. His work in construction-related energy and professional negligence matters is particularly notable. **Strengths:** "His written court work is outstanding." "His work is meticulous and of a very high standard." **Recent work:** Led by Marcus Taverner QC, he appeared before the TCC in a £7 million claim regarding negligent advice on the presence of asbestos in a substantial development in Wales.

Paul Bury (see p.608) Up-and-coming junior who is often led in major cases, including TCC litigation, adjudications and international arbitration. Has recently been instructed in large-scale energy and renewables disputes. **Strengths:** "He is able to penetrate difficult details and come out the other side with sensible answers." "Incisive, positive and a good communicator." **Recent work:** Led by Fionnoula McCredie QC in a £2.5 million adjudication concerning a subcontract for the communications system to certain London Underground tube lines in the run up to the Olympics. The adjudication enforcement was successfully resisted.

David Sheard (see p.763) Up-and-coming junior who has been led by prominent silks on several high-profile disputes. He has been instructed in litigation, arbitration and adjudications. **Strengths:** "He provides excellent drafting of pleadings." "He grasps complex, technical cases very quickly and makes them seem easy." **Recent work:** Advised contractor NTR Design and Build Ltd in its wrongful termination action against developer Buildrite Homes Limited. The action led to a summary judgment in favour of the clients.

Ben Sareen (see p.759) Up-and-coming junior who is lauded by instructing solicitors for his high-quality work. He frequently represents major contractors in disputes and arbitration both in the UK and abroad. **Strengths:** "Excellent attention to detail and notable drafting skills." "A fantastic junior who offers sensible and commercial advice." **Recent work:** Instructed as junior counsel for the defendant in Kier v Cameron Taylor, a £120 million dispute regarding defects in the construction of a shopping centre car park in Bournemouth.

Band 2

4 Pump Court
See profile on p.895

THE SET

A highly popular set that continues to be a natural choice for a range of clients across the construction sphere. Its members regularly act in disputes and arbitration both domestically and on the global stage. Notably, counsel from 4 Pump Court have provided advice to, and been instructed by, major players in a number of high-value infrastructure disputes in the Middle East. Its pre-eminent barristers have recently acted in the high-profile case Shangri-La Hotels v John Sisk & Son, and have been heavily involved in disputes concerning the construction of the Rolls Building.

Client service: Carl Wall and Stewart Gibbs are the primary contacts for the construction team. Sources enthuse: "Their client service and clerking is outstanding." "They're very approachable, responsible and accommodating." "I found the clerks excellent. They got on board very quickly, they were very sensible about billing and fees, and had a wonderfully hands-on approach."

SILKS

Sean Brannigan QC (see p.601) Top-drawer silk widely hailed for his courtroom presence. He regularly acts in high-value domestic cases and on major international arbitration seated worldwide, with an emphasis on work in the Far and Middle East. **Strengths:** "A very strong advocate with exceptional cross-examination skills." "He is superb on strategy and grabs a dispute with vigour." **Recent work:** Represented Fluor Limited in its major £400 million energy infrastructure dispute against Chinese contractors ZPMC.

Duncan McCall QC Excellent silk whose practice runs the full spectrum of construction and engineering claims. He has a particular focus on cases involving major infrastructure and commercial projects both nationally and abroad. **Strengths:** "Absolutely top-notch grasp of difficult, technical concepts in large, complex engineering disputes." "Calm, reassuring and measured: very good on his feet."

Jeremy Nicholson QC (see p.727) Highly experienced silk who offers particular expertise in large-scale international arbitration. He is also noted for his adroit handling of professional negligence and insurance-related construction disputes. **Strengths:** "Fabulous attention to detail. He has telescopic vision of the big picture." "An incredibly subtle thinker."

Rachel Ansell QC (see p.584) A highly lauded advocate with a burgeoning reputation for her high-quality casework, domestically and in the Middle East. She is regularly instructed by major clients, such as prominent contractors, on matters in the energy and infrastructure spheres. **Strengths:** "The quality of her advice and advocacy is excellent." "She ticks all the boxes that you want from a modern day QC." "Very bright and gives no-nonsense practical advice. A pleasure to work with and very responsive." **Recent work:** Acted for contractors, Carillion, in its high-profile claim concerning the Rolls Building construction. This was a multimillion-pound claim brought against the architects and the M&E consultants.

James Cross QC (see p.626) Highly regarded practitioner with a broad practice. He is particularly noted for his quality work in professional negligence-related construction matters. His clients include a wide range of prominent players in the construction industry, including government departments and major insurers. **Strengths:** "He's got a brain the size of a planet, he's able to find different angles to approach an issue. He's very much a person who we feel adds value to any matter." "He has an incredible eye for detail." **Recent work:** Represented risk management consultants HFL Risk Services Ltd in its defence of a multimillion-pound claim for damages arising from a catastrophic fire at a chemical plant in Yorkshire.

Anthony Speaight QC Senior silk with significant experience acting in the TCC on high-value claims relating to energy, infrastructure and upscale residential developments. **Strengths:** "An excellent advocate and extremely clever in his cross-examination." "His written work is absolutely superb." **Recent work:** Successfully represented the claimants in Mears Limited v Shoreline Housing Partnership. He triumphed in the Court of Appeal on points of law as to the sustainability of the client's case and issues of misrepresentation.

Benjamin Pilling QC (see p.738) Quality QC with a substantial practice in both the UK and the Middle East. He has worked on a number of large-scale construction disputes in the renewables, infrastructure and transport remits. **Strengths:** "Excellent barrister with a great deal of commercial awareness." "Brilliant at getting to the heart of really complex expert evidence in large construction and engineering disputes." **Recent work:** Acted for Hyde Housing Association in its multimillion-pound defective design and workmanship claim against contractors resulting from the destruction by fire of a sheltered accommodation.

Alexander Hickey QC (see p.670) New silk who wins praise from his fellow practitioners for his advocacy prowess. His domestic practice includes considerable experience in adjudication enforcement cases. **Strengths:** "A lot of tactical nous and a heavy-hitter in terms of legal firepower." "Outstanding service and clear, pragmatic advice." **Recent work:** Acted in Galliford Try v Estrua, an adjudication enforcement case in which it was argued that the leading case of ISG v Seevic was wrong.

David Friedman QC Hugely respected senior silk whose expansive practice covers all types of construction and engineering disputes, particularly those with a professional negligence aspect. **Strengths:** "He is an extremely strong advocate and particularly good at dealing with difficult situations." "A real heavyweight."

JUNIORS

James Leabeater (see p.698) Leading junior whose construction practice regularly sees him represent prominent contractors. He has acted in large claims nationally and in both Africa and the Middle East. **Strengths:** "He has an exceptional grasp of the facts." "A great advocate to have on your side." **Recent work:** Acted for Morgan Sindall in its defence of a £7.5 million claim brought by AMEC relating to the Malmaison Hotel in Liverpool.

Kate Livesey (see p.703) Prominentjunior who frequently appears unled in the TCC and before international tribunals, with a particular emphasis on construction-related professional negligence cases. She has represented an array of clients including contractors, subcontractors and insurers in a number of high-value disputes. **Strengths:** "She has a keen eye for detail and is utterly proactive." "An excellent senior junior." **Recent work:** Acted for subcontractor Seaway Heavy Lifting in its multiparty TCC dispute with Wood Group and East Anglia Offshore Wind. This was a £10 million claim relating to an offshore wind farm project.

James Bowling (see p.600) Excellent junior who regularly appears in both domestic and international arbitration and frequently advises on complex litigation and adjudications in the UK. **Strengths:** "Immense work rate. Very good with clients and judges." "He is a creative and tenacious advocate." **Recent work:** Successfully acted for the claimant in Fairhurst Ward Abbotts v 25 Culross Street Investments Ltd. The action concerned the termination of a building contract relating to a high-end Mayfair residential development.

Simon Henderson (see p.669) Widely respected senior junior who has acted in an impressive range of construction disputes and related professional negligence claims. His diverse client base includes major players in the energy, banking and telecoms sectors. **Strengths:** "He is extremely user-friendly and possesses excellent drafting skills." "One of the best senior juniors around, he's very hands-on, very calm on his feet and very good with clients. An excellent construction lawyer." **Recent work:** Defended M&E engineers in a multiparty dispute concerning allegedly defective air conditioning in a college building.

Lynne McCafferty (see p.711) Leading senior junior lauded for her skill in complex, highly technical construction disputes. Her robust domestic practice complements her impressive international arbitration offering, which is focused in the Middle East. **Strengths:** "Clear, pragmatic and able to grasp technically complex issues with ease." "Very thorough, strategically aware and commercial in her outlook." **Recent work:** Defended piling contractor Giken Europe BV against a multimillion-pound claim alleging that damage had been caused to neighbouring properties following extensive building works on a London residence.

Jessica Stephens (see p.772) Acclaimed junior with a heavyweight domestic practice and an international offering that includes disputes in construction markets worldwide. She has regularly appeared unled before the TCC in an impressive range of construction cases. **Strengths:** "Her written submissions are first-rate and she is wonderfully tough with the opposition." "She is particularly strong at devising workable strategies." **Recent work:** Successfully enforced an adjudicator's decision in a £2.5 million final account claim under a Term Partnering Contract in Rydon Maintenance v Affinity Sutton Homes Ltd.

Thomas Crangle (see p.625) Quality junior with a robust domestic offering and a burgeoning international arbitration practice centred in the Far East. He receives particular praise for his written advocacy. **Strengths:** "He is easy to work with and his drafting is absolutely excellent." "A calm operator; he's an old head on young shoulders." **Recent work:** Acted for AMEC in TCC proceedings regarding extensive cladding defects at the Malmaison Hotel and Apartments in Liverpool. The dispute was worth £7 million.

Jonathan Lewis (see p.701) Strong senior junior who regularly represents prominent clients such as major public bodies and large contractors. He has acted in high-profile disputes, adjudications and arbitrations. **Strengths:** "Superb written work." "He has a great style; both punchy and persuasive." **Recent work:** Led by Sean Brannigan QC in the £100 million dispute, Shangri-La Hotels Ltd v John Sisk & Son. The matter concerned the fit-out of a new hotel in the Shard skyscraper.

Claire Packman (see p.732) Robust senior junior who advises a diverse client base including major contractors, engineers and government departments. Her nationwide practice includes significant engagements in high-value adjudications and TCC cases. **Strengths:** "She has the ability to cut through the red tape and grasp the key issues with ease." "She is technically very competent and gives wonderful written advice." **Recent work:** Acted in Sir Roger de Haan v Gee, a claim relating to cladding in the construction of a private residence for the head of Saga Group. Issues included limitation and the construction of a direct warranty.

Luke Wygas (see p.800) Well-regarded junior who frequently advises on complex construction disputes, arbitrations and adjudications. He is able to draw upon his previous experience as a civil engineer to inform his burgeoning practice. **Strengths:** "His experience in the field and legal expertise makes him a formidable opponent." "He thinks things through very carefully and his advice is always very precise." **Recent work:** Acted unled in BMC v Tremco, a £50 million dispute involving a large retail car park. The case involved issues of jurisdiction, limitation and quantum.

Band 3

Crown Office Chambers

See profile on p.824

THE SET

A renowned construction chambers with an enviable track record of acting in large-scale engineering and infrastructure projects worldwide. The well-reputed set is regularly instructed by major developers and contractors in both the UK and abroad. Its skilled members demonstrate industry expertise across a number of sectors such as building, telecommunications and power. Members of Crown Office Chambers are increasingly active on the global stage and have recently handled matters in the Middle East and Africa.

Client service: "I found the clerks very personable, professional and reliable." "The clerks were very efficient and they did an excellent job." Chris Sunderland leads the construction clerking team.

SILKS

Roger ter Haar QC Acclaimed senior silk who is highly experienced across a broad spectrum of construction matters, with a particular emphasis on major projects in the Middle East. **Strengths:** "Briliant at cross-examination." "He's very good in court and clearly understands what judges and arbitrators want to hear."

Andrew Rigney QC Eminent silk who regularly acts in high-value litigation and arbitration in the UK and internationally. His work on construction cases throughout the energy sector elicits particular praise. **Strengths:** "He delivers pragmatic advice and his calm, measured style instils confidence in clients." "Technically excellent and exceptionally user-friendly." **Recent work:** Acted for Shangri La Hotels Ltd in its £90 million dispute with John Sisk & Sons Ltd. The case concerned the construction of the client's flagship hotel at The Shard.

David Sears QC Represents major clients from both public and private sectors in disputes covering the full range of construction matters. His significant professional negligence practice complements his lauded construction offering. **Strengths:** "An experienced advocate who is able to grasp complex and detailed matters quickly and effectively." "His written opinions have a real clarity about them." **Recent work:** Successfully acted for the appellant in Harding v Paice.

Ben Quiney QC Highly regarded silk who regularly appears before the TCC. He is particularly well known for his adroit handling of insurance-related construction cases, and demonstrates a growing focus on adjudications. **Strengths:** "Particularly good at oral advocacy." "His client care is excellent and he's always open to new ideas." **Recent work:** Appeared in Adprotel v Gleeds, a multimillion-pound adjudication arising from a fire during the construction of a hotel on the Strand, London.

Kim Franklin QC New silk who has recently been appointed the secretary of TECBAR. She has extensive experience appearing before the TCC and a burgeoning international practice based in Dubai. **Strengths:** "Terrific with clients." "Excellent for both contentious and non-contentious work."

JUNIORS

Anna Laney Impressive junior who is regularly instructed in large and technically complex litigation and arbitration. She has also advised on a number of notable and valuable disputes in the Persian Gulf. **Strengths:** "Highly skilled, fast-thinking and excellent on her feet." "Great at making the best of a difficult claim." **Recent work:** Defended contractors Willmot Dixon against a £7.5 million claim brought against them by Jockey Club Racecourses Limited. The matter concerned damages to Epsom Racecourse.

Charles Pimlott Talented junior who acts in arbitration, adjudications and adjudication enforcements in the TCC. He advises on matters in a wide range of sectors including utilities and commercial development. **Strengths:** "Highly intelligent and very articulate in his advice." "Very good commercial acumen." **Recent work:** Led by Andrew Rigney QC in Shangri-La Hotels v John Sisk & Sons. He acted for the claimants in a dispute over works at a luxury hotel in The Shard.

Crispin Winser Lauded junior whose practice extends from domestic residential development work and PFI matters to large-scale international arbitration. His drafting skill draws particular praise from market commentators. **Strengths:** "He is incredibly thorough and has an instant grasp of detail." "A good advocate who gives concise, practical advice." **Recent work:** Acted in Iouri Chliaifchtein v Wainbridge Estates Belgravia Ltd, a case involving several claims arising from a £250 million development in Knightsbridge.

James Medd Strong senior junior whose construction practice is complemented by his background in insurance law. He regularly advises contractors, subcontractors and suppliers in cases across the UK. **Strengths:** "He has real authority in the courtroom." "Good attention to detail, nothing slips by him." **Recent work:** Defended contractors J B Leadbitter Ltd against a substantial claim for flood damages to a hospital building in Swansea.

Jane Davies Evans (see p.630) Has a considerable international arbitration practice. She is regularly instructed in major disputes arising from infrastructure, energy and transportation projects worldwide. **Strengths:** "A sophisticated advocate." "She has great industry experience."

Rebecca Taylor Robust junior with a practice that sees her instructed as junior counsel in major disputes nationally and overseas. **Strengths:** "A pleasure to work with and has solid in-depth knowledge of construction law."

Cyril Chern Strong junior whose expertise lies in dispute resolution. He demonstrates particular prowess in adjudications and arbitration, and has a strong international practice. **Strengths:** "He is extremely well versed in international, heavy engineering disputes and adjudications."

39 Essex Chambers

See profile on p.840

THE SET

39 Essex Chambers is a construction set that packs a punch due to its impressive bench of formidable barristers. Commentators continue to rate it for the quality of its domestic and international litigation and arbitration work. It has two satellite offices in Singapore and Kuala Lumpur, reflecting its growing presence in Asia. Barristers from the set are frequently sought after to represent public bodies, developers and contractors, both at home and abroad. Recently, its members have been instructed in high-value energy and infrastructure arbitration in the Caribbean and the Middle East. The highly skilled team offers industry expertise across the oil and gas, utilities, insurance and energy sectors.

Client service: "One of the most dynamic clerks" David Barnes leads the clerking team with a "forward thinking," hands-on approach. "Their clerks are really commercial and focused on client delivery." "Very user-friendly, very prompt in response times and very good at getting fee quotes to you."

SILKS

Richard Wilmot-Smith QC Highly regarded senior silk who is particularly well known for his adroit handling of matters involving guarantees, performance bonds and related professional negligence claims. He has developed a sterling practice, both in the UK and abroad, which is supplemented by his regular work as an arbitrator. **Strengths:** "Incredibly tough, unequivocal in his advice and excellent with clients." "An inventive advocate."

Stuart Catchpole QC Masterful silk extolled for his courtroom presence and intellectual prowess. He has a renowned domestic practice and is widely respected for his international arbitration work. **Strengths:** "He's a devastating advocate and a fantastic cross-examiner, particularly of experts." "He has an unrivalled ability to work with instructing solicitors and clients as part of an integrated team." **Recent work:** Acted for the claimants in Kier Build Ltd v Cameron Taylor One Ltd, a claim in excess of £120 million arising from alleged design defects at the Castlepoint Retail Park.

Adrian Hughes QC Skilled silk with a robust domestic practice and a particular interest in infrastructure and PFI work. His international arbitration offering is notable, and he undertakes significant work in the Middle and Far East. **Strengths:** "A leader who is experienced and capable in the construction field." "He's got a perfect manner for arbitration."

Sean Wilken QC (see p.795) A formidable QC with a diverse practice, he regularly undertakes high-profile work in complex international arbitration and domestic litigation. His clients include public entities, contractors and developers. **Strengths:** "He really shone with his legal and commercial tactics." "Incredibly quick and a fabulous advocate." **Recent work:** Acted in Octagon Healthcare v John Laing Construction on a £52 million claim relating to the allegedly defective construction of a hospital.

Marion Smith QC (see p.769) Quality silk who is recognised for her prowess in domestic adjudications, TCC proceedings and international arbitration in Asia. She is frequently sought after to advise on a variety of matters, including PFI, energy and engineering disputes. **Strengths:** "Strong upbeat advocacy style: she certainly has the court's ear." "She provides clear and concise advice and has a wonderfully no-nonsense approach."

JUNIORS

Karim Ghaly (see p.651) Outstanding junior who regularly appears as sole counsel opposite prominent silks in high-value cases before the TCC. He is frequently instructed in multimillion-pound international arbitration, particularly in the energy sector. **Strengths:** "Effective at explaining complicated and technical legal issues to clients." "He is dynamic, energetic and hard-working." **Recent work:** Acted unled for the appellant in Iliffe & Anor v Feltham Construction Ltd & Others in the Court of Appeal.

Adam Robb Leading junior who is regularly sought after by household-name law firms to assist with high-value disputes. He is increasingly entrusted to act as sole counsel appearing opposite silks in court. **Strengths:** "Absolutely excellent on his feet and great at drafting." "He has a real eye for detail and is reliable in complex and highly technical cases." **Recent work:** Acted as sole counsel before the TCC in Community 1st v OMBC, a case concerning the operation of payment mechanisms in PFI and PFI type contracts.

Kate Grange Talented junior with a background in public law and procurement who regularly advises on complex construction litigation. Her impressive client base includes central government. **Strengths:** "Extremely good on the law, very thorough and very hard working."

Alexandra Bodnar (see p.598) Quality junior whose growing practice regularly sees her being led by prominent silks in big-ticket disputes. She offers expertise across litigation, arbitration and adjudication proceedings. **Strengths:** "She has a good grasp of technical detail and offers great support throughout a case." "She has a great work ethic." **Recent work:** Acted as sole counsel for the fourth party in a large, multiparty dispute, Borough of Barking and Dagenham Council v GLS Education Supplies Ltd v Stearn Electrical Co Ltd v RKW Ltd. The claim against the client was struck out and summary judgment granted.

Rachael O'Hagan (see p.729) Gifted junior increasingly instructed in valuable litigation and arbitration for a diverse client base including major contractors and government bodies. Her body of work includes significant matters in energy, infrastructure and residential development. **Strengths:** "She's unflappable; she deals incredibly well with pressure and demonstrates fantastic management skills." "She's extremely hard-working and takes a common sense approach."

Jess Connors Her wide-ranging practice covers domestic disputes and ADR alongside international arbitration. She has acted for prominent employers and contractors in litigious cases across the world. **Strengths:** "One of the most methodical barristers in the Temple." "Her attention to detail is quite phenomenal."

Patrick Hennessey Up-and-coming junior who elicits praise for his international arbitration work and often receives instruction as sole counsel in litigation and adjudications domestically. **Strengths:** "Impressive intelligence coupled with pragmatism." "Excellent analysis of technical issues, he is approachable, hard-working and bright." **Recent work:** Instructed as sole counsel in Carlo Kapp v Butlers, a multifaceted dispute arising from damage caused by refurbishment works.

4 New Square

See profile on p.880

THE SET

4 New Square has a long history of handling matters spanning the full spectrum of construction law. Its highly skilled barristers are regularly instructed by developers, contractors and insurers in both domestic litigation and international arbitration. Construction disputes relating to professional negligence and insurance claims are commonplace, with members demonstrating particular prowess in these complementary areas of law. The team has recently acted in a number of major cases such as Aspect Contracts (Asbestos) Ltd. v Higgins Construction and AMEC Group Limited v Ministry of Defence.

Client service: Senior clerk Lizzy Stewart leads the clerking and administration team. "Their clerks were very quick, very helpful and good value for money." "The clerking team is responsive and friendly to deal with."

SILKS

Roger Stewart QC (see p.773) Highly regarded senior silk with a strong reputation for work in construction-related professional negligence. He has acted for major clients in top-level disputes in the UK, Middle East and South America. **Strengths:** "He sees through to the heart of the issues in a very practical and pragmatic way." "Precise, strategic and very user-friendly."

Anneliese Day QC (see p.631) Standout silk with an enviable domestic practice that regularly sees her instructed in high-profile arbitration, litigation and adjudications. Her international offering includes work in the Far East, Middle East and the Caribbean. **Strengths:** "Technically astute, fantastic eye for detail and easy to work with." "Tough, tenacious and impressive on her feet." **Recent work:** Advised the claimants in Birmingham City Council v Amey on issues arising from work on the Birmingham road network.

Fiona Sinclair QC (see p.766) Impressive silk with an increasingly prominent practice that has seen her appear in the Court of Appeal and the Supreme Court. Her considerable domestic offering is supplemented by her involvement in large international arbitration. **Strengths:** "Fiona is charm personified, judges love her." "She is very pleasant to work with, calm, measured and a real team player." **Recent work:** Acted for the claimant in Merlin Attractions Operations Ltd v Speymill Plc and Allison Pike Partnership, a £10 million claim against the main contractor and architects of a new hotel, leisure and conference centre.

Mark Cannon QC (see p.611) Demonstrates particular prowess in professional negligence and insurance-related construction matters. He regularly acts for prominent contractors and consultants. **Strengths:** "His opinion is well respected by his peers and holds weight in any negotiation." "He is off-the-charts clever." **Recent work:** Represented contractor McLaughlin & Harvey Ltd in a dispute with its insurers, Allianz Plc. The case concerned damage caused to a new building at the Royal Victoria Hospital in Belfast.

Justin Fenwick QC (see p.644) Senior QC whose construction practice is focused on complex, high-value disputes, both in the UK and overseas. His considerable experience in the related fields of professional liability, professional negligence and civil fraud add further value to his offering. **Strengths:** "A doyen on the professional negligence side of the Construction Bar." "Highly intelligent, he reads tribunals well and is a very good linguist."

Ben Patten QC (see p.734) Strong silk who advises on big-ticket matters including all manner of domestic disputes and international arbitration. His practice is complemented by an acclaimed professional negligence offering. **Strengths:** "Strategically excellent." "Easy to work with and great with clients and judges." **Recent work:** Advised the claimants in Allen Todd Architecture v Capita Property, a £4 million claim arising from the allegedly negligent design of civic buildings in Barnsley.

JUNIORS

Richard Liddell (see p.701) Talented junior who demonstrates particular strength in cases concerning architects, specialist consultants and civil and structural engineers. He regularly acts as sole counsel in adjudications and arbitration and has appeared as junior counsel in the Court of Appeal and Supreme Court. **Strengths:** "Very thorough and user-friendly." "He doesn't miss a trick." **Recent work:** Led by Fiona Sinclair in Aspect Contracts (Asbestos) Ltd v Higgins Construction Plc. The matter concerned the interactions between construction adjudication, limitation, negative declarations and unjust enrichment.

Katie Powell (see p.741) Notable junior who frequently appears in significant litigation and complex multiparty actions before both the TCC and Court of Appeal. **Strengths:** "She gets down to the core detail of a case extremely quickly and her drafting is excellent." "One of the brightest and most capable juniors at the Bar." **Recent work:** Led by Fiona Sinclair QC in Rendelsham Estates & Others v Jeffrey Myers & Others, a complex claim arising from alleged defective construction of a block of flats in Liverpool.

Annabel Shaw (see p.763) In-demand junior who is often instructed by major clients in large, high-profile disputes and arbitration. She demonstrates particular strength in related technology matters. **Strengths:** "Has the ability to understand complex cases and to break down vast amounts of material at speed." **Recent work:** Led by Roger Stewart QC in Sir Robert McAlpine v DCA and Hoare Lea, a multi-party dispute concerning a luxury residential development in London.

Paul Cowan (see p.625) Fast-rising junior who was formerly a partner at prominent law firm White & Case. He has noted experience in major international arbitration concerning nuclear power, oil & gas. **Strengths:** "Someone who properly understands client relationships and can go well beyond legality into practicalities." "A very strong draftsman and powerful in the courtroom."

Band 4

Hardwicke

See profile on p.859

THE SET

A burgeoning construction chambers with noted strength in insurance-related construction disputes. Its members are instructed in a wide range of matters including high-value arbitration in the Middle East and significant domestic litigation. A recent highlight for the set has been acting for Orbit Heart of England housing association in its multimillion-pound dispute with Stratford-on-Avon District Council, a matter that hinged upon construction defects in 6,000 properties.

Client service: "The clerks were very commercially savvy and found innovative ways to help us be cost-effective." "Extremely efficient, good turnaround times and highly personable." Practice director Deborah Anderson leads the clerking team.

SILKS

Paul Reed QC Popular QC with a quality practice both domestically and in the Middle East. His offering is enhanced by his acknowledged expertise across the insurance sector. **Strengths:** "A very attractive advocate." "Methodical and commercial." **Recent work:** Advised in Grosvenor Estates v Carillion & Keller, a £25 million claim concerning damage to a building incurred during the reconstruction of a neighbouring property.

Nigel Jones QC Noted silk who draws praise for his advocacy. He counts several large housing associations among his most notable clients. **Strengths:** "Very strong in matters relating to negotiating financial settlements." "A devastatingly effective advocate." **Recent work:** Acted for Orbit Heart of England in its £12 million claim against Stratford on Avon District Council. The claim concerned over 6,000 properties transferred by the defendant to the claimant under a Large Scale Voluntary Transfer agreement in 1996, which were discovered to suffer from construction defects.

JUNIORS

David Pliener Highly regarded senior junior who regularly acts in litigation, arbitration and adjudications nationwide and abroad. He has advised on disputes in sectors as diverse as renewables, structural engineering and leisure. **Strengths:** "A very commercial problem solver who is brilliant with lay clients." "He is able to assert a commanding understanding of facts in the shortest time." **Recent work:** Provided strategic and legal advice on a multimillion-pound dispute arising from a tidal energy project in Ramsey Sound.

Michael Wheater Strong junior with a UK-focused practice who represents clients from across the construction industry, including designers, housing associations and contractors. **Strengths:** "Very strong knowledge of contractual law and matters relating to the negotiation of financial settlements." "Grasps issues quickly and is able to present advice to clients in a very clear, concise way." **Recent work:** Instructed as junior counsel for the respondent in Rydon Maintenance Ltd v Affinity Sutton Housing Ltd, a £3 million dispute arising from an adjudication enforcement.

Catherine Piercy Quality junior whose diverse practice includes regular appearances in adjudications, ADR and high-value litigation. **Strengths:** "Her written work is top class." "She is very commanding and highly effective when dealing with clients and the other side." **Recent work:** Acted for sports charity Cheriton Road Sports Ground Trust in its multimillion-pound final account adjudication against contractors ISG.

Sarah McCann Acts on a variety of domestic disputes including TCC claims and adjudications, with a particular focus on professional negligence and insurance-related construction work. **Strengths:** "A tenacious negotiator." "Extremely pragmatic and commercial." **Recent work:** Acted as junior counsel for Orbit Heart of England housing association against Stratford on Avon Council in a £12 million claim alleging breaches of warranty relating to a transfer agreement.

Brenna Conroy Up-and-coming junior who is increasingly taking on significant litigation, adjudications and international arbitration. Her burgeoning practice wins her the praise of solicitors and peers alike. **Strengths:** "Exceptional case management work." "She's good with clients and very easy to work with." **Recent work:** Led by Paul Darling QC in Henia Investments v Beck Interiors, a multimillion-pound TCC dispute concerning the interpretation of a standard form JCT contract in the context of the Housing Grants, Construction and Regeneration Act 1996.

Other Ranked Lawyers

Paul Letman (3 Hare Court) Highly experienced senior junior who regularly acts for leading house builders and developers in the UK. He also has a notable international practice with major clients in Gibraltar and the Caribbean. **Strengths:** "He is able to identify issues extremely quickly."

Michael Bowsher QC (see p.601) (Monckton Chambers) Experienced silk with a widely admired procurement and construction practice. His specialist work on EU procurement rules has drawn particular praise from industry sources. **Strengths:** "Very strategic. He knows judges well and can shape arguments based on that." "A great person to have because of his diverse practice."

Michael Black QC (XXIV Old Buildings) Highly regarded international arbitration specialist who is noteworthy for his work in Dubai and Africa. He advises on high-value disputes in the oil & gas sectors, among others. **Strengths:** "His attention to detail is superb and he has the court's ear." "He has an outstanding ability to distil and identify the main arguments to be grappled with and pursued."

Tom Montagu-Smith (XXIV Old Buildings) Noted international arbitration specialist who is particularly respected for his work in Dubai. His arbitration enforcement practice elicits praise from market sources. **Strengths:** "He is one of the leading counsel in Dubai International Finance Centre (DIFC) enforcement." "Proactive, user-friendly, totally committed and a clever tactician."

Joanna Smith QC (Wilberforce Chambers) Impressive QC with a strong construction practice and recognised skill in associated professional negligence matters. She regularly acts for prominent supplier-side clients in litigation and adjudications. **Strengths:** "Her written work is fantastic, her advocacy is first-class and she's excellent with clients." "Commercial and a great team player." **Recent work:** Represented a subcontractor in CIP Properties Ltd v Galliford Try, a high-value multiparty dispute concerning the redevelopment of Birmingham Children's Hospital.

MIDLANDS

Construction	
Leading Sets	
Band 1	
No5 Chambers *	
Leading Juniors	
Band 1	
Barrett Kevin	*No5 Chambers* [A]
Ensaff Omar	*No5 Chambers*

Band 1

No5 Chambers

See profile on p.931

THE SET

The pre-eminent construction set on the Midlands Circuit, No5 Chambers houses a team of experienced litigators who also offer expertise in arbitration and mediation proceedings. Members of the set routinely act on behalf of a diverse range of industry players, including developers, individuals, contractors, subcontractors and major construction companies. Its skilled advocates are frequently called upon to handle highly technical cases before the Birmingham TCC.

Client service: The clerking team is led by James Parks. "The clerks will bend over backwards to help." "A highly responsive team."

JUNIORS

Kevin Barrett Widely sought after construction specialist who represents a broad client base consisting of suppliers, consultants, guarantors, contractors and subcontractors. He demonstrates proficiency across an array of matters ranging from the valuation of building work to complex professional negligence claims. He draws on his prior experience as a construction solicitor to inform his burgeoning practice. **Strengths:** "No-nonsense and straightforward approach to issues." "He always comes up with practical solutions."

Omar Ensaff Respected junior whose busy construction practice sees him regularly appearing before the TCC. His broad-based expertise covers areas such as manufacturing, civil engineering, commercial property development and HVAC matters. **Strengths:** "Omar is a terrific advocate and and very tenacious." "He's fantastic, he clearly knows what he's talking about." **Recent work:** Represented the claimant in Saint Gobain Building Distribution v CA Blackwell & Tencate, a case concerning the design and construction of access roads at a wind farm.

NORTHERN/NORTH EASTERN

Construction	
Leading Juniors	
Band 1	
Singer Andrew	*Kings Chambers* *
Band 2	
Edwards Anthony	*St Philips Chambers*
Pennifer Kelly	*Kings Chambers* *

** Indicates firm / individual with profile.*

[A] direct access (see p.24).

Alphabetical order within each band. Band 1 is highest.

Ranked Lawyers

Andrew Singer (see p.766) (Kings Chambers) Widely sought after construction specialist whose practice is not limited to the Northern and North Eastern Circuits, but extends across the UK and Northern Ireland. He regularly appears before the TCC in complex construction disputes and professional negligence-related cases. **Strengths:** "Cuts to the heart of commercial and legal issues really quickly." "Andrew provides commercially focused advice, rolls up his sleeves and gets stuck in." **Recent work:** Represented the Northern Irish Housing Executive in numerous disputes against Healthy Buildings. The related cases centred around a contract for asbestos surveys.

Anthony Edwards (St Philips Chambers) Highly experienced construction specialist practising across a number of sectors including, utilities, transport and healthcare. He often appears before the TCC and routinely handles ICC arbitrations. **Strengths:** "He is very knowledgeable and thorough in his approach." "He is excellent; very clever and knows the system. A first port of call." **Recent work:** Acted as sole counsel in a case relating to the construction of a motorway in Uganda.

Kelly Pennifer (see p.736) (Kings Chambers) Well-regarded junior who regularly acts on behalf of a range of clients, including contractors and subcontractors. She frequently handles complex and extensive construction disputes at all judiciary levels, including in the House of Lords. **Strengths:** "Rapid and pragmatic with a thorough grasp of the legal issues." **Recent work:** Acted against national developer X Plc on behalf of 42 individual claimants who had purchased from them defective properties with circa £100,000 of repairs per unit.

WESTERN

Construction
Leading Sets
Band 1
St John's Chambers *
Leading Juniors
Band 1
Kearney Andrew *St John's Chambers*
Band 2
Sampson Graeme *3PB Barristers (ORL)* ◊
Stead Richard *St John's Chambers* Ⓐ
Taylor Rebecca *St John's Chambers*
* *Indicates firm with profile.*
Ⓐ *direct access (see p.24).*
◊ *(ORL) = Other Ranked Lawyer.*
Alphabetical order within each band. Band 1 is highest.

Band 1

St John's Chambers

See profile on p.941

THE SET

In terms of numbers, St John's Chambers has unmatched firepower in this area. It is the foremost specialist construction chambers on the Western Circuit, with a notable profile in the South Wales market. Its team of highly skilled advocates regularly acts in the most prominent, high-value and heavyweight disputes in the region under the instruction of some of the biggest industry players. Members of St John's demonstrate prowess across a broad range of construction matters including claims of defects, arbitration appeals and professional negligence-related cases.

Client service: "Extremely efficient, you invariably get an immediate response." "The team is always highly efficient and friendly." Robert Bocock leads the clerking.

JUNIORS

Andrew Kearney Widely regarded as the Western Circuit's leading barrister for construction and engineering disputes. A regular at the Bristol TCC, he is frequently instructed in sophisticated and high-profile cases. He routinely represents contractor clients, and is increasingly well known for his adroit handling of matters involving professional negligence elements. **Strengths:** "Andrew easily holds his own and is a talented advocate with exceptional writing skills." "Andrew is committed and tenacious, good on his feet, exceptionally hard working and very bright." **Recent work:** Represented Wheal Jane in a dispute arising from claims made by Linden Homes. The case concerned the discovery of a mine shaft beneath a newly built housing development which had previously received a 'clean bill of health'.

Richard Stead Respected barrister whose construction practice focuses on claims concerning the professional negligence of engineers, surveyors and architects. He also offers deep knowledge of the insurance elements of property damage cases. **Strengths:** "He's a very impressive figure with serious gravitas." "He has an excellent style in court." **Recent work:** Acted for the claimant in Croydon Hotels v Ardmore, a £1.1 million claim for liquidated damages and defective works.

Rebecca Taylor In-demand junior who frequently appears in construction adjudications and mediations. She demonstrates particularly notable ability in fraud-related cases. **Strengths:** "She is good with clients and her submissions to the judge are very mature." **Recent work:** Successfully defended a main contractor at the Cardiff TCC against a claim made by a subcontractor. The case concerned allegedly fraudulent documentation.

Other Ranked Lawyers

Graeme Sampson (3PB Barristers) Highly experienced barrister acting across all types of technically sophisticated construction disputes on behalf of contractors, subcontractors and employers. Regularly advises in adjudication, mediation and arbitration proceedings. **Strengths:** "Very accommodating, quick, dynamic and extremely good at cutting through any irrelevant material." "Very down to earth and always offers practical advice."

Contents:

LONDON

Consumer Law	
Leading Sets	
Band 1	
Gough Square Chambers *	
Band 2	
Henderson Chambers *	
Band 3	
5 Paper Buildings *	
Leading Silks	
Band 1	
Kirk Jonathan	*Gough Square Chambers*
Travers David	*6 Pump Court (ORL)* ◊ *
Waters Malcolm	*Radcliffe Chambers (ORL)* ◊ *
Band 2	
de Haan Kevin	*Francis Taylor Building (ORL)* ◊ 🄰
Hough Jonathan	*4 New Square (ORL)* ◊ *
Mawrey Richard	*Henderson Chambers* 🄰 *
New Silks	
Riley-Smith Toby	*Henderson Chambers* 🄰 *
Leading Juniors	
Star individuals	
Philpott Fred	*Gough Square Chambers*
Band 1	
Andrews Claire	*Gough Square Chambers*
Antrobus Simon	*Crown Office Chambers (ORL)* ◊ *
Barry Denis	*5 Paper Buildings* *
Bennett Miles	*5 Paper Buildings*
Goulding Jonathan	*Gough Square Chambers*
Hibbert William	*Henderson Chambers* *
Lomnicka Eva	*4 New Square (ORL)* ◊ *
MacDonald Iain	*Gough Square Chambers*
Popplewell Simon	*Gough Square Chambers* *
Smith Julia	*Henderson Chambers* *
Watson Mark	*6 Pump Court (ORL)* ◊
Band 2	
Crowe Cameron	*The 36 Group (ORL)* ◊
Douglas-Jones Ben	*5 Paper Buildings* *
Urell Kate	*Gough Square Chambers* *
Band 3	
Bala Ruth	*Gough Square Chambers* *
Falkowski Damian	*39 Essex Chambers (ORL)* ◊ 🄰
Fell Mark	*Radcliffe Chambers (ORL)* ◊ *
Gun Cuninghame Julian	*Gough Square Chambers*
Heller Richard	*Drystone Chambers (ORL)* ◊ *
Neville Stephen	*Gough Square Chambers* *
Rosenthal Dennis	*Henderson Chambers* *
Ross James	*Gough Square Chambers* *
Say Bradley	*Gough Square Chambers* *
Sumnall Charlene	*5 Paper Buildings* *
Warwick Henry	*Henderson Chambers* *
Up-and-coming individuals	
Johnson Andrew	*5 Paper Buildings* *

** Indicates set / individual with profile.*

🄰 direct access (see p.24).

◊ (ORL) = Other Ranked Lawyer.

Alphabetical order within each band. Band 1 is highest.

Band 1

Gough Square Chambers
See profile on p.855

THE SET

Consumer law is the lifeblood of this set that is equally adept at handling both civil and criminal consumer law cases. Its barristers are instructed on behalf of entities of every kind, from banks and corporations to government agencies and local councils, and are regularly involved in the most important cases of the day. By way of example, the set tackled the Supreme Court case of Beavis v ParkingEye Ltd, the leading decision on penalties and unfair terms in consumer contracts. It also handled Secretary of State for Business Innovation and Skills v PLT Anti-Marketing Limited, a matter concerning the application of the Consumer Protection From Unfair Trading Regulations 2008. Sources say of the set that it is "the foremost chambers for consumer credit," with one commenting: "I know that when I turn to them, I'll be supported by excellent QCs and senior juniors."

Client service: "The clerks are very helpful, and you get clear guidance on costs and timescales." "Senior Clerk Bob Weekes is a safe pair of hands, who ensures you have someone who gets the job done in a quality fashion and on time."

SILKS

Jonathan Kirk QC Regularly defends high-profile corporations against claims of mis-selling, and is an expert at advising companies nationwide on their regulatory and enforcement concerns. He is also the editor of the Pink Book on consumer law. **Strengths:** "He's respectful when working with solicitors and very practical with clients; he understands the law, and gets the commercial reality." "He's like a fine wine, and represents a real mark of quality. He's so accessible, and has a very easy manner which helps." **Recent work:** Acted for the parking company in the Supreme Court case of Parking Eye v Beavis, a matter concerning parking charges on private land.

JUNIORS

Fred Philpott Has been at the Bar throughout the lifetime of the Consumer Credit Act and is a foremost expert on it. He regularly advises on the regulatory aspects of the Act and routinely prosecutes banks and retailers accused of putting forward misleading prices. **Strengths:** "For the right case, he's just dynamite! He's prepared for a bit of a scrap, is creative in his legal arguments and what he doesn't know isn't worth knowing." "The guru of consumer law; he's pragmatic, commercial and good at applying his knowledge to the case." **Recent work:** Appeared for the claimant in Kay v Cameira, which concerned the defendant's refusal to repay a sizeable loan on the grounds that the interest rate made the relationship unfair.

Claire Andrews Head of chambers, who has an extensive track record of handling consumer law cases and advising, lecturing and writing on points of interest pertaining to consumer and food law. She is well versed in alternative dispute resolution and has experience of appearing as adjudicator, mediator and arbitrator. **Strengths:** "She was quick to understand the technical issues and imaginative in her counterarguments. She drafted very sensible and commercially realistic responses." "She gives extremely practical advice on what can and can't be done, and has a positive attitude." **Recent work:** Produced Enforcement of Consumer Rights and Protections, a comprehensive reference guide on the enforcement of consumer law, incorporating recent reorganisations and statutory changes within the field.

Jonathan Goulding Advises on both sides of consumer law, tackling criminal prosecutions as well as civil actions. His knowledge encompasses such diverse areas as food safety, consumer protection and unfair trading. **Strengths:** "His advice is practical, and his relationship with clients is good, but he can be firm when he needs to." "He's got a really good manner, and he's very good at simplifying things so everyone understands." **Recent work:** Succesfully acted for the prosecutor in R (Lincolnshire County Council) v Iftakhar Ahmed, in which the defendant was accused of overseeing the sale of counterfeit clothing.

Ruth Bala (see p.588) Has appeared in numerous cases right up to Supreme Court level. She has regularly represented local authorities in counterfeit goods and unfair trading cases, and has also acted for financial institutions in matters concerning enforceability disputes, alleged mis-selling and irresponsible lending. She is an expert on FCA compliance. **Strengths:** "Ruth has a great manner with the client, a quick grasp of the issues and gives detailed advice." "She's very thorough, nice to deal with and comes back to you quickly. She's happy to chat through any problems." **Recent work:** Prosecuted in Lincolnshire CC v Newbury, a case concerning two traders who had misrepresented the quality and price of drive resurfacings to elderly prospective consumers.

Julian Gun Cuninghame His practice has recently concentrated mainly on the representation of borrower entities in consumer credit litigation; he also regularly handles debtor work. **Strengths:** "Personable, knowledgeable and highly competent; he can quote the legislation in front of you. For finance and regulation, he's a first port of call." **Recent work:** Acted in Basinghall Finance Ltd v Momoh, pleading an unfair relationship defence in a case concerning a buy to let property.

Iain MacDonald His diverse consumer law practice takes in food law, trading standards and consumer credit matters in both the Crown and Magistrates' Courts. He regularly acts for well-known retailers, large-scale lending organisations and regulatory bodies. **Strengths:** "He's commercial, liked by clients, and very experienced and accommodating." **Recent work:** Acted for the Civil Aviation Authority in enforcing European Commission regulations against a number of airlines. The regulations concerned consumer compensation in the event of flight cancellations or delays.

Simon Popplewell (see p.740) Has handled regulatory and consumer credit matters throughout the duration of his career. His work typically ranges from representing lenders and drafting consumer credit agreements to advice on consumer contracts and protection. **Strengths:** "He sorts the wheat from the chaff, deals with matters in a succinct manner and has good judgement. His technical ability shines through." "He's very pragmatic in his advice, has a commercial outlook, and has fantastic knowledge of the Consumer Credit Act." **Recent work:** Appeared in The Secretary of State for Business Innovation and Skills v PLT Anti-Marketing Limited, defending the company against BIS's winding-up petition, citing Regulation 6 of the Consumer Protection from Unfair Trading Regulations.

Kate Urell (see p.786) Has a strong general consumer credit practice, having represented many leading financial institutions, and is an expert on due diligence relating to securitisation and licensing issues. Her non-credit practice sees her offering advice on product compliance, advertising and labelling issues. **Strengths:** "She is always on point and responsive. You go to her for precision." "She is able to get to grips with complex issues at great speed, has an impressive attention to detail, and a court manner that is always well received by the judges." **Recent work:** Advised Temple Finance on its consumer credit radio and television advertising campaign.

Stephen Neville (see p.726) Able to draw on over 25 years of experience in the field of consumer lending to advise on the regulatory aspects of large-scale consumer finance transactions. His client base includes a large number of high-profile banks and financial institutions. **Strengths:** "He was very responsive, engaged and easy to work with, and his content was of exceptional quality." "He gives clear, pragmatic and commercial advice." **Recent work:** In Projects Virage & Lagonda, he provided counsel to private equity investors TPG Capital and Blackstone, on FCA and CCA compliance relating to a £4 billion portfolio of secured consumer loans.

James Ross (see p.755) Handles a diverse array of work focused on consumer credit and finance issues generally. He has recently handled a number of mis-selling cases and advised on consumer protection regulatory compliance. **Strengths:** "He has a clear grasp of the credit industry's workings and concerns, and turns papers around very quickly." "A star of the future, he's easy to deal with, approachable, very commercial and pragmatic." **Recent work:** Acted for the claimant bank in the mortgage possession case of Santander UK plc v Harrison. The case concerned the definition of "credit in the form of a cash loan" in the context of the Consumer Credit Act.

Bradley Say (see p.759) Has a strong financial services and consumer credit practice but also handles a wide variety of other cases including those concerning food law and sale of goods in general. He is co-author of 'The Law of Consumer Credit and Hire'. **Strengths:** "Knows the good points from the bad and has a nice clear and simple advocacy style." **Recent work:** Instructed on behalf of the respondents in the test case of In re London Scottish Finance Ltd (in administration), Jack and another v Craig and others. The matter concerned the creditor's compliance with section 77 of the Consumer Credit Act.

Band 2

Henderson Chambers
See profile on p.864

THE SET

A deeply experienced team that tackles a vast range of consumer credit and consumer protection work. Its members are well versed in domestic and European legislation in this area, regularly draft credit and hire agreements, and advise on the enforceability of agreements under consumer credit legislation. Individuals here are well respected for their work in relation to regulatory prosecutions and are famed for their work concerning product recalls. Their extensive client base features financial bodies, government organisations and corporations, as well as private individuals. In recent months, barristers from this set have handled such cases as Burrell and others v Helical (Bramshott Place) Ltd, concerning the possible unfair nature of retirement flats' hidden exit fees, and the Seroxat group litigation, which questioned the possible defective nature of an anti-depressant. Instructors note that they "offer in-depth knowledge in a tricky area of law."

Client service: "Chief Clerk John White is a great practice manager, who is extremely polite and friendly on the phone." "The clerks understand the clients' needs, appreciate the importance of deadlines and promote confidence through the way in which they handle all matters."

SILKS

Richard Mawrey QC (see p.710) A highly accomplished silk in the field of consumer credit who has an extensive history of advising financial institutions on their documentation, new forms of credit and contentious cases. His portfolio of work includes consumer credit advice for the Bar itself. **Strengths:** "He presented extremely well, and did so with an excellent grasp of the facts, issues and practicalities." "He's very practical and commercial – an easy-to-use silk." **Recent work:** Instructed on behalf of the appellants in Southern Pacific Securities v Walker, which related to Consumer Credit Act legislation governing the content and format of regulated agreements. This was the first such case to reach the Supreme Court.

Toby Riley-Smith QC (see p.752) A new silk whose practice is strong on consumer finance and food safety issues. He has handled a number of class actions as well as matters concerning consumer credit and credit hire agreements and food product recall. His clients include banks, government and food-sector producers and importers. **Strengths:** "He gauges the tribunal well, is excellent with clients and is very patient as well." "He's very clearly spoken, technically gifted and a fine advocate."

JUNIORS

William Hibbert (see p.670) Has appeared in the highest courts on numerous occasions in connection with consumer credit matters; he is also deeply immersed in the field of consumer contract regulations. He is capable of handling everything from food labelling to pyramid selling cases. **Strengths:** "He's incredibly charming, unfailingly helpful, incisive and commercial as well." "His knowledge is second to none, and he has a great eye for detail." **Recent work:** Successfully defended GE Home Lending Limited against a number of claims including allegations of unfair relationships, breach of fiduciary duty and PPI mis-selling.

Julia Smith (see p.768) Brings to bear, comprehensive experience in financial and retail sector cases and is able to advise her clients on a broad spectrum of consumer credit issues. Such issues vary from disclosure obligations and unfair terms to non-compliance-related sanctions. **Strengths:** "She's clearly very knowledgeable, with significant experience and a genuine interest and passion for her subject." "She's a strong litigator who sees issues early and is authoritative and persuasive in court." **Recent work:** Successfully acted for the defendant in Ribchester v NRAM Plc and others, a claim concerning an interest only re-mortgage.

Henry Warwick (see p.790) His consumer law practice is strong on the finance side and he regularly deals with consumer credit agreements, personal loans and PPI policies. He is a former solicitor who also handles matters relating to the supply of services and sale of goods. **Strengths:** "Henry has impressed us with his straightforward approach and his thorough grasp of the complex and rapidly evolving law surrounding PPI mis-selling." "He is good if you need urgent advice as he can deal with issues quickly." **Recent work:** Represented the lender organisation in the case of Axton & Another v GE Money, a case concerning unfair lending relationships.

Dennis Rosenthal (see p.755) Able to provide guidance on a wealth of consumer law issues, from retail banking to data protection, Dennis focuses his practice on the drafting of credit and hire documentation, financial regulation and claims of unfair contract terms, amongst other issues. **Strengths:** "His main strength is his breadth of knowledge of Consumer Credit Law, and his ability to apply the law in commercial situations." "He knows his stuff, and his approach is practical." **Recent work:** Gave counsel to the Consumer Credit Trade Association over an extended period of time, and on a range of consumer law concerns. These included goods and services issues, the liability and release of joint debtors and unfair contract terms.

Band 3

5 Paper Buildings
See profile on p.889

THE SET

Members of 5 Paper Buildings are highly experienced in a broad array of consumer law areas, and have particular aptitude for matters concerning confiscation and restraint. Their client base encompasses prosecuting authorities and agencies, defendant individuals and brand-name businesses. Recent cases involving the set's members include Operation Canister, which concerned defendants implicated in widespread mobile phone insurance fraud, and Stanley Ashton v FACT LTD, which related to the use of a domestic services contract to show live sports on non-domestic premises. The highly adept barristers here are proficient at handling anything from trade descriptions and pricing offences to product safety, food safety and underage sales cases.

Client service: "The clerking team was very responsive and helped to accommodate our needs." "Dale Jones is a super senior clerk who is very smart and charming. He's the kind of clerk other clerks fear, in a good way."

JUNIORS

Denis Barry (see p.590) Handles consumer law as part of a wider criminal practice and has been involved in some of the most important matters around including the largest case ever prosecuted by the OFT. He obtained the largest consumer law confiscation order in a case ever, and has further established his credentials by becoming the lead editor of the main guide to the new Consumer Rights Act. He further acts in an advisory capacity for companies. **Strengths:** "He displays incredible attention to detail, is always well prepared and can get to grips with large volumes of paperwork." "A very capable advocate who quickly wins over juries with his charm." **Recent work:** Represented the prosecutors, Cambridge Trading Standards, in R v Murphy and Murphy, a money laundering and copyright case regarding the importing and sale of bootlegs. This case incorporated extensive expert evidence from copyright and trade mark holders.

Miles Bennett Highly experienced in relation to the regulatory and criminal aspects of consumer law as well as tangential areas of law such as product safety inquests, trade mark infringement matters and health and safety cases. He acts for prosecuting bodies and defends companies and directors. **Strengths:** "Exceptionally good at dealing with individuals; he allays their fears, explains the processes and owns the courtroom while he's there." "He's very experienced, is immensely affable and has an encyclopaedic knowledge of consumer law." **Recent work:** Appeared in R v Fox (and 10 others), representing the CMA in prosecuting a pyramid promotional scheme involving 11 defendants, nine of whom were convicted. These convictions were upheld at the Court of Appeal.

Ben Douglas-Jones (see p.635) Defends businesses and professionals against consumer-related claims and prosecutes on behalf of private entities, local authorities and the MHRA. His work takes in environment and food safety cases as well as trade mark and copyright matters. **Strengths:** "He's very good at explaining all the risks and requirements, and has a solid understanding of many areas of the law." **Recent work:** Provided counsel for the first defendant in Operation Cleo (R v Oliver et al), which concerned the alleged creation of a copycat website to deliberately resemble a government site in order to mislead consumers.

Charlene Sumnall (see p.776) Both prosecutes and defends consumer law cases in all levels of tribunals including the Court of Appeal. Her clients include local authorities, prosecution agencies, companies, directors and individuals, and she is an expert in everything from trading standards to copyright infringement. **Strengths:** "A strong personality who is a fierce performer in court. She's very knowledgeable, brings a lot of energy to a case, and is good with tricky clients." **Recent work:** Represented the director of a roof tile coating company who was accused of duping elderly consumers into purchasing a product that didn't work.

Andrew Johnson (see p.683) A skilled criminal lawyer who has cultivated a consumer law practice and now advises and acts for both defendants and prosecuting regulators. His client base includes several trading standards entities who turn to him for advice on the scope of their investigations. **Strengths:** "He's passionate and hard working, his turnaround time is very quick and I can call him any time." "He has a phenomenal knowledge of black-letter law." **Recent work:** Advised and later prosecuted on behalf of Hertfordshire Trading Standards in the case of R v Perry Waterman. In this matter the defendant was accused of selling counterfeit vehicle components and later found guilty of fraud and trade mark infringements.

Other Ranked Lawyers

Simon Antrobus (see p.584) (Crown Office Chambers) Boasts a high-profile national client following across the retail, food and hospitality sectors, and regularly defends criminal investigations of a highly sensitive nature. **Strengths:** "He gets to the heart of an issue and brings to bear a lot of knowledge as well as emotional intelligence." "He's attentive on the detail, and extremely well prepared." **Recent work:** Acted for Nutricia in R (on the application of Nutricia Ltd) v the Department of Health, which concerned the defendant's decision to classify a new product as a 'food supplement' rather than a 'medical food'.

Richard Heller (see p.669) (Drystone Chambers) Well versed in the prosecution of brand-name retailers, he tackles complex and large-scale regulatory crime cases. He frequently acts for Environmental Health Services and Trading Standards, and also has a strong defence practice. **Strengths:** "He knows the law and has done some good cases." **Recent work:** In the case of Princesse D'Isenbourg Co Limited, he represented the Royal Borough of Kensington and Chelsea in prosecuting the luxury foods trader on the grounds that it had been selling mislabelled caviar.

Damian Falkowski (39 Essex Chambers) Displays particular prowess in matters concerning mortgages and short-term finance and is often instructed, on the lender side, on issues concerning unfair relationships and mortgage fraud allegations. He also appears on investment mis-selling cases of high worth. **Strengths:** "He's a very reliable street fighter who goes the extra mile."

Kevin de Haan QC (Francis Taylor Building) Handles consumer law cases as part of a flourishing practice that also takes in health and safety, licensing and environment matters. He is an expert on enforcement and European legislation.

Jonathan Hough QC (see p.675) (4 New Square) Well versed in consumer credit matters, he provides representation for financial entities and their clients, and is an expert on consumer credit agreements and documentation. He also represents major motor insurers with regards to credit hire litigation. **Strengths:** "He has an excellent way of making the complicated understandable." "Very incisive, he's a very strong advocate who delivers exceptionally prompt and well-thought through advice." **Recent work:** In Baxendale-Walker v APL, he defended the solicitors against a Part 20 claim for negligent advice and drafting, brought by a lender which is itself under scrutiny for an alleged unenforceable loan agreement.

Eva Lomnicka (see p.703) (4 New Square) Both an academic who teaches at King's College London and an accomplished barrister who advises on consumer credit and other financial services issues. She is a noted expert on the legislation its impact on the provision of financial products in this area. **Strengths:** "She provides intelligent and thoughtful advice, she is always a pleasure to work with and she always gives matters her full attention." **Recent work:** Provided counsel to Edinburgh University with regards to whether FCA authorisation was necessary in order to furnish prospective employees with credit.

David Travers QC (see p.784) (6 Pump Court) Focuses his work around cases of a highly complex or sensitive nature, particularly in relation to food safety and consumer credit. He both defends and prosecutes, appearing on behalf of businesses and local and national government bodies. **Strengths:** "A silent assassin with a huge brain: in a contentious situation, he'll have spotted all the angles and witnesses don't see him coming." "He takes the pressure off due to his calm demeanour." **Recent work:** Acted for the defendants in R (London Borough of Havering) v Mitchells and Butlers Ltd and others. The case concerned widespread illness and one death caused by food poisoning from a Christmas lunch service.

Mark Watson (6 Pump Court) Highly experienced at both prosecuting and defending food and trading standards cases, he appears on behalf of companies and regulators such as the Food Standards Agency. He is also adept in matters regarding the enforcement of energy sector regulations. **Strengths:** "Very bright, very tenacious, highly efficient and very hard working." "He's technically astute, has a photographic memory and possesses an amazing ability to recall things." **Recent work:** Acted for the prosecutor in Food Standards Agency v Hala Abbatoirs Ltd, which concerned a number of hygiene and food safety regulations which had been violated.

Malcolm Waters QC (see p.790) (Radcliffe Chambers) Has strong financial services and retail banking knowledge and is often instructed to advise and act for a range of financial entities. He is particularly good at advising on unfair terms legislation relating to retail banking products. **Strengths:** "I was impressed with how approachable he was." "He was very familiar with the area and could give concise advice at short notice." **Recent work:** Represented NRAM in the test case of NRAM plc v McAdam and Hartley, regarding the recovery of interest on unregulated loan agreements that had been documented and processed as though they had been regulated by the CCA.

Mark Fell (see p.643) (Radcliffe Chambers) Advises financial sector organisations and regulatory bodies alike on a broad range of consumer finance and retail banking issues. He has experience of advising on sector-specific transactions and the redrafting of account terms. **Strengths:** "Shows meticulous attention to detail, together with clarity and precision in drafting, and has a patient, accessible and responsive manner." "He gets straight to the heart of the issue and is very user-friendly." **Recent work:** In Financial Conduct Authority v HFO, he assisted the FCA with its attempt to exclude a debt-collecting entity from from the consumer credit market.

Cameron Crowe (36 Bedford Row) Regularly tackles cases concerning money laundering, trading standards transgressions and related fraud, appearing on behalf of both the defence and the prosecution. He further provides advice to brand companies on their intellectual property concerns. **Strengths:** "He has strong knowledge of Trading Standards law, and presents cases in a clear and compelling way." "He's very commercial, highly approachable and takes a good attitude with solicitors." **Recent work:** Appeared in Northamptonshire County Council v Harpreet Garcha, acting for the council in bringing claims of fraudulent trading against the director of a letting company who had been accused, inter alia, of establishing a scam property maintenance organisation.

MIDLANDS

Consumer Law
Leading Juniors
Band 1
Berlin Barry *St Philips Chambers*
Band 2
Mills Ben *St Philips Chambers* Ⓐ *
Thorogood Bernard *No5 Chambers*
* *Indicates individual with profile.*
Ⓐ *direct access (see p.24).*
Alphabetical order within each band. Band 1 is highest.

Ranked Lawyers

Bernard Thorogood (No5 Chambers) Highly experienced at handling complex and severe health and safety cases, including those concerning fatalities. He has been instructed to defend, prosecute or advise clients as varied as NHS trusts, local authorities and large-scale businesses. **Strengths:** "He's meticulous, extremely hard-working, and definitely regarded as a leader in the field."

Barry Berlin (St Philips Chambers) A well-established presence in the regulatory field, who is instructed in environment and health cases as well as consumer law matters. He often receives briefs from governmental entities such as Ofcom, the HSE and local authorities. **Strengths:** "He's been doing regulatory law for a long time, and has a wealth of experience." "He's very forthright and direct." **Recent work:** Acted for the regulator in Office of Fair Trading v Furniture Village, where artificially inflated sofa prices designed to give the illusion of significant sale savings were alleged to have existed in contravention of the BIS Price Practice Guide.

Ben Mills (see p.718) (St Philips Chambers) His practice focuses on the nationwide prosecution of individuals for acts of money laundering, blackmail and other regulatory infringements within the financial sphere. He is also frequently instructed in cases relating to fire safety and consumer fraud. **Strengths:** "He's very cool, calm and collected, and able to answer even the most ridiculous questions." "He thinks through a case, and takes time to consider all the outcomes." **Recent work:** Represented the defendants in R v Nottingham Student Lettings Ltd and Robert Singh, addressing accusations that they had failed to provide adequate fire safety measures and risk assessments in new student housing.

Contents:

ALL CIRCUITS

Costs Litigation
Leading Sets
Band 1
Hailsham Chambers *
4 New Square *
Band 2
39 Essex Chambers *
Temple Garden Chambers *
Band 3
Kings Chambers *
Leading Silks
Band 1
Bacon Nicholas *4 New Square* *
Band 2
Browne Simon P *Temple Garden Chambers*
Holland David *Landmark Chambers (ORL)* ◊
Hutton Alexander *Hailsham Chambers* *
Band 3
Kirby PJ *Hardwicke (ORL)* ◊ Ⓐ
Post Andrew *Hailsham Chambers* *
Sachdeva Vikram *39 Essex Chambers* *
Williams Benjamin *4 New Square*
Leading Juniors
Star individuals
Mallalieu Roger *4 New Square* *
Band 1
Ayling Judith *39 Essex Chambers*
Carpenter Jamie *Hailsham Chambers* *
Marven Robert *4 New Square* *
Band 2
Brown Simon J *Crown Office Chambers (ORL)* ◊
Edwards Simon *39 Essex Chambers*
Friston Mark *Kings Chambers*
Hogan Andrew *Ropewalk Chambers (ORL)* ◊
James Mark *Temple Garden Chambers*
Lambert Sarah *1 Crown Office Row (ORL)* ◊
Saoul Daniel *4 New Square* *
Band 3
Hughes Paul *Kings Chambers* *
Laughland James *Temple Garden Chambers*
McDonald George *4 New Square* *
Munro Joshua *Hailsham Chambers* Ⓐ *
Ralph Craig *Kings Chambers* *
Stacey Dan *Hailsham Chambers* *
Wilkinson Richard *Temple Garden Chambers* *
Band 4
Benson Imran *Hailsham Chambers* *
Greaney Nicola *39 Essex Chambers* *
Joseph Paul *No5 Chambers (ORL)* ◊
Kapoor Shaman *Temple Garden Chambers*
Latham Kevin *Kings Chambers* *
Moore Oliver *Guildhall Chambers (ORL)* ◊
Scott Katharine *39 Essex Chambers*
Smith Matthew *Kings Chambers* *
Wibberley James *Guildhall Chambers (ORL)* ◊
Wignall Gordon *6 Pump Court (ORL)* ◊ Ⓐ
Up-and-coming individuals
Bedford Erica *Kings Chambers* *

** Indicates set / individual with profile.*

Ⓐ direct access (see p.24).

◊ (ORL) = Other Ranked Lawyer.

Alphabetical order within each band. Band 1 is highest.

Band 1

Hailsham Chambers
See profile on p.857

THE SET

Hailsham Chambers has an outstanding costs practice and boasts a strong bench of highly experienced specialist counsel. Its members handle a full range of costs disputes and have experience of representing a diverse body of clients in the High Court, Court of Appeal and Supreme Court. Interviewees say: "It's good to have a chambers you can rely on in such a specialist area, especially given the complexities of costs litigation and its constantly changing nature."

Client service: "We went to a costs seminar they put on, which was an excellent presentation." Stephen Smith leads a team that includes Michael Kilbey who is "very commercial, and always prepared to discuss fees."

SILKS

Alexander Hutton QC (see p.679) Described by interviewees as "the best advocate in the country for clinical negligence costs and funding." In addition to representing clients in contentious matters, he frequently advises solicitors on non-contentious matters relating to retainers and CFAs. **Strengths:** "He's a true specialist in this rather complex field and he's been a leader in it for many years so his knowledge is absolutely first class. He also does what not many counsel do in that he's equally good on paper as he is on his feet in court. In addition, he's a very effective member of a team – he has a very collegiate and collaborative approach." **Recent work:** Represented the defendant in Diann Blankley v Central Manchester Children's Hospital Healthcare NHS Trust, a complex conditional fee agreement appeal concerning the effect of loss of capacity on contracts.

Andrew Post QC (see p.741) Combines expertise in costs and clinical negligence, and is frequently instructed in cases of high value or matters where a point of principle may arise. He has considerable experience of matters relating to retainers and solicitor-client disputes. **Strengths:** "Andrew marries a wealth of expertise and experience with an approachable manner. He gives shrewd and commercial advice." **Recent work:** Acted in McGraw Hill v Deutsche Apotheker, a piece of large-scale cross-border litigation with major conflict of laws issues.

JUNIORS

Jamie Carpenter (see p.611) A standout costs practitioner who undertakes a full range of work in this sector including applications for wasted and non-party costs orders. He also drafts funding arrangements, and has a wealth of experience in heavyweight solicitor-client disputes. **Strengths:** "Extremely bright and clear in his advice, he is an expert on lawyer liability and costs issues, and is very relaxed with clients." "He is incredibly smart yet approachable, and has a great eye for detail." "He gives pragmatic, commercial advice and is always well prepared and eloquent." **Recent work:** Successfully represented the defendant in Omatov v Macaria Investments in an appeal against a judge's decision to refuse to set aside a default costs certificate.

Joshua Munro (see p.724) "A rising star in professional negligence and costs law," who has extensive experience as a litigator, and has appeared in costs cases at all levels including before the SCCO and the House of Lords. **Strengths:** "He is excellent at understanding the issues and provides relevant advice." **Recent work:** Represented Wiltshire PCT in a challenge against the reasonableness of CFA uplifts and insurance premiums in respect of clinical negligence claims.

Dan Stacey (see p.771) Has a full range of knowledge in costs cases including CFA disputes and solicitor-client disputes. He has represented clients in the High Court and Court of Appeal, and has also advised on DBAs and drafting CFAs. **Strengths:** "Dan is very reliable and gives us more confidence than we might have when we first go to him. He is very committed to the client and gives great advice when we find ourselves in stressful situations – he remains totally unfazed, which is very reassuring." "He is assured and unflappable in court." **Recent work:** Acted for Macpherson in a hearing involving a legal principle concerning a costs judge's discretion when finding that a solicitor must pay the client's costs, in particular when these costs have been reduced by more than a fifth.

Imran Benson (see p.594) Undertakes costs work as part of a busy commercial law practice. He assists clients with both contentious and non-contentious issues, and is increasingly taking on arbitration work. Recent cases handled have included own-client disputes and those dealing with issues rising from firm mergers. **Strengths:** "His advice is very practical and he gives us exactly what we need – good advice that is short and to the point." "He gave a really good, solid performance and demonstrated a good in-depth knowledge of costs law." **Recent work:** Advised Matthew Arnold Baldwin on the assignment of CFAs and the drafting of documents during its merger with Dentons.

4 New Square
See profile on p.880

THE SET

The pre-eminent set for costs litigation, it has members who offer market-leading expertise across the full range of costs cases and frequently handle high-profile and landmark matters in the Court of Appeal and Supreme Court. Recent examples of work undertaken include Coventry v Lawrence. One source states: "If the case is important, I wouldn't use any other chambers – any appeals or cases of significant value go to 4 New Square."

Client service: "The clerks, led by James Barrass, are helpful, friendly, organised and go out of their way to make the experience as easy as possible."

SILKS

Nicholas Bacon QC (see p.587) Recognised market leader whose "reputation goes before him." He heads the set's costs team and boasts an enviable résumé having led cases in the Supreme Court and handled other significant appeals. **Strengths:** "Superlatives can't describe how good he is – he's brilliant and always willing to put in extra time." "The only QC to instruct on anything costs related. Hands on and user-friendly, he's an excellent advocate and the standout leader in his field." **Recent work:** Represented Newsgroup Newspapers in Andrew Mitchell v Newsgroup Newspapers, a Court of Appeal case regarding the application of the new overriding objective and CPR 3.9 relief from sanction principles.

Benjamin Williams QC Skilled and well-respected advocate who draws praise for his in-depth knowledge of costs law. He frequently handles cases at the highest level, and has recently been active in a number of precedent-setting cases in the Court of Appeal and Supreme Court. **Strengths:** "If it's a technical point, Ben is your man." "He is extremely sharp witted, very good with clients and very accommodating." **Recent work:** Successfully represented Mr & Mrs Coventry and their insurers in Coventry v Lawrence, a high-profile Supreme Court decision regarding a challenge to the compatibility of the CFA funding regime with the ECHR.

JUNIORS

Roger Mallalieu (see p.706) "The best junior counsel in the field of costs," he frequently represents parties in solicitor-client disputes, third-party costs cases and CFA compliance matters. **Strengths:** "His knowledge and command of the material is spectacular." "He's superb. A master in his field, he doesn't waste time but gets to the point quickly and is wonderful in court. Excellent on both procedure and substantive law, he can confidently be recommended to any client." **Recent work:** Represented the Association of Costs Lawyers in Coventry v Lawrence, a high-profile Supreme Court decision regarding a challenge to the compatibility of the CFA funding regime with the ECHR.

Robert Marven (see p.708) Well versed in costs, CFAs, fixed fee regimes and litigation funding (including commercial funding for significant disputes). His client roster includes public bodies, insurers and private individuals. **Strengths:** "Very intelligent, excellent with difficult clients and very forensic." "If you need someone to really hit a point home, go with Robert – he isn't afraid to stick his neck out and fight the client's corner." "The thing that makes him stand out is the confidence he has in his own ability when making a difficult call on the merits of the case." **Recent work:** Acted in O'Brien v Shorrock & Motor Insurers Bureau, a High Court appeal concerning various issues in relation to the CFA between the claimant and his solicitors.

Daniel Saoul (see p.758) Previously qualified as a solicitor-advocate, he frequently handles solicitor-client costs disputes. He also boasts experience of practising as an attorney in the British Virgin Islands. **Strengths:** "In court he can be as aggressive as he needs to be whilst also being subtle and nuanced in how he handles things." "He was previously in private practice so has a very sympathetic and knowledgeable understanding of exactly what we as solicitors require – he combines an excellent grounding in costs with an understanding of why we do what we do, which he can then justify in detailed assessments." **Recent work:** Represented Addleshaw Goddard in respect of a claim brought by the firm to recover more than £12 million in unpaid legal fees from the Estate of their former client Boris Berezovsky.

George McDonald (see p.712) Represents a range of clients in complex costs disputes. He has particular experience of handling the specific costs issues relating to large group actions and complicated funding structures. **Strengths:** "He's a very pleasant guy – his customer service skills are excellent, his drafting is spot on, and his advocacy and delivery are very good." **Recent work:** Acted as costs counsel for Mirror Group Newspapers Limited in Gulati & others v MGN Limited, a high-profile phone hacking litigation.

Band 2

39 Essex Chambers

See profile on p.840

THE SET

39 Essex Chambers is well known for its multidisciplinary approach in costs advocacy, undertaking a full range of cases where these issues arise. The team has notable experience of advising on potential funding arrangements and of drafting costs documentation including legal expenses insurance policies. Members act for practitioners, insurers, funders and litigants, and are often to be seen in the appeal courts.

Client service: "The clerks, led by Alistair Davidson, are very amenable and flexible in helping to find counsel."

SILKS

Vikram Sachdeva QC (see p.757) Has considerable expertise in commercial costs and the disciplinary aspects of costs work, and also frequently appears in the Court of Appeal. Lately, he has impressed sources with his handling of notably complex cases. **Strengths:** "Has few peers when it comes to his knowledge of costs law and its practical application." **Recent work:** Acted for the successful appellant in Utilise v Davies, an important case marking the judiciary drawing back from decisions made in the Mitchell case of 40 years ago. The case concerned deviation from court directions.

JUNIORS

Judith Ayling Impressive senior junior with a substantial costs practice, who one source highlights as being a "costs guru." She regularly appears in detailed assessment hearings as well as appeals. Ayling is a popular choice of counsel for cases arising from personal injury and clinical negligence claims. **Strengths:** "I find her very approachable, reliable and sensible. She is very aware of the client's needs and is accurate and succinct in her advice." "Judith really understands complex litigation, and has a tremendous grasp of costs law." **Recent work:** Represented HMRC in a high-value case involving a VAT appeal. The case concerned the calculation of costs under a contingency fee agreement.

Simon Edwards Experienced advocate who is highly knowledgeable when it comes to conditional fee arrangements and other costs issues. His practice encompasses drafting solicitors' retainers, advising on third-party funding agreements and representing clients in litigious matters. **Strengths:** "He is a very bright chap." "In a detailed assessment hearing, he proved very helpful and practical." **Recent work:** Represented the claimant in Rylatt Chubb v Mengise, Solicitor's Act proceedings concerning the proper treatment of disbursements.

Nicola Greaney (see p.659) Regularly instructed in costs cases relating to clinical negligence and personal injury, and active in the recovery of costs against legally aided parties. As a member of the Attorney General's panel, she often represents the government in matters relating to this sector. **Strengths:** "She's very thorough, quick to respond and very bright as well." "Able to grasp the issues quickly, she gets to the nub of the matter without needing too much input." **Recent work:** Acted for the Secretary of State for the Home Department in a challenge to the government's use of the re Eastwood principle stating that in-house lawyers can recover the same costs as solicitors in private practice.

Katharine Scott Advises both claimants and defendants in all areas of costs litigation, undertaking party and party disputes as well as client and own-solicitor cases. In addition, she has significant expertise of matters relating to personal injury and clinical negligence. **Strengths:** "She's very clever and confident in what she does." "She's thorough, alive to issues and robust." **Recent work:** Successfully represented the paying party in Collis v Vision Express, which involved issues such as proportionality, hourly rates and success fee.

Temple Garden Chambers

See profile on p.919

THE SET

A highly regarded set with a notable team of costs barristers. Individuals here have been involved in numerous substantial cases involving matters such as conditional fee agreements and costs budgeting. Four of the practitioners are qualified to handle specialist costs mediation, a recent area of growth for the chambers. Members also provide regular lectures and costs training for clients. Clients say: "The chambers is very professional and efficient; it has excellent barristers and fine clerks."

Client service: "The clerks, led by senior clerk Dean Norton, are excellent and very accommodating." "They are very approachable, accommodating and personable. Nothing is too difficult for them."

SILKS

Simon Browne QC A standout individual who has considerable expertise in costs cases associated with heavy commercial and group litigation. He also sits on the Civil Justice Council for costs matters. **Strengths:** "Very approachable, down to earth and someone who offers top-quality advice. He's always very practical; he thinks through the consequences and is five steps ahead of everyone else." "He knows all the rules and regulations, and knows exactly which buttons to press." **Recent work:** Successfully represented a group of claimants against Mirror Group Limited in a damages and costs case.

JUNIORS

Mark James Undertakes a wide range of costs litigation including cases concerning champerty, solicitors' retainers and cost budgeting. He also regularly appears in applications for wasted and non-party costs. He has gained notable experience in claims against solicitors and barristers involving professional negligence. **Strengths:** "Very, very good in hearings and excellent in court. He's also clear and precise in his advice." **Recent work:** Assisted Chantel Investments with a professional negligence claim against its former solicitors that had resulted in major costs for the client.

James Laughland Experienced costs counsel who is habitually instructed in matters concerning costs budgeting and clinical negligence. He routinely acts on behalf of solicitors, clients and legal expense insurers. **Strengths:** "Very accessible and approachable, he is a lawyer who gives clear advice and builds up a good rapport with the client." "A leading costs junior who knows the law on ATE and success fees like the back of his hand." **Recent work:** Successfully represented the claimant in Nokes v Heart of England NHS Foundation Trust, defending a challenge to Nokes' clinical negligence ATE premium.

Richard Wilkinson (see p.795) Works with clients on a litigious and advisory basis, representing them in costs disputes in the SCCO and appellate courts. His areas of focus include commercial law, privacy, clinical negligence and personal injury disputes. **Strengths:** "Sensible, pragmatic and very responsive to the client's needs." "Efficient and excellent at identifying the costs arguments that really matter," he's "knowledgeable and provides practical advice." **Recent work:** Represented the claimant in Shannon v Global Tunnelling Experts UK Limited, proceedings to determine liability for costs contingent upon a discontinued personal injury claim.

Shaman Kapoor Handles costs matters, representing clients in both the SCCO and High Court. He has notable experience in international arbitration proceedings and is also a qualified costs mediator. **Strengths:** "Absolutely brilliant with the client." **Recent work:** Acted in Peters & Peters LLP v Mirchandani, a solicitor-client dispute about fees where fees had exceeded £2.3 million in circumstances where the defendant claimed the only estimate he received was for £300,000.

Band 3

Kings Chambers
See profile on p.968

THE SET

The go-to costs set on the Northern and North Eastern circuits, but also a chambers with a national presence. Its team of specialist junior barristers undertakes work in both an advisory and contentious capacity, handling appeals, fixed cost disputes, solicitor own-client disputes and allegations of misconduct. Members of the set regularly appear in the SCCO and appellate courts. Interviewees say: "The barristers here are easy to engage, have a genuine interest in the subject and are very pleasant people to deal with."

Client service: "The clerks, led by Stephen Loxton, are capable, efficient, flexible and easy to deal with."

JUNIORS

Mark Friston Highlighted by sources for his academic prowess and "encyclopaedic knowledge" of costs law, Friston handles a range of contentious and non-contentious matters. Notable areas of expertise for him include conditional fee agreements and cost sharing agreements. **Strengths:** "Probably the leading junior in terms of technical knowledge, he's on a par with any QC when it comes to costs and litigation funding."

Paul Hughes (see p.677) A costs and litigation funding practitioner who specialises in procedural law and the costs of actions based on negligence. He is regularly instructed in disputes relating to misconduct, wasted costs and non-party costs orders. **Strengths:** "Very knowledgeable in respect of the costs arena." **Recent work:** Represented the claimant in Flear v Reichert Jung, a case arising from a tranche of nearly 30 deafness claims.

Craig Ralph (see p.747) Handles costs and litigation funding cases, and has notable experience in costs budgeting, high-value claims and group litigation. Sources say he has a noted specialism in conduct relating to solicitor and own-client matters. He is also a qualified mediator. **Strengths:** "He is able to get to grips quickly with the key issues." "His knowledge is exceptional and he has the ability to present a case in a fashion that is appealing to varying levels of the judiciary." **Recent work:** Represented the claimants in a Kenyan group action claim against the Foreign and Commonwealth Office concerning allegations of serious mistreatment during the 'Mau Mau' rebellion.

Kevin Latham (see p.696) Undertakes both costs and personal injury cases, and boasts impressive experience in the courtroom. He regularly appears in solicitor and own-client disputes, and has handled a number of cases concerning wasted and third-party costs orders. Recently, he has also qualified as a mediator. **Strengths:** "He really fought the client's corner, worked hard and went the extra mile. He is a bright and competent lawyer." "A strong, sharp advocate with excellent technical knowledge." **Recent work:** Acted for YSL Beauté Limited & L'Oréal (UK) Limited as the defendant in an appeal regarding the effect the removal of a defendant company from the register has on the status of costs proceedings.

Matthew Smith (see p.769) Has wide experience in costs law including costs appeals, group litigations, matters regarding success fees and solicitor-client disputes. Additionally, he has significant knowledge of non-contentious costs and issues concerning retainers' contracts. **Strengths:** "Competent and personable, he's very sensible and can cut to the chase quickly with his advice." "Light on his feet, he reacts well to judges, and is responsive and accessible." **Recent work:** Acted in Jamadar v Bradford Teaching Hospitals NHS Trust, a case concerning whether CPR 3.13 required the filing of the costs budget where the claim was unallocated and the notice of proposed allocation had been revoked.

Erica Bedford (see p.593) An experienced junior barrister who maintains a specialist costs practice, appearing before the SCCO as well as the Court of Appeal and High Courts. **Recent work:** "A skilled advocate who is professional in her manner and convincing both in her presentation to the court and in her advice to the firm." "She is a strong advocate and a pleasure to work with." **Recent work:** Acted for the respondent in Hahn v NHS England. The appeal concerned questions such as whether the premium could be assessed with a broad brush, and the approach in applying proportionality.

Other Ranked Lawyers

Simon Brown (Crown Office Chambers) Leading barrister with an extensive costs and professional negligence practice who handles solicitor and client disputes and third-party costs orders, amongst others. Of late, he has been instructed in detailed assessment hearings as well as High Court appeals. **Strengths:** "Very knowledgeable on all aspects of costs law." **Recent work:** Appeared in the Court of Appeal representing the Official Solicitor in Wilsons Solicitor v Bentine and the Official Solicitor, regarding the one-fifth rule under s.70(9) of the Solicitor's Act.

Sarah Lambert (1 Crown Office Row) Well-regarded costs practitioner with wide-ranging experience in the field who is a popular choice for cases involving wasted costs, CFA compliance, success fees and costs capping. She regularly appears in the SCCO, County and High Courts, as well as the Court of Appeal. **Strengths:** "She gets to the root of the case very quickly and is excellent on her feet. She knows how to read a judge and take the points which need to be taken." **Recent work:** Represented the appellant in Cashman v Mid-Essex Hospital Services NHS Trust.

Oliver Moore (Guildhall Chambers) Specialising in personal injury claims and costs litigation, he has a caseload that sees him tackling detailed assessments in the SCCO, representing clients in costs settlements and handling costs appeals. Clients include both paying and receiving parties. **Strengths:** "Has a real interest in costs and always gets his facts and figures straight."

James Wibberley (Guildhall Chambers) Experienced in costs and litigation funding, he advises on such matters as own-client disputes and the enforceability of funding arrangements. He also assists with wasted costs and non-party costs applications. **Strengths:** "He's extremely knowledgeable and it's hard to beat him."

PJ Kirby QC (Hardwicke) An experienced commercial silk whose practice encompasses all areas of costs law. He is active in costs litigation in the SCCO, undertakes advisory work and drafts DBAs for firms. His skills are further demonstrated by his appointment as a High Court costs assessor. **Strengths:** "He is extremely user-friendly, very bright, commercial and a pleasure to work with." "He provides excellent, strategic legal advice." **Recent work:** Successfully acted for the appellant in Just Costs v Stone Rowe Brewer, a case that examined what constitutes "exceptional circumstances" with regard to Solicitors Act assessments.

David Holland QC (Landmark Chambers) An experienced litigator who is regularly instructed by the Law Society in complex costs disputes. Lately, he has been particularly involved in cases taken to the Court of Appeal, as well as in detailed assessment hearings. **Strengths:** "He's tenacious, he gives me support which is rare for a QC. He reads through the papers, challenges you, and picks you up on things, which I really like." **Recent work:** Handled an appeal for the claimant in MWP v Sinclair, which concerned the application of CPR Part 3.1(7) to an order.

Paul Joseph (No5 Chambers) A commercial practitioner who has a notable focus in the costs field. He has considerable experience of issues relating to pre-action protocols and the fixed cost regime, and also handles appeals and detailed assessments. **Strengths:** "He's very good and knows a lot about costs." **Recent work:** Assisted Michael Wilson and Partners Limited with a costs case concerning the recovery of USD5.9 million in fees.

Gordon Wignall (6 Pump Court) Costs specialist who frequently undertakes cases in both litigious and advisory capacities. In particular, he has recently been involved in group litigations; he has also advised on innovative EU principles relating to the remaining rules of champerty. **Strengths:** "He has extremely deep and extensive knowledge of costs topics." "He's very thorough, clear in his advice and friendly." **Recent work:** Recently involved in group litigation relating to a claim of costs recovery considered unlawful due to the breaching of cooling-off periods.

Andrew Hogan (Ropewalk Chambers) Represents paying and receiving parties in the County Court, High Court, Court of Appeal and Supreme Court. Recently, he has been involved in high-value detailed assessments, industrial deafness claims and cases involving the assignment of CFAs. Hogan is the author of an authoritative blog regarding the costs sector. **Strengths:** "A highly regarded practitioner who is very concise in his advice and gets to the heart of the issues very quickly." "Very personable, he understands the issues and is very good at explaining a particular legal point." **Recent work:** Represented the claimant in Jones v Spire Healthcare, looking at the question of whether a solicitor's CFA can be lawfully assigned.

COURT OF PROTECTION: An Introduction

Contributed by David Rees, Barrister at 5 Stone Buildings

The Court of Protection has very few judges assigned to it on a full-time basis. Most of the judges who exercise its jurisdiction are district, circuit or High Court judges who spend the majority of their time dealing with civil or family cases. The judges assigned to the court full time sit at its central registry at First Avenue House in Holborn, London, and that small team of full-time judiciary is headed by the Senior Judge, appointed under Section 46 of the Mental Capacity Act 2005 ("MCA 2005"). On 18 July 2016 Senior Judge Lush, who had held that post since the inception of the MCA 2005 on 1 October 2007, retired. Prior to his appointment as Senior Judge, Judge Lush had been Master of the old Court of Protection since April 1996. All those who practise regularly in the Court of Protection will be aware that throughout those 20 years, Judge Lush had been a champion for the rights and interests of those who lack capacity to make decisions for themselves. Within the property and affairs sphere he has produced a series of judgments removing defaulting deputies and attorneys and providing guidance on the limits of their powers to make gifts and other dispositions of the incapacitated person (or "P's") assets. His departure marks the end of an era for the court.

Further change has been afoot over the past year. On 1 July 2015 various changes to the Court of Protection Rules 2007 came into force. These are still bedding into place, particularly the new Rule 3A, which sets out various options by which the court can secure P's interests and position within the proceedings. These rule changes also permitted the introduction of pilot schemes to allow the testing of proposed rule and practice direction changes. The first of these, the transparency pilot, began on 29 January 2016 and has subsequently been extended to continue until 31 August 2017. This scheme was intended to address the allegations that had been made in the press about the Court of Protection operating as a "secret court" and provides for most Court of Protection hearings to take place in public (albeit subject to restrictions on identifying the persons involved in the proceedings). The initial impact of this pilot appears to be limited. It does not seem that either the press or the public have attended hearings in any great number, and the number of cases reported in the press appears to be much the same as before. A further important pilot scheme (the case management pilot) has been promulgated with a view to it coming into force on 1 September 2016 and running to 31 August 2017. This puts in place "case pathways" intended to apply to most personal welfare and property and affairs cases. Key changes include a requirement for a significant amount of pre-application investigation and evidence collation in most personal welfare cases, and the introduction of Dispute Resolution Hearings (modelled on Family Dispute Resolution Hearings) in contested property and affairs cases. The pilot scheme also seeks to limit the amount of expert evidence being placed before the court, changing the relevant test under the rules from evidence that is "reasonably required to resolve the proceedings" to evidence that is "necessary."

The fallout from the decision of the Supreme Court in the Cheshire West case ([2014] UKSC 19) as to what constitutes a deprivation of liberty continues. Where P is resident in a care home or hospital, the authorisation of deprivations of liberty takes place under the Deprivations of Liberty Safeguards (or "DoLS") provisions found in Schedules 1A and A1 MCA 2005. These safeguards have been considered by Parliament to be "not fit for purpose" and are currently the subject of an ongoing consultation exercise by the Law Commission. Where P is not in a hospital or care home, any deprivation of liberty must be specifically authorised by the Court of Protection under the MCA 2005. The procedure for doing so, and the steps needed to ensure that it complies with Article 5 of the ECHR, continues to be a matter of some controversy. The most recent guidance was provided by Mr Justice Charles (the Vice-President of the Court of Protection) in a series of judgments published in late 2015 and early 2016 (in particular Re NRA & Others [2015] EWCOP 59 and Re JM & Others [2016] EWCOP 15). The judge held that P does not have to be a party to all welfare applications intended to authorise a deprivation of liberty and that in some cases the procedural safeguards required by Article 5 of the ECHR could be met by appointing a relative or friend as a Rule 3A representative for P. However, the judge was concerned that in other cases where there was no friend or relative who could perform this role, there was at present no available means of obtaining appropriate representation for P. He therefore joined the Ministry of Justice and Department of Health as parties to the proceedings with a view to considering how a means of providing a procedure satisfying Article 5 could be provided. Further developments are awaited.

Another important decision (also by Mr Justice Charles) was that in Re PJV; PJV v The Assistant Director Adult Social Care Newcastle City Council & Another ([2015] EWCOP 87 and [2016] EWCOP 7). This was a property and affairs case in which the court explored the respective roles played by the Court of Protection and the Criminal Injuries Compensation Authority (CICA) in cases where compensation that has been awarded to a mentally incapacitated applicant under a Criminal Injuries Compensation Scheme is to be held upon trusts for that applicant. The decision made clear that the creation of such trusts is a matter for the CICA not the Court of Protection, and the role of the court would be limited to making a declaration as to whether it would be in the best interests of the applicant to accept the offer of compensation put forward by the CICA.

One Court of Protection case which did attract considerable press and public attention in the past year was that of Re C; King's College Hospital NHS Foundation v C [2015] EWCOP 80, in which Mr Justice Macdonald held that a woman, who was described in the press as a "socialite," retained capacity to refuse life-sustaining treatment. C died a few days after judgment was given. Demonstrating the lack of clarity often reflected in reporting of this area, the press coverage largely sought to categorise this as a "right to die" case, although in truth the issue for the court was simply C's capacity to make decisions about her own healthcare; this was not a case of assisted suicide. Nonetheless, the case and the attendant media interest highlights the importance of the issues dealt with by the Court of Protection.

Contents:

ALL CIRCUITS Health & Welfare

Court of Protection: Health & Welfare
Leading Sets
Band 1
39 Essex Chambers *
Band 2
Serjeants' Inn Chambers *
Band 3
Doughty Street Chambers *
Band 4
Garden Court Chambers *
1 Garden Court Family Law Chambers *
Kings Chambers *
No5 Chambers *
Outer Temple Chambers *
St Johns Buildings *
Leading Silks
Band 1
Lock David *Landmark Chambers (ORL)* ◊ [A]
Morris Fenella *39 Essex Chambers*
Mylonas Michael *Serjeants' Inn Chambers* *
Richards Jenni *39 Essex Chambers* *
Band 2
Bagchi Andrew *1 Garden Court Family Law Chambers*
Bowen Paul *Brick Court Chambers (ORL)* ◊ *
Gordon Richard *Brick Court Chambers (ORL)* ◊
Johnston Christopher *Serjeants' Inn Chambers* *
Khalique Nageena *No5 Chambers* [A]
Moon Angus *Serjeants' Inn Chambers* *
Sachdeva Vikram *39 Essex Chambers* *
Weereratne Aswini *Doughty Street Chambers* [A]
New Silks
Bretherton Kerry *Tanfield Chambers (ORL)* ◊ [A] *
Dolan Bridget *Serjeants' Inn Chambers* *
Horne Michael *Serjeants' Inn Chambers* *
** Indicates set / individual with profile.*
[A] direct access (see p.24).
◊ (ORL) = Other Ranked Lawyer.
Alphabetical order within each band. Band 1 is highest.

Court of Protection: Health & Welfare
Leading Juniors
Star individuals
Butler-Cole Victoria *39 Essex Chambers*
O'Brien Joseph *St Johns Buildings*
Ruck Keene Alexander *39 Essex Chambers* *
Band 1
Burrows Simon *Kings Chambers* *
Chisholm Malcolm *1 Garden Court Family Law Chambers* *
Fullwood Adam *39 Essex Chambers*
Greaney Nicola *39 Essex Chambers* *
Patel Parishil *39 Essex Chambers*
Street Amy *Serjeants' Inn Chambers* *
Band 2
Allen Neil *39 Essex Chambers* *
Burnham Ulele *Doughty Street Chambers*
Buttler Chris *Matrix Chambers (ORL)* ◊ [A]
Cavanagh Lorraine *St Johns Buildings*
Davidson Laura *No5 Chambers* [A]
Hallin Conrad *Serjeants' Inn Chambers* *
Hewson Barbara *1 Gray's Inn Square (ORL)* ◊ [A]
Miles Sophy E *Doughty Street Chambers*
Oscroft Jennifer *Cornerstone Barristers (ORL)* ◊
Paterson Fiona *Serjeants' Inn Chambers* *
Powell Debra *Serjeants' Inn Chambers* *
Reeder Stephen *Doughty Street Chambers*
Scolding Fiona *Outer Temple Chambers* [A]
Scott Katharine *39 Essex Chambers*
Weston Amanda *Garden Court Chambers*
Band 3
Clement Joanne *11KBW (ORL)* ◊ *
Dobson Catherine *39 Essex Chambers*
Greatorex Paul *11KBW (ORL)* ◊ [A] *
Hadden Rhys *Field Court Chambers (ORL)* ◊
Harris Bethan *Garden Court Chambers*
Hearnden Alexis *39 Essex Chambers*
Hirst Leonie *Garden Court Chambers*
Karim Sam *Kings Chambers* *
Mant Peter *39 Essex Chambers*
McCormack Ben *Garden Court North (ORL)* ◊
Meacher Alison *Hardwicke (ORL)* ◊
Mullins Mark *Outer Temple Chambers*
Pratley Michelle *39 Essex Chambers* [A] *
Rickard Susanna *Serjeants' Inn Chambers* *
Sharron Eliza *Kings Chambers* *
Van Overdijk Claire *No5 Chambers*
Up-and-coming individuals
Gardner Francesca P *Kings Chambers* *

Band 1

39 Essex Chambers

See profile on p.840

THE SET

39 Essex Chambers stands out as the market leader in this area both in terms of its breadth and depth of expertise. One impressed solicitor commented that "no one comes close to this set's depth of knowledge," while another added: "I always feel in incredibly safe hands – what they don't know, they find out quickly – they're just a cut above." The team is involved in many of the leading Court of Protection cases, including the only two cases that have reached the Supreme Court. Members here are adept at handling a full range of matters, and act for a diverse client group, including NHS bodies, the Official Solicitor and family members.

Client service: "The clerks are fantastic – they are easy to establish a relationship with and they go out of their way to help you, even with last-minute cases." Alastair Davidson is the senior clerk, and he works under David Barnes, director of clerking.

SILKS

Fenella Morris QC Top-quality silk who has a broad practice that encompasses Court of Protection, as well as health and community care matters. She is also increasingly involved in cases which involve disputes over property and financial affairs. She is an expert on capacity to consent to marriage and sexual relations, as well as on matters that concern urgent medical treatment and deprivation of liberty. Hers is a broad client base, ranging from individuals to NHS and private healthcare bodies. **Strengths:** "She's a very tough opponent who you can be sure knows what she's talking about." "She is extremely able, knowledgeable and hard-working."

Jenni Richards QC (see p.751) A standout silk who acts on behalf of public bodies and individuals. She is particularly adept at handling high-profile and complex cases under the Mental Capacity Act, many of which involve difficult issues around medical treatment, deprivation of liberty and capacity. **Strengths:** "She's really, really good and one of the very best silks in Court of Protection work." "She's very practical and very straightforward." **Recent work:** Instructed in A and Others v Hertfordshire NHS Foundation Trust, proceedings concerning a number of autistic adults and the question of whether they were deprived of their liberty.

Vikram Sachdeva QC (see p.757) Particularly adept at handling medical treatment cases due to his clinical background, which gives him an excellent understanding of the complex health issues involved. He has been involved in numerous high-profile and heavily scrutinised cases in the Court of Protection. One peer said of him: "He does the difficult cases and makes them look easy." **Strengths:** "He was a doctor before, so he knows the health issues very, very well." "A very smooth operator" who "is able to bring a different perspective to his cases." **Recent work:** Acted in the Supreme Court case of Aintree NHS Trust v James, a matter concerning the family of a seriously ill man and their attempts to force a hospital to keep treating him. This was the most important medical treatment case in the history of English law because it laid down the approach which must be applied in all cases.

JUNIORS

Victoria Butler-Cole Represents a broad range of clients including family members, health authorities, local authorities and the Official Solicitor. She is a top choice for a range of cases, including those relating to welfare, capacity and medical treatment disputes. She has been involved in a number of the leading cases concerning the application of Article 5 as well as those concerning the international jurisdiction of the Court of Protection. **Strengths:** "Victoria and Alexander Ruck Keene are the King and Queen of Court of Protection work." "It's her ability to get to the crux of the issues that impresses. She produces these amazing submissions and arguments that drill down to the nub of the matter, which is such a skill." **Recent work:** Acted for the Health Service Executive of Northern Ireland in Re PA, which concerned the placement in England of mentally disordered teenagers from Northern Ireland.

Alexander Ruck Keene (see p.756) Noted in the market for his academic excellence in the Court of Protection field. Peers consistently recognise his dedication to the area, citing his writing and involvement in the law as an indication of his pre-eminence. He edits and contributes to a number of leading publications dealing with the area, whilst also maintaining an enviable practice. **Strengths:** "He's like the father of the Court of Protection – he writes the rules, he's on every committee and he lectures on it. A real academic star – if you've got a complicated case, he's the person you would go to." "He's basically creating jurisprudence on his own, merging his forensic skills, his academic skills and his knowledge to develop the whole area of law." **Recent work:** Instructed by the Official Solicitor in Re MN in the Court of Appeal in a case concerning the limits of the Court of Protection's jurisdiction.

Adam Fullwood Has a broad practice that encompasses mental capacity, social housing and health and social care cases. He is highly regarded for his work for a broad range of clients, and regularly acts for private care providers, patients, service users and private litigants. **Strengths:** "He's an exceptional performer – he's very experienced, very reliable and a very persuasive advocate. He always delivers the goods." **Recent work:** Instructed in WS v Secretary of State for Defence, which concerned war pensions and attendance allowance payable to former members of the armed services who are disabled as a result of their service and in need of care and support.

Nicola Greaney (see p.659) An excellent practitioner who has a broad public law practice that encompasses community care, mental health and human rights. She is particularly adept at handling medical treatment cases, and is regularly involved in matters involving an overlap between mental capacity law and civil litigation. **Strengths:** "She is excellent; clients love her and she works hard for you." "She's not flashy or loud, but sensible and measured instead, which gains respect." **Recent work:** Instructed on behalf of Official Solicitor in a long-running case which started as a medical treatment matter about capacity to consent to contraception and developed into whether it was in a wife's best interests to continue to reside with her husband and also her capacity to consent to sexual relations.

Parishil Patel Leading junior who acts for a broad range of clients such as public bodies, family members and the Official Solicitor. He is particularly good at medical treatment disputes. **Strengths:** "He's extremely approachable, dependable and thorough in his work." "He's excellent on his feet and good at picking up complex matters at short notice." **Recent work:** Acted for M, the daughter of P, in a landmark judgment in which the court sanctioned the withdrawal of clinically assisted hydration and nutrition provided to a person in a minimally conscious state.

Neil Allen (see p.582) Excels at Court of Protection work that involves deprivation of liberty and other human rights issues. Peers point out his academic excellence as a distinguishing characteristic, citing his role as lecturer in Clinical Legal Education at the University of Manchester. **Strengths:** "His academic excellence in this field is a real strength, and he's brilliant." His ability to quickly identify those issues which may cause difficulties makes him a very helpful advocate." "The level of his ability is beyond his years of call." **Recent work:** Acted in Re X, which followed on from the Cheshire West decision. The case delivered guidance on devising a standardised system for dealing with cases where care arrangements for mentally incapacitated persons might amount to a deprivation of liberty.

Katharine Scott Instructed by a wide client base that includes local authorities, clinical commissioning groups (CCG), the Official Solicitor and others. She is particularly experienced at disputes that arise out of best interest decisions. **Strengths:** "She's so good with clients; she puts them at ease, highlights their issues and isn't afraid to tell them when they're wrong, albeit in a very sensitive and understanding way." "She's really on the ball, incredibly authoritative and very likeable. You've got to be able to be pragmatic in this field, and she's certainly that." **Recent work:** Acted in the appeal case of Re X (Deprivation of Liberty).

Catherine Dobson Increasingly well known in the market for her work handling welfare and medical treatment disputes. She acts for a broad range of clients including NHS trusts, CCGs and families. She is also well known for providing training and seminars on the Mental Capacity Act and the Mental Health Act. **Strengths:** "She's wonderful with clients. She thinks beyond the legal ramifications and considers what the personal impact on the client is." "She is able to pick up cases quickly and competently."

Alexis Hearnden Handles Court of Protection matters as a natural extension of her work in community care and mental health. She is adept at handling a range of cases, including those concerning deprivation of liberty, forced marriage and the relationship between the Mental Health Act and the Mental Capacity Act. **Strengths:** "She's very sensible and reasoned – an excellent person to have on board." "She's very confident and has excellent client-handling skills." **Recent work:** Acted for the local authority in LBC v RS, which was a contested capacity dispute around the capacity to marry.

Peter Mant Acknowledged as an expert in the field of health and welfare, and particularly proficient at handling cases on the overlap between the Mental Health Act and the Mental Capacity Act. Mant also regularly deals with deprivation of liberty matters. **Strengths:** "He's got a great academic mind and he's very good with clients – he's definitely rising." "He's a careful and thoughtful practitioner." **Recent work:** Instructed in the matter of PJ, a case that concerned both application of the Cheshire West acid test and the jurisdiction of the First-tier Tribunal to consider human rights issues when exercising its statutory function.

Michelle Pratley (see p.742) Has a noteworthy health and welfare practice, and particular experience in complex welfare disputes. She is frequently instructed across a broad spread of cases, including those concerning forced marriage, residence and deprivation of liberty. **Strengths:** "She's a flawless practitioner who is really approachable and liked by clients and judges." "She's a safe pair of hands who is very calming, very knowledgeable and erudite." **Recent work:** Instructed by Sandwell MBC in EWHC, which related to the marriage of incapacitated adults and capacity to sexual relations.

Band 2

Serjeants' Inn Chambers

See profile on p.907

THE SET

Serjeants' Inn stands out as a top choice for complex medical and healthcare cases, and has a very impressive track record of handling the leading and most publicised cases in the area. Recent highlights for the set include acting in Re MN, a significant case that concerned the provision of accommodation and a care package for a young man with cerebral palsy. The chambers is instructed by a wide range of clients, such as the Official Solicitor, NHS trusts and individuals, and solicitors say: "They've got some big hitters there." One commentator stated: "It is the strongest chambers for serious medical treatment cases in the Court of Protection in terms of the number of experienced counsel and the amount of work they undertake."

Client service: "The clerking is absolutely brilliant – they're my favourite clerks, actually. They're always very good at responding, they get back to you immediately and they go above and beyond to sort something out." The "absolutely brilliant" Lee Johnson is the senior clerk, and popular amongst those who instruct the set, as is the "effervescent and switched-on" Samantha Jones.

SILKS

Michael Mylonas QC (see p.725) Head of the Court of Protection team and a vastly experienced silk, who draws particular praise for his work handling medical treatment and welfare cases. He receives instructions from a broad range of clients, including NHS trusts, patients and the Official Solicitor, and is known for his sensitive and pragmatic handling of medical cases. **Strengths:** "He's incredibly well equipped to talk to clinicians and then translate that to the judge, and he does it in an incredibly unfussy, down-to-earth style." "He's a fantastic advocate and great all round. His grasp of medical work is second to none, and he gains the confidence of doctors completely." **Recent work:** Instructed by one of the CCGs in Re X, a matter which came out of the Supreme Court's judgment in Cheshire West.

Christopher Johnston QC (see p.684) Leading medical treatment practitioner who is often involved in the most complex cases. He is an expert on persistent vegetative state cases and is noted for his work as editor of 'Medical Treatment Decisions and the Law'. **Strengths:** "Methodical and very well prepared." "Confident and forthright."

Angus Moon QC (see p.720) Market-leading medical ethics practitioner who has been instructed in a number of high-profile cases. He is frequently involved in matters concerning the withdrawal of treatment including those relating to artificial nutrition and hydration. **Strengths:** "His expertise, knowledge and the way he conducts his advocacy are all very impressive. He's very commanding in court and has the attention of the judge and deals with unexpected difficult situations from witnesses superbly." "He has gravitas and he's very good at defining issues." **Recent work:** Instructed in Re Child JA which is an application to require provision of anti-retroviral therapy to a child with HIV.

Bridget Dolan QC (see p.635) Market leader for complex mental capacity issues, who had a previous life as a forensic psychologist. She is particularly adept at dealing with cases involving end of life decisions for people in minimally conscious states, and is also experienced at deprivation of liberty matters and those concerning capacity to consent to sexual relations. **Strengths:** "She's the most knowledgeable person on these cases. She is absolutely loved by her clients and she has the total respect of all the High Court judges that deal with this." "Her appointment to silk this year was hugely well deserved." **Recent work:** Represented the Official Solicitor in Re JM, AMY and Others, a significant and legally complex test case concerned with whether the use of the streamlined process for authorisation of a deprivation of liberty is a breach of the incapable person's Article 5 ECHR rights if they are not party to proceedings.

Michael Horne QC (see p.675) Principally known for his work in cases which relate to applications involving serious medical treatment. He is adept at acting for the full range of parties in Court of Protection proceedings, although the majority of his instructions come from NHS trusts and the Official Solicitor. He focuses on complex and high-value cases. **Strengths:** "He's fabulously well prepared and he leaves absolutely no stone unturned. He is a gentlemen who does everything absolutely properly and correctly – you know exactly where you stand with him." **Recent work:** Instructed in the much publicised 'sparkly socialite' case which concerned a woman who no longer wanted to continue dialysis.

JUNIORS

Amy Street (see p.775) Leading junior who has featured numerous times in cases dealing with the rise in social care placements that amount to a deprivation of liberty following the decision in the Cheshire West case. Deprivation of liberty is an area where she has particular experience, although she is also hugely adept at handling high-profile and urgent medical treatment matters. **Strengths:** "She's got a brain the size of a planet, and she's an extremely smooth and persuasive advocate." **Recent work:** Instructed in NCC v PB and TB as litigation friend to PB, a 79-year-old woman with a history of psychiatric ill health. The case revolved around whether she lacked capacity to make her own decision about where to live.

Conrad Hallin (see p.662) Has a breadth of experience in the Court of Protection, and is instructed by a broad range of clients including the Official Solicitor, local authorities and NHS trusts. He is particularly experienced at serious medical treatment cases, including applications for life-saving medical treatment, 'end of life' withdrawal of medical treatment and treatment of suicidal patients. He is also well versed in handling cases involving allegations of serious sexual assault against incapacitated adults. **Strengths:** "Conrad has a real interest and passion for the work. He is articulate and a good drafter, and also brave and willing to make difficult legal challenges." "He does medical treatment cases very thoroughly and very well, and is relentlessly persuasive." **Recent work:** Acted in Re JM and Others, a landmark Court of Protection case concerning deprivation of liberty.

Fiona Paterson (see p.734) Noted for her work handling cases concerning serious medical treatment and welfare decisions, she acts on behalf of a range of clients, including families, the Official Solicitor and NHS trusts. She spent eight years as a solicitor in Scotland practising medical law, and as a result has expertise beyond her year of call. **Strengths:** "She's got background in clinical negligence, medical law is her thing, and procedurally she's brilliant." "She's exceptionally professional and unflappable; she has a serenity about her when everything is going bonkers around her." **Recent work:** Instructed by a CCG in Re MN, which concerned the provision of an accommodation and care package for a young man with cerebral palsy.

Debra Powell (see p.741) Excels in health and welfare cases, and is particularly well known for handling matters concerning end of life care, and welfare decisions such as those concerning residence and contact. She frequently acts for health and social service bodies, as well as for private entities and the Official Solicitor. **Strengths:** "She's very calm in her advocacy, and her paperwork is very succinct." "She has undoubtedly got real ability, is extremely approachable and clients like her." **Recent work:** Instructed on behalf of L in Re L, a claim for damages for violation of Article 8 and Article 5 rights that was settled by a local authority.

Susanna Rickard (see p.751) Her wide-ranging experience in the Court of Protection encompasses cases relating to healthcare, welfare and financial decisions. She is known for her work in 'life and death' matters, as well as those concerning best interests decisions. She most frequently acts for families, patients and trusts. **Strengths:** "She's really intelligent and has a real grasp of complex legal issues. Her approach is very pragmatic, and she's able to deal with clients very easily." **Recent work:** Instructed in WBC v Z and Others, a case concerning a woman who appeared on a reality TV show and had a subsequent period of mental health problems.

Band 3

Doughty Street Chambers

See profile on p.828

THE SET

Doughty Street Chambers boasts a noteworthy breadth of expertise in Court of Protection work, being well versed in a number of areas including community care, housing and unlawful detention. Its members, who are all noted for their strong knowledge of human rights law, act for the full range of clients, including local authorities, family members and protected parties. One instructing solicitor commented: "The individuals here are right in the forefront of thinking on this subject, and are always trying to push the boundaries. They offer a range of skills and expertise and are high-calibre across the board."

Client service: "The clerks are very helpful. I've never had a problem with them in terms of chasing things up for me, getting fee notes out and negotiating fees." Sian Wilkins leads the clerking team for Court of Protection cases.

SILKS

Aswini Weereratne QC Acts for all parties in the Court of Protection, including the Official Solicitor, and is renowned for her work in cases concerning human rights, mental health and capacity. She is well versed in matters concerning the overlap between the Mental Capacity Act and the Mental Health Act, and is a noted deprivation of liberty expert. **Strengths:** "She is just brilliant, there are no other words. She has an amazing legal brain, and is very responsive, cool under pressure, and a highly intelligent lawyer." "Her written work and turn of phrase are excellent, and she can be dealing with something complex and academic and make it understandable." **Recent work:** Instructed in the significant Re MN case in the Court of Appeal, which concerned the jurisdiction boundary between the Court of Protection and the Administrative Court.

JUNIORS

Ulele Burnham Has a broad practice covering the law relating to mental capacity and mental health. She is also an expert in unlawful detention cases. **Strengths:** "She gets to grips with things very quickly and doesn't miss points." "She's particularly good with clients who are either vulnerable or concerned relatives, as she couches her advice well and takes on board their concerns."

Stephen Reeder Well-known specialist in welfare cases, who is adept at handling property and affairs matters. He is instructed by a broad range of clients including healthcare bodies, families and the Official Solicitor. **Strengths:** "He is really good at taking the heat out of emotional situations and looking at outcomes for a client, rather than getting bogged down in the law." "He's really an expert in his field so you feel you're in safe hands because you're confident that his advice is based on a lot of experience and really good knowledge of the law." **Recent work:** Instructed on behalf of a young woman with autism in a case which involved the issue of her long-term best interests in relation to her residence and care as she becomes a young adult.

Sophy Miles Was one of the leading national solicitors handling Court of Protection work before her move to the Bar in 2015. She is an expert on all health and welfare matters, and contributes to many of the leading texts in the area. **Strengths:** "She is extremely thorough, very responsive and very good with clients. Her cases are often reported, so she is at the cutting edge of legal developments." "She's incredibly knowledgeable and respected."

Band 4

Garden Court Chambers

See profile on p.851

THE SET

Garden Court Chambers draws on its experience and expertise in mental health, community care and public law matters to bolster a strong Court of Protection practice. Members are particularly well known for their work on deprivation of liberty cases, and those concerning disputed capacity. One recent highlight was W City Council v Mrs L, concerning the deprivation of liberty of a 93-year-old lady with Alzheimer's.

Client service: "The clerks are unbelievably good. You can call them up with a last-minute urgent application and they will find a way to do it for you." Senior civil clerk Phil Bampfylde "is quick to respond, helpful, humorous and a credit to the set."

JUNIORS

Amanda Weston Deeply experienced in mental capacity work, she is regularly instructed in deprivation of liberty and other welfare cases. She is well known for her work on safeguarding, and is able to handle highly emotional cases. **Strengths:** "She's a very persuasive advocate in court, who is also very good in pre-court discussions."

Leonie Hirst Acts for a full range of parties in the Court of Protection, and is adroit at handling best interests and deprivation of liberty matters. She is particularly experienced at handling disputes around mental health and safeguarding issues. **Strengths:** "Her drafting was very, very good. She did a position statement that was absolutely brilliant and also very easy for the client to understand, and she made the client feel extremely reassured about what would happen in court." **Recent work:** Instructed in W City Council v Mrs L, which concerned careful consideration of the 'acid test' and whether care arrangements in her home amounted to continuous supervision and control.

Bethan Harris Excels across a range of Court of Protection matters, including deprivation of liberty, Section 21A applications, and cases dealing with complex care packages. She acts for local authorities, family members and litigation friends. **Strengths:** "She's very good, very tempered, reasonable and insightful." "She's dogged and a fighter."

1 Garden Court Family Law Chambers

See profile on p.853

THE SET

1 Garden Court Family Law Chambers has a stellar team instructed by a range of clients. It frequently acts on behalf of the Official Solicitor and family members, but is probably best known for its work on behalf of local authorities. Members here are experienced in a broad range of matters, including cases concerning deprivation of liberty, forced marriage, residence and medical treatment.

Client service: "The clerks are helpful and understand the importance of providing a first-class service to solicitors, a point often overlooked by other chambers." Paul Harris is the senior clerk.

SILKS

Andrew Bagchi QC Market-leading practitioner who is particularly well known for his work in welfare cases, but who is also adept at handling finance and medical treatment matters. He is regularly instructed by the Official Solicitor, and excels at cases which involve the forced marriage of incapacitated adults. **Strengths:** "He's extremely effective, likeable, intelligent and sensible." "He's got the depth of knowledge to ensure he's going to be known as one of the best silks in this area."

JUNIORS

Malcolm Chisholm (see p.616) Leading senior junior who is best known for his work for local authorities and for parents. Praised in the market for his client-handling skills, he is an expert on cases concerning the overlap between the Mental Health Act and the Mental Capacity Act. **Strengths:** "He's well respected, logical and excellent with vulnerable clients." "His cross-examination is impressive."

Kings Chambers

See profile on p.968

THE SET

Kings Chambers has a thriving team of Court of Protection practitioners. Its members are particularly adept at advising professionals, including approved mental health professionals, medical practitioners and NHS trusts, but also frequently represent the protected party and regularly receive instructions from the Official Solicitor. They are adept across a range of matters, including those concerning capacity to consent to marriage and residence. They are also increasingly involved in property and financial affairs work. One impressed solicitor said: "They are the chambers that have the best reputation on circuit."

Client service: "The clerks are always really helpful and proactive. They are always available to speak to you." William Brown is chief clerk at the set.

JUNIORS

Simon Burrows (see p.607) A leading senior junior who is excellent with mental health and capacity issues. He is particularly adept at cases concerning the interplay between the Mental Health Act and the Mental Capacity Act, and remains a top choice for local authorities. **Strengths:** "He's excellent and brilliant with litigants in person." "He takes a pragmatic approach and provides thorough, robust advice." **Recent work:** Instructed in Re X, which dealt with the aftermath of the judgment in the Cheshire West case.

Sam Karim (see p.688) Highly regarded for his applications for urgent medical treatment, he is also adept at handling a range of welfare and deprivation of liberty matters. He is one of the leading practitioners in the North, and is regularly instructed by the Official Solicitor. **Strengths:** "He's a solid practitioner who is good with clients." "He is very adaptable and very good on his feet."

Eliza Sharron (see p.762) Experienced across a range of cases including those relating to best interest decisions and deprivation of liberty. She receives instructions from a broad client base that includes family members, local authorities and individuals who lack capacity. **Strengths:** "She is very thorough, capable in court and popular with solicitors." "She works incredibly hard, turns work around quickly, is very well prepared and equally at home acting for claimants as public authorities." **Recent work:** Instructed in Wigan Borough Council v CP and Others, which relates to the discharge plans for C, following a period of in-patient admission where C had sustained abuse.

Francesca Gardner (see p.650) Adept at handling the full range of Court of Protection matters, including serious medical treatment cases and welfare disputes. Her instructions come from a broad range of clients, including the Official Solicitor, private individuals and an array of public sector bodies. **Strengths:** "She has a clear grasp of complicated issues and the ability to convey that to clients." "She is very clear, concise and she cuts through all the nonsense."

No5 Chambers

See profile on p.931

THE SET

No5 Chambers has a strong team of Court of Protection specialists, who have particular skill handling serious medical treatment cases. Members receive instructions from a wide client base, including family members, health bodies, the Office of the Public Guardian and the Official Solicitor. Sources say that "the set is growing its Court of Protection offering" and "provides good service and good value." The team has been involved in A Local Authority v AG and DG, an appeal in the President's court concerning deprivation of liberty issues.

Client service: "The clerks are great and very responsive – especially down in Bristol." Tony McDaid is practice manager.

SILKS

Nageena Khalique QC Renowned silk who leads the Court of Protection team. She has a broad practice that encompasses cases concerning sexual abuse, forced marriage and financial abuse relating to vulnerable people. She is instructed by a range of clients including NHS trusts, clinical commissioning groups and the Official Solicitor. **Strengths:** "Her courtroom advocacy is lustrous and tenacious, earning her the respect of the client, opponents and the court. She has technical excellence and can distil legal and medical issues into clear and unambiguous advice. Clients like her because she establishes a positive relationship through her amenable and personable approach." **Recent work:** Instructed in KG v CW, MW and Nottingham County Council, which was a challenge to the removal of a young learning disabled girl from her mother. The case concerned deprivation of liberty in relation to her residence, property and contact with her mother.

JUNIORS

Laura Davidson Well regarded in the market, and noted for her academic excellence in human rights and mental health law. She is adept at handling serious medical treatment cases and disputes around the withdrawal of life-sustaining treatments. **Strengths:** "She's a doughty fighter."

Claire Van Overdijk Noted for having a broad Court of Protection practice and being strong on mental capacity issues generally. As well as having a strong practice, she has published a number of texts relating to the Court of Protection. **Strengths:** "She's very good, very approachable, very friendly and willing to provide advice outside of cases."

Outer Temple Chambers

See profile on p.887

THE SET

Outer Temple Chambers is "a growing team" with "some great names," increasingly known as being a top choice for NHS trusts and local authorities in Court of Protection work. Its quality practitioners are able to handle a range of Court of Protection matters, including those relating to residence, deprivation of liberty and capacity to consent to sexual relations. Recent highlights for them include acting in the much-publicised case of Kings College Hospital NHS Trust v C, where the court decided that C had the capacity to refuse life-sustaining kidney dialysis after 'losing her sparkle'.

Client service: "The clerks are very responsive and know who to offer me and who not to." Paul Barton is senior clerk.

JUNIORS

Fiona Scolding Instructed by family members, local authorities, NHS trusts and the Official Solicitor. She is particularly adept at handling cases that concern adults with learning disabilities, including those who have suffered familial abuse. **Strengths:** "She's very good on her feet and able to distil the issues very quickly to provide really clear advice." "She's got a really easy manner with clients and other parties. It gets a bit fraught in these cases, and she sets people at ease."

Mark Mullins Has a broad practice that encompasses cases involving mental health law, mental capacity and community care. He is experienced at handling end of life cases and other matters revolving around medical treatment. **Strengths:** "He's very knowledgeable about the court and very good at dealing with the other side, even when they're litigants in person." "Very experienced, unflappable and at ease when dealing with complex legal arguments. He's especially good on nasty sex cases." **Recent work:** Instructed in Bournemouth Borough Council v PS & DS which found that P was not deprived of his liberty as a result of care arrangements put in place for him by the local authority.

St Johns Buildings

See profile on p.970

THE SET

St Johns Buildings is a Northern set with a national presence in Court of Protection work. Members handle the full gamut of Court of Protection matters, including deprivation of liberty, termination of treatment and other welfare cases. They also undertake cases concerning property and financial affairs.

JUNIORS

Joseph O'Brien A leading junior in the market who is widely acknowledged as 'Mr Court of Protection'. He acts for a broad range of clients, including local authorities, CCGs and the Official Solicitor. He has a broad practice that encompasses medical, welfare and property and affairs matters, and is a noted expert in deprivation of liberty cases. **Strengths:** "He has a legally encyclopaedic knowledge of the Court of Protection. On top of this, he's fantastic at framing arguments, gives excellent advice, is brilliant with different clients and parties, and is fabulous on his feet." "He is the Grana Padano of Court of Protection law, having been involved in all of the big cases."

Lorraine Cavanagh Has expertise in cases concerning the marriage and sexual relations of incapacitated people, particularly involving concurrent matrimonial litigation. She is also experienced in matters relating to the transition from child to adult services. **Strengths:** "If you're representing family members and have a really difficult case that you're trying to win, she's perfect for it as she never gives up and thinks of really strategic and different ways of getting around problems." "She's so utterly committed and tenacious in what she does. She absolutely lives the case and fights incredibly hard for her clients."

Other Ranked Lawyers

Paul Bowen QC (see p.600) (Brick Court Chambers) Vastly experienced silk who is accomplished in both the High Court and the Court of Protection. He is an expert in capacity and mental health law, and is particularly active in cases that concern disputes around life-sustaining treatment and deprivations of liberty. **Strengths:** "Paul is a good operator, campaigner and lawyer, and he's fearless in the points he takes." **Recent work:** Instructed in the Cheshire West case. The Supreme Court accepted arguments he put forward, on behalf of the Equality and Human Rights Committee, that there had been a deprivation of liberty.

Richard Gordon QC (Brick Court Chambers) Top-quality silk renowned for his work in public, EU and human rights law. An expert on the Mental Capacity Act, he has been in many of the leading cases relating to that area. **Strengths:** "He is what you're looking for in a leader because he gives real strategic direction to a case."

Jennifer Oscroft (Cornerstone Barristers) Her solid grounding in community care and housing law assists her in her successful Court of Protection practice. She is experienced across a range of issues under the Mental Capacity Act, and handles matters relating to deprivation of liberty, capacity and best interests. **Strengths:** "She is possibly one of the best young barristers I've come across. She's excellent, extremely bright and extremely user-friendly." "She's years ahead of her call, and has the ability to analyse the most complex case law."

Rhys Hadden (Field Court Chambers) Experienced across a broad range of Court of Protection cases, including those concerning deprivation of liberty and areas of overlap with human rights law. **Strengths:** "He is incredible and liked very much by clients, who admire his manner and superior drafting." "With Rhys, you know 100% that he's reliable and will thoroughly prepare for the case. Rhys is excellent at talking to vulnerable adults, breaking down complex legal issues and making sure they can understand and participate as much as possible."

Ben McCormack (Garden Court North) He is regularly instructed in cases involving the Official Solicitor and is adept at dealing with mental capacity issues. He primarily acts for disabled adults and family members. **Strengths:** "He's a real pleasure to work with as he's very supportive and makes himself available to bounce ideas off all the way through a case. He provides clear and reliable advice every time, and is able to see the issues clearly." "He has an excellent understanding of the wider social welfare and public law issues accompanying Court of Protection cases, and takes a calm and practical approach that clients appreciate."

Barbara Hewson (1 Gray's Inn Square) Has a broad practice that includes Court of Protection, medical law, human rights and judicial review matters. Peers note her commitment to the work and her clients. **Strengths:** "Extremely intelligent and hard-working, she is eagle-eyed and able to deal with a case from different angles. She will go beyond the call of duty in order to succeed in a case."

Alison Meacher (Hardwicke) Has experience of forced marriage, capacity to marry and other issues surrounding mental capacity law. Historically, most of her instructions have come from local authorities, although she is increasingly acting for the Official Solicitor and family members. **Strengths:** "She's extremely thorough and knows the case inside-out. She's switched-on in court and you can really trust her." "Alison was fantastic and soon got the confidence of the client, who was very pleased."

Joanne Clement (see p.619) (11KBW) Often plays a central role in cases concerning mental capacity, welfare and finance, and also excels at local government, community care and housing work. **Strengths:** "She was really good when handling a case that was really, really important to the client. There was a lot of tension and she was excellent at defusing the historic problems and moving the matter forward." **Recent work:** Instructed by the Secretary of State for Health and Secretary of State for Justice in Re P and Others. This is a test case on the procedure to be adopted by the Court of Protection in deprivation of liberty cases following the Supreme Court decision in Cheshire West and the Court of Appeal's decision in Re X (a case in which she was also involved).

Paul Greatorex (see p.659) (11KBW) Has a broad practice that encompasses public, commercial and human rights law. He is particularly adept at mental capacity issues, and is frequently instructed by local authorities. Greatorex is a member of the Court of Protection User Group. **Strengths:** "A strong advocate who is highly persuasive in his arguments. He never gives up."

David Lock QC (Landmark Chambers) Negotiates an enviable Court of Protection practice as part of his wider public law work. An expert on NHS matters, he is regularly instructed on behalf of local authorities. **Strengths:** "His knowledge of the workings of the NHS is unparalleled. He deals with health across the board, and he's the guy you bring in when arguing jurisdiction." "David is unafraid to run difficult arguments." **Recent work:** Instructed in R v Secretary of State and Others, a Supreme Court case on the meaning of 'ordinary residence', which had implications for local authorities because it defined who had to pay to support these service users for life.

Chris Buttler (Matrix Chambers) Top-class practitioner who is held in high esteem for his work, and is strong on public law and human rights matters generally. He is instructed by a broad range of clients, including family members, NHS trusts and the Official Solicitor. **Strengths:** "He takes no nonsense and is very good on his feet."

Kerry Bretherton QC (see p.602) (Tanfield Chambers) A new addition to silk whose Court of Protection practice sees her acting for a broad range of clients, ranging from local authorities to families and deputies. **Strengths:** "Her commitment and persistence moved her client's position on very well. Without her purposefulness of mind, our client wouldn't have got the level of contact that he has with his adult children. She made a really big difference." **Recent work:** Instructed in Re MB which concerned an allegation of forced marriage and issues about the welfare of a vulnerable adult residing with her aunt.

ALL CIRCUITS Property & Affairs

Court of Protection: Property & Affairs
Leading Sets
Band 1
5 Stone Buildings *
Band 2
Radcliffe Chambers *
Leading Silks
Band 1
Rajah Eason *Ten Old Square (ORL)* ◊ *
Reed Penelope *5 Stone Buildings* *
Band 2
Angus Tracey *5 Stone Buildings* *
Leading Juniors
Star individuals
Rees David *5 Stone Buildings* *
Rich Barbara *5 Stone Buildings* *
Band 1
Goldsmith Joseph *5 Stone Buildings* *
Holmes Justin *Radcliffe Chambers* *
Band 2
Baxter Mark *5 Stone Buildings* *
Bedworth Georgia *Ten Old Square (ORL)* ◊ *
Edge Charlotte *5 Stone Buildings* *
Feltham Piers *Radcliffe Chambers* *
Haren Sarah *5 Stone Buildings* *
Hughes Ruth *5 Stone Buildings* *
McDonnell Constance *Serle Court (ORL)* ◊ *
McQuail Katherine *Radcliffe Chambers* *
Mullen Mark *Radcliffe Chambers* *
O'Sullivan Michael *5 Stone Buildings* *
Smith Howard *Radcliffe Chambers*
Staunton Ulick *Radcliffe Chambers*
Band 3
East William *5 Stone Buildings* *
Holland Jordan *5 Stone Buildings* *
Sartin Leon *5 Stone Buildings* *
Troup Alex *St John's Chambers (ORL)* ◊ [A]
Van Overdijk Claire *No5 Chambers (ORL)* ◊
** Indicates set / individual with profile.*
[A] direct access (see p.24).
◊ (ORL) = Other Ranked Lawyer.
Alphabetical order within each band. Band 1 is highest.

Band 1

5 Stone Buildings

See profile on p.914

THE SET

A leading chancery set that has top-class counsel able to handle the full range of Court of Protection property and affairs matters. Boasting unsurpassed expertise at both silk and junior level, it is "clearly the leader in this field" and has members who "are particularly good at Court of Protection with trust law aspects." Individuals here are involved in many of the leading financial cases and frequently act in matters at the cutting edge of the development of the law, including those that challenge the court's jurisdiction.

Client service: "The clerks are always very quick to come back to you. They're very easy to get on with and they will be helpful if you're trying to select a suitable barrister." Paul Jennings is the senior clerk at the set.

SILKS

Penelope Reed QC (see p.749) Top-class silk whose extensive chancery experience informs her excellent Court of Protection practice. She has been involved in numerous high-value, complex applications in the Court of Protection. **Strengths:** "She's an absolute pleasure to work with and frighteningly clever." "She's a staggeringly brilliant advocate."

Tracey Angus QC (see p.584) Has a broad practice that encompasses contentious probate, trusts and all sides of Court of Protection work, including both health and welfare, and property and affairs. She is instructed by a broad range of clients including charities, individuals and the Official Solicitor. **Strengths:** One solicitor commented: "If I could curtsy, I would – she's really clever." "She's obviously very clever and knowledgeable but one of her really good strengths is that she's incredibly user-friendly, accessible and very good at working collaboratively."

JUNIORS

David Rees (see p.750) "One of the leading lights in the field," he is an expert in matters that concern incapacity and elderly clients. He is noted for his unusual expertise in international and cross-border Court of Protection work that challenges the court's jurisdiction, and for handling cases that analyse orders made by foreign courts. **Strengths:** "The magnificent David Rees has forgotten more than most will ever know." "David always provides a thoughtful and detailed explanation of the issues in any case. He is able to look at matters from every conceivable angle and give holistic and pragmatic advice on problems put before him."

Barbara Rich (see p.750) Top-class Court of Protection barrister who has great experience in high-value, complex cases. She is also an expert on probate, the validity of wills and the administration of estates and trusts. **Strengths:** "Being against her in court is a challenge for any opponent because judges really trust her. She is compelling and has the ear of the court in a way which is totally deserved."

Joseph Goldsmith (see p.656) Successful traditional chancery lawyer whose practice takes in pensions, wills, probate and professional negligence matters. He is particularly adept at handling statutory wills and applications for lifetime gifts for people who lack capacity. **Strengths:** "He's very bright and always on top of the papers."

Mark Baxter (see p.592) Active Court of Protection barrister who handles a number of complex cases as part of his wide chancery practice. **Strengths:** "He's technically superb, is very good with clients, and is a very persuasive advocate who provides a tremendous service." "He's really measured in his advice, and both practical and pragmatic in his approach. His advocacy is also admirable."

Charlotte Edge (see p.639) Excels across the full range of matters, including applications for gifts, statutory wills applications, and other cases involving large estates and complex disputes between family members. **Strengths:** "She's very confident, she's very well prepared, she knows the law, and from the point of view of opposing barristers, she's very reasonable." "I was very reassured by her judgement, and she was reassuring, calm and got the job done."

Sarah Haren (see p.664) Her broad chancery practice encompasses both non-contentious and contentious work, and she is experienced in probate, inheritance claims and trusts matters. Haren has received instructions from a range of sources, including the Official Solicitor. **Strengths:** "She's very nice and has a good, commanding presence."

Ruth Hughes (see p.677) Instructed most frequently by the Official Solicitor, she handles cases involving statutory will applications, deputyships and divorce, amongst other things. She is well known for her work in cross-jurisdictional property and affairs matters, and has handled international matters arising under the Mental Capacity Act 2005. **Strengths:** "Very hard worker who is an extremely well organised and persuasive advocate. She isn't afraid to get stuck in, and she fights her clients' corner hard."

Michael O'Sullivan (see p.731) Noted junior with a wealth of experience in Court of Protection applications who is also adept at handling trusts and probate matters. He is also well known for his professional negligence practice and is often instructed in complex and high-value disputes. **Strengths:** "He is always sensible, realistic and user-friendly."

William East (see p.638) Well known for his breadth of experience in chancery matters, he's frequently involved in cases concerning statutory wills and contested deputyships, some of which are highly complex and involve challenging clients. **Strengths:** "He was amazing and got a really good settlement. Our client was a nightmare, but William managed to inject humour into conferences, and you could tell the client had real confidence in him."

Jordan Holland (see p.674) Has a thriving Court of Protection practice and receives an increasing number of his cases from the Official Solicitor. He's active in a variety of Court of Protection matters, ranging from statutory will applications to disputes over deputyships. **Strengths:** "His drafting is excellent, he works to very tight deadlines and he's able to give advice that the client doesn't want to hear but has to hear." "He's extremely knowledgeable and very good."

Leon Sartin (see p.759) Well-known counsel who is experienced in a range of matters, including those involving inheritance, ownership disputes, probate and statutory wills. **Strengths:** "He always takes a pragmatic approach to things."

Band 2

Radcliffe Chambers

See profile on p.903

THE SET

Radcliffe Chambers is a set with a fantastic private client base that has members skilled in handling the full range of property and affairs matters before the Court of Protection. Its talented silks and juniors are involved in some of the most high-profile reported cases in the sector, and regularly handle proceedings relating to the variation of trusts, lasting powers of attorney, deputyships and statutory wills. They also advise on personal welfare issues.

Client service: "The clerks are very good – they are always bending over backwards to help, and I've never had any issues with them. We have to have all bills assessed, and if there is a problem there's never been an issue having those bills knocked down or paid back where necessary." Keith Nagle and John Clark lead the clerking team.

JUNIORS

Justin Holmes (see p.674) Leading Court of Protection junior, who is particularly good at lasting and enduring powers of attorney, contested deputyships and applications for declarations of capacity. Instructions come from a broad range of sources, including the Public Trustee, private clients and the Official Solicitor. **Strengths:** "He is our preferred counsel for dealing with unusual and difficult cases. He's approachable, pragmatic and very responsive."

Piers Feltham (see p.643) Market-leading practitioner who remains a top choice for clients faced with a range of Court of Protection matters. He is particularly active on cases concerning the validity of powers of attorney and statutory wills. **Strengths:** "He has good experience, is sensible, and will always try and help people."

Katherine McQuail (see p.714) Has a good reputation for her work in mental capacity, and has been involved in cases relating to property, statutory wills and enduring powers of attorney. She works for a broad range of clients, and receives a number of instructions from the Official Solicitor. **Strengths:** "She is a very fair opponent who is courteous and friendly. If I have a case against her we can normally go a long way to narrowing the issues and coming to a fair conclusion."

Mark Mullen (see p.724) Has a broad range of expertise, and handles cases relating to capacity to marry, enduring powers of attorney and deputyship, among others. He is also experienced in personal welfare applications. **Strengths:** "He's always been very approachable and you can ask him things – he sees things through right to the end." **Recent work:** Instructed in London Borough of Haringey v CM, a contested application for the appointment of a property and affairs deputy.

Howard Smith Experienced Court of Protection specialist who practises mainly in property and affairs but is also adept at handling health and welfare matters. He is particularly active in cases concerning deputyships and best interests. **Strengths:** "He's very good at communicating with the solicitor, which is a must, especially in emergency applications. He's always very clear and concise in the advice he gives, and always happy to talk through something with you and amend if necessary."

Ulick Staunton Experienced in both contentious and non-contentious work, he is an expert in wills, estates, probate and Court of Protection work. **Strengths:** "He's very quick to respond and most helpful." "A doughty fighter and a forceful advocate, he'll push his client's position, but won't take bad points."

Other Ranked Lawyers

Claire Van Overdijk (No5 Chambers) Has a practice that encompasses both property and affairs and health and welfare matters. She acts for a range of clients, such as individuals, local authorities, the Official Solicitor and financial deputies. She is well known for her work in cases concerning statutory wills, gifts, trusts and disputed deputyships. **Strengths:** "She's very calm. We had an aggressive opponent, but Claire was very professional and a very good advocate."

Eason Rajah QC (see p.747) (Ten Old Square) Top-quality property and financial affairs silk with a fantastic reputation for his chancery work generally. **Strengths:** "Calm, sophisticated, smooth, highly intelligent and a shrewd strategist."

Georgia Bedworth (see p.593) (Ten Old Square) Noteworthy chancery barrister who is experienced in matters concerning probate, inheritance and the administration of estates. She is often involved in complex, high-value matters. **Strengths:** "She's quite an understated advocate but she gets her points across very well. Her style works well in the Court of Protection." "She's a very civilised opponent and a very clever person."

Constance McDonnell (see p.712) (Serle Court) Highly regarded for her work on probate and contentious trusts. When in the Court of Protection, she is frequently involved in cases concerning lifetime gifts, statutory wills, and enduring powers of attorney. **Strengths:** "She is extremely knowledgeable and comes across extremely well in court." "She's very clear, very authoritative and very clever."

Alex Troup (St John's Chambers) An exceptional chancery silk who is adept at handling Court of Protection work. He excels in cases concerning statutory wills, contested deputyship applications and lifetime gifts. **Strengths:** "Alex is a commanding advocate and has a no-nonsense style to negotiating, which makes him a very formidable opponent." "He's very impressive both on paper and in court, and his knowledge of cases is incredible. Understandable in the way he gives advice, he's very highly sought after." **Recent work:** Advised three children in relation to their concerns that their sister was financially abusing their father.

Contents:

LONDON

Crime
Leading Sets
Band 1
2 Bedford Row *
2 Hare Court *
6KBW College Hill
QEB Hollis Whiteman *
3 Raymond Buildings Barristers *
Band 2
25 Bedford Row *
Cloth Fair Chambers
Doughty Street Chambers *
Matrix Chambers *
Red Lion Chambers
Band 3
9-12 Bell Yard
Carmelite Chambers *
23 Essex Street *
Furnival Chambers *
Garden Court Chambers *
5 Paper Buildings *
Band 4
9 Bedford Row *
187 Fleet Street *
3 Temple Gardens
5 King's Bench Walk
5 St Andrew's Hill *
* *Indicates set with profile.*
Alphabetical order within each band. Band 1 is highest.

Band 1

2 Bedford Row
See profile on p.807

THE SET

"One of the top chambers in London in respect of criminal defence work," 2 Bedford Row is a "brilliant" set boasting a bench of "exceptional" criminal advocates who demonstrate "a real strength and depth of experience and skill." It has "a wide spectrum of specialisms, meaning that it can service all areas of crime, no matter how complex." Members regularly prosecute and defend the most complex and high-profile matters, including homicide, terrorism and sex offences, handling cases that are both privately and publicly funded.

Client service: The set's "friendly and efficient" clerks "provide an attentive and same-day service to every query" and "respond positively to any challenge." They are particularly praised for their "courtesy and efficiency in negotiating fees and recommending certain barristers for certain cases." "Legendary" senior clerk John Grimmer is credited for the set's impressive reputation in this regard, and is described by clients as "one of the key clerks at the Criminal Bar" and someone who is "second to none."

SILKS

Brian Altman QC (see p.583) Pre-eminent silk whose experience as former First Senior Treasury Counsel contributes to his status as a highly in-demand prosecutor of some of the most noteworthy murder and terrorism cases of recent years. He also boasts a flourishing defence practice, and undertakes work on murder and drug trafficking cases among others. Interviewees praise him for his meticulous preparation and attention to detail. **Strengths:** "His work is just outstanding and his judgement is impeccable, and he certainly deserves to be rated extremely highly." "What I found when I was in court is that he commands an awful lot of respect because it's deserved." "He's incredibly thorough and hard-working." **Recent work:** Led the prosecution in the high-profile case of John Downey, a suspected IRA terrorist charged with the Hyde Park bombing in 1982.

William Clegg QC (see p.618) A distinguished silk renowned for his criminal defence practice and his skills as an appellate advocate. Described as "one of the doyens of the Criminal Bar," he is singled out for his skilled defence of high-profile private individuals facing serious charges, including murder and rape. He is something of a fixture in reported cases, having appeared in a number of important matters before the Court of Appeal and the Supreme Court. **Strengths:** "He is a class act whose vast experience commands respect from everyone." "He has such an astute mind" and is "fantastic in court." **Recent work:** Represented Professor Gennadij Raivich, a 'professional' sperm donor, against allegations of sexual assault.

Mark Milliken-Smith QC (see p.717) Frequently instructed in complex and high-profile serious crime cases, he is a barrister with a particular expertise in defence work who is praised for his intellect. He is recognised for his work in cases involving violent crime including gang violence, sex offences and murder. He also has a particular specialism in criminal cases stemming from the sporting world. **Strengths:** "A powerful guy to have on your team. He is very imposing and commands massive respect in court and with clients." "He's sharp and concise." **Recent work:** Defended in a 'honey trap murder' case where the first defendant seduced the victim then conspired with others to rob and murder him.

Jim Sturman QC (see p.775) Specialises in defending high-profile individuals facing serious allegations, and attracts high praise for both his client-handling skills and smooth advocacy style. He often handles sexual offences cases and has developed a particular niche in the area of 'revenge porn.' **Strengths:** "He has consistently been at the top of his game for a number years, and is always in the first choice bracket in cases that are challenging. One of the Galácticos of the Bar." "A brilliant team member who it's great to have on board." "Incredibly hard-working with a bedside manner that gives huge confidence to clients and enormous support to instructing solicitors." **Recent work:** Represented Tania Clarence following the murder of her three seriously disabled children. The case focused on the argument of diminished responsibility, and Ms Clarence ultimately received a Hospital Order.

Richard Whittam QC (see p.795) Former First Senior Treasury Counsel renowned and respected by commentators for his tenacity, work ethic and superior jury advocacy. He is a leading prosecutor who has acted in several significant cases including matters of terrorism and allegations of historic sexual abuse. **Strengths:** "He has all the aptitude that you'd expect from someone who was Senior Treasury Counsel, and is efficient and well prepared." "He's extremely hard-working and prepares all of his cases extremely well." "I don't know if he kills people with kindness, but he's so reasonable and so fair that the jury wonder how he could possibly be wrong." **Recent work:** Prosecuted a well-known 'hate preacher' who was inciting support for terrorism and terrorist organisations.

Ian Stern QC Heads up the Regulatory Group at the chambers but also has a thriving criminal practice. He often acts in criminal proceedings in the regulatory and professional disciplinary sector. **Strengths:** "A go to guy for cases involving fatal shootings," he's "calm and fearless but not in a way which causes offense. Juries, witnesses and judges all warm to him." **Recent work:** Successfully acted for Anthony Long, the police marksman accused of killing Azelle Rodney, who was facing a murder charge relating to the incident.

JUNIORS

Dean George Notable criminal junior praised by the market for his intellectual acumen and advocacy skills. He is particularly experienced in handling complex, document-heavy serious crime cases, including murders and firearms offences. **Strengths:** "He's a clever defence advocate who is wise and wily." "He is a very accomplished junior who provided me with excellent support, ideas and arguments." "One of the hardest workers. He's underestimated by co-defendants and prosecution counsel and then, out of nowhere, he turns them over." **Recent work:** Defended a teenager accused of stabbing the son of a Ghanaian diplomat having allegedly identified him as a member of a rival gang.

Craig Rush Acclaimed criminal junior with a strong history of defending complex cases. He often undertakes high-profile, privately funded work, and is singled out by commentators for his experience in homicide cases and incidents involving serious organised crime. **Strengths:** "Very strong in serious crime." "He's a very good guy to work with." **Recent work:** Defended an individual within the Traveller community charged with carrying out an execution following a long-running feud.

2 Hare Court
See profile on p.861

THE SET

An "extremely experienced, well connected and personable" set "dedicated to providing honest advice," 2 Hare Court is made up of an "exceptional stable" of long-established silks and incredibly bright juniors. The individuals here are experienced in both prosecution and defence and have undertaken some of the most substantial and high-profile serious crime cases of the last year, including the defence of international cricketer Chris Cairns and the prosecution of Sarah Sands, who murdered an elderly paedophile who had been abusing her children. They have among

Crime

Leading Silks

Star individuals

Aylett Crispin *QEB Hollis Whiteman*
Emmerson Ben *Matrix Chambers*
Fitzgerald Edward *Doughty Street Chambers*
Gibbs Patrick *3 Raymond Buildings Barristers* [A] *
Heywood Mark *5 King's Bench Walk*
Kelsey-Fry John *Cloth Fair Chambers* *
Laidlaw Jonathan *2 Hare Court* *
Montgomery Clare *Matrix Chambers* *
Perry David *6KBW College Hill*
Pownall Orlando *2 Hare Court* *
Purnell Nicholas *Cloth Fair Chambers* *
Winter Ian *Cloth Fair Chambers* *

Band 1

Altman Brian *2 Bedford Row* *
Bajwa Ali Naseem *Garden Court Chambers*
Bennathan Joel *Doughty Street Chambers*
Bennett-Jenkins Sallie *2 Hare Court* *
Blaxland Henry *Garden Court Chambers*
Blunt Oliver *Furnival Chambers* *
Brown Edward *QEB Hollis Whiteman* *
Burke Trevor *3 Raymond Buildings Barristers* [A]
Cameron Alexander *3 Raymond Buildings Barristers* [A]
Chawla Mukul *9-12 Bell Yard* [A] *
Clegg William *2 Bedford Row* *
Dein Jeremy *25 Bedford Row* *
Etherington David *Red Lion Chambers*
Griffiths Courtenay *25 Bedford Row*
Hicks Martin *2 Hare Court* *
Hill Max *Red Lion Chambers* *
Horwell Richard *3 Raymond Buildings Barristers*
Jafferjee Aftab *Atkinson Bevan Chambers, (ORL)* ◊ [A]
Kamlish Stephen *Garden Court Chambers*
Keith Hugo *3 Raymond Buildings Barristers* *
Mendelle Paul *25 Bedford Row* *
Milliken-Smith Mark *2 Bedford Row* *
Moloney Tim *Doughty Street Chambers*
Owen Tim *Matrix Chambers*
Rees Jonathan *2 Hare Court*
Ryder John *6KBW College Hill*
Sturman Jim *2 Bedford Row* *
Whittam Richard *2 Bedford Row* *
Wood James *Doughty Street Chambers* [A]
Wright Peter *2 Hare Court*

Band 2

Borrelli Michael *3 Raymond Buildings Barristers* *
Bromley-Martin Michael *3 Raymond Buildings Barristers* [A]
Caplan Jonathan *5 Paper Buildings*
Carter-Stephenson George *25 Bedford Row*
Cottage Rosina *Red Lion Chambers*
Darbishire Adrian *QEB Hollis Whiteman*
Davies Hugh *3 Raymond Buildings Barristers* [A]
Denison Simon *6KBW College Hill*
FitzGibbon Francis *Doughty Street Chambers* [A]
Forshall Isabella *Doughty Street Chambers*
Forshaw Sarah *5 King's Bench Walk*
Healy Alexandra *9-12 Bell Yard* [A] *
Howker David *2 Hare Court*
Humphryes Jane *3 Raymond Buildings Barristers* *
Johnson Zoe *QEB Hollis Whiteman* *
Kelly Brendan *2 Hare Court* *
Khan Judy *Garden Court Chambers*
Lakha Abbas *9 Bedford Row* [A] *
Laws Eleanor *QEB Hollis Whiteman* [A] *
Lewis James *3 Raymond Buildings Barristers* [A] *
Macdonald Ken *Matrix Chambers*
Mansfield Michael *Mansfield Chambers (ORL)* ◊
Mayo Simon *187 Fleet Street* [A] *
O'Neill Brian *2 Hare Court*
O'Neill Sally *Furnival Chambers* [A] *
Penny Duncan *6KBW College Hill*
Rumfitt Nigel *7BR (ORL)* ◊
Russell Flint Simon *23 Essex Street*
Ryder Matthew *Matrix Chambers* *
Scobie James *Garden Court Chambers*
Spens David *QEB Hollis Whiteman* *
Stern Ian *2 Bedford Row*
Trowler Rebecca *Doughty Street Chambers* [A]
Turner Michael *Garden Court Chambers*
Vaughan Kieran *Garden Court Chambers*
Wass Sasha *6KBW College Hill*

Band 3

Ayling Tracy *2 Bedford Row* *
Bailin Alex *Matrix Chambers* *
Berry Anthony *9 Bedford Row* *
Bickerstaff Jane *9 Bedford Row* *
Bott Charles *Carmelite Chambers* *
Campbell-Tiech Andrew *Drystone Chambers (ORL)* ◊ *
Coffey John *3 Temple Gardens*
Hall Andrew *Doughty Street Chambers*
Higgs Jonathan *5 King's Bench Walk*
Jeremy David *QEB Hollis Whiteman*
Keleher Paul *25 Bedford Row* *
Kent Alan *Carmelite Chambers* *
Knowles Julian *Matrix Chambers*
Kovalevsky Richard *2 Bedford Row*
Lithman Nigel *2 Bedford Row* *
Malcolm Helen *3 Raymond Buildings Barristers* [A]
Metzer Anthony *Goldsmith Chambers (ORL)* ◊
Moore Miranda *5 Paper Buildings* *
Price John *23 Essex Street*
Sallon Christopher *Doughty Street Chambers* [A]
Sidhu Jo *25 Bedford Row* *
Smith Tyrone *25 Bedford Row* *
Trembath Graham *5 Paper Buildings*
Waterman Adrian *Doughty Street Chambers*
Wilding Lisa *Furnival Chambers*
Wolkind Michael *2 Bedford Row*

Band 4

Agnew Christine *2 Bedford Row* *
Brimelow Kirsty *Doughty Street Chambers* [A]
Bryant-Heron Mark *9-12 Bell Yard* [A] *
Christie Richard *187 Fleet Street* *
Christopher Julian *5 Paper Buildings*
Doyle Peter *25 Bedford Row*
Elliott Sarah *Doughty Street Chambers* *
Farrell Simon *3 Raymond Buildings Barristers* [A]
Fenhalls Mark *23 Essex Street* *
Friedman Danny *Matrix Chambers*
Grunwald Henry *Charter Chambers (ORL)* ◊ [A] *
Hislop David *Doughty Street Chambers* [A]
Hughes William *9-12 Bell Yard* *
Hynes Paul *25 Bedford Row* *
Lambert Nigel *Carmelite Chambers* [A] *
Lovell-Pank Dorian *6KBW College Hill*
Nathan David *33 Bedford Row (ORL)* ◊
Orchard Anthony *Carmelite Chambers* [A] *
Pople Alison *Cloth Fair Chambers* *
Rhodes Nicholas *Charter Chambers (ORL)* ◊ [A] *
Saxby Oliver *6 Pump Court (ORL)* ◊ [A]
Trollope Andrew *187 Fleet Street* *
Vullo Stephen *2 Bedford Row*
Wilcock Peter *Garden Court Chambers*

Band 5

Armstrong Dean *2 Bedford Row* *
Benson Jeremy *Red Lion Chambers*
Bentley David *Doughty Street Chambers* [A]
Bogan Paul *23 Essex Street*
Bourne Ian *Charter Chambers (ORL)* ◊ [A] *
Carter Peter *Doughty Street Chambers* *
Cooper John *25 Bedford Row*
Davis Adam *3 Temple Gardens* *
Finucane Brendan *Outer Temple Chambers (ORL)* ◊
Glen Ian *5 King's Bench Walk*
Godfrey Howard *2 Bedford Row* *
Harbage William *The 36 Group (ORL)* ◊
Heslop Martin S *2 Hare Court* *
Jefferies Andrew *Mansfield Chambers (ORL)* ◊
Jory Richard *9-12 Bell Yard* *
Lynch Jerome *Charter Chambers (ORL)* ◊ [A] *
Malik Amjad *The 36 Group (ORL)* ◊
McAtasney Philippa *Furnival Chambers* *
Peart Icah *Garden Court Chambers*
Power Lewis *7BR (ORL)* ◊ *
Richmond Bernard *Lamb Building (ORL)* ◊
Stein Sam *Mansfield Chambers (ORL)* ◊
Summers Mark *Matrix Chambers* *
Turner Jonathan *6KBW College Hill*
Whitehouse Sarah *6KBW College Hill*

Band 6

Aaronberg David *15 New Bridge Street (ORL)* ◊
Arlidge Anthony *Red Lion Chambers*
Dias Dexter *Garden Court Chambers*
Fortson Rudi *25 Bedford Row*
Goldberg Jonathan *North Square Chambers (ORL)* ◊
Hardy John *3 Raymond Buildings Barristers* *
Henley Christopher *Carmelite Chambers* *
Hines James *3 Raymond Buildings Barristers* [A] *
O'Connor Patrick *Doughty Street Chambers* [A]
Radford Nadine *3 Temple Gardens* [A] *
Tetlow Bernard *Garden Court Chambers*

New Silks

Atkinson Duncan *6KBW College Hill*
Cockings Giles *Furnival Chambers* *
Evans Philip *QEB Hollis Whiteman* *
Glasgow Oliver *2 Hare Court* *
Karmy-Jones Riel *Red Lion Chambers*
Moses Stephen *Furnival Chambers A* *
Rouse Justin *9 Bedford Row* *
Sibson Clare *Cloth Fair Chambers* *
Sweet Louise *Carmelite Chambers* *

** Indicates individual with profile.*
[A] direct access (see p.24).
◊ (ORL) = Other Ranked Lawyer.
Alphabetical order within each band. Band 1 is highest.

Crime

Leading Juniors

Star individuals

Saunders Neil *3 Raymond Buildings Barristers* [A] *

Band 1

Barnard Jonathan *Cloth Fair Chambers* *
Byrnes Aisling *25 Bedford Row* *
Dempster Jennifer *Red Lion Chambers*
Emlyn Jones William *3 Raymond Buildings Barristers*
Ferguson Craig *2 Hare Court* *
FitzGerald Ben *QEB Hollis Whiteman* *
Hill Miranda *6KBW College Hill*
Jones Gillian *Red Lion Chambers*
Ledward Jocelyn *QEB Hollis Whiteman*
Little Tom *9 Gough Square (ORL)* ◊ *
Mably Louis *6KBW College Hill*
Morgan Alison *6KBW College Hill*
Ray Simon *6KBW College Hill*
Whittaker David *2 Hare Court* *
Williamson Alisdair *3 Raymond Buildings Barristers* [A] *
Wormald Richard *3 Raymond Buildings Barristers* [A]

Band 2

Butt Matthew *3 Raymond Buildings Barristers* [A] *
Forster Tom *Red Lion Chambers*
George Dean *2 Bedford Row*
Gokani Rachna *QEB Hollis Whiteman* *
Hallam Jacob *6KBW College Hill*
Henry Edward *QEB Hollis Whiteman* *
Maguire Benn *QEB Hollis Whiteman* *
Naqshbandi Saba *3 Raymond Buildings Barristers* [A]
Newton Benjamin *Doughty Street Chambers*
Rush Craig *2 Bedford Row*
Taylor Paul *Doughty Street Chambers*
Thomas Richard *Doughty Street Chambers*
Ward Alexandra *9-12 Bell Yard* [A] *

Band 3

Ahmad Zubair *2 Hare Court* *
Aylott Colin *Carmelite Chambers* [A] *
Buchanan James *2 Hare Court* *
Bunyan Angus *2 Hare Court* *
Campbell Brenda *Garden Court Chambers*
Corsellis Nicholas *QEB Hollis Whiteman* *
Cotter Mark *5 St Andrew's Hill* *
Cray Timothy *6KBW College Hill*
Dineen Maria *2 Bedford Row* *
Eissa Adrian *25 Bedford Row* *
Evans Julian *QEB Hollis Whiteman*
Harries Mark *Carmelite Chambers* [A] *
Haughey Caroline *Furnival Chambers* [A] *
Heer Deanna *5 Paper Buildings* *
Jarvis Paul *6KBW College Hill*
Kazakos Leon *2 Hare Court* *
Kendal Timothy *2 Bedford Row*
Lewis Anya *Garden Court Chambers*
Lloyd Ben *6KBW College Hill*
Lownds Peter *2 Hare Court* [A] *
Lumsdon Kate *23 Essex Street* *
Marquis Piers *Doughty Street Chambers*
Munyard Terry *Garden Court Chambers*
Mylvaganam Paul *Goldsmith Chambers (ORL)* ◊
Nelson Michelle *Red Lion Chambers*
Pardoe Rupert *23 Essex Street*
Patterson Gareth *6KBW College Hill*
Piercy Arlette *25 Bedford Row* *
Polnay Jonathan *5 King's Bench Walk*
Przybylska Sarah *2 Hare Court* *
Ratliff Peter *6KBW College Hill*
Rowlands Peter *Garden Court Chambers*
Schutzer-Weissmann Esther *6KBW College Hill*
Strudwick Linda *QEB Hollis Whiteman* *
Wood David *Charter Chambers (ORL)* ◊ *

Band 4

Baker Simon *2 Bedford Row*
Bex Kate *2 Hare Court*
Cammerman Gideon *187 Fleet Street* *
Connolly Dominic *5 St Andrew's Hill* *
Gardiner Sebastian *25 Bedford Row*
Higgins Nichola *Doughty Street Chambers*
Howard Nicola *25 Bedford Row* *
Hughes David *9 Bedford Row* *
Ivill Scott *2 Hare Court* *
Jaffa Ronald *25 Bedford Row*
Kenyon Flavia *3 Temple Gardens* *
Ladenburg Guy *3 Raymond Buildings Barristers* *
Langley Charles *2 Bedford Row* *
Macdonald Alison *Matrix Chambers* *
Nathwani Rishi *5 King's Bench Walk*
Newell Charlotte *5 King's Bench Walk*
Payne Tom *Red Lion Chambers*
Phillips Paul *Charter Chambers (ORL)* ◊ [A] *
Poku Mary *9-12 Bell Yard* *
Ponte Luke *3 Raymond Buildings Barristers*
Rhodes David *Doughty Street Chambers*
Ritchie Shauna *2 Bedford Row* *
Rodham Susan *5 King's Bench Walk*
Rose Alex *Garden Court Chambers*
Smitten Ben *25 Bedford Row* *
Soertsz Lauren *Doughty Street Chambers*
Spiro Dafna *Garden Court Chambers*
Wakerley Paul *QEB Hollis Whiteman* *
Ware Christopher *2 Hare Court* *
Weekes Mark *6KBW College Hill*
Yeo Nicholas *3 Raymond Buildings Barristers* [A] *

Band 5

Alexis Fallon *QEB Hollis Whiteman*
Charbit Valerie *2 Bedford Row* *
Conway Charles *2 Bedford Row*
D'Cruz Rufus *Red Lion Chambers* *
Dunham Nicholas *9-12 Bell Yard* *
England William *Carmelite Chambers* *
Flanagan Julia *Charter Chambers (ORL)* ◊ *
Goudie Martin *Charter Chambers (ORL)* ◊ [A] *
Hawkins Quinn *2 Hare Court* *
Hill Rina-Marie *23 Essex Street*
Hunter Timothy *5 Paper Buildings* [A]
Huntley Clare *9-12 Bell Yard* *
Khan Ashraf *2 Bedford Row* *
Magee Samuel *2 Bedford Row*
Martin James *5 King's Bench Walk* *
Pons Gary *5 St Andrew's Hill* *
Price Roderick *187 Fleet Street* *
Rabaiotti Catherine *5 Paper Buildings*
Selby Lawrence *9 Bedford Row* *
Sherratt Matthew *Carmelite Chambers* [A] *
St Louis Brian *15 New Bridge Street (ORL)* ◊
Swain Jon *Furnival Chambers* [A] *
Warrington John *5 St Andrew's Hill* *
Wilkinson Kate *6KBW College Hill*
Wiseman Adam *Red Lion Chambers*
Zahir Hossein *Garden Court Chambers*

Band 6

Akuwudike Emma *25 Bedford Row* *
Arden Karina *9 Bedford Row* *
Carr Jamie *4 Breams Buildings (ORL)* ◊
Cohen Samantha *9 Bedford Row* *
Duncan Hannah *Atkinson Bevan Chambers (ORL)* ◊
Forte Timothy *3 Temple Gardens* *
Goodall Emma *Doughty Street Chambers*
Gottlieb David *Thomas More Chambers (ORL)* ◊
Hardy Max *9 Bedford Row* *
Horlick Fiona *Outer Temple Chambers (ORL)* ◊
Hossain Ahmed *23 Essex Street*
Hunter Allison *23 Essex Street* *
Levy Michael *2 Bedford Row* *
May Christopher *5 St Andrew's Hill* *
McGee Andrew *2 Bedford Row* *
McGhee Philip *QEB Hollis Whiteman* *
Mian Naeem *2 Hare Court*
Morgan Adam *Goldsmith Chambers (ORL)* ◊
Morrell Roxanne *Carmelite Chambers* *
Morris Robert *3 Raymond Buildings Barristers*
Neofytou Michael *25 Bedford Row* *
Oliver Heather *3 Raymond Buildings Barristers* *
Osman Osman *25 Bedford Row* *
Power Alexia *Furnival Chambers* [A] *
Richardson Alistair *6KBW College Hill*
Shroff Tessa *9 Bedford Row* *
Stott Philip *QEB Hollis Whiteman* *
Walbank David *Red Lion Chambers*
Walker Liam *Doughty Street Chambers*
Woodbridge Julian *1 King's Bench Walk (ORL)* ◊ *

Up-and-coming individuals

Buckley Joanna *Matrix Chambers*

* Indicates individual with profile.
[A] direct access (see p.24).
◊ (ORL) = Other Ranked Lawyer.
Alphabetical order within each band. Band 1 is highest.

their ranks numerous former and current Treasury Counsel, and are described as "fighters: they'll go in there and scrap for your client."

Client service: The set's clerking team is led by the "incredibly supportive and highly efficient" director of clerking Julian Campbell who is ably assisted by "fantastic" senior practice clerk Ben Heaviside. Both are praised for their dedication, and one impressed client states: "They have always gone beyond the call of duty to assist me when they can." Practice clerk Tara Johnson is also singled out for praise, and is described as "absolutely outstanding" by market commentators.

SILKS

Jonathan Laidlaw QC (see p.694) A "standout" silk with over 15 years of Treasury Counsel experience, he now specialises only in private defence work which spans the areas of general crime, business crime, fraud and regulatory work, among others. Sources are impressed by his ability and experience, labelling him "superb," "a class act" and "incredibly impressive." **Strengths:** "He is an excellent advocate. Calm and collaborative, he offers superb client care." "He is commendably straightforward in his approach yet commands huge authority and credibility in court. He is very hands-on and easy to work with." **Recent work:** Represented a notorious property developer in Liverpool who was alleged to be the financier and organiser of a sizeable countrywide heroin operation.

Orlando Pownall QC (see p.742) A "phenomenal" leading silk who, following a successful tenure as Treasury Counsel, now specialises in representing individuals charged in the most high-profile and significant cases, including the Chris Cairns perjury case. Considered a "legend" of the Criminal Bar by market observers, he attracts significant praise for his advocacy and client-handling skills. **Strengths:** "His advocacy is second to none and he is a delight to work with." "A very accomplished chap who is smooth and persuasive." "A man with a very bright mind." **Recent work:** Defended an individual who had been charged with murder as a result of a 'joint enterprise' stabbing.

Sallie Bennett-Jenkins QC (see p.594) An accomplished silk described by market observers as "the complete criminal barrister." A former Treasury Counsel, she now specialises in defending individuals against allegations of serious crime. She is highly praised for her attention to detail, and also lauded for her expertise in the cross-examination of expert witnesses across multiple disciplines. **Strengths:** "She has a fearless disposition and is academically very strong." "A streetfighting defence counsel who gets great results and is excellent with clients." "She is very skilled and very articulate. She's both very good on paper and very good in person." **Recent work:** Represented Paul Gadd (also known as Gary Glitter) for historic sexual abuse allegations against girls under the age of 15.

Martin Hicks QC (see p.671) A talented silk with a broad criminal practice that takes in both domestic and international cases. He has appeared in some of the most high-profile trials of recent years, including the trials of two Daily Mirror journalists. Described as an "impressive" practitioner, he is highly praised for his approach in court and his client communication skills. **Strengths:** "Martin provided me with constant reassurance and excellent legal advice." "He ran the show and we all had total confidence in him." "He has a very silky touch and is disarmingly languid. He is just the classic hand of steel in a velvet glove." **Recent work:** Prosecuted an individual claiming to belong to a religious sect who was charged with the murder of his mother and GBH of his partner. After a plea of guilty the defendant was sentenced to a minimum term of 20 years' imprisonment.

Jonathan Rees QC A highly regarded and experienced practitioner who in his time as Treasury Counsel was entrusted to prosecute highly complex and challenging cases, including the Sarah Sands murder. He is a "fantastic" barrister who is considered by commentators to be a "terrific asset" to his set. **Strengths:** "He's very thorough and always makes the time to go through everything. His legal analysis, his consideration of the relevant issues, and his ability to get on with the members of the team and focus on the relevant issues are very impressive. He is to be trusted with the most serious cases." **Recent work:** Successfully prosecuted an individual charged with the fatal stabbing of a 15-year-old boy in the course of an attempt to steal his bike.

Peter Wright QC Attracts praise for his determination and courtroom skills, and is extremely experienced in both prosecution and defence. He handles the full gamut of serious crime including terrorism, robbery and murder cases. **Strengths:** "He's a real fighter and a great barrister." "He's what I'd call a proper jury advocate."

David Howker QC A highly experienced practitioner who devotes his practice to the defence of individuals charged with serious criminal offences. Recent work has included complex and substantial cases involving major organised gang crime and murder. **Strengths:** "He is exceptionally approachable, which can be quite rare in a silk sometimes. He's very sharp as an advocate and very impressive all round." **Recent work:** Defended a man accused of murdering his girlfriend, before dismembering and concealing her body.

Brendan Kelly QC (see p.689) A highly praised silk who has tackled all manner of serious criminal work over the course of his career. He is singled out by market observers for his impressive courtroom presence and demeanour. **Strengths:** "Mr Kelly is a powerful advocate whom it is a delight to work with." "A man with big character who is fantastic on his feet." **Recent work:** Represented a defendant charged with a conspiracy to murder his wife. The case is currently awaiting appeal.

Brian O'Neill QC A strong silk who handles both prosecution and defence work. He has experience in all serious crime cases, with particular expertise in complex murder cases. **Strengths:** "He's very thorough. He reads his cases, he's very organised, and he shows great attention to detail." "He is incredibly conscientious and naturally charismatic." "An extremely robust prosecutor." **Recent work:** Defended an individual accused of four counts of murder following a revenge attack using a firebomb, which in a case of mistaken identity killed a mother and her three teenage children. The defendant was found guilty of manslaughter.

Oliver Glasgow QC (see p.654) A new silk considered by interviewees to be "a real star of the future." He is a current Senior Treasury Counsel with a varied criminal practice across all areas of serious crime. He often acts for high-profile individuals. **Strengths:** "He's a real class act and a really consummate prosecutor." **Recent work:** Prosecuted barrister Constance Briscoe for perverting the course of justice following the deliberate manufacture of evidence in a previous trial.

JUNIORS

David Whittaker (see p.794) Receiving instructions on both privately funded and legally aided work, he is praised by market observers for his vast experience across all areas of criminal law, from murder and manslaughter to complex fraud. He is also singled out for his experience in cases concerning terrorism and serious organised crime. **Strengths:** "One of the Bar's outstanding criminal juniors. He is extremely hard-working, meticulous, and someone who has both good judgement and great presence in court." **Recent work:** Represented a businessman accused of thefts of Chinese artefacts and rhinoceros horn libation cups at a value of more than £25 million.

Craig Ferguson (see p.644) A highly experienced and well-reputed junior with a varied practice spanning all areas of criminal defence. Well versed in advising and representing professional individuals facing criminal charges, he attracts praise for his advocacy style and his client-handling skills. **Strengths:** "Very client-friendly, very astute and a pleasure to work with." "An absolute class act." "Superb regulatory and criminal barrister."

6KBW College Hill

THE SET

A "well established" set "at the top of its game," which although perhaps best known for its prosecution work also boasts a flourishing defence practice, particularly in the private market. It houses an impressive collection of practitioners, and counts a vast number of treasury counsel among its ranks. The "first class" individuals here are regularly instructed in the most substantial and significant criminal cases, and have made numerous notable appearances before the Court of Appeal and Supreme Court. Sources say: "6KBW is bursting with counsel who are both good advocates and exceptional lawyers. It has huge depth of quality."

Client service: A "responsive" and "professional" clerks room that "goes way beyond the call of duty to provide an excellent service to clients." Senior clerk Andrew Barnes leads the "efficient" team, and comes highly recommended as he is "a pleasure to work with, reasonable and highly approachable." First junior clerk Richard Summerscales is also singled out for praise, and is described as "always polite, courteous, obliging and prompt. He is prepared to be flexible when required and has a refreshing 'can-do' mentality."

SILKS

David Perry QC A "stellar" advocate considered to be a "maestro" of the Criminal Bar, who is particularly renowned for having been instructed in the most significant appeals of recent times. He is highly experienced in acting for both the prosecution and the defence in only the most challenging and complex criminal matters, both domestically and internationally. **Strengths:** "You don't want to be on the other side against him. His reputation is fully deserved and there's no sign of his star waning." "The outstanding appellate advocate at the Criminal Bar" and "a go-to person for really difficult advisory work." **Recent work:** Instructed by the Government Legal Department to appeal a decision made by the Court of Appeal in the Cayman Islands regarding the acquittal of an individual charged with complex firearms offences.

John Ryder QC A well-regarded silk who specialises in defending the most complex and serious cases from violent crime to substantial fraud. He is also well known for his depth of experience in handling international criminal matters, particularly those in the Cayman Islands. **Strengths:** "An exceptional advocate who is skilled at taking both judge and jury with him." "He's incisive, right to the point and very articulate." **Recent work:** Successfully defended a Sun journalist charged with making payments to a prison officer in return for information regarding high-profile prisoner Jon Venables.

Simon Denison QC "Hugely experienced" practitioner and former Treasury Counsel who possesses in-depth knowledge of all areas of serious and complex crime, and has a particularly impressive understanding of challenging homicide and attempted murder briefs. He also has experience with gang-related and drug offences. **Strengths:** "He is very methodical in the way he prosecutes cases." "He's very effective and very tenacious." "A class act." **Recent work:** Prosecuted a joint enterprise murder with eight defendants on the indictment.

Duncan Penny QC Senior Treasury Counsel who is much admired by market observers for his approach to cases. He is extremely experienced in the prosecution of high-profile murders, and handled both the retrial of Barry George and the prosecution of those who murdered Ben Kinsella. **Strengths:** "A very passionate lawyer. He's very, very clever and excellent with clients." "A real star prosecutor." **Recent work:** Instructed in a case concerning the alleged murder of a Serco security guard committed by a prisoner in the cells of Blackfriars Crown Court.

Sasha Wass QC A renowned advocate instructed in many of the most high-profile cases of recent years, including those of Rosemary West and Rolf Harris. She is particularly au fait with briefs involving murder and sexual offences, and is praised by market commentators for her "skill over a range of different type of offences." **Strengths:** "She is a fearsome advocate who prepares thoroughly and effectively, but remains light on her feet. She is immensely clever and astute, and has the ability to charm a jury with her lively and engaging approach. It really is a winning combination. I will not hesitate to use her again when a client simply demands the best there is." **Recent work:** Defended a former senior political aide who was charged with the possession of indecent images of children.

JUNIORS

Miranda Hill A respected junior with significant experience of both serious crime and fraud. She is well versed in both prosecution and defence work and has handled complex cases including those relating to murder, perverting the course of justice and bribery. **Strengths:** "She's calm, clever, a delight to work with and a brilliant drafter." "Offers great client care." **Recent work:** Instructed on behalf of News UK to advise in respect of police investigations into the unlawful interception of voicemails.

Louis Mably "Strong" Senior Treasury Counsel with a broad experience of all areas of general crime, and a particular proficiency in corruption offences. Described as a "wonderful" practitioner, he has also been involved in matters centred on terrorism offences and assisted suicide. He also has a niche expertise in assisting European courts with various matters. **Strengths:** "If something intellectually is a problem, you turn to Louis Mably." "Clever, clever, clever and fantastically hard-working." **Recent work:** Represented the UK government at the ECHR in an appeal by the failed suicide bombers of 21 July 2005 in London.

Alison Morgan Well-regarded Junior Treasury Counsel who receives numerous plaudits from market observers for her ability as both prosecution and defence counsel. She has recently been instructed in multiple challenging and high-profile matters, including terrorism and firearms cases. **Strengths:** "Has outstanding attention to detail and the ability to take judges into her confidence with her command of evidence and applicable law." "Very sensible, very steady and very reliable indeed." **Recent work:** Successfully prosecuted a series of cases where individuals were charged with sending menacing and threatening messages to female MPs and campaigners, including threats to rape.

Simon Ray An "unflappable" junior with an "excellent reputation" who has regularly undertaken high-profile cases across the full spectrum of serious crime. He is also highly experienced in assisting City clients with criminal advice. Commentators praise him highly for his client-handling skills and jury advocacy. **Strengths:** "He's incredibly calm but authoritative, and inspires confidence in clients through his very measured and reasoned approach." "He has an understated yet extremely effective advocacy style and is superb with clients. He has sound judgement and is loved by clients." **Recent work:** Instructed to defend a senior barrister and former Recorder who had repeatedly breached a restraining order against his ex-wife. Despite being convicted on five out of six counts, he received only a suspended sentence following mitigation.

Jacob Hallam An "excellent" junior who is recognised for his efficacy acting on complex criminal matters, including cases which attract media attention. Recently, he has been instructed in numerous complex murder, sexual offence and corruption cases. **Strengths:** "He is a safe pair of hands in homicide work, capable of calm and devastating cross-examination." "A seriously good advocate." "He's very personable, an excellent drafter, and just a very, very bright man." **Recent work:** Prosecuted the Bishop of Lewes and his deputy for historic sex offences committed while they ran a scheme for aspirant clergymen. One defendant pleaded guilty, and another was convicted after trial.

QEB Hollis Whiteman

See profile on p.900

THE SET

An exceptional, "top-end" set with a long-standing reputation for professionalism and efficiency. It attracts the most significant and substantial criminal instructions on both the prosecution and defence sides, and has additional expertise in such areas as inquests, professional discipline and regulatory law, among others. The very talented barristers here are known for their superior advocacy skills and their approachability.

Client service: The clerks are led by the "very approachable and sensible" Chris Emmings. His "old-school criminal clerking team" is praised for its flexibility and efficiency. "They're very good at that personal touch and keeping up with the solicitors." Faye Patis is also singled out for praise, and is labelled "sensible" and "professional."

SILKS

Crispin Aylett QC An "excellent lawyer and a fine advocate" who is "devastatingly effective." He is particularly well known for his "superb" skills as a prosecutor, with one impressed source stating: "The best prosecutor in London in my opinion." In recent times he has undertaken several complex and high-profile murder cases, along with other matters such as terrorism and firearms offences. **Strengths:** "He's a brilliant, gifted advocate" and "an especially penetrating cross-examiner."

Edward Brown QC (see p.604) Well-regarded silk and a former Senior Treasury Counsel who attracts high praise for his advocacy skills. He's a highly experienced criminal practitioner who is also a strong regulatory lawyer. His recent work includes has seen him prosecute both a terrorist facilitator and a child murderer. **Strengths:** "Gloriously understated, he's a very, very effective advocate who gets great results." "A lovely advocate." **Recent work:** Successfully prosecuted a defendant accused of murdering a man who was acquitted 15 years previously of the murder of the defendant's sister.

Adrian Darbishire QC An "outstanding" barrister who specialises in serious cases including corporate crime, sexual offences and corruption cases. Described as "utterly brilliant" by sources, he is also highly experienced in health and safety work. **Strengths:** "A charming, sparkling advocate. He's a strong strategist and a terrific drafter." "He has the ability to understand the complexities of a case and ensure that a jury fully understands what is happening during a trial." "An imaginative and collaborative lawyer – working with him is a dream." **Recent work:** Successfully defended a consultant paediatrician charged with indecent assault on a young patient in the course of clinical examination.

Zoe Johnson QC (see p.684) An "up-and-coming" silk with expertise in both serious crime and professional discipline matters. She is praised by market commentators for her advocacy and strong work ethic, and has recently been instructed in matters relating to terrorism, homicide, child murder and gross negligence manslaughter. **Strengths:** "She is just awesome. She's so bright, so hard-working and she's got such good judgement."

Eleanor Laws QC (see p.697) A well-respected silk who specialises in serious crime and has particular expertise in murder and sexual offences. Her recent work includes acting as both prosecution and defence counsel in cases concerning historic sexual abuse and sex trafficking. **Strengths:** "Outstanding. Astonishing performance, breathtaking cross-examination and closing speech. I would have thought the go-to silk for all sexual allegations. Brilliant."

David Spens QC (see p.771) Praised for his advocacy, he has vast experience of both serious general crime and financial crime. He is a defence specialist who has represented those accused of murder and sex crime, as well as those charged with protest offences. A number of his cases have attracted media attention, one example of them being Operation Elveden, the investigation into allegations of inappropriate payments to police officers and other public officials. **Strengths:** "He's a very good tactician who is very good in front of the jury and very well respected by the judiciary." **Recent work:** Successfully defended an individual accused of murdering a man who had allegedly previously kidnapped and tortured him after the theft of a kilogram of cocaine.

JUNIORS

Ben FitzGerald (see p.645) A popular junior with in-depth experience across the full spectrum of criminal matters, who acts as both prosecution and defence counsel. Lauded by sources for his work ethic and "no-nonsense" approach to advocacy, he has been instructed in some of the most high-profile criminal cases of recent times. **Strengths:** "He has an outstanding ability to explain complex issues in a readily understandable way. There is a real sophistication to his advocacy." "He handled a client who could have been tricky extremely well, and had a very nice courtroom manner." **Recent work:** Prosecuted a teenage girl accused of infanticide having murdered her son seconds after his birth.

Jocelyn Ledward An "astonishingly capable" prosecutor and a very fine defence counsel who specialises in complex crime and fraud. She has been instructed in cases of murder, manslaughter and violent disorder. **Strengths:** "Very intelligent and able to think on her feet. She gains clients' trust very quickly and is tactically astute." "An extremely hard-working barrister. She puts in the hours at short notice and still turns things around very quickly." **Recent work:** Successfully prosecuted the three principal defendants accused of the murder of a professional poker player following a 'honey trap' plot.

Edward Henry (see p.670) A "terrific" junior with a "phenomenal" track record who specialises in all areas of general crime. He is particularly known for his expertise in serious organised crime, and is highly respected for his mastery of complex legal issues, including expert evidence and abuse of process. He regularly receives plaudits from market sources for his client-handling skills. **Strengths:** "He runs a silk's practice as a junior. He is extremely knowledgeable and a great jury advocate." "He has good legal skills and is convincing in court." **Recent work:** Acted in R v Brown, a complex drugs conspiracy case.

Rachna Gokani (see p.655) An "excellent" practitioner who is regularly entrusted with complex and challenging instructions, already having appeared before the Court of Appeal. She has handled matters across the full spectrum of serious crime, including cases of historic sexual assault, domestic violence and false imprisonment. **Strengths:** "She has fantastic judgement and is a delight to work with." **Recent work:** Successfully defended a newspaper tycoon charged with six counts of rape.

Benn Maguire (see p.706) A "strong junior" who specialises in defending those accused of serious crime, including cases of homicide, historic sex abuse and firearms offences. Highly regarded by his peers, he is also known for his work on appellate matters. **Strengths:** "Benn's a tremendous advocate. He's one of those barristers in court that everyone seems to spin around." **Recent work:** Represented Clive Goodman in the 'phone hacking' trial.

3 Raymond Buildings Barristers

See profile on p.904

THE SET

"A premiership set" with an "outstanding selection of advocates," its members provide stellar advocacy and advisory work, and excel in both legally aided and privately funded prosecution and defence work. They superbly handle the full gamut of serious criminal cases, and have great experience in the most high-profile terrorism and sexual offence work. Market observers particularly admire them for their attention to detail and their high-quality advocacy, with one individual commenting: "The thing that sums up 3RB barristers is their class. They are extremely polished in terms of the way they perfect and draft skeleton arguments and legal submissions. The level of thought and preparation is first-rate."

Client service: The set's clerking team, led by senior clerk Eddie Holland, is considered to be "highly efficient" and "flexible." Market observers state: "The clerking is great, and given that they're quite a big set that says an awful lot about the quality of that clerks room. Compared to some other sets of their size, they're just head and shoulders above the competition."

SILKS

Patrick Gibbs QC (see p.652) A "brilliant" silk with an excellent reputation across all areas of serious crime work. He has been instructed in some of the most significant cases in recent years, including Operation Elveden and the trial of Constance Briscoe. Well versed in both advisory work and litigation, he is highly respected for his intellectual acumen, and described by market observers as a "highly intelligent, superb all-round performer" who "grasps everything about a case very quickly." **Strengths:** "He is completely reliable, very calm under pressure and his judgement is just second to none." "He's a tremendous jury advocate, and his knowledge of the law is extraordinary." **Recent work:** Successfully defended one of the G4S security guards charged with the manslaughter of Angolan deportee Jimmy Mubenga.

Trevor Burke QC Specialising in all areas of serious crime and regularly advising high-profile individuals, he is described as a "very, very smooth and accomplished silk." He has substantial experience of both publicly and privately funded work, and has undertaken cases from murder to drug trafficking, both domestically and internationally. He has also been instructed in some of the most significant criminal investigations of recent years, including Operations Elveden and Pinetree. **Strengths:** "Tremendously versatile, polished, great with clients and someone with very good judgement." "He's hugely impressive in front of a jury and good at managing himself in the cut and thrust of the courtroom." **Recent work:** Responsible for the successful acquittal of a Sun journalist charged of corruption during Operation Elveden.

Alexander Cameron QC An outstanding and highly respected silk who attracts significant praise for his "hugely impressive" work ethic and excellent jury advocacy. Offering his services for both publicly and privately funded work, he has worked on numerous high-profile and complex cases, including those relating to homicide, drug and sexual offences. **Strengths:** "A complete star and has been throughout his career. He has an awful lot of charm, works very, very hard, and is a real performer in court." "Extremely astute QC whose strategic judgement is impeccable. A brilliant legal brain who has a commanding presence in court." "A go-to man for complex crime who is a great jury advocate and a wonderful speechmaker." **Recent work:** Defended a mentally vulnerable individual charged with the attempted murder of a police officer.

Richard Horwell QC A former First Senior Treasury counsel, who is instructed in complex and high profile cases. He has a practice rich in fraud, drugs, terrorism and sex cases, and has experience of representing the Crown in matters of national security. **Strengths:** "Very classy. His presentation and drafting are faultless. He's fantastic, and is meticulous both in his preapration and attention to detail. **Strengths:** Represented Max Clifford at his trial at Southwark Crown Court and at his appeal against sentence.

Hugo Keith QC (see p.689) Has a broad practice encompassing expertise in all areas of criminal law, including extradition and criminal public law alongside serious crime. Often undertaking the most challenging cases, he is praised for his courtroom presence and intellectual prowess. **Strengths:** "He's fantastic in front of a jury and his attention to detail is unparalleled." "An exceptional barrister with far-reaching expertise who is often instructed in some of the most challenging international cases." "Extremely clever and has a brilliant rapport with the judiciary."

Michael Borrelli QC (see p.599) Specialising in complex defence work, he has been party to some of the most high-profile criminal cases in recent times. He is particularly experienced in defending those charged with homicide offences that attract significant media attention. He is singled out by commentators for his advocacy and witness-handling skills. **Strengths:** "He's a very polished and stylish advocate who excels at cross-examination." "He's at the very top of his game and is universally respected by all solicitors." **Recent work:** Represented a gunman who had murdered an aspiring rapper in a case of mistaken identity.

Michael Bromley-Martin QC An "effective" silk who boasts vast experience across all areas of serious crime along with niche expertise in assisting police officers charged with criminal proceedings. He is praised for his advocacy style as well as his work ethic. **Strengths:** "He is one of the very best jury advocates around." "He was instructed at short notice and he was still completely on top of the facts." **Recent work:** Successfully defended a man accused of the attempted murder of an armed police officer.

Hugh Davies QC Experienced in both prosecuting and defending, and has developed expertise in the area of child sex exploitation via the internet or extra-jurisdictional contact. He also has an exceptional knowledge of the niche area of cybercrime. **Strengths:** "Very, very classy and very, very calm." "He's involved in the most serious and complex cases. If it is a high-profile, demanding case, with a high-profile, demanding client, then Hugh Davies is the one you would turn to." **Recent work:** Acted as leading counsel for a former chief reporter of the News of the World who was charged with phone hacking in a high-profile trial.

Jane Humphryes QC (see p.678) A "fearless advocate" who is "extremely diligent," she has vast experience of all areas of serious crime. She is particularly well known for her expertise in handling sex offences. Market observers comment on her approachability and her client-handling skills. **Strengths:** "Thorough, conscientious, passionate about defending her clients and extremely hard-working." "Extremely approachable and has a real knack with lay clients." **Recent work:** Represented an individual accused of sexual offences involving his young and vulnerable niece.

James Lewis QC (see p.700) "Incredibly experienced" silk whose practice includes serious criminal matters with an international angle, as well as extradition and fraud cases. Market observers are impressed with his intellectual acumen and say that he is "strong, smart and fearless." **Strengths:** "He has great authority and is very persuasive in court." "Very comprehensive, both in terms of reading around the case to understand it in greater detail and in thinking of all methods to meet the client's objectives." **Recent work:** Prosecuted an individual charged with the theft of extremely lucrative intellectual property.

JUNIORS

Neil Saunders (see p.759) A leading junior who is highly respected by his peers and described as "one of life's eternal geniuses." He both prosecutes and defends all areas of serious crime and fraud, and was heavily involved in Operation Elveden. Commentators single him out for his in-depth knowledge and shrewd approach in the courtroom. **Strengths:** "He's masterful and very well respected by judges and prosecutors alike, as well as co-defending counsel." "Neil Saunders has an unequalled practice as a leading junior and his knowledge of the law and presentation of legal arguments is universally respected. His breadth of practice attests to his versatility." **Recent work:** Defended a university student who was charged with growing cannabis in his halls of residence, among other offences. A non-custodial sentence was secured.

William Emlyn Jones An "excellent" junior barrister with experience of both prosecuting and defending criminal trials, who has a flourishing private practice. He has significant expertise in complex and high-profile murder trials, and also undertakes challenging terrorism work. He is praised by commentators for his advocacy and client-handling skills. **Strengths:** "He's a first-rate performer. He is good all round and particularly fantastic in his preparation." **Recent work:** Prosecuted a man accused of the murders of four young men whom he met on homosexual dating websites.

Alisdair Williamson (see p.797) A "majestic" practitioner with particular expertise in the defence of individuals, often high-profile, who have been charged with sexual assaults. He also regularly defends firearms and fraud cases, among other matters. He is particularly praised by sources for his jury and client manner. **Strengths:** "His quality of advocacy in cross-examination is of the first order." "Always the first choice for defendants facing allegations of rape or sexual assault." "He's got a very reassuring manner with clients, and an excellent jury manner." **Recent work:** Defended an individual charged with two acts of historic sex abuse, including homosexual child abuse and the rape and torture of his then wife. The defendant was acquitted of both charges.

Richard Wormald A "fantastic junior" who is extremely experienced in all matters of serious crime. He has experience of both prosecuting and defending, and has recently been instructed in highly significant cases involving multiple murder, firearms offences and perverting the court of justice. His advocacy skills come highly recommended. **Strengths:** "Absolutely first-class and a brilliant cross-examiner." "He's very accessible, works hard, has real flair in advocacy, and is someone who actually really cares about the clients." **Recent work:** Represented the Crown in the successful prosecution of a four-handed murder at Central Criminal Court.

Matthew Butt (see p.608) Skilled criminal defence practitioner with additional experience of prosecution work, who is considered to be a "rising star" by sources. He undertakes a broad spectrum of criminal briefs, and has recently been instructed in cases ranging from domestic violence to rape. Commentators further note his expertise in firearms offences and cases of universal jurisdiction. **Strengths:** "He's got really good judgement and is also a real fighter. He is the person you really want to have on your side." "A robust, fearless and persuasive advocate, with exemplary communication and client care skills." "He's thorough and bright." **Recent work:** Represented a former colonel of the Nepalese army charged with the commission of war crimes during Nepal's civil war in 2005.

Saba Naqshbandi Well-regarded junior with a varied practice that encompasses serious crime, international crime and fraud. She is regularly instructed to defend private prosecutions, and further undertakes an impressive amount of complex advisory work. **Strengths:** "Very polished and very versatile." **Recent work:** Advised on the production order applications that have arisen as a result of the phone hacking investigations.

Band 2

25 Bedford Row

See profile on p.810

THE SET

Specialist defence set 25 Bedford Row is known for the wide range of its criminal work and for being particularly strong in cases that are highly complex. Its barristers offer their services to both legally aided and publicly funded clients, and have defended individuals in some of the most high-profile cases of recent years, including Operation Elveden, the Poppy Day plot and the Marks & Spencer 'shopping trolley killing'. They are "counsel of very high calibre," both at silk and junior level, who are praised for their client-handling skills and effective courtroom performances. One interviewee states: "The advocacy at 25 Bedford Row has always been top-notch. I need them to command respect from the clients and they always deliver in that regard."

Client service: The "always accessible" Guy Williams leads a clerking team that receives plaudits for its service delivery. One source comments: "The communication from the clerks is particularly impressive and they are always accommodating." "When they deal with instructing solicitors, it's with respect." They attract further plaudits for their reliability and efficiency, and for "bringing order to what otherwise could be a chaotic existence."

SILKS

Jeremy Dein QC (see p.632) An "extremely charming" defence practitioner considered to be "a formidable and worthy opponent," who specialises in serious matters including murder, terrorism and organised crime. He is often entrusted with high-profile cases that have attracted significant media attention, including the 'shopping trolley killing'. He is highly recommended by commentators for his attention to detail and intellectual acumen. **Strengths:** "He's immensely reassuring when you've got a murder case with a strong forensic element as he's not at all frightened of facing scientific issues and leading them to the advantage of his client. A great jury advocate who is academically very bright." "He is very strong, has a very nice manner with the jury, and always gives his clients 100%." **Recent work:** Represented a defendant who had been charged with the murder of his partner and had proceeded to dispose of her body in a suitcase in a canal.

Courtenay Griffiths QC A "popular" silk with an impressive practice spanning both domestic and international criminal law. He is an expert in serious violent crime matters, and has handled numerous homicide and terrorism cases. He attracts significant praise for his approach in court, and is described as "a sensitive jury performer." **Strengths:** "A very powerful advocate who is eminently likeable, hugely talented, and someone who excels across a wide variety of different cases." "A super jury advocate." **Recent work:** Represented a defendant who strangled a trainee lawyer to death while he was staying as a lodger in her family home.

Paul Mendelle QC (see p.716) Respected silk with extensive experience of the most serious and high-profile criminal cases. He has handled numerous murder cases, including those relating to gangland warfare. He also played a significant part in Operation Elveden. **Strengths:** "A hard-working, excellent advocate who is very good with clients." "A very reliable performer who has good judgement." **Recent work:** Represented the principal defendant in a four-handed drug-related murder case. The case involved significant and complex legal arguments based on hearsay and bad character evidence.

George Carter-Stephenson QC Specialist crime and fraud practitioner with vast experience across a broad spectrum of criminal matters. He has recently been instructed in complex murder and conspiracy to commit murder cases. **Strengths:** "A real fighter and an attractive character who commands respect even from the most difficult to deal with clients." **Recent work:** Represented an individual accused of involvement in a multi-handed gangland murder of a 21 year old.

JUNIORS

Aisling Byrnes (see p.608) A strong junior who attracts praise from market observers for her handling of factually sensitive and emotive cases. She focuses her practice on all areas of serious crime, and has particular expertise in sexual offences and domestic violence cases. She is also singled out for her attention to detail, particularly in cases which involve complex pieces of evidence. **Strengths:** "Very sensitive, very passionate, very understanding but also tough when she needs to be. She gives very robust, direct advice and her advocacy style is very good." "She was very good with a client in horrendous emotional circumstances." **Recent work:** Represented an engineer charged with the sexual assault of a woman on the London Underground. The defendant was unanimously acquitted.

Cloth Fair Chambers

THE SET

A niche "superset" made up of six "fantastic individuals" who all possess "seriously excellent reputations." Members have experience of both pure crime and financial crime cases of the most serious and high-profile nature, the majority of which are privately funded. In recent times they have handled cases concerning murder, historic sexual offences and corporate manslaughter. A number of their clients are companies and individuals at risk of public exposure, such as 'fake sheikh' Mazher Mahmood and those involved in the 'phone hacking' trials.

Client service: A "bespoke service" is provided by the clerks, who are capably led by senior clerk Nick Newman. They are praised by sources for their organisation and their diary management.

SILKS

John Kelsey-Fry QC (see p.689) A pre-eminent silk considered by market sources to be "stellar." He is particularly known for his representation of private clients in the most serious general crime and financial crime cases. He has been instructed in some of the most headline-grabbing cases of recent years, handling cases relating to homicide, corruption, perverting the course of justice and affray. Commentators praise him for his brilliant advocacy and excellent legal mind. **Strengths:** "He's obviously fantastic and incredibly charismatic." "He is a superstar. In particular cases and areas he is second to none. He has a superb courtroom manner and an ability to see points that no one else would." "The best advocate in the land. He is brilliant on advisory work and also in court." **Recent work:** Provided pre-trial advice to Mazher Mahmood following his charge for perverting the course of justice following the Tulisa Contostavlos trial.

Nicholas Purnell QC (see p.745) "Hugely impressive" practitioner highly respected by market observers, who has vast experience of all areas of criminal law, both general and financial. Most recently he has handled some incredibly high-profile cases, including those involving historic sex abuse, terrorism, corporate manslaughter and perverting the course of justice. He attracts praise for his ability to work well with colleagues and provide straightforward advice. **Strengths:** "He's really excellent and has a great command about him." "Everyone knows his reputation and that he is fantastic to work with."

Ian Winter QC (see p.799) "Outstanding" silk handling purely privately funded cases. His recent work includes advising on charges ranging from blackmail to allegations of sexual offences. He is highly recommended by sources on account of his strategic approach to advice and his straightforward advocacy. **Strengths:** "Ruthlessly effective." "Analytical and user-friendly." "I think for certain clients he is the person that they want. He's no-nonsense, he gets to the point, he won't sugar-coat the advice, and that's what you need. If there's a way out in a case, he will find it." **Recent work:** Successfully defended a member of the Bar of Gibraltar charged with perverting the course of justice.

JUNIORS

Jonathan Barnard (see p.589) A "fantastic junior" considered by market observers to be among the leading legal minds at the Criminal Bar. He is highly experienced at handling both private prosecutions and private defence work, often as a leading junior. In recent times he has been instructed in matters including sexual offences and perverting the course of justice. **Strengths:** "He's completely reliable and has got a very impressive courtroom manner. His written work is fantastic and he's incredibly intelligent." "A polished performer who expertly dissects the other side both on paper and in court." **Recent work:** Defended a doctor facing a private prosecution regarding an illegal abortion clinic in Northern England. This was a landmark case on gender abortion issues.

Doughty Street Chambers

See profile on p.828

THE SET

A set with "a wealth of talent" that brings "an enlightened and aware approach to the work it does." Its members are "trustworthy and efficient" and offer expertise in all areas of criminal law, taking particular pride in their dedication to crime involving issues relating to human rights and civil liberties. They also have further expertise in areas such as extradition, civil law and public law. "Client-focused" in their approach, they act for both publicly and privately funded clients, and often appear before the Supreme Court and the Court of Appeal. Doughty Street Chambers also has an acclaimed international criminal law practice, and its advocates appear with regularity in cases before the ICC. Sources say: "The set has a fantastic reputation. Generally I'd expect anyone from there to be high quality."

Client service: A "high calibre" set of staff led by the "extremely helpful" business development director Maurice MacSweeney, who attracts high praise from sources. One commentator states: "Maurice is very business-minded, and I think he's a massive credit to Doughty Street." The clerks here are described as "user-friendly" and "organised."

SILKS

Edward Fitzgerald QC A pre-eminent figure at the Bar who comes highly recommended by market commentators for being "a fantastic lawyer and a fantastic human being" with a "brilliant reputation." He has considerable expertise in a vast array of criminal matters, including murder, and is also renowned for his international criminal law expertise. **Strengths:** "Hugely impressive, he has brought about changes in the law through his skilled and persuasive advocacy. He's very experienced and capable of handling the most difficult cases with meticulous care." "Once he gets himself involved in a client's cause, he takes it on as though the cause were personal to him and he is just relentless." **Recent work:** Represented an individual in an appeal against his conviction for the murder of his wife's lover.

Joel Bennathan QC A celebrated silk with in-depth experience across all areas of serious crime, who is particularly good at cases with complex legal arguments. He regularly handles appeal cases and is noted for his expertise in terrorism cases. Commentators say he is "conscientious" and praise him for his jury advocacy, client manner and intellectual acumen. **Strengths:** "His manner with clients is very personable. He can explain difficult legal and evidential points to clients so that they understand." **Recent work:** Represented an individual who had planned to decapitate a soldier or policeman on Remembrance Day.

Tim Moloney QC An "outstanding" practitioner who is highly praised for his exceptional advocacy skills, client-handling abilities and intellectual acumen. Considered a "true professional," he is particularly accomplished when it comes to handling serious criminal matters involving terrorism and murder. He is also well known for his niche experience in advising on reviews of death penalty decisions resulting from the actions of British government departments. **Strengths:** "A phenomenal academic lawyer with an incredible grasp of detail." "He is dedicated and passionate, has astonishing recall and attention to detail, and possesses a truly incisive mind. He is able to put people at ease immediately and approaches clients and professionals with courtesy and respect." **Recent work:** Involved in R v Jogee, the landmark case on the doctrine of joint enterprise before the Supreme Court.

James Wood QC A skilled practitioner who is highly sought after for terrorism cases. Committed to both private and publicly funded work, his practice also consists of challenging and complex cases relating to murder and drug offences. **Strengths:** "One of the all-time greats. At his best, he is a force of nature." "Has intellect and gravitas. He's very good with clients and taken seriously by judges." **Recent work:** Defended an individual accused of attempted murder, Section 18 GBH and possessing a weapon.

Francis FitzGibbon QC A "committed" silk with an "excellent" practice that is focused upon heavy crime and fraud. His recent matters have included cases relating to murder, joint enterprise and historic sex offences. Praised as a "fine academic lawyer," he is further noted for his expertise in cases involving complex medical and scientific expert evidence. **Strengths:** "He grasps the detail, does the work and in the right case comes across as being a man the jury can trust." "He seems to be someone who has the ear of the court." **Recent work:** Defended an individual who, while suffering from depression, murdered his next-door neighbour following a long-running dispute.

Isabella Forshall QC A "super" defence counsel described as "dedicated" and "hard-working," who is renowned for her handling of complex cases involving homicides, and in particular infanticide. She is also extremely well known for her mastery of substantial sexual offence cases. Her court manner and client-handling skills are highly acclaimed by sources. **Strengths:** "She's a lovely opponent who is very measured, very calm and very thoughtful." **Recent work:** Represented an individual tried as a result of Operation Bullfinch who had been accused by three vulnerable complainants of various sexual offences. He was acquitted of any direct sexual offending.

Rebecca Trowler QC A rising silk who is regularly instructed as defence counsel in high-profile and challenging criminal matters, including murder and gross negligence manslaughter cases. She is "a good tactician" who is "calm under pressure," and highly praised for her jury advocacy. Interviewees comment on her dedication to her clients: "I really admire the fact that she sees herself as a rock in support of her client's position." **Strengths:** "Strategic, intelligent and has a strong courtroom presence." "I liken her to a chess grand master in that she is always three moves ahead of the opposition." **Recent work:** Represented a transvestite with a severe personality disorder who was charged with the murder of her transsexual neighbour. The defendant was convicted with a life sentence, but the sentence was reduced after a successful appeal.

JUNIORS

Benjamin Newton An "incredibly diligent" junior highly regarded by solicitors who comes strongly recommended for his advocacy and preparation skills. He often acts as defence counsel, and has appeared in numerous headline-grabbing cases in recent years. By way of example, he acted for Trenton Oldfield, the man who disrupted the Boat Race, and Reverend Vickery House, who was charged with sexual offences. **Strengths:** "Tactically astute and a great advocate." "He is thoroughly prepared and excellent with the clients." "An excellent advocate in the higher courts" who is "very hard-working and very client-friendly." **Recent work:** Represented Tremeloes guitarist Rick Westwood, who was charged with a historic indecent assault on a girl then aged 16.

Richard Thomas An "absolutely fantastic" junior who was described by one impressed commentator as "one of the best junior counsel at the Bar." He is regularly instructed in extremely complex cases which attract significant media attention, including those relating to terrorism, burglary and corruption. **Strengths:** "So clever. He's great on the law and the speed at which he comes up with things is just fantastic." **Recent work:** Junior counsel in R v Doyle, also known as the Hatton Garden heist.

Paul Taylor An "outstanding" advocate who is highly regarded for his specialism and expertise in appellate work. He attracts plaudits for his preparation and intellect, and has been instructed in some of the most complex and challenging appeals of recent years, including those relating to fresh evidence, murders and historic sexual offences. He is also particularly renowned for his expertise in fitness to plead cases, particularly when related to psychiatric issues. **Strengths:** "He has an encyclopaedic knowledge of appeal authorities and is a very persuasive advocate." "He is ruthlessly well prepared and extremely committed." **Recent work:** Acted for an individual appealing a conviction for rape, kidnapping and false imprisonment on the grounds that the complainant retracted her evidence and failed to attend trial. Her evidence was allowed to be adduced at trial as hearsay.

Matrix Chambers

See profile on p.876

THE SET

A "cerebral and intellectual set" whose practice centres on complex, challenging and revolutionary criminal cases as opposed to traditional criminal matters. Its members are famed for their "modern and contemporary dynamic" and undertake a unique combination of constitutional and administrative criminal work, along with cases that relate to crime in the context of human rights and civil liberties. They are also known for their work on protest cases, international criminal law and extradition, with members regularly appearing before the ICC, the Court of Appeal and the Supreme Court. Commentators say that the individuals here are "client-focused, responsive and good to work with."

Client service: "The most friendly and professional set of clerks," according to one interviewee. Offering a unique business set-up, the clerks are known for placing their full focus on their allocated practice areas, and are considered to be "responsive and helpful" by those who encounter them. The criminal clerking team is capably led by practice manager Paul Venables.

SILKS

Ben Emmerson QC Famed for his involvement in some of the most high-profile cases of recent years, he is considered by those in market to be a "tremendous" and an "absolutely fantastic" practitioner. He is also renowned for his international criminal practice and regularly appears at the ICC. **Strengths:** "An absolute star." "Extremely authoritative."

Clare Montgomery QC (see p.720) An "exceptional" silk with experience of both defending and prosecuting, who has "an encyclopaedic knowledge of the law." She receives plaudits for her "innovative" and "inventive" approach, and is most often tasked with matters that involve substantial and challenging questions of law or fact. She is a noted criminal appellate lawyer and has further expertise in extradition work. **Strengths:** "She's a class act. She's amazingly quick to pick up on all of the issues but also just very, very good on her feet." "Incredibly bright and very clear-sighted." "She is one of the finest minds at the Bar, full stop." **Recent work:** Instructed by the DPP of the Bahamas in respect of an appeal made to overturn a murder conviction.

Tim Owen QC Has a practice encompassing the full spectrum of criminal law, be it general crime or fraud. He is applauded by sources for his exceptional advocacy, and impresses both as a jury advocate and an appellate advocate. He regularly appears before the Supreme Court. **Strengths:** "He is the consummate advocate and he commands tremendous respect from the Bench." "He's exceptional, very bright, very well respected and an extremely good barrister." **Recent work:** Represented Dennis Slade in a successful appeal against his conviction for conspiracy to murder, setting a precedent for the use of the Batvox voice recognition method.

Ken Macdonald QC A former Director of Public Prosecutions with vast experience of handling domestic and international crime. He is very good at assisting clients in strategically liaising with prosecution authorities. **Strengths:** "An extraordinarily polished trial advocate." **Recent work:** Advised an individual who had helped his father to commit suicide, subsequently making representations to the DPP as to why it would not be in the public interest to prosecute.

Matthew Ryder QC (see p.757) An experienced criminal advocate particularly highly regarded for his terrorism expertise. He regularly acts in high-profile cases and is extremely experienced in protest matters and cases relating to the actions of undercover police officers. **Strengths:** "Very, very clever, fantastic on the paperwork and someone with a very nice way about him in court." **Recent work:** Represented the defendant, a senior partner of a solicitors' firm, who was charged with immigration offences after being caught by an undercover sting operation conducted by BBC documentary 'Panorama'.

JUNIORS

Joanna Buckley An impressive young junior praised by market observers for her intellectual acumen. She is particularly well known for her exceptional work during the 'phone hacking' trials. **Strengths:** "Super bright, so clever, efficient and fantastic to work with." "She's very bright and is going to be a complete star." **Recent work:** Successfully defended an individual facing a charge of criminal damage and common assault. The common assault charge was dropped following a legal argument to exclude identification evidence under Section 78 of PACE.

Red Lion Chambers

THE SET

A set with an exceptional stable of "thoroughbred" advocates, both juniors and silks, who are "hard-working, excellent practitioners and very worthy opponents. You know that if you're up against Red Lion, you're going to get a decent fight." Members act for both the prosecution and defence, and regularly handle cases of the most challenging nature, some of which attract a significant amount of media. Instructing solicitors say: "The tenants, the quality of the results and their client service is always very good."

Client service: The set has an "efficient" and "responsive" clerking team known for being particularly appreciative of the needs of clients. Sources say: "They want to help you. They understand where you're coming from in terms of trying to avoid problems and are practical and easy to deal with."

SILKS

David Etherington QC Highly respected and experienced silk who is considered by commentators to be in a "league of his own." An "elegant wordsmith," he possesses in-depth knowledge of all areas of criminal law including fraud. Interviewees praise his jury advocacy in particular. **Strengths:** "He has real flair and is a very elegant advocate." "A class act with a great jury manner who knows how to handle a judge." "Good-humoured, succinct and to the point." **Recent work:** Represented an individual charged with the unlawful manslaughter of his friend during a game of Punch 4 Punch. The defendant was acquitted.

Max Hill QC (see p.671) Head of chambers Max Hill is "a quality performer" with a prosecution background, who now also represents the defence in some of the most serious and high-profile matters around, including murder and terrorism cases. He attracts praise from market commentators for his calm approach and his sound advocacy. **Strengths:** "He is thorough, unrelenting and he gets results." "He never wilts under pressure, he's brilliant on the law, and he's just so smooth in court." **Recent work:** Prosecuted a former Metropolitan Police firearms officer who was charged with the fatal shooting of Azelle Rodney.

Rosina Cottage QC An "excellent" practitioner and vastly experienced prosecution and defence counsel who is "meticulous" in her handling of the full spectrum of violent and sexual offences cases. She is particularly renowned for her handling of victims, witnesses and defendants who are subject to Special Measures, as well as those who are suffering from emotional vulnerability or mental impairment. **Strengths:** "An excellent cross-examiner who is firm but fair." "She has a lovely style in court -she's unassuming but powerful." "If you've got a case that involves vulnerable people, special measures or medical evidence relating to that vulnerable person, she's your person." **Recent work:** Prosecuted an extremely high-profile case of a cult leader charged with sexual offences, child neglect and false imprisonment. The defendant was convicted and jailed for 23 years.

JUNIORS

Jennifer Dempster A renowned junior specialising in the defence of those charged with counts of serious crime and fraud. She has recently been instructed in a wide variety of complex criminal cases, including those concerning murder, sexual offences and kidnapping. Described as "a superb advocate" with "amazing client care," she is particularly good at handling young defendants and witnesses. **Strengths:** "Excellent jury advocate who inspires the confidence of the client and the court and is a top-notch junior." "She's superb both with the clients and in front of juries." **Recent work:** Represented a defendant charged in a multi-handed conspiracy to murder. The case arose out of a campaign of harassment against the victim, who was ultimately shot in the chest but survived.

Gillian Jones A "brilliant" practitioner who is described by market sources as "bright, hard-working and fun." Often instructed as a leading junior, she is highly experienced in cases of murder and manslaughter, and also undertakes cold case work. She attracts plaudits for both her advocacy and her upbeat attitude. **Strengths:** "Hard-working, intelligent, highly capable and very amusing with it. She's going to go far." **Recent work:** Represented an individual charged with joint enterprise murder of an individual who was found in his basement.

Tom Forster A defence specialist who has undertaken numerous complex cases of the most serious nature, including matters relating to child prostitution and other serious organised crime. **Strengths:** "He is excellent with clients. He's really clever, hard-working and sensible. He's realistic about his cases and keeps people calm." "Very bright and a good all-rounder." **Recent work:** Defended a case involving an organised crime gang charged with kidnapping an individual at gunpoint and demanding money for his safe return.

Band 3

9-12 Bell Yard

THE SET

A highly regarded set with long-standing crime and fraud practices of a high standard. Its barristers undertake complex matters in all areas of general crime, including cases of misconduct in public office and corruption. They have also developed a growing expertise in cases of human trafficking and modern slavery. Members both prosecute and defend and tackle a regular diet of murder, manslaughter, sexual offences and child abuse cases.

Client service: The clerks, headed by Angela May, are "easy to deal with and efficient." They are highly regarded for their intuition, organisation and unfaltering promotion of the set's junior counsel.

SILKS

Mukul Chawla QC (see p.615) A highly respected silk who is a highly prominent figure at the Criminal Bar. A former standing counsel to HM Customs & Excise, he is heavily lauded for his jury advocacy and intellectual ability. He has experience of handling matters of significant public interest, including complex terrorism and corruption cases. **Strengths:** "He's a very, very polished performer who has a nice understated style which appeals to both judges and juries." **Recent work:** Instructed by the Home Office in a judicial review of a decision by the Home Secretary to refuse to accede to requests for mutual assistance from a US district court for materials held by MI5.

Alexandra Healy QC (see p.668) Both prosecutes and defends the most complex criminal and fraud cases. Recently she has handled challenging murder, sexual offences and child abuse cases, and was also involved in matters arising from Operation Elveden. Drug trafficking and serious organised crime cases are also a specialism. **Strengths:** "She is well prepared, takes absolutely no prisoners and is incredibly bright." **Recent work:** Defended an individual charged with the sexual abuse of six different child victims.

JUNIORS

Alexandra Ward (see p.789) Reputed junior who is particularly strong on sexual offences and road traffic incidents, along with fraud, bribery and corruption cases. She has been praised by judges and fellow practitioners alike for her impressive technical ability and her attention to detail. **Strengths:** "She is tenacious, forward-thinking and a tactical advocate. She is brilliant with clients and is an all-rounder." **Recent work:** Acted in R v Harold Chinegwundoh, a case concerning fitness to plead.

Carmelite Chambers

See profile on p.817

THE SET

A specialist defence set with a long-established history of handling serious criminal law cases, particularly those relating to financial crime. It possesses a strong bench of practitioners who carry out both international and domestic work, some of which is subject to intense media scrutiny. Recent work has included terrorism, murder and gross negligence manslaughter cases, and members have been involved in matters relating to Operation Elveden and Operation Weeting. They were also involved in R v Penton & Others, which concerned the murder of antique dealer and 'Antiques Roadshow' regular Michael Griffiths.

Client service: A highly regarded clerking team capably led by Marc King that is praised for its responsiveness and commerciality.

23 Essex Street

See profile on p.839

THE SET

A large set with a nationwide reputation that offers assistance to both privately and publicly funded individuals. Its members are noted for their dedication – "they afford each case the same level of effort and respect" – and handle both prosecution and defence work. Offering a "very high standard of advocacy," they undertake criminal cases of all different types, many of which attract high media interest. Murder, sexual offences and corporate manslaughter cases all form the staple diet of the set.

Client service: Led by their "tireless" chambers director Richard Fowler, this strong clerking team has earned a reputation for being "professional, helpful and reliable." They are respected for their intuition, with one source stating that "they're very helpful when it comes to identifying the right advocates for the personality of the client." Junior clerks Adam Chapman and Jack Shah are also singled out for praise for their strong organisational skills.

SILKS

Simon Russell Flint QC A "standout" silk who remains a leading figure at the Bar, and who has vast experience of both defending and prosecuting heavyweight criminal cases including homicides and serious drug offences. Known for his work both domestically and internationally, he is recognised by market observers for his "charming manner" and superior jury advocacy. **Strengths:** "A very stylish, well-rounded and experienced silk who has a very nice style with a jury." **Recent work:** Successfully prosecuted a gang-related murder with six teenage defendants. One defendant was convicted of murder, while five others were convicted of related offences.

Furnival Chambers

See profile on p.850

THE SET

A set with very fine barristers that handles everything from advisory work to appellate cases. Its members are praised for their client handling, with one interviewee stating: "If you instruct them you know the client will be looked after, and that they'll do a good job in terms of results." Members here have been entrusted with some of the most high-profile cases of recent times, including the prosecution of Rolf Harris, the murder of Sarah Payne and the case of 'M25 rapist' Antoni Imiela. They are known for their deft handling of terrorism, sexual offence and people-trafficking cases, and are good at all levels of call. An interviewee says: "We know their barristers well and feel assured that if one can't cover a case, there'll be another who will do it just as well."

Client service: Described by instructing solicitors as "one of the strengths of chambers," senior clerk Stephen Ball is the head of the clerking team. He and his team are noted for their innovation and dedication to providing a first-class service.

SILKS

Oliver Blunt QC (see p.598) Pre-eminent defence silk of vast experience who is "a quality performer," according to his peers. Praised for his attitude and his jury advocacy, he continues to excel in all areas of general criminal law including complex murders, multi-handed robberies and incidents stemming from serious organised crime. **Strengths:** "He displays impeccable charm with the jury and in the courtroom. Once he has his teeth in a case he doesn't let go until the fight is won." "An extremely talented and experienced silk."

Sally O'Neill QC (see p.730) An experienced practitioner who is highly acclaimed for her courtroom performances. An "astute advocate," she is particularly well known for her mastery of serious sexual offence and infanticide cases, most notably those involving 'baby shaking'. Her handling of the potentially vulnerable witnesses involved in such cases was much commented upon. She also excels in serious and complex murder and manslaughter cases, among others. **Strengths:** "She's very polished. Juries tend to like and trust her, because she has a direct way of communication with them which appeals to them." "She's a really formidable and fair opponent."

Garden Court Chambers

See profile on p.851

THE SET

A set with "a drive to assist the underdog," Garden Court Chambers is an "extremely capable set that has been at the forefront of many decisions which have changed criminal law." The full spread of criminal work is tackled and chambers has specialist knowledge of terrorism and protest cases. Evidencing this, members here acted in only the second ever prosecution for the possession of a chemical weapon, and represented the defendants of the Occupy Democracy protest. Murder, manslaughter and theft cases are also to the fore and individuals at the set recently had roles in the trial concerning the notorious Hatton Garden heist. Other areas of expertise include baby-shaking cases.

Client service: Senior clerk Colin Cook is particularly singled out for praise, with one solicitor stating: "One always feels that he is giving serious thought to appropriate counsel and one is being well looked after." He and his fellow clerks are praised for their "flexible" approach to fees, and they "regularly display no hesitation in assigning a matter to counsel on a pro bono basis."

SILKS

Ali Naseem Bajwa QC A renowned advocate with vast experience of all areas of serious crime, and particular expertise in handling criminal cases incorporating human rights issues. Highly proficient in conducting the most complex and challenging homicide and terrorism trials, he attracts praise from sources for his courtroom manner and intellectual acumen. **Strengths:** "A really charming and persuasive advocate." "He has a phenomenal legal brain that is perfectly suited for defence work." "His judgement on cases is excellent. He is great with clients and user-friendly to solicitors." **Recent work:** Represented a London university student, originally from Serbia, charged with preparing to travel to Syria to commit acts of terrorism.

Henry Blaxland QC A highly experienced defence specialist who attracts plaudits from market commentators for his dedication and attention to detail. A master of both serious crime and fraud cases, he comes particularly highly recommended for his expertise in terrorism matters and for his ability as an appellate advocate. **Strengths:** "Undoubtedly one of the leading criminal appeal lawyers in the country." "He has one of the best legal minds in the market and his attention to detail on cases is overwhelming." **Recent work:** Represented a woman who was jointly charged, alongside her lesbian partner, with the murder of that partner's eight year old daughter. The defendant was convicted of manslaughter, with the sentence reduced to 15 years on appeal.

Stephen Kamlish QC An "absolutely first-class" practitioner who has regularly been instructed in the most high-profile serious crime cases of recent years. As an example, he represented the family of Stephen Lawrence throughout the initial private prosecution of his alleged killers and acted for them in the inquiry which followed. He is a specialist in handling murder and terrorism cases, and is praised for both his combative advocacy style and his client-handling skills. **Strengths:** "He is beyond compare in terms of cross-examination." "Absolutely superb and very fluent." "I can't overstress how good Stephen was. He was that good that you would have actually paid to watch him." **Recent work:** Successfully represented a defendant charged in a gang-related eight-handed murder.

Judy Khan QC A "super practitioner" well versed in handling complex and high-profile criminal cases, who is highly praised for her "amazing" judgement and superior advocacy. She is particularly experienced in handling substantial murders and sex offences. **Strengths:** "She is one of the most accessible and plain-speaking QCs at the Bar. Clients love her straightforward, no-fuss approach." **Recent work:** Has spent the last two years leading a team of barristers on the Hillsborough inquests.

James Scobie QC A "popular" silk who is considered by sources to be "a real powerhouse in the courtroom." Described as an "excellent tactician," he is most highly praised for his ability to communicate with vulnerable clients. His practice encompasses all areas of serious crime, taking in murder and manslaughter cases as well as those relating to sexual offences. Many of the matters he handles attract significant media interest. **Strengths:** "Really enthusiastic, great with the clients, good to work with and just totally fearless." "A natural and gifted advocate who is confident and courageous in any situation." "His hard work stands out, and he has the ability to absorb and distil a lot of information very quickly. He's a great jury advocate and is loved by clients." **Recent work:** Represented one of four defendants charged with the premeditated murder of New Forest woman Pennie Davis.

Michael Turner QC A strong defence counsel specialising in serious crime. He is particularly renowned for his expertise in baby-shaking cases. **Strengths:** "Dedicated, incredibly hard-working and robust in court."

Kieran Vaughan QC A criminal heavyweight who comes highly regarded due to his exceptional legal mind and effective jury advocacy. He is a "pragmatic" individual with extensive experience in terrorism, homicide and sexual offence cases, who has been instructed in matters of significant public interest such as the Hatton Garden heist and the appeal of Ched Evans. **Strengths:** "Exceptionally bright, very sharp, and someone who combines intellectual talent with a very approachable manner." "Kieran is constantly working. He never stops thinking about the case and has an eye for detail which is second to none." **Recent work:** Represented a defendant who, having been charged with a murder committed on Christmas Day in Leicester Square, had fled to Jamaica for over a year. Despite being seen with a gun on CCTV moments before the murder, the defendant was acquitted in a 'cut-throat' defence.

5 Paper Buildings

See profile on p.889

THE SET

An impressive set that has been around for a century and more. It undertakes both privately and publicly funded work, and handles all types of serious crime from murder to perverting the course of justice. Commentators describe it as "a very, very proficient prosecution set that also offers fantastic defence counsel." Its members are regularly instructed in high-profile matters, as evidenced by their involvement in Operations Yewtree and Elveden, and handle cases concerning gang-related and serious organised crime. They are "reliable practitioners" who are "focused and attract good-quality work."

Client service: "The set is very well run, and the clerks are very pleasant and amenable." Instructing solicitors praise their organisation and treatment of clients. One particularly impressed source states: "The clerking is excellent. They remember that solicitors are the source of work, and they appreciate who we answer to. They cover any changes, and they are on top of their diaries." The highly experienced and equally highly respected senior clerk Dale Jones leads the team.

SILKS

Jonathan Caplan QC An "absolutely first-class" silk who is acclaimed by market commentators for his advocacy skills. Has a strong practice both domestically and internationally, and regularly appears before the Court of Appeal. Commentators praise him for his noteworthy efforts during the 'phone hacking' trials. **Strengths:** "Phenomenally good, particularly on his feet. He's a fantastic orator." "A very persuasive advocate who is very experienced." **Recent work:** Successfully defended famous radio DJ Neil Fox, who had been charged with historic sex offences.

Other Ranked Lawyers

Abbas Lakha QC (see p.694) A specialist defence advocate highly experienced in handling complex homicides and drugs offences, as well as fraud cases. He is also particularly familiar with the intricacies of appellate work. His recent cases have included the defence of the murderer of soldier Lee Rigby. **Strengths:** "A consummate operator." **Recent work:** Represented a defendant convicted of baby shaking. This was an appeal on the basis of fresh medical evidence.

Simon Mayo QC (see p.711) An "excellent" practitioner with capabilities as both prosecution and defence counsel. He continues to handle the most grave and complex cases, including multi-handed murders, robberies and sexual offences. He attracts particularly high praise from market observers for his attention to detail and fine jury advocacy. **Strengths:** "He is the most meticulous silk at the Criminal Bar, whose attention to detail is the reason why he wins cases. He has a succinct style to his cross-examination and closing speeches." "An accomplished advocate who has a sound legal mind and is very pleasant with it." **Recent work:** Defended Lewis Daynes in an extremely high-profile case concerning the murder of 14 year old Breck Bednar, whom Daynes had groomed online.

Mark Heywood QC The current First Senior Treasury Counsel and a man described by market sources as being "absolutely amazing." In his role he undertakes only the most serious and complex cases, and as a result has vast experience of homicide, organised crime and terrorism cases, to name but a few. He is also regularly called upon to advise on appellate matters. **Strengths:** "You can't get better than Mark Heywood. He's a beautiful advocate with great strategic awareness, who is lovely to work with and a very charming man." "One of the best lawyers, if not the best lawyer in the country." "A very steady, firm prosecutor." **Recent work:** Prosecuted an individual charged with multiple rapes of prostitutes. The defendant was convicted on every count and received life imprisonment.

Sarah Forshaw QC A "formidable" silk who is highly regarded by market commentators for her noteworthy practice, and who has acted in all manner of serious cases including those relating to murders and drug importation offences. She is particularly renowned for her expertise defending those charged with sexual offences, in particular historical sexual offences. She regularly handles cases concerning sexual assaults and gang rape. **Strengths:** "She's a silk who reads every piece of paper. She's demanding on those she works with and she's got great client rapport. Juries love her." "Brilliant. An amazing advocate who's comfortable with the clients, takes an uncompromising approach to case presentation and develops a very good rapport with the jury." **Recent work:** Successfully defended a young professional footballer accused of raping a teenage girl in a field during the early hours of the morning. The jury acquitted within 30 minutes.

Aftab Jafferjee QC of Atkinson Bevan Chambers, 2 Harcourt Buildings. A "very, very effective" prosecutor who continues to undertake all manner of serious criminal matters. He is highly respected by market observers for his incisive cross-examination and smooth advocacy style, and is masterful as both a trial and an appellate advocate. **Strengths:** "He's immaculate. He's an example of a very good lawyer and a very good advocate." "He's eloquent, smooth, and juries love him. It is difficult to spot a weakness in him."

Nigel Rumfitt QC (7BR) An experienced practitioner who is well known for his involvement in the 'phone hacking' trials. He is praised by market commentators for the quality of his advocacy. **Strengths:** "Pugnacious, direct, extremely effective and hard-working." **Recent work:** Successfully defended an individual in the final 'phone hacking' trial.

Tom Little (see p.703) (9 Gough Square) An exceptional Treasury Counsel who is "a real star in the making." Regularly appearing at the Old Bailey and the Supreme Court, often as a leading junior, he is entrusted with only the most serious and complex cases, including matters of homicide and terrorism. He is also extremely well versed in appellate work. **Strengths:** "He is highly intelligent, has good tactical and strategic nous, and is very good with opponents, judges and his leaders. He works extremely hard." "Strategically fantastic and a man with a lovely manner." **Recent work:** Prosecuted an ISIS-led conspiracy to murder soldiers and police officers on the streets of London.

Michael Mansfield QC (Mansfield Chambers) A pre-eminent figure at the Criminal Bar who has had an illustrious career acting in numerous celebrated cases. He was most recently in the news for his representation of the families in the Hillsborough inquest. In the past he has also acted for the families of Mark Duggan and Stephen Lawrence, and represented Barry George, the man cleared of the murder of Jill Dando. **Strengths:** "A complete fighter for his cause. Juries love him."

LONDON International Criminal Law

Crime: International Criminal Law	
Leading Silks	
de Silva Desmond	*Goldsmith Chambers*
Dixon Rodney	*Temple Garden Chambers*
Emmerson Ben	*Matrix Chambers*
Haynes Peter	*St Philips Chambers*
Hooper David	*25 Bedford Row*
Jordash Wayne	*Doughty Street Chambers*
Kay Steven	*9 Bedford Row* *
Khan Karim A. A.	*Temple Garden Chambers*
Moloney Tim	*Doughty Street Chambers*
Leading Juniors	
Ashraph Sareta	*Garden Court Chambers*
Bafadhel Sara	*9 Bedford Row* *
Butler Michelle	*Matrix Chambers* *
Cadman Toby	*9 Bedford Row* *
Clooney Amal	*Doughty Street Chambers* *
Edwards Iain	*1MCB*
Higgins Gillian	*9 Bedford Row* A *
Powles Steven	*Doughty Street Chambers* *
Reynolds Richard	*Garden Court Chambers*
Rogers Paul	*Outer Temple Chambers*

** Indicates individual with profile.*

A direct access (see p.24).

Alphabetical order within each band. Band 1 is highest.

Ranked Lawyers

Steven Kay QC (see p.688) (9 Bedford Row) Leading silk with a vast depth of experience of handling ICC proceedings, particularly those involving significant and high-profile political figures. He regularly defends those accused of war crimes and crimes against humanity. **Strengths:** "Absolutely fantastic." "He's like the Godfather of the ICC. He's the old-school kind of blue-chip lawyer you would want in a case." **Recent work:** Represented President Uhuru Kenyatta of Kenya, who was facing charges of crimes against humanity. The charges were ultimately withdrawn.

Sara Bafadhel (see p.587) (9 Bedford Row) Impressive junior known for her involvement in numerous cases before the ICC, in particular cases stemming from the Libyan conflict. She is also known for her consultancy work. **Strengths:** "She is a sound choice for even the most difficult of cases."

Toby Cadman (see p.609) (9 Bedford Row) "Absolutely brilliant" junior who is known for his complex advisory work. Specialising in international humanitarian law, he has represented numerous individuals charged with war crimes and is often entrusted to lead inquiries into mass genocide and acts of terrorism. **Strengths:** "A real mover and shaker in the field, and a suave advocate."

Gillian Higgins (see p.671) (9 Bedford Row) Noted by sources for her strong work ethic and knowledge of international criminal law, she is particularly adept at defending those charged with genocide, war crimes and crimes against humanity. She maintains a particularly strong affiliation with the African Court on Human and Peoples' Rights. **Strengths:** "Utterly fantastic." "She is very prominent, extremely hard-working and known as a very committed person who has done very well in all of her cases." **Recent work:** Represented the son of the first president of Kenya, who was charged with crimes against humanity due to alleged violence committed following the Kenyan election. The charges were ultimately dropped.

David Hooper QC (25 Bedford Row) Respected practitioner who attracts praise for his advocacy and his approach to international criminal law matters. Based at the ICC, he handles cases relating to war crimes or crimes against humanity that attract significant media interest. **Strengths:** "He is a very personable and open barrister who is able to deal with a wide range of people very effectively. He's able to win the trust and confidence of people from a wide range of different countries."

Wayne Jordash QC (Doughty Street Chambers) Prominent silk with a "wonderful reputation," who is noteworthy for his efforts in various high-profile ICL matters including those relating to human rights, war crimes and genocide. He has recently handled cases stemming from the ICTY and the International Criminal Tribunal for Rwanda (ICTR). **Strengths:** "He is great for talking through issues and working out a strategy of how to get around problems." "He is the person everyone mentions when you bring up international crime." **Recent work:** Acted at the ICTY for Stanišić, Milošević's intelligence chief and right-hand man during the civil war in Yugoslavia.

Tim Moloney QC (Doughty Street Chambers) "A remarkable barrister" who handles complex ICL matters in tandem with his crime and extradition practices. Highly respected by market commentators for his depth of knowledge, he is particularly renowned for undertaking death penalty cases and for training individuals across the globe in international human rights. **Strengths:** "His intellect and knowledge are matched only by his compassion and humanity." **Recent work:** Advised on a framework dealing with the detention and prosecution of children captured in areas of Africa who are, or have been, members of terrorist cell Boko Haram.

Amal Clooney (see p.619) (Doughty Street Chambers) Noted by commentators for her intellectual acumen and her approachability when handling complex international criminal law cases. A human rights expert, she regularly advises and represents individuals and governments who are facing charges of crimes against humanity. **Strengths:** "She's very skilled and very thoughtful in the way she approaches a case, and has a great understanding of ICC practices." "She is a very effective and focused advocate, and somebody who is able to work very effectively with people." **Recent work:** Successfully represented Mohamed Fahmy, a journalist originally convicted of spreading false news and collaborating with the Muslim Brotherhood. Fahmy was released on the basis that the trials did not comply with basic fair trial guarantees due to irrelevant evidence.

Steven Powles (see p.742) (Doughty Street Chambers) Experienced international criminal lawyer based in The Hague, who has assisted various parties and individuals in proceedings before the ICC, the SCSL and the ICTY, and has also advised the governments of Trinidad and Tobago and the Democratic Republic of the Congo. He is particularly well versed in handling matters relating to human rights, false imprisonment and war crimes. **Recent work:** Represented Silvio Berlusconi before the ECHR in challenging his conviction for tax fraud and the decision to prohibit him from standing for public office.

Sareta Ashraph (Garden Court Chambers) Known for her work as senior legal analyst on the UN Commission of Inquiry on Syria. Her wider international criminal law practice sees her advising on contraventions occurring during civil wars and national conflicts, as well as war crimes and crimes against humanity. **Strengths:** "Very diligent and a real asset to the team." **Recent work:** Represented three former members of the Revolutionary United Front charged with 18 counts of war crimes, crimes against humanity and other violations of international law.

Richard Reynolds (Garden Court Chambers) Strong practitioner known for his association with the UN and his expertise in human rights. His practice is particularly focused on fair trial rights in international criminal proceedings and investigations into deaths during incarcerations in international conflict zones. **Strengths:** "The brightest young lawyer I have come across. Extremely bright, committed and professional, he has an encyclopaedic knowledge of international criminal law and is an incisive and logical thinker." **Recent work:** Assisted on a case which arose out of the fatal shooting of civilians by

United Nations Mission in Kosovo Police (UNMIK) during a demonstration in 2007. It was found that UNMIK had violated Articles 2 and 11 of the ECHR.

Desmond de Silva QC (Goldsmith Chambers) Pre-eminent silk who is known for his involvement in the most high-profile inquiries into international criminal law issues. A former United Nations Chief War Crimes Prosecutor, based in Sierra Leone, he is praised for his vast depth of knowledge and intellectual acumen. **Strengths:** "He is a giant in the area. He's always one of the first people to turn to when you're looking at the very biggest cases and inquiries."

Iain Edwards (1MCB) International criminal law specialist who is praised for his approach with clients and his strong advocacy. He has spent a considerable amount of time representing individuals accused of genocide and crimes against humanity before the ICTR, and continues to be instructed by Rwandans facing similar charges. He has also appeared before the Special Tribunal for Lebanon in The Hague. **Strengths:** "He is extremely fair and will never state something that he knows to be untrue. "Ethical and very meticulous in his cross-examination," "he is an excellent barrister, who is very hard-working and shows great initiative." **Recent work:** Represented a Rwandan woman who sought to stand as an opposition candidate in presidential elections. She had been charged with offences relating to terrorism, genocide ideology and discrimination.

Ben Emmerson QC (Matrix Chambers) Masterful silk who attracts praise for his exceptional advocacy skills. He has been entrusted with the most serious and complex matters to come before the international criminal courts, including the ICJ and the International Criminal Tribunal for the former Yugoslavia (ICTY). His recent work includes representing Saif al-Islam Gaddafi and Abdullah al-Senussi before the ICC, looking at the question of where their criminal trials should be located. **Strengths:** "One of the leading lights in this field." "A superb lawyer."

Michelle Butler (see p.608) (Matrix Chambers) "Fantastic" junior who identifies as a specialist in international criminal law and attracts plaudits for her dedication and her technical ability. She has appeared before the ICTY and the Special Court for Sierra Leone (SCSL), and has represented governments, military officials and police officers, among others, who have been charged with war crimes and crimes against humanity. **Strengths:** "An outstanding barrister who has been involved in an array of fascinating cases." "She is extremely determined and dedicated to the field." **Recent work:** Acted as counsel for Libya in a matter relating to former prime minister Saif al-Islam Gaddafi and former intelligence chief Abdullah al-Senussi, who are charged with crimes against humanity and war crimes. The case looked at whether or not the trial should take place in Libya.

Paul Rogers (Outer Temple Chambers) Prosecution specialist noted for his advocacy skills, technical ability and dedication to international criminal law. He boasts vast experience of prosecuting war crimes and crimes against humanity including those involving genocide, torture and cruel treatment. Rogers has multiple years' experience as Senior Appeals and Trial Counsel for the Office of the Prosecutor at the ICTY. **Strengths:** "He is a very skilled criminal advocate with excellent analytical skills. He is both thorough and careful in reaching conclusions." "Very careful and very bright, he's dead serious about what he does and always takes pride in his work." **Recent work:** Led the prosecution response to appeals by three individuals charged with committing genocide, among other related offences, before the ICTY. The defendants were ultimately convicted.

Peter Haynes QC (St Philips Chambers) Highly recommended for his expertise in cases concerning war crimes, genocide and crimes against humanity, he represents both governments and heads of state. He practises exclusively in international criminal law and human rights, and has appeared before the ICTY, the ICC and the Special Tribunal for Lebanon. **Strengths:** "Knows how to handle difficult matters well and deal with the not inconsiderable pressures these cases bring." **Recent work:** Represented a former vice-president of the Democratic Republic of the Congo charged with war crimes and crimes against humanity.

Rodney Dixon QC (Temple Garden Chambers) Experienced practitioner who is well known for his representation of individuals, international governments and political leaders. He regularly appears before all international criminal courts, including the International Criminal Court (ICC), and also handles international criminal law matters before the UK courts. He boasts particular expertise in war crimes and humanitarian issues. **Strengths:** "An exceptional international lawyer." "He is extremely impressive, knowledgeable and responsive." "He's got clients on every continent," and is "a force to be reckoned with." **Recent work:** Acted as counsel for the UK government before the ICC in a preliminary examination investigating allegations of war crimes in Iraq.

Karim Khan QC (Temple Garden Chambers) Noted for his dedication and passion for international criminal law, he has represented clients in international courts across the world. As a prosecutor for the ICTY and ICTR, he has vast experience of handling complex matters such as crimes against humanity, war crimes and contempt of court disputes. **Strengths:** "Incredibly hard-working, extremely difficult to fight, passionate about his work and exceptional on his feet." "Always a gentleman and a tough advocate, he's a superb lawyer who is doing a great job for his clients." **Recent work:** Has acted for opposition leaders in Sudan at the ICC, and has also represented the deputy president of Kenya before the ICC.

MIDLANDS

Crime	
Leading Sets	
Band 1	
No5 Chambers *	
St Philips Chambers *	
Band 2	
7BR *	
Citadel Chambers	
No.1 High Pavement	
The 36 Group *	
Band 3	
KCH Garden Square	
St Ives Chambers *	
Leading Silks	
Star Individuals	
Crigman David	*St Philips Chambers*
Band 1	
Duck Michael	*No5 Chambers* [A]
Joyce Peter	*No.1 High Pavement*
Oldham Frances	*The 36 Group*
Smith Andrew	*St Philips Chambers* [A] *
Band 2	
Atkins Richard	*St Philips Chambers* [A] *
Brand Rachel	*Citadel Chambers*
Burrows Michael	*No5 Chambers*
Fisher Andrew	*Citadel Chambers*
Hotten Christopher	*No5 Chambers* [A]
Keeling Adrian	*No5 Chambers* [A]
Malik Amjad	*The 36 Group*
Mason David	*No5 Chambers*
Smith Shaun	*No.1 High Pavement*
Tedd Rex	*No5 Chambers*
Band 3	
Auty Michael	*No.1 High Pavement*
Evans Michael	*No.1 High Pavement*
Hankin Jonas	*No5 Chambers*
Heywood Mark	*No5 Chambers* [A]
Lloyd-Jones John	*The 36 Group*
Millington Christopher	*St Philips Chambers*
Power Lewis	*7BR* *

** Indicates set / individual with profile.*
[A] direct access (see p.24).
Alphabetical order within each band. Band 1 is highest.

Crime	
Leading Juniors	
Band 1	
Jackson Andrew	*St Philips Chambers* *
Way Ian	*KCH Garden Square*
Band 2	
Bradley Phillip	*No5 Chambers*
Cooper Peter	*St Ives Chambers* *
Dean Brian	*No5 Chambers* [A]
Garcha Gurdeep	*Citadel Chambers*
Heeley Michelle	*No5 Chambers* [A]
Kubik Heidi	*St Philips Chambers* *
Langdale Adrian	*7BR*
Reynolds Adrian	*No.1 High Pavement*
Band 3	
Gilchrist Naomi	*St Philips Chambers* [A] *
Hannam Timothy	*Citadel Chambers*
Horne James	*No.1 High Pavement*
Jackson David	*St Ives Chambers* *
Jacobs Amy	*St Ives Chambers* *
Liddiard Martin	*No5 Chambers* [A]
Mills Ben	*St Philips Chambers* [A] *
Morse Malcolm	*St Philips Chambers*
Pole Tim	*No5 Chambers*
Sandhu Harpreet Singh	*No5 Chambers* [A]
Saunders Kevin	*St Ives Chambers* *
Van der Zwart Mark	*KCH Garden Square*
Weetman Gareth	*7BR*

Band 1

No5 Chambers

See profile on p.931

THE SET

One of the foremost sets in Birmingham, No5 is home to an array of leading criminal advocates, from highly esteemed silks to a broad range of established and up-and-coming juniors. Members of the set handle the full ambit of criminal cases, including homicide, conspiracy, fraud and serious sexual offences. Commentators report: "Barristers from No5 Chambers have exceptional advocacy skills, and can provide whatever level of counsel you require in order to ensure that the defendant is at ease."

Client service: "The clerking is superb." "If instructed counsel is not available, you can guarantee that replacement counsel will be of a similar standing to counsel initially instructed. The clerks endeavour to ensure that this is the case." Tony McDaid is the practice director, while Andrew Trotter is the senior practice manager for crime and regulatory matters.

SILKS

Michael Duck QC An experienced barrister with noted expertise in fraud and serious organised crime and a strong track record in high-profile criminal cases. He works as both prosecution and defence counsel and is chair of the international committee of the Criminal Bar Association. **Strengths:** "He's a very keen prosecutor and he's excellent at defence too." "He is one of the best silks in the Midlands. He is hard-working, jury-friendly and he attracts the immediate trust of the most demanding of defendants – a genuine pleasure to work with." **Recent work:** Acted for the prosecution in R v Shafagat Hussain & Others which involved the importation of heroin from Pakistan over a two-year period.

Michael Burrows QC Established practitioner who is well versed in complex criminal law matters. He has experience acting for both the prosecution and defence and is regularly instructed in serious cases involving sexual offences, drug trafficking and murder.

Christopher Hotten QC Renowned criminal silk who is regularly called upon by both prosecution and defence due to his strong depth of experience in murder and manslaughter cases. He has specialist expertise in infant and child death cases involving non-accidental head injury. **Strengths:** "He is a Rolls-Royce practitioner who leaves no stone unturned." "He has a keen eye for the law and is meticulous in conference."

Adrian Keeling QC In high demand for his expertise in large-scale fraud and drug trafficking, Keeling also prosecutes and defends in major homicide cases. Recent cases have included multiparty conspiracies and significant international aspects. **Strengths:** "He is robust in court and gets very good results." "He is charming and persuasive and takes a superb tactical approach." **Recent work:** Successfully defended an individual charged with murder, where the cause of death was a severe traumatic brain injury.

David Mason QC Heavyweight criminal silk with an enviable reputation at the Midlands Criminal Bar. He is particularly well regarded for his work in infant death, child cruelty and murder cases and receives accolades for his skill in matters involving complex medical expert testimony. **Strengths:** "He is phenomenal in terms of his ability to assimilate medical information, and phenomenal in conference and on his feet. He creates a massive amount of confidence in the client because he's so approachable, but he's also an absolute demon in cross-examination."

Rex Tedd QC Deputy head of chambers and a highly respected presence on the Midland Circuit. He has well-honed capabilities in complex regulatory, fraud and corporate manslaughter cases. **Strengths:** "He is very high-profile and has terrific presence in court." "He is an excellent trial advocate."

Mark Heywood QC Highly regarded criminal silk who maintains a broad practice that comprises work on cases involving murder, driving offences and serious sexual crimes. He is regularly called upon as both prosecution and defence counsel. **Recent work:** Prosecuted R v Rosinke & Gmaj, a murder case which involved highly complex medical evidence.

Jonas Hankin QC Hankin recently joined No5 Chambers from St Philips Chambers. He specialises in major criminal litigation and has developed a particular niche in infant and child murder cases involving complex expert evidence.

JUNIORS

Michelle Heeley Experienced junior with expert knowledge of criminal fraud, drug trafficking, rape, murder and other serious criminal offences. She both defends and prosecutes high-profile and sensitive cases. **Strengths:** "She is tenacious, conscientious and thorough, and very reassuring with clients as well." **Recent work:** Lead counsel for the prosecution of nine individuals charged with conspiracy to supply class A drugs and firearms.

Phillip Bradley A CPS Grade 4 prosecutor who also takes on a significant amount of defence work on major criminal cases, including homicide, child abuse and large-scale fraud. **Strengths:** "He is very hard-working and prepares very well. He is also good with clients as well as an excellent advocate."

Brian Dean Experienced senior junior who is instructed in a broad array of cases, from gang violence, drug smuggling and murder cases to historic abuse proceedings. He is also well known for his expertise in financial crime matters. **Strengths:** "He is busy with all manner of work and well known as a hard grafter."

Martin Liddiard Highly regarded junior whose practice spans the full ambit of criminal law, with noted expertise in drug-related offences, commercial fraud and violent and sexual offences. **Strengths:** "He is a fearsome defence advocate."

Tim Pole Has an active Crown Court practice that slants towards regulatory and specialist crime areas. Road traffic collisions, health and safety prosecutions and confiscations all fall within his remit, though he also handles serious general crime cases as well. **Strengths:** "He's extremely good with clients, very hard-working and diligent. He is dogged in his representation of clients and has excellent advocacy skills." **Recent work:** Acted in the trial of notorious criminal Robert Knight, who was extradited from Spain in 2014 and charged with importation of class A drugs and cigarettes.

Harpreet Singh Sandhu Defends and prosecutes all manner of grave and complex drug, rape and murder cases. He is singled out for praise for his excellent manner when dealing with challenging or sensitive clients. **Strengths:** "He's extremely polished and well prepared." "He knows how to deal with clients at all levels, his drafting is second to none, and he has judges eating out of the palm of his hand." **Recent work:** Junior defence counsel in R v Santhosh Rajan, a case in which a nurse was charged with gross negligence following the death of a 91 year old woman.

St Philips Chambers

See profile on p.934

THE SET

Leading criminal set comprising a large number of talented silks and juniors. Members prosecute and defend an array of sensitive, high-profile cases and have wide experience appearing at inquiries, court trials and hearings. They are regularly involved in cases concerning historic and recent sex abuse allegations, homicide, drugs conspiracies and financial crime. Sources hold the set in high regard, with one solicitor commenting: "The counsel at St Philips Chambers are all proactive, approachable and knowledgeable."

Client service: "The clerks are very easy to work with and they are adaptable. They'll try and work round things. If a problem arises they're very good at coming up with solutions." Phil Jones, the senior criminal clerk, is reported to be "really efficient and slick."

SILKS

David Crigman QC Recognised as one of the most experienced and accomplished criminal barristers practising on the Midland Circuit. He is routinely instructed as both defence and prosecution counsel in prominent cases of murder and other violent crimes. **Strengths:** "An exceptional advocate, absolutely the best I've ever seen." **Recent work:** Acted in R v Dinobewei, a murder trial in Birmingham Crown Court.

Andrew Smith QC (see p.768) Experienced silk who is known for his ability to adroitly handle such grave charges as organised crime, fraud and homicide. Regularly acts on behalf of both sides in major cases, often involving high levels of documentation of complicated expert testimony. **Strengths:** "Often known as the cleverest in Birmingham, he really is exceptionally bright." "When you have a complex legal issue, then you go to Andrew." **Recent work:** Acted for the prosecution in R v Darrell Akins and Paul Clarke, a gang-related murder carried out with a sawn-off shotgun.

Richard Atkins QC (see p.586) An experienced advocate who has made many appearances in the Court of Appeal. He has led the defence and prosecution of many complex criminal trials covering such offences as murder, manslaughter, rape, fraud and drug importation. **Strengths:** "He is incredibly dedicated and hard-working." "He is a smooth silk who knows his law and is very good with clients." **Recent work:** Prosecuted the case of R v Somani, Somani, Green, Somani & Somani, which concerned tax evasion, Proceeds of Crime Act offences and tax credit fraud.

Christopher Millington QC Vastly experienced criminal silk who is regularly engaged in complex cases involving such allegations as homicide, rape and fraud. He has shown particular flair for murders related to gang violence and gross negligence manslaughter cases.

JUNIORS

Andrew Jackson (see p.681) Qualified Grade 4 prosecutor who has a long-standing reputation for handling serious criminal cases. He also defends cases, and is skilled at handling major drugs, fraud and sex offence charges. **Strengths:** "He is a great cross-examiner." "He is extremely well respected by judges and barristers. His advocacy is very thoughtful and persuasive." **Recent work:** Successfully defended Carolyn Keeling, a school teacher alleged to have sexually abused a male pupil in the 1980s.

Heidi Kubik (see p.693) A skilled advocate who acts for both the defence and the prosecution in serious criminal cases, with specialist expertise in those involving violence, sexual assault or conspiracy. **Strengths:** "She's good with lay clients and very knowledgeable about the law." "She is always well prepared and presents very good arguments." **Recent work:** Acted for the prosecution in a complex trial relating to the murder of a toddler.

Naomi Gilchrist (see p.653) An accomplished barrister who previously practised as a solicitor, and who has since built a very strong practice as both defence and prosecution counsel. She is valued for her input into a broad range of challenging criminal and regulatory matters. **Strengths:** "She's extremely fluent and good in court. She is accessible and gives good, quick advice." "She is professional and straight-talking." **Recent work:** Instructed in R v Beckford, a case relating to a failed shooting attempt outside a nightclub by a former gang member.

Malcolm Morse Specialises in high-level criminal cases concerning such issues as sexual offences and fraud. He has many years' experience and takes on both defence and prosecution work. **Strengths:** "He is one of the cleverest members on the circuit. He is a good performer and presents well."

Ben Mills (see p.718) Most often instructed in relation to financial crime, including such offences as blackmail, money laundering and counterfeiting. Also handles consumer fraud and fire safety matters with a criminal edge. **Strengths:** "He is good at explaining complex things and is hard-working but very personable." "He is approachable, amenable and good on paperwork." **Recent work:** Acted in R v Kevin Donaghey, a set of confiscation proceedings arising out of unlawful money lending.

Band 2

7BR

See profile on p.814

THE SET

7BR has a strong presence in Leicester and Nottingham, and is known for tackling heavyweight criminal work that encompasses violent offences, financial crime and large-scale fraud in equal measure. Its members possess extensive experience in defending against serious allegations, and are also adept at prosecuting cases. Recent instructions have involved the very gravest charges of murder, drug importation, rape and child abuse.

Client service: "Safe to say that they are very impressive and professional." Paul Eeles is senior clerk at 7BR.

SILKS

Lewis Power QC (see p.742) Prominent criminal barrister known for his handling of complex international cases relating to regulation, fraud, rape and murder. Sources commend his ability to manage and reassure clients in highly sensitive proceedings. **Strengths:** "The epitome of a modern silk. He is approachable, naturally charming and engaging, with a work ethic that is second to none. His client care skills leave the most apprehensive clients firmly reassured. His cross-examination is effortless and even in the most hopeless of cases, he fights tenaciously for the client and leaves no avenue unconsidered." **Recent work:** Appeared in R v Miles Headley, a high-profile attempted murder case linked to gang violence in south London.

JUNIORS

Adrian Langdale Respected practitioner focusing on white-collar and organised crime cases. Regularly appears in complex fraud proceedings on behalf of both the prosecution and the defence. **Strengths:** "A strong performer, he knows what he's doing."

Gareth Weetman Regularly instructed in complex criminal proceedings, where he represents defendants as well as prosecuting cases. He has considerable experience in handling violent and sexual offences as well as organised fraud matters. **Strengths:** "He's excellent: really impressive. Incredibly hard-working but really down-to-earth." **Recent work:** Part of the defence team in R v Hayley, Bevan, Savill and Others, a highly complex and extensive HMRC prosecution regarding fraudulent film investment schemes.

Citadel Chambers

THE SET

A highly regarded set that exhibits impressive strength in criminal cases on the Midland Circuit. Barristers at Citadel can provide multidisciplinary support across a range of matters, from complex HMRC fraud instructions to individual sex abuse claims.

Client service: Senior clerk Rodney Neeld leads the criminal clerking team.

SILKS

Rachel Brand QC Experienced silk known for her expertise in matters that concern forensic DNA evidence, including complex sexual abuse, rape and infant death cases. She regularly represents vulnerable clients, often with a history of mental health difficulties. **Strengths:** "She's the whole package; very down-to-earth, she really connects with the juries and she has a really impressive grasp of detail."

Andrew Fisher QC Versatile criminal barrister frequently instructed by government bodies in highly complex fraud, financial and white-collar crime cases containing large sums. He also takes on serious drug, murder and organised crime matters and is notably strong with technical legal issues. **Strengths:** "He's very confident, very smooth – he's a natural in silk, he's got that presence about him."

JUNIORS

Gurdeep Garcha Junior predominantly known for his defence work and who is frequently engaged in substantial cases concerning organised crime, drugs and complex fraud. He often acts on behalf of vulnerable and young individuals, and offers further experience in matters of asylum and immigration. **Strengths:** "He's very smooth in court, he has a practice above and beyond his year of call."

Timothy Hannam Regularly instructed by HMRC and the DWP on matters concerning smuggling, fraud and white-collar investigations, Hannam also has a particular interest in money-laundering cases. Offers regulatory and licensing expertise in matters revolving around potentially unlawful trading. **Strengths:** "A good prosecutor with an eye for detail."

No.1 High Pavement

THE SET

Specialist criminal set with a great deal of experience, prosecuting and defending on a wide array of serious criminal matters. Barristers at this set handle cases ranging from violent crime and murder to drug conspiracies and substantial fraud. One source comments: "They offer a premium service, anticipating all aspects of the case and remaining very available for both clients and instructors."

Client service: Senior clerk Nigel Wragg leads the set's clerking team.

SILKS

Peter Joyce QC Hugely experienced silk with many years working on serious crime cases and with a real expertise in homicide, having worked on a vast number of murder cases in his career. He is also highly adept at dealing with serious sexual offences against both adults and children, and also handles fraud and violent offences. **Strengths:** "He knows all the tricks of the trade; he is phenomenal, with real charisma."

Shaun Smith QC Joint head of chambers who has specialised in serious crime for 34 years. He is highly respected in the Nottingham market and handles many complex and high-profile cases including murder and manslaughter, sexual offences and serious fraud. **Strengths:** "He is excellent, very charismatic: he's very persuasive with juries, but also good with vulnerable clients, he just has that manner that makes him approachable."

Michael Auty QC A well-respected criminal law barrister with an extensive practice taking in a significant volume of murder cases as well as highly complex fraud work. He also acts in cases involving sexual offences and has additional expertise in regulatory matters. **Strengths:** "Michael is extremely hard-working, a phenomenal tactician and a superb cross-examiner."

Michael Evans QC Well-known defence lawyer who also has experience prosecuting cases. He regularly acts in murder and manslaughter cases, as well as those involving serious sexual abuse and complex fraud.

JUNIORS

Adrian Reynolds Well-respected and experienced junior barrister on the Midland Circuit who regularly acts in cases of murder as well as sexual offences and serious fraud. **Strengths:** "He has a good reputation in Nottingham."

James Horne Specialist criminal law barrister who has already accrued substantial experience on cases of historic sexual abuse, murder and serious violence.

The 36 Group

THE SET

Multidisciplinary set housing a growing criminal practice which covers the full range of serious crime matters across the Midlands and beyond. Recognised for its capabilities in handling weighty cases relating to sexual abuse, organised crime, homicide and conspiracy, among others. Commentators praise the strength "across the board" at The 36 Group and report that "the quality of their advocacy and their rapport with clients is what makes them stand out."

Client service: "I've worked closely with criminal practice manager Michelle Simpson, and with first criminal clerk Lloyd Hawkins: they are both excellent, and very supportive to us."

SILKS

Frances Oldham QC Highly regarded criminal silk specialising in complex matters of an extremely sensitive nature, with particular knowledge of historic sex abuse cases. Her practice extends to family and child law and she also sits as a Deputy High Court Judge in the Family Division. **Strengths:** "An enormously talented silk."

Amjad Malik QC Seasoned advocate practising predominantly in the field of high-profile commercial crime, handling matters relating to corruption, criminal confiscation and fraud. His expertise extends to serious offences of terrorism and murder. **Strengths:** "He is an exceptional advocate."

John Lloyd-Jones QC Criminal silk handling the full spectrum of serious cases, including murder, fraud and cybercrime. Sources commend his attention to detail and forensic preparation before a trial. **Strengths:** "He's always been an extremely professional and competent advocate and has obtained incredible results for his clients over the years." "He is no-nonsense, works very hard and his preparation is second to none."

Band 3

KCH Garden Square

THE SET

A full-service crime practice offering a range of experience in a diverse range of criminal matters. Members undertake both prosecution and defence work on everything from violent and sexual crimes, drugs and firearms offences through to serious fraud matters.

Client service: Anthony Krogulec is senior criminal clerk.

JUNIORS

Ian Way Has over 20 years of experience acting for both the prosecution and defence on the full gamut of criminal offences, with significant expertise in grave cases such as homicide, sexual assault and child abuse. He is also often instructed in drugs offences.

Mark Van der Zwart Head of chambers Mark Van der Zwart defends and prosecutes on many serious criminal cases. He has particular expertise in cases involving serious brain injuries to babies and children, as well as in sexual offences and drugs conspiracies involving multiple defendants. **Strengths:** "A very good guy and a steady operator."

St Ives Chambers

See profile on p.933

THE SET

A set with a growing reputation in the area of criminal law, that fields a strong contingent of highly capable junior barristers. Members of St Ives Chambers can claim a worthy caseload of criminal work that includes serious organised crime, sexual offences and gangland violence, acting for both the prosecution and defence. The set is praised in the market for its "excellent range" and described as an "incredibly professional outfit."

Client service: Philip Hidson leads the criminal clerks, described as "friendly, approachable and always happy to assist."

JUNIORS

Peter Cooper (see p.623) A highly experienced and well-respected senior junior on the Midland Circuit who acts on behalf of both the defence and prosecution. He is experienced in complex fraud and drug conspiracy cases, along with homicide and sexual offences. He also has significant experience working with complex medical evidence and expert witnesses. **Strengths:** "He has an excellent presence in court and his attention to detail is superb. He has real gravitas and inspires confidence in the client that he is somebody who will put forward their case very well." **Recent work:** Acted for the prosecution in R v Akeel Hussain, concerning a man who stabbed his partner to death while in the midst of a paranoid episode brought on by heavy use of recreational drugs.

Amy Jacobs (see p.681) Junior barrister who is instructed across a range of criminal matters, including violent, sexual and drugs offences. She has an increasing focus on defending clients accused of sexual crimes, particularly those in respect to family members. **Strengths:** "She has a very pleasant demeanour and presence in the courtroom and displays a very thorough knowledge of each case, thereby instilling confidence in clients during a difficult time."

David Jackson (see p.681) A Grade 4 prosecutor who has acted in many serious cases of violence, homicide and armed robbery, as well as large-scale drug conspiracies. He also has considerable experience of handling sexual offence cases involving children. **Strengths:** "He displays an exceptionally good all-round knowledge, and adopts more of a softly-softly approach in court, which can work wonders with clients."

Kevin Saunders (see p.759) Well-regarded defence lawyer with a great deal of experience working on high-profile and complex criminal law cases including homicide and serious sexual abuse. He is praised by clients for his knowledge and work ethic, and also for his regulatory expertise. **Strengths:** "He is good with a jury and with clients, approachable and responsive." "Very dedicated and extremely enthusiastic when a matter is handed to him. Also brilliant on his feet." **Recent work:** Acted for one of the defendants in R v Brown and Kauser, an infant death case in which the client was charged with allowing the death of her child while her co-defendant was charged with murder.

NORTH EASTERN

Crime
Leading Sets
Band 1
New Park Court Chambers
Park Square Barristers
Band 2
Bank House Chambers
Broadway House
Trinity Chambers *
Wilberforce Chambers
Leading Silks
Star individuals
Smith Robert *New Park Court Chambers*
Band 1
Greaney Paul *New Park Court Chambers*
Wright Richard *Park Square Barristers*
Band 2
Colborne Michelle *Broadway House*
Hedworth Toby *Trinity Chambers*
MacDonald Alistair *New Park Court Chambers*
Stubbs Andrew *St Pauls Chambers (ORL)* ◊
Band 3
Elvidge John *Dere Street Barristers (ORL)* ◊ *
Khan Tahir *Broadway House*
Moulson Peter *Park Square Barristers*
Pitter Jason *New Park Court Chambers*
Waterman Adrian *KBW (ORL)* ◊
Woodcock Robert *Dere Street Barristers (ORL)* ◊
New Silks
Makepeace Peter *Dere Street Barristers (ORL)* ◊
Melly Kama *Park Square Barristers*
Leading Juniors
Band 1
Drake Sophie *Broadway House*
Knox Christopher *Trinity Chambers*
McKone Mark D *Park Square Barristers*
Band 2
Brooke David *KBW (ORL)* ◊
de la Poer Nicholas *New Park Court Chambers*
Goddard Katherine L *Bank House Chambers*
Hussain Gul Nawaz Mahboob *Bank House Chambers*
Palmer Patrick *Park Square Barristers*
Silverton Catherine *Park Square Barristers*
Smith Andrew *Bank House Chambers*
Storey Tom *Zenith Chambers (ORL)* ◊
Thackray John *Wilberforce Chambers*
Band 3
Bennett Emma *Exchange Chambers (ORL)* ◊
Birkby Adam *New Park Court Chambers*
Collins Michael *Park Square Barristers*
Dixon David S *Park Square Barristers*
Grattage Stephen *Exchange Chambers (ORL)* ◊
Kealey Simon *Zenith Chambers (ORL)* ◊
* *Indicates set / individual with profile.*
◊ *(ORL) = Other Ranked Lawyer.*
Alphabetical order within each band. Band 1 is highest.

Band 1

New Park Court Chambers

THE SET

New Park Court Chambers is noted as one of the premier sets on the circuit housing both "leading juniors and exceptional silks." Its eminent members offer broad expertise across the full spectrum of criminal proceedings, covering areas such as terrorism, high-profile homicide cases, fraud and sexual offences. Given its formidable reputation, the set routinely attracts instructions in major criminal cases, and recently undertook R v Isabel Amaro, a highly publicised matter concerning a nurse who was charged with the manslaughter of a boy who was under her care at Leicester Royal Infirmary.

Client service: "They are efficient, friendly, approachable, and always swift to deal with any issues should they arise." The clerking team is led by Wayne Stevens.

SILKS

Robert Smith QC An exceptionally experienced silk who is a recognised expert in serious crime. He has significant expertise in homicide, corporate manslaughter and health and safety cases. He is also particularly well versed in medico-legal matters and demonstrates deep knowledge of human rights issues. **Strengths:** "He is the go-to silk for serious crime. He is extremely polished, authoritative and vastly experienced."

Paul Greaney QC Extremely well regarded on the circuit, market sources consider him one of the best silks in the country. He is routinely instructed in high-profile homicide and organised crime cases, and offers broader expertise in the areas of financial crime and sports law. **Strengths:** "Absolutely a leader in his field, a top-class advocate. He is extremely bright, excellent with clients and cerebral in his approach. He is always well prepared and was outstanding in Hillsborough: you'd struggle to find a better silk in this area." **Recent work:** Represented nurse Isabel Amaro who was charged, alongside two others, with the manslaughter of a boy who was under her care at Leicester Royal Infirmary in February 2011.

Alistair MacDonald QC Well established in the market, he has a stellar reputation for his deft handling of serious crime cases. He offers vast experience in complex homicide and major fraud matters, while his prior training as a biochemist only serves to strengthen his performance in matters containing a scientific element. He acted as chair of the Bar Council throughout 2015.

Jason Pitter QC Esteemed practitioner who routinely acts for both the defence and prosecution in a broad range of cases, including homicide, organised crime and fraud. He demonstrates particular skill when tackling drug importation cases and receives plaudits for his client relationship skills. **Strengths:** "Really experienced silk, one of best jury advocates around. He is very good with tribunals as well, and deals extraordinarily well with difficult clients. You're guaranteed to get top-quality representation with Jason." **Recent work:** Acted in R v Linden Smith, a case concerning alleged manslaughter as the result of an attack on the street. The matter involved complex issues of causation.

JUNIORS

Nicholas de la Poer Highly regarded junior with a flourishing practice. An acknowledged expert in serious fraud cases, he is experienced in homicide and sexual offence matters. He also receives regular instructions from an array of regulatory bodies, including the HSE, DEFRA, the FCA and the Environment Agency. **Strengths:** "His advocacy is excellent. He's wonderfully persuasive and informative in court and his written arguments are also highly impressive." "He immediately puts clients at ease, he's always fully prepared and can tackle the most complex cases." **Recent work:** Acted for the defence in Operation Tavernier, a significant multi-handed people-trafficking case. The defendant was a lawyer who organised immigration for a number of families from Pakistan and was alleged to have then exploited them upon their arrival in the UK.

Adam Birkby Routinely handles a wide range of serious crime cases, covering areas such as public disorder, sexual offences and homicide. He is particularly noted for his sensitive approach when dealing with young clients and defendants with mental health issues. **Strengths:** "Handles clients very well; he has a deft touch with both difficult and vulnerable individuals and an exceptional ability to put them at ease."

Park Square Barristers

THE SET

As one of the largest sets on the North Eastern Circuit, Park Square Barristers has vast capacity to undertake a full range of serious crime cases. The set houses a stable of highly respected barristers that market sources consider to be exceptionally capable, from juniors through to silks. Members of chambers are regularly instructed in all manner of complex and challenging criminal matters, including homicides, serious sexual offences and fraud. Well respected by peers and clients alike, Park Square continues to enjoy its reputation as a "fantastic set with a formidable team of barristers who are incredibly professional and highly conscientious."

Client service: "The excellent clerking certainly plays a part in winning them repeat instructions." The clerking team is led by Richard Sadler.

SILKS

Richard Wright QC Head of chambers, he is highly respected by peers and brings a great deal of experience to bear on his varied practice. He routinely acts for both the prosecution and the defence in serious crime cases and offers significant expertise in homicide and fraud matters. **Strengths:** "He is exceptional at what he does; he's incredibly approachable, brilliant in court and fantastic with clients." **Recent work:** Acted for the prosecution in Operation Reno, a historic child sex offence case involving 19 claimants who had attended a Catholic school and home for boys in East Yorkshire.

Peter Moulson QC Esteemed silk with a highly active practice, he is regularly called upon to handle high-profile murder cases involving complex medical issues, abnormal mental functioning or loss of self-control. He frequently tackles significant drug supply, money laundering and firearms cases. **Strengths:** "He's very conscientious and has a very nice manner, he gets on extremely well with clients and solicitors."

Kama Melly QC Respected criminal defence and prosecution barrister, she is recognised as an expert in sexual offence cases. She wins particular praise for her stellar advocacy and sensitive approach to matters involving vulnerable witnesses. **Strengths:** "She's very experienced in sex case work and highly approachable." **Recent work:** Acted in a case involving a teacher who was accused of the sexual abuse of four boys under the age of 12. The defendant was found not guilty of all charges.

JUNIORS

Mark McKone Highly regarded advocate who routinely appears for both the defence and prosecution. He handles a diverse range of significant matters, specialising particularly in serious sexual assaults and rape. **Strengths:** "He's a very gifted, excellent advocate." "He instils confidence in clients with his polished presentation in court." **Recent work:** Appeared for the prosecution in an attempted assisted suicide case. The defendant had purchased petrol and a lighter in order to aid a friend's planned self-immolation.

Patrick Palmer Well known for his broad-based practice, he offers notable expertise in areas such as serious sex offences, homicide and motor crimes. **Strengths:** "He's got a really nice, understated approach and is very good at identifying key issues." "When you're against Patrick, you know the case will be handled properly."

Catherine Silverton Dedicated criminal barrister who predominantly acts as defence. She is regularly instructed in serious crime cases such as murder, manslaughter, organised crime and serious sex offences. Silverton is particularly praised for her ability to skilfully cross-examine children and medical experts while advancing complex legal arguments. **Strengths:** "Very able practitioner and advocate." **Recent work:** Acted for a vulnerable woman suffering from paranoid schizophrenia who was accused of attempting to murder her boyfriend.

Michael Collins Respected junior whose deep expertise encompasses a diverse array of criminal matters. He is particularly noted for his expert handling of drug trafficking, motor crime and sexual abuse cases. **Strengths:** "He is absolutely reliable and trustworthy." "He is a very hard-working barrister who really commits to his cases."

David Dixon Experienced advocate who is highly respected for his prosecution work, especially in cases involving violent or sexual offences. **Strengths:** "He stays in contact, provides advice without being chased, is good with clients and is great at dealing with vulnerable witnesses."

Band 2

Bank House Chambers

THE SET

Bank House Chambers is a well-respected set for which criminal law remains a key focus. Its highly skilled members are capable of prosecuting and defending the most significant cases on the North Eastern Circuit, including murder, fatal driving offences, terrorism, rape and robbery. Housing a bench of "exceptionally good" practitioners, the set continues to attract instructions in highly significant cases on the circuit.

Client service: Led by senior clerk Wayne Digby, the clerking team are described by sources as "excellent and always willing to assist and help where possible. They're approachable and friendly."

JUNIORS

Katherine Goddard Specialises in serious sexual offence cases, often involving complex medical and forensic evidence. She is a grade four prosecutor and is routinely instructed by the CPS to prosecute in the Crown Court and Court of Appeal. **Strengths:** "She's got a really calm and reassuring manner." "She is very client-focused and strategically very strong." **Recent work:** Defended a 37-year-old woman accused of child cruelty, which allegedly led to the death of her four year old daughter. This matter involved mental health complexities.

Gul Nawaz Mahboob Hussain Maintains a busy practice acting for the defence in complex and serious crime cases. He has represented defendants in significant high-profile cases relating to terrorism, murder and armed robbery. **Strengths:** "A very talented individual." **Recent work:** Represented Manfu Asiedu, an offender who was convicted and incarcerated for his part in the 21/7 attempted suicide bombings. Asiedu was accused of attacking Jeremy Green, an ex-soldier, in prison.

Andrew Smith Smith is head of the criminal team at Bank House Chambers and is sought after for his vast experience of both prosecuting and defending in the Crown Court. He is particularly well known for his adept handling of matters involving historic sexual abuse and the abuse of children. **Strengths:** "He doesn't just toe the party line, he really fights the case."

Broadway House

THE SET

A burgeoning set housing an excellent stable of "growing young talent," Broadway House's skilled team of practitioners regularly appears before the Crown Court and the Court of Appeal. Offering its expert services to both legally aided and privately paying clients, the chambers is frequently called upon to handle the most serious criminal cases. Its members are particularly well versed in matters concerning historical and current sexual offences that often attract significant media attention.

Client service: The "reliably helpful" clerking team is led by Hayley Sanderson.

SILKS

Michelle Colborne QC Renowned for her wide-reaching work in criminal advocacy, Michelle specialises in cases concerning homicide, infant death and serious sexual offence. She is particularly noted for her deft handling of cases involving mental health complexities. **Strengths:** "She is a superb advocate, she does a lot of specialist murder and sexual offence work." **Recent work:** Served as lead counsel in a case named Operation Harehill, a 25-handed sexual grooming and exploitation case involving a vulnerable female complainant.

Tahir Khan QC Highly regarded silk who is esteemed for his criminal advocacy skills. He is frequently instructed by the CPS and HMRC and specialises in complex drug prosecutions, terrorism cases and matters involving serious violence.

JUNIORS

Sophie Drake Her dedicated practice focuses exclusively on criminal matters. She capably handles a wide range of complex cases, acting for both the prosecution and defence. She is an extremely experienced advocate who offers particular expertise in matters involving serious sexual offence. **Strengths:** "She is a wonderful advocate, a safe pair of hands and very well regarded."

Trinity Chambers

See profile on p.975

THE SET

Described by market sources as "a powerhouse in the North East," Trinity Chambers is particularly well known for its prominence in the Newcastle area. Its eminent barristers are capable of prosecuting and defending the most serious criminal offences, including terrorism, gangland murder, internet crime and motoring offences. While notably strong on the North Eastern Circuit, the set's distinguished team also routinely appears before the Court of Appeal and the Privy Council.

Client service: Criminal clerks Peter Finkill-Coombs and Liam Gorman run the clerks' room.

SILKS

Toby Hedworth QC A highly respected silk who has worked on an impressive variety of cases in the criminal and regulatory sphere. He is particularly recognised for his adept handling of complex judicial review proceedings. **Strengths:** "He's experienced and a good fighter in court." "He's a highly capable jury advocate."

JUNIORS

Christopher Knox Impressive junior with an extremely diverse practice, he has significant experience in homicide cases and matters concerning financial crime. While he regularly acts for defence counsel, he has also acted for the CPS and HMRC. **Strengths:** "He's a seasoned performer who leaves the court impressed."

Wilberforce Chambers

THE SET

Wilberforce Chambers remains a go-to set on the North Eastern Circuit, with market commentators highlighting its formidable presence in Hull and surrounds. Its eminent members have vast experience of handling significant, heavyweight criminal cases, and offer leading expertise in criminally related regulatory and health and safety matters. Housing a strong stable of advocates, they continue to hone their expertise in serious criminal matters, including sexual offences and human trafficking.

Client service: The highly organised and impressive Helen Goby leads the criminal clerking team.

JUNIORS

John Thackray Prosecutes and defends with equal regularity in a range of significant criminal cases. He is well respected for his stellar advocacy skills and specialism in cases concerning serious sexual assault and rape. He is also a regular fixture in the Court of Appeal. **Strengths:** "Well regarded by the judiciary and capable of getting on top of big cases with ease."

Other Ranked Lawyers

John Elvidge QC (see p.641) (Dere Street Barristers) Renowned for his expertise in cases involving homicide, serious and organised crime, commercial drugs supply and serious sexual offences. He has been instructed to prosecute and defend cases brought by the Crown Prosecution Service Complex Crime Unit. **Recent work:** Served as lead counsel in the prosecution of Martin Ruddy, an individual who was convicted of murdering his mother and father in their home. He claimed to have been the victim of a burglary in which he was stabbed and his parents murdered.

Robert Woodcock QC (Dere Street Barristers) Represents clients in cases across the spectrum of criminal law, making regular appearances both on the North Eastern Circuit and before the Old Bailey. He is widely respected for his sharp cross-examinations, eloquent courtroom performance and notable expertise in homicide cases. **Strengths:** "He's an impressive advocate with great client care skills." "He's very organised." **Recent work:** Successfully represented the defendant in a charge of conspiracy to traffic a vulnerable child into prostitution.

Peter Makepeace QC (Dere Street Barristers) Extensive experience both prosecuting and defending in a range of serious crime cases. He is a Grade 4 prosecutor and is particularly adept at dealing with cases concerning homicide or serious violence, as well as large-scale drug conspiracies. **Strengths:** "He is a wonderful silk who is rated highly by the market." **Recent work:** Acted in a high-profile case concerning 22 defendants who were accused of conspiracy to supply and distribute vast quantities of class A drugs nationwide. The matter hinged on decoded PGO encrypted messages.

Emma Bennett (Exchange Chambers) Has a formidable defence practice focusing on criminal and regulatory advocacy. She is sought after for her expertise in serious sexual offence cases, particularly those involving aspects of sexual grooming. **Strengths:** "Her relationship with clients is very good. She is a robust advocate, but in a reassuringly calm way." "She's great on her feet and can stand her ground." **Recent work:** Acted for one of 12 defendants charged with inciting a child to engage in sexual activity. The case involved the cross-examination of a young complainant regarding sensitive family and sexual issues.

Stephen Grattage (Exchange Chambers) Has a long-standing reputation in the market for his expertise in crime and fraud work. He is a Grade 4 prosecutor and has particular experience in computer-related crime. **Strengths:** "He does a lot of cross-country work and gets down to the real issues of a complex case quickly."

Adrian Waterman QC (KBW) Esteemed silk who practises almost exclusively in criminal law, specialising in sexual offences and homicides. **Strengths:** "He has a brilliant grasp of the evidence." "A highly impressive advocate in court." **Recent work:** Defended Mr Shaukat in a conspiracy to murder case. Waterman argued that there was insufficient evidence for the case to be put to a jury, to the effect that Mr Shaukat was found not guilty by order of the judge.

David Brooke (KBW) Long-standing practitioner in criminal law with impressive experience of handling cases relating to homicide, serious organised crime and sexual crime. He is especially well known for his ability to deal with complex multi-handed trials. **Strengths:** "He is a brilliant prosecutor." "He is a very safe pair of hands for sexual cases especially." **Recent work:** Prosecuted the adoptive parents of a ten year old child with foetal alcohol syndrome in a child cruelty case. The case was extremely complex given the background of sexual abuse and lack of capacity of the victim.

Andrew Stubbs QC (St Pauls Chambers) Experienced silk who regularly appears for both the prosecution and defence in significant criminal cases. He has particular expertise in fraud matters and has appeared in several highly sensitive murder cases.

Tom Storey (Zenith Chambers) Prominent criminal advocate who is frequently instructed on behalf of both the defence and prosecution. He specialises in large-scale, serious criminal matters and is well respected for his deft handling of highly sensitive cases. He has dealt with a wide range of criminal offences and offers a wealth of knowledge and experience in the sphere. **Strengths:** "He's absolutely unflappable." "He is terribly impressive in court, he's excellent." **Recent work:** Prosecuted an uninsured driver for causing death by dangerous driving and serious injury by dangerous driving. The defendant admitted to having taken cocaine on the day he collided with two schoolgirls who were crossing the road, killing one and seriously injuring the other. The defendant was sentenced to seven and a half years imprisonment.

Simon Kealey (Zenith Chambers) Specialist criminal law barrister who acts for both the defence and prosecution in a range of serious, multi-defendant cases. He is especially familiar with cases involving drugs conspiracy and people trafficking. **Strengths:** "He's very organised, very thorough and an incredibly hard worker." "He is absolutely brilliant when it comes to people trafficking cases." **Recent work:** Acted for the prosecution in a three-month, multi-defendant trial concerning people trafficking. The trial involved complex factual issues, non-English speaking complainants and a very large volume of evidence.

NORTHERN

Crime	
Leading Sets	
Band 1	
Exchange Chambers *	
7 Harrington St Chambers *	
Lincoln House Chambers	
Band 2	
Deans Court Chambers *	
23 Essex Street *	
Kenworthy's Chambers *	
St Johns Buildings *	
Leading Silks	
Band 1	
Wright Peter	*Lincoln House Chambers*
Band 2	
Denney Stuart	*Deans Court Chambers* Ⓐ
Johnson Nicholas	*7 Harrington St Chambers* *
Myers Benjamin	*Exchange Chambers*
O'Byrne Andrew	*St Johns Buildings*
Unsworth Ian	*7 Harrington St Chambers* *
Band 3	
Blackwell Kate	*Lincoln House Chambers*
George Mark	*Garden Court North (ORL)* ◊
Jones John Richard	*Exchange Chambers* *
Power Nigel	*7 Harrington St Chambers* *
Pratt Richard	*7 Harrington St Chambers* *
Roberts Lisa	*Lincoln House Chambers*
Weatherby Pete	*Garden Court North (ORL)* ◊
Leading Juniors	
Band 1	
Grennan Barry	*Kenworthy's Chambers* Ⓐ
Nolan Damian	*Exchange Chambers*
Simons Richard	*Lincoln House Chambers*
Band 2	
Ainsworth Mark	*Exchange Chambers*
Harrison Keith	*St Johns Buildings*
Lavery Michael	*Exchange Chambers*
McKee Hugh	*23 Essex Street*
Nuttall Andrew	*Lincoln House Chambers*
Parry Philip	*Exchange Chambers*
Band 3	
Andrews Philip	*St Johns Buildings*
Berkson Simon	*Exchange Chambers*
Cassidy Patrick	*Kenworthy's Chambers* Ⓐ
Duffy Jonathan	*7 Harrington St Chambers*
Emsley-Smith Rosalind	*Deans Court Chambers*
Farrow Adrian	*Exchange Chambers*
Greenhalgh Jane	*23 Essex Street* *
Harris Ian	*Exchange Chambers*
Hart Joseph	*Deans Court Chambers* *
Hayton Virginia	*Deans Court Chambers*
Judge Lisa	*Deans Court Chambers* Ⓐ
McMeekin Ian	*Lincoln House Chambers*
Metcalfe Ian	*Cobden House Chambers (ORL)* ◊
Riding Henry	*7 Harrington St Chambers*
Sastry Bob	*23 Essex Street*
Thompson Patrick	*23 Essex Street*
Toal David	*Exchange Chambers* *
Whitehurst Ian	*7 Harrington St Chambers* *

** Indicates individual with profile.*
Ⓐ direct access (see p.24).
◊ (ORL) = Other Ranked Lawyer.
Alphabetical order within each band. Band 1 is highest.

Band 1

Exchange Chambers
See profile on p.956

THE SET
A widely respected chambers boasting an impressively deep bench of experienced criminal practitioners. Members at Exchange Chambers demonstrate considerable ability across an array of serious criminal matters, including drug trafficking, sexual abuse and homicide, and the set also displays admirable strength in complex fraud and regulatory work. Equally adept at defending and prosecuting major crimes, sources praise the set as the "pinnacle" of representation on the Northern Circuit.

Client service: The clerks are commended for their "can-do" attitude and are highlighted as being "highly professional and very proactive." They are led by chambers director Tom Handley.

SILKS
Benjamin Myers QC A highly experienced criminal barrister with an emphasis on serious criminal matters such as homicide, drug trafficking, and organised crime. He is also very capable of taking on major cases concerning sexual and violent offences, including rape and armed robbery. **Strengths:** "An excellent lawyer with great courtroom skills." "He is a proper charismatic performer and comes across as genuine and thoughtful." **Recent work:** Defended a senior teacher at the Royal Northern College of Music against historic rape allegations made by a former pupil.

John Richard Jones QC (see p.685) Specialises in serious crime and fraud work, with particular expertise in money laundering, drugs and sexual offences. Regularly involved in cases arising out of domestic terrorism. **Recent work:** Successfully defended an individual employed at Heathrow airport against charges concerning the importation of contraband cigarettes and class A drugs.

JUNIORS
Michael Lavery An impressive junior known for his defence work, though he is also a CPS Grade 4 prosecutor. He regularly acts in serious murder and drugs cases, and also specialises in white-collar crime and health and safety proceedings. **Strengths:** "A very smooth speaker and operator, he is very client-friendly and very engaging." "A no-nonsense and very able barrister." "Charming, hard-working and diligent." **Recent work:** Successfully defended an individual charged with the importation of £60 million worth of cocaine through Liverpool. Acquittal secured pre-trial.

Mark Ainsworth Balances a thriving practice in general crime with an expertise in health and safety proceedings. He has experience prosecuting and defending serious cases including homicide, kidnapping and sexual offences. Also has a particular niche in electoral fraud. **Strengths:** "He's an extremely experienced, intelligent, organised individual who is authoritative in court." "He is very calm and measured, and gives difficult advice in a palatable manner." **Recent work:** Prosecuted an ice cream manufacturer for health and safety breaches after an employee lost her finger while cleaning a piece of machinery.

Philip Parry Junior who is well versed in both prosecuting and defending extremely serious crimes, including murder, sexual offences and human trafficking. He also offers significant knowledge of white-collar crime and fraud. **Strengths:** "Exceptionally good at connecting with clients from all different backgrounds, and intellectually he can get to grip with the most complex of cases." "He is fantastic, extremely communicative and very easy to engage with." **Recent work:** Defended Victorino Chua, a nurse responsible for poisoning 24 patients and murdering three by tampering with saline bags and ampoules.

David Toal (see p.781) Experienced criminal practitioner who regularly undertakes complex and substantial cases, including human trafficking, rape and other violent offences. He both prosecutes and defends cases, and has a particular emphasis on representing professionals facing criminal and regulatory proceedings. **Strengths:** "He is hard-working, intelligent, measured and an extremely safe pair of hands." **Recent work:** Successfully prosecuted a man charged with numerous sexual and violent offences, including firearms charges, over a sustained period of time and against four different women.

Ian Harris Particularly active on large-scale fraud matters, often tackling cases with a significant amount of highly technical and complex evidence to be considered. Also handles a range of serious crime work including drugs and violent offences. **Recent work:** Defended an individual who took part in an attack on a rival drug dealer. Successfully achieved a conviction of lesser wounding, while both co-defendants were convicted of attempted murder.

Simon Berkson Senior junior who is regularly engaged in defending complex fraud cases. He is also involved in a broad range of general crime matters concerning serious sexual and violent crimes, human trafficking and drugs conspiracies. **Strengths:** "One of the very best juniors on the circuit for me. He's a top lawyer." **Recent work:** Prosecuted a case concerning a Romanian national who was trafficked from Italy to the UK in order to work as a prostitute.

Adrian Farrow Highly experienced barrister who both prosecutes and defends criminal cases of the highest complexity. He balances his general criminal practice with health and safety and regulatory expertise, and is particularly well known for his local authority prosecution work. Also takes on serious cases of kidnap, robbery, drugs and firearms offences. **Strengths:** "He has brilliant judgement and is very measured." "He is hard-working, has a good eye for detail and a careful, meticulous approach." **Recent work:** Successfully defended an individual accused of being involved with the preparation and distribution of a large quantity of 'legal highs.'

Damian Nolan A "first-rate practitioner" and criminal specialist, he is highly experienced in handling criminal matters as well as regulatory offences. He has predominantly defended cases involving drugs, homicide and armed robbery, although he also takes on the prosecution of serious sexual offences. **Strengths:** "He is supportive of clients and appreciative of their difficulties, and he has a robust and open attitude both in chambers and in court. He is a courageous advocate." "He is a real fighter, but is also very easy to work with and is liberal with his advice." **Recent work:** Successfully defended an individual charged with the attempted murder of two individuals affiliated with a known crime family.

7 Harrington St Chambers

See profile on p.958

THE SET

A well-established set with a strong reputation on the Northern Circuit, 7 Harrington St Chambers fields a robust team of highly skilled criminal barristers. Members are equally adept at handling defence and prosecution proceedings that concern a broad range of serious crime and fraud matters. The set is regularly instructed in cases linked to organised crime, drug trafficking and homicide, and offers particular expertise in violent offences committed against members of the police force.

Client service: John Kilgallon is the practice director for the set.

SILKS

Nicholas Johnson QC (see p.684) Has considerable experience as both prosecutor and defender on a broad range of serious criminal cases. He is particularly known for his ability to handle challenging homicide cases, including murder, gross negligence manslaughter and gangland executions. **Strengths:** "He is absolutely meticulous, he's very impressive." "He is particularly good, destined for great things." **Recent work:** Acted for the prosecution in R v Donovan, Taylor and Spendlove, relating to the murder of Merseyside PC Neil Doyle and the serious assault of two other police officers.

Ian Unsworth QC (see p.786) Demonstrates considerable expertise across a range of serious crime matters, in which he acts as both prosecution and defence counsel. He regularly acts on high-profile murder cases as well as complex drug offences. **Strengths:** "He's extremely good and very fair." "He is solid and a safe pair of hands." **Recent work:** Acted for the prosecution in the high-profile case against Clayton Williams, who was convicted for killing PC Dave Phillips and attempting to harm another officer by running them over with a stolen truck.

Nigel Power QC (see p.742) Knowledgeable across the full spectrum of criminal law, Nigel Power QC exhibits notable strength in homicide cases, as well as large-scale fraud and criminal confiscations. **Recent work:** Successfully represented the defendant in R v Erskine against charges of murder, manslaughter and death by dangerous driving.

Richard Pratt QC (see p.742) Head of chambers and skilled as both prosecution and defence counsel for a range of criminal matters. He is particularly experienced in crimes of violence, including assault, manslaughter and murder. **Strengths:** "He is a very charismatic silk." **Recent work:** Successfully prosecuted the aunt and grandmother of a seven year old girl on charges of child cruelty and murder.

JUNIORS

Henry Riding Regularly instructed as both defence and prosecution counsel on an array of criminal matters, including major homicide cases.

Ian Whitehurst (see p.794) Experienced criminal advocate whose expertise in organised crime includes gang-related homicide, drug offences, corruption and armed robbery. He also takes on cases concerning sexual and violent crimes, and is equally adept at handling both prosecution and defence work. **Recent work:** Appealed in the High Court against a young man's conviction for assault.

Jonathan Duffy An experienced defence practitioner with a good number of Court of Appeal appearances under his belt. He is on the list of approved Counsel authorised to represent defendants and victims before The International Criminal Court at The Hague. **Recent work:** Appeared in the Court of Appeal, successfully appealing against a sentence imposed in respect of offences of rape and other sexual offences against a child.

Lincoln House Chambers

THE SET

Lincoln House Chambers houses a number of formidable criminal advocates known for both prosecuting and defending the most serious of criminal cases. Its members continue to appear in high-profile sexual abuse, firearms, organised crime and murder trials, and also take on significant white-collar crime and fraud matters. Sources attest to the wide spread of experience and specialism in chambers, with one describing it as "a dominant set that has always done top-end work."

Client service: "The clerking, led by director David Wright, is always good. They're attentive, they make sure everything is sorted out and come back with solutions. There's also a greater degree of flexibility on fees than from a London set."

SILKS

Peter Wright QC High-powered criminal silk whose profile on the Northern Circuit is "second to none." He has appeared in some of the most noteworthy trials of recent years and continues to defend and prosecute headline-grabbing murder, fraud and terrorism cases. **Strengths:** "It's always good news for me when I don't have to appear against Peter," says one peer. "His courtroom skills are par excellence." "Absolutely top drawer."

Lisa Roberts QC A skilled criminal advocate who prosecutes and defends a broad range of cases that includes significant health and safety and professional discipline work. She is also noted for her particularly tactful handling of challenging clients and difficult cases concerning sexual offences. **Strengths:** "A very capable, outstanding young silk." "She's just fabulous and clients adore her." "A really fantastic criminal barrister and advocate."

Kate Blackwell QC Regularly appears in complex white-collar and serious fraud cases, with noted experience in corruption and money laundering. She is also well known for her work on high-profile sexual offences, acting for both the prosecution and defence. **Strengths:** "She does high-profile work. She's very hard-working and committed to her clients."

JUNIORS

Richard Simons Leading junior who concentrates on defending clients facing allegations of serious criminal conduct. He has experience handling murder and firearms cases, including those relating to organised crime. He also handles significant fraud and confiscation matters. **Strengths:** "Great barrister, great with clients, hard-working and very experienced." "Clients just love him, brilliant in court and very good on tactical decisions."

Andrew Nuttall Senior junior who has recently been involved as counsel to members of the South Yorkshire Police in the Hillsborough inquiry. He has significant experience in multi-handed cases, and has prosecuted and defended numerous murder trials as well as complex fraud investigations. **Strengths:** "Extremely experienced across the board." "A really safe pair of hands."

Ian McMeekin Vastly experienced criminal practitioner with a reputation for strong defence advocacy and broad expertise of serious crime cases. He has handled murder, drug trafficking and sexual offences, as well as large-scale fraud and terrorism. **Strengths:** "A first-class performer, both in preparatory terms and as an advocate. Totally approachable, friendly and supportive, but with an incredible eye for detail and exceptionally hard-working. His written work is of the highest order."

Band 2

Deans Court Chambers

See profile on p.964

THE SET

An "excellent" set lauded for the quality of its "bright, hard-working, excellent barristers," Deans Court Chambers boasts a number of impressive individuals and a strong reputation for handling work at all levels of the court system. Members practise in all areas of serious crime, including major homicide and sexual offence cases, and are regularly involved in matters which attract significant media attention. They are also often the first port of call for cases that involve technically challenging medical and forensic evidence.

Client service: Capably led by senior criminal and regulatory clerk Peter Kelly, the clerking team at the set is described by one source as "brilliant, some of the best I've seen. They are very, very accommodating and easy to get hold of."

SILKS

Stuart Denney QC Highly respected silk described by sources as a "class act" and a "technically brilliant" advocate. Much of his practice is devoted to the defence of serious crime matters, including homicides, rapes and large-scale drug offences. He is also known for his expertise in handling health and safety cases with criminal elements. **Strengths:** "He's a first-rate all-round advocate. He has a very down-to-earth delivery, from the point of view of the jury. He is also highly intelligent and a first-rate lawyer." "He's amazing, very, very knowledgeable. He works very hard, and his expertise in court is just the best I've seen." **Recent work:** Defended an individual against allegations of attempted murder and rape arising out of a relationship begun on social media.

JUNIORS

Virginia Hayton A respected advocate with an impressive serious crime practice. She is particularly well versed in defending those charged with serious historic and current sexual offences, including rape, prostitution and child abuse. **Strengths:** "An excellent barrister who is bright, thoughtful and a safe pair of hands." "An effective advocate who has handled some really big cases." **Recent work:** Represented the first defendant in a case relating to historic sexual abuse claims which allegedly involved Jimmy Savile as a participant.

Rosalind Emsley-Smith A junior who comes highly recommended for her work ethic and her client care skills. She regularly handles serious crime and fraud matters, acting as both prosecution and defence counsel on cases concerning violent and sexual offences. She also has a thriving regulatory practice. **Strengths:** "A good lawyer who is hard-working and bright." "A very good advocate who can read the situation well in terms of the judge and who is very versatile and effective."

Joseph Hart (see p.666) Experienced counsel who regularly defends substantial cases of money laundering and fraud. His practice also encompasses the most serious violent crimes, including firearms offences and homicides, as well as human trafficking and sexual offences. **Strengths:** "He works hard to get the best for the client and is very thorough." "He's dealing with some increasingly complex work and he's naturally given to the job." **Recent work:** Represented an individual accused of murdering his partner's child, in which the Crown ultimately accepted a plea of manslaughter.

Lisa Judge Capable practitioner with a strong reputation in the health and safety space alongside her thriving criminal and regulatory practice. She is particularly known for her experience of handling cases involving sexual offences. **Strengths:** "She really fights hard for her clients." "She's highly persuasive and a good person to have on your side."

23 Essex Street

See profile on p.839

THE SET

23 Essex Street offers a strong team of criminal advocates specialising in both prosecution and defence, many of whom are senior juniors with many years' experience. The set offers a full range of services for serious crime, including noted expertise in murder, firearms and large narcotics cases. It wins praise from instructing solicitors for its ability to provide "quick and accurate advice" and "assured and confident accuracy."

Client service: "The clerks are accessible, available and sensible on fees. They are also flexible and always try to accommodate the client." Sean Hulston heads the clerking team and is described by one client as "without a shadow of a doubt the best clerk in Manchester."

JUNIORS

Patrick Thompson A seasoned criminal junior advocate who often acts unled for both the prosecution and defence in serious and high-profile criminal trials. Regularly handles murder, rape and drugs cases, with additional experience of fraud and regulatory offences. **Strengths:** "He is a very charismatic barrister." "A good jury advocate." **Recent work:** Defended the lead organiser of a conspiracy to supply the North East with £6 million worth of heroin.

Jane Greenhalgh (see p.660) Receives instructions from both defendant solicitors and the CPS for criminal litigation. She brings a wealth of experience in serious crime, and is also particularly strong with white-collar crime and fraud cases. **Strengths:** "Charming, down-to-earth and good with clients." "Impassioned where her clients are concerned, she is a natural defender." **Recent work:** Represented the defendant in R v Asif Yousaf, a case involving a gang-related murder in Sheffield.

Bob Sastry Focuses his practice on heavyweight crime, often involving serious violent and sexual offences. He also takes on cases involving complex conspiracies, drugs and money laundering. **Strengths:** "He's done some of the most serious cases I've had, he's a very good tactician." "Enthusiastic and conscientious." **Recent work:** Prosecuted a multi-handed conspiracy case concerning a number of armed robberies and burglaries.

Hugh McKee A popular choice for serious fraud cases, with extensive experience of carousel and commercial fraud. He has also handled serious criminal cases on behalf of both the defence and prosecution, including recent firearms, drug supply, and sexual abuse cases. **Strengths:** "I would trust him with absolutely any case of mine, exceptionally good with sensitive matters and witnesses. A fantastic advocate." "Technically brilliant, very good on paper. He's got a very good courtroom manner that commands respect." **Recent work:** Secured an acquittal for a client accused of the attempted murder of two men involved in drug importation.

Kenworthy's Chambers

See profile on p.967

THE SET

An "innovative, flexible and approachable" set with a long-standing reputation for excellence in criminal law. The team is praised by instructing solicitors, who see them as "keen to assist and deliver services in a modern and efficient manner." Barristers at Kenworthy's Chambers continue to receive instructions for both the prosecution and defence of serious criminal proceedings that range from white-collar crime and fraud through to major violent crimes, homicides and drugs offences.

Client service: Praised for their communication and their efficiency, the criminal clerking team is led by senior clerk Paul Mander.

JUNIORS

Barry Grennan Head of chambers and a highly respected criminal advocate who attracts plaudits for his work ethic and jury advocacy skills. He is vastly knowledgeable on all areas of serious crime, including gang-related murders, sexual offences, people trafficking and infanticide. He also boasts a thriving fraud and regulatory practice. **Strengths:** "Extremely busy, popular with clients, and passionate in front of a jury." "A hard-working, personable guy who's good in court." **Recent work:** Successfully achieved an acquittal for a client facing murder and manslaughter charges following the death of another man during a fight.

Patrick Cassidy A highly capable advocate with a broad practice encompassing the full spectrum of serious general and financial crime. He has experience of the most complex and challenging cases including sexual offences, child abuse and gangland crime. **Strengths:** "Shrewd and fearless, he is a dyed in the wool defender."

St Johns Buildings

See profile on p.970

THE SET

Boasts a sizeable bench of impressive specialist criminal practitioners who have a "vast amount of collective experience." They regularly undertake complex criminal matters, appearing before the judiciary in local Magistrates Court through to the Court of Appeal. Acting as both prosecutors and defence counsel, they are able to assist with the full spectrum of serious criminal cases, including murders, serious sex crimes, gangland violence and firearms offences.

Client service: Sources praise the clerking team, led by senior criminal and regulatory clerk Mark Heald, saying: "They strive to give me the barrister of my choosing and are consistently prepared to go the extra mile to ensure that my clients are well looked after."

SILKS

Andrew O'Byrne QC Head of the crime group and a leading silk who possesses an in-depth knowledge of all areas of criminal law. He continues to act in all areas of serious and complex crime, and has extensive experience of handling homicides, large-scale drug importations and historic sex allegations. **Strengths:** "He has consistently provided an excellent service and has a very good bedside manner." "He has a very good grasp of the details and is able to win over very difficult clients. His presence in court is exactly what you would expect from a top silk." **Recent work:** Represented an individual accused of murdering a woman whom he met on a dating website.

JUNIORS

Philip Andrews Highly experienced practitioner handling all manner of serious criminal cases. Exclusively acting for defendants, he is regularly instructed in cases concerning murder, violence, kidnap and sexual offences. **Strengths:** "Solid as a rock." **Recent work:** Represented the main defendant in a case where a group of businessmen were charged with kidnapping and assaulting men accused of criminal offences. The client was acquitted of all but one count.

Keith Harrison Receives very strong praise for his advocacy and experience as a criminal practitioner. While mainly acting for defendants, he is also a CPS Grade 4 prosecutor. His work regularly takes in cases regarding serious criminal acts, including homicide, sexual offences and large-scale drug conspiracies. **Strengths:** "Shrewd, fearless and extremely experienced." "Amazing, he's a brilliant lawyer and a brilliant advocate." **Recent work:** Represented the principal defendant in a case concerning charges of conspiracy to supply class A and B drugs as well as firearms offences.

Other Ranked Lawyers

Ian Metcalfe (Cobden House Chambers) Heading up the set's criminal team, he is highly experienced at both prosecuting and defending cases. He regularly undertakes the most serious of criminal matters, including murder, manslaughter, rape and sexual assault. **Strengths:** "Always well prepared."

Mark George QC (Garden Court North) A defence specialist with vast experience in the most complex and serious criminal offences, including large-scale drugs importation, historic sexual assault and murder. He has most recently been instructed on the Hillsborough Inquiry by families of those killed in the disaster. **Strengths:** "His cross examination is very good and very effective."

Pete Weatherby QC (Garden Court North) Leading expert in civil liberties and human rights law who has recently been engaged on the Hillsborough Inquiry on behalf of the families. He continues to maintain an active practice at the Criminal Bar, particularly in the appellate courts. **Strengths:** "Thorough, efficient and effective."

SOUTH EASTERN

Crime
Leading Sets
Band 1
Drystone Chambers *
Westgate Chambers
Band 2
Octagon Legal
6 Pump Court *
Red Lion Chambers
Leading Silks
Band 1
Khalil Karim *Drystone Chambers* *
Laws Eleanor *QEB Hollis Whiteman (ORL)* ◊ Ⓐ *
Band 2
Barraclough Richard *6 Pump Court* Ⓐ
Saxby Oliver *6 Pump Court* Ⓐ
Band 3
Coffey John *3 Temple Gardens (ORL)* ◊
Rafferty Angela *Drystone Chambers* *
Spence Simon *Red Lion Chambers*
* *Indicates set / individual with profile.*
Ⓐ *direct access (see p.24).*
◊ *(ORL) = Other Ranked Lawyer.*
Alphabetical order within each band. Band 1 is highest.

Crime	
Leading Juniors	
Band 1	**Thompson** Andrew *Red Lion Chambers*
Barton Richard *Westgate Chambers*	**Upton** Rebecca *Crown Office Row (ORL)* ◊
Carter William *Drystone Chambers* *	**Band 3**
Cherrill Beverly *Westgate Chambers*	**Ayers** Guy *Octagon Legal*
Clare Michael *Octagon Legal*	**Brady** Jane *Cornwall Street Chambers (ORL)* ◊
Hamblin Nicholas *Westgate Chambers*	**Daly** Nigel *Cornwall Street Chambers (ORL)* ◊
James Ian *Octagon Legal*	**Dyble** Steven *Red Lion Chambers*
Meredith Philip *Westgate Chambers*	**Farmer** John *Drystone Chambers* *
Shay Stephen *23 Essex Street (ORL)* ◊ *	**Gardner** Alan *23 Essex Street (ORL)* ◊
Band 2	**Gibbs** Georgina *The 36 Group (ORL)* ◊
James Rhodri *23 Essex Street (ORL)* ◊ *	**Gray** Jennifer *Lamb Building (ORL)* ◊
Lamb Jeffrey *Westgate Chambers*	**Krolick** Ivan *Lamb Building (ORL)* ◊
Morgans John *Octagon Legal*	**Lindop** Sarah *Westgate Chambers*
O'Higgins John *6 Pump Court*	**Matthews** Claire *Drystone Chambers* *
Paxton Chris *Red Lion Chambers*	**Perrins** Gregory *Drystone Chambers* *
Spence Stephen *Drystone Chambers* *	**Sadler** Rhiannon *9 Bedford Row (ORL)* ◊
Stephens Andrew *Westgate Chambers*	**Shaw** Andrew *Drystone Chambers* *
Taylor Simon *6 Pump Court* *	

Band 1

Drystone Chambers
See profile on p.829

THE SET

As one of East Anglia's leading criminal law sets, Drystone Chambers is known for handling some of the most noteworthy cases on the South Eastern Circuit. Barristers at Drystone are regularly instructed to both prosecute and defend major offences, including murder, rape and violent crime, as well as complex multi-handed sexual abuse and organised crime rings. One instructing solicitor comments on the broad reach of experience at the set, saying: "The reason I instruct them is that I know whatever barrister they send is going to be of a high calibre."

Client service: "The clerking is superb; they are extremely helpful and very approachable." "Their clerking service is excellent, and we know they'll do a good job for us." Mark Cornell and David Green are the senior clerks.

SILKS

Karim Khalil QC (see p.690) Standout criminal silk with established practices in London and the South East. He has a varied practice, prosecuting and defending major cases of actual and attempted murder, firearms possession and sexual offences. **Strengths:** "He is phenomenal." **Recent work:** Successfully led the prosecution against a defendant accused of stabbing a man to death in a drugs-related attack. Witnesses involved all sought to cover up their own or the defendant's involvement in the crime, making the presentation of the case extremely difficult.

Angela Rafferty QC (see p.746) Junior silk who is cultivating a high-profile criminal law practice in both defence and prosecution work, primarily with regard to sexually based offences. She commands particular proficiency in cases involving vulnerable witnesses and defendants, including those with psychiatric issues and learning difficulties. **Strengths:** "She would be my first choice for the most serious stuff." "Her written work is of an extremely high standard, and she's the sort of person everybody listens to." **Recent work:** Represented a paediatric consultant accused of multiple sexual offences against children. Following his conviction, successfully took the case to the Supreme Court in order to have the extended custodial sentence restructured.

JUNIORS

William Carter (see p.612) An experienced junior who is well versed in all areas of serious crime, including murder and sexual offences. Highly capable as both prosecuting and defence counsel, he also acts in large-scale cases relating to drugs and organised crime. **Recent work:** Led the successful prosecution of four members of an organised crime ring charged with conspiring to pervert the course of justice in an earlier trial involving the leader of the gang.

Stephen Spence (see p.770) A "marvellous" practitioner with a broad range of experience in criminal law that includes serious cases of murder, manslaughter and child sex offences. Also has a niche expertise in criminal matters related to aviation. **Strengths:** "He balances the gravitas of a very experienced member of the Bar with a friendly accessibility, and an ability to make my clients feel very comfortable with him. His ability to talk to the jury rather than at them is also very good indeed." **Recent work:** Instructed in R v Collins, a case linked to the investigation of a large-scale paedophile ring operating in Norfolk.

Claire Matthews (see p.709) Criminal law specialist who both prosecutes and defends a wide range of matters. She is particularly renowned for her expertise in cases concerning serious sexual offences, particularly those that involve children. **Strengths:** "A superb advocate, she is tenacious and she is also extremely good with clients." "Her preparation is very good, very high calibre. Any case that requires a high level of information and concentration is where she would shine." **Recent work:** Successfully represented the third defendant in a three-month trial concerning a paedophile ring. The defendant was acquitted on all counts but one of ABH.

Andrew Shaw (see p.763) Respected practitioner who is highly capable of handling a vast array of serious crime cases, including those that involve allegations of sexual assault, murder and attempted murder. He is also instructed in matters relating to drugs, firearms and fraud. **Recent work:** Successfully defended a teacher alleged to have abused a female student over an extended period of time.

John Farmer (see p.643) Highly experienced advocate whose practice extends from the South Eastern Circuit to London and beyond. He regularly handles the most serious cases of murder, manslaughter and rape, and is also highly experienced in large-scale drug offences and fraud.

Gregory Perrins (see p.736) A highly impressive barrister with a thriving criminal practice that takes in violent and serious crimes alongside heavyweight fraud cases. He is also well versed in handling health and safety and regulatory matters with a criminal edge. **Strengths:** "He's very good at bringing a very dry and boring case in a way that both the jury and the judge can understand. Equally he is able to communicate with clients of all backgrounds." **Recent work:** Successfully prosecuted a serving police officer for multiple counts of misconduct in public office, after he targeted victims of domestic violence for sex.

Westgate Chambers

THE SET

Based in Lewes, Westgate Chambers is able to provide both defence and prosecution counsel with equal skill, and tackles a full range of criminal and regulatory issues. Barristers at the set are instructed in major cases involving homicide, drug trafficking, child abduction, sexual abuse and fraud. Instructing solicitors praise the set and its members for being "incredibly approachable" and draw attention to their "wide-ranging experience and specialism."

Client service: "The clerks are friendly and approachable; they have a good knowledge of the set's members and their suitability for specific cases." James Still is the senior clerk.

JUNIORS

Richard Barton A "dedicated, articulate advocate" who is also joint head of chambers at Westgate. He continues to be instructed in highly complex and serious criminal cases, including murder, drug offences, child abduction and child sexual exploitation. **Strengths:** "He is an extremely adept advocate and is really intellectual. He grasps issues very quickly and his cross-examination is amazing." **Recent work:** Successfully led the prosecution of an organised crime group who trafficked millions of pounds worth of drugs across the South East.

Beverly Cherrill Renowned for her impressive expertise in cases concerning sexual offences, she is highly praised for her advocacy and witness-handling skills. She also boasts experience prosecuting and defending an array of other matters, including burglaries and drug offences. **Strengths:** "She is extremely experienced and knows the right tone to use in cross-examination. I get good advice from her as well, she's very good." **Recent work:** Instructed by a former school master to defend claims of numerous historical sexual offences brought by former pupils.

Nicholas Hamblin Respected junior praised for his attention to detail, intellectual acumen and persuasive courtroom manner. He is known for his ability to both prosecute and defend high-profile and complex criminal cases, including serious sexual offences and armed robberies. **Strengths:** "Very, very thorough and an excellent advocate." "He gets to grips with the file incredibly quickly and is a very good advocate. His experience is very apparent and his capability is second to none." **Recent work:** Defended an individual facing historical rape and abuse claims within his own family as well as from other parties.

Philip Meredith Highly experienced advocate with a range of experience in cases concerning serious violence, child and adult sexual offences and homicide. Handles cases as both prosecution and defence counsel. **Recent work:** Successfully defended a social worker charged with serious sexual offences against children under his care.

Jeffrey Lamb Handles a broad range of serious crime and fraud matters. A Grade 4 prosecutor, he also defends cases and can offer further assistance as a qualified mediator.

Andrew Stephens Junior with experience of the full gamut of complex criminal matters. He handles a significant amount of work relating to organised crime, money laundering and firearms possession, while also taking on cases concerning serious violent and sexual offences. **Recent work:** Successfully defended a client charged with attempted murder, where the incident was captured on CCTV.

Sarah Lindop Known for the quality of her practice defending clients facing serious sexual offence charges. She is adept at handling vulnerable witnesses and defendants, and is also extremely strong in managing cases with an international aspect. **Recent work:** Defended a man charged with sexual assault against two of his own children.

Band 2

Octagon Legal

THE SET

A Norwich-based set that is capable of prosecuting and defending a wide variety of criminal cases, and that has members experienced in appearing before courts of all levels. Barristers of Octagon Legal handle everything from violent crimes, murder and sex offences through to regulatory issues such as firearms licensing and health and safety.

Client service: Robert Gibson is the senior clerk.

JUNIORS

Michael Clare An experienced senior junior whose practice runs the full gamut of criminal matters. **Strengths:** "He essentially does all our criminal work, he is superb."

Ian James Has wide experience of acting in extremely challenging cases that concern serious crimes such as murder and armed robbery. He also specialises in cases involving firearms, and additionally takes on firearms licensing related work.

John Morgans Prosecutes and defends all areas of serious crime, and is particularly noted for his involvement in firearms cases, including appellate work.

Guy Ayers Noted practitioner who is experienced in handling all types of criminal offences, but is particularly well versed in handling firearms licensing and confiscation matters.

6 Pump Court

See profile on p.897

THE SET

6 Pump Court has a strong practice across the full spectrum of criminal law, and is particularly well recognised for its expertise in homicide and sexual offence cases. Its team of highly qualified silks and juniors are experienced in both prosecution and defence work and also regularly take on major cases relating to drug trafficking, fraud and animal cruelty. The set wins high praise overall from instructing solicitors, with one remarking: "The quality of the advocacy is very high, but their client manner is also excellent and the clerks will go out of their way to help you if they can."

Client service: "Senior clerk Richard Constable goes out of his way to assist, and probably goes further than most other clerks. The time and assistance that the clerks have been able to provide has been second to none."

SILKS

Oliver Saxby QC Practises extensively on both the London and South Eastern Circuits, and has notable expertise in cases of historic or multi-handed sexual abuse. He displays particular aptitude in handling multiple defendants or victims, and also regularly writes and speaks on the treatment of vulnerable witnesses. **Strengths:** "He went out of his way to be particularly helpful, very proactive and very quick in terms of his responses." "His preparation is outstanding and his court manner is excellent." **Recent work:** Led the prosecution of 11 members of the Aylesbury sex gang, who were accused of historic sex offences against two young girls. The trial resulted in a number of convictions.

Richard Barraclough QC Diverse criminal practice that includes prosecuting and defending serious crimes of violence, sexual assault and murder, as well as cases involving fraud and proceeds of crime. He has also taken on significant cases involving drugs and human trafficking. **Strengths:** "He's very hardworking and shows meticulous attention to detail. He's also a strong advocate in court, he comes across as a real fighter." **Recent work:** Defended a Slovakian national as one of several defendants facing serious allegations of human trafficking and sex offences against a vulnerable teenager. The case raised significant issues concerning the investigation of sex crimes and particularly the interview process for alleged victims.

JUNIORS

John O'Higgins As a senior junior who has significant experience prosecuting and defending cases, John O'Higgins focuses his practice on serious crimes including fraud, drug and sexual offences, violence and homicide. He has considerable experience in manslaughter and firearms cases. **Strengths:** "He's an extremely confident and commanding advocate, capable of undertaking the most serious work. His written work is also excellent: prompt and succinct." **Recent work:** Represented the third defendant on trial for the murder of a rival drug dealer in 2010, where the first two defendants were convicted. The client was acquitted of the murder charge and convicted for only one lesser offence.

Simon Taylor (see p.778) A leading junior for serious sexual offence or homicide cases, particularly those that involve highly challenging evidential concerns or vulnerable witnesses. Serves as both prosecution and defence counsel on heavyweight criminal matters. **Strengths:** "He's user-friendly for defendants, juries and judges, and his preparation is among the best I've seen from anyone." "He's very organised, very user-friendly and incredibly efficient." **Recent work:** Successfully prosecuted R v Holness, a case concerning the long-term historic sexual abuse of three individuals by their now elderly father.

Red Lion Chambers

THE SET

Red Lion Chambers provides specialist criminal and regulatory counsel from its Chelmsford annex, and also draws upon the strength its London base. Barristers at the set are highly capable of taking on serious cases of homicide, violence and sexual assault as well as major fraud and organised crime matters.

Client service: "Practice managers Andy Ioannou and Theresa Feeney are brilliant. They're prompt, they're pleasant, they get stuff done and they communicate with me straight away."

SILKS

Simon Spence QC Has experience defending and prosecuting high-profile criminal cases in London and the South East, including those involving serious sex offences, violence and drug trafficking. He has a growing practice in regulatory issues such as trading standards claims. **Strengths:** "He offers to the point, incisive advocacy, even at very short notice."

JUNIORS

Chris Paxton A highly regarded junior who has significant experience both prosecuting and defending serious crime. His broad practice also encompasses fraud, road transport and regulatory cases. **Strengths:** "He just dominates the courtroom. He's exceptional and the genuine article. I've seen him win cases that he shouldn't have won. He just has a knack for it." **Recent work:** Successfully prosecuted a man who stabbed his girlfriend to death, with the only witness to the event being a four year old child.

Andrew Thompson Prosecutes and defends a broad range of complex criminal cases, including murder, drug offences and child abuse. He is adept at handling vulnerable witnesses, such as very young children and individuals with mental health difficulties. **Recent work:** Acted in R v Lourenz, Luitjen and Others, which concerned the alleged importation of a substantial amount of class A drugs.

Steven Dyble Specialises in defence work that takes in serious cases involving violent and sexual offences, money laundering, drugs and homicide. He also has developed a niche in the law relating to assisted suicide. **Recent work:** Successfully defended an individual charged with brothel-keeping in a multi-defendant trial. The client was the only individual to be cleared of all charges.

Other Ranked Lawyers

Rhiannon Sadler (9 Bedford Row) Regularly instructed to prosecute cases concerning fraud as well as serious sexual and violent offences. She also defends a wide variety of cases, including child sexual abuse and multi-handed drugs conspiracies.

Jane Brady (Cornwall Street Chambers) Has a wide range of expertise in criminal law which includes significant cases of murder, burglary, sexual exploitation, fraud and drugs. She demonstrates particular skill in representing young or vulnerable clients, as well as individuals whose first language is not English.

Nigel Daly (Cornwall Street Chambers) Experienced criminal barrister who handles the full gamut of serious criminal matters, including murders and sexual offences.

Rebecca Upton (Crown Office Row) Capable of advising across a broad spectrum of criminal law matters. Notable cases include everything from dangerous driving and sex offences to arson and serious violence. **Strengths:** "She's very good at preparation, very good with clients and her cross-examination is second to none."

Stephen Shay (see p.763) (23 Essex Street) Well versed in handling matters of violent crime, including homicide and rape, as well as large-scale drug offences. Although he defends cases he is primarily a prosecutor, and is a member of the CPS specialist panels for serious crime and rape. **Recent work:** Successfully defended a father from the Pakistani community who had been charged with multiple counts of child cruelty.

Rhodri James (see p.682) (23 Essex Street) Praised by instructing solicitors for his availability, client manner and work ethic, Rhodri James offers a broad practice encompassing both general and financial crime. His recent caseload has included allegations of murder, rape and kidnapping, among others. **Strengths:** "He is probably one of the most hard-working advocates I know. He has a very impressive advocacy style, he's very good with clients, and he's very user-friendly." **Recent work:** Successfully represented the first defendant in a multi-handed case relating to charges of conspiracy to kidnap, blackmail and false imprisonment.

Alan Gardner (23 Essex Street) Focuses on prosecuting cases of violent crime, including those that involve sexual and firearms offences. He also has a significant understanding of complex fraud cases. **Recent work:** Successfully prosecuted a scout leader charged with grooming teenage boys over the internet.

Jennifer Gray (Lamb Building) An accomplished criminal advocate who is particularly adept at handling trials that involve multiple defendants or vulnerable clients. Handles both defence and prosecution of weighty serious crime matters including rape, murder and violent assault.

Ivan Krolick (Lamb Building) Highly experienced senior junior with a strong international slant to his practice. He boasts a strong appellate practice and has a particular niche in white-collar and proceeds of crime matters.

Eleanor Laws QC (see p.697) (QEB Hollis Whiteman) A well-established silk who tackles both defender and prosecutor work in relation to serious sexual offences including child sexual exploitation and abuse. She has recently been involved in a number of high-profile cases relating to historic and multi-handed abuse claims.

John Coffey QC (3 Temple Gardens) A veteran presence at the Criminal Bar in both London and the South East, John Coffey QC is valued for his experience across a range of matters, including drug-related offences, money laundering and murder. **Strengths:** "He's a presence around the court, and a gentleman."

Georgina Gibbs (The 36 Group) Has a strong practice in the field of serious and organised crime, with her recent work including attempted murder cases, sexual offences and large-scale drugs conspiracies. She is skilled in cases involving vulnerable individuals and complex medical evidence.

WALES & CHESTER

Crime	
Leading Sets	
Band 1	
Apex Chambers	
Farrar's Building *	
30 Park Place *	
9 Park Place *	
Band 2	
Iscoed Chambers	
Leading Silks	
Band 1	
Harrington Patrick	*Farrar's Building* *
Rees John Charles	*The Chambers of Mr J C Rees QC (ORL)* ◊
Band 2	
Clee Christopher	*Angel Chambers (ORL)* ◊
Evans Elwen Mair	*Iscoed Chambers*
Lewis Paul	*Farrar's Building* *
Mather-Lees Michael	*Farrar's Building* *
Leading Juniors	
Band 1	
Elias David	*9 Park Place*
Lewis Marian	*30 Park Place*
Rees Caroline	*30 Park Place*
Rees Jonathan	*Apex Chambers*
Richards Catherine	*Iscoed Chambers*
Band 2	
Edwards Heath	*9 Park Place*
Ferrier Susan	*Apex Chambers*
Griffiths Roger	*9 Park Place*
Pearson Elizabeth	*9 Park Place*
Band 3	
Crowther Lucy	*Apex Chambers*
Evans Huw	*30 Park Place*
Evans Timothy	*Apex Chambers*
Jeary Stephen	*30 Park Place*
Rees Christopher	*Apex Chambers*
Waters Sarah	*30 Park Place*

** Indicates set / individual with profile.*

◊ (ORL) = Other Ranked Lawyer.

Alphabetical order within each band. Band 1 is highest.

Band 1

Apex Chambers

THE SET

Very well-respected specialist criminal set whose members have particular expertise in serious and complex crime including fraud, dishonesty and violent offences. Commentators say that "it is the complete package" and "potentially the strongest single set doing criminal work in Cardiff at the moment."

Client service: Craig Mansfield is the senior clerk at Apex Chambers.

JUNIORS

Jonathan Rees Greatly esteemed by his peers for his work, he is an expert in white-collar fraud as well as the general range of complex criminal matters. He has significant expertise in misconduct proceedings held under police regulations, and in sports disciplinary work. **Strengths:** "He is extraordinarily able and exceptionally hard-working. The depth of his practice is quite amazing for someone of his call. He's really good for a young chap and has a great deal of potential."

Susan Ferrier Strong criminal practice with a focus on serious sexual offences. Demonstrates expertise in cases concerning historical sexual allegations and those where young and vulnerable witnesses are involved. She is also instructed across other areas of crime including cases relating to homicide and substantial drug conspiracies.

Lucy Crowther Respected by the judiciary on circuit, she has experience across a broad range of crime matters and particular expertise in defending and prosecuting sexual allegations cases. She also has experience working with local authorities on environmental and animal welfare cases. **Strengths:** "She's highly regarded. Sexual offences work is her particular strength at the moment; that's where she seems to be doing a great deal of work and she's very good."

Timothy Evans Has over 25 years of experience prosecuting and defending a full range of criminal offences, and has specific expertise in serious fraud and confiscation cases. He acts for HMRC, the CPS and the Wales Illegal Money Lending Unit. **Strengths:** "Good advocate with strong preparation and people skills."

Christopher Rees One of the founding members of the chambers, who is instructed in many high-profile serious and complex crime cases at all levels of court. He regularly acts on behalf of the Welsh Ministers and is also specialised in police disciplinary work.

Farrar's Building

See profile on p.843

THE SET

Highly regarded for its serious criminal work, Farrar's Building's members are instructed for the defence and prosecution in murder, sexual abuse, terrorism and firearms trials among others.

Client service: The senior clerk at the chambers is Alan Kilbey.

SILKS

Patrick Harrington QC (see p.664) Hugely experienced barrister on the Wales Circuit with significant experience in fraud and murder cases and who is highly praised by his peers. **Strengths:** "He's the top man. No one would say otherwise. He's very good." **Recent work:** Defended one of nine defendants charged with dealing in criminal property. The case involved the theft and sale from storage sites of BT equipment worth £1 million.

Paul Lewis QC (see p.701) Has appeared in over 100 homicide cases, regularly acting on either side of the docket. He is noted for his experience in child murder cases and complex fraud matters. **Strengths:** "He's an extremely competent advocate and very thorough. He's very good on his feet and he's got a very sound grasp of the law." **Recent work:** Successfully acted for a defendant charged with murdering a 22 month old child.

Michael Mather-Lees QC (see p.709) Regularly handles murder and manslaughter cases on behalf of both the prosecution and defence as part of a busy general crime practice. **Recent work:** Successfully defended a professional man charged with causing death by dangerous driving. The case involved complex scientific evidence and detailed cross-examination of expert witnesses.

30 Park Place

See profile on p.943

THE SET

A pre-eminent set on circuit that handles a full range of criminal work, prosecuting and defending both professional and lay clients in many high-profile cases including those relating to homicide, severe sexual offences and drug conspiracies. 30 Park Place houses an impressive group of expert barristers, and has particular strength among its juniors.

Client service: "I've been instructing them so I've known the clerks for years, and they often ring and consult and are very good." Phillip Griffiths is the senior clerk for the chambers and Tony Naylon heads up the criminal clerking team.

JUNIORS

Marian Lewis A strong practitioner known to sources for her expert handling of sexual offence cases and for her particular sensitivity with young or vulnerable witnesses. She has significant experience in a range of serious criminal cases including homicide, fraud and drug conspiracies. **Strengths:** "A very safe pair of hands, who is very, very cool and unflustered. She has good people skills and is a good advocate."

Caroline Rees A very experienced prosecution and defence barrister, with particular experience of acting in cases involving sexual abuse. Many of her cases arise from historical accusations or deal with multiple complainants or the trafficking of people for sexual exploitation. She also acts in homicide and drug conspiracy cases.

Huw Evans Known for his strength in case preparation on document-heavy cases and his expertise in cases concerning corruption and criminal fraud. He handles a mix of prosecution and defence tackling all manner of criminal cases as well as police disciplinary work. **Strengths:** "Very thorough. He's from a military background so his case preparation is brilliant. He has good people skills and is a formidable advocate."

Sarah Waters Acts for both prosecution and defence, handling a range of matters from motoring offences to serious sexual abuse and homicide cases. **Strengths:** "Her contributions to cases are excellent and she is someone who has a very, very bright future ahead of her." **Recent work:** Acted as sole counsel in R v Rabjohns, Battersby, Bridge and Hooper, representing the defendant in a six-week contested trial concerning three counts of conspiracy to murder. The case concerned a joint plan to ram a vehicle off the road.

Stephen Jeary He has a strong defence-based practice, and is sought out to handle serious fraud, homicide, drugs and sexual cases. **Strengths:** "A formidable advocate with a very good reputation."

9 Park Place

See profile on p.944

THE SET

Known as "a very strong set across the board" with over 30 dedicated criminal specialists who are instructed in relation to all aspects of criminal work. Barristers here have expertise in cases concerning sexual offences, child abuse, fraud, money laundering and homicide to name but a few areas.

Client service: Michael Lieberman is the senior clerk for the chambers and Nigel East heads up the criminal clerking team.

JUNIORS

David Elias Highly accomplished advocate with a strong practice in all aspects of criminal law, who acts in serious and complicated cases including those concerning sexual offences, homicide and drug conspiracies. **Strengths:** "Very well regarded by the judiciary and by his peers. He does the whole gamut of work."

Heath Edwards Broadly experienced criminal barrister who defends and prosecutes serious cases. He regularly handles large-scale drug and fraud cases. **Strengths:** "He's keen and eager, he prepares well, and he has very good people skills."

Roger Griffiths A Grade 4 prosecutor with over 30 years' experience as a criminal barrister who deals with highly sensitive cases including complex drug conspiracies and sexual offences. He has a particular specialism in covert surveillance cases.

Elizabeth Pearson Has an impressive reputation on both the defence and prosecution sides, and regularly handles cases concerning serious violence, drug conspiracies and proceeds of crime. He also handles serious sexual offence cases and works with young and vulnerable witnesses.

Band 2

Iscoed Chambers

THE SET

Iscoed Chambers has a strong criminal offering with 25 members offering expertise at all levels of seniority. Barristers from the set often act in complex and heavyweight crime matters for both the prosecution and the defence.

Client service: Avril Llewellyn is the chambers director.

SILKS

Elwen Mair Evans QC Head of Iscoed Chambers and a professor of law at the University of Swansea. She acts in high-profile criminal cases for both prosecution and defence.

JUNIORS

Catherine Richards She is highly regarded by her peers for her work on high-profile cases, and handles a range of cases including frauds and homicides. She is a Grade 4 CPS prosecutor and a specialist in rape and serious sexual offences. **Strengths:** "Prosecutes high-profile stuff." "Very well regarded – extremely good."

Other Ranked Lawyers

Christopher Clee QC (Angel Chambers) Head of Angel Chambers and a barrister with a dedicated criminal practice. He is regularly instructed to act in many high-profile criminal cases, and handles cases for both the prosecution and defence. **Strengths:** "Chris is a very good performer. He's solid and always prepares well."

John Charles Rees QC (The Chambers of Mr J C Rees QC) Specialist in violent crime and serious fraud with experience in high-profile murder cases. He has taken on HMRC and the SFO in high-profile MTIC and serious fraud cases respectively. **Strengths:** "He's still at the top of his game."

WESTERN

Crime	
Leading Sets	
Band 1	
Albion Chambers *	
Guildhall Chambers *	
3PB Barristers *	
Band 2	
Drystone Chambers *	
Pump Court Chambers *	
Leading Silks	
Star individuals	
Langdon Andrew	*Guildhall Chambers*
Smith Richard	*Guildhall Chambers*
Band 1	
Dunkels Paul	*Walnut House (ORL)* ◊
Lickley Nigel	*3PB Barristers*
Band 2	
Laws Simon	*Walnut House (ORL)* ◊
Meeke Martin	*Colleton Chambers (ORL)* ◊
Pascoe Nigel	*Pump Court Chambers*
Quinlan Christopher	*Guildhall Chambers*
Band 3	
Brunner Kate	*Albion Chambers* Ⓐ
Malcolm Alastair R	*Drystone Chambers* *
Parroy Michael	*3PB Barristers*
New Silks	
Feest Adam	*3PB Barristers*

** Indicates set / individual with profile.*
Ⓐ direct access (see p.24).
◊ (ORL) = Other Ranked Lawyer.
Alphabetical order within each band. Band 1 is highest.

Crime	
Leading Juniors	
Band 1	
Burgess Edward	*Albion Chambers*
Duval Robert	*Albion Chambers*
Jewell Matthew	*Drystone Chambers* *
Mooney Stephen	*Albion Chambers* Ⓐ
Row Charles	*Queen Square Chambers (ORL)* ◊
Tully Ray	*Guildhall Chambers*
Band 2	
Collins Rosaleen	*Guildhall Chambers*
Gerasimidis Nicolas	*Guildhall Chambers*
Jones Sarah	*Pump Court Chambers*
Lowe Rupert	*Guildhall Chambers*
Morgan Simon	*St John's Chambers (ORL)* ◊
Newton-Price James	*Pump Court Chambers*
Onslow Richard	*3PB Barristers*
Pakrooh Ramin	*Guildhall Chambers*
Band 3	
Beal Jason	*Devon Chambers (ORL)* ◊
Bradbury Timothy	*3PB Barristers*
Brown Anne	*Pump Court Chambers*
Bryan Robert	*Drystone Chambers* *
Cotter Nicholas	*3PB Barristers*
Evans David	*Walnut House (ORL)* ◊
Grey Robert	*3PB Barristers*
Haskell James	*Guildhall Chambers*
Horder Tom	*3PB Barristers*
Jones Samuel	*Guildhall Chambers*
McCarthy Mary	*Walnut House (ORL)* ◊
Nelson Giles	*Albion Chambers*
Reid David	*3PB Barristers*
Shellard Robin	*Queen Square Chambers (ORL)* ◊
Vigars Anna	*Guildhall Chambers*
Worsley Mark	*Guildhall Chambers*

Band 1

Albion Chambers

See profile on p.937

THE SET

A large team with a significant footprint on the Western Circuit that boasts consistent involvement in sophisticated criminal cases. Its barristers are instructed in high-profile matters that take in everything from violent crimes and multi-handed sexual offences to big-ticket frauds and regulatory violations.

Client service: The criminal clerking team is led by senior clerk Bonnie Colbeck.

SILKS

Kate Brunner QC A junior silk with a growing practice that regularly sees her instructed in serious violent crime, fraud and regulatory offences.

JUNIORS

Edward Burgess A widely respected junior with a sterling reputation for handling grave and complex criminal cases. He is a member of the CPS specialist rape panel and is frequently instructed as a prosecutor in addition to his defence work. **Strengths:** "Regarded as one of the leading juniors in Bristol, he's definitely up there with the best." "Unflustered with a very good command of detail."

Robert Duval A senior junior who is frequently called upon to both defend and prosecute the most serious of cases, including those that involve complex and high-profile violent offences.

Stephen Mooney An impressive practitioner with a strong defence practice as well as significant experience prosecuting on behalf of the Bar Standards Board. He is a Level 4 panel advocate for the CPS and also sits on its specialist serious crime group panel.

Giles Nelson Has a diverse criminal defence offering that is supplemented by his work as a CPS Level 3 prosecutor. He is regularly instructed on matters spanning the breadth of criminal law including drugs offences, sexual violence and health and safety cases with a criminal element.

Guildhall Chambers

See profile on p.938

THE SET

A highly respected set that remains dedicated to providing top-flight representation to both publicly and privately funded clients. Its members are known for their skilled handling of the full range of criminal matters, including cases that have attracted significant media interest, and are particularly well versed in advising and assisting on homicides and sex offences. The set's "capable and well organised" stable of barristers are praised for their "high-quality preparation, knowledge and advocacy."

Client service: The "proactive" and "experienced" clerks come highly recommended for their efficiency and client-handling skills. Lucy Northeast and Grant Bidwell in the criminal clerking team are singled out for praise, with one impressed referee stating: "They are capable and approachable. I would have no hesitation in commending the way in which both of them work."

SILKS

Andrew Langdon QC Maintains his reputation as one of the strongest criminal practitioners on circuit, demonstrated by his election as Vice Chairman of the Bar Council for 2016. He is particularly known for his involvement as both prosecution and defence counsel in extremely high-profile, serious crime matters, including multi-handed homicides and cases of false imprisonment. **Strengths:** "Andrew brings an unparalleled level of forensic intensity to his case preparation and advocacy." **Recent work:** Represented Shauna Hoare, who was jointly accused with her boyfriend of murdering Bristol teenager Becky Watts. Hoare was acquitted of murder and was instead convicted of manslaughter and other offences.

Richard Smith QC Highly experienced silk able to act as both prosecution and defence counsel in the most challenging and complex criminal cases, including those that feature vulnerable defendants accused of serious offences. **Strengths:** "An extremely competent and able advocate in cases at the very upper end of the spectrum." **Recent work:** Represented a former bishop charged with sexual offences and misconduct in public office.

Christopher Quinlan QC Noted for his ability to handle criminal matters of the utmost seriousness, including the defence of some particularly challenging cases of murder, manslaughter and sexual violence. **Recent work:** Represented an individual charged with the murder of her newborn baby. The defendant was convicted of manslaughter and was sentenced to probation.

JUNIORS

Ray Tully Head of the set's crime team and a CPS Grade 4 prosecutor, Ray Tully boasts experience in all areas of serious crime, including murder, manslaughter and rape. He is also an approved member of the CPS specialist rape and organised crime panels. **Strengths:** "A particularly outstanding individual who communicates clearly and sympathetically to clients, and prepares cases very thoroughly. He also has sound tactical judgement, and inspires confidence in both clients and the judiciary." **Recent work:** Successfully defended an individual who became involved in an altercation and struck a man who subsequently died as a result of his injury. The trial resulted in a hung jury and the defendant was found not guilty.

Rosaleen Collins Respected junior with in-depth knowledge of all areas of serious crime. She boasts a particular expertise in handling cases involving severe sexual allegations as well as vulnerable defendants and witnesses. **Strengths:** "She is sensitive to the needs of clients but robust as an advocate, dealing most competently with highly challenging sexual offences."

Nicolas Gerasimidis Described as "extremely thorough and intellectually astute," Nicolas Gerasimidis is highly praised for his attention to detail and jury advocacy. He specialises in complex crime and is regularly instructed in high-profile, serious cases of abuse, child injury and drug offences. **Strengths:** "Nicolas always seems to be head and shoulders above his opponents at trial. He has impeccable judgement when it comes to presenting his case and cross-examination, and handles the most difficult of cases and questions in a way that is obviously appreciated by the judge and jury." **Recent work:** Defended the first of four individuals indicted for a multi-handed historic child sex abuse case.

Rupert Lowe Noted junior with a broad practice in serious crime, fraud and health and safety. He specialises in defending and prosecuting sexual offence cases, including historic child abuse and rape, and also has experience of handling significant organised crime cases.

Ramin Pakrooh Extremely experienced in prosecuting and defending challenging matters such as firearms distribution, large-scale drug operations and violent crime, including homicide.

James Haskell Specialist criminal practitioner who is also regularly instructed on the criminal elements of professional disciplinary proceedings. He is also a Grade 3 CPS prosecutor and is appointed to the Crown's specialist rape panel. **Recent work:** Successfully defended an individual who was accused of the rape of a young woman, although both acknowledged that they were too drunk to remember the encounter.

Samuel Jones Focuses on defence work, and is particularly well versed in crimes involving serious violence and sexual offences. He also prosecutes cases, and is highly recommended overall for the strength of his courtroom advocacy. **Strengths:** "He is one of the most promising advocates I have come across. An excellent tactician, a capable lawyer, first class on paper and one of the most hard-working lawyers I have come across. If I was in trouble, I would go to him." **Recent work:** Defended an individual who caused the death of his partner in the course of trying to take his own life as part of an alleged suicide pact.

Anna Vigars Often instructed in heavyweight criminal cases, including those of murder and manslaughter. She boasts a particular expertise in cases involving serious sexual allegations and those with significant health and safety elements. **Recent work:** Successfully prosecuted an individual accused of murdering his landlady by pushing her down the stairs.

Mark Worsley Noted for his advocacy skills, Mark Worsley both prosecutes and defends serious crime cases. His practice runs the full gamut of criminal offences including sex crime, drugs and acts of violence. **Strengths:** "He's a very good advocate, very capable. He has a good eye for detail, he doesn't miss a lot, you can't get anything past him."

3PB Barristers

See profile on p.892

THE SET

3PB Barristers enjoys a sterling reputation on the Western Circuit for high levels of quality and consistency across its broad criminal practice. It has an enviable track record of handling high-profile and demanding criminal cases, including murder, fraud, drug and sex offences. Instructing solicitors single out the set's efficiency and excellent client service as strengths, observing that the practitioners are "extremely reliable with great diversity, and are able to get to grips with cases at a frightening speed."

Client service: "The clerking service is one of the main attractions of 3PB. It is the best that I have dealt with in 20-plus years of doing this work." Chambers director Stuart Pringle manages the criminal clerking team from Winchester.

SILKS

Nigel Lickley QC A leading criminal silk who is also head of chambers at 3PB. He has vast experience as both a prosecutor and defender on a wide range of cases including regulatory crime, white-collar fraud and violent offences. **Strengths:** "A very good jury advocate who is great on the human interest side of cases." "A very high-profile barrister with a really brilliant eye for detail who can think outside the box." **Recent work:** Acted for the prosecution in the case of a bigamous husband who killed his wife and other parties who perverted the course of justice by assisting him.

Michael Parroy QC Highly experienced barrister with a diverse criminal practice. He is instructed on a range of matters including drug cases, white-collar crime and serious violent offences, and has particular expertise in confiscation and restraint of assets. **Strengths:** "He is outstanding – a Rolls-Royce practitioner." **Recent work:** Instructed by the CPS to act in R v Dennis and Wilson, a major drug importation case.

Adam Feest QC New silk who both defends and prosecutes serious violent and sexual offences. He has additional experience acting in cases of drugs, fraud and deception. **Recent work:** Prosecuted a case of aggravated burglary of an elderly victim by a gang of masked intruders.

JUNIORS

Richard Onslow A very experienced senior junior who has appeared at tribunals ranging from local magistrates' courts all the way up to the Privy Council. He handles a broad spectrum of serious criminal cases including drug and sexual offences, human trafficking and violent crime, and also takes on police disciplinary matters. **Strengths:** "He is brilliant – hugely experienced and a consummate performer." **Recent work:** Successfully defended a client who was accused of participating in a gang rape.

Nicholas Cotter Has a general criminal and regulatory practice, and is active on both the Western and South Eastern Circuits. He has a track record of acting in cases involving fraud, organised crime and serious sexual offences. **Strengths:** "Completely unflappable, he has an extremely good temperament in court. Destined for great things." "A very capable advocate." **Recent work:** Represented the organised crime division of the CPS in Operation Greenless, a cross-border NCA prosecution involving indecent images of vulnerable individuals.

Robert Grey A well-regarded senior junior who is regularly instructed in complex drugs, fraud and sexual offences cases. He both prosecutes and defends, and also offers specialist expertise in proceeds of crime. **Strengths:** "He is extremely experienced and a very good advocate." "He provides an excellent service." **Recent work:** Successfully defended a former scoutmaster against charges arising from historic sex allegations.

Tom Horder Has a robust practice in regulatory offences that sees him instructed by a range of parties including public sector bodies, companies and private individuals. Also handles cases concerning violent crime and sexual abuse. **Strengths:** "Very able, a rising star." **Recent work:** Defended the then leader of Dorset County Council in the first ever prosecution brought under the Localism Act 2011, aimed at dealing with alleged political corruption.

David Reid A respected practitioner whose general crime practice sees him both defend and prosecute a wide range of matters. His recent work includes instruction in murder cases, serious sexual offences and drug-related crimes. **Strengths:** "The right man for a very serious case."

Timothy Bradbury Senior junior with a strong reputation for his skilful prosecutions on behalf of HMRC as well as other government bodies. He has expertise as a defender and prosecutor in all manner of tax cases, fraud and regulatory crime. **Recent work:** Instructed by the CPS Specialist Fraud Division in relation to a multi-handed cyber repayment fraud case involving an international organised crime group.

Band 2

Drystone Chambers

See profile on p.829

THE SET

Drystone Chambers has built up a strong reputation on the Western Circuit for its involvement in criminal cases of the utmost gravity. Members have a broad range of experience as both defence and prosecution counsel in proceedings involving violence, sexual offences, kidnapping and burglary. Respondents confirm the "very high calibre" of the advocates at the set and credit them with "a level of service which matches no other chambers we instruct in criminal matters."

Client service: Led by Mark Cornell and David Green, the clerking team is described as "truly outstanding," with one impressed interviewee stating: "Nothing is ever too much trouble, they will move heaven and earth to assist us."

SILKS

Alastair Malcolm QC (see p.706) Offers vast experience in a wide array of serious criminal matters, with a wealth of knowledge in handling cases of murder, fraud, robbery and serious sexual offences. **Strengths:** "A steady pair of hands." **Recent work:** Successfully defended a doorman against a charge of gross negligence manslaughter after his restraint of a customer resulted in their death.

JUNIORS

Matthew Jewell (see p.683) A leading junior for serious criminal matters, with excellent abilities in major fraud, drug conspiracy and violence cases. He frequently appears in court unled, and takes instruction as both prosecutor and defence counsel. **Strengths:** "I think he's an excellent advocate. If I were in trouble, I'd want him to defend me." **Recent work:** Appointed as leading junior to prosecute the case of R v Mullings and Others in a six-week trial over an alleged drugs conspiracy involving eight defendants.

Robert Bryan (see p.605) Covers the full gamut of serious criminal cases, including murder, sex offences, fraud and drug conspiracies. He is consistently praised among peers for his meticulous preparation and strong advocacy style. **Strengths:** "He is extremely thorough, he's good on the law and he takes good legal points."

Pump Court Chambers

See profile on p.898

THE SET

Pump Court offers a strong platform for trial advocacy within the Western Circuit, and has noted capabilities in a broad array of criminal work. Its members are frequently called upon to act on behalf of clients facing drugs, fraud, violence and sexual offence-related charges. The set's strong pool of criminal practitioners has been further augmented through the arrival of lateral hires within the past year.

SILKS

Nigel Pascoe QC A highly experienced criminal advocate with a distinguished reputation for prosecuting and defending high-profile murder cases. He is highlighted by peers for his courtroom oratory. **Strengths:** "A beautifully eloquent man." **Recent work:** Acted in R v Adam Cross, a landmark case where an individual convicted of grievous bodily harm was retried for murder following the victim's death subsequent to his conviction.

JUNIORS

Sarah Jones Has a strong reputation for her broad criminal expertise, and demonstrates considerable strengths in multi-complainant sexual offence matters and historic claims of sexual abuse. **Strengths:** "She's very tough. If you're against her she makes it difficult for you, in the best sense." **Recent work:** Defended a retired paediatric consultant facing historic claims of sexual assault and illegal abortions performed on child patients, uncovered by Operation Yewtree.

James Newton-Price An impressive performer who has over two decades of criminal advocacy experience on the Western Circuit. His practice includes acting in drug, robbery, money laundering and historic sex offence claims, and he also leads the set's crime and regulatory team. **Recent work:** Acted for the defendant in a case concerning allegations of human trafficking, forced marriage and prostitution in Banbury and London. He was convicted of a minor offence having been acquitted on all major charges.

Anne Brown A specialist in courts martial, with a wealth of experience in defending both senior and junior ranked military personnel. Her wider experience includes acting upon a broad range of sexual violence and child abuse cases. **Strengths:** "Very good indeed, she's very much in demand for historic sex offence cases." **Recent work:** Secured the acquittal of an officer at a court martial, following allegations that he raped a student visitor at an Officers' Mess.

Other Ranked Lawyers

Martin Meeke QC (Colleton Chambers) An impressive senior silk with strong credentials in prosecuting and defending sexual abuse and murder cases as well as acting in regulatory criminal proceedings.

Jason Beal (Devon Chambers) Jason Beal is head of Devon Chambers, and has over two decades of expertise which he extends to clients facing a broad range of criminal proceedings. He prosecutes and defends cases of fraud, financial crime, drug conspiracies and serious sexual offences.

Charles Row (Queen Square Chambers) A junior with a strong reputation in criminal matters, who focuses his practice on fraud and business crime, sexual abuse matters and murder. His regulatory work involves acting upon a range health and safety and trading standards cases. **Strengths:** "A really good practitioner. I have a huge amount of time for him, he's excellent." **Recent work:** Appointed to defend an individual with multiple business interests who was accused of fraud relating to PAYE and National Insurance payments totalling £1 million.

Robin Shellard (Queen Square Chambers) Specialises in handling sexual offence claims, particularly those that involve crimes against children and accusations of historic sexual abuse. He is also instructed on cases that concern drug conspiracies, fraud and matters involving firearm legislation. **Strengths:** "Robin is really good, a very strong practitioner who does a lot of defence work." **Recent work:** Acted for the CPS in an eight-week trial in Bristol Crown Court concerning 18 defendants alleged to have conspired to supply cocaine and cannabis.

Simon Morgan (St John's Chambers) Remains a prominent presence in proceedings involving regulatory offences, inquests and wider criminal matters. He also draws on his background as a criminal solicitor to provide in-depth experience in murder, manslaughter and rape allegations. **Strengths:** "A very experienced criminal practitioner who is well regarded in the courts."

Paul Dunkels QC (Walnut House) Highly experienced practitioner with an excellent track record of prosecuting and defending high-profile cases. He is particularly adept at taking on challenging and sensitive matters such as sudden infant death, murder with diminished responsibility and serious sexual offences. **Strengths:** "A class act." "He's got a very nice style."

Simon Laws QC (Walnut House) Centres his highly regarded practice on homicide, fraud and drug crime, with additional strengths in cases involving sexual offences.

David Evans (Walnut House) Exeter-based junior barrister who demonstrates considerable strength in a full range of criminal matters, with particular experience in handling serious child abuse cases, drug offences and fraud. **Strengths:** "Extremely good at criminal fraud work."

Mary McCarthy (Walnut House) Handles all kinds of criminal matters, with commendable experience acting in serious cases involving sexual offences, drugs, violence and fraud. She primarily acts as defence counsel, though she is also a CPS Grade 4 prosecutor. **Strengths:** "A formidable fraud advocate, certainly someone you want on your side." "She works really hard for her clients and she's got a great manner in court."

Contents:

LONDON

Data Protection	
Leading Sets	
Band 1	
11KBW *	
Band 2	
Blackstone Chambers *	
39 Essex Chambers *	
Matrix Chambers *	
Monckton Chambers *	
One Brick Court *	
Leading Silks	
Star individuals	
Pitt-Payne Timothy	*11KBW* *
White Antony	*Matrix Chambers* *
Band 1	
Caldecott Andrew	*One Brick Court* *
Coppel Philip	*Cornerstone Barristers (ORL)* ◊ 🄰
Grey Eleanor	*39 Essex Chambers*
Tomlinson Hugh	*Matrix Chambers*
Band 2	
Eadie James	*Blackstone Chambers*
Spearman Richard	*39 Essex Chambers* *
Steyn Karen	*11KBW* *
Swift Jonathan	*11KBW* *
Band 3	
Choudhury Akhlaq	*11KBW* *
Coppel Jason	*11KBW* *
Gallafent Kate	*Blackstone Chambers*
Williams Rhodri	*Henderson Chambers (ORL)* ◊ 🄰 *
New Silks	
Evans Catrin	*One Brick Court* *
Facenna Gerry	*Monckton Chambers* 🄰 *
Proops Anya	*11KBW* *
Leading Juniors	
Band 1	
Dunlop Rory	*39 Essex Chambers*
Eardley Aidan	*One Brick Court* *
Hopkins Robin	*11KBW* *
Skinner Lorna	*Matrix Chambers* *
Band 2	
Glen David	*One Brick Court* *
John Laura Elizabeth	*Monckton Chambers*
Knight Christopher	*11KBW* *
Milford Julian	*11KBW* *
Stout Holly	*11KBW* *
Band 3	
Barnes Jonathan	*5RB (ORL)* ◊
Cross Tom	*11KBW* *
Helme Ian	*One Brick Court* *
Kamm Rachel	*11KBW* *
Lask Ben	*Monckton Chambers* 🄰
Mansoori Sara	*Matrix Chambers*
Morrison Julianne	*Monckton Chambers*
Munden Richard	*5RB (ORL)* ◊
Sanders Oliver	*1 Crown Office Row (ORL)* ◊
Scherbel-Ball Jonathan	*One Brick Court* *
Sharland Andrew	*11KBW* 🄰 *
Up-and-coming individuals	
Emmerson Heather	*11KBW* *

** Indicates set / individual with profile.*
🄰 direct access (see p.24).
◊ (ORL) = Other Ranked Lawyer.
Alphabetical order within each band. Band 1 is highest.

Band 1

11KBW

See profile on p.855

THE SET

Widely regarded as the pre-eminent set for handling matters before the First-Tier and Upper Tribunals contesting decisions of the Information Commissioner. Since a large number of the set's barristers are members of the Attorney General's panels of counsel, 11KBW offers a significant depth of experience in representing the government and its ministers in an array of legal proceedings. The set is also highly regarded by instructing solicitors for its provision of its 'Panopticon' blog dedicated to information law.

Client service: "The clerks are efficient, responsive and professional." Lucy Barbet and Mark Dann are the joint senior clerks.

SILKS

Timothy Pitt-Payne QC (see p.727) Enjoys a stellar reputation as the silk of choice for the Information Commissioner and a number of other public bodies at all levels of Tribunal hearings. He excels in all areas of information law, including in matters addressing issues under FOIA, DPA and the EIR. **Strengths:** "He is brilliant. Really pragmatic, incredibly knowledgeable, responsive and commercial as well as being technically excellent." "Highly knowledgeable, experienced and very user-friendly." **Recent work:** Represented the Information Commissioner in a First-Tier Tribunal appeal brought by Google against an enforcement notice issued against it concerning the removal of certain website links on the basis of their publication constituting a breach of data protection legislation.

Karen Steyn QC (see p.761) Highly versatile silk with a deeply accomplished practice spanning a range of related areas, including local government, public and data protection law. She has further expertise in appearing in the European Courts in matters addressing information law points as they pertain to the ECHR. **Strengths:** "A wonderful advocate. She cuts to the heart of a matter, doesn't faff about and her arguments are beautifully written and expressed." "She is very well known and well respected for information law matters." **Recent work:** Represented the Attorney General in the Supreme Court stage of the challenge to the decision to veto the publication of letters from the Prince of Wales to government ministers.

Jonathan Swift QC (see p.765) Widely respected silk with a vast wealth of experience across a number of areas of law, including public law, information law, EU law and human rights. He is best known for his representation of government bodies, not least because he was once First Treasury Counsel. **Strengths:** "He is a very punchy and effective advocate. He knows his stuff inside out." "He gets across the detail of the case with remarkable speed and is a savvy court room operator, knowing when to push or to retreat from points. Charming to deal with." **Recent work:** Acted for the Attorney General in a judicial review of his decision to veto the publication under the FOIA of correspondence between government ministers and the Prince of Wales.

Anya Proops QC (see p.732) Took silk this year on the back of an exceptionally successful junior career representing both the Information Commissioner in Tribunal hearings, and public and private bodies in court proceedings dealing with significant points of information law. **Strengths:** "A first-class all-rounder and excellent on her feet." "Frighteningly clever – you want her on your side in court." **Recent work:** Represented the Information Commissioner as intervener in the Court of Appeal in the highly significant case of Google v Vidal-Hall, in which it was established that a claimant for damages under the DPA need not show pecuniary loss.

JUNIORS

Robin Hopkins (see p.662) Widely regarded as a leading junior for a wide range of matters turning on data protection and information law issues. Highly experienced at appearing in tribunal hearings of all levels, most often on behalf of the Information Commissioner. **Strengths:** "He is bright and articulate and clearly very familiar with issues in the DPA." "He is capable of absorbing huge amounts of detail quickly and reaching a legally correct but commercially sensible solution." **Recent work:** Acted for the Home Secretary in the Supreme Court case of Catt concerning the right of the police to retain data on an elderly peaceful protester who had not been charged with any offence.

Christopher Knight (see p.680) Increasingly seen as a highly skilled practitioner in data protection matters, with a large number of appearances in both First and Upper-Tier Tribunal hearings. He is a regular junior of choice for the Information Commissioner and has further experience in representing private corporations. **Strengths:** "He is smart, witty and delightful to work with." "He has all the technical details down pat and is very pleasant and charming." **Recent work:** Appeared on behalf of the Commissioner of Police of the Metropolis in a high-profile case dealing with a request for information concerning two individuals convicted in Thailand of the murder of two British backpackers.

Julian Milford (see p.705) Adept at handling employment and public law as well as data protection and freedom of information matters. He is a member of the A panel of treasury counsel and is experienced in appearing before the highest domestic and European courts. **Strengths:** "He is very knowledgeable, hard working and dedicated to achieving the best outcome." "A calm, courteous and effective barrister." **Recent work:** Acted as junior counsel for the Attorney General in an Upper Tribunal hearing addressing whether the Sovereign or other members of the royal household are public authorities for the purposes of the Environmental Information Regulations.

Holly Stout (see p.762) Wide-ranging expertise in a number of related areas, with particularly pronounced proficiency in the fields of public law, education and data protection law. She has further experience in handling matters arising in the realm of employment. **Strengths:** "She is intellectually exceptional in her handling of the law. A go-to for complex cases." **Recent work:** Represented the Information Commissioner in a case concerning access to court records and the application of the exemption in s.32 of FOIA.

Akhlaq Choudhury QC (see p.605) Established silk in the data protection and information law field with a track record of appearing in a number of leading cases in the area. He regularly appears on behalf of the government, charities and borough councils in both Tribunal and court hearings. **Strengths:** "He has a very clear, measured style and can present even a difficult case with flair." "His advice and approach to data protection is exemplary." **Recent work:** Acted for the Department of Energy and Climate Change in an Upper Tribunal hearing addressing the division between environmental and non-environmental information for the purposes of FOIA and the EIR.

Jason Coppel QC (see p.612) Acts frequently on behalf of the Information Commission and government ministers on a range of information law matters. He is especially experienced in handling cases dealing with issues in the context of the retention and disclosure of data relating to criminal records. **Strengths:** "He is thorough and technically excellent." **Recent work:** Represented the Home Secretary in a Supreme Court case challenging the retention of data by the police on the basis that it constituted a breach of Article 8 ECHR.

Tom Cross (see p.615) Represents both private media organisations and the Information Commissioner, and has had a number of recent cases heard in the Court of Appeal and the Upper Tribunal. He is particularly well versed in handling cases addressing the meaning and operation of statutory language. **Strengths:** "Tom has a razor-sharp intellect and a great feel for the forensic dynamics of a case." **Recent work:** Acted for the Information Commissioner in three test cases examining when a request for information may be "vexatious" under FOIA, or "manifestly unreasonable" under the EIR.

Rachel Kamm (see p.675) Enjoys a solid reputation as a junior with a versatile practice spanning information law, education, community care and local government matters. She is a member of the Attorney General's B panel of counsel as well as being a fee-paid judge of the Social Entitlement Chamber of the First-Tier Tribunal. **Strengths:** "A well-rounded, approachable and intelligent individual. She is very articulate, describing things well in a clear way." **Recent work:** Represented the Ministry of Justice in Upper Tribunal proceedings addressing whether the ambit of 'information' under FOIA extends to a CD recording of a hearing.

Andrew Sharland (see p.750) Well-respected junior with a diverse practice spanning education, public, human rights and information law. He has advocated before the Supreme Court and offers experience in representing public bodies, individuals and non-governmental organisations. **Strengths:** "A very effective, fluid and charming advocate." "He enthusiastically takes on FOIA and DPA work." **Recent work:** Represented the Cabinet Office in a First-Tier Tribunal hearing concerning a challenge to the decision not to release documents that had been declassified, in which the Tribunal dismissed the appeal on the basis of the costs limit detailed in s.12 FOIA.

Heather Emmerson (see p.629) Joins the junior listings in data protection this year on the back of a growing reputation in the field. Her work in information law most commonly arises in the context of human rights and public access to the reasoning behind decisions of public bodies and government ministers. **Strengths:** "She is fiercely bright." **Recent work:** Acted in a number of cases seeking the release of information regarding the decision-making surrounding the use of lethal drone strikes in Syria.

Band 2

Blackstone Chambers

See profile on p.801

THE SET

The pre-eminent set in public law matters, with a large number of silks and juniors widely considered to be the leading figures in that field, including in cases where public law overlaps with information law issues. Its impressive roster of counsel are additionally highly expert in appearing in human rights matters in both the domestic and European courts. Members often represent public bodies, NGOs and private corporations in a wide range of proceedings. **Client service:** "Blackstone Chambers is a class act. Gary Oliver is a shrewd, personable clerk and the team is always fun to deal with."

SILKS

James Eadie QC Appears for the government in its most significant and high-profile matters in the capacity of first treasury counsel and enjoys a position of some renown as an advocate of the highest order. His work in information law includes defending the compatibility of ministerial decisions with data protection and freedom of information legislation. **Strengths:** "He is an extremely good advocate with a lot of presence, a lot of gravitas and the ability to win the trust of the court." "He is a delight to work with and to be against. Even if you disagree with his argument you can't argue with its quality and the beauty of how it's expressed." **Recent work:** Acted for the Home Secretary in a Court of Appeal case brought by a number of MPs challenging DRIPA on the basis of incompatibility with EU law. The case resulted in the court making a reference to the CJEU for clarification of a previous judgment.

Kate Gallafent QC Highly respected silk with a broad ranging practice taking in public law and professional discipline matters as well as data protection and information law. She is additionally qualified as a CEDR mediator. **Strengths:** "She is excellent. She is fiercely bright but wears her learning lightly, striking the right balance between warmth and gravity." "Kate is approachable and easy to deal with. She responds promptly and keeps the client informed, an attitude of huge benefit to in-house lawyers."

One Brick Court

See profile on p.803

THE SET

The barristers of One Brick Court remain at the vanguard of this area, frequently being sought out to act in cases of the highest profile or utmost sensitivity. It has always been a leading set in defamation and reputation management matters and its members are particularly well placed to represent clients in cases where these areas overlap with information law. Its accomplished roster of counsel are accustomed to representing clients in both the public and private spheres, including major media organisations, government bodies and NGOs.

Client service: "Their clerks are very good. David Mace, their senior clerk is pragmatic, responsive and helpful. There's a lot more personal service from them than you get from most other chambers."

SILKS

Andrew Caldecott QC (see p.597) Highly experienced silk with an outstanding reputation in the field of defamation. He has been involved in a number of leading cases in data protection law, including the House of Lords case of Campbell v MGN. **Strengths:** "He is wonderful. He is incredibly bright and has his finger on the pulse. He has such good judgement." "He's a brilliant advocate and great to listen to." **Recent work:** Acted as lead counsel for a number of claimants under the final stages of the phone interception compensation scheme that was established in the wake of the phone hacking scandal.

Catrin Evans QC (see p.629) New silk who enjoys an excellent reputation as an intelligent advocate capable of handling the most nuanced arguments in information law. She is also an extremely well-regarded practitioner in the area of defamation and privacy. **Strengths:** "She is super brainy and a very pragmatic adviser. She has a great sense of what the client needs and completely understands the law and its complexities." "Catrin is modern in her approach, easy to work with and gets to the important points very quickly." **Recent work:** Acted as junior counsel for Google in the case of Vidal-Hall.

JUNIORS

Aidan Eardley (see p.626) Rises to the top rank of juniors this year in data protection and information law on the back of a growing appreciation of his expert counsel in a range of critical issues in the field, often on behalf of news media organisations. He is also well thought of in the related area of defamation/privacy. **Strengths:** "He is very good; he is very clever, very hard working and has supreme legal knowledge." "He is very knowledgeable in data protection and gives good advice on the options." **Recent work:** Acted for a Guardian journalist in an appeal to the Upper Tribunal by the Home Office against an ICO decision requiring the disclosure of the number of people who had been deprived of their citizenship on counter-terrorism grounds.

David Glen (see p.642) Versatile junior with a string of appearances in leading cases in the field of information law to his name. He is also well regarded for his expertise in defamation and public law as it applies to the media sector. **Strengths:** "One of the best juniors around and has more experience than most of contentious data protection work. He is very bright and great to work with." "He has an unstuffy and practical approach. He's extremely bright and he has all the cases at his fingertips. He is particularly helpful in dealing with complex issues." **Recent work:** Represented Elaph Publishing in defending a claim brought both in defamation and data protection with respect to an article published by the defendant about Prince Moulay Hicham on its website.

Ian Helme (see p.657) Enters the rankings this year on the back of a growing reputation as an expert junior counsel in data protection matters. He has already played an instrumental role in the establishment of certain principles in the field, including the 'right to be forgotten'. **Strengths:** "He is really smart. He cuts to the point quickly and is very commercial." "He is extremely knowledgeable, excellent on his feet and someone who gives firm opinions on the merits and chances of success, which puts clients at ease."

Jonathan Scherbel-Ball (see p.747) Well regarded for the strength of his representation in a number of areas in information law, especially where it interacts with principles of privacy and reputation management. He has additional expertise in cases dealing with the application of Articles 8 and 10 ECHR. Strengths: "He is very strong in the crossover between reputation management and data protection. Genuinely engaged, committed and hugely diligent." "The energy that he brings to a case is absolutely phenomenal. A great team player, his ability to come up with pretty much every available legal argument for assessment is incredibly impressive." Recent work: Acted as junior counsel for Google in Belfast High Court in defending a claim under the DPA brought by George Galloway MP, a matter dealing with the liability of internet intermediaries for online content.

39 Essex Chambers

See profile on p.828

THE SET

A versatile and well-staffed set of accomplished information law barristers who are particularly noted for their experience in cases relating to the FOIA. Its members are regularly sought out by public authorities and private individuals as well as media groups who require advice or representation in information cases, many of which have elements of privacy law.

Client service: "I like the clerks a lot. They are fair, reasonable and responsive." David Barnes is the director of clerking at the set.

SILKS

Eleanor Grey QC Robust and well-regarded silk with a great deal of experience in handling cases in the information law arena, most often for public and regulatory bodies. She has substantial further experience in inquiries work. **Strengths:** "A hugely impressive advocate and a delight to deal with."

Richard Spearman QC (see p.758) Experienced silk with a diverse practice spanning a number of areas besides data protection, including defamation and media law. His expertise in data protection is complemented by his knowledge of IP and insurance. **Strengths:** "He has great integrity and intellect. He gets on with every judge and is able to map a clear path to judgment in his client's favour." **Recent work:** Successfully acted pro bono for the daughter of a woman who died after refusing medical treatment in proceedings addressing whether a grant of lifetime anonymity expires upon death.

JUNIORS

Rory Dunlop Highly respected junior with a broad-ranging practice in data protection and information law. He has appeared in a number of recent cases addressing information law issues relating to badger culls and has further expertise in relation to human rights. **Strengths:** "He is calm under pressure, client-friendly and clever." "He is very practical and pragmatic and a congenial person to be against." **Recent work:** Acted for the Foreign and Commonwealth Office in an appeal brought by the charity Reprieve seeking the release of an OSJA assessment of the human rights risks posed by the provision of assistance in counter-narcotics policing in Pakistan.

Matrix Chambers

See profile on p.864

THE SET

Offers a roster of highly able silks and juniors with a great deal of experience in representing media organisations, corporations, private individuals and public bodies in data protection and freedom of information matters. Members of Matrix Chambers are especially well versed in cases addressing the border between traditional defamation actions and the provisions of the DPA.

Client service: "Fantastic. The clerking is excellent, very helpful, and they have a very good team set-up who look after you." Cliff Holland manages the clerking team dealing with this area of work.

SILKS

Antony White QC (see p.781) Exceptionally capable silk with a stellar track record of appearing on behalf of major media organisations and internet intermediaries in a number of the most high-profile matters of recent years. He is especially experienced in handling cases at the border of reputation management and data protection. **Strengths:** "Just brilliant. He has the necessary gravitas to deal with the most significant of points and is one of the most client-friendly, team-spirited barristers I've ever had the privilege of working with." "His intellect is matched by his manner. Very strong, very calm, assured, authoritative and precise." **Recent work:** Acted for Google in a high-profile case brought by Max Moseley challenging the availability of search results for images of a sado-masochistic sex party at which he was present.

Hugh Tomlinson QC Tremendously experienced and versatile silk with a central focus on media and information law, defamation and privacy matters. He is frequently instructed in the most high-profile cases. **Strengths:** "He is brilliant. Extremely versatile, extremely client-focused, a jolly nice person to work with and his depth of knowledge is extraordinary." "A pleasure to work with. A leader in the field and always practical and pragmatic." **Recent work:** Represented the claimants in the Court of Appeal in the landmark case of Vidal-Hall.

JUNIORS

Lorna Skinner (see p.755) Rises to the top tier of juniors this year amid growing acclaim for her expertise in handling information law matters, particularly those connected to the media industry. She has additional prowess in handling defamation and reputation management cases. **Strengths:** "She is very good on her feet and consistently gives sensible, pragmatic advice." "She is very good with clients and a very good advocate in court who judges tribunals well." **Recent work:** Acted for Times Newspapers in defending a claim brought under the DPA and misuse of private information, in which a central element of the defence was the protection afforded to media organisations under s.32 DPA.

Sara Mansoori An accomplished defamation junior who enjoys a growing reputation in the realm of information law and data protection. **Strengths:** "She is very considered, very good at thinking through the nuances of cases and has an extremely good mastery of the detail." "She has very good judgement and is extremely experienced." **Recent work:** Acted for six claimants in actions brought against the Home Secretary for damages arising from alleged breaches of the DPA as a consequence of the unintended publication of details of their immigration status.

Monckton Chambers

See profile on p.865

THE SET

Monckton offers an exceptionally accomplished roster of silks and juniors who are highly experienced in handling matters in the realms of European law, telecommunications and competition law. The work of the set in information law often arises in conjunction with one or more of these areas, and the barristers have further expertise in cases addressing the application of the Environmental Information Regulations. Members of Monckton are comfortable representing public bodies, individuals, corporations as well as the Information Commissioner in data protection proceedings in a variety of fora.

Client service: "Queries are dealt with promptly and professionally and the advice provided is very good." David Hockney is the senior clerk at the set.

SILKS

Gerry Facenna QC (see p.631) Takes silk this year on the back of a highly successful junior career, in which he gained significant expertise in a wide range of practice areas. His work in this area spans the full range of information law, and has a particular focus on cases with a public or EU law angle. **Strengths:** "He is a delightful advocate; tough, focused and engaging. His cross-examination of witnesses is pleasant for all in court and he gets to the heart of the matter." "He is good on his feet and good in writing, he speaks the clients' language and he cuts to the chase." **Recent work:** Represented charity Reprieve on behalf of two Burmese migrants sentenced to death in Thailand for the murder of two backpackers. This was a High Court case seeking to compel the release of data relating to the two men that was held by the Metropolitan Police.

JUNIORS

Laura Elizabeth John Experienced junior with a long track record of appearing successfully on behalf of the Information Commissioner in both tiers of the Tribunal. She has recently argued cases dealing with issues arising from the application of FOIA, the DPA and the EIR. **Strengths:** "She communicates well with clients and is an excellent advocate." "She is extremely able and can spin on a sixpence. She gets the right tone before the ICO." **Recent work:** Acted for the Information Commissioner in a case seeking the release of information concerning the contract under which West Ham United became the new 'anchor tenant' at the Olympic Stadium.

Ben Lask Acts for a range of clients, including public bodies, the Information Commissioner and private individuals and companies. He has further expertise in relation to telecommunications and competition law matters. **Strengths:** "He showed excellent technical knowledge on the issue at hand and explained the reasoning behind it very clearly." "He was very thorough, methodical and thoughtful in his advice."

Julianne Morrison Enters the numerical rankings this year amid growing appreciation from peers and clients alike for her adept handling of a range of cases in information law. She has further expertise in relation to competition and public law matters. **Strengths:** "Julianne is extremely knowledgeable on data protection and information law. She is able to think strategically and can quickly gain a foothold in new areas of law." "She can be relied upon to provide consistently impressive written and oral advice while remaining personable and approachable." **Recent work:** Appeared on behalf of Rights Watch UK in a case seeking the publication of the advice of the Attorney General concerning the legality of lethal drone strikes in Raqqah, Syria.

Other Ranked Lawyers

Philip Coppel QC (Cornerstone Barristers) Enjoys an excellent reputation both as a practitioner with a great deal of experience in appearing in a number of headline cases in the data protection realm and as the author of the leading textbook in the field. His work in information law matters often overlaps with his expertise in local government issues. **Strengths:** "He is thorough and technically excellent." "He is very personable, approachable and can look at issues in data protection with a problem-solving mind." **Recent work:** Represented the claimant in a case in the High Court brought under s.7 DPA requesting all data held on him by the directors of his apartment block and seeking compensation for breach of data protection principles.

Oliver Sanders (1 Crown Office Row) A solid junior in data protection matters, with experience in representing a number of government entities, charities and educational bodies in proceedings in a range of fora. He is a member of the Treasury A Panel of counsel. **Strengths:** "An extremely good lawyer. His paperwork is exceptional." "He is excellent on the law and on the tactics of a case." **Recent work:** Represented the Home Office in six linked test cases arising out of the accidental publication of the personal details of over 6,000 illegal immigrants online.

Rhodri Williams QC (see p.784) (Henderson Chambers) Experienced junior silk with deep expertise in acting on behalf of local government entities and public bodies in judicial review proceedings. His work in data protection often overlaps with the field of employment law. **Strengths:** "A very tenacious and determined advocate."

Jonathan Barnes (5RB) Joins the rankings this year on the back of increasingly recognised expertise in data protection matters. His practice centres on the intersection of media law, reputation management and information law. **Strengths:** "He is friendly and knows what he's talking about when it comes to data protection. It is reassuring to have him on board." "He is excellent; he is always a few steps ahead of the opposition." **Recent work:** Acted for a group of over 4,000 current and former employees of Morrisons seeking damages as a result of a data breach in which a disgruntled employee posted the details of thousands of employees' payroll information. The group contends that the supermarket is liable for the breach.

Richard Munden (5RB) Enjoys a reputation as a robust advocate with a great deal of experience of handling significant defamation and privacy matters as well as data protection cases. He has acted for police forces, private individuals and commercial organisations in matters alleging breaches of the DPA. **Strengths:** "He is very clear and has great judgement. It is great to have him on your side." "He is friendly, affable and you can talk quite frankly and confidently with him." **Recent work:** Acted for the claimant in a significant case combining arguments under libel and the DPA.

Contents:

LONDON

Defamation/Privacy
Leading Sets
Band 1
One Brick Court *
5RB *
Band 2
Matrix Chambers *
Leading Silks
Star individuals
Caldecott Andrew *One Brick Court* *
Band 1
Barca Manuel *One Brick Court* *
Browne Desmond *5RB*
Millar Gavin *Matrix Chambers*
Page Adrienne *5RB*
Price James *5RB*
Rampton Richard *One Brick Court* *
Rogers Heather *One Brick Court* *
Tomlinson Hugh *Matrix Chambers*
White Antony *Matrix Chambers* *
Band 2
McCormick William *Ely Place Chambers (ORL)* ◊
Nicklin Matthew *5RB*
Rushbrooke Justin *5RB*
Spearman Richard *39 Essex Chambers (ORL)* ◊ *
Band 3
Bailin Alex *Matrix Chambers* *
Garnier Edward *One Brick Court* *
Hudson Anthony *Matrix Chambers*
Thwaites Ronald *The Chambers of Ronald Thwaites (ORL)* ◊
New Silks
Evans Catrin *One Brick Court* *
Proops Anya *11KBW (ORL)* ◊ *
Vassall-Adams Guy *Matrix Chambers* [A] *
* *Indicates set / individual with profile.*
[A] *direct access (see p.24).*
◊ *(ORL) = Other Ranked Lawyer.*
Alphabetical order within each band. Band 1 is highest.

Defamation/Privacy
Leading Juniors
Star individuals
Sherborne David *5RB*
Band 1
Bennett William *5RB*
Dean Jacob *5RB* *
Eardley Aidan *One Brick Court* *
Glen David *One Brick Court* *
Marzec Alexandra *5RB*
Phillips Jane *One Brick Court* *
Skinner Lorna *Matrix Chambers* *
Speker Adam *5RB*
Wolanski Adam *5RB*
Band 2
Barnes Jonathan *5RB*
Busuttil Godwin *5RB* *
Helme Ian *One Brick Court* *
Mansoori Sara *Matrix Chambers*
Band 3
Jolliffe Victoria *5RB*
Michalos Christina *5RB*
Munden Richard *5RB*
Palin Sarah *One Brick Court* *
Reed Jeremy *Hogarth Chambers (ORL)* ◊ [A]
Silverstone Ben *Matrix Chambers*
Starte Harvey *One Brick Court* *
Wilson Kate *One Brick Court* *
Band 4
Addy Caroline *One Brick Court* *
Atkinson Timothy *One Brick Court*
Craven Edward *Matrix Chambers* *
Hirst David *5RB*
Scherbel-Ball Jonathan *One Brick Court* *
Shore Victoria *5RB*
Up-and-coming individuals
Ready Hannah *One Brick Court* *

Band 1

One Brick Court
See profile on p.815

THE SET

A premier libel and privacy set that is home to a raft of leading experts, including eminent silks and talented junior barristers. It houses members with an almost unparalleled depth of experience and expertise across the spectrum of media law, who handle data protection, libel, breach of confidence, privacy and contempt cases. The set gains fantastic acclaim from instructing solicitors who commend its "exceptional barristers" for being "very user-friendly and ever ready to help."

Client service: The clerking team is described as "very efficient and effective," and senior clerk David Mace is described as "pragmatic, responsive and helpful."

SILKS

Andrew Caldecott QC (see p.609) A runaway star of the Defamation and Privacy Bar, widely regarded as the leading silk in the area. He has unrivalled Supreme Court experience and is continually instructed in high-profile, precedent-setting cases. **Strengths:** "A genius. His knowledge is astonishing and his feel for a case is always spot-on. His advocacy is excellent." "He must be one of the top silks in the country. He's just amazing – a decent person and phenomenally clever." "Working with Andrew was the best moment in my career. He brings an electric focus to a case and has such charm and gravitas in court that judges are naturally inclined to what he has to say. A genuine talent." **Recent work:** Defended the BBC against a claim brought by a prominent Imam relating to use of the word 'jihad'.

Manuel Barca QC (see p.589) Highly sought-after media silk with expertise covering the full breadth of reputation management. He is instructed by major media organisations and broadcasters and is highlighted for his well-honed advocacy style. **Strengths:** "He gives consistently good advice and is very good with clients." "He is robust, gutsy and friendly." **Recent work:** Acted for AOL in a Court of Appeal case to test of the meaning of the s. 1 'serious harm' threshold.

Richard Rampton QC (see p.747) Considered a go-to senior counsel on complex libel claims who has a strong track record in precedent-setting cases. He continues to act for newspaper groups and publishers in defamation proceedings. **Recent work:** Acted for the defendant in the long-running Flood v Times Newspapers litigation.

Heather Rogers QC (see p.754) Superb media silk who maintains a busy libel and data protection and privacy practice. She is considered a go-to for defamation claims and film-related litigation. **Strengths:** "She is a leader; a really thoughtful and talented practitioner." "She has formidable forensic skills, gives cogent advice and is a pleasure to work with." **Recent work:** Defended Elaph Publishing against proceedings brought by His Highness Prince Moulay Hicham in the Court of Appeal.

Edward Garnier QC (see p.650) Accomplished media barrister with several decades of experience in defamation, confidence, contempt and freedom of information cases. His practice is underpinned by a parallel career in politics: he was Solicitor General in 2010-12 and has served as an MP since 1992. **Recent work:** Acted for Lord McAlpine in a successful libel claim against Sally Bercow.

Catrin Evans QC (see p.641) New silk who has a phenomenal reputation at the Defamation Bar and is frequently a top choice among instructing solicitors for sensitive libel and DPA claims. **Strengths:** "Her reputation as the top junior at the Defamation Bar was fully merited, and has now been recognised with her appointment as a QC this year. She is clever, hardworking and calm, and has extremely good tactical awareness and judgement." "She will clearly do very well – she's been brilliant for years." **Recent work:** Defended Associated Newspapers in proceedings brought by Ashton Kutcher and Mila Kunis under the DPA.

JUNIORS

Aidan Eardley (see p.638) Outstanding reputation for media law matters with a strong track record acting both for and against the media. He draws praise for his understanding of the DPA and his strong advocacy skills. **Strengths:** "He is very impressive and provides very good advice on privacy." **Recent work:** Acted for Katie Price in a libel claim against her ex-husband and former manager.

David Glen (see p.654) A barrister with a fine reputation for his libel and privacy work, who regularly acts as sole counsel as well as alongside leading silks on prominent cases. He represents a range of media organisations, tech companies and individuals in media disputes. **Strengths:** "He is extremely bright and someone you would want fighting your corner." "He is incredible and a great strategist." **Recent work:** Defended Associated Newspapers in a claim for defamation and malicious falsehood initiated by Optical Express.

Ian Helme (see p.669) Senior defamation junior who is particularly well regarded for data protection and freedom of information matters. **Strengths:** "He has an excellent grasp of the overlap between libel and data protection law and has excellent judgement. He is a very clear advocate and is not afraid to take on silks in court." **Recent work:** Represented the defendants in McGrath & Anr v Bedford & Anr, a dispute between two rival water purification companies involving claims for malicious falsehood and defamation.

Jane Phillips (see p.737) Well-regarded junior specialising in media litigation. She acts for a number of high-profile celebrity clients and media organisations in sensitive disputes. She also provides pre-publication advice to book publishers and broadcasters. **Strengths:** "I would recommend her for her clear, prompt, thorough and excellent advice." "She is very calm and has a sharp legal mind." "She is highly experienced and has an ability to grasp the key issues and deliver constructive advice. She is approachable, versatile and good at managing clients' expectations." **Recent work:** Acted for the BBC in a libel claim brought by a prominent Imam relating to the use of the word 'jihad'.

Sarah Palin (see p.732) Popular junior who draws praise for her advocacy skills and busy defamation and privacy practice. She is best known for acting on behalf of newspaper groups and media organisations. **Strengths:** "I have used her on defamation claims and have been very impressed." **Recent work:** Acted for Associated Newspapers in libel proceedings brought by J. K. Rowling.

Harvey Starte (see p.771) Highly experienced barrister who acts for both claimants and defendants in media disputes. He also provides advice on pre-publication to newspapers and magazines. **Strengths:** "He is hugely experienced and has good judgement. He delivers advice in a client-friendly manner and has excellent drafting skills." **Recent work:** Represented Oisin Tymon in a libel claim against Express Newspapers.

Kate Wilson (see p.798) Frequently involved in high-profile libel and privacy claims, with recent experience in the Supreme Court. She has niche expertise in online issues and claims involving public authorities. **Strengths:** "She is tremendous – her knowledge of the law is very impressive and she is able to act on instructions swiftly and in an unflappable manner." **Recent work:** Successfully defended St George's Healthcare NHS Trust against a libel claim brought by the mother of a former patient.

Caroline Addy (see p.579) Experienced practitioner who represents clients in cases involving media and information law, as well as human rights law. She has particular expertise in search engine and ISP liability issues. **Strengths:** "Has the confidence of the judges and is wonderful at handling difficult opponents with grace and charm." **Recent work:** Defended Abertawe Bro Morgannwg University Local Health Board in a libel claim brought by a surgeon employee.

Jonathan Scherbel-Ball (see p.759) Defamation and data protection practitioner who is well respected by broadcasters and other media organisations for defence work. His practice is augmented by his previous in-house experience at the BBC. **Strengths:** "He has a genuinely encyclopaedic knowledge of this area of law." "He's fantastic – incredibly responsive, really sharp and not afraid to give a frank view, which is refreshing." **Recent work:** Acted for Google in defamation proceedings initiated by MP George Galloway.

Hannah Ready (see p.749) Up-and-coming barrister who is quickly establishing a reputation as a leading junior at the Defamation Bar. She is well regarded for Supreme Court matters due to her previous experience as a judicial assistant. **Strengths:** "She's an exceptional junior; she's good at drafting, responsive and hard-working." "She is very impressive; gives excellent advice in conference and on paper. A rising star." **Recent work:** Defended Dai Havard MP in defamation proceedings initiated by one of his constituents.

5RB

See profile on p.905

THE SET

5RB is a formidable set that has long been respected for its position as a chambers at the forefront of this sector. It is known for its indisputable quality in the areas of defamation, privacy, contempt and data protection. Its members have a strong legacy of excellence in high-profile and landmark cases. Interviewees praise the barristers here for being "completely on top of the law," and say "they provide first-class advice, are commercially aware and a pleasure to deal with."

Client service: "The clerks are always very helpful in understanding a client's needs and delivering a fast, friendly and expert service. Jamie Clack is swift to respond, commercially minded and attentive." The clerking team is led by Andrew Love.

SILKS

Desmond Browne QC Former Chairman of the Bar and joint head of chambers, he has a phenomenal reputation in defamation and privacy circles. He is instructed in cutting-edge cases and injunctions. **Strengths:** "He is very approachable and judges like him." "Highly experienced and accomplished advocate with a keen sense of strategic appreciation. Knows the law inside-out. Respected by judges and feared by opponents." **Recent work:** Represented Tim Yeo in a libel claim against Times Newspapers.

Adrienne Page QC Highly experienced media silk with a broad practice spanning malicious falsehood, harassment, defamation and privacy. **Strengths:** "Adrienne Page is a brilliant legal mind and a pleasure to work with." "She is so precise and all over the facts." **Recent work:** Acted for Lachaux in a trial of preliminary issue to determine the threshold of the s. 1 'serious harm' test.

James Price QC A leading QC in all aspects of defamation. He is frequently instructed in seminal libel cases against newspapers. **Strengths:** "James Price QC is extremely bright and reliable." **Recent work:** Acted for Gary Flood in a libel claim against Times Newspapers.

Matthew Nicklin QC Highly sought after for his expertise and depth of experience in complex libel claims. He appears regularly before the Court of Appeal and the Supreme Court. **Recent work:** Acted for Mir Shakil-ur-Rahman in libel and harassment proceedings relating to a total of 25 TV broadcasts.

Justin Rushbrooke QC Relatively recent silk who is in continual high demand for his strong advocacy skills and understanding of the DPA. He has niche expertise in corporate libel claims and disclosure orders. **Strengths:** "He provides a very insightful view of cases." "He is fantastic with clients, putting them at ease and explaining legal concepts clearly." **Recent work:** Defended Piotr Tymula in libel proceedings initiated by Svetlana Lokhova.

JUNIORS

David Sherborne Star junior barrister who wins unanimous praise from peers for his privacy practice. He remains at the forefront of phone hacking litigation and continues to receive instructions in landmark libel and privacy cases. **Strengths:** "He has acted on many of the leading media decisions over the last 12 months. A true expert in his field and a pleasure to work with." "The go-to barrister on privacy cases, at the heart of phone hacking."

William Bennett Specialist media junior focusing on libel, breach of confidence and privacy. He regularly appears as sole counsel and is led by eminent silks in the field. **Strengths:** "One of the leading juniors at the Bar with a very busy practice. He is an excellent advocate who has conducted a number of trials. He's a pleasure to work with." **Recent work:** Acted for Gary Flood in a long-running libel claim against Times Newspapers.

Jacob Dean (see p.631) Premier junior in the media sector who frequently appears both as sole counsel in major cases and under the direction of leading silks. He has appeared before the Supreme Court and Court of Appeal on a number of occasions. **Strengths:** "He is absolutely brilliant. His intelligence and quick mind make him exceptionally good on his feet. A thoughtful strategist, full of common sense and very tactful with difficult opponents." **Recent work:** Acted for the defendant publisher in Rhodes v OPO which was heard by the Supreme Court.

Alexandra Marzec Has an enviable reputation in the area of libel and privacy litigation. She is particularly proficient in media defence, having acted for newspapers, private investigators and other members of the press in phone hacking claims. **Strengths:** "She is approachable and is tenacious when you want her to be."

Adam Speker Superb junior barrister with a broad media practice, encompassing all aspects of reputation management, privacy and media defence. He has appeared in the Privy Council unled, and led by top silks before the Supreme Court. **Strengths:** "He is always exceptionally well prepared and thinking well ahead of the game." "He is creative, has a good eye for detail and is very intelligent." **Recent work:** Acted as sole counsel in a successful appeal in the Privy Council overturning the Court of Appeal's judgement in the libel case of Kieron Pinard-Byrne v Lennox Linton.

Adam Wolanski Leading defamation junior who is valued by instructing solicitors for his client management skills and well-honed advocacy style. He acts for and against the major media organisations and newspapers in high-profile disputes. **Strengths:** "He has a certain way with the court and always ends up sounding like the core voice of authority." "He is a real expert in media and defamation, he does not mince his words and provides astute, honest and commercial advice to clients." **Recent work:** Defended Conde Nast against allegation of contempt following an article published in GQ during the Rebekah Brooks trial.

Jonathan Barnes Experienced junior acting mainly for claimants in claims concerning reputation, including libel, privacy and harassment proceedings. He is well regarded for his expertise in data privacy matters. **Strengths:** "He knows each section of complex areas of the law and how best to deploy them." "He is experienced in large data breaches and has an approachable and friendly manner." **Recent work:** Acted for Alvaro Sobrinho in a libel claim against Impresa Publishing.

Godwin Busuttil (see p.608) Top defamation junior counsel with a raft of expertise in privacy, conspiracy, data protection, online harassment and libel. He has co-authored much of the leading commentary on the practice area. **Strengths:** "He has an encyclopaedic knowledge of the law." **Recent work:** Represented Lachaux in a trial of preliminary issue relating to the meaning of the s. 1 'serious harm' test.

Christina Michalos Specialist media junior with additional expertise in IP and sports law. She has expert knowledge of defamation, freedom of information, the DPA and online issues. **Strengths:** "She is very good and very experienced."

Victoria Jolliffe Accomplished media law junior focusing on reputational matters for claimants and defendants. She has niche expertise in Norwich Pharmacal applications, and privacy and harassment injunctions. **Strengths:** "She is one of the best defamation juniors at the Bar." "She is very knowledgeable and a pleasure to work with." **Recent work:** Junior counsel representing Tim Yeo in his libel claim against Times Newspapers.

Richard Munden Experienced junior counsel with broad expertise in media matters, including claims involving the DPA and traditional libel matters. **Strengths:** "He is very client-friendly and delivers advice in a reassuringly confident manner." "He is a very able junior defamation expert." **Recent work:** Acted for seven professional footballers in a libel claim against News Group.

David Hirst Highly lauded defamation and privacy junior with a niche focus on online matters such as internet harassment, tracing and disclosure orders against ISPs. He also advises corporate entities and media organisations on pre-publication. **Strengths:** "I can't praise David Hirst highly enough. He is marvellous: incredibly clever, provides excellent advice and is a real expert in the fields of defamation and privacy." "His knowledge of ISP and online enforcement law is very impressive."

Victoria Shore Practises in the area of media law with expertise spanning libel, online harassment, privacy and breach of confidence. She also provides pre-publication advice to newspaper clients. **Strengths:** "She is a joy to work with – exceptionally fast in providing advice, clever, commercially aware, down-to-earth, good-humoured and practical."

Band 2

Matrix Chambers

See profile on p.876

THE SET

Matrix Chambers has a flourishing defamation practice that is home to a number of high-profile and in-demand barristers from senior to junior level. Its members act for claimants and defendants in a range of disputes concerning reputation management and privacy. The set is said to understand the increasing conflation of defamation and data protection law particularly well.

Client service: "They are a well-clerked set of chambers and have been since they were set up." "The clerks are very responsive and helpful, whilst the fees team are very pragmatic and reasonable to deal with when negotiating fees." Cliff Holland leads the clerking team that deals with these cases.

SILKS

Gavin Millar QC Premier defamation and privacy specialist who is often the media's first port of call for their most sensitive and important cases. He has wide-ranging media expertise in freedom of press, reporting restrictions and contempt cases and acts for all the major newspaper groups and their journalists. **Strengths:** "He is the best media silk currently practising." "He is the leading Article 10/ journalist's adviser and advocate. Particularly skilled in promoting Reynolds defences in complex cases." **Recent work:** Acted for the Sunday Times in Tim Yeo v Times Newspapers.

Hugh Tomlinson QC Widely regarded as a top-flight privacy silk who has been at the forefront of developments in the law in terms of privacy and defamation. He is frequently called upon for assistance on emergency injunctions. **Strengths:** "He is still the go-to privacy silk. He has led the era of reputation management." "He is excellent and very knowledgeable in his field. He is always able to give you a view on something quickly." **Recent work:** Acted for the claimant in the privacy case PJS v News Group Newspapers in the Court of Appeal.

Antony White QC (see p.793) Eminent media silk who is held in high regard for his knowledge of defamation law and the DPA. He is highlighted by instructing solicitors for his strong advocacy skills. **Strengths:** "He is extremely intelligent and a heavyweight on the most complex intermediary liability and data protection matters." "A very wise head with gravitas and deep knowledge – a go-to senior counsel when you are dealing with high-profile or complex areas." **Recent work:** Defended Associated Newspapers in a privacy action brought by Paul Weller.

Anthony Hudson QC Relatively new silk who offers expertise across the gamut of media law, including harassment, data protection and libel claims. **Strengths:** "He is fantastic – he is down-to-earth and he understands media law better than anyone. He is experienced, gets the big picture and advises clients well." **Recent work:** Defending Thomson & Ors in harassment and defamation proceedings brought by Issam Hourani.

Alex Bailin QC (see p.587) Well-regarded silk who maintains a broad practice encompassing media and criminal law. He is particularly well regarded for public law matters, open justice and reporting restrictions. **Strengths:** "He is extremely knowledgeable and gets on well with clients, who like his down-to-earth manner." **Recent work:** Represented a number of media organisations including the BBC, Guardian and the Mirror Group in the Litvinenko Inquiry.

Guy Vassall-Adams QC (see p.786) Media and information law specialist who took silk in 2016. He has a strong track record of success in high-profile media claims involving press intrusion and defamation. **Strengths:** "Displays unparalleled commitment, focus and energy." **Recent work:** Acted in the Google Oxford Mail case where the ICO has issued an enforcement notice against Google for refusing to remove search results from the Google search engine under the 'right to be forgotten'.

JUNIORS

Lorna Skinner (see p.767) Leading media and information law junior who is crafting a strong reputation in the fields of defamation, misuse of private information and data protection. She is highly experienced in injunctions, Supreme Court matters and high-profile disputes. **Strengths:** "She is incredibly bright, with a pragmatic and constructive approach to cases. She is excellent on human rights issues and good in conference and on her feet." **Recent work:** Acted for the mother of 'Jihadi John' in libel proceedings against The Times and The Telegraph.

Sara Mansoori Impressive media junior specialising in privacy, defamation and information law. She is experienced in phone hacking claims and regularly acts for celebrities and people in the public eye. **Strengths:** "Absolutely first-class. She has a very good manner with clients and shows exceptional attention to detail." "She has an impressive ability to digest complicated cases and cut to the key issues. She is excellent on privacy law." "She always makes herself available and her attention to detail is excellent." **Recent work:** Junior counsel for Meg Mathews in her phone hacking claim against MGN.

Ben Silverstone Impressive junior with a broad practice covering the full ambit of media law. He is regularly involved in high-profile defamation and data protection cases. **Strengths:** "A real up-and-coming star." "He's extremely good to work with and very intellectually capable. He's a lovely, genuine guy and that is reflected in the quality of his practice." **Recent work:** Junior counsel for Times Newspapers in a libel claim brought by Tim Yeo.

Edward Craven (see p.626) Junior barrister who has established an enviable reputation in the field of libel and privacy. He has a wealth of experience in phone hacking claims and is frequently instructed in a variety of other media disputes. **Strengths:** "He is a rising star in his area of expertise, whose opinion is highly valued by both solicitors and clients."

Other Ranked Lawyers

Ronald Thwaites QC (The Chambers of Ronald Thwaites QC) Highly experienced media silk who is famed for his superlative trial and jury skills. He has a versatile practice that sees him acting for both claimants and defendants in a variety of media disputes.

William McCormick QC (Ely Place Chambers) Considered a go-to practitioner for defamation and contempt matters. Highly valued for his cross-examination and advocacy skills. **Strengths:** "He is a first-class tactician and always impressive on his feet. He brings a magical touch to analysis and deployment of his skills." "He has a really lovely advocacy style." "He is charming, energetic and a master with the press." **Recent work:** Acted for Quindell in a libel claim against Gotham City Research.

Richard Spearman QC (see p.770) (39 Essex Chambers) Remains at the forefront of developments in the law in relation to privacy and injunctions. Continues to act for private clients and corporations on data privacy and commercial cases. **Strengths:** "He is a lovely advocate." **Recent work:** Represented News International in a claim against the police to recover data collected during the phone hacking investigation and prosecution.

Jeremy Reed (Hogarth Chambers) Well-regarded junior who is frequently instructed in phone hacking claims and a range of other privacy-related matters. **Strengths:** "A pleasure to work with. He is extremely knowledgeable, especially in relation to phone hacking. He is very approachable and easy to work with and really knows what's going on." **Recent work:** Acted for various claimants in phone hacking claims against MGN.

Anya Proops QC (see p.744) (11KBW) New silk who has an impressive depth of expertise in data protection, media and information law. She is widely viewed as spearheading the move towards the use of the DPA in the protection of reputation. **Strengths:** "An exceptional and very talented new silk. Knocks the competition out of the park. Likely to play a significant role in shaping the future of this practice area." "A first-class all-rounder and excellent on her feet." **Recent work:** Acted for Global Witness in a claim brought by Steinmetz regarding the DPA and journalistic freedom.

Contents:

LONDON

Education
Leading Sets
Band 1
11KBW *
Band 2
Matrix Chambers *
Band 3
39 Essex Chambers *
Senior Statesmen
Senior Statesmen: distinguished older partners
Beloff Michael *Blackstone Chambers (ORL)* ◊
Leading Silks
Band 1
Giffin Nigel *11KBW* *
Mountfield Helen *Matrix Chambers*
Oldham Peter *11KBW* *
Sheldon Clive *11KBW* *
Wolfe David *Matrix Chambers*
Band 2
Bowen Nicholas *Doughty Street Chambers (ORL)* ◊ Ⓐ
Goudie James *11KBW* *
Grodzinski Sam *Blackstone Chambers (ORL)* ◊
Band 3
Morris Fenella *39 Essex Chambers*
Pearce Robert *Radcliffe Chambers (ORL)* ◊ *
Warnock Andrew *1 Chancery Lane (ORL)* ◊ Ⓐ
Wise Ian *Monckton Chambers (ORL)* ◊ Ⓐ
New Silks
Squires Daniel *Matrix Chambers*
White Gemma *Blackstone Chambers (ORL)* ◊
* *Indicates set / individual with profile.*
Ⓐ *direct access (see p.24).*
◊ *(ORL) = Other Ranked Lawyer.*
Alphabetical order within each band. Band 1 is highest.

Education
Leading Juniors
Band 1
Clement Joanne *11KBW* *
Hannett Sarah *Matrix Chambers* Ⓐ
Lawson David *Serjeants' Inn Chambers (ORL)* ◊ Ⓐ *
Moffett Jonathan *11KBW* Ⓐ *
Band 2
Armstrong Nicholas *Matrix Chambers*
Broach Steve *Monckton Chambers (ORL)* ◊
Cornwell James *11KBW* *
Cross Tom *11KBW* *
Friel John *3PB Barristers (ORL)* ◊ Ⓐ
Hay Deborah *Deborah Hay (ORL)* ◊
Rawlings Clive *Doughty Street Chambers (ORL)* ◊ Ⓐ
Scolding Fiona *Outer Temple Chambers (ORL)* ◊ Ⓐ
Sharland Andrew *11KBW* Ⓐ *
Stout Holly *11KBW* *
Walker Amelia *1 Crown Office Row (ORL)* ◊
Band 3
Anderson Jack *39 Essex Chambers*
Auburn Jonathan *11KBW* Ⓐ *
Bicarregui Anna *39 Essex Chambers* Ⓐ
Darwin Claire *Matrix Chambers* *
Edwards Denis *Francis Taylor Building (ORL)* ◊ Ⓐ
Greatorex Paul *11KBW* Ⓐ *
Hyams Oliver *Devereux (ORL)* ◊ *
Kamm Rachel *11KBW* *
Luh Shu Shin *Garden Court Chambers (ORL)* ◊
McColgan Aileen *Matrix Chambers*
Purchase Mathew *Matrix Chambers* *
Ward Galina *Landmark Chambers (ORL)* ◊
Band 4
Amraoui Thomas *39 Essex Chambers*
Eddy Katherine *11KBW* *
Lawrence Anne *4-5 Gray's Inn Square (ORL)* ◊
Oldham Jane *11KBW* *
Pratley Michelle *39 Essex Chambers* Ⓐ *
Tkaczynska Anna *Arden Chambers (ORL)* ◊ *
Wilson Lachlan *3PB Barristers (ORL)* ◊
Up-and-coming individuals
Desai Raj *Matrix Chambers*
Prochaska Elizabeth *Matrix Chambers* *
Thelen Jennifer *39 Essex Chambers*

Band 1

11KBW

See profile on p.867

THE SET

11KBW stands alone as the best set for education law and handles cases covering nursery, primary, secondary and tertiary education. Its members act for both claimants and defendants including schools, teachers and local authorities. Recent work includes Al Furqan Trust v Al Furqan Primary School, a complex case concerning land held under UK Education legislation being used for an Islamic school, and H v A London Borough Council, a matter concerning special educational needs (SEN) provision. One enthusiastic source comments: "The barristers are superb and have a real depth of public law and local authority knowledge."

Client service: The clerking team is led by joint senior clerks Lucy Barbet and Mark Dann. "The clerks are very good and efficient – they are always very helpful and easy to contact. We have always had very positive involvement with them." "The clerks are brilliant – the speed of response is really good and they provide a really good service."

SILKS

Nigel Giffin QC (see p.653) Has over three decades of experience of advising on both education-specific matters and a vast array of issues that intersect with education law. He is particularly adept at judicial review cases. **Strengths:** "Has superb judgement as to the likely strength of a case and exudes real gravitas." "A joy to work with. He's incisive, completely on top of the law and a great advocate." **Recent work:** Represented the individuals in R (Morris and Thomas) v Rhondda Cynon Taf County Borough Council, a case challenging proposed austerity measures affecting nursery provision.

Peter Oldham QC (see p.729) Acts in all kinds of education-related litigation including discrimination, contract and admissions cases involving both schools and universities. He also has extensive expertise in governance and reorganisation matters. **Strengths:** "He is quick to see the main points of the argument and has a good analytical and practical approach to matters. He also has a good understanding of the client's position." "He takes the subject very seriously and is an attractive advocate." **Recent work:** Counsel in Delair v Manor Park School, a significant Article 9 ECHR claim relating to a pupil's right to pray in school.

Clive Sheldon QC (see p.763) An erudite silk who handles education law as part of a broad public law practice. He is frequently engaged in SEN, admissions and exclusions and discrimination claims. **Strengths:** "Excellent – he is very clear and quick in terms of his advice and has a very strong understanding of the issues." "He's very friendly and a very powerful advocate." **Recent work:** Advised in Davis v Westminster City School, a dispute involving a school's decision on moving an excluded pupil to another placement.

James Goudie QC (see p.657) An accomplished education practitioner with experience in a variety of other areas including administrative law, environmental law and employment law. He regularly advises local government and universities in challenges against admissions procedures and construction projects. **Strengths:** "A very knowledgeable and eloquent advocate who is well respected by the judges." "Technically excellent, well respected and someone who makes himself available at short notice." **Recent work:** Acted for the Schools' Adjudicator in a case involving the London Oratory School's admissions policy.

JUNIORS

Joanne Clement (see p.619) A dynamic education junior with particular expertise in cases concerning SEN, school reorganisations and academy conversions. She has a strong track record advising local authorities, universities and schools. **Strengths:** "Clearly a rising star, she is very knowledgeable and authoritative. A tough opponent." "She is very experienced in judicial review, a fact that comes across in the quality of the strategic advice she provides." **Recent work:** Represented the respondent in R (Foisal) v Glyndwr University, a judicial review challenging the exclusion of a student for failure to pay tuition.

Jonathan Moffett (see p.720) Has a burgeoning education practice and frequently handles disputes relating to school admissions, discrimination and educational provision for pupils with SEN. He has considerable court experience, having appeared before various courts including the ECHR. **Strengths:** "He is very approachable, easy to communicate with and extremely helpful. He has a really thorough knowledge of his subject." "He's able to pick matters up really late in the day, get up to speed and diagnose a strategy. All of this he does with a great sense of humour." **Recent work:** Acted as counsel to the UK government concerning an SEN matter before the ECHR. The case concerned an alleged lack of education provision for a schoolchild covering a period of almost twelve months.

James Cornwell (see p.624) Represents a range of public and private schools and universities in cases concerning admissions, exclusions and funding issues to name but a few. He has handled a number of judicial review, negligence, contract and discrimination claims for such clients and has also acted for central government. **Strengths:** "Clever and very experienced." **Recent work:** Junior counsel for the school in Mr and Mrs X v Governing Body of a School, an Upper Tribunal appeal concerning the interpretation of the Equality Act 2010 (Disability) Regulations 2010.

Tom Cross (see p.627) Has a thriving practice handling education, commercial law and human rights-related cases, and also has particular experience in religious matters. He is regularly instructed by individuals, schools and higher education institutions. **Strengths:** "He is incredibly user-friendly, extremely authoritative and very quick to get the issues." "A standout barrister, he fights the client's corner very hard, but in a way that results in settlement." **Recent work:** Represented the school in Billings v Hope Academy, a complex case relating to discrimination and physical abuse.

Andrew Sharland (see p.762) He is on the Attorney General's A Panel of counsel and routinely advises local authorities, schools and further education colleges. Sharland is highly praised for his knowledge of SEN, admissions and contract law. **Strengths:** "He is very down-to-earth, bright and incisive." "He gives pragmatic advice and is a measured advocate." "Recommended for judicial review work, he has brilliant client-handling skills and is a pleasure to work with." **Recent work:** Advised a university on an internal employment matter concerning a high-profile academic who was alleged to have bullied his then head of department.

Holly Stout (see p.774) Has extensive experience of acting in proceedings before the First-tier Tribunal, Upper Tribunal, Court of Appeal and High Court. She is adept at judicial review challenges, exclusions and school closure disputes. **Strengths:** "Intellectually exceptional," she is noted for her "depth of knowledge and deft handling of the law." "She is excellent for complex cases and very clear in her advice." "She processes and delivers matters very quickly, is user-friendly and is good on her feet." **Recent work:** Advised the university in Ramey v University of Oxford, a judicial review application to consider the lawfulness of the university's harassment policy.

Jonathan Auburn (see p.586) Advises an array of prominent clients in the education sector including public and private schools and colleges. Areas of particular interest include child protection, judicial review and discrimination claims. **Strengths:** "Extremely knowledgeable and approachable, and a barrister with good client care skills and a thorough grasp of the law. He inspires confidence." "Very efficient, he's extremely quick with the papers and machine-like in turning things around quickly." **Recent work:** Acted as counsel in a challenge at the Administrative Court relating to appropriate education provision for a child while out of school.

Paul Greatorex (see p.659) A popular choice for a number of different education cases including those concerning Equality Act claims, student disputes and academy conversions. **Strengths:** "A knowledgeable and forceful advocate who doesn't pull his punches but says it like it is. He is not afraid to express what is needed to get the best result in a case even if it doesn't sit too well with the client." "He is very good at communicating with clients and he understands the wider context of the sector."

Rachel Kamm (see p.687) A public law junior with a broad practice that combines expertise in education, data protection and community care law, among other areas. She has a strong track record acting for clients in highly contentious matters. **Strengths:** "A very clear and impressive advocate." "She provides practical solutions and doesn't watch the clock all the time. You don't feel pressurised." **Recent work:** Acted for an accountant at a maintained school in Brent who was accused of conspiring with other school employees to increase salaries and bonuses.

Katherine Eddy (see p.639) A well-known education practitioner with considerable experience in disputes, including those that involve aspects of public law, contract law and employment law. She is also well versed in Court of Protection issues and academy work. **Strengths:** "She is very good on the law and has a clear and direct advocacy style which is very persuasive." "Very sensible and commercial, she always displays good judgement, and is good at adapting to the level of service that we want." **Recent work:** Represented the Glyndwr University in several public law and contract disputes concerning fraudulent Test of English for International Communication certificates.

Jane Oldham (see p.729) Advises on a range of cases including judicial review challenges, local authority disputes, and matters relating to academies. Clients include a host of schools and higher and further education institutions. **Strengths:** "She gets straight to the heart of an issue and gives clear, concise advice. She has a particularly client-friendly manner and the ability to summarise complex issues."

Band 2

Matrix Chambers

See profile on p.876

THE SET

A cutting-edge set, known for its prowess in public law and human rights cases, that has extensive expertise in a wide range of education matters. Members here are well versed in handling issues relating to admissions, exclusions, SEN and discrimination. They advise an array of clients including individuals and institutions, acting for universities, NGOs, local authorities and the Department for Education. Recent work handled includes the landmark Supreme Court matter of R (Tigere) v Secretary of State for Work and Pensions, and St Mary Magdalene Academy v Secretary of State for the Home Department, two distinct cases concerning the crossover between immigration and education law. Instructing solicitors say: "The set is fantastic. All of the barristers are very approachable and you can easily talk through issues with them. They provide good, clear advice."

Client service: Lindsay Scott is the chief executive and Jason Housden is the senior practice manager. "Their clerks are fantastic – they are really efficient, responsive and well organised. Everyone seems to know what is going on and you don't always have to speak to the same clerk. They are very good at diarising."

SILKS

Helen Mountfield QC A pre-eminent education silk who regularly appears before the Supreme Court in high-profile litigation. She is a seasoned authority when it comes to equality law, safeguarding and forced academisation. **Strengths:** "A very experienced advocate who is insightful on the legal issues and has a keen eye for detail." "Her written work is amazing – she is able to cut through mounds and mounds of information and get all of it in, without annoying the judge." "She's very practical, clear-thinking and accessible."

David Wolfe QC A leading light in this market, who has been acting in significant education matters for over 20 years. He specialises in judicial review and frequently advises individuals, education groups and organisations. **Strengths:** "An excellent advocate who is great with clients and superb at drafting." "Just phenomenal – he will get a point straight away and just run with it. He's incredibly bright and at the pinnacle of his profession in terms of this area of the law." **Recent work:** Acted for the parents in Fox v Secretary of State for Education, a High Court case considering the lawfulness of the revised content for GCSE Religious Studies.

Daniel Squires QC A prominent education silk and a member of the Treasury A Panel. He is highly commended for his knowledge of community care and employment law and has appeared in several important education cases before the Court of Appeal, High Court and SEND tribunal. **Strengths:** "He has a very good intellect and is very experienced." "He's fantastic – he is willing to chat things through and he readily gives us his thoughts – he doesn't have to go away and think about things a great deal."

JUNIORS

Sarah Hannett Noted for her detailed understanding of SEN, human rights and exclusions matters. She is also extremely adept at advising clients on the implications of the Prevent duty. **Strengths:** "Extremely bright and easy to work with. She demonstrates a real commitment to education law and can be trusted to provide sound advice." "Very prompt and can deal with huge volumes of information in a small space of time. Her drafting is fantastic and she gets fantastic results. Her knowledge and expertise really make a difference to those that instruct her." **Recent work:** Advised Just For Kids Law in the leading Supreme Court case of R (Tigere) v Secretary of State for Business, Innovation and Skills, a matter concerning access to university funding for students without indefinite leave to remain in the UK.

Nicholas Armstrong Has a strong reputation in the education sector and routinely counsels schools, colleges and universities on a variety of issues. He is well versed in equality law, and issues relating to school reorganisation and the Prevent duty. **Strengths:** "Nick is a very strong, robust and determined individual who is a really good junior." "He is very tenacious and has a high degree of success. His arguments are always very compelling." **Recent work:** Acted in a Supreme Court case looking at the lawfulness of provisions excluding certain classes of migrant from student loan arrangements.

Claire Darwin (see p.629) An expert in education law, human resources and discrimination matters. She is also a member of the Attorney General's B Panel and is often engaged to advise on professional misconduct issues and judicial review proceedings. **Strengths:** "A real team player whose sector knowledge is excellent – she is able to tell you what is happening and she can quickly talk about strategy and the merits of the case." "She is very considerate, flexible and highly respected. A very good technical lawyer." **Recent work:** Acted in National College for Teaching and Leadership v Razwan Faraz, a complex, high-stakes employment and professional conduct case.

Aileen McColgan Has a growing practice that takes in SEN proceedings, equality law claims and other important advisory work. She acts for both claimants and defendants including prominent universities and local authorities. **Strengths:** "She has an excellent analytical mind and is a solid advocate and drafter. She is consistently reliable, she always listens, and she is a pleasure to instruct." "She uses her previous experience as an academic to advise on matters where academic practice and procedures are in dispute." **Recent work:** Junior counsel in R (Hunt) v North Somerset Council, a Supreme Court appeal concerning austerity measures and the duty imposed by the Education Act 1996.

Mathew Purchase (see p.745) An erudite education specialist with a deep knowledge of judicial review, contract law and school exclusion matters. He also represents a diverse list of clients in complex equality law claims. **Strengths:** "He is extremely clever and approachable and very reliable. He always does what he says he will do and he lets you know if he isn't going to meet a deadline. He is very sympathetic to clients' needs" but "has good judgement and is able to persuade clients not to run something if necessary."

Raj Desai Has good experience in the field of education law and is a sound choice for judicial reviews and SEN appeals. **Strengths:** "Very approachable, thorough and committed to the needs of vulnerable clients." "He offers very impressive advocacy and he is sharp when responding to comments being raised. His written work and analysis of the facts and legislation is really detailed." **Recent work:** Advised on the implications of the Supreme Court's landmark judgment in Tigere, a case looking at student loan eligibility for those without permanent immigration status. He was subsequently instructed to advise on and draft numerous post-Tigere urgent judicial reviews.

Elizabeth Prochaska (see p.744) A former judicial assistant to Baroness Hale and Lord Brown who is now enjoying a flourishing career at the Bar. She handles education cases as part of her wide-ranging public law and civil liberties practice. **Strengths:** "Exceptionally intelligent – her written work is of the highest standard." "She is responsive and able to obtain very successful outcomes. She makes you look at cases in a slightly different, but effective way."

Band 3

39 Essex Chambers

See profile on p.840

THE SET

A thriving set with a strong bench of experienced barristers, many of whom are members of the Attorney General's Panels of Counsel to the Crown. Equality Act, educational negligence and human rights matters feature prominently in its education law caseload. Members frequently represent clients before independent appeal panels and other specialist tribunals and are instructed by the full range of individuals and educational institutions across the sector. Their recent work has included Hancock v Birmingham City Council, a local authority matter concerning SEN provision, and McDonald v Birmingham City Council Independent Review Panel, a contentious exclusion dispute. Observers remark: "The barristers are really excellent – they are very communicative and quick in terms of their turnaround of papers."

Client service: David Barnes is the chief executive and director of clerking and Alastair Davidson and Michael Kaplan are senior clerks. "The clerks are extremely friendly and very willing to negotiate fees – they are very accommodating." "They are always quick to respond and very efficient."

SILKS

Fenella Morris QC A seasoned local government silk with wide-ranging expertise covering social care and procurement, as well as education law. She is particularly well known for her advocacy skills and frequently appears in major cases before the Supreme Court and ECHR. **Strengths:** "Highly respected and very sound." "She absolutely knows her stuff."

JUNIORS

Jack Anderson Handles complex and high-value SEN appeals and educational judicial reviews for both claimants and defendants. He often represents local authorities, the Department for Education, Ofsted and schools, and has extensive experience before the Administrative Court and Upper Tribunal. **Strengths:** "He is just super clever – he is quick and very attentive to detail. He is responsive and you can trust his judgement completely." "He is very precise and academic. On his feet he is very measured; he quietly takes everything in and challenges things in a non-confrontational way."

Anna Bicarregui A well-known public law junior with over a decade of experience. Her main areas of focus include education, human resources and Court of Protection matters. **Strengths:** "Highly knowledgeable, supportive and efficient." "She is very friendly and approachable."

Thomas Amraoui An impressive education lawyer with strong knowledge of the Equality Act who is an expert at admissions and exclusions disputes. He is frequently engaged by local authorities to handle complex judicial reviews. **Strengths:** "He is an impressive and confident junior who is very good at cross-examination." **Recent work:** Defence counsel in Myers v Stanford Junior School. This was a case challenging a school's decision to refuse a pupil leave of absence for a holiday.

Michelle Pratley (see p.742) Has a thriving practice in local government, community care and education law and has been practising in those areas for ten years and more. She routinely represents local authorities, schools, higher education institutions and individuals. **Strengths:** "She is brilliant – she is really fabulous with clients and has a nice gentle manner which works very well in the tribunal. She manages to impress the judges and when she needs to be tough she can be."

Jennifer Thelen Considered a solid option for those seeking counsel on SEN proceedings, discrimination claims or school exclusion disputes. She is also sought out for higher education matters involving contract law. **Strengths:** "She takes a really pragmatic and sensible approach and is very clear and straightforward about things." "She has very good knowledge of education law and is very thorough in her preparation." **Recent work:** Acted in Old Co Operative Day Nursery v Ofsted, a judicial review into an Ofsted inspection report that was brought by a nursery.

Other Ranked Lawyers

Anna Tkaczynska (see p.781) (Arden Chambers) Has strong skills in education law and also extensive expertise in housing, Court of Protection and local government law. She predominantly acts for individuals and local authorities. **Strengths:** "Extremely good at putting clients at ease and understanding complex issues quickly." "She always responds really quickly and has a clear understanding of the needs of the client." **Recent work:** Acted for the appellants in Mr & Mrs West v West Berkshire County Council, a case concerning whether a school was meeting a child's therapy needs.

Michael Beloff QC (Blackstone Chambers) Frequently acts in high-profile education, public law and EU law cases before the Supreme Court, ECJ and ECHR. He is well versed in disputes relating to prominent institutions in the higher education sector. **Strengths:** "An enormously impressive advocate who is highly persuasive and has a stellar reputation."

Sam Grodzinski QC (Blackstone Chambers) Has vast experience in civil liberties, education and local government work. He often acts in leading cases before the Court of Appeal and Supreme Court. **Strengths:** "A superb advocate who is great with clients." "He's very smart."

Gemma White QC (Blackstone Chambers) Represents both sides in contentious education cases, and handles employment and contract-related disputes concerning both schools and higher education institutions. She has additional experience in school admissions, human rights and Equality Act claims. **Strengths:** "Gemma is patient, unflappable and excellent with clients. She delivers speedy and incisive advice." "She really goes the extra mile, her advocacy is really good and she is generally a very steady hand."

Andrew Warnock QC (1 Chancery Lane) Offers a broad range of services to education clients, and also has expertise in crossover matters involving aspects of social care, safeguarding and professional negligence. He routinely advises major local government clients. **Strengths:** "He is very knowledgeable and calm and a very good advocate who is straightforward in his approach." **Recent work:** Acted for the respondent in Winstanley v Leeds University, a dispute relating to the marking of a PhD paper.

Amelia Walker (1 Crown Office Row) Maintains an excellent reputation in the market for her work across the fields of education, local government and regulatory law. She acts in a broad range of school-related matters, appearing in professional misconduct, SEN and abuse of process cases. **Strengths:** "Extremely knowledgeable and very competent." "She's a safe pair of hands who picks up cases very quickly. Her oral advocacy is very good."

Deborah Hay A sole practitioner who continues to impress with her outstanding knowledge of education law, and has represented an array of clients in highly contentious court and tribunal matters. **Strengths:** "She was very responsive and acted on our behalf very forcibly." "She is very committed and hugely experienced. She does huge amounts of appeal work for parents and family members."

Oliver Hyams (see p.679) (Devereux) Has a growing practice and deals regularly with judicial reviews and SEND tribunal appeals. He acts for a diverse list of clients including schools, universities and colleges. **Strengths:** "Absolutely excellent, he's very switched on and user-friendly." "He is a specialist in education who is technically very adept and strong on his feet." **Recent work:** Junior counsel in R (CD) v Westminster City School, an application for permission to review the lawfulness of regulations surrounding academy exclusions.

Nicholas Bowen QC (Doughty Street Chambers) Represents a range of clients including parents with disabled children, in fraught education disputes with local authorities. He also has significant expertise in Community Care and Court of Protection work. **Strengths:** "Really charming, he has a relaxed style of advocacy and is pragmatic and sensible. He's not an aggressive advocate."

Clive Rawlings (Doughty Street Chambers) Represents a range of clients in complex education cases including private individuals, education institutions and local authorities. He frequently appears in cases before the Court of Appeal, Administrative Court and First-tier Tribunal. **Strengths:** "Extremely knowledgeable and experienced, particularly in complex cases." "He is incisive in his analysis and good at drafting in a focused and user-friendly way."

Denis Edwards (Francis Taylor Building) Acts for both claimants and defendants in court and tribunal proceedings involving a number of different areas including education. He is particularly noted for his expertise in admissions and exclusions matters and equality law claims. **Strengths:** "A measured and thorough advocate."

Shu Shin Luh (Garden Court Chambers) A leading education and community care junior with a strong background advising vulnerable clients including children. She frequently advises parents in relation to complex equality claims. **Strengths:** "She is tenacious and very bright – she knows the law and is very committed." "Offers reliable, honest and clear advice and has an eye on strategy." **Recent work:** Counsel in R (SA) v Kent CC, a case considering the educational needs of migrant care leavers who have uncertain immigration status.

Anne Lawrence (4-5 Gray's Inn Square) An innovative education practitioner who is well versed in child protection, SEN provision and social care matters. She has impressive experience in cases concerning admissions and exclusions, and fitness to practice. **Strengths:** "Gets the bit between her teeth and is forceful."

Galina Ward (Landmark Chambers) An expert in SEN matters, amongst others, with over 15 years experience at the Bar. She routinely acts for individuals, schools and local authorities in complex education cases and judicial reviews. **Strengths:** "She is very thorough and provides very good technical arguments." "A powerful and effective advocate."

Ian Wise QC (Monckton Chambers) Has an active appellate practice and handles a wide range of important education, public law and human rights matters. He is routinely instructed by national charities and has strong knowledge of equality law. **Strengths:** "Always extremely impressive." "He's very knowledgeable and highly tactical in his approach." **Recent work:** Advised in R (Messenger Jones & Bell) v Secretary of State for Business, Innovation and Skills, a matter relating to the government's provision of Disabled Students Allowance.

Steve Broach (Monckton Chambers) A notable public law junior who acts for a number of prominent clients in the education sector. Much of his work is concerned with the educational needs of disabled children and those with SEN, as well as young people with learning difficulties and/or disabilities **Strengths:** "His knowledge of the law surrounding disabled children is hard to beat." "He always pushes new ideas to do with this area of the law and his attention to detail stands out as a definite strength." **Recent work:** Instructed in JH v Cheshire West and Chester Council, an application to appeal a decision to not provide an EHC Plan to a child with complex needs.

Fiona Scolding (Outer Temple Chambers) Maintains an excellent standing at the Education Bar and has over two decades of experience in education and public law. She is particularly adept at cases involving discrimination, and is also an expert at community care and Court of Protection work. **Strengths:** "A great advocate with a thorough grasp of the law. She is very skilled, extremely personable and is someone with a no nonsense approach to getting the right result for the client." "She is calm and gives clients very realistic and effective advice." **Recent work:** Represented a Greek Orthodox school in an application for judicial review which had been brought against it relating to the wearing of a headscarf whilst in school.

John Friel (3PB Barristers) An impressive junior at the cutting edge of legal reform in education. He often advises on matters relating to education and disability, and is highly sought after by educational institutions in both the private and public sector. He also represents charities and governing bodies. **Strengths:** "He is well organised and extremely good at advancing clients' cases." "He has an encyclopaedic knowledge of SEN in particular." **Recent work:** Advised in LW v Norfolk County Council, a case reported in The Educational Law Reports.

Lachlan Wilson (3PB Barristers) Head of the Public and Regulatory Law Group at his set, who has an active practice encompassing a multitude of education issues. He is frequently instructed by individuals, institutions and school governing bodies connected with primary, secondary and tertiary education provision. **Strengths:** "He is superb with clients and has the ability to instil confidence. He is super bright, quickly gets to the nub of the issue and is a really good strategist."

Robert Pearce QC (see p.735) (Radcliffe Chambers) A seasoned litigator and mediator with extensive expertise in education and charity law. He is frequently instructed by prominent universities and schools. **Strengths:** "Very good at succintly describing a legal case, he is extremely clever and always on top of his subject." "Very authoritative and able to provide good practical solutions." **Recent work:** Lead counsel for the University in University of London v Prag, a complex dispute concerning the Warburg Institute.

David Lawson (see p.697) (Serjeants' Inn Chambers) Undertakes a great deal of judicial review work involving schools, higher education institutions and local authorities. He also has significant expertise in cases concerning SEN provision. **Strengths:** "He is practical, focused and clearly very experienced." "He is really good with clients and makes them feel at ease – he really takes the time to explain what is happening and what he is doing." **Recent work:** Counsel in R (Nyoni) v Secretary of State for Business, Innovation and Skills, an access to university funding claim following the decision in Tigere.

Contents:

LONDON

Election Law	
Leading Silks	
Band 1	
Millar Gavin	*Matrix Chambers*
Mountfield Helen	*Matrix Chambers*
Price OBE Richard	*Littleton Chambers* *
Straker Timothy	*4-5 Gray's Inn Square*
Leading Juniors	
Band 1	
Dias Sappho	*4-5 Gray's Inn Square*
Hoar Francis	*Field Court Chambers* [A]

** Indicates individual with profile.*

[A] direct access (see p.24).

Alphabetical order within each band. Band 1 is highest.

Ranked Lawyers

Timothy Straker QC (4-5 Gray's Inn Square) Versatile public law silk with strong courtroom skills and experience. He routinely advises on issues relating to complex referenda, European and parliamentary elections. **Strengths:** "An excellent advocate who is thorough and a fine tactician." **Recent work:** Acted with regard to the Tower Hamlets mayoral election petition, the longest hearing of its kind for 25 years.

Sappho Dias (4-5 Gray's Inn Square) Well versed in a range of high-profile election matters, she has acted for several local authority returning officers regarding general and local elections. She was recently retained by the Electoral Commission for the Scottish Referendum and by several local authorities for the General Election. **Strengths:** "Incredibly user-friendly and knows election law inside out." **Recent work:** Acted in Williams v Patrick & others, creating and successfully arguing the principle that losing petitioners before Electoral Commissions must pay for the court costs.

Francis Hoar (Field Court Chambers) An expert in various aspects of election law and proceedings concerning political parties. He often advises in connection with major election petitions and regularly assists campaigning bodies on election issues. Hoar really came to prominence when he secured a High Court judgment that voided the election of Lutfur Rahman as Mayor of Tower Hamlets, despite being against two QCs. **Strengths:** "He was extremely thorough and he really had a great will to uncover anything that would assist the case." **Recent work:** Acted in Baxter v Fear & Ors, a petition arising from a mistake by a returning officer, whereby two wards received the wrong ballot papers.

Richard Price OBE QC (see p.743) (Littleton Chambers) Erudite litigator with an established career at the Bar spanning over four decades. Has significant expertise in media law, IP and election law, and regularly tries local government election petitions for the Election Commissioner. He also edits the leading textbook on electoral law. **Strengths:** "Always impresses with the professional and courteous way in which he conducts cases."

Gavin Millar QC (Matrix Chambers) A renowned election law specialist with over two decades of experience in this field. He has appeared in a number of ground-breaking electoral law matters over the years. **Strengths:** "He's a complete expert in the area of electoral law and he has been in most of the important cases so knows the area like the back of his hand." **Recent work:** Acted for the respondent, Nadine Dorries MP, in Ireland v Dorries (Mid-Bedfordshire Petition), a petition challenging her victory at the General Election.

Helen Mountfield QC (Matrix Chambers) A well-known election law silk with extensive experience in general election petitions and advisory work for candidates, parties and campaigning organisations. She regularly appears for clients in the Supreme Court and has strong expertise in civil liberties. **Strengths:** "She is very bright, diligent and knowledgeable. She is also excellent with clients and provides brilliant written work." **Recent work:** Instructed by NCVO to advise on the implications of the Transparency of Lobbying Bill.

Contents:

LONDON

Employment
Leading Sets
Band 1
Blackstone Chambers *
11KBW *
Littleton Chambers *
Matrix Chambers *
Band 2
Cloisters *
Essex Court Chambers *
Old Square Chambers *
Band 3
Devereux *
Outer Temple Chambers *
* Indicates set / individual with profile.
A direct access (see p.24).
◊ (ORL) = Other Ranked Lawyer.
Alphabetical order within each band. Band 1 is highest.

Employment	
Leading Silks	
Star individuals	Segal Oliver *Old Square Chambers* *
Cavanagh John *11KBW* *	**Band 3**
Goulding Paul *Blackstone Chambers*	Brennan Timothy *Devereux*
Hochhauser Andrew *Essex Court Chambers*	Ciumei Charles *Essex Court Chambers*
Jeans Christopher *11KBW* *	Ellenbogen Naomi *Littleton Chambers*
Linden Thomas *Matrix Chambers*	Ford Michael *Old Square Chambers* *
Reade David *Littleton Chambers*	Galbraith-Marten Jason *Cloisters* *
Rose Dinah *Blackstone Chambers*	Gott Paul *Fountain Court Chambers (ORL)* ◊ *
Band 1	Mountfield Helen *Matrix Chambers*
Allen Robin *Cloisters* *	Pitt-Payne Timothy *11KBW* *
Bloch Selwyn *Littleton Chambers* *	Randall Nicholas *Matrix Chambers*
Carr Bruce *Devereux*	Sheldon Clive *11KBW* *
Epstein Paul *Cloisters*	Sutton Mark *Old Square Chambers*
Hendy John *Old Square Chambers* *	White Antony *Matrix Chambers* *
Jones Seán *11KBW* *	Williams Heather *Doughty Street Chambers (ORL)* ◊
Laddie James *Matrix Chambers*	**Band 4**
McNeill Jane *Old Square Chambers* *	Bourne Charles *11KBW* A *
Monaghan Karon *Matrix Chambers*	Bryant Keith *Outer Temple Chambers*
Oudkerk Daniel *Essex Court Chambers*	Burns Andrew *Devereux* *
Short Andrew *Outer Temple Chambers*	Carss-Frisk Monica *Blackstone Chambers*
Stilitz Daniel *11KBW* *	Choudhury Akhlaq *11KBW* *
Band 2	Crasnow Rachel *Cloisters* *
Algazy Jacques *Cloisters* *	Duggan Michael *Littleton Chambers*
Brown Damian *Littleton Chambers*	Green Patrick *Henderson Chambers (ORL)* ◊ A *
Clarke Andrew *Littleton Chambers*	Howe Robert *Blackstone Chambers*
Craig David *Essex Court Chambers*	Lynch Adrian *11KBW* *
Devonshire Simon *11KBW* *	Romney Daphne *Cloisters* *
Glyn Caspar *Cloisters* *	Tolley Adam *Fountain Court Chambers (ORL)* ◊ *
Griffiths Martin *Essex Court Chambers*	**New Silks**
Mansfield Gavin *Littleton Chambers* *	Cohen Jonathan *Littleton Chambers*
Mulcahy Jane *Blackstone Chambers*	Collins Ben *Old Square Chambers* *
Nicholls Paul *Matrix Chambers*	Proops Anya *11KBW* *
Ritchie Stuart *Fountain Court Chambers (ORL)* ◊ *	Tatton-Brown Daniel *Littleton Chambers*

Band 1

Blackstone Chambers

See profile on p.813

THE SET

A leading employment set comprising a group of "supremely good barristers" who provide advice and guidance across the full range of employment law. Many practitioners have extensive experience of High Court litigation matters and they often handle highly complex tribunal cases. Specialisms within the group range from restrictive covenant and injunctive relief work to highly complex and highly sensitive discrimination and unfair dismissal claims. Its members have been involved in several key cases over the last year defining approaches to anti-suit injunctions and holiday pay disputes.

Client service: "The clerks are very responsive and incredibly approachable – they are always very keen to quote within the clients' means." "The clerking team is very efficient, well run and offers a slick service." Gary Oliver leads the clerking team.

SILKS

Paul Goulding QC Pre-eminent lawyer in restrictive covenants, with sources noting his "definitive knowledge" and "authoritative view." He is widely regarded as a leading light of the Employment Bar, handling the most complicated issues including team moves and whistle-blowing litigation. **Strengths:** "He is assured, enormously experienced and technically knowledgeable; he is a very reassuring presence to have in your camp." "He is ferociously clever, his attention to detail is second to none and he breaks down the most complicated issues piecemeal and explains them well to clients, who love him as a result." **Recent work:** Instructed in Petter v EMC Europe Ltd & EMC Corporation, a complex case on anti-suit injunctions and the Brussels I Regulation on jurisdiction.

Dinah Rose QC Has an established reputation as a formidable advocate who is incisive in her cross examination. Sources note her tactical approach to cases and her ability to command authority in tribunal and court settings. She is particularly strong in discrimination and equal pay cases. **Strengths:** "She has a crystal-clear way of thinking through very complex legal questions and is amazing on her feet. It is a lesson in advocacy when you instruct her." "Truly formidable – she combines incredible intellect and speed of thought with outstanding advocacy." **Recent work:** Represented trade union Usdaw in an appeal revolving around collective redundancies arising from the Woolworths insolvency.

Jane Mulcahy QC Highly experienced barrister praised by sources for her exceptional client skills and her impressive cross-examination in tribunal and Court of Appeal cases. She works across the whole breadth of employment law, with demonstrable expertise in discrimination and wrongful dismissal cases. **Strengths:** "She is extremely client-friendly and is good at putting the client at ease because she is unflappable." "She develops an excellent rapport with clients, is extremely responsive and her reputation as an immaculately prepared and excellent advocate is thoroughly deserved."

Monica Carss-Frisk QC Has extensive experience of employment law issues, with particular focus on injunctive relief matters and working time regulations. She is particularly adept at handling all manner of discrimination claims, including cases of sex, age, race and disability discrimination. **Strengths:** "Hugely impressive and knowledgeable." "Exceptionally calm and persuasive." **Recent work:** Instructed in Ministry of Defence v Fletcher, a complex Employment Tribunal case examining the power to award exemplary damages in a discrimination case.

Robert Howe QC Praised by sources for bringing a commercial edge to his employment work. Regularly instructed in High Court litigation, including difficult restrictive covenant issues and complex wrongful dismissal cases. **Strengths:** "He is fearsomely bright and brilliant on his feet in court." **Recent work:** Instructed by Ondra LLP in a £10 million dispute with a former senior executive over alleged ownership share of the LLP and notice pay.

Employment

Leading Juniors

Star individuals

- **Leiper** Richard *11KBW* *

Band 1

- **Cooper** Ben *Old Square Chambers* *
- **Kibling** Thomas *Matrix Chambers*
- **McCafferty** Jane *11KBW* *
- **Nawbatt** Akash *Devereux* *
- **Sen Gupta** Diya *Blackstone Chambers*
- **Sethi** Mohinderpal *Littleton Chambers* *

Band 2

- **Belgrove** Sophie *Devereux* *
- **Brittenden** Stuart *Old Square Chambers* *
- **Cheetham** Simon *Old Square Chambers* *
- **Coghlin** Thomas *Cloisters* *
- **Croxford** Thomas *Blackstone Chambers*
- **de Silva** Niran *Littleton Chambers*
- **Edge** Andrew *11KBW* *
- **Forshaw** Simon *11KBW* *
- **Jolly** Schona *Cloisters* *
- **Lewis** Jeremy *Littleton Chambers*
- **McCann** Claire *Cloisters* *
- **Mehrzad** John *Littleton Chambers* *
- **Michell** Paul *Cloisters* *
- **Milsom** Chris *Cloisters* *
- **Motraghi** Nadia *Old Square Chambers* *
- **Neaman** Sam *Littleton Chambers*
- **Newton** Katharine *Old Square Chambers* *
- **O'Dempsey** Declan *Cloisters* *
- **Pilgerstorfer** Marcus *11KBW* *
- **Quinn** Chris *Littleton Chambers* *
- **Rogers** Amy *11KBW* *
- **Solomon** Adam *Littleton Chambers*

Band 3

- **Barnett** Daniel *Outer Temple Chambers*
- **Bone** Lucy *Littleton Chambers* *
- **Brown** Edward *Essex Court Chambers*
- **Callaghan** Catherine *Blackstone Chambers*
- **Chudleigh** Louise *Old Square Chambers* *
- **Clarke** Gerard *Blackstone Chambers*
- **Darwin** Claire *Matrix Chambers* *
- **Davis** Carol *Littleton Chambers*
- **de Marco** Nick *Blackstone Chambers*
- **Edwards** Peter *Devereux* *
- **Fodder** Martin *Littleton Chambers*
- **Halliday** Patrick *11KBW* *
- **Martin** Dale *Littleton Chambers* *
- **Purchase** Mathew *Matrix Chambers* *
- **Sendall** Antony *Littleton Chambers* *
- **Shepherd** Jude *42 Bedford Row (ORL)* ◊
- **Sheridan** Matthew *Littleton Chambers* *
- **Stone** Judy *11KBW* *
- **Tuck** Rebecca *Old Square Chambers* *
- **Windle** Victoria *Blackstone Chambers*

Band 4

- **Allen** Andrew *Outer Temple Chambers*
- **Beale** Anna *Cloisters* *
- **Bell** Laura *Devereux*
- **Brown** Tom *Cloisters* *
- **Chan** Susan *42 Bedford Row (ORL)* ◊
- **Criddle** Betsan *Old Square Chambers* *
- **Davies** Charlotte *Littleton Chambers*
- **Donnelly** Kathleen *Henderson Chambers (ORL)* ◊ [A] *
- **Gardiner** Bruce *2TG - 2 Temple Gardens (ORL)* ◊ [A] *
- **Ling** Naomi *Outer Temple Chambers*
- **Masters** Dee *Cloisters* *
- **Mayhew** Alice *Devereux* *
- **Misra** Eleena *Littleton Chambers* *
- **Musgrave** Caroline *Cloisters* *
- **Omambala** Ijeoma *Old Square Chambers* *
- **Panesar** Deshpal *Old Square Chambers* *
- **Prince** Laura *Matrix Chambers* *
- **Rajgopaul** Craig *Littleton Chambers*
- **Reindorf** Akua *Cloisters* *
- **Robson** Alexander *Littleton Chambers*
- **Salter** Michael *Ely Place Chambers (ORL)* ◊ *
- **Scott** Ian *Old Square Chambers*
- **Seymour** Lydia *Outer Temple Chambers*
- **Shiu** Ming-Yee *Littleton Chambers* [A]
- **Smith** Andrew *Matrix Chambers* *
- **Stout** Holly *11KBW* *
- **Tether** Melanie *Old Square Chambers* *
- **White** Robin *Old Square Chambers* *
- **Williams** Ed *Cloisters* *
- **Wynne** James *Littleton Chambers* *

Band 5

- **Adkin** Tim *42 Bedford Row (ORL)* ◊
- **Barsam** Talia *Devereux* *
- **Bickford Smith** James *Littleton Chambers* *
- **Blake** Andrew *11KBW* *
- **Brook** David *Henderson Chambers (ORL)* ◊ [A] *
- **Casserley** Catherine *Cloisters* *
- **Cordrey** Thomas *Devereux*
- **Cunningham** Naomi *Outer Temple Chambers*
- **Davies** Jonathan *Serjeants' Inn Chambers (ORL)* ◊ *
- **Dobbie** Olivia-Faith *Cloisters* *
- **Dyal** Daniel *Cloisters* *
- **Hare** Ivan *Blackstone Chambers*
- **Harris** Lucinda *Devereux* *
- **Holloway** Orlando *42 Bedford Row (ORL)* ◊
- **Iyengar** Harini *11KBW* *
- **Kemp** Edward *Littleton Chambers* *
- **Lee** Michael *11KBW* *
- **Massarella** David *Cloisters* *
- **McColgan** Aileen *Matrix Chambers*
- **McNair-Wilson** Laura *Littleton Chambers*
- **Melville** Elizabeth *Old Square Chambers* *
- **Milford** Julian *11KBW* *
- **Mitchell** David *Ely Place Chambers (ORL)* ◊ *
- **Mitchell** Jack *Old Square Chambers*
- **Pritchard** Simon *Blackstone Chambers*
- **Robinson** Laura *Tanfield Chambers (ORL)* ◊ *
- **Russell** Jane *Essex Court Chambers* *
- **Stephenson** David *1MCB (ORL)* ◊
- **Stone** Christopher *Devereux* *
- **Toms** Nick *Doughty Street Chambers (ORL)* ◊
- **Wilson** Julian *11KBW* *
- **Winstone** Hilary *Old Square Chambers* *

Up-and-coming individuals

- **Balmer** Kate *Devereux* *
- **Banerjee** Lydia *Littleton Chambers* *
- **Fear Davies** Harriet *Devereux*
- **Gordon Walker** Emily *Outer Temple Chambers* *
- **Margo** Saul *Outer Temple Chambers*

** Indicates individual with profile.*

[A] direct access (see p.24).

◊ (ORL) = Other Ranked Lawyer.

Alphabetical order within each band. Band 1 is highest.

JUNIORS

Diya Sen Gupta An effective and incisive advocate who is well reputed for her commercial acumen. She is highly proficient in whistle-blowing and discrimination issues, with experience of complex team move cases and injunctive relief applications. **Strengths:** "She can very quickly grasp the issues and the importance of the case to the client – she instils confidence in the client and is able to establish a rapport with them quickly." "Her cross-examination is very thorough and effective." **Recent work:** Defended Citibank against claims by a former foreign exchange trader after he was dismissed from the bank after sharing confidential client information. Obtained a restrictive reporting order to prevent the employee from naming Citibank's clients.

Thomas Croxford Widely acknowledged as a strong High Court advocate, he often handles highly complex injunctive relief work and sophisticated discrimination claims. His multidisciplinary practice allows him to bring a commercial edge to his employment law analysis and he is identified by sources as personable and approachable. **Strengths:** "An experienced pair of hands who is a favourite for injunction work and restrictive covenants." "He is an excellent advocate with a remarkable understanding of the law." **Recent work:** Instructed in Tarazi v Virtu, a multi-jurisdictional High Court case claiming that claw-back entitlement and restrictive covenants in a former employee's long-term incentive plan were void.

Nick de Marco Handles a broad employment law practice, with expertise in complex discrimination issues and Employment Tribunal cases. He has experience of High Court litigation, regularly obtaining injunctions and restrictive covenant enforcements for his clients. **Strengths:** "He's excellent at cross-examination and he has real gravitas and presence." **Recent work:** Instructed in General Municipal and Boilermakers Union v Henderson, an appeal before the Employment Appeal Tribunal (EAT) which ruled that belief in left-wing democratic socialism is protected by the Equality Act.

Catherine Callaghan Has a wide employment law practice, which is bolstered by her knowledge of personal discipline issues and human rights law. She is experienced at handling unfair dismissal claims and breach of contract issues. **Strengths:** "She is very knowledgeable with a strong background in discrimination claims." "She is very client-friendly, very approachable and very hard-working." **Recent work:** Acted for a hedge fund in a complex High Court case surrounding the enforcement of restrictive covenants, an employee's breach of contract and the enforceability of revocation provisions in a deferred compensation scheme.

Gerard Clarke Highly experienced employment law practitioner recognised for his expertise in restrictive covenant cases and employee competition issues as well as his understanding of issues relating to garden leave. He regularly represents clients in the High Court and sources appreciate his commercial and pragmatic approach to cases. **Strengths:** "He is very good with clients, is fearless on his feet and is willing to fight for them." "His ability to condense and summarise in minimal paperwork is almost poetic – the judicial comments are always very positive about his skeleton arguments." **Recent work:** Acted in a High Court case concerning the misuse of confidential information and unlawful competition.

Victoria Windle Highly skilled employment law barrister with additional strength in commercial law. She is particularly adept at advising on cases which require knowledge of employee privacy rights and workplace monitoring to identify wrongdoing. Clients especially highlight her ability to work efficiently with difficult parties and her commitment to her cases. **Strengths:** "She is very articulate and confident and is very persuasive in her writing." "She is tremendously bright and hard-working and is someone who is always willing to roll up her sleeves." **Recent work:** Acted in Ignis v Heming, a claim for breach of contract, confidence and copyright against an employee on garden leave.

Ivan Hare Has extensive experience across the whole gamut of employment law issues, which is supplemented by his expert knowledge of professional discipline issues. He is recognised as a skilled tribunal advocate and often defends healthcare clients in complex employment disputes. **Strengths:** "He is very accessible, a good advocate and he always delivers – he understands our organisation very well." **Recent work:** Represented the General Medical Council (GMC) in an appeal as to whether regulatory and qualifications-driven bodies such as the GMC are liable under the Equality Act 2010.

Simon Pritchard Established by sources as a highly effective advocate, he focuses his employment practice on whistle-blowing and unfair dismissal claims. He is praised for his client service skills and sources are keen to highlight his proficiency in discrimination cases. **Strengths:** "He is exceptionally intelligent and is a fantastic advocate, particularly during cross-examination." "He is a very impressive advocate and is very good at highlighting weaknesses as well as strengths." **Recent work:** Acted in Mortimer v King and Others, a complex High Court case revolving around restrictive covenants and a team move dispute.

11KBW

See profile on p.867

THE SET

11KBW has a deep bench of eminent silks and juniors who offer high-quality advice across the whole gamut of employment law, and have extensive experience of High Court, Employment Tribunal and appellate court proceedings. Its members handle complex matters for senior individuals, large multinational employers and governmental institutions, tackling the usual diet of employment cases and further assisting with corporate governance issues, bonus disputes and remuneration matters. Clients value the fact that this is "a very supportive set whose barristers are always very friendly and approachable." **Client service:** "The clerking team are superb; they could not be nicer or more accommodating. They will do what they say and get back to you within a deadline – they are utterly brilliant. A Rolls-Royce service." Mark Dann and Lucy Barbet are the senior clerks at chambers.

SILKS

John Cavanagh QC (see p.613) Specialises in complex holiday pay issues but also has extensive experience in discrimination allegations and high-profile unfair dismissal claims. He regularly represents foreign governments, large organisations and senior individuals in all manner of cases in the Employment Tribunal and EAT. **Strengths:** "He has a huge amount of experience in equal pay work and is a specialist in the working time field. He is a very approachable silk." **Recent work:** Acted in the ECJ in Lock v British Gas, a complex case analysing whether commission should be considered when calculating holiday pay and how retrospectively claims can be included.

Christopher Jeans QC (see p.682) Acts across all levels of the justice system, handling complex employment issues at the Supreme Court, the High Court and at tribunals across the country. Well known for his expertise in holiday pay, discrimination and pensions cases, he often acts for high-profile individuals and large organisations. **Strengths:** "Chris is one of the all-time greats – he is indefatigable and has a very impressive all-round knowledge of employment law." "His cross-examination is very good and he is not afraid to ask difficult questions."

Seán Jones QC (see p.686) Renowned amongst peers and clients alike for his extensive employment law knowledge and robust advocacy style. He is regularly instructed in highly complex employment cases, handling everything from discrimination claims and unfair dismissal cases to holiday pay and equal pay matters. **Strengths:** "Seán's intellect and grasp of complex employment law problems is second to none – he is a straight talker who builds fantastic relationships." "He is authoritative and engaging in court, has very good strategic judgement and is great with clients." **Recent work:** Represented a canon of the Church of England in Pemberton v Bishop of Southwell and Nottingham, who sought to contest a decision to refuse him chaplaincy because he was in a same-sex marriage.

Daniel Stilitz QC (see p.773) Has extensive experience acting both for and against financial services and professional services employers across the whole gamut of employment law. He is singled out for his strong litigation style and he often handles difficult discrimination, whistle-blowing and constructive dismissal claims. **Strengths:** "He is excellent; he is very hardworking, very thoughtful and very pleasant to work with." "He is an excellent advocate and has very good cross-examination skills." **Recent work:** Acted for Goldman Sachs defending a high-profile claim of sex discrimination and unequal pay brought by a female banker employee.

Simon Devonshire QC (see p.633) Handles commercially sensitive employment law issues and has established himself as a notable advocate for restrictive covenant and confidentiality issues, and is experienced in acting before the High Court. His practice is strengthened by his knowledge of whistle-blowing and TUPE dispute complications. **Strengths:** "His advocacy skills were very good – he made mincemeat of his opponents and he did an extremely good job." "He is extremely responsive and very good with clients – we feel that we are in safe hands."

Timothy Pitt-Payne QC (see p.739) Well known for his overlapping employment law and information law knowledge, Pitt-Payne QC has established a niche practice around employee privacy issues and data protection matters in the workplace. His practice is bolstered by his strength in discrimination cases. **Strengths:** "A very good, very persistent and very considered barrister." **Recent work:** Defended the University of Leicester against a claim of victimisation and discrimination brought by a senior employee against other senior officers.

Clive Sheldon QC (see p.763) Undertakes a range of employment work with a focus on high-profile discrimination claims and complex boardroom disputes. He regularly represents both employers and employees, and his practice is strengthened by his public law work and education law knowledge. **Strengths:** "He is extremely good in employment law cases with a public law or education dimension, and he gives very practical, succinct advice." "He is great on detail and is a very cerebral, academic lawyer." **Recent work:** Successfully acted for Buckinghamshire Fire & Rescue Services against an appeal made by two fire fighters that they were unfairly dismissed for not complying with certain driving instructions.

Akhlaq Choudhury QC (see p.617) Admired by peers for his effective advocacy, he has vast experience of representing influential clients in the High Court, with particular strength in securing and resisting complex injunctions. **Strengths:** "He is very good, very user-friendly and he is very sensitive to our issues." "He has an instant rapport with the client and gets a good grasp of the issues in a short space of time." **Recent work:** Acted in Re-use Collections Ltd v Sendall, a complex restrictive covenant case in which a former employee helped his sons set up a rival company. Akhlaq proved that the covenant restrictions were not valid as the firm had failed to provide consideration over the terms, which were added to the employee's contract shortly before his termination.

Charles Bourne QC (see p.600) Acts across all aspects of employment law, with particular expertise in whistle-blowing, discrimination and equal pay issues. His practice is strengthened by his High Court litigation experience, advising individuals on injunction applications and obtaining or resisting them in court. **Strengths:** "He has a very understated manner in submissions which is effective." "He is an elegant advocate." **Recent work:** Acting in O'Brien and Others v Ministry of Justice, a multifaceted case encompassing thousands of claims, including discrimination, following the Supreme Court's ruling on part-time judges' rights to pensions.

Adrian Lynch QC (see p.704) Operates a wide employment law practice with added expert knowledge in public law issues. He is highly experienced in TUPE and its complications, often advising public bodies and large corporate companies on possible solutions to TUPE-related issues. **Recent work:** Instructed by the EHRC in Mrazek & Others v EHRC, addressing complications surrounding TUPE legislation and the transfer of the right to salary progression.

Anya Proops QC (see p.744) Praised by sources for her extensive knowledge of discrimination law and whistle-blowing issues. She is also recognised as a formidable advocate in tribunal settings. **Strengths:** "She is an excellent advocate who has a really calming influence on clients." "Whistle-blowing is her niche and something she is very well known for." **Recent work:** Successfully defended HSBC against allegations from a former employer that he had been dismissed because of his religion and race. The claimant was claiming over £10 million in damages.

JUNIORS

Richard Leiper (see p.699) He is widely identified by peers as an impressive advocate who is formidable in cross-examination. He has a very broad employment practice, with particular expertise in difficult restrictive covenant issues and high-profile discrimination claims. **Strengths:** "An excellent mind, an accomplished cross-examiner and a master of equal pay issues." "The leading junior at the Employment Bar without doubt – he is a QC in a junior's clothing."

Recent work: Acted for a claimant in a claim against Goldman Sachs, who threatened to expose alleged sex discrimination in the remuneration system at the firm.

Jane McCafferty (see p.711) Has established a reputation for handling complex employment issues including multi-jurisdictional team moves, restrictive covenant enforcement and multiparty litigation. She regularly supports high-profile financial services clients through sophisticated injunctive relief applications. **Strengths:** "She is very hard-working, a good strategist and she has very broad legal knowledge, with particular strength in financial services cases." "She is a joy to work with; assertive when necessary but always charming with clients."

Andrew Edge (see p.639) Repeatedly singled out by sources for his exceptional client handling skills and his approachability. Specialising in both employment and commercial law, he is recognised for his aptitude in handling complex injunctive relief issues and for having expertise in unfair dismissal claims. **Strengths:** "He is technically skilled and has a charming manner with clients – he is a pleasure to work with." "Andrew operates very much as a member of the client's team. He is friendly, determined and a good strategist." **Recent work:** Acted for easyJet against allegations brought by hundreds of its employees of underpaid holiday pay, which Andrew was able to restrict to a few days per worker at the initial preliminary hearing.

Simon Forshaw (see p.647) Admired for his impressive advocacy style, he has a strong reputation for his restrictive covenant and High Court litigation work. He has a developing commercial aspect to his employment practice, assisting clients with team moves and breach of contract disputes. **Strengths:** "An excellent junior who is on the rise. Clients never fail to be impressed by his advocacy." "Simon takes a robust stance in combative situations." **Recent work:** Successfully advised an NHS trust in an Employment Tribunal case contesting whether 'bank doctors' could be considered employees, ultimately finding that the claimant was self-employed.

Marcus Pilgerstorfer (see p.738) Handles a wide employment practice but he is particularly known for his expertise in all types of discrimination claims. Repeatedly instructed by individuals, financial institutions, SMEs and trade unions, he is admired amongst peers for his impressive employment law knowledge. **Strengths:** "He is very thorough, diligent and careful in the advice that he gives." "His advocacy is utterly courteous. He is forensic in his cross-examination and is as sharp as a razor; it is like watching a surgeon at work." **Recent work:** Acted in Hainsworth v Ministry of Defence, in a complex dispute revolving around whether reasonable adjustments can be made for someone who is not disabled but is associated with someone who is disabled.

Amy Rogers (see p.754) Widely reputed for her hard-working nature and intelligent approach and as such is instructed in many High Court commercial employment issues. She is especially recognised for her expertise in team move cases and employment matters with a competition element. **Strengths:** "She is extremely intelligent, very clear in her written arguments and is well liked and respected by her clients." "She is the junior of choice for lots of silks; she is fantastically hard-working, hugely experienced and has lots of experience of team move cases." **Recent work:** Instructed by a large national construction company alleging historic blacklisting in the construction sector.

Patrick Halliday (see p.662) Handles complex discrimination and whistle-blowing cases for clients across the banking, retail and healthcare sectors. He is experienced in both High Court cases and Employment Tribunal matters. **Strengths:** "He is reliably and consistently excellent. He is meticulously well prepared and is a calming presence to clients and witnesses." "He is clear-thinking and able to explain complex issues and present documents in a very logical way." **Recent work:** Acted in a significant equal pay case for ASDA store employees who are seeking the same wage as their warehouse counterparts.

Judy Stone (see p.774) Advises both claimants and respondents across a wide range of employment matters, with particular focus on whistle-blowing and discrimination issues. She is a skilled litigator, handling complex employment cases at both tribunal and appellate levels. **Strengths:** "She is very astute and is excellent at drafting whistle-blowing disputes." "She is absolutely fabulous, good with clients and really clever and committed."

Holly Stout (see p.774) Maintains a far-reaching employment practice giving advice to clients on everything from discrimination and whistle-blowing to restraint of trade and trade union matters. She is frequently instructed in complex Employment Tribunal cases and is praised for her clever and commercial approach to her cases. **Strengths:** "She is very productive and very collaborative in her approach." "Seriously clever."

Michael Lee (see p.698) Has an impressive employment law practice and is recognised for his strength in discrimination and whistle-blowing matters. Sources value his measured approach to sensitive matters. **Strengths:** "He is extremely hard-working, diligent and is able to pick up the facts of a case very quickly." "He is extremely thorough, very personable and good with the client." **Recent work:** Acted in a complex High Court case, concerning allegations of four employees orchestrating a team move and creating a new competing business. The case was complicated by breach of contract and restrictive covenant issues, including unlawful means conspiracy.

Andrew Blake (see p.597) Undertakes cases across the whole range of employment law on both respondent and claimant instructions. He has considerable experience representing clients at both the Employment Tribunal and the High Court, with focused attention towards discrimination and equal pay cases. **Strengths:** "He's good technically and can also explain things to the lay client."

Julian Milford (see p.717) Focuses his practice on tribunal representation, notably handling highly sensitive discrimination and whistle-blowing cases. Regularly instructed by large corporations, local authorities and trade unions, his employment practice is bolstered by his data protection and public law knowledge. **Strengths:** "Very meticulous in his approach and on a personal level he's always approachable and never too busy for a quick word of advice." **Recent work:** Handled a complex claim of sexual harassment by a senior executive against his employer. The matter was complicated by additional allegations of corporate malpractice.

Harini Iyengar (see p.680) Undertakes a wide range of employment law work with particular focus on complex disputes, including remuneration and restrictive covenant enforcement issues. Her employment practice is bolstered by her extensive knowledge of education and procurement law. **Strengths:** "She is extremely responsive and has a great attention to detail. She is also really client-friendly." **Recent work:** Represented a senior hedge fund saleswoman at an Employment Tribunal hearing who alleged sex and nationality discrimination and unfair dismissal against her employer Commerzbank.

Julian Wilson (see p.798) Particularly adept at advising on discrimination cases and partnership disputes. Sources recognise his strength in High Court matters, especially those containing elements of wrongful dismissal or breach of contract. **Strengths:** "He is an excellent adviser on injunctive relief work. He has a very clear and commercial approach." "He is a cerebral person who masters complexity with verve." **Recent work:** Acted for Duncan Bannatyne and Bannatyne Fitness in a claim for wrongful dismissal and unfair prejudice by a minority shareholder and former managing director.

Littleton Chambers

See profile on p.874

THE SET

An employment chambers at the forefront of the market, fully equipped to undertake the full gamut of complex and high-value matters, particularly in High Court cases with severe reputational risk. With its sizeable employment group Littleton offers enviable strength in depth across numerous sectors including financial services and healthcare, and its members are frequently sought out to undertake highly complex cases. Notable areas of strength include cases concerning whistle-blowing, Public Interest Disclosure Act, team moves and collective employment relations. The set's members have also been involved of late in ground-breaking cases relating to holiday pay, blacklisting and TUPE.

Client service: "The clerks are super-responsive and always willing to help. They are so good that you don't need to go anywhere else. They will cater to the client's needs and their budget – very user-friendly."

SILKS

David Reade QC A "heavyweight with a deservedly formidable reputation" who is known for leading landmark disputes in the UK and across Europe. His expertise includes TUPE and trade and extends to unique crossroads of disciplines, such as issues of partnerships and pensions. **Strengths:** "His advocacy skills are second to none; he has the ability to persuade without being aggressive. He seems to have an encyclopaedic knowledge of the law – it's incredible. Brilliant with the client; he is the ultimate team player and is always available, even when he's in the middle of cases." **Recent work:** Successfully represented the employer, Bidco 2, in a decision of the ECJ on the interpretation of 'establishment' under the Collective Redundancy Directive.

Selwyn Bloch QC (see p.597) An industry-leading restrictive covenant and restraint of trade specialist who has authored a textbook on the topic that is cited in courts. His international practice sees him acting as lead counsel to clients in the financial services sector in significant team move litigation. **Strengths:** "On restrictive covenants he is the go-to person, very impressive. He has great knowledge and expertise in the area and speaks with conviction; it's difficult to not be convinced by what he's saying." **Recent work:** Led concurrent proceedings in Massachusetts and the UK representing EMC Europe on a case concerning the forfeiture of employee stock options. The case raised issues of jurisdiction and anti-suit injunctions. It was heard in the Queen's Bench Division and Court of Appeal in 2015 and the Supreme Court has now granted permission to appeal.

Andrew Clarke QC Well-established silk with a history of appearing in industry-shaping employment disputes representing significant employers. His broad expertise extends across a range of matters including contractual disputes, industrial action, unlawful discrimination and employee status. **Strengths:** "A superb tactician, able to distil and convey complex legal issues, and is highly authoritative." **Recent work:** Acted for Reed in relation to disputed tax assessments of over £150 million coupled with judicial review proceedings. The case raised important questions about the employment status of agency workers, the mode of termination of their contracts of employment and the status of terms derived from statute relative to other terms.

Damian Brown QC An experienced practitioner whose expertise spans the range of employment law, with noteworthy experience in directors' duties, team moves and unlawful competition. He is recognised for his handling of significant industrial action and statutory claims matters. **Strengths:** "Very comfortable with dealing with clients directly and has a commanding presence in the tribunal room." **Recent work:** Appeared as lead counsel in a high-profile dispute between a consultant cardiac surgeon and his employer. The claimant was unwittingly the source of the worst known outbreak of prosthetic valve endocarditis, an infection related to cardiac valve surgery, which led to the deaths of five patients.

Gavin Mansfield QC (see p.707) Highly regarded silk handling high-profile restraint of trade and team move cases in the High Court. He possesses noted expertise in representing clients in the professional services and finance. **Strengths:** "He's a very impressive figure: he inspires confidence and he is very client-friendly and assured. He's very persuasive in his advocacy; he presents his case very logically and always delivers with real confidence and authority." **Recent work:** Acted for RBS defending claims brought by foreign exchange traders who were dismissed following the bank's inquiry into alleged market manipulation.

Naomi Ellenbogen QC Joint head of chambers who acts in high-value disputes on behalf of public and private clients including multinationals and governmental bodies. Peers and client alike commend her intelligence and sharp mind. **Strengths:** "Very competent, an excellent advocate and intellectually gifted." **Recent work:** Represented the Home Office in the Court of Appeal in an unfair dismissal and discrimination claim. This was the first case at appellate level to consider the requirements imposed by Section 15 of the Equality Act 2010. Ellenbogen identified and set out the appropriate approach to such claims, demonstrating the various errors which had been made by the tribunal in its very lengthy judgment before the appeal. Her approach was endorsed and adopted by the EAT.

Michael Duggan QC Provides expertise in disciplinary, commercial and employment law to employers facing all employment conflicts, including unfair dismissal, restrictive covenants and injunctions. He is known for his specialism in social media law. **Strengths:** "Impressive employment matters for his breadth of knowledge and effective advocacy. He has great instincts and is very user-friendly." **Recent work:** Acted for GDS Publishing in an application for injunction against a former employee and their new employer. The claim involves issues of confidential information, theft of information, soliciting clients and customers. The injunction was successfully obtained.

Jonathan Cohen QC A recently appointed silk who is highly praised by peers for his advocacy skills. His practice focuses on complex issues of fiduciary duties and serious fraud. **Strengths:** "He is completely smooth and nothing fazes him. He's a bit like a classical musician in the way that he prepares his cross-examination, it just flows beautifully. He inspires confidence in the client." **Recent work:** Acts on behalf of Barclays' EMEA chairman in a multi-million-pound employment claim as a result of the withholding of his bonuses, said by the bank to be justified on the basis of an SFO investigation into its present and former senior executives for fraud during the 2008 financial crisis, when Barclays was refinanced by Qatari investors.

Daniel Tatton-Brown QC New silk that focuses on complex and sensitive tribunal claims, competition litigation in the High Court and appellate work. Recognised for his knowledge of discrimination and whistle-blowing cases. **Strengths:** "Extremely measured and calm with a determined and proactive approach and very good client skills." **Recent work:** Acted on behalf of the claimant in an age discrimination case. Having won in the tribunal by successfully defending the claimant's discrimination claim, the decision was appealed in the EAT. The appeal was then successfully overturned and restored.

JUNIORS

Mohinderpal Sethi (see p.762) Well-regarded employment junior who frequently acts for some of the biggest clients in the financial services industry. He specialises in complex international business protection litigation in the context of restraint of trade and team moves. **Strengths:** "Very impressive; he is highly intelligent, quick, commercially astute and responsive to clients. He is very comfortable in dealing with clients and impresses them." **Recent work:** Representing Ms Mathur in the £20 million bonus and whistle-blowing claim as part of the global Libor/Euribor scandal. Deutsche Bank was fined a record-breaking USD2.5 billion to settle US and UK regulatory investigations into its role in manipulating the Libor/Euribor benchmark rates.

John Mehrzad (see p.715) Recognised for his sporting and employment practice that sees him representing senior executives and notable sporting figures in complex issues requiring in-depth industry knowledge. Appears frequently in the High Court and Court of Appeal on business and financial matters in the employment space. **Strengths:** "Very responsive, efficient and excellent with the law. He's also very strategic and tactical in the way he does things and is a very clear advocate; he's able to explain the law and break down complex issues." **Recent work:** Acted on behalf of Game Retail in a significant case concerning the misuse of Twitter, and other social media platforms, in the workplace. John led the client through a successful appeal and overturned the judgment made against it in the first instance.

Chris Quinn (see p.745) A seasoned practitioner that is regularly instructed in highly acrimonious and complex employment disputes. He provides forensic expertise in matters relating to breach of duty or dishonesty. **Strengths:** "Tactically astute and gets to grips with the detail. Robust and confidence-inspiring with clients." **Recent work:** Represented the defendant in a High Court claim said to be worth hundreds of millions of pounds arising out of the break-up of Marathon Asset Management.

Niran de Silva Utilises his experience as a derivatives broker to handle high-value employment conflicts relating to whistle-blowing, discrimination and restrictive covenants in the financial services sector. He is noted for his experience representing police forces in various matters. **Strengths:** "He's extremely thorough, diligent, knowledgeable and good with clients. His attention to detail is second to none and he's very good on his feet." **Recent work:** Acted for Surrey Police and Sussex Police in a claim for disability discrimination brought by a long-serving police firearms officer who had been removed from firearms duties because he had failed a hearing test. Following a three-day tribunal, all but one of the allegations were dismissed.

Jeremy Lewis Employment barrister that frequently engages in leading whistle-blowing claims and transfer of undertakings. Peers and clients commend his accessibility and dedication to his cases. **Strengths:** "He is focused and exacting in his work. Accessible at all hours and goes the extra mile." **Recent work:** Acted for the respondent employer in the Court of Appeal where the claimant contended that he was subjected to detriment on grounds of trade union and health and safety activities arising out of passing information said to be used for blacklisting. The claimant's appeal was successfully rejected.

Sam Neaman Acts for major corporate businesses in the High Court, Court of Appeal and Supreme Court, particularly in commercial and injunction employment matters. Additionally possesses recognised specialism in medical employment cases. **Strengths:** "A real heavyweight in cross-examination – unrivalled in that respect. Never leaves a stone unturned and is brilliant with confidential information and international business protection elements." **Recent work:** Featured in an EAT case, having won at first instance, which will have a considerable impact on the important question of whether an employer has an obligation to make permanent health insurance payments to employees on long-term sickness absence if the employer's insurance company does not do so.

Adam Solomon Represents both employees and employers in the EAT, High Court and Court of Appeal against notable QCs. He is recognised for his expertise in high-value team move and discrimination cases. **Strengths:** "An impressive advocate; charming but devastating in cross-examination. He is user-friendly and easy to work with." **Recent work:** Instructed on behalf of an employee of Rynda against the company in the Court of Appeal. The case concerned whether an individual could constitute an 'organised grouping' and thus whether her employment transferred under TUPE. This was the first time a case concerning TUPE had reached the Court of Appeal.

Lucy Bone (see p.598) Junior employment barrister offering overlapping knowledge in partnership and IP disputes. Handles the full range of employment issues and is sought after by groups in the financial services sector. **Strengths:** "Very responsive, willing to be flexible with availability, good to work with, good with clients and definitely knows her stuff." **Recent work:** Acted for a proprietary hedge fund in a substantial claim arising out of a team move dispute. The case concerned former employees who had allegedly taken computer code and specialised interest rate derivative trading algorithms and adapted them for use in their new business.

Carol Davis Handles complex tribunal cases, focusing particularly on sensitive whistle-blowing and discrimination cases. She also possesses noted experience in cases relating to termination and pay. **Strengths:** "She has a forensic attention to detail and identifies complex issues extremely quickly. She is an excellent strategist." **Recent work:** Represented the claimant, a former foreign exchange trader of RBS, dismissed for gross misconduct. It was alleged that the claimant was one of a number of foreign exchange traders across a number of banks who used online chatrooms to share confidential information about the trading activities of clients to manipulate the foreign exchange rate.

Martin Fodder Experienced practitioner who is a much-praised specialist in whistle-blowing cases, having written a leading textbook on the subject. He receives regular instructions from notable public bodies. **Strengths:** "Exceptional for whistle-blowing cases, he is good with clients and great with cross-examination. He is lovely to deal with and has a pool of knowledge." **Recent work:** Successfully defended an NHS trust in a claim of unfair dismissal by a consultant surgeon against his former employer. The case attracted considerable media attention because of the number of claims that have been brought by patients who were treated by the consultant.

Dale Martin (see p.708) Well versed in complex and high-value multi-claimant litigation and has a growing reputation in injunctive and appellate proceedings. He is also known by his peers for his expertise in holiday pay claims. **Strengths:** "Very commercial barrister who is well liked and respected by clients. He is very switched-on and provides a terrific service." **Recent work:** Successful appeal to EAT on behalf of 2 Sisters Food Group in November 2015, following two Employment Tribunal hearings earlier in 2015. Dealt with multiple equal pay claims brought by 65 employees at a food processing factory.

Antony Sendall (see p.761) Considerably experienced barrister renowned for his knowledge of injunction and whistle-blowing cases. He additionally handles mediation proceedings and sporting issues. **Strengths:** "Excellent overall pragmatic approach and has good client skills. He has an ability to cut through the detail and get to the core issues." **Recent work:** Acted on behalf of the claimants in a significant whistle-blowing and race discrimination case arising out of the Greek banking crisis. Represented the whistle-blowers in their claims against their former employer and the National Bank of Greece.

Matthew Sheridan (see p.764) Predominantly performs in disputes relating to unlawful competition and business protection matters. Peers commend the strength of his advocacy. **Strengths:** "An absolute standout junior for injunction work, he's able to take on High Court work at the drop of a hat. He is extremely intelligent and able to get to the crux of the legal argument very quickly. He is extremely reliable." **Recent work:** Acted as sole counsel for four defendants in claims for injunctive relief in support of post-termination restraints, springboard relief and damages. The defendants were alleged to have plotted over a period of years to, in effect, divert/re-create the claimants' entire business. A settlement was reached after the injunction stage.

Craig Rajgopaul Former solicitor offering a well-rounded perspective on complex employment proceedings. He is commended by sources for his client manner and commercial awareness. **Strengths:** "He is exceptionally bright, has an agile mind and very good client-handling skills. Highly impressive, particularly in discrimination and restrictive covenant matters, and he delivers things unbelievably quickly." **Recent work:** Acted for the claimant in a factually complex 15-day sex and pregnancy discrimination claim in the Employment Tribunal.

Alexander Robson Handles a swathe of employment matters in the High Court, including TUPE, discrimination claims and restraint of trade issues. He specialises in cases relating to bonus claims. **Strengths:** "An excellent junior; extremely approachable with incredible clarity of thought on how to run a case. He is able to construct an impressive legal argument – he's one to watch." **Recent work:** Acted for Premier League club Sunderland in a mixed Employment Tribunal and High Court £1.2 million bonus claim brought by a former club director alleging wrongful dismissal and unpaid bonus.

Charlotte Davies Specialises in High Court proceedings relating to restrictive covenants, unlawful competition and business protection. Peers and clients commend her abilities in complex sex discrimination cases. **Strengths:** "Brilliant advocacy – confident and competitive." **Recent work:** Acted for the claimant in a High Court case arising out of the departure of a senior employee who had set up a competitive business. The claimant contends that the employee has taken its confidential information to use for his new business, and that he acted in breach of his contractual and fiduciary duties.

Eleena Misra (see p.718) Practises broadly in public and private employment law with noted expertise in educational and healthcare-related issues. She demonstrates deep experience acting in disciplinary and regulatory matters. **Strengths:** "She instils a lot of confidence; she is very calm and measured in her approach, exceptionally prepared, very knowledgeable and knows her cases inside-out." **Recent work:** Acted for the successful respondent in an appeal which established two important principles in the context of an unfair dismissal and disability discrimination claim: how long an employer should reasonably wait before considering termination if an employee is on extended sick leave, and the dismissal of an employee on the grounds of disability.

Ming-Yee Shiu Recognised for her technical expertise in employment as well as her complementary commercial practice that often sees her in cases involving board members or senior executives of large organisations. She focuses mainly on injunctive relief and restrictive covenant matters. **Strengths:** "She is ferocious when she needs to be in court and very good at getting her views across." **Recent work:** Acted for the claimant in a contentious partnership/senior executive dispute. The claimant was a partner of a firm of property consultants who was requested to save a failing office in Dubai with the promise that he would return to the UK with his partnership intact. The firm, however, failed to keep its promise and dismissed him, leading him to issue the claim.

James Wynne (see p.801) Practises across the full spectrum of employment matters, including discrimination, contractual and team move disputes. He possesses noted experience in cases concerning strike action. **Strengths:** "An excellent advocate in a wide range of areas." **Recent work:** Succeeded at a ten-day Employment Tribunal concerning serious sex discrimination and harassment over six months by Unite the Union's most senior staff including its chief of staff.

James Bickford Smith (see p.596) Previously an academic at Oxford University who now frequently takes on complex employment disputes, often appearing in High Court injunctive relief cases. Clients and peers comment on his mental acuity and strategic approach to his advocacy. **Strengths:** "He is technically excellent, in some ways scarily bright, and for his level of call he gets involved in lots of very complex employment work. Terribly user-friendly, gets the result and gets it done, rolls up his sleeves and is not afraid to muck in." **Recent work:** Acted successfully for a former manager at a City fund in what is believed to be the first decided case in which a member of an LLP has been found to have been an 'employee' within the meaning of the Employment Rights Act.

Laura McNair-Wilson Rising junior barrister handling sensitive employment matters that stand to have lasting effects on the law. She is experienced in a wide variety of matters, most notably equality and unfair dismissal work. **Strengths:** "She's fantastic; her written work is fantastic, she's extremely good in meetings. She is a very safe pair of hands and completely calm under fire." **Recent work:** Acted for a senior member of the BBC in a high-profile unfair dismissal case after the claimant had been dismissed due to serious sexual assault allegations in connection with Operation Yewtree. The case concerned a claimant's right to anonymity in litigation and the balance between the claimant's Article 8 right to respect for his private life and the respondent's Article 10 right to open justice and freedom of expression.

Edward Kemp (see p.690) Offers cross-disciplinary expertise in employment, commercial and professional negligence matters. His practice is international, though his domestic practice has seen him in courts of all levels, up to the Supreme Court. **Strengths:** "Very good at drafting. He is calm, competent and deals with complicated issues with enthusiasm and diligence." **Recent work:** Acted for the London Borough of Brent in defence of a £1.5 million psychiatric injury claim by a former HR manager following findings of race discrimination. The case settled shortly after opening submissions on the first day of a three-day remedy hearing.

Lydia Banerjee (see p.589) Employment junior focusing on disability discrimination, restrictive covenants and bonus matters in the High Court. She bolsters her employment offering with a thriving sports and commercial practice. **Strengths:** "One of the brightest young barristers at the set; she is super-bright, extreme and faultless in her level of preparation and has a fantastic bedside manner."

Matrix Chambers

See profile on p.876

THE SET

Experienced team of highly skilled practitioners offering expert advice to employers, senior executives and employees. The bench has a varied range of specialisms and interests within employment law, ranging from whistle-blowing and discrimination claims to holiday pay disputes and restrictive covenant matters. The team's knowledge has been bolstered by the addition of Paul Nicholls QC from 11KBW, who specialises in wrongful dismissal and bonus disputes. Clients attest that Matrix "is a really dynamic and creative set who are looking ahead." **Client service:** "The clerking team is very good. They get back promptly and they are keen to give a good service." The clerking team is led by Cliff Holland.

SILKS

Thomas Linden QC He is lauded as a highly effective and impressive advocate, with clients and peers alike praising his sharp cross-examination skills and his forensic attention to detail. He takes a very commercial and pragmatic approach to his cases and handles highly complex employment cases in the High Court, including difficult zero hour contract litigation. **Strengths:** "He is an incredibly intelligent advocate who is extremely responsive and works well in a team. He has outstanding judgement and his skills, both commercially and legally, are immeasurable." "He is hugely clever, very hard-working and very strategic in his approach." **Recent work:** Instructed by almost 200 employees in a dispute with Sports Direct, concerning allegations that the company has breached its duty as it does not let them participate in share schemes because of their employment on zero hour contracts.

James Laddie QC Sources highlight not only his impressive advocacy and devastating cross-examination skills, but also his dedication to the case and his skilful handling of sensitive clients. He is widely reputed for his discrimination and whistle-blowing work, whilst also providing expert guidance in appellate cases and litigation in the High Court. **Strengths:** "He is a brilliant cross-examiner, very impressive with clients, and gauges the mood of the Tribunal very well." "He is someone you want on your side if doing a mediation; he is a great negotiator, brings a lot to the table and is able to break down deadlocks." **Recent work:** Instructed in Aloui-Belghiti v Jefferies International, a highly sensitive sexual harassment, discrimination and unfair dismissal claim brought by an employee against the bank. Laddie successfully defended the bank and the claimant withdrew her claim after cross-examination.

Karon Monaghan QC Established by many sources as a leading barrister for equality issues and discrimination claims. She is admired for both her fierce advocacy and her emotional intelligence, which allows her to form solid relationships with clients and solicitors alike. **Strengths:** "She has the attention of the court; she is a commanding presence and an exceptional advocate. She is a really experienced discrimination barrister." "She adopts a no-nonsense and pragmatic approach whilst at the same time remaining mindful of sensitivities." **Recent work:** Involved in a highly important judicial review, UNISON v Lord Chancellor, to challenge the requirement of claimants to pay tribunal fees to lodge a case.

Paul Nicholls QC Handles a wide practice, encompassing elements of employment, public and commercial law. Clients especially value the commercial acumen that he brings to employment issues, providing exceptional support in breach of contract and team move disputes. **Strengths:** "A fiercely bright and knowledgeable barrister who is good with solicitors as well as their clients and instils complete confidence." "He is very knowledgeable, practical and good at helping you achieve your commercial aim." **Recent work:** Acting for a United Arab Emirates company to restrain a team move of employees to a competitor company.

Helen Mountfield QC Widely recognised for her equality law and discrimination law knowledge, Helen incorporates this expertise into her employment practice. She is admired by clients for her ability to handle immense pressure and deliver imaginative solutions. **Strengths:** "She is fantastic, hugely knowledgeable and is a really attractive advocate in terms of her style and presentation to the court." "Her knowledge of equality law is second to none and she is passionate about her work." **Recent work:** Instructed in Big Brother Watch v United Kingdom, a complex case challenging the legal framework protecting the interception of communications data, raising issues of data privacy and confidentiality linked to employment.

Antony White QC (see p.793) Provides advice to public sector clients and trade unions, especially in cases which are highly sensitive or have a profound industrial action element. He maintains a broad employment practice, with additional strengths in privacy and data protection matters. **Strengths:** "He is brilliant and charming." "A very pleasant barrister who is exceptionally able." **Recent work:** Instructed in a highly complex pensions case, challenging the right for early retirement for certain individuals within the fire service on the grounds of age discrimination.

Nicholas Randall QC Regularly advises both employers and individuals from the financial services in complex employment law issues, including sophisticated discrimination claims. His employment law practice is bolstered by his expertise in pensions and sports law. **Strengths:** "He is efficient, responsive and reads the tribunal well." "He is calm and confident, has good client management skills and his tactics are sound." **Recent work:** Instructed in Pawel Szulc v The Charlemagne Capital Group, defending the group against a highly complex whistle-blowing claim launched by a former employee.

JUNIORS

Thomas Kibling Widely known for his strength in highly sensitive discrimination claims and whistle-blowing cases. Highly respected by sources for his impressive advocacy and refined client service. He brings a commercial edge to employment issues with knowledge of injunctive relief applications. **Strengths:** "Adept at handling difficult discrimination claims with reputational consequences." "He is excellent with clients, builds a very strong rapport with them and puts them at ease – he is a reassuring barrister." **Recent work:** Acted in Anastasiou v Western Union, a complex whistle-blowing and unfair dismissal claim that was passed to the EAT before remission to the Employment Tribunal.

Claire Darwin (see p.629) Highly experienced advocate who is commended by clients for her extensive attention to detail and preparation for her cases. She is well known for her strength in discrimination cases and her employment law practice is bolstered by her knowledge of education law. **Strengths:** "She's a fearsome advocate and is very approachable." "She is a well-prepared adviser and is an excellent cross-examiner." **Recent work:** Instructed in employment proceedings against teachers surrounding the alleged Islamification of some Birmingham schools.

Mathew Purchase (see p.745) Acts for employees, employers and trade unions across a wide range of employment law issues, representing clients in the High Court and the Court of Appeal. He is well regarded by clients for his intelligent approach to employment law issues and his effective advocacy. **Strengths:** "He gives amazing attention to detail and is extremely thorough. He is a safe pair of hands, intensely bright and a pleasure to work with." **Recent work:** Instructed in UNISON v Lord Chancellor, a challenge to whether claimants are required to pay fees to bring a claim to the Employment Tribunal. The matter has been escalated to the Court of Appeal and is pending entry to the Supreme Court.

Andrew Smith (see p.767) Focuses his employment practice on tribunal representation, guiding clients through complex Employment Tribunal, EAT and High Court cases. He has notable expertise in bonus disputes and other contractual issues. Clients praise his fantastic advocacy and his innovative approach to his cases. **Strengths:** "He quickly condenses factually complicated issues and provides a thorough and prompt service." "He gains a client's trust immediately with his interpersonal skills and his grasp of the key issues." **Recent work:** Instructed in Michallet v Mako Europe, a complex Employment Tribunal comprising claims of unfair dismissal, race discrimination and victimisation. Smith acted to successfully strike out all claims and additionally win a costs award for the respondent.

Laura Prince (see p.743) Has a far-reaching practice advising employers, employees and governmental bodies on all aspects of employment law, including equal pay and discrimination claims. She is recognised for her proficiency in complex TUPE matters and clients value her commercial acumen. **Strengths:** "She is very thorough and pays lots of attention to detail." "She is particularly impressive on the commercial side of a case, identifying the value and outcome early on and she makes sure that it is in tune with what the client wants." **Recent work:** Acted in Atkinson v Community Gateway Association, a highly complex case concerning whether an employee can bring a claim of constructive dismissal when they have themselves breached their contract of employment.

Aileen McColgan Focuses upon discrimination and equality issues, whilst maintaining an interest in the wider area of employment law. She has extensive experience handling complex holiday pay and restrictive covenant issues, appearing before the EAT and the High Court. **Strengths:** "She is really passionate about the case and the client and she really goes the extra mile. Once instructed she lives and breathes the case and she understands the academic side better than most." **Recent work:** Represented AG Carlisle against a claim of wrongful dismissal and holiday pay brought by a former employee.

Band 2

Cloisters

See profile on p.821

THE SET

Cloisters offers a solid collection of barristers who are highly experienced across all aspects of employment law. The employment group comprises a deep bench of respected silks and juniors offering specialisms in discrimination matters, equal pay disputes and unfair dismissals. The set is renowned for its employment litigation, with many silks undertaking complex cases in both High Court and Supreme Court settings. The set acts for both claimants and respondents, receiving instructions from individuals, trade unions, international employers and public institutions. Clients value the set's large, varied practice and its members' experience acting for many different types of clients.

Client service: "Head clerk Glenn Hudson is extremely helpful. They are all flexible and accessible, always very accommodating and helpful." "The clerks are really willing to help, they are responsive, will do things and are always looking for a way to help you out."

SILKS

Robin Allen QC (see p.582) Considerably experienced and eminent silk and head of chambers who frequently appears in the industry's most significant employment litigation. He is well reputed for his impressive track record in the House of Lords and the Supreme Court. **Strengths:** "One of the leading people, particularly in the field of discrimination, for 20 to 25 years. He gets the tribunal eating out the palm of his hand – he gives the impression that he could do it with his eyes closed, or in his sleep." **Recent work:** Featured in the largest piece of employment litigation currently in the UK, O'Brien vs Ministry of Justice, estimated to be worth over £2 billion. After going three times to the Supreme Court and once to the ECJ, there are now numerous final issues to be resolved.

Paul Epstein QC A talented advocate who handles high-profile employment and discrimination cases at both tribunal and High Court level. Clients value his creative and dedicated approach to cases, whilst others praise his extensive knowledge of restrictive covenant enforcement. **Strengths:** "He is a very good strategist; he combines amazing knowledge of the law with a very commercial and strategic approach to litigation." "He is an assured and authoritative silk who is a real team player and is popular with instructing solicitors and clients." **Recent work:** Acted in defence of ASDA in a widely reported mass equal pay claim brought against ASDA by thousands of its female employees.

Jacques Algazy QC (see p.581) A highly acclaimed advocate frequently sought out to act before both the High Court and employment tribunals, who is praised by clients and peers for his impressive cross-examination skills. He has established himself as an expert in jurisdictional disputes and international employment matters, often advising on cross-border elements of restrictive covenant enforcements. **Strengths:** "He is meticulous in his preparation, charming with clients but manages their expectations very cautiously. He is masterful in cross-examination – he is particularly good at teasing out inconsistencies in evidence." "He has a brilliant, tactical and forensic mind and he is not just a great barrister but a great winner of cases." **Recent work:** Acted for the employer in Shaw v Norbrook Laboratories, a claim by a former regional manager claiming that he was unfairly dismissed for protected disclosure or whistle-blowing matters.

Caspar Glyn QC (see p.655) Well-established silk recognised for his outstanding cross-examination skills and his adeptness in high-profile discrimination cases. Clients laud his high level of service and his approachability, especially valuing his pragmatic approach to difficult cases. He has expertise in industrial relations issues and is regularly instructed by both trade unions and employers. **Strengths:** "Scintillatingly good QC with a razor-sharp brain." "He is a highly capable barrister who has exceptional court presence; he commands the courtroom. He is a highly effective cross-examiner and fills the client with confidence." **Recent work:** Acted in Tracey v Foot Anstey, in which a lawyer alleged that he was not promoted to partner because he was over the age of 45. Caspar acted on the firm's behalf and successfully defended the claim.

Jason Galbraith-Marten QC (see p.649) Clients praise his exceptional advocacy, noting that he is able to steer witnesses in the direction he wants and that his cross-examination skills are highly impressive. He acts across all aspects of employment law, advising clients from local government, media organisations and employers from the motor industry. **Strengths:** "Very bright and persuasive. He has an excellent attention to detail, knows the materials in a bundle very well and is able to get to grips with the issues very quickly." "He is fiercely intelligent and very capable in the law but he complements that by being fantastic with clients and being very accessible." **Recent work:** Defended Pannone and several senior partners against claims of age and religious discrimination, whistle-blowing and unfair dismissal. He managed to secure a significant award for costs against the unsuccessful claimant.

Rachel Crasnow QC (see p.625) Recognised by peers and clients alike as a very strong advocate, praised for her killer cross-examination skills and her unflappable nature in the courtroom. She acts across the whole gamut of employment law and is often instructed by clients in the banking, media and education sectors. **Strengths:** "She has a very strong reputation in the disability discrimination field and is very knowledgeable." "Rachel is a gutsy advocate who is good on her feet and provides excellent tactical advice." **Recent work:** Instructed in O'Brien & Miller v Ministry of Justice, a highly complex case representing over one thousand judicial office holders in their fight for judicial pensions. The case has been deferred from the Court of the Appeal to the Supreme Court.

Daphne Romney QC (see p.754) Concentrates her practice on discrimination and equal pay matters, with additional strengths in wrongful dismissals and breach of contract issues. Clients highlight that she is a very effective advocate who has an aggressive approach to litigation that they really value. **Strengths:** "She is tenacious with an exceptional grasp of detail." "She is extremely bright, totally client-focused and a real fighter." **Recent work:** Acted in Adesokan v Sainsbury's, a claim of wrongful dismissal complicated further by the question of whether gross misconduct required deliberate intent.

JUNIORS

Schona Jolly (see p.684) Talented employment and discrimination lawyer who is widely admired by clients for her fierce advocacy and her ability to think quickly on her feet. Her employment practice is bolstered by her human rights knowledge. She is also a regular counsel for banking clients and trade unions. **Strengths:** "She is a fighter, collaborative and takes on board your input." "She is fantastic in cross-examination, really gets to the point of any legal dispute and is very sensible to deal with." **Recent work:** Acted for a large group of female Latin American cleaners who worked at the University of London and had formed an independent trade union which the university refused to recognise.

Thomas Coghlin (see p.619) Clients value his sensible, pragmatic advice and are impressed by his effective advocacy skills. He has extensive knowledge of employment law, bolstered by his experience as a part-time employment judge. He is instructed by employers, individuals and public organisations, including NHS trusts. **Strengths:** "He displays excellent technical knowledge and his cross-examination skills are impressive." "He works incredibly hard, is very incisive about how he thinks and he has a fantastic way about working with clients." **Recent work:** Acted in Longhurst v Beaver Management Services, a long-running dispute with a former managing director over years of unpaid bonuses that spanned the High Court, County Court and Employment Tribunal.

Claire McCann (see p.711) Has a wide practice spanning both employment and equality law issues, with expertise in discrimination claims and equal pay litigation. She is praised for her attention to detail and her superb client care. She has experience handling cases and large collective claims for all manner of clients. **Strengths:** "She is hard-working, bright and determined, with strong client care skills." "She is a very competent advocate who knows the case – in the tribunal she is very assured and confident and she is a very good cross-examiner." **Recent work:** Defended EEF against claims of unfair dismissal and indirect sex discrimination brought by two former employment solicitors at the firm.

Paul Michell (see p.716) Vastly experienced in employment law matters but particularly focuses on wrongful dismissal and discrimination cases, with knowledge of injunctive relief matters. Clients praise not only his incredible intellect but also his responsiveness and ability to turn around work very quickly. **Strengths:** "He has formidable forensic skills and his command of complex facts and scenarios is quite impressive." "He has an incredibly quick mind, and is very persuasive and powerful in court." **Recent work:** Instructed in Cordella v London School of Economics, a High Court case in which a professor alleged that he had been consistently denied promotion opportunities.

Chris Milsom (see p.718) Has a broad practice, covering the full spectrum of employment and discrimination disputes with specialist knowledge of gender reassignment and caste discrimination. Clients say that he is an impressive advocate with "encyclopaedic knowledge of employment law." **Strengths:** "He is a tenacious advocate and engenders confidence in clients both in conference and at trial." "He is terribly user-friendly and is very quick to evaluate the value and strength of a case." **Recent work:** Instructed in Bamieh v Foreign and Commonwealth Office, EULEX and Others, a claim of de-selection brought by a prosecutor seconded by the FCO to EULEX in Kosovo after she blew the whistle on systemic corruption in the Kosovan judiciary.

Declan O'Dempsey (see p.728) Widely recognised for his discrimination work, he has vast experience across the whole expanse of employment law. Clients praise his approachability, excellent client service and collaborative approach to his cases. **Strengths:** "His advocacy is impressive and his written advice and submissions are extremely comprehensive and knowledgeable." "He is the go-to person for tricky discrimination claims – he leaves no stone unturned." **Recent work:** Acted in Cordner v Chartered Institute of Taxation, a claim of disability discrimination brought by an individual who claimed that the institute had not made reasonable examination adjustments to meet their disability needs. Declan acted for the institute and proved that all reasonable adjustments had been made.

Tom Brown (see p.605) Highly experienced advocate appearing at both the High Court and tribunal in all manner of equality and employment disputes. He is praised by clients for his excellent cross-examination skills and he regularly acts in appellate cases. **Strengths:** "He is extremely sharp, has masses of experience and is great with clients." "He is first-class – he combines excellent intellect with tactical awareness and is great to work with." **Recent work:** Successfully defended the BBC against claims of race discrimination brought by a journalist who had been dismissed by the broadcaster. The case was also politically sensitive because it involved allegations that the BBC had reported events in Sri Lanka in a biased way.

Caroline Musgrave (see p.725) Employment law specialist with strong knowledge of whistle-blowing, discrimination and parental rights disputes. She is seen as a reliable, confident member of counsel who can hold her own against experienced senior barristers. **Strengths:** "She establishes a great rapport from day one with both solicitors and clients, and she exudes a persona of capability and confidence." "She is an outstanding junior who punches above her weight." **Recent work:** Successfully acted in Barry v University of Wales Trinity St David, an equal pay dispute where male workers, mostly caretakers and tradesmen, were claiming equal pay with female workers such as secretaries and library assistants.

Akua Reindorf (see p.750) Works primarily on highly complex discrimination cases, often representing trade unions and individuals at appellate cases and in Supreme Court matters. Clients especially rate her courtroom skills, noting that she is "a first-class advocate who sticks to her guns." **Strengths:** "She is very clear in the way that she presents her claims. She provides excellent analysis of the law and has excellent advocacy skills." "She is great with the client and is very calm, clear and intelligent." **Recent work:** Successfully represented a gay police officer at tribunal who brought allegations of discrimination, harassment and victimisation against his employers on the grounds of his sexual orientation.

Anna Beale (see p.593) Strong tribunal advocate representing employers and individuals in complex discrimination and whistle-blowing cases. Clients attest that she is an extremely hard worker who can quickly turn around large pieces of work. **Strengths:** "She really engages with the client and will go the extra mile – she will not give up for a client. She is very positive and determined." **Recent work:** Acted in Cullen v Boehringer Ingelheim, successfully acting for the claimant and securing a finding of unfair dismissal and compensation at the Employment Tribunal.

Dee Masters (see p.709) Has extensive knowledge of discrimination issues, with particular focus upon age discrimination issues. Clients praise her impressive client-handling skills, especially her ability to outline risks and explain concepts to lay clients. **Strengths:** "She is practical, diligent and thorough, with a good eye for the key issues at hand." "She is bright, responsive and commercially astute." **Recent work:** Instructed in Lorraine Robinson v Royal Borough of Greenwich, in which the claimant made allegations of institutional racism against the council. She successfully defended the council and several of its senior directors.

Ed Williams (see p.796) Skilled employment and discrimination law practitioner who is often instructed in appellate cases by public bodies and clients from the banking and education sectors. Clients are keen to highlight his masterful advocacy style. **Strengths:** "He is very thorough and shows outstanding commitment to the client's success." "He is very good, especially his skeleton arguments and his cross-examinations." **Recent work:** Represented a school in a lengthy unfair dismissal claim, in which four former teaching assistants claimed that the headteacher had forged their resignation letters.

Catherine Casserley (see p.612) Widely recognised in the market as an expert in disability discrimination law. She has vast experience in other aspects of employment law, acting at all levels including tribunal and Supreme Court cases. **Strengths:** "She is approachable, responsive and excellent with clients." "She is a leading expert in disability discrimination." **Recent work:** Instructed in Ackerman-Livingstone v Aster Communities, acting as a junior in a highly complex disability discrimination case brought before the Supreme Court, testing Section 15 of the Equality Act 2010.

Olivia-Faith Dobbie (see p.634) Handles a far-reaching employment practice, specialising in discrimination claims and working time disputes. Clients value her clear advice and professionalism, with many instructing her in restrictive covenant issues and injunctive relief matters. **Strengths:** "She is excellent at getting on top of the brief and provides strategic advice for success at tribunal." "She has a calm, structured approach to advice, providing absolute clarity in opinion." **Recent work:** Instructed by the respondents Conway AECOM and FM Conway defending against multiple claims brought by over 40 claimants in a large holiday pay dispute against their employers.

Daniel Dyal (see p.638) Has a solid employment and equality law practice, and is regularly instructed by large employers and significant trade unions. Clients admire his approachability and his ability to quickly grasp technicalities of cases. **Strengths:** "He is astute, assertive and he inspires client confidence." "He is very down to earth and client-friendly." **Recent work:** Successfully defended the NASUWT and its assistant general secretary against allegations of sex discrimination and bullying brought by a union member.

David Massarella (see p.709) Instructed by City law firms across a wide range of employment issues, including constructive dismissal cases and discrimination claims. Clients highlight his fantastic attention to detail when conducting cases. **Strengths:** "Fantastic senior junior with a meticulous approach. He is extremely supportive and willing to roll his sleeves up." **Recent work:** Defended Arriva against multiple whistle-blowing allegations brought against the company at Employment Tribunal.

Essex Court Chambers

See profile on p.836

THE SET

Essex Court houses a small but widely renowned group of barristers who are recognised for their experience of complex employment issues and their formidable advocacy in High Court litigation cases. Its members have a wide range of expertise, covering discrimination issues, partnership disputes and regulatory work amongst many other areas.

Client service: "The clerking team is good. They are certainly very quick at finding us counsel." "Joe Ferrigno is a fantastic clerk. He is very professional and also very engaging – he is practically working with you to get what the clients need." The clerking team is jointly led by David Grief and Joe Ferrigno.

SILKS

Andrew Hochhauser QC Has established a strong reputation in the market as a powerful, resolute advocate who will aggressively fight the client's case. He regularly handles sophisticated High Court litigation and is a trusted counsel for both large commercial organisations and senior individuals. **Strengths:** "He is an extremely skilled advocate who has a tremendous knowledge across the employment spectrum. He can be magical in the courtroom and is the best cross-examiner in the business." **Recent work:** Instructed in Paturel v Deutsche Bank Group Services, a breach of contract claim relating to a significantly large bonus which was brought against the bank.

Daniel Oudkerk QC Recognised for his strong commercial approach to complex employment matters. He has extensive experience of High Court litigation and is considered an expert in team move issues. Sources praise his technical approach to cases which is coupled with his "ferocious advocacy" skills. **Strengths:** "He is a very able advocate and has a good courtroom manner." "He is extremely bright and is the voice of reason in high-octane disputes." **Recent work:** Acted in Gallagher v Ross & Others, a complex team move case that encompassed elements of conspiracy claims, breach of fiduciary duty and garden leave issues.

David Craig QC Renowned by clients and peers alike as an exceptionally hard-working silk who is immensely dedicated to his cases. Sources also highlight his collaborative nature and intellectual prowess. He takes a notably commercial approach to both employment and partnership issues. **Strengths:** "He has the perfect combination of being technically brilliant and intellectually sharp, whilst being very good with clients." "He is immensely hard-working, is on top of the details and is a great team player."

Martin Griffiths QC Sources identify his expertise in handling complex employment issues, particularly in the financial services and sports sectors. Clients value his strategic approach and are impressed by both his written arguments and his courtroom advocacy. **Strengths:** "A razor-sharp mind and a superb tactician who is also a brilliant court performer." "Strategically strong and quick to get to the nub of the issue." **Recent work:** Acted in Simpkin v Berkeley Group Holdings, a high-value bonus and long-term incentive plan claim against a FTSE100 company brought by Berkeley's former financial director.

Charles Ciumei QC Handles sophisticated employment law issues, with particular proficiency in cross-jurisdictional matters. Sources highlight his tenacious advocacy and value his unfaltering support to the client and the case. **Strengths:** "His work is exceptional and very clever. He always raises his game and always gets you where you need to be." "He is superb – a very clever and tenacious advocate."

JUNIORS

Edward Brown Possesses considerable experience of High Court litigation cases, with additional expertise in representing financial services in complex Employment Tribunal disputes. Clients are keen to highlight his hard-working nature and dedication to the case. **Strengths:** "He is very supportive, a good team player and clearly very bright." "He is extremely bright, very responsive and is a persistent and persuasive advocate." **Recent work:** Acted for insurance brokers Arthur J Gallagher in a High Court injunctive relief and damages claim.

Jane Russell (see p.757) Junior Counsel to the Crown and an expert in both commercial employment cases and equalities-type litigation. **Strengths:** "A real enthusiast." "She has a way of building a good rapport with clients and keeping them focused on the key issues. She's also extremely good at putting them at ease in emotionally charged situations."

Old Square Chambers
See profile on p.886

THE SET

The set houses highly experienced practitioners with a wide range of specialities and interests, who handle all manner of cases relating to such issues as holiday pay, equal pay and whistle-blowing. Old Square is well established as a leading set for all manner of industrial relations issues, and has significant strength in discrimination claims. Clients attest that the chambers possesses an "excellent coverage of employment law, a very sensible attitude towards fees and great-quality people."

Client service: "The clerking is second to none. William Meade leads the team there and he does it very well; he's quite a proactive, forward-looking senior clerk and he instils that in the rest of the team. They're responsive and they always try and get you the barrister you want. It's very much a partnership we have with them."

SILKS

John Hendy QC (see p.669) Widely respected and admired by peers and clients alike for his expertise in industrial relations cases, including industrial action, collective bargaining and trade union rules. He also has extensive experience of blacklisting cases and clients attest that he has unparalleled knowledge of trade union injunctions. **Strengths:** "The top flight of industrial action lawyers – his understanding of the trade union landscape is among the best." **Recent work:** Instructed in RMT v Serco, a complex case regarding injunctions against industrial action.

Jane McNeill QC (see p.713) Highly experienced employment practitioner with expertise in discrimination claims and employment disputes within the healthcare sector. Her employment practice is bolstered by her personal injury knowledge and often advises where both disciplines intersect. Clients appreciate the high levels of clarity in both her advocacy and her written work, with others appraising her user-friendly nature. **Strengths:** "She is very user-friendly, very focused on what she is doing." **Recent work:** Acted in Chhabra v West London Mental Health NHS Trust, a Supreme Court case examining the rights of NHS trusts to discipline doctors and the extent to which the court may interfere.

Oliver Segal QC (see p.760) Specialist in discrimination law, with wider knowledge of employment law issues including breach of contract claims and equal pay matters. He is highly proficient in handling sophisticated collective disputes, including industrial action cases and TUPE complications. Clients value his hard-working approach and his ability to "cut through multifaceted cases and put his finger on the real nub of the issue." **Strengths:** "He gives excellent, commercial advice and is a highly impressive advocate who is fantastic with clients." "He has such a calming influence on claimants and clients and brings confidence to people." **Recent work:** Instructed in Deer v University of Oxford, a victimisation claim brought before the Court of Appeal by a lecturer who believed that her grievance had been handled unfairly.

Michael Ford QC (see p.646) Skilled practitioner handling highly complex Employment Tribunal matters, including discrimination claims and holiday pay disputes. Regularly acts before the Court of Appeal in industrial action cases and injunctive relief matters. **Strengths:** "He is technically brilliant and very quick at picking points up." "He has a wide range of experience and expertise and is very reliable." **Recent work:** Successfully assisted GMB in resisting an injunction against NHS employees to conduct a nationwide strike.

Mark Sutton QC Experienced practitioner who is widely reputed for his expertise in doctor disciplinaries and employment law issues arising from the healthcare sector. He is particularly skilled in handling whistle-blowing and TUPE matters, and has experience of injunctive relief applications before the Supreme Court. **Strengths:** "His written advice is excellent and he is good at delivering work on time." "He is our first choice advocate for doctors' disciplinary matters and complex appeals." **Recent work:** Instructed in Hayley Dare v WLMHT, a victimisation claim following a forensic psychologist whistle-blowing about patient safety at Broadmoor Hospital.

Ben Collins QC (see p.620) Recognised for his proficiency in sophisticated whistle-blowing claims and discrimination cases. He regularly acts for public sector employers and his employment practice is bolstered by his knowledge of personal injury law. **Strengths:** "He is a very punchy advocate who is good at robust cross-examination and the technical aspects of a case." "He gives clear, well-reasoned arguments so you can cut straight to the chase and have a structured, time-effective hearing." **Recent work:** Instructed in Beal v Care Quality Commission, a significant whistle-blowing claim brought by the former HR director of CQC.

JUNIORS

Ben Cooper (see p.622) Widely praised by clients and peers as an outstanding advocate who is incredibly hard-working and grasps the details incredibly quickly. He has expertise in injunctive relief issues and TUPE cases, among many other areas. Clients attest that he is "an excellent tactician who manages complex legal and sensitive employment issues with a relaxed manner." **Strengths:** "An all-round consummate employment lawyer who is incredibly capable and knowledgeable. He is able to picks up facts and run with them and he has excellent attention to detail." **Recent work:** Acted for members of Unite the Union who were victims of blacklisting by construction companies. Claimants are alleging unlawful means conspiracy, misuse of confidential information, defamation and potential career losses from the 1970s onwards.

Stuart Brittenden (see p.603) Offers expert advice to employers, individuals and trade unions with specialist knowledge of injunctive relief matters and discrimination cases. Clients are keen to highlight his highly impressive advocacy and written advice, with others praising his knowledge of difficult restrictive covenant issues. **Strengths:** "Excellent advocate with an eye for detail and commercially astute." "He is a delight to work with – he is approachable, hard-working and he knows everything back to front. You are assured that he will fight your corner." **Recent work:** Acted in Land Registry v Houghton & Others, successfully overturning an earlier tribunal decision that the employees should be disqualified from bonus entitlement following disability-related absences.

Nadia Motraghi (see p.723) Exceptionally skilled advocate who acts for both employers and senior executives. She also has significant experience representing governmental institutions and NHS organisations. Clients praise her dedication to cases and note her thoroughness and detailed approach. She has extensive experience of holiday pay claims and contractual disputes. **Strengths:** "She has a great combination of intellect, attention to detail and persistence, with a practical and focused approach – she is a pleasure to deal with." "She is a robust advocate who remains calm and composed at all times." **Recent work:** Instructed in Charlotte Monro v Barts Health NHS Trust, an unfair dismissal claim brought by a former trade union representative, alleging that she was wrongly dismissed for her whistle-blowing actions.

Simon Cheetham (see p.616) Widely respected by clients for his approachable manner and user-friendly nature, he is an expert on discrimination and industrial action matters. He regularly represents clients at all court levels, with significant experience of tribunal and High Court advocacy. **Strengths:** "He is a safe pair of hands on complex matters who has a robust and client-friendly approach." "He has an incredible rapport with the courts and the tribunal." **Recent work:** Acted in Lock v British Gas, a holiday pay case before the ECJ ruling that commission should be taken into account when calculating wages in respect of annual leave.

Katharine Newton (see p.727) Maintains a wide employment law practice, representing large employers and individuals from both the public and private sector. She is praised for her responsiveness and her advocacy skills. She regularly represents employers from the banking and financial services sectors, as well as large media organisations. **Strengths:** "She is sensible, bright and fantastic with clients and tribunals – clients adore her." "She is pragmatic, diligent and able to communicate with lay clients." **Recent work:** Defended East London NHS Foundation Trust against a disability discrimination claim brought by a former consultant psychiatrist, a claim of over £1.7 million.

Louise Chudleigh (see p.617) Experienced employment lawyer with expertise in discrimination, equal pay and whistle-blowing claims. Clients attest that she has a high level of client service and she is very quick at turning work around. Her extensive employment law knowledge is bolstered by her experience as an Employment Tribunal judge. **Strengths:** "She is really tough, really straightforward and really fights for her clients." **Recent work:** Defended the Commissioner of Police for the Metropolis against allegations of sexual orientation discrimination, made by a police constable whose sexuality was publicised in the press following the phone hacking scandal.

Rebecca Tuck (see p.784) Talented tribunal advocate with extensive knowledge of discrimination claims and unfair dismissal cases. Highly adept at handling complex employment litigation and she often conducts investigations into employees and advises grievance and disciplinary panels. **Strengths:** "She is fantastic in tribunals and is very client-friendly." **Recent work:** Instructed in Harrison v Institute of Psychoanalysis, an age discrimination case brought by the 76-year-old claimant after being rejected for a place at an institute course. Successfully won the claimant an apology and £15,000 in damages.

Deshpal Panesar (see p.733) Skilled advocate who regularly appears before the High Court and employment tribunals. He has extensive experience of handling difficult discrimination claims, including discrimination based on age, disability and religion. **Strengths:** "Deshpal is an excellent cross-examiner and you can rest assured that you have a real fighter in your corner." **Recent work:** Defended the University of Kent against an age discrimination claim brought against the university by a lecturer. Alleged that the requirement for admittance onto a PhD course was unlawful indirect age discrimination but this was successfully defended by Panesar at the EAT.

Betsan Criddle (see p.626) Has a broad employment law practice with notable experience in discrimination cases and injunction proceedings. She represents a wide range of clients including banks, independent schools, major charities, NHS trusts, trade unions and senior executives. **Strengths:** "She gets to grips with technical issues and breaks them down really well." "She is really good on her feet and she will absolutely fight your corner – she is a robust, optimistic lawyer." **Recent work:** Instructed in Annals v The Commissioner of Police for the Metropolis, a high-profile claim of sex discrimination after an officer was refused a career break to travel, despite his wife, also a police officer, being granted exactly the same leave.

Ijeoma Omambala (see p.730) Identified by peers as a strong discrimination lawyer who has expertise in wider employment law issues. Clients appreciate her approachable manner and personable nature. She is skilled in restrictive covenant issues, breach of contract matters and senior executive exits. **Strengths:** "A solid junior for discrimination cases." "She speaks in a very straightforward way and expresses herself succinctly and articulately, so you understand the points she is making both legally and factually." **Recent work:** Defended Shell against allegations brought by a former employee on the graduate trainee programme, including claims of race and disability discrimination and harassment.

Ian Scott Offers a wide employment law practice with particular interest in whistle-blowing and complex, multifaceted discrimination claims. Represents both employers and individuals, acquiring much experience assisting healthcare and local government clients. **Strengths:** "A heavy-hitting senior junior who is a formidable advocate." **Recent work:** Defended Ford against age discrimination claims brought by former employees receiving pensions from the company.

Melanie Tether (see p.779) Revered by clients for her thoroughness, attention to detail and her unflappable nature during tribunal proceedings. She regularly assists clients with complex disability discrimination cases and equal pay disputes. **Strengths:** "She is able to analyse vast quantities of information and distil it down to find the key strengths and weaknesses of the case." "She has a clinical approach to cases – she can cut through it and make it all seem so obvious." **Recent work:** Instructed in Ministry of Defence v Holloway and Others, a claim that the MoD had discriminated against spouses of armed forces personnel posted in Cyprus by employing them on less favourable contracts than their Cypriot counterparts.

Robin White (see p.794) Regularly tackles difficult discrimination and employment cases, with specific expertise in transgender issues within the workplace. She is often instructed by large clients from the transport and education sectors, and she is recognised for her effective advocacy style. **Strengths:** "She focuses on the key issues and hammers them home quickly and effectively. She is very good at reading what the tribunal is thinking and addressing it in a very concise way. She is a very feisty but very professional advocate." **Recent work:** Represented hundreds of government employees in a conflict over their contractual right to pay rises during the government pay freeze.

Elizabeth Melville (see p.715) Has a far-reaching employment practice with experience of harassment allegations, disability discrimination claims and equal pay disputes. Regularly represents clients from the education, finance and health sectors. **Strengths:** "She is extremely thorough and well prepared. She builds a good rapport with the clients." **Recent work:** Defended an NHS trust against allegations by a former consultant neurosurgeon of victimisation, unfair dismissal and detriments on grounds of having made protected disclosures.

Hilary Winstone (see p.799) Receives praise for being "a safe pair of hands" and having excellent client service skills. She is especially adept at handling employment and discrimination cases for public sector clients, including local authorities, police forces and NHS trusts. **Strengths:** "Excellent and practical barrister who gets to the heart of the matter straight away." "Excellent strategist and advocate who is very client-friendly and a real part of the team." **Recent work:** Instructed in Angela Bailey v Central and Northwest London NHS Trust, successfully defending the trust against claims of whistle-blowing, disability discrimination and victimisation.

Jack Mitchell He is well renowned for his work in high-profile whistle-blowing claims and regularly handles other sensitive employment cases for his clients. He has a notable interest in commercial aspects of employment law, advising on partnership issues and shareholder disputes. **Strengths:** "He is very responsive and is an absolute expert in his field, particularly whistle-blowing issues." "He is ideally suited to complex litigation cases such as equal pay matters and sex discrimination."

Band 3

Devereux

See profile on p.827

THE SET

A strong group of employment law practitioners who advise large multinational companies and governmental institutions on all aspects of employment law. The team has extensive experience of handling complex High Court matters and is widely recognised as a leader in industrial action and trade union disputes. Its members' individual specialisms help to strengthen the set's employment offering, and they demonstrate expertise where employment law intersects with other areas, including tax and personal injury. Chambers has strength at all levels of call, with sources noting that they are "a very good set of juniors and seniors, who are bright and intelligent."

Client service: "The clerking team at Devereux is very responsive and flexible in terms of pricing – they are a draw to use barristers at their set." "The clerking team are fantastic. They really get that it is a partnership and understand the client service level you have to deliver. They work very well together and have a very clear billing practice." Vince Plant serves as the chambers director.

SILKS

Bruce Carr QC A skilful advocate, widely recognised for his expertise in industrial relations and trade union matters. Sources also highlight his proficiency in whistle-blowing, discrimination and strikeout cases, alongside his high level of client service and determination that he brings to his cases. **Strengths:** "He is an exceptional advocate who is good at both closing submissions and cross-examination." "Very quickly gets to the nub of the issue and dispels very technical legal arguments from the other side that have no weight with the commercial realities." **Recent work:** Instructed in Lokhova v Sberbank, a high-profile sex discrimination case in which Carr obtained a £3.2 million award for the claimant.

Timothy Brennan QC Widely recognised for his strong tax knowledge, he is an established expert in employment law issues that have additional tax complications. He has extensive experience handling complex remuneration disputes and TUPE issues, often acting for large City clients and accountancy firms. **Strengths:** "He is competent in both employment and tax areas. He is incredibly quick, very good at knowing the answer and a very economic advocate." "He is very practical, very approachable and friendly and he is very good with the client."

Andrew Burns QC (see p.607) Advises clients on a broad range of employment matters, including complex industrial disputes and discrimination issues, among other areas. Sources praise his strong advocacy and cross-examination skills, noting that he is especially talented in injunctive relief and whistle-blowing matters. **Strengths:** "He is very bright, has got great attention to detail and has a good manner in tribunal and cross-examinations." "He is very good, but he is particularly good on strike injunctions and industrial action." **Recent work:** Successfully defended British Airways after 115 former BMI employees claimed automatic unfair redundancy, following BMI's takeover by British Airways. Claims were complicated by allegations of indirect sex and age discrimination.

JUNIORS

Akash Nawbatt (see p.725) Handles discrimination and whistle-blowing cases at all court levels, including the High Court and the Court of Appeal. He is regularly instructed by large banking clients and governmental institutions. Clients are impressed with his tribunal skills, noting his diligent and personable approach. **Strengths:** "He quickly grasps what the case is about and is insightful, technically strong and very client-friendly." "He is extraordinarily bright and very easy to work with – clients love him as he always puts the client at ease." **Recent work:** Instructed in Chu and Others v British Airways, a complex group race and age discrimination case brought by Hong Kong cabin crew surrounding the retirement age within British Airways.

Sophie Belgrove (see p.594) Recognised for bringing a commercial slant to her employment work, Sophie is regularly instructed in high-profile discrimination and whistle-blowing matters. Clients value her logical and sensible approach to cases and she is often instructed by leading financial institutions. **Strengths:** "She is very commercial, responsive and good on her feet; her cross-examination style is very effective but subtle and the claimant does not realise they are being undermined." "She is a very sensible person who steers a careful course and gets some really great results."

Peter Edwards (see p.639) Has a broad employment law practice, with extensive experience of High Court litigation and complex EAT claims. He specialises in industrial relations work and is often instructed by high-profile trade unions. **Strengths:** "He is very experienced across the whole employment field and good to work with – he gives helpful advice." **Recent work:** Instructed in O'Sullivan v TfL, a complex EAT case trying to ascertain whether a death in service benefit can be considered a loss following the redundancy and death of the claimant before the remedy hearing.

Laura Bell Experienced barrister who is respected by sources for her exceptional advocacy skills, particularly her ability to cross-examine thoroughly, robustly and sensitively. She operates a wide employment practice, which is bolstered by her personal injury law knowledge. **Strengths:** "She is very measured and calm, very organised and on her feet she is very impressive – she judges the mood of the tribunal very well." "She is extremely easy to work with as she is very helpful and responsive and very thorough in her approach."

Alice Mayhew (see p.710) An experienced High Court advocate who is highly knowledgeable in matters involving restrictive covenants, contractual rights and whistle-blowing. Clients attest that she has a high level of client service and is a confident and impressive advocate. **Strengths:** "She is excellent – she is extremely good with the client and really willing to get stuck in and be a team player." Solicitors note that "her advocacy is great" and that "she is robust when she needs to be." **Recent work:** Acted in Chesterton Global Limited and Neal Verman v Nurmohamed, a complex whistle-blowing case in which the tribunal sought to ascertain the proper interpretation of the term 'public interest' in the Employment Rights Act 1996.

Christopher Stone (see p.774) Clients praise him for his incredibly commercial approach to employment law matters, which may be attributed to his invaluable experience as a management consultant before joining the Bar. He focuses his employment practice on difficult discrimination tribunal claims, whilst operating a wider practice in tax and commercial law. **Strengths:** "He is practical, accurate and tactful where there are client sensitivities." "He can destroy witnesses in cross-examination whilst remaining very polite." "He does not leave any stone unturned and it is a huge comfort knowing that he is on your side." **Recent work:** Successfully acted in a complex disability discrimination, sexual orientation harassment and unfair dismissal claim. The case was complicated further by a personal injury claim and needing expert actuarial evidence to calculate pension loss.

Talia Barsam (see p.590) Praised for her approachability and client-handling skills, she has an extensive employment law practice advising on unfair dismissals, redundancies and TUPE issues. Regularly represents both private and public clients, with vast experience acting for healthcare trusts and local authorities. **Strengths:** "She is sharp, picks up facts quickly and is good at explaining matters and issues to clients." "She has the ability to gain the trust of the client very quickly and comes across as someone with great gravitas."

Thomas Cordrey Has established a strong employment practice, with notable expertise in complex TUPE issues and discrimination cases. Sources highlight his impressive advocacy in tribunal settings, most notably how he clearly delivers his submissions and arguments. **Strengths:** "He does not browbeat witnesses but can secure confessions from them by tactical questioning, and he has a very good manner with the tribunal." "He is extremely well organised; he gives first-rate legal analysis and his structured application to cases enables him to assimilate very complex facts." **Recent work:** Acted in a highly complex TUPE case on behalf of the Secretary of State for Health that considered an important estoppel point. The case has been heard in both the High Court and the EAT.

Lucinda Harris (see p.664) Continues to act for high-profile employers from both the public and private sectors, including large hospitality clients and influential banking institutions. She has a wide employment practice, offering expert advice on TUPE, discrimination and wrongful dismissal issues, among other areas. **Strengths:** "Gets up to speed with cases quickly and can build up a rapport with witnesses and clients."

Kate Balmer (see p.588) Represents high-profile employers and large banking institutions in all manner of employment matters, with specific focus on issues involving tax complications. She is highly regarded for her impressive client-handling skills. **Strengths:** "She is an excellent junior counsel who keeps on growing in her practice." "She is exceptionally good with clients – she puts them at ease and is responsive." **Recent work:** Successfully defended Network Rail in an equal pay and unlawful deductions claim brought by employees following contested job-banding after a TUPE transfer from Amey.

Harriet Fear Davies Frequently acts for both public and private sector clients. She is particularly experienced in handling matters of unfair and constructive dismissal, protected disclosure and discrimination. **Strengths:** "Exceptionally responsive and fully appreciative of the impact on a client's business." "Always well prepared." **Recent work:** Acted for a consultant surgeon in an unfair dismissal claim against a healthcare trust. The tribunal agreed with Harriet's assessment that the respondent's failure to properly constitute the dismissing panel in accordance with the national policy meant that her client had been unfairly dismissed.

Outer Temple Chambers

See profile on p.887

THE SET

Outer Temple provides an experienced team with an impressive breadth of expertise across a range of employment issues. Its barristers have particular strength in equal pay claims and cases where both employment and pension law intersects. The set has a growing reputation for its flourishing High Court practice, assisting high-profile clients with complex breach of contract and restrictive covenant claims. Barristers at the chambers regularly represent large employers and senior individuals, and are renowned for handling sizeable multiparty litigation in the public and police sectors.

Client service: "The clerking team is very responsive and easy to deal with – they give clear and sensible estimates." "The clerks are really helpful, always return calls, are very co-operative and quite understanding in terms of payment of fees." David Smith and Dave Scothern lead the team.

SILKS

Andrew Short QC Recognised for his expertise in complicated holiday pay matters and his highly praised advocacy in the EAT. His practice is bolstered by his renowned knowledge of pensions law and he is regularly instructed in pension-related discrimination claims. **Strengths:** "Andrew is a technically astute, but extremely down-to-earth QC, who breaks down the most complex of legal issues into client-friendly language." "Invaluable for his pragmatic, practical approach and his willingness to give clear and confident advice on difficult subjects." **Recent work:** Instructed in McCloud v Lord Chancellor & MoJ, a large multiple claims case challenging changes to judges' pension rights which is complicated by allegations of unlawfulness and discrimination.

Keith Bryant QC Handles a wide employment practice, enhanced by his extensive knowledge of pensions law. Regularly takes on high-profile discrimination cases and issues surrounding employment and national security vetting protocols. **Strengths:** "His responsiveness to client queries is very impressive, as is his range and depth of knowledge." **Recent work:** Acted for Swansea University against a disability discrimination claim concerning ill health retirement benefits from the university pension scheme.

JUNIORS

Daniel Barnett Acts for both employers and employees across a wide range of employment matters, with specific attention to restrictive covenants and age discrimination issues. Clients praise his incredibly high level of client service and responsiveness. He has considerable experience representing clients at all levels of the judicial system, including the High Court. **Strengths:** "He has a fast turnaround, is efficient and to the point." "His advocacy is good, he is a good cross-examiner and he can really pursue a point." **Recent work:** Acted for Gwyn Williams, former technical director of Leeds United FC, in a High Court claim for notice payment after he was dismissed from his role for gross misconduct.

Andrew Allen Has a multifaceted practice, complementing his extensive knowledge of employment law with expertise in both partnership and discrimination law issues. He is regularly instructed by both employers and employees from the legal sector and has notable specialism in injunctive relief cases. **Strengths:** "He is vastly experienced, immediately identifies the core issues in a case and is able to inspire complete confidence in both solicitors and the lay client." "His directness is refreshing; he will answer your question and nothing in what he says is unnecessary." **Recent work:** Represented a GlaxoSmithKline employee in a convoluted disability discrimination case against his employer.

Lydia Seymour Valued by clients for being "incredibly hard-working, strategic and insightful," with others highlighting her strong employment and pensions law crossover practice. She has extensive experience of discrimination cases and has a very detailed understanding of TUPE complications. **Strengths:** "She is a good team player who will fight the client's corner. She is also very thorough." "She leaves the client with the clear sense that they have had the best possible representation." **Recent work:** Instructed in Weerasinghe v Basildon & Thurrock University NHS Trust, a highly complex EAT case with claims of whistle-blowing, unfair dismissal and disability discrimination.

Naomi Ling Repeatedly instructed by clients to appear in complex tribunal and Court of Appeal cases across the whole gamut of employment law. She has extensive experience of restrictive covenants, bonus disputes and negotiating severance packages. **Strengths:** "She is on top of her stuff, calm and confident in her advocacy and is unfazed in tribunal." "She is very bright, very good with clients and very responsive." **Recent work:** Successfully represented University College NHS Trust in an appeal in the EAT, arguing that it had failed to make reasonable adjustments, and on disability-related discrimination.

Naomi Cunningham Focuses her employment practice upon discrimination matters, supported by extensive knowledge of mass equal pay litigation. She is recognised by sources for her commitment to her cases and her high quality of client service. **Strengths:** "She always makes clients feel at ease and explains things in a very clear way – she is very practical and pragmatic in her advice." "She has rare expertise in interim relief applications in union detriment cases." **Recent work:** Acted in Ahmed v Sainsbury's, a mass dispute revolving around the equal pay of female retail employees and male warehouse workers at Sainsbury's.

Emily Gordon Walker (see p.657) Primarily focused on Employment Tribunal cases, she assists both private and public sector employers in all manner of complex discrimination claims. She is adept at handling difficult TUPE issues and employment matters that have cross-jurisdictional elements. **Strengths:** "She made mincemeat of the opposition and slaughtered them in cross-examination." "A fantastic up-and-coming barrister." "Her advice was provided in a timely manner and was very concise and relevant."

Saul Margo Regularly represents clients in employment tribunals and is often instructed by governmental institutions and claimants. His employment practice is bolstered by his pensions law knowledge, which allows him to give expert advice in complex cases that incorporate both disciplines. **Strengths:** "He is one to watch – an excellent tactician." "He is conscientious and is always available at the end of the phone to deal with any questions as they arise." **Recent work:** Acted for over 7,000 police officers across the UK, in a case challenging the transitional protection given to older officers when the 2015 pension scheme was introduced. Claims included allegations of age discrimination and indirect race and sex discrimination.

Other Ranked Lawyers

Jude Shepherd (42 Bedford Row) Discrimination and employment lawyer who is widely lauded by clients and peers for her outstanding level of client service and support. She often acts at both the Employment Tribunal and EAT, and is highly knowledgeable in all aspects of employment law. **Strengths:** "She is very technical and always has time to speak with you about the issues." "She is very straightforward and down to earth, technically excellent and a brilliant advocate." **Recent work:** Acted in Deangate Ltd v Hatley and Others, in which the respondents appealed a decision that the claimants had applied for fee remission within the requisite time to proceed with their claim.

Susan Chan (42 Bedford Row) Experienced practitioner who has expertise in discrimination claims, especially cases involving disability and indirect discrimination. She is also adept at handling difficult restrictive covenant enforcements and Court of Appeal cases. **Recent work:** Successfully defended Lloyds Pharmacy against claims of unfair dismissal, wrongful dismissal and breach of contract by a former senior manager.

Tim Adkin (42 Bedford Row) Has a solid employment practice adeptly handling complex whistle-blowing and discrimination matters. Clients note that he has exceptional client-handling skills and that he is very approachable. **Strengths:** "He is very diligent and readily available to provide clear and pragmatic advice." "He does not sit on the fence and gives jargon-free advice and commentary." **Recent work:** Successfully defended Tesco against four claims of race discrimination, victimisation and unfair dismissal brought by former employees at Employment Tribunal.

Orlando Holloway (42 Bedford Row) Represents employees and employers from the transport, education and financial services sectors across all aspects of employment law. Clients value his robust advocacy style and his pragmatic approach to his cases. **Strengths:** "He always picks up the issues very quickly, is very pragmatic and good with the clients." "His key strengths are his interpersonal skills and his ability to read a tribunal and know when to make a particular point." **Recent work:** Defended Network Rail against claims by a former apprentice that the company failed to make reasonable adjustments for his disabilities, including dyspraxia and dyslexia, and thus were guilty of disability discrimination and unfair dismissal.

Heather Williams QC (Doughty Street Chambers) Highly reputed for her civil liberties knowledge which feeds into her strong employment practice, especially when tackling complex discrimination cases. Peers admire her skilful advocacy and attest that she is impressive when representing claimants. **Strengths:** "She is an absolute brainbox – she is extortionately intelligent and brings solid legal arguments which are difficult to break down in the courtroom." **Recent work:** Represented a high-profile news producer in a claim of sex and age discrimination against her former employer NBC News.

Nick Toms (Doughty Street Chambers) Experienced employment barrister with expert knowledge of unfair dismissal, redundancy and discrimination work. He is regularly instructed by claimants but also provides quality advice to trade unions.

Michael Salter (see p.758) (Ely Place Chambers) Highly knowledgeable lawyer who is instructed by both private companies and influential public sector employers. He is frequently sought out to handle cases involving discrimination and restrictive covenants. **Strengths:** "He is very user-friendly, very easy to deal with and he makes you feel like you are his only client." "He is an excellent and experienced Employment Tribunal advocate." **Recent work:** Acted in Sekon v London Heathrow Airports, an unfair dismissal claim lodged by a security officer at London Heathrow who stated that she was dismissed to avoid paying her a large redundancy payment.

David Mitchell (see p.719) (Ely Place Chambers) Has a wide employment law practice that is bolstered by his knowledge of media and public law. Clients praise his impressive knowledge and his dedication to his clients and their cases. **Strengths:** "He is a very bright guy and is very user-friendly for clients." "He works hard to get his head around complex law and delivers fantastic results for the clients." **Recent work:** Successfully acted in the Court of Appeal to reverse an earlier EAT decision, finding that his claimant had in fact been unfairly dismissed from Thames Water.

Stuart Ritchie QC (see p.752) (Fountain Court Chambers) Offers a unique blend of expertise of both employment and commercial law, with particular attention paid to matters involving fiduciary duties. He appears frequently in cases with senior executives and interim injunctions. **Strengths:** "Stuart is an excellent tactician, particularly in difficult and complex situations. He is extremely responsive and is a determined fighter who is highly effective in court." **Recent work:** Acted for the ex-chief technology officer of the BBC in his claims for unfair dismissal and whistle-blowing detriment. He claimed that he had been made a scapegoat for the failure of BBC's Digital Media Initiative. His unfair dismissal claim succeeded and the tribunal was critical of the BBC's conduct in dismissing him, following a 15-day hearing.

Paul Gott QC (see p.657) (Fountain Court Chambers) Experienced employment practitioner who is highly regarded for his extensive expertise in industrial relations and trade union issues. He regularly acts for large corporate employers from the retail, transport and public sectors. **Strengths:** "He has a very thorough grasp of both the law and commercial imperatives." "He is the go-to man for industrial relations work – his advice often helps resolve disputes behind the scenes without litigation or strike action." **Recent work:** Provided Morrisons with strategic legal advice when employees at its distribution centres threatened to strike.

Adam Tolley QC (see p.782) (Fountain Court Chambers) Maintains a wide employment practice, advising employers, governmental bodies and senior executives on all aspects of employment law. He is particularly skilled in handling complex holiday pay and injunctive relief matters. **Strengths:** "He is very responsive, creative and user-friendly. He is very tenacious on his feet and nothing fazes him." **Recent work:** Instructed in Allahditta v British Airways, a claim of religious discrimination and unfair dismissal brought by a former engineer. The case was further complicated by national security issues.

Patrick Green QC (see p.660) (Henderson Chambers) Well established in employment law with expertise in discrimination and whistle-blowing claims. Clients admire his advocacy skills and his creative approach to complex cases. **Strengths:** "He is extremely pleasant to deal with. He is proactive, creative and one of the best barristers I've ever dealt with." **Recent work:** Instructed in Shanks v Unilever Plc & Others, a complex employee patent compensation claim that was advanced to the High Court for further debate.

Kathleen Donnelly (see p.635) (Henderson Chambers) Talented practitioner with expertise in restrictive covenant matters, whistle-blowing and discrimination claims. Clients and peers alike highlight her impressive advocacy, noting that she is a formidable opponent in High Court cases. **Strengths:** "She is very confident, robust and clear in her advocacy." "She is highly intelligent and she has excellent attention to detail." **Recent work:** Instructed in Tshiaba v Dovetail, a race discrimination and wrongful dismissal claim brought by a former employee against the financial technology company.

David Brook (see p.604) (Henderson Chambers) Clients appreciate his commercial background and acumen which strengthen his solid employment practice. He advises both employers and senior executives across the whole gamut of employment law, with clients praising his strong communication skills. **Strengths:** "He is able to grasp issues quickly, summarise them succinctly and give the clients confidence in his knowledge of the subject." "He has very broad experience and is very good at looking at the commercial issues and what the client is trying to achieve." **Recent work:** Advised an employee on his claims of unfair dismissal, sex discrimination and sexual harassment against his former employer and colleagues.

David Stephenson (1MCB) An expert in all manner of discrimination claims with impressive knowledge across the wider aspects of employment law. He is instructed by both employers and senior executives, representing his clients in both tribunal and appellate cases. **Strengths:** "He is excellent with clients and he goes above and beyond." **Recent work:** Acted for a police officer who was promoted to sergeant by Hampshire Constabulary, yet her promotion was removed after the force posted her in a too distant location. The claimant argued that she could not work at that location due to childcare obligations and claimed that the refusal to make adjustments was indirectly discriminatory.

Jonathan Davies (see p.630) (Serjeants' Inn Chambers) Specialist employment lawyer who is an expert in restrictive covenants, discrimination claims and whistle-blowing cases amongst others. His clients include local authorities, the NHS, the police, companies and individuals. **Strengths:** "Very bright and very commercially switched-on." **Recent work:** Acted for around 80 police officers who were part of the Royal Protection Squad (known as SO14). This is a multiparty action where Davies's clients sought to obtain around £3,000,000 in unpaid allowances which they should have been paid following reforms to police pay in 2003.

Laura Robinson (see p.754) (Tanfield Chambers) A strong practitioner offering quality advice across thorny discrimination, whistle-blowing and unfair dismissal cases. Clients are keen to highlight her impressive advocacy style, noting that she is calm and unflappable under pressure but is equally able to push difficult points when necessary. **Strengths:** "A very competent and personable barrister who is able to delve to the heart of complex cases easily." "She really knows her stuff and is very down to earth."

Bruce Gardiner (see p.650) (2TG – 2 Temple Gardens) Handles complex discrimination claims and whistle-blowing cases for both employers and employees. His employment practice is bolstered by his personal injury knowledge and he is seen by clients as a reliable advocate. **Strengths:** "Very safe pair of hands and an impressive senior junior." "He is very capable, has a very good attitude and is good on paper and on his feet." **Recent work:** Acted for the former head of meat at ASDA, who brought unfair dismissal claims against his former employer.

MIDLANDS

Employment	
Leading Sets	
Band 1	
No5 Chambers *	
St Philips Chambers *	
Leading Silks	
Band 1	
Pepperall Edward	*St Philips Chambers* *
Leading Juniors	
Band 1	
Barney Helen	*No5 Chambers* [A] *
Beever Edmund	*St Philips Chambers* *
Hignett Richard	*No5 Chambers* [A]
Sadiq Tariq	*St Philips Chambers* [A]
Band 2	
Cooksey Nick	*River Chambers (ORL)* ◇
Crow Charles	*No5 Chambers* [A]
George Sarah	*St Philips Chambers* *
Gidney Jonathan	*St Philips Chambers* *
Hodgetts Elizabeth	*St Philips Chambers* *
Islam-Choudhury Mugni	*No5 Chambers*
Korn Anthony	*No5 Chambers* [A]
Maxwell David	*St Philips Chambers* *
Meichen Jonathan	*St Philips Chambers* [A] *
Roberts Gemma	*No5 Chambers* *
Sheppard Tim	*No5 Chambers* [A]
Band 3	
Feeny Jack	*No5 Chambers*
McGrath Andrew	*No5 Chambers* [A]
Owen Naomi	*No5 Chambers*
Powell Richard	*River Chambers (ORL)* ◇
Up-and-coming individuals	
Jennings Caroline	*No5 Chambers*

** Indicates set / individual with profile.*

[A] direct access (see p.24).

◇ (ORL) = Other Ranked Lawyer.

Alphabetical order within each band. Band 1 is highest.

Band 1

No5 Chambers

See profile on p.931

THE SET

No5 Chambers is renowned for its employment work, and acts for clients across the whole spectrum of the employment market, showing particular strength in discrimination claims and cases of unfair dismissal. The set regularly represents both private and public sector clients, and has extensive experience of working with NHS trusts, local authorities and large private employers. Recent cases handled by members of the set include Farmah & Others v Birmingham City Council, a large multi-claimant equal pay case, and Paul Beacham v West Midlands Ambulance Service, a complex unfair dismissal and disability discrimination claim. Clients state that the chambers has "a very impressive range of barristers who are highly skilled and very approachable."

Client service: "The chambers is administered very efficiently. I have always found the practice manager of the employment group, Martin Ellis, very approachable. He is extremely skilful at matching clients with barristers who have empathy and considerable expertise."

JUNIORS

Helen Barney (see p.590) Handles a wide range of employment issues, including complex discrimination tribunals and whistle-blowing matters. She is regularly instructed by large NHS trusts, local authorities and private employers. **Strengths:** "She offers very straightforward, understandable advice and excels in cross-examination of witnesses." "Her advocacy is detailed, she knows the papers inside out and her questioning is very focused – a highly skilled advocate." **Recent work:** Acted in Simon Mokwena v Midland Heart Ltd, a complex five-day race discrimination and whistle-blowing case.

Richard Hignett Head of the employment group and has extensive experience in a wide range of employment law matters. He is particularly skilled in handling highly complex discrimination claims and allegations of unfair dismissal. He also provides expert advice and counsel to high-profile employers in the retail, manufacturing and construction industries. **Strengths:** "He comes across as a very knowledgeable advocate and has a very good approach to witnesses on both sides." "He is softly spoken and polite in the employment tribunals, and is thoughtful and thorough in his advocacy too."

Mugni Islam-Choudhury Has experience of handling all aspects of employment law, and particular strength in complicated TUPE issues, high-value discrimination claims and whistle-blowing allegations. He acts for clients from both the private and public sectors, including NHS trusts, local councils and police forces. **Strengths:** "His grasp and analysis of the key elements of a case is hugely impressive, and he comes into his own when dealing with complex discrimination cases." "In tribunals he doesn't beat around the bush, he brings back the focus and is not one of those barristers who uses theatrics." **Recent work:** Acted in Dr FB Babapulle v Isle of Wight NHS Trust, defending the trust against allegations of unfair dismissal and whistle-blowing claims.

Charles Crow Regularly instructed by clients from the education, housing and police sectors to act in grievance and disciplinary matters. He has extensive experience of unfair dismissal cases and discrimination issues. **Strengths:** "He is an excellent advocate; he thoroughly prepares beyond anything I would expect and he gets on famously with lay clients." "His approachability is definitely a strength and he gets more out of the client. He is very persuasive and puts forward his argument in a professional way." **Recent work:** Acted in Rogers v United Care Limited, a seven-day complex disability discrimination and unfair dismissal case.

Tim Sheppard Focuses his practice on discrimination, whistle-blowing and unfair dismissal claims, making regular appearances in tribunals representing NHS trusts and national charities. He also has experience of representing clients in the High Court and the Court of Appeal. **Strengths:** "He excels in the cross-examination of witnesses and can react to all the nuances of a case that can develop." "He is an exceptional advocate who consistently delivers. He is very approachable and puts witnesses at ease." **Recent work:** Acted in Dr Shavnam Dosanjh v Nottinghamshire Healthcare NHS Trust, a complex unfair dismissal claim compounded by allegations of race discrimination, disability discrimination and whistle-blowing elements.

Gemma Roberts (see p.753) Regularly represents both private and public clients across the spectrum of employment issues, and has a particular focus upon discrimination matters. She is regularly instructed by NHS trusts and large multinational organisations for Employment Tribunal proceedings. **Strengths:** "She is very thorough, incredibly prepared and extremely intelligent. She also has a complete understanding of the healthcare sector and NHS clients." "She gets to the issue of the case very quickly and will know the case inside out and grasp the key issues very quickly." **Recent work:** Acted in Miss L Herlock v Black Country Partnership NHS Foundation, attempting to persuade the Employment Appeal Tribunal (EAT) that a previous case of unfair dismissal had been wrongly decided. She successfully overturned the previous verdict and the claimant withdrew her claims.

Anthony Korn Highly skilled in handling complex TUPE issues and equal pay cases, with further experience of sophisticated contentious work related to discrimination, whistle-blowing and restrictive covenant enforcement. **Strengths:** "He offers absolutely first-rate advocacy, and is measured and very detailed." "He is on point all the time; he knows what to ask and the answers that he wants." **Recent work:** Acted in Foolchand v Ministry of Justice, a complex unfair dismissal and disability discrimination case relating to the dismissal of an employee who had been involved in a car accident.

Jack Feeny Instructed by both public and private sector clients in cases related to TUPE issues and discrimination claims, among other issues. He regularly advises police institutions and claimants from the financial sector, and often appears in the EAT. **Strengths:** "He is not afraid to tackle difficult situations and challenge the evidence of the other side." "He presents his advocacy in a very calm and well-prepared manner and he never fails to make his points clearly." **Recent work:** Acted in The Chief Constable of Northumbria Police v Erichsen, a complex disability discrimination case.

Andrew McGrath Couples his employment practice with professional negligence work. He has vast experience of representing clients in tribunals in cases relating to whistle-blowing, unfair dismissal and alleged breaches of contract. **Strengths:** "He is calm in his advocacy and won't be hassled by either an opponent or the Bench: he makes sure that his point is made as he wants it." **Recent work:** Acted in SSC v Coltman, a complex alleged breach of contract case complicated by restrictive covenant issues.

Naomi Owen Regularly acts for both respondents and claimants in tribunal cases, advising on a wide range of employment matters ranging from all forms of discrimination and unfair dismissal to complex TUPE work. **Strengths:** "Good at managing clients who are upset or do not appreciate the legality of the situation, and is good at explaining things in simple terms that they can understand: she is really patient." "She is clearly conspicuously able and very pleasant to deal with." **Recent work:** Acted in Richardson v Arcola, a claim of whistle-blowing and unfair dismissal.

Caroline Jennings Regularly advises both respondents and claimants in matters relating to discrimination, unfair dismissal and redundancies, among other areas. She has experience of complex contentious work, representing clients in both the Employment Tribunal and EAT. She also assists clients with difficult internal investigations. **Strengths:** "She is very sensitive with confidential matters and she definitely gets the message and her case across." "She is very sensible and very approachable. She does not overcomplicate issues and makes my life as a solicitor easier." **Recent work:** Instructed in Ms Allen v BASF plc & Adecco UK Limited, a case concerning a high-value claim for unfair dismissal and added contractual disputes.

St Philips Chambers

See profile on p.934

THE SET

St Philips Chambers represents clients across the whole range of employment law, and has particular strength in wrongful dismissal, breach of contract issues and restrictive covenants, among other areas. The team also has extensive experience of representing clients in all manners of discrimination cases. Members often act for large employers and individuals across both the public and private sector, with some specialising in the representation of local governments and NHS trusts. Barristers from this set have been recently instructed in Joe Anderson v Chesterfield High School, an unfair dismissal based on alleged discrimination of an individual's philosophical beliefs, and Colin Weaver v Sainsbury's Supermarkets Ltd, a highly sensitive case involving allegations of discrimination based on sex, sexual orientation and national origins. They are described by clients as "an excellent employment team."

Client service: "Employment clerk Gary Carney is fantastic; he always makes you a priority and is quick to respond." "The clerk was great. He was very impressive and easy to deal with. He will always try to answer your queries and is entirely reasonable in term of fees."

SILKS

Edward Pepperall QC (see p.736) A leading commercial litigation silk who also tackles his fair share of employment work, often in the appeal courts. He has handled class actions and is a noted expert on discrimination and equal pay cases. **Strengths:** "Really sensible and easy to deal with, he fights his corner well." "A pragmatic and clinical advocate who is user-friendly and fantastic in front of clients."

JUNIORS

Edmund Beever (see p.594) Head of employment here and highly experienced at handling complex restrictive covenants and senior executive disputes and exits. He also has expertise in discrimination issues and whistle-blowing claims, and is frequently instructed by clients to represent them in substantial tribunal hearings. He brings added knowledge from his experience as a part-time employment judge. **Strengths:** "He is a very good advocate and a very effective cross-examiner; he is able to be forceful and also be in control without being aggressive. He is very composed." "He is exceptional in tribunal; he will not get the judge's back up and due to his presentation skills, he makes everybody listen." **Recent work:** Acted in Sarah Wickens v St Alberts RC Primary School, a multifaceted whistle-blowing claim that was further complicated by serious allegations of fraud.

Tariq Sadiq Operates a wide employment law practice, and has extensive experience of handling matters involving restrictive covenants, whistle-blowing claims and complex discrimination allegations. He has also established a niche expertise in national security employment disputes. Sadiq regularly acts for large public and governmental bodies. **Strengths:** "His committed and pragmatic approach to the case and immediate alignment to the client's values and objectives make him outstanding." "He is very down to earth and able to relate to the client. He is also very meticulous in his preparation for cross-examination." **Recent work:** Acted in Day v The Royal Bank of Scotland, a highly complex unfair dismissal case brought by a managing director, compounded by additional equal pay issues.

Sarah George (see p.651) An experienced advocate, who regularly represents clients in multi-day tribunal hearings involving whistle-blowing, unfair dismissal and equal pay issues, and also has added experience in complex discrimination work. She is often instructed by public authorities, including NHS trusts and universities, and further represents employers from the corporate sphere. **Strengths:** "She is always very well prepared and always gets all that she can out of a case." "She manages the tribunal very well; she gets them on board, breaks down the case very usefully and successfully, and gets positive reviews from clients."

Jonathan Gidney (see p.652) Has developed a specialised litigation practice, representing high profile clients in complex Employment Tribunal matters, and proving particularly strong in lengthy discrimination cases. He regularly represents both private and public clients, including NHS trusts, local authorities and large retailers, among others. **Strengths:** "He is very controlled and calm in court but he is always on the ball and knows what he is talking about. He does not need to be really aggressive or argumentative or have to adopt theatrical tactics." "He is a very formidable, bright chap and one of the go-to people for technical cases."

Elizabeth Hodgetts (see p.673) Operates a wide employment practice, and has extensive experience of representing clients in discrimination claims, whistle-blowing matters and equal pay disputes, among many other areas. She regularly represents public sector clients, including local authorities and NHS trusts, and acts for both claimants and respondents. **Strengths:** "She is intellectually savvy and very clued-up – there was never an issue which she could not unravel and simplify." "Very good with witnesses and she can deal with them across different levels of understanding. She also cross-examines very well." **Recent work:** Acted in Saunderson v Arriva Cymru, a case of unfair dismissal complicated by claims of age discrimination.

David Maxwell (see p.710) His practice encompasses the full spectrum of employment law litigation, with a particular focus upon unfair dismissal and many different forms of discrimination including maternity discrimination. He regularly represents clients from both the private and public sectors, and also conducts work for senior executives and employees. He has added expertise from his work as a part-time employment judge. **Strengths:** "He has very good advocacy skills – he does not over-argue the point but will take a strategic view on the case instead." "He is quite calm and deals with situations well in court, even when curveballs are thrown at him. I would highly recommend him for cases with difficult individuals, or where something needs to be handled carefully." **Recent work:** Acted in Hougton v NHS Business Services Authority, a sophisticated claim of sex and maternity discrimination.

Jonathan Meichen (see p.715) Acts for both larger private employers and local authorities in highly complex discrimination cases, and has particular expertise of discrimination in the education sector. He also has further experience of representing both individuals and trade unions in wider employment issues. Additional strengths include his investigative work into grievance and discrimination issues, as well as his work on unfair dismissals. **Strengths:** "He is very clever and his analysis is very logical and easy to understand." "He does not make it too technical. It is written in a way that meets the requirements of every audience." **Recent work:** Instructed in Vernon Allatt v Secretary of State for Justice, a complex unfair dismissal case involving a prison officer and the alleged use of excessive force.

Other Ranked Lawyers

Nick Cooksey (River Chambers) Represents both employers and individuals from the public and private sectors in complex employment litigation, and has extensive experience of both the EAT and Court of Appeal. He often handles discrimination cases and instances of unfair dismissal, and is regularly instructed by high-profile clients from the retail, car and energy sectors. **Strengths:** "He is very honest with his clients and does not sit on the fence." "He is good at putting the client at ease, cutting to the key issues and getting a handle on the main facts of the case."

Richard Powell (River Chambers) Has a broad employment practice, with particular focus on discrimination cases, whistle-blowing issues and unfair dismissal. He represents clients from the retail, banking and public sectors, and has experience of acting for governmental departments and large supermarkets. **Strengths:** "His style of questioning is very polite and gentle – he gently slices away at the witness to get what he needs from the cross-examination."

NORTH EASTERN

Employment	
Leading Juniors	
Star individuals	
Sweeney Seamus	*Parklane Plowden*
Band 1	
Bayne Dominic	*Parklane Plowden*
Bourne Colin	*Kings Chambers* *
Legard Edward	*Dere Street Barristers* *
Sugarman Andrew	*Parklane Plowden*
Band 2	
Callan Jane	*Trinity Chambers*
Goldberg Simon	*Trinity Chambers*
Jeram Kirti	*Parklane Plowden*
Serr Ashley	*Exchange Chambers*
Stubbs Richard	*Trinity Chambers*
Band 3	
Healy Samuel	*Dere Street Barristers* *
Kirtley Paul	*Exchange Chambers*
Morgan Jamie	*Trinity Chambers*
Tinnion Antoine	*Trinity Chambers*
Widdett Ceri	*Exchange Chambers*
Wilson Paul	*Broadway House*

* *Indicates individual with profile.*

Alphabetical order within each band. Band 1 is highest.

Ranked Lawyers

Paul Wilson (Broadway House) Noted for his experience which extends over the breadth of complex employment law matters including TUPE transfers and outsourcing. His peers favour him as a "talented" advocate and an "amiable opponent and fair negotiator." **Strengths:** "An excellent advocate with an incisive mind."

Edward Legard (see p.699) (Dere Street Barristers) Has an acclaimed full-service employment law practice which he provides to plcs, local authorities, health trusts, trade unions and individuals. His peers and clients praise him for his "excellent, well prepared and unflappable manner." **Strengths:** "Very personable, succinct and calm. The witnesses had great confidence in him and he definitely improved their tribunal experience." "Edward is fantastic to work with. He is very bright, quick to get to grips with issues, thorough, and responsive despite being very busy. He has a positive, can-do attitude and is committed to the case. He has a very nice manner and is a team player." **Recent work:** Represented the local authorities in a complex whistle-blowing and disability discrimination case and subsequent successful EAT appeal on the one unresolved matter.

Samuel Healy (see p.668) (Dere Street Barristers) A specialist employment advocate with a vast abundance of experience to offer to his clientele across the breadth of the practice area. He has been particularly commended by market commentators for his impressive experience handling TUPE and discrimination claims. **Strengths:** "I found him to be very friendly, approachable and tenacious as an advocate." "A pleasant and fair opponent." **Recent work:** Appeared for the local authority in Grosset v City of York Council a high-profile disability discrimination and unfair dismissal case which was deliberated over five days and addressed issues over the extent to which medical evidence not before the employer at the time of the act of discrimination is relevant to a justification defence.

Ashley Serr (Exchange Chambers) Respected for his holistic practice and expertise in TUPE, discrimination and unfair dismissal matters as well as his involvement in handling restrictive covenant and complex judicial review cases. He has extensive experience of appearing on behalf of high net worth and business clientele before employment tribunals, the ECHR and the Supreme Court. **Strengths:** "He's a very strong court performer and doesn't pull any punches. He's a good person to have on your side." "Intellectually strong and has a clear understanding of what is necessary for the client, whether it be an individual or organisation." **Recent work:** Appeared in Country Court Care and Others v Secretary of State for the Home Department, which discussed what extent the Human Rights Act is relevant when making considerations of whether to revoke Tier 2 Sponsorship licences of a care home facility when this may affect the welfare of the residents therein.

Paul Kirtley (Exchange Chambers) Has acquired an esteemed reputation as an advocate in employment law among other areas. He has a store of experience handling litigious matters across the scale, including discrimination, public interest disclosures, data protection and disciplinary cases for his public sector clients who include the NHS, police and local authorities. He also offers specialist services in mediation. **Strengths:** "A TUPE expert. In tribunal he is tenacious, confident and successful." "I have the highest regard for him, he's very capable and popular."

Ceri Widdett (Exchange Chambers) Sought after for her experience in discrimination claims, including equal pay. She has particular expertise in equality law and has been instructed to advise and act on behalf of numerous local authorities. **Strengths:** "Clients always love her approach as it gets to the root of the issues in a no-nonsense manner." "Her conduct in the tribunal is impeccable and of the highest standard." **Recent work:** Acted for a female claimant in the high-profile case of Crosse v Calderdale NHS Trust, concerning equal pay, breach of contract and constructive dismissal.

Colin Bourne (see p.600) (Kings Chambers) A long-term employment advocate, and draws on an impressive breadth and depth of experience from both his many years in practice and his former role as a trade union officer when assisting his broad client base in the full range of matters. His specialist areas include TUPE, whistle-blowing, trade union recognition and industrial law. **Strengths:** "He has compendious knowledge of the law, and is a tenacious and incisive advocate with a very user-friendly manner." "He is a robust individual and will always give full value to his clients." **Recent work:** Represented South Yorkshire Fire & Rescue Authority in a case with respect to claims under the Working Time Regulations alleging detriment by reason of a refusal to forgo rights under the WTR.

Seamus Sweeney (Parklane Plowden) A pre-eminent advocate who is widely respected in the North Eastern employment circuit. He regularly appears on behalf of a range of clients from large corporates and local authorities through to individual claimants. He is noted for his experience across the breadth of the practice area, and for his involvement handling collective employment and restructuring issues and equal pay claims. **Strengths:** "Incredibly personable, very good with clients and a very incisive legal brain. He's head and shoulders above everyone else." "He's very good and commands the respect of the tribunal. He's easy-going in his approach and that belies the fact that he's a very able practitioner who's rightly very highly regarded."

Dominic Bayne (Parklane Plowden) A well-trusted litigator with an impressive track record in all facets of employment law including discrimination and equal pay claims. He has a broad and diverse practice representing both private and public sector clients, ranging from large-scale organisations to individuals. **Strengths:** "He is very studious, very logical and a talented advocate." "He's very thorough, level-headed and straightforward." **Recent work:** Appeared in a ten-day discrimination claim, Aslam v Derby CC, which concerned around 25 allegations of discrimination over a period of seven years, inclusive of harassment, denial of opportunity of advancement through promotion and victimisation owing to prior grievances.

Andrew Sugarman (Parklane Plowden) Described as "rational, reasoned and experienced," Sugarman receives no shortage of praise in the market for his distinguished practice representing claimants and respondents. He acts for a diverse client base, from trusts, local authorities and large-scale corporates to individuals. **Strengths:** "A favourite with our team for all clients – he is personable, reliable and a fierce advocate." "A pragmatic barrister who gives commercial advice and counsel that can be relied on. He delivers positive outcomes, always with the client in mind." **Recent work:** Acted for several Immigration Appeal Tribunal judges in an ongoing case concerning part-time worker discrimination against the Ministry of Justice.

Kirti Jeram (Parklane Plowden) Recognised for her diligent practice representing public sector employers, which is inclusive of several local authorities. She has particular expertise in equal pay and unfair dismissal-related cases. **Strengths:** "Very competent and very capable advocate. She is a pleasure to work with." "She's level-headed and straightforward." "She is experienced and the tribunals listen to what she has to say." **Recent work:** Appeared in Richards v Manpower and Tynch v Manpower, cases concerning several claims involving harassment, race discrimination and disability discrimination among others.

Jane Callan (Trinity Chambers) Represents a diverse range of clients including local and health authorities, blue-chip companies and individuals, and offers specialist expertise in equal pay and discrimination cases. **Strengths:** "Always been known for her excellent standard of practice." "Her communication with clients is excellent and having access to such a renowned counsel helps: since she's so frequently in the courts, she is a known entity." **Recent work:** Acted in CED v DXC Trains Ltd + ASLEF & Others which was a case concerning claims of indirect and direct sex discrimination.

Simon Goldberg (Trinity Chambers) Peers heap praise on Goldberg for his impressive level of experience representing respondents and claimants nationally in the Employment Tribunal, EAT and High Court. He is noted for his depth of industry knowledge across the employment sphere. He offers niche services in post-termination restrictions and fiduciary duties. **Strengths:** "Simon is robust, he is extremely good with negotiations and is a strong competent court performer." "He has his clients' interests very firmly in his mind, and the other side has to be cautious dealing with him, he's a very good negotiator and practitioner." **Recent work:** Appeared on behalf of the MoD in an appeal against the registration of a COT3 agreement.

Richard Stubbs (Trinity Chambers) Best known for his experience advocating in complex employment matters and regularly appears for a variety of clients from individuals to local authorities and large corporates. He is well versed in handling multi-day hearings, TUPE, discrimination, equal pay and protected disclosures. **Strengths:** "Very impressive and he's quieter and more amicable in approach but he's tremendously effective. He's a very strong opponent." **Recent work:** Appeared on behalf of the respondent, DWP, in a five-day age and disability discrimination hearing with allegations of victimisation.

Jamie Morgan (Trinity Chambers) A diligent advocate who regularly appears for claimants and respondents in all conceivable reaches of the employment law practice area, from redundancies and dismissals to discrimination cases. He has a particularly esteemed reputation for handling equal pay litigation and acting for claimants in maternity-related claims. **Strengths:** "He has a very commercial and pragmatic view of a case. There's no ceremony, he gets straight to the heart of what the main issues are." **Recent work:** Represented the respondent in Thompson v Global Real Estate in relation to an unfair dismissal claim by a senior employee.

Antoine Tinnion (Trinity Chambers) Has an interesting depth of experience to draw upon, having accrued legal expertise in domestic and international matters in his long tenure as an advocate. He frequently represents respondents and claimants across the full spectrum of matters, including discrimination, unfair dismissal, wage disputes and TUPE matters. He is also a leading authority in the area of restrictive covenants. **Strengths:** "Very thorough and good at identifying issues and focusing on the ultimate objective."

NORTHERN

Employment
Leading Sets
Band 1
9 St John Street *
Band 2
Kings Chambers *
St Johns Buildings *
Leading Silks
Band 1
Gilroy Paul *9 St John Street*
Band 2
Gorton Simon *Atlantic Chambers (ORL)* ◊
* *Indicates set / individual with profile.*
◊ *(ORL) = Other Ranked Lawyer.*
Alphabetical order within each band. Band 1 is highest.

Employment
Leading Juniors
Band 1
Boyd James *Kings Chambers*
Brochwicz-Lewinski Stefan *9 St John Street*
Connolly Joanne *9 St John Street*
Gumbs Annette P *St Johns Buildings*
Morgan Edward *9 St John Street*
Quigley Louise *9 St John Street*
Wedderspoon Rachel *9 St John Street*
Woodward Joanne *9 St John Street*
Band 2
Draycott Paul *Doughty Street Chambers (ORL)* ◊
Gorasia Paras *Kings Chambers* *
Grundy Nigel *9 St John Street*
Mahmood Ghazan *St Johns Buildings*
Northall Daniel *Littleton Chambers (ORL)* ◊
Searle Jason *St Johns Buildings*
Siddall Nicholas *Littleton Chambers (ORL)* ◊ *
Band 3
Ali Kashif *St Johns Buildings*
Eeley Rebecca *9 St John Street*
Harwood-Gray Barry *Kenworthy's Chambers (ORL)* ◊
Niaz-Dickinson Anisa *Kenworthy's Chambers (ORL)* ◊ *
Trotter Helen *Kings Chambers* *
Williams Ben *Kings Chambers* *
Up-and-coming individuals
Daniels Laura *Kings Chambers* *

Band 1

9 St John Street

See profile on p.973

THE SET

9 St John Street's employment group is comprised of QCs and juniors who are capable of taking instructions on the full range of employment matters on behalf of employees, public and private employers, as well as trade unions. The set is particularly sought after for its experience with TUPE, unfair dismissal and discrimination claims. Its members' frequent activity in employment hearings, tribunals, High Court and appellate courts testifies to their strong, nationwide presence in the market.

Client service: Tony Morrissey is the senior clerk at 9 St John Street.

SILKS

Paul Gilroy QC Has wide-ranging experience in the field of employment law and is well versed in complex cases in the Employment Tribunal, Employment Appeal Tribunal (EAT) and the High Court. He is especially knowledgeable in employment issues in the sports industry and is highly regarded for his expertise in sports-related litigation and regulatory matters. **Strengths:** "Paul has a very robust and persuasive style." "He has a well-deserved reputation here in the North West."

JUNIORS

Louise Quigley Esteemed junior who is capable of handling a variety of employment matters, and particularly adept in whistle-blowing and maternity discrimination cases. **Strengths:** "Astute, personable and an excellent communicator." "She's very capable of distilling difficult legal issues into comprehensible language."

Stefan Brochwicz-Lewinski Has a wealth of experience in many areas of employment law and is well-regarded for his knowledge of TUPE, whistle-blowing and unfair dismissal issues, as well as his ability to seamlessly handle complex discrimination and equal pay claims. **Strengths:** "He is tenacious, a real battler." "He is willing to go the extra mile and works well as part of the team."

Joanne Connolly Has cultivated a reputation for her expertise in disability discrimination claims but is also notably experienced in unfair dismissal, whistle-blowing and equal pay claims. She is instructed by a variety of clients including those from local authorities, the education sector, corporate bodies and the NHS. **Strengths:** "She's an experienced advocate." "Always on top of the papers and someone with huge attention to detail, she never loses sight of the commercial goal."

Edward Morgan As an active advocate in the Emploment Tribunal and High Court, Morgan has a diverse employment practice. His experience in commercial law gives him a particular focus on restrictive covenants, shareholder disputes, breach of fiduciary duties claims and pension-related issues. **Strengths:** "He is extremely knowledgeable and experienced." "He has acute intelligence. He is a brilliant advocate and he excels with clients."

Rachel Wedderspoon Rachel is highly regarded for her knowledge of discrimination claims and is frequently instructed on behalf of police authorities, trade unions and NHS trusts.

Joanne Woodward Highly experienced in employment law, with strong expertise in complex discrimination work and appeals. She is also in high demand for her knowledge of TUPE and public interest disclosure claims, having worked with various high-profile public institutions throughout her career. **Strengths:** "She's a high-quality, well-prepared and well-respected advocate." "Clients are always impressed with her work."

Nigel Grundy Handles the full range of employment disputes for a variety of clients including NHS trusts, businesses, local authorities and clients from the education sector. He has experience of appearing in courts of all levels, including the Employment Tribunal, the EAT and the High Court. **Strengths:** "He is extremely client-friendly." "He delivers concise legal arguments and is an effective advocate."

Rebecca Eeley Rebecca is widely respected for her ability to handle complex discrimination cases. Her practice also includes matters relating to unfair dismissal, TUPE, whistle-blowing and equal pay.

Band 2

Kings Chambers

See profile on p.968

THE SET

The employment group at Kings Chambers acts on behalf of employers of all sizes as well as individual claimants. In recent years, its barristers have gained a reputation for their expertise in matters involving the NHS. Members continue to work on a number of significant, diverse cases at court, the Employment Tribunal and the EAT. Their current work includes matters relating to TUPE, discrimination and whistle-blowing.

Client service: Colin Griffin is the chief clerk at Kings Chambers for employment matters.

JUNIORS

James Boyd Leader of Kings Chambers' employment group, predominantly acting on behalf of employers. He does a substantial amount of work for NHS trusts as well as large multinational companies. **Strengths:** "James is exceptionally intelligent and quick-thinking." "He's always well prepared and has an excellent manner with clients." **Recent work:** Defended the University of Sunderland in a seven-day claim of race discrimination, disability discrimination and unfair dismissal.

Paras Gorasia (see p.657) Frequently works on high-value and complex claims involving discrimination, whistle-blowing and TUPE. His clients range from large multinational corporations to government departments. **Strengths:** "He is approachable, intelligent and great with clients. He is extremely responsive." "A persuasive advocate." **Recent work:** Instructed on behalf of the respondent, RBS, before Manchester Employment Tribunal in a ten-day disability discrimination and unfair dismissal claim. The value of the claim was approximately £500,000 and concerned over 100 allegations of discrimination. The claims were entirely dismissed by the tribunal.

Helen Trotter (see p.784) Renowned for her work relating to the Equality Act in both the tribunal and the civil courts. She has experience acting for several airlines, government departments and local authorities, in addition to individual claimants. **Strengths:** "Her strengths lie in her ability to analyse and process information quickly and deliver an opinion in a concise, clear, practical way." **Recent work:** Heavily involved with an appeal at the EAT on a test case regarding a vicar's loss of preaching licence following his same-sex marriage.

Ben Williams (see p.796) Ben regularly appears before tribunals to handle a range of employment issues, but deals particularly with unfair dismissal, TUPE and discrimination issues on behalf of respondent clients. **Strengths:** "I have been impressed by his attention to detail and very quick response to any question." **Recent work:** Represented the claimant, a former professional footballer who brought claims of whistle-blowing and breach of contract, in Eamonn O'Keefe v Whistledawn. Ben was able to expose significant untruths in the respondent's evidence. After the five-day tribunal, the claim resulted in a majority decision, ruling that Mr O'Keefe was unfairly dismissed due to whistle-blowing.

Laura Daniels (see p.628) Particularly noted for her interest and experience in TUPE, pregnancy discrimination and disability discrimination. She acts for both claimants and respondents in Employment Tribunal claims and employment-related civil court disputes. **Strengths:** "She is very good at getting to the crux of the case quickly and building an instant rapport with clients and instilling confidence." **Recent work:** Acted for the respondent, Crest Medical, in a three-day age discrimination and unfair dismissal claim before Liverpool Employment Tribunal. The allegations of age discrimination were dismissed and the parties resolved the dispute regarding unfair dismissal.

St Johns Buildings

See profile on p.970

THE SET

St Johns Buildings offers a bench of specialists whose combined expertise covers the full range of employment-related issues. It is a diverse set, skilled in representing both claimants and respondents, which has members who act for commercial employers as well as individual employees. Its barristers regularly appear in the Employment Tribunal, EAT and County and High Courts, in addition to disciplinary hearings.

Client service: "The clerks are always on hand to help out, and are willing to assist in meeting my clients' needs and/or budgets." The senior employment clerk at St Johns Buildings is Chris Shaw.

JUNIORS

Annette Gumbs Her background in personal injury and negligence cases means she is particularly esteemed for her knowledge of discrimination claims. She is also adept at handling issues involving restrictive covenants and frequently works on employment cases with a commercial element. **Strengths:** "She has an ability to cut through large amounts of information and paperwork and identify the important issues." **Recent work:** Instructed on behalf of the claimant in Turnball v Secretary of State for Health and Another, a complex case concerning the employment status of an NHS consultant.

Jason Searle Well versed in handling very high-profile employment cases and frequently appears in the Employment Tribunal, EAT and High Court. In recent years, he has become known for his expertise in the legal ramifications of social media in the workplace. **Strengths:** "He is succinct and articulate in his preparation of pleadings and advice." **Recent work:** Represented the claimant in a bullying and unfair dismissal case against Tameside NHS Trust. The nurse was given the maximum possible award for her claim.

Ghazan Mahmood Acts for both respondents and claimants, specialising in regulatory work and discrimination law. He regularly appears in the Employment Tribunal and the EAT, often working on cases involving the medical profession. **Strengths:** "Very quick and very bright." "He's an excellent barrister who gives very commercial advice."

Kashif Ali Experienced in representing both claimants and defendants in complex employment cases. He is frequently sought after for his insights into equal pay, whistle-blowing, unfair dismissal and discrimination law. **Recent work:** Represented the respondent in a race discrimination claim against the Chief Constable of Greater Manchester at the Manchester Employment Tribunal. After a three-week trial, the judge ruled in favour of the respondent.

Other Ranked Lawyers

Paul Draycott (Doughty Street Chambers) Previously an in-house advocate for a trade union firm of solicitors, Paul is particularly adept at handling matters relating to unfair dismissal, unlawful detriment, breach of contract, equal pay and discrimination on behalf of employees and unions. **Strengths:** "He's incredibly bright and has a really good grasp of the law." **Recent work:** Represented the respondent in Isherwood v Sale Grammar School, a whistle-blowing case questioning the claimant's dismissal after making protected disclosures regarding exam malpractice.

Simon Gorton QC (Atlantic Chambers) A seasoned performer in all areas of employment law, acting on behalf of clients ranging from trade unions and public bodies to high-profile companies and individuals. He has experience in both employment and personal injury law and is especially capable of handling matters relating to the Protection from Harassment Act. **Strengths:** "He's at the top of his game; he's very commercial and user-friendly." "Extremely knowledgeable, thorough and an excellent advocate."

Barry Harwood-Gray (Kenworthy's Chambers) Has noteworthy experience in high-profile discrimination cases as well as a host of other issues encompassing the full spectrum of employment law. He receives particular praise for his commercial, user-friendly style. **Strengths:** "Very personable and client-friendly and quick to grasp the key themes of the case." "Clients love him because of his personable style – his client manner is terrific." **Recent work:** Instructed on behalf of six respondent employees of the Bradford MDC at hearing, appeal and external mediation. The case, Mr Shamshuddin Ahmed v Bradford City Council and other, concerned public interest disclosure, disability, race discrimination and unfair dismissal claims. The claimant lost all his claims aside from the unfair dismissal one.

Anisa Niaz (see p.727) (Kenworthy's Chambers) Adept at handling complex and high-profile cases in the Employment Tribunal and the EAT. She is experienced in handling a wide range of employment concerns including whistle-blowing, unfair dismissal, discrimination and harassment. **Strengths:** "She takes everything in her stride. Hard-working and reliable, she is a great advocate who will fight to the bitter end." **Recent work:** Successfully represented the respondent in Mr Ian Banks v St Monica's RC High School, a case concerning claims of constructive unfair dismissal and disability discrimination.

Daniel Northall (Littleton Chambers) Regularly instructed on behalf of executives, high net worth individuals, large businesses and public sector bodies. Daniel is esteemed for his ability to handle complex, multi-day cases ranging from discrimination and whistle-blowing to wrongful termination and restrictive covenants. **Strengths:** "He consistently adopts great tactics to focus on the key points." "He is imaginative in his thinking and provides clear and practical advice." **Recent work:** Represented Virgin Media when 40 employees brought a claim against the company following a reorganisation exercise. The claim argued for a protective award and breach of contract.

Nicholas Siddall (see p.765) (Littleton Chambers) Has notable experience with TUPE, along with high-value discrimination claims and public interest disclosure cases. He is predominantly instructed on behalf of respondents but also works with trade unions and high net worth claimants. **Strengths:** "He's excellent on detail, extremely diligent and quick to respond." "Nicholas is a great advocate." **Recent work:** Acted for the respondent in Day v Health Education England, an Employment Tribunal claim of whistle-blowing. Nicholas argued that the claimant was not entitled to bring a claim against the respondent since, as a trainee placed at a London NHS trust, he held a contract of employment with the trust and not the respondent. The claim was struck out at tribunal and is now being appealed.

SOUTH EASTERN

Employment	
Leading Juniors	
Band 1	
Ashley Neil	*Octagon Legal*
Menzies Gordon	*6 Pump Court*
Band 2	
Singh Mukhtiar	*6 Pump Court* *
Up-and-coming individuals	
Cullen Grace	*6 Pump Court*
Godfrey Lauren	*Crown Office Row*

Ranked Lawyers

Lauren Godfrey (Crown Office Row) Known for his expertise in commercial chancery disputes, his work relating to employment is predominantly focused on matters of equal pay, restraint of trade, breach of fiduciary duties, confidential information and data protection. **Recent work:** Acted for the claimant in Admiral Recruitment v (1) James Doris & (2) Berkely Scott. Lauren argued on behalf of the claimant for breaches of express duties and implied duty of fidelity, misuse of confidential information and breaches of restrictive covenants.

Neil Ashley (Octagon Legal) Head of the employment group at Octagon Legal, Neil is sought after for his experience in representing claimants and respondents across a range of high-value disputes. He is noted for his knowledge of unfair dismissals, discrimination and equal pay claims, as well as TUPE. **Strengths:** "Neil is by far the best barrister I have ever worked with. He has a relaxed style which puts clients at ease and gives them great confidence. His advice is clear, succinct and highly commercial."

Gordon Menzies (6 Pump Court) Gordon acts for both respondents and claimants and is especially skilled in discrimination law. He has substantial experience with employment matters involving the medical profession, the education sector and social services. **Strengths:** "Gordon has a calm courtroom manner and highly tuned advocacy skills." **Recent work:** Acted on behalf of the respondent in Henneker v Kent Police, an unfair dismissal case. The case focused on the safeguarding of information held by state organisations; Henneker had been dismissed for abusing the police Genesis database.

Mukhtiar Singh (see p.766) (6 Pump Court) Instructed in all types of tribunal work and is particularly experienced in discrimination and whistle-blowing claims. Sources praise him for his personable nature and his ability to handle a diverse range of clients. **Strengths:** "He is extremely thorough, well prepared, hard-working and thinks outside the box. He is very commercially minded and really takes care of the client." **Recent work:** Acted for the claimant in an unfair dismissal case, Mr Colin Tritton v Instant Chimneys. Mukhtiar argued that Mr Tritton had been unfairly dismissed due to an injury he suffered in the workplace.

Grace Cullen (6 Pump Court) Frequently appears in the Employment Tribunal, Employment Appeal Tribunal and Court of Appeal, being instructed on behalf of companies, local authorities and individual claimants. Her work has covered a wide range of employment issues, including breach of contract, discrimination and unfair dismissal. **Strengths:** "She always gets back to me promptly, and is very knowledgeable." **Recent work:** Represented the respondent in Arya v Waltham Forest District Council in an unfair dismissal and discrimination claim. The claimant held strong anti-Semitic beliefs and Grace argued that his belief was not protected by the Equality Act.

WALES & CHESTER

Employment	
Leading Juniors	
Band 1	
Howells Chris	*Civitas Law* *
Band 2	
Vernon Robert	*9 Park Place*
Walters Jonathan	*River Chambers*
Band 3	
Bayoumi Mona	*Civitas Law* *
Vines Anthony	*Civitas Law* *
* *Indicates individual with profile.*	
Alphabetical order within each band. Band 1 is highest.	

Ranked Lawyers

Chris Howells (see p.676) (Civitas Law) A highly respected advocate for employers in appellate proceedings and noted for his abilities handling the defence of disability discrimination claims. He also has recent experience assisting with cases arising from bonus payment disputes and unfair dismissal allegations. **Strengths:** "He is brilliant: well spoken, comes across well in court and knows the law very well." "He is a very, very good advocate that is very good at thinking on his feet." **Recent work:** Instructed by Cardiff County Council to defend against claims of disability discrimination and unfair dismissal made by a former employee.

Mona Bayoumi (see p.592) (Civitas Law) Highlighted for her experienced representation of government organisations and other employers, she offers skilled counsel in Employment Tribunal proceedings and is noted for her abilities handling cases involving multiple claimants. She is recognised for her handling of discrimination allegations, unfair dismissal claims and redundancy disputes. **Strengths:** "She is friendly, efficient, knowledgeable and professional at all times." **Recent work:** Defended the Department of Work & Pensions against allegations of unfair dismissal and disability discrimination.

Anthony Vines (see p.787) (Civitas Law) Comes recommended for his effective representation for a range of parties, including unions, claimants and employers, in complex employment disputes. He is engaged for his counsel on regulatory compliance needs for employment terminations, and his recent experience includes handling cases arising from restrictive work covenants and racial discrimination allegations.

Robert Vernon (9 Park Place) Well-known advocate who comes recommended for his work on behalf of employers and for the quality of his client care skills and excellent courtroom presentation. He is noted for his experience in Employment Tribunal proceedings and is regularly sought after for his abilities in the defence of sexual, racial and disability discrimination claims. **Strengths:** "He is very personable, knowledgeable, authoritative and very effective in handling cross-examinations." "He is a good advocate who is good with clients." **Recent work:** Instructed by Kara to defend against allegations of unfair dismissal and racial discrimination made by a former employee.

Jonathan Walters (River Chambers) Regarded as a first port of call for police disciplinaries in the Welsh region and is also recognised for his experience representing government bodies and private organisations. He is highlighted for his effective handling of discrimination claims and for his counsel on both internal and Employment Tribunal hearings.

WESTERN

Employment	
Leading Sets	
Band 1	
Guildhall Chambers *	
Old Square Chambers *	
Band 2	
3PB Barristers *	
Pump Court Chambers *	
Band 3	
Albion Chambers *	
Leading Silks	
Band 1	
Ford Michael	*Old Square Chambers* *
Leading Juniors	
Band 1	
Cunningham Elizabeth	*Albion Chambers* [A]
Grennan Debbie	*Guildhall Chambers*
Smith Nicholas G	*Guildhall Chambers*
Band 2	
Allsop Julian	*Guildhall Chambers*
Dawson James	*3PB Barristers*
Dracass Timothy	*Pump Court Chambers*
Keen Spencer	*Old Square Chambers* *
Kempster Toby	*Old Square Chambers* *
Midgley Andrew	*Old Square Chambers* *
Mitchell Jack	*Old Square Chambers*
Self Gary	*Pump Court Chambers*
Whitcombe Mark	*Old Square Chambers*
Band 3	
Gower Helen	*Old Square Chambers*
Graham Gareth	*3PB Barristers*
Leach Douglas	*Guildhall Chambers*
Platt Heather	*Pump Court Chambers*
Roberts Allan	*Guildhall Chambers*
Roberts Stephen	*Albion Chambers*
Tether Melanie	*Old Square Chambers* *
Watson Graham	*Clerksroom Barristers Chambers (ORL)* ◊
Winstone Hilary	*Old Square Chambers* *
Wyeth Stephen	*3PB Barristers*
Up-and-coming individuals	
Emslie Simon	*Albion Chambers*
Gardiner Kerry	*Queen Square Chambers (ORL)* ◊
MacPhail Andrew	*3PB Barristers*
Staunton Suzanne	*Guildhall Chambers*

** Indicates set / individual with profile.*

[A] direct access (see p.24).

◊ (ORL) = Other Ranked Lawyer.

Alphabetical order within each band. Band 1 is highest.

Band 1

Guildhall Chambers

See profile on p.938

THE SET

A Bristol-based set that practises across the country and provides specialist advocacy and advisory services for employment and discrimination matters. The set works with a variety of firms and organisations, including local authorities. Its employment and discrimination group is composed of a bench of highly respected juniors who offer a depth of expertise capable of rivalling the set's London competitors. Its members regularly appear in the Employment Appeal Tribunal (EAT) and are also involved in a number of High Court applications and trials. Instructing solicitors comment: "The employment set has an outstanding array of barristers at all stages of experience, from very senior experienced barristers to those recently qualified."

Client service: Chris Checketts is the set's clerk for employment matters. "The clerking is first-class and this differentiates them from some of the other sets in the region."

JUNIORS

Debbie Grennan Highly regarded for her expertise in high-value and complex discrimination and whistle-blowing claims, as well as matters relating to equal pay and TUPE. She regularly receives instructions on behalf of respondent local authorities and the NHS. **Strengths:** "She has complete knowledge of her brief and is calmness personified." **Recent work:** Represented the claimants in a high-profile whistle-blowing case brought by two senior employees against two NHS trusts. The claims were successful, leading to a number of resignations and significant settlements.

Nicholas Smith As head of the set's employment and discrimination team, he is widely respected for his work on whistle-blowing and disability discrimination matters. He regularly gives lectures and seminars on employment issues across the country. **Strengths:** "Nick can deal with any situation and clients are immediately reassured by his manner and confidence." **Recent work:** Acted in Rhian Williams v ABMU Health Board, a disability discrimination case. Smith represented a recently dismissed senior midwife with chronic health issues.

Julian Allsop Handles employment matters in both the High Court and the tribunal, predominantly acting for employers. He is known for his expertise in complex injunction cases, discrimination, whistle-blowing and private sector equal pay litigation. **Strengths:** "Very articulate and able to grasp and convey complex issues." "Incredibly thorough, knowledgeable and approachable."

Allan Roberts Respected for his expertise in whistle-blowing and discrimination claims, and especially for dealing with complex police cases. **Strengths:** "He is astute, commercial and tenacious." "Clients find him approachable and inspiring of confidence." **Recent work:** Acted for two social workers, including the deputy head of social services, in a high-profile whistle-blowing claim. The claimants contend they were victimised for whistle-blowing and sought compensation of £500,000 and £170,000 respectively during the ten-day trial.

Douglas Leach Has a well-rounded practice which encompasses all areas of employment, discrimination and collective labour law. He is frequently instructed in long and technically complex TUPE and disability discrimination matters. **Strengths:** "His in-depth knowledge of complex areas of employment law is second to none." "He is confident and persuasive in his arguments and extremely reliable." **Recent work:** Successfully resisted an appeal in the EAT of Griffiths v Secretary of State for Work and Pensions. The claim concerned the difficult issue of attendance management and disability-related absence.

Suzanne Staunton Frequently undertakes multi-week, complex discrimination cases, often involving medical experts. She has also appeared successfully in the EAT and plans to expand her appellant practice. **Strengths:** "Her technical knowledge is excellent and she was a huge support throughout the case." **Recent work:** Acted for claimant in Mills v Pennine Care, involving multiple allegations of disability discrimination. The case is now proceeding to the EAT on the basis of some perversity and misdirection in the law.

Old Square Chambers

See profile on p.886

THE SET

A leading set on the Western Circuit that offers advocacy and advice across a wide range of employment issues. Its formidable expertise is clear from its members' leading roles in ground-breaking employment cases. Recent highlights include a case in the Employment Tribunal on whether holiday pay for UK workers should include commission payments, as well as multiple cases relating to the introduction of tribunal fees. Solicitors praise the chambers' "strong expertise in employment law." "They are very practical, down-to-earth lawyers who get to the heart of the matter very quickly."

Client service: "Very reliable set with helpful and well-informed clerks." William Meade is the set's senior clerk.

SILKS

Michael Ford QC (see p.646) Highly experienced silk who has worked on the full spectrum of employment issues. He is extremely active in the Court of Appeal and the Equality & Human Rights Commission. **Strengths:** "Fiercely bright silk." "Can see straight to the essence of the issue. He is very articulate and extremely impressive on his feet." **Recent work:** Instructed by the Equality & Human Rights Commission as intervener in a judicial review challenging the introduction of fees into the tribunal system.

JUNIORS

Andrew Midgley (see p.717) Particularly adept in matters of sex and race discrimination, as well as having an established practice in victimisation, whistle-blowing and holiday pay claims. **Strengths:** "He's fantastic with clients, a good advocate and a likeable character." **Recent work:** Successfully represented the Home Office in a five-day tribunal defending claims of unfair dismissal and disability discrimination.

Spencer Keen (see p.688) Highly regarded for his experience in complex and lengthy discrimination cases. He has particular knowledge of implementation of EU law in the UK with regard to disability discrimination. **Strengths:** "Spencer Keen is fantastic to work with and extremely well prepared." **Recent work:** Successfully defended Sports Direct against a discrimination and victimisation claim in Polujanczyk v Sports Direct. After the claim was struck out, he also successfully sought his client's wasted costs against the claimant's representative.

Toby Kempster (see p.690) Has crossover expertise in employment law and personal injury, with a wealth of experience in dismissal claims resulting from injury. He also handles contractual claims, especially restrictive covenants. **Strengths:** "He has a very pleasant manner with clients – he's calm and very considerate in the way he gives advice. I always feel he gives very sound advice." **Recent work:** Acted on behalf of the estate and independents of an employee who committed suicide subsequent to work-related issues in Yusva v Yeo Valley.

Jack Mitchell Frequently sought out to represent a variety of high-profile clients, he is highly regarded for his proficiency in matters of whistle-blowing and has co-written three of the leading textbooks on the subject. **Strengths:** "He's very quick to grasp complex issues and is great in cross-examination." **Recent work:** Represented 48 claimants in Thomas & Others v Quinn and Liberty. The case concerned holiday pay, terms and the conditions of employment among other issues.

Mark Whitcombe Sought after for his specialism in long and intricate discrimination cases, TUPE, equal pay and contractual disputes. He takes instructions from large trade unions, private individuals, government departments, NHS trusts and private sector companies. **Strengths:** "He is extremely knowledgeable and a confident advocate. He is well liked and respected by clients." **Recent work:** Represented the Environment Agency in its successful defence of a second appeal to the EAT in Carol Donnelly v The Environment Agency. The case concerned disability discrimination, harassment and unfair dismissal.

Helen Gower Helen is Legal Assessor for the Health & Care Professions Council and the General Pharmaceutical Council. She is experienced in complex claims of discrimination, whistle-blowing, TUPE, unfair dismissal and victimisation of trade union members. **Recent work:** Successfully represented the respondent in Boon v Reynards, defending a claim for unfair dismissal. The legal issue of whether it may be appropriate for a small company to use external HR as part of the decision-making in a disciplinary procedure was argued in this case.

Melanie Tether (see p.779) Has a well-rounded practice in all areas of employment law. She is also a leading expert on equal pay and has recently acted in multiple equal pay claims. **Strengths:** "A TUPE powerhouse with a meticulous sense of detail." "She is extremely hard-working and focuses on getting the best result." **Recent work:** Acted for the spouses of members of the armed forces posted in Cyprus in the discrimination claim Ministry of Defence v Holloway and Others. The complaint focused on unequal remuneration and conditions between British and Cypriot employees.

Hilary Winstone (see p.799) She has extensive experience with high-value corporate clients, along with police forces, the NHS and local authorities. She handles mediation in addition to internal and external disputes. **Strengths:** "Hilary is extremely responsive and what sets her apart is her natural ability to make clients and witnesses feel at ease and to work as a team with solicitors and clients alike." **Recent work:** Successfully defended an appeal in the EAT against Epsom & St Helier University Hospital NHS Trust.

Band 2

3PB Barristers

See profile on p.892

THE SET

The set's employment group consists of 28 barristers, offering advice and advocacy on all aspects of contentious employment issues. Its members regularly appear in the Employment Tribunal and EAT, as well as the High Court and the Court of Appeal. In recent years, they have developed particular expertise in employment issues related to local authorities, along with the healthcare and transport sectors. Solicitors describe them as "a well-run set of chambers with approachable and responsive barristers."

Client service: "We have always found the clerks in particular to be proactive, helpful and polite." "They are willing to go the extra mile." Russell Porter is the senior clerk.

JUNIORS

James Dawson Has a nationwide practice, representing both employers and employees with a focus on discrimination and unfair dismissal law. His crossover work in commercial law also contributes to his expertise in restrictive covenants and TUPE work. **Strengths:** "He is incredibly bright, has an encyclopaedic knowledge of TUPE and provides a first-class and responsive service." **Recent work:** Acted for a solicitor accused of gross misconduct in misleading the County Court. MacFarlane v BLM was a multi-day trial, including cross-examination of managing and senior partners in BLM. The Employment Tribunal found the claimant had been unfairly dismissed.

Gareth Graham Highly experienced in discrimination law and unfair dismissal. He is widely respected for his strategic approach to complex cases. **Strengths:** "As well as being technically competent on legal issues, he is also able to demonstrate a good understanding of a client's business and its commercial drivers." **Recent work:** Acted for the respondent in six cases of racial discrimination, harassment and victimisation against The Co-operative Group.

Stephen Wyeth Experienced in high-value discrimination cases and has had notable recent success in complex multi-day discrimination claims. He is also highly regarded for his knowledge of TUPE, as well as the enforceability of restrictive covenants and confidentiality clauses. **Strengths:** "He's an ex-solicitor and a part-time judge. He knows what he's doing and is good in presenting in a tribunal; he's had some phenomenal results for us." **Recent work:** Successfully acted for the respondent in Swarzenbach t/a Thames-side Court Estate v Jones at the EAT. Wyeth persuaded the tribunal to uphold the decision, arguing that the claimant was not eligible for continuity of employment to pursue a claim of unfair dismissal.

Andrew MacPhail Esteemed for his experience in a diverse array of employment law disputes, ranging from whistle-blowing, discrimination and harassment, to equal pay, unfair dismissal and TUPE. **Strengths:** "His experience at tribunal covers a wide range of employment law areas." "He is often instructed for complex multi-day discrimination and whistle-blowing hearings." **Recent work:** Acted for the respondent council in Ms Meade v Oxfordshire County Council, an appeal against the judgment of the Employment Tribunal. Ms Meade's claims for whistle-blowing detriment were dismissed at appeal.

Pump Court Chambers

See profile on p.898

THE SET

Pump Court Chambers is instructed on behalf of both employers and employees in a range of contentious and non-contentious employment matters. Its members appear at all levels of the judicial and tribunal hierarchy and are respected for their high quality of advocacy. In recent years they have acted for clients ranging from the London Borough of Southwark to the University of the Arts London. Market sources say: "Pump Court provides a London-comparable service on a local basis. It supplies a high level of expertise backed up by solid and flexible clerking."

Client service: "Their clerks are always very responsive." "If we're quoted something and we don't think it's market rate we'll have a conversation and it's usually a sensible outcome." David Barber is the chief clerk at Pump Court Chambers.

JUNIORS

Timothy Dracass An experienced tribunal and civil court advocate, he regularly represents claimants and respondents in a variety of employment matters such as unfair dismissal, discrimination, TUPE, whistle-blowing, equal pay and breach of contract. **Strengths:** "He has knowledge, experience and quiet efficiency." **Recent work:** Successfully represented a long-standing employee of Bovis Homes in an unfair dismissal case involving disputed allegations of fraud and bullying. Tribunal upheld the claimant's claim in the case of Plummer v Bovis Homes.

Gary Self Highly experienced at dealing with large respondent organisations and has consequently worked with a range of police forces. He is well versed in handling complex discrimination and victimisation cases. **Strengths:** "He gives straightforward, commercial advice and is very good with clients." "He's a real team player throughout the tribunal process." **Recent work:** Successfully acted for the respondent in Lowther v Wildbore and Gibbons, a factually complex whistle-blowing and victimisation case.

Heather Platt Represents a variety of clients on employment matters, including multinational corporations, public bodies and individuals. She is sought after for her experience in disability discrimination, whistle-blowing, unfair dismissal and TUPE. **Strengths:** "Heather is very good at giving an early opinion and sticking to it." "She gives prompt and comprehensive responses to requests for advice." **Recent work:** Represented the police in Markanday v The Chief Constable of Sussex Police, a claim involving multiple allegations of disability discrimination brought by a senior investigating officer.

Band 3

Albion Chambers

See profile on p.937

THE SET

Albion Chambers offers advice and advocacy services on employment matters to both employers and employees. Its members are capable of dealing with a full range of employment issues, most often for respondents. They have particular experience in disciplinary tribunals and are often instructed on behalf of trade unions and local authorities as well as private clients.

Client service: Stephen Arnold is the civil clerk at Albion Chambers.

JUNIORS

Elizabeth Cunningham Especially sought after for her expertise in disability discrimination, she has a wealth of experience in both the tribunal and High Court. A large proportion of her work is for local authorities but she is also instructed by private sector claimants and respondents. **Strengths:** "A very talented and clever advocate."

Stephen Roberts Stephen converted to the Bar from his work as a solicitor in 2002 and has since acquired a strong reputation as a specialist employment advocate. Typically, he deals with matters such as professional negligence, public interest disclosure, restrictive covenants and wrongful dismissal. **Strengths:** "Stephen is extremely knowledgeable and an exceptional advocate. He is respected by opponents and earns the trust of clients. He handles cases in a very professional and client-focused manner."

Simon Emslie Practises in both employment and personal injury law. He is frequently instructed on issues of unfair dismissal, whistle-blowing, TUPE and breach of contract. **Strengths:** "He presents himself in an assured way and presents our case in a confident fashion."

Other Ranked Lawyers

Graham Watson (Clerksroom Barristers Chambers) As head of Clerksroom's employment group, Watson advises on a range of employment matters such as TUPE, equal pay and whistle-blowing. He also practises in commercial law and is therefore especially knowledgeable on contractually based employment issues such as unfair dismissal. **Strengths:** "An employment specialist whose strengths lie in his advocacy. He's also very approachable and very good technically."

Kerry Gardiner (Queen Square Chambers) Advises both claimants and respondents on the full spectrum of employment law. She has notable experience in the EAT and frequently handles jurisdictional matters at pre-hearing reviews. **Strengths:** "She is very quick to respond." "She's very knowledgeable and is also good with clients."

Energy & Natural Resources

Contents:

LONDON

Energy & Natural Resources
Leading Sets
Band 1
One Essex Court *
Band 2
Atkin Chambers *
Brick Court Chambers *
Essex Court Chambers *
Keating Chambers *
4 Pump Court *
Band 3
39 Essex Chambers *
7 King's Bench Walk *
* Indicates / individual with profile.
◊ (ORL) = Other Ranked Lawyer.
Alphabetical order within each band. Band 1 is highest.

Energy & Natural Resources
Leading Silks
Band 1
Davies Helen *Brick Court Chambers*
Foxton David *Essex Court Chambers*
Gaisman Jonathan *7 King's Bench Walk*
Grabiner Anthony *One Essex Court*
Howard Mark *Brick Court Chambers*
McCaughran John *One Essex Court*
Onions Jeffery *One Essex Court*
Persey Lionel *Quadrant Chambers (ORL)* ◊
Rabinowitz Laurence *One Essex Court*
Rainey Simon *Quadrant Chambers (ORL)* ◊ *
Streatfeild-James David *Atkin Chambers*
Toledano Daniel *One Essex Court*
White Andrew *Atkin Chambers* *
Band 2
Blanchard Claire *Essex Court Chambers*
Brannigan Sean *4 Pump Court* *
Bryan Simon *Essex Court Chambers*
Catchpole Stuart *39 Essex Chambers*
Choo Choy Alain *One Essex Court*
Constable Adam *Keating Chambers* *
Dennison Stephen *Atkin Chambers*
Dennys Nicholas *Atkin Chambers*
Doerries Chantal-Aimée *Atkin Chambers* *
McMullan Manus *Atkin Chambers*
Mildon David *Essex Court Chambers*
O'Farrell Finola *Keating Chambers*
O'Sullivan Sean *4 Pump Court* *
Parkin Fiona *Atkin Chambers*
Schaff Alistair *7 King's Bench Walk*
Taverner Marcus *Keating Chambers* *
Tozzi Nigel *4 Pump Court* *
Band 3
Allen David *7 King's Bench Walk*
Bools Michael *Brick Court Chambers*
Buehrlen Veronique *Keating Chambers* *
Gunning Alexander *4 Pump Court* *
Matthews Duncan *20 Essex Street (ORL)* ◊
Rees Peter J *39 Essex Chambers*
Tromans Stephen *39 Essex Chambers*
Walker Steven *Atkin Chambers* *
Band 4
Hossain Sa'ad *One Essex Court*
Howe Timothy *Fountain Court Chambers (ORL)* ◊ *
Jacobs Richard *Essex Court Chambers*
Jowell Daniel *Brick Court Chambers* *
Kendrick Dominic *7 King's Bench Walk*
Malek Hodge M *39 Essex Chambers*
Masefield Roger *Brick Court Chambers* *
Matovu Harry *Brick Court Chambers* *
Moran Vincent *Keating Chambers* *
Parsons Luke *Quadrant Chambers (ORL)* ◊ *
Sharpe Thomas *One Essex Court*
Southern Richard *7 King's Bench Walk*
Vineall Nicholas *4 Pump Court* *
Wilken Sean *39 Essex Chambers* *
Wolfson David *One Essex Court*
New Silks
Hickey Alexander *4 Pump Court* *

Energy & Natural Resources
Leading Juniors
Band 1
Gledhill Orlando *One Essex Court* *
Lewis Christopher *Atkin Chambers* *
Band 2
Buckingham Paul *Keating Chambers* *
Midwinter Stephen *Brick Court Chambers*
Patton Conall *One Essex Court* *
Pilbrow Fionn *Brick Court Chambers*
Shapiro Daniel *Crown Office Chambers (ORL)* ◊ *
Band 3
Emmett Laurence *One Essex Court*
Garrett Lucy *Keating Chambers* *
Harris Christopher *3 Verulam Buildings (ORL)* ◊
Kramer Adam *3 Verulam Buildings (ORL)* ◊ *
Lazur Thomas *Keating Chambers* *
Ng Jern-Fei *Essex Court Chambers*
Sinclair Duncan *39 Essex Chambers*
Band 4
Brocklebank James *7 King's Bench Walk* *
Chennells Mark *Atkin Chambers*
Dhar Siddharth *Essex Court Chambers* *
Ghaly Karim *39 Essex Chambers* *
Hanna Ronan *Atkin Chambers* *
Healy Sandra *7 King's Bench Walk*
Jarvis Malcolm *20 Essex Street (ORL)* ◊
Leabeater James *4 Pump Court* *
Up-and-coming individuals
Jones Emma *One Essex Court* *
Watkins Michael *One Essex Court*

Band 1

One Essex Court

See profile on p.833

THE SET

A strong commercial set offering pre-eminent energy and natural resources expertise. Market sources highlight the chambers for having "excellent technical practitioners who give commercial advice and are very approachable. " Members are well versed in a wide range of energy work, and have particular expertise in North Sea oil cases and international contractual matters, as well as corporate and regulatory disputes. They are frequently instructed to appear in jurisdictions overseas and have significant experience of Russian oligarch cases.

Client service: The "excellent" Darren Burrows heads up a stellar clerking team which earns impressive praise from clients. One source stated: "I have to say, I have used the set more and more not just because of the barristers but because the clerks are extremely helpful. They are very responsive and much more attentive to clients' needs than most, and are open and frank about the strengths and skills of individual barristers. They are just very easy to deal with."

SILKS

Laurence Rabinowitz QC "He's a bit of a star" in the world of commercial energy work, earning a reputation as a go-to resource for a series of litigation and arbitration matters. Sources highlight him for his ability to take on the highest stake cases, and he can frequently be found dealing with contractual issues surrounding some of the biggest energy deals in the market. **Strengths:** "He has an outstanding ability to formulate a case in a way which will have maximum appeal." "First and foremost he is one of the nicest gentlemen at the bar. He is incredibly good with a solicitor or a client, and very, very hard-working and clever."

Anthony Grabiner QC One of the biggest names at the Bar, he possesses a stellar reputation across a series of commercial law areas. He brings esteem and gravitas to the biggest cases and has tackled large-scale energy matters as part of a hugely impressive portfolio. **Strengths:** "He is off the scale in terms of his ability to deal with difficult and serious matters. You get him out for the largest clients who need the best advice and he delivers it with great humour and aplomb. He can hold the board of a very large company in the palm of his hand." **Recent work:** Defended Blue Oil Trading against a wide array of claimants. The case concerned the delivery of naphtha cargoes.

John McCaughran QC An experienced litigator and arbitrator with great expertise both domestically and internationally, who is admitted to the BVI and Cayman Islands Bar. "One of the outstanding counsel at the Bar" according to sources who are familiar with his work in iconic recent cases like Talisman and Transocean Drilling. **Strengths:** "He's incredibly good with clients and conveys his advice in a way which is very well received. He's very much loved by the clients. He's very insightful, very good and dials in at the right level." "He's up there with the best oil and gas barristers and is really liked by clients." **Recent work:** Acted on behalf of Providence Resources in a matter concerning their hiring of a defective drilling rig. The case involved issues concerning the interpretation of pro forma remuneration and exclusion clauses.

Jeffery Onions QC "A very good commercial litigator" who earns praise for his work ethic and cross-examination skills. He has handled a broad range of commercial energy work in court and arbitration as both a litigator and an arbitrator. **Strengths:** "Phenomenally intelligent yet client-friendly." "He's a very good cross examiner and very hard-working." **Recent work:** Instructed in connection with the proper interpretation of a joint operation agreement between Eni UK and CNR International.

Daniel Toledano QC Experienced across a wide range of commercial energy issues including matters relating to joint ventures and other contractual disputes. He "commands respect" in the courtroom as well as in arbitration. Solicitors value his willingness to roll up his sleeves and work as part of the team. **Strengths:** "He just has a very calm, reassuring and economic way of conveying advice. He doesn't get flustered by tactics from the other side and is not fazed by pretty much anything whether on his feet or in correspondence. His ability to get people on board and help them understand the issues is second to none. He's been there, seen it and done it and inspires confidence in the clients." **Recent work:** Acted on behalf of British Gas in connection with a claim made by JPW Enterprises concerning the purchase of energy performance data.

Alain Choo Choy QC Operates both domestically and internationally across a spectrum of commercial energy matters. He is frequently instructed in arbitrations and has represented clients at all levels of court. His recent experience includes the Talisman case. **Strengths:** "Incredibly hard-working, very good and a very nice lawyer who is absolutely dedicated to his work." "He's a mathematical guy so he's very methodical, and a seriously good silk." **Recent work:** Represented a claimant in connection with a claim for misrepresentation made against Sumitomo, relating to the sale of interests in hydrocarbon blocks in the North Sea.

Thomas Sharpe QC An accomplished competition law practitioner with significant experience on the regulatory side of energy work. He represents a range of clients including utility companies, investment funds and regulatory bodies. **Strengths:** "He has a formidable track record and is excellent at delivering what the client needs." "He's a really good egg who is very active in EU work and is calm and measured in court." **Recent work:** Hired by OFWAT to offer advice on price review methodology.

Sa'ad Hossain QC A well-respected commercial barrister frequently involved in energy issues who has had recent involvement in the Talisman case. He has commonly represented clients in oil and gas cases, and is further praised for his all round energy industry expertise. **Strengths:** "He's quality, as he's so bright and capable. He's steeped in the industry and a real expert. He's also very responsive and user friendly." **Recent work:** Acted for two defendants in a Commercial Court dispute regarding North Sea Oil interests. The dispute involved parties with interests in neighbouring North Sea oil fields and concerned alleged overcharging under an agreement for the provision of transportation, processing and operating services.

David Wolfson QC Well known for his commercial acumen both in court and in arbitration. He is particularly adept at handling energy issues for international clients. **Strengths:** "He has a very broad practice in energy-related areas, and is a tenacious, never-say-die advocate. He will champion a cause beyond all others." **Recent work:** Represented Tullow Uganda as the claimant at both first instance and on appeal in relation to a USD113 million claim concerning petroleum exploration and development rights.

JUNIORS

Orlando Gledhill (see p.654) Handles significant energy cases across a wide range of areas, tackling matters concerning both traditional and non-traditional resources. His experience includes acting as sole counsel for British Gas in a contractual dispute. **Strengths:** "He's a very sophisticated barrister. He works very hard, spots the key points and is a very impressive opponent. He is someone you would want on your team." **Recent work:** Instructed to act for British Gas in defence of an £8 million claim concerning the distribution of shower regulators.

Conall Patton (see p.734) A "very good all-rounder" who is capable of dealing with both the commercial and regulatory aspects of energy work. He has experience of advising and representing clients both in court and in arbitration. **Strengths:** "He's very good and he does the crossover into regulatory work. He's clear, concise, incisive in his legal reasoning and someone with good judgement." **Recent work:** Led by Lord Grabiner QC in a 4-day preliminary issues trial relating to a claim for interest on arbitral awards.

Laurence Emmett Has amassed an impressive repertoire of energy cases including Talisman and Transocean Drilling. He earns praise for handling regulatory and commercial cases relating to both traditional and non-traditional sources of energy. Sources highlight him for his upstream and downstream oil and gas work. **Strengths:** "He's very good to deal with as he's very clever and pragmatic. He has a common-sense approach and is measured." "He's very engaged, helpful and enthusiastic." **Recent work:** Engaged by Providence to defend a claim relating to a drilling rig provided for Celtic Sea operations.

Michael Watkins One of the brightest junior prospects in energy work, who has a wide range of energy work under his belt and particular experience in international arbitration. Sources are quick to pick him out for his intelligence, collaborative approach and enthusiasm. **Strengths:** "He is very hard-working, extremely thorough and very bright but also very easy and approachable." "A team player and one to watch." **Recent work:** Led by Daniel Toledano QC he acted for British Gas defending a claim arising from a purchase agreement of energy performance data.

Emma Jones (see p.685) Draws impressive praise from peers and clients for her work across commercial energy matters. She has particular expertise in cases relating to gas sale, joint venture operation and services agreements. **Strengths:** "Her ability to turn out a submission in a short period of time at a ridiculously high standard is very impressive." **Recent work:** Acted for Talisman, led by Sa'ad Hossain QC, in a claim brought against them by Idemitsu Petroleum. The claim alleged a series of breaches of contract and fiduciary duty.

Band 2

Atkin Chambers

See profile on p.806

THE SET

A renowned construction set that is particularly strong on energy infrastructure work and the commercial issues surrounding it. It handles matters in a wide variety of energy sectors and undertakes cases concerning both traditional and renewable sources of energy. It is instructed by major oil and energy companies, and is active both domestically and internationally. By way of example, members have been recently involved in projects in Central Europe, Asia, the Middle East and the Caribbean to name but a few areas.

Client service: Justin Wilson heads the clerking team and is "a pleasure to deal with." Sources say: "The clerks are excellent. They are quick at informing you of developments and are very positive. They assist you with costs and budgets, and are very helpful and proactive."

SILKS

David Streatfeild-James QC Represents a wide range of energy clients both in litigation and in arbitration. He has earned a strong reputation among peers and clients for his ability to handle technically complex cases, and has frequently led cases involving overseas as well as domestic parties. **Strengths:** "He's analytical to the Nth degree, and for a big, important case there is no one better." "He's a straightforward, practical, easy to deal with guy who is always responsive, always wants to help and is a pleasure to deal with." **Recent work:** Represented Højgaard in the TCC in a design defects case concerning an offshore wind farm project.

Andrew White QC (see p.793) Heads the chambers and is acclaimed for his dedication to the area, having done "lots of the big energy cases." He has handled shipping and engineering matters amongst others, and is known for tackling both arbitration and litigation. **Strengths:** "He is a very calm advocate. If you were running a big case you would want him." "He has a very good strategic sense of how a case should be run." **Recent work:** Involved in case before the TCC in which a claim was brought by Fluor for USD400 million. The matter concerned an offshore wind farm.

Stephen Dennison QC Offers a broad spectrum of expertise and is effective at cases concerning engineering and infrastructure projects. He is well known for his ability to get on top of the details of a matter and his success in establishing a positive relationship with clients. **Strengths:** "He's very much hands on, he gets into the detail of a case and he is very, very supportive of his clients." "He has a very calm, measured, dignified and effective court manner."

Chantal-Aimée Doerries QC (see p.635) Her practice spans cases covering both traditional and non-traditional sources of energy and has a significant international element to it. She regularly undertakes construction and professional negligence work and is frequently instructed in arbitrations. **Strengths:** "She's always very well prepared in court, and is very articulate and calm when dealing with cases." "She's great – as well as being good on the law she is very user-friendly, has a quick turnaround and is a pleasure to work with. Her drafting is elegant and concise and she reads a tribunal really well."

Manus McMullan QC Handles matters relating to the renewables sector, but is most widely known for his work concerning the exploitation of oil and gas fields globally. His clients include both major and smaller oil companies, and he also represents national governments. **Strengths:** "He is a very fluent advocate, and is very, very bright so even when you are against him it's a pleasure to watch him in action." "His advocacy style is good. He presents very clearly and very precisely, and he comes across as genuine and trustworthy. He's an exceptional QC." **Recent work:** Led on a series of cases relating to the widening of the Panama Canal.

Fiona Parkin QC An advocate with "a real mastery of the detail," according to a number of sources. She is best known for handling large-scale infrastructure cases both domestically and internationally, and has represented a wide range of clients in both litigation and arbitration. **Strengths:** "Provides excellent technical analysis and really gets under the skin of the case from an early stage. She's a real team player who is client friendly and adopts an excellent strategic approach." **Recent work:** Acted in Re3 v Bracknell BC, a case concerning the proper operation of Paymec provisions in a waste-to-energy PFI contract for Reading.

Nicholas Dennys QC A construction, professional negligence and insurance expert who regularly handles energy-related cases. He is also regularly sought out as an arbitrator." **Strengths:** "He is superbly experienced, smooth and effective." "Willing and able to roll his sleeves up and dig into the detail of a case at short notice, he is strategic in his thinking and not scared to tell you what he thinks." **Recent work:** Represented the claimant, GBM Minerals, in a TCC case involving a phosphate mine in Guinea Bissau. The matter turned on claims of breach of contract and bribery.

Steven Walker QC (see p.788) "An expert on technically heavy energy cases" who has particular experience in power generation cases. A number of his cases have concerned offshore wind farms. **Strengths:** "He's technically excellent and really thinks around the issues to find a practical solution." "He's straight to the point – he tells us exactly what we need to do. He's always available, very responsive, prompt in his advice and just generally nice to work with." **Recent work:** Acted in Seaway Heavy Lifting v Wood Group v East Anglia Offshore Wind, representing Seaway Heavy Lifting. The case concerned a contractor's claims for additional payment arising from a contract for the supply and installation of met masts in connection with the development of an offshore wind farm.

JUNIORS

Christopher Lewis (see p.700) One of the leading lights of the junior Bar who has complementary construction and engineering expertise. He is frequently used for significant international arbitration matters. **Strengths:** "He's bright, on the ball and he gets stuck into the detail." "He's very bright and good at getting to the heart of a complex matter."

Ronan Hanna (see p.663) Represents a range of clients including contractors and engineers in both litigation and arbitration matters. **Strengths:** "He's ferociously bright, works incredibly hard and is really interested in the technical detail of a case. He makes sure he has a complete understanding of the technical points of a case and can explain them in simple terms. He's definitely a star in the making." **Recent work:** Led by Steven Walker in claims brought by Seaway Heavy Lifting, valued at around £10 million. The case concerned issues surrounding the development of an offshore wind farm.

Mark Chennells Experienced junior who acts in a variety of high-value energy disputes, many of which have a construction slant. He has recently been instructed in a number of major oil and gas cases relating to offshore drilling contracts. **Strengths:** "He got his mind around a really complicated issue and did a very good job with it." "He is hard-working and tenacious, crafts very clever arguments and is very good in terms of availability." **Recent work:** Acted for the defendant in Fluor v ZPMC, a USD400 million claim arising out of Greater Gabbard Offshore Wind Farm.

Brick Court Chambers

See profile on p.816

THE SET

One of the foremost sets at the Commercial Bar, Brick Court Chambers handles a broad range of high-end dispute work that includes major energy cases. Barristers at the chambers offer a broad array of commercial and regulatory expertise that extends to mining contracts, oil and gas work, renewables projects and trading agreements. They handle cases around the globe, with recent instructions coming from places as far flung as Brazil, Azerbaijan and Ghana. Sources say that the set "has some frankly brilliant practitioners" and are highly complimentary about the quality of client service they receive.

Client service: Julian Hawes and Ian Moyler co-lead the "very efficient clerking team." Sources describe them as: "Extremely efficient and very supportive."

SILKS

Helen Davies QC A highly rated competition lawyer with a significant amount of experience of handling complex commercial energy work. Sources praise her ability to handle some of the toughest and most technical cases, noting that she presents them in a "very persuasive and very fluent" manner. She possesses particular expertise in issues relating to oil and gas. **Strengths:** "A superb black letter lawyer who communicates very well. She's incredibly calm, highly responsive and someone who has huge gravitas in court." "If she says it can be done, it can; if she says it can't, it can't." **Recent work:** Represented BP in defence of a claim for £100 million brought by Scottish Power. The case concerned an alleged breach of contract.

Mark Howard QC One of those commercial silks who has a stellar reputation across a wide variety of areas. "If you stopped a hundred commercials silks and asked them who were the top silks, he'd be on the shortlist," said one peer. **Strengths:** "Sometimes you appear against someone and you're just instantly impressed at the way they get to the heart of the issues – he's one of those people." "What he says carries a lot of weight and he puts things across very clearly and concisely." "There are very few advocates who can give witnesses as difficult a ride as he can." **Recent work:** Appeared on behalf of the appellants in a Court of Appeal case concerning the payment of official adviser fees in the sale of a mining entity.

Michael Bools QC Has long experience of representing companies in oil and gas exploration disputes, but also handles other energy cases. Sources praise him for his "robust and excellent opinions." **Strengths:** "An intellectual heavyweight who is always thorough and detailed in his preparation. He's excellent on his feet and he always goes the extra mile." **Recent work:** Involved in an ICC arbitration concerning an investor's entitlement to information concerning a Kenyan oil exploration project.

Roger Masefield QC (see p.708) Praised by sources for his eagerness to engage with the case at hand and share the passion of his clients. An experienced litigator and arbitrator who is an expert in both the power and oil and gas sectors. **Strengths:** "He has a first-class mind, adopts an extremely flexible approach and is thoroughly committed to the case." "He's very hands on, really gets stuck into the detail and shows real enthusiasm for the cause." **Recent work:** Involved in a claim for damages brought in relation to four short-term loan facilities which financed an offshore oil and gas field in Ghana.

Harry Matovu QC (see p.709) A "very compelling advocate" who "presents a case extremely well." He handles a wide range of energy cases including those relating to LNG, power plants and oil and gas. He has previously acted in the high-profile Excalibur case. **Strengths:** "One of his key attributes is his ability to, with great wit and charm, metaphorically fix his hands around the throat of an opponent and slowly strangle them. He's quite beguiling, and also has a very, very detailed grasp of the facts and a thorough understanding of the law. Everything he does is done with charm, grace and style." **Recent work:** Instructed on behalf of an engineering group in a case relating to the construction and operation of a Tanzanian power plant.

Daniel Jowell QC (see p.687) Well regarded silk who is known for his commercial, competition and energy work. This range sees him represent both private businesses as well as corporate entities. Sources are impressed by his willingness to give firm and considered advice. **Strengths:** "He has a good range of work and can see issues in the wider context. He's very, very good and clients think very highly of him." **Recent work:** Represented Carillion in the Commercial Court in a matter concerning a contractual dispute over the performance of renewable energy services.

JUNIORS

Stephen Midwinter Garners praise for his work from sources who compliment him for his "commanding presence" and "user-friendly" attitude. **Strengths:** "He's one of the quickest juniors around. He has tremendous insurance knowledge and understands the energy business as well. He's an absolute pleasure to work with and his sheer speed of delivery is unsurpassed." **Recent work:** Involved in a claim concerning payment owed under a sale agreement relating to an iron ore mine in Brazil.

Fionn Pilbrow Strong on the commercial aspects of energy cases, he carries out his work in a "mature and dependable fashion," according to sources. Sources highlight him for his superior drafting skills, advocacy and knowledge of technical detail. **Strengths:** "He's intellectually astute, bright, charming and very good on his feet." "A great black letter lawyer who is hugely impressive in his ability to put forward something in a concise manner which gets to the heart of the case." **Recent work:** Led by Mark Howard QC in a West African crude oil trading case, he appeared on behalf of a group alleging fraud against former management.

Essex Court Chambers

See profile on p.836

THE SET

"One of the leading energy dispute commercial sets, Essex Court has a really, really good roster of individuals." Its practitioners frequently find themselves on cases abroad as well as at home, acting in a range of energy cases relating to power projects, renewables, and oil and gas. The set also possesses expertise in insurance issues relating to energy contracts.

Client service: The team is headed jointly by David Grief and Joe Ferrigno. Sources describe clerks as being "absolutely efficient," adding: "They are clear and responsive, and open and transparent in terms of people's availability."

SILKS

David Foxton QC An experienced silk with a very strong reputation for his work in a wide range of commercial cases involving energy issues. Impressed sources praise him for having a wide variety of attributes, saying: "He's bright, he's good on his feet and he's good with clients." **Strengths:** "Obviously a class act, he's an incredibly sophisticated barrister who knows exactly what the key points are. He has an understated manner which hides a really formidable ability to get to the heart of any legal issue." **Recent work:** Acted for the defendant in Arcadia Petroleum Limited v Bosworth and Miles, a USD325 million oil trading case that involves allegations of fraud and breach of fiduciary duty.

Claire Blanchard QC A very strong commercial litigator and arbitrator who is very much at home handling energy cases. She represents clients in international as well as domestic cases, and regularly tackles electricity and oil and gas matters. **Strengths:** "She takes a strong position for the client and is a good cross-examiner." "Possessed of a formidable command of the detail in a case, her written opinions are clear and concise. She has a wonderfully reassuring yet creditable manner with clients."

Simon Bryan QC Has a broad spectrum of complementary experience, being expert in shipping, insurance and general commercial matters. Clients feel assured that "he knows the case inside and out" and that "with him there won't be any surprises or mistakes." **Strengths:** "He has a great intellect and knows how to go for the jugular. If you're fighting a difficult case you very much want him on your side." "He's very clever, very hard-working and has a good sense of how to advance quite a complicated case." **Recent work:** Advised the Noble Group in relation to USD100 million supply contracts with Venezuelan aluminium producers, as well as on associated insurance issues.

David Mildon QC Experienced at handling an array of energy matters and someone with a strong overseas practice, he is an expert in electricity, carbon trading and renewable issues. Peers say: "He is very good as an arbitrator." **Strengths:** "When it comes to natural resources his industry knowledge is second to none. His analysis is brilliant and he has an ability to look at a very large document and find the best arguments in a short space of time."

Richard Jacobs QC A highly experienced silk with significant experience of cases where energy and insurance law overlap. He has significant experience of both acting as an advocate in arbitration and sitting as an arbitrator. **Strengths:** "He did a wonderful job of bringing himself up to speed in the case and was a very effective advocate. He actually sits and listens and understands what clients are looking for." **Recent work:** Represented an oil major in respect of a claim made in connection with the termination of a long-term crude oil supply contract.

JUNIORS

Jern-Fei Ng Has experience of cases involving some of the world's biggest energy traders. He has particular experience in coal, nickel and oil and gas matters, as well as those relating to the renewables sector. **Strengths:** "He never seems to sleep to be honest. He's incredibly responsive and works incredibly hard. He's got an encyclopaedic knowledge of case law and he's very good at drafting."

Siddharth Dhar (see p.633) A highly regarded barrister with wide-ranging commercial expertise who has experience in significant energy cases in both a courtroom and arbitration context. Sources were quick to highlight his impressive work ethic and intelligence. **Strengths:** "He's incredibly hard-working. He really rolls up his sleeves and gets stuck in, but he's incredibly down to earth as well. He gets involved as part of the team and is able to explain issues in a way which people, particularly international clients, will understand." **Recent work:** Sole counsel to the Republic of Albania in an ICSID arbitration concerning the construction of a renewable energy plant.

Keating Chambers

See profile on p.868

THE SET

A highly esteemed London construction set that is also valued for its expertise in energy and infrastructure work. It handles a broad spectrum of matters, regularly tackling power, renewables and oil and gas related cases, and is credited by one source as having "a hell of a lot of expertise in energy." The set houses a number of barristers with extensive engineering expertise, making it ideally placed to deal with highly technical issues relating to mining, extraction and construction projects.

Client service: "The clerks are fantastic as they are very responsive, very in tune with what clients require and very good on fees. They are flexible in what they can offer and when they can offer it." The team is headed by Declan Redmond.

SILKS

Adam Constable QC (see p.621) Has experience of handling infrastructure, shipbuilding and construction issues. Sources consistently praise him for his intellect, citing him as one of the cleverest people at the Energy Bar. **Strengths:** "He's incredibly intelligent, straight to the point and he gives very clear and concise advice. He doesn't mess around and he's very happy to give a view in a way which is readily understandable to the client." "He's brainy beyond belief, he's very good at probing the other side's case."

Finola O'Farrell QC An "extremely competent all-rounder," who has expertise in construction, engineering and energy disputes among other areas. Sources praise her for the fact that she is consistently "totally reliable and absolutely prepared." **Strengths:** "She is very, very bright and she does her homework. Extremely well prepared, she's a very skilled cross examiner who is charming in the way she presents her arguments."

Marcus Taverner QC (see p.778) Travels all over the world representing clients in energy disputes. Sources recommend him for being "a good trial lawyer" who "can get stuck into witnesses." His recent experience includes cases relating to LNG and pipeline issues. **Strengths:** "He has great vigour and he's very passionate about his cases. Meticulous in handling expert witnesses, he ensures that all his lines of cross-examination are well worked out." "He is incredibly commercial and great with clients."

Veronique Buehrlen QC (see p.606) Brings a commercial perspective to a spectrum of energy cases, proving both a good litigator and arbitrator. Clients describe her as "a careful thinker" who is "fully at home with the most technical of cases." **Strengths:** "She is really easy to work with, as she's on top of all the issues and good on her feet. She's a pleasure to work with and has a really good grip of the source material too." "Solicitors like her as she's good at managing clients' expectations."

Vincent Moran QC (see p.721) A highly capable performer in energy, professional negligence and construction cases. He has particular experience in offshore wind farm and domestic waste matters. **Strengths:** "Gives written advice that is absolutely spot on." "He manages strategy well and expertly masters the detail in a case." **Recent work:** Advised M+W High Tech Properties in their defence of claims brought by Biffa concerning potential defect and termination cost liability issues.

JUNIORS

Paul Buckingham (see p.606) Brings experience as a process engineer in the oil and gas sector to a practice that takes in engineering, construction and energy matters. He has particular expertise in issues involving international parties. **Strengths:** "As well as being a stunningly nice bloke, he puts on really, really great performances. He's very, very diligent and if you ask him for a view on something you know he's thought about all of the angles. His written work is very clear and no words are wasted." **Recent work:** Acted for E.ON in a defect dispute concerning the Robin Rigg offshore wind farm.

Thomas Lazur (see p.698) A well-regarded junior with experience in energy construction cases. Clients value him for his strong commercial outlook, his command of highly technical cases and his quality written work. **Strengths:** "He's extremely thorough and one for the very detailed cases that require intense knowledge of figures and claims. He has the ability to analyse a case expertly and produce excellent skeletons." **Recent work:** Acted for a claimant in a case of professional negligence brought against URS in connection with the design of a 72MW energy from waste power plant.

Lucy Garrett (see p.650) Wins admiring comments from peers and clients alike for her work in construction, energy and shipbuilding cases. Sources praise her for her "willingness to really pitch in and be very collaborative in her work." **Strengths:** "She is a force of nature. She manages to be both one of the hardest working and yet one of the most laid back people around. She gets on top of huge cases very, very quickly, and clients absolutely love her." **Recent work:** Acted in the Commercial Court in a case concerning an allegedly defective semi-submersible drilling rig.

4 Pump Court

See profile on p.895

THE SET

4 Pump Court brings its strength in commercial and construction law to bear when handling energy cases of the greatest value and complexity worldwide. A set that "always provides the right person for the right case," it has members who offer particular expertise in project and contractor-related matters. Individuals here are involved in each of the oil and gas, renewables and power production sectors, and have been involved in key matters such as Fluor Limited v ZPMC, a case concerning a wind farm in the North Sea.

Client service: "This is an excellently clerked set." Carl Wall, who primarily clerks the energy team, "stands out for wanting to build longer term relationships with solicitors."

SILKS

Sean Brannigan QC (see p.601) A titan in the construction arena who has significant experience in dealing with energy issues, particularly in the infrastructure and natural resource project field. He is consistently highlighted by clients for his teamwork and no-nonsense attitude, and is frequently involved in litigation involving overseas clients. **Strengths:** "He fights the case with passion and becomes part of the team. As he's down to earth, it's fun to work with him." "He is no nonsense, very intelligent but very easy to deal with. He's got that rare talent of being able to reduce the most complicated things to very, very simple concepts and as a result he goes down really well with tribunals." **Recent work:** Acted on behalf of Fluor in a Technology and Construction Court case concerning the construction of an offshore wind farm.

Nigel Tozzi QC (see p.783) Has a broad practice that takes in energy and construction matters, and is frequently appointed as an arbitrator. Clients really value his active involvement in the team and think of him as "a good all-round package." **Strengths:** "He's very, very effective as an advocate. He's got great tactical as well as forensic skill and judgement, and he's also very personable." **Recent work:** Represented the claimant Canapro in seeking damages against the Gambian Ministry of Petroleum. The case concerns a dispute centred around a contract for the supply of oil.

Sean O'Sullivan QC (see p.732) An "excellent advocate" with great knowledge of the energy industry. He specialises in drilling and offshore issues and has particular experience of representing drilling contractors. **Strengths:** "A fine advocate who gets to the issues extremely quickly. He's practical, always accessible and absolutely charming." "He just tells you the situation as it is and you feel completely safe letting him loose on clients." **Recent work:** Involved in an arbitration concerning shipbuilding defects, appearing on behalf of a parts manufacturer.

Alexander Gunning QC (see p.661) A "very fine advocate who has complete command of his case" according to his peers. He has frequently been involved in a range of energy infrastructure cases, and has also recently handled a spate of oil-related contract cancellation matters. **Strengths:** "He's extremely bright, hard-working, and seemingly available at all hours. An excellent leader of a team, he's easy to work with and also an excellent advocate and cross-examiner." **Recent work:** Instructed on behalf of the defendant in a dispute concerning the cancellation of an iron ore mining contract. The case was heard in Singapore.

Nicholas Vineall QC (see p.787) Carries a reputation for being able to handle some of the most technically challenging cases. He has been involved in numerous upstream issues including E&P and offshore construction contract matters. **Strengths:** "He's an excellent choice for document-heavy or detailed cases where you need someone to go through it all. He is particularly thorough and precise in his analysis." "He's very creative – he's good at making brick with only stubble." **Recent work:** Involved in an LMAA arbitration concerning a USD70 million claim brought by the purchaser of a drillship. The claim related to complex breach of contract issues.

Alexander Hickey QC (see p.670) A new and "much deserved" addition to silk according to peers, to whom he represents a "challenging opponent and very clever barrister." He specialises in oil and gas cases both onshore and offshore, and is an expert at matters relating to drilling and pipelines. **Strengths:** "He knows the industry really well. His cross examination and preparation for a hearing are excellent and his written work is very good as well. He recognises the strong points of the case." **Recent work:** Represented a party in a Commercial Court case relating to a joint venture agreement concerning a frontier oil exploration project in Kenya.

JUNIORS

James Leabeater (see p.698) A "bright, hard-working and user-friendly" barrister. He has well-rounded energy experience stemming from his construction, shipping and insurance expertise. **Strengths:** "He's intelligent and thorough in the way he works through a problem. An intellectual who can catch people out, he does an awful lot of work around a case, and looks at the wider issues including the state of the industry." **Recent work:** Acted on behalf of a broker in a commercial case arising out of the fact that a party had cancelled a contract concerning the construction of a deepwater drillship.

Band 3

39 Essex Chambers

See profile on p.840

THE SET

39 Essex Chambers is a set highly regarded for its expertise in commercial, regulatory and construction-related energy cases. The barristers here are well versed in more traditional energy work such as cases concerning oil and gas and electric power, but are also highly capable of dealing with matters relating to new and renewable energy sources. The set's regular client base encompasses regulatory and government bodies, refining companies and commodities traders, as well as insurers and financiers. Recently, members have advised on challenging issues concerning new sites for nuclear power stations, hydraulic fracking and solar parks, among other matters.

Client service: "Their clerks are excellent and good at co-ordinating all the work and providing support on all sorts of administrative affairs," according to market sources. The team is led by David Barnes. Another source said: "You can easily develop a trusting relationship with them. They are well structured and they are able to match the right people to the right job which is really important."

SILKS

Stuart Catchpole QC An "outstanding fellow in every respect" according to peers. He specialises in construction and design disputes concerning various facilities including power plants and water treatment infrastructure projects. He frequently represents clients in international arbitrations. **Strengths:** "He's very intelligent, very hard-working and very commercial. A good tactician and strategist, he's very good at getting the tribunal on his wavelength. In addition to being highly intelligent, he's also very easy to work with and he's a good team player."

Stephen Tromans QC An outstanding name in the environmental and planning spheres who brings his skills to the energy sector and is hailed as being "extremely eminent." **Strengths:** "He is without a doubt the best and most distinguished silk covering planning and environmental matters in the energy sector." "He just has a marvellous ability to cut through technically complex issues to get to the substance of the matter. He's someone who can think slightly differently and solve knotty problems." **Recent work:** Brought a claim on behalf of Total, challenging a decision of the European Commission over the allocation of emissions allowances.

Hodge M Malek QC A barrister well regarded for his broad commercial expertise, who is expert at handling significant energy cases. He has particular experience in representing major oil companies in disputes. **Strengths:** "It's hard to put into words what a seamless and easy process working alongside him is. He has that very rare talent of being both personable and yet able to give unvarnished advice, good or bad." **Recent work:** Involved in a series of corruption cases connected with the Omani oil and gas corruption investigation.

Peter J Rees QC Offers clients real depth of expertise in oil and gas matters, having been a solicitor and then, for three years, legal director of Royal Dutch Shell. He has also frequently acted as an arbitrator. **Strengths:** "He's very smart, extremely creative and very knowledgeable about energy and infrastructure law." "He really knows the industry, not just issues in the industry. He understands the commercial drivers of why the case is there to begin with."

Sean Wilken QC (see p.795) Has "thorough knowledge of upstream oil and gas work", and is frequently instructed in large-scale, international litigation. **Strengths:** "A very impressive and very clever man." "He really shone in his tactics both legally and commercially, and he was absolutely first class on his feet. He strikes the right balance between being forceful and gently persuasive."

JUNIORS

Duncan Sinclair Specialises in the regulatory and competition aspects of energy law and has frequently been involved in judicial review procedures. He handles both contentious and advisory work. **Strengths:** "Provides great practical, commercial advice and makes himself available. His prior experience of working at Ofgem means he offers a real insight into the regulator's processes and procedures." "He has a superb understanding of the regulatory framework affecting energy." **Recent work:** Acted for the claimant in R (RWE Generation UK Plc) v The Gas and Electricity Markets Authority (Ofgem), a case concerning discriminatory charges for the use of the National Grid.

Karim Ghaly (see p.651) Well regarded by clients for his technical expertise in the overlapping areas of construction, engineering and energy. He is frequently engaged by large-scale, international clients to deal with issues all over the world, and has experience of dealing with both traditional and non-traditional sources of energy. **Strengths:** "He's very good in terms of the strategy and technical side of the case. He's clearly very intelligent, very bright and he gets things quickly." "He's very calming, very sensible and very approachable."

7 King's Bench Walk

See profile on p.871

THE SET

Practitioners at 7KBW handle a significant amount of work relating to both onshore and offshore oil and gas projects, and are also adept at tackling construction, contract and trading disputes that arise in the energy sector. Their recent work examples include a USD19 billion arbitration concerning gas licensing rights in Kurdistan, as well as the SBM MOPUstor case, a major Commercial Court claim regarding a decommissioned oil rig in the North Sea.

Client service: Bernie Hyatt and Greg Leyden lead a team of "thinking clerks" who "pick barristers carefully to suit the needs of your case. "" They are high end and don't let you down."

SILKS

David Allen QC He is valued by clients for providing a "good understanding of the technical detail of the engineering aspects of energy cases." He specialises in a range of oil and gas issues including pipelines, drilling operations and offshore structures. **Strengths:** "He is spectacular to watch on his feet, as he's very engaging, very influential and highly persuasive. He's a tactician who is very good at analysing the position and advising which steps to take to get the best result. He's very passionate about what he does and aggressive when he needs to be."

Jonathan Gaisman QC An "absolutely outstanding commercial silk" who can handle the biggest energy cases. His recent experience includes the Excalibur case. **Strengths:** "He's a very effective advocate who can turn his hand to most any area. He's just an excellent barrister who is very clever at what he does." "He makes judges listen as he has a presence about him which commands attention. Not one to back off from taking difficult points, he's an excellent cross-examiner who can bully people into submission in an elegant way."

Alistair Schaff QC Has great experience of handling commercial energy work both in the litigation and arbitration contexts. He has particular expertise in cases involving professional negligence and pollution, and is noted for his skill in shipping and insurance cases. **Strengths:** "He's simply a class act. Hugely bright, hugely articulate and a real pleasure to work with, he has a wonderful ability to make a complex problem understandable and straightforward." "He has the knack of being able to make judges sit up and listen." **Recent work:** Instructed in a North Sea oil rig damage case.

Dominic Kendrick QC Handles a spectrum of commercial cases including insurance, shipping and commodities matters. Energy trading, power and offshore oil and gas matters all form part of his practice. **Strengths:** "His experience and knowledge speak for themselves. If I had a case where I wanted every inch of ground covered in an attractive way then I would use him." "He's very good for offshore energy. He has a very rigorous mind and he is always thinking two steps ahead. He is able to tie in the law with the technical side and use both to his advantage." **Recent work:** Advised Mopustor on a significant insurance claim made after a new oil rig was abandoned over safety concerns.

Richard Southern QC Has a wealth of experience of dealing with oil matters including over 40 representations of Glencore, but also handles other areas of energy work. Clients compliment him for his work ethic, intelligence and cross-examination skills. **Strengths:** "Incredibly smart and so responsive. Very easy to deal with and personable. He comes back to you very, very quickly. He works with you rather than dictates to you." **Recent work:** Involved in an oil trading dispute between Shell Trading Rotterdam and Motor Oil Corinth Refineries. The dispute related to a pricing clause concerning the delivery of diesel oil amongst other issues.

JUNIORS

Sandra Healy Covers a broad array of energy issues including upstream and downstream work. Her recent experience includes international arbitration cases concerning oil and gas exploration and development rights. **Strengths:** "She's a very good lawyer who is very down to earth and has no pretensions about her." **Recent work:** Involved in a case concerning the ownership of metal trading companies and the repayment of a loan.

James Brocklebank (see p.603) Has a wide commercial practice and significant experience in energy product liability, international trade and professional negligence cases. He is adept at handling international commercial arbitrations. **Strengths:** "Gives realistic advice on the merits of a case at an early stage, is very commercial in his approach, and alert to potential pitfalls." "He's responsive, insightful, clever and very thorough." **Recent work:** Involved in dispute concerning faults in the construction of gas pipelines connecting drilling rigs to the shore.

Other Ranked Lawyers

Daniel Shapiro (see p.762) (Crown Office Chambers) Offers a range of energy expertise and has a particular focus on oil installations and wind turbine issues. His energy expertise is complemented by his experience in professional negligence, insurance and general commercial matters. **Strengths:** "An excellent tactician who is clever and hard-working and makes himself available at all times. He's a real team player and one to have on your side when the going gets tough." **Recent work:** Acted on behalf of Total in connection with a claim for consequential losses and rebuilding costs after the explosion of an oil distribution terminal.

Duncan Matthews QC (20 Essex Street) A highly experienced practitioner who is his set's head of chambers. He focuses on international disputes across the range of up, mid and downstream energy work. Matthews has particular experience in the oil and gas sector and has handled cases concerning LNG issues, international trade and drilling disputes. He is frequently involved in matters involving civil fraud. **Strengths:** "He's not the man you want to be against. He's very effective and irritatingly good." "When he's on his feet in court he's very commanding and he has very good soft skills with the clients. He's effortless in the way he commands the court when he's in full flow." **Recent work:** Represented OMV Petrom in its case brought against Glencore. The issues centred around an accusation of fraud relating to the historic delivery of oil to Romania.

Malcolm Jarvis (20 Essex Street) Represents clients in high-stakes litigation and arbitrations concerning a range of energy sectors, and is particularly strong at cases involving oil, gas and mining concerns. He handles the full range of upstream and downstream work including matters relating to production sharing contracts, operating agreements and pollution issues. **Strengths:** "Very user friendly, hugely approachable, and highly intelligent, he delivers a high-quality product on time." **Recent work:** Acted in Ardila NV v ENRC NV, a dispute concerning payment obligations under a share purchase agreement. The case concerned a Brazilian iron ore mine.

Timothy Howe QC (see p.676) (Fountain Court Chambers) A capable practitioner who possesses a wide array of commercial expertise. He represents clients both domestically and abroad in major oil and gas disputes concerning exploration and trading rights. He also handles cases involving infrastructure projects and joint ventures. **Strengths:** "His insight into a case is always very good and he's excellent on strategy."

Lionel Persey QC (Quadrant Chambers) Highly regarded in the field for the depth of his energy expertise. He specialises in midstream and upstream cases including those relating to pipelines and ship construction as well as oil production and exploration. He is well versed at handling complex and high-value contractual disputes. **Strengths:** "Really does know the energy business inside and out." "A master tactician, he is an outstanding lawyer who works exceptionally hard." "He is good at managing a really big case and one of the leading examiners of experts in the business."

Simon Rainey QC (see p.746) (Quadrant Chambers) Handles high-profile energy work, and is an expert in insurance, maritime and shipping issues. Sources consistently highlight his willingness to master the detail of a case and provide high-level, technical input. **Strengths:** "He's quite outstanding as he's meticulous and just never misses an argument. He's always one step ahead of everybody." "He has an agile mind and is not afraid to push the boundaries of the law." **Recent work:** Advised Statoil in a case concerning re-determination of Nigerian oil field production shares.

Luke Parsons QC (see p.734) (Quadrant Chambers) Head of chambers and has a respected commercial and admiralty practice. He is praised for his ability to get on top of highly technical cases and for his excellent cross examination of experts. **Strengths:** "He's very hands on, shows impressive attention to detail and really engages with the case. A lawyer who tells it like it is without sugar coating it, he's involved from the start and can talk on a level playing field with the experts. In his advocacy he integrates excellent legal knowledge with an element of humour." **Recent work:** Defended TMT Asia in a Commercial Court dispute relating to competition and fraud issues. The case included allegations of market control and anti-competitive behaviour.

Christopher Harris (3 Verulam Buildings) "Someone who is definitely going places," and has a particular reputation in international arbitration. He wins acclaim for his "conversational advocacy style" and intelligence, and is experienced on both the technical side of oil and gas disputes and in financing issues. **Strengths:** "He's very robust, commercially minded and very good in front of a client. He provides a tailored approach and has the ability to prioritise the commercial imperatives of the client." "He's very smart, a very good oral advocate and someone with a very impressive practice."

Adam Kramer (see p.693) (3 Verulam Buildings) Frequently involved in energy cases and has a depth of experience in oil and gas issues. **Strengths:** "He is very strong intellectually and also a very good advocate. He prepares well and has a very sharp intellect, so he's quick and adaptable." **Recent work:** Acted for investment bank Renaissance Capital in its claim for fees plus interest from African Minerals Ltd, owners of an iron ore mine in Sierra Leone, after the company repeatedly failed to honour a fundraising fee arrangement.

Contents:

LONDON

Environment
Leading Sets
Band 1
39 Essex Chambers *
Francis Taylor Building *
Landmark Chambers *
6 Pump Court *
Band 2
Blackstone Chambers *
1 Crown Office Row *
Henderson Chambers *
Matrix Chambers *
Band 3
Brick Court Chambers *
Monckton Chambers *
Leading Silks
Star individuals
Tromans Stephen *39 Essex Chambers*
Band 1
Drabble Richard *Landmark Chambers*
Elvin David *Landmark Chambers*
Gibson Charles *Henderson Chambers* 🄰 *
Hart David *1 Crown Office Row*
Hermer Richard *Matrix Chambers*
Hockman Stephen *6 Pump Court* 🄰 *
Howell John *Blackstone Chambers*
Jones Gregory *Francis Taylor Building*
Lieven Nathalie *Landmark Chambers*
Maurici James *Landmark Chambers*
McCracken Robert *Francis Taylor Building* 🄰
Pleming Nigel *39 Essex Chambers*
Band 2
Fordham Michael *Blackstone Chambers*
Forsdick David *Landmark Chambers*
Harwood Richard *39 Essex Chambers* *
Nardell Gordon *20 Essex Street (ORL)* ◊
Pereira James *Francis Taylor Building* 🄰
Travers David *6 Pump Court* *
Turner Jon *Monckton Chambers*
Wolfe David *Matrix Chambers*
Band 3
Chamberlain Martin *Brick Court Chambers* *
de la Mare Thomas *Blackstone Chambers*
Ellis Morag *Francis Taylor Building*
Findlay James *Cornerstone Barristers (ORL)* ◊
McCullough Angus *1 Crown Office Row*
Sands Philippe *Matrix Chambers*
Smith Kassie *Monckton Chambers*
Strachan James *39 Essex Chambers*
Straker Timothy *4-5 Gray's Inn Square (ORL)* ◊
Webb Geraint *Henderson Chambers* *
New Silks
Busch Lisa *Landmark Chambers*
Facenna Gerry *Monckton Chambers* 🄰 *
Hyam Jeremy *1 Crown Office Row*
Riley-Smith Toby *Henderson Chambers* 🄰 *
Thornton Justine *39 Essex Chambers*
* Indicates / individual with profile.
🄰 direct access (see p.24).
◊ (ORL) = Other Ranked Lawyer.
Alphabetical order within each band. Band 1 is highest.

Environment
Leading Juniors
Band 1
Badger Christopher *6 Pump Court* *
Bates John H *Old Square Chambers (ORL)* ◊ *
Cook Kate *Matrix Chambers*
Dixon Emma *Blackstone Chambers*
Harris Mark *6 Pump Court*
Sheridan Maurice *Matrix Chambers*
Upton William *6 Pump Court*
Wald Richard *39 Essex Chambers*
Watson Mark *6 Pump Court*
Band 2
Banwell Richard *6 Pump Court*
Burton James *39 Essex Chambers*
Honey Richard *Francis Taylor Building* 🄰 *
Mehta Sailesh *Red Lion Chambers (ORL)* ◊
Band 3
Banner Charles *Landmark Chambers*
Collier Jane *Blackstone Chambers*
Galloway Malcolm *Crown Office Chambers (ORL)* ◊ *
Green Timothy *Outer Temple Chambers (ORL)* ◊ 🄰
Lewis Gwion *Landmark Chambers*
Macrory Richard *Brick Court Chambers*
Moules Richard *Landmark Chambers*
Riggs Samantha *25 Bedford Row (ORL)* ◊ *
Simons Zack *Landmark Chambers*
Westaway Ned *Francis Taylor Building*
Wignall Gordon *6 Pump Court* 🄰
Up-and-coming individuals
Blackmore Sasha *Landmark Chambers*
Dobson Catherine *39 Essex Chambers*
McGregor Claire *1 Crown Office Row*

Band 1

39 Essex Chambers

See profile on p.840

THE SET

A set with highly regarded members who handle all manner of environmental law cases in the High Court, Court of Appeal and Supreme Court, as well as in overseas jurisdictions. The individuals have a strong focus on the environmental implications of planning applications and infrastructure projects including HS2 and the expansion of Heathrow. They further represent clients suing companies such as BP and Shell for causing environmental damage and are well known for advising on environmental sentencing guidelines and air quality issues. One commentator says of the set: "If it is a really tricky issue, I would be going to 39 Essex."

Client service: "The clerks are very good and extremely responsive." Andrew Poyser leads the planning, environment and property law clerking team and is described as being "excellent and always good at picking the right barristers."

SILKS

Stephen Tromans QC Outstanding lawyer in the fields of environmental, energy, natural resources and planning law. He is highly esteemed for his work on air pollution and waste issues. **Strengths:** "He is a very shrewd operator with good judgement." "Amazing and peerless." "He is the star of the Environment Bar and nobody compares to him." "He has real gravitas and is always the first port of call for serious and complex matters." **Recent work:** Advised on air quality issues raised by the proposed expansion of Heathrow Airport.

Nigel Pleming QC Particularly strong when advising clients on environmental, energy and planning law. **Strengths:** "He handles really impressive work and is very robust and unflappable." "Bright and pragmatic, he has a strong understanding of local and central government."

Richard Harwood QC (see p.666) Advises on nuisance and criminal regulatory matters in environmental law; he is also an expert on Environmental Impact Assessments. **Strengths:** "Particularly good on judicial review in relation to environmental matters," he is "technically excellent." "Offers both thorough preparation and good advocacy." **Recent work:** Advised ministers on the Thames Tideway Tunnel project and represented the government in defending the scheme at four judicial reviews.

James Strachan QC Acts for airports, oil terminals, waste operations and wind farms faced with environmental litigation. He also advises development projects on environmental issues. **Strengths:** "He's extremely bright" and "he goes down very well in committee hearings." **Recent work:** Advised the government on the environmental law issues raised by HS2.

Justine Thornton QC Has a strong practice advising on claims for environmental damage. She also has wide-ranging experience of acting for corporate clients on waste, extraction and renewable energy cases. **Strengths:** "She is very sought after – particularly by claimants." "She has a fantastically charming and engaging advocacy style." "Her courtroom manner is terrific and she is dedicated, hard-working and cheerful in her approach." **Recent work:** Represented Colombian farmers in a case against BP for environmental damage caused by BP's oil production.

JUNIORS

Richard Wald A leading junior for claims of environmental damage who acts for both claimants and defendants. He is also an expert on the environmental law aspects of renewable energy projects. **Strengths:** "He gets straight down to business and drafts extremely quickly and accurately." "A great guy to work with, he's very down-to-earth." "His responses are quick and to the point." **Recent work:** Advised 200 claimants with regard to a compensation claim against the Upper Tribunal (Lands Chamber). The claimants alleged that their house had diminished in value following the expansion of Farnborough Airport.

James Burton Advises on the environmental law impacts of new transport route proposals, and has advised defendants facing the new sentencing guidelines for environmental offences. **Strengths:** "He is very personable and puts a lot of time and effort into cases." "Very thorough and intellectually bright," "he demonstrates meticulous preparation and has a keen eye for detail." **Recent work:** Represented petitioners seeking amendments to the HS2 bill.

Catherine Dobson Has a particular focus on nuclear law and the environmental law issues raised in the construction of nuclear facilities. **Strengths:** "She really understands and is sympathetic towards clients." **Recent work:** Assisted with a dispute concerning water extraction rights in the River Lea.

Francis Taylor Building

See profile on p.849

THE SET

"Undoubtedly a go-to set," Francis Taylor Building has a strong focus on cases concerning the overlap between environmental law and planning. They are experts on environmental regulation and criminal environmental liability, and regularly advise on matters relating to nuclear and renewable energy, airports, railways and oil and gas supply infrastructure. "The advice and expertise they give, in what is a niche area, are invaluable," according to one commentator. Clients include companies and developers in addition to regulators and environmental groups.

Client service: Paul Coveney leads an award-winning clerking team. "The clerking is exemplary, and all involved are approachable and reliable. They tick all the boxes in terms of client care."

SILKS

Gregory Jones QC Outstanding lawyer for all aspects of EU environmental law, who regularly advises developers and local planning authorities on planning and infrastructure projects. **Strengths:** "He is extremely responsive, very bright and aggressive in court." "He's very good at putting across his arguments to judges, and is a good courtroom practitioner." "Good with clients, he gives clear and innovative advice, and is tenacious in court."

James Pereira QC Advises on both environmental and planning law, and has a strong focus on pollution cases and those concerning compulsory purchase. **Strengths:** "He is a calm, authoritative and dogged advocate." "Clients love him as he is really personable but also a tough advocate."

Morag Ellis QC Acts on matters concerning planning, infrastructure, compulsory purchase, rights of way and green spaces. She also assists with matters concerning housing and retail developments, as well as waste and energy schemes. Commentators note that she has a particularly strong profile in Wales. **Strengths:** "She is extremely adaptable and very pleasant." "She's good at dealing with pressure." **Recent work:** Represented Welsh Ministers in a High Court challenge to planning permission for a wind farm in Mid Wales.

Robert McCracken QC Has a strong focus on EU environmental law and represents multinational enterprises as well as community groups in cases involving statutory nuisance and the protection of information and habitats. **Strengths:** "He is a bold and effective advocate who really will fight cases for his clients." "A really good performer and a creative barrister." **Recent work:** Acted for the Peak District National Park Authority on the suspension of mining extraction permission.

JUNIORS

Richard Honey (see p.674) Has a broad environment practice that sees him advising on matters relating to permitting, pollution liability, waste and land contamination, protected habitats and species and environmental crime and taxation. Natural England, the Environment Agency and water companies count among his clients. **Strengths:** "He offers high-quality legal analysis, has a very quick turnaround of papers and provides advice which is practical, easy to understand and useful." "Extremely thorough and very communicative, he's a dream for a solicitor." **Recent work:** Advised Severn Trent Water on whether the company was able to carry out pipe laying work on private land.

Ned Westaway Represents clients such as the Environment Agency, the Marine Management Organisation and Natural England in conservation law and protection of habitat cases. He further advises on matters relating to statutory nuisance, water law, waste law, contaminated land and environmental crime. **Strengths:** "He is very bright and very articulate." "Very responsive, hard-working and bright," he is "particularly good on flooding matters." **Recent work:** Advised in an inquiry about the accuracy of flood modelling.

Landmark Chambers

See profile on p.873

THE SET

A leading chambers for EU environmental law and habitat protection mandates, it is highlighted as having "barristers who are consistently excellent and user-friendly." They have advised, inter alia, on cases involving airport expansions, permitting law, developments and questions about nuclear power. They have further had significant involvement in the HS2 litigation.

Client service: Jay Fullilove heads the clerking team, which is described as being "really responsive." One satisfied commentator says that "they have commercial clerks who don't drag their feet and are very good and flexible to deal with."

SILKS

Richard Drabble QC Has an excellent reputation for advising on public law, planning and environment matters. He represents developers and local authorities in planning inquiries, and advises on European planning and EU environmental law. **Strengths:** "He's got a very gentle manner, is incredibly humble and there's not a lot he doesn't know about planning." **Recent work:** Acted for Associated British Ports regarding a judicial review of the Marine Management Organisation's refusal to make a harbour revision order.

David Elvin QC Well regarded for his work on planning, environmental and public law cases. He often advises on compulsory purchases and cases concerning the construction of highways. **Strengths:** "Incredibly clever and hard-working, he is a heavyweight presence."

Nathalie Lieven QC Esteemed for her environment and planning law practice, she has clients who include local authorities, central government bodies, private individuals and corporate entities. **Strengths:** "She is practical, commercial and reassuring when she needs to be, while also calling the shots and being very authoritative." "She is brilliant, especially when you're faced with an urgent situation." "Excellent for difficult matters where you need good, robust arguments." **Recent work:** Acted for Cuadrilla in an inquiry into planning permission for the exploration of fracking possibilities.

James Maurici QC A leading figure for matters involving climate change, fracking and marine environmental issues. He also advises clients on air quality, habitat and species protection, contaminated land and common law nuisance complaints. **Strengths:** "He's pretty persuasive and user-friendly." "He's ahead of the pack as an advocate as well as intellectually." **Recent work:** Acted for the Department of Transport on the response to the Airports Commission report into airport expansion.

David Forsdick QC Acts for claimants and defendants in environmental law litigation, and is strong on matters pertaining to climate change and air pollution. **Strengths:** "Offers excellent technical advice on biodiversity issues." "He has an attractive and persuasive advocacy style." **Recent work:** Represented the RSPB in a challenge to the consent granted to BAe Wharton for the culling of a protected species in a Special Protection Area.

Lisa Busch QC Advises on environmental and planning law issues in the High Court and Court of Appeal. **Strengths:** "She has a very detailed knowledge of the law relating to environmental and planning cases." **Recent work:** Advised the Secretary of State for Transport in relation to the Select Committee proceedings looking at the HS2 bill, particularly with regard to the Habitats Directive.

JUNIORS

Charles Banner Acts for the government on environmental law cases, and advises on EU environmental legislation. **Strengths:** "He has a quick brain, is very personable and has a great depth of knowledge of planning matters." "He is affable, approachable and client-friendly," and "really impressive in terms of his advocacy." **Recent work:** Advised Ashdown Forest Economic Development on a challenge to a policy prohibiting development within 7 km of the Ashdown Forest.

Zack Simons Focuses on planning, environmental and compulsory purchase law. His clients include developers, landowners, local authorities and central government. **Strengths:** "A good-quality, personable advocate with a strong ability to provide practical and commercial advice." **Recent work:** Acted for North Norfolk District Council in a challenge to planning permission for grain silos.

Gwion Lewis Represents clients in planning and environmental law cases including those concerning EU environmental law, public inquiries and judicial review. **Strengths:** "He picks up technical details very quickly and thoroughly, and is very good on his feet." **Recent work:** Advised the Environment Agency on challenges to the conditions set with regard to catching salmon in the River Wye.

Richard Moules Represents private developers, the government and other interested groups in planning and environmental law matters including flooding and waste disposal. **Strengths:** "His written work is excellent, he has a great manner with clients and he picks things up quickly and grasps the issues." "He researches issues very well and is very authoritative in conference." **Recent work:** Advised a gamekeeper on a judicial review of Natural England's refusal to provide a permit to kill buzzards in order to protect pheasants.

Sasha Blackmore Advises the government, house builders and NGOs on public and environmental law matters, especially those concerning marine issues. **Strengths:** "She is excellent on her feet, and produces great written work." "She is excellent at dealing with the political sensitivities of a case." **Recent work:** Advised the Northern Ireland government on a policy challenge brought by wind farm developers.

6 Pump Court

See profile on p.897

THE SET

"A first-rate chambers that is one of the best in terms of approachability and professionalism." It is particularly highly esteemed in the areas of statutory nuisance and environmental tort, and offers "a great spread of skill across all levels of seniority." Observers note that it is an outstanding set for flood management and species protection cases, and further admire it for its representation of clients in matters concerning climate change, emissions trading, waste and pollution.

Client service: Richard Constable's clerking team is widely praised, with sources saying the "clerks are great; they do quite a bit more than they have to." "One of the best clerking teams out there. The people there are very good at developing a relationship with you."

SILKS

Stephen Hockman QC (see p.673) Leading lawyer advising claimants and defendants on pollution cases, challenges to environmental decisions and environmental cases in the common law courts. **Strengths:** "He is the leading counsel for regulatory law, and is incredibly bright and great to deal with." "The speed of his understanding is amazing." **Recent work:** Acted for the Environment Agency in a judicial review into the powers of entry available to the Environment Agency.

David Travers QC (see p.784) Often acts for clients against the environmental regulators and has acted for a number of defendants facing allegations of environmental offences or permit revocations. He also advises on breaches of waste directives and those relating to environmental permits. **Strengths:** "He is meticulous in preparation and a great team player." "He has an exceptional skill level and his work is extremely good."

JUNIORS

Christopher Badger (see p.587) Leading lawyer for the regulatory aspects of environmental law, he advises the Environment Agency as well as corporate and individual clients. **Strengths:** "Advocacy-wise he is excellent as he's very calm and thinks before he speaks." "He takes a logical approach to the issues and has a deep knowledge of the law." **Recent work:** Advised on a judicial review challenging the implementation of the EU Emissions Trading System.

Mark Harris Highly regarded for his advice on regulatory matters in environmental law, he has an in-depth knowledge of cases concerning water, waste and the cross-border shipment of radioactive substances. He acts both for and against the Environment Agency. **Strengths:** "He is first-rate in terms of tactics and a shining example how to talk to a client rather than at a client." "He is very calm and fair as a prosecutor." **Recent work:** Represented Imerys Minerals when the company faced accusations of discharging chemicals into the River Par and the Rocks Stream in Cornwall.

William Upton Has a strong reputation for advising clients from both the public and private sectors on environmental law regulations and planning law. **Strengths:** "He is great to work with, user-friendly, down-to-earth and pragmatic." "Clients get on very well with him." **Recent work:** Acted for the defendant in a nuisance claim concerning light reflected from a wind turbine.

Mark Watson Well respected as a prosecution and defence barrister handling cases concerning pollution, waste deposits and nuisance claims. He acts for and against the Environment Agency and local authorities. **Strengths:** "He has got a photographic memory and is technically astute." "He has a great knowledge of environmental crime." **Recent work:** Acted for the Environment Agency in a claim against a waste contractor for the unlawful disposal of waste.

Richard Banwell Acts for and against the regulator on claims concerning waste treatment, disposal of radioactive waste, renewable energy issues, water management and permitting offences. **Strengths:** "Part of his skill lies in making something complicated simpler for the people he works with." "His relaxed style with the clients inspires confidence." **Recent work:** Assisted Tamar with compliance issues concerning breach of odour and noise conditions.

Gordon Wignall Has a practice with a strong focus on pollution claims and challenges to Environment Agency decisions. **Strengths:** "His knowledge of his area is extremely deep and extensive." **Recent work:** Represented Chadwick in a judicial review of a suspension notice served by the Environment Agency.

Band 2

Blackstone Chambers

See profile on p.813

THE SET

One of the very finest sets at the Bar, Blackstone has a large group of "excellent public lawyers with experience of environmental cases." Members have wide-ranging experience extending to public and private international law, EU regulation, climate change and human rights. They are also experts on commercial law issues and judicial reviews in this area. Their clients include a mixture of commercial bodies, private parties and the state, and they have recently been heavily involved in disputes relating to HS2 and air quality.

Client service: "Blackstone Chambers gives us a great service and the set is very amenable. All the barristers are people who will really pick up the phone and make themselves available to you and the chambers provides a real team operation." The genial and highly respected Gary Oliver leads the team.

SILKS

John Howell QC Held in high regard for his knowledge of public law and human rights, which he applies to environmental law cases, particularly at the EU level. **Strengths:** "He has a fantastic command of the facts and the law, and he is always thoroughly prepared for anything which may be thrown at him." "He is bright, intellectual, thorough and turns things around very quickly." **Recent work:** Appeared in the public inquiry into the 2010 Great Yarmouth Harbour Revision Order application.

Michael Fordham QC Particularly known for his expertise on judicial review and climate change issues relating to renewable energy. He also represents clients involved with planning appeals involving Environmental Impact Assessments. **Strengths:** "He is responsive, decisive and fiercely intelligent." "Authoritative and comprehensive, he engages quickly with a fact-heavy case, and immediately identifies key issues." **Recent work:** Acted for the claimants in a judicial review of the Secretary of State for Energy and Climate Change's decision to withdraw exemptions to the climate change levy.

Thomas de la Mare QC An experienced public lawyer with specialist expertise in the environmental information regulations. He frequently acts on international cases concerning these provisions. **Strengths:** "He is very polished and thoughtful, and a real enthusiast for this area of the law." "His grasp of cross-jurisdictional issues is really impressive and he shows a firm understanding of policy background and how things interrelate between domestic and international law." "He takes a critical approach to EU regulations and can see whether things have been properly implemented." **Recent work:** Acted for 20 water and sewage companies in a case revolving around the meaning of the term 'public authority' under various EU directives and regulations.

JUNIORS

Emma Dixon Offers broad environmental expertise, and acts in a mixture of contaminated land, water, fishing and air pollution cases. She also has exceptional experience of working with the state and is good on international issues such as climate change. **Strengths:** "She goes really in depth into the EU environmental law authorities and can easily dismantle the opposition's arguments." "A good team player, she is very robust and gives our clients confidence." **Recent work:** Represented the Environment Agency in a judicial review challenge against permitting decisions relating to two competing hydropower schemes on the River Avon.

Jane Collier An experienced junior barrister who advises on a range of EU environmental and information regulations, judicial reviews and planning law cases. **Strengths:** "She can master great swathes of technical detail and still be precise about the details of the brief." "She is very bright, has strong people skills," and is "very amenable to listening to what the client wants." **Recent work:** Acted for Natural England in an appeal by Walshaw Moor Estates against the modification of consents to carry out operations on a Site of Special Scientific Interest.

1 Crown Office Row

See profile on p.826

THE SET

A tight-knit set praised for its "real specialism in environmental law." It has great experience across many areas of the sector, has been instructed in some particularly notable cases involving waste and water, and has had roles in high-profile international litigation. Sources note that the chambers has become "an established brand in this area" and is known as "a really excellent environmental set which is very good, particularly on climate change issues."

SILKS

David Hart QC Advises across the range of environmental law, handling cases concerning contaminated land, nuisance, waste and water, and those with criminal aspects to them. **Strengths:** "He is user-friendly and simplifies very complex issues." "He has excellent technical knowledge." "He has a good grasp of the issues and you know you are in good hands when working with him."

Angus McCullough QC Represents clients predominantly with regard to public and regulatory law issues, and has handled many cases that involve environmental aspects. **Strengths:** "Very good on the planning side of environmental law."

Jeremy Hyam QC Focuses on the public law and regulatory aspects of environmental law including challenges against developments and environmental impact assessments. **Strengths:** "Very good at defending clients against Environment Agency prosecutions." "He is particularly strong on the public law aspects of environmental law."

JUNIORS

Claire McGregor Often acts for claimants in large group environmental actions as she has strong international experience and can speak multiple languages. **Strengths:** "She delivers very confident cross-examinations and has wide appeal as she has both great expertise and a great way of putting clients at ease." "A very bright junior and a rising star at the Bar, she is dedicated and a creative thinker." **Recent work:** Represented a group of 15,000 fishermen from the village of Bodo in their claims against Shell Nigeria relating to two oil spills in the local area.

Henderson Chambers

See profile on p.864

THE SET

A "top-notch" team for large international mass tort cases, it is praised for its complementary expertise overlapping areas such as health and safety, product liability and environmental law. It has represented several large international corporations facing class actions brought in the UK courts concerning allegations of pollution and environmental damage. Matters handled include the widely publicised Bodo litigation concerning the environmental impact of oil spills in the Niger Delta.

Client service: "In terms of the general approach of its clerking team, Henderson Chambers has a very sophisticated operation, which is difficult to beat." The well-respected John White leads the team.

SILKS

Charles Gibson QC (see p.652) A leading silk for large mass tort and group action claims who has appeared in extraordinarily large and demanding cases defending corporations against claims of environmental damage. **Strengths:** "A very good leader of a big team of people, he sees the wider strategic issues but also gets thoroughly into the details." "He's an effective operator with a very good courtroom manner." "A formidable leader who gives his heart and soul to any case, he is enthusiastic and committed, and clients really love him." **Recent work:** Defended BP against claims brought by a group of Colombian farmers alleging that the OCENSA oil pipeline in Colombia had caused nuisance and environmental damage to farms and waterways.

Geraint Webb QC (see p.791) A highly experienced silk who has defended clients in ground-breaking environmental mass tort cases, including claims relating to environmental damage caused by mining and oil operations. **Strengths:** "A great strategist who is very cool-headed and extremely reliable." **Recent work:** Led the defence team for Shell Nigeria against an action brought by 15,000 Nigerian claimants seeking damages as a result of two oil spills in the Niger Delta.

Toby Riley-Smith QC (see p.752) Specialises in the civil and criminal elements of cases relating to environmental disasters. He is an expert on nuisance and pollution claims linked to explosions, fires and waste operations. **Strengths:** "A very good advocate who gauges the tribunal well. He is excellent with clients, and very patient and thorough in his preparation." **Recent work:** Appeared in the Siraj v C Hall Limited case, concerning a private nuisance claim by a homeowner brought against a neighbouring farmer who had erected a wind turbine.

Matrix Chambers

See profile on p.876

THE SET

A chambers of choice for environmental claimants that is renowned for its strong commitment to human rights and international law. Much of the set's environmental law work centres on large group actions; however, it has diversified into a broader range of environmental work and is now often chosen to advise on other international issues such as climate change. Sources say the set is "efficiently run and has members with first-class legal brains who are deeply committed to the cases, going beyond what is expected and making significant sacrifices to achieve the client's ends."

Client service: "The clerking team is very good, particularly senior practice manager Jason Housden, who is really organised and helpful."

SILKS

Richard Hermer QC Praised for his highly impressive international credentials and commitment when tackling ground-breaking human rights and environmental damage cases. He has unparalleled experience of leading teams bringing cases on behalf of large groups of claimants in the developing world. **Strengths:** "Incredibly effective and a master tactician." "An excellent strategic thinker and legal brain whose commitment to human rights is second to none." "He has the courage to take on novel legal arguments and make a difference to the case." **Recent work:** Appeared as lead counsel for a huge number of individuals and communities in Nigeria in claims for damages and remedial action from Shell Nigeria following a large oil spill in the Niger Delta region.

David Wolfe QC An experienced silk with wide-ranging environmental expertise who has appeared in numerous cases involving EU and ECHR issues. Of late, he has handled a number of energy, habitats, waste and environmental information claims. **Strengths:** "He provides incredibly technical and detailed analysis on water cases." "He can draw out the more important, emotive points in a case and is fantastic with clients." "He never takes an easy case and usually finds extremely innovative and creative arguments." **Recent work:** Acted for Badger Trust in a Court of Appeal judicial review that examined challenges to the legality of the Secretary of State's policy of culling badgers.

Philippe Sands QC Advises on a broad scope of international environmental cases including marine boundary disputes, pollution claims and disputes over the use of natural resources. **Strengths:** "A deep thinker who is very considered and deserves a great deal of credit."

JUNIORS

Maurice Sheridan A leading junior who is especially recommended for his expertise in environmental law cases at EU level. He has handled a number of matters involving statutory appeals to the Secretary of State and permitting regulations. **Strengths:** "Very knowledgeable and an expert on water cases who has a long history and familiarity with this subject." "He is a highly strategic barrister who is excellent at European law." **Recent work:** Advised RE3 regarding environmental commercial claims in the Commercial Court and in private adjudication proceedings.

Kate Cook An experienced and authoritative junior barrister who offers exceptional knowledge of public law environmental cases. She often represents clients in international cases involving fishing regulation and carbon trading. **Strengths:** "She is extremely authoritative, has a good track record and is well regarded." "Her contextual knowledge of public and environmental law is extremely impressive." **Recent work:** Advised and provided detailed analysis on the legality of EU proposals in relation to the trade and conservation of Atlantic bluefin tuna.

Band 3

Brick Court Chambers

See profile on p.816

THE SET

Offers exceptional depth and experience of public law and regularly handles multifaceted cases requiring expertise in public, competition, EU and environmental law. Members regularly advise on cases concerning emissions, air quality and the environmental impact of energy developments.

Client service: "The set is highly professional, well clerked and always very amenable and helpful." Julian Hawes and Ian Moyler are the joint senior clerks.

SILKS

Martin Chamberlain QC (see p.614) Specialises predominantly in human rights, EU and public administrative law including high-profile judicial review challenges brought on environmental grounds. **Strengths:** "He is very deserving of his phenomenal reputation." "He is measured and understated in conference and discussions but a hugely impressive and persuasive advocate when on his feet."

JUNIORS

Richard Macrory A highly respected and experienced barrister and professor of environmental law who is frequently consulted by the UK government on environmental sanctions and regulation. **Strengths:** "A first port of call on tricky public law issues."

Monckton Chambers

See profile on p.877

THE SET

Widely recognised for its exceptional EU law practice, this set offers strong expertise in international cases concerning energy conservation, emissions trading and access to environmental information. It also advises on a wide range of domestic environmental matters including those concerning contaminated land, agriculture and permitting.

Client service: "The set exudes a very easy, down-to-earth style, and the clerks are absolutely super and extremely user-friendly." David Hockney leads the clerking team.

SILKS

Jon Turner QC Has an extremely strong reputation for his work on behalf of NGOs, action groups and commercial clients. He is an expert on issues such as pollution control and the protection of natural habitats. **Strengths:** "He gave us a clear indication of what we needed to do and what we couldn't do and left a very strong impression with the client." "He is a fabulous leader of a team; he will keep things down-to-earth and he doesn't have any trace of arrogance or pomposity." **Recent work:** Acted on behalf of an electrical waste recycling group on a claim against several electrical lamp producers. The case concerned alleged breaches of the EU WEEE electrical waste regulations.

Kassie Smith QC Advises on cases involving numerous private parties and NGOs as well as on environmental issues concerning UK government departments and the application of EU regulations. **Strengths:** "She has excellent legal qualifications and is very helpful to the solicitor in the preparation of cases." **Recent work:** Acted for the Secretary of State for Environment, Food and Rural Affairs in a judicial review challenge relating to the government's failure to comply with EU emission limits of nitrogen dioxide in London.

Gerry Facenna QC (see p.643) Recognised as an expert junior for cases relating to the EU regulation of, and access to, environmental information. He often acts for NGOs and campaigning groups. **Strengths:** "He is a superstar who is really good on cases concerning the environment and the protection of information. He has that EU law angle that really helps in this area, and is held in high esteem." **Recent work:** Represented the Environment Agency in the first applications for commercial 'fracking' licences.

Other Ranked Lawyers

Samantha Riggs (see p.752) (25 Bedford Row) Has a background in criminal law and has developed an impressive specialism in defending clients being prosecuted for criminal charges in relation to breaches of environmental law. **Strengths:** "She is extremely tenacious, incredibly hard-working and someone who invests enormous effort and attention to detail in each case she fights. She is fierce in her cross-examination and passionate in her defence of clients." **Recent work:** Defended SITA UK against charges of breaching its environmental permits for Connon Bridge landfill site.

James Findlay QC (Cornerstone Barristers) Offers wide experience of planning and environmental issues, and has significant experience in cases concerning the impact of wind farm developments. **Strengths:** "He is very approachable and commercial in his advice. He is a team player in his approach and very collaborative." **Recent work:** Represented Hackney London Borough Council in a judicial review challenge to a planning consent granted for the demolition of buildings in a conservation area.

Malcolm Galloway (see p.650) (Crown Office Chambers) Represents the Environment Agency and defendants, including corporate defendants and individual parties, in criminal prosecutions for breaches of environmental legislation. **Strengths:** "An excellent criminal law barrister in relation to environmental, health and safety work." **Recent work:** Acted for the Environment Agency in the prosecution of individuals illegally disposing of end of life tyres at various sites in the South West of England.

Gordon Nardell QC (20 Essex Street) An experienced QC who has a reputation for grasping technical issues, he focuses mainly on the environmental aspects of energy, utilities and waste cases. **Strengths:** "He knows how the regulator thinks and has excellent presentation skills. He takes a commercial and considered approach." **Recent work:** Appeared on behalf of the Civil Aviation Authority in judicial review proceedings brought by a resident complaining about Gatwick Airport aircraft noise.

Timothy Straker QC (4-5 Gray's Inn Square) Highly regarded for his knowledge of environmental issues relating to the planning of large infrastructure projects, particularly those relating to coastal ports and shipping. **Strengths:** "A fine tactician and an excellent advocate." **Recent work:** Represented several parties, including county councils and the National Trust, on HS2 issues.

John Bates (see p.591) (Old Square Chambers) A highly recommended expert on the law of nuisance who has a strong portfolio of multiparty claims and contaminated land cases, many of which are technically and scientifically complicated in nature. **Strengths:** "A real heavyweight. There is nothing he doesn't know about the law of private nuisance, and his advice is solid and sound." "Although he is quite quiet, he knows the law inside out, and his mind is amazing." **Recent work:** Represented multiple claimants in nuisance claims relating to odour from a composting operation.

Timothy Green (Outer Temple Chambers) Represents the Environment Agency and corporate clients in cases relating to alleged permit breaches and criminal activity in the waste management industry. Also advises on EU regulation of manufacturing and extraction processes. **Strengths:** "He is very tenacious, sees the bigger picture and spots the good points." **Recent work:** Represented the Environment Agency in its prosecution of a group of companies and individuals for an unlawful waste operation.

Sailesh Mehta (Red Lion Chambers) Acts in numerous cases involving the prosecution of environmental criminal charges. He both acts for defendants and appears on behalf of the Environment Agency. **Strengths:** "He is bright, pragmatic, thoroughly prepared and clearly respected by both judges and opponents." **Recent work:** Acted in R v Ezeemo, Benson, Vengelov and Others, the Environment Agency's largest ever investigation into alleged illegal exports of waste electrical equipment from the UK to Nigeria.

MIDLANDS

Environment
Leading Sets
Band 1
No5 Chambers *
Leading Silks
Band 1
Cahill Jeremy *No5 Chambers* Ⓐ
New Silks
Kimblin Richard *No5 Chambers*
Leading Juniors
Band 1
Berlin Barry *St Philips Chambers (ORL)* ◊
Green Timothy *Outer Temple Chambers (ORL)* ◊ Ⓐ
Wignall Gordon *6 Pump Court (ORL)* ◊ Ⓐ
** Indicates set with profile.*
Ⓐ direct access (see p.24).
◊ (ORL) = Other Ranked Lawyer.
Alphabetical order within each band. Band 1 is highest.

Band 1

No5 Chambers

See profile on p.931

THE SET

The leading set for environmental law on the Midland Circuit, with barristers regularly appearing in technically and legally complex cases before a variety of tribunals. Members have expertise in multiple areas including renewable energy, waste and pollution, and have been instructed recently in water quality cases under the Environmental Damage Regulations and the Water Framework Directive.

Client service: Tony McDaid is the set's practice director.

SILKS

Jeremy Cahill QC A highly experienced silk and head of the set's environmental and planning group. He has extensive experience of representing clients at public inquiries, with specific expertise in minerals, renewable energy and waste. **Strengths:** "A good advocate in the planning and regulatory law fields."

Richard Kimblin QC Regularly instructed in leading environmental cases throughout England and Wales, including before the High Court and Court of Appeal, and highlighted for his strength in issues concerning Environmental Impact Assessment, permitting and Habitats Regulations issues. **Strengths:** "Great on his feet. He is very astute and often brings a calmness to a situation which provides the clarity needed." **Recent work:** Represented the Secretary of State for Communities and Local Government in a case concerning the definition of 'tree' and the scope of legal protection for woodlands.

Other Ranked Lawyers

Timothy Green (Outer Temple Chambers) A specialist in regulatory investigations and environmental law. He is particularly noted for his prosecution work on behalf of the Environment Agency, and was recently instructed in a precedent-setting case concerning use of the regulator's powers to prosecute for fraud and money laundering arising out of serious environmental harm. **Strengths:** "Very co-operative and takes a sensible approach."

Gordon Wignall (6 Pump Court) A junior with many years of experience of acting in strict liability pollution claims in group litigation, as well as in regulatory proceedings challenging decisions by the Environment Agency. He also provides advice in non-litigious regulatory cases. **Strengths:** "A junior of choice for environment and a real heavyweight for private nuisance matters." **Recent work:** Acted for Chadwick in a judicial review in the Administrative Court in respect of a suspension notice served by the Environment Agency.

Barry Berlin (St Philips Chambers) An experienced environmental prosecutor who is regularly instructed by the Environment Agency and other public bodies on matters including environmental planning, hazardous substances, minerals, waste management and contaminated land. **Recent work:** Led the successful prosecution team in the Court of Appeal in a case concerning the pollution of a watercourse by Thames Water due to its failure to respond properly to untreated sewage leaking from a blocked pumping station.

NORTH EASTERN

Environment
Leading Juniors
Band 1
Morgan Charles *4-5 Gray's Inn Square***

Ranked Lawyers

Charles Morgan (4-5 Gray's Inn Square) An experienced junior, widely regarded as an expert in water-related environmental issues. He also regularly advises on waste and noise issues. His national client base includes landowners, developers, local authorities and water level management organisations. **Strengths:** "He brings natural enthusiasm to projects and cases. He is a very solid professional who communicates well, is an excellent technician and has an excellent brain." "He is an expert in water and drainage law. A great man for attention to detail and he really gets to the bottom of arguments." **Recent work:** Acted for the defendant in Environment Agency v Scott, successfully gaining acquittal on two of the four remaining environmental permitting breach charges.

NORTHERN

Environment
Leading Sets
Band 1
Kings Chambers *
Senior Statesmen
Senior Statesmen: distinguished older partners
Sauvain Stephen *Kings Chambers* *
Leading Silks
Band 1
Fraser Vincent *Kings Chambers* *
Manley David *Kings Chambers* *
Leading Juniors
Band 1
Barrett John *Kings Chambers* *
Hart Joseph *Deans Court Chambers (ORL)* ◊ *
Stockley Ruth *Kings Chambers* *
** Indicates set / individual with profile.*
◊ (ORL) = Other Ranked Lawyer.
Alphabetical order within each band. Band 1 is highest.

Band 1

Kings Chambers
See profile on p.968

THE SET

Kings Chambers maintains its position as the leading environment set on the Northern Circuit. Members act for a broad spectrum of clients, from individuals to corporates to developers. Its highly esteemed barristers offer a broad array of expertise, including local authority enforcement work and the auditing of Environmental Statements, and regularly represent clients in the magistrates' courts through to the High Court and Court of Appeal. The set houses particular expertise in the waste, water and renewable energy spaces.

Client service: "The clerks are very good, and very good at being interchangeable: they were au fait with the case and able to pick up as and when needed, which really impressed." "The clerking is very, very good. The clerks come into their own and they can turn things around quickly. It's a very efficient service." Bill Brown is the senior clerk.

SILKS

Stephen Sauvain QC (see p.759) An exceptional silk, highly regarded for his expertise in the areas of environment, planning, local government and public law. Receives high praise for the quality of his advisory work, with clients including national developers, local authorities and government agencies. **Strengths:** "He is an excellent advocate, capable of digesting volumes of information quickly. He has an easy-going, practical manner and he gives clearly communicated guidance." "He is very good. His attention to detail is excellent and he gives sound advice."

Vincent Fraser QC (see p.648) A highly regarded silk particularly adept at handling disputes involving environmental permitting and Environmental Impact Assessments. He handles a broad array of matters ranging from contaminated land to sewers and water law. **Strengths:** "He is a very skilled cross-examiner and an excellent person to have on your side." "His knowledge is encyclopaedic; he truly is a first-class QC." **Recent work:** Successfully represented Wainhomes at a planning appeal against the refusal of permission for a residential development. The matter involved weather and noise considerations.

David Manley QC (see p.706) A prominent silk with an abundance of experience in environmental matters. He is particularly adept at handling cases in the waste, renewable energy and animal rendering industries. Manley is also regarded as a specialist in the niche areas of nuclear and fracking. **Strengths:** "He is well prepared and analyses the issues, and provides punchy, straightforward advice." "He is an excellent source of local advice, an exceptional advocate and easy to talk to." **Recent work:** Acted for Lancashire County Council in Elizabeth Warner v Lancashire County Council, a case involving the highly contentious issue of fracking.

JUNIORS

John Barrett (see p.590) Maintains an excellent reputation as an accomplished junior in the areas of planning, administrative and public law and environmental law. He is noted for his adept handling of matters pertaining to the minerals, waste and renewables sectors. He acts for house builders, local authorities and agricultural clients. **Strengths:** "He has an excellent rapport with clients and is very empathetic." "He is a solid performer." **Recent work:** Successfully represented JG Pears at a planning appeal for a biofuel facility for burning chicken litter.

Ruth Stockley (see p.773) A well-regarded junior with a broad practice spanning areas such as environment, and town and country planning. She has a wealth of public inquiry experience and regularly advises developers, local authorities and other parties. **Strengths:** "She is excellent – very good and effective, with considerable experience. She is always very, very reliable." **Recent work:** Acted for Durham County Council in a public inquiry concerning proposals for the surface mining of coal from agricultural land.

Other Ranked Lawyers

Joseph Hart (see p.666) (Deans Court Chambers) Offers a broad environmental law practice with niche expertise in the developing field of fire safety law. **Strengths:** "He is hard-working, has an excellent attention to detail, is great with clients and is good at adapting to situations." "He is excellent on his feet – a gifted and intuitive advocate. He is pragmatic and commercial in his approach and works incredibly hard to get the best result possible. He clearly cares about results and is the person you want on your team." **Recent work:** Acted for the defence in R v Rodrigues, concerning allegations that a waste management company had been dumping waste in a public sewer.

Henderson Chambers
online application form
Midday deadline 31 March 2018 for May - July 2018
Midday deadline 27 July 2018 for Sept - Dec 2018

WESTERN

Environment	
Leading Silks	
Band 1	
Vaitilingam Adam	*Albion Chambers*
Leading Juniors	
Band 1	
Moorhouse Brendon	*Guildhall Chambers*

Alphabetical order within each band. Band 1 is highest.

Ranked Lawyers

Adam Vaitilingam QC (Albion Chambers) Prominent silk on the Western Circuit with a broad environmental law practice. He is well regarded for his regulatory practice and noted for his experience in handling contaminated land and pollution cases. **Strengths:** "He is very good on his feet, responsive, commercial and an accomplished advocate."

Brendon Moorhouse (Guildhall Chambers) A highly regarded junior with particular expertise in environmental law and regulatory matters. He has a wealth of experience handling noise abatement, watercourse pollution, waste packaging and illegal deposits of waste cases. **Strengths:** "The main environmental junior on the Western Circuit." "His criminal background provides him with a wide knowledge base. Clients count on his experience to know how to proceed with a case."

extrapolating from webpages for 2017

preference to candidates to come up to mid April year they begin BPTC

Blackstone Mini Pupillage (compulsory)

apply asap after 1 Sept 2018
window closes beginning Jan 2019
mini-pupillage period 1 Sept - mid April
(Gateway offers first week May)
(Gateway application period 2nd week Jan - 2nd week Feb)

spend a week in Chambers, attached to one or two members
undertake a set piece of work
two academic references, from undergraduate / postgraduate

Brick Court Chambers Mini Pupillage (compulsory)

spend a week in Chambers, mini pupil supervisor
carry out a standard piece of assessed work
assessed anonymously by reference to Chambers' selection criteria
interview for mini-pupillage
apply (and undertake) mini pupillage before applying for pupillage through the Gateway system

"as soon as you have started your GDL course"
if just apply through Gateway, will be treated as both mini + pupillage appl.

Contents:

LONDON

European Law
Leading Sets
Band 1
Blackstone Chambers *
Brick Court Chambers *
Monckton Chambers *
Band 2
11KBW *
Senior Statesmen
Senior Statesmen: distinguished older partners
Beloff Michael *Blackstone Chambers*
Vaughan David *Brick Court Chambers*
Leading Silks
Star individuals
Anderson David *Brick Court Chambers*
Band 1
Dashwood Alan *Henderson Chambers (ORL)* ◇ [A] *
Demetriou Marie *Brick Court Chambers*
Mercer Hugh *Essex Court Chambers (ORL)* ◇
Pannick David *Blackstone Chambers*
Rose Dinah *Blackstone Chambers*
Stratford Jemima *Brick Court Chambers*
Ward Tim *Monckton Chambers* [A] *
Band 2
Bacon Kelyn *Brick Court Chambers*
Beal Kieron *Blackstone Chambers*
Beard Daniel *Monckton Chambers*
Chamberlain Martin *Brick Court Chambers* *
Coppel Jason *11KBW* *
de la Mare Thomas *Blackstone Chambers*
Fordham Michael *Blackstone Chambers*
Hoskins Mark *Brick Court Chambers* *
Jowell Daniel *Brick Court Chambers* *
Moser Philip *Monckton Chambers* [A] *
Randolph Fergus *Brick Court Chambers*
Robertson Aidan *Brick Court Chambers*
Rogers Ian *Monckton Chambers*
Smith Kassie *Monckton Chambers*
Swift Jonathan *11KBW* *
Thompson Rhodri *Matrix Chambers (ORL)* ◇
Turner Jon *Monckton Chambers*
New Silks
Facenna Gerry *Monckton Chambers* [A] *
Harris QC (Hon) Jonathan *Serle Court (ORL)* ◇ *
Kennelly Brian *Blackstone Chambers*
Lester Maya *Brick Court Chambers* *
Leading Juniors
Band 1
Rhee Deok Joo *39 Essex Chambers (ORL)* ◇
Wakefield Victoria *Brick Court Chambers*
Band 2
Banner Charles *Landmark Chambers (ORL)* ◇
Blakeley Richard *Brick Court Chambers* *
Blundell David *Landmark Chambers (ORL)* ◇
Holmes Josh *Monckton Chambers*
Scannell David *Brick Court Chambers*
Tridimas Takis *Matrix Chambers (ORL)* ◇
* Indicates set / individual with profile.
[A] direct access (see p.24).
◇ (ORL) = Other Ranked Lawyer.
Alphabetical order within each band. Band 1 is highest.

Band 1

Blackstone Chambers

See profile on p.813

THE SET

Blackstone Chambers is a pre-eminent set advising government bodies, corporations, NGOs and individuals on the full range of European law. The chambers covers judicial reviews and litigation, handling anything from tobacco and gambling regulation to human rights-related cases. Recent cases have included ClientEarth v Secretary of State for the Environment, Food and Rural Affairs and R (Imperial Tobacco & ors.) v Secretary of State for Health. One instructing solicitor enthused: "The set has a stable of outstanding public law and regulatory barristers and would be first choice in that area."

Client service: "I have found the clerks to be incredibly helpful. We had discussions on fees and they made an effort to be accommodating." Senior clerk Gary Oliver heads the clerking team.

SILKS

Michael Beloff QC Boasts enviable experience in the field of European law in addition to his expertise in administrative, professional discipline and sports law. He is a hugely experienced litigator and arbitrator whose track record is second to none. **Strengths:** "He's exceptionally bright and is able to grasp points quickly and run with them."

David Pannick QC Has a broad practice encompassing all aspects of EU law as well as UK administrative law and human rights. He is universally admired for his exceptional advocacy skills. **Strengths:** "The opportunity to see him in full flow is one that has to be taken – to see his advocacy is an incredible experience." **Recent work:** He represented the Gibraltar government in a judicial review challenging new gaming laws imposing restrictions on services provided from Gibraltar to the UK.

Dinah Rose QC Receives widespread praise for her advocacy. She has a broad practice and has represented clients before the UK and EU courts on cases concerning gambling, tobacco and the environment. Undoubtedly one of the superstars of her generation at the Bar. **Strengths:** "She is a good persuader of judges, very down-to-earth and easy to work with." **Recent work:** She acted for ClientEarth in ClientEarth v Secretary of State, a case before the ECJ concerning air quality in London.

Kieron Beal QC Has acted recently in high-profile judicial reviews with EU law elements. He represents companies, NGOs and government bodies. **Strengths:** "He is pragmatic, thoughtful and always on the money – an excellent combination when one is looking for cutting-edge advice." **Recent work:** He represented Western Sahara Campaign in a judicial review against HMRC and Defra relating to the failure of EU legislation to recognise the independence of Western Sahara from Morocco.

Michael Fordham QC Has a broad practice acting on everything from cases in the utilities sector to those with human rights and migration elements. He is a popular choice for instructing solicitors in judicial review cases. **Strengths:** "He is just a guru of judicial review cases and always thinks how to intervene to best effect." **Recent work:** He represented SSE as an intervener in RWE Generation's challenge to the Gas and Electricity Markets Agency's changes in calculating electricity transmission system charges.

Thomas de la Mare QC Experienced in EU and competition law. He is widely praised for his energy and creativity. **Strengths:** "We have really tested his ability to come up with novel ideas to help the clients, and I think he's done that very well." **Recent work:** He acted for the appellant members of the Criminal Bar in a judicial review challenging the legality of the Quality Assurance Scheme for Advocates.

Brian Kennelly QC New silk with a broad EU law practice covering sanctions, telecoms and competition law. He is praised by instructing solicitors for being user-friendly and is lauded as a star of the future. **Strengths:** "He is very technical, client-friendly and easy to work with. Instructing him is always a very positive experience." **Recent work:** Led by Dinah Rose QC, he acted for Imperial Tobacco in its challenge to the EU's Second Tobacco Directive.

Brick Court Chambers

See profile on p.816

THE SET

Brick Court provides a top-flight European law offering that is sought out by prestigious law firms seeking advice in areas as diverse as tax, free movement and EU-wide IP. The barristers receive instructions from multinational corporations, government bodies and individuals, and are increasingly active in the expanding area of EU sanctions. Of late, members have handled a number of headline-grabbing matters, as illustrated by their appearance in the Tobacco Directive judicial reviews. Instructing solicitors say: "All the barristers are efficient, bright and know the law, and the clerks are easy to deal with."

Client service: "The clerks are everything you would hope for – responsive and great at handling communication with the courts." Senior Clerks Julian Hawes and Ian Moyler head the clerking team.

SILKS

David Vaughan QC Renowned practitioner with vast experience of all aspects of EU law. He is well regarded for his work before both UK and EU courts and has over 50 years of experience in the field. **Strengths:** "He is the éminence gris of EU law."

David Anderson QC Experienced at working in both Brussels and Washington, DC, he has highly developed expertise in all aspects of EU law. He is the government's Independent Reviewer of Terrorism Legislation. **Strengths:** "He is highly respected by the EU judiciary and his fellow barristers. Combines adept client-handling skills with an exceptionally strong strategic instinct – he's a delight to work with." **Recent work:** He represented Japan Tobacco in R(JTI) v Secretary of State for Health challenging the legality of legislation requiring the plain packaging of cigarettes.

Marie Demetriou QC Handles a broad range of EU law matters concerning the internal market, free movement, pharmaceuticals and EU-wide IP. **Strengths:** "Very responsive and very approachable, she is quick to get to grips with the complex facts of a case and gives very clear and pragmatic advice." **Recent work:** She represented Phillip Morris in its UK and EU challenges to plain packaging legislation concerning tobacco.

Jemima Stratford QC Acts in cases covering a wide range of EU law matters, handling issues as varied as data protection, tax and free movement. She has been active of late in telecoms and pharmaceuticals litigation. **Strengths:** "Jemima has excellent judgement, is very responsive, highly proactive and incredibly hard-working." **Recent work:** She represented Astellas in declaration proceedings against Accord concerning the ability of Accord to market a leukaemia drug.

Kelyn Bacon QC Has notable experience in pharmaceuticals and tobacco-related EU cases. She is experienced at acting before the EU and UK courts. **Strengths:** "Kelyn is great as she's efficient, bright and helpful." **Recent work:** Appeared in a judicial review acting as leading counsel for the Tipping Paper Claimants in their challenge to the Standardised Packaging of Tobacco Products Regulations 2015

Martin Chamberlain QC (see p.614) Represents individuals and companies before EU and UK courts. He has recently acted on discrimination and tobacco regulatory cases. **Strengths:** "He is very easy to get along with and a proper modern silk. He is one of the team when we instruct him. He takes a relaxed approach, focuses on the detail and is strong advocacy-wise." **Recent work:** He represented the Legal Services Board before the Supreme Court defending an EU law challenge to the Quality Assurance Scheme for Advocates.

Mark Hoskins QC (see p.675) An experienced EU and competition law practitioner, with notable experience of representing the government and companies before UK and EU courts. Sources highlight his punchy advocacy style. **Strengths:** "Very commercial and very impressive, he's a man who believes in the quality of his advice." **Recent work:** Acted for the Department of Health in various high-profile challenges to the validity of EU Tobacco Directives relating to tobacco packaging and e-cigarettes.

Daniel Jowell QC (see p.687) Experienced in tax restitution and has recently been involved in high-profile tobacco-related litigation. He is well regarded for his judicial review work and for EU law in general. **Strengths:** "He is exceptional all round." **Recent work:** He acted for Benkert as intervener in Philip Morris v Secretary of State for Health, a challenge to the Tobacco Directive.

Fergus Randolph QC Renowned EU law practitioner who is particularly well regarded for his work in commercial agency cases. He has recently been involved in various EU sanction matters. **Strengths:** "He is very experienced and he gives sensible and pragmatic advice because he knows his area so well." **Recent work:** He acted for Islamic Republic of Iran Shipping Lines with regard to its challenge to EU sanctions imposed upon it.

Aidan Robertson QC Esteemed EU lawyer with experience in areas as diverse as telecoms, taxation and free movement. He is also a well-regarded academic. **Strengths:** "He is a fantastic team player, who is very responsive." **Recent work:** He acted for Barnfield Construction in Barnfield Construction v Department for Communities and Local Government, a judicial review challenge to retrospective revocation of a European Regional Development Fund grant.

Maya Lester QC (see p.700) New silk with an exceptionally broad EU law practice that covers cases concerning competition law, sanctions and fundamental rights. She is exceptionally well regarded for her work on EU sanctions. **Strengths:** "She is happy to answer queries at all hours and really knows her stuff." **Recent work:** She represented the Chagos Islanders in a judicial review of the FCO's decision to impose a Marine Protection Zone around the Chagos Islands.

JUNIORS

Victoria Wakefield Acts in a wide range of EU law cases before UK and EU courts, and has a focus on competition law, agricultural law and fundamental rights. **Strengths:** "She combines common sense, intellectual rigour and a real willingness to roll up her sleeves." **Recent work:** Led by David Anderson QC, she appeared in a judicial review acting for Roche in a matter concerning the pharmaceuticals Penalties Regulation.

Richard Blakeley (see p.597) Experienced in all aspects of EU law, and has recently appeared in a number of EU sanctions cases. He also has experience of handling EU-wide IP cases. **Strengths:** "Richard excels at getting in the mindset of the clients and understanding the matter from their point of view." **Recent work:** He represented the Premier League in various actions enforcing its copyright.

David Scannell A well-regarded junior who recently acted on the various tobacco judicial reviews. He is also experienced before the European Chemicals Agency Board of Appeals. **Strengths:** "He is measured, chooses his points selectively and delivers them well." **Recent work:** He acted for Grace in an appeal against a decision of the European Chemicals Agency.

Monckton Chambers

See profile on p.877

THE SET

Monckton Chambers boasts a stellar European law offering and has barristers experienced in all aspects of European law, including discrimination, tax, free movement and financial regulation. Many counsel are leading experts in European competition law. The set acts for private companies, NGOs, public bodies and EU institutions. Recent cases include the Tobacco judicial reviews and ClientEarth v Defra. An impressed client states: "They are at the top of their game, they are responsive and they are very good communicators."

Client service: "The clerks are very proactive and sensible on fees." Senior clerk David Hockney heads the clerking team.

SILKS

Tim Ward QC (see p.789) Excellent EU law advocate with experience of handling the full range of EU law mandates. He has recently been active in free movement, discrimination and EU sanctions cases. **Strengths:** "Tim is a very adept and able strategist who is decisive and consistently delivers sound and forthright advice." **Recent work:** He acted for the Icelandic Deposit Guarantee Scheme against the UK and Dutch governments before the European Free Trade Association court. This was a matter following on from the famous 'Icesave' case in 2013 which decided that the Icelandic state was not liable for deposits in failed banks.

Daniel Beard QC Has vast experience of handling European law cases. His practice covers competition and regulatory matters, and he is particularly renowned for his work in telecoms litigation. **Strengths:** "He has good insight into the regulator's thinking, is a very fluent advocate and is good on his feet." **Recent work:** Acted in a major EU constitutional case before the CJEU looking at whether the EU could sign up to the ECHR. He represented the UK.

Philip Moser QC (see p.722) EU law expert with specific expertise in public procurement and VAT. He has been active of late on various Francovich damages claims. **Strengths:** "Philip is a hugely impressive and knowledgeable advocate who wins the confidence of judges. He's both a very seasoned court performer and someone who is good at negotiation and mediation situations." **Recent work:** He represented the UK government in a £415 million Francovich damages case arising from the licensing obligation for GSM Gateways.

Ian Rogers QC Specialist in non-competition EU law, noted for his expertise in cases concerning free movement, labour law, public health regulation and fundamental rights. He has recently been instructed in tobacco-related cases. **Strengths:** "He offered commercially minded advice in what was a very delicate situation, and he quickly identified the fatal flaws in our opponent's case." **Recent work:** He acted for the UK on a challenge to the validity of the Revised Tobacco Products Directive before the CJEU.

Kassie Smith QC Has a broad EU law practice that covers areas as diverse as environmental, discrimination and competition law. She is a sought-after counsel for NGOs, government departments and private companies. **Strengths:** "Her advocacy is effective and to the point." **Recent work:** She represented Defra in a judicial review brought by ClientEarth concerning the government's failure to comply with EU nitrogen dioxide emission limits in London.

Jon Turner QC Boasts expertise in a wide range of EU law subjects from environmental law to criminal justice. He is best known for his competition law expertise and is experienced in acting before both UK and European courts. **Strengths:** "Jon is highly regarded and has a keen insight into the client's commercial objectives." **Recent work:** He acted in a judicial review challenge by the European Low Fares Airline Association against the EU carbon trading regime.

Gerry Facenna QC (see p.643) Frequently instructed by the UK government, he is experienced in international relations, citizenship and environmental issues. He acts regularly before the UK and EU courts. **Strengths:** "He is truly superb in all aspects of the job. Obscenely clever, he's a great strategist and a superb advocate. He reads the situation perfectly and is a commercially aware perfectionist. I would not want to be against him." **Recent work:** He acted on a challenge to the UK's protection of pensioners who are former employees of companies that become insolvent.

JUNIORS

Josh Holmes Particularly well-regarded junior, who worked as a referendaire to the CJEU. He has a broad EU law practice and has recently been active handling cases concerning public law, criminal justice and financial regulation. **Strengths:** "He is a very strong EU law practitioner" who "can more than hold his own when pitted against a bunch of silks."

Recent work: He represented the UK government in a challenge to the lawfulness of rules permitting the export of data by companies from the EU to the USA.

Band 2

11KBW

See profile on p.867

THE SET

11KBW is a strong European law set drawing strength from its leading administrative and public, employment and public procurement law practices. The barristers are adept at non-competition European law and are frequently instructed by government entities to act before both UK and European courts. The chambers has recently been instructed in litigation related to prisoners' voting rights.

Client service: Lucy Barbet and Mark Dann are joint senior clerks of what is "an excellent clerking team."

SILKS

Jason Coppel QC (see p.624) An expert in non-competition EU law, who has experience before both UK and EU courts. His recent cases have covered areas such as welfare, agriculture and human rights. **Strengths:** "His written arguments are always excellent and his advocacy is clear and compelling. He has a clear grasp of the issues." **Recent work:** He acted for the government in litigation related to prisoners' voting rights.

Jonathan Swift QC (see p.777) Former First Treasury Counsel, a position he held for nearly a decade, he remains a popular choice for government departments. He is experienced in human rights, constitutional law, data protection and regulation cases, among many other areas. **Strengths:** "He has a razor-like ability to get to the heart of the issue." **Recent work:** He acted for HMRC in Littlewoods v HMRC, a case concerning whether there is a right to recover compound interest on overpaid VAT.

Other Ranked Lawyers

Hugh Mercer QC (Essex Court Chambers) Well regarded for his expertise in a wide range of European matters, including cases relating to damages, environmental law and free movement. **Strengths:** "He is technically strong and also very pragmatic." **Recent work:** He represented the National Union of Farmers as an intervener in Syngenta v EC and Bayer v EC, which related to the EC ban on the use of neonicotinoids as pesticides.

Deok Joo Rhee (39 Essex Chambers) Specialises in EU economic and social policy covering areas such as immigration, employment and public procurement. She is frequently instructed by the Government Legal Service. **Strengths:** "She is exceptionally hard-working, and her preparation for cross examination is incredibly detailed." **Recent work:** She represented the UK in a treaty-based challenge to part of an EU regulation adopted in the field of transport/trans-European rail network.

Alan Dashwood QC (see p.629) (Henderson Chambers) Vastly experienced EU law expert who was a director in the Council of Europe's legal service. In addition, he is an active academic. **Strengths:** "He has an excellent understanding of technical detail and takes a very commercial approach." **Recent work:** He acted for Viorel Micula against the EC in a case concerning the interplay between arbitral awards, EU law and state aid.

Charles Banner (Landmark Chambers) Acts for a range of clients including private clients, NGOs and the government. He is on the Attorney General's A panel. **Strengths:** "He has an incredibly detailed knowledge of EU law and shows real skill in applying it." **Recent work:** He represented the UK in M'Bodj v. État Belge concerning the entitlement of a seriously ill asylum seeker to benefits under the EU Qualification Directive.

David Blundell (Landmark Chambers) An expert in all aspects of EU law, who is on the Attorney General's A Panel. He advises on cases relating to such areas as environment and social security. **Strengths:** "His ability to identify key points and advance unique arguments is impressive." **Recent work:** He acted in two recent referrals to the CJEU concerning the scope of citizenship rights and the Zambrano decision.

Rhodri Thompson QC (Matrix Chambers) Acclaimed for his work in major telecoms disputes. He has a broad EU law practice, with a strong competition and state aid element to it. **Strengths:** "A strong lawyer who produces particularly good paperwork." **Recent work:** He acted in James Craig and ors. v R, a case relating to a fisherman over-fishing his quota.

Takis Tridimas (Matrix Chambers) Particularly well regarded as an academic and author on the subject of EU law. His practice covers judicial reviews, financial law and human rights. He is experienced in acting before both the EU and UK courts. **Strengths:** "He is exceptionally intelligent and incisive when advising on matters of EU free movement and citizenship law." **Recent work:** He acted in Chrysostomides, Agroton and ors. v EU in which 51 depositors and shareholders of Cypriot banks sought compensation for loss suffered as a result of the 'haircut' imposed by the Cyprus bail-in programme.

Jonathan Harris (see p.665) (Serle Court) Specialises in European private international law and sits on the Lord Chancellor's Advisory Committee on the subject. In addition, he is an active academic. **Strengths:** "He is accessible and easy to deal with, and the work he does is of a very high standard." **Recent work:** He acted for the Central Bank of Italy in successfully challenging the jurisdiction of the English courts to determine the liability of the bank for refusing to permit the exchange of lira.

Monckton Mini Pupillage

9th April deadline for May - July 2018

CV and covering letter with available dates + 'Monitoring' Form

three days, attached to junior barrister

11 KBW mini pupillage (compulsory)

one week in Chambers

piece of work assessed by two members

asked Qs about work produced and offered constructive feedback

-> assessed on both written work and oral discussion

application form, deadline approx 9 Nov 2018

interview for place on mini-pupillage

final round interview and make pupillage offer on basis of interview

Contents:

LONDON

Extradition	
Leading Silks	
Band 1	
Fitzgerald Edward	*Doughty Street Chambers*
Keith Hugo	*3 Raymond Buildings Barristers* *
Knowles Julian	*Matrix Chambers*
Lewis James	*3 Raymond Buildings Barristers* A *
Montgomery Clare	*Matrix Chambers* *
Perry David	*6KBW College Hill*
Summers Mark	*Matrix Chambers* *
Band 2	
Garlick Paul	*Furnival Chambers* A
Hardy John	*3 Raymond Buildings Barristers* *
Hines James	*3 Raymond Buildings Barristers* A *
Jones Alun	*Great James Street Chambers*
Josse David	*5 St Andrew's Hill* *
Malcolm Helen	*3 Raymond Buildings Barristers* A
Leading Juniors	
Band 1	
Brandon Ben	*3 Raymond Buildings Barristers*
Caldwell Peter	*Drystone Chambers* *
Cooper Ben	*Doughty Street Chambers* A
Dobbin Clair	*3 Raymond Buildings Barristers* *
Keith Benjamin	*5 St Andrew's Hill* *
Lloyd Ben	*6KBW College Hill*
Smith Joel	*Furnival Chambers* *
Watkins Aaron	*Matrix Chambers*
Watson Ben	*3 Raymond Buildings Barristers* A *
Band 2	
Barnes Rachel	*3 Raymond Buildings Barristers* A *
Draycott Natasha	*5 St Andrew's Hill* *
Grandison Myles	*Drystone Chambers* *
Hill Rebecca	*5 St Andrew's Hill* *
Weekes Mark	*6KBW College Hill*
Band 3	
Butt Matthew	*3 Raymond Buildings Barristers* A *
Collins Louisa	*5 St Andrew's Hill* *
Cumberland Melanie	*6KBW College Hill*
Ezekiel Adina	*6KBW College Hill*
Hawkes Malcolm	*Doughty Street Chambers* A
Hearn Nicholas	*Furnival Chambers* *
Lindfield Gemma	*5 St Andrew's Hill* *
Nice Amelia	*5 St Andrew's Hill* *
Scott Rachel	*3 Raymond Buildings Barristers* *
Stansfeld James	*Furnival Chambers* *
Sternberg Daniel	*9-12 Bell Yard* *
Townshend Saoirse	*The 36 Group*
Westcott Mary	*Doughty Street Chambers*

** Indicates individual with profile.*
A direct access (see p.24).
Alphabetical order within each band. Band 1 is highest.

Ranked Lawyers

Daniel Sternberg (see p.772) (9-12 Bell Yard) Prosecution specialist with strong experience of handling European Arrest Warrants and assisting European governments with extradition requests regarding individuals based in the United Kingdom. He is praised for his ethical approach and his dedication to his clients' cause. **Strengths:** "A very nice, very calm, measured advocate" who is "a first-rate prosecutor." **Recent work:** Represented the Italian government in its extradition request for three men accused of having links to IS in Syria and planning to carry out terrorist activities.

Edward Fitzgerald QC (Doughty Street Chambers) Pre-eminent silk with a varied practice, who regularly represents the most high-profile defendants such as Gary McKinnon and Boriz Berezovsky. He comes highly recommended by commentators for his vast intellectual acumen and his impressive courtroom manner. **Strengths:** "One of the best extradition silks around, he's extraordinarily hard-working and enthusiastic." "One of the cleverest and most interesting advocates to listen to. He's absolutely at the top of his game, and judges have the most complete respect for him." **Recent work:** Advised the government of Ecuador on the international law and extradition aspects relating to the grant of diplomatic asylum to Wikileaks creator Julian Assange.

Ben Cooper (Doughty Street Chambers) Attracts plaudits for his passionate and relentless approach to his cases. "A live wire" who is "utterly and completely engaged in his cases," he is particularly experienced at handling US extradition requests. He is also highly capable of conducting extradition cases relating to complex human rights issues. **Strengths:** "Very tenacious." "He thinks things through in a great deal of depth and he's very good on his feet." "He is absolutely determined, will never give up" and "has an incredible reputation with clients." **Recent work:** Successfully defended an individual facing extradition to Dubai on the grounds that he would be at increased risk of torture due to his homosexuality.

Malcolm Hawkes (Doughty Street Chambers) Extradition specialist praised for his technical ability. He is adept at conducting complex cases relating to European Arrest Warrants that encompass human rights issues. He is also extremely experienced at handling Interpol Red Notices. **Strengths:** "He's just fantastic and really very experienced." "He's really dedicated and will work really hard." **Recent work:** Represented a doctor facing extradition to the USA having been accused of child rape. The challenge was based on a contravention of Article 5 and the fact that the defendant would face an indefinite sentence if returned to the USA.

Mary Westcott (Doughty Street Chambers) Dedicated practitioner who utilises her expertise in the European Convention of Human Rights and public law proceedings to undertake complex extradition matters. Praised for her work ethic and her devotion to clients, she is particularly experienced in handling matters involving inhumane prison conditions, human trafficking and children's rights. **Strengths:** "Intelligent and articulate, she really excels in the technical areas of extradition law." "She cares about each individual, and puts long hours and extreme effort into fighting the extradition process." **Recent work:** Represented an individual in a test case as to whether extradition to Hungary should be barred due to inhuman and degrading prison conditions.

Peter Caldwell (see p.609) (Drystone Chambers) Highly capable as both a prosecutor and a defence counsel, he handled numerous complex and high-profile extradition requests, including European Arrest Warrant matters and individual cases of British citizens facing extradition to international jurisdictions. He also has experience of advising financial corporations and government agencies. **Strengths:** "He's experienced, very technical and highly knowledgeable." "A really good and calm advocate whose opinions carry weight with the judges." **Recent work:** Represented a businessman facing extradition to Ireland following accusations of fraud in collusion with a corrupt police officer.

Myles Grandison (see p.658) (Drystone Chambers) Up-and-coming extradition practitioner who is noted for his strong work ethic and client-handling skills. He regularly defends individuals facing complex extradition proceedings, most often involving European governments. **Strengths:** "He is just absolutely dedicated to his clients." "He has a thriving defence practice, and is somebody that's quite meticulous in his preparation." **Recent work:** Successfully defended an individual whose extradition was sought by both Romania and Germany. The case was won on the grounds of prison conditions, the validity of the European Arrest Warrant issued by Romania and issues of double jeopardy in Germany.

Paul Garlick QC (Furnival Chambers) Vastly experienced advocate with an expert knowledge of civil liberties. He is extremely familiar with handling extradition requests involving human rights violations, particularly those stemming from Turkey and Russia. **Strengths:** "Has enormously wide international experience, and he never fails to impress." "Very able and understanding with a deep knowledge of the law."

Joel Smith (see p.768) (Furnival Chambers) Praised for his intellectual acumen and efficiency, he has a practice that encompasses both criminal law and extradition. He often represents individuals who have been requested due to convictions for serious crimes, including murder and terrorism. In addition he acts for foreign governments who have placed said extradition requests. **Strengths:** "An extremely impressive young lawyer." "He's understated, extremely clever and no-nonsense." "Very personable. He has the respect of the court and is very sensible." **Recent work:** Represented an individual who is the subject of a US extradition request, having been accused of causing a "flash crash" as a result of 'spoof' trading and fraud.

Nicholas Hearn (see p.668) (Furnival Chambers) Impressive junior instructed as both prosecution and defence counsel in a number of complex extradition matters. He is an expert on European Arrest Warrants and the human rights aspects of extradition cases. **Strengths:** "Very experienced and very technically sound." "Imaginative in the issues he raises," "he has a deep understanding of the law and can properly evaluate issues as they arise." **Recent work:** Represented the Hungarian government with regard to the sufficiency of assurances offered by the Hungarian authorities in respect of prison conditions.

James Stansfeld (see p.771) (Furnival Chambers) Praised by sources for his advocacy skills, he has appeared before both the Supreme and the Divisional Courts. He has developed a particular expertise in assisting Greece in its extradition requests, and has further represented both private individuals and other European governments. **Strengths:** "Very, very bright and academically very impressive." "He has great drafting skills, is extremely good at the technical aspects of the law, and is good at communicating complex problems in a very clear way." **Recent work:** Appeared before the Supreme Court in a case questioning the validity of European Arrest Warrants issued by Poland. The case considered whether or not a warrant needs to include details of the activation of a suspended sentence.

Alun Jones QC (Great James Street Chambers) Renowned silk who is known for his years of extradition experience, and has handled cases all the way to the Supreme Court. On past occasions, he has represented individuals charged with genocide, murder and manslaughter. **Strengths:** "He's a very difficult opponent and you've got to be on your mettle if you're against him."

David Perry QC (6KBW College Hill) Leading silk with vast experience of representing numerous foreign governments in extremely high-profile extradition cases. He is particularly experienced in advising on extradition matters relating to financial issues, including fraud, corruption and bribery. **Strengths:** "He is undoubtedly the most respected QC in any court he goes into." "A masterful advocate." **Recent work:** Represented a former JP Morgan trader accused by the US government of being responsible for synthetic credit trading which led to trading losses that surpassed USD6.2 billion.

Ben Lloyd (6KBW College Hill) "Intellectually sound" junior with "good analytical skills" who has considerable experience of both prosecuting and defending European and international governments. Highly praised for his advocacy and client care skills, he is also regularly instructed privately to advise companies and individuals on extradition matters. **Strengths:** "One of the most eloquent barristers at the Extradition Bar." "His approach to work is meticulous, he is thoroughly prepared and he's good with clients." "A really smooth advocate." **Recent work:** Represented the Spanish government, which had issued an extradition request for a man convicted for the 1986 terrorist attacks in Madrid.

Mark Weekes (6KBW College Hill) "Outstanding" practitioner with a broad practice who is extremely well-versed in extradition matters stemming from criminal charges of the utmost seriousness. He is particularly experienced in representing foreign governments and individuals who are seeking or fighting extradition requests related to war crimes and crimes against humanity. **Strengths:** "He's really bright and drafts really excellent, solid skeletons." "An absolutely ideal junior" whose "clarity of thought is very impressive." **Recent work:** Represented an individual facing extradition for his alleged involvement in the Rwandan genocide, which left 800,000 dead in 100 days.

Melanie Cumberland (6KBW College Hill) Specialises in handling extradition matters arising out of allegations of terrorism, and has particular experience of assisting with extradition requests from North America. She also regularly advises foreign governments on conducting extradition matters within the United Kingdom. **Strengths:** "She is completely and utterly dependable, and absolutely brilliant when it comes to skeleton arguments."

Adina Ezekiel (6KBW College Hill) Particularly experienced in the prosecution of extradition matters, she most notably represents foreign governments and judicial authorities. She has in-depth understanding of advising and representing the US government in extradition matters based in the UK. **Strengths:** "Very sound." "A terrier with a first-class brain." **Recent work:** Represented the US government in a long-running extradition case of a British man who is alleged to have murdered an individual during the course of a robbery before fleeing back to Britain.

Julian Knowles QC (Matrix Chambers) High-calibre silk with a broad practice, who represents high-profile individuals, governments and corporate clients. He regularly assists European governments in requesting those persons convicted or accused of crimes including terrorism and murder. **Strengths:** "Highly innovative, he conjures up points from nowhere in the most imaginative way." "A brilliant silk who is especially good at defending extradition requests, as he's tenacious and leaves no stone unturned in terms of case preparation. He's a silk that likes to draft his own submissions and really engage with the arguments." **Recent work:** Represented the Italian government in seeking the extradition of three men accused of involvement in ISIS related terrorism.

Clare Montgomery QC (see p.720) (Matrix Chambers) Respected silk who is considered "devastatingly intelligent" by those in the extradition market. She is known for her involvement in incredibly high-profile cases, and is particularly well versed in assisting individuals who are being sought for extradition by international governments as a result of alleged criminal offences. **Strengths:** "She is just overwhelmingly clever." "She is a superstar of the extradition world." **Recent work:** Represented a former senior banker facing an extradition request from the government of Iraq.

Mark Summers QC (see p.776) (Matrix Chambers) Described as "extraordinarily talented," he comes highly recommended for his impressive courtroom manner. He is an expert in mutual legal assistance, and represents individuals as well as European and international governments in all manner of extradition cases. He has particular experience in handling US extradition matters. **Strengths:** "He has what is pretty much unrivalled expertise in the field and a really detailed knowledge of the case law." "He has an encyclopaedic knowledge of this area, his written work is amazing and he's an incredibly effective advocate." **Recent work:** Represented a UK national facing extradition to the USA having been accused of the trafficking of chemical weapons detection equipment to Syria against US arms control.

Aaron Watkins (Matrix Chambers) Highly praised for his ability as an advocate and a draftsman, he both defends individuals and represents governments in complex extradition proceedings, often appearing before the Supreme Court. He also boasts an impressive advisory practice. **Strengths:** "He's unflappable and his written work is just excellent. He's equally as brilliant when it comes to technical arguments." "He's a fearless advocate in court and a real fighter." **Recent work:** Represented Spain in its high-profile extradition request relating to the head of Rwanda's security services who was alleged to be involved in the Rwandan genocide.

Hugo Keith QC (see p.689) (3 Raymond Buildings Barristers) An "absolutely outstanding" extradition specialist who is "head and shoulders above the majority of the pack." He handles the most complex and high-profile extradition proceedings, and is praised by market commentators for his advocacy skills and client manner. **Strengths:** "He's exceptionally good as he's very smooth with clients and very well prepared." "Extraordinarily well-regarded and someone with a huge intellect." **Recent work:** Represented the Republic of South Africa in relation to the extradition of Shrien Dewani, who is alleged to have arranged the murder of his wife while on their honeymoon.

James Lewis QC (see p.700) (3 Raymond Buildings Barristers) Outstanding silk with in-depth experience of the most complex and challenging extradition cases who has particular experience of extradition requests stemming from United States legislation. He comes highly recommended for his colourful advocacy and intellectual acumen. **Strengths:** "A terrific opponent who is extraordinarily able. He is very enthusiastic, has lots of energy and never misses a point." "Strong, smart and fearless," he has "very good understanding of extradition and international law, and is delightful to work with." **Recent work:** Represented an individual facing an extradition request to the United States from Trinidad following allegations of FIFA corruption.

John Hardy QC (see p.664) (3 Raymond Buildings Barristers) Respected practitioner highly familiar with European Arrest Warrants and matters involving complex Article 8 issues who regularly acts for both the prosecution and defendants. He attracts further plaudits for his client-handling skills. **Strengths:** "An absolute star who is extraordinarily hard-working, wonderful with clients, extraordinarily personable and a very fair minded opponent." "An absolutely lovely advocate."

James Hines QC (see p.672) (3 Raymond Buildings Barristers) Noted silk who maintains a broad criminal and commercial practice, and is particularly known for his advisory work on the extradition front. He is highly experienced at assisting governments and foreign fugitives in various different courts. **Strengths:** "Very able" and "good at getting clients to confront difficult issues." **Recent work:** Represented an individual who had been the subject of repeated European Arrest Warrants from Belgium. All previous EAW attempts have been refused.

Helen Malcolm QC (3 Raymond Buildings Barristers) Extradition specialist with particular expertise in European extradition matters. She combines her mastery of extradition with her capabilities in fraud law, and often represents individuals facing extradition as a result of financial crime. She also boasts experience of handling Requested Person cases and extradition allegations relating to genocide. **Strengths:** "She has gravitas and commands a lot of respect from other counsel and the court." "The most hard-working QC and just so dependable, she is absolutely the safest set of hands you could ever want and very clever." **Recent work:** Instructed by the Republic of Kenya to front their request to extradite an individual for trial. The individual is responsible for defrauding financiers and other companies through sales of mortgaged oil.

Ben Brandon (3 Raymond Buildings Barristers) Praised by sources for his innovative arguments and his intellectual acumen, he is experienced at handling both the prosecution and defence of individuals in extradition matters. He also regularly represents foreign governments. **Strengths:** "Really respected by the Westminster judges." "His written work is probably the best I've seen in terms of his skeleton submissions." "Very confident and very forthright." **Recent work:** Represented an individual facing extradition to the United States despite never having visited the country. The case centred around images of serious sexual offences against children which had been shared over the internet with individuals based in the United States.

Clair Dobbin (see p.634) (3 Raymond Buildings Barristers) "Phenomenal" junior with a broad practice encompassing public law and human rights as well as extradition. She has undertaken some of the most high-profile and sensitive extradition work of recent years, and has appeared in cases in the Supreme Court and the European Court of Human Rights. She is highly praised for her courtroom and client-handling skills. **Strengths:** "Amazing. She's really thorough and prepares great arguments." "Her written submissions are great, her oral presentation of arguments is very persuasive, and she's excellent with clients." **Recent work:** Represented a number of high-profile defendants resisting their extradition to the United States, where they face a whole life term of imprisonment (an alternative to the death penalty).

Ben Watson (see p.790) (3 Raymond Buildings Barristers) Has vast experience in cases concerning European Arrest Warrants and extradition relating to international terrorism issues. This "phenomenally bright" practitioner is also well versed in the area of mutual legal assistance, and is experienced in both prosecuting and defending individuals and foreign governments. **Strengths:** "Judges really, really love him and his legal analysis is brilliant." "He has a great degree of charm as an advocate, but he can be steely when necessary." **Recent work:** Successfully resisted, on health grounds, the extradition of a married couple to Greece following their conviction and sentencing for fraud.

Rachel Barnes (see p.590) (3 Raymond Buildings Barristers) Criminal law specialist with an extremely strong extradition practice. Having acted as both a lead junior and a junior alone, she is particularly experienced in handling extradition issues for both governments and requested persons. She is also an expert on Interpol Red Notices. **Strengths:** "Very thorough barrister who ensures she's really researched the issue before giving her advice. Her work is very well written, well structured and well referenced." "Lovely, thorough, very smart, and hard-working." **Recent work:** Successfully represented an individual who was subject to an extradition request following a conviction for murder in Ghana, a crime which carries a mandatory death penalty.

Matthew Butt (see p.608) (3 Raymond Buildings Barristers) Undertakes highly complex and sensitive extradition proceedings. He has represented requested persons who have been convicted of offences including fraud, torture and murder. **Strengths:** "He certainly knows what he's doing, an intricate knowledge of case law serves him really well." **Recent work:** Successfully defended an individual facing extradition to India, following charges of historical sexual abuse in an orphanage in Goa. The appeal was rejected on the basis that the extradition would be unjust and oppressive due to the defendant's mental health.

Rachel Scott (see p.760) (3 Raymond Buildings Barristers) Represents both requesting states and requested persons, and is highly regarded for her intellectual acumen and her work ethic. She is particularly experienced in extradition matters involving Russia and the Ukraine, and is also well versed in judicial review and appellate proceedings relating to extradition. **Strengths:** "Rachel is extremely intelligent, hard-working and an excellent lawyer. She also possesses great practical sense and is extremely personable." "Very concise, highly efficient and incredibly intelligent." **Recent work:** Represented a banker facing a Russian extradition request arising out of the takeover of the Bank of Moscow.

David Josse QC (see p.687) (5 St Andrew's Hill) Experienced silk with in-depth knowledge of extradition and international criminal law. He is particularly well known for his expertise in handling international war crimes and matters of genocide. He also boasts an impressive insight into cases on prison conditions. **Strengths:** "He has extensive international experience and is good for highly complicated cases." **Recent work:** Acted in the leading case on Romanian Article 3 prison conditions, examining issues including the reliability of assurances given by Romanian authorities and overcrowding.

Benjamin Keith (see p.689) (5 St Andrew's Hill) Described as a "strong advocate" by market sources, he attracts extremely high praise for the depth of his knowledge of extradition law. As well as vast experience of handling European Arrest Warrants, war crimes and cases involving political corruption, he boasts particular expertise in matters stemming from Russia and the Ukraine. **Strengths:** "Gifted, very diligent and up-to-date on the law." "He is unafraid to raise challenges on all sorts of issues, and has his finger on the pulse." "He is a really clear, straight-to-the-point advocate." **Recent work:** Represented the CPS and the National Crime Agency in a test case on whether an individual can be extradited to the United Kingdom to serve a sentence for a confiscation order.

Natasha Draycott (see p.637) (5 St Andrew's Hill) Praised for her abilities as an advocate, particularly when dealing with vulnerable or difficult clients. She is renowned for her knowledge of European Arrest Warrants, as well as her experience of handling matters relating to the standard of prison conditions in international domains. **Strengths:** "She's always shown full commitment to her cases." "Knowledgeable and experienced," she's "excellent with clients and her work product is always on time." **Recent work:** Represented an appellant in a landmark case relating to the compliance of European Arrest Warrants in relation to Section 20 of the Extradition Act 2003.

Rebecca Hill (see p.671) (5 St Andrew's Hill) Extradition specialist who prosecutes and defends individuals in all jurisdictions, and boasts particular knowledge of human rights issues. She is particularly well versed in European extradition issues and appellate proceedings. **Strengths:** "Very knowledgeable and a quality counsel." "Her advice and advocacy are on-point and focused." **Recent work:** Represented a homosexual Lithuanian man convicted of sexually assaulting another male and who was subject to an extradition request to serve his sentence. It was argued that the level of homophobia in Lithuania was so rife that the individual was uniquely vulnerable.

Louisa Collins (see p.620) (5 St Andrew's Hill) Appreciated by market commentators for her professional approach and her abilities as an advocate. She is highly experienced in a variety of challenging extradition matters, having represented both foreign governments and requested persons. She is also well equipped to handle vulnerable individuals. **Strengths:** "Her skeletons are just so professional and she is one of those people that when she goes before a judge she commands the respect of all the judges there." "Very persuasive and very knowledgeable, she's firm in her approach when necessary." **Recent work:** Represented the US government in requesting the extradition of a man sought to be prosecuted for allegations of rape and historical sexual abuse against his daughter.

Gemma Lindfield (see p.702) (5 St Andrew's Hill) Specialises in extradition, and has particular expertise in complex genocide cases. She is also highly experienced at handling extremely high-profile European Arrest Warrants and abuse of process applications. **Strengths:** "She gives clear, robust advice to the clients, especially the difficult ones." "She's very hard-working, and has a good grasp of the broad landscape." **Recent work:** Represented Rwanda in its extradition requests against five individuals sought for genocide and crimes against humanity.

Amelia Nice (see p.727) (5 St Andrew's Hill) "Excellent" practitioner renowned for her combined interests of family law and extradition matters. She has developed a subsequent expertise in handling extradition matters involving children, particularly those concerning child abduction and trafficking. Sources praise her for the way she communicates with vulnerable witnesses and defendants. **Strengths:** "She's got a lovely style of advocacy and, knowing a lot about family law, is particularly good with vulnerable clients." **Recent work:** Represented an individual, who was highly vulnerable both mentally and physically, in a case which concerned a complex Article 3 prison conditions argument.

Saoirse Townshend (The 36 Group) Up-and-coming junior developing an impressive extradition practice both as a jury and an appellate advocate. She is particularly well versed in European Arrest Warrant cases, and acts for both requesting government and requested persons. **Strengths:** "She's a very bright and meticulous counsel who has great attention to detail and is very clear and concise in her written work." "Saoirse is a creative barrister who is diligent." **Recent work:** Represented a 17 year old individual who had been requested by the government of Albania to serve a sentence for two burglaries committed when he was 14. The individual fled Albania having been forced into gang activity.

FAMILY/MATRIMONIAL: An Introduction

Contributed by 1 Garden Court Family Law Chambers

To set the family matrimonial context, 2016 saw a number of interesting facts emerge in data published by the Office for National Statistics, revealing that marriage continues to be in decline. 50.6% of the population aged 16 and over were married in 2015, in contrast to 54.8% in 2002. This was coupled with an increase in more people remaining single (up from 29.6% in 2002 to 34.5% in 2015) and an increase in the number of cohabiting couples (from 6.8% in 2002 to 9.5% in 2015). Given the political lack of enthusiasm to adopt the Law Commission recommendations set out in the 2007 report 'Cohabitation: The Financial Consequences of Relationship Breakdown', this increase in cohabitation figures might suggest the report should be revisited.

The year has seen a number of developments aimed at modernising and streamlining the family justice system. There were attempts to introduce a private member's bill providing for a "no fault" divorce, with strong support from Resolution and other family law groups. Although time ran out for passage of the bill, it is anticipated that it will be reintroduced in coming sessions of Parliament. Given that a recent Resolution poll established that over a quarter of divorcing couples falsify their petition claims, this is clearly a reform that needs to be made. Meanwhile, all divorce petitions are now issued out of regional centres (some of which, such as the London and South East Divorce Centre, have struggled to cope with the anticipated levels of petitions). The Statement on the Efficient Conduct of Financial Remedy Cases allocated to a High Court Judge provided revised guidance for the procedure to the adopted in such cases – including strict limits on the length of skeleton arguments. It is likely that such guidance will be extended to apply in due course to all financial remedy cases. Meanwhile the President of the Family Division envisages that within four years the Family Court will be both digitised and paperless (digital online divorce is planned for initial implementation in early 2017). The President predicts that a digital revolution will enable a radical revision of both court forms and court orders. This is certainly a brave new world and will mean a huge change to working practices, which the President exhorts the profession to embrace.

The Family Justice Council has produced two very helpful guides. The first, 'Sorting out Finances on Divorce', is aimed at litigants in person (given that 79% of family cases now involve at least one unrepresented party). Although no substitute for individual legal advice, it is a timely and valuable aid to those who cannot afford representation. By contrast, the second guide, 'Guidance on Financial Needs on Divorce', is aimed at the judiciary and legal advisers and focuses on the cases where the available assets do not exceed the parties' needs. It originated from concerns that there appeared to be significant regional differences in the level of needs-based support likely to be awarded in different courts and the lack of transparency in this area of the law. The aim of this guide is to ensure that there is a greater clarity and consistency of approach across the jurisdiction in such cases. It is likely to become a standard reference and all practitioners (and judges) will need to become familiar with its guidance.

It is of note that the family courts in England and Wales are still currently considered more likely to provide generous ongoing financial support compared to other international jurisdictions (as established in Pennington Manches LLP's 'From Dependency to Self-Sufficiency: The International Spousal Maintenance Barometer'). It may be that the publication of the Family Justice Council guide, advocating "a rigorous and disciplined approach consistent with the objective of enabling a transition to independence," will mean that England and Wales will in the future no longer be automatically considered the jurisdiction for ongoing financial support claims.

Meanwhile, the members of the judiciary continue to endorse support for the use of arbitration as an alternative to court-based resolution of disputes. Mostyn J noted that arbitration gives divorcing couples the same advantages as have been made available to commercial people for over a century and that there are only limited challenges to arbitral awards. In DB v DJ [2016] EWHC 324 (Fam) Mostyn J establishes a fast-track procedure within the High Court in the event of there being any challenge to such awards to enable a speedy determination of the issues. It will be interesting to see whether this sort of judicial support will lead to an increased take-up in arbitration among divorcing couples. It may be that the extension of arbitration to children cases, through the Children Arbitration Scheme launched in July, will boost the take-up of such services.

With regard to children, in May the education secretary announced that there would be changes to existing legislation to make it "crystal clear" that councils and courts must place children with the person best able to care for them throughout their minority. This came in the context of the number of decisions for adoption made by courts and councils having fallen by around 50% over the preceding two years.

In children public law proceedings, 2016 saw increasing criticism of local authorities that are failing families by abusing the use of Section 20 agreements, with children having been left in foster placements and scant regard paid to the requirement for a speedy resolution of proceedings. The President gave clear guidelines on such agreements in N (Children) (Adoption: Jurisdiction) [2015] ESCA Civ 1112. The misuse has led not just to criticism of local authorities by the judiciary, but also a significant increase in costs sanctions.

The number of surrogacy cases continues to grow, as does the call for reform. In Re Z [2016] EWHC 1191 (Fam) the President made a formal declaration of incompatibility under the Human Rights Act, ruling that the law discriminated against single parents through surrogacy and breached their human rights. As yet it remains unclear what will be done to address this.

In terms of changes ahead, there is the introduction of "Settlement Conferences", which have been used for some years now in Canada. Similar to the FDR in financial remedy cases, they have been trialled in courts here and could be set to expand in the future.

Looking forward to 2017, the EU referendum result will undoubtedly produce great uncertainty in the future development of family law and will also raise serious questions over the continued applicability of instruments such as Brussels IIa – in relation to uniform jurisdictional rules for divorce proceedings and maintenance agreements. It is far too early to predict how these issues will develop, but it is certain that family law will remain dynamic, challenging and, above all, interesting.

Contents:

LONDON

Family: Matrimonial Finance
Leading Sets
Band 1
1 Hare Court *
Band 2
29 Bedford Row Chambers *
1 King's Bench Walk *
Queen Elizabeth Building QEB *
Band 3
4 Paper Buildings *
Leading Silks
Star individuals
Marks Lewis *Queen Elizabeth Building QEB* *
Pointer Martin *1 Hare Court*
Todd Richard *1 Hare Court*
Band 1
Amos Tim *Queen Elizabeth Building QEB* *
Bishop Timothy *1 Hare Court*
Cayford Philip *29 Bedford Row Chambers* [A] *
Chamberlayne Patrick *29 Bedford Row Chambers* *
Cusworth Nicholas *1 Hare Court*
Dyer Nigel *1 Hare Court*
Howard Charles *1 King's Bench Walk* *
Leech Stewart *Queen Elizabeth Building QEB* *
Marshall Philip *1 King's Bench Walk* *
Peel Robert *29 Bedford Row Chambers* [A] *
Scott Timothy *29 Bedford Row Chambers* [A] *
Southgate Jonathan *29 Bedford Row Chambers* *
Stone Lucy *Queen Elizabeth Building QEB* *
Turner James *1 King's Bench Walk* *
Band 2
Balcombe David *1 Crown Office Row (ORL)* ◊
Bangay Deborah *1 Hare Court*
Eaton Deborah *1 King's Bench Walk* *
Hale Charles *4 Paper Buildings*
Harrison Richard *1 King's Bench Walk* *
Pocock Christopher *1 King's Bench Walk* *
Warshaw Justin *1 Hare Court*
Wilson John *1 Hare Court*
Band 3
Anelay Richard *1 King's Bench Walk* *
Cohen Jonathan *4 Paper Buildings*
Davidson Katharine *1 Hare Court*
Hussey Ann *1 Hare Court*
Le Grice Valentine *The 36 Group (ORL)* ◊
Sternberg Michael *4 Paper Buildings*
Trowell Stephen *1 Hare Court*
Wagstaffe Christopher *29 Bedford Row Chambers* *
New Silks
Ewins James *Queen Elizabeth Building QEB* *
* Indicates set / individual with profile.
[A] direct access (see p.24).
◊ (ORL) = Other Ranked Lawyer.
Alphabetical order within each band. Band 1 is highest.

Family: Matrimonial Finance	
Leading Juniors	
Star individuals	**Bates** Richard *29 Bedford Row Chambers* *
Clarke Elizabeth *Queen Elizabeth Building QEB* *	**Batt** Charanjit *Queen Elizabeth Building QEB* *
Molyneux Brent *29 Bedford Row Chambers* *	**Blatchly** Phillip *Fourteen* *
Oliver Harry *1 King's Bench Walk* *	**Budden** Rosemary *Queen Elizabeth Building QEB* *
Webster Simon *1 Hare Court*	**Calhaem** Simon *29 Bedford Row Chambers* *
Band 1	**Cassidy** Sheena *3PB Barristers (ORL)* ◊
Allen Nicholas *29 Bedford Row Chambers* [A] *	**Chapman** Nicholas *29 Bedford Row Chambers* *
Bentham Daniel *Queen Elizabeth Building QEB* *	**Domenge** Victoria *29 Bedford Row Chambers* *
Brooks Duncan *Queen Elizabeth Building QEB* *	**Firth** Matthew *Queen Elizabeth Building QEB* *
Campbell Alexis *29 Bedford Row Chambers* *	**Fox** Nicola *1 King's Bench Walk* *
Castle Richard *1 King's Bench Walk* *	**Johnston** Justine *4 Paper Buildings*
Cowton Catherine *Queen Elizabeth Building QEB* *	**Kenny** Christian *1 Hare Court* *
Faggionato Marina *Queen Elizabeth Building QEB* *	**Kisser** Amy *Queen Elizabeth Building QEB* *
Glaser Michael *Fourteen* [A] *	**Langridge** Niki *The 36 Group* *
Gray Nichola *1 Hare Court*	**Lister** Caroline *1 King's Bench Walk* *
Kingscote Geoffrey *1 Hare Court*	**Newman** Peter *1 King's Bench Walk* *
Nagpal Deepak *1 King's Bench Walk* *	**Sheridan** Amber *29 Bedford Row Chambers* *
Roberts James *1 King's Bench Walk* *	**Teacher** Petra *29 Bedford Row Chambers* [A] *
Sear Richard *1 Hare Court* *	**Band 4**
Yates Nicholas *1 Hare Court* *	**Boyd** Kerstin *Tanfield Chambers (ORL)* ◊
Band 2	**Cameron** Gillon *Fourteen* *
Bailey-Harris Rebecca *1 Hare Court*	**Carter** Tom *1 Hare Court*
Bojarski Andrzej *The 36 Group (ORL)* ◊	**Collins** Ken *29 Bedford Row Chambers* [A] *
Bradley Michael *1 Hare Court*	**Cook** Katherine *1 Hare Court* *
Burles David *1 Garden Court Family Law Chambers* *	**Emanuel** Mark *29 Bedford Row Chambers* *
Cade Davies Lynsey *29 Bedford Row Chambers* [A] *	**Heppenstall** Claire *1 Garden Court Family Law Chambers*
Carew Pole Rebecca *1 Hare Court* *	**Jackson** Sally *New Court Chambers* *
Chandler Alexander *1 King's Bench Walk* *	**Jefferson** Helen *2-3 Hind Court (ORL)* ◊
Cook Ian *1 King's Bench Walk* *	**Lyon** Stephen *4 Paper Buildings*
Heaton Laura *29 Bedford Row Chambers* [A] *	**Max** Sally *29 Bedford Row Chambers* *
Kelsey Katherine *1 King's Bench Walk* *	**Roberts** Patricia *Fourteen*
Lazarides Marcus *Queen Elizabeth Building QEB* *	**Tambling** Richard *29 Bedford Row Chambers* *
Mitchell Peter *29 Bedford Row Chambers* *	**Tyzack** William *Queen Elizabeth Building QEB* *
Murray Judith *4 Paper Buildings*	**Wilkinson** Nicholas *1 Hare Court*
Phipps Sarah *Queen Elizabeth Building QEB* *	**Woodham** Samantha *4 Paper Buildings*
Singer Samantha *Queen Elizabeth Building QEB* *	**Up-and-coming individuals**
Sirikanda Morgan *Queen Elizabeth Building QEB* *	**Calnan** Ella *Fourteen*
Sumner Emma *1 Hare Court*	**Clapham** Penelope *1 Garden Court Family Law Chambers* *
Thorpe Alexander *Queen Elizabeth Building QEB* *	**Clayton** Henry *4 Paper Buildings*
Tod Jonathan *29 Bedford Row Chambers* *	**Hartley** Charlotte *1 King's Bench Walk* *
Band 3	**James** Byron *Fourteen* *
Amaouche Sassa-Ann *29 Bedford Row Chambers* *	**Williams** Helen *29 Bedford Row Chambers* *
Anderson Nicholas *1 King's Bench Walk* *	**Wiseman** Naomi *Garden Court Chambers (ORL)* ◊

The editorial is in alphabetical order by firm name.

42 Bedford Row

See profile on p.811

Large common law set with a family team that demonstrates particular strength in complex public law care proceedings. It has over 30 years of experience of acting for local authorities and handles complex cases involving issues such as non-accidental injuries, neglect and sexual and emotional abuse. Its members also undertake international child law matters, including cases concerning forced marriages and child abduction, and have growing expertise in matrimonial finance cases.

Client service: "Their clerks are very good at managing, diarising and co-ordinating a lot of stuff and there will always be plenty of good barristers available. They communicate well together and so remove the stress of changing barristers at the last minute." James Tidnam leads the family clerks. He benefits from having access to the sage advice of Alan Brewer, former senior clerk and now consultant to the set who has enjoyed the respect of his peers over a number of decades.

SILKS

Tina Cook QC Well-regarded children practitioner who is known for her expertise in public law care work. Her practice consists of cases involving sensitive issues relating to deceased children, sexual abuse and vulnerable parents. She is particularly good at cases involving children with learning disabilities. **Strengths:** "A local authority silk of choice who takes an absolute no-nonsense approach to cases. She is a forensic cross-examiner and knows her cases inside out."

JUNIORS

Family: Children
Leading Sets
Band 1
4 Paper Buildings *
Band 2
1 Garden Court Family Law Chambers *
1 King's Bench Walk *
Band 3
29 Bedford Row Chambers *
Coram Chambers *
Harcourt Chambers *
Band 4
42 Bedford Row *
Fourteen *
New Court Chambers *
Leading Silks
Star individuals
Eaton Deborah *1 King's Bench Walk* *
Setright Henry *4 Paper Buildings*
Storey Paul *29 Bedford Row Chambers* *
Verdan Alex *4 Paper Buildings*
Band 1
Bazley Janet *1 Garden Court Family Law Chambers* *
Delahunty Jo *4 Paper Buildings* *
Feehan Frank *1 King's Bench Walk*
Geekie Charles *1 Garden Court Family Law Chambers* *
Gupta Teertha *4 Paper Buildings*
Harrison Richard *1 King's Bench Walk* *
Morgan Sarah *1 Garden Court Family Law Chambers* *
Pressdee Piers *29 Bedford Row Chambers* *
Turner James *1 King's Bench Walk* *
Williams David *4 Paper Buildings*
Wood Catherine *4 Paper Buildings*
Band 2
Connolly Barbara *7BR (ORL)* ◊
Cook Tina *42 Bedford Row*
Fottrell Deirdre *1 Garden Court Family Law Chambers* *
Hale Charles *4 Paper Buildings*
Howard Charles *1 King's Bench Walk* *
Judd Frances *Harcourt Chambers*
Langdale Rachel *7BR (ORL)* ◊ *
Tyler William *The 36 Group (ORL)* ◊ *
Band 3
Bagchi Andrew *1 Garden Court Family Law Chambers*
Ball Alison *1 Garden Court Family Law Chambers*
Crowley Jane *1 Garden Court Family Law Chambers*
Grief Alison *4 Paper Buildings*
Hames Christopher *4 Paper Buildings*
Kirk Anthony *1 King's Bench Walk* *
Scott-Manderson Marcus *4 Paper Buildings*
Scriven Pamela *1 King's Bench Walk* *
Sternberg Michael *4 Paper Buildings*
Tughan John *4 Paper Buildings*
Vater John *Harcourt Chambers*
New Silks
Markham Hannah *The 36 Group (ORL)* ◊
** Indicates set / individual with profile.*
🄰 direct access (see p.24).
◊ (ORL) = Other Ranked Lawyer.
Alphabetical order within each band. Band 1 is highest.

Family: Children	
Leading Juniors	
Star individuals	**Jefferson** Helen *2-3 Hind Court (ORL)* ◊
Devereux Edward *Harcourt Chambers*	**Jones** Maggie *Garden Court Chambers (ORL)* ◊
Band 1	**Jones** Richard *1 Garden Court Family Law Chambers*
Brereton Joy *4 Paper Buildings*	**Jubb** Brian *4 Paper Buildings*
Cover Martha *Coram Chambers* *	**Khan** Hassan *4 Paper Buildings*
Gration Michael *4 Paper Buildings*	**Lister** Caroline *1 King's Bench Walk* *
Johnston Justine *4 Paper Buildings*	**McCormack** Philip *42 Bedford Row*
King Samantha *4 Paper Buildings*	**Phillips** Katie *42 Bedford Row*
McKenna Anna *1 King's Bench Walk* *	**Selman** Elizabeth *1 King's Bench Walk* *
Mills Barbara *4 Paper Buildings*	**Sprinz** Lucy *1 Garden Court Family Law Chambers* *
Murray Judith *4 Paper Buildings*	**Stone** Sally *1 Garden Court Family Law Chambers* *
Renton Jacqueline *4 Paper Buildings*	**Taylor** Gemma *42 Bedford Row*
Segal Sharon *1 Garden Court Family Law Chambers* *	**Vindis** Tara *9 Gough Square (ORL)* ◊ *
Band 2	**Woodward-Carlton** Damian *42 Bedford Row*
Arnot Lee *29 Bedford Row Chambers* *	**Band 4**
Bain Giles *New Court Chambers* *	**Anderson** Nicholas *1 King's Bench Walk* *
Bennett Jonathan *42 Bedford Row*	**Briggs** Laura *9 Gough Square (ORL)* ◊ *
Cudby Markanza *1 King's Bench Walk* *	**Cabeza** Ruth *Field Court Chambers (ORL)* ◊
Forster Sarah *Garden Court Chambers (ORL)* ◊ 🄰	**Cameron** Gillon *Fourteen* *
Fox Nicola *1 King's Bench Walk* *	**Clapham** Penelope *1 Garden Court Family Law Chambers* *
Jarmain Stephen *1 King's Bench Walk* *	**Cronin** Kathryn *Garden Court Chambers (ORL)* ◊
Jenkins Catherine *1 Garden Court Family Law Chambers*	**Drew** Jane *Coram Chambers* *
Kelsey Katherine *1 King's Bench Walk* *	**Edwards** Michael *4 Paper Buildings*
Poole Christopher *New Court Chambers* *	**Fletcher** Matthew *1 Garden Court Family Law Chambers*
Ramsahoye Indira *29 Bedford Row Chambers* *	**Gartland** Dorothea *4 Paper Buildings*
Reardon Madeleine *1 King's Bench Walk* *	**Geddes** Gillian *2-3 Hind Court (ORL)* ◊ *
Tod Jonathan *29 Bedford Row Chambers* *	**George** Susan *Coram Chambers* *
Band 3	**Hughes** Daisy *1 Garden Court Family Law Chambers*
Amiraftabi Roshi *29 Bedford Row Chambers* *	**Jackson** Sally *New Court Chambers* *
Chaudhry Mehvish *Harcourt Chambers*	**Kirby** Ruth *4 Paper Buildings*
Chokowry Katy *1 King's Bench Walk* *	**Miller** Christopher *Fourteen* *
Foulkes Rebecca *4 Paper Buildings*	**Parker** Timothy *9 Gough Square (ORL)* ◊ *
Glaser Michael *Fourteen* 🄰 *	**Roberts** James *1 King's Bench Walk* *
Guha Anita *7BR (ORL)* ◊	**Tyzack** William *Queen Elizabeth Building QEB* *
Habboo Camille *Fourteen*	**Wan Daud** Malek *Garden Court Chambers (ORL)* ◊
Heppenstall Claire *1 Garden Court Family Law Chambers*	**Wiseman** Naomi *Garden Court Chambers (ORL)* ◊
Jarman Mark *4 Paper Buildings*	

Jonathan Bennett Acts on behalf of all parties in care proceedings and specialises in non-accidental injury cases with complex forensic evidence. He has recently appeared in both the High Court and the Court of Appeal in contested adoption proceedings. **Strengths:** "He's excellent with clients and in terms of his advocacy."

Gemma Taylor Renowned for her handling of serious public law cases relating to severe injury, abuse and adoption. She exhibits strength representing local authorities in matters with complex medical evidence. **Strengths:** "She has an enormously strong and well-deserved reputation. She is often against leading silks in proceedings with local authorities, and is the kind of advocate those local authorities have great confidence in."

Philip McCormack Public law specialist with experience in civil and criminal proceedings. He mainly represents children in complex proceedings across a range of matters including infant death, head injury and abuse. **Strengths:** "He's a good, solid advocate who's thorough and diligent."

Katie Phillips Exhibits expertise in family issues concerning vulnerable children and adults in complex care proceedings. She acts for all parties and specialises in non-accidental injury cases. **Strengths:** "She has an exceptionally thorough and fair approach. When it comes to local authorities, it's hard to find someone who does it better than her."

Damian Woodward-Carlton An experienced children barrister who focuses on sensitive international public proceedings, representing all parties. His caseload typically involves cases concerning complex issues surrounding allegations of non-accidental injury, abuse and, more recently, radicalisation. **Strengths:** "He's got a lovely client manner. He is unflappable and a genuinely nice man."

29 Bedford Row Chambers

See profile on p.812

THE SET

Formidable specialist family set offering strength at every level in proceedings relating to relationship breakdown and children. It is renowned for its expertise in handling enormous financial disputes for high net worth and high-profile figures.

Client service: "The clerks are more than helpful and make working with set a pleasure." The senior clerk is James Shortall.

SILKS

Paul Storey QC (see p.774) Standout children specialist who is renowned for his formidable advocacy and involvement in highly complex public and private cases in the Supreme Court and Court of Appeal. His expertise extends to non-accidental injury, death and abuse issues, and he has handled a number of old cases revived following new evidence. **Strengths:** "He is one of the best silks for medical cases, and there is no one in England who knows more about traumatic infant brain injury. He is a most formidable and ferocious opponent."

Jonathan Southgate QC (see p.770) Recently appointed silk who has rapidly developed a formidable practice representing household names and high net worth individuals in tremendously high-value matrimonial finance proceedings. He is commended for his tenacity in court and his commercial awareness during divorce. **Strengths:** "He is measured, astute and wise beyond his years. A very impressive court performer who is already garnering plaudits in silk as a class act."

Philip Cayford QC (see p.613) Represents high-profile clients in significant financial remedy proceedings. He is regarded highly for his knowledge, and his experience covers the full range of high-value disputes, including those concerning issues of Schedule 1, TOLATA and trusts. **Strengths:** "One of the most experienced financial silks. He has tremendous judgement, is hugely experienced and is a formidable advocate in whose hands both clients and solicitors feel very comfortable." **Recent work:** Featured in a leading case in the Supreme Court on strike-out, delay, the relationship between CPR and FPR, case management, legal costs and funding.

Patrick Chamberlayne QC (see p.614) Has earned a fine reputation for tackling substantial financial remedy proceedings involving complex trust, business structures and Inheritance Act claims. His practice is mainly international and is notable for its connections to the Middle East. **Strengths:** "Wise and clever, he is brilliant with solicitors and clients alike. Meticulous and methodical in his analysis and advice, he is utterly strategic in his approach and a most impressive and persuasive advocate." **Recent work:** Represented Nicole Appleton in her divorce from Liam Gallagher.

Robert Peel QC (see p.736) Family silk with notable expertise in high-value matrimonial disputes on behalf of high-profile individuals of significant wealth. His specialism lies in cases with complex business and trust structures located internationally. **Strengths:** "His advice is hugely authoritative. He is clear, concise and inspires absolute confidence from both professionals and clients. His advocacy is delivered with the assurance of a Court of Appeal judgment."

Piers Pressdee QC (see p.743) Expert private law children practitioner instructed by London's top firms for complex international disputes. He demonstrates strength in leave to remove and abduction cases and is noted for his knowledge of alternative family and assisted reproduction issues. **Strengths:** "He is approachable, thorough and a consummate tactician and strategist who takes a pragmatic approach to complex children cases. Excellent at managing clients and the court, he is absolutely the right choice for cases involving leave to remove, same-sex parentage, surrogacy and sperm donor agreements." **Recent work:** Acted in Re C, an important case concerning judgment publication in private children law proceedings.

Timothy Scott QC (see p.760) Renowned international matrimonial finance specialist who demonstrates impressive knowledge of all matters relating to jurisdiction. He has frequently appeared in the Court of Appeal, House of Lords and Supreme Court on cross-border issues. **Strengths:** "He's very good on obtuse points of law, and it's hard to think of anyone better on international cases." **Recent work:** Led an appeal from Scotland to the UK Supreme Court under the Hague Convention on International Child Abduction. Scott represented the International Academy of Matrimonial Lawyers, which had been given permission to intervene in the appeal, in order to let the court know how the point under appeal had been looked at in a range of jurisdictions around the world.

Christopher Wagstaffe QC (see p.787) Financial practitioner with a focus on representing high net worth individuals in international cases, particularly those situated in the Isle of Man, the Channel Islands, Gibraltar and the Caribbean. He is further known for his knowledge of how Schedule 1 of the Children Act relates to cohabitation. **Strengths:** "A remarkable advocate whose advice is sound, pragmatic and results-driven." **Recent work:** Achieved a resolution by consent in a complex application to vary 4 separate Jersey settlements.

JUNIORS

Brent Molyneux (see p.720) Well-regarded senior junior handling highly complex financial disputes for an enviable international clientele of prominent public figures. He is lauded for his understated advocacy style and conciliatory approach. **Strengths:** "A dynamic and inventive advocate who is also extremely practical. Humorous, excellent with clients, and someone who can be relied upon for clear and concise advice and brilliant strategy. He has a steeliness that makes him a tenacious negotiator." **Recent work:** Acted in RAPP v RAPP, appearing for an appellant husband on the hearing of his appeal against the final orders made in financial remedy proceedings.

Alexis Campbell (see p.610) Family finance junior with a solid reputation for assisting high net worth business clients with matters involving complex company, trust and pension issues. **Strengths:** "A senior junior with an assured manner who is technically very sound. Clients appreciate her empathy and well-honed advocacy skills."

Nicholas Allen (see p.582) High-value financial specialist who regularly handles cases using the collaborative process having trained as collaborative counsel. He is commended for his attention to detail and his sympathetic manner with clients. **Strengths:** "He reads absolutely everything he's sent and knows the papers inside out. He instils a huge amount of confidence in clients, he is an extremely charming advocate and he can disarm difficult cases."

Lynsey Cade Davies (see p.608) An international divorce specialist who focuses on complex financial matters for high net worth clients following relationship breakdown. She has a particular interest in trust and business structures in matrimonial proceedings. **Strengths:** "Lynsey is enormously helpful and constructive in her approach to cases. She's hard-working, detailed and focused on what is important in a case – she's a good tactician." **Recent work:** Acted in a highly publicised case in which the wife received an uplift in her settlement four years after the death of her divorced husband.

Indira Ramsahoye (see p.747) Children law practitioner, well regarded for her considerable experience handling complex international children matters. She possesses a noted specialism in matters concerning external relocation and abduction. **Strengths:** "She is hugely experienced, highly effective and has a terrific client manner." **Recent work:** Acted in a complex High Court case involving a committal application made within wardship proceedings and entailing consideration of orders made in a foreign court precluding the removal of children.

Lee Arnot (see p.585) Offers clients a dual money and children service, and has extensive experience in both the public and private spheres. He is noted for his attention to detail when handling complex children proceedings. **Strengths:** "He's very smart and his analysis is excellent. He is a brave advocate."

Laura Heaton (see p.669) A mediator and collaboratively trained junior who specialises in a wide range of financial proceedings and is recognised for her prowess in ADR. Her cases mainly consist of matters with complex business and trust elements, many of which involve a third party. **Strengths:** "She is thorough and detail-focused in her approach. Ever the negotiator, if a case can be settled she will settle it. Gives sensible advice and backs it up with a persuasive negotiation style and compelling advocacy."

Peter Mitchell (see p.719) Experienced matrimonial junior with a versatile practice covering all complex issues relating to financial remedy following relationship dissolution. He has particular expertise in the law as it relates to nuptial agreements, cohabitants and TOLATA issues. **Strengths:** "Peter's preparation and attention to detail are second to none. He prepares cases with flair and expertise, is charismatic and is intellectually at the top of his game." **Recent work:** Acted in a non-disclosure case where a seven-judge Supreme Court unanimously overturned the Court of Appeal, allowing the appeal of Mrs Sharland, setting aside the final order and remitting the case to the High Court.

Jonathan Tod (see p.782) Family barrister proficient at handling both sophisticated financial and children matters. He specialises particularly in Schedule 1 Children Act cases, often those occurring in conjunction with high-value divorce proceedings. **Strengths:** "His Schedule 1 work is some of the best in the country. He is a brilliant money practitioner." **Recent work:** Featured in the representation of an artist, advising her on a prenuptial agreement in her marriage to the future Earl of Plymouth.

Roshi Amiraftabi (see p.583) Specialist public and private children law junior who demonstrates great expertise when it comes to jurisdictional issues. Her caseload consists of complex relocation, abduction, enforcement and leave to remove cases, some of which are highly acrimonious. **Strengths:** "A brilliant and tireless Children Act specialist and go-to counsel for advice on leave to remove and child abduction cases."

Victoria Domenge (see p.635) Handles both private substantial financial and sensitive children matters for a range of clients. She is commended for her constructive approach, which stems from her experience as a mediator and collaborative counsel. **Strengths:** "She has a very considered style, is thoughtful and has a sophisticated approach. She's impressive but doesn't showboat or strut. She has no ego."

Petra Teacher (see p.779) Versatile junior who covers a broad range of private children and matrimonial finance cases. She is noted in particular for her expertise in relation to nuptial agreements and Schedule 1 matters. **Strengths:** "She is increasingly impressive and authoritative."

Sassa-Ann Amaouche (see p.583) Family junior who is in high demand for her expertise in sophisticated divorce proceedings involving significant assets, complex business structures and issues of non-disclosure. She is regarded for her manner and tenacious and no-nonsense advocacy style. **Strengths:** "Intelligent and dynamic counsel. A brilliant advocate and negotiator who is able to provide practical advice in complex financial cases, especially those involving non-disclosure or litigation misconduct." **Recent work:** Acted for the wife in a heavily contested separation in which the husband repeatedly attempted to use press intervention as an intimidation tactic.

Richard Bates (see p.592) Handles mainly matrimonial finance cases on behalf of wealthy individuals, especially those involving complex business structures. He additionally engages in Schedule 1 children proceedings and exhibits knowledge in matrimonial-related farming issues. **Strengths:** "An unflappable character whom opponents take lightly at their peril. He's very hard-working and good on the detail." **Recent work:** Handled a complex financial remedy case involving around £54 million and an offshore trust.

Simon Calhaem (see p.609) Finance specialist who handles a broad range of related matters, including complex trust, inheritance, probate and divorce cases. His practice extends internationally, in particular to the Cayman Islands and Gibraltar. **Strengths:** "Punchy and bright, a tactician who is always looking at the longer game." **Recent work:** Acted in Wyatt v Vince, representing the successful appellant in the Supreme Court.

Nicholas Chapman (see p.615) Considerably experienced practitioner who tackles contested divorce proceedings of high net individuals. He additionally sits as a Deputy District Judge on the Western Circuit. **Strengths:** "He is popular, efficient, and combines many years of experience with a very 'can-do' attitude. He's very user-friendly."

Amber Sheridan (see p.764) Young matrimonial finance junior with a growing reputation for handling high-value financial remedy proceedings for high-profile international clients. Despite being of relatively recent call, she is recognised for the complexity of the matters she undertakes. **Strengths:** "A shrewd negotiator and one to watch for the future. She is cool and level-headed."

Sally Max (see p.710) Family junior practising mainly in the high net worth matrimonial finance arena. She has particular expertise in issues concerning cohabitation, the Schedule 1 Children Act and cases concerning complex business and trust structures. **Strengths:** "Detail-focused, patient and surgically precise in her advice and advocacy. She's an excellent negotiator and advocate."

Ken Collins (see p.620) Private family barrister who mainly handles high-value financial disputes following divorce. He additionally maintains a caseload of children matters, and has a focus on cases dealing with relocation. **Strengths:** "He is astute, quick on his feet, personable and feisty."

Mark Emanuel (see p.641) Offers representation in a range of family cases following relationship dissolution. He is best known for his knowledge of business, trust and child residence issues in high-value proceedings. **Strengths:** "He's a barrister who has gravitas in court and an attention to detail that is second to none."

Richard Tambling (see p.777) Matrimonial finance junior who handles a wide variety of issues surrounding divorce, including matters concerning Schedule 1, TOLATA and significant wealth. His practice predominantly focuses on cross-border cases, often those involving offshore assets. **Strengths:** "He's excellent at finance, puts clients at ease and is a nice opponent to be against. A true expert."

Helen Williams (see p.796) Finance practitioner noted for her previous experience as a chartered accountant, which she brings to bear in matrimonial proceedings concerning complex tax, company and trust structure issues. Her cases often involve valuation issues and corporate non-disclosure. **Strengths:** "A star in the making. She offers extremely good client care and has a superb knowledge of the law." **Recent work:** Involved in a precedent-setting case concerning whether valid consents to legal parenthood had been given by seven same and opposite sex unmarried couples who had conceived using donor sperm.

Coram Chambers

See profile on p.822

THE SET

Specialised set that handles public and private children law and finance work, and related Court of Protection, human rights and alternative family cases. It is recognised for its commitment to providing an affordable service to vulnerable and disadvantaged clients and regularly handles pro bono work.

Client service: "The clerks are efficient and creative. They have a shared vision and ethos and they tell you exactly what the position is. They're also really good on billing, which is increasingly important." The senior clerk is Paul Sampson.

JUNIORS

Martha Cover (see p.625) Widely respected and highly experienced practitioner who is head of chambers and has a reputation as a specialist in complex children law matters. She covers a wide range of sensitive matters including cases concerning serious injury, abuse, international adoption and wardship. **Strengths:** "She is a stalwart favourite in the field of public children law and shows an unwavering commitment to the welfare of children both in her casework and beyond. Her manner with clients is firm but compassionate and she delivers top-quality advice in a no-nonsense manner."

Jane Drew (see p.637) A committed children law practitioner specialising in acting for children removed from care. She practises widely in public and private law, handling cases involving severe issues of mental health, abuse, domestic violence and neglect. **Strengths:** "She has a real sense of gravitas about her, and everyone always defers to her in a room. She is also an utterly fair cross-examiner."

Susan George (see p.651) An international children specialist handling complex cases mainly relating to mental health, neglect, abuse and vulnerable adults. She represents all parties though largely acts on behalf of adoptive parents and guardians. **Strengths:** "She's a very balanced lawyer; in court she is an excellent judge of when to press forward and when to hold back. She is very caring towards clients and gives excellent advice."

Fourteen

See profile on p.848

THE SET

Family chambers offering services across the range of children and matrimonial finance law. It has a recognised high net worth divorce practice that increasingly extends internationally.

Client service: "The clerks, led by Geoffrey Carr, are brilliant. I really enjoy dealing them; they're always extremely helpful and so cheerful. The barristers are an accessible and extremely capable bunch."

JUNIORS

Michael Glaser (see p.653) Prominent family junior in high demand for his expertise in complex matrimonial finance proceedings, who typically acts for an impressive high net worth and high-profile clientele. He also acts in children law matters and is recognised for the persistence and quality of his advocacy. **Strengths:** "He's the most tenacious of barristers. He knows the law inside out; the amount of knowledge he has at his fingertips is insane. He's a great tactician, is persuasive and really fights a client's corner."

Phillip Blatchly (see p.597) Handles matters in the private client sphere relating to family breakdowns and focuses on complex cases involving trust structures and non-disclosure of assets. His advocacy is notable for its utilisation of technical legal points to progress cases. **Strengths:** "A very good advocate who is excellent at explaining legal points in a comprehensible way and is prepared to take a judge on." **Recent work:** Represented the wife in a long-running divorce case where both the parties and their respective assets were based in Australia and Thailand.

Camille Habboo Primarily a public law children practitioner known for her involvement in severe cases relating to abuse and non-accidental injury. Her work sees her representing a wide range of vulnerable clients and local authorities and often includes an international element. **Strengths:** "She's a really good pusher for the client – she will keep going."

Gillon Cameron (see p.610) Predominantly practises in ancillary relief proceedings and has experience of handling applications relating to TOLATA. He additionally handles children work and is an expert on Hague Convention abduction issues. **Strengths:** "Very able and offers quality representation."

Christopher Miller (see p.717) Practises exclusively in family finance disputes following relationship dissolution. His areas of expertise include matters relating to TOLATA and the Inheritance Act. **Strengths:** "His attention to detail and preparation stand out as does the clarity with which he presents his case in court."

Patricia Roberts Specialises in complex family finance matters, particularly disputes concerning interveners, trust structures, third party interests and Schedule 1 Children Act. Her children practice consists of handling cases involving issues of non-accidental injury, abuse and mental health. **Strengths:** "She's extremely good and very down-to-earth. She also has very god attention to detail."

Ella Calnan Family junior with a mixed practice of high-profile finance and children work. Her caseload includes cases relating to private international disputes over children and high-value divorce proceedings. **Strengths:** "She's phenomenally bright and empathetic, down-to-earth and sensible. She's definitely one to watch for the future."

Byron James (see p.682) Up and coming junior with a growing reputation in complex financial remedy proceedings. His specialism extends to offshore trust, private children and cohabitation matters. **Strengths:** "He's a very intelligent and talented advocate. He will always go the extra mile to ensure a client's case is presented and advanced in the best way possible. He will achieve great things."

1 Garden Court Family Law Chambers

See profile on p.853

THE SET

Highly regarded family set offering specialised expertise in every area of child law, including international abduction, complex care proceedings and surrogacy. It additionally provides a growing financial practice, aiding clients in the distribution of assets post-divorce.

Client service: "Excellent service. The clerks are very helpful and even if you have just a query and need a quick opinion they will readily find someone in chambers for you to speak to." Paul Harris is the senior clerk in chambers.

SILKS

Janet Bazley QC (see p.593) Co-head of chambers and regarded highly for her extensive experience of complex, law-making children cases. She has notable expertise in cases involving technical medical or forensic evidence. **Strengths:** "She has an extraordinary work ethic and is utterly committed to trying to achieve the best results for the client. She came in at the last minute in our case and dominated in court."

Sarah Morgan QC (see p.721) Manages a full caseload of heavy-hitting public and private law children matters, from severe non-accidental injury cases to private child relocation. She acts in cases that garner significant media attention and so routinely offers the utmost discretion to her clients. **Strengths:** "She swiftly analyses the issues in a case and delivers some of the best cross-examination around." **Recent work:** Represented a father in one of the first cases in which a judge in the Family Division was asked to remove children from the care of their parents because of a risk of harm to children from radicalisation and recruitment to terrorist activity.

Charles Geekie QC (see p.651) Renowned for his handling of extremely complex and sensitive children matters, public and private, such as international adoption, relocation and abduction. He co-leads chambers and routinely engages in cases relating to sexual, emotional and physical abuse. **Strengths:** "Charles is an absolute leader in the field of children work. He is a great strategist who is highly intelligent, charming and reassuring to clients in difficult situations. He commands the greatest respect from both solicitors and the court."

Andrew Bagchi QC Routinely represents local authorities in highly sensitive public law cases relating to child abuse. His private law practice covers both contentious matrimonial disputes and child relocation cases. **Strengths:** "Well thought of by his peers and by the Bench, he has excellent client care skills and is an effective, organised and decisive advocate who always gets to the root of the problem." **Recent work:** Involved in the first set of care proceedings where live reporting was permitted. The case was a rehearing of circumstances of the death of a sibling.

Deirdre Fottrell QC (see p.647) A recent silk who is recognised for having international expertise that covers child adoption, relocation and abduction matters. She additionally has a growing surrogacy practice and regularly appears in cases involving a complex application of the Human Rights Act. **Strengths:** "Deirdre Fottrell has made her mark this year as a silk. She has an intricate knowledge of the most complex international and domestic law and she is a magnetic and powerful advocate. Her pro bono work fighting for children's rights is especially commendable."

Alison Ball QC Known for her representation of local authorities in public law cases involving allegations of domestic violence and abuse. Additionally handles cases concerning wardship of vulnerable children. **Strengths:** "Tenacious and thorough, she uses her broad reserves of knowledge to the client's benefit."

Jane Crowley QC Focuses her public children law practice on cases concerning infant death, domestic violence and complex medical circumstances. She is additionally noted for her strength in representing vulnerable individuals or parents with learning disabilities. **Strengths:** "An amiable silk who is very straightforward in her approach."

JUNIORS

Catherine Jenkins Public law specialist who represents children, parents and local authorities in cases involving abuse and non-accidental injury. She also offers expertise in international adoption proceedings. **Strengths:** "She's hugely experienced" and "someone who fights her cases with skill."

David Burles (see p.607) A well-regarded matrimonial finance lawyer who focuses on disputes concerning the distribution of proprietary and monetary assets after relationship breakdown. He has a specialism representing cohabitants in unmarried couples, and also handles some private children work. **Strengths:** "He is an absolute pleasure to work with; he is personable with clients, persuasive, and precise in drafting. He will regularly alight on the solution that everyone else has missed. He is unfailingly courteous and judges obviously respect him."

Claire Heppenstall Handles complex financial and children law work and often leads proceedings concerning both. She is commended for her tactical approach when handling cases involving issues of abuse and education. **Strengths:** "A great advocate. She's an iron fist in a velvet glove when needed but is always pragmatic and gently but firmly reminds clients of the need to consider what is best for the children. She goes out of her way to explain tactical decisions and is a pleasure to work with for solicitors and clients alike."

Sharon Segal (see p.761) Highly regarded practitioner who specialises in dealing with vulnerable clients in private and public law cases including issues of sexual and physical abuse, non-accidental injury and 'honour violence'. She is routinely instructed by high-profile individuals across many jurisdictions. **Strengths:** "She's fabulous and the most organised scheduler on the planet. Fantastically hard-working, she is a very effective senior junior who has a great way with clients."

Lucy Sprinz (see p.771) Covers the full spectrum of children issues, specialising in particular in the representation of parents faced with allegations of abuse and neglect. She additionally has a burgeoning practice dealing in cases concerning alternative families. **Strengths:** "Lucy is exceptionally bright and extremely personable with clients. She deals with the most complex cases and is always prepared. She's a pleasure to work with."

Richard Jones Recognised for his expertise in challenging private law children proceedings and noted for his effective client manner. He handles a large volume of complex cases relating to parents seeking contact with their children and exhibits strength in the growing area of surrogacy. **Strengths:** "One of the loveliest and most effective advocates; he's so erudite and handles sensitive cases perfectly, taking exactly the right approach. He also has great technical expertise."

Sally Stone (see p.774) Mainly acts in public adoption and care proceedings representing local authorities, children and parents. She is noted for her specialism in cases concerning injured children and surrounding issues of mental health and technical medical evidence. **Strengths:** "She's an excellent lawyer who shows brilliant attention to detail, doesn't miss anything and is very reliable."

Penelope Clapham (see p.617) Has a mixed practice and handles both high-value matrimonial finance and sensitive children matters, both of which often feature a strong international element. She is noted for her deft handling of challenging abuse cases. **Strengths:** "Fearless advocate with excellent legal knowledge and a fantastic way with her clients. Her court documents are superb."

Matthew Fletcher Offers clients a multidisciplinary approach, having a background in both children and immigration law. His practice is internationally focused, and he is particularly known for his work aiding vulnerable clients in proceedings against local authorities. **Strengths:** "He's really good at getting to the crux of the case and at getting clients to focus in on their case. He's particularly good for clients with cost constraints."

Daisy Hughes An experienced child practitioner who handles all manner of adoption and Children Act cases. She is noted for her expertise in acrimonious cases involving same-sex couples, religious conflict and non-accidental injury. **Strengths:** "She's fantastic, very methodical in approaching complicated cases and excellent on areas of law that are not part of the everyday. Her client care is just wonderful. She's very compassionate to her clients whilst being an outstanding advocate. Judges are incredibly complimentary about her."

Garden Court Chambers

THE SET

A predominantly public law chambers with an expanding group of barristers well versed in children proceedings involving the state. The set has recently been instructed in major cases concerning allegations of abuse and radicalisation and its barristers are particularly adept at representing vulnerable parties. Its members are well placed to draw on Garden Court's wide-ranging expertise across other disciplines including immigration and social housing.

Client service: "The clerks are welcoming, helpful and are keen to offer alternative counsel should your chosen barrister be unavailable. They deal with requests for fee notes in a timely fashion and will respond to calls promptly." Colin Cook and Phil Bampfylde lead the clerking team.

JUNIORS

Sarah Forster (Garden Court Chambers) Recently moved from Fourteen, she has a wealth of experience of handling grave public law cases concerning vulnerable clients. She is also recognised for her management of challenging mediation proceedings. **Strengths:** "She's a hugely respected junior who fights cases excellently. She really gets the best out of a case; she's tenacious and has a good grasp of the issues."

Maggie Jones (Garden Court Chambers) Known for her representation of parents in complex public care proceedings as well as her skill in acting for vulnerable parties. She notably engages in cases relating to post-adoption contact, abuse allegations and immigration. **Strengths:** "She's very clever and very good with vulnerable people. She really thinks on her feet."

Kathryn Cronin (Garden Court Chambers) Extensively experienced junior renowned for her dual immigration and family practices, who handles complex international issues at the cross-section of the two areas. She is particularly noted for her cross-border adoption and surrogacy expertise. **Strengths:** "A go-to advocate for complex international adoption and surrogacy cases and any family placement where there is an immigration crossover. She is highly skilled and great with clients."

Malek Wan Daud (Garden Court Chambers) Public law practitioner handling complex care work on behalf of all parties, with a particular interest in representing minority individuals. He is known for his participation in serious cases involving allegations of sexual abuse, domestic violence and neglect. **Strengths:** "He's just brilliant – one of the best negotiators around. He keeps to the issues and he nails it forensically."

Naomi Wiseman (Garden Court Chambers) Up-and-coming junior family barrister with a diverse portfolio of public and private children law cases as well as financial remedy proceedings. Her cases are typically high-value and are increasingly international in nature. **Strengths:** "She has a terrific work rate and clients like her no-nonsense style."

Harcourt Chambers

See profile on p.858

THE SET

Family and civil chambers notably handling the most complex public law care and international children work. As well as handling children law, the members here are committed to matrimonial finance work.

Client service: "The Harcourt clerks are helpful, great at what they do and are organised. They go above and beyond." Simon Boutwood is chambers director in London.

SILKS

Frances Judd QC Highly experienced silk focusing on children matters, whose practice has an emphasis on complex public law cases involving non-accidental injury, sex abuse, forced marriage and child trafficking. Commentators note her expertise in international abduction, relocation and surrogacy matters. **Strengths:** "She is a popular advocate with a strong nationwide following."

John Vater QC A public law specialist known for his expertise in medical cases containing extensive expert evidence. He is commended for his technical knowledge and skill at cross-examination. **Strengths:** "An all-round excellent character who impresses clients with his advocacy and negotiating skills. He is one of the best public children law parents' advocates in the country."

JUNIORS

Edward Devereux Renowned family junior considered to be a leading expert in the international movement of children, particularly through abduction. He has been involved in landmark cases that have shaped the country's laws and appears in the most complex cases in the Supreme Court, the ECJ and the US Supreme Court. **Strengths:** "His extensive knowledge of EU law is impeccable. He has a great strategic mind and will have a good plan from day one. He is probably now the leading junior in international children's work." **Recent work:** Featured in the first case on the 1996 Hague Convention to come before the Supreme Court. The Supreme Court considered the workings of that Convention in the context of a child abduction from Morocco to England and Wales.

Mehvish Chaudhry Junior family barrister renowned for her expertise in international child movement, who regularly appears in the High Court, Court of Appeal and Supreme Court. She possesses a wealth of knowledge of child abduction, forced marriage and care cases in South Asia. **Strengths:** "She has quickly established herself as one of the best young barristers in the child abduction field. She is a superb junior who punches way above her weight."

1 Hare Court

See profile on p.860

THE SET

Leading specialist family set recognised for its strength in handling international matrimonial finance cases for high-profile clientele. It houses talent in depth and offers specialists in TOLATA, Schedule 1 Children Act, Inheritance Act and off-shore trust issues.

Client service: "The set has an extremely responsive chambers at every level and a particularly pleasant and efficient clerks room led by senior clerk Steve McCrone."

SILKS

Richard Todd QC Extremely well-regarded financial practitioner who handles disputes relating to significant assets and trusts structures following relationship breakdown. He has unique expertise in international cases, in particular those relating to the Cayman Islands and Hong Kong, where he has been called to the Bar. **Strengths:** "One of the best silks: he's so down-to-earth, phenomenal and charming. He's spot-on in his judgement, supremely confident and very accurate." **Recent work:** Acted as lead counsel for the successful wife in a leading Supreme Court case concerning nuptial agreements. It produced a decision that remains the benchmark throughout the Common Law world on matters of nuptial agreements.

Martin Pointer QC A leading figure in the field of complex matrimonial finance disputes who frequently appears in the very biggest and most high-profile cases. He handles major domestic and international disputes, many of which have astronomical monetary assets at stake. **Strengths:** "He is exceptional and remains the leading light of the Family Bar. He is head and shoulders above the majority of his contemporaries, and is the very best trial advocate there is." **Recent work:** Acted in the largest divorce case ever in Hong Kong, which was also one of the biggest in the world.

Timothy Bishop QC Regularly engages in the most substantial of matrimonial financial cases across multiple jurisdictions. He has a varied client base that includes, among others, high-profile media and business people. **Strengths:** "He is a highly experienced, elegant advocate. Knowledgeable and thoughtful, he will look at a problem from a 360-degree perspective."

Nicholas Cusworth QC Highly respected practitioner who is head of chambers and specialises in large-scale financial remedy proceedings for high-profile and high net worth individuals worldwide. He is additionally noted for his involvement in complex private law children proceedings. **Strengths:** "One of the best silks in the UK. He has remarkable knowledge and is at the cutting edge of new developments in financial remedies."

Nigel Dyer QC An expert in multi-jurisdictional divorce who has led landmark cases in the area. He has particular interest in cases with complex asset tracing and business structures to unpick. **Strengths:** "He's got such good judgement, is so impressive in court and also has a really good client manner. He deals equally well with savvy businessmen and nervous or distressed clients."

Justin Warshaw QC Newly appointed silk with an impressive clientele of high-profile individuals and public figures. He mainly handles international work and regularly appears before the High Court and the Court of Appeal. **Strengths:** "Brilliant on his feet, he instinctively cuts through a case to the killer points, bringing the judges with him. He gets unbelievable results."

Deborah Bangay QC A practitioner who is well respected for her handling of financial divorce proceedings on behalf of high net worth individuals and the excellence of her private children law practice. She is noted for her tenacity in court. **Strengths:** "A remarkable advocate with impeccable attention to detail. She always effectively fights her client's cause."

John Wilson QC Experienced family lawyer who is particularly good at handling complex divorce proceedings with professional negligence or TOLATA elements. Typically handles financial remedy cases for high net worth individuals. **Strengths:** "He's got a stellar brain and his knowledge is tremendous. He's a winner of clients, a real gentleman and is loved by judges."

Stephen Trowell QC A predominantly matrimonial finance practitioner who participates in significant financial remedy proceedings relating to unique matters of jurisdiction and ownership. He also has a private law children practice, handling matters of relocation and abduction. **Strengths:** "Extremely intelligent, very numerate and always comprehensively prepared for a case. He has an uncanny ability to destroy the opposition's position before they get on their feet." **Recent work:** Handled a case conducted in the media spotlight involving a US lawyer and entrepreneur and his Russian beauty queen wife.

Katharine Davidson QC A matrimonial practitioner with a background in banking who brings her technical expertise to bear when handling complex financial disputes involving third party businesses, trusts and tax. Her practice extends abroad and she has experience of handling cases in the Cayman Islands. **Strengths:** "Confident, engaging and always committed to the case."

Ann Hussey QC Has a wide-ranging clientele but is particularly noted for her expertise in handling disputes relating to farming and agricultural issues. She regularly tackles high-value divorces with off-shore assets, representing both interveners and trustees in proceedings. **Strengths:** "A superb tactician with great attention to detail. She is a truly gifted advocate who is extraordinarily responsive and never fails to find the best solution."

JUNIORS

Simon Webster Eminent senior junior who is instructed by the nation's leading firms in some of the most substantial financial remedy proceedings globally. His private children practice sees him handling international residence and leave to remove disputes for high net worth clients. **Strengths:** "A complete all-round top-class performer who is difficult to fault in any respect."

Nichola Gray Extensively experienced family practitioner focusing on financial disputes, who regularly represents wealthy individuals. She has expertise in asset tracing as it relates to offshore trusts and other concealed wealth. **Strengths:** "A fearless fighter who is a formidable and persuasive advocate." **Recent work:** Undertook the first civil partnership financial remedy case to be heard by the Court of Appeal.

Geoffrey Kingscote Matrimonial practitioner with extensive experience of complex financial remedy proceedings, who has a particular interest in nuptial agreements and cases concerning non-disclosure. His contentious work is bolstered by an active mediation practice. **Strengths:** "He's always in demand. He has a wonderful client manner, great judgement and the ability to simplify complex issues." **Recent work:** Featured in one of the most valuable ever divorces, securing USD530 million for the client.

Richard Sear (see p.760) A widely regarded junior who often handles financial remedy proceedings for high net worth business people with assets in offshore trust and company structures. He is also a qualified arbitrator and mediator. **Strengths:** "He's an excellent junior who punches well above his weight. A very talented and intelligent advocate for complicated financial cases. His practice is on fire and he's a future star."

Nicholas Yates (see p.801) Focuses on the financial side of relationship dissolution, handling complex cases relating to significant assets and Inheritance Act and Schedule 1 Children Act applications. He additionally leads negotiations in high-value nuptial agreements. **Strengths:** "He's astonishingly good; he thinks in a very interesting way and very strategically. He slots right into a team and gets some incredible results."

Rebecca Bailey-Harris Former professor of law and French-speaking matrimonial practitioner who specialises in cases across borders. She has an interest in disputes concerning cohabitants and unmarried couples. **Strengths:** "She's excellent on jurisdictional disputes."

Michael Bradley Appears in complex international ancillary relief proceedings on behalf of high net worth individuals, and has particular experience in the Cayman Islands. His expertise extends to cases concerning the relocation of children and the Inheritance Act. **Strengths:** "He's a super silky smooth advocate. Judges love him." **Recent work:** Acted as junior for a wife in a £150 million case, where the High Court decided that wife was entitled to a full 50%.

Rebecca Carew Pole (see p.611) Focuses her matrimonial practice on contested financial disputes, mostly for high net worth clients. Additionally handles complex leave to remove applications for notable individuals. **Strengths:** "Rebecca is a powerful advocate with real presence and has a wonderful way with clients. She offers quick, insightful analysis of complex issues and innovative solutions."

Emma Sumner Acts in high net worth Schedule 1 children and ancillary relief proceedings, and is a specialist at navigating complex trust and tax structures. She often represents high-profile international individuals in the entertainment, sporting and banking industries. **Strengths:** "Calm and measured with superb judgement and excellent client care skills. She inspires confidence and is an excellent advocate."

Christian Kenny (see p.690) Robust financial lawyer who has experience of handling ancillary relief cases with offshore trust structures and undisclosed assets. He is additionally noted for his knowledge in Schedule 1 and TOLATA family cases. **Strengths:** "His forensic attention to detail and ability to get all over the numbers very rapidly are huge assets when dealing with complex financial affairs."

Tom Carter Mainly handles complex, high-value financial remedy work for high-profile figures. His cases are often international in nature, hotly contested and centred on substantial assets. **Strengths:** "His attention to detail is fantastic and he is really thorough in his preparation for court. He's also very good on his feet."

Nicholas Wilkinson Handles both private matrimonial finance and children law matters for a high-profile clientele. His cases are often complex and involve technical aspects relating to tax and trusts. **Strengths:** "Does a great job of making the seemingly unarguable a tempting proposition, and is always prepared to go toe to toe with the opposition."

Katherine Cook (see p.622) An all-round family barrister that is noted for her matrimonial finance practice that consists of high-value divorce and nuptial agreement proceedings. Her clientele is international, with notable work being done in South Africa, the Cayman Islands, the UAE and Gibraltar. **Strengths:** "She's definitely the right person to go to when you're trying to settle; she keeps very calm under pressure."

1 King's Bench Walk

See profile on p.870

THE SET

Prominent all-round set offering the highest level of expertise in both high-value divorce and complex children cases. Its barristers act in the most significant cases of the hour and are no strangers to the Supreme Court.

Client service: "The clerks are amazing at 1 King's Bench Walk; they're always happy and willing to assist. It's a well-run set." The senior clerk at chambers is David Dear.

SILKS

Deborah Eaton QC (see p.639) Pre-eminent silk in family law renowned for her tremendous knowledge of private law children matters, having been instrumental in landmark cases in the field. She also possesses an active financial remedy practice representing high net worth individuals. **Strengths:** "Deborah Eaton is in a class of her own. There is no one with a greater court presence and she is the best cross-examiner in children proceedings. She is the go-to barrister for children." **Recent work:** Acted on behalf of a high-profile family in immensely difficult proceedings requiring complicated psychiatric intervention.

James Turner QC (see p.785) Universally acclaimed practitioner recognised for the strength of both his finance and children work. Handling complex matters at the highest level, he undertakes work in multiple jurisdictions, and is noted for his expertise in child abduction. **Strengths:** "A polymath who is able to advocate on the widest of subjects. A consummate lawyer with a significant and wide-ranging skill set that makes him an extremely well respected and highly sought-after advocate."

Frank Feehan QC Highly experienced family silk with demonstrable expertise in severe public law children matters involving complex medical evidence. He has recently taken significant matters to the Supreme Court and has also engaged in some high net worth divorce work. **Strengths:** "He is extremely tenacious and takes every point worth taking." **Recent work:** Acted in Re R, in both the High Court and Court of Appeal, representing a Moroccan father in complex habitual residence and abduction proceedings.

Richard Harrison QC (see p.666) Versatile practitioner who is widely regarded for his expertise in complex international child abduction cases. He is also sought after for the strength of his high-value matrimonial finance practice and has appeared in matters with a value of a billion pounds plus. **Strengths:** "He's very clever, very modest, user-friendly and well respected by judges. An absolute expert." **Recent work:** Featured in the first case concerning the 1996 Hague Convention to reach the Supreme Court.

Charles Howard QC (see p.675) Heavy-hitting family practitioner who demonstrates notable expertise in significant matrimonial finance and complex private children matters. He has extensive experience of handling international matters, particularly in Gibraltar and Hong Kong. **Strengths:** "He has a superlative intellect and is a devastating advocate. You get Rolls-Royce quality with him."

Philip Marshall QC (see p.708) Highly regarded finance silk who handles high-value divorce litigation for an enviable clientele of wealthy individuals. He is commended for his conciliatory approach and his ability to settle hotly contested cases. **Strengths:** "Very clever and a real class act. A first-class advocate with an encyclopaedic knowledge of financial remedies law."

Christopher Pocock QC (see p.739) A highly experienced financial silk who routinely handles multi-jurisdictional proceedings for high net worth individuals. He is noted for his expertise in complex tax, corporate and asset structures as they relate to family law. **Strengths:** "He's very down-to-earth, personable and really good with numbers. He's also a brilliant advocate."

Richard Anelay QC (see p.584) Extremely experienced family practitioner handling mainly large-scale matrimonial disputes with significant assets at stake. He additionally practises in private children proceedings and sits as an FDR judge and mediator. **Strengths:** "Extremely experienced." **Recent work:** Represented a husband in a family dispute where violence was alleged by both sides.

Anthony Kirk QC (see p.692) An expert in cases concerning severely injured and abused children. He also possesses a thriving mediation practice that focuses on private children settlements. **Strengths:** "An extremely effective mediator with a wealth of experience."

Pamela Scriven QC (see p.760) Manages a specialised children practice focusing on highly sensitive cases with elements of abuse, non-accidental injury and complex medical evidence. She also handles private international disputes, involving relocation and abduction. **Strengths:** "She can turn her hand to any children's case, is so reliable and can deal with the most difficult matters."

JUNIORS

Harry Oliver (see p.729) Leading junior in the field of divorce law who routinely handles significant financial remedy proceedings for extremely high-profile individuals. His work is mainly international and often involves complex issues relating to businesses and offshore trusts. **Strengths:** "He knows the law backwards and gets all the detail in no time. A real fighter who thrives on complex cases."

Richard Castle (see p.613) A well-known financial barrister who is respected for his handling of high-value matrimonial disputes for wealthy business people and company owners. He is additionally noted for his work in the Cayman Islands, where he conducts significant cases. **Strengths:** "Very commercial and no-nonsense, he is gentle and softly spoken but this belies a steely approach. His manner with clients, his opponents and the judge serves him very well. He is able to grasp very complex financial matters fantastically quickly, especially where there is a corporate angle." **Recent work:** Acted in a financial remedy claim involving assets of over USD200 million.

Anna McKenna (see p.713) Specialist children law practitioner who is commended for her strength in handling severe matters including issues of child trafficking, abuse and death. She has appeared in the Supreme Court handling children cases and routinely leads complex proceedings. **Strengths:** "An excellent barrister for children's cases. Charming and persuasive but can be tough when required. However nightmarish the case, there's a sense of relief when she's on your side." **Recent work:** Instructed at three hours' notice to respond, for a mother, to an application for permission to terminate life support medical treatment for a horrifically injured six week old baby facing certain death.

Deepak Nagpal (see p.725) Frequently leads in substantial financial remedy proceedings, acting on behalf of public figures and other high net worth clients. He is also the sole family Treasury Counsel and so advises and represents the government on significant issues. **Strengths:** "One of the most razor-sharp brains at the Bar. He thinks outside the box at all times."

James Roberts (see p.753) Highly regarded family practitioner whose practice is divided between the very largest financial disputes and complex multi-jurisdictional child matters. His financial remedy practice sees him representing extremely high-profile figures in enormous divorce proceedings with labyrinthine assets to navigate. **Strengths:** "A go-to option; he's robust, very quick at getting to the root of issues and consequently in great demand." **Recent work:** Acted in the most recent authority case on the circumstances in which an award can be set aside following a "Barder" event. The case involved the suicide of the husband after payment of half of the initial settlement.

Alexander Chandler (see p.614) Maintains a specialised matrimonial practice, acting for high net worth individuals in substantial disputes over assets. He is noted for his handling of complex issues surrounding Schedule 1 and TOLATA applications. **Strengths:** "He's absolutely the most fabulous detail merchant; he never misses a trick."

Markanza Cudby (see p.627) Children practitioner who focuses on sensitive public law work concerning non-accidental injury and infant fatality. She also has a thriving international private law caseload. **Strengths:** "She is extremely experienced, well respected and impressive."

Ian Cook (see p.622) Handles complex divorce proceedings in London and abroad for a range of clients. His cases often involve vast assets held within complex trust structures. **Strengths:** "Tenacious, client-friendly and pragmatic. He doesn't pull his punches and is a great all-rounder."

Nicola Fox (see p.647) Brings her experience as a psychologist to complex and acrimonious matrimonial and private children disputes. She has a particular expertise in relocation cases. **Strengths:** "She has a good grasp of the issues, is thorough in her research, relates well with the client and is calm and straightforward. She's an effective advocate."

Stephen Jarmain (see p.682) Practises across a wide spectrum of family issues, handling complex private children and ancillary relief proceedings. He has experience of representing high-profile individuals in international disputes. **Strengths:** "A very thorough junior whose preparation is second to none. He has an excellent client manner and is a delight to work with. He's very bright and always approachable." **Recent work:** Represented the respondent mother in an appeal brought to clarify the law on internal relocation.

Katherine Kelsey (see p.689) Appears in complex divorce proceedings for notable individuals of significant wealth. She also acts in private children cases, in particular contractual and international relocation cases. **Strengths:** "She is immensely user-friendly and a very sound family lawyer whose all-round skills belie her relatively low level of call. She produces first-class paperwork and will go far."

Madeleine Reardon (see p.749) Experienced family barrister with deep expertise in complex children cases, both public and private. She handles the full breadth of issues, including those concerning Schedule 1, relocation and social parentage. **Strengths:** "Client-friendly and a powerful advocate in court. She is excellent at quickly winning the confidence and respect of clients and judges alike."

Katy Chokowry (see p.616) Specialises in cross-border child abduction, leave to remove and relocation proceedings and has appeared in both the Court of Appeal and the Supreme Court. She is additionally noted for her knowledge of wardship and forced marriage. **Strengths:** "She sticks to her guns and is not afraid to take points even in front of a hostile judge."

Caroline Lister (see p.702) Has a broad practice covering both high net worth ancillary relief and international private children cases. She is recognised for her skilful handling of particularly acrimonious proceedings. **Strengths:** "She fights very hard, and is poised and articulate. She can be quite tough and is very secure in her handling of a judge."

Peter Newman (see p.727) Widely respected family junior specialising in matters involving complex corporate and offshore trust structures with significant assets. He has particular experience of navigating technical jurisdictional issues. **Strengths:** "He is absolutely meticulous and persuasive. He has an amazingly organised brain, and his work is incredibly well written."

Nicholas Anderson (see p.583) Has a mixed practice that covers a range of private family issues. His areas of focus include international child abduction and relocation cases and asset disputes between cohabitants. **Strengths:** "Excellent advocate who is calm and unflappable and always spot-on with his advice." **Recent work:** Represented a father following Hague Convention proceedings where the judge had initially ordered the return of four children to Australia. The mother applied to commit the father for breach of undertakings, but all applications were resisted.

Elizabeth Selman (see p.761) Focuses on private proceedings following relationship dissolution, on both the financial and children sides. Her children practice covers all related issues, including leave to remove and prohibited steps orders. **Strengths:** "A master of the papers who has complete command of her brief in court. She's really forthright and not afraid to argue a point if she believes in it."

Charlotte Hartley (see p.666) Junior barrister with noted ability in complex international financial remedy cases. She additionally possesses a growing practice relating to alternative family structures, including those concerning same-sex parentage. **Strengths:** "She is a very good advocate who is thorough and is gaining an enviable reputation."

New Court Chambers

See profile on p.878

THE SET

Specialist family set acting on the London and South Eastern Circuits in cases across the gamut of family finance and children law. The chambers is noted for its strength in public children law work, and handles complex matters involving serious abuse and injury to vulnerable children and adults.

Client service: "The clerks, led by Paul Bloomfield, are very accommodating and will bend over backwards to get something done. They are extremely well organised."

JUNIORS

Giles Bain (see p.588) Co-head of chambers who focuses on complex public law children cases, representing parents, children, local authorities and third parties. His practice sees him engaged in serious matters including those relating to sexual abuse and non-accidental injury. **Strengths:** "He's a very calm, measured and intuitive advocate. He's very easy to work with in a high-pressure environment and his technical ability and client manner are very good. He's enormously well respected by judges."

Christopher Poole (see p.739) Handles the whole spectrum of children-related issues, from international adoption to abuse and neglect cases. He acts as co-head of chambers and is commended for his work on behalf of guardians and local authorities in serious matters. **Strengths:** "I think he's a supremely confident advocate who certainly knows his stuff in public law. He has a quiet, authoritative manner that gets to the heart of things."

Sally Jackson (see p.681) Covers the full range of family cases, from complex children proceedings to high-value divorce disputes. Her public law practice sees her representing all parties, including parents, children and local authorities. **Strengths:** "She has a meticulous mind and her advice is second to none. She's very clear with the clients when explaining quite technical stuff relating to the law. She goes above and beyond her brief."

4 Paper Buildings

See profile on p.888

THE SET

A powerhouse of family law that offers unparalleled depth in all public and private law children-related issues, both international and domestic. The set further has a growing matrimonial finance practice, and its members service high net worth clients in complex disputes concerning large assets.

Client service: "The clerks are incredibly user-friendly; they're great for solicitors, they're flexible, they're reasonable on fees, and they're prepared to adapt. They know their barristers really well." The senior clerk is Michael Reeves.

SILKS

Henry Setright QC Extraordinarily experienced children law specialist who is widely regarded as the ultimate expert on international children matters, particularly abduction. He is routinely in the Supreme Court, leading the most significant, law-changing cases. **Strengths:** "The supreme master of all aspects of abduction law. He has unparalleled knowledge of the law, tactical supremacy and an advocacy style that none can match." **Recent work:** Achieved a successful application in a landmark 1980 Hague Convention/Article 8 human rights case run for an Argentine father against a Romanian wife.

Alex Verdan QC Head of chambers and indubitably a force in the field of children law. His expertise encompasses all issues, including the most severe and complex of children issues, and he is routinely instructed by the top family firms. **Strengths:** "A fierce advocate who is very efficient on his feet and whose cross-examination is off-the-scale impressive: he already knows the answers to all his questions."

Jo Delahunty QC (see p.632) Highly sought-after specialist children silk entrusted with the most significant and demanding national cases. She has particular expertise in matters concerning a large amount of complex expert evidence following investigation. **Strengths:** "She is exceptional in every way and has an attention to detail beyond any other silk right now."

Teertha Gupta QC Focuses on international children disputes, both public and private, many of which involve forensic investigation. He is universally commended for his personable advocacy style and his prowess in the courtroom. **Strengths:** "He's charm personified, is fantastic with clients and is very friendly. He's also a brilliant strategist and tactician."

David Williams QC A leading silk widely respected for his knowledge regarding complex applications of the Hague Convention. He has appeared in both the Supreme Court and the ECJ. **Strengths:** "He is completely meticulous and is an extremely able advocate. One of the best Hague Convention specialists." **Recent work:** Engaged in a Supreme Court case seeking to establish a new legal framework for the exercising of wardship jurisdiction based upon the nationality of a child.

Catherine Wood QC Recognised for her expert international children practice, particularly when it comes to matters concerning abduction, parental alienation and sexual abuse. She brings her experience as a judge to bear when handling complex cases. **Strengths:** "An excellent advocate with superb judgement who is at home dealing with complicated children's cases. She never gets it wrong; she absolutely nails it in one sentence."

Charles Hale QC Renowned family silk who specialises in complex matters in both the private children and matrimonial finance spheres. He routinely handles significant cases on behalf of an impressive client base of high-profile individuals. **Strengths:** "A very commanding presence in the courtroom. He's wonderfully pragmatic, very persuasive and very thorough. He has one of the best client manners going."

Alison Grief QC Children law specialist who offers services in complex children cases and demonstrates noted expertise in those matters requiring expert medical evidence. She has a strong private law practice and is noted for her handling of alleged sexual abuse cases. **Strengths:** "She works exhaustively to ensure the very best result for her client. She is a specialist in non-accidental medical cases."

Christopher Hames QC Has a notable international children practice and deep expertise in matters concerning the application of the Hague Convention. His growing financial practice sees him representing high net worth individuals in divorce proceedings. **Strengths:** "He's easy to work with, relentless in court, fearless, incredibly knowledgeable and very persuasive. A superb advocate." **Recent work:** Acted in Cambra v Jones, a case concerning the failure to return two children to Spain under the Hague Convention.

John Tughan QC Has expertise in both public and private children proceedings. He possesses great experience of handling complex cases concerning abuse and relocation. **Strengths:** "Tenacious, hard-working and willing to push the boundaries for his clients."

Jonathan Cohen QC Financial silk with a wealth of experience of handling high-value disputes for clients following relationship breakdown. He sits as both Recorder and Deputy High Court Judge in the family courts and is widely commended for his judgement. **Strengths:** "She's smart, clever, tactical and a pleasure to listen to in court. Judges really pay attention to him and he has excellent judgement in financial cases."

Marcus Scott-Manderson QC Private children law specialist who is recognised for his extensive experience and knowledge of issues concerning the Hague Convention. He mainly focuses on international cases and is solid in proceedings concerning expert evidence. **Strengths:** "If you have a Hague Convention problem, he has encyclopaedic knowledge."

Michael Sternberg QC Extremely experienced family practitioner who focuses on complex ancillary relief proceedings for high net worth individuals. He is additionally noted for his specialism in matters relating to pensions. **Strengths:** "He's very thorough and meticulous in his preparation. He's a thoughtful strategist who focuses on the best interests of the client."

JUNIORS

Joy Brereton Highly experienced children law barrister who is recognised for her work in cases concerning the movement of children internationally. She additionally exhibits strength in matters concerning issues of criminal offences and abuse. **Strengths:** "She's marvellously authoritative, and can deal with both clients and the judge beautifully."

Michael Gration Family junior fast developing a strong children practice with a focus on complex abduction cases. He has appeared before the Supreme Court and the ECHR despite his relatively junior level of call. **Strengths:** "Unflappable and brilliant with clients and judges alike, he has knowledge, subtlety and a highly persuasive style of advocacy. Truly an expert within a highly specialised field, he knows how to pitch a case in a way that is far above his year of call." **Recent work:** Represented an appellant father who had sought the summary return of his child to Morocco.

Judith Murray Balanced practitioner who divides her practice between representing high net worth individuals in complex financial remedy and cross-jurisdiction children proceedings. She routinely handles acrimonious proceedings concerning alleged sexual abuse. **Strengths:** "She's a ferocious advocate who is very punchy but calm in a crisis. She's a number one choice for finance and children cases and has a wealth of experience in both."

Justine Johnston Renowned for her expertise in both complex family finance and children matters, she handles all issues flowing from relationship breakdown. She is recognised in particular for international leave to remove cases. **Strengths:** "She is a real fighter and a ferocious advocate who is incredibly well thought of. Her advocacy and preparation skills are extremely good."

Samantha King Renowned family junior in high demand due to her deep knowledge of public and private law cases, both at home and abroad. She exhibits strength in public law cases concerning non-traditional families and surrogacy. **Strengths:** "She is widely known as the best advocate around in children cases. Her cross-examination skills and eloquent submissions are second to none. She is direct and clear in her advice but caring and empathetic towards her clients."

Barbara Mills Highly regarded family barrister with recognised expertise in private children proceedings, in particular cross-border cases in the High Court. She also demonstrates strength in mediation and is a private judge. **Strengths:** "Her preparation is excellent, her cross-examination is second to none and she is absolutely magical in court." **Recent work:** Represented the father in contested proceedings concerning the future care of a seven year old girl. The case involved allegations of maternal mental health, drug misuse, and both domestic and physical violence against the girl.

Jacqueline Renton Focuses her specialised children practice on sophisticated conflicts centring on jurisdiction, relocation and abduction. She regularly appears in the High Court and the Supreme Court. **Strengths:** "She is brilliant on children law and holds herself extremely well in court against much more senior barristers."

Rebecca Foulkes Manages a diverse children practice that sees her appearing in the Court of Appeal and the Supreme Court in significant proceedings. She also has a growing reputation with regard to cases concerning assisted reproduction. **Strengths:** "A leading junior in her field, particularly in public law. A tenacious and smooth advocate who is very intelligent." **Recent work:** Represented a mother who had sought to prevent the father from spending time with the children in Dubai, where he was based, for fear that he would seek to wrongfully retain the children there. The case involved consideration of expert evidence as to the safeguards that would be available within the legal system of the UAE and highly contentious oral evidence from each parent.

Brian Jubb Brings extensive experience to bear in complex children proceedings. He has a specialism in public law cases representing vulnerable adults. **Strengths:** "He's a true gentleman. His detailed, understated advocacy gets him the ear of the court."

Hassan Khan Experienced children law junior who handles the full range of public and private children law cases. He is noted for his strength in matters relating to wardship and cross-border child abduction. **Strengths:** "A real fighter and a high-quality advocate. He combines charm with great knowledge of the law."

Mark Jarman A cross-jurisdictional specialist who represents notable individuals in private children disputes. He mainly acts in cases concerning relocation, abduction and enforcement orders. **Strengths:** "He is highly intelligent, calm, persuasive and very good with clients."

Michael Edwards Children law junior with a growing practice, who has handled a number of highly complex abduction cases in the Court of Appeal and the Supreme Court. His public law practice consists of the most sensitive and severe cases concerning matters such as infant death and abuse. **Strengths:** "A rising star with a packed diary of complicated children cases. He's a bright, well prepared and thoughtful advocate."

Dorothea Gartland Private and public law lawyer focusing on complex children issues, domestically and abroad. She is noted in particular for her expertise in cases involving issues of parentage. **Strengths:** "She is a tenacious advocate who readily gets to grips with tricky, gritty cases. She is particularly recommended for her work with alternative family structures." **Recent work:** Represented the intervener Health Trust Barts in a case in which the applicant sought a declaration of parentage that he was the father of the child his partner had conceived at a fertility clinic.

Ruth Kirby Experienced family and Court of Protection practitioner who has expertise in sensitive matters. She is praised for the strength of her advocacy and for the tenacity she shows on behalf of her client in court. **Strengths:** "Quick on her feet and fantastic at client care. She's always best in a fight; she sees the client's interests and goes for it."

Stephen Lyon Respected senior junior who possesses a deep knowledge of matrimonial finance proceedings and services clients of significant wealth. He is additionally a qualified family arbitrator and sits in ADR proceedings. **Strengths:** "His client care skills are phenomenal and he really has the ear of the court."

Samantha Woodham Family practitioner handling a variety of private law matters relating to both family finance and children. Her specialism lies in high-value matrimonial disputes, Schedule 1 and leave to remove cases. **Strengths:** "She has a fantastic manner and goes above and beyond the call of duty."

Henry Clayton Up-and-coming family finance junior who handles matters including maintenance orders, Schedule 1 and CSA appeals. He routinely services high net worth clients and is commended for his grasp of complex issues despite his junior level of call. **Strengths:** "He's impressive for his years. He's meticulous in his approach, produces incredible paperwork, is super bright and knows how to deal with senior silks. He shines in financial cases where his judgement stands out." **Recent work:** Featured in a case in the ECJ concerning the meaning of the word 'established' in the Brussels IIA regulation.

Queen Elizabeth Building QEB

See profile on p.902

THE SET

Extremely good matrimonial finance outfit routinely involved in the sector's most significant disputes in addition to more moderate proceedings. Members here have a strong focus on international work and a growing offering in children law.

Client service: "Very professional and client-facing, the clerks are exceptionally well organised, efficient, very professional and people who provide a wonderful service." The senior clerk is Howard Rayner.

SILKS

Lewis Marks QC (see p.707) One of the prime leaders in London family law, who acts as head of chambers and handles the most significant financial cases for the highest-profile clients. He is renowned for his technical proficiency and superior courtroom skills. **Strengths:** "A go-to adviser in complex money disputes involving ultra high net worth individuals." **Recent work:** Represented the claimant wife in a complex financial relief claim, arising from the breakdown of what was the husband's fifth marriage, and the wife's second. There was a substantial issue as to the valuation of the husband's business.

Tim Amos QC (see p.583) Highly experienced and respected money practitioner with a specialism in high-value Anglo-German disputes owing to his expertise in the field and fluency in the language. He is additionally noted for his position as both collaborative counsel and resolution mediator. **Strengths:** "He is a beautiful advocate who has a superb manner with clients. He has meticulous attention to detail and first-class command of his brief." **Recent work:** Acted for an appellant wife, winning in London at the Privy Council after 16 years of delays and adverse judgments emanating from the Jamaican justice system.

Stewart Leech QC (see p.698) Leading family silk known for his Anglo-French practice, who represents extremely wealthy clients in complex nuptial agreement and financial remedy proceedings. He is also noted for his work with trustees and cohabitants. **Strengths:** "He has superb client care skills and offers quietly persuasive advocacy. He has a real ability to cut to the core of the issues and to present complex arguments in an accessible way."

Lucy Stone QC (see p.774) Eminent financial practitioner who represents ultra high net worth individuals in substantial financial remedy proceedings. Her practice spans the globe, with a particular focus on cases surrounding the Isle of Man and Hong Kong. **Strengths:** "She's highly experienced, and has the right balance of legal and commercial understanding. She has an incredible grasp of the detail and is one of the best cross-examiners around."

James Ewins QC (see p.642) Newly appointed Queen's Counsel specialising in large-scale financial remedy proceedings concerning complex international wealth and trust structures. **Strengths:** "James can cut through a brief to identify the magic number for settlement in lightning-quick time. Happily, his extraordinary intelligence combines with a down-to-earth nature and clients feel very safe in his hands."

JUNIORS

Elizabeth Clarke (see p.617) Leading financial junior specialising in high net worth divorce cases of high technical complexity, many of which involve issues of tax and offshore trusts. She is commended for her sharp and assertive advocacy. **Strengths:** "She is steely, intelligent and someone who commands respects from judges. She gives clear and concise advice to clients, and is at the top of her game."

Duncan Brooks (see p.604) Family junior offering deep expertise in significant financial remedy cases and private children matters. He is also widely regarded for his growing arbitration, FDR and wider dispute resolution practice. **Strengths:** "He has superb judgement; he doesn't overcomplicate a case and he wins it with confidence. He's a great advocate who has superb client care skills and is leading the way in arbitration and dispute resolution." **Recent work:** Represented a wife in a complex case where the husband had declared himself bankrupt owing substantial debts to his son. The preliminary issues were whether the son had a beneficial interest in the matrimonial home, and whether the husband and wife owed the son money.

Marina Faggionato (see p.643) Family junior recognised for the growing strength of both her complex high net worth finance and private children practices. She is commended for her efforts in tackling cases of an international nature. **Strengths:** "She has a maturity and gravitas in excess of her call and excels at international cases, being assisted by her impressive language skills. She is destined for great things."

Daniel Bentham (see p.594) Financial remedy specialist noted for his understated yet precise advocacy. He mainly represents high net worth clients in complex matters involving business interests and trusts. **Strengths:** "A charming client manner masks a shrewd brain. He's a sure-footed adviser who is a polished and persuasive advocate." **Recent work:** Acted for a wife in a case involving committal of her husband to prison for breach of court orders and breach of an undertaking to lodge share certificates as security for payment of a lump sum.

Catherine Cowton (see p.625) Expert family finance practitioner who is well respected for her high-profile practice, which consists of both significant litigation and private FDR hearings. Her expertise additionally extends to substantial nuptial agreements and Schedule 1 cases. **Strengths:** "She's clearly very sharp but also emotionally intelligent; she knows what a client needs and connects with them. Incredibly tenacious and fearless in court, she's very thorough and has everything at her fingertips."

Morgan Sirikanda (see p.767) Family practitioner focusing on complex high-value matrimonial finance cases, often including an international element. He is noted for his TOLATA expertise and regularly represents unmarried couples and cohabitants. **Strengths:** "He's seriously impressive. Very elegant and capable, he has a way of cutting right to the heart of the matter and taking the client along with him. He writes brilliantly and is obviously immensely knowledgeable." **Recent work:** Acted for the husband, the CEO of an AIM-listed investment company, in a high-value financial remedy case where the wife was a former Russian model. The judge refused to hear the case in private and it sparked debate over whether such cases should be heard openly.

Marcus Lazarides (see p.697) Dual practitioner covering both complex private children and family finance work. He is particularly noted for his financial remedy cases where he navigates intricate corporate and trust structures containing significant assets. **Strengths:** "He's charming and calm under pressure, he prepares thoroughly and he is delightful with clients. He brings a balanced approached to advice and negotiations and is also a persuasive advocate."

Sarah Phipps (see p.737) Experienced family junior frequently instructed by London's leading firms on high net worth financial remedy proceedings and private children cases. She mainly handles divorce cases but can turn her hand to complex Schedule 1 and leave to remove matters. **Strengths:** "Sarah is determined and fantastically able. Clients love her as she fights so hard for them in court, whilst also giving sound advice."

Samantha Singer (see p.766) Has a practice comprising high-value divorce proceedings and private children matters undertaken on behalf of high-profile individuals. She is noted for her routine instruction by high-ranking London solicitor firms. **Strengths:** "Samantha is so incredibly charming that clients adore her. As you would expect from those at QEB, she is thorough, knowledgeable and working at the forefront of family law."

Alexander Thorpe (see p.781) Practises exclusively in financial remedy proceedings upon relationship dissolution. He is particularly adept at high-value cases concerning large quantities of forensic evidence and questions of non-disclosure. **Strengths:** "He's got a good bedside manner, has great poise and is able to absorb a lot of information at short notice. He always makes the points in the right way and shows very good instinct in his advocacy."

Rosemary Budden (see p.606) Focuses on matrimonial proceedings on behalf of wealthy clients, often involving complex corporate, trust and tax elements. Her practice is mainly international and she also handles private children work. **Strengths:** "She's tenacious but fair, has a great intellect and is adored by her clients." **Recent work:** Handled a high-profile, complex, international financial remedy High Court case which received front-page press coverage. It concerned a Russian beauty queen who was divorcing her US attorney husband.

Amy Kisser (see p.692) Family practitioner handling a mixture of both financial and private children cases. She is noted for her specialism in representing international clients, particularly cohabitants or unmarried couples. **Strengths:** "She is extremely able and has a great client manner. She is meticulous in her preparation and is very good at guiding clients towards a realistic outcome."

Charanjit Batt (see p.592) Predominantly a financial practitioner handling moderate and high net worth divorce proceedings. She is noted for her international expertise, particularly when it comes to jurisdiction issues. **Strengths:** "She is tenacious, fantastic on the detail and someone who doesn't miss any relevant points."

Matthew Firth (see p.645) Focuses his family practice on financial remedy proceedings, engaging in high-value disputes on behalf of wealthy individuals. He is notable for his prior experience in other areas of the law including personal injury, property and crime. **Strengths:** "He is fastidious and meticulous – perfect for complicated financial cases requiring mastery of the detail."

William Tyzack (see p.785) Versatile family junior with a mixed practice comprising both international finance and children proceedings. He handles matters including those relating to leave to remove, abduction and divorce. **Strengths:** "Very calm and unflappable, he doesn't get riled easily. He also really knows the law."

Other Ranked Lawyers

Barbara Connolly QC (7BR) Hugely experienced family silk who handles complex and severe children law cases. She is renowned for her expertise in cases concerning alternative families and assisted reproduction. **Strengths:** "She has unrivalled knowledge at silk level of surrogacy and cases involving alternative family structures. She's also an excellent cross-examiner; she's dynamite on her feet."

Rachel Langdale QC (see p.695) (7BR) A highly regarded children practitioner who handles complex cases in both the public and private arenas. She is noted for her expertise in cases involving expert medical evidence, and is particularly good at international matters relating to non-accidental head injuries. **Strengths:** "She's well thought of in her field, forms an extremely good rapport with her clients and is really good to work with. She is massively hard-working, always prepared and tenacious in her advocacy."

Anita Guha (7BR) Child law expert who utilises her experience in immigration and refugee matters to represent vulnerable clients in complex international proceedings. She further has particular expertise in forced marriage cases. **Strengths:** "She's fantastically well prepared, excellent on her feet, a great strategist and someone who has a wonderful manner with clients. She thinks creatively outside the box and the court loves her."

David Balcombe QC (1 Crown Office Row) Manages a unique practice, exhibiting expertise in matrimonial finance, professional discipline and clinical negligence work. His family finance cases range in value from moderate to high net worth and often have an international element to them. **Strengths:** "He never loses sight of what someone actually needs from a case and gives really good advice early on. He's the person you go to if you want sane, objective judgement."

Ruth Cabeza (Field Court Chambers) Highly regarded children law barrister sought after for her expertise in international children law matters including adoption, surrogacy and abduction. She has been involved in landmark cases that have advanced the law. **Strengths:** "She is the go-to person for cases involving inter-country adoption and has notable skills in child trafficking and Hague Convention abductions." **Recent work:** Acted in a unique case involving a surrogacy, whereby the mother of a single male agreed to be the surrogate for his child.

Tara Vindis (see p.787) (9 Gough Square) Handles children law cases, many of which involve complex medical evidence and expert witnesses. She is known for her experience in handling cases involving non-accidental injury. **Strengths:** "She's excellent. She has incredible client care, is very sensitive with vulnerable individuals, and is a very good advocate who is particularly skilful in cross-examination."

Laura Briggs (see p.602) (9 Gough Square) Children law barrister focusing on complex public law matters including sexual abuse and non-accidental injury cases, often with an international element. She also sits as a recorder on the south eastern family circuit. **Strengths:** "She has amazing attention to detail, is brilliant with clients, is a great advocate, has a very calm persona and is very effective."

Timothy Parker (see p.734) (9 Gough Square) Acts as head of chambers and is known for his care practice handling some of the most severe cases involving non-accidental injury and sexual abuse. He also has a strong family finance practice and is an arbitrator. **Strengths:** "He's very effective; he asks all the killer questions you wish you'd asked. He has a really good client manner and is often instructed by silks in heavyweight care cases."

Gillian Geddes (see p.651) (2-3 Hind Court) Has extensive experience in sensitive public law matters pertaining to children, including those concerning non-accidental injury and abuse. She is additionally noted for her specialism in handling cross-border cases with an immigration aspect to them. **Strengths:** "She is great for advocacy and you can really see her level of expertise come through. She exudes experience."

Helen Jefferson (2-3 Hind Court) Family junior handling both children and matrimonial finance issues for a range of clients. She has a broad practice and has experience of cases with Schedule 1, TOLATA and Hague Convention aspects attached to them. **Strengths:** "She's so adaptable; it's rare that you find a barrister who can appreciate every kind of client. She's a confident performer who is very forthright."

Sheena Cassidy (3PB Barristers) Deputy head of chambers and a matrimonial finance practitioner specialising in complex cases involving issues of tax and trust structures. She is noted for her experience in cases involving non-disclosure and fraud. **Strengths:** "She's so measured, thorough, committed and unflappable."

Kerstin Boyd (Tanfield Chambers) Matrimonial finance junior who handles all manner of proceedings following relationship dissolution, including those relating to TOLATA and the Schedule 1 Children Act. She is committed to providing an affordable service to a wide range of clients. **Strengths:** "She is very personable and professional. She's great with clients and good at explaining things very simply, especially when dealing with financial reports."

William Tyler QC (see p.785) (The 36 Group) Well-regarded QC specialising in both public and private children law proceedings, who is an expert on jurisdiction issues. He is noted for his experience in handling proceedings concerning serious allegations. **Strengths:** "He's highly intellectual and provides understated yet assertive advocacy."

Valentine Le Grice QC (The 36 Group) Focuses his financial practice on high-value matters concerning complex trust structures in and out of the context of marriage. He also devotes a portion of his time to private children cases and arbitration proceedings. **Strengths:** "Technically and tactically brilliant, he's an excellent advocate."

Andrzej Bojarski (The 36 Group) A well-regarded family practitioner specialising in complex, high-value financial disputes following relationship breakdown, who has particular expertise in cases involving offshore trusts. He also acts as a family arbitrator in finance proceedings. **Strengths:** "Andrzej is excellent for financial work. His expertise in complicated offshore finances is second to none, and he is a barrister who offers strong advice."

Hannah Markham QC (The 36 Group) Focuses on sensitive children matters in the public and private spheres. Her practice has a strong international focus and she is fluent in Spanish. **Strengths:** "She's very sensitive to what her clients are experiencing and has superb client care skills. Outside court she has a no-nonsense, unpretentious manner. Inside court she gets all her points across forcefully and effectively." **Recent work:** Featured in a case where a mother claimed that her children had been subjected to torture and ritualistic sex abuse by their father, the leader of a cult.

Niki Langridge (see p.695) (The 36 Group) Exclusively practises in the matrimonial finance sphere, handling moderate to high net worth financial remedy cases, many of which have fact-finding or tax issues attached to them. She is additionally a qualified collaborative counsel and mediator, offering services in ADR. **Strengths:** "She's absolutely brilliant at big money cases and is on the ball in complex work. She's an excellent advocate and negotiator and her settlement success rate is second to none."

MIDLANDS

Family/Matrimonial
Leading Sets
Band 1
No5 Chambers *
St Ives Chambers *
St Philips Chambers *
Band 2
St Mary's Chambers *
Leading Silks
Band 1
Meyer Lorna *No5 Chambers*
Weston Jeremy *St Ives Chambers* *
Band 2
Isaacs Elizabeth *St Ives Chambers* *
McGrath Elizabeth *St Philips Chambers* *
Vater John *Harcourt Chambers (ORL)* ◊
* *Indicates set / individual with profile.*
Ⓐ *direct access (see p.24).*
◊ *(ORL) = Other Ranked Lawyer.*
Alphabetical order within each band. Band 1 is highest.

Family/Matrimonial
Leading Juniors
Band 1
Abberley Stephen *St Philips Chambers*
Adams Christopher *St Philips Chambers* *
Bond Leisha *St Philips Chambers* *
Brown Stephanie *No5 Chambers* Ⓐ
Carter Rosalyn *St Philips Chambers* *
Friel Michele *No5 Chambers*
Hadley Richard *No5 Chambers*
James Christopher *No5 Chambers* Ⓐ
McCabe Louise *St Philips Chambers* Ⓐ *
Meachin Vanessa *St Philips Chambers* Ⓐ *
Messling Lawrence *St Philips Chambers* *
Mullen Jayne *St Ives Chambers* *
Nosworthy Jonathan *St Philips Chambers* Ⓐ *
Starks Nicholas *St Ives Chambers* *
Walker Elizabeth *St Philips Chambers* *
Wynne Ashley *No5 Chambers* Ⓐ
Band 2
Allen Juliet *No5 Chambers*
Bache Nina *St Ives Chambers* *
Bojarski Andrzej *The 36 Group (ORL)* ◊
Brown Kristina *No5 Chambers*
Chavasse Ann *St Ives Chambers*
Claxton Judith *St Mary's Chambers*
Clifford Victoria *No5 Chambers*
Day Andrew *St Ives Chambers* *
Fothergill Francesca *St Philips Chambers*
Gallacher Kirsty *No5 Chambers*
Gilead Beryl *St Mary's Chambers*
Grant Orla *No5 Chambers*
Hodges Victoria *St Mary's Chambers*
Kingerley Martin *The 36 Group (ORL)* ◊
Lakin Tracy *St Ives Chambers* *
Maynard Matthew *St Ives Chambers* *
Nuvoloni Stefano *No5 Chambers*
Page Nigel *St Mary's Chambers*
Pemberton Yolanda *St Philips Chambers* *
Pritchard Sarah *St Ives Chambers* *
Reece Jason *St Mary's Chambers*
Rogers Gregory *St Ives Chambers* *
Smallwood Anne E *No5 Chambers*
Brown Kristina *No5 Chambers*
Up-and-coming individuals
French Lucie *St Philips Chambers* *
Jackson Charmian *St Ives Chambers* *
Jacques Gareth *St Mary's Chambers*

Band 1

No5 Chambers

See profile on p.931

THE SET

No5 Chambers is a set with a national reach that has a wealth of highly experienced individuals who undertake a broad spectrum of family work. The renowned matrimonial finance team is frequently instructed in high net worth cases, and also undertakes complex private and public law children matters. Sources note the team's professionalism and the clerks' helpful approach, describing No5 as an "impressive, forward-looking set."

Client service: "The clerks, led by Russell Hobbs, are very helpful and accessible. The go-to chambers in the Midlands." "The set is efficiently run, customer-friendly and good at liaising with the courts."

SILKS

Lorna Meyer QC Exceptional silk dealing with a range of children law matters, from international adoption to complex physical and sexual abuse cases. Interviewees praise her as an impressive intellectual and an excellent advocate. **Strengths:** "Lorna is a reassuring presence in any case, has a good command of her material and a composed style that judges like." "A very clever, hugely conscientious lawyer who has a good rapport with both clients and judges." **Recent work:** Presented an application to use High Court inherent jurisdiction to disrupt the activity of a group of men engaged in the child sexual exploitation of a teenager. The case is believed to have been the first of its kind.

JUNIORS

Stephanie Brown Highly experienced and a leader in matrimonial finance cases, she is regularly instructed in high-value financial remedy work involving complex assets, such as family businesses. Of late, her caseload has featured a strong emphasis on disputes that involve multi-jurisdictional issues. **Strengths:** "A first-class barrister, thorough and conscientious." "She has a wonderful combination of empathy, technical knowledge and a robust approach when needed."

Michele Friel A standout practitioner specialising in private law children work, she has extensive experience in issues ranging from fostering and adoption to external relocation. Sources highlight her as the go-to individual for complex children cases. **Strengths:** "Michele is simply the best for complex Children Act matters. She has a wealth of knowledge and applies this in a robust and effective manner." "Spot-on with her preparation, and her cross-examination is second to none."

Richard Hadley An impressive junior who focuses exclusively on children matters. His practice encompasses a range of the most sensitive care proceedings, with notable skill at handling complex medical evidence. He also undertakes immigration and abduction-related issues. **Strengths:** "Absolutely first-class and delightful to work with. He is thorough and effective." "Really knows his stuff, good attention to detail and very meticulous. A very good advocate."

Christopher James Specialist family barrister focusing on complex financial claims. He frequently undertakes high net worth cases involving family businesses, professional partnerships and pension issues, as well as disputes between unmarried couples. **Strengths:** "He has a certain perspicacity which reassures clients, he feels like a safe pair of hands and is also very approachable."

Ashley Wynne A highly rated advocate focused on high-value matrimonial finance cases and cohabitee disputes. He has specialist knowledge of cases involving trusts, corporate interests and third-party claims. Sources are impressed with his in-depth technical knowledge. **Strengths:** "A real specialist in financial remedy proceedings, an expert in negotiations and able to remain calm under pressure." "Personable, succinct and gives honest, pragmatic advice."

Victoria Clifford Well-regarded practitioner undertaking a broad range of family law work such as complex public and private children issues, domestic abuse injunctions and financial disputes. She often takes on cases that require careful handling of vulnerable and challenging clients. **Strengths:** "A very strong and robust advocate, excellent at managing client expectations." "My first port of call for complex matters. A tough litigator who fights tooth and nail for her client."

Kirsty Gallacher Continuing to impress with expertise beyond her call, Kirsty Gallacher handles care matters involving the most severe abuse allegations, whether physical, sexual or emotional. Other notable areas of expertise include child abduction cases and jurisdictional issues. **Strengths:** "A real rising star, Kirsty is patient with her clients and communicates well." "She is extremely prepared and thorough, gets on well with clients and always fights for them." **Recent work:** Represented a mother facing all her children being placed into care.

Orla Grant A strong junior with a mixed practice covering both public and private children law, as well as ancillary relief and other matrimonial finance work. She regularly represents clients in cases involving examples of serious abuse, including domestic violence. In financial matters, she is often instructed on cases with high-value assets. **Strengths:** "A go-to individual for children work. She is superb and very good with clients." "An excellent advocate who cuts to the chase and is good at resolving issues." **Recent work:** Represented the husband in a financial remedy dispute that concerned approximately £6.6 million worth of assets.

Stefano Nuvoloni Senior junior practising in all areas of childcare law, from cases of severe injury or fatality to the most contentious residence and relocation disputes. He has an expanding practice advising local authorities on human rights issues, and has been involved in recent ground-breaking work on the disruption of child sexual exploitation. **Strengths:** "Very hard-working, fair in his representation and well prepared." "Really impressive, he was able to build up trust with a very difficult client. He really stands out."

Anne Smallwood A very experienced family finance practitioner specialising in ancillary relief following divorce or separation. Regularly instructed on cases of substantial value involving corporate assets, foreign property or land and farming issues. **Strengths:** "Anne is very good, very dependable and great with clients. I have a lot of confidence in her."

Juliet Allen Focuses on private law children work, with her practice also encompassing disputes over land, inheritance and complex business arrangements. Lately, cases have included significant multi-jurisdictional elements. **Strengths:** "Extremely easy to work with, a very good advocate and very affable." "Good with her clients, robust and always clear and realistic with her advice."

Kristina Brown An established practitioner in both public and private children law who focuses on serious cases of child abuse involving complex medical and factual evidence. She acts for parents and children as well as local authorities. **Strengths:** "Smart, insightful and someone with a phenomenal work rate, she has the makings of a future silk." "She can take a case that is drifting and pin it down." **Recent work:** Represented the father of an 11-year-old child whose mother asserted parental alienation and opposed any contact between father and child.

St Ives Chambers

See profile on p.933

THE SET

St Ives Chambers continues to excel in all aspects of family law, with its barristers leading the way in children matters and family finance cases. While the team remains particularly noteworthy for the breadth of its public and private children work, it does regularly take on high-value matrimonial finance cases, many of which have specialist elements to them such as international assets or offshore trusts. Market commentators praise the clerking as efficient, approachable and organised.

Client service: "The team has a variety of experience and a breadth of knowledge. Both clerks and counsel are helpful and accommodating." The clerking is led by chambers director Jackie Maskew, with Sarah Robinson and Clare Radburn heading the family teams.

SILKS

Jeremy Weston QC (see p.792) Head of chambers and a brilliant family silk who focuses exclusively on children matters. His caseload includes the most complex care cases, including sexual abuse, serious injuries and fatalities. Sources cite his excellent bedside manner and preparation for cases. **Strengths:** "Specialist children's counsel, highly regarded and tactically astute." "Jeremy is approachable, easy to work with, affable with the client and gives good advice."

Elizabeth Isaacs QC (see p.680) Impressive silk with an excellent reputation in complex care proceedings that is reinforced by her former career in child protection social work. She is regularly instructed in cases involving death or serious injury, and also handles the more intricate aspects of private law such as surrogacy and same-sex parenting issues. **Strengths:** "We worked very closely as a team, she is competent and approachable." "She is just really, really excellent and very nice."

JUNIORS

Jayne Mullen (see p.723) Leading family junior focused on high-value matrimonial finance cases, with notable experience in issues concerning complex pensions and business accounts. Of late, her work has focused on large divorce settlements that often involve complex financial structures and division of assets. **Strengths:** "Arguably the leading ancillary relief barrister in the West Midlands. A wonderfully calm and collected manner coupled with a keen mind and formidable approach to advocacy." "A very experienced, capable barrister. Excellent on financial dispute cases."

Nicholas Starks (see p.771) An excellent advocate who continues to impress with his detailed approach to cases and thorough preparation. He largely focuses on multifaceted financial provision cases arising from divorce as well as under TOLATA, Schedule 1 applications and the Civil Partnership Act. He is regularly instructed on disputes of a high-value and complex nature. **Strengths:** "His legal knowledge is second to none on financial matters, he is very experienced in ancillary relief and achieves excellent results." "Outstanding attention to detail and excellent case preparation. He has strong strategic skills when looking at cases and communicates well with both solicitor and lay client."

Nina Bache (see p.587) Child law specialist and experienced advocate who receives instructions in public and private law cases that regularly involve severe abuse. She has a particular interest in representing children, although she also works with parents, guardians and local authorities, and is known for taking on cases that concern particularly vulnerable parties. **Strengths:** "Excellent client manner, a hard-working and perceptive advocate." "Extremely thorough in her preparation of cases and analysis of reports. A confident and able advocate."

Ann Chavasse Well-regarded practitioner focused on care and adoption cases, who frequently undertakes matters involving physical and sexual abuse or neglect. She has gained significant expertise in matters involving complex medical evidence, serious injuries and infant death. **Strengths:** "Ann is a very knowledgeable and passionate advocate." "Very robust in representing parents in difficult care matters. In the face of adversity she copes extremely well."

Andrew Day (see p.630) Noted by sources for his meticulous approach and attention to detail, he maintains a strong reputation for financial and property disputes. He has notable experience handling cases with onshore and offshore trust assets, businesses and pensions, and those arising from criminal confiscation proceedings. **Strengths:** "Andrew is very knowledgeable, strategic and a good negotiator." "His detailed preparation is second to none on finance, he is reassuring to clients with a real desire to achieve the best outcome."

Tracy Lakin (see p.694) A Children Act specialist, representing local authorities, guardians, parents and children in public and private childcare proceedings. Past cases have included aspects such as shaken baby syndrome, sexual abuse and chronic neglect. **Strengths:** "Excellent, really hard-working and someone with a great eye for detail. Good with vulnerable clients."

Matthew Maynard (see p.710) Represents parents, local authorities and children in complicated care proceedings, which often concern severe non-accidental injuries, sexual abuse and child death. Also noted for his private law practice, which has a particular slant towards surrogacy matters and international movement of children. **Strengths:** "Very robust, no nonsense and straight-talking." "Good on his feet but also caring with wonderful client skills."

Sarah Pritchard (see p.744) Junior barrister with an excellent childcare practice encompassing both public and private law issues. She has extensive experience handling cases that entail elements such as factitious illness, serious head injuries and child fatality. **Strengths:** "Excels in her profession, has a keen eye for detail, is an excellent advocate and is approachable." "She's excellent in court, very impressive indeed."

Gregory Rogers (see p.754) Focuses on childcare work and, of late, has handled many cases of severe non-accidental injury. His practice also includes family financial matters. **Strengths:** "Excellent advocate, very diplomatic and good with clients. A well-respected barrister in court."

Charmian Jackson (see p.681) Continues to impress interviewees as a standout up-and-comer, with a practice that encompasses public and private family law. Lately, she has gained particular experience in handling financial remedies cases which involve individuals with disabilities, debt and state benefits considerations. **Strengths:** "A rising star who is not only a safe pair of hands but is showing a true flair for advocacy. She is clear in her advice to clients and has confidence when articulating her case before the court."

St Philips Chambers

See profile on p.934

THE SET

Eminent family law team with a wide breadth of expertise in public and private law matters. The children law specialists have extensive experience of complex proceedings, from severe care cases to adoption and international child abduction. The financial remedies team also distinguishes itself by having impressive knowledge of issues such as pension arrangements, foreign assets, trusts of land and inheritance. Sources commend the skills the set's barristers bring to bear on the most complex cases and also praise the "standout " clerking.

Client service: "Senior family clerk Mark Mansell is extraordinarily helpful. I know I can always get good people there." "The clerks are excellent, they are caring and hospitable. The service is second to none."

SILKS

Elizabeth McGrath QC (see p.713) An expert family law practitioner with a broad range of experience. In children work, she has handled cases of abduction and relocation, as well as serious injury and sexual abuse. She also takes on complex financial remedy cases concerning high net worth individuals. **Strengths:** "An excellent silk. Her client care skills are second to none and she is robust in the face of difficult opponents." "A brilliant tactician and outstanding negotiator."

JUNIORS

Stephen Abberley Respected for both his undertaking of public and private children law work and complex financial proceedings, he continues to receive praise from interviewees, who highlight his impressive technical skill and analysis. **Strengths:** "Stephen is very pleasant, doesn't mess about, gets on with clients and says it like it is." "He has a great track record of getting the findings he's looking for and has a very good, individual style of advocacy and client care as well."

Christopher Adams (see p.579) A well-known junior and public children law specialist who represents local authorities, parents and children in often serious and medically complex proceedings. His recent caseload has featured the most severe cases of non-accidental injury and child death, including murder cases. **Strengths:** "Absolutely excellent, capable, competent and well prepared." "He is amazing, super bright, quiet and calm but makes his points well. He has everyone's respect."

Leisha Bond (see p.598) A standout financial provision practitioner, she represents clients in high-value cases, often involving complex property portfolios, businesses and large pensions. She has further experience of TOLATA, Schedule 1 applications and Children Act matters. **Strengths:** "Very well prepared, good with clients and polished in her presentation." "Strong, direct and no-nonsense barrister."

Rosalyn Carter (see p.612) Renowned children law specialist with expertise covering both public and private law proceedings. Care and adoption work is a notable specialism, with matters habitually involving international elements. She also handles serious injury and child death matters, and regularly takes on cases with disputed or contradictory medical evidence. **Strengths:** "Rosalyn is very good on children work, her service and commitment is second to none and she will always go the extra mile." "She's in a class of her own, she reads absolutely everything and will know everything in the bundle."

Louise McCabe (see p.711) Standout practitioner specialising in high-value financial remedies, with recent cases including complexities of farming land, company assets and tax issues. Sources are full of praise for her technical ability and forensic skill set. **Strengths:** "Destined for great things. A wonderful advocate, negotiator and communicator on all levels." "Gives sensible, pragmatic advice and also enjoys the detail of complex issues."

Vanessa Meachin (see p.714) Prominent family law specialist with a broad practice range encompassing matrimonial finance, care, adoption and private children work. Recent cases have included serious allegations of physical and sexual abuse, as well as the death of a child. **Strengths:** "Absolutely excellent, her preparation is second to none and her advocacy is excellent." "Forensic, detailed and good with clients."

Lawrence Messling (see p.716) Senior junior who focuses exclusively on serious public law children cases, in which he is regularly instructed by local authorities, parents and guardians. His caseload includes complex fact-finding cases, fabricated illnesses and multi-jurisdictional aspects. **Strengths:** "Lawrence is excellent, extremely courteous, unruffled and very hard-working." "Always well prepared and a lovely manner. I just think he's brilliant."

Jonathan Nosworthy (see p.728) Highly regarded financial practitioner specialising in high net worth financial remedy claims and TOLATA cases. His broad experience encompasses overseas assets, complicated business arrangements, pensions and third-party interveners. **Strengths:** "Jonathan is exceptionally good. He is a fierce advocate but has a great bedside manner." "Excellent client manner, thorough knowledge and preparation."

Elizabeth Walker (see p.788) Experienced family law advocate focusing on care and adoption proceedings. Her caseload includes the more serious aspects of public children law such as abuse allegations and fatalities. **Strengths:** "Incredibly bright, very personable, really on the ball and a good strategic thinker." "She is always very well prepared and good with clients."

Francesca Fothergill Extremely competent matrimonial finance advocate, with a significant reputation for her grasp of issues relating to farming and landed estates. She is frequently instructed in cases with complex forensic accountancy evidence and in international matters such as foreign prenuptial agreements. **Strengths:** "A formidable advocate, very good with agricultural cases and very approachable." "Her practical knowledge is great and she's also very bright. She has a good brain and is good at grasping the intricacies of the case."

Yolanda Pemberton (see p.736) Junior practitioner who impresses with her work on public law cases involving induced illness, serious injuries and historic or long-standing examples of sexual abuse. Particularly experienced in representing local authorities as well as parents and guardians. **Strengths:** "Very well prepared and unflappable, I have absolute confidence in her abilities."

Lucie French (see p.649) Well-reputed up-and-coming junior whose family law practice encompasses a full range of matters, including public and private children work. She also has a notable interest in TOLATA and other family finance proceedings. **Strengths:** "She is sensible, has good cross-examination technique and instils confidence." **Recent work:** Represented the defendants in a contested TOLATA trial following the death of their mother.

Band 2

St Mary's Chambers

See profile on p.977

THE SET

Based in Nottingham and specialising in family law, St Mary's Chambers houses a number of well-regarded tenants handling a full spectrum of cases. The team is highly skilled in financial cases involving high net worth assets and complex financial issues, including family businesses and agricultural interests. Additionally, the set's children law practitioners are frequently involved in the most complex and serious cases of injury, abuse, fabricated illness and child death. Interviewees are impressed, describing St Mary's as "a well-run chambers and definitely the go-to set in Nottingham."

Client service: "An excellent set, the clerks are efficient and incredibly organised. As a set they present a very united front and have good leadership on all sides." Scott Baldwin is the senior clerk.

JUNIORS

Judith Claxton Experienced family law practitioner, focusing exclusively on public children matters. She has extensive expertise in complex multiple injury cases, as well as those where allegations of sexual abuse have been made. **Strengths:** "She is excellent, thorough and hands-on." "I really rate her very highly. If I was up against it, I would go to her."

Nigel Page A highly regarded financial remedy advocate, he undertakes significant high net worth matters which frequently involve multiple properties, trusts, businesses or agricultural issues. He is highlighted by sources for his strength on complex ancillary relief cases. **Strengths:** "He is very thorough, good with clients and with the financial side of things." "He is excellent, his preparation is second to none."

Beryl Gilead Specialises in public law children work where she deals with the most complex care matters such as severe non-accidental injury claims and cases with unusual medical aspects. She represents local authorities, parents and guardians and is often appointed to take the lead on cases as sole counsel. **Strengths:** "Beryl is highly intelligent, extremely good with clients and works very hard." "She is just phenomenal, very approachable, always willing to help and happy to go the extra mile."

Jason Reece Respected barrister known for undertaking complicated children work and who is also joint head of chambers. He takes on public care cases involving emotional abuse, chronic neglect or fatal injuries, as well as private law cases such as international child abduction. His practice also covers financial remedy matters. **Strengths:** "He's very thorough, always well prepared and personable." "Very good bedside manner, very helpful and sensible in his outlook. Good on his feet and gives robust advice."

Victoria Hodges Joint head of chambers with a broad family law practice encompassing children matters such as sexual abuse allegations, non-accidental and fictitious injuries. She also handles a range of high net worth financial cases. **Strengths:** "Very enthusiastic about her work, passionate and a safe pair of hands." "Gets to grips with cases very quickly and is exceptional at cross-examination."

Gareth Jacques Practises in all areas of family law, with an equal ability to take on matrimonial finance matters and complicated children law disputes. He is further experienced in handling divorce cases involving large agricultural estates. **Strengths:** "Gareth is really competent, very skilful and a fluent advocate." "Excellent advocacy skills and tenacious in cross-examination."

Other Ranked Lawyers

John Vater QC (Harcourt Chambers) An impressive advocate who specialises in the field of children's law. He undertakes the most serious care cases such as those involving allegations of serious injury and murder. He also handles sensitive and complex private children matters. **Strengths:** "He is excellent, he got to grips with the case quickly and ran it successfully. I went to him for his medical knowledge and understanding." "Excellent in medical cases, and robust."

Andrzej Bojarski (The 36 Group) Wins praise for his financial remedies practice in which he represents clients in high-value disputes. He is frequently instructed in matters involving business assets, trusts and international aspects. **Strengths:** "Go-to individual for financial work. I know I can trust him and he will cut to the chase. He is brilliant with the client too." "A very accomplished advocate. Good on paper and in court."

Martin Kingerley (The 36 Group) Highly regarded for his expert handling of complex, high-profile children law matters, both public and private. His expertise also covers assisted conception and surrogacy. **Strengths:** "Excellent, Martin is a cut above the rest." "Professional, charming and helpful."

NORTH EASTERN

Family/Matrimonial
Leading Sets
Band 1
Zenith Chambers
Band 2
Broadway House
Dere Street Barristers
Trinity Chambers *
Leading Silks
Band 1
Lee Taryn *37 Park Square Chambers (ORL)* ◊
Band 2
Hayes John *Zenith Chambers*
Stonor Nicholas *Trinity Chambers*
Leading Juniors
Star individuals
Hajimitsis Anthony *Zenith Chambers*
Band 1
Cole Robert *Broadway House* *
Isaacs Paul *Broadway House*
Richardson James *Trinity Chambers*
Saxton Nicola *St Pauls Chambers (ORL)* ◊
Spain Timothy *Trinity Chambers*
Wood Martin *Broadway House*
Band 2
Allman Marisa *Zenith Chambers*
Astbury Joanne *Parklane Plowden (ORL)* ◊
Bickerdike Roger *Zenith Chambers*
Campbell Diane *Dere Street Barristers*
Garnham Clare *Zenith Chambers*
Hargan James *Park Square Barristers (ORL)* ◊
McCallum Louise *Zenith Chambers*
Murden Claire *Park Square Barristers (ORL)* ◊
Myers John *Zenith Chambers*
Oliver Crispin *Dere Street Barristers*
Power Nick *Broadway House*
Shaw Nicola *Trinity Chambers*
Stanistreet Penelope *St Johns Buildings (ORL)* ◊
Swiffen Guy *Zenith Chambers*
Todd Martin *Dere Street Barristers*
Band 3
Anning Sara *Parklane Plowden (ORL)* ◊
Armstrong Kester *Dere Street Barristers*
Darlington Elizabeth *Zenith Chambers*
Donnelly Lewis *Zenith Chambers*
Glover Stephen J *37 Park Square Chambers (ORL)* ◊
Gray Justin *Trinity Chambers*
Henley Carly *Dere Street Barristers*
Knox Christopher *Trinity Chambers*
Lennon Karen *Dere Street Barristers*
Moulder Pauline *Dere Street Barristers*
Shaw Elizabeth *37 Park Square Chambers (ORL)* ◊
Shelton Gordon *Broadway House*
Smith Jennie *Dere Street Barristers*
Whittaker Dornier *Zenith Chambers*
Up-and-coming individuals
Maxwell-Stewart Duncan *Parklane Plowden (ORL)* ◊
** Indicates set / individual with profile.*
◊ (ORL) = Other Ranked Lawyer.
Alphabetical order within each band. Band 1 is highest.

Band 1

Zenith Chambers

THE SET

A sizeable and high-profile set offering experts in children law, financial matters and adult care. Its barristers are regularly instructed in high net worth divorce proceedings and cases concerning TOLATA, same-sex families and surrogacy law, while the designated children team handles both public and private matters. In addition to its sterling reputation for advocacy, Zenith Chambers also offers strength in ADR such as collaborative law and mediation.

Client service: "Senior family clerk Rebecca Hartley is incredibly efficient, really helpful and will always go the extra mile." "The clerks are exceptionally organised and always keep us informed."

SILKS

John Hayes QC Regularly instructed to handle complicated care proceedings, including cases concerning allegations of serious abuse and neglect. He specialises in public law, representing parents, guardians and local authorities alike, and is particularly experienced in managing complex legal and medical evidence. **Strengths:** "He is great, you couldn't fault him." "He did a very capable job in a difficult case, and is able to explain very complex medical issues." **Recent work:** Represented Leeds City Council in the first reported case concerning female genital mutilation heard by the English family courts.

JUNIORS

Anthony Hajimitsis An enormously popular and respected senior junior who specialises in high-value matrimonial finance and divorce proceedings. He is widely praised for his strong intellect and calm manner in court, as well as his ready command of the technical details of a case. **Strengths:** "He absolutely knows his stuff. He's so thorough, he knows the case inside out and has great attention to detail. He's also absolutely fantastic with clients, and handles difficult cases very well."

Clare Garnham Previously practised as a solicitor and now acts in a range of high-profile public law cases. Her chief focus is on representing children in cases centring on abduction and abuse claims, while she also handles a number of serious non-accidental injury and child death cases. **Strengths:** "Your go-to family lawyer, she has a broad range of expertise and really knows what she's doing."

Louise McCallum Covers public and private law matters, representing parents, guardians and local authorities in challenging care proceedings. She has notable expertise in forced marriage cases and is also experienced in dealing with serious claims of non-accidental injury and sexual abuse. **Strengths:** "She is bloody fantastic, very calm, composed and civil, irrespective of how unreasonable your opponent can be."

Marisa Allman An expert on the modern family, Marisa Allman offers impressive knowledge on the law surrounding such matters as surrogacy, fertility and same-sex relationships. She also has considerable expertise in the financial repercussions arising from family breakdown, including those cases with an international aspect. **Strengths:** "Outstanding attention to detail, incredibly thorough, really calm and professional. I just cannot fault her." **Recent work:** Served as advocate to the court in a case where a donor father was seeking declaration of parentage.

Roger Bickerdike An authority on matrimonial finance and private law children work, who is particularly adept at handling complicated and high-value financial remedy proceedings. He is commended for his cross-examination skills, technical abilities and effective communication with clients and instructing solicitors. **Strengths:** "Technically excellent with a really good eye for detail. He's very good on his feet and able to offer sensible advice."

John Myers A fierce advocate who remains a popular choice for tough children cases. He has over 30 years' experience in family law and is regularly instructed on difficult public and private law cases concerning allegations of abuse and neglect. **Strengths:** "A tenacious and committed advocate who is also good on client care."

Guy Swiffen A dedicated children specialist whose remit spans both the public and the private spheres. He has experience acting on behalf of local authorities as well as parents and guardians on complex cases concerning neglect, sexual abuse and child death. **Strengths:** "He is superb in his advocacy skills and his knowledge of the law – he's absolutely excellent."

Dornier Whittaker Extremely skilled in private law work relating to children as well as financial family disputes. She has previously advised on complicated separations involving farming and corporate assets, in addition to complex child relocations. **Strengths:** "She is sensible, charming and empathetic, and really excellent at managing difficult people."

Elizabeth Darlington Highly regarded for her expertise in property and chancery law, she is frequently the top choice for solicitors handling TOLATA and cohabitation disputes. **Strengths:** "She has an excellent knowledge in the complex area of trusts of land work, has a good client manner, and is calm, thorough and well prepared." **Recent work:** Represented the proprietor of a residential property and cafe whose former cohabitee was seeking an interest in both.

Lewis Donnelly Dedicated to defending individuals and families in complex children law cases, including those relating to permanence orders, serious injury and religious radicalisation. He is extremely well practised in public law care proceedings, with recent experience before the High Court and the Court of Appeal. **Strengths:** "His attention to detail and knowledge of the law is second to none." **Recent work:** Acted on behalf of a father, successfully appealing an order of the family court stating that foster carers should be granted party status in care proceedings.

Band 2

Broadway House

THE SET

Broadway House fields a broad spread of barristers covering the full range of financial and children matters. Especially respected for its money work, the set boasts some of the region's leading experts in ancillary relief, and also has individuals who are well capable of handling complex TOLATA and inheritance proceedings.

Client service: "They're really professional: the barristers we use are all excellent, and the clerks manage everything we send them very well." Robin Slade is the set's senior civil and family clerk.

JUNIORS

Robert Cole (see p.620) A noted expert in high-value ancillary relief cases, who also deals with TOLATA and Inheritance Act claims. His previous time in practice as an accountant makes him a sure hand in managing difficult financial and business issues arising from divorce and separation. **Strengths:** "A confident and impressive advocate with good client skills."

Paul Isaacs A renowned authority on big money cases, Paul Isaacs is one of the most experienced senior juniors on the North Eastern Circuit. Much of his practice centres on high-stakes separations involving ultra high net worth individuals, where he is singled out for his intelligence and the strength of his advocacy. **Strengths:** "He has great intellectual skills, and I don't think I've seen anyone better at cross-examination – he's the guy you want on your side at the final hearing."

Martin Wood Maintains a strong reputation in the market as a leading finance expert, particularly in the field of ancillary relief. He is eminently capable of taking on the most complex financial disputes involving business assets, offshore trusts, pensions and inheritance claims. **Strengths:** "He's at the top of the tree on the finance side of things." "One of the safest pairs of hands for really complex matters."

Nick Power A former solicitor, Nick Power is becoming a first-choice junior for many solicitors handling money work. He is also commended for his expertise on child law and, in particular, his ability to handle emotionally fraught cases with sensitivity and tact. **Strengths:** "He has very good technical ability and a great client manner, I would recommend him without hesitation." "He tends to be my go-to because of his experience and his ability with clients."

Gordon Shelton A highly regarded and established family law barrister who offers impressive experience on a mix of children and finance cases. He is noted for his skilled handling of complex and high net worth matrimonial finance disputes. **Strengths:** "Very knowledgeable and friendly with clear straightforward advice. He is an excellent advocate."

Dere Street Barristers

THE SET

Dere Street has chambers in York and Newcastle and houses barristers who cover the full range of family law, and have an exceptional reputation for public and private children work. Barristers at the set regularly handle complex childcare and Court of Protection proceedings, including those that concern substantial international interests and medical elements. The set also takes on a range of financial work that covers marital and cohabitation disputes, many of which are of substantial value.

Client service: "Efficient and reliable. The clerks are excellent and attentive, and will always help us out." The head clerk is Kevin Beaumont and the senior family clerk is Neil Gibson.

JUNIORS

Diane Campbell An expert on complex childcare matters, she regularly acts in cases concerning neglect or abuse, including many that involve accompanying criminal proceedings. She is also extremely good at handling cases which require an understanding of complicated medical evidence, such as fabricated illness or non-accidental injury. **Strengths:** "She is very careful in ensuring her client understands and is comfortable with everything." "Tenacious and thorough."

Crispin Oliver Well-respected senior junior who is also head of chambers. He specialises in financial orders and high-value ancillary relief, and wins praise for his client communication skills and ability to tackle cases concerning complex and international assets. **Strengths:** "Very experienced, he picks things up quickly and is good at getting into the subtleties of the case." "In a complicated case, he knew which areas to focus on and was very easy to work with. We were so glad to have him on board."

Martin Todd Known for the quality of his expertise in difficult children work, including claims of sexual abuse, factitious illness and serious head injuries. Represents parents and local authorities on both sides of cases which are often factually and medically challenging. **Strengths:** "He has a good eye for detail and very calm manner, which judges like."

Kester Armstrong An established figure praised for her rigorous representation and in-court skills. Her experience spans a range of complex children matters, and she recently acted on a significant cross-border care case.

Karen Lennon Has a broad family practice incorporating both financial and children work. She is very familiar with care and wardship proceedings, and has experience handling complex cases of injury, abuse and neglect on behalf of parents, children and local authorities. **Strengths:** "A real battler who makes clients feel she's on their side, and never lets them get steamrollered into something they're not comfortable with."

Pauline Moulder A very experienced senior junior who is known for her collaborative approach. Exceptionally well versed in childcare law, she represents parents, children and local authorities alike in complex cases of serious injury, child relocation and stillbirth. **Strengths:** "I can recommend her without reservation. The advice, support, guidance and experience you gain from working with her is great."

Jennie Smith Experienced in public and private family law matters, with a particular focus on cases involving vulnerable adults. Also manages a substantial caseload of finance work, including ancillary relief and cohabitation disputes. **Strengths:** "Good at high net worth money cases." "I would instruct her if I wanted someone to rigorously present a case."

Carly Henley A public law specialist, she regularly acts on child abuse and serious non-accidental injuries cases. Her role as an assistant coroner means she is particularly adept at handling highly technical medical and factual evidence on a case. **Strengths:** "Always well prepared. A courageous and accomplished advocate." "She is top class: extremely hard-working and very forensic in her approach. I would choose Carly for a case where the issues are technically difficult."

Trinity Chambers

See profile on p.975

THE SET

A well-regarded set for both finance and children work, operating from Newcastle and Middlesbrough. Provides robust advocacy at all levels of the court system and also has ample expertise in ADR, boasting as it does several accredited arbitrators and mediators in its ranks. Members of Trinity Chambers have recently been instructed in novel matters pertaining to issues of radicalisation and child harm, as well as high-value ancillary relief cases.

Client service: "We find the clerks very accommodating, helpful and easy to get hold of. They do all they can to help us, even at the last minute or at short notice." Simon Stewart is the practice director, while Kevin McLafferty and Steven Preen are the civil and family clerks.

SILKS

Nicholas Stonor QC Head of the family group, he is widely admired for his work on complex childcare proceedings. He regularly acts in the public sphere on cases involving complex medical, religious and cultural issues, including forced marriage. In addition to this, he also advises on divorce and private law children matters. **Strengths:** "He is a superb performer, his preparation is fantastic and his manner with everyone is excellent: frankly, he's your dream silk!" "Such an excellent advocate, he's always thoroughly prepared and he offers fantastic courtroom presence and excellent cross-examination skills."

JUNIORS

James Richardson Focuses his practice on family finance work, including cohabitation claims as well as traditional ancillary relief work. He regularly represents high net worth individuals in complicated disputes involving substantial business, property and financial concerns. **Strengths:** "Always thoroughly prepared, very good in court, and his points are very thorough." "A very diligent, detailed man who knows his law." **Recent work:** Acted for the applicant in a financial remedies case which centred on a considerable personal injury award.

Timothy Spain Known for his expertise in money and children work, he is a strong advocate who is also an accredited family arbitrator. He has handled a number of complex financial cases involving farms, insolvency and hidden wealth, and has considerable familiarity with TOLATA claims. **Strengths:** "If you've got a tricky case and need someone to go in and fight your corner, he will do it." "For both complex children and financial matters, he's a go-to if you need anything technical or difficult with regard to the law."

Nicola Shaw An experienced junior who is praised for her straightforward and thorough approach, and who is highly knowledgeable in ancillary relief and TOLATA proceedings. Known for her excellent negotiation skills, she is a qualified arbitrator and has additional training in collaborative law. **Strengths:** "She's precisely what you need in any aggressive case; sensible, pragmatic and even-handed." "She is erudite, clever, very good with clients and a strong negotiator."

Justin Gray A respected advocate who handles the full range of children law, and has particular specialisms in adoption, surrogacy, forced marriage and international relocation. Also handles cases concerning vulnerable adults and other Court of Protection matters. **Strengths:** "He has a good brain and is very good on complex technical issues." "Great in court, really excellent."

Christopher Knox Vastly experienced senior junior who has an excellent reputation for money work. He specialises in high-value ancillary relief cases with corporate issues, and receives praise for his tenacious approach in court. **Strengths:** "A terrific cross-examiner, he'll fight our corner to the end of the earth." "He's been doing it for years but he's so enthusiastic, he makes every client feel they're his only case."

Other Ranked Lawyers

Taryn Lee QC (37 Park Square Chambers) Experienced family silk who is also joint head of chambers. She has a huge amount of expertise in children law, which extends to same-sex adoptions, paternity disputes and child relocation as well as severe cases of child abuse and injury. **Strengths:** "A very senior silk who is very well thought of in her field."

Stephen Glover (37 Park Square Chambers) Joint head of chambers and a specialist in financial remedy work, he is praised for his tactical skills and offers considerable courtroom experience. He is known for advising on complex property, trust and inheritance issues. **Strengths:** "A recognised practitioner for matrimonial finance who is very good at what he does."

Elizabeth Shaw (37 Park Square Chambers) Senior junior who is an established expert on children matters specialising in complicated care proceedings. She has significant experience of public and private law and regularly acts for children, parents and local authorities.

Joanne Astbury (Parklane Plowden) Head of the family team at Parklane Plowden, Joanne Astbury focuses her practice on public children law and care proceedings. She has particular experience representing children as well as clients of all ages who have mental health and learning difficulties. **Strengths:** "Very well regarded. She's excellent, you can't fault her."

Sara Anning (Parklane Plowden) A specialist in children work, who acts for guardians, children and local authorities and has particular experience in cases concerning allegations of severe harm, including physical and sexual abuse. Also takes on cases concerning same-sex parenting and artificial insemination. **Recent work:** Acted for the maternal grandmother in a High Court case concerning the death of a disabled mother and the subsequent care of her disabled son.

Duncan Maxwell-Stewart (Parklane Plowden) Has a diverse practice covering finance and children work. He handles a range of public and private children law cases, including abuse and injury claims, while also taking on matrimonial finance matters that cover issues such as inherited wealth, farms, trusts, foreign assets and pensions. **Strengths:** "I've used him on both children and finance stuff. Clients love him and I'm really impressed by him." **Recent work:** Represented the mother in a finding of fact hearing concerning an alleged non-accidental injury, which resulted in her exoneration.

James Hargan (Park Square Barristers) Handles a wide range of complex public childcare proceedings, although he is especially adept at cases concerning serious non-accidental injury. He is noted for his excellent client communication and particularly for his careful management of challenging parental figures. **Strengths:** "Highly experienced counsel with excellent technical skills and the ability to reassure clients in difficult and challenging circumstances."

Claire Murden (Park Square Barristers) Deputy head of the family team, she wins praise for her reassuring demeanour and excellent trial preparation. She regularly advises parents, guardians and local authorities in care proceedings and is often instructed on cases with complex medical and legal aspects. **Strengths:** "She has a calm, reassuring and persuasive manner which complements her excellent technical skills."

Pennie Stanistreet (St Johns Buildings) Specialist child law expert who typically acts for parents and local authorities. She has a background in criminal as well as family law, and many of her most significant cases have concerned complex injuries and medical concerns. **Strengths:** "An oracle, she is absolutely the person you'll go to with any query." "Down-to-earth, tenacious and always fights clients' corners effectively."

Nicola Saxton (St Pauls Chambers) Senior junior who is well known for her expertise in ancillary relief and other financial work. She frequently advises high net worth individuals on cases involving significant corporate assets as well as foreign and domestic trusts. Also takes on applications under the Schedule 1 Children Act and TOLATA. **Strengths:** "She's just brilliant, extremely good technically and she will really fight your corner for you."

NORTHERN

Family/Matrimonial
Leading Sets
Band 1
Deans Court Chambers *
St Johns Buildings *
Band 2
Exchange Chambers *
Leading Silks
Band 1
Harrison Sally *St Johns Buildings*
Band 2
Cross Jane *Deans Court Chambers*
Grocott Susan *Deans Court Chambers*
Heaton Frances *St Johns Buildings*
Rowley Karl *St Johns Buildings*
* Indicates set / individual with profile.
◊ (ORL) = Other Ranked Lawyer.
Alphabetical order within each band. Band 1 is highest.

Family/Matrimonial
Leading Juniors
Band 1
Brody Karen *Deans Court Chambers*
Eastwood Charles P *St Johns Buildings*
Fordham Judith *Exchange Chambers*
Kloss Alexander W *St Johns Buildings*
Murray Ashley *Ashley Murray Chambers (ORL)* ◊
Band 2
Bennett Abigail *St Johns Buildings*
Bowcock Samantha *15 Winckley Square (ORL)* ◊
Deas Susan *Deans Court Chambers*
Guirguis Sheren *Exchange Chambers*
Hillas Samantha *St Johns Buildings*
Reade Kevin *7 Harrington St Chambers (ORL)* ◊ *
Woodward Alison *Deans Court Chambers*
Band 3
Bennett Martyn *Oriel Chambers (ORL)* ◊
Birtles Samantha *18 St John Street (ORL)* ◊ *
Cavanagh Lorraine *St Johns Buildings*
Dawar Archna *Deans Court Chambers*
Greenhalgh Emma *9 St John Street (ORL)* ◊
Gregg Rebecca *Deans Court Chambers*
Gregory Karen *Exchange Chambers*
Heppenstall Rachael *9 St John Street (ORL)* ◊
Hobson Heather *Deans Court Chambers*

Band 1

Deans Court Chambers

See profile on p.964

THE SET

This highly respected set fields an exceptional team of barristers with significant family law experience, particularly in the area of child protection. Its members are accustomed to taking on highly complex public and private cases that often concern difficult issues such as induced illness, sexual abuse and serious head injuries. The set is also adept at handling matrimonial finance cases, including significant high-value financial remedies. Barristers at the set are described by sources as "approachable, with an excellent reputation for advocacy," and the set also receives high praise for its levels of client care.

Client service: "Their clerking team is the best in Manchester, no doubt. They're always clear on fees, and they make sure you get the barrister you want." "A very good, strong set with excellent clerking." Matthew Gibbons is the set's senior clerk and Martin Leech is head of the family clerking team.

SILKS

Jane Cross QC Highlighted for her expertise in handling public children matters, including serious injury and death cases. She is also well known for her involvement in difficult disputes regarding neglect and sexual abuse. **Strengths:** "I rate her highly, she's meticulous in her preparation." "Excellent on childcare."

Susan Grocott QC Has a diverse practice, advising on a range of finance issues in addition to public and private children work. Her caseload includes an emphasis on negligence, serious injuries and induced illness. **Strengths:** "Provides robust, pragmatic and client-centric advice. She is a pleasure to work with." "She is very driven to meeting her client's needs and a pleasure to work with."

JUNIORS

Karen Brody Highly respected for her work in the private child and matrimonial finance spaces. She is especially proficient at handling disputes involving hidden, dissipated or missing assets. **Strengths:** "She has an incisive grasp of key issues, pragmatic negotiation skills and very strong advocacy." "A superb advocate who is no-nonsense and practical."

Susan Deas Provides advice on financial remedy matters arising from divorce and relationship breakdowns, regularly acting for high net worth individuals. She is additionally able to handle private children cases. **Strengths:** "Has a very good manner with clients and is very pragmatic." "I can commend Susan for her professionalism, conscientiousness, helpfulness and impressive client focus."

Alison Woodward Best known for her expertise in representing parents and children on public children matters, although she can also take on private disputes. She regularly undertakes cases involving neglect, serious injury and sexual abuse. **Strengths:** "She is undoubtedly extremely experienced at children work. Well respected by judges, and user-friendly for both professional and lay clients." "Really good for children work."

Rebecca Gregg Primarily handles children law cases, tackling public and private work. She acts for parents, guardians and local authorities in neglect, sexual harm and non-accidental injury cases. **Strengths:** "Careful, considered, immaculately prepared, and brings new perspectives to cases." "An excellent advocate, very popular among solicitors."

Archna Dawar Handles complicated children matters as well as high-value financial remedy work, and has a solid reputation for advising on cross-cultural issues. She is experienced at taking on cases concerning cohabitation and property division. **Strengths:** "Really great for children work." "Her ability to absorb vast quantities of information in a short time is very impressive. She gets to the nub of the case quickly, and she is equally as good on children cases as she is on finance cases."

Heather Hobson Acts for parents, children and local authorities on public and private family law, and has experience working on international cases. She also regularly advises on financial remedy disputes. **Strengths:** "Deals very thoroughly with large quantities of information and presents it in a manageable form." "Extremely articulate and impressive advocate in complex private children cases."

St Johns Buildings

See profile on p.970

THE SET

St Johns Buildings boasts a very deep and experienced bench that one instructing solicitor credits with "a spread and depth of talent in family law unrivalled in the North West." Members offer a broad array of expertise that includes cases involving inherited wealth, bankruptcy, occupation orders, prenups and TOLATA disputes. The set also adopts a notably modern approach to its work and is mentioned by one source as "a forward-thinking super set designed for the 21st century."

Client service: "Their clerks are generally responsive and realistic when agreeing fees." "The clerks are helpful, responsive to our needs and are flexible." Paul Laverty leads the family clerking team.

SILKS

Sally Harrison QC Hugely respected for her skill at taking on high-profile and high-value matrimonial finance matters. She recently took a significant financial remedy case to the Supreme Court, representing the wife's interests in the dispute. **Strengths:** "Combines excellent client care skills with pragmatic advice, rigorous attention to detail, effective negotiation and fearsome advocacy." "Sally is a sparkling advocate who is commanding and charismatic both inside the courtroom and outside."

Karl Rowley QC A children law specialist who has a wealth of experience advising on private and public cases. His areas of expertise include international adoptions and child death. **Strengths:** "He is thorough and has a calm court manner." "He finds unusual arguments and angles to cases and uses them very skilfully."

Frances Heaton QC Focuses her practice on children law, representing parents, children and local authorities on private and public matters. She has worked on numerous cases involving sexual abuse and serious injury, and also has expertise in international adoption and surrogacy. **Strengths:** "She is wonderful on surrogacy work."

JUNIORS

Charles Eastwood Specialises in taking on financial remedy work, and has experience representing high net worth individuals on cases concerning pensions, trusts and businesses. He also has considerable knowledge of issues surrounding inheritance. **Strengths:** "A thorough, good communicator with excellent advocacy skills." "His knowledge and experience make him suitable for the most complex of cases."

Alexander Kloss Senior junior who focuses on representing clients on high-value financial remedy matters. He has a particular flair for disputes that involve the negotiation of prenuptial agreements, business valuations and farm ownership. **Strengths:** "Intelligent, calm and reassuring for clients. He has the rare gift of knowing when to do the deal and when to fight." "He is thorough, liked by clients and an excellent advocate."

Abigail Bennett Best known for her work on matrimonial finance issues, Abigail Bennett is also a trained collaborative lawyer. Her practice extends to work in private children law, where she has experience in surrogacy, same-sex parenting and donor conception. **Strengths:** "Very polished and good with complex money cases." "Quickly grasps the issues and is confident in managing client expectations."

Samantha Hillas Very well thought of in the market for her experience handling notable matrimonial finance cases, often of considerable value. She was recently involved in the high-profile Gohil v Gohil case heard in the Supreme Court. **Strengths:** "A robust character; she tells it like it is, but is very clever and analytical." "She has a wonderful manner with clients and is able to instil confidence from the outset. The case preparation is detailed and well presented. She is great on her feet and a very strong advocate."

Lorraine Cavanagh Focuses on representing clients in children law cases, and has notable expertise in fatal and serious non-accidental injury matters. She also advises on wardship for children with major psychological issues. **Strengths:** "Lorraine Cavanagh is a hugely experienced barrister who brings an enormous amount of technical knowledge and empathy to her child law cases." "She is bright and extremely hard-working, and has a keen eye for detail."

Band 2

Exchange Chambers

See profile on p.956

THE SET

Based in Leeds, Liverpool and Manchester, Exchange Chambers houses a solid group of barristers experienced in a wide variety of family law matters. The set has real strength in advising on matrimonial finance issues and has recently been engaged on a number of significant high-value divorce disputes. Members are also well equipped to deal with children law cases, and the group wins praise overall for its "great legal experience and excellent client care."

Client service: "The clerking is amazing, I rate theirs as the best in Liverpool." "The clerks are always happy to assist with any issues and will go above and beyond to try and resolve any issues." The clerking team is led by chambers director Tom Handley, and the civil law team in Liverpool by Rachel Williams and Sarah Rotherham.

JUNIORS

Judith Fordham Focuses on handling difficult matrimonial finance matters, and is also head of the set's family team. She is skilled at taking on TOLATA, inheritance and ancillary relief cases, and demonstrates particular understanding of disputes involving farms. **Strengths:** "Very competent and thorough practitioner known for her tenacious approach to her cases." "Highly experienced and very well respected."

Sheren Guirguis Specialises in private children law, as well as finanical remedy and inheritance matters, and also has notable experience in trusts work. She wins praise for her pragmatic and sensitive approach to cases. **Strengths:** "Very well prepared, good with clients and a good advocate." "Strikes a good balance between being firm and doing what the client needs."

Karen Gregory Best known for her experience in taking on high-value ancillary relief and matrimonial finance cases, with over 20 years' experience in the field. She often advises on complex matters concerning pensions, businesses and overseas assets. **Strengths:** "Very thorough and detailed." "Meticulous in her preparation, and always knows her cases inside and out."

Other Ranked Lawyers

Ashley Murray (Ashley Murray Chambers) Specialises in advising on divorce and related financial remedy issues. He also represents clients in cases concerning cohabitation and ancillary relief. **Strengths:** "Ashley is unflappable and always impeccably prepared." "One of the most experienced counsel in the North West. His preparation is second to none."

Kevin Reade (see p.749) (7 Harrington St Chambers) Well known for his diverse practice, representing clients in both matrimonial finance and private children cases. **Strengths:** "Excellent reputation as a tenacious advocate."

Martyn Bennett (Oriel Chambers) Highly experienced at taking on major complex finance cases. He regularly acts for high net worth individuals on financial remedies matters and also takes on ancillary relief work and some private children cases. **Strengths:** "I find him extremely thorough and very good."

Samantha Birtles (see p.596) (18 St John Street) Enjoys a solid reputation for her children law work and advises on public and private matters. **Strengths:** "Extremely experienced. Very popular with both professionals and lay clients."

Emma Greenhalgh (9 St John Street) Focus on children cases, with childcare issues being a particular specialism. She also acts for children, parents and local authorities in sexual abuse, non-accidental injury and induced illness matters. **Strengths:** "She is thorough and passionate about her cases." "Personable, intelligent and really thinks about her cases."

Rachael Heppenstall (9 St John Street) Specialises in matters regarding childcare, and also has a solid reputation for her skill in handling claims of factitious illness and physical and sexual assault.

Samantha Bowcock (15 Winckley Square) Children law specialist who advises parents, children and local authorities on both public and private matters.

SOUTH EASTERN

Family/Matrimonial
Leading Sets
Band 1
Harcourt Chambers *
Band 2
Crown Office Row *
Leading Silks
Band 1
Judd Frances *Harcourt Chambers*
Vater John *Harcourt Chambers*
Band 2
Goodwin Nicholas *Harcourt Chambers*
New Silks
Vine Aidan *Harcourt Chambers*
Leading Juniors
Band 1
Hay Fiona *Harcourt Chambers*
Sampson Jonathan *Harcourt Chambers*
Sharghy Pegah *Crown Office Row*
Band 2
Adamson Louisa *Becket Chambers (ORL)* ◊
Battie Eleanor *Crown Office Row*
Carrodus Gail *Huntercombe Chambers (ORL)* ◊
Farrington Gemma *Stour Chambers (ORL)* ◊
Hall Jeremy *42 Bedford Row (ORL)* ◊
Kefford Anthony *Fenners Chambers (ORL)* ◊
Mehta Anita *Crown Office Row*
Porter Joanne *Stour Chambers (ORL)* ◊
Smith Adam *Crown Office Row* [A]
Spinks Roderick *Fenners Chambers (ORL)* ◊
Tahir Perican *1 King's Bench Walk (ORL)* ◊ *
Walden-Smith David *29 Bedford Row Chambers (ORL)* ◊ *
Watson Duncan *1 Garden Court Family Law (ORL)* ◊ *
Band 3
Brooke-Smith John *Trinity Chambers (ORL)* ◊
Bundell Katharine *Fenners Chambers (ORL)* ◊
Campbell Jane *6 Pump Court (ORL)* ◊
Claridge Rachael *Crown Office Row* [A]
Hancock Maria *Westgate Chambers (ORL)* ◊
Topping Caroline *6 Pump Court (ORL)* ◊
Wall Christopher *Becket Chambers (ORL)* ◊
Up-and-coming individuals
Kochnari Kate *Stour Chambers (ORL)* ◊
Slee Lydia *Stour Chambers (ORL)* ◊
Spence Elizabeth *Stour Chambers (ORL)* ◊
* *Indicates set / individual with profile.*
[A] *direct access (see p.24).*
◊ *(ORL) = Other Ranked Lawyer.*
Alphabetical order within each band. Band 1 is highest.

Band 1

Harcourt Chambers

See profile on p.858

THE SET

Harcourt Chambers enjoys an outstanding reputation in the South East for children matters, and also benefits from its significant presence in London. Its pre-eminent team tackles complex proceedings, handling, among others, cases concerning physical and sexual abuse and child abduction. The set also boasts a team of financial specialists who regularly tackle high-value cross-border cases involving highly complicating factors such as trusts, company arrangements and convoluted pensions provision. Many of the cases handled by the barristers here are international in nature.

Client service: "The set is well managed by Simon Boutwood. They are always asking how they could do better, if they could be any more accommodating and accessible." "They are easy to use, the barristers and clerks are all very user-friendly, and they make sure of their availabilities."

SILKS

Frances Judd QC An expert in private and public children law matters, Frances Judd QC handles cases relating to surrogacy and parental responsibility, sudden infant death and child sexual abuse. She is much admired for her knowledge of international and domestic relocation law, and is regularly briefed by guardians, parents and local authorities. **Strengths:** "Frances remains our first-choice children silk. She addresses subjects with finesse and sensitivity, but is calm and reassuring with clients." "She sees the long-term, not the short-term, gain for a client and is a voice of wisdom and experience."

John Vater QC Focusing on public children law matters, Vater is particularly adept at handing sensitive cases containing complex medical evidence. He is skilled at representing local authorities and parents in cases concerning relocation and surrogacy, while also taking on private international adoption work. **Strengths:** "He has wonderful in-depth knowledge of medical issues, he is exceptionally well prepared, and fights his client's corner." "He's a fearsome and superb advocate."

Nicholas Goodwin QC An extremely experienced silk who regularly handles public and private children law proceedings as well as financial remedy work. He is highly regarded for his participation in cases concerning non-accidental injury and infant fatalities, while also advising adopters and local authorities in international adoption cases. **Strengths:** "He is cerebral and well organised, he's good on the science and medical evidence." "His attention to detail is second to none; nothing escapes him. He is a worthy silk, and client-friendly with it."

Aidan Vine QC Vine is a skilled advocate who is experienced in matrimonial finance and children cases, often with an international element. He has appeared with regularity in the High Court and Court of Appeal, and also regularly lectures and publishes on family law matters. **Strengths:** "His skill lies in his intellectual approach to law." "He has an excellent manner with clients."

JUNIORS

Jonathan Sampson Specialising in high net worth matrimonial finance, Jonathan Sampson is particularly adept at handling finance cases involving significant trust and business assets, as well as those with international aspects. He also takes on public care cases relating to children and vulnerable adults. **Strengths:** "He really thinks about cases and is superb in court." "Very polished but devastating in cross-examination."

Fiona Hay Senior junior who is esteemed for her expertise in financial relief and particularly sought after for her knowledge of cases involving pensions. A published expert on this subject, she wins praise for her ability to get to grips with the complexities of difficult financial arrangements. **Strengths:** "Remarkably effective, she gets results." "Her strength lies in her analytical skills and expertise in pensions, which is second to none."

Band 2

Crown Office Row

See profile on p.826

THE SET

Known for its strength and breadth of expertise in the area of family law, Crown Office Row boasts an impressive group of barristers in its flourishing Brighton office. The team has extensive experience in cases that concern children and vulnerable adults, and regularly handles matters concerning care and supervision orders, Section 8 applications, domestic violence hearings and Court of Protection issues. They also undertake a full range of family finance issues arising from divorce and civil partnership dissolution as well as cases concerning TOLATA and the Inheritance Act.

Client service: "The clerking is very professional and helpful. They are happy to discuss fees with clients. Not all sets have such attentive and responsive clerks, they go over and above!" David Bingham is the senior clerk at Crown Office Row.

JUNIORS

Pegah Sharghy Acclaimed for her specialism in family finance, Peggy Sharghy is able to handle the most complex of financial proceedings involving inheritance, company and children aspects. Sources laud her strong advocacy skills and outstanding technical ability. **Strengths:** "She is the best for complex advice in tricky situations." "A winning advocate. She is concise, clear and well liked by clients and judges."

Eleanor Battie Instructed in private and public children matters in every tier of the family court; she is also developing a growing practice in Court of Protection work. She regularly represents parents and local authorities in care proceedings, often involving difficult international aspects or abuse allegations. **Strengths:** "She has excellent advocacy skills, she prepares thoroughly and really fights the client's case." "She is a very tenacious and fearsome opponent."

Anita Mehta Specialises in private family law, concentrating on financial remedy matters that often include complicated company, pensions and international aspects. She also boasts a particular expertise in Schedule 1 Children Act applications. **Strengths:** "She's a very energetic, resourceful and enthusiastic advocate in financial provision." "She has a good eye for detail and takes a very pragmatic approach, which clients appreciate."

Adam Smith With over 25 years of experience in family law, Adam Smith is highly respected for his expertise in children matters. He is instructed on behalf of parents, children and their guardians on a variety of issues but is especially esteemed for his handling of non-accidental injury cases. **Strengths:** "He is hard-working and dedicated to obtaining the very best result for the client."

Rachael Claridge Junior who practises in all areas of family law but is particularly focused on child protection issues. She has significant experience in public law matters and is a sought-after advocate for parents, local authorities and guardians. She is equally capable of handling private law cases such as contact disputes and child relocation. **Strengths:** "Really good childcare lawyer." "Explains very complicated matters to clients in a straightforward way."

Other Ranked Lawyers

Louisa Adamson (Becket Chambers) A highly experienced family lawyer and mediator who is particularly esteemed for her work in public law children cases, including care and adoption proceedings. She is adept at dealing with cases involving parents who exhibit learning difficulties or challenging behaviour. **Strengths:** "Her client care is excellent, especially with vulnerable individuals." "She is efficient and thorough."

Christopher Wall (Becket Chambers) Junior who is predominantly instructed in matrimonial finance matters and public law children work. He has distinguished experience of complex disputes concerning private companies, trusts and international assets, and also regularly tackles difficult children cases involving abuse and neglect. **Strengths:** "Highly experienced and has great depth of knowledge." "He is a very sensible barrister, the sort who will tell clients exactly how it is and will manage their expectations. He has a calm, reassuring manner and is very experienced."

Jeremy Hall (42 Bedford Row) An exclusively family law practitioner with over 20 years' experience, Jeremy Hall has a highly regarded practice in public law children cases and financial remedy work. The majority of his instructions are on behalf of parents but he also represents local authorities and children, often in serious cases of alleged abuse. **Strengths:** "He's friendly and approachable with clients but stands by his advice." "Good to work with, helpful and his legal knowledge is excellent."

David Walden-Smith (see p.788) (29 Bedford Row Chambers) Highly regarded family finance specialist with a strong expertise in matters involving complex company valuations, assets, trust and tax issues. He also takes on Schedule 1 applications as well as a range of other private children work. **Strengths:** "An exceptional advocate, pragmatic and focused. He's authoritative, effective, and assertive in the courtroom." "A particular specialist in financial and children matters, his depth of preparation is second to none."

Anthony Kefford (Fenners Chambers) Highlighted for his expertise in matrimonial finance, trust and inheritance disputes and prenuptial agreements. He also regularly handles matters relating to TOLATA and Children Act cases. **Strengths:** "Simply excellent. Very thorough and very knowledgeable. Clients have absolute faith in him." "He is consistently strong in his advice and approach."

Roderick Spinks (Fenners Chambers) Highly regarded for his knowledge of TOLATA proceedings, financial remedy cases and prenuptial and post-nuptial agreements. Often acts for high net worth individuals on cases that involve complicated assets, trusts and international concerns. **Strengths:** "He is meticulous in his presentation and brings charm and charisma to the presentation of cases." "He is very well regarded in finance and a terrific negotiator in court."

Katharine Bundell (Fenners Chambers) Diverse practice in family law, providing advice on all matters relating to financial remedy and trusts of land disputes, in addition to a wide range of public and private children work. She often takes on financial cases concerning tricky jurisdictional and company-related issues. **Strengths:** "Her knowledge of the law is second to none and always up to date." "Katharine is capable of putting even the most nervous of clients at their ease, and is a joy to work with from the point of view of a solicitor."

Duncan Watson (see p.791) (1 Garden Court Family Law Chambers) Focuses on family finance matters, and is an expert in financial remedies concerning divorce, cohabitation disputes and Schedule 1 applications. He is noted for his ability to handle complex cases relating to partnerships, companies, trusts and assets. **Strengths:** "He is extremely good on money cases, very particular and good at addressing the detail." "He is good with demanding clients, very patient and unshakable in his views, and also very methodical."

Gail Carrodus (Huntercombe Chambers) Specialises in complex financial matters and has noteworthy, far-reaching experience in financial remedy cases. She is frequently instructed on behalf of high net worth clients who have international financial interests.

Perican Tahir (see p.777) (1 King's Bench Walk) Strong reputation as a specialist in matrimonial finance, cohabitation disputes and Schedule 1 applications. She also has extensive experience with private law children matters, particularly in cases involving child abduction. **Strengths:** "A determined and efficient advocate, Perican's pragmatic, analytical and incisive approach achieves consistent success and makes her one of our first choices for counsel."

Jane Campbell (6 Pump Court) Widely respected for her expertise in financial remedies, Jane Campbell also works on private law children cases. Recently, she has been involved in advising on an overseas divorce, as well as cases protecting vulnerable clients in residence disputes and financial remedy proceedings. She has also been appointed to sit as a Deputy District Judge. **Strengths:** "Very empathetic with clients but also able to provide clear, hard advice." "She has a remarkable skill in building a rapport with clients."

Caroline Topping (6 Pump Court) Senior junior who is renowned for her expertise in family law relating to children. She is primarily instructed in care proceedings as well as special guardianship and placement order applications, representing parents, guardians and children alike. Her private law practice extends to child relocation and protection, including contact disputes. **Strengths:** "She is good with difficult clients, she provides clear and robust advice and her cross-examination is really good." "She fights to the end for her clients."

Gemma Farrington (Stour Chambers) Specialises in complex care proceedings, usually acting on behalf of parents but sometimes representing children. She is also well versed in private law cases, and has significant experience in taking cases to the Court of Appeal. **Strengths:** "She has a methodical and thorough approach." "Excellent in cross-examination."

Joanne Porter (Stour Chambers) A former solicitor with experience in private and public law matters who is especially knowledgeable when it comes to public cases concerning adoption and care proceedings. She is praised for her understanding of international issues, particularly in relation to Eastern European families. **Strengths:** "Sympathetic, professional and knowledgeable. She works well with vulnerable clients and has expertise in Eastern European care cases."

Kate Kochnari (Stour Chambers) Acts exclusively in family law and Court of Protection matters. She specialises in care and adoption proceedings, cohabitation disputes and financial remedy, and is particularly praised for her impeccable client care and communication. **Strengths:** "She has a very nice manner with parents and very good experience of dealing with children and guardians. She is approachable, good with written work and always keeps you up to date."

Lydia Slee (Stour Chambers) Junior with noteworthy experience in public and private law children matters. She has been instructed in complex issues involving non-accidental injury and abuse, and is adept at handling vulnerable clients and complicated factual and legal evidence. **Strengths:** "She has a lovely manner with clients. She is very sympathetic and knowledgeable, tells them what their case is and flags any problems up straight away." "Very bright and a real fighter."

Elizabeth Spence (Stour Chambers) Well known for her expertise in complex public and private children law matters, including non-accidental injury and factitious illness cases. She also regularly represents clients in financial proceedings which involve complicated business arrangements or inherited assets. **Strengths:** "Very on the ball, forthright in court even with difficult parties on the other side. She comes across as experienced beyond her call." "Elizabeth is thorough and a very strong advocate."

John Brooke-Smith (Trinity Chambers) Senior junior who has extensive expertise in financial remedy cases relating to divorce, cohabitation disputes and children matters. He is often engaged on behalf of high net worth individuals. **Strengths:** "He is an excellent advocate."

Maria Hancock of Westgate Chambers. Seasoned children law practitioner who regularly handles matters involving complex medical evidence and care proceedings. She is instructed on behalf of parents and guardians as well as children in cases that concern abuse, non-accidental injury and adoption. **Strengths:** "An experienced family lawyer who can handle very complicated casework."

WALES & CHESTER

Family/Matrimonial
Leading Sets
Band 1
30 Park Place *
Band 2
9 Park Place *
Leading Silks
Band 1
Henke Ruth *30 Park Place*
Tillyard James *30 Park Place*
Band 2
Crowley Jane *30 Park Place*
Hopkins Paul *9 Park Place*
Leading Juniors
Band 1
Felstead Christopher *9 Park Place*
Radcliffe Sheila *Cathedral Chambers (ORL)* ◊
Sandercock Natalie *30 Park Place*
Taylor Rhys *30 Park Place*
Thomas Owen *9 Park Place*
Band 2
Allen Mark *30 Park Place*
Barry Matthew *9 Park Place*
Edmondson Harriet *30 Park Place*
Heyworth Catherine Louise *30 Park Place*
Hughes Kate *30 Park Place*
John Catrin *30 Park Place*
Leader Lucy *Angel Chambers (ORL)* ◊
Thomas Lisa *9 Park Place*
Band 3
Douglas Colin *30 Park Place*
Harrington Rebecca *30 Park Place*
Kirby Rhian *30 Park Place*
Miller Richard *9 Park Place*
Parry Siân *9 Park Place*
Williams Claire *30 Park Place*
Up-and-coming individuals
Daniel Hayley *Cathedral Chambers (ORL)* ◊
Evans David Gareth *9 Park Place*
Jones Rhian *30 Park Place*
* *Indicates set with profile.*
◊ *(ORL) = Other Ranked Lawyer.*
Alphabetical order within each band. Band 1 is highest.

Band 1

30 Park Place

See profile on p.943

THE SET

30 Park Place maintains its standing as a leading family law set, with its experienced individuals able to provide a broad range of expertise. The renowned childcare team is known for covering serious cases of abuse and neglect, while the matrimonial finance practitioners regularly handle complex, high net worth matters. Sources highlight the set's strength in depth, as well as the knowledge and understanding of both the barristers and the clerks, saying: "There are a lot of serious, reliable advocates there that I would trust on family matters, and they also have a very good support staff who are quick, helpful and loyal."

Client service: "The clerks, led by senior clerk Phillip Griffiths, are a credit to them. They are very honest, will always try to accommodate you and are very approachable."

SILKS

Ruth Henke QC A prolific silk who is highly respected for her expertise in care cases involving children and vulnerable adults. She frequently deals with sensitive Children Act matters, in both public and private law proceedings. Interviewees note her skilled handling of the most complex matters. **Strengths:** "Ruth Henke is fantastic, there is no one else in Wales that I would choose over her. She is extremely thorough and has excellent preparation; you always feel like she is streets ahead." "A very safe pair of hands, well prepared and conscientious."

James Tillyard QC Highly respected family practitioner with an exceptional reputation in financial matters. Regularly undertakes high-value work with complex asset issues, including international elements. Sources praise his problem-solving abilities during heavyweight cases. **Strengths:** "He provides clear advice, good representation and reasonable solutions." "Very able in money and child law work. He is tenacious and a good fighter – you would want him in your corner."

Jane Crowley QC Continues to be a leading individual for cases involving serious physical abuse to children, particularly those that require a strong grasp of complex medical evidence. Her private law practice also includes a particular interest in forced marriage and child relocation matters. **Strengths:** "Well respected for Children Act matters."

JUNIORS

Natalie Sandercock Experienced junior who is particularly well known for taking on high net worth financial remedy cases. She also handles local authority care work, with notable expertise in cases involving the Court of Protection and Deprivation of Liberty Safeguards. **Strengths:** "She has extensive knowledge and a high-level understanding of business and complex pensions. Clients like that she hits the ground running." "A tenacious advocate."

Rhys Taylor A well-respected barrister, known for his financial family practice with significant expertise in trusts of land and Inheritance Act cases. He is regularly instructed in disputes involving agricultural and farming elements. **Strengths:** "The leading junior for money and TOLATA cases." "Very good on trusts of land cases, and very much has his finger on the pulse."

Mark Allen Senior junior who is highly regarded for his expertise in both public care and private family work. Of late, his caseload has included serious physical and sexual abuse cases. Sources praise him for his manner with vulnerable clients including those with mental health problems. **Strengths:** "He is very knowledgeable and able in cases involving complex legal and medical issues, and good in extremely sensitive cross-examinations."

Harriet Edmondson Specialising in care work, she is recommended for her handling of sensitive cases involving vulnerable individuals. She is experienced in representing parents, guardians, children and local authorities during proceedings relating to non-accidental injury, death and sexual abuse. **Strengths:** "She is extremely able and thorough. Good with clients, diligent in her preparation and skilled in her advocacy."

Catherine Louise Heyworth Highlighted by sources for her depth of experience in complex injury cases, Catherine Heyworth undertakes a range of care work including serious physical and sexual abuse matters. She has notable expertise in cases involving complicated head injuries. **Strengths:** "I have always been impressed with her ability to empathise with the clients and her knowledge of areas outside the legal remit, such as medical knowledge."

Kate Hughes An experienced advocate with a strong childcare practice, who also takes on financial remedy matters. She frequently represents local authorities but also has experience acting for guardians, parents and prospective adopters in complex care cases. **Strengths:** "I find her very professional, she always knows her case well and is an excellent advocate."

Catrin John Highly regarded in the public law children field, she specialises in representing local authorities and guardians in heavyweight sexual and physical abuse matters. She has further notable experience in cases where parenting has been affected by mental illness. **Strengths:** "She is very capable, experienced in complex cases, is good with the clients and takes a very sensible approach to what she does."

Colin Douglas Handles public and private law cases involving children, with a particular emphasis on care matters. He has extensive experience of representing vulnerable clients in cases of serious physical, sexual and emotional abuse. **Strengths:** "He is very good and does well on children matters."

Rebecca Harrington Undertakes a full range of family finance work, including ancillary relief and enforcement cases, often involving owner-run companies and foreign assets. Also advises on complex immigration and asylum issues concerning children. **Strengths:** "She is very competent, a great junior barrister."

Rhian Kirby Strong junior with a varied care practice, representing local authorities, guardians and parents in non-accidental injury and abuse cases, among others. Interviewees note her excellent manner with vulnerable clients and her handling of complex issues. **Strengths:** "She is extremely patient, has excellent preparation, is very approachable and experienced. More than a safe pair of hands."

Claire Williams Respected junior frequently instructed by local authorities in a range of serious physical and sexual abuse cases. She also represents parents and guardians, and her extensive experience has been further cemented by undertaking cases in the High Court and the Court of Appeal. **Strengths:** "She is extremely bright, an excellent advocate and has a good approach with clients."

Rhian Jones Specialises in Children Act cases, particularly public law proceedings involving domestic abuse, sexual abuse and severe non-accidental injuries. Also handles private children work and has significant appellate experience. **Strengths:** "Ridiculously well prepared, pragmatic in her approach and gives the clients confidence."

Band 2

9 Park Place

See profile on p.944

THE SET

9 Park Place boasts a highly regarded family team, well versed in all areas of both public and private family law. Its practitioners regularly undertake high-value financial cases, including ancillary relief,

TOLATA and cohabitation matters. They also deal extensively with Children Act cases, representing all parties in complex care cases and private disputes. Interviewees praise the set's efficiency and professionalism.

Client service: "The family clerk, Lesley Haikney, is great to deal with. The clerking there is particularly good and they are always able to accommodate." "They are proactive in providing training, which is always helpful."

SILKS

Paul Hopkins QC Head of chambers Paul Hopkins QC is an experienced advocate who handles public and private children matters. He regularly acts for parents, local authorities and interveners in cases that concern serious sexual abuse allegations, non-accidental injuries and fatalities. **Strengths:** "I would struggle to find a better trial advocate, he is fantastic at cross-examining. He is also very approachable and very good at working as a team, and the quality of his paperwork is second to none."

JUNIORS

Christopher Felstead A standout junior who specialises in family finance with a significant focus on complex ancillary relief. He is well versed in dealing with high-value settlements, family businesses and farming cases. **Strengths:** "He is my first choice in Cardiff for his robust style and firm but fair approach." "A very good finance practitioner who is very focused and organised."

Owen Thomas A highly respected junior whose broad knowledge covers the full family law spectrum. Of late, his focus has been on public law children work where he regularly represents local authorities in serious sexual abuse or injury cases. **Strengths:** "A wonderful advocate." "A safe pair of hands who is approachable and very good at his job."

Matthew Barry Well-regarded family advocate focusing on financial remedy proceedings, as well as handling complex private law children issues. He has gained significant experience in cases that combine civil and family law, such as Inheritance Act matters and cohabitee disputes. **Strengths:** "Matthew Barry is excellent on his feet and gets to grips with cases very quickly."

Lisa Thomas An impressive junior who is frequently instructed by local authorities, guardians and parents in heavyweight public law cases, including those that involve allegations of murder or abuse. Her practice further covers private law children and ancillary relief work. **Strengths:** "She has a cool unflappability that is quite impressive, and she is always up to speed with everything."

Richard Miller An experienced practitioner specialising in children work who has a particular focus on public law matters. Recent work includes undertaking cases involving severe injuries to children, as well as sexual abuse and fatalities. **Strengths:** "He is extremely experienced and someone I would trust and rely upon." "Very good at dealing with clients in very difficult situations."

Siân Parry A senior junior with extensive experience and who has recently been appointed a Deputy District Judge. She has a broad practice covering both public and private law, and has recently handled several complex adoption and special guardianship orders. **Strengths:** "Good with clients, and always fair and reasonable." "A very good advocate."

David Gareth Evans Well-rounded barrister undertaking a full spectrum of family law cases, from private and public law children applications to ancillary relief and cohabitation disputes. In 2015, he was appointed a Deputy District Judge. **Strengths:** "He is exceptionally good with clients and very thorough."

Other Ranked Lawyers

Lucy Leader (Angel Chambers) Has a strong Children Act practice, representing individuals in public and private law matters. Her practice also encompasses matrimonial finance cases and enforcement proceedings. **Strengths:** "Lucy is able to assimilate a lot of factual detail very quickly, is consistent and always well prepared."

Sheila Radcliffe (Cathedral Chambers) Specialises in public law children work, and is praised by sources for her work ethic and attention to detail. She is especially adept at handling cases that concern adoption and guardianship proceedings. **Strengths:** "Very capable, an excellent advocate and always prepared to fight the client's corner."

Hayley Daniel (Cathedral Chambers) Has a wide range of experience in family law work, both public and private, including ancillary relief and trusts of land disputes. Also regularly represents parents and local authorities in children cases concerning serious allegations of abuse. **Strengths:** "Excellent, very professional and well liked by clients."

WESTERN

Family/Matrimonial
Leading Sets
Band 1
Albion Chambers *
Pump Court Chambers *
St John's Chambers *
Band 2
3PB Barristers *
Leading Silks
Star individuals
Sharp Christopher *St John's Chambers* [A]
Band 1
Hyde Charles *Albion Chambers*
Jacklin Susan *1 Garden Court Family Law (ORL)* ◊ [A] *
Band 2
Ekaney Nkumbe *Albion Chambers*
Wills-Goldingham Claire *Colleton Chambers (ORL)* ◊ [A]
Band 3
Samuels Leslie *Pump Court Chambers* *
Skellorn Kathryn *St John's Chambers*
** Indicates set / individual with profile.*
[A] direct access (see p.24).
◊ (ORL) = Other Ranked Lawyer.
Alphabetical order within each band. Band 1 is highest.

Family/Matrimonial	
Leading Juniors	
Band 1	**Duthie** Catriona *St John's Chambers*
Boydell Edward *Pump Court Chambers*	**Elliott** Colin *KBG Chambers (ORL)* ◊
Dinan-Hayward Deborah *Albion Chambers* [A]	**Evans** Judi *St John's Chambers*
Leafe Daniel *Albion Chambers*	**Godfrey** Christopher *Colleton Chambers (ORL)* ◊
Miller Nicholas *St John's Chambers*	**Goodall** Rachael *3PB Barristers*
Sproull Nicholas *Albion Chambers* [A]	**Griffiths** Hayley *3PB Barristers*
Band 2	**Ingham** Liz *Colleton Chambers (ORL)* ◊
Commins Andrew *St John's Chambers* [A]	**Iten** Corinne *Pump Court Chambers*
Dixon Ralph *Clerksroom Barristers Chambers (ORL)* ◊	**Martin** Nicola *3PB Barristers*
Hunter Susan *St John's Chambers* [A]	**Mashembo** Carol *St John's Chambers* [A]
Kelly Geoffrey *Pump Court Chambers*	**Pope** Sarah *Albion Chambers* [A]
Naish Christopher *Magdalen Chambers (ORL)* ◊	**Reed** Lucy *St John's Chambers*
O'Neill Louise *St John's Chambers* [A]	**Saunders** Zoë *St John's Chambers*
Roberts Stephen *Albion Chambers*	**Small** Gina *KBG Chambers (ORL)* ◊
Whitehall Mark *Colleton Chambers (ORL)* ◊	**Ward** Annie *Pump Court Chambers*
Band 3	**Zabihi** Tanya *3PB Barristers*
Atkinson Jody *St John's Chambers* [A]	**Up-and-coming individuals**
Chapman John *Pump Court Chambers*	**Norman** Richard *St John's Chambers*

Band 1

Albion Chambers

See profile on p.937

THE SET

Albion Chambers is a Bristol mainstay for family law, with a strong and deep bench capable of taking on a wide range of matters. The set is especially well known for its work in matrimonial finance, with members regularly handling cases that include highly complex elements such as businesses, pensions, farming and trusts. It also has a number of children law specialists active in the public and private spheres.

Client service: Michael Harding is the set's senior family clerk.

SILKS

Charles Hyde QC Head of chambers who has over 25 years' experience acting for clients in complex matrimonial finance disputes, and is also able to advise on private children cases. Known particularly for his pragmatism, he is described by more than one source as a "class act." **Strengths:** "He prepares meticulously, is responsive to work with and has an excellent client manner." "Expert in high net worth financial matters, well liked by clients, a very smooth operator."

Nkumbe Ekaney QC Represents parents and children in public and private child law cases, with particular expertise advising on matters concerning serious non-accidental injuries. He is also experienced at handling matters that concern sexual assault, neglect and child death. **Strengths:** "A children lawyer through and through." "Very well thought of."

JUNIORS

Deborah Dinan-Hayward Best known for her financial remedy work, with experience representing high net worth clients and a knack for cases involving overseas assets and interests. In addition to handling litigation, she is also able to guide clients through ADR. **Strengths:** "Deborah has an excellent manner with clients, instilling in them confidence and reassurance that they are in safe hands." "Great rapport with nervous or uncertain clients, and a no-nonsense approach in court."

Daniel Leafe Widely respected for his expert handling of complex financial disputes, Daniel Leafe focuses on cohabitation and matrimonial finance issues. He wins warm praise for the strength of his advocacy and ability to "think outside the box." **Strengths:** "A determined and skilled advocate with a vast knowledge of case law." "He is always thoroughly prepared and has a stylish approach to his advocacy that impresses clients and solicitors alike."

Nicholas Sproull Junior who is highly experienced in acting for high net worth individuals on financial remedy matters. He also has considerable expertise on associated cross-border issues. **Strengths:** "Amazing advocate, incredibly approachable for clients." "Excellent with clients and a joy to watch in court. His attention to detail is second to none and he never fails to impress."

Stephen Roberts Maintains a diverse practice, frequently advising on ancillary relief matters, and also able to take on complex public children law work. He is experienced at handling cases involving serious neglect, sexual assault and complicated care issues. **Strengths:** "Stephen is extremely knowledgeable and an exceptional advocate. He is respected by opponents and earns the trust of clients. He handles cases in a very professional and client-focused manner."

Sarah Pope Often acts for guardians on public children law cases. She has experience in a wide variety of issues, including FGM, international relocation, child death and sexual abuse.

Pump Court Chambers

See profile on p.898

THE SET

An extensive team with vast experience representing clients on all aspects of family law. It is active on a range of matrimonial finance matters, and has members who are regularly instructed in cases concerning high net worth individuals and complicated financial arrangements or cross-border interests. The set also takes on public and private children law cases, and is adept at handling issues such as sexual abuse, abduction as well as applications for adoption and placement orders.

Client service: "Responsive in returning calls and offer a really good service." "I continue to be impressed by their clerks." Tony Atkins is the senior clerk.

SILKS

Leslie Samuels QC (see p.758) Advises on the full range of family law issues, representing clients in public and private children matters, as well as in matrimonial finance cases. He is able to oversee ADR procedures as well as handle litigation. **Strengths:** "He is highly authoritative, especially when it comes to cases concerning non-accidental injury in children." "He is hard-working, conscientious and a quietly assertive advocate."

JUNIORS

Edward Boydell Head of the family finance team, with over two decades' experience advising on matrimonial finance. He regularly represents high net worth clients in cases involving challenging assets such as farms, family companies and overseas trusts. **Strengths:** "Always exceptionally prepared, he is a fantastic negotiator and advocate who suits almost every client due to his versatile personality." "Excellent client-handling and thorough analytical skills."

Geoffrey Kelly A specialist in matrimonial finance matters who is best known for working on financial remedies resulting from marriage and relationship breakdown. He also advises on disputes regarding Schedule 1 of the Children Act. **Strengths:** "Geoff works very hard on his cases and is liked by clients, who feel reassured by his representation." "Always exceptionally prepared, he knows the law inside out, is a superb advocate, is very commercial in his approach and is always on hand to guide you through the process."

John Chapman Fields a broad practice covering private child and matrimonial finance disputes. He regularly acts for high net worth individuals on complex cases involving overseas property, trusts and businesses. **Strengths:** "Effective and well prepared." "He is very user-friendly, has a great manner with clients and is an excellent advocate."

Corinne Iten Well respected for her work on complicated public children law matters, in which she represents parents, children and local authorities. She is especially experienced at taking on sexual assault and serious non-accidental injury cases. **Strengths:** "Corinne Iten is an exceptional advocate orally and in written argument. She remains calm, is attentive to the client's instructions and gives clear advice." "Well respected, effective and well researched."

Annie Ward Specialises in taking on finance disputes and is able to aid clients as a mediator as well as an advocate. She is experienced at taking on matrimonial cases involving inheritance, businesses and children issues. **Strengths:** "Has an eye for detail, gives sound advice and is tenacious as an advocate." "Has a no-nonsense approach combined with pragmatic and sensible advice. She's always reassuring to anxious clients."

St John's Chambers

See profile on p.941

THE SET

A very strong Bristol-based team capable of representing clients across the full spectrum of family law matters. Offers a robust matrimonial finance practice and has also built up significant experience in private and public ADR proceedings. The set is also highly regarded for its forward-thinking approach to client service.

Client service: "A really busy set, but the clerks never leave you hanging, they always seem to be extremely organised." "Quality of clerking is very good. I think they are capable of getting the right person for the job and they work with you to make sure you get the service you want." Practice manager Luke Hodgson is in charge of the family team.

SILKS

Christopher Sharp QC Leader of the set's family team and hugely respected for his experience of representing high net worth clients in major ancillary relief and TOLATA cases. He regularly acts in matters with an international element to them. **Strengths:** "Has a keen eye for detail and an ability to grasp complicated issues with great ease." "Preeminent. He's been around forever. He's brilliant on the detail, very clever, very thorough, and he doesn't give up – he's a classic QC."

Kathryn Skellorn QC Specialises in handling complicated children work in both a public and a private context. Her cases frequently concern highly sensitive and difficult issues, as well as complex medical elements. A number of them concern brain trauma, torture, sexual abuse and child death. She also regularly handles disputes regarding surrogacy and same-sex parenthood. **Strengths:** "Very forensic and eloquent in court." "Tenacious, thorough and impressive."

JUNIORS

Nicholas Miller Senior junior whose practice at the Bar is bolstered by his ten years' previous experience as a solicitor. He is highly thought of for his work in the ancillary relief sphere, representing clients in cases with complex pension, farm and company elements. **Strengths:** "He's a rock on whom one can depend for any financial case." "Utterly reliable for outcomes, he always calls it right. Settles where he can, fights where he must."

Andrew Commins Well known for representing high net worth clients on significant matrimonial finance issues, and is experienced at handling cases involving pensions, companies and trusts. In addition to his litigation practice, he also works as a mediator. **Strengths:** "Clients like his straightforward and practical approach to cases." "Very calm and reasonable, and has an excellent client manner."

Susan Hunter Head of St John's Chambers, she focuses her practice on financial remedy issues and is especially skilled at advising on cases involving third-party interests. She also acts for clients in private children cases. **Strengths:** "Very analytical, forensic and user-friendly." "Her no-nonsense approach gains clients' confidence immediately."

Louise O'Neill Highly regarded for her expertise in complex private and public children law matters, and has represented clients in international abduction, wardship and inherent jurisdiction cases. **Strengths:** "She is an approachable and proactive advocate." "Really empathises with clients and brings real insight into the whole case."

Jody Atkinson Focuses his practice on matrimonial finance issues, and is skilled at taking on inheritance and probate cases. Also active in matters related to child support. **Strengths:** "Brilliant, bright, very good on child support agency work." "Very knowledgeable."

Catriona Duthie Practises across the full spectrum of family law matters, and is best known for her work acting for clients in private and public children law matters. She is noted by sources for being a tenacious litigator. **Strengths:** "Excellent and an impressive advocate."

Judi Evans Heads the family practice group at the set, and enjoys a solid reputation for her work in the public sphere, particularly on non-accidental injury cases. She has additional experience acting as a mediator. **Strengths:** "Judi Evans has a great rapport with clients and is quick on her feet."

Carol Mashembo Has a diverse family practice encompassing cohabitation disputes, financial remedies and private children law. She has over 15 years' experience and is used to handling cases that involve dealing with litigants in person. **Strengths:** "Good at looking at the wider picture, being pragmatic and finding the best solution for clients." "Extremely impressive – she's strong, sensible and very insightful. Her advice on when to fight and when not to fight undoubtedly helped the client enormously."

Lucy Reed Specialises in children work, and is able to act for clients on a wide variety of public and private cases. She regularly advises on matters involving challenging or vulnerable parties, such as parents with substance abuse or mental health issues, and children with disabilities and learning difficulties. **Strengths:** "Lucy is humane, sensible and crafts her submissions with precision and insight." "Combines a massive intellect with really meticulous forensic preparation, and has enormous humanity as well."

Zoë Saunders A junior best known for her work on cohabitation disputes, including TOLATA and Schedule 1 applications. She is also skilled at taking on matrimonial finance litigation, handling cases concerning pension, insolvency and land issues. **Strengths:** "She gives robust and compassionate advice, and clients love her humour and real-world approach. Her technical and commercial knowledge is excellent and she is above all practical and realistic in all matters."

Richard Norman Acts in a wide variety of family law matters, including those concerning financial remedies following relationship breakdowns, and complicated private children cases. **Strengths:** "He has great energy and an ability to absorb and distil huge amounts of information. He has a very good ability to read a case and call the right settlement offer." "Excellent, he is very measured when dealing with particularly difficult litigants in person."

Band 2

3PB Barristers

See profile on p.892

THE SET

3PB Barristers enjoys a strengthening reputation in the area of family law, and fields an experienced group with a history of acting for clients in a wide range of matters. Members are engaged on significant public and private children law cases and the set also offers a dedicated family financial and property team. In addition to its litigation prowess, 3PB is also skilled at taking clients through the process of ADR. **Client service:** "The clerks are always ready and willing to help." "If there is anything that concerns me, I know I can bring it to the clerks' attention and it is dealt with discreetly and efficiently." Russell Porter is the family clerk.

JUNIORS

Rachael Goodall Primarily works on financial remedy and TOLATA disputes, especially those arising from relationship breakdown. She is also able to advise on private children matters. **Strengths:** "A great all-rounder, whose manner with clients is commendable as she is sensitive yet strong. Her advice is top class." "Offers excellent knowledge of matrimonial financial law and proceedings, thorough and prompt preparation, superior attention to detail, and great empathy with clients in difficult circumstances."

Hayley Griffiths Has over two decades of experience advising on a range of children law work, acting for children, parents and local authorities in public and private matters. She is especially well known for her work on cases involving complex care proceedings. **Strengths:** "She's a super hard-working advocate, with a really personable manner." "Hayley has a calm and professional style which is reassuring to clients."

Nicola Martin Highly thought of for her work taking on difficult childcare cases, including those involving serious injury or death. Additionally well respected for her work on matrimonial finance cases.

Tanya Zabihi Has over 25 years of experience representing parents, guardians and local authorities on complicated children matters. She has expertise in care proceedings, especially where the children have special educational needs. **Strengths:** "Very tenacious and good on complex cases." "Really good with clients and a very robust, strong advocate."

Other Ranked Lawyers

Ralph Dixon (Clerksroom Barristers Chambers) A senior junior best known for his experience acting for high net worth clients on financial remedy matters. **Strengths:** "Very able and tenacious, a tough negotiator."

Claire Wills-Goldingham QC (Colleton Chambers) Has over 25 years' experience in family law, advising on public and private child matters including serious non-accidental injury and child death cases. She is also able to advise on high-value financial remedies involving farms and family companies. **Strengths:** "A robust and tenacious advocate who fights hard for clients." "She's excellent on complex high net worth cases."

Mark Whitehall (Colleton Chambers) Specialises in taking on children law cases that involve complex medical evidence and serious injuries. Also well known for his expertise in cases involving adoption and children being placed into care. **Strengths:** "Calm and unflappable in even the most volatile situations – his ability to defuse situations is unique and a great asset." "An incredibly safe pair of hands who is very well respected by other counsel and solicitors that undertake this type of work."

Christopher Godfrey (Colleton Chambers) Focuses his practice on public children law work, and devotes the majority of his time to care matters. Also skilled at taking on private disputes involving child relocation and surrogacy. **Strengths:** "Chris is straight-talking and down-to-earth. He tells it as it is." "Well mannered and good with both professional and lay clients."

Liz Ingham (Colleton Chambers) Leads the family group at the set, and has over 25 years' experience across a wide range of family law matters. She is especially well versed in handling cases involving factitious illness and serious injury to babies. **Strengths:** "Very thorough, competent and quietly persuasive." "She has an uncanny ability to remember the most obscure pieces of information in cases and is always able to get to the relevant point with minimum fuss or delay."

Susan Jacklin QC (see p.680) (1 Garden Court Family Law Chambers) Enjoys a very strong reputation for her work across the spectrum of family law. She acts for clients facing difficult financial remedy and private children matters. **Strengths:** "Very approachable, her clients like her, and she distils complex legal and factual concepts in a manner they understand." "Calm, one of the most thorough people I've ever met, and someone with the most remarkable tactical brain."

Colin Elliott (KBG Chambers) Specialises in acting for high net worth individuals in complex issues of financial remedy and ancillary relief. He is experienced at taking on cases that involve pensions, trusts and farms, as well as those with international aspects to them. **Strengths:** "The best money practitioner in Cornwall. Judges like him enormously." "A very good finance barrister."

Gina Small (KBG Chambers) Best known for her work advising on difficult care and adoption cases. She is also very capable when it comes to ancillary relief, and has further experience of handling inheritance issues. **Strengths:** "Very thorough and experienced in both public law and private Children Act matters."

Christopher Naish (Magdalen Chambers) Has a broad practice, acting for guardians, parents and local authorities on private and public children law matters, as well as being able to handle complex financial remedy cases. **Strengths:** "Christopher Naish is very highly experienced and has a wealth of knowledge of family law. He also is very good at establishing a good relationship with clients and putting them at their ease." "A commanding presence, with good attention to detail, and great in cross-examination."

FINANCIAL CRIME: An Introduction

Contributed by Cloth Fair Chambers

This is now the third year in which this specialism has been characterised in this guide as Financial Crime, and alongside it the sub-specialism Financial Crime: Corporates. Many financial crime investigations and prosecutions will not involve a corporate entity under investigation. Many would be recognisable as what used to be described as "white-collar crime": individuals charged with various species of fraud, bribery or money laundering offences.

The SFO, self-described as "the specialist prosecuting authority tackling the top level of serious or complex fraud, bribery and corruption," has had an increased overall budget year upon year for the last four financial years, reflecting an appetite for the investigation and prosecution of significant and high-profile corporates and individuals. Other agencies with criminal prosecutorial powers, such as the CMA and the FCA, continue to show a preparedness to prosecute serious allegations of financial crime, namely criminal cartel offences and insider dealing offences, which also fall within this specialism. The perceived deterrent effect of criminal prosecution is well regarded by these prosecution agencies. The SFO, in particular, indicates an ongoing keenness to participate as a key player on the global stage of criminal investigation and prosecution, particularly in partnership with the US agencies.

Inevitably it is the multi-jurisdictional, multi-defendant and multi-faceted investigations and prosecutions which produce the most significant developments in the field of financial crime for those representing both individuals and corporates. Notably, in the last twelve months two deferred prosecution agreements (DPAs) have been offered by the SFO, approved by the court, and signed by two corporates: SFO v Standard Bank plc (30 November 2015) and SFO v XYZ Ltd (8 July 2016). Publication of the full judgment in XYZ Ltd awaits the conclusion of criminal proceedings against a number of former employees of XYZ.

However, there have also been timely reminders in a number of high-profile financial criminal jury trials that a significant number of cases in the UK will still go all the way to a jury trial and verdict, with everything at stake for an individual or, occasionally, a corporate client. This specialism therefore demands the skill and expertise of an advocate who can offer insightful strategic advice from the initial phone call at the start of an internal investigation into suspected criminal conduct, but also deliver a potent closing jury speech should the case go that far, and everything else in between. 'End to end' representation remains the hallmark of best practice in this field.

As criminal investigations become more complex, the 'everything else in between' list grows longer each year. For example, the relationship between legal professional privilege and a self-report of an internal investigation to a prosecution agency by lawyers on behalf of a corporate client continues to generate issues requiring expert advice on a case-by-case basis.

DPAs now form part of landscape upon which a corporate client must be advised, but by no means the totality of it. There will be some cases where a self-report is not required and is not otherwise in the best interests of the corporate. There will be some cases where a DPA is less desirable than other possible outcomes of a criminal investigation. In both Standard Bank plc and XYZ Ltd, there were features of the corporate structure and ownership at the time a DPA was on offer that are likely to have rendered it a more attractive outcome than it otherwise might have been.

Undoubtedly, the SFO was keen to establish that the legislation could and would work. The extent to which this will continue beyond Standard Bank plc and XYZ Ltd in the circumstances of the offer of further DPAs remains to be seen (Leveson LJ described XYZ Ltd as an "exceptional" case). So it is that the future development of DPAs remains uncertain.

What is clear is that decisive strategic advice is essential at an early stage, even more so now that a DPA will be one of the options under active consideration. In both Standard Bank plc and XYZ Ltd, the promptness of the self-report to the SFO in each case was critical to the outcome, as was the extent and manner of co-operation with the SFO. Once the possible criminality is brought to the attention of the corporate and its lawyers, and the clock starts ticking, the corporate needs step-by-step advice to best preserve its position in relation to the range of possible outcomes that exist at that stage. The advocate will be particularly mindful of how to tailor that advice to best protect the corporate in any negotiation for a DPA, or in any potential criminal proceedings which may follow.

Advising and representing individuals under investigation or charged with financial crime remains an integral and important part of this specialism. For an individual under threat of criminal prosecution, the past year has also seen significant developments. For example, the SFO has indicated an increased preparedness to charge non-UK nationals living outside the UK with criminal offences arising from their conduct whilst also working outside the UK, should the criminal law permit it. Public sentiment in relation to a perceived lack of probity and appropriate standards in corporate affairs and the financial markets illuminates recent history and the current position.

A jury trial, along with its many other features, allows for an interesting test of another aspect of public sentiment, namely the question of prosecutorial policy decisions. These include a decision to grant immunity from prosecution to individuals who have admitted crime and are prepared to give evidence against others charged, a decision to prosecute only junior employees for what is alleged to be systemic criminal conduct, and a decision to prosecute an individual employee of a company for the commission of criminal offences for the benefit of his/her employer while making a court-approved DPA with the corporate employer.

It remains to be seen whether there are significant impairments to a prosecution agency's ability to discharge its disclosure obligations or other impairments to an individual's right to a fair trial, when s/he is prosecuted on the basis of evidence produced by an internal investigation designed to procure a DPA in the best interests of the company. While this might be an inexpensive way for a prosecutor to proceed in monetary terms, it may come with other costs. 'Delegation' of its disclosure obligations has proved problematic for the SFO in the past, in other circumstances, although it rejected those criticisms at the time. Representing individuals who have been 'sold' as part of the self-report process requires the expertise of advocates who understand exactly what has gone on in that process and what consequences it has produced. 'End to end' representation is as important for an individual client as it is for a corporate one. As ever, there are interesting and challenging times ahead for the specialists in this field and their clients.

Contents:

LONDON

Financial Crime
Leading Sets
Band 1
2 Bedford Row *
Cloth Fair Chambers
2 Hare Court *
QEB Hollis Whiteman *
3 Raymond Buildings Barristers *
Band 2
25 Bedford Row *
9-12 Bell Yard
Carmelite Chambers *
The Chambers of Andrew Mitchell QC *
23 Essex Street *
Doughty Street Chambers *
6KBW College Hill
Matrix Chambers *
5 Paper Buildings *
Red Lion Chambers
* Indicates set / individual with profile.
[A] direct access (see p.24).
◊ (ORL) = Other Ranked Lawyer.
Alphabetical order within each band. Band 1 is highest.

Financial Crime
Leading Silks
Star individuals
Cameron Alexander *3 Raymond Buildings Barristers* [A]
Gibbs Patrick *3 Raymond Buildings Barristers* [A] *
Keith Hugo *3 Raymond Buildings Barristers* *
Kelsey-Fry John *Cloth Fair Chambers* *
Montgomery Clare *Matrix Chambers* *
Perry David *6KBW College Hill*
Purnell Nicholas *Cloth Fair Chambers* *
Winter Ian *Cloth Fair Chambers* *
Band 1
Bott Charles *Carmelite Chambers* *
Bowes Michael *Outer Temple Chambers (ORL)* ◊
Boyce William *QEB Hollis Whiteman* *
Caplan Jonathan *5 Paper Buildings*
Carter-Stephenson George *25 Bedford Row*
Chawla Mukul *9-12 Bell Yard* [A] *
Darbishire Adrian *QEB Hollis Whiteman*
Ellison Mark *QEB Hollis Whiteman* *
Fisher Jonathan *Red Lion Chambers*
Healy Alexandra *9-12 Bell Yard* [A] *
Laidlaw Jonathan *2 Hare Court* *
Larkin Sean *QEB Hollis Whiteman* *
Lissack Richard *Fountain Court Chambers (ORL)* ◊ *
Mayo Simon *187 Fleet Street (ORL)* ◊ [A] *
Milliken-Smith Mark *2 Bedford Row* *
Mitchell Andrew *The Chambers of Andrew Mitchell QC* *
Nelson Cairns *23 Essex Street*
Owen Tim *Matrix Chambers*
Radcliffe Andrew *2 Hare Court* *
Shaw Antony *Red Lion Chambers*
Sturman Jim *2 Bedford Row* *
Band 2
Bailin Alex *Matrix Chambers* *
Burke Trevor *3 Raymond Buildings Barristers* [A]
Carter Peter *Doughty Street Chambers* *
Clegg William *2 Bedford Row* *
Coltart Christopher *2 Hare Court* *
Doyle Peter *25 Bedford Row*
Farrell Simon *3 Raymond Buildings Barristers* [A]
Hackett Philip *New Square Chambers (ORL)* ◊ *
Hawes Neil *Charter Chambers (ORL)* ◊ [A] *
Kelly Brendan *2 Hare Court* *
Knowles Julian *Matrix Chambers*
Kovalevsky Richard *2 Bedford Row*
Lewis James *3 Raymond Buildings Barristers* [A] *
Macdonald Ken *Matrix Chambers*
Pople Alison *Cloth Fair Chambers* *
Pownall Orlando *2 Hare Court* *
Russell Flint Simon *23 Essex Street*
Thompson Collingwood *7BR (ORL)* ◊ *
Band 3
Allen Tom *5 Paper Buildings*
Armstrong Dean *2 Bedford Row* *
Blaxland Henry *Garden Court Chambers (ORL)* ◊
Bogan Paul *23 Essex Street*
Carlile of Berriew Alex *9-12 Bell Yard* *
Fenhalls Mark *23 Essex Street* *
Finnigan Peter *QEB Hollis Whiteman* *
Hines James *3 Raymond Buildings Barristers* [A] *
Jones John Richard *Carmelite Chambers* *
Malcolm Helen *3 Raymond Buildings Barristers* [A]
Malek Hodge M *39 Essex Chambers (ORL)* ◊
Penny Duncan *6KBW College Hill*
Price Tom *25 Bedford Row*
Sallon Christopher *Doughty Street Chambers* [A]
Sangster Nigel *25 Bedford Row* *
Sherrard Charles *Furnival Chambers (ORL)* ◊ [A] *
Smith Leonard *Carmelite Chambers* *
Trollope Andrew *187 Fleet Street (ORL)* ◊ *
Wass Sasha *6KBW College Hill*
Webster Alistair *The Chambers of Andrew Mitchell QC* *
Band 4
Benson Jeremy *Red Lion Chambers*
Bowers Rupert *Doughty Street Chambers* *
Brodie Graham *The Chambers of Andrew Mitchell QC*
Brompton Michael *5 Paper Buildings* *
Christopher Julian *5 Paper Buildings*
Darlow Annabel *6KBW College Hill*
Etherington David *Red Lion Chambers*
Griffiths Courtenay *25 Bedford Row*
Hales Sally-Ann *Red Lion Chambers*
Hicks Martin *2 Hare Court* *
Horwell Richard *3 Raymond Buildings Barristers*
Kane Adam *Carmelite Chambers* *
Kinnear Jonathan S *9-12 Bell Yard* [A] *
McGuinness John *9-12 Bell Yard* *
Miskin Charles *23 Essex Street*
Pinto Amanda *The Chambers of Andrew Mitchell QC* *
Rainsford Mark *The Chambers of Andrew Mitchell QC* *
Ryder John *6KBW College Hill*
New Silks
Ashley-Norman Jonathan *3 Raymond Buildings* [A] *
Deacon Emma *5 Paper Buildings* *
Grey Siobhan *Doughty Street Chambers*
Sibson Clare *Cloth Fair Chambers* *

Band 1

2 Bedford Row

See profile on p.807

THE SET

A set that performs at the top of the market, 2 Bedford Row has quality members who regularly appear in the most high-profile cases, acting for corporates as well as individuals. Matters relating to financial services, false accounting and corruption are of particular interest. Recent key cases handled include the defence of Jean-Daniel Lainé. His arrest resulted from the SFO's investigation of Alstom for alleged bribery in overseas jurisdictions.

Client service: "The clerks are superbly responsive and very helpful. They always put the solicitor's mind at rest." Senior clerk John Grimmer is "a very trusted pair of hands."

SILKS

Mark Milliken-Smith QC (see p.717) An acclaimed team player with 30 years of experience at the Bar. He wins plaudits for his pragmatic and sensitive approach with those facing criminal and fraud charges, and is an expert in SFO, bribery and tax matters. **Strengths:** "He cuts through complex issues very quickly and identifies the key strategic points at an early stage. There were unique delicate political dimensions to the case we were handling, and his advice was invaluable. The client loved him as he has great interpersonal skills, and he was very popular amongst our team as he has a relaxed yet authoritative way about him."

Jim Sturman QC (see p.775) Advises corporate entities as well as individuals, including company executives and professional staff. He is an experienced adviser in jurisdictions outside the UK, including the Turks and Caicos Islands. **Strengths:** "Has an excellent manner with clients and is a first-rate advocate. He goes the extra mile to get the best possible result." "He fought a hard case for us, proving a fantastic team player and a great strategist." **Recent work:** Acted in R v Tim O'Sullivan, representing a legal professional implicated in a case concerning allegations of conspiracy to evade tax by way of a property transaction.

William Clegg QC (see p.618) Heads up the set and has extensive experience with juries going back decades. He is an attractive advocate, with a charismatic and persuasive manner, who is called on when the stakes are high. **Strengths:** "A fantastic advocate who is old school in a good way, and thoroughly charming and funny." "You can't argue with his ability to charm the jury." **Recent work:** Defended Jean-Daniel Lainé, a director of Alstom Network UK Ltd who was charged with corruption following an SFO investigation.

Richard Kovalevsky QC Offers cogent advice to corporates and individuals facing allegations of insider dealing and bribery amongst others. He is acclaimed for his focused approach, as well as his engaging and approachable manner. **Strengths:** "His

Financial Crime

Leading Juniors

Leading Juniors
Star individuals
Saunders Neil *3 Raymond Buildings Barristers* [A] *
Band 1
Barclay Robin *Fountain Court Chambers (ORL)* ◊ *
Barnard Jonathan *Cloth Fair Chambers* *
Bodnar Andrew *Matrix Chambers*
Forster Tom *Red Lion Chambers*
Hill Miranda *6KBW College Hill*
Kendal Timothy *2 Bedford Row*
Little Tom *9 Gough Square (ORL)* ◊ *
Mansell Jason *QEB Hollis Whiteman* [A] *
Rudolf Nathaniel *25 Bedford Row*
Tanchel Vivienne *2 Hare Court*
Band 2
Aylott Colin *Carmelite Chambers* [A] *
Baker Simon *2 Bedford Row*
Brandon Ben *3 Raymond Buildings Barristers*
Clare Allison *Red Lion Chambers*
Clarke Sarah *Serjeants' Inn Chambers (ORL)* ◊ *
Ferguson Craig *2 Hare Court* *
Ferguson Stephen Michael *2 Bedford Row*
Furlong Richard *Carmelite Chambers* *
Gokani Rachna *QEB Hollis Whiteman* *
Harries Mark *Carmelite Chambers* [A] *
Howard Nicola *25 Bedford Row* *
Irwin Gavin *Drystone Chambers (ORL)* ◊ *
Jones Gillian *Red Lion Chambers*
Lennon Jonathan *Carmelite Chambers* *
Riggs Samantha *25 Bedford Row* *
Summers Ben *3 Raymond Buildings Barristers* *
Wells Colin *25 Bedford Row*
Wheeler Andrew *7BR (ORL)* ◊ *
Wong Natasha *187 Fleet Street (ORL)* ◊ [A] *
Band 3
Barnes Rachel *3 Raymond Buildings Barristers* [A] *
Convey Christopher *The Chambers of Andrew Mitchell QC* *
Davison Eleanor *Fountain Court Chambers (ORL)* ◊ *
Dineen Maria *2 Bedford Row* *
Hammond Sean *2 Bedford Row*
Mitchell Keith *The Chambers of Andrew Mitchell QC* *
Payne Geoffrey *25 Bedford Row* *
Ramasamy Selva *QEB Hollis Whiteman* *
Raudnitz Paul *QEB Hollis Whiteman* *
Stern David *5 St Andrew's Hill (ORL)* ◊ *
Whittaker David *2 Hare Court* *
Willcocks Hannah *Red Lion Chambers*
Yeo Nicholas *3 Raymond Buildings Barristers* [A] *
Band 4
Burge Edmund *5 St Andrew's Hill (ORL)* ◊ *
Carter-Manning Jennifer *7BR (ORL)* ◊ [A]
Douglas-Jones Ben *5 Paper Buildings* *
FitzGerald Ben *QEB Hollis Whiteman* *
George Dean *2 Bedford Row*
Gillespie Christopher *2 Hare Court* *
Goldring Jenny *5 St Andrew's Hill (ORL)* ◊ *
Guest Peter *187 Fleet Street (ORL)* ◊ *
Hillman Gerard *Carmelite Chambers* [A] *
Hopper Stephen *5 Paper Buildings*
Khan Ashraf *2 Bedford Row* *
Marshall Andrew *Red Lion Chambers*
Mawrey Eleanor *9 Gough Square (ORL)* ◊ *
Osman Faisal *The Chambers of Andrew Mitchell QC* *
Patterson Gareth *6KBW College Hill*
Payne Tom *Red Lion Chambers*
Schutzer-Weissmann Esther *6KBW College Hill*
Scott Rachel *3 Raymond Buildings Barristers* *
Thacker James *9 Gough Square (ORL)* ◊ *
Ward Alexandra *9-12 Bell Yard* [A] *
Weeks Janet *5 Paper Buildings*
Wormald Richard *3 Raymond Buildings Barristers* [A]
Up-and-coming Individuals
Doble Tom *QEB Hollis Whiteman* *

* *Indicates individual with profile.*

[A] *direct access (see p.24).*

◊ *(ORL) = Other Ranked Lawyer.*

Alphabetical order within each band. Band 1 is highest.

Financial Crime: Corporates

Leading Silks
Band 1
Cameron Alexander *3 Raymond Buildings Barristers* [A]
Gibbs Patrick *3 Raymond Buildings Barristers* [A] *
Keith Hugo *3 Raymond Buildings Barristers* *
Kelsey-Fry John *Cloth Fair Chambers* *
Montgomery Clare *Matrix Chambers* *
Perry David *6KBW College Hill*
Purnell Nicholas *Cloth Fair Chambers* *
Winter Ian *Cloth Fair Chambers* *
Band 2
Altman Brian *2 Bedford Row* *
Bailin Alex *Matrix Chambers* *
Bowes Michael *Outer Temple Chambers (ORL)* ◊
Clegg William *2 Bedford Row* *
Kovalevsky Richard *2 Bedford Row*
Lissack Richard *Fountain Court Chambers (ORL)* ◊ *
Malek Hodge M *39 Essex Chambers (ORL)* ◊
Pople Alison *Cloth Fair Chambers* *
Sturman Jim *2 Bedford Row* *
New Silks
Sibson Clare *Cloth Fair Chambers* *

Leading Juniors
Band 1
Hill Miranda *6KBW College Hill*
Saunders Neil *3 Raymond Buildings Barristers* [A] *
Summers Ben *3 Raymond Buildings Barristers* *
Band 2
Barnard Jonathan *Cloth Fair Chambers* *
Barnes Rachel *3 Raymond Buildings Barristers* [A] *
Davison Eleanor *Fountain Court Chambers (ORL)* ◊ *
Mansell Jason *QEB Hollis Whiteman* [A] *
Medcroft Nicholas *Fountain Court Chambers (ORL)* ◊ *

subtlety, emotional intelligence and quick wit make him very effective." "A nice guy and a very capable advocate, he has a laid back advocacy style and good rapport with juries. He's a good cross-examiner and argues the law really convincingly." **Recent work:** Advised on R v Larcombe, a retrial of a journalist at The Sun newspaper, a case concerning alleged corrupt payments for information relating to the British Royal Family.

Dean Armstrong QC (see p.585) An accomplished silk who has real-world commercial experience garnered in the City of London. Sources applaud him for his superior client service, mastery of the facts in a case, and effective advocacy. **Strengths:** "He worked very well in conference, had prepared extremely well, and dealt very competently with a number of legal arguments. His advocacy skills are sublime and he is a class act."

Brian Altman QC (see p.583) Having had a long tenure as Treasury Counsel at the Central Criminal Court, he has deep insight into the mechanics of prosecuting criminal cases. He is frequently sought out by global corporations to advise on the potential criminal ramifications of officer conduct and corporate transactions. **Strengths:** "Has fabulous prosecution experience." "Definitely a hard hitter."

JUNIORS

Timothy Kendal A noted senior junior who remains in high demand due to the impressive strategic input he offers. His experience includes advising on international bribery matters and real estate-related frauds. **Strengths:** "A good tactician who comes up with very novel ideas." "Impeccably prepared, he produced a model skeleton argument." **Recent work:** Acted for the lead defendant in R v Banner-Eve and Others, a case concerning conspiracy to defraud via land banking.

Simon Baker A well-trained junior with experience of regulatory and financial crime work. He is acclaimed for his impressive skill in mastering the facts of document-heavy cases. Strengths: "His knowledge of the cases he works on and his ability to have every word of the brief at his fingertips is extremely impressive." "We call him 'The Machine' because he can churn out work. He's one of the most efficient working barristers that we know."

Stephen Ferguson A dedicated defence counsel with a strong work ethic and a reassuring client manner. Key mandates he has advised on include allegations of insurance fraud. **Strengths:** "A very talented barrister who is hard working and able to understand the most complex of cases with ease. Stephen is excellent with clients, who warm to his charm immediately."

Maria Dineen (see p.634) A proven junior counsel with notable experience of prosecuting cases, who also regularly defends in company and investment fraud cases. Her areas of strength include confiscation work. **Strengths:** "Her jury speeches are effective and certainly not bog standard." "One of the brightest barristers around, she is meticulously prepared and knows the case better than anyone else in the room." **Recent work:** Acted as lead counsel in the high-profile SFO prosecution of former JJB Sports CEO Chris Ronnie.

Sean Hammond Noted for his interpersonal skills in and out of court, he handles high-value matters such as boiler room frauds and money laundering investigations. **Strengths:** "He always brings a high level of subtlety and intelligence to his work. He is very adept at getting the best out of others, including co-defendants, almost without them realising what's going on." **Recent work:** Acted for the lead defendant in R v Dosanjh and Others, a prosecution for conspiracy to defraud, relating to the international trading of carbon credits.

Dean George An accomplished adviser in the criminal defence sphere, who regularly handles cross-border fraud cases. **Strengths:** "He's obviously going to be a star in the future, as he works really hard and is very good tactically." **Recent work:** Defended a G4S security van driver, alleged to have stolen £800,000 through fraud/theft.

Ashraf Khan (see p.691) Recognised for advising on serious financial crime matters. He regularly defends cases of mortgage, tax and investment fraud. **Strengths:** "His written work is particularly good."

Recent work: Advised a defendant in R v Bellwood and Others, the Operation Bamburgh 2 prosecution for mortgage fraud.

Cloth Fair Chambers

THE SET

A small chambers with top-drawer practitioners who are market leaders in privately funded criminal work, acting for individuals and corporations at home and abroad. Its members are specially selected to advise on the most high-profile matters of the day, including major FCA and SFO investigations into market manipulation, corporate mis-statement and corruption. Commentators note their sensitivity to client needs, saying, "they just get the way corporate solicitors think."

Client service: "The administration is excellent here and the clerks are very good as they understand the cases the barristers are instructed in." Nick Newman is the senior clerk and is described as "great at what he does and highly efficient."

SILKS

John Kelsey-Fry QC (see p.689) A star player on account of his truly remarkable performances as a jury advocate. He is regularly selected to advise on high-stakes matters, such as high-profile investigations and prosecutions by the SFO and FCA. **Strengths:** "An exceptional advocate, who is hard working and a natural orator with superb jury appeal. Watch him, the way he cross-examines and the way a jury reacts, and you appreciate he has the ability to hold the jury in the palm of his hand." "A very forthright individual who takes no prisoners and is highly effective." **Recent work:** Advised Olympus Corporation in defending a charge of making misleading statements to auditors.

Nicholas Purnell QC (see p.745) A highly respected and accomplished silk who continues to impress the market with his performance on leading cases, and who is noted for breaking new ground in the area of Deferred Prosecution Agreements. His recent matters have seen him advising on mis-statement of corporate results and manipulation of rates. **Strengths:** "One of the most accomplished QCs in the corporate crime field. He is an impressive advocate and a great strategist who is very client-friendly. He is our counsel of choice when dealing with complex and sensitive matters that involve our most important clients." "Silky smooth, he makes his point not through aggression but through intellect. He is the only member of the Bar I've seen do a four-month trial and never use notes to make his speeches, which is awe-inspiring." **Recent work:** Acted for Standard Bank in securing the first UK Deferred Prosecution Agreement in relation to suspected bribery.

Ian Winter QC (see p.799) A popular choice of senior counsel for advisory matters at the pre-charge stage of criminal matters. He is acclaimed for his aggressive and effective client advocacy. **Strengths:** "He always has his finger on the pulse and effectively addresses issues in advance of trial." "A first port of call when you need early stage strategic input. He is great at giving advice and very clever." **Recent work:** Provided advice to a former finance officer at Tesco, in a matter concerning a mis-statement of the company's profits.

Alison Pople QC (see p.740) Enjoys rising market acclaim for her fluent interpersonal skills and methodical courtroom manner. Her cases involve allegations of insider dealing, corporate mis-statement and corruption. **Strengths:** "She was very diplomatic in dealing with a number of difficult issues, and a real source of support in a way you wouldn't necessarily expect a barrister to be, navigating many difficult aspects of the cases." "Her carefully structured cross-examination was understated but very damaging to the opposition's case." **Recent work:** Advised a senior banking professional in relation to Operation Tabernula, an investigation into alleged insider trading.

Clare Sibson QC (see p.764) Equally popular for her advice on general serious crime as well as financial crime. Her intelligence and prowess were recognised when she was appointed to silk in February 2016. **Strengths:** "A very talented barrister, who produces clear, concise advice on a variety of criminal fraud matters." "Her legal analysis is first rate and she is a good blue-sky thinker. She has an incredibly quick mind and looks at things that might not have been considered previously." **Recent work:** Acted as lead counsel in the high-profile Olympus litigation concerning suspected corporate corruption.

JUNIORS

Jonathan Barnard (see p.589) The sole junior counsel at this chambers, albeit one with experience of acting unled in hotly contested criminal and quasi-criminal matters concerning corruption, mis-statement of financial figures and fraud. He wins plaudits for being a practical and clever advocate who performs at a level akin to that of a QC. **Strengths:** "He's very intelligent, very hard working, very confident and highly competent. Highly sophisticated and professional clients are immediately won over and he operates at the highest end of the market." "He has wonderful judgement and powers of analysis." **Recent work:** Advised the former Finance Director of Tesco with regard to an investigation into an overstatement of profits by the company.

2 Hare Court

See profile on p.861

THE SET

A leading crime and fraud set that also has enviable skills in regulatory areas such as health and safety and professional discipline. Its members are a popular choice for those seeking cogent and effective advice on all manner of financial crime cases, including those relating to issues such as illegal manipulation of rates, tax fraud and corruption. Significant recent work includes HMRC's prosecution of Michael Richards for conspiracy to evade £300 million in tax. According to one source, 2 Hare Court is "accepted by everyone as a really high-quality set that has a very good quality of tenant from top to bottom."

Client service: "The clerks are business-minded and clearly have their counsels' interests at heart; they match the best counsel to the case. They are not lazy, and are happy to arrange court listings for you and to do liaising. They are also friendly and approachable." Julian Campbell, the director of clerking, is very well respected and known for his commerciality, as is senior practice clerk Ben Heaviside, who is in charge of the financial crime side of things.

SILKS

Jonathan Laidlaw QC (see p.694) Shines in the area of crime, having had 15 years of experience as Treasury Counsel at the Old Bailey. He acts for companies bringing private prosecutions and for individuals facing potential criminal sanctions. **Strengths:** "A very persuasive advocate with a sure touch. He's very, very user-friendly and very good with all the members of my team." "Easy to work with, very responsive and extremely straightforward." **Recent work:** Retained by the Bank of England to advise in respect of SFO, FCA and DoJ investigations, including those relating to LIBOR.

Andrew Radcliffe QC (see p.746) A proven expert in the field of white-collar crime whose practice extends to overseas territories, including the Turks and Caicos Islands. He is particularly experienced at advising on money laundering and cartel work. **Strengths:** "A Rolls-Royce performer whose judgement is excellent. He put an enormous amount of work into the case, and his ability to judge the tribunal and get it right in front of the jury was spot on. He did his research and had a great grasp of the file. Delightful to work with, he's a barrister who provides no drama or fuss. He just gets to the point in a no-nonsense way." **Recent work:** Advised a defendant in R v O'Sullivan and Kerr, a Turks and Caicos Islands prosecution relating to taxation on the transfer of a high-end property.

Christopher Coltart QC (see p.621) Serves as head of the set's business crime and financial services practice group. He is able to call upon valuable prior experience as a corporate solicitor when handling his cases. **Strengths:** "He is terrific, because he's very calm and, having worked in the City, he has a good grasp of the system. He's very responsive, extremely clever and easy to work with." "He is very well prepared, knows his stuff inside-out and is very experienced."

Brendan Kelly QC (see p.689) A very measured advocate who commands considerable respect. He is a popular choice for individuals facing charges of fraud, money laundering and bribery. **Strengths:** "Extremely unflappable." "He's very good if you're seeking a barrister who can handle demanding clients very well." **Recent work:** Advised the defence in R v Michael Richards, a prosecution for conspiracy to defraud HMRC of £300 million.

Orlando Pownall QC (see p.742) Wins plaudits for smooth and sophisticated advocacy. Tax fraud, insider dealing and postal fraud matters all feature on his work roster. **Strengths:** "He's unflappable under fire and nothing ruffles him. Lots of people at his level tend to rely on their natural ability to let them get away with it and thus don't work as hard. But he does, and he is a deadly opponent." "A great jury advocate with a lovely style." **Recent work:** Advised car dealer Sarju Popat with regard to an HMRC prosecution for tax evasion relating to second hand vehicles.

Martin Hicks QC (see p.671) A broadly accomplished QC who applies his wide knowledge of criminal legal procedure to financial crime case. His recent cases have seen him representing journalists accused of using corrupt practices in order to acquire information, and acting for professionals charged with market abuse. **Strengths:** "He is a fantastic advocate. In court he's very funny and very persuasive in his arguments. Juries really like him as he's very down to earth and can explain complicated concepts quite simply." **Recent work:** Advised the defence in R v Ben O'Driscoll, a case arising from the Operation Elveden investigation into alleged bribery of individuals by the UK media.

JUNIORS

Vivienne Tanchel As a former finance professional who later retrained as a barrister, she has enviable real-world experience to bring to financial crime cases. She is a popular choice for defence work involving allegations of market abuse and regulatory breaches. Strengths: "One of those people who is both a brilliant junior and an expert, she is a former foreign exchange ('forex') trader, so has an understanding of the financial world and trading floor which other barristers just can't match." "Has an expertise that is way beyond that of many criminal barristers, and is extremely hard working and conscientious." Recent work: Acted for Danny Forsyth in a Financial Conduct Authority ('FCA') prosecution for boiler room fraud.

Craig Ferguson (see p.644) Good on his feet in court and skilled at handling difficult personalities in an effective manner. Serious crime, including fraud and professional disciplinary cases, forms the mainstay of his practice. **Strengths:** "Very good on paper and very, very good in court." "He isn't one of those barristers that falls out with other barristers – he will try and charm them into submission." **Recent work:** Acted for fashion industry professional Natasha Ramlogan, who was implicated in an allegedly fraudulent VAT reclaim scheme.

David Whittaker (see p.794) Frequently appears as leading counsel on financial crime cases as part of his well-rounded and broad criminal defence practice. He attracts market attention for his highly fluent and convincing advocacy in court and his calm demeanour. **Strengths:** "A very smooth operator who has a relaxed style and a very good client manner. Great strategically, he picks up the key points and acts on them." "A well-prepared, effective cross-examiner who is very in command." **Recent work:** Advised former company director Gary West following his prosecution by the SFO on a number of charges, including fraudulent trading and bribery.

Christopher Gillespie (see p.653) A reassuring counsel to nervous clients negotiating the criminal justice system for the first time. He is an expert in health and safety and professional discipline, as well as financial crime. **Strengths:** "He was the best advocate in the trial we had. He had to negotiate a tricky cut-throat issue, and whilst others went off-piste or didn't put the work in, he shone. He knew the case well and had fully thought through the line he was going to take." "He's hard working, fearless and he gets results."

QEB Hollis Whiteman

See profile on p.900

THE SET

Highly respected set that has considerable understanding of the interplay between crime and regulatory work. It is regularly sought out to handle high-profile matters, and has recently been involved in both LIBOR manipulation cases and those arising from Operation Tabernula, the insider dealing investigation. A number of its members have prior or current experience of prosecuting financial crime cases, which affords them valuable insight into the best approach to take when defending such actions.

Client service: "The clerks are 'on it' and take responsibility for matters. They get back to you quickly and if they don't know something they will always call." Chris Emmings is the senior clerk.

SILKS

Adrian Darbishire QC A junior silk attracting growing recognition for his winning approach in white-collar crime cases. According to commentators, he is excellent on the paperwork and has strong advocacy skills. They further praise him for his lateral thinking and superb interpersonal skills. **Strengths:** "A charming, sparkling advocate, who's a strong strategist and a terrific drafter." "An extraordinary hard worker who is prepared to think strategically and do things out of the ordinary in a good way. Working with him is a dream as he doesn't talk down to you and you can have lots of fun." **Recent work:** Acted as lead defence counsel for former Barclays trader Ryan Reich, advising him in connection with the SFO investigation into the manipulation of LIBOR.

William Boyce QC (see p.601) A highly effective silk with an impressively persuasive manner in front of judges and juries. Although a former senior treasury counsel at the Central Criminal Court, he now has a strong defence practice and has been instructed in some major cases, including Operation Tabernula, the largest and most complex insider-dealing case prosecuted by the FCA. **Strengths:** "A wonderful cross-examiner, who is utterly tenacious, modest to a fault, and someone with supremely good judgement." "An amazing jury advocate who is very good with complex cases and has a great manner with clients." **Recent work:** Represented chartered accountant Andrew Hind with regard to Operation Tabernula, a high-profile insider dealing investigation.

Mark Ellison QC (see p.640) Head of chambers and a highly experienced criminal prosecutor who was a former first senior treasury counsel. Nowadays, he tackles a broad mix of publicly and privately funded criminal defence work, including SFO prosecutions concerning suspected bribery and insider dealing. **Strengths:** "Extremely hard working, he takes it upon himself to do a lot of detailed preparation. He's a fantastic all-rounder and a pleasure to work with as he's delightful and easy-going." "Has great commercial judgement." **Recent work:** Advised on R v Hind and Others, a prosecution arising from the Operation Tabernula insider dealing investigation.

Sean Larkin QC (see p.695) Both prosecutes and defends high-value money laundering, investment and tax frauds. **Strengths:** "Extremely thorough in his advice and case preparation, he's a good barrister who is great on his feet." "He's a fine cross-examiner who presents well and has a good rapport with the jury." **Recent work:** Led the prosecution in R v Hill, a case concerning allegations of money laundering via forex bureaus.

Peter Finnigan QC (see p.645) A former standing counsel to HMRC, who has broad experience of cases concerning bribery, money laundering and Missing Trader Intra-Community ('MTIC') frauds. **Strengths:** "He is meticulous in his preparation, calm, effective, and someone you can trust with any brief." **Recent work:** Had a lead role for a broker in R v Cryan and Others, an SFO prosecution for alleged manipulation of LIBOR.

JUNIORS

Jason Mansell (see p.707) His background as both a solicitor at a magic circle firm and a regulator at the FSA means that he has great insight into how best to approach financial crime cases. He has recently advised a number of corporates on cross-border corruption issues, and counselled financial institutions facing inquiries into rate manipulation. **Strengths:** "Very good at the intricacies of financial crime, he is bright, good with clients and someone with great strategic vision." "Having him on board is fantastic as he knows how the FCA think; he is not a pushover in any way and has taken cases against them all the way."

Rachna Gokani (see p.655) Exhibits capabilities beyond her years and has an attractive advocacy style, as well as an extremely impressive ability to recall the facts of the matter at hand. Allegations of corruption and accounting fraud are a regular feature of her caseload. Strengths: "One of the best junior members of the Bar currently, who has expertise beyond her years, and an incredible mastery of detail in a case. She is able to step into complex matters in a way not all juniors would be able to." Recent work: Represented a former officer of oil and gas company Swift Technical Group in an SFO prosecution for alleged bribery of Nigerian tax officials.

Selva Ramasamy (see p.747) Prosecutes and defends cases involving professionals and companies charged in criminal, regulatory and disciplinary proceedings. He is particularly good at financial crime cases involving doctors and other healthcare professionals. **Strengths:** "Incredibly able and extremely calm, he glides around the courtroom." "He's extremely thorough, very responsive and has very sound judgement. He is very pleasant to work with too."

Paul Raudnitz (see p.748) A sound and dependable barrister who prosecutes and defends, and regularly provides companies with pre-charge advice. Investment fraud, bribery and money laundering cases all form part of his practice. **Strengths:** "A safe pair of hands, who is sensible and down to earth." **Recent work:** Acted for the FCA in R v Crawley and Others, a prosecution concerning an alleged £4.3 million land banking fraud.

Ben FitzGerald (see p.645) Lauded for his great command of the facts in a case, his strong work ethic, and his leadership skills when part of a team. Cases involving money laundering, banking and tax frauds feature regularly in his workload. **Strengths:** "Fantastic in terms of his advocacy and his ability to control very difficult clients." "He's very commercial and thoughtful in his approach, and never talks down to anyone so he's good in a team." **Recent work:** Advised on the defence of Evdoros Demetriou, a director of a key company implicated in the Operation Amazon prosecution, which centred around carbon credit trading fraud.

Tom Doble (see p.634) A younger counsel with a rising profile due to his high-quality work in the financial criminal arena. He is an expert on cases involving interest rate manipulation and tax fraud. **Strengths:** "A fantastic lawyer, who is able to deal with cases of considerable complexity. He has judgement and the ability to read a situation that belies his quite recent call." **Recent work:** Advised a defendant in R v Ryan Reich and Others, a case relating to alleged criminal manipulation of LIBOR by employed financial traders.

3 Raymond Buildings Barristers

See profile on p.904

THE SET

A hugely renowned criminal chambers that is "packed to the rafters with very, very clever lawyers." Its members are highly sought after for both prosecution and defence work, and regularly handle high-value corporate fraud matters and cases relating to corruption and market manipulation. Its high-calibre silks, in particular, come in for a lot of praise. Key work examples include the representation of a number of parties implicated in the high-profile LIBOR and EURIBOR prosecutions. Members have also been involved in the widely reported investigation into transport company Alstom, looking at the company's overseas contracts. Alstom was subsequently prosecuted for suspected corruption.

Client service: Eddie Holland is the senior clerk. He's "a very friendly chap who really takes time to understand the nature of the case, so he can select the right barrister to recommend."

SILKS

Alexander Cameron QC Regularly sought out by individuals as well as household-name corporations to advise on high-profile and high-stakes financial criminal matters. He is lauded as the consummate silk, and is a committed team player who dispenses passionate and authoritative advocacy. **Strengths:** "Works very, very hard, and takes almost a surgical approach to litigation. He thinks everything through in minute detail and doesn't make a move until he has thought of the consequences many times." "An immense jury advocate who captivates his audience. He's super charming." **Recent work:** Acted for two divisions of multinational company Alstom, representing them in a widely reported investigation into alleged bribery.

Patrick Gibbs QC (see p.652) Highly intelligent and persuasive, he acts on behalf of corporations, as well as individuals, facing potential criminal sanctions. **Strengths:** "Very well liked and respected by judges, solicitors and clients. He invariably identifies some fresh approach to cases in which he is involved." "He gets the ear of the court, his tone is just right, and he's both courageous and diplomatic." **Recent work:** Advised on SFO v Kappauf, a case regarding a Deutsche Bank financial trader accused of illegal manipulation of the Euro Interbank Offered Rate ('EURIBOR').

Hugo Keith QC (see p.689) An in-demand silk who regularly acts for corporate clients, including financial institutions. He is praised for his clear and sharp mind as well as his smooth advocacy style. **Strengths:** "He is one of the few people at the Bar who combines expertise in criminal and public law. A versatile, clever lawyer who is very easy to work with, super bright and particularly good for appellate work." "Corporates are more interested in appellate skills and he has those in abundance." **Recent work:** Acted for a former employee of a financial institution, in the high-profile investigation and prosecution concerning LIBOR manipulation.

Trevor Burke QC Popular both domestically and in jurisdictions outside the UK such as the Cayman Islands. He advises on a broad range of financial crime cases, including those relating to theft, tax evasion and bribery. **Strengths:** "Extremely good in front of the jury, he's good at managing himself in the cut and thrust of the courtroom. There were lots of big egos in court and he handled it all really well." "Tremendously versatile, polished, great with clients and someone with very good judgement." **Recent work:** Advised Michelle Bouchard who was accused of a multimillion-dollar bank fraud and theft in the Cayman Islands.

Simon Farrell QC Has proven skill in financial crime and Proceeds of Crime Act ('POCA') cases, and acts for the prosecution as well as the defence. **Strengths:** "He's very solid, has a good client manner, and is thorough in his approach." **Recent work:** Acted for Michael Elsom, a city broker implicated in a film finance tax fraud.

James Lewis QC (see p.700) Relied upon by an impressive client base, including the SFO. He is experienced at advising on potentially criminal conduct such as rate manipulation. **Strengths:** "A smooth, clever advocate who inspires confidence. He is academically excellent, and has considerable experience in international cases." "Very comprehensive, both in terms of reading around the case to understand it in greater detail and in thinking of all methods to meet the client's objectives." **Recent work:** Had a lead role on behalf of the SFO in the investigation into alleged illegal manipulation of forex rates.

James Hines QC (see p.672) Known for his effective advocacy style, he emphasises his strongest arguments well and communicates clearly with his audience. He is sought out to advise on high-stakes matters, and had a key role in the widely reported investigations surrounding LIBOR. **Strengths:** "Very fluid, he manages to put things in a way which is easily understood, and I think he hits well above his experience as a silk." "Equally good on paper as he is an advocate, he grasps the essential points remarkably quickly, even when deluged with papers, and cuts through the chaff to get to the important points." **Recent work:** Led the prosecution of a number of Barclays Bank employees for alleged LIBOR manipulation, acting on behalf of the SFO.

Helen Malcolm QC A renowned expert in crime, fraud and extradition cases. She is regularly called upon to advise on the defence of individuals accused of corruption. **Strengths:** "She comes into her own for appellate proceedings, is pleasant to work with and responsive, especially out of hours." "Extremely clever and extremely hard working, she instils considerable confidence in clients. When complex issues are to be addressed, she stands out as a result of her great intelligence." **Recent work:** Advised the defence in R v Dixon, an SFO prosecution involving an alleged £17 million fraud relating to arbitrage gambling.

Richard Horwell QC Regularly handles appeals following convictions in fraud and broader financial crime cases. He is renowned for his calm and reassuring style. **Strengths:** "One of the top-rated barristers in the country as far as Court of Appeal work is concerned." "His presentation, drafting and construction of arguments are all faultless, and he shows a meticulous level of preparation and attention." **Recent work:** Advised on the appeal of Jason Hollier, an individual previously convicted of perjury and fraudulent trading.

Jonathan Ashley-Norman QC (see p.585) One of the newest silks at the set, he has a practice that is heavy on cases concerning internal disciplinary matters and allegations of cross-border fraud. **Strengths:** "He has just been made up to silk, and deservedly so." "He's quick to grasp the salient issues in a case." **Recent work:** Acted in R v Yeomans, Yeomans and Clarke, a case involving suspected VAT fraud and money laundering relating to the sale of controlled substances.

JUNIORS

Neil Saunders (see p.759) A senior junior who is instructed by individuals, corporations and public bodies. He is an experienced adviser in relation to high-level investigations into insider dealing, company fraud and bribery. **Strengths:** "He has got tremendous client care skills and makes the client feel safe. He's a very eloquent advocate, and you know if you instruct him on a case he's as good as many silks." "He is incredibly client-friendly, and good at conveying unwelcome advice when he has to." **Recent work:** Advised Orit Eyal-Fibeesh, a company director prosecuted for false invoicing and fraud.

Ben Brandon An accomplished junior whose capability in financial crime matters is complemented by his market-leading extradition practice. He has defended senior company employees embroiled in corporate, insurance and Ponzi frauds. **Strengths:** "Intelligent, hard working and someone who offers good all-round client care." **Recent work:** Advised on Government of Greece v Kyriakos Griveas, representing a media company officer on criminal and extradition proceedings concerning an alleged EUR21.7 million fraud on the Greek National Bank.

Ben Summers (see p.776) A highly competent and well-organised barrister with laudable experience of advising on bribery, fraud and regulatory issues. Corporations and public bodies, as well as individuals, feature highly on his client roster. **Strengths:** "A star of the future, who is very diligent and interested in his cases." "He is meticulous and knows his onions. No page in a brief goes unread, and every single avenue in the case is pursued and analysed." **Recent work:** He advised the FCA on its regulatory investigation into, and prosecution of, a number of financial institutions implicated in the illegal manipulation of LIBOR.

Rachel Barnes (see p.590) An accomplished junior whose international crime and fraud practice is complemented by her expertise in extradition. Although she often advises individuals, she is also increasingly sought out by companies that are dealing with internal investigations, or are accused of potential sanctions breaches and illegal manipulation of benchmark rates. **Strengths:** "A very thorough barrister who ensures she's really researched the issues before giving advice. Her work is very well written, well structured and well referenced." "Very strong, very detailed on the case, and very good with clients who may be extremely stressed." **Recent work:** Acted in R v Thomas Campbell, a case concerning a large-scale alleged theft of hydrocarbon oil from the national pipeline network.

Nicholas Yeo (see p.801) Specialises in fraud and has noted expertise in money laundering, an area he regularly writes about in various texts. He has recently been acting in Operation Tabernula, the FCA's largest and most complex insider dealing investigation. **Strengths:** "He's very personable with clients and willing to take on board their opinions. If they want a particular aspect of the case developed he's always willing to take it on board." "Masters the detailed legislative landscape, and has great command of mutual assistance legislation." **Recent work:** Acted in SFO v Saleh, a case concerning an application to discharge a real estate freezing order, arising from the sale of shares by the wife of a diplomat.

Rachel Scott (see p.760) Counts extradition and financial crime cases as cornerstones of her practice. She is an experienced junior counsel for the prosecution, and her enviable client list includes the SFO. **Strengths:** "Shows great attention to detail, and is very good at talking through difficult points of law." **Recent work:** Acted as first junior counsel for the SFO in its prosecution of Alstom for alleged corruption and bribery.

Richard Wormald A leading junior in serious crime, able to turn his hand to cases of corruption, fraud and market abuse. **Strengths:** "Just a great all-rounder. Bright, good with a jury and good with clients, he's easy to work with, and fun with it." **Recent work:** Acted for a number of directors of Rolls-Royce in the wake of the SFO's investigation into suspected bribery.

Band 2

25 Bedford Row

See profile on p.810

THE SET

A set that enjoys considerable market acclaim for its skills handling many types of criminal cases. Its financial crime team has handled many high-profile cases relating to tax and investment fraud, as well as a number of bribery and corruption matters, both at home and abroad.

Work highlights for the chambers include R v Dartnell and Others, a £142 million fraud and corruption case involving a Belgian bank, and Operation Bamburgh, a large-scale mortgage fraud concerning over £100 million of losses sustained by three mortgage providers.

Client service: "The clerks are superb and form a friendly close-knit team. They ensure every hearing is covered, and that you have the opportunity to discuss a case before the hearing happens." Guy Williams leads the clerking team, assisted by deputy senior clerk Emma Makepeace.

SILKS

George Carter-Stephenson QC A leading silk who impresses interviewees with his passion and persuasiveness when addressing a jury, as well as his meticulous case preparation. He has proven expertise in cases involving alleged tax frauds, corrupt payments and rate manipulation. **Strengths:** "A leader of choice for anybody at the top of the indictment. He has a level of knowledge, experience and input that you rarely see in other silks." "One of the best jury advocates at the Criminal Bar, he adopts a very good tactical approach to cases, and knows how to talk to juries." **Recent work:** Advised the defence in R v Robert Gold, a prosecution arising from the Operation Amazon investigation into suspected tax fraud relating to carbon credits.

Peter Doyle QC Provides high-quality defence counsel, and regularly handles boiler room frauds and cases involving tax fraud and bribery. **Strengths:** "A composed figure who always has the facts at his fingertips." **Recent work:** Acted for the principal defendant in R v Nicholas Smith and Others, a case concerning allegedly corrupt agreements to pay government department officials in a number of African states.

Tom Price QC Noted for his polished advocacy and excellent interpersonal skills when dealing with lay clients, opposing counsel and judicial figurers. **Strengths:** "He has an excellent manner and I don't know of any case he's been involved with where he hasn't got on with the client very well. He knows how to deal with the court, the judge, the prosecution and the jury." **Recent work:** Represented a defendant in R v Goldsmith, which concerned alleged mortgage fraud relating to high-end London properties.

Nigel Sangster QC (see p.758) An experienced defence silk who attracts praise for the calming influence he has on clients facing stressful criminal proceedings. He regularly defends in tax and investment fraud cases. **Strengths:** "Extremely personable, very approachable, and a very good listener who observes a situation and then comes in with measured comments. He exudes confidence and takes control of the conference when he needs to." "Extremely thorough in his preparation and robust in his advocacy." **Recent work:** Advised in R v Kimberly Murphy and Others, a £1.6 million film finance tax fraud.

Courtenay Griffiths QC Enjoys an enviable reputation both at home and abroad for his work handling high-profile and high-value financial crime and corruption cases, some of which involve public servants. He is praised for his taut and commanding advocacy style. **Strengths:** "His written work is excellent and only surpassed by his oral advocacy which is superb. He's obviously ferocious – you need to be when you're a criminal barrister – but he always does things in a decent manner." **Recent work:** Acted in R v Misick and Others, a case before the Turks and Caicos Islands Supreme Court. The former First Minister of the Turks and Caicos Islands faced allegations of having been involved in corruption and money laundering during his time in office.

JUNIORS

Nathaniel Rudolf A recognised junior counsel in financial crime and the related field of POCA work. His key instructions include advising on allegations of rate manipulation and insider dealing. **Strengths:** "Very analytical and very switched on when it comes to all aspects of financial crime and POCA. A real expert, he has written leading books, and is a walking, talking 'anorak' on the subject, given his phenomenal knowledge." "He's great on details and has the stamina required to handle these long fraud cases." **Recent work:** Advised on the defence of Colin Goodman, an interdealer broker, who faced a high-profile SFO prosecution for manipulation of LIBOR.

Nicola Howard (see p.675) A well-organised, highly dependable junior counsel who applies herself effectively and communicates well with both clients and judges. She is experienced at acting in a range of financial crime cases, including those relating to tax fraud and rate manipulation. **Strengths:** "Extremely good on the organisation front, she shows great attention to detail and is firm when clients need to have a little pressure applied." "She is lovely to work with, clearly respected and a consummate junior who gets on very well with judges in London." **Recent work:** Acted in R v Zemmel and Others, a prosecution for an alleged £1 million VAT fraud connected with broadcast licensing of cage fighting events.

Samantha Riggs (see p.752) Attracts market acclaim for her skill in cases where environmental law and financial crime overlap. She has handled a number of high-value financial crime cases relating to land banking and carbon credits. **Strengths:** "A fearless, leading junior." "Has knowledge beyond almost everyone else in her area, and shows a willingness to fight hard for the client's case." **Recent work:** Acted in R v Linda Noad, a prosecution for suspected money laundering, following alleged land banking and carbon credit frauds committed by members of her family.

Colin Wells A committed and diligent junior counsel who has deep experience of handling cases relating to money laundering, boiler room fraud and bribery. **Strengths:** "A very experienced advocate who works very hard." "The client really engaged well with him, and was very complimentary." **Recent work:** Advised in R v Linda Noad, a case involving suspected laundering of proceeds of land banking investment and carbon credit fraud.

Geoffrey Payne (see p.735) Counts high-value financial crime, such as tax and investment fraud, as a cornerstone of his practice. He is noted for his superior tactical awareness, cogent analysis of facts and strong client service skills. **Strengths:** "An extremely hard-working junior who produces work of the highest quality, always on time." "Brilliant to work with, he is fantastic in his analysis of a case and the speed with which he responds to professional clients is second to none." **Recent work:** Appeared in R v Kimberly Murphy and Others, a film finance tax fraud case.

9-12 Bell Yard

THE SET

A superior criminal set that attracts praise for its impressive work acting for the prosecution in suspected corruption, insider dealing and corporate fraud cases. Testament to its skills, it was involved in one of the most prominent financial industry criminal misconduct cases of recent years, namely the SFO's high-profile action regarding alleged criminal manipulation of LIBOR.

Client service: "The clerks are very accommodating, very responsive and people who find you what you need." Angela May is the senior clerk.

SILKS

Mukul Chawla QC (see p.615) Head of chambers, who is acclaimed for his superb judgement and meticulous preparation when advising on marquee cases. He both prosecutes and defends cases, and has been involved in some of the major cases of recent years. **Strengths:** "He has a wonderful ability to deal with very large and complex matters and represent them brilliantly in front of the jury." "A formidable presence in court." **Recent work:** Led the prosecution of a number of individuals, notably Tom Hayes, charged in connection with the SFO's high-profile action concerning alleged criminal manipulation of LIBOR.

Alexandra Healy QC (see p.668) Displays excellent communication and presentation skills, and is a highly confident performer, even when the facts seem stacked against her. She is experienced in prosecution and defence cases involving suspected fraud relating to bribery of public officials, company insolvency and insider trading. **Strengths:** "She is very intelligent, has a great rapport with the client and really appreciates the issues in a case." "She's easy to deal with, very amiable and extremely sensible." **Recent work:** Advised the prosecution in R v John Clifton Davies, a case concerning an insolvency adviser who allegedly defrauded companies in difficulty.

Lord Carlile of Berriew QC (see p.611) An experienced practitioner who regularly handles tax and commercial fraud cases. He is noted for his reassuring presence, and is a fluent public speaker, even when under pressure. **Strengths:** "A very good orator." "An exceptional advocate who has great presence in court."

Jonathan Kinnear QC (see p.691) Regulatory, criminal and confiscation issues feature prominently in his caseload, and he has handled a number of matters involving allegations of MTIC fraud, money laundering and corruption. **Recent work:** Advised the SFO on Operation Dynamo, an investigation into suspected corruption involving mineral exploitation rights on the part of Mykola Zlochevsky, the high net worth former ecology minister of the Ukraine.

John McGuinness QC (see p.713) Retained as leading counsel in cases such as those concerning allegations of multi-jurisdictional tax fraud. He is noted for his strong work ethic and persuasive advocacy style. **Strengths:** "Extremely diligent and hard working."

JUNIORS

Alexandra Ward (see p.789) A popular figure who has a sterling reputation as a junior counsel acting for the prosecution. She is applauded for her enthusiastic and responsive client service, and the careful, methodical analysis she applies to document-heavy cases. **Strengths:** "She is fantastic on the detail and leaves no stone unturned. She can pore over thousands of documents and draw out the facts." **Recent work:** Acted as junior counsel for the prosecution in Operation Tabernula, a large and widely reported FCA action concerning alleged insider dealing in the City of London.

Carmelite Chambers

See profile on p.817

THE SET

A defence-minded chambers that regularly handles high-end financial crime work. Areas of strength for the set include cases concerning manipulation of rates, mortgage fraud and corruption. Key instructions include R v Read and Others, a high-profile prosecution arising from the extensive investigation into financial traders' alleged rigging of LIBOR.

Client service: "They always try to get you who you want, and know the right people to offer. In advance of hearings they keep us apprised of matters so you never get a situation where a barrister has been told something and you haven't. We always get their personal mobile and e-mail, and they keep us fully abreast." Marc King is the head clerk and, according to one source, "the most responsive clerk I've ever dealt with."

SILKS

Charles Bott QC (see p.599) A popular choice of silk for the defence of a variety of financial criminal charges, including those relating to rate manipulation, tax fraud and corruption. He is known for his superior intellect, careful attention to detail and great communication skills. **Strengths:** "If you've got silks who start to be guided by their ego, there can start to be quite a lot of posturing that not only wastes time but which can elevate the temperature and make things really quite difficult. There's no ego with him, even though he's entitled to have it." "A lawyer with a brilliant mind and an understated advocacy approach. He's a devastating talent in and out of court." **Recent work:** Acted for a defendant in R v Read and Others, a case connected with the high-profile criminal prosecutions for alleged manipulation of LIBOR.

John Richard Jones QC (see p.685) A senior silk who has enviable experience of handling SFO and CPS prosecutions. His key instructions involve advising on suspected insider dealing, tax fraud and money laundering matters. **Strengths:** "Very attentive to both clients and solicitors."

Leonard Smith QC (see p.768) A criminal defence silk who commands respect for the pains he takes with his preparation, and for the persuasive advocacy he delivers in court.He regularly handles cases involving allegations of mortgage fraud, breach of sanctions and overseas corruption. **Strengths:** "Very industrious and someone with superb technical knowledge. He is prepared for most eventualities and is definitely a great courtroom advocate." **Recent work:** Acted for the lead defendant in R v David Purdie and Others, a prosecution for mortgage fraud of circa £300 million involving around 2,400 properties.

Adam Kane QC (see p.687) An effective experienced silk who has a rising market profile. He handles matters involving suspected corruption, tax evasion and money laundering. **Strengths:** "An accomplished advocate who is a regular in high-calibre fraud cases." **Recent work:** Advised on Operation Hayrack, a prosecution for alleged bribery relating to contracts to maintain the Royal Palaces.

JUNIORS

Colin Aylott (see p.587) A dependable junior popular with instructing solicitors for defending complicated fraud cases. He acts in matters concerning allegations of rate manipulation, money laundering and mortgage fraud. **Strengths:** "Straightforward in his approach and not a man to panic." **Recent work:** Acted in R v James Gilmour, a high-profile SFO prosecution for alleged manipulation of LIBOR.

Richard Furlong (see p.649) A reliable choice for matters where numerous documents need to be considered, he is acclaimed for his cogent case interpretation and affable client manner. **Strengths:** "Very analytical, very good at looking at the detail of the case, and good at challenging the client's instructions where necessary. He is great at getting into the detail of a case." **Recent work:** Advised the defence in the Operation Galion prosecution, which involved the allegedly fraudulent sale of advertising space in non-existent publications.

Mark Harries (see p.664) Known for his measured, careful analysis of the facts and persuasive court advocacy style. Criminal defence work forms the mainstay of his practice and he regularly handles cases involving embezzlement, mortgage fraud and corruption. **Strengths:** "Cool, calm, collected and gets on well with clients. He can handle complex issues with ease and make it all look easy." "A junior counsel of some promise who is a good advocate and an extremely confident individual." **Recent work:** Advised on R v Richard Gilliland and Steven Davies, a case concerning alleged criminal and financial impropriety in the running of a school.

Jonathan Lennon (see p.699) Heavyweight fraud and POCA work lie at the heart of his practice. He has the ability to swiftly analyse complex cases with large volumes of documents and produce sound advocacy. **Strengths:** "He is of huge practical assistance to those who instruct him. He is very good at guiding professional clients through difficult cases, produces excellent written work, and has put so much into cases over years." "One of the best juniors in financial crime, and someone with a phenomenal brain and a capacity for hard work. He leaves court at the end of a long day and overnight produces a brilliant skeleton argument."

Gerard Hillman (see p.672) A proven defence advocate who handles high-value financial crime work, including money laundering, MTIC and investment fraud cases. **Strengths:** "An excellent advocate with a great breadth of knowledge." **Recent work:** Acted for Buddika Kadurugamuwa, a solicitor accused of money laundering in a EUR100 million shipping fraud.

The Chambers of Andrew Mitchell QC

See profile on p.819

THE SET

A chambers renowned not only for financial criminal work, but also for the confiscation proceedings that frequently follow successful prosecutions. Interviewees praise its members for their strategic thinking, focused action and friendly service. Key areas of strength include cases involving tax and investment fraud, and allegations of rate manipulation. Individuals here are also well used to tackling matters concerning corruption overseas.

Client service: "There's a small but very well run team of clerks there." Martin Adams is the practice director, and is "very helpful and very fair."

SILKS

Andrew Mitchell QC (see p.719) A well-known heavyweight silk who is a great choice of leading counsel for high-value matters connected with financial wrongdoing. His reputation has spread far and wide, ensuring he is instructed to advise on marquee matters both at home and abroad. **Strengths:** "He really highlights his client's strongest points whilst rubbing in the other side's defective ones. His oral submissions are extremely impressive." "He's hugely organised, hard working and someone who deserves his reputation." **Recent work:** Advised on the Turks and Caicos Islands prosecution of Missick and Others. The case concerned public servants suspected of bribery, corruption and money laundering.

Alistair Webster QC (see p.792) A barrister with great interpersonal skills who gets the best out of clients and the judiciary, and is noted for his attractive advocacy style. Strengths: "Very user-friendly, and his advocacy shines." "He produces excellent performances in the Court of Appeal." Recent work: Led the defence of Trevor McClintock, a Belfast businessman accused of defrauding a number of banks.

Graham Brodie QC A newer silk noted for his attractive presentation style in court and for being a good team player. He regularly advises on allegations of money laundering and overseas corruption, and he is also experienced in related POCA work. **Strengths:** "He has civil and criminal experience, and is technically very able." "Exceptionally smooth in his delivery." **Recent work:** Defended Sandeep Gill who was accused of laundering the proceeds of MTIC fraud by way of a bank which was specifically established for that purpose.

Amanda Pinto QC (see p.738) Acts for the prosecution and the defence in serious financial crime cases, including those involving mis-statement of financial accounts, investment frauds and money laundering. Interviewees reserve special mention for her easy-going manner and clear commitment to obtaining the best result for her client. **Strengths:** "Very clever. She is a real warrior who cannot be knocked off her perch; she just comes back again and again." "Produces pithy oral and written advocacy." **Recent work:** Defended Emma Farmer who faced prosecution and later confiscation proceedings related to Operation Steamroller, an investigation into suspected share fraud and consequent money laundering.

Mark Rainsford QC (see p.746) Has superb legal knowledge and great judgement in how best to advance the client's cause. He regularly handles corruption cases and all manner of investment frauds, including those relating to Ponzi schemes. **Strengths:** "A very good, strategic and tactical thinker who is great with clients. He's easy to deal with and gets right to heart of a problem." **Recent work:** Acted in R v Sutherland, a case concerning an individual who was previously employed in financial services and was then implicated in the alleged laundering of USD 120 million arising from boiler room fraud.

JUNIORS

Keith Mitchell (see p.719) Puts clients in stressful situations at ease and speaks to them in a style they can readily understand, according to those who instruct him. He frequently acts unled, acting for the defence in high-value cases. **Strengths:** "Very industrious, very reassuring, and very articulate in communicating complicated legal concepts." "He handles a lot of high-level financial criminal work, he is great with juries, and he wins a lot of cases." **Recent work:** Advised the defence in a case arising from the Operation Cactus Hunt investigation into an alleged £12 million pensions and carousel fraud.

Christopher Convey (see p.622) Recognised for his diligence, great attention to detail and fine advocacy skills. Rate rigging and corporate theft matters feature highly in his caseload. **Strengths:** "A prolific worker who really gets into the detail. We had a tremendous volume of material at short notice but he was exceptional on the paperwork." "He's tenacious and bright." **Recent work:** Acted for Tom Hayes in the high-profile SFO case concerning alleged manipulation of LIBOR.

Faisal Osman (see p.731) A careful barrister with great powers of factual recall and a highly supportive junior counsel, who adds clear value to proceedings. His experience includes advising on high-value allegations of tax fraud and international money laundering. **Strengths:** "Able to get up to speed in complex cases very quickly, he has an in-depth knowledge of all the material in the brief. " **Recent work:** Advised Samuel Tree on his prosecution and confiscation proceedings relating to the alleged advertising and sale of worthless bomb detection devices to buyers worldwide.

Doughty Street Chambers

See profile on p.828

THE SET

A set with enviable bench strength at silk level that is strong in the defence of serious financial crime. One source said of it: "I think it's got a lot stronger in recent years. It's weathered the legal aid storm well and is still getting some interesting cases." Its members are sought out to act in cases concerning high-profile insider dealing, international corruption and tax allegations.

Client service: "The clerks are realistic and approachable, and the billing is very straightforward." Tom Street is the crime team leader.

SILKS

Peter Carter QC (see p.612) An experienced practitioner on the defence and the prosecution side who handles insider dealing, share fraud and tax evasion cases. Sources applaud him for his thorough approach to case preparation, and note that he is able to command respect from all who deal with him. **Strengths:** "Up there with the best, he's very good on the detail and a very sensible advocate who is authoritative in the way he deals with things. Everyone likes and respects him." "A very good forensic lawyer." **Recent work:** Advised on R v James Sanders and Others, a case arising from the Operation Kronos investigation into alleged transatlantic insider dealing.

Christopher Sallon QC A well-liked and highly respected senior silk with the necessary gravitas to secure the best results whatever the circumstances. Sources speak of his persuasive advocacy style and ability to motivate the teams he works with in difficult situations. His clients include high-level bank executives. **Strengths:** "He is just a joy to work with, not only because he's a lovely, gentle, persuasive advocate, but also because he's got the most amazing sense of humour."

Rupert Bowers QC (see p.600) Regularly defends white-collar crime cases, and has handled a number of cases concerning tax evasion, parliamentary expenses and money laundering. **Strengths:** "A real problem solver who is excellent at challenging search warrants." **Recent work:** Acted in R v Gurmail Singh Dosanjh and Others, a case concerning an alleged £11 million VAT fraud relating to the trading of carbon credits.

Siobhan Grey QC Appointed to silk in 2016 following years of successful practice as a dependable, committed junior. She is a dedicated defence barrister whose work includes advising on high-value financial and business crime involving such issues as export control and insider dealing. **Strengths:** "Very, very good, and not afraid to ruffle feathers in court – she's not afraid to take the judiciary on if necessary." "She took every point, fought tooth and nail for the client but was very charming with it. I was very impressed with her commitment, which was extraordinary." **Recent work:** She advised on R v Joan Tree, an alleged fraud related to the marketing, sale and export of fake bomb detection devices.

23 Essex Street

See profile on p.839

THE SET

A large set of accomplished barristers that "can provide a suitable barrister for every job." Members practise across a range of areas relating to financial crime, and are praised for both their willingness to act as part of a team and their diligent case preparation. As well as prosecuting and defending criminal cases, the set also has broad regulatory expertise and advisory capacity. Recent work handled by 23 Essex Street includes cases stemming from Operation Amazon, a high-value carbon credit fraud investigation.

Client service: "The diary clerks are very accessible." Richard Fowler is the chambers' director, and "very good at putting people together in a team."

SILKS

Cairns Nelson QC Co-head of the set, and recognised for his confident, reassuring and rallying manner, even when the facts of the case appear unfavourable. He has built a sterling reputation acting for both the prosecution and the defence in cases concerning matters such as carbon credits, professional reporting fraud and export control. **Strengths:** "He's got a really good grasp of the law and no fear at all. Sometimes you have a case which is not looking too good, or doesn't seem to be able to go anywhere, and some people shy away from that. He doesn't. He grabs the bull by the horns and embraces the situation. He's an imposing character but a man with a huge amount of warmth to whom clients listen and fully respect." **Recent work:** Acted in R v Rivers and Others, a trading standards prosecution concerning 13 individuals charged with newspaper fraud.

Simon Russell Flint QC Former head of the set and an experienced criminal silk on the London scene. He has led in a huge array of financial crime cases, including those involving overseas corruption, film investment schemes and identity theft. **Strengths:** "A stylish, well-rounded and experienced silk." **Recent work:** Appeared in R v Griffiths, defending charges of criminal misrepresentation in relation to investment in media production companies.

Mark Fenhalls QC (see p.644) Current chair of the Criminal Bar Association of England and Wales, and a high-profile practitioner. His wide practice has seen him handle, inter alia, cases involving tax fraud and corruption with regard to public contracts. **Strengths:** "He is extremely sensitive to clients in a tough spot, and knows how best to work with instructing solicitors to make them feel comfortable." "Very good at one of the more underrated skills in the job, namely persuading the client to accept the lawyer's advice." **Recent work:** Advised Jeremy Garrett, an unqualified tax professional, in connection with a prosecution arising from irregularities in his personal tax returns.

Paul Bogan QC A dedicated defence silk with notable experience in the realm of serious crime and fraud. His experience includes advising on cases relating to mortgage fraud, money laundering and the awarding of public service contracts. **Strengths:** "A very good advocate who works very hard." **Recent work:** Advised Nicholas Hill, the proprietor of a bureau de change, on charges relating to the suspected laundering of £300,000.

Charles Miskin QC A former standing counsel to the precursor to HMRC, and thus highly experienced in advising on tax-related cases including MTIC and carbon credit frauds. **Strengths:** "He's dynamic and shows leadership." **Recent work:** Acted as prosecution counsel in the high-profile Operation Amazon matter, concerning allegations of a massive tax fraud in relation to carbon credits.

6KBW College Hill

THE SET

A leading set with great pedigree that offers a selection of individuals, well versed in handling all manner of general crime, fraud, bribery and POCA-related cases. Although historically associated with prosecution work, it is nowadays just as well known for acting for defendants. Its members are noted for being "diligent and individuals who provide great gravitas in court." They regularly handle big-ticket work, as evidenced by their involvement in cases arising from the investigation into former city professionals for alleged illegal manipulation of LIBOR.

Client service: The support staff at the set are "attentive, responsive, professional and polite." Andrew Barnes is the senior clerk and is highly respected. "He doesn't tell you what you want to hear, but tells you how it is instead. He doesn't try to push unsuitable barristers at you."

SILKS

David Perry QC A star player and a highly accomplished silk who is at the apex of the Criminal Bar. Interviewees were effusive in their praise of his intellect, judgement and gravitas, and lauded him for his efforts in high-stakes criminal matters such as those concerning overseas bribery and corruption investigations into household-name companies. **Strengths:** "In the top two or three criminal counsel in the country. He's just unflappable, has an encyclopaedic knowledge of case law, and is supremely clever. He's a marvellous advocate, and when you listen to him it's like having your ears rubbed in velvet." "The counsel of choice for governments and large financial institutions, he has absolutely unrivalled expertise, and can present the most technical criminal cases with ease."

Duncan Penny QC Senior treasury counsel who handles high-profile prosecutions involving overseas corruption and company law breaches, amongst others. **Strengths:** "A very passionate lawyer, who is very, very clever, and excellent with clients." **Recent work:** Acted in R v Gyrus Group Limited and Olympus Corporation, a high-profile Companies Act 2006 prosecution concerning the alleged misleading of a company auditor.

Sasha Wass QC A renowned force in the criminal law world who is regularly sought out by the CPS and SFO to lead on high-profile prosecutions. She regularly handles money laundering and investment and banking fraud cases. Strengths: "Obviously has an excellent legal mind, but is also able to communicate in a very personable way." Recent work: Advised the SFO in connection with Tesco's widely reported misstatement of accounts.

Annabel Darlow QC A well-established performer who receives repeat instructions from prosecuting authorities such as the SFO. Her work experience includes advising on alleged frauds relating to mortgages and the provision of public services. **Recent work:** Assisted the SFO in an investigation into government contracts with G4S & Serco, following widely reported allegations of fraudulent conduct at those companies.

John Ryder QC Lauded for his charming and effective style, he is a man who commands obvious respect in court. Examples of his high-value financial criminal defence work are numerous and include cases concerning rate manipulation, cartels and insider dealing. **Strengths:** "Has a robust style and is great to have on board when the facts in your case aren't looking too encouraging." "His presentation is second to none. He speaks to the jury in an easy, palatable and digestible manner." **Recent work:** Acted in R v Terry Farr and Others, advising a former City broker charged with alleged criminal manipulation of LIBOR.

JUNIORS

Miranda Hill Increasingly sought out to advise corporations implicated in financial crime, and has acted for some household names from the media, manufacturing and financial services sectors. She is a level-headed and thoughtful barrister, who assimilates large quantities of data in order to give best advice. **Strengths:** "We in the commercial sphere value someone who can turn things around in short order when there's a high volume of material and pressure from the clients to get advice out quickly. Miranda is a wise head, and a calm and considered person under pressure." "She is very effective, has excellent drafting skills, and produces clear, cogent advice." **Recent work:** Junior counsel to News UK and News Group Newspapers, advising on matters relating to the high-profile phone hacking investigations and associated allegations of bribery of public servants in exchange for information.

Gareth Patterson A versatile performer accustomed to acting for the SFO in criminal investigations and prosecutions. He is also recognised for representing defendants accused of fraud and rate manipulation. **Strengths:** "Industrious and can be relied upon to absorb every fact in the case." **Recent work:** Acted as junior counsel to Terry Farr, in a case brought by the SFO for alleged criminal manipulation of LIBOR.

Esther Schutzer-Weissmann Regularly acts for the prosecution, handling cases relating to allegations of investment fraud, mis-statement of financial accounts and money laundering. **Strengths:** "Extremely hard working and thorough." **Recent work:** Junior counsel to the prosecution in R v Rommell Brown and Others, a case concerning an alleged multihanded £1.5 million boiler room investment fraud.

Matrix Chambers

See profile on p.876

THE SET

Recognised for its defence of high-level, privately funded financial crime cases, including those relating to tax frauds, rate rigging and corruption. The calibre and expertise of its members are such that instructing solicitors entrust them with the most complex matters, some of which involves work in jurisdictions overseas. Notable instructions include advising on the high-profile investigation by the SFO into alleged illegal manipulation of the EURIBOR.

Client service: "Bills are timely and detailed, and it's a smooth running operation." Paul Venables heads up the team for this practice area.

SILKS

Clare Montgomery QC (see p.720) A widely acclaimed top-drawer silk whose talents are in considerable demand both at home and abroad. She acts for individuals and corporations, and is an elite practitioner whose "pitch perfect advocacy" is employed to great effect in appellate cases. **Strengths:** "One of the biggest brains at the Bar and an amazing appellate lawyer." "She thinks of every angle and comes up with clever stuff. Clients absolutely love her as she's plain talking, reassuring and very clear about what will happen." **Recent work:** Acted for Thomas Kwok, appealing a finding of misconduct related to payments made to the Chief Secretary of Hong Kong.

Tim Owen QC Financial crime is but one strand of this silk's impressively broad practice. He is particularly good at advising listed companies on potential bribery charges. **Strengths:** "He's very good with the lay client as he can make difficult concepts easily intelligible." "His real talent is as an appellate advocate. He is very good in the senior courts, gets respect from the appeal judges, and everything that he does is beautifully prepared."

Alex Bailin QC (see p.587) A popular choice of adviser for financial market-related matters, who is no stranger to finance having had a career in derivatives trading before coming to the Bar. He is applauded for being quick to grasp the facts at hand as well as for his winning interpersonal skills with solicitors and lay clients. **Strengths:** "He is really good at judicial review challenges to the SFO, is very user-friendly and very good to work with." **Recent work:** Provided advice in the ongoing SFO investigation into alleged rigging of the EURIBOR.

Julian Knowles QC His financial crime work sees him handling tax evasion and confiscation matters, amongst others, as well as cases involving allegations of rate manipulation. His is an international practice and he regularly handles overseas frauds and associated extradition work. **Strengths:** "A terrific appellate lawyer." **Recent work:** Acted in R v Boyle Transport, an appeal examining the treatment of company profits in relation to criminal confiscation.

Ken Macdonald QC A former Director of Public Prosecutions ('DPP') and thus no stranger to the intricacies of serious criminal cases, including frauds. His client roster includes high net worth individuals. **Strengths:** "His advocacy skills and ability to express himself succinctly are like nobody else's."

JUNIORS

Andrew Bodnar Applauded for his ability to come up with clear strategies when facing document-heavy cases. He is an expert in cases involving money laundering and asset tracing, and takes on the most complex, multi-jurisdictional cases. **Strengths:** "Produces outstanding analysis of documents, particularly in complex financial matters." "Very responsive and practical." **Recent work:** Acted in R v Noad, a prosecution for money laundering arising from a land banking fraud valued in excess of £11 million.

5 Paper Buildings

See profile on p.889

THE SET

Has proven expertise advising on a broad range of general crime, financial crime and regulatory matters. Its members are called upon to both defend and prosecute cases involving such issues as rate manipulation, corruption and false invoicing. Recently, the set has been involved in high-profile prosecutions relating to alleged LIBOR manipulation, and has also advised with regard to overseas bribery allegations surrounding the Sweett Group.

Client service: "They are very, very organised and provide a great service. The clerking is excellent and you don't have to chase them; they remember that solicitors are the source of their work, and they appreciate who we answer to. I don't think they could improve, that's how good I think they are." Dale Jones is the senior clerk. "He is very responsive, no-nonsense, and commercial without being too sharp in his approach."

SILKS

Jonathan Caplan QC Extremely highly regarded and noted for his impressive strategic input to a case and appealing advocacy style. High-profile matters he has advised on include those relating to charges of corporate mis-statement, as well as alleged manipulation of benchmark rates. **Strengths:** "A terrific advocate, who is a brilliant speech maker." "A tactical genius."

Tom Allen QC A fairly new silk with deep experience of financial crime, who has handled cases relating to rate manipulation, film finance and bribery. He is noted for his clear communication skills and approachable manner. **Strengths:** "He's quite young for a silk but has lots of presence and ability, and the tone of his delivery is very convincing." "He possesses excellent judgement and great client-care skills." **Recent work:** Had a lead role for the defence in R v Pabon, a case involving a former trader with Barclays Capital who was accused of LIBOR manipulation.

Michael Brompton QC (see p.604) Lauded in equal measure for his interpersonal skills as eye for detail. He is regularly sought out to advise on high-value corruption and investment fraud matters, and generally acts on the prosecution side. **Strengths:** "A really practised litigator who shows great judgement. He's very confident and he doesn't mess around, so clients love him. He tries to find a way to make it work, rather than just saying 'no' which is annoying." "He really does get into the detail and doesn't delegate everything." **Recent work:** Had a lead role on behalf of the SFO in its prosecution of construction services company Sweett Group. The case concerned bribery in a number of Middle Eastern countries.

Julian Christopher QC A popular choice of lead counsel for prosecuting authorities, including the CPS. He is often selected to advise in cases relating to organised crime, including those concerning alleged corruption of public servants. Strengths: "A consummate barrister who is very incisive and very logical. He deals with complex problems well, gets to the heart of the issue and articulates things well. He shortens rather than lengthens the process, which is great." Recent work: Advised the prosecution in R v Chris Pharo & Jamie Pyatt, a retrial of two journalists accused of making payments to a police officer in exchange for information.

Emma Deacon QC (see p.631) Regularly handled serious cases unled before taking silk in 2016. She is a committed and smart criminal prosecution barrister, who is also capable of handling defence work. **Strengths:** "She is extraordinarily hard working, really tactical and quite aggressive." "Definitely a force to be reckoned with, she's very thorough, doesn't give much away, and is a proper opponent." **Recent work:** Advised the SFO in R v Johnson and Others, a case concerning former Barclays Bank employees implicated in alleged manipulation of LIBOR.

JUNIORS

Ben Douglas-Jones (see p.635) A junior with a strong work ethic, who is a level four criminal prosecutor. He regularly handles confiscation cases, as well as mortgage and tax frauds. **Strengths:** "A real rising star, whose industriousness is extraordinary to behold. The speed and accuracy of his work is outstanding, and he has exceptionally good judgement." **Recent work:** Lead prosecution counsel in R v Nicholas Marcou and Others, a case concerning the Operation Abacus investigation into alleged factoring and false invoicing fraud.

Stephen Hopper Prosecutes and defends financial cases of varying degrees of seriousness. He regularly advises on cases relating to VAT reclaims, money laundering and NHS suppliers. **Strengths:** "Very measured and able to structure a case well." **Recent work:** Advised the CPS on R v Rasheed and Hussain, a prosecution at the Old Bailey for alleged money laundering via a money transfer business in London.

Janet Weeks A grade four prosecutor, and a popular choice of barrister for serious high-value fraud matters. She has handled a number of notable corruption, insider dealing and employment fraud cases. **Strengths:** "She is meticulous and always in command of her brief." **Recent work:** Acted on the SFO's prosecution of Alstom, which concerned alleged bribery relating to bids to construct overseas infrastructure projects.

Red Lion Chambers

THE SET

A first port of call for heavyweight criminal and fraud matters, Red Lion Chambers has members who both prosecute and defend fraud cases of all shapes and sizes. Barristers at the set are sought out to advise on many extremely high-profile matters, and can be regularly sighted in rate rigging, investment fraud and money laundering cases. Recent work examples include R v Jacobs and Others, a case concerning four defendants charged with making corrupt payments to Nigerian tax officials, and R v Rohit Jha, an alleged ETF trading fraud by an employee at Credit Suisse.

Client service: "Out to impress, this is a very solid set and the clerks will bend over backwards to assist. We are delighted with their performance." Mark Bennett is the practice director.

SILKS

Jonathan Fisher QC User-friendly, easy to work with, and a great team player. He wins plaudits for his technical knowledge and persistence when tackling high value accounting fraud and bribery cases. **Strengths:** "He is very dogged, incredibly knowledgeable, and someone with a good sense of humour. He gets across complex messages in a very entertaining way, and can make the convoluted readily understandable." "Exhibits a rare depth of knowledge and expertise in relation to money laundering matters, and his advice is both insightful and highly practical." **Recent work:** Advised on the case of Olympus Corporation and the Gyrus Group, an alleged USD 1.7 billion accounting fraud.

Antony Shaw QC An unflappable and highly convincing jury advocate who advises on high-stakes criminal matters, including alleged rate manipulation and tax fraud. **Strengths:** "Scholarly and someone with an incredible work ethic, he has a nice touch with judges and juries." "He has a great presence in court, is bright and works very hard." **Recent work:** Advised on the defence of Danny Wilkinson, a financial trader involved in the second round of SFO prosecutions concerning alleged manipulation of LIBOR.

David Etherington QC Well known for his astute and effective counsel across a variety of criminal matters, he regularly defends in high-value investment fraud cases. Interviewees praise him for his attractive advocacy style and diligent case preparation. **Strengths:** "One of the most well-known and best prepared barristers around," who "produces advocacy of the highest standard." **Recent work:** Defended company director Peter Benstead against Ponzi fraud-related charges stemming from a currency exchange business.

Jeremy Benson QC An experienced silk who handles serious general crime, including murders, as well as financial crime. MTIC and other VAT frauds form a cornerstone of his practice. **Strengths:** "He knows his law and is very personable when dealing with clients and the judge." **Recent work:** Advised on matters connected with the Operation Borzoi and Operation Bayweek investigations, which concerned large-scale money laundering and tax fraud.

Sally-Ann Hales QC A fairly new silk recognised for her mixed prosecution and defence practice. She handles bribery, tax fraud and money laundering cases, amongst others. **Strengths:** "Delightful, down to earth and sensible." **Recent work:** Acted as lead prosecution counsel in the Swift Group case of R v Jacobs & Others, which involved the suspected making of corrupt payments to Nigerian tax officials.

JUNIORS

Tom Forster A barrister on the SFO's A panel who is lauded for going above and beyond the call of duty to secure great results in financial criminal cases. He acts for both the defence and prosecuting authorities. **Strengths:** "Fantastic to work with, he's realistic and has an exceptional grasp of the key issues in a case." "He's hard working, clear in his advice, and his written and oral presentations are beyond reproach." **Recent work:** Acted for the defence in R v Anwyl, a case arising from the Operation Amazon investigation into suspected tax fraud via carbon trading.

Allison Clare Renowned for her lengthy experience advising on financial crime. Recent cases handled have involved the trading of financial instruments and allegations of market manipulation or corruption. **Strengths:** "Really strong intellectually and the master of her brief." **Recent work:** Advised on R v Rohit Jha, the prosecution of a former Crédit Suisse employee for alleged fraud relating to ETF trading.

Gillian Jones An assiduous junior and a quick-thinking, aggressive advocate, whose cases involve allegations of insider dealing, rate rigging and investment fraud. **Strengths:** "An outstanding senior junior with very good judgement, who is very hard working, intelligent and capable." **Recent work:** Appeared in R v Read and Others, advising the prosecution on this high-profile case concerning alleged manipulation of LIBOR.

Hannah Willcocks A level-headed and reliable junior counsel with proven advocacy and case management skills. She is sought out by regulatory and prosecuting authorities, including the CPS, for such matters as suspected insider trading, tax fraud and corruption cases. Strengths: "Incredibly calm under fire." "She is so on top of things, and her mastery of an inordinate amount of material is very impressive." Recent work: Advised on R v Jasvinder Mahal and Kulsum Ashoush, a prosecution for submitting allegedly fraudulent VAT returns.

Andrew Marshall A noted CPS grade four advocate with extensive experience of prosecuting high-value matters, including alleged tax frauds. He is an expert on document-heavy cases involving complex technical evidence. **Strengths:** "Has impeccable judgement and makes complicated things sound simple." **Recent work:** Prosecuted a number of barristers charged with VAT fraud.

Tom Payne A seasoned prosecution counsel who complements his serious general crime practice with a specialism in financial crime-related matters such as money laundering. **Strengths:** "He knows the law, is confident and self assured." **Recent work:** Acted in R v Momodu Uduojie and Others, a prosecution for alleged money laundering following a number of suspected advanced fee frauds.

Other Ranked Lawyers

Collingwood Thompson QC (see p.780) (7BR) A senior silk with the skills and experience to handle high-stakes, document-heavy fraud work. He is sought out to advise high-profile entities at home and abroad, and has previously advised the Attorney General of Jersey. **Strengths:** "The full package QC." "He's extremely able and does a lot of large cases."

Andrew Wheeler (see p.793) (7BR) Regularly prosecutes and has been on a number of panels, including the SFO's A panel. He engenders respect for his great manner in court and is known for his highly effective cross-examination style. He has advised on a number of suspected tax and accountancy frauds. **Strengths:** "He is excellent at picking up the threads of a case, and has great client-care skills." "He is a good performer, who understands technical and financial accounting issues, and presents cases well."

Jennifer Carter-Manning (7BR) Has a broad practice in financial crime which takes in money laundering, corruption and financial regulatory work at home and abroad. **Strengths:** "A very tenacious advocate who really fights her corner."

Neil Hawes QC (see p.667) (Charter Chambers) A quality advocate who is sought out to advise on leading cases involving rate rigging, corruption and mortgage fraud. **Strengths:** "Very reliable and very hard working, he's innovative and will push the boundaries of legal arguments in court." "He has a fabulous presence in court and fights for the clients." **Recent work:** Acted for the defence in R v Tom Hayes, arguably the highest profile prosecution to date for alleged manipulation of LIBOR.

Gavin Irwin (see p.680) (Drystone Chambers) An advocate who is clear and polite in court, and a skilled manager of challenging personalities. He has handled a number of money laundering cases. **Strengths:** "A sure, friendly, intelligent, sensible advocate who is direct with the judge." "His tactical awareness is very good, and he has excellent knowledge of the law." **Recent work:** Provided advice relating to National Trading Standards' prosecution of Peter Hall, connected with the creation of 'copy-cat' websites for submitting tax returns.

Hodge Malek QC (39 Essex Chambers) A highly accomplished senior practitioner with enviable experience of handling civil and criminal fraud. He regularly tackles cases concerning such matters as rate manipulation and overseas corruption in the oil and gas sector. Lauded for his sensible and commercially sensitive advice, he advises individuals and companies. **Strengths:** "One of the leading silks in the area of financial crime and regulatory investigations. He is very good at presenting to clients and is great to have on the team as he has gravitas and great judgement." "Very knowledgeable about the interface between civil and criminal litigation, and the risks and pitfalls that lie therein. He's vastly experienced." **Recent work:** Advised inter dealer broker ICAP on civil and criminal matters arising from the LIBOR rate rigging scandal.

Simon Mayo QC (see p.711) (187 Fleet Street) Noted for his great appreciation of factual detail and strong advocacy skills. He regularly acts in cases involving tax, finance and investment fraud. **Strengths:** "An excellent barrister who produces strong legal arguments and is an efficient cross-examiner." **Recent work:** Advised on the defence on HMRC's Operation Amazon investigation, concerning suspected carbon credit trading fraud.

Andrew Trollope QC (see p.784) (187 Fleet Street) An accomplished silk who prepares diligently and puts in a spirited performance in court. His experience includes advising on fraud and tax evasion charges. **Strengths:** "He's careful to read the papers in detail and fights hard on behalf of his clients."

Natasha Wong (see p.799) (187 Fleet Street) A highly diligent junior counsel who exhibits clear communication skills and has great sensitivity to client concerns. High-value money laundering, rate rigging and corporate theft matters feature in her caseload. **Strengths:** "A complete joy to work with, she is extremely client-friendly and well liked by judges. She works very hard and is an ideal junior." **Recent work:** Acted for the defence in R v Jamshed Abidi and Others, a prosecution for alleged money laundering.

Peter Guest (see p.661) (187 Fleet Street) An experienced junior who handles a broad range of serious crime, including fraud. He has advised on tax frauds, money laundering and subsequent POCA work. **Strengths:** "A proper courtroom advocate."

Richard Lissack QC (see p.702) (Fountain Court Chambers) An adroit silk who is sought out to advise companies as well as individuals and employees on matters such as rate rigging, corporate transactional fraud and false accounting allegations. Sources were enthusiastic about his practical and business-friendly ethos, and clear presentation skills. **Strengths:** "Instils enormous confidence in clients, and is a terrific advocate whether in the boardroom or the courtroom." "He's extremely commercial, very client-friendly and focused on the strategic outcome." **Recent work:** Led for the defence in the SFO's investigation into Barclays Bank's 2008 Qatar capital raising.

Robin Barclay (see p.589) (Fountain Court Chambers) Known for his expedient strategic advice, practical approach and provision of great client service. His practice sees him advising on corporate regulatory compliance matters as well as white-collar crime cases concerning corruption and market manipulation. **Strengths:** "He is very good on the detail and focused on client needs and client objectives. He takes a very common sense, pragmatic approach to things." **Recent work:** Acted as junior defence counsel in FCA v Benjamin Anderson & Others, a case arising from the FCA's insider dealing investigation and prosecution, Operation Tabernula.

Nicholas Medcroft (see p.715) (Fountain Court Chambers) A highly experienced junior, well-versed in representing significant financial institutions in investigations brought by the SFO and FCA. He frequently handles cases relating to money laundering and tax fraud as well as regulatory failure. **Strengths:** "He is very bright indeed and very hard-working." "He is forthright and honest in his advice." **Recent work:** Successfully defended RBS against allegations of conspiracy to defraud brought by an aggrieved liquidator.

Eleanor Davison (see p.630) (Fountain Court Chambers) A strong team player with superb communication skills who provides high-quality input under challenging conditions. **Strengths:** "Very responsive and not in any way hierarchical – she doesn't see her role as only one narrowly defined thing. She's very prepared to help with disclosure and drafting skeleton arguments, and more than willing to get her hands dirty. " **Recent work:** Has been advising on three public corporate criminal and regulatory global investigations

Charles Sherrard QC (see p.764) (Furnival Chambers) Wins plaudits for being a highly switched-on silk whose criminal defence practice spans the range of privately funded and legal aid work. Tax and boiler room frauds feature in his key caseload. **Strengths:** "Fantastic at what he does," he's both "bright and very able." **Recent work:** Acted for Stuart Jones, a former director of JJB Sports, who was implicated in the alleged forging of bank statements.

Henry Blaxland QC (Garden Court Chambers) Brings superior advocacy skills and substantial gravitas to proceedings. He has advised on high-stakes matters involving allegations of rate rigging and tax fraud. **Strengths:** "A very experienced silk, who is extremely approachable and has a great rapport with clients. He's very good on technical arguments." "An intellectual heavyweight who delivers fantastic closing speeches." **Recent work:** Acted for the defence in R v Darrell Read, a case concerning alleged manipulation of LIBOR.

Tom Little (see p.703) (9 Gough Square) A high-profile treasury counsel, and a popular choice for advising on the prosecution of an array of criminal cases. In the financial criminal arena he acts on cases involving allegations of rate rigging, international corruption and film finance fraud. **Strengths:** "He is a real class act who is able to remain cool under pressure." **Recent work:** Has been advising the SFO in relation to LIBOR rigging at RBS.

Eleanor Mawrey (see p.710) (9 Gough Square) Has extensive experience of financial crime work and has acted as first prosecution junior in a number of high-value insider trading cases. **Strengths:** "She is very easy to work with and connects well with those instructing her. She has great soft skills."

James Thacker (see p.779) (9 Gough Square) A broadly skilled junior who handles a variety of serious crime cases. He regularly tackles complex fraud work and is a grade three specialist fraud prosecutor. **Strengths:** "A clever advocate who is highly strategic and always eyeing the opportunity to trap his opponent." **Recent work:** Acted for the CPS in R v Samuel Kayode, the prosecution of a former finance manager of an educational charity for alleged financial irregularities.

Philip Hackett QC (see p.661) (New Square Chambers) A confident barrister who presents well and is noted for being prepared to take novel positions, in order to further his client's interests. **Strengths:** "A very brave advocate," who "brings a great sense of humour to court, and is fearless in his pursuit of the client's cause." **Recent work:** Acted for the defence in SFO v Goodman, a case arising from the high profile investigation and prosecutions for alleged illegal manipulation of LIBOR.

Michael Bowes QC (Outer Temple Chambers) A barrister who offers practical advice and understands the commercial and practical implications of serious financial crime cases. He acts for corporations and individuals, and has broad experience of representing parties affected by allegations of rate manipulation, corruption and insider dealing. **Strengths:** "Very clever and has wide expertise, so is comfortable with criminal and civil work." "He is an old-school barrister but has learned new tricks on how to give the credible and relevant commercial advice that is required. He delivers that advice in the best and most commercial way, and is responsive and clear-minded."

Sarah Clarke (see p.618) (Serjeants' Inn Chambers) A former in-house counsel at the FSA, the precursor to the FCA, who is completely au fait with the financial world. She frequently acts unled on matters involving investment fraud and insider dealing. **Strengths:** "She has real ability, and is a very conscientious and strong court performer. She is very good at insider dealing cases, having written the leading work on the law and practise of their prosecution." **Recent work:** Acted in R v Hope and Von Badlo, a case arising from an alleged large-scale forex investment fraud.

David Stern (see p.772) (5 St Andrew's Hill) Stern is the key business crime and financial regulation barrister at the set. His areas of expertise include advising on rate rigging, corruption and investment fraud cases. **Strengths:** "He's incredibly hard working. He makes sure he knows everything about the case that he's instructed on, and he's involved in the case at a very early stage." "A talented and pragmatic defence counsel," he "will work with the team in guiding the strategy and tactics." **Recent work:** Acted in SFO v Read and Others, a case concerning the alleged illegal manipulation of LIBOR.

Edmund Burge (see p.607) (5 St Andrew's Hill) A popular and highly experienced junior counsel who frequently leads for the prosecution. His high-value financial criminal cases include a number relating to MTIC, VAT and diversion fraud. **Strengths:** "A star in the making." "He's tough but fair, and always knows the case inside-out. He has a good jury manner and is not intimidated by anybody or anything." **Recent work:** Acted as lead prosecuting junior in R v Ahmed, Shearer and Azzopardi, a case arising from the Operation Modcons investigation into a suspected fraudulent VAT and PAYE tax scheme perpetrated by company officers and accountants.

Jenny Goldring (see p.655) (5 St Andrew's Hill) Handles cases concerning bribery allegations as well as multihanded MTIC prosecutions. Her tax and fraud capabilities mean that she has also regularly appeared in the VAT Tribunal. **Strengths:** "Reads the papers thoroughly, prepares her arguments well and sees points that other people would miss." **Recent work:** Acted for the appellant in Rioni Limited v HMRC.

THE REGIONS

Financial Crime	
Leading Silks	
Band 1	
Csoka Simon	*Lincoln House Chambers*
Gozem Guy	*Lincoln House Chambers*
Howker David	*2 Hare Court*
Pickup James	*Lincoln House Chambers*
Sangster Nigel	*St Pauls Chambers*
Webster Alistair	*Lincoln House Chambers*
Band 2	
Enoch Dafydd	*New Park Court Chambers*
Harrington Patrick	*Farrar's Building* *
New Silks	
Johnson Nicholas	*Exchange Chambers*
Leading Juniors	
Band 1	
Bridge Ian	*No5 Chambers*
Grattage Stephen	*Exchange Chambers*
MacAdam Jason	*Exchange Chambers*
Band 2	
Jebb Andrew	*Exchange Chambers*
Kelly Mark	*No5 Chambers* Ⓐ
Whitehurst Ian	*7 Harrington St Chambers* *

* *Indicates individual with profile.*

Ⓐ *direct access (see p.24).*

Alphabetical order within each band. Band 1 is highest.

Ranked Lawyers

Andrew Jebb (Exchange Chambers) Recognised for his expertise in criminal defence work. His areas of strength include advising on suspected pension and mortgage frauds. **Strengths:** "He is exceptionally good. He is very organised and has extremely good judgement." **Recent work:** Acted in R v Gary Quillan and Others, representing the lead defendant charged with a multimillion-pound pension tax relief fraud.

Nicholas Johnson QC (Exchange Chambers) Courts high-level recognition for his handling of complex financial crime cases. Key mandates include advising on allegations of money laundering, MTIC fraud and corporate corruption. **Strengths:** "Lots of people say they can do white-collar crime, but he is a real expert in it." "He took silk recently, which was deserved definitely. He is very busy but always on top of everything." **Recent work:** Advised the defence in R v Habib and Others, concerning alleged laundering of funds arising from suspected diversion fraud relating to UK public bodies such as NHS trusts.

Stephen Grattage (Exchange Chambers) Continues to impress in the financial crime space, handling complex fraud cases as part of a broader criminal and regulatory practice that also encompasses matters such as corporate Environmental and Trading Standard prosecutions. **Strengths:** "Extremely efficient and extremely pleasant to deal with. In some very difficult situations he smoothed the path and enabled the case to progress." "A strong advocate with excellent analytical ability."

Jason MacAdam (Exchange Chambers) Offers a strong track record in serious financial fraud cases. MacAdam handles such matters as part of a broader criminal and regulatory practice.

Patrick Harrington QC (see p.664) (Farrar's Building) Renowned for his skill in handling the prosecution and defence of high-value financial crime, including alleged tax frauds related to film finance, mortgages and carbon credits. **Strengths:** "One of the best jury advocates in the UK in my opinion. Juries just love him. He plays the jury like a really good musician; he knows exactly what's right for the jury, strips the case down to bare essentials whether prosecuting or defending a serious crime, and is very good at pretending to the jury that he's just coming to terms with the facts of the case as the case is developing, even though you know he's got an encyclopaedic knowledge of the case." **Recent work:** Acted for the prosecution arising from the Operation Bulkhead investigation, involving a suspected £275 million film finance tax fraud.

David Howker QC (2 Hare Court) An acclaimed barrister for criminal fraud work such as alleged pension frauds and tax evasion, with noted experience of defending complex cases against HMRC. **Strengths:** "A fantastic jury advocate, who makes things interesting as criminal fraud cases can be very dry. He had lots of cross-examination of witnesses to do. I don't know how but he managed to keep it fresh so he never lost the jury while he was on his feet."

Ian Whitehurst (see p.794) (7 Harrington St Chambers) Instructed in a raft of financial crime cases, such as those involving allegations of Ponzi schemes and advanced fee fraud. He also handles broader criminal cases such as those involving allegations of homicide and sexual offence. **Strengths:** "A very good performer. He is fearless and defendants love him. He will get stuck in but knows when not to lock horns with witnesses. A very good tactician."

Simon Csoka QC (Lincoln House Chambers) A highly respected figure in the Criminal Defence Bar, who handles a range of complex and high-value fraud cases. Areas of strength include cases involving allegations of missing trader intra-community (MTIC) fraud. **Strengths:** "Very good on issues such as disclosure and dismissal. He is very active pre-trial, looking for anything which can bring an end to the case before it gets anywhere near a jury." "Great, extremely intelligent. A very good approach to matters." **Recent work:** Acted in R v Anthony O'Neill, regarding long-running allegations of missing trader fraud and income tax fraud in relation to the construction industry.

Guy Gozem QC (Lincoln House Chambers) A highly regarded silk with a proven track record advising on fraud cases with aspects of regulatory law. Sources are fulsome in their praise of his style, and his ability to engage effectively with juries. **Strengths:** "He is very calm in the face of adversity, which is great in this area." "I certainly recommend him for his skills – an excellent performer."

James Pickup QC (Lincoln House Chambers) A strong presence on the Northern circuit. He is recognised for his handling of complex financial crime and commercial fraud cases, such as alleged tax frauds. **Strengths:** "Excellent paperwork, very pragmatic and a common-sense approach. He presents in a clear and concise manner." "A superb advocate and tactician. Diligent and hard-working." **Recent work:** Acted for the defendant in R v Arif Patel, a highly complex case involving aspects of charity fraud, missing trader fraud and commercial fraud.

Alistair Webster QC (Lincoln House Chambers) A highly experienced silk who excels in complex cases involving allegations of loan, tax and pension fraud, among other matters. He regularly represents the SFO in both fraud and proceeds of crime cases. **Strengths:** "He is very clever, very hard-working and he has very good judgement." "A fantastic QC." **Recent work:** Acted as lead defence counsel in R v McClintock, a Northern Ireland High Court case concerning alleged fraud by false representation, related to real estate bank loans.

Dafydd Enoch QC (New Park Court Chambers) Noted for his broad experience of financial crime cases, including suspected pension and tax frauds. Enoch acts for both prosecution and defence. **Strengths:** "A very good practitioner. He is extremely approachable and loves to get involved with a case at an early stage in proceedings."

Ian Bridge (No5 Chambers) Excels in matters such as significant tax and investment frauds. Particular areas of strength include cases involving allegations of money laundering and corporate corruption. **Strengths:** "Very, very good on his feet. He is extremely busy but always has time for cases and for clients. I find him very effective; he is enormously helpful." "He is a very good advocate and has a good understanding of tax tribunal procedures." **Recent work:** Acted for the defence in R v Conroy, concerning a major MTIC fraud. Bridge also handled the later confiscation proceedings.

Mark Kelly (No5 Chambers) Noted for his representation of accountants and other professionals in complex fraud cases. **Strengths:** "A good, analytical lawyer. He worked incredibly hard and devised legal submissions which won the case." **Recent work:** Acted as junior counsel to Harpal Singh Gill, who stood accused of laundering £32 million, a sum allegedly acquired through the supply of controlled substances.

Nigel Sangster QC (St Pauls Chambers) Has a fine track record in sophisticated financial crime cases, including those involving allegations of film and MTIC fraud. Other areas of strength include cases involving money laundering and confiscation proceedings. **Strengths:** "A good operator. He is a big beast in both general crime and financial crime, and he is good in both. A very confident advocate." "He is totally unflappable and presents as a calm individual, which impresses juries." **Recent work:** Advised on R v Kimberly Murphy and Others, a case concerning an allegedly fraudulent film investment scheme.

Contents:

LONDON

Financial Services
Leading Sets
Band 1
Blackstone Chambers *
Fountain Court Chambers *
Band 2
3 Verulam Buildings *
Band 3
Outer Temple Chambers *
South Square *
4 Stone Buildings *

Financial Services	
Leading Silks	
Star individuals	
Blair Michael	*3 Verulam Buildings*
Brindle Michael	*Fountain Court Chambers* *
Flint Charles	*Blackstone Chambers*
Herberg Javan	*Blackstone Chambers*
Lissack Richard	*Fountain Court Chambers* *
Band 1	
Crow Jonathan	*4 Stone Buildings* *
Malek Ali	*3 Verulam Buildings*
Malek Hodge M	*39 Essex Chambers (ORL)* ◇
Thanki Bankim	*Fountain Court Chambers* *
Vineall Nicholas	*4 Pump Court (ORL)* ◇ *
Zacaroli Antony	*South Square* *
Band 2	
Bowes Michael	*Outer Temple Chambers*
Eadie James	*Blackstone Chambers*
Green Andrew	*Blackstone Chambers*
Philipps Guy	*Fountain Court Chambers* *
Saini Pushpinder	*Blackstone Chambers*
Band 3	
Allison David	*South Square* *
Bompas George	*4 Stone Buildings* *
Coleman Richard	*Fountain Court Chambers* *
Dohmann Barbara	*Blackstone Chambers*
Dutton Timothy	*Fountain Court Chambers* *
Fisher Jonathan	*Red Lion Chambers (ORL)* ◇
George Andrew	*Blackstone Chambers*
Hunter Andrew	*Blackstone Chambers*
Mitchell Andrew	*Fountain Court Chambers* *
Odgers John	*3 Verulam Buildings*
Peacock Nicholas	*Maitland Chambers (ORL)* ◇ *
Robertson Patricia	*Fountain Court Chambers* *
Russen Jonathan	*Maitland Chambers (ORL)* ◇ *
Strong Benjamin	*One Essex Court (ORL)* ◇

** Indicates set / individual with profile.*

[A] direct access (see p.24).

◇ (ORL) = Other Ranked Lawyer.

Alphabetical order within each band. Band 1 is highest.

Financial Services	
Leading Juniors	
Band 1	
Assersohn Oliver	*Outer Temple Chambers*
Jaffey Ben	*Blackstone Chambers*
Khan Farhaz	*Outer Temple Chambers*
Marquand Charles	*4 Stone Buildings* *
Purchas James	*4 Pump Court (ORL)* ◇ *
Purves Robert	*3 Verulam Buildings*
Band 2	
Brent Richard	*3 Verulam Buildings*
Hattan Simon	*Serle Court (ORL)* ◇ *
Lomnicka Eva	*4 New Square (ORL)* ◇ *
Mansell Jason	*QEB Hollis Whiteman (ORL)* ◇ [A] *
Mayhew David	*39 Essex Chambers (ORL)* ◇
Medcroft Nicholas	*Fountain Court Chambers* *
Pritchard Simon	*Blackstone Chambers*
Band 3	
Al-Attar Adam	*South Square* *
Barclay Robin	*Fountain Court Chambers* *
Clarke Sarah	*Serjeants' Inn Chambers (ORL)* ◇ *
Davison Eleanor	*Fountain Court Chambers* *
Eborall Charlotte	*3 Verulam Buildings*
Hall Taylor Alex	*4 New Square (ORL)* ◇ *
Hanif Saima	*39 Essex Chambers (ORL)* ◇ [A] *
King Henry	*Fountain Court Chambers* *
Mallinckrodt Sophie	*3 Verulam Buildings*
McClelland James	*Fountain Court Chambers* *
Shivji Sharif	*4 Stone Buildings* *
Up-and-coming individuals	
Temple Adam	*4 Pump Court (ORL)* ◇ *

Band 1

Blackstone Chambers

See profile on p.813

THE SET

Blackstone Chambers is a leading set for the full range of financial services work, with a group of barristers at all levels who bring unrivalled experience in the biggest and most complex suits in the sector. Its strong relationships with both regulators and major institutions, born of long-standing advisory roles as well as regular secondments from chambers, ensure a top level of market awareness and commercial sensibility. **Client service:** "The clerks, led by Gary Oliver, are very good and efficient."

SILKS

Charles Flint QC Revered figure on the financial services scene, highly respected both for his deep technical understanding of the matters at hand and his skills as an advocate in the courtroom. He is broadly considered to lend weight and credence to a case by reputation alone. **Strengths:** "Absolutely brilliant. So sure-footed, so calm, and judges just love him because he's so reliable and he gets it right." "He's the doyen of advice work whenever there's an intersection with the FCA." **Recent work:** Advised the FCA on whether interest rate swap agreements used by banks fell under their regulatory jurisdiction.

Javan Herberg QC Highly reputed in all aspects of regulatory and enforcement action, and much in demand as both an adviser and advocate. **Strengths:** "He is mega clever, and undoubtedly one of the three or four leading names in the field." "He's our primary port of call for anything really complex." **Recent work:** Acted for KPMG on a claim for judicial review of its decision-making as a skilled person in respect of Barclays Bank's decisions on the small business structured interest rate products redress scheme.

James Eadie QC The primary contact for the Treasury in a range of matters of which financial services comprises one facet. His all-round strength and experience across a variety of areas make him a leading choice for those seeking the most comprehensive representation. **Strengths:** "He is quite simply stunning in his ability to know exactly what the good point is in a mass of detail. " **Recent work:** Acted for the SFO in a £300 million claim by the Tchenguiz brothers suing for misfeasance in respect of false allegations of financial misconduct and fraud.

Andrew Green QC Highly regarded for his work for a variety of financial institutions under the scrutiny of the FCA as well as his provision of advice for the regulatory body itself. Recent work has also included significant representations of individuals undergoing investigation for market activities. **Strengths:** "Extremely bright and analytical, and ferocious in cross-examination." "A very knowledgeable and skilled strategist." **Recent work:** Represented African Land during a claim for injunctive relief by the FCA, determining whether the company's scheme is a collective investment scheme as defined by Section 235, FSMA 2000.

Pushpinder Saini QC Skilled advocate who wins praise for his handling of clients as well as his prowess in the courtroom. Particularly noted for his recent work on sanctions and fraud matters. **Strengths:** "He stepped in at short notice and was highly impressive, a very good advocate on his feet." **Recent work:** Advised on an application to the ECHR against the UK in respect of the nationalisation of shares in Northern Rock.

Andrew George QC Recognised specialist in the financial services field, and particularly praised for his skill and expertise in dealing with the intricacies of the FCA investigation and enforcement process. Especially experienced in the representation of individuals, as well as financial institutions. **Strengths:** "He's very incisive and intelligent, grasps facts quickly and is great with clients." "He provides excellent strategic and legal advice." **Recent work:** Advised the Libyan Investment Authority on its USD2 billion claim in the Commercial Court alleging bribery by Société Générale.

Barbara Dohmann QC Well-established figure in the market who enjoys a great reputation for her long experience of dealing with a wide range of financial services issues. Particularly noted for her work on international multi-jurisdictional cases. **Strengths:** "She's perfect for very complex cases which require a heavyweight."

Andrew Hunter QC Relatively young silk who is nonetheless widely seen as being able to stand up to the most battle-hardened advocates thanks to a combination of deep sector knowledge and a sophisticated courtroom manner. He acts for the FCA as well as for those undergoing regulatory proceedings. **Strengths:** "Has a charming way of speaking, and his intellect and breadth of practice are exceptional." "Phenomenally bright and wins even under very testing circumstances." **Recent work:** Acted for a trader against allegations by the FCA of fixing of Euribor interest rates, successfully appealing to the Upper Tribunal for third party rights to challenge an FCA notice against a major bank.

JUNIORS

Ben Jaffey A first-choice junior for many for representation before a range of financial regulatory bodies and tribunals including the FCA, PRA and Upper Tribunal. Alongside working on disputes arising from the Libor and forex proceedings, he has also been engaged on cases concerning accusations of financial misreporting. **Strengths:** "Very bright, able and has good judgement. Clearly impressive." **Recent work:** Represented Barclays in a judicial review of the decision by KPMG as the independent reviewer of the sale of interest rate hedging products by Barclays.

Simon Pritchard Highly regarded younger junior who works on the full array of financial regulations matters for both institutions and individuals including collective investment schemes, market abuse and insider trading issues. Sources praise his level of insight into the nuanced detail of the regulations. **Strengths:** "A very, very bright young lawyer who is very well versed in the regulatory framework." "Someone who thinks through all the positions and comes up with good answers. He's worth his weight in gold." **Recent work:** Represented the FCA in the first case to go to trial in which the FCA has requested that the court impose penalties for market abuse.

Fountain Court Chambers

See profile on p.847

THE SET

Recent top-level reinforcements have elevated this set to ever more dizzying heights of financial regulatory work, making it a top choice for some of the biggest clients in the sector. Broad experience at all levels makes Fountain Court a safe and effective choice for both retail banks and the more rarefied operators in the sector. Its barristers have notable experience in representing clients on foreign and multi-jurisdictional matters.

Client service: "The clerks are very approachable and very responsive. They understand the value of the commercial relationship and they try to match the right counsel for the right jobs. They're not salesmen; they want to offer quality where they can at the right price, which is very much appreciated." The clerks are led by Alex Taylor.

SILKS

Michael Brindle QC (see p.603) A widely revered silk whose experience and expertise have made him a regular choice for the FCA whenever they are looking to pursue the largest and most complex instances of enforcement action. He is also extremely popular with those seeking the most effective defence against the regulator. **Strengths:** "He does a lot of work for the FCA and is obviously extremely good. He's totally trusted as a major figure by everyone." **Recent work:** Acted for the FCA in a successful appeal against a decision notice of the regulator on the grounds that it contained inadequate reasons.

Richard Lissack QC (see p.702) A recent arrival at Fountain Court, who brings with him widely perceived excellence in financial and commercial advocacy. Qualified to practise in New York, Dubai, Northern Ireland and the Caribbean, he is much valued for his skill in handling proceedings with major multi-jurisdictional concerns. **Strengths:** "An all-round highly polished product. He is completely adept at handling civil litigation. He also has the sweep of skills that make him a very rare advocate and a very good one." "A rambunctious powerhouse of an advocate."

Bankim Thanki QC (see p.780) Much valued by banks, on both the retail and investment sides, for his ability to construct a highly sophisticated defence in response to regulatory inquiries by the FCA, PRA and SFO. A strong background in commercial litigation combined with extensive international experience makes him a powerful choice for City institutions. **Strengths:** "Very in demand by banks for defence work." "Very good and very measured." **Recent work:** Acted for Deloitte in a successful appeal against a decision by the FRC, obtaining a reduction in the fine levied from £14 million to £3 million.

Guy Philipps QC (see p.736) Highly regarded for his work for the full range of financial institutions including insurance and reinsurance companies as well as retail and investment banks. Broad commercial expertise ensures that he is capable of handling the most esoteric financial services matters with aplomb. **Strengths:** "Extremely accomplished on tribunals and matters before the FCA." **Recent work:** Acted for Angela Burns in her appearance before the Upper Tribunal to contest accusations of a failure to disclose conflicts of interest.

Timothy Dutton CBE QC (see p.638) A doyen of the Bar who is able to draw upon almost peerless levels of experience of handling a range of financial services matters at all levels. His parallel expertise in professional discipline makes him an especially good representative of individuals in the financial industry undergoing investigation. **Strengths:** "Extremely experienced. His strategy, advice and respect all set him apart."

Andrew Mitchell QC (see p.719) Especially well thought of for his work defending banks from investigations into matters of interest rate swaps, currency derivatives and the mis-selling of financial products, including PPI. As well as for his knowledge, he wins praise for his particularly effective style of advocacy. **Strengths:** "He's got a very nice courtroom manner, with a very effective way of presenting his points in a way that's easy to understand." **Recent work:** Acted for RBS in the defence of a complex claim regarding contractual estoppel in a retail and regulatory context.

Patricia Robertson QC (see p.753) Acts in a wide array of significant financial services regulatory matters, particularly in instances of alleged mis-selling of financial products. Her in-depth knowledge of the operational proclivities of the FCA ensures that she is in high demand by institutions seeking the most effective defence in the area. **Strengths:** "Fantastic, a very strong advocate who is very strong on her feet."

JUNIORS

Henry King (see p.691) Drawing upon his past life as a qualified chartered accountant, he is able to adroitly handle the most complex and technical aspects of regulatory disputes between financial institutions and the FCA. He is especially noted for his work helping banks sift through the fallout from the financial crisis. **Strengths:** "Very experienced and a pleasure to work with." "Very diligent and knows what he's talking about." **Recent work:** Represented the Financial Reporting Council against Deloitte and the former finance director over the audit of Aero Inventory.

James McClelland (see p.711) A much-admired junior with a significant and growing practice in financial services regulation, particularly on issues involving FSMA directives and European regulations. He has been involved in some of the highest-profile and highest-value cases in the sector over the last few years. **Strengths:** "Brilliant. So on top of the detail, and a very nice guy. The client really likes him." **Recent work:** Acted for RBS and its former directors defending a multibillion-pound group action alleging a breach of the statutory regulations governing share prospectuses.

Richard Coleman QC (see p.620) A well-regarded figure across the City, who is appreciated for his talent and experience in both litigation and other modes of dispute resolution. **Strengths:** "A thorough cross-examiner and technically very good. He grasps complex issues immediately and has a good manner with clients." **Recent work:** Advised the FCA on new rules concerning payday lenders.

Nicholas Medcroft (see p.715) Particularly admired for his strength in handling commercial litigation in a regulatory context, where he advises clearing banks and individuals who are undergoing FCA investigation and enforcement proceedings. **Strengths:** "He's very strong and very much liked on the prosecution side." **Recent work:** Represented a bank in a case concerning whether a bank can deal with what may be the proceeds of fraud.

Robin Barclay (see p.589) A leading junior in many areas of financial services, whose widely acknowledged expertise in financial crime, fraud and other regulatory matters makes him an increasingly popular choice for both individuals and companies. His experience in civil and criminal matters means that he is often called upon to advise on a range of cross-border issues. **Strengths:** "It's his ability to work well in a team as well as being unafraid to give an opinion, his experience which comes across in his advice, his great technical judgement and especially his emotional intelligence that make a huge difference." "A very, very good performer and incredibly responsive."

Eleanor Davison (see p.630) Highly experienced at handling issues concerning the whole gang of regulatory bodies including the FCA, CTFC, SEC and JFSA. Her involvement in recent major enforcement proceedings across the continent, including Libor and forex, means that she brings an excellent overview and perception of the market to her clients. **Strengths:** "Very responsive, and clearly an expert in her field, so we feel entirely comfortable dealing with her." "Very user-friendly, very organised, very clever." **Recent work:** Acted for Barclays in a dispute with PCP Capital over an £800 million claim for consultancy services.

Band 2

3 Verulam Buildings

See profile on p.924

THE SET

It is able to bring major expertise to bear on complex and multi-jurisdictional financial regulatory issues. Thanks to its deep bench of barristers well versed in the intricacies of banking law and litigation in a wider context, the set is appreciated by clients for its particular commercial and market awareness. Many members of chambers have spent time working for the regulators or as solicitors specialising in the field, granting them particular insight into the vast array of financial regulation legislation.

Client service: "The clerks are really responsive. They always get back to you quickly and always do what they say they will. They're extremely efficient." "I am impressed with the client care and attention to matters whether large or small." The clerks are led by Stephen Penson.

SILKS

Michael Blair QC A leading light of the financial regulatory scene thanks to his extensive experience not only at the Bar but also within many regulatory bodies through their various iterations. Now working primarily in an advisory capacity, he is highly valued for the strength of the counsel which he can offer on pan-European matters. **Strengths:**

"Fantastic. He clearly has an encyclopaedic knowledge of the area." "His strength is that he has a very, very detailed knowledge and understanding of the legislation, so when he makes submissions he does so with great authority and persuasiveness."

John Odgers QC Drawing on his private sector experience as an investment banker, he is highly regarded for his technical ability in both an advisory capacity and as a courtroom advocate. He acts for clients seeking advice on matters of compliance with regulations concerning derivatives, securities and commodities. **Strengths:** "An amazing technical lawyer with an extraordinary work rate." "He has a very thorough and detailed approach to everything and he is very enjoyable to work with." **Recent work:** Acted for Companhia Carris de Ferro de Lisboa, along with other Portuguese public transport corporations, in a £1.1 billion dispute over structured interest rate swaps.

JUNIORS

Robert Purves A very highly regarded junior whose much sought-after advice ranges from technical advisory work on the applications of existing legislation to representation on contentious matters of investigation and enforcement. He offers particular expertise in the insurance sector. **Strengths:** "He's a fantastic barrister who can get under the skin of an issue, which is what you need." "He knows what he's talking about when it comes to interpretation and can speak authoritatively on the issues."

Richard Brent Has a broad practice across the worlds of banking and finance, insurance and EU law, making him a popular choice for those seeking advice on a broad range of regulatory issues informed by a high level of market awareness. **Strengths:** "He's an expert in the field – very precise and analytical, and practical as well."

Charlotte Eborall Coming from secondment at the FCA, she brings cutting-edge insight into the workings of the regulator along with her own expertise in the sector. Recent work has particularly focused on Part VII transfers, as well as operating in the regulatory space between consumer credit and financial services more generally. **Strengths:** "Approachable, knowledgeable and hugely responsive. She is great to work with and fabulously client-facing." "Very thorough, friendly and knows her stuff. Turnaround time is also very quick." **Recent work:** Represented the FCA to make submissions at the final hearing of the sanction of a Part VII insurance business transfer.

Sophie Mallinckrodt A highly regarded junior with a broad practice covering some of the most technical aspects of financial regulation, particularly in collective investment schemes and the mis-selling of financial products. **Strengths:** "Sure-footed and definite in her advice, commercial and user-friendly." "Offers clear advice, strong analysis and good client-handling skills." **Recent work:** Advised the SFO on the legal professional privilege asserted by a third party regarding the criminal proceedings brought against Tom Hayes.

Ali Malek QC A powerful advocate in the financial services sector, respected both for his highly effective and technical advice and for his forceful representation of clients facing investigation and enforcement proceedings. He is particularly noted for his strength and experience operating internationally. **Strengths:** ""A very, very class act. Very refined and very, very bright." **Recent work:** Represented Lafayette and others in its action against Nationwide, alleging breaches of regulatory requirements.

Band 3

Outer Temple Chambers

See profile on p.887

THE SET

A particularly strong base in criminal law contributes to this set's notable reputation in handling a wide range of financial services matters, from mis-selling and fraud to insider dealing and money laundering. Similarly renowned civil capabilities enable its members to effectively deal with a wide array of regulatory and banking issues for their clients. The set has a global presence, and its members are heavily involved in some of the most significant multi-jurisdictional cases in the area.

Client service: "The clerks have been very good in terms of accommodating our needs. It's a nice place with nice facilities." "They're always very efficient to deal with." They are led by David Smith and Dave Scothern.

SILKS

Michael Bowes QC A heavy-hitting silk whose prowess in handling some of the most significant financial regulatory cases of recent times, including Libor, forex and other instances of pan-European financial litigation, is highly praised. His criminal law background stands him in particularly good stead when he's representing individuals and managers. **Strengths:** "Superb knowledge, extremely hard-working and excellent instinct." "He's clever, understands the issues and gives good, practical advice."

JUNIORS

Oliver Assersohn A highly regarded junior who is an expert at handling complex issues relating to mis-sold investments and breaches of the perimeter. Having been on secondment to the FCA, he has highly valuable insight into the workings of the regulator. **Strengths:** "His written work is always excellent, he provides clear and practical advice and he deals with clients in a very empathetic manner." **Recent work:** Advised the RDC on a novel enforcement action against a hedge fund and its CEO and compliance manager, alleging market abuse.

Farhaz Khan An increasingly admired junior with a growing following among the largest corporations and institutions in the sector. Instructed by both private clients and the regulator, and combining his knowledge in this area with a broader commercial and civil practice, he is well able to contend with the most complex and multifaceted issues in the space. **Strengths:** "I'd genuinely say he's probably the best junior at the Bar for financial services work, he's just excellent. He's sensible, his judgement is impeccable and he will bring proper imaginative solutions." "He is proactive, helpful, very pragmatic and has the client's best interests at heart." **Recent work:** Represented former Keydata compliance officer Peter Johnson in the Upper Tribunal.

South Square

See profile on p.910

THE SET

South Square leverages its acclaimed strength in insolvency to advise administrators on the regulatory aspects of financial restructuring. The set has a strong history in the financial services sector having been active in a number of leading cases since the financial crisis including the Lehman Brothers "Waterfall Application" and the unravelling of derivatives broker MF Global. Its members advise a variety of clients including financial institutions and private equity groups as well as public bodies such as the FCA and the Treasury.

Client service: "They are really good, very responsive, helpful and timely. They are very reasonable with things and realistic." The clerks are led by Mike Killick and Dylan Playfoot.

SILKS

Antony Zacaroli QC (see p.802) A standout commercial silk, held in much esteem for his skill and expertise in handling matters for some of the largest financial institutions across the globe. His superlative technical ability holds him in good stead when he is advising. companies, banks and regulatory bodies. **Strengths:** "He's incredibly bright and very technical, as well as user-friendly and personable." **Recent work:** Advised the special administrators in the special bank administration of MF Global on the regulatory aspects of client classification.

David Allison QC (see p.583) Has a commercial and banking practice which encompasses a broad swathe of the financial services scene, and he is often called upon to handle matters of extremely high value. **Strengths:** "He's very determined and fights his corner quite strongly." **Recent work:** Advised Lehman Brothers on the interpretation of the FCA standard form agreement pursuant to which a USD2 million subordinated loan was made by the shareholders of Lehman Brothers.

JUNIORS

Adam Al-Attar (see p.581) An increasingly prominent junior at the Financial Services Bar who enjoys a growing practice arising from his work on insolvencies. He has recently been particularly active in the banking sector, advising on exchange and clearing house regulations. **Strengths:** "He's technically excellent." **Recent work:** Advised the liquidators regarding the collapse of the Dubai bank of the Espirito Santo Group follow allegations of fraud.

4 Stone Buildings

See profile on p.913

THE SET

4 Stone Buildings is a popular choice for those seeking a rounded and holistic legal offering, as it has barristers with extensive commercial experience who are equally conversant in the finer points of banking, company and insolvency law. Its members regularly represent clients before the full range of regulatory bodies including the RDC and the FSMT.

Client service: "Their clerking, led by David Goddard, is the best in the City. The guys over there are excellent. They are always on top of things, always friendly, and always in tune with your client's objectives." "The clerking is excellent, they're very user-friendly and very easy to speak to."

SILKS

George Bompas QC (see p.598) Renowned for the quality of his representation in court, and is particularly praised for his cross-examination technique. His strong performances are supported by a comprehensive knowledge of the regulations, and he has particular experience in working for international clients in Hong Kong, the Cayman Islands and the British Virgin Islands. **Strengths:** "A brilliant guiding light providing strategy and valuable expertise. He is calm and measured and should come with the warning: 'Opposition beware.'" "He is bright, commercial and solutions-focused." **Recent work:** Represented Richard Desmond against Credit Suisse and GLG Partners in a case concerning complex derivative transactions which were heavily loss-making during the financial crisis.

JUNIORS

Charles Marquand (see p.707) A highly regarded senior junior who is especially valued for his expertise in non-contentious advisory work acting for clients in the financial services sector. He shows impressive technical skill and an in-depth knowledge of regulations across the EU. **Strengths:** "He's always very responsive, pragmatic and clear in his advice." "Very good technically, and very user-friendly and commercial."

Sharif Shivji (see p.764) His previous background as a derivatives trader allows him to bring a wealth of direct and professional experience to his highly rated work advising on a range of domestic and international financial regulatory issues. He is also well regarded as an advocate and regularly appears before the Upper Tribunal. **Recent work:** Successfully acted for the FCA against Timothy Roberts and Andrew Wilkins regarding the marketing of 'death bonds'.

Jonathan Crow QC (see p.627) An increasingly major figure on the financial services scene thanks to his widely perceived excellence in both written and courtroom advocacy, deep knowledge of the intricacies of the subject and broad base of experience in commercial litigation and public law. **Strengths:** "Absolutely stellar. His opinions are clear, incisive and well reasoned. People assume that they're right just because they come from him." "He's intellectually brilliant and manages to make complicated issues seem unbelievably simple and straightforward." **Recent work:** Represented the FCA in a Supreme Court appeal arising from the London Whale trial, resulting in J.P. Morgan being fined £137 million.

Other Ranked Lawyers

Benjamin Strong QC (One Essex Court) Has a strong banking and finance practice and is often called upon to advise on an array of financial services issues both at home and abroad. His recent caseload has had a particular focus on developments in the Libor proceedings as well as securitisation issues more generally. **Strengths:** "First rate in swaps and derivatives. He's very, very clever and analytical." **Recent work:** Acted for the FCA against the former chairman of Capital Markets at J.P. Morgan.

Hodge Malek QC (39 Essex Chambers) A towering figure in the financial services sector thanks to his work on a series of high-profile international cases on behalf of financial institutions as well as regulatory bodies. He is well versed in the rules concerning the operations of mergers and acquisitions and consumer credit programmes. **Strengths:** "He has gravitas and wise judgement on issues with wide implications." "He's strategic and very good at presenting to clients. He's great to have on your team." **Recent work:** Advised Conlon in a Court of Appeal case concerning the decision in Harrison v Black Horse regarding the question of whether payment protection insurance amounted to an unfair credit bargain.

David Mayhew (39 Essex Chambers) Has longstanding expertise and experience in the area, and draws upon his past experience as head of enforcement at the FCA. He handles the full gamut of complex financial services issues. **Strengths:** "He comes with a huge body of expertise and experience behind him."

Saima Hanif (see p.663) (39 Essex Chambers) A well-respected junior who represents both individuals and institutions undergoing investigation and enforcement proceedings by financial regulators. **Strengths:** "Incredibly thorough, intelligent, quick to respond and someone with incredible analysis." **Recent work:** Represented Tim Roberts, formerly CEO of Catalyst, in an appeal against an FCA decision banning him from working in the financial services industry.

Nicholas Peacock QC (see p.735) (Maitland Chambers) Often called upon by the FCA to advise on particularly novel or complex matters, and has recently advocated for the regulator in the Supreme Court. **Strengths:** "He has a very cool, calm head and does an excellent job in the line of fire."

Jonathan Russen QC (see p.757) (Maitland Chambers) Well thought of for his work advising on the regulatory requirements involved in the investment sector. He is an expert on both the structure of vehicles and disputes between asset/fund managers and regulatory bodies. He is experienced in acting in both a domestic and international capacity. **Strengths:** "He's responsive, brings clarity to what is contentious and recognises the different perspectives in a case." **Recent work:** Acted for Arizona Investments in a claim against a bank which had recommended an investment that had been lost as a result of the Madoff fraud.

Eva Lomnicka (see p.703) (4 New Square) An intellectual heavyweight at the Bar, as much renowned for her publishing and academic record as for her role as a go-to adviser on complex and cutting-edge financial services questions. **Strengths:** "One of the go-to academics for banking and financial services." **Recent work:** Advised Edinburgh University on whether it needed to obtain authorisation from the FCA in order to provide credit to potential employees.

Alex Hall Taylor (see p.662) (4 New Square) A hard-working senior junior who represents a wide range of financial institutions and individuals. He is involved in such diverse matters as fraud, bank collapses and business acquisitions. He is also experienced in conducting cases in a range of offshore territories. **Strengths:** "He is smart, always on the ball, very hard-working and great to work with." **Recent work:** Advised FD Financial, the financial advisers of the claimant, in a case concerning the impact of fixed interest rate early redemption clauses in a multimillion-pound loan used to purchase a property portfolio.

Nicholas Vineall QC (see p.787) (4 Pump Court) A first round pick for many looking for regulatory representation thanks to his deep understanding of the sector combined with his thorough knowledge of the inner workings of the regulator. He is also often called upon to advise the FCA itself. **Strengths:** "A standout choice of counsel if you want someone who cuts the mustard technically but also really gets the regulator." "He is crisp and analytical, and his advocacy is clear and succinct." **Recent work:** Acted for the claimants in a class action claim against Capita, seeking £40 million of compensation for Capita's role as authorised corporate director in the collapse of the Arch Cru investment funds.

James Purchas (see p.745) (4 Pump Court) An outstanding junior with prowess not only in the strictly regulatory aspects of financial services but also in complementary areas such as insolvency and payments. He is often called upon to advise on issues without precedent. **Strengths:** "Has good response times and engages with understanding the client's objectives." **Recent work:** Instructed by the FCA on a case involving the laundering of proceeds from land-banking operations to a Panamanian company.

Adam Temple (see p.779) (4 Pump Court) An increasingly prominent junior in the financial services sector, with solid experience of advising both the regulators and a range of banking and corporate institutions. He has recently been particularly active working for private clients on regulations concerning peer-to-peer lending and interest rate swaps. **Strengths:** "Adam is very pleasant to work with. He offers good, clear, practical advice." **Recent work:** Acted for the FCA in a case to determine whether investment schemes promoted to members of the public are unauthorised collective investment schemes.

Jason Mansell (see p.707) (QEB Hollis Whiteman) A highly regarded junior whose widely acknowledged expertise in financial crime is matched by his increasingly impressive efforts in dealing with cases concerning financial regulatory issues. He acts particularly for those whose activities have come to the attention of the regulatory bodies. **Strengths:** "Extremely hard-working, and has fantastic judgement and great client care."

Jonathan Fisher QC (Red Lion Chambers) Particularly valued for his advice on the criminal aspects of financial services, often providing support on matters of money laundering and economic sanctions. His strong enforcement credentials mean that he is often seen advising on multi-jurisdictional market abuse cases. **Strengths:** "He's very knowledgeable in his areas of expertise and has strong opinions which are obviously well reasoned, well thought out and therefore reliable." **Recent work:** Advised Mineworld Ltd. in its dealings with the FCA when the regulatory body sought a permanent injunction against market traders using high frequency trading and algorithmic trading.

Sarah Clarke (see p.618) (Serjeants' Inn Chambers) Highly valued by the FCA, which often instructs her in major investigatory matters with significant technical aspects. Her previous experience working for the regulator, as well as her work for a variety of financial institutions, affords her notable experience in cases of fraud, insider dealing and market abuse. **Strengths:** "She is extremely well prepared, very knowledgeable and puts the client at the heart of her advice." "If it's really technical she comes to the fore." **Recent work:** Acted for the FCA against Westwood Independent Financial Planners in an allegation of mis-selling of geared traded endowment policies.

Simon Hattan (see p.667) (Serle Court) An impressive junior lauded for the strength of his intellectual drive and the particular perception and skill set which his well-renowned commercial chancery practice grants him. His previous career as an investment banker ensures he has a strong commercial view of the workings of the City. **Strengths:** "He has a deep background and understands issues from a business perspective."

Fraud: Civil

Contents:

LONDON Fraud: Civil

Fraud: Civil
Leading Sets
Band 1
Blackstone Chambers *
Brick Court Chambers *
One Essex Court *
Essex Court Chambers *
Fountain Court Chambers *
Maitland Chambers *
Serle Court *
4 Stone Buildings *
3 Verulam Buildings *
Band 2
XXIV Old Buildings *
Wilberforce Chambers *
* Indicates set / individual with profile.
◊ (ORL) = Other Ranked Lawyer.
Alphabetical order within each band. Band 1 is highest.

Fraud: Civil
Leading Silks
Band 1
Anderson Robert *Blackstone Chambers*
Beltrami Adrian *3 Verulam Buildings*
Girolami Paul *Maitland Chambers* *
Howard Mark *Brick Court Chambers*
McGrath Paul *Essex Court Chambers*
McQuater Ewan *3 Verulam Buildings*
Miles Robert *4 Stone Buildings*
Peto Anthony *Blackstone Chambers*
Rabinowitz Laurence *One Essex Court*
Smith Stephen *Erskine Chambers (ORL)* ◊ *
Smouha Joe *Essex Court Chambers*
Thanki Bankim *Fountain Court Chambers* *
Band 2
Boyle Alan *Serle Court* *
Brindle Michael *Fountain Court Chambers* *
Browne-Wilkinson Simon *Fountain Court Chambers* *
Collings Matthew *Maitland Chambers* *
Crow Jonathan *4 Stone Buildings* *
Croxford Ian *Wilberforce Chambers*
de Garr Robinson Anthony *One Essex Court* *
Dougherty Charles *2TG - 2 Temple Gardens (ORL)* ◊ *
Freedman Clive *7 King's Bench Walk (ORL)* ◊ *
Gourgey Alan *Wilberforce Chambers*
Grabiner Anthony *One Essex Court*
Hill Richard G *4 Stone Buildings* *
Hunter Andrew *Blackstone Chambers*
Jones Philip *Serle Court* *
Kitchener Neil *One Essex Court*
Marshall Philip *Serle Court* *
Montgomery Clare *Matrix Chambers (ORL)* ◊ *
Norbury Hugh *Serle Court* *
Onslow Andrew *3 Verulam Buildings*
Rubin Stephen *Fountain Court Chambers* *
Steinfeld Alan *XXIV Old Buildings*
Tolaney Sonia *One Essex Court*
Toledano Daniel *One Essex Court*
Trace Anthony *Maitland Chambers* *
Wardell John *Wilberforce Chambers*
Band 3
Chapman Jeffrey *Fountain Court Chambers* *
Choo Choy Alain *One Essex Court*
Cohen Lawrence *Wilberforce Chambers*
Dohmann Barbara *Blackstone Chambers*
Dowley Dominic *Serle Court* *
Goodall Patrick *Fountain Court Chambers* *
Levy Robert *XXIV Old Buildings*
Lord Tim *Brick Court Chambers*
Malek Ali *3 Verulam Buildings*
Malek Hodge M *39 Essex Chambers (ORL)* ◊
Matovu Harry *Brick Court Chambers* *
Matthews Duncan *20 Essex Street (ORL)* ◊
Mill Ian *Blackstone Chambers*
Morgan Richard *Maitland Chambers* *
Moverley Smith Stephen *XXIV Old Buildings*
Pillow Nathan *Essex Court Chambers*
Quest David *3 Verulam Buildings*
Ritchie Stuart *Fountain Court Chambers* *
Saini Pushpinder *Blackstone Chambers*
Samek Charles *Littleton Chambers (ORL)* ◊
Stanley Paul *Essex Court Chambers*
Weisselberg Tom *Blackstone Chambers*
Band 4
Adkin Jonathan *Fountain Court Chambers* *
Auld Stephen *One Essex Court*
Ayres Andrew *Maitland Chambers*
Brisby John *4 Stone Buildings* *
Davenport Simon *3 Hare Court (ORL)* ◊
Davies-Jones Jonathan *3 Verulam Buildings*
Dunning Graham *Essex Court Chambers* *
Fenwick Justin *4 New Square (ORL)* ◊ *
Fraser Orlando *4 Stone Buildings* *
George Andrew *Blackstone Chambers*
Howe Robert *Blackstone Chambers*
Howe Timothy *Fountain Court Chambers* *
Jones Elizabeth *Serle Court* *
Lowenstein Paul *3 Verulam Buildings*
Moeran Fenner *Wilberforce Chambers*
Newman Catherine *Maitland Chambers* *
Odgers John *3 Verulam Buildings*
Salzedo Simon *Brick Court Chambers* *
Sutcliffe Andrew *3 Verulam Buildings*
Swainston Michael *Brick Court Chambers*
Talbot Rice Elspeth *XXIV Old Buildings*
Thompson Steven *XXIV Old Buildings*
Waller Richard *7 King's Bench Walk (ORL)* ◊
New Silks
Casey Aidan *3 Hare Court (ORL)* ◊
Head David *3 Verulam Buildings*
Mumford David *Maitland Chambers* *
Penny Tim *Wilberforce Chambers*
Phelps Rosalind *Fountain Court Chambers* *
Valentin Ben *Fountain Court Chambers* *

Band 1

Blackstone Chambers

See profile on p.813

THE SET

Influential commercial litigation set comprising a number of the best silks and juniors in the market. "The barristers at all levels have always been outstanding," remarks one market source. They act for both claimants and defendants, including companies, banks and individuals, in high-value fraud disputes that frequently span multiple jurisdictions. Allegations handled include bribery, conspiracy, forgery, dishonesty, deceit, misappropriation, misrepresentation and breach of contract.

Client service: "The clerks at Blackstone are extremely user-friendly. You can call them any time and they will go out of their way to be of assistance." "They understand how solicitors work and the pressures that we are under from our clients." Gary Oliver is the senior clerk.

SILKS

Andrew Hunter QC Has a dynamic civil fraud practice, and is instructed by claimants and defendants in trials and applications, many of which are multi-jurisdictional. **Strengths:** "He is strategically very aware and highly intelligent." "Andrew Hunter is a very astute guy. He knows his way around civil fraud litigation." **Recent work:** Represented one of the co-defendants in a claim by the Libyan Investment Authority, worth over USD1 billion, against Société Générale and a number of individuals.

Andrew George QC Undertakes significant fraud litigation as part of a wider commercial practice that also takes in financial services, media and professional negligence matters. **Strengths:** "He well deserved his appointment to silk this year. He has excellent judgement and his written work is very good. He is persuasive and while he has a close attention to detail focuses on the pertinent points." "He is outstanding on FSMA issues and is a deceptively forceful advocate." **Recent work:** Represented the Libyan Investment Authority in filing a claim for in excess of USD1 billion against Société Générale concerning alleged bribery.

Robert Anderson QC Puts a flair for cross-examination to use in fighting challenging fraud cases. A large bulk of his practice has an international component. **Strengths:** "He is a persuasive advocate. Very few people have as much experience as he has. He is all over this space and knows the law very well. I've seen him turn judges on several occasions when they weren't with us. He's very clever and great to work with." **Recent work:** Represented Dubai Islamic Bank in a USD1.2 billion claim brought by Plantation relating to a loan that was restructured in the aftermath of a commercial credit fraud.

Anthony Peto QC In addition to heading the set, he continues to manage a substantial commercial fraud caseload. He receives accolades for his work on injuctions freezing, tracing and recovering assets. **Strengths:** "He's incredibly courteous and he's got a very good sense for tactics." "He is tremendously charismatic, confident and intelligent. He is able to grasp important, complex issues very quickly and is impressively committed to clients and their cause." **Recent work:** Represented more than six defendants in a USD170 million action brought by Otkritie, the Russian bank, alleging fraud.

Barbara Dohmann QC A seasoned silk who continues to robustly represent defendants and claimants in instances of alleged fraud. She also serves in the International Court in Qatar as a judge. **Strengths:** "She's fabulous, astute, sharp as anything and a brilliant cross-border strategist." **Recent work:** Acted for Ms Baturina, a wealthy Russian businesswoman, in pursuing a USD100 million claim against

Fraud: Civil
Leading Juniors
Band 1
Drake David Serle Court *
Higgo Justin Serle Court *
Hutton Louise Maitland Chambers *
Parker Matthew 3 Verulam Buildings *
Pilbrow Fionn Brick Court Chambers
Powell Leona Blackstone Chambers
Willan James Essex Court Chambers
Band 2
Akkouh Tim Erskine Chambers (ORL) ◊ *
Atrill Simon Fountain Court Chambers *
den Besten Ruth Serle Court *
Denton-Cox Gregory 4 Stone Buildings *
Dilnot Anna Essex Court Chambers
Elliott Steven One Essex Court
Harrison Christopher 4 Stone Buildings *
Harrison Nicholas Serle Court *
Haydon Alec Brick Court Chambers
John Laura Fountain Court Chambers *
Lazarus Michael 3 Verulam Buildings *
Mallin Max Wilberforce Chambers
Midwinter Stephen Brick Court Chambers
Nambisan Deepak Fountain Court Chambers *
Polley Alexander One Essex Court *
Sinclair Paul Fountain Court Chambers *
Weekes Robert Blackstone Chambers
Zellick Adam Fountain Court Chambers *
Band 3
Davies David Essex Court Chambers
Gillett Emily Erskine Chambers (ORL) ◊ *
Hall Taylor Alex 4 New Square (ORL) ◊ *
Hattan Simon Serle Court *
Hayman George Maitland Chambers *
Hood Nigel New Square Chambers (ORL) ◊
Hubbard Mark New Square Chambers (ORL) ◊
Kramer Adam 3 Verulam Buildings *
Ng Jern-Fei Essex Court Chambers
Pester Iain Wilberforce Chambers
Peters David Essex Court Chambers
Pillai Rajesh 3 Verulam Buildings
Singla Tony Brick Court Chambers *
Smith Ian The Chambers of Andrew Mitchell QC (ORL) ◊ *
Band 4
de Mestre Andrew 4 Stone Buildings *
de Verneuil Smith Peter 3 Verulam Buildings *
Fulton Andrew 20 Essex Street (ORL) ◊
Gledhill Orlando One Essex Court *
Goldsmith Jamie One Essex Court
John Benjamin Maitland Chambers *
King Edmund Essex Court Chambers
Morrison Matthew Serle Court *
Newton Laura Brick Court Chambers *
Robins Stephen South Square (ORL) ◊ *
Up-and-coming individuals
Dudnikov Anton Essex Court Chambers *
Sheehan James Maitland Chambers *
* Indicates individual with profile.
◊ (ORL) = Other Ranked Lawyer.
Alphabetical order within each band. Band 1 is highest.

Mr Chistyakov relating to investments in Moroccan real estate.

Ian Mill QC An authority in commercial litigation who is comfortable handling the full sweep of fraud allegations. **Strengths:** "Ian is undoubtedly one of the leading advocates of his generation in fraud work. He is a massive courtroom personality and a good cross-examiner who really commands the room." "He is presentationally brilliant and very good with clients." **Recent work:** Represented Bonhams, the auction house, in four Commercial Court claims relating to the sale of a rare 1954 Ferrari.

Pushpinder Saini QC Has litigated a number of noteworthy fraud disputes, many of which are multi-jurisdictional. **Strengths:** "He is a very good and delightful advocate." "He's got a very sharp mind and is not afraid to roll his sleeves up either."

Robert Howe QC Maintains an extensive practice across the fields of commerce, banking and finance, media and entertainment, sport and employment. He has appeared in many domestic and international civil fraud cases. **Strengths:** "He is measured but also quite strident. He hits the notes just right." "He is very friendly, excellent on his feet and very bright." **Recent work:** Represented Kazakhstan Kagazy, a paper, cardboard and packaging manufacturer, and other claimants in bringing a USD200 million fraud action against two of its former directors.

Tom Weisselberg QC A quality advocate who attracts weighty fraud instructions, many of which emanate from foreign jurisdictions. **Strengths:** "He is a very good advocate and has excellent judgement." "He's a good, user-friendly strategist who knows his law and is great to instruct and work with." "He is smart, personable and user-friendly." **Recent work:** Defended HMRC in a claim brought by Bernie Ecclestone, the head of Formula One, and his ex-wife Slavica, relating to over USD1 billion in unpaid tax and interest that HMRC demanded, allegedly in breach of an agreement.

JUNIORS

Leona Powell Deals with challenging fraud trials and arbitrations in the context of a commercial practice that also incorporates contractual disputes, commodities cases and professional negligence matters. **Strengths:** "She is very efficient and heavily relied on by QCs as a reliable junior. People trust her." **Recent work:** Defended T&L Sugars in a EUR30 million claim brought by ED&F Man alleging that a shipment of sugar was deliberately diverted to a third party in breach of contract.

Robert Weekes Lauded for his technical knowledge of the law when appearing in civil fraud trials and arbitrations, both single-handedly and led by senior counsel. **Strengths:** "He has an excellent eye for detail." "He is approachable, likeable and a pleasure to work with." **Recent work:** Successfully defended Mishcon de Reya in claims brought by Kwok Choon Chiang and other investors in a hotel resort alleging that the law firm dishonestly assisted an individual who defrauded them.

Brick Court Chambers

See profile on p.816

THE SET

A set replete with market-leading QCs and juniors accustomed to handling high-value fraud matters. Instructions are often international and multi-jurisdictional in nature, stemming from such regions as the CIS, the Caribbean and, increasingly, Africa. "Brick Court has a wealth of talent and expertise in the area and good strength in depth," observes one instructing solicitor. "The barristers are intellectually impressive and user-friendly."

Client service: "The clerks are efficient and provide good client service." "They are commercial and well connected at court. They're easy to deal with and responsive." Ian Moyler and Julian Hawes are joint senior clerks.

SILKS

Harry Matovu QC (see p.709) Has a proven track record in civil fraud, having handled numerous high-value actions with cross-border elements to them. **Strengths:** "He is a charming and unflappable advocate. He has developed a real expertise in complex jurisdictional battles." **Recent work:** Acted for VIP Engineering & Marketing in pursuing a claim of nearly USD500 million in damages against Standard Chartered and other defendants relating to a power plant project in Dar es Salaam that became unprofitable as a result of alleged fraud.

Mark Howard QC A stalwart of the Bar who exudes confidence when handling high-profile fraud matters, many of which have an international dimension. His decision-making and cross-examination skills earn him plaudits from peers and clients alike. **Strengths:** "Mark Howard is just a force of nature. He pulls it out of the hat every time." "He penetrates all the surrounding noise and is very good at getting to the key points. He also reads the court and judges very well." **Recent work:** Acted for Arcadia Petroleum in bringing a claim for over £250 million against Peter Bosworth, its former CEO, and Colin Hurley, its former CFO, alleging that they engaged in fraudulent trading to divert profits away from the oil company.

Michael Swainston QC An experienced advocate instructed in complex fraud disputes. He offers specialist expertise in the countries of the CIS. **Strengths:** "A tough cross-examiner and a brilliant strategist." **Recent work:** Defended Peter Bosworth, the former CEO of Arcadia Petroleum, in a claim brought by the oil company alleging that he and other employees diverted profits away from the oil company.

Tim Lord QC A barrister of considerable versatility whose civil fraud practice is bolstered by his know-how in such areas as banking and finance, energy, professional negligence and insurance. **Strengths:** "He has an excellent client manner. He is a forceful and compelling advocate." "His advocacy is superb and he is fearless in his approach to a case."

Simon Salzedo QC (see p.758) Brings and defends valuable claims relating to such allegations as bribery, fraudulent misrepresentation and dishonesty. **Strengths:** "He's extremely well known on the civil fraud circuit." "He is very available, very hardworking, clear and a good tactician." **Recent work:** Defended Sushovan Hussain, the former CFO of Autonomy, in a USD5 billion claim brought by HP against him and Michael Lynch, the former CEO of Autonomy, alleging that they fraudulently misrepresented the state of Autonomy's finances before its takeover by HP.

JUNIORS

Alec Haydon A much-heralded litigator who acts for both claimants and defendants in complicated fraud actions involving such issues as asset tracing and freezing injunctions. **Strengths:** "He's quick, sensible, engaging, tough and committed." **Recent work:** Defended Gennady Bogolyubov in a claim brought by Victor Pinchuk against him and Igor Kolomoisky alleging that they did not hand over ownership of an iron ore mining company in Ukraine after having taken payment for it.

Fionn Pilbrow An in-demand senior junior with a reputation for taking tough domestic and international fraud cases to trial. **Strengths:** "Fionn is personable and enjoyable to work with. He is very responsive and easily contactable." "His advice is clear and logical." "Judges listen to him. He has the court's attention and that's important." **Recent work:** Acted for Arcadia and other oil companies in bringing a claim against two former executives who allegedly siphoned off profits.

Stephen Midwinter A well-regarded senior junior who enjoys a busy fraud practice, often undertaking advocacy unled. **Strengths:** "He's excellent and has a very good manner about him. He picks really good points and really hammers home on them." **Recent work:** Defended Merchantbridge in a fraud action brought by a former employee who alleged that when he left the company he was not paid enough for his shares.

Tony Singla (see p.766) Centres his practice on heavyweight commercial and banking litigation. He receives regular instructions in complex fraud disputes. **Strengths:** "He's absolutely fantastic and no doubt destined for great things. He is very hard-working, incredibly clear in his advice. very efficient, and has seriously impressed when on his feet in court." "He is attentive to detail and produces really good work." **Recent work:** Represented the Bank of St Petersburg in a USD500 million dispute with Vitaly Arkhangelsky, a Russian businessman, relating to a loan repayment and involving serious allegations of fraud and conspiracy.

Laura Newton (see p.727) A commercial practitioner instructed, often as sole counsel, in multiparty international fraud actions arising out of various allegations. **Strengths:** "She is very personable and very diligent, and has judgement beyond her years." "She grasps material and produces high-quality work in very quick time." **Recent work:** Acted in Terra Raf Trans Traiding Ltd v Assaubayev, a dispute in which it was alleged that loan documentation was a sham.

One Essex Court

See profile on p.833

THE SET

One of London's leading commercial sets and a force to be reckoned with in the fields of corporate, chancery and banking and finance law. Its large team of high-calibre silks and junior advocates deals with complicated civil fraud disputes arising out of such allegations as bribery, conspiracy, breach of fiduciary duty and misrepresentation. The lawyers are active both at home and abroad, appearing in many different jurisdictions, and "can turn their hands to most things as their quality is so high." Recent successes include Libyan Investment Authority v Société Générale and the Dar Al Arkan litigation.

Client service: "The clerking operation is first-rate." "Their clerks are phenomenal." Darren Burrows is the senior clerk.

SILKS

Anthony de Garr Robinson QC (see p.631) Runs a busy commercial chancery practice and takes on significant fraud litigation and arbitration work, much of which originates offshore in regions such as the Caribbean and the Middle East. **Strengths:** "He is a great advocate who has an excellent bedside manner with clients." "He's impressive and thorough." **Recent work:** Defended a Portuguese bank in a USD77 million claim brought by RP Explorer Master Fund against various defendants alleging that they took part in a conspiracy to defraud investors.

Alain Choo Choy QC A junior QC with a broad banking and finance, energy and general commercial practice who has appeared in a range of weighty civil fraud cases. He is deeply familiar with the legal issues that different jurisdictions present. **Strengths:** "Very bright and a pleasure to work with." **Recent work:** Represented Clyde & Co, formerly the solicitors of Mukhtar Ablyazov, in regard to whether documents they held belonging to him could be withheld owing to legal professional privilege.

Anthony Grabiner QC An experienced commercial advocate with a broad practice covering civil fraud, banking and finance, energy and other areas. He is a legendary figure at the Bar who has dealt with many difficult domestic and international disputes. **Strengths:** "Tony has got the most amazing judgement. I really value his integrity, his judgement and his experience." "Lord Grabiner remains one of the most eminent counsel at the Bar. He has great personal force and presence in court, and commands considerable respect from the Bench." **Recent work:** Instructed by the Bank of England to investigate the alleged involvement of bank officials in the rigging of the foreign exchange market.

Daniel Toledano QC An amiable advocate instructed in relation to complicated civil fraud matters. He has a wide-ranging commercial practice that covers a variety of areas including banking and finance, sport and energy. **Strengths:** "Daniel's a very calm, measured advocate. It's easy to get fazed by what the other side are doing but he never does." "He is very approachable and is a pleasure to work with." **Recent work:** Acted for Deutsche Bank as a co-defendant in a claim brought by Bilta alleging fraud and dishonest assistance surrounding carbon emissions trading.

Laurence Rabinowitz QC A leading litigator with a commercial practice encompassing civil fraud, energy, competition, professional liability and banking and finance. Solicitors seek him out to handle high-profile fraud cases. **Strengths:** "He masters the detail of cases incredibly quickly and always adds significant value both with his advice and as a tactician. He is very good with clients too." "He has an incredibly incisive analytical mind, coupled with hugely reassuring client-handling skills." **Recent work:** Represented Autonomy and Hewlett-Packard Vision in bringing USD5 billion claims against Lynch and other defendants relating to false accounting.

Neil Kitchener QC Tackles a great many cases involving allegations of fraud. His commercial practice also touches on arts and antiques, banking and finance, sports and energy law. **Strengths:** "He sees technical points which other barristers may not pick up and he is extremely hard-working." "Neil Kitchener is a very clear advocate who gives good, robust advice." "He is confident, self-assured and a very skilled, aggressive cross-examiner." **Recent work:** Defended Ilya Yurov in Commercial Court claims brought by Oleg Kolyada relating to a trust deed and a sale of shares.

Sonia Tolaney QC A standout silk who is particularly adept at dealing with instances of alleged banking fraud. **Strengths:** "She is very user-friendly, formidably clever and also very engaged." "She quickly earns the respect of solicitors and clients alike." **Recent work:** Defended RBS and former directors in group litigation stemming from a 2008 rights issue of shares.

Stephen Auld QC Sweeps up impressive instructions in a number of areas and handles cases concerning civil fraud, banking and financial services, sports, media and commodities. **Strengths:** "He is a charming and confident advocate. He is great with clients and quick to grasp complex issues and identify commercial solutions." **Recent work:** Represented Highland Financial Partners, a Texan hedge fund, in successfully blocking an anti-suit injunction that would have prevented it from suing RBS for alleged fraud.

JUNIORS

Alexander Polley (see p.739) An experienced senior junior involved in many fraud cases of complexity and significance. **Strengths:** "He's amazingly responsive and he's also very creative in the ideas that he comes up with." "He presents things very clearly and is very good in court. His drafting is excellent." "He is extremely good at getting very quickly to the heart of huge volumes of information and complex issues." **Recent work:** Defended members of Société Générale in high-profile litigation brought by the Libyan investment Authority relating to favourable deals that were allegedly procured through bribery.

Jamie Goldsmith Has developed a vibrant civil fraud practice and attracts many high-profile instructions. **Strengths:** "He is extremely hard-working. His attention to detail is outstanding, as is his advocacy." "He has excellent judgement and is a very good, safe pair of hands." **Recent work:** Represented 14 investors in McGraw-Hill International v Deutsche Apotheker & Others, a EUR130 million dispute relating to fraudulent misrepresentations allegedly made by RBS and Standard & Poor's.

Orlando Gledhill (see p.654) Called upon to act in leading fraud cases arising out of such allegations as misrepresentation, misappropriation of assets and misuse of information. **Strengths:** "Orlando is a fantastic lawyer and one of the best draftsmen I've come across. His ability to say things in a short number of words is unparalleled. He captures things in a punchy way." "His drafting and strategic advice are exemplary." **Recent work:** Represented IMR Management Services and Jai Krishna Saraf in a disclosure application by EuroChem Volga-Kaliy, as part of a substantial fraud claim relating to the construction of a Siberian mine.

Steven Elliott Sought after for his persuasive advocacy in challenging fraud disputes. **Strengths:** "He is one of the cleverest juniors at the Commercial Bar. He is user-friendly and has a relaxed manner. His written work is of the highest quality." **Recent work:** Defended Mercuria Energy in a fraud claim concerning the trading of carbon emission allowances.

Essex Court Chambers

See profile on p.836

THE SET

Home to a number of acclaimed silks and juniors participating in landmark instances of fraud litigation. Members deal with all manner of allegations including conspiracy, bribery and breach of contract. They have a wealth of experience in obtaining emergency injunctions, both domestically and internationally in offshore jurisdictions. Respondents regard them as "the market leaders in fraud," remarking: "They've just got such strength in depth."

Client service: "Essex Court has superb clerks. They are the gold standard." The senior clerks David Grief and Joe Ferrigno are viewed with particular favour. "David Grief will bend over backwards to make sure you get whatever you need whenever you need it." "Joe Ferrigno is a delight to deal with."

SILKS

Paul McGrath QC A prominent figure renowned for his knowledge of fraud legislation and for having authored a much-read book on the subject. He takes part in high-value disputes, both in the UK and in offshore jurisdictions such as the British Virgin Islands (BVI), the Cayman Islands and the Isle of Man. **Strengths:** "Paul is phenomenal. He doesn't have to look stuff up. He just seems to know everything about civl fraud. Clients and judges like him." **Recent work:** Defended Maksat Arip, one of the co-defendants in a USD200 million fraud claim brought by Kazakhstan Kagazy, a paper supplier, relating to funds that were allegedly misappropriated.

Joe Smouha QC A skilled commercial silk who champions clients' interests in domestic and international courtroom trials and arbitrations. **Strengths:** "He is very user-friendly, bright and a good tactician for heavyweight litigation." **Recent work:** Represented Blue Tropic and Coppella Ventures, two BVI companies belonging to the Patarkatsishvili family, in a fraud claim against Ivane Chkhartishvili alleging that he requisitioned shares from them without obtaining permission.

Paul Stanley QC Roundly recognised for his ability to prosecute and defend significant fraud actions. **Strengths:** "He's clever and very familiar with this sort of work." "He has a brain the size of a planet."

Nathan Pillow QC A personable advocate who since taking silk in 2015 continues to pick up steam and is seen acting in heavyweight fraud trials and tribunals. He is adept at handling cross-border cases that potentially raise conflicts of laws. **Strengths:** "He is seriously impressive. He is commercial but knows the law inside out as well. When he's on his feet you feel very comfortable that he will not come unstuck at any point. He is also very personable and impresses our clients face to face." **Recent work:** Represented Otkritie in ongoing proceedings against 19 former employees alleged to have participated in a conspiracy to defraud the Russian financial services provider.

Graham Dunning QC (see p.637) Handles fraud disputes as part of a broad-ranging commercial practice with an international character. **Strengths:** "He has a clear advocacy style that instils confidence." **Recent work:** Acted for the third defendant in Arcadia v Bosworth & Others, a USD250 million claim against former senior executives of the oil company alleging that they engaged in fraudulent trading to divert profits.

JUNIORS

Anna Dilnot A former solicitor who has had involvement in some major pieces of fraud litigation including those relating to Prince Jefri and Bernie Madoff. **Strengths:** "Anna is simply excellent. She is very good at judgement and drafting, and also very responsive and available." **Recent work:** Defended Maksat Arip and Shynar Dikhanbayeva, two former directors of Kazakhstan Kagazy, a paper manufacturer, implicated in a USD200 million alleged fraud.

David Davies An experienced senior junior who centres his commercial practice on fraud and has contested many significant cases. **Strengths:** "He is a tremendous lawyer who shows good judgement and is easy to work with. He remains calm under pressure." **Recent work:** Successfully defended Sergey Maksimov, the former president of PJSC VAB, a Ukrainian bank, in contempt proceedings, in which it was alleged that he breached freezing injunctions taken out against him.

David Peters A brilliant junior who places an emphasis on fraud within a productive commercial practice. He has appeared as sole counsel in several major matters. **Strengths:** "David Peters is phenomenally bright and incisive. He has perspicacity and can slice through mountains of material to get to the point." "He's a barrister for the 21st century – he's utterly enthusiastic and brilliant with the clients." **Recent work:** Acted for Dynami SPC IV and Intervisatrade in bringing a USD35 million claim against Pablo Fernando Chiriboga Bechdach and other defendants relating to the purchase of an Ecuadorian power-generating barge.

Anton Dudnikov (see p.637) Regularly instructed to act in high-value fraud cases involving such issues as conspiracy, bribery and contempt of court. A native Russian speaker, he is well qualified to handle litigation in Russia and the CIS. **Strengths:** "He is hard-working, great on the detail and someone who drafts well. He is very intelligent and perceptive on the legal issues and easy to work with." **Recent work:** Represented Otkritie, a Russian bank, in claims against George Urumov and other defendants arising from alleged misappropriation of assets.

Edmund King Handles fraud instructions, both in court and in arbitration, as part of his comprehensive commercial practice. **Strengths:** "He is innovative, energetic and creative in his approach to unusual problems."

James Willan A go-to junior who has participated in a number of landmark fraud cases and is particularly knowledgeable about freezing orders. **Strengths:** "He is phenomenally bright and hard-working." "James Willan is a walking brain. He gets to grips with the most complex points you could imagine. If you've got some hideous case based on foreign law he's the man to throw all the experts' reports at and say, 'What's going on?'" **Recent work:** Defended Abourahman Boreh in proceedings brought by the Republic of Djibouti alleging that he committed fraud while head of the country's Ports and Free Zones Authority.

Jern-Fei Ng Maintains a busy civil fraud practice and acts in major, multiparty proceedings. **Strengths:** "He impresses with his willingness to roll up his sleeves and on a personal level he is very approachable and very friendly." "He is exceptionally hard-working and phenomenally clever, but at the same time the most courteous barrister you could ever hope to have the pleasure of instructing."

Fountain Court Chambers

See profile on p.847

THE SET

A commercial litigation set with a fine bench of experienced silks and juniors. Members have fought and won many high-profile fraud disputes, and have clout in related fields such as banking and finance and conflict of laws. "You can always be comfortable that you're getting very good advice," remarks one market observer. Proceedings frequently have an international dimension and span multiple jurisdictions.

Client service: "The clerks are always approachable and will get back to you as soon as they can." "The clerking at Fountain Court is exceptional. They're very professional and proactive, and try and understand the needs of the clients." Alex Taylor is the senior clerk.

SILKS

Bankim Thanki QC (see p.780) Runs a busy practice that includes regular instructions in civil fraud arbitrations and litigation. He also serves as deputy head of chambers. **Strengths:** "Bankim is an extremely impressive silk who allies mastery of the law with excellent strategic and commercial thinking. He is exceptionally responsive and user-friendly, and always very willing to get into the detail." "Bankim is a genuine all-rounder who has the universal respect of his clients, his opponents and the judiciary." **Recent work:** Represented Teva Pharma and Cephalon, its subsidiary, in a £100 million fraud action against Wockhardt relating to a manufacturing contract for a leukaemia drug.

Ben Valentin QC (see p.786) A promising new silk who has amassed extensive experience of handling complex cases of alleged fraud. **Strengths:** "Ben is exceptionally hard-working, methodical and completely unflappable." "Undoubtedly a rising star at the Bar, he has a razor-sharp intellect and is very practical, commercial, easy to work with and charming with clients." **Recent work:** Defended HSH Nordbank in claims brought by the liquidators of the Saad Investments Group relating to reverse payments.

Michael Brindle QC (see p.603) A veteran commercial practitioner who continues to pack a punch in fraud disputes, many of which are international and multi-jurisdictional in nature. **Strengths:** "He's fantastic on his feet." "A supremely assured advocate." **Recent work:** Represented Novoship in an appeal by Mr Mikhaylyuk, a former employee, against a Commercial Court decision to award Novoship USD169 million in damages for alleged chartering contracts fraud.

Simon Browne-Wilkinson QC (see p.605) Handles high-value fraud claims both domestically and internationally across multiple jurisdictions. **Strengths:** "He was brilliant. He helped us to come up with a strategy to get from back foot to front foot quickly and then to chase the bad guys down the road. It was a pleasure working with him and he became one of my favourite silks as a result." **Recent work:** Represented a witness in a large-scale dispute between BTA Bank and Mukhtar Ablyazov, its former chairman, regarding an alleged misappropriation of assets.

Stephen Rubin QC (see p.756) An exceptional commercial advocate instructed in multimillion-pound fraud litigation and arbitrations. His work often has an international aspect, involving such jurisdictions as Russia, the CIS and the Caribbean. **Strengths:** "He has a keen and creative mind, and is superb at getting out of tricky spots. He reads the court exceptionally well and always ensures his client's case is presented as attractively as possible." "He is a pugnacious sort in court." **Recent work:** Represented Patokh Chodiev in bringing, together with business partners Alexander Machkevitch and Alijan Ibragimov, a fraud claim against Kirill Stein.

Jeffrey Chapman QC (see p.614) A standout silk with a broad commercial and banking practice who appears on behalf of claimants and defendants in fraud-related claims. **Strengths:** "He is meticulous, concise and someone with an effective and persuasive style of advocacy." "He's great on his feet under pressure in court and comes up with creative solutions." **Recent work:** Successfully pursued a EUR100 million claim on behalf of Group Seven against Allied Investment and others alleging that they persuaded it to invest in a fraudulent scheme.

Patrick Goodall QC (see p.656) Has scored wins in numerous high-profile fraud claims. **Strengths:** "He's very commercial and very sensible, and has very balanced views on everything. He is a good advocate who is extremely easy to work with and very user-friendly."

Stuart Ritchie QC (see p.752) A broad commercial practitioner who takes on high-level fraud work covering all manner of issues including trusts, dishonest assistance and breach of duty. **Strengths:** "Stuart has a sharp mind and very good knowledge of the law." "He is undoubtedly one of the best silks around for complex fraud disputes and big-ticket litigation. His star keeps rising in this field. He's super clever and the judges listen to him as he's a voice of reason." **Recent work:** Represented the defendant in Dar al Arkan Real Estate Development Co v Al Refai & others, an action seeking the enforcement of two judgments in Bahrain.

Jonathan Adkin QC (see p.579) An impressive advocate who has acted in a large number of prominent, multi-jurisdictional fraud disputes. **Strengths:** "He's very commercial. He cuts through nonsense and provides very crisp and clear analysis of a case. "Adkin is very effective. He sticks to the issues and puts his case plainly and simply." **Recent work:** Acted for the applicants in a USD1.3 billion claim brought by JSC Mezhdunarodniy Bank and the Deposit Insurance Agency of Russia against Sergei Pugachev. The case concerned the alleged misappropriation of assets.

Timothy Howe QC.(see p.676) An experienced silk with a global practice who is routinely engaged to act in multimillion-pound fraud disputes. Many of his cases since the financial crisis have concerned banking fraud. **Strengths:** "He was absolutely brilliant. He got stuck in and gave fantastic strategic direction. He wasn't scared of getting his arms around the case and seemed to know everything there is to know." "He is exceptionally hard-working, a team player and an extremely gifted advocate." **Recent work:** Defended a syndicate of banks led by RBS in a claim brought by Marme Inversiones regarding funds that were allegedly lost as a result of Euribor rigging.

Rosalind Phelps QC (see p.736) Awarded silk in 2016 in acknowledgement of her exemplary commercial and banking practice. She has acted in a variety of complex fraud disputes. **Strengths:** "She's exceptional in terms of both her commitment and tenacity. She deals well with judges and is good with clients." "She is very measured and gives good tactical advice." **Recent work:** Acted for Cephalon in bringing a high-value claim against CP Pharmaceuticals concerning a manufacturing contract for a leukaemia drug.

JUNIORS

Adam Zellick (see p.802) At ease handling large-scale, high-value fraud litigation that often involves freezing injunctions. **Strengths:** "He is very clever. He gets to the issues at hand and is very good at connecting the issues with the evidence and drawing out what's salient." "He is a cracking fraud lawyer and a remarkably good advocate." **Recent work:** Acted for the third defendant in a £175 million fraud action brought by Kazakhstan's Alliance Bank.

Deepak Nambisan (see p.725) Instructed in complicated disputes containing serious allegations of fraud. His practice is both domestic and international, crossing into such jurisdictions as Russia and the Cayman Islands. **Strengths:** "He is a master of detail but a persuasive advocate." **Recent work:** Successfully defended Investcorp, a financial services provider, in a USD300 million claim brought by Riad Tawfiq Al Sadik, a wealthy Middle Eastern businessman regarding alleged breaches of contract and fiduciary duty.

Simon Atrill (see p.586) A well-regarded junior who has deployed his talents in several major multi-million-pound fraud trials. **Recent work:** Acted for Group Seven in initiating fraud proceedings against various defendants relating to a EUR100 million investment.

Laura John (see p.683) An experienced junior who has a solid grasp of banking-related fraud. Solicitors extol her commercial awareness and user-friendliness. **Strengths:** "Her drafting is very good." "She is extremely bright, dedicated and approachable." **Recent work:** Defended RBS in a claim brought by Morris Group that alleged fraudulent misrepresentation.

Paul Sinclair (see p.766) Deals effectively with major fraud claims stretching across multiple jurisdictions. **Strengths:** "Paul Sinclair is bright and commercial." "He is very clever and user-friendly." **Recent work:** Successfully represented the defendants in Parish v Danwood. The defendants were alleged to have misrepresented the value of shares.

Maitland Chambers

See profile on p.875

THE SET

An outstanding commercial set featuring a number of silks and juniors engaged in civil fraud litigation. Sources draw attention to the "incredible strength in depth" in chambers and find the barristers "easy to deal with, responsive and available." Members are capable of pursuing large matters, many of which concern overseas jurisdictions. Recent instructions include JSC BTA Bank v Ablyazov and Dar Al Arkan v Al Refai.

Client service:

"The clerking is very slick. If you ask them to fix a date in a diary or to call you back it happens." "John Wiggs, the senior clerk, is great. He's very responsive if there's an issue that needs to be resolved and is good at keeping things moving forward on a balanced, friendly basis."

SILKS

Andrew Ayres QC Enters the table for the first time having taken silk in 2015. He is skilled at prosecuting and defending weighty cross-border and UK-based fraud cases. **Strengths:** "He is someone who inspires confidence and can be trusted with whatever's at hand." "He is very clever and has a very good manner with clients." **Recent work:** Acted for the second and third defendants in a £9 million action brought by Stephen Hunt, the liquidator of Autogas, alleging missing trader fraud.

Paul Girolami QC (see p.653) A popular silk whose civil fraud work is reinforced by his deep knowledge of commercial chancery, company and insolvency law. **Strengths:** "He is ideally suited for complex fraud claims." "Paul Girolami is absolutely brilliant. He is extremely effective in court." **Recent work:** Acted for one of the defendants in the Libyan Investment Authority's USD1.5 billion action against Société Générale concerning alleged bribery.

Matthew Collings QC (see p.620) Routinely instructed in significant cases of alleged fraud, including courtroom trials and arbitrations. **Strengths:** "He is knowledgeable and creative." "He is a tenacious operator who is hugely committed to the client's cause." **Recent work:** Acted for Cedar Capital Partners, a hotel investment consultancy, in a dispute with FHR relating to a secret EUR10 million fee that Ramsey Mankarious, the founder of Cedar, allegedly took in return for finding a buyer of the Monte Carlo Grand Hotel.

Anthony Trace QC (see p.783) A senior silk and a fine cross-examiner who is regularly entrusted by major City law firms with fraud cases of the highest value and importance. **Strengths:** "His cross-examination is impressive and he is very capable on his feet. He knows how to talk to a judge and get across the key points quickly and effectively, and he's always full of energy." **Recent work:** Acted for Ekaterina Berezovskaya, daughter of the late Boris Berezovsky, in Aeroflot v Berezovsky, a widely reported attempt to have a Russian ruling enforced in the UK.

Richard Morgan QC (see p.721) Applies an expert understanding of the law to fraud disputes, particularly when it comes to freezing, tracing and recovering assets. He is deeply familiar with jurisdictional issues, having acted in a number of cross-border cases. **Strengths:** "He's very good, quick and responsive. A great team player who's pretty aggressive, he's extraordinarily thoughtful in terms of thinking of potential solutions." "He has an encyclopaedic knowledge and grasp of the technicalities and procedure in this field." **Recent work:** Represented Russtech, the third defendant in Erste v Red October & Others, a case concerning an alleged conspiracy to induce insolvency.

Catherine Newman QC (see p.727) Has an extensive commercial chancery practice that encompasses many civil fraud instructions, including ones with an international dimension. **Strengths:** "Catherine's a superstar in the courtroom. She's incredibly well prepared." "Catherine has the ability to take the temperature of the situation and read the court. She is well regarded by the judiciary and easy to get on with. Clients really like her and she's extremely bright. She really is a tour de force." **Recent work:** Acted for Sait Salam Gutseriev, a Russian businessman, in BTA Bank v Dregon Land, a complex case of alleged fraud.

David Mumford QC (see p.724) Even before taking silk in 2016 was appearing unled as sole counsel in substantial pieces of civil fraud litigation arising out of such issues as dishonest assistance and the misappropriation of assets. **Strengths:** "He's very calm and authoritative." "He is a first-rate advocate whose written work is turned around with amazing speed." **Recent work:** Acted for Asia Resource Minerals, a mining company, in a raft of legal proceedings relating to allegedly misappropriated assets.

JUNIORS

Louise Hutton (see p.679) Sought after for her advice and advocacy in major pieces of fraud litigation incorporating the full spectrum of allegations. **Strengths:** "She is very experienced." "She is thoughtful and analytical."

George Hayman (see p.667) A well-liked junior who takes on challenging fraud cases as part of a practice that also encompasses wider commercial chancery and media law. **Strengths:** "You can trust his judgement. When George says 'I know you'll be angry but don't do this' I listen." **Recent work:** Represented Latvijas Krājbanka in a claim for USD80 million against Vladimir Antonov, the majority owner of the bank.

Benjamin John (see p.683) An accomplished senior junior frequently instructed in large-value fraud proceedings involving various allegations including corruption and bribery. **Strengths:** "He has a sharp mind, is a lovely person to deal with and is a good team player." "He is an excellent draftsman and tactician." **Recent work:** Represented Nomura International in a USD3 billion action relating to the enforceability of transactions made by executives at Banca Monte dei Paschi di Siena, the Italian lender, which are alleged to have concealed losses and enabled the misrepresentation of its financial situation.

James Sheehan (see p.763) An up-and-coming junior operating a fine civil fraud and commercial chancery practice. His workload includes major actions in the UK and abroad. **Strengths:** "James is incredibly hard-working and very pleasant to work with. He delivers well thought out and well-reasoned written products in good time." "His manner is calm and reassuring, so he's perfect for clients in crisis. He is wise beyond his years of call." **Recent work:** Represented Dar Al Arkan Real Estate Development Company and Bank Alkhair in a USD1 billion Commercial Court claim relating to the online publication of serious corporate malpractice allegations.

Serle Court

See profile on p.908

THE SET

A large commercial set hosting a plethora of talented QCs and juniors at all levels of call. Its members are more than capable of dealing with the most serious and complex fraud proceedings, and are applauded for their wealth of experience. One solicitor comments: "The set gives me such good service. The barristers are so experienced on the civil fraud stuff that they can just pick up cases and run with them. They don't have to waste time getting to grips with things because this work is bread and butter to them."

Client service: "It is an extremely professional and well-run set. The service we have received has always been excellent." Steve Whitaker, the head clerk, is "always approachable" and "truly excellent."

SILKS

Alan Boyle QC (see p.601) A distinguished commercial silk who has handled a range of important fraud cases. His practice covers several areas of law including company, insolvency and trusts. **Strengths:** "He is absolutely top-notch. He devotes himself to the client's cause and always impresses with his ability to convert volumes of paper and vastly complex issues into clear, pragmatic advice. He is a brilliant advocate." **Recent work:** Acted for the trust defendants in Kingate Global Fund v Kingate Management, a fraud claim relating to assets that two feeder funds transferred to Bernard L Madoff Investment Securities.

Hugh Norbury QC (see p.728) An excellent young silk instructed in high-profile and high-value civil fraud cases involving allegations such as breach of fiduciary duty and conspiracy. **Strengths:** "He's incredibly dedicated to detail." "He has an understated way of presenting his case which really has you listening to him. He holds the attention of the judge." **Recent work:** Successfully acted for Coca-Cola Enterprises in proceedings against various defendants to recover over £6 million in misappropriated assets.

Philip Jones QC (see p.686) Provides carefully crafted advice in difficult fraud disputes and is adept at addressing jurisdiction issues. **Strengths:** "He is really solid as an opponent. He's absolutely delightful and a very safe pair of hands." **Recent work:** Acted for Kazakhstan's BTA Bank in bringing a USD6 billion fraud claim against Mukhtar Ablyazov and others.

Philip Marshall QC (see p.708) A specialist fraud advocate instructed in significant pieces of litigation involving the full range of allegations. **Strengths:** "He absorbs documentation impressively quickly and is formidable and aggressive when he needs to be." **Recent work:** Represented the respondents in an application by Ras Al Khaimah Investment Authority for interim relief involving freezing and receivership orders.

Dominic Dowley QC (see p.636) Works on pivotal fraud cases within the context of an international commercial practice that also covers banking and financial services, professional negligence and trusts work. **Strengths:** "He's a very cerebral barrister who pays strong attention to detail." **Recent work:** Acted in Novoship v Mikhaylyuk, a multi-jurisdictional fraud claim arising out of bribes paid to a former manager of Novoship for the chartering of oil tankers.

Elizabeth Jones QC (see p.685) An experienced commercial practitioner frequently instructed in major fraud matters. She is also a skilled mediator. **Strengths:** "She has outstanding tactical judgement and the ability to co-ordinate numerous parties to work together." "She's very careful and forensic."

JUNIORS

Justin Higgo (see p.671) An admired junior with a broad commercial chancery practice. He receives a steady supply of significant fraud instructions. **Strengths:** "He has an impressive reputation." **Recent work:** Represented Aeroflot, Russia's state airline, in bringing a claim for damages against the estate of Boris Berezovsky relating to the alleged misappropriation of assets.

David Drake (see p.636) Advises in complex cases of civil fraud, and is an expert on freezing and document preservation orders. "He has a high degree of technical skills and can express the most complex matters in simple, direct terms." **Recent work:** Acted for the defendants in Coll v Floreat Merchant Banking.

Nicholas Harrison (see p.666) Has handle high-value fraud claims emanating from all around the globe. Jurisdictions in which he has appeared include Bermuda, the Bahamas, the Isle of Man and the BVI. **Strengths:** "Efficiently prepares first-rate written submissions, and masters complex factual cases." **Recent work:** Handled the Blickle litigation in Bermuda and the BVI. This was an ownership dispute between rival trusts in Jersey and Bermuda that centred on allegations of fraudulent misappropriation of trust assets.

Ruth den Besten (see p.632) An accomplished barrister who focuses on sizeable commercial fraud litigation. **Strengths:** "She's user-friendly and supportive of her instructing solicitors. In her approach she's very calm and measured and she inspires confidence. "She provides good, clear analysis and is excellent at cross-examination and in court generally." **Recent work:** Acted for a majority of defendants in successfully resisting an application for interim relief made by Ras Al Khaimah Investment Authority.

Simon Hattan (see p.667) Manages a general commercial and chancery practice and is regularly instructed on fraud matters involving such allegations as breach of fiduciary duty and dishonesty. **Strengths:** "He is pragmatic, experienced and brilliant." "He is very bright, thorough, tenacious and commercial." **Recent work:** Represented the defendants in group claims against RBS valued in excess of £3 billion relating to a 2008 rights issue.

Matthew Morrison (see p.722) Prosecutes and defends high-profile fraud proceedings concerning such issues as unfair prejudice, conspiracy and misappropriated assets. **Strengths:** "Matthew Morrison is extremely responsive and user-friendly. He is able to assimilate complex facts and plead very detailed statements of a case. He is also very good on his feet." **Recent work:** Defended Charles Ridley in a claim brought by Dubai Islamic Bank alleging that he put the proceeds of a fraud into a trust on the island of Jersey.

4 Stone Buildings

See profile on p.913

THE SET

4 Stone Buildings has a breadth of expertise that enables its members to pick up many of the most prestigious fraud instructions. A force to be reckoned with in related areas such as trusts and insolvency, it regularly secures instructions with an international flavour, and has members who are highly adept at worldwide asset tracing and recovery. Testament to its pedigree in this area it has, over the years, been involved in such celebrated cases as Guinness, Polly Peck, BCCI, Maxwell, Enron and Madoff.

Client service: "I know all the clerks there and find them to be extremely responsive." "The clerking service is efficient and sensible." Senior clerk David Goddard is hugely popular with those that instruct the set. "He's old-school in the best sense. Every day of the hearing he would come to court and he would check in on his barristers in court that day, hang around, shake the hands of the solicitors. I've never seen it with anybody else. He's just a nice person who it's easy to deal and negotiate with."

SILKS

Robert Miles QC Handles the most serious civil fraud and asset recovery cases, and is one of the most celebrated barristers at today's commercial chancery Bar. Leading instructing solicitors constantly seek out his services and he has been in some headline-making cases such as Equitable Life, Lehman Brothers and MF Global. **Strengths:** "What's really nice about him is how down-to-earth and user-friendly he is, notwithstanding his stellar reputation." "Robert Miles is a star of the Bar who combines fantastic technical ability, strategic judgement and user-friendliness with powerful and incisive advocacy. He is full of ideas and inspires huge confidence in clients." **Recent work:** Represented the liquidators of Singularis in bringing legal proceedings against Daiwa alleging breach of duties.

Jonathan Crow QC (see p.627) An experienced advocate whose fraud work forms part of a wider company, commercial and public law practice. **Strengths:** "Jonathan Crow QC is a great wordsmith and delightful to work with." **Recent work:** Acted for Victor Pinchuk in bringing a USD2 billion claim against Igor Kolomoisky and Gennadiy Bogolyubov that included allegations of fraud.

Richard Hill QC (see p.671) A junior silk with a reputation for producing robust advocacy in civil fraud disputes. He has particular expertise in City-based litigation and has handled some headline-grabbing cases such as Meridien Constantin v Bernie Ecclestone. **Strengths:** "He's very bright and quick to grasp an issue." "He's easy to work with and he has a very good track record." **Recent work:** Represented Victor Pinchuk in a USD2 billion fraud claim against two other Ukrainian businessmen.

John Brisby QC (see p.603) An experienced silk who has taken on hefty fraud cases both at home and in many offshore jurisdictions including the Isle of Man, Gibraltar, Bermuda, Guernsey and the Bahamas. **Strengths:** "He has an impressive eye for detail and really scoured the papers. He was an extremely effective advocate on his feet, and very good at reading his audience and understanding the judge." **Recent work:** Acted for Peak Hotels and Resorts in a very high-profile shareholder battle for control of Aman Resorts, a group of ultra-luxury hotels worth around USD358 million.

Orlando Fraser QC (see p.648) Handles leading fraud cases as part of a domestic and international commercial chancery caseload. He is noted for his cross-examination and negotiation skills. **Strengths:** "Orlando is an excellent silk who turns work around quickly and is a very reliable sounding board." **Recent work:** Represented the fourth defendant in legal proceedings brought by the Republic of Djibouti relating to alleged mismanagement of the country's main port. He was successful in having freezing injunctions in the British Virgin Islands and Singapore discharged.

JUNIORS

Christopher Harrison (see p.665) An accomplished senior junior who tackles fraud-related litigation as part of a broader commercial practice. His instructions originate both in the UK and overseas. **Strengths:** "He gives very straightforward, nonsense advice. He's very approachable and very amenable to the idea of talking things through. He makes himself available and is a good member of the team." **Recent work:** Represented Michele Hope, the fashion outlet, in bringing a claim against its bookkeeper to recover stolen funds.

Andrew de Mestre (see p.631) An expert in cases concerning dishonesty and fraudulent misrepresentation, he is proficient at tracing and recovering misappropriated assets. **Strengths:** "As well as being a top advocate, he is someone who understands the technical aspects of a case and can lead the discussions with clients on those points sensibly."

Gregory Denton-Cox (see p.632) A skilled senior junior with a wide commercial chancery practice who has appeared in many headline-grabbing fraud cases. **Strengths:** "He's terrific, hard-working and really user-friendly." **Recent work:** Defended Goldman Sachs in a USD1.2 billion claim brought by the Libyan Investment Authority contending that it bribed LIA officials in return for securing lucrative deals.

3 Verulam Buildings

See profile on p.924

THE SET

A leading civil fraud set, noted for its superior knowledge of the banking sector, that is "always a serious contender for the juiciest fraud cases." Members have appeared in many significant and high-value cases, including Vincent Tchenguiz v Grant Thornton and Libyan Investment Authority v Société Générale.

Client service: Solicitors remark that the set is "well run and efficient" and find the clerks, led by Stephen Penson, to be "modern, easy to deal with and commercial."

SILKS

Adrian Beltrami QC An acclaimed commercial litigator who focuses in particular on financial disputes, many of which involve allegations of fraud. **Strengths:** "He is someone whom judges respect." "He's got a very nice courtroom manner, and he presents things clearly and crisply." "Adrian Beltrami is a very polished advocate." **Recent work:** Defended Société Générale against a £1.5 billion claim brought by the Libyan Investment Authority alleging that it bribed officials in return for securing favourable deals.

Ewan McQuater QC Has a varied caseload strong on banking and finance cases as well as general commercial chancery matters. He is routinely called upon to act in multi-jurisdictional civil fraud cases. **Strengths:** "He's very sensible, very commercial and very easy to work with." "He has vast experience in civil fraud matters." **Recent work:** Defended Nick and Christian Candy, the property developing brothers, in a claim brought by Mark Holyoake alleging that they employed fraudulent misrepresentation and other means to force him to repay, earlier than agreed, a loan that they had made to him.

Andrew Onslow QC A redoubtable advocate with a wide commercial practice who is sought out for his ability to prosecute and defend multibillion-pound claims. **Strengths:** "He's very measured and very sensible." "Very punchy in his advocacy and down-to-earth in his opinions," "He is a first-class advocate who can get to grips with the thorniest of issues." **Recent work:** Defended the NCA against a compensation claim brought against it by Israel Perry alleging that it illegally froze his assets worldwide.

Ali Malek QC An accomplished practitioner who manages a weighty commercial caseload. He is renowned for the effectiveness of his cross-examination. **Strengths:** "He is very well respected in his field, good at the big points and extremely skilled at informing case strategy." "He is a smooth operator." **Recent work:** Defended Threadneedle, the asset management firm, in a USD120 million claim brought by Otkritie, the Russian bank, relating to fraud committed by employees of both institutions.

David Quest QC Maintains a broad commercial practice with an international reach. He graduated in mathematics before turning to law and provides sought-after advice in instances of complex financial fraud. **Strengths:** "David Quest is diplomatic and super clever." **Recent work:** Acted for Todaysure Matthews, a British manufacturer of incinerators, in bringing proceedings against Marketing Ways Services, a Saudi Arabian company, alleging that it received only part of an agreed payment due to a fraudulent demand having been made on the performance guarantee.

Jonathan Davies-Jones QC Has a fantastic track record in fraud-related litigation. He is particularly good on cases with financial complexities. **Strengths:** "He is extraordinarily clever but retains a pragmatic approach. Very user-friendly, he is one of the best trial advocates at the Bar." **Recent work:** Defended Niranjan Hiranandani, an Indian entrepreneur, against a £350 million claim brought by Hirco, a real estate investment company, which lent money to him to fund real estate projects in two Indian cities that were not completed due to alleged fraud.

Paul Lowenstein QC A dedicated commercial advocate who has taken to trial many cases containing allegations of civil fraud. He ordinarily acts for banks. **Strengths:** "The presence in a courtroom he has is phenomenal." **Recent work:** Defended LLB Verwaltung, a Swiss bank, in two separate actions arising out of the same alleged fraud.

John Odgers QC Well equipped to litigate fraud-related disputes particularly in the realm of banking and finance. **Strengths:** "He's a very clever man and he's got a scientific background that comes through. He's very measured and precise." **Recent work:** Defended Nobahar-Cookson and Barclays Private Bank and Trust in a dispute with The Hut Group about alleged breaches of warranties in a share purchase agreement.

Andrew Sutcliffe QC A popular choice for fraud disputes whose portfolio of cases extends to banking and finance, professional negligence and media law. Since 2004 he has sat part-time as a Chancery Division judge. **Strengths:** "He's such a joy to work with." "He is clear-thinking, wise and approachable." "He is a real team player." **Recent work:** Represented the NCA in bringing civil recovery proceedings against Mr Ghulam, Mr Jardine and other defendants relating to alleged fraud.

David Head QC Took silk in 2016 and continues to take on prominent civil fraud instructions as part of an expansive commercial practice. **Strengths:** "Razor-sharp and a fine strategist. He is a considered tactician and a robust advocate who does not shy away from a difficult decision or a forceful point." **Recent work:** Represented the defendants in Alliance Bank v Zhunus and others, a case arising from the alleged misappropriation of USD160 million.

JUNIORS

Adam Kramer (see p.693) A highly regarded commercial practitioner adept at handling disputes in such areas as fraud, insurance, energy and banking. **Strengths:** "He's extremely nice to work with and extremely bright." **Recent work:** Represented the Candy brothers in a £120 million action brought by Mark Holyoake alleging losses due to renegation on a loan agreement.

Matthew Parker (see p.733) Prosecutes and defends serious fraud claims, routinely appearing unled. **Strengths:** "Matt is an incisive written advocate with a meticulous eye for detail and is very easy to get along with. His drafting rarely requires editing and he always cover every point, and in style." "He is an excellent team player." **Recent work:** Represented the Central Bank of Ecuador and other appellants in a successful Privy Council appeal against Conticorp and other respondents that resulted in them being awarded in excess of USD500 million.

Michael Lazarus (see p.697) A talented commercial practitioner who handles fraud cases as part of a wide-ranging practice that also takes in banking and finance, professional negligence and IT matters. **Strengths:** "He is extremely diligent." "Michael Lazarus is very approachable and is a great pleasure to work with. He has a very sharp mind and can identify complex issues extremely quickly." **Recent work:** Defended Threadneedle, the asset manager, in a USD100 million action brought by Otkritie, the Russian bank, alleging vicarious liability for a conspiracy entered into by employees of both organisations.

Rajesh Pillai Litigates and arbitrates domestic and international fraud cases on behalf of corporations and individuals. He has an intimate understanding of financial regulations. **Strengths:** "Rajesh Pillai is very bright, very easy to work with and quick at getting on top of complex facts." He "provides clear analysis" and is "hard-working, very bright and accessible." **Recent work:** Defended Niranjan Hiranandani, an Indian entrepreneur, in a £350 million fraud claim brought by Hirco relating to investments in Indian real estate.

Peter de Verneuil Smith (see p.631) A skilled senior junior whose mandate of commercial cases extends beyond the UK to such jurisdictions as Singapore and Hong Kong. **Strengths:** "Peter is the most responsive junior member of counsel I've ever worked with. No matter when, he is always available. He's very intelligent and comes up with creative solutions. He is a very impressive character." **Recent work:** Represented a Swiss bank in a USD90 million fraud action brought by Group Seven against various defendants.

Band 2

XXIV Old Buildings

See profile on p.884

THE SET

Comprises a number of leading silks and juniors successful at achieving victories for clients in major fraud disputes. Barristers concentrate on cases with millions or billions of pounds at stake and deal with complex allegations ranging from bribery and money laundering to breach of duty and undue influence. They are a strong force both domestically and internationally and benefit from their know-how in financial services regulation and trusts and insolvency law. Recent cases of significance include Libyan Investment Authority v Société Générale and Arcadia Petroleum v Bosworth.

Client service: "The clerks are extremely helpful. They get back to you quickly and always provide you with the information you need. They are very well organised and have a strong working relationship with their barristers. There is never any slip between cup and lip." Sue Medder, the chambers director, is reported to have "brought a fantastic breath of fresh air to the set. Having previously worked at Withers she knows the pressures solicitors are under."

SILKS

Alan Steinfeld QC A respected silk well known for his work in the fields of offshore trusts, company law and civil fraud. He has conducted actions in a host of jurisdictions beyond the UK for many years. **Strengths:** "He has such an incredible feel for the law. A difficult question came from the Bench and he batted the answer right back at them. As a result the judges had this unbelievable confidence in him and wanted to know what he thought." "He is fantastically intelligent and charming." **Recent work:** Acted in Phillips v Symes, a complex multi-jurisdictional dispute involving various fraud allegations to do with assets at the Gibraltar branch of a French bank.

Stephen Moverley Smith QC Handles substantial civil fraud litigation as part of a practice that also covers trusts, finance and insolvency. **Strengths:** "He's very effective indeed." "Stephen is very clever and quick to grasp both commercial and legal points and articulate them in a way that is particularly persuasive." **Recent work:** Represented the applicants in RAK Investments v Bestfort Development, an application for interim relief to aid a USD42 million fraud claim brought in Georgia.

Steven Thompson QC Has run a successful commercial practice in silk since being appointed in 2015, appearing in cases arising out of fraud in a number of jurisdictions. **Strengths:** "He is very good on his feet." "He is a bright, punchy advocate with real expertise in cross-border fraud work. "He is very hands-on and just picks the client up and takes them along on the journey." **Recent work:** Represented a defendant in Arcadia v Bosworth, a high-value fraud action concerning alleged fraudulent trading of oil.

Robert Levy QC An experienced commercial silk who has fought and won major civil fraud cases for clients located across the world including in the Caribbean, South America and Russia. **Strengths:** "He's got an excellent nose for fraud and he's fearless in pursuing those cases." **Recent work:** Represented a defendant in JPSPC 4 and JPSPC 1 v Schools & Others, a dispute relating to a Cayman fund that became insolvent.

Elspeth Talbot Rice QC Effective at dealing with large, multimillion-pound fraud and asset-tracing claims. Her practice also encompasses general commercial dispute resolution and traditional chancery. **Strengths:** "She is mightily impressive and very composed. She cuts to the chase very quickly, and people don't doubt her judgement. She's on the money." "She's good at building pressure and keeping the litigation moving. She's an incredibly smooth and an extremely pleasant advocate." **Recent work:** Instructed in Wood v Add, a claim brought by a woman against her ex-boyfriend to recover tens of millions amassed by him while they were together.

Wilberforce Chambers

See profile on p.925

THE SET

A growing team comprising "lots of talented barristers" catering to clients caught up in alleged fraud. Cases span onshore and offshore jurisdictions and are frequently valued at billions of pounds. Members are adept at locating, freezing and recovering the proceeds of fraud.

Client service: "The clerks are very good and it is a very user-friendly chambers." "The set is well served by its clerks, who have got things well organised." Nicholas Luckman is the practice director and Mark Rushton is the head clerk.

SILKS

Alan Gourgey QC Routinely called upon to deal with difficult, fast-moving fraud litigation and arbitrations involving such allegations as breach of contract, deceit, bribery and misappropriation. He is successful at obtaining freezing and search orders. **Strengths:** "He's excellent and his cross-examination is superb." "Alan Gourgey is very balanced, very good and very clever." **Recent work:** Acted in Bank of Moscow v JFC BVI & Others, a USD150 million misappropriation of assets claim.

Ian Croxford QC A tenacious silk regularly engaged in high-profile commercial disputes in which fraud is alleged. **Strengths:** "He is hugely versatile and able, and he is extremely good to work with." "He is a mature, sensible silk."

John Wardell QC An outstanding leader with a wide-ranging practice who is accustomed to fighting complex fraud disputes. **Strengths:** "He is user-friendly and a good fighter." "Great with clients, he's very hands-on and approachable. He understands and speaks the language that business people understand and is not afraid to give a view." **Recent work:** Acted for PCP in bringing a deceit claim against Barclays relating to the refinancing of the bank in 2008.

Lawrence Cohen QC Has been involved in a number of complex, high-value cases such as those arising out of the liquidation of BCCI, and is noted for the international reach of his practice. **Strengths:** "He is very incisive, very clever and very tactical." **Recent work:** Acted in Planck v Tinsel Group and Vitol Holdings, a dispute concerning one of the world's largest energy traders.

Fenner Moeran QC A versatile barrister who maintains a broad practice covering civil fraud, pensions and trusts work among other things. He provides clients with well-considered advice and is particularly good on fraud cases with financial services aspects. **Recent work:** Represented a company's liquidators in an action against a former director relating to property that allegedly went missing.

Tim Penny QC An excellent advocate who solicitors are pleased to see has recently taken silk. He has handled a number of significant fraud cases, and is especially knowledgeable in the realm of injunctive relief. **Strengths:** "He's got a great courtroom presence and knows how to do the best for his clients in tricky situations." "He is an expert in this field and works well with clients." **Recent work:** Successfully brought a £15 million claim on behalf of JSC VTB Bank against various defendants.

JUNIORS

Iain Pester Has worked on a number of high-profile civil fraud cases and, being a fluent Russian speaker, is an expert in work emanating from that country. **Strengths:** "He has a good, analytical mind and is a strong advocate whose Russian language skills are of enormous benefit." **Recent work:** Represented JSC Bank of Moscow in making a committal application against Vladimir Kekhman after he had breached a USD250 million freezing order.

Max Mallin Instructed in heavyweight fraud claims, especially those with international or banking elements. **Strengths:** "He is very good and very knowledgeable." "He's exceptional. I would go to him if I was in trouble." **Recent work:** Represented Nextam Partners in bringing a contempt claim against Mohamed Sarwar Mughal and others for breaching various interlocutory orders.

Other Ranked Lawyers

Ian Smith (see p.768) (The Chambers of Andrew Mitchell QC) A civil and criminal fraud specialist comfortable managing complex proceedings involving such issues as asset recovery and money laundering. **Strengths:** "Ian is meticulous in his preparation." "He is an excellent communicator."

Stephen Smith QC (see p.769) (Erskine Chambers) A heavyweight commercial advocate sought after for his advocacy in global fraud proceedings involving the freezing, tracing and recovery of stolen assets. **Strengths:** "He is very user-friendly, very knowledgeable and very effective." "Stephen Smith is a fount of knowledge. He is very experienced, easy to work with and also a very good advocate." **Recent work:** Acted on behalf of BTA Bank in a dispute with Mukhtar Ablyazov, its former chairman, concerning an alleged misappropriation of assets.

Tim Akkouh (see p.580) (Erskine Chambers) An excellent commercial advocate routinely instructed in big-stakes civil fraud proceedings. He is adept at dealing with interim relief and committal orders. **Strengths:** "Tim is extremely bright and thoughtful. He's lots of fun to deal with and absolutely on the ball." **Recent work:** Successfully acted for BTA Bank in a Supreme Court case against Mukhtar Ablyazov.

Emily Gillett (see p.653) (Erskine Chambers) Handles high-value fraud cases, some of which are multi-jurisdictional and involve complex foreign law. She is especially good at interim relief applications and the obtaining of contempt of court orders. **Strengths:** "A lateral thinker who is incredibly hard-working and has good ideas." "She works very hard and produces good written work." **Recent work:** Acted for BTA Bank in substantial litigation against Mukhtar Ablyazov including opposition to an appeal concerning estoppel, privity of interest and abuse of process.

Duncan Matthews QC (20 Essex Street) An ideal counsel for international fraud disputes who has extensive experience of handling matters both at home and in offshore jurisdictions such as BVI and Nevis. He was lead defence counsel in the substantial Mukhtar Ablyazov litigation which was freighted with allegations of fraud. **Strengths:** "He's phenomenal. If you've got something that's a bit tricky he's brilliant." "He commands the court with ease." **Recent work:** Acted for the claimant in OMV Petrom SA & SC Petrolexportimport SA v Glencore International Aktiengesellschaft, an action relating to allegedly low-grade crude oil that was delivered in the 1990s.

Andrew Fulton (20 Essex Street) A gifted senior junior handling significant banking and finance, energy and commercial fraud litigation. **Strengths:** "He is quick to grasp complex issues and identify commercial solutions. He provides practical advice and is a great team player." **Recent work:** Won damages of over USD100 million for Petrom in a large fraud claim against Glencore relating to the delivery of allegedly low-quality oil to Romania in the 1990s.

Hodge Malek QC (39 Essex Chambers) A renowned commercial silk instructed in relation to complex, high-value civil and criminal fraud disputes. He has strong international credentials and is especially knowledgeable about the Middle East and South Asia. **Strengths:** "Hodge Malek QC goes from strength to strength. He is a persuasive, hard-working advocate who can engage and get on well with his clients and put them at ease, and he is exceptionally good on his feet." "He is an astute tactician who gives clear strategic advice." **Recent work:** Represented KPMG in a USD10 million claim brought by Al-Jizzi involving elements of fraud.

Simon Davenport QC (3 Hare Court) A dedicated practitioner active in high-profile cases arising out of international and domestic fraud. He possesses a deep knowledge of Russian and CIS legal systems. **Strengths:** "He is very knowledgeable and an exceptional advocate. He is extremely bright and very commercial." **Recent work:** Successfully represented a number of defendants in a £50 million action brought by NGM Sustainable Developments involving various allegations including fraudulent conspiracy.

Aidan Casey QC (3 Hare Court) A much-heralded new commercial silk who excels in civil fraud cases involving injunctive relief and asset recovery. **Strengths:** "He is so clever and yet so personable. Aidan's written work is outstanding. His advocacy is clear, well put together and persuasive." **Recent work:** Successfully represented Phillip Wallis, the first defendant in a £50 million claim brought by NGM Sustainable Developments involving numerous allegations including fraudulent conspiracy.

Clive Freedman QC (see p.648) (7 King's Bench Walk) A fantastic commercial counsel for high-profile fraud trials with international elements. **Strengths:** "He is very experienced and creative in fraud cases and considers all the angles." "His depth of thought, analysis and creativity make him an exceptional civil fraud lawyer. He also has the ability to put across complex arguments in a persuasive manner." **Recent work:** Acted for the Bank of Moscow in a £150 million claim against Andrey Valerievich Chernyakov seeking the enforcement in England of Russian judgments to recover the proceeds of fraud.

Richard Waller QC (7 King's Bench Walk) A leading silk with a broad commercial practice that also covers energy, insurance and shipping. He is adept at handling high-value, multiparty civil fraud litigation involving jurisdictional issues. **Strengths:** "A real powerhouse in court." "He is very persuasive, and a fearless advocate and ferocious cross-examiner." **Recent work:** Defended Abourahman Boreh in a claim brought by the Republic of Djibouti alleging that he committed fraud while head of the country's Ports and Free Zones Authority.

Charles Samek QC (Littleton Chambers) A sound choice for high-profile fraud claims with multi-jurisdictional complexities. He is especially effective at applying for and obtaining interim relief in the form of freezing and disclosure injunctions. **Strengths:** "He's an oustanding advocate. He has real presence in court and you can see that the judges really listen to him. He came across really well." "He is extremely bright, hard-working and responsive." **Recent work:** Acted for Ilyas Khrapunov in a dispute between BTA Bank and various defendants concerning allegations of conspiracy and frustration of enforcement.

Clare Montgomery QC (see p.720) (Matrix Chambers) A well-known advocate with a multi-jurisdictional criminal and civil practice who is used to dealing with difficult disputes. **Strengths:** "She operates at the very top of the market." "She's a star of the Bar."

Justin Fenwick QC (see p.644) (4 New Square) Manages an impressive commercial litigation caseload and deals with numerous UK and offshore fraud disputes involving all sorts of allegations. **Strengths:** "He gets involved in a way that I haven't experienced a leader get involved before. His advocacy is amazing, as is his knowledge of the documents." "He has a brilliant courtroom manner and good judgement." **Recent work:** Instructed in Weavering v Ernst & Young, a high-value claim relating to a hedge fund audit that was allegedly fraudulent.

Alex Hall Taylor (see p.662) (4 New Square) A busy senior junior frequently instructed in complex, multimillion-pound actions arising from alleged fraud. He is commended for his expertise in pre-emptive relief. **Strengths:** "He was easy to deal with, thorough and did a good job." "He's a good trial lawyer and a very safe pair of hands." "He is very smart and very hard-working." **Recent work:** Acted for HRH Prince Abdulaziz of Saudi Arabia in a large-scale fraud dispute with Apex Global Management.

Nigel Hood (New Square Chambers) Represents claimants and defendants in headline-grabbing civil fraud claims arising from allegations of money laundering, conspiracy and breach of fiduciary duty. **Strengths:** "He is extremely knowledgeable, hard-working and helpful. He presented the case in a very clear and persuasive manner, while keeping a very collected and even humble composure." "When he does something it's always really sensible and his written work is very strong." **Recent work:** Successfully acted for an appellant in the Court of Appeal as part of the Otkritie International Investment Management litigation which involved allegations of conspiracy, deceit and money laundering.

Mark Hubbard (New Square Chambers) Has a vibrant commercial practice and regularly handles complex international civil fraud matters. **Strengths:** "He is a very assured senior junior who is quick to grasp issues." **Recent work:** Succeeded in obtaining USD20 million for the claimants in Abela v Badaraani, a multi-jurisdictional civil fraud claim also taking place in Lebanon and Italy.

Stephen Robins (see p.753) (South Square) Capable of handling major fraud-related litigation across multiple jurisdictions. **Strengths:** "Stephen has produced some great written work for us and gives practical advice." "Stephens Robins is very bright, very capable and an excellent draftsman." **Recent work:** Defended Johannes Runar Johannsson in a claim for over £1.3 billion in damages brought by Vincent Tchenguiz alleging that multiple defendants conspired to bring about his arrest by providing the SFO with false information.

Charles Dougherty QC (see p.635) (2TG – 2 Temple Gardens) A relatively new commercial silk who appears for claimants and defendants in cases of alleged fraud, many of which have cross-border aspects to them. He is adept at swiftly deploying interlocutory procedures such as disclosure and freezing orders. **Strengths:** "He is extremely client-friendly, decisive in his views and very measured and sensible in his tactical advice. His client handling and knowledge of his subject are excellent. He's very nice and easy to work with because he's both friendly and attentive." **Recent work:** Successfully represented the Federaltive Republic of Brazil as claimant in a corruption case involving the tracing and recovery of public money alleged to have been stolen by the former mayor of São Paulo and routed out to such jurisdictions as the BVI and Jersey.

HEALTH & SAFETY: An Introduction

Contributed by James Maxwell-Scott QC of Crown Office Chambers

Sentencing after the Definitive Guideline

The Sentencing Council's Definitive Guideline for Health and Safety Offences, Corporate Manslaughter and Food Safety and Hygiene Offences was published on 3 November 2015 and came into force on 1 February 2016. The Guideline was widely expected to have most impact on large organisations (defined as those with a turnover of £50 million and over) and individuals; the starting points proposed in the Guideline for individuals would be likely to see significant numbers of cases crossing the custody threshold that would not previously have done so.

There is no doubt that fines imposed since 1 February have been higher than before, although perhaps not quite as high as many predicted. In February, ConocoPhillips (UK) was fined a total of £3 million following gas leaks on a gas platform which created a risk of explosion, albeit that the sentencing hearing was originally started in January 2016 and the judge considered he was not thereby bound to have regard to the new Guideline. In May, a Balfour Beatty company was fined £2.6 million following a fatal accident in which a trench collapsed on a worker. In April, Travis Perkins was fined £2 million after a customer was fatally crushed by a company vehicle at a builders' merchants' yard. It is unlikely that any of those fines would have reached close to those levels before the Guideline.

However, two cases involving British Telecom (a very large organisation for the purpose of the Guideline) illustrate the fact that fines over £1 million are not inevitable for very large organisations. In those cases, both in summer 2016, the fines were £500,000 and £600,000.

The significant differences in starting point based on culpability level and harm category, particularly for large and very large organisations, mean that there is a greater incentive for defendants to challenge the prosecution case at a Newton hearing if the appropriate categories cannot be agreed. Although it is early days, it does seem that the Guideline has fuelled a trend towards more contested trials and more contested sentencing hearings.

Corporate and gross negligence manslaughter

The most significant corporate manslaughter case of 2016 was R v Maidstone and Tunbridge Wells NHS Trust, in which Coulson J ruled that the defendant had no case to answer. The defendant hospital trust is the largest organisation prosecuted for this offence to date. Coulson J had ruled before the trial that the prosecution should particularise its case on who constituted senior management and the prosecution case was that the clinical director was the lowest tier of senior management involved on the facts of the case. At the close of the prosecution case, Coulson J ruled that there was no evidence to support the allegations of breach of duty relating to the appointment of two anaesthetists or the appraisal and supervision of them generally. Further, there was no evidence that the alleged failures in their supervision on the date of the fatality had caused or contributed to the death. The case confirms the commonly held view that the larger the defendant, the more difficult it is to prosecute it for corporate manslaughter. It will be interesting to see how the argument in relation to senior management is framed in a large private sector organisation.

In the first corporate manslaughter case sentenced under the Guideline, a care home company was fined £30,000 but, notably, a director of the company was sentenced to imprisonment for over three years for gross negligence manslaughter, and the manager of the home was sentenced to two years' imprisonment for a health and safety offence.

There appears to be a renewed enthusiasm on the part of prosecutors to pursue gross negligence manslaughter charges rather than corporate manslaughter charges. The outcomes of the two cases discussed above suggest a possible explanation for that trend.

Conclusion

The Definitive Guideline has undoubtedly raised the stakes in this specialist area of practice, in particular for large organisations and individual defendants. The need for expert advice and high-quality advocacy has never been greater. Those in need of such assistance will find all the help they need in these pages.

Contents:

LONDON

Health & Safety
Leading Sets
Band 1
Crown Office Chambers *
Henderson Chambers *
Band 2
2 Bedford Row *
6 Pump Court *
Band 3
2 Hare Court *
Outer Temple Chambers *
3 Raymond Buildings Barristers *
Temple Garden Chambers *
Leading Silks
Star individuals
Matthews Richard *2 Bedford Row*
Band 1
Compton Ben *Outer Temple Chambers*
Darbishire Adrian *QEB Hollis Whiteman (ORL)* ◊
Lissack Richard *Fountain Court Chambers (ORL)* ◊ *
Morton Keith *Temple Garden Chambers* *
Popat Prashant *Henderson Chambers* [A] *
Sturman Jim *2 Bedford Row* *
Band 2
Ageros James *Crown Office Chambers*
Campbell Oliver *Henderson Chambers* [A] *
Caplan Jonathan *5 Paper Buildings (ORL)* ◊
Cooper John *Crown Office Chambers* *
Laidlaw Jonathan *2 Hare Court* *
Travers David *6 Pump Court* *
Band 3
Forlin Gerard *Cornerstone Barristers (ORL)* ◊ *
Gibson Charles *Henderson Chambers* [A] *
Hockman Stephen *6 Pump Court* [A] *
Walsh Stephen *3 Raymond Buildings Barristers* [A] *
New Silks
Ashley-Norman Jonathan *3 Raymond Buildings* [A] *
Maxwell-Scott James *Crown Office Chambers*
Riley-Smith Toby *Henderson Chambers* [A] *
** Indicates set / individual with profile.*
[A] direct access (see p.24).
◊ (ORL) = Other Ranked Lawyer.
Alphabetical order within each band. Band 1 is highest.

Health & Safety
Leading Juniors
Star individuals
Antrobus Simon *Crown Office Chambers* *
Kay Dominic *Crown Office Chambers* *
Band 1
Balysz Mark *Crown Office Chambers*
Watson Mark *6 Pump Court*
Band 2
Adamson Dominic *Temple Garden Chambers*
Atkins Mike *Crown Office Chambers* *
Bates Pascal *6 Pump Court* [A] *
Bennett Lee *6 Pump Court* [A]
Buchanan James *2 Hare Court* *
Canby Fiona *Temple Garden Chambers*
Galloway Malcolm *Crown Office Chambers* *
Harris Mark *6 Pump Court*
Le Fevre Sarah *3 Raymond Buildings Barristers* [A] *
Leonard James *Outer Temple Chambers*
McGee Andrew *2 Bedford Row* *
Naqshbandi Saba *3 Raymond Buildings Barristers* [A]
Ritchie Shauna *2 Bedford Row* *
Band 3
Dickason Robert *Outer Temple Chambers* *
Du Cann Christian *39 Essex Chambers (ORL)* ◊
Ferguson Craig *2 Hare Court* *
Heer Deanna *5 Paper Buildings (ORL)* ◊ *
Hunt Quentin *2 Bedford Row* *
Kendrick Julia *Crown Office Chambers*
McLoughlin Kevin *Temple Garden Chambers*
Mehta Sailesh *Red Lion Chambers (ORL)* ◊
Menzies Gordon *6 Pump Court*
Rush Craig *2 Bedford Row*
Sanderson Eleanor *2 Bedford Row* *
Tampakopoulos Alexandra *2 Hare Court* *

Band 1

Crown Office Chambers

See profile on p.824

THE SET

Crown Office Chambers has long been home to a quality team of barristers, highly respected in the market for their health and safety work. As commentators say, the set comprises "a very strong group of like-minded, exceptional individuals" who routinely handle the most important cases in the market. "Generally all of their barristers are excellent. They possess great knowledge of the law and are good on service as well." The set represents both companies and individuals facing criminal prosecutions by such bodies as the Environment Agency and The Health and Safety Executive, and handle all manner of health and safety matters including high-profile corporate manslaughter cases. They are regularly involved in well-publicised matters of the day, such as the Maine Place electric gates fatality case in Manchester. The set also represented Serco in a matter concerning the death of a prison custody officer killed whilst on duty.

Client service: Andy Flanagan leads the clerking team, assisted by Toby Sparrow and Steve Purse. The clerks are "on the ball" and "give you a very good service. They are good at getting you out of a sticky spot." Flanagan is noted for being "very helpful and responsive" and is someone who "runs a tight ship."

SILKS

James Ageros QC A specialist health and safety practitioner, instructed to undertake both prosecution and defence work of the utmost complexity. **Strengths:** "He's got a great depth of experience in this field" and is "always impressive." "He's very level headed and calm, and can handle very difficult clients well, even in the most turbulent situations." **Recent work:** Instructed to represent Linley Development Limited in a corporate manslaughter prosecution. The case concerned the death of an employee who was killed when a retaining wall collapsed.

John Cooper QC (see p.623) Regularly instructed by directors and major corporations in significant health and safety cases, and often sought out to appear at inquests. **Strengths:** "He is an incredibly capable health and safety lawyer" who is "extremely tenacious and skilful." "Great regulatory lawyer, who is a superb attack weapon. When you know you're in a fight he's your man." **Recent work:** Defended the director of Cheshire Gates Automation Ltd in a gross negligence case concerning a girl who had been crushed by electric gates and subsequently died.

James Maxwell-Scott QC A renowned health and safety lawyer with specialist expertise, who advises clients in both civil and criminal matters pertaining to fatal and non-fatal accidents. **Strengths:** "He is a class act. He's fantastically bright, has a great manner with his clients and has an excellent legal head on him." **Recent work:** Prosecuted Dynamiq Cleaning & Metroline in a case where an employee of the cleaning company sustained serious injuries as a result of being crushed between two buses.

JUNIORS

Simon Antrobus (see p.584) A well-regarded barrister, praised by his peers for his remarkable intellect and market expertise. He is regularly instructed to undertake significant heavyweight cases on behalf of the defence but also has a wealth of experience handling high-profile prosecutions across a range of industry sectors. **Strengths:** "He's absolutely outstanding." "He's exceptional, he's attentive on the detail and he's extremely well prepared." "Absolutely first-class regulatory lawyer." **Recent work:** Advised Brighton & Sussex NHS University Hospital in an investigation regarding the death of a patient who had been poisoned by the hospital's contaminated water supply.

Dominic Kay (see p.688) A barrister with a formidable reputation, who is noted for excellence when defending large companies and directors in cases relating to fatal and non-fatal accidents in the workplace. **Strengths:** "He's excellent with clients, great on the paperwork and very knowledgeable." **Recent work:** Acted on behalf of Huntley Mount Engineering Limited defending a corporate manslaughter prosecution. The case concerned an apprentice who had become trapped in a metal lathe and was subsequently killed.

Mark Balysz Highly esteemed advocate, regularly instructed to defend corporate entities and directors in cases of the utmost severity. Testament to his skills, in 2015 he successfully obtained acquittals for all of the defendants he represented. **Strengths:** "He has great presence in court and is very authoritative." "A flamboyant performer and a great jury advocate." **Recent work:** Successfully defended Francis Brown Ltd in a case relating to the death of an employee who was electrocuted.

Julia Kendrick Manages complex health and safety cases on behalf of clients facing prosecution and investigation by local authorities, the HSE and other regulatory bodies. **Strengths:** "Has a good business like approach," and is "a fine advocate." "She has extensive knowledge and a very calming manner."

Mike Atkins (see p.586) Has significant expertise in criminal regulatory law and regularly represents individuals and companies facing charges of corporate and gross negligence manslaughter. He is an expert in both fatal and non-fatal accident cases. **Strengths:** "He is massively well prepared and extremely thorough." "Absolutely excellent and so hardworking, he's fully switched on." **Recent work:** Defended Maidstone and Tunbridge Wells NHS Trust in a corporate manslaughter prosecution, the first of its kind against an NHS trust.

Malcolm Galloway (see p.650) Acts for both the prosecution and defence handling high-profile cases of the utmost complexity, which often stem from inquests or investigations relating to health and safety. **Strengths:** "He's got very good tactical insight." "He's a great jury advocate, who is very, very personable and extremely sharp." **Recent work:** Prosecuted DS Smith in relation to safety breaches which consequently led to the death of a senior manager, killed as a resulted of being entangled in a pressing machine.

Henderson Chambers

See profile on p.864

THE SET

Henderson Chambers houses a host of highly skilled practitioners in this field, each one of whom is expert in the criminal, regulatory and civil aspects of health and safety law. Members here are consistently sought out to undertake high-profile cases, whether they be prosecutions and appeals, inquests, such as Re Vauxhall Helicopter Crash, or corporate manslaughter trials, such as R v CAV Aerospace. They also provide regulatory and operational advice on health and safety issues for the likes of the London Fire and Emergency Planning Authority. Commentators say: "They are excellent people to have in your corner and make you feel as if you're the only person for whom they're acting."

Client service:

"The clerks are very helpful and very efficient. They understand the product and are very helpful in terms of recommending people." The chief clerk is John White who receives praise for being "timely and responsive"

SILKS

Prashant Popat QC (see p.740) Regularly receives instructions covering all aspects of health and safety law. He is an expert in both regulatory and criminal matters and also handles public inquiries and inquest work. **Strengths:** "A very, very impressive character. He's got the experience having won some outstanding cases. He is high quality, no question." "He's very thorough and masterful in his advocacy." **Recent work:** Acted in R v Falcon Crane Hire and Doug Genge, a case regarding two people who were killed as a result of a crane collapse.

Oliver Campbell QC (see p.610) A leading practitioner specialising in the defence of clients facing prosecution or investigation in relation to fatal accidents or corporate manslaughter. He is highly regarded for his extensive knowledge of health and safety law. **Strengths:** "A very competent and very capable advocate." **Recent work:** Defended Veolia and John Fowler & Sons in a prosecution by the HSE involving the death of a welder, who had been killed whilst repairing a lorry.

Toby Riley-Smith QC (see p.752) Routinely instructed by large businesses to undertake complex criminal or civil proceedings following serious or fatal accidents within the workplace. **Strengths:** "He is a man who displays consummate attention to detail." "A great advocate who is thoroughly well prepared." **Recent work:** Acted for Tesco Stores in a matter concerning an old aged pensioner who died in a Tesco Express store after slipping on rainwater in one of the aisles and suffering a heart attack.

Charles Gibson QC (see p.652) Represents public bodies and corporate entities involved in a wide range of industry sectors, on health and safety matters including product safety, risk assessment and corporate manslaughter. **Strengths:** "A very poised advocate with enormous experience who is very good with clients." **Recent work:** Acted for UK Power in a case brought by the HSE relating to the death of a pedestrian electrocuted by a live electricity cable.

Band 2

2 Bedford Row

See profile on p.807

THE SET

A fine set noted for its advanced expertise in criminal law and its depth of knowledge and experience in the health and safety market. It handles an ever increasing caseload of high-profile health and safety cases, acting for both the defence and prosecution, and remains a set of choice for many large corporations and regulatory bodies including the HSE. Its barristers are sought out by FTSE companies to handle an array of cases across multiple industry sectors.

Client service: "The clerks are excellent and very easy to get hold of." One particular clerk, Paul Rogers, was commended by one source for being "exceptional and very good at looking after his solicitors." The clerking team is led by the well-respected senior clerk John Grimmer.

SILKS

Richard Matthews QC A leading authority with an impressive reputation who both acts for the HSE and undertakes private defence instructions. He is consistently sought out by leading companies and directors in need of expert representation. **Strengths:** "His depth of knowledge is second to none. He's exemplary" "He's a champion in his chosen field with an innate ability to see the path to success." "He is the gospel on health and safety." **Recent work:** Defended Pyrahna Mouldings in a corporate manslaughter prosecution. The case concerned a senior supervisor who was accidentally locked in a mouldings oven by his son-in-law and subsequently died.

Jim Sturman QC (see p.775) Well-regarded silk recognised for his vast experience in matters involving multiple fatalities and regulatory breaches. As well as representing businesses facing prosecution by the HSE, he is also instructed to appear at inquests. **Strengths:** "He's a very good advocate in court, and particularly impressive when acting for individuals." "He is very good and a real trial lawyer." **Recent work:** Acted in a case brought by the HSE where an employee was entangled in rotating machinery and had to undergo a leg amputation at the scene.

JUNIORS

Andrew McGee (see p.712) Handles all manner of health and safety work for both the prosecution and the defence. He is frequently called upon by companies and individuals across a range of industries to provide advice or representation. **Strengths:** "He is a fantastic advocate, who has criminal experience in spades." "An avuncular and perceptive advocate." **Recent work:** Represented Rooftop Rooms Ltd in a fatal accident case where an apprentice fell from a significant height.

Shauna Ritchie (see p.752) Has developed a notable health and safety practice, and is regularly instructed to undertake both prosecution and defence matters involving fatal and non-fatal incidents. **Strengths:** "She is a formidable prosecutor," and "a heavyweight practitioner in this field." **Recent work:** Instructed by the HSE in an inquest regarding the death of four employees of Hazewood Construction who had died whilst working at Claxton Engineering.

Quentin Hunt (see p.678) Prosecutes and defends a broad spectrum of health and safety cases, and has significant expertise in handling matters pertaining to fatalities at work. **Strengths:** "A terrific advocate," who is "a very measured prosecutor." **Recent work:** Acted on behalf of the HSE in a case regarding a fire which occurred on a ship and resulted in a welder sustaining serious burn injuries.

Eleanor Sanderson (see p.758) Manages a complex caseload comprising matters relating to corporate manslaughter, gross negligence manslaughter and regulatory breaches. She is also recognised for her significant capability in fire safety cases. **Strengths:** "She's very smart and quick on the uptake." **Recent work:** Defended Temple Lifts in a HSE prosecution where several tourists sustained severe injuries after being a lift which plummeted into a service shaft as a result of failures in the lift's mechanism.

Craig Rush Handles an array of regulatory matters and has been instructed in numerous health and safety cases across a range of sectors. He regularly acts on behalf of major leading companies . **Strengths:** "Formidable, bright and has good judgement." **Recent work:** Representing the HSE in a prosecution against 777 Environmental Limited regarding a fatal accident which occurred during a demolition on the site of Strata Building.

6 Pump Court

See profile on p.897

THE SET

6 Pump Court is home to a large team of dedicated barristers, specialising in the full range of health and safety cases. It hosts a fine group of barristers, two of whom are Standing Counsel to the HSE and nine of whom are listed as members of the Regulatory list. Individuals here both defend and prosecute high-profile regulatory matters, and are routinely instructed in matters of the utmost significance. By way of example they were involved in proceedings arising out of both the steel collapse at Claxton Engineering and the explosions at Buncefield.

Client service: "The clerks are efficient and work hard to build up good relationships with instructing solicitors." The clerking team is headed by senior clerk, Richard Constable.

SILKS

David Travers QC (see p.784) Highly sought after by leading companies across a range of business sectors who are facing prosecution. He undertakes high-profile regulatory cases, often involving serious accidents and regulatory breaches. **Strengths:** "He's a silent assassin with a huge brain" and is "absolutely charming." **Recent work:** Acted on behalf of the owner of a large hotel in London in a case concerning a long list of fire safety violations and offences.

Stephen Hockman QC (see p.673) A well-respected practitioner sought out by clients to assist with health and safety and environmental regulatory issues. He is extremely experienced, as evidenced by his key roles in both the Buncefield litigation and the Hillsborough inquest. **Strengths:** "A lawyer with a first-class brain who has first-class judgement." **Recent work:** Acted in the case of Royal Borough of Kensington and Chelsea v Aggreko plc. In this matter the defendant was facing prosecution following an incident where a worker sustained burn injuries as a result of exposed wires on the site.

JUNIORS

Mark Watson A leading authority in the health and safety market, who is renowned for his extensive capabilities across the full range of health and safety law. He acts for both the prosecution and defence, handling serious cases, many of which involve corporate manslaughter or matters arising from major disasters. **Strengths:** "He's a quality act who is well respected." "An expert in fairground cases," he is "just excellent and another good all rounder." **Recent work:** Represented Greenwood Forest Park Ltd and its director regarding a case where an 11 year old fell from a zip wire and subsequently died.

Pascal Bates (see p.592) Expert prosecutor, regularly called upon by both the HSE and local authorities to handle high profile cases often involving fatalities. **Strengths:** "He is insanely meticulous. How he retains all the information he does is unbelievable." "A man of detail." **Recent work:** Prosecuted a case involving a fire which occurred in co-joined terraced properties and left extensive damage to properties but no fatalities or seriously injured individuals.

Lee Bennett Experienced advocate who routinely handles complex cases, primarily on behalf of companies, directors and public bodies being prosecuted by the HSE or other regulatory authorities. **Strengths:** "Standout health and safety junior. There's nothing he doesn't know about the law, and he's a brilliant tactician." "He is excellent on inquests and health and safety." **Recent work:** Spent much of the last year heavily involved in the Hillsborough Inquest.

Mark Harris Specialist regulatory practitioner, with a wealth of experience and expertise across the full breadth of health and safety law. He is renowned for his capabilities across many sectors, and handles cases relating to anything from railways and construction projects to explosive substances and lifting equipment. **Strengths:** "He's a careful, detailed advocate with very good judgement." "He's very bright, tenacious, efficient and hard working, as well as a good advocate." **Recent work:** Instructed by HSE in the prosecution of Grundfos Pumps Ltd. The case concerned a trainee electrocuted whilst testing the circuit boards for managing pump controls.

Gordon Menzies Handles both prosecution and defence matters, acting on behalf of regulatory authorities such as the HSE and multinational corporations. **Strengths:** "He has a very gentle and thoughtful advocacy style which is very effective. He relaxes people and is very disarming." "Calm and elegant," he "develops an excellent rapport with our clients." **Recent work:** Prosecuted transport company David Transport Ltd in a case concerning the death of a lorry driver who fell from an unsecured ladder when unloading a lorry.

Band 3

2 Hare Court

See profile on p.861

THE SET

A set noted for its broad depth of expertise and extensive experience within the health and safety market. It is regularly instructed by clients across a range of sectors (most notably the engineering and construction industries). Members frequently undertake highly complex cases, predominantly on the defence side, though there are also a number of eminently capable prosecutors among the set's ranks. Cases regularly involve corporate manslaughter, and non-fatal and fatal accidents in the workplace. Individuals here offer advice and representation to directors and large corporate organisations facing prosecution or investigation by regulatory bodies.

Client service: The director of clerking, Julian Campbell, has a formidable reputation. "He is innovative and drives the barristers on his books to be more proactive. He's been a success as a result of that." "It's down to him that we instruct Hare Court now," said one leading solicitor. He and his team are "pragmatic and efficient."

SILKS

Jonathan Laidlaw QC (see p.694) A seriously impressive criminal silk who has a thriving health and safety defence practice. He undertakes all manner of health and safety work for a host of clients, and has acted for US corporations. **Strengths:** "A proper advocate in court, who has so much gravitas." **Recent work:** Instructed in the case of HSE v Siemens and Fluor UK Ltd where the defendant faced prosecution for breaching health and safety legislations following a death at the Greater Gabbard Wind Farm Project.

JUNIORS

James Buchanan (see p.606) Handles defence work on behalf of large corporate entities, handling cases that often involve fatal and non-fatal accidents in the workplace. **Strengths:** "Charming, knowledgeable and justifiably established as one of the leading juniors for health and safety." **Recent work:** Instructed in the case of HSE v Freight First Ltd where an employee died attempting to connect a cab to a lorry, having not received the training to do this.

Craig Ferguson (see p.644) Concentrates his practice on the defence of clients across various business sectors. His cases often involve fatalities and catastrophic injuries sustained in the workplace. **Strengths:** "He is a very strong and passionate advocate." "He's very calm, authoritative and knowledgeable." **Recent work:** Represented Bayer Cropscience in relation to an accident involving a contractor who sustained facial burns after drilling into a live electricity supply.

Alexandra Tampakopoulos (see p.778) Draws on her experience as a general criminal practitioner to defend clients in a wide range of health and safety cases, many of which involve fatalities or regulatory breaches. **Strengths:** "Really good at inquest work and very thorough." **Recent work:** Represented the driver of a forklift truck that collided with a co-worker, killing him.

Outer Temple Chambers

See profile on p.887

THE SET

The highly skilled barristers at Outer Temple Chambers are greatly experienced in all manner of criminal and regulatory health and safety cases, and have additional experience in handling inquests and inquiries. They are regularly instructed by leading law firms to undertake the most complex of cases including those relating to gross negligence manslaughter, industrial explosions and serious workplace accidents and fatalities. Instructing solicitors praise the set for its commercial approach and expertise, with one saying: "They are my go-to set for health and safety as they have a good range of counsel who have a distinct lack of ego, which makes my job that bit easier."

Client service: "The clerks are efficient, organised and very nice to deal with." "They're always very good at helping me with an alternative barrister if the ones I like aren't available." The business development director of the health team, Graham Woods, manages this area.

SILKS

Ben Compton QC Expert health and safety advocate, applauded for his wealth of experience and mastery when defending corporate bodies and directors in both the civil and criminal courts. **Strengths:** "He is the genuine article. He is very, very polished, highly professional and an absolute pleasure to work with." "One of the best jury advocates" and "without a doubt fantastic for corporate manslaughter cases." **Recent work:** Defended Linley Development Ltd in a corporate manslaughter case where an employee was killed by a collapsing wall.

JUNIORS

James Leonard A leading health and safety barrister, widely regarded for his far-reaching practice which encompasses the full range of regulatory and criminal liability matters pertaining to health and safety. **Strengths:** "He's a fantastic tactician and incredibly charming." **Recent work:** Acted for the Princes Sporting Club regarding an 11 year old who died in a fatal accident involving a banana boat.

Robert Dickason (see p.633) Has significant expertise conducting both regulatory and criminal defence cases. He has handled a number of high-profile matters including the Sterecycle manslaughter case. **Strengths:** "Professional and very thorough," he's "very intelligent, down to earth and easy to work with." **Recent work:** Instructed in a case involving Lakanal House where six residents died as a result of a fire in a London tower block. Also handled the Sterecycle manslaughter case, a matter concerning a high profile fatal explosion at a waste recycling plant.

3 Raymond Buildings Barristers

See profile on p.904

THE SET

A set of chambers with a formidable reputation in criminal law but which is also very strong in regulatory work. Its members are routinely instructed by individuals and regulated organisations, as well as leading companies and numerous regulatory bodies. They provide advice and representation with regard to all aspects of health and safety law including inquests and enforcement proceedings. Cases handled include those relating to fatal and non-fatal workplace accidents, and matters arising from major disasters.

Client service: One enthusiastic source commended the clerking of this set, commenting that "the clerking and administration has always been impressive. Deadlines are kept to, they are approachable and fee notes are provided promptly when requested." The clerks are led by senior clerk Eddie Holland.

SILKS

Stephen Walsh QC (see p.789) Has a broad practice covering all aspects of health and safety legislation. He has particular expertise in construction and fire safety matters. **Strengths:** "A go-to individual for health and safety, who is a great advocate and good on the law." **Recent work:** Represented a construction company facing prosecution by the HSE in relation to a fatal accident which occurred in a sewage plant.

Jonathan Ashley-Norman QC (see p.585) Instructed in cases of the utmost severity and sensitivity, and called upon by the likes of the Office of Road and Rail and the HSE. He is also a silk of choice for the Environment Agency. **Strengths:** "He has good judgement, is particularly skilled in re-examination and has very good technical knowledge of the subject matter." **Recent work:** Instructed in HSE v Balfour Beatty, Norland and Mark King, a case concerning a fatal electrocution which occurred at a data centre managed by a global bank.

JUNIORS

Saba Naqshbandi Recognised in the health and safety market for her extensive work and particular expertise in the fire safety space. She has been involved in a number of high-profile matters including a case relating to a fire at a New Look retail store. **Strengths:** "She's a sensible, smart prosecutor" and "someone who is brilliantly friendly with clients. She also has a very strategic mind and an excellent grasp of the law." **Recent work:** Acted as defence counsel for a company and its director facing a fire safety prosecution relating to a care home.

Sarah Le Fevre (see p.698) Has a far-reaching health and safety practice that encompasses key areas of the law including workplace, food and fire safety. She has further developed a specialism in the water safety market, and counts major companies such as Thames Water Utilities Ltd and Anglian Water Services Ltd as being amongst her clients. **Strengths:** "She's done a significant amount of enforcement work and has a very good brain." **Recent work:** Acted for the HSE in an investigation regarding the death of a butler who suffered fatal injuries at Burghley House when he was crushed by a lift.

Temple Garden Chambers

See profile on p.919

THE SET

Temple Garden Chambers is widely known for its specialist breadth of expertise and depth of experience in health and safety law. Members here appear on behalf of individuals, organisations and public bodies facing prosecution or enforcement proceedings. They have offered advice and representation in some of the most significant cases in the last ten years including R v Southampton University Hospital Trust and R v Cotswold Geotechnical.

Client service: The clerks, under the leadership of senior clerk Dean Norton, "always try to accommodate your needs." They are "responsive, helpful, polite and efficient."

SILKS

Keith Morton QC (see p.722) Principally acts on behalf of defendants in complex, high-profile matters relating to health and safety, many of which involve fatalities or major accidents. He is frequently instructed in the most prominent cases, and acted in the Stockwell shooting case. **Strengths:** "He is extremely thorough, meticulous in his preparation and tactically astute." "Keith Morton has an excellent manner with clients," and is "very experienced and incredibly intelligent." **Recent work:** Defended John Lewis Plc in a case involving an employee who had fallen from the roof of a store.

JUNIORS

Fiona Canby Has an exclusively defendant-based practice, and is regularly instructed by individuals, large companies and governmental bodies such as the Ministry of Justice. She has particular experience of representing companies in the construction industry. **Strengths:** "She shows very good attention to detail." "She's got a really nice manner and is good in court." **Recent work:** Acted on behalf of the Highways Agency in a case concerning the death of a traffic officer.

Kevin McLoughlin Expert in a range of health and safety cases, and acts for both the defence and prosecution. He also sits as a coroner, appearing at inquests in relation to fatalities in the workplace. **Strengths:** "He knows his stuff and has stacks of experience." "A bright guy and a really good presenter of cases." **Recent work:** Defended Oscars Wine Bar Ltd in a case concerning a young woman who had to undergo emergency surgery to have her stomach removed as a result of being served a drink containing liquid nitrogen.

Dominic Adamson Has an extensive health and safety practice principally focused on defendant work, and regularly handles inquests and cases involving fatalities. He is experienced in handling a wide range of matters for individuals and companies from a range of different industry sectors. **Strengths:** "Hard working, very pleasant and personable." "He is technically very astute across a broad range of areas." **Recent work:** Instructed by Tata Steel UK Limited regarding an incident where an explosion occurred on site, resulting in an employee suffering serious injuries.

Other Ranked Lawyers

Gerard Forlin QC (see p.646) (Cornerstone Barristers) Specialist regulatory barrister, who is highly expert in the full range of health and safety law. He is experienced in transport, environmental and product liability matters. **Strengths:** "He's a powerful advocate." "He is equipped with a laser-focused mind and has a great depth of knowledge in health and safety law."

Christian Du Cann (39 Essex Chambers) Devotes much of his practice to the representation of individuals and businesses facing investigation or prosecution. He handles all manner of health and safety cases including those relating to workplace fatalities and transport accidents. **Strengths:** "He's very solid, knows his stuff and has a very good relationship with clients." "Christian Du Cann is a lovely advocate and he's so smooth." **Recent work:** Instructed on behalf of a transport company facing prosecution by the HSE for the death of an employee who was crushed by one of the company's HGV lorries.

Richard Lissack QC (see p.702) (Fountain Court Chambers) Renowned practitioner who handles health and safety work as part of a very wide ranging practice, and has been involved in some of the very biggest cases in the market. **Strengths:** "A class act." "He's helpful, forthright, bullish and highly efficient." **Recent work:** Acted in an investigation involving Conoco Phillips North Sea Oil & Gas relating to a gas leak at a landing station.

Jonathan Caplan QC (5 Paper Buildings) Regularly instructed by individuals, directors and corporate bodies across the full range of health and safety matters. He is thoroughly experienced at handling cases concerning a number of sectors, including the construction, rail and transport sectors. **Strengths:** "Cool under pressure, astute, clever and imaginative."

Deanna Heer (see p.669) (5 Paper Buildings) Well-regarded barrister, who draws on her experience as a criminal practitioner to prosecute and defend health and safety cases. She is regularly instructed by individuals and organisations facing investigation or prosecution for health and safety offences or regulatory breaches. **Strengths:** "She's extremely able." "Mainstream criminal practitioner and a very formidable opponent." **Recent work:** Currently acting in the prosecution of a site manager for gross negligence relating to the death of an employee who fell from a great height.

Adrian Darbishire QC (QEB Hollis Whiteman) Highly regarded and has an enviable caseload of high-profile defence instructions. He has significant expertise in the areas of fraud, crime and professional regulation. **Strengths:** "He's an extremely talented criminal barrister and he's brought that experience to health and safety." "Adrian Darbishire is a fantastic advocate." **Recent work:** Acted in the case of R v Hi-Fold Doors Ltd & Naylor, a manslaughter case regarding the death of two shanty singers who were crushed at a music festival.

Sailesh Mehta (Red Lion Chambers) Acts for both the prosecution and defence in significant regulatory health and safety matters and is regularly sought out to handle cases pertaining to environmental law and fire safety law. **Strengths:** "A very fine performer," who is "a tenacious fighter." **Recent work:** Instructed by HSE to prosecute Siemens PLC and Fluor PLC in a case concerning the death of an employee on a wind turbine site.

MIDLANDS

Health & Safety
Leading Sets
Band 1
No5 Chambers *
St Philips Chambers *
Leading Silks
Band 1
Tedd Rex *No5 Chambers*
Leading Juniors
Band 1
Berlin Barry *St Philips Chambers*
Gilchrist Naomi *St Philips Chambers* [A] *
Thorogood Bernard *No5 Chambers*
Band 2
Farrer Adam *No5 Chambers*

Band 1

No5 Chambers

See profile on p.931

THE SET

The "excellent" No5 Chambers is respected for the high quality of its regulatory barristers at silk and junior levels. Its leading practitioners have significant expertise in complex health and safety and environmental matters for both the prosecution and the defence. Members are regularly sought out by individuals, regulatory bodies, local authorities and major businesses to handle high-profile cases.

Client service: "Their members and clerks are not pompous and go about their business in ensuring the provision of an excellent quality service." The regulatory clerking team is led by Andrew Trotter.

SILKS

Rex Tedd QC An experienced silk who is renowned for his involvement in high-profile health and safety cases. He frequently appears for the HSE in significant prosecutions. **Strengths:** "He is a regulatory silk with a national reputation. He has huge capacity to digest mammoth quantities of evidence and disseminate its significance in a particular case. He is a superlative advocate who has immense charisma coupled with necessary gravitas." "He is an excellent trial advocate."

JUNIORS

Bernard Thorogood Handles a wide range of regulatory matters and is particularly well known for his work prosecuting and defending serious health and safety cases. **Strengths:** "He is exceptional. His work ethic is incredible. I don't know how he keeps the hours he keeps and has the output he does." "He is fastidious in his preparation." **Recent work:** Acted for the HSE in a case concerning the death of a worker who died while repairing an industrial cooker.

Adam Farrer Regularly defends and prosecutes complex health and safety cases and acts at inquests concerning workplace fatalities. **Strengths:** "He's a very thorough practitioner and gets the job done." "He is a very capable performer."

St Philips Chambers

See profile on p.934

THE SET

Members of St Philips Chambers regulatory group are noted for their ability to prosecute and defend complex cases. It boasts a wide range of clients, including local authorities, regulatory bodies and businesses. The set's talented practitioners handle all manner of health and safety work, and are regularly involved in proceedings concerning fatal and non-fatal accidents.

Client service: "All contact with chambers is extremely professional and all members of staff are approachable, responsible and extremely competent." Sam Collins is the senior regulatory clerk.

JUNIORS

Barry Berlin A well-known regulatory heavy hitter who is routinely instructed to prosecute and defend significant health and safety cases. **Strengths:** "We appreciate his approachability, respect his advice and value his judgement implicitly." "He is accessible, hard working and knowledgeable. He goes beyond the extra mile." **Recent work:** Prosecuted Hugo Boss in relation to an accident at its Bicester Village shop which resulted in the death of a four-year-old boy.

Naomi Gilchrist (see p.653) Represents clients in criminal regulatory matters and complex health and safety work. Her cases often involve fatalities and catastrophic injuries. **Strengths:** "She's extremely fluent, good in court and has a sense of humour."

NORTHERN/NORTH EASTERN

Health & Safety
Leading Silks
Band 1
Horlock Timothy *Deans Court Chambers*
Band 2
Kennedy Christopher *9 St John Street*
Lawrence Nigel *7 Harrington St Chambers* *
Pitter Jason *New Park Court Chambers*
Leading Juniors
Band 1
Judge Lisa *Deans Court Chambers* [A]
Smith Peter *Deans Court Chambers*
Band 2
Donnelly Kevin *Lincoln House Chambers*
Hart Joseph *Deans Court Chambers* *
McKeon James *7 Harrington St Chambers*
* *Indicates set / individual with profile.*
[A] *direct access (see p.24).*
Alphabetical order within each band. Band 1 is highest.

Ranked Lawyers

Timothy Horlock QC (Deans Court Chambers) A highly regarded regulatory silk who is frequently instructed by clients involved in heavyweight health and safety cases. He acts for both the prosecution and the defence, and is comfortable handling matters arising from a broad range of industry sectors. **Strengths:** "As an advocate he's excellent."

Lisa Judge (Deans Court Chambers) Regularly defends individuals and companies in major health and safety cases brought by various regulatory bodies. **Strengths:** "She's a practical operator and a good tactician." "Lisa Judge does quite a bit of health and safety work and I highly rate her."

Peter Smith (Deans Court Chambers) A specialist defence barrister who represents individuals and notable companies in enforcement actions brought by the HSE and local authorities. **Strengths:** "He is very impressive. His practice alone would allow him to take silk." "He's always got the client's best interest and outcomes in mind, and his preparation is highly detailed." "He's very competent and has very good technical knowledge."

Joseph Hart (see p.666) (Deans Court Chambers) Instructed by both the defence and the prosecution in cases concerning breaches of health and safety regulations. His work also includes fire safety matters and he represents clients at inquests. **Strengths:** "He is reliable, a really safe pair of hands." **Recent work:** Represented a client at an inquest into the death of a diver.

Nigel Lawrence QC (see p.697) (7 Harrington St Chambers) Regularly prosecutes health and safety cases concerning non-fatal injuries and workplace deaths for the HSE and other regulatory entities. He also represents defendants and acts at inquests. **Strengths:** "He's very knowledgeable and very engaging." "Nigel Lawrence QC is very highly regarded." **Recent work:** Represented the defendant in a case concerning the death of a man in an industrial oven.

James McKeon (7 Harrington St Chambers) Has specialist expertise in a wide range of health and safety matters. He is frequently instructed by the HSE in enforcement proceedings.

Kevin Donnelly (Lincoln House Chambers) Criminal law practitioner with a significant regulatory caseload. He is regularly instructed by public sector clients on a range of health and safety issues.

Jason Pitter QC (New Park Court Chambers) Acts for the prosecution and defence in cases concerning fatal and non-fatal accidents and regulatory breaches. He also advises individual and corporate clients on compliance matters. **Strengths:** "He's very good in court and he has a very easy manner in conferences. He's very efficient in what he does."

Christopher Kennedy QC (9 St John Street) A leading regulatory practitioner who devotes his practice to the defence of individuals and companies in health and safety prosecutions. **Strengths:** "He has the knowledge and presence to have clients eating out of the palm of his hand."

WESTERN

Health & Safety	
Leading Silks	
Band 1	
Langdon Andrew	*Guildhall Chambers*
Band 2	
Haggan Nicholas	*12 College Place*
Leading Juniors	
Band 1	
Dixey Ian	*Guildhall Chambers*
Morgan Simon	*St John's Chambers*
Band 2	
Bennett James	*Guildhall Chambers*
Lowe Rupert	*Guildhall Chambers*
Vigars Anna	*Guildhall Chambers*
Up-and-coming individuals	
Jones Samuel	*Guildhall Chambers*

Alphabetical order within each band. Band 1 is highest.

Ranked Lawyers

Nicholas Haggan QC (12 College Place) Handles both criminal and regulatory work and is instructed on a wide range of health and safety matters. He acts for both the prosecution and the defence in cases concerning workplace accidents and exposure risks. **Strengths:** "Nick is just stellar on his feet and he has a wonderful way with witnesses."

Andrew Langdon QC (Guildhall Chambers) A renowned criminal silk who is regularly instructed to handle heavyweight health and safety matters, including those concerning fatalities. He defends and prosecutes cases, frequently appearing for the HSE and the Environment Agency. **Strengths:** "Andrew Langdon is extremely bright and extremely competent."

Ian Dixey (Guildhall Chambers) Brings a wealth of experience to his strong practice prosecuting and defending major health and safety cases. He is on the HSE's A-list of approved prosecuting counsel. **Strengths:** "He is very competent and certainly an opponent to be reckoned with." "He is extremely experienced and very calm under pressure." **Recent work:** Prosecuted London Fenestration Trades and Sir Robert McAlpine Ltd after an employee died following a fall.

James Bennett (Guildhall Chambers) Represents regulatory bodies and companies in the full spectrum of health and safety matters concerning fatal and non-fatal incidents. He frequently handles cases involving electrocutions. **Recent work:** Acted for the defence in a case concerning the death of an electrician at a data centre.

Rupert Lowe (Guildhall Chambers) Has developed a notable health and safety practice and has specialist expertise handling matters relating to workplace fatalities. **Strengths:** "Rupert Lowe has a fine head for detail and is a very bright lawyer."

Anna Vigars (Guildhall Chambers) Both prosecutes and defends large corporate clients and individuals in an array of significant health and safety cases. **Strengths:** "She's extremely personable." "Sees the wood for the trees and presents cases in an attractive way to juries."

Samuel Jones (Guildhall Chambers) Acts for both the prosecution and the defence in relation to a wide range of health and safety cases. He is also adept at handling matters concerning environmental and fire safety issues. **Recent work:** Represented the HSE against a construction company in a case concerning a fall at one of its sites.

Simon Morgan (St John's Chambers) A respected practitioner with a notable crime practice who also enjoys a fine reputation for his health and safety work. He receives instructions from defendants in addition to the HSE and the Environment Agency. **Strengths:** "He has got very good tactical insight and a very good grasp of the technicalities of health and safety law." "He's very capable, practical and user-friendly."

Contents:

LONDON

Immigration
Leading Sets
Band 1
Garden Court Chambers *
Band 2
Blackstone Chambers *
Doughty Street Chambers *
Matrix Chambers *
Band 3
39 Essex Chambers *
Landmark Chambers *
1 Pump Court *
Senior Statesmen
Senior Statesmen: distinguished older partners
Macdonald Ian *Garden Court Chambers*
Leading Silks
Star individuals
Fordham Michael *Blackstone Chambers*
Fransman Laurie *Garden Court Chambers*
Husain Raza *Matrix Chambers*
Band 1
Carss-Frisk Monica *Blackstone Chambers*
Eadie James *Blackstone Chambers*
Giovannetti Lisa *39 Essex Chambers*
Harrison Stephanie *Garden Court Chambers*
Knafler Stephen *Landmark Chambers*
McCullough Angus *1 Crown Office Row (ORL)* ◊
Tam Robin *Temple Garden Chambers (ORL)* ◊
Band 2
Farbey Judith *Doughty Street Chambers* Ⓐ
Pannick David *Blackstone Chambers*
Rose Dinah *Blackstone Chambers*
Southey Hugh *Matrix Chambers* *
Band 3
Bourne Charles *11KBW (ORL)* ◊ Ⓐ *
Johnson Jeremy *5 Essex Court (ORL)* ◊ *
Kovats Steven *39 Essex Chambers*
* Indicates set / individual with profile.
Ⓐ direct access (see p.24).
◊ (ORL) = Other Ranked Lawyer.
Alphabetical order within each band. Band 1 is highest.

Immigration	
Leading Juniors	
Star individuals	**Band 3**
Dubinsky Laura *Doughty Street Chambers*	**Bazini** Daniel *No5 Chambers (ORL)* ◊ Ⓐ
Band 1	**Blundell** David *Landmark Chambers*
Ahluwalia Navtej Singh *Garden Court Chambers*	**Brewer** Michelle *Garden Court Chambers*
Berry Adrian *Garden Court Chambers*	**Dunlop** Rory *39 Essex Chambers*
Buley Tim *Landmark Chambers*	**Hickman** Tom *Blackstone Chambers*
Chapman Rebecca *Garden Court Chambers*	**Hirst** Leonie *Garden Court Chambers*
Chirico David *1 Pump Court*	**Hodgetts** Glen *Glen Hodgetts (Barrister-at-Law) (ORL)* ◊
Cronin Kathryn *Garden Court Chambers*	**Jegarajah** Shivani *Mansfield Chambers (ORL)* ◊
Henderson Mark *Doughty Street Chambers*	**Jones** David *Garden Court Chambers*
Seddon Duran *Garden Court Chambers*	**Nicholson** Edward *No5 Chambers (ORL)* ◊
Toal Ronan *Garden Court Chambers*	**Ó Ceallaigh** Greg *Garden Court Chambers*
Weston Amanda *Garden Court Chambers*	**O'Callaghan** Declan *Landmark Chambers*
Band 2	**Palmer** Robert *Monckton Chambers (ORL)* ◊ Ⓐ
Armstrong Nicholas *Matrix Chambers*	**Band 4**
Chandran Parosha *1 Pump Court* Ⓐ	**Braganza** Nicola *Garden Court Chambers*
Chelvan S *No5 Chambers (ORL)* ◊	**Buttler** Chris *Matrix Chambers* Ⓐ
Denholm Graham *Landmark Chambers*	**Hooper** Louise *Garden Court Chambers*
Fripp Eric *Lamb Building (ORL)* ◊	**Kiai** Gilda *1 Pump Court*
Goodman Alex *Landmark Chambers* Ⓐ	**Knorr** Michelle *Doughty Street Chambers*
Haywood Philip *Doughty Street Chambers* Ⓐ	**Kohli** Ryan *Cornerstone Barristers (ORL)* ◊ *
Jorro Peter *Garden Court Chambers*	**Laughton** Victoria *1 Pump Court*
Khubber Ranjiv *1 Pump Court* Ⓐ	**Lemer** David *Doughty Street Chambers* Ⓐ
Kilroy Charlotte *Doughty Street Chambers*	**Meredith** Catherine *Doughty Street Chambers*
Knights Samantha *Matrix Chambers*	**Moffatt** Rowena *Doughty Street Chambers*
Lewis Patrick *Garden Court Chambers*	**Poole** Tom *3 Hare Court (ORL)* ◊
Mackenzie Alasdair *Doughty Street Chambers*	**Poynor** Bryony *Garden Court Chambers*
Middleton Joseph *Doughty Street Chambers* Ⓐ	**Robinson** Catherine *1 Pump Court*
Naik Sonali *Garden Court Chambers*	**Rothwell** Joanne *No5 Chambers (ORL)* ◊ Ⓐ
Payne Alan *5 Essex Court (ORL)* ◊ *	**Sheldon** Neil *1 Crown Office Row (ORL)* ◊
Sayeed Sadat *Garden Court Chambers*	**Vaughan** Anthony *Garden Court Chambers*
Smith Abigail *Garden Court Chambers*	**Waite** John-Paul *5 Essex Court (ORL)* ◊ *
Symes Mark *Garden Court Chambers*	**Ward** Galina *Landmark Chambers*
Walsh John *Doughty Street Chambers*	**Up-and-coming individuals**
Yeo Colin *Garden Court Chambers* *	**Loughran** Gemma *Garden Court Chambers*

Band 1

Garden Court Chambers

See profile on p.851

THE SET

The foremost set leading the way at the London Immigration Bar, Garden Court Chambers houses an unsurpassable team of advocates who handle the full gamut of immigration matters. Its practitioners, from top-quality juniors to renowned QCs, appear in the highest courts acting on behalf of vulnerable clients and high net worth private individuals alike. Many of them have recently been leading the way on policy and casework to relieve the refugee crisis in Calais and across Europe.

Client service: "The clerking is very good, they always respond to things extremely promptly. The clerks are friendly, efficient and will go out of their way to help." Colin Cook leads the clerking team.

SILKS

Ian Macdonald QC A vastly knowledgeable and highly respected silk who has a long history of assisting asylum seekers and others facing immigration and nationality issues. He offers a wealth of experience and routinely undertakes Tribunal, High Court and Court of Appeal work. **Strengths:** "A giant of the field of immigration law." "He is recognised as a leading author in this area."

Laurie Fransman QC A celebrated silk with market-leading knowledge of nationality and asylum law. He enjoys a glowing reputation, both domestically and internationally, thanks in part to his significant contribution to leading literature in the area. His areas of expertise within asylum law include complex protection and exclusion cases. **Strengths:** "The guru of nationality law." "The authority on immigration law who deftly handles the most challenging points." **Recent work:** Acted for Dmytro Firtash, successfully challenging a US extradition request on behalf of the Ukrainian oligarch, who was on bail in Austria.

Stephanie Harrison QC Highly esteemed barrister who is particularly well known for her adroit handling of the most complex immigration and asylum matters. She frequently appears in the highest courts in landmark immigration cases, such as human rights claims, unlawful detention matters and deportation appeals. **Strengths:** "Almost unrivalled when it comes her deep knowledge of detention issues." "She is a legend at the Bar with a famed refugee practice." **Recent work:** Successfully responded to the Home Secretary's review of a Special Immigration Appeals Commission (SIAC) decision on the correct approach to disclosure of judicial review proceedings under new statutory review provisions.

JUNIORS

Navtej Singh Ahluwalia An impressive junior with considerable experience who is often instructed in judicial review proceedings in relation to EU free movement law and deportation. He has significant knowledge of, and has written on, the points-based system (PBS). **Strengths:** "Very approachable and prepares meticulously for Immigration Tribunal hearings." "A charismatic and highly persuasive advocate." **Recent work:** Appeared in R (Selim Macastina) v SSHD, a test case considering whether an amendment to the Immigration (EEA) Regulations was contrary to EU free movement law.

Adrian Berry An exceptionally skilled junior, whose practice is heavily focused on British nationality and EU free movement law. He routinely receives instructions from large-scale corporations in major commercial immigration matters. **Strengths:** "An absolutely brilliant brain and a delightful personality – always a pleasure to work with." "One of the finest legal minds of our time." **Recent work:** Instructed in R (Deelavathi Bondada) v SSHD, a case establishing the necessary criteria to prove that an individual is a British citizen by descent, and therefore entitled to a British passport.

Rebecca Chapman Offers broad immigration expertise and specialist insight into international human rights law. She regularly handles third-country and asylum cases and was appointed a Deputy Judge of the Upper Tribunal in 2015. **Strengths:** "She is very compassionate and strong on children or family cases." "An absolutely fantastic advocate."

Kathryn Cronin A first-class advocate with a wealth of immigration knowledge. She is regularly instructed in asylum and family law cases and has notable expertise in matters concerning gender persecution, trafficking and child-related immigration. Cronin is admitted to practice in both the UK and Australia. **Strengths:** "Kathryn is exceptionally bright and academic, but also down-to-earth." "Very approachable, a fantastic advert for the Bar in general."

Duran Seddon A leading junior with an impressive case history, having been involved in a number of high-profile immigration, asylum and human rights matters before SIAC, the House of Lords and the Strasbourg Grand Chamber. He routinely acts for senior political and business figures in highly sensitive cases. **Strengths:** "Duran is very bright and very experienced." "He is extremely clever and has an amazing eye for detail." **Recent work:** Appeared in the Supreme Court in HA (Iraq) v SSHD, a case considering the immigration rules in relation to public interest and Article 8 of the ECHR.

Amanda Weston Leading immigration barrister who routinely acts for overseas, high-profile clients in complex citizenship and inbound-travel matters. Distinguished for her commitment to the representation of migrants, she also weights her caseload towards unlawful detention work on behalf of vulnerable adults and children. **Strengths:** "She is an absolute standout claimant barrister." "She does lots of complex work for vulnerable clients and always does an excellent job." **Recent work:** Acted in Bosov v SSHD, successfully overturning the Home Office's decision to exclude Dmitry Bosov, a well-known Russian businessman, from the UK.

Ronan Toal Much respected for a practice that has seen him become a favourite among fellow barristers and solicitors alike. His caseload is varied, with a particular focus on human trafficking and Country Guidance matters. **Strengths:** "His knowledge is incredibly impressive, he takes interesting approaches and makes them work." "He has an encyclopaedic knowledge of immigration and asylum law."

Peter Jorro Highly experienced practitioner with a varied practice covering areas such as the PBS, asylum and EEA law. He counts high net worth individuals, businesses and asylum applicants among his broader clientele. **Strengths:** "Excellent on complex EU matters for high-profile clients." "He has a profound knowledge of refugee issues."

Patrick Lewis A truly experienced practitioner, he regularly appears before the Court of Appeal and Administrative Court. He is a commercial immigration specialist who regularly advises both private individuals and large corporations. **Strengths:** "He's very approachable and always listens with avid attention, which inspires confidence." "His immigration knowledge and the way he works with clients are very impressive." **Recent work:** Appeared in BD v ECO (Moscow), a case regarding a high net worth individual whose application was refused on account of an allegation that he had provided false information in respect to a previous application.

Sonali Naik Esteemed senior junior with a wealth of experience appearing before Tribunals and in judicial review proceedings. Her practice focuses on Article 8 ECHR and deportation matters. While largely publicly funded, she also acts for private clients. **Strengths:** "Naik is technically very good and highly persuasive." "She is able to master detail and break down concepts with ease." **Recent work:** Acted in BM and Others, a Country Guidance appeal in the Upper Tribunal concerning returns to the Democratic Republic of Congo for foreign national criminals, refused asylum seekers and those involved in opposition political movements.

Sadat Sayeed Routinely handles politically sensitive cases on behalf of high-profile individuals within the political, business and sporting worlds. He is particularly noted for his deep knowledge of human rights and refugee law, regularly advising clients from Eastern European countries. **Strengths:** "He is absolutely committed to each and every case." "His written pleading is top-notch. He sets out arguments extremely clearly and persuasively." **Recent work:** Instructed in R (ILPA) v Tribunal Procedure Committee and Lord Chancellor, a matter regarding the legality of the new First-tier Tribunal procedure rules which permit a 'secret evidence' procedure.

Abigail Smith Draws on her prior experience as a solicitor, and previous engagement with various NGOs, to offer excellent immigration advice to a diverse clientele. She frequently appears in the First-tier and Upper Tribunals in complex asylum and immigration matters. **Strengths:** "Great in both technical cases and Article 8 matters." "Incredibly responsive and has a friendly and welcoming manner with clients." **Recent work:** Acted in Aziza Tahir & Abdulhamid Ibrahim v SSHD, a case regarding the right of family reunion for a child recognised as a refugee in the UK.

Mark Symes A quality advocate offering an all-round immigration service. Before coming to the Bar he worked at the Refugee Legal Centre and he is now best known for appearing in various landmark Country Guidance asylum cases. **Strengths:** "Encyclopaedic knowledge and innovative approach to legal issues." "He is fiercely intelligent and strikes up good relationships with clients." **Recent work:** Acted in Zhegrova, the lead case regarding the extent to which cohabitation between spouses is required before retained rights of residence accrue under EU law.

Colin Yeo (see p.801) An esteemed and popular immigration barrister, he is particularly highly regarded by peers and widely recognised for his editorship of the Free Movement blog. His client base is varied, and includes high net worth private individuals, law centres and businesses of all sizes. **Strengths:** "Extraordinary energy and commitment." "Very responsive. He offers highly detailed advice and comprehensive knowledge of case law." **Recent work:** Successfully appeared on behalf of the appellant in Saif Ullah v SSHD. This was an appeal against refusal of status to a man who had been a resident in the UK for 15 years, but who had previously been deported for a large-scale fraud offence and re-entered the country illegally.

Michelle Brewer Acts primarily for victims of human trafficking and unlawful detainment, representing clients in public law, immigration and criminal appellate proceedings. She regularly advises organisations such as the Equality and Human Rights Commission on anti-trafficking measures. **Strengths:** "Excellent with vulnerable clients, she provides first-class, family-based immigration advice." "Very impressed with how quickly she digests information and turns it into a compelling argument." **Recent work:** Instructed in PA v SSHD, a judicial review considering the Home Secretary's decision to detain a pregnant woman.

Leonie Hirst A stellar immigration practitioner with a busy caseload encompassing detention, EEA law and trafficking matters. She is noted for her work with vulnerable individuals, including clients who lack mental capacity and those who have been victims of torture. **Strengths:** "She's hard-working and committed." "An excellent junior: easy to work with and a very good advocate." **Recent work:** Instructed in R (ASK) v SSHD, a case challenging the Home Secretary's failure to secure transfer to a psychiatric hospital for a detainee with schizophrenia who lacked mental capacity.

Greg Ó Ceallaigh A budding junior, he continues to impress peers and clients alike with his flourishing immigration and asylum practice. He offers great experience in areas such as EU law-related judicial reviews, third-country removal and detention matters. **Strengths:** "He is completely on top of Italy third-country case litigation." "He fights extraordinarily hard on detention and asylum cases." **Recent work:** Successfully argued that an Italian national who had committed numerous offences had acquired a right of permanent residence in SSHD v Vassallo.

Louise Hooper A promising immigration junior who has garnered peer respect for her expertise regarding sexual orientation and gender-based claims. She routinely acts on behalf of vulnerable clients who have been victims of unlawful detention and trafficking. **Strengths:** "She has standout knowledge of unaccompanied minors." "She's fantastic – when you have her on side you're instantly more confident. She gets straight to the point and has an amazing analytical brain." "Committed, driven, a pleasure to work with and thoroughly effective in the High Court." **Recent work:** Acted in HN v SSHD, a case concerning the deportation of refused Afghan asylum seekers on charter flights.

David Jones An accomplished public lawyer, who is adept at handling immigration, asylum and human rights law at all levels, from the First-tier Tribunal to the ECHR. Market commentators highlight his strong track record of securing substantial damages for individuals who have been unlawfully detained. **Strengths:** "Words cannot describe how brilliant his work is." "An absolutely wonderful, charming advocate." **Recent work:** Acted in BB v SSHD, a high-value unlawful detention and personal injury claim concerning a seriously mentally ill Algerian man who had repeatedly been detained under immigration powers.

Nicola Braganza A rising junior who continues to receive praise for her work with vulnerable appellants and their families. Her caseload includes complex work regarding trafficking, domestic abuse cases and asylum-seeking children. She regularly appears before the Upper Tribunal and the Court of Appeal.

Strengths: "Nicola has particular expertise with complex immigration cases." "She has amazingly in-depth knowledge and is prepared to go the extra mile for clients."

Bryony Poynor A top immigration junior with a broad caseload encompassing all areas of asylum, nationality, deportation, EU free movement and human rights law. She frequently acts for vulnerable clients in sensitive, complex cases concerning trafficking and persecution. **Strengths:** "Very dedicated, it's an absolute pleasure to work with Bryony." **Recent work:** Acted in HN v SSHD, a case challenging the government's removal of refused asylum seekers to Afghanistan.

Anthony Vaughan Hailed by peers, he routinely acts on behalf of high-profile individuals in challenges against decisions of the Home Office, particularly regarding deportation or removal actions. His burgeoning career sees him making regular appearances before the Supreme Court and SIAC. **Strengths:** "He is very organised and very good to work with." "You always know he will prepare a case to the highest possible standard and give pragmatic advice." **Recent work:** Instructed in AA (Afghanistan) v SSHD, a test case clarifying the UK's obligations to unaccompanied asylum-seeking children.

Gemma Loughran Popular among peers, Loughran routinely appears before a range of judicial fora, including the First-tier and Upper Tribunals and the High Court. She has significant experience of handling complex detention and removal cases and is particularly noted for her provision of expert advice to Somali nationals and victims of trafficking. **Strengths:** "She really gets to grips with the material, has a good knowledge of the law and is concise, calm and considered." "Extremely able lawyer who is prepared to take difficult cases and handle them with panache."

Band 2

Blackstone Chambers

See profile on p.813

THE SET

Blackstone Chambers is renowned for its esteemed immigration practitioners who routinely undertake the most significant, complex and widely publicised judicial reviews on behalf of the Home Office. Its barristers appear in the highest domestic and European courts and are able to draw upon their extensive public international law expertise when appearing in major immigration matters. One commentator remarks: "The set has some absolutely brilliant barristers who are regulars in the Supreme Court."
Client service: "The clerks are very good. Their communication is excellent and they are very easy to work with." Senior clerk Gary Oliver heads up the team.

SILKS

Michael Fordham QC Pre-eminent immigration silk with outstanding expertise encompassing complex judicial review proceedings and high-profile human rights cases. A regular feature in the Supreme Court, he offers unrivalled advice concerning civil liberties, EU law and Country Guidance. **Strengths:** "A star silk who does a great deal of heavyweight work." "The court sits up and listens when he talks."

Monica Carss-Frisk QC Joint head of chambers, she is a brilliant public law and immigration silk who is distinguished by her masterful handling of matters concerning unlawful imprisonment and the ECHR. She regularly acts on behalf of the government in the most prominent EU courts. **Strengths:** "She has the ear of the court." "She is patient, knowledgeable and committed."

James Eadie QC Extraordinary immigration barrister with many strings to his bow. As First Treasury Counsel, he is the government's silk of choice for the most complex public law, immigration and human rights cases. **Strengths:** "One of the absolute best barristers at the Bar, he is a standout individual with a wonderful practice." "When James stands up, he receives avid attention from the entire court."

David Pannick QC A public law legend praised by peers for his deep knowledge and broad-based expertise. He has an impressive track record of appearing before the highest European courts in the most complex asylum and civil liberties cases. **Strengths:** "An amazing public lawyer." "He is brilliant at what he does."

Dinah Rose QC Highly esteemed throughout the market, she has a broad immigration practice with a significant emphasis on human rights, civil liberties and EU law. She routinely appears in the Court of Appeal, the Supreme Court and the ECJ. **Strengths:** "She is just fantastic, incredibly bright."

JUNIORS

Tom Hickman Has considerable expertise across a wide range of practice areas. A regular presence in SIAC and the ECHR, he has acted against the government in significant citizenship and national law matters. **Strengths:** "He's doing the really complex work. He will go a long way in the legal world."

Doughty Street Chambers

See profile on p.828

THE SET

Doughty Street Chambers is a renowned, claimant-focused immigration set offering expert advocacy and advice to a diverse clientele. Peers hold the set in high regard for its full-service immigration offering, and are quick to highlight the breadth and depth of its advocates' expertise. The set continues to tackle the most complex, high-profile detention and trafficking cases, while its barristers are also recognised for their provision of expert advice to educational establishments on sponsorship licence compliance. One source says: "Doughty Street is right in the thick of the most contentious policy points; its members are involved in many of the biggest, landmark cases."
Client service: "The clerking is efficient and prompt. They provide good access to counsel and are good at arranging listings and passing on relevant material in a timely fashion." Richard Bayliss leads the clerking team.

SILKS

Judith Farbey QC A high-calibre immigration silk who is highly sought after by businesses and educational institutions for her wide expertise, particularly regarding Tier 2 and Tier 4 of the PBS. Her broad practice also sees her acting in judicial review proceedings regarding nationality law and highly sensitive human rights issues, often on behalf of high-profile individuals. **Strengths:** "Strong strategic thinker, she is ever practical and down-to-earth, with a very engaging and amiable manner." "Her submissions are stupendous, she's a very, very thorough lawyer."

JUNIORS

Laura Dubinsky A leading light at the Immigration Bar, Dubinsky is famed among peers and clients alike for her nous and insight into complex asylum and detention law. Her depth of knowledge is reflected by her routine appearances in the highest courts, where she frequently advises on landmark litigation concerning detention and removal. **Strengths:** "She's phenomenal on immigration detention." "Extremely passionate about her work and really willing to push the boundaries for clients, to great effect." **Recent work:** Acted for the appellant in CS v SSHD, a case considering how the protections EU citizens enjoy from expulsion from EU territory apply in the context of threats to public security.

Mark Henderson A leading claimant-focused immigration barrister, he is regularly instructed by top-tier solicitors given his vast expertise encompassing asylum, human rights and EU law. He routinely appears in the highest domestic and European courts on behalf of vulnerable clients. **Strengths:** "He can digest an amazing amount of information and can be relied upon to set out persuasive arguments in court." "He's very frank and realistic about the merits of a case; that's important and really valued by the client." **Recent work:** Acted in R (Babbage) v SSHD, a definitive case concerning the detainment of foreign national prisoners.

Philip Haywood An immigration stalwart, he is highly regarded for his extensive experience and expertise. He routinely represents clients at all levels, from the tribunal to the ECHR. His recent work has involved complex unlawful detention and deportation claims. **Strengths:** "He always produces absolutely insightful arguments." "Able to grasp very complex issues immediately, he has an incredible ability to pare things down to the bare essentials." **Recent work:** Appeared before the Upper Tribunal in a case considering the implications of the use of social media and the internet by Iranian asylum seekers.

Charlotte Kilroy A public law practitioner, Kilroy weights her caseload heavily towards human rights and immigration matters. She is particularly well regarded for her work with vulnerable migrants, including those who have been unlawfully detained and are facing deportation. **Strengths:** "She is knowledgeable and experienced in detained fast track procedures." "An outstanding advocate with a keen intellect and an absolute commitment to fighting her client's case. You want her in your corner."

Alasdair Mackenzie Prior to joining the set in 2005, Mackenzie co-founded the charity Asylum Aid. He is now a high-profile immigration barrister frequently appearing at all levels of tribunal, SIAC and the Court of Appeal. His noted areas of expertise include family law and human rights. **Strengths:** "He is extremely bright and one of the most responsive barristers around." "He is very knowledgeable and has learned the art of putting complex cases to the judge clearly and persuasively." **Recent work:** Appeared in R (MM and Others) v SSHD, a case considering whether the Home Secretary can take the character of family members into account when refusing to naturalise someone otherwise entitled to be granted citizenship.

Joseph Middleton Established practitioner handling a plethora of immigration matters for prominent firms. His caseload is geared towards corporate immigration matters, and has a notable focus on blue-chip companies, banks and high net worth clients. **Strengths:** "Great to work with and has a very measured approach. He is very strong on Russian-related cases." "He has excellent attention to detail." **Recent work:** Appeared in R v SSHD, a judicial review of the revocation of the London School of Business and Finance's Tier 4 sponsor licence.

John Walsh A seasoned immigration barrister, he routinely undertakes public access work as well as legal aid and privately funded matters. He has notable experience of advising on family-related immigration and unlawful detention cases. He draws on his EU and prison law expertise to offer a finely tuned service. **Strengths:** "Excellent knowledge of EU free movement law." "He stands out as an engaging advocate."

Michelle Knorr Focuses predominantly on claimant-side immigration and public law, and is a particularly experienced representative of victims of trafficking and other vulnerable individuals. Her recent work has seen her acting in judicial review proceedings concerning unlawful detention. **Strengths:** "She's incredibly bright and a very persuasive advocate." "She has an encyclopaedic knowledge of trafficking law."

David Lemer Popular and respected barrister with a broad practice spanning immigration, employment and civil liberties. A regular feature in the High Court, Court of Appeal and European courts, he demonstrates particular skill in public authority disputes. **Strengths:** "He's brilliant: incredibly organised and approachable." "He has a multidisciplinary approach, he will often do immigration cases that involve other elements of law." **Recent work:** Appeared in R (McCarthy) v SSHD, a judicial review case regarding the scope of powers granted to the government by the Frontiers Protocol and Article 35 of the Citizens Rights Directive.

Catherine Meredith An enterprising and experienced immigration barrister, she is highly regarded for her handling of complex cases involving trafficking, children and sexual and gender-based violence. Her broad practice has a noted focus on EU and ECHR law. **Strengths:** "She's completely dedicated to every single case she takes on." "If I had a trafficking case I'd go to her in a heartbeat." **Recent work:** Instructed in Y & Others, a test case forming part of the detained fast track litigation. The matter concerned potential victims of trafficking and sexual minorities.

Rowena Moffatt Public law specialist with experience in judicial review proceedings, human rights matters and EU law disputes. She is regarded for her ability to undertake the full suite of immigration matters on behalf of both private individuals and large businesses. **Strengths:** "She's very bright, thorough and offers excellent knowledge of EU law." "A calm and assured all-rounder with the ability to handle PBS matters and complex human rights appeals with aplomb."

Matrix Chambers

See profile on p.876

THE SET

This lauded immigration chambers is recognised for its extensive expertise encompassing a plethora of areas, including a growing focus on the fields of sports and business immigration. Its members receive regular instructions in both the domestic courts and further afield in areas such as the Cayman Islands and British Virgin Islands. The set utilises its crossover experience in areas such as equality, community care, mental health and immigration detention to continue to offer dedicated, publicly-funded work to a range of clients. One market source describes the chambers as "extremely professional and forward-thinking. It has good research support and an impressive array of barristers, from juniors right through to silks."

Client service: "The clerking is really spot-on at Matrix Chambers, they are one of the sets where the clerks are really on top of things." The clerking team is led by senior practice manager Jason Housden.

SILKS

Raza Husain QC A world-class public law practitioner held in the highest esteem by peers and clients alike. He is particularly renowned for his adroit handling of human rights and asylum cases. As a regular feature in the Supreme Court and increasingly in EU courts, his caseload includes complex work for refugees and prominent, high-value individuals. **Strengths:** "An absolute star of the Bar in this area." "Absolutely exceptional, a pre-eminent silk in immigration." **Recent work:** Instructed in HA (Iraq) v SSHD, the first individual immigration Article 8 case to be heard in the Supreme Court for eight years.

Hugh Southey QC (see p.770) Exceedingly popular among top-flight solicitors, he specialises in human rights and immigration matters. He regularly appears in the highest courts on test cases regarding SIAC, EU law and unlawful detainment. His immigration practice is complemented by his broader prison law expertise. **Strengths:** "An absolutely excellent QC who is extremely clever and tenacious." "Brilliant, he is masterfully on top of all areas in immigration." **Recent work:** Acted in Pham v SSHD, a claim which raised the issue of whether there is 'European citizenship' and whether that status gives rise to rights.

JUNIORS

Nicholas Armstrong Has a wide-ranging immigration practice that routinely sees him appearing in test cases regarding national security. He demonstrates further skill in deportation cases, and is well known for his provision of expert advice to businesses on matters such as Tier 2 sponsorship licences and illegal working. **Strengths:** "Incredibly clever, he's an innovative thinker who is highly valued." **Recent work:** Acted in ZZ v SSHD, a case which established a core minimum disclosure required in immigration proceedings, even those which are outside Article 6 ECHR.

Samantha Knights Comes highly recommended by peers and solicitors, who recognise her work in ground-breaking immigration cases. Recently, she has appeared in the Court of Appeal in a test case concerning the legal aid available to refugees. She also offers expertise across national security and deportation matters. **Strengths:** "She is extremely responsive and her written submissions are absolutely first-class." **Recent work:** Acted in Al-Jedda v SSHD, a case concerning deprivation of nationality in the context of an individual who is believed to have links to terrorism.

Chris Buttler An established public law barrister, he is noted for his work in detention and removal cases. He regularly acts on behalf of individuals in the High Court and Court of Appeal, and is particularly highly regarded for his adept representation of vulnerable clients. **Strengths:** "He's very clued up on novel points of law." "He's very sharp in court and articulates points better than most." **Recent work:** Successfully acted for the victim of trafficking in R (FM) v SSHD, a challenge brought against the Home Office's refusal to grant the victim leave to remain in order that they might recover from the ordeal.

Band 3

39 Essex Chambers

See profile on p.840

THE SET

39 Essex Chambers is a respected immigration set that remains a popular choice for complex judicial review proceedings concerning removal, detention and control orders. While traditionally strong advocates on behalf of the defence, it continues to grow its claimant-side practice, with members regularly appearing in significant asylum cases. It is routinely engaged in high-profile matters, not least due as a result of their ever-increasing offering in the field of business immigration.

SILKS

Lisa Giovannetti QC An immigration specialist with a vast and varied practice consisting of government, public body and private individual work. Her caseload encompasses the full spectrum of human rights, national security and asylum matters, and she routinely appears in the highest domestic and EU courts. **Strengths:** "The Godmother of immigration and the go-to person for government-related work. Incredible." "She somehow combines being a really charming advocate with being very steely underneath." **Recent work:** Instructed by the government on R (Giri) v SSHD, a case considering the ambit of the 'precedent fact' approach in immigration cases.

Steven Kovats QC Previously a member of the Attorney General's A Panel before taking silk, he is a public law specialist offering in-depth expertise across the board. He predominantly acts for central and local government bodies, but is also instructed by private individuals and migrants. He routinely appears in the highest domestic and EU courts in prominent matters, such as those centring on naturalisation and false imprisonment.

JUNIORS

Rory Dunlop Esteemed junior offering capabilities that cover the full range of immigration law. He routinely acts both for and against the government and is a familiar face in the High Court. **Strengths:** "Honourable and intelligent – when I think of exemplary counsel for the Secretary of State, it's him who springs to mind." **Recent work:** Acted for the Home Secretary in JS (Nepal) v SSHD, a case investigating whether the 'historic injustice' of government policy towards Gurkhas was relevant to the Article 8 rights of a Gurkha's son.

Landmark Chambers

See profile on p.873

THE SET

A popular set which is well respected for its formidable team of immigration practitioners. Key strength in this area forms part of Landmark Chambers' broader offering in the field of administrative and public law. Its advocates are regularly called upon to act on behalf of claimants, as well as the government, in high-profile immigration disputes and complex judicial review proceedings. Market commentators value the set's "approachable ethos; as a chambers it is unpretentious, sensible, practical and pragmatic."

Client service: "The clerks are brilliant, absolutely wonderful: they can't do enough for you." Jay Fullilove leads the clerking team.

SILKS

Stephen Knafler QC A highly regarded public law barrister, he draws on his extensive knowledge to offer clients a well-rounded immigration service. He is often instructed to act on behalf of vulnerable clients and frequently appears against the government in important test cases regarding the Home Secretary's obligations. **Strengths:** "He brings such a sense of authority and clarity to a case. He has a real willingness to take into account different views." "A great public law lawyer, which can really enhance pleadings in immigration cases because he is able look at a case more broadly." **Recent work:** Acted in R (Hysaj, Bakijasi, Kaziu) v SSHD, a case considering whether citizenship obtained as a result of fraudulent representations is void or voidable.

JUNIORS

Tim Buley A leading junior, he is highly regarded for his public law knowledge and immigration expertise. He routinely acts for claimants in a diverse range of cases, including deportation and detention matters. **Recent work:** Appeared in R (Gudanavicienev, Reis) v Director of Legal Aid Casework, a test case considering the duty to provide legal aid in immigration and deportation cases under the ECHR and the EU Charter of Fundamental Rights.

Graham Denholm Experienced barrister with notable expertise in asylum and deportation matters. He is a recognised immigration detention expert who is routinely called upon to act for clients in judicial review proceedings against the Home Office. **Strengths:** "Excellent barrister, he has particularly good knowledge when it comes to detention. He reads cases extremely." "Denholm is one of the best claimants representatives for immigration detention. He's extremely careful and very proper in the way he presents cases." **Recent work:** Instructed in TH (Bangladesh) v SSHD, a case regarding the deportation of a Bangladeshi national following a conviction of attempted murder .

Alex Goodman Acting exclusively for claimants, he appears in courts at all levels, including the immigration tribunal, the Supreme Court and the ECHR. Peers acknowledge his depth of expertise, particularly highlighting his aptitude in matters concerning deportation and detention. **Strengths:** "He knows unlawful detention inside and out." "He is superb. He uses inventive arguments and is brilliant on his feet, often winning supremely complex cases."

David Blundell Well respected by peers and clients alike, he sits on the Attorney General's A Panel and regularly appears in the highest domestic and overseas courts, including the Supreme Court, ECHR and ECJ. He demonstrates notable skill in EU law-related cases. **Strengths:** "He is an extraordinarily impressive advocate." "An outstanding junior: he is totally reliable and dedicated to his cases." **Recent work:** Appeared in Singh and Khalid v SSHD. This was a challenge to the interpretation of transitional provisions in two sets of changes to the Immigration Rules, which brought Article 8 ECHR more fully within the scope of the Rules.

Declan O'Callaghan Routinely acts for claimants, who are often highly vulnerable individuals, in challenges against government deportation orders. Vastly experienced, he has been instructed in significant matters in both domestic and EU courts. **Strengths:** "Very user-friendly, he takes a great interest in the client and is highly attuned to the wider implications of his advice." "He's brilliant: very to the point, a sterling advocate and his drafting is excellent, he really knows his stuff." **Recent work:** Appeared in R (Vipasa) v SSHD, a case considering the refusal to grant an Indian national indefinite leave to remain.

Galina Ward Has a broad public law practice and notably strong knowledge of the education and property sectors. She specialises in the representation of migrants and families who are subject to immigration control, regularly appearing in the First-tier and Upper Tribunals. **Strengths:** "Excellent barrister, she's a go-to for appeals, opinions and judicial review. She's on the ball and has an excellent understanding of both the law and how it is applied." **Recent work:** Acted in R (Syed Shah) v SSHD, a judicial review of the refusal to issue a British passport to a man who may have been the victim of identity theft.

1 Pump Court

See profile on p.894

THE SET

A well-established set with traditional strength in the immigration sphere, 1 Pump Court continues to expand its burgeoning practice. Chambers predominantly handles claimant work, with an emphasis on legal aid cases, and is particularly noted for its members' aptitude in, and adroit handling of, complex judicial review proceedings. Its advocates handle the full range of immigration work, covering areas such as gender-related persecution, trafficking, unlawful detention, business immigration and complex protection claims. The set's complementary strength in the related fields of social welfare, family and EU law only serves to buttress its robust presence in the market. Its esteemed barristers make regular appearances in the Court of Appeal, Supreme Court and ECHR.

Client service: "The clerks are very responsive and very accommodating. They're flexible on fees, too. Organisationally, they are sound." Senior clerk Ian Burrow heads up the team.

JUNIORS

David Chirico A highly respected practitioner who continues to handle a broad range of matters, including complex deportation and removal cases, often on behalf of vulnerable clients. He demonstrates particular skill in immigration claims relating to social support entitlements. **Strengths:** "A leading junior in this area." "He is an individual that simply gets on with it without fanfare or nonsense. He is superbly committed and experienced." "He's undoubtedly extremely clever, but it's his tenacity that makes him really stand out." **Recent work:** Instructed in R (Kannathasan) v SSHD, a judicial review considering whether a person's removal from the UK would constitute a breach of Article 3 rights in light of the real risk of suicide.

Ranjiv Khubber A judicial review stalwart, he comes highly recommended by peers for his expert challenging of public authority decisions. He takes a notably multidisciplinary approach to his practice, with cases often involving human rights and EU law considerations. **Strengths:** "Very approachable and easy to deal with." **Recent work:** Acted in Essa v SSHD, a test case considering the correct approach to rehabilitation and integration where the Home Office sought to deport an EU national with a permanent right to reside in the UK.

Parosha Chandran Works extensively with victims of trafficking and other vulnerable individuals in a range of human rights cases. Her exceptional experience has also led to her advising the likes of the UK government and the UN. **Recent work:** Appeared in Shipitko, a complex trafficking case involving a highly vulnerable Ukrainian victim.

Gilda Kiai A sought-after immigration barrister who is lauded for her work with vulnerable individuals, particularly victims of trafficking. She is noted for her adroit handling of deportation and asylum matters, while her respected criminal practice only serves to strengthen her offering in the sphere. **Strengths:** "She's just fantastic: really approachable, easy to communicate with and very good with vulnerable clients." "I will always choose her on vulnerable client cases – she really feels what you feel for the client."

Victoria Laughton Offers clients a complete immigration, human rights and public law service. Her caseload covers unlawful detention work for individuals and advisory work for businesses, including how to overturn 7B bans. She recently appeared in an intervention in the Supreme Court concerning minimum income requirements. **Strengths:** "She is simply excellent and a delight to work with. She is always on point, dedicated and never fails to impress." "She is extremely well respected. A true master of advocacy and persuasion." **Recent work:** Instructed in Abunasir v SSHD, a judicial review challenge to the detention of a foreign national who was a former prisoner. The case considered the impact of deliberate obstruction on the 'reasonable period'.

Catherine Robinson Respected junior who regularly acts in complex, high-profile judicial review proceedings concerning deportation. Her impressive caseload covers areas such as asylum and refugee law. **Strengths:** "She really sees her client's point of view, really listens." "She's incredibly intelligent and excellent on trafficking and deportation." **Recent work:** Acted in BXS v SSHD, a case regarding the Home Secretary's refusal to consider an in-country application to revoke a deportation order from an EEA national.

Other Ranked Lawyers

Ryan Kohli (see p.692) (Cornerstone Barristers) An immigration barrister with a highly respected practice. He regularly acts in significant judicial review proceedings, often in relation to unlawful detention. **Recent work:** Appeared on behalf of the Home Secretary in R (on the application of Zeka) v SSHD, a permission hearing concerning a judicial review challenge to the Secretary's decision that an asylum applicant's claim was unfounded.

Angus McCullough QC (1 Crown Office Row) An esteemed public law silk, he is renowned for his adept handling of SIAC work, which often centres on national security matters. He routinely acts for both claimants and the government in complex, high-profile cases.

Neil Sheldon (1 Crown Office Row) Esteemed junior who demonstrates notable skill in national security and public law matters relating to immigration. **Strengths:** "Just fantastic, he works incredibly hard and handles a lot of big work for the Home Office." "Undoubtedly a first-class advocate."

Jeremy Johnson QC (see p.684) (5 Essex Court) Well regarded for his broad-based public law practice. He utilises his human rights, police and prison law experience to offer top-quality advice on immigration and asylum challenges. **Strengths:** "If Jeremy's on your team you know you're going to be well looked after."

Alan Payne (see p.735) (5 Essex Court) Accomplished silk who routinely acts for the government in immigration and human rights cases. His broad public law knowledge only serves to strengthen his work in the field. **Strengths:** "He is a very pugnacious opponent, produces quality written work and is always clear in his courtroom presentations." "He's frustratingly good." **Recent work:** Acted in SSHD v SS (Congo) & 5 Others, a three-day appeal considering the correct approach to Article 8 in the context of immigration rules.

John-Paul Waite (see p.787) (5 Essex Court) Particularly well known for adroit representation of the Home Secretary. His broad immigration practice sees him regularly handling a variety of high-profile matters, often before the Court of Appeal. He continues to demonstrate particular skill in unlawful detention cases. **Strengths:** "John-Paul is a sound-minded opponent. He's an excellent advocate and produces high-quality written work." **Recent work:** Instructed in SR (Algeria) v SSHD, a matter considering whether a person who has been involuntarily removed from the UK is deemed to have abandoned their appeal.

Glen Hodgetts of Glen Hodgetts (Barrister-at-Law) A sole practitioner who is well known for his immense experience and expertise across the immigration sphere. His diverse clientele ranges from high net worth individuals and legal aid clients to large businesses and educational establishments. **Strengths:** "An absolute pleasure to work with. He's organised, methodical and reliable." "Stands out in judicial review proceedings; he's very impressive at getting positive outcomes in the early stages."

Tom Poole (3 Hare Court) Regularly acts for the Home Secretary in complex immigration cases. His practice has a notable focus on human rights law, and he is often instructed in judicial review proceedings concerning detainment and deportation. **Recent work:** Appeared on behalf of the Home Secretary in MD Haider Ali v SSHD, a claim concerning the detention of a foreign national suffering from mental illness.

Charles Bourne QC (see p.600) (11KBW) A highly experienced silk who draws upon his broad expertise in the areas of employment, public law and local government to offer both claimants and the Home Office stellar, well-rounded immigration advice. **Strengths:** "He is parachuted in on the most complex immigration matters." **Recent work:** Acted in JE Jamaica, a test case heard in the Court of Appeal considering the point at which long residence entitles a migrant to remain under Article 8.

Eric Fripp (Lamb Building) A leading immigration junior with considerably deep knowledge of refugee and human rights law. He routinely appears in significant cases on behalf of persecuted minorities and continues to advise NGOs on matters such as statelessness and nationality. **Strengths:** "An excellent lawyer with an incredible understanding of asylum law."

Shivani Jegarajah (Mansfield Chambers) An established immigration lawyer who is held in particularly high regard for her in-depth knowledge of human rights issues. Her varied caseload includes prominent yet niche cases, such as major challenges to refusal of entry clearance decisions and complex freedom of speech matters. **Strengths:** "She's very popular and much in demand. A fantastic advocate." **Recent work:** Acted in Sehwerert, a case concerning the refusal of entry clearance to one of the 'Cuban Five' who wished to meet with UK MPs to discuss his case.

Robert Palmer (Monckton Chambers) Regularly appears in the higher domestic and EU courts in significant national security, EU freedom of movement and human rights cases. His stellar reputation is reflected by his position on the Attorney General's A Panel of counsel. **Strengths:** "Highly skilled advocate, he has handled complex, flagship immigration cases." **Recent work:** Acted in W (Algeria) & Others v SSHD, a matter regarding the government's 'Deportation with Assurances' programme.

S Chelvan (No5 Chambers) An esteemed and highly respected immigration barrister who is particularly recognised for his LGBTQ rights work. His work is international in its scope, while his diverse client base includes many individuals who are fleeing persecution. **Strengths:** "He is extremely well regarded for his work in LGBTQ asylum seeker cases." "He is very committed and knows everything there is to know about same-sex asylum seeker cases. Always pushes to get the best results for his clients."

Daniel Bazini (No5 Chambers) Acts for a variety of clients, such as private individuals, educational institutions and employers. His areas of expertise include complex sponsor licence issues and the PBS. **Strengths:** "Excellent knowledge of the points-based system, great with clients and reliably on hand to provide ad hoc assistance." "He is thorough and pragmatic in his approach and gets to the heart of the matter at top speed."

Edward Nicholson (No5 Chambers) Respected immigration specialist with prior experience as a legal officer for the Refugee Legal Centre. He routinely appears in judicial review proceedings concerning significant deportation and human rights matters. **Strengths:** "He deals with cases absolutely thoroughly and with a keen eye for detail. He has won very complex cases and has a good rapport with clients." "He has the ability to think outside the box and find creative solutions."

Joanne Rothwell (No5 Chambers) Routinely acts for highly vulnerable clients, including minors and individuals with mental health issues. Her broad caseload regularly sees her acting in complex immigration, asylum and nationality matters. **Recent work:** Appeared in Sawsan Chakra, a matter regarding a Syrian national who was refused UK entry clearance to visit family members.

Robin Tam QC (Temple Garden Chambers) Leading counsel to the Home Office, he is sought after for his expertise across a range of national security matters, such as control order and deportation cases. **Recent work:** Appeared in R (ZS (Afghanistan)) v SSHD, a case considering the requirements for the lawful immigration detention of children.

MIDLANDS

Immigration
Leading Sets
Band 1
No5 Chambers *
Number 8 Chambers
* *Indicates set / individual with profile.*
[A] *direct access (see p.24).*
◊ *(ORL) = Other Ranked Lawyer.*
Alphabetical order within each band. Band 1 is highest.

Immigration
Leading Juniors
Band 1
De Mello Ramby *No5 Chambers*
Mahmood Abid *No5 Chambers* [A] *
Vokes Stephen *Number 8 Chambers*
Band 2
Mandalia Vinesh *No5 Chambers* [A]
Muman Tony *43templerow Chambers (ORL)* ◊
Pipe Adam *Number 8 Chambers*
Rutherford Emma *Number 8 Chambers*
Sadiq Tariq *St Philips Chambers (ORL)* ◊ [A]

Band 1

No5 Chambers

See profile on p.931

THE SET

A well-respected national practice that is recognised for its extensive experience before the Upper Tribunal, Court of Appeal and the Supreme Court. Its roster of skilled advocates is well equipped to handle the full range of both personal and corporate immigration matters and is sought after as counsel to high net worth individuals and entrepreneurs on complex Points-Based System (PBS) issues.

JUNIORS

Ramby De Mello Receives attention for his excellent advocacy and experience acting for clients in the European Court of Justice and the Supreme Court. He is able to handle a range of immigration, asylum and nationality matters.

Abid Mahmood (see p.706) Recognised for his broad experience of immigration cases, including matters concerning questions of asylum or human rights. Mahmood heads the immigration group at No5 Chambers. **Recent work:** Instructed as lead counsel in a Supreme Court appeal against the Secretary of State for the Home Department. The case concerned the government's evidential flexibility policy for its points-based immigration system.

Vinesh Mandalia Impressive experience before the Administrative Court and the Upper Tribunal with respect to immigration law cases. Regularly instructed by the Government Legal Department. **Strengths:** "He is user-friendly, knows the law inside and out and his advocacy skills are second to none." **Recent work:** Represented the Secretary of State for the Home Department in a judicial review regarding the handling of proceedings following the issuance of a supplementary decision letter.

Number 8 Chambers

THE SET

Number 8 Chambers offers an impressive depth of immigration law talent in the Midlands Circuit. The set is noted by observers for its deep bench of seasoned barristers and experience across a broad spectrum of immigration matters, including asylum, nationality and refugee issues.

JUNIORS

Stephen Vokes A well-regarded immigration law specialist who is admired for his depth of experience and excellent case preparation. He is a seasoned counsel for both High Court and Court of Appeals proceedings, with experience of a broad range of immigration and asylum cases. **Strengths:** "He is extremely experienced, well prepared and able to find solutions to complex legal arguments."

Adam Pipe Handles a broad range of immigration and asylum law cases. He regularly handles cases before the Immigration Tribunal, the Administrative Court and the Court of Appeal.

Emma Rutherford Offers a respected immigration law practice, while also impressing in criminal law matters and civil litigation. **Strengths:** "She is a brilliant advocate who is well liked by clients and judges."

Other Ranked Lawyers

Tony Muman (43templerow Chambers) A well-regarded junior who is noted for his counsel on immigration law, asylum and EU and nationality law. **Strengths:** "A safe pair of hands."

Tariq Sadiq (St Philips Chambers) Recognised for his representation of the government in immigration proceedings with national security and terrorism aspects. He is also noted for his handling of Special Immigration Appeals Commission (SIAC) cases and judicial reviews related to matters such as human rights, discrimination and EEA free movement.

NORTHERN/NORTH EASTERN

Immigration
Leading Sets
Band 1
Kenworthy's Chambers *
Band 2
Garden Court North
Leading Juniors
Band 1
Brown George *Kenworthy's Chambers*
Frantzis Roxanne *KBW (ORL)* ◊
Nicholson John *Kenworthy's Chambers*
O'Ryan Rory *Garden Court North*
Schwenk Mark *Kenworthy's Chambers*
Band 2
Jagadesham Vijay *Garden Court North*
Khan Shazia *Kenworthy's Chambers* Ⓐ
Mair Lucy *Garden Court North*
Patel Gita *Kenworthy's Chambers* Ⓐ
Pickering Rebecca *Kenworthy's Chambers*
* *Indicates set with profile.*
Ⓐ *direct access (see p.24).*
◊ *(ORL) = Other Ranked Lawyer.*
Alphabetical order within each band. Band 1 is highest.

Band 1

Kenworthy's Chambers

See profile on p.967

THE SET

The leading immigration set in the Northern Circuit, Kenworthy's Chambers offers the full suite of immigration and asylum law services with advocates drawing on their family law experience to offer a more complete service to clients. Its members frequently appear in the Upper Tribunal and at judicial review.

Client service: Courtney Soden is the set's immigration clerk. "Courtney is great – she's very quick to respond, and confirmations, bookings and fee notes are sent out quickly. The clerks are very user-friendly and very easy to get hold of."

JUNIORS

Mark Schwenk Capable of handling the full range of immigration and asylum matters at judicial review, the Upper Tribunal and the High Court. Schwenk is well versed in complex human rights and unlawful detention issues. **Strengths:** "Mark is an experienced immigration advocate with excellent legal knowledge of the civil penalties system and grounds for appeal."

George Brown A high-calibre immigration lawyer with an extensive immigration, asylum and nationality practice. **Strengths:** "He's very approachable and has a legal brain." "There is a very high standard in any work he does for you."

John Nicholson A leading immigration barrister with impressive experience of handling deportation and destitution cases for vulnerable clients. He also regularly advises on general immigration and asylum matters. **Strengths:** "Very experienced, extremely thorough and up to date with case law." "He fights to the death."

Shazia Khan Enjoys a fine reputation in the immigration law space, handling a broad range of matters including asylum and nationality law matters and cases with a human rights component. **Strengths:** "She is consistently one of our first-choice barristers for all types of cases. She is particularly good in complex matters like deportation."

Gita Patel A highly experienced barrister with a good reputation in the region. She has a broad immigration practice regularly appearing in the Court of Appeal and Administrative Court, and has notable expertise acting for vulnerable appellants. **Strengths:** "She is very knowledgeable in terms of case law."

Rebecca Pickering A reliable immigration lawyer who regularly appears before the First and Upper Tiers. Her practice covers matters such as deportation and the Points Based System (PBS). **Strengths:** "She's excellent with vulnerable clients and minors." "She always goes the extra mile and is extremely approachable."

Band 2

Garden Court North

THE SET

Garden Court North is an important presence in the immigration and human rights sector. The set offers expertise in connection with the full range of immigration law, including asylum and nationality law, while members are also noted for their ability to draw on knowledge of complementary areas such as prison, employment and discrimination law. Interviewees comment that the set's "attitude and dedication to asylum and immigration applicants is tremendous."

Client service: Sarah Wright is the set's senior clerk.

JUNIORS

Rory O'Ryan Covers a broad range of matters including asylum applications, human rights, PBS issues and trafficking. He regularly acts in judicial reviews, and appears before the Court of Appeal and the Supreme Court.

Vijay Jagadesham Undertakes a wide range of immigration and asylum work, most notably on behalf of vulnerable adults and children. He is experienced before the Administrative Court and draws on his public law experience to advise on detention and sponsorship matters. **Strengths:** "He is practical and good on the law." "He is pragmatic in the face of difficult judges."

Lucy Mair Has a broad immigration practice that takes in trafficking, asylum and human rights cases. **Strengths:** "A first-choice barrister." "She is extremely conscientious and thorough. Excellent on trafficking cases, she is very approachable and responsive."

Other Ranked Lawyers

Roxanne Frantzis (KBW) A leading immigration and public law barrister. She has a broad practice and is particularly adept at handling deportation and trafficking cases for vulnerable clients. **Strengths:** "Impressive specialist immigration barrister." "She is very knowledgeable and has a good level of expertise." **Recent work:** Acted in Secretary of State for the Home Department v KJ Angola and Others, a series of conjoined appeals in which the Court of Appeal will provide guidance on the application of Section 117 of the Nationality Immigration and Asylum Act 2002 to deportation appeals.

Contents:

LONDON

Information Technology
Leading Sets
Band 1
4 Pump Court *
Band 2
Atkin Chambers *
Henderson Chambers *
8 New Square *
11 South Square *
3 Verulam Buildings *
Leading Silks
Band 1
Alexander Daniel *8 New Square* *
Charlton Alex *4 Pump Court* *
McCall Duncan *4 Pump Court*
Meade Richard *8 New Square* *
Storey Jeremy *4 Pump Court* *
Streatfeild-James David *Atkin Chambers*
Band 2
Akka Lawrence *20 Essex Street (ORL)* ◊
Douglas Michael *4 Pump Court* *
Gourgey Alan *Wilberforce Chambers (ORL)* ◊
Howe Martin *8 New Square* *
Silverleaf Michael *11 South Square*
Susman Peter *Henderson Chambers* 🄰 *
Tozzi Nigel *4 Pump Court* *
Vanhegan Mark *11 South Square*
Band 3
Baatz Nicholas *Atkin Chambers*
Burkill Guy *Three New Square (ORL)* ◊ *
Croall Simon *Quadrant Chambers (ORL)* ◊ *
Dennys Nicholas *Atkin Chambers*
Howells James *Atkin Chambers* *
Lowenstein Paul *3 Verulam Buildings*
Mawrey Richard *Henderson Chambers* 🄰 *
O'Sullivan Zoe *One Essex Court (ORL)* ◊
Pilling Benjamin *4 Pump Court* *
Speck Adrian *8 New Square* *
New Silks
Bergin Terence *4 Pump Court* *
Campbell Douglas *Three New Square (ORL)* ◊ *
Moody-Stuart Thomas *8 New Square* *
* *Indicates set / individual with profile.*
🄰 *direct access (see p.24).*
◊ *(ORL) = Other Ranked Lawyer.*
Alphabetical order within each band. Band 1 is highest.

Information Technology
Leading Juniors
Star individuals
Lazarus Michael *3 Verulam Buildings* *
Band 1
Henderson Simon *4 Pump Court* *
Lavy Matthew *4 Pump Court* *
Nicholson Brian *11 South Square*
Saunders Nicholas *Brick Court Chambers (ORL)* ◊
Band 2
Freedman Clive *3 Verulam Buildings* *
Hicks Michael *Hogarth Chambers (ORL)* ◊
McCafferty Lynne *4 Pump Court* *
Onslow Robert *8 New Square* 🄰 *
Osborne Richard *4 Pump Court* *
Band 3
Kulkarni Yash *Quadrant Chambers (ORL)* ◊ *
Lewis Christopher *Atkin Chambers* *
Richardson Matthew *Henderson Chambers* *
St Ville James *8 New Square* *

Band 1

4 Pump Court
See profile on p.895

THE SET

A peerless group of silks and juniors who are able to bring unrivalled expertise to a range of IT issues including the emerging fields of cloud computing and cyber security. Members are involved in some of the largest copyright and contractual cases, and regularly act for major industry figures. Clients include governments internationally, global IT consultancies and multinational corporations, as well as the emergency services and small software houses

Client service: "The clerks are great and I always get a great service from them. They are proactive and always do what they can to make people available for me." Chambers' Chief Executive Carolyn McCombe leads the clerking and administration team.

SILKS

Alex Charlton QC (see p.615) Has a rounded and highly respected IT practice, and acts for major private and public entities in the most significant disputes, bringing his technical expertise to bear. He has recently been involved in software licensing disputes as well as cases concerning contractual disputes and terminations. **Strengths:** "A very knowledgeable and powerful advocate." "He can cut through the rhetoric and provide pragmatic legal advice that takes into account the client's commercial considerations." **Recent work:** Defended Damco against a £9 million claim by U-2-ME alleging poor quality software and delays in the provision of services.

Duncan McCall QC Renowned as much for his approachable and user-friendly style of advocacy as for his clear-cut and expertly informed commercial legal advice. He has recently bolstered the international side of his practice and has been engaged in matters in the Dubai International Financial Centre courts. **Strengths:** "He is thorough in his approach and analysis, has a relaxed but persuasive style of advocacy and is unflappable." "Very user-friendly and commercial, he's excellent on difficult issues of contractual interpretation." **Recent work:** Represented P&O Ferries in the termination of an outsourcing contract with Getronics.

Jeremy Storey QC (see p.774) Long-standing figure at the top end of the IT Bar who has extensive experience and handles some of the most significant disputes in the field. He is as equally adept at arbitrations as he is at straight litigation. **Strengths:** "A very seasoned operator who delivers an excellent product." "He's a very well-prepared advocate with a good eye for detail." **Recent work:** Acted for BT in a dispute with Ciena Communications regarding charges for the supply and support of networking equipment.

Michael Douglas QC (see p.635) Particularly recognised for acting for governmental organisations and major corporations in resolving contractual disputes, especially those concerning defence-related systems. He also tackles a range of outsourcing and software licensing matters, employing his technical skill as both an arbitrator and a litigator. **Strengths:** "Very capable and very likeable, with a nice reassuring manner for clients." "He doesn't come in with big guns and massive noise, but just quietly gets on with it." **Recent work:** Acted for Fujitsu in actions brought against IBM for breach of contract concerning the supply and maintenance of IT systems for the DVLA.

Nigel Tozzi QC (see p.783) A widely talented silk who brings a broad range of expertise to bear when tackling his varied technology practice. He is especially recognised for handling IT software disputes for libraries, airports, hotels and universities. **Strengths:** "An extremely impressive opponent who is irrepressibly energetic." "He's no-nonsense, user-friendly and super smart."

Benjamin Pilling QC (see p.738) Noted for representing cross-border clients, particularly Asian and American companies and individuals. He has a practice that takes in both traditional commercial cases and highly technical matters. **Strengths:** "A very clear thinker, a good cross-examiner and someone who is good on paper." "He's very quick to pick up the complex facts of a case and get to grips with the technical aspects of the IT system and software in issue." **Recent work:** Appeared for the defendant in the technically complex case of BGL Group v Ciboodle, concerning a project to replace a legacy IBM 'green screen' system used by a company.

Terence Bergin QC (see p.595) Took silk this year having had an outstanding career as a junior involved in some of the most challenging technology cases. He has breadth and depth of technical expertise and represents suppliers and consumers. Clients include retailers, government bodies and global telecoms providers. **Strengths:** "Massively experienced in this area and a very well-known name." "He's pragmatic, confident and good on his feet." **Recent work:** Defended DCML against a £2 million claim by AFD Software/Zipaddress regarding the excessive use of a software licence.

JUNIORS

Simon Henderson (see p.669) A highly regarded junior who is equally experienced at acting in both litigation and arbitration for clients on the supplier and consumer side of technology disputes. He has recently acted for some of the biggest global retailers and software companies. **Strengths:** "Exceptionally good, he's a very commercially minded chap." "Very pragmatic and very likeable." **Recent work:** Advised on the IT aspects of claims totalling £100 million arising from Nokia's sale of Vertu.

Matthew Lavy (see p.696) Drawing on technical expertise gained in his previous life as a software developer, he is able to advise on the most sophisticated technology disputes and projects. Lavy is especially valued by clients for his knowledge of cyber security and data protection matters, and is well versed in business critical systems for corporate and banking entities. **Strengths:** "So versatile in the tech space, he really understands the forensic detail." **Recent work:** Advised in a dispute between T-Systems and EE, arising from an extensive IT transformation and modernisation project.

Lynne McCafferty (see p.711) Representing clients ranging from specialist software providers to large-scale government bodies, she is recognised for her ability to make complex technical aspects of cases comprehensible. She also acts in litigation and arbitration for clients including IT suppliers and consultants. **Strengths:** "Very clever and really adds value and strategic guidance to cases." "Very hard-working and well organised."

Richard Osborne (see p.731) A well-regarded junior whose flourishing IT practice was built on his involvement as part of the government's team in the largest ever IT arbitration in the UK. He now also represents suppliers and consumers in the sector. **Strengths:** "An excellent junior with great drafting skills. He's very responsive and easy to work with." **Recent work:** Defended IBM against a £25 million breach of contract claim brought by the National Trust. The case concerned hosting services for the Trust's membership infrastructure.

Band 2

Atkin Chambers

See profile on p.806

THE SET

A set with a broad team of silks who can offer assistance with numerous aspects of information technology law. Members handle disputes between major suppliers and customers in both the public and private spheres, and also handle cases concerning telecommunications outsourcing and online banking and money transfer systems. A number of the cases handled have significant cross-border elements.

Client service: The "energetic and engaging" Justin Wilson is the senior clerk.

SILKS

David Streatfeild-James QC Very highly regarded practitioner who has acted for some of the most significant players in the information technology market. He is praised for his ability to represent a broad range of clients in this sector including contractors, government bodies and private employers. **Strengths:** "Has a very good big picture view of litigation and doesn't get lost in the details." "He's masterful."

Nicholas Dennys QC Frequently acts for major household name companies in relation to international software and hardware disputes. He brings his experience in construction and infrastructure, professional negligence and energy cases to best serve his technology clients. **Strengths:** "He is very knowledgeable and skilled in the field, and acts with consummate skill."

Nicholas Baatz QC Excels in information technology law disputes involving mass transit, power plants and cross-border telecommunications. He is also an experienced arbitrator and mediator. **Strengths:** "A very effective and impressive advocate."

James Howells QC (see p.676) Especially recognised for his skill in handling energy and power disputes with attendant technological and technical complications. His practice also covers IT issues such as software licensing and data protection, and he is well versed in alternative dispute resolution methods such as arbitration and mediation. **Strengths:** "An excellent lateral thinker with a pragmatic approach to solving clients' problems." "Astonishingly hard-working." **Recent work:** Represented PTT defending £9 million of claims brought by Triple Point Technology relating to the termination of a technology contract.

JUNIORS

Christopher Lewis (see p.700) Well recognised for his activity in the construction and energy sectors. He is instructed by suppliers and customers in cases concerning hardware, software and telecoms. **Strengths:** "A barrister with a very powerful mind who has great analytical capabilities."

Henderson Chambers

See profile on p.864

THE SET

Henderson Chambers has members who are well regarded for their work handling some of the biggest technology disputes. Cases handled involve the provision of major IT systems by suppliers, software licensing and contracts, and the technological aspects of engineering and construction projects. The set also has strength in data protection and multi-jurisdictional hacking cases.

Client service: John White is the chief clerk.

SILKS

Peter Susman QC (see p.776) Esteemed silk with a particular specialisation in disputes arising from alleged software defects. He is highly regarded for his work for private developers, customers and major government bodies. **Strengths:** "Extremely nice and friendly, and really gets to grips with things." **Recent work:** Acted for the the claimant in a case regarding the use of mechanised price information extraction software on a rival company's website that caused the site to crash.

Richard Mawrey QC (see p.710) An established figure at the Technology Bar who has long experience of handling a range of IT matters including disputes concerning faulty software and the alleged failure of major IT projects. He is also noted for his expertise in the area of public procurement in the IT sector. **Strengths:** "He won the client's confidence very quickly due to his very pragmatic approach."

JUNIORS

Matthew Richardson (see p.751) Offers a sophisticated technical background as well as legal expertise. He is especially expert in cases concerning cyber crime and data protection, and is also well versed in the emerging field of crypto-currencies. **Strengths:** "Incredibly good at marrying the legal side of things with the very technical side." "He has an innovative approach, is punchy and is hard-working." **Recent work:** Acted for the claimant in an action to secure the removal of content from a BitTorrent site through the use of injunctive relief.

8 New Square

See profile on p.881

THE SET

This set has significant strength in intellectual property and media law as well as a diverse information technology practice. Members are noted for the technical expertise they bring to bear when handling complex cases regarding software licensing or matters concerning data protection or cyber security.

Client service: John Call leads the clerking team. A man of vast experience, he has been senior clerk at the set for over 30 years.

SILKS

Daniel Alexander QC (see p.581) Highly respected silk whose information technology work practice covers a broad range of contractual disputes and issues relating to rights. He is also experienced at handling biotechnology, telecommuncations and system design matters. **Strengths:** "A very strong practitioner who is very fluent, thoughtful and strategic." "He's excellent both on a personal level and in terms of his advocacy and legal insight."

Richard Meade QC (see p.715) Especially noted for his experience of handling technology patent issues, he is an expert on trademarks and design rights. **Strengths:** "Very quick, very smart and a lethal opponent." "He's massively talented and an intellectually awesome person to work with."

Martin Howe QC (see p.676) Well regarded for his skill in navigating the intersection between information technology, intellectual property and European Union law. His recent work has been particularly focused on internet broadcasting rights and violations. **Strengths:** "As well as being a leader in the field generally, he has a detailed technical grasp of computing and digital technology."

Adrian Speck QC (see p.770) Commended for his mature and intelligent handling of cases concerning technology patent licensing, telecommunications and computer gaming. He is also active in pharmaceutical and biotechnology law. **Strengths:** "A fantastic advocate." "A bright man who will always try to find a clever point."

Thomas Moody-Stuart QC (see p.720) Has recently taken silk following a successful career as a junior specialising in the trade mark and patent aspects of information technology law. **Strengths:** "He has an impressive grasp of the detail in a case."

JUNIORS

Robert Onslow (see p.730) A well-respected senior junior whose practice covers the full range of information technology matters but has a special focus on data and software protection issues. His advice is lent particular weight due to the fact that he has a background in software development. **Strengths:** "Thorough, detailed and impressive."

James St Ville (see p.771) Especially noted for his skill in handling cases with dominant mathematical and technical elements. He is active across the full range of patent and registered design, computer contract and database rights cases; he is also proficient in matters concerning computer hacking.

11 South Square

See profile on p.909

THE SET

A notable and growing presence at the IT Bar. The set is able to draw upon its market-leading reputation in the intellectual property space to inform its work in the internet trading, software patent and licences and telecommunications sectors. Members are equally active in resolving disputes through litigation and arbitration.

Client service: Ashley Carr is the head of the clerking team and has been at the set for over 20 years.

SILKS

Michael Silverleaf QC Handles the most complex aspects of both information technology and intellectual property law, and is able to advise clients on the commercial and technical considerations of cases including software licensing disputes. He also acts as a mediator. **Strengths:** "Very tenacious and very effective." **Recent work:** Represented Interflora in its dispute with Marks & Spencer over the use of Google Adwords.

Mark Vanhegan QC Has a broad practice covering the technology aspects of patent, telecommunications and media law. He is also an experienced mediator and arbitrator, drawing on his strong technical knowledge to aid resolution. **Strengths:** "He's got a very judge-like way about him and comes across as very calm and thoughtful." **Recent work:** Continues to act for Samsung in the company's patent disputes with Unwired Planet.

JUNIORS

Brian Nicholson A highly regarded junior who has particular strength in handling patent and trademark disputes. He is especially valued by technology clients as he has both commercial awareness and a comprehensive understanding of the technical aspects of his cases. His recent work in the telecommunications sector has been particularly notable. **Strengths:** "Extremely bright and extremely sound on both the technology and the law." "He's very versatile and has very broad experience." **Recent work:** Acted for IPCom in its action against Nokia over infringement of a software patent.

3 Verulam Buildings

See profile on p.924

THE SET

A well-regarded chambers whose expertise in IT is increasingly in demand at home and abroad. The set's significant knowledge of the banking sector means it is a regular presence in disputes concerning financial technology, internet trading and electronic currency. **Client service:** "Led by Stephen Penson, the clerking is excellent and extremely helpful."

SILKS

Paul Lowenstein QC Acts in cases concerning contractual telecommunication issues and domain disputes, amongst other areas. He has long experience in financial and business litigation, and is particularly adept at cross-examination. **Strengths:** "Brilliant on his feet, he's really hard-working and a real team player." "A very effective and very tenacious kind of opponent." **Recent work:** Represented Heming against accusations of business secrets theft and breach of confidence. The case involved the alleged theft of investment analysis software from Ignis Asset Management.

JUNIORS

Michael Lazarus (see p.697) Leading junior at the IT bar with a peerless reputation for both his courtroom advocacy and for his deep technical understanding of the issues at hand. He is an expert on the technology aspects of the sale and purchase of business assets, and is also highly adept at banking and finance, fraud and professional negligence cases. **Strengths:** "Has the ability to take a complex set of facts and technical issues and translate them into straightforward advice." "He's incredibly bright."

Clive Freedman (see p.648) Respected junior whose information technology practice centres particularly on cases concerning online banking and e-commerce. His technical expertise also comes into play in his parallel role as a mediator and arbitrator for technology disputes. **Strengths:** "Really good, and knows his technical stuff well." **Recent work:** Acted for the customer in Allfiled UK Ltd v Eltis & Ors, a case concerning software intellectual property rights and the duties of employees.

Other Ranked Lawyers

Nicholas Saunders (Brick Court Chambers) A leading junior in the field who is able to assist clients whose IT disputes concern significant contractual disputes and notable cross-border aspects. He also has prowess in intellectual property and European law. **Strengths:** "Really focused and calm, he's unbelievably on top of the detail and all the strategic issues."

Zoe O'Sullivan QC (One Essex Court) Has a growing IT practice that sees her handling cases concerning software development and licensing, major contractual disputes and outsourcing issues. She is also experienced at handling media tech issues. **Strengths:** "She's formidably bright, writes very well and has a good balance of gravitas and humour." "She's able to have very practical and pragmatic conversations and to communicate effectively with clients."

Lawrence Akka QC (20 Essex Street) Active in a wide range of information technology cases, from those involving data security and database rights to cutting-edge work concerning satellites and advanced telecommunications. His commercial sensibility makes him a popular choice for high-value technology disputes. **Strengths:** "He doesn't just look at the law but gets involved in the underlying merits, which is very important." "Clearly a man who knows his IT, he had a very comprehensive grasp of the issues in the case." **Recent work:** Represented T-Systems against Everything Everywhere in an £80 million IT services dispute regarding the the migration and management of Orange and EE's legacy IT infrastructure.

Michael Hicks (Hogarth Chambers) A senior junior well regarded for his work across the spectrum of information technology law who has handled matters ranging from disputes over software and hardware failures to cases involving database security. **Strengths:** "He's very impressive and has a really deep knowledge and understanding of the subject." **Recent work:** Acted for SAS Institute in its claim against World Programming Ltd. concerning copyright for computer software and the legality of 'drop in' replacements for software.

Guy Burkill QC (see p.607) (Three New Square) Particularly admired for his technical grasp of complex technology matters, evidenced by his recent engagement to act in major smartphone and telecoms cases. He is also an expert in the intellectual property aspects of software and hardware disputes. **Strengths:** "A fantastic mathematical and technical talent." "He can grasp the key issues in the case very quickly and come up with creative solutions."

Douglas Campbell QC (see p.610) (Three New Square) A new silk whose skill in intellectual property and copyright issues feeds in effectively to an information technology practice that covers software and hardware disputes including those involving consumer and professional products, digital media players and automotive technology. **Strengths:** "His knowledge is really great and he's a really committed advocate." **Recent work:** Represented the Office of National Statistics defending allegations of copyright infringement related to records management software.

Simon Croall QC (see p.626) (Quadrant Chambers) Has significant experience of handling cases arising from large-scale IT projects. He is particularly noted for the international scope of his work and has acted in numerous cross-border arbitrations. **Strengths:** "He's clever, sensible and good with clients." **Recent work:** Appeared in De Beers v Atos Origin, a high-profile dispute relating to a failed IT project for the world's largest diamond trader.

Yash Kulkarni (see p.693) (Quadrant Chambers) Handles IT as part of a wider commercial practice and has been in a number of reported cases such as De Beers v Atos Origin. **Strengths:** "Clearly on top of his material, he's a very good cross-examiner and an impressive performer all round." **Recent work:** Acted for the owner of a number of financial journalism websites in a claim against a website developer. The case concerned alleged deficient coding and architecture design relating to websites.

Alan Gourgey QC (Wilberforce Chambers) A chancery law leader who is well regarded for his skill in handling the commercial aspects of information technology disputes. He is noted for his ability in court, and is also recognised for his quality as an arbitrator. **Strengths:** "He's great on his feet. Judges really appreciate being addressed by him because they have the feeling that they will now get to the bottom of the issue."

Inquests & Public Inquiries

Contents:

ALL CIRCUITS

Inquests & Public Inquiries
Leading Sets
Band 1
1 Crown Office Row *
Band 2
Doughty Street Chambers *
5 Essex Court *
3 Raymond Buildings Barristers *
Band 3
Garden Court Chambers *
Matrix Chambers *
Serjeants' Inn Chambers *
Temple Garden Chambers *
Leading Silks
Band 1
Barton Fiona *5 Essex Court* *
Beer Jason *5 Essex Court* *
Beggs John *Serjeants' Inn Chambers* *
Eadie James *Blackstone Chambers (ORL)* ◊
Emmerson Ben *Matrix Chambers*
Gibbs Patrick *3 Raymond Buildings Barristers* 🄰 *
Hough Jonathan *4 New Square (ORL)* ◊ *
Lambert Christina *1 Crown Office Row*
Morton Keith *Temple Garden Chambers* *
Band 2
Davies Hugh *3 Raymond Buildings Barristers* 🄰
Grey Eleanor *39 Essex Chambers (ORL)* ◊
Horwell Richard *3 Raymond Buildings Barristers*
Johnson Jeremy *5 Essex Court* *
Keith Hugo *3 Raymond Buildings Barristers* *
Leek Samantha *5 Essex Court* *
Mansfield Michael *Mansfield Chambers (ORL)* ◊
Phillips Rory *3 Verulam Buildings (ORL)* ◊
Tam Robin *Temple Garden Chambers*
Thomas Leslie *Garden Court Chambers*
Band 3
Dias Dexter *Garden Court Chambers*
Francis Robert *Serjeants' Inn Chambers* *
Friedman Danny *Matrix Chambers*
Giffin Nigel *11KBW (ORL)* ◊ *
Glasson Jonathan *Matrix Chambers* *
Greaney Paul *New Park Court Chambers (ORL)* ◊
Green Samuel *New Park Court Chambers (ORL)* ◊
Griffin Nicholas *QEB Hollis Whiteman (ORL)* ◊ *
Hill Henrietta *Doughty Street Chambers* 🄰
Kark Tom *QEB Hollis Whiteman (ORL)* ◊ *
Laidlaw Jonathan *2 Hare Court (ORL)* ◊ *
Lissack Richard *Fountain Court Chambers (ORL)* ◊ *
O'Connor Andrew *Temple Garden Chambers*
O'Connor Patrick *Doughty Street Chambers* 🄰
Richards Jenni *39 Essex Chambers (ORL)* ◊ *
Weatherby Pete *Garden Court North (ORL)* ◊
Williams Heather *Doughty Street Chambers*
New Silks
Bradley Clodagh *1 Crown Office Row*
Dolan Bridget *Serjeants' Inn Chambers* *
McGahey Cathryn *Temple Garden Chambers*
Skelton Peter *1 Crown Office Row*
Thomas Owain *1 Crown Office Row*
** Indicates set / individual with profile.*
🄰 direct access (see p.24).
◊ (ORL) = Other Ranked Lawyer.
Alphabetical order within each band. Band 1 is highest.

Inquests & Public Inquiries
Leading Juniors
Band 1
Dobbin Clair *3 Raymond Buildings Barristers* *
Hewitt Alison *5 Essex Court* *
Hill Matthew *1 Crown Office Row*
Moss Nicholas *Temple Garden Chambers*
Sheldon Neil *1 Crown Office Row*
Straw Adam *Doughty Street Chambers*
Band 2
Antrobus Simon *Crown Office Chambers (ORL)* ◊ *
Ballard Briony *Serjeants' Inn Chambers* *
Campbell Brenda *Garden Court Chambers*
Gallagher Caoilfhionn *Doughty Street Chambers* 🄰 *
Band 3
Beattie Kate *Doughty Street Chambers*
Bunting Jude *Doughty Street Chambers*
Butt Matthew *3 Raymond Buildings Barristers* 🄰 *
Cartwright Sophie *Deans Court Chambers (ORL)* ◊ *
Cumberland Melanie *6KBW College Hill (ORL)* ◊
Gerry Alison *Doughty Street Chambers*
Horstead Sean *Garden Court Chambers*
Matthewson Scott *42 Bedford Row (ORL)* ◊
Mellor Christopher *1 Crown Office Row*
Naqshbandi Saba *3 Raymond Buildings Barristers* 🄰
Powell Debra *Serjeants' Inn Chambers* *
Saunders Neil *3 Raymond Buildings Barristers* 🄰 *
Tampakopoulos Alexandra *2 Hare Court (ORL)* ◊ *
Uberoi Michael *Outer Temple Chambers (ORL)* ◊
Williams Vincent *9 Gough Square (ORL)* ◊ *
Up-and-coming individuals
Heaven Kirsten *Garden Court Chambers*
Nicholls Jesse *Doughty Street Chambers*
Williamson Oliver *Serjeants' Inn Chambers* *

Band 1

1 Crown Office Row

See profile on p.826

THE SET

1 Crown Office Row is "a very impressive set with a large collection of very high-calibre barristers," commentators enthuse. The chambers is often the first choice for inquests arising in the context of clinical negligence. Its wide-reaching expertise also encompasses deaths in prison, police custody, psychiatric institutions and military deaths. Members also frequently appear in high-profile, politically-charged public inquiries. This leading set accepts instructions from state agents, bereaved families and other participants, and has several members who have experience of appearing as counsel to the inquest or inquiry. Recently, the set has played a prominent role in the inquest into the Hillsborough Stadium disaster in 1989.

Client service: "1 Crown Office Row is in a league of its own for clerking. They are efficient, slick, quick and never let you down. A very efficient set of chambers." Chambers director Andrew Meyler leads the team.

SILKS

Christina Lambert QC A popular choice for large, politically-charged inquests and public inquiries. She receives extensive praise for her sensitive handling of bereaved families and other vulnerable parties, and for her notably deep knowledge of clinical negligence. Strengths: "Her combination of high intellect, smooth advocacy and sensitivity towards families is absolutely superb and invaluable." "Her work ethic and ability to deal with expert evidence is astonishing." Recent work: Appointed by Lord Justice Goldring as lead counsel to the renewed inquests into the deaths of 96 spectators at Hillsborough.

Clodagh Bradley QC Predominantly represents bereaved families at inquests into deaths caused by clinical negligence. She is capable of handling complex factual circumstances and difficult causation arguments. **Strengths:** "She combines intelligence with tenacity. She's good at keeping many balls in the air, and the effort that she puts into cases is formidable." "She is very thorough in her cross-examination and a wonderful advocate on behalf of her clients." **Recent work:** Represented the family at the inquest into the neonatal death of a first-born twin, who died at five days of age. The baby sustained a severe brain injury during the neonatal period immediately following his delivery, when attention was diverted to the second-born twin.

Peter Skelton QC Frequently instructed as counsel to large inquests and inquiries, which are often under considerable media scrutiny. He also routinely represents participants in inquests involving clinical negligence. **Strengths:** "He comes up with novel ideas, provides a realistic and sensible evaluation of cases and deals with difficult clients well. He just navigates the course through." "Great on his feet, thinks quickly, sharp as a razor and very articulate." **Recent work:** Served as counsel to the Coroner at the inquest into the Birmingham pub bombings in 1974, which resulted in the deaths of 21 people.

Owain Thomas QC Regularly appears in high-profile inquests as part of his broader clinical negligence and professional discipline focused practice. He is often instructed by healthcare providers, prisons and other public bodies. **Strengths:** "He's great, incredibly clever and gets amazing results. He gets right to the heart of problems, is very insightful and offers good legal analysis." "He is super bright and his attention to detail is incredible." "He gives very well thought out, honest views of cases and grasps the medical facts with ease."

JUNIORS

Matthew Hill Has extensive experience of acting as counsel to inquiries or inquests, and is also recognised for his adept representation of implicated state agents. His significant expertise in public law matters complements his flourishing practice, and he is particularly highly praised for his ability to marshal large amounts of information. **Strengths:** "He is intellectually one of the most able people practising at the Bar. Where he is particularly strong is mastering a lot of difficult facts and concepts. He offers a unique perspective." "Extremely intelligent, very hard-working, an incredible eye for detail and an extremely capable advocate, even in the most complex cases." **Recent work:** Served as First Junior Counsel to the Coroner, Sir John Goldring, in the new inquests into the deaths of 96 people at Hillsborough.

Neil Sheldon Predominantly acts in public inquiries on behalf of state agents and routinely serves as counsel to the inquiry. His experience includes proceedings arising from national security and armed conflicts, prison deaths and institutional negligence. **Strengths:** "A good advocate with very good people skills." "He is just completely in control of the brief. He is very, very calm under fire and a very reassuring presence, judges love him." "Incredibly approachable, he really goes above and beyond. His advice is always easy to follow and he is particularly brilliant with difficult clients and sensitive matters. An all-round pleasure to work with." **Recent work:** Represented the Home Secretary in an inquest into the death by poisoning of former Russian spy Alexander Litvinenko.

Christopher Mellor Habitually represents NHS Trusts, healthcare professionals and other participants in complex inquests. He specialises in proceedings arising from deaths occurring in mental heath institutions. **Strengths:** "Extraordinary skill in managing difficult clients." "Always on top of all the detail, he is incredibly diligent in his role."

Band 2

Doughty Street Chambers

See profile on p.828

THE SET

Doughty Street Chambers remains dedicated to representing bereaved families in inquests and public inquiries. The set also receives praise for the quality of its barristers – "the advocates there are totally reliable, easy to get hold of and highly responsive." Its members are particularly strong in Article 2 proceedings which involve deaths in police custody, prisons and hospitals, including mental health institutions. The set demonstrates further strength in public law cases relating to inquests, such as applications for funding and challenges against coronial decisions. Sources comment: "Of the sets that represent bereaved families, they are the most impressive in terms of quality."

Client service: "The clerks are always helpful, they make the effort to get to know you and do their best to resolve any problems in good time. They are clear in their communications, kind-spirited and helpful." "Always prompt in their responses, the clerks really go the extra mile for you." Richard Bayliss leads the clerking team.

SILKS

Henrietta Hill QC Appears on behalf of bereaved families and other participants in high-profile inquests and inquiries scrutinising the actions and omissions of the state. She also offers expert advice to clients who are seeking to obtain an inquiry or inquest. **Strengths:** "Phenomenally well organised, bright and very, very engaging." "Her written work is outstanding." **Recent work:** Acted in an inquest representing Hermitage Capital, the victim of a USD230 million fraud which whistle-blower Alexander Perepilichny exposed shortly before he died in suspicious circumstances.

Patrick O'Connor QC Specialises in the representation of bereaved families in inquests, including Article 2 proceedings, which arise from deaths in prisons and police custody. He has also appeared in complex inquiries involving miscarriages of justice and the state's actions during armed conflicts. **Strengths:** "Wonderfully experienced, persistent and determined."

Heather Williams QC Draws on her substantial expertise in police law to represent bereaved families and victims of alleged misconduct in inquests and inquiries. She also provides expert advice and representation to clients in related civil proceedings. **Strengths:** "An impressively clever lawyer. She has a really acute mind for new legal points and produces wonderful written advocacy." **Recent work:** Represented one of the bereaved families in the inquest into the Hillsborough Stadium disaster, raising specific issues about policing errors.

JUNIORS

Adam Straw Has a strong track record of being instructed in major, high-profile inquests and inquiries, typically on behalf of bereaved families. He receives considerable praise for his legal knowledge and admirable work ethic. **Strengths:** "Hard-working and cerebral, he is in high demand because he's so good to work with." "Bright and wonderfully knowledgeable." **Recent work:** Represented Neville Lawrence, the father of Stephen Lawrence, in the Undercover Policing Inquiry chaired by Sir Christopher Pitchford. He was also instrumental in challenging the initial timetable which delayed the inquiry until 2020, instead securing a 2015 start date.

Caoilfhionn Gallagher (see p.649) Frequently appears for bereaved families in significant inquests which are often at the centre of broader social justice campaigns. She is particularly proficient in proceedings which scrutinise the adequacy of police investigations. **Strengths:** "Incredibly bright, intelligent, very good tactically and superb in writing. She is on the ball, organised and detailed." "A formidable advocate, she is very creative in terms of how to assist clients, incredibly determined and exceptionally bright. She understands the wider issues around a case and is clearly very committed to her clients." **Recent work:** Represented the family of Joseph Lawton, who committed suicide while in police custody, in an inquest into his death. Central to the inquest was the law governing the treatment of 17 year olds in police custody and specific failings by Greater Manchester Police.

Kate Beattie Recently joined Doughty Street Chambers, where she maintains her focus on inquests and public inquiries. Her wide-reaching expertise includes proceedings arising in the healthcare setting and the criminal justice system. **Strengths:** "Knowledgeable, empathetic, loved by clients and a pleasure to work with." "A very creative thinker." **Recent work:** Served as junior counsel to the Dame Janet Smith Review, which was established by the BBC to conduct an impartial, thorough and independent review of the culture and practices of the organisation during Jimmy Savile's tenure.

Jude Bunting Has wide-reaching experience which includes inquests arising from deaths in prison, deaths in police custody and proceedings arising from the Troubles in Northern Ireland. His deep expertise in public and administrative law means he is well placed to advise on judicial reviews concerning coronial decisions. **Strengths:** "An extremely tenacious and clever advocate." **Recent work:** Represented the family of Robert Richards in an inquest into his death by hanging while an inmate in Wandsworth Prison. Possible systemic failures of the prison were scrutinised due to its exceptionally high incidence of prisoner deaths.

Alison Gerry Brings her deep expertise in human rights law to bear on her inquests practice. She typically acts in Article 2 proceedings which involve deaths in prisons, police custody and mental heath institutions. **Strengths:** "Incredibly well prepared, she gets down to the important issues quickly, is very businesslike, highly competent and an effective cross-examiner of witnesses." "Very experienced, kind and good to work with. She will go the extra mile and is excellent with clients and families." **Recent work:** Represented the family of a woman who died following an overdose while undergoing mental health treatment.

Jesse Nicholls Extremely well regarded for his detailed knowledge of inquests. He frequently acts on behalf of bereaved families in high-profile inquests, including Article 2 proceedings. He is also routinely instructed by families and NGOs in judicial reviews arising from inquests. **Strengths:** "Has an exceptional command of the law and drafts phenomenal legal submissions. He has a huge capacity for completing exceptionally difficult work within a short amount of time, and getting it right." "Very junior to be as good an advocate as he is. He really knows and understands the nature of inquests law." "He has a really lovely manner with distressed clients and is a calm presence in court." **Recent work:** Appeared on behalf of the families of 77 victims in an inquest into the Hillsborough Stadium disaster.

5 Essex Court

See profile on p.834

THE SET

5 Essex Court is a go-to set for police forces involved in inquests and inquiries. Its highly skilled members are also routinely instructed by coroners, public and private prisons and other state agents. According to commentators, its barristers are "incredibly knowledgeable in the field and a real pleasure to work with." Several members of the set have recently been instructed in the inquest into the deaths of 96 fans in the Hillsborough Stadium disaster of 1989 and the Undercover Policing Inquiry being chaired by Sir Christopher Pitchford.

Client service: Mark Waller leads the clerking team, which "reliably provides exceptional service."

SILKS

Fiona Barton QC (see p.591) A strong choice for the representation of police constables who are facing significant exposure in controversial inquests and inquiries. A police law specialist, she offers expert advice on all aspects of police policy and operational issues. **Strengths:** "Very good command of the detail." "She has the capacity to deal with huge quantities of work and turn it around in a short timescale." **Recent work:** Instructed to act on behalf of the Chief Constable of South Yorkshire Police in the inquests into the deaths of 96 fans at the Hillsborough Stadium in 1989.

Jason Beer QC (see p.593) Established silk who habitually appears in highly publicised public inquiries and inquests. He demonstrates expertise across a broad range of areas, such as coronial law and issues concerning the operation of the criminal justice system. **Strengths:** "Produces very effective legal submissions, and he cross-examines with the panache of a top-flight criminal silk. Just a great all-rounder." "He has a fantastic capacity for hard work." "He handles difficult briefs wonderfully and has an extremely effective manner of advocacy. He makes the best of every point and has a great deal of experience as counsel to the inquiry." **Recent work:** Served as counsel to the Commissioner for Police of the Metropolis in the Independent Inquiry into Child Sexual Abuse chaired by Hon. Lowell Goddard.

Jeremy Johnson QC (see p.684) Applauded for his expertise in factually-complex inquests and public inquiries. He receives instructions from police forces, constables, commissioners and the IPCC. He also frequently advises on public law challenges against refusals to hold public inquiries. **Strengths:** "A brilliant academic mind, he knows all the arguments that can be raised to get the best result for clients. He has the respect of courts and is very calm when faced with difficult situations." "He is an extremely clever lawyer and a quality performer." **Recent work:** Represented the West Midlands Police in a renewed inquest into the Birmingham pub bombings in 1974.

Samantha Leek QC (see p.698) Typically acts for police and other state agents in emotionally-charged inquests and inquiries, including proceedings which arise from deaths abroad. She also frequently acts as counsel to the inquest. **Strengths:** "She has the ability to remain impartial and to manage process effectively in the most sensitive cases, which is a very great skill." "Incredibly charming, which is important with judges. She's also very tough: if she were representing you, you would be over the moon." **Recent work:** Appeared in the inquests investigating the death of 30 British nationals who were shot in a terrorist attack in Sousse, Tunisia, on 26 June 2015. Leek served as counsel to the inquests.

JUNIORS

Alison Hewitt (see p.670) Habitually represents police constables in inquests considering the adequacy of police responses. She has substantial experience in proceedings which invoke Article 2 of the ECHR. **Strengths:** "She has the right balance in making sure that her clients' interests are protected, but also facilitating the rights of families to the truth." "Extremely experienced and very knowledgeable about coronial law. She handles difficult briefs with tenacity without being too aggressive." **Recent work:** Represented the Chief Constable of Devon and Cornwall Constabulary in an inquest into the death of a vulnerable adult with serious mental health problems. Days prior to his death, the deceased had sought the help of the police and mental health services.

3 Raymond Buildings Barristers

See profile on p.904

THE SET

3 Raymond Buildings fields a large number of key barristers specialising in inquests and public inquiries. Solicitors value its "provision of quality advocates, from top to bottom." The set demonstrates particular strength in matters which overlap with professional misconduct or criminal law. It also caters to proceedings which involve health and safety, clinical negligence and road traffic accidents. Its esteemed members are habitually instructed by state agents, particularly police forces, as well as bereaved families. The advocates housed in chambers also routinely serve as counsel to inquests and inquiries. Recently, a particular case highlight has been the high-profile inquest, which was subsequently converted into an inquiry, into the death of ex-KGB agent Alexander Litvinenko.

Client service: "The clerks reliably provide a good service and are always helpful." Head clerk Eddie Holland "is brilliant. He is not just efficient, which you would expect, but also incredibly nice. He has a wonderfully reassuring manner."

SILKS

Patrick Gibbs QC (see p.652) Has a strong track record of being instructed in the highest-profile inquests and inquiries, particularly where police conduct is under scrutiny. He routinely appears on behalf of all participants, including state agents and bereaved families. **Strengths:** "A wonderful advocate. He's phenomenally bright and a proper intellect. He also writes wonderfully well, his drafting is spot-on." "Offers excellent advice, is a brilliant advocate and has great client skills." **Recent work:** Served as lead advocate for the Investigative Committee of the Russian Federation at the inquiry into the death of Alexander Litvinenko, an ex-KGB agent.

Hugh Davies QC Highly popular choice for politically-charged inquests. He is particularly noted for his adroit representation of police forces in proceedings involving deaths in custody and deaths caused by firearms. His broad capabilities also regularly see him serving as counsel to inquests. **Strengths:** "He is extremely intelligent and his technical knowledge is first class. He is able to absorb huge amounts of detail and knows the case inside out before it's even started." **Recent work:** Represented a firearms officer who, as part of a pre-planned operation, shot dead an individual who was allegedly linked to organised crime. The proceedings were complicated by the possibility of the officer being charged with murder.

Richard Horwell QC Predominantly represents police forces in sensitive and politically-charged public inquiries. He also advises clients in the aftermath of inquiries, offering guidance through the Maxwellisation process and assisting with the implementation of recommended reforms. He is also highly experienced in inquests relating to self-inflicted deaths. **Strengths:** "He is a solid practitioner, thorough in his approach and very experienced." **Recent work:** Served as counsel to the Commissioner of the Metropolitan Police at the inquiry into the death of former KGB agent Alexander Litvinenko, who was poisoned by radioactive polonium-210.

Hugo Keith QC (see p.689) Habitually represents individuals, state agents and other participants in sensitive public inquiries and inquests, usually under considerable media attention. As a renowned criminal silk, he is a particularly popular choice for inquests which involve parallel criminal proceedings. **Strengths:** "A versatile, incredibly bright advocate who is very easy to work with." **Recent work:** Represented the Metropolitan Police Service in an inquest into the death of Mark Duggan, whose shooting by an armed police officer was one of the causes of the London riots of 2011.

JUNIORS

Clair Dobbin (see p.634) Frequently instructed to represent the most exposed parties in high-profile public inquiries and inquests. Her practice has a particular emphasis on inquests relating to prison and police custody deaths. She is also adept at appearing in related civil and professional misconduct proceedings. **Strengths:** "She has a breadth of experience that belies her year of call. Very supportive and approachable." "She is an effective advocate. She is calm and restrained but also knows when to go for the jugular." **Recent work:** Appointed by the Independent Inquiry into Child Sexual Abuse to lead three of its high-profile investigations into children's homes in Lambeth, Nottinghamshire and the Rochdale area.

Matthew Butt (see p.608) Respected practitioner with a wide-ranging inquests and inquiries practice. He demonstrates notable strength in proceedings concerning police conduct, clinical negligence and education, and specialises particularly in the representation of Silver Commanders in inquests relating to police firearms use. **Strengths:** "Thorough in court, he is always precise and careful and considers every angle in advance." "He is noted for his forensic and careful questioning, and has a wonderfully calm manner." "He is a very impressive and able advocate who is also highly likeable." **Recent work:** Instructed on behalf of two police officers in the inquest into the death of Philmore Leonard Mills, an individual who died in hospital after being restrained.

Saba Naqshbandi Considerable experience representing police forces in factually-complex inquests and public inquiries. She is also noted for her expertise in proceedings which involve health and safety, and is particularly good on fire safety related matters. **Strengths:** "Brilliantly friendly with clients and solicitors, but she also has a very strategic mind and an excellent grasp of the law." "Her attention to detail is second to none." "She is very professional and always presents really well." **Recent work:** Instructed by the Metropolitan Police Service from an early stage in the high-profile inquest, which has since been converted into a public inquiry, concerning the death of Alexander Litvinenko.

Neil Saunders (see p.759) Held in high regard for his adroit representation of bereaved families in complex inquests and inquiries. He is also adept at advising both institutions and individuals on the procedure surrounding inquests. **Strengths:** "He achieves fantastic results. A very nice person to deal with and very straightforward in his approach." **Recent work:** Advised the family of a man who died as the result of a road traffic accident, offering advice throughout the subsequent police investigation and the coronial process.

Band 3

Garden Court Chambers

See profile on p.851

THE SET

Garden Court Chambers is noted for its expert representation of bereaved families in a broad range of inquests, including proceedings brought under Article 2 of the ECHR. The set is a particularly popular choice for inquests concerning the operation of the criminal justice system and police shootings, as demonstrated by its members' recent appearances in the inquests into the deaths of both Mark Duggan and Azelle Rodney. Several of the set's advocates have also been involved in the inquest into the deaths of 96 football fans in the 1989 Hillsborough Stadium disaster. Market sources comment that the barristers at Garden Court are "brilliant, able to deftly handle bereaved clients and extremely knowledgeable."

Client service: "The clerks have been excellent, quick to respond and very flexible." The "helpful, humorous and responsive" Phil Bampfylde leads the clerking team.

SILKS

Leslie Thomas QC Strong track record representing bereaved families in highly contentious inquests, including Article 2 proceedings. He has particular expertise in inquests which concern police conduct, such as deaths by police restraint and police shootings. **Strengths:** "A renowned expert on the law in this area. He fights extremely hard for the interests of families." **Recent work:** Secured a verdict of unlawful killing for the family of two children who died while on a Thomas Cook holiday having been overcome by fumes from a faulty boiler.

Dexter Dias QC Predominantly instructed in inquests arising in the criminal justice setting, including deaths in prisons and deaths resulting from police conduct. He routinely receives instructions from bereaved families and NGOs. **Recent work:** Represented the family of 17 year old Jake Hardy in an inquest into his death by hanging while in prison custody.

JUNIORS

Brenda Campbell Qualified to appear in inquests across England, Wales and Northern Ireland. She typically acts for bereaved families in matters involving police conduct and state collusion. **Strengths:** "Her advocacy is punchy, effective and well judged for the environment." "A really excellent cross-examiner." **Recent work:** Represented 14 of the bereaved families in the fresh inquests into the Hillsborough Stadium disaster.

Sean Horstead Represents bereaved families in highly publicised inquests. His expertise involves inquests into deaths resulting from police conduct and deaths in prison custody. **Strengths:** "Very pleasant, but underneath his charm he's very steely." **Recent work:** Represented the family of Arthur Cave in a highly publicised inquest into his death following a fall from cliffs in Brighton.

Kirsten Heaven Has extensive experience of appearing in inquests, and has a particular focus on Article 2 proceedings concerning individuals in the care of the state who commit suicide. She routinely appears in inquests in both England and Wales. **Strengths:** "A tenacious and formidable advocate." "An incredible jury advocate. She has a really good style which gets the jury on board." "Really creative in her approach and a thoughtful tactician." **Recent work:** Represented the family of a young girl in an inquest into her self-inflicted death following a rape allegation and failed prosecution, in which there had been multiple failures by social services, adult mental health services and the CPS.

Matrix Chambers

See profile on p.876

THE SET

Matrix Chambers houses a number of renowned barristers with considerable experience of appearing in public inquiries and inquests. Its esteemed advocates are regularly called upon to handle the most significant, high-profile cases, such as the recent Independent Inquiry into Child Sexual Abuse. Members are regularly instructed by state agents and bereaved families, and frequently appear as counsel to inquests and inquiries. The set's broader human rights offering makes it a particularly popular choice for matters which invoke Article 2 of the ECHR. Its wide-reaching expertise also encompasses proceedings involving deaths that occur abroad, such as in the context of armed conflict. Barristers at Matrix Chambers are notably well versed in public law claims related to inquests and inquiries.

Client service: "The clerks provide a really high level of service." Jason Housden leads the clerking team, which is praised for its "efficient, organised and welcoming approach."

SILKS

Ben Emmerson QC Highly esteemed barrister who is renowned for his experience appearing in major, high-profile inquiries. He is capable of representing core participants as well as acting as counsel to the inquiry. **Strengths:** "A very good strategic mind and a good understanding of what the inquiry is trying to achieve; he never gets lost in the detail." "A fearless advocate, he is very confident and direct." **Recent work:** Served as counsel to the Independent Inquiry into Child Sexual Abuse conducted by Hon. Lowell Goddard.

Danny Friedman QC Brings his considerable expertise in human rights law to bear on public inquiries and inquests, including proceedings under Article 2 ECHR. He is often instructed in judicial reviews arising in the course of inquests. **Strengths:** "Very impressive, he is a very professional practitioner who's good at seeing the big picture and very straightforward in his approach. A consummate professional and an extremely persuasive advocate." "Incredibly well prepared and he judges his cross-examinations perfectly." **Recent work:** Represented the mother of a soldier in an inquest into his death, which was caused by heat illness as a result of drill and physical exercise, an illegal form of military punishment.

Jonathan Glasson QC (see p.654) Experienced in a broad array of inquests and public inquiries, with a notable emphasis on matters involving an overlap with criminal law. His recent instructions have concerned police shooting, terrorism and armed conflict. **Strengths:** "Very charming, knowledgeable and pleasant to work with." "Excellent courtroom advocacy." "An in-depth knowledge of the subject area." **Recent work:** Represented the UK government in the inquests into the deaths of Captain Tom Sawyer and Corporal Danny Winter, who died as a result of friendly fire while on an operation to clear a known Taliban stronghold.

Serjeants' Inn Chambers

See profile on p.907

THE SET

Serjeants' Inn Chambers offers expertise in a broad range of public inquiries and inquests, and has a notable emphasis on those relating to the healthcare sector. Its members routinely represent bereaved families, healthcare professionals, NHS trusts, local authorities and other state agents in complex clinical negligence inquests, including proceedings invoking Article 2. The set is also well known for its adept representation of police officers in inquests. Recently, members have acted in the inquests into the death of 96 fans in the Hillsborough Stadium disaster, as well as the inquest into the death of Private Cheryl James at the Deepcut Army Barracks in 1995.

Client service: "Approachable, amenable and quick at responding." "Very professional and organised, but also personable." Senior clerk Lee Johnson leads the clerking team, and is described by clients as "lovely, down-to-earth and highly efficient."

SILKS

John Beggs QC (see p.594) Standout silk who typically acts for police forces facing considerable scrutiny in highly publicised inquests. He habitually advises on the adequacy of police investigations, as well as deaths resulting from actions or omissions made by the police. **Strengths:** "He is an absolutely tireless fighter for his clients' interests, and a fearless advocate." "His ability to digest cases and present all the key points succinctly is hugely impressive. His work ethic is exceptional, he always meets deadlines and responds to clients without delay." **Recent work:** Acted for Surrey Police in the fresh inquest into the death of Private Cheryl James at the Deepcut Army Barracks in 1995.

Robert Francis QC (see p.648) Has extensive experience of appearing in, and chairing, public inquiries. He is particularly adept at handling proceedings in the healthcare context. **Strengths:** "Highly competent, highly able and very experienced." **Recent work:** Chaired the Freedom to Speak Up Review, which was established by the government to consider whistle-blowing in the NHS.

Bridget Dolan QC (see p.635) Highly regarded advocate who regularly appears in complex inquests, including proceedings invoking Article 2 of the ECHR. In addition to her experience representing bereaved families and state agents, she frequently serves as counsel to the inquest. **Strengths:** "Absolutely excellent and incredibly clever, she knows how the coroner will approach a matter. She's very clear and precise, and has a good approach with witnesses. One of the best cross-examiners at the Bar." "Relates to families in a very caring and sensitive way. She's up to date with her legal knowledge, very approachable and professional at all times." **Recent work:** Served as counsel to the inquest into the death of Cheryl James, a soldier who was found at the Deepcut Barracks in Surrey with a single gunshot wound to her head.

JUNIORS

Briony Ballard (see p.588) Predominantly acts in inquests, including Article 2 proceedings, which involve clinical negligence. She routinely receives instructions from healthcare professionals, NHS Trusts and bereaved families. **Strengths:** "Substantial knowledge of inquests law and very approachable." "An amazing advocate, she is fiercely intelligent and gets right to the heart of the case." **Recent work:** Represented the family of a woman who committed suicide the day after she was discharged from a hospital that had been treating her for self-inflicted injuries.

Debra Powell (see p.741) A popular junior who is frequently instructed in inquests concerning clinical negligence. She habitually represents bereaved families, healthcare professionals, NHS trusts and other state agents. Her broad practice also sees her regularly appearing in public inquiries. **Strengths:** "Very effective counsel, she is stellar on inquests law. She is able to build a good rapport with bereaved families and to express legal matters in layman's terms."

Oliver Williamson (see p.797) Highly regarded junior counsel who regularly represents police officers, healthcare professionals and NHS trusts in a broad range of inquests. He receives considerable praise for his reasonable approach and sound judgement in highly controversial proceedings. **Strengths:** "Very impressive, he works hard at all hours, gives very careful consideration to documents and is a wonderful tactician. He is approachable, has a good eye for detail and thinks outside the box." "A lawyer with a nice manner and good judgement whose standard of cross-examination is excellent." **Recent work:** Represented three retired police superintendent match commanders at the fresh inquest into the Hillsborough Stadium disaster.

Temple Garden Chambers

See profile on p.919

THE SET

Temple Garden Chambers offers an impressive depth of expertise in the field of inquests and inquiries, and is especially strong in proceedings which arise in the context of national security. It frequently fields instructions from various government departments, including the Ministry of Defence, as well as regulators and other state agents. Several of the highly regarded practitioners housed in chambers also routinely appear as counsel to inquiries and inquests. Members are habitually instructed in the largest public inquiries taking place in the UK, including the recent Undercover Policing Inquiry and the Independent Jersey Care Inquiry. An additional area of focus for the set is inquests concerning health and safety, with a recent highlight being its instruction in the inquest into the Vauxhall helicopter crash.

Client service: Senior clerk Dean Norton's clerking team offers an "efficient, friendly and helpful service."

SILKS

Keith Morton QC (see p.722) Highly regarded silk who frequently handles inquests involving regulatory and national security law. He receives instructions from state agents, including regulators, alongside private companies and bereaved families. **Strengths:** "A fantastic grasp of the law. He has a great jury manner and is a wonderful cross-examiner, which becomes immediately apparent." "A lovely manner in court. It is important in inquests not to be too combative, and he does it beautifully. The witnesses hardly realise they're being cross-examined given his deftness of touch." "He is thorough, bright, intelligent and a pleasure to work with." **Recent work:** Acted for the Civil Aviation Authority in a high-profile inquest into the death of a pilot and pedestrian in the Vauxhall helicopter crash.

Robin Tam QC Known for his broad practice, he represents a range of participants and routinely serves as counsel to the inquest or inquiry. He is frequently sought out by the UK government to appear in sensitive proceedings concerning national security. **Strengths:** "Very, very, very good on the law." "Very confident. An impressive performer. Very hard-working." **Recent work:** Served as counsel to the inquest, and later the inquiry, into the death by poisoning of former Russian spy Alexander Litvinenko.

Andrew O'Connor QC Incredibly knowledgeable about inquests and public inquiries. He typically acts on behalf of state agents in highly publicised inquests of national and international significance. He is also adept at advising coroners when serving as counsel to the inquest or inquiry. **Strengths:** "Very experienced, he has a good grasp of the detail and is very easy to work with." "Very clever and a brilliant advocate. He understands incredibly complex issues which arise in inquiries and can cope with difficult, sensitive matters with seeming ease." **Recent work:** Instructed to act for the National Crime Agency in the Undercover Policing Inquiry being led by Lord Justice Pitchford.

Cathryn McGahey QC Routinely instructed as counsel to large public inquiries, she also demonstrates great aptitude when appearing on behalf of participants. She is a skilled representative of state agents in inquests, and has a particular focus on proceedings involving deaths in custody. **Strengths:** "She is exceptionally bright and an excellent advocate." "A really nice manner when conducting proceedings, which is ideal for harrowing inquiries." "She is a master at acting for an inquiry and managing a large case." "Extremely deft witness-handling, she is very astute, strategically minded and calm in court." **Recent work:** Served as counsel to the Independent Jersey Care Inquiry chaired by Frances Oldham QC. This was an investigation of alleged abuse and a possible cover-up by senior politicians, lawyers and police officers.

JUNIORS

Nicholas Moss Extremely well-regarded junior who is frequently instructed in complex inquests by government departments, including the Ministry of Defence. He demonstrates noteworthy aptitude in proceedings involving national security. **Strengths:** "Tremendous intellect." "A delight to watch in court. He is so well prepared he has everything at his fingertips. The submissions are beautifully pitched and persuasive and he has wonderful court etiquette." "A very smooth, persuasive style. He deals with complex matters with great clarity. His forensic examination of expert witnesses is absolutely exceptional." **Recent work:** Instructed to represent the Ministry of Defence in the second inquest into the death of Private Cheryl James, the second of four deaths that occurred at the Deepcut Army Barracks between 1995 and 2002.

Other Ranked Lawyers

Scott Matthewson (42 Bedford Row) Focuses predominantly on representing private contractors in inquests arising from deaths in prisons. He is also adept at inquest proceedings which involve clinical negligence. **Strengths:** "Superb. He has a brain the size of a planet." "A highly effective cross-examiner." "Really good judgement." **Recent work:** Represented G4S in an inquest into the death of Gary Douglass, an individual who attempted to behead two students and disembowel himself with a samurai sword. Despite having undergone life-saving surgery, he later died in prison from internal bleeding.

James Eadie QC (Blackstone Chambers) In his capacity as First Treasury Counsel, he regularly advises the UK government on complex legal issues which arise in the course of inquests and public inquiries. He also appears in public law claims that shape the boundaries of the law on inquests and inquiries. **Strengths:** "He is probably the best advocate at the Bar." "He can digest and master briefs in astronomically short amounts of time and presents cases in court better than anyone."

Simon Antrobus (see p.584) (Crown Office Chambers) Specialises in inquests which involve an overlap with health and safety law. He typically acts on behalf of commercial clients in inquests and in any related health and safety prosecutions. **Strengths:** "Great ability to quickly absorb huge quantities of information and use it to best effect. He is very persuasive in his arguments and has a very good client manner." "Attentive on the detail and extremely well prepared." **Recent work:** Acted for BP in the two-month inquest into the terrorist attack at BP's In Amenas oil refinery in Algeria.

Sophie Cartwright (see p.612) (Deans Court Chambers) Revered for her knowledge of coronial law. She frequently acts for interested parties, coroners and NGOs in inquests and judicial reviews which determine the boundaries of coronial law. **Strengths:** "Encyclopaedic knowledge of the law, sound judgement and extremely good at dealing with people." **Recent work:** Served as counsel to the inquest into the death of two employees of G4S in Iraq who were shot by their colleague, an individual who had been deployed without proper criminal and health checks.

Eleanor Grey QC (39 Essex Chambers) Brings her considerable expertise in healthcare law to bear on her impressive work in public inquiries and independent reviews. She remains a popular choice for major, high-profile cases given her stellar reputation. **Strengths:** "A highly sensitive advocate who is wonderfully thorough." **Recent work:** Chaired the Independent Review of Children's Cardiac Care in Bristol.

Jenni Richards QC (see p.751) (39 Essex Chambers) Renowned public law and human rights expert, she wins extensive praise for her expertise in inquiries and inquests concerning ill-treatment and fatalities. She remains a popular choice for public bodies and families in inquests. **Strengths:** "Intellectually fantastic. Her ability to move through complex issues and documents is phenomenal. She is a wonderful advocate who can handle high-profile, complex and sensitive cases really well." **Recent work:** Represented the Yorkshire Ambulance Service at the inquest into the deaths of 96 people following the Hillsborough Stadium disaster.

Richard Lissack QC (see p.702) (Fountain Court Chambers) Offers experience across a broad range of inquests and public inquiries. He has appeared in diverse proceedings concerning areas such as clinical negligence, health and safety and financial services. **Strengths:** "Brilliant, incisive and intelligent. He gets to the point quickly and is excellent in court, a very impressive advocate." "Very calm and has a good way with clients. Really user-friendly and good to work with."

Pete Weatherby QC (Garden Court North) Committed to representing bereaved families in high-profile inquests. He is also adept at judicial reviews involving coronial law. **Strengths:** "Measured as an advocate, which makes him popular with juries. He is a great leader and great lawyer." "Very good strategically." **Recent work:** Represented 20 families in the fresh inquests into the Hillsborough Stadium disaster.

Vincent Williams (see p.797) (9 Gough Square) Typically acts for bereaved families in inquests concerning clinical negligence, criminal justice and health and safety. He also represents state agents, such as police commissioners. **Strengths:** "Very calm and measured. Well thought out advice and he's absolutely at home in the Coroner's Court." "Really good with clients and very sensitive." "A fair minded barrister and a good advocate." **Recent work:** Instructed on behalf of a bereaved family in an inquest concerning the failure of a hospital to recognise a serious cardiac condition in a ten month old child.

Jonathan Laidlaw QC (see p.694) (2 Hare Court) Experienced criminal and regulatory silk who is frequently instructed in significant inquests and public inquiries. He has considerable experience of inquests involving health and safety. **Strengths:** "Enormous deftness of touch and skill in questioning." "Great client care and amazing gravitas. He is very good on his feet and very good in conference." **Recent work:** Acted for Hugo Boss in a highly publicised inquest into the death of a four year old child who was crushed by a falling mirror at its Bicester Village store.

Alexandra Tampakopoulos (see p.778) (2 Hare Court) Highly sought after for complex inquests and inquiries, often involving an international aspect. She is also noted for her expertise in health and safety inquests. **Strengths:** "A good and steady advocate and excellent to work with." "Very good client-relationship skills. She is also very intelligent, sympathetic and compassionate." **Recent work:** Instructed as counsel to the Independent Inquiry into Child Sexual Abuse, which is investigating whether public bodies and other non-state institutions failed to protect children from sexual abuse in England and Wales.

Nigel Giffin QC (see p.653) (11KBW) Well known for his wide-ranging practice, which includes considerable experience of inquests and public inquiries. He routinely acts on behalf of core participants and regularly appears as counsel to inquiries. **Strengths:** "Great attention to detail and good judgement." "A joy to work with. He is incisive, hard-working, completely on top of the law, personable, a team player and a great advocate on his feet." **Recent work:** Represented the Church of England in the Independent Inquiry into Child Sexual Abuse being chaired by Justice Goddard.

Melanie Cumberland (6KBW College Hill) Appears in significant public inquiries and inquests involving national security and international relations. She typically acts for the UK government and other state agents. **Strengths:**"Phenomenally hard-working and diligent." "A real attention to detail and ability to collate information in a very clear, intelligent way." **Recent work:** Instructed by the Secretary of State for the Home Department in the public inquiry into the death of former KGB agent Alexander Litvinenko.

Michael Mansfield QC (Mansfield Chambers) Respected advocate who represents bereaved families in highly publicised and sensitive inquests. He is particularly experienced in inquests which concern police conduct, including police shootings. **Strengths:** "He was a very impressive cross-examiner. Very well judged, pretty tough and robust. Effective, thorough, incisive and low-key advocacy." **Recent work:** Represented the families of 74 victims of the Hillsborough Stadium disaster.

Paul Greaney QC (New Park Court Chambers) Brings his in-depth knowledge of criminal law to the inquests sphere. He receives considerable praise for his superb cross-examination and advocacy skills. **Strengths:** "He's absolutely brilliant, and has both excellent judgement and brilliant natural authority, as well as great questioning skills." "He put the client's case forward in a crystal-clear way. A very, very effective cross-examiner and a very good lawyer all round." **Recent work:** Represented the rank and file officers of the Police Federation at the Hillsborough inquests.

Samuel Green QC (New Park Court Chambers) Well known for his broad practice, which includes inquests arising in the criminal and regulatory sphere. He is particularly adept at inquests involving police conduct. **Strengths:** "He is a great advocate: fair, sensible and reasonable." **Recent work:** Appeared in the inquest into the Hillsborough Stadium disaster on behalf of the rank and file officers of the Police Federation.

Jonathan Hough QC (see p.675) (4 New Square) Recommended for his phenomenally deep knowledge of coronial law. He offers expert advice to coroners on all aspects of inquests and is regularly called upon to handle the most high-profile cases. **Strengths:** "He is the oracle for inquest work, he is just brilliant. His written submissions are particularly strong, they are so well formulated that they become almost unanswerable. His preparation is meticulous, he thinks like a judge." **Recent work:** Served as counsel to the inquiry in the inquests into the Hillsborough Stadium disaster chaired by coroner Lord Justice Goldring.

Michael Uberoi (Outer Temple Chambers) Extensive experience of large public inquiries involving criminal justice, healthcare and financial services. He often represents the UK government in legacy inquiries related to the Northern Ireland Troubles. **Strengths:** "Exceptionally good. Very, very hard-working, incredibly incise, lots of panache and confidence. A really good advocate." **Recent work:** Represented a consultant paediatric anaesthetist in a public inquiry established by the Secretary of State to investigate a number of paediatric deaths in the Royal Belfast Hospital which involved hyponatraemia.

Nicholas Griffin QC (see p.660) (QEB Hollis Whiteman) Regularly involved in significant public inquiries on behalf of participants and as counsel to the inquiry. He has also appeared as an expert witness in major public inquiries. **Strengths:** "Great intelligence, integrity and commitment. He brings an astute, tactical approach to problems as well as a determination to solve them." "A fantastic advocate. He is fluent, charming and persuasive." **Recent work:** Instructed as counsel to the public inquiry chaired by Hon. Lowell Goddard investigating the extent to which institutions have failed to protect children from sexual abuse.

Tom Kark QC (see p.688) (QEB Hollis Whiteman) Appears in a wide array of public inquiries and inquests. His recent instructions involve healthcare regulation as well as health and safety. **Strengths:** "Very thorough in his preparation, he is a supremely hard worker." "A reasonable and sensible advocate." **Recent work:** Served as counsel to the Mid Staffordshire NHS Foundation Trust Public Inquiry, which was commissioned by the Secretary of State for Health and chaired by Robert Francis QC.

Rory Phillips QC (3 Verulam Buildings) Extensive experience of large public inquiries and investigations. His recent instructions have concerned areas such as press regulation, financial services and national security. **Strengths:** "A huge brain and an amazing ability to deal with vast amounts of information at top speed." "A highly persuasive advocate." **Recent work:** Advised the Ecclesiastical Insurance Office in relation to the Goddard Inquiry's investigation into the Anglican Church.

INSURANCE: An Introduction

Contributed by 7 King's Bench Walk

This year has been dominated by the pending impact of the Insurance Act 2015 and the Enterprise Act 2016 on insurance law. The 2015 Act enters into force in August 2016 and the 2016 Act enters into force in May 2017. This legislation occupies the thoughts of many legal practitioners and many professionals in the market, because while it solves some problems, it involves issues and uncertainties which will require clarification before the Court.

The new legislation is introduced against the background of the steady beat of insurance and reinsurance litigation across all markets and products. Natural disasters, crime, computer fraud, economic sanctions, financial losses, corporate liabilities, business interruption and property damage are only a few of the causes giving rise to very substantial losses and very substantial insurance claims. Marine, energy, financial institutions, professional indemnity, global liability, commercial property and consumer insurance policies are the protections designed to deal with these problems.

The Insurance Bar continues to deal with a broad range of insurance and reinsurance disputes. The choice of London as a forum for these disputes and the choice of English law remain prevalent, reflecting the depth of expertise and experience of the Insurance Bar. Its practice is not limited to coverage disputes under insurance and reinsurance policies, but also extends to subrogated proceedings and defence of claims, and claims against other insurance professionals, such as brokers.

Insurance litigation encompasses both marine and non-marine insurance. There have been a number of notable marine insurance disputes over the past year. Hull claims, including total loss claims, continue to dominate (including *The Renos*, *The Galatea*, and *The Brillante Virtuoso*). The Court of Appeal has heard a number of marine insurance cases, including the interaction of liability insurances (P&I) and claims under direct action statutes (*The Yusuf Cepnioglu*) and the operation of a war risks policy (*The B Atlantic*). The Court of Appeal also clarified the law concerning the use of fraudulent devices in *VerslootDredging v Gerling*, and the result of an appeal to the Supreme Court, at the time of writing, is expected imminently.

There remains, as ever, a broad spectrum of non-marine insurance cases within the work of the Insurance Bar. There have been disputes concerning risk presentation (*Brit UW Ltd v F&B Trenchless Solutions Ltd, Mutual Energy Ltd v Starr Underwriting Agents Ltd*), cover under professional indemnity policies (*Arc Capital Partners Ltd v Brit UW Ltd, Ocean Finance & Mortgages Ltd v Oval Insurance Broking Ltd*), rectification of policies (*Equity Syndicate Management Ltd v GlaxoSmithKline plc*), employers' liability policies and asbestos-related illnesses (*Cape Distribution Ltd v Cape Intermediate Holdings Plc*). There have been significant decisions of the Court of Appeal dealing with cover under a property and business interruption insurance policy (*Milton Furniture Ltd v Brit Insurance Ltd*), cover under a professional indemnity policy (*AIG Europe Ltd v OC320301 LLP*), and motor insurance and subrogation (*Sobrany v UAB Transtira*). The Supreme Court has made an important ruling on damages available against the police for the London riots (*Mitsui Sumitomo Insurance Co (Europe) Ltd v Mayor's Office for Policing and Crime*).

In addition, there continues to be reinsurance litigation, arising out of issues of risk presentation (*AXA Versicherung AG v Arab Insurance Group (BSC)*, and policy interpretation (*Teal Assurance Co Ltd v WR Berkeley Insurance (Europe) Ltd*).

A large number of insurance and reinsurance disputes are resolved by means of arbitration. Very substantial claims under policies of liability and commercial property insurance, as well as treaty reinsurance claims and claims relating to the reinsurance of mass insurance products, continue to be dealt with by international arbitration under the aegis of most arbitral institutions (including LCIA, ICC, SIAC and HKIAC). Numerous claims are also dealt with by ad hoc arbitration. Arbitration, in particular international arbitration, has proved to be a popular choice of forum for insurance cases. This is an international practice in which the Insurance Bar continues to play a major part.

Many insurance disputes are commercial or international in character. There remain a large number of cases concerning consumer insurance claims, focusing mainly on motor insurance, personal injury claims and household policies. There have also been numerous small business claims under property, business interruption and professional indemnity policies. Indeed, professional indemnity claims both against insurers and insurance brokers continue to occupy the work of the Insurance Bar.

Most insurance and reinsurance disputes continue to be litigated in the Commercial Court. The Queen's Bench Division and the Technology and Construction Court continue to hand down decisions in insurance cases, with an emphasis on commercial property, liability, professional indemnity and consumer insurance policies. A number of appeals have been heard in the Supreme Court, Privy Council, and the Court of Appeal in insurance and reinsurance cases over the past year, with important legal developments being recorded in the process. When the Insurance Act 2015 and the Enterprise Act 2016 enter into force, it is anticipated that a number of provisions of this new legislation will have to be tested before the Courts.

Contents:

LONDON

Insurance
Leading Sets
Band 1
7 King's Bench Walk *
Band 2
Brick Court Chambers *
Essex Court Chambers *
Fountain Court Chambers *
Band 3
Devereux *
20 Essex Street *
4 New Square *
Band 4
Crown Office Chambers *
4 Pump Court *
2TG - 2 Temple Gardens *
3 Verulam Buildings *
* Indicates set / individual with profile.
[A] direct access (see p.24).
◊ (ORL) = Other Ranked Lawyer.
Alphabetical order within each band. Band 1 is highest.

Insurance
Leading Silks
Star individuals
Edelman Colin *Devereux* *
Band 1
Butcher Christopher *7 King's Bench Walk*
Crane Michael *Fountain Court Chambers* *
Edwards David *7 King's Bench Walk*
Foxton David *Essex Court Chambers*
Gaisman Jonathan *7 King's Bench Walk*
Kealey Gavin *7 King's Bench Walk*
Kendrick Dominic *7 King's Bench Walk*
Lockey John *Essex Court Chambers* *
Railton David *Fountain Court Chambers*
Schaff Alistair *7 King's Bench Walk*
Weitzman Tom *3 Verulam Buildings*
Band 2
Adam Tom *Brick Court Chambers*
Berry Steven *Essex Court Chambers*
Bryan Simon *Essex Court Chambers*
Calver Neil *Brick Court Chambers*
Cannon Mark *4 New Square* *
Christie Aidan *4 Pump Court* *
Edey Philip *20 Essex Street*
Eklund Graham *4 New Square* *
Elkington Ben *4 New Square* *
Goodall Patrick *Fountain Court Chambers* *
Hancock Christopher *20 Essex Street*
Healy Siobán *7 King's Bench Walk* *
Howard Mark *Brick Court Chambers*
Hunter Andrew *Blackstone Chambers (ORL)* ◊
Jacobs Richard *Essex Court Chambers*
MacDonald Eggers Peter *7 King's Bench Walk*
Moody Neil *2TG - 2 Temple Gardens* *
Moriarty Stephen *Fountain Court Chambers* *
Mulcahy Leigh-Ann *4 New Square* *
Neish Andrew *4 Pump Court* *
Reed Paul *Hardwicke (ORL)* ◊ [A]
Stanley Paul *Essex Court Chambers*
Thanki Bankim *Fountain Court Chambers* *
Band 3
Blackwood Andrew Guy *Quadrant Chambers (ORL)* ◊ *
Blanchard Claire *Essex Court Chambers*
Davies Helen *Brick Court Chambers*
Dougherty Charles *2TG - 2 Temple Gardens* *
Fenton Adam *7 King's Bench Walk*
Fenwick Justin *4 New Square* *
Green Andrew *Blackstone Chambers (ORL)* ◊
Hirst Jonathan *Brick Court Chambers*
Hofmeyr Stephen *7 King's Bench Walk*
Hough Jonathan *4 New Square* *
Howe Timothy *Fountain Court Chambers* *
Hubble Ben *4 New Square* *
Lord David W *Three Stone (ORL)* ◊
Masefield Roger *Brick Court Chambers* *
Matovu Harry *Brick Court Chambers* *
Palmer Howard *2TG - 2 Temple Gardens* *
Phillips Rory *3 Verulam Buildings*
Quiney Ben *Crown Office Chambers*
Rigney Andrew *Crown Office Chambers*
Sabben-Clare Rebecca *7 King's Bench Walk*
Salzedo Simon *Brick Court Chambers* *
Scorey David *Essex Court Chambers*
Smith Jamie *4 New Square* *
Stewart Roger *4 New Square* *
Tozzi Nigel *4 Pump Court* *
Wales Andrew *7 King's Bench Walk*
Waller Richard *7 King's Bench Walk*
Band 4
Ansell Rachel *4 Pump Court* *
Bailey David *7 King's Bench Walk*
Burns Andrew *Devereux* *
Cogley Stephen *XXIV Old Buildings (ORL)* ◊
Day Anneliese *4 New Square* *
Hext Neil *4 New Square*
Houseman Stephen *Essex Court Chambers*
Jones Nigel *Hardwicke (ORL)* ◊ [A]
Miller Andrew *2TG - 2 Temple Gardens* *
Mitchell Andrew *Fountain Court Chambers* *
Moger Christopher *4 Pump Court* *
Moore Martin *Erskine Chambers (ORL)* ◊ *
Moxon Browne Robert *2TG - 2 Temple Gardens* *
O'Sullivan Sean *4 Pump Court* *
Swainston Michael *Brick Court Chambers*
Webb Geraint *Henderson Chambers (ORL)* ◊ *

Band 1

7 King's Bench Walk

See profile on p.871

THE SET

A set that is "insurance top to bottom," 7KBW has a formidable offering of barristers who cover insurance disputes of all kinds and in virtually all sectors. Considered "the first port of call" for insurance, members are regularly instructed by parties from around the globe in matters of the utmost complexity and magnitude. Recent international cases have involved insurance losses arising from natural disasters in Asia and political upheaval in the Middle East. The set has also had significant involvement in major Bermuda Form arbitrations.

Client service: "We have a very close relationship with senior clerk Bernie Hyatt and the others. We trust them to know our preferences and we feel as though we can talk to them honestly about fees as well." "The clerks are always highly responsive and helpful."

SILKS

Christopher Butcher QC Leading insurance silk and an "incredibly impressive individual" who is widely praised for his understanding of the field and his great standing at the Bar. He is regularly involved in litigation and arbitrations concerning claims of the highest value. **Strengths:** "A total class act and one of the leading insurance and reinsurance coverage specialists. He has an exceptional intellect and total command of the insurance field." **Recent work:** Represented first-layer insurers in Single Buoy Mooring v Zurich, a USD800 million claim relating to the alleged total loss of an oil rig.

David Edwards QC An outstanding silk known for his forensic attention to detail and meticulous preparation. "A formidable advocate who is as good on his feet as he is on paper," he has an impressive international practice and notable expertise in New York law and Bermuda Form work. **Strengths:** "Undoubtedly one of the next generation of real stars. His insurance expertise is very broad, he is bright, very direct, meticulous and prepared to roll his sleeves up and get stuck into the detail."

Jonathan Gaisman QC A silk who is considered "one of the cleverest people at the Bar full-stop" and who receives numerous plaudits for the strength of his advocacy. He has extensive arbitration expertise, both as an advocate and as arbitrator, and is an expert in Bermuda Form work. **Strengths:** "Simply excellent. His advocacy is second to no one." "He's extraordinarily diligent and effective in dealing with any large and complex commercial dispute."

Gavin Kealey QC Highly regarded advocate and arbitrator who is head of chambers. In addition to his wealth of experience in insurance law and commercial disputes, he is lauded as a "very dynamic lawyer who is also fun to work with." **Strengths:** "Intellectually powerful, rigorous and fearless." "He is brilliant, extraordinarily disciplined in his thinking and someone who challenges others to raise their game and to think as clearly as they can."

Dominic Kendrick QC An "extremely user-friendly" silk who is also considered an "excellent insurance and commercial leader." He is well known for handling high-value commercial disputes, including prominent insurance litigation, arbitrations and appeals. **Strengths:** "Very good, very technical, and good at handling sophisticated legal points." "Somebody who gets to grips with issues very quickly, and who can take both an intuitive and analytical approach." **Recent work:** Instructed in an appeal of the 'Ocean Victory' case concerning the total loss of a vessel at a Japanese port.

Alistair Schaff QC Standout silk for both insurance and reinsurance disputes, who is also an undoubted leader in the field of international arbitration. As an arbitrator, he is described as "extremely methodical and very, very good." He has an extremely active practice and has argued cases in courts of the highest level in the UK and abroad. **Strengths:** "Possesses outstanding analytical and advocacy skills, and is a first choice for any complex reinsur-

Insurance
Leading Juniors
Band 1
Cutress James *Fountain Court Chambers* *
Lynch Ben *Fountain Court Chambers* *
Midwinter Stephen *Brick Court Chambers*
Padfield Alison *4 New Square* *
Ratcliffe Peter *3 Verulam Buildings*
Shapiro Daniel *Crown Office Chambers* *
Band 2
Brocklebank James *7 King's Bench Walk* *
Harrison Richard *Devereux* *
Kerr Simon *7 King's Bench Walk*
Khurshid Jawdat *7 King's Bench Walk*
Pliener David *Hardwicke (ORL)* ◊ 🄰
Band 3
Craig Nicholas *3 Verulam Buildings*
Holmes Michael *7 King's Bench Walk*
Kramer Adam *3 Verulam Buildings* *
MacDonald Alexander *7 King's Bench Walk*
Medd James *Crown Office Chambers*
Nolten Sonia *2TG - 2 Temple Gardens* *
Pilbrow Fionn *Brick Court Chambers*
Purchas James *4 Pump Court* *
Singla Tony *Brick Court Chambers* *
Sutherland Jessica *7 King's Bench Walk*
Band 4
Chalmers Suzanne *Crown Office Chambers*
Edwards Patricia *20 Essex Street*
Green Alison *2TG - 2 Temple Gardens* 🄰 *
Parker Benjamin *7 King's Bench Walk*
Patel Shail *4 New Square*
Troman Carl *4 New Square* *
Up-and-coming individuals
Morcos Peter *4 New Square* *
Wright Harry *7 King's Bench Walk*
* *Indicates individual with profile.*
🄰 *direct access (see p.24).*
◊ *(ORL) = Other Ranked Lawyer.*
Alphabetical order within each band. Band 1 is highest.

ance dispute." "He's incredibly perceptive and a very shrewd tactician." **Recent work:** Represented insurers in a successful bid to avoid policy coverage for a superyacht due to the over-valuation of the vessel's true worth.

Siobán Healy QC (see p.668) Highly regarded for her work in the insurance industry, particularly when it comes to professional indemnity matters. She has strong experience in arbitrations and international disputes, and also acts in an advisory capacity for insurance companies on an ongoing basis. **Strengths:** "She's very good, very user-friendly and really good at going the extra mile." "Hard working, technically excellent, very responsive and easy to work with."

Peter MacDonald Eggers QC A "very user-friendly and commercial" silk who is a go-to for high-value matters. He is involved in a wide array of international insurance cases arising from complex issues such as piracy, trade sanctions, and natural disasters. **Strengths:** "Exceptionally knowledgeable and intelligent." "Always delivers a first-class work product. He is very user-friendly and provides commercial legal advice without sitting on the fence." **Recent work:** Acted for the shipbuilder and mortgagee bank in a case concerning the constructive total loss of the vessel 'Brillante Virtuoso', where a claim of USD85 million was being contested on the grounds of owner misconduct and breach of warranty.

Adam Fenton QC Known for his "enormous attention to detail" and strength in professional negligence as well as insurance. He acts as both advocate and arbitrator, often in cases relating to the financial sector. **Strengths:** "He is an excellent lawyer, who is very thoughtful and able to assist with the early resolution of matters."

Stephen Hofmeyr QC Recognised for his wide-ranging insurance expertise and strong track record in handling international insurance disputes arising from significant global crises. He is also noted for his prominence in marine insurance. **Strengths:** "Very cerebral and effective," "he is very good with clients and offers very good common sense analysis." One source comments: "When the going gets rough, bring in the Hof!"

Rebecca Sabben-Clare QC Has considerable insurance expertise and is "an excellent advocate who establishes a good rapport with the judge." Political and war risks, professional indemnity and reinsurance disputes form key components of her practice. **Strengths:** "She's got the complete package – she has a very good head on her, excellent judgement when it comes to running cases, and a very persuasive manner when dealing with the courts." **Recent work:** Instructed by Insurance Company of the State of Pennsylvania in a claim against Equitas concerning reinsurance liability.

Andrew Wales QC Takes on insurance work covering a range of different areas, including disputes in the pharmaceutical industry, major D&O claims and international cases involving political unrest. He is highly regarded for his intellect and for the fact that "he has all the detail at his fingertips." **Strengths:** "A very proactive and hard working QC, who is not afraid to roll his sleeves up." "Very thorough and extremely knowledgeable silk, who can clarify even the most complex point." **Recent work:** Represented the Romanian insurers of a Taiwanese cargo vessel that was lost in a typhoon off the coast of Vietnam. The case settled favourably.

Richard Waller QC Specialises in political risk cases but also handles a wider range of international insurance and reinsurance work, particularly disputes with a large element of fraud. Other recent instructions have included business interruption and property damage claims arising out of natural disasters. **Strengths:** "Has excellent analytical and advocacy skills and is very easy to work with. Richard is proactive and flexible and gets on well with clients." "He's very smart and very commercial."

David Bailey QC Handles a broad spectrum of insurance work across numerous sectors, including shipping, transport and construction. He is experienced in all manner of dispute work and has significant arbitration expertise. **Strengths:** "Hard working and very thorough. He's a considered advocate who gets his message across through being restrained and measured." **Recent work:** Represented Hill Dickinson in Starlight v Allianz and others, a successful appeal regarding jurisdictional issues.

JUNIORS

James Brocklebank (see p.603) Handles insurance claims arising out of a wide range of commercial matters, with a particularly strong reputation in professional negligence cases and in the energy sector. **Strengths:** "He's got a very good style, he's very concise, he doesn't go on too long and he's got the ear of the judge." **Recent work:** Successfully defended OAMPS Special Risk against a multimillion-euro brokers, negligence claim concerning damage to the superyacht M.Y. 'Galatea'.

Simon Kerr Acts for both insurers and insureds in high-value cases, including Bermuda Form arbitrations. Handles claims arising out of underlying disputes in the energy, construction, shipping and commodities sectors, among others. **Strengths:** "He's great, very personable, very easy to get along with, very effective and good on his feet."

Jawdat Khurshid Tackles high-value, complex disputes in the insurance industry as part of a broader commercial practice. He is often engaged in arbitrations and his work has a significant international focus. **Strengths:** "Extremely user-friendly and a good tactician."

Michael Holmes Junior with a solid reputation in the market, particularly for reinsurance disputes, where he is a noted specialist. He is regularly involved in international arbitrations, particularly in the construction and energy sectors. **Strengths:** "Hugely knowledgeable, particularly in the reinsurance space, a terrific team player and a very engaging person who gets on very well with clients." "Very bright, with an encyclopaedic knowledge of insurance law." **Recent work:** Acted for AXA Versicherung AG in a case relating to a first-loss treaty which covered a book of energy construction risks.

Alexander MacDonald Has notable expertise in marine insurance as well as in claims arising out of financial crime and reinsurance disputes. As well as acting as an advocate in court and arbitration, he is also regularly instructed in an advisory capacity. **Strengths:** "Sensible, pragmatic and good with clients." **Recent work:** Represented primary and excess insurers in a constructive total loss claim concerning the YME MOPUster oil platform in the North Sea.

Jessica Sutherland Handles a broad insurance practice taking in brokers' negligence claims and reinsurance matters, in addition to coverage disputes. She has notable experience in Bermuda Form arbitrations. **Strengths:** "An exceptionally clever and able junior." "She's on top of the detail and willing to muck in." **Recent work:** Instructed by defendant brokers in a claim for alleged negligence when placing property damage cover.

Benjamin Parker Has significant involvement with insurance litigation and arbitration in domestic and international markets. **Strengths:** "A rising star and a class act. He has a superb grasp of detail, provides excellent advice and support quickly and efficiently and is, quite simply, a delight to work with." **Recent work:** Acted for shipowners in a Commercial Court case claiming total loss of a vessel in the Pacific Ocean due to fire.

Harry Wright Up-and-coming junior who "performs significantly above his year of call" and who has developed an impressive reputation for his knowledge of the 2015 Insurance Act, among other things. **Strengths:** "Intelligent, quick witted, hard working and a pleasure to work with." "Great with clients, very personable, very enthusiastic and really efficient."

Band 2

Brick Court Chambers

See profile on p.816

THE SET

Sophisticated commercial set that excels in handling disputes at the higher end of the insurance and reinsurance market. Has excellent strength in depth and the ability to take on big-ticket claims and esoteric points of insurance law with equal aplomb. The set's involvement in the Single Buoy Moorings case, valued at over £1 billion, showcases its prominence in truly top-drawer insurance matters. Additionally, members are instructed in all types of marine and non-marine insurance matters and can also collectively boast a broad range of other specialisms.

Client service: "The clerks, led by senior clerks Julian Hawes and Ian Moyler, are very good and very responsive. They will be very straight with you on both timing and cost."

SILKS

Tom Adam QC Undertakes substantial work in the insurance industry, and has been especially active in handling reinsurance disputes, particularly arbitrations. He has recently handled a number of insurance claims relating to the financial and construction sectors. **Strengths:** "His cross-examination is sublime and a joy to behold. Also, despite being diabolically bright, he is a good person to work with and helps get things done." "Gets stuck in and enthuses clients with his committed approach." **Recent work:** Acted in a property damage claim brought against insurer Starr regarding an undersea electricity cable running between Northern Ireland and Scotland.

Neil Calver QC An experienced insurance practitioner who is highly regarded for his arbitration and advocacy skills. He has considerable expertise in a range of areas and boasts a strong practice in the aviation and banking sectors. **Strengths:** "He is very commercial, very clever and can be relied upon to give advice on complex issues in a straightforward and uncomplicated manner. He is also very good with clients and good at assessing the merits of a case and coming up with tactical litigation strategies." **Recent work:** Represented Brit in a policy avoidance case relating to underground tunnelling works which led to a train derailment.

Mark Howard QC "A top-quality commercial leader with very good insurance experience," who is noted for his superior advocacy. His insurance work is consistently of high quality and value and draws on his strengths in numerous other commercial disciplines. **Strengths:** "Brilliant cross-examiner, who has the respect of the court – judges really listen to what he has to say." "A powerful, senior silk, who is the right man to turn to for the important occasion." **Recent work:** Represented Gard Marine in a USD130 million insurance claim for loss of vessel.

Helen Davies QC Joint head of chambers who is regarded highly for her advocacy skills and commercial acumen. Her insurance practice has a strong focus on international arbitration, and she takes on significant reinsurance and professional negligence cases. **Strengths:** "Phenomenally quick and incredibly impressive both in conference and as an advocate." "She is amazingly good – she's incredibly clever, great in court and has a really great client manner."

Harry Matovu QC (see p.709) Takes on a broad range of insurance work that includes cases in the London and Bermuda markets, and covers such diverse areas as credit insurance, political risk, aviation and professional indemnity. **Strengths:** "He is a total joy to work with, and his cross-examination is absolutely amazing. He can charm answers out of witnesses and decisions out of arbitrators."

Jonathan Hirst QC Vastly experienced silk who is also joint head of chambers. He is experienced in numerous areas, including shipping, banking, competition law and arbitration. High-value insurance and reinsurance cases form a key part of his commercial practice. **Strengths:** "A real heavyweight with whom it is easy to work." **Recent work:** Lead counsel to the International Oil Pollution Compensation Funds which sought immunity to a suit regarding incidents of pollution.

Simon Salzedo QC (see p.758) Well known for his ability as a commercial barrister and specialist in professional negligence. His practice has a significant focus on insurance work, particularly regarding marine, financial and political lines. **Strengths:** "He is highly intelligent and very sharp witted."

Roger Masefield QC (see p.708) Involved in a range of high-value insurance work that includes substantial claims arising out of natural disasters and offshore energy projects, as well as instances of broker's negligence. **Strengths:** "Hugely impressive: he punches above his weight and has real charisma." "He's very sensible and extremely diligent."

Michael Swainston QC Versatile commercial barrister who takes on significant international cases, and has experience in multiple jurisdictions, including Bermuda, Hong Kong, Dubai and Qatar. **Strengths:** "Unflappable both in court and with clients."

JUNIORS

Stephen Midwinter Extremely well-regarded junior known for his "really exceptional reinsurance brain." His practice involves a high degree of international focus, with cases often originating abroad, and he is particularly strong in the energy and banking spheres. **Strengths:** "A go-to junior with brilliant analytical capacity." "Hugely intelligent and able to cut straight to the key aspects of a matter. He has excellent turnaround times and is able to provide advice which hits the perfect level of detail and formality every time." **Recent work:** Acted for Single Buoy Moorings in a USD1 billion construction all risks claim in the Commercial Court.

Tony Singla (see p.766) Specialised in marine insurance and handles numerous cases dealing with damage and total loss of vessels. He also handles cases arising out of offshore energy and construction projects. **Strengths:** "An outstanding junior who is extremely responsive, very bright and very good on tactics." "He has an extremely impressive personality and exudes confidence." **Recent work:** Instructed by AXA in a multimillion-pound coverage dispute relating to the sinking of a yacht.

Fionn Pilbrow Continues to have a broad commercial practice featuring significant amounts of high-value insurance work. He also has additional expertise in fraud and international arbitration. **Strengths:** "Incredibly bright and an absolute pleasure to work with." **Recent work:** Acted for System 2 Security and the owners of the Grand Pier at Weston-super-Mare in an insurance claim resulting from the total destruction of the pier's pavilion in 2008.

Essex Court Chambers

See profile on p.836

THE SET

Essex Court Chambers is engaged in insurance and reinsurance work to an extremely high level in multiple jurisdictions around the world, and demonstrates exceptional capability when handling international arbitrations. The set boasts "a number of very impressive insurance lawyers," particularly in silk, and has some of the field's foremost experts in Bermuda Form cases. Major instructions typically come from industries with global or cross-border concerns, such as the energy, mining and shipping sectors, although members are active on the full range of insurance claims.

Client service: "The clerking is absolutely first rate, the service they provide is brilliant. Senior clerk David Grief has been around a very long time and is right up there as one of the legends of clerking: he gets a similar standard out of the rest of his team." The extremely well-respected Joe Ferrigno is Grief's joint senior clerk and a popular figure among instructing solicitors.

SILKS

David Foxton QC Considered "a Rolls-Royce performer" widely acknowledged as a "brilliant" lawyer of outstanding intellect. He is a top-level commercial litigator and international arbitration expert of universal renown. **Strengths:** "He's got an immense breadth of knowledge and is a genuine intellectual." "He's incredibly easy to work with and very clear on what his opinion is and the reasons for having it."

John Lockey QC (see p.703) Known for the breadth of his international practice, particularly in Hong Kong, where he was recently involved in two significant insurance arbitrations. Instructing solicitors consider him a "wise and experienced insurance silk," who "always delivers a first-class service." **Strengths:** "Exceptionally constructive in his advice, he's very clever and knows insurance from top to bottom. He understands it both from a legal and practical point of view, is extremely responsive and always makes himself available when needed." **Recent work:** Represented a panel of insurers seeking to repudiate a D&O claim relating to a tax penalty.

Steven Berry QC A highly effective advocate who takes on a range of hefty commercial cases. He has significant experience in major insurance and reinsurance disputes. **Strengths:** "He's extremely no-nonsense and gets to the heart of the question quickly."

Simon Bryan QC Has considerable expertise in handling insurance cases relating to shipping and commodities disputes, and also regularly takes on complex reinsurance work in the energy sector. **Strengths:** "He's excellent, very user-friendly, very bright, hard working and an excellent advocate." **Recent work:** Successfully defended Arab Insurance Group in its Commercial Court claim against AXA for alleging attempted avoidance of energy reinsurance treaties.

Richard Jacobs QC Co-head of chambers who also has a significant and wide-ranging insurance practice. He is well versed in international arbitration, and known for his familiarity with the Bermuda Form in particular. **Strengths:** "As well as having excellent expertise, he is eminently approachable and a very good teamplayer. He is quite happy to roll his sleeves up and get involved not just with substantive elements of the case but also procedural aspects. He thinks outside the box and brings a fresh approach to the issue we are presented with."

Paul Stanley QC A silk known for being "one of the cleverest barristers at the Bar" and a "fount of knowledge" for cases involving the Bermuda Form, a subject on which he is a published expert. He is highly regarded for his skills as both advocate and arbitrator. **Strengths:** "He is just superb, is incredibly personable and is a very good advocate. He will be one of the standout insurance barristers in years to come." "He cuts through to the important issues in a case and keeps in mind the client's commercial drivers."

Claire Blanchard QC Very experienced commercial barrister who is known for taking on disputes in the marine insurance sector, as well as non-marine cases, including construction and energy arbitrations. **Strengths:** "Very impressive, extremely bright and very quick witted."

David Scorey QC A junior silk with a "very good insurance brain on him," who is building a strong reputation for Bermuda Form work. He also handles a wide range of other commercial insurance disputes, a number of which involve jurisdictional issues. **Strengths:** "He is our go-to junior silk for insurance. A rising star who is phenomenally good, he knows insurance well and is very good on his feet. He has an authority which eludes many silks senior to him."

Stephen Houseman QC Regularly involved in insurance and reinsurance disputes that arise out of the energy and mining industries. He is skilled at handling international cases with a multi-jurisdictional aspect or which otherwise involve foreign law. **Strengths:** "Extremely clever, but still down to earth and easy to work with." "He is very user-friendly, offers quick turnaround times and is commercial." **Recent work:** Defended a Barbados-based insurance provider against a claim by a private equity house. The equity house sought to recover due diligence costs after an unsuccessful bid to acquire managing agent Sagicor Europe and an associated Lloyd's syndicate.

Fountain Court Chambers

See profile on p.847

THE SET

A market-leading banking and commercial law set that is highly regarded for its commitment to the insurance sector. Members are regularly instructed in high-value cases arising out of the financial services industry but also generate substantial professional indemnity, property damage and product liability work. They further provide insurance expertise in niche sectors such as political risk, aviation and travel. Instructing solicitors particularly highlight the set's proficiency at highly technical matters.

Client service: "The clerks, led by Alex Taylor, are really helpful and efficient, and they know the courts inside-out."

SILKS

Michael Crane QC (see p.625) "An absolutely top insurance and reinsurance silk" who offers "premier-league quality and has a great manner." He is very well known for his expertise in aviation, product liability and pharmaceutical matters, and takes on an increasing number of cases as an arbitrator. **Strengths:** "He's exceptionally good at establishing an instant rapport with clients and understanding their key commercial objectives, whilst at the same time being an effective advocate." "Top of the tree for coverage advice, he is clear, authoritative and a pleasure to work with." **Recent work:** Acted for insurers in Mitsui Sumitomo v Mayor's Office of Police & Crime, a case concerning compensation claims against the Metropolitan Police for damages caused (and subsequent losses of rent and profits) at the Sony warehouse in Enfield during the London riots of 2011.

David Railton QC Silk known for his "top-level preparation and advocacy," who is involved in a wide variety of complex insurance cases. He has particular specialism in financial lines but also handles significant property damage and business interruption claims. **Strengths:** "He is meticulous in his planning, incredibly bright and is also a lovely man as well." "An excellent senior silk suited to the most complex cases."

Patrick Goodall QC (see p.656) Has a growing reputation for his work handling substantial insurance and reinsurance disputes. His practice is international in nature and he has handled a number of complex cross-border claims. **Strengths:** "He's dynamic, he's got energy and he's a good courtroom presence." "Very forceful and convincing on his feet."

Stephen Moriarty QC (see p.721) Respected insurance silk who is also head of chambers. Moriaty manages a strong domestic and international practice as an advocate and has also recently taken on the role of arbitrator in a number of high-value reinsurance disputes. **Strengths:** "Never fails to impress with his intellectual abilities when facing the obvious difficulties of the cases he deals with." "He is exceptionally bright, and once he takes you on, he is really committed and gives 100% to the client."

Bankim Thanki QC (see p.780) Deputy head of chambers particularly well known for taking on major insurance cases in the financial sector. **Strengths:** "He is just fantastic: tough, clever, smooth, he's the complete package." "A top-rate commercial lawyer." **Recent work:** Continued to represent Sequana SA in a very significant claim against BAT arising out of the contamination of the Fox River in Wisconsin.

Timothy Howe QC (see p.676) "A very sound advocate" who has an extremely broad commercial practice, which extends to an impressive array of international insurance disputes, particularly in the financial sector. **Strengths:** "He is certainly clever and a good advocate, but he is also approachable and very easy to work with." "Very good and very meticulous." **Recent work:** Represented Morgan Stanley in multimillion-pound credit risk claims against Mitsui Sumitomo that related to a failed commercial real estate project in the USA.

Andrew Mitchell QC (see p.719) Continues to advise on significant insurance cases, representing insurers, reinsurers and underwriters as well as brokers and policyholders. He offers particular insight into claims affecting the banking industry. **Strengths:** "Pragmatic, with excellent response times." "A good commercial barrister." **Recent work:** Represented QBE in a case testing an insured's right to claim on after-the-event insurance even though it was known to have committed VAT fraud.

JUNIORS

James Cutress (see p.628) An "extremely bright" junior who receives warm praise for his intelligence and work ethic. He is involved in a considerable range of insurance and reinsurance disputes, including Bermuda Form arbitrations. **Strengths:** "Very bright, responsive and someone with a good eye for detail." "An excellent, well-rounded individual who provides first-class service." **Recent work:** Instructed in a complex £1 million claim under an equine insurance policy.

Ben Lynch (see p.704) A leading junior who moved to Fountain Court from Devereux in October 2015. He enjoys an excellent reputation at the Bar for his work on highly complex coverage disputes and also writes and speaks extensively on insurance law. **Strengths:** "He is the junior I would go to with my next coverage dispute: he's very good on his feet and very, very bright." **Recent work:** Acted for the insurers in a high-value D&O insurance claim arising out of alleged fraud concerning two substantial Indian property schemes.

Band 3

Devereux

See profile on p.827

THE SET

A highly commercial set that can claim consistent involvement in sophisticated insurance and reinsurance disputes. He acts on behalf of a wide range of clients, including major insurers and reinsurers, as well as insurance brokers and banks. Its members are also known for their deep understanding of insurance law and regulation, and have recently provided key advice to the industry on the implementation of the 2015 Insurance Act.

Client service: "The clerks, led by Vince Plant, are terrific: they're really good, super responsive, and can never do enough."

SILKS

Colin Edelman QC (see p.639) Renowned leader at the Insurance Bar, described by one source as "the best barrister in the market by far" and by another as a "star performer, who raises the game for the entire set." He wins praise both for his strength as an advocate and as an arbitrator, and continues to be involved in insurance and reinsurance disputes of the highest order. **Strengths:** "The doyen of the insurance and reinsurance world, he has such excellent judgement and a real presence." "The biggest insurance brain at the Bar, but also such a kind and generous advocate." **Recent work:** Instructed in a dispute between shipowners and the underwriters of a hull and machinery insurance policy after the flooding of a vessel. The case involved the affirmation of the principle that otherwise valid insurance claims may be rendered void by the use of a 'fraudulent device' in the making of the claim.

Andrew Burns QC (see p.607) A silk who can claim a growing insurance practice that includes a strong focus on cases arising out of employer liability and professional negligence. **Strengths:** "He is knowledgeable, clever and a good advocate." "He's easy to work with and a safe pair of hands." **Recent work:** Advised Bar Mutual Indemnity Fund on insurance issues arising out of a professional negligence case relating to the settlement of a discrimination claim.

JUNIORS

Richard Harrison (see p.666) Senior junior whose practice entails handling a significant international caseload of highly complex insurance and reinsurance disputes. His deep involvement with the industry has led to him providing opinions on amendments to the 2015 Insurance Act. **Strengths:** "Simply superb. He gives clear, focused advice and is a pleasure to work with." "Extremely sensible, very commercial, very measured and easy to deal with, he knows his insurance and reinsurance inside and out." **Recent work:** Defended Enterprise Insurance against allegations of repudiation of a claims management agreement concerning 12,000 third-party insurance claims.

20 Essex Street

See profile on p.838

THE SET

Specialist marine and shipping set engaged in high-level insurance work in these sectors. Its members were recently instructed in a number of substantial claims concerning the damage, seizure and total loss of vessels. They are further experienced in a wide range of insurance cases beyond the shipping sector, and advise insurers, reinsurers and policyholders on coverage disputes, subrogated recoveries and Bermuda Form arbitrations. The set has been increasingly involved in handling cases that debate the construction and drafting of policies, particularly in the D&O space.

Client service: "They are very commercial in terms of fees, and eager to assist those instructing them." Neil Palmer is the senior clerk.

SILKS

Philip Edey QC Familiar with insurance claims across a broad range of business areas, and well regarded as "an extremely impressive and appealing advocate." He also acts in an advisory capacity and has a strong track record of representing clients in international arbitrations. **Strengths:** "A man to have on your side and someone who makes you feel you are his only client." "He has a very pleasant, effective manner and a formidable intellect."

Christopher Hancock QC Co-head of chambers and an experienced insurance silk who regularly takes on high-value and complex international claims. He was recently involved in several cases focusing on significant losses in the marine industry. **Strengths:** "Very able, very thorough and highly experienced. He's a really safe pair of hands." **Recent work:** Instructed on behalf of Legal Risk Solutions in a Commercial Court claim concerning the validity of an insurance policy when the assured's business practices faced allegations of fraud.

JUNIORS

Patricia Edwards Maintains a diverse commercial practice that takes instructions in high-value insurance cases, typically in the marine industry. **Strengths:** "She is very intelligent and very thorough when supporting a QC in a case." **Recent work:** Acted on behalf of the underwriters in the case of the vessel 'Brilliante Virtuoso', which was lost after a pirate attack in 2011.

4 New Square

See profile on p.880

THE SET

Although undoubted leaders in professional negligence, 4 New Square also marshals an impressive insurance offering, and has a strong bench of silks and juniors tackling high-value disputes in the area. As well as leading the way on matters regarding professional indemnity, members handle big-ticket construction and property damage claims, and also specialise in broker disputes. In addition to the quality of its barristers, the set receives glowing accolades for its "outward-looking, modern approach" and its focus on customer service.

Client service: "The clerks, led by Lizzy Stewart, are very helpful, friendly and accommodating. They are a strong team who offer very good service."

SILKS

Mark Cannon QC (see p.611) Renowned expert on professional indemnity, who has additional expertise in construction coverage disputes. His regularly undertakes highly complex cases, such as those involving multiple layers of insurance or aggregation issues. **Strengths:** "Bright, erudite and incisive." **Recent work:** Achieved a favourable result on behalf of Click Netherfield, who sought coverage for loss of goods after a fire at a warehouse in Qatar.

Graham Eklund QC (see p.640) Known for his involvement in substantial insurance disputes, not least those involving allegations of fraud or dishonesty. Instructing solicitors regard him as "someone you want on your side when something gets a bit knotty" and particularly praise his skill in handling expert witnesses on a case. **Strengths:** "He's absolutely superb and a pleasure to work with – a really, really sharp man." **Recent work:** Successfully assisted Equity Red Star in rectifying an insurance policy, thereby ensuring that the company was not liable for contributions sought by AXA in a motor insurance claim involving a hire car.

Ben Elkington QC (see p.640) Well-regarded silk who is known for being an insurance coverage specialist. He is instructed by both insurers and insureds on a regular basis, and has a notable focus on property damage cases, although he is well versed in all types of non-marine policies. **Strengths:** "He is one of those people who's got a brain the size of a planet." "He is assured, user-friendly and makes a real difference to the outcome of cases." **Recent work:** Represented Allianz as the insurer in a claim arising out of the confiscation of an aircraft in Brazil due to alleged failure to pay customs duties.

Leigh-Ann Mulcahy QC (see p.723) Boasts strong credentials in professional negligence and product liability. Her insurance work often originates in these areas, and she has key experience acting as an advocate, arbitrator and mediator. **Strengths:** "Very thorough, very concise and a formidable opponent." "One of the brightest young leaders around, who is well organised and always on top of a case. She cuts to the key issues and is also very approachable." **Recent work:** Appointed to advise National Grid on seeking indemnity from former employers' liability insurer Excess. The case concerned asbestos-related disease claims brought by employees.

Justin Fenwick QC (see p.644) Active in a wide range of insurance disputes, particularly professional negligence claims involving an element of dishonesty. Instructing solicitors and fellow barristers alike highlight him for his superb advocacy skills and describe him as a "fearsome cross-examiner." **Strengths:** "He is absolutely superb on the detail, especially with cases involving figures. He also has a sixth sense about issues of fraud and dishonesty." "He is unbelievably experienced; he's done so many trials that nothing fazes him." **Recent work:** Defended Cape against claims brought by insurers to recover settlements paid out in mesothelioma cases where Cape was the parent company to a manufacturer.

Jonathan Hough QC (see p.675) Takes on the full spectrum of coverage disputes, handling both litigation and arbitration cases, and is also regularly instructed in disputes between insurers and reinsurers. He receives strong praise for his advocacy skills and his ability to remain contactable despite his heavy workload. **Strengths:** "He provides careful, comprehensive advice in a very timely manner, is particularly responsive and works in a collaborative manner." "He just makes everything easy for you. You ask him something and you get chapter and verse action points – it's amazing." **Recent work:** Represented Motorplus, an underwriter of legal expenses insurance, in a £7.5 million claim brought against it by a law firm with which it had a referral arrangement.

Ben Hubble QC (see p.677) Respected professional negligence and insurance silk who is also head of chambers. His professional indemnity work features a strong element of cases concerning solicitors' firms as well as those with a financial regulatory aspect to them. **Strengths:** "Technically very proficient and also very approachable." "Pragmatic and commercial." **Recent work:** Acted for AIG in asserting that thousands of claims against a law firm should be aggregated as one claim under a professional indemnity policy.

Jamie Smith QC (see p.768) Since taking silk "he continues to go from strength to strength" handling a practice that combines professional negligence and insurance work. He enjoys an extremely positive reputation and is known for being personable, extremely hard working and very good on his feet. **Strengths:** "Even with an incredibly wide and busy caseload, he seems able to turn his attention to a case and make you feel like it's the only one he's dealing with. His work ethic is absolutely faultless, he is very personable to deal with and, as an advocate, you feel very safe in his hands." "He's so hard working, and the quality of his advice is superb." **Recent work:** Advised RSA on policy response when faced with a USD287 million fraud claim brought against one of its insureds.

Roger Stewart QC (see p.773) A highly knowledgeable silk in the professional negligence and construction spheres who regularly turns his hand to major insurance disputes. Known for being "extremely good when you've got a complex coverage matter," he is also singled out for his client-friendly approach. **Strengths:** "A great cross-examiner who is absolutely razor sharp and has an amazing facility in court." "He prepares extremely well and has a very calming approach with clients. They feel very at ease with his advice."

Anneliese Day QC (see p.631) Very well-regarded silk who is "a charming, intelligent and ruthlessly brilliant advocate." Advising on a wide array of insurance work, she regularly tackles complex cases that take in significant issues surrounding aggregation, dishonesty and jurisdiction. **Strengths:** "Apart from giving sound legal advice as one would expect, she is commercially aware and demonstrates an excellent understanding of the pressures insurers face." "Has an incredible work ethic and is excellent with clients." **Recent work:** Represented Hiscox in a claim arising out of the destruction of a stately home by fire, which was ultimately settled in mediation.

Neil Hext QC A silk known for the quality of his advice and who is described as "technically excellent and a real fighter." He is actively engaged in a whole host of insurance-related work, including the full range of coverage and policy issues, as well as significant disputes involving brokers. **Strengths:** "Incredibly bright and hard working, and particularly good on highly technical insurance issues." "He's an absolutely brilliant teamworker and someone who looks at the detail and picks up points other people would miss." **Recent work:** Acted for Homeserve in a £30 million claim against RSA to recover the costs of the mandated compensation scheme linked to the mis-selling of financial products.

JUNIORS

Alison Padfield (see p.732) A very highly thought-of junior who is "just a joy to work with" and experienced in both insurance and professional negligence cases. She is noted for her methodical and meticulous approach. **Strengths:** "She is outstandingly user-friendly: nothing I put her way seems to floor her. Always calm and in control, she's good at rolling up her sleeves and making you feel you're all in this together." "Technically brilliant and with an eye for detail." **Recent work:** Represented Adana Construction in a coverage dispute that resulted from the catastrophic collapse of a crane in Liverpool in 2009.

Shail Patel A very highly thought-of junior who has developed a robust insurance practice that focuses particularly on professional indemnity and disputes involving a significant element of fraud. **Strengths:** "Very good, very bright, with a very good head on his shoulders." "He is good at seeing all the pieces and identifying the key issues. In court he is great on his feet and a fine cross-examiner, who is good at picking up discrepancies." **Recent work:** Appointed to defend Onsite Group in a dispute with its liability insurers arising out of a £4.3 million subrogated claim relating to a flood at a hospital that was under construction.

Carl Troman (see p.784) Considered a "go-to junior for professional indemnity," he is appreciated for his technical capabilities as well his user-friendly approach. He has recently handled cases involving complex issues such as aggregation, misrepresentation and non-disclosure. **Strengths:** "Gives good robust advice, sticks to his guns, and is very thorough and very helpful." "He's extremely approachable and a very charming individual who has a good touch with clients." **Recent work:** Represented Hiscox in a claim brought by an insured for property damage sustained during an earthquake: the claim was denied by the insurers on the grounds that the indemnity claim was advanced via fraudulent means.

Peter Morcos (see p.721) An up-and-coming junior whose broadly commercial practice has a significant focus on insurance law. He has involvement in substantial coverage disputes, aggregation claims and issues of non-disclosure. **Strengths:** "Gives clear, considered and strategic advice. He gets straight to the nub of the issue and is very hard working and responsive."

Band 4

Crown Office Chambers

See profile on p.824

THE SET

A set known for its strength in the area of physical risk that fields major insurance claims that arise out of construction and property damage on the one side, and complex personal injury and clinical negligence on the other. Members are instructed to represent insurers, policyholders and brokers on difficult coverage issues, subrogated claims and cases involving fraud, often in the context of multiparty litigation. As well as representing clients in disputes, they also regularly act in an advisory capacity for insurers seeking clarification on policy interpretation and other commercial concerns.

Client service: "The clerks, led by senior clerk Andy Flanagan, is excellent: they are user-friendly, pragmatic and keen to help."

SILKS

Ben Quiney QC A silk who is "particularly good on matters that combine insurance law and construction issues," and one who is noted for his effective presence in court. As well as construction cases, he handles a broad remit of insurance work that extends to D&O claims, property damage, subrogated recovery and coverage disputes. **Strengths:** "Intelligent and strategic," he's "clever, practical and easy to work with." **Recent work:** Defended Chubb against a multimillion-pound Commercial Court claim relating to a fire at a property on The Bishops Avenue.

Andrew Rigney QC Handles a broad range of insurance disputes, including cases arising out of major construction projects and claims relating to product liability and professional indemnity policies. He is recognised for his tireless work ethic and his user-friendly approach, and was described by one instructing solicitor as "an excellent lawyer able to reduce an enormous amount of material down to manageable chunks." **Strengths:** "Although he is very busy, he constantly makes himself available. He rolls his sleeves up, gets straight into the detail and provides sound, sensible, commercial advice. He's ahead of everybody else in the room." **Recent work:** Acted in Bache v Zurich Insurance, representing insurers on claims relating to a building guarantee insurance scheme.

JUNIORS

Daniel Shapiro (see p.762) An insurance and reinsurance specialist who demonstrates particular acumen in handling property damage cases, brokers disputes and professional indemnity. **Strengths:** "He is totally user-friendly, excellent on his feet, very bright and very open to having a debate about things – he seems to thrive on that." "He's quick, efficient and decisive." **Recent work:** Acted for tunnelling contractor F&B Trenchless Solutions in a dispute over coverage under its public liability policy after a tunnelling job under a railway line led to the derailment of a freight train.

James Medd Senior junior who is very highly thought of for his expertise in construction-related insurance disputes. He is well versed in all aspects of the industry. **Strengths:** "Technically excellent and highly experienced," he's "an extremely able guy who is very approachable." **Recent work:** Represented contractors JB Leadbitter in a property damage claim brought by the occupiers of a hospital building for flood damage allegedly caused by drain blockage on an adjacent site.

Suzanne Chalmers Experienced in a broad spectrum of insurance work and regularly instructed by many of the leading insurance providers as well as Lloyd's syndicates. Coverage disputes, subrogated recoveries, issues of fraud and property damage all represent key aspects of her practice. **Strengths:** "She shows brilliant attention to detail, and takes a human approach to litigation. She has the ability to cut through complex documents and arrive at the correct answer." **Recent work:** Appointed to represent four insurers in co-ordinated subrogation claims against flood risk consultants, flood defence engineers and property developers, in the wake of flooding at the Glasdir Estate in Ruthin.

4 Pump Court

See profile on p.895

THE SET

A set actively involved in a broad array of insurance work that displays a high degree of expertise when tackling sophisticated domestic and international disputes. Members distinguish themselves with their handling of financial lines, construction, property and professional negligence cases, to name a few, and are experienced advocates and advisers held in high esteem. The set also receives plaudits for the strength of its service, with one instructing solicitor remarking that "the best clerks I deal with are at 4 Pump Court."

Client service: "The clerks are really good and incredibly well run by Carolyn McCombe: they really think about how they can help."

SILKS

Aidan Christie QC (see p.617) An "unflappable" silk who is considered a "great tactician." He has vast experience of handling insurance and reinsurance cases of some magnitude in domestic and international markets. **Strengths:** "Very user-friendly silk with a hands-on and commercial approach. He is a consummate professional, who is a polished performer who never appears ruffled." "Technically excellent, he provides valuable foresight and critical thinking ability and gives very accessible advice on even the most complicated of issues." **Recent work:** Instructed in Aldridge & Others v Liberty Mutual Insurance & Arch Insurance, which concerned a breach of warranty claim related to a professional indemnity policy.

Andrew Neish QC (see p.726) Has an insurance practice that is truly international in focus, as evidenced by his involvement in recent matters involving Mexican, Australian and US interests, to name a few. He is known for being a tough advocate, and instructing solicitors say he is someone they would go to with difficult coverage points. **Strengths:** "His provision of robust commercial advice on credit insurance disputes makes him a go-to guy." "If you want someone who's just on top of every aspect of insurance law, he's your chap."

Nigel Tozzi QC (see p.783) A versatile commercial silk who frequently turns his hand to high-end insurance and reinsurance disputes, and who is head of chambers at 4 Pump Court. Considered a "blindingly good advocate," he is known for his extremely thorough preparation and his expertise in providing strong coverage advice. **Strengths:** "He is quick, to the point and very good in court." "He is incredibly enthusiastic and good with clients, and has a terrific bedside manner." **Recent work:** Advised a major bank on a USD90 million claim under a fidelity policy that related to losses arising out of advances that were secured inappropriately.

Rachel Ansell QC (see p.584) A highly capable silk who has already established credentials in the professional negligence, construction and property damage fields. She has a growing reputation for insurance work among instructing solicitors, with one saying: "My first question, if we need a silk, is: 'Why haven't we instructed Rachel already?'" **Strengths:** "She is tenacious and a forceful advocate." "Impressive in court and fearsome in cross-examination, she provides clear and well-structured arguments. She's bright, effective, commercially astute, strategically sound and a delight to work with." **Recent work:** Represented Brit in a claim under a commercial combined insurance policy for a warehouse fire where cover was denied due to security-related precedents.

Christopher Moger QC (see p.720) Highly experienced silk with a strong track record of representing insurers in sensitive, high-end disputes. His recent work has featured increasing involvement in arbitration and mediation work on an international level. **Strengths:** "Very calm and measured, and strong on his feet." "He is a really good advocate, as he is so authoritative."

Sean O'Sullivan QC (see p.732) Combines his robust practices in the shipping and energy sectors with high-level insurance expertise and a strong facility for international arbitration work. He is regularly instructed in major marine insurance and reinsurance cases that involve significant loss around the globe. **Strengths:** "He works very hard, is very personable and a very good advocate." "Very sharp and very good on his feet." **Recent work:** Instructed in Hyundai Marine v Houlder, a USD15 million claim for negligence against a reinsurance broker arising out of the failure to discover an instance of fraud.

JUNIORS

James Purchas (see p.745) Senior junior regarded as being "sharp on technical and tactical issues," particularly when it comes to cases involving financial services regulation. He is well regarded for his insurance practice, which sees him particularly advising insurers on major coverage disputes and professional indemnity claims, as well as commercial disputes between insurance providers. **Strengths:** "Offers top-quality analysis and clear, firm advice. He is easy to work with and very good with clients." "Very hard working, very bright and very reliable." **Recent work:** Instructed on behalf of a Guernsey-based insurer in a legal expenses insurance dispute with a firm of solicitors.

2TG – 2 Temple Gardens

See profile on p.920

THE SET

A chambers with excellent bench strength in the form of both silks and juniors, all of whom engage in a broad array of insurance work. The set has a focus on property and casualty risks, and professional negligence claims, but also boasts recognised experts in more specialised areas such as life and motor insurance fraud. It is applauded for the strength of its education programme, which sees it providing numerous training seminars and events for insurers and their solicitors.

Client service: "The set has very efficient clerking led by senior clerk Lee Tyler. Their bills come in promptly and, if I need a response, I usually get one within an hour."

SILKS

Neil Moody QC (see p.720) Highly respected silk who is also head of chambers. He is extremely well versed in the area of property damage and frequently advises on insurance coverage disputes arising after significant incidents of fire and flood. **Strengths:** "He is very experienced, has a very commercial approach, and is straightforward and easy to work with." "He understands what clients want and then he implements it." **Recent work:** Advised on a claim arising from a large electrical fire that was alleged to be fraudulent on the grounds of material non-disclosure and breach of warranty.

Charles Dougherty QC (see p.635) Widely known for his expertise in professional negligence, he also takes on high-value insurance work that covers a huge range of claims, including those relating to major instances of art theft, financial crime and property damage. **Strengths:** "Instantly inspires confidence. He is razor sharp in his analysis but down to earth with clients." "An exceptionally intelligent man, who just gets things and runs with them."

Howard Palmer QC (see p.732) A very experienced silk with a significant international element to his practice. His broad insurance expertise extends, particularly, to construction, professional negligence, property damage and motor insurance claims. **Strengths:** "Howard is highly approachable and a pleasure to deal with. He is very thorough in his approach and this is reflected in his advice." "He is great at understanding the issues, knowing what the client needs to understand and making sure that they do understand it."

Andrew Miller QC (see p.717) Regularly instructed in high-value insurance disputes, a number of which concern property damage, particularly as the result of fire. **Strengths:** "He's got a friendly, non-pompous approach. He's good with clients and he just gets his head down and works."

Robert Moxon Browne QC (see p.723) A silk who is described by instructing solicitors as "excellent on coverage and very client-facing." He is very experienced at dealing with insurance coverage issues and claim repudiation, and has a niche specialism in contested life insurance claims – an area in which he does a lot of work on behalf of reinsurers. **Strengths:** "Extremely helpful, pragmatic and quick to get to grips with complex insurance issues."

JUNIORS

Sonia Nolten (see p.728) Maintains a strong insurance practice dominated by work in the life and health spheres, and often takes on exceedingly complex cases. Her wide-ranging capabilities also extend to property damage cases. **Strengths:** "Approachable, practical and commercial." "She's one of those people who is exceedingly clever and down to earth with it. She's practical in terms of not wasting time on peripheral stuff and being good at cutting to the key issues."

Alison Green (see p.659) Respected senior junior with a firm command of insurance and reinsurance law. She gives expert advice to both insurers and insureds on the wording and interpretation of policies, and also regularly deals with claims arising as a consequence of fire damage. **Strengths:** "She is a true expert in the field of English insurance law. I would doubt there is anyone who knows it as well." "She is incredibly user-friendly."

3 Verulam Buildings

See profile on p.924

THE SET

Offers considerable insurance expertise in cases involving banking and financial services, which are core areas of focus for the set as a whole. Its members are adept at handling professional negligence and indemnity claims of some scale, and are also known for their expertise in product liability cases and sophisticated broker disputes. The set also has a prominent practice handling insurance business transfers and other regulatory matters.

Client service: "The set has impressive client care, takes a reasonable and flexible approach to rates and fees, and devotes due attention to matters whether small or large." Stephen Penson is the set's senior practice manager.

SILKS

Tom Weitzman QC Prominent insurance silk known for his involvement in significant product liability and professional indemnity cases. Although he represents clients from all corners of the market, he is particularly renowned as "the go-to QC for coverage disputes involving brokers." **Strengths:** "His advice is delivered in a practical, accessible and user-friendly way that the clients love. He delivers pragmatic solutions to complex problems." "He's got a great manner with the court and can be very tough when he wants to be."

Rory Phillips QC Very well regarded for his growing practice in public law, but also continues to be involved in numerous insurance cases, particularly those concerning sophisticated regulatory matters. **Strengths:** "Very effective on his feet." "He's very good with clients and in conference, and he gets to the nub of what we're going to do with a case." **Recent work:** Represented UK regulators in a Part VII FSMA transfer of business to Hong Kong that was the first of its kind.

JUNIORS

Peter Ratcliffe A very highly respected junior known for his involvement in major insurance and reinsurance disputes, and who is especially in demand for his expertise in claims of broker negligence. **Strengths:** "He is brilliant with the detail on cases. You can be sure he's read every page and has taken it all on board." "User-friendly, works hard and knows his stuff." **Recent work:** Instructed by a major insurer in a USD80 million dispute concerning property reinsurance and professional negligence resulting from a significant industrial incident at a petrochemical plant in the Netherlands.

Nicholas Craig Has a broadly international practice that takes in a wide array of insurance and reinsurance cases. He has particular recent experience in a number of high-value professional negligence claims. **Strengths:** "Very good in court." **Recent work:** Instructed on behalf of insurer HDI-Gerling in a professional negligence claim brought against an insured, Rentokil.

Adam Kramer (see p.693) Manages the full spectrum of insurance and reinsurance work and is also known for his sterling reputation in the banking sector. **Strengths:** "Very clever indeed and highly responsive. He's a junior barrister who performs at a more senior level than his call suggests." "He is very confident and gives very strong advice."

Other Ranked Lawyers

Andrew Hunter QC (Blackstone Chambers) Highly rated for his advocacy skills, he is said to "float like a butterfly, sting like a bee" in court. He undertakes a variety of work in the insurance industry but his core expertise lies in handling Bermuda Form arbitrations. **Strengths:** "Very user-friendly, hugely intellectual and fantastic on his feet, he really does have the court in his hands when he speaks." "A real street fighter, who will not let a point go."

Andrew Green QC (Blackstone Chambers) Handles a whole range of insurance and reinsurance work, and tackles major domestic and international arbitrations as well as commercial court disputes. **Strengths:** "A very commercially minded litigator." "He is an excellent advocate who is extremely good at cross-examination." **Recent work:** Successfully defended Victoria Banking Services on a matter regarding commission claimed under an "affinity" marketing scheme by a major trade union.

Martin Moore QC (see p.721) (Erskine Chambers) Recognised as "the go-to barrister for Part VII transfer work," he also advises across the full spectrum of insurance regulatory and compliance issues, increasingly so in the areas of new product development and company reorganisation. **Strengths:** "Has outstanding technical knowledge and takes a pragmatic approach." "He provides robust support and is willing to engage on matters raised by the regulator in a firm but sensible manner." **Recent work:** Represented Excess Insurance during the Part VII transfer of its insurance business, which included significant company reorganisation.

Paul Reed QC (Hardwicke) Noted for the breadth of his expertise in property damage and construction, he typically takes on high-value insurance cases arising out of these areas of specialism. His cases often involve major international projects. **Strengths:** "Paul is steeped in the insurance market and highly regarded. He has a first-rate understanding of insurance and is very commercial in his approach." "He's always robust in his views and meticulous as to detail." **Recent work:** Instructed in Lagan Homes v MV Kelley & The Millward Partnership, an £8 million dispute regarding the negligent design of an underground car park.

Nigel Jones QC (Hardwicke) Takes on significant insurance claims arising from a broad array of underlying incidents, including construction disputes, professional negligence and sports injuries. He is known for his skill in handling litigation involving multiple parties and/or jurisdictional issues. **Strengths:** "His knowledge and ability to simplify even the most complex insurance arguments are second to none. He is a real teamplayer, who is highly accessible and really gets stuck into the facts and law. He basically answers the questions that you haven't even asked yet." **Recent work:** Represented Keller in seeking indemnity under public liability and professional indemnity policies following a significant construction dispute.

David Pliener (Hardwicke) A highly capable insurance junior who also has considerable property damage and construction expertise. He regularly represents many of the leading insurers in complex coverage and policy disputes. **Strengths:** "Incredibly client-friendly and someone with an excellent grasp of complex documents. He is able to extract information from the client with great skill, and always gives good commercial advice." **Recent work:** Instructed in Vaughan v Zurich, a £5 million professional indemnity coverage dispute relating to the redevelopment of Belfast's Royal Victoria Hospital.

Geraint Webb QC (see p.791) (Henderson Chambers) Excels at handling major insurance cases arising out of product liability issues, and also manages significant property damage claims. He is also involved in providing coverage opinions and advice to both prominent insurers and claimants. **Strengths:** "Has an excellent understanding of insurance and a sharp forensic mind. He is an amazing teamplayer, with an impressive intellect and an approachable manner. He is counsel to have on your side in a fight."

Stephen Cogley QC (XXIV Old Buildings) A notable commercial litigator who has recently moved from Quadrant Chambers. He frequently acts for policyholders on major insurance matters, but also represents brokers and insurers. **Strengths:** "His advocacy is absolutely superb and his understanding and mastery of the brief is peerless. Not only that, he is also commercial and talks the client's language." **Recent work:** Advised the National Iranian Tanker fleet on insurance aspects of a USD1.5 billion refinancing dispute.

Andrew Guy Blackwood QC (see p.596) (Quadrant Chambers) Engaged in significant insurance and reinsurance work that focuses particularly on the energy sector. He also handles major political and war risk claims. **Strengths:** "Bright, user-friendly and quick to turn things round, he's very effective as an advocate." "A very good analytical lawyer who displays great attention to detail." **Recent work:** Defended Arab Insurance Group in reinsurance litigation brought by AXA, who sought to avoid energy reinsurance treaties they had entered into during the 1990s.

David Lord QC (Three Stone) Has a wide international commercial practice that focuses consistently on significant insurance and reinsurance cases. He gets involved in coverage disputes as well as complex multi-party disputes. **Strengths:** "He has great antennae for the right courtroom arguments. His advice and delivery are really client-focused, and he wraps issues and solutions in user-friendly bite-size parcels." "He's a common-sense, down-to-earth, sensible insurance specialist." **Recent work:** Continued to represent Lloyd's brokers as parties in a coverage dispute arising out of a robbery of a West End jewellery shop.

Contents:

LONDON

Intellectual Property
Leading Sets
Band 1
Three New Square *
8 New Square *
11 South Square *
Band 2
One Essex Court *
Hogarth Chambers *
Band 3
Blackstone Chambers *
Leading Silks
Star individuals
Alexander Daniel *8 New Square* *
Hobbs Geoffrey *One Essex Court* [A]
Meade Richard *8 New Square* *
Band 1
Bloch Michael *Blackstone Chambers*
Burkill Guy *Three New Square* *
Mellor James *8 New Square* *
Purvis Iain *11 South Square*
Speck Adrian *8 New Square* *
Tappin Michael *8 New Square* *
Vanhegan Mark *11 South Square*
Waugh Andrew *Three New Square* *
Wyand Roger *Hogarth Chambers*
Band 2
Acland Piers *11 South Square*
Edenborough Michael *Serle Court (ORL)* ◇
Himsworth Emma *One Essex Court*
Howe Martin *8 New Square* *
Lykiardopoulos Andrew *8 New Square* *
Mitcheson Thomas *Three New Square* *
Silverleaf Michael *11 South Square*
Turner Justin *Three New Square* *
Wilson Alastair *Hogarth Chambers*
Band 3
Bacon Kelyn *Brick Court Chambers (ORL)* ◇
Baldwin John *8 New Square* *
Cuddigan Hugo *11 South Square*
Howe Robert *Blackstone Chambers*
May Charlotte *8 New Square* *
Mill Ian *Blackstone Chambers*
Miller Richard *Three New Square* *
New Silks
Abrahams James *8 New Square* [A] *
Campbell Douglas *Three New Square* *
Hinchliffe Thomas *Three New Square* *
Malynicz Simon *Three New Square* *
Moody-Stuart Thomas *8 New Square* *
* *Indicates set / individual with profile.*
[A] *direct access (see p.24).*
◇ *(ORL) = Other Ranked Lawyer.*
Alphabetical order within each band. Band 1 is highest.

Intellectual Property
Leading Juniors
Band 1
Hicks Michael *Hogarth Chambers*
Hollingworth Guy *One Essex Court*
Nicholson Brian *11 South Square*
Roberts Philip *One Essex Court* [A]
Band 2
Brandreth Benet *11 South Square*
Chacksfield Mark *8 New Square* *
Copeland Miles *Three New Square* *
Delaney Joe *Three New Square* *
Edwards-Stuart Anna *11 South Square*
Jamal Isabel *8 New Square* *
Lane Lindsay *8 New Square* [A] *
Norris Andrew *Hogarth Chambers*
Saunders Nicholas *Brick Court Chambers (ORL)* ◇
St Quintin Thomas *Hogarth Chambers*
Tritton Guy *Hogarth Chambers* [A]
Ward Henry *8 New Square* *
Whyte James *8 New Square* *
Band 3
Alkin Tom *11 South Square*
Baran Stuart *Three New Square* *
Berkeley Iona *8 New Square* *
Davis Richard *Hogarth Chambers*
Harbottle Gwilym *Hogarth Chambers* [A]
McFarland Denise *Three New Square* *
Michaels Amanda *Hogarth Chambers*
Pickard Kathryn *11 South Square*
Pritchard Geoffrey *Three New Square* *
St Ville James *8 New Square* *
Band 4
Aikens Chris *11 South Square*
Bowhill Jessie *8 New Square* *
Chapple Malcolm *New Square Chambers (ORL)* ◇
Engelman Mark *Hardwicke (ORL)* ◇ [A]
Hall Chris *11 South Square*
Heal Madeleine *New Square Chambers (ORL)* ◇ [A]
Heald Jeremy *Three New Square*
Hill Jonathan *8 New Square* [A] *
Longstaff Benjamin *Hogarth Chambers*
Moss Jonathan *Hogarth Chambers*
Reed Jeremy *Hogarth Chambers* [A]
Reid Jacqueline *11 South Square*
Up-and-coming individuals
Riordan Jaani *8 New Square* *

Band 1

Three New Square

See profile on p.879

THE SET

A top-flight set admired for its excellent roster of both silks and juniors, and also celebrating several new Queen's Counsel appointments this year. Members are recommended for patent disputes arising in the telecommunications and life sciences sectors, including infringement claims, SPC disputes and invalidation attempts. It is also highlighted for its assistance with contentious trade mark proceedings. The set continues to stand out for its pragmatic and commercial approach.

Client service: The clerking team is "charming and very helpful," and is distinguished for its "consummately professional service." Senior clerk Nick Hill is "excellent" and "very easy to work with."

SILKS

Guy Burkill QC (see p.607) Highlighted for his excellent advice and his strong courtroom presentation. He is recognised for his expertise in mechanical and electronic patent disputes. His recent experience also includes trade mark infringement claims and disputes concerning allegations of the misappropriation of confidential information. **Strengths:** "Clients really like his technical knowledge. He is very user-friendly and service-oriented too." "He is hard-working, user-friendly and also incredibly academic." **Recent work:** Instructed by Flynn Pharma in its trade mark action against DrugsRUs. The case arose from the parallel importation of pharmaceutical products.

Andrew Waugh QC (see p.791) Tenacious and detail-oriented advocate with a strong reputation for patent litigation in the biotechnology field. He handles a range of contentious proceedings including invalidation attempts, opposition actions and Swiss-type claims. **Strengths:** "He is just brains, brains and more brains. He is incredibly hard-working, incredibly thorough and, my God, is he well prepared! He really takes the fight to the other side." "He is a high-energy advocate with a forceful style in the courtroom." **Recent work:** Acted for Idenix in its patent infringement action against Gilead relating to Sovaldi, a hepatitis C treatment.

Thomas Mitcheson QC (see p.719) A very popular recent silk recommended for his calm demeanour, excellent client service and strong cross-examination skills. He is noted for his handling of patent and trade mark litigation, including oppositions and infringement claims. **Strengths:** "He is particularly good at reading the judges and predicting what points they will be interested in." "He is very client-friendly and highly strategic." **Recent work:** Represented Cadbury in its successful opposition to Nestlé's application to register a trade mark for a four-finger chocolate bar shape, representing its Kit-Kat product.

Justin Turner QC (see p.785) A well-regarded barrister with a strong technical background in the life sciences sector and substantial experience in biotechnology patent litigation. He is also noted for his experience acting in EPO proceedings, as well as copyright and design rights disputes. He earns praise for his strong courtroom presentation, especially with regard to cross-examination. **Strengths:** "He is very useful for technically complicated and scientific matters." "He is very well prepared in court and does an excellent job with cross-examinations." **Recent work:** Represented Gilead in its high-profile dispute with Idenix regarding a hepatitis C medication.

Richard Miller QC (see p.717) Head of the chambers and a calm, authoritative presence in the courtroom. He has experience handling pharmaceutical and telecommunications patent litigation, including licensing disputes and infringement claims. **Strengths:** "Obviously a very good operator who thinks strategically." "A very skilful advocate that is a pleasure to work with." **Recent work:** Appeared in a royalties dispute between the Medical Research Council and Celltech regarding the Lucentis and Avastin products.

Douglas Campbell QC (see p.610) A tenacious, talented and quick-witted new silk. He stands out for his capabilities acting in patent, design right and trade mark infringement disputes. He is also noted for his experience handling proceedings in the IPEC and the Court of Appeal. **Strengths:** "He is very easy to work with and incredibly client-focused." "He has a brilliant mind, and is outstandingly commercial and incisive." **Recent work:** Appeared in the appellate proceedings between Fox and The Glee Club regarding claims of trade mark infringement for use of "glee."

Thomas Hinchliffe QC (see p.672) Newly appointed silk highlighted for his abilities handling biotechnology and pharmaceutical patent litigation matters. Sources are quick to highlight his polished advocacy, his incisiveness and his commercial awareness. **Strengths:** "He is a strong advocate who is extremely well organised and very service-oriented." "He is extremely personable, commercial, thorough and responsive." **Recent work:** Successfully represented Teva in relation to a patent revocation attempt by Synthon for the patents covering Copaxone.

Simon Malynicz QC (see p.706) A new silk recognised for his strong focus on contentious trade mark matters, including infringement claims and opposition proceedings. He is esteemed for his practical and tactically minded counsel, as well as his experience acting in CJEU and Court of Appeal proceedings. **Strengths:** "He has an in-depth knowledge of soft IP matters and offers practical solutions." "He is very impressive on trade mark matters and knows the law inside-out." **Recent work:** Instructed by Nestlé in relation to its application to trade-mark the shape of its four-finger KitKat chocolate bar. The matter has received significant media coverage.

JUNIORS

Miles Copeland (see p.623) User-friendly and highly responsive barrister noted for his excellent client service. He is experienced advising on patent litigation involving pharmaceutical companies, including secondary use and infringement claims. **Strengths:** "He is very hard-working, really enthusiastic, good on his feet and provides excellent support throughout cases." "He is commercial and astute counsel." **Recent work:** Represented Shionogi in a patent dispute with Merck regarding the latter's new HIV treatment.

Joe Delaney (see p.632) Highlighted for his persuasive written work and his command of technical detail in complex patent cases. He is particularly active in relation to infringement claims concerning biotechnology and telecommunications patents. **Strengths:** "He is very bright and good at synthesising simple-looking arguments from complex facts and law." "He is very personable and has a good, practical sense of strategy." **Recent work:** Instructed by Regeneron in its patent infringement action against Kymab. The case concerned a method for creating genetically modified rodents for use in human antibody production.

Stuart Baran (see p.589) Continues to impress instructing solicitors with his work ethic, client care, commerciality and intelligence. He is recognised for his experience in trade mark litigation, and is also well known for his representation of life sciences companies in high-value patent and SPC litigation. **Strengths:** "He is really user-friendly, smart and extremely hard-working." "He has a very mature and sensible manner that belies his years." **Recent work:** Instructed by Teva in its dispute with Boehringer Ingelheim regarding the SPIRIVA inhaler product.

Denise McFarland (see p.712) A "natural advocate," McFarland receives consistent praise for her client-facing skills and responsiveness as well as her courtroom skill. She is noted for her work in anti-counterfeiting actions and trade mark infringement claims. She has additional experience advising on patent invalidation actions and mediations. **Strengths:** "She is super-smart, very strategic and really knows her way around the system." "She is hugely knowledgeable and clients really love her." **Recent work:** Appeared in trade mark proceedings initiated by Autobrokers against defendants alleged to have produced counterfeit car parts.

Geoffrey Pritchard (see p.743) Noted for his pragmatism, client services and strong courtroom presentation, as well as a superb intellect. He has experience handling trade mark and patent infringement cases, with additional abilities acting in EPO opposition proceedings. **Strengths:** "He is incredibly hard-working, user-friendly and easy to get on with." "He gives clear, straightforward and user-friendly advice." **Recent work:** Appeared in SDL Hair v Next Row, an enquiry as to damages following a successful patent infringement action.

Jeremy Heald A calm and considered advocate who is well known for his experience in assisting pharmaceutical clients in patent revocation actions. He is also highlighted for his work in trade mark disputes, including infringement actions. **Strengths:** "He is very thorough, intellectual and gets right into the details." "He is a pleasure to work with. His unassuming nature belies his first-rate intellect." **Recent work:** Appeared as junior counsel for Lilly in defence of a patent revocation proceeding initiated by Actavis regarding the use of the drug atomoxetine in the treatment of ADHD.

8 New Square

See profile on p.881

THE SET

Regarded as a top-quality patent chambers, 8 New Square is home to some of the leading lights of the Intellectual Property Bar at silk level. Its juniors maintain busy patent litigation practices in the technical, industrial and life sciences industries, with members also highlighted for design right, trade mark and copyright expertise. Beyond its "fantastic roster of talent," it is recommended for being "very modern, forward-thinking and providing sound commercial advice," as well as offering instructing solicitors "a very broad skill set in the soft IP space." **Client service:** The "very focused and proactive" clerking team led by John Call are "always very accommodating, approachable and friendly." Others add: "The clerks are always helpful, a good source of information and always contactable."

SILKS

Daniel Alexander QC (see p.581) A market-leading silk enjoying an exceptional reputation for his advocacy in patent litigation involving pharmaceutical and TMT companies. He is also distinguished for his abilities in assisting with cross-border trade mark infringement disputes involving digital retailers. **Strengths:** "He has got an incredible mind, he is wonderfully articulate and he is incredibly accessible." "A smooth-as-silk silk who is willing and able to take a difficult case and find winning points in it. He sees the bigger picture, and clients like him because he's a great cross-examiner with a very delicate touch." **Recent work:** Appeared in Vringo v ZTE, a telecommunications patent dispute with significant FRAND aspects.

Richard Meade QC (see p.715) A measured and very effective silk handling complex patent litigation involving life sciences companies. He assists with a range of contentious matters including infringement claims, invalidation attempts and Swiss-type claims. **Strengths:** "A very senior patent barrister and an excellent performer. He is level-headed and cool under pressure." "One of the pre-eminent patent barristers in the UK right now. He is just incredibly calm, thoughtful and strategic." **Recent work:** Instructed by Actavis in its patent invalidity claim against Warner-Lambert, relating to the drug pregabalin.

James Mellor QC (see p.715) A reassuringly smooth and confident advocate recommended for trade mark litigation and copyright disputes. As well as disputes concerning online platforms, Mellor also handles TMT and life sciences patent litigation matters. **Strengths:** "He is very bright, user-friendly, practical and provides well-analysed advice." "He is experienced and unflappable. A go-to QC for telecommunications and electronics cases." **Recent work:** Acted for Ericsson in its patent action against Apple, alleging infringement of patents related to mobile device internet connectivity.

Adrian Speck QC (see p.770) A technically brilliant, practical and commercially minded barrister recognised for representing telecommunications companies in high-value patent litigation. His other areas of expertise include second-use medical claims and trade mark infringement actions involving online vendors. **Strengths:** "He is terribly clever, works incredibly hard, is really good at taking responsibility for the case and spots weaknesses really quickly. A real talent." "An extremely approachable QC who is very bright and quickly grasps complex matters." **Recent work:** Instructed by Actavis in its dispute with Warner-Lambert over the pregabalin drug. The dispute includes a claim for patent infringement as well as for secondary medical use claims.

Michael Tappin QC (see p.778) Enjoys an excellent reputation for his courtroom presentation and capabilities handling highly technical life sciences patent disputes. He is also noted for his experience acting in TMT patent infringement cases. **Strengths:** "He is the complete package. He gets all over the detail and is really accessible." "His advocacy style is fantastic. It strikes the balance between confident and friendly, and judges really respond well to the delivery." **Recent work:** Represented HTC in appellate proceedings brought by Gemalto, which alleges that various of HTC's smartphones infringe a patent covering the use of the Java programming language with a microcontroller or smart card.

Martin Howe QC (see p.676) User-friendly and cerebral advocate recognised for his abilities handling high-profile copyright litigation. He is also praised for his strong courtroom presentation and drafting, and has substantial experience acting in patent and SPC disputes arising in the life sciences sector . **Strengths:** "He always does a good job and is very effective in court. He is highly persuasive and always clear and rational." "He is really user-friendly and judges respect him. He is a bright, enthusiastic and committed barrister." **Recent work:** Instructed by Rihanna in her action against Topshop alleging copyright infringement for the use of her likeness on a T-shirt. The Court of Appeal confirmed the verdict in favour of the claimant.

Andrew Lykiardopoulos QC (see p.704) A likeable and popular silk who is consistently praised by instructing solicitors for his client-facing skills and his willingness to get to grips with the technical details of a case. He is regularly called upon for multi-jurisdictional trade mark infringement disputes, as well as high-end patent litigation involving TMT and pharmaceutical companies. **Strengths:** "He is incredibly sharp and insightful. His work is always of high quality and well thought through." "A barrister who is incredibly organised, very good on his feet and gives great strategic advice." "He is just an excellent QC and a real pleasure to work with." **Recent work:** Successfully defended ASOS in a trade mark infringement action initiated by ASSOS, a Swiss clothing manufacturer. The client was held to have a valid own-name defence and permission to appeal to the Supreme Court was denied.

John Baldwin QC (see p.588) Recognised as a staunch courtroom advocate who excels at cross-examination, as well as a hugely knowledgeable and very strategic counsellor. He is noted for his abilities acting for media clients in breach of confidence disputes, and has additional strength assisting with trade mark and patent litigation. **Strengths:** "In court, he is a very prepared, determined and persuasive advocate. It is lovely to hear him talk as he puts arguments together very well." "He is a senior operator who brings experience and intelligence to bear on cases." **Recent work:** Appeared for The Sofa Workshop in its action against Sofaworks in the IPEC alleging trade mark infringement.

Charlotte May QC (see p.710) Well-regarded silk, praised for the quality of her client care and commerciality, as well as her calm and controlled advocacy. She is recognised for her broad practice with recent experience handling TMT and pharmaceutical patent disputes and trade mark infringement claims involving retailers and digital platforms. **Strengths:** "She has amazing experience for someone of her call and a good rapport with judges. She is a good advocate with a nice way of presenting things." "She is very thorough and very strong technically. She has an excellent manner with clients." **Recent work:** Successfully represented Thomas Pink in its trade mark and passing-off action again Victoria's Secret UK, concerning the sale of clothing under the name Pink.

James Abrahams QC (see p.579) A new silk commended for his extremely efficient, tenacious and forthright advocacy and his depth of experience acting in TMT patent litigation. He is also experienced assisting with trade mark infringement and database rights disputes. **Strengths:** "He is incredibly intelligent. He is a street-fighter advocate who gets down to the nitty-gritty and rolls his sleeves up. He always puts in the effort and is unafraid of the difficult cases – he gets the best out of them." "He is fantastic on paper and a very logical thinker. He is extremely hard-working, has never let me down and makes it an easy working relationship." **Recent work:** Appeared in the long-running and high-profile patent dispute between Huawei and Unwired Planet, concerning telecoms patents.

Thomas Moody-Stuart QC (see p.720) A seasoned and calm courtroom advocate who took silk this year, in an appointment that has been widely approved of by the wider market. He is admired for his practicality, responsiveness and tactical strength. He handles trade mark and patent infringement claims, as well as misuse of confidential information disputes. **Strengths:** "He is very quick on the uptake, able to provide very comprehensive advice and makes great suggestions on how to proceed." "He is very good on the strategy. He's a street fighter and is good for bad-tempered squabbles." **Recent work:** Represented Take Two Interactive in its trade mark and copyright dispute with the BBC, concerning the BBC's film about the making of Grand Theft Auto.

JUNIORS

Mark Chacksfield (see p.613) Enjoys a strong following among instructing solicitors, who praise his analytical and creative approach, as well as his excellent client service skills. He is particularly adept at representing pharmaceutical clients, particularly in revocation actions and EPO proceedings. **Strengths:** "He is really great with clients and is very solid, commercial and creative." "He is enormously bright and diligent, with a keen focus on client demands." **Recent work:** Appeared for Genentech in the final first instance trial of a long-running patent dispute with Hospira, concerning Genentech's patent for a combined Herceptin and taxoid treatment regimen.

Isabel Jamal (see p.682) An extremely conscientious and talented junior who impresses instructing parties with her commercial focus and responsiveness. She is recommended for her experience acting in high-value litigation connected to pharmaceutical, telecommunications and engineering patents. **Strengths:** "She is a bright, hard-working and thoughtful junior." "She is a star in the making who is wise beyond her years." **Recent work:** Represented Actavis in its revocation action against Lilly regarding the use of atomoxetine in manufacturing an ADHD medication.

Lindsay Lane (see p.695) Well-regarded junior highlighted for her pragmatic advice and efficiency. She is known for her representation of media clients in copyright disputes arising from unsanctioned broadcasts, and also has experience in patent infringement disputes and comparative advertising injunctions. **Strengths:** "She is an experienced counsel with a comprehensive and detailed knowledge of copyright law." "She has a very clear approach and is good at cutting through to what really matters." **Recent work:** Advised Imperial Tobacco on the IP aspects of a judicial review of legislation to introduce plain packaging for cigarettes.

Henry Ward (see p.789) Impresses sources with his realistic and commercial advice, his innovative approach to IP litigation and his experience assisting with IPEC proceedings. He is recognised for his skill handling patent infringement and invalidation claims in the telecommunications, pharmaceutical and engineering sectors. **Strengths:** "He is a very clear, direct and no-nonsense barrister." "He is astute, tactically excellent and has great drafting skills." **Recent work:** Acted for MobileIron in defence of a claim brought by Good Technology Corporation, concerning a patent for mobile communications system architecture.

James Whyte (see p.795) Regarded as a star of the future, Whyte is a technically brilliant junior with a background in the biotechnology field. He is also noted for his abilities representing electronics and telecommunications clients in patent infringement claims **Strengths:** "He had a wonderful understanding of the technical aspects of the case. Clients like his clear and concise advice, and his cool and calm manner." "He combines a rigorous and thorough command of technical detail with clear and patient advocacy – a highly recommended junior for both technology and life sciences work." **Recent work:** Acted for Siemens in defence of a patent infringement claim by Wobben relating to wind turbine control. Wobben's patent was found to be invalid and, in any event, not infringed.

Iona Berkeley (see p.595) Seasoned junior with experience assisting with IPEC, IPO and Court of Appeal proceedings. She is known for her expertise in soft IP matters. Her recent work includes advising on a design rights infringement claim. **Strengths:** "She is thorough and very accomplished." **Recent work:** Instructed as junior counsel by Doncaster Pharmaceuticals in its parallel imports dispute with Specialty European Pharma. The court found that enforcement of Speciality European Pharma's trade mark to prevent Doncaster's rebranding of pharmaceuticals would constitute a discriminatory restriction on imports from member states.

James St Ville (see p.771) A very experienced junior who is well regarded for his attention to detail and commerciality. His recent work includes the handling of copyright, patent and trade mark infringement disputes. His other areas of ability include database rights and design rights litigation. **Strengths:** "He is an absolute perfectionist with a real eye for detail, which is really useful for trade mark infringement cases." "He is extremely thorough and leaves no stone unturned. His preparation on every case is superb and detailed, and he has first-class drafting." **Recent work:** Instructed to defend Open College Network Credit4Learning against a trade mark infringement and passing-off claim made by NOCN, regarding the use of the OCN acronym. It was ruled that this trade mark was invalid and the claimant had no entitlement.

Jessie Bowhill (see p.600) A responsive and practical junior noted for her commerciality. She has expertise in trade mark matters, including infringement and passing-off claims. She is also experienced advising on copyright disputes arising from digital broadcasts. **Strengths:** "She provides really objective advice and has a great attention to detail." "She is a fierce advocate who is very intelligent, straight-talking and no-nonsense." **Recent work:** Instructed by higher education organisation NOCN in its action against Open College Network Credit4Learning, alleging trade mark infringement and passing-off.

Jonathan Hill (see p.671) Impresses instructing solicitors with his intelligence, user-friendliness and accomplished courtroom advocacy. He is experienced handling patent litigation related to licensing agreements and infringement allegations. His additional areas of expertise include trade mark, copyright and database rights. **Strengths:** "He works extremely hard, gets a good practical understanding of cases and is a very effective cross-examiner." "He is amazingly bright with an encyclopaedic knowledge of case law. He is deeply commercial and brings a brilliantly analytical focus on the points that really matter." **Recent work:** Acted as sole counsel to Document Management Solutions in defence of a patent infringement claim brought by Everseal Stationery Products. A counterclaim successfully invalidated the patent in question.

Jaani Riordan (see p.752) A rising star of the junior IP Bar, he is praised for his attention to detail, his commerciality and his responsiveness. He has experience acting in a broad range of contentious IP matters including trade mark infringement claims involving high-street retailers and online services, and patent litigation in the telecommunications and pharmaceutical sectors. **Strengths:** "He offers astute, commercial and tactical advice." "He impresses with his wealth of knowledge and his ability to distil very complex issues and ideas down into bite-sized, comprehensible chunks." **Recent work:** Instructed by Unwired Planet in its patent infringement action against Huawei, Samsung and Google concerning 4G mobile phones.

11 South Square

See profile on p.909

THE SET

An excellent set, regarded as a leader for IP matters due to its "strength and depth at all levels." It is host to a skilled bench of impressive QCs and juniors, who are well known for their client care, courtroom presentation and abilities handling complex patent litigation. Members are also highlighted for their representation of TMT and pharmaceutical clients, as well as those embroiled in high-profile copyright, design right and trade mark disputes.

Client service: "The clerks have got a really good manner and are obviously excellent at dealing with solicitors. They know their way around the court and how to get things done." Ashley Carr is the senior clerk and is praised for being "unfailingly commercial" and "really good to deal with because he knows the industry inside-out."

SILKS

Iain Purvis QC One of the most sought-after silks at the Intellectual Property Bar, and regarded as an extremely bright and effective barrister. He is well known for his skill in trade mark litigation and is also recommended for patent disputes involving hi-tech and pharmaceutical companies. **Strengths:** "He is at the top of his game: he has great analytical skills and presents cases in a way that judges want to listen to." "He is a first choice for 'bet the company' litigation. He is enormously clever and very well respected in the highest courts." **Recent work:** Acted for IPcom in its patent infringement action against telecommunications manufacturer HTC.

Mark Vanhegan QC A knowledgeable and incredibly bright silk highlighted for his client care skills, his practical advice and the strength of his courtroom advocacy. He is known for his abilities handling high-profile TMT patent disputes, and is also fully conversant with claims of design right and trade mark infringement. **Strengths:** "He is a very experienced litigator and a very persuasive cross-examiner." "He is incredibly bright, whilst also being down-to-earth and very easy to work with. He has an excellent bedside manner with clients." **Recent work:** Appeared for PMS International in appellate proceedings arising from its long-running dispute with Magmatic over ride-on children's suitcases. The dispute concerns the alleged infringement of a Community registered design, a UK unregistered design right and a copyright.

Piers Acland QC A hands-on and very approachable silk, highlighted for his client care skills and the quality of his courtroom advocacy, particularly in cross-examination. He is sought after for his experience representing life sciences companies in high-value patent litigation. **Strengths:** "He is really quick to identify the legal points and winnow out the critical arguments." "He is absolutely brilliant. He is very end goal-oriented and he gets the best result. He has a relaxed style in court, and is very succinct and clear. He is very persuasive and very successful." **Recent work:** Represented Idenix Pharmaceuticals in its dispute with Gilead Sciences, in which Idenix alleged patent infringement by Gilead in relation to its hepatitis C treatment, Solvadi.

Michael Silverleaf QC An authoritative silk renowned for his oral presentation and his tenacious advocacy. He has substantial experience of assisting with trade mark and patent litigation matters, including infringement, invalidation and passing-off claims. **Strengths:** "His advocacy skills are exactly what you would expect for someone of his level, and his input before the hearings is just as valuable. He is good at identifying the critical points to focus on." "He is phenomenal. He gets straight to the nub of the issues and gives absolutely correct advice." "He is fiercely intelligent – you want him on your side." **Recent work:** Represented Starbucks (HK) in its trade mark dispute with BSkyB regarding the use of the mark NOW TV. The case reached the Supreme Court, which considered the extent to which an overseas business can rely upon the goodwill in its name to restrain acts of passing-off in the UK.

Hugo Cuddigan QC A very commercial recent silk, distinguished for his tactical ability, work ethic and user-friendliness. He is comfortable handling litigation involving pharmaceutical, mechanical and hi-tech patents, and his recent work also includes a high-profile copyright infringement case. **Strengths:** "He has got excellent judgement and is very good on his feet as well." "He has got a very good court manner and is incredibly hard-working." **Recent work:** Successfully acted for singer Rihanna in her copyright infringement action against high-street retailer Topshop, concerning a T-shirt featuring her likeness.

JUNIORS

Brian Nicholson Extremely sharp and thorough senior junior recommended for his abilities assisting with hi-tech patent litigation proceedings involving telecommunications companies. His other areas of experience include Community design right disputes and pharmaceutical patent infringement claims **Strengths:** "He has got an excellent grasp of IP law and can apply his brilliance to it. He is a real pleasure to work with." "He combines his technical background with legal skills very effectively. A prodigiously hard worker, with a real eye for detail and strategic planning." **Recent work:** Acted for Dr. Reddy's Laboratories in its patent infringement dispute with Warner-Lambert regarding the drug pregabalin, which is used to treat epilepsy and generalised anxiety disorder.

Benet Brandreth Efficient, pragmatic and responsive barrister recommended for his commercial advice. He enjoys a strong reputation for trade mark and copyright infringement disputes. He also has experience in litigation concerning mechanical patents. **Strengths:** "He is really good to deal with. He is very clever and persuasive, and has a great advocacy style." "He has strong oral advocacy skills and is very knowledgeable about trade marks." **Recent work:** Represented a Swiss manufacturer of cycling clothing, ASSOS, in its trade mark and passing-off claim against ASOS. The appellate proceedings of this long-running case hinged on the application of an own-name defence.

Anna Edwards-Stuart A very experienced senior junior, highlighted for her responsiveness, pragmatic advice and strong written opinion work. She has experience of invalidation and infringement actions relating to patents and trade marks, as well as IPEC proceedings. **Strengths:** "She is an up-and-coming star who is a great favourite with clients." "She is great to have on big cases because she works extremely hard and is not fazed by enormous tasks." **Recent work:** Represented Ono Pharmaceuticals in its patent dispute with Merck Sharp & Dohme concerning an oncology treatment using anti-PD-1 antibodies.

Tom Alkin A quick-thinking and forthright junior praised for his courtroom presentation. He is particularly effective in patent litigation involving life sciences and technology sector clients. He also has experience assisting with trade mark invalidation actions and royalties disputes. **Strengths:** "He is very impressive on his feet." "He is very thorough and quick-thinking. He grasps the facts and the commercial requirements of clients very quickly." **Recent work:** Acted for Convatec in its patent dispute with Smith & Nephew, concerning the silverising of fibres used in wound dressings.

Kathryn Pickard Noted for her representation of life sciences companies in litigation arising from second medical use claims, infringement allegations and market authorisation applications. She also assists media clients in passing-off disputes. **Strengths:** "I am very impressed with her: she has good judgement and gives fast responses." "She has an excellent knowledge of design law, is responsive and good to work with." "She is an exceptionally sensible and user-friendly junior." **Recent work:** Represented Mylan in high-profile patent revocation proceedings brought against Warner-Lambert regarding the drug pregabalin.

Chris Aikens Well liked by instructing solicitors, with a good reputation for IPEC proceedings and contentious design rights matters. He is also noted for his assistance with patent entitlement disputes, Community trade mark infringement claims and allegations of passing-off. **Strengths:** "He impresses with his expertise, his understanding of patent law and his ability to grasp the details of the case." "He is detailed, responsive, bright and technically sound. He is great to bring in on complex patent disputes." **Recent work:** Represented Premium Interest in the defence of a trade mark passing-off claim made by internet company Pinterest.

Chris Hall A rising star at the Junior Bar, recommended for design right, copyright and trade mark infringement claims. He is also noted for his experience assisting with IPEC and IPO proceedings. Instructing solicitors highlight him as incisive, hard-working and practical. **Strengths:** "He is obviously really smart and really helpful. He's always available, really responsive and shows a great grasp of legal and commercial issues." "He is very tenacious and has a good attention to detail." "He is a young man who is going places." **Recent work:** Represented Kenilworth Funding in its patent infringement claim against BlackBerry and Microsoft relating to visual voicemail interface technology.

Jacqueline Reid A very bright junior noted for her robust courtroom presentation and her expertise in design rights matters. She is also noted for her experience assisting with mechanical patent disputes and IPEC proceedings arising from trade mark infringement claims. **Strengths:** "She is very bright; her advice is spot-on and very commercial. She has an annoying habit of always being right." "She is very experienced and combines a thorough and methodical approach with a combative attitude in court. Clients have the confidence that she is fighting their corner." **Recent work:** Instructed by Giordano Poultry to act in its patent infringement dispute with Crocker Enterprises over the design of a water supply device for poultry.

Band 2

One Essex Court

See profile on p.833

THE SET

A set best known for its commercial work but capable of supplying top-flight silks and juniors to manage high-profile intellectual property cases. Members are frequently called upon to handle trade mark and copyright disputes, as well as disputes concerning online platforms. The set is consistently recognised for its modern and user-friendly approach, an attitude reflected by its helpful and well-liked clerking team.

Client service: Members of the clerking team, led by senior clerk Darren Burrows, are "excellent, very experienced and try to help whenever they can." Deputy senior clerk Jackie Ginty is singled out as "very approachable and really helpful."

SILKS

Geoffrey Hobbs QC Hobbs is an exceptionally talented IP litigator and is particularly highly thought of for his work in trade mark disputes. His recent activity includes advising on judicial reviews, online advertising and multi-jurisdictional infringement claims. **Strengths:** "He is a brilliant strategist at the top of his game." "He just knows the law inside-out." **Recent work:** Represented BAT in a judicial review of the introduction of plain packaging regulations for cigarettes.

Emma Himsworth QC Recognised as an expert on trade mark law, with a strong work ethic and a user-friendly approach. As well as handling high-end and technically complex trade mark litigation, she is effective in digital platform infringement claims, invalidation attempts and licensing disputes. **Strengths:** "She is patient, hard-working and manages client expectations well." "She is encyclopaedic on trade mark law and you can have absolute confidence in her opinion." **Recent work:** Represented Sports Direct International in its trade mark infringement and validity dispute with Boxing Brands concerning the use of a "Queensbury" mark.

JUNIORS

Guy Hollingworth A popular junior among instructing solicitors for his composure, polished courtroom presentation and first-rate knowledge of trade mark matters. He regularly handles infringement and opposition claims, with additional expertise in copyright and design rights disputes. **Strengths:** "He is a very clever and measured advocate." "He is smart, diligent and easy to work with." **Recent work:** Instructed by Chelsea Football Club in its dispute with Chelsea Man concerning the registration of the Chelsea Supporters Trust trade mark.

Philip Roberts Known for his technical background and his skill representing clients in sensitive database rights litigation. He is also experienced in trade mark disputes involving media clients and retailers. **Strengths:** "He is technically fantastic and gives spot-on advice." "He is very bright, good on his feet and easy to work with. Clients like his knowledge of IP law and technology." **Recent work:** Defended Zynga against a claim by JW Spear & Sons that the game "Scramble with Friends" infringed on the "Scrabble" trade marks. The case resulted in the invalidation of the "tile" mark previously possessed by the claimant.

Hogarth Chambers

See profile on p.866

THE SET

Home to an impressive selection of IP practitioners which is particularly strong at the junior level. Sources are quick to highlight the quality of its senior juniors, whilst also noting the polished advocacy and commercial awareness of the silks. Members are instructed on a broad range of trade mark, copyright and design right disputes, and are also recognised for their expertise in electrical and mechanical patent matters.

Client service: The clerking team is "very good and very responsive." The "excellent" senior clerk Clive Nicholls is praised as someone "who goes out of his way to assist solicitors and gives a really good insight into the market."

SILKS

Roger Wyand QC Well regarded by sources for his strong courtroom presentation and his abilities handling high-stakes litigation, including appellate proceedings. He has significant experience in trade mark and patent litigation infringement disputes. **Strengths:** "He is a brilliant asset with exceptional knowledge of everything IP-related. He is an unassuming, relaxed and calming influence, and he never gets flustered." "He is user-friendly and commercially savvy." **Recent work:** Acted for Pal International in a passing-off dispute with Gamma Healthcare, concerning medical wipe products.

Alastair Wilson QC A seasoned silk, distinguished for his extensive experience in, and creative approach to, copyright litigation. His recent activity also includes trade secrets misappropriation claims, patent invalidation actions and patent infringement actions. **Strengths:** "He is a man for hard cases. He thinks laterally and dynamically, and challenges the norms." "He has very impressive technical knowledge and legal expertise." **Recent work:** Instructed by TDY Industries in its dispute with Pramet Tools over the alleged infringement of a mechanical patent.

JUNIORS

Michael Hicks A highly regarded senior junior who earns plaudits for his client care and excellent courtroom advocacy. He acts in litigation arising from the parallel importation of goods and the misuse of confidential information. He is also experienced in patent and trade mark infringement claims. **Strengths:** "He is fantastic on paper, has really good judgement and is incredibly adept at handling questions from the bench. He is very gentle but redoubtable before the court." "He is extremely personable and very good with clients." **Recent work:** Represented Jaguar Land Rover in its successful interim injunction application for the restraint of DGT Wheels' importation and sale of replica wheels.

Andrew Norris Recognised for his excellent manner with clients, his commerciality and his experience handling IPEC proceedings. He is known for his representation of luxury brands and entertainment clients, including in trade mark and copyright infringement disputes. He also has experience acting in cases involving mechanical patents. **Strengths:** "He is a very experienced and savvy trade mark specialist." "He is helpful, keen, very bright and hard-working. He has a lot to offer on difficult cases." **Recent work:** Acted for Jack Wills in its High Court action against House of Fraser, regarding the use of a logo similar to that of Jack Wills on a House of Fraser clothing range.

Thomas St Quintin Offers commercially minded advice and takes a strategic approach to litigation, attracting praise from peers and solicitors for the quality of his courtroom presentation. He handles trade mark, design right and copyright litigation, including infringement claims and ownership disputes. **Strengths:** "He ticks all the boxes – he is technically outstanding, responsive, approachable, commercial and clearly has a razor-sharp mind. He understands the principles of client service and helps solicitors deliver exceptional service to their clients." "He is very thorough, always thinks very commercially, and is very bright. He makes things clear for clients and puts them at ease." **Recent work:** Acted for Bhopal Productions UK in a dispute with Akhtar, concerning copyright ownership in a feature film.

Guy Tritton A highly responsive barrister with excellent client service skills, who stands out for his knowledge of pan-European trade mark matters. He has experience handling anti-counterfeiting actions, passing-off claims, database rights disputes and patent infringement claims. **Strengths:** "He is a very forthright, direct and commercial barrister." "He is very responsive, very helpful in turning cases around and very experienced." **Recent work:** Acted for Domestic & General Insurance in its passing-off action against Secure My Goods.

Richard Davis Well regarded for his advocacy skills and technical knowledge. He is recognised for his involvement in high-value electronics, pharmaceutical and electrical patent infringement disputes. **Strengths:** "He is very helpful, pragmatic and clients have huge respect for him." "He is very user-friendly and very knowledgeable in the IP arena." **Recent work:** Represented British Gas in its dispute with Vanclare concerning patent infringement claims connected to smart metering devices.

Gwilym Harbottle Recognised for his experience acting in copyright proceedings for clients in the recording industry. He also has experience assisting with trade mark and design right infringement claims, as well as and multi-jurisdictional licensing disputes. **Strengths:** "He is intelligent, available and very down-to-earth. He provides high-quality work and is very professional." "He is very academic and detail-oriented." **Recent work:** Acted for Motivate Publishing FZ in its dispute with the owners of Hello Magazine over a trade mark licence for the Middle East edition of the magazine.

Amanda Michaels Highly experienced and pragmatic junior highlighted for her expertise in trade mark law. She is experienced handling IPEC, IPO and appellate High Court proceedings. She is recommended for the quality of her courtroom advocacy and is sought after for opinion work. **Strengths:** "She is an ideal choice for opinion work. Her oral presentation is forthright and persuasive." "She is extremely practical, very commercial, tells it at is it is, and is great with clients." **Recent work:** Acted for the defendant to a claim by Procter & Gamble of design right infringement regarding the design of cosmetics packaging.

Benjamin Longstaff A respected junior with abilities beyond his year of call, and a strong reputation for trade mark disputes. He is also noted for his presence in high-value patent infringement proceedings involving electronics companies. **Strengths:** "He is a real talent whose experience, advice and approach are far beyond his years." "He is a very focused and clever barrister, and is extremely good to work with." **Recent work:** Instructed by Vringo as junior counsel in its patent infringement and validity dispute with ZTE over the handover of mobile data between radio network subsystems. The case had significant FRAND aspects.

Jonathan Moss Forthright and practical junior noted for his involvement in high-profile Community trade mark litigation. He has additional experience handling passing off claims and revocation actions, as well as pharmaceutical patent disputes and misuse of confidential information cases. **Strengths:** "He is always very helpful and pragmatic in the advice he gives." "He is very commercial and has an excellent depth of experience." **Recent work:** Instructed by Rolex in its trade mark revocation action against Ralph Lauren for its registration of the trade mark RLX for use in relation to watches.

Jeremy Reed Admired for his strategic approach and his experience acting in disputes arising from misappropriation of trade secrets allegations. Reed is regularly involved in trade mark application and opposition matters arising in the retail industry. **Strengths:** "He is very sharp, very measured and clients like him." "He is extremely knowledgeable, very approachable and easy to work with." **Recent work:** Acted for Skechers USA in its opposition to an attempt by Go Outdoors to trade mark the phrases "Go Run" and "Go Walk." The opposition rested on the question of whether the marks were descriptive or distinctive.

Band 3

Blackstone Chambers

See profile on p.813

THE SET

Fields a number of silks with specialist IP knowledge and a strong reputation in the media and entertainment sector. Members are recognised for their extensive experience representing television, sports and recording industry clients. They are regularly called upon for copyright litigation, including licensing disputes, ownership claims and claims of online platform infringement. The set also has an increasing presence in contentious patent matters involving telecommunications and pharmaceutical clients, including FRAND trials and EPO oppositions.

Client service: Gary Oliver leads the clerking team. Sources say: "The clerking team at Blackstone is excellent, very efficient and very responsive."

SILKS

Michael Bloch QC An incredibly bright, tactical and commercially aware silk recommended for complex trade mark litigation. He has substantial experience in opposition actions and infringement claims involving digital retailers. His recent work also includes acting in pharmaceutical patent disputes. **Strengths:** "He is phenomenally smart, very aware of how judges might approach particular problems, and is not only logical but good with strategy." "He is a heavyweight. He is fiercely bright, very affable and a very good advocate." **Recent work:** Appeared in the dispute between Cadbury and Néstle concerning the registration of the KitKat shape trade mark.

Robert Howe QC A media and sports specialist known for handling high-end licensing and infringement disputes, including cases involving the use of content on digital platforms. He is well versed in copyright law and experienced handling trade mark litigation. **Strengths:** "He is a tough and very tenacious opponent." "He is an excellent advocate with absolute attention to detail." **Recent work:** Represents Sky and the England and Wales Cricket Board in copyright infringement action against Fanatix. The dispute concerned the broadcast of cricket match clips online.

Ian Mill QC A very well-known and respected advocate whose work in this area involves representing recording and television industry clients in high-value copyright litigation. He handles rights ownership disputes and anti-piracy actions involving digital platforms. **Strengths:** "He is an excellent and very authoritative barrister who you'd rather have on your team than against you." "If you need a warrior to go into battle on a difficult case, then he is your guy." **Recent work:** Defended Blue Mountain Music against proceedings initiated by Cayman Music, concerning the ownership of copyright in certain Bob Marley songs.

Other Ranked Lawyers

Kelyn Bacon QC (Brick Court Chambers) Recognised for her life sciences sector expertise and her knowledge in pan-European regulatory matters, including orphan medical product authorisations. She stands out for her depth of experience handling Supplementary Protection Certificate disputes. **Strengths:** "She is sensible, gives pragmatic advice and is very accessible." "She is exceptionally well regarded and seen as a really serious opponent." **Recent work:** Instructed by Astellas in defence of an action initiated by Accord regarding the eligibility for generic marketing authorisations of the cancer drug bendamustine.

Nicholas Saunders (Brick Court Chambers) Frequently handles complex telecommunications and pharmaceutical patent infringement disputes. He is also experienced advising on trade mark disputes. **Strengths:** "He has a very calming manner and good instincts on what points to run." "He is very strong intellectually and user-friendly." **Recent work:** Instructed by Samsung in defence of a high-profile patent infringement claim brought by Unwired Planet, concerning 4G and 3G mobile phones.

Mark Engelman (Hardwicke) Recommended for contentious trade mark matters, and particularly sought after by media and entertainment clients. He is also experienced handling cross-border and high-profile disputes. **Strengths:** "He impresses with his creative thinking, technical ability and legal arguments, both written and in hearings." "He is always helpful and practical." **Recent work:** Appeared in the dispute between the Ukulele Orchestra of Great Britain and The United Kingdom Ukulele Orchestra concerning claims of Community trade mark infringement.

Malcolm Chapple (New Square Chambers) A seasoned litigator highlighted for the strength of his advocacy and his experience in the IPEC. His recent work includes the handling of trade mark and patent infringement claims, as well as database rights disputes. **Strengths:** "He is a very experienced barrister and an effective opponent in IP cases." "Clients love him and judges have a lot of respect for him." **Recent work:** Acted for Bestway Cash and Carry in its long-running action against Bestway Technology concerning claims of trade mark infringement and passing off.

Madeleine Heal (New Square Chambers) Maintains a broad litigation practice taking in patent infringement, copyright ownership and database rights disputes. She is particularly noted for her representation of media sector clients. **Strengths:** "She is an excellent advocate who really knows her stuff and inspires confidence." "She provides excellent advice." **Recent work:** Instructed by BSI Enterprises as sole counsel in its action against Blue Mountain Music, concerning the ownership of music that Bob Marley produced between 1973 and 1976.

Michael Edenborough QC (Serle Court) A seasoned silk highlighted for his deep expertise in trade mark law. He has additional expertise in patents, trade marks and design rights disputes. He is recognised for his experience assisting government agencies and abilities handling appellate proceedings. **Strengths:** "He is very experienced and always provides careful and considered advice." "He is brilliant in court and his knowledge base is second to none." **Recent work:** Appeared in the trade mark infringement dispute between social networking platform Pinterest and Premium Interest, a digital news service.

THE REGIONS

Intellectual Property
Leading Juniors
Band 1
Cook Christopher *Exchange Chambers*
Jones Victoria *3PB Barristers*
Lambert Jane *4-5 Gray's Inn Square*
Alphabetical order within each band. Band 1 is highest.

Ranked Lawyers

Christopher Cook (Exchange Chambers) Particularly well known for his skill in patent, licensing and design right matters, alongside passing off and trade mark issues. Sources are quick to praise his commercially astute approach and strong grasp of the technical aspects of complex IP law.

Jane Lambert (4-5 Gray's Inn Square) Well regarded for her burgeoning, UK-wide IP practice which has its roots in the North of England. She is notably active on behalf of emerging businesses and regularly assists start-ups with a range of matters including trade marks, copyright and patents. **Strengths:** "Very good on strategy, tactics, drafting and client management. She is effective, helpful and always willing to go the extra mile." "Passionate about IP and very proactive." **Recent work:** Appeared in Playboy Enterprises International, Inc. v Michael Ross, an application for transfer of a domain name that was the same as, or confusingly similar to, the complainant's trade mark.

Victoria Jones (3PB Barristers) Enjoys a strong reputation in the field for her broad-based knowledge and significant expertise. Her diverse practice covers areas such as passing off, breach of confidence and trade mark disputes. **Strengths:** "Excellent in court with a very friendly manner that puts clients at ease. She has an impressive intellect and an excellent eye for detail." "First-class, she adopts a commercial approach, manages client expectations and is remarkably quick to respond." **Recent work:** Acted on behalf of the claimant in Victoria's Secret Stores Brand Management Inc v (1) Cornucopia Entertainment Limited (2) Minesh Vohra. The claim centred around passing off, trade mark infringement and breach of contract after the defendants allegedly sold unauthorised tickets to the annual Victoria's Secret Fashion Show.

International Arbitration

Contents:

LONDON Arbitrators

International Arbitration: Arbitrators
Star individuals
Hoffmann Lord *Brick Court Chambers*
Veeder V V *Essex Court Chambers*
Band 1
Bartlett Andrew *Crown Office Chambers*
Black Michael *XXIV Old Buildings*
Blackburn John *Atkin Chambers* *
Boswood Anthony *Fountain Court Chambers* *
Brynmor Thomas David *39 Essex Chambers (ORL)* ◊
Calver Neil *Brick Court Chambers*
Edelman Colin *Devereux* *
Fernyhough Richard *Keating Chambers* *
Furst Stephen *Keating Chambers* *
Gaitskell Robert *Keating Chambers* *
Glick Ian *One Essex Court*
Gruder Jeffrey *Essex Court Chambers* *
Harding Richard *Keating Chambers* *
Heilbron Hilary *Brick Court Chambers*
Hirst Jonathan *Brick Court Chambers*
Jacobs Richard *Essex Court Chambers*
Joseph David *Essex Court Chambers* *
Kealey Gavin *7 King's Bench Walk*
Landau Toby *Essex Court Chambers*
Langley Sir Gordon *Fountain Court Chambers* *
Leaver Peter *One Essex Court* *
Lew Julian D. M. *20 Essex Street*
Marrin John *Keating Chambers* *
Matthews Duncan *20 Essex Street*
Moger Christopher *4 Pump Court* *
Redfern Alan *One Essex Court* *
Reichert Klaus *Brick Court Chambers*
Rix Bernard *20 Essex Street*
Rokison Kenneth *Kenneth Rokison QC - International*
Rowley William J *20 Essex Street*
Siberry Richard *Essex Court Chambers*
Smouha Joe *Essex Court Chambers*
Sutton David *20 Essex Street*
Style Christopher *One Essex Court*
Symons Christopher *3 Verulam Buildings*
Tackaberry John *39 Essex Chambers*
* *Indicates individual with profile.*
Alphabetical order within each band. Band 1 is highest.

Ranked Lawyers

John Blackburn QC (see p.596) (Atkin Chambers) Best known for his expertise in international construction and engineering-related arbitrations. He accepts appointments in ad hoc and institutional arbitrations under the auspices of the ICC, the LCIA and UNCITRAL. He has acted as co-arbitrator, chair and sole arbitrator of tribunals with seats in Geneva, Paris, Stockholm, Singapore and Dubai. **Strengths:** "Immensely experienced, very well organised, and a man with a good incisive brain."

Lord Hoffmann QC (Brick Court Chambers) Possesses a prestigious reputation as an arbitrator in disputes relating to intellectual property rights and public international law, among others. Throughout his long-standing career, he has been appointed as an arbitrator in proceedings governed by many leading arbitral bodies including the ICC, SIAC, KLRCA and the LCIA. **Strengths:** "He is everything that you can possibly want from an arbitrator: he's merit driven, fast and in control of the proceedings."

Neil Calver QC (Brick Court Chambers) His multifaceted practice as a barrister serves him well when he sits as an arbitrator, and he handles a variety of matters including those relating to banking and finance, aviation, professional negligence, commercial law and insurance and reinsurance. He has accepted appointments under major arbitral bodies including the LCIA, the ICC and the PCA in The Hague. **Strengths:** "He has a great mind, particularly for insurance. He is also very personable and great to work with."

Hilary Heilbron QC (Brick Court Chambers) Widely considered to be a heavyweight in international arbitration who has expertise in cases concerning the energy, banking, telecommunications and pharmaceutical industries. She has been appointed under the rules of the ICC, AAA, ICDR and LCIA and has considerable experience of acting as an ad hoc and emergency arbitrator. **Strengths:** "An intelligent arbitrator and a steady hand on the tiller."

Jonathan Hirst QC (Brick Court Chambers) Accomplished arbitrator with experience in hearing a wide array of disputes including Bermuda Form arbitrations. He specialises in a range of disputes including maritime, insurance and reinsurance matters. **Strengths:** "Very conscientious and fair arbitrator with a very sound approach." "Very good with witnesses, particularly in terms of making them feel at ease."

Klaus Reichert (Brick Court Chambers) Has accepted appointments as a chair, co-arbitrator and sole arbitrator of tribunals with seats around the globe. He is especially well regarded in the USA, Brazil, Paris and London. He has heard a wide range of cases under the auspices of the ICC, LCIA, ICDR, AAA and DIFC, among others. **Strengths:** "Very fair and commercially minded." "Good at coming up with pragmatic and interesting solutions to problems."

Andrew Bartlett QC (Crown Office Chambers) Has long-standing experience of acting as an arbitrator in a wide range of disputes including those relating to the insurance, financial services, construction and engineering sectors. He has sat on arbitration panels in London, Paris and Hong Kong. **Strengths:** "He is an excellent arbitrator, who is decisive, hard-working and clear-thinking."

Colin Edelman QC (see p.639) (Devereux) Renowned in the field of international arbitration for his wealth of expertise in the full range of arbitral disputes, he specialises in commercial matters, especially insurance and reinsurance claims. He regularly acts as sole arbitrator under the rules of leading institutions and has handled hearings taking place across the globe. **Strengths:** "Second to none in the insurance sector." "An excellent arbitrator who is responsive and pragmatic. He conducts himself in an extremely professional fashion."

Ian Glick QC (One Essex Court) Highly respected for his expertise in disputes concerning construction, company acquisitions, joint ventures, oil and gas, shipbuilding and trade finance, amongst others. He has sat as a co-arbitrator, chair and sole arbitrator on both ad hoc and institutional arbitrations including those under the auspices of the LCIA, ICC and SCC. He has heard cases in London, New York, Singapore and Lusaka, to name but a few locations. **Strengths:** "He is intelligent, has a great capacity to listen and a measured and careful style that works well in the international context."

Peter Leaver QC (see p.698) (One Essex Court) Accomplished international commercial arbitrator, focusing his practice on corporate matters as well as claims arising in the insurance, IP and energy sectors. Recently, he has been particularly active in disputes emerging from the oil and gas industry. He is experienced in sitting in tribunals governed by ad hoc and institutional rules. **Strengths:** "A standout arbitrator who is clever, knowledgeable and commercially minded."

Christopher Style QC (One Essex Court) Recommended for his international arbitration practice, he acts as an arbitrator in ad hoc and institutionally governed hearings with seats in London, Singapore, Dubai, Stockholm, The Hague, Copenhagen and Zürich, among others. He has notable experience in commercial disputes including those concerning oil and gas projects, joint ventures, financing and infrastructure. **Strengths:** "Very responsive. He has a pleasant demeanour, is open to both parties and makes you feel you're getting a very fair hearing."

Alan Redfern (see p.749) (One Essex Court) Widely respected for his expertise as an arbitrator in the domestic and international commercial arenas. He has a wealth of experience in hearing disputes governed by the rules of prominent arbitral institutions such as the ICC, AAA and LCIA. His comprehensive practice covers a wide range of issues including insurance and reinsurance concerns, international construction projects, oil and gas claims and joint venture matters. **Strengths:** "He has a lovely, light touch while always remaining in charge." "A man with good commercial sense."

V V Veeder QC (Essex Court Chambers) Widely celebrated as one of the most distinguished international arbitrators. His deep expertise in this area sees him regularly appointed as arbitrator in commercial arbitrations as well as investment treaty disputes. **Strengths:** "One of the most sought-after arbitrators in the world. He's been doing it for a very long time and is really good at running a tribunal."

Jeffrey Gruder QC (see p.661) (Essex Court Chambers) Distinguished for his expertise in acting as an arbitrator in a number of high-value international disputes both in an ad hoc context and governed by the rules of the Swiss Chamber, UNCITRAL and the LCIA. He has recently been appointed in tribunals with seats in Zürich, Geneva, Singapore and Toronto handling claims relating to insurance policies, shipbuilding contracts and patent licensing, amongst others. **Strengths:** "Extremely impartial, efficient, on the ball and very well prepared."

Richard Jacobs QC (Essex Court Chambers) Sits as an arbitrator in disputes concerning a vast range of issues, and has handled matters relating to insurance and reinsurance, shipbuilding, joint ventures, power projects and distribution agreements. He has been appointed as arbitrator in ad hoc arbitrations and under the auspices of the DIFC, the LCIA, the ICC and SIAC. **Strengths:** "Very skilful in navigating complex legal technical issues."

David Joseph QC (see p.686) (Essex Court Chambers) Formidable practitioner with wide-ranging expertise spanning a variety of sectors such as insurance and reinsurance, construction, aerospace and joint ventures. He has been appointed in ad hoc proceedings and hearings governed by the rules of the ICC, LCIA and LMAA. **Strengths:** "Very intellectually strong and able to cope with the most complex cases."

Toby Landau QC (Essex Court Chambers) Highly recommended international arbitrator with substantial experience in international trade, energy, shipping and infrastructure project disputes. He has been appointed as a sole arbitrator, co-arbitrator and chair in ad hoc and institutional proceedings under the rules of major arbitral bodies including the ICC, the LCIA, the CRCICA and ARIAS.

Richard Siberry QC (Essex Court Chambers) A formidable international arbitrator with considerable experience in the commercial sector, who covers a full range of disputes, including those relating to the insurance and reinsurance, shipping, oil and gas and commodities sectors. He has acted as a sole and co-arbitrator for various arbitral bodies, including the ICC, LMAA, LCIA, and has also handled matters under the (Railtrack) Access Dispute Resolution Rules. **Strengths:** "He works incredibly hard no matter how big or small the case is. He gets into the details and writes excellent comprehensive awards."

Joe Smouha QC (Essex Court Chambers) Highly reputed international arbitrator, appointed in ad hoc arbitrations, as well as under principal arbitral bodies such as the ICC, AAA and LCIA. He specialises in hearing commercial disputes of every stripe. **Strengths:** "Very clever and great to work with."

Julian Lew QC (20 Essex Street) Possesses over 30 years of experience as an arbitrator and is sought after for his wealth of expertise in disputes arising in a wide range of spheres. He has handled a number of arbitrations concerning joint ventures, oil and gas, construction contracts and trading agreements. He has sat as a sole arbitrator, co-arbitrator and chair on tribunals with seats in Zürich, Paris, Canada and Prague among others. **Strengths:** "Very fair, pragmatic and on top of the procedure."

Duncan Matthews QC (20 Essex Street) Possesses long-standing experience in international arbitrations and has expertise in a broad spectrum of sectors including banking and finance, international trade, carriage of goods, oil and gas, and insurance and reinsurance. He accepts appointments under leading arbitral institutions with seats around the world. **Strengths:** "He knows the case and is very balanced and fair."

William Rowley QC (20 Essex Street) Highly regarded for his expertise in this arena, having chaired or co-chaired tribunals governed by the laws of a range of jurisdictions including China, Poland, Dubai, Uganda, England and New York. He has participated in various tribunals handling disputes concerning a range of matters such as oil and gas contracts, trade mark licensing, defence industry contracts and joint ventures. **Strengths:** "He is incredibly sensible and manages the parties extremely well."

Bernard Rix (20 Essex Street) Possesses a deep commercial law expertise, having acted as a judge at the Commercial Court and subsequently at the Court of Appeal. He is experienced in acting as an arbitrator in proceedings concerning a wide range of commercial issues including banking and finance, energy and natural resources and insurance and reinsurance. **Strengths:** "Excellent as an arbitrator."

David Sutton (20 Essex Street) Pre-eminent international arbitrator with a wealth of expertise in the construction and engineering, environment, energy and IP sectors. Over the course of his career, he has been appointed as an arbitrator under the rules of the leading arbitral bodies, including the ICC, LCIA, AAA and HKIAC. **Strengths:** "A pleasure to work with. He's meticulous, intelligent and diligent."

John Tackaberry QC (39 Essex Chambers) Acclaimed international arbitrator with considerable expertise in the areas of construction, commercial and energy law. His substantial experience as an advocate in international arbitrations has afforded him a deep understanding of disputes arising in both common law and civil law jurisdictions. **Strengths:** "He is a pragmatist and likes to cut to what really counts."

David Brynmor Thomas (39 Essex Chambers) A respected name for international arbitration who regularly acts as counsel as well as sits as arbitrator in significant commercial disputes. He has particularly deep expertise in infrastructure matters and is well versed in the LCIA and UNCITRAL rules. **Strengths:** "Thorough, careful and analytical in his approach."

Anthony Boswood QC (see p.599) (Fountain Court Chambers) Noted international arbitrator appointed in disputes in various regions including Kenya, Germany, South Africa and Ukraine. He has solid experience of acting as a co-chair and sole arbitrator in ad hoc arbitrations and those governed by the rules of the ICC and LCIA. **Strengths:** "Fantastic arbitrator. He's absolutely no nonsense, and just gets to the point quickly and concisely."

Sir Gordon Langley QC (see p.695) (Fountain Court Chambers) Highly reputed former High Court judge currently concentrating on acting as an arbitrator in disputes arising in a number of spheres including insurance and reinsurance, energy, shipping, commercial contracts and joint ventures. He acts as a party-appointed arbitrator in ad hoc hearings and under the rules of SIAC, the LCIA and the ICC. **Strengths:** "Brilliant, incisive, quick and charming."

Richard Fernyhough QC (see p.644) (Keating Chambers) Leading arbitrator in construction and engineering disputes who has handled cases concerning hotels, power stations, railways and airports. He is vastly experienced in acting as an arbitrator under the rules of various prominent arbitral bodies including the LCIA, SIAC, DIAC, the Cairo Regional Centre for Commercial Arbitration and the ICC. **Strengths:** "Clever, diligent and hard-working."

Stephen Furst QC (see p.649) (Keating Chambers) Widely praised for his expertise in highly complex disputes concerning the oil and gas and construction industries, as well as computer software and hardware. He has recently been appointed under a range of arbitral institutions including the LCIA, ICC, DIAC and HKIAC. **Strengths:** "Extremely experienced and patient."

Robert Gaitskell QC (see p.649) (Keating Chambers) A chartered engineer, widely respected for his work as an arbitrator in highly technical multi-jurisdictional construction, engineering and technology disputes. He undertakes cases concerning a range of issues, and has handled matters relating to power stations, oil and gas plants and petrochemical projects. He is regularly appointed under a number of arbitral institutions such as the ICC, KLRCA, EDF, LCIA, SIAC and Dubai RTA. **Strengths:** "Very strong on technical disputes because of his background as an engineer."

Richard Harding QC (see p.663) (Keating Chambers) Multilingual arbitrator with substantial experience of acting under the rules and laws of numerous jurisdictions in the Middle East especially Egypt, Qatar, the UAE, Kuwait and Jordan. He possesses expertise in various types of construction and engineering matters, and has handled a number of project related disputes concerning railways, roads, factories, water infrastructure and high-rise developments. **Strengths:** "The go-to person for construction arbitrations with a Middle Eastern element." "Highly skilled in ensuring that the arbitration process is conducted quickly, efficiently and cost-effectively."

John Marrin QC (see p.708) (Keating Chambers) Best known for his expertise in international construction cases, but also regularly sits as an arbitrator on disputes relating to technology, energy, PFI, rail and software projects. His experience is of a truly international character, as is evidenced by his participation in tribunals concerned with disputes in more than 34 jurisdictions. **Strengths:** "Incredibly bright, pleasant to work with and an exceptionally hard worker."

Kenneth Rokison QC (Kenneth Rokison QC – International Commercial Arbitrator) A man with impressive experience of handling major commercial disputes, as a barrister, a judge and latterly an arbitrator. His areas of expertise include insurance and reinsurance, commodity trades and oil and gas. He accepts ad hoc appointments as well as those made under the auspices of the LCIA and ICC. **Strengths:** "Superb. He's very quick and grasps the points immediately."

Gavin Kealey QC (7 King's Bench Walk) Prominent arbitrator in the international commercial disputes sphere, best known for his expertise in insurance and reinsurance matters. He builds on many years of experience as counsel, arbitrator and deputy High Court judge. His practice is of a truly international nature, as evidenced by his appointment to chair tribunals in places as far afield as Italy, New Zealand, Dubai, Singapore and the USA. **Strengths:** "Very well prepared and very good at handling the dispute, the parties and the counsel." "Gives timely, well-reasoned decisions."

Michael Black QC (XXIV Old Buildings) Specialises in hearing commercial, insurance, construction and oil and gas related arbitrations particularly in the Middle East, India and Africa. He has been part of international tribunals with seats across a variety of jurisdictions including New Delhi, Bucharest and London.

Christopher Moger QC (see p.720) (4 Pump Court) An arbitrator with a burgeoning reputation for handling a range of commercial disputes including those concerning joint ventures and share sale agreements. He is particularly well thought of for his expertise in Sino-foreign disputes and he is a noted member of the HKIAC, as well as SIAC, KLRCA and CIETAC. **Strengths:** "He is fiercely intelligent and has a tremendous work ethic, as well as a great mind for detail. He is an excellent advocate, and he has been able to transfer his skills seamlessly into his role as an arbitrator."

Christopher Symons QC (3 Verulam Buildings) Best known for his expertise in insurance and reinsurance disputes. He is also recommended for construction, telecommunications, shipping, pharmaceuticals and commodities arbitrations. He acts as a chair and co-arbitrator in cases under the auspices of the ICC, the LCIA and UNCITRAL among others. **Strengths:** "A calm authority." "He makes sure that the Tribunal addresses all the issues raised."

LONDON Construction/Engineering

International Arbitration Construction/Engineering Leading Sets
Band 1
Atkin Chambers *
Keating Chambers *
Band 2
Crown Office Chambers *
39 Essex Chambers *
4 Pump Court *

Leading Silks	
Band 1	
Boulding Philip	*Keating Chambers* *
Brannigan Sean	*4 Pump Court* *
Catchpole Stuart	*39 Essex Chambers*
Darling Paul	*Keating Chambers* *
Dennison Stephen	*Atkin Chambers*
Harding Richard	*Keating Chambers* *
McMullan Manus	*Atkin Chambers*
Streatfeild-James David	*Atkin Chambers*
Taverner Marcus	*Keating Chambers* *
ter Haar Roger	*Crown Office Chambers*
White Andrew	*Atkin Chambers* *
Band 2	
Ansell Rachel	*4 Pump Court* *
Ashcroft Michael	*20 Essex Street (ORL)* ◊
Black Michael	*XXIV Old Buildings (ORL)* ◊
Buehrlen Veronique	*Keating Chambers* *
Constable Adam	*Keating Chambers* *
Dennys Nicholas	*Atkin Chambers*
Doerries Chantal-Aimée	*Atkin Chambers* *
Elliott Timothy	*Keating Chambers* *
Furst Stephen	*Keating Chambers* *
Goddard Andrew	*Atkin Chambers* *
Gunning Alexander	*4 Pump Court* *
Lemon Jane	*Keating Chambers* *
Lofthouse Simon	*Atkin Chambers* *
Moran Vincent	*Keating Chambers* *
Parkin Fiona	*Atkin Chambers*
Reed Paul	*Hardwicke (ORL)* ◊ 🄰
Rigney Andrew	*Crown Office Chambers*
Thomas David	*Keating Chambers* *
Wilken Sean	*39 Essex Chambers* *
New Silks	
Hickey Alexander	*4 Pump Court* *
Hussain Riaz	*Atkin Chambers* *

** Indicates set / individual with profile.*
🄰 direct access (see p.24).
◊ (ORL) = Other Ranked Lawyer.
Alphabetical order within each band. Band 1 is highest.

International Arbitration Construction/Engineering Leading Juniors	
Band 1	
Chern Cyril	*Crown Office Chambers*
Ghaly Karim	*39 Essex Chambers* *
Lewis Christopher	*Atkin Chambers* *
Band 2	
Buckingham Paul	*Keating Chambers* *
Bury Paul	*Keating Chambers* *
Chennells Mark	*Atkin Chambers*
Garrett Lucy	*Keating Chambers* *
Lamont Calum	*Keating Chambers* *
Pimlott Charles	*Crown Office Chambers*
Robb Adam	*39 Essex Chambers*
Thompson James	*Keating Chambers* *

Band 1

Atkin Chambers

See profile on p.806

THE SET

Atkin Chambers is celebrated for its deep bench of members, who have experience of handling a wide range of international arbitrations concerning construction and engineering projects in South East Asia, Central Asia, Europe, the Middle East, North and South America, Africa and the Caribbean. The set represents large contractors and developers, shipping corporations and drilling service providers, among others, in arbitrations under the auspices of the ICC, SIAC, HKIAC, LCIA and DIAC. The expertise of its barristers is regularly sought after for high exposure matters. One recent example of the work they have done is Grupo Unidos per el Canal v Autoridad del Canal de Panamá, said to be the largest infrastructure project dispute in history, valued at USD5.2 billion. The matter concerned the expansion of the Panama Canal. A solicitor instructing the set commented: "They are very much hands-on lawyers and good team players, who clearly know their area well."

Client service: "The clerking staff is very helpful and responsive." Justin Wilson, the set's senior clerk "does a very effective job and is particularly impressive."

SILKS

Stephen Dennison QC Widely praised for his expertise in handling international arbitrations, primarily in connection with matters of civil engineering, construction, transport, energy and utilities. He is particularly sought after for arbitrations governed by the rules of the ICC, SIAC and the LCIA. **Strengths:** "He's a very good analyst – he has a very good grasp of the key legal and factual issues and takes a very meticulous approach to the case."

Manus McMullan QC One of the leading practitioners in the area who has a stellar reputation in the sphere of infrastructure disputes. He is sought after by governments, professional advisers, individuals and international contractors in connection with national and foreign disputes concerning a wide array of issues including construction, engineering, energy and utilities. **Strengths:** "He's very bright, hardworking and an excellent advocate. He is very good with the tribunal, excellent in arbitration matters and very user-friendly." **Recent work:** Acted on behalf of the claimant, a large cladding contractor, with regard to a USD300 million claim relating to the termination of a contract concerning the construction of ultra-high luxury first-class and business lounges for a new airport in Doha, Qatar.

David Streatfeild-James QC A pre-eminent silk who attracts incredible praise for his advocacy. He handles challenging, high-value international arbitrations with seats in London and abroad, appearing on behalf of contractors, professionals, private employers and governments from around the world. **Strengths:** "An incredible advocate. He is an absolute master of the 'magical mystery tour' in which he walks an expert witness through an extended series of seemingly innocuous questions that invariably end with a crippling admission." "Unquestionably a top choice for any bet-the-company construction disputes."

Andrew White QC (see p.793) Specialises in international arbitrations concerning the full spectrum of construction and engineering-related disputes including those concerning shipbuilding, rail, and oil and gas projects. He represents a myriad of clients including manufacturers, contractors, governments and professional advisers. **Strengths:** "He makes himself available at short notice, thinks quickly and is really good at developing strategies."

Nicholas Dennys QC Possesses solid expertise in the sphere of international arbitration particularly with respect to construction, road and rail transport, infrastructure, IT and oil and gas-related concerns. He is experienced in appearing before tribunals around the world governed by the rules of the ICC, HKIAC, LCIA and SIAC. **Strengths:** "He's incredibly bright – razor sharp."

Chantal-Aimée Doerries QC (see p.635) Best known for her expertise in representing clients in international arbitrations concerning energy, infrastructure projects and construction. She has significant experience in ad hoc arbitrations as well as those held under the auspices of the LCIA, ICC, SIAC, LMAA and SCMA. **Strengths:** "She's good on the law and very user-friendly. She turns work around quickly and is a pleasure to work with."

Andrew Goddard QC (see p.655) Acts on behalf of a range of clients including contractors, professionals, employers and sub-contractors in international arbitrations administered by the HKIAC, LCIA, LMAA and the ICC. **Strengths:** "He is very imaginative and finds solutions that others wouldn't necessarily come up with."

Simon Lofthouse QC (see p.703) Concentrates his practice heavily on complex international construction arbitrations, but also possesses expertise in disputes regarding energy and construction-related professional negligence issues. He represents professionals, governments and corporations in hearings taking place in Africa, the Middle East, Asia, Europe and the Caribbean. **Strengths:** "Very pleasant to work with. He engaged very efficiently right from the outset. He got directly involved, went into considerable detail in order to understand the dynamics of the case, and gave very commercial advice." "He is hands-on, very experienced and unflappable."

Fiona Parkin QC Particularly sought after for her international arbitration expertise, specifically handling disputes in connection with large infrastructure projects. She acts on behalf of governments, public bodies, international corporations and professionals in arbitrations administered by leading arbitral bodies, including the ICC, IBA, UNCITRAL and LCIA. **Strengths:** "Has amazing attention to detail and masters the case completely."

Riaz Hussain QC (see p.679) Considerably experienced in appearing as a sole counsel in large construction and engineering, energy, natural resources and utilities-related international arbitrations, governed by prominent institutions, such as the LCIA, DIAC and ICC. **Strengths:** "Gets to grips with the details of a case quickly and gives clear direction."

JUNIORS

Christopher Lewis (see p.700) Has an international practice covering disputes relating to matters of construction, information technology and energy across Asia, the USA, the Middle East and Europe. He has a particular interest in disputes relating to conflict of laws. **Strengths:** "He is very good at working with a team. He's very down to earth and pragmatic. He knows how best to resolve things from a commercial point of view as well as a legal point of view."

Mark Chennells Known for his prowess in international arbitration concerning the technology and construction sectors. He assists clients on a broad array of contentious issues, and is an expert in property construction, infrastructure disputes and energy disputes. He is particularly experienced in appearing before tribunals with seats in Europe and the Far East. **Strengths:** "He has a first-class intellect and a charming approach."

Keating Chambers

See profile on p.868

THE SET

Keating Chambers is a true heavyweight set with extensive experience in the construction, infrastructure and energy sectors. It is particularly recommended for its expertise in handling technically complicated cases, due to the dual qualification of many of its members as engineers and barristers. Its silks and juniors provide robust representation in disputes concerning projects across the world, and have particularly strong practices in the Middle East. They handle the full range of institutional arbitrations, including SIAC, DIAC, LCIA, ICC, KLRAC and HKIAC matters. Observers note: "Keating is a go-to set for construction and engineering disputes, and you know you will get a good operator."

Client service: "The clerks are extremely patient, efficient and helpful." Declan Redmond is the director of clerking.

SILKS

Philip Boulding QC (see p.600) Sought after by a range of clients including governments and leading construction and energy companies. His formidable international arbitration practice has a focus on the engineering, construction and technology sectors, and is particularly experienced in handling arbitrations in the Far East. **Strengths:** "He is very impressive, hands-on and client friendly."

Paul Darling QC (see p.629) Distinguished for his expert handling of construction and engineering related international arbitrations, he has been involved in matters heard under the rules of many leading arbitral institutions including the ICC, HKIAC, DIAC, LCIA and SIAC. His forte lies in handling hearings that require considerable cross-examination of various expert witnesses. **Strengths:** "He is a tenacious and effective cross-examiner. His cross-examination made a key difference to the outcome of the hearing." "He is constantly able to come up with clear and strong arguments no matter how complicated, document-heavy or weak a case is. His solutions are both creative and commercially sensible."

Richard Harding QC (see p.663) Represents a wide variety of clients including governments, professionals, private employers and contractors in construction and engineering disputes, particularly in the Middle East. He has significant experience in cases that engage various Middle Eastern laws, such as those of Egypt, Qatar, Jordan, Kuwait and the UAE. **Strengths:** "He is always outstanding when it comes to providing advice and representation."

Marcus Taverner QC (see p.778) Highly regarded for his extensive knowledge of construction and engineering matters and his legal and strategic guidance on international arbitrations concerning disputes in various countries including Australia, China, Egypt, Nigeria, Brazil and Russia. He acts on behalf of a wide range of clients including contractors, developers, employers and state affiliated organisations. **Strengths:** "We think he's an outstanding silk in London for international arbitration – he's a phenomenal advocate."

Veronique Buehrlen QC (see p.606) Commended for her international arbitration practice which covers disputes arising in the construction, infrastructure and shipbuilding sectors. She is particularly recommended for her prowess in assisting with energy, and oil and gas-related contentious matters, and has experience in ICC and LCIA arbitrations concerning projects in Asia and West Africa, among others. **Strengths:** "Extremely thorough and very capable of handling very technical cases."

Adam Constable QC (see p.621) Specialises in international construction, shipbuilding, infrastructure and energy related arbitrations. He represents a wide range of clients in connection with projects based around the world, including those in Nigeria, Greece, Spain and the Cayman Islands. Constable regularly tackles ICC, SIAC, SCC, DIAC and LMAA arbitrations. **Strengths:** "He is very calm and confidence-inspiring."

Timothy Elliott QC (see p.640) Well regarded for his expertise in handling disputes arising from construction, engineering and energy projects, as well as professional negligence matters. He possesses longstanding experience of acting on behalf of a wide spectrum of domestic and foreign clients, including public authorities, contractors, funding institutions, sub-contractors, engineers, surveyors and architects. **Strengths:** "He is hugely experienced, very calm and organised. He's a good operator."

Stephen Furst QC (see p.649) Recommended for handling complex international arbitrations concerning a wide array of construction, engineering, technology, shipbuilding and energy issues. He has recently appeared before tribunals in connection with disputes arising out of projects in Hong Kong, Thailand, the UAE, Europe, the Republic of Ireland and Russia. **Strengths:** "He is very thorough and intellectually very able. He is definitely a person in whom you can have great confidence."

Jane Lemon QC (see p.699) Recommended for her international arbitration expertise in cases regarding engineering, construction, technology, shipbuilding and energy issues. She has recently been acting on behalf of a range of clients, including contractors, sub-contractors, developers and designers, in arbitrations taking place primarily in the UAE, the Middle East and Asia. **Strengths:** "She is incredibly bright, hard-working and thorough."

Vincent Moran QC (see p.721) Has an international arbitration practice that encompasses disputes relating to the fields of construction, engineering, IT, energy and transport. Recently he has been involved in various cases in Dubai and Hong Kong regarding road and wind farm projects, commercial property and high rise building developments. **Strengths:** "He is quick on his feet and very articulate in court."

David Thomas QC (see p.780) Noted for his international arbitration practice focusing on construction disputes in the Middle East, Africa and Asia-Pacific, and a barrister with considerable experience of appearing before the Dubai World Tribunal. He has handled a vast number of arbitrations regarding a broad range of projects including power and water disposal plants and reservoirs, among others. **Strengths:** "He can cut through and get to the heart of the matter."

JUNIORS

Paul Buckingham (see p.606) A qualified Chartered Engineer who is particularly adept at technically complex international construction, engineering and energy arbitrations. He is experienced in handling arbitrations covered by ad hoc rules, or the rules of the ICC, UNCITRAL and LCIA, that deal with projects based in Europe, the Middle East, the Caribbean, Africa and the Far East. **Strengths:** "His technical ability marries very well with his legal aptitude."

Paul Bury (see p.608) Specialises in construction and energy related international arbitrations. He possesses considerable experience in handling LCIA, ICC and Hong Kong Ordinance arbitrations concerning projects in a variety of countries, including Russia, Nigeria, Qatar and Hong Kong. **Strengths:** "He is incredibly sharp and very switched on. He works incredibly hard and always has a really good grasp of the detail."

Lucy Garrett (see p.650) A barrister noted for her expertise in construction and engineering-related international arbitrations, who has significant experience of handling disputes in the Middle East. She has appeared in arbitrations governed by the rules of the ICC, LCIA and other arbitral institutions involving high-value claims in connection with the construction of hospital complexes, ports, airports and metro stations, among other projects. **Strengths:** "She has impressed clients with her ability to strip away the less meaningful information to get to the crux of the matter."

Calum Lamont (see p.694) A highly regarded international arbitration barrister, specialising in infrastructure and maritime disputes, who has particular expertise in projects arising in the Middle East. He is especially sought after for claims involving Chinese, Korean, Qatari and Emirati elements. **Strengths:** "He is committed, bright and responsive." "He is very strategic. He thinks through how things are going to play out. He's very logical and very helpful." **Recent**

work: Represented Nakheel, a Dubai state contractor, in a dispute before the Dubai World Tribunal concerning the facilities management services on the Palm in Dubai.

James Thompson (see p.781) His practice encompasses a range of international arbitrations, and has a particular emphasis on construction and engineering, infrastructure, technology and energy disputes. He has been involved in arbitrations governed by various bodies and is something of an expert in Qatari, Omani and UAE-related matters. **Strengths:** "He's exceptionally bright, excellent at streamlining the arguments and very good at breaking up huge amounts of evidence in order to get to what's crucial to the client's case."

Band 2

Crown Office Chambers

See profile on p.824

THE SET

Acclaimed set with talented barristers who specialise in arbitrations concerning the energy and construction sectors. Its members possess extensive experience and have a strong understanding of proceedings and claims arising in foreign jurisdictions, including the Middle East, Latin America, Japan and the USA. They have particular experience in arbitrations concerning the construction of canals, power stations, airport terminals and roads. Market sources describe Crown Office Chambers as "a flexible set that brings a lot of industry knowledge."

Client service: "The clerks are most helpful and they are a pleasure to deal with at all levels." Andy Flanagan is the set's senior clerk.

SILKS

Roger ter Haar QC A well respected leading silk acclaimed for his expertise in disputes concerning engineering and construction matters. He is a popular choice for authorities, governments, contractors and employers, and has a wealth of experience in connection with projects across the globe, in areas such as Pakistan, Kuwait, India, Dubai, Saudi Arabia and Australia. **Strengths:** "He is the most approachable and easy to work with silk that I've ever met. He's easy to get in touch with, constantly available and a team player – he's a terrific advocate."

Andrew Rigney QC Noted international arbitration practitioner, who is highly experienced in handling high-value disputes across a range of sectors. He has in recent years handled matters concerning infrastructure projects, renewables, oil and gas and process plants. He is sought after by clients around the globe in relation to claims arising in North and South America, Europe, Africa and the Middle East. **Strengths:** "Very diligent. He gets stuck into the detail and is very user-friendly."

JUNIORS

Cyril Chern Highly regarded within the international arbitration market for his understanding of complex engineering matters and for his superb knowledge of construction law. Chern has years of experience of handling large-scale construction disputes, involving a myriad of projects such as public buildings, nuclear power plants, bridges, tunnels and airports. **Strengths:** "Possesses the keen intellect and ability to deal with all parties, no matter what their background, nationality or experience."

Charles Pimlott Concentrates on disputes arising in the construction and energy sectors, and also handles insurance and professional negligence claims that arise out of major projects. Pimlott has been involved in cases concerning high-profile projects around the world, including those in Italy, Cyprus, Kuwait and Dubai. He has regularly appeared before arbitral tribunals with various international seats. **Strengths:** "Very good on construction claims."

39 Essex Chambers

See profile on p.840

THE SET

39 Essex Chambers has a talented team of silks and juniors specialising in international arbitrations concerning high-value construction and engineering disputes in a number of regions, including the Caribbean, Saudi Arabia, Russia, China and Indonesia. The set is noted for its ability to provide robust international representation and has offices in Kuala Lumpur and Singapore, as well as several members based in Australia, Canada, Hong Kong and South Africa. It was recently instructed in a TCC claim, worth EUR150 million regarding the development of a Bulgarian power plant. A commentator says of the barristers here: "They are very dynamic and have strength in depth."

Client service: "Superior in terms of clerking services." "Their director of clerking David Barnes has been very influential in making a very dynamic set of chambers." "David is really good with relationships and is always contactable and available."

SILKS

Stuart Catchpole QC A pre-eminent silk who is renowned for his expertise in international arbitration, specialising in construction and engineering disputes, but also covering cases arising in the transport, power generation and energy industries. He provides robust representation in ad hoc arbitrations, as well as arbitrations under the auspices of the ICC, LCIA, DIAC, ADCCAC, HKIAC and UNCITRAL. **Strengths:** "Very intelligent, hard working, and commercial. He's a nice guy with it too."

Sean Wilken QC (see p.795) Concentrates his practice on high exposure international arbitrations, particularly in relation to the energy, infrastructure and construction sectors. He has a wealth of experience of handling disputes relating to projects in various parts of the world, including the Middle East, Africa and the Caribbean, and has appeared before tribunals governed by the rules of the ICC, HKIAC, SCC, DIAC, SIAC and the LCIA. **Strengths:** "He is very switched-on and has a great analytical mind."

JUNIORS

Karim Ghaly (see p.651) Regularly appears as sole counsel in various international arbitrations for a number of significant international clients. He is particularly impressive when handling construction and engineering disputes in China, Africa, South America and Europe. **Strengths:** "He's very intelligent and gets things done quickly."

Adam Robb A talented international arbitration junior whose practice has a substantial emphasis on engineering, construction and infrastructure disputes. He has handled a number of matters in Europe, Africa and the Middle East concerning airport constructions, transport works and energy ventures. **Strengths:** "Very hard-working, bright, and user-friendly. He works well as part of a team."

4 Pump Court

See profile on p.895

THE SET

The barristers at 4 Pump Court are noteworthy for their wealth of expertise in the spheres of construction, shipping, technology and professional negligence and are regularly instructed on international arbitrations resulting from disputes in those areas. The members handle a wide array of claims in Eastern Europe, Africa, the Middle East and the Far East in connection with power stations, reclamation projects, oil fields, shipyards, wind farms and football stadiums, among others. A solicitor states: "They are very helpful. All of them, however senior, roll up their sleeves and get involved."

Client service: "Their clerks are first rate – they manage expectations well." Stewart Gibbs and Carl Wall are the set's senior clerks.

SILKS

Sean Brannigan QC (see p.601) Widely considered as one of the leading practitioners in this field, he is particularly noted for his work in infrastructure, engineering and construction disputes in connection with projects in Africa, the Far East and the Middle East. **Strengths:** "Very user-friendly and fights the case with passion." "He has a dogged style of cross-examination." **Recent work:** Represented a Malaysian contractor in a significant claim, in excess of 1 billion UAE dirhams, against a Dubai government entity regarding a flagship development.

Rachel Ansell QC (see p.584) Highly respected for her expertise in handling engineering, construction and energy-related international arbitrations in the Middle East. Ansell has been involved in projects concerning gas pipelines, residential developments and airports. **Strengths:** "She is willing to get her hands dirty when it comes to getting to know the details of the dispute and being part of the legal team." **Recent work:** Represented an oil pipeline operator in an ICC arbitration against a contractor in connection with six oil pumping stations in Africa.

Alexander Gunning QC (see p.661) Highly regarded for his international arbitration practice focusing on matters of construction and energy. He is particularly well known for his expertise in handling disputes regarding the cancellation of construction projects abroad. **Strengths:** "A very good team player, who is highly intelligent. He understands what is required and delivers." **Recent work:** Acted for the Ministry of Transport of a Central Asian state in an arbitration relating to a cancellation of an intercontinental rail project.

Alexander Hickey QC (see p.670) Specialises in construction, engineering and energy disputes arising in the Middle East, Europe, Asia and Africa and is experienced in handling arbitrations governed by the civil and common laws of such regions. **Strengths:** "His key strength is his inventiveness – he will find arguments that no one else would find. He is really good at finding an interesting way of looking at something." **Recent work:** Acted in a case encompassing a number of claims in excess of USD500 million in connection with the design and construction of oil processing facilities for three oil fields.

Other Ranked Lawyers

Michael Ashcroft QC (20 Essex Street) A hugely intelligent practitioner best known for his shipping and commodities work, who also handles a good deal of off shore oil and gas construction arbitrations. These often involve very high stakes and extremely technical legal points. **Strengths:** "He's got a good, easy advocacy style and comes across well. His is an easy, free-flowing delivery."

Paul Reed QC (Hardwicke) An experienced silk noted for his wealth of expertise in the construction sector, who is also recommended for his strengths in insurance disputes. He is regularly engaged in arbitration proceedings both domestically and overseas, and particularly noted for his work concerning the Caribbean and the Middle East. **Strengths:** "He is absolutely methodical in his preparation, he works very hard and he gives sound advice."

Michael Black QC (XXIV Old Buildings) An accomplished practitioner who is good at construction and engineering disputes, and has a fine track record in the oil and gas sector. He often undertakes work concerning the Middle East and is also developing a particular renown for handling matters relating to India, China and Africa. **Strengths:** "His ability to rapidly pick out the most important points and have an accordingly practical approach is something that is very much valued." **Recent work:** Represented IPCO Nigeria in the Court of Appeal against Nigerian National Petroleum. The matter concerned the enforcement of a New York Convention Award acquired through fraudulent means.

LONDON General Commercial & Insurance

International Arbitration General Commercial & Insurance
Leading Sets
Band 1
Essex Court Chambers *
Band 2
One Essex Court *
20 Essex Street *
7 King's Bench Walk *
Band 3
Brick Court Chambers *
Fountain Court Chambers *
3 Verulam Buildings *
* Indicates set / individual with profile.
◊ (ORL) = Other Ranked Lawyer.
Alphabetical order within each band. Band 1 is highest.

International Arbitration: General Commercial & Insurance	
Leading Silks	
Star individuals	
Landau Toby *Essex Court Chambers*	
Band 1	
Crane Michael *Fountain Court Chambers* *	
Dunning Graham *Essex Court Chambers* *	
Edelman Colin *Devereux (ORL)* ◊ *	
Flynn Vernon *Essex Court Chambers*	
Foxton David *Essex Court Chambers*	
Joseph David *Essex Court Chambers* *	
Kealey Gavin *7 King's Bench Walk*	
Malek Ali *3 Verulam Buildings*	
Rabinowitz Laurence *One Essex Court*	
Smouha Joe *Essex Court Chambers*	
Band 2	
Brindle Michael *Fountain Court Chambers* *	
Edey Philip *20 Essex Street*	
Edwards David *7 King's Bench Walk*	
Howard Mark *Brick Court Chambers*	
Kimmins Charles *20 Essex Street*	
Matthews Duncan *20 Essex Street*	
Millett Richard *Essex Court Chambers*	
Rainey Simon *Quadrant Chambers (ORL)* ◊ *	
Schaff Alistair *7 King's Bench Walk*	
Stewart Roger *4 New Square (ORL)* ◊ *	
Thanki Bankim *Fountain Court Chambers* *	
Tozzi Nigel *4 Pump Court (ORL)* ◊ *	
Wolfson David *One Essex Court*	
Band 3	
Berry Steven *Essex Court Chambers*	
Black Michael *XXIV Old Buildings (ORL)* ◊	
Bright Robert *7 King's Bench Walk*	
Butcher Christopher *7 King's Bench Walk*	
Calver Neil *Brick Court Chambers*	
Catchpole Stuart *39 Essex Chambers (ORL)* ◊	
Green Andrew *Blackstone Chambers (ORL)* ◊	
Gruder Jeffrey *Essex Court Chambers* *	
Gunning Alexander *4 Pump Court (ORL)* ◊ *	
Hossain Sa'ad *One Essex Court*	
Howe Timothy *Fountain Court Chambers* *	
Jacobs Richard *Essex Court Chambers*	
O'Sullivan Sean *4 Pump Court (ORL)* ◊ *	
Parsons Luke *Quadrant Chambers (ORL)* ◊ *	
Persey Lionel *Quadrant Chambers (ORL)* ◊	
Salzedo Simon *Brick Court Chambers* *	
Toledano Daniel *One Essex Court*	
Band 4	
Baker Andrew *20 Essex Street*	
Choo Choy Alain *One Essex Court*	
Collett Michael *20 Essex Street*	
Collins James *Essex Court Chambers*	
Diwan Ricky *Essex Court Chambers*	
Douglas Zachary *Matrix Chambers (ORL)* ◊	
Gaisman Jonathan *7 King's Bench Walk*	
Healy Siobán *7 King's Bench Walk* *	
Hofmeyr Stephen *7 King's Bench Walk*	
Hunter Andrew *Blackstone Chambers (ORL)* ◊	
Kendrick Dominic *7 King's Bench Walk*	
Key Paul *Essex Court Chambers*	
Lewis David *20 Essex Street*	
Pillow Nathan *Essex Court Chambers*	
Qureshi Khawar *Serle Court (ORL)* ◊	
Railton David *Fountain Court Chambers*	
Selvaratnam Vasanti *St Philips Stone Chambers (ORL)* ◊ *	
Swainston Michael *Brick Court Chambers*	
Waller Richard *7 King's Bench Walk*	
Wordsworth Samuel *Essex Court Chambers*	
New Silks	
Moollan Salim *Essex Court Chambers*	
Valentin Ben *Fountain Court Chambers* *	

Band 1

Essex Court Chambers

See profile on p.836

THE SET

Essex Court is the pre-eminent international arbitration set, particularly sought after for its deep bench and historical expertise in representing high-profile clients in disputes arising under the remit of numerous arbitral bodies including the ICC, SIAC, the LMAA and the LCIA. Barristers of the set frequently gain instruction in international cases of great complexity and value, as evidenced by their recent involvement in Pinchuk v Bogolyubov & Kolomoisky. Commentators say: "They are at the top of the league when it comes to international arbitration and they don't disappoint. They deliver high-quality advice quickly and in a way which is accessible to clients."

Client service: "They have some of the best clerks in the city." "They have very good clerks who are very helpful whenever you contact any of them." The senior clerks are Joe Ferrigno and David Grief.

SILKS

Toby Landau QC Widely acclaimed as "a superstar" for his expertise in acting as counsel and arbitrator in national and international courts and tribunals. He is frequently called on for high-value and complex cases involving commercial entities and sovereign states. **Strengths:** "Absolutely brilliant in arbitration; he knows it inside out and is one of the best readers of the tribunal." "Phenomenally smart and incredibly thoughtful and reflective. You know he's always ten steps ahead of everybody else." **Recent work:** Acted in Astro Nusantara v PT First Media, which concerned the enforcement of a foreign award under the New York Convention 1958 in the Court of First Instance in Hong Kong.

Graham Dunning QC (see p.637) A heavyweight of international commercial arbitration with long-standing experience of appearing before courts and arbitration panels domestically and abroad. He often represents high net worth individuals, financial institutions and large companies, among others. **Strengths:** "Dunning is a fantastic trial advocate. He is incredibly well prepared, has an encyclopaedic knowledge of the law and is very good at jurisdictional matters."

Vernon Flynn QC Known for his significant expertise in handling domestic and international commercial disputes, including multi-jurisdictional arbitration. He has appeared before courts and tribunals in various jurisdictions including Dubai, Singapore, Stockholm and the Cayman Islands, acting on behalf of prominent individuals and major corporations.

International Arbitration General Commercial & Insurance
Leading Juniors
Star individuals
Harris Christopher *3 Verulam Buildings*
Band 1
Dhar Siddharth *Essex Court Chambers* *
Midwinter Stephen *Brick Court Chambers*
Willan James *Essex Court Chambers*
Band 2
Byam-Cook Henry *20 Essex Street*
Dudnikov Anton *Essex Court Chambers* *
Holmes Michael *7 King's Bench Walk*
Pilbrow Fionn *Brick Court Chambers*
Pillai Rajesh *3 Verulam Buildings*
Quirk Iain *Essex Court Chambers*
Riches Philip *20 Essex Street*
Spalton George *4 New Square (ORL)* ◊ *
Walker Damien *Essex Court Chambers*
Wood Emily *Essex Court Chambers*
Yeginsu Can *4 New Square (ORL)* ◊ *
Yeo Nik *Fountain Court Chambers* *
Band 3
Aswani Ravi *St Philips Stone Chambers (ORL)* ◊ *
Baloch Tariq *3 Verulam Buildings*
Brocklebank James *7 King's Bench Walk* *
Brynmor Thomas David *39 Essex Chambers (ORL)* ◊
Hubbard Daniel *One Essex Court*
King Edmund *Essex Court Chambers*
Pearce Luke *20 Essex Street*
Welsh Angeline *Matrix Chambers (ORL)* ◊
Up-and-coming individuals
Ho Edward *Brick Court Chambers*
Shah Nehali *One Essex Court*
Sloboda Nicholas *One Essex Court* *
* *Indicates individual with profile.*
◊ *(ORL) = Other Ranked Lawyer.*
Alphabetical order within each band. Band 1 is highest.

Strengths: "He has a persuasive charm that makes every member of the team feel valued."

David Foxton QC Widely acclaimed as a "standout performer" who handles a host of arbitration issues including jurisdictional challenges under Section 68 and applications to appeal under Section 69 of the International Arbitration Act 1996. He appears before tribunals under the LCIA, LMAA, ICC, SIAC and ARIAS rules. **Strengths:** "Absolutely amazing, he's an absolute supersilk. He has a phenomenal intellect and I've never seen anyone deal so well with difficult, stressed-out clients. He has a wonderful bedside manner." "Extremely clever, creative, and fantastic to work with." **Recent work:** Acted in a high-profile multimillion-dollar dispute between Ukrainian oligarchs Viktor Mikhaylovich Pinchuk, Gennadiy Borisovich Bogolyubov and Igor Valeryevich Kolomoisky.

David Joseph QC (see p.686) Comes highly recommended for his broad commercial international arbitration practice that covers a wide array of industries including the energy, telecoms, construction, insurance, shipping and aerospace sectors. **Strengths:** "A smooth, confident advocate." "A sound strategist and good at developing case theory." **Recent work:** Acted on behalf of Astro All Asia Networks in its claim against PT First Media and FM and others. This was an arbitration and subsequent enforcement court proceedings arising from the split of an Indonesian satellite TV joint venture.

Joe Smouha QC Widely considered as one of the strongest practitioners at the International Arbitration Bar due to his extensive experience in handling notable commercial disputes under a number of prominent arbitral institutions including the ICC and LCIA. **Strengths:** "An incredibly clever lawyer, he's an absolutely first-rate advocate and brilliant at cross-examination." **Recent work:** Represented Raytheon in its dispute with the Home Office concerning the remission of a £224 million arbitral award previously granted to it.

Richard Millett QC Highly regarded for his handling of high-value international arbitrations for financial clients, significant individuals and international corporations. He handles institutional and ad hoc arbitrations and frequently appears in offshore jurisdictions. **Strengths:** "He is a bright fellow; he is creative, accessible and easy to work with as part of the team." "He brings a huge amount of experience to his analysis of the situation and he has a good way of seeing the issue the way the Bench is likely to see it. You don't only get a strict legal analysis but also a judicial view of how it is likely to go."

Steven Berry QC Provides solid representation in international arbitration disputes concerning matters of commodities, shipping and insurance and reinsurance. He is experienced in appearing before tribunals governed by the rules of the LMAA, SIAC, the LCIA and the ICC. **Strengths:** "Few people at the English Bar are as good at cross-examination as he is. He is good for particularly difficult cases and topics."

Jeffrey Gruder QC (see p.661) Handles arbitrations governed by the LCIA, ICC and LMAA, SIAC and the Swiss Chamber as well as ad hoc arbitrations and court applications in connection with arbitration issues. He is particularly well placed to represent insurers and international conglomerates. **Strengths:** "I was impressed by the way, when dealing with complex issues, he manages to get to the heart of the issue very quickly and communicate his opinions with great clarity."

Richard Jacobs QC Acts on behalf of a number of domestic and foreign clients in a variety of multi-jurisdictional arbitrations. He handles ICC, SIAC, LCIA and ad hoc arbitrations and is particularly good at those cases concerning insurance and reinsurance, maritime, oil and gas and sale of goods issues. **Strengths:** "Personable, very hard-working, diligent and reliable."

James Collins QC Noted for an international arbitration practice focusing on representing clients, including high-profile and foreign corporations, before domestic and international tribunals. He is particularly strong on financial transaction and international trade disputes. **Strengths:** "Collins is very responsive, bright and not taken aback by difficult technical points." "His advocacy is really exceptional. He makes difficult concepts sound easy."

Ricky Diwan QC Highly regarded for his international arbitration practice, which concentrates on commercial and investment issues. He has significant experience of arguing cases under a variety of laws and regulations and representing clients before national and international arbitral tribunals. **Strengths:** "Ricky is meticulous, extremely hard-working and always on top of all the details."

Paul Key QC Specialises in international arbitrations arising in a variety of sectors including oil and gas, shipping, foreign investments and telecommunications. He has an impressive track record of representing large corporate clients in high-profile cases. **Strengths:** "A very clever and hard-working lawyer. He did an excellent job in particular in the context of the legal analysis, strategy and cross-examination." "Has astonishing intellectual ability." **Recent work:** Successfully represented National Iranian Gas Corporation in its ongoing successful defence of two parallel arbitrations brought by Botas, the Turkish state gas company.

Nathan Pillow QC Has a practice that focuses on matters of finance and international trade arising in the sectors of commodities, transport, shipping, telecommunications and energy. He is experienced in representing clients before tribunals both domestically and abroad, and has handled a number of matters in Paris, Singapore and the Middle East. **Strengths:** "He is calm, collected and organised. He understands how a team works and is mindful of all aspects of the workings of a large and complex matter."

Samuel Wordsworth QC Praised by peers for his advocacy skills in the sphere of international arbitration. He has a strong background in commercial and jurisdictional issues and often appears before tribunals acting under the rules of the ICC and LCIA. **Strengths:** "He's a very talented cross-examiner. He's very forceful in his presentation, without being a showman."

Salim Moollan QC Acts on behalf of a range of clients including pharmaceutical corporations, communication companies and state-owned organisations in commercial arbitrations and related court applications under domestic and international law. **Strengths:** "A smooth and assured advocate." "Fantastic and excellent on his feet."

JUNIORS

Siddharth Dhar (see p.633) Highly distinguished junior who is frequently instructed as lead counsel in cases very rarely seen being undertaken by a barrister of his call. He has established himself as a go-to name for energy sector and investment treaty arbitrations. **Strengths:** "Absolutely amazing junior; he is very hands-on and informed. He is accessible, friendly, and very quickly gets the confidence of the client." **Recent work:** Acted as the sole lead advocate for the Republic of Albania in Albaniabeg & Others v Republic of Albania. This was a EUR450 million Energy Charter Treaty claim.

James Willan Provides robust representation when handling international arbitrations governed by ICC and LCIA rules. He is also well versed in oil rig disputes under the SCMA and LMAA rules. **Strengths:** "Clearly frighteningly bright, he's very on the ball and understands very complex issues." "A real rising star." **Recent work:** Defended Nigerian National Petroleum Corporation against the efforts of IPCO to enforce an arbitration award for over USD400 million under the New York Convention.

Anton Dudnikov (see p.637) Regularly instructed as sole counsel on various disputes by enviable clients such as state governments and high-profile individuals. He often works on prominent and high-value cases arising in the Middle East and Central Asia. **Strengths:** "His written advocacy is very precise and persuasive, and he has a very methodical and effective oral advocacy style." "He's always on top of everything, and seems to absorb information at an incredible rate." **Recent work:** Acted in Pearl Petroleum Company v The Kurdistan Regional Government of Iraq which concerned the enforcement of a USD100 million order.

Iain Quirk Respected for providing robust representation in international arbitrations under the remit of the ICC, LMAA, AAA and LCIA among other arbitral institutions. His international arbitration experience covers a wide array of industries, and he regularly handles matters concerning the oil and gas, construction and telecommunications sectors. **Strengths:** "Efficient, responsive, good with clients, and someone with a huge in-depth knowledge of all arbitration matters – he really is a specialist."

Damien Walker Well regarded for having an arbitration practice that covers truly international commercial disputes, many of which give rise to issues of conflicts of law. He is experienced at handling proceedings governed by the majority of leading institutional rules. **Strengths:** "He was a huge help in pulling together the factual and legal information and assisting with the pleadings." **Recent work:** Represented three Cypriot companies, large shareholders of Ukrnafta, in an LCIA arbitration against Naftogaz in connection with a shareholder agreement.

Emily Wood Concentrates her practice on high-value, complex international commercial arbitration and has particular expertise in handling challenges to arbitral awards. She has substantial experience of arbitrations conducted under the ICC, LCIA and UNCITRAL rules. **Strengths:** "Very clever, sharp and knowledgeable about the law." "Her written advocacy is beautiful and her oral advocacy is pretty spectacular. She's really going from strength to strength." **Recent work:** Represented Raytheon Systems in a case initiated against it by the Home Office challenging the arbitration award granted to the company for £224 million.

Edmund King Experienced in handling international arbitrations, ad hoc as well as in connection with a range of arbitral institutions, such as the LCIA, LMAA, LME and SIAC. He undertakes a broad range of cases concerning banks, shareholders, telecoms companies and energy suppliers. **Strengths:** "Very impressive and a good cross-examiner." "A robust and strong advocate, who is very user-friendly and easy to work with."

Band 2

One Essex Court

See profile on p.833

THE SET

One Essex Court is widely praised for its broad international arbitration practice, representing clients before tribunals based around the world including in Dubai, Geneva, London, Singapore and Hong Kong. Its barristers possess solid expertise in matters connected to a broad range of sectors such as energy, health, aviation, insurance and telecommunications. The set attracts praise from instructing solicitors, who say: "They provide great support and I wouldn't hesitate to go there for my biggest and most difficult cases."

Client service: Darren Burrows is the set's senior clerk. According to market sources, the clerking team is "outstanding and proactive." "The clerks are really superbly on the ball. They don't push the wrong sort of person on you. They don't push on fees. They're absolutely spot-on."

SILKS

Laurence Rabinowitz QC Widely considered by clients and peers as a "legend of his generation." He is celebrated for his broad international arbitration practice, and has long-standing expertise in issues relating to the energy and financial sectors among others. **Strengths:** "Laurence is a completely stellar barrister. He has an outstanding ability to formulate a case in a way which will have a maximum appeal to the tribunal."

David Wolfson QC Respected for his expertise in banking and commercial dispute resolution, including expertise in litigation and arbitration. He is well versed in handling arbitrations under the ICC and LCIA. **Strengths:** "David is a powerful advocate who communicates well with the tribunal and knows how to deal with difficult points."

Sa'ad Hossain QC Handles a range of commercial disputes, including international arbitrations of significant value, particularly in the oil and gas and petrochemical sectors. He is well versed in ICC and LCIA proceedings, and attracts an international client base. **Strengths:** "A very user-friendly lawyer, who is intellectually and legally adept."

Daniel Toledano QC Handles international arbitrations governed by the rules of various arbitral bodies, including the LME, LCIA and ICC. He also undertakes related court applications such as injunctive relief, ancillary relief, enforcement of awards and stay of proceedings. **Strengths:** "He gets up to speed with things and assimilates very quickly. He is very user-friendly, highly intelligent, and has great analytical ability." **Recent work:** Acted on behalf of Nigerian Agip Exploration, a subsidiary of Eni SpA, in appeals brought against it under Sections 67 and 68 of the Arbitration Act 1996. The matter concerned disputes over oil mining leases.

Alain Choo Choy QC Provides solid advice and representation in commercial arbitrations, particularly those in connection with questions of jurisdiction and conflicting laws. **Strengths:** "Bright, dynamic, intelligent and user-friendly." **Recent work:** Acted on behalf of MRI Trading in an LME arbitration regarding a contractual dispute over the delivery of 40,000 WMT of copper concentrates.

JUNIORS

Daniel Hubbard Frequently acts as sole counsel in high-value international arbitrations with particular emphasis on disputes regarding issues of oil and gas. **Strengths:** "Very sharp, detailed and has a strategic mind."

Nehali Shah An up-and-coming junior who assists in high-stakes international arbitrations under the rules of institutions such as the LCIA, LMAA, ICC and SIAC, as well as enforcement proceedings ancillary to such arbitrations. **Strengths:** "Very responsive, very smart and just a pleasure to work with." **Recent work:** Acted on behalf of Cruz City in a jurisdictional dispute initiated against it by Arsonovia under Section 67 of the Arbitration Act 1996.

Nicholas Sloboda (see p.767) Boasts significant experience in LCIA, ICC and SIAC arbitrations, and has, on occasion, acted as the lead on a number of them. **Strengths:** "He is excellent: he is very pragmatic, cuts through all the nonsense and reads and absorbs long documents very quickly." **Recent work:** Acted for Nigerian Agip Exploration in appeals brought against it under Sections 67 and 68 of the Arbitration Act 1996 in connection with disputes with Allied Energy over oil mining leases.

20 Essex Street

See profile on p.838

THE SET

20 Essex Street is celebrated for its strong focus on international arbitration covering disputes governed by leading arbitral bodies including the LMAA, LCIA, ICC, HKIAC and SIAC. Its members act on behalf of clients from the Middle East, Europe, the USA, Latin America and Asia and are particularly renowned for their expertise in challenging arbitration awards under Section 69 of the International Arbitration Act. The set impresses commentators with its "very high calibre of barristers." Recently, it was involved in a jurisdictional challenge regarding whether a dispute would be heard before the English High Court or in arbitration in Lebanon.

Client service: "The senior clerk, Neil Palmer, always bends over backwards to provide you with the right barrister at short notice, at the right price depending on the dispute, the client and what you're looking for."

SILKS

Philip Edey QC Well regarded for his expertise in international arbitrations, ad hoc or under various arbitral rules, such as the ICC, LMAA and LCIA. His diverse client base spans the globe and includes companies and individuals in an ever-growing list of jurisdictions including China, Singapore, India, Russia and the USA. **Strengths:** "He's someone to whom I take difficult matters where I need a barrister with ferocious intellect and great cross-examination skills. Traditionally he's a man I go to when I can't think my way out of a problem." **Recent work:** Involved in a challenge over whether a joint venture dispute should be resolved by the means of arbitration in New York or litigation in Jersey.

Charles Kimmins QC Formidable international arbitration counsel, concentrating on arbitrations under the LCIA, LMAA and ICC. He is sought after for his significant experience in appeal applications under Sections 67, 68 and 69 of the Arbitration Act 1996. **Strengths:** "He had perfect recollection; he seemed to be extremely sharp and extremely adept at understanding the issues, the relevant law and how it would be in applied."

Duncan Matthews QC Provides robust international arbitration representation in disputes across a broad spectrum of industries. He regularly handles energy, banking and finance, joint venture, insurance and reinsurance, and international trade matters. **Strengths:** "Incredibly bright and approachable." "Has backbone and is certainly tough."

Andrew Baker QC Specialises in international commercial arbitrations concerning a wide spectrum of matters including sale of goods, commodities, shipping, insurance and reinsurance. **Strengths:** "He has a good brain – he's able to deal with cases where there's a lot of heavy lifting on the legal principle side." **Recent work:** Acted in the Clipper Monarch case which involved a question of whether a time charterer could enforce its arbitration awards against the voyage charterer and the shipper.

Michael Collett QC Handles international arbitrations in connection with a wide range of issues including energy, commodities, general commercial and international trade. **Strengths:** "Really good at unravelling a very complicated picture." "He is good at identifying and analysing tricky issues and conflicts of law. He's also very approachable and a pleasure to work with." **Recent work:** Acted in Aston FFI v

Louis Dreyfus Commodities, where he defended an appeal under Section 69 challenging a GAFTA appeal award.

David Lewis QC Experienced in appearing before courts and arbitral tribunals including the DIFC, ICC and LCIA. He has handled arbitrations taking place in a number of cities including Dubai, Hong Kong, London and Singapore. **Strengths:** "Very responsive, very easy to interact with and someone who provides measured and thoughtful analysis." **Recent work:** Acted in the Cayman Court of Appeal in MNC Media Investment v Ang Choon Ben & Ang Siong Kiat, which concerned the interpretation of a New York Convention arbitration award.

JUNIORS

Henry Byam-Cook Has a practice which covers a broad range of commercial matters including shipping and insurance. He has experience in handling arbitrations governed by the rules of a number of bodies including the ICC, LMAA, FOFSA and LCIA. **Strengths:** "Very bright. A really good advocate, who is hard-working and just a very straightforward individual."

Philip Riches Undertakes a wide array of disputes, with particular emphasis on shipping matters. His practice also takes in telecoms, trade, pharmaceuticals and energy arbitrations. **Strengths:** "He's somebody who rolls up his sleeves and is also creative with his ideas about how to do things on cases." "Extremely user-friendly and clients like him. He writes very quickly and very well and knows arbitration inside out."

Luke Pearce Handles a range of international arbitrations and ancillary applications under the Arbitration Act 1996. He is well versed in commercial arbitration relating to shipping and insurance matters. **Strengths:** "He is adept at gripping technical cases. He's not afraid of difficult, mathematically based bits of analysis. He's not just a lawyer; he's someone with a good grasp of numbers, which is obviously very useful." **Recent work:** Acted as sole counsel on behalf of the appellant in Libero Commodities SA v Alexandre Augustin.

7 King's Bench Walk

See profile on p.871

THE SET

Historically known for its insurance expertise, 7KBW's general international arbitration practice is equally highly regarded by peers and clients, who state: "7KBW is very much at the heart of commercial arbitration." The set handles a wide array of court proceedings related to arbitration issues including applications under the Arbitration Act 1996 and disputes over the validity of arbitration agreements, as well as requests for the enforcement of arbitration awards.

Client service: "The clerking is excellent. I have never seen more supportive clerks in my life. Whether it be responding to questions, requests for numbers, or availability, they really seem to care about their people." The senior clerks are Greg Leyden and Bernie Hyatt.

SILKS

Gavin Kealey QC A celebrated counsel in international arbitration best known for his focus on contractual disputes arising in a wide array of industries, ranging from shipping and insurance to oil and gas. He has recently appeared before numerous foreign tribunals such as those in Dubai, New Zealand and Bermuda. **Strengths:** "His mastery of the facts allowed him to demonstrate his very lucid writing skills and flawless oratory to a very impressed arbitral tribunal that was, frankly, spellbound."

David Edwards QC Well regarded for his international arbitration practice, with prowess in handling disputes relating to banking and finance, international trade, insurance and reinsurance and professional negligence issues. He is adept at advising on or advocating foreign law cases, particularly when New York law is involved. **Strengths:** "Very sharp and an excellent advocate, both in terms of his written and oral addresses to the court. An excellent cross-examiner."

Alistair Schaff QC An acclaimed international arbitration advocate and adviser with significant experience in insurance, energy and shipping-related disputes. He is experienced in acting as counsel and as arbitrator in institutional and ad hoc arbitrations **Strengths:** "He is very user-friendly, hard-working and an impressive lawyer."

Robert Bright QC Possesses considerable charter party and trade expertise, and attracts a global client base. He is experienced in appearing before tribunals in Europe, Hong Kong, Singapore and Malaysia. **Strengths:** "He is patient, logical, persuasive and always makes himself available out of hours."

Christopher Butcher QC Provides robust international representation, and has recently been involved in LCIA, LMAA and ICC related arbitrations. He is often a first port of call for international insurer clients. **Strengths:** "A highly intellectual advocate who will pursue something legally difficult and win." "He's an excellent advocate; he is authoritative and has great experience in insurance."

Jonathan Gaisman QC Handles a comprehensive international arbitration practice covering a range of issues, including energy and insurance-related disputes. He also handles proceedings before courts in matters linked to arbitration. **Strengths:** "His legal analysis is first-rate and thorough."

Siobán Healy QC (see p.668) Well-reputed QC for international arbitration in connection with a range of sectors spanning shipping, commodities and insurance. He is also a proficient arbitrator in shipping disputes concerning delays, demurrage, safe ports, grounding and sinking of tugs, as well as in shareholder and reinsurance disputes. **Strengths:** "Considerate, thorough and presents arguments very firmly."

Stephen Hofmeyr QC Appears before arbitral tribunals in London, Europe, South-East Asia and the Caribbean. A number of the matters he undertakes concern insurance and reinsurance, shipping, share sale and pharmaceutical related concerns. **Strengths:** "He has a sharp mind – he thinks everything to an end and comes up with alternatives as well."

Dominic Kendrick QC Acts as counsel in international arbitrations, and has particular expertise in disputes regarding matters of jurisdiction and conflicts of law, insurance and reinsurance, finance, shipping and commercial fraud. **Strengths:** "He has a very rigorous mind; he is always thinking two steps ahead and is able to tie together the legal and technical sides of an issue."

Richard Waller QC Has a practice that covers a spectrum of disputes concerning insurance and reinsurance and shipping issues under the rules of various governing bodies including the LCIA, the LMAA and ARIAS. **Strengths:** "He rolls up his sleeves and is a terrific cross-examiner. He's brave and doesn't give up."

JUNIORS

Michael Holmes Provides robust representation in international arbitrations and related court applications, and has particular expertise in the spheres of insurance and reinsurance, international trade and shipping. **Strengths:** "Hugely knowledgeable and a terrific team player."

James Brocklebank (see p.603) Assists on a wide range of international arbitrations, with emphasis on insurance and reinsurance. He is experienced in advising and acting in cases concerning contractual and tortious disputes. **Strengths:** "James has an outstanding intellect. He is very diligent and commercial."

Band 3

Brick Court Chambers

See profile on p.816

THE SET

Brick Court is known for its expertise in handling international arbitrations regarding a wide spectrum of subject matters, and is particularly expert in insurance and energy related disputes. The set's barristers are experienced at appearing before tribunals with seats in the EU, Bermuda, Switzerland, Singapore, the USA, Hong Kong and the Middle East. Recently, members of Brick Court have been engaged in energy treaty arbitrations and bilateral investment treaty arbitrations as well as some high-value instructions relating to IP and software disputes.

Client service: "The clerks are pragmatic and polite. The experience has been nothing but very professional." Julian Hawes and Ian Moyler are the set's senior clerks.

SILKS

Mark Howard QC Acclaimed for his significant experience in handling a wide range of arbitrations including those relating to the banking, energy, fraud, professional negligence and insurance and reinsurance sectors. **Strengths:** "A fantastic cross-examiner, who prepares really well and gets on top of the detail."

Neil Calver QC Provides assistance with various types of international arbitrations including Bermuda Form, ICC and LCIA matters. He often acts on behalf of international businessmen and oligarchs. **Strengths:** "Very pleasant and very sensible." "He inspires confidence in his clients."

Simon Salzedo QC (see p.758) Noted for his international arbitration expertise, particularly in disputes under the auspices of the ICC and LCIA. His practice covers a wide range of matters including insurance and reinsurance cases, joint ventures, defence contracts and ship sales. **Strengths:** "A very compelling advocate who is absolutely accessible."

Michael Swainston QC Handles an international practice that covers various types of arbitration, including LCIA, Bermuda Form and ICC matters. He is particularly experienced at handling disputes linked to Russia and CIS countries. **Strengths:** "Very knowledgeable about all aspects Russian, and a very persuasive advocate who fights hard."

JUNIORS

Stephen Midwinter Acts as an adviser and advocate

in international arbitrations, either ad hoc or under the rules of a range of institutions, including the LCIA, ICC and Stockholm Chamber of Commerce. He handles a wide array of disputes, with a strong emphasis on insurance and reinsurance claims. **Strengths:** "Exceptionally strong in both litigation and arbitration."

Fionn Pilbrow Acts on behalf of a variety of individuals and organisations including oil companies, telecommunication operators, insurers and reinsurers. He is experienced in disputes conducted under the ICC, LCIA, LMAA, ARIAS, the Swiss International Rules of Arbitration and the Stockholm Chamber of Commerce. **Strengths:** "He's very tenacious and a pleasure to work with."

Edward Ho A rising star who provides representation in ad hoc and institutional arbitrations, under the auspices of various arbitral bodies such as HKIAC, the LMAA and the LCIA. He has recently worked on disputes regarding fraud, energy, shipping and commodities, among others. **Strengths:** "An excellent junior; very bright, quick and responsive."

Fountain Court Chambers

See profile on p.847

THE SET

Fountain Court is recommended for handling arbitrations of a truly international nature, governed by a range of foreign laws and the rules of numerous leading arbitral institutions, including the ICC, LMAA, LCIA, SIAC and DIAC. The set also possesses expertise in arbitration-related court proceedings and its members regularly act in multi-jurisdictional cases in a diverse range of jurisdictions including the UAE and Russia. The set is also able to leverage its expertise in fraud to take on substantial arbitrations concerning dishonesty and forgery.

Client service: "Sian Huckett in particular is great. She is incredibly responsive, very easy to get on with and very helpful. You can't ask for much more." Senior clerk Alex Taylor leads the team.

SILKS

Michael Crane QC (see p.625) Has long-standing experience in handling commercial disputes by means of international arbitration. He is further noted for his expertise in product liability, particularly in relation to the aviation and pharmaceutical industries. **Strengths:** "He's excellent – a delight to work with and extremely smooth." "A very polished performer." **Recent work:** Represented the Czech Republic in its successful attempt to resist enforcement against it in England under the New York Convention of an arbitration award issued in Prague in favour of the claimant.

Michael Brindle QC (see p.603) Highly regarded advocate for international arbitration, whether ad hoc or under the rules of governing arbitral bodies, including the LCIA, SIAC, the ICC and the City Disputes Panel. He is also noted for his experience sitting as an arbitrator in the UK and abroad. **Strengths:** "Someone that you would trust to run the case properly, effectively and make the call strategically."

Bankim Thanki QC (see p.780) Well regarded for the breadth of his expertise in relation to international arbitration, he has handled a number of LCIA, SIAC and HKIAC arbitrations. **Strengths:** "He is exceptionally good and brilliant at everything he does." **Recent work:** Defended Sonera in an appeal by Çukorova Telecom challenging the enforcement of a Swiss ICC arbitration award.

Timothy Howe QC (see p.676) Handles a wide array of disputes resolved by the means of international arbitration, and has noted expertise in finance and energy matters. He has appeared in various arbitral venues, including London, Singapore, Dubai and Hong Kong. **Strengths:** "He's a very tenacious advocate, very dogged in his cross-examination and on top of the detail."

David Railton QC Noted for having a solid arbitration practice that focuses on insurance-related disputes. He has particular expertise in Bermuda Form arbitrations. **Strengths:** "A first-class insurance and general commercial barrister." "He is meticulous in his planning, incredibly bright and a lovely man as well."

Ben Valentin QC (see p.786) Handles an international arbitration practice that focuses on contractual disputes arising in the insurance and aviation industries. He is also an expert on matters concerning M&As and energy and carbon emissions. **Strengths:** "He is absolutely terrific. He's terribly calm, and is understated but really quite impressive." **Recent work:** Acted for Hellenic, a Greek energy corporation, seeking to set aside an arbitration award through a Section 67 Arbitration Act 1996 application.

JUNIORS

Nik Yeo (see p.802) Provides solid assistance in international arbitrations concerning a variety of contentious matters including disputes across the IP, energy and insurance sectors. **Strengths:** "Gets to grips with the issues of a case very quickly." "He is very committed and hard-working, and is articulate and quick thinking on his feet."

3 Verulam Buildings

See profile on p.924

THE SET

3 Verulam Buildings is respected for its international arbitration practice, which has recently been strengthened as a result of the addition of two experienced arbitration counsel in the last two years. Its members provide representation on a wide array of issues before arbitral tribunals, and also handle ancillary applications in the courts. An instructing solicitor notes: "They are very quick to respond, very commercial and they understand where we and ultimately the clients are coming from."

Client service: "The clerks were very accommodating, helpful and practical." Stephen Penson leads the clerking team. As part of its client service programme the set provides seminars on international arbitration.

SILKS

Ali Malek QC Handles a broad range of international arbitration disputes regarding oil and gas, infrastructure and joint venture matters among others. He has considerable experience of appearing before tribunals in numerous cities including Amsterdam, The Hague, London and Stockholm. **Strengths:** "His oversight, years of experience and gravitas are his main strengths. He's an excellent strategist." "A very smooth and persuasive advocate." **Recent work:** Acted for the government of Egypt in its long-running dispute with Malicorp arising out of the termination of a 'turnkey' contract for the construction of an airport near the Red Sea.

JUNIORS

Christopher Harris Highly regarded for his expertise in representing clients in disputes relating to a wide array of industries. He is an expert in aircraft leasing, oil and gas matters, and infrastructure projects. **Strengths:** "His advocacy is very well presented, sleek and convincing." **Recent work:** Represented Russia, resisting enforcement of arbitral awards for USD50 billion obtained by former shareholders of Yukos under the Energy Charter Treaty.

Rajesh Pillai Provides robust assistance in international arbitrations, and is often sought after for his expertise in offshore and foreign law disputes, particularly in connection with India. **Strengths:** "He balances a huge workload with incisive strategic input; he is never too busy to help and excels as a problem solver."

Tariq Baloch Represents an enviable array of clients including international corporations in multi-jurisdictional arbitrations governed by the rules of leading institutions, including the ICC, SCC, LCIA and DIAC. He handles insurance and reinsurance, energy, oil and gas, banking and telecommunications matters, to name but a few. **Strengths:** "He has an extraordinarily strong legal mind. He used to be an academic and he has a really good knowledge of the law and a very solid work ethic. He is very reliable." "He has a grasp of the law which is bullet-proof so having him in your corner is a massive reassurance."

Other Ranked Lawyers

Andrew Green QC (Blackstone Chambers) Focuses on oil and gas disputes, and has significant experience in proceedings taking place in India. He has solid knowledge of arbitration governed by the rules of various arbitral bodies, including the LCIA and ICC. **Strengths:** "He is excellent on his feet and great when you need someone to stick up for the client in a difficult situation." **Recent work:** Represented one of the largest Russian corporations in an ICC arbitration concerning the shares sale in an oil exploration company.

Andrew Hunter QC (Blackstone Chambers) Highly respected for his expertise in a range of areas, and particularly good at insurance, sports and investment arbitrations. He is also well versed in Bermuda Form arbitrations and is praised for his devastating cross-examination. **Strengths:** "A really quick study who has good presence in court. He is unflappable and reads the pulse of the tribunal perfectly."

Colin Edelman QC (see p.639) (Devereux) Sought after for his expertise in representing clients in high-value international arbitrations in connection with matters of insurance and reinsurance, energy and life sciences. He has experience of appearing before tribunals around the world including Bermuda, the Far East, Africa and the USA. **Strengths:** "He is one of the smartest people I have come across." "He is hugely experienced, user-friendly and tenacious."

Stuart Catchpole QC (39 Essex Chambers) Noted for his handling of international arbitration in connection with insurance and energy matters. He is experienced in arbitrations under the rules of various arbitral bodies and is familiar with international laws, having acted in arbitrations governed by the laws of Dubai, Ireland, Hong Kong, Jordan and Nigeria. **Strengths:** "Very bright and analytical, a great strategist and a formidable presence in court. He combines a superb understanding of the law with a very commercial approach."

David Brynmor Thomas (39 Essex Chambers) Provides advice and representation in connection with international arbitrations, especially when such disputes concern issues relating to major projects, energy, IP rights and insurance. **Strengths:** "Very able. Shows great attention to detail and is very articulate."

Zachary Douglas QC (Matrix Chambers) Possesses a wealth of expertise in international disputes, having appeared before various arbitral tribunals governed by the rules of many major arbitral institutions, such as the ICC, the LCIA and UNCITRAL. Being fluent in Russian and French, he is experienced in carrying out arbitrations in both of these languages. **Strengths:** "Very responsive, knowledgeable and helpful."

Angeline Welsh (Matrix Chambers) Possesses a wide international arbitration practice, covering a range of commercial claims, including those concerning investment treaties and the energy, telecommunications and construction sectors. She is especially sought after for her expertise in handling disputes arising in emerging markets and in court proceedings related to arbitrations, such as enforcement of arbitral awards and anti-suit injunctions.

Roger Stewart QC (see p.773) (4 New Square) Well respected for his international arbitration practice, which covers a wide range of disputes for numerous clients across the globe. He is particularly noted for his expertise in construction and insurance. **Strengths:** "He is a formidable advocate who gets to the heart of matters quickly." **Recent work:** Successfully set aside an arbitration award for the Home Office and obtained remission to a new tribunal in the case of Home Office v RSL.

George Spalton (see p.770) (4 New Square) Recommended for his expertise in international arbitration and his ability to work on disputes heard by national as well as international tribunals. **Strengths:** "He's very well travelled – he's one of those barristers whose practice doesn't just operate out of London."

Can Yeginsu (see p.801) (4 New Square) Assists with the full gamut of international arbitration including those governed by the rules of the LMAA, the LCIA, the ICC and UNCITRAL. He is experienced in disputes relating to conflicts of law and jurisdiction and is well versed in matters concerning a wide range of industries including the IT, energy, insurance, shipping and financial services sectors. **Strengths:** "He is fiercely clever but also a true team player; he knows arbitration inside out and is a very elegant and effective advocate."

Michael Black QC (XXIV Old Buildings) Known at the International Arbitration Bar for his long-standing experience in different types of disputes including those relating to company law and energy. His expertise in Middle Eastern matters is well recognised within the market, as is his ability to represent national and international clients in arbitrations under the auspices of various arbitral bodies including the LCIA, ICC and DIFC. **Strengths:** "He is very much a team player and has an exceptional ability to see the core issues."

Nigel Tozzi QC (see p.783) (4 Pump Court) Has a wide-ranging international arbitration practice representing clients in disputes in a variety of areas, including shipping, energy and insurance. He carries an enviable reputation, particularly for the quality of his advocacy. **Strengths:** "A blindingly good advocate." "He's really organised, really methodical, highly logical and very thorough." **Recent work:** Acted on behalf of an aerodynamic enhancements design company in its challenge against an aircraft manufacturer for breach of confidentiality and wrongful use of its designs.

Alexander Gunning QC (see p.661) (4 Pump Court) Handles a number of complex international arbitrations, regularly appearing before tribunals based in Hong Kong, London and Singapore. He is particularly well versed in disputes relating to the shipping and energy sectors. **Strengths:** "He's extremely easy to work with; he's completely hands-on and always on top of everything." **Recent work:** Represented a prominent Russian individual in an LCIA arbitration regarding a hijacked website.

Sean O'Sullivan QC (see p.732) (4 Pump Court) Provides solid representation in various commercial disputes including those concerning shipping, reinsurance and commodities. **Strengths:** "An excellent lawyer, who is a great advocate and one of the most user-friendly barristers I've worked with." **Recent work:** Acted on behalf of a Korean shipyard in an LCIA arbitration against a thruster manufacturer. The matter concerned construction delays to a series of drillships caused by the alleged defects in their thrusters.

Simon Rainey QC (see p.746) (Quadrant Chambers) Highly regarded for his expertise in handling high-profile international arbitrations in connection with complex oil and gas, banking and finance and trade issues. He is well known for his prowess in advising and representing clients in disputes in countries as far flung as Turkey, Russia, the USA, China and India. **Strengths:** "An extremely accomplished advocate." "He has always been first-class. He has a specialism in international trade and delivers top-quality work." **Recent work:** Acted on behalf of Stemcor, one of the leading global coal and mineral traders, in an LCIA arbitration in connection with a long-term coking coal contract.

Luke Parsons QC (see p.734) (Quadrant Chambers) Concentrates his practice on arbitrations with a cross-border component. He is best known for his expertise in representing clients in enforcement of arbitration awards under the New York Convention as well as in court proceedings concerning the challenging of awards. **Strengths:** "He's charming but at the same time incisive. He really drills down to the bottom of points."

Lionel Persey QC (Quadrant Chambers) Instructed by clients for his expertise in handling a gamut of international arbitrations, including under the auspices of the ICC, LMAA, LCIA, LOF and ad hoc. His areas of expertise include jurisdictional disputes and conflicts of law, and he is experienced across multiple sectors including the shipping, insurance, reinsurance, energy and natural resources fields. **Strengths:** "A master tactician. He's an outstanding lawyer who works exceptionally hard."

Khawar Qureshi QC (Serle Court) Experienced at representing clients in commercial arbitrations governed by leading institutions, such as the ICC, LCIA, LMAA and DIAC. He is also regularly instructed in court proceedings regarding issues arising under the Arbitration Act 1996. **Strengths:** "He's very smart, user-friendly and a good team player. He's good at dealing with clients in court hearings, he can think on his feet rapidly and he's particularly good at cross-examination."

Vasanti Selvaratnam QC (see p.761) (St Philips Stone Chambers) Handles a practice covering a broad spectrum of disputes in connection with a number of issues including force majeure, conflict of laws and all forms of interim urgent relief. She has notable experience in both dry and wet shipping and commodities. **Strengths:** "She is very impressive as well as being a very strong team player." "She is always accessible and maintains her good humour and equanimity in the most difficult circumstances."

Ravi Aswani (see p.586) (St Philips Stone Chambers) Concentrates on commercial disputes, particularly joint venture claims, arising in the shipping, energy, and insurance and reinsurance sectors among others. He is experienced in representing domestic and foreign clients. **Strengths:** "Tremendously skilled and empathetic towards the client."

Contents:

LONDON

Licensing
Leading Sets
Band 1
Francis Taylor Building *
Band 2
3 Raymond Buildings Barristers *
Band 3
Cornerstone Barristers *
Leading Silks
Star individuals
Gouriet Gerald *Francis Taylor Building* Ⓐ *
Walsh Stephen *3 Raymond Buildings Barristers* Ⓐ *
Band 1
de Haan Kevin *Francis Taylor Building* Ⓐ
FitzGerald Susanna *One Essex Court (ORL)* ◊ *
Kolvin Philip *Cornerstone Barristers* *
Matthias David *Francis Taylor Building*
Band 2
Bromley-Martin Michael *3 Raymond Buildings Barristers* Ⓐ
Findlay James *Cornerstone Barristers*
Heslop Martin S *2 Hare Court (ORL)* ◊ *
Leading Juniors
Star individuals
Le Fevre Sarah *3 Raymond Buildings Barristers* Ⓐ *
Rankin James *Francis Taylor Building* Ⓐ *
Band 1
Grant Gary *Francis Taylor Building* Ⓐ *
Naqshbandi Saba *3 Raymond Buildings Barristers* Ⓐ
Phillips Jeremy *Francis Taylor Building* Ⓐ
Ranatunga Asitha *Cornerstone Barristers* *
Band 2
Butt Matthew *3 Raymond Buildings Barristers* Ⓐ *
Cannon Josef *Cornerstone Barristers* *
Charalambides Leo *Francis Taylor Building*
Band 3
Clarke Rory *Cornerstone Barristers*
Glenser Peter *9 Bedford Row (ORL)* ◊ *
Kapila Rachel *3 Raymond Buildings Barristers* Ⓐ *
Ladenburg Guy *3 Raymond Buildings Barristers* *
Monkcom Stephen *Tanfield Chambers (ORL)* ◊
Whale Stephen *Landmark Chambers (ORL)* ◊ Ⓐ *
* *Indicates set / individual with profile.*
Ⓐ *direct access (see p.24).*
◊ *(ORL) = Other Ranked Lawyer.*
Alphabetical order within each band. Band 1 is highest.

Band 1

Francis Taylor Building

See profile on p.849

THE SET

Maintains its status as the set of choice for licensing law. With a raft of stellar juniors and silks, it is able to handle all levels of licensing work. Its practice is impressively broad, with practitioners acting for both local authorities and licensees in cases involving sexual entertainment venues, nightclubs and restaurants, among other matters. The set attracts an abundance of praise for its bench strength.

Client service: The clerking team, headed by Paul Coveney, is described as "exceptionally professional" and "superb at every level."

SILKS

Gerald Gouriet QC (see p.657) A lawyer with a stellar track record who is often chosen to act in licensing appeals of varying complexity. His client base is diverse and includes local authorities, late-night venues and gambling establishments. **Strengths:** "He is able to cut through the issues to hone in on the critical aspects of a case." "Far and away the most impressive on his feet; there is no one else in this market who is more skilful as an advocate." "His eye for detail is a strength."

Kevin de Haan QC A well-regarded gambling and e-commerce licensing expert, noted for his ability to deal with domestic licensing cases and those involving multiple jurisdictions. He also receives recognition for his work in alcohol licensing. **Strengths:** "He has a wealth of knowledge concerning the gambling, alcohol and entertainment industries; he is a first-class lawyer." "He has been steeped in the industry and his opinion is well thought of by authorities."

David Matthias QC Go-to licensing barrister for local authorities in London, particularly Westminster City Council. He frequently appears on the highest-profile matters concerning intricate questions of licensing law. Judicial reviews are a special area of expertise. **Strengths:** "He is a force of nature and incredibly effective in court." "Judges are convinced by his arguments." **Recent work:** Acted for Westminster City Council on R (Hemming and Others) v Westminster City Council, a Supreme Court case concerning the licence fees levied on operators.

JUNIORS

James Rankin (see p.748) Able to advise on all aspects of licensing law as a result of his extensive experience in this sector. He is sought after for his outstanding advocacy skills, regularly appearing for the trade, local authorities and Metropolitan Police in applications and appeals. **Strengths:** "He is a safe pair of hands, especially when you are dealing with some of the large local authorities." "He is very eloquent and his arguments are very well thought out; he is quite formidable." **Recent work:** Successfully acted for the London Borough of Redbridge in opposing an application for permission of judicial review by Spanish restaurant La Sala.

Gary Grant (see p.658) Deals with the full range of issues stemming from premises licence applications, particularly those involving significant variations and reviews. He represents prominent bars and restaurants, but can also be found on the side of the local authority. **Strengths:** "Gary is determined and competitive, fair and honest in his appraisal of the strengths and weaknesses of a case. He is able to charm a tribunal." "His skeleton arguments are really precise, detailed and thorough. He comes across straight away as if he knows what he is talking about." **Recent work:** Acted for the Royal Borough of Kingston upon Thames in a High Court case concerning the inaccurate naming of the appellant, Essence, and the impact this has on the interpretation of the relevant time limits.

Jeremy Phillips Especially valued for his academic knowledge of the breadth of licensing law, which he employs to advise large-scale corporations and community groups. He is also active on the contentious side, and has expertise in licensing judicial review matters. **Strengths:** "He turns papers around with impressive speed and has proved to be helpful beyond the advice requested." "He's thorough, has excellent attention to detail and is very persuasive." "An extremely experienced counsel who brings a very commercial perspective and is very approachable." **Recent work:** Represented the London Borough of Barnet in an appeal concerning the revocation of a premises licence due to breaches of food safety regulations.

Leo Charalambides Enjoys a flourishing licensing practise and handles instructions from across the country. He works on behalf of local authorities on a range of issues, including those relating to alcohol and taxi licensing. **Strengths:** "He gives commercially minded advice and listens to the client's needs." "He's very accomplished and technically astute."

Band 2

3 Raymond Buildings Barristers

See profile on p.904

THE SET

A set with wide-ranging regulatory expertise which regularly handles matters in the licensing sphere. Its substantial team of licensing experts includes juniors and silks who are able to work across the full spectrum of cases. Alcohol, gambling and taxi licensing cases are all areas of focus, as are licensing cases concerning the security industry.

Client service: The clerking team, led by senior clerk Eddie Holland, is "very responsive," "understanding of clients" and generally of the "very highest standard."

SILKS

Stephen Walsh QC (see p.789) Handles licensing applications for prominent casinos, late-night venues and restaurants, and is also adept at dealing with judicial reviews, licence reviews and appeals. He receives praise for his ability to adapt his advocacy style to accommodate the needs of different tribunals. **Strengths:** "He understands the industry from the operator's point of view; he has a commercial head on his shoulders." "He is very conscientious and puts the client first." **Recent work:** Acted for Boujis Nightclub in a review of its licence, after a series of disturbances at the premises.

Michael Bromley-Martin QC Acts for both local residents and licensees in various proceedings. He brings his criminal law expertise to bear in contentious matters, representing clients in appeals and judicial reviews. **Strengths:** "He is the barrister to go for when you need a fighter." **Recent work:** Represented Essence in a judicial review of the Royal Borough of Kingston upon Thames's refusal to renew its nightclub licence.

JUNIORS

Sarah Le Fevre (see p.698) Regularly involved with some of the highest-profile cases involving premises licences. She chiefly represents operators but is also able to assist local authorities. Her practice encompasses both contentious and advisory work. **Strengths:** "Her manner with clients is second to none and her attention to detail and preparation are faultless; hand her the brief and she will master it." "Very client-focused and very good at turning around papers quickly." **Recent work:** Acted for the London Borough of Islington in an appeal by Fabric Nightclub concerning the use of drug dogs at its premises.

Saba Naqshbandi Frequently advises well-known names and is called on to appear in challenging tribunal hearings. She represents licensees from many industries, including the retail and restaurant sectors. **Strengths:** "When she prepares, she really does make sure that no stone is left unturned." "She has a very sound knowledge of all matters of licensing law. Very measured in her approach, she is very client-focused and also a very capable advocate."

Matthew Butt (see p.608) Advises various players in the market, such as the police, Transport for London and late-night venues. He has a broad practice and his work ranges from taxi licensing issues and new premises licence applications to judicial reviews. **Strengths:** "He is academically outstanding – every time he asks a question it's always the most pertinent point. "His cases are thoroughly prepared and presented in a logical format. He is very good for the more technical cases." **Recent work:** Acted for stripping establishment Charlie's Angels in an appeal against the refusal of its application for a sexual entertainment licence.

Rachel Kapila (see p.687) Attracts prestigious clients from the security, retail and restaurant sectors. Clients hold her in high regard, and note that she has in-depth knowledge of the full scope of licensing law matters. **Strengths:** "She is superbly bright, tenacious and willing to go the extra mile for her clients." **Recent work:** Advised restaurant Hors D'Oeuvre on the extension of hours of its bar and restaurant within a cumulative impact zone.

Guy Ladenburg (see p.693) Boasts a broad practice acting for the police, licensees and local authorities. Contested licence applications are a key area of focus, and he is an expert in alcohol licensing, betting and gaming, as well as a number of related regulatory areas. **Strengths:** "A very intelligent and charming man who is as bright as a button and handles tremendous amounts of work very quickly." **Recent work:** Successfully represented Crownmead Stores in an appeal against the revocation of its licence.

Band 3

Cornerstone Barristers

See profile on p.823

THE SET

"Extremely high-quality barristers," according to one impressed client, who also notes that "you can have complete faith that the members here will provide a value-for-money service." It has substantial experience of acting for a variety of local authorities and the Metropolitan Police in a large number of licensing matters. Its members cover all manner of licensing cases including those involving gambling, alcohol, taxis and street trade.

Client service: Ben Connor heads the clerking team. Clients universally agree that the clerks are "really helpful and always knowledgeable."

SILKS

Philip Kolvin QC (see p.693) Routinely instructed to act in the most significant of licensing matters. His practice encompasses both gambling and premises licence concerns and he remains the preferred barrister for a number of clients from many sectors. **Strengths:** "He is calm, gives clear and concise advice, and is fantastic on his feet. He is essentially an encyclopaedia on licensing." "He is simply in the top rank in the licensing field and has been for a while." "The go-to guy for all licensing matters. He is determined and frighteningly bright. He is able to assess the key issues in any case with speed and precision." **Recent work:** Lead counsel for the licensees in R (Hemming and Others) v Westminster City Council, a Supreme Court case concerning the licence fees levied on operators.

James Findlay QC Brings general public law expertise to bear when representing governmental bodies in licensing disputes. He deals with various licensing issues including those relating to taxis, gambling and street trading. **Strengths:** "He is very thorough and knows his stuff." **Recent work:** Advised Sheffield Council on its gambling licensing policy in the face of a number of potential judicial review challenges to it.

JUNIORS

Asitha Ranatunga (see p.748) Client base predominantly consists of local authorities. He regularly works on appeals and summary review proceedings involving the revocation of licences or the denial of licence applications. **Strengths:** "He is extremely hard working, well prepared and very thorough." "His written work is excellent – it's to the point, relevant and easy to understand." **Recent work:** Successfully represented the London Borough of Islington in an appeal against its decision to revoke a premises licence for a nightclub.

Josef Cannon (see p.611) Handles a diverse array of work including judicial reviews, local authority prosecutions, taxi licence matters and premises licence applications. Sources are quick to compliment him on his client-friendly approach. **Strengths:** "He is an extremely effective cross-examiner." "He always provides a first-class service. He has the local knowledge, is politically aware and adds value." **Recent work:** Advised Red Mantra, a bar based within a cumulative impact zone, on an application for an extension of its opening hours. The application, which was opposed by the local authority, was granted.

Rory Clarke Best known for his taxi licensing work and, recently, has also been active in cases involving the premises licences of late-night venues. He frequently appears in summary review proceedings, acting for both the Metropolitan Police and the licensee. **Strengths:** "He is very approachable, helpful and capable. He is good in court and very easy to work with." **Recent work:** Represented the Metropolitan Police in a review of the premises licence of Boujis, a popular London nightclub.

Other Ranked Lawyers

Peter Glenser (see p.654) (9 Bedford Row) Has cornered the market in firearms licensing, and regularly defends private clients who have breached firearm licence requirements. He is praised for the depth of his knowledge of this area. **Strengths:** "He is the pre-eminent lawyer with regard to any cases involving firearms, particularly in the context of country sports. His knowledge of the complicated laws and guidance that apply in this tricky area means that he is always the most knowledgeable person in the courtroom."

Susanna FitzGerald QC (see p.645) (One Essex Court) Endorsed by peers and clients for her experience with gambling and gaming licensing matters, she often appears in the most significant cases in these areas. She advises offshore platforms and domestic operators. **Strengths:** "She is extremely talented and clearly a leader in the field of gambling licensing. She has excellent understanding of complex gambling legislation and can swiftly reconcile the relevant regulations with the client's objectives." A gambling guru, who is a pleasure to instruct."

Martin Heslop QC (see p.670) (2 Hare Court) Long-established advocate working exclusively on behalf of the trade. Especially noted for his licensing work in the gambling sector, counting some of the most prominent names in this sector as clients. **Strengths:** "Exceptional advocate. He has a keen interest in the sector and long experience of advising the casino industry in particular."

Stephen Whale (see p.793) (Landmark Chambers) Primarily deals with judicial reviews and appeals. He has experience of issues relating to premises licences and is often instructed in matters which reach the High Court. **Strengths:** "He has a very good background in licensing law and a really down-to-earth advocacy style." **Recent work:** Acted for the claimant in R (Akin) v Stratford Magistrates' Court, a judicial review claim concerning the procedural irregularity surrounding the revocation of a snooker club's licence.

Stephen Monkcom (Tanfield Chambers) Has a strong advisory licensing practice, with special emphasis on the gaming and gambling sectors. He has an enviable reputation in this area and is widely known for his academic prowess. **Strengths:** "He is a really clever chap with immensely sound judgement." "He provides extremely thorough and considered advice."

MIDLANDS

Licensing
Leading Juniors
Band 1
Clover Sarah *Kings Chambers*
Evans Andrew *St Philips Chambers* *
Williams Ben *Kings Chambers* *

Ranked Lawyers

Sarah Clover (Kings Chambers) A popular choice for a range of licensees, who is also able to act for local authorities. She often handles complex licensing matters, handling judicial reviews, prosecutions and appeals. **Strengths:** "An excellent advocate with a keen eye for detail, who is always willing to take on a challenge." "She is a formidable advocate and phenomenal at written work." "Very approachable, knowledgeable and easy to work with." **Recent work:** Successfully represented Jimann in appeals brought by Bedford Borough Council against its licence variation.

Ben Williams (see p.796) (Kings Chambers) Advises both authorities and licensees on licensing reviews and variation matters. He is particularly well regarded for taxi licensing work. **Strengths:** "I have been impressed by his attention to detail and very quick response to any question." "His written advice is analytical and a joy to read." **Recent work:** Advised DeVere Venues on a licence variation application to increase its hours, despite prior noise complaints.

Andrew Evans (see p.641) (St Philips Chambers) Barrister of choice for Birmingham City Council in licensing appeals. Of late, he has enjoyed a varied practice, handling matters as wide-ranging as boat and zoo licensing cases. **Strengths:** "He is very knowledgeable – he grasps the points and he is pragmatic in his advice." "He has the ability to make himself a part of the team without losing his objectivity." **Recent work:** Represented Birmingham City Council in an appeal against its decision to withdraw the premises licence of a community social club.

NORTH EASTERN

Licensing
Leading Juniors
Band 1
Holland Charles *Trinity Chambers*
Band 2
Smith Joan *Trinity Chambers*

Ranked Lawyers

Charles Holland (Trinity Chambers) Licensing forms a large part of his broad civil practice and he has developed expertise across the full range of licensing matters. He is respected both for his tenacity and his strong advocacy skills. **Strengths:** "Charles has a gift for dealing with the uncomfortable truth head on. He pulls no punches in his advice, and is highly valued for that."

Joan Smith (Trinity Chambers) Regularly advises various clients on all aspects of taxi licensing. She also works on alcohol, gambling and zoo licensing cases. **Strengths:** "Joan has a real understanding of both the law and the practicalities of a case. Her advice is always clear. Her manner with clients and in court is impeccable."

WESTERN

Licensing
Leading Juniors
Band 1
Light Roy *St John's Chambers* [A]
* *Indicates individual with profile.*
[A] *direct access (see p.24).*
Alphabetical order within each band. Band 1 is highest.

Ranked Lawyers

Roy Light (St John's Chambers) Principally acts for operators in appeals across the country. Recently, he has spent much of his time dealing with late-night alcohol and taxi licensing matters. **Strengths:** "Very hands-on, he breaks down complex issues in a client-friendly way." **Recent work:** Acted for Exeter City Council in R (on the application of Valleywood Resources) v Exeter City Council, a case involving a decision to refuse to renew a sexual entertainment venue licence.

Contents:

LONDON

Local Government
Leading Sets
Band 1
11KBW *
Landmark Chambers *
Band 2
Cornerstone Barristers *
39 Essex Chambers *
Band 3
Francis Taylor Building *
Leading Silks
Star individuals
Giffin Nigel *11KBW* *
Howell John *Blackstone Chambers (ORL)* ◊
Band 1
Drabble Richard *Landmark Chambers*
Goudie James *11KBW* *
Lieven Nathalie *Landmark Chambers*
Morris Fenella *39 Essex Chambers*
Sheldon Clive *11KBW* *
Straker Timothy *4-5 Gray's Inn Square (ORL)* ◊
Band 2
Elvin David *Landmark Chambers*
Lowe Mark *Cornerstone Barristers* *
Maurici James *Landmark Chambers*
Band 3
Arden Andrew *Arden Chambers (ORL)* ◊ *
Bhose Ranjit *Cornerstone Barristers* *
Coppel Jason *11KBW* *
Coppel Philip *Cornerstone Barristers* [A]
Findlay James *Cornerstone Barristers*
Glover Richard *Francis Taylor Building*
Grodzinski Sam *Blackstone Chambers (ORL)* ◊
Harwood Richard *39 Essex Chambers* *
Hockman Stephen *6 Pump Court (ORL)* ◊ [A] *
Knafler Stephen *Landmark Chambers*
Mountfield Helen *Matrix Chambers (ORL)* ◊
Oldham Peter *11KBW* *
Richards Jenni *39 Essex Chambers* *
Roots Guy *Francis Taylor Building* *
Steyn Karen *11KBW* *
Westgate Martin *Doughty Street Chambers (ORL)* ◊
Williams Rhodri *Henderson Chambers (ORL)* ◊ [A] *
Wise Ian *Monckton Chambers (ORL)* ◊ [A]
Band 4
Béar Charles *Fountain Court Chambers (ORL)* ◊ *
Bourne Charles *11KBW* [A] *
Clayton Richard *4-5 Gray's Inn Square (ORL)* ◊
Forsdick David *Landmark Chambers*
Kolinsky Daniel *Landmark Chambers* *
Mould Timothy *Landmark Chambers*
Strachan James *39 Essex Chambers*
Swift Jonathan *11KBW* *
Warnock Andrew *1 Chancery Lane (ORL)* ◊ [A]
Wolfe David *Matrix Chambers (ORL)* ◊
New Silks
Busch Lisa *Landmark Chambers*
* *Indicates set / individual with profile.*
[A] *direct access (see p.24).*
◊ *(ORL) = Other Ranked Lawyer.*
Alphabetical order within each band. Band 1 is highest.

Local Government
Leading Juniors
Band 1
Sharland Andrew *11KBW* [A] *
Band 2
Baker Christopher *Arden Chambers (ORL)* ◊ *
Hutchings Matthew *Cornerstone Barristers* *
Manning Jonathan *Arden Chambers (ORL)* ◊ *
Moffett Jonathan *11KBW* [A] *
Oldham Jane *11KBW* *
Band 3
Auburn Jonathan *11KBW* [A] *
Clement Joanne *11KBW* *
Kinnier Andrew *Henderson Chambers (ORL)* ◊ [A] *
Band 4
Beglan Wayne *Cornerstone Barristers* *
Blundell David *Landmark Chambers*
Buley Tim *Landmark Chambers*
Greatorex Paul *11KBW* [A] *
Hannett Sarah *Matrix Chambers (ORL)* ◊ [A]
Harrop-Griffiths Hilton *Field Court Chambers (ORL)* ◊
Lawson David *Serjeants' Inn Chambers (ORL)* ◊ [A] *
Scolding Fiona *Outer Temple Chambers (ORL)* ◊ [A]
Up-and-coming individuals
Emmerson Heather *11KBW* *

Band 1

11KBW

See profile on p.867

THE SET

11KBW is a stellar local government set housing a deep bench of silks and juniors who regularly attract instructions in high-stakes cases. Its eminent members routinely litigate both for and against local government, with recent work highlights including R (Sky Blue Sports and Leisure Ltd) v Coventry City Council – a matter concerning state aid and the acquisition of Coventry City's football ground – and L & P v Warwickshire County Council and Another – a judicial review relating to proposed local authority cuts to funding for social care services. According to market commentators, 11KBW is a go-to set "when you need heavyweight advice and representation as it fields an array of advocates with enormous experience in local government matters."

Client service: "The clerking is always very helpful and user-friendly. They go the extra mile to assist and are incredibly supportive. They have no trouble negotiating fees and are very good at resolving any queries promptly." Lucy Barbet and Mark Dann head the clerking team.

SILKS

Nigel Giffin QC (see p.653) Seasoned public law silk with extensive expertise encompassing social care, housing and education matters. He regularly appears in significant cases with complex civil liberties and human rights aspects. **Strengths:** "He is extremely bright and experienced." "He reliably provides authoritative and comprehensive advice, no issue is too complex." **Recent work:** Acted for the local authority in R (Morris and Thomas) v Rhondda Cynon Taff CBC, a case regarding the local authority's decision to stop the provision of nursery education to three-year-olds.

James Goudie QC (see p.657) An erudite silk with a broad practice, he handles all manner of administrative and public law cases and is a noted expert in employment law. His significant contributions in the field have earned him the nickname of 'Godfather of local government'. **Strengths:** "A very distinguished leader in the field." "He knows everything and he will articulate it in a way that is always helpful. Very responsive, and the advice he provides is extremely practical." **Recent work:** Represented the claimants in Liverpool BC and Others v Secretary of State for Health. This was a multibillion-pound challenge to the level of funding allocated to local authorities in order for them to fulfil their obligations to detainees.

Clive Sheldon QC (see p.763) Esteemed practitioner whose top-tier advocacy is lauded by peers and clients alike. He has vast experience of acting on behalf of a wide range of government departments. **Strengths:** "He has a very robust way of dealing with things and is very strong in written submissions. His advice is always clear and concise." "A real pleasure to work with, he is adaptable, flexible and provides pragmatic advice." **Recent work:** Acted in Secretary of State for Health v Cornwall County Council, a Supreme Court case concerning funding for the residential care of disabled young people.

Jason Coppel QC (see p.624) Highly regarded practitioner with noted local government expertise. He handles this work as part of his broader practice, which encompasses areas such as public procurement and human rights. **Strengths:** "He is extremely clever and can be very bold in his advocacy, where necessary." "Thorough and technically excellent." **Recent work:** Acted as lead counsel in R (Moore, Trebar and Wakeling) v Secretary of State for Communities and Local Government, a significant judicial review challenging the Secretary of State's discretion to allow local authorities to appropriate allotments for redevelopment.

Peter Oldham QC (see p.729) A renowned advocate in the field of public law who brings the full weight of many years' experience to bear when undertaking cases. He regularly handles complex education, equality law, procurement and state-aid matters. **Strengths:** "He provides practical and pragmatic advice and real world solutions." **Recent work:** Represented the local authority in R ota Robson v Salford BC, a challenge concerning the provision of transport to disabled adults.

Karen Steyn QC (see p.773) Popular choice for local authorities, claimants and other public bodies in the most significant local government cases. Her broad practice encompasses such areas as social security, education, community care and human rights. **Strengths:** "She is excellent- very calm and particularly good at producing detailed pleadings from complex mounds of information." "Extremely clever, she is a super local government lawyer with a broad public law background. Incredibly energetic and fights hard for her clients." **Recent work:** Acted in R (SG previously JS) v Secretary of State for Work and Pensions, a major case concerning the legality of the government's 'benefit cap' policy under human rights legislation.

Charles Bourne QC (see p.600) A recognised expert in public law, employment and local government. He regularly advises government bodies, regulators and private individuals, and is an accomplished mediator. **Strengths:** "An impressive and compelling advocate." **Recent work:** Appeared in Jones v London Borough of Southwark, a High Court challenge concerning whether local authorities are permitted to collect water rates from their tenants.

Jonathan Swift QC (see p.777) An extremely well-respected public lawyer whose cases often touch upon civil liberties, constitutional law and environmental issues. He is a familiar face in the Court of Appeal and Supreme Court. **Strengths:** "His attention to detail is very high and he's a wonderful strategist. His advice is extremely high quality and he's a pleasure to deal with." **Recent work:** Instructed in R (Tilley) v Vale of Glamorgan Council – a challenge to the decision to transfer the management of local library services to voluntary bodies.

JUNIORS

Andrew Sharland (see p.762) Dynamic junior with considerable expertise in local government, community care and employment law. He is well known for his adroit representation of a range of clients, including public authorities and NGOs. **Strengths:** "He has an excellent legal brain and excellent knowledge of the area. He is tactically astute and aggressive in court when you need him to be." "His advice is comprehensive and pragmatic." **Recent work:** Recently advised in R (Law) v Essex County Council, a case considering the decision to grant planning permission to a £5 million primary school in Colchester.

Jonathan Moffett (see p.720) Leading junior tackling a wide range of complex public law matters involving local government issues. He demonstrates notable skill in cases pertaining to EU and environment law, and is a member of the Attorney General's A panel of counsel to the Crown. **Strengths:** "He continues to impress with his encyclopaedic knowledge of the law and his ability to set out complex legal matters with real clarity. His commitment to his client's cause is sensational which, when combined with a highly affable personality, make him one of the finest junior counsel in his field." **Recent work:** Acted for the Fire Authority in R (London Borough of Southwark) v London Fire and Emergency Planning Authority, a case concerning potential liability for the Lakanal House tower block fire in which six people lost their lives.

Jane Oldham (see p.729) Has a fine track record of handling sophisticated public, information and education law matters. She is particularly adept at representing clients in major appeals, while market commentators underscore her capability in complex procurement cases. **Strengths:** "She is razor sharp, very approachable and particularly well-informed. She is good at sorting the wheat from the chaff." "Extremely helpful and thorough."

Jonathan Auburn (see p.586) Highly praised junior with extensive knowledge of local government matters, particularly those relating to the provision of health services. He offers expert representation and guidance to both local authorities and claimants, and demonstrates notable insight into cases concerning complex issues of mental health and capacity. **Recent work:** Appeared in a significant test case which determined the type of authorisation required to deprive an individual of their liberty within a healthcare setting.

Joanne Clement (see p.619) Continues to run a thriving public law, human rights and community care practice. She routinely acts both for and against local authorities in complex, high-profile cases, and has broad experience in claims for judicial review. **Strengths:** "She is extremely intelligent. Her experience is very extensive, particularly in terms of public law challenges against local authorities." **Recent work:** Junior counsel in R (Tilley) v Vale of Glamorgan County Borough Council, a case concerning the future management of local library services.

Paul Greatorex (see p.659) Seasoned local government practitioner with additional experience of handling antisocial behaviour cases and employment matters. He habitually acts for a range of prominent public authorities in major challenges to administrative decisions. **Strengths:** "He strikes a nice balance between being fair and being aggressive where necessary." "He has a very common-sense approach to matters. He will put forward the best options for his clients with clarity and take a rounded, holistic approach." **Recent work:** Advised in C v Northumberland County Council, an information and human rights law matter concerning the storage of child protection records by a local authority. The records pertained to a case which had closed 35 years ago.

Heather Emmerson (see p.641) Up-and-coming junior who exhibits strength across a number of areas, including healthcare, immigration and judicial review proceedings. She is noted for her highly effective advocacy style, and frequently appears as junior counsel in significant cases heard before the High Court, Court of Appeal and Supreme Court. **Recent work:** Represented the London Fire Commissioner and the London Fire and Emergency Planning Authority in R (London Borough of Islington and others) v Mayor of London, a major judicial review concerning the mayor's decision to close several fire stations in London.

Landmark Chambers
See profile on p.873

THE SET

Outstanding set with significant expertise in planning, administrative and public law and local authority disputes. Its practitioners have a strong track record in matters involving complex local government, human rights and housing issues. Recent work includes R (Spitalfields Historic Buildings Trust Ltd) v Mayor of London – a judicial review of the mayor's powers to take over the planning functions of London local planning authorities – and Turner v SSCLG, a Court of Appeal case concerning allegations that a Planning Inspector's inquiry was unlawful due to apparent bias. One market commentator describes the set as "an impressive group of counsel with a range of experience and practice areas."

Client service: "They provide very good, efficient clerking, and are totally reliable." Jay Fullilove heads the clerking team.

SILKS

Richard Drabble QC Fine local government barrister who is universally respected by his peers. He is held in particularly high esteem for his advocacy skills and makes regular appearances before the Administrative Court, Court of Appeal and Supreme Court. He is also well versed in European law, and routinely represents clients before the European Court of Justice and the European Court of Human Rights. **Strengths:** "He is a very good technician on statutory interpretation and deals with planning, marine planning and bespoke private legislation. He is absolutely superb." "Richard has formidable intellect and is extremely highly regarded for his expertise across a wide range of subject areas. He has vast experience to draw from and is a persuasive advocate with an absolute command of the subject matter." **Recent work:** Advised the Brighton Marina Company in Powell v Brighton Marina Co, a Court of Appeal case concerning the potential redevelopment of Brighton Marina under a private Act of Parliament.

Nathalie Lieven QC Highly sought-after local government silk with a wide-ranging practice encompassing matters relating to civil liberties, planning and environment law. Acts for a diverse client base including public authorities, central government, NGOs and private clients. **Strengths:** "Nathalie is a brilliant and fearless advocate with a great ability to present complex issues in a compelling and cogent way." "Very approachable with a remarkable grasp of the technical aspects of a case. Clearly very highly rated. "**Recent work:** Served as counsel to the two individuals in Re X Court of Protection, a matter concerning deprivation of liberty involving human rights issues arising from the seminal Cheshire West judgement.

David Elvin QC Has over three decades of experience at the Bar, practising in a wide range of areas including local government, civil liberties and European law. Particularly adept at handling complex highways and real estate matters. **Strengths:** "He provides clear, effective advice on planning and regeneration work. He is also vastly experienced in judicial review proceedings." "He is very good, he has an encyclopaedic knowledge and is always completely on top of his game."

James Maurici QC Experienced public law silk with a fine track record of advising public authorities on complex matters arising within the context of housing and education. He is regularly instructed in high-stakes local government disputes and has a solid understanding of EU law and funding issues. **Strengths:** "Thorough in his evaluation of cases, and confident and inspiring in providing advice and conducting advocacy." **Recent work:** Advised the council in Nicholas v Trafford Council, a judicial review of the council's decision to approve the award of a contract to replace all existing street lights with LED luminaires.

Stephen Knafler QC Handles some of the most significant cases in the sphere involving complex aspects of public, commercial and criminal law. He is a highly experienced representative of healthcare bodies, regulators and care homes. **Strengths:** "He is very capable in court and regularly tackles the most difficult and complex cases. The advice he sends through is very clear and concise."

David Forsdick QC Renowned local government silk with extensive expertise across a plethora of public and environment law issues. He routinely acts as lead counsel for public authorities involved in high-stakes vires disputes. **Strengths:** "He is a good public lawyer and a robust advocate. He is a firm, forceful and courageous advocate." **Recent work:** Represented the objectors in a judicial review, R (Ball) v London Borough of Lambeth, regarding planning permission for the construction of the Garden Bridge in Central London.

Daniel Kolinsky QC (see p.693) Acts for a range of clients in important local government matters, including public authorities, individuals and NGOs. Well known for his advocacy skills and is a familiar face in the High Court, Court of Appeal and Upper Tribunal. **Strengths:**" He is very personable, efficient and, in terms of drafting, he delivers very quickly." "He is reliable and has a good rapport with clients." **Recent work:** Advised the valuation officer in Woolway (VO) v Mazars LLP, a Supreme Court case giving radical new guidance on how property should be shown in the non-domestic rating list.

Timothy Mould QC Has over two decades' experience in this sector advising on an array of matters, including public sector law, environmental law and infrastructure projects. He is also highly adept at handling civil liberties, community law and tax disputes for a number of prominent clients. **Strengths:** "He is a very impressive advocate with great attention to detail and the ability to impart advice in a way that is straightforward and easy to understand." **Recent work:** Served as counsel in Tesco Stores Ltd v Valuation Office Agency, a tribunal proceeding concerning the rateability of cash machines at supermarket stores.

Lisa Busch QC Regularly instructed in public law and local government matters, including major challenges to local authority decisions at the High Court and Court of Appeal. She is well versed in civil liberties issues and is a member of the Attorney General's A Panel of counsel. **Strengths:** "Lisa has very detailed knowledge of the law, particularly as it relates to environmental and planning matters." **Recent work:** Advised the Secretary of State in Select Committee proceedings concerning the HS2 rail project bill.

JUNIORS

David Blundell Acts for both sides in complex local authority disputes and is a seasoned advisor to government departments in a range of civil and EU matters. He is a particularly experienced representative of clients at the upper levels of the UK judicial system, as well as the European Court of Human Rights and the European Court of Justice. **Strengths:** "Incredibly clever, very thorough and very good in terms of drafting. He has a notable sympathy for the client and just gets it. He is easy to work with and highly responsive." **Recent work:** Served as counsel in R (Project Seventeen) v London Borough of Lewisham, a test case concerning local authority policy on support provided to families under the Children's Act 1989.

Tim Buley Impressive junior with strong experience in public law and public sector matters, particularly cases arising within the context of community care, social housing and planning. Advises a range of clients, including individuals, commercial entities and pressure groups. **Strengths:** "Fantastic. He is very straightforward to deal with, listens to what you say and is realistic. A good drafter." "Excellent on local authority land disposal issues and judicial review proceedings." **Recent work:** Advised the local authority in Reverend Paul Nicolson v Grant Thornton UK LLP and the London Borough of Haringey, a challenge relating to an audit and the recovery of legal fees by Haringey council.

Band 2

Cornerstone Barristers

See profile on p.823

THE SET

Cornerstone Barristers garners significant praise in the local government sector due to its members' adroit handling of a range of issues for local authorities across the UK. The set demonstrates particular strength in matters involving environment, licensing and information law. Recent highlights for the chambers include advising the HS2 Select Committee on compensation and compulsory purchase issues, and Couves v Gravesham BC, a complex planning matter which involved a decision based on vires and procedural issues. Market observers remark that "the quality of the barristers' advice and work, and the standard of their advocacy, is absolutely excellent. They instil total confidence in the client and are wonderful at providing practical solutions to complex issues."

Client service: "The clerks are very helpful, they're always accommodating, highly responsive and willing to negotiate on fees." Ben Connor is the senior clerk.

SILKS

Mark Lowe QC (see p.703) A highly experienced silk with extensive expertise spanning the fields of public sector, planning and environment law. He is often instructed in landmark cases due to his stellar reputation and is a familiar face in the Supreme Court. **Strengths:** "He can digest huge volumes of information very quickly and is always very well prepared. He gives sensible advice and is very clear in managing expectations." "He is very measured and has a fantastic sense of humour. He is great to work with." **Recent work:** Served as lead counsel for Hertfordshire County Council in an inquiry into a project for the treatment of municipal waste.

Ranjit Bhose QC (see p.595) Expert in a variety of high-stakes public sector disputes, he is regularly called on by a diverse range of local authority clients. He has significant experience at the Bar and is particularly well versed in discrimination, licensing and antisocial behaviour law. **Strengths:** "Excellent, a super advocate who really has the ear of the court: he is to the point, concise and punchy." "The service he provides is always of the highest quality." **Recent work:** Represented the local authority in Royal Borough of Kensington and Chelsea v Pond House lessees, an Upper Tribunal application dealing with the question of whether EU procured framework agreements for construction services were compatible with landlord and tenant service charge legislation.

Philip Coppel QC A highly popular choice of local government counsel who is particularly well known for his appellate practice. His broad expertise encompasses further areas, such as information law and commercial disputes. **Strengths:** "A very robust advocate." **Recent work:** Served as lead counsel in Perry v London Borough of Hackney & Others, a planning dispute concerning the lack of information provided to one of the council's officers by a property developer.

James Findlay QC Leads the chambers and garners significant praise for his knowledge of administrative and public law, local government and environment matters. He habitually handles judicial reviews and statutory appeals at many of the highest courts in the UK, including the Supreme Court. **Strengths:** "His preparation is superb." "Very persuasive advocacy, very pleasant." **Recent work:** Acted in Harrier Developments v Fenland DC, a challenge to a planning decision raising issues of committee decision making and planning judgments.

JUNIORS

Matthew Hutchings (see p.679) A civil and commercial litigation specialist who offers further expertise in real estate, housing and public sector law. He is highly sought after by private individuals, public authorities and commercial entities. **Strengths:** "He provides a high-quality service which encompasses great preparation of files, robust skeleton arguments and stylish presentation in court."

Wayne Beglan (see p.594) Versatile junior handling a broad range of local government work, including planning and employment matters and major challenges to administrative decisions. He regularly represents clients in tribunal proceedings in the High Court and is a familiar face in the Court of Appeal. **Strengths:** "Very thorough and excellent on his feet." "He provides really good skeleton arguments and is a wonderfully articulate advocate who makes compelling arguments." **Recent work:** Advised Ealing in R (HA) v Ealing London Borough Council, a significant housing matter relating to criteria used by local housing authorities when considering allocation of homes.

39 Essex Chambers

See profile on p.840

THE SET

39 Essex Chambers is a versatile set taking on a large number of local government cases for over 130 local authorities. It houses esteemed members who are particularly known for their expertise in disputes relating to community care, education, planning and procurement. Its barristers have recently appeared in R (Silus Investments) v London Borough of Hounslow – a judicial review of the decision to designate a conservation area –and R (Joicey) v Northumberland County Council – a leading case relating to access to information in advance of council meetings under the Local Government Act 1972. One market source says: "They are a leading set in this area of law, especially in relation to mental capacity and administrative law cases. One of the advantages of using them is that, if your first choice is unavailable, someone equally capable will be."

Client service: "In terms of clerking, they are very helpful and always have someone available when needed. They are sensible with fees and they turn work around in time. They are also very approachable." Alastair Davidson and Michael Kaplan are the senior clerks for the team.

SILKS

Fenella Morris QC Erudite local government silk advising local authorities and individuals in complex cases incorporating various aspects of both public and private law. She is also well known for her deep knowledge and understanding of healthcare, procurement and real estate-related work. **Strengths:** "She is extremely bright, very likeable and instils trust in the court. She has very good experience and knowledge of local government work – she really gets the culture." "She is an effective advocate who always puts her case across well."

Richard Harwood QC (see p.666) Well-known public sector practitioner with aptitude and previous experience as a London borough councillor. He is particularly adept at judicial review work and frequently represents local authorities in high-profile disputes. **Strengths:** "He offers a real specialism in planning matters and is particularly good with policy work." **Recent work:** Represented Councillor Golds in London Borough of Tower Hamlets v Councillor Golds, an Upper Tribunal claim concerning the standards regime for councillors.

Jenni Richards QC (see p.751) Enjoys a solid reputation for her work in public law, including matters relating to local authority vires, civil liberties and regulatory law. A highly experienced practitioner, she acts predominantly for local government bodies and public interest groups. **Strengths:** "Good all-round knowledge of many areas and extremely well liked by clients. She comes up with novel and interesting arguments." "A formidable opponent; she is very good at presenting things in a very clear way that makes them easy to take in." **Recent work:** Advised the local authority in Multiple Tenants of Salisbury Independent Living v Wirral Borough Council, a series of challenges relating to the allocation of housing benefit.

James Strachan QC A dynamic local government silk with an excellent track record in local authority disputes and vast experience in judicial review proceedings. Routinely advises on high-profile infrastructure projects and is a member of the Attorney General's A Panel of counsel. **Strengths:** "Very, very clever. He is one of the hardest working silks at the Bar and has a great client manner." **Recent work:** Acted as lead counsel for the Government and HS2 in promoting the new high-speed railway from London to Birmingham, a project with an estimated cost of £43 billion.

Band 3

Francis Taylor Building
See profile on p.849

THE SET

A distinguished set which is widely respected for its adept handling of contentious public sector matters, including cases concerning council tax, funding and procurement issues. Its highly regarded practitioners predominantly act for public authorities and deal with issues surrounding education, housing and community care. Members of the set recently acted in Cardiff Stevedoring and Cargo Handling Ltd v Craig Jones and Associated British Ports Ltd, a complex rating matter involving land and buildings at Cardiff Docks. They also appeared in Trustees of Jonton Executive Pension Fund, J A Fenessey and Mcfen Haulage & Plant Ltd v Greater London Authority, a case concerning compensation for the compulsory purchase of land for the Olympic Games in 2012. Market observers comment: "Francis Taylor Building has an excellent spread of barristers to cover any public law, environment, planning, highways or local government issue. The chambers has quality in depth and is very able, even at short notice, to provide an appropriately experienced barrister."

Client service: Paul Coveney leads the clerking team.

SILKS

Richard Glover QC Erudite public sector specialist who is routinely called on to represent clients in tribunal proceedings and inquiries. He is lauded for his breadth of expertise, encompassing such areas as planning, rating and compensation matters. **Strengths:** "He is an excellent advocate who can put up a proper fight in court. "**Recent work:** Served as counsel in Total Lindsey Oil Refinery Ltd v Sykes, concerning an assessment of the rateable value of an oil refinery for business rates.

Guy Roots QC (see p.754) Highly sought after for his expert advice across a range of areas, including local government, environment and land valuation. He habitually undertakes national and international work, making regular appearances before tribunals and appeal courts across the UK, Hong Kong and the Caribbean. **Strengths:** "An extremely able advocate with a wealth of experience, he really gets to the heart of any matter and presents cases with clarity." "A fount of information due to his experience." **Recent work:** Advised in E M Watts Development Company Ltd v Government of British Virgin Islands, a valuation case concerning compensation for the compulsory purchase of land.

Other Ranked Lawyers

Andrew Arden QC (see p.584) (Arden Chambers) Has an impressive reputation in the market for his knowledge of administrative, constitutional and local government law. He is particularly adept at advising on local authority funding, competitive tendering and procurement issues. **Strengths:** "A leader in this field, he is extremely well known and produces a lot of the case law in this area." **Recent work:** Led in R (Edwards & Others) v Birmingham City Council, a judicial review proceeding concerning the local authority's discharge of homelessness functions.

Christopher Baker (see p.588) (Arden Chambers) Has a broad practice covering various aspects of public sector law, such as strategic administration and policy work. He routinely leads in high-stakes matters at the upper levels of the courts and tribunal system. **Strengths:** "Extremely well versed in complicated areas of the law. His instincts have proven very reliable." **Recent work:** Acted in Mohamoud v Royal Borough of Kensington & Chelsea, a case concerning local authority housing provision for children under the Children's act 2004.

Jonathan Manning (see p.707) (Arden Chambers) Experienced public law junior who is often instructed in local government vires, funding and civil liberties cases. He also has deep knowledge of antisocial behaviour law, and landlord and tenant issues. **Strengths:** "He is excellent. He has a really good understanding of how local authorities work organisationally and is an absolute pleasure to work with. He is a very sound advocate." **Recent work:** Advised Shelter in R (SG) v Secretary of State for Work and Pensions, a Supreme Court case concerning the legality of the overall benefit cap.

John Howell QC (Blackstone Chambers) Notable public law silk offering expertise across a broad range of matters, including civil liberties, local government and public procurement. He also has in-depth knowledge of social care, environment and European law issues. **Strengths:** "He has a deeply impressive grasp of very complex legal points and is incredibly clever."

Sam Grodzinski QC (Blackstone Chambers) Has a wealth of experience, specialising in public law, civil liberties and commercial issues. He predominantly advises central government and local authority clients in high-stakes disputes. **Strengths:** "A very well-respected lawyer." **Recent work:** Advised several local authorities on threatened budget cuts to care services for disabled adults and children.

Andrew Warnock QC (1 Chancery Lane) A highly respected personal injury specialist who regularly handles complex local authority matters. He has deep knowledge of duty of care cases and is routinely instructed in high-value claims concerning social care and education. **Strengths:** "He is scarily clever and a fierce advocate, but also very approachable and user-friendly." **Recent work:** Appeared in Edwards v London Borough of Sutton, an occupiers' liability claim relating to an ornamental footbridge in a London park.

Martin Westgate QC (Doughty Street Chambers) Erudite silk with vast experience at the Bar and a broad practice encompassing public sector law, housing and social care. He demonstrates particular strength in appellate work, and regularly appears before the Administrative Court. **Strengths:** "He is very pleasant and charming. His caseload is both complex and interesting." "A fabulous advocate."

Hilton Harrop-Griffiths (Field Court Chambers) Has a strong track record in local government matters and regularly handles cases concerning social care, immigration and asylum issues. He is frequently instructed in judicial review proceedings and has a deep understanding of children's law and mental health. **Strengths:** "He is highly responsive and very knowledgeable." **Recent work:** Acted in R (CO) v Surrey County Council, a dispute between a local authority and the grandmother of a child in need regarding eligibility for fostering allowance.

Charles Béar QC (see p.593) (Fountain Court Chambers) A highly sought-after advocate with expertise in high-value commercial disputes, employment and judicial review proceedings. He frequently represents clients in complex matters before the High Court and Court of Appeal.

Timothy Straker QC (4-5 Gray's Inn Square) A leading light in the field of public sector law, he routinely appears in complex, high-profile local authority disputes. He acts for London-based public authorities involved in major infrastructure and development projects, such as the construction of cycle superhighways. **Strengths:** "His strength lies in the authoritative nature of his crystal-clear advice." "He is highly responsive and works wonderfully under pressure." **Recent work:** Advised in Eliterank v Royal Borough of Kensington and Chelsea, a dispute concerning the future of garden squares in the borough.

Richard Clayton QC (4-5 Gray's Inn Square) Has a particular interest in contentious local authority matters, advising both claimants and defendants, and is well versed in community care, information law and equality act claims. He also sits as Deputy High Court Judge. **Recent work:** Acted in R (Bridgerow) v Chester West, a challenge regarding the refusal of Chester West Council to renew the licence of a lap-dancing lounge in a historic area of the city.

Rhodri Williams QC (see p.796) (Henderson Chambers) Public sector law expert with deep knowledge covering all aspects of EU public procurement. He is routinely instructed by local authorities, regional governments and government departments across the UK. **Strengths:** "Rhodri is responsive and practical and provides robust advice that sticks to the point without exaggerating." **Recent work:** Served as lead counsel for UHB and the Welsh Health Specialised Services Committee in Dyer v Welsh Ministers

& Abertawe Bro Morgannwg UHB & Another. This was a judicial review of the local health board's decisions under Section 3 of the National Health Service (Wales) Act 2006.

Andrew Kinnier (see p.691) (Henderson Chambers) Dynamic public sector law practitioner with extensive knowledge of procurement, infrastructure projects and arbitration. His practice focuses primarily on complex advisory work. **Recent work:** Advised the Secretary of State in The Queen (Hull City Council) v Secretary of State for Business & Newcastle City Council, a judicial review in which Hull City Council challenged the operation of the primary authority scheme.

Helen Mountfield QC (Matrix Chambers) A highly accomplished silk taking on a range of high-stakes administrative and public law matters, including local authority disputes. She deals with cases involving various aspects of equality, regulatory and education law. **Strengths:** "She is a well-respected high flyer in the field." "She is very likeable and a sterling advocate." **Recent work:** Advised in Kanu v London Borough of Southwark, an appeal concerning the point at which homeless people are classed as 'vulnerable' under the Housing Act 1996.

David Wolfe QC (Matrix Chambers) Outstanding local government silk with a wealth of experience. He predominantly advises claimants, including individuals and various organisations involved in high-profile actions against local authorities. **Strengths:** "He is an incredibly good advocate and can present cases concisely with all of the details at his fingertips." "Fantastic. He understands the technical side of things and knows the law inside out." **Recent work:** Acted for the claimant in Aaron Hunt v North Somerset Council. This was a Supreme Court challenge concerning the right of successful claimants in judicial review proceedings to recover reasonable costs.

Sarah Hannett (Matrix Chambers) Highly active in major local authority disputes, including matters involving human rights and education issues. She acts for both claimants and councils and has represented over 75 public authorities across the country. **Recent work:** Served as lead counsel in R (Cornwall County Council) v Secretary of State for Health. This was a judicial review application brought by Cornwall Council regarding residency provisions afforded to a young person with significant community care needs.

Ian Wise QC (Monckton Chambers) Well versed in complex local authority disputes, including matters relating to the duty to support children and families in need. He regularly acts for claimants and has deep knowledge of social care law. **Strengths:** "Clients are always extremely impressed with him." **Recent work:** Advised in Robson and Barrett v Salford City Council, a case brought by two severely disabled adults challenging the council's decision to halt provision of a direct transport service for disabled people to get to day centres and respite care.

Fiona Scolding (Outer Temple Chambers) Recognised for her knowledge and experience in local authority disputes, she routinely takes instructions from major public sector clients across the country. She is highly regarded for her broad practice, which encompasses education, housing and social care. **Strengths:** "She's very approachable and her knowledge of this area of law is right up there. She reliably delivers what you need in a palatable way." "She is very experienced; a great tactician and a highly persuasive advocate." **Recent work:** Acted in T v London Borough of Brent and Royal Free Hospital Trust, a case investigating whether an Italian national was owed any duty of care by the local authority or NHS Trust when he refused to return to Italy.

Stephen Hockman QC (see p.673) (6 Pump Court) Accomplished silk with expertise in all aspects of local government law, including planning, environment and senior officer's tenure matters. He regularly advises on health and safety, and regulatory issues. **Strengths:** "Really nice to work with as he is down to earth, thorough and knowledgeable. He puts lay clients at ease straight away, gives realistic advice, and is very approachable, available and responsive." **Recent work:** Advised in R (William McLennan) v Medway Council and Rochester Airport Limited, a judicial review concerning planning permission for a paved runway at Rochester Airport.

David Lawson (see p.697) (Serjeants' Inn Chambers) Has impressive expertise across a range of complex public sector matters, including those relating to the provision of healthcare and community care services. **Strengths:** "He is very communicative and his advocacy is fantastic. He can just cut through very complex cases and he proactively listens to everyone's ideas. He also spots points others would miss and has a very creative approach." **Recent work:** Appeared in R (SD) v Lincolnshire, a procurement dispute regarding the precise interpretation of which services the council was obliged to put out to tender.

NORTHERN

Local Government
Senior Statesmen
Senior Statesmen: distinguished older partners
Sauvain Stephen *Kings Chambers* *
Leading Silks
Band 1
Fraser Vincent *Kings Chambers* *
Leading Juniors
Band 1
Burns Paul *Exchange Chambers* *
O'Brien Sarah *Exchange Chambers*
** Indicates individual with profile.*
Alphabetical order within each band. Band 1 is highest.

Ranked Lawyers

Paul Burns (see p.607) (Exchange Chambers) Fine local government and social housing specialist, who routinely handles high-stakes litigation for a range of prominent public sector clients. He is well versed in a variety of issues relating to public law, regulatory law and human rights. **Strengths:** "Paul is excellent to work alongside and is a client favourite. His knowledge is exceptional and he is extremely approachable and accommodating. He is always on hand to provide advice when required, nothing's ever too much trouble." **Recent work:** Acted for the council in Metropolitan Borough of St Helens v Paige Leyland, a high-profile closure order obtained under new anti-social behaviour legislation.

Sarah O'Brien (Exchange Chambers) Highly regarded junior with vast experience of acting for local authorities in complex disputes. She is particularly adept at handling cases relating to housing, civil liberties and discrimination.

Vincent Fraser QC (see p.648) (Kings Chambers) Erudite public sector silk with a robust practice in local government vires, funding and administration matters. He is routinely involved in compensation claims resulting from compulsory purchase and real estate development projects. **Recent work:** Acted as lead counsel for the local authority in Mohammed v Newcastle City Council, an upper tribunal matter involving five compensation claims totalling more than £8 million. The claims raised multiple complex issues with respect to land compensation principles, rights to light, accountancy evidence and land valuation.

Stephen Sauvain QC (see p.759) (Kings Chambers) Leading silk with a broad practice encompassing such areas as highways, road traffic regulations and environmental work. He frequently advises clients in complex judicial review proceedings and is held in particularly high esteem by his peers. **Strengths:** "He is excellent, his attention to detail is superb and he provides sound advice." **Recent work:** Advised in R (on the application of Bedford Land Investments Limited) v Secretary of State for Transport v Bedford Borough Council. This case concerned the construction of Section 250 of the Local Government Act 1972, the power to award costs at public inquiries.

Contents:

LONDON

Media & Entertainment
Leading Sets
Band 1
Blackstone Chambers *
Band 2
8 New Square *
Band 3
Hogarth Chambers *
Leading Silks
Star individuals
Mill Ian *Blackstone Chambers*
Band 1
Baldwin John *8 New Square* *
Cullen Edmund *Maitland Chambers (ORL)* ◊ *
Howe Robert *Blackstone Chambers*
Saini Pushpinder *Blackstone Chambers*
Spearman Richard *39 Essex Chambers (ORL)* ◊ *
Band 2
Mellor James *8 New Square* *
Weisselberg Tom *Blackstone Chambers*
Band 3
Alexander Daniel *8 New Square* *
Anderson Robert *Blackstone Chambers*
Cuddigan Hugo *11 South Square (ORL)* ◊
Davies Helen *Brick Court Chambers (ORL)* ◊
de la Mare Thomas *Blackstone Chambers*
Hobbs Geoffrey *One Essex Court (ORL)* ◊ Ⓐ
Howe Martin *8 New Square* *
Hunter Andrew *Blackstone Chambers*
May Charlotte *8 New Square* *
Pannick David *Blackstone Chambers*
Silverleaf Michael *11 South Square (ORL)* ◊
Speck Adrian *8 New Square* *
Sutcliffe Andrew *3 Verulam Buildings (ORL)* ◊
New Silks
Malynicz Simon *Three New Square (ORL)* ◊ *
Moody-Stuart Thomas *8 New Square* *
Leading Juniors
Star individuals
Vinall Mark *Blackstone Chambers*
Band 1
Harbottle Gwilym *Hogarth Chambers* Ⓐ
Hicks Michael *Hogarth Chambers*
Lane Lindsay *8 New Square* Ⓐ *
Michaels Amanda *Hogarth Chambers*
Norris Andrew *Hogarth Chambers*
Band 2
Alibhai Ari *QEB Hollis Whiteman (ORL)* ◊ *
Cleaver Tom *Blackstone Chambers*
Deacon Robert *Thomas More Chambers (ORL)* ◊
Groome David *QEB Hollis Whiteman (ORL)* ◊
Hickman Tom *Blackstone Chambers*
Quirk Iain *Essex Court Chambers (ORL)* ◊
Ratcliffe Peter *3 Verulam Buildings (ORL)* ◊
Richards Tom *Blackstone Chambers*
Segan James *Blackstone Chambers*
Singla Tony *Brick Court Chambers (ORL)* ◊ *
St Quintin Thomas *Hogarth Chambers*
Tritton Guy *Hogarth Chambers* Ⓐ
* *Indicates set / individual with profile.*
Ⓐ *direct access (see p.24).*
◊ *(ORL) = Other Ranked Lawyer.*
Alphabetical order within each band. Band 1 is highest.

Band 1

Blackstone Chambers

See profile on p.813

THE SET

Blackstone is a formidable media and entertainment set, combining unrivalled strength in contractual media disputes with expertise in copyright, administrative and regulatory matters. Its members act for clients in a range of sectors, including the film and TV, broadcasting, publishing and music industries. Noteworthy cases from this year include acting for BASCA and the Musicians' Union in a judicial review challenging the government's private copying exception and defending Karl Sydow in proceedings brought by Jeffrey Archer. A solicitor comments: "They are far and away the leading entertainment chambers."

Client service: "I am absolutely impressed. Their QCs are first-rate and the clerks are very available." "The clerks are very quick to get back to you, and are very helpful and polite." The set's senior clerk is Gary Oliver.

SILKS

Ian Mill QC A runaway star of the Media and Entertainment Bar who is widely regarded as the leading silk for music industry clients. He continues to be instructed in cutting-edge commercial and intellectual property cases and has expert knowledge of Section 97A internet blocking orders. **Strengths:** "He is creative in approach and adept at finding interesting routes through complex problems." **Recent work:** Acted for music industry bodies in a successful judicial review challenging the government's private copying exception.

Robert Howe QC Highly regarded media and entertainment silk who acts for both claimants and defendants in the music, television and broadcasting sectors on both commercial and intellectual property matters. Commentators highlight his strong oral advocacy and presentation skills. **Strengths:** "He can read a judge or a tribunal extremely well, so his judgement in terms of how to pitch things is spot-on in terms of tone." "Robert Howe is an excellent advocate and cross-examiner." **Recent work:** Defended PRS in a broadcasting licence dispute brought by ITV.

Pushpinder Saini QC Renowned for a diverse practice that includes acting for major record companies, production companies and other media organisations in commercial and contractual disputes. **Strengths:** "He is extremely intelligent and builds good rapport with instructing solicitors and clients." **Recent work:** Acted for the government in a judicial review challenging its private copying exception.

Tom Weisselberg QC A relatively new silk who is held in high esteem for his broad entertainment practice. He is praised for his technical ability, and he represents claimants and defendants in complex contractual, copyright and patent litigation and arbitrations. **Strengths:** "He is extremely sharp, very personable and clever and quick at turning documents around." "He is technically excellent and incredibly easy to work with." **Recent work:** Represented Virgin Media as intervener in the Court of Appeal case ITV v TV Catchup.

Robert Anderson QC Leading silk who maintains a broad commercial practice, encompassing sports litigation in addition to media and entertainment claims. He combines long-standing expertise in phone hacking claims with experience in high-profile media disputes for clients in the theatre, publishing, music and telecoms sectors, among others. **Strengths:** "I rate him very highly for work in the commercial context." **Recent work:** Represented theatre producer Karl Sydow in proceedings brought by Jeffrey Archer relating to the worldwide 'Dirty Dancing' theatre tour.

Thomas de la Mare QC Commands an excellent reputation as a leading media law barrister, with expertise in advertising and broadcasting law, among other areas. His media practice is complemented by additional expertise in regulatory, intellectual property and EU law. **Strengths:** "Tom de la Mare is very smart with an impressive brain." "Amazingly talented, a great lateral thinker." **Recent work:** Acted for BASCA in a successful judicial review challenging the government's private copying exception.

Andrew Hunter QC Recognised commercial and media law expert who attracts praise for his calm manner when dealing with clients. He is renowned for his expertise in royalties cases. **Strengths:** "He is excellent, has good judgement and is very bright and easy to work with." **Recent work:** Acted for Liberty Investment in proceedings relating to revenues from the 'Dirty Dancing' stage musical.

David Pannick QC Celebrated public law barrister with experience in high-profile media disputes. He maintains a strong privacy practice, regularly advising clients on regulatory and criminal aspects of press phone hacking. **Strengths:** "He is one of the top barristers in London." **Recent work:** Acted for MGN in a Court of Appeal case to determine the amount of damages to be awarded to victims of phone hacking.

JUNIORS

Mark Vinall Star junior Mark Vinall has forged a distinguished practice in the field of media and entertainment law. He regularly appears on his own and alongside leading silks in high-value, cutting-edge cases involving TV and film production companies, broadcasters and talent and record companies. **Strengths:** "Mark Vinall is a rising star." "A very talented junior: he is very down-to-earth, bright and hard-working. He is very user-friendly." **Recent work:** Sole counsel for the Really Useful Group in proceedings relating to the cancellation of the 'Jesus Christ Superstar' US arena tour.

Tom Cleaver Quickly establishing a reputation as a leading media and entertainment junior. He is in increasingly high demand for his expertise in complex music, emerging media and gaming disputes. **Strengths:** "He is a go-to barrister on video games and digital entertainment matters. He is calm, considered and intimately knowledgeable about video games industry matters." **Recent work:** Acted as sole counsel for numerous artists, including Sam Smith and Disclosure, in a copyright dispute relating to song lyrics.

Tom Hickman Has a flourishing reputation at the Media and Entertainment Bar and receives particular accolades for his skill in navigating music-related contractual cases. He has additional expertise at appellate level. **Strengths:** "He is a down-to-earth barrister who instils confidence." **Recent work:** Represented Ali Campbell, Mickey and Astro, members of music group UB40, in a dispute relating to use of the band name.

Tom Richards Has an established media law practice that is complemented by expertise in EU law, IP and public law. He has appeared before a variety of courts and tribunals, and is particularly well regarded for copyright and contractual disputes arising in the music industry. **Strengths:** "He is very nice to work with, very receptive and clear in his analysis." **Recent work:** Defended Parlophone Records in a digital royalties claim brought by band members of Radiohead.

James Segan Maintains a broad practice which spans media and entertainment, EU and public law. He also has significant experience in Copyright Tribunal matters. **Strengths:** "He is excellent and the clients trust his advice. He produces well thought out written advice and is happy to get stuck in. He is excellent in particular with his written and closing submissions." **Recent work:** Represented PRS in a Copyright Tribunal hearing relating to ITV's blanket licence.

Band 2

8 New Square

See profile on p.881

THE SET

8 New Square is a leading intellectual property chambers with significant skill and expertise in copyright, licensing and performing rights disputes that intersect with media and entertainment law. Members of the set have a variety of sector-specific expertise, and regularly act for broadcasters, print and online media companies, artists and record labels, and other media entities.

Client service: John Call is 8 New Square's senior clerk.

SILKS

John Baldwin QC (see p.588) A leading intellectual property silk who continues to receive instructions in media cases with an IP element, particularly licensing, copyright and comparative advertising disputes. **Strengths:** "He is an excellent heavyweight QC."

James Mellor QC (see p.715) Experienced intellectual property barrister who often acts for broadcasters, computer software companies, music and literary artists and other media and entertainment entities. **Strengths:** "He is excellent for trade mark and passing off."

Daniel Alexander QC (see p.581) Highly regarded silk with a historical involvement in many cutting-edge media and intellectual property cases. He is known for his expertise in commercial licensing. **Strengths:** "A barrister with a great mind who is very friendly."

Martin Howe QC (see p.676) Commands a reputation as an accomplished copyright silk with noted expertise in EU law matters. He regularly appears before the ECJ. **Strengths:** "He has in-depth knowledge of copyright in broadcasts, EU copyright law and great commercial understanding of the client's objectives. He provides clear strategic advice."

Charlotte May QC (see p.710) A relatively recent silk who wins accolades from clients for her in-depth knowledge of trade mark and passing-off, copyright and patent law. **Strengths:** "We rate her very highly and would be quick to turn to her for assistance with advertising and media disputes."

Adrian Speck QC (see p.770) An intellectual property specialist who acts for a range of media and entertainment clients, including private authors, broadcasters and TV production companies. He is particularly well regarded for his expertise in television formats and Section 97A blocking orders. **Strengths:** "He's the real deal and punches above his weight."

Thomas Moody-Stuart QC (see p.720) A new silk who practises a range of intellectual property law, and is particularly strong in trade mark disputes. **Strengths:** "He is very good and definitely deserved to take silk."

JUNIORS

Lindsay Lane (see p.695) Has a high level of experience in comparative advertising disputes, in addition to trade mark and passing-off cases, television format cases and copyright infringement. She has appeared before the Copyright Tribunal on numerous occasions. **Strengths:** "Clever and efficient and delivers pragmatic advice."

Band 3

Hogarth Chambers

See profile on p.866

THE SET

Hogarth is an impressive intellectual property and chancery set whose junior members act for a range of media and entertainment clients in the film and TV, advertising, publishing and music industries. Its members are well versed in handling a variety of complex trade mark and copyright infringement claims, image rights cases and licensing disputes.

Client service: Clive Nicholls is the set's senior clerk.

JUNIORS

Gwilym Harbottle Advises on a wide complement of media law issues and has expertise in both IP and chancery law. His caseload for this year is particularly impressive and features a range of cases for music industry clients including collecting societies and artists. **Strengths:** "He is razor sharp, with an impressive grasp of substantive and highly complex detail." "He is very experienced in the field of copyright across the board and provides clear and concise advice." **Recent work:** Acted for New Order bassist Peter Hook in initiating proceedings relating to the grant of a trade mark licence to use the New Order band name.

Michael Hicks Has expertise in cases involving emerging media, video games software houses, e-commerce businesses and online publishers, among other more traditional media entities. He is an expert in a range of intellectual property law, particularly copyright. **Strengths:** "He is a very approachable barrister who has an excellent manner with clients, and quickly puts them at their ease. He prepares very thoroughly, his written and oral style is accessible, and he is a pleasure to work with." **Recent work:** Instructed in Cassie Creations v Blackmore, a case concerning eBay's VeRO take-down programme.

Amanda Michaels Experienced IP junior who assists media entities in protecting their copyright, design rights and database rights. She has noted sector-specific expertise in the publishing industry, music and record industry and art world. **Strengths:** "She finds solutions that get to the heart of the client's concerns." "She gives very solid and pragmatic advice and has deep experience in trade mark and passing-off matters."

Andrew Norris Proficient in a variety of intellectual property law, particularly in copyright, image and design rights protection that is of concern to media entities. He has additional expertise in contractual disputes. **Strengths:** "He is straight-talking and commercial." **Recent work:** Successfully represented Rihanna in the High Court and Court of Appeal in a dispute with Topshop relating to the unauthorised use of her image on an item of merchandise.

Thomas St Quintin Increasingly in demand for his wide-ranging intellectual property law expertise. He is known for his strong technical ability and is particularly skilled in acting for film and TV production companies and broadcasters. **Strengths:** "He is extremely bright and prepared to roll up his sleeves to get the job done." **Recent work:** Acted for Bhopal Productions in a dispute relating to the copyright of a feature film.

Guy Tritton Has a wide-ranging intellectual property practice encompassing patent litigation, complex trade mark infringement cases and copyright disputes. **Strengths:** "He is highly experienced and a fantastic advocate. He is excellent at client management and has a calm authority about him whatever the situation."

Other Ranked Lawyers

Helen Davies QC (Brick Court Chambers) Well-respected commercial silk with particular expertise in media and broadcasting rights, in addition to competition and EU law. She is frequently instructed by the Premier League. **Strengths:** "She is a formidable litigator." "She is excellent for media work, particularly with a competition element." **Recent work:** Represented the Premier League in litigation before the Competition Appeal Tribunal.

Tony Singla (see p.766) (Brick Court Chambers) Has a growing reputation as a top commercial junior, with expertise in complex competition and EU law and media and entertainment, particularly those in the online gambling sector. **Strengths:** "He is a top-class junior." "He's a very good commercial barrister." **Recent work:** Represented ITV in a contractual licensing dispute with Scottish Television.

Geoffrey Hobbs QC (One Essex Court) Esteemed IP specialist who receives accolades for his skill in trade mark law and copyright infringement cases. His media clients include publishers, authors and other media entities. **Strengths:** "He is a fantastic IP barrister." "He is masterful in trade marks and passing off."

Iain Quirk (Essex Court Chambers) Impressive commercial barrister who acts alongside silks and as sole counsel for a broad range of clients in the media and entertainment sphere, including film studios, collecting societies and other media entities. **Strengths:** "He has a confident, easy style of oral advocacy and his written advocacy is concise. He picks up the issues very quickly."

Richard Spearman QC (see p.770) (39 Essex Chambers) A force in media cases involving copyright infringement, with a particular focus on disputes arising in the film sector. Clients highlight his advocacy skills and courtroom presence. **Strengths:** "In his specialist zone of media he is very authoritative." "He is excellent in court, extremely responsive and in control of his papers."

Edmund Cullen QC (see p.628) (Maitland Chambers) Has a first-class reputation in the world of IP and media and entertainment law, and a superb track record of appearing in significant music cases. He acts for a range of high-profile artists, in addition to collecting societies and trade bodies. **Strengths:** "He is one of the leading media silks at the Bar. He gives clear advice and is excellent at both cross-examination and in submissions to the judge." "His judgement, drafting and advocacy are all superb." **Recent work:** Acted for PRS in a copyright infringement claim against SoundCloud.

Simon Malynicz QC (see p.706) (Three New Square) Took silk this year following a distinguished career as junior counsel. His media practice centres on trade mark disputes and copyright cases and he regularly appears before the General Court and ECJ. **Strengths:** "He's down-to-earth and happy to roll his sleeves up and engage with solicitors on tactics. He's good with clients and a real all-rounder." **Recent work:** Acted for The Specials in a dispute relating to the rights of the band name.

Ari Alibhai (see p.581) (QEB Hollis Whiteman) Criminal practitioner who is highly regarded by industry bodies for his expertise in private prosecutions of criminal copyright infringement offences. **Recent work:** Instructed by the DPP Northern Ireland in the prosecution of a film link aggregation website.

David Groome (QEB Hollis Whiteman) Expert in private criminal intellectual property infringement prosecutions. He acts for music, film, sports and broadcasting media entities. **Recent work:** Successfully prosecuted the directors of Digicams, a company which operated numerous false Sky TV accounts.

Hugo Cuddigan QC (11 South Square) An IP specialist with expertise in all aspects of intellectual property law, including copyright and trade mark. He has a wealth of experience in representing music industry clients in complex copyright disputes. **Strengths:** "He's good with clients: he's polished, commercial and astute." "He is clever and tenacious and good even with the most challenging clients." **Recent work:** Acted for The Prodigy in copyright infringement proceedings initiated by Anthony James.

Michael Silverleaf QC (11 South Square) The head of chambers, with far-reaching expertise in intellectual property and IT law. He receives instructions from prestigious design houses, broadcasters, social media companies and other media entities, who value his expertise in brand and image rights protection. **Strengths:** "There are few if any people who are as authoritative as him." **Recent work:** Acted for Fresh Trading in a copyright ownership claim against Deepend relating to an Innocent Smoothies logo.

Robert Deacon (Thomas More Chambers) Experienced commercial and chancery barrister, with noted expertise in the digital media sector. He has substantial experience of handling complex royalties disputes. **Strengths:** "He is highly experienced and confidence inspiring, quick to respond, thorough and commercial in his approach."

Andrew Sutcliffe QC (3 Verulam Buildings) Offers expert counsel on an array of media issues, as part of a broader practice. He has long-standing involvement in many significant music, film and publishing cases. **Strengths:** "He is extremely bright and has clear strategic thinking."

Peter Ratcliffe (3 Verulam Buildings) Highly regarded commercial barrister who acts primarily for insurers, reinsurers and brokers. He also has significant media sector expertise due to his successful career as a film producer prior to joining the Bar. **Strengths:** "He is thorough, conscientious and user-friendly." **Recent work:** Represented Citi in a dispute with Terra Firma relating to the acquisition of EMI Music Group.

Contents:

ALL CIRCUITS

Mediators
Leading Silks
Band 1
Jackson Rosemary *Keating Chambers* *
Kallipetis Michel *Independent Mediators*
Lomas Mark *Independent Mediators*
Sturrock John *Core Solutions Group*
Wood William *Brick Court Chambers*
Band 2
Glasgow Edwin *39 Essex Chambers*
Ruttle Stephen *Brick Court Chambers*
Band 3
Jones Elizabeth *Serle Court* *
Kershen Lawrence *Doughty Street Chambers*
Band 4
Flint Charles *Blackstone Chambers*
Methuen Richard *12 King's Bench Walk* *
Leading Juniors
Band 1
Rogers Beverly-Ann *Serle Court* *
Band 2
Willis Tony *Brick Court Chambers*
Band 3
Arkush Jonathan *Enterprise Chambers*
Johnson Paul *Kings Chambers* *
Manning Colin *Littleton Chambers* *
Shane Michael *Atkin Chambers* *
Band 4
Birch Elizabeth *3 Verulam Buildings*
Evans Robert *Keating Chambers* *
Vara Beverley *Maitland Chambers* *
* *Indicates individual with profile.*
Alphabetical order within each band. Band 1 is highest.

Band 1

Rosemary Jackson QC
Keating Chambers

Former construction silk Rosemary Jackson QC is the "ideal facilitator" according to market sources, who now employs her vast experience at the Bar as a full-time mediator. She regularly handles high-value and multi-party disputes in the construction and engineering sector, including those with professional negligence and insurance elements. She draws praise for her "gravitas" and her "shuttle diplomacy in difficult circumstances."

Michel Kallipetis QC
Independent Mediators

Michel Kallipetis QC is a widely admired mediator who draws particular praise from fellow legal professionals for his "huge gravitas." He handles a range of cases from areas as diverse as trusts, employment, professional indemnity and insurance, and he is frequently sought out for mediations "with big numbers involved, big personalities involved and when the mediator needs to hold his own."

Mark Lomas QC
Independent Mediators

Mark Lomas QC is a highly sought-after mediator who is regularly chosen for complex and high-value disputes. He is acclaimed for his work in professional negligence matters and has substantial experience in commercial contract and insurance disputes. Market sources identify his "forensic style" and "intellectual weight and rigour" as his most impressive qualities.

Beverly-Ann Rogers
Serle Court

Beverly-Ann Rogers is a "very effective" mediator with an expertise in trusts, probate, property, company and partnership disputes. She has drawn praise from her fellow legal professionals for her "great strategies to move people towards compromise." She is also known for her work in professional negligence and employment disputes.

John Sturrock QC
Core Solutions Group

John Sturrock QC, regarded by some in the market as Scotland's leading mediator, is praised for his "impressive and involved style of mediating" and his "absolute command of the room." His diverse practice includes mediating professional negligence, employment and commercial contract disputes in a broad range of sectors, both in the United Kingdom and overseas.

William Wood QC
Brick Court Chambers

"Highly experienced and creative" mediator and arbitrator William Wood QC is praised by solicitors for his "friendly and constructive style," and is noted for his large and diverse practice. He is regularly chosen for difficult and high value matters, particularly those with insurance or financial services elements, and is equally adept at mediating both international and domestic disputes.

Band 2

Edwin Glasgow QC
39 Essex Chambers

Senior silk Edwin Glasgow QC is considered a "first choice mediator, particularly for complex multi-party mediations" according to market commentators. He has experience in a broad spectrum of areas including insurance, construction, professional negligence and employment. He has appeared as a mediator in a number of different jurisdictions and has several big ticket disputes on his résumé.

Stephen Ruttle QC
Brick Court Chambers

Stephen Ruttle QC is singled out by sources as being "in the top echelons of mediators in the country." Fellow legal professionals note his expertise in insurance and professional negligence disputes and he has additional experience in construction, banking and shipping matters.

Tony Willis
Brick Court Chambers

The "excellent" Tony Willis is an experienced mediator with a strong background in litigation. Market sources consider him to be "very authoritative." He has notable experience in professional negligence claims, construction and engineering disputes, as well as cases in the energy sector.

Band 3

Jonathan Arkush
Enterprise Chambers

Experienced mediator Jonathan Arkush has a robust practice focused on chancery, property and inheritance disputes. One source states that "he can turn his hand to pretty much anything in the mediation world." He has mediated in multi-party disputes and has additional experience in professional negligence claims.

Paul Johnson
Kings Chambers

"Well regarded" mediator Paul Johnson has continues to build upon his Manchester-based practice. He has significant experience as a commercial litigation solicitor, having transferred to the bar in 2006. He has undertaken mediations in a number of areas including employment, healthcare and insurance disputes. One source states that his "switched on, astute approach" is particularly effective.

Elizabeth Jones QC
Serle Court

Elizabeth Jones QC combines her robust litigation practice with frequent sittings as a mediator, covering a broad range of areas including chancery, commercial, and offshore disputes. One admiring fellow mediator states that, "She is intelligent, self-confident and not afraid of telling everyone what the law is."

Lawrence Kershen QC
Doughty Street Chambers

Lawrence Kershen QC is an experienced full-time mediator whose background as an advocate in civil, commercial and criminal litigation gives him a strong base for his ADR practice. He has been appointed on a number of complex disputes arising from commercial contracts, construction, property, IP and professional negligence.

Colin Manning
Littleton Chambers

Colin Manning has spent over 45 years as a commercial litigator, giving him a substantial expertise in dispute resolution. He is frequently appointed on especially difficult matters in fields as diverse as healthcare, tax and partnership. One market source states that he "made an extremely difficult mediation look effortless," while another praised him as "effective" and a "good communicator."

Michael Shane
Atkin Chambers

Michael Shane is a "very commercial" mediator with a worldwide practice that has seen him appointed on matters in Europe, the USA and the Far East. The focus of his practice is on engineering, construction and energy disputes, with other areas of expertise including insurance and finance. He attracts particular praise for his ability to take "a very global and complex case and break it down into smaller pieces."

Band 4

Elizabeth Birch
3 Verulam Buildings

Elizabeth Birch is an experienced barrister with expertise in multi-party, cross-border disputes. She is described by one admirer as having "that skill of getting people, despite their prejudices, to see that there is a better way forward for them and all parties." Another praises her as "very patient, thoughtful and thorough." She has significant experience in the construction, shipping, insurance and energy sectors, among others.

Robert Evans
Keating Chambers

Robert Evans utilises his strong civil engineering specialism in his ADR practice and is frequently instructed in highly technical construction, engineering and energy disputes. He has particular expertise in cases in these sectors involving professional negligence claims. He wins praise from market commentators for his "understated style" and for his "extremely pragmatic and very user friendly" approach.

Charles Flint QC
Blackstone Chambers

Charles Flint QC is a highly regarded senior silk whose "malleable approach" wins praise from sources in the market. He is frequently instructed in cross-border mediations, with one admiring practitioner stating "he went the extra mile to encourage settlement and did a lot of research to ensure he was equipped to deal with the different parties." He has expertise in financial services and banking disputes, with additional experience in professional negligence and chancery cases.

Richard Methuen QC
12 King's Bench Walk

Richard Methuen QC is "extremely good at facilitating the coming together of people to achieve a satisfactory outcome," according to one commentator. His ADR practice is centred on personal injury, clinical negligence and professional negligence claims, with observers noting: "He is extremely adept at mediating difficult cases."

Beverley Vara
Maitland Chambers

Beverley Vara is a "very supportive and helpful" mediator who is regularly appointed to property disputes and cases involving professional negligence. One impressed observer stated that "she was very good and skilled in moving the parties to settle" and "she was instrumental in getting the parties out of their entrenched positions."

Motor Insurance Fraud

Contents:

ALL CIRCUITS

Motor Insurance Fraud
Leading Sets
Band 1
Temple Garden Chambers *
Leading Silks
Band 1
Kennedy Christopher *9 St John Street (ORL)* ◊
Band 2
Featherby William *12 King's Bench Walk (ORL)* ◊ *
Leading Juniors
Band 1
Crapper Sadie *39 Essex Chambers (ORL)* ◊
Dawson Judy *Park Square Barristers (ORL)* ◊
Grant Marcus *Temple Garden Chambers* *
Higgins Paul *Deans Court Chambers (ORL)* ◊
Laughland James *Temple Garden Chambers*
McCann Simon *Deans Court Chambers (ORL)* ◊ Ⓐ
McCluggage Brian *9 St John Street (ORL)* ◊
Wilson Peter J *Park Square Barristers (ORL)* ◊
Band 2
Davies George *Temple Garden Chambers* *
Furness Corin *Parklane Plowden (ORL)* ◊
Glassbrook Alex *Temple Garden Chambers* *
Sharpe Tim *Temple Garden Chambers* *
Snarr Matthew *9 St John Street (ORL)* ◊ *
Symington Anna *St John's Chambers (ORL)* ◊ Ⓐ
* Indicates set / individual with profile.
Ⓐ direct access (see p.24).
◊ (ORL) = Other Ranked Lawyer.
Alphabetical order within each band. Band 1 is highest.

Band 1

Temple Garden Chambers
See profile on p.919

THE SET

Temple Garden Chambers offers leading expertise in the area of motor insurance fraud, and possesses some of the most accomplished juniors in the market. The set's very active practice encompasses an impressive range of fraud work including staged and contrived accidents, phantom passenger claims, contempt of court and sham credit hire arrangements. As well as handling individual dishonest claims, many of its members also have considerable talent in uncovering and exposing wider networks of fraud.

Client service: "The clerks, led by Dean Norton, are absolutely brilliant and they go out of their way to assist. They will always try to find you someone, and they make sensible recommendations. They take the time to get to know fee earners. When I call they know what my preferences are and they know who I will use."

JUNIORS

Marcus Grant (see p.658) Leading junior for motor insurance fraud cases, particularly those that involve contempt of court. **Strengths:** "He is the genius for me. He is gifted, he truly takes care of his cases and he's a master in his area of practice, especially when it comes to contempt of court." "He has an incredible ability to see the wood for the trees, and he builds cases without making them into War and Peace, getting the critical points across calmly." **Recent work:** Successfully proved contempt of court in a case where four individuals were accused of staging a 'crash for cash' incident in April 2011.

James Laughland Has a practice that focuses on personal injury and costs litigation alongside motor insurance fraud. He demonstrates a notable talent for cases that rely on the exposure of wider fraud networks. **Strengths:** "He is very good on his feet and on paper, and he understands the nuances of fraud rings." "He's a great all-rounder who is quick at turning papers around. You know he'll fully consider them and look at every bit of detail. His advocacy is great as well." **Recent work:** Represented the defendant in an induced slam-on collision case where the claimant ultimately admitted to credit hire fraud.

George Davies (see p.629) A junior who is "not afraid to take on a fight" and whose experience at the Bar is bolstered by his former career as a City solicitor handling international fraud litigation. He has a range of motor fraud expertise that he applies to cases involving staged accidents, bogus passengers and fraud rings. **Strengths:** "He is a brilliant all-rounder and he has outstanding advocacy skills. He's always willing to test the boundaries and have a go. He delivers excellent service and has a real can-do attitude." **Recent work:** Represented a group of insurers facing four supposedly unconnected RTA claims which seemed to be linked by similar factual evidence in each case. After allegations of fraud were made, all four claims were discontinued.

Alex Glassbrook (see p.654) His work in the motor insurance field features a strong emphasis on handling dishonest claims on behalf of insurance companies. **Strengths:** "He's prompt, detailed and comprehensive in his advices."

Tim Sharpe (see p.762) Acts for claimants and defendants in motor insurance fraud cases including induced and staged collisions, fraud rings and contempt of court. **Strengths:** "He is brilliant at putting the facts together with the law." "He's well prepared, doughty and knows the points to run." **Recent work:** Defended an insurance company against a litigant who brought a dishonest claim for a genuine accident in which he was not involved.

Other Ranked Lawyers

Paul Higgins (Deans Court Chambers) Fields a strong practice in motor insurance fraud and regularly defends insurers against claimants looking to defraud them. Has appreciable experience in handling committal proceedings and putting cases before the Court of Appeal. **Strengths:** "He has a national reputation for this type of work and his cross-examination is phenomenal."

Simon McCann (Deans Court Chambers) An experienced junior specialising in motor insurance fraud claims. He has advised on all aspects of fraud, including contempt proceedings, and is also deeply involved in assisting insurers and local authorities on how best to investigate and uncover fraud rings. **Strengths:** "He's very good and has a reassuring, natural manner before the judge."

Sadie Crapper (39 Essex Chambers) Known for her strong work in motor insurance fraud, which sits alongside her estimable personal injury practice. She has considerable experience of acting for defendant insurers facing issues such as staged accidents, phantom passengers and exaggerated claims. **Strengths:** "A barrister at the top of her game."

William Featherby QC (see p.643) (12 King's Bench Walk) Notable personal injury silk with significant civil fraud expertise who takes on a healthy amount of work related to motor fraud. He is well known for his impressive command of cases involving contempt of court. **Strengths:** "Meticulous in document preparation and a ruthless and thorough advocate."

Corin Furness (Parklane Plowden) Strong practice handling the defence of fraudulent motor insurance claims relating to staged and deliberately induced accidents, bogus passengers, exaggerated claims and fraud rings. **Strengths:** "Has the skills to get to the bottom of the most complex cases."

Judy Dawson (Park Square Barristers) A dedicated specialist in motor insurance fraud who is especially involved in working with insurers to expose large fraud rings. Her busy caseload often features dishonest claims that are highly sophisticated and complex. **Strengths:** "She's always prepared to tell us not what we want to hear but the actual facts of the case in front of us. Her pleadings are second to none, she sets up the cases perfectly and she explains the positions very well." "She's got a tremendous ability to absorb very difficult and complex cases."

Peter Wilson (Park Square Barristers) Staunch defender of insurance companies facing fraudulent personal injury claims. He has experience in a wide range of work relating to staged and induced collisions, faked injuries and bogus passenger claims. **Strengths:** "He's really thorough. He will go through instructions with a fine toothcomb, and prepare to within an inch of his life. If you've got a high value or very technical claim, you know he will be ready." **Recent work:** Defended an insurance company against two separate RTA claims in which it was discovered that both claimants were supposed to have had possession of the same hire vehicle simultaneously.

Anna Symington (St John's Chambers) Acts for both claimants and defendants, although many of her instructions come from leading insurers. Her experience in personal injury, costs litigation and fraud work positions her well to take on significant claims of motor insurance fraud. **Strengths:** "Very quick to pick up on issues and robust in her desire to follow up a case and run with it."

Christopher Kennedy QC (9 St John Street) An expert in personal injury law who also has considerable knowledge of road traffic accident cases. He frequently represents insurers faced with large and potentially fraudulent claims. **Strengths:** "Single-minded in pursuit of his case and quite prepared to dig his heels in where necessary."

Brian McCluggage (9 St John Street) Takes on a number of cases related to road traffic accidents as part of his wider personal injury practice. He is known for his involvement in high-value cases and those involving an element of insurance fraud. **Strengths:** "Incredibly knowledgeable and highly reliable."

Matthew Snarr (see p.769) (9 St John Street) Specifically acts for defendants in cases of fraudulent motor insurance claims. He has a particular specialism in high-value proceedings and those relating to organised fraud rings. **Strengths:** "Thorough, sensible and can talk to the client in a way that they can understand."

Contents:

LONDON

Offshore
Leading Sets
Band 1
Maitland Chambers *
XXIV Old Buildings *
Serle Court *
Wilberforce Chambers *
Band 2
New Square Chambers *
South Square *
4 Stone Buildings *
* Indicates set / individual with profile.
◊ (ORL) = Other Ranked Lawyer.
Alphabetical order within each band. Band 1 is highest.

Offshore	
Leading Silks	
Band 1	**Marshall** Philip *Serle Court* *
Atherton Stephen *20 Essex Street (ORL)* ◊	**McQuater** Ewan *3 Verulam Buildings (ORL)* ◊
Boyle Alan *Serle Court* *	**Miles** Robert *4 Stone Buildings*
Brownbill David *XXIV Old Buildings*	**Mowschenson** Terence *Wilberforce Chambers*
Cooper Gilead *Wilberforce Chambers* *	**Quest** David *3 Verulam Buildings (ORL)* ◊
Crow Jonathan *4 Stone Buildings* *	**Rajah** Eason *Ten Old Square (ORL)* ◊ *
Dicker Robin *South Square* *	**Smith** Stephen *Erskine Chambers (ORL)* ◊ *
Girolami Paul *Maitland Chambers* *	**Thanki** Bankim *Fountain Court Chambers (ORL)* ◊ *
Green Brian *Wilberforce Chambers*	**Todd** Michael *Erskine Chambers (ORL)* ◊ *
Ham Robert *Wilberforce Chambers*	**Band 3**
Le Poidevin Nicholas *New Square Chambers*	**Alexander** David *South Square* *
Millett Richard *Essex Court Chambers (ORL)* ◊	**Allison** David *South Square* *
Moverley Smith Stephen *XXIV Old Buildings*	**Ayliffe** James *Wilberforce Chambers*
Parker Christopher R *Maitland Chambers* *	**Barlow** Francis *Ten Old Square (ORL)* ◊ *
Steinfeld Alan *XXIV Old Buildings*	**Black** Michael *XXIV Old Buildings*
Talbot Rice Elspeth *XXIV Old Buildings*	**Chivers** David *Erskine Chambers (ORL)* ◊ *
Taube Simon *Ten Old Square (ORL)* ◊ *	**Davis-White** Malcolm *XXIV Old Buildings*
Warnock-Smith Shân *5 Stone Buildings (ORL)* ◊ *	**Dowley** Dominic *Serle Court* *
Band 2	**Flynn** Vernon *Essex Court Chambers (ORL)* ◊
Adkin Jonathan *Fountain Court Chambers (ORL)* ◊ *	**Fraser** Orlando *4 Stone Buildings* *
Brisby John *4 Stone Buildings* *	**Hubble** Ben *4 New Square (ORL)* ◊ *
Collings Matthew *Maitland Chambers* *	**Legge** Henry *5 Stone Buildings (ORL)* ◊ *
Fenwick Justin *4 New Square (ORL)* ◊ *	**McCall** Christopher *Maitland Chambers* *
Furness Michael *Wilberforce Chambers*	**McGrath** Paul *Essex Court Chambers (ORL)* ◊
Hacker Richard *South Square* *	**Newman** Catherine *Maitland Chambers* *
Hapgood Mark *Brick Court Chambers (ORL)* ◊	**Thom** James *New Square Chambers*
Hinks Frank *Serle Court* *	**Trace** Anthony *Maitland Chambers* *
Hollington Robin *New Square Chambers*	**Tregear** Francis *XXIV Old Buildings*
Howard Mark *Brick Court Chambers (ORL)* ◊	**New Silks**
Jones Elizabeth *Serle Court* *	**Hilliard** Jonathan *Wilberforce Chambers*
Levy Robert *XXIV Old Buildings*	**Mumford** David *Maitland Chambers* *
Lord David W *Three Stone (ORL)* ◊	**Wilson** Richard *Serle Court* *
Lowe Thomas *Wilberforce Chambers*	

Band 1

Maitland Chambers

See profile on p.875

THE SET

Members of Maitland Chambers make regular appearances in key offshore jurisdictions, and have notable experience of handling cases in the British Virgin Islands (BVI), the Bahamas and the Cayman Islands, amongst others. They undertake major commercial litigation, often acting for companies in insolvency matters and shareholder disputes. Individuals from the set represented banks and trustees following the Madoff affair and have also been acting in the high-profile Nina Wang probate dispute in Hong Kong.

Client service: "The clerks are excellent. They are always responsive, they try their utmost to help, and they are not difficult to deal with over fees." John Wiggs sets the tone as the senior managing clerk.

SILKS

Paul Girolami QC (see p.653) Has a formidable reputation for his work handling insolvency, fraud and company litigation. He is admitted in the BVI and has also attained significant experience appearing in Gibraltar and the Dubai International Financial Centre (DIFC). **Strengths:** "He's incredibly smooth and has proven himself to be imaginative and able to think outside the box."

Christopher Parker QC (see p.733) Maintains his premiere standing in offshore dispute work and regularly handles insolvency and company litigation, including shareholder disputes and breach of fiduciary duty claims. He has been called to the BVI Bar, and also has experience of court proceedings in Hong Kong, Bermuda, Dubai and the Channel Islands. **Strengths:** "He is a robust and forceful advocate who carries the court with him. He is not afraid of making big judgement calls and he gets them right."

Matthew Collings QC (see p.620) Regularly appears for clients in both initial and appellate proceedings across the BVI, the Cayman Islands and Hong Kong. He is skilled in a diverse array of company, insolvency and company litigation matters. **Strengths:** "I think he's just great to work with. He's responsive, he gets the right answer very quickly and he's thoroughly reliable. He very much rolls his sleeves up and gets involved in all aspects of the case." **Recent work:** Successfully acted for Staray Capital in a shareholder dispute in the BVI.

Christopher McCall QC (see p.711) Hugely experienced in trust and private client dispute work, and also an expert in charity law. His practice regularly takes him across key Caribbean jurisdictions and to Hong Kong. **Strengths:** "He's a great figure who is really top-class."

Catherine Newman QC (see p.727) A practitioner with over 35 years' experience who has noted ability in company, banking and insolvency cases and business disputes generally. She is a senior and much-respected figure at the Bar who is much in demand both at home and abroad. **Strengths:** "A great cross-examiner and an absolute delight." **Recent work:** Successfully acted for Cayman company Acorn International in a shareholder dispute which resulted in a winding-up petition.

Anthony Trace QC (see p.783) Has gained a wealth of experience advocating before the courts in Gibraltar, Hong Kong and several Caribbean jurisdictions. As well as being a fine litigator, he is a noted figure in ADR, having served as an arbitrator. **Strengths:** "He's highly persuasive and carries the court with confidence." **Recent work:** Engaged by a private individual to successfully obtain a freezing order against the Bank of St Petersburg in the Dominican Court of Appeal.

David Mumford QC (see p.724) Took silk in 2016 and continues to go from strength to strength in international commercial litigation. He has recently been active handling trust and breach of duty claims across the BVI, Jersey and Singapore. **Strengths:** "He can take something very complicated and make it seem straightforward – he is great at getting to the heart of big, complex matters." **Recent work:** Represented CCIF defending audit negligence claims brought by Topping Chance Development, following the collapse of a food exporting company.

XXIV Old Buildings

See profile on p.884

THE SET

A loyal following of instructing solicitors frequently turns to this chambers due to its offering of renowned barristers who have a strong track record in offshore trusts and commercial cases. Members here regularly act in traditional Caribbean and European jurisdictions, and further extend their reach to such areas as Cyprus, Liechtenstein and the wider Middle East. Market sources are quick to commend the set for its world-wide presence, revealing that "this is pretty much the number-one chambers operating in Dubai " and also "a serious player in the Channel Islands." The set has recently had key roles in matters arising from the collapse of Carlyle Capital and has also been involved in the high-value Crociani trust litigation.

Client service: "I like the clerks there; they're always very honest over who can do what, particularly Paul Matthews. I'm always very confident that when I pick the phone up, they'll be very helpful to me."

Offshore
Leading Juniors
Band 1
Brightwell James *New Square Chambers*
Hagen Dakis *Serle Court* *
Richardson Giles *Serle Court* *
Singla Nikki *Wilberforce Chambers*
Tucker Lynton *New Square Chambers*
Band 2
Cloherty Adam *XXIV Old Buildings*
Cumming Edward *XXIV Old Buildings*
Halkerston Graeme *Wilberforce Chambers*
Harrison Nicholas *Serle Court* *
Hubbard Mark *New Square Chambers*
Mold Andrew *Wilberforce Chambers*
Shah Bajul *XXIV Old Buildings*
Shivji Sharif *4 Stone Buildings* *
Weaver Elizabeth *XXIV Old Buildings*
Willan James *Essex Court Chambers (ORL)* ◊
Band 3
Child Andrew J *Wilberforce Chambers*
Holden Andrew *XXIV Old Buildings*
Langlois Nicole *XXIV Old Buildings*
O'Mahony David *7BR (ORL)* ◊ [A] *
Parker Matthew *3 Verulam Buildings (ORL)* ◊ *
* Indicates individual with profile.
[A] direct access (see p.24).
◊ (ORL) = Other Ranked Lawyer.
Alphabetical order within each band. Band 1 is highest.

Paul Matthews and Dan Wilson are senior practice managers.

SILKS

David Brownbill QC A natural choice for the most complex and contentious trusts litigation, he is frequently called upon to handle work in the Channel Islands, the BVI and the Cayman Islands. His specialism lies in multi-jurisdictional and high-value traditional and commercial chancery work. **Strengths:** "His legal knowledge, particularly in relation to offshore trusts, is second to none, and he is excellent in conference and when dealing with the client." **Recent work:** Instructed by the Jersey offices of Carey Olsen to act in the Crociani trust litigation which involved claims of more than USD100 million.

Stephen Moverley Smith QC Impressed commentators affirm his position at the forefront of BVI and Cayman Island litigation. He is well versed in a range of commercial cases, including those concerning restructuring, fraud and insolvency. **Strengths:** "A wonderful choice of counsel for offshore litigation, who has a high level of expertise in local BVI and Cayman law. He garners great respect from the offshore judiciary." **Recent work:** Acted for two shareholders of Shansui Cement opposing the appointment of provisional liquidators.

Alan Steinfeld QC Solicitors flock to him due to his wide commercial and traditional chancery expertise and his profound knowledge of trust disputes. He has broad offshore experience across the Channel Islands, the Caribbean and Hong Kong; he is also a mediator. **Strengths:** "A genius who is unbelievably clever and a real pleasure to deal with. He's no doubt the cleverest person in a room." **Recent work:** Acted as defence counsel to Carlyle Capital-related entities in connection with a USD1 billion breach of contract and fiduciary claim, following the collapse of Carlyle Capital.

Elspeth Talbot Rice QC A highly regarded and much sought-after expert handling a full spectrum of commercial and traditional chancery work. She has experience of acting in jurisdictions spanning the BVI, Bermuda and the UK Crown dependencies. **Strengths:** "An incredibly hard-working and bright individual. She has a very commercial approach and a deep knowledge of insolvency principles and how they can be applied." **Recent work:** Acted for the beneficiaries and new trustees in Walker v Egerton Vernon. This was a £100 million breach of trust claim.

Robert Levy QC A leading silk for complex, high-value insolvency claims, particularly within the Caribbean jurisdictions. He has been called to the Bar of the Eastern Caribbean in the BVI, and the Bars of Anguilla and St Vincent, and he is also admitted ad hoc in the Cayman Islands. **Strengths:** "His written submissions are a model of clarity, which is what you particularly need in offshore jurisdictions." **Recent work:** Acted for several companies in appeals to the Eastern Caribbean Supreme Court regarding the financial collapse of the Cap Juluca luxury resort in Anguilla.

Michael Black QC Marked out by interviewees for his work in Dubai and the wider Middle East. His practice encompasses banking and general commercial litigation, and he is further noted for his strength in arbitration. **Strengths:** "Truly a global advocate, and one of the best appearing in the DIFC." **Recent work:** Acted in Al Sadik v Investcorp, a USD100 million claim alleging breach of fiduciary and other duties.

Malcolm Davis-White QC A noted practitioner in the fields of insolvency and company disputes, who is an expert in matters involving directors' duties. His recent activity has included advising on several contentious trust matters in Guernsey. **Strengths:** "He gives you brainpower and information-crunching skills, which then translates into very usable strategy and usable bits of information." **Recent work:** Acted for Millard against the government of the Commonwealth of the Northern Mariana Islands in respect of that government's appeal against the making of bankruptcy orders on debtors' petitions.

Francis Tregear QC Well known for his liquidation work, he has acted for clients in Bermuda, the BVI and the Cayman Islands. He offers additional expertise in trust disputes, and has recently been active in Jersey and Bermuda. **Strengths:** "User-friendly, clever and responsive." **Recent work:** Acted for the additional liquidator of the Herald Fund, a major Madoff feeder fund, in claims against the Madoff estate in the Cayman Islands.

JUNIORS

Adam Cloherty Impresses sources with his courtroom advocacy skills, and has particular experience of BVI and Cayman Islands cases. He has also handled matters in Jersey, Guernsey and the Isle of Man. **Strengths:** "An effective cross-border insolvency expert, who is particularly useful in BVI matters. He is easy to work with and a team player." **Recent work:** Acted as sole counsel to Exemplary Holdings against Soneva Fushi, a BVI-incorporated luxury resort operator. The case revolved around claims of unfair prejudice and breach of shareholders' agreements.

Edward Cumming Highly regarded amongst peers for his excellent advocacy skills, he frequently appears in trust, company and general commercial litigation. He has a substantial offshore practice, and appears in Singapore, South Africa and Mauritius, alongside more traditional jurisdictions in the Caribbean and Channel Islands. **Strengths:** "Charming to work with and a provider of incisive legal advice. For a junior of his level he's a solicitor's dream." **Recent work:** Acted in the Crociani trust litigation in Jersey, which involved breach of trust claims valued at more than USD100 million.

Bajul Shah Has an enviable offshore practice, and handles cases in Cyprus, the Caribbean and the Channel Islands. He offers expertise in a broad range of commercial chancery areas, including insolvency, trusts, probate and civil fraud. **Strengths:** "His comprehensive understanding of asset management and the workings of the Caribbean jurisdictions make him a potent force in fund management disputes." **Recent work:** Advised First Caribbean Bank in connection with the receivership and insolvency of BVI-based Bobby's Supermarket.

Elizabeth Weaver A deeply experienced junior barrister, well versed in professional negligence and general chancery matters. She is routinely called upon for her expertise in international trusts disputes and high-value commercial litigation. **Strengths:** "A very articulate, impressively persuasive and effective barrister." **Recent work:** Acted in Credit Suisse v Haggiag, advising trustees in a claim that challenged the validity of Guernsey trusts in Italian proceedings.

Andrew Holden Receives consistent praise for his deep level of experience in trust litigation work. His experience extends to the Channel Islands, BVI and Cayman Islands, amongst others. **Strengths:** "His power of reason and depth of knowledge are very good. He is confident and good on his feet, and he's also got an engaging personality." **Recent work:** Instructed by Withers LLP in a case concerning the disputed removal of the protector of a private family trust in Guernsey.

Nicole Langlois A respected junior with considerable credentials in commercial contractual and trust litigation. She is called to the Bar in both the UK and in Jersey. **Strengths:** "Very approachable and practical, but also very astute on the more technical aspects of the case. There were some real complexities attached to the matter she handled, and she displayed a real enthusiasm for getting to the bottom of them." **Recent work:** Acted for the fifth defendant in the Crociani trust litigation in Jersey.

Serle Court

See profile on p.908

THE SET

Serle Court offers unrivalled expertise for those with cases in the Channel Islands and is also a key player in Bermuda and the wider Caribbean offshore jurisdictions. Its top-drawer silks and juniors are often to be found acting for high net worth individuals and multinational companies in a wide array of commercial and chancery disputes. They are at a set that is hailed for having "a strong, positive reputation." It is "a definite go-to chambers for contentious trust work."

Client service: Steve Whitaker is head clerk at the set. "A good clerk knows when to say, 'No, we can't do it.' Most clerks only say yes, but Steve is refreshingly honest in his views."

SILKS

Alan Boyle QC (see p.601) Widely praised as a leading light of the Offshore Bar, Alan Boyle is highly sought after for trusts, insolvency and probate litigation amongst other things. He serves as head of chambers at Serle Court. **Strengths:** "A true grandee of the Chancery Bar and an absolute pleasure to work with. He has unparalleled experience in trust, company and commercial cases and brings genuine gravitas." **Recent work:** Acted for a private individual in a ten-week trial in the Cayman Islands. The case concerned an alleged breach of trust following the restructuring of a major trust fund.

Frank Hinks QC (see p.672) Has long-standing experience of handling litigation across numerous offshore jurisdictions, having appeared in a wide range of locations both across the Caribbean and in Hong Kong. He is particularly adept at co-ordinating complex and multi-jurisdictional litigation. **Strengths:** "Very experienced and a tremendously hard worker who is detail-oriented. He is willing to think creatively to solve problems."

Elizabeth Jones QC (see p.685) Excels in complex, multi-jurisdictional litigation, and has in-depth expertise in company and commercial law generally. She regularly advises on disputes in the Channel Islands, and is also called to the Bar of the BVI. **Strengths:** "She's fierce on her feet and the clients absolutely love her. She gets to grips with the intricate detail of a case in a short space of time."

Philip Marshall QC (see p.708) Demonstrates strong credentials in asset recovery and civil fraud cases, and has additional strength in restructuring and insolvency disputes. He has appeared or advised in courts in jurisdictions including Hong Kong, Bermuda and the BVI. **Strengths:** "One of the best strategists at the Bar. He constantly thinks of new angles in a case and is good at fighting the client's corner in the face of real adversity." **Recent work:** Acted in ISIS Investments v McHarrie, representing directors alleged to have breached their duty following the collapse of Icelandic bank Kaupthing.

Dominic Dowley QC (see p.636) A commercial chancery expert, with a deep level of experience of contentious trust and investment structure disputes. He is active across the BVI, the Cayman Islands and Bermuda. **Strengths:** "He's commercial, reliable and user-friendly." **Recent work:** Acted in Salem v Salem, a major international trust dispute in Guernsey.

Richard Wilson QC (see p.798) Enjoys a strong reputation in traditional and commercial chancery litigation, and has particular expertise in trusts, probate and partnership disputes. He has appeared for clients in Gibraltar, the Cayman Islands and the Eastern Caribbean Supreme Court. **Strengths:** "Well-known trusts specialist who continues to impress with his service delivery and skill set."

JUNIORS

Dakis Hagen (see p.661) A junior with an outstanding reputation for handling international trust, fraud and asset tracing matters. He regularly appears in Bermuda and Jersey, as well as the wider Caribbean jurisdictions. **Strengths:** "Incredibly polished and very easy to work with. He's obviously immensely smart, but also very straightforward and his advice is always user-friendly and clear." **Recent work:** Advised the YT Charitable Foundation on the proposed winding-up of its USD500 million charitable fund.

Giles Richardson (see p.751) A key player in contentious international trusts cases, who has acted for both trust companies and personal trustees in places as far-flung as the Channel Islands, the BVI and St Kitts & Nevis. **Strengths:** "An outstanding tactician, who is charming, very easy to work with and technically very gifted." **Recent work:** Acted for Barclays Wealth Trustees against Equity Trust. This matter concerned £50 million worth of claims against the former trustees of property unit trusts.

Nicholas Harrison (see p.666) Has experience of practising in Bermuda, the Bahamas, Jersey and the Isle of Man, amongst others. He has had notable roles in several high-value, cross-jurisdictional disputes. **Strengths:** "He is wonderful to work alongside if you're a solicitor, and his written work is exemplary." **Recent work:** Acted in the Wang probate litigation in Bermuda, which involved claims upon assets valued at up to USD17 billion held in Bermuda trusts.

Wilberforce Chambers

See profile on p.925

THE SET

Widely considered a standout set of chambers for offshore and international disputes, Wilberforce Chambers offers dedicated strengths in such areas as trusts, banking and finance, company law and asset tracing. The set boasts a deep and multi-talented pool of expert barristers who are members of, or have been called to, the Bars of the Bahamas, the BVI, the Cayman Islands, Dubai, Singapore and the UK Crown dependencies. Instructing lawyers are quick to highlight the set's pre-eminent position, revealing that "Wilberforce is one of the standout names for offshore work, and really is the set to beat." **Client service:** "The clerks are very helpful and always responsive, and the chambers is very well run." Mark Rushton is the head clerk.

SILKS

Gilead Cooper QC (see p.623) Has a great standing in offshore litigation, and noted ability in trusts, fraud, breach of fiduciary duty and professional negligence disputes. He has appeared in court proceedings in the BVI, Bermuda, the Cayman Islands and Hong Kong. **Strengths:** "His real value lies in his ability to communicate clearly and concisely, and in a language that is easy to understand. That's a real skill."

Brian Green QC A market leader in chancery work, who is regularly instructed by solicitors due to his ability to handle the most complex and high-profile litigation. He has a wide-ranging practice but proves particularly adept at cases concerning trusts and pensions. **Strengths:** "He's outstandingly able and practical in his application of very complex legal principles."

Robert Ham QC Robert Ham is a star of the trusts world, and receives effusive praise for his outstanding efforts in private client work, tax law and pensions. **Strengths:** "An absolutely brilliant trusts lawyer, who knows that very fine line between protecting the trustee and minimising costs."

Michael Furness QC An impressive silk, who is especially knowledgeable in trusts and tax disputes, as well as contentious and non-contentious pension scheme work. His practice regularly leads him to appear in Bermudian trust cases, and he has experience of acting in Hong Kong's Court of Final Appeal. **Strengths:** "A really quite formidable and wonderfully smooth advocate."

Thomas Lowe QC Has a wealth of experience of appearing in the Cayman Islands and BVI, acting in a wide range of private client disputes and contentious trust matters. He has a particular forte in handling litigation following the collapse of investment structures. **Strengths:** "Powerful and clear on his feet. He can explain the most complicated principles and reduce them to their basic elements very effectively."

Terence Mowschenson QC A popular and much-admired chancery silk, who has undertaken a range of banking, finance, company and insolvency cases worldwide. He has appeared in a wide range of jurisdictions, including Gibraltar, the Isle of Man, the Cayman Islands and the BVI. **Strengths:** "A serious figure in the offshore market," who is "charming and effective."

James Ayliffe QC A very strong chancery commercial performer who is proficient in banking, civil fraud, partnership, real estate and trusts cases. Truly international in his scope, he has handled matters in many offshore jurisdictions, as well in a host of countries such as South Africa and the USA. **Strengths:** "He has an excellent legal brain and he really knows how to take a matter forward."

Jonathan Hilliard QC His appointment as Queen's Counsel in early 2016 demonstrated his excellent reputation in trusts and commercial litigation work. His practice has led him to act in the Isle of Man, Gibraltar and the BVI, amongst other jurisdictions. **Strengths:** "Exceptionally bright and clearly destined for great things. He's very easy to use, and someone you can just pick up the phone to and have a chat with in order to resolve issues."

JUNIORS

Nikki Singla A very highly regarded junior with experience of appearing for clients in the Cayman Islands, Bermuda and Dubai. Solicitors turn to him for advice on a wide range of commercial and business cases, and admire him for his specialist trusts expertise. **Strengths:** "He states things in a clear and clever way, is sensible and doesn't take bad points."

Graeme Halkerston Very well acquainted with the offshore market, having worked for several years as a partner in a leading firm in the Cayman Islands. He maintains a diverse and dynamic commercial litigation practice, and has strengths in banking and financial disputes and cross-border fraud. **Strengths:** "He has an encyclopaedic knowledge of all things to do with insolvency and company law. His depth and breadth of offshore knowledge is something that really makes him stand out."

Andrew Mold Adroitly handles a diverse range of traditional and commercial chancery matters, demonstrating considerable strength in cases concerning trusts, professional liability and company law. His practice has led him to litigate or advise on matters in the Cayman Islands, Jersey, the Isle of Man, Bermuda and Singapore. **Strengths:** "Quick, good on his feet and someone who can see the wood for the trees. He can explain matters in a way clients understand."

Andrew Child Has a strong offshore practice and noted experience of handling civil fraud and trusts matters. He joined the set from Three Stone Buildings in October 2015. **Strengths:** "Displays good commercial acumen in solving trust disputes."

Band 2

New Square Chambers

See profile on p.882

THE SET

A highly popular choice for commercial litigation work across the Caribbean and UK Crown dependencies. Members are principally instructed to act on behalf of corporate entities, but also act for ultra-high net worth individuals in a diverse array of commercial disputes. The set continues to attract high-profile roles in landmark matters, and worked on the long-running Alhamrani v Alhamrani case which determined the ownership of Chemtrade. They have also handled numerous claims linked to the collapse of Kaupthing Bank.

Client service: "We greatly appreciate the time and trouble that the clerks take with us." Phil Reeves leads the clerking team at the set.

SILKS

Nicholas Le Poidevin QC Considered one of the standout names at the Offshore Bar, he has outstanding capabilities in contentious trust, estate and probate work. He has been active in the Channel Islands and Isle of Man and throughout the Caribbean. **Strengths:** "Technically astute and someone with excellent skills." **Recent work:** Retained by a plaintiff in the Crociani trust litigation, challenging payments made to the settlor and appointment of a new trustee.

Robin Hollington QC His offshore practice encompasses work in jurisdictions across the western Atlantic, and he has made appearances in the BVI, the Cayman Islands and New York, whilst also acting in Hong Kong and Singapore. He has a wealth of knowledge of company and insolvency litigation. **Strengths:** "He literally wrote the book on shareholder disputes and is someone judges listen to." **Recent work:** Acted in YM Holdings v Paragon Securities in the Turks & Caicos Islands, to strike out a petition to appoint a liquidator.

James Thom QC Handles cases in a number of offshore jurisdictions, and is called to the Bar of the BVI and the Bar of St Vincent and the Grenadines. He has particular expertise in cases relating to hedge funds. **Strengths:** "Methodical in his approach; he's calm even in the face of the most violent of storms." **Recent work:** Has spent a good deal of his time recently handling Weavering Macro Fixed Income Fund Ltd v Ernst & Young, a large case concerning a hedge fund that had been defrauded by its investment manager.

JUNIORS

James Brightwell Acclaimed by market sources for his work in trusts and estates litigation. He is frequently called upon to represent clients in the BVI and the Channel Islands, and has garnered accolades for his role in the Tchenguiz trust litigation. **Strengths:** "He has a mastery of all the facts when handling complicated and complex cases. He's user-friendly and incredibly bright, and his knowledge of trusts law is encyclopaedic." **Recent work:** Acted for Investec against Rawlinson & Hunter Trustees and Oscatello, defending claims connected with £180 million of loans owed within the Tchenguiz Discretionary Trust.

Lynton Tucker A respected and seasoned litigator with a wealth of experience in trust law, who has an offshore practice encompassing work across the Channel Islands, the Cayman Islands, the BVI and Hong Kong. **Strengths:** "Brilliant at conducting arguments in difficult cases, he is a go-to senior junior for the most complex cases." **Recent work:** Acted in Alhamrani v Alhamrani, a BVI case in the Privy Council to determine the ownership of a Middle Eastern oil company.

Mark Hubbard Has a wide-ranging offshore practice, and displays considerable skill handling trusts, company, civil fraud and insolvency litigation. The Bahamas, the Isle of Man and the Channel Islands are jurisdictions he has particular experience of practising in. **Strengths:** "Very sensible and practical," "he's a delight to work with and is a good authoritative adviser to clients." **Recent work:** Acted for two companies in litigation to gain control of Crowd Shout, obtaining urgent injunctions in Malta and advising on claims in the Isle of Man.

South Square

See profile on p.910

THE SET

Although traditionally celebrated for its unrivalled strength in corporate insolvency work, the set has expertise in a wider range of commercial offshore matters, and has acted in a number of banking and financial, company law and professional negligence disputes. Members regularly appear across the Caribbean jurisdictions, and an impressive number of them are called to the Bar of the BVI and, ad hoc, to the Bar of the Cayman Islands. They have acted in a number of substantial litigation cases, including the USD9 billion Saad fraud case and a USD1 billion professional negligence claim against HSBC brought by a Madoff feeder fund. Sources say: "This is an excellent set of chambers. You could pluck anyone out of there and expect them to be amongst the very best in the market."

Client service: "Their clerks are excellent. They're very attentive and make sure you don't have to chase too much." Mike Killick and Dylan Playfoot are senior practice managers.

SILKS

Robin Dicker QC (see p.633) A star of the offshore world with outstanding credentials in financial and restructuring litigation. His distinguished insolvency background led to him acting for the now-defunct Lehman Brothers and the Icelandic commercial bank Landsbanki in restructuring and insolvency disputes. **Strengths:** "Very clever, very helpful to the court and someone who inspires confidence in the judge. He's a very thorough and charming advocate."

Richard Hacker QC (see p.661) Amasses accolades for his work in the Channel Islands, the Isle of Man, Bermuda, the BVI and the Cayman Islands. He specialises in commercial dispute resolution, and tackles shareholder disputes, fraud, asset tracing and insolvency work. **Strengths:** "A level-headed practitioner who brings a good commercial view to bear."

David Alexander QC (see p.581) An impressive silk with a broad offshore practice who handles company, restructuring, trusts and general commercial work. He has recently been involved in major insolvency litigation. **Strengths:** "Provides clear, definitive advice in a client-friendly form and is a good strategist."

David Allison QC (see p.583) A seasoned litigator with considerable strength in company and insolvency law, who often handles high-value claims with multi-jurisdictional implications. His thriving offshore practice has seen him handling cases in Dubai, Guernsey and the Cayman Islands to name but a few jurisdictions. **Strengths:** "Just superb on technical insolvency work." "He offers a good balance between commerciality and legal expertise." **Recent work:** Acted for the Hong Kong branch of Raiffeisen Bank in the BVI, handling claims brought against Asia Coal Energy over the purchase of a coal company.

4 Stone Buildings

See profile on p.913

THE SET

A new entrant to the table that handles a good deal of offshore litigation in commercial and corporate disputes. 4 Stone Buildings enjoys a strong reputation in offshore jurisdictions, and is regularly instructed in matters before the courts of the Caribbean and the Channel Islands. It has further experience in emerging markets within Eastern Europe, Africa and South-East Asia. Members continue to undertake highly significant cases worldwide, recently acting in Al Khorafi v Bank Sarasin-Alpen, a high-profile mis-selling case before the DIFC.

Client service: "I get spectacular client service from them. They're attentive and can be contacted at any time of day or night, and if I need them to step up they always deliver." David Goddard leads the clerking team.

SILKS

Jonathan Crow QC (see p.627) A formidable offshore advocate with an outstanding track record in heavyweight commercial, company and public law cases. The broad geographic spread of his work takes him to Hong Kong, the Channel Islands and several Caribbean jurisdictions. **Strengths:** "His best trait is that he's a very effective advocate whose thoughts are very well marshalled. He's very direct and gets to the point quickly – he has a great style." **Recent work:** Acted for the estate of an Eastern European oligarch in Blue Tropic v Chkhartishvili, seeking USD10 million in restitution for the misappropriation of assets.

John Brisby QC (see p.603) John Brisby's busy commercial practice sees him tackle work in Gibraltar, the Isle of Man, Bermuda and the Cayman Islands, amongst other jurisdictions. He has attained a fine reputation for his excellent courtroom advocacy, and has acted in cases relating to the collapses of Enron, Barings, Maxwell and Barlow Clowes. **Strengths:** "The overall breadth and depth of his knowledge is very useful. He finds things that everyone else has overlooked before they have the chance to become bigger problems." **Recent work:** Acted in Re Viking River Cruises, a USD1 billion claim in the Bermudian Supreme Court.

Robert Miles QC Prized by solicitors for his expert ability in offshore financial, commercial and corporate disputes, he has advised on, or appeared in, high-profile financial services litigation throughout his distinguished career. He is admitted ad hoc in the Isle of Man, the Seychelles, the Cayman Islands and Bermuda, and is also a member of the BVI Bar. **Strengths:** "Down to earth and user-friendly notwithstanding his superb reputation." **Recent work:** Acted for the defendant in Barclays Bank v Red Oak Operations, a USD10 million claim alleging fraud perpetrated on the bank.

Orlando Fraser QC (see p.648) Has a great reputation for commercial litigation, having appeared in disputes concerning fraud, trusts, insolvency and company law. His offshore practice incorporates work in the BVI, Dominica, Nevis and the USA. **Strengths:** "A vivacious and punchy junior silk who is incredibly able and confident." **Recent work:** Acted for the fourth defendant against claims brought by the Republic of Djibouti concerning the ownership and management of the main port of Djibouti.

JUNIORS

Sharif Shivji (see p.764) An eminent junior with a background as a former derivatives trader. He delivers standout performances in financial services litigation, and has a highly international practice that sees him work in places such as Dubai, the BVI and Trinidad & Tobago. **Strengths:** "Extremely knowledgeable about financial services issues. He is really on top of everything." **Recent work:** Acted in Al Khorafi v Bank Sarasin-Alpen (ME) Limited and others, a landmark banking and financial services case, and one of the highest-profile investment mis-selling cases in the Middle East.

Other Ranked Lawyers

David O'Mahony (see p.730) (7BR) Highly regarded for his financial regulatory, money laundering and international criminal work. He has been called to the Bar in the Turks & Caicos Islands and has acted in the DIFC. **Strengths:** "Offers first-rate advice and can be trusted with the most difficult cases." **Recent work:** Acted for Mr Bhojwani in his application to the ECHR challenging his conviction for laundering USD43 million of the proceeds of corruption in Jersey.

Mark Hapgood QC (Brick Court Chambers) Prized for his distinguished track record in commercial law matters, he has deep expertise in banking, insurance and professional negligence claims. He has recently been active in numerous proceedings in the BVI. **Strengths:** "Bright and hard working, he's very commercial and devastating on his feet." **Recent work:** Appeared in ABN AMRO Fund Services (Isle of Man) Nominees v Krys, a four-day application in the BVI seeking to restrain liquidators from pursuing USD6 billion of claims in the USA.

Mark Howard QC (Brick Court Chambers) A respected commercial silk with a wealth of knowledge in banking, fraud, insurance and energy litigation. He has acted in several prominent cases in the courts of the BVI. **Strengths:** "He'll blow away someone in a commercial case as easily in the BVI as he does in London" **Recent work:** Acted in Akers v Samba, a case concerning the determination of a Cayman trust fund and a dispute over jurisdictional issues.

Stephen Smith QC (see p.769) (Erskine Chambers) Offers clients almost unparalleled expertise in civil fraud litigation and asset-freezing matters. His offshore practice incorporates work in the BVI, Cayman Islands, Bahamas and UK Crown dependencies. **Strengths:** "The master of the freezing injunctions field." "He's a good tactician and also a disarmingly good advocate."

Michael Todd QC (see p.782) (Erskine Chambers) Extremely highly regarded for his cerebral approach and vast expertise in company law disputes. **Strengths:** "He has a comprehensive knowledge of company law. He's a very good advocate and a completely safe pair of hands. He's really quite magnificent." **Recent work:** Acted for a shareholder in the Al Dobowi Group presenting winding-up petitions in respect of the group's BVI holding companies.

David Chivers QC (see p.616) (Erskine Chambers) Boasts a strong following in the Caribbean, having been called to the Bar of the BVI and ad hoc to the Bars of the Cayman Islands and Bermuda. His practice comprises a great deal of corporate and company litigation. **Strengths:** "He has a comprehensive knowledge of company law, and is very well versed in shareholder disputes." **Recent work:** Defended Swedish bank SEB against the liquidators of the Weavering Macro Fixed Income Fund in the Cayman Islands. The case concerned claims brought to recover USD9 million of preferential payments received by the bank.

Richard Millett QC (Essex Court Chambers) Boasts an excellent track record in commercial litigation and arbitration matters, and is good at financial services and banking work. His is admitted to the Bars of the BVI and Anguilla, and is also called ad hoc to the Bars of the Cayman Islands, Bermuda, Nevis, the Isle of Man and the Bahamas. **Strengths:** "A master of offshore technical work." "Passionate and very detailed, he is very innovative and a great advocate."

Vernon Flynn QC (Essex Court Chambers) A strong commercial silk, who is well versed in big-ticket offshore matters across the Caribbean, Hong Kong, Dubai and the Seychelles. **Strengths:** "He's user-friendly, sensible and he listens to you. He's quite calm, which is obviously reassuring." **Recent work:** Acted for Taaleem against the National Bonds Corporation in the DIFC. This was a USD100 million property dispute which involved an alleged breach of trust.

Paul McGrath QC (Essex Court Chambers) Often appears in, or advises on, high-value commercial claims, and is also highly adept at international arbitration. His offshore practice includes work in the Cayman Islands, the BVI, Dubai and Singapore. **Strengths:** "Extremely talented, he has a forensic knowledge of the law and is a measured and effective advocate." **Recent work:** Acted in Kazakhstan Kagazy v Maksar Arip, a case concerning trusts litigation in Cyprus and Switzerland.

James Willan (Essex Court Chambers) Attracts consistently excellent praise from peers and instructing solicitors, who commend him as a "top-notch commercial junior." He has been called to the Bar of the BVI, and is also admitted in the DIFC, the Isle of Man and the Cayman Islands. **Strengths:** "Exceptionally bright. Instructing him is like instructing a QC." "Very gifted, he's one of the most intellectually brilliant counsel you could come across." **Recent work:** Acted for an individual defendant in proceedings brought in the BVI by Kazakh uranium company Kazatomprom, alleging misappropriation of interests in uranium mines.

Stephen Atherton QC (20 Essex Street) A towering figure in insolvency, civil fraud and company litigation, with a wide-ranging offshore practice that takes in work in Singapore, the Caribbean and the Channel Islands. He is also frequently called upon to advise on insolvency matters in Hong Kong. **Strengths:** "Stephen is every bit as good as his richly deserved reputation, and has a great manner to boot." **Recent work:** Acted for Aurelius Investments in its disputed attempt to appoint liquidators to two insolvent BVI companies, which comprise part of the now-collapsed OAS Group.

Jonathan Adkin QC (see p.579) (Fountain Court Chambers) Highly regarded in the area of contentious trust work, with additional experience in civil fraud, insolvency and partnership matters. He is called to the Bar in Gibraltar, Bermuda and the Cayman Islands. **Strengths:** "Remarkably confident on his feet and a young silk who punches well above his weight." **Recent work:** Acted in Al Mojil v Protiviti, a claim in the DIFC surrounding the IPO of a Saudi Arabian company.

Bankim Thanki QC (see p.780) (Fountain Court Chambers) A skilled silk with an excellent pedigree in commercial litigation and regulatory work across the Caribbean, Channel Islands and Far East. He is also a skilled international arbitrator. **Strengths:** "He's very effective, as he's strategically thoughtful and penetrating in his analysis. He has a natural charm and an easy-going attitude that makes him easy to work with."

Justin Fenwick QC (see p.644) (4 New Square) An excellent advocate for cases concerning professional negligence, who has additional capabilities in civil fraud and commercial litigation generally. His practice is heavily weighted towards offshore litigation, and he has experience in both Caribbean and Far Eastern jurisdictions. **Strengths:** "He's just an amazing advocate, whose ability to make an incredibly complex case seem simple is really good. He had the trial judge eating out of the palm of his hand." **Recent work:** Acted in Orient Power v Ernst & Young, a claim brought by liquidators alleging the auditors had failed to notice fraudulent trading.

Ben Hubble QC (see p.677) (4 New Square) Has noted expertise in pensions and professional liability cases, and additional capabilities in wider commercial litigation. His offshore work is focused on the Caribbean, and he has recent experience of Cayman Islands and Antiguan proceedings. **Strengths:** "Clever, calm and confident. He's notable for his incredible memory for detail." **Recent work:** Represented Spectacular Holdings in bringing claims against company directors and registered agents in the BVI, alleging they wrongly sold the company's property on instructions from the owner's former personal assistant.

Simon Taube QC (see p.778) (Ten Old Square) A go-to silk for major trusts, estates and tax issues, who handles contentious and non-contentious work. His practice also incorporates charity, professional negligence and property matters. **Strengths:** "For trusts law he is head and shoulders above the vast majority at the Bar. He is phenomenally clever, and clients regard him as an obvious choice for the really, really big cases." **Recent work:** Advised on a case relating to the Tchenguiz Family Trust in the Guernsey Court of Appeal.

Eason Rajah QC (see p.747) (Ten Old Square) An exemplary practitioner who receives abundant chancery-related offshore instructions, and has noted skill in contentious trusts matters. He provides clients with a deep level of experience in Jersey court proceedings. **Strengths:** "A leading light in trusts and private client work." "He's incredibly articulate and precise, and his arguments are very punchy and convincing." **Recent work:** Acted in the Crociani trust litigation, successfully obtaining a ruling on exclusive jurisdiction clauses for his client in the Privy Council.

Francis Barlow QC (see p.589) (Ten Old Square) Highly regarded amongst peers for his chancery practice, he is particularly noted for his work in contentious trust, probate and succession matters. He serves as head of chambers at Ten Old Square. **Strengths:** "There aren't too many QCs around with his level of experience in trusts, wills and estates. He is very knowledgeable and he writes and speaks eloquently."

Shân Warnock-Smith QC (see p.790) (5 Stone Buildings) A dominant presence in high-profile offshore litigation, who has outstanding credentials in private client and wealth structuring work. She also practises at ITC Chambers in the Cayman Islands, and offers a wealth of experience of acting in Cayman cases and those in the wider Caribbean jurisdictions. **Strengths:** "What she does is bring clarity to a case; she makes complicated cases very simple, and it's a great skill to have. Judges love it and clients love it."

Henry Legge QC (see p.699) (5 Stone Buildings) Enjoys a thriving chancery practice, and is an expert in disputes concerning trusts, estates, pensions and art. His offshore practice includes a significant amount of trusts work in Jersey. **Strengths:** "He's a real pleasure to work with, and that's really important. He's very good at what he does."

David Lord QC (Three Stone) A pre-eminent silk with an excellent profile in corporate insolvency cases, who has handled landmark litigation surrounding the collapses of the Fairfield and Weavering funds. He is called to the Bar of the BVI, and continues to tackle cases in the Cayman Islands, Bermuda, Brunei and the Channel Islands. **Strengths:** "Has a quick grasp of details, is excellent with clients and is excellent on tactics." **Recent work:** Advised liquidators in bringing claims against the Weavering Capital Fund for breach of directors' duties, following the collapse of the fund.

Ewan McQuater QC (3 Verulam Buildings) Interviewees commend him for his strategic direction of a case and his strength in court and in arbitration. He has a strong commercial chancery practice, and is noted for his strength in banking disputes. **Strengths:** "Provides really clear direction and strategy." **Recent work:** Advised Turkish state bank Ziraat in connection with an ownership dispute over Turkish mobile services provider Turkcell in the BVI.

David Quest QC (3 Verulam Buildings) Devotes a large part of his work to international arbitration matters and offshore litigation, and has particular expertise in Cayman Islands proceedings. His broad commercial practice encompasses fraud, finance, insurance and professional negligence disputes. **Strengths:** "He's got a phenomenal analytical mind. He really pulls apart a case using his forensic mind and fierce intellect. He makes it all look relatively easy." **Recent work:** Represented AHAB in bringing a USD9 billion fraud claim against the Saad Group in the Cayman Islands.

Matthew Parker (see p.733) (3 Verulam Buildings) A respected junior with experience in a broad spectrum of commercial litigation. He has recently represented clients in the BVI, the Cayman Islands, the Bahamas and Anguilla. **Strengths:** "Extremely user-friendly and great with clients." **Recent work:** Acted for the Central Bank of Ecuador against Conticorp in the Privy Council. This matter concerned the collapse of an Ecuadorian bank.

Contents:

LONDON

Partnership
Leading Sets
Band 1
Ten Old Square *
Partnership Counsel *
Serle Court *
Band 2
Maitland Chambers *
XXIV Old Buildings *
Leading Silks
Star individuals
Machell John *Serle Court* *
Band 1
Jones Philip *Serle Court* *
Steinfeld Alan *XXIV Old Buildings*
Band 2
Ritchie Stuart *Fountain Court Chambers (ORL)* ◊ *
Talbot Rice Elspeth *XXIV Old Buildings*
Tipples Amanda *Maitland Chambers* *
Band 3
Blayney David *Serle Court* *
Mill Ian *Blackstone Chambers (ORL)* ◊
Newman Catherine *Maitland Chambers* *
Thompson Andrew *Erskine Chambers (ORL)* ◊ *
New Silks
Mumford David *Maitland Chambers* *
Leading Juniors
Star individuals
Callman Jeremy *Ten Old Square* *
I'Anson Banks Roderick *Partnership Counsel* *
Band 1
Gavaghan Jonathan *Ten Old Square*
Haywood Jennifer *Serle Court* *
Jelf Simon *Partnership Counsel* *
Band 2
Blackett-Ord Mark *5 Stone Buildings (ORL)* ◊ *
King Michael *XXIV Old Buildings*
Mather James *Serle Court* *
Band 3
Braithwaite Thomas *Serle Court* *
Keller Ciaran *Maitland Chambers* *
Roseman Gideon *Ten Old Square* *
Winston Naomi *Ten Old Square* *
** Indicates set / individual with profile.*
◊ (ORL) = Other Ranked Lawyer.
Alphabetical order within each band. Band 1 is highest.

Band 1

Ten Old Square

See profile on p.885

THE SET

This chambers, a pioneer in the development of a specialised partnership offering, continues to maintain a team dedicated to the resolution of issues arising from partnerships established across the full range of professional service, financial, medical, property and agricultural structures. Also well known for its thought leadership and prompt provision of advice, it enjoys particularly close relationships with several of the leading law firms practising in this area. Commentators speak of Ten Old Square as "a fabulous set" and "one of the standout sets for partnership law," one interviewee particularly emphasising the fact that it is "very generous in the education of partnership practitioners generally, inviting the partnership community to seminars of the highest standard."

Client service: "The clerks are well organised by Keith Plowman, price sensibly and are immediately responsive." "The clerks are friendly, approachable and easy to talk to and particularly good when it comes to discussing fees in advance."

JUNIORS

Jeremy Callman (see p.610) Universally acknowledged for his unsurpassed combination of exhaustive technical knowledge, thoroughness of approach, formidable courtroom presence and excellence of client rapport. He acts almost exclusively in partnership and LLP matters, representing both partnerships and individual partners and maintaining a strong focus on the litigation of matters for clients from the professional services, financial and medical spheres. **Strengths:** "One of the best minds at the Partnership Bar, with the highest service level I have ever experienced. His relentless cross-examination is a joy to behold and his thoroughness, intellectual rigour and sheer determination come through when the pressure is on and at trial." "He's like gold dust. He's very pragmatic, has in-depth understanding and adapts his approach to the matter in hand." **Recent work:** Led for the claimant in Reinhard v Ondra LLP, a key High Court case which established that an individual cannot be both a member and an employee of an LLP at one and the same time.

Jonathan Gavaghan Attracts special praise for his blend of deep knowledge, client-friendliness and particularly high degree of accessibility. He is noted for his handling of issues affecting individual solicitors or their firms, and offers especially extensive experience as an arbitrator of, or arbitration counsel in, partnership disputes. **Strengths:** "As bright as you could wish: authoritative, thorough and reliable." "Very practical, down to earth and knows his stuff." **Recent work:** Acted in a multiparty arbitration concerning the dissolution of a solicitors' firm.

Gideon Roseman (see p.755) Devotes a sizeable proportion of his chancery and commercial practice to the litigation of partnership disputes on behalf of clients from not only the legal sector, but also from such spheres as property development and recruitment consultancy. He also acts extensively in an advisory capacity and draws praise for his approachability, practicality and responsiveness. **Strengths:** "A really hard worker with bucket-loads of passion: he's good on his feet, good at the paperwork, full of energy and liked by clients." "Absolutely fantastic: he drills down into the detail very well, explains and advocates in a clear way, and if the other side has got it wrong, he makes sure the judge knows it!" **Recent work:** Acted for a corporate partner in a set of separate but related proceedings combining issues of partnership, insolvency and high-value loan agreements in the luxury holiday accommodation sector.

Naomi Winston (see p.799) Is a highly active and very well-regarded barrister with an established reputation as a junior counsel in key partnership cases who is now attracting increasing attention as a leading advocate and adviser in her own right. She operates across an impressively broad range, acting for individuals and partnerships in the professional services, financial and medical sectors. **Strengths:** "Extremely bright, with a deep and detailed knowledge of all things partnership and LLP, she brings huge enthusiasm and energy to all her cases." "Has an enthusiastic manner, is client-friendly and is clearly talented." **Recent work:** Advised parties on both sides in a dispute between the former components of a dissolved GPs' partnership that were continuing to share two properties. She helped to broker a complex settlement on the first day of a scheduled trial.

Partnership Counsel

See profile on p.891

THE SET

A uniquely specialised set, exclusively concerned with partnership issues, that actively seeks resolution by means other than litigation where possible, but nevertheless offers top-flight advocacy capability. Although especially noted for the representation of solicitors' firms and LLPs, or their individual members, the chambers is becoming increasingly active in matters involving hedge and other funds or cases concerning family partnerships. The two-barrister team also acts extensively in an advisory capacity. More than one source praises the set for having "the greatest degree of specialisation around," and it is further described as being "very well regarded by solicitors" and "at the top of the game."

Client service: "Practice manager Tyroon Win is very personable and has very good interpersonal skills." "He is very efficient, able to understand the sensitivities of a case and very sensible and pragmatic."

JUNIORS

Roderick I'Anson Banks (see p.680) Has focused exclusively on partnership and LLP law since the 1980s and is consistently cited by sources for his exhaustive and unsurpassed knowledge of the area. Respected as a courtroom opponent of great tactical skill, he is nevertheless distinguished by his ability to find alternatives to litigation. He acts particularly prominently for solicitors' firms and individual solicitors. **Strengths:** "Absolutely masterful: he not only knows the theory, but is also able to explain the practice and is so self-contained and capable." "At the top of the tree, particularly for advisory work." **Recent work:** Instructed at short notice during the closing stages of Ingenious Film Partners LLP v HMRC to provide specialist partnership-related expertise on questions raised by the First-Tier Tax Tribunal in connection with the case.

Simon Jelf (see p.683) Highly recommended for both contentious and advisory matters, particularly those affecting solicitors – both individually and collectively – or trading partnerships. He also offers specialised knowledge of medical partnership issues and of questions of LLP formation and dissolution. **Strengths:** "Focused, professional, charming and at the top of his game technically." "Polite and unassuming, but with the most impressive knowledge of the law of partnership, he is able to provide excellent commercial advice."

Serle Court

See profile on p.908

THE SET

Serle Court maintains a particularly large and impressive team of barristers operating prominently in the partnership sphere who are respected both for pure, black-letter expertise in traditional partnership matters and cutting-edge insights into the expanding area of investment vehicle partnership. The affairs of family wealth and business, farming, medical and property partnerships are also covered and the set is further noted for its specialist expertise in LLP issues. Sources characterise Serle Court as a "very serious Chancery set of real depth" and a "forward-looking practice." It is particularly distinguished by the additional value conferred by its "useful seminar programme" and "excellent academic publications."

Client service: "The clerking is good: the clerks are very smooth, very prompt and very easy to use." "They deal with things in a quick and efficient way." Steve Whitaker is the head clerk.

SILKS

John Machell QC (see p.705) Receives extensive and enthusiastic praise from across the market as the go-to silk for the most complex or intractable pure partnership or LLP matters, his mastery of the latter being cited particularly frequently. Sources also pay tribute to his superb advocacy, strategic eye for a likely outcome and complete command of structuring questions. **Strengths:** "The only specialist partnership silk, and far and away the best QC handling this type of work." "The counsel of choice in this area, particularly in respect of LLP issues. He is authoritative, excellent in conference and user-friendly." **Recent work:** Successfully led for the respondents in Flanagan v Liontrust Investment Partners LLP, widely acknowledged as one of the most significant partnership cases of recent years. The High Court found that the doctrine of repudiatory breach of contract cannot apply to LLP agreements involving more than two parties.

Philip Jones QC (see p.686) Stands out for his clarity of thinking, straightforwardness of exposition and high level of user-friendliness, founded on many years' experience in the handling of partnership and LLP issues, often acting for HMRC in cases involving taxation aspects. He is also prominent in the representation of solicitors' firms and property partnerships, and has acted as counsel in many partnership-related arbitrations. **Strengths:** "Provides perfect analysis, and is very quick and very good at dealing with the client and explaining things to the layman." "We use him regularly, principally when clients are looking for a more heavyweight name with sound commercial judgement."

David Blayney QC (see p.597) Specialises, in the partnership sphere, in complex and often contentious financial and accounting matters, and is also experienced in cases concerning the dissolution of solicitors' partnerships. He acts regularly as an arbitrator of partnership disputes. **Strengths:** "A brain the size of a planet." "Superb on accounting issues."

JUNIORS

Jennifer Haywood (see p.668) Combines extensive and varied commercial chancery experience with a record of in-depth involvement in an exhaustive range of contentious and non-contentious partnership issues. Active in both the legal and financial services spheres, and a noted authority on LLP issues, she attracts particular praise for her excellent, candid and common sense-based client service. **Strengths:** "Her greatest asset is her practical, commercial advice. What you want is expertise relevant to what your best next steps are, and you will always get a straight answer from Jennifer." "A great all-rounder, and immensely able technically." **Recent work:** Acted, led by John Machell QC, for the successful respondent parties in the significant LLP-related case, Flanagan v Liontrust Investment Partners LLP.

James Mather (see p.709) Singled out by sources for his clear, responsive and thoroughly dependable advocacy and advice in the partnership sphere, particularly where the operations of solicitors' firms, private equity houses and other financial services providers are concerned. He also offers notable expertise and experience on LLP documentation issues. **Strengths:** "Clever, thoughtful and incisive. His reputation continues to grow." "He's particularly solid on partnership and boardroom disputes." **Recent work:** Acted for businessman Miten Dutia in High Court proceedings concerning the existence of an alleged partnership with Sir Bob Geldof to invest in African businesses through the private equity firm 8 Miles.

Thomas Braithwaite (see p.601) A versatile commercial chancery barrister with particularly extensive partnership experience in the legal and medical spheres, and in matters concerning partnerships established outside the UK. He is further noted for his familiarity with arbitration and mediation procedures and is valued for his pragmatic, dependable advice on the merits of claims. **Strengths:** "Very bright, quick on the uptake and good at identifying and explaining problems." "A highly intelligent, fine advocate who thinks things through from first principles."

Band 2

Maitland Chambers

See profile on p.875

THE SET

Maitland Chambers both advises and litigates on all aspects of partnership law, providing multidisciplinary expertise to address issues raised by legal, financial, commercial and medical partnerships. Notable areas of well-honed experience include the representation of individual solicitors or accountants and the handling of matters concerning particularly high-value funds partnerships, often those structured as LLPs. Interviewees rate the chambers as "obviously in the magic circle of Chancery practices," one describing it as "my go-to set – they are very commercial and very professional in the way they run things."

Client service: "The clerking has always been very good: they're really proactive and helpful, you're able to have a frank discussion about fees and they're ready to help where they can." "Fantastic from the clerking point of view: they're always willing to assist." John Wiggs is the much respected senior clerk.

SILKS

Amanda Tipples QC (see p.781) Regularly handles complicated, high-stakes partnership disputes with major commercial, agricultural or other real estate aspects, being particularly well known for her assured handling of matters involving trusts and contention within families. Sources testify extensively and enthusiastically to her extreme user-friendliness and the consistent excellence of her advice. **Strengths:** "Brilliant, accessible and so easy to work with." "On partnership and trust disputes, she's absolutely amazing – there's no other way to put it – and she goes the extra mile over and over again." **Recent work:** Acted for two parties in a complex family dispute revolving around the construction of a partnership agreement and whether or not a particular farm constituted a partnership asset.

Catherine Newman QC (see p.727) A highly experienced commercial chancery silk with an extensive record of involvement in high-value partnership disputes, particularly those with a strong commercial or financial element. She also regularly advises solicitors' firms on such contentious, or potentially contentious, issues as team moves and changes or projected dissolutions. **Strengths:** "An excellent, very diligent advocate and cross-examiner who's also able to speak to clients in plain English, which is very helpful in the throes of a trial." "An absolute delight and a great cross-examiner." **Recent work:** Acted for the defendant in the British Virgin Islands (BVI) High Court case Stephen Plant v Pickle Properties, which concerned a dispute between former partners over bank guarantee contribution rights.

David Mumford QC (see p.724) Specialises in the litigation or arbitration of partnership-related disputes arising in a commercial context, including matters involving LLP structures. He frequently advocates in both litigation and arbitration, or advises, on partnership issues in such offshore jurisdictions as Jersey and the Cayman Islands. **Strengths:** "Very pragmatic, practical and unflappable, and always in charge of the brief." **Recent work:** Acted for two of the parties in Adler v Adler, a multimillion-pound dispute arising from the dissolution of a 30-year-old family property development partnership.

JUNIORS

Ciaran Keller (see p.689) Offers extensive experience in the handling of complex or very high-value partnership matters with a strong international element. He is further noted for his knowledge and experience of the high-end accountancy sector and is a source of sound advice on global partnership restructuring questions. **Strengths:** "Extremely intelligent, incredibly user-friendly, responsive, practical and really good on paper: he always manages to fit everything in." "An excellent and hugely competent leading junior." **Recent work:** Acted for New World Value Fund, the successful respondents in Privy Council proceedings concerning entitlements to the assets of a BVI-based limited partnership worth over USD1 billion.

XXIV Old Buildings

See profile on p.884

THE SET

XXIV Old Buildings combines a full service with regard to traditional professional service and financial partnership issues with niche expertise in catering to the contentious or advisory requirements of partners and partnerships operating in such areas as film finance, hospitality and cross-jurisdictional joint venture structures. A commitment to the avoidance of litigation and the securing of out-of-court settlements where possible remains a strong distinguishing characteristic of this set.

Client service: "One of the better-run sets, and one with incredibly efficient clerks." Paul Matthews and Dan Wilson are the senior practice managers.

SILKS

Alan Steinfeld QC Commands tremendous respect as one of the London Bar's most active and redoubtable commercial and chancery silks, being particularly well known for his handling of partnership matters with a strong commercial or financial services aspect. He regularly acts in complex partnership issues considered in the courts of a number of British offshore territories or dependencies and of Hong Kong. **Strengths:** "Incredibly bright, knows this stuff like the back of his hand and is a go-to for difficult problems in this space." "He's very, very experienced, and has sound understanding and an ability to identify an issue that inspires confidence in clients." **Recent work:** Retained in Aeris Capital Blue Ocean SARL v Silver Reel GP Ltd, a Grand Court of the Cayman Islands case concerning the terms of redemption applying to a partnership interest.

Elspeth Talbot Rice QC Noted for combining a formidable courtroom presence with a widely admired clarity of exposition when dealing with especially complex and highly contentious partnership matters. Her experience covers the full range of partnership types, and she has particular familiarity with issues affecting commercial, financial services or family-owned structures. **Strengths:** "She did an incredibly good job of making the whole of a complex matter very straightforward, and she convinced the judge." "She is the sort of silk who you are happy to have on your side, but apprehensive about having against you." **Recent work:** Acted for celebrity hypnotist Paul McKenna in a dispute with former partner Clare Staples involving, inter alia, cross-jurisdictional issues concerning the dissolution of their business partnership.

JUNIORS

Michael King Seasoned senior junior, widely respected, both for his hands-on experience with an impressive range of partnership types and as one of the leading academic authorities in this sphere. He is particularly well known for advising on matters involving farming partnerships and for counselling individuals on projected departures from partnerships. **Strengths:** "Very experienced and very good." **Recent work:** Acted in a matter regarding a dispute between a solicitor and former partners that raised the question of whether a coroner's pension partnership constitutes a partnership asset.

Other Ranked Lawyers

Ian Mill QC (Blackstone Chambers) Specialises in the litigation of partnership disputes originating in the media and entertainment sector in general and the music industry in particular, and of those concerning offshore limited or quasi-partnerships. He also advises on matters affecting legal partnerships, including those operating in offshore territories. **Strengths:** "He is a brilliant, very hard-working and responsive advocate who gives clear and firm advice to clients who love him." "Some just go through the motions; he really lives and breathes the case." **Recent work:** Continued to act in a complex and multifaceted case, considered by several tribunals, including the Privy Council, both in the UK and the BVI, and concerning entitlements to the assets of Salford Capital Partners.

Andrew Thompson QC (see p.780) (Erskine Chambers) Noted for his expertise in LLP law and in particular with regard to the resolution of disputes arising from the nature of LLP agreements and structures. He also acts in matters concerning traditional professional services partnerships, winning praise for his application of valuable cross-disciplinary skills. **Strengths:** "Extremely impressive. Has the ability to knit together perfectly the law and commercial considerations. He has a great ability to steer a matter through the legal maze to the right destination." "Offers superb analysis and expertise and has a number of successful high-profile cases behind him."

Stuart Ritchie QC (see p.752) (Fountain Court) Stands out for his mastery of matters concerning LLPs or fiduciary duties or those affecting individuals holding senior executive positions in commercial or asset management partnerships. Particularly active in the territory where company, agency, partnership and employment law intersect, he receives especially enthusiastic praise for the quality and determination of his advocacy. **Strengths:** "Fantastic on his feet and a match for any partnership law barrister out there." "Always accessible, commercial and clear in his advice." **Recent work:** Acted for the former chief financial officer in a major transport sector company in a dispute with that company concerning, inter alia, the question of his entitlement to equity in a claim against a Luxembourg special investment partnership.

Mark Blackett-Ord (see p.596) (5 Stone Buildings) Consistently identified by sources as one of the leading academic authorities on all aspects of partnership law and receives comparable praise for the skilful practical application of his knowledge. He is active across a broad range of issues, including, in addition to matters concerning traditional professional services firms, cases involving medical partnerships and funds structured as limited partnerships. **Strengths:** "Few can claim the kind of specialist partnership knowledge that he can and he deals with things in a very pragmatic and sensible way." "The go-to partnership dispute barrister, and someone who is excellent with clients."

MIDLANDS

Partnership	
Leading Silks	
Band 1	
Randall John	*St Philips Chambers* *
Zaman Mohammed	*No5 Chambers*
Leading Juniors	
Band 1	
Dean Paul J	*St Philips Chambers* *
Najib Shakil	*No5 Chambers*
Whitaker Stephen	*No5 Chambers*

* *Indicates individual with profile.*

Alphabetical order within each band. Band 1 is highest.

Ranked Lawyers

Mohammed Zaman QC (No5 Chambers) Regularly acts, on a national basis, in high-stakes cases affecting family or other commercial partnerships, winning high praise, not only for his tenacious advocacy, but also for his well-honed negotiation and mediation skills. He also advises extensively on matters involving traditional solicitors' and accountancy practices. **Strengths:** "He's right up there, totally outstanding." "Very able and knows what he's doing."

Shakil Najib (No5 Chambers) Advises on and litigates a comprehensive range of partnership cases. These cover everything from questions concerning the initial establishment of partnerships through to issues arising from their dissolution. He is particularly at home handling matters involving partnerships in the accountancy, commercial property and hospitality sectors and is particularly respected for his determined and persuasive advocacy. **Strengths:** "Realistic and practical, commercial in his approach, not overly legalistic and someone a businessman would warm to." "He certainly knows his way around both the law and process." **Recent work:** Acted for the claimant in a legally and factually complex case concerning an alleged breach of an agreement settling the final accounts of an accountancy partnership and the allegedly unlawful transfer of its business to a new LLP.

Stephen Whitaker (No5 Chambers) A highly respected chancery barrister with long-standing and extensive experience in the partnership sphere who brings a wealth of corporate and commercial law expertise to his work in the area. His tactical skill in the courtroom and the excellence of his submissions attract equal praise. **Strengths:** "A very senior junior who certainly knows his onions." "A very, very clever man and a safe pair of hands who wouldn't need a leader."

John Randall QC (see p.748) (St Philips Chambers) A multi-talented silk with an established track record in the partnership arena, who is particularly good at representing parties in disputes involving partnerships or quasi-partnerships in the real estate sector. He is an expert at providing advice to clients on how best to avoid litigation and keep out of the courtroom, but once in court, he proves to be a formidable advocate. **Strengths:** "One of the great commercial silks outside London and often active on partnership cases: I'm always happy to work with him."

Paul Dean (see p.632) (St Philips Chambers) Having formerly been a solicitor, he brings personal experience of partnership issues to the table when handling factually and procedurally complex cases in this sector. **Strengths:** "He has one of the best junior partnership practices in Birmingham and is more experienced in it than anyone else I know: a go-to man for partnership." "Always a port of call for me: I trust him when it comes to partnership law and he's involved in the big cases."

NORTHERN

Partnership
Leading Sets
Band 1
Kings Chambers *
Leading Silks
Band 1
Anderson Lesley *Kings Chambers* *
Band 2
Chaisty Paul *Kings Chambers* *
New Silks
Harper Mark *Kings Chambers* *
Leading Juniors
Band 1
Berragan Neil *Kings Chambers* *
Band 2
Cadwallader Neil *Exchange Chambers (ORL)* ◊

Band 1

Kings Chambers

See profile on p.968

THE SET

Kings Chambers continues to draw praise as the go-to set for partnership and LLP issues in the North. It maintains an impressive team of chancery specialists and has practice area expertise extending across the fullest range of issues affecting not only professional service partnerships, but also partnership structures operating in the agricultural, commercial and financial sectors. Especially noted for its discreet handling of matters for individual solicitors, the chambers receives an exceptionally enthusiastic level of feedback, with one source reporting: "They're the set I go to for anything in the North; I can't think of another set of chambers with that level of expertise."

Client service: "I've been dealing with chief clerk Colin Griffin for 20 years and he's absolutely first-class and extremely efficient. The clerking generally is first-class: they're sensible, work with us and provide a really solid service."

SILKS

Lesley Anderson QC (see p.583) An eminent commercial silk with especially noteworthy partnership expertise, particularly in the professional services sphere, who regularly advises solicitors, financial advisers, surveyors and estate agents. She brings to her work valuable personal experience of working in a training capacity for an international law firm. **Strengths:** "She advises on complicated partnership disputes and is excellent in her field."

Paul Chaisty QC (see p.614) Regularly acts in partnership cases within the context of a broad chancery and commercial litigation practice, focusing primarily on matters affecting professional services structures and LLPs, including restrictive covenant and springboard injunction issues. Sources testify to the formidable nature of his courtroom performances. **Strengths:** "A great advocate, who is good on paper, very thorough and excellent in every respect." "Determined, dogged and ferocious in cross-examination."

Mark Harper QC (see p.664) A new silk with an increasingly prominent litigation practice who attracts specific attention for his assured handling of partnership matters, particularly those covering such areas as relationship breakdown, projected expulsion or equality questions. Issues concerning the division or protection of partnership assets is another significant area of focus. **Strengths:** "An excellent trial advocate who excels at tough cross-examination." "He's always a very safe pair of hands. He's excellent, good with clients, and short and succinct in his advice which goes down well."

JUNIORS

Neil Berragan (see p.595) Offers over 20 years' specialised experience in the partnership sphere and is particularly familiar with contentious issues arising from within solicitors' partnerships and LLPs. Sources speak with consistent enthusiasm of his particularly impressive courtroom manner. **Strengths:** "Realistic and commercial, and quickly gains the trust of clients." "Provides knowledgeable, solid and pragmatic advice." **Recent work:** Acted for parties involved in a dispute generated by the failure of a Manchester law firm and concerning the entitlements of former members, for tax purposes, to shares in that firm's losses.

Other Ranked Lawyers

Neil Cadwallader (Exchange Chambers) Specialises in matters affecting partnerships in the commercial sphere, particularly where property issues are involved, and is also noted for his frequent representation of doctors' and dentists' partnerships. In addition to a much-admired litigation practice, he also advises on transactional matters. **Strengths:** "Extremely clever, very good with clients, as good on paper as he is on his feet and someone who has immense gravitas before the court." **Recent work:** Acted in a factually complex dispute between a former member of a medical practice and the practice itself. The member claimed that he was invalidly expelled from the partnership at will, whilst those opposing him maintained that he retired voluntarily having clearly breached both professional standards and the terms of the partnership deed.

WESTERN

Partnership
Leading Sets
Band 1
Guildhall Chambers *
St John's Chambers *
Leading Silks
Band 1
Sims Hugh *Guildhall Chambers*
Leading Juniors
Band 1
Maher Martha *St John's Chambers* 🄰
Band 2
Marsden Andrew *Commercial Chambers (ORL)* ◊ 🄰
Warner Malcolm *Guildhall Chambers*
* *Indicates set / individual with profile.*
🄰 *direct access (see p.24).*
◊ *(ORL) = Other Ranked Lawyer.*
Alphabetical order within each band. Band 1 is highest.

Band 1

Guildhall Chambers

See profile on p.938

THE SET

Guildhall Chambers combines specialist chancery knowledge with exhaustive commercial experience and insight to provide a comprehensive service covering professional service, financial, medical and commercial partnerships. Key areas of expertise include alleged breaches of duty, accounting questions and quasi-partnership matters. The set also offers advisory and drafting services, covering both traditional partnerships and LLPs.

Client service: "Continues to provide a London-quality service (both at clerking and at barrister level) at regional prices." Commercial clerk Mike Norton is a key contact for partnership matters.

SILKS

Hugh Sims QC An exceptionally versatile commercial silk, praised for his advocacy, advice and client-handling skills across an impressive range of practice areas. In the partnership sphere, he regularly handles high-stakes issues with a strong commercial flavour, including those concerning real property or family partnerships, or quasi-partnership structures. He also advises extensively on matters affecting solicitors' firms. **Strengths:** "Always in demand, and a great practitioner in the field of partnership law." "He's exceptionally hard-working, very bright and innovative."

JUNIORS

Malcolm Warner A well-known and respected senior junior in the partnership space who draws on a wealth of experience in the commercial and, in particular, property sectors to inform the matters he handles. He is especially noted for his handling of issues involving medical and farming partnerships. **Strengths:** "Very much a partnership specialist – which gives him an edge – and my go-to to bounce things off."

St John's Chambers

See profile on p.941

THE SET

St John's Chambers fields a substantial team, covering all the main contentious and non-contentious partnership bases and offering not only litigation, but also arbitration and mediation expertise. The set is especially noted for its handling of insolvency issues and is also particularly skilled in the farming, property and technology partnership spheres.

Client service: "They provided a very good service: they were all very professional and did everything you'd expect." Robert Bocock is the practice manager.

JUNIORS

Martha Maher Commands widespread recognition as one of the region's leading partnership specialists and is active across the full range of practice area issues, with particularly keen skills where medical and commercially-focused partnership structures are concerned. Admired for her tough courtroom advocacy, she is also noted for her openness to alternative dispute resolution processes and is prominent in the mediation of partnership disputes. **Strengths:** "She is definitely up there as a true specialist when it comes to partnership work." "Absolutely excellent."

Other Ranked Lawyers

Andrew Marsden (Commercial Chambers) Draws profitably on previous experience as a solicitor to advise and advocate on issues affecting not only professional services partnerships, but also those operating in, amongst others, the financial, medical and real estate sectors. He frequently acts in matters where partnership structures have been undermined by irreparable breakdowns in personal relations, bringing to this aspect of his work the skills of a CEDR-trained mediator. **Strengths:** "A leading light in the area of shareholder and partnership disputes." "You can call him up and just pick his brains which is very helpful."

Contents:

LONDON

Pensions
Leading Sets
Band 1
Wilberforce Chambers *
Band 2
Outer Temple Chambers *
Band 3
Radcliffe Chambers *
5 Stone Buildings *
Leading Silks
Star individuals
Green Brian *Wilberforce Chambers*
Simmonds Andrew *5 Stone Buildings* *
Band 1
Furness Michael *Wilberforce Chambers*
Newman Paul *Wilberforce Chambers*
Rowley Keith *Radcliffe Chambers* *
Spink Andrew *Outer Temple Chambers*
Stallworthy Nicolas *Outer Temple Chambers*
Tennet Michael *Wilberforce Chambers*
Band 2
Ham Robert *Wilberforce Chambers*
Short Andrew *Outer Temple Chambers*
Band 3
Agnello Raquel *Erskine Chambers (ORL)* ◊ *
Bryant Keith *Outer Temple Chambers*
Hitchcock Richard *Outer Temple Chambers*
Legge Henry *5 Stone Buildings* *
Moeran Fenner *Wilberforce Chambers*
Tidmarsh Christopher *5 Stone Buildings* *
New Silks
Hilliard Jonathan *Wilberforce Chambers*
* *Indicates set / individual with profile.*
◊ *(ORL) = Other Ranked Lawyer.*
Alphabetical order within each band. Band 1 is highest.

Pensions
Leading Juniors
Band 1
Grant David E *Outer Temple Chambers*
Mold Andrew *Wilberforce Chambers*
Sawyer Edward *Wilberforce Chambers*
Band 2
Campbell Emily *Wilberforce Chambers*
Clifford James *Maitland Chambers (ORL)* ◊ *
Goldsmith Joseph *5 Stone Buildings* *
Khan Farhaz *Outer Temple Chambers*
McKechnie Emily *Wilberforce Chambers*
Ovey Elizabeth *Radcliffe Chambers* *
Rickards James *Outer Temple Chambers*
Walmsley James *Wilberforce Chambers*
Band 3
Faulkner Benjamin *Wilberforce Chambers*
Ling Naomi *Outer Temple Chambers*
Margo Saul *Outer Temple Chambers*
Mathers Wendy *Radcliffe Chambers* *
Robinson Thomas *Wilberforce Chambers*
Band 4
Allen Sebastian *Wilberforce Chambers*
Burroughs Nigel *4 New Square (ORL)* ◊
Friedman Bobby *Wilberforce Chambers*
McCreath James *Wilberforce Chambers*
Seaman Jennifer *Outer Temple Chambers* *
Seymour Lydia *Outer Temple Chambers*
Seymour Thomas *Wilberforce Chambers*
Up-and-coming individuals
Chew Jonathan *Wilberforce Chambers*
Hill Nicholas *Outer Temple Chambers*

Band 1

Wilberforce Chambers

See profile on p.925

THE SET

Wilberforce Chambers is widely regarded as the leading set for pensions law issues. Its members bring impressive knowledge to traditional pension matters, as well as to cases intersecting with trust and insolvency issues. They enjoy a wealth of experience representing both employers and trustees, as well as scheme members, the Pensions Regulator and the Pensions Protection Fund. Members of Wilberforce frequently appear in the most high-profile pensions disputes, including IBM v Stuart Dalgleish, which concerned the employer's power to close a scheme against the opposition of its members. The group is also acting on both sides of British Airways v Trustees of the Airways Pension Scheme in a dispute concerning the Trustees' use of a discretionary power to grant pension increases. Respondents enthuse about the set's "very good array of silks" and its "list of outstanding juniors that just goes on and on."

Client service: "They're very accommodating, always ready to help out, and they make sure you get what you need." Mark Rushton is the head clerk.

SILKS

Brian Green QC One of the leading lights in the pensions industry, he is frequently seen on some of the most high-profile and significant pieces of litigation. He brings well-honed advocacy skills to his litigation and offers expertise in tax and trusts law. **Strengths:** "He has an incredible brain and makes sense of complex issues in an authoritative and sensible way." "When he's working on a case he gives absolutely everything. He's incredibly committed, hard-working and really experienced." **Recent work:** Represented Stena and the other employers of the Merchant Navy Pension Fund in ongoing litigation concerning a new contributions scheme.

Michael Furness QC Enjoys broad expertise in occupational pensions and other relevant areas, including tax law and trust litigation. He is well known for engaging in international litigation in offshore jurisdictions. **Strengths:** "Because he's very intellectual he usually manages to stave off any attacks on the argument from the judge." "I'd particularly go to him when we have intricate, technical pension issues that might require assessment from the court." **Recent work:** Represented ITV in the Court of Appeal in an attempt to strike out part of the opposition's pleading.

Paul Newman QC Highly regarded in the industry, he acts in the full range of pension matters and is particularly recommended for high-profile, intricate cases. He acts for a diverse set of clients, including employers, trustees, the Pensions Regulator and the Pension Protection Fund. **Strengths:** "He's very impressive on the technical pensions analysis and also has a litigator's instinct." "He's a creative thinker; he's one of the people we would go to with a problem that needs to be solved." **Recent work:** Acted for the members of the Merchant Navy Pension Scheme in a three-week trial after the proposed increase to the number of employers contributing to the scheme funds.

Michael Tennet QC One of the leading silks for pensions, he is a master in regulatory matters and additionally specialises in actuarial issues. He is regularly seen in some of the pension industry's most high-profile and contentious cases. **Strengths:** "He has a very nice, calm and measured advocacy style and he's a good cross-examiner." "He's someone to go to if you want a commercial steer, but he's also got the technical ability to back up that instinct." **Recent work:** Secured, on behalf of the Trustees of the Merchant Navy Ratings Pension Fund, a declaration on the legality of a recovery plan to ensure the funding of a £200 million deficit.

Robert Ham QC A much-admired silk with a very strong reputation in the field of chancery. He is frequently sought out to provide counsel on complex pension scheme matters. He also offers expertise in associated professional negligence issues. **Strengths:** "He's very good at reading the court." "It was an incredibly complicated matter and he was able to break it down into very simple terms for our client."

Fenner Moeran QC An impressive advocate, particularly well versed in pension liberation, fraud and moral hazard disputes. He frequently represents trustees and employers, as well as the Pensions Regulator and the government. **Strengths:** "He's very good at thinking laterally and he brings a novel argument." "He's really good on his feet and at taking a commercial view." **Recent work:** Acted on behalf of the Secretary of State for Defence in an Ombudsman appeal concerning the incorrect administration and potential public liability of the Army pension scheme.

Jonathan Hilliard QC Widely regarded as the go-to barrister for technical pensions issues, he represents parties in a broad array of cases. He has significant experience in liberation, moral hazard and professional negligence matters. **Strengths:** "He invariably makes the right call and is an encyclopaedia in the pensions fraud context." "He has a ferocious intellect and gets to the bottom of problems very effectively." **Recent work:** Represented the trustee of Box Clever before the Court of Appeal in a case brought by the Pensions Regulator to consider the Upper Tribunal's powers when dealing with financial support directions.

JUNIORS

Andrew Mold Highly regarded junior who receives praise for his measured approach in court and his ability to simplify complex pension issues. He often appears unled in significant cases and specialises in professional negligence and regulatory aspects. **Strengths:** "He is outstandingly intelligent, incredibly easy to work with and flexible. He has a really fabulous manner and is supremely intelligent." "He struck the right balance between technical advice and tactical advice." **Recent work:** Instructed for the administrators of the Nortel Networks Pensions Scheme on the powers of the Pensions Regulator to compel other companies to fund the scheme.

Edward Sawyer A gifted and experienced pensions barrister who has appeared in several high-profile cases affecting the industry. He is often involved in long-running litigation with international elements concerning pension schemes and the Regulator. **Strengths:** "He sees the big picture and thinks of innovative strategies for taking things forward." **Recent work:** Acted for the Trustee of the IBM Pension Plan following a major trial and ruling that determined that IBM had breached its duty of good faith.

Emily Campbell Maintains an impressive reputation for her handling of pension matters that contain financial, actuarial or tax aspects. She is also experienced in regulatory, professional negligence and rectification issues. **Strengths:** "She's able to cut through the detail on complex academic pensions law questions and come to working practical solutions." "Her mathematical brain is almost as impressive as her legal brain, which is of huge benefit when dealing with pension cases that involve complex maths issues." **Recent work:** Represented the proposed representative beneficiary in a dispute regarding a mistake in a scheme's early retirement arrangement.

Emily McKechnie A well-reputed chancery lawyer whose expertise in pensions is complemented by her burgeoning reputation in professional negligence. **Strengths:** "She's very adept at finding practical solutions around very difficult and complex issues." "She's very good with clients and extremely professional. She's a good orator and very good at conveying things verbally in an understandable manner." **Recent work:** Acted for the BBC in a case brought by a member complaining that a capped pay rise was contrary to Section 91 of the Pensions Act 1995 and breached the trust rules.

James Walmsley An established pensions junior who is highly reputed for his diligent work ethic. He is well versed in regulatory investigations. Strengths: "He's extremely clever, easy to work with and makes himself available." "He's a really autonomous junior who will just run with a case on his own until the leader is available." Recent work: Assisted the Trustee of the Merchant Navy Pension Scheme in a trial for the approval of the handling of a large deficit.

Benjamin Faulkner Promising junior with a broad commercial chancery practice. He specialises in pensions and related professional negligence disputes. **Strengths:** "He's very easy to work with, he's very calm and he produces very good work very quickly." "He puts the work in and is prepared to get into the detail, and all that with an easy-going friendly manner." **Recent work:** Assisted with the high-profile IBM litigation, challenging significant pension cuts at trial and acting in the consequential issues hearing.

Thomas Robinson Enjoys a wealth of experience in regulatory, moral hazard and insolvency cases. Highly valued by the Pensions Regulator. **Strengths:** "He's very considered, level-headed and a good strategist." "He's very good in court; he's very calm and won't be pushed around." **Recent work:** Acted in Re Desmond & Sons, a case that sought Contribution Notices against the former directors of a manufacturer and distributor.

Sebastian Allen A well-regarded junior with experience in the full spectrum of pensions cases. Has advised and advocated on some of the most large-scale pensions disputes, including Silentnight and Nortel. Strengths: "He was always approachable and willing to help." "A massive brain." Recent work: Acted for British Airways in a challenge against the trustees' decision to utilise an unusual discretionary power and make pension increases.

Bobby Friedman A respected pensions junior with considerable regulatory experience. He has acted in some of the most high-profile pensions disputes and trials. **Strengths:** "A rising star. He's unafraid to make difficult calls and he portrays a confidence that belies his years." "He's been very consistent and authoritative in the advice he's provided." **Recent work:** Acted for the Pensions Regulator in proceedings concerning Section 7 of the Pensions Act 1995 in relation to the appointment of a trustee to an occupational pension scheme.

James McCreath Acts for employers, trustees and scheme members in a variety of pension disputes. He has gained particular exposure to Section 75 debt claims and regulatory cases. **Strengths:** "He's a great team player, who is very smart and has excellent drafting skills." "He masters his brief very well and works very effectively with his leader." **Recent work:** Defended two Russian companies against the Pensions Regulator, who sought high value contribution notices.

Thomas Seymour Has a broad commercial chancery practice encompassing both pensions and trusts. **Strengths:** "He has a strong instinct about what the right thing is to do and he builds an intellectual case around that." "He's incredibly thoughtful and can be relied upon to get the right answer."

Jonathan Chew Enjoys a busy and broad pensions practice. He has acted in regulatory cases concerning moral hazard, liberation and debt issues. **Strengths:** "His opinions and written submissions were excellent." "He's very hard-working, bright and a really good team player." **Recent work:** Acted for the trustees in a dispute concerning Capgemini's obligation to pay towards the debt on leaving the scheme.

Band 2

Outer Temple Chambers

See profile on p.887

THE SET

Outer Temple Chambers is an imposing presence in the pensions arena. The set is renowned for the dual expertise held by many of its barristers, who are well equipped to advise where pensions intersects with employment or financial services law. It additionally offers strength representing the Pensions Regulator, the Pension Protection Fund and the Pensions Ombudsman, as well as trustees and employers. Its members have often appeared in prominent cases in the industry, including in IBM UK Ltd v Dalgleish and Merchant Navy Ratings Pension Trustees v P&O. Instructing solicitors rave about its "top-notch" barristers and appreciate their "pragmatic and commercial" approach when handling cases and talking to clients.

Client service: "The clerks are very responsive and easy to work with if you're up against tight deadlines." The barristers are clerked by business development managers David Smith and Dave Scothern.

SILKS

Andrew Spink QC An authoritative and experienced advocate well known for his handling of high-profile pension disputes. Frequently undertakes professional negligence, regulatory and Part 7 and 8 claims in relation to pensions. **Strengths:** "Any opinion of his carries weight with the other side." "He takes everything into account, thinks outside the box and thinks commercially." **Recent work:** Represented P&O Group in a challenge against the Merchant Navy Ratings Pension Trustees' deficit reduction proposition.

Nicolas Stallworthy QC Stands out for his impressively broad pensions practice, covering regulatory, professional negligence and tax implications. He is widely recommended for complex pensions issues and often acts in sensitive cases. **Strengths:** "If anyone can win you a slightly unwinnable argument, he is your man." "He has a first-class mind and he masters the evidence to a very impressive degree." **Recent work:** Acted for the representative beneficiaries in the high-profile IBM litigation concerning IBM's breach of duty to employees.

Andrew Short QC Highly sought after for his specialism in matters where pensions intersects with employment law issues. He is seen to act in some of the most significant pension disputes, often with discrimination or equalisation aspects. **Strengths:** "He has that pension-employment crossover expertise which is very valuable." "Very down-to-earth, straight-talking and good at finding solutions." **Recent work:** Acted for over 200 judges disputing pension changes on grounds of age, sex and race discrimination.

Keith Bryant QC Highly rated by respondents for his skill in high-value, complex matters, particularly regarding rectification, equalisation and Part 8 claims. Strengths include representing public sector organisations, trustees and individual scheme members. **Strengths:** "He writes fabulous opinions and can really dissect difficult things and put them into simple language." "He's not only a good technical expert, but he presents his thoughts in a way clients can understand." **Recent work:** Led a Part 8 claim raising equalisation and construction issues where he acted for the representative beneficiary.

Richard Hitchcock QC Well-respected advocate with extensive experience in regulatory cases, in particular concerning equalisation and the reach of the Pension Regulator's powers. He frequently acts for trustees, members, unions and employers. **Strengths:** "He's incredibly knowledgeable on pensions but he manages to convey his legal knowledge in a very understandable way for clients." "He has a very down-to-earth attitude and is good when dealing with people who are not experienced in pensions." **Recent work:** Represented the Appellant Trustee in Garvin Trustees v Denis Desmond, which disputed the capacity of the Pensions Regulator to grant Contribution Notices.

JUNIORS

David Grant The go-to junior for Part 8 and professional negligence claims concerning pension schemes. He frequently appears before the Court of Appeal and High Court and often leads his own cases. **Strengths:** "He's got very good analytical abilities and he's a good advocate too." "He gave very pragmatic and robust advice which helped to get the matter to a successful settlement." **Recent work:** Acted in Grolier International & Anor v Capital Cranfield Trustees, which concerned the approval of a compromise around Part 8 proceedings.

Farhaz Khan Highly sought-after barrister for pensions matters concerning the financial services industry and investments. He regularly appears in cases with an international element and has a growing regulatory practice. **Strengths:** "He's very good at marshalling information and cutting through the complexity." "He's a good go-to person when a matter straddles pensions and financial services." **Recent work:** Acted in Philips Pension Trustees & Philips Electronics UK v Aon Hewitt & AllianceBernstein, a case challenging the investment of trust assets, worth £2 billion, which caused massive losses during the credit crunch.

James Rickards Well versed in both financial services and pensions law, he is instructed on a wide array of disputes and regulatory cases. **Strengths:** "He's got that mix of commercial and pensions experience and he marries the disciplines very well." "He's very easy to deal with, quite tenacious and commercially minded." **Recent work:** Continued to act for the Trustees of the Carrington Wire Defined Benefit Scheme in a case brought by the Pensions Regulator to seek Contribution Notices.

Naomi Ling Specialising in both pensions and employment law, she is an expert in professional negligence, discrimination and rectification disputes. She is particularly strong at representing public sector organisations, as well as private employers and trustees. Strengths: "She's very thorough and user-friendly." "She's very bright and super-reliable." Recent work: Acted in McCloud v Ministry of Justice, a discrimination case raised by over 200 judges concerning changes to their pension entitlements.

Saul Margo An experienced junior offering expertise at the intersection of pensions and employment law. He regularly advises government departments and the Pensions Regulator. **Strengths:** "Saul has been extremely good operating in a team of leading counsel and solicitors to conclude extremely complex cases to the clients' satisfaction." **Recent work:** Acted as part of a team representing the trustee in the significant IBM litigation concerning a breach of duty of good faith.

Jennifer Seaman (see p.760) Well respected in the pensions arena, she offers expertise in a wide range of cases, including civil fraud, professional negligence and regulatory matters. She has represented clients solely before the High Court and appeared in the Supreme Court and Court of Appeal. **Strengths:** "She is absolutely fabulous. She has the ear of the judge when she speaks." "She's a good advocate; she has a very calm understated manner." **Recent work:** Assisted in Ballinger & Antheor v Mercer Ltd & Another, successfully arguing limitation on behalf of the defendants in a professional negligence claim.

Lydia Seymour Recommended for her specialisation in the pension and employment crossover, but is additionally well versed in pure pension disputes. She frequently acts for the Pensions Regulator, employers, trade unions and individuals. **Strengths:** "She is a very good communicator and has the benefit of good experience in both pensions and employment law." "She manages to translate pension issues into layman's terms." **Recent work:** Acted in Secretary of State for Communities and Local Government v Fire Brigades Union, a Part 8 claim concerning the potential age discrimination of certain scheme provisions.

Nicholas Hill An up-and-coming junior with significant expertise in financial services law. He can boast extensive experience in Part 8 claims, professional negligence and contribution disputes. **Strengths:** "He's very practical and gets straight to the point." **Recent work:** Assisted in Philips Pension Trustees & Philips Electronics UK v AON Hewitt & AllianceBernstein, a case regarding the investment of trust assets, worth £2 billion, which caused massive losses during the financial crisis.

Band 3

Radcliffe Chambers

See profile on p.903

THE SET

Radcliffe Chambers offers far-reaching experience into the professional negligence, trusts and corporate insolvency issues that intersect pensions. It handles both litigious and advisory matters for a variety of schemes, including SSASs, SIPPs and Local Government Pension Schemes. The set acts for the usual parties in pension disputes, and also represents insurers, advisers and regulatory bodies. Its members have recently defended the trustees of the Airlines Pension Scheme in British Airways v Spencer & Others, which is a high-profile case surrounding the power of trustees to make discretionary pension increases.

Client service: "We've found the clerks to be helpful, particularly Keith Nagle. He's extremely understanding of a particular client's needs and suggesting which counsel is best placed to deal with it." The senior clerks at Radcliffe Chambers are Keith Nagle and John Clark.

SILKS

Keith Rowley QC (see p.756) A leading silk handling the full breadth of pensions issues from Part 8 claims to equalisation matters. He also commands expertise in pension disputes with professional negligence elements. **Strengths:** "He's very hands-on and he has gravitas and knows what goes down well with judges." "He's very analytical and he masters complex issues and sees a way forward very well." **Recent work:** Acted in Buckinghamshire v Barnardo's & Others, a Part 8 claim which sought to clarify whether trustees had the power to switch from RPI to CPI.

JUNIORS

Elizabeth Ovey (see p.732) An experienced chancery lawyer, who has expertise in pension disputes, as well as related professional negligence and financial services issues. **Strengths:** "She is technically very strong and she's thorough in her advice and clear in her conclusion." "She is very measured and has a good style of communicating with clients; she gets points across in a way we can all live with given our different perspectives." **Recent work:** Acted for the Trustees of the Moores Furniture Pension Scheme in a rectification claim followed by a claim that the deed was invalid.

Wendy Mathers (see p.709) A rising pensions and commercial chancery junior. She is popular with respondents for her knowledge in Part 8 claims and professional negligence disputes. **Strengths:** "She's not simply a street fighter, she's a good technical trusts and pensions lawyer." "She's very attentive to the client's commercial requirements and is also a technically excellent barrister." **Recent work:** Acted as sole counsel counsel in Auguste v Ascham Homes, an appeal against a decision of the Deputy Pensions Ombudsman.

5 Stone Buildings

See profile on p.914

THE SET

5 Stone Buildings offers a breadth of expertise in pension disputes and is particularly experienced in matters concerning trust law and professional negligence. Its members act for a wide range of clients ranging from individual private members and trustees to employers and the Pensions Regulator. The set is regularly instructed in the most headline-grabbing cases, including the long-running matter concerning the closure of two defined benefit pension schemes by IBM.

Client service: "The clerking is good; they're responsive and give me what I need when I need it." Paul Jennings is the senior clerk.

SILKS

Andrew Simmonds QC (see p.765) An authority on the full spectrum of pension issues, including those matters with professional negligence and financial services dimensions. He advises and litigates for an impressively diverse set of clients and is an asset on some of the most contentious pension cases. **Strengths:** "He's exceptionally good on his feet, he's very popular with judges and he's a very attractive advocate so he garners their attention." "He's fantastically analytical, incredibly clever and commercial." **Recent work:** Played a central role in IBM UK Holdings v Dalgleish litigation and its consequent remedies calculation.

Henry Legge QC (see p.699) Trusted by a diverse range of clients to represent them in high-profile pensions litigation, particularly concerning construction disputes and professional negligence. He is also highly valued for his foreign law and actuarial expertise. **Strengths:** "He's brilliant in terms of his intellectual and legal analysis." "He's very forensic and analytical but he brings a commercial, practical angle as well." **Recent work:** Acted in Re Nortel Networks Canada as an expert witness on UK pensions and construction of contracts in Canadian courts.

Christopher Tidmarsh QC (see p.781) Respondents emphasise his top-drawer advice on highly technical matters, particularly on those with a tax or professional negligence crossover. He regularly acts for the Pension Protection Fund and the Pensions Regulator. **Strengths:** "He has a very considered in-depth analysis of the law, particularly on very complex technical issues where you're looking for a practical way through." "He has a really nice understated manner in court but can be really steely when he needs to be."

JUNIORS

Joseph Goldsmith (see p.656) Well-established chancery junior with extensive experience counselling clients on high-profile pension disputes and appearing in the courts, including the Court of Appeal. His practice also encompasses professional negligence elements of pensions matters. **Strengths:** "He's a very technically strong junior and he's got a very good drafting style." "He does very high-quality written work to a high technical standard with a very precise and well laid out style."

Other Ranked Lawyers

Raquel Agnello QC (see p.580) (Erskine Chambers) Prized by clients for her expertise in the pensions and insolvency fields. She is highly knowledgeable when it comes to regulation and frequently advises on moral hazard and restructuring cases. **Strengths:** "The crossover point between insolvency and pensions is where she has her strength." "She is very tenacious, quick-thinking and an all round good advocate." **Recent work:** Acted for the Pensions Regulator in its first Contribution Notice case against the directors and shareholders of the Desmond Pension Scheme.

James Clifford (see p.619) (Maitland Chambers) An experienced pensions barrister enjoying a strong reputation in this field. His broad practice encompasses the full spectrum of pension issues, including interpretation of scheme rules, professional negligence and liberation. **Strengths:** "He's particularly good at adapting his advice to the particular client." "He is very thorough and very helpful." **Recent work:** Represented scheme members in a prominent, high-value case concerning the administration of the Gleeds Pension Scheme.

Nigel Burroughs (4 New Square) Highly recommended for his professional negligence expertise in the crossover with pension administration. He frequently advises lawyers in relation to scheme amendments. **Strengths:** "He's very user-friendly, he rolls his sleeves up and he straddles professional negligence with pensions." "He's very concise and clear." **Recent work:** Represented Blake Lapthorn against Abbey Life Trust Securities in a dispute concerning the drafting of a consolidated trustee deed and bringing into play Section 37 of the Pensions Scheme Act 1993.

PERSONAL INJURY: An Introduction

Contributed by 12 King's Bench Walk

"It is the aim of an award of damages in the law of tort, so far as possible, to place the person who has been harmed by the wrongful acts of another in the position in which he or she would have been had the harm not been done: full compensation, no more but certainly no less."

In February this year, the Supreme Court delivered its judgment in *Knauer v Ministry of Justice*, less than a month after hearing argument. The very first sentence of the judgment restates the "full compensation" principle that underlies personal injury litigation.

In reversing a decades-long practice of using the date of death to calculate future loss multipliers, a practice which was, since *Wells v Wells*, obviously wrong to any numerate personal injury lawyer, the Supreme Court reinforced the common law's commitment to ensuring that injured persons are justly compensated for their injuries. It is unfortunate that so obvious a correction took so long to make. The common law is usually nimble when tackling obvious unfairness, and that reputation for flexibility needs to be preserved if the common law, and in particular the principle of full compensation, is to be protected.

The profession faces the challenge of protecting that principle, most immediately in persuading the new Lord Chancellor in the new government that fixed costs will fundamentally cripple the process that seeks to achieve it. This will require dialogue and patient persuasion.

Personal injury lawyers will have to accept that spiralling costs cannot and will not be tolerated but, equally, the government and the judiciary must accept that there will be cases where the cost of properly investigating the cause of an accident or the extent of injuries caused will approach, or even exceed, damages recovered. Whilst costs at such a level are obviously undesirable, the commitment to full compensation will occasionally require nothing less. Proportionality is now a valuable ingredient of our legal system, but it should not trump the assessment of damages according to the common law.

There are several areas where changes can easily be made to keep costs reasonable. Experts' fees and waiting lists, particularly in catastrophic cases, are out of control. This is partly the product of a risk-averse unwillingness on the part of solicitors to try anyone new. There is also a tendency to write off possible experts on the basis of second hand descriptions of a testing cross-examination. The resulting high demand for the few experts that experienced litigators are prepared to use inevitably pushes up fees. If this impasse is not broken, there is little chance of keeping substantial personal injury litigation out of the cost cutters' spotlight. The net urgently needs to be cast wider to include younger experts – particularly medical experts – who may be inexperienced in medico-legal work, but who have the advantage of being in current clinical practice. This is easy to say but harder to do when a client's claim or defence depends on expert opinion, but unless the profession is brave in this area, the consequences are obvious. The imposition of single joint experts in whom neither party has confidence would not benefit anyone.

The abolition of cost budgeting would also save time and costs. Never has a procedural innovation been less popular with the judiciary and lawyers alike. The broad brush reductions applied by busy District Judges and Masters with better things to do inevitably encourage excessive budgets from claimants. The effect of QOCS and the rock bottom hourly rates squeezed out of panel solicitors by insurers inevitably encourage artificially low budgets from defendants. Counsel instructed to appear at CCMCs rarely have the expertise required to attack or defend budgets. The time and expense spent briefing them to do so or sending a costs draftsman/fee earner to help pushes up costs further. The entire process has become artificial and time consuming, and is increasingly avoided where possible. Reform is required.

The fixed costs battle has already been lost in relation to low-value claims and the junior personal injury Bar is replete with stories of the rough-and-ready justice which has resulted, and which impacts on claimants and defendants alike. The Bar must call on its powers of persuasion and innovation to make the case against ever higher limits below which fixed costs bite.

In that regard, the personal injury Bar is already admirably involving itself in the Briggs review of the civil court structure. While online courts are unlikely to be workable in much of personal injury litigation (problems with testing evidence and ensuring that disclosure obligations are met without the supervision of legal representatives immediately spring to mind), accepting a greater role for schemes such as the Ministry of Justice claims portal and working to make those as effective a means of justly compensating injured persons as possible, is a pragmatic way forward for personal injury barristers.

Lastly, although the consequences of Brexit will be wide-ranging, its impact on personal injury litigation is not obviously profound. The Enterprise Act has already neutered the six-pack Regulations – but those Regulations have irreversibly changed the course of employer's liability law over the last 20 years, and cases such as *Kennedy v Cordia* in the Supreme Court earlier this year (see the section on common law liability at paragraph 107) suggest the common law is willing to replace what has been lost, at least to some extent.

And as the Brexit process matures, there will be uncertainty and difficulty determining how personal injury liabilities and judgments are to be treated outside the detailed framework provided by the EU. The personal injury Bar should see this as an opportunity to prepare to advise the many claimants and insurers likely to be embarking upon European litigation outside the EU in the not too distant future.

Contents:

LONDON

Personal Injury
Leading Sets
Band 1
Crown Office Chambers *
39 Essex Chambers *
9 Gough Square *
12 King's Bench Walk *
Outer Temple Chambers *
Band 2
7BR *
1 Chancery Lane
Cloisters *
1 Crown Office Row *
Devereux *
Temple Garden Chambers *
2TG - 2 Temple Gardens *
Band 3
Doughty Street Chambers *
Farrar's Building *
Old Square Chambers *
** Indicates set / individual with profile.*
[A] direct access (see p.24).
◊ (ORL) = Other Ranked Lawyer.
Alphabetical order within each band. Band 1 is highest.

Personal Injury
Senior Statesmen
Senior Statesmen: distinguished older partners
Purchas Christopher *Crown Office Chambers*
Leading Silks
Star individuals
Block Neil *39 Essex Chambers* *
Burton Frank *12 King's Bench Walk* *
Gumbel Elizabeth-Anne *1 Crown Office Row*
McDermott Gerard *Outer Temple Chambers*
Ritchie Andrew *9 Gough Square* *
Weir Robert *Devereux* *
Band 1
Aldous Grahame *9 Gough Square* *
Browne Benjamin *2TG - 2 Temple Gardens* *
Cory-Wright Charles *39 Essex Chambers*
Glancy Robert *Devereux* *
Hogarth Andrew *12 King's Bench Walk* *
Jeffreys Alan *Farrar's Building* *
Killalea Stephen *Devereux* *
Lynagh Richard *Crown Office Chambers*
Maskrey Simeon *7BR*
Norris William *39 Essex Chambers*
Rodway Susan *39 Essex Chambers*
Russell Paul *12 King's Bench Walk* *
Westcott David *Outer Temple Chambers*
Worthington Stephen *12 King's Bench Walk* *
Band 2
Bishop Edward *1 Chancery Lane*
Browne Simon P *Temple Garden Chambers*
Donovan Joel *Cloisters* *
Featherby William *12 King's Bench Walk* *
Ford Steven *7BR*
Foy John *9 Gough Square* *
Levy Jacob *9 Gough Square* *
McCaul Colin *39 Essex Chambers*
Methuen Richard *12 King's Bench Walk* *
Platt David *Crown Office Chambers*
Readhead Simon *1 Chancery Lane*
Rose Paul *Old Square Chambers* *
Ross John *1 Chancery Lane*
Walker Ronald *12 King's Bench Walk* *
Warnock Andrew *1 Chancery Lane* [A]
Watt-Pringle Jonathan *Temple Garden Chambers* *
Wilson-Smith Christopher *Outer Temple Chambers* *
Band 3
Antelme Alexander *Crown Office Chambers*
Audland William *12 King's Bench Walk* *
Hitchcock Patricia *Cloisters* *
Kent Michael *Crown Office Chambers*
McNeill Jane *Old Square Chambers* *
Nolan Dominic *Hailsham Chambers (ORL)* ◊ *
Oppenheim Robin *Doughty Street Chambers*
Picton Julian *Hailsham Chambers (ORL)* ◊ *
Porter Martin *2TG - 2 Temple Gardens* [A] *
Stevens Howard *3 Hare Court (ORL)* ◊
Sweeting Derek *7BR* [A]
New Silks
Latimer-Sayer William *Cloisters* *
O'Sullivan Derek *39 Essex Chambers*
Steinberg Harry *12 King's Bench Walk* *
Weitzman Adam *7BR*
Witcomb Henry *1 Crown Office Row*

Band 1

Crown Office Chambers

See profile on p.824

THE SET

Crown Office Chambers can count many of the UK's leading catastrophic injury and industrial disease specialists among its ranks. Its barristers are regularly chosen by claimants and defendant insurers in precedent-setting, maximum severity cases. One market commentator notes that the set "provides a consistently high level of service, and its members consistently deliver excellent results."

Client service: Greg Frewin's team of clerks are commended for being "spot-on, incredibly attentive and always helpful: they really stand out."

SILKS

Christopher Purchas QC Veteran personal injury silk known for skilfully handling catastrophic injury litigation. He has notable experience in EL/PL claims, fatal accidents and maximum severity cases. **Strengths:** "He's a long-standing, heavyweight private injury silk."

Richard Lynagh QC Head of chambers at the set and a tremendously well-respected senior silk. He is described as a formidable opponent by peers given his adept representation of both claimants and defendants in the largest catastrophic injury claims. **Strengths:** "He is exceptional. You want him on your side." "Masterful: he's vastly experienced and just a top-notch advocate." **Recent work:** Acted for the defence in Hicks v Young, a claim brought by a passenger who sustained a severe brain injury by jumping out of the defendant's moving taxi. The matter involved complex issues of causation, the tort of false imprisonment and contributory negligence about which there is no clear authority.

David Platt QC Prominent silk with notable expertise encompassing traditional asbestos claims and the burgeoning field of industrial disease litigation. Instructed by both claimant and defendant solicitors, he also has extensive experience in military and catastrophic injury claims. **Strengths:** "He's formidably intelligent and very well organised, with knowledge that cuts to the heart of issues." "Superb at strategy and a brilliant advocate. There's no one better when it comes to asbestos litigation. Easy to work with, clients appreciate his expertise and he delivers stunning results." **Recent work:** Acted in Heneghan v Manchester Dry Docks and others before the Court of Appeal. The case concerned the application of the Fairchild test of causation for lung cancer cases.

Alexander Antelme QC Particularly highly thought of for his adept representation of defendant and insurer clients in catastrophic injury claims. He is noted for his expertise in fatal accident claims in which the deceased was a high earner and for his deep knowledge of complex medical causation issues. **Strengths:** "He's one of the best advocates around. Very good with clients, he puts them at ease instantly. He's very bright and has incredible medical knowledge."

Michael Kent QC Esteemed practitioner with an impressively broad practice that includes industrial disease, historic child abuse and catastrophic personal injury claims. He frequently appears before the highest courts in the UK, including the ECJ and Supreme Court, and has acted in numerous test and group actions. **Strengths:** "He's a brilliant advocate." "Urbane, pleasant and very clever." **Recent work:** Acted for the defence in Saunderson v Sonae Industria (UK Ltd), a group action brought by over 16,000 claimants seeking damages for the alleged effects of smoke and toxic emissions from a factory fire that burned for two weeks in Liverpool.

JUNIORS

Patrick Blakesley Heavy-hitting senior junior who is instructed by both claimant and defendant solicitors in catastrophic injury claims. He is singled out by clients for his incisive cross-examination of medical experts. **Strengths:** "Exceptionally eloquent, he's a superb advocate with a lot of flair." "He's absolutely on top of all the issues and is very persuasive. He achieves an awful lot for clients."

Catherine Foster Splits her practice between complex industrial disease, historic child abuse and serious personal injury litigation. She is the first choice for many large insurer clients in high-profile group actions. Her strategic expertise and courtroom prowess are especially highly valued by clients. **Strengths:** "She is a superb advocate and a formidable opponent in court." "Always thoroughly examines the issues in dispute and provides clear advice on how best to proceed. A go-to counsel on complex disease claims." **Recent work:** Acted for the defendant solicitors in Procter v Raleys Solicitors, a negligence allegation brought by a group of ex-miners against various law firms for their handling of miners' indemnification claims under the BCC HAVS compensation scheme.

Personal Injury	
Leading Juniors	
Star individuals	
Grant Marcus	*Temple Garden Chambers* *
Band 1	
Bagot Charles	*Hardwicke (ORL)* ◊
Begley Laura	*9 Gough Square* *
Blakesley Patrick	*Crown Office Chambers*
Charles Henry	*12 King's Bench Walk* *
Doherty Bernard	*39 Essex Chambers*
Du Cann Christian	*39 Essex Chambers*
Evans Lee	*Farrar's Building* *
Foster Catherine	*Crown Office Chambers*
Freeman Peter	*Temple Garden Chambers*
Goolamali Nina	*2TG - 2 Temple Gardens* *
Hillier Nicolas	*9 Gough Square* *
Lawson Daniel	*Cloisters* *
Levinson Justin	*1 Crown Office Row*
Lewers Nigel	*12 King's Bench Walk* *
Matthews Julian D	*7BR*
McKechnie Stuart	*9 Gough Square* *
Sanderson David	*12 King's Bench Walk* *
Silvester Bruce	*Devereux* *
Snowden Steven	*Crown Office Chambers* *
Tavares Nathan	*Outer Temple Chambers*
Vincent Patrick	*12 King's Bench Walk* *
Woodhouse Charles	*Old Square Chambers* *
Woolf Eliot	*Outer Temple Chambers*
Band 2	
Ayling Judith	*39 Essex Chambers*
Baldock Nicholas	*6 Pump Court (ORL)* ◊
Bate-Williams John	*Temple Garden Chambers* *
Bell James	*Temple Garden Chambers*
Bennett Daniel	*Doughty Street Chambers*
Brown Catherine	*12 King's Bench Walk* *
Brown Geoffrey	*39 Essex Chambers*
Cartwright Richard	*Devereux* *
Chapman Matthew	*1 Chancery Lane*
Davis Andrew	*Crown Office Chambers*
Dignum Marcus	*12 King's Bench Walk* *
Dyer Simon	*Cloisters*
Ferris Shaun	*Crown Office Chambers* *
Ford Jeremy	*9 Gough Square* *
Formby Emily	*39 Essex Chambers* *
Furniss Richard	*42 Bedford Row (ORL)* ◊
Glynn Stephen	*9 Gough Square* *
Gregory Richard	*42 Bedford Row (ORL)* ◊
Hamill Hugh	*12 King's Bench Walk* *
Harris Roger	*2TG - 2 Temple Gardens* [A] *
Johnson Laura	*1 Chancery Lane* [A]
King Simon	*7BR*
Laughland James	*Temple Garden Chambers*
Matthewson Scott	*42 Bedford Row (ORL)* ◊
McCormick Alison	*Outer Temple Chambers*
McDonald John	*2TG - 2 Temple Gardens* [A] *
Mendoza Colin	*Devereux* *
Mooney Giles	*9 Gough Square* *
Phillips Matthew	*Outer Temple Chambers* *
Roy Andrew	*12 King's Bench Walk* *
Russell Christopher	*2TG - 2 Temple Gardens* *
Samuel Gerwyn	*Doughty Street Chambers*
Stephenson Christopher	*9 Gough Square* *
Todd James	*39 Essex Chambers* *
Trusted Harry	*Outer Temple Chambers*
Wilkinson Richard	*Temple Garden Chambers* *
Williams A John	*Crown Office Chambers* *
Band 3	
Adamson Dominic	*Temple Garden Chambers*
Aldridge James	*Outer Temple Chambers*
Boyle Matthew	*Crown Office Chambers* *
Crapper Sadie	*39 Essex Chambers*
Cummerson Romilly	*39 Essex Chambers*
Dawson Adam	*9 Gough Square* *
Edwards Peter	*Devereux* *
Hand Jonathan	*Outer Temple Chambers* *
Hiorns Roger	*9 Gough Square* *
Hunter Robert	*Devereux* *
Kellar Robert	*1 Crown Office Row*
Kemp Christopher	*Outer Temple Chambers*
Kilcoyne Paul	*Temple Garden Chambers*
Meakin Timothy	*7BR* [A]
Piper Angus	*1 Chancery Lane*
Rivers David	*Old Square Chambers* *
Stagg Paul	*1 Chancery Lane* [A]
Walker Adam	*7BR* *
Walker Christopher	*Old Square Chambers* *
Waters Julian	*1 Chancery Lane*
Wille Andrew	*Farrar's Building* *
Up-and-coming individuals	
Dobie Lisa	*1 Chancery Lane*
Hughes Anna	*2TG - 2 Temple Gardens* *
Maclean Niall	*12 King's Bench Walk* *

** Indicates individual with profile.*

[A] direct access (see p.24).

◊ (ORL) = Other Ranked Lawyer.

Alphabetical order within each band. Band 1 is highest.

Steven Snowden (see p.769) Personal injury and occupational illness specialist. He regularly handles maximum severity claims on behalf of insurers and claimants. He routinely appears unled in complex actions concerning brain and spinal injuries and cancers caused by asbestos exposure. **Strengths:** "Very smooth advocate, very urbane. He has a gentle but highly effective manner." **Recent work:** Defended London Fire and Emergency Planning Authority against claims brought by a firefighter who allegedly suffered serious spinal injuries during a training exercise.

Andrew Davis Regularly instructed by defendant solicitors in significant brain and spinal injury claims. He is often chosen for cases where there are novel or unusual legal complications. His broader practice includes insurance and commercial disputes. **Strengths:** "He's extremely bright, cuts through the issues quickly and is extremely good in court." "He is disarmingly charming, bright, able and a wonderful negotiator."

Shaun Ferris (see p.644) Highly regarded senior junior whose personal injury practice includes product liability disputes. He frequently acts for insurers and defendants in catastrophic injury claims and has notable experience in brain and spinal injury cases involving sports accidents. **Strengths:** "He's very good at managing clients and lay witnesses. He's got a very relaxed demeanour and doesn't get in a flap, he deals with everything with composure." "Able to digest a large amount of documentation very quickly and assimilate the key issues."

John Williams (see p.796) An authority on occupational illness litigation with a pre-eminent asbestos disease and catastrophic injury defence practice. He has extensive experience in psychiatric injury, fatal accidents and complex workplace injury claims. **Strengths:** "He's excellent, a formidable opponent." "He is extremely robust; as a trial advocate he can really go for the jugular when called for." **Recent work:** Acted in Cassley v GMP Securities Europe Ltd & Sundance Resources Ltd. Successfully defended a £7 million fatal accident claim arising from a plane crash in the Congo.

Matthew Boyle (see p.601) Specialises in serious injury and RTA cases, offering broad experience in both fatal and catastrophic claims. He is noted for his able cross-examination and adroit handling of complex technical evidence. **Strengths:** "He will reliably do a good job, plus he's thorough and utterly approachable." **Recent work:** Acted for the claimant in Spring v Maps Fast Foods, a case in which the claimant suffered multiple injuries as a result of two RTAs.

39 Essex Chambers

See profile on p.840

THE SET

39 Essex Chambers is a distinguished set that prides itself on its provision of the highest-quality representation in complex personal injury disputes. The set's impressive client base is composed primarily of insurer and defendant clients. The chambers houses numerous leading counsel who offer broad expertise across the full spectrum of personal injury matters. Market sources confirm that "their strength in depth and knowledge of the subject matter is superb."

Client service: Practice manager Ben Sundborg leads "a very good bunch of clerks who are commercially oriented." The clerks are credited for their "forward-moving, forward-thinking, dynamic approach that serves clients and solicitors very well."

SILKS

Neil Block QC (see p.598) Head of chambers and a true leading light of the defendant personal injury market. He regularly acts in high-stakes litigation of the utmost complexity on behalf of a raft of loyal insurer clients. He has recently been involved in prominent cross-jurisdictional and conflict of laws cases. **Strengths:** "A pleasure to work with. No matter how busy he is, he will always find the time to answer questions and assist on a case." "Clients love him, he has the gravitas that gives them comfort as he's a huge name in the market. If you've got him acting for you the other side know you're serious." "He's superbly clever and absolutely charming. Pragmatic and realistic." **Recent work:** Acted for the defence in Rudd v Taylor, a case in which the claimant was in a minimally conscious state which caused great difficulties regarding the calculation of life expectancy and cognition.

Charles Cory-Wright QC Highly sought after for his experience representing both claimants and defendants in serious RTA claims. He focuses on catastrophic injuries, both physical and psychiatric, and has a leading nervous shock practice. **Strengths:** "He has a very good bedside manner and is able to deal very effectively with cases of a sensitive nature. He shows empathy with claimants when he needs to but can put up a fierce fight when necessary." "His advocacy skills are amazing." **Recent work:** Acted in McCormick v Corcodel, successfully securing £1.7 million for a claimant who was seriously injured after being hit by a car.

William Norris QC An extremely well-regarded and experienced defendant silk who is often called upon in complex liability and catastrophic injury cases. He is highly praised for his heavy-hitting advocacy and impressive knowledge of personal injury litigation. **Strengths:** "He's very impressive on his feet. If you want somebody to fiercely fight your corner, you go to him." "He's charm itself, a real smooth operator." **Recent work:** Instructed by the defendant in the High Court trial of Kolasa v Ealing Hospital. The case concerned the duty of care owed by a hospital to an outpatient.

Susan Rodway QC Splits her impressive personal injury and clinical negligence practice between representing large insurers and claimants in catastrophic injury matters. Her client care, tenacity and willingness to run difficult cases all elicit glowing market praise. **Strengths:** "She's an outstanding QC, very tenacious, excellent in terms of client relationships and very approachable and friendly." "She is great, she gets straight to the crux of what you need in the case and focuses on building the evidence. She is completely committed and a great team player."

Colin McCaul QC His practice runs the gamut of personal injury claims, from industrial disease to catastrophic injury. He is also known for his expertise with complex liability and causation disputes, in both personal injury and clinical negligence. **Strengths:** "He's a real class act." "He's a very good advocate, good with judges, clever and forceful when necessary." **Recent work:** Acted in Lear v Hickstead Ltd, appearing for a client who had been rendered paraplegic after the ramp of a horse lorry struck him while parked in the defendant's car park.

Derek O'Sullivan QC A standout silk who regularly appears in high-value catastrophic injury cases. He elicits stellar market praise for his technical abilities and client care, and is one of the few barristers to have been instructed in a corporate manslaughter case. **Strengths:** "Phenomenally good, his pleadings are a work of art." "He's completely on the ball, excellent with clients and an excellent all-rounder." "Excellent relationships with the lay clients and very good at handling expert witnesses."

JUNIORS

Bernard Doherty Regularly instructed by defendant clients in the most complex spinal and brain injury claims. He is a well-respected authority on insurance disputes, especially those involving conflict of laws issues arising from accidents in Europe and further abroad. **Strengths:** "He's a stellar advocate with excellent client skills." "He is really the top person for complex issues. He has absolute encyclopaedic knowledge of the area." **Recent work:** Represented the defendant insurance provider in Various Claimants v Kooperativa Poistovna, a case involving multiple claims arising from a serious RTA.

Christian Du Cann One of the most respected juniors in the market with a well-earned reputation given his exceptional courtroom abilities. Regularly acts for claimants and defendants in extremely high-value catastrophic injury cases. **Strengths:** "He really is outstanding." "Absolutely first-class, he just wipes the floor with people, his advocacy skills are first-rate." "He is just brilliant on his feet, great with clients and great at negotiating with defendants." **Recent work:** Represented the defendant in Laws v Pooley, a £4 million claim brought by a partially paralysed claimant.

Judith Ayling Well known for her adroit handling of complex quantum and costs issues for both claimant and defendant clients. Her expertise encompasses catastrophic brain and spinal injuries, in both a personal injury and clinical negligence context. **Strengths:** "She's first-rate and has a very measured style." "She is outstanding." **Recent work:** Appeared on behalf of the defendant in Moorcock v Clyde Builders, a £500,000 workplace accident claim that involved issues of exaggeration and dishonesty.

Geoffrey Brown Respected senior junior with notable expertise in stress at work, amputations and high-value catastrophic brain injury cases. He is regularly instructed as sole counsel by defendant insurers and routinely appears against esteemed silks. **Strengths:** "An iron fist in a silk glove." "He is great with clients and always delivers."

Emily Formby (see p.646) Brings a comprehensive understanding of technical legal and medical issues to her personal injury cases. She is well versed in catastrophic and fatal injury claims and demonstrates particular strength in cases concerning human rights law. **Strengths:** "Her analysis of the issues is very good and she has a particularly strong understanding of medical evidence." "She's an outstanding junior, excellent attention to detail and very client-friendly."

James Todd (see p.782) Splits his practice between catastrophic injury and industrial disease, acting for both sides. He has further, niche expertise in sporting injury claims, especially those concerning skiing or horse-riding accidents. **Strengths:** "Very approachable, pragmatic and client-friendly." "He's always able to get to the nub of the matter very quickly and can digest huge amounts of material at top speed. He's got an exceptional skill set." **Recent work:** Acted for a third party defendant in the case of Belfitt v Foreign Commonwealth Office and Morson Human Resources. The case concerned an accident at an overseas UK embassy. The claim failed at trial and costs were recovered.

Sadie Crapper Continues to gain praise for her growing personal injury practice. She routinely handles quantum and liability disputes for claimants and defendants. She is noted for her experience with complex fraud cases and employers' liability disputes, having previously practised at the Employment Bar. **Strengths:** "One of the rising stars at 39 Essex Street." "She's absolutely excellent." **Recent work:** Secured the pre-trial abandonment of the case of Rosarti v Fairview Holdings Ltd, which alleged that a claimant required full-time care for his wife.

Romilly Cummerson Recently joined from Hardwicke Chambers and brings a practice focusing on RTAs and serious injuries alongside extensive experience handling inquests. Her approachable manner draws particular praise from interviewees. **Strengths:** "She's extremely intelligent and technically amazing – she's great at distilling the issues. She's a brilliant advocate and is persuasive in her arguments."

9 Gough Square

See profile on p.854

THE SET

9 Gough Square is a standout personal injury chambers offering top-tier advice and representation to clients. Its regular instruction in significant cases frequently sees its members appearing before the Supreme Court and Court of Appeal. The set is particularly highly regarded for its exceptional advocacy on behalf of claimants, who form the core of its client base. Its members include some of the most esteemed practitioners in the catastrophic injury and industrial disease market. One interviewee singles them out as "an excellent set of chambers with incredible breadth and depth of experience in all areas of personal injury work."

Client service: Clients describe the clerking team, led by Michael Goodridge, as "outstanding, commercially astute and quick to resolve any issues that arise." "They bend over backwards to help."

SILKS

Andrew Ritchie QC (see p.752) Head of chambers and an undoubted leader in the field. He is universally praised for his advocacy style and notable flair when arguing technical quantum points, especially in cases involving the MIB. Clients also highlight his measured handling of fatal accident claims and command of liability disputes. **Strengths:** "He's incredible, no waffle to him at all. He knows exactly what needs to be done, he's totally precise and concise." "He is fantastic and commands the whole courtroom. He's a very skilful advocate, authoritative and fantastic with clients." "A real superstar." **Recent work:** Represented the families in the In Amenas inquest into the death of the hostages taken by Al Qaeda terrorists at a BP gas facility in Algeria.

Grahame Aldous QC (see p.581) A tremendously gifted advocate who regularly acts for clients in multimillion-pound brain and spinal injury claims. He is singled out for his capability in cross-border cases, particularly those involving maritime accidents and complicated quantum points. **Strengths:** "Particularly excellent, brilliant at cross-examining expert witnesses." "He makes the unarguable sound plausible."

John Foy QC (see p.648) Regularly sought out by major claimant personal injury firms and widely commended for his expert client management. His esteemed practice focuses on brain and spinal injuries and fatal accidents. He is also notably well versed in costs litigation. **Strengths:** "He's fantastic, very confident yet down-to-earth. He's a joy to work with and fosters really collaborative relationships." "His ability to cut through a lot of information and get to the salient point is extraordinary to watch, and he's exceptional with clients." **Recent work:** Appeared for the claimant in Hart v Woodcock, a matter regarding serious head injuries sustained by a cyclist in an RTA.

Jacob Levy QC (see p.700) Market sources characterise him as an extremely accomplished and able advocate with an industrious and personable approach to claimant-side personal injury litigation. He is also an expert on RTAs and clinical negligence. **Strengths:** "He is possibly the hardest-working barrister there is. He is completely thorough and leaves no room for confusion in his arguments." "His negotiating skills are wonderful, it doesn't matter who he's up against, he will always do a great job and get wonderful results."

JUNIORS

Laura Begley (see p.594) Routinely instructed in the most complex, high-value personal injury litigation. She is commended by interviewees for her analytical and technical approach and is recognised as a leading expert in criminal injury compensation and brain injury claims. **Strengths:** "Excellent advocate and litigator who gives clear advice." "She's just brilliant, her technical capability is quite outstanding."

Nicolas Hillier (see p.672) Outstanding reputation for representing claimants who have suffered life-changing catastrophic injuries. He receives praise from market commentators for both his excellent technical nous and compassionate client care. **Strengths:** "One of the top senior juniors out there. He's always well prepared and a fantastic advocate." "He's exceptional, he's excellent in court and gives very realistic and sympathetic advice to clients."

Stuart McKechnie (see p.713) Heralded as a true specialist in quantum, he regularly appears unled for claimants in multimillion-pound cases. His expansive knowledge spans the full spectrum of catastrophic injuries, and he is well known for his command of maximum severity brain injury claims. **Strengths:** "Almost legendary in terms of maximising claims for his clients." "Has an amazing knowledge of spinal injury cases, he really does add a lot of value to cases." "He's incredibly hard-working and extraordinarily bright." **Recent work:** Represented the claimant in Fletcher v BT PLC, a case concerning a young shipbroker who was struck with a BT telegraph pole and suffered multiple serious brain and spinal injuries.

Jeremy Ford (see p.646) Heads up the personal injury team at the set. He is a noted senior junior who routinely acts for both claimants and defendants. His expert handling of catastrophic brain and spinal injury claims elicits broad market praise. **Strengths:** "On his feet he is absolutely brilliant, he really takes command of the whole case." "He's very intellectual and a lethal cross-examiner." **Recent work:** Represented the estate of the deceased in Anghel & Gheorghe Milosavlevici v Siday Construction Limited. The case concerned the death of a construction worker who was crushed by a concrete slab while excavating a residential property. Also appeared in a separate action brought by the father of the deceased, who developed PTSD after witnessing the event. Damages of £650,000 were agreed at a joint settlement meeting.

Stephen Glynn (see p.655) Routinely called upon by claimant solicitors in catastrophic injury, sexual abuse and industrial disease cases. He is particularly recognised for his deftness of touch with especially vulnerable clients. **Strengths:** "He's fantastic and always does an excellent job." "As far as asbestos is concerned, he is one of the leading juniors." **Recent work:** Instructed by the claimant in Houselander v Port of London Authority, a living mesothelioma claim where the claimant was exposed to asbestos as a docker at the Royal Docks, London.

Giles Mooney (see p.720) Regularly acts for both claimants and defendants and is one of the foremost experts for cases involving injuries caused by animals. He has vast experience in multimillion-pound catastrophic injury claims and complex liability disputes. **Strengths:** "He's excellent: very down-to-earth, personable and gets on well with clients. An all-round excellent advocate." "Personable, accessible and available when you need him." **Recent work:** Appeared in Carrick & Lee v Bromley Mytime Limited on behalf of both claimants. The case centred on allegations that serious psychiatric injury was sustained when the claimants were held hostage and threatened at knifepoint during the robbery of the golf club at which they worked.

Christopher Stephenson (see p.772) Has an excellent grasp of technical medical points and routinely takes instructions in both clinical negligence and personal injury matters. Claimant solicitors regularly choose him for catastrophic injury cases and highlight his meticulous attention to detail. **Strengths:** "He's a great advocate and exceptionally good with clients – professional and sympathetic." "He's got a very good understanding of the law and always phrases his advice in ways that are helpful." **Recent work:** Appeared in Madison v Oliver on behalf of the claimant, who lost his arm in an RTA.

Adam Dawson (see p.630) Has a personal injury practice that includes mesothelioma claims and fatal accident, brain and spinal injury cases. This broad base of expertise also serves his predominantly claimant clients extremely well in areas such as EL/PL claims and RTAs. **Strengths:** "He's pragmatic and he very much works as a team. He is approachable and his client care is excellent." **Recent work:** Settled on behalf of the claimant in Vladimir o Capano (deceased) v Bennett for over £500,000. The claimant was an Italian citizen working in the UK who was killed while crossing a country road.

Roger Hiorns (see p.673) Respected senior junior with considerable expertise in industrial disease cases. He has experience handling RTAs that result in serious injuries and is well versed in technical medical points. **Strengths:** "He's got a fabulous client manner – what they really like about him is that he distils really complex legal arguments into very straightforward advice in plain English." **Recent work:** Successfully acted for the claimant in Hayton v Iggesund Paperboard, a case concerning the claimant's noise-induced hearing loss.

12 King's Bench Walk

See profile on p.872

THE SET

12 King's Bench Walk comes highly recommended and is described as "the gold standard of chambers for personal injury work." It offers an almost unparalleled bench of leading juniors and silks who accept instructions from both claimant and defendant clients. Its members are equally as well versed in catastrophic injury cases as they are in industrial disease work.

Client service: The "excellent" clerks are widely praised for being "efficient and very approachable." One client highlights the fact that "you can pick up the phone, tell them your problem and they'll sort it out for you almost immediately. They'll always work to fit you in, even when they're busy." Graham Johnson leads the clerking team.

SILKS

Frank Burton QC (see p.608) Widely considered to be one of the best claimant silks, he shows equal deftness of touch across the most complex catastrophic personal injury matters and industrial disease claims. He has appeared in numerous high-profile cases and has a fantastic reputation among both peers and clients. **Strengths:** "Sheer genius." "He's unbelievable, he's amazing. Completely trustworthy, fantastic with clients and utterly charming." "He's astoundingly personable, and as such he builds fantastic client relationships. He pushes boundaries without presenting unnecessary risk – everything you expect from a top QC." **Recent work:** Secured victory in the Supreme Court in Knauer v Ministry of Justice. This precedent-setting matter decided that the multiplier for future loss is calculated from the date of trial, not the date of the claimant's death.

Andrew Hogarth QC (see p.673) Receives near-universal acclaim for his mixed claimant/defendant practice, with market-leading expertise in occupational stress and employers' liability disputes. He is also highly experienced in industrial disease and catastrophic injury cases. **Strengths:** "Someone who is immensely skilled and knowledgeable." "He's a very tough negotiator, highly intelligent, and produces excellent results in difficult cases." **Recent work:** Appeared before the Court of Appeal on behalf of the defendant in Thompson v Thompson. The case concerned the calculation of multipliers for damages.

Paul Russell QC (see p.757) Continues to handle premium cases for insurer and defendant clients facing large-loss claims and complex issues of quantum or liability. A silk whose star continues to rise, he has experience in a wide range of personal injury matters and is known for offering clients a "Rolls-Royce service." **Strengths:** "He's absolutely brilliant and engenders absolute respect." "He's as bright as you'd expect a leader at the Bar to be; he's calm, to the point and technically brilliant." **Recent work:** Defended in Knibbs v Rai, a case in which the claimant suffered brachial plexus, head and spinal injuries.

Stephen Worthington QC (see p.800) An extremely highly regarded defendant practitioner, it comes as no surprise that he is the preferred counsel for numerous leading motor insurers. He regularly represents clients in large-loss and catastrophic injury defences and in cases that are policy and precedent-setting. **Strengths:** "He has a vast wealth of experience in terms of MIB work and he's a go-to person for CAT loss cases from a motor perspective." "He's incredibly user-friendly and excellent on liability and quantum."

William Featherby QC (see p.643) Regularly represents clients in high-value personal injury matters, with a focus on brain and psychiatric injuries. He is praised for his formidable courtroom abilities and is a noted specialist for contempt of court and fraud cases. **Strengths:** "He's a fearsome advocate and a very powerful representative." "He's great on strategy, really brilliant." **Recent work:** Represented a youth professional footballer in Hamed v Mills and Tottenham Hotspur Ltd. The claim was brought against the football club's doctor and a cardiologist for failing to spot a pre-existing heart condition which caused the claimant to collapse and suffer catastrophic brain damage during his first match for the football club.

Richard Methuen QC (see p.716) Personal injury practitioner who defends claims on behalf of insurance clients facing large-loss litigation, with deep expertise in road traffic and head injury cases. Boasts a market-leading mediation and arbitration practice. **Strengths:** "He is calm, fiercely clever and quite brilliant on complex quantum." "He's willing to take on more difficult cases than many would, and has achieved some fantastic results over the years."

Ronald Walker QC (see p.788) Provides his clients with a service of the highest quality in both personal injury and industrial disease matters. He is known to be a thorough and fearless litigator who commands wide respect at the Bar. **Strengths:** "He's a go-to because he has a thorough understanding of the issues involved and the complexities of industrial disease. Great at the big picture." "For a QC he is amazingly accessible and provides straightforward advice, which is highly reassuring for the client. He leaves no stone unturned and considers everything."

William Audland QC (see p.586) Has an impressively broad practice that includes catastrophic, brain and spinal injuries in addition to cross-border claims. He is equally comfortable with complicated quantum or liability disputes. **Strengths:** "He's got an extremely forensic approach to evidence and finds solutions very effectively." "He's a fighter when it's appropriate, but he's also personable and good with clients. He prepares meticulously." **Recent work:** Acted for the insurer in Gurung v Gurung, a £4 million claim. The case concerned the father of a young Nepalese family who suffered catastrophic injuries and, as a result, was wheelchair-bound, but did not have permanent leave to remain in the UK.

Harry Steinberg QC (see p.772) Recently appointed silk who has carved out an incredibly impressive name for himself at the industrial disease and catastrophic Personal Injury Bar. He boasts an exhaustive knowledge of asbestos disease issues and makes regular appearances before the Supreme Court. **Strengths:** "He is superb on his feet and his written work is out of this world. He cuts out all of the nonsense." "In terms of his knowledge and advocacy, he's second to none." "He's incredibly clever and willing to take on cases involving particularly difficult points of law." **Recent work:** Acted in the Supreme Court case of Knauer v Ministry of Justice, successfully arguing that damages multipliers should be calculated from the date of trial not the date of the claimant's death.

JUNIORS

Henry Charles (see p.615) Represents claimants and defendants in the most significant and complex of injury claims, with specific expertise in psychiatric injuries, brain injuries and workplace stress. Sources praise his ability to efficiently and effectively handle the largest cases. **Strengths:** "He's excellent, really good with the clients, great on his feet and provides meticulous attention to detail. He's also very supportive, helpful and flexible in terms of contact hours." **Recent work:** Appeared in the Robertson inquest, an investigation into the deaths of two young women who were volunteering with Lattitude Global Volunteering in South Africa.

Nigel Lewers (see p.700) Has developed expertise across a variety of personal injury matters and is an experienced representative of both claimants and high-profile insurer clients. He is noted for his adroit handling of claims involving complex spinal injuries and industrial disease cases. **Strengths:** "He gets to very difficult causation points and he doesn't get flustered; the clients absolutely love him." "He's a master technician, very thorough and very meticulous." **Recent work:** Acted for the defence in Polidano v Balfour Beatty Rail, a case concerning a rail worker whose leg was amputated as a result of a severe railway accident.

David Sanderson (see p.758) A highly regarded practitioner with a loyal client following, he routinely acts for both sides in high-value brain and spinal injury cases. He is widely praised for his able handling of complex liability disputes and grasp of technical evidence. **Strengths:** "He's first-rate and his advocacy is excellent, judges absolutely love him."

Patrick Vincent (see p.787) Enjoys a stellar reputation among both defendant and claimant clients for his adept handling of high-value brain and spinal injury cases. He is singled out for his keen eye for detail and grasp of technical insurance issues. **Strengths:** "Very clever, able to absorb a lot of information and distil it down to focus on the salient points very quickly. He's very good on his feet and is a brilliant advocate." "He's one of the top counsel for motor policy work."

Catherine Brown (see p.604) Widely recognised for her broad expertise and delicate handling of psychiatric injury, stress at work and sexual abuse claims. She regularly defends educational institutions and council bodies and is an experienced actor in complicated liability disputes. **Strengths:** "She very quickly picks out the key details from vast swathes of information." "She's excellent, a joy to work with." **Recent work:** Acted for the police in ABC v Northumbria Police, a claim for psychiatric injury allegedly caused by the Raoul Moat shootings.

Marcuș Dignum (see p.633) Primarily defends insurance clients in catastrophic injury claims that involve large financial exposure. He focuses on RTAs involving difficult liability, causation and quantum issues. **Strengths:** "He's brilliant on road traffic accident liability and deals with some of the highest-value cases. He's got a good manner and he'll fight when he needs to." "Always keeps his commercial hat on and he'll push for a commercial settlement." **Recent work:** Acted in Michelle Duff v Service Ins. Co., representing the claimant, who had suffered an alleged traumatic brain injury following an RTA. This was a claim for £6.7 million.

Hugh Hamill (see p.662) Regularly receives instructions from insurers and public authorities in catastrophic injury claims. He is an esteemed, leading practitioner in the field of chronic pain and fibromyalgia who is particularly praised for his courtroom prowess. **Strengths:** "His preparation is very good. He is excellent on his feet – a fantastic advocate." "Takes a refreshingly robust approach to cases." **Recent work:** Acted for the defence in Corcoran v Richards. The claimant alleged that a 'near miss' RTA with the defendant triggered their fibromyalgia.

Andrew Roy (see p.756) Has a personal injury practice that continues to grow in scope and stature. He has recently been instructed in complex industrial disease litigation and is an expert on limitation in personal injury claims. **Strengths:** "He's quite happy doing complex brain and spinal cases and frequently appears against QCs. He's very thorough and a good negotiator with confidence in the courtroom. He's someone who's prepared to take risks and go the extra mile for clients on CFAs." **Recent work:** Acted for the claimant in the widely publicised case of Flint v Tittensor. An actor in the television series 'Shameless' allegedly hit the claimant with his car, causing the claimant to go blind in one eye.

Niall Maclean (see p.705) Impressive junior with a growing profile at the Personal Injury Bar. He has experience handling catastrophic and fatal injury claims on behalf of both defendants and claimants, and receives particular praise for his representation of government departments. **Strengths:** "He sets out the entire range of options clearly, leaving clients with no confusion as to what the possible outcomes are. He's fantastic from an evidence-gathering point of view." "His attention to detail is excellent and he's willing to fight fiercely when necessary." **Recent work:** Acted for the defence in Scott v Gavigan, a case in which the claimant had sustained severe injuries as a result of a motorcycle accident.

Outer Temple Chambers

See profile on p.887

THE SET

Outer Temple Chambers is well known for its excellence in travel and cross-border claims, and is described by clients as an "exceptional set for personal injury." Its highly esteemed members routinely take instructions from both claimant and defendant solicitors in an impressive array of matters, with a particular focus on catastrophic injury cases. Its pre-eminent barristers also tackle more specialist areas of personal injury law, including sexual abuse, aviation and industrial disease claims.

Client service: The clerks at Outer Temple Chambers "will move heaven and earth to help you," according to its clients. Paul Barton leads the team and receives praise across the board: "He just makes things happen – he's an excellent clerk, second to none. He never lets you down."

SILKS

Gerard McDermott QC Pre-eminent silk who is one of the finest personal injury barristers on the circuit. He focuses on the largest catastrophic injury cases and routinely acts in precedent-setting, cross-border litigation. He is widely praised for his fantastic track record in particularly unpromising or challenging cases. **Strengths:** "He's excellent. I don't think I've ever seen a better barrister on his feet." "He has the most incredible people skills, everyone loves him." "He's a top operator. His judgement is excellent, he always makes sure he gets the best result for clients." **Recent work:** Appeared in Young v AIG on behalf of a claimant who suffered a heart attack and stroke and was left paraplegic after an RTA.

David Westcott QC Urbane and accomplished personal injury silk who focuses on catastrophic injury, international injury litigation and clinical negligence. He primarily, but not exclusively, acts for claimants, and comes highly recommended for his grasp of highly complex quantum points. **Strengths:** "He's in a different league for technical or cerebral points." "He brings gravitas – he's affable, charming, able to get on well with claimants and respected by both sides of the courtroom." **Recent work:** Successfully resisted appeal on behalf of the the claimant in Thompson v Thompson & Colonial, a claim for damages in Bermuda.

Christopher Wilson-Smith QC (see p.798) Consummate personal injury silk with decades of experience acting for claimants and defendants. His caseload frequently includes maximum severity catastrophic injury claims, often complicated by breaches of duty of care in the subsequent medical treatment of the injuries. **Strengths:** "An excellent advocate on his feet." "He's excellent: excellent judgement, extremely hard worker, does what needs to be done." **Recent work:** Represented a gymnast claimant who fractured their spine while unsupervised, leaving them paralysed, in Jay Young v SGA Productions Limited.

JUNIORS

Nathan Tavares Continues to appear in significant, high-value catastrophic injury cases in which damages often exceed £1 million. He is praised for his impressive command of quantum issues and marked attention to detail. **Strengths:** "He's got real gravitas and is clearly a silk in the making. He's a real technician, a real brain." "He's approachable, thorough and detailed. He gives good, in-depth advice on how to pursue a claim." **Recent work:** Acted in Menendez v Metal Processing Limited on behalf of a claimant whose hands were severed by a metal processing machine.

Eliot Woolf Known for his impressively broad practice which encompasses cross-border and travel claims, catastrophic injury and military accidents. He elicits praise for his forensic approach to complex evidence, particularly when it concerns issues of quantum. **Strengths:** "He's very good and fantastic with clients. Always cool as a cucumber." "He is extremely well prepared and he seems to always know what the other side is thinking – he's always three chess moves ahead, it's amazing."

Alison McCormick Has a claimant-side practice that focuses on industrial disease, spinal and brain injuries and fatal accidents. She is singled out by numerous solicitors for her sensitive handling of matters on behalf of vulnerable clients and for her attention to detail with complex quantum issues. **Strengths:** "She's very calm and measured in the advice that she gives, her advice is always very clear and concise and reasoned." "Her client care skills and bedside manner are superb and really put clients at ease." **Recent work:** Achieved a settlement of £4.2 million for a claimant who sustained a serious spinal injury and was left paraplegic after an RTA.

Matthew Phillips (see p.737) Has an impressive record representing claimants in catastrophic injury and industrial disease cases. Equally well versed in quantum and liability disputes, and offers niche expertise in cases concerning contact sports accidents. **Strengths:** "Well liked, he always provides thorough advice at the appropriate level. He's able to explain the most complex legal issues in the most straightforward manner." "A confident advocate with a keen eye for detail."

Harry Trusted Receives instructions from claimant and defendant solicitors in catastrophic injury cases, with specific expertise in paraplegic, tetraplegic, amputation, serious burns and brain injury matters. He is also applauded for his capable handling of quantum points. **Strengths:** "He's very efficient, very disciplined and has a real sense of urgency – gets on with things promptly and efficiently." "Continues to produce the goods for a loyal client base." **Recent work:** Achieved a settlement of more than £3 million for a claimant who was left tetraplegic following an accident at work in Jay Young v SGA Productions.

James Aldridge RTA and liability specialist with extensive experience in catastrophic, brain and spinal, and psychiatric injury cases. His practice is evenly split between claimant and defendant work. **Strengths:** "Performs well in complex matters; he quickly gets to grips with issues and is good to work with."

Jonathan Hand (see p.663) A leading junior in the niche area of catastrophic injuries caused by equestrian accidents. He is highly regarded for his adroit handling of RTA cases and routinely acts on behalf of both claimant and defendant solicitors in major personal injury and clinical negligence matters. **Strengths:** "His preparation is meticulous. He has a very calm manner and is extremely practical and sensible. Clients love him."

Christopher Kemp Has a broad, predominantly claimant-focused personal injury practice. He offers expertise in matters involving chronic pain, sexual abuse, sporting accidents and brain and spinal injuries. He is noted for his adroit handling of cases in which there is an intersection between clinical negligence and personal injury law. **Strengths:** "Sympathetic with clients, thorough and always adds value. He has excellent medical knowledge and is good with experts." **Recent work:** Acted for a claimant injured at work in Louise Mennell (Alldiss) v Phones 4U Ltd. A minor injury lead to catastrophic chronic pain and psychiatric injury.

Band 2

7BR

See profile on p.814

THE SET

7BR provides expert legal advice and advocacy to claimants and defendants, whether institutions or individuals, in complex, high-value personal injury litigation. Catastrophic brain and spinal injury litigation forms the backbone of the practice, but increasingly the set is considered to be a major player in high-profile historic sexual abuse claims.

Client service: The "first-class" clerking team is led by Mark Waterson. "They are always willing to put themselves out for you, their client care is exceptionally good."

SILKS

Simeon Maskrey QC Leading silk who is heralded as one of the most gifted advocates handling precedent-setting personal injury, clinical negligence and product liability litigation. He routinely acts for both sides, and has a particular focus on maximum severity brain and spinal injury cases. **Strengths:** "He's a force of nature, a very astute and practical litigator." "A standout practitioner, people who encounter him are left in awe." **Recent work:** Appeared on behalf of the claimant in Jack Smith v Mushtaq. The case concerned an RTA which left the claimant with severe brain injuries.

Steven Ford QC Has an outstanding reputation for his defence work in historic sexual abuse cases, an area that forms part of his specialist practice which focuses almost exclusively on psychiatric injuries. He also represents defendants in occupational stress, bullying and harassment matters. His clients are often educational or religious institutions, youth organisations or local authorities. **Strengths:** "He's excellent, he's been involved in some of the most complex and public work in the area and gives great client care." "Very calm and measured, he obviously knows his stuff." **Recent work:** Represented the Scout Association in JL v Archbishop Michael Bowen and Scouts Association. The case considered the meaning of consent in sexual assault claims.

Derek Sweeting QC Widely acclaimed for his personal injury work in the Iraqi Civilian Group Litigation. He is instructed by claimants and defendants in catastrophic injury cases and has considerable experience in group actions. **Strengths:** "Very bright, extremely calm and reassuring."

Adam Weitzman QC One of the leading lights for defendant sexual abuses cases, he is singled out for his robust advocacy and efficient approach. His catastrophic injury practice is exclusively claimant-focused and centres on serious brain and spinal injuries, fatal accidents and amputations. **Strengths:** "He's very pragmatic in terms of finding sensible solutions, great with difficult clients and technically incredibly able." "His cross-examination of experts is sublime." **Recent work:** Acted for the defence in A v Trustees of Watchtower Bible Society, an historic child abuse claim.

JUNIORS

Julian Matthews Accomplished and hugely experienced senior junior who handles catastrophic injury cases of the utmost severity. He primarily acts for defendants and major insurers, offering specific expertise in medically complex brain injuries and RTAs involving significant liability issues. **Strengths:** "He's absolutely superb, able to cut through all the blather and get to the nub of the issue – his gravitas is amazing." "His client-facing skills are excellent, he puts them at ease and talks to them at the appropriate level." **Recent work:** Acted for the defendant in CJM v Vital Pet Products, a case concerning a lorry that struck a cyclist who suffered significant brain and psychiatric injuries.

Simon King Routinely receives instructions from claimants and defendants in catastrophic injury cases. He is highlighted for his masterful cross-examination of expert witnesses and for his thorough analysis of technical evidence. **Strengths:** "Personable, very thorough, good in court and fights his corner fiercely." "He's incredibly experienced in brain and spinal injury cases." **Recent work:** Represented the claimant in Foster v Duff, a case concerning multiple injuries following an RTA. The establishment of health and life expectancy for causation was complicated by the claimant's pre-existing cancer.

Adam Walker (see p.788) Has a rapidly developing personal injury practice that encompasses catastrophic injury and industrial disease matters, among other areas. He routinely acts on behalf of claimants and defendants, and is increasingly sought out by members of the armed forces in personal injury claims brought against the Ministry of Defence. **Strengths:** "He's excellent, extremely thorough and forensic in his approach. A great strategist and an excellent advocate." **Recent work:** Acted for the claimant in Fletcher v Ministry of Defence. The case concerned a soldier who alleged that their noise-induced hearing loss resulted from the MoD's failure to provide adequate hearing protection.

Timothy Meakin His esteemed practice covers a diverse range of personal injury areas, including catastrophic injury, industrial disease and sexual abuse cases. He routinely acts on behalf of insurers and claimants, and is especially well versed in complex employers' liability and workplace injury disputes. **Strengths:** "Very methodical, thorough, analytical and very supportive. Good with clients too." **Recent work:** Appeared on behalf of the claimant in Graham v Commercial Bodyworks Ltd, a high-value workplace injury case that was heard in the Court of Appeal.

1 Chancery Lane

THE SET

1 Chancery Lane is a renowned set brimming with barristers who are experienced in handling high-profile matters for both defendants and claimants. Its strengths lie in catastrophic injury, particularly with regard to maximum severity brain, spinal and psychiatric claims, and industrial disease. The set elicits particular praise for its pragmatic approach to the ongoing legal reforms in personal injury law.

Client service: Clark Chessis leads a team of clerks who receive unanimous praise from the market. "Brilliant, some of the best clerking in the country without a shadow of a doubt." "An excellent team, they always find exactly the right counsel who will fit the bill."

SILKS

Edward Bishop QC Maintains an impressive, multidisciplinary practice comprising catastrophic personal injury, clinical negligence and police law. He is regularly instructed in cases wherein the victim makes allegations against the state regarding its failure to protect against criminal acts. **Strengths:**

"He's terribly bright, intelligent and fantastic with clients. He really rolls his sleeves up and he communicates well." "A very able trial advocate who masters his brief, holds his nerve and delivers when it matters." **Recent work:** Acted for the defence in Williams v Newport Gwent Police and Others, a case where the claimant was shot by her former partner at a hairdressing salon. She alleged that the police force did not properly protect her from attack and claimed damages under common law and the Human Rights Act 1998.

Simon Readhead QC Experienced silk with extensive experience handing complex, high-value catastrophic injury and clinical negligence litigation. He is picked out by numerous clients for his superb schedules and expert handling of difficult quantum and causation issues. **Strengths:** "He deftly handles complex cases and is a very determined, excellent advocate." "Always one step ahead of his opponent."

John Ross QC Head of chambers who receives plaudits from numerous clients for his intellect, manner in court and client skills. He has tremendous experience in catastrophic head injury cases and is noted for his specific expertise in acquired brain injuries. He is routinely instructed by leading claimant solicitors. **Strengths:** "He's sociable, pleasant and impresses clients. You know when barristers are truly heard by the court, and he is." "A brilliant advocate – he's exceptional at pulling out the real issues in what are often very complex pieces of litigation." **Recent work:** Secured £4.3 million in damages for the claimant in Mitchell v Sommerville. His client, a passenger in a vehicle, had suffered a catastrophic acquired brain injury as a result of an RTA.

Andrew Warnock QC Prominent defence counsel for serious historic sexual abuse cases, often involving multiple claimants and famous defendants. He is also a regular feature in the most complex and precedent-setting public liability cases. A go-to choice for many major insurers. **Strengths:** "Probably #1 in terms of developing the law in duty of care." "He is someone who has an excellent academic grasp of the law and an extremely good bedside manner." **Recent work:** Represented the defendant in AAA v British Airways PLC. The case involved multiple child claimants in Kenya and Uganda who were allegedly abused by a BA pilot.

JUNIORS

Matthew Chapman Best known for his work in cross-border personal injury litigation. His leading reputation in this area is built upon his pronounced expertise in English catastrophic personal injury law. He is particularly experienced in RTA claims that involve the MIB. **Strengths:** "He's hugely knowledgeable, a superb advocate, very good with clients and very responsive." **Recent work:** Appeared in Charlie Ireson v MIB on behalf of a child claimant who suffered catastrophic brain injuries in an RTA in Lithuania.

Laura Johnson Has a respected claimant practice focusing on spine and brain injuries. She also routinely acts for the defence in sex abuse, EL/PL and stress at work cases. Clients are consistent in their high praise of her advocacy skill and technical ability. **Strengths:** "Very approachable, good with witnesses, cuts to the chase and is extremely bright."

Angus Piper Routinely instructed by leading defendant solicitors and insurers in complex catastrophic injury cases. He offers notable insight in high-value quantum disputes and receives praise for his robust and forthright approach to courtroom litigation. **Strengths:** "He's very user-friendly, realistic and calm: impressive on his feet." **Recent work:** Secured dismissal, with costs, for the defendant in Roberts v Brighton CC. The claimant suffered head injuries and a heart attack after a cycling accident on council-owned parkland.

Paul Stagg Demonstrates notable skill in catastrophic personal injury cases, particularly those containing state care or EL/PL elements. He acts for both sides in litigation and has extensive experience in defendant-side historic sexual abuse cases. **Strengths:** "He's got a fierce intellect and is very user-friendly." **Recent work:** Acted for the defence in Elgie v Commissioner of Police of the Metropolis. The case concerned a police officer who suffered a serious injury during an exercise, resulting in below-the-knee amputation.

Julian Waters Senior junior with a catastrophic injury practice that includes complex claims involving the Human Rights Act, inquests and the police. He is noted for formidable courtroom presence and strong client skills. **Strengths:** "He's excellent on his feet: I've seen him reduce opponents to quivering wrecks."

Lisa Dobie A respected name at the defendant Personal Injury Bar, she regularly handles inquests and serious injury cases, particularly on behalf of local authorities and other public bodies. She has also developed a claimant-side practice, a recent highlight of which has been her representation of multiple clients in Highways Act claims against Essex County Council. **Strengths:** "She's very accessible, down-to-earth and shows great empathy. On her feet she consistently asks the right questions on behalf of clients." **Recent work:** Successfully represented a defendant foster carer in Nash v Remington. In this case, a baby suffered a fractured pelvis after falling while the carer heated its bottle in the kitchen.

Cloisters

See profile on p.821

THE SET

Cloisters is recognised as a highly significant set in the claimant catastrophic injury market. The chambers houses a bench of both flourishing and well-established advocates who are regular features in some of the most high-profile cases in the sector. Practitioners at the set share a core expertise in brain, spinal and psychiatric injury claims, and are regularly called upon to handle multimillion-pound disputes on behalf of their varied client base.

Client service: Glenn Hudson leads the "superbly efficient and smooth" clerking team.

SILKS

Joel Donovan QC (see p.635) Concentrates on maximum severity psychiatric, spinal and brain injury cases for claimants. His practice includes work in clinical negligence and he is praised by sources for his strategic nous and vast medical knowledge. **Strengths:** "Very good on complex technical issues, he's very supportive and approachable." **Recent work:** Appeared in the Supreme Court on behalf of the appellant in Mohamud v Morrisons Supermarkets, a case considering the vicarious liability of a retailer following a workplace assault committed by one of its employees.

Patricia Hitchcock QC (see p.673) Praised for her reassuring client manner and impressive command of high-end catastrophic injury cases. Her expertise in complex RTAs is lauded, as is her attention to detail and formidable courtroom experience. **Strengths:** "She's very good at brain work, understands the issues and sticks to her guns. She's clear, good with clients and down-to-earth." "She is one of the groundbreaking leaders in the quantum field. Excellent client manner."

William Latimer-Sayer QC (see p.696) Widely considered to be a leading light in the area, his practice is at the cutting edge of personal injury quantum. He receives universal praise for his technical knowledge, empathetic client manner and diligent work ethic. **Strengths:** "He is one of the brightest stars at the personal injury and clinical negligence Bar. He's excellent on the very big cases and has an encyclopaedic knowledge of quantum." "He's just a class apart – he'll fly as a silk." **Recent work:** Acted in Ingham v Bashir, achieving a settlement of more than £5 million for a claimant who suffered tetraplegia following an RTA.

JUNIORS

Daniel Lawson (see p.697) Recognised by the market as a leading claimant junior who often appears unled against silks in complex catastrophic injury, chronic pain and stress at work claims. Clients readily endorse his grasp of employers' liability disputes and matters concerning the police. **Strengths:** "Seeing him in court is incredible. He's an amazing advocate, not a single word is wasted." "An immensely bright, well-prepared barrister." "His attention to detail is fantastic. He gets on incredibly well with clients, turns papers around quickly and is wonderfully passionate." **Recent work:** Represented the claimant in Joshua Senior v Rock UK Adventure Centres Ltd. The claimant sustained a severe spinal cord injury and underwent below-the-knee amputation as a result of equipment failure at the activities centre.

Simon Dyer Focuses on personal injury and clinical negligence for claimants who have suffered catastrophic injuries. His disarming style in joint settlement meetings and negotiations elicits praise from clients, and he is regularly instructed in multimillion-pound claims. **Strengths:** "He puts clients at ease and is a phenomenal performer on his feet." "A go-to guy for high-value claims." **Recent work:** Appeared in Gosford v French on behalf of a claimant who suffered severe brain injuries after being knocked off his motorbike.

1 Crown Office Row

See profile on p.826

THE SET

1 Crown Office Row houses an "eminent team of fantastic personal injury practitioners," market sources attest. Its respected members handle defendant and claimant catastrophic injury litigation of the highest standard, and are frequently instructed in cases with complex issues of medical causation. The set is particularly well known for its experience and expertise in historic child abuse cases, an area of specialism that routinely sees its members appearing in high-profile actions such as the Mau Mau litigation and cases related to Jimmy Savile, Grafton House Children's Home and the Elm Guest House.

Client service: Senior clerk Matthew Phipps leads the clerking team. "They're utterly great, always friendly and co-operative." "Just brilliant, really responsive and effective."

SILKS

Elizabeth-Anne Gumbel QC Commands universal respect for her unrelenting work ethic, mastery of personal injury law and total devotion to her cases. Her practice focuses on claimant-side, maximum severity catastrophic injury matters, group actions and sexual abuse work. **Strengths:** "She's hugely compassionate with clients and passionate about getting the right results. She has an incredible legal brain." "She's willing to take on Herculean legal tasks in very complex cases, and she's successful in it." "She is just phenomenal, she's got a brain the size of the Shard and works extremely hard on behalf of her clients."

Henry Witcomb QC An advocate of tremendous renown given his compelling advocacy in complex group actions and historic sexual abuse claims. He is a leading clinical negligence practitioner and is well versed in catastrophic personal injury claims. He acts for defendants and claimants and receives praise for his sensitive approach in matters concerning vulnerable clients. **Strengths:** "He is extremely good with clients, creative and provides really innovative solutions. A brilliant negotiator." "There aren't many words to describe him other than superb. You can always trust him to take a holistic approach to the case and look at the bigger picture." **Recent work:** Acted on behalf of the estate in Various Claimants v Estate of Sir James Savile under the instruction of Savile's professional executor.

JUNIORS

Justin Levinson Leading senior junior for claimant-side child abuse litigation. He has an exceptional reputation and practically unrivalled experience in claims against the Anglican and Catholic churches. He routinely represents clients in actions brought against nearly every class of defendant, including individuals, educational institutions, social services departments, schools, care homes and youth organisations. **Strengths:** "He is excellent, probably the preeminent practitioner in the field. Very able on his feet and in court and has an excellent manner all round. You couldn't wish for a better advocate." **Recent work:** Acted for the claimant in the unique case of ABC v West Heath 2000 Limited. Legal precedent was set in this case, which concerned an underage pupil who was encouraged by her teacher to take and send indecent images of herself.

Robert Kellar Has a wide-ranging personal injury practice with an emphasis on abuse litigation and cases concerning military accidents. He takes instructions from defendants and claimants and often represents the Ministry of Defence and other government departments. **Strengths:** "I find him very easy to deal with, very pragmatic and a good communicator. He always turns things around on time." **Recent work:** Represented the MoD in a claim brought under the Fatal Accidents Act 1976, Griffiths v Ministry of Defence. The case concerned the death of a soldier who was accidentally shot during an army exercise.

Devereux

See profile on p.827

THE SET

Devereux continues to be instructed by leading claimant firms for high-value personal injury cases. Its valued members provide expert guidance in catastrophic, psychiatric and fatal injury matters, and regularly appear in the appellate courts litigating the most legally challenging cases.

Client service: Director Vince Plant's clerks are described as "personable, affable, efficient, pragmatic and very user-friendly."

SILKS

Robert Weir QC (see p.792) Towering presence at the Personal Injury Bar and one of the most respected and successful barristers in the market. He is regularly instructed by leading claimant and defendant solicitors in maximum severity catastrophic brain and spinal injury cases. **Strengths:** "Absolutely top-notch. He really is gold-standard." "He's got a massive intellect." "His approach is incredibly precise. He provides fantastic and realistic advice and is able to push the boundaries." **Recent work:** Represented an employee of the prison service who was injured by a prisoner in the Supreme Court case Cox v Ministry of Justice.

Robert Glancy QC (see p.653) Masterful advocate and vastly experienced personal injury specialist. His caseload is full of claimant instructions for the most life-changing brain and spinal injury cases. He is one of the first arbitrators for the recently established Personal Injury claims Arbitration Service. **Strengths:** "He's awesome. As a court advocate he is phenomenal, a real tour de force." "He's brilliant with clients, they love him."

Stephen Killalea QC (see p.691) Has an outstanding reputation in maximum severity spinal injury cases and for his adroit handling of the most complex liability disputes for claimants who have suffered life-changing injuries. He receives plaudits for his excellent client care, powerful advocacy and standout negotiation skill. **Strengths:** "He's very affable and great with clients. He's a real street fighter and very tenacious." "He's very approachable, highly intelligent and a ferocious cross-examiner." "Just the most persuasive advocate." **Recent work:** Appeared in Bridie Young (by her Mother and Litigation Friend Frances Young) v Goldern Coast Sporting Villas Limited. Represented the claimant, who suffered a brain injury when she was nine years old after falling off a zip wire in a pub garden. A settlement of £3.5 million was reached.

JUNIORS

Bruce Silvester (see p.765) Hugely experienced senior junior with an enviable caseload of multimillion-pound catastrophic injury instructions, predominantly from claimant solicitors. Sources value his ability to be very direct in his dealings with the opposition while remaining entirely sympathetic and approachable for the client. **Strengths:** "Very calm, very confident in his own abilities, not afraid of difficult cases." "Incredibly tenacious and single-minded in his pursuit of the client's objectives. He is very creative and always prepared to think outside the box." **Recent work:** Represented the claimant in David O'Mahoney v Derek Stratton. A trooper in the Household Cavalry was struck by the defendant's taxi and suffered near-fatal brain injuries. Achieved £1.5 million at a joint settlement meeting.

Richard Cartwright (see p.612) Brings an attention to detail that few can match and is regularly instructed in complex quantum disputes. His practice focuses on claimant-side catastrophic injury and clinical negligence litigation. **Strengths:** "He's rated extremely highly, he just gets it." "Very organised, excellent client skills." **Recent work:** Appeared for the claimant in Amy Werner v Geoffrey Lederman. The matter concerned an elderly driver who injured nine pedestrians, one of whom was an American student who suffered brain damage and lost sight in one eye.

Colin Mendoza (see p.716) Handles the full spectrum of personal injury work for both claimants and defendants, with significant expertise in life-changing brain and spinal injuries, catastrophic psychiatric injuries and amputations. He comes particularly recommended for handling complex quantum issues. **Strengths:** "He's a junior in name only. He's very good with clients, he puts them at ease, he prepares well for conferences and doesn't need anyone holding his hand." "Pragmatic and provides sensible solutions."

Peter Edwards (see p.639) Routinely appears in high-profile inquests and maximum severity catastrophic injury cases. His employment law practice complements his personal injury offering, especially in complex EL/PL disputes and quantum calculations. **Strengths:** "He's excellent. If it's a difficult case he'll handle it with absolute aplomb." **Recent work:** Acted for the claimant in a 25-day inquest investigating whether the police used excessive force when arresting the deceased in Jordan Begley (deceased) v Greater Manchester Police.

Robert Hunter (see p.678) Instructed by numerous leading claimant solicitors for catastrophic injury cases. He is best known for his excellent work in fatal accident matters and for his expert handling of the unique quantum issues associated with such cases. Clients particularly praise his work ethic, bedside manner and schedules. **Strengths:** "Fiercely intelligent and a great tactician." **Recent work:** Appeared in Hicks v Young on behalf of the claimant. The case concerned catastrophic brain injuries sustained by the client after jumping out of a moving taxi.

Temple Garden Chambers

See profile on p.919

THE SET

Temple Garden Chambers provides high-calibre personal injury representation to claimants, defendants and insurers. Its notably deep bench of highly skilled practitioners offers experience across the full spectrum of catastrophic injury cases, in addition to notable expertise in chronic pain, subtle brain injury and military claims.

Client service: Dean Norton's clerking team comes highly recommended. "The clerks are absolutely fantastic. They're absolutely reliable and remove stress for the client."

SILKS

Simon Browne QC Noted for expertise in catastrophic brain and spine injuries, which he regularly handles on behalf of major insurers and leading claimant solicitors. Over the course of his celebrated career, he has also developed a strong reputation for aviation accidents, clinical negligence cases and cross-border litigation. **Strengths:** "He was very good with the clients and very efficient. A pleasure to instruct." "He's very smooth. Clients like him, he's approachable." **Recent work:** Acted for the defence in Abdulah Alasow v Redcorn Limited. The case concerned a five year old boy who lost his leg after being run over by a lorry.

Jonathan Watt-Pringle QC (see p.791) Receives instructions from defendants, insurers and claimants in catastrophic brain and spinal injury cases. His practice includes health and safety, clinical and professional negligence and inquests. Market commentators particularly highlight his meticulous attention to detail. **Strengths:** "He has incredible verve and a rare ability to think about all elements of a case and bring something new to the table every time. His technical ability and commerciality are great." "I'd use him without hesitation, he's incredibly likeable on top of being very clever." **Recent work:** Represented the claimant in JX MX v AX SX, a case involving a 16 year old claimant who suffered catastrophic brain injuries and spastic tetraplegia after an RTA. Settled for a lump sum of £4.35 million.

JUNIORS

Marcus Grant (see p.658) A pioneer in the areas of complex subtle brain injury and chronic pain syndrome. He has been at the cutting edge of fibromyalgia litigation for many years, and is a vigorous advocate for its recognition by courts and insurers. His tremendous medical knowledge and unwavering commitment are singled out by solicitors, while he is also instructed by insurers for committal proceedings for dishonest litigants. **Strengths:** "A brain the size of a planet, incredible on his feet and a lethal cross-examiner." "At the forefront of the field. Not only does he have an absolutely first-class intellect, he is engaging and a real pleasure to work with. He is a master tactician and an outstanding advocate." "Very approachable, clients are at ease with him." **Recent work:** Appeared in Kashif v Simpson on behalf of a claimant who developed a chronic pain syndrome following a low-speed car crash.

Peter Freeman Top-performing counsel for claimant and defendant solicitors seeking detailed advice and robust advocacy in catastrophic injury cases, particularly RTAs. His clients praise his prowess both in the courtroom and at joint settlement meetings, and he is frequently instructed in cases involving aviation and sporting accidents. **Strengths:** "He's extremely user-friendly and has incredible empathy." "Go-to counsel for complex and catastrophic personal injury matters, he's extremely approachable and very realistic in terms of what can be achieved."

John Bate-Williams (see p.592) Veteran catastrophic personal injury and fatal accident practitioner with extensive experience handling maximum severity cases. He is primarily instructed by defendant insurers but has increasingly been sought out by claimant solicitors in a range of areas, including aviation catastrophes. **Strengths:** "Always willing to go the extra mile – gets to the heart of problems quickly and presents innovative but realistic solutions." "Superb negotiator, he provides wonderful attention to detail and excellent client skills."

James Bell Has a highly reputable, mixed claimant and defendant personal injury and clinical negligence practice, with a focus on catastrophic injuries. He is noted for his experience in cross-border matters and EL/PL cases. **Strengths:** "You don't need a QC with a junior of his ability." "He's very practical, can give a great academic legal answer and can then translate that into practical steps for implementation. He has a very good bedside manner with clients." **Recent work:** Acted for the defence in Lucchesi v Kelly, a highly complex fibromyalgia claim.

James Laughland Has a multidisciplinary practice focusing on personal injury and costs litigation. He is instructed by claimants and insurers alike, often in cases involving allegations of fraud or dishonesty. He is particularly praised by clients for his tact and clarity. **Strengths:** "He tailors his advice to the client. A very good advocate, very well prepared and very good tactically." **Recent work:** Acted for the defence in Paul Brown v Logoplaste Limited, a case in which the claimant suffered a minor blow to the head and subsequently developed temporary paraplegia, requiring a hospital stay of six weeks and a spinal fusion operation. The claimant had an undiagnosed congenital spine defect making him susceptible to such trauma.

Richard Wilkinson (see p.795) Consummate professional who is mainly instructed by large insurers in catastrophic injury, fatal accident and costs cases. His experience in chronic pain litigation is particularly noteworthy, as is his expert handling of employers' liability disputes. **Strengths:** "He's very calm and very forensic. He's always thinking of the counterarguments and he's always prepared to fight fiercely when necessary. Clients like him as he's very down-to-earth." **Recent work:** Defended both parties in Kaufhold v (1) Gough (2) Aviva Insurance. The claimant advanced a £1.4 million claim for chronic pain brought on by an RTA. The matter settled for £263,000 pre-trial.

Dominic Adamson Splits his time between representing defendant and claimant clients in catastrophic injury litigation as well as handling dishonest injury claims for insurers. He is known for his specialist product liability and health and safety expertise. **Strengths:** "I rate him highly, he's very experienced but he's also hugely client-focused and brings a huge amount of comfort to them." **Recent work:** Acted for the defence in Cardarello v John Atwell & Others, a case in which the claimant was in three RTAs. He claimed in excess of £5.7 million and recovered less than £40,000.

Paul Kilcoyne Concentrates on representing claimants who have suffered catastrophic injuries and is a leading choice for clients bringing claims against the Ministry of Defence. His expertise in representing members of the armed forces comes highly praised by numerous instructing solicitors. **Strengths:** "He's first-rate and very proactive. His advice is always concise and to the point, he's good in conference and a brilliant negotiator." "Clients like him because he speaks their language, which is so important for clients in the military." **Recent work:** Acted in Soni Mills v Ministry of Defence on behalf of a claimant who suffered spinal injuries after participating in a 'team building' exercise in the Officers' Mess.

2TG – 2 Temple Gardens

See profile on p.920

THE SET

2 Temple Gardens houses a deep roster of well-known personal injury practitioners. Its members routinely provide expert advice to both claimants and defendants, and continue to be a particularly popular choice for major insurers. The set's specialisms include catastrophic injuries, occupational stress and bullying, travel personal injury, chronic pain and industrial disease.

Client service: The clerks, led by Lee Tyler, are described as "slick, efficient and seamless." "They are very impressive: always helpful and accommodating."

SILKS

Benjamin Browne QC (see p.605) Acts for both claimants and defendants and continues to enjoy a particularly stellar reputation among insurers. Catastrophic brain and spinal injuries make up the bulk of his personal injury practice. He is also expert in cases concerning serious injuries suffered abroad. **Strengths:** "A pleasure to be against, never misses a trick, he's really first-rate." "Meticulous with his paperwork and extremely approachable."

Martin Porter QC (see p.740) One of the leading claimant's counsel for personal injury litigation concerning cycling accidents. He also represents both defendants and insurers in serious brain and spinal injury, clinical negligence and occupational stress cases. **Strengths:** "He's great in negotiations and is exceptionally thorough. He gives people a great feeling of confidence, which is exactly what you want in leading counsel."

JUNIORS

Nina Goolamali (see p.657) A well-respected junior with an impressive defendant-side caseload composed primarily of maximum severity catastrophic injury cases. She often appears as sole counsel against silks in complex disputes. Her broad expertise covers areas such as sports accidents, with a particular emphasis on motor sports, and cases concerning EL/PL. **Strengths:** "One of the most knowledgeable and personable barristers around, she's ridiculously clever." "Incredibly user-friendly, handles the opposition well. Good with clients and good on her feet." **Recent work:** Acted on behalf of the defendant in Buswell v Symes & Motor Insurers Bureau, a £1 million claim concerning an RTA.

Roger Harris (see p.665) Although best known for his defendant-side practice, he is also a highly proficient representative of claimant clients. He is a regular feature in complex catastrophic injury cases and also regularly handles matters concerning occupational stress and harassment. **Strengths:** "He's technically brilliant, a catastrophic injury specialist." "Incredibly charming and doesn't get fazed or agitated with opponents, even in difficult cases." **Recent work:** Appeared for the respondent in Mohamud v Wm Morrison PLC, a case considering whether a retailer ought to be vicariously liable if one of its employees assaults a customer.

John McDonald (see p.712) Highly experienced in both personal injury and industrial disease cases, he has a particularly strong occupational stress, bullying and harassment practice. He has been instructed in arbitrations across Europe and Africa and elicits praise for his exhaustive case preparation. **Strengths:** "He's excellent: incredibly prompt, pragmatic and very astute when it comes to risk management."

Christopher Russell (see p.757) Esteemed practitioner who counts an impressive range of high-profile defendant law firms and major insurers among his clientele. He receives enthusiastic praise for his skilled handling of joint settlement meetings and for his masterful cross-examination of witnesses. **Strengths:** "Very intelligent, he is an excellent advocate who holds his own against any leading silk in the personal injury field." "He's not an aggressive cross-examiner. In court, there's more of the rapier than the cudgel about him."

Anna Hughes (see p.677) A junior with a flourishing personal injury practice. She has experience in complicated liability disputes and serious injury cases, and a particular flair for quantum issues. She routinely appears on behalf of defendant clients in cases concerning suspected fraudulent claims. **Strengths:** "She's my preferred counsel when I need someone robust and forensic. She can deconstruct a claimant's claim without getting flustered in the face of resistance." **Recent work:** Successfully represented the applicant in Royal & Sun Alliance PLC v Fahad. In this case, the respondent had brought a fraudulent claim for damages against the applicant, which was dismissed.

Band 3

Doughty Street Chambers

See profile on p.828

THE SET

Doughty Street Chambers is a progressive set housing personal injury and industrial disease advocates with a particularly strong reputation for civil liberties work. Its esteemed members regularly receive instructions from both claimants and defendants. The chambers is well known for handling group actions, often involving faulty medical products, trade unions or migrant workers.

Client service: "The clerking is really good, they go the extra mile to get things sorted." "They're some of the friendliest clerks, they can't do enough for you." The clerking team is led by Kevin Kelly.

SILKS

Robin Oppenheim QC Prominent silk with broad civil expertise that includes personal injury, clinical negligence, and a market-leading product liability practice. He primarily handles catastrophic brain and spinal injury cases and complex group actions. **Strengths:** "He really is superb." "He really is a cut above."

JUNIORS

Daniel Bennett Robust personal injury and industrial disease specialist who routinely accepts instructions from claimant solicitors. He is well known for his adroit handling of complex and unusual employers' liability cases. Clients praise his tenacity and pragmatism, while his prior experience as a personal injury solicitor informs his burgeoning practice. **Strengths:** "He's very brave, he's on the ball, he gets it. He's very good with clients and can be aggressive in court because he knows the law inside out." **Recent work:** Appeared on behalf of the deceased's family in the inquest of a worker who died after falling from a great height in Ansquer (Maxwell Deceased) v Cooper B-Line Limited.

Gerwyn Samuel Highly respected and sought-after senior junior with great experience in maximum severity brain and spinal injury cases. He demonstrates further proficiency in particularly high-value claims and quantum disputes. **Strengths:** "He's sharp, inventive, strong on tactics and extremely thorough." "Excellent grasp of the medicine and a total understanding of the complex needs of clients. Prepared to push legal boundaries where necessary." **Recent work:** Represented the claimant in Reece Clarke v Chief Constable of Essex, a case that settled for a £5 million lump sum and £225,000 periodical payments. The claimant had suffered catastrophic injuries leaving him tetraplegic and with severe cognitive impairment.

Farrar's Building

See profile on p.843

THE SET

Farrar's Building is a set with a long-standing reputation for its high-quality representation of both claimant and defendant clients. It also remains a favoured chambers for household names in the insurance market. Its members are experts in catastrophic injury, dishonest or fraudulent claims, policy litigation and industrial disease.

Client service: Senior clerk Alan Kilbey's team "work like clockwork." "They are realistic on fees and very accommodating."

SILKS

Alan Jeffreys QC (see p.683) Distinguished catastrophic injury silk with a practice that encompasses maximum severity and large-loss brain and spine injuries. He routinely acts on behalf of insurers, public authorities and private defendants. His expertise in complex liability disputes is especially noteworthy. **Strengths:** "He's among the top silks for major catastrophic injury work." "Quiet, cerebral, and when he talks you listen. He's got a very powerful way of putting his view across without antagonising people."

JUNIORS

Lee Evans (see p.642) A leading senior junior who has an incredibly impressive caseload of numerous, multimillion-pound, maximum severity catastrophic injury cases. He is a natural choice for the leading road traffic insurers and industry players. Clients commend his accomplished grasp of both complex liability and quantum disputes. **Strengths:** "Has a great, down-to-earth manner which means he gets along well with both witnesses and insurers." "His attention to detail is really second to none and he's not scared of getting his hands dirty." "I think he's fantastic, he's an all-court player and he's really going places." **Recent work:** Appeared for the defence in Searle v London Bus Company, a case involving a city solicitor who was hit by a bus.

Andrew Wille (see p.795) Accepts instructions from both claimants and defendants in his specialist area of life-changing brain and spinal injuries. He is also routinely involved in amputation cases and matters concerning serious accidents involving animals. **Strengths:** "He's really good with clients, an excellent communicator and really good at achieving the desired outcome." **Recent work:** Acted for the claimant in Spencer v Terry. The claimant had been thrown off her horse after being chased by the defendant's dog.

Old Square Chambers

See profile on p.886

THE SET

Old Square Chambers provides expert counsel to a diverse range of clients. The set is continuing to develop its defendant and insurer practice, having already established itself as a highly proficient claimant chambers. Its members handle the full range of personal injury claims, and have expertise in catastrophic brain and spine injuries, occupational diseases, accidents at work and employers' liability.

Client service: "Their whole package is very good, from point of contact to the end of the case." "Value for money is outstanding." William Meade leads the clerking team.

SILKS

Paul Rose QC (see p.755) Highly experienced silk offering expertise across catastrophic injury cases and complex employment litigation. He regularly receives instructions from leading claimant solicitors, and is particularly well known for his proficiency in complex liability disputes and military claims. **Strengths:** "Incredible eye for detail, he's excellent." "He's extremely thorough and he's got a very nice manner with clients."

Jane McNeill QC (see p.713) Established silk who is a go-to for claimant solicitors seeking counsel in catastrophic injury cases, especially when they overlap with employment law. Her caseload has included high-value RTAs, abuse cases and fatal accident claims. **Strengths:** "She's someone you want on your side, a fearsome opponent." "Hugely client-friendly." "She's always pragmatic and not afraid to take on difficult cases."

JUNIORS

Charles Woodhouse (see p.800) Robust defence advocate who regularly appears unled against leading silks for claimants or defendants in catastrophic injury litigation. He is noted for his expertise in amputation and chronic pain cases and has experience representing military personnel in claims against the Ministry of Defence. **Strengths:** "Commanding in court, with a good presence and an astute appreciation of where the strengths of a case lie." "Sharp legal brain who gives clear advice. He's sympathetic but measured when advising clients. Very approachable and likeable." **Recent work:** Acted for the defence in Doyle v Papamichael, a case in which the claimant had suffered serious leg injuries requiring multiple surgeries.

David Rivers (see p.752) Handles a broad range of personal injury claims, with notable expertise in complex quantum and employers' liability disputes. His claimant-focused practice comes highly recommended by sources who are keen to highlight his in-depth understanding of technical evidence and difficult legal points. **Strengths:** "He's excellent. He's willing to take on risky cases under CFAs, he's timely with his advice and it's always very clear." **Recent work:** Represented the claimant in Moreton v Dreamworks, a case concerning a complex spinal injury which was further complicated by underlying spondylosis.

Christopher Walker (see p.788) Personal injury specialist who focuses on catastrophic brain and spinal injuries, amputations and fatal accidents. Receives instructions from claimant and defendant solicitors and is particularly praised for his adroit handling of employers' liability disputes. **Strengths:** "He's really good with clients, has a great manner and really puts them at ease. He's very bright." "Extraordinarily calm and very charming."

Other Ranked Lawyers

Richard Furniss (42 Bedford Row) Knowledgeable senior junior who comes highly recommended by clients for catastrophic personal injury and professional and clinical negligence cases. His lateral thinking is praised by instructing solicitors, as is his polished management of difficult negotiations. He is also experienced in inquests and Court of Protection matters. **Strengths:** "He has an uncanny ability to zero in on key issues in an instant, giving clarity and focus to the most complex matters, without sacrificing attention to detail. He has phenomenal intellect, immense knowledge and vast wisdom." **Recent work:** Acted for the claimant in Wastell v Chaucer Insurance Services. In this case, the claimant was on a motorbike that collided with a negligent pedestrian, who died, and left the claimant with serious injuries.

Richard Gregory (42 Bedford Row) Recognised for his abilities in catastrophic injury and costs litigation on behalf of claimant clients. He has deep knowledge of the Fatal Accidents Act and vast experience in industrial disease cases, lower limb amputations and complex spinal injuries claims. **Strengths:** "Fantastic attention to detail and you can always rely on his technical expertise." "He is well prepared, confident and capable."

Scott Matthewson (42 Bedford Row) Receives instructions in high-value fatal accident and catastrophic injury cases for an even split of defendant and claimant solicitors. He has experience in high-profile public liability litigation, often involving the armed forces or the police, and in complex RTAs, with specific expertise in motorcycle accidents. **Strengths:** "He's incredible in terms of knowledge and experience." "He's very good, very personable and has a lovely manner with clients. He's an excellent advocate." "Extremely diligent with a profoundly strong knowledge of statute and common law." **Recent work:** Represented the claimant in Campbell v Ministry of Justice, a case concerning a prison officer who sustained a severe brain injury following multiple incidences of prisoner violence.

Dominic Nolan QC (see p.728) (Hailsham Chambers) Recognised for his assiduous care of both lay and insurer clients and his able handling of multimillion-pound catastrophic injury claims. He primarily represents defendants and is experienced across the most serious RTAs and psychiatric injury cases. **Strengths:** "He's premier league, he's really good." "He has a very brilliant brain. He prepares extremely thorough advice and takes a highly pragmatic approach."

Julian Picton QC (see p.738) (Hailsham Chambers) Defendant-focused practitioner who routinely handles high-value catastrophic injury cases, with a particular emphasis on RTAs, and professional negligence matters. He offers expert insight into highly complex quantum issues and has authored a leading textbook on the subject. **Strengths:** "He has a wonderfully crisp style and is unquestionably intelligent."

Charles Bagot (Hardwicke) Leading senior junior with an excellent reputation for personal injury litigation. He has developed a practice, primarily acting for defendants and insurers, that focuses on catastrophic injury, psychiatric shock and allegations of fraud. He is particularly lauded for his expert knowledge of quantum and for his exceptional technical ability. **Strengths:** "He's tremendously technically gifted, really first-class." "He is dogged in his approach and has one of the sharpest minds I've ever seen, his ability to analyse a case forensically and with a human touch is incredible." "He just always delivers, he's absolutely immaculate." **Recent work:** Appeared in the Court of Appeal in Padley v CDI Anderselite Ltd for the appellant. The case investigated whether it is an abuse of process to reissue a second identical claim where a first claim has been struck out for breach of an 'unless order'.

Howard Stevens QC (3 Hare Court) Tackles a diverse range of catastrophic injury cases and cross-border litigation for both claimant and defendant clients. His vast appellate experience and calm, collected approach to joint settlement meetings and negotiations were praised by sources. **Strengths:** "He is great, down-to-earth and deals with everything in his stride." "He is massively thorough and is a very calm, reasoned advocate."

Nicholas Baldock (6 Pump Court) Handles work for both claimants and defendants in cases involving life-changing brain injuries, amputations and chronic pain syndromes. He is regularly instructed by clients in the Channel Islands and has a particular interest in sports accidents. **Strengths:** "He is very level-headed and pragmatic, measured and thoughtful."

ALL CIRCUITS Industrial Disease

Personal Injury: Industrial Disease
Leading Silks
Burton Frank *12 King's Bench Walk (ORL)* ◊ *
Kent Michael *Crown Office Chambers (ORL)* ◊
Limb Patrick *Ropewalk Chambers (ORL)* ◊ *
Melton Christopher *Byrom Street Chambers (ORL)* ◊ *
Platt David *Crown Office Chambers (ORL)* ◊
Rawlinson Michael *Kings Chambers (ORL)* ◊ *
Adams Jayne *Ropewalk Chambers (ORL)* ◊ *
Kilvington Simon *Byrom Street Chambers (ORL)* ◊ *
Steinberg Harry *12 King's Bench Walk (ORL)* ◊ *
Leading Juniors
Bennett Daniel *Doughty Street Chambers (ORL)* ◊
Bowley Ivan *Lincoln House Chambers (ORL)* ◊
Brace Michael *12 King's Bench Walk (ORL)* ◊ *
Cooper Douglas *Deans Court Chambers (ORL)* ◊ *
Cowan Peter *Oriel Chambers (ORL)* ◊
Feeny Charles *Complete Counsel (ORL)* ◊
Foster Catherine *Crown Office Chambers (ORL)* ◊
Glynn Stephen *9 Gough Square (ORL)* ◊ *
Hiorns Roger *9 Gough Square (ORL)* ◊ *
Levene Simon *12 King's Bench Walk (ORL)* ◊ *
MacPherson Alexander *Crown Office Chambers (ORL)* ◊
McDonald John *2TG - 2 Temple Gardens (ORL)* ◊ [A] *
O'Leary Robert *Crown Office Chambers (ORL)* ◊
Phillips Matthew *Outer Temple Chambers (ORL)* ◊ *
Scott Gemma *12 King's Bench Walk (ORL)* ◊ *
Snowden Steven *Crown Office Chambers (ORL)* ◊ *
Todd James *39 Essex Chambers (ORL)* ◊ *
Williams A John *Crown Office Chambers (ORL)* ◊ *
* *Indicates individual with profile.*
[A] *direct access (see p.24).*
◊ *(ORL) = Other Ranked Lawyer.*
Alphabetical order within each band. Band 1 is highest.

Ranked Lawyers

Alexander MacPherson (Crown Office Chambers) Primarily acts in the defence of clients in significant industrial disease and personal injury cases. He has an impressively deep understanding of areas stretching beyond asbestos diseases, offering enviable expertise in cases involving noise-induced hearing loss and hand-arm vibration syndrome. **Strengths:** "He's a tough yet pleasant opponent." **Recent work:** Secured the dismissal of all claims against his client in Meredith v ADM Services, a case involving allegations of an upper limb disorder caused by vibrating tools.

Michael Brace (see p.601) (12 King's Bench Walk) Has vast experience handling a wide range of cases across the areas of industrial disease, clinical negligence and personal injury. He has a particular focus on asbestos disease claims, specifically those concerning mesothelioma and pleural plaques. **Strengths:** "He's a first port of call for mesothelioma work. He's got a great handle on the principles, an excellent empathetic manner with clients and the academic rigour to get to the heart of things." **Recent work:** Acted for the claimant in Kenneth Henley v Ministry of Defence, a case concerning the exposure of an MoD employee to asbestos at work. During the trial the claimant passed away and damages of almost £300,000 were awarded.

Simon Levene (see p.700) (12 King's Bench Walk) Respected industrial disease and personal injury practitioner bringing decades of experience to the table. He routinely handles high-value claims and is well known for his grasp of complex quantum issues. **Strengths:** "He's a good all-rounder with excellent knowledge of disease work."

Gemma Scott (see p.760) (12 King's Bench Walk) Up-and-coming junior barrister who is widely praised for her adroit handling of industrial disease claims and empathetic bedside manner. She often appears as sole counsel in high-value claims. **Strengths:** "She's very bright and her in-depth knowledge of asbestos work is particularly remarkable given her call." "She's fantastic with clients." **Recent work:** Successfully acted in Pugh v GPT Realisations Ltd., securing £280,000 for the wife of a claimant who died of mesothelioma caused by asbestos exposure at work.

Christopher Melton QC of Byrom Street Chambers Please see editorial on p.407.

Simon Kilvington QC of Byrom Street Chambers Please see editorial on p.408.

Charles Feeny of Complete Counsel Please see editorial on p.410.

Michael Kent QC of Crown Office Chambers Please see editorial on p.393.

David Platt QC of Crown Office Chambers Please see editorial on p.393.

Catherine Foster of Crown Office Chambers Please see editorial on p.393.

Robert O'Leary of Crown Office Chambers Please see editorial on p.411.

Steven Snowden of Crown Office Chambers Please see editorial on p.394.

John Williams of Crown Office Chambers Please see editorial on p.394.

Douglas Cooper of Deans Court Chambers Please see editorial on p.408.

Daniel Bennett of Doughty Street Chambers Please see editorial on p.413.

James Todd of 39 Essex Chambers Please see editorial on p.395.

Stephen Glynn of 9 Gough Square Please see editorial on p.396.

Roger Hiorns of 9 Gough Square Please see editorial on p.396.

Frank Burton QC of 12 King's Bench Walk Please see editorial on p.396.

Harry Steinberg QC of 12 King's Bench Walk Please see editorial on p.397.

Michael Rawlinson QC of Kings Chambers Please see editorial on p.409.

Ivan Bowley of Lincoln House Chambers Please see editorial on p.410.

Peter Cowan of Oriel Chambers Please see editorial on p.411.

Matthew Phillips of Outer Temple Chambers Please see editorial on p.398.

Patrick Limb QC of Ropewalk Chambers Please see editorial on p.405.

Jayne Adams QC of Ropewalk Chambers Please see editorial on p.405.

John McDonald of 2TG – 2 Temple Gardens Please see editorial on p.401.

MIDLANDS

Personal Injury	
Leading Sets	
Band 1	
No5 Chambers *	
Band 2	
Ropewalk Chambers *	
Leading Silks	
Band 1	
Bleasdale Paul	No5 Chambers [A]
Limb Patrick	Ropewalk Chambers *
Band 2	
Bright Christopher	No5 Chambers *
Hunjan Satinder	Kings Chambers (ORL) ◊ *
Jones Jonathan	No5 Chambers *
New Silks	
Adams Jayne	Ropewalk Chambers *
Leading Juniors	
Band 1	
Cox Jason	Ropewalk Chambers
Moat Richard	No5 Chambers
Band 2	
Brunning Matthew	No5 Chambers [A]
Campbell Stephen	No5 Chambers [A]
Coughlan John	No5 Chambers
Cursham Georgina	Ropewalk Chambers *
Dean Peter	No5 Chambers
Duthie Malcolm	No5 Chambers
Evans Paul	No5 Chambers
Gregory Richard	Ropewalk Chambers
Herbert Douglas	Ropewalk Chambers
Jaspal Kam	Ropewalk Chambers *
McNamara Andrew	Ropewalk Chambers *
Mitchell Jonathan	Ropewalk Chambers *
Pitchers Henry	No5 Chambers
Rochford Thomas	St Philips Chambers (ORL) ◊ *
Stewart Toby	Ropewalk Chambers
Turton Philip	Ropewalk Chambers *
Xydias Nicholas	No5 Chambers

* Indicates set / individual with profile.
[A] direct access (see p.24).
◊ (ORL) = Other Ranked Lawyer.
Alphabetical order within each band. Band 1 is highest.

Band 1

No5 Chambers

See profile on p.931

THE SET

No5 Chambers covers the full gamut of personal injury matters including industrial disease, employers' liability, occupiers' liability and RTA claims. It assists both claimants and defendants. Recently it has advised on the inquest into Seren Bernard's death which examined the actions of a local authority in relation to a teenager who died while living with foster parents. One impressed source notes: "The quality of the work is great. The barristers are incredibly professional, they know their stuff. I have no doubt that when I instruct them that I'm getting the best."

Client service: "The clerks are efficient and helpful." "They are friendly and approachable." Martin Hulbert and Zoe Tinnion are the senior practice managers for personal injury matters.

SILKS

Paul Bleasdale QC Highly experienced in catastrophic injury and fatal accident claims. He also has expertise in industrial disease cases. **Strengths:** "One of the best and most experienced serious injury silks in the Midlands. He doesn't shy away from difficult cases. A powerful advocate in court." "His wealth of experience, pragmatic advice and excellent client manner make him a go-to personal injury QC." **Recent work:** Advised the defendant on a quantum dispute in the case of Sarwar v IBC Vehicles. This involved a claimant who had an accident at work.

Christopher Bright QC (see p.603) Regularly assists claimants and defendants with catastrophic injury and fatal accident cases. He also has significant experience in RTA claims. **Strengths:** "He is able to marshal the facts of the most complex of cases and provide practical advice in all circumstances. He is a model of clarity in court and is able to relate well to clients." "Chris is very well organised and has a methodical approach. He is meticulous."

Jonathan Jones QC (see p.685) Highly esteemed silk with particular expertise in quantum and brain injuries. He also has vast experience in employers' liability and road traffic accident claims. **Strengths:** "His exceptional analytical skill translates into real results for clients. He is the barrister you want on your side in the most technically challenging cases." "Quick-thinking, tactically astute, careful and good with clients." "Thorough and forensic. Great on his feet with first-class technical skills." **Recent work:** Advised on quantum issues in the case of Andrew Goff v Tarver and QBE Insurance.

JUNIORS

Richard Moat Handles a broad range of personal injury matters including fatal accident, chronic pain, brain damage and psychiatric claims. **Strengths:** "He often comes up with unique strategies to resolve cases." "Provides realistic, balanced advice which gets to the heart of the matter." "Excellent advocacy skills." **Recent work:** Assisted a claimant after he suffered a severe injury to his leg in a road traffic accident.

Matthew Brunning Well-known junior with expertise in a variety of personal injury matters including fatal and catastrophic injury claims as well as disease cases. Sources repeatedly commend his attention to detail. **Strengths:** "Superb on detail and can dissect even the most complex evidence into understandable formats." "Provides balanced advice to achieve the best outcome." **Recent work:** Represented the defendant in Worthington v 03918424 Ltd, a chronic pain case. Managed to obtain an order that the claimant pay the defendant's costs after it was discovered he had exaggerated his suffering.

Stephen Campbell Often advises both defendants and claimants on cases involving brain damage, amputation and paralysis. Solicitors note his excellent client manner. **Strengths:** "Stephen's big strength is the way he develops a rapport with clients." "He's very approachable and has a good bedside manner with clients." "He has a good reputation for attention to detail. He is very thorough." **Recent work:** Advised the defendant in the case of Lloyd v European Car Services Ltd and Kiely Bros and others. This was a paraplegia claim arising out of an RTA.

John Coughlan Experienced in disease cases and psychiatric claims. He is noted for having strong negotiation skills. **Strengths:** "Exceptionally sharp but also has a way of making clients feel utterly at ease. He is a fantastic litigator, always prepared and incredibly pragmatic with real tactical nous." "John is a very astute practitioner. He is a really good negotiator." **Recent work:** Advised the claimant in the case of Sarah Dodd. The claimant suffered a simple ankle injury at work which led to much wider issues.

Peter Dean Continues to be an esteemed personal injury practitioner. He handles a wide spectrum of matters including sexual abuse, fatal accident, RTA and employers' liability claims. **Strengths:** "An all-round performer, he is good with papers and good in court." **Recent work:** Successfully advised the claimant in the case of Stephenson v Secretary of State for Energy, Newcastle County Court, a hearing loss case.

Malcolm Duthie Strong junior regularly handling spinal injury, psychiatric and amputation claims. Much of his work is high-value in nature. His advocacy skills are praised by sources. **Strengths:** "He has an excellent work ethic, great attention to detail and is very good with clients." "He has a strong approach to negotiation and a focus on truly representing his clients." "An intelligent, articulate and a skilled advocate." **Recent work:** Successfully assisted a claimant with establishing liability after he suffered an electric shock while working.

Paul Evans Experienced in numerous different personal injury issues including pain disorders, brain and spinal injuries and amputations. Clients repeatedly praise his ability to remain calm in difficult circumstances. **Strengths:** "Clients absolutely love him." "Approachable, efficient and dependable. His advocacy skills are impressive." **Recent work:** Advised a claimant who sustained a spinal injury after he fell from a high area on a construction site.

Henry Pitchers Strong personal injury practice centred on high-value and complex claims. Sources highlight his excellent client skills. **Strengths:** "Excellent attention to detail and an easy but confident manner with clients." "Client-friendly manner."

Nicholas Xydias Broad range of expertise encompassing industrial disease, fatal accident and spinal injury claims. **Strengths:** "Thorough, proactive and approachable." "Very knowledgeable and good in court." **Recent work:** Assisted a prison officer after he developed tuberculosis by coming into contact with a prisoner suffering from the illness.

Band 2

Ropewalk Chambers

See profile on p.976

THE SET

Ropewalk Chambers continues to go from strength to strength. It blends its strong expertise in disease work with skill in a variety of other areas including child abuse and stress claims. The chambers advises a number of major insurers as well as claimants. Recent cases dealt with by the set include Zurich Insurance v IEGL, a Supreme Court judgment granting insurers a new right when it comes to recovering costs in mesothelioma claims. Sources note that the barristers at Ropewalk Chambers are "uniformly good."

Client service: "The clerks are very personable and helpful." "Tony Hill is fantastic. If you ever need anything, he will deal with it for you." Tony Hill is the senior clerk at the set.

SILKS

Patrick Limb QC (see p.702) Highly regarded personal injury silk with vast experience in disease claims. He has particular expertise in matters involving occupational cancer and is praised by solicitors for his straightforward approach to issues. **Strengths:** "Impeccable standards." "His manner is very user-friendly. He gets to the point very clearly and in a manner that the client can understand." **Recent work:** Acted for the defendant in Zurich Insurance v IEGL, a landmark Supreme Court appeal establishing a new right concerning the recoverability of costs for insurers in mesothelioma claims.

Jayne Adams QC (see p.579) Recent silk highly esteemed for her experience in industrial disease claims. She frequently handles matters involving fraud and is commended for her client care. **Strengths:** "Jayne has excellent attention to detail, is robust and concise in her advice and is able to come up with practical solutions." "Very thorough and good on her feet." **Recent work:** Advised the defendant in a case concerning multiple fire and rescue workers claiming suffering due to contaminated water.

JUNIORS

Jason Cox Excellent junior with expertise in a wide variety of personal injury claims including those relating to industrial disease. Sources repeatedly note his attention to detail. **Strengths:** "Jason is an extremely capable lawyer who is able to quickly grasp the relevant issues in a case. His advice is always provided without delay and shows great attention to detail." "Straightforward and effective." **Recent work:** Acted for the defendant in a case concerning a claimant who suffered a back injury after two different accidents.

Georgina Cursham (see p.628) Widely esteemed for her expertise in claims involving the Animals Act. She assists both claimants and defendants. **Strengths:** "Very prompt, has an eye for detail, good on her feet and efficient." "Has a very good way of explaining the complexities of the Animals Act to clients." **Recent work:** Advised a woman seeking compensation after a bull fatally attacked her husband and caused her serious injuries.

Richard Gregory Particularly skilled in employers' liability and occupiers' liability claims. Also has experience in disease matters. Solicitors cite the strength of his client skills. **Strengths:** "Extremely thorough and very experienced. Very good with clients and very methodical." "Approachable and helpful. Great with clients and very good on his feet." **Recent work:** Successfully advised the claimant in the case of Keywood v Chief Constable of Nottinghamshire, which concerned a teenage boy bitten by a police dog.

Douglas Herbert Strong junior skilled at handling high-value personal injury claims. Sources note his vast experience in this area of the law. **Strengths:** "People are able to trust him and rely on his judgement."

Kam Jaspal (see p.682) Enters the rankings in recognition of his excellent market feedback. Specialises in disease work frequently advising on hand-arm vibration syndrome, noise-induced hearing loss and mesothelioma. He is praised by solicitors for his cross-examination skills. **Strengths:** "Very good on his feet and with cross-examination of the claimant." **Recent work:** Successfully acted for the defendant in Eric Smith v Wormald Holdings, a hearing loss claim.

Andrew McNamara (see p.713) Expertise in the full spectrum of personal injury matters including industrial disease and employers' liability claims. He assists both claimants and defendants. **Strengths:** "Very good at explaining matters to clients. He is reliable and goes the extra mile." **Recent work:** Acted for the defendant in Pickles v Calico Housing, a case concerning hand-arm vibration.

Jonathan Mitchell (see p.719) Well-regarded junior with capabilities in all manner of personal injury issues including RTAs and employers' liability claims. **Strengths:** "Jonathan has very good advocacy skills." "Thoroughly experienced." **Recent work:** Successfully represented the defendant in the case of Graham v Commercial Bodyworks which examined whether the claimant's employer was vicariously liable for injuries inflicted by a work colleague.

Toby Stewart Well-regarded barrister with a wealth of experience in disease claims. Solicitors draw attention to his excellent interpersonal skills. **Strengths:** "Toby is very thorough, has a tremendous bedside manner with clients and is very approachable." "Toby is excellent with clients: he has a nice, reassuring manner and a clear and calm approach." **Recent work:** Successfully represented the defendant in the case of Gibbs v Western Landscapes Limited, a disease case.

Philip Turton (see p.785) Advises both claimants and defendants on an array of issues including child abuse, stress and occupational disease claims. **Strengths:** "An extremely good advocate. He is excellent on his feet and extremely thorough in his preparation." **Recent work:** Advised on a case involving an outbreak of legionella in South Wales.

Other Ranked Lawyers

Satinder Hunjan QC (see p.678) (Kings Chambers) Well regarded for his catastrophic injury work. He frequently handles claims arising in a sports context. Many of his cases have international aspects and concern spinal and brain injuries. **Strengths:** "Tactically brilliant, approachable, excellent with clients, pragmatic, robust and unflappable." "Very approachable, reliable and intelligent."

Thomas Rochford (see p.754) (St Philips Chambers) Has a strong claimant personal injury practice but also assists defendants in this area of the law. He is also experienced at dealing with schedules of loss. **Strengths:** "He has good attention to detail." "Very astute and knowledgeable." **Recent work:** Advised the family of a man who killed himself while in hospital.

NORTH EASTERN

Personal Injury
Leading Sets
Band 1
Parklane Plowden
Leading Silks
Band 1
Lewis Andrew *Park Square Barristers (ORL)* ◊
Leading Juniors
Band 1
Axon Andrew *Parklane Plowden*
Copnall Richard *Parklane Plowden* *
Exall Gordon *Zenith Chambers (ORL)* ◊
Murphy James *Parklane Plowden*
Band 2
Ditchfield Michael *Kings Chambers (ORL)* ◊
Edwards Daniel *Dere Street Barristers (ORL)* ◊ *
Elgot Howard *Parklane Plowden*
Friday Stephen *Parklane Plowden*
Furness Corin *Parklane Plowden*
Jamieson Stuart *Parklane Plowden*
Kirtley Paul *Exchange Chambers (ORL)* ◊
Nossiter Tom *Parklane Plowden*
Souter Catherine *Parklane Plowden*
Turner Steven *Parklane Plowden*
Williams Christopher *Parklane Plowden*
Up-and-coming individuals
Armstrong Hylton *Parklane Plowden*
* *Indicates individual with profile.*
◊ *(ORL) = Other Ranked Lawyer.*
Alphabetical order within each band. Band 1 is highest.

Band 1

Parklane Plowden

THE SET

As the leading personal injury set in the North East, Parklane Plowden regularly represents claimants and defendants in complex, catastrophic and high-value claims. It has an exceptionally deep bench and a broad raft of expertise among its barristers, making it a favourite set for regional and national law firms as well as insurers, trade unions and self-insured companies.

Client service: "The clerks give you results not problems. They understand the difficulties in managing a catastrophic injury case load." "They bend over backwards; if they can do anything to facilitate the case then they'll do it." The "absolutely brilliant" practice director Michael Stubbs leads the clerking team.

JUNIORS

Andrew Axon Head of chambers who combines his outstanding personal injury practice with his work in clinical negligence, and excels in catastrophic cases relating to brain and spinal injury as well as amputations. He is typically instructed in very high-value cases, and is noted for his excellent advocacy and client-care skills. **Strengths:** "He has a lot of experience of dealing with brain injury claims. He puts clients at ease and explains difficult legal issues thoroughly. He's very confident and a strong advocate during joint settlement meetings." "Bright, good with the client and someone who picks up the crucial issues in a case very quickly."

Richard Copnall (see p.623) Known for his commanding presence at trial and in negotiations, making him a powerful representative for clients. He principally acts in high-value catastrophic injury cases, though he also represents clients during inquests, and has additional experience in human rights issues. **Strengths:** "He's very assertive, very robust and straight to the point. He doesn't waste his words; he's the man you want on a difficult negotiation settlement." "Very authoritative. He's the person you want in court if you had a very intricate legal argument to be put before a judge."

James Murphy A well-respected junior and head of the personal injury team at Parklane Plowden. He is equally capable of handling both industrial disease and catastrophic injury claims, and also has a specialist focus on employer's liability. He represents claimants and defendants, both at first instance and on appeal. **Strengths:** "He's very knowledgeable and robust. He has a very positive approach towards litigation: he always sees the solution and works towards it." **Recent work:** Acted in Hall v CPL Ltd, a claim arising out of a sidewall mining accident where liability was disputed.

Howard Elgot Senior junior known for his superb grasp of claims involving serious spinal and brain injuries. Praised for his technical acumen, he often acts in complex, high-value paralysis cases, representing both claimants and defendants. **Strengths:** "Very good on the technical side of medical evidence." "Has a strong reputation for complex claims of significant value. He is approachable and good with clients."

Stephen Friday Retains a broad practice representing defendants and claimants alike. He is particularly experienced in cases concerning chronic pain, brain injury and amputation, as well as others arising in a clinical setting. He also takes on claims relating to fatal traffic accidents, most notably those involving motorcyclists. **Strengths:** "Bright, intellectual and robust, he has good judgement." "He gives off a persona of confidence that is not misplaced. He's very good on technical points and prepared to stand up and really fight for his clients."

Corin Furness Very well versed in employment and public liability, and also noted for his fraud expertise. He also regularly handles claims concerning serious injuries and fatalities caused by RTAs. **Strengths:** "The guy I'd turn to when I had difficult issues which require attention to detail and lots of documents. He's very thorough and meticulous." "Extremely methodical, he really gets into the detail and he won't let things go until he has a full understanding."

Stuart Jamieson Junior whose flourishing practice sees him representing both claimants and defendants in complex personal injury cases. He regularly acts for clients with life-altering injuries arising from accidents at work as well as serious traffic accidents. He is also noted for his work recovering costs. **Strengths:** "He provides a very thorough and prompt service." "We rely on counsel to have a good understanding of both personal injury and clinical negligence, as well as costs, all of which he does." **Recent work:** Acted for the defendant NHS trust in a multi-track claim concerning a workplace accident where the claimant had subsequently been given early retirement against her wishes.

Tom Nossiter Receives high praise for his exceptional client-care skills, which lend strength to his claimant-focused practice. He acts in high-value occupiers' and public liability claims as well as complex employment liability cases. **Strengths:** "A very bright guy who is excellent at managing clients expectations. He is very straightforward with clients and lays the risks out for them, but he is also very sympathetic and has a good bedside manner." **Recent work:** Acted in Mario Poathy-Pratha v Leeds City Council, a public liability claim concerning a cyclist who hit a pothole in the road.

Catherine Souter Represents claimants and defendants in multi-track as well as fast-track cases. She has a broad range of experience but is particularly knowledgeable on personal injury arising out of health and safety breaches, and is well versed in employment, occupiers and public liability cases. **Strengths:** "Clients love her; she's very much on their side. Impressive in conference and an excellent advocate." "A safe pair of hands who is pragmatic and very good in court."

Steven Turner Predominantly acts for defendants, though he also represents claimants in catastrophic injury cases arising out of road traffic accidents. Highly knowledgeable on credit hire, fraud and costs work, he also has a very strong sports law practice. **Strengths:** "Exceptional in matters of legal compliance." "He is practical and logical, even if we don't instruct him on a particular case we will always go to him for advice."

Christopher Williams Has a broad practice that combines expertise in personal injury and professional negligence. He acts in a wide range of cases, representing both claimants and defendants in employer's liability matters, including those concerning industrial disease and injuries in the workplace. **Strengths:** "He is great in court, particularly in cross-examination. He knows how to win a case in front of a judge." **Recent work:** Defended Shell UK against an occupier's liability claim, where liability was admitted but the value of the claim was disputed.

Hylton Armstrong Has a broad personal injury practice, acting in fast-track and multi-track claims as well as representing clients at inquests. He regularly undertakes cases arising out of RTAs and incidents occurring on construction sites. **Strengths:** "His advice is very succinct and he is brilliant in court." "He is a safe pair of hands, bright and well prepared." **Recent work:** Represented the family of a self-employed painter at the inquest into his death, which occurred while he was painting windows on a developer's site.

Other Ranked Lawyers

Daniel Edwards (see p.639) (Dere Street Barristers) A highly regarded barrister who maintains a broad personal injury practice. He is best known for his experience in employers' liability, including industrial disease cases, where he acts for both claimants and defendants on complex claims. **Strengths:** "A good operator who is very personable, very thoughtful and very careful." "A very good advocate and a very well-prepared opponent."

Paul Kirtley (Exchange Chambers) Acting principally for claimants, he is known for his involvement in high-value, complex claims including chronic pain, amputation and traumatic brain injuries. **Strengths:** "He's a very well-thought of and experienced practitioner who has a very good manner with clients." "He has a thoughtful approach to complex claims and excellent client-care skills."

Michael Ditchfield (Kings Chambers) A specialist in industrial disease, including claims concerning asbestos, hand arm vibration and noise induced hearing loss. He regularly acts for defendant parties in cases that involve complex questions of causation and liability. **Strengths:** "A very dogged and determined cross-examiner." **Recent work:** Acted in Lowe v Amec plc, in which the claimant alleged the onset of hand arm vibration syndrome after only a week of using workplace tools.

Andrew Lewis QC (Park Square Barristers) Leading silk who maintains an unparalleled practice in the North East. He focuses his skills on multimillion-pound cases and has an outstanding reputation for acting for defendants. His experience extends to catastrophic injury claims relating to brain and spinal cord injuries as well as industrial disease matters. **Strengths:** "A standout advocate who gives clear advice." "Andrew is a safe pair of hands. He always provides sound advice, is down to earth and so easy to deal with, always putting clients at their ease."

Gordon Exall (Zenith Chambers) Renowned for his written work and opinions in complex cases, particularly fatal accident claims. He is also praised for his unrivalled technical insight and empathetic client skills. **Strengths:** "His knowledge and experience is phenomenal and he is extremely personable with clients, especially when difficult decisions have to be made." "He's very thorough, with a good eye for the law and detail." **Recent work:** Acted in Strazds v National Probate Directorate, regarding a claimant who was injured doing work which was imposed by a probation order.

NORTHERN

Personal Injury
Leading Sets
Band 1
Byrom Street Chambers *
Band 2
Deans Court Chambers *
Exchange Chambers *
Band 3
Kings Chambers *
9 St John Street *
Band 4
Cobden House Chambers *
St Johns Buildings *
Leading Silks
Star individuals
Melton Christopher *Byrom Street Chambers* *
Band 1
Allen Darryl *Byrom Street Chambers* *
Braithwaite Bill *Exchange Chambers*
Grime Stephen *Deans Court Chambers*
Hartley Richard *Cobden House Chambers* *
Heaton David *Byrom Street Chambers* *
Horlock Timothy *Deans Court Chambers*
Hunter Winston *Byrom Street Chambers* *
Kennedy Christopher *9 St John Street*
Machell Raymond *Byrom Street Chambers*
McDermott Gerard *9 St John Street*
Rawlinson Michael *Kings Chambers* *
Rowley James *Byrom Street Chambers* *
Waldron William *Exchange Chambers*
Yip Amanda *Exchange Chambers*
Band 2
Braslavsky Nicholas *Kings Chambers* *
Hinchliffe Nicholas *9 St John Street*
Jones Rhiannon *Byrom Street Chambers* *
Martin Gerard *Exchange Chambers*
Poole Nigel *Kings Chambers* *
Redfern Michael *St Johns Buildings*
Willems Marc *Cobden House Chambers* *
New Silks
Kilvington Simon *Byrom Street Chambers* *
* Indicates set / individual with profile.
🅐 direct access (see p.24).
◊ (ORL) = Other Ranked Lawyer.
Alphabetical order within each band. Band 1 is highest.

Personal Injury
Leading Juniors
Star individuals
Grace Jonathan *Deans Court Chambers*
Band 1
Burns Peter *Byrom Street Chambers* *
Cowan Peter *Oriel Chambers (ORL)* ◊
Feeny Charles *Complete Counsel (ORL)* ◊
Knifton David *Exchange Chambers* *
Little Ian *9 St John Street*
Whitehall Richard *Deans Court Chambers*
Band 2
Ashworth Fiona *Kings Chambers* *
Bowley Ivan *Lincoln House Chambers (ORL)* ◊
Cooper Douglas *Deans Court Chambers* *
Grimshaw Nicholas *Deans Court Chambers*
Grundy Philip *St Johns Buildings*
Harrison Peter *St Johns Buildings*
Howells Catherine *Exchange Chambers* *
Jones Michael *Cobden House Chambers* *
Laprell Mark *18 St John Street (ORL)* ◊
Lemmy Michael *9 St John Street*
Luck Julie-Anne *Kenworthy's Chambers (ORL)* ◊
Maguire Stephen *Kings Chambers*
McCann Simon *Deans Court Chambers* 🅐
McCluggage Brian *9 St John Street*
Paul Daniel *Deans Court Chambers*
Snarr Matthew *9 St John Street* *
Stockwell Matthew *Outer Temple Chambers (ORL)* ◊
Ward Andrew *Exchange Chambers* *
Up-and-coming individuals
Gutteridge Chris *Exchange Chambers* *

Band 1

Byrom Street Chambers

See profile on p.960

THE SET

Offering unrivalled expertise and a strong team of highly qualified practitioners, Byrom Street Chambers is the leading set on the Northern Circuit for personal injury work. Barristers here represent both claimant and defendants and are often instructed by leading national law firms and insurers. With a deep bench of leading silks, the set acts principally in extremely high-value and catastrophic cases, including those concerning serious brain and spinal injuries, fatal accidents and industrial disease. Sources comment on the set's excellent clerking and also draw attention to the strength of the "superb" silks, who are "as good as anyone you could get in London."

Client service: The "faultless" clerking team, led by Steven Price, is famed for its responsiveness, flexibility and accommodating nature, and is described by one solicitor as "the best in Manchester." Other sources note the clerks' "innovative and well-organised" approach and say that "they have an amazing knack of making problems go away."

SILKS

Christopher Melton QC (see p.715) Standout silk who excels at representing claimants in high-value catastrophic injury and fatal accident cases, particularly those involving minors. He is praised for his superb client-care skills alongside his exceptional oral advocacy. **Strengths:** "Going into any claim with Christopher will put you at an advantage, regardless of who you are up against: technically he's superb and his experience is unparalleled." "He shows great attention to detail going through documents and is very good at presenting his points too. He's good at getting to the root of nuanced, difficult cases." **Recent work:** Acted in a trial determining liability in favour of a teenage claimant who ran across a dual carriageway in darkness and was knocked down by the defendant's vehicle.

Darryl Allen QC (see p.582) A highly respected silk who maintains an outstanding catastrophic injury practice. He acts for both claimants and defendants and is known for his technical precision and meticulous case preparation. **Strengths:** "Probably the most razor sharp barrister you'll ever come across; he's really top-notch, very calm and collected." "His preparation is second to none, he always has a complete handle on the case." **Recent work:** Acted for the defendant in a complex claim relating to a life-changing spinal cord injury.

David Heaton QC (see p.668) Known for his prodigious practice in catastrophic spinal and brain injury cases, Heaton is eminently capable of representing both claimants and defendants on highly challenging claims. A highly regarded trial advocate, he is also known for his pragmatic approach to settlement negotiations. **Strengths:** "He demonstrates superb attention to detail and commerciality in catastrophic cases." "He provides clear, unequivocal advice, and he is both very easy to contact and client friendly." **Recent work:** Represented the first defendant in ABC v Merritt and a hospital NHS trust, in which the claimant alleged that a brain injury sustained during an RTA had significantly worsened as the result of surgical and medical mismanagement.

Winston Hunter QC (see p.678) A catastrophic injury specialist who also has extensive knowledge of issues surrounding loss of earnings and insurance indemnity. Renowned for the high calibre of his advocacy and technical expertise, he acts for both claimants and defendants in high-value, complex cases. **Strengths:** "He has a encyclopaedic knowledge of catastrophic injury work and his breadth of experience is incredibly wide. He's also got the ability to assimilate a huge amount of information and deliver high-quality advice at very short notice." "Inspires confidence in all that he does: he is a superb advocate and a real team player." **Recent work:** Represented the claimant, a former senior partner at a global law firm, in a high-value claim for loss of career following injuries sustained in an accident.

Raymond Machell QC A formidable advocate who acts in multimillion-pound cases involving injuries of maximum severity and complexity. He maintains a stellar reputation for his claimant work while also regularly representing defendants in high-value cases. **Strengths:** "If I had a seriously tricky liability or causation matter I would go to him. He has a very no-nonsense approach and is taken very seriously by his opponents." "A QC of unrivalled excellence. His attention to detail is exceptional and he keeps the whole legal team on their toes." **Recent work:** Acted for the claimant in Wilshaw v Viridor Waste Management, a catastrophic injury claim arising out of an RTA.

James Rowley QC (see p.756) Maintains a balanced practice representing both claimants and defendants in catastrophic injury cases. Deals with claims of the utmost severity, including amputations along with brain and spinal injuries. He is lauded for his technical proficiency and attention to detail, in addition to his advocacy skills. **Strengths:** "A heavyweight practitioner; he's amazing in the courtroom as well as being understanding and sympathetic with clients." "He is known particularly for his encyclopaedic knowledge of case law, and is also very good at maximising a claim." **Recent work:** Achieved a favourable settlement on behalf of a claimant farm worker who had lost both legs above the knee after being run over by a reversing tractor.

Rhiannon Jones QC (see p.686) Appears for both claimants and defendants in catastrophic injury and chronic pain cases, and increasingly for claimants in historic sexual abuse cases. She has an active inquests practice and her instructing solicitors praise her handling of difficult clients and meticulous case preparation. **Strengths:** "She's tactically brilliant." "She is very incisive and good at getting to grips with the particulars of a case with a heavy volume of paperwork." "She's absolutely fantastic, full of empathy for the clients and always puts them first." **Recent work:** Appeared for the family of a pedestrian killed by a speeding police car responding to a 999 call in Gibson v Northumbria Police.

Simon Kilvington QC (see p.691) New silk who has an outstanding practice handling industrial disease and serious injury claims. He is well known for his expertise in asbestos-related cases, and is widely praised for his advocacy skills and clear, straightforward advice. **Strengths:** "He is able to summarise the key issues of a case in very clear terms for the client. He's also tactically astute and a good negotiator." "A thoughtful, detailed barrister who is meticulous in his preparation of detailed work."

JUNIORS

Peter Burns (see p.607) Specialises in personal injury and industrial disease claims, with additional expertise in insurance matters. He is very able to handle cases related to injuries of some severity, including high-value claims for brain and spinal injury. **Strengths:** "He adds value; he introduces new angles you might not have thought of, and always gives a little bit extra." "Without exception he provides thorough, precise and coherent advice cutting directly to the crux of the matter."

Band 2

Deans Court Chambers

See profile on p.964

THE SET

Deans Court Chambers enjoys significant renown on the Northern circuit for its personal injury expertise. The team acts in a wide range of claims relating to severe injuries and accidents, including specialist areas such as accidents abroad and fraudulent claims. Often instructed by trade unions, national and international law firms and insurers, as well as individual claimants, the set has earned its reputation as an attractive choice for all parties involved in complex personal injury litigation.

Client service: "The clerks are swift and very slick: they've never let us down, either on booking counsel when we need it or getting back to us on fees." The clerking is lead by the "incredibly commercially astute" Matt Gibbons who, sources say, "understands what is needed to enhance and develop a working relationship."

SILKS

Stephen Grime QC An outstanding personal injury silk who regularly acts in multimillion-pound severe injury claims, including accidents abroad. Alongside his technical skill, sources also extol his ability to put clients at ease, especially claimants in catastrophic injury cases. **Strengths:** "An intellectual powerhouse. Always well prepared and good with clients." "He's probably the most capable personal injury silk on the circuit, and a pre-eminent civil advocate." "A highly intelligent silk with extensive knowledge and experience, capable of great innovation and extremely good with clients."

Timothy Horlock QC A seasoned practitioner known for his expertise in catastrophic injury, employers' and public liability and serious RTAs. He represents both claimants and defendants and can also advise on cases concerning psychological damages and sports injuries. **Strengths:** "A proper leader, he always impresses and is a genuine pleasure to work with, taking a like-minded team approach." "An outstanding QC and an excellent negotiator, who is extremely good on his feet."

JUNIORS

Jonathan Grace Pre-eminent senior junior at the Northern Personal Injury Bar. He represents claimants and defendants alike in difficult cases regarding serious injury and fatal accidents. He is known for his ability to negotiate complex issues of liability and quantum, as well as for his calm, measured advocacy style. **Strengths:** "He's so calm, he just doesn't get ruffled. He's very warm and charming, but he's also as cool as a cucumber." "Extremely experienced and very economical in negotiations and pleadings. He is a very good tactician."

Richard Whitehall An experienced junior who handles all areas of personal injury, primarily focusing on multi-track cases of significant value. He regularly acts in catastrophic injury, RTA and industrial disease claims, and is also very well versed in issues of employers' and public liability. **Strengths:** "One of the finest barristers I've had the pleasure to be against. His cross-examination was flawless and devastating, absolutely lethal." "He handles difficult cases very well: he's very good in court and always well prepared."

Douglas Cooper (see p.622) Highly qualified to advise on a broad range of industrial disease claims, Cooper is particularly well regarded for his exceptional practice in noise-induced hearing loss cases. He principally represents defendants, including insurers and corporate clients. **Strengths:** "A very skilled junior who specialises in occupational disease cases and who has a keen eye for detail." "He is the best defence lawyer for deafness cases around right now."

Nicholas Grimshaw Principally represents defendants in a broad range of personal injury claims, including industrial disease, fatal accidents and serious injuries. He also has a niche practice in cases related to farming and equestrian activities.

Simon McCann Primarily represents defendants, including insurers, corporate clients and local authorities, particularly those who are facing potentially fraudulent claims. He also has significant experience in catastrophic accident and industrial disease cases. **Strengths:** "He has a very good manner in court, he is a very reassuring and natural presence in front of the judge." **Recent work:** Represented the defendant's insurer in a civil fraud case regarding multiple fraudulent claims made by one individual.

Daniel Paul Junior who is well regarded for his work in catastrophic injury cases, including fatal accident claims. He has extensive expertise in matters pertaining to employers', occupiers' and public liability, as well as RTAs. **Strengths:** "He is an incredibly able advocate, who is well prepared but who also doesn't seem to feel stress in the court room, he's always very quick to deal with anything thrown at him." "Extremely approachable, engaging and prepared to work very flexibly to meet his instructing solicitors and clients' needs."

Exchange Chambers

See profile on p.956

THE SET

Based in Liverpool, Exchange Chambers is renowned throughout the Northern circuit for its expertise in catastrophic brain and spinal injury claims. The set principally acts for claimants, and is regularly instructed by leading law firms and trade unions, though it can also claim a strong defence practice. Sources commend the set's barristers for being "very accessible and supportive, with the more senior counsel having the specialist skills required for catastrophic injury cases."

Client service: "The service you get is excellent: you get responses from the clerks promptly and they go out their way to help you with just about anything." "The speed of response is very good, alternative arrangements are always set up if diaries clash and they're good if something is quirky or difficult. The clerks are very good at figuring out how to solve problems." Chambers director Tom Handley leads the clerking team.

SILKS

Bill Braithwaite QC The leading claimant silk for catastrophic brain and spinal injury cases on the Northern circuit. Alongside his superlative advocacy skills he is praised for his extensive medical knowledge, as well as his sensitive approach to working with brain-injured clients. **Strengths:** "Bill is an immensely experienced barrister who has the ability to put clients at ease whilst simultaneously being a fierce advocate for them." "A QC of formidable experience and expertise." "He very much looks outside the box and takes a wider view of the case, always doing what's best for the client."

William Waldron QC Primarily acts in traumatic brain and spinal injury cases, with a particular focus on claims concerning significant loss and those involving minors. He represents both claimants and defendants and is highly praised for his client care and advocacy skills. **Strengths:** "A top-class advocate, he's very good in the court room." "Thorough, analytical, clever. Everything you would expect of a leading QC in the field coupled with a very user-friendly approach and understated manner."

Amanda Yip QC Maintains her position as a leading catastrophic injury barrister, specialising in multi-track claims of significant value concerning brain and spinal injuries and amputations. Interviewees highlight her negotiation and advocacy skills along with her ability to put worried or difficult claimants at ease. **Strengths:** "She's easy going but very firm. She knows her stuff but is approachable and willing to listen as well." "She demonstrates an outstanding level of knowledge and experience, has an excellent manner with clients and is an impressive negotiator. Always maintains her professionalism even in the most testing of situations."

Gerard Martin QC Regularly instructed on behalf of claimants in multimillion-pound catastrophic brain injury cases, though he also has considerable knowledge concerning amputation claims. He has a notable interest in issues of litigation capacity, particularly when it comes to children. **Strengths:** "An organised and accessible QC who understands the benefits of a structured plan for cases." "Not only reliable, but exceptional in terms of results. It's always a positive experience for clients due to his exceptional bedside manner, and his track record speaks for itself."

JUNIORS

David Knifton (see p.692) Senior junior praised for his attention to detail and strategic approach to complex cases, alongside his supportive and sympathetic manner with clients. He specialises in acting for claimants who have suffered catastrophic injuries, notably those with complicating factors such as disputed liability and contributory negligence. **Strengths:** "Just supreme in his technical ability, though his best asset is the way he can take something that appears indecipherable and break it down into manageable terms, not only for the solicitor but for the client." "He takes no nonsense and gets the job done. Meticulous in his preparation and strong in negotiation, he is a calm but strong and reassuring presence." **Recent work:** Represented a claimant who became tetraplegic when the taxi he was travelling in skidded on ice and collided with another vehicle.

Catherine Howells (see p.676) Acts in a broad range of personal injury and clinical negligence cases on behalf of both claimant and defendant parties. She is noted for her strength in serious injury matters, and also handles claims arising out of industrial disease, fatal accidents and chronic pain conditions. **Strengths:** "She gives excellent, clear advice, and can adapt to the needs of the client." "An excellent junior who is very helpful, flexible and accommodating. She demonstrates empathy with clients but is tough in negotiations."

Andrew Ward (see p.789) Experienced junior who acts for claimants and defendants alike in cases relating to serious and fatal accidents. Well versed in RTAs and injuries sustained at work, he also has considerable expertise in military claims, and has represented the MOD on a number of occasions. **Strengths:** "He is very accessible and good with the clients, and he takes a good common-sense approach." "He is very smooth, very knowledgeable, and always in control."

Chris Gutteridge (see p.661) Continues to develop a strong practice in personal injury, which encompasses serious injury and fatal accident claims along with those concerning psychological damages. He is noted for his natural advocacy skills and his approach to client care. **Strengths:** "He is really good at understanding the issues in a case and getting to grips with them quickly. He is also excellent at relating to lay clients and putting them at their ease." "He is pragmatic and insightful, with excellent client-facing skills."

Band 3

Kings Chambers

See profile on p.968

THE SET

Offers a broad range of personal injury expertise to a wide client base that includes trade unions, insurers and companies as well as local and national law firms. Barristers at the set variously specialise in claims relating to asbestos exposure, military service and chronic pain conditions. They are also well versed in catastrophic brain and spinal cord injuries, particularly those sustained as the result of RTAs. Sources describe Kings Chambers as "a very commercially minded set that understands the environment we're operating in" and also add "few sets are at the cutting edge of asbestos litigation in the same way as Kings Chambers."

Client service: "The clerking is a well-oiled machine. Steve Loxton is very approachable, very accommodating. The team is always in the right place at the right time." "They are a very modern set, with very efficient clerks."

SILKS

Michael Rawlinson QC (see p.749) Renowned silk with a dual focus on industrial disease claims along with injuries sustained during military service. Acts mainly on behalf of claimants though he also advises insurers on legal strategy, particularly with relation to asbestos liability. **Strengths:** "A very well-prepared and hard-working advocate who gives practical and clear advice to clients." "He's like a legal encyclopaedia; his knowledge of case law is incredible." "He provides useful analysis which brings a unique perspective. He's the standout silk for a difficult case against the MOD." **Recent work:** Represented a marine who became tetraplegic following a misjudged dive from his ship into the sea off Gran Canaria.

Nicholas Braslavsky QC (see p.602) Vastly experienced silk who represents claimants and defendants alike in catastrophic cases of neurological injury. He is regularly instructed in claims of high value and complexity that arise out of RTAs, industrial accidents, sports and outdoor pursuits. **Strengths:** "He combines everything you want in a QC, he's clever, a good advocate, tactical and easy to work with." "He is forensic in his attention to detail, he will know a case inside-out." **Recent work:** Represented defendant insurer in Neild v Gullivers World, a case involving the alleged collapse and subsequent tetraplegia of an individual who had ridden on a wooden roller coaster at a UK theme park.

Nigel Poole QC (see p.740) Widely admired silk who represents both claimants and defendants. He specialises in claims concerning catastrophic brain and head injuries, most often those associated with RTAs, however he also has expert knowledge of cases concerning the military. His trial work includes significant appellate experience, including appearances in both the Court of Appeal and the Supreme Court. **Strengths:** "He is incredibly astute, and also quite ingenious; he's always thinking about different angles." "He's extremely focused and incredibly collaborative, with excellent client-care skills." **Recent work:** Appeared in the Court of Appeal in Billet v MOD, concerning the assessment of damages for loss of earning capacity and the definition of disability.

JUNIORS

Fiona Ashworth (see p.585) A national leader for cases concerning fibromyalgia and other chronic pain conditions, in which she principally represents claimants. As well as her exhaustive knowledge of this subject, she also receives plaudits for her impeccable client care and robust advocacy. **Strengths:** "The doyenne of chronic pain cases, she knows that subject inside-out." "She's very authoritative; she has a detailed grasp of the issues and articulates them well." "She is thorough, analytical and generally very good." **Recent work:** Represented a woman who stubbed her toe at work and subsequently developed a chronic pain condition which ultimately led to her fracturing her other ankle due to a lack of mobility.

Stephen Maguire Junior who is applauded as a tenacious and determined representative for clients in catastrophic and life-altering injury cases. He regularly handles claims that arise out of RTAs, workplace accidents and defective products. **Strengths:** "He gets very good results in negotiations, often beyond our expectations." "His robust and uncompromising approach to litigation is inspiring. He is brave and willing to take on and win cases with difficult causation issues or where liability is in dispute."

9 St John Street

See profile on p.973

THE SET

9 St John Street occupies a strong position as a well-regarded set for a broad range of personal injury work. The barristers here are regularly instructed by both claimants and defendants to act in multi-track and fast-track personal injury claims relating to catastrophic injuries, RTAs and industrial disease. The set also offers expertise in more specialist areas such as fraudulent claims, accidents abroad and cases involving psychological damages.

Client service: "The clerks, led by Tony Morrissey, are very efficient and friendly, and very quick to get back to you. They're also good at providing added value, and will really go out on a limb for you." "The clerks are brilliant and really sensible in who they recommend to you. They will talk through the options and give you a choice, letting you know a bit more about each barrister, which is really useful."

SILKS

Christopher Kennedy QC Principally represents defendants, often on significantly high-value claims, though he also undertakes claimant work. His caseload encompasses catastrophic brain injury, RTAs and industrial disease claims, among others. **Strengths:** "Detail-driven and an effective negotiator." "An incisive thinker with an approachable and emphatic manner with clients. He is superb at breaking down the complex components of policy issues and his attention to detail in catastrophic personal injury claims is outstanding."

Gerard McDermott QC Vastly experienced silk who practices in London as well as in the North. He handles a wide array of catastrophic injury matters, particularly those with complex issues relating to liability and causation. He also has notable expertise in cases with a cross-border element. **Strengths:** "He has that judgement you are looking for from a senior QC, and also has a good feel for the complexities of foreign law." "He sees the psychology and tactics of things as well as the law." "Very astute on liability issues and not afraid to take risky cases to trial if necessary. **Recent work:** Acted for the claimant in Young v AIG, concerning an RTA in Portugal which resulted in one fatality and a catastrophic injury leading to paraplegia.

Nicholas Hinchliffe QC Frequently acts for insurers dealing with potentially fraudulent claims, while also representing claimants in catastrophic injury and industrial disease cases. **Strengths:** "Able, experienced and does a very good job." "An excellent lawyer in the courtroom."

JUNIORS

Ian Little Highly respected junior who acts predominantly for claimants. He regularly represents trade unions in employment liability cases concerning industrial accident and disease claims. Also handles a substantial volume of RTA and clinical negligence matters. **Strengths:** "He has a very laconic and laid back style which is very effective." "He is a reassuring presence. He's not afraid to tackle complex and challenging cases with aplomb."

Michael Lemmy Regularly represents claimants and defendants alike in multi-track cases of significant value. He has extensive experience in employment liability and RTA claims, and is particularly knowledgeable on brain and spinal injuries. **Strengths:** "A very experienced, good quality senior junior counsel. He's very switched on, commercial and practical." "He's very thorough, very good with witnesses and excellent at cross-examination." "He shows good attention to detail and works extremely hard." **Recent work:** Acted for one of the defendants in Griffiths v TSS & GBS, a multiparty case concerning an alleged traumatic brain injury for which the liability and quantum were in dispute.

Brian McCluggage Specialist personal injury and insurance practitioner with a strong track record of acting in high-value catastrophic injury claims. He is very familiar with cases that concern amputations, psychological damages and chronic pain conditions, and also acts in matters involving allegations of fraud or dishonesty. **Strengths:** "Pro-active, client-focused, professional and approachable." "He is a good, hard-working, competent opponent."

Matthew Snarr (see p.769) Focuses his practice on personal injury and health and safety matters, with considerable expertise in employment liability. He has significant advocacy experience at both trial and appellate level, and regularly acts for clients in high-value claims. **Strengths:** "He's very capable and a good opponent, he does a good job for his clients." "A very good and very straightforward barrister."

Band 4

Cobden House Chambers
See profile on p.961

THE SET

Highly capable Manchester-based set with a robust personal injury offering. Barristers at Cobden House Chambers take on a broad range of cases, including those relating to catastrophic brain and spinal injuries, RTAs and chronic pain disorders. They can also provide expertise in employers' and public liability, and are regularly instructed by clients faced with potentially fraudulent or dishonest claims. The set receives warm praise overall, with one source saying: "The barristers are technically excellent, and they also offer a very personal service, which can be lacking in larger sets."

Client service: "I can't think of a time when the clerks have ever let me down: they're very good at organising diaries and when it comes to making sure people and things are where they need to be, and they're flexible on fees as well." Steven Tobias is the senior civil clerk in charge of personal injury.

SILKS

Richard Hartley QC (see p.666) Highly regarded personal injury silk who is also head of chambers. His practice focuses significantly on catastrophic injury cases, including sports injuries, as well as chronic pain conditions. He represents both claimants and defendants and receives wide acclaim for his advocacy and ability to build rapport with clients. **Strengths:** "His extensive knowledge of the law and of the tactics involved with litigating catastrophic injury claims mean he is someone I would always want on my side. He has the ability to make even the most complex legal issues seem straightforward." "He has excellent expertise and brilliant ideas. He is also very good at dealing with difficult family dynamics and complicated situations."

Marc Willems QC (see p.795) Acts for claimants and defendants alike in heavyweight cases concerning catastrophic brain and spinal injury as well as amputations. He receives praise for his technical skills and his highly cerebral approach. **Strengths:** "He is very considered, and he has the ability to think outside the box. He's also very empathetic which is good for the clients."

JUNIORS

Michael Jones (see p.686) Principally instructed in severe brain injury cases, representing both claimants and defendants. He also undertakes a wide range of other work, including claims relating to industrial disease and chronic pain. Regularly acts on behalf of major insurers as well as government bodies. **Strengths:** "The law and advocacy just come naturally to him: he doesn't need to put on a show, he just gets the job done." "A top-notch junior."

St Johns Buildings
See profile on p.970

THE SET

Based in Liverpool and Manchester, St Johns Buildings provides a broad range of services to both claimants and defendants on the personal injury front. Adept at handling all manner of claims, barristers at the set take on cases regarding RTAs and work-related accidents, catastrophic injuries, industrial disease and psychological harm including PTSD. They are praised by sources as "a good commercially minded chambers with a number of first-rate counsel."

Client service: "The clerks are very accommodating: they are prepared to take a commercial view with regards to fees, and also do things for the benefit of the lay client. They go above and beyond." Chris Shaw is the senior civil clerk.

SILKS

Michael Redfern QC Maintains a strong reputation as a specialist in catastrophic injury. He is known for his experience acting in cases concerning severe brain injury, which is bolstered by his additional expertise in clinical negligence matters.

JUNIORS

Philip Grundy Vastly experienced junior with an impressive practice in catastrophic personal injury. He acts for claimants and defendants in a variety of cases and has particular expertise in accidents and conditions associated with the workplace. This includes everything from industrial workers suffering from hand-arm vibration syndrome through to military personnel affected by PTSD. **Strengths:** "A creative thinker who is calm, unflappable and very patient with difficult clients." "Always accommodating, deeply committed to his clients and families interests, pursues cases with vigour."

Peter Harrison Acts in a variety of high-value catastrophic injury claims, including those resulting from military service and claims for psychological damage. Represents both claimants and defendants in high-value, complex cases. **Strengths:** "If there's a joint settlement meeting which requires silk gloves he can be extremely amenable. If there are negotiations or a trail where a fight is needed he can be aggressive as well." **Recent work:** Represented the defendant in a case concerning a subtle brain injury sustained when the claimant was five years old. The claim featured complex issues of causation as well as consideration of the claimant's future prospects for employment and independent living.

Other Ranked Lawyers

Charles Feeny (Complete Counsel) An accomplished practitioner who splits his focus between industrial disease and catastrophic injury claims. As well as his expertise in asbestos-related diseases, he also handles high-value injury cases relating to RTAs and product liability issues. **Strengths:** "He is able to cut through the most complicated of matters and quickly arrive at the nub of any dispute." "An acknowledged expert in occupational disease cases who can always be relied upon to have the right answer in complex and high-value cases."

Julie-Anne Luck (Kenworthy's Chambers) An impressive junior who previously practiced for over 10 years as a solicitor. She has a growing reputation for her personal injury work, which includes significant employers' liability and high-value traumatic injury cases. She is also an accredited mediator. **Strengths:** "She offers a very proactive, thorough and personable service and is always on hand to assist despite being extremely busy. Her analytical skills and keen eye for detail helps her to quickly get to grips with the main issues in a case and she is reassuring in her practical approach."

Ivan Bowley (Lincoln House Chambers) Focuses on representing claimants in cases concerning workplace accidents and industrial disease. He wins plaudits for his comprehensive knowledge of asbestos-related disease and noise-induced hearing loss, among other areas. **Strengths:** "An exceptional junior for disease and illness claims, with an encyclopaedic knowledge of hearing loss and asbestos cases. Intellectual, but compassionate with clients." "Determined, bright and vastly experienced in industrial disease."

Peter Cowan (Oriel Chambers) "A simply brilliant industrial disease lawyer" who has an outstanding national reputation for his expertise in this field. In addition to his top-notch understanding of asbestos-related conditions, he also handles a broad range of other disease and personal injury-related cases. **Strengths:** "He has a wealth of experience and judgement that is close to unerring." "He is incredibly able on his feet and always comes over very well with clients. A real standout personality."

Mark Laprell (18 St John Street) A well-regarded senior junior who represents clients in a broad range of cases arising out of serious injury and fatal accidents. He is broadly praised for his depth of experience at the Personal Injury Bar. **Strengths:** "It's always great to have him on your team." "A veteran player who does high-value, high-quality catastrophic injury work." "Very capable and hugely experienced."

WALES & CHESTER

Personal Injury	
Leading Sets	
Band 1	
Civitas Law *	
30 Park Place *	
Leading Silks	
Band 1	
Williams Lloyd	*30 Park Place*
Leading Juniors	
Band 1	
Arentsen Andrew	*Farrar's Building (ORL)* ◊ *
Davies Ben	*30 Park Place*
Harrison Robert	*30 Park Place*
Jones Nicholas David	*Civitas Law* *
O'Leary Robert	*Crown Office Chambers (ORL)* ◊
Thomas Bryan	*Civitas Law* *

Band 1

Civitas Law

See profile on p.942

THE SET

Civitas Law is at the forefront of personal injury law in Wales. It is instructed by national law firms, trade unions, private companies and insurers in the most complex and high-value of cases in the area. The set has an exceptional catastrophic injury practice, and its barristers represent both claimants and defendants. Industrial disease experience is also on offer here. Sources say: "It has good strength in depth from the senior practitioners down to the more junior members, so any value of work can be covered."

Client service: Andrea Mclean is the senior clerk, and is praised for her responsiveness and helpful manner. The clerks in her team "go out of their way to be accommodating." "Andrea is very approachable, amenable and very friendly. She always gets back to you straight away."

JUNIORS

Nicholas David Jones (see p.686) Has a well-developed practice in high-value, catastrophic brain and spinal injury cases, where he acts for both claimants and defendants. He is considered pre-eminent in this field in the region. **Strengths:** "He is thoughtful in the advice he gives, very good with clients, approachable, hard-working and accessible." "He's very cerebral, and the go-to for difficult questions of liability." "He shows great attention to detail and his knowledge of brain injury is second to none."

Bryan Thomas (see p.780) Has a strong personal injury practice focusing on traumatic brain injury cases. In addition he is adept at employment liability, covering cases concerning accidents at work as well as industrial disease claims. **Strengths:** "He's thoughtful in his advice and pragmatic as well."

30 Park Place

See profile on p.943

THE SET

30 Park Place is a significant regional presence in personal injury. Acting on behalf of claimants and defendants, the set represents clients in both multi-track and fast-track cases. Members have a broad range of expertise, and are regularly instructed by law firms, insurers and trade unions.

Client service: Phillip Griffiths is the senior clerk at the set.

SILKS

Lloyd Williams QC Leading practitioner for catastrophic and fatal accident claims. He is applauded by the market for his high-value brain and spinal injury practice, representing claimants and defendants alike, and is noted for his quality client care. **Strengths:** "Calm and methodical, he is a strategic thinker who is excellent with clients from all walks of life." "A go-to barrister on fatal accident cases."

JUNIORS

Ben Davies Has a claimant-focused practice and acts in high-value, often multimillion-pound claims, on behalf of traumatically injured claimants. He also represents fast-track claimants. He is noted for his excellent client care skills. **Strengths:** "He's very careful and considered."

Robert Harrison Maintains a well-developed employment liability practice that takes in industrial disease claims and fatal accident cases. He is also experienced in a wide range of non-employment claims, including cases involving minors. **Strengths:** "Takes a very friendly and conscientious approach to dealing with claims. He has meticulous attention to detail and is tactically astute." "He's bright and sensible, and his experience manifests itself in his understanding of a case." "Has a very good bedside manner with clients and is impressive in court."

Other Ranked Lawyers

Robert O'Leary (Crown Office Chambers) An employment liability expert, who has experience of complex matters of significant value. He has handled group action litigations, industrial disease claims and cases relating to stress. **Strengths:** "Very bright and very experienced as well."

Andrew Arentsen (see p.585) (Farrar's Building) Continues to act in Wales-focused cases from London. He represents claimants and defendants in a range of catastrophic injury cases, and is noted for his dedication and client-oriented approach. **Strengths:** "He clearly has a great intellect, is very good with clients, is very approachable, and is very good at explaining things in lay language." "He's a very hard-working junior, who puts a lot of time into his practice."

WESTERN

Personal Injury	
Leading Sets	
Band 1	
Guildhall Chambers *	
St John's Chambers *	
Band 2	
Old Square Chambers *	
Leading Silks	
Band 1	
Palmer Adrian	*Guildhall Chambers*
Sharp Christopher	*St John's Chambers* [A]
Leading Juniors	
Star individuals	
Edwards Glyn	*St John's Chambers*
Band 1	
Benson Julian	*Guildhall Chambers*
Lomas Mark	*3PB Barristers (ORL)* ◊
McLaughlin Andrew	*St John's Chambers* [A]
Reddiford Anthony	*Guildhall Chambers*
Snell John	*Guildhall Chambers*
Stead Richard	*St John's Chambers* [A]
Walker Christopher	*Old Square Chambers* *
Band 2	
Bennett Daniel	*Doughty Street Chambers (ORL)* ◊
Farmer Gabriel	*Guildhall Chambers*
Grice Timothy	*St John's Chambers*
Isherwood John	*Unity Street Chambers (ORL)* ◊
Kempster Toby	*Old Square Chambers* *
Risoli Andreá	*Old Square Chambers* *
Symington Anna	*St John's Chambers* [A]
Taylor Christopher	*Queen Square Chambers (ORL)* ◊
Woodhouse Charles	*Old Square Chambers* *
Zeb Emma	*St John's Chambers* [A]
Band 3	
Chippindall Adam	*Guildhall Chambers*
Haines David	*Doughty Street Chambers (ORL)* ◊
Haven Kevin	*Pump Court Chambers (ORL)* ◊
Horner Robert	*3PB Barristers (ORL)* ◊
Panton Tom	*Guildhall Chambers*
Stamp Abigail	*Guildhall Chambers*
White Matthew	*St John's Chambers* [A]

** Indicates individual with profile.*
[A] direct access (see p.24).
◊ (ORL) = Other Ranked Lawyer.
Alphabetical order within each band. Band 1 is highest.

Band 1

Guildhall Chambers

See profile on p.938

THE SET

Barristers at Guildhall Chambers have a versatile skill set spanning industrial disease, RTA and employers' liability claims. Its members act for both claimants and defendants, with a number of prominent insurance companies forming part of its client base. Guildhall's members handle cases across the UK. One impressed source observes: "The quality of the advice is the main thing I like about the set. You know you're in good hands with them."

Client service: Heather Bidwell and Wendy Shaw clerk the personal injury barristers at the set. "Wendy is great. She's easy to get hold of and nothing is too much trouble." "The clerks are friendly and efficient." "The quality of the training they provide is exceptional and driven by what their clients ask for. They know their customer base very well."

SILKS

Adrian Palmer QC Outstanding silk with a strong defendant practice. He frequently assists insurance companies with policies as well as cases. **Strengths:** "Adrian's depth of intellectual ability and dexterity are matched by few other silks. He's at the very top of the tree." "A superb tactician. If I have highly technical issues on insurance or personal injury matters, I go to him."

JUNIORS

Julian Benson Highly esteemed junior adept at handling catastrophic injury claims. He has significant experience in chronic pain cases and is repeatedly praised for his client skills. **Strengths:** "Extremely hard-working, dynamic and has an excellent manner with clients." "An excellent court advocate. He can be trusted to take on complicated matters and to consistently achieve the best outcomes for clients." **Recent work:** Acted for the claimant in a fatal accident claim raising issues relating to both quantum and liability.

Anthony Reddiford Excellent junior specialising in asbestos and chronic pain claims. He also has a wealth of experience in matters involving brain, spinal and psychiatric injuries. He often handles cases with a fraud aspect. **Strengths:** "A top-quality barrister. He is very thorough and has a very good court manner." "He is very straight-talking and manages client expectations incredibly well. Nothing fazes him and he is utterly dedicated to every case he deals with." **Recent work:** Assisted two boys who were injured as infants with a criminal injuries compensation claim.

John Snell Focuses on personal injury cases relating to animals, particularly equine claims. He often handles matters involving brain injuries, spinal injuries and regional pain syndrome. **Strengths:** "John has a first-class grasp of the Animals Act and is a real expert in his field." "Excellent understanding of Animals Act claims. Unparalleled for his knowledge and close attention to the issues." **Recent work:** Acted for the defendant in a horse-riding accident case in which the claimant alleged she suffered a spinal injury due to her horse being hit by a whip by the defendant riding instructor.

Gabriel Farmer Handles cases involving spinal, brain and limb injuries. He frequently advises on high-value RTAs and fatal accident claims. **Strengths:** "Extremely thorough in his preparation, and knowledgeable of the relevant law." "Always on top of the detail."

Adam Chippindall Experienced in RTA and fatal accident claims. His workload consists of complex and high-value matters for both claimants and defendants. **Strengths:** "He is extremely experienced and knowledgeable." "Adam has an excellent eye for the finer details." **Recent work:** Acted for the claimant in the case of Co-operative Group (CSW) v Pritchard, a Court of Appeal case which examined medical causation and assessed whether or not contributory negligence is available as a partial defence in assault claims.

Tom Panton Significant expertise in employers' liability claims. He also has vast experience in industrial disease claims including hand-arm vibration syndrome, noise-induced hearing loss and asbestos cases. **Strengths:** "A very safe pair of hands, very pragmatic and very easy to engage with. He provides practical, commercial advice." "Pleasant, professional and straightforward."

Abigail Stamp Wide-ranging expertise covering public liability, employers' liability, industrial disease, RTAs and fatal accident claims. She assists both claimants and defendants. **Strengths:** "Very good with clients." **Recent work:** Acted for the claimant in an RTA claim. The victim suffered physical and psychological injuries.

St John's Chambers

See profile on p.941

THE SET

St John's Chambers has a wealth of experience in personal injury work. The set handles all manner of matters for claimants and defendants including accident at work and RTA claims. It has recently seen a sharp increase in industrial disease cases. Sources note that "they are very user-friendly and will always go the extra mile for you."

Client service: "The clerks are very efficient and supportive." "They are helpful, friendly and approachable." Annette Bushell leads the clerking team supporting the personal injury group.

SILKS

Christopher Sharp QC Highly esteemed silk who acts for both defendants and claimants. He frequently handles cases involving local authority negligence. **Strengths:** "Christopher is exceptionally bright, has fantastic attention to detail and is a very strong advocate." "He is extremely astute and excellent with the client."

JUNIORS

Glyn Edwards Outstanding barrister widely lauded for his expertise in personal injury matters. He advises both claimants and defendants and focuses his practice on serious and catastrophic injury claims. Sources repeatedly draw attention to his excellent manner with clients. **Strengths:** "Brilliant on his feet in court; he absorbs the detail but cuts through to the salient issues. He puts clients at ease." "He is intellectually excellent; he's able to guide clients through the most challenging of cases."

Andrew McLaughlin Leading personal injury barrister in the Western Circuit, adept at handling a variety of issues including stress, RTA and industrial disease claims. **Strengths:** "A very good advocate at trial. He thinks well on his feet and has an amiable personality." "Andrew gets straight to the heart of what a case is about and has a very good manner with clients." **Recent work:** Successfully acted for the defendant in Forrester v Clydesdale Bank and MOD which concerned an employee injured on an assault course he attended for leadership training purposes.

Richard Stead Highly experienced in a variety of issues including Animals Act claims and construction site accidents. He focuses on matters involving brain and spinal injuries. **Strengths:** "Richard possesses a high degree of courtroom skill and extraordinary tactical acumen." "He cuts to the issues quickly and is very approachable." **Recent work:** Advised the defendant on a claim brought by a widow whose husband was killed by a bullock.

Timothy Grice Well known for his expertise in military claims. He largely assists claimants who have suffered catastrophic injuries. **Strengths:** "Hugely knowledgeable, extremely clear in his advice and strategic thinking, and excellent on paper, in conference and in court." "Really good at complex military claims. He is meticulous and a calm, measured individual." **Recent work:** Advised on a non-freezing cold injury claim.

Anna Symington Adept at handling matters involving fraud. She assists both claimants and defendants. **Strengths:** "She is tactically brilliant and robust in court." "She is willing to go that extra mile to get results." **Recent work:** Advised the defendant in Morrison v Finglands & QBE which concerned a fraudulent claim by a woman involved in a staged bus crash.

Emma Zeb Continues to impress the market with her skill in the personal injury field. She often handles cases involving catastrophic brain injuries. She also has strong expertise in Highway Act claims. **Strengths:** "Very knowledgeable, approachable and great with clients." "She cross-examines with extreme skill." **Recent work:** Acted for a claimant who suffered a number of internal injuries affecting her dancing career.

Matthew White Advises both claimants and defendants on a variety of issues including asbestos, stress, accident at work and Highway Act claims. **Strengths:** "He has a talent for thinking on his feet whilst offering considered and robust advice in cases of a complex nature." "Matthew has a very keen eye for detail and is extremely thorough. He is enthusiastic and works very hard for the best result for the client." **Recent work:** Advised the defendant on a highway claim in which the claimant ran into a pillar fire hydrant without a cover.

Band 2

Old Square Chambers

See profile on p.886

THE SET

The barristers of Old Square Chambers advise clients on a myriad of personal injury issues including employers' liability, sexual abuse and RTA claims. Its members are particularly adept at handling matters involving fatal accidents and catastrophic injuries. The chambers has traditionally focused on claimant work but now also frequently advises defendants. Sources observe that the barristers are "friendly, client-focused and have a huge range of experience in personal injury work."

Client service: "The clerks are really good. They're very user-friendly and efficient." "The clerking is brilliant. They're always happy to try and help. A couple of times, I've instructed at the last minute and they've been efficient and swift in getting us a barrister." William Meade is the senior clerk at the set. Liane Ratcliffe is the set's manager in its Bristol annexe.

JUNIORS

Christopher Walker (see p.788) Well-respected barrister with a wealth of experience in fatal accident and catastrophic injury claims. He also has expertise in product liability and employers' liability cases. **Strengths:** "He has a great manner about him and puts clients at ease. He's very bright and can pick things up pretty quickly." "Urbane, personable and inspires confidence." **Recent work:** Advised a claimant who was rendered paraplegic when he fell off his motorbike in an attempt to move away from another vehicle.

Toby Kempster (see p.690) Strong expertise in employers' liability cases with a particular focus on stress claims. He often handles asbestos-related matters. **Strengths:** "Toby Kempster is incredibly approachable and clients really like him." "Very good with clients, very personable and very thorough." **Recent work:** Acted in Halfpenny v Leek Construction & Others, a case concerning asbestos exposure leading to pleural thickening.

Andreá Risoli (see p.752) Frequently handles CICA appeals relating to sexual abuse and assaults at work. He is skilled at dealing with catastrophic injury claims. **Strengths:** "He has a coherent, resolute style. His structured approach and experience has reaped rewards." "Great attention to detail and a good lateral thinker."

Charles Woodhouse (see p.800) Handles a versatile practice encompassing fatal accident, brain injury and spinal cord injury cases. He is well versed in RTAs and workplace injuries. **Strengths:** "He's very pragmatic and a barrister of choice for clients with chronic pain cases." **Recent work:** Advised a claimant who suffered serious injuries in an RTA.

Other Ranked Lawyers

Daniel Bennett (Doughty Street Chambers) Highly regarded barrister specialising in workplace injuries and occupational disease. He also handles product liability cases. **Strengths:** "Daniel's knowledge of employers' liability is well rounded and thorough. He gives practical and commercially perceptive advice and has an approachable style." "His employers' liability and disease knowledge is excellent." **Recent work:** Acted for the family of a man who died at work after he fell from a height.

David Haines (Doughty Street Chambers) Benefits from being a qualified doctor. His practice covers a wide range of personal injury matters including industrial disease, product liability, public liability, RTA and occupiers' liability claims. **Strengths:** "He is always thorough in his advice and is extremely approachable and willing to help." **Recent work:** Advised a prisoner who was seriously injured by guards who believed he had been party to a fight.

Mark Lomas (3PB Barristers) Has a broad skill set encompassing industrial disease, occupiers' liability, historic sex abuse and employers' liability claims. He is adept at handling cases involving fatal accidents and catastrophic injuries. **Strengths:** "A superb advocate with meticulous attention to detail." "He is extremely good at analysing complex issues." **Recent work:** Acted for the claimant, who had suffered a serious brain injury, in an RTA claim.

Robert Horner (3PB Barristers) Handles all manner of personal injury matters for both claimants and defendants. He frequently advises on fatal accident claims. **Strengths:** "He provides good, concise, common-sense advice." "Robert is thorough and organised. He is approachable and deals with clients well. He is flexible and supportive."

Kevin Haven (Pump Court Chambers) Regularly handles matters involving young people who have suffered psychiatric damage. He also has significant experience in yacht racing and motorcycle claims. **Strengths:** "Kevin always deals with matters very promptly and thoroughly. He builds a good rapport with clients and explains difficult concepts in simple terms." "He identifies issues very quickly and provides pragmatic, logical solutions."

Christopher Taylor (Queen Square Chambers) Has broad capability in the personal injury field encompassing spinal injury, head injury and fatal accident claims. He also has significant expertise in industrial disease cases. **Strengths:** "A great barrister to have on board for high-value claims which also require an understanding approach." "Christopher Taylor is very thorough and has excellent client care. He is great working as part of a team and his tenacity has helped him secure some excellent results for his clients." **Recent work:** Acted for the defendant in an occupiers' liability case in which the claimant broke his neck at an indoor climbing centre.

John Isherwood (Unity Street Chambers) Receives widespread recognition for his skill in personal injury law. His broad practice covers industrial disease, employers' liability and RTA claims. **Strengths:** "He has a great rapport with clients and a common-sense, no-nonsense approach." "An extremely good trial advocate."

Contents:

LONDON

Planning
Leading Sets
Band 1
Landmark Chambers *
Band 2
Francis Taylor Building *
Band 3
39 Essex Chambers *
Band 4
Cornerstone Barristers *
Band 5
6 Pump Court *
* *Indicates set / individual with profile.*
Ⓐ *direct access (see p.24).*
◊ *(ORL) = Other Ranked Lawyer.*
Alphabetical order within each band. Band 1 is highest.

Planning	
Leading Silks	
Star individuals	**Stinchcombe** Paul *39 Essex Chambers* Ⓐ
Corner Timothy *Landmark Chambers*	**Strachan** James *39 Essex Chambers*
Elvin David *Landmark Chambers*	**Warren** Rupert *Landmark Chambers*
Humphries Michael *Francis Taylor Building* Ⓐ *	**Band 3**
Katkowski Christopher *Landmark Chambers*	**Ash** Brian *39 Essex Chambers*
Kingston Martin *No5 Chambers (ORL)* ◊	**Drabble** Richard *Landmark Chambers*
Lieven Nathalie *Landmark Chambers*	**Edwards** Douglas *Francis Taylor Building* *
Purchas Robin *Francis Taylor Building* Ⓐ	**Findlay** James *Cornerstone Barristers*
Band 1	**Glover** Richard *Francis Taylor Building*
Brown Paul *Landmark Chambers*	**Karas** Jonathan *Falcon Chambers (ORL)* ◊ *
Clarkson Patrick *Landmark Chambers*	**McCracken** Robert *Francis Taylor Building* Ⓐ
Ellis Morag *Francis Taylor Building*	**Phillpot** Hereward *Francis Taylor Building*
Harris Russell *Landmark Chambers*	**Price Lewis** Rhodri *Landmark Chambers*
King Neil *Landmark Chambers*	**Straker** Timothy *4-5 Gray's Inn Square (ORL)* ◊
Lockhart-Mummery Christopher *Landmark Chambers*	**Tait** Andrew *Francis Taylor Building* *
Lowe Mark *Cornerstone Barristers* *	**Tromans** Stephen *39 Essex Chambers*
Mould Timothy *Landmark Chambers*	**Band 4**
Village Peter *39 Essex Chambers*	**Boyle** Christopher *Landmark Chambers*
Band 2	**Hobson** John *Landmark Chambers* Ⓐ
Bird Simon *Francis Taylor Building* *	**Kolinsky** Daniel *Landmark Chambers* *
Cameron Neil *Landmark Chambers*	**Litton** John *Landmark Chambers*
Forsdick David *Landmark Chambers*	**Nardell** Gordon *20 Essex Street (ORL)* ◊
Harwood Richard *39 Essex Chambers* *	**Ornsby** Suzanne *Francis Taylor Building* Ⓐ *
Hicks William *Landmark Chambers*	**Sheikh** Saira Kabir *Francis Taylor Building* Ⓐ
Hill Thomas *39 Essex Chambers*	**White** Sasha *Landmark Chambers*
Howell Williams Craig *Francis Taylor Building* Ⓐ *	**Willers** Marc *Garden Court Chambers (ORL)* ◊
Jones Gregory *Francis Taylor Building*	**New Silks**
Mauricì James *Landmark Chambers*	**Bedford** Michael *Cornerstone Barristers* *
Pereira James *Francis Taylor Building* Ⓐ	**Booth** Alexander *Francis Taylor Building* Ⓐ *
Phillips Richard *Francis Taylor Building*	**Busch** Lisa *Landmark Chambers*
Roots Guy *Francis Taylor Building* *	**Ground** Richard *Cornerstone Barristers* *
Steel John *39 Essex Chambers* Ⓐ *	

Band 1

Landmark Chambers

See profile on p.873

THE SET

Landmark Chambers stands out from the rest at the top of the market and attracts an immense number of London's leading planning solicitors and high-profile clients. Its members are engaged in some of the most high-level and complex cases the planning world has to offer, dealing with issues such as compulsory purchase, regeneration and planning policy. Several of them have been engaged in the past year by the government or other interested parties in shaping the direction of the ongoing HS2 rail project, the UK's largest infrastructure undertaking.

Client service: "Clerks at Landmark are really helpful and approachable and excellent to deal with." "The overall impression is of a very strong planning chambers with an abundance of talent, supported by a very friendly, good-humoured and enthusiastic set of clerks, well led by Jay Fullilove."

SILKS

Timothy Corner QC Regarded as one of the strongest QCs in the planning arena. He sits as a Deputy High Court Judge in the Administrative Court, as well as on a plethora of advisory panels. He is frequently instructed in critical appeals and reviews, both for and against challengers to high-profile developments. **Strengths:** "He possesses that skill of being able to read a situation and see what is required as a response. He thinks very deeply about what should and shouldn't be said in any given situation – a very shrewd tactician is Tim." "He is brilliant on his feet and quick to adapt to changing situations. It's like watching a masterclass in advocacy." **Recent work:** Secured victory for the Canary Wharf Group and Qatari Diar in the final appeal of a long-running case regarding the development of new offices and housing on the South Bank. Development begun once the challenge was overturned.

David Elvin QC Known for putting his outstanding intellect to work on complicated cases that often involve specialist planning criteria. Compulsory purchase matters, environmental impacts on planning and deep knowledge of EU law make up just part of his repertoire. He has worked on some of the most significant and trying infrastructure cases in the country over the last several years. **Strengths:** "David Elvin's intellectual rigour is second to none, something that he combines with clear commercial, strategic advice." "At the top of the tree in terms of his grasp of issues and experience of previous projects. He has a very firm handle on strategy in what are fast-moving and dynamic situations." **Recent work:** Engaged on multiple fronts with the controversial HS2 litigation. Represented petitioners on several occasions before the House of Commons Select Committee and challenged the directions of the project at several critical junctures.

Christopher Katkowski QC Universally regarded as a leading silk, Christopher Katkowski QC is a planning specialist with a remarkable track record of success at inquiry or in judicial review. Clients and peers, who speak warmly and at length of his creativity, sound judgement and concise advice, assert that he remains a leader at the Bar for complex planning cases. **Strengths:** "Very imaginative approach to the presentation of our evidence. Very good control of the proceedings, and he managed to completely demolish the opposing witnesses. Completely on top of his game, frankly." "Very practical, calm and accessible. Just phenomenal." **Recent work:** Defended the compulsory purchase order (CPO) for Tottenham Hotspur FC's new stadium. The challenge was successfully dismissed without appeal.

Nathalie Lieven QC Regularly appears in the High Court on both public inquiries and planning challenges. Her client base includes a number of central government departments as well as NGOs and various corporate entities. In planning, she frequently represents both local authorities and developers across a range of challenging cases. **Strengths:** "She has got an A1 mind and is razor sharp – sharpest in the box. Good on difficult matters where you need good robust arguments put forward by a strong personality." "She is amazing. Not a hint of pomposity – she really relates to clients, witnesses and inspectors well." **Recent work:** Represented Network Rail in three separate Transport and Works Orders cases regarding railway extensions for the Northern Hub. Two of the schemes run through central Manchester and one caused controversy due to its impact on two Grade I listed buildings.

Paul Brown QC A skilled High Court and Court of Appeal advocate who has served in a number of government advisory roles. Paul is a former member of the Treasury A Panel and also contributed to the 2013 review of national planning policy. Recently, he has been involved in the high-profile London 'basement wars'. **Strengths:** "He is responsive and has an

Planning	
Leading Juniors	
Star individuals	
Cook Mary	*Cornerstone Barristers* *
Band 1	
Banner Charles	*Landmark Chambers*
Beard Mark	*6 Pump Court* Ⓐ
Cosgrove Thomas	*Cornerstone Barristers* *
Lyness Scott	*Landmark Chambers*
Reed Matthew	*Landmark Chambers*
Band 2	
Burton James	*39 Essex Chambers*
Honey Richard	*Francis Taylor Building* Ⓐ *
Williams Guy	*Landmark Chambers*
Band 3	
Lewis Meyric	*Francis Taylor Building* Ⓐ *
Morgan Stephen	*Landmark Chambers*
Murphy Melissa	*Francis Taylor Building* *
Tabachnik Andrew	*39 Essex Chambers*
Wald Richard	*39 Essex Chambers*
Walton Robert	*Landmark Chambers*
Whale Stephen	*Landmark Chambers* Ⓐ *
Band 4	
Clay Jonathan	*Cornerstone Barristers* *
Colquhoun Celina	*No5 Chambers (ORL)* ◊
Green Robin	*Cornerstone Barristers* *
Moules Richard	*Landmark Chambers*
Pike Jeremy	*Francis Taylor Building* Ⓐ *
Ranatunga Asitha	*Cornerstone Barristers* *
Shadarevian Paul	*Cornerstone Barristers* *
Simons Zack	*Landmark Chambers*
Turney Richard	*Landmark Chambers*
Upton William	*6 Pump Court*
Westmoreland Smith Mark	*Francis Taylor Building*
Williams Anne	*6 Pump Court* *
Zwart Christiaan	*39 Essex Chambers* *
Band 5	
Banwell Richard	*6 Pump Court*
Beglan Wayne	*Cornerstone Barristers* *
Darby Jonathan	*39 Essex Chambers* *
Dehon Estelle	*Cornerstone Barristers*
Flanagan Hugh	*Francis Taylor Building*
Graham Paul Annabel	*Francis Taylor Building* *
Grant Edward	*6 Pump Court*
Helme Ned	*39 Essex Chambers*
Keen Graeme	*Landmark Chambers*
Kohli Ryan	*Cornerstone Barristers* *
Lambert Emmaline	*6 Pump Court* *
Lewis Gwion	*Landmark Chambers*
Parry Clare	*Cornerstone Barristers* *
Pugh-Smith John	*39 Essex Chambers* *
Thomas Megan	*6 Pump Court*
Townsend Harriet	*Cornerstone Barristers* *
Westaway Ned	*Francis Taylor Building*
Wills Jonathan	*Landmark Chambers*
Up-and-coming individuals	
Clutten Rebecca	*Francis Taylor Building*
Grogan Rose	*39 Essex Chambers* *
Hutton Victoria	*39 Essex Chambers* *
Sackman Sarah	*Francis Taylor Building*
Stedman Jones Daniel	*39 Essex Chambers*

** Indicates individual with profile.*

Ⓐ direct access (see p.24).

◊ (ORL) = Other Ranked Lawyer.

Alphabetical order within each band. Band 1 is highest.

amazing eye for detail, which makes him a perfect choice for our judicial review work, particularly in the environment sector." "A very good inquiry and High Court advocate who is brilliant with clients and a very down-to-earth, practical counsel." **Recent work:** Acted in Republic of France v Royal Borough of Kensington and Chelsea, successfully resisting a challenge brought by the French government to the grant of a lawful development certificate for the construction of a large basement at 10 Kensington Palace Gardens, which is adjoined to the home of the French ambassador.

Patrick Clarkson QC Veteran of the Planning Bar with decades of experience at his command. He has represented both public and private entities, often in the realm of retail and housing development. He also advises on strategy development in the early stages of project promotion. **Strengths:** "Provides clear, prompt advice and is very approachable." **Recent work:** Acted in Re Clean Power Properties, a case concerning a recycling plant.

Russell Harris QC A barrister with over 30 years of experience, who handles major planning cases. He frequently acts on matters relating to significant regeneration projects and is known for both his intellectual range and fierce advocacy. **Strengths:** "One of the leading barristers on urban development, particularly in London, and particularly involving tall buildings." "Absolutely formidable in advice and very enjoyable to work with. Clients of all natures and styles respond well to his confidence and clarity. He can express complicated concepts clearly, and he almost always wins." **Recent work:** Secured consent for the development of the Circuit of Wales, the site of a proposed motor circuit, business park and hotel and leisure complex, in a move that included the release of 830 acres of common land for the project.

Neil King QC An experienced hand for both infrastructure and traditional planning cases. He is well versed in the minutiae of compulsory purchase, environmental and compensation law and appears frequently at inquiries, at tribunals and in the higher courts. **Strengths:** "A very good advocate on town centre regeneration schemes particularly." "A really charming, graceful advocate." **Recent work:** Provided advice on the submissions by Gatwick Airport to the Airports Commission and the government to promote the second runway project.

Christopher Lockhart-Mummery QC A planning specialist for more than 30 years, he has handled a remarkable range of disputes and schemes, including some of the most significant cases in infrastructure, retail, office and residential development. His experience is complemented by his qualifications as a mediator and examiner of neighbourhood plans. **Strengths:** "His style is far less aggressive than many silks and is much more effective as a result. Most importantly, however, he has laser-like precision when it comes to framing a case. Christopher has the confidence to identify the one or two critical points that he thinks will achieve a win and to focus on them to the exclusion of the others. This shows a degree of confidence and ability that few of his competitors have." **Recent work:** Represented the appellant party, Mr Champion, against North Norfolk District Council in a case that raised critical questions about EIA and habitat concerns in planning processes. Following the determination of an unlawful EIA, planning permission went ahead.

Timothy Mould QC Has spent the last few years as one of the government's chosen counsel promoting the HS2 bill in the Parliamentary Select Committee. He continues to manage a broad practice of planning cases including those with environmental, ratings or community law elements. **Strengths:** "He has that technique for putting across complex questions in simple language, and coming up with forensic solutions to problems." "An outstanding advocate with a very good style. He really gets on like a house on fire with the committee, as he does with judges. He doesn't feel a need to do anything other than elegantly and clearly present the case." **Recent work:** Led a claim in judicial review against the mayoral decision to grant permission to a major residential/ mixed-use development at the Mount Pleasant Royal Mail site. Permission was refused following the argument that the Mayor had failed to secure necessary affordable housing yield.

Neil Cameron QC Comes highly recommended for his forensic and forthright style. His workload of planning and environmental cases has included enforcement notices, infrastructure, heritage issues and energy development. He often represents local authorities. **Strengths:** "He's very measured, authoritative, calm and likeable. He can understand the private and public perspective as well, and he's also got a very strong specialism in technical areas such as compulsory purchase and appropriation schemes." "He is a very strong black-letter lawyer who has excellent range." **Recent work:** Stood for the London Borough of Camden at a planning inquiry regarding the proposal of a 24-storey residential tower and associated heritage and design issues.

David Forsdick QC Has taken on a number of eye-catching planning cases in recent years, engaging with both housing and infrastructure matters of national importance and novel construction. Instructing solicitors enjoy his open and affable work dynamic. **Strengths:** "A really very frighteningly astute barrister" "Absolutely first-rate from a legal analysis point of view. Chases down the points and is a very effective operator." **Recent work:** Defended the conversion of the listed house of Sir Arthur Conan Doyle into a specially equipped school by a charitable foundation. The case questioned the circumstances in which listed building conversion is viably secured and how development should be approached.

William Hicks QC Has a strong history working on retail development schemes across the country, but also undertakes the full range of planning matters. He has three decades' experience of dealing with work involving transport, energy, housing and listed buildings among others. **Strengths:** "I love working with him. He's a tremendous operator." **Recent work:** Led an objection to the Bank Station upgrade works, citing issues such as noise, tunnelling and construction methodology.

James Maurici QC A respected advocate well equipped to act in a broad range of planning cases for developers and public entities. The long list of areas in which he is experienced includes advising on EU matters and state aid issues related to planning or compulsory purchase. **Strengths:** "He is extremely clever, incisive and gets to the point. His knowledge and understanding of planning, compulsory purchase and a range of related public law matters is unparalleled. He is also easy to work with, down-to-earth and approachable, and he is an excellent advocate both orally and in writing." "He gets thoroughly involved and immersed in the work that he does. When you instruct James, he is full-blooded and full-hearted." **Recent work:** Lead counsel to the Department of Transport with regard to the significant and highly publicised governmental decision on the Airports Commission report.

Rupert Warren QC A rising force in the planning field who is noted for his extensive advice regarding rewrites of the NPPF. He continues to advise the government on high-profile planning matters, and also to act for developers. **Strengths:** "A really, really outstanding lawyer, a master of contentious planning and a tremendously nice guy." "The most impressive of the new generation." **Recent work:** Promoted a 28-storey tower scheme for Essential Living through recovered inquiry. The case included a number of challenges including residential amenity and heritage issues and is set to be a benchmark for similar schemes in Camden.

Richard Drabble QC A strong advocate in court work of all levels. Sources highlight the energy and intellectual firepower he brings to instructions on behalf of developers and local authorities. He also takes on international cases, and has particular experience of appearing before the European courts. **Strengths:** "Intellectually ahead of the pack." **Recent work:** Appeared for Associated British Ports in a judicial review regarding the refusal of a harbour revision order by the Marine Management Association as part of an ongoing dispute. The refusal had significant value impact on the running of a major refinery.

Rhodri Price Lewis QC Known for his successes in village green cases and for a practice that focuses on a core of environmental planning matters including energy, transport, waste and mineral work. He is an infrastructure specialist and also more than capable of handling traditional development cases. **Strengths:** "A very likeable and effective advocate with many years of successful practice behind him." "What's always refreshing is that he may speak softly with a client but he always rams the message home about the case. He is conscious of sensitivities but gets the message across." **Recent work:** Instructed by Tandridge District Council in two challenges to the council's development plan, including one of the first cases to bring the Community Infrastructure Levy into consideration.

Christopher Boyle QC Has more than two decades of experience in town and country planning, including expertise with environmental considerations, compulsory purchase and infrastructure projects. He primarily represents landowners, developers and promoters of residential and infrastructure schemes. **Strengths:** "Christopher is a formidable advocate both in the courts and at inquiries. He is particularly adroit at getting on well with judges and inspectors. He is highly intelligent, very hardworking and has a down-to-earth personality, which makes him an ideal choice to lead a multidisciplinary public inquiry team." "Forensic in his assessment of the detail and brilliant in cross-examination." **Recent work:** Acted for the trustees of the Riverine Centre in the High Court challenging the Secretary of State's refusal of planning permission for a conservative Tabligi Jamaat Muslim 'mega-mosque', in a case combining planning and human rights concerns.

John Hobson QC Worked as a solicitor in private practice and for local authorities before being called to the Bar. In silk, he has extensive experience of appearing on behalf of local government and the Mayor of London's office in relation to significant planning cases. Also holds the distinction of having a seat on several panels and committees of importance to the sector, and is Special Adviser to the House of Commons Select Committee reviewing Northern Irish planning law. **Recent work:** Represented Lincolnshire County Council in the Court of Appeal regarding a judicial review of quashed planning permission for the Grantham Relief Road. The case involved the environmental statement's compliance with EU law.

Daniel Kolinsky QC (see p.693) An impressively experienced advocate who has handled a broad variety of cases in the High Court and Court of Appeal. He often acts on behalf of London authorities as well as NGOs, developers and individual claimants, and is well versed in the complexities of affordable housing and other local government matters. **Strengths:** "A brilliant advocate who is assertive in court without coming across as difficult. He is extremely approachable and very down-to-earth." "Exceptionally talented advocate and a master of detail. He is extremely practical and works exceptionally well with retail clients. His unfussy and clear approach is appreciated by clients and those instructing in equal measure." **Recent work:** Acting for the Secretary of State, he successfully defended claims of bias regarding planning permission granted to a Broadview Energy Developments wind turbine project.

John Litton QC A QC with multi-jurisdictional experience, having been admitted to the Hong Kong Bar and the Supreme Courts of the Eastern Caribbean and Northern Ireland. His practice sees him handling a wide range of cases including those relating to country planning, compulsory purchase and highways law. **Strengths:** "John is completely dedicated. I'm guessing it is partly because of his practice in Hong Kong, where he is not doing just planning work; he has a fairly broad approach to everything and manages to find innovative ways around problems." "He really understood our clients' drivers – not just legal but also commercial drivers." **Recent work:** Represented Gleeson Developments in their challenge to the Secretary of State's decision to recover a Section 78 appeal for his own determination after a decision had been issued by the inspector for a housing scheme. The interpretation of the Secretary of State's recovery powers was called into question.

Sasha White QC An incredibly active silk who is frequently instructed on behalf of the largest names in retail and residential development. He garners high praise from his instructing solicitors. **Strengths:** "Sasha is incredibly clear, incredibly concise and a lovely, lovely guy to work with. Very trustworthy." "Undoubtedly a man with a fantastic brain and a great team player."

Lisa Busch QC A new silk with an extensive history of high-end government work. Lisa has sat on the Attorney General's Panel for over a decade and has attracted the praise of peers and clients for her involvement in some of the most high-profile recent planning debates, including HS2. She is noted as a go-to barrister for High Court matters. **Strengths:** "Lisa is very conscientious, very hard-working, very thorough and very passionate." "She has very detailed knowledge of the law relating to environmental and planning cases." **Recent work:** On the team of counsel dealing with HS2.

JUNIORS

Charles Banner Takes on a wide variety of High Court, inquiry and advisory work for commercial and government clients. He is a member of the Attorney General's A Panel and engages with some of the government's most complex planning cases. Peers and clients alike rate him very highly for his performance. **Strengths:** "He is excellent on the client service front and a very bright guy with great expertise in many aspects of the law." "Very commercial as well as academic, and with a nice advocacy style." **Recent work:** Acted as sole counsel for the Secretary of State in a high-profile challenge to a CPO issued to aid the redevelopment of Shepherd's Bush Market. The claim was successfully defended against several opposing silks, with the decision now pending appeal.

Scott Lyness Has a fantastic reputation for his wide-ranging planning practice, acting for developers, planning authorities and other parties at all levels. He has experience with a variety of cases dealing with such matters as listed buildings, compulsory purchase and technical or environmental issues. He has acted in some of the most significant large-scale infrastructure and energy developments of recent years. **Strengths:** "One of the best barristers I have had the pleasure of working with, including QCs." "Scott's ability to understand technical scientific evidence is to be commended, as is his ability to calmly ensure that all that is needed is covered." **Recent work:** Appeared on behalf of Northern Ireland Electricity at a major infrastructure project inquiry, regarding their interconnector crossing the Northern Ireland/Republic border.

Matthew Reed Regarded as one of the top planning juniors currently working in the field. He excels in a wide range of cases including appeals at all levels, enforcement matters and the promotion of or objection to development in the residential, retail and industrial sectors. His work for both government bodies and private corporations has earned him an excellent profile in the market. **Strengths:** "One of the most hard-working, determined barristers around. He has a very good knowledge of planning law, especially with environmental issues, and is extremely capable in advocacy and cross-examination – you know you have given your client the best shot. A very good choice for the difficult cases." "A leading junior, excellent at leading detailed cases at inquiry, and charming with clients." **Recent work:** Lead advocate in a decade-long case surrounding the decision to grant permission for approximately 3 million sq ft of warehouse space and a rail freight terminal in the green belt. The challenge considered the materiality of similar decisions and whether a quashed decision is material to a later decision.

Guy Williams Handles a practice that touches on all aspects of planning law, and has recently handled a number of inquiry appearances dealing with energy, infrastructure, housing and retail matters. He is also seasoned in statutory challenges and judicial reviews with local government involvement. He is sought after for his CPO expertise and sits on the advisory panel to Crossrail and TfL for such matters. **Strengths:** "An excellent junior and very strong on CPO/compensation cases. He is destined to take silk." "Very thorough and thoughtful and quite a strategist. He has a very gentle manner but is very effective." **Recent work:** Acted for Goodman Logistics, seeking permission to develop a large strategic rail freight interchange consisting of two terminals and warehousing of over 200,000 sq m in the green belt between London and Slough.

Stephen Morgan Has specialised in planning since his training days, having graduated in both planning and law. He is extensively experienced in all aspects of the sector, from applications to enforcement and appeals, and has a special interest in village greens, neighbourhood plans, challenges and judicial reviews. He tries to avoid litigation for his clients where possible by finding creative solutions with all the tools at his disposal. **Strengths:** "Excellent on both planning matters and applications for registration of land as a town or village green. He is very knowledgeable and deploys his knowledge and experience in a very user-friendly way." "He is very approachable, very friendly and puts minds at ease in what can sometimes be uncomfortable situations at public inquiries." **Recent work:** Defended Chichester District Council in a challenge from landowner Crownhall Estate on the lawfulness of the Loxwood Neighbourhood Plan crafted and promoted by the local authorities. The case raised fundamental questions about the scope of neighbourhood planning legislation in the government's plans derived from the Localism Act 2011.

Robert Walton Counsels and acts for a wide variety of clients in hearings, public inquiries and higher court cases. He has expertise in all areas of planning law including enforcement notices, promotion or objections to development and policy, and the judicial review and challenges process regarding planning decisions. **Strengths:** "Very good in terms of witness preparation. He has a very calm, relaxed style at inquiry, and is able to keep the inspector onside and get what we want from the witnesses. A good one for dealing with large, complex inquiries." "He has that very avuncular manner, and he guides clients through difficult commercial problems very nicely." **Recent work:** Provided promotion for Gatwick Airport's second runway via the Airports Commission process.

Stephen Whale (see p.793) Recently promoted to the London A Panel of the Attorney General's Panel of Counsel, on which he has sat since 2007. He represents a large number of local authority, government and private clients across almost all types of planning law cases, including those with environmental or criminal components. **Strengths:** "He is excellent and well liked by clients. He is totally unflappable and really helps to calm clients during difficult contentious matters. He's also well liked by judges and inspectors and manages to be firm without being aggressive or hostile." "He has got a very pleasing manner. He is very down-to-earth and says it like it is." **Recent work:** In a case that has generated national news coverage, he successfully represented Reigate & Banstead Borough Council in charging Robert Fidler with contempt of court regarding the construction and occupation of his mock 'castle'.

Richard Moules Au fait with a wide range of planning areas, including CPOs, policymaking and enforcement, and a barrister with a specialism in highways and rights of way matters. He has lectured and published a number of works on planning law, and regularly appears in the High Court representing developers, the government and community groups. **Strengths:** "Very good at getting to grips with things quickly and standing up to the opposing QC." "Has superb knowledge of the law and is very user-friendly." **Recent work:** Appeared for the GLA in a three-week inquiry promoting a CPO made by the Mayor under Section 333ZA of the Greater London Act 1999 – the first of its kind. The CPO enables the regeneration of the former Southall gasworks brownfield site into a mixed-use scheme.

Zack Simons A popular name at the Planning Bar. He focuses on planning, compulsory purchase and environmental work, and has appeared in leading cases on current contentious planning issues such as environmental impact and housing need. He represents landowners, central government, private developers and local authorities for all types of work in the field. **Strengths:** "Always provides clear written advice, is very well informed and knowledgeable on planning and CPO issues." "He has a practice beyond his call. He is often in the higher courts and big inquiries, whether he is being led or not – a very capable barrister." **Recent work:** Acted for the promoters of the West Hendon CPO, which was successfully confirmed by the Secretary of State after a two-week inquiry. The CPO facilitates the regeneration of the estate to provide up to 2,000 new homes, a school and additional community and commercial elements.

Richard Turney He has gained a great reputation for his regular court and inquiry appearances tackling statutory challenges, judicial reviews and criminal or environmentally implicated planning cases. He also has a broad advisory practice and is well versed in infrastructure matters relating to a wide variety of sectors. **Strengths:** "A really technically excellent barrister who is very helpful and responsive towards his instructing solicitors." **Recent work:** Aiding the London Borough of Croydon in promoting a CPO for its major town centre retail scheme. Also successfully defended a challenge to planning permission for the project, backed by Westfield and Hammerson, in a High Court judicial review.

Graeme Keen An expert in both planning and environmental law whose experience ranges from local plan examinations through to major infrastructure projects. He also handles a number of cases relating to housing, retail and highways. **Strengths:** "Excellent in all he does: he's very thorough, he gets the points very quickly and he provides very accurate advice to lay clients, who are helped to understand what to expect." "Thorough, diligent and extremely hard-working." **Recent work:** At a four-day inquiry called by the Secretary of State, promoted the residential development of a large greenfield site on the edge of a West Sussex village. The inquiry involved a number of issues, including heritage, housing land supply, visual impact and the contrary Neighbourhood Plan.

Gwion Lewis Boxes with some of the heavyweights of the planning world in public inquiries, judicial reviews and challenges to a diverse range of projects. He has a particular specialism in infrastructure advice, and is an expert in port-related development and energy projects. He is also qualified in Wales and edits the Wales segment of the Planning Encyclopaedia. **Strengths:** "He picks up technical detail very quickly and thoroughly, and is very good on his feet." "Provides excellent advice and is approachable. We have great confidence in him." **Recent work:** Acting as sole counsel for an alliance of some 12 local authorities, including Chiltern District Council and Camden Borough Council, opposing HS2 on environmental grounds, mainly relating to noise impact, but also raising issues pertaining to air quality and landscape harm.

Jonathan Wills A seasoned inquiry advocate, having represented developers and local authorities in a broad spectrum of cases. He is also a regular at the High Court and Court of Appeal and has appeared in some of the most high-profile enforcement cases of recent years. He is available to advise on issues ranging from environmental impact assessment to listed buildings and use class matters. **Strengths:** "An enforcement specialist. He does a lot of it and did very well running some difficult arguments. A good choice for that kind of work." "Very conscientious, and has an incisive and persuasive legal mind. He is willing, without any pressure being applied, to respond to a client's needs as and when required." **Recent work:** Acted for developer Miaris in challenging an inspector's decision on a planning enforcement appeal. The High Court was convinced that, contrary to the opinion set out in the Planning Encyclopaedia, it did have the power to grant permission to appeal on a Section 289 challenge. Also represented the client at the subsequent appeal.

Band 2

Francis Taylor Building

See profile on p.849

FTB effortlessly maintains its reputation as a market leader when it comes to infrastructure. The set offers a diverse range of planning expertise and handles NSIPs and similarly massive projects with ease. Its barristers represent developers, landowners, central and local government and action groups. They have been involved with some of the capital's most significant cases as well as those branching out to all edges of the country. Instructing solicitors mark them out for their "consistency of quality."

Client service: "The clerks are always very approachable. Overall the set seems to be commercially minded and understands the differing requirements of its clients. Being able to match style to the differing requirements of commercial and private clients is quite a task to pull off consistently. Paul Coveney's team at FTB does this very well."

SILKS

Michael Humphries QC (see p.678) Known to all as the leading name in infrastructure planning law. He has an excellent reputation for working on projects of all types, especially the often vast NSIPs. He is also heralded for his compulsory purchase work and edits leading publications in both areas. He is a deeply experienced advocate across the entire space, advising and acting for utilities, objectors, landowners, developers and public entities. **Strengths:** "The guru of infrastructure work. Always has been, always will be." "Michael is the go-to barrister for major infrastructure projects. He has an amazingly powerful intellect and an incredible grasp of detail, which he distils into commercial, client-friendly advice. He is a dream to work with and a real team player."

Robin Purchas QC Has a long-standing reputation as one of the finest planning QCs at the Bar. His specialisms include compulsory purchase, compensation and valuation. He has a strong track record of promoting and objecting to major public planning matters including the Channel Tunnel and Crossrail. His infrastructure experience extends to aviation, energy and other fields. **Strengths:** "The professor of planning law." "Robin is a class act. He's tireless and gives every job everything he's got. He's extraordinary."

Morag Ellis QC Holds an enviable position in the market both as a barrister well versed in the broadest aspects of planning law and as a rare expert in some of its most unique and evolving areas. She is chair of the Planning and Environment Bar Association and also sits on the panel of silks to the Welsh government. **Strengths:** "In court, sometimes what is required is to say very little and then sit down. That's a ballsy call for anyone to have to make, so you have to be very confident that you'll be right – and she invariably is." "Pragmatic, calm, approachable and a very effective advocate." **Recent work:** Responded on behalf of Welsh ministers to a High Court challenge to their grant of planning permission for a wind farm on mountain upland at Garreg Lwyd, Mid Wales. The scheme came just under the NSIP threshold and was considered under the Town and Country Planning Act 1990.

Simon Bird QC (see p.596) A member of both the Planning and Environmental Bar Association and the National Infrastructure Planning Association. He has an impressive track record of appearing on behalf of ports, airports, house builders, and central and local government agencies at major inquiries. **Strengths:** "Simon can make the most complex problems sound simple and easy to understand. He is a great choice for clients. Very commercial and focused on the things that really matter." "He is really calm, measured and very accessible. He makes himself available and is a team player; he takes into account the views from the team and is just a pleasure to work with." **Recent work:** Resisted five appeals promoting residential development within the setting of St Osyth Priory (an assemblage of Grade I, II* and II listed buildings, a Scheduled Ancient Monument and a Registered Park and Garden). Each of the schemes was proposed as enabling development to fund essential repairs to the nationally important heritage assets.

Craig Howell Williams QC (see p.676) A traditional development and infrastructure specialist highly experienced in planning, environment and related public law matters. His case history demonstrates his expertise in matters involving large projects such as urban extensions and transport. He also handles substantial commercial work in the leisure and retail sectors. **Strengths:** "An incredibly diligent operator who is very calm under pressure and controls proceedings to the advantage of his clients." "Incredibly thorough and also incredibly well liked by clients. A true gent." **Recent work:** Represented Lakeland Estates against Rutland Council over the course of several appeals over 15 years, related to the planning permission granted to a controversial golf course on Rutland Water.

Gregory Jones QC A silk renowned for his expertise in planning and administrative law. His practice spans town and country planning, DCO-scale projects, environmental impact and other complex cases at all levels of review. He has carved out an additional niche in offshore marine spatial planning, and is well versed in EU law. **Strengths:** "The thinking man's QC." "Not just the meat-and-two-veg planning silk. He can deal very comfortably with European issues and complexity across the board."

James Pereira QC James Pereira QC's practice covers all areas of planning. His excellent reputation as an advocate comes from his frequent appearances at inquires and in the High Court. He also promotes and resists CPOs. **Strengths:** "Very thorough and considered, he gives logical and pragmatic advice and is not afraid to have difficult conversations." "James is a delight to work with – he's clever, fast, efficient and an excellent advocate on his feet."

Richard Phillips QC A QC characterised by his deep experience in a variety of areas of planning law. He has tackled cases relating to historic buildings and major residential, retail and leisure developments. He is an Assistant Parliamentary Boundary Commissioner for England. **Strengths:** "Forensic attention to detail. Gives insightful, straightforward advice." "Very thorough, highly respected."

Guy Roots QC (see p.754) A long-time trusted adviser and advocate for private and public organisations. His planning acumen extends to green belt development, energy projects, retail, housing, regeneration and major public works. He also maintains a strong reputation for compulsory purchase and related compensation work. **Strengths:** "A very thorough advocate who presents cases with diligence." "When you look at his closing remarks, you read it and think: how can we lose?" **Recent work:** Opposed, on behalf of ITV, the proposed route of the Trafford Park tram extension. The argument was based primarily on noise objections concerning interference, created at the line corner and via speaker system announcements, which would conflict with the filming of programmes at a recently built £50 million studio.

Douglas Edwards QC (see p.639) Douglas Edwards QC's robust practice is built around planning, environmental, CPO, highways law, government and infrastructure work. He is an expert in commons and village greens matters and is also frequently consulted on land assembly matters by local authorities. He represents both public and private clients at all levels in the courts and at inquiries. **Strengths:** "Has a fantastic grasp of planning knowledge and is exceptionally good at condensing complex information for clients." "He is able to provide clear and straightforward strategic advice as he grasps issues exceptionally quickly and is able to focus on the key aspects of a case." **Recent work:** Acted jointly for the Mayor of London and Lambeth LBC, as supporters of the Shell Centre redevelopment scheme, in an appeal against the dismissal of the Secretary of State's decision to grant planning permission to the project.

Richard Glover QC Well equipped to resolve disputes of all natures and an expert in compulsory purchase, ratings and local government work. He specialises in non-mainstream planning matters that may require valuation and compensation experience. **Strengths:** "He's got a special talent for how cases ought to be presented to the tribunal." "His biggest strength is his technical expertise. He can come up with an argument that the other side hasn't thought of, and he has the confidence to stick to his guns on it." **Recent work:** Acted for Hovis regarding the effects of the Trafford Park tramline extension which threatened the closure of a 24-hour flour mill in Trafford, Manchester.

Robert McCracken QC Acts for regulators, utilities, authorities and community groups across all planning and environmental matters. He engages in planning law cases from the most local level to the international, and is experienced in EU law. **Strengths:** "His strength is that he is able to cut right to the chase. Not somebody who, if you like, throws everything at an issue. He gets right to it and is very focused." "Robert is very thorough and acts very much in the client's interest, being a very skilled cross-examiner as well as someone with a mastery of the law." **Recent work:** Acted for CPRE during its challenge to the granting of permission for a large housing block scheme on the edge of Port Meadow which obscured views of the 'dreaming spires' in Oxford.

Hereward Phillpot QC A star as a junior who has continued to win the admiration of peers and clients in silk. Hailed as one of the top barristers acting in infrastructure matters, he frequently appears at inquiries, hearings and higher court cases. Many of the complex development cases he takes on pertain to particularly large or high-profile projects. **Strengths:** "He is succinct, clear and pragmatic. He focuses on solutions. He is cool and calm at all times and has a wonderfully reassuring manner during periods of high stress for clients." "In years to come, without a doubt, he is going to be one of the leaders of the Planning Bar." **Recent work:** Represented Navitus Bay Development at an examination under the Planning Act 2008 into their controversial offshore wind park. The development, proposed for just off the Jurassic Coast in Dorset, is the largest of its type to go through the process, and its sensitive location near to shore meant a variety of environmental impact issues needed to be addressed.

Andrew Tait QC (see p.777) Head of chambers who has promoted a raft of major infrastructure projects in London. He has also acted in relation to high-profile transport schemes. His practice further extends to waste matters, land valuation, new settlements and major mineral proposals. **Strengths:** "He is incredibly thorough and detailed, clients hugely respect his input and he is excellent on his feet." "He is extremely good at handling the largest cases and making them seem more straightforward than they are." **Recent work:** Promoted the Bank Station Capacity Upgrade on behalf of London Underground at public inquiry. The upgrade marks a significant addition to the transport infrastructure in the City.

Suzanne Ornsby QC (see p.731) Frequently involved in top cases involving strategic environmental assessment and neighbourhood planning. Her practice covers public inquiries relating to electricity and water supply, minerals and waste, as well as commercial and residential development. **Strengths:** "An excellent mind that can grapple with very difficult concepts." "Suzanne is really strong on development plan policy advice and lots of fun to work with." **Recent work:** Acted in the Court of Appeal on the first case on the discretion of local authorities to determine the extent of a neighbourhood area, as set out under sections 61F and 61G of the Town and Country Planning Act, inserted by the Localism Act 2011.

Saira Kabir Sheikh QC Frequently sought out as an advocate for appeals, inquiries, High Court challenges, Crown and Magistrates' Courts proceedings. She is experienced in all aspects of planning and environmental law. Her remit includes compulsory purchase, highways, Transport and Works Orders and other parliamentary matters. **Strengths:** "She has a manner that enables her to deliver hard messages very diplomatically." "Her skills as an advocate and the quality of her advice always inspire tremendous confidence and respect." **Recent work:** Appeared for Kestrel Hydro in its appeal against the inspector's decision to uphold an enforcement notice requiring the removal of various structures to comply with a separate notice against change of use to Kestrel's green belt development. The case questioned the scope of enforcement powers.

Alexander Booth QC (see p.599) A new silk already impressing as a QC. He engages with all kinds of planning work, notably NSIP cases and valuation or compensation proceedings related to compulsory purchases. He appears for both public and private bodies and recently took on cases related to the Thames Tideway Tunnel, the London Olympics and Crossrail. **Strengths:** "One of those barristers that goes the extra mile in terms of client care – he's very good, very thorough and a provider of excellent advice." "He has everything he needs to make a success of it in silk."

JUNIORS

Richard Honey (see p.674) Regularly appears in the High Court, and is an expert on compulsory purchase and infrastructure cases. He also features frequently in the Upper Tribunal (Lands Chamber). He is called to the Bars of England and Wales and Northern Ireland and represents defendants and claimants of all kinds. **Strengths:** "Richard is extremely good, very thorough and someone who inspires confidence in the instructing solicitor and the client." "He is meticulous, has a very good eye for detail and is very impressive on his feet." **Recent work:** Appeared for the Secretary of State as the respondent in a Court of Appeal challenge to the granting of planning permission for the construction of a wind turbine at Shipmeadow, close to the Norfolk Broads. The appeal was rejected on all grounds after considering a number of interlinked issues.

Meyric Lewis (see p.701) Specialises in planning and related environmental issues, being an expert in environmental impact assessment and CPOs among many other matters. He is well recognised for his advice and advocacy in cases regarding major infrastructure proposals. He represents clients ranging from individual objectors to high-end developers. **Strengths:** "As well as being very knowledgeable, he is really good at understanding the whole picture of the project and coming up with solutions. He is a very practical person and is willing to really commit to the case." "Meyric is very quick to grasp the issues and his attention to detail is second to none. He never fails to deliver." **Recent work:** Appeared before the Select Committee for HS2 on behalf of various petitioners. The matters raised included the CPO to acquire the Stratford Sail and challenges regarding disturbance to a Grade II* listed building as well as routes into the West End.

Melissa Murphy (see p.724) An experienced junior with a strong track record in a number of areas of planning law. She focuses her practice primarily on infrastructure and compulsory purchase cases, but also handles residential schemes, heritage issues and public authority matters, on both the local and the parliamentary scale. **Strengths:** "A real pragmatist. Especially on planning inquiries, she is very, very persuasive." "Very pleasant and approachable, he has a detailed knowledge of the environmental aspects of planning in particular." **Recent work:** Led by Craig Howell Williams QC, she represented the triumvirate of the Mayor of London and the London Boroughs of Hillingdon and Hounslow in a Section 78 appeal concerning works at Heathrow Airport to allow full runway alternation. She handled specialist evidence areas concerning environmental impact assessment, air quality and airport operations.

Jeremy Pike (see p.738) Experienced with various planning law considerations including commons and village greens, judicial reviews or challenges, Transport and Works Orders and compulsory purchases. His areas of focus include renewable energy, infrastructure and environmental impact assessment cases. He advises clients of all kinds in the public and private sectors, and also sits as an inspector for commons registration authorities. **Strengths:** "A very solid, safe pair of hands. He is approachable and accessible, and clients relate well to him." **Recent work:** On behalf of Halite Energy Services, challenged the decision to refuse consent for the Peesall Underground Gas Storage Facility. Worked with Michael Humphries QC to secure the first and only successful High Court challenge to a government NSIP refusal and advised in the following redetermination for the development consent application.

Mark Westmoreland Smith Concentrates his practice on cases concerning the delivery of essential energy (including renewables), waste and transport infrastructure. He typically acts for local authorities or promoters in these schemes. **Strengths:** "Well organised and unflappable. He's highly professional, very easy to deal with and a very pleasant individual with a good sense of humour." "He's got a natural ability to focus quickly on the real issues, and is very pragmatic and sensible about how to deal with them. He's easy to work with and very effective." **Recent work:** Promoted a controversial overhead power line scheme in North Wales designed to connect onshore wind farms but which will necessarily pass through countryside and nearby cultural heritage areas.

Hugh Flanagan A barrister dedicated to planning and compulsory purchase cases. He is a member of the Attorney General's C Panel of Counsel, and also acts for local authorities and developers. Retail, heritage, residential, enforcement and residential planning work are all areas in which he is particularly knowledgeable. **Strengths:** "A very talented junior who can more than hold his own in the company of QCs, and who gives valuable support and insight." **Recent work:** Acted for London City Airport in an appeal against the Mayor's refusal of planning permission for development of the airport's infrastructure, including terminal and taxiway extensions. The project had the support of the local planning authority, but was rejected by the Mayor on noise grounds.

Annabel Graham Paul (see p.658) Has acted in a number of significant, complex or otherwise novel infrastructure, compulsory purchase and mainstream planning cases in the High Court and Court of Appeal. Her practice reaches into all corners of planning law, and takes in inquiries and local plan examinations. **Strengths:** "She is not afraid to roll her sleeves up and get stuck in. She is very approachable, good to work alongside and is well liked by clients." "She works incredibly hard, and you can go to her and she will quickly and without pretence give you a view. She's never uncomfortable if put on the spot." **Recent work:** Acted for the South Warwickshire NHS Trust in a High Court challenge arguing that the organisation should receive funding for its hospitals from developers of new housing schemes. The High Court challenge settled with the developer agreeing to pay the NHS the money sought.

Ned Westaway Acts for local authorities, planning applicants and objectors, handling a broad range of cases, including those relating to major development proposals, complex enforcement and significant infrastructure projects. He is also an expert in environmental law. **Strengths:** "Very bright indeed, very articulate and not afraid to go to court with a case that is out of the ordinary – he is very environmentally minded and has a good sense of the principles." "Very reliable, personable and very good at what he does." **Recent work:** Acted for the London Borough of Camden in its resistance to a challenge made to the decision by the Secretary of State to reject permission for the redevelopment of a large residential property in Hampstead. The key issues included the approach to evidence on viability and costings, as well as interpreting the NPPF regarding the green belt.

Rebecca Clutten Continues to develop a practice in major infrastructure and compulsory purchase. She has experience of working for both promoters and claimants in CPO matters. Her client list and track record feature a number of high-profile names and projects. **Strengths:** "Very fast, astute and client-friendly." "Articulates extremely complex issues superbly, and has a great approach with the clients." **Recent work:** Acted for London Underground at a public inquiry concerning the Bank Station capacity upgrade. The project's aim is to alleviate overcrowding and circulation problems in the station in order to accommodate growth in the City.

Sarah Sackman A rising junior with experience of appearing in the Supreme Court, who is a regular in judicial reviews and planning inquiries of all kinds. She engages with a broad range of cases and, as a member of the Attorney General's C Panel of Counsel, regularly represents the government as well as local authorities, NGOs and other institutions. **Strengths:** "She has a very thorough strategic grasp and a light touch; she's very good with clients." **Recent work:** Appeared on behalf of the claimants in a judicial review of planning permission granted for a multimillion-pound golf course to be built in an Area of Outstanding Natural Beauty. The case raised key questions about whether the supporting text to a planning policy forms part of the development plan.

Band 3

39 Essex Chambers

See profile on p.840

THE SET

A growing set that continues to be a major contender in the planning law market, taking on new talent and a substantial caseload of top mandates in the sphere. Clients and instructing solicitors agree that "the level of service, from clerk to counsel, is excellent. Administratively it works very well, and turnaround time on instructions is generally excellent." There is extensive expertise on offer, with capability in every aspect of planning law. Members handle residential, retail, infrastructure and energy cases as well as matters relating to village greens and environmental concerns.

Client service: "The overriding theme running through most of their barristers and staff is one of approachability, practicality and responsiveness. Once you've instructed them, they remember your name and the last job you instructed them on, which provides a feel of familiarity." "Generally my go-to because if I don't know who to instruct, the chief clerk Andrew Poyser always gives a very good steer. I've never got a bum recommendation off him."

SILKS

Peter Village QC Widely considered to be one of the best at the Planning Bar, especially when it comes to residential and retail development or other cases of substantial size and profile. He has acted successfully for objectors, developers and landowners in examinations, inquiries and appeals for more than three decades. **Strengths:** "A force of nature – the man to go to if you have a very difficult case." "Very robust and committed to the client's cause. A real street fighter when the chips are down." **Recent work:** Acted for the claimant landowner in a complex five-week inquiry into the Port of London's CPO of Orchard Wharf on the north bank of the Thames. The case was tangled with an inquiry into the appeal against Tower Hamlets' refusal of permission to develop the Wharf.

Richard Harwood QC (see p.666) A silk whose reputation and profile are fast on the rise. He has authored a number of standard texts on planning and environmental law and frequently appears in the courts in high-profile cases. He acts for developers and landowners as well as government authorities and interest groups. **Strengths:** "He is extremely clever and gets to the heart of the issue in no time at all. His knowledge is encyclopaedic across planning and heritage matters." "He very easily inspires confidence in clients and his cross-examination is absolutely forensic. He isn't aggressive – he just quietly picks people apart." **Recent work:** Defeated four important judicial reviews concerning the Thames Tideway Tunnel. The project is the largest to go through the nationally significant infrastructure regime.

Thomas Hill QC A consistently highly thought-of silk who concentrates his practice on major infrastructure work over a range of sectors. He has expertise in airports, ports and energy projects including renewables. **Strengths:** "The quality of his advice and the way he conducted himself on our behalf was very professional. He has such a clear understanding of this area of the law." "He has a special expertise in the area of renewable energy development as well as aviation matters." **Recent work:** Acted for Hallam Land Management in a long-running public inquiry regarding a new neighbourhood development at Aylesbury, heavily opposed by the local community.

John Steel QC (see p.772) Due to his complementary practice in aviation, John Steel often acts on major infrastructure cases regarding airports, but he is just as comfortable engaging with other significant infrastructure, leisure, retail or residential development matters as well as cases covering mineral or waste concerns. His technical nous enables him to tackle complex cases, whether they are in relation to engineering, environmental or compulsory purchase complications. **Strengths:** "Knowledgeable and tactically aware, particularly on CPO matters." "Has a good grasp of the issues and provides excellent advice on tactics and procedures." **Recent work:** Provided extensive advice to Cornwall County Council regarding policy development in relation to the regeneration of St Austell, Blaise and the formerly polluted Clay Area in north-west Cornwall.

Paul Stinchcombe QC A strong advocate in matters ranging from compensation cases and inquiries to judicial reviews. He has extensive experience of both promoting and opposing large-scale development projects. **Strengths:** "He's very honest and candid: as much as you might not want to hear it, he'll tell you what you should hear, and that is what you need." "He will go the extra mile in preparation and ensure that he has the fullest understanding of the client's instructions and requirements so as to be best able to represent them." **Recent work:** Acting for Eastleigh Borough Council, resisted four applications for housing developments of differing sizes and at separate locations. The cases raised important issues as to whether countryside protection policies can be rendered out of date by reason of housing shortfall.

James Strachan QC A tactically and technically minded QC who has won a strong reputation both at the Bar and among his clients for his work on major developments. His infrastructure résumé includes a substantial appointment promoting the HS2 rail project for the government. He is also well versed in the housing, retail, highways and urban design fields. **Strengths:** "A surgical strategist – starts with the big picture then immerses himself in the detail to deliver the winning blows at inquiry." "A real tactician who is able to steer a clear course through the most complex disputes." **Recent work:** Appeared for the Forge Field Society in its challenges to two separate planning applications relating to the historic village of Penshurst. Both permissions for new housing developments were successfully quashed based on consideration of the statutory requirements when dealing with conservation areas and listed buildings.

Brian Ash QC Appears regularly at major inquiries, in judicial reviews and in the courts tackling a host of diverse planning matters. He is extremely experienced in cases relating to compulsory purchase, highways law, environmental issues, retail development and infrastructure projects. **Strengths:** "He is friendly, with a relaxed manner, but robust when required to make representations to the inquiry. He makes his advocacy look effortless."

Stephen Tromans QC Formerly a solicitor for nine years before being called to the Bar. Throughout his career he has specialised in energy, environment and planning law, and he frequently acts in nuisance claim cases, judicial reviews, appeals and other instances where his specialisms converge. He is also well versed in international (particularly EU) cases. **Strengths:** "Still one of the leading brains in environment and planning law at the Bar." "He's very authoritative and very clever but also approachable and able to explain himself clearly and persuasively. He's one of those old-fashioned persuasive advocates who speaks the judges' language." **Recent work:** Advised Cuadrilla on the development of exploration sites for hydraulic fracturing (commonly known as "fracking").

JUNIORS

James Burton Over the past year, he has worked on some of the most high-profile cases in the market. His expertise in environmental law proves useful in a number of the matters he handles. **Strengths:** "I am impressed by his breadth of knowledge, efficiency and thoroughness. He is extremely committed and hard-working, as well as personable, always approachable and patient in explaining complex matters to clients." "An excellent planning barrister, with strength in associated areas, who is a good all-rounder." **Recent work:** Represented the landowner in a complex five-week inquiry into the Port of London's CPO of Orchard Wharf, opposite the O2 Arena.

Andrew Tabachnik An expert in residential promotion, regeneration and retail development among other areas. A seasoned advocate in inquiry and High Court scenarios that may involve additional considerations such as green belt impact, compensation or listed buildings, he frequently appears for big-name developers, as well as local authorities and other interested parties. **Strengths:** "A barrister with a very powerful intellect." "A real black-letter lawyer who can really get down into the rules and regulations, and who is particularly good at cross-examination." **Recent work:** Represented developers Grainger in a fraught battle concerning the redevelopment of land above Seven Sisters tube station, which requires the demolition of a locally listed building in order to go ahead. He assisted the developers in successfully resisting a judicial review of the planning application, in both the High Court and the Court of Appeal.

Richard Wald Has written extensively on his specialisms of planning, environmental, energy and administrative law and is a member of the Attorney General's B Panel of Junior Counsel. He acts for both public and private clients. **Strengths:** "He's very clear in his written opinions, but his real advantage is that you can put Richard in front of a client and he is able to distil the legal facts and put them into language that clients and developers really understand." "Top-notch advice every time – he's strategically aware and gives solution-focused advice time and time again." **Recent work:** Acted for William Davis Ltd and Hallam Land Management in an appeal against Warwick District Council's refusal to grant planning permission to a 1,000-home scheme. Issues of heritage and conservation were at the heart of the debate, given the proposed site's close proximity to Warwick Castle and surrounding parkland.

Christiaan Zwart (see p.802) Has ability and experience in niche areas including development finance, DCO infrastructure cases and Community Infrastructure Levy matters, the last of which he has particular expertise in. His client base extends internationally and he is a regular advocate in High Court and Supreme Court cases as well as Lands and Tax Chambers. **Strengths:** "The phrase that springs to mind is 'very collaborative'. We could bounce ideas off each other and get to a practical solution rather than him being very dictatorial." **Recent work:** Instructed by the Examining Authority for the UK's first tidal wave electricity generating station at Swansea Bay. His role involved advising on terms of the draft order as well as the procedure to reduce the risk of a judicial review challenge.

Jonathan Darby (see p.628) Acts in all aspects of planning processes for domestic and international clients, including landowners, developers, third parties and local authorities. He is also well versed in environmental law, and his practice takes in criminal proceedings related to planning and the Environmental Protection Act 1990. **Strengths:** "A clear advocate, who is persistent and tenacious and does very well with the court." "John is extremely competent, very good in conference and someone who gives pragmatic advice on issues. Rather than stick strictly to the legal position, he can offer other potential options to explore." **Recent work:** Acted pro bono for the appellant Mr Turner in an appeal challenge brought against the Secretary of State with regard to the apparent bias of a planning inspector. The case attracted much attention as it arose out of an inquiry into the promotion of major development for the South Bank and the Shell Tower.

Ned Helme Has a diverse planning practice and a good reputation among clients drawn from a number of sectors. His broad areas of expertise encompass environmental, financial regulatory and public law, making him very knowledgeable on cross-disciplinary matters. He frequently prepares and acts for clients in inquiries and judicial reviews. **Strengths:** "Goes the extra yard for the client. I'm very impressed by the effort he has been willing to make." **Recent work:** Acted successfully for Valley Grown Nurseries in a judicial review of a decision to grant the organisation planning permission for a 92,000 sq m glasshouse in the Lee Valley. Issues raised include the implementation of NPPF green belt policy, Environmental Impact Assessment, habitats and the Lee Valley's own development plan.

John Pugh-Smith (see p.744) Focuses his practice on town and country planning law and environmental law, and is also an accomplished mediator. He most frequently represents local or central government authorities and interested parties such as objectors or claimants in a variety of planning cases. **Strengths:** "Approachable and calm. As safe a pair of hands as you'd expect from such an experienced practitioner." "Really good with clients: he's not afraid of taking the bull by the horns and getting to the facts, giving the right advice even if he thinks that advice will be unpopular." **Recent work:** Acted for the claimant, a local farmer, in a High Court judicial review of planning permission granted by Cornwall County Council to allow a hard-rock quarry to reopen on Lizard Peninsula. Environmental Impact Assessment was a central element of the argument.

Rose Grogan (see p.660) Offers planning expertise to an enviable roster of clients, and has a number of high-profile house builders and universities among her clientele. As well as being led by QCs in inquiries and appeals, she also acts as sole counsel. She also has burgeoning expertise in complementary areas of construction, environmental and energy law. **Strengths:** "When cross-examining in an inquiry she has a punch that belies her very pleasant exterior." "She's very helpful and positive in her approach." **Recent work:** Appealed against refusal of planning permission for the University of Sussex's campus masterplan. Heritage issues, landscape impact and the consideration of student housing were all prominent elements of the case.

Victoria Hutton (see p.679) A relatively new face at the Bar and already considered one of the most capable juniors in the market for representing developers, individual objectors and local authorities in varied planning law cases. She has led cases as sole counsel in the Court of Appeal. **Strengths:** "She gets stuff done with a quick turnaround and makes herself available and accessible. A good junior to have on board." "She's very quick to pick up on points of weakness and help clients through those." **Recent work:** Appeared for an interested party of local citizens opposed to the construction of a 9,000-capacity mosque in West Ham. A high-profile and controversial development which was opposed for a number of reasons, most notably the scale and sustainability of the project along with concerns about traffic, contamination and social cohesion.

Daniel Stedman Jones Came to the Bar with government experience and a dedicated focus on planning and environment law. He represents clients of all kinds, both public and private, in the full range of tribunals, inquiries, appeals and other court matters, and has a strong track record in judicial reviews. He is also knowledgeable on town and village greens, highways and rights of way laws. **Strengths:** "He is a pleasure to work with, as he is dynamic, commercially aware and thinks outside the box. He is an outstanding advocate who continually impresses when faced with tough opposition." **Recent work:** Appeared for the claimant developer in a judicial review challenge to the lawfulness of the Loxwood Neighbourhood Plan and an associated planning appeal. The appeal regarded the refusal of planning permission for reasons of prematurity and alleged non-compliance with the neighbourhood plan. This appeal was recovered for determination by the Secretary of State, and the two reviews ran concurrently.

Band 4

Cornerstone Barristers

See profile on p.823

THE SET

Cornerstone boasts a highly capable set of barristers who apply their skills to all elements of planning law. It has a number of deeply experienced silks, as well as some of the most promising juniors at the Bar, many of whom are familiar with matters that require a specialist touch. Members handle inquiries, judicial reviews, hearings, High Court and Court of Appeal cases for a wide range of clients.

Client service: "The clerks are very helpful and will accommodate you. They're very responsive and will bend over backwards. They are excellent and always willing to negotiate fees. They do training for us too." "Always receive excellent assistance from Ben Connor's practice management team. They are efficient and effective in the service they provide."

SILKS

Mark Lowe QC (see p.703) A prominent silk in the planning sphere who has practised in the field for over 30 years. He maintains a strong general practice with capability across all types of planning and environmental law and continues to appear in major cases, including those concerning infrastructure projects. **Strengths:** "Incredibly friendly and good to work with, and has a huge amount of respect. You can really sense when judges lean into people, and Mark has that gravitas to make your client's case as strong as possible." "Absolutely excellent; the service is second to none." **Recent work:** Represented a consortium of Buckinghamshire authorities in front of the HS2 Select Committee, whose case concerned improved mitigation where the route passes through the county. Planning issues on the table included green belt policy, landscape, heritage, highways and traffic, waste, environmental and community impact.

James Findlay QC Operates a substantial planning practice in Scotland as well as in England and Wales. He is particularly adept at dealing with controversial or complex cases with a high profile. His work for local authorities often concerns housing or energy projects. He also frequently represents developers in these matters as well as in cases relating to CPOs and retail and leisure development. **Strengths:** "James is very quick to understand complex legal situations and advise on the best way forward in sensitive situations." "He is a consummate team player and he commands authority in a calm, quiet manner. He gives the whole team confidence." **Recent work:** Appeared in an appeal before the Supreme Court challenging the decision by Scottish ministers to grant permission to an Aberdeenshire offshore wind farm. The proposed farm would be in direct view of Trump International, Scotland, the golf course owned by client Donald Trump.

Michael Bedford QC (see p.593) A new silk with an established practice who acts in cases concerning developments of all kinds. He is particularly seasoned in inquiries and often promotes major infrastructure cases. He has assisted with a diverse host of schemes, including those relating to castles and tank farms, and is an expert in the more standard residential and retail schemes. **Strengths:** "Impeccably prepared, calm and unflappable. Quietly brilliant." "He has an amazing ability to combine forensic analysis and fine-grained understanding of the real nitty-gritty details of a case with a view of the bigger picture. He is good at anticipating where objectors may spot weakness." **Recent work:** Defended Teinbridge District Council against a challenge to the adoption of its plan for local development on the basis of alleged breaches of the Habitats Directive and Strategic Environmental Assessment Directive.

Richard Ground QC (see p.660) Extensively experienced in planning inquiries, both major and local, and also an expert in planning, village greens, local government and environmental law. His skill extends to challenging cases concerning enforcement, infrastructure and more. **Strengths:** "He's a very good judge of situations and he's very sensible. One of those people you instinctively trust." "On the ball, extremely professional, and very well prepared." **Recent work:** Represented local authorities in Slough in the inquiry into SIFE Railfreight terminal, which would be the largest development of its kind in London's green belt for some years. The proposed buildings of 2 million sq ft were pitched for a site that was also proposed for a third runway for Heathrow and was additionally entangled with the HS2 project.

JUNIORS

Mary Cook (see p.622) Continues to stand out at the junior Bar for her wealth of planning expertise. Developers and landowners turn to her to promote complex, high-value cases and offer advice on pre-applications through to appeal. **Strengths:** "Clear, incisive and sharp, she actually manages to be pleasant while being an aggressive advocate." "She is top-quality, has an eye for detail, is incredibly supportive of the team, and is very good at giving guidance. You feel as though you're in safe hands all the way through the process." **Recent work:** Advised the London Borough of Southwark throughout several regeneration projects involving the Elmington Estate. Assisted in a number of aspects including checking over the applications and Section 106 agreements, setting up three CPOs and subsequently acting at inquiry for one of the three.

Thomas Cosgrove (see p.624) Acts for an array of clients ranging from interest groups to house builders and retailers, and is a regular feature at residential and heritage development inquiries. He is also expert in the field of renewable energy projects. **Strengths:** "Not only is he good on the papers, but he is a fearsome and extremely capable advocate. Without fear of exaggeration or contradiction, he would be one of the best senior junior planning barristers anyone could get in the country. He should be a QC." "A rigorous cross-examiner. He gives people a hard time in the best possible way." **Recent work:** Fought for Powys County Council in the biggest ever onshore wind farm public inquiry in the UK, concerning proposals for five farms. The case raised questions on energy policy, visual impact, ecology and heritage.

Jonathan Clay (see p.618) An able and experienced advocate who acts for major players in residential and infrastructure development cases. His areas of expertise also include enforcement, renewable energy, village greens and commercial development. **Strengths:** "The perfect example of a barrister who can deliver a successful case without any drama." "A very effective advocate who's excellent at identifying key issues." **Recent work:** Acted for the Suffolk District Council in Hopkins Homes v Suffolk Coastal DC, one of the most prominent cases concerning interpretation of the NPPF.

Robin Green (see p.660) Advises and appears for developer and local authority clients at inquiry and in the High Court. His practice encompasses all aspects of planning law and he has niche experience in such areas as planning-related professional negligence. **Strengths:** "Worth his weight in gold. He provides very clear, practical advice, often reducing complex issues to easily understandable summaries. His advocacy is like his approach to providing advice in that it very clearly focuses on the issues at hand." "He is thorough and painstaking, and he emanates assurance." **Recent work:** Acted for the Roseacre Awareness Group in the first planning inquiries into proposals for fracking in the UK. Exploration in aid of this controversial gas extraction method was opposed by both local residents and the council in Roseacre Wood, Lancashire.

Asitha Ranatunga (see p.748) Frequently handles wind farm cases and other renewable energy proposals, but is an expert in all manner of planning cases. He often represents local authorities regarding their development plans, and appears at examinations and challenges. **Strengths:** "He has an efficient and effective approach to work and problem solving. His ability to take in information and act upon it under time-limited conditions is very impressive." "Quick and clear advice." **Recent work:** Acted for South Norfolk District Council in defending its decision to refuse outline planning permission for a scheme for up to 650 houses at Cringleford.

Paul Shadarevian (see p.762) A former solicitor who represents public and private entities of all kinds in inquiries and High Court appearances. He has a wealth of appeals experience, especially acting for local authorities, and has handled a number of major infrastructure cases. **Strengths:** "Very knowledgeable in planning law and extremely focused on securing the best for the client." "He is invaluable as he gets straight to the key points in conference, he wins his points calmly without showboating, and he keeps tight control of the case." **Recent work:** Assisted Gloucester City Council at appeal in defending their position against Peel Holdings. The company had been refused an application for an out-of-town retail redevelopment as it threatened the viability of the town centre and the council's own town centre regeneration plans. Advice given in the lead-up to the inquiry led to the withdrawal of the appeal and a second refusal for the scheme.

Wayne Beglan (see p.594) Handles planning cases as part of his wide-ranging local government practice. He represents both local authorities and private clients. **Strengths:** "A strong advocate in the High Court who is very well structured in terms of his arguments and very clear on what his case is." "A tough cookie." **Recent work:** Represented Welwyn Hatfield Council in both stages of a public inquiry, along with a subsequent High Court challenge to the Secretary of State's refusal of planning permission for a proposed recycling and energy recovery facility to be located in the town.

Estelle Dehon Dedicates a significant portion of her practice to planning law, frequently representing interest groups, individuals and local authorities in sometimes controversial cases. She regularly appears in public inquiries concerning substantial development proposals. **Strengths:** "Intellectually outstanding and also pleasant and personable." "Her work rate is impressive, and her attention to detail and tenacity are equally so." **Recent work:** Advised Friends of the Earth from the committee stage on four connected appeals regarding objections to fracking at two sites in Lancashire. The client was granted Rule 6 status to appear at the inquiry regarding the one outstanding appeal, which they will provide with evidence on environmental and climate change factors, waste and public health.

Ryan Kohli (see p.692) Typically undertakes work for local authorities and the Secretary of State, and has notable experience in inquiries that throw up technical issues. He is also familiar with appeals against enforcement notices. **Strengths:** "Very succinct and gets to the point quickly. His written advice is very good and clients love him – he's charming." **Recent work:** Acted as sole counsel to the Secretary of State in resisting a Section 289 challenge against the decision of an inspector to refuse an appeal against an enforcement notice issued by Guildford Borough Council.

Clare Parry (see p.734) Has crossed swords with some of the Bar's top planning barristers in judicial reviews and inquiries. She is appointed to the Attorney General's C Panel. **Strengths:** "She always delivers a first-class service. She turns jobs around very efficiently and often when faced with very difficult time constraints." "She has good knowledge and is excellent in court." **Recent work:** Appeared on behalf of Lewes District Council in a judicial review challenge against the council's formation of a new neighbourhood plan. Claims included breaches of the Strategic Environmental Impact Directive and Habitats Directive, as well as a breach of the common law standards of fairness. The challenges were rejected, with permission granted to appeal on one point only.

Harriet Townsend (see p.783) Has a strong track record of handling CPO cases, development inquiries, enforcement appeals and other hearings. She has recently been tackling matters relating to high-end basement proposals and cases involving heritage or preservation concerns. **Strengths:** "She has excellent knowledge of planning and environmental law. A very surefooted advocate who is without arrogance. She shows good judgement when presenting cases and is very thorough in her preparation." **Recent work:** Acted for Denbighshire County Council in an inquiry brought by the owner of the Denbigh Hospital, a Grade II listed building. The owner objected to compulsory acquisition of the site, raising a number of arguments including allegations of fraud and conspiracy against the council, habitat concerns over bat populations, and the disclosure of funds claimed by the owner but used by the council for necessary works on the property.

Band 5

6 Pump Court

See profile on p.897

THE SET

A smaller but undeniably effective chambers well liked by local authority clients, as demonstrated by its appointment to the London Boroughs Legal Alliance panel for planning law. Members of the set also frequently represent private developers, landowners and third parties. Members here have high levels of experience in enforcement matters, environmental considerations, appeals and local plan advice. They are also experts on planning policy and planning-related criminal proceedings. Clients say that this is "an intimate and approachable set."

Client service: "A very professional set of chambers that provides a comprehensive service which includes a regular programme of planning law update seminars and public inquiry training. The clerks, led by Peter Constable and supported by Ryan Barrow, give flexible and professional support in arranging procedural matters. In particular, I frequently use the chambers for Direct Access instructions, and they are well geared up to deal with this approach."

JUNIORS

Mark Beard A leading junior known for his holistic planning practice that covers residential, energy, retail and leisure development, as well as matters of enforcement and planning policy. He has experience with diverse technical cases in the sector, including those involving housing supply, conservation and green belt issues. **Strengths:** "Great all-rounder, a skilled advocate and a calm head in a storm." "Local authorities trust him. He's got a very sensible head on his shoulders." **Recent work:** Instructed by Countryside Properties to advise on and promote a large residential development within the High Weald Area of Outstanding Natural Beauty. Due to the location, local opposition was high and the LPA withdrew initial support for the scheme. Following two appeals, planning permission has been granted.

William Upton Secretary of the Planning and Environment Bar Association, with over 20 years of experience in the field at his command. He represents both developers and local authorities and also frequently engages with planning policy. He is called upon by LPAs to advise on core strategies and also has the technical nous to handle niche cases (especially those with environmental overlap) as well as broad mainstream matters. **Strengths:** "His intelligence is just amazing. Somehow you'll give him the papers and he seems to have a wide understanding of the whole issue in a very short time. He focuses on the pertinent issues immediately." "He's a powerful advocate who is able to reveal the weakness in an appellant case." **Recent work:** Represented the Exmoor National Park Authority in the Divisional Court against appellant Mr Wilmot's challenges to his conviction for eight listed building offences. The allegations included that the NPA were guilty of contempt and that Wilmot's convictions were based on false evidence. Judges rejected his appeal, having decided there was no justification for setting aside the earlier decision.

Anne Williams (see p.796) Receives praise for her consistently high-quality client service as well as her keen legal skills. A qualified planner and regular inspector at village green inquiries as well as a barrister, she is able to apply her extensive experience to high-profile and complex cases of all types. She represents developers and public authorities. **Strengths:** "A consistently reliable and solid barrister. Her greatest strength is her adaptability and flexibility in being able to approach each case differently as the circumstances require." "She is thorough, patient, understanding and forceful when necessary." **Recent work:** Successfully defended against an appeal regarding the refusal of planning permission for residential development in Moddershall Valley, Stafford. The valley, set to be designated as a World Heritage Site, contains a large number of "heritage assets" including 12 flint mills which originally supplied the Potteries.

Richard Banwell Known for his environmental expertise, he is particularly adept at handling cases where planning and environmental law overlap. He specialises in renewable energy projects and complex enforcement inquiries for both local authorities and developers. He is also experienced in large-scale inquiries of many kinds, including those regarding tall buildings in central London. **Strengths:** "He has particular expertise in drainage issues and similar water-related matters." "He is very straightforward, and there's not a lot of pomp and circumstance with him. He's very easy to talk to and clear in his advice." **Recent work:** Advised Dover District Council on the updated planning application of the Lydden Hill Racing Circuit. The circuit had operated subject to permission from 1986 with inadequate controls, and an abatement notice had to be served after submission of the updated application due to noise nuisance concerns.

Edward Grant Maintains a diverse client base of developers, local authorities and interested third parties whom he advises and acts for in inquiries. He is familiar with all aspects of planning law and in particular has experience in large housing cases and criminal proceedings arising from enforcement prosecutions. **Strengths:** "Tenacious advocate who is incisive and able to get the heart of the case." "He has written a textbook on enforcement so he knows the procedures thoroughly." **Recent work:** Represented the London Borough of Haringey at inquiry, resisting a proposal to build around 100 new homes on sites designated as part of ecological corridor and safeguarded Crossrail land.

Emmaline Lambert (see p.694) Respected as a strong junior in the field who has broad experience of inquiries, enforcement matters and High Court challenges. She represents a diverse range of clients and has also co-authored a book on her specialist subject of enforcement. **Strengths:** "She is sensitive but very confident and sharp, particularly in advocacy. She's always calm and focused, and clients are always impressed by her client care and attention. She has the ability to see issues others haven't thought of." **Recent work:** Acted for the London Borough of Hackney in a highly publicised case concerning a block of flats built by Yusuf Sarodia and his company Garland Development. Permission was granted for 14 flats and commercial floor space, but instead 34 flats were constructed with no commercial space and the building measuring higher than granted. An initial enforcement notice was not complied with. Eventual confiscation proceedings resulted in a historic fine handed down by the borough.

Megan Thomas Has over 20 years of experience of handling a wide range of cases including those relating to enforcement, local plan advice, conservation and housing. She is well versed in infrastructure projects. **Strengths:** "Has a particularly good grasp of the environmental elements. She is quietly very good at what she does." **Recent work:** Instructed by Epping Forest District Council in a judicial review of their decision to grant planning permission to a nursery extension in the green belt and regional park. The case raised the question of whether new agricultural buildings in the belt must be assessed for their impact on its openness, as well as whether ecological assessment would be required for impact on nearby protected areas.

Other Ranked Lawyers

Gordon Nardell QC (20 Essex Street) Known for his environmental credentials, which he applies to planning cases concerning development projects at home and abroad. He also has a burgeoning reputation in the energy sector. **Strengths:** "He's just super-intelligent. He's very good on highly technical issues: things like habitat regulations and complex challenge work. He's able to give very good technical but strategic advice."

Jonathan Karas QC (see p.687) (Falcon Chambers) A noted land law practitioner who regularly handles planning cases. He has particular expertise in highway law as well as cases concerning the compulsory acquisition of property rights. He has recently been involved in a number of high-value compulsory purchase cases. **Strengths:** "It's quite a niche area where real estate and planning combine, but he is fantastic and as good as any I've worked with in terms of his responsiveness and his engagement. He was very clear with the client as to the strengths and weakness of the case." "Has an outstanding ability to break down tricky issues, and provides clear and practical advice." **Recent work:** Acted for United Utilities in promoting a CPO to acquire land for substantial environmental improvements needed for the Eccles Waste Water Treatment Works.

Marc Willers QC (Garden Court Chambers) A leading specialist in Gypsy, Traveller and Roma law who has edited a number of books on the subject. He generally represents individual and group objectors against local or national authorities. **Strengths:** "In his delivery, he makes you feel comfortable and then of course he trips you up, which is a good skill. Not that he's trying to make you fall over but he will get the point out of you that you're trying to steer clear from." **Recent work:** Represented claimants challenging the Secretary of State's refusal to revoke the appeal decisions made in their cases, despite the fact that the recovery of those decisions for his own determination had been found to be unlawfully discriminatory in Moore and Coates v SSCLG. The claim went through to appeal.

Timothy Straker QC (4-5 Gray's Inn Square) Has a history of acting for London authorities on large-scale projects in both public law and planning contexts. He has promoted major infrastructure projects and acted on regeneration schemes for public and private clients. He also has related experience with environmental impact assessment. **Strengths:** "Very patient, thorough and great to work with." "Absolutely excellent. He goes the extra mile, is tactical, and will give you the advice as it is." **Recent work:** Instructed by authorities in Buckinghamshire, Hillingdon, Kensington and Chelsea along with the National Trust concerning the parliamentary proceedings for HS2, the UK's largest infrastructure development.

Martin Kingston QC (No5 Chambers) A discerning silk remarkably well respected both at the Bar and by instructing solicitors. He regularly takes on large-scale, high-profile cases and has been involved in a number of major infrastructure and energy projects in recent years. He is very active in the Planning Court and Court of Appeal. **Strengths:** "His knowledge knows no bounds. He's also client-friendly and solution-focused." "He has set the standard at the Planning Bar for the last 20 years."

Celina Colquhoun (No5 Chambers) Has a practice with infrastructure cases at its core, and has handled a number of matters concerning major projects in the transport sector in particular. She further undertakes CPO, waste management and local impact matters among others. **Strengths:** "In court, she has an ability to withstand quite intense questioning. She doesn't get flustered, she is very calm, and she stands firm." **Recent work:** Undertook a challenge to the Neighbourhood Plan of Chiltern District Council. The absence of rigour in the plan was challenged on several fronts, including an argument that the council had been wrong to reject inspector recommendations and had applied the wrong approach to basic conditions. In a rare successful outcome, the entire plan was overturned.

MIDLANDS

Planning
Leading Sets
Band 1
No5 Chambers *
Leading Silks
Star individuals
Kingston Martin *No5 Chambers*
Band 1
Cahill Jeremy *No5 Chambers* Ⓐ
Crean Anthony *Kings Chambers (ORL)* ◊ *
New Silks
Kimblin Richard *No5 Chambers*
Leading Juniors
Band 1
Goatley Peter *No5 Chambers* Ⓐ
Young Christopher *No5 Chambers*
Band 2
Choongh Satnam *No5 Chambers* Ⓐ
Clover Sarah *Kings Chambers (ORL)* ◊
Jones Timothy *No5 Chambers* Ⓐ
Richards Hugh *No5 Chambers*
Up-and-coming individuals
Corbet Burcher James *No5 Chambers*
Osmund-Smith Thea *No5 Chambers*
Pindham Nina *No5 Chambers*
Smyth Jack *No5 Chambers*
* *Indicates set / individual with profile.*
Ⓐ *direct access (see p.24).*
◊ *(ORL) = Other Ranked Lawyer.*
Alphabetical order within each band. Band 1 is highest.

Band 1

No5 Chambers

See profile on p.931

THE SET

No5 maintains its reputation as the leading planning set in the Midlands, and is home to an impressive list of silks and juniors. It offers wide-ranging expertise across planning law from compulsory purchase orders to energy and infrastructure matters, and has an excellent reputation for High Court challenges and judicial review work. Members of the set regularly act for national developers and house builders and are instructed by prominent consultancies. Sources remark on them being a "heavyweight in planning," noting that "No5 does some incredible work in the planning sector."

Client service: "The clerks are very usable and honest, and they will work with you and stay in touch to keep you updated. They are very responsive and I feel like I am well looked after and in safe hands." "Andy Bisbey is absolutely great. He will bend over backwards to do what he can and will always accommodate regardless. He always finds someone really helpful, and it's guys like Andy that make a chambers." Andrew Bisbey is the practice manager for planning.

SILKS

Martin Kingston QC A pre-eminent planning silk, with a highly regarded practice, noted for his involvement in high-profile and complex energy and infrastructure cases. He has particular expertise in nuclear matters. **Strengths:** "One of the best lawyers of his generation and a star individual nationally, not just in the Midlands. He is a class act." "Exceptional, a delight to work with and a first-rate silk, ideal for complex cases. He's clear-thinking at all times."

Jeremy Cahill QC Extremely well-regarded silk, highly regarded for his expertise in all matters relating to five-year land supply. His sector expertise encompasses retail, commercial and care home cases. **Strengths:** "A good old-fashioned street-fighting advocate who you want in your corner." "An excellent advocate with an incisive and commercial approach who has considerable experience across the spectrum of planning and environmental law."

Richard Kimblin QC An esteemed silk who acts for clients including developers, public sector organisations and the government. He regularly handles cases involving energy, infrastructure and residential schemes. **Strengths:** "A perfect blend of knowledge and pragmatism. Richard is excellent both in his advice and on his feet." "He is knowledgeable in both planning and environmental law. He has a real attention to detail and leaves no stone unturned." **Recent work:** Acted for the Secretary of State in Oxfordshire County Council v Secretary of State for Communities and Local Government and Others, a case examining planning obligations and requirements, as well as monitoring fees.

JUNIORS

Peter Goatley Commended by sources for his expertise in both an advisory and litigation context. He typically acts for impressive clients, including those in the public sector. **Strengths:** "Excellent and eloquent advocate who is a good strategist and an asset to any client team." "He is a robust junior, a good lawyer and someone with a lovely manner. He is a genuinely nice person and very good at what he does."

Christopher Young Enjoys an excellent reputation for his practice dedicated to the fields of town and country planning, compulsory purchase and highways law. He is often instructed in inquiry and High Court proceedings for developers, national house builders and major retailers. **Strengths:** "Works tirelessly at planning inquiries to cover all possible issues and is very strong on five-year housing land supply and viability issues." "He has a great client base and is very good on residential work, displaying an amazing attention to detail." **Recent work:** Represented DLA Delivery in DLA Delivery v Lewes DC and Newick Parish Council, a High Court challenge to the Newick Neighbourhood Plan.

Satnam Choongh Well regarded for his broad expertise spanning planning and environment law, he has particular prowess in the retail, residential and waste sectors. He garners praise from peers and clients for both his strategic advisory and advocacy abilities. **Strengths:** "He has a lot of gravitas and loads of commercial experience." "He is clever, highly motivated and good-humoured." **Recent work:** Represented Richborough Estates on the promotion of 113 residential units at Gateway Avenue, Baldwins Gate, Newcastle-under-Lyme, outside a village boundary.

Timothy Jones Widely regarded in the market for his niche expertise in Gypsy and Traveller planning cases. He is additionally skilled at handling matters regarding neighbourhood plans, compulsory purchase, highways, the Community Infrastructure Levy, and town and village greens. **Strengths:** "He is just all-round brilliant." "One of the most expert barristers representing Gypsies and Travellers. His expertise in this area is second to none, particularly when it comes to interpreting statutory provisions." **Recent work:** Acted for the lead claimant in R (Moore) v Secretary of State for Communities and Local Government and Bexley LBC, a successful application for judicial review of the Secretary of State's decision to recover Gypsy planning appeals for determination by him.

Hugh Richards Attracts praise from market sources for his wide-ranging experience of handling High Court litigation and inquiry work, acting for both local authorities and developers. He is noted for his adept handling of infrastructure and energy matters. **Strengths:** "He inspires confidence in his team and he will get right to the point in a case and get it across nicely and firmly. He just inspires confidence." "He is a forceful advocate and looks after his clients' interests very effectively. "

James Corbet Burcher An up-and-coming junior frequently highlighted for his client-friendly approach who is developing a strong reputation in the market. He is commended by sources for his adept handling of assets of community value and for his work in neighbourhood planning and residential development matters. **Strengths:** "He has a good style and intellectual approach." "He comes back very quickly, lets you know what he is doing and doesn't leave you hanging. He is very capable and very keen."

Thea Osmund-Smith Noted for her strong inquiry practice, she regularly advises major clients including energy providers, house builders and local authorities. She attracts a wealth of praise from market sources, who cite her as one to watch due to her dedication and enthusiasm. **Strengths:** "She is very, very good, and has a lovely manner. She is client-friendly and pursues points very thoroughly." "She is enthusiastic and an excellent junior."

Nina Pindham New entrant to the table who is highlighted by commentators for her intellectual and diligent approach to cases. She frequently represents landowners, developers and local authorities on an array of planning matters. She is experienced in acting for clients at inquiry, in the High Court and the Court of Appeal. **Strengths:** "She is only a junior barrister but her ability to crack intellectually challenging issues is unbelievable. If you think of it as chess, she is always three or four moves ahead of the opposition." "She has proved very responsive within short timescales when dealing with urgent work."

Jack Smyth Attracts praise for his confident advocacy style and client manner. He has experience of appearing in the High Court, acting on a number of high-profile cases. He is also developing emerging expertise in planning injunction matters, regularly advising local authorities. **Strengths:** "His planning expertise is second to none, especially for someone so junior. He's a confident advocate, clients are always happy, and I can't fault him." "He has clarity of thought, engages well, is really interested in the case and makes it easier as a result of his good insight into matters. He is also incredibly quick." **Recent work:** Represented Harborough District Council in Crane v Secretary of State for Communities and Local Government and Harborough District Council. In this matter he resisted a statutory challenge under Section 288 of the 1990 Planning Act.

Other Ranked Lawyers

Anthony Crean QC (see p.626) (Kings Chambers) Highly respected planning silk who garners praise for his High Court experience and his flair for advocacy. He frequently represents well-known developers in high-profile planning inquiries and regularly acts for clients in the Court of Appeal. **Strengths:** "He is an innovative and strategic thinker who is good with clients." "He's an imaginative and able lawyer." **Recent work:** Acted for Oxford City Council, successfully defending a judicial review brought by GRA Acquisition.

Sarah Clover (Kings Chambers) Able to handle a diverse range of planning disputes, and has particular expertise in development and enforcement matters. She has a wealth of experience in housing land supply issues and in planning challenges in the High Court. **Strengths:** "Her sense of humour, professionalism, confidence and unquestionable planning expertise just shine through." "A very good team player who gels excellently with everyone. She is very organised and a very good advocate." **Recent work:** Acted for Bromsgrove District Council in relation to the successful refusal of a planning appeal at Whitford Road and associated works.

NORTHERN

Planning
Leading Sets
Band 1
Kings Chambers *
Senior Statesmen
Senior Statesmen: distinguished older partners
Sauvain Stephen *Kings Chambers* *
Leading Silks
Band 1
Crean Anthony *Kings Chambers* *
Fraser Vincent *Kings Chambers* *
Manley David *Kings Chambers* *
Tucker Paul *Kings Chambers* *
Leading Juniors
Band 1
Barrett John *Kings Chambers* *
Cannock Giles *Kings Chambers* *
Carter Martin *Kings Chambers* *
Ponter Ian *Kings Chambers* *
Band 2
Easton Jonathan *Kings Chambers* *
Hunter John *Kings Chambers* *
Reid Sarah *Kings Chambers* *
Stockley Ruth *Kings Chambers* *
Up-and-coming individuals
Gill Anthony *Kings Chambers* *
Humphreys Freddie *Kings Chambers* *
** Indicates set / individual with profile.*
Alphabetical order within each band. Band 1 is highest.

Band 1

Kings Chambers
See profile on p.968

THE SET

Kings Chambers continues to be the standout set for planning in the region, and has unparalleled strength and depth among its members. It offers broad expertise and has impressive advocates who regularly act for clients in high-profile appeals, inquiries and hearings. Its members also have extensive judicial review experience and are particularly adept at handling village green matters. Kings Chambers' barristers frequently act on behalf of an array of clients including local authorities, major developers, house builders and national retailers. Sources particularly praise the size and diversity of the set's offering, with one interviewee stating: "They continue to offer the strongest service outside of London in planning and environment matters."

Client service: "They have friendly, approachable clerks who go the extra mile to help out. It is very helpful having the option of a Leeds base as well as Manchester." "The clerking is extremely efficient. The clerks are always courteous and very helpful and understand your needs. They give you options not problems." William Brown is the senior clerk for planning concerns.

SILKS

Stephen Sauvain QC (see p.759) Lauded as a leading silk in planning and universally regarded as an expert in all areas of highways law. He maintains an excellent advisory practice and is noted for his complementary expertise in environment and local government matters. **Strengths:** "He is the go-to barrister for all matters related to highways and his knowledge in this area is unsurpassed. He has an easy-going manner with both his instructing solicitors and clients which creates a good working relationship." "A brilliant planning QC and an excellent orator." **Recent work:** Acted in Timmins v Gedling BC concerning whether a cemetery is an appropriate development in a green belt after the publication of the National Planning Policy Framework.

Anthony Crean QC (see p.626) Commands an excellent reputation for his broad planning expertise, and is particularly noted by sources for his work in the residential sector. He acts for clients across the public and private sectors and is praised for his smooth and innovative advocacy style. **Strengths:** "He is incredibly smooth and one of the leading silks in the area." "He is an excellent advocate in the planning and environment sector. He can synthesise difficult stuff and really articulate it all very well indeed." **Recent work:** Acted for Cheshire East Council, successfully bringing a Section 288 claim against the Secretary of State for Communities and Local Government and Richborough Estates.

Vincent Fraser QC (see p.648) Widely recognised as a standout silk in the field of renewable energy, and regularly acts in some of the most prominent cases regarding solar, wind and biomass energy. He has additional expertise in the residential and retail sectors, and advises on significant development projects. **Strengths:** "He is very thorough and very prepared. He is a tenacious cross-examiner and prepares his team well for inquiry." "He is a skilled advocate and gets to the heart of the matter." **Recent work:** Represented REG Windpower in its successful appeal in respect of an application for five wind turbines up to 100 metres in height.

David Manley QC (see p.706) Highly regarded planning silk with impressive environmental crossover capabilities, who has a wealth of experience of advising national house builders and retailers on a broad array of planning matters. He has an esteemed inquiry practice and is also adept at handling judicial review cases. **Strengths:** "He provides both pragmatic and extremely comprehensive legal advice. He is a highly effective advocate with a very client-focused approach." "He carries a lot of respect; when he speaks everybody listens and his reputation goes before him. He is very effective at thinking on his feet. Because of his experience and knowledge he is a force to be reckoned with." **Recent work:** Acted for Yorkshire Water in its successful appeal regarding substantial alterations to the listed Butterley Reservoir Spillway.

Paul Tucker QC (see p.785) Praised as a key figure in planning with noted expertise in inquiries. He is highlighted for his adept handling of significant complex development matters for residential, infrastructure and retail clients. He has additional expertise acting for public sector organisations. **Strengths:** "He gives pragmatic advice and has a way of simplifying legal principles and practical ramifications so that clients are in a position to give instructions with confidence." "He is always very approachable and down-to-earth. He is direct in his advice, and is a hard-hitting QC who is very popular." **Recent work:** Acted for Gallagher Estates in its successful appeal for permission for 450 dwellings on land at Heathcote, Warwick.

JUNIORS

John Barrett (see p.590) Widely praised for his residential expertise and his abundance of planning experience. He frequently acts for national house builders and developers, and has particular strength in judicial and statutory reviews and Local Plan adoption cases. **Strengths:** "He is phenomenally knowledgeable, extremely personable and easy to work with. He is firm but fair and is very clever at addressing weak points in the case." "He is exceptional." **Recent work:** Acted for Tensi Homes in relation to an appeal for a large residential development on a greenfield site on the edge of a Cheshire village.

Giles Cannock (see p.611) Commended by sources for his wide-ranging planning expertise and thorough approach to cases. He is especially adept at handling energy infrastructure, residential development, compulsory purchase order and highways matters. **Strengths:** "He is very thorough and thinks a lot about a case in terms of strategy and getting the detail right. On the professional side the quality of his work is exemplary, and he is assertive and firm, but not aggressive. He is very good with clients, and is a good team player as he gets the best out of people." "A bright, strong advocate, very good on tactics in difficult judicial review cases." **Recent work:** Successfully acted for the developers in promoting a highly controversial residential development of up to 250 homes on a greenfield site, as an urban extension to Middleton St George in Darlington.

Martin Carter (see p.612) Well known for his appeals work on behalf of housing developer clients. Additionally, he is held in high regard for his significant experience in town and village green cases and is praised by sources for his thoughtful and diligent approach. **Strengths:** "He works hard for clients and takes a pragmatic approach." "He is considered and calm, with a good eye for detail and sound judgement." **Recent work:** Successfully acted for a landowner resisting an application to register land as a village green, in order to protect its development prospects.

Ian Ponter (see p.739) Esteemed for his planning and environmental expertise, he regularly acts for developers and land promoters. He has noted expertise in statutory challenges, judicial review and compulsory purchase matters. He is regarded as an excellent advocate and praised by sources for his commercial sensitivity. **Strengths:** "He is quite formidable in his intellectual capacity and approach to jobs. The insight he brings reduces complex cases to quite simple points. Intellectually he is very good and he has an easy charm about him." "He is an excellent advocate who is quick-thinking on his feet." **Recent work:** Acted for the developer in a planning inquiry against the refusal of planning permission for the proposed residential development of a greenfield in a village in Nottinghamshire.

Jonathan Easton (see p.638) Valued for his practical approach and drive to go the extra mile for clients. He centres his well-regarded practice on residential development and social housing matters. He is also adept at handling a range of highways and compulsory purchase matters. **Strengths:** "He is a very effective advocate and really stretches the team to find all of the angles. He is very creative and innovative in his approach, and doesn't just do what you would expect – he thinks outside the box." "He is articulate and a good team player. He is great to kick ideas around with to reach a pragmatic solution."

John Hunter (see p.678) Well regarded for his advocacy skills and High Court work, he has a wealth of experience in planning inquiries and related court proceedings. He frequently acts for developers, local authorities and other interested parties. **Strengths:** "He is very professional and his written work is very good. He understood and clarified our position perfectly and was able to summarise it in a really concise and clear manner that put our case across perfectly." "He is a very good advocate to work with, and has an incredibly good memory and a genuine interest and enthusiasm about the law and its detail." **Recent work:** Acted successfully as junior counsel for the claimant in R (Robert Hitchins Ltd) v Worcestershire CC, allowing it to avoid further payment towards new highways infrastructure.

Sarah Reid (see p.750) Attracts plentiful praise for her wide-ranging planning practice, and frequently acts on behalf of developers and local authorities. She is noted for her expert strategy and effective advocacy style. **Strengths:** "She is one of the most thorough lawyers that I have ever come across. She is extremely good on matters of detail and fact, very insightful when it comes to the law and someone who manages to put the most complex of matters in ways that clients understand." "She shows a very great attention to detail and is very, very focused. She is very good at motivating and is a good leader of a team." **Recent work:** Represented Shropshire Council in the case of The Stew, Frankwell Quay, Shrewsbury, a five-week inquiry into an application to demolish an 18th century building in a Conservation Area.

Ruth Stockley (see p.773) Respected planning junior, widely regarded as an expert in highways law. Her practice also spans environment, compulsory purchase, village greens and judicial review matters. **Strengths:** "She is excellently prepared, performs well on her feet, and is an absolute pleasure to work with." "She is alive to the angles and issues in a case and thinks two steps ahead. She is very user-friendly, and very patient with both instructing solicitors and clients." **Recent work:** Acted for Wigan Council in relation to two co-joined planning appeals seeking to resist the grant of planning permission on two greenfield sites for nearly 400 new houses.

Anthony Gill (see p.653) An up-and-coming junior with a broad planning offering, who acts for clients in residential, retail, renewables, highways and enforcement matters. He is commended by sources for his thorough and organised attitude to a case. **Strengths:** "He is a hard-working, incisive and commercial operator." "He is a friendly character and makes sure you cover everything. He picks up on things you might not have thought of."

Freddie Humphreys (see p.677) New entrant to the table who is praised by sources for his fresh and collaborative approach. He has experience in a range of inquiries, and regularly handles enforcement prosecution and appeals work. **Strengths:** "A rising star, relatively recently called to the Bar, but who seems to understand what it is all about, and has a good grasp." "He is a good junior who is well prepared and personable."

WESTERN

Planning
Leading Juniors
Band 1
Wadsley Peter *St John's Chambers (ORL)* ◊

Ranked Lawyers

Peter Wadsley (St John's Chambers) Experienced in cases at the intersection between environmental and planning law. He is highly experienced in inquiries and appeals, as well as in judicial review proceedings, and frequently acts on behalf of local authorities and developers. **Strengths:** "Extremely knowledgeable and has a huge amount of experience. He is very approachable and a lot of authorities instruct him directly because they have such a good relationship with him." "He has a wealth of experience and an innate ability to think on the hoof, whether in conference or in court. He is a real master of his craft – he's seen it all before and he knows law and policy inside out." **Recent work:** Acted in R (Port Regis School) v North Dorset District Council, a case regarding planning applications where Masonic activities were involved. Two of the councillors determining the applications were Masons, and the case considered whether there was apparent bias in the decision process.

POCA WORK & ASSET FORFEITURE: An Introduction

Contributed by The Chambers of Andrew Mitchell QC

POCA Introduction: Renewal, Reform; Renaissance?

The evolution of the world of asset forfeiture continues apace and the provisions of the Proceeds of Crime Act 2002 continue to engage the attentions of the appellate courts and Parliament like a bothersome wasp. The late Lord Bingham's valiant attempt to clarify the law in relation to confiscation proceedings, seems, sadly, to have had little impact. The 'proliferating case law', (*R v May* [2008] 1 A.C. 1028), which in his judgment added little comprehension to the statutory provisions in question, continues to flow from the appellate courts. In the first half of 2016 the Court of Appeal Criminal Division considered more than a dozen cases in relation to the restraint and confiscation provisions of POCA alone.

The reverberations of the Supreme Court's statement of the importance of the application of Article 1 Protocol 1 of the ECHR to confiscation proceedings in the case of *R v Waya* [2013] 1 A.C. 294 continue to be felt. The Supreme Court, at least at first blush, appeared to uphold the approach of removing all sums received by a defendant in connection with their crime. Consideration of the outcome of the Court's decision may give reason to pause: what Mr Waya had removed from him was his profit from the transaction, not the turnover. Retrenchment usually takes place in careful stages.

Change, or at least development, continues in other corners of the field. The re-statement of the principles in relation to the existence and surmounting of the corporate veil, in *Petrodel* [2013] 2 A.C. 415, found its place in the confiscation landscape in *R v Boyle Transport* [2016] 4 W.L.R. 63. The correct approach to addressing such issues was set out in the authoritative ruling of Davis LJ on behalf of the Court of Appeal. At the same time, Davis LJ addressed another thorny issue: how does the court calculate benefit in circumstances where the underlying activity was lawful? The reference to a 'rogue trader', lawfully employed by a multinational merchant bank, who engages in an unlawful conspiracy to manipulate a benchmark for gain was as timely as it was insightful. It came just a few weeks before the commencement of the confiscation hearing in *R v Hayes*, the UBS trader convicted of LIBOR manipulation. *R v Hayes* also saw the ruling of Cooke J, sitting in the Central Criminal Court, in relation to the POCA s.10A application made by Mr. Hayes' wife. The new s.10A of POCA took effect mid 2015. It introduced a power to criminal courts dealing with confiscation proceedings to make binding determinations of ownership of assets, as between defendants and third parties. How much it will be used, and indeed should be used, is open to debate and argument. In *R v McCormick*, also heard at the Old Bailey this year, s.10A was utilised in a cross-border case, to bring both individual and corporate third parties into confiscation proceedings that were ultimately the subject of a compromise agreement. By way of contrast, the decision in *Hayes* went against the spouse, blocking her attempt to engage with the court. In the event, the confiscation order made in *Hayes* was for a sum far below that which was initially sought by the prosecution. The final judgment focused on the identification and removal of that which was identified in *Boyle* as the 'ill-gotten' gains obtained by the defendant; again considerations of proportionality were to the fore.

The theme of reform was evident elsewhere, as the House of Commons Home Affairs Select Committee reported, in June, upon its inquiry into the effectiveness of POCA. In particular, the inquiry focused upon the effectiveness of confiscation orders. Its recommendations included the creation of a 'properly resourced' specialist confiscation court, the creation of a new offence of failing to pay a confiscation order and an enhanced role for the private sector in collecting unpaid confiscation orders. The Select Committee did not accept the submissions to it for the reform of the criminal lifestyle provisions and the removal of the 'assumptions' from the confiscation process. Likewise, it made no recommendation for the enhancement of the existing civil recovery process. Some will regard these as missed opportunities for further, but much needed, reform.

The Government also pursued its own reform agenda. With the launch of the UK "Action Plan for anti-money laundering and counter-terrorist finance" in April, two consultations were issued: one in relation to legislative reform and a second in respect of AML Supervision. By far the most radical, and controversial, of these was the suggestion in the legislative reform consultation that the Suspicious Activity Report 'Consent' regime be abolished. The proposal that it be replaced with enhanced information sharing, both with law enforcement and across private institutions, met with critical responses, in particular from the representatives of the legal profession, concerned as to both the increased burdens it would place upon their clients and the threat of inroads into a client's legal professional privilege. The outcome of the consultation is awaited, but in times of straitened public finances it is possible to detect a strong motivation to remove the operative cost of the consent regime from the public purse.

In Europe, proceeds of crime reform initiatives come hard on the heels of their predecessors. The 4th EU Money Laundering Directive came into force in EU law on 26 June 2015, with domestic legislatures obliged to implement it within two years. Before the UK government had commenced its consultation in relation to it, the EU Commission issued, in July 2016, a formal Proposal for the amendment of the Directive. Changes to the disclosure of beneficial ownership information, increased powers to obtain information for FIUs and an enhanced due diligence regime for entities in high-risk jurisdictions are amongst the new measures. The Proposal also sought the acceleration of the deadline for implementation by 6 months, to January 2017. A 5th AML Directive had been anticipated; the Commission would appear to have preferred to push the implementation of its most urgent reforms via an amendment instead.

This, of course, leads to perhaps the greatest potential area of reform of them all. What will occur if, or when, the United Kingdom excises itself from the European Union, and potentially the Council of Europe's Convention on Human Rights and Fundamental Freedoms? Which laws will remain on the statute books, which will be amended, and which will be wholly replaced are questions that are yet to be addressed. The Money Laundering Regulations are a case in point. Prescribed by EU law, they exist as domestic legislation. The need for, and utility of, counter-money laundering and terrorist financing laws is manifest: a theme taken up by the Home Affairs Select Committee. However, what form they should take, their scope and the degree to which they should burden the businesses to which they apply, remain areas of continued and forceful debate. Would the UK government introduce different, perhaps more relaxed, standards from those required by Europe? Would continued trade require a level playing field? Or would the UK government see it as important to have the most rigorous levels of regulation? There is some reason to believe that the latter may be the option taken – see its previous 'gold-plating' approach to regulation in this field.

Asset forfeiture and proceeds of crime therefore remains an area for continued renewal, reform and, in the event of a departure from the EU, maybe even a renaissance in the common law.

It is the quintessential specialist area, yet it requires the ability to command disparate disciplines: from crime to property law and equity, from commercial law to receivership. It demands of its practitioners the insight and judgement obtained from hard won experience.

Clients will need, and with this Guide will find, those practitioners who possess the required abilities to lead them through the hazards that are inherent in litigation in this field.

ALL CIRCUITS

POCA Work & Asset Forfeiture
Leading Sets
Band 1
The Chambers of Andrew Mitchell QC *
Band 2
6KBW College Hill
Matrix Chambers *
3PB Barristers *
3 Raymond Buildings Barristers *
5 St Andrew's Hill *
Leading Silks
Star individuals
Mitchell Andrew *The Chambers of Andrew Mitchell QC* *
Perry David *6KBW College Hill*
Band 1
Farrell Simon *3 Raymond Buildings Barristers* [A]
Fisher Jonathan *Red Lion Chambers (ORL)* ◊
Hall Jonathan *6KBW College Hill*
Owen Tim *Matrix Chambers*
Band 2
Brodie Graham *The Chambers of Andrew Mitchell QC*
Campbell-Tiech Andrew *Drystone Chambers (ORL)* ◊ *
Fisher Richard *Doughty Street Chambers (ORL)* ◊ [A]
Montgomery Clare *Matrix Chambers* *
Peto Anthony *Blackstone Chambers (ORL)* ◊
Rainsford Mark *The Chambers of Andrew Mitchell QC* *
Shaw Antony *Red Lion Chambers (ORL)* ◊
New Silks
Ashley-Norman Jonathan *3 Raymond Buildings Barristers* [A] *
Talbot Kennedy *The Chambers of Andrew Mitchell QC* *
** Indicates set / individual with profile.*
[A] direct access (see p.24).
◊ (ORL) = Other Ranked Lawyer.
Alphabetical order within each band. Band 1 is highest.

POCA Work & Asset Forfeiture
Leading Juniors
Star individuals
Bird Andrew *5 St Andrew's Hill* *
Band 1
Bodnar Andrew *Matrix Chambers*
Cassidy Sheena *3PB Barristers*
Evans Martin *The Chambers of Andrew Mitchell QC* *
Fletcher James *5 St Andrew's Hill* *
Jackson Fiona *The Chambers of Andrew Mitchell QC* *
Smith Ian *The Chambers of Andrew Mitchell QC* *
Band 2
Convey Christopher *The Chambers of Andrew Mitchell QC* *
Hays William *6KBW College Hill*
Jarvis Paul *6KBW College Hill*
Lennon Jonathan *Carmelite Chambers (ORL)* ◊ *
Stancombe Barry *The Chambers of Andrew Mitchell QC* *
Band 3
Dennison James *5 St Andrew's Hill* *
Freeman Lisa *Furnival Chambers (ORL)* ◊ *
Green Timothy *Outer Temple Chambers (ORL)* ◊ [A]
Krolick Ivan *Lamb Building (ORL)* ◊
Osman Faisal *The Chambers of Andrew Mitchell QC* *
Powell Oliver *Outer Temple Chambers (ORL)* ◊
Rudolf Nathaniel *25 Bedford Row (ORL)* ◊
Small Penelope *The Chambers of Andrew Mitchell QC* *
Yeo Nicholas *3 Raymond Buildings Barristers* [A] *

Contents:

Band 1

The Chambers of Andrew Mitchell QC

See profile on p.819

THE SET

Widely regarded as the pre-eminent set for proceeds of crime and asset forfeiture matters, this chambers boasts a market-leading team of specialist silks and juniors who handle cases across the full spectrum of POCA work. Members act on behalf of prosecuting authorities, defendants, regulatory bodies, receivers, companies and third parties, and have recently been instructed in some of the most significant precedent-setting cases in this field, including R v Harvey. This case established that when making a confiscation order and assessing the benefit obtained by the offender, any VAT which has already been accounted for to HMRC should not be included. The strength of the team has recently been bolstered by the addition of Ian Smith from 11 Stone Buildings.

Client service: "The clerks can't do enough for you. They're excellent, and very helpful whether on the phone, over e-mail or in person. They are very easy to talk to and negotiate with, and great at arranging telephone conferences – they take all the pressure off you and just go ahead and sort everything out." Practice manager Martin Adams "is just phenomenal – he will move mountains to get you the hearing you need, and he has a personal touch with both the staff and barristers."

SILKS

Andrew Mitchell QC (see p.719) Frequently cited as "the godfather of POCA," Mitchell has great experience in this area and is frequently instructed in precedent-setting cases. **Strengths:** "He really is a leader in the field and a cut above the rest because of his experience of dealing with cases at the highest level. His advocacy skills are exemplary because they are matched with a deep knowledge of both civil and criminal POCA matters." "He could charm the birds from the trees – his manner in court is impeccable." **Recent work:** Appeared in the Supreme Court on behalf of the appellant in R v Harvey, which established that when calculating the amount of a confiscation order, any VAT which has been accounted for to HMRC should not be included.

Graham Brodie QC Acts for claimants and defendants in proceedings relating to allegations of commercial wrongdoing. He handles cases concerning restraint, freezing and confiscation of assets in both the civil and criminal spheres. **Strengths:** "He's an extremely able barrister who is easy to work with, communicative, responsive, and hard-working. He thinks through issues in a detailed and methodical manner, and is also willing and able to come up with novel and effective solutions to problems." **Recent work:** Represented a former Goldman Sachs banker in confiscation proceedings following a conviction for money laundering in Nigeria.

Mark Rainsford QC (see p.746) Handles specialised financial crime, proceeds of crime and asset recovery cases. He boasts particular expertise in money laundering matters. **Strengths:** "He's a lovely guy to work with and a good lawyer, who is also very experienced in civil fraud, meaning he brings an extra dimension to his cases. He has a good rapport with the judges." "Mark is sensible, practical and knows what he's doing." **Recent work:** Acted for the principal defendant in a privately funded case concerning allegations that the client had laundered the proceedings of a number of boiler room frauds based in the UK and abroad.

Kennedy Talbot QC (see p.777) A highly specialist practitioner who "lives and breathes POCA" according to sources. He is well versed in all aspects of civil recovery, disclosure, restraint, receivership and asset confiscation. **Strengths:** "Kennedy has a brilliant, brilliant mind and fantastic drafting skills." "He is extremely knowledgeable and one of the longest-established practitioners in this area, so he really knows his stuff." "One of the foremost experts in confiscation and restraint law, he is extremely erudite and very good with clients."

JUNIORS

Martin Evans (see p.642) Boasts expertise in both POCA and criminal fraud matters. He has recently represented the prosecuting authorities in a number of high-level restraint, money laundering and confiscation cases. **Strengths:** "He is very good and very knowledgeable, and has a great eye for detail. His written work is extremely good, and he is very approachable and a real team player." "Clever, engaged, personable and very knowledgeable, he's a pleasure to work with." **Recent work:** Acted for the CPS in the Supreme Court case of R v Harvey, which determined that the VAT element of sums should be discounted when calculating the benefit figure in confiscation proceedings.

Fiona Jackson (see p.681) Experienced criminal counsel who assists defence and prosecution clients with fraud, POCA and asset recovery matters. She is also regularly instructed in cases with international elements, including those relating to international mutual legal assistance and international regulatory work. **Strengths:** "Her knowledge of the law and ability to express arguments is as good as it gets – plus she is great to talk to and very user-friendly." "A really good, hard-working barrister with mature judgement. You need someone whom you can trust and whose judgements stand up in court, and hers do." **Recent work:** Instructed by the CPS in confiscation proceedings concerning the failure of the defendant to comply with a confiscation order made for several million pounds' worth of assets acquired through a long-running VAT fraud scheme.

Ian Smith (see p.768) Commercial litigator and criminal lawyer who has a specialist knowledge of POCA. **Strengths:** "He's someone you can turn to for a quick answer, who is very direct and pragmatic in his approach." "Ian is very good at handling the civil/criminal interplay in POCA matters." "He is hard-working, utterly committed, great with clients, and someone who sees the big picture."

Christopher Convey (see p.622) Frequently acts for defendants and third parties in POCA proceedings relating to allegations of business crime and corporate wrongdoing. He has particular experience of advising offshore trusts on money laundering and compliance issues. **Strengths:** "Very smart, and very thoughtful in his approach to cases – he has a strategic overview of the case. He brings intellectual rigour to a case, and is tough as well – he's not afraid to make unpopular arguments." **Recent work:** Acted for the CPS in proceedings surrounding the imposition, appeal against and subsequent enforcement of a confiscation order made in relation to the proceeds of tax credit fraud.

Barry Stancombe (see p.771) POCA and asset forfeiture specialist with noteworthy experience in civil recovery and receivership. He acts for receivers and prosecuting authorities amongst others. **Strengths:** "His technical knowledge of POCA work is fantastic. The strategy and tactics he employs are impressive – he thinks well ahead and guesses what the opponents will do." "He is a very polished professional from a civil law background, who is a great asset when you're dealing with asset forfeiture where crime and civil proceedings overlap." **Recent work:** Acted for the SFO in confiscation proceedings against the former director and chief executive of JJB Sports.

Faisal Osman (see p.731) Enters the rankings this year in recognition of his growing expertise and reputation in this space. He regularly advises claimants and third parties on asset recovery matters, and also handles confiscation, fraud and regulatory enforcement. **Strengths:** "He is delightful, highly intelligent and someone with a prodigious appetite for work, who is a real rising star in both the civil as well as the criminal fields." "For a young and upwards moving junior he is fantastic – he's very intelligent, very good at paperwork and he produces fantastic skeleton arguments with great attention to detail. If you instruct him as a junior you get silk-standard advice without the price." **Recent work:** Instructed as specialist confiscation counsel on behalf of the defendant in R v Bostock, a complex cross-border case regarding a benefit sought of over £250 million.

Penelope Small (see p.767) A new entry to the rankings this year, who is recognised for her specialist expertise in POCA proceedings, asset recovery and restraint orders in both the civil and criminal spheres. **Strengths:** "Penny is dynamic, works extremely hard and is very client-focused and proactive." "She is very, very clever and has a very deep understanding of POCA matters." **Recent work:** Instructed by the SFO as specialist counsel for the restraint and confiscation proceedings following conviction in Operation Steamroller. This case involved the theft of over USD100 million through a major boiler room fraud operation.

Band 2

6KBW College Hill

THE SET

The barristers of 6KBW College Hill regularly advise clients on civil recovery mandates and represent them in judicial reviews. They are frequently involved in international POCA work, and recently acted on behalf of the Kuwaiti authorities in international restraint proceedings. One client described the set as being "strong from top to bottom; you know you're getting quality." Another source remarked that "the members go the extra mile".

Client service: Clients comment that Andrew Barnes's clerking team is "always very helpful, and very keen to assist." Deputy senior clerk Mark Essex was picked out by a client as "one of the best clerks there" and someone who "just can't do enough for you".

SILKS

David Perry QC Market leader for advice on restraint and money-laundering matters, most notably for clients based abroad, including those in Hong Kong. **Strengths:** "He remains the consummate performer, and if you are lucky enough to get him to appear in a case then you are fortunate indeed." "From an academic point of view he is the best in the business, and he is someone who takes a holistic view of the law." **Recent work:** Represented the Foreign & Commonwealth Office in a confiscation order case.

Jonathan Hall QC Highly esteemed for his work in civil recovery, and an expert on freezing and disclosure orders. He also advises on domestic and international restraint and receivership in confiscation cases. **Strengths:** "Hall is an established player who is well beyond his year of silk in terms of his gravitas and the cases he deals with." "He's really clever, he writes well and he's a great advocate." **Recent work:** Acted for the UK government in a case concerning the calculation of benefit from organised crimes.

JUNIORS

William Hays Boasts particular strength in the field of financial crime, and regularly advises companies, international governments and prosecuting authorities. **Strengths:** "He's so bright he puts everyone around him to shame – he's a very clever young up-and-coming guy whose technical ability is second to none." "He really knows his way around this area of law." **Recent work:** Assisted the Italian government with a request to freeze assets held in a UK bank account.

Paul Jarvis Both defends and prosecutes in confiscation hearings and enforcement proceedings. He is an expert on cash forfeiture and restraint cases. **Strengths:** "His drafting skills are brilliant, and he's so clever it's ridiculous. He has a wonderful bedside manner with clients, and makes everyone feel quite tranquil." "His technical knowledge is sound, he's a good strategist and he handles complicated POCA matters." **Recent work:** Acted for Gurchuran Singh in defending a claim of possessing counterfeit goods and an appeal against a confiscation order.

Matrix Chambers

See profile on p.876

THE SET

A source describes this set as being "responsive, good with clients and home to some serious brainpower." Members have a focus on advising corporate and individual clients on allegations of money laundering and civil fraud, and assist international clients, particularly those from Hong Kong, with asset recovery matters. Recent cases include an appeal to the Supreme Court concerning joint benefit and apportionment.

Client service: The clerking team, which is lead by Paul Venables, is "always a real pleasure to deal with" and is "responsive and proactive."

SILKS

Tim Owen QC Key figure for confiscation and asset recovery cases, who is also well regarded for his advice on money laundering cases. **Strengths:** "He's exceptional – very bright, very well respected and an extremely good barrister." "He's perfect – he's really down to earth, extremely clever and not pompous in the least." **Recent work:** Advised the defendant GH on an appeal by the DPP concerning money laundering and criminal confiscation.

Clare Montgomery QC (see p.720) A key name at the Criminal Bar with a stellar financial crime practice strengthened by her expertise in asset forfeiture. She acts on domestic and international POCA matters. **Strengths:** "She's just top-drawer; she grasps things very quickly and gives easy-to-digest, no-nonsense advice." "She adds a huge amount of value, is terribly efficient and extremely user-friendly." **Recent work:** Instructed to represent ex-Birmingham City owner Carson Yeung in a money laundering case in the Hong Kong Court of Final Appeal.

JUNIORS

Andrew Bodnar Leading junior referred to by some instructing solicitors as 'Mr Asset Recovery', who assists with multi-jurisdictional restraint and asset forfeiture matters. He attracts praise for both his written and oral advocacy. **Strengths:** "He is capable of thinking both swiftly and outside the box, and is very confident and seemingly unflappable." "One of the best juniors in confiscation these days, he's had a clear focus on this area for a long time and knows it so well that he has the case law on the tip of his tongue." **Recent work:** Acted in SOCA/NCA v Kalsoom Amir/Sanam, a civil recovery claim under Part 5 of POCA against a man found to be an international drug dealer.

3PB Barristers

See profile on p.892

THE SET

Individuals here advise both claimants and defendants on cash seizures and freezing orders, as well as mainstream POCA work. They are involved in leading cases and recently represented the wife of a convicted money launderer in the Supreme Court

matter of Gohil v Gohil, assisting with all POCA issues which arose in the case. Members assist private individuals as well as government departments, financial institutions and tax advisers amongst others. A good proportion of their work is international in nature and a number of the counsel here have been called to the Bar in overseas jurisdictions. One client says of the set: "The barristers are always very accurate in their advice and invariably willing to be commercial when they need to be."
Client service: "The clerks are always very keen to help, willing to accommodate our needs and quick to get back to you." Chambers director Stuart Smith leads the clerking team.

JUNIORS
Sheena Cassidy According to sources, Cassidy is "undoubtedly the leading family law practitioner in asset forfeiture work." She is a leading figure for restraint and confiscation proceedings, and acts for the CPS, SFO and individual clients. **Strengths:** "She displays excellent attention to detail in complex confiscation and enforcement matters, and has an eye for detail when producing written submissions." "Second to none in terms of her work ethic, case engagement and advice." **Recent work:** Appeared in Re White; Re Gangar, instructed by the SFO. The case concerned an application for a certificate of inadequacy by defendants found guilty of a Ponzi scheme fraud.

3 Raymond Buildings Barristers
See profile on p.904
THE SET
Well-known set that acts for both individuals and agencies in cases concerning allegations of fraud, money laundering and insider dealing. Members appear as both prosecution and defence counsel in restraint, confiscation and civil recovery proceedings, and assist with search and seizure orders and receivership applications. The set was recently instructed in the Court of Appeal case of R v Gray and Doran regarding the defendants' liability to pay excise duty upon smuggled goods. Sources say that "the set is full of very bright people who work at a high level."
Client service: "The clerking team is stellar, it's a Rolls-Royce operation. They not only solve problems quickly but anticipate them and get ahead of issues before we've even thought of them. They're a class apart and the best of any chambers I've worked with." Eddie Holland is senior clerk at the set.

SILKS
Simon Farrell QC Has particular expertise in money laundering, corporate crime and tax fraud which informs his POCA practice. **Strengths:** "Highly respected for his knowledge of the area and the strategic steer he gives on cases." "He's a very personable gentleman and a really good advocate who has broken into the top echelons of POCA work." **Recent work:** Instructed by the CPS in the Court of Appeal case of Lambert & Walding, a leading case on the division of benefit between defendants in confiscation cases.

Jonathan Ashley-Norman QC (see p.585) Has a strong focus on fraud and regulatory mandates. He advises on civil recovery and confiscation proceedings, often acting for the defence. **Strengths:** "He is a good opponent – he is pragmatic, charming and fights well for his client." "He is a class act." **Recent work:** Represented the appellants in R v Gray and Doran, an appeal against a conviction for massive excise evasion in respect of 20 million smuggled cigarettes and the associated benefit figure of £4.4 million.

JUNIORS
Nicholas Yeo (see p.801) Frequently represents clients in money laundering, confiscation and cash recovery cases, and advises on restraint order applications. **Strengths:** "He's very good with clients, very articulate, very bright, and has a great ability to grasp a brief." "He's a feisty advocate and a nice guy who knows what he's doing." **Recent work:** Acted as junior counsel in Malabu Gas & Oil, an application to discharge a restraint order made in respect of monies said to be the proceeds of corruption involving the government of Nigeria and two of the world's largest oil companies.

5 St Andrew's Hill
See profile on p.912
THE SET
The set has a particular focus on asset forfeiture, confiscation orders and money laundering cases. Members frequently advise on search and seizure warrants, and act for the NCA in challenges to search warrants and POCA Production Orders in the context of money laundering investigations. They further appear for and against receivers in fraud and asset recovery matters. Cases handled include R v Hayes, where the set advised Hayes' wife on confiscation proceedings regarding marital assets following Libor fraud. Market sources say the individuals here are "creative, commercial and not afraid to roll up their sleeves and get involved."
Client service: Commentators report that "overall the clerking is brilliant." The chambers director Wayne King is singled out for particular praise, with sources saying "he is top-notch" and "he runs a very tight ship."

JUNIORS
Andrew Bird (see p.596) Outstanding junior in the fields of asset recovery and police powers, including search warrants and production orders. He is highly sought after by government bodies. **Strengths:** "He straddles the divide between civil and criminal law with comfort, and he's fantastic at judging a tribunal. He really knows his onions. You can put a point to him and he'll come up with creative solutions quickly, which is what you want in a barrister. He's good strategically, good on his feet and good on paper." **Recent work:** Represented HMRC in a case involving the forfeiture of a statue looted from Libya.

James Fletcher (see p.646) Assists the CPS and SFO with asset forfeiture and restraint cases. He regularly advises HMRC and specialist defence bodies on freezing and confiscation orders, and acts in cases concerning enforcement, money laundering and search warrants. **Strengths:** "He has so much knowledge about fraud and POCA, and is always willing to help, answer questions and discuss things with us." "He's excellent – he's very bright, thorough, pleasant and good to work with." **Recent work:** Represented the NCA in civil recovery proceedings relating to five properties.

James Dennison (see p.632) Acts for the CPS and the SFO in asset recovery and civil fraud cases. He also advises on confiscation and restraint mandates. **Strengths:** "He is very well organised and tactically astute." "James Dennison is the prosecutor's choice."

Other Ranked Lawyers

Nathaniel Rudolf (25 Bedford Row) Enters the rankings this year in recognition of the glowing reviews he receives from clients, who praise both his vast knowledge and client skills. His practice covers serious fraud, high-value confiscation proceedings and related matters. **Strengths:** "He's the guy you can call with a tricky issue and he will immediately give you sound, knowledgeable, level-headed advice. He has a phenomenal capacity to deal with large, complex cases and complex data. He's a bit like a walking encyclopaedia." **Recent work:** Represented the defendant in R v Roewal and Others, both with regard to allegations of international money laundering and the subsequent confiscation proceedings.

Anthony Peto QC (Blackstone Chambers) Handles a range of POCA and civil recovery matters as part of his commercial advisory and civil fraud practice. He has recently been active on a number of matters for government agencies. **Strengths:** "He's very proactive and displays excellent analytical skills."

Jonathan Lennon (see p.699) (Carmelite Chambers) Regularly handles POCA matters arising from criminal fraud trials including those concerning money laundering, tax evasion and conspiracy to fraud. He acts for prosecuting authorities including the SFO, and also defends professional individuals and business owners. **Strengths:** "He's extremely articulate and intelligent, and impresses with his advocacy skills – he certainly manages to get the attention of the court and the judge." "Very conscientious and someone with great drafting skills." **Recent work:** Represented the SFO against Yemen's former president Ali Abdullah Saleh in a case revolving around bribery allegations and the subsequent freezing of the defendant's UK-based assets.

Richard Fisher QC (Doughty Street Chambers) Primarily assists defendants in cases involving allegations of fraud and money laundering, assisting with all stages from pre-trial advice and restraint orders to post-conviction confiscation proceedings. **Strengths:** "He's very charming, very bright, very hard-working and obviously a specialist in financial crime, POCA work and tax fraud." "He is strong in court and has a good presence in front of the judge."

Andrew Campbell-Tiech QC (see p.610) (Drystone Chambers) Has extensive experience of handling POCA matters including restraint and confiscation proceedings arising from criminal trials. **Strengths:** "He has an exceptional level of intellect and first-rate experience within this field, demonstrated by the quality and accuracy of his advice. On a personal level he is completely honest and direct in his approach – he is completely straightforward, says it as he sees it and is wholly transparent." "His intellect and judgement are first-rate, and he gets straight to the point in POCA matters." **Recent work:** Represented the defendant in Kakkad, a case considering whether the existing precedent on the calculation of benefit with relation to seized drugs is compatible with the ECHR principle of proportionality.

Lisa Freeman (see p.648) (Furnival Chambers) Recognised as a strong advocate in POCA proceedings, who regularly handles asset restraint and civil recovery cases. She also advises on anti-money laundering regulation and compliance. **Strengths:** "Lisa has a great legal mind," and is "a formidable opponent in court."

Ivan Krolick (Lamb Building) Has long-standing experience in the POCA, asset forfeiture and financial crime sector. He has particular experience of handling confiscation proceedings. **Strengths:** "Ivan is very clever and has appeared in some of the field's leading cases."

Timothy Green (Outer Temple Chambers) Has a substantial POCA practice, and handles money laundering, cash forfeiture, restraint and confiscation proceedings on behalf of defendants, third parties and prosecuting authorities. **Strengths:** "He has a very good reputation, and he makes well-structured, attractive submissions where everything is very well thought through." "He has great oral advocacy skills, he's very good in court, and he has good strategic nous as well. He thinks of different ways of presenting the case and explores different angles so as to present it in the best possible way." **Recent work:** Acted in Re Timothy Baker, advising the defendant on the review of a confiscation order relating to offshore assets.

Oliver Powell (Outer Temple Chambers) Represents the Crown and defendants in freezing injunctions, restraint, confiscation and civil recovery matters. He is also experienced in advising on cash seizure and money laundering cases. **Strengths:** "He's brilliant with clients, very bright, really quick to grasp things and has really good communication skills." "The quality of work that he does is exceptional and he punches above his weight – he'll often be against silks and leading juniors even though he's less senior because he's such an expert in this area of the law. What it comes down to is that he just works harder than anyone else – he's completely committed to his client's cause."

Jonathan Fisher QC (Red Lion Chambers) Has a well-respected practice and frequently assists high-profile individuals, City firms and US firms with money laundering issues. **Strengths:** "He's always very responsive, and he understands our business – he's a leader in this field but he is also down to earth and understands commercial concerns as well as the law." "He's highly intelligent, very responsive, easy to work with, and a person whom clients quickly grow to trust."

Antony Shaw QC (Red Lion Chambers) Handles high-value confiscation matters as part of a specialised serious fraud practice that sees him tackling money laundering, white-collar crime and corruption litigation. **Strengths:** "He is an excellent silk to work with, not least because of his ability to give incisive written opinions. He also has excellent advocacy skills, and is very good at using new technology to aid case management." **Recent work:** Acted in R v Perrin & Faichney, appearing on behalf of a third party in confiscation proceedings against the defendants.

Contents:

ALL CIRCUITS Mainly Claimant

Police Law: Mainly Claimant	
Leading Sets	
Band 1	
Doughty Street Chambers *	
Band 2	
Garden Court Chambers *	
Matrix Chambers *	
Leading Silks	
Star individuals	
Kaufmann Phillippa	*Matrix Chambers*
Williams Heather	*Doughty Street Chambers*
Band 1	
Cragg Stephen	*Monckton Chambers (ORL)* ◊
Hill Henrietta	*Doughty Street Chambers* [A]
Southey Hugh	*Matrix Chambers* *
Band 2	
Bowen Nicholas	*Doughty Street Chambers* [A]
Hermer Richard	*Matrix Chambers*
Laddie James	*Matrix Chambers*
Metzer Anthony	*Goldsmith Chambers (ORL)* ◊
Owen Tim	*Matrix Chambers*
Ryder Matthew	*Matrix Chambers* *
Thomas Leslie	*Garden Court Chambers*
Leading Juniors	
Star individuals	
Brander Ruth	*Doughty Street Chambers*
Band 1	
Bunting Jude	*Doughty Street Chambers*
Law Helen	*Matrix Chambers*
Macdonald Alison	*Matrix Chambers* *
Sikand Maya	*Garden Court Chambers*
Straw Adam	*Doughty Street Chambers*
Band 2	
Brown Nick	*Doughty Street Chambers*
Gallagher Caoilfhionn	*Doughty Street Chambers* [A] *
Gask Alex	*Doughty Street Chambers*
Gerry Alison	*Doughty Street Chambers*
Hemingway Sarah	*Garden Court Chambers*
Morris Anna	*Garden Court Chambers*
Murphy Fiona	*Doughty Street Chambers*
Simblet Stephen	*Garden Court Chambers*
Stanage Nick	*Doughty Street Chambers* [A]
Thacker Rajeev	*Garden Court Chambers*
Up-and-coming individuals	
Desai Raj	*Matrix Chambers*
Minetta Morris Una	*Garden Court Chambers*
Nicholls Jesse	*Doughty Street Chambers*

** Indicates set / individual with profile.*
[A] direct access (see p.24).
◊ (ORL) = Other Ranked Lawyer.
Alphabetical order within each band. Band 1 is highest.

Band 1

Doughty Street Chambers

See profile on p.828

THE SET

Described by a source as "the go-to chambers" in this field, Doughty Street advises on a range of actions against the police, including those concerning data retention, police negligence and the wrongful arrest of protestors. One interviewee states that the set "has always been the obvious place for police law." Of late, its members have been involved in the Hillsborough Inquest and the Pitchford Inquiry into undercover policing. Commentators enthuse that the barristers here are "top-class" and that Doughty Street is an "outstanding set."

Client service: Richard Bayliss is responsible for the actions against the police practice area. Sources are keen to highlight that the clerks are "invariably very helpful."

SILKS

Heather Williams QC A leading figure for abuse of police powers cases, especially those relating to disability discrimination and Article 3 abuses. She has a very strong reputation for her work representing protestors and the victims of undercover policing. **Strengths:** "She brings cleverness and simplicity to a case; her skill lies in turning complicated matters into a narrative people can understand." "Phenomenally bright, she will grasp the issues quickly and make excellent decisions." "She has an astonishing ability to produce excellence every time." **Recent work:** Represented a man shot by a Metropolitan Police officer in a claim alleging assault, police negligence and Article 2 violations.

Henrietta Hill QC Highly regarded for her work acting for families in inquests into police-related deaths. She also assists the victims of police discrimination. **Strengths:** "Her work is immaculate and her attention to detail is unimpeachable." "She goes the extra mile and gives you practical, very good advice." **Recent work:** Advised the Equality and Human Rights Commission in an investigation into the treatment of female, black and minority ethnic and homosexual officers by the Metropolitan Police.

Nicholas Bowen QC Handles claims against the police and other public bodies within the criminal justice system relating to negligence, malicious prosecution and misfeasance. **Strengths:** "He is a very bright and innovative lawyer." "He is very personable in his approach and good with clients." **Recent work:** Acted for 15 police officers bringing a claim against South Wales Police for false imprisonment, malicious prosecution and misfeasance following the murder of Lynette White.

JUNIORS

Ruth Brander An exceptional lawyer when it comes to actions against the police, inquests and cases concerning prisoners' rights. **Strengths:** "She is a dream junior to have; her arguments are perfectly honed and she is a delight to work with." "She has a real gift for identifying key issues in a case and how to exploit them." "She is exceptionally bright, hard-working and meticulously thorough." **Recent work:** Appeared in R (Hicks) v Commissioner of Police of the Metropolis in a challenge to arrests on the day of the Royal Wedding.

Jude Bunting Highly regarded for his advice on the legality of police investigations, and the duty of care owed to detainees to investigate their cases quickly. **Strengths:** "A very charming advocate." "His cross-examination is intuitive and skilled." "He is absolutely brilliant with clients, works extremely hard and has great attention to detail." **Recent work:** Acted in Zenati v Commissioner of Police of the Metropolis, which found that under Article 5 of the European Convention the police owe a duty to investigate criminal offences quickly.

Adam Straw Esteemed for his work representing clients in inquests, human rights cases and issues arising from police surveillance. **Strengths:** "He has an outstanding intellect and work ethic and is one of the best juniors around." "He is very good, and both understanding and accommodating." **Recent work:** Acted for Neville Lawrence in the inquiry into undercover policing.

Nick Brown Advises clients on wrongful arrests and injuries or deaths in police actions. He has additional expertise in medical and clinical negligence claims. **Strengths:** "Impressively thorough in his analysis, and someone with an exceptional eye for detail." "He is extremely hard-working and very bright." **Recent work:** Represented 77 of the families involved in the Hillsborough Inquest.

Caoilfhionn Gallagher (see p.649) Represents clients in inquests into deaths in police custody, and is no stranger to the Supreme Court. A number of her cases are sensitive and raise national security issues. **Strengths:** "She is ferociously hard-working" and "a really good lawyer with good judgement." "She puts everything into a case for her clients," "has an exceptional legal mind and is tenacious." **Recent work:** Acted for the family of 17-year-old Joseph Lawton, who took his life while in police custody. The case has led to greater support measures being introduced for 17-year-olds who have been detained.

Alex Gask Assists with claims against the police, particularly those relating to civil liberty infringements and human rights breaches. He is also an expert on inquests and prison law. **Strengths:** "He is very thorough in his preparation and takes a measured approach." "He was empathetic with the client and good tactically in the case." "He is client-focused and his client care is really good." **Recent work:** Acted for Dossett v Commissioner of Police, a claim for malicious prosecution arising out of the failed prosecution of three men for the murder of journalist Daniel Morgan.

Alison Gerry Acts in cases concerning breaches of the Human Rights Act and misfeasance in public office. She is particularly strong on malicious prosecutions and false imprisonment matters. **Strengths:** "She is incredibly bright, knowledgeable, personable and good with clients." "She has a fantastic ability to grasp and develop complex cases." **Recent work:** Represented three claimants in a claim against the Metropolitan Police for false imprisonment, assault and racial discrimination.

Fiona Murphy Represents clients in inquests and inquiries, particularly those relating to deaths in contact with police. **Strengths:** "Knowledgeable and approachable," "she is very aware of the right tactical approach to take." "She is really good at procedure and is sharp on her feet." **Recent work:** As part of the Pitchford Inquiry, she advised five women who were duped into deceptive relationships with police officers who were undercover. She also represented the families of deceased children whose identities were appropriated as part of the officers' cover.

Nick Stanage Advises on malicious prosecutions, the misuse of tasers and police discrimination. He has represented several political protestors in their actions against the police. **Strengths:** "Good at dealing with a fraught situation, and has a calming approach." "An astute and quick-witted advocate with excellent analytical skills and the ability to empathise with clients and explain legal issues clearly to them." **Recent work:** Represented several political and pacifist groups in the Pitchford Inquiry.

Jesse Nicholls Has a strong focus on claims against the police, inquests and judicial reviews. **Strengths:** "He is incredibly detailed, very thorough." "Exceptionally hard-working," and "incredibly thorough in his preparation – clients adore him." **Recent work:** Acting for 77 of the families involved in the Hillsborough Inquest.

Band 2

Garden Court Chambers

See profile on p.851

THE SET

A set with a "good depth of quality" that advises on claims for assault, false imprisonment and malicious prosecution. Members assist claimants with human rights breaches, inquest-related cases and equality law matters. They have further acted in precedent-setting cases concerning strip searches and those looking at the question of whether the police can claim immunity from liability when it comes to misfeasance. One source says "the senior juniors are very good," whilst another describes the members here as being "street-fighting jury advocates." They are "good advocates, who have a strong rapport with clients and offer superior client care."

Client service: Colin Cook heads a team of "excellent, professional clerks."

SILKS

Leslie Thomas QC An extremely strong trial advocate, who often handles claims relating to deaths during or following police contact and data retention. He has been active on several historic cases, including those involving police shootings. **Strengths:** "He is a genie of a trial advocate, who is superb with juries." "A fearsome cross-examiner," who is "absolutely amazing in court." "He is well respected for his fearless and devastating cross-examination." **Recent work:** Acted for the family of Dean Joseph, who was shot by the police following an armed siege.

JUNIORS

Maya Sikand Well respected for advising the victims of false imprisonment, assault, malicious prosecution and human rights breaches. She also acts in inquests and judicial reviews, and is an expert on closure orders. **Strengths:** "Her advocacy skills are good, she gives a detailed analysis and is a tenacious cross-examiner." "Passionate and robust," "she brings energy and enthusiasm and has a can-do approach." **Recent work:** Appeared in the Pitchford Undercover Policing Inquiry, acting for the whistle-blower Peter Francis, who had been part of the Met's Special Demonstration Squad.

Sarah Hemingway Acts for claimants in cases concerning false imprisonment, assault and malicious prosecution. She also handles police discrimination claims and judicial reviews. **Strengths:** "She knows her stuff and turns the paperwork around very quickly." "She will go the extra mile to help clients," and "is very detailed and thorough."

Anna Morris Has a strong focus on inquests and actions against the police following protests. **Strengths:** "She has a good advocacy style." "She is thorough, helpful, diligent and has a specialist knowledge of protest law." **Recent work:** Represented a member of the Critical Mass Cycle Ride in a claim for false imprisonment.

Stephen Simblet Frequently advises on inquests into deaths in custody and psychiatric detention claims. **Strengths:** "He is good on his feet, he's got the case law at his fingertips and can argue a case well." **Recent work:** Acted for Daniels and Gillard in a claim against the Chief Constable of South Wales alleging misconduct.

Rajeev Thacker Specialises in discrimination claims against the police, as well as human rights cases. **Strengths:** "He specialises in police cases involving discrimination and has good judgement." "He brings a very intellectual but accessible approach and is easy to work with." "He cares about clients, is really collaborative and courts and judges like him."

Una Minetta Morris Advises on human rights claims, data retention issues, failure to intervene claims and deaths in police contact. She also represents clients in inquests and judicial reviews. **Strengths:** "A no-holds-barred cross-examiner, who is fearless." "She has excellent attention to detail and great technical knowledge." "She is tenacious and a real fighter." **Recent work:** Acted in Crook v Chief Constable of Essex Police, a case alleging breaches of the Data Protection Act and Human Rights Act arising out of the unlawful disclosure of Mr Crook's photograph and name in connection with a rape allegation.

Matrix Chambers

See profile on p.876

THE SET

A set of "great depth and expertise" that is made up of "heavyweight lawyers." Its police law team has a strong focus on advising the victims of police discrimination, and is highly effective at handling inquests, inquiries and civil liberties claims. The set has acted on the Duggan inquest and inquiry, the Pitchford Inquiry and the Edward Snowden disclosures. Members here also act for forces in claims against the police.

Client service: Jason Housden heads the clerking team at Matrix and is noted for his acute knowledge of the practice area and sunny disposition.

SILKS

Phillippa Kaufmann QC One of the outstanding lawyers in the area, she is a leading figure for advising claimants on false imprisonment, malicious prosecution, misfeasance and negligence claims. She also assists with Human Rights Act claims and inquests into deaths in police custody. **Strengths:** "She is one of the leading lawyers of her generation, who presents issues beautifully and is a blistering advocate." "She is both inventive and perceptive, and her advocacy is top-class." **Recent work:** Represented eight women in claims for invasions of their right to privacy and personal integrity following relationships with undercover police officers.

Hugh Southey QC (see p.770) Well-regarded barrister with a broad practice incorporating human rights breaches, actions against the police, prison law and immigration issues. **Strengths:** "He is a fantastic prison lawyer, who is really on top of privacy and good at building a case." "He is very sharp, always on top of his brief and very responsive." **Recent work:** Acted in a claim that stop-and-searches without reasonable suspicion are incompatible with the Human Rights Act.

Richard Hermer QC Advises on claims against the police, particularly in the field of counter-terrorism. He also has considerable experience of acting in cases regarding police shootings. **Strengths:** "He is highly respected as a civil litigator." **Recent work:** Advised the family of Mrs Groce, who was shot during the Brixton riots, in a claim against the police.

James Laddie QC Has a long-standing practice in the field of police malpractice, particularly focusing on claims of police discrimination. **Strengths:** "He has a flair for advocacy and a passion for the rights of victims, and is excellent both with clients and in negotiation." "He is a thorough and experienced trial advocate." **Recent work:** Acted for Edric Kennedy-Macfoy, a black fireman tasered by police officers while helping them at a scene of violent disorder.

Tim Owen QC Assists clients with first-instance trials, appeals and judicial reviews relating to police law. He has extensive experience of both criminal and public law. **Strengths:** "He is excellent with clients and is very good at cross-examining professional witnesses." "He is extremely well known and highly regarded." **Recent work:** Brought a claim against Merseyside Police for negligence and a breach of the Data Protection Act. Owen acted on behalf of a family whose address and identification details were accidentally revealed to criminal defendants.

Matthew Ryder QC (see p.757) Has a strong focus on cases concerning undercover policing, and also advises on the rights of journalists, police misconduct claims and human rights cases. **Strengths:** "He is hard-working and diligent." "He is very good at private law discrimination claims against the police, and his pleadings are both succinct and compelling." **Recent work:** Advised Liberty and seven other NGOs in relation to a challenge to surveillance powers used by GCHQ and the police.

JUNIORS

Helen Law A leading lawyer for actions against the police and claims against other prosecuting bodies. Her practice covers public, civil and criminal law, and has a strong focus on the criminal justice system. **Strengths:** "She is fantastic on the advice side and with clients, and is also excellent on her feet." "She is good at identifying key issues and quickly providing detailed and accurate advice." **Recent work:** Represented a claimant in a claim that the Crown Prosecution Service had abandoned an investigation into grooming and sexual abuse, breaching the claimant's rights to Articles 3 and 8 of the Human Rights Act.

Alison Macdonald (see p.705) Has a strong reputation for matters concerning human rights within the criminal justice system. She advises on both public law and civil damages claims. **Strengths:** "She has a relaxed and measured style that is compelling." "She presents complex arguments in a simple way, and is a pleasure to work with." "She provides frank advice when needed." **Recent work:** Represented John Catt in a challenge about the retention of information about him on the Domestic Extremism Database.

Raj Desai Has acted in civil actions against the police and judicial review challenges. He also advises on the Human Rights Act and on prison law. **Strengths:** "He is extremely wise, great to work with and clever as hell." "He instils confidence in you." "He has a very calm manner, both in terms of dealing with families and in his questioning of witnesses." **Recent work:** Acted for the claimants in a claim for racially motivated assault and false imprisonment brought against the Commissioner of the Metropolitan Police.

Other Ranked Lawyers

Anthony Metzer QC (Goldsmith Chambers) Frequently advises on police misfeasance claims and inquests into deaths in police custody. He has also assisted officers with claims against their own forces. He has experience of both criminal and civil cases, as well as medical, pharmaceutical and financial law. **Strengths:** "He is extremely reliable, responsive and conscientious." "He is excellent on his feet, and is tough but likeable." "An outstanding jury advocate with unmatched cross-examination skills."

Stephen Cragg QC (Monckton Chambers) Has a strong focus on human rights cases, and is celebrated for his representation of clients in inquests. **Strengths:** "He has an encyclopaedic knowledge of the law on biometric data retention," and is "very thorough and keen." **Recent work:** Acted in a claim for assault by the police brought against the Metropolitan Police.

ALL CIRCUITS Mainly Defendant

Police Law: Mainly Defendant
Leading Sets
Band 1
5 Essex Court *
Serjeants' Inn Chambers *
Band 2
1 Chancery Lane
Leading Silks
Star individuals
Beggs John *Serjeants' Inn Chambers* *
Band 1
Barton Fiona *5 Essex Court* *
Beer Jason *5 Essex Court* *
Johnson Jeremy *5 Essex Court* *
Band 2
Leek Samantha *5 Essex Court* *
Studd Anne *5 Essex Court* *
Waldron William *Exchange Chambers (ORL)* ◇
Warnock Andrew *1 Chancery Lane* [A]
Band 3
Basu Dijen *5 Essex Court* *
de Bono John *Serjeants' Inn Chambers* *
Keeling Adrian *No5 Chambers (ORL)* ◇ [A]
Whyte Anne *Atlantic Chambers (ORL)* ◇
* *Indicates set / individual with profile.*
[A] *direct access (see p.24).*
◇ *(ORL) = Other Ranked Lawyer.*
Alphabetical order within each band. Band 1 is highest.

Police Law: Mainly Defendant
Leading Juniors
Band 1
Boyle Gerard *Serjeants' Inn Chambers* *
Ley-Morgan Mark *Serjeants' Inn Chambers* *
Thomas George *Serjeants' Inn Chambers* *
Waters Andrew *5 Essex Court*
Band 2
Berry James *Serjeants' Inn Chambers* *
Branston Barnabas *5 Essex Court* *
Buckett Edwin *9 Gough Square (ORL)* ◇ *
Daniels Iain *Ely Place Chambers (ORL)* ◇
Fortt Russell *5 Essex Court*
Holdcroft Matthew *5 Essex Court* *
Johnson Laura *1 Chancery Lane* [A]
Morley Stephen *Serjeants' Inn Chambers* *
Simcock Sarah *Serjeants' Inn Chambers* *
Stagg Paul *1 Chancery Lane* [A]
Ventham Charlotte *5 Essex Court* *
Weddell Geoffrey *1 Chancery Lane*
Wells Graham *Oriel Chambers (ORL)* ◇
Wolfe Georgina *5 Essex Court* *
Wynn Toby *KBW (ORL)* ◇
Band 3
Clemens Adam *7BR (ORL)* ◇
Collier Beatrice *5 Essex Court* *
Cornell Kate *5 Essex Court* *
Dixey Jonathan *5 Essex Court* *
Dobie Lisa *1 Chancery Lane*
Gold Elliot *Serjeants' Inn Chambers* *
Hare Ivan *Blackstone Chambers (ORL)* ◇
Mortimer Sophie *1 Chancery Lane*
Sandhu Harpreet Singh *No5 Chambers (ORL)* ◇ [A]
Skelt Ian *KBW (ORL)* ◇
Williams Vincent *9 Gough Square (ORL)* ◇ *
Williamson Oliver *Serjeants' Inn Chambers* *
Up-and-coming individuals
Hayward Cicely *5 Essex Court* *
Rathmell Aaron *Serjeants' Inn Chambers* *
White Cecily *Serjeants' Inn Chambers* *

Band 1

5 Essex Court
See profile on p.834

THE SET

Acts for police forces across the UK on high-profile matters such as Hillsborough and David Miranda. Its members also undertake misfeasance and false imprisonment claims, such as Mouncher, Daniels, Gillard & Others v The Chief Constable of South Wales, a case arising out of the investigation into the death of Lynette White. Sources say that "the barristers are personable and skilled at engaging with police officers" and that "the quality of counsel on offer is second to none." One commentator adds: "5 Essex is a set immersed in police law; its barristers are at the cutting edge of everything."

Client service: "The clerks are friendly and easy to deal with" and "provide a very good service – they will try to alter things so you get the barristers you want." One commentator notes: "The support offered by the clerking team, and in particular the head clerk Mark Waller, is unsurpassed."

SILKS

Fiona Barton QC (see p.591) Standout lawyer who assists forces with judicial reviews, inquests, public inquiries, misconduct proceedings and public interest immunity issues. **Strengths:** "She displays great sensitivity and has a great client manner." "She is incredibly experienced and pleasant to work with," and "her knowledge base is extensive – she has gravitas and commands confidence." "One of the finest police law barristers in the country." **Recent work:** Represented Chief Constable Creedon in an investigation into the quashing of a conviction following allegations of non-disclosure of informant-linked material.

Jason Beer QC (see p.593) A leading lawyer who advises police forces across England and Wales on civil claims, misconduct proceedings, inquests and inquiries. **Strengths:** "He is unflappable, he's practical, clients like and respect him, and his advocacy is second to none." "His ability to review and take in the central features of a case is brilliant.""He goes the extra mile when needed." **Recent work:** Advised the Metropolitan Police as an interested party on the phone hacking claims.

Jeremy Johnson QC (see p.684) An exceptional barrister for disciplinary proceedings, misfeasance and data protection matters. He is highly regarded by forces, which he advises on covert policing techniques and represents in public inquiries. **Strengths:** "He is a genuine police law specialist" and "an extremely good barrister." "He is a first-rate, efficient, clear-thinking silk of the highest quality" who is "super-clever, seems to know everything, and has a brain the size of a planet." **Recent work:** Acted for the Commissioner of Police of the Metropolis in a judicial review of a stop and search.

Samantha Leek QC (see p.698) Has a particular focus on police shootings and deaths in custody. She also assists forces with judicial reviews, inquests, police negligence and claims of assault, false imprisonment and malicious prosecution. **Strengths:** "She has a great client manner, and is good at dealing with bereaved families." "She facilitated discussion and put the chief constables at their ease with a very relaxed manner." "She is level-headed, fantastic with clients and an expert on police shootings." **Recent work:** Advised the Chief Constable of Avon and Somerset Constabulary on the inquest into the death of Bijan Ebrahimi. It was alleged that the police failed to take steps to protect him despite being alerted to the fact that he was in danger.

Anne Studd QC (see p.775) Advises forces on judicial reviews, misfeasance claims, inquests, police discrimination and Article 2 matters. **Strengths:** "She has a great bedside manner and is down-to-earth and sensible." "She is very decisive and steadfast." "She is able to cut through the myriad of information and get to the heart of the issue in cases." **Recent work:** Acted for the Chief Constable of the West Midlands Police on the inquest into the death of Kingsley Burrell while in police custody.

Dijen Basu QC (see p.591) Assists clients with policing protests and events, data protection questions and claims of assault, false imprisonment and malicious prosecution. He has a strong focus on counter-terrorism policing and judicial reviews. **Strengths:** "He is incredibly eloquent, he goes the extra mile all the time and his work ethic is immense." "The jury likes his style, and he is intelligent and well prepared." "His advice is spot-on and he provides a very quick turnaround of papers." **Recent work:** Advised the Chief Constable of Devon and Cornwall on officers' entitlement to overtime payment.

JUNIORS

Andrew Waters Prominent figure in the market for police discipline, police law inquiries and inquests into deaths in police custody. He also represents forces in claims of false imprisonment, assault, malicious prosecution and negligence. **Strengths:** "Preeminent for police conduct and discipline cases." "His laid-back, calm approach instils you with the confidence that you have the right person." "He is liked by clients and witnesses alike." **Recent work:** Advised on the Hillsborough inquest.

Barnabas Branston (see p.602) He is highlighted for his experience with inquests, and his work relating to police disciplinary hearings and civil law actions. **Strengths:** "He has a great rapport with officers and a really practical approach." **Recent work:** Acted for West Midlands Police in the independent investigation of the Hillsborough disaster, which formed part of the inquest.

Russell Fortt Has represented a large number of forces in relation to claims of assault, false imprisonment, wrongful disclosure and malicious prosecution. He also has experience of judicial reviews and inquests into deaths in custody. **Strengths:** "He has good experience and is regarded as a safe pair of hands." **Recent work:** Advised the Chief Constable of Surrey Police on disclosure issues in the case of Starr v Ward.

Matthew Holdcroft (see p.674) Often defends forces in claims for wrongful arrest, assault and malicious prosecution. He also assists with allegations of discrimination. **Strengths:** "Outstanding on police misconduct matters." "He's particularly strong on his feet where his thorough analysis pays off." "He is very efficient and knowledgeable, and has sound judgement." **Recent work:** Acted for the police in Bates v Cleveland Police, a case concerning a police officer who had sexually assaulted a woman while on duty.

Charlotte Ventham (see p.787) Represents chief constables and the IPCC with regard to judicial reviews, inquests, human rights breaches and data protection issues. She also acts on civil actions. **Strengths:** "She is very thorough, pre-empts well and knows the papers inside out." "Her effort on cases is tireless." "She is approachable and knowledgeable" and "is good on her feet." **Recent work:** Advised the Chief Constable of Norfolk Police on an allegation of a malicious prosecution.

Georgina Wolfe (see p.799) Frequently assists forces and the IPCC with judicial reviews, public inquiries and inquests. She also advises on the retention of data and human trafficking issues. **Strengths:** "Her drafting is fantastic." "She is a real hard worker and very bright." **Recent work:** Represented the Metropolitan Police in a judicial review of a stop and search.

Beatrice Collier (see p.620) Has a broad police practice, advising on wrongful arrest, assault, false imprisonment, malicious prosecution, disciplinary proceedings, inquests and employment claims. **Strengths:** "She is well educated, well qualified and bright." **Recent work:** Acted for the Chief Constable of South Wales defending a claim for malicious prosecution, false imprisonment and misfeasance in public office brought by 15 former officers.

Kate Cornell (see p.624) Assists clients with all types of civil claims, including deaths in custody and police negligence. She often acts on cases involving human rights issues, especially those arising out of protests. **Strengths:** "She is good on paperwork, has good attention to detail and is approachable." **Recent work:** Advised Merseyside Police on a claim for negligence and breach of Articles 2 and 8 of the Human Rights Act following the disclosure to the defendants of the address of prosecution witnesses.

Jonathan Dixey (see p.634) Advises forces on claims for misfeasance, wrongful arrest and false imprisonment, and is an expert on judicial reviews and inquests. He has particular expertise in disclosure matters. **Strengths:** "He has a good manner and deals with challenging issues very well." **Recent work:** Represented the Commissioner of the Metropolitan Police in a challenge to the force obtaining communications data from three journalists during the 'Plebgate' affair.

Cicely Hayward (see p.667) Assists with defences against claims of assault, malicious prosecution and false imprisonment. She also advises on the retention of DNA and fingerprints. **Strengths:** "She is well prepared and has the ability to build up an immediate rapport with witnesses." "She is well liked, very thorough and her defences are robust." "She is really tough and really able." **Recent work:** Advised the Chief Constable of South Wales on claims for unlawful arrest, malicious prosecution, misfeasance in public office and breach of Article 8 brought by former officers.

Serjeants' Inn Chambers

See profile on p.907

THE SET

An exceptional set that handles a wide range of police law matters such as discipline hearings, civil actions, restraining orders and judicial reviews, it is "an excellent resource for police work." Members of the set also provide advice on operational matters, and have represented the police in the Hillsborough and Deepcut inquests as well as in several high-profile claims for wrongful arrest. One interviewee enthuses: "The barristers are tactically aware and alive to possibilities."

Client service: Lee Johnson's team of clerks are extremely well thought of by interviewees, with one source saying: "The service is second to none." Another praises them as being "flexible, approachable and responsive," while one source comments that "the clerks are superb – the good working relationship between them and counsel is reflected in the quality of service you get."

SILKS

John Beggs QC (see p.594) An outstanding barrister who acts for forces and chief constables on judicial reviews, inquiries, inquests and misconduct hearings. He also advises on police employment matters and claims arising out of allegations of police negligence. **Strengths:** Competitors see him as "the devil incarnate, as he is so devastatingly good." "He is Mr Police Law" and is "tactically astute, impressive with clients and head and shoulders above the rest." "Top of the tree and first-class," he is "the guy to go to." **Recent work:** Represented the Commissioner of the Metropolitan Police in claims for assault, false imprisonment and racial abuse.

John de Bono QC (see p.631) Has a particular focus on police misconduct hearings, especially allegations of police corruption. **Strengths:** "He has a no-nonsense style, is approachable and tells it like it is." **Recent work:** Advised Merseyside Police on the misconduct hearing of an officer dismissed for gross misconduct.

JUNIORS

Gerard Boyle (see p.601) Leading lawyer in the field of inquests and police misconduct trials. He frequently represents clients in Police Appeals Tribunal cases, and also offers operational advice. **Strengths:** "He has excellent knowledge of police disciplinary procedures and is very good in conferences with clients." **Recent work:** Acted for the Chief Constable of Kent on a claim for false imprisonment.

Mark Ley-Morgan (see p.701) Key lawyer for inquests into deaths in police custody, judicial reviews and misconduct proceedings. He also acts for clients in civil claims, and has a strong focus on medical issues within police cases. **Strengths:** "He is a great trial advocate, and is excellent with clients and officers." "He has the Midas touch; clients love him as do judges, and for jury trials he is excellent." "He is relaxed, calm, approachable, down-to-earth and robust." **Recent work:** Represented an officer charged with misconduct for failing to avert the death of a man who was killed by his neighbour. The neighbour had suspected that the victim was a paedophile.

George Thomas (see p.780) Highly regarded for his knowledge of civil actions, inquests, disciplinary matters, discrimination claims and judicial reviews. He also advises on operational matters. **Strengths:** "He is down-to-earth, experienced, gets on with witness and clients, and gets the jury and judges on side." "He is a must-have for mass arrest cases" and "is fantastic for jury trials." **Recent work:** Assisted the Metropolitan Police Commissioner with a defence against claims of false imprisonment brought by English Defence League members.

James Berry (see p.595) Focuses on judicial reviews, inquests, inquiries, false imprisonment cases, human rights claims and misconduct hearings. **Strengths:** "He offers an extremely thorough analysis of all the pertinent issues in a case, and is tenacious when on his feet." "He is thorough, robust, popular with officers, very efficient on his feet and someone with a keen forensic eye."

Stephen Morley (see p.722) Acts for forces on police misconduct hearings, disciplinary proceedings and Police Appeals Tribunal hearings. **Strengths:** "His understanding of policing is very strong, he's very approachable and he's completely reliable in meeting deadlines." "He is excellent, affable and has the ability to both reassure clients and intimidate the other side." **Recent work:** Represented the Commissioner of the Metropolitan Police in the Police Appeals Tribunal hearing of a Detective Chief Superintendent dismissed for misconduct.

Sarah Simcock (see p.765) Acts for the police on claims of false imprisonment, assault, malicious prosecution, race discrimination and negligence. She often advises on disciplinary hearings for serious misconduct. **Strengths:** "She is no-nonsense, very diligent and someone who knows the papers backwards." **Recent work:** Represented Thames Valley Police in an inquest into a death following restraint used in a stop and search.

Oliver Williamson (see p.797) Advises on several high-profile inquests and public interest matters, and also assists forces with operational questions. **Strengths:** "He has a good brain and is a good drafter who is popular with clients." **Recent work:** Advised North Yorkshire Police on claims of false detention and breach of Article 8 brought by football supporters held on coaches while returning from a match.

Elliot Gold (see p.655) Frequently acts for forces in misconduct cases and in Police Appeals Tribunal hearings. **Strengths:** "You can be confident he has read everything, he has a good way in conference and his understanding of police law is exceptional." "He is exceedingly bright and thinks outside the box." "Has a precise, prepared and considered approach." **Recent work:** Represented Avon and Somerset Constabulary in respect of allegations of failure to investigate bullying by other officers.

Aaron Rathmell (see p.748) Advises on judicial reviews, human rights claims and claims for assault, negligence and defamation. He also has experience of advising on covert policing operations. **Strengths:** "Excellent across the board." "His academic drafting and people skills are exceptional." "He has a textbook knowledge and knows all the answers." **Recent work:** Acted for Northumbria Police on a negligence claim relating to 'heat of the moment' decision-making by officers.

Cecily White (see p.794) Has assisted with claims for assault, unlawful stop and search, police discrimination, false imprisonment, malicious prosecution, misfeasance in public office and failure to investigate Human Rights Act breaches. **Strengths:** "Her written work is superb." "She is very clever and explains her points well so that laypeople can understand." **Recent work:** Advised Surrey Police on the inquest into the death of Cheryl James at Deepcut Barracks.

Band 2

1 Chancery Lane

THE SET

The set "has a strong group of junior counsel with genuine expertise in this sector" and a particular focus on fatal shootings, deaths in custody, false imprisonment, malicious prosecutions and police discipline matters. Members of the set have of late acted on Hasanovic v Sussex Police, Metro Inns v Gloucestershire Constabulary and Rawson v Hampshire Constabulary. Interviewees say that "the barristers are very helpful," "have a commitment to police law" and "represent a good mix of juniors and seniors." Members here are noted for being "keen to go the extra mile."

Client service: Senior clerk Clark Chessis is, according to one interviewee, "absolutely exceptional; he has great knowledge, and can get you just the right person."

SILKS

Andrew Warnock QC Advises police forces on personal injury issues and police law claims, including human rights breaches and failures to investigate. **Strengths:** "His quiet manner belies a steely determination and intellectual rigour." **Recent work:** Represented Sussex Police in a claim under Article 2 of the Human Rights Act concerning failure to protect a woman who was murdered by her husband.

JUNIORS

Laura Johnson Advises forces on misfeasance claims as well as liability issues and disclosure queries, and has experience of representing clients in inquests. **Strengths:** "She's very good on paperwork and her pleadings are very good."

Paul Stagg Represents clients in inquests, tribunals and in civil courts. He acts on cases involving human rights issues, police shootings, deaths in custody and police discipline. **Strengths:** "His paperwork is really good and you can trust he'll be better prepared than the other side." **Recent work:** Advised the Commissioner of the Metropolitan Police on a claim for false imprisonment, malicious prosecution and racial discrimination.

Geoffrey Weddell Has a strong practice advising forces on false imprisonment, assault and malicious prosecutions. **Strengths:** "He is good at handling trials and getting the confidence of officers." "He is good at keeping morale up and fighting in court."

Lisa Dobie Acts for police forces on inquests and civil claims, such as wrongful arrest, assault and unlawful detention. She also advises forces on employers' liability. **Strengths:** "She gives excellent practical advice, is realistic, is good with clients and is also great with juries and at trial." "She is very thorough, provides excellent defence and her paperwork is good."

Sophie Mortimer Has considerable experience of representing police forces in jury trials and advising on procedural matters. **Recent work:** Acted for the Metropolitan Police Commissioner on claims for trespass, assault, false imprisonment and post-traumatic stress disorder.

Other Ranked Lawyers

Anne Whyte QC (Atlantic Chambers) Often represents clients in judicial reviews and inquests, as well as in civil claims against the police. She also has a strong focus on assisting police forces with personal injury claims and liability issues. **Strengths:** "She offers detailed guidance, and has good technical and commercial awareness." "She is eloquent and calm, and is good on Article 2 inquests and civil actions."

Ivan Hare (Blackstone Chambers) Often acts for the IPCC on judicial reviews, particularly those involving protests and deaths in police custody. **Strengths:** "He organises things well, invariably understands the case and regularly delivers."

Adam Clemens (7BR) Represents police forces in human rights claims and judicial reviews, particularly those involving the policing of protests. He also assists forces with data protection and information sharing. He has further experience of advising on counter-terrorism measures and search warrants. **Strengths:** "He is a safe pair of hands and very down-to-earth." "He's very knowledgeable on public disorder." "He is very user-friendly, he works well with solicitors and witnesses."

Iain Daniels (Ely Place Chambers) Acts for police forces and private prison providers in claims of malicious prosecution, false imprisonment and assault. He is also celebrated for his work on judicial reviews. **Strengths:** "He is very pleasant, hospitable and accommodating." "His advocacy skills are excellent" and "his attention to detail and willingness to work in a team are plain for all to see." "His demeanour in court is very good." **Recent work:** Advised Sussex Police on claims of false imprisonment, assault and breaches of Articles 10 and 11 of the Human Rights Act brought by protesters.

William Waldron QC (Exchange Chambers) Has a strong focus on assisting police forces with severe personal injury claims. **Strengths:** "A top-class advocate who is very pragmatic and a very easy chap to get along with."

Edwin Buckett (see p.606) (9 Gough Square) Acts for police forces and the Police Federation on police misconduct matters and deaths in custody. Also advises on matters involving police informers. **Strengths:** "He communicates effectively, and is likeable and down-to-earth." "He has got very good knowledge and experience." **Recent work:** Advised Hertfordshire Constabulary on a claim for damages arising from an alleged failure to investigate a multiple rape, assault and harassment claim.

Vincent Williams (see p.797) (9 Gough Square) Advises police forces on judicial reviews, and cases involving deaths in police contact, and injuries suffered by officers. He is also an expert on disclosure matters and misfeasance in public office. **Strengths:** "He fights his corner constructively and sensibly." "He is very experienced, and is both responsive and informal in his approach." **Recent work:** Represented Hertfordshire and Bedfordshire Police in a judicial review into an alleged IPCC failure to investigate a murder carried out by a serving officer.

Toby Wynn (KBW) Acts for chief constables in relation to claims of misfeasance in a public office and police discipline. He also assists with operational issues. **Strengths:** "He is very user-friendly, responds quickly, and is pragmatic and robust when he needs to be." "He is excellent on his feet and in cross-examination and is good with juries." **Recent work:** Advised the Chief Constable of Northumbria Police on a claim for misfeasance in a public office brought by the victim of an assault.

Ian Skelt (KBW) Advises on contentious and non-contentious police law matters, and handles both litigation and advisory matters. **Strengths:** "Technically sound, with thoroughness and a common-sense approach." "His written work is fantastic, and he is a very persuasive advocate." **Recent work:** Represented the Chief Constable of North Yorkshire Police in a judicial review into the disclosure of information on a criminal records certificate.

Adrian Keeling QC (No5 Chambers) Represents police officers in matters before misconduct panels and Police Appeals Tribunals. He advises on inquests and cases concerning deaths in custody, claims of fabricated evidence and excessive use of force. **Strengths:** "He is thorough, eloquent and polite." "He reassures clients, is charming and persuasive and has a superb tactical approach." **Recent work:** Acted for an officer charged with dangerous driving while on duty.

Harpreet Singh Sandhu (No5 Chambers) Assists members of the Police Federation with misconduct proceedings. He also represents officers in Appeals Tribunal hearings. **Strengths:** "He is extremely thorough, his judgement is spot-on, he is polite and courteous before the judge and he is great with clients." "He is always well prepared, and a man of great charm."

Graham Wells (Oriel Chambers) Acts for the police cases concerning judicial review, inquests into deaths following police contact, liability questions and disciplinary issues. **Strengths:** "He is precise, thorough, robust and trusted."

Contents:

LONDON

Product Liability
Leading Sets
Band 1
Henderson Chambers *
Band 2
7BR *
Crown Office Chambers *
Doughty Street Chambers *
Band 3
Fountain Court Chambers *
4 New Square *
Serjeants' Inn Chambers *
2TG - 2 Temple Gardens *
Leading Silks
Star individuals
Gibson Charles *Henderson Chambers* [A] *
Oppenheim Robin *Doughty Street Chambers*
Band 1
Maskrey Simeon *7BR*
Popat Prashant *Henderson Chambers* [A] *
Preston Hugh *7BR* [A]
Waite Jonathan *Crown Office Chambers*
Webb Geraint *Henderson Chambers* *
Band 2
Antelme Alexander *Crown Office Chambers*
Block Neil *39 Essex Chambers (ORL)* ◊ *
Brook Smith Philip *Fountain Court Chambers* *
Dougherty Charles *2TG - 2 Temple Gardens* *
Johnston Christopher *Serjeants' Inn Chambers* *
Mulcahy Leigh-Ann *4 New Square* *
Prynne Andrew *Temple Garden Chambers (ORL)* ◊
Spencer Michael *Crown Office Chambers*
Band 3
Campbell Oliver *Henderson Chambers* [A] *
Crane Michael *Fountain Court Chambers* *
Eklund Graham *4 New Square* *
Lawson Robert *Quadrant Chambers (ORL)* ◊ *
Moody Neil *2TG - 2 Temple Gardens* *
Shah Akhil *Fountain Court Chambers* *
Sheehan Malcolm *Henderson Chambers* [A] *
Turner David *4 New Square*
New Silks
Riley-Smith Toby *Henderson Chambers* [A] *
* Indicates set / individual with profile.
[A] direct access (see p.24).
◊ (ORL) = Other Ranked Lawyer.
Alphabetical order within each band. Band 1 is highest.

Product Liability
Leading Juniors
Band 1
Kinnier Andrew *Henderson Chambers* [A] *
Korn Adam *7BR*
Medd James *Crown Office Chambers*
Pilgerstorfer Marcus *11KBW (ORL)* ◊ *
Band 2
Dilworth Noel *Henderson Chambers* *
Feldschreiber Peter *4 New Square* *
Knight Heidi *Serjeants' Inn Chambers* *
Power Eloise *Serjeants' Inn Chambers* *
Power Erica *Crown Office Chambers* *
Purnell James *Henderson Chambers* [A] *
Band 3
Andrews Claire *Gough Square Chambers (ORL)* ◊
Bennett Daniel *Doughty Street Chambers*
Bradley Matthew *Henderson Chambers* [A] *
Matthews Julian D *7BR*
Philpott Fred *Gough Square Chambers (ORL)* ◊
Powell Katie *4 New Square* *
Up-and-coming individuals
Lambert Harry *Crown Office Chambers* *

Band 1

Henderson Chambers
See profile on p.864

THE SET

Few would question the position of Henderson Chambers as "the foremost chambers for product liability." The set enjoys universal acclaim for its "weight of numbers" and "genuine expertise" in the area, and is credited amongst instructing solicitors for having barristers who "really have their fingers on the pulse" of trends and developments in the market. The group boasts numerous specialists in this field, including some of the very best at the Bar, and can offer comprehensive defence against the most challenging and sensitive claims faced by corporate clients, and particularly product manufacturers. Its members are deeply involved in all of the most high-profile group actions, including those relating to metal-on-metal hips, PIP breast implants and numerous pharmaceutical products.

Client service: "Fantastic clerking led by senior clerk John White who is very proactive and always stays in touch. The clerks bend over backwards to maintain a relationship and to understand what's going on in your litigation. They know who you know, who you've seen, they keep track of everything. They are very polished, slick and charming to deal with."

SILKS

Charles Gibson QC (see p.652) Star performer who is regarded as "a master of strategy in defending product liability group claims." His superb practice stands as one of the most prolific when it comes to defending corporate clients on cases stemming from faulty medical devices and pharmaceuticals, as well as other consumer products. He is readily acknowledged by the market as a go-to silk who is "absolutely first class in all aspects and easy to work with." **Strengths:** "If you had a major product liability case, you'd want him leading it. He really sees the big picture in terms of where you want to get to." "One of the most charismatic barristers that I've ever come across. He is very energetic and will fight your corner to the end." **Recent work:** Instructed on behalf of the Medical Protection Society regarding claims brought in the metal-on-metal hip litigation.

Prashant Popat QC (see p.740) A "class act" who conveys "sheer gravitas" as one of the foremost product liability specialists at the bar. He is eminently capable of leading on major group litigation and also handles unitary claims that resolve through both criminal and civil proceedings. **Strengths:** "Very effective and excellent technical knowledge; balanced and practical approach." "Superb attention to detail and a great advocate." **Recent work:** Instructed on behalf of the defendant in the hip implant litigation brought against Smith and Nephew.

Geraint Webb QC (see p.791) Considered "a rising star in the ranks of leading counsel," Geraint Webb QC continues to strengthen his impressive product liability practice with participation in many of the major medical device and pharmaceutical cases arising in recent years. His practice also extends into property damage claims resulting from faulty products and issues surrounding product recalls. **Strengths:** "He knows the law inside out, he's got a nice calm manner in his oral advocacy and a nice spare style in his written work as well." "Outstandingly bright, clear advice and client-friendly." **Recent work:** Represented BMI Healthcare in the PIP breast implant litigation.

Oliver Campbell QC (see p.610) Very experienced in product safety and liability, with the added benefit of his expertise in health and safety law. Regularly instructed on major group actions and also advises on regulatory matters. **Strengths:** "Really impressed with him on product safety: he's got all the diligence and thoroughness you'd expect from a senior junior, and he's kept all of that as silk." "He will go far; he is academic, thoughtful, prompt and good to work with in a team." **Recent work:** Represented US manufacturer Wright Medical Technology for its part in the ongoing metal-on-metal hip litigation.

Malcolm Sheehan QC (see p.763) A recent silk with a thriving product liability practice who continues to impress with his client-friendly manner. His expertise encompasses medical devices as well as pharmaceutical and automotive products, and he has in-depth knowledge of the issues surrounding product liability insurance and product recall. **Strengths:** "He is just such a detailed, analytical barrister; you know he just doesn't drop the ball on anything." "Extremely thorough, outstanding client manner and is an absolute pleasure to work with." **Recent work:** Retained to defend manufacturer Biomet in the metal-on-metal hip litigation.

Toby Riley-Smith QC (see p.752) New silk who previously enjoyed an outstanding reputation as a junior and who continues to be regarded highly for his product liability expertise. His recent caseload has included significant group actions arising in the medical and pharmaceutical spheres; he can also claim notable proficiency in cases involving healthcare and consumer products as well as property damage. **Strengths:** "Fantastic to work with and such a grafter: he is really hard-working, he thinks nothing of coming into our offices, rolling up his sleeves, getting stuck in and helping." "Very impressive chap and very effective, he's always exceedingly pleasant to deal with as well." **Recent work:** Instructed in the Bodo litigation, representing Shell and its Nigerian subsidiary against a group action alleging damages caused by a faulty oil pipeline to over 15,000 claimants in Nigeria.

JUNIORS

Andrew Kinnier (see p.691) "A rising star" who receives very high praise for his involvement in complex product liability cases, particularly those concerning defective medical devices and pharmaceuticals. He is a sought-after junior amongst many leading silks as well as instructing solicitors, all of whom regard him as a pleasure to work with.

Strengths: "He is a very stylish advocate. He is confident, articulate and persuasive." "A first-class junior with broad product liability experience and a real team player." **Recent work:** Defended GlaxoSmithKline against claims brought by over 100 individuals regarding discontinuing use of the antidepressant Seroxat.

Noel Dilworth (see p.634) Senior junior who fields a wide-ranging product liability practice that straddles both claimant and defendant work. He advises on individual claims as well as significant group litigation arising from a number of different sectors. **Strengths:** "Combines his great intellect with a practical approach." "Very knowledgeable and easily gets to grips with complicated factual issues." **Recent work:** Defended a former subsidiary of BP against a group action alleging that the defective design of an oil pipeline led to damage at the farms of over 100 Colombian nationals.

James Purnell (see p.745) Highly regarded junior who has had recent involvement in high-profile group action cases relating to metal-on-metal hip implants and gynaecological mesh. His broad product liability practice also encompasses an eclectic range of other work including claims related to electrical devices and agricultural equipment. **Strengths:** "Amazing service delivery, gets to the point and thinks quickly on his feet." "Attentive and well versed in product liability and recovery issues. He applies his mind to the matter." **Recent work:** Appointed as junior counsel to Biomet who faces group action against them in the metal-on-metal hip litigation.

Matthew Bradley (see p.601) Offers very strong understanding of the Consumer Protection Act and is known for his ability to turn his hand to both civil and criminal product liability defence. He is qualified to advise on a wide range of product liability matters and is considered to be "excellent on paper and tigerish in court." **Strengths:** "A robust, engaging barrister." "Technically very strong and exudes confidence." **Recent work:** Represented a consultant surgeon in the metal-on-metal hip litigation who was deemed, under the Consumer Protection Act, to have become a producer of the implants due to having combined components from different manufacturers.

Band 2

7BR

See profile on p.814

THE SET

A very capable set whose core focus is on representing claimants in major group litigation stemming from defective medical products and devices. Its members are acclaimed for their advocacy skills and knowledge of product liability, and have been instructed in many of the most high-profile cases seen recently in the market, including those regarding vaccines, hip and breast implants. The set also maintains an active involvement in claims concerning household consumer goods, acting for both claimants and defendants.

Client service: "The clerks are fantastic, I can't fault them at all. Paul Eeles, the senior clerk, is great at keeping instructing solicitors happy, he is very engaging and very quick to repsond, and really has his barristers under a tight whip: if he calls they will answer."

SILKS

Simeon Maskrey QC An esteemed silk dedicated to the representation of claimants, he is considered a "fantastic" and "formidable" advocate and is also highly prized for his judicial expertise. He specialises in medical and pharmaceutical claims and frequently takes a leading role in complex multiparty actions. His work in product liability has elevated him to arenas as prestigious as the Supreme Court and the European Court of Justice. **Strengths:** "Strategically brilliant. Gets on top of the most complex cases with incredible speed. A superb advocate." "Fearsomely bright but approachable and easy to work with."

Hugh Preston QC Boasts an extremely strong reputation as one of the best claimant barristers around, and known for being "creative with sound judgement, a silk you want on your side." His prominence in the product liability space is typified by his instruction in landmark cases such as the metal-on-metal hip implant and PIP breast implant litigation. **Strengths:** "He is an absolutely excellent advocate. He is someone who, I think, always has the ear of the court and who pitches his submissions very well and very reasonably so the judges listen." "Highly experienced and a safe pair of hands. Accessible and well liked by clients." **Recent work:** Instructed in the DePuy ASR group litigation to represent hundreds of claimants who received hip implants, not only those in the UK but in various international jurisdictions across the world.

JUNIORS

Adam Korn Top quality junior whose fantastic product liability practice dovetails neatly into his equally impressive work in clinical negligence. He takes instructions from claimants in cases that arise from all kinds of medical procedures, devices and vaccine programmes, amongst other areas. **Strengths:** "He basically does the work of a QC without the title. He's just great, you can go to him with anything at any time and he'll sort you out." "He grasps issues very quickly. As an advocate he is very accommodating in terms of his prior preparation, he's very quick to think on his feet as well."

Julian Matthews Senior junior specialising in cases that feature the intersection of product liability, clinical negligence and personal injury. Takes on matters involving very severe injury to claimants and those concerning complex points of causation and liability.

Crown Office Chambers

See profile on p.824

THE SET

Prominent set with an emphasis on representing defendants in substantial group actions and unitary product liability cases, although members also take instruction from claimants as well. The set's experience in the area of physical risk, taking in insurance and property damage work, is put to good use on major claims concerning a range of commercial and industrial products, as well as domestic and household consumer goods. Members are also involved in major medical and pharmaceutical cases, and win general acclaim for the quality of their expertise from silk through to junior level.

Client service: "They are an excellent chambers. You get to know the clerks and barristers on a first name basis, even the receptionist knows you! They seem to have that customer care that no matter how busy they are they still respond and return emails very quickly." The clerking team is led by Andy Flanagan.

SILKS

Jonathan Waite QC Widely thought of as one of the leading silks in this area, Jonathan Waite QC is known as a true product liability specialist. He has outstanding knowledge of medical and pharmaceutical cases and has been involved in many of the most-high profile group litigation cases in recent times. **Strengths:** "He is all the things a top QC should be: intellectually rigorous, calm in a crisis whilst also pragmatic and commercial." "Very gutsy counsel; he puts absolutely everything into any case, very experienced and bright, good advocate."

Alexander Antelme QC Since taking silk, Antelme's reputation has flourished as a leader in the area of product liability, where he is involved in major cases concerning defective medical devices, domestic appliances and industrial equipment. Although he acts for parties on both sides of these disputes, he is best known for representing defendants. **Strengths:** "Heavyweight product liability silk with oodles of specialist experience." "A first-class advocate who pays great attention to detail." **Recent work:** Instructed by DePuy International in the metal-on-metal hip litigation, including both the ASR and Pinnacle cases, the latter of which now includes a GLO.

Michael Spencer QC Veteran leader in the product liability space who is admired for his consummate understanding of the sector. He also retains an excellent reputation for his advocacy, with one instructing solicitor calling him "a class act whose abilities in the courtroom leave others trailing behind." **Strengths:** "A leader in the field; he has vast experience. His tactical and procedural knowledge is excellent." "Probably the most experienced senior counsel at the bar in this area: he's very sensible and easy to work with, he has a good rounded view of matters."

JUNIORS

James Medd Considerable construction and property damage expertise which extends to serious cases of product liability in these areas. He also bolsters his practice with strong insurance credentials which he brings to bear on product liability policy disputes. **Strengths:** "A very safe pair of hands in this area." **Recent work:** Instructed in Bell v Northumbrian Water Limited, a claim brought by householders who alleged that disrepair of a sewage pipe had led to the land underneath their homes to subside.

Erica Power (see p.742) A "top-quality junior" who is highly sought after for major group actions in the medical and pharmaceutical sectors. Instructing solicitors praise her attention to detail, her work ethic and her thorough and considered approach to cases. **Strengths:** "Assured and thorough with excellent experience of medical device and healthcare-related products disputes." "She is excellent, very straightforward, very intelligent and detail-oriented. Her help has been invaluable." **Recent work:** Retained as a senior junior in the metal-on-metal hip litigation on behalf of Finsbury Orthopaedics and Finsbury Instruments.

Harry Lambert (see p.694) Considered "one to watch" at the product liability bar, Harry Lambert recently arrived at the set from Doughty Street Chambers. He has had involvement in major group cases as well as individual claims concerning household goods and appliances. **Strengths:** "Extremely dedicated and hard-working, Harry's astute intellect allows him to handle difficult cases and tricky legal issues with aplomb. Rightly regarded as a leading junior in product liability." "Excels in whatever he turns his hand to. Fabulously clever and innovative lawyer." **Recent work:** Instructed to represent a large group of claimants in the ASR hip litigation.

Doughty Street Chambers

See profile on p.828

THE SET

Doughty Street Chambers offers streamlined yet heavyweight representation to claimants involved in large-scale litigation arising from significant product liability claims, and has notable strength in cases in the medical industry. Its members' participation in the recent metal-on-metal hip implants litigation is well noted, as well as their part in numerous key group actions over the years concerning both physical devices as well as pharmaceutical products.

Client service: Kevin Kelly leads Doughty Street's team of civil clerks.

SILKS

Robin Oppenheim QC At the pinnacle of claimant representation sits Robin Oppenheim QC who is revered by instructing solicitors as "the best in the business." His experience in clinical negligence and personal injury matters strengthens his product liability practice, which has most prominently seen him involved in high-profile group litigation related to medical devices. **Strengths:** "Before you even start with him he wants to know how you're going to cross the finish line, he's impressive in every way." "Supremely intelligent and experienced product liability silk with a great eye for detail." **Recent work:** Continues to lead a team of counsel representing claimants in the metal-on-metal hip litigation against DePuy.

JUNIORS

Daniel Bennett A highly capable junior with valuable former experience as a solicitor at a leading claimant law firm. He fields a broad product liability practice which includes defective medical devices and drugs as well as cosmetics and other high street consumer goods. **Recent work:** Represented a former Paralympic athlete who suffered extensive burns due to a Thermos flask with a defective two-part lid.

Band 3

Fountain Court Chambers

See profile on p.847

THE SET

Fountain Court fields a product liability group best known for its ability to manage highly technical cases that originate in the aviation, marine and industrial sectors. In addition to their skill in understanding the complex technical evidence involved in these claims, they also have the ability to identify tricky points of contract law and exclusions, conflicts of law and jurisdictional issues. Members take a similarly sophisticated approach to major litigation arising in the pharmaceutical industry and medical device claims.

Client service: "The clerks, led by Alex Taylor, are very attentive and very approachable."

SILKS

Philip Brook Smith QC (see p.604) Maintains an active product liability practice that includes ongoing instruction in the PIP breast litigation, amongst other things. Offers a strong mathematical background which enables him to take on cases with highly technical or statistical aspects. **Strengths:** "Excellent strategic overview and court presence."

Michael Crane QC (see p.625) Renowned for his aviation and insurance experience, Michael Crane QC's product liability practice is a component of his formidable commercial practice. He regularly acts for manufacturers of whole aircraft and component parts, as well as taking on claims concerning mining and drilling equipment. **Recent work:** Represented the first defendant in a commercial court claim after a fire on board a parked Boeing 787 Dreamliner at Heathrow Airport, which was said to be caused by a defective lithium battery.

Akhil Shah QC (see p.762) Specialises in highly technical product liability claims, particularly in the aviation sector, although his skills also lie in contract law and professional negligence. He offers niche expertise in cases concerning design and manufacturing defects in both commercial aircraft and helicopters. **Strengths:** "He's an incredibly intelligent, very astute barrister, whose written product is one of his strongest points. He drafts pleadings incredibly well."

4 New Square

See profile on p.880

THE SET

4 New Square's sterling reputation for professional negligence work is complemented by its efforts in the insurance and property damage spheres, and all three form a strong basis for taking on significant product liability cases. The set can claim a strong bench of capable practitioners whose expertise range from the medical and pharmaceutical sectors to cases involving commercial products such as electrical devices and industrial equipment. In addition to the expertise of its barristers, the set receives warm praise for the quality of its clerking service.

Client service: "They always provide a very responsive service, and they are a modern, outward-looking chambers." Lizzy Stewart and Dennis Peck lead the clerking team.

SILKS

Leigh-Ann Mulcahy QC (see p.723) Known for her strength in the pharmaceutical and medical sectors, she also demonstrates command of commercial cases related to industrial products. Her practice involves not only high-level advocacy and appellate expertise, but also significant advisory work relating to pharmaceutical regulation. **Strengths:** "Very knowledgeable, measured, great with clients." "Hard-working, bright and user-friendly." **Recent work:** Represented Cape in a case involving a number of subrogated claims relating to asbestos products.

Graham Eklund QC (see p.640) A highly regarded QC whose product liability practice focuses on property damage resulting from allegedly defective industrial and commercial products. He is often the first port of call in cases concerning significant fire damage and frequently acts for both claimants and defendants. **Strengths:** "His legals are first-rate and he's also calm and unflappable which instills confidence." "Client-friendly and an excellent advocate." **Recent work:** Advised on a claim alleging that a serious fire in a hotel sauna was caused by a defective light fitting.

David Turner QC Undertakes a range of commercial product liability work with a notable focus on fire-damage cases. He has also recently undertaken a number of claims relating to the use of defective concrete at airports and motorways. **Strengths:** "Excellent at reading opponents." **Recent work:** Acted for the defendant against a claim alleging that a factory fire was caused by a faulty air conditioning unit.

JUNIORS

Peter Feldschreiber (see p.643) Specialist in the medical industry, known for his ability to provide outstanding regulatory advice on product liability cases. A superbly academic lawyer who is well reputed for his understanding of every aspect of the pharmaceutical sector, thanks to his previous career in medicine and in pharmaceutical regulation. **Strengths:** "He is a wonderful character. He has the experience on the medical and pharmaceutical sides, he's also done the regulatory side, then he decided he was interested in the legal side. Fantastic chap, very nice as well. That combination is genuinely unique, nobody else has got that sort of background." **Recent work:** Provided advice on the duties of the regulator to provide commercial confidentiality in relation to a clinical trial relating to an arthritis treatment.

Katie Powell (see p.741) Concentrates primarily on product liability disputes which stem from a construction or technical standpoint, and bolsters this with her professional negligence expertise. She has a niche specialism in cases concerning plastic polymer products. **Strengths:** "Great with clients, excellent service on product liability cases." **Recent work:** Represented Oasis Air Conditioning in a case alleging that a heating system installed in a BMW showroom was defective.

Serjeants' Inn Chambers

See profile on p.907

THE SET

Specialists in medical and pharmaceutical matters, members at Serjeants' Inn are known for their skill at representing claimants on cases that straddle the line between clinical negligence and product liability. This year, the set can claim deep involvement in many of the ongoing group actions arising in regard to defective hip implants, as well as claims relating to a range of other medical devices. The set also has a growing focus on claims involving other kinds of consumer products and takes on an increasing amount of defendant work in this regard.

Client service: Lee Johnson is the senior clerk at Serjeants' Inn.

SILKS

Christopher Johnston QC (see p.684) Enjoys a strengthening reputation as a claimant silk who is methodical and well prepared in everything he does. He has been involved in a number of recent, highly publicised group actions relating to medical devices, on which he can also bring to bear his top-notch clinical negligence expertise. **Strengths:** "He has a no-nonsense approach to everything and everyone, and cuts through the peripheral issues that often plagues high-profile group litigation. He is a hands-on silk and is fantastic with clients."

JUNIORS

Heidi Knight (see p.692) A junior who is very highly thought of for her technical and legal abilities as well as her client care skills, with one instructing solicitor describing her as "frighteningly bright but incredibly approachable." She is instructed on behalf of claimants involved in significant pieces of group litigation as well as those taking individual action in cases of defective medical devices. **Strengths:** "Her preparatory work is superb and she inspires confidence in clients and solicitors who can relax knowing that the case has been fully prepared. Very easy to work with and responsive." "Technically astute and very able. A real team player."

Eloise Power (see p.741) Demonstrates a high level of technical ability in medical matters as well as a thorough understanding of product liability law. Her standing as a junior has ensured her involvement in many eye-catching cases including those dealing with trans-vaginal mesh, metal-on-metal hip implants and pharmaceutical products. **Strengths:** "She is passionate and razor sharp on her feet. She has a sensible approach to what can often seem like a complicated case." "A persuasive and determined advocate. Always impressive."

2TG – 2 Temple Gardens

See profile on p.920

THE SET

Has a particular reputation for handling multi-track product liability disputes where one or more parties are based abroad, or which involve other intrinsic cross-border aspects. As well as providing strong expertise in jurisdictional law, members specialise in related areas such as insurance, property damage and personal injury, and have seen increasing instruction in product liability cases as a result. Recent instructions have come with regard to a huge range of product types including medical devices, industrial equipment, consumer products and construction materals.

Client service: "The clerks are very good and they are competitive in their pricing. They will listen to any sort of discussion you have on fees and are always very accommodating with that side of things." Lee Tyler is the senior clerk.

SILKS

Charles Dougherty QC (see p.635) A skilled product liability silk with a respectable insurance practice who is especially well known for his considerable international focus. His product liability practice stems primarily from the medical and pharmaceutical industries but also takes on property damage claims that arise from faulty products. **Strengths:** "An excellent advocate who is extremely knowledgeable on international jurisdiction and conflicts issues." "He has such a good brain, he has a really rapid grasp of the issues. His advocacy is great as well, he gets just the right tone."

Neil Moody QC (see p.720) Head of chambers who also takes on major cases of product liability that relate to property damage, particularly in the industrial sector. His work also benefits from his additional proficiency as a professional negligence and insurance specialist. **Strengths:** "He instils a great sense of authority and confidence." "Offers well-respected, considered advice." **Recent work:** Represented a supplier of industrial flooring coatings in a claim relating to a car park in a Dubai mall.

Other Ranked Lawyers

Neil Block QC (see p.598) (39 Essex Chambers) Specialises in product liability claims that have resulted in serious personal injury or property damage. His practice also sees him acting on high-profile group litigations relating to defective household products and medical devices. **Strengths:** "A quiet advocate who has a lot of sound judgement." "He is extremely good, very able and has really excellent negotiation skills." **Recent work:** Represented NHS surgeons in the metal-on-metal hip litigation.

Claire Andrews (Gough Square Chambers) Highly regarded for her expertise in consumer law, she offers specialist knowledge to clients facing complex product liability cases in the food industry. Instructing solicitors praise her "encyclopaedic" knowledge of the area, saying "what she doesn't know isn't worth knowing." **Strengths:** "She always provides very intelligent and very authoritative input into discussions." "Excellent product safety knowledge and a good commercial head."

Fred Philpott (Gough Square Chambers) Very experienced senior junior who is considered "a bit of a guru" on the subject of consumer law, an area in which he has written and published extensively. He also has considerable knowledge of food safety and product liability claims, and is a go to person for such specialist work. **Strengths:** "He is very good and very user-friendly with clients. You give him a job and you'll get back a fully thought out and good answer."

Marcus Pilgerstorfer (see p.738) (11KBW) A highly knowledgeable junior whose immersion in the product liability space is demonstrated by his decision to take a PhD on the subject. His legal work remains focused on representing claimants, and he has been involved in both individual cases as well as in a number of the high-profile group actions arising out of defective hip implants. **Strengths:** "He is brilliant. He gets the law right every time, he's a detail person and the perfect junior to have working with you." "For novel issues he is fantastic, and in terms of paper-based work his advice is detailed, clear and fully justified, covering periphery issues as well as the black letter of instructions." **Recent work:** Represented numerous claimants in the ongoing PIP breast implant litigation.

Robert Lawson QC (see p.697) (Quadrant Chambers) An expert in aviation and travel law who focuses his attention on major product liability cases in these areas. He has been instructed by defendants in a number of significant claims arising from defective equipment alleged to have contributed to aircraft fires, crashes and serious personal injury. **Strengths:** "He is very enthusiastic, proactive and user-friendly, and he knows his subject inside out." **Recent work:** Defended the manufacturers of a lithium battery that was held partially responsible for a fire that caused substantial damage to a parked Boeing 787 Dreamliner at Heathrow Airport.

Andrew Prynne QC (Temple Garden Chambers) Veteran silk regarded as a "pioneer" of the area and who can claim involvement in many highly significant product liability cases. His work in this field sits neatly within his larger common law and commercial practice which also involves an emphasis on many complementary areas of law such as insurance, personal injury and health and safety. **Strengths:** "He has a huge amount of product liability experience."

Contents:

LONDON

Professional Discipline
Leading Sets
Band 1
Blackstone Chambers *
1 Crown Office Row *
39 Essex Chambers *
Serjeants' Inn Chambers *
Band 2
Fountain Court Chambers *
2 Hare Court *
Outer Temple Chambers *
QEB Hollis Whiteman *
Band 3
2 Bedford Row *
23 Essex Street *
Hailsham Chambers *
4 New Square *
3 Raymond Buildings Barristers *
Band 4
5 Essex Court *
Old Square Chambers *
* *Indicates set / individual with profile.*
[A] *direct access (see p.24).*
◊ *(ORL) = Other Ranked Lawyer.*
Alphabetical order within each band. Band 1 is highest.

Professional Discipline	
Leading Silks	
Star individuals	
Dutton Timothy	*Fountain Court Chambers* *
Band 1	
Beggs John	*Serjeants' Inn Chambers* *
Coonan Kieran	*1 Crown Office Row*
Edis William	*1 Crown Office Row*
Forde Martin	*1 Crown Office Row*
Foster Alison	*39 Essex Chambers* *
Francis Robert	*Serjeants' Inn Chambers* *
Gibbs Patrick	*3 Raymond Buildings Barristers* [A] *
Hopkins Adrian	*Serjeants' Inn Chambers* *
Hubble Ben	*4 New Square* *
Kark Tom	*QEB Hollis Whiteman* *
Lambert Christina	*1 Crown Office Row*
Malek Hodge M	*39 Essex Chambers*
Miller Stephen	*1 Crown Office Row*
O'Rourke Mary	*Old Square Chambers*
Shaw Mark	*Blackstone Chambers*
Stern Ian	*2 Bedford Row*
Sutton Mark	*Old Square Chambers*
Treverton-Jones Gregory	*39 Essex Chambers*
Band 2	
Davies Hugh	*3 Raymond Buildings Barristers* [A]
Glynn Joanna	*1 Crown Office Row*
Hugh-Jones George	*Serjeants' Inn Chambers* *
Johnson Zoe	*QEB Hollis Whiteman* *
Larkin Sean	*QEB Hollis Whiteman* *
Moon Angus	*Serjeants' Inn Chambers* *
Pannick David	*Blackstone Chambers*
Pittaway David	*Hailsham Chambers* *
Robertson Patricia	*Fountain Court Chambers* *
Rose Dinah	*Blackstone Chambers*
Williams Geoffrey	*Farrar's Building (ORL)* ◊ *
Band 3	
Barton Fiona	*5 Essex Court* *
Beer Jason	*5 Essex Court* *
Booth Richard	*1 Crown Office Row*
Coleman Richard	*Fountain Court Chambers* *
Flint Charles	*Blackstone Chambers*
Grey Eleanor	*39 Essex Chambers*
Herberg Javan	*Blackstone Chambers*
McLaren Michael	*Fountain Court Chambers* *
McPherson Graeme	*4 New Square* [A] *
Morris Fenella	*39 Essex Chambers*
Mylonas Michael	*Serjeants' Inn Chambers* *
Band 4	
Aaronberg David	*15 New Bridge Street (ORL)* ◊
Beloff Michael	*Blackstone Chambers*
Chawla Mukul	*9-12 Bell Yard (ORL)* ◊ [A] *
Gallafent Kate	*Blackstone Chambers*
Havers Philip	*1 Crown Office Row*
Hendy John	*Old Square Chambers* *
Hutton Alexander	*Hailsham Chambers* *
Lawrence Patrick	*4 New Square* *
Lewis Adam	*Blackstone Chambers*
Milliken-Smith Mark	*2 Bedford Row* *
Monty Simon	*4 New Square* *
Price Richard	*Littleton Chambers (ORL)* ◊ *
Richards Jenni	*39 Essex Chambers* *
Sachdeva Vikram	*39 Essex Chambers* *
Winter Ian	*Cloth Fair Chambers (ORL)* ◊ *
New Silks	
Bradley Clodagh	*1 Crown Office Row*
Gollop Katharine	*Serjeants' Inn Chambers* *
Hyam Jeremy	*1 Crown Office Row*
Ozin Paul	*23 Essex Street*
Thomas Owain	*1 Crown Office Row*

Band 1

Blackstone Chambers

See profile on p.813

THE SET

Remains a go-to set for all manner of professional discipline disputes given its extensive industry expertise which encompasses areas such as finance, accountancy, sports, education, law and healthcare. Blackstone Chambers provides clients with "spot-on, practical guidance and advice." Its esteemed members are particularly highlighted for their deft handling of appellate matters before the High Court, while clients appreciate the set's provision of an impressive "depth and range of high-quality, persuasive and well-measured advocates."

Client service: Senior clerk Gary Oliver "understands clients' needs, and is approachable and very attentive." Market sources say that the clerking team "are friendly, responsive and always willing to help."

SILKS

Mark Shaw QC Well-known and highly respected advocate who focuses on disciplinary matters involving healthcare professionals. He is frequently instructed by a wide variety of medical regulators, including the GMC, NMS and GOC. **Strengths:** "He has an exceptional mind, particularly in relation to regulation and professional discipline work. His knowledge is encyclopaedic, he's personable and can understand the law and apply it in a creative manner." "Mark is both very bright and very personable. He is one of the go-to counsel for complex, high-profile cases involving public law issues." **Recent work:** Appeared in R (Kinnersley) v GMC & Antoniou, successfully appearing for the GMC to resist a High Court judicial review challenge to the disclosure of expert reports to complainants in medical disciplinary cases.

David Pannick QC Public law specialist with a fine reputation in the professional discipline sphere. He routinely handles an impressive range of matters in overseas courts such as Bermuda and the British Virgin Islands, appearing for clients in the financial sector. **Strengths:** "Lives up to his considerable reputation. He demonstrates client relationship skills of the very highest order and is able to distil even the most complex case into three or four apparently simple issues." "One of the most brilliant silks, he has an incredibly fierce intellect."

Dinah Rose QC Impressive barrister with a formidable reputation. She routinely represents claimants across several professions, most notably handling complex cases concerning the financial sector. **Strengths:** "Dinah Rose is a fearless and impressive advocate who you would always want on your side." **Recent work:** Represented various claimants in a challenge to a new quality assurance scheme for criminal advocates. The case centred on breaches of the principle of the independence of the advocate and breaches of EU law.

Charles Flint QC Respected leader in the field of financial services regulation. He is routinely called upon by both regulators and regulated organisations, such as investment banks. **Strengths:** "A very experienced practitioner who's highly personable in his approach." "Charles Flint is the doyen of financial services regulatory investigations and excels in matters where public and regulatory law overlap."

Javan Herberg QC Focuses his esteemed practice on financial services regulation, regularly appearing on behalf of both professionals and regulatory bodies. **Strengths:** "He's insightful, gets to the heart of a matter and understands the key issues. He's quick on his feet, and a very smooth advocate with a measured delivery that lands very well." **Recent work:** Acted for RBS in connection with FCA and PRA regulatory proceedings arising from a major IT malfunction in 2012 which led to nationwide failures in processing accounts and payments at RBS, NatWest and Ulster Bank.

Michael Beloff QC One of the most senior and experienced advocates in the field of public law. He is held in particularly high esteem for his expert handling of disciplinary matters relating to the health and legal professions, and he also demonstrates prowess in the education, sports and financial sectors. **Strengths:** "He has a mind like a trap. He comes up with unbelievable points, works really hard and goes to incredible lengths in his preparation." **Recent work:** Acted for NHS England in a major case challenging its ability to meet its statutory financial duties.

Kate Gallafent QC Accomplished silk with vast experience in the sporting, telecommunications and

Professional Discipline
Leading Juniors
Star individuals
Bradly David *39 Essex Chambers* *
Brassington Stephen *2 Hare Court* *
Band 1
Barnfather Lydia *QEB Hollis Whiteman* *
Boyle Gerard *Serjeants' Inn Chambers* *
Colman Andrew *2 Hare Court* *
Ferguson Craig *2 Hare Court* *
Foster Charles *Serjeants' Inn Chambers* *
Haycroft Anthony *Serjeants' Inn Chambers* *
Hockton Andrew *Serjeants' Inn Chambers* *
Holl-Allen Jonathan *Serjeants' Inn Chambers* *
Horlick Fiona *Outer Temple Chambers*
Hurst Andrew *2 Hare Court* *
Jenkins Alan *Serjeants' Inn Chambers* *
Kennedy Andrew *1 Crown Office Row*
Lambis Marios *2 Hare Court*
Leonard James *Outer Temple Chambers*
Morris David *Serjeants' Inn Chambers* *
Neale Fiona *Hailsham Chambers* *
Partridge Richard *Serjeants' Inn Chambers* *
Peacock Nicholas *Hailsham Chambers* *
Ramasamy Selva *QEB Hollis Whiteman* *
Tabachnik Andrew *39 Essex Chambers*
Watson Claire *Serjeants' Inn Chambers* *
Band 2
Baumber Kevin *3 Raymond Buildings Barristers*
Campbell Sarah *23 Essex Street*
Carpenter Chloe *Fountain Court Chambers* *
Counsell James *Outer Temple Chambers*
Cridland Simon *Serjeants' Inn Chambers* *
Hamer Kenneth *Henderson Chambers (ORL)* ◊ [A] *
Hare Ivan *Blackstone Chambers*
Harris Rebecca *QEB Hollis Whiteman* *
McCartney Kevin *5 Paper Buildings (ORL)* ◊
McDonagh Matthew *Outer Temple Chambers*
Rahman Shaheen *1 Crown Office Row*
Sheldon Neil *1 Crown Office Row*
Singh Sandesh *2 Bedford Row*
Band 3
Allen Rupert *Fountain Court Chambers* *
Bex Kate *2 Hare Court*
Butt Matthew *3 Raymond Buildings Barristers* [A] *
Callaghan Catherine *Blackstone Chambers*
Fortune Malcolm *Serjeants' Inn Chambers* *
Ley-Morgan Mark *Serjeants' Inn Chambers* *
McClelland James *Fountain Court Chambers* *
Pardoe Rupert *23 Essex Street*
Parker Paul *4 New Square* *
Powell Giles *Old Square Chambers* *
Uberoi Michael *Outer Temple Chambers*
Band 4
Dobbin Clair *3 Raymond Buildings Barristers* *
Emlyn Jones William *3 Raymond Buildings Barristers*
Greaney Nicola *39 Essex Chambers* *
Hearnden Alexis *39 Essex Chambers*
Hobcraft Gemma *Doughty Street Chambers (ORL)* ◊
Hodivala Jamas *2 Bedford Row*
Medcroft Nicholas *Fountain Court Chambers* *
Newman Philip *42 Bedford Row (ORL)* ◊
Przybylska Sarah *2 Hare Court* *
Sleeman Susan *Doughty Street Chambers (ORL)* ◊
Band 5
Atchley Richard *3 Raymond Buildings Barristers*
Barnes Matthew *1 Crown Office Row*
Brandon Ben *3 Raymond Buildings Barristers*
Colin Giles *1 Crown Office Row*
Criddle Betsan *Old Square Chambers* *
Geering Christopher *2 Hare Court* *
Hanif Saima *39 Essex Chambers* [A] *
Holdcroft Matthew *5 Essex Court* *
Jones Tristan *Blackstone Chambers*
Ladenburg Guy *3 Raymond Buildings Barristers* *
Lazarus Robert *39 Essex Chambers*
Levey Edward *Fountain Court Chambers* *
Mant Peter *39 Essex Chambers*
Motraghi Nadia *Old Square Chambers*
Newbegin Nicola *Old Square Chambers* *
Price Louise *Doughty Street Chambers (ORL)* ◊
Saunders Neil *3 Raymond Buildings Barristers* [A] *
Spencer Paul *Serjeants' Inn Chambers* *
Whitelaw Francesca *5 Essex Court* *
Williamson Alisdair *3 Raymond Buildings Barristers* [A] *
Up-and-coming individuals
Emmerson Heather *11KBW (ORL)* ◊ *
Nesterchuk Tetyana *Fountain Court Chambers* *
Rich Ben *2 Hare Court* *
** Indicates individual with profile.*
[A] direct access (see p.24).
◊ (ORL) = Other Ranked Lawyer.
Alphabetical order within each band. Band 1 is highest.

healthcare sectors. She routinely acts for both the regulators and the regulated. **Strengths:** "Her teamwork and supportive nature is particularly notable. She is very user-friendly and comes up with pragmatic solutions." **Recent work:** Appeared for Ofcom in a challenge to its refusal to extend a community radio service licence following breaches of licence conditions.

Adam Lewis QC Highly thought of in the field of sporting regulation, he is frequently involved in significant and complex disciplinary matters concerning sports such as snooker and tennis. He receives particular praise for his technical expertise and depth of knowledge. **Strengths:** "He is a fantastic advocate who phrases matters in a way which really hits home; he knows just which nerve to strike and does so in an elegant way." "He has an encyclopaedic knowledge of sports law jurisprudence." **Recent work:** Acted for the Football League in the prosecution of QPR's breach of financial fair play rules.

JUNIORS

Ivan Hare Experienced junior who routinely undertakes complex disciplinary cases regarding the police and health services. **Strengths:** "He is very polished and extremely skilful." **Recent work:** Acted in GMC v Adeogba and Visvardis, a series of related appeals concerning the circumstances in which a Fitness to Practise Panel can proceed in the absence of a doctor, and the admissibility of fresh evidence on appeal to the High Court.

Catherine Callaghan Highly proficient barrister whose broad industry expertise is widely praised, covering sectors such as healthcare, law, accountancy and advertising. She regularly represents both regulatory bodies and the regulated. **Strengths:** "She analyses the strengths and weaknesses of cases very quickly and incisively, coming up with novel responses. She picks up on technical points very quickly and prepares thoroughly." "A smart and capable lawyer with total command in the fields of professional discipline and public law." **Recent work:** Acted for the GMC in a judicial review considering the proper construction of the GMC's 'five-year rule' and the GMC's power to reconsider a decision under that rule.

Tristan Jones Demonstrates expertise in the areas of sport, education and healthcare regulation. He is regularly instructed to both defend and prosecute professional individuals. **Strengths:** "An impressive junior, he works very effectively under great pressure and is a fine analyst and draftsman."

1 Crown Office Row

See profile on p.826

THE SET

1 Crown Office Row boasts an impressive array of "high-calibre barristers" offering top-tier advice and representation to a diverse clientele. The set is sought after by a wide range of professional individuals, including solicitors, doctors, nurses, vets, surveyors, engineers and brokers, and has vast experience appearing before their respective regulatory bodies. The chambers continues to be highly thought of by market commentators, who underscore its provision of "quality across the board," from juniors through to silks. Its esteemed members are well versed on both sides of the disciplinary process, and remain a popular choice for regulators, such as the GMC, GOC, SDT and FCA. In particular, its annexe in the same building as the MPTS makes a highly convenient choice for those involved in medical disciplinary hearings.

Client service: The clerking team, led by Matthew Phipps, "cannot be faulted," according to market sources. "They are efficient, user-friendly and always prompt. Administratively, they are certainly an impressive group."

SILKS

Kieran Coonan QC Esteemed silk with a stellar reputation in the remit of healthcare regulation. He regularly appears on behalf of both claimants and defendants before the GMC and GDC. **Strengths:** "He's been doing this forever and has an encyclopaedic knowledge." "He's a very assured advocate who is brilliant at handling difficult clients in difficult cases."

William Edis QC Distinguished healthcare practitioner who routinely receives instructions in high-value disputes. His broader practice sees him making regular appearances before the Disciplinary Committee of the Royal College of Veterinary Surgeons, demonstrating notable skill in cases concerning fraud. **Strengths:** "One of the more cerebral advocates; he brings the power of intellect to cases, which has proven invaluable to clients." "One of the leading silks in this area of work, with a gift for knowing how to cut to the chase and get to the real issue." **Recent work:** Appeared before the Court of Appeal in Michalak v GMC, a challenge to various GMC decisions on the grounds of discrimination.

Martin Forde QC Respected advocate who is frequently sought after by chiropractors, dentists, doctors and osteopaths, alongside their regulators. Given his sterling reputation, he is regularly instructed in high-profile, significant disciplinary proceedings. **Strengths:** "He has a very smooth and persuasive oral advocacy style and is a very tough opponent." "A clear and straightforward advocate with very good judgement as to how to pitch a case and what arguments to run with."

Christina Lambert QC Experienced practitioner who is renowned for her adroit representation of professionals appearing before the GMC. In particular, she offers deep expertise in matters concerning medical practitioners who have been charged with sexual assault. **Strengths:** "An extremely experienced silk, she has a strong pedigree in healthcare professional discipline work and an enviable attention to detail." "She possesses spot-on judgement and is able to pitch her submissions in a way which is most persuasive."

Stephen Miller QC Experienced medical specialist whose broad healthcare expertise spans across disciplinary matters, healthcare-related criminal cases, multiparty actions and significant inquiries. **Strengths:** "Excellent drafting and superb preparation, he is certainly well equipped to handle complex regulatory cases."

Joanna Glynn QC Well known for her representation of regulators, particularly in healthcare matters. She is also highly regarded for her disciplinary work in the legal and financial sectors. **Strengths:** "A strong, well-known and highly respected silk." "She's been doing this work for years and is extremely proficient."

Richard Booth QC Recognised primarily for his vast experience in the healthcare and veterinary remits, though he also demonstrates aptitude in cases concerning sports regulation. He typically represents professional individuals before their regulatory bodies. **Strengths:** "A hugely effective advocate who is right up there in terms of tactical nuance." "A first-rate, impressive advocate who is regularly retained on challenging cases." **Recent work:** Appeared before the MPTS on behalf of a consultant cardiologist who faced serious allegations of dishonesty.

Clodagh Bradley QC Established medical law specialist whose disciplinary cases have predominantly involved the GMC, though she also has experience of appearing before the GDC, GOC and NMC. She frequently handles complex cases involving alcohol and opiate misuse, rape, fraud and practitioners' physical and mental health issues. **Strengths:** "A skilled, forceful and highly effective advocate, she always has her clients' best interests at heart and never fails to impress." "She combines intelligence with tenacity; she's good at keeping many balls in the air and is absolutely dedicated to her cases." **Recent work:** Appeared on behalf of paediatric neuropathologist Dr Waney Squier in GMC v Squier. The GMC brought misconduct charges against Squier after she allegedly provided misleading evidence in her capacity as an expert witness in seven highly contentious cases concerning 'shaken baby syndrome'.

Philip Havers QC Highly regarded silk with notable expertise in the professional discipline remit. He routinely handles regulatory work in the healthcare and sports sectors, among others. **Strengths:** "Very experienced silk; he is a formidable opponent in healthcare disciplinary matters."

Jeremy Hyam QC An impressive healthcare advocate who is recognised for his deft handling of complex cases on behalf of medical practitioners. **Strengths:** "A highly innovative lawyer, he is inventive in how he applies the law and demonstrates an impressive grasp of emerging legal trends." "He is an incredibly thoughtful, intelligent and committed advocate whose advice is invariably reliable." "He is always helpful and effective as an advocate, and he works extremely well to a tight timescale."

Owain Thomas QC Held in high esteem for his adroit representation of various professional individuals facing disciplinary proceedings, including architects, solicitors, medical practitioners and engineers. **Strengths:** "Very good on his feet, he has excellent instincts when it comes to hearings. He's decisive and a wonderful strategist, even when under pressure." "He is reliably calm and considered during complex and lengthy cases."

JUNIORS

Andrew Kennedy Offers broad expertise in the disciplinary arena with a specialist focus on healthcare matters. He is a familiar face in complex, high-profile GMC and GDC proceedings. **Strengths:** "He's a genius, he gets brilliant results and has the ability to turn challenging cases around." "Andrew grabs the case by the scruff of the neck; he knows the tribunals well and knows how to handle them."

Shaheen Rahman Routinely tackles complex, high-profile and long-running cases before healthcare regulatory bodies. She is also noted for her deft handling of significant judicial review proceedings and sophisticated appellate work. **Strengths:** "She has the ability to command a room and nearly always manages to pull a result out of the bag, even in cases that initially appear to be unwinnable." "She has a wonderfully precise approach to regulatory matters, and is extremely well prepared, tenacious and thorough."

Neil Sheldon Respected for his highly effective representation of doctors and dentists. His busy practice sees him regularly appearing before the GMC, the GDC and the High Court. **Strengths:** "He exhibits a really high level of skill and steely determination. He is absolutely focused on delivering the desired outcome for the client in complex cases." "A standout junior, his simplification of complex matters is exemplary."

Matthew Barnes Medical specialist offering broad-based experience and expertise. He is regularly called upon to appear before a range of regulators, including the GDC, NMC and British Acupuncture Council. He is also noted for his aptitude in matters concerning NHS trust employment issues. **Strengths:** "He is a very relaxed yet direct advocate with a refreshing style. He's very good at identifying the approach that should be taken in a case and is an excellent strategist." **Recent work:** Represented a dentist who was charged by the GDC with clinical failures concerning the preparation and fitting of a bridge. The allegations included failure to receive consent from the patient and failure to communicate clinical mistakes.

Giles Colin Accomplished junior who is recognised for his high-quality work in the healthcare sector. He focuses particularly on the representation of doctors and dentists, while remaining a popular choice for hospital trusts and the ambulance service. **Strengths:** "He's excellent: he knows this area inside out, is exceptionally experienced and is able to deal with matters proficiently by getting right to the point."

39 Essex Chambers

See profile on p.840

THE SET

39 Essex Chambers distinguishes itself by its breadth of industry expertise and remains a highly popular choice across the medical, media, sports, legal and environment sectors. Its accomplished members routinely appear on behalf of both regulators and professional individuals in significant disciplinary hearings, complex judicial review proceedings and High Court appeals. They also provide expert advice on risk and compliance to clients who are seeking to prevent disciplinary or regulatory issues from developing. Market sources regard the chambers as "expert and a true leaders in its field. It has a broad range of counsel available, from most experienced QCs to very willing and highly capable juniors."

Client service: The clerking team, led by Peter Campbell, is regarded as "responsive, reliable and highly practical."

SILKS

Alison Foster QC (see p.647) Hugely experienced silk offering deep expertise in the legal, medical and veterinary sectors. She routinely appears before the higher courts, and is particularly recognised for her deft handling of complex judicial review proceedings and statutory appeals. **Strengths:** "An incredibly astute, very intelligent and extremely perceptive practitioner. She is very effective at drawing out the real, key issues." "A highly effective and confident advocate who is listened to by judges at all levels. She is supremely knowledgeable in regulatory law." **Recent work:** Represented a clinical psychologist who faced multiple serious allegations. These included false claims for fees, refusal to disclose clinical records, false representations about patients' mental health and inadequate treatment.

Hodge Malek QC Respected advocate who brings significant commercial experience to bear upon his established disciplinary practice. He offers particular expertise across the financial, legal and sports sectors. **Strengths:** "He's quick on the uptake, exceptionally thorough and ultra-confident." "He is a highly effective advocate who very rarely fails to deliver on his chosen strategy." **Recent work:** Acted in ICAP plc, a case concerning the Libor rigging scandal. The matter involved both financial regulators, such as the FCA, and criminal bodies, including the SFO.

Gregory Treverton-Jones QC Renowned and exceptionally experienced advocate who specialises in the representation of solicitors facing significant disciplinary proceedings. He is also noted for his adept representation of barristers and surveyors. **Strengths:** "He is extremely knowledgeable and highly respected by the SDT." "He's excellent and authoritative in the area of solicitors' regulation." **Recent work:** Successfully represented a solicitor in a High Court application seeking to set aside an intervention into his practice.

Eleanor Grey QC Demonstrates notable skill in regulatory and disciplinary matters concerning the health and social care sectors. Market sources are quick to praise her courtroom advocacy skills. **Strengths:** "She is brilliant, really calm and incisive, and she has a great manner with clients." "She engenders absolute confidence." **Recent work:** Acted for the former Healthcare Commission and its chair in the Mid-Staffordshire Public Inquiry into NHS standards.

Fenella Morris QC Skilled advocate whose broad practice encompasses a number of professional remits, including healthcare, accountancy and finance. She enjoys a long track record of providing significant policy advice to regulators and disciplinary bodies. She regularly acts for both the prosecution and defence. **Strengths:** "Fenella is straight-talking, assertive and obviously very knowledgeable about the regulation of healthcare professionals." "If you want someone who will debate issues for you zealously, stick to their guns and present legal arguments robustly, she's the person to go to."

Jenni Richards QC (see p.751) Highly respected silk, her practice covers a wide range of sectors, including finance, healthcare, education and social care. She is routinely called upon to act on behalf of both claimants and defendants, and draws upon her deep knowledge of public law to inform her regulatory work. **Strengths:** "She is a proven winner and an absolute pleasure to work with." "She is absolutely tenacious and very dedicated to her clients." **Recent work:** Acted in Human Fertilisation & Embryology Authority v St Jude's Women's Clinic, a regulatory appeal regarding the suitability of the clinic to hold a licence.

Vikram Sachdeva QC (see p.757) Renowned silk whose highly active practice sees him regularly appearing before a range of regulatory bodies, including the GMC, GDC, NMC, SDT and Care Standards Tribunal. He is an adept representative of both respondents and applicants. **Strengths:** "He is qualified as both a doctor and a lawyer, which gives him great insight. He's intellectually able and a very strong advocate." "He is intelligent, brings lateral thinking to cases and is very industrious." **Recent work:** Successfully acted on behalf of a GP in Dr Sampson Asare v NHS England. This was a matter concerning a doctor who had been threatened with a twelve-month suspension from practice while allegations of sexual misconduct were investigated.

JUNIORS

David Bradly (see p.601) Exceptional advocate who regularly assists both regulators and professional individuals in the healthcare sector. He is also highly regarded for his deft handling of complex cases on behalf of accountants, architects, psychologists and counsellors before their respective regulatory bodies. **Strengths:** "Incisive and persuasive, he knows how to get to the heart of a case and how to bring the committee with him." "He has first-class judgement and is a go-to lawyer in complex, sensitive and high-profile cases." **Recent work:** Appeared in PSA v Nursing and Midwifery Council & Jozi. This was an appeal brought by the PSA regarding what was deemed to be an unduly lenient sanction handed down to a care home nurse.

Andrew Tabachnik Highly regarded junior who is recognised for his capable handling of complex professional discipline matters. He regularly appears both for and against regulators, and focuses his practice on the legal, financial and sporting sectors. **Strengths:** "He takes a measured, intellectual approach and is highly capable of persuading judges on the nuances of conflicts." "Andrew is an exceptional junior who provides high-quality legal advice and pragmatic, strategic contributions to matters. He is a precise and thorough draftsman and a highly persuasive advocate." **Recent work:** Acted for the regulator in SRA v Pauline Twist, successfully resisting Ms Twist's application to set aside the intervention into her practice.

Nicola Greaney (see p.659) Routinely appears in significant disciplinary matters, frequently on behalf of professional individuals in the veterinary and healthcare sectors. She is able to draw upon her deep knowledge of clinical negligence and personal injury law to inform her well-respected regulatory practice. **Strengths:** "She is really responsive to her clients' needs and turns work around really quickly. She's a delight to work with." "Her advice is always practical, sensible and to the point." **Recent work:** Acted in Davies v RCVS, a judicial review challenge to the decision of the RCVS to close two complaints made by a veterinary surgeon against two veterinary nurses.

Alexis Hearnden Highly regarded for her effective representation of both professional individuals and their regulators, focusing primarily on the healthcare sector. She has acted for the GOC, GDC, HCPC, GOsC and RCVS, and regularly appears before the NMC. **Strengths:** "I'm always impressed with Alexis; she's clever, good on technical points and never misses a trick." "She is a well-respected junior who is both thorough and approachable." **Recent work:** Acted for the GDC in a fitness to practise case concerning a dentist who was accused of conducting unnecessary and incompetent root canal work.

Saima Hanif (see p.663) Accomplished junior who is particularly well known for her adroit representation of financial services professionals. She is also called upon to tackle significant healthcare matters, often handling cases on behalf of public bodies, doctors, dentists and pharmacists. **Strengths:** "A pleasure to work with, she is a very smart advocate who really understands how FCA enforcement investigations work." "She packs a punch as an advocate given her polite yet assertive manner. She's ultra-professional and conscientious in her conduct." **Recent work:** Acted in Paivi Grigg v FCA, a case concerning a risk management director who failed to ensure that an IFA network's risk management framework was adequate.

Robert Lazarus Highly thought-of advocate who is particularly noted for his adroit representation of healthcare professionals. His broader client base includes architects and solicitors. **Strengths:** "An absolute pleasure to work with; he's analytical, precise, extremely knowledgeable and fantastic with clients." "He has a significant background knowledge of the healthcare world which is extremely helpful." **Recent work:** Successfully defended an educational psychologist in Health & Care Professions Council v Davies, a matter centring on the inappropriate use of psychometric assessments.

Peter Mant Sought after for his expert knowledge of matters in the healthcare regulatory remit. He routinely acts on behalf of the PSA, the GMC and the GDC, and is a familiar face in the High Court. **Strengths:** "Peter is well regarded for his strong grasp of complex legal issues, attention to detail and straightforward approach." "A go-to junior, he has excellent judgement and is a pleasure to work with." **Recent work:** Acted in Ariyanayagam v GMC, an appeal brought by a top consultant arguing against his erasure. The MPTS found that the consultant had dishonestly failed to comply with his contractual obligations over a period of several years.

Serjeants' Inn Chambers

See profile on p.907

THE SET

Outstanding set that continues to excel in the field of profession discipline, and has particular prominence in the healthcare sector. Market commentators consider Serjeants' Inn Chambers to be "strong and skilled throughout," housing an extensive selection of advocates who are experienced representatives of numerous professionals, from accountants, actuaries and architects, to solicitors, social workers and sportsmen. Interviewees explain that it is "reassuring to know that there is a set whose members have such a thorough understanding of professional regulation and such an ability to always get to the heart of a matter."

Client service: Senior clerk Lee Johnson oversees a strong clerking team. "They are extremely calm and resourceful."

SILKS

John Beggs QC (see p.594) Renowned advocate with a wealth of experience in disciplinary police proceedings. He specialises particularly in the prosecution of senior officers in high-profile cases. **Strengths:** "A leading counsel in his field, he offers excellent advocacy, careful preparation and phenomenal attention to detail." "He's very practical and extremely thorough, he never backs down and is a very persuasive and articulate advocate." **Recent work:** Prosecuted a chief constable facing numerous allegations of misconduct, prior to acting in the first ever Section 38 'removal of chief constable' process.

Robert Francis QC (see p.648) Esteemed silk who draws particular praise for his deft handling of complex judicial review proceedings. He primarily focuses his respected practice on the healthcare sector, regularly appearing on behalf of regulatory bodies. **Strengths:** "An experienced, clear advocate who knows the area inside out." "An absolutely first-rate advocate." **Recent work:** Acted in GMC v Squier, a highly publicised matter concerning a consultant neuropathologist accused of providing misleading pathological evidence in several cases concerning 'shaken baby syndrome'.

Adrian Hopkins QC (see p.674) Well-known healthcare specialist with vast experience in the professional discipline field. He is held in particularly high regard for his finely tuned advocacy before the GMC, where he regularly represents individual practitioners, and for his advisory role regarding reforms to regulatory frameworks and guidelines on ethical standards. **Strengths:** "He is excellent, his preparation is second to none, he's superb on his feet and he can get panels eating out of his hand. Just a class act." "He's one of the best all-round healthcare silks around."

George Hugh-Jones QC (see p.677) Regarded as a particularly strong advocate in healthcare regulatory matters. He routinely represents medical practitioners before the GMC and GDC, as well as in complex appeals in the Administrative Court. He regularly tackles matters concerning sexual indecency, including allegations of rape. **Strengths:** "I'm staggered by the short length of time it takes him to get up to speed with issues, regardless of their complexity. He's an incredibly impressive advocate." "His grasp of complex legal arguments and quick identification of salient issues is exemplary." **Recent work:** Secured the acquittal of a surgeon who had been accused of defective surgery, forgery and misogynistic behaviour.

Angus Moon QC (see p.720) Esteemed practitioner who is particularly highly regarded for his standout representation of healthcare professionals before the GMC and MPTS. He is regularly called upon to handle the most high-profile, precedent-setting cases in the sector. **Strengths:** "Very down-to-earth and extremely experienced. Essentially, he's one of the leading silks in the country for disciplinary and regulatory proceedings." "He's very on the ball and knows his stuff." **Recent work:** Acted for the defence in GMC v Monro, a case centring on allegations of lead poisoning.

Michael Mylonas QC (see p.725) Frequently represents doctors facing the most serious, career-threatening allegations. He routinely undertakes complex First-tier and Upper Tribunal disciplinary proceedings for primary care trusts. **Strengths:** "He takes a direct, proactive approach and is always aware of the key issues in a case. He's a highly effective advocate all round." "He is a first-class lawyer and an exceptional advocate with extensive experience of professional discipline work." **Recent work:** Acted for a successful senior dental surgeon who was accused of committing character assassination of a colleague in order to prevent them from obtaining a job.

Katharine Gollop QC (see p.656) Esteemed silk with a particularly strong reputation in the field of professional discipline. She regularly represents doctors, dentists, chiropractors and other healthcare professionals at interim and full hearings. **Strengths:** "She's incredibly tenacious and has the ability to pitch things in the perfect manner to get the right result." "She's quiet but effective; a formidable opponent." **Recent work:** Represented a medical practitioner accused of needlessly prescribing opiates to a large number of vulnerable patients. The panel found no misconduct and declined to impose a warning.

JUNIORS

Gerard Boyle (see p.601) Standout practitioner in the professional discipline sphere, he is recognised as a specialist in the fields of both medical and police law. He also frequently represents the BSB in disciplinary proceedings against barristers. **Strengths:** "He is particularly highly regarded for his ability to digest vast amounts of information at speed." "In terms of advocacy, he takes a reasoned and measured approach which is wholly appropriate and pragmatic." "He's razor-sharp, incredibly thorough and very efficient." **Recent work:** Appeared in Merseyside Police v Stubbs, prosecuting a PC accused of being a sexual predator towards female victims of crime.

Charles Foster (see p.647) A specialist in the field of healthcare regulation, he draws upon his broad experience to deftly represent the interests of medical professionals facing disciplinary proceedings. **Strengths:** "He is extremely bright, articulate and charming to clients and professional panels alike." "He's an entertaining and effective advocate."

Anthony Haycroft (see p.667) Highly respected senior junior with vast knowledge of disciplinary proceedings in the healthcare sector. He is an accomplished representative of doctors and dentists, regularly appearing on their behalf in complex regulatory and criminal cases. **Strengths:** "He is a shrewd and tactical barrister with a forensic, meticulous approach to cases. His retention of detail is phenomenal, while his background as a prosecutor in the most serious criminal cases means he can cross-examine with finesse and polish." "He always steers clients through tricky situations and choppy waters extremely well."

Andrew Hockton (see p.673) Acknowledged professional discipline specialist, he is habitually instructed in the most serious regulatory cases in the medical and dental fields. He often defends leading medical practitioners in complex disciplinary proceedings and significant criminal cases. **Strengths:** "A very senior and experienced junior barrister with extensive knowledge of the GMC and GDC. He has a calm, professional approach in the most difficult cases." "He has incredibly broad experience and delivers results." **Recent work:** Successfully acted on behalf of two doctors who were accused of assaulting a policeman in Spain.

Jonathan Holl-Allen (see p.674) Prominent and highly respected practitioner who regularly appears in GMC and GDC proceedings in the defence of professionals. He is also highly experienced in employment law matters. **Strengths:** "He is very sharp, bright and takes a forensic approach, which makes him extremely good in complex clinical cases." "One of the most meticulous barristers you could hope to instruct. His biggest strength is his eye for detail; he's incredibly thorough and never misses a thing." **Recent work:** Acted for a dentist who was facing allegations of dishonesty. This was a significant case as it considered the correct legal test for dishonesty in disciplinary proceedings.

Alan Jenkins (see p.683) Exceptionally experienced and knowledgeable advocate in the field of healthcare regulation. He continues to be instructed in high-profile, significant GMC and GDC cases. **Strengths:** "There are only a few barristers with his deep knowledge of UK healthcare regulation or his experience before the GMC and GDC. A highly experienced advocate, he has a light touch that works its magic with both witnesses and panels." "He can smooth over very tricky issues for clients. He presents cases seamlessly, nothing fazes him and he remains completely calm under pressure."

David Morris (see p.722) His expertise in disciplinary and regulatory cases in the healthcare sector is unquestionable. He focuses his practice on the representation of healthcare practitioners, regularly appearing before their disciplinary bodies and in the Administrative Court. **Strengths:** "David is a barrister whose experience of the GMC and GDC is almost unrivalled, and for whom complex cases are second nature." "He's very thorough and has an incredible eye for detail. He's excellent on complex, paper-heavy cases and is phenomenally experienced."

Richard Partridge (see p.734) An esteemed junior, he regularly appears in landmark GMC cases. He continues to be instructed on behalf of medical practitioners in the GMC, the GDC and other healthcare regulators. **Strengths:** "He has a very technical and perceptive mind and gets to grips with complex medical matters very quickly." "He was himself a doctor, which gives him an edge in understanding the medical side of things, while his tactical decision-making is always highly impressive."

Claire Watson (see p.790) Regularly acts on behalf of healthcare professionals before their regulatory bodies in disciplinary hearings. She is also an accomplished representative of the police in proceedings before misconduct panels and the Police Appeals Tribunal. **Strengths:** "Her ability to master the detail of a case is almost second to none. Her aptitude for understanding clinical issues is exceptional, her cross-examinations are well structured, her submissions well reasoned, persuasive and measured and she fiercely safeguards the interests of her clients." "When cross-examining expert witnesses, she has a real knack of asking the right questions." **Recent work:** Acted on behalf of a GP who was initially found guilty of misconduct, having engaged in an affair with one of his patients. Successfully had the GP's previously imposed suspension lifted.

Simon Cridland (see p.626) Both GMC and GDC proceedings are familiar territory to Cridland, who has a burgeoning reputation in the field of healthcare regulation. In addition to fitness to practise hearings, he has experience of challenging the decisions of regulators in the Administrative Court. **Strengths:** "He's very good; I nearly trust him to fill my teeth, such is his understanding of dentistry." "He is relaxed yet can be direct and robust when necessary; he's an extremely bright barrister who gets to crux of issues quickly." **Recent work:** Successfully represented a paediatrician facing allegations of clinical incompetence and dishonesty.

Malcolm Fortune (see p.647) An exceptionally experienced advocate who frequently appears before the Fitness to Practise Panels of the GDC and GMC. Market commentators underscore his exceptional experience and depth of knowledge when it comes to the regulation of medical professionals. **Strengths:** "He's very experienced in the field, he prepares well and is highly professional. He understands the process and knows exactly what it's all about." "A seasoned advocate who is particularly strong in contested hearings."

Mark Ley-Morgan (see p.701) Experienced advocate who regularly offers expert advice to police forces facing misconduct allegations. He has considerable experience of appearing before Police Appeal Tribunals and regularly presents cases on behalf of the chief constable. His aptitude in inquests is also highly praised, as is his skilled defence of various healthcare professionals. **Strengths:** "Robust and fearless advocate with a heavy punch that will only be delivered when the time is right." "His cross-examination is excellent, and he has a particular skill for getting fact from fiction."

Paul Spencer (see p.770) Respected advocate who is particularly noted for his adroit handling of complex inquests. His broad-based expertise covers areas such as social work, health and safety regulations and policing matters. **Strengths:** "He's very good and is a genuine expert in this area." "He is very well prepared and knowledgeable in inquests due to his vast experience."

Band 2

Fountain Court Chambers

See profile on p.847

THE SET

Fountain Court Chambers is an established set housing a distinguished team of barristers. The set is noted for its adept representation of various regulated professionals, notably auditors and accountants, but also architects, solicitors, barristers, sportsmen and healthcare professionals. As "a tour de force of brain power and commerciality," the chambers also remains a popular choice for a range of regulatory bodies. Market sources underscore its members' "reassuringly deep understanding of professional discipline in all its guises."

Client service: Senior clerk Alex Taylor leads "a professional, slick operation that is very responsive to the needs of its clients." "Both counsel and clerks have been enormously accommodating when we've needed to get advice at short notice."

SILKS

Timothy Dutton CBE QC (see p.638) Pre-eminent advocate who is exceptional in the field of professional discipline. He has the absolute respect of the market, who deem his advocacy and advice to be of the highest quality. His considerable experience in relation to financial services, medical and legal regulation makes him highly sought after for high-profile, high-value matters. **Strengths:** "The doyen of the Regulatory Bar, he is wonderfully calm and has great poise in court. He can sell the most implausible case to the hardest-hearted individuals." "Everyone else is a distant second in terms of effectiveness and competence." "He can pluck an incredible argument out of nowhere." "An exceptional advocate who has tremendous authority in the courtroom. He is able to cut through complex issues in a pragmatic and insightful manner." **Recent work:** Instructed in FRC v Deloitte and Einollahi, a case regarding the collapse of MG Rover. The FRC alleged that Deloitte and Einollahi acted without regard to their duties of objectivity and without managing conflicts.

Patricia Robertson QC (see p.753) Respected silk with vast experience of handling complex professional discipline matters in the medical, legal, financial and accountancy sectors. She regularly appears in proceedings heard before the FRC and in the SDT. **Strengths:** "She is meticulous, incredibly bright and really gets into the detail of cases." "She has masses of intellect, application and energy." "Incredibly bright and intellectually rigorous, she's good at getting to the point and providing effective analysis."

Richard Coleman QC (see p.620) An experienced and effective silk who is particularly au fait with legal and financial disciplinary proceedings. He frequently represents the FSA and SRA in high-profile matters. **Strengths:** "Richard is an extremely able barrister who provides a thorough overview of complex legal and disciplinary issues in a concise and pragmatic manner. His judgement and contribution to cases are highly valued." "He has a very thorough approach to cases and an excellent eye for detail." **Recent work:** Acted on behalf of the regulator in SRA v Vaux, a successful application to the Divisional Court to strike out Mr Vaux's appeal against being struck off the register.

Michael McLaren QC (see p.713) Highly skilled and commercially minded advocate whose deep knowledge of administrative law complements his distinguished professional discipline practice. He is frequently instructed by professional individuals, law firms and the SRA in significant cases. **Strengths:** "A first-rate advocate, he is a commercial lawyer with deep knowledge of solicitors' discipline." "He always provides extremely clear and helpful advice." **Recent work:** Instructed by the SRA in a matter involving a solicitor who was challenging the SRA's intervention into their practice.

JUNIORS

Chloe Carpenter (see p.611) Junior with a strong reputation in the field of professional discipline, particularly as it relates to solicitors and barristers. She habitually acts for the SRA and is especially adept at advisory work on behalf of both regulators and the regulated. **Strengths:** "She is well placed to handle challenging matters. Her detailed analysis and balanced, well-written opinions are of great assistance to clients." "She demonstrates strong analytical skills, high levels of intellect and commercial acumen." **Recent work:** Instructed by the SRA in a disciplinary case against a solicitor who was alleged to have dishonestly removed money from a client's account.

Rupert Allen (see p.582) Respected advocate who is frequently instructed by the SRA in relation to contested interventions and complex judicial reviews. **Strengths:** "A junior with considerable experience before the SDT. He prepares extremely thoroughly for hearings and has a talent for spotting clever arguments to advance on behalf of his clients." "Rupert is impressive; he's extremely bright and able. He has a good analytical mind and an eye for detail. He is also a persuasive advocate who is well liked by clients." **Recent work:** Acted for the Law Society in relation to a claim brought by a firm of solicitors alleging that the Law Society was negligent in registering a bogus law firm created by a fraudster.

James McClelland (see p.711) Enjoys a strong reputation for his regulatory practice, which focuses on legal services regulation. He is typically involved in significant judicial review proceedings that define the powers and duties of disciplinary bodies in the legal sector. **Strengths:** "He brings clarity to complex cases and deals with them brilliantly. As an advocate, he is always available and friendly." "He is very bright, charming and a straight-talking individual." **Recent work:** Acted for the regulator in SRA v Lawson, an appeal concerning the two-year suspension of a solicitor.

Nicholas Medcroft (see p.715) A specialist in professional discipline cases in the financial services sector, he regularly prosecutes bankers, accountants and corporate finance advisers. He has acted for the FRC in matters involving highly complex regulatory and compliance issues. **Strengths:** "He's completely industrious, very sensible, very sound, very hard-working and a persuasive advocate." "He's a tenacious master of detail."

Edward Levey (see p.700) Respected junior who continues to develop his expertise in disciplinary matters involving solicitors. He frequently tackles significant cases on behalf of the SRA, both before the Solicitors Disciplinary Tribunal and in the Administrative Court. **Strengths:** "He's building a real name for himself in complex cases where his tenacious and assertive advocacy is a real asset." "His relaxed style puts clients and witnesses at ease and he's very bright and responsive." **Recent work:** Acted in a three-day disciplinary hearing in the SDT involving a solicitor who had dishonestly taken money from an elderly and vulnerable client.

Tetyana Nesterchuk (see p.726) Accomplished representative of legal regulators, she is regularly called upon by both the BSB and the SRA. She also advises individual practitioners and law firms, often in complex and unusual cases. **Strengths:** "She has the most incredible work ethic and a phenomenal ability to absorb detail and assimilate facts." "She is an invaluable presence on any case; she is hard-working, diligent, completely on top of documentation and has an excellent grasp of the crucial details of the case." **Recent work:** Acted in a test case determining the scope of the SRA's territorial jurisdiction to bring disciplinary proceedings against non-SRA-regulated lawyers practising in SRA-regulated firms.

2 Hare Court

See profile on p.861

THE SET

2 Hare Court is an esteemed set which is particularly well known for its adroit handling of disciplinary matters in the healthcare sector, though many of its accomplished barristers offer industry expertise in the legal, sports, policing and financial sectors. The set houses a formidable team of practitioners who are recognised for their "well-polished, professional" representation of professional individuals before a range of regulators, including the GMC, GDC, NMC and GPhC. As it is a particularly strong criminal law set, members of 2 Hare Court excel in cases in which there is an overlap between crime and professional discipline, such as gross negligence manslaughter. Market commentators highlight the "forensic knowledge and high standard of advocacy" provided by the chambers.

Client service: "They're outstanding. They bend over backwards to help us and have an incisive understanding of specialist areas of law." Tara Johnson leads the team, and is characterised as "one of the best clerks to work with; you can't fault her."

JUNIORS

Stephen Brassington (see p.602) Outstanding advocate with a varied practice, who focuses particularly on the defence of medical professionals. He offers further industry expertise in the sports and education sectors, regularly prosecuting on behalf of the NCTL and The FA. **Strengths:** "A spellbinding advocate who achieves astounding results for his clients. Add relentless hard work, fierce intellect and natural charisma all together, and you get Stephen Brassington." "The best cross-examiner I have ever come across, due to his ability to pick people apart. He beats experts in their own area of expertise, pouncing on any comment in a way that changes the game." "A charismatic, dynamic advocate who is also an extremely skilled, strong strategist." **Recent work:** Defended an internationally renowned dentist who was accused of incompetently placing implants without the informed consent of patients.

Andrew Colman (see p.621) Recognised for his adept defence of doctors, dentists and other healthcare professionals in major, complex fitness to practise cases. His varied practice regularly sees him prosecuting on behalf of the NCTL, while he also demonstrates deep knowledge of legal sector regulation. **Strengths:** "A go-to for really detailed, document-heavy cases; when you need someone to absorb huge quantities of information quickly, he manages it with ease." "He's cerebral, bright on the law and academically astute." "A master of detail. His submissions are works of genius." **Recent work:** Served as lead counsel in the presentation of the regulatory cases against the teachers implicated in the 'Trojan Horse' scandal.

Craig Ferguson (see p.644) Renowned for his skilled representation of professional individuals, he remains a highly popular choice for doctors, but also dentists, pharmacists and solicitors. His criminal experience regularly sees him appearing for medical professionals in associated criminal proceedings. **Strengths:** "He puts forward the most persuasive, compelling submissions and has an almost incomparable ability to think on his feet." "He's at the top of his game; he's hugely empathetic, creative in his legal arguments and flexible in terms of his approach to cases." **Recent work:** Defended a GP facing multiple allegations of sexually motivated touching of female patients.

Andrew Hurst (see p.679) Respected junior with an excellent reputation in the field. He focuses his practice on the representation of medical professionals, regularly handling complex clinical and sexual disciplinary matters at the GMC and GDC. **Strengths:** "His advocacy is simply exceptional, not just in terms of tone and style, but the way he frames an argument is extraordinary. He can think outside the box to find unique arguments others might miss."

"Always fully on top of the facts, he has a measured style that invariably finds favour with panels." **Recent work:** Represented a doctor facing two allegations of sexual touching during patient consultations.

Marios Lambis Possesses particular expertise in the field of healthcare regulation. He remains a popular choice for the defence of medical practitioners, regularly appearing in GMC and GDC fitness to practise hearings, alongside associated criminal cases. **Strengths:** "Utterly charming, he could talk the birds out of the trees. He's an incredible asset in front of tribunals." "An excellent advocate who is brilliant with clinical cases." **Recent work:** Acted in a case involving a GP who allegedly bullied and pressured a vulnerable older patient to drop a complaint.

Kate Bex Well known for her adept handling of complex cases, including High Court proceedings and significant inquests. She regularly acts both for and against the main healthcare regulators, including the GMC, NMC, GDC and GPhC. **Strengths:** "She's very efficient, flexible and certainly very experienced." "She's always well prepared and on top of her papers."

Sarah Przybylska (see p.744) Acts for an extensive range of healthcare professionals before their regulators. She is noted for her appellate work, and is regularly called upon to supervise and co-ordinate complex investigations on behalf of regulators. **Strengths:** "A senior junior with authoritative knowledge of regulatory law; she gets fantastic results."

Christopher Geering (see p.651) Has developed a stellar reputation in the disciplinary sphere, focusing on the healthcare, social care and education sectors. He routinely appears before the GMC, GDC, ACCA and NCTL, acting on behalf of both regulators and the regulated. He habitually deals with multi-handed, factually complex and high-profile cases. **Strengths:** "He impresses with his ability to digest, retain and manage a large volume of documentation." "A really systematic thinker who gets to the heart of a matter quickly and presents persuasively." **Recent work:** Represented a doctor accused of performing an unnecessary vaginal examination of a patient.

Ben Rich (see p.751) Both defends and prosecutes at the NMC, GDC, NCTL and ACCA. He is recognised for his deft handling of complex judicial review proceedings and quality appellate work. **Strengths:** "Ben is a very calm, wise lawyer who has a proven track record of allaying the fears of clients, enabling them to engage in proceedings effectively." "Thorough, knowledgeable and great at keeping his clients informed." **Recent work:** Represented a nurse accused of multiple clinical errors, including allowing a patient to receive toxic levels of opiates. Successfully secured a dismissal of the charges.

Outer Temple Chambers

See profile on p.887

THE SET

Respected set housing a formidable team of barristers offering extensive knowledge and expertise in the field of professional discipline. Particular strength can be found in the healthcare sector, while its esteemed advocates also offer specialist advice and representation in the legal, transport and finance sectors. Sources consider them to be "experts in what they do," which is typically to advocate on behalf of professional individuals before various regulatory bodies. The set's annexe in the St James's Building in Manchester makes it a highly popular choice for complex GMC work.

Client service: Market sources consider the clerking at the set to be "very efficient and very helpful." Paul Barton is the senior clerk at the set.

JUNIORS

Fiona Horlick Respected junior who regularly prosecutes and defends professional individuals. Her extensive criminal experience complements her burgeoning practice. **Strengths:** "Her advocacy skills are second to none; most would hate to be subjected to a cross-examination by her because she's just so good. She grasps technical issues extremely quickly and is an extremely effective advocate." "She has a phenomenal understanding of her cases and is always able to pick up on the key issues, regardless of the volume of information." **Recent work:** Acted in PSA v (1) GMC (2) Uppal, an important High Court decision on the interaction between a finding of dishonesty and the question of impairment in fitness to practise hearings.

James Leonard Noted for his broad professional discipline practice which encompasses fitness to practise hearings, Crown Court trials and complex judicial review proceedings. He focuses his practice on the healthcare sector and regularly appears before the GMC, GDC and GPhC. **Strengths:** "His easy-going nature puts clients at ease and he has a wonderfully analytical mind. He's able to get on the right side of tribunals and carry them with him. A wonderfully persuasive advocate." "He is always clear, concise and totally on the ball."

James Counsell Accomplished advocate with an extensive history of appearing in significant High Court appeals. He has an excellent knowledge of professional discipline in relation to dentists, accountants, solicitors, barristers and actuaries. **Strengths:** "He's very detail-focused, he picks up on absolutely everything and he's very good at digesting large quantities of information in a very short period of time." "James is one of the elder statesmen of the junior Bar whose unflappable exterior makes him a really polished performer before the panels. He is well received whenever he appears." **Recent work:** Acted in GMC v Pool, a case concerning a consultant psychiatrist who faced misconduct allegations after appearing as an expert witness in a case when he allegedly did not have sufficient expertise to do so.

Matthew McDonagh Esteemed professional discipline junior offering deep expertise in the healthcare and legal sectors. He routinely acts on behalf of both professional individuals and their regulators. **Strengths:** "He is an able and persuasive advocate, very bright and good on his feet. In his defence work, he develops a good relationship with clients and works committedly on their behalf. Clients relate well to him and respect his supportive but sensible advice." "A persuasive advocate who is popular with clients. He has very pragmatic, sound judgement." **Recent work:** Assisted with the coroner's inquest into the death of a young child who had been prescribed the wrong inhaler by a GP.

Michael Uberoi Highly thought-of junior who excels at representing medical professionals before their regulators, including the GMC and GDC. He also represents professionals before the FCA Enforcement Division, and is often called upon by sportsmen and sportswomen in disciplinary proceedings. **Strengths:** "Analytical, calmly persuasive and thorough; when you send him papers, you know he'll have read, analysed and carefully prepared every aspect of the case." "Michael is a very impressive junior barrister who is knowledgeable and accomplished beyond his years. He is sensible, realistic and pragmatic in his advice, whilst his care in presenting a case is notable."

QEB Hollis Whiteman

See profile on p.900

THE SET

QEB Hollis Whiteman is a well-respected set housing an accomplished team of practitioners. Its skilled members regularly attract instructions in high-value, complex matters in the field of professional discipline, offering assistance to both claimants and defendants. The chambers is a particularly popular choice for a range of regulatory bodies, such as the BSB, SRA, British Horseracing Authority, Metropolitan Police Service and numerous healthcare regulators, for whom they frequently prosecute significant cases. Market sources value the set's versatility, praising its ability to offer "first-class advice and advocacy across a variety of areas."

Client service: Chris Emmings leads the team and "knows the market extremely well," according to market sources. "Their clerks are the best. They really understand their client base, always make an effort and are very accessible. Dealing with any of them is extremely easy."

SILKS

Tom Kark QC (see p.688) Respected silk with extensive experience in the professional regulatory field; he focuses particularly on complex healthcare issues. He is typically instructed by the GMC and is well known for his adept handling of significant inquests. **Strengths:** "Tom is often the first choice for high-profile cases. He is an authoritative and commanding advocate who is easy to work with." "He's someone who's at the very top of this area of work. He's very good in long-running, complex regulatory cases and is always a pleasure to work with." **Recent work:** Acted in GMC v Squier, a highly publicised matter concerning a consultant neuropathologist accused of providing misleading pathological evidence in several cases concerning 'shaken baby syndrome'.

Zoe Johnson QC (see p.684) Combines deep knowledge of both the criminal and regulatory fields to offer a real depth of expertise in professional discipline matters, especially those concerning psychiatric and medical causation issues. She is frequently involved in cases relating to 'shaken baby syndrome' as well as gross negligence manslaughter. **Strengths:** "She is an effective communicator and an accomplished practitioner who leads by example and not just direction. She is one of the finest jury advocates out there." **Recent work:** Instructed in a case involving a senior registrar, against whom allegations of gross negligence manslaughter were brought.

Sean Larkin QC (see p.695) Highly respected practitioner who has a real depth of experience acting on behalf of both defendants and prosecutors. His broad expertise includes sexual offences, clinical failings and serious dishonesty. **Strengths:** "Sean is an impressive barrister and an excellent advocate. He always provides high-quality, level-headed advice and a clear strategy." **Recent work:** Prosecuted a case against a doctor accused of performing female genital mutilation.

JUNIORS

Lydia Barnfather (see p.590) A go-to practitioner for many major healthcare regulatory bodies, including the GMC, GOC and GDC. She regularly appears before tribunals as well as on appeal, and specialises particularly in conduct, health and performance-related issues. Market sources highlight her ability to distil complex cases and relay them comprehensively to her client. **Strengths:** "Clients absolutely love her; she's very clever and has wonderful judgement. You feel very lucky if she's in your corner." "A brilliant trial advocate who manages her cases with minimum fuss. She'll sort the wood from the trees, even on the most technical of cases, and presents superbly." "She's equally at ease with complex clinical issues and probity cases." **Recent work:** Instructed to prosecute a Harley Street dentist in relation to allegations of gross clinical errors. Appeared successfully in front of the GDC and on appeal.

Selva Ramasamy (see p.747) Habitually handles matters on behalf of professional individuals and regulated companies, offering extensive expertise in serious fraud matters. His further areas of expertise encompass both the health and policing sectors. **Strengths:** "He's very good, extremely experienced and very calm under pressure. He's very adept at cross-examination and it takes a lot to ruffle him. He's one of the most polished advocates out there: suave without being pretentious." **Recent work:** Appeared on behalf of an osteopath who specialises in treating dancers. Successfully defended him against allegations of sexual assault.

Rebecca Harris (see p.665) Established practitioner who has experience of acting both for the defence and for the prosecution before a range of tribunals. She is routinely instructed by an array of healthcare regulators, while sources highlight her ability to handle delicate situations with tact and charm. **Strengths:** "She is extremely able and gives highly effective, practical solutions to complex legal issues. She is also charming and good-humoured as well as a very clever and pragmatic advocate." "She is excellent. She really combines scrupulous manners with complete competence, and she has the ability to make any committee realise that." **Recent work:** Acted in GDC v DT, a case concerning a dentist accused of numerous clinical deficiencies and of making dishonest claims for NHS remuneration.

Band 3

2 Bedford Row

See profile on p.807

THE SET

2 Bedford Row is an esteemed set which handles a broad range of professional discipline work, notably on behalf of regulators, though it is also well equipped to assist regulated professionals. The chambers offers notable strength in the healthcare sector, counting the GDC, GMC, NMC and Health Professions Council among its diverse client base. The set also has a respected profile in sporting discipline matters, as well as financial services and solicitors' regulation. Market sources highlight that 2 Bedford Row's practitioners "give 100% of their effort and time to understand the challenges facing their clients."

Client service: "The clerks are great, they all have a wonderful attitude. It's a very smooth operation: efficient, friendly and it works well." According to sources, what lead clerk John Grimmer "doesn't know about clerking isn't worth knowing."

SILKS

Ian Stern QC Exceptional advocate offering expertise across numerous fields of regulation. He is particularly noted for his adroit representation of police officers and healthcare professionals, while his thorough cross-examination and smooth advocacy style are also highlighted. **Strengths:** "He is an excellent lawyer and an excellent advocate who is absolutely at the top of his game." "It's hard to see any weaknesses: he's good with clients, hard-working, thorough, and very good at getting answers out of people without them knowing they're being asked a question." **Recent work:** Successfully secured the acquittal of the police marksman who faced the charge of murdering Azelle Rodney, a suspected armed robber.

Mark Milliken-Smith QC (see p.717) Esteemed silk specialising in the areas of healthcare and sporting regulation. He routinely appears before the GMC, GDC, GOC and ACCA, and is known for his adept representation of high-profile sportsmen and sportswomen. **Strengths:** "He works extremely hard, he has good judgement and an excellent advocacy style." "He's excellent, he exudes friendliness and confidence. As a client you would know you are in safe hands. He's a red-hot lawyer." **Recent work:** Acted in RBS 6 Nations v Pascal Pape, an appeal concerning a citing complaint regarding an admitted act of foul play in an RBS 6 Nations Rugby Championship 2015 match.

JUNIORS

Sandesh Singh Accomplished advocate who is particularly well known for his adroit representation of a range of medical professionals. He is a regular fixture in the GDC and GOC. **Strengths:** "He's an extremely impressive individual. Thorough is an understatement. He is bright, super-knowledgeable, measured, reasonable and easy to deal with. He's a detail-oriented man with strong advocacy skills."

Jamas Hodivala An advocate who has impressed commentators with his adept representation of professionals in the healthcare, legal and sporting sectors. He frequently handles complex cases before various regulators, including the GDC, GOC and SRA. **Strengths:** "He is really charming, very precise and very smooth. He's always impressive and measured." "He's very, very good, clients feel they are in safe hands with him." **Recent work:** Acted in GDC v Slee, a case concerning a dentist whose clinical standards and practice facilities were allegedly unsatisfactory.

23 Essex Street

See profile on p.839

THE SET

An established set offering "a really excellent, wide range of skills" in the professional discipline sphere. Its respected barristers have extensive experience of representing regulators across a broad spectrum of industries, including the healthcare, financial services and policing sectors. While traditionally recognised for its sterling work on behalf of the prosecution, 23 Essex Street continues to develop and grow its defence practice, regularly acting on behalf of professional individuals before the SRA, ACCA, GDC and RCN.

Client service: "The clerking is grand. They are very approachable, you get a quick response and they fully understand the regulatory constraints at play. The fees are flexible and competitive." Richard Fowler leads the clerking team.

SILKS

Paul Ozin QC Continues to impress individuals in the field of professional discipline, where he is best known for his stellar work in the field of financial regulation. He regularly handles complex cases on behalf of the ACCA and enjoys a formidable reputation for his prosecution of healthcare professionals. **Strengths:** "He's technically very astute, he has a forensic brain and very quickly grasps complex clinical issues. He can glide through really complex reports and distil them down expertly." "He's intelligent, articulate and well liked by clients." **Recent work:** Instructed in a clinical case brought against a dentist accused of misleading patients. In one scenario, the dentist is alleged to have told the patient that a synthetic bone implant was being used in place of a cow artefact.

JUNIORS

Sarah Campbell Focuses her respected professional discipline practice on the area of healthcare regulation. She is routinely called upon to prosecute healthcare professionals, such as doctors and dentists, and offers particular expertise in matters concerning sexual assault and young children. **Strengths:** "Sarah is an experienced junior and a pleasure to work with. She is personable, hard-working and very measured in her approach." "A very fine advocate with a good style when appearing before tribunals."

Rupert Pardoe A knowledgeable and experienced advocate, he frequently serves as legal adviser in police disciplinary misconduct hearings. He is also regularly called upon to represent professional individuals at inquests, notably doctors and police officers. **Strengths:** "A real street fighter, he is a very powerful, very senior and very effective advocate." "Rupert is very knowledgeable about police discipline; he is an outstanding advocate who has a charming and engaging style." **Recent work:** Represented a police officer accused of failures in timekeeping, and then with lack of truthfulness in covering it up.

Hailsham Chambers

See profile on p.857

THE SET

Hailsham Chambers is a highly regarded set with broad expertise spanning numerous areas subject to regulation, including the healthcare, financial and legal sectors. Its diverse client base includes both regulatory bodies and numerous regulated individuals, such as dentists, nurses, surveyors, solicitors and opticians, among others. Its esteemed members are regularly called upon to appear in significant public inquiries, inquests and tribunals, and are particularly familiar faces in the NMC.

Client service: Stephen Smith leads the "highly effective, reasonable and flexible" clerking team.

SILKS

David Pittaway QC (see p.738) Prominent figure in the field of professional discipline, whose esteemed practice focuses particularly on the legal and healthcare professions. Given his stellar reputation, he is frequently called upon by regulators to advise on potential changes to their regulatory procedures. **Strengths:** "David is forensic and comprehensive in his preparation and masterful in his advocacy. He is especially devastating in cross-examination." **Recent work:** Assisted with the Browne Review of the Bar's disciplinary tribunal service, which was set up to ensure a proper degree of independence from the BSB.

Alexander Hutton QC (see p.679) Highly respected silk offering deep expertise in the field of healthcare regulation. He is regularly called upon to assist with significant, high-profile disciplinary proceedings on behalf of doctors, dentists and other clinical practitioners. **Strengths:** "He is a wonderful cross-specialist who is very charming and very able."

JUNIORS

Fiona Neale (see p.726) Prominent practitioner who is highly respected for her healthcare regulatory work. She typically handles complex cases on behalf of dentists and doctors, while her professional discipline practice is buttressed by complementary expertise in the field of clinical negligence. **Strengths:** "She's brilliant. She has a lovely manner with clients, particularly the difficult ones, and demonstrates fantastic knowledge of the area." "She has more common sense than anyone I've ever met at the Bar and gets amazing results, particularly for doctors and dentists. She's a stellar senior junior." **Recent work:** Instructed in a GDC case concerning the delayed diagnosis of ovarian cancer in 35 patients.

Nicholas Peacock (see p.735) Established practitioner who is particularly well regarded for his adept representation of medical professionals. He routinely handles complex fitness to practise hearings on behalf of dentists before the GDC. **Strengths:** "He really knows the law inside out, he has an encyclopaedic knowledge and he's very hard-working. His robust advocacy style is also something panels really appreciate, and he goes above and beyond in his preparation." **Recent work:** Defended a dentist against allegations of clinical misconduct in a matter concerning the treatment of prisoners.

4 New Square

See profile on p.880

THE SET

4 New Square is well respected for its provision of professional discipline expertise across many sectors, excelling particularly in matters concerning the actuarial, accountancy, financial and legal professions. Its highly skilled members routinely appear before a variety of regulatory bodies, such as the FRC, BSB and SDT, acting on behalf of both prosecutors and defendants. The set is particularly noted for its deep knowledge of regulatory matters related to horse-racing.

Client service: "The clerks provide an outstanding service." Lizzy Stewart leads the clerking team.

SILKS

Ben Hubble QC (see p.677) Incredibly highly regarded silk who is known for his deft handling of disciplinary matters, particularly those concerning the accountancy and legal professions. He routinely attracts instructions in high-profile cases and regularly assists global law firms in complex regulatory proceedings. **Strengths:** "Absolutely at the top of his game and excellent to work with." "He is a very good advocate who demonstrates wonderful judgement." **Recent work:** Represented the former partner of an accountancy firm who was accused of incompetence in auditing and of misleading the public in relation to an IPO.

Graeme McPherson QC (see p.714) Renowned for his deft handling of disciplinary proceedings in the sporting sector, he is a recognised specialist in the niche remit of horse-racing regulation. He is also an accomplished advocate in relation to the veterinary and legal professions. **Strengths:** "He's a fantastic barrister who can be ruthless in the defence of cases where necessary." "He's a very good advocate who comes from a horse-training background. He's a very good lawyer who is always very well prepared." **Recent work:** Successfully appeared on behalf of Qatar Racing to appeal a decision made by racecourse stewards to disqualify the horse Simple Verse from a race.

Patrick Lawrence QC (see p.697) Esteemed silk who regularly undertakes disciplinary actions against auditors. He is recognised for his adroit handling of complex judicial review proceedings, and offers further expertise in matters concerning the financial and legal sectors. **Strengths:** "He's a really polished advocate who is always on top of the facts. He's a class act and a nice chap." **Recent work:** Instructed by the FRC Conduct Committee in disciplinary proceedings brought against a chartered accountant as well as Ernst & Young.

Simon Monty QC (see p.720) A barrister of long standing with vast experience in the field of professional discipline. He regularly appears on behalf of regulated individuals in the accountancy and legal sectors. **Strengths:** "He is excellent with clients and very strong on strategy." "He's a really nice man but an incredibly tough opponent. He goes the extra mile for his clients and is incredibly thorough." "He's very user-friendly, responsive and always sticks to deadlines." **Recent work:** Instructed in SRA v Dennison, a seven-week SDT hearing arising out of the collapse of The Accident Group.

JUNIORS

Paul Parker (see p.733) Respected junior with a notably broad disciplinary practice, he is regularly called upon to assist with challenges concerning the misapplication of conduct rules by various regulatory bodies. He draws particular praise for his regulatory work concerning the accountancy and legal professions. **Strengths:** "He's a wonderful advocate: tenacious, brave and prepared to roll his sleeves up. You feel very confident in his services." "He's forthright and forceful in submissions whilst being respectful, and clients love him." **Recent work:** Appeared before the Actuaries Disciplinary Tribunal Panel to defend a client in relation to pension equalisation actuarial work.

3 Raymond Buildings Barristers

See profile on p.904

THE SET

A very highly respected chambers, 3 Raymond Buildings Barristers is well known for its capability in professional discipline, an area of expertise which is only buttressed by its additional strength in the remits of crime and public law. The set is particularly recognised for its deep knowledge of police misconduct, with members regularly acting on behalf of both officers and police authorities. Its hugely skilled practitioners are also routinely called upon by regulators in the sporting industry, such as The FA and the International Cricket Council.

Client service: Eddie Holland leads the "spot-on" clerking team. "The clerks are good and communicate well, and you know you're getting superb quality for the price."

SILKS

Patrick Gibbs QC (see p.652) Esteemed practitioner with a thriving practice focusing on the defence of barristers, solicitors and police officers. He offers particular expertise in disciplinary matters containing criminal elements, and excels at significant inquests and in complex inquiries. **Strengths:** "He's spectacularly good." "He's amazing, he's a respected silk with perhaps the nicest touch in advocacy of anyone at the Bar. He's an immaculate advocate, just terrific." **Recent work:** Handled a case regarding a barrister and part-time judge who faced allegations of perverting the course of justice and document forgery in relation to the prosecution of Chris Huhne MP.

Hugh Davies QC A specialist representative of police officers in major misconduct hearings and inquests, alongside related judicial review proceedings. He is an adroit representative of police forces and individuals in matters concerning police-related fatalities, and offers particularly deep knowledge of the functioning of the IPCC and Police Reform Act 2002. **Strengths:** "He is one of the best in the business in the field of police discipline and is often involved in the most serious and complex cases. If it's a high-profile, demanding case, he's a go-to because there are so many strings to his bow." **Recent work:** Acted in PC Birks v MPS, a judicial review brought by an officer who was due to become a church minister, but was prevented from resigning in order for the IPCC to complete its investigation into a death in custody.

JUNIORS

Kevin Baumber Highly experienced in matters relating to the regulation of police officers. He routinely appears on behalf of officers in disciplinary hearings, Police Appeals Tribunals and significant judicial reviews, offering particular experience in cases involving general crime and fraud. **Strengths:** "He's very thorough and very good strategically. His written work is excellent and he has a real ability to out-think the opposition." "He's always meticulously prepared for a case. He's very self-assured and has a likeable advocacy style, so juries invariably warm to him." **Recent work:** Represented a police officer in an IPCC-directed gross misconduct hearing, successfully achieving stay of proceedings on behalf of his client.

Matthew Butt (see p.608) Particularly highly regarded for his adept representation of police officers in serious misconduct hearings. He is vastly experienced in matters relating to the deployment of armed officers, and regularly appears on officers' behalf in complex regulatory proceedings and high-profile, significant inquests. **Strengths:** "He's certainly on his way to becoming a top practitioner. He has a commanding presence in court, and when he makes submissions, you know the tribunal is fully listening." **Recent work:** Acted on behalf of a PC in an appeal against dismissal from the force.

Clair Dobbin (see p.634) Respected junior who is regularly called upon to act on behalf of police officers in complex disciplinary proceedings. She is particularly noted for her skilled handling of major inquests and is an expert in cases concerning deaths in custody. **Strengths:** "She's excellent, a totally conscientious and dedicated practitioner." "She's just class, an absolutely first-rate advocate." **Recent work:** Represented the MPS in an Article 2 inquest investigating the death of an individual suffering from 'acute behavioural disorder' who had been restrained by the police.

William Emlyn Jones Criminal law specialist with a strong track record in disciplinary cases concerning police misconduct. He is particularly well known for his adroit representation of officers in matters concerning deaths in custody and police pursuits. **Strengths:** "He's excellent and he has a very nice courtroom manner. He's way beyond his call in terms of demeanour and presentation." "He's intellectually rigorous and a very serious practitioner." **Recent work:** Acted for a PC facing allegations of use of excessive force during the stop and arrest of a suspected burglar.

Richard Atchley Knowledgeable advocate who is renowned for his adept representation of police officers. His broad areas of expertise encompass serious criminal offences, major inquests and inquiries. **Strengths:** "He is superb and particularly wonderful when it comes to complex cases. He can be positive even in difficult circumstances, and he's fearless in court." "He has this lovely, laid-back presentation style. His clients love him to bits and he's completely unflappable." **Recent work:** Led a successful appeal against the dismissal of a police constable.

Ben Brandon A skilled representative of police officers facing serious criminal and professional discipline proceedings. Much of his work is highly publicised, and often relates to international legal issues. **Strengths:** "He's very clever, astute and always precise in his approach. He's good at technical arguments, particularly on the issue of police surveillance." "He's technically a very capable advocate." **Recent work:** Instructed in a misconduct hearing relating to the death of a mentally ill prisoner who died shortly after being restrained by several police officers.

Guy Ladenburg (see p.693) Known for his expert representation of police officers in unsatisfactory performance matters, criminal cases and gross misconduct proceedings. He routinely acts for the police in coroners' inquests into deaths in custody and other suspicious deaths. **Strengths:** "A very popular, robust all-rounder in police discipline cases." "He has a very nice touch, a wonderful turn of phrase and he demonstrates excellent judgement in court." **Recent work:** Successfully secured the acquittal of an officer who was accused of breach of duty. The case concerned the death of an individual who had been detained under the Mental Health Act.

Neil Saunders (see p.759) As a specialist criminal advocate and experienced disciplinary barrister, Saunders is well placed to advise police officers facing an array of charges. He is noted for his depth of knowledge in the areas of sports and financial crime. **Strengths:** "Just a superb operator." "He's an absolutely standout barrister. He has a very good courtroom manner and is a very reassuring advocate, whichever side he's on. He projects confidence, not just in himself but in his case."

Alisdair Williamson (see p.797) Regularly defends police officers before criminal courts and regulatory panels. His strategic, measured management of cases is particularly underscored by market sources. **Strengths:** "He's very good at getting his head around a case quickly, and from there he makes the right strategic calls. A highly experienced, unflappable advocate, he's always calm and able to think on his feet." **Recent work:** Successfully defended an Asian police officer in relation to comments he posted on the Commissioners Forum which highlighted perceived racism within the Met.

Band 4

5 Essex Court

See profile on p.834

THE SET

One of the premier sets for police professional misconduct issues, the team is well versed in handling work on behalf of chief constables, the IPCC and police authorities. 5 Essex Court's highly regarded practitioners are capable of dealing with the full range of police disciplinary work alongside regulatory matters affecting the healthcare sector.

Client service: Mark Waller leads the clerking team.

SILKS

Fiona Barton QC (see p.591) Renowned silk who possesses a wealth of experience in matters relating to police discipline. She is regularly called upon to handle significant, highly publicised inquests. **Strengths:** "She is often instructed in sensitive cases and specialises in police work. She brings an invaluable decisiveness to any case."

Jason Beer QC (see p.593) Respected silk who is notably adept in disciplinary and regulatory matters concerning administrative, public and police law. He is best known for his adroit representation of police officers in complex misconduct proceedings. **Strengths:** "He's very, very bright and has a nice manner with the court. He's an impressive advocate and his written work is very good. He's the real deal."

JUNIORS

Matthew Holdcroft (see p.674) Dynamic junior who is well known for his representation of police officers in fitness to practise hearings and inquests. He offers deep expertise in matters concerning unlawful arrest, assault, malicious prosecution, misfeasance and allegations of discrimination. **Strengths:** "He is outstanding in police misconduct matters." "A very clever and highly astute tactician, he's a very affable man and an extremely effective advocate." **Recent work:** Represented a chief constable who sought to quash an IPCC report which criticised his conduct.

Francesca Whitelaw (see p.794) A dedicated representative of police forces across the country who handles all aspects of civil law relating to the police. She frequently appears in significant misconduct hearings before the Police Appeals Tribunal and is recognised for her deft handling of complex judicial review proceedings. **Strengths:** "She is hard-working and always well prepared. Her written submissions are comprehensive and she manages her hearings with confidence. She's a highly likeable advocate." **Recent work:** Appeared in the 'Plebgate' scandal on behalf of the Chief Constable for the Warwickshire Police. This matter centred on accusations that Inspector MacKaill had made dishonest and misleading statements to the press.

Old Square Chambers

See profile on p.886

THE SET

Old Square Chambers boasts an impressive professional discipline practice, augmented by its members' extensive experience in the employment sphere. The team's expertise is further complemented by established strength in the areas of personal injury and clinical negligence. The set attracts instructions from a wide range of clients, including professional individuals, regulators and NHS trusts. It houses a dynamic team of barristers who are particularly well versed in matters concerning healthcare, alongside those relating to the financial, education and law enforcement services.

Client service: The "absolutely brilliant" senior clerk William Meade "goes the extra mile for clients." "The clerks are always super-helpful and absolutely trustworthy, and they take the time to get to know their clients."

SILKS

Mary O'Rourke QC Prominent figure in the field of healthcare regulation. She is held in high regard, by both peers and the healthcare professionals she represents, given her robust style and formidable presence in court. **Strengths:** "She's exceptional. I think she's one of, if not the, leading silk in the country for the defence of medical practitioners. She's an outstanding advocate who is often the barrister of choice for doctors who are facing difficulties." **Recent work:** Instructed in a judicial review concerning the GMC's refusal of a doctor's application for reinstatement.

Mark Sutton QC Exceptional advocate who is well known for his provision of expert advice and representation to professionals, NHS trusts and medical defence organisations. His advocacy style and extensive knowledge of employment matters are particularly praised by market sources. **Strengths:** "He's an exceptional cross-examiner, a fantastic barrister, and one of the best in the country in this field. He's a robust advocate and a nice man too." "He's among the first-class advocates. You enjoy listening to him because he's powerful and persuasive in his presentations. He captures a legal point both straightforwardly and elegantly. It's almost art." **Recent work:** Assisted the BMA with a major consultation conducted by the GMC regarding the reform of its fitness to practise procedures.

John Hendy QC (see p.669) Esteemed silk offering vast experience in the field of healthcare regulation. Alongside his specialism in the defence of various medical professionals, he is regularly called upon by barristers and solicitors to assist with disciplinary proceedings in the legal sphere. **Strengths:** "He's absolutely first-class, one of the top advocates for complex medical and employment-related disciplinary cases. If you want someone to really go for it, he's first-rate and hugely experienced." "He's a forceful and robust advocate, and tremendously authoritative." **Recent work:** Successfully obtained an injunction in the Court of Appeal to restrain disciplinary proceedings against a consultant psychiatrist.

JUNIORS

Giles Powell (see p.741) Offers experience across the board in the field of professional discipline. He is known primarily for his representation of professionals in the healthcare, financial, police and legal sectors. **Strengths:** "He's very well respected and clients like him, he's a silk in waiting and a real expert in this field. He's a fierce cross-examiner and has an excellent client manner." "He's responsive, robust, helpful and has a good rapport with clients."

Betsan Criddle (see p.626) A junior who is particularly noted for her medical regulatory and disciplinary work. She routinely acts on behalf of dentists and other healthcare professionals in complex fitness to practise proceedings. **Strengths:** "She's very robust, incredibly hard-working and performs at a much higher level than her year of call would suggest. She's a real star for the future." "She's supremely professional, very well read and always prepared. A dynamic advocate, she's very client and committee-friendly, and she has a huge gravitas when presenting." **Recent work:** Represented a dentist in fitness to practise proceedings concerning allegations that patient confidentiality had been breached.

Nadia Motraghi Impressive practitioner who is dedicated to the representation of professionals in disciplinary proceedings within the healthcare sector. She is praised particularly for her robust advocacy and polished presentation in court. **Strengths:** "She's excellent, a very well-prepared advocate who is excellent on her feet. She's very confident and great at cross-examining and presenting cases." "She's excellent at handling tricky individuals and is absolutely unflappable. Her case handling skills are incredible, she's a very bright practitioner who never stops working." "A formidable barrister who consistently punches above her weight." **Recent work:** Successfully appeared on behalf of a nurse in an appeal against an NMC decision regarding professional misconduct.

Nicola Newbegin (see p.726) Well-regarded advocate with experience in a range of disciplinary proceedings, particularly those before the GDC, HCPC and NHS trusts. She is highly acclaimed for her representation of both trusts and doctors in a large number of High Court and Court of Appeal cases. **Strengths:** "She's one to watch, an extremely hard-working and very bright practitioner."

Other Ranked Lawyers

Philip Newman (42 Bedford Row) Possesses comprehensive knowledge of disciplinary proceedings, having acted for both regulators and regulated professionals across a diverse range of areas. He offers notable experience of appearing before a variety of regulators, such as the GDC and the Institution of Structural Engineers. **Strengths:** "He's a very impressive advocate." **Recent work:** Instructed in a case concerning allegations of serious incompetence brought against an orthodontist.

Mukul Chawla QC (see p.615) (9-12 Bell Yard) An established specialist in both criminal and disciplinary matters. He is routinely instructed by the FRC to deal with public interest cases brought against accountants, and by the Police Federation in relation to police misconduct cases. **Strengths:** "A delightful opponent and very able, he is very laid back and has a charming advocacy style, which is a real asset." "A very able and persuasive advocate with great presence. He would instil complete confidence in any panel." **Recent work:** Acted for the executive counsel to the FRC in FRC v Mazars and Richard Karmel. This was a disciplinary proceeding brought against Mazars and one of its partners concerning the Members Pension Covenant Review of the Threshers group of off-licences.

Ian Winter QC (see p.799) (Cloth Fair Chambers) An established expert in the field of financial crime and fraud, he is noted for his superior advocacy skills in disciplinary hearings. **Strengths:** "He's energetic, fizzing with ideas, passionate about cases and produces wonderful briefs." "He's a fabulous silk and a superb advocate for big cases." "The best in the business, he's the bee's knees."

Gemma Hobcraft (Doughty Street Chambers) Versatile junior who routinely represents a wide range of medical professionals before numerous regulators, including the GDC, NMC and GPhC. She has extensive experience of guiding professional individuals through all stages of disciplinary proceedings. **Strengths:** "She provides top-level, practical advice. If it's a tricky case containing particularly complex issues, she's the go-to counsel as she's able to cut through the issues and think of an innovative way forward." "She's particularly good at advising on technical issues." **Recent work:** Represented a nurse at a conduct and competence committee hearing before the NMC. The defendant was facing charges of clinical misconduct and aggressive behaviour.

Susan Sleeman (Doughty Street Chambers) A dedicated representative of healthcare professionals facing disciplinary proceedings, she has vast experience acting on behalf of nurses, physiotherapists and pharmacists. Her professional discipline expertise is complemented by her deep knowledge of employment law. **Strengths:** "She's a pleasure to work with and has an excellent knowledge of healthcare regulation." "Her advocacy skills, attention to detail and client care are all highly impressive." "Panels like her because she's very charming and personable in the way she addresses them." **Recent work:** Prosecuted a case on behalf of the NMC against a registrant who was accused of carrying out a manual bowel evacuation inappropriately and despite the protestations of the patient.

Louise Price (Doughty Street Chambers) Renowned junior with vast experience of representing healthcare professionals before most of the major regulators. She also regularly attracts instructions from teachers, on behalf of whom she frequently appears before the NCTL. She is particularly noted for her adroit handling of matters concerning serious allegations of dishonesty or sexual misconduct. **Strengths:** "She takes a pragmatic approach to cases and is really good at keeping the client on track. She's very likeable and wonderfully easy to work with." **Recent work:** Appeared before the NCTL on behalf of a teacher who was accused of involvement with the Birmingham 'Trojan Horse plot'.

Geoffrey Williams QC (see p.796) (Farrar's Building) Respected silk who is noted for his proficiency in the field of solicitors' regulation. He regularly acts on behalf of regulators, such as the SRA, and is developing a highly respected defence-side practice. He wins the praise of peers for his first-rate advocacy. **Strengths:** "He embodies good judgement and always knows where to draw the line." "He knows everything there is to know about solicitors' regulation. His slow, measured, calm delivery can really hold a tribunal's attention." **Recent work:** Represented the SRA in a four-day hearing before the SDT. The case concerned two solicitors, one of whom was fined £10,000 and the other of whom was struck off.

Kenneth Hamer (see p.662) (Henderson Chambers) Standout practitioner with a breadth of expertise encompassing numerous areas of professional regulation. In particular, he is known for his adept representation of accountants and for his sterling prosecution work on behalf of the GPhC. **Strengths:** "He has almost unparalleled knowledge of regulatory case law." "His grasp of the detail is nearly unequalled, together with his encyclopaedic knowledge of regulators."

Heather Emmerson (see p.641) (11KBW) A skilful advocate who routinely prosecutes on behalf of the SRA, the GMC and the Gambling Commission. She is a regular feature in the High Court and receives praise for her meticulous approach to her work. **Strengths:** "She is incredibly bright, practical and user-friendly. She's a wonderful advocate." "A genuine rising star, she is a consummate professional in terms of application, preparation and presentation." **Recent work:** Acted for the SRA in disciplinary proceedings brought against a solicitor who was accused of dishonesty and scheming.

Richard Price OBE QC (see p.743) (Littleton Chambers) An advocate of considerable reputation, he offers expert advice and representation to both regulators and the regulated in the legal sphere. **Strengths:** "He is authoritative, pragmatic and commands huge respect. He knows the world of professional regulation inside out." "He's a very safe pair of hands and an absolutely thorough practitioner."

David Aaronberg QC (15 New Bridge Street) An esteemed criminal barrister with vast experience of regulatory matters, particularly those concerning the pharmaceutical industry.

Kevin McCartney (5 Paper Buildings) An accomplished advocate, he primarily represents defendants in fitness to practise hearings. He is noted for his deep knowledge of regulation in the pharmaceutical sphere, and frequently appears before the FTP Committees of the GPhC. **Strengths:** "His breadth of expertise in relation to pharmacy law really stands out. He is a very strong advocate with a great client manner, and that makes him a joy to work with." "A very thorough, hard-working and approachable individual."

THE REGIONS

Professional Discipline	
Leading Sets	
Band 1	
Deans Court Chambers *	
Band 2	
New Park Court Chambers	
Leading Silks	
Band 1	
Keeling Adrian	No5 Chambers (ORL) ◊ [A]
O'Rourke Mary	Deans Court Chambers
Sephton Craig	Deans Court Chambers
Band 2	
Pitter Jason	New Park Court Chambers
Roberts Lisa	Lincoln House Chambers (ORL) ◊
Leading Juniors	
Band 1	
Atherton Peter	Deans Court Chambers
Baxter Bernadette	Lincoln House Chambers (ORL) ◊
Beattie Sharon	New Park Court Chambers
Cartwright Sophie	Deans Court Chambers *
Kitching Robin	Deans Court Chambers [A]
Band 2	
Crossley Steven	Exchange Chambers (ORL) ◊ *
Cundy Catherine	9 St John Street (ORL) ◊
Dudley-Jones Elizabeth	Deans Court Chambers
Grundy Nigel	9 St John Street (ORL) ◊
MacAdam Jason	Exchange Chambers (ORL) ◊
Morgan Edward	9 St John Street (ORL) ◊
Tyson Richard	3PB Barristers (ORL) ◊

* Indicates set / individual with profile.
[A] direct access (see p.24).
◊ (ORL) = Other Ranked Lawyer.
Alphabetical order within each band. Band 1 is highest.

Band 1

Deans Court Chambers
See profile on p.964

THE SET
Deans Court Chambers retains its reputation as the leading regional chambers for professional discipline cases, offering a strong bench of silks and juniors handling both disciplinary and regulatory matters. Members are strong in both defence and prosecution, regularly appearing before the GMC, the Police Federation and NHS trust foundations.

Client service: "Senior clerk Matt Gibbons and the team are outstanding – extremely helpful, very accommodating and fair."

SILKS
Mary O'Rourke QC Has a highly regarded professional discipline practice with a focus on the defence of doctors in matters before the GMC and other disciplinary bodies. She is also regularly instructed by dentists and nurses in regulatory matters, gaining respect in this area from interviewees for her "encyclopaedic knowledge of healthcare regulation." **Strengths:** "She's exceptional. I think she is one of the leading silks in the country for what she does in the defence of medical practitioners." "A leading silk – formidable and very knowledgeable." "She is clearly one of the leading silks in this field. She has a wide expertise, long experience and is extremely practical and effective." **Recent work:** Acted for a doctor in B v GMC, a case concerning the doctor's application for restoration after voluntary erasure several years ago.

Craig Sephton QC Noted for his expertise in professional discipline defence work, acting for a number of doctors and solicitors as part of a broader practice that also covers professional negligence defence. He is also regularly instructed by the GMC in cases brought before both the Fitness to Practise Panel and the Administrative Court. **Strengths:** "He is an extremely bright, extremely effective and balanced advocate – he can be ferocious when he wants to be and is a very powerful presence in tribunals." "He gives no-nonsense, straightforward advice."

JUNIORS
Peter Atherton Gains regular instruction from the GMC in medical tribunal cases, drawing on his wealth of experience handling civil and criminal cases when acting in court. He is also skilled at handling inquests concerning self-harm cases and Human Rights Act applications, among other matters. **Strengths:** "He is a hugely experienced, long-standing prosecution performer." "He has the style and ability to do consistent consecutive and long-running cases, which he does with aplomb. He knows how to handle panels and is a very proficient advocate who knows the business." "He is extremely charming and nothing fazes him – a really safe pair of hands." "A very experienced practitioner – measured and meticulous." **Recent work:** Acted for the GMC in GMC v Dr Y, concerning the English language skills of a forensic medical examiner.

Sophie Cartwright (see p.612) Experienced prosecutor on behalf of the GMC and handler of high-profile public inquiry police cases. Her professional discipline practice also takes in the representation of individual professionals, local authorities and NHS trusts. **Strengths:** "She has an encyclopaedic knowledge of the relevant area of law. She has sound judgement and is extremely good at dealing with people." "She is extremely knowledgeable in relation to healthcare crime and regulation. A team player who impresses clients with a personable manner and effective advocacy." **Recent work:** Acted as counsel in the inquest into the death of PM. This was an inquest concerning the death of two men shot by DF in Iraq while working for G4S as an armed security contractor.

Robin Kitching Known for his work for the GMC on sensitive and high-profile cases, with expertise in handling fitness to practise cases. He handles professional discipline matters as part of a broader practice that also encompasses criminal law work. **Strengths:** "He is outstanding. A very incisive, sharp advocate." "His knowledge of regulation is just fantastic – encyclopaedic."

Elizabeth Dudley-Jones Has a broad professional discipline and employment law practice, with a notable focus on handling cases concerning medical and healthcare law. She regularly prosecutes cases for the GMC, including several cases before the Fitness to Practise Panel. **Strengths:** "She has a very good bedside manner with clients and meticulous preparation." "She is very bright and has impressive knowledge of professional regulation – I have been impressed with her approach and depth of knowledge."

Band 2

New Park Court Chambers

THE SET
New Park Court Chambers is highly regarded for its strong team of barristers and varied professional discipline practice. Its barristers are often instructed by members of the police force and healthcare professionals, and also regularly act on behalf of the GMC in fitness to practise cases.

Client service: "The clerking is always efficient, friendly and approachable. If we have an issue, it is sorted swiftly." Wayne Stevens is the senior criminal clerk.

SILKS
Jason Pitter QC A vastly experienced silk noted for handling misconduct hearings before the GMC, the NMC and police misconduct panels. He receives recognition for his expertise in both the defence and prosecution of healthcare and police force professionals. **Strengths:** "A really experienced silk and one of the best jury advocates I have seen. His main strength is the way he deals with clients and difficult individuals. You are guaranteed to get good representation with Jason." "He is a very polished advocate, his cross-examination technique is impressive and effective. A high-calibre advocate."

JUNIORS
Sharon Beattie Respected junior focusing her practice on representing clients in the medical profession, who regularly presents complex and sensitive professional discipline cases before the GMC. She complements her professional discipline practice with experience in handling serious criminal cases. **Strengths:** "She's really impressive, a fantastically organised advocate. She is completely on top of the information and the case as a whole." "She is very experienced and has dealt with some high-profile complex cases." "She's a big hitter – I am very comfortable instructing her on quite serious and challenging allegations."

Other Ranked Lawyers

Steven Crossley (see p.627) (Exchange Chambers) Focuses his professional discipline practice on police cases, acting for his clients in inquests and tribunals and before the High Court. Crossley also handles private client criminal work. **Strengths:** "A leading junior in every sense of the word. He is a reliable, dependable, very professional and excellent advocate. He is brilliant with clients." "He is a good advocate – very pragmatic and sharp." "He is an outstanding operator who is very calm, measured, well prepared and quietly effective." **Recent work:** Acted for PC Joanne Parr in a police misconduct case in which the defendant was accused of deliberately failing to assist a member of the public during an assault.

Jason MacAdam (Exchange Chambers) Has a reputable practice handling cases involving the police force and healthcare professionals. He receives regular instruction in matters before tribunals including the GMC, the Health and Care Professions Council and police discipline tribunals. **Strengths:**

"Jason is great at dealing with difficult clients and at carefully managing their expectations." "He is a very concise, understandable and to-the-point advocate." "Very down-to-earth, sensible and has good judgement."

Lisa Roberts QC (Lincoln House Chambers) Experienced in both the defence and prosecution of police and medical professionals, with experience in handling regulatory offences. She complements her professional discipline practice with expertise in criminal law. **Strengths:** "Lisa has an extremely powerful advocacy style and will fight for clients, especially in difficult cases. She is very committed to her work and her clients, and always ensures that their best interests are met. She is approachable and always makes herself available when she is needed."

Bernadette Baxter (Lincoln House Chambers) A strong junior regularly gaining instructions for professional discipline cases within the police force and medical profession, with her clients including several police officers and the GMC. **Strengths:** "Her legal knowledge is excellent, her technical knowledge is excellent and her advocacy is first-class." "She's at the top of her game – she is very capable, tenacious, has good judgement and, on top of that, she's easy to work with and gets on with it."

Adrian Keeling QC (No5 Chambers) A highly regarded silk with a focus on the representation of police officers at all levels of the disciplinary process, including Police Appeals Tribunals, misconduct panels and the High Court. He is also known for his expertise in handling cases concerning misconduct in public office. **Strengths:** "He has a nice, easy-going style but is robust in court and gets very good results." "He is reassuring to clients, charming and persuasive, and has a superb tactical approach." **Recent work:** Acted in the inquest into the death of Lloyd Butler, representing several police officers charged with the death of a mentally ill man taken into custody.

Richard Tyson (3PB Barristers) Recognised for his advocacy in healthcare-related professional discipline matters, including both the defence and prosecution of healthcare professionals. He is also experienced in prosecuting on behalf of the GMC, and advocating for clients before Fitness to Practise Panels. **Recent work:** Acted for the GMC in GMC v Dr Grant, a case concerning a GP's involvement in a child sexual abuse case.

Catherine Cundy (9 St John Street) Continues to impress in professional discipline cases in the healthcare profession, drawing on her previous role as in-house counsel at the GMC. She regularly prosecutes on behalf of the GMC in fitness to practise cases concerning clinical and sexual misconduct. **Strengths:** "She's very good. She can see the holes in a defence case very easily, is very good at cross-examination and has an excellent manner in tribunals. She works very hard and is extremely well prepared. I've never seen anything less than 100% preparation from her." "She is courteous and extremely efficient." **Recent work:** Acted for the GMC in GMC v Dr C S. The case concerned allegations of misconduct against a doctor who had had a sexual relationship with a patient.

Nigel Grundy (9 St John Street) Particularly impresses in healthcare-related professional discipline matters, regularly handling GMC fitness to practise hearings and receiving regular instruction from the Ambulance Service and several NHS trusts. **Strengths:** "He is a very sensible and sound practitioner." "He is fair and easy to get on with – everything you need in a prosecutor."

Edward Morgan (9 St John Street) Experienced in handling professional discipline matters and related employment cases. He represents clients in Employment Tribunals and a range of disciplinary proceedings. **Strengths:** "He is extremely good: very cerebral, very eloquent and very impressive."

Professional Negligence

Contents:

LONDON

Professional Negligence
Leading Sets
Band 1
4 New Square *
Band 2
Hailsham Chambers *
Band 3
Brick Court Chambers *
Fountain Court Chambers *
4 Pump Court *
3 Verulam Buildings *
Wilberforce Chambers *
Band 4
1 Chancery Lane
Crown Office Chambers *
7 King's Bench Walk *
Band 5
Hardwicke *
Maitland Chambers *
XXIV Old Buildings *
Serle Court *
2TG - 2 Temple Gardens *
* Indicates set / individual with profile.
[A] direct access (see p.24).
◊ (ORL) = Other Ranked Lawyer.
Alphabetical order within each band. Band 1 is highest.

Professional Negligence	
Leading Silks	
Star individuals	*Chambers*
Fenwick Justin	4 New Square *
Pooles Michael	Hailsham Chambers *
Stewart Roger	4 New Square *
Band 1	
Brindle Michael	Fountain Court Chambers *
Davidson Nicholas	4 New Square *
Day Anneliese	4 New Square *
Edelman Colin	Devereux (ORL) ◊ *
Gaisman Jonathan	7 King's Bench Walk
Howard Mark	Brick Court Chambers
Hubble Ben	4 New Square *
Lawrence Patrick	4 New Square *
McPherson Graeme	4 New Square [A] *
Moger Christopher	4 Pump Court *
Patten Ben	4 New Square *
Rowley Keith	Radcliffe Chambers (ORL) ◊ *
Salzedo Simon	Brick Court Chambers *
Simpson Mark	Fountain Court Chambers *
Tozzi Nigel	4 Pump Court *
Weitzman Tom	3 Verulam Buildings
Band 2	
Adam Tom	Brick Court Chambers
Butcher Christopher	7 King's Bench Walk
Cannon Mark	4 New Square *
Christie Aidan	4 Pump Court *
Croxford Ian	Wilberforce Chambers
Douglas Michael	4 Pump Court *
Elkington Ben	4 New Square *
Flenley William	Hailsham Chambers *
Halpern David	4 New Square *
Harvey Michael	Crown Office Chambers
Hollander Charles	Brick Court Chambers
Newman Paul	Wilberforce Chambers
Onslow Andrew	3 Verulam Buildings
Powell John L	4 New Square *
Smith Joanna	Wilberforce Chambers
Steinfeld Alan	XXIV Old Buildings
Turner David	4 New Square
Wardell John	Wilberforce Chambers
Band 3	
Ayliffe James	Wilberforce Chambers
Brannigan Sean	4 Pump Court *
Chapman Graham	4 New Square *
Cousins Jeremy	Radcliffe Chambers (ORL) ◊
Dale Derrick	Fountain Court Chambers *
de Waal John	Hardwicke [A]
Dougherty Charles	2TG - 2 Temple Gardens *
Dutton Timothy	Fountain Court Chambers *
Eklund Graham	4 New Square *
Grant Thomas	Maitland Chambers
Howe Timothy	Fountain Court Chambers *
Jones Nigel	Hardwicke [A]
Jones Philip	Serle Court *
Lord Tim	Brick Court Chambers
Neish Andrew	4 Pump Court *
Sabben-Clare Rebecca	7 King's Bench Walk
Seitler Jonathan	Wilberforce Chambers
Sinclair Fiona	4 New Square *
Smith Jamie	4 New Square *
Symons Christopher	3 Verulam Buildings
Thanki Bankim	Fountain Court Chambers *
Trace Anthony	Maitland Chambers *
Band 4	
Cross James	4 Pump Court *
Goodall Patrick	Fountain Court Chambers *
Hilliard Lexa	Wilberforce Chambers
Marshall Philip	Serle Court *
Moriarty Stephen	Fountain Court Chambers *
Mulcahy Leigh-Ann	4 New Square *
Pilling Benjamin	4 Pump Court *
Robertson Patricia	Fountain Court Chambers *
Ross John	1 Chancery Lane
Stanley Clare	Wilberforce Chambers
Tregear Francis	XXIV Old Buildings
Wales Andrew	7 King's Bench Walk
New Silks	
Head David	3 Verulam Buildings
Mitchell Paul	Hailsham Chambers *
Plewman Thomas	Brick Court Chambers

Band 1

4 New Square

See profile on p.880

THE SET

4 New Square has for many years enjoyed a pre-eminent reputation at the Professional Negligence Bar, and the set continues to impress with both the size of its team and the quality of its advice. Members are instructed by claimant and defendant parties in cases involving all kinds of professionals, and often appear against one another in the Commercial Court, Court of Appeal and Supreme Court. Recent work highlights include Gemini v CBRE, a claim for negligent valuation totalling over £100 million, and Khanty-Mansisyk v Forsters regarding the execution of a deal for oil reserves in Russia. One instructing solicitor remarks: "4 New Square are a Rolls-Royce service at Chevrolet prices. The breadth and depth of their expertise is unparalleled."

Client service: "The clerks are always able to deliver someone at the right level and with the right expertise, regardless of the issues and how unusual they may be. They have a good understanding of the barristers' particular strengths and weaknesses and they are not afraid to make a recommendation and push it." Lizzy Stewart is the senior clerk.

SILKS

Justin Fenwick QC (see p.644) A standout professional negligence silk who is well versed in both UK-based and offshore commercial litigation. A formidable advocate, he is particularly adept at handling professional negligence and related insurance matters that involve significant elements of fraud or dishonesty. **Strengths:** "He has a sixth sense about strategy, and is a fantastic cross-examiner." "Justin Fenwick is a majestic and authoritative advocate who is also great to work with." **Recent work:** Acted in Gemini v CBRE, concerning a substantial property portfolio that was allegedly overvalued for a loan syndication.

Roger Stewart QC (see p.773) An exceptionally well-respected silk whose broad professional negligence practice particularly focuses on claims in the construction industry. He also maintains an impressive insurance practice, and is additionally instructed in complex international arbitration and appellate work. **Strengths:** "He has seen and done it all, but his enthusiasm and skills are as fresh as ever." "Tough, practical, commercial and clever." **Recent work:** Successfully appealed Gabriel v Little, a solicitors' negligence claim where it was found that the damages initially awarded actually exceeded the scope of the duty.

Nicholas Davidson QC (see p.629) Offers vast experience in the professional negligence sphere across his more than 40 years of practice at the Bar. Regularly takes on high-profile negligence cases arising from complicated issues such as corporate governance breakdown, institutional fraud and downturns in the property market. **Strengths:** "He's extremely thorough and detailed in his assessment, with a real enthusiasm for the law." "He's a great leader on complex cases who is always calm and measured." **Recent work:** Acted for the claimant in Wright v Lewis Silkin, who alleged that the law firm had left him unprotected and therefore unable to properly enforce a previous judgment against another defendant.

Anneliese Day QC (see p.631) With a strong reputation for her courtroom advocacy and commercial savvy, Anneliese Day QC is very often called

Professional Negligence	
Leading Juniors	
Star individuals	
Charlwood Spike	*Hailsham Chambers* *
Band 1	
Bacon Francis	*Hailsham Chambers* *
Hall Taylor Alex	*4 New Square* *
Holwill Derek	*Hailsham Chambers* *
Livesey Kate	*4 Pump Court* *
Mirchandani Siân	*4 New Square* *
Phipps Charles	*4 New Square* *
Savage Amanda	*4 New Square* *
Shapiro Daniel	*Crown Office Chambers* *
Wilton Simon	*Hailsham Chambers* [A] *
Band 2	
Allen Scott	*4 New Square* *
Brocklebank James	*7 King's Bench Walk* *
Carpenter Jamie	*Hailsham Chambers* *
Evans Hugh	*4 New Square* *
Evans-Tovey Jason	*Crown Office Chambers*
Howarth Simon	*Hailsham Chambers* *
Parker Matthew	*3 Verulam Buildings* *
Yeo Nik	*Fountain Court Chambers* *
Band 3	
Collett Ivor	*1 Chancery Lane*
Dixon Clare	*4 New Square* *
Dumont Thomas	*Radcliffe Chambers (ORL)* ◊ *
Evans Helen	*4 New Square* *
Jackson Hugh	*Selborne Chambers (ORL)* ◊ *
Liddell Richard	*4 New Square* *
Lynch Ben	*Fountain Court Chambers* *
Oppenheimer Tamara	*Fountain Court Chambers* *
Powell Katie	*4 New Square* *
Troman Carl	*4 New Square* *
Band 4	
Chelmick Timothy	*4 New Square* *
Colter Lucy	*4 New Square* *
Ferguson Eva	*Hailsham Chambers* *
Hall James	*Hardwicke*
Harris Miles	*4 New Square* *
Jackson Matthew	*Hailsham Chambers* *
McCann Sarah	*Hardwicke* [A]
Munro Joshua	*Hailsham Chambers* [A] *
Parker Paul	*4 New Square* *
Polley Alexander	*One Essex Court (ORL)* ◊ *
Ratcliffe Peter	*3 Verulam Buildings*
Rushton Nicola	*Hailsham Chambers* *
Shuman Karen	*1 Chancery Lane* [A]
Simpson Jacqueline	*Hailsham Chambers* *
Spalton George	*4 New Square* *
Spencer Andrew	*1 Chancery Lane*
Stacey Dan	*Hailsham Chambers* *
Weaver Elizabeth	*XXIV Old Buildings*
Wood Benjamin	*4 New Square* *
Wygas Luke	*4 Pump Court* *
Yates David	*Pump Court Tax Chambers (ORL)* ◊ *
Up-and-coming individuals	
Patel Shail	*4 New Square*
Pugh Helen	*3 Hare Court (ORL)* ◊ *
Ryan Michael	*7 King's Bench Walk*
Smiley Ben	*4 New Square* *
Thomas David	*2TG - 2 Temple Gardens* *

** Indicates individual with profile.*

[A] direct access (see p.24).

◊ (ORL) = Other Ranked Lawyer.

Alphabetical order within each band. Band 1 is highest.

upon to handle high-value professional negligence and insurance disputes. She is regularly instructed by both sides in complex multiparty litigation arising from major construction projects. **Strengths:** "She's tough, tenacious and impressive on her feet." "She's a supremely intelligent litigator with the perfect balance between charm and incisiveness." **Recent work:** Acted for the claimant in Barnsley College v White Young & Green & Galliford Try, a multimillion-pound claim brought against engineering consultants and contractors involved in the design and build of the college.

Ben Hubble QC (see p.677) Head of chambers and a specialist in professional liability, Ben Hubble QC is highly regarded for his ability to take the lead in complex, multiparty litigation. He has a strong track record of handling claims against lawyers, surveyors, accountants and actuaries, particularly in the wake of challenging situations such as market collapse or wide-scale fraud. **Strengths:** "He's accessible, articulate and an excellent advocate who is very easy to work with." "Quickly identifies the key issues and provides practical and commercial advice." **Recent work:** Acted in Hawksford v Halliwells LLP on behalf of the claimant, an offshore Jersey trust, which alleged that solicitors had wrongly drafted a sale and purchase agreement that exposed the trust to litigation.

Patrick Lawrence QC (see p.697) Esteemed practitioner who has a long history of acting in professional negligence cases, particularly in the financial sector. He is eminently capable of handling litigation at first instance all the way up to appellate level, including the Supreme Court. **Strengths:** "He's extremely good on cross-examination in court, and also very good with clients in conference." "A highly persuasive advocate who can make complicated arguments understandable." **Recent work:** Acted in Titan v Colliers, a EUR70 million claim concerning the valuation of property in Germany.

Graeme McPherson QC (see p.714) Known for the great strength of his professional negligence and discipline practice, Graeme McPherson QC expertly handles complex commercial litigation as well as mediation and arbitration proceedings. He is most often involved in cases concerning financial advisers and solicitors, although he has also advised on claims relating to the conduct of professionals in the art, sport and intellectual property arenas. **Strengths:** "An experienced professional negligence specialist giving clear advice, ensuring the thorough preparation of disputes." "Excellent analysis and a common-sense approach." **Recent work:** Acted in Marrache and Others v Baker Tilly Ltd, defending the accountants and auditors at Gibraltar's largest law firm against claims that they failed to notice senior partners' thefts from client accounts.

Ben Patten QC (see p.734) A specialist in professional negligence and construction matters, Ben Patten QC has experience handling cases in the Commercial Court, TCC and Chancery Division, as well as through arbitration. He is very highly regarded for his expertise in claims concerning negligent advice on the part of solicitors, valuers and financial advisers. **Strengths:** "My number one choice for advice on technical points, and someone who provides excellent strategic advice." "What he doesn't know about professional negligence isn't worth knowing." **Recent work:** Acted for Persimmon Homes in a professional negligence claim against its former solicitors concerning conveyancing of a large development site.

Mark Cannon QC (see p.611) Well-regarded silk who offers the benefit of his broad experience in construction and insurance as well as professional negligence. While he is especially known for his expertise in construction and property-related claims, he also advises on a diverse range of other matters, from healthcare to financial services. **Strengths:** "Phenomenally clever, with practical and commercial sense as well." "Not only charming and friendly, he has an almost encyclopaedic knowledge of complex areas of law which he applies in a way that is easy to understand." **Recent work:** Represented Goldsmith Williams against claims brought by numerous 'right to buy' council tenants who alleged that they completed property purchases based on negligent advice.

Ben Elkington QC (see p.640) Diverse practice taking in extensive insurance and property damage work alongside professional negligence cases. His expertise in insurance brokers' negligence is well noted, and he also tackles claims relating to solicitors, tax advisers, valuers and barristers. **Strengths:** "Ben is always on top of the finer details while keeping in mind the bigger picture." "He's very engaged, reliable and personable, a fantastic asset on your side." **Recent work:** Defended tax advisers Afortis against claims that they had provided negligent advice to investors on the risks of certain tax avoidance schemes.

David Halpern QC (see p.662) A highly experienced silk whose broad commercial chancery experience feeds into his sophisticated professional negligence practice. He handles a broad range of claims arising from business and property disputes, and also takes on cases involving insurance elements. **Strengths:** "He's a first-rate analyst of the facts, and an impressive authority in chancery law. He provides excellent, clear delivery to clients." "Very technically gifted on property matters." **Recent work:** Instructed by the claimant in the appeal of Hughes-Holland v BPE, a case concerning the proper measure of damages that are awarded for solicitors' negligence claims.

John Powell QC (see p.741) Vastly experienced in both domestic and international advisory work concerning the financial sector, with a particular emphasis on fraud and professional negligence matters. He often sits as an arbitrator and is also qualified to practise in a number of offshore jurisdictions. **Recent work:** Advised Capita Financial Managers on claims of investment mis-selling brought by Connaught Income Fund, which allegedly resulted in the fund's collapse.

David Turner QC Handles professional negligence claims brought against construction professionals, insurance brokers and solicitors, among others. Particularly adept at advising on cases of allegedly negligent tax and auditing advice, including pre-packaged schemes for tax mitigation. **Strengths:** "His real strength is being able to cut through all the rubbish to get to the relevant point extremely quickly." "Incredibly knowledgeable, practical and commercial." **Recent work:** Defended accountancy firm Lowick Rose LLP on appeal against an £18 million claim brought against it by a lender.

Graham Chapman QC (see p.614) Highly regarded commercial barrister who acts for claimants and defendants on a range of professional negligence matters. Advises on cases of auditors', solicitors' and valuers' negligence, particularly in relation to substantial financial and property concerns. **Strengths:** "He consistently provides robust and commercial advice, as well as advocacy of the highest quality." "Graham is very user-friendly and an excellent team player." **Recent work:** Acted for the claimants in Fortelus Special Situations Master Fund v Fried Frank, which concerned legal advice given by the Paris office of Fried Frank on French insolvency procedures.

Graham Eklund QC (see p.640) Veteran practitioner Graham Eklund QC has extensive experience, including impressive professional negligence expertise, stretching back four decades. His work in this area is augmented by his strong practices in insurance, product liability and property damage. **Strengths:** "Clients value his direct, no-nonsense approach and judgement." "His legal skills are first rate, but he's also calm and unflappable." **Recent work:** Acted in McLughlin & Harvey Ltd v Zurich Professional and Financial Lines, in which contractors sought indemnity from their insurer regarding defects in the design and construction of a Scottish building.

Fiona Sinclair QC (see p.766) Particularly strong on claims relating to tax and investment advice delivered by solicitors and accountants, as well as professionals in the property and construction spheres. She regularly handles litigation of substantial value and complexity, often involving a large number of parties. Also offers considerable expertise in professional indemnity issues. **Strengths:** "She knows how the courts work inside-out, provides pithy, down-to-earth advice, and gets on top of the details quickly." "Fiona is charm personified; judges love her." **Recent work:** Acted for a group of 48 firms of solicitors in the Concord Street litigation, defending a £24 million claim for damages brought by 104 claimants with regard to defects in a residential property development.

Jamie Smith QC (see p.768) Estimable barrister whose already outstanding professional negligence practice has only strengthened since taking silk. He is a go-to adviser and advocate for high-value negligence claims, particularly those involving solicitors and valuers. He also has a commendable reputation for his work on insurance-related cases. **Strengths:** "He is highly analytical and able to see through complicated issues." "Jamie is thoughtful, approachable and efficient, with an impressive grasp of lengthy facts." **Recent work:** Successfully represented a barrister in Chinnock & Schumann v Rea, defending misconduct claims regarding a previous clinical negligence suit.

Leigh-Ann Mulcahy QC (see p.723) Frequently instructed in high-value professional liability matters concerning accountants, lawyers and insurance brokers. She has broad advocacy experience, including significant appellate work, and is also known for her expertise in alternative dispute resolution. **Strengths:** "She has a very good manner about her, and she's very technically able." "I found her to be very responsive, and she cuts right to the chase." **Recent work:** Defended DWF LLP against a £12 million claim for negligence brought in relation to previous product liability litigation.

JUNIORS

Alex Hall Taylor (see p.662) Highly regarded junior with a thriving professional negligence practice that incorporates claims concerning a wide range of professionals, including lawyers, accountants, valuers and tax advisers. Frequently involved in cases with significant chancery, offshore or tax elements. **Strengths:** "His analysis is second to none and he is tremendous with clients." "He offers sound written advice and is happy to give a commercial steer on how to move a case forward or what to look for in a settlement. Clients are always happy for us to instruct Alex." **Recent work:** Advised fine art dealers Hazlitts Gooden & Fox on a claim against a solicitors' firm for defective drafting of documents during the sale of a Monet painting.

Siân Mirchandani (see p.718) Regularly instructed in negligence claims concerning financial, legal and construction professionals, acting for both claimant and defendant parties. Her scientific background before being called to the Bar enables her to handle highly technical claims with aplomb. **Strengths:** "She's very user-friendly, good with clients and gets to the point quickly." "With a sharp mind and excellent attention to detail, Siân is the senior junior of choice for surveyors' negligence claims." **Recent work:** Defended law firm Mathew & Mathew in a multiparty dispute concerning claims from right-to-buy council tenants that they had been given negligent conveyancing advice on property purchases.

Charles Phipps (see p.737) Represents a broad range of clients, most often defendants, including insolvency practitioners, surveyors, valuers and financial services professionals. He has a particular specialism in claims relating to obligations of confidentiality and privilege. **Strengths:** "He's a wonderful, steady pair of hands who always remains calm." "He's obviously hugely intelligent, approachable, and works well as part of a team." **Strengths:** Represented law firm Ward Hadaway against allegations brought by multiple claimants concerning breach of fiduciary duty and negligence regarding buy-to-let property purchases.

Amanda Savage (see p.759) Amanda Savage has a strong practice handling claims against valuers, financial sector professionals and lawyers, and also additional experience in wasted costs cases. She is regularly instructed in claims arising from legal advice given on property and matrimonial finance matters. **Strengths:** "A brilliant lawyer, hard working and approachable, and a wonderful team member." "She's thorough, pragmatic and easy to work with." **Recent work:** Represented solicitors in Evans v Challinors, concerning allegations that they mishandled an ancillary relief settlement.

Scott Allen (see p.582) Experienced barrister who is instructed in cases featuring a diverse selection of professionals, including accountants, insurance brokers, solicitors and architects. He has handled several high-profile cases in recent years, and is well known for the practical tenor of his advice and meticulous approach. **Strengths:** "He shows huge attention to detail and had a fantastic grip on the issues of the case, despite their complexity." "Very bright, but equally commercial and pragmatic. He's also very user-friendly." **Recent work:** Advised Shorts Financial Services LLP on a claim that could potentially extend the principle laid down in White v Jones to professionals other than solicitors.

Hugh Evans (see p.641) Highly experienced in the field of professional negligence, with additional experience in insurance matters and costs litigation. Represents claimants and defendants alike, and has a particular focus on claims against solicitors and other parties involved in property transactions. **Strengths:** "Hugh demonstrates wit and energy, and is tremendously likeable too." "Hugh knows professional negligence inside-out, and is great to work with." "He is phenomenally bright and gives very practical advice." **Recent work:** Acted for claimant lender Mortgage Agency Services Number One in a £5 million claim for fraudulent misrepresentation against a borrower's solicitors on a remortgage transaction.

Clare Dixon (see p.634) Broad expertise in professional negligence matters, encompassing a wide range of claims against solicitors, barristers, insurance brokers and valuers. She often takes on cases that involve additional elements of fraud or wasted costs. **Strengths:** "She's extremely intelligent, and gives her advice in a very understandable way." "She is fantastic to work with and quickly grasps the detail in large cases." **Recent work:** Acted for the defendant law firm in Begum v Neejam LLP and Mallick, a claim related to an employment dispute that was allegedly under-settled.

Helen Evans (see p.641) Regularly instructed on high-profile professional negligence cases against insurance brokers, surveyors, lawyers and financial professionals. She demonstrates particular proficiency in large-scale litigation involving multiple parties. **Strengths:** "She's very attentive and thorough, and very good at managing expectations in terms of what she can do." "She is an extremely skilled tactician and a joy to watch in court." **Recent work:** Sole counsel to the defendant trustee companies in a group claim from 160 investors, regarding advice on investments in Brazilian teak plantations.

Richard Liddell (see p.701) Manages a healthy caseload of professional negligence work that includes claims against civil and structural engineers, accountants, barristers and solicitors. Takes on claimant and defendant work and has advocacy experience that extends all the way up to the Supreme Court. **Strengths:** "Rick Liddell is very thorough and brings a rational approach to cases." "He's very capable, extremely hard working, very approachable and user-friendly." **Recent work:** Acted for defendant solicitors in response to a British company's allegations of negligent tax advice concerning the reconstruction of a French company.

Katie Powell (see p.741) Highly adept at handling claims brought against lawyers for allegedly mishandled litigation and other legal matters. She is also regularly instructed in cases concerning independent financial advisers, construction professionals and valuers. **Strengths:** "She is very good at thinking on her feet, even at short notice." "She's user-friendly, always available and able to grasp the details of a case swiftly." **Recent work:** Acted in Antonio Caliendo & Barnaby Holdings LLP v Mishcon de Reya LLP, a claim that law firm Mishcon de Reya LLP failed to negotiate or note the lack of certain terms in a share sale agreement.

Carl Troman (see p.784) Focuses particularly on professional negligence claims relating to solicitors, accountants, construction professionals and insurance brokers. Regularly instructed on complex and high-value litigation concerning a large number of parties. **Strengths:** "He is very good at drafting and very good on his feet." "An accomplished advocate who has the confidence to hold his ground against far more senior barristers." **Recent work:** Acted for the claimant in Ponsonby v Farmers & Mercantile, who alleged negligence on the part of insurance brokers in relation to a personal injury claim for which they were underinsured.

Timothy Chelmick (see p.616) Can claim proficiency in a comprehensive array of professional negligence claims, acting for claimants and defendants. Widely encompassing cases concerning legal, financial and construction professionals, his practice has an increasing focus on international work, particularly in the Middle East. **Strengths:** "He is extremely commercial, and clients love him for his no-nonsense approach." "He has excellent advocacy skills." **Recent work:** Defended a number of independent financial advisers against claims that they had given negligent advice with regard to various investment schemes.

Lucy Colter (see p.621) Has a flourishing practice in the professional liability space that includes cases concerning insurance brokers, investment managers and barristers, among others. Also adept at handling claims against a range of construction professionals, including project managers, architects and quantity surveyors. **Strengths:** "She is extremely hard working, very bright and has an exceptional mastery of the detail of complex matters. Even as a junior member of the team, she provides valuable input." "She's thorough and tenacious in extracting information from clients." **Recent work:** Acted in Boliari EAD and George Christoph v Rana Bains and Rabinder Senghera, bringing claims for negligence and breach of trust and fiduciary duty against two solicitors.

Miles Harris (see p.665) Tackles professional liability matters relating to a broad range of financial and legal service providers, as well as disputes concerning professional indemnity insurance. He is capable of acting for both claimants and defendants and regularly undertakes alternative dispute resolution as well as litigation. **Strengths:** "He's utterly charming, with very efficient and polished drafting, and he is strategically far-sighted." "He gives brilliant advice, and is just a joy to work with." **Recent work:** Acted for the claimant in Fitness First Clubs Limited v Shoosmiths and Brodies LLP. It was alleged that solicitors had omitted certain commercial leasing liabilities from a company voluntary agreement.

Paul Parker (see p.733) Highly experienced senior junior whose practice in professional liability encompasses claims against virtually all non-medical professions. Recent claims have concerned negligence in relation to commercial conveyancing, audit planning and financial mis-selling, among other areas. **Strengths:** "He's very good to work with, very approachable, deals with matters promptly and he's good both on paper and on his feet in court." "He gives clear, robust advice." **Recent work:** Acted for the defendant law firm in Paragon Mortgages Ltd v GM Wilson Solicitors, which concerned lenders' claims that the firm had conducted the conveyance of a housing development with a defective title.

George Spalton (see p.770) Very capable of handling professional negligence claims against lawyers, accountants, auditors and actuaries, among others. In addition to his wide experience in the Commercial Court and Court of Appeal, where he often appears unled, he also has a strong reputation for his arbitration work. **Strengths:** "George is good on his feet, and clients like him." "He provides clear, commercial advice." "A very bright and thorough junior who is a great team player." **Recent work:** Defended a firm of accountants in Harlequin v Wilkins Kennedy, against claims relating to a Caribbean property scheme.

Benjamin Wood (see p.799) Draws upon his previous career as a corporate financier to advise on complex professional liability issues in the financial sector. Has experience acting for both claimants and defendants in major litigation and has appeared in the High Court and Court of Appeal, both as junior counsel and unled. **Strengths:** "He's a rising star, with experience and attitude which belie his years." "Ben has the ability to identify the key issues in a case quickly, and deliver clear and pragmatic advice." **Recent work:** Acted for Harding Homes in a claim against Bircham Dyson Bell, alleging that the defendant allowed its investors to conduct a compromising debt deal that involved wider than usual personal guarantees.

Shail Patel Specialises in high-end commercial disputes, including significant professional negligence and related insurance cases. He has advised on cases concerning property investments, trusts and tax advice, and regularly acts for both claimant and defendant parties. **Strengths:** "Shail has a lot of insurance experience. He is bright, accessible and an excellent team player." "He's impressive in terms of his speed of response and commercial advice." **Recent work:** Sole counsel to claimant valuers Esurv in a Contribution Act claim for conveyancing negligence against Goldsmith Williams Solicitors.

Ben Smiley (see p.767) Up-and-coming junior who has cultivated a practice spanning an extensive array of professional negligence work, with a focus on claims against financial advisers and insurance brokers, as well as legal professionals. He has additional expertise in financial regulatory matters. **Strengths:** "He's incredibly charming, hands-on and always responds. He's flexible in his methods and modern in his approach." "An impressive junior with strong analytical skills." **Recent work:** Advised the defendants in Berntsen and Richardson v Tait and Rayment, at first instance and in the Court of Appeal, on a case concerning alleged dishonest conspiracy and misconduct among company administrators.

Band 2

Hailsham Chambers

See profile on p.857

THE SET

Hailsham Chambers is firmly established as a go-to set at the Professional Negligence Bar, with its members acting in a wide array of high and low-value disputes. The set is instructed by claimants and defendants hailing from almost every sector and including lawyers, clinicians, accountants and surveyors. Recent work highlights include Wellesley v Withers, in which the Court of Appeal ruled on causation principles in tort, and E Surv v Goldsmith Williams, a case on the duties of conveyancing solicitors. Sources describe the set as "the best of the Bar" and "near the top of the market, without a doubt." **Client service:** "The clerking at Hailsham is proficient, expeditious and user-friendly." "The clerks very much want to work with you and assist whenever they can." Stephen Smith is the senior clerk.

SILKS

Michael Pooles QC (see p.740) Described by one source as "the best professional indemnity barrister there is," Michael Pooles QC is renowned for his skill in handling indemnity claims and related coverage matters. He acts for a comprehensive range of clients, but has particular focus on claims concerning surveyors, accountants and lawyers. **Strengths:** "If we need to win a case, we instruct Michael. What he doesn't know about professional indemnity isn't worth knowing." "Confident, inspiring and reassuring: a superb lawyer with a refined and smooth style." **Recent work:** Advised the defendant in Jackson v Thompsons and Prescott, an £80 million claim arising from the defeat of a group litigation order application.

William Flenley QC (see p.646) Well versed in the full spectrum of professional liability work, William Flenley QC serves as an arbitrator and a mediator as well as an advocate. He specialises particularly in solicitors' negligence, on which subject he has co-authored a leading reference text. **Strengths:** "He brings immaculately detailed preparation combined with an exhaustive knowledge of the law." "William Flenley is very concise, and incredibly likeable as well." **Recent work:** Defended law firm Giambrone against more than 100 solicitors' claims for breaches of trust and contract relating to the conveyancing of property in Southern Italy.

Paul Mitchell QC (see p.719) New silk who has considerable expertise in professional liability cases relating to financial advisers, accountants and solicitors. He represents claimants and defendants alike in court as well as in alternative dispute resolution proceedings. **Strengths:** "Charming and incisive, with a real knack for thinking on his feet. A cool strategist who adds class to any team." "Phenomenally bright and the advice that he provides is very commercial." **Recent work:** Acted for the second defendant in a claim brought by the beneficiaries of a will who accused its executors of conspiracy and breaches of trust and contract.

JUNIORS

Spike Charlwood (see p.615) Standout junior who is typically instructed in higher-value professional negligence claims regarding financial professionals, lawyers and valuers. Noted expertise in cases with elements of dishonesty or fraud. He is widely praised for the strength of his "no-nonsense advocacy" and intellectual approach. **Strengths:** "He gives really excellent, practical advice and he is frighteningly intelligent." "He turns things around very fast, he's really reliable and he's not afraid to say what he thinks." **Recent work:** Part of the defence team for Gateley in a £100 million commercial court claim for solicitors' negligence brought against the firm.

Francis Bacon (see p.587) Centres his practice on professional negligence cases and insurance coverage disputes, particularly those with an element of fraud. Often takes on high-value solicitors' negligence claims with significant international aspects. **Strengths:** "A senior junior who is very sharp, very good with clients and extremely good on his feet. One thing I really like is that he will come to a view and then stick to it." "Unflappable under pressure, he never backs down from difficult work." **Recent work:** Defended Notable Solicitors against a EUR100 million money laundering claim.

Derek Holwill (see p.674) With more than 25 years' experience at the Professional Negligence Bar, Derek Holwill is well placed to counsel claimants and defendants, most commonly in the financial and legal sectors. He also advises on professional indemnity coverage issues. **Strengths:** "His attention to detail and his ability to be resolute and approachable make him a force to be reckoned with." "When he speaks in court, everyone listens." **Recent work:** Defended a financial adviser against a £5 million claim relating to a misappropriated premium for an insurance policy intended to cover a failed investment.

Simon Wilton (see p.798) Head of the professional negligence group at Hailsham and an impressive practitioner in the field. He is most often instructed by professionals and indemnity insurers in the real estate and financial sectors, where he takes on high-profile multiparty cases. **Strengths:** "He has excellent technical knowledge, a great grasp of the law and a very commercial approach." "Thorough, charming and quick on his feet." **Recent work:** Represented a firm of surveyors facing a multimillion-pound claim for negligence with regard to a compulsory purchase of a warehouse and offices prior to the London 2012 Olympics.

Jamie Carpenter (see p.611) Largely concentrates on representing defendants in professional negligence cases, though he also has a growing reputation for claimant work. He is best known for his work with claims against solicitors, and he can also provide the benefit of his strong practice in costs litigation. **Strengths:** "His advice, his proactivity and his response time are second to none." "He dissected an extremely complex area of law with precision and intelligence, and then managed to explain it all in a clear and straightforward manner for the lay client." **Recent work:** Represented an Italian solicitors' firm facing claims from would-be purchasers of off-plan property in Calabria who lost their deposits following failed transactions.

Simon Howarth (see p.676) With an extensive practice in handling claims of solicitors' and barristers' negligence, Simon Howarth is also able to advise on claims regarding insurance brokerage disputes. He is also regularly instructed in complex, high-value claims arising in the financial sector. **Strengths:** "He applies his formidable intellect in a way that makes his knowledge and advice accessible." "A real expert in professional negligence who understands all the nuances and who is an excellent tactician." **Recent work:** Defended a solicitor in a dispute arising from the contested purchase of a fish farm, which called for a defence alleging the illegal manipulation of financial matters to the claimants' advantage.

Eva Ferguson (see p.644) Specialises in solicitors' negligence claims and is able to handle a wide array of matters, including mishandled litigation, disputes over wills and trusts, lenders' claims and negligent conveyancing. She also represents clients in the financial sector, including valuers, receivers and investors. **Strengths:** "She grasps the key issues quickly, she's very user-friendly and has an excellent bedside manner with clients." "Responsive, bright, comes up with interesting views and then has confidence in her convictions." **Recent work:** Successfully defended the law firm Wolferstans against a claim that it had lost a client the chance to sue an NHS trust for alleged negligence.

Matthew Jackson (see p.681) Senior junior with a strong track record in defending a range of professionals, including accountants, valuers and solicitors, as well as professional indemnity insurers. Often takes on high-value claims against law firms arising from prior personal injury or clinical negligence litigation. **Strengths:** "He's very thorough, provides solid, practical advice, and knows the area very well." "He's a pugnacious and effective advocate who's good with clients and excellent on policy issues." **Recent work:** Defended a number of law firms against allegations that claims for government-funded compensation made by miners suffering from "vibration white finger" were undervalued.

Joshua Munro (see p.724) A junior who has many years' experience in the field of professional negligence, Joshua Munro is typically involved in claims against surveyors, lawyers and independent financial advisers. He complements his practice with experience in insurance and costs work. **Strengths:** "He's a firm and persuasive advocate who shows attention to detail and has a really good manner with the court." "Clear and robust, and always willing to back his own judgement." **Recent work:** Successfully defended law firm Preston Mellor Harrison against negligence claims brought by a property developer with regard to advice on an option agreement.

Nicola Rushton (see p.756) A go-to junior for professional negligence work arising in the financial sector, Nicola Rushton regularly provides counsel to banks, lenders, accountants and mortgage brokers. She is especially well versed in complex claims relating to the restructuring or securitisation of loans. **Strengths:** "She cuts through to the nub of a case to develop solutions that work well, and to advise in down-to-earth terms." "An exceptionally safe pair of hands who also innovates in terms of strategy and practical suggestions. The advice she provides is robust and concise." **Recent work:** Advised Barclays Bank on a negligence claim concerning the valuation of a care home.

Jacqueline Simpson (see p.765) Serves a comprehensive professional client base with particular focus on accountants, financial advisers, surveyors and solicitors. She is very well thought of for the quality of both her advice and her advocacy, as well as her approachability. **Strengths:** "She gives excellent advice and is very commercially minded." "She has a good ability to see the wood for the trees and is also a pleasure to deal with." **Recent work:** Successfully acted for the defendant in an appeal concerning the extent of a solicitor's retainer in ancillary relief proceedings.

Dan Stacey (see p.771) Frequently provides counsel to clients facing major High Court and Court of Appeal proceedings. His work includes acting for and against accountants, surveyors and solicitors, and he has a particular flair for cases involving issues of limitation. **Strengths:** "There's no area of professional negligence he doesn't know about. His written and oral advice is very clear, and he's genuinely very good to work with. He's a go-to person." "A very good advocate who is prepared to knuckle down and do the work." **Recent work:** Acted for the defendant solicitors in a High Court claim alleging that the client had failed to provide an exclusive jurisdiction clause in a share purchase agreement.

Band 3

Brick Court Chambers

See profile on p.816

THE SET

A leading commercial set which can claim an impressive number of heavyweight litigators among its ranks. The highly regarded silks at Brick Court Chambers are often instructed in high-profile and high-value negligence disputes on behalf of claimant and defendant parties alike. Recent work highlights include National Trust v IBM, concerning the provision of software and project management services, and the £1.6 billion audit negligence litigation which arose from the failure of subprime lender Cattles, in which members represented PwC. Commentators highlight the set as one to turn to with tough cases. **Client service:** "They are very well run." "The clerks are easy to work with and to contact." Julian Hawes and Ian Moyler are the senior clerks.

SILKS

Mark Howard QC Considered "right at the top" for major litigation, Mark Howard QC is best known for his extensive experience in banking and civil fraud cases. He also takes on considerable work in the professional negligence sphere, particularly in relation to financial services. **Strengths:** "A legend at the Bar who is big in commercial and financial services and who is consistently rated for his cross-examination." "He's really strong in court, a very good analyst and examiner who would be one of the first you'd look to for a heavy hitter." **Recent work:** Acted in an unusual dispute between two competing hedge fund entities that involved allegations of negligent fund management.

Simon Salzedo QC (see p.758) Centres his professional negligence practice on cases relating to accountancy as well as other financial services. Also known for his strength in handling high-value insurance disputes, as well as his robust practice in banking and fraud matters. **Strengths:** "Very bright, pre-eminent on difficult accounting issues and a pleasure to deal with." "The combination of his accountancy background and his formidable knowledge of the law is a real strength." **Recent work:** Acted for the liquidator of an investment fund who brought a claim of £100 million against KPMG for negligent auditing of the fund.

Tom Adam QC Typically advises on professional negligence matters relating to solicitors, insurance brokers and accountancy firms. He is known for the breadth of his commercial practice and wins praise for his ability to handle highly complicated cases. **Strengths:** "He continues to impress on large complex litigation, and he's the first choice for challenges to existing law." "He has a great ability to break down complex issues." **Recent work:** Defended Blake Morgan (previously Morgan Cole) as one of three law firms facing charges of conspiracy with automotive consultants Autofocus to provide misleading evidence relating to credit hire charges.

Charles Hollander QC An experienced silk who is admitted to practise at both the Hong Kong and UK Bars. He is frequently called upon for professional negligence cases involving solicitors' firms, and has particular specialist expertise in issues surrounding professional privilege and conflicts of interest. **Strengths:** "He has the ability to provide focused and practical solutions." "He is massively persuasive; it's very clear from a very early stage that he knows what he's talking about." **Recent work:** Advised Dechert as the former solicitors of ENRC over whether a costs assessment arising from an alleged breach of retainer should be heard in open court.

Tim Lord QC Takes on a highly varied stream of work in the professional negligence ambit, although he is particularly valued for his work on claims relating to financial and banking professionals. **Strengths:** "A brilliant advocate who is able to get to the heart of a dispute very quickly." **Recent work:** Leading counsel in the Court of Appeal on UBS v KWL, LBBW and Depfa, a banking dispute which includes significant professional negligence claims against a portfolio manager.

Thomas Plewman QC SC New silk at the London Bar who also has many years' experience practising as senior counsel in South Africa. He is most often appointed to act in cases of accountants' and auditors' negligence, and is also experienced in a range of other general commercial claims. **Strengths:** "He is fantastic value, with a great track record on accountancy cases." **Recent work:** Defended Grant Thornton against claims of negligence in its role as reporting accountant, after the collapse of an American Leisure Group business following its IPO.

Fountain Court Chambers

See profile on p.847

THE SET

Fountain Court Chambers is a leading set for claims against financial services professionals, including investment managers and insurance brokers. Members are in demand not only for their dispute resolution experience but also for their knowledge of regulatory matters. Recent case highlights include the Bank Sarasin litigation in Dubai, a significant mis-selling claim, and LBF v HSBC Private Bank (Suisse), a USD50 million claim by the administrators of Lehman Brothers. Instructing solicitors report: "The quality of the set is very impressive. Their individuals are extremely bright and the advice given is highly commercial."

Client service: "The clerks, led by Alex Taylor, are generally very good and helpful."

SILKS

Michael Brindle QC (see p.603) Having cultivated a commercial law practice of international scope, Michael Brindle QC works on negligence claims alongside company law, banking and arbitration matters, among others. He focuses his negligence work in the financial area, including several multi-jurisdictional cases. **Strengths:** "He's a great all-rounder and a fabulous advocate." "He's an absolute trooper." **Recent work:** In the cross-border case of Al Khorafi v Bank Sarasin, defended a number of claims, including breach of contract, negligent investment advice and misrepresentation.

Mark Simpson QC (see p.765) Highly regarded for the forcefulness of his advocacy and for his deep familiarity with negligence claims in the financial and legal sectors. As well as taking on high-profile litigated claims, he also regularly counsels businesses and firms on regulatory concerns and investigations. **Strengths:** "Mark Simpson is a real heavyweight, a leader and a fantastic cross-examiner." "Very hands-on, tactically astute and very enthusiastic; I was impressed with him on his feet." **Recent work:** Acted in Mortgage Agency Services Number One Ltd v Edward Symmons LLP, which queried whether lenders can recover hedging costs from negligent valuers.

Derrick Dale QC (see p.628) Typically takes on cases involving claims against financial service providers, solicitors and barristers and has provided counsel to City and mid-market law firms, as well as insurers. Augments his professional negligence practice with his strong reputation in banking and general commercial work. **Strengths:** "He has a fantastic eye for detail, and is good at seeing things as the court would." "I don't think I've ever met a harder-working member of the Bar." **Recent work:** Defended Simons Muirhead Burton against a claim for wasted costs relating to alleged unreasonable conduct by the law firm during previous litigation.

Timothy Dutton CBE QC (see p.638) Can claim a high level of expertise in regulated market sectors, which sees him regularly instructed in highly complex negligence claims involving financial, legal and accountancy professionals. His work in this space has seen him appear in the Court of Appeal and the Supreme Court, and even the House of Lords. **Strengths:** "He's extremely authoritative in court, he's good with clients, gives clear advice and gets to the heart of issues." "A doyen in relation to professional conduct." **Recent work:** Defended Herbert Smith Freehills against London Underground's claim that they were negligently advised to exercise a put option in which they overpaid by £148 million.

Timothy Howe QC (see p.676) Commands almost 30 years' experience at the Bar, including recurrent involvement in complex, high-profile professional negligence cases. He is especially adept at handling claims arising out of the recent financial crisis, and has acted for banks and financial institutions around the world. **Strengths:** "He is a very able advocate and is very good with the law." "He's approachable and very easy to work with." **Recent work:** Represented HSBC in a USD50 million claim brought by the administrators of the Lehman Brothers, alleging negligence during the close-out of a portfolio of ISDA swaps.

Bankim Thanki QC (see p.780) An experienced commercial barrister with a focus on banking disputes, Bankim Thanki QC also centres his professional negligence work on the financial sector. He has dealt with numerous claims relating to insurance, fund management and financial mis-selling. **Strengths:** "Bankim is technically excellent, very responsive and popular with the insurance market." "He doesn't sit on the fence: he gives very clear advice and isn't afraid to put his neck on the block." **Recent work:** Represented Goldman Sachs against claims brought by two ultra high net worth individuals that the bank was negligent in realising certain margin securities.

Patrick Goodall QC (see p.656) Known for the scope of his commercial practice which takes in a considerable amount of international work as well as UK cases. Regularly handles large-scale professional negligence matters that carry a significant level of exposure. **Strengths:** "Very bright, easy to work with, clients are calmed by him." "He's very user-friendly." **Recent work:** Represented the defendant in Bradbury v Mercer Limited, a claim for breach of duty and negligence in relation to the provision of pension consultancy services.

Stephen Moriarty QC (see p.721) Head of chambers and a respected silk who maintains a broad commercial practice. His work includes significant professional negligence and insurance claims, most often concerning financial and legal services. **Strengths:** "Once he takes you on he is really committed and gives 100% to the client. He has a policy to only ever make credible arguments and points worth making, so that now when he speaks, judges and arbitrators pay attention." **Recent work:** Defended an aviation finance entity against claims by a lender that mortgaged aircraft were sold at an undervalue, in breach of duty.

Patricia Robertson QC (see p.753) Handles the full length and breadth of professional liability concerns, including significant regulatory work. She is particularly familiar with claims in the banking and finance sphere, although she regularly handles cases concerning solicitors, accountants and auditors. **Strengths:** "She's tenacious, quick-witted and on top of all the detail." "A superb advocate, she rolls her sleeves up and gets involved." **Recent work:** Defended US law firm Fried Frank against high-value claims brought against its Paris office by a hedge fund that alleged it had received negligent advice relating to insolvency and restructuring proceedings.

JUNIORS

Nik Yeo (see p.802) Can claim a strong practice in financial sector professional negligence matters, often providing counsel in cases with high exposure. His recent work has included a number of large-scale claims against valuers, banks and liquidators. **Strengths:** "Nik Yeo is technically superb, practical, client-friendly and very responsive." "Gets to grips with the issues of a case very quickly." **Recent work:** Represented the claimant in Gemini (Eclipse 2006-3) v CBRE and King Sturge, a £173 million claim alleging the negligence undervaluation of over £1.2 billion of commercial property in the UK.

Ben Lynch (see p.704) Highly regarded junior who recently moved to Fountain Court Chambers from Devereux. He is regularly instructed in high-exposure and high-value cases of professional negligence, and is also well known for his outstanding expertise in insurance matters. **Strengths:** "He's client-friendly, responsive, and one of the hardest-working junior counsel around." "He's fabulous on coverage stuff, providing incredibly detailed, intelligent analysis." **Recent work:** Represented the claimant in AIG Europe Ltd v OC320301 LLP, querying the impact of the aggregation clause within a solicitor's professional indemnity insurance.

Tamara Oppenheimer (see p.730) A high-profile junior with a broad commercial practice and who has been appointed to the Attorney General's B-Panel of Counsel. She regularly takes on high-value professional negligence cases arising in the financial sector, including recent work advising banks on claims of financial mis-selling. **Strengths:** "She was all over the detail, gave a very thorough review of the papers and had a very good understanding of the factual matrix." **Recent work:** Defended RBS against a £200 million claim regarding the alleged mis-selling of an interest swap in the context of a securitisation. The case includes not only claims of negligence, but also allegations of fraud and Libor-related issues.

4 Pump Court

See profile on p.895

THE SET

A set that is highly regarded for its experience in professional negligence, 4 Pump Court handles claims in a truly diverse range of sectors. Members take on cases involving accountants and auditors, solicitors and barristers, surveyors and valuers, financial advisers and insurance professionals. They are able to advise on cross-border disputes and claims with an element of alleged fraud. Recent cases include Maharaj v Johnson, in which the Privy Council reviewed certain principles of limitation in tort, and a claim against risk management consultants following a chemical plant fire. "The people I go to there are all at the top of their game," remarks one instructing solicitor. "They are bright and know what they are doing."

Client service: "The clerks are brilliant. Nothing is too much for them. They go out of their way to make sure we are happy." "They are on the ball in terms of offering in-house training and inviting us to their events." Chief executive Carolyn McCombe runs the set's clerking and administration team.

SILKS

Christopher Moger QC (see p.720) A silk with more than 30 years' experience at the Bar, Christopher Moger QC often advises on professional negligence disputes that are international in nature. He works for and against financial and legal professionals such as insurance brokers, actuaries, accountants and solicitors. **Strengths:** "He's a safe pair of hands, a clever and silky smooth advocate."

Nigel Tozzi QC (see p.783) A highly versatile commercial silk who handles a diverse range of professional negligence cases. He regularly acts for major insurers as well as clients in the financial sector, and also has niche expertise in shipping-related disputes. **Strengths:** "He's really fantastic in court, really organised and really methodical." "Nothing is too much trouble for him, he's also incredibly thorough and his preparation is amazing." **Recent work:** Defended a firm of solicitors against claims that they had failed to correctly advise ship buyers on a decision to terminate two shipbuilding contracts.

Aidan Christie QC (see p.617) Primarily handles negligence claims relating to the financial and insurance sectors, although he is eminently capable of tackling cases concerning almost every major profession. He regularly acts in high-profile cases, where he stands for and against clients that include brokers, underwriters, financial advisers, auditors and hedge fund directors. **Strengths:** "He gives good, commercial and pragmatic advice. He's someone I'd go to to get things quickly analysed, he's very effective." "He's technically excellent, provides a great level of service and gives very accessible advice." **Recent work:** Acted in Connaught Income Fund v Capita Financial Matters and Blue Gate Capital, relating to the mis-selling of an unregulated collective investment scheme.

Michael Douglas QC (see p.635) Handles a broad spread of professional negligence matters that includes a particular focus on representing construction professionals. He also takes on cases that involve lawyers, valuers and insurance brokers, and is involved in a growing amount of work with international aspects. **Strengths:** "A brilliant partner during tough litigation." "He's an excellent advocate and user-friendly." **Recent work:** Represented a firm of surveyors facing allegations of dishonestly overvaluing a number of newly built harbour properties.

Sean Brannigan QC (see p.601) Specialises in professional negligence cases arising in the energy and construction arenas, although he also handles claims involving accountants, solicitors, brokers and insurers. He has a growing reputation for his international work, particularly in the Middle and Far East. **Strengths:** "Sean is great with clients, and can assimilate key technical issues so that they can understand." "If you need a fighter on your side, he is your man." **Recent work:** Acted in Shangri-La Hotels v Sisk, a £45 million dispute arising from the construction of a hotel in the Shard building.

James Cross QC (see p.626) Diverse negligence practice with a particular slant towards disputes arising in the construction sector. He regularly advises on high-value claims that relate to catastrophes such as collapse, flooding and fire. **Strengths:** "He's got a brain the size of a planet and he can find different angles from which to approach an issue." "He has an incredible eye for detail and picks up points that others miss. When you have a complex multiparty issue, he is great." **Recent work:** Represented the defendant HFL Risk Services in a high-value negligence case concerning a catastrophic fire at a Yorkshire chemical plant.

Andrew Neish QC (see p.726) Strong insurance and reinsurance practitioner who is well placed to advise on disputes involving insurance brokers' negligence. He is also active on a range of other claims that include legal and financial professionals as well as those in the property sector. **Strengths:** "I'll go to him when I want someone to take on a difficult coverage point." "Robust commercial advice on credit insurance disputes makes him the go-to guy for us." **Recent work:** Acted in Brit UK Limited et al v BDO Canada LLP, a dispute relating to advice given to BDO Canada regarding tax avoidance schemes and coverage issues.

Benjamin Pilling QC (see p.738) Previously a leading junior for construction and technology-related disputes, Ben Pilling QC continues to build a very strong professional negligence practice in silk. In addition to advising architects, engineers and surveyors, he is also adept at handling claims relating to legal, financial and property services. **Strengths:** "He demonstrated an impressive and detailed knowledge of the factual and commercial issues." "A wonderfully calm advocate who makes the complex appear simple." **Recent work:** Represented Hyde Housing Association in bringing claims of defective design and workmanship against contractors after the destruction by fire of a sheltered accommodation building.

JUNIORS

Kate Livesey (see p.703) Very highly regarded junior who handles a wide array of professional negligence claims, including those brought against financial advisers, auctioneers, lawyers and many others. A significant amount of her work also comes from the construction sector. **Strengths:** "She is excellent, she shows great attention to detail and is very personable." "She is a standout junior who is destined for the top. She always seems to make time to deal with our cases and puts so much extra effort in." **Recent work:** Acted in Francis Bradshaw Partnership v AECOM, advising engineering consultants on a subrogated claim arising from allegedly negligent advice given by a geotechnical expert.

Luke Wygas (see p.800) Junior with an engineering background who is particularly adept at handling highly technical professional negligence claims. He dedicates much of his practice to acting for individuals in the construction industry, but also advises on claims relating to surveyors, accountants and solicitors. **Strengths:** "Inventive, bold and tenacious, he's very user-friendly with a quick turnaround." "He works hard to get the right result; he's great with clients and confident in court." **Recent work:** Represented the claimant in Lloyds Bank v McBains, which set legal precedence on the duties required of a bank monitoring surveyor.

3 Verulam Buildings

See profile on p.924

THE SET

An outstanding set for claims against financial services professionals, due to its noted strength in banking litigation and financial matters. In addition to representing accountants and investment brokers, its members act in disputes involving software designers, veterinary surgeons and chartered surveyors. Recent work highlights include McGraw-Hill v Deutsche Apotheker, concerning the duties of rating agencies, and Zurich Insurance v Aon UK, an £80 million reinsurance dispute following an incident at a petrochemical complex in the Netherlands. Market sources refer to 3 Verulam Buildings as a "prominent and well-established set."

Client service: "Practice manager Stephen Penson is a joy to deal with." "Stephen isn't just a clerk. He understands our industry and is always a welcome port of call for advice. He is very approachable, very personable and works as hard as we do."

SILKS

Tom Weitzman QC A formidable practitioner who has an equally strong reputation for his professional negligence and insurance expertise. As well as regularly representing professional indemnity insurers and brokers, he also works with a wide array of other professionals, including architects, engineers, solicitors, accountants and actuaries. **Strengths:** "He's an excellent practitioner with great organisational and advocacy skills." "He has wide experience and good attention to detail." "Extremely intelligent, precise and a team player."

Andrew Onslow QC Has a strong financial services and fraud practice which sits alongside his professional negligence work. As well as financial professionals, he also handles cases involving solicitors' negligence, and has niche expertise in representing auction houses in high-profile art disputes. **Strengths:** "Andrew was incredibly easy to work with, which is important when you are working under intense pressure. On his feet you could see he had the trust of the tribunal." "A very accomplished practitioner and advocate who works very well in the financial area." **Recent work:** Acted in Thwaytes v Sotheby's, defending the auction house against allegations of negligence relating to the appraisal of a Caravaggio painting.

Christopher Symons QC Represents a broad spectrum of professionals, including barristers, insurance brokers and financial advisers. He balances his work in professional negligence arbitration with a particularly impressive practice in handling major arbitrations. **Recent work:** Advised in SIAT v GMT Marine and Offshore Surveys Ltd, litigation brought against ship surveyors after a fire broke out in a shipyard.

David Head QC A new silk who is frequently instructed in a broad range of professional negligence work, David Head QC also boasts strong expertise in fraud, insurance and banking. He regularly advises clients in the financial sector, including brokers, accountants and auditors, along with solicitors and surveyors and a range of other professionals. **Strengths:** "He was very personable, instantly easy to work with, and at ease with the complex and scientific underlying factual substance of the dispute." "He's bright, and delivers a quick turnaround."

JUNIORS

Matthew Parker (see p.733) Handles a range of high-profile professional negligence cases on behalf of claimant and defendant parties. He is particularly well known for advising on cases alleging negligence on the part of accountants and solicitors. **Strengths:** "An impressive up-and-comer and an excellent advocate." **Recent work:** Appeared in NatWest Bank v Healys, acting for the defendant solicitors' firm, which faced negligence claims from the bank in relation to a property development venture.

Peter Ratcliffe Has considerable experience handling high-value claims relating to insurance brokers' negligence. His work in this area also regularly encompasses claims made against financial advisers and investment managers. **Strengths:** "He is thorough, conscientious and user-friendly." **Recent work:** Sole counsel for the defendant in Sanlam Securities v Merchant Cavendish Young, brought by a discretionary fund manager in relation to negligent fund management.

Wilberforce Chambers

See profile on p.925

THE SET

Leading commercial and chancery set with an enviable reputation at the Professional Negligence Bar. Members at Wilberforce Chambers are often instructed to act for and against legal and construction professionals, including solicitors, engineers and architects. Recent cases include CIP Properties v Galliford Try, concerning the redevelopment of Birmingham Children's Hospital, and Accolade Wines v VolkerFitzpatrick, a £170 million claim in respect of defective concrete flooring at a drinks distribution warehouse. Instructing solicitors comment on the "good spread of specialists" at the set and say: "They are difficult to beat, frankly."

Client service: "The clerking team is very helpful and goes above and beyond those of other sets I have used." "The clerks at Wilberforce are very commercial and very responsive." Nicholas Luckman is the practice director and Mark Rushton is the head clerk.

SILKS

Ian Croxford QC An impressive advocate who boasts an extensive track record of dealing with large-scale professional liability cases. Takes on claims involving a wide range of professionals, including civil engineers, stockbrokers, solicitors and management consultants, among others. **Strengths:** "He's robust, very good with clients, and one of the best cross-examiners I've ever seen." "His attention to detail and ability to identify alternative and sustainable arguments, combined with his pragmatic advice, is invaluable."

Paul Newman QC Best known for his pensions expertise, Paul Newman QC also has a wealth of experience in handling professional negligence claims relating to pension schemes and other financial services. **Strengths:** "Paul is very committed as an advocate, very confident and energetic." "An absolutely outstanding advocate, who fights with a passion which seems to be lacking in many others." **Recent work:** Acted in Strawson v Berkeley Burke, concerning an alleged failure to maintain accurate trust records as well as allegedly negligent tax advice.

Joanna Smith QC Highly thought of for her advocacy and her technical skills, Joanna Smith QC takes on a full spectrum of professional negligence claims, although she is especially well versed in cases concerning the construction industry. **Strengths:** "Her written work is fantastic, her advocacy is first class and she's excellent with clients." "By far the best and most supportive barrister I've ever worked with. She is down to earth and really values the importance of having a good relationship with her clients." **Recent work:** Acted for a subcontractor as one of the defendants in CIP Properties (AIPT) Limited v Galliford Try and Others, a multiparty claim alleging negligence in the redevelopment of Birmingham Children's Hospital.

John Wardell QC Maintains a strong commercial practice with a steady emphasis on professional negligence matters in which he acts for both claimants and defendants. He regularly takes on cases relating to legal, financial and property services, and also regularly defends other barristers against claims of negligence. **Strengths:** "He's very experienced, with an unerring instinct for what is important in a case." "I like the fact that he's bold and he sticks to his guns, he never sits on the fence." **Recent work:** In PB Limited v Watson Burton, defended a silk and junior facing negligence claims relating to advice they had given on the construction of an asset sale agreement.

James Ayliffe QC An experienced practitioner who regularly takes on high-value professional negligence claims. Particularly active on cases arising in the property and legal sectors, he also handles claims relating to accountants, actuaries and financial advisers, among others. **Strengths:** "He calms the clients down; he's very good at putting people at their ease." "James is very measured, and prepared to stick his neck out when it's the right thing to do." **Recent work:** Acted in Royal Mail Estates v Maples Teesdale, representing the defendant against a claim concerning a contract for the sale of a high-value development site in Kensington.

Jonathan Seitler QC Commands an impressive professional negligence practice in the property sector, often advising on claims relating to very high-value transactions. Regularly advises on cases brought as the result of allegedly faulty advice given by solicitors and valuers. **Strengths:** "He's very personable, gives good practical advice and is not scared to jump off the fence." "If it's a property-based claim, he would be the first person I'd think to go to." **Recent work:** Acted in Barker v Baxendale Walker, defending a solicitor against a £19 million professional negligence claim regarding tax advice.

Lexa Hilliard QC Although she is most often called upon to handle claims regarding accountants and insolvency practitioners, Lex Hilliard QC also regularly takes on a range of other professional negligence work. She regularly advises and litigates claims concerning auditors, investment advisers and solicitors, among others. **Strengths:** "Very good on complicated, cross-border matters, she's provided some concrete opinions on what are really complicated issues." "Widely experienced in the field, she has excellent client skills, is a pleasure to work with and is an extremely good advocate."

Clare Stanley QC Represents a broad range of professionals in high-value negligence claims, including legal, financial, accountancy and insolvency practitioners. She is often involved in cases featuring highly complex and technical elements, as well as allegations of fraud. **Strengths:** "With a very high level of technical ability, she's able to see a lot of the nuances in the case." "Clare provides highly intelligent, strategic and commercial advice." **Recent work:** Successfully defended the law firm Mishcon de Reya against claims that they acted negligently in the drafting of documents pursuant to the sale of Queens Park Rangers FC.

Band 4

1 Chancery Lane

THE SET

1 Chancery Lane boasts a commendable team of silks and juniors who practise in diverse areas of professional negligence. Its members are particularly experienced in claims involving the insurance, healthcare and construction industries, and can provide direct advice to clients under the Public Access Scheme. Recent case highlights include Sugar Hut Group v AJ Insurance, which concerned the limits of a fire insurance policy, and Bank of Scotland v Anglo Law Solicitors, in which a firm of lawyers was alleged to have acted negligently in with an impostor.

Client service: Jenny Fensham is the practice administrator, and Clark Chessis leads the clerking team.

SILKS

John Ross QC Venerable practitioner with over 40 years' experience practising at the Bar. Although he is highly experienced in handling negligence claims of all kinds, he typically focuses his work on cases involving surveyors, accountants, lawyers and insurance brokers. **Recent work:** Acted in Sugar Hut Group v AJ Insurance, a claim alleging that an insurance broker had provided a client with inadequate protection in a fire insurance policy.

JUNIORS

Ivor Collett A well-regarded junior who regularly handles claims relating to professionals in the construction and legal sectors. He also has considerable insurance expertise and regularly acts for insurers as well as defendants in professional indemnity litigation. **Strengths:** "His advice was succinct and he was never on the fence." "He is forensic in his consideration of documents and able to explain complex legal principles to lay clients with ease." **Recent work:** Acted in Santander v Fernandez, representing the defendant valuer against allegations of professional negligence, which also included claims of fraud.

Karen Shuman Combines her specialist chancery practice with a broad range of professional negligence expertise. Particularly well versed in claims that involve significant underlying property or probate issues in addition to claims of negligence. **Strengths:** "Karen has a breathtaking command of the practice area, combined with top-drawer client service and an ability to get to the heart of the matter with peerless acumen."

Andrew Spencer Focuses his practice on claims against surveyors and solicitors, and has notable expertise in handling property-related professional negligence claims. In particular, he is regularly instructed in claims concerning mishandled litigation and lenders' claims against solicitors and valuers. **Strengths:** "His ability to turn work around is incredible, he's very good at coming back with quick and considered certainty, and he's also a very commercial individual."

Crown Office Chambers

See profile on p.824

THE SET

Crown Office Chambers has a broad practice which covers a wide range of professions, including construction, legal and financial services. Members are highly regarded for their knowledge and litigation experience, and receive instructions from both claimant and defendant parties in complex and high-value disputes. Recent work highlights include Involnert Management v Aprilgrange, a EUR13 million claim against Lloyd's insurers for a superyacht destroyed by fire, and a claim against an expert witness alleged to have given faulty evidence at trial.

Client service: "They deal with things efficiently and promptly and with a great deal of flexibility." "They are responsive and get things done." Andy Flanagan is the senior managing clerk and Steve Purse is the senior team clerk.

SILKS

Michael Harvey QC Has a strong reputation for handling negligence issues in the arenas of construction and finance, and is often called upon to provide advice on the duties of professionals facing complex and difficult situations. He is also well known for his ability to handle claims against solicitors and insurance brokers. **Strengths:** "He really seems to know the law inside-out, and will always turn up fully prepared." "He's meticulous and user-friendly."

JUNIORS

Daniel Shapiro (see p.762) Top-level junior handling a broad spectrum of professional negligence cases that concern the actions and advice of lawyers, surveyors and insurance brokers, among others. He is able to act for both claimants and defendants, and has trial experience reaching all the way up to the Supreme Court. **Strengths:** "I consider his particular strengths to be his technical knowledge and expertise, his views and recommendations on case strategy, and his thoroughness." "Highly intelligent, responsive and tactically astute." **Recent work:** Appeared unled in the Commercial Court on behalf of the Greek brokers in Involnert Management Inc v Aprilgrange Ltd, concerning the destruction of a superyacht by fire.

Jason Evans-Tovey Regularly advises on matters arising from insurance disputes, including both property damage and professional negligence claims. He is frequently instructed in cases concerning a range of professionals including valuers, solicitors, financial advisers and planning consultants. **Strengths:** "He's very easy to work with, commercial, robust and practical, and he can be a bruiser in court when required." "I've used him on cases where I would have been happy to instruct a silk. He is a pleasure to work with and he doesn't just sit on the fence, he gives us an answer for where he thinks the case should go." **Recent work:** Acted in Metropolitan Venues Limited v Watson Burton LLP, which concerned negligence and breach of contract claims regarding a large property development in the North East.

7 King's Bench Walk

See profile on p.871

THE SET

A distinguished commercial set with a superb reputation in the insurance sector, 7 King's Bench Walk also offers robust representation on professional negligence matters. In particular, its members are regularly instructed on behalf of financial professionals including accountants, independent advisers, banks and hedge fund managers. Recent case highlights include Cattles v PwC, a £1.6 billion claim for audit negligence, and Sebry v Companies House, concerning the duty of care owed by the registrar to those on the UK register of companies.

Client service: "The clerks are very helpful. They take as much off your hands as they can." "We found the clerks easy to deal with, and we could always get hold of someone." Bernie Hyatt and Greg Leyden are the joint senior clerks.

SILKS

Jonathan Gaisman QC Displays particular strength in handling professional negligence claims in the financial sector, most often those of especially high worth or exposure. He has handled a number of very substantial auditors' negligence claims, and is also known for his extremely strong insurance practice. **Strengths:** "He's a very charismatic advocate and a great team player who knows when to be aggressive." "He is a terrifying advocate and very, very well established." **Recent work:** Represented claimant Cattles Plc in its claim for over £1.6 billion against PwC, alleging negligent auditing of financial statements in 2006 and 2007.

Christopher Butcher QC An insurance heavyweight who is also a well-established figure in the professional negligence world. He regularly acts on cases concerning insurance brokers, solicitors and accountants, with particular expertise in claims that arise out of allegedly faulty financial and auditing advice. **Strengths:** "I find him a very careful and persuasive advocate, and a very good predictor of what the judge will think. He has a tremendously sharp intellect which can cut right through difficult issues." **Recent work:** Defended Grant Thornton against Renewable Power & Light's claim that the firm breached its duty in affirming that the company was appropriate for AIM admission.

Rebecca Sabben-Clare QC Well-respected silk who has developed an established presence in the professional negligence field alongside her broadly commercial practice. Her work in this space encompasses a wide variety of claims concerning insurance brokers and solicitors, auditors and accountants. **Strengths:** "Clever, hard working and hands-on, she relishes responsibility and is fearless." "She has really good experience in the auditor negligence field and was able to get a good grasp of a fiendishly complicated case. She is extremely technical and very user-friendly." **Recent work:** Acted for Manchester Building Society in its claim against former auditors Grant Thornton, for negligence which allegedly cost the company £50 million in losses.

Andrew Wales QC Provides counsel to professional indemnity insurers as well as professionals facing negligence claims. Recent cases have involved claims against auditors, solicitors and manufacturers, among others. He is known for the international breadth of his practice, particularly in Asia. **Strengths:** "He has a huge intellect and is great on the detail." **Recent work:** Defended PwC against allegations that for six years they had negligently audited a company complicit in fraudulent gold trading.

JUNIORS

James Brocklebank (see p.603) Noted for his professional negligence and insurance expertise, James Brocklebank regularly handles major negligence claims relating to insurance brokers, financial advisers and accountants. **Strengths:** "James Brocklebank does terrifically good skeleton arguments, and is a tremendously talented practitioner." **Recent work:** Defended an insurance broker in the high-value Commercial Court claim concerning MY 'Galatea', a superyacht that was destroyed by fire.

Michael Ryan Up-and-coming junior who advises on high-profile negligence issues across a comprehensive array of professions, with a particular focus on claims concerning solicitors and auditors. He has appeared regularly on high-value Commercial Court claims and in complex, multiparty litigation. **Strengths:** "Michael Ryan is very approachable, and maintains a good knowledge of the case and the documents, even in complex matters." "He shows excellent attention to detail." **Recent work:** Represented Mishcon de Reya in a £34 million claim brought against the firm by liquidators following the collapse of a property investment company.

Band 5

Hardwicke

See profile on p.859

THE SET

Hardwicke demonstrates strength and depth across the professional negligence spectrum, and handles cases in the financial services, insurance, property and construction. The set's client base typically encompasses defendant solicitors, estate agents, architects and other professionals, as well as those on the claimant side. Members of this set have recently been instructed in Blakemores LDP (in admin) v Scott and Others, representing the claimant firm in pursuit of £700,000 in unpaid legal fees, on the grounds that the claim itself had been dealt with negligently. Those who instruct them observe that barristers at the set are "very commercial, very efficient and very smart."

Client service: "The clerks are extremely helpful, and always prepared to be flexible." "The clerks are very responsive, and alive to commercial and time pressures." Deborah Anderson is the practice director.

SILKS

Nigel Jones QC Draws on his extensive experience in commercial litigation and insurance law to bolster his robust professional negligence practice. Regularly instructed in cases that concern accountants, solicitors and surveyors, among others. He is also co-head of chambers at Hardwicke. **Strengths:** "He's absolutely charming, with an incredible intellect, and he made us feel at ease straight away." "He's a superb advocate, a great black letter lawyer on paper, and he has great commercial instinct as well." **Recent work:** Represented Wright Hassall in a claim for unpaid fees as well as the firm's defence of a professional negligence claim brought by a former client.

John de Waal QC Handles a broad range of professional negligence cases, most often on behalf of defendants, and is particularly well versed in claims concerning solicitors. He also maintains a broad advisory practice, largely catering to insurer clients. **Strengths:** "He gives sound advice and is quick to respond: he is commercial and understands the work that we do." "He is technically very good, and he really understands the client's commercial needs and wants." **Recent work:** Acted for defendant solicitors in Ivor Ferreira v Lloyd & Associates LLP, a £2 million negligence claim in relation to property investment.

JUNIORS

James Hall A junior who moved to Hardwicke in 2015, James Hall takes on substantial negligence claims relating to surveyors, architects and solicitors. He is also able to draw upon his previous experience as an employed barrister in the financial services department of a national law firm. **Strengths:** "He has an innovative approach to problem solving and gives commercial and pragmatic advice at a level clients love." "He's one of the most commercially minded barristers I've come across." **Recent work:** Acted for the claimant in Freemont (Denbigh Ltd) v Knight Frank LLP, an £8 million claim for negligent overvaluing of a commercial property.

Sarah McCann Highly capable junior who advises on professional negligence claims in the construction industry as well as the financial, property and legal sectors. Advises both claimant and defendant parties and also takes on matters concerning professional indemnity insurance. **Strengths:** "She filtered through all the information to produce a great response that pulled everything together." "Fastidious in her preparation and extremely generous with her time." **Recent work:** Acted for the defendant valuer in EGT Finance Ltd v Stocker & Roberts and Others, a £1.5 million claim relating to the alleged overvaluation of a property.

Maitland Chambers

See profile on p.875

THE SET

Maitland Chambers is a leading commercial chancery set with a distinguished reputation, handling high-profile professional negligence cases. As leading practitioners in areas such as real estate and insolvency, members combine specialist knowledge of professional negligence matters with an expert command of the underlying law. Recent cases include Lloyds Bank v Nattrass Giles, a dispute regarding the proceeds of a global settlement with a negligent professional, and Instant Access Properties v Rosser, a £35 million claim against the directors and advisers of a property investment company.

Client service: Stewart Thompson is the chambers director and John Wiggs leads the clerking team.

SILKS

Thomas Grant QC Acts mainly on financial and legal sector negligence claims, with broad experience in the courts all the way up to appellate level. He wins praise for the strength of his advocacy and is considered "a barrister you'd much rather have on your side than against you." **Strengths:** "Powerful and persuasive in his advocacy." "Tom Grant is very forthright, and also extremely popular with his clients." **Recent work:** Acted for the respondent bank in the Court of Appeal concerning Lloyds Bank v Nattrass Giles, which challenged the allocation of proceeds after a settlement with a negligent individual.

Anthony Trace QC (see p.783) Typically called upon to handle complex professional negligence cases involving solicitors, and often on behalf of high-profile City law firms. He is a respected advocate who displays a notable proficiency in matters requiring extensive cross-examination. **Strengths:** "He's a real whirlwind, incredibly punchy and very, very enthusiastic." "He's a first-rate advocate and a leader."

XXIV Old Buildings

See profile on p.884

THE SET

XXIV Old Buildings acts in a large number of high-value and complex professional negligence matters. Members are known for their expertise in financial mismanagement cases, and typically act in claims against trustees, fiduciaries and professional advisers. Recent work highlights include Jackson & Money v Gershinson, a claim against the directors of a company in liquidation, and Choicezone v Barclays Bank, a dispute in respect of a mis-sold interest rate swap.

Client service: Sue Medder is the chambers director.

SILKS

Alan Steinfeld QC Seasoned practitioner who regularly advises on professional negligence cases of a highly complex nature as part of his wider commercial litigation practice. His work in this space is bolstered by his fine credentials in fraud, insolvency and company law. **Strengths:** "He just gets the law; he's got something you can't teach. He's relentless, and judges defer to him on points of law." "He's brilliant in court." **Recent work:** Acted in Crest Nicholson v Regional, a claim for rectification and professional negligence.

Francis Tregear QC Experienced silk who offers comprehensive experience in the domain of professional negligence. He handles a vast array of claims arising from breaches of trust, contract and fiduciary duty, as well as misrepresentation and defective documentation. **Strengths:** "Very good on shareholder disputes." **Recent work:** Acted in Jackson and Money v Gershinson and Others, involving allegations that directors of a liquidated company breached fiduciary duty in their tax planning measures.

JUNIORS

Elizabeth Weaver Senior junior Elizabeth Weaver has extensive experience in professional negligence cases and focuses particularly on claims in the financial sector. She is particularly adept at tackling negligence issues in the context of disputed trusts. **Strengths:** "A senior junior who is very good and very reliable."

Serle Court

See profile on p.908

THE SET

Serle Court is noted for its strength in professional negligence disputes, particularly those with significant chancery elements. Members at the set are especially adept at handling claims for and against financial professionals, including banks, insurers and insolvency practitioners. Recent work highlights include Thwaytes v Sothebys, concerning a painting misattributed to Caravaggio, and Walker v Stuart Smalley, which arose from a tax avoidance case.

Client service: John Petrie is the chief executive of chambers, and Steve Whitaker is the head clerk.

SILKS

Philip Jones QC (see p.686) Regularly instructed by both sides on professional negligence cases relating to a broad range of business professionals, including accountants, lawyers, company administrators and tax advisers. His practice benefits from his comprehensive understanding of commercial chancery law. **Strengths:** "He gets to the point very quickly, takes a very clear approach to the case and in the interlocutory hearings he's good on his feet." **Recent work:** Defended Monaco-based accountants and service providers against a negligence claim following the collapse of an investment fund in the Cayman Islands.

Philip Marshall QC (see p.708) A commercial chancery barrister with a notable focus on professional negligence matters, Philip Marshall QC can also bring to bear his familiarity with insolvency, banking and civil fraud issues. He serves as both a Recorder and a Deputy High Court Judge. **Strengths:** "His handle on the law and his advocacy are both incredible." **Recent work:** Acted in Dickson v Christies, regarding the misattribution and inaccurate valuation of a painting by Titian.

2TG – 2 Temple Gardens

See profile on p.920

THE SET

2 Temple Gardens is a common and commercial law set with a reputation for excellence in complex, high-value and sensitive professional negligence claims. Its members have diverse strengths covering areas such as insurance, healthcare and construction. Recent case highlights include Gaze v Harcus Sinclair, a £15 million claim against solicitors and barristers arising out of unsuccessful litigation, and Towergate Risk Solutions v Bluebon, concerning the alleged negligence of insurance brokers following a catastrophic hotel fire.

Client service: "The clerks are very good at picking the right people. They have been patient with us and kept diaries as clear as possible." Lee Tyler is the senior clerk.

SILKS

Charles Dougherty QC (see p.635) Charles Dougherty QC is regularly instructed in negligence issues concerning a diverse range of professionals, including financial intermediaries, insurance brokers and other barristers. He complements this work with strong practices in insurance, fraud and product liability, and also has a broad focus on international work. **Strengths:** "He is very thorough, clear and measured, as well as being user-friendly and easy to work with." "Absolutely razor sharp and confidence-inspiring." **Recent work:** Acted for a firm of solicitors bringing a negligence claim against the Law Society for including the details of a firm on their website which turned out to be fake.

JUNIORS

David Thomas (see p.780) An up-and-coming barrister who frequently tackles professional negligence claims relating to surveyors, brokers and solicitors. He has considerable expertise in commercial fraud, meaning that he often acts for defendants on claims involving fraudulent or dishonest behaviour. **Strengths:** "He's easy to work with, very reliable and hard-working; he can take the lead when he needs to." "He turns things around quickly and always gives good-quality work."

Other Ranked Lawyers

Colin Edelman QC (see p.639) (Devereux) An esteemed silk who is an expert in insurance and reinsurance brokers' negligence claims. He also takes on extensive work relating to other kinds of professional negligence, including acting for and against lawyers, architects and financial advisers, to name a few. **Strengths:** "He's a prodigious and astonishing individual whose knowledge of the law is phenomenal, as is his ability to grasp the facts of a case." "He provides extremely clear and thorough advice."

Alexander Polley (see p.739) (One Essex Court) Highly capable junior who is regularly involved in complex, multiparty litigation, often with an international aspect. His professional negligence practice has a particular focus on handling claims against solicitors and auditors. **Strengths:** "He's calm, assured, and he's got a modesty about him that belies how smart he is." "Very impressive, commercial and good at drafting." **Recent work:** Defended PwC against claims by financial services group Cattles that auditors had failed to recognise fraudulent activity within the company over several years.

Helen Pugh (see p.744) (3 Hare Court) Up-and-comer Helen Pugh increasingly focuses her practice on professional negligence disputes, in which she acts both for and against lawyers, accountants and surveyors, among others. She also takes on a significant amount of work in an advisory capacity as well as handling alternative dispute resolution proceedings. **Strengths:** "A real asset to our team who worked incredibly hard and who clearly knows this area well." "She comes well prepared, she is very good at announcing right at the beginning what the main issues are going to be." **Recent work:** Acted for the claimant in Symrise AG v Baker & McKenzie, a case involving allegations of negligent Mexican tax advice in connection with a USD1.5 billion merger.

David Yates (see p.801) (Pump Court Tax Chambers) Has a niche specialism in tax and finance-focused professional negligence claims, which is greatly enhanced by his former career as a corporate financial analyst. He has advised on a wide range of financial claims relating to film finance schemes and offshore trusts, as well as faulty tax, accountancy and legal advice. **Strengths:** "With an absolute command of the most complex technical issues, and a matched ability to distil them for those less familiar, David provides a top-drawer service with style."

Keith Rowley QC (see p.756) (Radcliffe Chambers) Highly respected silk who acts for and against professionals ranging from financial advisers and stockbrokers to actuaries, accountants and barristers. His work encompasses the full extent of professional negligence, although he is particularly well known for his strength in pensions-related cases. **Strengths:** "He's very thorough and very experienced. He often appears in hotly contested professional negligence claims."

Jeremy Cousins QC (Radcliffe Chambers) Has almost four decades of experience at the Bar which includes considerable involvement in major professional negligence cases. Regularly takes on claims relating to solicitors' negligence, although he also handles issues arising from breach of fiduciary duty and other financial issues. **Strengths:** "He is excellent: he has an eye for detail, is incredibly thorough and looks at things in a very calm way." **Recent work:** Acted in AIB v Redler & Co, bringing a claim against a solicitor accused of breaching trust by releasing funds without authority during a property transaction.

Thomas Dumont (see p.637) (Radcliffe Chambers) A vastly experienced senior junior who is a veteran at the Chancery Bar, Thomas Dumont is also very active in the field of professional negligence. His main area of focus is in representing accountants and solicitors in negligence claims arising out of tax and estate planning disputes. **Strengths:** "He has a practice balanced between professional negligence and chancery, which is a rare thing. He's an experienced advocate but he's also fun to work with and makes our clients feel relaxed."

Hugh Jackson (see p.681) (Selborne Chambers) Impressive senior junior who undertakes a significant number of professional negligence cases involving property and chancery elements. Regularly acts for clients on both sides of complex, multiparty litigation, especially with regard to allegedly negligent advice from solicitors, tax and financial advisers. **Strengths:** "He's a pleasure to work with, commercial and a good tactician." "An extremely hard worker with great client skills, he's a real team player who goes the extra mile." **Recent work:** Continues to represent Mishcon de Reya against a high-value claim of professional negligence by the former trustee in a case of personal bankruptcy.

LONDON Technology & Construction

Professional Negligence Technology & Construction
Leading Sets
Band 1
Atkin Chambers *
Keating Chambers *
4 Pump Court *
Band 2
Crown Office Chambers *
39 Essex Chambers *
4 New Square *
* Indicates set / individual with profile.
◊ (ORL) = Other Ranked Lawyer.
Alphabetical order within each band. Band 1 is highest.

Professional Negligence: Technology & Construction	
Senior Statesmen	
Senior Statesmen: distinguished older partners	
Friedman David *4 Pump Court*	
Leading Silks	
Band 1	**Moran** Vincent *Keating Chambers* *
Brannigan Sean *4 Pump Court* *	**Nissen** Alexander *Keating Chambers* *
Catchpole Stuart *39 Essex Chambers*	**Rawley** Dominique *Atkin Chambers* *
Douglas Michael *4 Pump Court* *	**Sears** David *Crown Office Chambers*
McMullan Manus *Atkin Chambers*	**Sinclair** Fiona *4 New Square* *
Rigney Andrew *Crown Office Chambers*	**Williamson** Adrian *Keating Chambers* *
Stewart Roger *4 New Square* *	**Band 3**
Streatfeild-James David *Atkin Chambers*	**Bowdery** Martin *Atkin Chambers*
Taverner Marcus *Keating Chambers* *	**Cannon** Mark *4 New Square* *
ter Haar Roger *Crown Office Chambers*	**Constable** Adam *Keating Chambers* *
White Andrew *Atkin Chambers* *	**Dennys** Nicholas *Atkin Chambers*
Wilmot-Smith Richard *39 Essex Chambers*	**Hargreaves** Simon *Keating Chambers* *
Band 2	**Lemon** Jane *Keating Chambers* *
Ansell Rachel *4 Pump Court* *	**Marrin** John *Keating Chambers* *
Baatz Nicholas *Atkin Chambers*	**Nicholson** Jeremy *4 Pump Court* *
Cross James *4 Pump Court* *	**Parkin** Fiona *Atkin Chambers*
Darling Paul *Keating Chambers* *	**Pilling** Benjamin *4 Pump Court* *
Day Anneliese *4 New Square* *	**Quiney** Ben *Crown Office Chambers*
Dennison Stephen *Atkin Chambers*	**New Silks**
Doerries Chantal-Aimée *Atkin Chambers* *	**Hickey** Alexander *4 Pump Court* *
Lofthouse Simon *Atkin Chambers* *	**Hussain** Riaz *Atkin Chambers* *
Moody Neil *2TG - 2 Temple Gardens (ORL)* ◊ *	

Band 1

Atkin Chambers

See profile on p.806

THE SET

A go-to set for virtually any kind of construction dispute, Atkin Chambers can also claim to have one of the foremost teams for professional negligence work in this field. Members represent claimant and defendant parties and are instructed on behalf of individual professionals, their employers and indemnity insurers based domestically and abroad. Recent work highlights include Wellesley v Withers, a claim for losses caused by the drafting of a partnership agreement, and Accolade Wines v VolkerFitzpatrick, pertaining to the defective construction of a floor slab at a drinks warehouse. Instructing solicitors refer to the "undoubted technical excellence" of the barristers, while also praising their ability to work together smoothly as a team.

Client service: "The clerks are always available, always willing to help, proactive and prompt in responding." "The clerks are very capable and very good at doing deals on fees." Fay Gillott is chief executive of the set and Justin Wilson leads the clerking team.

SILKS

Manus McMullan QC Advises on a wide array of professional negligence claims in construction and technology contexts, including an increasing number of an international nature. He handles cases relating to architects, surveyors and engineers as well as software developers, systems analysts and computer programmers. **Strengths:** "Outrageously clever, he puts other lawyers to shame with his legal knowledge." "He's brilliant with clients, excellent on his feet, self-sufficient and very calm."

David Streatfeild-James QC Brings to bear his 30 years' experience at the Bar when handling complex and often high-profile negligence claims regarding contractors, architects and other construction professionals. He is able to serve as an arbitrator or ad-

Professional Negligence Technology & Construction
Leading Juniors
Band 1
Henderson Simon *4 Pump Court* *
McCafferty Lynne *4 Pump Court* *
Band 2
Collings Nicholas *Atkin Chambers* *
Coplin Richard *Keating Chambers* *
Garrett Lucy *Keating Chambers* *
Ghaly Karim *39 Essex Chambers* *
Hanna Ronan *Atkin Chambers* *
Lamont Calum *Keating Chambers* *
Leabeater James *4 Pump Court* *
Pliener David *Hardwicke (ORL)* ◊ 🄰
Robb Adam *39 Essex Chambers*
Slow Camille *Atkin Chambers* *
* *Indicates individual with profile.*
🄰 *direct access (see p.24).*
◊ *(ORL) = Other Ranked Lawyer.*
Alphabetical order within each band. Band 1 is highest.

judicator as well as an advocate. **Strengths:** "Astute, perceptive and imaginative, David picks things up incredibly quickly, and his advice is practical as well as technical." **Recent work:** Represented the defendant contractor in a TCC action alleging defects in the design and construction of a guided busway in Cambridgeshire.

Andrew White QC (see p.793) Head of chambers Andrew White QC handles a wide range of domestic and international disputes, including negligence claims arising from major construction, oil and gas, shipbuilding, rail and engineering projects. He regularly tackles matters in the High Court and also handles a significant number of arbitrations both in the UK and abroad. **Strengths:** "His advice is very straightforward and delivered in a manner that is easy to understand and follow."

Nicholas Baatz QC Vastly experienced barrister who is deeply familiar with handling cases through the TCC as well as in adjudication. He undertakes claims against engineers, architects and contractors, acting for claimants and defendants. **Strengths:** "An excellent lawyer with absolutely brilliant client skills." "Extremely good on a case where the issues are very difficult." **Recent work:** Advised CIP Property in its claims against architects, engineers and contractors involved in the design and construction of a residential, retail and leisure complex in Birmingham.

Stephen Dennison QC Seasoned practitioner whose varied practice takes in construction and engineering, energy, transport and utilities work alongside associated insurance, professional negligence and public procurement matters. Continues to handle major litigation as well as domestic and international arbitrations. **Strengths:** "Very able. Provides clear commercial advice that clients readily understand. An excellent advocate who is always cool, calm and collected." **Recent work:** Acted for the defendant in Newcastle NHS Trust v Healthcare Services Newcastle and Laing O'Rourke, regarding claims relating to the construction of clinical support offices in a hospital renewal plan.

Chantal-Aimée Doerries QC (see p.635) Undertakes a considerable amount of professional negligence work, most often in large construction and infrastructure projects. She has recently been instructed in claims against engineers, quantity surveyors and architects, among others. **Strengths:** "A well-respected QC at the Construction Bar who is also carving out a real niche for herself in international arbitration."

Simon Lofthouse QC (see p.703) Frequently instructed in complex professional negligence disputes on behalf of both claimant and defendant parties. He is equal to handling any number of highly technical claims relating to major residential and commercial developments, engineering projects and IT installations. **Strengths:** "He is ferociously intelligent, an absolutely formidable advocate and immensely well prepared on his paperwork. By the time you instruct him, he's already three steps ahead of you."

Dominique Rawley QC (see p.748) Acts in a wide array of high-value engineering and construction matters, including professional negligence cases, often revolving around complicated technical and contractual aspects. He regularly appears in the TCC and also handles adjudications and arbitrations. **Strengths:** "A very clever advocate who can make a bad case look like a shining diamond." "Dominique has an eye for detail and enthusiasm for the case." **Recent work:** Acted for the defendant in Hyde Housing Association v Osborn, concerning claims that negligent fire protection design at a sheltered accommodation building allowed a fire to spread.

Martin Bowdery QC Specialises in professional negligence claims relating to major construction and engineering projects, including everything from power stations and reservoirs to IT systems and motorways. He acts for domestic and international parties in litigation as well as ADR proceedings. **Strengths:** "An extremely bright barrister who is imaginative, creative and prepared to give strong advice." "Offers a very commercial approach and is a good lateral thinker." **Recent work:** Defended Cumbria County Council in a PFI dispute relating to allegedly defective highway works.

Nicholas Dennys QC Acts as advocate and adviser to a wide range of clients facing domestic and international disputes in construction, engineering, IT and infrastructure projects. His practice involves a significant proportion of professional negligence cases, including a number of recent instructions in the transport sector. **Strengths:** "Nick Dennys is superb: a great performer and a talented advocate."

Fiona Parkin QC Instructed on behalf of professionals, multinational companies, government and public bodies facing a wide range of professional negligence claims. He regularly advises on matters emerging out of major international infrastructure projects. **Strengths:** "An excellent lawyer who is very much a details person and who creates a good rapport with clients." **Recent work:** Represented executive search agency Wellesley Partners, who brought a claim against law firm Withers LLP for losses incurred as a consequence of a negligently drafted partnership agreement.

Riaz Hussain QC (see p.679) A new silk who focuses his practice on the construction and engineering sectors, Riaz Hussain QC also has significant international arbitration experience. He is regularly instructed in negligence claims pertaining to design and construction defects in major building works, including PFI projects. **Strengths:** "Gets to grips with the details of the case quickly: he is easy to work with and gives clear direction." **Recent work:** Acted in Brunel v SSE and Aecom, a TCC case brought against a contractor concerning the allegedly negligent design of an electrical system.

JUNIORS

Nicholas Collings (see p.620) Has a busy professional negligence practice encompassing the IT, construction, natural resources and energy sectors. He is instructed in domestic and international disputes, and represents designers, developers, contractors and other construction professionals, as well as insurers and brokers. **Strengths:** "An excellent advocate." **Recent work:** Acted for the claimant in G&J Stone Group v Markel and Others, a claim against insurers and brokers for negligent litigation advice on a large residential development project.

Ronan Hanna (see p.663) Has wide-ranging expertise in engineering and construction disputes, and significant experience in professional negligence cases involving engineers, contractors and architects, among others. Adept at managing claims through the courts, he also regularly undertakes adjudication and arbitration work. **Strengths:** "User-friendly and a team player, with a fantastic work ethic." **Recent work:** Acted in Persimmon Homes v Arup, involving claims against an engineer arising out of the contamination of a development site in South Wales.

Camille Slow (see p.767) An experienced junior who specialises in construction and professional negligence, often taking on multiparty claims of significantly high value. She is particularly well versed in social housing and PFI project disputes. **Strengths:** "A real team player who is prepared to roll up her sleeves and get stuck into the evidence, She comes up with compelling and well thought through arguments." **Recent work:** Acted in Newlon Housing Trust v Sir Robert McAlpine and Buro Happold and Populous, a case concerning defects in a social housing development in the new Emirates Stadium.

Keating Chambers

See profile on p.868

THE SET

Keating Chambers enjoys a leading reputation at the Construction Bar and its specialist knowledge extends to professional negligence matters. Members act for and against construction professionals of all types, including architects, contractors, surveyors and project managers. Recent work highlights include Buchan v Hyder, a £30 million claim against engineering consultants relating to a commercial car park, and a £20 million dispute over the renovation of 125 Old Broad Street in the City of London. It is a go-to set for many instructing solicitors faced with complicated construction claims.

Client service: "I have always enjoyed working with the clerks at Keating. They are professional, reasonable, sensible and proactive. When I have issues regarding fees, they do their best to resolve them." Declan Redmond is CEO and director of clerking.

SILKS

Marcus Taverner QC (see p.778) Has an exceptional reputation as a construction silk; he also possesses deep expertise in professional negligence and international arbitration generally. He regularly acts for blue-chip clients around the world in extremely high-profile cases, many of which involve catastrophic design and construction defects. **Strengths:** "Supremely clever and enthusiastic, he has the ability to see around corners. He is also a brilliant advocate." **Recent work:** Acted in Buchan v Hyder, a negligence claim brought against consultant engineers involved in the design of a large car park.

Paul Darling QC (see p.629) A silk who has cultivated an impressively global practice, particularly in energy and construction-related disputes. He has significant experience in professional negligence matters, and has brought such cases to the TCC and High Court as well as the appellate courts. **Strengths:** "He is constantly able to come up with clear and strong arguments no matter how complicated, document-heavy or weak a case is. His solutions are creative and commercially sensible."

Vincent Moran QC (see p.721) Well known as an experienced advocate and adviser on a wide range of professional negligence matters connected to the construction industry. He regularly represents contractors, architects and designers, among other parties, as both claimants and defendants in high-value multiparty disputes. **Strengths:** "He's extremely hard working, imaginative, safe and commercial." "He is a tenacious fighter for his clients." **Recent work:** Advised defendant architects in Carillion Construction Ltd v Woods Bagot, AECOM Ltd and Emcor Ltd, a negligence-related claim pertaining to the design and construction of the new High Court building.

Alexander Nissen QC (see p.728) Seasoned practitioner mainly representing professionals in the energy, engineering and construction spheres, but also regularly appearing in legal and property services cases. **Strengths:** "If I have a challenging or technical question, I go to him straight away." "He has exceptional analytical skills, and is strategically very good." **Recent work:** Acted in Accolade v VolkerFitzpatrick and Others, a multiparty dispute relating to the defective design and construction of a large wine warehouse in Bristol.

Adrian Williamson QC (see p.797) Highly experienced in construction law and related professional negligence matters. He is regularly instructed to act for claimant and defendant parties in project manager, architect, engineer and quantity surveyor cases. **Strengths:** "He really rolls his sleeves up and gets into the detail." "Always efficient and quick to respond with high-quality advice. A hugely persuasive and highly skilled advocate." **Recent work:** Acted in the appeal of West v IFA, concerning the powers conferred by a net contribution clause.

Adam Constable QC (see p.621) Particularly adept at handling technical claims relating to large-scale or intricate engineering and construction work, including negligence disputes. His practice involves acting for and against professionals, including project managers, engineers and architects. **Strengths:** "He's incredibly intelligent, gets straight to the point and provides clear, concise advice." "He is commercially minded, and always provides practical and user-friendly advice." **Recent work:** Acted in Costain v Jacobs and URS, pursuing claims for negligent design checking in the construction of a waste management centre.

Simon Hargreaves QC (see p.664) Has extensive experience of negligence claims against professionals across an array of industries, including the technology, engineering and construction sectors. A talented litigator, he also handles all forms of ADR and is regularly instructed in complex multiparty disputes. **Strengths:** "He's a very good advocate, and he's prepared to roll up his sleeves and get involved." **Recent work:** Acted in Liberty Mercian Limited v Cuddy Civil Engineering Limited, a dispute arising from a landslip at a retail development.

Jane Lemon QC (see p.699) Continues to build a strong practice in silk as a construction and professional negligence specialist,; she also excels in the field of international arbitration. She handles claims relating to such diverse areas as engineering, shipbuilding and energy, and is also adept at acting on behalf of professional indemnity insurers. **Strengths:** "Incredibly bright, thorough and hard working, she is just a joy to work with. In terms of her advocacy, she's not at all afraid to go for the jugular, and can be very effective in her cross-examination." **Recent work:** Acted for Leeds City Council in bringing claims for negligence in the construction of a retaining wall that resulted in several landslips and a major highway closure.

John Marrin QC (see p.708) Vastly experienced silk who appears regularly in the High Court and Court of Appeal, but also takes on the full range of ADR, including significant international arbitration work. He is familiar with the full extent of energy, engineering and construction law, and is frequently retained on complex professional liability claims in these areas.

JUNIORS

Richard Coplin (see p.623) A qualified engineer who previously worked in the renewable and alternative energy sectors, Richard Coplin can provide highly specialised advice on technology and construction negligence matters. He regularly handles claims involving engineers, architects and surveyors, and is adept at litigation and ADR such as arbitration and adjudication. **Strengths:** "Dealing with engineering claims comes as second nature to him; he's also good on his feet." "He's a part of the team, and a real can-do lawyer." **Recent work:** Acted in CIP v Galliford Try, a high-value multiparty dispute regarding defects at a shopping centre.

Lucy Garrett (see p.650) Practises across the sectors of energy, construction and shipbuilding, and handles significant professional negligence disputes in these areas. She is often called on to litigate high-value matters in the Commercial Court and the TCC, and also gets involved in major arbitrations. **Strengths:** "She's an absolutely first-class lawyer who works phenomenally hard, and her client skills are second to none." "Highly commercially astute." **Recent work:** Acted for the claimant in Warburtons Limited v CH Babb Co. Inc, a case resulting after a large oven installed by the defendant caused significant fire damage to the claimant's factory.

Calum Lamont (see p.694) A well-established junior at the Construction Bar who has a rapidly expanding practice in the field of professional negligence and related insurance issues. He regularly handles high-value matters not only in the UK but also in the Middle East. **Strengths:** "He's a great adviser and you get the feeling he knows exactly what he's doing." "Calum is very hard working, very commercial, good with clients and quick on his feet." **Recent work:** Represented the claimant in the high-profile case of Accolade Wines v GJ3 and Others, regarding allegedly defective flooring at a Bristol wine warehouse.

4 Pump Court

See profile on p.895

THE SET

Although 4 Pump Court has a broad professional negligence practice, the quality of its work in construction and technology matters stands out. Members represent claimants and defendants, together with their insurers, and are noted for their international experience in the Middle and Far East. Recent work highlights include Shangri-La Hotels v Sisk, a £45 million dispute arising from the construction of the Shard building in London, and a significant DIAC arbitration concerning a landmark building in Dubai. "I really value the approach taken by their barristers," says one instructing solicitor, "they are very pragmatic and clients readily understand them." **Client service:** "The standard of their clerks is a cut above other sets." "Not every case is the same and they know that." Carolyn McCombe is chief executive and head of clerking at 4 Pump Court.

SILKS

David Friedman QC Highly esteemed for the strength of his construction practice, David Friedman QC is also well equipped to handle professional negligence disputes in this sector. His work often involves claims connected to substantial international projects in the energy sector. **Strengths:** "He is very considered in his approach, very analytical and a good advocate. He is also very user-friendly for both clients and instructing solicitors."

Rachel Ansell QC (see p.584) A very capable junior silk who has an impressive and wide-reaching practice taking in major construction, insurance and property damage cases alongside professional negligence. As well as her strong domestic practice, she has built a considerable presence in the UAE and regularly handles cases in the Middle East. **Strengths:** "She's unbelievably thorough, very responsive, aware of the commercial realities and not afraid to put her name to a recommendation." "She's very commercially astute and tough." **Recent work:** Acted for the structural engineers and their insurers in an arbitration case appertaining to the construction of an international exhibition centre in the Middle East.

Jeremy Nicholson QC (see p.727) Vastly experienced silk who focuses on negligence claims relating to construction projects, particularly those with significant multiparty interests. He is eminently capable of handling highly technical cases concerning architects, engineers, surveyors and other construction professionals. **Strengths:** "He's very proactive in the advice he gives, he's got a keen eye for detail and he's good with clients." "He's an incredibly subtle thinker who is very bright and approachable." **Recent work:** Acted in Francis Bradshaw Partnership v AECOM, a claim against consultant engineers for negligent advice following the collapse of a retaining wall at a retail park.

Alexander Hickey QC (see p.670) New silk who is capable of advising on either side of claims relating to surveyors', architects' and engineers' negligence. He is regularly instructed in complex litigation proceedings regarding new developments, environmental risk assessment and property finance. **Strengths:** "Very incisive, he cuts to the chase on an issue, he's excellent with witnesses and he has a very quick turnaround speed." "Commercially minded, he inspires confidence in his clients." **Recent work:** Acted in Tuita International v De Villiers Surveyors, defending a valuer against allegations that they negligently revalued a project where a borrower sought further funding.

James Cross QC (see p.626) Please see editorial on p.460.

Benjamin Pilling (see p.738) Please see editorial on p.460.

Michael Douglas (see p.635) Please see editorial on p.460.

Sean Brannigan (see p.601) Please see editorial on p.460.

JUNIORS

Simon Henderson (see p.669) A strong performer in the areas of construction and information technology, Simon Henderson is able to advise comprehensively on professional negligence matters within these fields. His direct experience of working in the IT sector means he is especially well placed to assist in technology claims. **Strengths:** "He's very hands-on, and has a great in-depth knowledge of construction. A very good advocate who is calm on his feet, he is also very good with clients." "He's clever, no-nonsense, and gets to the point." **Recent work:** Acted in Barnsley College v WYG Engineering & Galliford Try, defending mechanical and electrical engineers against claims relating to alleged defects in the air conditioning of a new college facility.

Lynne McCafferty (see p.711) Counsels a broad range of construction and technology-based clients on negligence claims, and represents surveyors, architects, computing consultants and software designers. She also has wide experience of dealing with professional indemnity insurers on associated coverage matters. **Strengths:** "She's very detailed, very user-friendly and very efficient; she can assimilate very detailed technical matters very quickly." **Recent work:** Acted for the defendant in Francis Bradshaw Partnership v AECOM Infrastructure Partnership, a high-value contribution claim against a firm of geotechnical engineers arising from earlier TCC litigation.

James Leabeater (see p.698) Handles the full gamut of construction-related professional negligence, including cases against engineers and architects, project managers, valuers and quantity surveyors. His varied practice sees him handling claims arising from high-end residential developments to major international and offshore energy projects. **Strengths:** "James Leabeater has an impressive intellect." "He is bright, hard working and very user-friendly." **Recent work:** Acted in Yeomans Row Partners v Michael Barclay Partnership LLP and Other, a case against structural engineers with regard to two residential developments in Kensington.

Band 2

Crown Office Chambers

See profile on p.824

THE SET

Highly respected for its construction and insurance expertise, Crown Office Chambers can also claim involvement in many of the most significant professional negligence cases to reach the TCC. These have included substantial claims arising out of major transport, energy, infrastructure and development projects. Members have recently acted in Iliffe v Feltham Construction, a £6 million claim resulting from the destruction by fire of a mansion on a private island, and Arije SAS v Albany Interiors, a £2 million dispute over the quality of the security devices installed in a jewellery shop that was robbed. Sources characterise Crown Office as "a quality set with plenty of experience to hand and a variety of specialisms."

Client service: Senior managing clerk Andy Flanagan leads the clerking team, which wins plaudits for its responsiveness and transparency on billing arrangements. Steve Purse, senior clerk in charge of the professional negligence team, is singled out for particular praise: "Steve is excellent. Nothing is too much for him. He understands the need to provide good service, manage fees and get everything organised."

SILKS

Roger ter Haar QC Widely experienced in professional liability of all types, Roger ter Haar QC regularly represents claimants and defendants in cases alleging negligence of construction professionals such as architects, engineers and surveyors. He is also able to advise on cases with significant insurance aspects. **Strengths:** "He is flexible, practical, approachable and appears with some distinction in the higher echelons of court." "He's a very tough and tenacious litigator."

Andrew Rigney QC Highly regarded silk who is known for handling large-scale negligence cases that emerge from significant construction projects. He is well versed in issues surrounding claims against architects, surveyors and engineers, to name a few. Rigney also has robust insurance and property damage practices. **Strengths:** "He's somebody you want in your corner in a complex case, and he's very good at doing the legwork." "He's fun and hard working, and he has a very practical approach." **Recent work:** Acted for Shangri-La in its claims against Sisk for negligence during the construction of a new hotel in the Shard building.

David Sears QC Provides an impressive breadth and depth of experience spanning all aspects of engineering and construction negligence. He is familiar with claims involving project managers, architects and quantity surveyors, among other professionals. **Strengths:** "He's relaxed, charming and confident in what he does, and his written opinions have a real clarity about them." "He's user-friendly and gets on very well with clients." **Recent work:** Acted in Munkenbeck & Partners Urbanism Ltd v The Vinyl Factory Ltd and Others, representing an architecture firm that sought unpaid fees for its contribution to a Westminster development and was subsequently hit with a counterclaim for negligence.

Ben Quiney QC Very capable of advising on a range of professional negligence matters, although he primarily focuses on claims against construction professionals and insurance brokers. He is regularly instructed in cases concerning multimillion-pound losses and high-end commercial developments. **Strengths:** "He delivers very good client care, he's open to new ideas and he's easy to discuss matters with." **Recent work:** Defended the engineers in Carillion v AECOM against negligence claims relating to the Rolls Building, which houses the High Court of Justice.

39 Essex Chambers

See profile on p.840

THE SET

This highly regarded set fields a well-respected construction practice, and a significant proportion of its work also involves negligence allegations against engineers, architects, builders and other construction professionals. The chambers receives high praise for its client service model, with one source saying: "It is probably one of the most forward-looking sets across the whole of the Bar."

Client service: "They are one of the best clerking teams I have ever come across." "Director of clerking David Barnes is something else really. He is extremely good at making contacts and he also understands the business."

SILKS

Stuart Catchpole QC Has a strong practice in the construction and technology sectors, and is often instructed in large-scale and highly complex professional negligence claims in both areas. As well as being an advocate, he is also a qualified adjudicator, mediator and arbitrator who handles disputes around the world. **Strengths:** "He has a very analytical mind, he's also very commercial and thinks about what the client wants to achieve." "A great strategist and a formidable presence in court." **Recent work:** Defended Kier against sizeable negligent design claims relating to a shopping centre car park. He also advised on a recovery action against the consultant structural engineer.

Richard Wilmot-Smith QC Can claim almost 40 years of experience handling a comprehensive spectrum of engineering and construction concerns, and has a substantial focus on international work. He is regularly engaged on major professional negligence cases and can smoothly turn his hand to litigation, arbitration and other forms of ADR. **Strengths:** "He is hugely knowledgeable, always perfectly prepared and gives a seemingly effortless performance in court." **Recent work:** Acted in Harrison v Maison Blanc, representing a shop owner who sought recovery from both a contractor and a surveyor who failed to notice and rectify a faulty sign that fell and caused injury.

JUNIORS

Karim Ghaly (see p.651) Continues to undertake significant professional negligence work as part of his busy construction law practice. He appears for and against construction and engineering professionals both at first instance and on appeal, and also has a strong reputation for handling international arbitrations. **Strengths:** "A very laid-back and able junior, with good judgement." "He is really good on paper and really good on his feet; his cross-examination is absolutely devastating." **Recent work:** Acted for the main contractor in Iliffe and Another v Feltham Construction and Others, defending claims that the destruction of a property on a private island was due to negligent design.

Adam Robb An experienced junior who focuses his attention on professional negligence matters in substantial infrastructure, construction and engineering projects. He provides counsel to engineers, contractors and architects, among others, and is regularly instructed in very high-value, multiple party disputes. **Strengths:** "He gets stuck in and becomes part of the team, epitomising the modern approach to a barrister-solicitor relationship." "Technically excellent and very user-friendly." **Recent work:** Represented the contract administrator and architect in Cwm Taf v Nightingale, a TCC dispute involving claims of defect and delay in the construction of a South Wales' hospital.

4 New Square

See profile on p.880

THE SET

4 New Square has a formidable reputation in professional negligence matters, including those with a construction or technology element. It enjoys a strong relationship with many of the main profes-

sional indemnity insurers, but also receives instructions from all manner of defendant and claimant parties to negligence claims. Members have recently acted in Sir Robert McAlpine v David Chipperfield Associates, a £25 million claim against architects and engineers, and Lagan Homes v MV Kelly, a substantial dispute in regard to the specification of a basement car park.

Client service: "The set is pretty slick. Senior clerk Lizzy Stewart is particularly impressive. The front of house is friendly yet efficient."

Other Ranked Lawyers

David Pliener (Hardwicke) Instructed extensively on cases of professional negligence in the construction industry. He regularly represents property owners, contractors and engineers, as well as their insurers, and has wide experience of handling litigation, adjudication and arbitration. **Strengths:** "He can be tenacious without irritating the judge; he delivers his points incredibly capably and he is very cool under pressure." "He is sharp, keen-minded and very capable." **Recent work:** Acted in Sanderson Homes v Franki Foundations, a case alleging that negligent underpinning caused a slaughterhouse to collapse.

Neil Moody QC (see p.720) (2TG – 2 Temple Gardens) Head of chambers and a very well-respected silk who undertakes a considerable amount of work in the professional negligence space. A substantial proportion of his cases result from utilities or construction projects, where he is also able to bring to bear his extensive experience in property damage, insurance and product liability matters. **Strengths:** "He's very experienced and has a very commercial approach. I like that he understands what clients want and then implements it." **Recent work:** Acted in Willmott Dixon v Robert West, which involved claims against a consulting engineer for defective design at a hotel development in Clapham.

Roger Stewart (see p.773). Please see editorial on p.454.

Annieliese Day (see p.631). Please see editorial on p.454.

Fiona Sinclair (see p.766). Please see editorial on p.456.

Mark Cannon (see p.611). Please see editorial on p.455.

MIDLANDS

Professional Negligence
Leading Silks
Band 1
Anderson Mark *No5 Chambers* 🄰
Pepperall Edward *St Philips Chambers* *
Randall John *St Philips Chambers* ◊ *
Leading Juniors
Band 1
Brennan John *St Philips Chambers* *

Ranked Lawyers

Mark Anderson QC (No5 Chambers) Has an esteemed practice advising on claims against solicitors, banks, accountants and architects. He often assists with claims for negligence involving fraud and conveyancing transactions. **Strengths:** "He has the ability to grasp the facts and get to the heart of the problem immediately. He's very incisive and very clear in his advice." "He is an extremely impressive advocate." **Recent work:** Acted in a claim for negligence against an architect involved in the design and restoration of a building.

Edward Pepperall QC (see p.736) (St Philips Chambers) Well reputed for representing claimants in actions against solicitors and barristers for negligently under settling cases. He is also experienced in bringing claims against accountants relating to general accountancy services and failed tax mitigation schemes. **Strengths:** "Excellent on paper and on his feet, and has a fantastic manner with clients." "The man to go to when you have tricky procedural issues. He is very practical and gets to grips with cases very quickly."

John Randall QC (see p.748) (St Philips Chambers) Leading silk for actions against solicitors and engineers, particularly in the field of property development. He is also well versed in accountants' liability cases. **Strengths:** "A very impressive advocate with close attention to detail who is impressive in conference." "He is hugely intelligent and good with clients. He manages to combine an encyclopaedic knowledge of the law with a first-rate appreciation of strategy and an excellent eye for detail." **Recent work:** Acted in a counterclaim for fees brought against a firm of solicitors. The matter stemmed from a contingency fee arrangement.

John Brennan (see p.602) (St Philips Chambers) Noted for his broad chancery and commercial law practice; especially strong at handling professional negligence claims brought against solicitors. He has experience of appearing in courts of all levels, right up to the Supreme Court. **Strengths:** "He is very approachable, very helpful and very user-friendly." **Recent work:** Advised on a claim against a solicitor for the unauthorised release of a mortgage advance.

NORTHERN

Professional Negligence
Leading Silks
Band 1
Anderson Lesley *Kings Chambers* *
Cawson Mark *Exchange Chambers* *
Chaisty Paul *Kings Chambers* *
New Silks
Harper Mark *Kings Chambers* *
Leading Juniors
Band 1
Berragan Neil *Kings Chambers* *
Lawrenson Sarah *Kings Chambers* *
* *Indicates individual with profile.*
🄰 *direct access (see p.24).*
Alphabetical order within each band. Band 1 is highest.

Ranked Lawyers

Mark Cawson QC (see p.613) (Exchange Chambers) Continues to impress in the professional negligence sector, handling a range of claimant and defendant work pertaining to the legal profession. **Strengths:** "He is excellent, he has good manners with clients and he is very user-friendly, responsive and very capable in the courtroom."

Lesley Anderson QC (see p.583) (Kings Chambers) Handles professional negligence matters as part of a broader commercial and chancery practice. She is widely considered to be one of the outstanding practitioners on the Northern Circuit. **Strengths:** "Lesley Anderson QC is a joy to instruct on a variety of issues. She is a very impressive and powerful advocate who is also extremely approachable." "She has great ability in conference and is fantastic with our clients." **Recent work:** Represented the claimants in Hinchliffe v Linder Myers LLP, a case concerning the failure of solicitors to obtain deeds of covenant and to subsequently register the title to a number of investment properties.

Paul Chaisty QC (see p.614) (Kings Chambers) Noted for his representation of professionals such as solicitors and accountants, as well as corporate clients and commercial lenders, in a range of professional negligence matters. He offers particular strength in cases pertaining to property transactions. **Strengths:** "His advocacy skills are second to none. He is incredibly quick and methodical. He cuts through and is able to get to the core of the issues quickly." **Recent work:** Instructed in Halsall v Champion Consultancy, a high-value claim for breach of contract and negligence in relation to tax mitigating schemes in the context of film schemes.

Neil Berragan (see p.595) (Kings Chambers) Experienced in handling professional negligence matters against legal professionals, financial advisers and accountants. He represents both claimants and defendants. **Recent work:** Appeared in Footballers v Afortis, acting for a number of Premier League footballers who brought a case concerning negligent advice regarding investments in film schemes.

Sarah Lawrenson (see p.697) (Kings Chambers) Handles professional negligence matters pertaining to construction law, as well as wills, trusts and probate matters. Her clients include trustees, solicitors and construction professionals.

Mark Harper (see p.664) (Kings Chambers) Handles professional negligence disputes in the legal, investment advisory and accountancy spheres, among others. Also handles a broader range of chancery and commercial disputes. **Recent work:** Acted in Michael Coatman v Coutts & Co, a professional negligence case alleging negligent investment advice.

WESTERN

Professional Negligence
Leading Silks
Band 1
Palmer Adrian *Guildhall Chambers*
Sims Hugh *Guildhall Chambers*
Leading Juniors
Band 1
Pearce-Smith James *St John's Chambers*
Virgo John *Guildhall Chambers*
Band 2
Dickinson John FH *St John's Chambers* 🄰 *
** Indicates individual with profile.*
🄰 direct access (see p.24).
Alphabetical order within each band. Band 1 is highest.

Ranked Lawyers

Adrian Palmer QC (Guildhall Chambers) Highly regarded for his strong focus on professional negligence in the field of financial services, particularly tax and accountancy negligence. **Strengths:** "He is very hands-on, very clear and fantastic under pressure." "He has an astonishing ability to assimilate detailed information and identify the core issues." **Recent work:** Advised on a claim resulting from a breach of contract on a development site.

Hugh Sims QC (Guildhall Chambers) A leading figure for advising on claims against solicitors, surveyors, accountants and construction companies. **Strengths:** "Exceptionally bright and user-friendly across a broad range of practice areas." "He's very good on the detail and very quick at coming to conclusions. He really does inspire confidence and talks at a level clients understand." **Recent work:** Represented a lender in a claim against a firm of accountants concerning a negligent due diligence report for the purchase of a US medical home care company.

John Virgo (Guildhall Chambers) Specialises in professional negligence disputes relating to the financial services including claims concerning financial mis-selling, the fraudulent manipulation of rates and negligent investment advice. **Strengths:** "Ever reliable and hard working." "He's extremely pragmatic and always a team player – it is always really good to work with him." **Recent work:** Acted for the claimants in a claim against RBS involving the mis-selling of hedging products.

James Pearce-Smith (St John's Chambers) Well known for representing banks in professional negligence lender claims. He also acts in claims against solicitors, valuers, accountants and architects. **Strengths:** "He is extremely thorough and robust in his advice; he is also an impressive advocate." **Recent work:** Advised on a claim against a solicitor for the negligent conduct of a previous negligence claim arising from the reverse takeover of a company.

John Dickinson (see p.633) (St John's Chambers) Advises on professional negligence claims in the banking, accountancy and fraud sectors. He also assists with claims against engineers and solicitors. **Strengths:** "He is very good with the clients and has a very keen commercial awareness." "He is very measured and very thorough; he leaves no stone unturned and one would always trust his advice."

Contents:

LONDON

Property Damage	
Leading Sets	
Band 1	
Crown Office Chambers *	
2TG – 2 Temple Gardens *	
Leading Silks	
Band 1	
Eklund Graham	*4 New Square (ORL)* ◊ *
Elkington Ben	*4 New Square (ORL)* ◊ *
Moody Neil	*2TG – 2 Temple Gardens* *
Reed Paul	*Hardwicke (ORL)* ◊ 🄰
Rigney Andrew	*Crown Office Chambers*
Band 2	
Ansell Rachel	*4 Pump Court (ORL)* ◊ *
Cross James	*4 Pump Court (ORL)* ◊ *
Moxon Browne Robert	*2TG – 2 Temple Gardens* *
Palmer Howard	*2TG – 2 Temple Gardens* *
Band 3	
Antelme Alexander	*Crown Office Chambers*
Miller Andrew	*2TG – 2 Temple Gardens* *
Quiney Ben	*Crown Office Chambers*
Sinclair Fiona	*4 New Square (ORL)* ◊ *
ter Haar Roger	*Crown Office Chambers*
Waite Jonathan	*Crown Office Chambers*
Webb Geraint	*Henderson Chambers (ORL)* ◊ *
Leading Juniors	
Band 1	
Brown Geoffrey	*39 Essex Chambers (ORL)* ◊
Crowley Daniel	*2TG – 2 Temple Gardens* *
Green Doré	*2TG – 2 Temple Gardens* *
Band 2	
Boon Elizabeth	*Crown Office Chambers* *
Field Julian	*Crown Office Chambers* *
Nolten Sonia	*2TG – 2 Temple Gardens* *
Pliener David	*Hardwicke (ORL)* ◊ 🄰
Shapiro Daniel	*Crown Office Chambers* *
** Indicates set / individual with profile.*	
🄰 direct access (see p.24).	
◊ (ORL) = Other Ranked Lawyer.	
Alphabetical order within each band. Band 1 is highest.	

Band 1

Crown Office Chambers
See profile on p.824

THE SET

Crown Office Chambers fields a deep bench of property damage experts at both silk and junior level, many of whom can draw on impressive strength in areas of complementary specialism such as insurance, product liability and professional negligence. Members handle a huge array of claims, including many that involve highly complex or novel points of law, and regularly cover cases involving both domestic and overseas losses associated with major construction and development projects.

Client service: "The clerks, led by Andy Flanagan, go above and beyond. They are always asking how they can help and we find them to be very proactive."

SILKS

Andrew Rigney QC A leading silk who is "somebody you want in your corner on a difficult, complex case." He is regularly instructed in highly technical cases concerning damage caused by fire, collapse or construction defect. His practice has a significant international element to it. **Strengths:** "Technically excellent, but also exceptionally user-friendly, he is somebody who rolls his sleeves up and gets stuck in."

Alexander Antelme QC Increasingly handles a significant number of high-value claims, including those relating to catastrophic fire, flood and landslip damage, particularly at commercial and industrial properties. Strengths: "He is brilliant, and has a really good attitude towards working with both juniors and clients."

Ben Quiney QC Brings to bear a wide level of experience in related areas, such as construction, professional negligence and insurance. He is regularly instructed in claims arising out of fire, flood and other disasters, and possesses deep expertise in coverage issues and subrogated recovery. Strengths: "He has a very relaxed manner, but he also cuts to the chase and doesn't mess around."

Roger ter Haar QC Veteran silk with many years' experience in this area of law, and who also demonstrates considerable construction and insurance expertise. **Strengths:** "He absolutely knows his way about this area of the law, and is extremely experienced and very good."

Jonathan Waite QC Known primarily for his outstanding product liability expertise, he also manages numerous property damage cases particularly those relating to fire and flood damage. **Strengths:** "He is formidable on his feet and incredibly well prepared. He's good when it comes to complex policy wording or interpretation and he deals with matters with consummate professionalism.

JUNIORS

Elizabeth Boon (see p.599) Manages a fine property damage practice which incorporates her strong knowledge of professional negligence and product liability. She also demonstrates key insurance expertise, which she brings to bear on fire, flood and subsidence claims, among others. **Strengths:** "Her attention to detail is impressive; she turns things around quickly, and she really rolls her sleeves up and gets involved." **Recent work:** Represented the defendant in a claim arising out of a fire at a plastics factory, which raised significant questions about the ability of PVC to self-combust.

Julian Field (see p.644) A senior junior who "knows his way around" property damage and frequently gets involved in multiparty cases and those involving highly technical aspects. He is highly sought after for multimillion-pound claims involving fire, flood and explosions. **Strengths:** "A very experienced and very senior junior, who is well regarded and good in court." **Recent work:** Acted for Aviva as insurers of a post-production film studio whose basement premises were damaged by water leaking from a restaurant in the building upstairs.

Daniel Shapiro (see p.762) "A silk in the making," who is known for his "ability to just cut through the issues." He has an impressive commercial practice that involves significant focus on property damage work, and he often stands as sole counsel in significant recovery actions, particularly subrogated claims. **Strengths:** "He has a great way about him and provides clear and concise opinions and answers." **Recent work:** Defended Ashworth Frazer in a flood damage claim linked to the alleged supply of an incorrect part which was incorporated into a sprinkler system.

2TG – 2 Temple Gardens
See profile on p.920

THE SET

A robust group highly respected for its deep engagement with the sector, and one that, as well as handling major cases, also offers regular training seminars to solicitors and insurance industry professionals. The set is instructed in a broad range of property damage work handling everything from major fire and flood cases to challenging construction disputes and matters concerning damage arising from defective products.

Client service: "The clerks have been very amenable, and senior clerk Lee Tyler has worked hard to accommodate what we want."

SILKS

Neil Moody QC (see p.720) Elected as head of chambers in July 2015, he also remains leader of the property damage group. He is known for being an "incredibly user-friendly" silk who displays complementary strengths in areas such as insurance and product liability. His practice is particularly focused on disputes arising out of construction and utilities projects. **Strengths:** "He brings a quiet confidence to the case without being brash or arrogant. We felt we were on solid ground with him."

Robert Moxon Browne QC (see p.723) A "first-rate" property damage silk who is incredibly experienced in the sector. He is especially well known for his expertise in handling catastrophic fire cases, particularly those relating to the failure of fire suppression devices. **Strengths:** "He's seen everything and been everywhere. He knows every case."

Howard Palmer QC (see p.732) Experienced in a broad range of property damage work, ranging from complex construction disputes through to subsidence and flood claims. He is known for his ability to handle cases with highly technical aspects, such as those involving medical or engineering issues. **Strengths:** "Very methodical, very detailed and quite a cerebral character but also someone who it's easy to work with."

Andrew Miller QC (see p.717) Has a strong practice and regularly defends against high-value claims for fire and flood damage to luxury residential properties and hotels. He also handles substantial property damage disputes arising out of construction and engineering projects. **Strengths:** "Very savvy, with good client skills and a commercial approach. He's astute and responsive."

JUNIORS

Daniel Crowley (see p.627) A junior who "definitely earns his slot" in the property damage rankings, and who bolsters his capability in the area with strong knowledge of the Defective Premises Act. He's highly regarded for his strength when it comes to handling tree root subsidence claims. **Strengths:** "He is excellent, really thorough and very clever." "He is very bright and spot-on legally."

Doré Green (see p.659) A highly respected senior junior known for his "phenomenally forensic" approach and his understanding of complex insurance as well as property damage issues. He specialises in construction-related cases whilst also handling a wide range of fire and flood claims, amongst others. **Strengths:** "He is an insurance specialist with a science background, who is good for highly technical insurance and property damage disputes."

Sonia Nolten (see p.728) Possesses deep experience in insurance and property damage, which she brings to bear on a wide range of claims, including those concerning fire and water damage to residential and commercial property. She is also an expert on construction disputes. **Strengths:** "Extremely hard-working and reliable, she has a good understanding of the technical and evidential issues relating to claims involving land movement."

Other Ranked Lawyers

Geoffrey Brown (39 Essex Chambers) A very experienced senior junior known particularly for his measured approach to proceedings. He handles claims arising out of fire and flood as well as subsidence and landslip. **Strengths:** "A QC in all but title, who is good for very tricky cases. He is a safe pair of hands and brings a calming effect to more emotive matters."

Paul Reed QC (Hardwicke) A highly respected property damage silk whose "energy is simply unbelievable" and who wins praise for his considerable expertise in construction and insurance matters. He is regularly instructed in substantial, high-profile claims concerning multiple parties. **Strengths:** "He has the ability to cut through everything very quickly, but he is also approachable and gets on very well with clients." **Recent work:** Represented Grosvenor Street in a £20 million claim arising out of the negligent design and construction of a new commercial development that led to the destruction of adjacent properties.

David Pliener (Hardwicke) A "sharp, keen-minded and very capable" senior junior, who is known for handling disputes of a highly technical nature with aplomb. He also possesses invaluable understanding of the construction industry and is often instructed in cases with an international aspect. **Strengths:** "He is a brilliant advocate, who is incredibly impressive and also one of those lawyers who has a real mastery of details and numbers as well." **Recent work:** Represented shipping company Stema in a £2 million dispute regarding ground failure at Tilbury Docks.

Geraint Webb QC (see p.791) (Henderson Chambers) Demonstrates high levels of capability in handling group actions and mass torts, and has shown particular flair for cross-border disputes regarding environmental contamination. She also handles a wide range of cases arising out of major fires and explosions, as well as those resulting from faulty products. **Strengths:** "He is extremely capable, very cool-minded, a great strategist and someone who is extremely reliable." **Recent work:** Defended a London-domiciled client in two separate mass tort actions over land contamination in Africa allegedly caused by copper mining.

Graham Eklund QC (see p.640) (4 New Square) Considered a "go-to man for insurance," he also maintains a significant practice in property damage that is particularly focused on handling fire claims. His reach extends to cases involving fires that have arisen out of professional negligence and defective equipment. **Strengths:** "He sees the heart of the issue immediately and never loses focus." "He enjoys a tremendous popularity based on his thorough application to his instructions, his courteous style and his great client awareness." **Recent work:** Retained in the case of Georgia Pacific v Corlett, which concerned a fire at a paper warehouse allegedly caused by the negligent maintenance of electrical systems.

Ben Elkington QC (see p.640) (4 New Square) Handles a broad range of property damage work, including fire claims in particular, and also regularly gets involved in surrounding insurance, contract and negligence issues associated with such cases. He is adept at managing difficult multiparty claims through to successful outcomes. **Strengths:** "Very engaged, reliable and approachable, he's a pleasure to work with and a great asset to have on your side." "Commercially aware, he's really nice to work with and really concise in his advice." **Recent work:** Represented Wagamama in a multiparty claim regarding a fire at one of the company's restaurants.

Fiona Sinclair QC (see p.766) (4 New Square) Possesses significant strength in the areas of construction and professional negligence, all of which she brings to bear on property damage cases of significant value and complexity. She demonstrates particular skill in handling cases involving catastrophic building collapse. **Strengths:** "She's excellent. She turns things around very quickly and everything we get from her is very good." **Recent work:** Represented Merlin Attractions in a £10 million claim against the main contractor and architects responsible for a new hotel and leisure centre at its Legoland theme park in Windsor.

Rachel Ansell QC (see p.584) (4 Pump Court) A relatively recent silk with an admirable property damage practice, who also has strength in professional negligence and construction matters and a robust understanding of insurance cases. She is noted for her experience of handling subrogated claims as well as fire damage claims. **Strengths:** "She is tenacious. She will take a matter by the scruff of the neck and you know she'll cover every angle. You get advice that covers the full spectrum of what you need to know." **Recent work:** Defended Brit Insurance against a claim for a fire at a warehouse where two security-related precedents had been breached.

James Cross QC (see p.626) (4 Pump Court) Takes on cases that cover a broad range of property damage work, including everything from fire and flooding to building collapse and other man-made or natural catastrophic damage. He also has invaluable experience in construction and professional negligence law which assists him well in this area. **Strengths:** "He's got a very collaborative style, in terms of both his manner and his willingness to roll up his sleeves and work as part of a team to get a fast turnaround."

Public International Law

Contents:

LONDON

Public International Law	
Leading Sets	
Band 1	
Essex Court Chambers *	
Band 2	
Blackstone Chambers *	
20 Essex Street *	
Matrix Chambers *	
Senior Statesmen	
Senior Statesmen: distinguished older partners	
Berman Franklin	*Essex Court Chambers*
Leading Silks	
Star individuals	
Lowe Vaughan	*Essex Court Chambers*
Band 1	
Bethlehem Daniel	*20 Essex Street*
Sands Philippe	*Matrix Chambers*
Shaw Malcolm	*Essex Court Chambers*
Wordsworth Samuel	*Essex Court Chambers*
Band 2	
Landau Toby	*Essex Court Chambers*
Mendelson Maurice	*Blackstone Chambers*
Otty Timothy	*Blackstone Chambers*
Band 3	
Chamberlain Martin	*Brick Court Chambers (ORL)* ◊ *
Douglas Zachary	*Matrix Chambers*
Qureshi Khawar	*Serle Court (ORL)* ◊
Steyn Karen	*11KBW (ORL)* ◊ *
New Silks	
Fatima Shaheed	*Blackstone Chambers*
Leading Juniors	
Star individuals	
Wood Michael	*20 Essex Street*
Band 1	
Sarooshi Dan	*Essex Court Chambers*
Verdirame Guglielmo	*20 Essex Street*
Band 2	
Boyle Alan	*Essex Court Chambers*
Macdonald Alison	*Matrix Chambers* *
Olleson Simon	*Three Stone (ORL)* ◊
Sander Amy	*Essex Court Chambers*
Band 3	
Bastin Lucas	*Quadrant Chambers (ORL)* ◊ *
Goodwin-Gill Guy	*Blackstone Chambers*
Ní Ghrálaigh Blinne	*Matrix Chambers*
Patel Naina	*Blackstone Chambers*
Staker Christopher	*39 Essex Chambers (ORL)* ◊
Wells Jessica	*Essex Court Chambers*
Up-and-coming individuals	
Butler Michelle	*Matrix Chambers* *

** Indicates set / individual with profile.*
◊ (ORL) = Other Ranked Lawyer.
Alphabetical order within each band. Band 1 is highest.

Band 1

Essex Court Chambers
See profile on p.836

THE SET

The foremost chambers for PIL matters, Essex Court offers a deep bench of eminently qualified silks and juniors, several of whom are appointed to the panel for the Attorney General. Its members have extensive experience of handling sophisticated cases, and appear regularly in the ICJ as well as the International Tribunal for the Law of the Sea. They are often involved in major inter-state disputes and investment treaty work, and have further specialist knowledge of human rights cases and international arbitration.

Client service: "The service is very proactive, without being over the top. It is a well-run commercial and practical set of chambers." David Grief and Joe Ferrigno, the senior clerks, are praised for being "very user-friendly and highly approachable."

SILKS

Sir Frank Berman QC An immensely experienced PIL lawyer who has exceptional depth of knowledge. Routinely called upon as an arbitrator as reflected in his recent caseload comprised of notable international arbitrations. **Strengths:** "Deep wealth of experience and very erudite." "One of the greats. Someone who I eagerly try to get when PIL issues are at the heart of the issue for arbitral appointment."

Vaughan Lowe QC A leader in the PIL field who is renowned for his fierce intellect. He regularly appears in front of international tribunals and is a noted expert in boundary disputes and investment treaty work. **Strengths:** "One cannot praise his intellect, his academic prowess and his professional skills highly enough. He is highly respected by the bench and his peers, and is a leading authority on his subject." He is noted for his "excellent strategic awareness." **Recent work:** Acted for Nicaragua in ICJ proceedings against Colombia concerning delimitation of maritime boundaries.

Malcolm Shaw QC Has a strong academic background and is well respected for the brilliant advice he gives to governments and international organisations. He has an interesting spread of cases in the English courts and before international tribunals. **Strengths:** "Well known for the quality of his advocacy and very learned too." "A very nice guy who is brilliant and very easy to get along with."

Samuel Wordsworth QC Handles a broad spectrum of PIL cases, proving an expert on both bilateral investment treaties (BIT) and inter-state disputes. He frequently represents the UK government in domestic courts on international disputes and is "an effective advocate who always has the ear of the court." **Strengths:** "Sam is on an upward trajectory." "He's very bright, shows great attention to detail and produces very technical but practical advice."

Toby Landau QC Highly respected for being "whip-smart" on all matters regarding investor/state arbitrations and state-on-state disputes. He regularly appears before international tribunals and has a strong client base made up predominantly, but not exclusively, of governments. **Strengths:** "An arbitration guru who is exceptionally good." "He is right at the top of his game: a fine advocate who deals with difficult and challenging situations with great aplomb, and who knows his topic absolutely back-to-front." **Recent work:** Represented Singapore in a significant inter-state dispute regarding the Malaysia-Singapore Railway. He also represented Libya in a high-profile case looking at the extent of state immunity pertaining to foreign embassy employees in the UK.

JUNIORS

Dan Sarooshi Has the academic knowledge and practical experience to make him a popular choice in the PIL sphere. He has an excellent track record of representing governments, international organisations and FTSE 100 companies. **Strengths:** "Very efficient and quick to grasp and identify solutions to complex issues." "He's very personable and outgoing and is an extremely bright advocate." **Recent work:** Successfully acted for the State Oil Marketing Company of the Iraqi Ministry of Oil in resisting the enforcement of an arbitral award brought against it.

Alan Boyle A seasoned practitioner who continues to take on an interesting spread of state-on-state disputes. He regularly represents the UK government. **Strengths:** "Brilliant and knows the law inside out. He has a deep academic understanding of the law and has good awareness of the challenges and demands of PIL work."

Amy Sander Garners praise from clients for her "exceptional intellect" and the extremely hard work she puts into cases. She advises both governments and multinationals and is an expert in BITs and boundary disputes. **Strengths:** "She flawlessly analyses and handles extremely complex issues. She is an excellent team player, who is extremely hard-working and very effective even when handling the most urgent matters." **Recent work:** Instructed by Republic of Kenya in proceedings before the ICJ brought by the Federal Republic of Somalia regarding the delimitation of maritime space.

Jessica Wells Junior with a growing practice in PIL who has a strong level of experience as both an adviser and an advocate. She also has a strong commercial disputes practice and is an expert on conflict of law issues. **Strengths:** "She writes some very impressive submissions and is very good to work with." **Recent work:** Represented the Foreign & Commonwealth Office in a claim brought against the UK and eight other nuclear power states, alleging a breach of their obligations to pursue nuclear disarmament.

Band 2

Blackstone Chambers
See profile on p.813

THE SET

Possesses a deep well of barristers who have a particularly strong reputation on the human rights side of PIL. Areas of strength include international disputes, constitutional affairs, immigration and diplomatic immunity issues. This is a "really professional" set that is "very easy to work with and full of helpful support staff." "It gives clients the right impression," according to commentators. Typical of the work it does, it represented the Russian Federation against Georgia in a case before the ECHR concerning alleged serious human rights violations.

Client service: The set has "proficient clerks" led by Gary Oliver who are "good, professional, proactive and courteous."

SILKS

Maurice Mendelson QC A very well-regarded silk who advises governments, commercial entities and private investors on international law and investment arbitration. **Strengths:** "Very knowledgeable and has been around for a very long time. He's excellent for bouncing ideas off and discussing strategy." "He is uncommonly responsive and breathtakingly fast – it never fails to amaze me how quickly he puts together an opinion. He is also far more creative and open-minded than most barristers of his vintage." **Recent work:** Advised an investor on the international law elements of the USD40 billion Grand Nicaragua Inter-Oceanic Canal Project.

Timothy Otty QC Particularly good at PIL cases relating to human rights and international sanctions, he typically acts for claimants. He is regularly instructed in matters arising in areas of conflict, most notably Africa and the Middle East. **Strengths:** "He has a sharper insight and better perspective than most, and has been involved in some of the most high-profile matters on the international human rights side." "A very bright and measured advocate, who is excellent with clients." **Recent work:** Acted for a claimant in a Supreme Court challenge to sanctions imposed by the UN Security Council in relation to Al-Qaeda.

Shaheed Fatima QC Has a formidable reputation for her excellence in handling sensitive PIL matters in domestic courts. She is seen as very much "a rising star" in PIL. **Strengths:** "She's very bright and has an impressive style." "She's simply brilliant and a joy to work with." **Recent work:** Sole counsel to the claimant in Djakishev v Kazakhstan. Djakishev alleged a number of serious human rights violations, including arbitrary detention and breach of fair trial rights.

JUNIORS

Guy Goodwin-Gill Has a strong academic background and is well respected for his specialist knowledge of refugee law. He's a seasoned practitioner who is an established name in both domestic and international courts and tribunals. **Strengths:** "Fantastic. He is a world leader in international refugee law."

Naina Patel "A young, extremely talented barrister who is on the path to stardom." She has a comprehensive knowledge of PIL matters and regularly advises corporate and government clients on compliance with human rights. **Strengths:** "Very thorough, reliable and helpful. She is extremely hard-working, bright and committed." **Recent work:** Acted in AH (Algeria) v Secretary of State for the Home Department, a case concerning the application of the exclusion clauses in Article 1F of the Refugee Conventions to a conviction for participating in an association of terrorists.

20 Essex Street

See profile on p.838

THE SET

A set brimming with barristers who have experience of handling PIL cases both in English courts and before international tribunals. Members often act for the Foreign & Commonwealth Office (FCO) as well as international governments, companies and individuals. They provide a full-service offering and handle interstate arbitration, boundary disputes, investment treaty work and diplomatic immunity cases. The set was formerly home to the recently retired Sir Elihu Lauterpacht CBE QC LLD, one of the towering figures of the PIL Bar, whose legacy lives on in the form of the talented members he leaves behind.

Client service: "All at the set are very flexible and open to working with us in any way." "They have some incredible people and are very prominent in the area." Senior clerk Neil Palmer is praised for his smooth running of chambers.

SILKS

Sir Daniel Bethlehem QC A benchmark to which others aspire, he handles high-profile state-on-state, diplomatic immunity and BIT cases. He has strong ties to the FCO, and has vast experience of both acting and sitting as an arbitrator. **Strengths:** Dubbed "a legend" by peers and clients alike, he is "a terrific lawyer, who is a strategic thinker at the top of his field." **Recent work:** Represented the Marshall Islands in its claim that the UK, along with other nuclear states, breached its obligations to pursue negotiations for nuclear disarmament.

JUNIORS

Sir Michael Wood Active in all areas of PIL and someone who devotes much of his time to advising the FCO. He is well versed in complex land and maritime boundary disputes, and other international government disputes, and has great experience of appearing before international courts and tribunals. **Strengths:** "His role for some 35 years as a lawyer with the FCO, including as its Principal Legal Adviser, gives him unique and valuable experience and insight. He is a pleasure to work with, and his advocacy is measured but compelling." **Recent work:** Acted in Kimanthi and Others v Foreign and Commonwealth Office, a tort claim in relation to the handling of the Mau Mau emergency in Kenya.

Guglielmo Verdirame Active in a broad spectrum of PIL work, he tackles cases dealing with international human rights, BITs and inter-state disputes. He is a noted academic in this area who also has significant court experience, having handled domestic PIL cases all the way up to appellate level. **Strengths:** "Predominantly an academic, very very good and also manages to span a fairly broad practice area – nothing but praise for him." "He's excellent and very well versed in PIL." **Recent work:** Advised the Russian Federation on a claim made by Exxon Neflegas before an arbitral tribunal under the UNCITRAL Rules. Acted for Italy in ICJ proceedings against India concerning the latter's detention in custody of two Italian marines after an incident in 2012.

Matrix Chambers

See profile on p.876

THE SET

Matrix has a high-calibre, multidisciplinary team that has expertise in environmental cases, maritime disputes, international humanitarian law and investment treaty arbitration. Its members frequently appear in domestic and international courts at all levels and "impress with their level of scholarship and knowledge, as well as their intelligence and commitment." They are "incredibly responsive, very helpful and always friendly. They run cases in the way they should be run."

Client service: "The practice manager, Paul Venables, organises the set very well, and keeps things moving along with good humour."

SILKS

Philippe Sands QC Peers sees him as "a great standard bearer for the PIL cause" and note that he is highly respected by the ICJ and a host of other international tribunals. He has deep expertise in maritime delimitation, international environmental law and investment treaty cases, and also increasingly acts as an arbitrator. **Strengths:** "His work is both detailed and expert." "He's a very senior, important and respected figure with a great public profile and a strong practice."

Zachary Douglas QC A fluent Russian speaker and an expert in international human rights cases, investment treaty work and interstate boundary disputes. Market sources all agree he has a "very fine reputation in the market." **Strengths:** "He's calm, he's relaxed and he listens. He can explain things in everyday English and is just a delight." "Very good and very smart, he is always on top of things." **Recent work:** Appeared before the Supreme Court appealing the decision not to order an inquiry into the 1948 'Batang Kali massacre' in Malaysia.

JUNIORS

Alison Macdonald (see p.705) Has a broad practice and has extensive experience of operating across criminal, commercial and international law, acting as both adviser and advocate. Widely regarded at the Bar, she regularly represents states in ICSID arbitrations. **Strengths:** "She is widely regarded at the Bar for being a very good advocate." **Recent work:** Instructed by Ghana in a maritime boundary dispute against Côte d'Ivoire. She also represented the Hashemite Kingdom of Jordan in an ICSID arbitration brought by a Kuwaiti telecommunications company.

Blinne Ní Ghrálaigh A strong up-and-coming junior "carving a real niche for herself," who handles a growing PIL workload. Experienced in acting before domestic and international courts and tribunals, she represents a range of clients from states to NGOs. She also has impressive academic credentials, and has recently been a visiting fellow at Harvard University's international human rights programme. **Strengths:** "She is always meticulous in her research and digs deep into the case." **Recent work:** Advised on the UK's PIL obligations with regard to the sale of arms to Saudi Arabia in light of that country's defiance of international humanitarian law.

Michelle Butler (see p.608) "A strong candidate in the field" who is well versed in a range of PIL matters. She is experienced in acting for governments in substantial inter-state disputes, and regularly appears before international courts and tribunals such as the ICJ and ECJ. **Strengths:** "Technically brilliant on a wide range of human rights issues. She does meticulous research, gives really good advice and is very good at managing expectations." **Recent work:** Represented the applicants in Chiragov v Armenia, heard before the ECHR's Grand Chamber. The case was brought by Kurdish citizens forced to leave their homes due to Armenian occupation of the region in 1992.

Other Ranked Lawyers

Martin Chamberlain QC (see p.614) (Brick Court Chambers) Has a wealth of experience advising an impressive set of government clients on inter-state disputes. He is an expert on human rights law in both international and domestic courts. **Strengths:** "An impressive and persuasive advocate, who offers great assurance and superior intelligence."

Christopher Staker (39 Essex Chambers) His wide practice takes in investment treaty arbitration work, international criminal law matters and human rights cases before domestic and international courts and tribunals. As well as having significant experience in European cases, he has additional expertise in Australian and African matters. **Strengths:** "Has expert knowledge of both public international law and international organisations." "His drafting skills are excellent and he's a pleasure to work with." **Recent work:** Represented victims in the 'Kenya 1 case', which concerned violence perpetrated in the country following the 2007 election.

Karen Steyn QC (see p.773) (11KBW) An expert on the ECHR convention and international humanitarian law (IHL) who handles high-profile and sensitive political cases. She has extensive experience of representing the British government in PIL matters. **Strengths:** "When it comes to IHL and military matters abroad she's the go-to person." "Seen on high-profile and difficult cases involving international law points, she is an exceptional barrister, who is very diligent." **Recent work:** Appeared in the Supreme Court in Serdar Mohammed v Ministry of Defence, a case regarding the detention of insurgents in Afghanistan that raised complex points of international law. She was also the only government counsel to act in both Belhaj & Others v Straw & Others, and Rahmatullah v MOD. These were cases concerning serious allegations of the rendition, detention and mistreatment of persons during the Iraq war.

Simon Olleson (Three Stone) "Very erudite and hard-working," he has a strong academic background in PIL and a keen interest in the law of state responsibility. He has recently advised on the PIL angles of environmental disputes and shown himself to be an expert in maritime delimitation cases, BIT disputes and inter-state arbitration. **Strengths:** "He's very good at absorbing a lot of information quickly and turning things around efficiently."

Lucas Bastin (see p.591) (Quadrant Chambers) A seasoned practitioner with regard to PIL matters, who is particularly good at investment treaty work and commercial arbitrations under ICSID, SCC, LCIA ICC, UNCITRAL and ad hoc rules. His wider PIL work sees him handling cases involving state immunity and inter-state sanctions. **Strengths:** "He is a go-to junior for investment treaty arbitration, and has superb drafting and communication skills. He has a background as a solicitor in this area, giving him the ability to step into teams and make a real contribution." "He's extremely eloquent" and "very very personable – he does the client-facing stuff at the drop of a hat and combines charm with a powerful brain." **Recent work:** Acted in A11Y Ltd v Czech Republic, a case alleging the state's discriminatory conduct against the company during a complex investment treaty arbitration.

Khawar Qureshi QC (Serle Court) A prominent presence in the PIL sphere with a broad range of expertise, but who is especially good at work concerning investment treaties and trade agreements. **Strengths:** "A pure PIL lawyer who covers a huge span of public international law."

Contents:

LONDON

Public Procurement	
Leading Sets	
Band 1	
11KBW *	
Monckton Chambers *	
Band 2	
Keating Chambers *	
Band 3	
Blackstone Chambers *	
Henderson Chambers *	
Leading Silks	
Star individuals	
Bowsher Michael	*Monckton Chambers* Ⓐ *
Giffin Nigel	*11KBW* *
Hannaford Sarah	*Keating Chambers* *
Band 1	
Coppel Jason	*11KBW* *
Goudie James	*11KBW* *
Howell John	*Blackstone Chambers*
Moser Philip	*Monckton Chambers* Ⓐ *
Band 2	
McCredie Fionnuala	*Keating Chambers* *
Williams Rhodri	*Henderson Chambers* Ⓐ *
Band 3	
Béar Charles	*Fountain Court Chambers (ORL)* ◊ *
Choudhury Akhlaq	*11KBW* *
Herberg Javan	*Blackstone Chambers*
Lewis Adam	*Blackstone Chambers*
Leading Juniors	
Band 1	
Barrett Joseph	*11KBW* *
Sloane Valentina	*Monckton Chambers* Ⓐ
West Ewan	*Monckton Chambers* Ⓐ
Williams Rob	*Monckton Chambers*
Band 2	
Gollancz David	*Keating Chambers* *
Lamont Calum	*Keating Chambers* *
Segan James	*Blackstone Chambers*
Taylor Simon	*Keating Chambers* *
Band 3	
Blackwood Anneliese	*Monckton Chambers*
Gray Margaret	*Brick Court Chambers (ORL)* ◊
Kinnier Andrew	*Henderson Chambers* Ⓐ *
Osepciu Ligia	*Monckton Chambers*
Up-and-coming individuals	
Banks Fiona	*Monckton Chambers* Ⓐ
Johnston Tim	*Brick Court Chambers (ORL)* ◊

** Indicates set / individual with profile.*

Ⓐ direct access (see p.24).

◊ (ORL) = Other Ranked Lawyer.

Alphabetical order within each band. Band 1 is highest.

Band 1

11KBW

See profile on p.867

THE SET

A set held in high esteem for its wider expertise in judicial review and public law, 11KBW is a real trail-blazer in the public procurement sphere. Its growing team of "exceptional barristers" acts on behalf of public authorities, tenderers and other claimants and has significant experience in handling cases relating to both public and private sector contracts. The set offers a comprehensive service that ranges from preliminary advice through to High Court claims, judicial reviews and disputes heard in the ECJ.

Client service: "The clerking is excellent: they understand the pressures of being a solicitor and the need to give a quick response. They take the trouble to understand the work we are doing and are particularly well aligned to our practice area." Lucy Barbet and Mark Dann are the joint senior clerks.

SILKS

Nigel Giffin QC (see p.653) A leading silk who receives considerable praise for the outstanding expertise and judgement he shows when handling public procurement matters, which form a significant part of his robust public law practice. Sources say that he is highly approachable and client-friendly counsel. **Strengths:** "He's got a brain the size of a planet. He's very incisive and also immensely practical. He is perfect if you want someone to roll up their sleeves, absorb a huge amount of information in a small amount of time and give the right advice." "A specialist in public procurement law who is able to provide quick answers to difficult questions."

Jason Coppel QC (see p.624) Represents both claimants and defendants in high-profile procurement challenges. He takes on work relating to contracts in a wide variety of areas including medicine, legal aid, childcare and non-profit. **Strengths:** "His written work is brilliant. He's really clear, helpful and practical and not overly academic. A great advocate, he's very measured when he speaks and not showy, and you can't help but listen to him." "He has a background rooted in European law, and is a top-drawer silk for frontline cases." **Recent work:** Acted on behalf of the non-profit organisation Bristol Missing Link in successfully resisting an application to lift an automatic suspension that would have prevented conclusion of a support services contract.

James Goudie QC (see p.657) A hugely respected veteran of the Bar who is regularly instructed by local authorities to provide advice on complex procurement issues. His writings on public law have been published widely. **Strengths:** "He is formidable."

Akhlaq Choudhury QC (see p.617) Has considerable experience in the public procurement space, where he advises on commercial contracts as well as government agreements. He has extensive court experience and can handle large-scale challenges and trials as well as urgent interim applications. **Strengths:** "He is such a gentleman. He's so calm under pressure, and he approaches cases with real care and concern." **Recent work:** Represented a number of criminal legal aid firms in a large-scale challenge to the procurement process undertaken by the Legal Aid Agency which determined the awarding of criminal duty solicitor contracts.

JUNIORS

Joseph Barrett (see p.590) Well-regarded junior who has a growing practice in public procurement law, and particular expertise in EU procurement and state aid. He wins praise for his tenacity in court and his vigorous work ethic. **Strengths:** "He likes a good fight and is a hard worker. He's great at giving a clear steer in a case, and he never sits on the fence." **Recent work:** Acted on behalf of DWF in a High Court challenge concerning the Insolvency Service's procurement of legal services in England, Wales and Scotland.

Monckton Chambers

See profile on p.877

THE SET

An impressive number of procurement experts work at Monckton Chambers, a set with a greater pedigree and history in public procurement than any other. Its strength in depth ensures that all manner of procurement cases are handled, from non-contentious matters to complex litigation. Commentators say that "the silks and juniors here understand that it is not simply about the law; it's about knowing how court processes work, it's about knowing the correct strategy, and it's about understanding the judge."

Client service: "This is an incredibly professional and slick outfit, and it is always reassuring to speak to one of the clerks there." "The clerks are very responsive and personable" and "easy, relaxed and friendly." David Hockney leads the clerking team.

SILKS

Michael Bowsher QC (see p.601) A venerable silk with roots in the origins of procurement legislation itself. Having been at the forefront of this area from its inception, he is an advocate revered by both claimants and defendants faced with high-value and important procurement challenges. **Strengths:** "Very commercial and pragmatic, as well as highly personable. It gives our clients peace of mind to know they've instructed one of the very best." "He is without a doubt superb. He is Mr Procurement and you'd struggle to find someone with greater knowledge and experience. Very client-friendly, he's not afraid to challenge client thinking or pose difficult questions." **Recent work:** Represented Associated British Ports in its legal challenge against the decision by the Ministry of Defence to award Solent Gateway a contract to run Marchwood Military Port.

Philip Moser QC (see p.722) Highly regarded for his expertise in procurement, commercial agent cases and EU law. A significant portion of his work arises from instructions received from the government. **Strengths:** "He's exceptional. Judges and clients all think really highly of him, and he's a very persuasive advocate and a very formidable opponent." "A go-to silk whose advice is always focused and creative. Clients always feel they are in safe hands with him." **Recent work:** Advised Deutsche Flugsicherung following a challenge to its successful bid to take on Gatwick Airport's air traffic control contract.

JUNIORS

Valentina Sloane A highly respected junior who handles procurement cases as part of her wider European law practice. She is regularly instructed by top law firms and the government. **Strengths:** "She's technically very strong and great for high-value procurement matters." "She is willing to test the boundaries of the law to get the right result for the client." **Recent work:** Acted for the Cabinet Office in defeating a challenge regarding a framework agreement for locum doctor services.

Ewan West Previously a civil servant in the Department for Transport, this well-respected barrister has a public procurement practice that covers transport, utilities and health. He has worked on many significant and high-profile challenges. **Strengths:** "Ewan is exceptional and goes beyond the call of duty." "Having worked within the government, he understands the machinery of it, which is very helpful." **Recent work:** Acted for Blue Water Recoveries as the claimant in a case concerning the validity of an already passed procurement. The successful tenderer had amended its tender after submission.

Rob Williams A go-to barrister for both public sector and utilities work, who has been instructed in a number of leading procurement cases. **Strengths:** "He's one of those barristers who actually seems to care about what the outcome is and works really hard to get you where you need to be." **Recent work:** Acted on behalf of the Home Office in the high-profile case of Airways Solutions Limited v Secretary of State for the Home Department.

Anneliese Blackwood A knowledgeable junior who handles contentious and non-contentious matters, and has been involved in a significant percentage of the leading procurement cases that have gone to trial in recent years. **Strengths:** "She is very commercially minded and very quick to understand client concerns. An effective junior with a great understanding of the law." "Anneliese is extremely user-friendly and very strong tactically." **Recent work:** Acted for the defendants in the ground-breaking case of EdenRed (UK Group) Limited v Her Majesty's Treasury & Others.

Ligia Osepciu A talented junior who has experience in competition law, public procurement and utilities regulation. She has worked on a number of important cases, often unled. **Strengths:** "She is so good, and never makes you feel like you're a burden on her time." "She's bright, friendly and flexible." **Recent work:** Acted as sole counsel for Milton Keynes Council in a challenge to the awarding of an asbestos removal contract.

Fiona Banks An able barrister with a far-reaching client list. As well as having a flourishing practice, she also contributes pieces on public procurement to various law publications. **Strengths:** "Fiona has an exceptional work ethic." **Recent work:** Acted on behalf of non-profit Counted4 in a challenge to a procurement process undertaken by Sunderland City Council for the provision of a substance misuse service.

Band 2

Keating Chambers

See profile on p.868

THE SET

Keating Chambers fields a very strong public procurement group and has a growing reputation for taking on high-profile cases in both the public and private sectors. Its members demonstrate a firm command of EU law and are involved at all stages of the procurement process, providing strategic advice to bidders as well as handling disputes. In addition, the set is praised for being "very proactive and commercially minded" in both its advice and approach to client service.

Client service: "The clerks are friendly and accessible, and keen to build a relationship with you." "If you want to know about counsel availability, they come back to you very quickly. Everything runs like clockwork there." Declan Redmond is director of clerking.

SILKS

Sarah Hannaford QC (see p.663) A superb silk who is respected across the board. She is instructed in procurement cases of the highest importance, in terms of both their monetary worth and legal significance. **Strengths:** "She's unbelievable in terms of her knowledge and her ability to cut through things and get right to the core of the issue." "User-friendly, phenomenally clever and a fantastic advocate." "As good as her superb reputation suggests." **Recent work:** Acted for the Legal Aid Agency in defending challenges from over 100 firms concerning the procurement process for contracts for criminal legal aid work.

Fionnuala McCredie QC (see p.712) Held in high esteem and with a busy procurement practice, she acts for both contracting authorities and challengers. **Strengths:** "A barrister who has a great manner with lawyers and clients, she cuts through everything and gives clear explanations." "Extraordinarily bright and unstuffy." "She's a force to be reckoned with."

JUNIORS

David Gollancz (see p.656) A former solicitor who brings a pragmatic approach to his procurement practice. His clients range from national and local government bodies to national and international companies. **Strengths:** "He's very detailed in his approach, has a great understanding of procurement law, and is good at making connections between cases and bringing everything together." "He's like the terminator of procurement law. He just doesn't stop until he's found you a solution or an argument." **Recent work:** Advised on the procurement of contracts for the new emergency services network, and defended a challenge brought by the incumbent supplier of said services.

Calum Lamont (see p.694) A junior who, thanks to his sophisticated approach to public procurement challenges, is in high demand by solicitors. **Strengths:** "Very diligent and hard-working, he is good at rolling up his sleeves, getting involved and coming up with ideas." **Recent work:** Acted for the appellant in Silverhill v Gottlieb, a much publicised case in which local councillor Kim Gottlieb took legal action against his own council.

Simon Taylor (see p.779) Handles public procurement cases as part of his strong competition and EU law practice. He handles both contentious and non-contentious work, and is also experienced in mediation. **Strengths:** "A great authority on competition law in the health service." "He's very client-friendly and bends over backwards to help you." **Recent work:** Acted for NHS England in successfully defending an application for judicial review of its decision not to contract a provider of stereotactic radiosurgery services.

Band 3

Blackstone Chambers

See profile on p.813

THE SET

Blackstone Chambers has an excellent reputation for its public law practice and handles high-profile work in the public procurement sector. The set's strong commercial outlook sees its members advising significant clients in the private sector including multinational companies, sports clubs and property developers. It also receives instruction from local authorities and government bodies on complex public sector disputes.

Client service: "Senior clerk Gary Oliver understands client needs, and is approachable and very attentive to us. We know all the clerks very well: they are a really cohesive team and know what their barristers can and cannot deliver."

SILKS

John Howell QC An experienced silk with an impeccable understanding of public law. He regularly appears in the High Court, Court of Appeal and Supreme Court, acting for clients from both public and private sectors. **Strengths:** "He comes from a public law background and is absolutely brilliant. He is a very persuasive advocate, both his analysis of the law and his skeletons are as good as you would ever get."

Javan Herberg QC An esteemed silk who handles public procurement cases as part of a much wider and highly successful public law and commercial practice. His procurement clients include airports, utilities and local authorities. **Recent work:** Acted in the Supreme Court for insurance brokers Risk Management Partners in a challenge to the decision of local authorities to award insurance contracts without a procurement process.

Adam Lewis QC A silk who is an expert in sports-related procurement. He acts for both private and public bodies. **Strengths:** "He is the best at what he does. There's none better in the sports law world." **Recent work:** Defended UK Sport against a challenge by British Swimming concerning the decision to reject a bid to fund synchronised swimming.

JUNIORS

James Segan An extremely able barrister who practises in EU, public and commercial law. He has key clients in the telecoms, IT and housing sectors. **Strengths:** "An experienced junior who is highly regarded throughout the sector." **Recent work:** Acted as leading counsel for Fujitsu in a damages claim against the Department for Transport concerning a major UK government IT contract.

Henderson Chambers

See profile on p.864

THE SET

Henderson Chambers has an established reputation in European law and is an attractive proposition for clients with procurement-related cases. Its barristers engage in both contentious and non-contentious work, and often appear in high-value procurement disputes. Members advise a varied client base consisting of government departments, NHS Trusts and defence contractors among others.

Client service: Head clerk John White impresses with his "attentiveness and professionalism." The other clerks under him are "friendly, good and quick."

SILKS

Rhodri Williams QC (see p.796) A silk with significant EU and public procurement law experience. He is regularly instructed by local and regional government bodies. **Strengths:** "He is hard-working and knows procurement law extremely well. He has gravitas, produces well-reasoned arguments and has always got us great results." **Recent work:** Acted for Triumph Furniture as the claimant in a high-value damages claim concerning a breach of public contracts regulations in relation to furniture supply and interior design services.

JUNIORS

Andrew Kinnier (see p.691) A junior who is known for his work on large-scale service agreements and regeneration projects, and who has considerable expertise in both court and arbitration proceedings. He also stands as junior counsel to the Crown and the Welsh government. **Strengths:** "He's a fantastic team player who's incredibly bright and insightful, and who always provides commercially driven advice." **Recent work:** Acted for Prime in a challenge to the procurement of healthcare-related construction projects.

Other Ranked Lawyers

Margaret Gray (Brick Court Chambers) A highly intelligent junior who regularly handles public procurement cases in the European courts. She is experienced in procurement cases relating to infrastructure, healthcare and construction. **Strengths:** "She is a very senior junior. You could compare her to a silk in terms of her ability and depth of experience." **Recent work:** Successfully defended Fermanagh District Council in a procurement challenge brought by a construction firm regarding a million-pound contract award.

Tim Johnston (Brick Court Chambers) A junior with a growing profile who is active in competition and European law, and is no stranger to procurement cases. **Strengths:** "He combines intelligence and sensitivity with an incredible work ethic. A proactive lawyer who has an excellent sense of humour." "Tim is a team player who will work all hours to get the job done. He is on a fantastic upward trajectory with his public procurement practice." **Recent work:** Defended the Ministry of Defence against a claim that it had unlawfully awarded a contract to a commercial rival.

Charles Béar QC (see p.593) (Fountain Court Chambers) Acts for both public and private sector clients in a range of high-profile procurement work. He is equally capable of taking on advisory and advocacy roles, and has trial experience that extends all the way up to the highest appellate courts. **Strengths:** "He's one of the few barristers who is both a brilliant black-letter lawyer and also fantastic on his feet." "He has an encyclopaedic knowledge of the law." **Recent work:** Represented claimants in the UK's largest ever procurement challenge. It had been brought by 11 firms of solicitors against the Lord Chancellor and concerned his award of criminal defence duty contract work.

Real Estate Litigation

Contents:

LONDON

Real Estate Litigation
Leading Sets
Band 1
Falcon Chambers *
Band 2
Landmark Chambers *
Maitland Chambers *
Wilberforce Chambers *
Band 3
Enterprise Chambers *
Selborne Chambers *
Serle Court *
Tanfield Chambers *
Band 4
Hardwicke *
Radcliffe Chambers *
* *Indicates set / individual with profile.*
Ⓐ *direct access (see p.24).*
◊ *(ORL) = Other Ranked Lawyer.*
Alphabetical order within each band. Band 1 is highest.

Real Estate Litigation
Leading Silks
Star individuals
Dowding Nicholas *Falcon Chambers* *
Band 1
Bhaloo Zia *Enterprise Chambers*
Fancourt Timothy *Falcon Chambers* *
Fetherstonhaugh Guy *Falcon Chambers* *
Gaunt Jonathan *Falcon Chambers* *
Johnson Edwin *Maitland Chambers* *
Jourdan Stephen *Falcon Chambers*
Karas Jonathan *Falcon Chambers* *
Male John *Landmark Chambers*
McGhee John *Maitland Chambers* *
Rainey Philip *Tanfield Chambers* Ⓐ *
Reynolds Kirk *Falcon Chambers* *
Seitler Jonathan *Wilberforce Chambers*
Small Jonathan *Falcon Chambers*
Wicks Joanne *Wilberforce Chambers*
Band 2
Barnes Michael *Wilberforce Chambers*
Bhose Ranjit *Cornerstone Barristers (ORL)* ◊ *
Holland David *Landmark Chambers*
Holland Katharine *Landmark Chambers*
Hutchings Martin *Wilberforce Chambers*
Morshead Timothy *Landmark Chambers*
Pymont Christopher *Maitland Chambers* *
Walker Andrew *Maitland Chambers* *
Wonnacott Mark *Maitland Chambers*
Band 3
Ayliffe James *Wilberforce Chambers*
Driscoll Michael *Maitland Chambers* *
Dutton Timothy C *Maitland Chambers* *
Elvin David *Landmark Chambers*
Furber John *Wilberforce Chambers*
Laurence George *New Square Chambers (ORL)* ◊ *
Stevens-Hoare Brie *Hardwicke* Ⓐ
Stoner Christopher *Serle Court* *
Tager Romie *Selborne Chambers* *
Warwick Mark *Selborne Chambers* *
Band 4
Bignell Janet *Falcon Chambers* *
Blaker Gary *Selborne Chambers* Ⓐ *
de Waal John *Hardwicke* Ⓐ
Grant Thomas *Maitland Chambers*
Halpern David *4 New Square (ORL)* ◊ *
Pearce Robert *Radcliffe Chambers* *
Reed Rupert *Wilberforce Chambers*
Sheehan Malcolm *Henderson Chambers (ORL)* ◊ Ⓐ *
Tipples Amanda *Maitland Chambers* *
Trace Anthony *Maitland Chambers* *
New Silks
Clarke Ian *Selborne Chambers* *
Davey Jonathan *Wilberforce Chambers*
Johns Alan *Maitland Chambers*
Shea Caroline *Falcon Chambers*
Weekes Tom *Landmark Chambers*

Band 1

Falcon Chambers

See profile on p.842

THE SET

Falcon Chambers continues to display an unparalleled level of expertise and dominance in the Bar's property litigation sector. Known for having one of the finest real estate benches in the market, it has several pre-eminent silks and juniors. The set demonstrates its prowess across the full spectrum of real estate issues, and boasts barristers with specific knowledge of niche areas such as manorial rights, village greens and agriculture. Sources praise it, saying: "It absolutely leads the market in terms of the breadth of experience that it has. If it's something niche and tricky, it seems that Falcon always has someone there that has the relevant expertise to tick the box that you need. To have someone on your side with their barristers' level of expertise is priceless." **Client service:** Steve Francis is the senior clerk.

SILKS

Nicholas Dowding QC (see p.636) Remains the top-ranked silk in the Real Estate Litigation Bar. He is an expert in all areas of property law and is regularly selected to act as an arbitrator. **Strengths:** "Nick's in a league of his own." "He remains a firm favourite. He has an outstanding brain and an excellent client manner." "He is clever and an incredibly persuasive advocate, who is kind and courteous. Judges listen to him and clients trust him." **Recent work:** Handled a five-day valuation arbitration linked to a major distribution centre in Hong Kong.

Timothy Fancourt QC (see p.643) His practice encompasses leasehold obligations and development agreements, commercial leases and appeals, and he has further expertise in protest and occupation matters. He is well reputed for his proven track record of handling high-profile matters. **Strengths:** "He is certainly one of the leading QCs in the property litigation field. He has an extremely good reputation and he's someone we trust with high-level work." "He is a very persuasive advocate and a good opponent. He gets to the bottom of the issues." **Recent work:** Acted in an appeal surrounding a contract which was key to the sale of a shopping complex located in Windsor.

Guy Fetherstonhaugh QC (see p.644) Acts as the joint head of chambers and is widely respected in the market. His areas of expertise include rent review, easements and restricted covenants. **Strengths:** "Aside from his outstanding legal abilities, he has fantastic client skills and a great sense of humour which helps." "He's the go-to person for rent interpretations." **Recent work:** Acted in the high-profile Marks & Spencer v BNP Paribas break clause case.

Jonathan Gaunt QC (see p.651) Regularly represents clients in matters concerning enfranchisement, rent review and enforcement of covenants. **Strengths:** "He is a true heavyweight." "At trial, I felt completely in safe hands. It was almost like he didn't need to speak. He never made me feel stressed and he very much had the ear of the court." **Recent work:** Acted in a case involving a boundary dispute between two neighbours which concerned the implications of the hedge and ditch rule.

Stephen Jourdan QC Has an extremely wide property and agricultural law practice and also handles property-related insolvency, partnership and professional negligence claims. **Strengths:** "He is excellent. He is very intelligent, and he gets right to the heart of the issues very quickly." "Stephen's vast experience shines through when he is advising." **Recent work:** Successfully achieved summary judgment application for the defendant in a case that was an interpretation of Section 36C of the Companies Act 1985.

Jonathan Karas QC (see p.687) Has a practice that is predominantly centred around land law. He specialises in the crossover of planning, agriculture and property law, and is an expert in right to light. **Strengths:** "Jonathan's practice is very broad and he is one of those rare advocates who advises on both planning and property litigation, which makes him very useful indeed." **Recent work:** Provided right-to-light advice to developers looking to construct a significant structure in Tower Hamlets.

Kirk Reynolds QC (see p.750) Maintains his standing as a leading property silk, and operates across the full range of property law matters. **Strengths:** "He writes the book on dilapidations and is a very good operator." "Absolutely outstanding, he is very clever and clients love him." "He never ceases to amaze with his ability to think outside the box – he's your man when you're really up against it."

Jonathan Small QC Focuses on a variety of legal matters linked to development, and regularly handles overage, rights of way and purchase disputes. **Strengths:** "Excellent commercial understanding." "Fantastic at contractual disputes relating to property."

Janet Bignell QC (see p.596) Regularly instructed in high-value development disputes. Her practice has a strong focus on landlord and tenant law, but she handles the full range of real estate disputes, including leasehold and contractual issues. **Strengths:** "Offers strong commercial advice on landlord and tenant, and general property matters, and is good in court." "Incredibly bright, accessible and someone who gets to grips with a matter quickly." **Recent work:** Acted in a case with elements of land registration law. She successfully rebuked claimants' dam-

Real Estate Litigation

Leading Juniors

Band 1

- **Clark** Wayne *Falcon Chambers*
- **Radevsky** Anthony *Falcon Chambers* *
- **Rosenthal** Adam *Falcon Chambers* *
- **Sefton** Mark *Falcon Chambers*
- **Stacey** Myriam *Landmark Chambers*
- **Taggart** Nicholas *Landmark Chambers*
- **Tanney** Anthony *Falcon Chambers* *
- **Tozer** Stephanie *Falcon Chambers* *

Band 2

- **Bruce** Andrew *Serle Court* *
- **Cowen** Gary *Falcon Chambers* *
- **Denehan** Edward *9 Stone Buildings (ORL)* ◇
- **Dray** Martin *Falcon Chambers* *
- **Duckworth** Nathaniel *Falcon Chambers*
- **Fieldsend** James *Tanfield Chambers* Ⓐ *
- **Francis** Andrew *Serle Court* *
- **Greenhill** Julian *Wilberforce Chambers*
- **Harpum** Charles *Falcon Chambers* *
- **Healey** Greville *Falcon Chambers* *
- **Heather** Christopher *Tanfield Chambers* *
- **Hornett** Stuart *Selborne Chambers* Ⓐ *
- **Jefferies** Thomas *Landmark Chambers*
- **Kitson** Justin *Selborne Chambers* *
- **Lamont** Camilla *Landmark Chambers*
- **Peters** Edward *Falcon Chambers* *
- **Pryor** Michael *Maitland Chambers* *
- **Scott** Tiffany *Wilberforce Chambers*
- **Windsor** Emily *Falcon Chambers* *

Band 3

- **Buckpitt** Michael *Tanfield Chambers* *
- **Calland** Timothy *Maitland Chambers*
- **Chorfi** Camilla *Selborne Chambers* *
- **Fitzgerald** Elizabeth *Falcon Chambers*
- **Gunaratna** Kavan *Enterprise Chambers*
- **Hutton** Caroline *Enterprise Chambers*
- **Kalfon** Olivier *Maitland Chambers* *
- **Letman** Paul *3 Hare Court (ORL)* ◇
- **Muir** Nicola *Tanfield Chambers* Ⓐ *
- **Ollech** Joseph *Falcon Chambers* *
- **Polli** Timothy *Tanfield Chambers* Ⓐ *
- **Radley-Gardner** Oliver *Falcon Chambers*
- **Rolfe** Patrick *5 Stone Buildings (ORL)* ◇ *
- **Steinert** Jonathan *Henderson Chambers (ORL)* ◇ Ⓐ *
- **Taskis** Catherine *Falcon Chambers* *
- **Trompeter** Nicholas *Selborne Chambers* Ⓐ *
- **Watkin** Toby *Landmark Chambers*

Band 4

- **Bates** Justin *Arden Chambers (ORL)* ◇ *
- **Bickford-Smith** Stephen *Landmark Chambers*
- **Braithwaite** Thomas *Serle Court* *
- **Bredemear** Zachary *1 Chancery Lane (ORL)* ◇ Ⓐ
- **Butler** Andrew *Tanfield Chambers* Ⓐ *
- **Clegg** Richard *Selborne Chambers* Ⓐ *
- **Crampin** Cecily *Falcon Chambers* *
- **Demachkie** Jamal *Hardwicke*
- **Denyer-Green** Barry *Falcon Chambers* *
- **Dovar** Daniel *Tanfield Chambers* *
- **Gatty** Daniel *Hardwicke* Ⓐ
- **Gibbons** Ellodie *Tanfield Chambers* Ⓐ *
- **Harrison** Philomena *Maitland Chambers* *
- **Isaac** Nicholas *Tanfield Chambers* Ⓐ *
- **Kokelaar** Sebastian *Three Stone (ORL)* ◇
- **Mendoza** Neil *Selborne Chambers* *
- **Shuman** Karen *1 Chancery Lane (ORL)* ◇ Ⓐ
- **Sissons** Philip *Falcon Chambers*
- **Smith** Adam *Maitland Chambers* *
- **West** Mark *Radcliffe Chambers* *
- **Williams** Simon *Radcliffe Chambers* *

Band 5

- **Barton** Zoe *Selborne Chambers* *
- **Bleasdale** Marie-Claire *Radcliffe Chambers* *
- **Cox** Tamsin *Falcon Chambers* *
- **Darton** Clifford *Ely Place Chambers (ORL)* ◇ *
- **Fain** Carl *Tanfield Chambers* Ⓐ *
- **Falkowski** Damian *39 Essex Chambers (ORL)* ◇ Ⓐ
- **Faulkner** Benjamin *Wilberforce Chambers*
- **Francis** Edward *Enterprise Chambers*
- **Glover** Marc *Tanfield Chambers* *
- **Helmore** Katie *Landmark Chambers*
- **Hicks** Edward *Radcliffe Chambers* *
- **Loveday** Mark *Tanfield Chambers* *
- **Moffett** William *Radcliffe Chambers* *
- **Palfrey** Monty *Hardwicke*
- **Selway** Kate *Radcliffe Chambers* *
- **Walder** Aaron *Landmark Chambers*
- **Walsh** Michael *Tanfield Chambers* *
- **Ward** Galina *Landmark Chambers*
- **Yates** Katrina *Landmark Chambers*

Up-and-coming individuals

- **Holmes** Harriet *Tanfield Chambers* *

* *Indicates individual with profile.*

Ⓐ *direct access (see p.24).*

◇ *(ORL) = Other Ranked Lawyer.*

Alphabetical order within each band. Band 1 is highest.

ages claims related to a marketing issue in the sale of the Vauxhall Cross development site.

Caroline Shea QC Handles commercial and residential landlord and tenant disputes, many of which are complex in nature. She has a great deal of expertise in the appellate courts. **Strengths:** "She is absolutely outstanding. She is not only a great lawyer but she has excellent client skills." **Recent work:** Acted in Winterburn v Bennett, a legally sensitive appeal involving important questions to do with the law of easements.

JUNIORS

Wayne Clark Handles a good deal of commercial property disputes, and is an expert on business tenancies. He also advises on development, joint venture agreements and overage provisions. **Strengths:** "He knows the area inside out, and he's very good on paper." "He is charming but deadly. He stuck the knife in, in a very charming way."

Anthony Radevsky (see p.746) Has a practice that combines property law with real estate-related professional negligence. He is noted for his expertise in leasehold enfranchisement. **Strengths:** "Has a massive reputation as a towering academic and a walking encyclopaedia on certain property law areas. He has an unnerving ability to explain in one sentence what it takes ten pages for others to explain." **Recent work:** Acted in Snowball Assets Ltd v Huntsmore House (Freehold), which involved the valuation of freehold in collective enfranchisement.

Adam Rosenthal (see p.755) Widely recognised as a high-level junior in his field. His main areas of focus include landlord and tenant litigation, restrictive covenants and insolvency issues. **Strengths:** "He is very bright, he knows his stuff, and he is very good on his feet in court." "Ticks every box and I strongly suspect that he will be a QC before too long." **Recent work:** Successfully represented Prince Evans LLP in a land registration and professional negligence claim brought against it by A2 Dominion Homes.

Mark Sefton Widely acknowledged as one of the leading juniors in his field. His practice has a focus on property-related insolvency, as well as commercial and residential landlord and tenant disputes. **Strengths:** "Hugely brainy – he's very insightful." "A major strength is his approachability – he is always happy to assist with even obscure queries. His advice is always down to earth, sensibly reasoned and practical." **Recent work:** Advised clients on a recovery dispute concerning a £21 million development site in Romford.

Anthony Tanney (see p.778) Continues to be sought out for his exemplary work across a range of real property matters. His specialisms include rent review, rights of way and land registration. He is also known to take on cases related to easements and professional negligence. **Strengths:** "He's a very solid performer – he knows his stuff inside and out, no question about that." "Anthony Tanney has been excellent; his written opinions are fantastic and really clear. He is very good tactically." "Consistently provides high-quality advice."

Stephanie Tozer (see p.783) Handles a plethora of property-related disputes, and is recognised for her skill in handling residential and commercial landlord and tenant disputes. **Strengths:** "Extremely bright and as thorough in her preparation of her cases as anyone we have worked with." "She has an incisive mind and is a robust advocate." "Hard-working and efficient, she provides quality advice and excellent paperwork and is very easy to work with." **Recent work:** Settled a £40 million claim for compensation against TfL concerning Farringdon station.

Gary Cowen (see p.625) Frequently advises on complex litigation, and has a great deal of experience in the Court of Appeal. Real estate forms the core of his chancery practice and he has notable experience in restrictive covenants and leasehold enfranchisement. **Strengths:** "He is incredibly together and calm." "He's quick, responsive and able to deal with numerous questions arising out of very complex scenarios." "Gives clear and practical advice." **Recent work:** Instructed in Blackwell & Another v Bailey & Another, a case concerning an injunction designed to prevent the defendant pursuing a business venture in their home.

Martin Dray (see p.636) A highly sought-after junior, with a specialism in high-profile property cases. He covers a range of matters including boundary disputes, lease renewals and adverse possession disputes. He also sits as a judge in the First-tier Tribunal. **Strengths:** "He's a brilliant lawyer – but he's also very funny and charming." "Martin is excellent to work with. He's approachable and quick to turn matters around." **Recent work:** Acted in Paton v Cordrey, a long-running boundary dispute.

Nathaniel Duckworth An expert in real property, and residential and commercial landlord and tenant work. He is an expert in everything from boundary disputes and adverse possession claims to easements and restrictive covenants. **Strengths:** "Offers excellent, pragmatic advice, which is quickly turned around."

Charles Harpum (see p.664) Receives plaudits for his extensive knowledge of property law and his ability to handle complex matters. His areas of focus include conveyancing law, land registration, and landlord and tenant law. **Strengths:** "Frankly he's absolutely magnificent, he's quite simply faultless. It's a pleasure to give him something hugely complex." **Recent work:** Has recently acted on a number of cases related to fishing rights, including a very complex case about the title to fishing rights in Derbyshire.

Greville Healey (see p.668) His practice is centred around rights of way and rights of light issues, as well as landlord and tenant law. Clients appreciate his ability to handle complex matters. **Strengths:** "Continues to prove himself an excellent advocate. He is exceptionally popular with clients and very much treated by them as part of their wider legal team." "He is very creative. He turned what was a pretty hopeless claim into something quite formidable." **Recent work:** Acted in a two-day rights of light trial at County Court which raised interesting and difficult legal questions regarding the court's jurisdiction to grant damages in lieu of an injunction.

Edward Peters (see p.736) Has cultivated a reputation as a property litigation specialist, and is praised by peers for his intelligent approach to his cases. His practice takes in dilapidations, covenants and possession claims. **Strengths:** "Meticulous and likeable." "Very competent, very quietly spoken and intellectually good." "Excellent – a clear adviser on restrictive covenant claims and agricultural property disputes." **Recent work:** Acted for the claimant, a hotel company, in its claim for damages arising from the negligent drafting of a lease.

Emily Windsor (see p.798) Has a practice which spans all facets of property litigation, and particular experience with regard to development agreements, rent review and leasehold enfranchisement. **Strengths:** "Emily is a delightful person to deal with." "She provides excellent, thorough, practical and commercial advice – she is part of the team." **Recent work:** Acted in Benyatov v Redrow Homes, resisting an order for specific performance of two sale contracts.

Elizabeth Fitzgerald Advises her clients on both commercial and residential landlord and tenant matters. She is also adept at handling compulsory purchase orders and professional negligence cases. **Strengths:** "She's at the junior end of Falcon, but somebody who needs to be taken seriously; she's very good." "You would want Elizabeth on your side. She is a very good advocate who is popular with clients."

Joseph Ollech (see p.730) Has a robust real estate litigation practice and wide experience of disputes arising under the 1954 Act, the Rent Acts and the Housing Acts. He is particularly strong on restrictive covenants, easements, adverse possession claims and boundary disputes, and is also an expert in property-related company and insolvency law. **Strengths:** "He is very approachable, very bright and highly responsive." "In a chambers where everyone is clever, one always senses that Joe, even though still junior, would rank amongst the very cleverest. His advisory work is outstanding." **Recent work:** Acted in a case that dealt with riparian rights, negligence, nuisance and abstraction of water.

Oliver Radley-Gardner Acknowledged for his diverse property practice that incorporates proprietary estoppel, negligence issues, and landlord and tenant litigation. He also has a burgeoning reputation in telecoms. **Strengths:** "Of the crop of outstanding youngsters at Falcon Chambers, Oliver is our favourite. He has a first-class intellect." "He is very strong, has a lot of experience with enfranchisement and right-to-manage cases, and a vast knowledge of property law generally."

Catherine Taskis (see p.778) Noted for her far-reaching expertise in both residential and commercial landlord and tenant real property law. Clients seek her out for her specialism in agricultural law. **Strengths:** "It is always a pleasure instructing her." "She is user-friendly, bright and a go-to real estate specialist." **Recent work:** Successfully represented the applicant in Kerrai v Radia, an attempt to modify a restrictive covenant that would have prevented building on land.

Cecily Crampin (see p.625) Widely acknowledged as an exceptionally promising property junior, with a sophisticated practice. Her focuses include landlord and tenant, mortgage and real property work. **Strengths:** "She is very able and very much a rising star." "She is brilliant at property litigation and someone to really watch for the future." "She is very bright and very imaginative when it comes to producing creative solutions to problems." **Recent work:** Instructed in a multi-claim dispute involving a group of developers and a leaseholder. The case concerned interpretation of contracts and land registration.

Barry Denyer-Green (see p.632) A strong performer in compulsory purchase and compensation cases. He also has experience in the Lands Tribunal. **Strengths:** "Possesses strong legal understanding and an excellent bedside manner." "Extremely knowledgeable when it comes to CPO claims and very user-friendly." **Recent work:** Acted in a compulsory purchase case in the Upper Tribunal and handled the subsequent claim for compensation.

Philip Sissons Handles a range of real estate litigation matters including landlord and tenant issues, and is widely recognised for his formidable expertise in the High Court, County Courts and the Court of Appeal. **Strengths:** "Really approachable and straightforward." "Philip is one of the brightest of the youngsters and will go a long way." **Recent work:** Acted for Lynn Shellfish in its appeal to the Court of Appeal. The case has now been allowed to proceed to the Supreme Court.

Tamsin Cox (see p.625) Predominantly focuses on landlord and tenant cases in both commercial and residential settings. **Strengths:** "Amongst the juniors, she has always stood out and has always been excellent. She's very good on her feet and very reliable." "She's a confident advocate who gives superb written advice in a client-friendly form." **Recent work:** Advised on a claim to enfranchise made by the representatives of deceased tenants on a large West London estate.

Band 2

Landmark Chambers

See profile on p.873

THE SET

Landmark Chambers packs a punch due to its expertise in handling high-profile property disputes. The set offers a vast array of legal services and has a multidisciplinary group with expertise in planning and environmental work. Its members continue to be praised by clients as leaders in real estate litigation and are supported by a strong clerking team. "They understand my firm, my practice and what I need. They are largely considered to be one of the top real estate chambers, and I use them because they are specialists," a source says. Individuals here are frequently called upon to take on cases ranging from contractual disputes and nuisance claims to trespass and rights of light cases.

Client service: "The clerking is really good and really responsive. The service is very good." Jay Fullilove is the senior clerk.

SILKS

John Male QC Has extensive experience dealing with rent reviews and business tenancies, and is noted for his skill as an arbitrator. He is highly sought after for his knowledge of landlord and tenant property litigation. **Strengths:** "An exceptional intellect and someone who always goes the extra mile. His calm and reassuring manner is popular with clients." "He is always a favourite with real estate clients. John is responsive and has real gravitas."

David Holland QC A skilled property litigator, who is known for working closely with property developers, individual householders and landowners. His expertise extends to property-related professional negligence. **Strengths:** "He is a pleasure to work with – very no-nonsense and straight-talking, which is great." "David inspires confidence. He is decisive and robust. He knows the details and is good with sophisticated clients." **Recent work:** Acted for Vodafone in a claim by a developer seeking to force the company to vacate a development site in central Manchester.

Katharine Holland QC Garners praise for her broad practice and her user-friendly approach. She has a strong track record of acting in high-profile cases including disputes relating to landmarks and football clubs. **Strengths:** "She has fantastic protester expertise; she would be our first choice in this area. She is fantastically user-friendly." "Devastating in court, and leaves no stone unturned in her preparation for key court applications." **Recent work:** Acted in Cabot Carbon v Manchester Ship Canal Company, in which a challenge to an arbitration award was successfully resisted.

Timothy Morshead QC An accomplished property silk, with a practice which incorporates chancery and public law litigation. He is notable for his ability to expertly analyse and advise on the interpretation of leases and overage agreements. **Strengths:** "Extremely clever and very quick. You ring him and within two hours you get back accurate written advice. He is very good on his feet too, with great communication skills." "He's rigorous and clever and he's got a very nice style orally – he's a very effective advocate." **Recent work:** Conducted the appeal in Woolway (VO) v Mazars, a case related to rating law.

David Elvin QC A highly capable property silk, with particular expertise in public law, planning and environmental law. The cases he undertakes range from compulsory purchase and compensation matters to those involving highways and human rights. He is known for his extensive work in the Court of Appeal, High Court and ECHR. **Strengths:** "He is astonishing; he is readily available, has a brilliant mind and is very clear in his advice." **Recent work:** Acted in R (Gottlieb) v Winchester City Council, a case concerning a city centre regeneration scheme.

Tom Weekes QC Noted for having an exceptional property litigation practice, and has been elevated to Queen's Counsel this year. His practice takes in landlord and tenant disputes, as well as commercial property litigation. **Strengths:** "He is excellent in every regard, user-friendly, knowledgeable and someone who gives good pragmatic advice." "He gets straight to the point." **Recent work:** Acted on a successful appeal pertaining to a dispute between neighbouring owners of a commercial premises.

JUNIORS

Myriam Stacey Covers a broad range of real estate litigation issues, and has a diverse skill set, handling matters relating to service charges, conveyancing, restrictive covenants and adverse possession. **Strengths:** "She is frighteningly bright." "She's intelligent, attentive and personable." "She gives spot-on, clear advice." **Recent work:** Acted for the landlord in Carlos Place v Timothy Taylor Gallery, a case concerning a property in Mayfair undergoing redevelopment. The tenant brought claims of interference and breach of covenant.

Nicholas Taggart A leading property junior, who is regularly sought out for his expertise in landlord and tenant cases, and issues arising from commercial property disputes such as rent reviews and dilapidations. **Strengths:** "Easy-going, dependable barrister with a wealth of experience across the property sector. He is always a delight to work with and well liked by clients. He anticipates the next step and you find he'll have already prepared before you have finished instructing him." **Recent work:** Acted in Osborne (Bournemouth) Ltd. v Bournemouth District Council, a multimillion-pound claim by a developer against a local authority following the termination of a joint venture agreement between them.

Thomas Jefferies A talented property litigation junior renowned for his work in enfranchisement, planning and commercial landlord and tenant cases. His practice also extends to mediation and he is well versed in handling planning inquiries and appeals. **Strengths:** "He is extremely clever."

Camilla Lamont A well-respected property barrister with expertise pertaining to service charge litigation, mixed-use schemes and commercial property disputes. She is also known for her work in environmental litigation. **Strengths:** "She is unbelievably bright. She can put things into layman's terms for clients." "She is approachable, always available on the phone and able to work things through." **Recent work:** Acted for the National Bank of Greece enforcing a multimillion-pound judgment handed down by a Cypriot court.

Toby Watkin Advises landowners, local authorities and developers on restrictive covenant and enforcement issues. **Strengths:** "He's intelligent, attentive and personable. Clients like him." "He is very knowledgeable and easy to work with. He's commercially minded." **Recent work:** Represented Homebase and Argos in relation to several complex 1954 Act issues affecting their various outlets.

Stephen Bickford-Smith Known for his focus on real property and construction disputes. He regularly takes on development agreement, boundary and easement law cases. **Strengths:** "He is the author of the leading book on the subject of rights of light. He knows the subject inside out and gives very good advice." **Recent work:** Represented the defendants in Patel v Griffiths, a declaratory relief claim. He argued with success that the proposed work by the claimants would breach several of the defendants' rights.

Katie Helmore Recognised for her versatile property practice that covers a wide scope of property law issues. She has specialist knowledge of both aviation and protester injunctions. **Strengths:** "She's brilliant; she's very robust and very commercial which always impresses my clients." "Brilliant. She knows how to manage clients' problems." **Recent work:** Represented a client in a High Court claim for a possession order of a £42 million listed property in Pall Mall that had been invaded by 30 trespassers.

Aaron Walder Highly capable property junior with experience across a diverse range of areas, who is an expert in agricultural matters, forfeiture and breach of covenant. He also handles enfranchisement, rights of light and development cases. **Strengths:** "He is good at giving a view or informed opinion, and we see him as an extra member of the team. He is very good at communication." **Recent work:** Represented the developer in a dispute with the purchaser of two flats in the Orion building in Birmingham City Centre.

Galina Ward Handles property litigation as part of a broad practice that also encompasses public law, immigration and ratings cases. She is known for her work in social housing as well as commercial and residential landlord and tenant disputes. **Strengths:** "A powerful and effective advocate." **Recent work:** Instructed in Dudley MBC v Dudley Muslim Association, a claim by the local authority for specific performance of a re-transfer clause in a transfer of land.

Katrina Yates Garners praise for her diligent approach and her expertise when it comes to land registry matters. Other areas of focus include landlord and tenant disputes and real property cases. **Strengths:** "Very commercial and very responsive." "Thorough and concise in her advice." **Recent work:** Acted in Ameen Adam v Salim Adam, a case where the applicant was seeking a beneficial interest in Yates' client's property.

Maitland Chambers

See profile on p.875

THE SET

Maitland Chambers is well known for its real estate expertise and can handle every facet of property law. Its members have a number of Supreme Court and a host of Court of Appeal cases under their belts and are "very knowledgeable about the industry. They have a lot of experience, are all very approachable, and don't talk down to the client." Aside from pure property work, they are also adept at property-related insolvency disputes.

Client service: "They have very good levels of service and the clerking is always very helpful." John Wiggs is the set's senior clerk.

SILKS

Edwin Johnson QC (see p.684) Receives praise from the market for his skill as an advocate. His practice is predominantly focused on professional negligence claims arising from real estate. **Strengths:** "He is particularly good on his feet, and a very smooth operator who is incredibly intelligent and prepared to get stuck in. He's a silk who doesn't mind getting his hands dirty." "He has an amazing brain and he is user-friendly and clear."

John McGhee QC (see p.712) A leading property silk, whose practice takes in property-related professional negligence matters as well as general real estate cases. He is admired for his tactical approach. **Strengths:** "A first choice for rights of light." "He is technically very strong and, importantly, fits in well and works well with our clients." **Recent work:** Acted in Tindall Cobham v Adda Hotels, a high-profile Landlord and Tenant Act case regarding a number of Hilton hotels.

Christopher Pymont QC (see p.745) Head of Maitland Chambers who counts restrictive covenants, break clauses and leases as just some of his areas of expertise. **Strengths:** "Excellent under pressure and great with clients." **Recent work:** Successfully acted for the claimants in the Supreme Court case of FHR v Mankarious.

Andrew Walker QC (see p.788) Handles real estate-related litigation, arbitrations and expert determinations. His recent work has seen him dealing with planning obligations, contract disputes and rent review. He garners praise for his multifaceted practice. **Strengths:** "Good attention to detail and commercially minded." "First choice for heavyweight matters requiring more seniority."

Mark Wonnacott QC An established property silk with a practice involving complex property litigation, who regularly handles landlord and tenant, and dilapidations cases. He has appeared at all levels of the domestic courts up to the Supreme Court. **Strengths:** "He is so level-headed and he gives direct advice." "He's a no-nonsense, straight-talking QC and he's very smart." "He is a class apart and he will do things his way."

Michael Driscoll QC (see p.637) Regularly handles a plethora of real estate matters, and is particularly known for advising building societies and banks on cases concerning negligence and breach of trust. His expertise extends to telecommunications, rent review and property development matters. **Strengths:** "Exceptionally thorough and clear in his opinion."

Timothy Dutton QC (see p.638) Receives much praise for his client-friendly approach, and his knowledge of property-related disputes. His work concentrates on enfranchisements, equitable remedies and contractual disputes. **Strengths:** "Tim is an excellent barrister who has a good rapport with clients and a real feel for landlord and tenant disputes. He is particularly strong on rent review matters and his advice is always excellent." **Recent work:** Acted in Dooba Developments v McLagan Investments, a case concerning a conditional contract to buy land for a supermarket.

Thomas Grant QC A respected property silk with a focus on landlord and tenant matters. His practice specialises in chancery litigation and he regularly appears in the Court of Appeal. **Strengths:** "Tom's advocacy is excellent and he has a very good client manner." "Highly impressive advocate who cuts through complex issues to give sound, commercial advice." **Recent work:** Acted in Heaselands v Crest Nicholson, a case that centred around overage payments arising from a development agreement.

Amanda Tipples QC (see p.781) Covers a broad range of property and commercial chancery litigation and is a regular choice for clients faced with very knotty problems. **Strengths:** "She knows her onions and clients love her, as she is an effective advocate." "She is consistently brilliant." **Recent work:** Represented a company acting as the proprietor of a West London property, against a third party who claimed interest in the property by means of proprietary estoppel.

Anthony Trace QC (see p.783) Predominantly focuses on property litigation cases, many of which are highly publicised. He works frequently with City firms, and is known for the superior quality of his cross-examinations. **Strengths:** "A first-rate advocate."

Alan Johns QC Elevated to Queen's Counsel earlier this year, he is known for his decisiveness and his impressive tactical mind. His work is focused on property law, and he is an expert in retail and leisure developments. **Strengths:** "He is tactically shrewd, quick-thinking and extremely personable – a great all-rounder." "Commercial and extremely sharp-witted." **Recent work:** Represented the lessee in a high-profile forfeiture trial concerning the Kensington Park Hotel.

JUNIORS

Michael Pryor (see p.744) A highly praised senior junior, with a dedicated real estate litigation practice. He has devoted much of his time to enfranchisement work as well as property-related professional negligence. **Strengths:** "He has a massive sense of humour, is really good fun and is absolutely brilliant on the detail." "Allies enthusiasm with real forensic ability." **Recent work:** Instructed in BG Penny v European Metal Recycling, a case concerning a scrap metal yard, which looked at issues including nature of access and drainage rights.

Timothy Calland Has a commercial chancery practice with an impressive property law focus. His practice covers the full gamut of real estate issues. **Strengths:** "A fantastic advocate who remains calm in a crisis and provides sharp, commercially focused advice on all instructions. A force to be reckoned with in the courtroom." "Very able and knows his stuff inside and out." **Recent work:** Acted in Slough Borough Council v (1) Orange Personal Communications Ltd, (2) EE Ltd, advising the landowner in a dispute between the two phone companies regarding the removal of a telecoms mast.

Olivier Kalfon (see p.687) Regularly handles contentious property matters including residential and commercial landlord and tenant disputes. He often advises on property-related insolvency. **Strengths:** "A strong advocate and a respected adviser. He is always calm and considered, and is good with clients."

Philomena Harrison (see p.666) Widely acknowledged as a prominent property junior with experience in break option disputes and property-related professional negligence. She works closely with investment funds and banks. **Strengths:** "Very impressive." "Very hands-on, commercial and extremely approachable and knowledgeable." "She's a force to be reckoned with." **Recent work:** Represented Samuel Smith Old Brewery in a case concerning proceedings to fix the price of the freehold of a property.

Adam Smith (see p.767) Specialises in real estate litigation, concentrating on leasehold enfranchisement, commercial lease renewals and service charge disputes. **Strengths:** "His advice is always spot-on and he has pulled a couple of rabbits out of the hat this year. He is quite gentle in court. Judges like him and he has had some great results." **Recent work:** Successfully achieved a judgment in favour of Barclays Bank against Poling Worldwide. This was a dispute concerning a charge over a mixed residential and commercial property.

Wilberforce Chambers

See profile on p.925

THE SET

Wilberforce demonstrates a mastery of property work, attracting work ranging from advising on real estate transactions and development proposals to high-value disputes for prominent clients. Its members are regarded as a tough proposition to come up against in court, with sources saying: " Wilberforce is difficult to beat, frankly. Everybody there is at the top of their game." The set is widely acclaimed for its widespread expertise in cases concerning adverse possession, trusts of lands, village greens, easements and restricted covenants.

Client service: "Mark Rushton is the clerk there and he gives great service. He's brilliant at clerking and he's my go-to person for bigger stuff. He's very good at finding people within my budget for all my needs."

SILKS

Jonathan Seitler QC Continues to be considered one of the top property litigation silks of the Bar. He frequently handles a broad caseload of high-profile, complex real estate disputes. **Strengths:** "He's in a different league." "He has immense flair." "Jon Seitler is a standout individual – he's very down to earth and he's super-bright." **Recent work:** Represented Stella McCartney in a Landlord and Tenant Act 1954 case relating to the proposed development of a flagship store on Bond Street.

Joanne Wicks QC Has a fine reputation as a top real estate QC, and has a practice centred around property transactions and professional negligence. She has recently seen an increase in arbitration and expert determination work. **Strengths:** "She's really smart and knows her stuff." "The way she picks up facts is very impressive. She is very astute and you always feel like she knows what's going on in the case." **Recent work:** Acted for Josephs of Bond Street in a Landlord and Tenant Act 1954 case against fashion designer Stella McCartney, resisting the proposed development of a flagship store on Bond Street in premises occupied by Josephs.

Michael Barnes QC Well known for his work in administrative and property law. His primary focus is on cases concerning estoppel, laws of natural justice, and landlord and tenant disputes. His recent work has seen him acting in cases in the Cayman Islands and Hong Kong. **Strengths:** "Highly intellectual and has a strategic mind for litigation."

Martin Hutchings QC Noted for his impressive property practice spanning contentious and non-contentious matters and professional liability. His areas of specialism include landlord and tenant matters, dilapidations and lease issues. **Strengths:** "Technically excellent and very commercial." "Very easy to work with, clever and thoughtful." **Recent work:** Represented the claimant in London & Regional v Corradi, a 1954 Act redevelopment case which also had elements of highway and trespass law.

James Ayliffe QC Often praised for his approach to property cases and his effectiveness as a communicator. He is the editor of a leading landlord and tenant practitioner text and he regularly handles high-value property disputes. **Strengths:** "He's very bright and he's very good at putting people at ease." "Superb, gives detailed but practical advice." **Recent work:** Successfully defended a £55 million claim against a company for losses caused by breach of options.

John Furber QC Particularly adept at handling landlord and tenant disputes, and is an expert on development and commercial property cases. His practice also incorporates matters relating to easements and restricted covenants. **Strengths:** "Well respected by the court. His advice is spot-on and very rarely changes throughout the process." "Hands-on and helpfully clear and firm in his directional steer of cases." **Recent work:** Successful claim for a declaration on behalf of the leaseholder of a commercial premises in West London that the landlord's consent for alterations to the premises to create 16 or 17 flats had been unreasonably withheld.

Rupert Reed QC Well known for his extensive property practice, he regularly undertakes disputes concerning the management and development of commercial properties. **Strengths:** "His written work is very good. He is very approachable and you can go to him for ad hoc advice." "Hands-on and very proactive." **Recent work:** Represented DAMAC in the DIFC Court of Appeal. This was a case concerning the ability of a developer to add additional office units on to the floor plan of a tower.

Jonathan Davey QC Has extensive experience of working in the Court of Appeal. He is an expert in real property and landlord and tenant disputes. **Strengths:** "Very good with clients, and someone with a very calm manner." "A brilliant Treasury counsel, in massive demand for good reason." **Recent work:** Acted in a high-value landlord and tenant dispute between a commercial landlord and tenant concerning Centre Point, New Oxford Street.

JUNIORS

Julian Greenhill A major player at the Property Bar known for his expertise in handling real property and landlord and tenant cases. **Strengths:** "Very commercially focused and very good with clients. He has an excellent bedside manner." "When you ask him to do something, he does exactly what you want – his drafting and teamwork are really impressive." **Recent work:** Represented GLH Hotels in its defence against an indemnity claim.

Tiffany Scott Has a highly visible practice in the property litigation sector. She has become known for her work in the full spectrum of real estate cases and handles matters relating to rights of light, trespass and adverse possession. She also regularly tackles development disputes. **Strengths:** "Technically very sharp and engaging with clients." "Bright and considered." **Recent work:** Successfully achieved an expedited trial and subsequent settlement of a dispute surrounding the sale, purchase and development of land that had increased in value after the initial agreement.

Benjamin Faulkner Focuses on high-profile, complex property litigation. He is noted for his user-friendly approach and attention to detail. His expertise extends to tenancy agreements and property statutes. **Strengths:** "He's thoughtful, very bright and he's a pleasure to work with." "He has great attention to detail. He is also good from a tactical perspective too, and you see that he cares about the cases he deals with." **Recent work:** Represented Gordon Ramsay in Ramsay v Love, a high-profile case concerning a major London pub.

Band 3

Enterprise Chambers

See profile on p.950

THE SET

Enterprise Chambers is a formidable property set with substantial expertise in landlord and tenant disputes that has a strong bench of junior counsel and a number of highly respected silks. Catering to a client base of mid-tier City and regional firms, it has recently handled a number of cases relating to development projects and further handled matters concerning the enforceability of leases and mortgage agreements. Those that instruct the set appreciate the level of specialism it has: "The barristers at Enterprise have a high level of knowledge of the issues surrounding real estate law. Whatever it is we need, they have people there that can deal with it across the board."

Client service: "Enterprise is a set that is hungry to impress." "Its clerks are great. They are really transparent on fees and commercial in their approach." Antony Armstrong leads the clerking team.

SILKS

Zia Bhaloo QC A well-established property silk with a long-standing reputation as one of the top landlord and tenant barristers. She also has niche expertise in telecoms work, and the interface between landlord and tenant and insolvency work. **Strengths:** "She's amazing. She's very cool, calm and collected and she's so smooth she makes it look effortless. Amazing to watch, she's very persuasive in the courtroom and has gravitas." "She is clearly very experienced and she knows her stuff, and for a QC, she is incredibly user-friendly. She doesn't rely on juniors too much – she gets stuck in herself." **Recent work:** Lea on Lynn Shellfish v Loose in the Supreme Court, representing the owner of a private fishery. The case involved the extent of a right established by prescription.

JUNIORS

Kavan Gunaratna Lauded for his user-friendly and positive approach to insolvency and property litigation. His practice includes business tenancy litigation, service charge disputes and property claims. **Strengths:** "He is a delight to work with, and is unflappable and creative." "Clients love him. He is great, he's thorough, he's very good on his feet and he's very charming." **Recent work:** Acted for the owner of Pointwest Building in a high-value service charge claim brought by the tenants.

Caroline Hutton Known for her specialist real property and agriculture practice, as well as her pragmatic approach to cases. She is also a trained mediator and arbitrator. Her work sees her tackling complex rural and agricultural issues. **Strengths:** "Brilliant on agricultural matters, she's succinct and speedy." "She is exceptionally able. She is a battleship amongst yachts."

Edward Francis Has a versatile property practice and regularly handles cases concerning easements, mortgages, and commercial landlord and tenant disputes. **Strengths:** "He is very quick at turning around work, and is on top of everything." "On his feet, he is patient and relentless and also extremely economical. His written work is thorough and creative." **Recent work:** Represented the defendant in Cottsway Housing Association Ltd v Ibis Healthcare Ltd, a dispute concerning the return of a deposit after non-completion of a sale agreement.

Selborne Chambers

See profile on p.906

THE SET

Selborne Chambers houses a skilled bench of silks and juniors who have great collective expertise in real estate litigation. Its members handle the full gamut of property matters and have a particularly fine reputation for their expertise in property disputes which contain a professional negligence or fraud element.

Client service: "They have good responsiveness, and their clerks are like having an additional member on your team. They're really good and they really add value. They save you a lot of time." Greg Piner is the senior clerk.

SILKS

Romie Tager QC (see p.777) A veteran of numerous significant, high-profile property cases who is in demand by a host of leading instructing solicitors. He is praised for his creative and proactive approach to complex cases. **Strengths:** "When we have an issue that nobody else can solve for us, he's the man we go to. He also has the most astonishing capability to get to grips with complex issues, whether they be technical or factual issues. His cross-examination technique should be emulated by all members of the Bar." **Recent work:** Successfully represented the claimant in a seven-day trial concerning an oral agreement made several years prior. The case ended with an award to the claimant of more than £15 million.

Mark Warwick QC (see p.790) A highly respected silk whose work regularly consists of high-profile and highly complex real property litigation. He is praised for his dedication and his exceptional level of experience. **Strengths:** "He brings huge experience to all cases. He tells you as it is, which is what clients need to hear." "He is incredibly responsive and turns around papers faster than anyone I have come across." **Recent work:** Acted in Skelwith (Leisure) Ltd v Armstrong, a multi-party dispute over a defunct golf course in Yorkshire.

Gary Blaker QC (see p.597) Earns praise for his approachability and practical work style. Easements, mortgages and boundaries are some of his areas of speciality. **Strengths:** "He's accommodating and open to other ideas." "Very approachable, and very new school rather than old school. He knows his stuff and he's up for a fight – he's willing to push if the argument has got merit but won't fight for the sake of it."

Ian Clarke QC (see p.617) A recent silk noted for his exceptional client service, who handles property work alongside his private client and professional negligence matters. **Strengths:** "Confident, tough and plain-speaking but good with the lay client and someone with excellent drafting skills." "He is very knowledgeable in relation to land registration issues." **Recent work:** Acted for BP Oil in defence of its right to establish a right of way over its leasehold property.

JUNIORS

Stuart Hornett (see p.675) Concentrates on real property, with a particular focus on landlord and tenant disputes. His practice also takes in general commercial litigation and chancery disputes. **Strengths:** "Stuart gives robust commercial advice and is prepared to go the extra mile when needed." "An excellent senior junior growing in stature each year." **Recent work:** Represented the owners of a property next to a proposed development in a case concerning breach of freehold covenants and right to light.

Justin Kitson (see p.692) Has a great deal of expertise in property-related professional negligence, and regularly handles high-value property disputes generally. His recent cases have involved easements, sales contracts and restrictive covenants. **Strengths:** "Extremely good junior barrister, who is bright, thorough and a great team player." **Recent work:** Recently acted for SL Construction in a complex commercial dispute concerning commercial contracts of housing development schemes in the West Indies.

Camilla Chorfi (see p.616) Known for her diverse property practice, she has made a name for herself with her impressive advocacy and advisory work. She regularly appears in the High Court, and is noted for her focus on cases concerning freehold covenants, the Rent Act and insolvency. **Strengths:** "She has been awesome." "She's very good and we work well together." **Recent work:** Handled a dispute between a management company, a majority lessee and a freeholder concerning entitlement to manage a block of flats in Manchester.

Nicholas Trompeter (see p.784) Applauded for his clear and concise advice, he handles top-level property work as part of a wider commercial chancery practice that is heavy on professional liability and asset recovery work. **Strengths:** "He's very detailed and the sort of person that you'd want on your team. He has very quick response times and turns around his papers swiftly. He'll tell you from the beginning the up-sides and down-sides of the cases." **Recent work:** Acted for a landlord in a case to oppose a second appeal, in a matter pertaining to an uncontested lease renewal.

Richard Clegg (see p.618) A property specialist with a focus on commercial litigation and arbitration. He handles both residential and commercial land property issues, as well as cases concerning easements and restrictive covenants. His recent work has involved a significant number of cases relating to the 1925 Law of Property Act and land registration law. **Strengths:** "Very bright and very talented." "He is good with clients and somebody who just rolls his sleeves up." **Recent work:** Instructed in a contentious trust dispute between family members concerning the ownership of a number of family assets.

Neil Mendoza (see p.716) Acknowledged for his commitment to his clients and his never-say-die attitude. He is a respected commercial litigator and has expertise in land and property matters. He exhibits great talent for commercial landlord and tenant property litigation, and is also often called upon by mortgage lenders to take charge of complex repossessions. **Strengths:** "He gets things done quickly and properly, and he will fight his client's cause all day every day." **Recent work:** Acted in Frontier Estates v Berwin Leighton Paisner, a dispute concerning issues of professional negligence in the context of a complicated joint venture property agreement.

Zoe Barton (see p.591) Has a practice that combines property, trusts and estates with other chancery work. She is known for taking on cases with elements of fraud, and for acting for high-street retailers. **Strengths:** "She's absolutely fabulous and is very persuasive before the court. I would not want to be on the end of a cross-examination by her." **Recent work:** Acted for four trustees who were looking to be registered as the proprietor of freehold land upon its registration. He successfully obtained first registration for the trustees.

Serle Court

See profile on p.908

THE SET

Serle Court is respected for its property work, and has broad expertise in handling complex litigation and non-contentious issues. Its silks and juniors offer sophisticated and tailored real estate counsel, focusing on such matters as restrictive covenants, rights of light and boundary disputes as well as break notices, dilapidations and adverse possession. They have a further niche specialism in the law relating to waterways.

Client service: "Steve Whitaker's clerking team is very responsive."

SILKS

Christopher Stoner QC (see p.774) Has garnered recognition for his expertise in water and canal law, and is known as one of the leading silks practising riparian rights. His practice also takes in service charge and landlord and tenant disputes. **Strengths:** "Knowledgeable, efficient and a clear advocate." "Easy to work with and a real team player, he's extremely thorough and impressive on his feet." **Recent work:** Acted in R Square Properties Ltd v Nissan Motors (GB) Ltd, successfully obtaining a judgment that rights contained in a lease were in fact defined as easements.

JUNIORS

Andrew Bruce (see p.605) Has a high-quality property practice, with an emphasis on landlord and tenant law and property litigation. **Strengths:** "His written work is superb." "His breadth of knowledge on property-related professional negligence makes him an easy choice for any such dispute." **Recent work:** Instructed in several recent property cases including a business tenancy dispute, and a multi-million-pound development case linked to Manchester airport.

Andrew Francis (see p.648) Has a fine reputation at the Bar for his dedicated property litigation practice. He is acknowledged for his work in restricted covenants and rights of light, and is also recognised for his knowledge of party wall law. **Strengths:** "The go-to man for right to light cases." "He's the first port of call on restrictive covenant disputes." **Recent work:** Acted in Scott v Winter, a restricted covenant case to determine whether damages or an injunction were the necessary course of remedy.

Thomas Braithwaite (see p.601) Noted for having a diverse practice that spans franchise rights, development rights and negligence claims amongst other matters. He is regularly instructed by major bodies such as The Crown Estate. **Strengths:** "He is very persuasive on his feet and judges like him. He has a winning advocacy style." "He is authoritative, gives clear advice and doesn't sit on the fence." **Recent work:** Instructed in Zero-C v Dragonsway Wales, a dispute over a development heard before the High Court.

Tanfield Chambers

See profile on p.917

THE SET

Tanfield is a highly regarded set with an established reputation as enfranchisement and residential property specialists. It is noted for its skill in handling a range of real estate issues from land registrations, village greens and rights of light to easements and boundaries. All manner of real estate clients are catered for including a number of high-profile developers and landowners. Sources say of it: "It is a fine set that is particularly good at enfranchisement and lease extension claims."

Client service: "The clerking is good. They're sensibly priced and they have a lot of good barristers at junior to mid-junior level." Eamonn Kelly is the set's chief executive.

SILKS

Philip Rainey QC (see p.746) Continues to be regarded as one of the Bar's finest property silks, and has an excellent reputation for his enfranchisement work. His practice is also centred around expert determination, fraud claims and easements. **Strengths:** "Superb for enfranchisement leasehold. He is clever, articulate and robust as well." "He drives them from the top – I think he is one of the top five in the country in enfranchisement." **Recent work:** Acted in Menelaou v Bank of Cyprus, a Supreme Court case concerning a mortgagee's rights of subrogation to an unpaid vendor's lien when it transpires that their legal charge is void.

JUNIORS

James Fieldsend (see p.645) Offers pragmatic advice to his clients regarding service charge disputes and leasehold enfranchisement. He is a published author, who is known for his work applying human rights conventions to property disputes. **Strengths:** "Always commercial and focused and great with clients." **Recent work:** Acted in Howard de Walden Estates Ltd v Accordway and Kateb, a case concerning the scope of an intermediate landlord's right to represent its own interests in a tenant's claim to a new lease.

Christopher Heather (see p.668) Handles cases concerning easements, boundaries, industrial estates and restaurants, amongst others. He is especially noted for his professional negligence and enfranchisement work. **Strengths:** "He was very sensible in providing realistic advice and doing what he felt was appropriate to manage expectations." "Pragmatic, technically sound and extremely helpful and proactive." **Recent work:** Acted in Snowball Assets Ltd v Huntsmore House Freehold Ltd, a two-day appeal in the Upper Tribunal in a case concerning the requirements of the Leasehold Reform, Housing and Urban Development Act 1993.

Michael Buckpitt (see p.606) A prominent property junior, with a practice that focuses on landlord and tenant law. He is also noted for his dedication to leasehold enfranchisement and his close relationship with London Estates. **Strengths:** "He gives good, down-to-earth, practical advice and gets on well with and communicates well with developer clients." **Recent work:** Successfully represented Harvey Nichols in obtaining injunctions restricting the activities of fur protesters.

Nicola Muir (see p.723) Focuses her practice on residential and commercial landlord and tenant disputes, and has significant experience in the Court of Appeal. **Strengths:** "Very good on service charges, and landlord and tenant work." **Recent work:** Acted in a landlord and tenant dispute case concerning whether proposed refurbishments were chargeable to the lessees of a building.

Timothy Polli (see p.739) Noted for his expertise spanning contract and commercial law, as well as his professional negligence work and his handling of development disputes. He comes highly praised for his advocacy. **Strengths:** "An experienced junior and a good trial lawyer for property-related matters." "He is very impressive and holds the court's attention. He is a real specialist in the field and good on the detail." **Recent work:** Was instructed in a complex £2.2 million professional negligence claim concerning an Estate Management Deed.

Andrew Butler (see p.608) A well-reputed real estate barrister, who focuses on commercial and professional negligence disputes. He is noted for his work in property damage, service charge and joint venture claims. **Recent work:** Acted for Church Motors in a dispute involving the renewal of a 1954 Act protected tenancy.

Daniel Dovar (see p.636) Has a diverse commercial and residential property practice, specialising in contentious landlord and tenant matters. He is frequently sought out by clients for guidance on leasehold disputes, as well as conveyancing disputes and professional negligence matters. **Strengths:** "He is very persuasive and intelligent." "His opinion was one of the most refreshing I'd ever read. The advice he gave was very simple to follow and constructive."

Ellodie Gibbons (see p.652) A widely respected property junior known for advising on commercial and residential landlord disputes. Her practice includes service and administration charge issues, right to manage cases and enfranchisement claims. **Strengths:** "She is very knowledgeable on leasehold enfranchisement, and is approachable and pragmatic." "Ellodie gives practical advice in a plain-speaking manner and has a well-deserved reputation for her enfranchisement work." **Recent work:** Acted for a landlord in a case heard in the Court of Appeal concerning alleged breaches of covenant and tortious duty leading to disrepair.

Nicholas Isaac (see p.680) An authority on the full range of issues arising in disputes involving party walls. His real estate practice also incorporates easement and boundary matters. **Strengths:** "He is a really good property litigator." "He is a compelling advocate and I don't know anyone better at managing a challenging client." **Recent work:** Instructed in a Party Wall Act case concerning basement developments in London.

Carl Fain (see p.643) A talented property barrister with expertise in business tenancy renewals, service charge disputes and dilapidation claims. His practice also takes in landlord and tenant matters. **Strengths:** "Has excellent knowledge of property law and is a safe pair of hands for any property dispute. He has an ability to see the big picture and achieve a cost-effective resolution, and is a pleasure to deal with." "An extremely able and approachable barrister who provides practical advice." **Recent work:** Acted on a collective enfranchisement case, successfully arguing that an Initial Notice served via e-mail was valid.

Marc Glover (see p.654) Garners praise for his user-friendly approach. He regularly handles cases involving easements, boundary disputes and property development. **Strengths:** "He breaks down difficult concepts and has a very good eye for detail, as well as strategy." "He is a real pleasure to work with, and is a very engaging person with an excellent knowledge of the court." **Recent work:** Was instructed in a case at the Court of Appeal concerning the right of a squatter to claim title to land where he was illegally squatting.

Mark Loveday (see p.703) Maintains a diverse commercial and residential property litigation practice. He has recently acted on multiple dilapidations cases, as well as contentious rent reviews and forfeitures. **Strengths:** "He provided excellent advice. He was very thorough and is obviously very knowledgeable in his field." "A bright and intelligent guy you take difficult problems to." **Recent work:** Took on an advisory role in Romulus City v International Financial Reporting Standards Foundation. This was a dispute concerning a £3 million window replacement in an office block.

Michael Walsh (see p.789) Acts for landlords, developers, local government bodies and large institutional lenders in a broad range of property-related cases. He regularly handles matters concerning development issues, agricultural land and commercial property. **Strengths:** "He rose to the challenge at short notice and got a fantastic result for our client." **Recent work:** Instructed in a case for Vale Royal Methodist Church relating to an error made in the registration of the church's title.

Harriet Holmes (see p.674) Frequently appears at the High Court and County Courts, taking on a diverse range of matters, including adverse possession, enfranchisement and party wall issues. She is noted for her dedication to her clients. **Strengths:** "She gave the client a great deal of confidence and is intellectually very able." "She is genuinely committed to the client's interests." **Recent work:** Appeared as junior counsel for the respondents in the Court of Appeal in a dispute concerning trespass, right of way and adverse possession issues.

Band 4

Hardwicke

See profile on p.859

THE SET

A high-quality set that handles the full range of real estate disputes, including residential lease cases and commercial landlord and tenant matters. Its members are noted for their far-reaching property expertise and ability to advise clients in related insurance, professional negligence and construction cases. The set is recognised for its robust team: "They have some top property performers," market observers report.

Client service: "The clerks are responsive, commercial and do not shy away from giving sensible fee quotes which they stick to. They proactively manage the relationship between instructing solicitors and the barristers, and understand the important part they play in the process. They have gone 'over and above' for me in the past." Deborah Anderson is the set's practice director.

SILKS

Brie Stevens-Hoare QC Regularly works with property developers and owners on significant professional negligence litigation matters, as well as disputes arising from real estate transactions. She is recognised for her user-friendly approach. **Strengths:** "Her service levels are excellent and her communication is great." "A very good advocate, who is calm, clear, concise and responsive to client needs." "She's a top performer." **Recent work:** Acted in Coope v Ward, an easement case arising out of the collapse of an ancient wall following heavy snowfall.

John de Waal QC A prominent real estate litigation silk who frequently works with insurers on contentious real estate mandates. He is renowned for his leading advisory practice working with clients on a range of construction and property issues. **Strengths:** "Great with clients and very easy to work with." "Offers clear, confident advice, and extremely flexible working arrangements. He has a charming and reassuring client manner and represents good value for money." "Very client-friendly; he has a good manner about him. A confident, clear thinker; he is measured in his approach and he always looks for the solution." **Recent work:** Acted in Parking Eye v Beavis, a high-profile Supreme Court case concerning the circumstances in which a landowner or his agent could lawfully impose a charge of £85 on a trespasser who had overstayed his permitted time in a car park on private land.

JUNIORS

Jamal Demachkie Recognised for his work in commercial and property law. His practice concentrates on commercial disputes, chancery litigation and landlord and tenant claims. **Strengths:** "Jamal is a superb advocate with a really good manner in court." "He has a charming way with judges and clients. He is a very good advocate and a go-to guy." **Recent work:** Handled an agricultural tenancy claim relating to the interpretation of the service provisions in the Agricultural Tenancies Act 1995.

Daniel Gatty Handles a wide range of property matters, and has a strong focus on professional negligence disputes arising from real estate issues. He is also known for his work in cases involving land registration, secured lending and mortgages. **Strengths:** "He is extremely knowledgeable." "Down to earth, unassuming and has a very nice approach with clients." **Recent work:** Acted in a dispute between four brothers concerning co-owned shops and investment properties.

Monty Palfrey A highly popular choice for a wide variety of commercial and residential property mandates. He regularly represents clients in court in numerous landlord and tenant, easement and boundary disputes. **Strengths:** "He is very willing to give off-the-cuff advice and he points out the pitfalls in a case at an early stage. He's extremely helpful, sympathetic and understanding." **Recent work:** Recently acted in a case defending a restaurant tenant against a landlord's claims that the client was trespassing after the end of a six-month licence.

Radcliffe Chambers

See profile on p.903

THE SET

Radcliffe demonstrates strength in a broad array of property matters, and has a team of highly talented and respected specialists, who handle cases both domestically and in overseas jurisdictions. They are regularly embroiled in major pieces of litigation, and, when not in court, advise and undertake drafting in connection with development proposals and other transactional work. Clients include solicitors, local authorities and a range of property professionals such as chartered surveyors, architects and structural engineers.

Client service: "The clerks were very helpful, amenable and swift in responding." Keith Nagle and John Clark are the joint senior clerks.

SILKS

Robert Pearce QC (see p.735) Recognised for his extensive work at the Chancery Bar, and is an expert in landlord and tenant disputes and real property litigation. Particular areas of focus include cases involving land registration, leasehold enfranchisement and adverse possession claims. **Strengths:** "Very personable, experienced and authoritative." **Recent work:** Represented the claimants in a High Court dispute pertaining to an agricultural estate.

JUNIORS

Mark West (see p.792) Demonstrates strength across the full spread of contentious property work. Leasehold enfranchisement, restrictive covenants and easements are among his areas of expertise. His recent work has seen him acting for clients in matters relating to agricultural land law. **Recent work:** Acted on behalf of two members of a family farm in a matter concerning their succession to an agricultural tenancy.

Simon Williams (see p.796) Acts for property professionals, private individuals and companies on a range of real estate disputes. He is acknowledged for his advisory work and expertise in professional negligence cases. **Strengths:** "He is a very solid performer." **Recent work:** Acted in the Court of Appeal contesting an award of damages for the landlord's breach of covenants with regard to a luxury mansion block in Marylebone.

Marie-Claire Bleasdale (see p.597) A highly experienced property junior whose practice includes advising on cases involving conveyancing and real property issues. She is frequently instructed in landlord and tenant disputes. **Recent work:** Represented Broadley Investments in relation to an injunction to prevent works that would breach the Party Wall Act 1996.

Edward Hicks (see p.670) Demonstrates strength in a range of disputes concerning property law. He has experience of representing clients in high-value residential landlord and tenant matters. **Strengths:** "Easy to work with and good with clients." "Ed is great. He is very knowledgeable and I completely trust that what he's saying is true. He is clear and articulate in court, and professional but lovely with it." **Recent work:** Defended the tenants in a claim for damages concerning a breach of covenant and trespass, among other allegations.

William Moffett (see p.720) Predominantly focuses on matters concerning beneficial ownership of land, options and easements. He also possesses expertise in landlord and tenant cases. **Strengths:** "Very knowledgeable and extremely helpful. He goes above and beyond when handling his cases and always expresses himself in easy-to-understand language." "Shows very good attention to detail."

Kate Selway (see p.761) Has a diverse property practice, which includes disputes involving agricultural tenancies, landlord and tenant law and real property issues. She is regularly sought out for work pertaining to propriety estoppel, easements and mortgages, among other issues. **Strengths:** "Provides prompt and pragmatic advice, and is not afraid to give a definitive opinion." **Recent work:** Acted in an agricultural tenancy and inheritance tax matter connected to succession tenancies under the Agricultural Holdings Legislation.

Other Ranked Lawyers

Justin Bates (see p.592) (Arden Chambers) Has a strong reputation as a leading property junior. His experience at tribunal is well noted, and he is often instructed to take on rent charge enforcements and general property litigation. **Strengths:** "No one better for service charge disputes." "His knowledge of the rules is fantastic." **Recent work:** Acted in Assethold Ltd v Watts, a case concerning interpretation of service charge covenants.

Zachary Bredemear (1 Chancery Lane) Has a significant property practice, with a specific focus on property-linked professional negligence cases. He often appears on behalf of developers acting against surveyors, architects and solicitors. **Strengths:** "He is very tenacious and works out a strategy as to how to play the litigation, which is very helpful." **Recent work:** Acted for a beneficiary in a claim for transfer of property subject to a trust deed.

Karen Shuman (1 Chancery Lane) Garners recognition as a promising real estate junior who advises on mortgages, lender claims and commercial leases. She regularly acts for solicitors and insurers. **Strengths:** "A skilled, effective negotiator."

Ranjit Bhose QC (see p.595) (Cornerstone Barristers) Works closely with landlords in both the public and private sectors, and has a particular specialism in property-related professional negligence cases. **Strengths:** "Fantastically smart and a man with a huge brain. He is very good at taking an awful lot of information and coming back with the right answers." **Recent work:** Instructed in a service charge dispute relating to the Chelsea Harbour Estate.

Clifford Darton (see p.629) (Ely Place Chambers) Has a specialist practice focused on property litigation connected to water law and pollution issues. He also has experience of representing clients in claims related to mortgages and restrictive covenants. **Strengths:** "He is suave, sophisticated and someone with a razor-sharp intellect." **Recent work:** Appeared in a three-week trial that concerned the beneficial ownership of certain commercial and residential properties in the West Midlands.

Damian Falkowski (39 Essex Chambers) A property specialist with expertise across a range of issues, who receives high praise for his advocacy. Particular areas of strength include planning and development litigation. **Strengths:** "He gets straight to the point, and his advice is reliable and clear. He's very controlled and calm, yet authoritative." **Recent work:** Instructed in a claim concerning a boundary development dispute at a property in Battersea.

Paul Letman (3 Hare Court) Specialises in real estate litigation, covering the full range of property matters. He is an expert in restrictive covenants, environmental issues and professional negligence cases. **Strengths:** "Paul Letman is a pleasure to be against. He presents his case strongly but in a very affable manner."

Malcolm Sheehan QC (see p.763) (Henderson Chambers) Recognised for his expertise at the Property Bar and sits as a part-time judge in the Property Chamber of the First-tier Tribunal. His clients include developers and local authorities. **Strengths:** "Very calm and clear and can get his head around complicated issues quickly. He is very good at articulating difficult points to clients." "He's extremely thorough and is an absolute pleasure to work with." **Recent work:** Represented the Secretary of State in a dilapidations case, valued at £5 million.

Jonathan Steinert (see p.772) (Henderson Chambers) Has over 20 years' experience of handling the contentious and non-contentious elements of property law. His practice includes advising on construction issues. **Strengths:** "Provides robust and decisive advice."

David Halpern QC (see p.662) (4 New Square) Displays excellence in both professional negligence and property litigation. His practice has a particular emphasis on property law and the principles of valuation. **Strengths:** "Has an excellent manner, is great to work with and meets tight deadlines. He is very intelligent, pragmatic and commercial." **Recent work:** Defended Gala Coral against a claim from a landlord that alleged a breach of a keep-open covenant.

George Laurence QC (see p.696) (New Square Chambers) Handles a broad array of property mandates, excelling in specialist matters such as village green issues. His work frequently also includes cases relating to easements and restrictive covenants. **Recent work:** Appeared before the Court of Appeal in a case to establish the ability of the claimant to set out public footpaths under the General Inclosure Act 1801.

Patrick Rolfe (see p.754) (5 Stone Buildings) Represents defendants and claimants in professional negligence cases arising from property issues. He frequently handles mandates relating to easements, acquisitions and restrictive covenants. **Strengths:** "He is a really excellent barrister and knows the law inside out. He really fills you with confidence and knows what he is talking about. He is good on his feet as well." "Very practical in his approach and good to deal with."

Edward Denehan (9 Stone Buildings) Devotes his practice to real property cases, taking on both contentious and non-contentious matters. His work typically includes property valuation, rights of way and conveyancing issues. **Strengths:** "Brilliant with clients, very easy to deal with and an exceptionally strong advocate. His cross-examination skills are second to none." "Robust, bullish and very clear in his advice." "He is very bright and very persuasive." **Recent work:** Recently acted on the enforcement of an option that resulted in the acquisition of a commercial property.

Sebastian Kokelaar (Three Stone) A formidable property junior with expertise in commercial property and restricted covenants. His areas of focus also include landlord and tenant cases. **Strengths:** "Gave very concise and particular advice and was able to guide the client with a defined strategy." "Thorough, balanced and user-friendly." "An impressive junior with a growing reputation."

MIDLANDS

Real Estate Litigation
Leading Sets
Band 1
St Philips Chambers *
Band 2
No5 Chambers *
Leading Silks
Band 1
Randall John *St Philips Chambers* *
Leading Juniors
Band 1
Verduyn Anthony *St Philips Chambers* Ⓐ *
Band 2
Caney Michelle *St Ives Chambers (ORL)* ◊ *
Mitchell David *No5 Chambers* Ⓐ
Taylor David *No5 Chambers* Ⓐ
Band 3
Brennan John *St Philips Chambers* *
Owen Jonathan *Ropewalk Chambers (ORL)* ◊ *
* *Indicates set / individual with profile.*
Ⓐ *direct access (see p.24).*
◊ *(ORL) = Other Ranked Lawyer.*
Alphabetical order within each band. Band 1 is highest.

Band 1

St Philips Chambers

See profile on p.934

THE SET

This leading set maintains a stellar reputation for commercial property litigation. The team has notable experience handling a variety of complex disputes between landlords and tenants, and substantial expertise in matters pertaining to easements and rights of way. Notable cases include Heaselands v Crest Nicholson, a rights of access dispute regarding aspects of a Section 106 agreement, and Balevents v Sartori, a retrial at the High Court raising issues of fiduciary duty and adverse possession. Its members represent landlords, property owners and developers.

Client service: "I like their accessibility, ease of engagement and technical competence." "They are always very helpful, return calls very quickly and arrange conferences efficiently." Joe Wilson is the set's chief clerk.

SILKS

John Randall QC (see p.748) An exceptionally well-recognised silk whose property expertise comes highly recommended. His substantial experience includes handling rights of way disputes for landlords and developers. **Strengths:** "Hugely intelligent and good with clients, John manages to combine an encyclopaedic knowledge of the law with a first-rate appreciation of strategy and an excellent eye for detail." "An excellent advocate who presents his argument very succinctly and logically." **Recent work:** Acted for Regency Villas in Regency Villas v Diamond Resorts, a case concerning the enforceability of rights purportedly granted to the various members of a time-share scheme over an adjoining golf course and other leisure facilities by a deed which is now lost.

JUNIORS

Anthony Verduyn (see p.787) Widely lauded for the depth of his knowledge of property law. He acts in a variety of cases ranging from leasehold disputes to possession claims and allegations of professional negligence. **Strengths:** "He thinks outside the box and looks at novel approaches." "Extremely bright, down-to-earth and great with clients." **Recent work:** Represented Birmingham City Council in Al-Furqan Educational Trust v Birmingham City Council. His role involved handling the rent and possession claims connected with the running of Islamic schools at the Birmingham site.

John Brennan (see p.602) Experienced in commercial property and chancery matters. His broad practice includes acting for private clients on easements and propriety estoppel claims. **Strengths:** "He is very good on his feet." "Very responsive with tremendous client-handling skills." **Recent work:** Acted in Gardner v Sayce, a dispute between the owner of a converted barn and the farmer pertaining to the owner's rights to restrictive covenants and easements.

Band 2

No5 Chambers

See profile on p.931

THE SET

No5 Chambers is a well-established set whose clientele includes developers, landlords, private clients and local authorities. Its barristers have extensive experience of handling a broad range of property-related disputes encompassing landlord and tenant matters, restrictive covenants and easements. The set has a strong reputation for its track record on disputes arising from development projects and probate matters. Recent cases include Rosefair Limited v Butler & Os, in which issues were raised concerning the interests of sub-purchasers.

Client service: "Their clerks are very, very accommodating. They will go out of their way to assist in whatever way they can." "Very efficient, very approachable and really, really helpful." Tony McDaid is the set's practice director.

JUNIORS

David Mitchell Has a strong chancery practice with particular expertise in real estate disputes. In addition to his experience in contentious probate matters, his practice includes acting on possession orders, restrictive covenants and professional negligence claims. **Strengths:** "He is clear and detailed, and a very good advocate." "Insightful and intelligent." **Recent work:** Acted for the claimant in Mitchell v Watkinson & Williams, an adverse possession claim relating to the ownership of part of a cricket ground.

David Taylor Highly respected junior and First-tier Property Tribunal judge with broad experience acting for landlords in tenancy disputes and representing developers in contentious rights of way matters. He also handles restrictive covenants and high-value professional negligence claims. **Strengths:** "Commercially minded and gets to the heart of the matter quickly." "The quality of his knowledge is excellent." **Recent work:** Represented the landlord in Calthorpe Estates v VCSL & Dale, an injunctive relief claim brought against the tenant.

Other Ranked Lawyers

Jonathan Owen (see p.732) (Ropewalk Chambers) An experienced junior with broad experience in chancery and real estate matters. He has a significant record representing his clients in boundary disputes, possession claims and trespass issues. **Strengths:** "He is exceptionally intelligent."

Michelle Caney (see p.611) (St Ives Chambers) Highly praised for her advocacy skills in court. In addition to her strong social housing practice, she handles a range of commercial property matters and has notable experience in boundary disputes, possession claims and allegations of mortgage fraud. **Strengths:** "Very conscientious, very thorough, and you always know you are in safe hands with her." "Superb advocate with extremely detailed preparation in trials." **Recent work:** Acted for the respondent in Ingleby-Oddy v Farmar, a First-tier Tribunal application for the registration of a right of way over a piece of agricultural land.

NORTH EASTERN

Real Estate Litigation	
Leading Sets	
Band 1	
Enterprise Chambers *	
Leading Juniors	
Band 1	
Klein Jonathan	*Enterprise Chambers*
Band 2	
Fletcher Stephen	*Dere Street Barristers (ORL)* ◊ *
Jarron Stephanie	*Enterprise Chambers*
Rodger Jonathan	*Enterprise Chambers*
Walker Bruce	*Exchange Chambers (ORL)* ◊
Band 3	
Crossley Dominic	*St Philips Chambers (ORL)* ◊ *
Griffin Margaret	*Enterprise Chambers*
Up-and-coming individuals	
Heath Duncan	*Enterprise Chambers*

** Indicates set / individual with profile.*
◊ (ORL) = Other Ranked Lawyer.
Alphabetical order within each band. Band 1 is highest.

Band 1

Enterprise Chambers

See profile on p.950

THE SET

Enterprise Chambers continues to be recognised as the leading set in the North East for property litigation. The team has extensive experience of representing commercial landlords in tenancy-related issues and handles a significant number of boundary disputes. Notable recent cases include Network Rail Infrastructure Ltd v Bowring, a boundary dispute raising questions regarding adverse possession, and Mark v Charter Properties, whereby the landlord sought lease forfeiture against a tenant. The set is also known for its strength in chancery and commercial litigation, and has significant expertise assisting private clients with contentious trusts.

Client service: "The clerking team is really excellent, very user-friendly and easy to get on with." "The clerks are very good at defining what the timescale is for doing the work." Key contacts are Joanne Caunt in Leeds and Bethany Thompson in Newcastle.

JUNIORS

Jonathan Klein Highly renowned for his strength in property litigation, with a practice covering a wide range of issues. He has substantial expertise in rent valuations, boundary disputes and contentious lease renewals. **Strengths:** "He is meticulous, prepares beyond belief, and will know the papers inside out before he sets foot inside the court." "Always on top of the legal issues and formidable to be against." **Recent work:** Acted for the landlords on the rent valuation and lease terms of a venue in Halifax, West Yorkshire.

Stephanie Jarron Well known as a highly experienced property barrister. Her areas of expertise include right of way issues and complex landlord and tenant disputes. Her clients include public organisations and private clients. **Strengths:** "A tenacious advocate always willing to fight her client's corner." **Recent work:** Successfully fixed her client's proposed boundary line in a boundary dispute between neighbours.

Jonathan Rodger Highly regarded junior with extensive experience in disputes arising from real estate developments and transactions. In addition to representing clients in boundary disputes and professional negligence claims, he also specialises in insolvency matters. **Strengths:** "He combines strong technical skill with commercial judgement." "Very good at mitigating situations and great at managing client relations." **Recent work:** Acted in Nicholson v Bamigbade, a boundary dispute relating to a disparity between the property deed and the reality of the build.

Margaret Griffin Has a strong track record of acting in complex landlord and tenant disputes. Other areas of expertise include professional negligence and chancery law cases, particularly those concerning probate and trusts. **Strengths:** "As well as being available to talk, she is down-to-earth in presenting quite difficult concepts to clients." "She is switched on and bright." **Recent work:** Defended a solicitor against an allegation of professional negligence pertaining to a real estate transaction.

Duncan Heath An up-and-coming junior whose expertise in contentious real estate forms one facet of his broad commercial chancery practice. His experience also encompasses trusts disputes and insolvency cases. **Strengths:** "A rising star." "Refreshingly approachable and easily builds a rapport with clients." **Recent work:** Acted for the claimant in McCleary v Allied Irish Bank, a lawsuit relating to allegations of forgery and involving elements of Irish banking law and English real estate law.

Other Ranked Lawyers

Stephen Fletcher (see p.646) (Dere Street Barristers) Newcastle-based junior with a strong reputation among clients for his experience handling a range of complex cases in court. His broad-ranging practice includes contentious lease renewals, break clauses and high-value dilapidation claims. **Strengths:** "He is capable and commercial." **Recent work:** Represented the claimant in Finalcertain Ltd v Peckvale Ltd, a claim to enforce repairing covenants of the client's property.

Bruce Walker (Exchange Chambers) Highly respected junior who handles landlord and tenant disputes, and also acts for private clients on right of way issues. He is also known for his expertise in probate and trust matters. **Strengths:** "He is incredibly bright, incredibly thorough, and incredibly knowledgeable about his area." "He has strong advocacy skills." **Recent work:** Represented the defendant in Willow Design v London Ebor & RBDA. The case concerned claims of liquidators regarding beneficial interest in land.

Dominic Crossley (see p.627) (St Philips Chambers) Well recognised in the market for the strength of his real estate litigation practice. He has broad experience covering issues connected to easements, possession claims and land disputes. **Strengths:** "A very able advocate who also relates well to the clients." "He is one to watch."

NORTHERN

Real Estate Litigation
Leading Sets
Band 1
Kings Chambers *
Leading Silks
Band 1
Anderson Lesley *Kings Chambers* *
Chaisty Paul *Kings Chambers* *
Leading Juniors
Band 1
Horne Wilson *Kings Chambers* *
Lander Richard *Kings Chambers* *
Band 2
Green David *Atlantic Chambers (ORL)* ◊
Hall Matthew *Kings Chambers* *
Halliwell Mark *Kings Chambers* *
Wheatley Geraint *Kings Chambers* *
Band 3
Clayton Nigel *Kings Chambers* *
Foster Ian *Exchange Chambers (ORL)* ◊
** Indicates set / individual with profile.*
◊ (ORL) = Other Ranked Lawyer.
Alphabetical order within each band. Band 1 is highest.

Band 1

Kings Chambers
See profile on p.968

THE SET

A pre-eminent set with a broad offering in property litigation that covers dilapidations, insolvency issues and landlord and tenant disputes. One impressed source notes that "they have a full range of highly skilled barristers, from juniors up to silk." Members have vast experience of acting for national retailers, local authorities and financial corporations. Notable recent cases include CJS Investments v Zagora, a substantial claim relating to the entitlement of majority leaseholders, management companies or freeholders to manage a block of 100 apartments in central Manchester, and Laver Leisure Ltd v Crowtrees Farm, a case concerning the possession of a farm from a sitting tenant under the Agricultural Holdings Act 1986.

Client service: "The administrative side of things is very professional. From the reception to clerking, they are very good and able to get things done." Colin Griffin leads the clerking team.

SILKS

Lesley Anderson QC (see p.583) Has an enviable reputation in the sector and is recognised for her considerable strength in commercial property cases, particularly those relating to insolvency. She is an experienced representative of clients before the Supreme Court and routinely advises local authorities on development-related issues. **Strengths:** "She exhibits an encyclopaedic knowledge of the law." "Very good on her feet, unstoppable, very responsive and always offers a strategic angle." **Recent work:** Acted for the intervener in Rosemary Scott v Southern Pacific Mortgages in the Supreme Court. This matter related to whether a purchaser of land subject to a sale-and-leaseback arrangement was able to create a proprietary interest in the land that was capable of being an overriding interest.

Paul Chaisty QC (see p.614) Earns praise for his outstanding corporate and insolvency capabilities in the real estate sector. He is a highly experienced barrister with expertise in commercial leases and conveyancing matters. He regularly represents clients in landlord and tenant disputes and is highly regarded for his adept handling of complex and high-value matters. **Strengths:** "He has a rare ability that combines great intellect with commercial acumen." "He is seriously good: he gets to the crux of things very, very quickly, he is very sharp in court and he can be ferocious when he needs to be."

JUNIORS

Wilson Horne (see p.675) Well-respected barrister with a specialist focus on planning and construction. His extensive experience in the sector includes handling arbitration cases and he is regularly instructed to represent landlords and surveyors in property disputes. **Strengths:** "He is a tenacious advocate. His performance on his feet and his ability to deal with incredibly tense atmospheres in court are second to none." **Recent work:** Defended the administrators in Saw, Wilson v O'Keefe and Others, Nationwide BS against claims for damages in excess of £1 million brought by unsecured creditors who also requested a declaration to state that the administration was void.

Richard Lander (see p.695) Demonstrates notable strength in real estate matters containing professional negligence, insolvency and probate elements. He is recognised for his capable handling of disposals and regularly acts for clients in boundary disputes. He has experience representing developers and frequently appears before the property tribunal. **Strengths:** "Shows a masterful grasp of the issues. Great on his feet and will drive points home." "Very impressed, he is highly intelligent." **Recent work:** Acted for Ripple Developments in Ripple Developments Limited v Potts, a six-day trial involving the client's claim for damages. Obtained a successful ruling along with a seven-figure sum.

Matthew Hall (see p.662) Highly regarded barrister who demonstrates prowess in the property sector. He is recognised for his adroit handling of property acquisition cases and routinely acts for landlords and property developers. His expertise also encompasses land law and residential management. **Strengths:** "Excellent junior with a keen eye for detail." "Very good, assertive and user-friendly." **Recent work:** Successfully defended RTM Company in Malloney v Chancery Gardens (Salford) RTM Company Limited against a challenge to the service charge arising out of the large-scale replacement of windows at the development.

Mark Halliwell (see p.662) Valued for his expertise in the sector and for his deep knowledge of trusts. He has a wealth of experience with contracts and regularly handles title and lease issues. He frequently appears in the High Court and regularly represents landowners in property disputes. He is also experienced in dealing with construction and development matters. **Strengths:** "Highly impressive. He is a busy guy but he is very responsive; he always goes out of his way." "Extremely knowledgeable and versatile." **Recent work:** Successfully appeared on behalf of Burnley Borough Council in a case regarding forfeiture possession proceedings.

Geraint Wheatley (see p.793) Commended for his strength in dilapidations and service charge disputes. He is frequently instructed by clients from the financial sector to handle property litigation cases. He also has experience in high-value litigation and frequently acts for borrowers in commercial repossession claims. He also routinely advises on trespass and trusts issues. **Strengths:** "Very commercially astute, he gets the job done." "Exceptional property litigator, very commercial, someone I would be happy to put in front of any client." **Recent work:** Represented a mortgage lender in Mortgage Express & Baker v Giwa regarding a title rectification claim filed by the client.

Nigel Clayton (see p.618) Highly experienced in the areas of land law and professional negligence-related claims. He is frequently sought out for his considerable expertise in mortgages and demonstrates further strength in commercial and banking matters. **Strengths:** "He provides excellent written advice. Clients comment on his professional and approachable manner." "Very thorough and good with detail."

Other Ranked Lawyers

David Green (Atlantic Chambers) Has a diverse real estate practice that includes commercial, professional negligence and insolvency-related issues. He is an experienced representative of clients in mortgage-related cases and routinely handles matters related to trust litigation. **Strengths:** "A very well-respected barrister who interacts well with clients and is very user-friendly."

Ian Foster (Exchange Chambers) Has a broad property practice that takes in boundary disputes, right of way issues and professional negligence cases. He has extensive experience with tribunals and has handled cases in the Court of Appeal. **Strengths:** "A safe pair of hands."

SOUTH EASTERN

Real Estate Litigation	
Leading Juniors	
Band 1	
Clargo John	*Hardwicke*
Sinnatt Simon	*Crown Office Row*
Band 2	
Demachkie Jamal	*Hardwicke*
Gore Andrew	*Fenners Chambers*
Redmayne Simon	*East Anglian Chambers*
Wilson Alasdair	*Fenners Chambers*
Worton Louise	*3PB Barristers*
Up-and-coming individuals	
John Charlotte	*Crown Office Row*

Ranked Lawyers

Simon Sinnatt (Crown Office Row) Highly respected property practitioner who frequently undertakes instructions from developers, local governments and private clients. His expertise covers proprietary estoppel cases, landlord and tenant issues and collective enfranchisement. **Strengths:** "Simon is user-friendly, very accessible, and someone who works as a team with the solicitors. He has a good creative mind when considering the many solutions and ways to resolve issues." "He's very clear and concise on paper." **Recent work:** Acted in Achieving Perfection Ltd v Gray at Brighton County Court, which concerned the validity of service of notice via e-mail.

Charlotte John (Crown Office Row) Property-focused barrister with a wider chancery practice. She undertakes instructions on residential and commercial landlord and tenant matters as well as land and boundary disputes. **Strengths:** "Very clever and very committed to her cases. Very personally involved."

Simon Redmayne (East Anglian Chambers) Highly respected advocate whose practice encompasses property work, land disputes and trusts. He is also recognised for his work on contested probate matters. **Strengths:** "He is a very good barrister: good with clients, good on his feet, and mediator-qualified." "He is very thorough and commercially minded."

Andrew Gore (Fenners Chambers) Well-known property barrister with a diverse practice. He routinely handles development issues alongside land ownership and land use matters. Offers additional expertise in property-related professional negligence and agricultural law. **Strengths:** "Very experienced and always shows great attention to detail. Excellent drafting and negotiating skills." **Recent work:** Advised the respondents in Kember & Sexton v Gill, a dispute concerning land ownership and rights of way.

Alasdair Wilson (Fenners Chambers) Well-recognised barrister with a strong reputation for his property practice. His expertise covers trust matters and commercial and residential landlord and tenant work. **Strengths:** "Thorough and always quick to deal with ongoing issues." "He has a strong intellect combined with genuine determination to succeed." **Recent work:** Successfully represented the defendant in a case concerning a constructive trust and a proprietary estoppel claim.

John Clargo (Hardwicke) Well-regarded junior who heads the property and chancery group at the chambers. His practice encompasses commercial and residential landlord and tenant work, property-related professional negligence cases and real property issues. **Strengths:** "He is very user-friendly. He is commercial as well as legal." "He is an excellent advocate, unflappable." **Recent work:** Acted in Bethell v St John's College, a much-publicised dispute between a retired architect and the Oxford college concerning repairs to a dilapidated hedge.

Jamal Demachkie (Hardwicke) Skilled barrister with a diverse property practice covering landlord and tenant disputes and real property work. He also undertakes instructions concerning co-ownership and constructive trust matters. **Strengths:** "He is very good and has a very charming way with judges and clients." "Very strong barrister, who is a very good advocate and a go-to guy." **Recent work:** Successfully concluded a Court of Appeal case on behalf of the respondent concerning establishment of causation for an instance of fire damage to a property.

Louise Worton (3PB Barristers) Strong junior who handles property matters within her broader chancery practice. She specialises in landlord and tenant matters, advising both residential and commercial clients. **Strengths:** "Exceptional barrister with fantastic advocacy skills. Her written work is always extremely helpful." "She speaks in plain English, and has an ability to break down extremely complex issues into simple language." **Recent work:** Successfully acted for the landlord in Chaplair Limited v Kumari, a Court of Appeal case concerning recovery of legal costs under the terms of a lease.

WESTERN

Real Estate Litigation	
Leading Sets	
Band 1	
St John's Chambers *	
Band 2	
Guildhall Chambers *	
Leading Silks	
Band 1	
Blohm Leslie	*St John's Chambers*

** Indicates set with profile.*
[A] direct access (see p.24).
◊ (ORL) = Other Ranked Lawyer.
Alphabetical order within each band. Band 1 is highest.

Real Estate Litigation	
Leading Juniors	
Band 1	
Sharples John	*St John's Chambers* [A]
Band 2	
Auld Charles	*St John's Chambers*
Jones Christopher	*St John's Chambers*
Paton Ewan	*Guildhall Chambers*
Sahonte Rajinder	*Guildhall Chambers*
Troup Alex	*St John's Chambers* [A]
Wales Matthew	*Guildhall Chambers*
Walsh Tim	*Guildhall Chambers*
Band 3	
Adams Guy	*St John's Chambers* [A]
Berkley Michael	*Magdalen Chambers (ORL)* ◊
Up-and-coming individuals	
Brown Matthew	*Guildhall Chambers*

Band 1

St John's Chambers
See profile on p.941

THE SET

This outstanding set houses a dedicated team of property practitioners who work across a broad spectrum of commercial and residential property matters, handling such matters as development issues and agricultural disputes. The set undertakes cases for a variety of clients, including investors, landowners, local authorities and private clients. Of late, its members have appeared in significant property cases such as Hoyl Group v Cromer Town Council, which concerned estoppel and rights of way issues relating to a listed council building, and Saunders v Caerphilly County Borough Council. "I find that they just go a bit further for the client. They dig deep, try hard for the clients, are thorough and look for a solution," market commentators enthuse.

Client service: "The clerks are excellent. They are very efficient, very thorough and very understanding." Derek Jenkins heads the clerk team.

SILKS

Leslie Blohm QC Leading silk who wins plaudits from peers and solicitors alike for his exceptional property practice. He heads the set's commercial and chancery group and has particular expertise in town and village greens work. **Strengths:** "He is excellent with clients, good on the paperwork, very thorough and excellent in his advice." "He has an amazing way of explaining the most complicated issues in an easy and understandable manner." "Shows calmness under pressure and has good analytical skills." **Recent work:** Acted for Bristol City Council in obtaining possession of an allotment required for the development of the city's dedicated bus lane.

JUNIORS

John Sharples Pre-eminent junior with an outstanding reputation for his property disputes practice. He is very well versed in handling a variety of complex cases, and takes instructions from landowners, public authorities and private clients, amongst others. **Strengths:** "He combines formidable intellect with being very down to earth, very user-friendly and very approachable. He provides a terrific service." "He has great people skills but is also an intelligent and tenacious advocate. That's a rare combination, he's a real pleasure to work with and good on his feet in court." **Recent work:** Acted in an arbitration case relating to an unusual rent review clause concerning the calculation of profit rental and proper interpretation of contractual assumptions.

Charles Auld Respected barrister with expertise in land registration and land-related cases, in addition to more traditional chancery matters. His broad practice runs the full gamut of commercial property issues. **Strengths:** "Charles is extremely personable, client-friendly, supportive and pragmatic." "Good at putting clients at ease." **Recent work:** Acted on behalf of a farm owner in a dispute concerning possession and eviction orders for squatters occupying part of his land.

Christopher Jones Strong junior who handles property-related matters within his broader chancery practice. His areas of expertise encompass probate matters, landlord and tenant disputes, and real property litigation. **Strengths:** "He is user-friendly, proactive, accurate and technically very good. He really rolls his sleeves up." "He offers very pragmatic advice, and appreciates the commercial realities facing the defendant." **Recent work:** Acted for the defendants in a three-day trial regarding a dispute with neighbours over rights of access to a driveway.

Alex Troup Highly regarded chancery barrister who specialises in property litigation, but also remains active in contentious trusts and probate matters. **Strengths:** "Client-friendly, very impressive on paper and in court and a fantastic advocate – he is a formidable opponent." **Recent work:** Successfully acted for the claimant in a dispute over rights to access a moor in Cornwall.

Guy Adams Experienced chancery practitioner with a strong focus on property work. His expertise covers commercial and residential landlord and tenant matters as well as development issues. **Strengths:** "A most inventive thinker. You think you cover all the angles in court, and then he comes up with something completely novel." "He's keen, driven and is a self-motivator." **Recent work:** Acted for the claimant, a farmer, in a case regarding compensation for compulsory purchase barred by limitations.

Band 2

Guildhall Chambers

See profile on p.938

THE SET

Guildhall Chambers is a highly regarded set that provides expert assistance in real property, landlord and tenant, wills and estates, and trusts cases. The chambers serves a broad range of clients including private individuals, developers, landowners and housing associations. Market sources describe the members here as having "a real feel for the need for practical answers in the busy legal world," and as being "user-friendly, personable and easy to deal with."

Client service: "The clerks are reliable and you always get a response." Justin Emmett is the principal civil clerk, whilst Charlie Ellis and Maggie Pearce clerk for the property team.

JUNIORS

Ewan Paton Strong property junior with significant experience in residential landlord and tenant matters and real property law. He comes highly recommended for his probate expertise, and has notable insight into professional negligence-related claims. **Strengths:** "He is very academic, and very good at ploughing through a lot of detailed documents. His written advice is always interesting." **Recent work:** Successfully acted for the defendant in a registered land dispute concerning adverse possession of a courtyard.

Rajinder Sahonte Traditional chancery practitioner with expertise in commercial and residential real estate and contentious probate work. He is also active on professional negligence cases relating to property. **Strengths:** "He is extremely approachable, very user-friendly, and nothing is too much trouble for him. He always fights your corner." **Recent work:** Successfully acted for the claimants in Shaw v Grouby, a boundary dispute concerning rights of way and restrictive covenants.

Matthew Wales A renowned barrister offering a great deal of expertise across the field of property law. He routinely handles property-related insolvency and professional negligence work. He has vast experience in matters relating to trusts alongside landlord and tenant cases. **Strengths:** "He is a quality act, who is smart, diligent, sensible, and someone who gives good advice to the clients." "Clear and considered: he is excellent at giving sound, practical advice." **Recent work:** Successfully represented Morningside Residents Association in relation to an adverse possession claim against the owner of an adjoining piece of land.

Tim Walsh Highly regarded barrister who handles both real property and probate work. His expertise covers trusts and estate matters, landlord and tenant issues, and inheritance claims. **Strengths:** "Very thorough on the facts, he is able to go from the detail to the bigger picture with ease." "He is brilliant and good at explaining matters to lay clients." **Recent work:** He advised in Entwistle v Waring, a dispute involving will contract and proprietary estoppel.

Matthew Brown A well-recognised practitioner with a growing reputation for both property and probate work. He has experience of handling cases concerning real property and trusts and estates, as well as those relating to landlord and tenant issues. **Strengths:** "Clever and diligent." "He is pleasant, effective and ambitious." "He's a balanced guy with a great sense of humour."

Other Ranked Lawyers

Michael Berkley (Magdalen Chambers) Joint head of chambers who has a wide-ranging property practice that covers both real property and commercial landlord and tenant disputes. He also undertakes matters concerning trusts and wills and probate. **Strengths:** "He has an excellent manner when dealing with clients. He's totally pleasant and very likeable."

Contents:

LONDON

Restructuring/Insolvency
Leading Sets
Band 1
South Square *
Band 2
Enterprise Chambers *
Erskine Chambers *
Maitland Chambers *
4 Stone Buildings *
Band 3
New Square Chambers *
XXIV Old Buildings *
Serle Court *
* Indicates set / individual with profile.
◊ (ORL) = Other Ranked Lawyer.
Alphabetical order within each band. Band 1 is highest.

Restructuring/Insolvency
Leading Silks
Star individuals
Dicker Robin *South Square* *
Moss Gabriel *South Square*
Trower William *South Square* *
Zacaroli Antony *South Square* *
Band 1
Arden Peter *Erskine Chambers* *
Chivers David *Erskine Chambers* *
Crow Jonathan *4 Stone Buildings* *
Miles Robert *4 Stone Buildings*
Phillips Mark *South Square* *
Band 2
Atherton Stephen *20 Essex Street (ORL)* ◊
Davis-White Malcolm *XXIV Old Buildings*
Girolami Paul *Maitland Chambers* *
Hilliard Lexa *Wilberforce Chambers (ORL)* ◊
Jones Philip *Serle Court* *
McQuater Ewan *3 Verulam Buildings (ORL)* ◊
Toube Felicity *South Square* *
Band 3
Agnello Raquel *Erskine Chambers* *
Alexander David *South Square* *
Allison David *South Square* *
Bompas George *4 Stone Buildings* *
Brisby John *4 Stone Buildings* *
Collings Matthew *Maitland Chambers* *
Crystal Michael *South Square* *
Hill Richard G *4 Stone Buildings* *
Marshall Philip *Serle Court* *
Mortimore Simon *South Square* *
Pascoe Martin *South Square* *
Steinfeld Alan *XXIV Old Buildings*
Band 4
Davis Glen *South Square* *
Gibbon Michael *Maitland Chambers* *
Hollington Robin *New Square Chambers*
Isaacs Barry *South Square* *
Moverley Smith Stephen *XXIV Old Buildings*
Parker Christopher R *Maitland Chambers* *
Potts James *Erskine Chambers* *
Shekerdemian Marcia *Wilberforce Chambers (ORL)* ◊
Smith Tom *South Square* *
Stubbs Rebecca *Maitland Chambers* *
Tolaney Sonia *One Essex Court (ORL)* ◊
Trace Anthony *Maitland Chambers* *
Band 5
Arnold Mark *South Square* *
Beltrami Adrian *3 Verulam Buildings (ORL)* ◊
de Garr Robinson Anthony *One Essex Court (ORL)* ◊ *
Gledhill Andreas *Blackstone Chambers (ORL)* ◊
Goldring Jeremy *South Square* *
Hardwick Matthew *3 Verulam Buildings (ORL)* ◊
Thompson Andrew *Erskine Chambers* *
Thompson Steven *XXIV Old Buildings*
New Silks
Bayfield Daniel *South Square* *
Lightman Daniel *Serle Court* *

Restructuring/Insolvency
Leading Juniors
Band 1
Addy Catherine *Maitland Chambers* *
Al-Attar Adam *South Square* *
Fisher Richard *South Square* *
Robins Stephen *South Square* *
Shaw Peter *9 Stone Buildings (ORL)* ◊
Stonefrost Hilary *South Square* *
Tamlyn Lloyd *South Square*
Band 2
Boardman Christopher *Radcliffe Chambers (ORL)* ◊
Briggs John *South Square* *
Kalfon Olivier *Maitland Chambers* *
Leahy Blair *20 Essex Street (ORL)* ◊
Page Rebecca *Maitland Chambers* *
Band 3
Curl Joseph *9 Stone Buildings (ORL)* ◊
Eaton Turner David *New Square Chambers* *
Goodison Adam *South Square* *
Griffiths Ben *Erskine Chambers* *
Groves Hugo *Enterprise Chambers*
Haywood Marcus *South Square*
Ife Linden *Enterprise Chambers*
Kyriakides Tina *Radcliffe Chambers (ORL)* ◊
McCulloch Niall *Enterprise Chambers*
Pester Iain *Wilberforce Chambers (ORL)* ◊
Ritchie Richard *XXIV Old Buildings*
Robinson Thomas *Wilberforce Chambers (ORL)* ◊
Band 4
Adair Stuart *XXIV Old Buildings*
Bailey James *New Square Chambers*
Barker James *Enterprise Chambers*
Beswetherick Anthony *20 Essex Street (ORL)* ◊
Deacock Adam *Radcliffe Chambers (ORL)* ◊
Nersessian Tiran *4 Stone Buildings* *
Prentis Sebastian *New Square Chambers*
Riley Jamie *Littleton Chambers (ORL)* ◊
Zelin Geoffrey *Enterprise Chambers*
Band 5
Burton Paul *Three Stone (ORL)* ◊
de Mestre Andrew *4 Stone Buildings* *
Fulton Andrew *20 Essex Street (ORL)* ◊
Gunaratna Kavan *Enterprise Chambers*
Harrison Christopher *4 Stone Buildings* *
Hinks Philip *3 Verulam Buildings (ORL)* ◊
Johnson Clara *3 Hare Court (ORL)* ◊
Jordan Ruth *Serle Court* *
Lewis Daniel *3 Hare Court (ORL)* ◊
Markham Anna *4 Stone Buildings* *
McCambley Dawn *Radcliffe Chambers (ORL)* ◊
Meyer Birgitta *1 Essex Court (ORL)* ◊
Pickering James *Enterprise Chambers*
Shepherd Tom *4 New Square (ORL)* ◊
Start Angharad *3 Verulam Buildings (ORL)* ◊
Thornley Hannah *South Square* *
Up-and-coming individuals
Cooke Charlotte *South Square* *

Band 1

South Square

See profile on p.910

THE SET

South Square is "at the top of its game" in the insolvency field and enjoys a stellar reputation for pure insolvency work. The set continues to be seen as the "first stop for all insolvency and restructuring work" by market commentators, who highlight the dedicated expertise of its members. Its pre-eminent barristers remain highly popular among clients for high-value and cross-border work, including the ongoing Waterfall Applications I and II following the Lehman Brothers administration, and demonstrate considerable strength in areas such as schemes of arrangement, enforcement planning and offshore litigation. Sources celebrate the set's crop of standout silks alongside its "frighteningly bright juniors."

Client service: "Excellent clerking, really top-notch. Very professional and modern." The "brilliant clerking team" is led by senior practice managers Mike Killick and Dylan Playfoot.

SILKS

Robin Dicker QC (see p.633) A leading insolvency silk who is widely recognised for his work on headline cases. His busy practice sees him regularly appearing before the Court of Appeal and Supreme Court in complex, cross-border cases. Sources draw attention to his approachable manner and intellectual ability, lauding him as a "superstar." **Strengths:** "He is right at the top of the tree." "He always adds value given his insight into complex legal issues."

Gabriel Moss QC An outstanding, highly experienced advocate who routinely tackles the most significant insolvency cases. Interviewees hail him as a "leader in his field," citing his "encyclopaedic knowledge" and ability to provide "well-prepared, clear advice." He regularly appears in high-value, cross-border insolvency cases. **Strengths:** "He remains the doyen of the Insolvency Bar." "One of the absolute best in the field." **Recent work:** Acted for PHS Group in successfully obtaining an order sanctioning a high-value and complex scheme of arrangement with its lenders.

William Trower QC (see p.784) Held in high esteem for his adroit handling of the full range of insolvency matters, both in the UK and overseas. He has recently played a key part in the Waterfall Applications I and II, among other high-profile cases. **Strengths:**" He is a first choice for the most difficult intellectual assignments in the restructuring and insolvency arena." "He's super-friendly, helps out at short notice and fully understands clients' needs." **Recent work:** Acted on behalf of an insolvent Icelandic bank in Landsbanki v UBS, a closeout and set-off dispute with a trading counterparty.

Antony Zacaroli QC (see p.802) Esteemed practitioner who is particularly praised for his ability to undertake highly technical cases. He brings deep experience to bear on complex international disputes and is lauded for his commercially astute approach. **Strengths:** "He's very good to work with and exceptional at what he does; he's one of the best insolvency lawyers at the Bar." "He provides timely, pragmatic advice and instils absolute confidence in clients." **Recent work:** Appealed against the dismissal of a winding-up petition and the removal of the provisional liquidators of a British Virgin Islands company.

Mark Phillips QC (see p.737) A respected silk offering deep expertise across the full spectrum of insolvency law. He excels in areas such as schemes of arrangement and multi-jurisdictional disputes. **Strengths:** "He's very bright, client-friendly and unafraid to pursue difficult arguments to great effect." "When you want someone who really rolls up their sleeves and is a formidable operator, he's great." **Recent work:** Acted for an Abu Dhabi wealth fund and Edgeworth in a series of related claims arising out of the collapse of the deal to finance the Santander headquarters in Madrid.

Felicity Toube QC (see p.783) Combines her vast experience and expertise in contentious insolvency cases, particularly those involving fraud, with an excellent courtroom presence. She frequently turns her hand to offshore disputes, and is well recognised for her strength in international proceedings. **Strengths:** "She's incredibly bright and capable but also very down-to-earth and unbelievably accessible. I can't recommend her highly enough." **Recent work:** Involved in the MFG litigation. This was a leading case on extraterritoriality of private examination under Section 236 of the Insolvency Act 1986.

David Alexander QC (see p.581) Stands out for his provision of expert counsel to clients in major litigation proceedings, both at home and further afield. He is widely acclaimed for his persuasive advocacy style and strategic nous. **Strengths:** "He's astute and a brilliant trial attorney." "He offers clear, definitive advice in client-friendly form." **Recent work:** Advised on a significant litigation involving a EUR22 million claim by Landsbanki against the founder of fashion chain Karen Millen and former CEO of retailer All Saints.

Michael Crystal QC (see p.627) A highly capable insolvency barrister who is a prominent feature in cross-border cases brought by a range of clients. He is also a familiar face in offshore jurisdictions. **Strengths:** "He's good at what he does and absolutely great in court." "He has a fantastic reputation and practice."

Simon Mortimore QC (see p.722) Has an impressive restructuring and insolvency practice, with a particular emphasis on directors' duties. Commentators draw attention to his broad expertise, which covers areas such as contested winding-up and complex liquidation proceedings. **Strengths:** "He is outstanding." "The absolute authority on points of contract law." **Recent work:** Acted for Lloyds Bank in the contentious Angel Group administration and its conversion to liquidation.

Martin Pascoe QC (see p.734) Frequently sought out to handle complex insolvency disputes. Commentators draw particular attention to his adroit handling of international deals. **Strengths:** "Martin is an experienced QC. He is extremely knowledgeable and is a calm, clear and assured presence." **Recent work:** Served as lead counsel for the administrators of the MF Global UK investment bank insolvency.

David Allison QC (see p.583) A flourishing silk who acts on behalf of a range of clients in both domestic and offshore matters. He regularly advises on informal insolvency cases, and is characterised as commercially and technically adept by market sources. **Strengths:** "He's very commercial, pragmatic, responsive and ever-helpful." "David is thorough, affable and articulate with excellent technical knowledge." **Recent work:** Acted for one of the respondents to the Waterfall II Application brought by the administrators of Lehman Brothers to resolve the outstanding issues relating to the distribution of Lehman's assets.

Glen Davis QC (see p.630) Attracts instructions from a diverse range of clients and offers specialist insight into commercial issues involving an insolvency aspect, particularly in the financial services sector. He is routinely called upon to assist with fund collapses and international shipping insolvencies. **Strengths:** "He is good for complex issues as he reliably comes up with clever points. It's helpful to have someone with complete integrity who can put a case forward in the most convincing way possible." "He is thorough and highly analytical." **Recent work:** Acted for the company and subsequently the Special Administrators of WorldSpreads. Provided expert advice on client money distribution issues.

Barry Isaacs QC (see p.680) Highly recommended for his insight into reconstruction and insolvency law, and for his further, complementary expertise in the areas of company, commercial litigation and banking and finance. His broad practice consists of both domestic and international work. **Strengths:** "A very clever lawyer, he really knows his stuff." **Recent work:** Acted for the APCOA Parking group of companies in relation to a multimillion-dollar restructuring which involved a scheme of arrangement.

Tom Smith QC (see p.769) A popular silk with an impressive caseload including substantial domestic and international matters. He stands out for his work on schemes of arrangement, and is considered particularly noteworthy for his responsiveness and efficiency on cases. **Strengths:** "Tom is an advocate with gravitas that belies the fact that he is a fairly junior silk, and combines the skills of a top-notch commercial litigator with those of a highly experienced insolvency lawyer." "He is a behemoth of intelligence who can deliver incisive and commercial advice." **Recent work:** Acted for Deloitte as the liquidators of Espirito Santo Banks Dubai, the Dubai operations of the Portuguese bank Espirito Santo, which was subject to bank resolution proceedings.

Mark Arnold QC (see p.585) Focuses his practice on restructuring and insolvency cases both in the UK and further afield. He places particular emphasis on clients in the financial services sector as part of his wider practice. **Strengths:** "Mark is very intelligent and very thorough." "He gives clear, measured advice." **Recent work:** Served as counsel in a high-value cross-border insolvency dispute concerning the enforceability of a third-party set-off clause contained in a USD100 million loan facility agreement.

Jeremy Goldring QC (see p.656) Has substantive experience in commercial litigation, restructuring and insolvency and company law. He has a sterling reputation for his adroit handling of offshore matters, and is frequently called to the Bar in the Cayman and British Virgin Islands. **Strengths:** "He is one of the best junior silks practising in this area." **Recent work:** Acted for Kaupthing in an application concerning the effect of the Credit Institutions Regulations 2004 on proceedings in England.

Daniel Bayfield QC (see p.592) Attracts commendations for his strong knowledge of insolvency law and for his particularly skilled handling of scheme work. Sources draw attention to his commercial sense and confident advocacy style. **Strengths:** "He has an excellent knowledge of insolvency law and is wonderful at applying it in practice." "He is very capable and a responsive presence on the most complex and urgent engagements." **Recent work:** Played a key role in the Waterfall I Application proceedings arising out of the Lehman Brothers administration.

JUNIORS

Adam Al-Attar (see p.581) Standout junior exhibiting great strength in bank and fund insolvencies. He regularly attracts instructions in headline cases and demonstrates notable skill in contested restructurings. **Strengths:** "He does wonderfully in mediation and negotiates well in settlement meetings. He has good experience and is developing a sterling practice." **Recent work:** Advised Apcoa Parking Holdings, a major restructuring of a group of German companies, in a contested scheme case involving the negotiation of limits of creditor obligations.

Richard Fisher (see p.645) Accomplished junior active on behalf of an impressive client base including major banks and hedge funds. He is held in high esteem by market sources, who describe him as "persuasive in court" and "one of the best juniors in the city." **Strengths:** "He's bright, cheerful, forthright and unflappable." **Recent work:** Acted for the scheme company in respect of the billion-dollar restructuring of the Codere group.

Stephen Robins (see p.753) A leading junior who regularly appears before the Supreme Court and Court of Appeal in high-profile cases. His broad client base includes winding-up boards, administrators and Chapter 11 and foreign trustees. **Strengths:** "Stephen is a rising star – he's extremely bright and thorough and has an outstanding knowledge of insolvency law." "He is very bright, creative and prolific." **Recent work:** Instructed by the administrators of oil exploration and production company Afren. Appeared in multiple hearings, including one concerning an application for the appointment of administrators in respect of a Nigerian subsidiary group.

Hilary Stonefrost (see p.774) Excels in matters involving schemes of arrangement as part of her wide-ranging practice, which encompasses both domestic and international insolvencies. **Strengths:** "Hilary provides solid advice and has reassuring gravitas." "She is incredibly good at accommodating our requests at short notice." **Recent work:** Appeared in a dispute concerning the removal, replacement, remuneration and expenses of administrators appointed to a number of shipowning companies in the North Sea Base Investments group.

Lloyd Tamlyn Divides his practice between corporate and personal insolvency cases. He routinely takes instructions from a diverse range of clients, including both private individuals and large-scale organisations. **Strengths:** "He is fiercely intelligent and pugnacious, someone you want in your corner and not against you." "Authoritative, commercial, exceptionally bright and hard-working." **Recent work:** Advised in relation to a public interest winding-up petition in which it was alleged that the respondents had committed a breach of the Financial Services and Markets Act 2000.

John Briggs (see p.602) Undertakes a diverse array of instructions given his impressively broad expertise. He regularly handles insolvency cases concerning debtors, pensions, partnerships and professional negligence claims. **Strengths:** "He has this ability to take a highly complex case and cut to the core issues with ease." "Concise, commercial and charming." **Recent work:** Appeared in McCarthy v Tann, a matter concerning proof of debt in company liquidation.

Adam Goodison (see p.656) Well-established practitioner who frequently acts in restructuring and business disputes on behalf of an impressive range of clients. He is habitually instructed by state governments and office holders in addition to corporations and trustees. **Strengths:** "Adam knows his stuff and is well regarded in this field." **Recent work:** Acted in the successful USD1 billion restructuring of fleet tanker group TORM.

Marcus Haywood Well respected in the restructuring and insolvency field, he regularly features in high-profile cases in the Supreme Court and Court of Appeal. He exhibits pronounced capability in both domestic cases and sophisticated international liquidations. **Strengths:** "He's fantastic at explaining things at a level that clients can understand and he has a total grasp of the law." "Marcus is extremely user-friendly and flexible. He offers charming and absolutely on-the-money advice and advocacy." **Recent work:** Appeared before the Supreme Court in a case considering the meaning of the term 'establishment' under the Insolvency Regulation.

Hannah Thornley (see p.781) Litigation expert who receives instructions from a broad range of clients, among whom she is able to count the Secretary of State. She is highly recommended for her technical aptitude and pragmatic approach. **Strengths:** "Hannah clearly knows the law inside out."

Charlotte Cooke (see p.622) Respected insolvency barrister who routinely receives instructions in major disputes which often contain an offshore element. She is singled out as a junior who is well equipped to handle sophisticated cases on behalf of both private individuals and large corporations. **Strengths:** "Charlotte adopts a clear-thinking and no-nonsense approach to insolvency matters. She is an impressive operator who reliably provides commercial and innovative advice." "She is impressive in court and always concise and accurate in her arguments. She has an impressive grasp of the most complex issues." **Recent work:** Assisted a large Ukrainian energy company with its proposal for an English scheme of arrangement to restructure debts.

Band 2

Enterprise Chambers

See profile on p.950

THE SET

Members of Enterprise Chambers have a strong track record in the insolvency field and demonstrate notable capability in cross-border cases. Its highly esteemed members offer expertise across a broad range of areas, and tackle high-profile insurance insolvencies with increasing regularity. Barristers at the set attract impressive instructions, featuring on headline matters such as MF Global and Clydesdale Financial Services v Smailes in the past year.

Client service: "The clerks are excellent. They're very proactive and there's no issue in relation to fees. They're very responsive and easy to deal with." "The clerks make it easy for the user with their can-do, positive attitude. They don't put obstacles in the way of getting the job done; one quick call and they will move mountains." The clerksroom is led by senior clerk Antony Armstrong.

JUNIORS

Hugo Groves Handles a mixed caseload featuring both company and insolvency litigation. His recent assignments have included claims against directors and shareholder disputes. **Strengths:** "He is very knowledgeable and easy to work with, in addition to being excellent in court."

Linden Ife Insolvency litigation specialist with a track record of acting in cases concerning the unlawful conduct of directors. Her robust advocacy style is particularly celebrated by interviewees. **Strengths:** "Linden provides superb support and is able to analyse very knotty legal problems quickly and effectively." "She is tenacious and able to hold her own in difficult circumstances." **Recent work:** Acted for the lenders in the liquidation of former claims management company Claims Direct, which suffered losses of around £200 million.

Niall McCulloch Attracts abundant praise from commentators, many of whom pinpoint his thorough preparation and impressive courtroom presence. He concentrates his practice on company insolvency. **Strengths:** "He's a practical, sensible, pleasant opponent who knows his stuff." "He's tenacious in court and his skeletons are excellent." **Recent work:** Acted for the liquidator in a case concerning breach of fiduciary duty in relation to distributions made before and after the insolvency of the company.

James Barker Handles the full scope of insolvency-related instructions, including matters regarding director's misfeasance, wrongful trading and the payment of unlawful dividends. He is regularly sought out by accountancy firms, who continue to value his expert advice and representation. **Strengths:** "He continues to provide very thorough, well thought out opinions. He's a great tactician who gives an excellent and timely service, in addition to being a formidable advocate who is always well prepared." "He always goes the extra mile and will roll his sleeves up at trial." **Recent work:** Acted on behalf of the liquidator in a litigation arising out of a £2.5 million share buy-back arrangement involving the former director and majority shareholder of NAL Realisations.

Geoffrey Zelin A popular choice for big-ticket insolvency cases owing to his "immense experience and superb intellect." His broad client base includes liquidators, receivers and administrators. **Strengths:** "He's a superb intellect and works well in a team." "He brings intellectual rigour and is a pleasure to work with." **Recent work:** Advised the liquidators in a claim for breach of duty brought by the former directors of East Midlands Renewable Energy.

Kavan Gunaratna Advises primarily on insolvency matters with a commercial or property slant. He is well liked by clients, who applaud his intelligence and top-quality advocacy. **Strengths:** "He is one of the best barristers in this area. He can apply the law in a second and doesn't panic, whatever the situation." **Recent work:** Advised HSBC in a High Court litigation arising out of the £5 million insolvency of the Park Group Care Homes network.

James Pickering Highly sought-after practitioner at the Insolvency Bar who regularly handles high-profile, multimillion-pound disputes. His areas of expertise include guarantee claims and fraud trials, alongside the developing remit of crypto-currency debt. **Strengths:** "He is a brilliant cross-examiner, offers excellent client service and delivers every single time." "He is personable, easy to work with and responsive." **Recent work:** Instructed by the creditors of crypto-investors Mintpal in a groundbreaking crypto-currency case. Successfully obtained the appointment of provisional liquidators.

Erskine Chambers

See profile on p.832

THE SET

A highly regarded company law set that fields a number of key restructuring and insolvency advocates. Its members routinely handle major disputes on behalf of high-calibre clients, particularly in the areas of banking and finance and civil fraud, and regularly provide expert advice in cross-border corporate insolvency cases. The chambers earns praise for its high-quality caseload and approachable clerks.

Client service: "The clerks are responsive and highly accommodating, with a very clear sense of client needs." The clerking team is led by senior clerk Mike Hannibal.

SILKS

Peter Arden QC (see p.584) Prominent insolvency silk who excels in international insolvency matters. He is highly popular with a range of clients, notably those in the financial sector. **Strengths:** "He's incredibly clever, turns work around quickly and is user-friendly and flexible. Anything that requires an intellectual powerhouse, he's at the front of the queue."

David Chivers QC (see p.616) Esteemed practitioner who offers expert counsel and representation to clients across a range of areas, with an emphasis on company law and commercial restructuring and insolvency. He has vast experience handling complex matters at both the domestic and international level. **Strengths:** "He very quickly grasps the situation and has an ability to respond extremely quickly to complex questions." "He has wonderful gravitas, can explain complicated issues with clarity, and is calm and unflappable in court." **Recent work:** Appeared before the Court of Appeal in Trustees of Olympic Airlines SA Pension & Life Assurance Scheme v Olympic Airlines SA. The case investigated the meaning of the term 'establishment' under the Insolvency Regulation.

Raquel Agnello QC (see p.580) Distinguished silk who receives widespread commendation for her sharp mind and commercial sense. She has a particularly strong reputation in the areas of personal and corporate insolvency and pensions. **Strengths:** "Raquel is extremely bright and has a great ability to keep things focused. She is always able to break down complex matters and provide clear, strategic advice."

James Potts QC (see p.741) Highly respected dispute resolution specialist who focuses his practice on insolvency and company law. His busy caseload features both contentious and non-contentious work, and he is particularly well versed in the area of misfeasance claims. **Strengths:** "He has great technical ability and won't run away from a fight." "His legal analysis is insightful and fearless." **Recent work:** Acted for the claimant liquidator of Mezhprombank in its successful application to the Court of Appeal to maintain a USD2 billion worldwide freezing order which had been previously been secured against a former Russian oligarch in 2014.

Andrew Thompson QC (see p.780) Respected silk who undertakes company law and insolvency cases on behalf of a broad range of clients. He has a strong track record of handling significant insolvency disputes.

JUNIORS

Ben Griffiths (see p.660) Has a broad insolvency practice featuring both litigious and advisory work. He specialises in corporate insolvency and, in recent years, he has appeared in some of the highest-profile cases in the market, including the Lehman Brothers administration, Kaupthing and MF Global. **Strengths:** "He is a fantastic, extremely intelligent junior. He's incredibly hard-working and consistently produces work of an excellent quality." **Recent work:** Assisted the liquidators of Carlyle Capital Corporation with their claims against the company's former directors and investment managers.

Maitland Chambers

See profile on p.875

THE SET

Maitland Chambers is a prestigious set housing an impressive team of restructuring and insolvency practitioners. The quality of representation and advice offered by its barristers receives widespread praise from market commentators. Its members are frequently instructed in significant cross-border insolvency disputes and have become a regular feature in the Caribbean courts recently. Commended as fielding "impressive players, " the set continues to benefit from the addition of new experts in this area, which has only served to buttress its reputation as a vibrant, dynamic set.

Client service: "The clerking is excellent. They're all very capable people, and a very nice bunch. " The clerking team is led by senior clerk John Wiggs.

SILKS

Paul Girolami QC (see p.653) Has a substantial practice advising companies and individuals in financial distress. His caseload features both domestic instructions and complex cross-border disputes. **Strengths:** "He's very capable and can handle anything that's thrown at him. He's particularly strong in cases with an offshore element."

Matthew Collings QC (see p.620) Highly proficient practitioner who demonstrates great skill in offshore insolvency matters. He routinely handles cases that are complex, high-value and high-profile. **Strengths:** "Matthew is strategic and fun to work with." "A highly capable and extremely bright advocate." **Recent work:** Successfully defended Ticketus in a well-publicised battle with the owner and largest shareholder of Glasgow Rangers, Craig Whyte, resulting in his bankruptcy.

Michael Gibbon QC (see p.652) Draws on his prior experience as a financier to inform his highly regarded insolvency practice. He is well known for his adept representation of stakeholders in commercial insolvency cases, while his key clients, HMRC and BIS, continue to benefit from his expertise. **Strengths:** "Michael's strengths are that he can effectively translate the law to clients, he is highly commercial, he doesn't get caught on esoteric points of law, and he is an effective advocate in court." **Recent work:** Acted in Jetivia SA v Bilta (UK) Ltd, a case considering whether liquidators can pursue the directors of one-man companies for breach of fiduciary duty.

Christopher Parker QC (see p.733) Commercial chancery silk with a strong following for contentious work in the insolvency and fraud arenas. Commentators note his technical excellence and down-to-earth approach. **Strengths:** "He's very clever and an exceptional appeal advocate." "A formidable opponent with an engaging court manner."

Rebecca Stubbs QC (see p.775) Appears in high-profile matters, regularly representing clients in the Supreme Court and before the Privy Council. She is recognised for her broad-based experience and expertise in the field. **Strengths:** "Rebecca has a wonderful reputation, very strong."

Anthony Trace QC (see p.783) Respected silk who is a regular feature in high-profile restructuring and insolvency cases. His recent work highlights include the Lehman, Landsbanki and Woolworths cases. **Strengths:** "He is an energetic and creative advocate, versatile and fearless." **Recent work:** Appeared in the Waterfall Application on behalf of the administrators of one of the two shareholders in Lehman Brothers International.

JUNIORS

Catherine Addy (see p.579) Standout junior who is deemed a "restructuring and insolvency guru." She enjoys a number of prestigious appointments, including Junior Counsel to the Crown and Bencher of the Middle Temple, and exhibits skill across the full range of insolvency matters. **Strengths:** "Catherine is a superb advocate, extremely approachable, highly intellectual and pragmatic." "What she doesn't know about insolvency could be written on a postage stamp. She's absolutely superb on her feet, really impressive." **Recent work:** Successfully acted for the Secretary of State in directors' disqualification proceedings brought against the CEO and financial director of Pritchards Stockbrokers.

Olivier Kalfon (see p.687) Offers a broad practice with notable strength in the areas of insolvency, banking and finance and dispute resolution. Sources hail his skilled advocacy and composure in cases. **Strengths:** "Olivier will make himself available as soon as he can, his written work is fantastic and clients love him. He's the full package."

Rebecca Page (see p.732) Represents a significant gain for the set, bringing with her substantial experience of company and insolvency disputes. She regularly handles major cases in the High Court and Court of Appeal. **Strengths:** "Rebecca is quick to grasp the issues and to turn around written advice. She is excellent, both in conference and on her feet in court." "She's industrious and reliable – a rising star." **Recent work:** Appeared in the Supreme Court in a case concerning breach of duty claims which were brought by insolvent company Bilta UK against its former directors.

4 Stone Buildings

See profile on p.913

THE SET

A highly impressive set whose experienced members handle matters spanning the full spectrum of insolvency work, with a particular focus on contentious insolvency cases. Market commentators highlight the number of silk-level "big hitters" housed by the set, alongside its wealth of up-and-coming juniors whose practices are flourishing. 4 Stone Buildings is habitually called upon to advise the government on insolvency matters, and maintains a solid reputation for its strength in the associated field of company law. Its members are routinely sought after to tackle highly publicised international cases such as Enron, Yukos, Transocean and Elektrim.

Client service: The clerking team, led by senior clerk David Goddard, "provide spectacular client service: they're attentive and can be contacted at any time of the day or night. They always deliver and never disappoint."

SILKS

Jonathan Crow QC (see p.627) Manages a busy caseload, splitting his time evenly between commercial and public law litigation. He frequently appears in the Supreme Court, Court of Appeal and ECHR, and is singled out by market commentators as a persuasive advocate. **Strengths:** "He is a standout silk in this area." "Fabulous on his feet." **Recent work:** Led an appeal in the Supreme Court arising from the insolvency of a large bunker supplier. The matter investigated the application of the Sale of Goods Act to contracts.

Robert Miles QC Renowned silk offering expertise across a full range of financial, corporate and commercial disputes. He remains a popular choice for an array of high-profile, big-ticket insolvency cases, with recent highlights including the Greek sovereign debt restructuring. **Strengths:** "He is consistently excellent and thinks outside the box. He's a huge resource." "Robert is a standout silk with a great intellect and good advocacy skills." **Recent work:** Acted on behalf of the Cayman Islands-appointed liquidators of Singularis Holdings in Singularis Holdings Limited v Daiwa Capital Markets Europe Limited.

George Bompas QC (see p.598) Leading insolvency practitioner who is recognised for his expert handling of major, sophisticated insolvency disputes alongside his significant experience in ADR proceedings. He is regularly called upon to assist with international matters and multimillion-pound claims. **Strengths:** "George is obviously a very experienced and reputable silk. Any opinion from him will be worth its weight in gold." "He's in a league of his own." **Recent work:** Instructed in the administration of MF Global Services.

John Brisby QC (see p.603) Has substantial experience advising in big-ticket litigation. He has appeared before the courts of the Isle of Man, Gibraltar and Bermuda, among others. **Strengths:** "He is very good at managing clients and coming up with novel legal arguments. At times, cases require a robust approach, which he is capable of providing." "A formidable advocate and superb cross-examiner." **Recent work:** Advised the opposing creditor in high-value personal bankruptcy proceedings concerning property investor Glenn Maud.

Richard Hill QC (see p.671) Highly sought after by an array of clients for his extensive expertise in complex insolvency disputes and for his specialist insight into various forms of ADR. His established restructuring and insolvency practice is further complemented by deep knowledge across the areas of civil fraud, commercial and company law. **Strengths:** "Excellent on the detail and easy to deal with, along with being straightforward and giving practical advice." "Faced with a particularly knotty problem, he's your man." **Recent work:** Represented the claimant, Peak Hotels and Resorts, in a well-publicised shareholder battle for control of the multimillion-dollar celebrity retreat Aman Resorts.

JUNIORS

Tiran Nersessian (see p.726) Habitually attracts instructions from both private clients and government officials owing to his strong track record in this area. His flourishing practice regularly sees him appearing as sole counsel in cases up to the Court of Appeal. **Strengths:** "Tiran deals with instructions swiftly and efficiently: he's hard-working, very approachable and a tenacious advocate." "He is extremely thorough and deeply impressive." **Recent work:** Instructed as sole counsel by the defendant directors in Brooks v Armstrong, a liquidators' claim for wrongful trading and misfeasance.

Andrew de Mestre (see p.631) Has considerable experience across the full gamut of restructuring and insolvency law. He regularly acts on behalf of an array of clients, including bondholders, issuers and corporate trustees, and routinely appears as sole counsel in high-profile cases. **Strengths:** "He is an undoubtedly bright guy who is highly capable." "A hard-working and sensible advocate." **Recent work:** Acted for the defence in The Liquidators of Hellas Telecommunications (Luxembourg) II SCA v Apax Partners LLP & Others, a claim brought by the liquidators of Hellas II who sought recovery of sums in excess of EUR900 million.

Christopher Harrison (see p.665) Has developed a highly regarded insolvency practice which is complemented by his wider strength in chancery commercial matters. He features regularly in high-profile cross-border cases and complex shareholder disputes. **Strengths:** "He's very bright, accessible and commercial." "He is 100% reliable and dedicated to going the extra mile." **Recent work:** Instructed to defend a multimillion-pound insolvency-related claim by the former wife of the late Russian oligarch and billionaire Boris Berezovsky.

Anna Markham (see p.707) Habitually instructed in significant insolvency and company law matters, she has a strong reputation for her skill and style as an advocate. She is an experienced representative in court and has appeared both for and against government departments in a range of insolvency-related disputes. **Strengths:** "Anna is practical and hands-on, as well as being upbeat and fun to work with." **Recent work:** Successfully secured the withdrawal of a winding-up petition that had been brought against the client, Leeds United FC.

Band 3

New Square Chambers

See profile on p.882

THE SET

New Square Chambers provides high-calibre counsel and representation to both corporations and private individuals in complex insolvency cases. Its barristers are well versed in administrations, receiverships and voluntary arrangements, among other areas, and are regularly called upon to act in challenging cross-border cases. The chambers provides robust advocacy at all levels, with market sources drawing particular attention to the New Square's promising crop of juniors.

Client service: "I can't fault the clerks at all – they're very, very good." "The clerks at New Square get back to you quickly and are sensible when discussing costs." Phil Reeves is head of clerking at the set.

SILKS

Robin Hollington QC Impressive silk with a wide-ranging company, insolvency and litigation practice. He continues to feature as an expert witness in courts and arbitral tribunals owing to his robust reputation in this area. **Strengths:** "He is extremely authoritative in his responses, you get a great level of comfort when he's on board. I'd recommend him for particularly complex questions and for precedent-setting disputes that will change the law." **Recent work:** Acted for the petitioner in Caldero v Beppler & Jacobson, a long-running dispute relating to two prestigious hotels in Montenegro. The case centred on whether sums invested in Beppler & Jacobson were invested by way of loan or capital.

JUNIORS

David Eaton Turner (see p.639) Well-established junior undertaking significant domestic and cross-border work. He regularly acts on behalf of both private individuals and large corporations. **Strengths:** "A brilliant technical lawyer with a good understanding of insolvency matters. He reliably delivers results." **Recent work:** Appeared on behalf of the trustee in bankruptcy in Raithatha v Williamson, a landmark case considering a trustee's rights to claim part of a bankrupt's pension entitlements for the estate in bankruptcy.

James Bailey A "user-friendly, focused and astute" practitioner with a strong practice encompassing commercial chancery, company and insolvency law. He frequently plays a key role in major, high-profile cases. **Strengths:** "James is exceptionally bright and anticipates every possible angle in a case." **Recent work:** Assisted the primary creditor, and subsequently the liquidators, with the complex liquidation of S. Simon & Co. The case involved ten separate actions by the office holders against various creditors and its directors.

Sebastian Prentis Recognised for his expertise in personal and corporate insolvency law. Interviewees particularly praise his strong client relationship skills and adroit handling of complex restructuring matters. **Strengths:** "For a junior, he is exceptionally skilled. He is capable of handling the most heavyweight cases with aplomb." "An excellent advocate and always a pleasure to work with." **Recent work:** Acted for the successful Greek liquidators in the high-profile case of Olympic Airlines. The matter centred around the meaning of 'establishment' in the Insolvency Regulation.

XXIV Old Buildings

See profile on p.884

THE SET

A respected chambers with a "great reputation in the insolvency space," according to market commentators. XXIV Old Buildings houses a team of robust insolvency advocates, from juniors through to silks. The set provides in-depth expertise and experience in offshore matters as part of its broad offering, which also encompasses areas such as shareholders' disputes, corporate insolvencies, directors' disqualification proceedings and unfair prejudice petitions.

Client service: "The clerking is very good. They understand markets outside of London and accommodate them, and they're a very progressive set. " The clerking team is led by senior practice managers Dan Wilson and Paul Matthews.

SILKS

Malcolm Davis-White QC A pre-eminent practitioner who is frequently instructed in complex, high-value insolvency matters, both domestically and abroad. He receives particular accolades for his adroit handling of directors' disqualification proceedings. **Strengths:** "He is clear, concise, authoritative and confidence-inspiring." **Recent work:** Successfully acted on behalf of the ACCA in its case against the insolvency practitioner who dealt with the CVA of fashion retailer Miss Sixty.

Alan Steinfeld QC Stands out for his active practice in offshore jurisdictions, notably the British Virgin Islands and Cayman Islands. He also routinely advises clients in significant domestic litigation. **Strengths:** "Alan has the ability to think outside of the box in some very difficult circumstances. He is always impressive."

Stephen Moverley Smith QC Attracts major international instructions owing to his deep experience in cross-border matters. He has a particularly robust reputation in the area of offshore work and trusts. **Strengths:** "He's an energetic, hard-working lawyer as well as an impressive advocate who makes an impression on the courtroom." **Recent work:** Acted for two significant shareholders in a Cayman Islands-based shareholder battle.

Steven Thompson QC Newly appointed silk with a stellar reputation for his effective advocacy style. He frequently advises clients based in the Middle East, and his deft handling of cross-border matters wins notable praise. Sources characterise him as a "precise and innovative thinker who provides punchy advice." **Strengths:** "He is incredibly smart, easy-going and responsive. He fills clients with huge amounts of confidence and reliably delivers fantastic results." "Absolutely outstanding, he can run rings around the other side." **Recent work:** Acted for the defendant in VTB v Parline, a RUB1 billion Russian insolvency claim.

JUNIORS

Richard Ritchie Well-regarded senior junior who is relied upon by long-standing clients, including the BIS and Treasury Solicitor, for his broad expertise. He also remains busy handling complex international and offshore work. **Strengths:** "Richard is very good at getting his head around large and complex issues." **Recent work:** Advised Powerhouse International in connection with the collapse of the group and directors' disqualification proceedings.

Stuart Adair A popular choice for clients seeking quality advice on both contentious and non-contentious matters in the insolvency arena. Commentators note that he is "fantastic on his feet before the court." **Strengths:** "He's excellent – excels in written work and is super-friendly." **Recent work:** Advised on all insolvency aspects of Anthony James Cole v Liam Howlett and others, a complex intellectual property dispute.

Serle Court

See profile on p.908

THE SET

Serle Court houses a strong team of practitioners who offer quality counsel and representation to both corporate and personal insolvency clients. The set prides itself on its ability to combine insolvency expertise with strength and depth in allied areas of law, such as fraud, partnership and banking and finance. Its members demonstrate robust technical expertise and regularly appear in high-profile matters in the area.

Client service: "Their clerking is excellent and highly effective." "The clerks are always responsive." Steve Whitaker leads the clerking team.

SILKS

Philip Jones QC (see p.686) A well-known advocate who is highly praised by market commentators for his breadth of expertise, encompassing insolvency, fraud and financial services. He remains a particularly popular choice in complex offshore insolvency cases and counts the Secretary of State among his diverse clientele. **Strengths:** "He possesses analytical ability and can think outside the box. He's robust, user-friendly and very helpful." **Recent work:** Acted for the Cabinet Office in its claim to recover a grant of £3 million following the insolvency of the charity Kids Company.

Philip Marshall QC (see p.708) Impressive silk who routinely receives instructions in offshore cases in addition to complex domestic disputes. He is highly recommended for his strength in restructuring and insolvency matters, which is buttressed by wider expertise in areas such as company, civil fraud and banking. **Strengths:** "He's an outstanding advocate, extremely diligent and very well regarded." **Recent work:** Represented the directors of Mazey Properties in a significant claim made in Guernsey. The case concerned the collapse of a company trading in asset-backed securities.

Daniel Lightman QC (see p.701) Widely admired for his vast experience and adept representation of all parties in bankruptcy and insolvency cases. Interviewees particularly highlight his standout technical ability and deft handling of complex cases. **Strengths:** "He is very helpful on complex matters and businesslike to deal with – a consummate professional." "Very clever and very technical – he is an advocate with a loyal following." **Recent work:** Successfully acted on behalf of the claimants in Munday v Hilburn, a claim brought against financial advisers alleging misrepresentation and fraud.

JUNIORS

Ruth Jordan (see p.686) Well known for her adroit handling of cases on behalf of the government. She offers broad expertise across the insolvency space, with notable strength in matters containing financial services and fraud elements. **Strengths:** "Ruth is a clear-headed and intellectual advocate." **Recent work:** Acted for the respondents in an appeal heard before the Privy Council. This was a multimillion-pound banking fraud and dishonest assistance claim arising out of the insolvency of Banco Continental.

Other Ranked Lawyers

Andreas Gledhill QC (Blackstone Chambers) A newly appointed silk who is variously hailed as "incisive," "thorough" and "able to see through the most complex legal issues." He is a regular feature in high-profile, international insolvency matters. **Strengths:** "He has a marvellous style, is very persuasive and gets the job done." "He's supremely clever and client-sensitive." **Recent work:** Advised the applicant bondholders in an application to set aside recognition of the Brazilian restructuring proceedings in respect of OGX.

Birgitta Meyer (One Essex Court) Regularly handles complex insolvency cases as part of her broader commercial litigation practice. Market commentators are quick to highlight her authoritative manner in court and her ability to present arguments with absolute conviction. **Strengths:** "She has a meticulous approach and a wonderful manner with clients. She's a great advocate, easy to work with and extremely proactive." **Recent work:** Acted for Johannes Martin in its successful application to set aside statutory demand based upon a US judgment which was not registered in the UK.

Sonia Tolaney QC (One Essex Court) Has significant experience acting for diverse parties in bankruptcy and insolvency matters. She is recognised for her adroit handling of complex, cross-border disputes. **Strengths:** "She has an amazing brain and is an incredibly charming person. She combines rare common sense with a considerable intellect, making her advice highly valuable."

Anthony de Garr Robinson QC (see p.631) (One Essex Court) An expert in corporate insolvency matters as part of his broader commercial chancery practice. He routinely handles both complex, domestic cases and those with an international dimension.

Stephen Atherton QC (20 Essex Street) A highly experienced silk who routinely tackles both domestic and cross-border matters. He excels in cases containing fraud elements and is a familiar face in offshore jurisdictions. Sources praise his "commercial and pragmatic" approach. **Strengths:** "He's very bright and down-to-earth, a great advocate." **Recent work:** Instructed by Sahaviriya Steel Industries UK in relation to its attempted restructuring and proposed administration.

Blair Leahy (20 Essex Street) Has a practice centred on international and domestic insolvencies. She remains popular among clients for cases involving allegations of fraud and breach of duty. **Strengths:** "She's very bright, reliable and thorough." "Blair knows the technical side of the law inside out and is a wonderful tactician." **Recent work:** Appeared in Pioneer Freight Futures (PFF) v Diana Chen, a substantial and complex BVI Insolvency Act claim against PFF's former director, and, reputedly, China's wealthiest woman.

Anthony Beswetherick (20 Essex Street) Concentrates his busy practice on cross-border insolvency cases, demonstrating particular prowess in those containing a fraud element. **Strengths:** "He will find a straight path through a difficult legal argument which is easy for the judge to follow. He excels in insolvency matters, he really does." **Recent work:** Advised a Chinese secured lender on possible challenges to an English administration order.

Andrew Fulton (20 Essex Street) Well respected for his expert representation of clients seeking advice on restructuring and insolvency cases. He is regularly instructed in offshore matters and habitually handles major domestic disputes. **Recent work:** Acted in Kaupthing Singer & Friedlander Ltd (In Administration) v UBS AG on behalf of EY as administrators.

Clara Johnson (3 Hare Court) A junior with a flourishing practice who is well acquainted with the full gamut of insolvency cases. She regularly handles instructions on behalf of office-holders, directors, bankrupts and creditors, among others. **Strengths:** "She is personable and provides practical, timely advice." **Recent work:** Prepared an application against multiple respondents in a matter concerning "creditor resistance" fraud perpetrated against major utility companies.

Daniel Lewis (3 Hare Court) Highly popular in the market for his advocacy style and personable manner. He undertakes wide-ranging insolvency work with a particular emphasis on claims arising from participation in tax avoidance schemes. **Strengths:** "Can't recommend highly enough: he's pragmatic, user-friendly, clever and deals with different personalities sensitively. A totally impressive advocate." **Recent work:** Served as supporting counsel to US attorneys in a case in which a Chinese construction company applied to dismiss Chapter 11 proceedings in Delaware in favour of proceedings in the Bahamas.

Jamie Riley (Littleton Chambers) Especially well regarded in the area of corporate insolvency. He is equally adept at handling domestic and offshore cases, and has featured in a number of significant matters. **Strengths:** "Jamie is a smooth operator, collected and thorough. He's even-tempered on his feet, but also quite devastating. He's a class act." **Recent work:** Acted for a company registered in the Cayman Islands which owned a hotel near Hyde Park. The company was the respondent to an administration application which had been brought by The Co-operative Bank pursuant to a £35 million facility.

Tom Shepherd (4 New Square) Possesses a wealth of experience advising on multimillion-pound deals, both in the UK and further afield. He offers expertise in both corporate and personal insolvency cases and exhibits particular strength in matters involving a fraud element. **Strengths:** "He is good on his feet and very robust. A pleasure to work with." **Recent work:** Advised the liquidator in a successful claim to recover a yacht that had been misappropriated by the former directors of a company.

Christopher Boardman (Radcliffe Chambers) Attracts glowing praise from market commentators, who commend his "phenomenal delivery" in court. He undertakes the full scope of insolvency work, acting on both contentious and non-contentious cases. **Strengths:** "He's very on the ball with his advice and is an excellent advocate. He has a calm and convincing manner, even in the trickiest of cases." "He is someone you want on your side in a difficult fight." **Recent work:** Acted for the directors of a large building company in a multimillion-pound wrongful trading claim.

Tina Kyriakides (Radcliffe Chambers) Rated highly in the insolvency space, where she is noted for her pragmatism and flair in court. Her insolvency expertise is wide-ranging, including administration, voluntary arrangements and directors' disqualification proceedings. **Strengths:** "She's extremely thorough, personable, tenacious and excellent on her feet." **Recent work:** Defended Changtel Solutions against a winding-up petition for over £15.5 million brought by HMRC.

Adam Deacock (Radcliffe Chambers) Handles the full spectrum of insolvency work. He regularly appears in court and offers expert counsel to a diverse range of clients in an advisory capacity. **Strengths:** "Adam is great with complex litigation and has a very commercial approach." **Recent work:** Acted for Eco Measure Market Exchange in an application to strike out a winding-up petition relating to sums allegedly due for carbon reduction measures.

Dawn McCambley (Radcliffe Chambers) Enjoys a strong reputation in the insolvency arena given her evident expertise in areas such as misfeasance, wrongful trading, contractual disputes and transaction avoidance. She is notably strong in matters centring around fraud. **Strengths:** "She's extremely competent and well thought of." "She's an excellent junior and a good all-rounder." **Recent work:** Acted in Christopher Josife v Summertrot Holdings Limited, successfully defeating an application to set aside a statutory demand made on behalf of the debtor.

Peter Shaw (9 Stone Buildings) Advises on a mixture of corporate and personal insolvency cases, and has a significant focus on matters containing a fraud element. **Strengths:** "He's realistic, takes the right points in court and doesn't waste time." "He is very user-friendly and able to think outside the box." **Recent work:** Instructed by HMRC in a high-value dishonest conspiracy claim.

Joseph Curl (9 Stone Buildings) A well-recognised barrister highlighted for his dedicated corporate and personal insolvency practice. He regularly acts in high-value deals on behalf of prominent clients. **Strengths:** "He's clever, commercial and reliable." **Recent work:** Acted for Longmeade's liquidator in a £16 million claim against the Official Receiver.

Paul Burton (Three Stone) Makes a frequent appearance in complex cross-border cases, standing out in particular for his trial advocacy. He is particularly adept at advising on issues relating to the administration of insolvent estates. **Strengths:** "Paul is a tough, no-nonsense advocate who can cut through complex issues with ease." **Recent work:** Acted on behalf of an action group of former investors in IAP Action Group v Rosser & Others. The case centred on suspected fraud in connection with IAP's insolvency.

Ewan McQuater QC (3 Verulam Buildings) Renowned barrister who is regularly instructed on big-ticket insolvency cases. His broader areas of associated expertise include commercial dispute resolution and civil fraud, among others. **Strengths:** "He is very user-friendly and doesn't pontificate. Clients like him because he can speak their language." **Recent work:** Appeared as lead counsel in Lehman Brothers International v DZ Bank AG and Bank of New York, a case concerning multiple claims triggered by Lehman's collapse and its default on a whole series of high-value tri-party repo positions.

Adrian Beltrami QC (3 Verulam Buildings) Acts for insolvency clients as part of his broader commercial practice, which also encompasses banking, financial services and fraud. **Strengths:** "He is cerebral and very tactical." **Recent work:** Acted for the liquidators of Kingate in proceedings arising out of the high-profile Madoff fraud case.

Matthew Hardwick QC (3 Verulam Buildings) Roundly praised by market commentators as "focused, incredibly attentive to detail and extraordinarily committed." He habitually appears in both contentious and non-contentious insolvency cases for a diverse range of clients. **Strengths:** "He's incredibly sharp and possesses excellent drafting skills." **Recent work:** Acted for Asia Coal Energy Ventures in the defence of parallel insolvency proceedings brought by the Raffeisen Bank in the Commercial Court of the British Virgin Islands and in the UK.

Philip Hinks (3 Verulam Buildings) An esteemed practitioner with a broad-ranging practice. He regularly handles high-value, major insolvency disputes, demonstrating particular skill in matters containing a fraud element. **Strengths:** "Philip exudes authority, he has an amazing ability to grasp complex issues quickly and he performs well beyond his year of call." **Recent work:** Acted for Renault Sport SAS, the purchaser of the entire shareholding in Lotus F1, in circumstances where HMRC was seeking to place Lotus into administration.

Angharad Start (3 Verulam Buildings) A standout junior who is recognised for her quality contribution to a number of high-profile insolvency cases. She demonstrates expertise across the board, regularly acting in matters such as shareholder disputes, wrongful trading litigation and misfeasance claims. **Strengths:** "She's smart, thorough and tenacious – a highly impressive practitioner." **Recent work:** Acted in a case involving multimillion-pound misfeasance claims concerning the sale of an extremely high-profile retailer.

Lexa Hilliard QC (Wilberforce Chambers) Esteemed practitioner offering an impressive breadth of experience and expertise across all areas of insolvency law. She regularly takes instruction at both the domestic and international level, while her respected practice focuses predominantly on advisory work. **Strengths:** "She is absolutely superb. She is a first choice for complex restructuring work. She's very user-friendly, easy to deal with and will turn work around very quickly." **Recent work:** Acted for former joint liquidators in the Supreme Court of Antigua in connection with their claim for remuneration.

Marcia Shekerdemian QC (Wilberforce Chambers) Regularly approached by clients seeking advice on corporate and personal insolvency cases. She has carved out a niche in the area of fraud and asset recovery work, and regularly acts in cross-border cases. **Strengths:** "She is exceptionally good at drafting and offering strategic advice. She's a tenacious adviser who punches well above her weight." **Recent work:** Represented a large group of bondholders following the collapse of a Luxembourg investment company dubbed the 'death bond' company.

Iain Pester (Wilberforce Chambers) Routinely handles insolvency instructions on behalf of distressed corporates and individuals. His areas of skill include directors' disqualification proceedings and shareholder disputes. **Strengths:** "Iain knows his subject inside out and is diligent with research – he's an excellent all-round junior." **Recent work:** Advised the trustee of bankruptcy of two directors of Weavering Capital. The matter concerned a USD459 million fraud.

Thomas Robinson (Wilberforce Chambers) Inspires confidence in clients, who rate him as "unflappable and eloquent." He is well known for his adept representation of the Pensions Regulator, and continues to be a popular choice for international insolvency matters. **Strengths:** "He's highly competent – he's undoubtedly going to go a long way."

MIDLANDS

Restructuring/Insolvency
Leading Sets
Band 1
St Philips Chambers *
Leading Silks
Band 1
Khangure Avtar *St Philips Chambers*
* Indicates set / individual with profile.
Alphabetical order within each band. Band 1 is highest.

Restructuring/Insolvency
Leading Juniors
Band 1
Morgan James *St Philips Chambers* *
Band 2
Brown Marc *St Philips Chambers* *
Weaver Matthew *St Philips Chambers* *

Band 1

St Philips Chambers

See profile on p.934

THE SET

St Philips Chambers remains the premier insolvency set in the Midlands, boasting an experienced team of insolvency specialists. The set receives particular praise for its highly commercial approach and "depth of knowledge, which goes right down to the junior members," and is also commended for its excellent client service. The team's formidable reputation is founded upon the broad-ranging expertise of its members, which includes cross-border issues, liquidation and misfeasance claims.

Client service: "The clerking was very good. They are clear with their fee estimates and very easy to deal with. They make my life easier rather than harder." The clerking team is headed by Joe Wilson.

SILKS

Avtar Khangure QC Top-tier silk whose capabilities span the full spectrum of insolvency work. He frequently handles complex cases on behalf of a range of clients, with notable experience in the financial sector. Market sources are quick to highlight his strength in oral advocacy and measured approach in court. **Strengths:** "The most notable person in this market, he is a very impressive operator with a nice style and a balanced, smooth approach." "I would have no hesitation using him again; he is particularly good on his feet and good with judges."

JUNIORS

James Morgan (see p.721) Hugely experienced

junior who is highly regarded for his work in all aspects of personal and corporate insolvency and commercial dispute resolution. **Strengths:** "Comfortably the leading junior counsel in the region, James is intelligent, pragmatic and commercial. He also has a terrific bedside manner with both clients and judges." **Recent work:** Continued to act for liquidators in a multimillion-pound misfeasance and avoidance claim against former directors and other connected parties.

Marc Brown (see p.604) A junior who is regularly instructed on high-value and complex matters, Marc Brown is vastly experienced in both personal and corporate insolvency work. He acts on behalf of individuals, companies and insolvency practitioners. **Strengths:** "Marc is a very bright, up-and-coming junior counsel who shows a lot of promise in the area." "His technical abilities and his thoroughness are both extremely impressive." **Recent work:** Successfully acted on behalf of debtors who sought an adjournment of a bankruptcy order in a long-running case in the Court of Appeal.

Matthew Weaver (see p.791) A well-known barrister who also has previous experience working as a solicitor at a City law firm. He regularly takes instructions on both personal and corporate insolvency matters, and advises a healthy mix of clients including liquidators, administrators and trustees in bankruptcy. **Strengths:** "He is my first port of call. He's very commercial, good in conference and good on his feet. I can't recommend him highly enough." **Recent work:** Continued to advise the former administrators of B W Estates in a dispute with a creditor.

NORTH EASTERN

Restructuring/Insolvency	
Leading Sets	
Band 1	
Enterprise Chambers *	
Band 2	
Exchange Chambers *	
Kings Chambers *	
Leading Silks	
Band 1	
Jory Hugh	*Enterprise Chambers*
Leading Juniors	
Band 1	
Groves Hugo	*Enterprise Chambers*
Temple Eleanor	*Kings Chambers* *
Band 2	
Bond Kelly	*Enterprise Chambers*
d'Arcy Eleanor	*Kings Chambers* *
Linklater Lisa	*Exchange Chambers* *
Rodger Jonathan	*Enterprise Chambers*
Up-and-coming individuals	
Heath Duncan	*Enterprise Chambers*

* *Indicates set / individual with profile.*

Alphabetical order within each band. Band 1 is highest.

Band 1

Enterprise Chambers

See profile on p.950

THE SET

Enterprise Chambers is a leading insolvency and restructuring set in the North East with offices in both Newcastle and Leeds. It handles an array of insolvency work including complex personal cases as well as larger commercial matters. The set regularly acts for companies, directors and individuals regarding restructuring administrations, liquidations and bankruptcies. It is also noted for its national reach and cross-border insolvency experience.

Client service: "The clerking is excellent and very responsive, helpful and highly organised. They are always very commercial and pragmatic on fee negotiations." Joanne Caunt heads up the clerking team in Leeds and Bethany Thompson leads the clerking in Newcastle.

SILKS

Hugh Jory QC A leading silk in the North East who is also regularly instructed to act in the London courts. He takes on a broad range of contentious corporate and personal insolvency, and has clients including businesses, office holders and high-value individuals. **Strengths:** "He is very bright, very good tactically at trial and he also understands the commercial needs of the client." "Provides extremely technical advice delivered in a client-friendly manner."

JUNIORS

Hugo Groves A highly experienced insolvency practitioner who has particular expertise in dealing with business, partnership and commercial disputes, often with a cross-border element. He receives praise for his commercial knowledge and practical advice. **Strengths:** "Hugo is one of the leading cross-border insolvency barristers in the UK." "He is very commercial and very pragmatic."

Kelly Bond Has considerable experience in restructuring and insolvency cases relating to both individual and corporate clients. She regularly advises insolvency practitioners on all aspects of bankruptcy, liquidation and administration. **Strengths:** "Her work is consistently of a high standard; she is very competent and approachable." **Recent work:** Continued to act for an English trustee against a bankrupt who is the subject of a previous bankruptcy in Scotland, raising complex issues around the application of legislation.

Jonathan Rodger Undertakes complex corporate and personal insolvency work as part of his mixed commercial and chancery practice. He has particular expertise in complex, high-value bankruptcy proceedings. **Strengths:** "He provides sound advice and is extremely well thought of in the Newcastle area." **Recent work:** Acted for a trustee in a subsidiary action to recover possession of the bankrupt's matrimonial home.

Duncan Heath Enters the rankings this year as the result of high praise from both peers and instructing solicitors. Handles all aspects of personal and corporate insolvency, with particular experience in bankruptcy and winding-up petitions. **Strengths:** "He is really easy to get on with. He offers great knowledge of insolvency procedures and excellent practical advice."

Band 2

Exchange Chambers

See profile on p.956

THE SET

Exchange Chambers is known for the scope of its insolvency and restructuring experience, and draws particular praise for its corporate insolvency offering. The set frequently acts on behalf of office holders and individuals in connection with insolvency-specific claims.

Client service: Jonathan I'Anson is the set's practice manager in Liverpool, while Ian Spencer leads the clerking operations in Leeds and Nick Buckley heads up the team in Manchester.

JUNIORS

Lisa Linklater (see p.702) An experienced junior frequently instructed in the full range of personal and corporate insolvency cases including those relating to administrations, bankruptcy and liquidation. **Recent work:** Advised a high net worth individual in opposing an application to suspend their discharge from bankruptcy.

Kings Chambers

See profile on p.968

THE SET

A compact set with a strong reputation for insolvency, Kings Chambers has a number of well-regarded barristers handling the full spread of insolvency and restructuring work. It is frequently involved in difficult administrations, personal bankruptcies and partnership insolvencies. Members regularly take instructions from companies, directors, office holders and debtors, and handle both contentious and non-contentious matters.

Client service: "I think that the clerks at Kings Chambers are the best clerks. They are very efficient, friendly and helpful." Gary Smith is the senior clerk in Birmingham, Colin Griffin leads the team in Manchester and Rory Davis heads up the clerking in Leeds.

JUNIORS

Eleanor Temple (see p.779) A leading barrister on the North Eastern Circuit, Eleanor Temple is frequently instructed in high-value personal and corporate insolvency and restructuring matters. **Strengths:** "She is a wonderful advocate who is great on her feet, and gets to the bottom of problems immediately." **Recent work:** Represented a claimant facing a High Court fraud claim that resulted in a freezing injunction, costs claims and a bankruptcy petition.

Eleanor d'Arcy (see p.628) Maintains a broad chancery and commercial practice which incorporates significant insolvency and restructuring work. She regularly acts for both individuals and companies and is noted for her experience in insolvency cases relating to property. **Strengths:** "She is thorough, well organised and very competent." **Recent work:** Represented claimants in a dispute with their tenant. The case concerned unpaid rent and property dilapidations.

NORTHERN

Restructuring/Insolvency
Leading Sets
Band 1
Exchange Chambers *
Kings Chambers *
Leading Silks
Band 1
Anderson Lesley *Kings Chambers* *
Cawson Mark *Exchange Chambers* *
Band 2
Casement David *Kings Chambers* *
Chaisty Paul *Kings Chambers* *
New Silks
Mohyuddin David *Exchange Chambers*
Leading Juniors
Band 1
Doyle Louis *Kings Chambers* *
Maynard-Connor Giles *Exchange Chambers*
Band 2
Berragan Neil *Kings Chambers* *
Sandbach Carly *Exchange Chambers*
Walmisley Lisa *Kings Chambers* *
* *Indicates set / individual with profile.*
Alphabetical order within each band. Band 1 is highest.

Band 1

Exchange Chambers

See profile on p.956

THE SET

Exchange Chambers is a market-leading set which continues to attract high-value instructions from office-holders and individuals owing to its stellar reputation. Its eminent members offer expertise across the full spectrum of restructuring and insolvency matters, regularly advising in areas such as the recovery of assets, freezing injunctions and transactional avoidance provision. The set remains highly regarded on the Northern Circuit, with market commentators describing it as "a very strong chambers that is well known for its chancery work. It continues to be a preferred choice for insolvency."

Client service: "The clerks are very efficient, very accommodating and always willing to help." "You reliably get a sensible recommendation from the clerks at Exchange, and in terms of cost they'll be as flexible as they possibly can." "The clerks are highly commercial and they turn matters around quickly."

SILKS

Mark Cawson QC (see p.613) Stands out for his adept representation of both corporates and individuals in complex insolvency cases. He numbers banks, office-holders and government departments among his impressive roster of clients, and is commended for his "measured, calm manner and formidable legal mind." **Strengths:** "His drafting skills are excellent. He's calm on his feet, but ruthless when he needs to be." **Recent work:** Defended the former directors of the Burnden Group in a multimillion-pound misfeasance claim brought by the liquidator.

David Mohyuddin QC As an insolvency expert, he is particularly well equipped to handle matters across the board, such as public interest winding-up petitions and directors' disqualification proceedings. Market sources characterise him as "confidence-inspiring," adding that he "demonstrates impressive adversarial skills which are supported by great technical knowledge." **Strengths:** "Decisive and thorough, he displays an intricate knowledge of the law and applies it brilliantly." "An excellent strategist." **Recent work:** Instructed on behalf of the Official Receiver and liquidator to assist with the wind-down of Sahaviriya Steel Industries.

JUNIORS

Giles Maynard-Connor Primarily handling corporate fraud and contentious insolvency cases, he is regularly instructed in high-profile, complex matters. Impressed sources praise his vast experience and meticulous approach, commenting that "he leaves no stone unturned." **Strengths:** "He is not only a technically strong barrister, but a commercial and tenacious advocate." **Recent work:** Acted for Lemma in a successful appeal before the Supreme Court contesting a decision by the liquidator of a foreign insurance company.

Carly Sandbach Undertakes contentious corporate and personal insolvency work as part of her broader commercial litigation practice. She demonstrates skill in areas such as breach of directors' duties and cases containing fraud elements. **Strengths:** "She is a superb advocate who is very sharp and always adds value." " A tenacious advocate who is extremely well versed in this area." **Recent work:** Instructed by the Secretary of State in connection with the proposed winding-up of Dalton & Dalton Tax Consultants on public interest grounds.

Kings Chambers

See profile on p.968

THE SET

Kings Chambers is a premier restructuring and insolvency set on the Northern Circuit featuring high-quality advocates throughout, from juniors through to silks. Its eminent members are well equipped to handle a diverse range of instructions, covering areas such as liquidation, receiverships, company voluntary arrangements and an array of insurance-related matters. Market sources commend the chambers as "a pre-eminent insolvency set outside of London: they're absolutely bloody marvellous."

Client service: "The clerks reliably offer a good service, they are highly responsive and very helpful." "Always helpful and proactive in their approach." The clerking team is led by Colin Griffin.

SILKS

Lesley Anderson QC (see p.583) A top restructuring and insolvency silk offering expertise across the board. She is well equipped to handle both corporate and personal insolvency matters of the utmost complexity. **Strengths:** "She is very bright, good with clients and tireless in getting the right result." **Recent work:** Acted on behalf of the appellant landlord of a shopping centre in a dispute with a tenant over the service charge and insurance rents.

David Casement QC (see p.612) Routinely handles big-ticket restructuring and insolvency cases, especially in the sports sector. **Strengths:** "An absolutely first-rate barrister." **Recent work:** Instructed to act for the Trustee in Bankruptcy in connection with the insolvency of Al Midani. The case involved the complex process of tracing assets throughout Europe and the Middle East.

Paul Chaisty QC (see p.614) Habitually represents lenders and company-side clients in recovery and insolvency cases. His broad industry expertise covers sectors such as real estate and sports. **Recent work:** Handled complex directors' disqualification proceedings in connection with the administration of Magnus Properties.

JUNIORS

Louis Doyle (see p.636) Focuses on asset recovery, breach of duty claims and general insolvency work. He receives glowing praise from the market and demonstrates particularly deep knowledge of the Insolvency Act 1986. **Strengths:** "Louis is an excellent all-rounder." "He is down-to-earth, well informed and very good with clients." **Recent work:** Acted for the administrators of a collapsed high street retailer, the Burdens Group.

Neil Berragan (see p.595) Handles matters spanning the full spectrum of insolvency work and habitually opposes respected silks in court. He routinely tackles contentious matters both for and against administrators and liquidators. **Recent work:** Defended a substantial claim for misfeasance brought by the liquidators against the former director of Market Reach Solutions.

Lisa Walmisley (see p.788) Represents a wide array of parties to bankruptcy, and has a practice with a particular emphasis on transaction avoidance litigation. She is well equipped to handle both corporate and personal insolvency cases. **Strengths:** "She is friendly, knowledgeable and a strong advocate in court."

WESTERN

Restructuring/Insolvency
Leading Sets
Band 1
Guildhall Chambers *
Leading Silks
Band 1
Davies Stephen *Guildhall Chambers*
Sims Hugh *Guildhall Chambers*
Leading Juniors
Band 1
Bamford Jeremy *Guildhall Chambers*
Brockman Christopher *Guildhall Chambers*
French Paul *Paul French - Independent barrister (ORL)* ◊
Passfield Simon *Guildhall Chambers*
Ramel Stefan *Guildhall Chambers*
Band 2
Ascroft Richard *Guildhall Chambers*
Brown Daisy *Guildhall Chambers*
Doyle Holly *Guildhall Chambers*
Levy Neil *Guildhall Chambers*
Maher Martha *St John's Chambers (ORL)* ◊ Ⓐ
* *Indicates individual with profile.*
Ⓐ *direct access (see p.24).*
◊ *(ORL) = Other Ranked Lawyer.*
Alphabetical order within each band. Band 1 is highest.

Band 1

Guildhall Chambers
See profile on p.938

THE SET

Based in Bristol, Guildhall Chambers offers leading insolvency advice, and fields one of the foremost specialist teams outside of London. Its members provide advice and advocacy on all aspects of contentious insolvency law and are also able to take on non-contentious insolvency issues, corporate recovery and turnaround. The set is known for its "proactive and dynamic set-up" which sees it engaging directly with clients by providing a range of educational seminars. **Client service:** "The clerks are helpful, efficient, friendly and responsive. They understand what we need and what works for us." Justin Emmett leads the civil clerking team.

SILKS

Stephen Davies QC A standout silk who has also published widely on insolvency law and practice. In addition to corporate and personal insolvency, he has a particular niche in asset recovery and directors' liability. He has also been noted for his recent work advising on the restructuring of solicitors' firms. **Strengths:** "He never ceases to amaze me with his commercial awareness, lateral thinking and approachability. He is a joy to work with and intellectually fantastic." "He is fierce and incredibly hands-on. It is very reassuring when you have him on a case." **Recent work:** Instructed to resist bankruptcy proceedings arising from a dispute connected to the headquarters of Santander in Madrid.

Hugh Sims QC A strong commercial barrister who specialises in corporate insolvency work. He acts in claims for and against insolvency practitioners, and also has expertise in directors' disqualification proceedings. **Strengths:** "He is very thorough and reliable, his advocacy is excellent and he has a great style. He is extremely precise and user-friendly." "Tactically excellent and great to work with." **Recent work:** Successfully acted in a validation application concerning the post-petition transfer of commercial property in Hatton Garden, London.

JUNIORS

Jeremy Bamford Noted for specialising in insolvency litigation concerning both individuals and companies. Also handles disciplinary and regulatory proceedings involving insolvency practitioners and directors' disqualifications. **Strengths:** "Technically outstanding and user-friendly. If you have a real technical matter he is a good man to have on the team." "Jeremy is our first port of call for any insolvency issues. He continues to impress with his clear, concise and effective advice. **Recent work:** Successfully represented HMRC in relation to recovering unpaid PAYE/NIC against the Lotus Formula 1 racing team, to the value of £2.3 million.

Christopher Brockman Dedicated insolvency specialist who is also head of the insolvency team at Guildhall Chambers. He is regularly instructed by insolvency practitioners and government departments, appearing in both local and London courts, and he is also an accredited mediator. **Strengths:** "He has been there and done it many times before and brings his experience and pragmatism to every case." "He provides services in a very commercially sensitive way, and gives advice and constructive views on the way forward." **Recent work:** Acted for HMRC in relation to an application which reinforced the principles upon which the court will appoint a provisional liquidator.

Simon Passfield A highly sought-after junior who is active in all areas of corporate and personal insolvency. He wins praise from sources, who highlight not only his technical knowledge and work ethic, but also the strength of his written and oral advocacy. **Strengths:** "He is a very bright, perceptive individual and the quality of his analysis is first-class." "He has a very strong understanding of the technical elements of the law, and is very accomplished on his feet." **Recent work:** Acted for the trustee in a high-value bankruptcy case that was complicated by allegations of professional misconduct as well as the disputed ownership of valuable chattels initially concealed by the bankrupt.

Stefan Ramel Handles personal and corporate insolvency matters, and also writes and speaks broadly on a variety of insolvency topics. A multilinguist, he is widely respected for his impressive command of cross-border issues. **Strengths:** "Goes beyond his level of call in terms of expertise, particularly when handling cross-border, technical insolvency issues." "Very user-friendly and incredibly bright. His written opinions are very good as they are detailed and yet commercial." **Recent work:** Successfully acted for an individual looking to annul a bankruptcy order obtained against him.

Richard Ascroft Has a substantial practice covering all areas of corporate and personal insolvency law. He is an expert in directors' duties and is regularly instructed in transaction avoidance claims and directors' misfeasance proceedings. **Strengths:** "He is thorough and a great advocate." **Recent work:** Acted in a claim by a company in liquidation that alleged professional negligence on the part of its former accountants.

Daisy Brown Focuses significantly on insolvency as part of her broader chancery practice, which extends to commercial litigation and advisory work. She is an experienced junior who has appeared in court at all levels, including the Court of Appeal.

Holly Doyle Has a broad range of experience that encompasses winding-up and bankruptcy petitions as well as complex misfeasance cases and transaction avoidance claims. She is regularly involved in high-value cases appearing before the County and High Courts. **Strengths:** "She is very thorough." **Recent work:** Represented a trustee in a contested application for possession and sale of a property held by the bankrupt under a deed of trust, which it transpired was a sham.

Neil Levy A noted banking and finance specialist who also advises on insolvency work. He has key expertise in handling insolvency disputes related to professional negligence. **Strengths:** "He is very good and thorough, and the way he delivers advice is easy to understand."

Other Ranked Lawyers

Paul French An independent insolvency barrister who can advise, advocate and consult on a wide variety of insolvency-related matters, and who has a particular focus on personal insolvency cases. **Strengths:** "He has got an encyclopaedic knowledge of personal insolvency law."

Martha Maher (St John's Chambers) An expert in regulatory work relating to insolvency practitioners, who is also adept at handling high-profile partnership disputes that feature an insolvency element. **Strengths:** "Puts clients at ease, is very proactive and has great drafting skills." **Recent work:** Represented Malaysian investors in the UK solar industry in a performance claim against a company in liquidation.

Contents:

ALL CIRCUITS

Sanctions	
Leading Silks	
Band 1	
Otty Timothy	*Blackstone Chambers*
Randolph Fergus	*Brick Court Chambers*
Saini Pushpinder	*Blackstone Chambers*
New Silks	
Kennelly Brian	*Blackstone Chambers*
Lester Maya	*Brick Court Chambers* *
Leading Juniors	
Band 1	
Pobjoy Jason	*Blackstone Chambers*
* *Indicates individual with profile.*	
Alphabetical order within each band. Band 1 is highest.	

Ranked Lawyers

Jason Pobjoy (Blackstone Chambers) Leading junior in the field. He has a background in public international law and frequently appears before European courts. He is often instructed to advise on asset-freezing regimes and on sanctions compliance. **Strengths:** "He has a great turnaround time, a keen eye for detail, and he provides sharp analysis." **Recent work:** Led by Brian Kennelly QC, he represented Ahmed Ezz and his wives before the General Court in an application to unfreeze their assets.

Timothy Otty QC (Blackstone Chambers) Has a broad public law and human rights practice. He is experienced in acting for individuals and financial institutions in judicial reviews opposing freezing orders. He has advised on numerous countries' sanctions regimes, as well as Al-Qaeda. **Strengths:** "He is a very careful advocate and makes extremely well thought-through submissions. He is always well prepared for cases." "He is outstanding." **Recent work:** He acted for a Russian journalist and broadcaster whose assets were frozen by the EU because of alleged support for Russian action in Ukraine.

Pushpinder Saini QC (Blackstone Chambers) Displays expertise in sanctions regimes affecting numerous jurisdictions. His reputation in the field stems from his having acted in Kadi v Council, the leading sanctions case. **Strengths:** "A really strong advocate and utterly reliable." **Recent work:** He acted for Rosneft in Rosneft v Council. In this case, Rosneft challenged the EU Russian sanctions regime.

Brian Kennelly QC (Blackstone Chambers) Involved in a large number of cases that cover a wide range of sanctions regimes. He acts for a range of clients, regularly advising individuals on delisting procedures, and advising companies on compliance. **Strengths:** "He is good at dealing with clients and sorting the wheat from the chaff. He knows how to get to the nub of the matter as quickly as possible." **Recent work:** He represented four Ukrainian individuals, including former politicians whose assets have been frozen by the EU, in challenges to those freezing orders.

Fergus Randolph QC (Brick Court Chambers) Has a very broad EU law practice, of which sanctions law is a significant part. He has acted on some of the seminal cases in the field and has been active of late advising Iranian companies that are subject to listing. **Strengths:** "He is extremely good: he's flexible, hard working and has enormous technical knowledge." **Recent work:** He acted for IRISL on IRISL v EU Council, challenging sanctions imposed on the Iranian company.

Maya Lester QC (see p.700) (Brick Court Chambers) New silk receiving universal praise for her expertise in sanctions cases. She has vast experience of handling numerous high-profile cases, representing individuals and companies. She also co-writes a well-regarded sanctions blog. **Strengths:** "Queen of the Sanctions Bar without a doubt. She is just phenomenal." "Beyond responsive. First-class." **Recent work:** She acted for National Iranian Tanker Company in a challenge to its relisting on an EU sanctions list.

SHIPPING & COMMODITIES: An Introduction

Contributed by Simon Rainey QC and Nevil Phillips of Quadrant Chambers

The legal market for the Commercial Bar: looking back

The legal market, from the perspective of the Commercial Bar, has remained characteristically busy. Some familiar themes endure, as cases which made the news in earlier periods progressed to the appellate stages in late 2015 and 2016. At the same time, shipping and commodities are areas which continue to generate new areas of dispute, having given rise to some notable new decisions over the last twelve months.

The physical markets: now and looking forward

In terms of the physical markets, the period has been one of conflicting pictures.

Halfway through 2016, some commodity values are enjoying an uplift. However, the improvement is patchy, with upward movements in sugar, crude and gold, but with declines in coal and other industrial commodities – a reflection of the fact that global trade is slowing, with shipowners continuing to be affected by falling demand for coal, iron ore and associated products. Most of the decline is because China, as the world's biggest buyer of coal and iron ore, continues to see its own economy and industrial output slow.

This continues to send shipping rates to new lows, furthered by an apparent oversupply of ships ordered as the world's economies recovered from the earlier, post-2008 recession. As a result, the shipping industry is scaling back fleets and consolidating. That is likely to be a feature going forward. The trade in iron ore is expected to grow moderately over the next few years, but coal shipments to China are anticipated to continue in decline (although India offers greater possibilities as a market for the latter, as its consumption and imports of coal for power generation are rising more quickly than it can meet domestically).

The consequence is that the shipping market is gradually changing in response. There is a perceptible increase in scrapping, with the gradual effect of reduced competition and increased prices. However, some analysts suggest that it will be five years or so before the surplus of tonnage that lies behind some of the rate decline will be gone.

The legal market: outlook

The effect of the physical markets has been arguably to reduce the number of new instructions coming into the legal market, at least on the shipping side. Many of the specialist shipping solicitors' firms are reporting reduced activity as a consequence of the state of the physical market, and even the P&I clubs are suggesting that claim numbers are reduced (as members prefer to resolve their disputes "at the coalface" rather than invoke a claim which may impact upon their claims record). However, London's pre-eminence as a centre of excellence for legal services in the shipping and commodities fields (together with the willingness of the London firms and the Commercial Bar to adopt more flexible business and fee practices in order to adapt to the times and to be sensitive to the position of the clients) means that it continues to hold its own, despite these challenges.

The foregoing appears especially true of the Commercial Bar in these fields, aided as it is by its comparatively small number of specialist practitioners, its ability (eg via its lateral seniority structures within every chambers) to cater flexibly for a variety of case types and demands, and its high reputation in the international context. It is these factors which have kept it busy over the last twelve months and which may be anticipated to keep it so over the next year, despite the fact that the legal market is possibly more challenging than it was in 2015.

Developments of particular note

As a reflection of the existing themes and the new developments referred to above in the shipping and commodities sector for the Commercial Bar, the following are among the developments:

Existing themes

The fallout from the well-publicised collapse of the OW Bunkers Group continued to make the headlines via the litigation in respect of the 'Res Cogitans'. With some expedition, that matter reached the Supreme Court, which gave judgment in May 2016 ([2016] 2 WLR 1193).

On the same date, the Supreme Court also gave judgment in The Global Santosh [2016] 1 WLR 1853, holding that, while parties beneath the charterers in a contractual charter chain could count as their agents under the head charter party, that was only so where they were carrying out the charterers' obligations under that charter.

In 2015, in Spar Shipping AS v Grand China Logistics [2015] EWHC 718 (Comm), Popplewell J held (opposite to the conclusion of Flaux J in The Astra [2013] 2 Lloyd's Rep. 69) that the obligation to make punctual advance payment of hire under a time charter was not a condition. In June 2016, the Spar Shipping decision was heard before the Court of Appeal, from which judgment is awaited on this critical issue.

New developments

In Yemgas FZCO & Others v Superior Pescadores SA [2016] EWCA Civ 101, the Court of Appeal held that in any case where: (i) a bill of lading is issued incorporating the Hague Rules as enacted in the country of shipment; and (ii) the country of shipment has enacted the Hague-Visby Rules, this should be considered as incorporating the latter.

In The Wehr Trave [2016] EWHC 583 (Comm), the Commercial Court determined the scope of a charterer's right of employment of a vessel under a trip time charter.

In MSC Mediterranean Shipping Co SA v Cottonex Anstalt [2016] EWCA Civ 789, the Court of Appeal determined that a carrier recovered demurrage in respect of the detention of shipping containers up to the date when the commercial purpose of the adventure was deemed to have become frustrated, by reason of the shipper's continuing breach of contract in failing to redeliver the containers within the free time allowed, which thereby became repudiatory.

Brexit: situation normal

One development which cannot escape mention is Brexit, following the result of the UK referendum on 23 June 2016.

Many have questioned whether this will impact upon shipping and commodities work in the London legal market. However, the overwhelming consensus is that it will not.

Such work derives almost entirely from the express choice of English law and jurisdiction (either High Court or arbitral). There is no reason why this should change. The attractions of such a choice remain. Indeed, as regards arbitration, there is no risk of change. Even as regards enforcement of English High Court judgments within the EU (which has not, historically, been a compelling factor in the choice of English jurisdiction), the situation is unlikely to alter in practice (in light of the 2005 Hague Convention on Choice of Court Agreements, to which all EU Member States are already a party, and the UK's likely accession to that in any event).

Thus, there is no feature of Brexit which should result in any negative impact upon the legal market for shipping and commodities in England and Wales. On the contrary, at the time of writing, the only effect of Brexit is likely to be a positive one for this market: the change in the value of sterling renders litigation/arbitration in the UK even better value and more attractive for overseas clients than was already the case before.

Contents:

LONDON

Shipping & Commodities
Leading Sets
Band 1
20 Essex Street *
Quadrant Chambers *
Band 2
7 King's Bench Walk *
Band 3
Essex Court Chambers *
4 Pump Court *
St Philips Stone Chambers *
* *Indicates set / individual with profile.*
◊ *(ORL) = Other Ranked Lawyer.*
Alphabetical order within each band. Band 1 is highest.

Shipping & Commodities	
Leading Silks	
Star individuals	**Cooper** Nigel *Quadrant Chambers* *
Rainey Simon *Quadrant Chambers* *	**Gunning** Alexander *4 Pump Court* *
Band 1	**Kverndal** Simon *Quadrant Chambers* *
Ashcroft Michael *20 Essex Street*	**Lewis** David *20 Essex Street*
Berry Steven *Essex Court Chambers*	**MacDonald Eggers** Peter *7 King's Bench Walk*
Bright Robert *7 King's Bench Walk*	**Masters** Sara *20 Essex Street*
Edey Philip *20 Essex Street*	**Melwani** Poonam *Quadrant Chambers* *
Goldstone David *Quadrant Chambers*	**Nolan** Michael *Quadrant Chambers* *
Hancock Christopher *20 Essex Street*	**O'Sullivan** Sean *4 Pump Court* *
Kendrick Dominic *7 King's Bench Walk*	**Russell** Jeremy *Quadrant Chambers* *
Matthews Duncan *20 Essex Street*	**Saloman** Timothy *7 King's Bench Walk*
Parsons Luke *Quadrant Chambers* *	**Selvaratnam** Vasanti *St Philips Stone Chambers* *
Persey Lionel *Quadrant Chambers*	**Smith** Christopher *Essex Court Chambers* *
Schaff Alistair *7 King's Bench Walk*	**Turner** James M *Quadrant Chambers* *
Young Timothy *20 Essex Street*	**Vineall** Nicholas *4 Pump Court* *
Band 2	**Band 4**
Baker Andrew *20 Essex Street*	**Butcher** Christopher *7 King's Bench Walk*
Blackburn Elizabeth *St Philips Stone Chambers*	**Davey** Michael *Quadrant Chambers*
Croall Simon *Quadrant Chambers* *	**Dias** Julia *7 King's Bench Walk*
Dunning Graham *Essex Court Chambers* *	**Eaton** Nigel *Essex Court Chambers*
Hill Timothy *20 Essex Street*	**Flynn** Vernon *Essex Court Chambers*
Jacobs Nigel *Quadrant Chambers* *	**Gruder** Jeffrey *Essex Court Chambers* *
Kimmins Charles *20 Essex Street*	**Healy** Siobán *7 King's Bench Walk* *
Lord Richard *Brick Court Chambers (ORL)* ◊	**Hirst** Jonathan *Brick Court Chambers (ORL)* ◊
Southern Richard *7 King's Bench Walk*	**Hofmeyr** Stephen *7 King's Bench Walk*
Thomas Robert *Quadrant Chambers* *	**Karia** Chirag *Quadrant Chambers* *
Waller Richard *7 King's Bench Walk*	**Kenny** Stephen *7 King's Bench Walk*
Band 3	**Kimbell** John *Quadrant Chambers* *
Allen David *7 King's Bench Walk*	**Passmore** John *Quadrant Chambers*
Bailey David *7 King's Bench Walk*	**Pillow** Nathan *Essex Court Chambers*
Blanchard Claire *Essex Court Chambers*	**Russell** John *Quadrant Chambers* *
Bryan Simon *Essex Court Chambers*	**Tozzi** Nigel *4 Pump Court* *
Coburn Michael *20 Essex Street*	**New Silks**
Collett Michael *20 Essex Street*	**Kenny** Julian *20 Essex Street*

Band 1

20 Essex Street

See profile on p.838

THE SET

This distinguished set provides market-leading representation across a wide range of dry shipping and commodities matters, marshalling acclaimed and significantly experienced barristers, including the authors of prominent industry textbooks. Sources commend the "versatility, strength and depth" of the chambers. Its members regularly act in high-value matters in the Commercial Court, and are also active in arbitration and mediation. 20 Essex Street maintains an outstanding presence in the field, and has recently acted in a raft of important cases including Bunge v Nidera in the Supreme Court and 'The Prestige', which concerned a very large oil spill.

Client service: Led by senior clerk Neil Palmer the "extremely user-friendly" team is "very easy to deal with and takes a commercial approach."

SILKS

Michael Ashcroft QC A distinguished barrister with an enviable reputation for his work across shipping and commodities matters. He is particularly highlighted for his outstanding ability in complex arbitrations. **Strengths:** "Has the ability to think in a very transforming way, really easy to work with and very diligent." "A very powerful advocate." **Recent work:** Successfully acted for the respondent owners in Trafigura Beheer v Navigazone Montanari, a dispute arising from the hijacking of an oil/chemical tanker and subsequent discharge of fuel oil cargo. The case concentrated on the proper meaning of an 'in transit loss' clause.

Philip Edey QC An exceptional advocate with considerable shipping and commodities expertise. His broad practice includes charter party disputes, cargo claims and bills of lading cases. **Strengths:** "A good man to have on side in a legally difficult case. He is very willing to work as part of a team and always brings added intellectual weight." "He has an amazing delivery and a real ability to get to the nub of the case and pull out all of the points. He's an amazing cross-examiner and very focused on all the details." **Recent work:** Acted in defence of HNA Group in a case concerning a claim made by Shagang Shipping in relation to a long-term charter party. Underlying issues include allegations of bribery and torture.

Christopher Hancock QC Joint head of chambers with Duncan Matthews QC. An admired practitioner, he is frequently lauded for his "encyclopaedic knowledge of the law." His wide-ranging practice covers both shipping and commodities disputes and arbitrations. **Strengths:** "He has a knowledge of case law which is frankly incredible." "He is the go-to guy for anything super-intellectually demanding and high stakes. He is one of the sharpest minds at the Commercial Bar." **Recent work:** Represented the claimant London Steam-Ship Owners' Mutual Insurance Association in arbitration against The Kingdom of Spain and the French State concerning compensation for pollution damage relating to a large oil spill. The case involved consideration of the application of time limits under the Arbitration Act 1996 and further questions of state immunity.

Duncan Matthews QC Joint head of chambers with Christopher Hancock QC. An "utterly outstanding advocate," Matthews has an established reputation as a leading silk at the Shipping and Commodities Bar. He acts in dry bulk and tanker charter party disputes, affreightment matters and cargo claims, and is particularly notable for his expertise in civil fraud cases. **Strengths:** "Very verbally polished and with a sense of humour. He can be both quite aggressive and effective." "A very serious and very clever guy, he can squeeze a killer argument out of nothing, it seems." **Recent work:** Defended the underwriters of the 'Brillante Virtuoso' in a claim arising from a piracy attack off Yemen relating to the alleged constructive total loss of the vessel.

Timothy Young QC A highly esteemed barrister who combines marked ability in shipping and commodities matters with specialist expertise in several related areas including international trade and sale of goods. **Strengths:** "If I need a huge legal brain to get

Shipping & Commodities
Leading Juniors
Band 1
Phillips Nevil *Quadrant Chambers* *
Priday Charles *7 King's Bench Walk*
Smith Christopher M *Quadrant Chambers* *
Band 2
Aswani Ravi *St Philips Stone Chambers* *
Buckingham Stewart *Quadrant Chambers* *
Byam-Cook Henry *20 Essex Street*
Jones Mark *St Philips Stone Chambers* *
Leabeater James *4 Pump Court* *
Macey-Dare Thomas *Quadrant Chambers* *
Parker Benjamin *7 King's Bench Walk*
Pounds Caroline *Quadrant Chambers* *
Whitehead Thomas *St Philips Stone Chambers* *
Wright Alexander *4 Pump Court* *
Band 3
Bovensiepen Daniel *20 Essex Street*
Craig Nicholas *3 Verulam Buildings (ORL)* ◊
Healy Sandra *7 King's Bench Walk*
Henton Paul *Quadrant Chambers* *
Holmes Michael *7 King's Bench Walk*
Jones Susannah *20 Essex Street*
Moore Natalie *Quadrant Chambers*
Pearce Luke *20 Essex Street*
Toms Paul *Quadrant Chambers* *
Toney Rachel *St Philips Stone Chambers* *
Walsh David *Quadrant Chambers* *
Watthey James *4 Pump Court* [A] *
Band 4
Brier Jeremy *Essex Court Chambers*
Casey N G *7 King's Bench Walk*
Davies Josephine *20 Essex Street*
Debattista Charles *St Philips Stone Chambers*
Henderson Neil *4 Pump Court* *
Hopkins Philippa *Essex Court Chambers*
Hosking Ruth *Quadrant Chambers* *
King Edmund *Essex Court Chambers*
Kulkarni Yash *Quadrant Chambers* *
Lightfoot Jeremy *St Philips Stone Chambers*
Mander Marcus *7 King's Bench Walk*
Morgan Gemma *Quadrant Chambers* *
Riches Philip *20 Essex Street*
Sarll Richard *7 King's Bench Walk*
Shirley James *St Philips Stone Chambers* *
Stevenson Peter *Quadrant Chambers* *
Sutherland Jessica *7 King's Bench Walk*
Turner Adam *7 King's Bench Walk* *
Warrender Nichola *Quadrant Chambers* *
Up-and-coming individuals
Barrett Stephanie *Quadrant Chambers* *
Coffer Benjamin *Quadrant Chambers*
Gardner Ben *Quadrant Chambers* *
Lahti Liisa *Quadrant Chambers* *
Stiggelbout Mark *Quadrant Chambers* *
Tan Charlotte *20 Essex Street*
* *Indicates individual with profile.*
[A] *direct access (see p.24).*
◊ *(ORL) = Other Ranked Lawyer.*
Alphabetical order within each band. Band 1 is highest.

me out of a hole, I go to Tim Young. He is unique, extraordinarily bright and fun to use." "A very difficult opponent because he is intellectually so imaginative and he is always jumping around, keeping you on your toes." **Recent work:** Acted for Continental Lines in the first case to consider the meaning of cargo being loaded and discharged at the expense and risk of the shippers/charterers.

Andrew Baker QC A prominent silk, well known for his excellent capability in commodities and dry shipping cases. He has related strength in international trade cases and arbitration. **Strengths:** "Obviously very bright, extremely academic and knows the law very well." "One of the first names in dry shipping work, he authors one of the main shipping reference texts." **Recent work:** Acted for the claimant in Castleton Commodities Shipping v Silver Rock Investments relating to questions of recovery of proceeds from the sale of an iron ore cargo after non-payment problems.

Timothy Hill QC An exceptionally skilled barrister recently arrived from Stone Chambers, who brings with him considerable ability in shipping matters. Well known for his expertise in wet shipping cases, he has a broad practice that also covers charter parties, shipbuilding and bills of lading disputes. **Strengths:** "He is really good at cross-examination and is a tough advocate." "Tim is excellent for salvage, shipping litigation and insurance matters. He is user-friendly, very sharp and doesn't waste your time."

Charles Kimmins QC A respected silk with notable experience concerning charter parties, bills of lading and MOAs. He is known for his expertise across the full range of shipping and commodities issues. **Strengths:** "Very bright intellectually and he also has a very persuasive manner and good judgement." "He sets the standard which all should aspire to but very few achieve." **Recent work:** Acted for the PDVSA in a dispute with CH Offshore over unpaid sums due under various charters.

Michael Coburn QC A highly regarded practitioner commended for his expertise in shipping and commodities matters and his additional capability in international trade matters. He is frequently praised by solicitors in interviews for being "very pleasant and incredibly obliging." **Strengths:** "He exudes confidence and it is always a pleasure working with him." "He has particular strength in providing prompt advice when it's required. He is very calm and self-assured and also has a keen eye for detail." **Recent work:** Represented Grand China Logistics in a time charter dispute with Spar Shipping. A key question was whether the obligation to pay hire was a condition.

Michael Collett QC Commended for being "very practical and user-friendly," Collett has marked expertise in shipping, commodities and international trade matters. Widely regarded as an advocate, he also accepts appointments as an arbitrator. **Strengths:** "A quiet, undemonstrative advocate and very effective for it, he has a deadly quietness to him and can spin coils around you and net you. He has a very good technique." **Recent work:** Acted in MTM Hong Kong v MT Maritime Management regarding an appeal of an arbitration decision concerning the difference between a vessel's actual and hypothetical earnings up to the end of substitute employment.

David Lewis QC A "very committed and user-friendly" barrister with a strong advocacy and advisory practice. He marshals his shipping and commodities knowledge in international arbitrations and private international law disputes. **Strengths:** "A very likable individual and a very dedicated and excellent lawyer." "His cross-examination is good, and he is easy to work with, quick to respond and accessible." **Recent work:** Acted in Shipowner's Mutual P&I Association v Containerships Denizcilik Nakliyat Ve Ticaret, a case concerning anti-suit injunctions against third parties suing in a non-EU court.

Sara Masters QC An experienced barrister with a broad practice covering international trade and sanctions issues alongside shipping and commodities matters. She is also well known as an arbitrator and mediator. **Strengths:** "Fantastic to work with." "She's clearly very clever and she understands what needs to be done for the client. I find her approachable and user-friendly with a good sense of humour." **Recent work:** Acted in Newland Shipping and Forwarding Limited v Toba Trading and Others in relation to a claim concerning the alleged fraudulent procurement of contracts for the sale of petroleum products to Iran.

Julian Kenny QC A well-known and highly recommended new silk. He is a commercial law specialist with an established reputation for shipping and commodities work. **Strengths:** "Impressive, concise, bright and excellent on paper." "He is very witty and gets the Tribunal laughing along with him, very effective at steering them along the way he wants to go." **Recent work:** Acted in the Supreme Court on an appeal concerning the issue of whether a contract for the supply of bunkers is a contract of sale.

JUNIORS

Henry Byam-Cook A strong junior with a broad commercial disputes practice. He has experience in sale contract issues, ship finance and charter party disputes. **Strengths:** "Charming, affable and loved by clients. He is very good and very dependable." "He is very bright, incisive in his legal work and one of those people that is very approachable." **Recent work:** Acted in a one-day appeal hearing before the Court of Appeal relating to a novel point on the incorporation of a jurisdiction clause into a bill of lading.

Daniel Bovensiepen Frequently acts in collision, shipbuilding and ship sale disputes covering multiple shipping industry sectors. He has further experience of commodities matters. **Strengths:** "He has a razor-sharp intellect and a fantastic written style. He's superbly hard-working and a terribly nice person to work with." "He had a very measured manner and had good analysis of the case." **Recent work:** Acted in NYK Bulkship v Cargill International, concerning the proper application of Rainy Sky and Arnold v Britton, and liability or responsibility for acts of agents under charter parties.

Susannah Jones An experienced junior with expertise in shipping, commodities and additional areas covering insurance, banking and civil fraud matters. **Strengths:** "A brilliant junior who is very strong on the law, legal writing and getting into the detail of things." "A strong performer, who is good on a difficult case." **Recent work:** Acted in Seagrain v Glencore, an arbitration appeal on the GAFTA prohibition clause.

Luke Pearce A prominent junior recognised by sources for his advocacy skills. He deals with shipping and commodities matters as well as banking and derivatives issues. **Strengths:** "A master of detail, an outstanding advocate and a pleasure to work with." "A star in the making." **Recent work:** Acted in MSC v Cottonex, a Commercial Court trial concerning a claim for demurrage for detention of shipping containers.

Josephine Davies Regularly instructed in challenging commodities and shipping disputes. Her practice includes freight agreements, charter parties and bills of lading. **Strengths:** "She is highly intelligent, very hard-working and very user-friendly." "A very strong advocate, very willing to go in to bat hard for her clients." **Recent work:** Acted for Engen Petroleum in two linked cases concerning questions of causality relating to the contamination of a gasoil cargo.

Philip Riches Recently arrived from Stone Chambers bringing expertise in shipping disputes as well as mining, energy and trade matters. He also has experience in shipbuilding arbitrations. **Strengths:** "A decent reputation and a diverse work profile."

Charlotte Tan An "extremely bright and charming" junior with expertise in shipping, commodities and commercial dispute resolution. She acts in charter party, shipbuilding and joint venture disputes. **Strengths:** "She is a really effective and hard-working junior. 'Getting involved' is an understatement, I felt she had become part of our team." "I have seen her at a hearing outmatch an opposing QC with ease and elegance. She is proactive and often comes up with smart ideas for arguing a case which are not immediately obvious but which stand up on analysis." **Recent work:** Acted in a dispute relating to an oil spill and the attempts by France and Spain to recover compensation for extensive pollution damage. The case included novel points relating to state immunity and the interaction between English arbitration law and Brussels regulation.

Quadrant Chambers

See profile on p.901

THE SET

Quadrant Chambers is a set at the forefront of the Shipping and Commodities Bar. Sources say "of all the sets that do this work, you immediately think of them." Its members are highly acclaimed for their impressive advocacy and exceptional client service. Bolstered by multiple new arrivals, the set has increased its ability to offer leading capability in sophisticated wet shipping actions, as well as across dry shipping matters and commodities disputes. In addition to mustering popular and renowned silks, Quadrant is particularly recommended by solicitors for its extremely deep bench of highly able juniors. Notable recent instructions include the 'Res Cogitans' OW Bunkers test case, 'Kairos Shipping' Court of Appeal action concerning limitation action and 'The Sea Miror', a case considering the meaning of cargo being handled "at the expense of the shippers/ charterers."

Client service: The "incredibly good" Simon Slattery and the "legendary" Gary Ventura lead an impressive team commended as "excellent, approachable and practical – the clerks' room is extremely helpful."

SILKS

Simon Rainey QC (see p.746) A renowned and venerable silk universally acclaimed for "masterful" work across shipping and commodities matters. His exceptional practice covers diverse matters including shipbuilding, dangerous cargo and charter party disputes. **Strengths:** "Very impressive and focused – he thinks fast on his feet. He is fantastic both on the technical law and also as an advocate. He is easy to work with and charming, and remains calm and collected when under pressure." "He is stellar. He has a brain the size of a planet." **Recent work:** Acted in Bunge v Nidera for the successful appellant Bunge in a landmark Supreme Court decision relating to the GAFTA Default Clause and sale of goods damages.

David Goldstone QC An outstanding barrister with marked ability in shipping law. His practice covers wet and dry work such as salvage, unsafe ports and bills of lading disputes. **Strengths:** "A very clever brain, he gets straight to the nub of the point and advises clearly and concisely." "Incredibly cerebral and really excellent." **Recent work:** Instructed by various Lloyds underwriters in a constructive loss claim under a war risks policy.

Luke Parsons QC (see p.734) Esteemed head of chambers who is well respected for his broad shipping and commodities practice covering issues such as shipbuilding, ship sale and charter party disputes. **Strengths:** "Exceptionally bright and very good on his feet. He is a master of getting the tone and the content of his delivery just right no matter the audience." "A real street fighter, he fights the points and wins even if it starts off looking difficult." **Recent work:** Acted in Shagang Shipping v HNA Airlines in a charter party dispute involving allegations of bribery and torture.

Lionel Persey QC An excellent silk, deputy High Court judge and Lloyds arbitrator. He has a first-rate practice covering shipping matters including charter parties, bills of lading, salvage and collisions. **Strengths:** "Incredibly experienced and knows his stuff backwards." "He knows the law inside-out, understands the legal and technical issues and is absolutely user-friendly." **Recent work:** Acted in the case of Nordlake and Sea Eagle, a collision action in Admiralty Court arising from the sinking of an Indian navy vessel.

Simon Croall QC (see p.626) A highly regarded barrister with a superb practice that takes in shipping, commodities and international trade matters. He has significant arbitration experience frequently acting for Far Eastern clients. **Strengths:** "Razor sharp and very good on his feet." **Recent work:** Acted for a large Spanish travel company in a dispute concerning early termination of a charter party for a cruise vessel.

Nigel Jacobs QC (see p.682) An esteemed practitioner who frequently tackles collision, salvage and marine insurance matters as well as dry shipping work. **Strengths:** "He is of high intellectual calibre. He is to-the-point and is a very effective advocate and arbitrator." "He was very easy to work with, incredibly hard-working, passionate and dedicated to the case." **Recent work:** Acted for the cargo interests in Kairos Shipping v Enka involving a limitation claim where the shipowner's right to limit under the Limitation Convention is to be tried.

Robert Thomas QC (see p.780) A well-known barrister frequently commended for his "intellectual firepower." His varied and notable practice includes shipping and commodities matters and advice on anti-suit injunctions and freezing orders. **Strengths:** "A class act, very assured and hard-working, accessible and a joy to work with." "If there is a novel or difficult application where we need to persuade a judge, he is very good at that." **Recent work:** Acted in 'The Sea Miror' case, a bill of lading dispute concerning the meaning of the term that cargo is to be loaded and discharged "at the expense and risk of the shippers/ charterers".

Nigel Cooper QC (see p.623) A well-known silk engaged in both wet and dry shipping work as well as insurance and international trade matters. He frequently advises on shipbuilding and yacht-related disputes. **Strengths:** "Practical and a sensible guy, a good advocate." "He is very approachable and he has been able to take very complex legal problems and condense that in writing to a very understandable presentation." **Recent work:** Acted in consolidated action in the Commercial Court with six parties arising from alleged mis-delivery of cargo in China and subsequent claims under letters of indemnity.

Simon Kverndal QC (see p.693) A shipping specialist with recognised ability in shipping litigation and arbitration. He acts in disputes arising from ship financing, salvage and port safety issues. **Strengths:** "A very attractive style of advocacy and pleasant to work with." "Very thorough, thinks outside the box." **Recent work:** Acted for third-party carriers in The South West Strategic Health Authority v Bay Island Voyages, a case concerning the Athens Convention.

Poonam Melwani QC (see p.716) A well-regarded silk and "impressive advocate" with a prominent shipping and commodities practice. She is regularly instructed in charter party, bill of lading and general contract disputes. **Strengths:** "Incredibly hard-working, she will leave no stone unturned to fight your case." **Recent work:** Acted in a dispute arising from the alleged mis-delivery of cargo and breaches of an exclusive jurisdiction clause due to the commencement of 23 sets of proceedings by Chinese freight forwarders.

Michael Nolan QC (see p.728) A "very intellectual and very experienced" silk with an extensive shipping practice covering litigation, arbitration and advice. He deals with charter party, bills of lading and shipbuilding contract disputes. He has particular knowledge of the sea-fishing industry. **Strengths:** "He has great attention to detail whilst not losing sight of the core issues. His clear communications skills, his approachability and teamwork are also worthy of mention." **Recent work:** Acted for the owners of a vessel in an appeal of an arbitration award relating to a charter party dispute over liability for costs of transiting the Suez Canal as a result of amended voyage orders.

Jeremy Russell QC (see p.757) A barrister with significant experience in dry shipping and commodities work. He has a particularly strong maritime arbitrations practice. **Strengths:** "He's been around the block and knows it all."

James Turner QC (see p.785) A highly recommended barrister regularly instructed in shipbuilding, salvage and marine casualties. He also covers charter parties and trade finance matters including bills of exchange and letters of credit. **Strengths:** "He has an amazing ability to crunch through the details of a very technical case." "An excellent advocate; he is very high quality." **Recent work:** Acted in Moran Yacht & Ship v Pisarev and Another in a dispute over commission relating to the sale of a yacht.

Michael Davey QC Well regarded for his ability in wet and dry shipping disputes including charter parties, bills of lading, salvage and collisions. He also covers related insurance and conflicts of law matters. **Strengths:** "He is fast and intelligent, he can break a problem and rebuild it." "Very straightforward, very user-friendly and exceptionally bright."

Chirag Karia QC (see p.688) A barrister with a significant shipping and commodities practice who undertakes work in a variety of areas including cargo claims, collisions and marine insurance disputes. **Strengths:** "He is very user-friendly, a very good advocate and excellent at cross-examining. He is a pleasure to work with." "He is very bright, very commercial, and his advice was spot on." **Recent work:** Acted on behalf of one of China's largest oil companies in a claim for damages from other international oil companies, arising from excessive salt content of Angolan oil cargoes purchased from those companies.

John Kimbell QC (see p.691) Recognised "for his approachability and clear-cut opinions." His practice encompasses wet and dry shipping work, and he appears in both litigation and arbitration proceedings. **Strengths:** "He is very approachable, very commercial and excellent on his feet as an advocate." "He has a good way of quietly dropping the bad points and ambushing you with a good point: he's good on strategy and tactics."

John Passmore QC A highly able silk with a broad practice covering wet and dry shipping as well as commodities disputes. He also takes on ship sale and purchase, shipbuilding and offshore construction matters. **Strengths:** "He is absolutely excellent, very sensible, very considered and very measured." "He unravels the complex to make it simple." **Recent work:** Acted in a jurisdiction dispute in two cargo claims. A leading case on the interpretation of jurisdiction regimes in shipping, transport and aviation conventions.

John Russell QC (see p.757) A tough advocate whose shipping practice includes charter parties, shipbuilding and piracy claims. He has particular acumen in both cargo claims and yacht-related disputes. **Strengths:** "The kind of barrister you would want to have on your side. He's not afraid to challenge anyone on anything." "He's bright, commercial, user-friendly and he delivers when you need it." **Recent work:** Acted in the Supreme Court on behalf of Sea Shepherd UK against Fish & Fish in a dispute arising from the releasing of a catch of allegedly illegally caught bluefin tuna.

JUNIORS

Nevil Phillips (see p.737) An outstanding junior with an excellent and long-standing reputation who frequently appears unled against QCs. He has marked experience covering wet and dry shipping disputes and he authors a leading text on the Merchant Shipping Act 1995. **Strengths:** "He is tenacious and a terrier, incredibly user-friendly and someone with an incredibly good sense of humour. He can take the intensity and pressure out of a situation, and works as a complete extension of your office." **Recent work:** Acted for owners in Spar Shipping v Grand China Logistics Holding, a complex charter party dispute. It is a notable case for the question of whether a failure to pay hire under a time charter party constitutes a breach of condition and/or a repudiatory/renunciatory breach.

Christopher Smith (see p.768) A top junior highly praised by interviewees as "personable and commercially minded." He has a wide-ranging practice encompassing dry shipping, commodities, transport and insurance disputes. He often acts unled in court and arbitration proceedings. **Strengths:** "High intellectual calibre, effective with commercial and procedural practicalities and a highly effective advocate." "An excellent user-friendly advocate who has a great command of detail, is great on his feet and is excellent to work with." **Recent work:** Acted in a dispute concerning whether it was permissible to commence in rem proceedings for the purposes of obtaining security in support of foreign arbitration proceedings.

Stewart Buckingham (see p.606) Demonstrating considerable expertise across a wide practice area, he takes on work in energy commodities, shipbuilding, and wet and dry shipping law. He has notable experience of highly technical arbitrations. **Strengths:** "Practical and level headed to work with." "He's going to be a notable player in the future."

Thomas Macey-Dare (see p.705) A highly commended practitioner specialising in wet and dry shipping, international trade and insurance disputes. He has particular strength in emergency applications as well as technical issues related to navigation and seamanship. **Strengths:** "Exceptionally good with the technical aspects." "His understanding of the maritime and commercial law was spot-on and he is able to direct a case to the right issues. He was completely unflappable, he kept his head no matter what was thrown our way." **Recent work:** Acted for the owners and P&I insurers in Kairos Shipping and Another v Enka & Co and Others in a limitation claim arising from the total loss of the 'Atlantic Confidence'. The case deals with questions of importance to the industry around the owners' right to limit their liability.

Caroline Pounds (see p.741) A sought-after junior regularly engaged on a broad range of high-profile wet and dry shipping disputes and commodities cases. She is highly commended for her ability in the High Court and in arbitration, frequently appearing on a sole basis. **Strengths:** "She is clearly very knowledgeable on shipping and provides good, accurate, timely and commercial advice." "A preferred junior on very big and complex cases." **Recent work:** Acted in a charter party claim involving allegations of bribery and torture. The case is of additional note for raising questions as to the appropriate approach to the calculation of discounts relating to damages.

Paul Henton (see p.670) An experienced junior with capability in a range of Commercial Court and arbitration actions. His practice encompasses both wet and dry shipping cases. **Strengths:** "His work product is excellent, he is very hard-working and very user-friendly. I see him as a rising star." "Extremely bright, diligent and reliable." **Recent work:** Acted for the buyers in disputes relating to CIF sale of coking coal which arrived off-specification.

Natalie Moore An accomplished junior with capability to act in international trade, wet and dry shipping matters in Commercial Court and in arbitration. She has handled cases relating to piracy as well as bills of lading and charter party disputes. **Strengths:** "Very clever, thorough and reliable." "A rising star, she is bright, tough and good on her feet. She can stand up to any QC." **Recent work:** Acted for the claimant in Spar Shipping v Grand China Logistics Holding, a charter party dispute relating to a failure to pay hire.

Paul Toms (see p.782) A highly regarded junior with marked capability in shipping and commodities actions in the High Court, London Mercantile Court and in arbitration. He acts in piracy and charter party disputes among other areas. **Strengths:** "He has great attention to detail and great tactical awareness." "Extremely diligent and his attention to detail is very good. He is very nice to work with and a very straightforward advocate." **Recent work:** Acted in Mitsui & Co v Beteiligungsgesellschaft LPG Tankerflotte a dispute looking at the interpretation of Rule F of the York Antwerp Rules in the context of ransom piracy payments.

David Walsh (see p.789) Acts on a range of dry shipping cases and is frequently recommended for his advocacy. His practice includes charter parties, demurrage disputes and marine insurance matters. **Strengths:** "Very quick to understand what you want and very easy going about life." "He displayed good advocacy skills and had a complete grasp of the issues." **Recent work:** Represented Tate & Lyle in a dispute relating to a long-term raw sugar supply agreement involving allegations of unlawful means of conspiracy.

Ruth Hosking (see p.675) Commended for her practice covering bills of lading, charter parties and commodities disputes as well as anti-suit injunctions. She appears in the Commercial Court and in arbitrations, and is regularly instructed directly. **Strengths:** "She is very quick thinking, gets straight to the point and has excellent attention to detail." "Her particular strength is her ability to cut through the detail and focus on the relevant issues." **Recent work:** Acted for insurers in claims related to a cargo lost following a fire and subsequent sinking of a vessel.

Gemma Morgan (see p.721) Has a practice covering wet and dry shipping work as well as matters concerning commodities and international carriage of goods. She has a prominent arbitration practice, regularly undertaking shipbuilding and technical disputes. **Strengths:** "Good on her feet, nice to work with and easily fits in as part of the team." "Decisive, smart and user-friendly."

Peter Stevenson (see p.773) An able junior recently arrived from Stone Chambers. His practice covers wet and dry shipping work as well as marine insurance and shipbuilding disputes. **Strengths:** "Very commercial and very responsive, he really gets to the nub of things." "He is good when we are struggling, he comes up with good ideas." **Recent work:** Acted in Aquavita International v Ashapura Minechem, a case concerning a contract of affreightment dispute. It is notable for being the first case where a judgment on the meaning of 'fairly evenly spread' in contracts of affreightment was given.

Nichola Warrender (see p.790) An experienced junior with expertise in wet and dry shipping, international trade and commodity matters. She also tackles shipbuilding cases and other commercial disputes. **Strengths:** "She was thorough, thoughtful and had prepared the case beautifully." "Easy to work with, likeable and good on detail." **Recent work:** Acted for various Lloyds underwriters in a constructive loss claim made under a war risks policy following the alleged boarding of a vessel by armed men and detonation of an incendiary device, causing an engine room fire.

Stephanie Barrett (see p.590) A "rising star" with experience across a range of shipping matters. She demonstrates strong ability in shipbuilding and cargo claims as well as charter party disputes including demurrage and unsafe port issues. **Strengths:** "She was very diligent, proactive and her response times were very swift." **Recent work:** Acted for the appellant in a case concerning the availability of capital allowances on two LNG tankers including examination of anti-avoidance issues in the Capital Allowances Act 2001.

Benjamin Coffer A standout shipping and commodities junior highly praised as a "star of the future." He has expertise in charter party, shipbuilding and ship finance disputes as well as in both hard and soft commodities including oil, coal, steel, sugar and grains. **Strengths:** "He is the best junior I have come across in my career, he can get to grips with every legal question we have thrown at him." "I go to him because he can do everything." **Recent work:** Acted for the claimants in Volcafe Limited v CSAV in a cargo claim notable for considering the relationship between inherent vice defence and the duties of a carrier under the Hague Rules.

Ben Gardner (see p.650) A "very impressive" junior with a broad practice covering commodities, shipping matters as well as insurance and conflict of laws. He regularly receives direct in-house instructions from industry clients. **Strengths:** "Very helpful, sensible and willing to get stuck in as much as required." "He is a great junior counsel and very user-friendly. He is solution driven, helps you make a decision and is very personable." **Recent work:** Acted in a carriage of goods dispute which included a question relating to whether the Hague or the Hague-Visby rules are incorporated by the clause paramount in a bill of lading.

Yash Kulkarni (see p.693) A "technically adept and tactically aware" junior with an active shipping and commodities practice. He has marked experience in freezing, search and asset preservation orders as well as anti-suit injunctions. **Strengths:** "Highly intelligent, approachable, commercial and user-friendly." "He continues to provide solid legal advice with a firm grasp of the commercial aspects of a dispute." **Recent work:** Appeared for the defendant in an appeal against the findings of arbitrators in a charter party dispute relating to damages awardable for a repudiatory breach.

Liisa Lahti (see p.693) A highly capable junior with experience in shipping, commodities and international trade disputes. She is commended by sources for her commercial approach bolstered by her background as a solicitor. **Strengths:** "Enthusiastic, hard-working and very easy to deal with." "An amazingly user-friendly individual, very down to earth and bright. I think she is a star of the future." **Recent work:** Acted for various shipowners in relation to claims arising from the insolvency of OW Bunkers including issues of retention of title clause, construction contracts and the sale of goods.

Mark Stiggelbout (see p.773) A well-regarded shipping and commodities practitioner with additional faculty in insurance, energy and insolvency disputes. He acts in court and arbitration proceedings and has experience obtaining urgent injunctive relief. **Strengths:** "He provided comprehensive and compelling advice." "He is well ahead of his years; his drafting skills are amazing, he is very precise, clear and he is always there to step up if you are in trouble." **Recent work:** Acted in Bunge v Nidera, a dispute concerning an anticipatory breach of a one-off sale of goods contract.

Band 2

7 King's Bench Walk

See profile on p.871

THE SET

This exemplary set provides consummate service to clients in sophisticated dry shipping, commodities and insurance disputes. Its esteemed members are highly regarded for their deft handling of international trade, marine insurance and shipbuilding disputes. The chambers has enjoyed a particularly impressive year acting in high-profile matters, including the main 'OW Bunker' litigation and 'Brillante Virtuoso', concerning the constructive loss of a vessel after being boarded by pirates. Sources claim that "if you have a case you need to win with very high stakes, you can't really go wrong with them."

Client service: Solicitors say "the clerks are excellent, very stable, professional and very accommodating." The team is led by senior clerks Bernie Hyatt and Greg Leyden.

SILKS

Robert Bright QC An outstanding silk with an exceptional reputation for the quality of his advocacy. He regularly handles some of the foremost cases in the industry and is well versed in charter party, commodities, shipbuilding and ship sale disputes. **Strengths:** "A very polished advocate and very effective." "A hard opponent, he takes no prisoners." **Recent work:** Represented a banking consortium seeking to recover USD900 million in multiple disputes following the bankruptcy of OW Bunkers.

Dominic Kendrick QC An eminent silk with a practice of the highest calibre, "who always seems to be right." He has considerable expertise in sophisticated shipbuilding cases and charter party disputes. **Strengths:** "What he says is very well received in tribunals because he adopts a very down-to-earth and sensible, measured style. He is extremely courteous and extremely pleasant." "He is always thinking two steps ahead. He is able to tie the law and the technical side together and use both to his advantage." **Recent work:** Acted in a USD200 million charter party dispute relating to the total loss of a vessel in a Japanese port.

Alistair Schaff QC A leading commercial barrister renowned for his ability in shipping, insurance and international trade disputes. He is an admired advocate but he is also regularly called on to act as an arbitrator. **Strengths:** "A phenomenal mind, an excellent and subtle advocate, a real pleasure to work with and totally reliable." **Recent work:** Acted for insurers in a dispute related to the overvaluation of a superyacht.

Richard Southern QC An excellent barrister with marked ability in shipping and commodities matters with particular focus on shipbuilding and charter party disputes. An accomplished advocate, he also accepts instruction as an arbitrator. **Strengths:** "He is always very impressive, he has an excellent forensic mind and deploys his arguments well." "He is very gentle with clients and has very good written submissions and oral advocacy." **Recent work:** Acted in a dispute involving claims of deceit and conspiracy related to 32 cargoes of crude oil sold and delivered to Romania.

Richard Waller QC A highly regarded practitioner with experience in a range of shipping disputes acting in both litigation and arbitration. He easily turns his hand to charter party disputes, piracy cases and port nominations. **Strengths:** "He is excellent in every department, very bright, incredibly hard working and really obtains the faith and trust of clients."

David Allen QC A tough and technically knowledgeable barrister sought after for his forthright advocacy style. His practice encompasses a range of shipping and commercial disputes and he has particular expertise in offshore matters. **Strengths:** "A strong advocate, he has a no-nonsense but pleasant attitude." "A personable chap and a really aggressive cross-examiner, I want him on cases that require someone really robust." **Recent work:** Acted for a private client in a copyright and construction dispute relating to the alleged copying of a bespoke gigayacht.

David Bailey QC A strong practitioner with capability in a range of shipping matters in both litigation and arbitration. He is recognised for his experience in shipbuilding and yacht-related disputes. **Strengths:** "He is very intelligent, experienced and also commercially sensible." "He has an ability to get hold of the whole case in the round and find a commercial solution." **Recent work:** Acted for the buyers and financiers of a ship in arbitration and litigation relating to allegations of fraud and illegality.

Peter MacDonald Eggers QC A dynamic commercial barrister with capability across shipping, commodities, insurance and energy matters among other areas. He has experience in piracy, sanctions, charter party and sale of goods disputes. **Strengths:** "He's very approachable, very understanding and very happy to get his hands dirty and help us if need be." **Recent work:** Acted for the shipowner and the mortgagee bank in a dispute concerning a claim under a war risks policy, involving issues of terrorism and piracy arising from the total loss of the 'Brillante Virtuoso'.

Timothy Saloman QC A superb barrister, recognised for his skilful advocacy. He tackles bills of lading, charter party, shipbuilding and P&I disputes in court and in arbitration. **Strengths:** "He is very passionate, committed, strategic and thoughtful. He is almost always contactable and provides prompt advice." **Recent work:** Represented Sinochart in an unsafe port claim arising from the total loss of a vessel in a Japanese port.

Christopher Butcher QC Has a broad commercial practice with strength in shipping and commodities being complemented by expertise in insurance and professional negligence. He has particular experience in shipbuilding disputes. **Strengths:** "A real powerhouse in terms of intellect."

Julia Dias QC A highly proficient silk experienced in dry shipping, sale of goods and international trade matters. She has a busy arbitration practice and also acts as a mediator. **Strengths:** "Very good and very bright, user-friendly and very hard-working." "She's excellent on her feet." **Recent work:** Acted for the shipowners in a demurrage claim met with a counter claim for damages for cargo contamination.

Siobán Healy QC (see p.668) A notable silk specialising in shipping, commodities and international trade matters including dangerous cargoes, demurrage and shipbuilding disputes. She regularly acts in arbitrations as an advocate and is frequently appointed as an arbitrator. **Strengths:** "She was a pleasure to work with; she was considered, thorough and she presented the arguments very firmly."

Stephen Hofmeyr QC An experienced barrister with expertise in a range of shipping matters including shipbuilding disputes, yacht-related litigation and charter party disputes. He appears as an advocate in Commercial Court and arbitration and also engages in advisory work. **Strengths:** "He is excellent, he gives a really thorough academic analysis." " A marine insurance heavyweight."

Stephen Kenny QC Regarded as an "extremely approachable silk" with expertise in shipping, commodities and international trade disputes. He has noteworthy experience of cases involving allegations of fraud. **Strengths:** "He is scholarly, highly intelligent and gentlemanly." "He gets to the point and deals with things in a very client-friendly manner." **Recent work:** Appeared in a dispute relating to a contract for the sale of a shipment of Ebok crude oil.

JUNIORS

Charles Priday A highly accomplished and respected junior with an admirable practice covering dry shipping, shipbuilding and international trade disputes. He regularly acts on a sole basis against QCs in litigation and arbitration. **Strengths:** "He is ferociously hard-working and delivers excellent client service together with sound legal advice." "He is enormously experienced and is very reliable and sensible in the advice that he gives."

Benjamin Parker A highly regarded junior, adept at handling a range of commercial shipping disputes. He regularly appears in Commercial Court, in arbitration and also has a burgeoning advisory practice. **Strengths:** "A very knowledgeable, detailed and smart lawyer." "Good at condensing complex issues into a much more manageable format." **Recent work:** Acted in British American Tobacco v Exel Europe, a case in the Supreme Court on jurisdiction concerned with the international carriage of goods.

Sandra Healy A strong junior regularly instructed in shipping and commodities matters in litigation and arbitration. She has marked ability in charter party and cargo claim disputes and has expertise in interim relief and jurisdiction matters. **Strengths:** "She is charming to work with and extremely bright and capable." "She is ahead of her call; she's bright, user-friendly, quick and reliable." **Recent work:** Acted for the shipowners in a dispute arising from the collision of a vessel and a superyacht.

Michael Holmes A highly proficient junior whose practice includes cargo claims, international carriage of goods-related issues and a range of charter party disputes including unsafe ports, quarantine and dangerous cargoes. He also acts in yacht-related actions. **Strengths:** "I found him to be extremely diligent and hard-working. He is very quick to pick up on the salient points in a case and produces first-class work. He is a pleasure to work with." **Recent work:** Acted in a dispute involving allegations of tortious interference and conspiracy relating to a multiparty agreement to charter VLCCs.

N G Casey An experienced junior with strength in a range of disputes in litigation and arbitration. He frequently tackles charter party disputes and superyacht-related cases. **Strengths:** "Quick, accurate and knowledgeable." "He's always very confident and easy to work with. He tends not to be fazed by anything. He is good at identifying the crucial detail which has to be nailed down in order to get what you want."

Marcus Mander A capable practitioner who undertakes cases across the whole range of commercial shipping litigation. He takes on shipbuilding and ship finance disputes in litigation and arbitration. **Strengths:** "Intellectually he is very good and has a great manner with the whole team. He is very responsive and very thorough." "He is exceptionally good at managing time and expectation." **Recent work:** Acted for ING Bank in multiple disputes stemming from the bankruptcy of OW Bunkers.

Richard Sarll An adroit junior who acts in both commercial shipping and admiralty law. He is instructed in charter party disputes, general average cases and collisions. **Strengths:** "His written work is excellent and his advice is top-notch." "He is quick, intellectually sharp and great to work with." **Recent work:** Acted successfully in several cases on the extension of time for commencement of collision proceedings.

Jessica Sutherland An effective barrister whose practice covers shipping litigation and arbitration. She acts in matters arising from charter party disputes and general average claims. **Strengths:** "She is client friendly, ready to assist and someone who provides prompt advice." "She is very easy to work with." **Recent work:** Acted for the shipowners in disputes over the proper construction of on demand and performance guarantees.

Adam Turner (see p.785) An experienced junior who is well versed in dry shipping matters as well as international trade and insurance. He has expertise in cases involving commercial fraud, jurisdictional issues and interim relief. **Strengths:** "He is very sharp and does not miss anything." "He has an extremely good sense of humour, is a delight in a stressful situation and is wonderful at dealing with clients." **Recent work:** Acted in Glory Wealth Shipping v Shandong Iron & Steel, a dispute concerning liability under long-term contracts of affreightment.

Band 3

Essex Court Chambers

See profile on p.836

THE SET

Shipping and commodities remain a core practice area for this highly regarded set, well known for its strength in this sector. Its members are in demand as advocates covering litigation and international arbitrations in a range of areas including marine insurance, shipbuilding and dry shipping disputes. Solicitors say "the all-round service they provide is of such a high standard." Recent cases include the 'Ocean Victory' in an important unsafe port action and 'Valle di Cordoba' regarding in-transit loss.

Client service: "The clerks are terrific, always on the look out and always proactive," reports one source. The senior clerks are David Grief and Joe Ferrigno.

SILKS

Steven Berry QC A renowned barrister and regarded as "a seriously impressive advocate" with a leading dry shipping practice. He is recognised for his significant expertise in charter party, marine insurance and bill of lading disputes. **Strengths:** "Undoubtedly a silk that strikes terror into the hearts of his opponents."

Graham Dunning QC (see p.637) Co-head of chambers and a highly respected silk well known for his distinguished advocacy. He has extensive experience across a broad spectrum of shipping and commodities matters including charter party and bill of lading disputes. **Strengths:** "An absolutely outstanding master of the courtroom, extraordinarily user-friendly and very good with clients. The type of silk you want in a very difficult case." **Recent work:** Acted in Commercial Court proceedings to prevent vessels from being arrested.

Claire Blanchard QC A highly regarded practitioner with experience in a range of shipping and international trade matters. She acts as an advocate and also accepts appointments as an arbitrator. **Strengths:** "An exceptional barrister, she delivers thoroughly considered advice in clear terms and offers keen strategic insight at all stages of a dispute." **Recent work:** Acted in multiple arbitrations concerning charter party disputes.

Simon Bryan QC An experienced barrister with a strong shipping and commodities practice. He is praised as an advocate, acting both in arbitrations and in Commercial Court. **Strengths:** "Very bright, commercial, approachable and reliable." "His advocacy was great and his cross-examination was first-class, he knew what he needed to get and got it." **Recent work:** Represented the shipowners of the 'Kriti Filoxenia' in an appeal to the Commercial Court from an arbitration award relating to a charter party dispute.

Christopher Smith QC (see p.768) A commercial silk with a reputable wet and dry shipping practice. He has expertise in collisions, towage, charter party and bill of lading disputes and additional ability in shipbuilding matters. **Strengths:** "His understanding of the subject matter was extremely good." "Very user-friendly, approachable, bright and hard-working." **Recent work:** Acted in two arbitrations and subsequent court actions relating to a shipbuilding dispute over two vessels.

Nigel Eaton QC A knowledgeable and technically capable silk with a broad-based shipping and commodities practice. He tackles charter party, contract of affreightment and shipbuilding actions as well as hard and soft commodity disputes. **Strengths:** "He is extremely methodical, and a very clear and clever advocate who is very composed. I use him on cases where we need to understand technical expert evidence." "He has incredible attention to detail and is really strong analytically. He is an all-round impressive performer." **Recent work:** Acted for a large shipping company in a case in the High Court relating to attempts to raise finance for new ships.

Vernon Flynn QC Acts in a range of commercial shipping and commodities matters including both wet and dry shipping. He is regularly instructed in the Commercial Court, in arbitration proceedings and in cases before civil tribunals. **Strengths:** "An outstanding legal brain, coupled with excellent client-handling skills."

Jeffrey Gruder QC (see p.661) A well-known barrister with a broad commercial law practice. He has recently been involved in several high-profile shipping disputes. **Strengths:** "One of the wise old men of the Commercial Bar." "He is very clever, very quick to respond and very commercial in his approach. A first-class resource." **Recent work:** Acted in a charter party dispute relating to the total loss of a vessel in a Japanese port.

Nathan Pillow QC Has a practice covering bareboat, time and voyage charter party disputes as well as other shipping industry contract disputes. He has particular ability in cases containing allegations of fraud. **Strengths:** "A good advocate, clear and focused." "A talented and polished performer." **Recent work:** Continued to act in Fiona Trust & Holding Corp. v Privalov and others, a long-running shipping dispute.

JUNIORS

Jeremy Brier A noteworthy junior with considerable ability across wet and dry shipping matters including shipbuilding and marine insurance disputes. He has experience of jurisdiction and fraud issues. **Strengths:** "He is very pleasant and provides a good sounding board for ideas." **Recent work:** Acted for Greek shipowners in a dispute in the Commercial Court involving issues of fraud and jurisdiction.

Philippa Hopkins A proficient junior with a wide commercial dispute resolution practice that has a particular focus on shipping matters. She regularly acts as an advocate in court as well as in arbitration forums. **Strengths:** "Extremely reliable." "An outstanding advocate, who is very sharp and tends to frighten the opposition with her intellect and drive."

Edmund King A commercial junior who includes shipping as a key component of his wider practice. He has noted expertise in obtaining interim relief. **Strengths:** "He is effective and knowledgeable."

4 Pump Court

See profile on p.895

THE SET

The set is seen to be "making a big play to move into the shipping world" and continues to cement a growing reputation for excellence in the sector. It has maintained its upward trajectory in shipping to offer clients expertise across wet and dry matters and disputes covering hard and soft commodities. The set regularly acts in complicated high-value confidential shipbuilding disputes. Both the silks and juniors are frequently recommended for their legal and commercial acumen and attract particular praise for their approachability and user-friendly style.

Client service: The clerking team is praised by solicitors as particularly accommodating. Sources comment: "Their clerking room as a whole is excellent," and "the clerks are quick in response." Carolyn McCombe is the set's chief executive and leads the clerking team.

SILKS

Alexander Gunning QC (see p.661) A "very user-friendly and able" barrister with a strong shipping and commodities practice. He has marked expertise in charter party, shipbuilding and offshore construction disputes. **Strengths:** "A tremendous all-rounder with great technical knowledge who is an extremely good advocate." "A very good team player and highly intelligent. He understands what is required and delivers."

Sean O'Sullivan QC (see p.732) A highly commended barrister with expertise in dry shipping matters including demurrage, charter party and sale of goods disputes. He stands out for his deft handling of shipbuilding disputes in litigation and arbitration. **Strengths:** "A very proficient lawyer who is very economical and a very safe pair of hands." "He is, in a quiet and undemonstrative way, extremely effective."

Nicholas Vineall QC (see p.787) Often highlighted for his technical acumen, he has particular experience in offshore construction and shipbuilding disputes. **Strengths:** "He is particularly thorough and precise in his analysis. For document-heavy or detailed cases where you need someone very thorough to go through it all, he is an excellent choice." "He has a nice approach with a lot of gravitas, he takes the Tribunal with him." **Recent work:** Acted in a dispute in the Commercial Court over an inordinate delay in a maritime arbitration award.

Nigel Tozzi QC (see p.783) A respected commercial shipping barrister, he acts as both an advocate and arbitrator. He handles a variety of matters including ship conversion and repair, shipbuilding and ship sale disputes. **Strengths:** "He really is a team player, a pleasure to deal with and a very good and charming advocate." "Very friendly, hugely experienced and very commercial."

JUNIORS

James Leabeater (see p.698) An excellent junior with notable capability across dry shipping, shipbuilding and offshore construction disputes. He regularly appears in both Commercial Court and arbitration forums. **Strengths:** "He is bright, hard-working and very user-friendly." "A junior who is in demand for being able to plough through the details." **Recent work:** Acted in a USD10 million claim arising from the sale of three liquefied gas tankers.

Alexander Wright (see p.800) An outstanding junior with a dynamic practice including charter party, contract of affreightment and international carriage of goods disputes. He is also instructed in complex shipbuilding disputes and a range of wet shipping matters. **Strengths:** "He is brilliant, absolutely outstanding and extremely clever. I think he will be silk in a very short time, his written advocacy is extremely strong and for someone relatively junior, he is excellent on his feet too. He can gauge where the judge is going." **Recent work:** Acted in a charter party dispute involving allegations of bribery and torture.

James Watthey (see p.791) Regarded as "a tenacious counsel" with recognised capacity in both wet and dry shipping matters. He is particularly notable for his work in superyacht disputes. **Strengths:** "He is highly intelligent and his advice is commercial and practical. He is extremely good on his feet, he knows when to bite and when not to." **Recent work:** Acted in a dispute arising from a claim for a declaration of non-liability arising out of damage to a vessel in Turkey.

Neil Henderson (see p.669) Has a strong practice covering wet and dry shipping disputes as well as commodities matters. He has experience appearing in the High Court, Admiralty Court and in arbitration forums. **Strengths:** "Excellent and commercial." "A tenacious counsel. He is very dynamic and shows a good understanding of the marine market which enables him to bring a commercial approach to disputes." **Recent work:** Acted for the shipowner of the 'Bao Yue' in a dispute concerning the duties/obligations on a shipowner when discharging a cargo and a shipowner's right to return of the bill of lading.

St Philips Stone Chambers

See profile on p.934

THE SET

A robust set with a sterling reputation in the sector, that has particular ability in high-profile wet shipping disputes. Its members are well versed in specialist admiralty matters including collisions, salvage and general average, while also receiving regular instruction in dry shipping, commodities and marine insurance matters. Solicitors commend the set as "hugely experienced." Recent cases of note include Nordlake v Seaeagle, a collision involving five vessels and 'Stolt Kestrel' concerning important issues of admiralty practice and procedure.

Client service: The clerks are "friendly and prompt" and highly responsive. The chief point of contact is chambers executive officer Luke Irons.

SILKS

Elizabeth Blackburn QC An experienced and highly regarded silk with specialist expertise in wet shipping disputes. Her diverse practice includes marine insurance, pollution, collision and salvage actions as well as shipbuilding and international maritime law. **Strengths:** "She is on top of the detail." "She is very good at setting up from the outset where the case needs to go, she will prepare a very comprehensive strategy." **Recent work:** Acted in a complicated collision action involving five vessels.

Vasanti Selvaratnam QC (see p.761) An experienced barrister with considerable ability in wet and dry shipping matters as well as commodities disputes. She regularly acts as an arbitrator when not acting in court and arbitration settings. **Strengths:** "Very impressive and a very pleasant person to liaise with." "She has a very comforting manner that is extremely good for nervous clients and has tremendous presence in court." **Recent work:** Acted in a dispute relating to the construction of an Interim Funding Agreement, the meaning of Rule F of the York Antwerp Rules 1994 and estoppel issues.

JUNIORS

Ravi Aswani (see p.586) An excellent practitioner with a wide ranging shipping, commodities and international trade practice. He has notable experience acting as an advocate, arbitrator and mediator. **Strengths:** "A junior with experience beyond his years. He is unerringly dependable, provides pragmatic commercial advice and has an excellent manner with clients."

Mark Jones (see p.685) A prominent junior with a strong international trade, commodities and shipping practice regularly handling charter party disputes, collisions and general average. He has further expertise in complex shipbuilding and ship sale and purchase disputes. **Strengths:** "He is frighteningly intelligent and has great people skills. I think he is a class act and the kind of person destined to take silk." **Recent work:** Acted for Navigators Insurance Company in a claim under a P&I policy relating to the total loss of a vessel between Papua New Guinea and China.

Thomas Whitehead (see p.794) A top junior with a broad wet and dry shipping practice that encompasses issues of salvage, collisions, charter party disputes and general average. He has recognised expertise in jurisdictional and conflict of laws matters. **Strengths:** "He is very good at detail and I think he is very good at cross-examination because he can really pack all of the facts into his head." "When we thought there was a brick wall, he got us around it. He is a very good advocate." **Recent work:** Acted for PDV Marina in a Commercial Court dispute over claims for hire under alleged charter parties and guarantees.

Rachel Toney (see p.782) A highly recommended junior with ability across wet and dry shipping matters including collisions, indemnity claims and charter party actions. She has a flourishing shipbuilding disputes practice. **Strengths:** "She pulls out all the stops and is really nice to deal with." "She can absorb a great amount of technical detail." **Recent work:** Represented the owners of a bulk carrier in a dispute arising from an allision in an enclosed dock system of a port.

Charles Debattista Acts as both an advocate and an arbitrator in shipping matters such as charter party, letters of credit and ship management disputes. He is particularly well known for his large advisory practice. **Strengths:** "He is able to immediately home in on what is important and give the matter his full and undivided attention. He is totally dedicated to his brief and one feels that one is in a very safe pair of hands." **Recent work:** Appeared in an application before the High Court relating to multiple cargo claims for perishable cargo aboard an idle vessel.

Jeremy Lightfoot Covers a range of shipping matters as part of his commercial law practice. He handles both litigation and arbitration and is noted for his technical knowledge. **Strengths:** "Very sharp with fantastic concise drafting skills." "He is able to provide timely and precise analysis of the strengths of a case in clear and effective terms."

James Shirley (see p.764) A "very approachable" junior with a burgeoning shipping practice. He has experience in charter party disputes, demurrage and unsafe port claims. **Strengths:** "His written advocacy and oral advocacy are excellent." "He is very approachable and a great person to have as part of the team. He really puts in a lot of work for the client and the case."

Other Ranked Lawyers

Richard Lord QC (Brick Court Chambers) An acclaimed and highly respected barrister with an extensive shipping practice. He acts on cargo claims, shipbuilding and charter party disputes. **Strengths:** "He is prudent and meticulous in his preparation of cases and is extremely persuasive at hearings."

Jonathan Hirst QC (Brick Court Chambers) Highly regarded at the Commercial Bar, Hirst has significant experience in shipping disputes having practised in the area for 40 years. He is a strong advocate and also acts as a deputy High Court judge. **Strengths:** "A grand old man of the Commercial Bar, he makes very concise, clear submissions and is very effective in court." "A very big hitter, who is a confident advocate."

Nicholas Craig (3 Verulam Buildings) A recognised junior with experience as an advocate and arbitrator in shipping and commodities disputes. He is experienced in issues relating to conflict of laws and jurisdiction. **Strengths:** "His assistance was informed, prompt, thorough and thoughtful." "He is very good; he's very user-friendly and has a measured approach to being counsel. He's an outstanding junior." **Recent work:** Acted for Samsung Heavy Industries in a shipbuilding dispute involving a claim for monies due from a large Turkish shipping line.

Contents:

LONDON

Social Housing
Leading Sets
Band 1
Arden Chambers *
Cornerstone Barristers *
Doughty Street Chambers *
Garden Court Chambers *
Band 2
Hardwicke *
Five Paper *
Leading Silks
Star individuals
Arden Andrew *Arden Chambers* *
Band 1
Knafler Stephen *Landmark Chambers (ORL)* ◊
Westgate Martin *Doughty Street Chambers*
Band 2
Bhaloo Zia *Enterprise Chambers (ORL)* ◊
Bhose Ranjit *Cornerstone Barristers* *
Drabble Richard *Landmark Chambers (ORL)* ◊
Rutledge Kelvin *Cornerstone Barristers* *
Band 3
Lieven Nathalie *Landmark Chambers (ORL)* ◊
New Silks
Bretherton Kerry *Tanfield Chambers (ORL)* ◊ [A] *
Grundy Nicholas *Five Paper*
** Indicates set / individual with profile.*
[A] direct access (see p.24).
◊ (ORL) = Other Ranked Lawyer.
Alphabetical order within each band. Band 1 is highest.

Social Housing	
Leading Juniors	
Star individuals	**Shepherd** Jim *Doughty Street Chambers*
Bates Justin *Arden Chambers* *	**Tweedy** Laura *Hardwicke* [A]
Davies Liz *Garden Court Chambers*	**Vanhegan** Toby B *Arden Chambers*
Band 1	**Band 3**
Baker Christopher *Arden Chambers* *	**Baldwin** Timothy *Garden Court Chambers*
Burton Jamie *Doughty Street Chambers*	**Beckley** John *Garden Court Chambers*
Dymond Andrew *Arden Chambers* *	**Beglan** Wayne *Cornerstone Barristers* *
Fitzpatrick Edward *Garden Court Chambers*	**Bennett** Morayo Fagborun *Hardwicke*
Holbrook Jon *Cornerstone Barristers* *	**Blackmore** Sally *Ely Place Chambers (ORL)* ◊ *
Hutchings Matthew *Cornerstone Barristers* *	**Bowen** James *Garden Court Chambers*
Johnson Lindsay *Doughty Street Chambers* [A]	**Brown** Robert *Arden Chambers* *
Lane Andrew *Cornerstone Barristers* [A] *	**Brownhill** Joanna *Five Paper*
Manning Jonathan *Arden Chambers* *	**Compton** Justine *Garden Court Chambers*
Nabi Zia *Doughty Street Chambers*	**Davis** Adrian *Field Court Chambers (ORL)* ◊
Paget Michael *Cornerstone Barristers* *	**Hodgson** Jane *Five Paper*
Preston Dominic *Doughty Street Chambers*	**Johnston** Connor *Garden Court Chambers*
Underwood Dean *Cornerstone Barristers* [A] *	**Lintott** David *Cornerstone Barristers* *
Band 2	**Madge-Wyld** Sam *Arden Chambers* *
Beecham Sara *Five Paper*	**Meacher** Alison *Hardwicke*
Bhogal Kuljit *Cornerstone Barristers* *	**Orme** Emily *Arden Chambers* *
Carter David *Doughty Street Chambers*	**Peacock** Ian *New Square Chambers (ORL)* ◊ *
Cattermole Rebecca *Tanfield Chambers (ORL)* ◊ *	**Reeder** Stephen *Doughty Street Chambers*
Chataway Ben *Doughty Street Chambers*	**Salmon** Sarah *Arden Chambers* *
Colville Iain *Arden Chambers* *	**Sergides** Marina *Garden Court Chambers*
Davies Sian *39 Essex Chambers (ORL)* ◊	**Smith** Stephanie *Arden Chambers*
Evans Stephen *Five Paper*	**Tueje** Patricia *1 Pump Court (ORL)* ◊ *
Gallivan Terence *Five Paper* [A]	**Up-and-coming individuals**
Harris Bethan *Garden Court Chambers*	**Adams** Brynmor *Five Paper*
Kohli Ryan *Cornerstone Barristers* *	**Cullen** Clare *Arden Chambers* *
Nicol Nicholas *1 Pump Court (ORL)* ◊ [A]	**Glenister** Leon *Landmark Chambers (ORL)* ◊
Oscroft Jennifer *Cornerstone Barristers*	**Steinhardt** Sarah *Doughty Street Chambers*
Osler Victoria *Five Paper*	**Tkaczynska** Anna *Arden Chambers* *
Rowlands Catherine *Cornerstone Barristers*	

Band 1

Arden Chambers

See profile on p.805

THE SET

Arden Chambers is a pre-eminent set which routinely receives instruction in the most significant, high-profile social housing matters. Its sought-after members frequently provide top-level counsel to policy makers across the UK. The chambers is renowned for its highly skilled team of practitioners, whose broad-based expertise regularly sees them acting on behalf of a varied client base, including social landlords, tenants and homeless applicants. Its members' sector knowledge runs the full gamut of social housing law, and they are experienced representatives before all levels of court and tribunal, including the Court of Appeal and Supreme Court.

Client service: "The clerks are very easy to work with." "Fees are very reasonable and they're happy to negotiate based on instructions and the complexity of the matter. " Elton Maryon leads the clerking team.

SILKS

Andrew Arden QC (see p.584) A highly experienced and well-regarded housing silk. A master in his field, he has made over 25 appearances in the Supreme Court and is a regular feature in the most high-profile social housing cases. His significant contribution to the field includes long-standing positions as editor of the Encyclopaedia of Housing Law and Practice, the Housing Law Reports and the Journal of Housing Law. **Strengths:** "Very impressive. A housing law expert with a national reputation." **Recent work:** Appeared before the Supreme Court on behalf of the local authority in Haile v LB Waltham Forest, a significant case considering the pertinent factors for determining whether a person is 'intentionally homeless'.

JUNIORS

Justin Bates (see p.592) Distinguished by the depth of his experience acting for social landlords, tenants and long leaseholders in particular. Routinely appears in cases, both for and against local authorities, concerning landlord licensing schemes. He is increasingly active in policy work, with a recent highlight being his drafting of the Homes (Fitness for Human Habitation) Bill 2015 for Karen Buck MP. **Strengths:** "He is technically and academically one of the leading barristers in the trade." "Absolutely on top of the law and always willing to try inventive approaches." **Recent work:** Provided expert evidence to a House of Lords committee concerning the impact of the Equality Act 2010 on disabled persons.

Christopher Baker (see p.588) Founder member of Arden Chambers and a specialist in housing with "a comprehensive knowledge of local government law." He owes his strong reputation in the sector to his many appearances in high-profile cases which are often heard before the Supreme Court. He is recognised for the quality of his advisory work on matters such as policy making and strategic administration. **Strengths:** "One of the best social housing lawyers around." "Enormous breadth of knowledge in housing, social care and local authority issues." **Recent work:** Led for the local authority in Mohamoud v Kensington & Chelsea RLBC, a leading case in the Court of Appeal concerning whether a child's interests must be assessed before eviction from homelessness accommodation.

Andrew Dymond (see p.638) Considered an extremely powerful practitioner in technically complex cases. His written advocacy wins particular praise, as does his insight into matters concerning proposed housing schemes and their statutory compliance. He also authors and edits key housing law commentary. Strengths: "Extremely good on his feet and hugely robust." "He is extremely bright and beautifully analytical." Recent work: Acted for a young mother in temporary accommodation in judicial review proceedings to establish the legality of the council's threat to evict her for having visitors after hours.

Jonathan Manning (see p.707) Known particularly for his local government and judicial review work, he regularly appears for individual applicants and tenants as well as local authorities and registered providers. He is increasingly involved in cases relating to housing benefits, including the 2012 benefit cap. **Strengths:** "Incisive, precise, approachable and easy to work with." "Has the ability to get to the salient point very quickly and is respected by judges. A standout practitioner." **Recent work:** Successfully represented Birmingham City Council in Samuels v Birmingham CC, a homelessness appeal concerning the scope of benefits to be taken into account when determining whether accommodation is affordable.

Iain Colville (see p.621) Primarily handles housing cases and homelessness appeals on behalf of public authorities and individual applicants. He is regularly instructed in cases in the lower and higher courts and has made several recent appearances in the Supreme Court. His complementary knowledge of the wider aspects of local government renders him a formidable opponent. **Recent work:** Successfully resisted an application by East Midlands Property Owners to overturn Nottingham City Council's decision to designate certain areas in the city as subject to the additional licensing regime under the Housing Act 2004.

Toby Vanhegan Talented junior who is highly thought of for his innovative approach. He is sought after by both landlords and tenants, and demonstrates particular strength in housing cases containing human rights or immigration elements. His sterling practice regularly sees him appearing before the High Court, the Court of Appeal and the ECHR. **Strengths:** "He knows the law inside out and his cross-examination is a treat to watch." **Recent work:** Served as junior counsel for both appellants in Mohamoud v Kensington & Chelsea LBC and Saleem v Wandsworth LBC. These were significant test cases to determine whether children's interests must be considered in decisions to repossess accommodation.

Robert Brown (see p.604) Praised for his relaxed and confident court manner. He is an impressive junior who has appeared in courts at all levels, and has experience of handling both multi-track and fast-track cases. Strengths: "When handling more complex cases, he projects a real air of confidence and gives the best possible advice." "Completely on top of the law and a calm, careful advocate." Recent work: Successfully acted on behalf of the respondent local authority in Evans v Royal Borough of Kensington & Chelsea, an appeal against a ruling that a claimant had made herself intentionally homeless due to antisocial behaviour.

Sam Madge-Wyld (see p.705) Regularly acts on behalf of both tenants and landlords in a wide range of social housing disputes, and has particular experience of appearing in judicial reviews. Market commentators consider him to be "very technically able," while his considerable knowledge of immigration law complements his highly thought-of practice. **Strengths:** "He understands the brief, masters it quickly and comes up with reasonable proposals for the client's position." "Thoroughly reliable, quick thinking and good on his feet. He's not caught out by anything in court and is completely on top of the law." **Recent work:** Successfully appeared before the First-tier Tribunal on behalf of the leaseholders of St Saviour's Estate. It was decided that considerable costs from major works across several estates were not recoverable by Southwark LBC as some of the works carried out were improvements and not repairs.

Emily Orme (see p.730) Well known for her adept representation of clients across the public and private sectors, including social landlords, local authorities, tenants and the homeless. Her impressive breadth of expertise encompasses areas such as business tenancies, antisocial behaviour, disrepair and possession claims and housing benefits. **Strengths:** "I admire her attention to detail and how swiftly she is able to find solutions to even the most complicated cases. She is very experienced and knowledgeable and has a sharp mind. She is also very good with clients." **Recent work:** Acted for the local authority in Islington LBC v Elugbadebo. This was a claim for possession on the basis of no right to succeed to the tenancy due to the continuity of occupation having been broken by the deceased tenant's two-month absence from the property prior to their death.

Sarah Salmon (see p.757) Well versed across all aspects of landlord and tenant law, with particular expertise in antisocial behaviour cases. She is widely praised for her advocacy skills and highly respected for her leading commentary on housing law and judicial review proceedings. Her complementary acumen in public law matters buttresses her enviable practice. **Strengths:** "She's an excellent advocate: unfazed, likes a complex case, likes a challenge." "Very able, she's very good with clients, manages cases well and is a very solid advocate." **Recent work:** Assisted Tai Ceredigion, a Welsh non-profit housing association, with its successful possession of a property under the Housing Act 1988. The case centred on the defendant's persistent harassment towards the association and its staff.

Stephanie Smith Regularly instructed on behalf of local authorities and is well respected for her adroit handling of complex leasehold disputes. She demonstrates prowess across all areas of landlord and tenant law, including residential and commercial possession matters and homelessness appeals. **Strengths:** "Great all-rounder, she'll pick up anything and do a very good job with it." "Absolutely excellent: clients and solicitors love her alike." **Recent work:** Served as junior counsel in BCC v Norma Wilson, a homelessness appeal concerning the scope of inquiries in light of the Equality Act 2010.

Clare Cullen (see p.627) Up-and-coming junior with considerable experience in the space, covering areas such as possession claims, homeless applications and antisocial behaviour injunctions. She routinely acts for both public and private clients, including tenants, social landlords and local authorities. **Strengths:** "She has a lot of experience, very thorough. You can always rely on her to be thoroughly prepared for a hearing." **Recent work:** Acted for one of the tenants in Shah v Folkes and Green, a claim for possession and counterclaim for an award under the Housing Act 2004. The cased centred on the alleged failure to serve prescribed information on a "relevant person."

Anna Tkaczynska (see p.781) Routinely represents landlords and tenants in possession proceedings and disrepair claims. Market commentators laud her deft handling of cases involving particularly difficult clients. Strengths: "Really efficient, on the ball, bright and pleasant to deal with." "Her legal knowledge is fantastically in-depth, and she's extremely dedicated to this area of law." Recent work: Acted for Leicester City Council in a trial for possession on the grounds of antisocial and criminal behaviour committed by the defendant and his family.

Cornerstone Barristers

See profile on p.823

THE SET

Cornerstone Barristers is a standout social housing chambers with a formidable reputation for its work on behalf of public authorities, housing associations and registered landlords. Members of the set have appeared before the Supreme Court and Court of Appeal in numerous major cases, including complex and high-profile homelessness matters. The chambers houses high-quality advocates at all levels, from juniors through to silks. Its barristers' broad expertise encompasses areas such as statutory nuisance, repossessions and allocations, human rights and public law defences. A recent highlight for the set has been its engagement in The Royal Borough of Kensington and Chelsea v Lessees of 1-124 Pond House. The matter resulted in a landmark decision that multiparty framework agreements entered into by, or on behalf of, a public authority qualified as long-term agreements, meaning full service charges can be recovered from leaseholders.

Client service: "The clerks are responsive and make sure everything is where it needs to be." "Very prompt and efficient to deal with. " Ben Connor leads the clerking team.

SILKS

Ranjit Bhose QC (see p.595) Well-respected silk with a broad housing practice that encompasses possession actions, housing finance and large-scale regeneration schemes for local authority and housing association clients. He is particularly commended for his expertise in complex leaseholder issues and service charges. **Strengths:** "One of the best in the social housing sector. He knows and understands the law very well and is always very calm." "A brilliant lawyer – highly intelligent and always goes right to the issue. He has very good interpersonal skills with clients." **Recent work:** Acted on behalf of the local authority in Tachie v Welwyn Hatfield DC in the Court of Appeal. The case involved complex public procurement issues and regulatory concerns.

Kelvin Rutledge QC (see p.757) Highly experienced silk with a particular focus on matters concerning local government. He offers respected expertise in a range of cases, such as those involving homelessness allocation schemes and outer borough placements. He also makes frequent appearances before the Court of Appeal and Supreme Court. **Strengths:** "Blown away by him, one of the most tenacious advocates around." **Recent work:** Led for both local authorities in Hotak v Southwark LBC and Johnson v Solihull MBC, two highly significant cases in the Supreme Court concerning the definition of "vulnerability" in the context of homelessness.

JUNIORS

Jon Holbrook (see p.673) Routinely represents local authority landlords and housing associations in a broad range of housing disputes, including matters relating to community care, the Court of Protection and public law. He is widely praised for his thorough technical knowledge of the sector. **Strengths:** "Always brilliant. He combines remarkable understanding of the law with standout client relationship skills." "Terribly good – you get a QC service when you go to him." **Recent work:** Successfully defeated an appeal against a landlord's possession claim of a large central London house.

Matthew Hutchings (see p.679) Highly regarded, passionate advocate with a broad housing practice. He is known for his adept representation of local authorities, tenants and homeless applicants before all levels of court. Strengths: "Very good advocate. When he explains something, it's always presented in clear terms and in an attractive way." "An absolutely brilliant lawyer."

Andrew Lane (see p.695) Talented advocate who is praised for his unwaveringly dedicated approach, regardless of whether he is handling high-profile cases in the Court of Appeal and Supreme Court or more routine County Court possession claims. His practice encompasses all areas of social housing law, including welfare reform, housing fraud and advisory work for registered providers. **Strengths:** "He's got a very good presence in court, affable but very able." "Excellent client skills and very good on his feet. He's particularly good with vulnerable residents who require a more sensitive form of cross-examination." **Recent work:** Successfully obtained possession of a property for the London Borough of Sutton on the basis that the defendant had unlawfully sublet the premises.

Dean Underwood (see p.786) Housing and administrative specialist and current chair of the Social Housing Law Association. He is praised for his "methodical" advocacy and adept representation of local authorities and social landlords at all levels of court and tribunal. **Strengths:** "Exceptional understanding of housing issues, he is a thoroughly nice person and great with clients." "Very responsive and solution-oriented." **Recent work:** Represented the respondent housing association in Werrett v Evesham & Pershore Housing Association in the High Court. Successfully defeated Mr Werrett's appeal against possession proceedings and injunction orders on the basis that he did not, as he claimed, lack mental capacity.

Michael Paget (see p.732) Offers top-quality advice to an array of clients, including local authorities and housing associations. He is also highly regarded for his direct access and pro bono work on behalf of tenants. Interviewees particularly note his adroit handling of homelessness applications and leasehold disputes. **Strengths:** "A fantastic barrister." **Recent work:** Acted for Wandsworth LBC in a judicial review of the council's decision to refuse accommodation to a claimant.

Kuljit Bhogal (see p.595) Considered an expert in areas such as antisocial behaviour, public defence and the Equality Act. She is frequently sought out by housing clients for her insight and advice on major policy matters. **Strengths:** "Very robust but also highly reasonable with defendants." "She's very personable and a highly impressive oral advocate." **Recent work:** Acted for the London Borough of Wandsworth in a successful application for a closure order due to persistent antisocial behaviour.

Ryan Kohli (see p.692) Talented junior who receives regular instruction in antisocial behaviour injunctions, homelessness appeals and possession claims. He is highly experienced at tribunal level and has served as sole counsel in the Court of Appeal. **Strengths:** "An impressive advocate who provides good skeleton arguments in complex cases." "A very firm opponent." **Recent work:** Obtained an outright possession order for the Peabody Trust against a tenant who had used the premises for serious drug-related antisocial behaviour.

Jennifer Oscroft Specialises in defending local housing authorities and social landlords against public law challenges, offering particularly valuable insight into the housing implications of the Public Sector Equality Duty. She frequently appears in highly significant cases, often before the Supreme Court. **Strengths:** "She is incredibly thorough, calm and approachable." "Exceptionally well prepared and brilliant with clients." **Recent work:** Acting for the London Borough of Lewisham in a homelessness appeal concerning the implications of current immigration rules on a person's right to homelessness assistance.

Catherine Rowlands Predominantly advocates on behalf of local authorities and housing associations. She offers expertise across all areas of housing law, including succession disputes, possession claims and unlawful eviction. Interviewees are particularly quick to highlight her tenacity in court. **Strengths:** "A very tough opponent and really fights her corner." "Very quick, very clever. An excellent advocate." **Recent work:** Acted for Southwark LBC in an appeal concerning intentional homelessness and domestic violence.

Wayne Beglan (see p.594) Routinely undertakes housing work on behalf of local authorities and registered providers. He offers notable expertise across the areas of planning, regeneration and procurement. He has considerable experience appearing before the High Court and appellate courts. **Strengths:** "Brilliant paperwork. He drafts letters which close down complex queries and result in the other side's lawyers waving the white flag." **Recent work:** Represented Ealing in R (on the application of HA) v Ealing London Borough Council, a landmark case concerning the scope of residence requirements that councils are able to include in their allocation schemes.

David Lintott (see p.702) Known particularly for his expertise in homelessness matters, he regularly makes successful presentations before the Court of Appeal. He is habitually instructed on behalf of local authorities, among his broader client base. **Strengths:** "He will always give a practical answer and show you the way forward." **Recent work:** Successfully appeared on behalf of the London Borough of Croydon in a major eligibility case before the Court of Appeal. The case concerned the compliance of English housing and homelessness regulations with EU law.

Doughty Street Chambers

See profile on p.828

THE SET

Doughty Street Chambers is one of the foremost housing sets in the country and continues to be a highly popular choice for both tenants and applicants. This burgeoning chambers is held in high esteem for its provision of a fully comprehensive service in housing law. It is known particularly for its regular involvement in complex cases that cross over with community care, human rights and social welfare issues. Members frequently appear in leading cases and are routinely called upon to present before the Supreme Court.

Client service: "Really easy to deal with, the clerks are extremely helpful and efficient." "Absolutely professional, they respond to things promptly and are consistently helpful. A good bunch." Sian Wilkins leads the clerking team.

SILKS

Martin Westgate QC Respected leader of the housing and public law teams and widely considered to be a go-to silk for tenants and applicants. His recent work highlights include high-profile cases concerning the housing benefit cap and the so-called 'bedroom tax'. **Strengths:** "Prodigious work ethic. His analysis is excellent and his reputation superb." "Brilliant lawyer with a beautiful ability to reduce complex legal issues." **Recent work:** Acted in MG v SSHD, a case concerning an asylum seeker's challenge to the decision to place him in accommodation in Portsmouth and to refuse to provide him with travel expenses to enable him to visit his young son, a British citizen who lived with his mother in Canterbury.

JUNIORS

Jamie Burton Well-respected litigator with a strong reputation for his judicial review work. He is held in esteem for his adroit handling of homelessness cases and landlord and tenant disputes, and offers particularly in-depth knowledge of the Housing Act 1996. **Strengths:** "Incredibly intelligent, strategic and very well respected." "He's great, fights hard for his clients and has real presence in court." **Recent work:** Acted in Poshteh v Royal Borough of Kensington and Chelsea, a major case in the Court of Appeal concerning how local authorities should consider mental health issues when making decisions regarding homeless assistance.

Lindsay Johnson Housing specialist known for his strong track record in judicial reviews and in public law challenges covering a range of issues, such as failure to comply with homelessness duties, antisocial behaviour policies and failure to follow allocation policies. His diverse practice also includes areas such as stock transfers, unlawful eviction and possession proceedings. **Strengths:** "A dogged advocate. He is thorough and reliably puts forward interesting arguments." "Very approachable and extremely tenacious." **Recent work:** Appeared in Manchester Ship Canal Developments v Persons Unknown, a case concerning possession proceedings arising from protest camps established to protest against fracking.

Zia Nabi Housing and social welfare specialist with significant experience advocating in the Court of Appeal and the Supreme Court. He routinely handles public law challenges with regard to community care, social housing and human rights law. **Strengths:** "Very concise and clever, he has incredible knowledge. He is both down-to-earth and eloquent." **Recent work:** Successfully represented the appellant in Fryars v Crawley Borough Council, overturning the County Court's prior ruling that the council did not have a duty to accommodate Ms Fryars.

Dominic Preston Elicits praise for his homelessness expertise, encompassing priority need and intentionality cases, Court of Protection and antisocial behaviour work. His is able to draw on broader knowledge of human rights, EU and immigration law to inform his burgeoning housing practice. **Strengths:** "His thinking is quick and decisive, but inclusive and very approachable." "Extremely thoughtful. He's a real specialist and very well regarded in the housing community." **Recent work:** Successfully represented the appellant in Farah v Hillington LBC at the Court of Appeal, an intentional homelessness case based on failure to pay rent which raised important issues concerning the government's recent changes to welfare benefits.

David Carter Widely praised for the high quality of his written arguments. He has substantial experience of advocating on behalf of both private and public sector clients in a range of cases, covering areas such as landlord and tenant and local government issues. **Strengths:** "Knows when to push hard in cases." "A very good advocate." **Recent work:** Represented the applicant in Wilson v Birmingham City Council, an appeal against the council's denial of homelessness duty due to Wilson's refusal to accept high-rise accommodation as her son has claustrophobia and is scared of heights.

Ben Chataway Experienced housing lawyer and part-time Tribunal Judge whose practice is informed and enhanced by his knowledge of welfare and social security benefit matters. He typically handles housing cases involving public law and discrimination issues. **Strengths:** "He has a very methodical approach to casework, always very clear and concise." "A fantastic junior: hard working, co-operative and very reliable." **Recent work:** Represented a homeless 17-year-old in an urgent challenge by judicial review of Wandsworth social services' refusal to accommodate.

Jim Shepherd Housing and property specialist known for his work on behalf of law centres and vulnerable tenants. He is lauded by market commentators as a personable, sensitive but tenacious advocate. **Strengths:** "Offers all-round solid advice, and is pragmatic and good at negotiation." "A straightforward, no-nonsense advocate. Composed, on top of things, unflappable and charming." **Recent work:** Successfully defended a tenant with schizophrenia from eviction proceedings brought on grounds of rent arrears.

Stephen Reeder A specialist in homelessness and social housing allocation cases concerning vulnerability and intentionality issues, particularly with regard to mental health. As such, he is regularly instructed by the Official Solicitor on behalf of litigants lacking capacity. **Strengths:** "Universally liked by clients and opponents." "Great opponent to have, very measured and clear."

Sarah Steinhardt Effective, up-and-coming advocate with pronounced expertise in mental capacity and Equality Act issues in the context of social housing. She regularly handles disability discrimination matters in relation to the 'bedroom tax' as part of her diverse practice. **Strengths:** "A rising star, able to think outside the box, who is quick on her feet, covers all bases and never loses sight of the prize." "Very knowledgeable. She will always look for an innovative argument and push the client's case." **Recent work:** Acted for the claimant in two linked judicial reviews regarding the London Borough of Brent's failure to provide suitable accommodation.

Garden Court Chambers

See profile on p.851

THE SET

Garden Court Chambers continues to be instructed in significant and varied social housing matters. Its pre-eminent team of highly skilled barristers renders the set a highly popular choice for tenants, occupiers and homeless applicants in particular. The set's unwavering commitment to publicly funded work on behalf of vulnerable clients has made it a go-to set for law centres and legal-aided housing cases across the UK. The chambers is routinely involved in precedent-setting cases, with members making regular appearances before the Court of Appeal and Supreme Court.

Client service: "The clerks are exceptionally great, they respond immediately and are unflappable. They clearly have a good relationship with the barristers and are good at juggling things around." "Very good client care, they get back to you quickly and have a well-organised system." Tim Hempsted leads the clerking team.

JUNIORS

Liz Davies Has vast experience in the social housing sector and is recognised for her outstanding knowledge of homelessness law, which she demonstrates in court and in her authoritative writing on the subject. She draws on her broader expertise in the fields of community care and administrative law to buttress her highly esteemed housing practice. **Strengths:** "A real star of the housing team. She brings confidence and experience to the courtroom and has a real passion for housing and the rights of tenants." "Has an encyclopaedic knowledge of homelessness law and is a really good advocate as well." **Recent work:** Appeared in a successful homelessness appeal against Westminster City Council. The case involved interpretation of the Hotak v Southwark LBC Supreme Court decision on the definition of 'vulnerable' in councils' homelessness duties.

Edward Fitzpatrick Handles a wide range of housing and property matters for tenants and applicants. He earns consistent praise for his measured and meticulous approach to complex homelessness and antisocial behaviour litigation. **Strengths:** "Has a very calm manner and tends to put agitated clients at ease by explaining things in a clear, concise way." "Very good in court, realistic and pragmatic. He has tenacity measured with realism." **Recent work:** Acted in a homelessness case concerning the suitability of accommodation offered by Solihull MBC to a defendant with mental health problems who had suffered discrimination and abuse in the area following gender reassignment.

Bethan Harris Specialises in cases with combined housing, capacity and community care aspects, often for disabled and otherwise vulnerable clients. She sits on the Panel of Counsel for the Equality and Human Rights Commission and regularly speaks on developments in social housing law. **Strengths:** "An experienced tenant lawyer with 100% commitment to any case she takes on. Her preparation is second to none and she brings a real interest in equality and disability legislation to her work."

Timothy Baldwin Dedicated junior with a reputation for taking on challenging and legally complex social housing work. His practice typically concerns homelessness and allocation cases for tenants with mental health issues or specialist community care needs. **Strengths:** "Very intelligent. Broad and thorough understanding of the law." "Highly intellectual, extremely helpful, always up to the challenge." **Recent work:** Appeared on behalf of a homeless claimant in a High Court test case, successfully arguing that Westminster City Council's housing allocation scheme was unlawful .

John Beckley Practises a broad range of social housing law, with particular expertise in defending vulnerable clients threatened with possession or accused of antisocial behaviour. He is also well regarded for his work in homelessness appeals and disrepair cases. **Strengths:** "A brilliant barrister, really good with the clients and approachable." "He can formulate an argument very clearly and inspires confidence in others."

James Bowen Experienced social housing specialist who is praised for his calm and confident manner when dealing with clients. His practice comprises all aspects of antisocial behaviour, possession, unlawful eviction and homelessness. **Strengths:** "Clearly very experienced and puts clients at ease." "A very strong housing lawyer."

Justine Compton Up-and-coming housing junior with specialist knowledge of Traveller law. In addition to her advocacy, she routinely writes and lectures on various aspects of social housing legislation. **Strengths:** "Justine's excellent. I find her very good on disrepair cases. She's very clear, does good tables and is a good advocate as well." "She's very sympathetic to the client; they really like her." **Recent work:** Successfully defeated the City of Westminster in an appeal concerning whether the client was intentionally homeless having left her husband who had caused her psychological harm.

Marina Sergides A "persistent and tenacious" advocate with a broad social housing practice, encompassing areas such as homelessness, unlawful eviction and disrepair. She offers enviable experience in possession claims, particularly as they relate to Article 8 and public law. **Strengths:** "In court she's just a great advocate, she really fights the client's corner." "She will take on unusual and challenging cases, and I like her approach with clients." **Recent work:** Defended a vulnerable tenant with serious mental health problems who faced eviction on the basis of antisocial behaviour.

Connor Johnston Recognised housing and homelessness specialist with a growing reputation for technically complex possession cases and judicial review. He won the 2015 Legal Aid Lawyer of the Year award for his commitment to publicly funded social housing work. **Strengths:** "Provides thorough, clear advice and acts quickly when it's needed." "Clients love him. He's very approachable and understands all the legal issues with ease." **Recent work:** Represented a young mother in a complex homelessness appeal concerning the eligibility for homelessness assistance with regard to Article 8 of the ECHR.

Band 2

Hardwicke

See profile on p.859

THE SET

The social housing team at Hardwicke is distinguished by its expertise in property and public law. Members practise in all areas of social housing litigation, including possession and disrepair claims, right-to-buy matters and landlord and tenant disputes. They are regularly instructed on behalf of housing associations and local authorities in County Court proceedings and have appeared at all court levels up to the Supreme Court.

Client service: "They deserve praise for clerking. The clerks give us the impression that they value us." "They're efficient, very easy to get on with and really helpful." Paul Horsfield is the senior practice manager.

JUNIORS

Morayo Fagborun Bennett Handles a wide range of social housing matters, with a particular emphasis on homelessness and disrepair cases. Her esteemed work in the area is complemented by her substantial property practice. **Strengths:** "She's excellent, incredibly thorough." **Recent work:** Successfully obtained an outright possession order for East Thames Homes against a disabled assured tenant who had let out parts of the property to lodgers.

Laura Tweedy A "go-to barrister" for many large housing associations. She elicits praise for her deft client-handling and cross-examination skills and makes regular appearances before the Supreme Court and Court of Appeal. **Strengths:** "She goes down very well with the clients, knows her stuff and gets the results." **Recent work:** Successfully appealed to the Court of Appeal on behalf of the appellant in Haile v the London Borough of Waltham Forest, a homelessness case in the Supreme Court.

Alison Meacher A specialist in housing work which crosses over with Court of Protection, mental capacity and other social welfare matters. She habitually acts on behalf of local authorities, registered providers and vulnerable tenants. **Strengths:** "Great for Court of Protection and housing-related work, she's robust and clear thinking." **Recent work:** Represented the defendant tenant in Moat Homes v Bastow, a case concerning an application for possession and an application for an Anti-Social Behaviour Injunction with respect to the tenant.

Five Paper

See profile on p.890

THE SET

Clients praise the housing team at Five Paper for its "very professional and highly skilled" team of barristers. Members routinely provide counsel to, and advocate on behalf of, housing associations, registered social landlords and local authorities. Commentators rate the breadth of experience and expertise on offer at the set, covering areas such as antisocial behaviour, housing management and unlawful eviction cases.

Client service: "Absolutely excellent clerking, no issues with fees at all and they are very flexible." "They always deal with issues quickly and work hard to keep our level of trust in them." David Portch is the senior clerk.

SILKS

Nicholas Grundy QC Head of chambers and an experienced senior advocate with a specialism in social housing cases that interact with real property, European law or discrimination issues. He regularly advises local housing authorities on policy matters and earns praise for his dedication to clients. **Strengths:** "He does a brilliant job, he's right on the money. His response times are frightening and his level of client care is a cut above." "Absolutely excellent advice. He has a real depth of knowledge but has also retained a very down-to-earth manner." **Recent work:** Successfully represented the housing association in Akerman-Livingstone v Aster Communities Ltd, a case that was heard in the Supreme Court.

JUNIORS

Sara Beecham Acts on behalf of local authorities and registered providers in a wide range of social housing matters, including antisocial behaviour injunction and possession claims. She has a particular interest in cases involving human rights and discrimination issues. **Strengths:** "Very experienced, confident and approachable." "Technically excellent and a pleasure to deal with." **Recent work:** Acted for London Quadrant Housing Trust in a successful possession claim against protesters who were occupying a former university campus.

Stephen Evans Considered an authority on the Equality Act and disability discrimination in relation to social housing. He is also experienced in judicial review of homelessness decisions, leasehold valuation and dilapidation claims. **Strengths:** "Sound, practical advice which comes with a thorough knowledge of the law." "His knowledge of court procedure is second to none." **Recent work:** Successfully acted for the local council in Mohamoud v Kensington and Chelsea Royal London Borough Council, a County Court possession claim which went to the Court of Appeal.

Terence Gallivan Acts primarily for housing associations and local authorities, although he is also recognised for his representation of legal aid clients in the sector. Much of his housing practice involves human rights and mental health issues. **Strengths:** "What he doesn't know about housing law isn't worth knowing." "He is clever and charming and has that confidence which comes from having done this for many years." **Recent work:** Represented Lambeth LBC in claims to adverse possession of short-life properties brought by occupiers who had been there for 30 years.

Victoria Osler Well known for her diverse practice which covers areas such as possession actions and homelessness cases, among others. Routinely handles matters in the High Court and Court of Appeal. She impresses clients with the high quality of her written advice as well as her oral advocacy. **Strengths:** "An excellent technical lawyer. I have a huge respect for her mind, she is an amazing legal brain." "She's wonderful with clients, very personable and friendly but also very clear on where the case is at and what needs to be done."

Joanna Brownhill A property barrister with significant experience acting for both landlords and tenants in social housing cases. She has a thorough knowledge of leasehold matters and service charge disputes; she also sits as a part-time judge in the First-tier Tribunal. **Strengths:** "Technically excellent and a pleasure to deal with." "A very robust advocate, highly knowledgeable and very approachable." **Recent work:** Successfully obtained an outright possession order against a joint tenant in a sheltered persons' scheme.

Jane Hodgson Routinely handles a broad range of housing, landlord and tenant cases, encompassing areas such as unlawful eviction, succession rights and antisocial behaviour. **Strengths:** "An excellent social housing barrister and a tough advocate." "Sensible, very effective and not someone to be brow-beaten." **Recent work:** Represented London Borough of Redbridge in a homelessness appeal.

Brynmor Adams Talented up-and-coming junior who is particularly well known for his adroit handling of social housing cases that contain property and public law elements. He offers significant experience in Environmental Protection Act prosecutions. Strengths: "His ability to read a document and pull it apart is way beyond his years." "He achieves fantastic results and offers incredibly sound advice." Recent work: Acted for Notting Hill Housing Trust in a tenancy fraud case brought against a tenant whose brother was living in the property illegally.

Other Ranked Lawyers

Sally Blackmore (see p.596) (Ely Place Chambers) Represents landlords and tenants in all areas of social housing law, with particular expertise in dilapidation matters and cases involving public law and human rights issues. **Strengths:** "She's very thorough and cares about the cases she takes on, leaving no stone unturned."

Zia Bhaloo QC (Enterprise Chambers) A leading silk for property and commercial real estate, her social housing practice primarily involves high-value planning and development issues as well as landlord and tenant disputes. **Strengths:** "Very strategic. She doesn't just give you the law, she explains the practical effects of what you can and cannot do within that law."

Sian Davies (39 Essex Chambers) Advises and advocates for local government, social services and housing departments on a wide range of public law matters. Her social housing practice is further strengthened by her knowledge of immigration, asylum and EU law.

Adrian Davis (Field Court Chambers) Advocates at all levels of court and tribunal on behalf of landlords, tenants and homeless applicants. He is highly experienced in possession claims and homelessness appeals. **Strengths:** "An excellent barrister and a first choice for dealing with difficult housing cases. He can quickly make sense of, and advise on, complex issues." **Recent work:** Represented the defendant in a possession claim brought on grounds of rent arrears, and in a counterclaim for compensation due to the claimant's failure to protect her tenancy deposit.

Stephen Knafler QC (Landmark Chambers) Experienced housing and public law specialist with a thorough knowledge of immigration, judicial review and community care law. He regularly leads in housing cases in the Court of Appeal and Supreme Court. **Strengths:** "He is one of the best community care lawyers in the country. If you've got a community services element to your case, he is the man you go to." "A great housing and public law lawyer." **Recent work:** Represented the appellant in Rehana Hussain v Waltham Forest LBC at the Court of Appeal. The case concerned the requirement for authorities to accommodate victims of psychological and not just physical abuse.

Richard Drabble QC (Landmark Chambers) A local government and planning specialist with extensive knowledge and experience of housing benefits and social welfare cases, including work concerning the recent benefit cap. He routinely appears at all levels of domestic and European courts. **Strengths:** "Commands authority and has prodigious mental agility and ability." "He has an all-round ability to see the law from a much wider perspective."

Nathalie Lieven QC (Landmark Chambers) Highly regarded for her expertise across a broad range of public law matters, she regularly acts on behalf of central and local government clients. She has appeared in several high-profile social housing and homelessness cases, including Sharif v LB Camden in the Supreme Court. **Strengths:** "A very successful practitioner."

Leon Glenister (Landmark Chambers) A rising star with a wide-ranging public and property law practice. He is frequently instructed by local authorities, housing associations and tenants on cases concerning human rights and equality issues. **Strengths:** "His submissions are fantastic and his advocacy skills are brilliant." **Recent work:** Represented a secure tenant in a successful challenge to Lambeth Council's plans to demolish and regenerate the Cressingham Gardens Estate.

Ian Peacock (see p.735) (New Square Chambers) Well known for his work appearing unled on behalf of Westminster Council in multiple cases concerning housing allocation schemes, homelessness and outer-borough placements. He has significant experience of appearing in key housing cases at the Court of Appeal and Supreme Court. **Strengths:** "He is extremely thorough, thoughtful, and he puts the client's case across well." **Recent work:** Acted as sole counsel for Westminster in R (Alemi) v Westminster City Council.

Nicholas Nicol (1 Pump Court) A social welfare and public law specialist who is noted for his strength in homelessness, leasehold and disrepair matters. He regularly acts in publicly funded cases for tenants and also sits as a part-time First-tier Tribunal judge. **Strengths:** "A brave barrister, who is very calm under pressure and unfazed." "Very popular on the tenant side, and deservedly so."

Patricia Tueje (see p.785) (1 Pump Court) A dedicated and experienced housing and community care lawyer. Her record for defending tenants and applicants in difficult possession claims and homelessness appeals is held in high esteem by her peers. **Strengths:** "Very good with clients and excellent at cross-examination."

Rebecca Cattermole (see p.613) (Tanfield Chambers) A landlord and tenant specialist with an enviable understanding of the property aspects of social housing law, as well as antisocial behaviour and housing management issues. **Strengths:** "Her paperwork is superb. She is bright and tenacious." **Recent work:** Represented the tenant in a possession claim against Hyde Housing Association concerning the terms of a shared ownership lease.

Kerry Bretherton QC (see p.602) (Tanfield Chambers) Has a long-standing reputation for public law and real estate litigation, and regularly acts on behalf of social housing tenants and homeless applicants. She has significant experience of appearing before the Court of Appeal and Supreme Court. **Strengths:** "She goes the extra mile for clients and thinks outside the box." **Recent work:** Appeared in an appeal concerning the implications of Article 8 for possession orders brought by private landlords.

MIDLANDS

Social Housing
Leading Sets
Band 1
Arden Chambers *
St Ives Chambers *
Leading Silks
Band 1
Arden Andrew *Arden Chambers* *
Leading Juniors
Band 1
Caney Michelle *St Ives Chambers* *
Manning Jonathan *Arden Chambers* *
Singleton Michael *St Ives Chambers* *
Band 2
Diggle Mark *Ropewalk Chambers (ORL)* ◊
McNamara Andrew *Ropewalk Chambers (ORL)* ◊ *
Newman Anya *St Ives Chambers* *
Vanhegan Toby B *Arden Chambers*
Up-and-coming individuals
Lawal Tom *St Ives Chambers* *
** Indicates set / individual with profile.*
◊ (ORL) = Other Ranked Lawyer.
Alphabetical order within each band. Band 1 is highest.

Band 1

Arden Chambers

See profile on p.805

THE SET

Arden Chambers is among the foremost specialist social housing sets in the country and, having opened its Birmingham office in 2014, is an increasingly prominent force in the Midlands. Its members frequently advise on high-level housing policy matters and make regular appearances in the Court of Appeal and the Supreme Court. Its skilled team of advocates enjoys a formidable reputation in the sector due to its adroit handling of complex, high-profile cases on behalf of local authorities, housing associations and tenants.

Client service: "The clerks are very easy to work with." "Approachable and hands-on, the clerks are reliably helpful at Arden." Elton Maryon leads the clerking team.

SILKS

Andrew Arden QC (see p.584) Prominent in the social housing sphere given his undisputed technical skill and regular appearances before the Supreme Court. He enjoys a reputation as one of the UK's authoritative social housing silks due to his highly praised advocacy style and influential contributions to major publications in the field. **Strengths:** "Provides authoritative advice on difficult technical areas." **Recent work:** Acted for the local authority in Haile v LB Waltham Forest, an influential case determining which factors to consider when deciding whether someone is "intentionally homeless."

JUNIORS

Jonathan Manning (see p.707) A founding member of Arden Chambers, he is praised for his commercial approach and his ability to handle complex technical matters, including cases arising out of the recent bedroom tax. He frequently advocates before the Court of Appeal. **Strengths:** "A fountain of knowledge in the social housing sector. A key player who regularly formulates important points of principle in this practice area. He cuts through issues with ease and is great with clients." **Recent work:** Successfully represented Birmingham City Council in a homelessness appeal concerning whether local authorities can take into account income derived from welfare benefits other than housing benefits.

Toby Vanhegan Housing specialist with a thorough grasp of immigration and asylum law. He is regularly sought after by tenants and homeless applicants given his formidable reputation. Interviewees commend him for his efforts to progress the law and for his deft handling of client relationships. **Strengths:** "Knows the law inside-out and his cross-examination is a treat to watch." **Recent work:** Appeared for the appellant in Scott v Croydon LBC, one of a number of test cases heard in the Court of Appeal. The case considered whether the exclusion of migrant carers from homelessness assistance and welfare benefits was contrary to EU law.

St Ives Chambers

See profile on p.933

THE SET

St Ives Chambers is committed to providing top-tier advice to a diverse clientele. It is routinely called upon by landlords, local authorities and housing associations, and frequently accepts publicly funded work on behalf of tenants. Its highly experienced barristers offer broad expertise across the full range of social housing matters, and regularly handle anything from cases arising from antisocial behaviour legislation to possession and disrepair claims. "The entire team is fantastic; they all go out of their way to accommodate our needs," interviewees enthuse.

Client service: "Absolutely excellent to deal with the clerks." "The clerks are brilliant, they will negotiate on fees and are really prompt in coming back to you." Clare Radburn, practice manager, and Ross Hands, assistant practice manager, lead the clerks.

JUNIORS

Michelle Caney (see p.611) Singled out for her expertise in cases involving disability, mental capacity and human rights issues. She is instructed in matters ranging from possession and injunction claims to judicial review claims and service charge disputes. She accepts instructions on behalf of landlords and tenants and has appeared in the Court of Appeal as sole counsel. **Strengths:** "She's forensic in preparation, goes way above and beyond and has an utterly thorough grasp of every detail of the case." "Superb advocate with extremely detailed preparation in trials." **Recent work:** Represented Sustain UK in its successful Anti-Social Behaviour Injunction claim against an evicted former tenant who had returned to harass vulnerable tenants.

Michael Singleton (see p.767) Long-standing, esteemed member of this set who has recently demonstrated great insight and skill in matters pertaining to the Anti-Social Behaviour, Crime and Policing Act 2014. He is also distinguished by his regulatory work in areas such as unlawful eviction, planning enforcement and the Environmental Protection Act. **Strengths:** "Excellent with difficult defendants, thorough on complex legal issues and dogged in court." "An absolute specialist in his area, he knows the whole range of issues in housing law and his knowledge of case law is second to none." **Recent work:** Successfully defended Shepherds Bush Housing Association against a prosecution by a tenant alleging Statutory Nuisance based on damp and vermin infestation.

Anya Newman (see p.726) Routinely undertakes complex property disputes, antisocial behaviour litigation and possession claims involving human rights issues and the Equality Act. She makes regular appearances in the High Court. **Strengths:** "Has an excellent rapport with clients and is always prepared to argue fiercely for the outcome desired by those instructing her." **Recent work:** Represented Bromford Housing Association in a successful possession claim against a tenant alleged to have breached their tenancy agreement.

Tom Lawal (see p.697) Enjoys a growing reputation as a robust, up-and-coming housing specialist with excellent client skills. Strengths: "He's a real fighter, who is very vivacious and very protective of his clients and witnesses when he's in court." "He has a great rapport with clients and offers sound, pragmatic advice."

Other Ranked Lawyers

Mark Diggle (Ropewalk Chambers) Respected advocate who routinely provides advice and representation to tenants, local authorities and housing associations. His broad range of expertise covers areas such as possession, demotion and disrepair claims. He has significant insight into right-to-buy, licensing and management matters as they relate to the Housing Act. **Strengths:** "He has a fantastically wide spectrum of knowledge and his use of tactics is quite fascinating." "Not afraid to think outside the box." **Recent work:** Successfully obtained a possession order for Lincolnshire County Council against a tenant who had allowed its premises to be used for the trading of illegal cigarettes.

Andrew McNamara (see p.713) (Ropewalk Chambers) Advises on homelessness policy, introductory tenancy schemes and right-to-buy for landlords, local councils and tenants. He also sits as a judge of the First-tier Tribunal and is an assistant coroner for Nottinghamshire. **Strengths:** "He has vast experience with both tenants and local authorities." "Very good in court in terms of cross-examination of witnesses and attention to detail." **Recent work:** Represented Newark and Sherwood District Council in the defence of a possession claim.

NORTHERN

Social Housing	
Leading Silks	
Band 1	
Bartley Jones Edward	*Exchange Chambers*
Leading Juniors	
Band 1	
Burns Paul	*Exchange Chambers* *
Fullwood Adam	*39 Essex Chambers*
McCormack Ben	*Garden Court North*
Stark James	*Garden Court North*
Band 2	
Byles Andrew	*Garden Court North*
Cawsey Laura	*Garden Court North*
Hobson John S	*Doughty Street Chambers*
O'Brien Sarah	*Exchange Chambers*
Willock Gary	*Garden Court North*

** Indicates individual with profile.*

Alphabetical order within each band. Band 1 is highest.

Ranked Lawyers

John Hobson (Doughty Street Chambers) Manchester-based practitioner who specialises in the representation of tenants and homeless individuals. He is frequently sought after to handle possession proceedings concerning antisocial behaviour, unlawful eviction, disrepair and Traveller law. **Strengths:** "Reliable, pragmatic and an excellent team player." **Recent work:** Defended a tenant against a possession claim brought against her due to her sons' alleged criminal activity.

Adam Fullwood (39 Essex Chambers) Recognised for his strength across all areas of public and administrative law. He is particularly adept at handling housing matters containing human rights, immigration, mental capacity and mental health elements. **Strengths:** "Very thorough, he isn't scared of taking novel points and making them work, which clients love."

Edward Bartley Jones QC (Exchange Chambers) Widely considered to be the go-to silk in the region for social landlords. He is respected for his expertise in human rights and judicial review, which complements his established social housing practice.

Paul Burns (see p.607) (Exchange Chambers) Head of the local government and social housing department since 2010. His specialist practice includes housing management and antisocial behaviour cases. He routinely handles matters concerning the Mental Capacity Act 2005 and Equality Act 2010. **Strengths:** "Nothing's ever too much for him, I've not come across anyone comparable in terms of knowledge and expertise." "He is thorough, doesn't patronise clients, provides great advice on risk and guides clients of all degrees of knowledge through the legal process effectively." **Recent work:** Acted on behalf of Wigan Council in an escalating dispute with a tenant. The matter concerned the definition of "antisocial behaviour" under new legislation for civil injunctions. He was ultimately successful on all points of law, with the authority being granted injunctive relief and costs.

Sarah O'Brien (Exchange Chambers) Advises and represents social landlords in matters ranging from possession and injunction claims to those concerning housing management, tenancy policies and governance. She draws upon extensive knowledge of human rights, mental capacity and equality issues to inform her flourishing practice. **Strengths:** "Fantastic to work with and very knowledgeable, she incisively cuts through irrelevant material." "Hyper-intelligent and very good at complex homelessness cases, especially when they involve immigration issues." **Recent work:** Acted for Rochdale Boroughwide Housing in a possession and injunction claim based on threats of violence. The case involved mental health and capacity issues.

Ben McCormack (Garden Court North) Regularly instructed in statutory homelessness appeals in the County Court. His vast expertise covers all aspects of housing law, including homelessness, possession proceedings, discrimination cases and housing benefit disputes. **Strengths:** "He has one of the most effective court manners of anybody I've come across. He's very down to earth and judges really like his approach." "Knowledgeable, approachable and always willing to go the extra mile."

James Stark (Garden Court North) Regularly advocates before the Court of Appeal and enjoys a formidable reputation in the sector. In addition to his in-depth knowledge of public and private landlord and tenant law, he has broad experience in trespasser and Traveller cases, and frequently takes instructions from the Official Solicitor to represent those with diminished capacity and mental health issues. **Strengths:** "Not afraid to go for the difficult argument. He is a very bright lawyer, academically impressive and able to bring an informed chancery slant to his landlord and tenant work." "He is one of the most authoritative, experienced advocates on the circuit."

Andrew Byles (Garden Court North) Has significant experience of acting on behalf of tenants and other occupiers across a diverse range of housing matters. He is a particularly skilled representative of vulnerable clients, including the homeless, those with mental health issues and individuals who speak little or no English. **Strengths:** "Very good at articulating his arguments, pragmatic and sensible when it comes to trial." "He will take what might be described as unusual points and run them well. He is very good at managing the clients."

Laura Cawsey (Garden Court North) Well versed in all aspects of housing law, with particular experience in homelessness cases, unlawful evictions and antisocial behaviour injunctions. She is also highly regarded for her in-depth knowledge of Equality Act appeals. **Strengths:** "She is very approachable and goes out of her way to make clients feel at ease."

Gary Willock (Garden Court North) His broad experience in the sector encompasses areas such as possession proceedings, mandatory and restraining injunctions, succession disputes and unlawful eviction cases. **Strengths:** "Well prepared and sensible, he will always strive to achieve the best outcome for the client."

Contents:

LONDON

Sport
Leading Sets
Band 1
Blackstone Chambers *
Band 2
2 Bedford Row *
Monckton Chambers *
4 New Square *
Leading Silks
Star individuals
Lewis Adam *Blackstone Chambers*
Band 1
Harris Paul *Monckton Chambers*
McPherson Graeme *4 New Square* [A] *
Mill Ian *Blackstone Chambers*
Randall Nicholas *Matrix Chambers (ORL)* ◊
Sturman Jim *2 Bedford Row* *
Band 2
Hunter Andrew *Blackstone Chambers*
Pannick David *Blackstone Chambers*
Band 3
Beloff Michael *Blackstone Chambers*
Gallafent Kate *Blackstone Chambers*
Mulcahy Jane *Blackstone Chambers*
Phillips Mark *South Square (ORL)* ◊ *
Band 4
Green Andrew *Blackstone Chambers*
Hollander Charles *Brick Court Chambers (ORL)* ◊
Howe Robert *Blackstone Chambers*
Milliken-Smith Mark *2 Bedford Row* *
Saini Pushpinder *Blackstone Chambers*
Band 5
Brown Damian *Littleton Chambers (ORL)* ◊
Glyn Caspar *Cloisters (ORL)* ◊ *
Goulding Paul *Blackstone Chambers*
Jeans Christopher *11KBW (ORL)* ◊ *
Jones Seán *11KBW (ORL)* ◊ *
Stoner Christopher *Serle Court (ORL)* ◊ *
New Silks
Bayfield Daniel *South Square (ORL)* ◊ *
Kennelly Brian *Blackstone Chambers*
* *Indicates set / individual with profile.*
[A] *direct access (see p.24).*
◊ *(ORL) = Other Ranked Lawyer.*
Alphabetical order within each band. Band 1 is highest.

Sport
Leading Juniors
Star individuals
de Marco Nick *Blackstone Chambers*
Band 1
Crystal Jonathan *Goldsmith Chambers (ORL)* ◊
Saoul Daniel *4 New Square* *
Weston Louis *3PB Barristers (ORL)* ◊
Band 2
Liddell Richard *4 New Square* *
Meakin Ian *XXIV Old Buildings (ORL)* ◊
Segan James *Blackstone Chambers*
Band 3
Banks Fiona *Monckton Chambers* [A]
Mehrzad John *Littleton Chambers (ORL)* ◊ *
Richards Tom *Blackstone Chambers*
Band 4
Draper Owain *One Essex Court (ORL)* ◊ *
Hickman Tom *Blackstone Chambers*
Mountford Tom *Blackstone Chambers*
Band 5
Butler Rupert *3 Hare Court (ORL)* ◊ [A]
Dean Jacob *5RB (ORL)* ◊ *
Smith Andrew *Matrix Chambers (ORL)* ◊ *

Band 1

Blackstone Chambers

See profile on p.813

THE SET

Home to the leading collection of sports barristers in the market, Blackstone offers a truly formidable combination of specialist knowledge and fearless advocacy. As well as offering superior representation, a number of the set's silks and juniors appear as arbitrators or panel members on major tribunals, appeal boards and ethics committees.

Client service: "They're very strong and well regarded in the sports sector. The clerking team is excellent and makes dealing with the set very easy." Gary Oliver is the senior clerk at the set.

SILKS

Adam Lewis QC Widely regarded as the leading sports barrister in the UK thanks to his singular focus on the practice area, "encyclopaedic" knowledge of judgments and extensive list of high-profile clients. **Strengths:** "He's obviously top-notch. He knows all the cases because he's been in most of them. His knowledge of the area is unparalleled." "Adam Lewis is the safest pair of hands in the sports sector." **Recent work:** Acted for Premier Rugby and the Football League in various proceedings involving EU competition and free movement law issues.

Ian Mill QC Involved in a plethora of disputes across tennis, boxing, football and other sports, he acts as advocate, arbitrator and panel chairman. He is known for being a tenacious cross-examiner. **Strengths:** "The ideal choice for heavyweight contentious sporting disputes." "A very strong lawyer and tough cross-examiner who fights hard for his clients." **Recent work:** Successfully obtained an award for F1 driver Guy van der Garde in an arbitration against his team, Sauber. The team was ultimately ordered to honour their contractual obligations to him.

Andrew Hunter QC Becoming increasingly prominent as an advocate for parties involved in sports-related complex contractual disputes. **Strengths:** "He's just a delight to have in front of you because he's very measured and very concise – there's no unnecessary drama in his delivery and no stamping of feet or banging of fists on the table." **Recent work:** Acted as lead counsel for Asian Football Confederation president Mohamed Bin Hammam in his continuing dispute with FIFA.

A towering figure at the Bar, **David Pannick QC** is instructed in sports law matters of the highest importance, particularly those relating to football. **Strengths:** "A class act generally." "He straddles numerous areas of the law like a god, including sport." **Recent work:** Acted for the Association of Football Agents in its complaint to the European Commission regarding new disciplinary regulations imposed by UEFA and the FA.

Michael Beloff QC A pioneer of sports law who is one of the most experienced and respected barristers in the UK. Sources praise him for his brilliant intellect and authoritative presence, qualities that serve him well as committee chairman for governing bodies. **Strengths:** "He remains the market leader for difficult sports disputes." "Michael has a brilliant mind and is very good on his feet." **Recent work:** He has been advising the Gibraltar Football Association as they attempt to obtain membership of FIFA.

Kate Gallafent QC Singled out for her exemplary skills as an advocate on matters involving anti-doping and disciplinary hearings. She is heavily involved in panels for child protection in sport. **Strengths:** "She is not afraid to stand up to senior judges and is excellent in her research." "Kate Gallefant is incredibly sharp but also very personable and client-friendly." **Recent work:** Advised the Lawn Tennis Association in relation to disciplinary proceedings against a junior tennis player. She further defended the body against subsequent race discrimination claims brought against it in the County Court and Court of Appeal.

Jane Mulcahy QC A personable but authoritative advocate who handles disputes and disciplinary hearings concerning doping, discrimination and unfair dismissal. **Strengths:** "Jane gives clear and frank advice. She is someone you actively want to work with on a matter, and is absolutely excellent with clients." "Her reputation affords her a deserved seat at the top table of advisers in the industry."

Andrew Green QC Highly rated for his work on sports disciplinary matters, particularly in the world of rugby. **Strengths:** "He's fantastic" and is noted for his "superior strategic skills." **Recent work:** Represented the RFU in disciplinary proceedings brought against Leicester Tigers' director of rugby, Richard Cockerill.

Robert Howe QC An in-demand advocate for contract matters with a media or copyright angle, who is hailed as a calm and reassuring presence in the courtroom. **Strengths:** "Whenever we've got a tricky issue, he's the one to go to. He's a very smart guy who's very accessible and takes a practical approach to things." **Recent work:** Acted for the ECB and Sky in a copyright infringement claim against online service Fanatix.

Pushpinder Saini QC Versatile commercial silk acknowledged for his handling of high-profile sports matters, some of which he undertakes on a pro bono basis. **Strengths:** "He's a very well-respected guy, and totally charming."

Paul Goulding QC A leading figure in the employment law world, he is instructed in a variety of employment law-related sports matters, including those relating to contract disputes and discrimination. **Strengths:** "He's brilliant and has got a lovely way with clients." **Recent work:** Acted for the engine manufacturer of the Mercedes F1 team in a dispute with an employee who resigned to join a competitor.

Brian Kennelly QC New silk acknowledged for his superior advocacy skills and his considerable experience of appearing before CAS arbitrations.

Strengths: He's very sharp-witted and very helpful in putting a case together." **Recent work:** Represented Chelsea in resisting a challenge by Juventus to the UEFA rule that makes the Italian club liable to pay a £14 million damages award made against Adrian Mutu.

JUNIORS

Nick de Marco An outstanding practitioner with a widely held reputation at the Bar for being the foremost expert on football regulatory matters. **Strengths:** "Nick is head and shoulders above all the juniors. He is truly exceptional all round, knows the area inside-out, is good on the law and is good in court." "Extremely good on sports-related litigation, he has a thorough knowledge of football regulatory provisions at all levels." **Recent work:** Represented footballer Jake Livermore in his successful reduction of a ban brought by the FA for a positive cocaine test.

James Segan Has attracted attention for his growing list of instructions in both commercial and regulatory matters, especially those involving competition law. **Strengths:** "James is an experienced junior who is highly regarded throughout the sector." "He's very, very accomplished." **Recent work:** Represented the RFU as sole counsel in its disciplinary prosecution of Leicester Tigers' defence coach Philip Blake under World Rugby's new anti-corruption rules.

Tom Richards A valued adviser on football and rugby disputes with a competition law aspect, who has acted as sole counsel in several recent arbitrations. **Strengths:** "Incredibly bright, personable, hard-working and the first choice for complex legal disputes in sport." "He's seriously bright and a very strong advocate."

Tom Hickman Talented junior who receives regular instructions in major contractual disputes. He also acts as an adviser on anti-doping issues. **Strengths:** "He gets good results and is both tactically and intellectually astute." **Recent work:** Represented an Indian broadcasting company that had purchased broadcasting rights in its defence against a claim brought by a national cricket authority.

Tom Mountford Becoming increasingly active in the area both as an advocate and through his involvement as legal secretary of the IAAF Ethics Commission. **Strengths:** "His written work is excellent and his grasp of the law is very, very good." "An up-and-coming sports barrister, he is bright, hard-working and someone who produces excellent quality work." **Recent work:** Acted for the Federation Internationale de Gymnastique in its successful application to strike out a personal injury claim brought against it by Adeva Bryan.

Band 2

2 Bedford Row

See profile on p.807

THE SET

A noteworthy group with significant talent in sports law, particularly at silk level. The set's noted expertise in criminal law provides it with a strong grounding for disciplinary proceedings in rugby and football. Barristers here are experts on anti-doping, match fixing and corruption.

SILKS

Jim Sturman QC (see p.775) An outstanding criminal lawyer widely regarded as the go-to barrister for football disciplinary hearings, with experience of acting for both defendants and governing bodies. His expertise in criminal matters is a boon as he has been acting as an advocate for a senior IAAF executive being investigated by WADA. **Strengths:** "Very experienced in the Court of Arbitration for Sport, he's easy to speak with, accessible and down-to-earth." "A true professional" whose criminal law background really assists him on sports disciplinary matters." **Recent work:** Represented Rotherham United FC in FDC proceedings against the club for fielding an ineligible player.

Mark Milliken-Smith QC (see p.717) Experienced silk with a background in criminal law, who has carved out a niche as an advocate in rugby disciplinary proceedings. **Strengths:** "Has great knowledge of the sports disciplinary system," and is "a very trusted advocate." **Recent work:** Represented a French rugby player in respect of an off-field incident at Twickenham during the 2015 Rugby World Cup.

Monckton Chambers

See profile on p.877

THE SET

Monckton Chambers is a go-to set for clients with sports issues, especially those involving questions of commercial and competition law. Its members frequently appear in CAS proceedings, the FIFA Dispute Resolution Chamber and FA arbitrations and disciplinary hearings. They are instructed by governing bodies, clubs and athletes on matters in a broad range of sports.

Client service: "Monckton Chambers is well run, with a good clerking team headed up by David Hockney. He is a pleasure to deal with and he has a good team behind him."

SILKS

Paul Harris QC Renowned for his excellent knowledge of regulatory frameworks and the broader sporting environment, as well as his robust advocacy style. He is frequently instructed in sports matters involving competition law aspects. **Strengths:** "He's incredibly bright and very good on his feet. A very forceful advocate, he doesn't give up." "He's the doyen of competition law and competition sports work."

JUNIORS

Fiona Banks Emerging junior who receives instructions across a variety of sports including football, rugby, motor racing and cycling. **Strengths:** "Fiona is an extremely safe pair of hands. She is responsive and thorough and thinks strategically." "A strong junior who is extremely user-friendly."

4 New Square

See profile on p.880

THE SET

Barristers at 4 New Square cover an array of sports matters, and act on behalf of governing bodies, athletes, clubs and agents. Members of the set are particularly active at the Court of Arbitration for Sport and regularly appear for clients on anti-doping, disciplinary, governance and commercial mandates.

Client service: "The set has very personable clerks and barristers with an ever-increasing reputation in the sector." Lizzie Stewart is the senior clerk at the set.

SILKS

Graeme McPherson QC (see p.714) Admired for his remarkable knowledge of horse racing and its regulations, he has an excellent track record of acting for governing bodies in disciplinary hearings. He also advises on rugby-related matters. **Strengths:** "He knows everything you need to know about horse racing and the law." "He's very straightforward and he lets you know what he needs." **Recent work:** Acted for the Qatari Royal Family in its successful appeal against the demotion of its filly, Simple Verse, as victor of the St Leger, the world's oldest classic horse race.

JUNIORS

Daniel Saoul (see p.758) Has a broad list of instructions in cases concerning rugby, boxing, darts, table tennis and football. He has a strong reputation as an advocate on anti-doping matters. **Strengths:** "Absolutely outstanding. He is the complete counsel: he has a brilliant intellect, he's always able to find one extra first-rate point of argument, he's excellent at paperwork and he's a particularly outstanding advocate. Having been a solicitor, he understands the commercial drivers of the client better than most." **Recent work:** Acted for former darts world champion Richie Burnett in successfully reducing the standard ban after Burnett tested positive for cocaine at a world tour event.

Richard Liddell (see p.701) Identified as a rising star for sports matters involving employment law, contractual issues and regulatory aspects. His practice sees him handle high-profile football, rugby, horse racing and athletics cases. **Strengths:** "Has very good technical knowledge and is extremely effective at client service. He takes a rigorous approach to his work."

Other Ranked Lawyers

Charles Hollander QC (Brick Court Chambers) Has a long history of involvement in the anti-doping sphere and remains in demand for difficult disputes in motor sport and horse racing. **Strengths:** "Charles has an excellent understanding of sports law and a great feel for tactics and the wider picture. He has great authority but remains highly approachable."

Caspar Glyn QC (see p.655) (Cloisters) Continues to be active and is well regarded for his work on employment contract disputes for clubs and individuals. **Strengths:** "He is a fantastic contractual lawyer. Clients love him. He really is rising fast." "Enthusiastic, intelligent and great to work with on employment matters." **Recent work:** Reached an out-of-court settlement on behalf of snooker referee Michaela Tabb, following allegations of sexual discrimination brought against World Snooker.

Owain Draper (see p.636) (One Essex Court) Instructed in cases involving competition law and commercial issues, most often appearing for individuals and organisations related to football. **Strengths:** "Technically very sound and offers practical advice." **Recent work:** Acted for Comtec Racing in proceedings arising from terminated driver and sponsorship agreements.

Jonathan Crystal (Goldsmith Chambers) Enjoys a long-standing reputation as an adviser to high-profile sportspeople, agents, governing bodies and rights holders. **Strengths:** "He has an encyclopaedic knowledge of sports law and has represented the very best parties. And he's a street fighter, which some clients really like."

Rupert Butler (3 Hare Court) An experienced junior with a impressive record acting for governing bodies and individuals on commercial matters. **Strengths:** "Very user-friendly and a good man to have on the team. He's got a lot of experience."

Christopher Jeans QC (see p.682) (11KBW) A star figure at the Employment Bar, Christopher Jeans QC provides counsel on high-profile contractual disputes to do with the sports world. **Strengths:** "He's very good at cases where reputational issue is at stake."

Seán Jones QC (see p.686) (11KBW) A highly rated practitioner who is often instructed in rugby matters with an employment aspect. **Strengths:** "Tactically brilliant and very client-friendly. He's able to explain difficult legal concepts in clear terms to lay clients."

Damian Brown QC (Littleton Chambers) Highly experienced in employment-related sports disputes, especially those with freedom of movement issues. **Strengths:** "He really gets on top of the papers and focuses on the issues at hand. He has a very nice style and is never aggressive or blustery."

John Mehrzad (see p.715) (Littleton Chambers) Has developed a good name in the sports law arena, having received frequent instructions in regulatory and contractual disputes. He is an FA Rule K arbitrator and has been appointed to the FA Chairman's Anti-Discrimination Panel. Recently he has been appointed to the British Cycling Review Panel following widely publicised criticism of discrimination within UK Cycling and the resignation of the organisation's technical director. **Strengths:** "John Mehrzad is excellent as he's practical, authoritative, confident and very responsive." "He's probably the go-to junior on agents work." **Recent work:** Acted without a leader for Forest Green Rovers FC in the club's appeal against a League Conference decision not to order a replay after an ineligible player had been fielded in a tie.

Nicholas Randall QC (Matrix Chambers) Noted for his presence as a quietly authoritative counsel and arbitrator for the FA and for his exemplary knowledge of the football industry and its regulations. **Strengths:** "A superb tactician with superior employment law knowledge who understands the sports sector and in particular the soccer industry." "He's a go-to silk for football in particular, who regularly acts against regulatory bodies." **Recent work:** Represented Hull City FC in a successful challenge against the FA's decision to refuse to permit the club to change its name to Hull Tigers.

Andrew Smith (see p.767) (Matrix Chambers) A dedicated junior who continues to attract attention from the market due to his securing of instructions in employment-related matters. Those that seek his services include FIFPro, UEFA and other governing bodies. **Strengths:** "He is very impressive in terms of both the persuasiveness of his written submissions, and, in particular, his advocacy skills. **Recent work:** Acted for Newmarket Equine Hospital in its defence of an unfair dismissal and disability discrimination claim brought by a former staff member.

Ian Meakin (XXIV Old Buildings) Based in Geneva, Ian Meakin is frequently called on to act in disputes and commercial matters involving F1 teams and other motor sports bodies. **Strengths:** He's very well known for getting a lot of sports-related work. He's very good to work with, very user-friendly and a charming fellow."

Louis Weston (3PB Barristers) Manages a blossoming sports practice and has key knowledge of match-fixing cases. He receives instructions relating to snooker, motor racing and horse racing. **Strengths:** "An excellent barrister in all respects. He is extremely bright and has a keen analytical mind." "He has a great sense of humour in front of panels, but he still takes the work seriously." **Recent work:** Acted for the World Professional Billiards and Snooker Association to prosecute match-fixing allegations against an amateur snooker player.

Jacob Dean (see p.631) (5RB) Noted for his work representing sporting bodies in a variety of contentious matters. He has niche expertise in defamation and privacy law.

Christopher Stoner QC (see p.774) (Serle Court) Heavily involved in commercial matters relating to swimming and football, and also an adviser in disciplinary proceedings. **Strengths:** "He has the perfect blend for a barrister in that he's both authoritative and approachable. He gives very clear advice that I'm happy to rely on, and my clients are too."

Mark Phillips QC (see p.737) (South Square) A respected practitioner valued for his expertise and track record in major sport-related restructuring and insolvency mandates. **Strengths:** "A tenacious advocate who is both direct and tactically astute."

Daniel Bayfield QC (see p.592) (South Square) Known for his excellent football knowledge and restructuring and insolvency expertise. **Strengths:** "He is very bright and able, and combines a sound legal approach with pragmatic advice."

THE REGIONS

Sport	
Leading Silks	
Band 1	
Casement David	*Kings Chambers* *
Quinlan Christopher	*Guildhall Chambers*
Smith Richard	*Guildhall Chambers*
Band 2	
Gilroy Paul	*9 St John Street*
Greaney Paul	*New Park Court Chambers*
Unsworth Ian	*7 Harrington St Chambers* *
Leading Juniors	
Band 1	
Budworth Martin	*Kings Chambers*
Leach Robin	*3PB Barristers*
Band 2	
Berragan Neil	*Kings Chambers* *
Moore Craig	*Parklane Plowden*
Sadiq Tariq	*St Philips Chambers* Ⓐ
Turner Steven	*Parklane Plowden*

** Indicates individual with profile.*

Ⓐ direct access (see p.24).

Alphabetical order within each band. Band 1 is highest.

Ranked Lawyers

Christopher Quinlan QC (Guildhall Chambers) Leading criminal silk with a wide-ranging sports practice who has recognised expertise in anti-doping matters. He is frequently called upon to sit as a tribunal chairman. **Strengths:** "He's very well organised and has a fantastic work ethic." **Recent work:** Appointed as Judicial Officer for the 2015 Rugby World Cup final, and also advised on other matters throughout the tournament.

Richard Smith QC (Guildhall Chambers) Valued for his advice on sports disciplinary matters, particularly in connection with rugby. He is often called upon to advise on the drafting of sports regulations. **Strengths:** "As far as rugby is concerned, he's the best in the world." **Recent work:** Continues to advise the RFU on various issues including in-tournament disciplinary hearings and pre-emptive media planning.

Ian Unsworth QC (see p.786) (7 Harrington St Chambers) Works extensively in sports and serious crime, serving as a leading advocate in anti-doping matters. Also instructed by the RFU for rugby disciplinary hearings. **Strengths:** "A very able criminal silk who does a lot of disciplinary work."

David Casement QC (see p.612) (Kings Chambers) Highly experienced barrister with one of the most impressive sports offerings outside London. He is recognised for his diverse practice as an arbitrator, counsel and panel chairman. **Strengths:** "He is an extremely good sports lawyer who is technically brilliant and forceful before any tribunal." **Recent work:** Continues to sit as chairman of various disciplinary hearings, panels and sports arbitrations.

Martin Budworth (Kings Chambers) Promising junior praised for his approachability, commerciality and intricate understanding of the sports industry. He's well versed in employment-related disputes, especially those relating to football. **Strengths:** "A real star and a sports nut who gets some great results for players." **Recent work:** Advised the Football League on its prosecution of Blackpool FC regarding a pitch invasion by fans.

Neil Berragan (see p.595) (Kings Chambers) Known for his advocacy throughout specialist business courts in the north as well as the High Court in London. He is experienced in professional negligence claims involving individuals in football. **Recent work:** Acted for Bolton Wanderers in their successful defence of allegations brought by an agent alleging 'switching' of a representation contract.

Paul Greaney QC (New Park Court Chambers) Gifted criminal barrister with an excellent record for handling regulatory and serious crime, inquests and public law. Frequently called upon by the Football Association to advise on high-profile disciplinary proceedings. **Recent work:** Represented the FA after they charged Benoit Assou Ekotto with improper conduct over his Tweet congratulating Nicolas Anelka on his use of the quenelle gesture.

Craig Moore (Parklane Plowden) Specialises in sport-related personal injury and insurance matters, and acts for individuals and governing bodies in the worlds of both football and rugby. Sits as an arbitrator and mediator for the Sports Dispute Resolution Panel.

Steven Turner (Parklane Plowden) Represents sporting clubs and individuals in complex insurance and contractual disputes, as well as personal injury cases. Clients have included parties involved in rugby, football, cricket and darts. **Strengths:** "He's innovative in his approach, very thorough and very knowledgeable."

Robin Leach (3PB Barristers) Recognised as a leading junior in horse racing disputes who gets frequent appointments from the Jockey Club, BHA and HRA. Has recently represented jockeys in high-profile matters involving accusations of corruption.

Paul Gilroy QC (9 St John Street) Prominent employment silk with a wealth of experience, who acts for football manager clients in cases of appointment and dismissal. Also valued for his work on discrimination and breach of contract cases. **Strengths:** "If you've got a case you need to fight he's an excellent choice."

Tariq Sadiq (St Philips Chambers) Maintains a busy practice acting for clients dealing with rugby, cricket, equestrian and football disputes, amongst others. Has a focus on cases involving issues of discrimination and frequently sits as an arbitrator for the FA Arbitration Panel. **Strengths:** "He's very committed and builds up a rapport with people quickly." **Recent work:** Acted for Professional Game Match Officials Referees Ltd in an age discrimination claim brought by a group of well-known Premiership referees.

Contents:

LONDON

Tax
Leading Sets
Band 1
Pump Court Tax Chambers *
Band 2
Gray's Inn Tax Chambers *
Band 3
Devereux *
Field Court Tax Chambers *
11 New Square
Temple Tax Chambers *

Tax
Leading Silks
Star individuals
Gardiner John *11 New Square*
Goldberg David *Gray's Inn Tax Chambers*
Milne David *Pump Court Tax Chambers* *
Peacock Jonathan *11 New Square* *
Prosser Kevin *Pump Court Tax Chambers* *
Band 1
Baker Philip *Field Court Tax Chambers* *
Ewart David *Pump Court Tax Chambers* *
Flesch Michael *Gray's Inn Tax Chambers*
Gammie Malcolm *One Essex Court (ORL)* ◇
Ghosh Julian *Pump Court Tax Chambers* *
Goy David *Gray's Inn Tax Chambers*
Shaw Nicola *Gray's Inn Tax Chambers*
Band 2
Baldry Rupert *Pump Court Tax Chambers* [A] *
Brennan Timothy *Devereux*
Cullen Felicity *Devereux*
Furness Michael *Wilberforce Chambers (ORL)* ◇
Goodfellow Giles W J *Pump Court Tax Chambers* [A] *
Thornhill Andrew *Pump Court Tax Chambers* *
Way Patrick *Field Court Tax Chambers* *
Band 3
Fisher Jonathan *Red Lion Chambers (ORL)* ◇
Fitzpatrick Francis *11 New Square*
Gibbon Michael *Maitland Chambers (ORL)* ◇ *
Green Michael *Fountain Court Chambers (ORL)* ◇ *
Hardy Amanda *Old Square Tax Chambers (ORL)* ◇ *
Jones Philip *Serle Court (ORL)* ◇ *
Maugham Jolyon *Devereux* *
Thomas Roger *Pump Court Tax Chambers* *
Venables Robert *Old Square Tax Chambers (ORL)* ◇
New Silks
Sykes Laurent *Gray's Inn Tax Chambers*
* *Indicates set / individual with profile.*
[A] *direct access (see p.24).*
◇ *(ORL) = Other Ranked Lawyer.*
Alphabetical order within each band. Band 1 is highest.

Tax
Leading Juniors
Band 1
Bremner Jonathan *Pump Court Tax Chambers* *
McCarthy Hui Ling *11 New Square*
Nathan Aparna *Devereux* *
Ridgway Philip *Temple Tax Chambers* *
Rivett James *Pump Court Tax Chambers* *
Schwarz Jonathan S *Temple Tax Chambers* *
Sherry Michael *Temple Tax Chambers*
Thomas Michael *Pump Court Tax Chambers*
Vallat Richard *Pump Court Tax Chambers* [A] *
Woolf Jeremy *Pump Court Tax Chambers* [A] *
Yates David *Pump Court Tax Chambers* *
Band 2
Henderson James *Pump Court Tax Chambers* [A] *
James Alun *Temple Tax Chambers* *
Jones Michael *Gray's Inn Tax Chambers*
Lemos Marika *Devereux* *
McDonnell Conrad *Gray's Inn Tax Chambers*
Murray Rebecca *Temple Tax Chambers* *
Nawbatt Akash *Devereux* *
Soares Patrick *Field Court Tax Chambers* *
Band 3
Akin Barrie *Devereux*
Brinsmead-Stockham John *11 New Square* *
Chacko Thomas *Pump Court Tax Chambers* *
Mehta Nikhil *Gray's Inn Tax Chambers*
Ripley Michael *11 New Square*
Walford Philip *11 New Square*
Yang Zizhen *Pump Court Tax Chambers* *
Up-and-coming individuals
Afzal Imran *Field Court Tax Chambers* *
Stone Christopher *Devereux* *

Band 1

Pump Court Tax Chambers

See profile on p.899

THE SET

Pump Court Tax Chambers "represents the very pinnacle of tax expertise," and has some of the best tax counsel around at both silk and junior level. It is heavily involved in weighty income and corporate tax matters and high-profile avoidance cases, including those relating to film finance schemes. A significant number of the set's silks and juniors are on the Treasury panels. "The set is made up of excellent individuals who are superbly well managed," market commentators say.

Client service: "The clerks are always courteous and helpful." Nigel Jones leads the team.

SILKS

David Milne QC (see p.718) An iconic presence at the Tax Bar who is highly sought after for his expertise on both the contentious and the non-contentious side. He regularly handles Supreme Court and ECJ briefs and wins praise for his strong advocacy in these tough cases. **Strengths:** "An excellent advocate with a great mind. He has the ability to make the complex simple." **Recent work:** Acted for HMRC in its challenge to a tax scheme devised by EY and implemented by Greene King which involved loan relationship provisions.

Kevin Prosser QC (see p.744) A pre-eminent silk who acts for the Revenue and taxpayers on a range of tax issues, including challenges to major schemes. He has appeared at all levels of court and also maintains a highly respected advisory practice. **Strengths:** "He's so very quick to react, very responsive, very flexible and very proactive in giving advice. He is an experienced, leading silk with an amazing brain, who's the ultimate failsafe option." "A true heavyweight tax counsel whose opinions command respect and carry significant force." **Recent work:** Involved in an income tax case relating to shares given as part of a bonus. The key issue being whether shares counted as restricted shares for income tax purposes if the conditions under which they would be forfeited had been hedged against such that the recipient did not stand to lose out either way.

David Ewart QC (see p.642) Handles some of HMRC's most important test cases, and also regularly represents the Revenue in group litigations. He further acts for taxpayers on significant matters in an advisory capacity and in court. **Strengths:** "His advice was clear, unequivocal and extremely helpful." **Recent work:** Represented HMRC in the Franked Investment Income GLO test case, concerning dividends paid into the UK by international subsidiaries of UK companies.

Julian Ghosh QC (see p.651) Regularly appears before the highest courts both in England and Wales and in Scotland, acting for taxpayers and the Revenue. He is particularly well regarded for his work involving loan relationships and EU law. **Strengths:** "Incredibly sharp. He's client-friendly, switched on and practical." **Recent work:** Acted for HMRC in a corporate tax scheme case involving transfer pricing issues and the creation of an artificial loss on derivatives.

Rupert Baldry QC (see p.588) Although best known for HMRC work, he also has an impressive taxpayer practice and has handled a number of group litigations. Many of his cases involve transfers between international arms of multinational businesses, and deal with issues such as loans to foreign subsidiaries and the taxation of foreign dividends. **Strengths:** "Very commercial and very forensic. His work is very, very impressive." **Recent work:** Acted for HMRC in defence of a group litigation challenge to the UK's corporate manufactured overseas dividend scheme.

Giles Goodfellow QC (see p.656) A "frighteningly clever" expert on income tax and employee benefits matters. He regularly provides advice on corporate reorganisations, tax-related professional negligence and tonnage tax. **Strengths:** "Offers excellent, practical insights and has a first-rate knowledge of tax. Makes himself available at short notice." **Recent work:** Acted for the taxpayer in a case regarding the use of restricted shares in a subsidiary company to pay employees without incurring income tax or NIC liabilities. The value of the shares was realised on liquidation, which was not a chargeable event for tax purposes.

Andrew Thornhill QC (see p.781) Best known for his particular expertise in employee benefit trusts and disguised remuneration matters. He also advises on corporate reorganisations and the use of offshore structures to hold UK property assets. **Strengths:** "Exceptionally intelligent and reassuringly confident advice." **Recent work:** Successfully appeared in the Supreme Court on behalf of the taxpayer in John Mander Pension Trustees v HMRC, a transfer of funds between pension schemes case.

Roger Thomas QC (see p.780) Has extensive experience of handling challenging corporate tax matters before the highest courts. His particular area of expertise is stamp duty, and he is regularly instructed on the most complex SDLT cases. **Strengths:** "His approach is direct and straightforward – he sees the argument and presents it." **Recent work:** Acted for the taxpayer in a large-scale SDLT case concerning the acquisition of the Chelsea Barracks site.

JUNIORS

Jonathan Bremner (see p.602) Leading junior with an impressive track record of acting in heavyweight litigation. He is often instructed in major employee benefit trust cases and group litigations. **Strengths:** "He is very, very bright. He is thoughtful, impressive, engaging and he shares things well. He always brings interesting things to the table." **Recent work:** Junior counsel in the Liberty tax scheme case.

James Rivett (see p.753) Highly regarded tax junior with a broad-based corporate tax practice. He acts with a leader on many significant instructions and also leads his own cases, often appearing against silks. **Strengths:** "He has been extraordinary in terms of his kindness and patience. He also had a complete understanding of all aspects of the case." **Recent work:** Junior counsel in BT Pension Trustees v HMRC, a case concerning the tax treatment of dividend payments from shares in foreign companies.

Michael Thomas Taxpayer-side practitioner with a broad-based advisory and contentious tax practice. He is particularly well versed in property tax matters, including stamp duty, development matters and agricultural and business property relief from inheritance tax. **Strengths:** "A strong junior counsel with good all-round knowledge who gives strong commercial advice. He's particularly strong on real estate-related tax matters." **Recent work:** Acted on a pro bono case with the potential to set a number of important precedents. One of the issues concerned a tribunal's right to determine time limits to reclaim overpaid tax.

Richard Vallat (see p.786) Frequently acts for HMRC on challenges to avoidance schemes and is an expert on corporate tax and capital allowances issues. He also takes instructions on the taxpayer side in cases concerning corporate tax schemes, employee benefit trusts and tax-related professional negligence. **Strengths:** "Leading junior, who is a lateral thinker with a commercial approach. He has excellent technical understanding." **Recent work:** Junior counsel on two conjoined appeals before the Supreme Court. At issue were schemes using supposedly restricted shares to pay employees free of income tax and NIC, where the circumstances under which the shares would be forfeited had been hedged against such that the employees could not lose out regardless.

David Yates (see p.801) Often appears unled against silks in cases for the Revenue, and also has a solid taxpayer-side practice. He has niche expertise in advising insurers on tax-related professional negligence matters. **Strengths:** " Easy to deal with, he gets into court and fights for his client." **Recent work:** Successfully represented HMRC in a case concerning the tax treatment of the taxpayer's grant of an option over shares in a subsidiary company to an employee benefit trust.

Jeremy Woolf (see p.800) Senior junior with extensive experience in a range of complex corporate tax litigation and advisory mandates. He is particularly strong on income tax and employee benefit trusts issues. **Strengths:** "He is very client-friendly, almost impossibly nice and charming, and very tenacious. He will pull out all the stops and will work frighteningly hard to win." **Recent work:** Junior counsel in John Mander Pension Trustees v HMRC before the Supreme Court, concerning the transfer of funds between pension schemes.

James Henderson (see p.669) Junior counsel on some of the most significant corporate tax cases of recent years. He also has a thriving advisory practice, and receives regular instructions in cases regarding business reorganisations. **Strengths:** "An authoritative advocate who prepares carefully and conscientiously for the case." **Recent work:** Junior counsel in Bristol & West v HMRC, a case concerning group mismatches in derivative contracts.

Thomas Chacko (see p.613) An "excellent" junior with a growing reputation in employment tax matters. He also has experience of cases involving partnership structures. **Recent work:** Acted in Anson v HMRC, a Supreme Court appeal concerning double taxation relief on profits from a Delaware LLC.

Zizhen Yang (see p.801) Appears with leading silks in major litigation and also handles her own cases unled. She has recently appeared in matters regarding double taxation relief, business reorganisations and loan relationships and derivative contracts. **Strengths:** "Industrious, user-friendly, and someone who produces outstanding drafting. She is well liked and highly regarded." **Recent work:** Acted in a transfer of assets between group companies case. The case turns on whether the paying off of a debt can be construed as a transfer of the debt to the creditor.

Band 2

Gray's Inn Tax Chambers

See profile on p.856

THE SET

Gray's Inn Tax handles the full spectrum of tax issues, having direct tax, indirect tax and private client specialists at the set. Its members handle high-profile litigation for taxpayers and the Revenue before the domestic courts and in Europe, and they are also able to take matters to trial before the Hong Kong courts. Its barristers have flourishing advisory practices, and regularly counsel a range of clients, including blue-chip corporates on highly complex tax issues.

Client service: "Absolutely fantastic. They're flexible and nothing is too much trouble. The clerks are very, very good. Down to the receptionist it's an incredibly friendly and excellent place," say sources. The "fantastic" Chris Broom heads the team.

SILKS

David Goldberg QC A hugely well-respected figure at the Tax Bar, held in high regard for his innovative arguments and technical acumen. He has incredible experience in the most complex tax cases. **Strengths:** "Good, solid, reliable. Excellent in a fight." "Good client handling."

Michael Flesch QC Maintains a broad litigation and advisory practice covering the whole spectrum of tax-related issues. He specialises in big-ticket corporate transactions and offshore matters. **Strengths:** "Exceptional and just gives fantastic advice."

David Goy QC Has extensive experience of taxation of real estate transactions, and a wider practice that encompasses a variety of direct and indirect tax-related advisory and advocacy work. He is a regular in high-profile litigation and provides sage advisory counsel. **Strengths:** "Good at handling clients and very good at saying no to people when they need to be told no. He is a high-quality adviser, and someone who is always on our list of people to instruct." "One of the greats at the Tax Bar. He is a very good, solid barrister who you always get a reasoned view from."

Nicola Shaw QC An eminent QC who is experienced in representing both the taxpayer and the Revenue. She has represented clients at all levels of domestic courts and tribunals, including the Supreme Court, and has also taken cases to the ECJ. **Strengths:** "She is a delight to work with. She is practical, sensible, has good judgement, and is undoubtedly going to be one of the leaders of the Tax Bar in years to come."

Laurent Sykes QC New silk with a corporate and employment tax litigation practice, who is active predominantly on the taxpayer side. He also has a solid advisory practice that caters to a number of leading corporate clients. **Strengths:** "Very thorough and diligent, and a great communicator."

JUNIORS

Michael Jones A highly respected junior experienced in a broad range of tax issues, who has a focus on corporate and commercial matters, including shareholder taxation and employment tax issues. He is regularly instructed in high-value litigation both for the taxpayer and for HMRC. **Strengths:** "I always find him really easy to work with and very on top of all the issues. He gets to the point really easily and quickly." "He's very good: he's very smart, clear, sensible and responsive. He just ticks lots of boxes." **Recent work:** Acted in a judicial review brought by Bernie Ecclestone against HMRC related to the Revenue's decision to issue assessments against him for tax and penalties totalling over £1 billion.

Conrad McDonnell Concentrates his practice on VAT and corporate tax issues, along with employee taxation and pension schemes. He is usually instructed on the taxpayer side. **Strengths:** "He is very, very clever indeed."

Nikhil Mehta An experienced practitioner who previously worked as a solicitor in London and a barrister in Mumbai. He carries out contentious and advisory work on behalf of corporate and private clients. **Strengths:** "He has the advantage of having been a solicitor, so he's used to dealing with clients. He knows what it's like to face the client and tailors his advice with that in mind." **Recent work:** Represented the taxpayer in a dispute as to whether the full carry-forward of trading losses is permitted on a trade succession in common ownership.

Band 3

Devereux

See profile on p.827

THE SET

Devereux is a set making a real push in the tax market that distinguishes itself from the competition by having a distinct focus on tax litigation. Whilst many sets handle bulk advisory or tax planning work, this chambers offers individuals with strong advocacy skills, a number of whom are on the Attorney General's panel of junior counsel. Members are well versed in a number of tax areas and have a distinct specialism in employment-related tax matters. Recent

high-profile cases handled by them include Eclipse Film Partners v HMRC, and John Mander Pension Scheme Trustees Limited v HMRC, an employment pension scheme case heard at the Supreme Court.
Client service: Vince Plant is director of chambers. The team has "always been exceptional," according to market sources, who say that the clerks are "very friendly and good at recommending barristers."

SILKS
Timothy Brennan QC A highly experienced practitioner with extensive knowledge of corporation tax and employment taxes. His cases often involve complex issues of employment law and the taxation of employee remuneration. **Strengths:** "Very user-friendly and responsive, he has great technical knowledge which he applies commercially." **Recent work:** Instructed in a judicial review brought by users of a marketed tax avoidance scheme challenging HMRC's withdrawal of access to the Liechtenstein Disclosure Facility.

Felicity Cullen QC Well respected for her extensive experience of advising clients on complex tax issues. She also appears in litigation relating to all aspects of revenue law, acting for taxpayers and HMRC. **Strengths:** "Absolutely excellent. She gave us very balanced, clear advice, and weighed up different courses of action. She was particularly alert to the sensitivities involved."

Jolyon Maugham QC (see p.710) A well-known expert on tax avoidance matters with a robust litigation practice. He often represents taxpayers in high-value scheme challenges. **Strengths:** "An excellent advocate, who's very calm and measured and deals well with judges' questions. He is an extremely good writer who is able to add a lot of colour to his arguments. He's going to be one of the stars of the future." **Recent work:** Acted for Eclipse Film Partners in a case against HMRC before the Supreme Court.

JUNIORS
Aparna Nathan (see p.725) Has expertise in the full range of corporate tax cases and is an expert in inheritance tax and trusts matters. She maintains a strong advisory practice and is involved in many large-scale tax litigation matters. **Strengths:** "Always brings something interesting to the table and is willing to share her experiences. She is very experienced, very organised, very user-friendly and someone who's prepared to think around the issue."

Marika Lemos (see p.699) Has wide-ranging tax expertise. She tackles advisory mandates and has a growing litigation practice, acting for taxpayers and HMRC. **Strengths:** "Very able junior, who is exceptionally good with clients and advisers." **Recent work:** Acted for a taxpayer in a dispute with HMRC as to whether the Revenue was out of time to raise a duty assessment.

Akash Nawbatt (see p.725) Specialises in tax and employment law, and is a strong choice for employment tax and disguised remuneration matters. He also handles the full range of corporate tax issues. **Strengths:** "Has an agile legal mind and is a very confident and measured advocate."

Barrie Akin He has extensive experience of advising on a wide range of Revenue law issues. Sources highlight his advocacy and technical skills. **Strengths:** "He would be my first port of call if I wanted to ask a technical question of anyone. He has a photographic memory of all the authorities, and is incredibly able when dealing with technical points of law. He is very nimble on his feet when it comes to cross-examination. It comes quite naturally to him." **Recent work:** Represented Wiltonpark in a case regarding the VAT status of vouchers redeemed by dancers in lap dancing clubs.

Christopher Stone (see p.774) Specialises in employment taxation and income tax issues, acting for the Revenue and for taxpayers, handling advisory work and litigation. **Strengths:** "He's very good, very on-the-point, highly articulate, and everything you would expect of an up-and-coming advocate." **Recent work:** Acted unled in Raftopoulou v HMRC on behalf of the taxpayer. On appeal, the Upper Tribunal considered the scope of the First-tier Tribunal's jurisdiction to extend time limits.

Field Court Tax Chambers

See profile on p.844

THE SET
Field Court Tax is a close-knit set of experienced specialists handling the full range of tax mandates. "They are a nice set to deal with," says one market commentator. Field Court Tax barristers have particular expertise in international tax, double taxation and tax matters involving human rights issues.
Client service: The "very, very helpful" Marie Burke is the practice manager and Stephanie Talbot is assistant practice manager. One source describes them as "the best clerks of any chambers I work with."

SILKS
Philip Baker QC (see p.588) Has a particular focus on international and EU tax law, and expertise in corporate and private client matters. He often acts in cases before the ECJ. **Strengths:** "He is really superb, and is very analytical and very friendly. He has an EU background as well." **Recent work:** Involved in a case concerning whether or not the exit tax imposed on trustees contravenes EU law.

Patrick Way QC (see p.791) Maintains a strong practice in tax litigation and advisory work for taxpayers and HMRC. He has experience of acting at all levels of the tax tribunal and court appellate system. **Strengths:** "If you're looking for a good-quality tax QC, you can't do better than going to Patrick. He has a well-deserved reputation both for his technical work and his performances as an advocate." **Recent work:** Successfully acted for the taxpayer in Glyn v HMRC, the first win for a taxpayer in a residence case for more than 30 years.

JUNIORS
Patrick Soares (see p.770) Sought after for his depth of experience in tax advisory work. He is experienced in dealing with a great variety of cases, including those concerning property transactions, offshore issues and VAT. **Strengths:** "He gnaws away at a problem until he gets a solution. He produces the goods and goes the extra mile for you. In what had beforehand been a foggy matter he was able to give clear advice. He provided clarity in the context of confusion."

Imran Afzal (see p.580) Has a growing reputation for his handling of a range of domestic and international tax issues. He represents a wide array of clients in litigation and also has a robust advisory practice. **Strengths:** "Incredibly thorough and really on the ball." **Recent work:** Led in a case concerning whether or not individual members of a partnership could claim tax relief in respect of disputed losses.

11 New Square

THE SET
11 New Square is a long-established specialist tax set with a number of well-known and hugely respected silks among its ranks. These silks are ably supported by junior counsel who have been recently joined at the set by the well-respected Hui Ling McCarthy. Commentators say of chambers: "It is smaller than others but by golly it is good." Its members represent taxpayers and HMRC before all levels of domestic courts and in Europe. They also advise on taxation issues in international jurisdictions, including Hong Kong, Malaysia, Singapore and India.
Client service: The "avuncular and always very pleasant" John Moore heads the clerking team.

SILKS
John Gardiner QC Has earned a reputation as one of the absolute top tax practitioners. He has extensive experience of representing taxpayers, particularly financial institutions, in litigation before all levels of domestic courts and internationally. **Strengths:** "He is absolutely fantastic: he has fine judgement, huge gravitas and is as sharp as anything."

Jonathan Peacock QC (see p.735) Deeply experienced in advising financial institutions, multinationals and high net worth individuals on a range of tax matters. He is seen as a standout figure at the Tax Bar with the gravitas to handle the most sophisticated and significant cases. **Strengths:** "He has a real command of the court and a really good eye for strategy, and for how to play the hearing. He is an advocate judges very much like listening to as he's very clear and has a light touch. He also works very, very hard." **Recent work:** Acted in Anson v HMRC, a double tax relief and UK tax treatment of Delaware companies case.

Francis Fitzpatrick QC Recent silk with a strong advisory and litigation practice. He frequently acts for financial institutions, blue-chip companies and private individuals in a range of cases concerning such issues as employee remuneration, corporate finance, venture capital and domicile. **Strengths:** "He's bright and user-friendly and technically very strong. He has always produced good results in terms of turning things around in a helpful way. He's very good at strategy."

JUNIORS
Hui Ling McCarthy Highly rated junior who specialises in VAT, corporate and business tax matters. She has represented clients at every level of the domestic courts. **Strengths:** "Excellent, she's just so bright and so on top of everything. She is really direct and cuts through all the issues." **Recent work:** Instructed in Lobler v HMRC, a case regarding the taxation of partial withdrawals from insurance policies.

John Brinsmead-Stockham (see p.603) A new entrant in this year's rankings. He has a growing reputation having worked on a number of significant tax cases in recent years, including big-value litigation and matters which set important precedents. **Strengths:** "He leaves no stone unturned in getting to grips with every aspect of the dispute." "He's very capable, well informed and clear." **Recent work:** Junior counsel for the taxpayer before the Supreme Court in Anson v HMRC, a case relating to the double taxation treaty between the UK and the USA and the UK treatment of Delaware companies.

Michael Ripley Takes instructions in the full range of direct tax matters, handling litigation and advisory mandates. He is a qualified chartered accountant and a former visiting tutor at City University on European law. **Strengths:** "He is technically brilliant and exceptionally good in advisory matters." **Recent work:** Instructed in HMRC v Lloyds Bank Leasing. The case concerned the scope of anti-avoidance rules in tax legislation and the application of the 'main purpose' test.

Philip Walford Experienced in dealing with a wide variety of tax cases, including those relating to income tax, capital gains tax, VAT and corporation tax. He has particular expertise in oil and gas tax matters, tax arbitrage and double taxation issues.

Temple Tax Chambers

See profile on p.921

THE SET

Temple Tax has specialists in all areas of direct taxation. Its members also have expertise in VAT and other indirect taxes. Temple Tax barristers handle a wide range of work before domestic and international courts, acting for taxpayers and HMRC. Its counsel also have strong advisory practices.

Client service: Claire James is the senior clerk. Market sources describe the service as "very good and very responsive."

JUNIORS

Philip Ridgway (see p.751) Corporate tax specialist with particular expertise in business reorganisations. He also acts in SDLT cases, and is increasingly called on to advise on the tax consequences of high-value divorce matters. **Strengths:** "An ex-accountant and a good person for technical tax questions."

Jonathan Schwarz (see p.759) Highly regarded for his expertise in international tax matters. His particular areas of expertise include double tax relief, tax treaties and cross-border transactions. **Strengths:** "He's a good, solid adviser with a lot of experience." "He provides excellent cross-border advice."

Michael Sherry Head of chambers and a well-regarded practitioner for all aspects of tax. As well as corporate taxes, he has significant experience in VAT, private client taxation and back duty. **Strengths:** "We find Michael attentive to detail and he offers pertinent and salient advice."

Alun James (see p.682) Focuses on corporate tax matters, including transactions, corporate reorganisations and debt restructures. He has expertise in all direct tax matters, and is also an experienced VAT practitioner. **Strengths:** "Alun is technically very good but is also aware of the commercial dynamics of transactions. He is user-friendly and often able to add real value when advising on technical issues."

Rebecca Murray (see p.724) A recent addition to the Attorney General's panel, who has a growing reputation at the Tax Bar for private client, VAT and corporate tax issues. She has recently appeared unled in the Court of Appeal. **Strengths:** "She is quickly up and coming. She's a very nice person, who is active at the Revenue Bar and earning a good reputation." **Recent work:** Instructed unled for the taxpayer in Donaldson v HMRC before the Court of Appeal. The case concerned whether the Revenue's automated daily penalties system complies with two necessary legislative conditions.

Other Ranked Lawyers

Malcolm Gammie QC (One Essex Court) A widely respected silk with extensive experience in tax litigation and advisory work. He is frequently involved in a range of international and commercial taxation issues. **Strengths:** "He is outstandingly good technically and also very sensible so clients find him very reassuring." "Malcolm has justifiably earned the trust of the HMRC and taxpayers alike. He has been particularly useful recently in helping to cut through seemingly intractable disputes with HMRC, allowing both sides to reach a pragmatic but also technically justified settlement." **Recent work:** Acted for HMRC in one of the Ingenious tax scheme cases.

Michael Green QC (see p.659) (Fountain Court Chambers) Handles large-scale tax litigation on behalf of the government, and regularly undertakes tax avoidance and transfer pricing cases He has extensive experience of handling high-profile cases which are factually and legally complex. **Strengths:** "He appeals to judges due to his soft spoken approach and brilliant grasp of the arguments in a case."

Michael Gibbon QC (see p.652) (Maitland Chambers) Frequently instructed by HMRC but also represents the taxpayer. He has a strong corporate tax and substantial trusts practice. **Strengths:** "An outstanding practitioner. He has done a lot of tax for the Revenue and is immensely talented." **Recent work:** Acted in a case concerning £30 million of tax which a banking group (Bank of Scotland) had sought to save by a complex series of transactions which involved buying losses from outside the group.

Amanda Hardy QC (see p.663) (Old Square Tax Chambers) Maintains a broad tax practice across corporate, VAT and private client matters. She has strong expertise in representing clients at tribunals and in appeals. **Strengths:** "She is very practical, very good with clients and someone who commands attention. She is very clear and direct but also very good at getting to the crux of what a client wants and assessing the situation in terms of personalities."

Robert Venables QC (Old Square Tax Chambers) A highly experienced tax lawyer who has represented clients at the highest level. His particular expertise includes offshore tax planning, inheritance tax and employee remuneration. **Strengths:** "He is fantastic. He is very, very thorough and a very bright tax lawyer. He is in a class of his own." "He is very clever and has interesting technical views."

Jonathan Fisher QC (Red Lion Chambers) Specialises in representing individual and corporate taxpayers in HMRC investigations. Sources highlight his previous experience as standing counsel to the Inland Revenue as being particularly helpful. **Strengths:** "I use him because of his experience advising the Revenue before he moved to private practice. He knows how the Revenue ticks, and is very approachable and very good with clients." **Recent work:** Advised the taxpayer on an investigation into an alleged film scheme tax fraud.

Philip Jones QC (see p.686) (Serle Court) Regularly appears for HMRC in tax disputes, and has recently started taking cases on the taxpayer side. He also advises on professional negligence matters relating to tax advice. **Strengths:** "He has a calm manner and an extremely incisive mind."

Michael Furness QC (Wilberforce Chambers) Specialises in trust work and an array of related issues. He possesses particular expertise in occupational pensions, tax litigation and onshore and offshore trust matters. **Strengths:** "If anyone can win a tax avoidance claim, Furness can." "He's excellent, always well prepared and someone who gives clear advice. He makes well-argued and clearly expressed points at tribunal." **Recent work:** Engaged to deal with an issue concerning film scheme relief.

LONDON Indirect Tax

Tax: Indirect Tax
Leading Sets
Band 1
Monckton Chambers *
Pump Court Tax Chambers *
Band 2
Essex Court Chambers *
Band 3
Blackstone Chambers *
39 Essex Chambers *
Gray's Inn Tax Chambers *
Temple Tax Chambers *
Leading Silks
Star individuals
Cordara Roderick *Essex Court Chambers* *
Milne David *Pump Court Tax Chambers* *
Band 1
Hall Melanie *Monckton Chambers*
Hitchmough Andrew *Pump Court Tax Chambers* *
Peacock Jonathan *11 New Square (ORL)* ◊ *
Pleming Nigel *39 Essex Chambers*
Prosser Kevin *Pump Court Tax Chambers* *
Shaw Nicola *Gray's Inn Tax Chambers*
Band 2
Baldry Rupert *Pump Court Tax Chambers* Ⓐ *
Beal Kieron *Blackstone Chambers*
Eadie James *Blackstone Chambers*
Foster Alison *39 Essex Chambers* *
Ghosh Julian *Pump Court Tax Chambers* *
Grodzinski Sam *Blackstone Chambers*
Lyons Timothy *39 Essex Chambers* Ⓐ
Scorey David *Essex Court Chambers*
Thomas Roger *Pump Court Tax Chambers* *
Band 3
Conlon Michael *Temple Tax Chambers* *
Goy David *Gray's Inn Tax Chambers*
Key Paul *Essex Court Chambers*
Moser Philip *Monckton Chambers* Ⓐ *
Peretz George *Monckton Chambers*
New Silks
Thomas Owain *1 Crown Office Row (ORL)* ◊
** Indicates set / individual with profile.*
Ⓐ direct access (see p.24).
◊ (ORL) = Other Ranked Lawyer.
Alphabetical order within each band. Band 1 is highest.

Tax: Indirect Tax
Leading Juniors
Band 1
Mantle Peter *Monckton Chambers* Ⓐ
Sloane Valentina *Monckton Chambers* Ⓐ
Band 2
Hamilton Penny *Pump Court Tax Chambers* Ⓐ *
Hill Raymond *Monckton Chambers*
Mitrophanous Eleni *Matrix Chambers (ORL)* ◊
Thomas Michael *Pump Court Tax Chambers*
White Jeremy *Pump Court Tax Chambers* *
Band 3
Bremner Jonathan *Pump Court Tax Chambers* *
Brinsmead-Stockham John *11 New Square (ORL)* ◊ *
Henderson James *Pump Court Tax Chambers* Ⓐ *
Macnab Andrew *Monckton Chambers*
McCarthy Hui Ling *11 New Square (ORL)* ◊
Murray Rebecca *Temple Tax Chambers* *
Ng Jern-Fei *Essex Court Chambers*
Rivett James *Pump Court Tax Chambers* *
Sherry Michael *Temple Tax Chambers*
Singh Sarabjit *1 Crown Office Row (ORL)* ◊

Band 1

Monckton Chambers

See profile on p.877

THE SET

A market-leading set, Monckton Chambers possesses a sizeable team of dedicated specialists with deep expertise in all areas of indirect tax. With an unrivalled breadth of talented silks and juniors, it continues to impress in the market with its expertise in the areas of VAT, EU law and customs and excise duties law. Members are experienced in their representation of both the taxpayer and the Revenue, and regularly appear in courts from the First-tier Tribunal to the Supreme Court.

Client service: "The clerking has been absolutely perfect. I think head clerk David Hockney runs a very sharp operation there. They like to find a way to facilitate all pockets and be pragmatic. They're willing to accommodate you and in turn you keep going back for more."

SILKS

Melanie Hall QC A "real player" in the field of indirect tax, she is well known for her expertise in VAT matters in particular. She regularly takes substantial and high-value instructions from HMRC and from taxpayers. She is praised by market observers for her impressive ability as a litigator and her client-handling skills. **Strengths:** "She is very user-friendly." "She is a good old-fashioned street fighter. She just litigates properly." **Recent work:** Represented The Wellcome Trust in the first case of its kind, questioning whether charities should be permitted input tax deductions on buildings they utilise for charitable purposes.

Philip Moser QC (see p.722) Highly respected for his expertise in EU-related tax matters in the areas of both VAT and customs, and regularly appears before the ECJ. He is trusted with sophisticated and substantial instructions from HMRC and high-profile corporations. He also has long-standing experience of handling MTIC fraud cases. **Strengths:** "He gives practical, tactical advice." "He is an excellent advocate before the CJEU and very able." **Recent work:** Represented HMRC before the ECJ, which led to the extension of the Kittel test for MTIC VAT fraud to other areas of tax fraud.

George Peretz QC Well known for his VAT practice in particular. He is often trusted by HMRC with the most complex and challenging of VAT cases, and has a wealth of experience of appearing before the Supreme Court and the ECJ. **Strengths:** "He's exceptionally quick at getting to the heart of the issue." **Recent work:** Represented HMRC in Rio Tinto v HMRC, which is the leading case on the use of 'price adjustments' to claim refunds on VAT.

JUNIORS

Peter Mantle An "excellent" lawyer with vast expertise in all areas of indirect tax. He is most frequently retained by HMRC to assist in complex litigation and advisory matters; he also has broad experience of acting for private clients. He is well versed in indirect tax disputes emanating from EU law issues. He is praised by market commentators for his abilities, with one source describing him as "an ideal junior." **Strengths:** "For representing HMRC he's the best of the best of juniors." "Incredibly hard working and very reliable." **Recent work:** Represented HMRC in a test case as to whether taxpayers have an EU law right to recover compound interest on overpaid VAT.

Valentina Sloane A leading junior who is considered to be "an extraordinary VAT specialist" by market commentators. She specialises in representing taxpayers while simultaneously holding a position on the Treasury A-Panel. She regularly appears before the Supreme Court, the Court of Appeal and the ECJ. She is further praised by instructing solicitors for the clarity and practicality of her advice on indirect tax matters. **Strengths:** "She is incredibly intelligent, always impeccably prepared and thinks on her feet. The advice is always excellent – nothing has ever come unstuck with her advice – and she is thoroughly professional at all times." "She is very user-friendly and very sharp. A great asset to the team, and a great advocate." **Recent work:** Represented Pendragon in a test case before the Supreme Court regarding when the principle of abuse can be used to challenge tax avoidance schemes.

Raymond Hill An indirect tax specialist who is singled out for his vast experience of representing clients before the ECJ. He is particularly well known for his command of complex VAT matters. **Strengths:** "He is fair, able and knowledgeable about VAT. He is a very, very pleasant and an honourable opponent." "He was able to really give the client the advice they needed." **Recent work:** Represented HMRC in a case before the Court of Appeal which considered whether a provider of business education within a higher education institution should benefit from the exemption of VAT.

Andrew Macnab Can call upon broad indirect tax expertise spanning VAT, excise duties and customs duties, among other matters. He continues to act regularly for HMRC, handling complex and high-profile test cases particularly in the field of VAT. **Strengths:** "He's a great paper advocate and has a very nice writing style." **Recent work:** Representing HMRC in Littlewoods Retail and Others v HMRC, relating to the issue of compound interest on overpaid VAT.

Pump Court Tax Chambers

See profile on p.899

THE SET

Pump Court Tax Chambers boasts an incredibly strong stable of experienced silks and juniors, contributing to its steadfast reputation as one of the leaders in this area. While members continue to be trusted with the largest VAT reclaim cases in the market, it also regularly receives challenging and high-profile briefs in areas such as landfill tax, gaming duty and VAT mitigation schemes.

Client service: "I have been impressed with the clerking service at Pump Court Tax Chambers. I have found the clerks to be friendly and approachable, as well as being efficient at keeping diary dates and facilitating conference calls." "I have found Pump Court to be a very helpful set, dealing quickly with fee requests and assisting greatly with the preparation of court bundles." The team is led by senior clerk Nigel Jones.

SILKS

David Milne QC (see p.718) Highly praised by commentators who describe him as "brilliant" and a "giant" of the Tax Bar. He has expertise in all areas of indirect tax, and is experienced in both complex advisory work and high-value litigation. He is frequently trusted with the most high-profile and substantial cases, and has represented clients before both the ECJ and the Supreme Court. **Strengths:** "He's clearly one of the leading lights of the Tax Bar. He's very good with clients and provides first-rate advice." "He has an exceptional reputation." **Recent work:** Representing HMRC in an appeal regarding its challenge to a tax scheme devised by a high-profile professional services firm.

Andrew Hitchmough QC (see p.673) An indirect tax specialist who is highly praised by commentators for his polished advocacy and user-friendly approach. He attracts attention for his vast expertise in the area and has represented the taxpayer and HMRC in some of the most high-profile VAT cases of recent years. **Strengths:** "He blends technically rigorous advice with commercial acumen and smooth client-handling skills." "He's a great orator, great in court, and he's very skilled at putting across his arguments." **Recent work:** Acted for a group of trust companies in a case involving the supply of investment management services to investment trusts.

Kevin Prosser QC (see p.744) Considered by market observers to be the "doyen of tax QCs," he continues to advise high-profile individuals and companies on complex direct and indirect tax issues stemming from corporate transactions. He is praised for his breadth of knowledge and depth of expertise across the area. **Strengths:** "He has an ability to grasp the detail, but also his courtroom style is fantastic and his grasp of the arguments is unparalleled." "He remains at the top of his game. The depth of his experience shines through when dealing with complex case strategy matters." **Recent work:** Acted for Mercedes-Benz in the Court of Appeal regarding whether the hire purchase of cars counts as supply of goods or services for the purposes of VAT.

Rupert Baldry QC (see p.588) Described as a "thoughtful" and "understated" individual, he has a broad range of expertise in indirect tax, including customs, excise duties and aggregates levy. He undertakes advisory and litigation work for the Revenue and the taxpayer. **Strengths:** "He approaches it as a team effort, which is great. He really involves his instructing solicitors so it's a collaborative effort to get the right result." "He is always careful to give that extra little bit of thought to something." **Recent work:** Assisted Hanson UK in a case relating to whether the movement of rocks within the construction site of a reservoir qualifies for aggregates levy.

Julian Ghosh QC (see p.651) Maintains a broad practice encompassing all areas of tax, including indirect tax matters, in which he represents the taxpayer and the Revenue. **Strengths:** "He is exceptionally bright." "He brings an invaluable perspective to any case." **Recent work:** Represented Ocean Finance in the restructuring of its group to make it more VAT-efficient, which HMRC declared abusive.

Roger Thomas QC (see p.780) Experienced practitioner who is highly praised for assisting charities with their indirect tax needs. He is very well versed in matters involving stamp duty land tax. He is lauded by market commentators as being "a very balanced and cautious adviser, corrective to some of the other advisers who are out there." **Strengths:** "He was very impressive, and gave the client the clear steer that was needed. A masterful performance." **Recent work:** Acting in Longridge on the Thames v HMRC in a case questioning whether supplies made in relation to the construction of a training centre were zero-rated on the basis that the centre was intended for charitable purposes rather than business activities.

JUNIORS

Michael Thomas Maintains a broad tax practice, including business tax, VAT and private client work. Specialising in representing the taxpayer, he is particularly highly regarded by market commentators as "the go-to man for stamp duty land tax." **Strengths:** "Michael is an extremely articulate advocate and focuses on the key points in a case, narrowing the issues to ones which are winnable and most easily understood by the judge. When giving opinions, Michael is frank about the prospects and has usefully discouraged litigation in favour of dialogue with HMRC on a number of occasions, saving clients considerable costs and uncertainty." **Recent work:** Representing the taxpayer in Portland Gas Storage v HMRC, apropos the right to appeal a decision relating to stamp duty issues.

Penny Hamilton (see p.662) Enjoys an impressive indirect tax practice which includes vast experience in the climate change levy, customs and excise duties, aggregates levy and VAT. She attracts particular praise from market observers for her "authoritative" expertise in complex landfill tax matters. **Strengths:** "She is competent, able and diligent." "She is incredibly knowledgeable." **Recent work:** Acting for the taxpayer in Devon Waste Management Ltd v HMRC, a complex appeal concerning whether or not landfill tax should be paid on soft waste.

Jeremy White (see p.794) Considered to be an "extremely knowledgeable" individual, he is highly regarded by market commentators for his significant expertise in issues involving customs and duties. He also has vast knowledge of trade barriers, appearing regularly in the ECJ in cases involving numerous international customs authorities. **Strengths:** "I am impressed by his vast retention of technical knowledge. Combined with his sharp mind and exceptional intelligence, he has the edge with customs matters." "He was particularly easy to work with. He has a great deal of experience and knowledge in the niche area of customer international trade." **Recent work:** Acting for B&M Retail in the leading case relating to the burden of proof in connection with excise duty on spirits.

Jonathan Bremner (see p.602) Considered a very able junior by market sources, he enjoys a rapidly growing practice in the area of indirect tax with extensive experience representing taxpayers and the Revenue. He is often entrusted with complex VAT and customs cases, appearing before the Supreme Court and the Upper Tribunal. **Strengths:** "He is very bright, able and personable." "He's very personable and certainly, in light of correspondence with him, he has an acute and forensic intelligence. He's good on points of detail." **Recent work:** Represented PwC in a substantial VAT case considering which of two companies within a business group can bring a VAT claim.

James Henderson (see p.669) Offers an impressive indirect tax practice within an overall tax expertise. He is experienced in all areas of indirect tax, and is particularly well versed in complex VAT matters. **Strengths:** "He's very smooth and straightforward in court. He puts across his case with great skill and simplicity." **Recent work:** Represented the taxpayer in a matter of overpaid VAT and failure to appeal within the time limit.

James Rivett (see p.753) Has a growing indirect tax practice with a particular expertise in VAT, often appearing before the Upper Tribunal. He attracts high praise from market commentators for his intelligence and litigation skills. **Strengths:** "He is very bright." "He is an excellent litigator." **Recent work:** Represented the taxpayer in a case challenging the compatibility of the UK VAT regime with EU Directives.

Band 2

Essex Court Chambers

See profile on p.836

THE SET

A renowned set with a tight-knit group of pre-eminent practitioners offering expertise in areas across indirect tax. Members are able to offer an incredibly high standard of advisory work and litigation in all courts. Recent matters undertaken include issues of VAT, insurance premium tax, and customs and excise duties.

Client service: "The clerking team is responsive, approachable and happy to have sensible discussions on fees." Joe Ferrigno leads the clerking team at the set.

SILKS

Roderick Cordara QC (see p.624) An indirect tax specialist highly praised by market commentators for his advocacy and expertise. He is described as an "exceptional advocate" with a "huge reputation." He has featured in some of the most significant indirect tax cases in recent years, particularly complex VAT matters, before the Supreme Court and the ECJ. **Strengths:** "He's a very able advocate, he's formidably intelligent and very, very good with clients." "He is an outstanding advocate and excellent with clients. He is very good at conveying complex or difficult messages tactfully but clearly, and he brings insightful analysis to complex problems." "He gets to the point and he delivers added-value advice."

David Scorey QC Distinguished silk whose extensive indirect tax expertise is encompassed within an impressive commercial practice. He is particularly commended by market observers for his litigation skills in complex VAT and MTIC fraud cases. **Strengths:** "He is highly committed, industrious, conscientious and an excellent draftsman." "He is incredibly experienced and presents exceedingly well, which is of great reassurance to the client."

Paul Key QC Renowned by the market for his expertise in matters of contentious litigation relating to VAT, having appeared before the Court of Appeal and the ECJ. He has represented the Revenue and taxpayers, including high-profile multinational corporations. **Strengths:** "Paul is excellent. He is incredibly bright and incredibly personable." **Recent work:** Acted for EMI in a leading case on the three-year cap, pertaining to the recovery of overpaid output tax on compact disc samples of around £1.5 million.

JUNIORS

Jern-Fei Ng Prominent for his VAT expertise, he has successfully represented taxpayers and HMRC, appearing before the ECJ as an unled junior. Described as "assiduous" by market commentators, he is highly praised for his client-handling skills and work ethic. **Strengths:** "He is one of the most industrious people I've ever come across." "He is very good, with a good forensic mind." **Recent work:** Represented the taxpayer in claims for compound interest arising from a wrongful refusal to allow recovery of input tax due to allegations of MTIC fraud.

Band 3

Blackstone Chambers

See profile on p.813

THE SET

A highly regarded set in a multitude of practice areas, Blackstone Chambers houses multiple outstanding individuals who specialise in the area of indirect tax. Their caseload regularly includes substantial VAT, SDLT, customs and tax mitigation issues, among other more niche areas such as air passenger duty. Members are particularly renowned for their expertise in EU and international indirect tax matters.

Client service: "The clerks are polite, approachable and efficient in their diary timing, arranging conferences and negotiating fees. They will always look for fee compromise, making it easier for me to deal with client expectations." Senior clerk Gary Oliver leads the team.

SILKS

Kieron Beal QC An experienced silk held in high regard by market commentators for his in-depth knowledge of EU law. Representing both HMRC and taxpayers, he attracts praise for his advocacy and his professional approach. Recent matters relate to VAT and customs duty classifications, among others. Strengths: "He is very charismatic in his advocacy, really easy to work with, meets deadlines and is a real pleasure to work with." "He has shown strong, intelligent advocacy skills when before the tribunal and a thorough understanding of his briefs." Recent work: Represented HMRC following a challenge to the compatibility with EU law of the introduction of a new gambling duties regime.

James Eadie QC Eadie is extremely well regarded in the market and is particularly noted for being the government's Treasury Devil. He is well versed in matters concerning criminal tax issues and tax avoidance schemes. **Strengths:** "He has a very good reputation and is obviously very highly regarded." **Recent work:** Undertook a case challenging the application of air passenger duty to continental flights.

Sam Grodzinski QC A celebrated silk who attracts unreserved praise for his assured advocacy style. He has a vast depth of expertise and can handle the most complex and challenging VAT, stamp duty land tax and customs matters. **Strengths:** "He has barrels of intellectual firepower, a devastatingly excellent style of advocacy and there is an economy about his submissions that less able barristers would be unable to carry off." "His performance is consistently stunning in court and with clients. He is firmly established as one of the leading silks in indirect tax matters and the standout choice for matters involving public law issues." **Recent work:** Acted for Telefónica in a VAT case, on roaming charges outside the EU.

39 Essex Chambers

See profile on p.840

THE SET

What it lacks in quantity, 39 Essex Chambers makes up for in the quality of its indirect tax silks. They regularly undertake instructions from HMRC and taxpayers in domestic and European matters, including complex cases in VAT, SDLT and customs and excise duties. They are also well versed in tax mitigation issues.

Client service: "An excellent set with an excellent reputation." "The clerks are fair, reasonable and responsive. That is very much appreciated." David Barnes is the director of clerking at the set.

SILKS

Nigel Pleming QC Considered to be "outstandingly good" by commentators, Pleming is particularly known for his advisory work. He continues to represent HMRC and taxpayers in complex and substantial VAT cases, with a particular focus on tax mitigation issues. **Strengths:** "He is first class." "He is bright and pragmatic, with a strong understanding of local and central government." "He is very well regarded and great to work with." **Recent work:** Represented HMRC before the Court of Appeal in a case concerning the margin of VAT in relation to the sale of cars, in the context of the EU law principle of abuse of rights.

Alison Foster QC (see p.647) Complements her public law practice with her expertise in indirect tax. She has significant experience acting in challenging VAT cases, particularly when representing HMRC. She has previously appeared before the Court of Appeal and the ECJ, and is praised by the market for her ability to combine competition and tax law in her advice. **Strengths:** "She is a very serious heavyweight advocate." "She's great to work with. She's a very, very charming advocate and clients love her."

Timothy Lyons QC Highly experienced in indirect tax law with a noteworthy specialism in international customs matters and EU law. His impressive client roster includes foreign governments, multinational corporations and high-profile individuals with significant net worth. **Strengths:** "He was commercial and produced an excellent work product." "He's brilliant. He wrote the book on customs duty and knows everything about it."

Gray's Inn Tax Chambers

See profile on p.856

THE SET

A specialist tax set handling domestic and international issues, and assisting the Revenue and the taxpayer. The set prides itself not only on its litigation prowess but also on its particularly high standard of advisory work. Members are specifically noted for their expertise in VAT, particularly in terms of the recovery of overpaid tax.

Client service: "They've been very accommodating, they've always tried to meet my expectations, and they're one of my first ports of call when I come to a matter that I need assistance on." "The clerking is very good. Everyone appreciates the pressure that solicitors are under, and are always willing to accommodate our needs on funding or other issues. They make sure the barristers are adequately prepared. You are always reassured that, when you pick up the phone to Gray's Inn Tax Chambers, you are going to get a very good service." The team is led by senior clerk Chris Broom.

SILKS

Nicola Shaw QC Devoting a significant portion of her broad tax practice to indirect tax instructions, she regularly represents taxpayers and HMRC in contentious matters, particularly in the area of VAT. Described as "brilliant" and "impressive" by market observers, she is further lauded for her charismatic advocacy. **Strengths:** "I think she's an excellent advocate, and she is very cool under pressure." "She's really personable, she rolls her sleeves up and works with us and the client in a very collaborative way." **Recent work:** Representing Prescription Eyewear in a case regarding VAT liability of supplies of prescription glasses by internet retailers.

David Goy QC An extremely well-regarded silk singled out for his niche expertise in VAT issues within land and property. He is also well equipped to advise on a vast number of other areas within indirect tax. **Strengths:** "He is utterly charming, delightful and very articulate." "A well-known name on the circuit."

Temple Tax Chambers

See profile on p.921

THE SET

A dedicated tax set with full and varied expertise in indirect tax matters, often representing clients from high-profile and high net worth corporations. Its members are particularly well versed in complex litigation issues within VAT and MTIC frauds, as well as input and output tax issues. Individuals regularly appear before justices in tribunals all the way up to the Supreme Court.

Client service: The clerking team is led by Claire James.

SILKS

Michael Conlon QC (see p.621) Made a much-anticipated return to the Bar in 2015, following his three-year tenure as head of indirect tax at Hogan Lovells. He is known for his vast expertise and impressive depth of knowledge in indirect tax, in particular VAT matters. **Strengths:** "He is very knowledgeable in VAT matters." "If there's something going on in the VAT world, he will know about it." "He is extremely well known."

JUNIORS

Rebecca Murray (see p.724) Leading junior with a broad practice encompassing indirect tax, perhaps best known for her litigation abilities. She regularly represents the taxpayer in substantial VAT cases and also undertakes complex and challenging pro bono work. **Strengths:** "An enthusiastic character." "We have a huge regard for Rebecca Murray." **Recent work:** Acted for Westinsure Group in an appeal concerning the scope of insurance exemption from VAT for a company acting as an intermediary.

Michael Sherry Head of chambers with a wide-ranging practice and a strong interest in indirect tax. He has experience handling VAT matters in relation to private education facilities and distance learning materials, as well as customs and excise duty matters. **Strengths:** "He's very clever, very knowledgeable and he has a very commercial approach."

Other Ranked Lawyers

Sarabjit Singh (1 Crown Office Row) Well-regarded junior who possesses a broad civil practice, which encompasses an in-depth indirect tax expertise. An A-panellist for the Treasury, he is particularly well known for his representation of the Revenue and has previously appeared before the Court of Appeal and the Upper Tribunal. **Strengths:** "He is very good and very able."

Owain Thomas QC (1 Crown Office Row) A new silk already considered to be a "standout" individual at the Bar, combining his tax practice with an impressive public law background. He regularly represents the Revenue and is extremely experienced in handling complex VAT cases, among other matters. **Strengths:** "He is a truly excellent practitioner." "He's very able."

Eleni Mitrophanous (Matrix Chambers) Often represents multinational companies, handling multimillion-pound mandates for international corporations. She is also recognised for her knowledge of EU law. **Strengths:** "She is very able, very personable and a very elegant draftswoman." **Recent work:** Represented HMRC in a case concerning the VAT due regarding the provision of temporary staff to clients.

Jonathan Peacock QC (see p.735) (11 New Square) A "genius" of the Indirect Tax Bar, singled out for his intellectual acumen and his wealth of experience in the area. He regularly advises multinational corporations and high net worth individuals on indirect tax issues, and is particularly well versed in tax mitigation issues. He also regularly provides expert opinions on overseas litigation. **Strengths:** "He has a huge amount of gravitas. He works high-stakes and stressful conferences very astutely and is very thorough." "He is very, very clever, provides excellent advice to the clients and is a very good advocate." **Recent work:** Represented the National Exhibition Centre in a case relating to VAT liability of booking fees and the scope of exemption for payment-handling services.

John Brinsmead-Stockham (see p.603) (11 New Square) A go-to junior for HMRC, he is particularly well equipped to handle complex VAT litigation. He also has extensive experience in managing customs duty cases of impressive complexity. **Strengths:** "He's very capable, very clear and very well informed." **Recent work:** Represented Reed Employment in a case involving the recovery of £60 million worth of VAT overpaid by an employment bureau.

Hui Ling McCarthy (11 New Square) A highly praised up-and-coming junior who is lauded for her dedication to tax matters. She is particularly well known for her expertise in complex, high-value VAT and stamp duty land tax matters. She regularly represents HMRC in some of its most significant indirect tax issues. **Strengths:** "She's diligent, eloquent, intelligent and fascinated by the subject." "She is a phenomenally perceptive junior." **Recent work:** Represented HMRC in a case considering the treatment of SDLT following the sale of Chelsea Barracks by the MoD.

LONDON Private Client

Tax: Private Client	
Leading Sets	
Band 1	
Pump Court Tax Chambers *	
Band 2	
Old Square Tax Chambers *	
Wilberforce Chambers *	
Band 3	
Devereux *	
Field Court Tax Chambers *	
Gray's Inn Tax Chambers *	
5 Stone Buildings *	
Leading Silks	
Star individuals	
Massey William	*Pump Court Tax Chambers* *
Prosser Kevin	*Pump Court Tax Chambers* *
Band 1	
Kessler James	*Old Square Tax Chambers* *
McCall Christopher	*Maitland Chambers (ORL)* ◊ *
Band 2	
Ewart David	*Pump Court Tax Chambers* *
Flesch Michael	*Gray's Inn Tax Chambers*
Ghosh Julian	*Pump Court Tax Chambers* *
Green Brian	*Wilberforce Chambers*
Band 3	
Furness Michael	*Wilberforce Chambers*
Hardy Amanda	*Old Square Tax Chambers* *
New Silks	
Davey Jonathan	*Wilberforce Chambers*

* *Indicates set / individual with profile.*
🄰 *direct access (see p.24).*
◊ *(ORL) = Other Ranked Lawyer.*
Alphabetical order within each band. Band 1 is highest.

Tax: Private Client	
Leading Juniors	
Star individuals	
Chamberlain Emma	*Pump Court Tax Chambers* 🄰 *
Band 1	
Nathan Aparna	*Devereux* *
Rivett James	*Pump Court Tax Chambers* *
Whitehouse Christopher	*5 Stone Buildings* *
Wilson Elizabeth	*Pump Court Tax Chambers* *
Band 2	
Lemos Marika	*Devereux* *
Soares Patrick	*Field Court Tax Chambers* *
Vallat Richard	*Pump Court Tax Chambers* 🄰 *
Band 3	
Afzal Imran	*Field Court Tax Chambers* *
Akin Barrie	*Devereux*
Poots Laura	*Pump Court Tax Chambers* 🄰 *
Richards Ian	*Pump Court Tax Chambers* *
Sartin Leon	*5 Stone Buildings* *

Band 1

Pump Court Tax Chambers
See profile on p.899

THE SET

Pump Court is a well-known personal tax and private client set that has particular expertise in offshore and onshore trust reorganisations and inheritance tax, and is a leader in employee benefit trusts. The team has experience of advising on entrepreneur's, business property and agricultural property relief. Pump Court's broad group consists of 22 barristers, eight of whom are silks.

Client service: "A leading set. The first people I would think of going to for private client tax. Beyond their expertise, the administration of the set is great; the clerks are very user-friendly and efficient. It's a slick operation." Nigel Jones is the head clerk.

SILKS

William Massey QC (see p.709) A leading silk in the Private Client Tax Bar, who is extremely experienced in a variety of areas, including tax and estate planning, agricultural property, BPR and APR. He has represented clients in the High Court and Supreme Court. He continues to grow his practice in matrimonial finance-related work. **Strengths:** "Famously 'the best in town' when it comes to tax and landed estates." "He is very masterful when it comes to dealing with the taxation issues affecting landed estates. To find a QC who can steer you around the law is absolutely essential, and Massey is one of the most capable landed estate tax barristers." **Recent work:** He provided beneficiaries with an opinion on the Variation of Trusts Act 1958 and successfully argued an extension of a trust period does not amount to a new settlement for tax purposes.

Kevin Prosser QC (see p.744) His reputation and expertise lie in highly complex and litigious personal tax and income tax cases. He is increasingly representing individuals in cases relating to tax avoidance schemes. **Strengths:** "Kevin is exceptional. His drafting is superb and he picks up points very quickly in conference." "He is able to explain difficult concepts well, and is very persuasive. In addition to being very smart and knowing his way around tax, he gives practical guidance but can translate that convincingly and clearly in a court setting." **Recent work:** He represented UBS on an income tax issue relating to receiving shares in a company as bonuses.

David Ewart QC (see p.642) As an accomplished private client tax practitioner, he advises clients on trust legislation, BPR and inheritance tax planning. **Strengths:** "He is technically a superstar – pragmatic, thorough and imaginative." "He is sensible, approachable, down-to-earth, low-key but clearly intelligent." **Recent work:** He represented Andrew Chappell, who claimed a deduction for overseas manufactured dividends which was challenged by HMRC.

Julian Ghosh QC (see p.651) A QC in England and Scotland, he advises the taxpayer and Revenue on personal tax matters; he has a particular expertise in BPR and APR work. **Strengths:** "He really is excellent, superb." **Recent work:** He represented a US LLC client on its right to not pay UK income tax on profits as a result of double tax relief.

JUNIORS

Emma Chamberlain (see p.614) Her practice focuses on private client tax, on matters such as trust reorganisation, the structuring of offshore trusts and companies, and IHT and CGT planning for UK-domiciled clients. Personal tax issues on divorce and employee benefit matters increasingly feature in her caseload. **Strengths:** "She is the pre-eminent expert on all matters to do with tax of trusts and offshore trusts. She is top of the tree for that – an absolute star." "She has extensive knowledge of the field and you know if you get an opinion from her, it's going to be very difficult for the Revenue to argue against it." **Recent work:** Continued to represent a client in a residential dispute pertaining to time spent in Monaco.

Elizabeth Wilson (see p.797) Advises and litigates on IHT, CGT and offshore trust planning, and assists non-domiciliaries on planning matters. She also has experience of advising on tax-efficient investment vehicles such as partnerships and trust structures. **Recent work:** Represented a client on the exemption of inheritance from IHT, and specifically argued the transaction was not a transfer of value.

James Rivett (see p.753) An impressive personal tax junior, he advises HMRC and private client firms on tax issues, including innovative trusts techniques. He represents landed estates on BPR, APR and IHT matters. **Strengths:** "I would swear by him. He can master the most arcane areas of tax law and create a road map of how you get from A to B. He is particularly good with non-domicile clients." "We really appreciate how nimble he is. He takes it all in his stride. He's really fantastic." **Recent work:** Relitigated the Shiner & Sheinman v HMRC case in the First-tier Tribunal, regarding retrospective application of UK legislation in relation to personal rights under EU law.

Richard Vallat (see p.786) An experienced advocate advising clients on IHT, CGT, offshore trust estate planning and income tax matters. His practice sees him representing HMRC in alleged tax avoidance cases. **Strengths:** "He is highly knowledgeable. He has the advantage that he understands the corporate side of things, so is a reliable pair of hands." "He is completely charming outside court, and formidable as opposition once you cross through the door. He is clever and high quality – a strong tax litigator." **Recent work:** Represented HMRC on a late filing penalty relating to a self-assessment tax form. Successfully argued the wording in the form could be considered "proper notice."

Laura Poots (see p.740) Focuses her practice on personal tax issues, including offshore tax structures and family partnerships aimed at minimising exposure to IHT, CGT and other taxes. She represents HMRC on tax issues with increasing regularity. **Strengths:** "She's a delight. She's very much to the point, she's clear, concise and makes things pretty easy." "She is excellent on response times, and very knowledgeable on private client." **Recent work:** Represented HMRC on personal tax issues related to an owner-managed property company.

Ian Richards (see p.751) Significant experience representing a broad range of private clients, including ultra high net worth individuals, international sporting individuals and entertainers. He assists his clients with residency status matters, offshore trusts and techniques to preserve and protect wealth and future gains.

Band 2

Old Square Tax Chambers

See profile on p.918

THE SET

The set possesses expertise representing many national and international ultra high net worth clients in advisory and litigious capacities. The barristers assist with private client tax matters such as trusts, inheritance tax and high-profile divorce cases. **Client service:** "I find the clerks very good: they're very helpful and always willing to assist you and guide you to the right person. It is a very well-run chambers." Tony Hall is the senior clerk at the set.

SILKS

James Kessler QC (see p.690) Head of chambers James Kessler QC is an experienced practitioner in the areas of trusts, wills and charities. He has notable experience advising non-domiciliaries on their tax affairs. **Strengths:** "He is a very strong practitioner. He is known for his excellent academic work on drafting." "I rate his intellect and I have a great deal of respect for him."

Amanda Hardy QC (see p.663) Continues to represent clients in litigation, which include trusts and tax aspects in divorce. She assists with individuals' personal tax planning and has expertise in pension taxation, as well as offshore domicile and residency issues. **Strengths:** "Amanda Hardy has been providing exceptionally good tax advice. She has excellent writing skills and she has provided clear, concise advice." "She is very practical and good with clients – she commands their attention. She's direct and to the point but also very good at getting to the nuance of what a client wants."

Wilberforce Chambers

See profile on p.925

THE SET

Barristers at this set are adept at dealing with highly complex offshore trusts, estate and inheritance tax planning matters. Its members represent private clients in a range of litigious personal tax disputes. **Client service:** "The clerking is superb and obviously top-notch. They've worked on that to make sure it's an easy and friendly system." The head clerk is Mark Rushton.

SILKS

Brian Green QC An experienced private client and chancery barrister, Green advises on trusts and estates as well as pension tax issues. Strengths: "The brilliant thing is his ability to see through complex matters; he is ingenious and very creative. His writing is clear and his drafting is clever." "He has been an absolute gem: he has given amazing advice and is coming up with great solutions."

Michael Furness QC Experienced in advising private clients and the Revenue on personal tax and inheritance matters. He also represents clients on offshore trust and tax litigation. **Strengths:** "He is a good technician." **Recent work:** Advised on a range of issues relating to film scheme reliefs.

Jonathan Davey QC Having taken silk in 2016, Jonathan Davey QC has expertise representing high net worth clients in complex private tax matters. His practice also sees him representing the Crown in personal tax disputes. **Strengths:** "He's very good: personable and on the ball. He's a real team player. He was a pleasure to work with." "He has been extremely impressive."

Band 3

Devereux

See profile on p.827

THE SET

Devereux's barristers advise and litigate complex, cross-border private client tax matters. Inheritance tax, capital gains tax and income tax are all areas the set has expertise in. The set's practice also encompasses UK and international tax and trusts issues relating to charities and relevant donations. **Client service:** "The clerks were great. They were on the ball all the time, and went the extra mile to make sure the barrister was always on hand. They have one clerk allocated to a case – it's streamlined." The head clerk is Vince Plant.

JUNIORS

Aparna Nathan (see p.725) An adept barrister with well-established advisory and litigation practices. She has particular expertise in revenue law, offshore structures and tax planning for UK and non-UK domiciled entrepreneurs. **Strengths:** "She's always delightful to deal with. She gives very good, practical commercial advice. Inheritance tax is her particular strength." "Every opinion has the rigour of being extremely well prepared. She's very thorough and exhaustive on tax analysis; she gives good, robust views." **Recent work:** Represented HMRC in the Court of Appeal on the interpretation of procedural provisions for loss of claims.

Marika Lemos (see p.699) Advises a broad client base, including individuals, trustees and public bodies, on private client tax matters. She is highly experienced in international and offshore trust litigation. **Strengths:** "She is absolutely brilliant and extremely nice. She writes a very good letter, which will be technical but very readable and understandable. She provides clear advice in an approachable manner." "Her attention to detail is unbelievably good; if you are missing anything she will bring it to light."

Barrie Akin A former chartered tax accountant, Barrie Akin has a unique perspective on tax matters. His practice includes advising foreign and domestic high net worth individuals on capital gains tax planning, including the use of residency rules. He has represented clients against HMRC on offshore trust and tax disputes. **Strengths:** "His knowledge is fantastic, as he was ex-Revenue before he went to the Bar. He is also very accessible." "He has a brilliant mind in terms of tax planning. Not only does he have an amazing understanding, but he has the number-crunching accountancy style. He is absolutely excellent."

Field Court Tax Chambers

See profile on p.844

THE SET

Field Court has a broad client base ranging from governments and multinational enterprises to high net worth individuals and celebrities. Its expertise extends to international matters, with some members having appeared in foreign court proceedings. **Client service:** "I rate the practice managers at Field Court very highly. They are the best clerks of any chambers I work with. They manage cases exceptionally well, and are easy and personable to get on with." Marie Burke is the set's practice manager, and Stephanie Talbot is the assistant practice manager.

JUNIORS

Patrick Soares (see p.770) Head of chambers Patrick Soares is frequently called on to represent both private clients and HMRC on international and domestic private client tax matters. **Strengths:** "He has a malleable mind to think around problems and to make very interesting tax structures."

Imran Afzal (see p.580) Possesses knowledge on international and domestic tax matters. He represents high-profile clients on litigious matters, and has appeared before domestic and foreign courts. **Strengths:** "He is a very bright man. He is wise beyond his years in terms of knowledge of the law, judgement and how to take particular matters forward." "He is a very talented lawyer and very clever." **Recent work:** Represented HMRC in the Icebreaker case and on whether partnership members could claim tax relief as a result of partnership losses.

Gray's Inn Tax Chambers

See profile on p.856

THE SET

Gray's Inn's private client work has seen its barristers represent clients in UK and Hong Kong courts. Members draw on their expertise in personal and business tax to represent both the Revenue and taxpayers, including high net worth individuals and entrepreneurs. They also frequently advise non-domiciled individuals on estate planning and residence issues.

Client service: "The clerks are absolutely fantastic. They're flexible and nothing is too much trouble. Chris Broom is fantastic - very social and very approachable." Chris Broom is the senior clerk.

SILKS

Michael Flesch QC An experienced practitioner adept in representing UK and non-UK domiciled clients on private client tax matters. He has strong litigation and advisory practices. **Strengths:** "He is exceptional and top of the line. He just gives fantastic advice." "He is a really wonderful private client silk. A very good, charming guy."

5 Stone Buildings

See profile on p.914

THE SET

Members of this well-known chancery set are frequently called on to represent clients in advisory and litigious capacities. The set's broad private client taxation offering extends to trusts, inheritance tax and pension matters.

Client service: "The head clerk Paul Jennings is particularly good at making sure of responses and keeping us informed."

JUNIORS

Christopher Whitehouse (see p.794) A leading junior whose expertise lies in tax, trusts and estates work. He also has experience in APR and BPR claims for farmhouses and landed estates. **Strengths:** "He is exceptionally bright and understands the complexities of landowning trusts." "Landed estate work and the Settled Land Act is a rarefied area that he is big in. He always gives incredibly good advice."

Leon Sartin (see p.759) Possesses a broad chancery practice. His expertise includes trusts, tax and inheritance planning, and he acts for clients in both advisory and litigious capacities. His practice includes professional negligence and Court of Protection work. **Strengths:** "His analysis is extremely good, he's practical and his application is even better. He gets down to what things really mean in practice, and doesn't leave you with just one page of theory." "He is calm and has a nice amount of gravity, people listen to him."

Other Ranked Lawyers

Christopher McCall QC (see p.711) (Maitland Chambers) A highly experienced tax barrister known for advising private individuals on trusts and tax law. He has particular experience with the planning of trusts upon divorce. **Strengths:** "He is thorough, pleasant and very careful."

THE REGIONS

Tax	
Leading Juniors	
Band 1	
Bridge Ian	*No5 Chambers*
Graham-Wells Alison	*St John's Chambers* *
Puzey James	*St Philips Chambers* *
Rowell George	*St John's Chambers*

** Indicates individual with profile.*

Alphabetical order within each band. Band 1 is highest.

Other Ranked Lawyers

Ian Bridge (No5 Chambers in Birmingham) Leverages his background in civil and criminal fraud matters to provide skilful representation in VAT and excise duties cases. He is further noted for his experience handling tax issues in connection with insurance premiums and construction projects. **Strengths:** "He is very tenacious and committed." **Recent work:** Acted on behalf of several construction companies in cases against HMRC regarding VAT assessment and penalties related to fraudulent VAT losses.

Alison Graham-Wells (see p.658) (St John's Chambers) Has a broad commercial chancery practice and noteworthy experience of handling tax-related litigation. Her recent cases include acting for private clients on matters pertaining to inheritance tax, tax avoidance schemes and VAT returns. **Strengths:** "She is a very tenacious and skilled courtroom advocate." **Recent work:** Acted on behalf of the taxpayer in Mr Robert Huitson v HMRC, appealing entitlement to trust income.

George Rowell (St John's Chambers) Highly recommended for his extensive experience of handling tax disputes, especially those involving VAT, PAYE and inheritance tax. He is frequently instructed on behalf of both taxpayers and HMRC. **Strengths:** "He is an impressive and persuasive advocate who is quick on his feet." **Recent work:** Continues to represent HMRC in a long-standing VAT appeal related to denied input tax of more than £7 million.

James Puzey (see p.745) (St Philips Chambers in Birmingham) Highly reputed for his expertise in indirect tax matters, he is especially well known for his work on VAT, excise and duty cases. He is regularly engaged on cases connected to MTIC fraud, and is an expert on the seizure and restoration of goods. **Strengths:** "He is well regarded for his experience and commitment to hard work." **Recent work:** Provided counsel on behalf of the taxpayer in Fonecomp Ltd v HMRC, a Court of Appeal case related to MTIC VAT fraud.

Telecommunications

Contents:

LONDON

Telecommunications
Leading Sets
Band 1
Blackstone Chambers *
Monckton Chambers *
Band 2
Brick Court Chambers *
Leading Silks
Band 1
Beard Daniel *Monckton Chambers*
Carss-Frisk Monica *Blackstone Chambers*
Rose Dinah *Blackstone Chambers*
Saini Pushpinder *Blackstone Chambers*
Turner Jon *Monckton Chambers*
Band 2
Crow Jonathan *4 Stone Buildings (ORL)* ◊ *
de la Mare Thomas *Blackstone Chambers*
Herberg Javan *Blackstone Chambers*
Lowenstein Paul *3 Verulam Buildings (ORL)* ◊
Pannick David *Blackstone Chambers*
Read Graham *Devereux (ORL)* ◊ *
Ward Tim *Monckton Chambers* [A] *
Levy Juliette *Cerulean Chambers (ORL)* ◊
Band 3
Bacon Kelyn *Brick Court Chambers*
Beal Kieron *Blackstone Chambers*
Charlton Alex *4 Pump Court (ORL)* ◊ *
Demetriou Marie *Brick Court Chambers*
Howe Timothy *Fountain Court Chambers (ORL)* ◊ *
Pickford Meredith *Monckton Chambers* [A]
Smith Kassie *Monckton Chambers*
Thompson Rhodri *Matrix Chambers (ORL)* ◊
New Silks
Facenna Gerry *Monckton Chambers* [A] *
Kennelly Brian *Blackstone Chambers*
Lee Sarah *Brick Court Chambers*
* *Indicates set / individual with profile.*
[A] *direct access (see p.24).*
◊ *(ORL) = Other Ranked Lawyer.*
Alphabetical order within each band. Band 1 is highest.

Telecommunications
Leading Juniors
Band 1
Holmes Josh *Monckton Chambers*
Segan James *Blackstone Chambers*
Woolfe Philip *Monckton Chambers* *
Band 2
Bates Alan *Monckton Chambers* [A] *
Chapple Malcolm *New Square Chambers (ORL)* ◊
Ford Sarah *Brick Court Chambers*
Howard Anneli *Monckton Chambers* [A] *
Jones Tristan *Blackstone Chambers*
Lazarus Michael *3 Verulam Buildings (ORL)* ◊ *
Lynch Ben *Fountain Court Chambers (ORL)* ◊ *
O'Donoghue Robert *Brick Court Chambers*
Palmer Robert *Monckton Chambers* [A]
Band 3
Gibson Nicholas *Matrix Chambers (ORL)* ◊
Lask Ben *Monckton Chambers* [A]
Lavy Matthew *4 Pump Court (ORL)* ◊ *
Mussa Hanif *Blackstone Chambers*
Richards Tom *Blackstone Chambers*
Vinall Mark *Blackstone Chambers*
Up-and-coming individuals
Hirsch Georgina *Devereux (ORL)* ◊

Band 1

Blackstone Chambers

See profile on p.813

THE SET

A top-notch set with a commanding reputation in the telecoms sector, Blackstone offers an impressive array of barristers with telecoms expertise and is the set of choice for operators and regulatory bodies alike. A public law powerhouse, it is known for its regulatory expertise in particular. Standout work for the set has involved key issues such as Ethernet charges, net neutrality and network sharing arrangements, and recent prominent cases have included Lebara Mobile v Lycamobile UK, TalkTalk v Ofcom and Vodafone v British Telecommunications.

Client service: "The clerks are incredibly helpful and make every effort to be accommodating." "They are always professional and take a lot of pride in the work they do." The clerking team is led by the very experienced, highly respected and well-liked Gary Oliver.

SILKS

Monica Carss-Frisk QC Has a superb reputation in the telecoms sectors, and impresses with her calm and composed manner in court. **Strengths:** "She is extremely capable and very good at dealing with difficult clients." "She is very persuasive and judges like her as she's calm, logical and effective." **Recent work:** Acted in Recall Support Services Ltd v Secretary of State for Culture, Media and Sport, appearing for number of claimants in a large 'Francovich' damages claim.

Dinah Rose QC An outstanding barrister with a ferocious intellect who is known for her likeability among clients. She is particularly well versed in telecoms regulatory matters. **Strengths:** "A truly exceptional barrister who is a treat to instruct. Her formidable reputation is thoroughly deserved." "She will really muck in on every aspect of the case and is a formidable advocate." **Recent work:** Represented Cable & Wireless and other network operators in an appeal concerning overcharging by BT for Ethernet services.

Pushpinder Saini QC Highly reputed for his work on the intersection between telecoms issues and EU and competition law, he is one of the counsels of choice for Ofcom. **Strengths:** "He's an excellent advocate who always comes across as totally reasonable, which is a real plus-point." **Recent work:** Represented the government in BASCA v Secretary of State, a case regarding a challenge to the introduction of the private copying exception.

Thomas de la Mare QC A strong competition lawyer who is regularly instructed in telecoms regulatory matters. He is highly praised for his creative approach to complex issues. **Strengths:** "He has a quick brain, is robust in his advice and always a gentleman." "He is able to grasp complex issues, come up with very pragmatic advice, and take a very business-friendly approach." **Recent work:** Advised Lebara in a case with Lyca surrounding Lyca customers' access to Lebara's website and services. The dispute covered issues including net neutrality, consumer protection and data protection.

Javan Herberg QC Gifted silk noted for being a go-to counsel for Ofcom. He is commended for his personable manner with clients and business-friendly approach to matters. **Strengths:** "He is a statesman-like silk with dashes of charm and humility." "He is understated but very clever. You can rely on him to explore different angles and he's very easy to work with." **Recent work:** Represented Ofcom in a case relating to BT's tiered pricing of non-geographic numbers.

David Pannick QC A towering authority when it comes to administrative and public law, he is as strong on telecoms regulatory matters as he is in the many other fields he practises in. **Strengths:** "Always brilliant to work with, he's very approachable, very clever, very practical and highly pragmatic." **Recent work:** Furnished HKT with advice on a telecoms-related judicial law review in Hong Kong.

Kieron Beal QC Noted for being an affable lawyer who provides pertinent and on-point advice. He has a fine reputation in the EU and competition sector. **Strengths:** "He's responsive and knows his stuff when it comes to telecoms and judicial reviews. He's personable, easy to deal with and flexible." **Recent work:** Represented Sky as intervener in a Competition Appeal Tribunal (CAT) appeal relating to the BT and TalkTalk v Ofcom case. The case concerned issues surrounding BT's supply of wholesale VULA services.

Brian Kennelly QC Newly appointed silk who is highly regarded for both his in-depth knowledge of the telecoms regulatory sphere and his client-friendly manner. **Strengths:** "There is no bluster with Brian, only crystal clear, expertly delivered explanation and interpretations of cases, presented with a strong persuasive edge." "He is absolutely brilliant and very highly regarded by clients." **Recent work:** Successfully persuaded Ofcom to delay the release of public sector spectrum until the Three/O2 merger decision had been taken by the EC.

JUNIORS

James Segan A talented junior noted for his dexterity handling cases concerning the interface between IP and telecoms. He furnishes advice on a range of FRAND and net neutrality cases, among others. **Strengths:** "A brilliant advocate with very clear thought processes. He's a real pleasure to work with." **Recent work:** Obtained a mandatory injunction from the High Court on behalf of Packet Media which ensured that O2 continued its service pending an abuse of dominance case.

Tristan Jones A dedicated and conscientious junior with great writing skills and a wealth of experience of acting for telecoms regulatory bodies. **Strengths:** "He is bright, sensible and easy to get on with." "A very practical, hard-working junior who handles clients extremely well." **Recent work:** Acted for Ofcom in both BT's and TalkTalk's appeals to the CAT regarding their 'Fixed Access Market Review'.

Hanif Mussa Well versed in acting for telecoms regulatory bodies and operators. He is appreciated by solicitors for his strong drafting skills and the excellence of his client relations. **Strengths:** "He is very smart, very savvy and very presentable." **Recent work:** Represented Telecom2 as sole counsel in cases relating to termination charges for calls on networks of a number of mobile operators.

Tom Richards Impressive junior with a strong track record on cases pertaining to mobile spectrum licensing. Sources extol his clear and eloquent style of communication. **Strengths:** "He is very user-friendly, very helpful and very timely in his advice. He has a clear drafting style as well, which is very important when you're dealing with technical telecoms issues." "He's very decisive, very bright and very thorough. He's also very eloquent and gets to the issues quickly."

Mark Vinall Elicits praise for his work as a go-to junior for Ofcom. He demonstrates particular skill in telecoms regulatory matters with competition and EU law aspects. **Strengths:** "An extremely competent junior who obviously knows the telecoms industry very well." "He's very competent and certainly has the technical expertise." **Recent work:** Represented Ofcom as sole counsel in CAT proceedings relating to non-geographic numbers.

Monckton Chambers

See profile on p.877

THE SET

This dynamic set is lauded for its impressive track record in prominent cases in the telecoms sector. A first choice for many blue-chip operators in the telecoms space, Monckton Chambers bolsters its offering with a wealth of experience in the EU and competition sphere. Significant cases for the set of late have included Telefonica O2 and Others v BT in the 08 numbers appeals, and TalkTalk and BT v Ofcom, which related to VULA appeals.

Client service: "The clerks are always very good there, which takes a lot of the pain out of matters." David Hockney leads the team.

SILKS

Daniel Beard QC A leading market authority on competition law who brings his expertise to bear in telecoms cases for both public and private entities. Solicitors extol his ability to distil complex technical telecoms issues into clear, persuasive arguments. **Strengths:** "He has the ability to focus in on one or two intuitive points for the judges. Dan is very good at encapsulating your case in one neat idea, which is very useful." **Recent work:** Represented the Home Secretary in a claim by telecoms companies that the government had mis-implemented EU law.

Jon Turner QC Multi-talented silk endorsed as a counsel of choice for high-end mobile operators faced with telecoms regulatory litigation. Sources enthuse about his top-notch client skills. **Strengths:** "He's quite fearless in that he will take difficult points on, and he enjoys the thrill of trying to get judges to change their minds on something difficult." "Jon is brilliant: he's incredibly clever and a great advocate." **Recent work:** Instructed by Samsung in patent infringement litigation concerning mobile phone technology.

Tim Ward QC (see p.789) Counsel of choice for a variety of mobile and fixed-line telecoms operators. He draws upon his expertise in EU and public law to provide a comprehensive assessment of telecoms matters for clients. **Strengths:** "A very adept and able strategist who is decisive and who consistently delivers sound and forthright advice." "A very accessible barrister, he is fantastic at getting into the detail and is very good in front of clients." **Recent work:** Represented Telefonica O2 as lead counsel in BT v Ofcom, a case regarding non-geographic number charges.

Kassie Smith QC Has a wealth of experience in cases pertaining to the interplay between IP and telecoms. Sources are highly complimentary of her affable manner and approachability. **Strengths:** "She has a clarity and focus about her in court which brings simplicity to the complex." "She's very clever, extremely talented and very user-friendly." **Recent work:** Acted for Huawei in Unwired Planet v Huawei Technologies, Samsung Electronics and Google. The dispute concerned an abuse of dominance claim in relation to standard essential patents.

Meredith Pickford QC Wins plaudits for his user-friendly approach and impressive advocacy skills. Solicitors consider his background in economics to be a key advantage when he provides telecoms regulatory advice. **Strengths:** "It's a technical and specialist field and he gets to grip with it easily." "He's very good at cross-examining technical experts." **Recent work:** Acted for Samsung in Unwired Planet v Samsung and Huawei, a case relating to FRAND issues.

Gerry Facenna QC (see p.643) New silk highlighted for his strong track record in the Phonepay Plus litigation. Aside from telecoms expertise, he is adept at both data protection and environment law. **Strengths:** "He is truly superb in all aspects of the job. He's obscenely clever, a great strategist and a superb advocate. He reads the situation perfectly and is a commercially aware perfectionist." **Recent work:** Acted for Optimus Mobile and Oranduu in a judicial review challenge to the regulatory framework used by Phonepay Plus.

JUNIORS

Josh Holmes An attractive choice for both regulators and operators in the telecoms sector. He boasts a standout reputation in competition law and has experience of acting for major players at a national and international level. **Strengths:** "He is outstanding and incredibly good to work with. He's ultra-sensible and you know you'll end up with a case that is really well thought through." "An absolute gentleman and a very able advocate." **Recent work:** Instructed by Ofcom in a case against BT pertaining to charges for superfast broadband products.

Philip Woolfe (see p.800) Well versed at handling telecoms cases before the CAT and Court of Appeal. He is highly endorsed for his strong work ethic and hands-on approach to cases. **Strengths:** "An absolutely fantastic junior who is extremely bright and knowledgeable about telecoms. He works well with a range of QCs." "He's very energetic and turns the paperwork around very quickly." **Recent work:** Acted for EE, Vodafone and O2 in CAT appeals in relation to BT's non-geographic number charges.

Alan Bates (see p.591) Telecoms regulation remains a key area of expertise for a lawyer who also has strong suits in public law generally and utilities regulation in particular. Solicitors point to level-headedness and attention to detail as being his key attributes. **Strengths:** "He's really intelligent but very unassuming; it's very interesting seeing him as an advocate. He has a diffident manner but is actually extremely forceful." **Recent work:** Acted for Sky in a dispute with Ofcom pertaining to BT's duty to supply competitors with wholesale access to broadband for retail customers.

Anneli Howard (see p.675) A diligent junior with a strong awareness of commercial considerations. Clients appreciate her personable manner and comprehensive approach to cases. **Strengths:** "She is very hard-working, ferociously bright and she really does do a great job at getting the client's case in the best possible order." "She understands the commercial realities of our business, the rationale of our objective and the wider environments in which we work." **Recent work:** Advised BT on its response to OFCOM's discussion document on digital communications.

Robert Palmer Enjoys a strong track record in Ofcom appeals and cases in front of the CAT and Administrative Court. His command of EU and competition law makes him a popular choice for operators embroiled in regulatory disputes. **Strengths:** "His technical skill and knowledge of competition and EU law are very good." "He's a very highly thought-of junior who will continue to thrive." **Recent work:** Represented BT in a dispute with Ofcom over the decision to limit charges for the provision of number portability services to other providers.

Ben Lask Offers expertise across a whole gamut of regulatory, commercial and contractual telecoms issues. He is noted particularly for his work for major operators before the CAT. **Strengths:** "He is very responsive, very commercial and able to manage difficult clients. He provides clear advice and is always at the end of the phone when we need to speak to him." "Ben is very clear, methodical and thoughtful in his advice." **Recent work:** Represented Naka AG in a commercial dispute with Cloud 9 Mobile Communications pertaining to the sale of airtime for mobile phone calls.

Band 2

Brick Court Chambers

See profile on p.816

THE SET

A robust set particularly well regarded for its strength in handling the commercial side of telecoms cases, Brick Court Chambers has a strong reputation for acting on behalf of private companies in competition-related telecoms disputes. Its members regularly act for operators and regulatory bodies both national and internationally, covering jurisdictions including Hong Kong, Ireland, Mauritius and Slovakia, to name but a few. Its work highlights of late include BT v Ofcom (the Ethernet appeals), Vodafone v Infineon (the smart card chips cartel) and Lebara v Lycamobile, a net neutrality case.

Client service: "The set has small armies of clerks to handle your matters expertly." Ian Moyler and Julian Hawes lead the team.

SILKS

Kelyn Bacon QC A true telecoms expert who handles everything from competition law to intellectual property issues, she is recognised for her work for telecoms operators. **Strengths:** "She's got a terrific brain and is good under seige."

Marie Demetriou QC Acts for telecoms operators in a range of matters involving competition, EU and administrative and public law. **Strengths:** "She's jolly good and does a lot of telecoms work." "A very able advocate." **Recent work:** Represented Philips Electronics in Vodafone v Infineon, a case which arose after the EC found a cartel in the telecoms smart card chips market.

Sarah Lee QC Newly appointed silk who is a go-to counsel for BT in appeals against Ofcom and in the CAT. She is highly respected for her commercial awareness and in-depth consideration of business objectives. **Strengths:** "She's very passionate, very involved in cases and understands the commercial aspects incredibly well. She grasps our objectives and is able to come up with the key arguments." "Phenomenally hard-working and phenomenally bright." **Recent work:** Instructed by BT in relation to Gamma v Ofcom, a case concerning cost orientation obligations.

JUNIORS

Sarah Ford Admired by silks and solicitors as a gifted junior in the telecoms sector who is recognised for her work in front of the CAT in particular. **Strengths:** "A great all-round barrister who has done a number of telecoms cases and knows how to put her client's case across." "An outstanding junior whose drafting is really excellent. She possesses extremely good judgement and is very sensible and down-to-earth." **Recent work:** Instructed by Unwired Planet in a telecoms patent enforcement case.

Robert O'Donoghue Very highly regarded for his work on a variety of cases pertaining to mobile termination rates, as well as net neutrality. Sources point to his understanding of both telecoms regulations and competition law as being his key attributes. **Strengths:** "Extremely impressive and an absolute pleasure to work with. He's incredibly hard-working, highly intelligent and articulate, and has a great grasp of the economic arguments." "A very thorough adviser who knows case law inside out." **Recent work:** Represented Lycamobile in Lebara v Lycamobile, a case concerning net neutrality rules and the interplay with traditional tort.

Other Ranked Lawyers

Juliette Levy QC (Cerulean Chambers) A prominent figure acting for service providers in contentious network sharing and telephone mast cases. She is admired by interviewees for her depth of knowledge, attention to detail and client-friendly manner. **Strengths:** "She's very user-friendly, pragmatic and unbelievably dedicated – the full package." "Blessed with really good technical knowledge, she was very quick to think of answers to the client's wacky questions. Her ability to turn a technical area into something easy to understand is highly impressive."

Graham Read QC (see p.749) (Devereux) Commercial disputes between telecoms operators consitute a core area of expertise, and he is admired by sources for his wealth of experience in the sector. Read is particularly noted for his work with BT. **Strengths:** "He has incredible telecoms expertise and knows our business inside out." "He's personable and knowledgeable and has a lot of valuable experience. He's also very bright and easy to work with." **Recent work:** Instructed by BT in litigation with Funeven concerning the valuation of wayleaves.

Georgina Hirsch (Devereux) Brings to bear 15 years' experience as a solicitor. She acts on behalf of operators in disputes in the CAT regarding telecoms regulatory and competition matters. **Strengths:** "She's extremely likeable and a really excellent team player." "She's very diligent and very good at researching."

Timothy Howe QC (see p.676) of Fountain Court Chambers Particularly strong on the commercial and joint venture side of telecoms work but also an expert in cases with a competition and/or regulatory dimension. He regularly leads large litigation teams in telecoms related disputes and is known for his industrious and collegiate approach to his work. **Strengths:** "A great choice for big ticket commercial work." **Recent work:** Acted in Piksel v Filmflex, a high value dispute between competitors in the hi-tech Video On Demand market.

Ben Lynch (see p.704) (Fountain Court Chambers) Endorsed for his experience in commercial telecoms litigation, particularly in artificial inflation of traffic (AIT) cases. Silks point to him as an industrious and approachable junior of choice. **Strengths:** "He's incredibly hard-working and gets into the detail incredibly well. He is really able to distil the evidence down to its key parts and apply it to our objectives. He's very good at unusual arguments and can think outside of the box." "He is an extremely diligent and hard-working person who is very popular." **Recent work:** Instructed as sole counsel to BT in an AIT dispute with major mobile network operators.

Rhodri Thompson QC (Matrix Chambers) His expertise in EU and competition law along with regulatory financial matters make him a counsel of choice for major telecoms operators in a range of matters within the sector. He attracts praise as a particularly convincing advocate. **Strengths:** "He's a charming and effective advocate with very good experience. His clients clearly love him. He commands significant respect and is a well-established name." "He has a sharp intellect and a deep understanding of the telecoms framework, and is very good at applying that detail to the argument." **Recent work:** Instructed by BT in BT v Ofcom VULA, a case concerning BT's charges to competitors for superfast broadband.

Nicholas Gibson (Matrix Chambers) Assists both public and private sector companies on contentious regulatory, competition and commercial mandates pertaining to the telecoms industry. He is well versed in acting before the CAT and Court of Appeals. **Strengths:** "He picks up a heavy workload and is a big asset to the case." "He provides good commercial, pragmatic advice." **Recent work:** Furnished advice as sole counsel to BT on potential ways to challenge Ofcom's statement on porting charges.

Malcolm Chapple (New Square Chambers) Highly respected for his advice on contractual disputes and intellectual property infringement cases between major telecoms operators. **Strengths:** "He's a very effective advocate and very good overall." "He's extremely knowledgeable on telecoms matters." **Recent work:** Advised Truancy Call on internet and telephone network service agreements with schools and public organisations.

Alex Charlton QC (see p.615) (4 Pump Court) A commanding figure in the IT landscape who has great telecoms expertise. He acts for major operators in contractual cases dealing with issues ranging from network sharing agreements to facilities management. **Strengths:** "He likes getting his hands dirty and really gets stuck into the issues." "Leads the case from the start and takes a pragmatic and incisive approach." **Recent work:** Instructed by EE in a dispute with Mundio Mobile concerning the terms of a wholesale telecommunications supply agreement.

Matthew Lavy (see p.696) (4 Pump Court) Comes recommended for his commercial telecoms offering, and acts on high-end disputes relating to telecoms systems. He is especially impressive on cases involving the interplay between IT and telecoms software. **Strengths:** "He's brilliantly clever and gets to things very quickly. He's very funny and affable too." "He's an extremely gifted junior on the commercial side of things." **Recent work:** Advised EE in a contractual dispute with T-Systems following the transformation of Orange and T-mobile into a single estate.

Jonathan Crow QC (see p.627) (4 Stone Buildings) A gifted silk whose telecoms offering is matched by his expertise in the financial, commercial and administrative spheres, among others. **Strengths:** "He's very well versed on the regulatory side. He's had a stellar career and is a wonderful bloke who is an absolutely fantastic advocate." "He's an excellent, top-notch advocate and all-rounder." **Recent work:** Represented Telefónica in the BT v Telefónica Supreme Court appeal regarding 08 number charges.

Paul Lowenstein QC (3 Verulam Buildings) Enjoys a solid reputation for cases involving commercial contract disputes between fixed and mobile operators. **Strengths:** "He's a very good advocate and bloody aggressive. He's particularly punchy in terms of the language he uses." **Recent work:** Represented Joshua Heming in a dispute with Ignis Asset Management regarding breach of confidence and theft of business secrets surrounding investment analysis software.

Michael Lazarus (see p.697) (3 Verulam Buildings) Impresses with his work on commercial contractual issues in the telecoms space. He brings an impressive knowledge of IT, banking and finance and fraud law to bear when working for major mobile operators. **Strengths:** "He doesn't sit on the fence, and helps you decide what to do." "The breadth of his practice is very impressive."

Contents:

LONDON International Personal Injury

Travel: International Personal Injury
Leading Sets
Band 1
1 Chancery Lane
3 Hare Court *
2TG – 2 Temple Gardens *
Band 2
Devereux *
Outer Temple Chambers *
Band 3
Quadrant Chambers *
Leading Silks
Band 1
Palmer Howard *2TG – 2 Temple Gardens* *
Weir Robert *Devereux* *
Band 2
Block Neil *39 Essex Chambers (ORL)* ◊ *
Browne Benjamin *2TG – 2 Temple Gardens* *
Dougherty Charles *2TG – 2 Temple Gardens* *
McDermott Gerard *Outer Temple Chambers*
Stevens Howard *3 Hare Court*
Band 3
Audland William *12 King's Bench Walk (ORL)* ◊ *
Killalea Stephen *Devereux* *
Ross John *1 Chancery Lane*
Russell John *Quadrant Chambers* *
Leading Juniors
Star individuals
Chapman Matthew *1 Chancery Lane*
Deal Katherine *3 Hare Court*
Kinsler Marie Louise *2TG – 2 Temple Gardens* *
Mead Philip *Old Square Chambers (ORL)* ◊ *
Band 1
Crowther Sarah *Outer Temple Chambers*
Doherty Bernard *39 Essex Chambers (ORL)* ◊
McParland Michael *Quadrant Chambers* *
Prager Sarah *1 Chancery Lane*
Woolf Eliot *Outer Temple Chambers*
Band 2
Harding Jack *1 Chancery Lane*
Howells Katherine *Old Square Chambers (ORL)* ◊ *
Janusz Pierre *3 Hare Court*
Saxby Dan *3 Hare Court* *
Silvester Bruce *Devereux* *
Wyles Lucy *2TG – 2 Temple Gardens* *
Young Andrew *3 Hare Court*
Band 3
Bradley Ben *Outer Temple Chambers*
Candlin James *12 King's Bench Walk (ORL)* ◊ *
Clarke Daniel *Outer Temple Chambers*
Hunter Robert *Devereux* *
McTague Meghann *2TG – 2 Temple Gardens* *
Pugh Helen *3 Hare Court* *
Reeve Matthew *Quadrant Chambers* *
Spencer Andrew *1 Chancery Lane*
Wijeyaratne Asela *3 Hare Court* *
Up-and-coming individuals
Hughes Anna *2TG – 2 Temple Gardens* *
* *Indicates set / individual with profile.*
◊ *(ORL) = Other Ranked Lawyer.*
Alphabetical order within each band. Band 1 is highest.

Band 1

1 Chancery Lane

THE SET

1 Chancery Lane deals with the full gamut of multi-jurisdictional travel cases from individual illness claims to catastrophic injuries and fatalities overseas. Members are lauded for their skill in breaking down complex issues concerning liability, jurisdiction and applicable law, and regularly advise defendant tour operators and insurers as well as individual claimants. Recent landmark cases handled include Lady Brownlie v Four Seasons, where the Court of Appeal upheld the claimant's claim for breach of contract against the defendant hotel. Interviewees describe the chambers as "a go-to set in travel law which is at the top of its game and provides very straightforward advice."

Client service: Satisfied clients comment that senior clerk Clark Chessis "runs a very organised team extremely well" and is "exactly what you want in a clerk." "They absolutely know what they're doing and are great to deal with."

SILKS

John Ross QC Instructed in significant catastrophic injury and fatal accident claims, and has long-standing experience of acting for claimants and insurers on the defendant side. His cases regularly involve employer liability, indemnity and international safety standards. **Strengths:** "He's an incredible strategist, who is calm under pressure and has the gravitas you'd expect from an experienced silk." "He's in and out of court so much that he makes dealing with judges look so easy." **Recent work:** Represented the defendant employer in Cassley v GMP Securities & Sundance, a claim brought by the family of an employee killed in an air crash in Africa while on business.

JUNIORS

Matthew Chapman Acclaimed by market commentators as "an absolute superstar in travel law," he distinguishes himself through his tremendous knowledge of key travel law directives and private international law. His caseload encompasses a broad spectrum of high-profile fatal accidents and catastrophic injury claims. He represents both claimants and defendants in complex cases that often raise novel points of law under Rome II. **Strengths:** "He has an encyclopaedic knowledge of travel law cases and has been involved in some of the most important cases in a very fast-changing landscape." "Nothing stumps him; there's no case you could put before him that he wouldn't be able to tackle." "The pre-eminent travel law junior of his generation, unsurpassed in pure travel law, who expresses himself clearly, is very good with clients and can be trusted to get something right." **Recent work:** Acted for the claimant in Hulse v Virgin Holidays Limited, a case arising from a fatal quad bike crash in Morocco, which hinged on tour operator liability for excursions run by third-party companies.

Sarah Prager Commended for her impressive advocacy skills, she handles sensitive fatal accident and catastrophic injury cases that often result in precedent-setting decisions and create new legislation. She is a popular choice amongst leading solicitor firms on both the claimant and defendant side. **Strengths:** "Sarah is a delight to work with as she's realistic and pragmatic in her advice but not afraid to take risks when necessary." "She stands her ground and knows when to push the opponent." "Her sense of humour is second to none, and you can always rely on her to bring it into play, but at the same time she knows what she's talking about and will put up the very best fight to get results for the client." **Recent work:** Represented the claimant in Howes v MIB, a case centring on an RTA in Greece caused by an untraced driver. The case looked at the possibility of a UK national living abroad being able to recover and claim damages under English law.

Jack Harding Well regarded for his thoroughness, he has wide-ranging expertise that covers private international law, aviation accidents and package travel. He represents claimants and defendant tour operators, airlines, hotels and insurers in cases arising from aircraft incidents and outbreaks of illness. **Strengths:** "Jack has an incredible ability to view a case from all angles and often pre-empts issues before they even arise." "He turns things around very quickly, gets to the nub of the issue and gives strong advice."

Andrew Spencer Acts for and against tour operators in group actions and package travel claims relating to illness and accidents suffered overseas. He is highlighted for his knowledge of jurisdiction, applicable law and local standards. **Strengths:** "Andrew is organised, approachable and has a great knowledge of travel claims, which has delivered some excellent results." "He has terrific client care skills; he's always available to assist and nothing is ever too much trouble." "I really like how he interacts with judges in court cases. He's bright and personable."

3 Hare Court

See profile on p.863

THE SET

Renowned for the long-standing experience of its silks and bench strength at junior level, the team at 3 Hare Court enjoys an exceptional reputation for complex travel cases. Members predominantly specialise in high-value package travel claims on behalf of tour operators, as well as catastrophic and fatal injury cases on both claimant and defendant side. Barristers are also in demand for jurisdictional and choice of law issues, having appeared in key cases including Panagaki v Minetta & Others. One impressed solicitor notes: "3 Hare Court is one of the foremost chambers in terms of travel law. I can't speak highly enough of its flexibility and customer-focused approach."

Client service: "The clerks are brilliant, from the seniors all the way down to the juniors. They know which barrister is suitable for which case." "It's a great set of clerks, and it shows because they're all consistent. I feel like I can tell them what I need and they will move heaven and earth to supply it." James Donovan is the senior clerk.

SILKS

Howard Stevens QC Has a long-standing reputation for acting in catastrophic injury cases which incorporate jurisdiction and applicable law questions. He is also a regular fixture in high-profile inquests and group litigation arising from multiple fatalities during package holidays. **Strengths:** "He's brilliant; he cuts to the chase very quickly, and has a great manner with clients and the courts." "Howard is extremely thorough, knows every little detail and is a calm, reasoned and effective advocate." "He's a real stickler for detail who's very good with clients." **Recent work:** Advised TUI as the defendant tour operator in the inquest into the Sousse terrorist attacks in June 2015.

JUNIORS

Katherine Deal Attracts widespread commendation for her overarching knowledge of travel law and her ability to advocate in court on complex and often novel issues. She acts for claimants and defendants in equal measure, and is regularly involved in high-value claims arising from RTAs and package holiday incidents resulting in fatality or catastrophic injury. **Strengths:** "She's clearly trusted to take on difficult cases and does a very good job at taking these through to trial." "Katherine is a hard-nosed, no-nonsense litigator who is very well respected and very adept at managing the client's expectations." "What she doesn't know about travel law isn't worth knowing." **Recent work:** Represented the catastrophically injured claimant in Keefe v MAPFRE & Hoteles Piñero Canarias, a seven-figure claim complicated by questions of the insurer's limit on policy.

Pierre Janusz Instructed by both claimants and defendants in complex travel personal injury cases involving conflicts of law questions. His expertise encompasses various types of incidents, ranging from RTAs to accidents at hotels and workplaces abroad. **Strengths:** "He is a very intelligent man who thinks deeply about things and is thorough with his work." "Pierre has great attention to detail and is always up for a jurisdictional battle." "He is vastly experienced and a tough negotiator." **Recent work:** Represented the claimant in Williams v MAPFRE, in which the defendant contested English jurisdiction on the grounds of policy territorial limits.

Andrew Young Specialises in holiday claims, including group actions, and has a strong focus on cases related to accidents taking place during outdoor excursions such as skiing or exploring. He also assists clients with claims brought following injuries sustained on military service. **Strengths:** "He's passionate, thorough, great with clients and he demonstrates extensive knowledge of jurisdictional issues." "Andrew is great at cutting through detail and getting to the heart of the case in a very short timescale." **Recent work:** Advised the claimant on questions of inadequate safety measures in Reid v BSES, a case arising from a fatal polar bear attack on a remote Norwegian island.

Dan Saxby (see p.759) Frequently instructed by claimants and defendant tour operators, travel agents and airlines. He focuses on package travel litigation, leading group actions in catastrophic injury claims and advising on questions of jurisdiction and scope of liability. **Strengths:** "He's very bright, persuasive, quick-witted and a safe pair of hands in front of a judge. His experience in foreign law cases is useful." "He is a hugely experienced advocate who knows how to win in court." "Dan is able to achieve tremendous results for his clients in court and is very popular amongst travel lawyers and clients alike." **Recent work:** Acted for the defendant in Hurley v TUI, a case which raised questions of the claim's credibility and potential breaches of local standards.

Asela Wijeyaratne (see p.795) Primarily acts for claimants in cases emerging from a variety of transport accidents including RTAs and aircraft crashes. He assists with evidence concerning local standards, applicable law issues and treaties such as the Montreal and Athens Conventions. **Strengths:** "He has a sensible commercial view, turns papers around quickly and is beyond his years in terms of experience and effectiveness." "He is calm, approachable and provides sound, clear advice." "Not only is his written work good, he can also be both mild and aggressive as an advocate." **Recent work:** Advised a claimant on liability matters and recoverable damages under the Montreal Convention after she sustained injuries during the evacuation of flight BA2276.

Helen Pugh (see p.744) Represents claimants and defendants in package travel, aviation and cruise claims. She advises on cases of illness, including group actions, and those relating to injuries sustained in hotels. **Strengths:** "Helen is a talented junior who prepares thoroughly, keeps an open mind and welcomes input from those instructing her." "She is a very profound advocate and her written advice is always spot-on." "She is pleasant to deal with, hardworking and knowledgeable." **Recent work:** Acted for defendant cruise liner Sunshine Cruises against 28 claimants who initiated a group action after suffering illness. The case turned on the defendant's duty of care and scope of responsibility in preventing norovirus outbreaks.

2TG – 2 Temple Gardens

See profile on p.920

THE SET

Boasting an abundance of quality at silk level and a group of highly rated juniors, 2 Temple Gardens is consistently involved in the most influential travel cases. In the last year, its members have played key roles in Marshall v MIB and Wall v Mutuelle de Poitiers, both of which raised significant questions of applicable law under Rome II. The team stands out for its knowledge of private international law and its skill in contesting jurisdiction and quantum issues, being described by one instructing solicitor as "up there with the very best." Members act for both claimants and defendants handling predominantly high-value claims arising from accidents overseas resulting in death or catastrophic injury.

Client service: According to interviewees, "the clerks are very accommodating when helping organise conferences" and "they talk about fees realistically." "They give you confidence in chambers and make sure they provide their clients with a quality service." Lee Tyler heads the team.

SILKS

Howard Palmer QC (see p.732) Praised for the high quality of his written advice, he is especially adept at leading complex, multi-jurisdictional cases which address foreign law and applicable law issues. He is regularly instructed by defendant tour operators, insurers and hotels in high-profile claims arising from RTAs and other types of accident abroad resulting in catastrophic injury or fatality. **Strengths:** "He gets to the crux of the matter easily, deals with the relevant material and can separate the good points from the bad points." "His advocacy is calm and assured." "Howard is highly experienced and knowledgeable in cross-border personal injury cases." **Recent work:** Represented the appellant hotel chain in the appeal of Brownlie v Four Seasons Holdings, a case arising from a fatal accident during an excursion in Egypt. A key point that arose was the ability of claimants to bring proceedings domestically against foreign holding entities that incorporate hotel chains based in multiple jurisdictions.

Benjamin Browne QC (see p.605) Deals with cases arising out of RTAs and serious accidents at transportation hubs. He is well regarded for his international experience which encompasses applicable law matters and cost recovery pursuits on behalf of foreign insurers. **Strengths:** "He has good intellect and good presence in court." "He always makes himself amenable in negotiation, which results in a good settlement for the client."

Charles Dougherty QC (see p.635) Has carved out a strong reputation for handling landmark Rome II and private international law cases which turn on jurisdiction and applicable law points. He predominantly acts for defendant tour operators and insurers in complex fatal and catastrophic injury cases. **Strengths:** "Charles is extremely bright and very on the ball." "He is very analytical and confident in his judgement." "He's a hugely effective advocate, who's likeable and knows which points to take and which not to pedal so hard."

JUNIORS

Marie Louise Kinsler (see p.692) Has a formidable standing in the market having been involved in an array of key cases concerning EU law and Rome II. She receives tremendous praise for her profound understanding of private international law, and is instructed by both claimant and defendant solicitors in complex RTA cases. **Strengths:** "She is like an authority in herself, so you know you can stand behind the advice she gives. Tactically, she's very shrewd but fair." "She can cut through issues that seem impenetrable and come to a constructive conclusion." "I know I can pick up the phone to her and run something by her, and she usually knows the answer immediately. She's right at the top of her game." **Recent work:** Instructed to act for the catastrophically injured claimants in Arnott & Hughes v CARE USA, a case arising from an RTA in Ethiopia which concerned complex liability and heads of loss issues. Damages were issued in line with English law.

Lucy Wyles (see p.801) Noted for her knowledge of EU legislation and applicable law, she primarily handles catastrophic injury cases concerning RTAs. Impressed solicitors highlight her quick turnaround times. **Strengths:** "She grabs difficult cases with both hands and proves exemplary as far as assimilating knowledge is concerned." "I find her clear and concise, and she takes a practical approach." "She is very intelligent, grasps things very quickly and gives clear, decisive advice."

Meghann McTague (see p.714) Has considerable experience in illness claims, handling anything from group actions under the package travel regulations to cases concerning passengers taken ill on board aircraft. She has extensive knowledge of the Montreal and Athens Conventions. **Strengths:** "She is very down to earth and fights the right points in a case." "Clients immediately warm to her as she has the ability to assimilate facts and give straightforward advice." "She is feisty and prepared to argue difficult cases." **Recent work:** Represented the first defendant in Leek v NP Insurance and Aigaion which concerned a fatal RTA in Greece and the risk period for insurance cancellation under Greek law.

Anna Hughes (see p.677) Handles a wide range of claims following overseas accidents. She is mainly instructed by defendants to draft defences of package travel claims and advise on jurisdictional issues. **Strengths:** "Anna is very good; a real rising star." "I'm impressed by her approachability, familiarity with papers and firm grasp of the key issues in a case." **Recent work:** Acted for the defendant in H Findlay v TTAFS, a food poisoning claim turning on the tour operator's status as an organiser under the package travel regulations.

Band 2

Devereux

See profile on p.827

THE SET

With two well-reputed travel silks at its disposal, Devereux is regarded as "a top-quality chambers of real experts." The set's silks focus on jurisdiction, applicable law and quantum issues in relation to high-value claims following accidents overseas. Landmark cases involving the team include Wigley-Foster v MIB, which concerned a claimant's right to bring proceedings against the MIB due to the insolvency of the defendant's insurer. Juniors are also well respected for their competence in group illness claims.

Client service: "The clerks are first-rate and they give a great service." "The clerking service is very good. Paperwork is fast and efficient, and the individual clerks are approachable." "The clerks are very easy to work with and do the best they can to accommodate our needs and those of our clients."

SILKS

Robert Weir QC (see p.792) Enjoys a stellar reputation as a leading travel barrister. He is instructed by claimants and defendants in high-value travel claims raising complex and novel points of law under Rome II and the Human Rights Act. His scope of expertise encompasses applicable law, jurisdictional questions and issues relating to quantum. **Strengths:** "Robert is razor-sharp in his analysis and has a wonderfully calm yet forceful nature when in court." "He's arguably the go-to silk in an international case; he deals with ground-breaking issues, is hugely thorough, is totally assured and is someone with unsurpassed knowledge." "The breadth of his intellect is extraordinary. He tells things as they are, is very ingenious and he's dedicated to the client's cause." **Recent work:** Represented the claimant in Humphrey v Aegis Defence Services, a case concerning injury sustained during a military training exercise in Iraq.

Stephen Killalea QC (see p.691) An outstanding personal injury lawyer who acts for catastrophically injured claimants in high-value, sensitive cases. He is notably good at complex RTA and hotel claims. **Strengths:** "He is very good with clients and has a real eye for detail on quantum." "He cuts to the chase and addresses the important matters whilst also identifying novel issues that others wouldn't have thought of." "He's particularly clued up on jurisdiction issues." **Recent work:** Acted in Emslie v RII, representing a claimant who was catastrophically injured in an RTA in the USA. The claimant alleged that the vehicle was unsafe to drive on the terrain in question.

JUNIORS

Bruce Silvester (see p.765) Focusing his practice on travel litigation, he appears frequently in large-scale group actions on both the claimant and defendant side. He handles claims arising from a range of transport accidents, both on road and at sea. **Strengths:** "He is a great advocate, well respected by clients and judiciary alike, who has a wealth of knowledge and takes a tenacious approach to litigation." "Bruce is incredibly single-minded in his pursuit of the client's objective, and always prepared to think outside the box with liability arguments." "He gets a grasp of cases very quickly and is a bullish advocate." **Recent work:** Successfully represented the claimant in the appeal of Gillian McIlhagga v Abdul Majid, which arose from a quad biking accident in Spain resulting in catastrophic injury.

Robert Hunter (see p.678) Joins the rankings due to excellent feedback from peers and instructing solicitors. He mainly handles serious illness and catastrophic injury cases, including group actions, and regularly acts for claimant holidaymakers. **Strengths:** "He's an extremely good, passionate advocate who's great with clients and demonstrates specialist knowledge." **Recent work:** Appeared in Perkins v TUI UK, representing a claimant who suffered kidney damage on holiday in Turkey. The case was settled on the basis of potential future damages claims due to the longevity of the claimant's illness.

Outer Temple Chambers

See profile on p.887

THE SET

Outer Temple Chambers' experienced team has considerable strength in depth, and continues to make headway, boosted by recent key additions at junior level. The set offers noteworthy expertise in catastrophic injury, taking on cross-border cases ranging from RTAs and skiing accidents to clinical negligence. Its barristers receive significant instructions, having appeared in Moreno v MIB, which raised issues of applicable law and damages in the context of Rome II and the Motor Insurance Directive. Members predominantly act for private individuals, large claimant groups and insurers.

Client service: "The clerking team is very slick." "The clerks are very good and offer a high level of client care." "They are always ready to help out, and you feel like you have someone on your side when you need to get things done." Paul Barton is the senior clerk.

SILKS

Gerard McDermott QC Visible in complex, high-value cross-border claims relating to RTAs and outdoor pursuits. He is highlighted for his understanding of Rome II, and advises on quantum and applicable law issues both in Europe and further afield. **Strengths:** "Gerard has a real zeal for international law issues and a great understanding of the needs of catastrophically injured claimants." "He is very experienced, always well prepared and excellent on his feet." "He's one of the top barristers for catastrophic injury; he's very good at mediating and settling high-value cases because he knows how much money someone should get." **Recent work:** Led in Vann & Others v Ocidental-Companhia De Seguros, a fatal RTA in Portugal in which Portuguese law applied with proceedings taking place in the English Courts.

JUNIORS

Sarah Crowther Regularly undertakes complex cross-border claims which hinge on issues of jurisdiction, MIB responsibility and package travel regulations. She has established an impressive profile in fatality and catastrophic injury cases, representing both claimants and defendants. **Strengths:** "Sarah is excellent on technical points of law and is a persuasive and tenacious advocate." "She's extraordinarily bright, has a good bedside manner with clients and is both tough and pleasant." "She's a real specialist in jurisdiction and applicable law, who knows the legislation like the back of her hand." **Recent work:** Represented the deceased claimant's widow in Marshall & Pickard v MIB & Others, a fatal RTA case which raised key points of law on causation, applicable law and the scope of ability to claim against the MIB when the defendant driver is responsible.

Eliot Woolf Widely regarded as a top choice for gastric illness claims, in which he primarily represents claimants. He has a robust track record of leading large-scale group actions against tour operators, travel agents and hotels. A number of his cases involve complex jurisdictional points. **Strengths:** "Eliot is an exceptionally knowledgeable, personable and approachable litigator, a wonderful advocate and a great team player." "He's very pleasant to work with due to having a great way with clients and an ability to explain difficult concepts in simple terms." "Eliot's client care is fantastic and he can deal with tricky situations in a sensitive, palatable way that the client understands." **Recent work:** Acted for 599 claimants against First Choice Holidays following a mass outbreak of illness at a resort in Turkey.

Ben Bradley Has an extensive knowledge of clinical negligence and is a popular choice for claimants injured working abroad, during package holidays or in RTAs. He regularly appears in cross-border claims contested under the package travel regulations. **Strengths:** "An up-and-coming star with a real eye for detail and a great deal of knowledge in the area of package travel regulations." "He is brilliant on package travel cases and has a very good academic understanding of the law." "Ben is a very good technician; his legal skills and understanding of case law in terms of package travel is phenomenal." **Recent work:** Successfully settled the Cobb & 8 Others v Touchdown Travel case on behalf of the claimants. The defendant's argument that the holiday was not governed by the package travel regulations was dismissed.

Daniel Clarke Handles a broad range of international personal injury claims and has expertise in package travel and the Athens and Montreal Conventions. He represents seriously and catastrophically injured claimants in direct actions against foreign insurers, airlines and tour operators. **Strengths:** "He gives difficult advice very openly and honestly, and is capable of spotting tricky issues." "Daniel is an experienced practitioner in travel claims and has an especially good manner with minors." "Daniel is always just an e-mail away and you can have a sensible discussion around the case." **Recent work:** Represented the claimant in Holliday v Unipol SAI Assicurazioni, an RTA case resulting in catastrophic injury which addressed assessment of damages under Italian law.

Band 3

Quadrant Chambers

See profile on p.901

THE SET

A well-rounded team with formidable regulatory and commercial expertise at silk and junior level, Quadrant Chambers is regarded as "a standout set for aviation work that most importantly wins trials." On the aviation side, barristers are highly sought after by airlines and tour operators for flight delay disputes under Regulation 261, in addition to package travel regulations and ATOL licensing matters. Further expertise lies in shipping and personal injury claims, where members typically act on large-scale group litigation arising from illness outbreaks during package holidays. The set's international reach is characterised by its involvement at silk level in the Jetstar Hong Kong Airways case, in which the airline was denied permission to operate in Hong Kong.

Client service: The clerking team headed by Gary Ventura wins considerable praise for its efficiency: "I can't fault them, they're extremely prompt when coming back to you." "The clerks are awesome; they always turn things around, are very user-friendly and always happy to run across the road and make calls if necessary."

SILKS

John Russell QC (see p.757) Offers strong capability in the aviation and marine industries, where his advice encompasses contentious, regulatory and commercial matters. He is present in group litigation cases arising from fatal accidents and advises on contractual obligations and regulatory compliance. **Strengths:** "He's commercial, effective and knows how to win." "He has the gift of the gab on the personal injury side." "John is very well known in the aviation field." **Recent work:** Acted in the Norman Atlantic case concerning a ferry that caught fire leading to a number of deaths on board. He represented the charterers in a dispute with the shipowner over causation.

JUNIORS

Michael McParland (see p.714) Has an excellent reputation for international personal injury work, where he regularly handles claims arising from RTAs, aviation and marine accidents. He is highlighted for his top-quality advice on comparative law and conflicts of law matters. **Strengths:** "Michael has an unrivalled knowledge of international law issues and is a ferocious advocate." "He is very straightforward, never afraid of a fight and incredibly incisive during cross-examinations." "His advice is very easy to read, well structured and practical." **Recent work:** Acted for the claimants in Dusek & Others v Stormharbour Securities, a fatal helicopter crash in Peru which turned on the extent of employer liability.

Matthew Reeve (see p.750) Highlighted for his superb knowledge of the aviation industry, his expertise ranges from regulatory and commercial advice under EU law to representing claimants and defendants in air crash cases. He also deals with hotel food poisoning claims. **Strengths:** "Matthew combines legal prowess with a remarkable degree of insight into the technical aspects of aviation incidents." "He is highly empathetic and very good with clients." **Recent work:** Represented the claimant in Cassley v GMP Securities & Sundance, a case which arose from a fatal aviation accident in Congo. The court held the defendant employer to be in breach of its obligations to employees in distant jurisdictions.

Other Ranked Lawyers

Neil Block QC (see p.598) (39 Essex Chambers) Benefiting from a distinguished personal injury and clinical negligence background, he focuses on significant RTAs abroad and claims involving overseas nationals injured in UK territory. He ably acts for claimants, defendants and insurers. **Strengths:** "He is very bright, authoritative, charming with clients and an excellent advocate." "He is tough in court and very constructive in a settlement meeting." "Neil really gets to grips with complex cases, he can see the wood for the trees and disregard the issues that will lead nowhere." **Recent work:** Acted for the insurer in Chavda v Suncorp Metway Insurance Company, a case concerning an RTA in Australia resulting in multiple fatalities and catastrophic injuries.

Bernard Doherty (39 Essex Chambers) Wins extensive praise for his strength in dealing with private international law questions in complex travel claims. He regularly appears on the claimant and defendant side in cases arising from RTAs and alleged negligence. **Strengths:** "He is a top barrister for complex issues who is always willing to give a view up front and who has an encyclopaedic knowledge of the area." "Bernard is very responsive and knows his way around the European legislation." "He can run cases from the outset without silk supervision, and his cross-examination skills are something to behold." **Recent work:** Acted in Syred v PZU, representing a claimant who suffered a catastrophic brain injury after an RTA. The case concerned the interpretation of Polish law in the English courts.

William Audland QC (see p.586) (12 King's Bench Walk) Active on a range of complex travel cases arising from RTAs and package holiday incidents resulting in death or catastrophic injury, representing both claimants and defendants. He also advises domestic tour operators and insurers on recovery actions against third parties. **Strengths:** "He gives straightforward, practical and commercial advice, and is a master of cross-examination." "William is very bright and great at identifying and addressing the key issues in complex cases." "He is very analytical and has excellent attention to detail." **Recent work:** Represented the catastrophically injured claimant in Pina v Fidelidade Seguros, a case arising from an RTA in Portugal; it addressed complex questions of applicable law, liability and quantum.

James Candlin (see p.611) (12 King's Bench Walk) Frequently called upon for cases centring on jurisdiction and foreign law questions. He has significant experience of dealing with cross-border food poisoning, serious illness, catastrophic injury and other more sensitive claims. **Strengths:** "Because of his in-depth knowledge of medical issues, he's a safe person to turn to for issues of causation, such as illness outbreaks in foreign hotels." "He has very good attention to detail and can absorb significant facts from large volumes of papers." "James is very protective of his client whilst simultaneously remaining realistic." **Recent work:** Acted in Cave v Red Sea Holidays, advising the defendant on causation and subsequent settlement of the case. The claimant had contracted severe gastric illness on a package holiday in Egypt.

Philip Mead (see p.714) (Old Square Chambers) Praised for being "completely on top of the myriad of European and international regulations," he is often instructed in high-value claims arising from RTAs and package holidays. He predominantly acts for claimants against insurers, compensation bodies and employers. **Strengths:** "He knows the area inside out and back to front." "He is extremely experienced, well known and well recognised." "Philip is an excellent advocate who has been involved in some of the leading cases on private international law and jurisdiction." **Recent work:** Advised the defendant hotel on jurisdictional issues under the Brussels Regulation in Keefe v MAPFRE & Hoteles Piñero Canarias.

Katherine Howells (see p.677) (Old Square Chambers) Handles claims arising from accidents resulting in serious injury and death overseas. She has a strong focus on the aviation industry and handles, amongst others, matters concerning air accidents and airport and airfield-related incidents. **Recent work:** Represented the claimant in Bianco v Bennett, a fatal RTA in England involving an Italian citizen, complicated by the issue of the recoverability of employee benefits.

LONDON Regulatory & Commercial

Travel: Regulatory & Commercial
Leading Sets
Band 1
Fountain Court Chambers *
Quadrant Chambers *
Leading Silks
Band 1
Crane Michael *Fountain Court Chambers* *
Lawson Robert *Quadrant Chambers* *
Shah Akhil *Fountain Court Chambers* *
Band 2
Russell John *Quadrant Chambers* *
Shepherd Philip *XXIV Old Buildings (ORL)* ◊
Thanki Bankim *Fountain Court Chambers* *
Band 3
Kimbell John *Quadrant Chambers* *
New Silks
Phelps Rosalind *Fountain Court Chambers* *
Leading Juniors
Band 1
Marland Timothy *Quadrant Chambers*
Reeve Matthew *Quadrant Chambers* *
Band 2
Shah Bajul *XXIV Old Buildings (ORL)* ◊
* *Indicates set / individual with profile.*
◊ *(ORL) = Other Ranked Lawyer.*
Alphabetical order within each band. Band 1 is highest.

Band 1

Fountain Court Chambers
See profile on p.847

THE SET

Fountain Court Chambers has a long-established reputation as an eminent travel and aviation set. A top choice on the commercial front, it is also a leading player when it comes to matters concerning key regulatory questions. Members represent large airlines and regulatory authorities in cases concerning passenger travel claims and tour operator insolvencies. They also advise on non-contentious issues such as airport operations. According to sources, "the set attracts work due to its headline-grabbing silks," a fact underlined by members' appearances in Ethiopian Airlines v Honeywell & Others and Huzar v Jet2.com. The set has boosted its silk ranks in the last year with the appointment of Rosalind Phelps, enhancing its already enviable profile in the sector.

Client service: "The clerking service has always been reliable and of high quality." Alex Taylor leads a team of people who are "always responsive in relation to the instructions given to them."

SILKS

Michael Crane QC (see p.625) Consistently instructed on landmark and high-profile claims concerning product liability and causation questions in relation to air crashes and major incidents. He also ably assists with regulatory matters including airline licensing applications. **Strengths:** "Michael is an absolute star in aviation and a very pleasant person." "He is very experienced and judges listen to him." "He's the number-one silk in aviation matters; he can do anything on the contentious and regulatory side." **Recent work:** Acted for Virgin Atlantic regarding a product liability claim against Mitsubishi and Koito, which centred on doctored test results and non-compliant designs of airline seats.

Akhil Shah QC (see p.762) Enjoys a strong track record in key travel cases concerning flight delay claims and passenger rights. Many of these cases have set new legal precedents. In addition, he advises on new market entries and questions arising from the Denied Boarding Regulations. He acts for airlines, tour operators and regulatory bodies. **Strengths:** "He is a subtle advocate with a very broad practice." **Recent work:** Represented the claimant in Dawson v Thomson Airways, a Court of Appeal case which confirmed the six-year limitation period for compensation under Regulation 261.

Bankim Thanki QC (see p.780) A leading aviation lawyer who advises airlines, contractors and regulators. He handles commercial disputes over airport development and operation, and offers regulatory assistance with regard to liabilities in the context of tour operator bankruptcy. **Strengths:** "He's extremely client-friendly, very commercial and an excellent lawyer." **Recent work:** Represented GMR as contractor in a claim against the Maldivian government for unlawful termination of a project to develop Maldives International Airport.

Rosalind Phelps QC (see p.736) Her travel law expertise is widespread, and she is well acquainted with ATOL licensing applications, travel litigation and disputes involving airlines. She acts for both airline companies and regulatory authorities. **Strengths:** "She is extremely knowledgeable about aspects of aviation law which non-experts would miss." "She has developed a reputation for complex aviation commercial disputes." "I found her extremely pleasant to deal with and efficient." **Recent work:** Represented Belfast International Airport in a damages claim against Aer Lingus after the airline's decision to switch its operations to Belfast City Airport on financial grounds.

Quadrant Chambers
See profile on p.901

THE SET

A well-rounded team with formidable regulatory and commercial expertise at silk and junior level, Quadrant Chambers is regarded as "a standout set for aviation work that, most importantly, wins trials." On the aviation side, barristers are highly sought after by airlines and tour operators for flight delay disputes under Regulation 261, as well as cases concerning package travel regulations and ATOL licensing matters. Further expertise lies in shipping and personal injury claims and large-scale group litigation arising from illness outbreaks during package holidays. The set's international reach is characterised by its involvement at silk level in the Jetstar Hong Kong Airways case concerning refusal of permission to operate in Hong Kong.

Client service: The clerking team, headed by Gary Ventura, wins considerable praise for its efficiency: "I can't fault them; they're extremely prompt when coming back to you." "The clerks are awesome; they always turn things around, are very user-friendly and are always happy to run across the road and make calls if necessary."

SILKS

Robert Lawson QC (see p.697) An illustrious figure in the regulatory and commercial domain who is a top choice for complex and landmark travel cases in the aviation industry. He acts for claimants, regulators and leading airlines on matters ranging from operating licences to ticketing disputes. **Strengths:** "He has the ability to cut through all the chaff and get to the wheat, making things easy that, on the face of it, appear quite complicated." "He knows his way around the international conventions better than anyone else and is very user-friendly." "He responds very promptly to instructions and always gives good advice in plain English that lay clients find easy to understand." **Recent work:** Successfully represented Cathay Pacific Airways in a dispute against Jetstar Hong Kong Airways over the airline's application for a licence to operate in Hong Kong.

John Russell QC (see p.757) Offers strong capability in the aviation and marine industries, where his advice encompasses regulatory and commercial matters. He is present in group litigation cases arising from fatal accidents and regularly advises on contractual obligations and regulatory compliance. **Strengths:** "He's commercial, effective and knows how to win." "He has the gift of the gab on the personal injury side." "John is very well known in the aviation field." **Recent work:** Acted in the Norman Atlantic case which concerned a ferry that caught fire leading to a number of deaths on board. He represented the charterers in a dispute with the shipowner over causation.

John Kimbell QC (see p.691) Specialises in high-profile aviation disputes, handling fatal air crash cases as well as sensitive matters arising from serious injury on-board aircraft. He is highlighted for his international knowledge and often advises on complex jurisdictional and foreign law issues. **Strengths:** "He distils very complex issues and breaks them down into simple ones, winning trials as a result of his fearlessness in front of judges." "He has a great advocacy style and builds his cases brick by brick to give you a beautiful wall of arguments." "John is very knowledgeable in aviation cases and a tenacious lawyer." **Recent work:** Successfully represented the defendant in Stott v Thomas Cook. The Supreme Court upheld the decision to dismiss the claimant's claim for discrimination.

JUNIORS

Timothy Marland Regularly defends international airlines in disputes with claimant passengers over flight cancellations, ticketing errors and various other ATOL-related issues. He also advises on regulatory and commercial matters in the aviation and shipping industries. **Strengths:** "He is bright, robust and tenacious when it comes to aviation and liability questions." "Timothy is extremely well known in the aviation and commercial field." **Recent work:** Appeared in the case APTA v PIA, a dispute over commission paid for fuel surcharges.

Matthew Reeve (see p.750) Highlighted for his superb knowledge of the aviation industry, his expertise ranges from regulatory and commercial advice under EU law to representing claimants and defendants in air crash cases. He also deals with hotel food poisoning claims. **Strengths:** "Matthew combines legal prowess with a remarkable degree of insight into the technical aspects of aviation incidents." "He is highly empathetic and very good with clients." **Recent work:** Represented the claimant in Cassley v

GMP Securities & Sundance, a case arising from a fatal aviation accident in Congo. The court held the defendant employer to be in breach of its obligations to employees in distant jurisdictions.

Other Ranked Lawyers

Philip Shepherd QC (XXIV Old Buildings) Makes frequent appearances in aviation-related disputes, acting for travel agents and airlines. An experienced commercial litigator and arbitrator, he also benefits from having a strong background in private international law and advises on jurisdiction and foreign law issues. **Strengths:** "He's at the top of the tree in aviation, and is a very well-known name who is well regarded amongst top solicitors." **Recent work:** Represented Jet2.com against Blackpool Airport in a dispute over opening hours to accommodate flights, which turned on the contract's best endeavours clause.

Bajul Shah (XXIV Old Buildings) Undertakes commercial disputes in the aviation industry, and has substantial aircraft leasing and maintenance knowledge. He also advises on product liability and potential engineering negligence issues. **Strengths:** "A clear thinker with a comprehensive understanding of the law." **Recent work:** Acted on Jet2.com v Tarom, defending a Romanian maintenance organisation against a claim for breach of contract brought by the airline.

Contents:

LONDON

Trusts	
Leading Silks	
Band 1	
Angus Tracey	*5 Stone Buildings* *
Barlow Francis	*Ten Old Square* *
Boyle Alan	*Serle Court* *
Brownbill David	*XXIV Old Buildings*
Cooper Gilead	*Wilberforce Chambers* *
Green Brian	*Wilberforce Chambers*
Ham Robert	*Wilberforce Chambers*
Hinks Frank	*Serle Court* *
Le Poidevin Nicholas	*New Square Chambers*
Legge Henry	*5 Stone Buildings* *
McCall Christopher	*Maitland Chambers* *
Moeran Fenner	*Wilberforce Chambers*
Rajah Eason	*Ten Old Square* *
Reed Penelope	*5 Stone Buildings* *
Steinfeld Alan	*XXIV Old Buildings*
Talbot Rice Elspeth	*XXIV Old Buildings*
Taube Simon	*Ten Old Square* *
Warnock-Smith Shân	*5 Stone Buildings* *
New Silks	
Hilliard Jonathan	*Wilberforce Chambers*
Wilson Richard	*Serle Court* *
Leading Juniors	
Band 1	
Bedworth Georgia	*Ten Old Square* *
Brightwell James	*New Square Chambers*
Campbell Emily	*Wilberforce Chambers*
Child Andrew J	*Wilberforce Chambers*
Dumont Thomas	*Radcliffe Chambers* *
Hagen Dakis	*Serle Court* *
Henderson William	*Serle Court* *
Hubbard Mark	*New Square Chambers*
Meadway Susannah	*Ten Old Square* *
Richardson Giles	*Serle Court* *
Studer Mark	*Wilberforce Chambers*
Tucker Lynton	*New Square Chambers*
Up-and-coming individuals	
Holden Andrew	*XXIV Old Buildings*
* *Indicates individual with profile.*	
Alphabetical order within each band. Band 1 is highest.	

Ranked Lawyers

Christopher McCall QC (see p.711) (Maitland Chambers) Hugely experienced trusts barrister who has served on The Trust Law Committee since its inception. He regularly handles the largest cases both domestically and internationally and is an expert on the trusts aspects of divorce. **Strengths:** "He sees issues from new angles and readily identifies what is worth pursuing in a case."

Nicholas Le Poidevin QC (New Square Chambers) Trusts specialist who is widely admired for the scope of his knowledge and experience. He is instructed on all manner of trust-related litigation. **Strengths:** "Bright, up to speed, and a lawyer with a very nice, persuasive advocacy style. He's absolutely substance and not show." **Recent work:** Advised the trustees in Riches v Pullan, a case concerning a group of property companies valued at around £117 million.

Henry Legge QC (see p.699) (5 Stone Buildings) Advises on trustee and beneficiary disputes, and has far-reaching experience of cases in offshore jurisdictions. **Strengths:** "Carries the case and has a charming advocacy style. He's tactical, he shows good judgement and is good with clients. Clients feel comfortable as he explains things clearly."

James Brightwell (New Square Chambers) Handles both contentious and non-contentious trusts work, and is instructed in high-value matters in a variety of jurisdictions around the world. **Strengths:** "Modest and unassuming, he is always excellent on paper and with clients. He explains matters clearly, calmly and succinctly and is right when it comes to predicting the outcomes of cases." **Recent work:** Acted for the President of India in a dispute over funds settled by the Nizam of Hyderabad in 1948.

Mark Hubbard (New Square Chambers) Busy both in the UK and overseas, he has handled a plethora of trusts cases of considerable value. He is instructed in both contentious and non-contentious matters. **Strengths:** "He provides advice which is of the highest quality, dealing with the legal technicalities of a matter, and can be applied practically. He is excellent in conference and is well liked by clients." **Recent work:** Advised a widow in a matter involving complex international trusts and estates. The case involved proceedings in Jersey, Switzerland and France.

Lynton Tucker (New Square Chambers) Leading trusts junior who is praised for his extraordinary depth of knowledge. He has a large advisory practice and frequently deals with offshore matters. **Strengths:** "The guru of trusts law generally. Everyone looks up to him for the ultimate answer. He is the editor of 'Lewin on Trusts', and his knowledge is second to none. He is unbelievably talented." **Recent work:** Acted in Orb ARL v Ruhan, a case concerning profits made under an alleged joint venture that were supposed to have found their way into an Isle of Man trust.

David Brownbill QC (XXIV Old Buildings) Trusts law specialist and editor of 'International Trust Laws'. Brownbill is routinely instructed in high-value trusts matters in a variety of jurisdictions. **Strengths:** "An absolute expert in his field who knows his way round trusts as well as anyone." **Recent work:** Acted in Akers and Others v Samba, a £300 million claim concerning the insolvency of a Cayman Islands company. The matter involved a validity of trusts question.

Alan Steinfeld QC (XXIV Old Buildings) Widely respected figure at the Bar who handles trusts cases domestically and overseas. **Strengths:** "Has a remarkable ability to distil a lot of information into the most important points in a very short time. He's very concise, clear in his thinking, and great at drawing the strings of a case together." **Recent work:** Appeared in The Z Family Trusts, acting for the beneficiary of a number of very large discretionary trusts established in Gibraltar. These trusts held the wealth of two brothers engaged in extensive property development in London.

Elspeth Talbot Rice QC (XXIV Old Buildings) Experienced and much-admired chancery silk with a wealth of experience in trusts related matters. She is particularly strong in offshore work. **Strengths:** "Elspeth has such vast knowledge and understanding, and the level of respect for her in the offshore world is more or less unparalleled." **Recent work:** Acted for the beneficiaries in Walker v Egerton Vernon, a £100 million grossly negligent breach of trust case.

Andrew Holden (XXIV Old Buildings) Acts in a variety of trust law matters, both as a litigator and in an advisory capacity. He has good experience in international trust law, and is an expert in trust structuring and trust protectors. Recently, he has been retained by the government of Bermuda to assist in the revision of its Trustee Act. **Strengths:** "He has carved a niche for himself giving advice on the removal of trustees and protectors. At a very young age, he has become the authority on that area. He provides very succinct and very good advice." **Recent work:** Acted in Re Piedmont & Riviera Trusts, where he successfully persuaded the court to set aside the appointment of both the trustees and protectors of Jersey law trusts worth in excess of £25 million.

Francis Barlow QC (see p.589) (Ten Old Square) Head of chambers who handles matters both domestically and overseas. He is highly experienced at drafting trusts and advising on their construction, and also expert at handling contentious trusts and succession matters. **Strengths:** "The king of the variation trust world. He really is very good at it and knows how to read the court. He's got so much experience and he is such a safe pair of hands."

Eason Rajah QC (see p.747) (Ten Old Square) Operates both domestically and overseas, and has particular experience regarding applications under the Variation of Trusts Act 1958. **Strengths:** "A very quick thinker who has a silky delivery in court." "He's super-impressive, tremendous with clients and an absolute delight to work with." **Recent work:** Lead counsel on a breach of trust claim involving English, Jersey, US, Dutch and Mauritian trusts and tax law.

Simon Taube QC (see p.778) (Ten Old Square) Hugely experienced and respected barrister who is an expert in both contentions and non-contentious trusts cases, and has appeared in a wide number of jurisdictions. **Strengths:** "Remarkably erudite and authoritative," he is "brilliant at masterminding the strategy in a case." "He knows the law backwards and if he says something is right you'd be unwise to challenge it." **Recent work:** Acted in Labrouche v Frey and Others, a seven-week trial involving breach of trust claims and involving the interplay between English, Swiss and Liechtenstein trust laws.

Georgia Bedworth (see p.593) (Ten Old Square) Experienced in both contentious and non-contentious trusts, and often sought out to handle high-value matters, some of which relate to landed estates. **Strengths:** "Provides clear, balanced opinions and is not one to sit on the fence." "She's very empathetic and inspires confidence from the beginning." **Recent work:** Handled an application under Section 57 Trustee Act 1925 for additional powers to be given to trustees of the funds of Portman Estate, which owns a large part of Central London.

Susannah Meadway (see p.715) (Ten Old Square) Particularly strong on cases concerning landed estates, she frequently advises on applications to extend the lifetime of trusts under the Variation of Trusts Act 1958, and secures rectification by the court of trust documents in marginal cases. **Strengths:**

"Technically excellent, clear in her opinions and not one to engage in esoteric language. Clients find her to be very pleasant and very reassuring."

Thomas Dumont (see p.637) (Radcliffe Chambers) Highly sought-after senior junior with over three decades of experience. He has extensive Court of Appeal experience and many of his cases have assisted in establishing modern analyses of constructive trusts. **Strengths:** "Clear, robust and incisive. He's approachable, very ready to work collaboratively and it is always a pleasure to work with him. In a scrap, he is a great friend to have at your side."

Alan Boyle QC (see p.601) (Serle Court) Head of chambers and a barrister with long experience of handling trust and probate litigation. He has specific expertise in handling the trusts elements of high-value divorce cases. **Strengths:** "Never ceases to impress, and when he gets his teeth into a case he is unstoppable. He really throws his all into his clients' cases and is meticulous in his preparation."

Frank Hinks QC (see p.672) (Serle Court) Handles contentious and non-contentious matters in a variety of jurisdictions, and has advised several high-profile figures. **Strengths:** "He's learned and highly responsive, with a quick turnaround time when it comes to the papers. The man is utterly reliable and very bright."

Dakis Hagen (see p.661) (Serle Court) Has a truly international practice and handles cases of great value and complexity. He is an expert in both the trusts elements of divorce and in professional negligence matters relating to trust structuring. **Strengths:** "Particularly strong on complex, technical points. He has proved himself time and again to be exceptionally hard working and accessible." **Recent work:** Advised a trustee in a £100 million claim relating to an alleged major breach of trust.

William Henderson (see p.669) (Serle Court) Advises a wide range of clients in domestic and international trust disputes, and is experienced in both contentious and non-contentious cases. He is also an expert on trusts-related professional negligence claims. **Strengths:** "When he stands up, judges and opponents really listen. His views are held in great esteem."

Giles Richardson (see p.751) (Serle Court) Handles both advisory and litigious trust matters, and is active both in the UK and offshore. **Strengths:** "One of the lead experts in Jersey trust matters, and a barrister whose work rate is phenomenal." **Recent work:** Acted in Fiduciare v Investec Trustees, appearing for successor trustees in proceedings against former trustees alleging negligent investment in hedge funds.

Richard Wilson QC (see p.798) (Serle Court) Handles a large trusts practice and is active worldwide. He has appeared in high-level trusts cases in the Channel Islands, the British Virgin Islands and the Cayman Islands. **Strengths:** "A demolition ball in court. He's one of the true trial barristers, who is always game for the fight." **Recent work:** Acted in Fielden v Christie-Miller, appearing for the trustees of the Swyncombe Settlement defending a claim brought against them for proprietary estoppel by a beneficiary.

Emily Campbell (Wilberforce Chambers) Has experience of tackling complex private client litigation and is an expert in drafting trust documentation. Her practice takes in both contentious and non-contentious matters. **Strengths:** "She clearly analyses all the problems in a case, and comes up with creative ways of solving them."

Tracey Angus QC (see p.584) (5 Stone Buildings) Experienced Chancery barrister with wide expertise whose practice incorporates both onshore and offshore matters. **Strengths:** "She's a whirlwind of energy who's very sensible and has good judgement. She gets on very well with clients, and really fights for them." **Recent work:** Acted in a multi-jurisdictional dispute over an estate and an alleged forged will.

Penelope Reed QC (see p.749) (5 Stone Buildings) Acts in high-value trust and property matters both domestically and offshore. She also has experience in family provision cases, and contentious wills and probate matters. **Strengths:** "She has a great following and gets in lots of big cases." "She is super smart and a wise, guiding hand. She strategically steers the case beautifully."

Shân Warnock-Smith QC (see p.790) (5 Stone Buildings) Advises on, and represents clients in, trusts, estate and charity cases, and has a particular focus on wealth structuring. She has vast experience of practising both domestically and overseas, and is heavily involved in major offshore matters. **Strengths:** "What she does is bring clarity to a case. She makes complicated cases very simple. Judges love it and clients love it."

Gilead Cooper QC (see p.623) (Wilberforce Chambers) Handles trusts work as part of his wide-ranging chancery practice and appears in a multitude of jurisdictions. **Strengths:** "He is a shrewd litigator, who is tenacious and thoughtful." **Recent work:** Acted in a Lebanese family dispute involving trust arrangements in the UK, Guernsey and Lebanon.

Brian Green QC (Wilberforce Chambers) Hugely respected chancery silk who is regularly instructed in complex high-value matters both domestically and in offshore jurisdictions. **Strengths:** "He sees a way through very complex matters which seem to be beset with intractable problems. Ten other silks wouldn't see what he sees, he's that ingenious and creative."

Robert Ham QC (Wilberforce Chambers) Handles trusts cases both in a litigious and advisory capacity, and is also a noted expert in trusts-related professional negligence cases. **Strengths:** "A doyen of the contentious trusts world, who's one of the strongest when it comes to the paperwork."

Fenner Moeran QC (Wilberforce Chambers) Handles trusts cases that are high in value and of a sensitive nature. He has experience in matters resulting from matrimonial breakdown and intricate family disputes. **Strengths:** "His commercial acumen is phenomenal, and his ability to work with offshore lawyers, onshore lawyers and a large wider team is second to none." **Recent work:** Acted in a high-profile will dispute involving a wealthy Pakistani family. The will was contested on the grounds of possible forgery.

Andrew Child (Wilberforce Chambers) Frequently represents trustees and beneficiaries in breach of trust claims, and has a busy practice both at home and abroad. **Strengths:** "He is technically excellent in contentious trust and probate matters, particularly those with a foreign element."

Mark Studer (Wilberforce Chambers) An expert at drafting and advising on trusts who has a strong private client following. In demand both at home and abroad, he has advised on matters in Hong Kong, the Bahamas, Bermuda, Guernsey and Scotland. **Strengths:** "He has a really very precise and intellectual approach to trust law and is extremely knowledgeable on the case law side of things and in terms of drafting."

Jonathan Hilliard QC (Wilberforce Chambers) Active in a wide variety of jurisdictions, and someone with expertise in high-profile divorce matters involving offshore trusts. He is well versed in the intricacies of complex offshore trust structures. **Strengths:** "Exceptionally bright, and clearly destined for great things." **Recent work:** Acted for a Gibraltar law firm in its defence against claims of dishonesty regarding its management of a large trust.

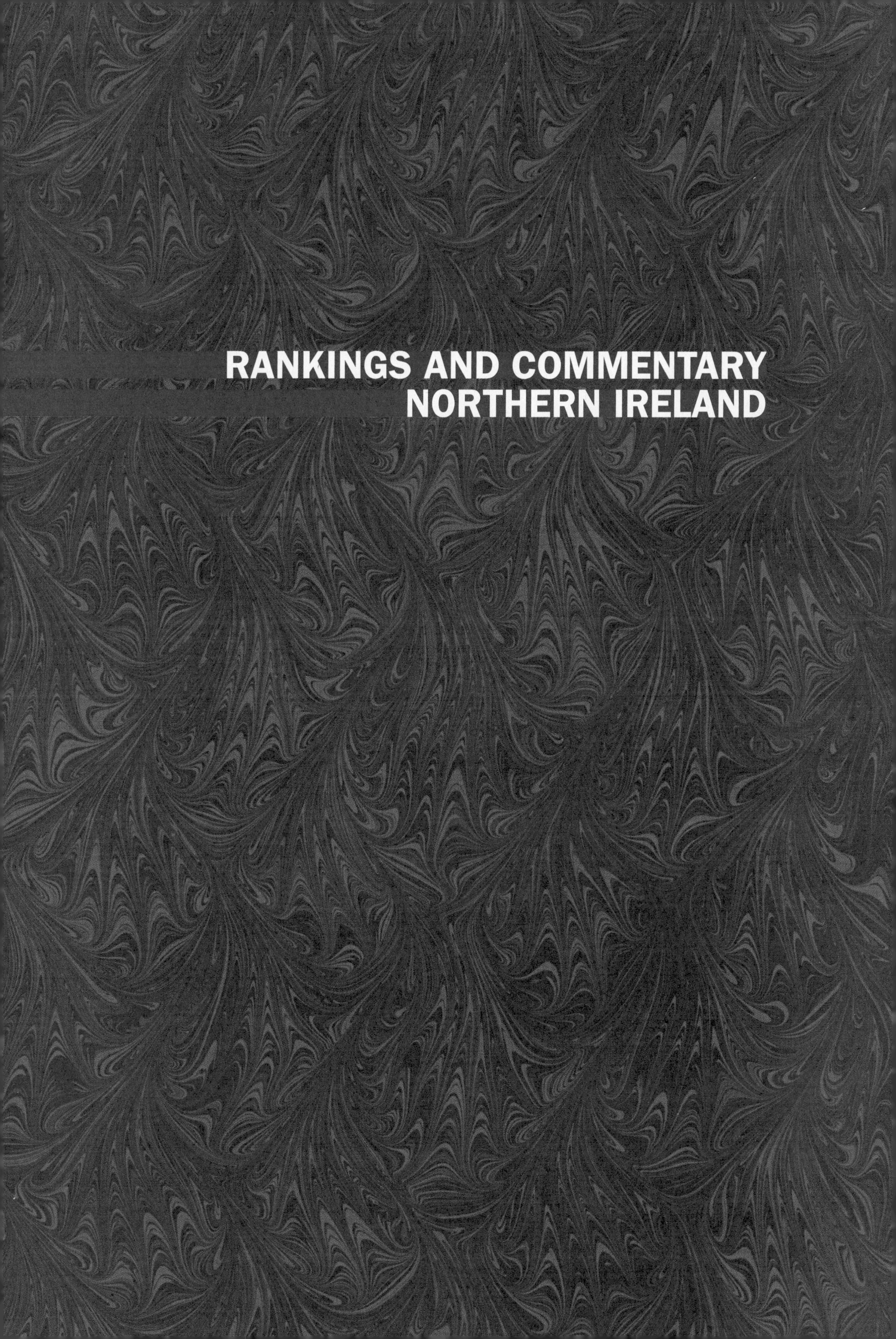

RANKINGS AND COMMENTARY NORTHERN IRELAND

Contents:

COMMERCIAL DISPUTE RESOLUTION

Commercial Dispute Resolution
Leading Silks
Band 1
Fee Brian
Hanna Nicolas
Humphreys Michael
O'Donoghue Francis Philip
Orr Mark
Shaw Stephen
Simpson Gerald
Band 2
Anyadike-Danes Monye
Good Patrick
Lockhart Brett
Scoffield David
Simpson Jacqueline
Leading Juniors
Band 1
Colmer Adrian
Dunlop David
Gibson Keith *
MacMahon James Hugh
Millar Robert
Band 2
Atchison Wayne
Coghlin Richard
Dunford Craig
Dunlop Jonathan
Egan Michael
Flanagan Donal
Girvan Peter
Gowdy William
Hopkins Peter
Stevenson Douglas
Up-and-coming individuals
Fee Fiona
Fletcher Alistair
Neeson Michael
Sinton William
** Indicates individual with profile.*
Alphabetical order within each band. Band 1 is highest.

Ranked Lawyers

SILKS

Brian Fee QC A highly regarded individual whose practice encompasses a wide spectrum of commercial disputes, such as breaches of agreement and misrepresentation, as well as chancery and negligence matters. He receives positive commentary on his role as mediator and regularly acts for both defendants and plaintiffs in high-value disputes. **Strengths:** "He was very capable at identifying the points we should focus on. He explains points simply to clients and he's very effective. A really respected pillar of the Bar." "He ticks all the boxes: he's incredibly clever, he can relate to clients, he can break down complex legal issues, he puts people at ease and the way he handles witnesses and judges is superb." "He is someone you look forward to working with because you know he will cut through all the irrelevancies and bring a sense of reality to disputes that are getting out of control."

Nicolas Hanna QC Receives the utmost praise for his industrious approach to matters, and is known in the field for his excellent client service. Other noted strengths include mediation, and he regularly acts for clients in matters arising from claims of professional negligence and defamation, as well as frequently being called upon to handle judicial reviews. **Strengths:** "He is one of our finest lawyers, he's absolutely superb in written form." "He is very experienced and good at analysing and presenting an argument."

Michael Humphreys QC A fantastic choice for all manner of commercial disputes, his practice regularly covers construction, shareholder disagreements and corporate matters, among others. He is known in the field for his academic skill and abilities on his feet, and he is highly praised for his negotiation and tenacity in court. He regularly practises litigation, arbitration and mediation. **Strengths:** "He is a heavyweight in Northern Ireland, our top senior counsel, an excellent advocate who is very good at breaking down complex matters to make them look simple, straightforward and concise." "He has good commercial instincts in terms of being able to assess the merits, and where others procrastinate, he zones in quickly." "He is robust, bright and capable of fighting a case pretty forcefully."

Frank O'Donoghue QC Has an enviable reputation in the field for his capacity to turn his hand to anything, and proves particularly strong on detailed shareholder and construction disputes. He frequently acts as mediator and also practises criminal law. **Strengths:** "Frank's grasp of all areas of the law is unparalleled; he's so capable of covering different areas." "An excellent senior counsel with an amazing appetite for hard work and a great relationship with the client. He will put himself out to facilitate the needs of the client in whatever urgent situation may arise." "He is extremely talented, quick at getting up to speed and has a great degree of common sense."

Mark Orr QC Has a glowing reputation among peers for his work in chancery and tax matters as well as commercial cases. He is known for his expertise and skill in instructions which include matters related to trusts, shareholder disputes and claims of unfair prejudice. Market sources describe him as "very knowledgeable." **Strengths:** "His technical knowledge is what makes him stand out. He's very calm, experienced and reassuring – he just looks like you want to trust him." "His advisory work is very strong and he is trusted by the judges."

Stephen Shaw QC Held in very high regard for his communication abilities and presence in court, he is regularly instructed by solicitors in high-value mandates spanning commercial disputes, judicial reviews and company matters. He has experience in litigation as well as ADR, and he frequently acts in land matters such as planning appeals and rent reviews. **Strengths:** "He has gravitas and is well regarded by the judges. It demonstrates intent when he is brought in." "He is clear-minded and switched-on."

Gerald Simpson QC Extremely well-respected member of the Bar, particularly praised for his work in IP disputes. He is typically instructed in complex litigation, and has a proven track record in matters of defamation. He also receives recognition for his work as a mediator and for his "excellent service." **Strengths:** "His statement of the case was exceptionally well drafted." "His advice is clear and succinct and he very much has a no-nonsense approach."

Monye Anyadike-Danes QC Combines her commercial practice with family and construction law work, and is also an expert in judicial review. She is praised for her meticulous preparation of cases. **Strengths:** "She is extremely hard-working, very capable, pleasant to deal with, accommodating and approachable." "Monye is industrious and has a lovely manner with clients."

Patrick Good QC Known for his experience, he regularly acts on the defence side of professional negligence matters. He is also noted for his expertise in chancery, real estate and more general commercial disputes. **Strengths:** "He's an excellent advocate and he's very good on his papers as well." "He is meticulously prepared and a very good operator." "Affable and highly skilled in negotiation."

Brett Lockhart QC Practises a broad range of commercial matters and is also heavily involved in IP, defamation and clinical law. He is increasingly instructed as a mediator in partnership disputes and regularly acts in criminal law cases defending government entities. **Strengths:** "Brett really invests in a case and he's happy to allow for plenty of leading-in time." "He's very reliable and you know you will get the unvarnished truth from him, which is really important." "He is particularly understanding of clients in a sensitive situation."

David Scoffield QC Mainly known for handling procurement work and judicial reviews, but is developing an increasingly strong reputation in the world of commercial disputes. Sources praise his high commitment to cases and note that he particularly excels in complex matters. **Strengths:** "He is very analytical and reads heavily into the papers." "He is a very intelligent guy but approachable, and he has a measured and realistic approach to his work." "He is bright, hard-working and also motivated and interested. His paperwork is brilliant."

Jacqueline Simpson QC Known for her expertise in banking law, she also regularly handles chancery and personal injury cases. She enjoys high praise for her people skills. **Strengths:** "She's very hard-working, a very well-prepared and capable counsel, and she's quite commercially minded. She has a sensible, pragmatic approach." "She is excellent with clients, direct and effective."

JUNIORS

Adrian Colmer Highly praised junior with a great commercial practice, who has particular strength in land law and chancery disputes. He is known both for his ability to see the detail in a case and for his commercial know-how, and has a wealth of experience across many different types of contentious proceedings. **Strengths:** "He is extremely good at cutting through to the core points of the cases, and knows how to analyse and prioritise matters." "He is very candid and forthright."

David Dunlop Renowned senior junior known for practising across a wide spectrum of commercial instruction; his practice includes financial, construction, company and property disputes. He is highly regarded by market sources for his detailed preparation of cases, his efficiency in court and his commercial savvy. **Strengths:** "He has the capacity to take on volumes of information very quickly." "He's terrific and has an amazing capacity for work." "He's like a senior counsel wrapped up in a junior. He's extremely able in court and can hold his own with anybody."

Keith Gibson (see p.652) A tremendous choice for complicated, high-value commercial matters as well as those of a chancery, IP or banking nature. He has a reputation for having a straightforward approach and more than one source highlights the clarity of his advice. He regularly appears in multi-party disputes. **Strengths:** "He is dynamic and very focused, as well as being excellent at getting back in a timely manner and great at driving things on." "He is responsive, pragmatic and understanding."

Hugh MacMahon Experienced practitioner with an enviable reputation in the field, who is particularly renowned for his work on solicitors' negligence and defamation claims. Clients of his include a range of insurance companies. **Strengths:** "He's thorough in his early advice – it's clear that he takes a sharp, tactical stance from early on." "A hard-working, perceptive and conscientious lawyer with good insight." "His advisory work is first-class."

Robert Millar Held in high regard among peers and instructing solicitors for his wide-ranging commercial, chancery and clinical negligence practice. Sources note his capacity to handle complex cases and lengthy experience in the field. **Strengths:** "A very experienced, able, bright guy." "He is great on paper and very good at grasping the detail of the cases."

Wayne Atchison Acts across a range of different disputes including those of a financial, contractual and company nature. He is praised for his well-structured and timely advice. **Strengths:** "His response time is excellent, and he's someone who understands the relationship a solicitor has with a client – he understands the pressures that a solicitor has, so he advises accordingly, and he goes the extra mile to make sure you are well serviced." "He is good on paper and good on his feet."

Richard Coghlin Covers a range of public procurement, construction and professional negligence cases. Sources highlight his preparation and in-depth understanding of the matters at hand. **Strengths:** "He has all the attributes of an academic lawyer: he's a very hard worker, he's strong in court and his advisory work is quite superb."

Craig Dunford Noted for his skills particularly in written advices, he regularly acts for solicitors in insolvency, chancery and more general commercial cases. **Strengths:** "He is very forthright and properly stands his ground." "He is quite academic and cautious in a good sense."

Jonathan Dunlop Has experience in several key areas of commercial disputes, and is noted for his particular expertise in partnership-related matters. Sources praise his negotiation skills. **Strengths:** "He has a very incisive mind; he gets straight to the point." "He has a prolific commercial and chancery practice and is personable and able."

Michael Egan Holds a reputation for providing a value-added service. **Strengths:** "He is really excellent with clients, and pragmatic. He brings that kind of problem-solving ability to the equation."

Donal Flanagan Recognised for his activity on behalf of English insurers and recommended for banking matters. **Strengths:** "He is approachable, pragmatic and he delivers client-focused results. Clients find him to be very impressive."

Peter Girvan Tends to focus on technology, social media and privacy disputes. He is known in the field for his practice on behalf of claimants. **Strengths:** "I don't think anybody could question his ability." "He is bright, ambitious and he really extends the boundaries."

William Gowdy Handles a range of commercial disputes as well as insolvency matters. He is commended for his academic prowess and preparation. **Strengths:** "He's extremely good, a very bright, able guy doing a wide range of work and one of the most commercially able juniors." "He will always fight for his client but he's very straight."

Peter Hopkins A former solicitor who has the ability to offer alternative insights into cases. His practice encompasses insolvency and personal injury actions, among others. **Strengths:** "He's excellent in terms of advisory and drafting work." "Peter's experience of both sides of the legal profession is an invaluable benefit to him in dealing with cases and clients."

Douglas Stevenson An increasing presence in the Commercial Court. As an ex-solicitor, he is noted for his ability to see the other side and offer a different perspective. **Strengths:** "He is very diligent; he has very solid judgement and a common-sense approach." "His skeleton argument and approach to the case was just first-class."

Fiona Fee Recommended for her upfront approach to practicalities and her background in media law, she is known for her ability to unpick complex evidence. **Strengths:** "She's an all-rounder in terms of delivering advice, distilling information and explaining matters to clients in a practical way. She has strong advocacy skills." **Recent work:** Acted for defendants Porsche in a contested freedom of information claim, in which the client did not want to disclose commercially sensitive vehicle testing results.

Alistair Fletcher Handles commercial cases as well as chancery and personal injury matters, on top of defamation and judicial reviews. **Strengths:** "He is ambitious and hungry, and receptive to taking things on at short notice."

Michael Neeson Well versed in banking litigation and also regularly handles matters involving land law, professional negligence and licensing. **Strengths:** "He has an excellent rapport with clients and is able to concisely present quite complex issues." "He is affable and intelligent, with great advocacy skills."

William Sinton Divides his practice between commercial, chancery, insolvency and land law cases. **Strengths:** "He has great attention to detail. He is very considered in his approach and tough in negotiation."

PERSONAL INJURY

Personal Injury
Leading Silks
Band 1
Fee Brian
Montague Turlough
O'Donoghue Francis
Band 2
Keenan Colm Joseph
McGuinness Andrew
Ringland David
Leading Juniors
Band 1
Potter Gary
Band 2
Dunlop David
Up-and-coming individuals
Fee Fiona

Ranked Lawyers

SILKS

Brian Fee QC Adept at advising both claimants and defendants on complex personal injury issues. He shows expertise in a variety of matters including product liability claims and psychiatric injury cases. **Strengths:** "Brian is excellent with clients; he's extremely good at explaining what can be quite complex matters in a straightforward manner that allows clients to understand what the issues are."

Turlough Montague QC A top silk who is well known for his skill in defending personal injury claims. He has a particular reputation for representing government departments during litigation and is also regularly involved in public inquiries. **Strengths:** "He's very astute. One of the premier barristers in Northern Ireland. He's also a very good negotiator."

Frank O'Donoghue QC Leading silk in the Northern Irish market noted for his abilities in a broad range of matters including industrial disease, employers' liability and RTA claims. **Strengths:** "Frank is a leading QC with extensive experience in a range of matters." "He is approachable and very good with clients. He is also very good on his feet."

Colm Joseph Keenan Well-regarded silk with experience in a broad range of personal injury work. He is consistently noted for his great skill in handling noise-induced hearing loss cases. **Strengths:** "Very experienced in deafness cases." "A very able lawyer."

David Ringland Prominent silk who enjoys a thriving personal injury defence practice. He acts for a number of well-known insurers, and is praised by commentators for his collaborative approach during a case. **Strengths:** "David is very thorough." "He is efficient in court."

JUNIORS

Gary Potter Highly esteemed barrister able to advise both claimants and defendants, including insurance companies. He shows strong expertise in a broad range of industrial disease work that encompasses claims for asbestos conditions, hand-arm vibration syndrome and RSI, among others. **Strengths:** "Meticulous in his preparation. He is very good at adapting his style of advocacy to the occasion." "A well-established junior with a diverse practice."

David Dunlop A busy senior junior who is applauded for the careful attention he shows to every case. Market sources also attest to his extensive experience in personal injury matters. **Strengths:** "A very strong junior counsel, held in very high regard."

Andrew McGuinness Experienced personal injury junior noted for his thorough approach to matters. He bolsters his practice with his additional expertise in professional negligence. **Strengths:** "Andrew's meticulous approach and attention to detail ensure that he is an essential component of any legal team." "He prepares extremely thoroughly and identifies issues well ahead of time."
Recent work: Acted for the claimant, a primary school student, in a loss of eyesight claim. The boy lost the sight in one of his eyes after a peer hit him in the eye with a wand during a school play.

Fiona Fee Advises both claimants and defendants on a wide range of different matters including workplace and RTA claims. Also regularly acts on cases involving significant public liability, including those that concern government departments. **Strengths:** "Fiona has sound judgement and is skilled at dealing with clients." "Confident on her feet and meticulous in her work. She is approachable, intelligent, good with clients and great with attention to detail."

REAL ESTATE LITIGATION

Real Estate Litigation
Leading Silks
Band 1
Humphreys Michael
Leading Juniors
Band 1
Colmer Adrian
Band 2
Dunlop David
Alphabetical order within each band. Band 1 is highest.

Ranked Lawyers

SILKS

Michael Humphreys QC Well-recognised QC with a broad chancery and commercial practice that encompasses property matters and construction disputes. He also takes on professional negligence claims against surveyors and architects. **Strengths:** "An experienced barrister who is well respected by judges and colleagues alike. A skilled advocate." "Clear and concise in his advice, he provides an exceptionally high level of service."

JUNIORS

Adrian Colmer Very well-regarded chancery barrister with an excellent reputation for his property practice. His expertise covers landlord and tenant disputes, estates matters, repossessions and land issues. **Strengths:** "A very pleasant guy to work with who is very diligent. His written work is excellent and he is good in court." "Has an extensive chancery practice, and is a go-to name for land and property advice." "He is a leading junior in real estate litigation; he has gravitas at the Bar."

David Dunlop Experienced practitioner singled out for his property expertise. Areas of particular interest cover landlord and tenant issues as well as matters relating to land law. **Strengths:** "He is highly efficient and gets through a phenomenal amount of work." "An extremely diligent counsel with an eye for detail and a high level of technical competence."

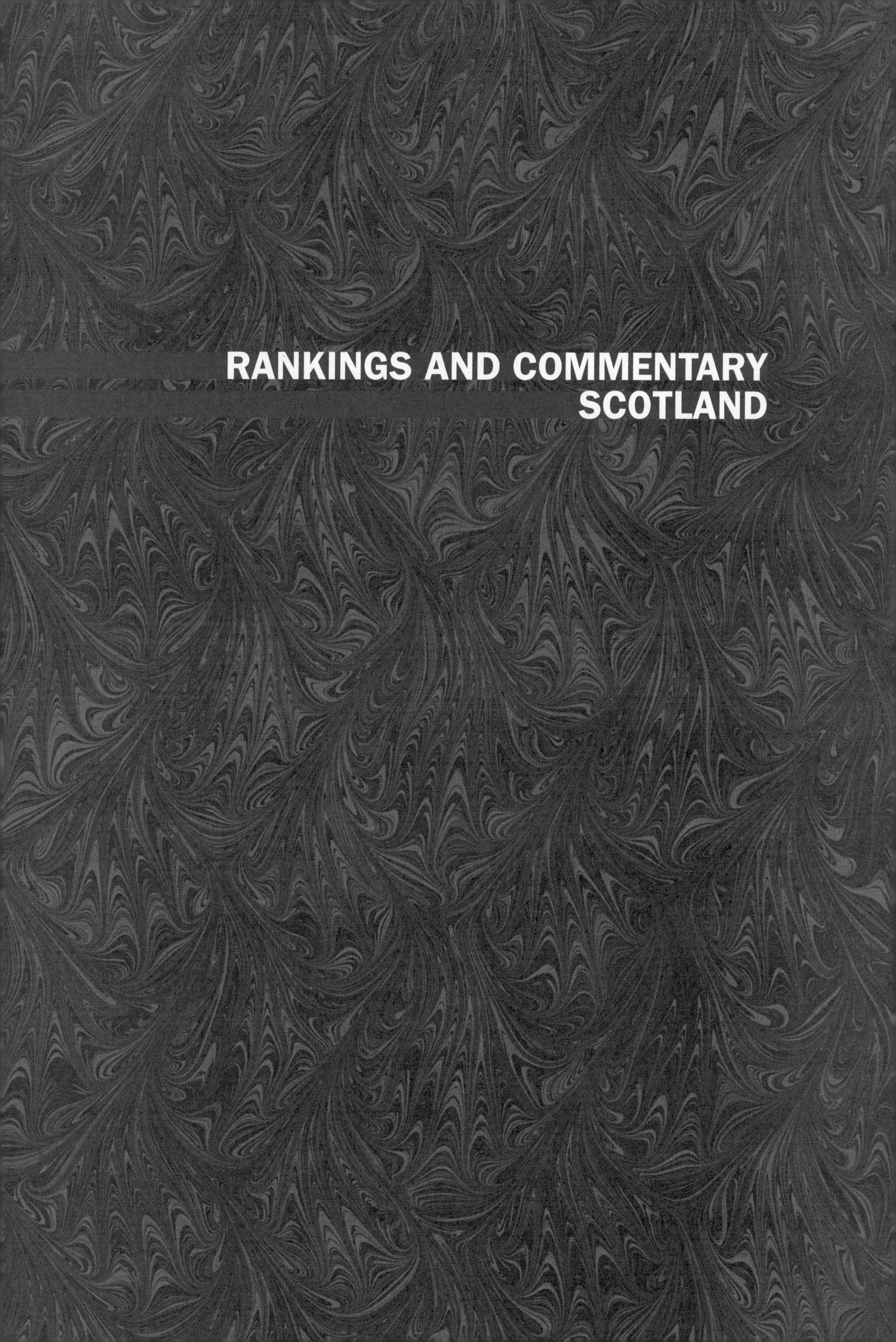

RANKINGS AND COMMENTARY
SCOTLAND

Contents:

ADMINISTRATIVE & PUBLIC LAW

Administrative & Public Law
Leading Stables
Band 1
Axiom Advocates *
Band 2
Ampersand *
Leading Silks
Band 1
Carmichael Ailsa J *Ampersand*
Johnston David *Axiom Advocates*
Lindsay Mark *Axiom Advocates*
Mitchell Jonathan J *Arnot Manderson (ORL)* ◊
Moynihan Gerry *Axiom Advocates*
O'Neill Aidan *Ampersand*
Band 2
Bovey Mungo *Hastie Stable (ORL)* ◊
Crawford Ruth *Axiom Advocates*
Findlay James *Terra Firma Chambers (ORL)* ◊
Mure James *Axiom Advocates*
Poole Anna *Axiom Advocates* *
Thomson Malcolm *Ampersand*
Leading Juniors
Star individuals
Ross Morag *Axiom Advocates*
Band 1
MacGregor John *Axiom Advocates*
Pirie Chris *Hastie Stable (ORL)* ◊
Webster Andrew G *Hastie Stable (ORL)* ◊
Band 2
Burnet Alasdair J *Terra Firma Chambers (ORL)* ◊
Byrne Daniel *Axiom Advocates* [A]
** Indicates set / individual with profile.*
[A] direct access (see p.24).
◊ (ORL) = Other Ranked Lawyer.
Alphabetical order within each band. Band 1 is highest.

Band 1

Axiom Advocates

See profile on p.946

THE SET

Axiom Advocates offers an unrivalled depth of public law expertise and houses high-quality practitioners at every level. Clients comment that it is "without a doubt the top stable in this area," explaining that "you can be assured that their advocates will be at the top of their game. They are academically brilliant and there is a real sense of quality across the board." Members tackle all aspects of administrative and public law, including commercial, EU, planning, procurement, human rights and immigration. A recent highlight was Ross v Lord Advocate, a case concerning the publication of clear guidelines on prosecutions arising from assisted suicide. This matter featured members of Axiom acting for both the petitioner and respondent.

Client service: "The clerking at Axiom is great. They are very responsive, helpful, friendly and accommodating. They are great at coming up with the best lawyer when you're not seeking out someone specific." Practice manager Lesley Flynn leads the team.

SILKS

David Johnston QC Strong choice for administrative and public law cases involving novel questions of law. He regularly represents the Scottish government and other public bodies in legislative and regulatory challenges. **Strengths:** "Consistently high standard of advice and effective advocacy." "He has a very intellectual approach to matters and really thinks things through." **Recent work:** Represented the Scottish Information Commissioner in an appeal examining the scope of the personal data exemption under the Freedom of Information (Scotland) Act 2002.

Mark Lindsay QC Has extensive experience of acting for petitioners and respondents in high-profile public and administrative law challenges. He also advises public bodies on freedom of information responses and the implications of legislative reform. **Strengths:** "Has an incredible analytical mind, produces very detailed submissions and is good with the clients." "Great breadth of experience. He is also very easy to deal with. Even when he is on the opposing side, he is very reasonable, approachable and pragmatic." **Recent work:** Acted for the Law Society of Scotland in an appeal to the Inner House which considered whether or not the Court of Session had an inherent common law power to grant an English barrister ad hoc rights of audience.

Gerry Moynihan QC Offers a breadth of administrative and public law expertise, which includes commercial, human rights and regulatory challenges. He is also experienced at acting in public inquiries. **Strengths:** "He is very pragmatic in his approach and has the ear of the court." "An astute lawyer with a sharp mind, who has a concise and measured delivery in court and an assured manner with clients." **Recent work:** Represented the Scottish government in a case which considered whether the Scotch Whisky Association's challenge to Alcohol (Minimum Pricing) (Scotland) Act 2014 was a breach of EU provisions on the free movement of goods.

Ruth Crawford QC Often seen in challenging and complex judicial reviews and regulatory appeals. She is also frequently instructed to advise public bodies on legislative interpretation. **Strengths:** "A wealth of experience – her ability to take the court with her is one of her great strengths." "Very good in court and delivers clear, organised submissions. She has a willingness to roll up her sleeves and can assimilate huge amounts of information. Very good drafting and great turnaround times." **Recent work:** Represented the Financial Conduct Authority in a challenge against the sanctions regime applicable to perpetrators of mortgage fraud.

James Mure QC Predominantly handles public law challenges which turn on the interpretation of EU law. He receives instructions from the Scottish government, local authorities and other clients in the public sector. **Strengths:** "Highly intelligent." "He is very strong on technical details. He gives clear opinions and doesn't sit on the fence." **Recent work:** Led a challenge brought by Angus Growers against the withdrawal of its recognition as a producer organisation supporting the fruit and vegetable sector and a related claim for damages under Francovich state liability principles.

Anna Poole QC (see p.739) Represents petitioners, respondents and interested parties in judicial reviews, statutory appeals and regulatory challenges. Her broad, substantive expertise includes planning, community care, devolution and other aspects of local authority law. **Strengths:** "She is very thorough and also very good at thinking of how to present to the court, not just legally but also tactically." "She is very well prepared, very clever and also very good at putting arguments across to the bench." **Recent work:** Acted for Milton Keynes Council in its judicial review challenging the Scottish ministers' approach to the meaning of ordinary residence and therefore, the liability for the care costs of an individual who had moved from England to Scotland.

JUNIORS

Morag Ross Widely regarded as one of the top juniors at the Scottish Bar. She acts in significant public law challenges across a wide range of subjects, including commercial, human rights, EU and planning law. **Strengths:** "Very persuasive advocacy. She is more than a safe pair of hands. Extremely bright and able to make very incisive arguments." "Her written advice is extremely well thought out, logically drafted and presented in a way that makes difficult subject matter easily digestible. She is very bright." **Recent work:** Represented the Lord Advocate in a judicial review brought by a petitioner seeking publication of a policy outlining the circumstances in which a prosecution will be brought against a person who is involved in assisted suicide.

John MacGregor Acts for petitioners, respondents and interveners in a wide range of judicial reviews and regulatory appeals. He is expert in a number of areas, and especially well regarded for his handling of procurement disputes. **Strengths:** "Excellent advocacy, advice and attention to detail." "A thoroughly good lawyer. What I really like is that he is absolutely candid. He knows which points are rubbish and won't try to pull the wool over your eyes." **Recent work:** Represented the Equality and Human Rights Commission as interveners in a petition for judicial review concerning the failure of the Scottish ministers to lay regulations under the mental health legislation.

Daniel Byrne Draws on his deep expertise in human rights law to represent petitioners and respondents in administrative and public law challenges. He is particularly strong in the context of immigration and asylum appeals. **Strengths:** "One of the most intelligent advocates at the Bar." "Good presentation. He knows to pick good points, which makes him effective." "He is very thorough, business-like and easy to put before clients, including corporate clients." **Recent work:** Represented one of the respondents in a judicial review challenging the Secretary of State over the Home Department's use of Swedish company Sprakab in assessing the reliability of asylum claims.

Band 2

Ampersand

See profile on p.945

THE SET

Ampersand offers expertise across a diverse range of public and administrative law cases, notably in the areas of commercial, planning, EU and human rights law. Within the public sector, the stable receives instructions from local authorities as well as the Scottish and UK governments. Advocates also represent corporations, charities and individual petitioners seeking to challenge legislation and public body decision-making. Recently, members have been involved in a high-profile judicial review concerning the 'Named Person' provisions in the Children and Young Persons (Scotland) Act 2014.

Client service: "The clerks are very responsive and able to put forward good counsel." "A good clerking team. They are helpful, friendly and accommodating." Practice manager Alan Moffat leads the team.

SILKS

Ailsa Carmichael QC Maintains a broad administrative and public law practice, representing petitioners and respondents in significant judicial reviews. She also advises local authorities about their funding obligations, especially where responsibility for the provision of a particular service is being contested by another local authority. **Strengths:** "Excellent, reasonable and pragmatic." "A nice manner in court." "She offers both clarity of analysis and clarity of presentation, which makes her an effective advocate and means that she has the ear of the court." **Recent work:** Represented one of the interveners involved in the Christian Institute's high-profile challenge to the introduction of regulations requiring every child in Scotland to be assigned a named person with responsibility for overseeing their welfare under the Children and Young Persons (Scotland) Act 2014.

Aidan O'Neill QC Frequently involved in cases of significance before the highest courts in the UK and EU. He specialises in challenges against legislation and government policy on the grounds of human rights and EU law. **Strengths:** "His sheer scope of knowledge and intellectual capacity is astounding." "He is tenacious and takes on points others wouldn't think of." **Recent work:** Represented the appellants in a judicial review against the Lord Advocate concerning the right of prisoners to vote in the Scottish independence referendum.

Malcolm Thomson QC Has extensive experience of appearing in administrative and public law cases. He is particularly noted for representing clients in both the private and public sectors in planning appeals and inquiries. **Strengths:** "Very nice to deal with and very knowledgeable." "He takes a well thought-through and thorough approach to his cases."

Other Ranked Lawyers

Jonathan Mitchell QC (Arnot Manderson) Frequently involved in controversial and precedent-setting litigation before the administrative and appellate courts. He is particularly experienced in cases involving human rights, information, political and constitutional law. **Strengths:** "He is highly intelligent. He finds interesting arguments and is a confident advocate at appellate levels." **Recent work:** Represented the petitioners in a landmark challenge to the election of Alistair Carmichael MP following the emergence of evidence that he had lied about his knowledge of a memo concerning Nicola Sturgeon which was leaked to the press.

James Findlay (Terra Firma Chambers) Has considerable experience of acting in judicial reviews relating to planning, infrastructure and environmental law. He also offers expertise in protective costs orders. **Strengths:** "I have always found him highly effective on paper and in court." "Very approachable, knowledgeable and pragmatic about finding solutions. Accessible at all hours." "Very user-friendly and straightforward to deal with. Although he's very busy, he does turn work around very quickly and is very good with clients." **Recent work:** Represented the petitioner, St Andrews Environmental Protection Association, in a challenge against the grant of planning permission for the relocation of a secondary school onto green belt land.

Mungo Bovey QC (Hastie Stable) Particularly proficient in administrative and public law cases involving complex arguments about human rights and equality. He has considerable experience of public law cases arising in the context of immigration and asylum. **Strengths:** "Very experienced, especially on the claimant side, and excellent at immigration cases."

Chris Pirie (Hastie Stable) Noted for his deep expertise in public law cases involving immigration and social welfare. As standing junior to the Advocate General for Scotland, he has considerable experience of representing the UK government and particularly the Department for Work & Pensions. **Strengths:** "Very well organised and effective on his feet."

Andrew Webster (Hastie Stable) Continues to serve as First Standing Junior Counsel to the Advocate General for Scotland, a role which sees him act for the UK government in a wide range of administrative and public law cases. His expertise in immigration and human rights is of particular note. **Strengths:** "An effective advocate with a wealth of experience."

Alasdair Burnet (Terra Firma Chambers) Noted for his broad public and administrative law practice, which encompasses EU, procurement and planning law. He is also involved in complex cases regarding the powers and duties of public bodies. **Strengths:** "Good at thinking laterally." "A very effective advocate. He is very knowledgeable about planning but also practices in other areas of public law. He has the ear of the court." **Recent work:** Appointed by the Supreme Court to advise on an unopposed challenge brought by Scottish ministers against a declaration by the Inner House that parts of the Agricultural Holdings (Scotland) Act were in breach of the ECHR and beyond the legislative competence of the Scottish Parliament.

AGRICULTURE & RURAL AFFAIRS

Agriculture & Rural Affairs
Leading Stables
Band 1
Terra Firma Chambers *
Westwater Advocates *
Leading Silks
Star individuals
Agnew of Lochnaw Bt Crispin *Westwater Advocates* *
Band 1
Reid J Gordon *Terra Firma Chambers*
Leading Juniors
Band 1
Cameron Donald *Westwater Advocates*
Maclean Iain *Terra Firma Chambers*
Sutherland Robert *Terra Firma Chambers*
Up-and-coming individuals
MacDougall Neil *Westwater Advocates*
* *Indicates set / individual with profile.*
Alphabetical order within each band. Band 1 is highest.

Band 1

Terra Firma Chambers

See profile on p.948

THE SET

Terra Firma Chambers is renowned for its strong agricultural and rural affairs practice and can also provide specialist expertise in property, planning, commercial and administrative law. The stable is led by a number of Scotland's foremost advocates with a plethora of experience in representing clients before the Scottish Land Court, the Court of Session and Sheriff Courts in a wide range of matters. The members of the stable are also well known for regularly speaking at major conferences on agricultural and crofting law and have also had numerous articles published on agricultural holdings and related matters. Advocates represent farmers, estates and commercial landowners for a number of matters ranging from crofting issues and rent reviews to agricultural subsidies and livestock issues.

Client service: "The administrative side of things ticks along like clockwork; everything is run exactly the way it should be." Emma Potter is the practice manager at the stable and is assisted by two deputy clerks, Tracy Whitelaw and Andrew Veitch.

SILKS

Gordon Reid QC A well-established commercial silk with extensive experience of dealing with a range of agricultural and land law disputes. He is considered as one of the foremost advocates in this area of law and has recent experience of dealing with a number of disputes connected to agricultural and commercial tenancies. **Strengths:** "He is absolutely brilliant and he is really reliable. You know what you are getting with him." "He radiates gravitas and instils confidence in clients."

JUNIORS

Iain Maclean He specialises in property-related work, with a particular focus on matters connected to landed estates and rural property. He is also recognised for his expertise on crofting matters and has the ability to represent clients in a broad range of issues including sporting rights, sheep stock valuations and tenancy rights under the Agricultural Holdings Act. **Strengths:** "He really knows his stuff and is well thought of in the legal industry." "He is a very sharp guy and a very insightful chap; a heavy hitter with a great wealth of knowledge."

Robert Sutherland He is a very experienced advocate with specialist expertise in agricultural and crofting law and also practises in the areas of property, planning, environmental and public and administrative law. He has represented clients in a wide variety of cases before the Scottish Land Court, the House of Lords and the Supreme Court. **Strengths:** "He is a very intellectual person and has a great grasp of the complexities of the law." "He is very bright and has a lot of experience in this field. He has a very broad practice across the whole spectrum of rural matters." **Recent work:** Acted for the trustees of an inter vivos trust in a professional negligence action arising from an unsuccessful attempt to remove an agricultural tenant.

Westwater Advocates

See profile on p.949

THE SET

Westwater Advocates has extensive experience in representing clients in both agricultural and crofting matters and is known as one of the leading stables in Scotland. Its practice covers all landed estates matters as well as landlord and tenant issues, renewable energy and compulsory purchases. The stable has experience of arguing property and agricultural cases before the Sheriff Courts, the Scottish Land Court, the Lands Tribunal for Scotland and the ECJ. The advocates also represent public bodies, local authorities and governmental organisations in a number of matters connected to agricultural law.

Client service: "They are a very well-run set and they have always provided me with a helpful as well as friendly service." Sheila Westwater is the principal clerk, assisted by deputy clerks Christina Ballantyne and Jane Morrison.

SILKS

Sir Crispin Agnew of Lochnaw Bt QC (see p.580) He is one of the foremost experts in rural property law and has extensive experience in dealing with all issues facing landed estates and estate owners. He also advises on many other issues in connection with agricultural and environmental law including crofting matters, conveyancing issues, renewable energy and European law issues. **Strengths:** "He is a real leading light and one of the leading senior practitioners. He has written influential academic books on the subject and has a really huge amount of knowledge in his area." "He is absolutely outstanding in his field and covers a broad range of agricultural and crofting matters." **Recent work:** Appealed to the Court of Session for a complicated legal issue without prior precedent on the meaning of the word 'landlord' in the Crofters (Scotland) Act 1993.

JUNIORS

Donald Cameron He is an experienced advocate and regularly represents clients in cases concerning both employment and agricultural law. Cameron has a strong history of arguing cases in front of a variety of courts including the Court of Session, the Supreme Court and the ECJ. **Strengths:** "He has a real interest and understanding of rural matters and he has vast knowledge of this industry as he comes from farming background." "He is very good and I rate his skills highly." **Recent work:** Acted for the Scottish government in Feakins v Scottish Ministers with regard to the amount and rate of interest due on outstanding sums due to the appellant.

Neil MacDougall Represents clients in a broad range of practice areas which include commercial, employment and agricultural law. He has developed significant experience in dealing with all aspects of agricultural and rural property matters and has argued cases in the Scottish Land Court, the Lands Tribunal for Scotland and the ECJ. **Strengths:** "He is a very eloquent speaker and can make his point forcefully." "He is very smart and he knows what he is doing."

CIVIL LIBERTIES & HUMAN RIGHTS

Civil Liberties & Human Rights
Leading Stables
Band 1
Axiom Advocates *
Band 2
Ampersand *
Leading Silks
Band 1
Carmichael Ailsa J *Ampersand*
Mitchell Jonathan J *Arnot Manderson (ORL)* ◊
O'Neill Aidan *Ampersand*
Band 2
Bovey Mungo *Hastie Stable (ORL)* ◊
Band 3
Lindsay Mark *Axiom Advocates*
Poole Anna *Axiom Advocates* *
Leading Juniors
Band 1
Pirie Chris *Hastie Stable (ORL)* ◊
Webster Andrew G *Hastie Stable (ORL)* ◊
Band 2
MacGregor John *Axiom Advocates*
Band 3
Byrne Daniel *Axiom Advocates* 🄰
Komorowski Julius *Terra Firma Chambers (ORL)* ◊
Ross Douglas *Ampersand*
Ross Morag *Axiom Advocates*
* *Indicates set / individual with profile.*
🄰 *direct access (see p.24).*
◊ *(ORL) = Other Ranked Lawyer.*
Alphabetical order within each band. Band 1 is highest.

Band 1

Axiom Advocates

See profile on p.946

THE SET

Axiom Advocates remains at the forefront of the field of civil liberties and human rights in Scotland. In terms of firepower, the stable is unrivalled in this area and houses many high-calibre practitioners, from juniors through to silks. Its highly skilled members have vast experience of appearing before the Inner and Outer House of the Court of Session, Sheriff Courts, the UK Supreme Court and the ECHR. Its advocates are recognised for their deft handling of highly complex judicial review proceedings, and have recently acted in a number of market-leading cases, such as Gordon Ross v Lord Advocate, a case concerning the lawfulness of assisted suicide. Instructing solicitors describe this stable's advocates as "available, approachable and helpful."

Client service: "The clerks are very polite, willing to help, and they always get back to you quickly." "All the clerks are quick and efficient." Lesley Flynn is the practice manager.

SILKS

Mark Lindsay QC A market-leading silk with a well-established practice, he is regularly called upon to challenge the decisions of tribunals, regulatory bodies and local and central government. Given the high calibre of his instructions, he is a regular feature before all levels of domestic court and the ECJ. **Strengths:** "He has an incredibly analytical mind, he reliably provides very detailed submissions and he's good with the clients."

Anna Poole QC (see p.739) Operating at every level of court, from the Sheriff Court to the ECHR, she has been instructed in a number of high-profile, policy-changing matters. Her broad expertise covers areas such as freedom of information, access to justice, prisoners' rights and child protection. **Strengths:** "She is very good at putting her case across persuasively, and not the least bit daunted by the highest levels of court." "She's completely up-to-date and knows all the latest cases. She really has the ear of the court." **Recent work:** Acted in Carroll v Scottish Borders Council, a case concerning the placement of a wind farm. The matter considered the compatibility of local review decisions with the EU Charter of Fundamental Rights.

JUNIORS

John MacGregor Respected junior with a strong track record of assisting local government and other public bodies with administrative appeals and judicial review proceedings. His broad client base includes institutions such as Police Scotland, Glasgow City Council, the Mental Health Tribunal for Scotland and the Serious Organised Crime Agency. **Recent work:** Assisted the Equality and Human Rights Commission with its intervention in LS v Scottish Ministers, a judicial review petition concerning the failure of ministers to lay regulations under the mental health legislation.

Daniel Byrne Represents a variety of petitioners and respondents, including public bodies, individuals facing deportation and the Scottish government. He demonstrates expertise across diverse areas, such as prison, mental health, energy and planning law, and is dedicated to the protection of vulnerable groups. **Strengths:** "You know he'll make a good job of any instruction; he's got good judgement and can formulate arguments excellently." "He clearly knows what he's doing and he's a real pleasure to work with."

Morag Ross Routinely assists both respondents and claimants, including public authorities. She is well versed in judicial review proceedings, procurement law, government litigation and complex aspects of EU legislation. **Strengths:** "She's meticulous in her preparation and delivery and is always listened to by the Bench." "She's top-drawer: efficient, thorough and able to pick things up at short notice."

Band 2

Ampersand

See profile on p.945

THE SET

An esteemed stable that exhibits key strengths in the areas of employment, equality and EU law. Ampersand fields a formidable team of well-respected advocates who offer expert assistance and representation in complex civil liberties and human rights cases. Given its stellar reputation, Ampersand regularly wins instructions in the most high-profile, significant cases, as evidenced by its recent handling of R (Sandiford) v Foreign and Commonwealth Office. This case considered whether the FCO is obliged to fund advocacy for British citizens facing the death penalty abroad.

Client service: Alan Moffat is the practice manager.

SILKS

Ailsa Carmichael QC Highly experienced silk who routinely appears in the Supreme Court and the Court of Session. She habitually assists with matters relating to immigration, asylum and professional negligence, and wins praise for her deft handling of complex judicial review proceedings, statutory appeals and public inquiries. **Strengths:** "She's sensible, reasonable and thorough. When she speaks, the court pays full attention because they know she'll add something that's worth saying." "She's very well respected by the market."

Aidan O'Neill QC As a barrister practising across England, Wales and Scotland, he is well placed to advise on the impact of complex aspects of EU law upon British human rights. He is highly regarded for his finely tuned advocacy skills, and makes regular appearances before the Supreme Court. **Strengths:** "He's very inventive, knowledgeable and academic. He's completely up-to-date and is a bold advocate on behalf of his clients." **Recent work:** Appeared in Hainsworth v MoD, a case concerning an employer's obligations to accommodate the disability requirements of an employee's child.

JUNIORS

Douglas Ross Draws upon his prior experience as a UN legal adviser to better assist his clients in significant cases. His highly active practice sees him making regular appearances before the Supreme Court, the Mental Health Tribunal and the High Court of Justiciary. His burgeoning civil liberties and human rights practice is complemented by further expertise in the areas of personal injury and medical negligence. **Strengths:** "He's a very steady, reliable advocate and he's really got the ear of the court."

Other Ranked Lawyers

Jonathan Mitchell QC (Arnot Manderson) Esteemed human rights silk with particularly significant experience in appellate proceedings. His broad-based expertise encompasses areas such as employment, commercial and family law, and he is regularly called upon to assist with complex social security matters. **Strengths:** "Jonathan is a definite leader in the field, who is very clever and a particularly good choice for tricky constitutional cases at the cutting edge of the law." "Brilliant in his oral advocacy, his courtroom presence can't be overstated."

Mungo Bovey QC (Hastie Stable) Highly experienced silk who regularly handles major human rights cases before the Privy Council and the Supreme Court. He is a popular choice for matters containing complex aspects of discrimination and equality law and a recognised expert in employment cases. **Strengths:** "He fights the whole way and is totally committed to human rights." "He's a hugely important silk with a well-deserved reputation."

Chris Pirie (Hastie Stable) Well known for his wide-reaching expertise, covering areas such as equality and public law, disciplinary matters and significant criminal cases. **Strengths:** "He has punched well above his weight since the day he started." "He's incredibly capable and wonderful to work with. He's a thoroughly reliable, intellectually able junior."

Andrew Webster (Hastie Stable) Widely respected for his varied practice, he offers expert human rights advice and representation across areas such as immigration, family and social security law. He is held in high esteem for his adroit handling of complex judicial review proceedings and statutory appeals. **Strengths:** "He's well regarded, easy to work with and takes a comfortingly relaxed approach with clients." "He's been around the block a few times, so he really knows his stuff."

Julius Komorowski (Terra Firma Chambers) Accomplished junior who is highly sought after for his deep knowledge of civil liberties and human rights law. He regularly appears against the UK government, Scottish ministers and local authorities in matters involving prison law, asylum or mental health elements. **Strengths:** "A big brain, he's a deep thinker and also a very good speaker." "He's really broken through in the field of civil liberties and human rights, not least because of his wonderful personality."

CLINICAL NEGLIGENCE

Clinical Negligence
Leading Stables
Band 1
Ampersand *
Compass Chambers *
Band 2
Arnot Manderson
Axiom Advocates *
Leading Silks
Band 1
Caldwell Marion *Compass Chambers* *
Dunlop Laura *Hastie Stable (ORL)* ◊
Dunlop Roddy *Axiom Advocates*
Ferguson Iain *Axiom Advocates*
MacAulay Colin *Arnot Manderson*
Maguire Maria *Ampersand*
Smith Andrew *Compass Chambers*
Band 2
Anderson Rory *Compass Chambers*
Bowie Simon *Ampersand*
Clancy Ronald *Ampersand*
Duncan Alastair *Axiom Advocates*
Haldane Shona *Arnot Manderson*
McLean Alan *Hastie Stable (ORL)* ◊
Milligan Robert *Compass Chambers* *
Stephenson David *Ampersand*
Young Andrew R W *Arnot Manderson*
Leading Juniors
Star individuals
Smart Astrid *Compass Chambers*
Band 1
Henderson Lisa *Ampersand*
Mackenzie Euan *Ampersand*
MacSporran Archie *Ampersand*
McGregor Malcolm *Compass Chambers*
Sutherland Lauren *Ampersand*
Band 2
Drysdale Fiona *Ampersand*
Khurana Vinit *Ampersand*
Tait Arabella *Arnot Manderson*
Band 3
Dawson Jamie *Ampersand*
Devaney Catherine *Ampersand*
Doherty Una *Ampersand*
Fitzpatrick Mark *Ampersand*
Mackenzie Neil *Arnot Manderson*
Paterson Chris *Axiom Advocates*
Pugh Richard *Compass Chambers* *
Ross Douglas *Ampersand*
Stuart Philip *Ampersand*
Up-and-coming individuals
Reid Paul *Ampersand*
* *Indicates set / individual with profile.*
◊ *(ORL) = Other Ranked Lawyer.*
Alphabetical order within each band. Band 1 is highest.

Band 1

Ampersand

See profile on p.945

THE SET

A prominent stable in the clinical negligence domain, Ampersand possesses a solid bench of highly experienced silks and juniors. Its members handle the full spectrum of matters including high-value and complex cases for both pursuers and defenders. Members acted in the landmark Montgomery v Lanarkshire Health Board case which has had a huge impact on laws of consent in this field.

Client service: "Excellent clerking team – Alan Moffat is always willing to help us in any respect." "Very good, they will try and accommodate us and the clients as much as possible. The senior clerk, Alan Moffat, is very proactive."

SILKS

Maria Maguire QC Unanimously regarded as a standout advocate in this arena, Maria is constantly in high demand. Of late, she has been focused on acting for pursuers in cases of the utmost complexity and severity. **Strengths:** "An absolute star at clinical negligence." "She carries a great deal of weight in the court."

Simon Bowie QC He possesses a wide-ranging practice and is praised in particular by market sources for his medical negligence defence work for both institutions and individuals. **Strengths:** "He's got a level of charisma that works with judges. He inherently has the ear of the court." "Excellent at defending cases."

Ronald Clancy QC An established name in the field of medical negligence, who possesses a depth of experience of taking cases of significant value to court. **Strengths:** "Good at high-value, complex stuff." "He's highly experienced, able to give clear advice and is someone with a lot of experience in court."

David Stephenson QC A formidable opponent on the medical negligence defence side, who frequently receives instructions from a range of health boards. **Strengths:** "Very highly regarded as a defender." "Very competent." **Recent work:** Instructed to defend a claim of negligence relating to the storage of cryogenically frozen sperm.

JUNIORS

Lisa Henderson Market commentators are extremely impressed by the work Lisa does in the clinical negligence sphere. She acts for both pursuers and defenders in high-value cerebral palsy and spinal injury cases. **Strengths:** "Her standard of work is excellent." "A go-to counsel for cerebral palsy. Her grasp of even the smallest detail is incredible."

Euan Mackenzie Highly regarded by peers who note his excellent attention to detail. He is frequently seen on both the defenders' and pursuers' side of medical negligence cases and possesses additional expertise in public inquiries. **Strengths:** "Fantastic; he always goes beyond what you need him to do and goes through everything with a fine-tooth comb." "A very experienced senior junior."

Archie MacSporran Experienced at taking civil cases in the Court of Session. In addition to defending clinical negligence matters, he is also well reputed in fatal accident inquiries and mental health tribunals. **Strengths:** "A joy to work with and a first-rate junior." "Very fair and even handed."

Lauren Sutherland A well-known figure in medical negligence, who is frequently instructed in a diverse range of high-value cases. **Strengths:** "Her knowledge of the legal and medical aspects of the cases she handles is phenomenal." "Absolutely superb at medical negligence cases. She goes the extra mile to understand the expert knowledge." **Recent work:** Acted for the pursuer in a case related to the suicide of a girl and the psychological effects of this on her mother.

Fiona Drysdale Birth and brain injury cases are an important area of her expertise. She often represents those of limited capacity such as children and the vulnerable. **Strengths:** "Thorough, clever, efficient and responsive." "A very dedicated counsel; you can see that she really cares about the case." **Recent work:** Acted in a cerebral palsy case involving complex causation and a lengthy proof.

Vinit Khurana As a former GP, Vinit brings a wealth of expert medical knowledge to his practice. He represents a wide range of clients in clinical negligence cases and is particularly knowledgeable in fatal accident inquiries. **Strengths:** "Very able and methodical." "Insightful and very responsive."

Jamie Dawson A junior with an extensive civil practice with a focus on clinical negligence. He is recognised in the market for his work in fatal accident inquiries. **Strengths:** "He is very good at picking up on things and running with them."

Catherine Devaney She possesses experience in several aspects of medical negligence work including cases involving periodical payments and cerebral palsy. **Strengths:** "Very hard-working." "She is someone who I can trust to get to grips with the detail on the case." **Recent work:** Instructed in a matter in which the claimant, who suffered from a negligent infertility procedure, passed away mid-case.

Una Doherty A former litigation solicitor who regularly acts for the defence in medical negligence cases. Claims related to cerebral palsy are a key area of expertise. **Strengths:** "Very able and efficient. She's insightful and good at analysing cases." "She's always very well prepared." **Recent work:** Acted on behalf of the NHS Central Legal Office in a case relating to the suicide of a prison inmate.

Mark Fitzpatrick Reputed for his work in medical negligence defence, he is often instructed in matters involving fatalities and catastrophic injuries. **Strengths:** "A senior junior on the defence side; he's instructed time and again because he does so well for them." "Works well in a team."

Douglas Ross An extremely experienced junior in the area of personal injury and medical negligence, who is particularly knowledgeable in cases involving fatalities. **Strengths:** "A top advocate." "Very thorough, efficient and quick at getting back to you."

Philip Stuart An established junior with significant expertise in the areas of birth damage and brain injuries. He frequently acts in cases that are both high value and complex. **Strengths:** "Has a great deal of experience in high-value defence work." "Responds within timescales."

Paul Reid An up-and-coming junior with a particular focus on cauda equina. He frequently acts on behalf of both pursuers and defenders and was instructed by NHS Scotland in the high-profile vaginal mesh cases. **Strengths:** "He stands out." "He is robust and he sticks to his guns." **Recent work:** Instructed by the insurers of the Society of Radiographers in a claim alleging professional negligence on the part of a radiographer.

Compass Chambers

See profile on p.947

THE SET

Compass Chambers has an established reputation for handling the full spectrum of medical negligence cases for both claimants and defendants. Its members are frequently engaged to handle both sensitive and high-value claims. The set receives instructions from various Scottish health boards including the Medical and Dental Defence Union of Scotland and the NHS Central Legal Office.

Client service: "The clerks are very good, Gavin Herd runs a tight ship. You can rely on them to get the job done. You can't fault them." "Gavin Herd is always willing to help out. The whole team works together really well. The seminars they run for general advice are outstanding."

SILKS

Marion Caldwell QC (see p.609) A highly regarded silk whose clinical negligence practice is complemented by her strong expertise in personal injury. She is especially experienced in brain aneurysm cases and claims for catastrophic injury. **Strengths:** "She is incredibly hard-working and dedicated to the cause. Once she gets her teeth into a case, she doesn't let go." "She is very approachable and is a really good communicator."

Andrew Smith QC Well placed to handle a range of brain injury claims as he is particularly noted for his strength in cases relating to neurology. He is also experienced in cases concerning injury at birth as well as high-value patrimonial loss cases. **Strengths:** "An extremely committed and efficient advocate."

Rory Anderson QC A seasoned figure who is especially noted for his clinical negligence defence work. He is experienced in judicial reviews and public inquiries and has additional expertise acting for pursuers in contamination cases. **Strengths:** "He is experienced, straightforward and very pleasant to deal with." "He is a very senior figure at the Bar."

Robert Milligan QC (see p.717) Interviewees praise his abilities in cases involving fatalities and catastrophic injury. He receives instructions from both claimants and defendants and attracts praise for his strategic approach. **Strengths:** "If you've got a tricky case, he's good at knowing how to deal with the tactics of the other side." "A highly intelligent, skilled advocate. He's a good person to have in your corner."

JUNIORS

Astrid Smart Unanimously regarded as a standout junior in her field who is regularly engaged to handle a range of medical and dental negligence claims. She also has a niche interest in employer and occupier liability. **Strengths:** "A go-to junior in Scotland for clinical negligence." "She is brilliantly knowledgeable, has a wonderful way with clients and is a very good all-round advocate." **Recent work:** Acted in a claim of failure to diagnose cervical cancer due to a misinterpreted smear test. The case involved complex issues of quantum and causation.

Malcolm McGregor A very well-reputed advocate with a strong track record in defending a range of medical professionals in claims of negligence. His enviable client base includes doctors, nurses, dentists and surgeons. **Strengths:** "Very good attention to detail and excellent with clients." "He acts for both claimants and defendants which means he can give a rounded view." **Recent work:** Appeared in a fatal accident inquiry in Glasgow, acting in defence of the GPs of a bin lorry driver who killed six people when he lost control and crashed.

Richard Pugh (see p.744) An active junior who is frequently sought out for high-value and complex medical negligence cases. He is noted for his complementary expertise in personal injury and is praised for his medical knowledge and personable nature. **Strengths:** "An excellent advocate, one who knows his medicine inside out." "He is very involved with his work and also very good with clients." **Recent work:** Acted in defence of a health board in a case regarding delay in diagnosis of a brain aneurysm resulting in cognitive limitations for the pursuer.

Band 2

Arnot Manderson

THE SET

Arnot Manderson is frequently engaged by both pursuers and defenders to act on matters involving the full range of medical professionals. Its members are particularly knowledgeable on catastrophic injury and fatal claims, handling matters that are both high value and complex. The stable is frequently called on by health boards as well as individuals.

Client service: "The clerking team is both very helpful and accommodating." "They are very good – Andrew Sutherland has been doing it for a long time." Andrew Sutherland and Elizabeth Manderson are the senior clerks at the stable.

SILKS

Colin MacAulay QC A highly regarded silk known for wide civil practice and notable experience in catastrophic injury claims. He is lauded by interviewees for his cross-examination and strong rapport with clients. **Strengths:** "A fantastic senior counsel. He is calm and very good at managing client expectation." "His cross-examination skills are second to none, it's like watching a master at work."

Shona Haldane QC A silk who is well versed on both the pursuer and defence side. She has experience chairing NHS disciplinary fact finding panels and is well placed to defend health boards and medical product manufacturers. **Strengths:** "She's always on top of the facts and very pragmatic. She is able to command the attention of the board." "She is sympathetic, which is a necessity in this field. She's good at explaining difficult things to the clients."

Andrew Young QC Recognised by peers for his expert handling of complex matters of catastrophic injury for both pursuers and defenders. He possesses an in-depth understanding of brain and spinal injury cases. **Strengths:** "He has a level of gravitas that gives your case added credibility." "He is calm and efficient."

JUNIORS

Arabella Tait She represents both pursuers and defenders in the full spectrum of medical negligence issues including dental, nursing and midwifery claims. She is particularly experienced in the area of catastrophic injury. **Strengths:** "She is very experienced and good on her feet." "She's robust, she tells clients the truth but in a nice way." **Recent work:** Instructed on a failure to diagnose pneumonia claim which resulted in the death of the patient who was a carer for his disabled wife.

Neil Mackenzie Regularly seen in the Court of Session, he is capable of handling both the pursuer and defender sides of medical negligence claims. His wide civil practice also encompasses personal injury, particularly disputes relating to industrial disease and asbestos. **Strengths:** "Superb legal brain and brilliantly analytical." "Great attention to detail." **Recent work:** Acted in defence of Lanarkshire Health Board, in a case involving complex causation of a brachial plexus injury.

Axiom Advocates

See profile on p.946

THE SET

Axiom is a solid stable in the area of clinical negligence with a wealth of advocates who are regularly sought after to act on a range of defence matters on behalf of the MDDUS and NHS Legal Office. Its members are also equipped to handle work for pursuers, including claims made with the help of legal aid.

Client service: "The clerks are very user-friendly and efficient." "They are available, approachable and helpful and their response times are very good." Lesley Flynn is the practice manager at the stable.

SILKS

Roddy Dunlop QC Well regarded for his work in defending a variety of medical professionals as well as health boards in claims of negligent care, as such he is regularly engaged by the NHS Central Legal Office. **Strengths:** "Very highly respected." "He's popular and well regarded, a fighter." **Recent work:** Defended the Scottish Ambulance Service against a claim of causing a heart attack by sending a patient to the wrong facility.

Iain Ferguson QC An experienced silk who regularly defends hospitals and GPs against a range of claims with particular experience in those relating to neurosurgery and obstetrics. **Strengths:** "He's very exacting, very well prepared and precise." "He's outstandingly good." **Recent work:** Acted in defence of Lothian Health Board in a case concerning allegations of negligence on the part of neurologists and a neurosurgeon. The pursuer was paralysed following spinal surgery to remove a benign tumour when he was a teenager.

Alastair Duncan QC Frequently engaged by medical professionals to defend against claims of negligence and also possesses experience in handling inquiries. **Strengths:** "Well-respected, steady counsel. Peer respect is very much there." **Recent work:** Represented Great Glasgow and Clyde Health Board in an inquiry into the death of an infant.

JUNIORS

Chris Paterson With an interest in professional liability, Chris is well placed to defend claims against medical and dental professionals such as GPs and surgeons. He is noted for his experience in judicial review proceedings. **Strengths:** "He is particularly good at working with the MDDUS." "He is very capable and his eye for detail is phenomenal." **Recent work:** Acted in defence of a surgeon against claims of negligent mastectomy and reconstruction surgery.

Other Ranked Lawyers

Laura Dunlop QC (Hastie Stable) A highly regarded silk with a wealth of experience in complex clinical negligence matters. She is regularly engaged to handle significant public inquiries in this practice area. **Strengths:** "An all-round great performer." "She is very thorough, experienced and she has a great way of dealing with difficult clients."

Alan McLean QC (Hastie Stable) An experienced silk in the clinical negligence sphere acknowledged by peers for his handling of large scale cases for health boards. He is noted for his experience in complex disputes relating to cerebral palsy. **Strengths:** "He conducts cases with meticulous care." "He is incredibly able; he's very thorough – you know that no stone will be left unturned."

COMMERCIAL DISPUTE RESOLUTION

Commercial Dispute Resolution
Leading Stables
Band 1
Axiom Advocates *
Band 2
Ampersand *
Leading Silks
Band 1
Borland Garry *Axiom Advocates* *
Currie Heriot *Axiom Advocates*
Dunlop Roddy *Axiom Advocates*
Ellis Nick *Westwater Advocates (ORL)* ◊ *
Howie Robert *Ampersand*
Lake Jonathan C *Axiom Advocates*
Martin Roy *Terra Firma Chambers (ORL)* ◊
McBrearty Kenneth *Axiom Advocates*
Moynihan Gerry *Axiom Advocates*
Sandison Craig *Ampersand*
Band 2
Clancy Ronald *Ampersand*
Davidson of Glen Clova Neil *Axiom Advocates*
Duncan Alastair *Axiom Advocates*
Lindsay Mark *Axiom Advocates*
MacNeill Calum H S *Westwater Advocates (ORL)* ◊ *
Reid J Gordon *Terra Firma Chambers (ORL)* ◊
Sellar David *Ampersand*
Band 3
McNeill James W *Axiom Advocates*
Mure James *Axiom Advocates*
Young Andrew R W *Arnot Manderson (ORL)* ◊
New Silks
Higgins Roisin *Axiom Advocates*
* *Indicates set / individual with profile.*
◊ *(ORL) = Other Ranked Lawyer.*
Alphabetical order within each band. Band 1 is highest.

Commercial Dispute Resolution
Leading Juniors
Band 1
Delibegović-Broome Almira *Axiom Advocates*
MacColl Gavin L *Hastie Stable (ORL)* ◊
Richardson Martin H *Axiom Advocates*
Thomson David *Axiom Advocates* *
Band 2
Barne Jonathan *Axiom Advocates*
O'Brien Paul *Axiom Advocates*
Ower Susan *Axiom Advocates*
Ross Morag *Axiom Advocates*
Walker Gavin *Axiom Advocates*
Band 3
Brown Jonathan *Axiom Advocates*
Duthie Euan *Axiom Advocates*
Hawkes Graeme I *Ampersand*
MacGregor John *Axiom Advocates*
McClelland Ross *Axiom Advocates*
Paterson Chris *Axiom Advocates*
Robertson Eric W *Arnot Manderson (ORL)* ◊
Up-and-coming individuals
Anderson Ross G. *Ampersand*
Massaro David *Axiom Advocates*

Band 1

Axiom Advocates

See profile on p.946

THE SET

There is broad consensus among market commentators that Axiom remains the foremost stable in Scotland for commercial disputes. Individual members are acknowledged as go-to advocates in a diverse range of specialist fields, including banking, contract, insolvency, construction, IP and real estate. A key recent highlight saw advocates from the stable instructed on both sides of SSE Generation v HOCHTIEF Solutions and HOCHTIEF (UK) Construction, a multimillion-pound dispute relating to the collapse of an intake tunnel at a hydroelectric power station in the Scottish Highlands. The stable's typical client list features leading corporates and financial institutions, as well as local authorities and the Office of the Solicitor to the Advocate General. The stable's advocates are regularly instructed in cutting-edge and high-profile matters before the Court of Session.

Client service: "The clerks are very approachable and knowledgeable on the availability and likely feelings of an advocate towards taking a case." "You can place a lot of trust in the clerks – they have a very commercial approach and appreciate the need for a quick turnaround." "The clerks are accessible and contactable. They bill promptly and are on top of counsel's availability." Lesley Flynn is the practice manager and leads the clerking team.

SILKS

Garry Borland QC (see p.599) Regularly cited as a standout advocate for construction and engineering disputes. Also frequently instructed in insolvency, tax and professional liability proceedings, in addition to general commercial matters. He is renowned for his depth of analysis, his grasp of complex technical issues and his attention to detail. **Strengths:** "He is an excellent strategist who always strives for the best commercial result for the client." "He identifies the crux of an issue very quickly, communicating well with the client in plain English." "When it comes to thoroughness, he is unrivalled in his willingness to immerse himself in the complexity of cases. He has real clarity of thought and precision of delivery." **Recent work:** Representing engineering firm AL Daines in a £26 million dispute arising from the terms of a wind farm contract.

Heriot Currie QC A senior silk whose immense experience covers all aspects of commercial dispute resolution. He is very well respected within the profession, and is highlighted by solicitors as a go-to advocate for exceptionally complex or novel cases. He maintains a broad practice, but is especially well reputed in the fields of construction and IP. **Strengths:** "He is very responsive and willing to work to tight deadlines on complex new instructions." "He is obviously at the top of the Bar, and is very good on his feet."

Roddy Dunlop QC Noted for the breadth of his expertise, as well as his assertive and persuasive advocacy before the Bench. He receives especially high praise for his handling of media and professional discipline matters. Market commentators also note his success in major banking litigation. **Strengths:** "One of the most effective court performers at the Scottish Bar; he has a real skill for compelling and persuasive arguments." "He is very good at drilling down and making complex pictures a lot simpler – he picks up the details of a wide range of disputes very quickly." **Recent work:** Successfully defended Glasgow City Council against a multimillion-pound claim relating to one of its contracts.

Jonathan Lake QC Principally represents clients in real estate, IP and contract litigation. He is also praised for his work in construction and professional negligence matters. Commentators highlight the ease with which he grasps complex issues of law, as well as the strength of his opinion work. **Strengths:** "He's commercial and very good at speaking the client's language." "He has a real passion for technical legal issues, and an ability to wrestle with those issues and produce an authoritative opinion." "He is a really accomplished and assured senior who embraces complex arguments and is extremely persuasive on his feet."

Kenneth McBrearty QC Has a breadth of expertise spanning a wide variety of commercial disputes, including partnership and IP cases. He earns particular recognition for his handling of major real estate and professional negligence matters. Instructing solicitors highlight his client-friendly manner and clear communication style. **Strengths:** "He has a nice combination of being very forensic on the detail as well as being personable and relating well to clients." "He is really user-friendly and speaks in a way that clients can understand – he's very clear in terms of expressing what the options are." "He is one of the most pragmatic guys at the Bar, but he doesn't substitute his pragmatism for the quality of his advice – on technical details and the nitty-gritty he is outstanding." **Recent work:** Acted for Tor Corporate in a high-value dispute with Sinopec Group Star Petroleum over the management of a drilling rig.

Gerry Moynihan QC Maintains a strong reputation in the market for his considerable experience in construction, planning, public law and professional liability matters, in addition to purely commercial disputes. He is regarded by instructing solicitors as a client-friendly silk who communicates in a clear and down-to-earth manner. **Strengths:** "I'm always impressed by Gerry's ability to take six or seven lever-arch files and absorb the information really quickly when there's a time bar coming up." "He's very good at understanding where the client is coming from, and is commercial in his approach. He also works well in a team setting – he understands what solicitors need from him."

Lord Davidson of Glen Clova QC Highlighted for his strong tactical sense and formidable cross-examination abilities. His experience covers litigation in the Court of Session and ECJ, as well as the representation of clients in mediations and arbitrations. In addition to his legal work, he is a member of the Labour front bench in the House of Lords. **Strengths:** "He has a huge level of experience and insight." "He's someone to use for trickier cases – he's very switched-on and is very good at getting to the nub of a situation very quickly."

Alastair Duncan QC A leading silk in the field of professional negligence, whose abilities are also in high demand for commercial contract disputes. He is regarded as a strong team player with sound commercial judgement. **Strengths:** "Clients like him because in consultations he is able to speak with them directly, in their own terms." "He is able to pick up and run with complex contractual disputes at short notice." **Recent work:** Successfully defended IT services company Capgemini against a breach of contract claim.

Mark Lindsay QC Able to call upon broad commercial litigation experience, including in several major shareholder and contractual disputes. He also possesses considerable experience in public and administrative law, having been a standing junior to the Home Secretary prior to taking silk. **Strengths:** "A pleasant, softly spoken and considered man with a fantastic analytical mind." "He has a keen intellect which is displayed in his written opinions and advice at consultations, which clients find easily comprehensible. These abilities are matched by strong advocacy skills." "He is a great all-rounder." **Recent work:** Acted for the trustee and general partner of Gyle Shopping Centre in a dispute with Marks & Spencer over the interpretation of the terms of a commercial lease.

James McNeill QC Senior silk acknowledged as a leading authority on issues relating to trusts and pension schemes. His broader commercial expertise covers tax and contentious insolvency. He also regularly sits as a mediator. **Strengths:** "He has an unrivalled knowledge of complex trust and tax issues."

James Mure QC Acts for clients in major contractual and commercial property disputes. His expertise in these areas is complemented by in-depth knowledge of public law, procurement and planning issues. **Strengths:** "He has a very persuasive, eloquent style before the court." "He's highly intelligent and demonstrates meticulous attention to detail, but at the same time he is very engaging, approachable and down-to-earth." **Recent work:** Acting for the pursuer in a dilapidations claim relating to a major industrial site in Glasgow.

Roisin Higgins QC Maintains an impressive reputation as one of the Bar's leading authorities on IP-related issues. She has additional expertise in construction and property disputes. Market commentators highlight her impressive combination of robust advocacy and in-depth intellectual insight. **Strengths:** "She takes things away and really mulls them over. When she comes back to you, she has a very well-considered and thorough answer." "She takes a forthright, pragmatic and commercial approach; she's easy to work with and responsive." "She is an advocate who has the ear of the court."

JUNIORS

Almira Delibegović-Broome Acts for clients across the full spectrum of commercial disputes. She is developing an especially strong reputation in relation to high-value insolvency proceedings. Complex evidential hearings form a major part of her practice. **Strengths:** "Almira will fight hard for you. She has a huge brain and is very committed." "She has a keen intellect and isn't afraid of a fight." **Recent work:** One of several counsel acting for SSE Generation in a major dispute arising from the collapse of a hydropower tunnel in the Scottish Highlands.

Martin Richardson Exceptionally popular among instructing solicitors due to his combination of approachability and rigorous intellectual analysis. Construction and engineering cases are a key area of focus for this bright and hard-working junior. **Strengths:** "Martin, perhaps because he used to be a solicitor, understands what we're looking for, offering strategic guidance as well as a clarity of thought around a particular point. He's great with clients too – they always respond well to him. He's very personable and always on top of the detail." "He is extremely sought after for his careful analysis and effective court performance." **Recent work:** Defending HOCHTIEF Solutions and HOCHTIEF (UK) Construction against claims brought by SSE Generation in relation to a tunnel collapse at the Glendoe hydroelectric project.

David Thomson (see p.781) An experienced junior in particularly high demand for insolvency, real estate and company litigation. Sources emphasise his impressive advocacy skills and outstanding grasp of technical points of law. **Strengths:** "He is very clever, methodical and good at arguing a point, but very commercial as well." "He is very good at digesting complicated contracts and getting to the nub of an issue where there's a lot of technical input." "He combines commercial acumen with strong advocacy skills to great effect." **Recent work:** Representing the Advocate General for HMRC in a dispute with the former Rangers FC over its use of an employee benefit trust scheme.

Jonathan Barne Meticulous preparation and a robust style of advocacy see Barne instructed on cases ranging from contractual disputes to construction, engineering and commercial property matters. He is regarded as a team player who excels at both written opinions and oral advocacy. **Strengths:** "He is very, very thorough in presenting his arguments; he's always incredibly well prepared." "He is extremely hard-working, and is prepared to roll his sleeves up and be part of the team." **Recent work:** Instructed on behalf of Aberdeen Asset Management in a complex dispute with the Trustees of Strathclyde Pension Fund. The claimant alleges that Aberdeen Asset Management breached the terms of its discretionary investment mandate by investing in a substantial office property.

Paul O'Brien Consistently rated by sources as one of the most intellectually able juniors at the Scottish Bar. His key areas of focus are IP and general commercial litigation. In addition, he has also been instructed on complex commercial property and insolvency matters. **Strengths:** "You know he will cover everything very accurately – he is immensely intelligent." "He is highly analytical and extremely hard-working. He brings real intellectual firepower and can get to the heart of the matter very quickly." "He is very bright; his great strength lies in legal analysis and opinion work." **Recent work:** Acting for the defenders in a complex warranty claim brought by the purchasers of a whisky distillery.

Susan Ower Praised by sources as a multi-talented advocate who relates well to clients and is a strong performer in court. Contractual disputes and insolvency form a large part of her practice. **Strengths:** "Where she really stands out is as a court advocate. On her feet, she is superb at guiding a witness through a complicated narrative, as well as keeping the client on track and focused on the evidence." **Recent work:** Acted for Marine Harvest (Scotland) in overturning an interim interdict preventing it from releasing a significant quantity of salmon into a loch in north-west Scotland.

Morag Ross A specialist in public and administrative law, particularly noted for her detailed knowledge of public procurement issues. She is well respected within the legal community for her clear and detailed advice. **Strengths:** "She is exceptionally clever, and also very diligent, approachable and good with clients." "She has a very comprehensive knowledge of her subject area and is very respected by the Bench."

Gavin Walker A senior junior often instructed as lead counsel. His quick turnaround and team-oriented approach make him a popular choice among instructing solicitors. He has developed a strong reputation in a number of areas, including construction, real estate, IP and professional negligence. **Strengths:** "He's strong on his feet in court as well as in his written work." "He is a focused and determined advocate with real punch." "He is good at thinking outside the box." **Recent work:** Acted for Glen Clyde in a breach of contract dispute with a Russian importer.

Jonathan Brown Active in professional negligence cases, as well as contractual, partnership and shareholder disputes. He also represents clients in insolvency and commercial property matters. Market commentators highlight his depth of experience and detailed preparation. **Strengths:** "He is very well prepared – he produces logical and coherent notes of argument." "His attention to detail is excellent." **Recent work:** Sole counsel for the pursuer in partnership litigation with a mid-tier firm of chartered accountants.

Euan Duthie Regularly instructed in relation to insolvency proceedings and professional negligence matters. He continues to develop an impressive following in the market, with sources emphasising his robust court presence and pragmatic advice. **Strengths:** "He is very practical in his advice and he's not scared to tell a client if he thinks they're taking an unreasonable approach." "His advice is detailed and precise. He takes a commercial overview and works with the client to achieve their objectives." **Recent work:** Instructed by the administrators of Heritable Bank in a dispute with the winding-up board of Landsbanki, Heritable's Icelandic parent company.

John MacGregor Maintains a broad commercial dispute resolution practice, complemented by his strong focus on public law. He is increasingly noted for representation of financial institutions in disputes concerning financial products. Sources note his impressive powers of analysis and ability to engage well with clients. **Strengths:** "He is probably the go-to junior in Scotland for swaps and financial services litigation." "He makes himself available at all times and is a trusted name for clients." **Recent work:** Representing BAM Properties in a contractual dispute with IVG Glasgow Partnership, concerning the distribution of funds held in a retention account.

Ross McClelland An in-demand junior who represents clients in litigation and various forms of ADR. He frequently represents clients in commercial property and professional negligence proceedings, but is equally adept at complex contractual disputes. **Strengths:** "His attention to detail is meticulous and he always gives clients clear and well thought-out advice." "He is very good at communicating with the client what the situation is and what their options are." **Recent work:** Instructed on behalf of Restaurantdiary.com in its dispute with the former Australia and New Zealand distributor of its restaurant booking software.

Chris Paterson Best known for his expertise in the professional liability sphere, defending healthcare, legal and construction professionals – among others – in a wealth of high-stakes proceedings. He also has notable experience in contractual disputes and commercial property litigation. **Strengths:** "He's someone who'll pick up the phone when you call him and is always happy to talk through any issues you might have." "He is easy to work with and just very, very bright." **Recent work:** Defended ACE Winches against a EUR9 million claim resulting from its provision of an allegedly defective winch product to Open Hydro.

David Massaro A recent call to the Bar and a former solicitor at a well-known firm, whose reputation in insolvency and commercial property litigation continues to grow. He is recommended by several market sources as an advocate to watch, with his client-handling skills singled out for particular praise. **Strengths:** "He is an excellent technical lawyer." "He is a bright and diligent advocate with a growing practice." "He is definitely a star of the future."

Band 2

Ampersand

See profile on p.945

THE SET

Ampersand is noted for the broad range of specialisms held by its members. The stable is home to market-leading experts in planning and medical negligence law, alongside several respected advocates whose principal focus is commercial dispute resolution. Within this field, members have particular expertise in insolvency, construction, real estate, shipping, media and IP matters. Members of the stable typically act for leading corporates and financial institutions, and are popular choices with leading solicitors in the market.

Client service: "Alan Moffat is courteous, efficient and very straightforward and informative to deal with." "The clerks are responsive and can give fairly candid advice about who is the right advocate to go to." "The clerks are always helpful at putting you in touch with the right counsel, and very easy to deal with." The practice manager is Alan Moffat.

SILKS

Robert Howie QC Undertakes instructions in all areas of commercial law, but is especially highly regarded for complex construction, insolvency and shipping disputes. Sources remark on his formidable intelligence, encyclopaedic knowledge of the law and impressive powers of court advocacy. **Strengths:** "He has a fabulous command of the English language, as well as of every matter that passes in front of him: he has a magnificent ability to pick up things almost instantaneously." "If you want an unusual argument, he thinks outside the box and can come up with a novel solution. He's someone you want on your side if you have a tricky case."

Craig Sandison QC A much in-demand advocate noted for his keen intelligence and highly persuasive powers of argument. He is primarily focused on commercial disputes, with expertise in this area complemented by a depth of experience in real estate and IP matters. His tenacious courtroom style has secured him a loyal following among instructing solicitors. **Strengths:** "He is always willing to put an argument forward, and has an ability to do so eloquently and persuasively." "He is tenacious, brilliantly clever and doesn't get fazed by anything." "He is immensely intelligent, a formidable advocate and certainly one of the top commercial silks in Scotland."

Ronald Clancy QC Continues to attract instructions on a significant number of high-value commercial disputes. He maintains a leading reputation in personal injury and media cases, and is also noted for representing clients in professional conduct cases, including before the disciplinary panels of major sporting bodies. **Strengths:** "He is extremely easy to work with, terrific at analysis and a very good advocate." "He is exceptionally good on his feet."

David Sellar QC Numerous sources highlight Sellar as Scotland's leading advocate for company and insolvency matters. He is frequently engaged for cases of unusual complexity or those turning on novel points of law. **Strengths:** "He is a hugely experienced guy who is very intelligent and good with clients." "He has very strong technical knowledge and is also really responsive and good to work with."

JUNIORS

Graeme Hawkes A well-regarded and experienced junior who is recommended by market commentators as a sound choice for banking and real estate litigation, in addition to purely commercial matters. Sources are impressed by his advocacy skills and manner with clients. **Strengths:** "He is commercial in his approach." "He is good on his feet, sensible and user-friendly."

Ross Anderson A recent call who is cementing a very strong reputation in the market. Approachability, a strong technical grasp of the law and an ability to think strategically are among the characteristics noted among Anderson's particular strengths. **Strengths:** "A young advocate, but an extremely good lawyer who is very easy to deal with. He is prompt and thorough, and a really good addition to the stable." "He has a fantastic ability to get to grips with the commercial reality of a dispute, as well as the legal and factual issues." "A rising star at the Commercial Bar." **Recent work:** Acted for First Marine Scotland in proceedings arising from allegations of breaches of fiduciary duty by a former director.

Other Ranked Lawyers

Andrew Young QC (Arnot Manderson) Attracts instructions on numerous commercial and private law matters, including contractual, tax and professional negligence disputes. He continues to be well respected within the profession. **Strengths:** "He has a great reputation." "He is careful, considered and highly respected."

Eric Robertson (Arnot Manderson) Has a wide commercial and property law litigation practice. He continues to act in a range of contractual, company law, IP and reparation disputes. **Strengths:** "He is dependable, easy to work with and understands the issues." "He is very approachable and personable." **Recent work:** Representing Marks & Spencer in a dispute with Gyle Shopping Centre General Partners relating to the terms of a commercial lease.

Gavin MacColl (Hastie Stable) Commands enormous respect throughout the market, and is widely considered one of Scotland's leading juniors for commercial disputes. He is highly experienced and noted as a formidable opponent in court. His practice has an emphasis on commercial contract disputes, but also encompasses insolvency, construction, property and professional negligence. **Strengths:** "He puts up a good fight in court. He also reads judges quite well, and is able to give you a quick view in terms of where he sees the case going." "He is an excellent senior commercial junior who is tenacious yet pragmatic. He wins clients' trust easily."

Roy Martin QC (Terra Firma Chambers) Seasoned advocate whom sources regularly cite as Scotland's pre-eminent planning silk. His expertise extends to commercial property and related matters. He is described by interviewees as a figure who lends great gravitas to any argument he presents in court. **Strengths:** "A very senior QC who is highly respected by the Scottish courts." "He is very quick at picking up issues, and has an excellent manner about him, especially in court."

Gordon Reid QC (Terra Firma Chambers) A veteran silk who remains highly sought after for real estate and construction cases. His vast experience adds considerable insight to his handling of major commercial disputes. He is regularly appointed as an arbitrator and as a tribunal judge. **Strengths:** "Manages client expectations very well and is quietly spoken but very effective on his feet." "Very thorough and pleasant to deal with." **Recent work:** Acting for Highlands & Islands Airports Limited in proceedings against Shetland Islands Council relating to alleged defects in an airport runway.

Nick Ellis QC (see p.640) (Westwater Advocates) Possesses broad commercial expertise incorporating professional negligence and media. He is particularly sought after for complex construction disputes. Sources recognise his pragmatism, commerciality and thoroughness, while also noting the high esteem in which he is held by the Bench. **Strengths:** "He has got the ear of the court and is very quick to get a grasp on the issues, even if they are complex." "He is very thorough, very able, in touch with commercial reality and willing to get off the fence."

Calum MacNeill QC (see p.705) (Westwater Advocates) Holds recognised expertise in clinical negligence and employment issues, alongside pure commercial matters. He regularly acts for clients in mediation and also appears as a chairperson in disciplinary appeals for the Scottish Police Service. **Strengths:** "He is very calm and measured; gives sound and practical advice." "He is good to work with, straightforward and down to earth." **Recent work:** Defending a firm of surveyors against a substantial claim for breach of contract and professional negligence relating to the valuation of a commercial property in central Glasgow.

COMPANY

Company	
Leading Stables	
Band 1	
Axiom Advocates *	
Leading Silks	
Band 1	
Sellar David	Ampersand (ORL) ◊
Band 2	
Currie Heriot	Axiom Advocates
Howlin Michael P	Terra Firma Chambers (ORL) ◊
Leading Juniors	
Band 1	
Thomson David	Axiom Advocates *
Thomson Fergus	Terra Firma Chambers (ORL) ◊

Band 1

Axiom Advocates
See profile on p.946

THE SET

Axiom Advocates remains the leading Scottish stable for commercial matters, and is known for handling the full spectrum of both company law disputes and non-contentious company matters. The advocates are also highly regarded for their advisory work concerning directors' duties, and the stable has a number of members who are past and present Standing Juniors to the United Kingdom government.

Client service: "The leaders in the field." The commercial clerking team is led by Colleen Adams.

SILKS

Heriot Currie QC A respected commercial silk, with a recognised expertise in handling company cases concerning breach of fiduciary duty. His broad practice also includes disputes related to construction, intellectual property and professional negligence, among other commercial matters. **Strengths:** "He is very experienced and an English barrister down south. He has a quality practice."

JUNIORS

David Thomson (see p.781) Held in high regard for his commercial litigation practice, he is regularly instructed by the Secretary of State to handle director disqualification claims. Instructing solicitors appreciate that he is "very easy to work with," reporting that "he works collaboratively with you as a team." He complements his company practice with additional expertise in property and insolvency matters. **Strengths:** "He is very user-friendly, he makes himself available and he's very good with clients. I would say he's a very safe pair of hands; if I instruct David I know I'm going to get a very good job done." **Recent work:** Acted for respondent Hornbuckle Mitchell Trustees in Gray and others v Braid Group, a case concerning an unfair prejudice action.

Other Ranked Lawyers

David Sellar QC (Ampersand) Garners market-wide recognition and is praised as "an outstanding silk" for his highly specialised company and insolvency practice. He is regularly instructed by clients in matters relating to takeovers and capital structures, in addition to being instructed by several banks in consolidation and insurance scheme cases. **Strengths:** "He is just an outstanding company and insolvency practitioner at the Bar generally. He is seen as the go-to guy for many of the big company and insolvency cases. He specialises in that area and devotes his practice to it." "A first-rate commercial silk. His ability, knowledge and experience in this area sets him apart."

Michael Howlin QC (Terra Firma Chambers) A well-regarded silk with a strong focus on company, commercial and corporate insolvency law. On the company side, he is experienced in unfair prejudice disputes, directors' disqualifications and reductions of capital cases, and is also frequently instructed in insolvency cases with a cross-border element. **Strengths:** "He is a seasoned and highly experienced practitioner. He is very impressive in the clarity of his thinking. He's quite decisive in the sense that he won't sit on the fence – he'll get the point and be very clear about what his point is." "Very good, proactive counsel. His background as a solicitor means he understands the practical realities and identifies a pragmatic commercial solution very quickly."

Fergus Thomson (Terra Firma Chambers) Brings a wealth of experience as a finance solicitor to his practice in company, banking, insolvency and professional negligence work. He gains instruction from several leading financial services clients in business transfer matters, and also regularly handles company disputes involving partnerships and unfair prejudice claims. **Strengths:** "I was very impressed by his oral presentation and his arguments in court. He's seen as someone with experience in corporate and banking and he has confidence and is assured in court." "He's very experienced and has been both a solicitor and an advocate so is pretty knowledgeable."

CONSTRUCTION

Construction	
Leading Stables	
Band 1	
Axiom Advocates *	
Leading Silks	
Band 1	
Borland Garry	Axiom Advocates *
Currie Heriot	Axiom Advocates
Howie Robert	Ampersand (ORL) ◊
Reid J Gordon	Terra Firma Chambers (ORL) ◊
Band 2	
Ellis Nick	Westwater Advocates (ORL) ◊ *
Lake Jonathan C	Axiom Advocates

* Indicates set / individual with profile.
◊ (ORL) = Other Ranked Lawyer.
Alphabetical order within each band. Band 1 is highest.

Construction	
Leading Juniors	
Band 1	
Richardson Martin H	Axiom Advocates
Walker Gavin	Axiom Advocates
Band 2	
Barne Jonathan	Axiom Advocates
Broome Jonathan	Axiom Advocates
MacColl Gavin L	Hastie Stable (ORL) ◊
McKenzie Alasdair	Axiom Advocates

Band 1

Axiom Advocates
See profile on p.946

THE SET

Axiom Advocates is regarded as the pre-eminent construction stable at the Scottish Bar. Its practitioners are routinely instructed in the country's most prestigious construction disputes and related arbitration proceedings. The stable frequently offers specialist counsel across major infrastructure, energy and engineering projects, demonstrating particular insight into professional negligence and construction defect claims. One market commentator remarks that Axiom is "widely considered to be the most commercial stable in Scotland."

Client service: Practice manager Lesley Flynn leads the clerking team. "The clerks are always very helpful and respond to queries quickly. Every clerk within the stable can be relied on to effectively assist." "A highly responsive team."

SILKS

Garry Borland QC (see p.599) Recognised advocate with a broad-based practice running the full gamut of construction and engineering matters. He regularly represents clients in complex, high-profile disputes, such as expense and defect claims. **Strengths:** "He masters the detail, but also has a strategic and commercial approach." "He brings the full weight of experience to his cases, and he has a speed and accuracy of analysis that few can match." **Recent work:** Acted for the main contractor, Lend Lease Construction, in a number of complex, multimillion-pound claims brought by a sub-contractor. The set of claims all related to the construction of the Hydro arena, a new concert venue in Glasgow.

Heriot Currie QC Hugely experienced senior counsel with an internationally recognised practice. He habitually handles the most complex, significant disputes in the construction industry, and is lauded for his deft handling of technically complex PFI contracts. **Strengths:** "He's hugely impressive in court and has great gravitas, being one of the most senior QCs." "He is very straightforward and effective." **Recent work:** Acted in Prospect Healthcare v Keir Build and Carillion Construction in a claim arising from allegations of defectively manufactured products. The £11 million claim concerned the embrittlement of plastic pipework in a hospital.

Jonathan Lake QC A leading silk in the Scottish construction market who can boast a history of appearances in the country's most sophisticated and high-profile cases. He represents a diverse array of clients in major instances of litigation and arbitration, and demonstrates notable skill in matters containing professional negligence elements. Sources further praise his strong grasp of technically complex contractual issues. **Strengths:** "Very good at looking at things commercially and has a keen eye for detail." "He's excellent, very down-to-earth and able to explain things with absolute clarity." **Recent work:** Acted for the defendant in SGL Carbon Fiber vs Stork Technical Services (RBG), a complex arbitration arising from a multimillion-pound engineering contract dispute.

JUNIORS

Martin Richardson Widely respected advocate who is recognised for his commercial nous. A regular feature at the Court of Session, he is frequently instructed by top-flight industry players in all manner of construction disputes. **Strengths:** "He is very knowledgeable, he understands the construction world and he provides reliable and consistent advice from the outset." "One of the most impressive juniors at the Scottish Bar." **Recent work:** Acted as sole counsel in Huntaven Properties v Hunter Construction, a multimillion-pound claim relating to defective concrete at a pipe storage yard in Aberdeenshire.

Gavin Walker Former solicitor and leading junior in the sector, he is regularly instructed by contractors and developers in heavyweight construction disputes. He demonstrates particular ability in professional negligence-related matters. **Strengths:** "Very user-friendly and he always has a clear idea on strategy." "He's highly intelligent, good on his feet and excellent on complex legal issues." **Recent work:** Acted for the defence in Dumfries & Galloway v Kier Construction, a £12 million claim regarding alleged design and workmanship failures in the construction of a leisure centre complex.

Jonathan Barne Well-regarded advocate with an impressively broad practice encompassing the professional negligence, insolvency and administrative elements of construction law. He is often instructed in multimillion-pound disputes and matters of significant prestige. **Strengths:** "He's got a wonderful eye for detail and will pull out all the stops to deliver in tight timescales." "Can cut through a lot of information to get to the crux of an issue very quickly." **Recent work:** Appeared in SSE Generation v HOCHTIEF, an immensely large-scale and high-value case concerning the collapse of a tunnel which had formed part of an hydro-electric scheme built by the defenders.

Jonathan Broome Experienced practitioner in the field of construction who offers particular expertise in matters with a professional negligence overlap. As director of the Scottish Arbitration Centre, and as a former solicitor, he is also well-versed in all forms of ADR. **Strengths:** "Extremely switched-on, with a keen eye for detail and considerable construction expertise." "Brilliant legal mind, very thorough and able to pick up on the smallest of details." **Recent work:** Instructed in Bouygues E&S Contracting v Vital Energi Utilities, a high-value claim concerning the termination of mechanical and electrical subcontracts.

Alasdair McKenzie An in-demand advocate who regularly appears on behalf of contractors, subcontractors, employers and professional individuals. He exhibits aptitude across various forms of ADR and has broad experience in judicial review proceedings. **Strengths:** "You know you've got a good advocate when Alasdair's on board." "He provides extremely thorough interrogation of details and demonstrates capability across all areas of construction law." **Recent work:** Acted in Stewart Milne Westhill v Halliday Fraser Munro, a high-value claim regarding design defects in a multi-use development in Aberdeen which had caused flooding.

Other Ranked Lawyers

Robert Howie QC (Ampersand) Outstanding construction silk with a sterling reputation and notable technical expertise. He is a formidable figure who regularly appears before all levels of judiciary in Scotland and across the UK, handling matters that run the full gamut of construction law. **Strengths:** "A construction guru in Scotland, the advocate of choice on construction matters." "He's a real specialist in construction and knows the subject inside-out."

Gavin MacColl (Hastie Stable) Director of the stables and a highly praised construction specialist. His commercial approach and tenacious courtroom demeanour are particularly highlighted by market sources. **Strengths:** "Highly trusted and dependable." "He has a thorough and intelligent approach to his work."

J Gordon Reid QC (Terra Firma Chambers) A stalwart of the Scottish Bar who has vast experience and expertise. He routinely appears in major construction cases, and offers complementary abilities in the fields of real estate, rural affairs and commercial disputes. **Strengths:** "He's very thorough, very good." "Quickly gets to grips with difficult issues."

Nick Ellis QC (see p.640) (Westwater Advocates) Highly esteemed advocate whose experience in construction disputes is extensive. He demonstrates notable skill in complex contractual matters and in cases that overlap with professional negligence. **Strengths:** "Very thorough, incredibly commercial and pragmatic." "Gives clear, consistent advice in a timely manner."

EMPLOYMENT

Employment
Leading Stables
Band 1
Westwater Advocates *
Leading Silks
Star individuals
Napier Brian *Hastie Stable (ORL)* ◊
Band 1
MacNeill Calum H S *Westwater Advocates* *
* *Indicates set / individual with profile.*
◊ *(ORL) = Other Ranked Lawyer.*
Alphabetical order within each band. Band 1 is highest.

Employment
Leading Juniors
Band 1
Stobart Alice *Westwater Advocates* *
Band 2
Hardman Alasdair *Hastie Stable (ORL)* ◊
Hay David *Westwater Advocates* *
McGuire Kenneth *Westwater Advocates*
Band 3
Cameron Donald *Westwater Advocates*
Grant-Hutchison Peter *Terra Firma Chambers (ORL)* ◊ *

Band 1

Westwater Advocates

See profile on p.949

THE SET

Westwater Advocates continues to assert itself as the pre-eminent employment law set in Scotland. The stable boasts a depth of experience and specialities, ranging from complex discrimination issues to unfair dismissals and whistle-blowing complications. Its members regularly represent both employers and individuals and are experienced in acting for clients in the Supreme Court, Court of Session, and in employment tribunals across the United Kingdom.

Client service: "The clerking team is excellent – they always try to match the service to my budget." "The team continually impress with their standard and confidence." Sheila Westwater leads the clerking team.

SILKS

Calum MacNeill QC (see p.705) An experienced practitioner instructed in all aspects of employment law, with expertise handling complex restrictive covenant and unfair dismissal claims. He has represented clients in courts across the land, ranging from employment tribunals to complex cases in the Supreme Court. **Strengths:** "He is a very gifted advocate and very able counsel." "He is very direct and gives you a clear steer on what he thinks of your case." **Recent work:** Acted in McBride v Scottish Police Authority, a Supreme Court case in which he argued that the claimant, a fingerprint officer, was unfairly dismissed following an alleged misidentification.

JUNIORS

Alice Stobart (see p.773) Provides expert advice across the whole range of employment issues, with added strengths in professional discipline matters. She regularly handles complex discrimination issues and is particularly adept at supporting clients with difficult unfair dismissal cases. **Strengths:** "She is extremely capable and gives first-class opinions and advocacy work. She produces exceptional written work which is presented in a user-friendly way." "She is an excellent advocate and is concise and quick to respond to queries." **Recent work:** Acted in the Employment Tribunal case of Mr Padia & Mrs Padia v Sainsbury's, representing individuals over alleged race discrimination and unfair dismissal from their positions.

David Hay (see p.667) Regularly represents individuals, large organisations and local authorities across the whole range of employment law. His particular areas of interest include holiday pay issues, discrimination law and working time regulations. **Strengths:** "His ability to grasp the finer details of a case quickly and get to the heart of the issue is impressive." "He is technically very good and knowledgeable. He has a very good advocacy style and gets the ear of the court in even the most complicated court settings." **Recent work:** Acted in Truslove v Scottish Ambulance Service, a case looking at whether time spent by paramedics at remote locations constitutes working time under the Working Time Regulations and therefore European case law.

Kenneth McGuire An advocate with experience across the whole range of employment law, with particular strengths in discrimination and equal pay issues. He regularly represents clients in both employment tribunals and the Court of Session. **Strengths:** "He is extremely accommodating of clients' expectations, has a genuine enthusiasm for working in a wide range of areas, and is extremely skilful." "He is very thorough in court, has a very good attention to detail and puts the claimants at ease." **Recent work:** Acted in Mrs J Campbell & Others v Fife Council, a complex equal pay claim brought against Fife Council by hundreds of different claimants.

Donald Cameron Appears in all levels of court including the EAT, Inner House and Court of Session, often in complex unfair dismissal cases. His practice is bolstered by additional experience of public law. **Strengths:** "His advocacy skills are excellent." "He is really good at tailoring his style and manner to the individual client; he can change his phrasing or style to suit individual circumstances." **Recent work:** Acted in Sharkey v Lloyds Bank, a case in the Employment Appeal Tribunal where he represented the employee in an unfair dismissal dispute.

Other Ranked Lawyers

Brian Napier QC (Hastie Stable) Widely recognised as a pre-eminent member of the Employment Bar in Scotland, with additional experience of acting in courts across England. He operates a wide employment law practice, with a particular strength in discrimination matters. He is a well-known advocate at both the Employment Tribunal and the Supreme Court. **Strengths:** "He is an absolute pleasure to work with. He is very bright and has an encyclopaedic knowledge of the law." "He has an unparalleled reputation in Scotland – he is extremely helpful and intuitive at addressing clients' needs."

Alasdair Hardman (Hastie Stable) Commands a wide employment law practice, with significant experience in discrimination matters and trade union disputes. **Strengths:** "In the tribunal, he is very experienced, very measured and has a gentle approach which is very effective." "He just argues simply and effectively and seems to have a good rapport with the Bench."

Peter Grant-Hutchison (see p.659) (Terra Firma Chambers) Has extensive experience of employment law issues, with expertise in discrimination matters and complex TUPE regulations. He has strengths in handling trade union disputes and has regularly represented clients at both the Employment Tribunal and the High Court.

FAMILY/MATRIMONIAL

Family/Matrimonial
Leading Stables
Band 1
Westwater Advocates *
Leading Silks
Star individuals
Scott Janys M *Westwater Advocates* *
Band 1
Dowdalls Catherine *Arnot Manderson (ORL)* ◊
Mitchell Jonathan J *Arnot Manderson (ORL)* ◊
* *Indicates set / individual with profile.*
◊ *(ORL) = Other Ranked Lawyer.*
Alphabetical order within each band. Band 1 is highest.

Band 1

Westwater Advocates

See profile on p.949

THE SET

Westwater Advocates is widely acknowledged as Scotland's "pre-eminent family law stable." It boasts an unrivalled group of experts, enabling it to cover financial issues and children law at every level. Many of its advocates offer impressive expertise in international work, including complex abduction and child relocation cases as well as divorce proceedings with cross-border aspects. The stable is considered a go-to for almost any kind of family case, with one source saying: "I feel there's great breadth and depth in the set generally; they will have an advocate who fits the type of case and the type of client."

Client service: "The clerks there are superb: they're friendly, flexible and work with us very well." Sheila Westwater serves as the stable's principal clerk.

Family/Matrimonial
Leading Juniors
Star individuals
Brabender Lynda J *Westwater Advocates*
Innes Ruth *Westwater Advocates*
Band 1
Clark Marie H *Arnot Manderson (ORL)* ◊
Hayhow Robert *Westwater Advocates*
Jack David *Hastie Stable (ORL)* ◊
Malcolm Kirsty *Westwater Advocates* *
Speir John *Westwater Advocates*
Band 2
Wild Alison *Westwater Advocates* *
Band 3
Ennis Isabella *Westwater Advocates*
Loudon Mary *Westwater Advocates*
McAlpine Scott *Westwater Advocates*
Up-and-coming individuals
Gilchrist Nicola *Arnot Manderson (ORL)* ◊
MacLeod Ceit-Anna *Arnot Manderson (ORL)* ◊
Shewan Rachel *Westwater Advocates*

SILKS

Janys Scott QC (see p.760) "The queen of family law," she is firmly established as a leading advocate and has acted in some of Scotland's most significant cases. Her remit spans extremely high-value financial provisions in addition to complex child law cases. She is also a published expert on education law and has successfully argued cases all the way up to the Supreme Court. **Strengths:** "She has incredible attention to detail and is very tenacious – her reputation speaks for itself." "The leading QC in Scotland: technically fantastic and always willing to think outside the box."

JUNIORS

Lynda Brabender Widely respected as one of the leading juniors for family cases in both the financial and children spheres. Much of her caseload involves public law, with a particular emphasis on childcare cases. She is also highly regarded for her ability to negotiate complex financial provisions, predominantly in the Court of Session. **Strengths:** "Good attention to detail, she gives clients confidence that she's really fighting for them and standing up for them." "She has fantastic advocacy skills and also does good written work. Extremely likeable and very experienced."

Ruth Innes A former family solicitor who is an authority on complex divorces and financial provisions, particularly those that concern the ownership of farms and agricultural land. Her varied experience also spans cross-border cases, cohabitation disputes, adoption, child abductions and relocations. **Strengths:** "Talented, bright, diligent and very reliable, she's my first port of call." "She is excellent: she has great attention to detail, and is very good on the law and in court." **Recent work:** Acted for the respondent in a case which centred on the return of two children to France under the Hague Convention.

Robert Hayhow A heavyweight in the field of financial provision who is also experienced in child relocation and abduction cases. He garners much praise for his interpersonal skills, with market sources citing his ability to reassure clients and persuade courtrooms. **Strengths:** "He's thorough, prepared and organised; you feel like you're in a safe pair of hands." "Even at short notice you can rely on him to be very good."

Kirsty Malcolm (see p.706) Junior who is building a solid reputation as an expert on cohabitation issues. Very well versed in handling complex, high-value divorce proceedings and is also noted for her skilled handling of child abductions, relocations and contact disputes. **Strengths:** "Well regarded and well instructed: clients like her and she's approachable." "She's excellent at going through the details. For complex cohabitation cases, it would be Kirsty every time." **Recent work:** Acted for the pursuer in an appeal concerning the relevance of a pension to the financial provision awarded in a divorce.

John Speir An experienced advocate who is also an accredited family arbitrator and mediator. He offers a broad range of skills and experience, with some of his most impressive cases focusing on cohabitation disputes, financial provisions and child relocations. **Strengths:** "He is very easy to work and communicate with – you have the sense with him that you are running things together." "A fearless litigator who commands a lot of confidence with clients. He is friendly, approachable and businesslike." **Recent work:** Acted in the Sheriff Court in what is thought to be the first contested evidential hearing brought under the Forced Marriage Act 2011.

Alison Wild (see p.795) A former solicitor whose practice at the Bar encompasses a range of children and money matters. Her experience includes cases under the Hague Convention, cohabitation disputes, freeing orders and financial provisions. **Strengths:** "A very talented advocate who is very good with people and confidence-inspiring." "Alison's just so hands-on and so speedy in her turnaround. She totally commits to a case."

Isabella Ennis Maintains a broad focus, acting in cases concerning children law and matrimonial finance. She is notably respected for her expertise in repatriation and compulsory care proceedings, where she acts for local authorities and parents. Recent work has included a number of complex divorces and child contact cases. **Strengths:** "She's always approachable and good technically." "A very good advocate."

Mary Loudon A family law specialist who has previous experience as a solicitor and mediator. She handles cohabitation disputes and high-value divorce proceedings, and is also able to take on adoption and child abduction cases. **Strengths:** "She is knowledgeable and very pleasant to work with." "Very easy to deal with, she always stays calm."

Scott McAlpine A junior who is rapidly establishing a reputation as a leading advocate for both children and financial cases. Sources commend his calm approach and effective courtroom advocacy. He offers especially deep knowledge of cases concerning international relocation, adoption and cohabitation law. **Strengths:** "A very experienced, very competent barrister whose writing is amazing." "Straightforward in his approach, smart and very helpful throughout." **Recent work:** Successfully acted for the petitioner on three applications for permanence orders concerning children of various ages, one of whom had complex needs.

Rachel Shewan Recently called to the Bar after working almost 20 years as a solicitor, she is already making an impression with her practice in children law. She offers notable expertise in child relocation, abduction, adoption and contact disputes. **Strengths:** "Very easy to deal with, she gives clear advice." "She has particular expertise in childcare matters." **Recent work:** Acted for the respondent in a Hague Convention case successfully opposing the return of children from Scotland to Australia.

Other Ranked Lawyers

Catherine Dowdalls QC (Arnot Manderson) A revered expert on both money and children law, Catherine Dowdalls QC is an accredited family law arbitrator who is also lauded for her advocacy skills. She offers considerable experience before the courts all the way up to appellate level, and is regularly instructed in a wide array of matters including high-value divorces, permanence orders, cohabitation disputes and adoptions. **Strengths:** "An outstanding family advocate: great with clients, good at analysing information and robust in court." "Thoroughly switched-on, well prepared, fantastic attention to detail, and she really thinks on her feet." **Recent work:** Acted for the father in an appeal to the Supreme Court for the return of his children to France.

Jonathan Mitchell QC (Arnot Manderson) Maintains a broad focus on public law issues and is extremely well versed in high-value divorce cases in addition to other family matters. His practice is further bolstered by a deep understanding of the technicalities of human rights, mental health and immigration law. **Strengths:** "He is a polymath – one of these people who can bend their mind to anything." "He's very experienced and very effective in court, very persuasive."

Marie Clark (Arnot Manderson) A multi-talented advocate whose practice is bolstered by her former experience as a solicitor. She is frequently instructed in divorce cases, cohabitation disputes, child law and civil partnership matters, and has most recently been engaged in a number of child abduction cases. **Strengths:** "An absolute delight! She's very gentle, knows what she's doing, and I'm consistently impressed by her."

Nicola Gilchrist (Arnot Manderson) Junior who is building a very strong practice handling both complicated matrimonial and children law disputes. She has acted in a wide array of cases that often include sensitive cross-cultural issues, including permanence orders, child abductions, forced marriage and financial provision. **Strengths:** "I cannot recommend her highly enough; this was a complicated case and she took it all in her stride." "Very impressed with her advocacy and ability." **Recent work:** Successfully acted for the wife in a financial provision dispute in which the husband argued that he had pronounced a talaq divorce and therefore they were no longer married at the date of proof.

Ceit-Anna MacLeod (Arnot Manderson) Previously practised as a solicitor and is becoming a go-to junior for a broad range of family cases, including those relating to financial provision, permanence orders, Hague Convention applications and residence disputes. She is commended for her client management, courtroom composure and pragmatism. **Strengths:** "Capable, cool-headed and extremely good with clients – she goes above and beyond in terms of service." "She has cogent opinions and an excellent knowledge of family law."

David Jack (Hastie Stable) A highly respected advocate with experience that runs the full gamut of family matters, and who is regularly instructed in both the Sheriff Court and the Court of Session. He is especially well regarded for his expertise in child law, but also takes on a range of family finance work. **Strengths:** "He was a joy to watch on his feet, he really nailed things in the courtroom – he is a proper court lawyer." "He is always really well prepared, really helpful and easy to deal with. He makes it easy for clients to understand things too."

HEALTH & SAFETY

Health & Safety
Leading Stables
Band 1
Compass Chambers *
Leading Silks
Star individuals
Gray Peter *Compass Chambers* *
Band 1
Macleod Murdo *Compass Chambers*
Leading Juniors
Band 1
Anderson Gavin *Westwater Advocates (ORL)* ◊
Duff Susan *Compass Chambers* *
Smith Barry *Compass Chambers* *
** Indicates set / individual with profile.*
◊ (ORL) = Other Ranked Lawyer.
Alphabetical order within each band. Band 1 is highest.

Band 1

Compass Chambers

See profile on p.947

THE SET

As the leading health and safety stable in Scotland, Compass Chambers has a strong reputation for its specialist expertise in this area. Advocates here demonstrate real prowess in complex, high-profile matters and are eminently capable of handling serious criminal and regulatory issues arising out of the most grievous health and safety infractions. Examples of this include the stable's recent involvement in fatal accident inquiries (FAIs) relating to the Glasgow bin lorry crash and the death of firefighter Ewan Williamson. Impressed sources praise Compass for its "excellent service and readiness to offer solutions."

Client service: "The service from the clerks is first-class, and on the inevitable occasions when minor difficulties or administrative issues arise they are rectified quickly and cheerfully." The clerking team is led by practice manager Gavin Herd.

SILKS

Peter Gray QC (see p.659) Standout silk with an enviable reputation at the Scottish Health and Safety Bar. He is an expert in all aspects of regulatory crime and has a particularly strong focus on health and safety and environmental matters. He is frequently involved in the most headline-grabbing prosecutions and inquiries in Scotland. **Strengths:** "Peter is recognised as the pre-eminent regulatory lawyer in Scotland and has an encyclopaedic knowledge of the relevant authorities." "He is an excellent trial lawyer: he communicates so well with the jury, the Bench and the client." **Recent work:** Represented the local authority in the Glasgow bin lorry FAI, concerning the death of six individuals and injury of 15 others in December 2014 when a lorry collided with pedestrians in the city centre.

Murdo Macleod QC Specialising in criminal work, Macleod maintains an enviable practice comprising all manner of regulatory and health and safety matters. He is regularly instructed to act in public and fatal accident inquiries. **Strengths:** "His strengths are his ability to communicate with the Bench and how well he works in a team."

JUNIORS

Susan Duff (see p.637) Well-regarded barrister who is skilled in regulatory and enforcement matters relating to significant health and safety breaches. She specialises in undertaking defence work on behalf of both individuals and corporate clients. **Strengths:** "Susan delivers clear and concise advice, explaining complex legal issues to clients in a way they can easily understand. She provides a vigorous and fearless defence with outstanding advocacy skills, and can be relied upon to reassure the most anxious or demanding of clients." **Recent work:** Instructed in HMA v Transpan Ltd, the prosecution of an animal feed transportation company after an employee died as the result of negligent safety procedures in operating the rear door of a tipper truck.

Barry Smith (see p.768) A respected junior barrister with growing expertise in regulatory crime, including health and safety matters. He is regularly instructed on cases arising out of fatal road traffic and workplace accidents. **Strengths:** "An able advocate who is really on top of his game." "He has quickly established himself as impressive and reliable in regulatory matters; he takes a balanced approach and clients respond well to his reasoned analysis of a case." **Recent work:** Acted on behalf of the Scottish Fire and Rescue Service during the FAI into the 2009 death of a serving firefighter, Ewan Williamson.

Other Ranked Lawyers

Gavin Anderson (Westwater Advocates) Has significant experience of handling the defence and prosecution of complex health and safety matters, most often those arising out of serious or fatal accidents in the workplace. **Strengths:** "He maintains very high standards in his court advocacy, his written work and how he relates to both clients and instructing solicitors." "He has very deep knowledge and is great to work with." **Recent work:** Acted in HM Advocate v Bruce of the Broch 1886 Ltd, a case concerning an employee's fall through a fragile roof during demolition works.

IMMIGRATION

Immigration
Leading Silks
Band 1
Lindsay Mark *Axiom Advocates*
Leading Juniors
Band 1
Bryce Joseph *Hastie Stable*
Byrne Daniel *Axiom Advocates* [A]
Caskie Alan *Hastie Stable*
Winter Stephen *Terra Firma Chambers*

Ranked Lawyers

Mark Lindsay QC (Axiom Advocates) A respected advocate who is regularly sought after for his handling of immigration-related judicial reviews and statutory appeals in the Court of Session. He also offers experience handling appellate proceedings at the First-tier Tribunal and the Supreme Court. **Recent work:** Acted for the appellant in an Inner House proceeding concerning the approach to be adopted when assessing the credibility of certain asylum seekers.

Daniel Byrne (Axiom Advocates) A formidable junior who impresses with his excellent command of the courtroom and strong client care skills. He is also noted for his handling of cases with EU law and human rights components. **Strengths:** "He is excellent with clients, easy-going and able to deal with very complex work."

Joseph Bryce (Hastie Stable) Earns market praise for his abilities in immigration cases involving refugees and asylum law. He represents both petitioners and the government. **Strengths:** "He will always find a solution for the most complex of issues and is great value for money." "He is my first choice when I need an advocate."

Alan Caskie (Hastie Stable) A well-known and well-regarded advocate who is highly sought after and prized for his innovative case strategies. He is distinguished for his experience representing petitioners in complex immigration cases. **Strengths:** "He has a real can-do attitude and he is really prepared to fight cases." "One of the big names for immigration in Scotland. He is one of the first names people would think of for petitioner work."

Stephen Winter (Terra Firma Chambers) Distinguished for his assistance with judicial reviews and his abilities acting in cases with significant human rights aspects. He is recognised for his experience of appearing in Court of Session, Asylum and Immigration Tribunal and ECHR proceedings. **Strengths:** "He is very good and the advice we get from him is really high-quality." "A friendly and approachable advocate who turns around work very quickly." **Recent work:** Acted in Mirza v Secretary of State for the Home Department in a case clarifying the approach to assessing a case in terms of Article 8 of the ECHR.

INFORMATION TECHNOLOGY

Information Technology
Leading Silks
Band 1
Mitchell Iain G *Arnot Manderson*
[A] *direct access (see p.24).*
Alphabetical order within each band. Band 1 is highest.

Ranked Lawyers

Iain Mitchell QC (Arnot Manderson) Highly regarded for his expert handling of complex matters across the IT law spectrum. He has vast experience in such areas as outsourcing, commercial contracts and software licensing. His complementary expertise in employment and business law informs his high-quality work in the space. **Strengths:** "He's very practical, pleasant to work with and he's got an impressive ability to take a large amount of information and distil it to its original essence."

INTELLECTUAL PROPERTY

Intellectual Property
Leading Stables
Band 1
Axiom Advocates *
Leading Silks
Band 1
Currie Heriot *Axiom Advocates*
Lake Jonathan C *Axiom Advocates*
Sandison Craig *Ampersand (ORL)* ◊
Band 2
Mitchell Iain G *Arnot Manderson (ORL)* ◊
New Silks
Higgins Roisin *Axiom Advocates*
Leading Juniors
Band 1
O'Brien Paul *Axiom Advocates*
Band 2
Pickard Kathryn *Axiom Advocates*
Walker Gavin *Axiom Advocates*
Up-and-coming individuals
Tariq Usman *Ampersand (ORL)* ◊
* *Indicates set with profile.*
◊ *(ORL) = Other Ranked Lawyer.*
Alphabetical order within each band. Band 1 is highest.

Band 1

Axiom Advocates

See profile on p.946

THE SET

Axiom Advocates remains the benchmark for intellectual property work at the Scottish Bar, given its unrivalled team of pre-eminent advocates who routinely attract instructions in the most sophisticated, high-value matters. Its esteemed members demonstrate expertise across such areas as patent infringement and trade mark disputes. The skilled advocates at Axiom remain a popular choice for a diverse client base, which comprises manufacturers, government entities and multinational corporations, among others. The stable is highly respected by market commentators, who particularly highlight its proactive and commercial approach.

Client service: "The clerks are very professional and very thorough." Lesley Flynn leads the clerking team.

SILKS

Heriot Currie QC A distinguished presence at the Scottish Bar, he is noted for his vast experience and gravitas in court. He regularly handles a broad range of high-value disputes, with particular strength in complex patent infringement claims. **Strengths:** "He's the man you want for complicated, high-value disputes. He is very experienced, eminent and widely respected by judges, given his seniority." "Remains one of the leading silks in IP and for commercial matters generally."

Jonathan Lake QC Highly sought after for his proficiency across an array of IP matters, he exhibits considerable knowledge and expertise in the field. He is regularly instructed on behalf of large corporate clients and is praised for his strategic approach to complex cases. **Strengths:** "A go-to advocate for IP disputes. He is excellent, very commercial, sensible and extremely bright. He's amazingly sharp and delivers wonderful arguments, both in writing and in court." "Jonathan is an excellent senior counsel who has a detailed, in-depth knowledge of his cases and broad IP knowledge which is second to none. He never loses sight of the bigger commercial picture ."

Roisin Higgins QC Newly minted silk who is widely respected for her broad expertise and adroit handling of complex IP disputes. Her areas of skill include passing-off, copyright and trade secret matters. **Strengths:** "Huge amount of IP experience across the board, she produces good written work and is excellent on her feet." "Very commercial, she has a good sense of the wider context of her advice and is extraordinarily knowledgeable."

JUNIORS

Paul O'Brien Well-regarded junior counsel known for his technical expertise and breadth of knowledge. He is regularly called on to handle a wide range of IP disputes, including patent, copyright and restrictive covenant matters. **Strengths:** "His real skill is his attention to detail. He is very bright and very thorough in his preparations." "He has an ability to really understand detailed technical information and to form a clear view of how to proceed. He is very bright, clear and persuasive." **Recent work:** Acted for the defence in Clark v TripAdvisor LLC, successfully resisting an application by two hoteliers for disclosure of details of the authors of allegedly defamatory reviews of their B&B.

Kathryn Pickard Dual-qualified English advocate with extensive experience dealing with sophisticated IP disputes. She is recognised for her adept handling of a range of matters, such as patent and trade secret litigation. **Strengths:** "The best IP junior in Scotland. Kathryn brings experience and expertise from the London Bar." "She's great, client-friendly and really willing to roll her sleeves up."

Gavin Walker Skilled practitioner whose broad expertise in the field covers such matters as passing-off, copyright infringements and trade mark issues. He is a regular feature in high-profile IP disputes. **Strengths:** "He has built up a specialism in the space. He is very personable and impressive in court." **Recent work:** Instructed by the Football Association in brand protection and enforcement proceedings against various pubs which were streaming live matches from abroad to avoid payment.

Other Ranked Lawyers

Craig Sandison QC (Ampersand) Highly rated for his standout courtroom presence and adroit handling of the full range of IP disputes. His broad client base includes private individuals and international corporations. **Strengths:** "Really excellent, he's very intelligent and really understands IP at a very technical level. He demonstrates great skill in court and really fights his client's corner." "Tenacious, brilliantly clever and doesn't get fazed by anything."

Usman Tariq (Ampersand) Junior counsel with a highly active IP practice, who demonstrates acumen in such areas as design rights, trade mark disputes and passing off matters. He is highlighted for his skill in enforcement proceedings and demonstrates particular industry expertise in the music and media sphere. **Strengths:** "A junior counsel with a flourishing reputation in IP matters, especially copyright infringement." **Recent work:** Represented Sky PLC in enforcement proceedings regarding unlicensed broadcasting of the company's sport channels.

Iain Mitchell QC (Arnot Manderson) Seasoned advocate at the Scottish Bar with experience across the full spectrum of IP disputes. He is noted for his complementary expertise in IT and technology law and is routinely called on to tackle complex copyright infringement, design rights and data protection issues. **Strengths:** "Very intelligent and willing to go for ambitious arguments with great success. He will push the boundaries where necessary." **Recent work:** Defended Stepper Technology against alleged software copyright infringement claims concerning the production of silicon chips.

MEDIA LAW

Media Law	
Leading Silks	
Band 1	
Clancy Ronald	*Ampersand*
Dunlop Roddy	*Axiom Advocates*
Leading Juniors	
Band 1	
Campbell Ewen	*Axiom Advocates*
Hamilton Duncan	*Arnot Manderson*

Ranked Lawyers

Ronald Clancy QC (Ampersand) Perennial presence at the Scotland Media Bar and counsel of choice for a number of media organisations. He is particularly well regarded for pursuers' media work and his expertise in reporting restrictions. **Strengths:** "He is one of those people who inspires confidence. He has a great presence in court, a calm and firm manner and is very much recognised as being a specialist in reporting restrictions." "He is easy to work with and experienced and he doesn't shy away from a fight."

Duncan Hamilton (Arnot Manderson) Established junior with a broad practice in the media field, frequently instructed by defenders, including the BBC and SNP. Particularly well regarded for his reputation management and defamation skills. **Strengths:** "He is very good with clients and has technical knowledge at the tip of his tongue." "He has a broad church in terms of media work and is recognised as one of the leading lights in the field." **Recent work:** Provided pre-publication advice to BBC Scotland in connection with a programme exploring drug abuse in athletics.

Roddy Dunlop QC (Axiom Advocates) Esteemed media practitioner, frequently instructed by defenders and pursuers in addition to a host of regional and national newspaper groups. He regularly appears in major defamation claims and is a top choice for other high-profile media work. **Strengths:** "He is terrific and is widely regarded as the best defamation senior by some margin." "He is a key player in the media industry." **Recent work:** Acted for the SNP in defamation proceedings initiated by a property developer.

Ewen Campbell (Axiom Advocates) Well-regarded junior receiving frequent instructions on media cases. Acts for both defender and pursuer clients who benefit from his prior experience at a media solicitors' firm in Scotland. **Strengths:** "He is very professional, organised and works well with clients." "He is a very fastidious worker and very clever." **Recent work:** Junior counsel to News Group in appeal proceedings brought by Tommy Sheridan MSP regarding his conviction for perjury.

PENSIONS

Pensions	
Leading Silks	
Band 1	
Martin Roy	*Terra Firma Chambers*
McNeill James W	*Axiom Advocates*
Sellar David	*Ampersand*
Leading Juniors	
Band 1	
Cunningham Greg	*Westwater Advocates*

Ranked Lawyers

David Sellar QC (Ampersand) A leading insolvency barrister who brings unparalleled expertise to pensions issues concerning the financial services industry. **Strengths:** "He's very good technically, very quick and thorough."

James McNeill QC (Axiom Advocates) A highly regarded silk with extensive experience in occupational pension schemes, trusts and tax issues. He is also recognised for his mediation practice. **Strengths:** "He's the main QC we go to and he's very helpful." "One of the real recognised experts in this field."

Roy Martin QC (Terra Firma Chambers) An experienced planning and real estate silk, who is also famed for his handling of pensions equalisation litigation. **Strengths:** "Outstanding on the interpretation of scheme documentation and equalisation."

Greg Cunningham (Westwater Advocates) Enjoys a wide practice which encompasses employment and professional negligence aspects of pensions law. He frequently handles Ombudsman cases and is knowledgeable in Local Government Pension Schemes. He acts for trustees, local authorities and corporates. **Strengths:** "He is very pragmatic and knows pensions inside-out."

PERSONAL INJURY

Personal Injury
Leading Stables
Band 1
Compass Chambers *
Band 2
Ampersand *
Band 3
Arnot Manderson
** Indicates set / individual with profile.*
◊ (ORL) = Other Ranked Lawyer.
Alphabetical order within each band. Band 1 is highest.

Band 1

Compass Chambers
See profile on p.947

THE SET

Compass Chambers is unanimously considered a market-leading stable for personal injury work in Scotland. Its advocates have considerable expertise across the whole gamut of personal injury matters including catastrophic injury, industrial disease and employers' liability claims. The stable attracts praise from several instructing solicitors including one who notes that "they have a very good collection of people who are all real experts in their respective fields."

Personal Injury	
Leading Silks	
Star individuals	
Milligan Robert	*Compass Chambers* *
Band 1	
Caldwell Marion	*Compass Chambers* *
Clancy Ronald	*Ampersand*
Clarke Geoff	*Compass Chambers*
Di Rollo Simon	*Ampersand*
Hanretty Gerald	*Arnot Manderson*
Mackay Ian	*Compass Chambers* *
Maguire Maria	*Ampersand*
Primrose Graham	*Ampersand*
Shand Lesley	*Compass Chambers*
Band 2	
Bain Dorothy	*Ampersand*
Dunlop Roddy	*Axiom Advocates (ORL)* ◊
Grahame Angela	*Compass Chambers* *
Murphy Laurence	*Arnot Manderson*
Smith Andrew	*Compass Chambers*
Young Andrew R W	*Arnot Manderson*

Client service: "I have always had a very good experience with the clerks there. They are all very diligent and they get back to you very quickly." Gavin Herd is the senior practice manager at the stable.

SILKS

Robert Milligan QC (see p.717) Widely revered and considered one of Scotland's most eminent personal injury advocates. He is considered to be an authority on catastrophic injury, occupational stress and product liability claims and acts for both pursuers and defenders. **Strengths:** "He conveys real gravitas, and has an excellent legal mind that does not detract from his ability to explain things fully and simply to clients." "He is excellent to bring into cases to tackle some major roadblock. He just seems to find a solution which other advocates haven't thought of."

Marion Caldwell QC (see p.609) Highly regarded for her expertise in occupational stress and catastrophic injury claims, in particular those involving brain injuries. She is acknowledged as a leading figure in medical negligence claims and regularly acts for both pursuers and defenders. **Strengths:** "I would put her in the top bracket of advocates for personal injury work in Scotland. She just has that reputation and is someone you can't help but respect."

Geoff Clarke QC Considered one of the foremost experts in industrial disease claims. He is capable of handling a whole range of matters including fatal accident, medical negligence and employers' liability claims. **Strengths:** "Excellent technical knowledge,

Personal Injury
Leading Juniors
Band 1
Galbraith Amber *Compass Chambers* *
Love Steve *Compass Chambers*
Mackenzie Neil *Arnot Manderson*
McGregor Malcolm *Compass Chambers*
Middleton Graeme *Compass Chambers* *
Pugh Richard *Compass Chambers* *
Smart Astrid *Compass Chambers*
Band 2
Balfour Gordon *Arnot Manderson*
Christine Kenneth *Compass Chambers*
Henderson Lisa *Ampersand*
Laing Steve *Compass Chambers*
Lamont Gordon *Compass Chambers* *
Lloyd Preston *Compass Chambers*
Mackenzie Euan *Ampersand*
Marney Christian *Ampersand*
McNaughtan David *Compass Chambers*
Tait Arabella *Arnot Manderson*
Band 3
Charteris Ruth *Arnot Manderson*
Davie Isla *Ampersand*
Dawson Jamie *Ampersand*
Fitzpatrick Brian *Ampersand*
MacMillan Andrew *Westwater Advocates (ORL)* ◊
Thornley Gavin *Compass Chambers*
Wilson Calum *Compass Chambers* *
Wray Laura *Westwater Advocates (ORL)* ◊ *
** Indicates individual with profile.*
◊ (ORL) = Other Ranked Lawyer.
Alphabetical order within each band. Band 1 is highest.

good at providing clients with clear, uncomplicated advice in difficult cases and has very good tactical awareness." **Recent work:** Represented the pursuer on the Young v McVean case in which the son of the pursuer was killed by a dangerous driver.

Ian Mackay QC (see p.705) Capable of handling cases across the whole spectrum of personal injury, he has a particular specialism in stress and catastrophic injury work. He acts for both pursuers and defenders, and he is known for his expertise in examinations. **Strengths:** "He is one of the best personal injury silks in Scotland. He has an incredibly strong intellect and combines it with so much experience." **Recent work:** Represented the pursuer and appellant in the high-profile employers' liability case Kennedy v Cordia in the Supreme Court.

Lesley Shand QC Has a broad practice encompassing both industrial disease and catastrophic injury cases. She regularly works for insurers and she also represents pursuers and has experience of participating in fatal accident inquiries. **Strengths:** "She has a formidable reputation for being particularly thorough in the way she approaches cases. No stone is left unturned when she is involved." **Recent work:** Represented the pursuer on the case of Scott Forbes v Wishaw Abattoir Ltd in which the pursuer had suffered a serious eye injury.

Angela Grahame QC (see p.658) Has a varied practice spanning road traffic accident, employers' liability, catastrophic injury and industrial disease claims. Sources appreciate her approachable nature and experience in personal injury matters. **Strengths:** "She is incredibly detailed and excellent in court. No matter what happens in court, she always handles it superbly." **Recent work:** Represented the pursuer on the John McShane v Burnwynd Racing Stables case in which a horse trainer sustained a serious shoulder injury after a fall.

Andrew Smith QC Has particular expertise in cases involving brain injuries and complex quantum issues and is also well versed in high-value road traffic accidents and disease cases. He is known for his robust approach to representing pursuers and he also has considerable experience working on the defendant side. **Strengths:** "He is an excellent court technician and he is the guy to go to if you want someone to put up a good fight."

JUNIORS

Amber Galbraith (see p.649) A leading junior who is known for her work for both pursuers and defenders. She shows expertise in catastrophic injury and has a burgeoning reputation in employment liability claims attracting praise for her dilligence on cases. **Strengths:** "Her attention to detail is outstanding and she always puts clients at ease." "Very thorough and knowledgable. Just a really useful person to have on a case." **Recent work:** Represented the pursuer on the Veronica McCreery v Terence Letson case in which the pursuer suffered a severe brain injury in a road traffic accident.

Steve Love Maintains an excellent reputation for road traffic accident claims, particularly for his expertise on cases involving motorcycle-related injuries. He also has experience in aviation matters and is known for his tenacity on cases. **Strengths:** "He is incredibly experienced, and when you need someone to hammer home an argument he is the man to use." **Recent work:** Involved in Graeme Neill v G1 Group, a high-value case in which the pursuer claimed to have suffered psychological injury in the workplace.

Malcolm McGregor Acts primarily for defenders and is a specialist in catastrophic injury and industrial disease claims, particularly in asbestos-related actions. He is also a recognised expert in clinical negligence claims. **Strengths:** "He is technically astute. When you need him to be, he is very combative and good at taking a strong line." **Recent work:** Acted for the insurer on the case of Jacqueline Gillespie v CIS Insurance, involving a brain injury suffered in a road traffic accident.

Graeme Middleton (see p.716) Has a broad practice which encompasses a range of personal injury matters including employment liability, industrial disease, road traffic accidents and fatal claims. He is also a prominent figure in professional and clinical negligence matters. **Strengths:** "He is very well organised, very professional and very good with clients. You can trust him with just about any type of case and any type of complexity." **Recent work:** Acted in Robert Fraser v Kitsons Insulation Contractors, a case related to pleural plaques from asbestos.

Richard Pugh (see p.744) Has expertise in a wide array of personal injury matters including industrial disease and road traffic accident claims with complementary skill in employment liability. He acts for both pursuers and defenders on complex, high-value claims. **Strengths:** "He is very experienced and knowledgable. He knows all the ins and outs of personal injury practice." **Recent work:** Acted for the defender in the case Docherty v ICI, involving an asbestos-related death.

Astrid Smart A standout junior in both personal injury and clinical negligence matters. She is acknowledged as a towering figure in claims related to employment liability, public liability, occupiers' liability and road traffic accidents. **Strengths:** "I have seen her on her feet, her input behind the scenes and her interactions with clients, and she really scores top marks on every measure." "An incredibly gifted advocate with superb negotiating skills. One of the top juniors in the business." **Recent work:** Represented Ellen Mitchell, guardian of Scott Stewart, in a claim against EUI Insurance, a catastrophic injury case following a road traffic accident.

Kenneth Christine Known primarily for representing pursuers and attracts praise for his experience across the whole range of personal injury matters. His areas of expertise include road traffic accidents and industrial disease claims, in particular asbestos-related matters. **Strengths:** "His strength as a lawyer for me would be how hard he fights for his clients. He is just really good at getting deals done."

Steve Laing Highly regarded for his ability to handle fatal and catastrophic injury claims, in particular those relating to road traffic accidents. He commands respect for his work in numerous aspects of personal injury including employers' liability and occupiers' liability matters. **Strengths:** "He is really very detailed and excellent at picking his way through every nook and cranny. He is also not scared to take things to court and is really good on his feet."

Gordon Lamont (see p.695) Has a broad practice that spans a wide range of personal injury matters including public liability and aviation accidents. He also has experience of undertaking fatal accident inquiry work. **Strengths:** "He has good technical knowledge and can handle pursuer and defender work equally well."

Preston Lloyd Handles the full gamut of personal injury matters ranging from road traffic accidents to employers' liability. He is also experienced in cases involving property damage and insurance claims. **Strengths:** "He provides excellent and detailed advice in relation to complex personal injury cases. He is also very good in court."

David McNaughtan Has an expansive practice and is proficient in matters relating to occupiers' liability, road traffic accidents and industrial disease. He attracts praise for his organisation and attention to detail. **Strengths:** "He is extremley hard-working and really feels the pulse of his cases. He is very friendly and empathic to his clients but is not afraid to be straight with them when required."

Gavin Thornley Focuses on fatal and catastrophic injury claims. He is capable of handling matters involving offshore accidents, employment liability, industrial disease and road traffic accidents. **Strengths:** "He has such a nice manner and is just very pleasant to work with. He is fantastic with all the number crunching and really drills into the specifics of the evidence."

Calum Wilson (see p.797) Known by solicitors and advocates alike for his impressive knowledge in disease claims. He is also proficient in claims involving road traffic accidents. **Strengths:** "He enjoys the difficult cases and is always willing to tackle them." "He has a certain gravitas and is always very practical."

Band 2

Ampersand

See profile on p.945

THE SET

An impressive stable possessing a number of advocates who are skilled across the whole spectrum of personal injury claims. It has an impressive record in terms of its work on catastrophic and fatal injury cases. Several of Ampersand's advocates also command respect in the spheres of industrial disease and clinical negligence. One impressed solicitor notes: "Ampersand is a top stable with plenty of advocates who you cannot help but respect."

Client service: "The clerks are very dilligent and get back to you very quickly. You can't fault them." "I have always found them to be very approachable, responsive and they find solutions to my problems quickly." The clerking team at the stable is headed by Alan Moffat.

SILKS

Ronald Clancy QC An expert in catastrophic injury claims including road traffic accidents as well as those with a connection to employers' liability and clinical negligence. He primarily represents pursuers and is widely considered to be one of the top personal injury advocates in Scotland. **Strengths:** "Ronnie is a force of a nature. He is the go-to guy for personal injury." "He has this sort of gravitas where he can just hold the ear of the Bench."

Simon Di Rollo QC A specialist in high-value and complex catastrophic injury claims. He has a broad practice covering industrial disease, employers' liability and medical negligence claims. **Strengths:** "He is eloquent and good on his feet, delivering his point very well." "He has a very good commercial head on him which insurers appreciate." "He is excellent at knowing the tactics the other team will employ."

Maria Maguire QC A towering figure in both personal injury and clinical negligence matters. She specialises in complex catastrophic injury claims as well as fatal accidents, abuse claims and psychiatric injuries. Her competitors agree that she is a formidable opponent in court. **Strengths:** "She is one of the best advocates, if not the best, in Scotland. She is very nice and approachable with clients but in a courtroom she is just fierce." "She doesn't give in easily. She is very robust and formidable on cases."

Graham Primrose QC Acts for both pursuers and defenders and is considered an expert on aviation-related cases. He attracts praise for his technical skill and his eye for commercial considerations. **Strengths:** "He is flawless. His paperwork is always neat and you just know that he will have done a very thorough job." "He is an excellent silk. He's really knowledgeable; he knows all the ins and outs of personal injury and he really keeps on top of his cases."

Dorothy Bain QC Noted for a caseload that encompasses a whole range of matters including industrial disease and catastrophic injury claims. She is hailed for her meticulous and tenacious nature. **Strengths:** "She has a knack for getting surprisingly good results in very difficult cases." "She is very strong in court. She is the kind of person that you want in your corner. Some people claim to be tenacious in court but she really is."

JUNIORS

Lisa Henderson Has a varied practice, often handling employers' liability, product liability and road traffic accident claims. She is respected for her medical knowledge and her ability to apply these to catastrophic injury and cerebral palsy claims. **Strengths:** "She is extremely good and able to take on a variety of complex cases and run with them. She is able to handle vast quantities of cases and get to the nub of the issues." "I am always confident she will be aware of the issues and she has a lot of experience in medical and high-value cases."

Euan Mackenzie He is skilled in a number of areas relating to personal injury including employers' liability, catastrophic injury and fatal accident claims. He has recently been active in several public inquiries. **Strengths:** "He is very able and prides himself on efficiency." "He is a very experienced junior who is very good to work with. The standard of his work is excellent." **Recent work:** Acted for the pursuer on Frances MacLaughlin v Morrison and Esure involving a catastrophic injury following the pursuer being deliberately run down.

Christian Marney Acts primarily for defenders on a wide range of personal injury cases including occupiers' liability, public liability and industrial disease claims. He is routinely instructed by major insurers as well as solicitors and construction professionals. **Strengths:** "He is a good guy – a very talented individual." "It is always a challenge when you come up against him."

Isla Davie Experienced junior who acts for both pursuers and defenders. She has a wide-ranging civil practice which spans both personal injury and medical negligence matters. She has a reputation for taking a methodical and considered approach to cases. **Strengths:** "Her thorough, precise and methodical approach to written work and her measured style in court ensure that she has the ear of the judge."

Jamie Dawson He has a varied civil practice that includes matters ranging from industrial disease to road traffic accidents and public liability claims. He is singled out for his proactive approach to the cases he is involved in. **Strengths:** "He is very good at picking up on things and running with them." "I would describe him as very proactive. He was very good in the case I was on and made a very positive contribution to its conclusion."

Brian Fitzpatrick An authority on catastrophic injury claims, including brain and spinal injuries. He specialises in high-value road traffic accidents and is praised for the strength of his advocacy in court. **Strengths:** "It doesn't matter what the case is, he will fight your corner." "He is very experienced. He has dealt with all the issues before and works hard on difficult, unusual cases."

Band 3

Arnot Manderson

THE SET

A well-regarded stable with gifted advocates capable of handling a diverse range of personal injury cases including industrial disease, employers' liability, catastrophic injury and road traffic accident claims. The stable also possesses advocates with experience of featuring in a number of public inquiries. One impressed lawyer notes that "everyone there is of a certain mould where they are all very calm and collected. They are very good at coping with difficult cases and they are just a very professional outfit."

Client service: "I have always had a good experience with the clerks there. They are very dilligent and they get back to you very quickly. You really can't fault them, any problems are dealt with quickly and they keep you informed of what the situation is." Elizabeth Manderson and Andrew Sutherland are the head clerks at the stable.

SILKS

Gerald Hanretty QC Renowned for his tenacity on high-value cases involving catastrophic and fatal injuries. He primarily represents defenders and is known for taking a robust line on issues of liability. **Strengths:** "He is highly intelligent and assimilates facts very quickly. He is excellent at cross-examinations even with the most difficult of witnesses. He is solid, dependable, reliable and really is one of the standout advocates at the Scottish Bar."

Laurence Murphy QC A prominent advocate in a variety of practice areas. His personal injury practice is complemented by his ancillary experience in professional negligence and property damage litigation. **Strengths:** "Laurence is great in court and is excellent on his feet. He is very effective and calm in difficult situations. He is exceptionally talented and a very clever individual."

Andrew Young QC An authority on brain and spinal injuries. His workload includes a number of clinical negligence, employers' liability and commerical matters. **Strengths:** "He is great tactician and always gets to the nub of the case very quickly. He is always very pragmatic but he is tough and certainly no pushover."

JUNIORS

Neil Mackenzie A standout junior for industrial disease cases, in particular those involving asbestos-related claims. He is highly regarded for his experience in both personal injury and clinical negligence claims. **Strengths:** "For me, he is really a bit of a shining star. He is one of the most thorough, intelligent and innovative advocates I have ever come across." **Recent work:** Acted in Gail Gordon v Grampian Health Board, a mesothelioma case. The matter involved the potential exposure of a nurse to asbestos in a hospital corridor.

Gordon Balfour Acknowledged for his diverse workload, predominantly for defenders, across a range of areas including disease claims, employers' liability and catastrophic injury matters. **Strengths:** "He is just exceptional and has really good technical knowledge. He is also very good on his feet and is extremely approachable." **Recent work:** Represented the defender in the Dean Holgate v The Advocate General for Scotland case. The case involved a fatal friendly fire incident in Afghanistan which the pursuer claims led to the development of PTSD.

Arabella Tait Represents both pursuers and defenders in high-value, complex matters including road traffic accidents, catastrophic injury and industrial disease claims. She has considerable experience in asbestos-related cases. **Strengths:** "Efficient, organised and experienced in all aspects of personal injury claims. A strong negotiator." "She really is my go-to advocate. You just know what you're going to get in terms of quality and know you will not have any problems at all." **Recent work:** Acted in Craig Harrison v Aquashield Thermal Coating, a case involving a catastrophic injury stemming from a workplace accident.

Ruth Charteris Held in high esteem for her work on road traffic accident claims, in particular those involving catastrophic brain injuries. She is known primarily for representing defenders and also has considerable experience in clinical negligence. **Strengths:** "She is excellent on complex technical points and can analyse the details very well. She is also very approachable with clients and gets on very well with insurers." **Recent work:** Acted in O'Brien v Bonnar, a case in which the guardian of a severely brain-injured man sought several million pounds for his injuries, particularly with respect to his future care.

Other Ranked Lawyers

Roddy Dunlop QC (Axiom Advocates) Has a wide-ranging practice that extends beyond personal injury. He is a highly esteemed advocate and is particularly respected for handling catastrophic injury and fatal claims. **Strengths:** "Dilligent and impressive on his feet."

Andrew MacMillan (Westwater Advocates) Primarily represents pursuers. He is able to handle a wide range of personal injury matters including employers' liability, road traffic accidents and industrial disease claims.

Laura Wray (see p.800) (Westwater Advocates) Represents both defenders and pursuers. She has experience working on road traffic accidents, employers' liability and industrial disease claims. **Strengths:** "She has a wealth of personal injury experience and a fantastic manner with clients. She works very hard to achieve an excellent result in every case."

PLANNING & ENVIRONMENT

Planning & Environment	
Leading Stables	
Band 1	
Terra Firma Chambers *	
Leading Silks	
Star individuals	
Martin Roy	*Terra Firma Chambers*
Thomson Malcolm	*Ampersand (ORL)* ◊
Band 1	
Agnew of Lochnaw Bt Crispin	*Westwater (ORL)* ◊ *
Armstrong Douglas	*Terra Firma Chambers*
Mure James	*Axiom Advocates (ORL)* ◊
Wilson Ailsa	*Ampersand (ORL)* ◊
Band 2	
Campbell John D	*Hastie Stable (ORL)* ◊
Crawford Ruth	*Axiom Advocates (ORL)* ◊
Findlay James	*Terra Firma Chambers (ORL)* ◊
Steele Gordon	*Terra Firma Chambers*
Leading Juniors	
Band 1	
Burnet Alasdair J	*Terra Firma Chambers*
Band 2	
McKay Marcus	*Ampersand (ORL)* ◊
van der Westhuizen Laura-Anne	*Ampersand (ORL)* ◊
Up-and-coming individuals	
Sutherland Alasdair	*Terra Firma Chambers*
** Indicates set / individual with profile.*	
◊ (ORL) = Other Ranked Lawyer.	
Alphabetical order within each band. Band 1 is highest.	

Band 1

Terra Firma Chambers

See profile on p.948

THE SET

Terra Firma remains very much the principal stable in Scotland for planning and environmental law. It has a bench of highly distinguished silks and juniors who act in many high-profile cases and regularly appear in judicial reviews and statutory appeals. Its advocates represent a wide range of clients, handling cases relating to retail and housing developments, as well as infrastructure projects. They are also strong in the energy sector, proving particularly effective at matters relating to renewables. Clients include developers, local councils, and objectors. Members of the stable recently acted in Gibson v Scottish Ministers, defending a decision to grant permission for a £79 million wind farm development.

Client service: "Terra Firma stands out as having the best clerking in Scotland. They are the quickest to get back to you, and are most helpful and approachable." "Emma Potter, the clerk at Terra Firma, is fantastically helpful."

SILKS

Roy Martin QC Considered to be at the forefront of planning in Scotland due to his exceptional strength across the spectrum of planning work. He is commended by sources for his work in high-profile complex litigation concerning strategic land and development. **Strengths:** "He is still at the top of his game and second to none for planning challenges." "He has top planning knowledge and quite often people go to him for who he is." **Recent work:** Represented the City of Edinburgh Council in the Edinburgh Tram public inquiry, which related to both the delay in provision and cost of the construction of the tram line.

Douglas Armstrong QC Highly respected for his work across a range of planning matters and has a particular expertise in matters relating to renewable energy and large-scale infrastructure projects, particularly those concerning highways and road bridges. He is praised by sources for his broad planning knowledge. **Strengths:** "He is very approachable and excellent in consultations with clients." "One of Scotland's leading planning seniors. He builds a good rapport with clients, is thorough and accurate in his analysis, and is widely respected by his peers." **Recent work:** Acted for the Scarborough Muir Group in its case against the Scottish Ministers in relation to a dispute about the Forth Crossing Act.

James Findlay QC Renowned for his experience, knowledge and gravitas, he brings a strong level of skill and experience to his role as a standing junior to the Scottish Ministers. He has enviable experience across the full range of planning and environmental law, and often appears in inquiries and in higher courts at all levels. **Strengths:** "His knowledge and understanding of the law are amongst the best at the Scottish Bar." "He has a good breadth of knowledge and he is very hard-working. He is always well organised and is an especially skilful cross-examiner." **Recent work:** Acted in an appeal to the Supreme Court, appearing on behalf of Trump in a case concerning a wind farm.

Gordon Steele QC Highly commended for his public inquiry work, he is a long-standing planning and environment advocate who handles high-profile and highly complex retail development matters as well as compulsory purchase cases. **Strengths:** "Has excellent advocacy skills, and is very commercial and focused on achieving the best result for the client. He also demonstrates a very good understanding of the technical issues." "One of the best cross-examiners in Scotland at public inquiry. He is great with clients and a pleasure to work with."

JUNIORS

Alasdair Burnet A standing junior to the Scottish Government who frequently appears in appeals and inquiries relating to residential, retail, and leisure developments. He also handles renewable energy and infrastructure work. **Strengths:** "He has extensive knowledge and experience in planning matters. He is very approachable and is very good at thinking on his feet." "Clients love him; he is insightful and able to convey decisions in a clear, uncomplicated way. His preparation in court is excellent, and he has a calm and measured delivery." **Recent work:** Appeared in Carroll v Scottish Borders Council, acting for a local authority defending the first challenge to the decision of a local review board since they were set up following the Planning (Scotland) Act 2006.

Alasdair Sutherland A junior who, prior to coming to the Bar, worked as a solicitor at a top Scottish firm. He often handles cases concerning renewable energy projects, compulsory purchase and land planning. He also has experience acting for Traveller communities. **Strengths:** "Hugely impressive; he is thorough, quick, responsive and very approachable. He is a pleasure to work with." "He has a great breadth of knowledge and a very thorough approach." **Recent work:** Acted for the respondent in Christine Hunt & Others v Moray Council, opposing a challenge to the council's decision to grant planning permission for the erection of beach huts at Findhorn.

Other Ranked Lawyers

Malcolm Thomson QC (Ampersand) Acknowledged as a leading expert across the gamut of planning and environmental law matters. He acts for both developers and objectors and is especially experienced in tackling cases relating to retail development and renewable energy. **Strengths:** "He's immensely experienced and has a superb knowledge of planning and environmental law. He's an outstanding performer, who is thorough and someone who explores all the options. He allies his legal knowledge with great experience and commercial sense to provide the client with as many options as possible." **Recent work:** Acted for the promoter in a matter regarding a compulsory purchase order for St James Quarter, Edinburgh, the site of a major retail led development.

Ailsa Wilson QC (Ampersand) Highly regarded for her work across a whole range of planning matters and particularly praised for her impressive efforts in public inquiries. She is considered to be one of the leading QCs in terms of energy work, and she regularly represents energy providers. She is also highly experienced in handling cases concerning infrastructure projects, appearing on behalf of local authorities and government bodies. **Strengths:** "She is very thorough and always has an excellent grasp of the underlying law as well as the facts of the case. She is excellent in inquiries and at court hearings." "She's a top choice for both opinion work and court and inquiry work. She has great experience across a whole range of planning work and her legal knowledge is excellent." **Recent work:** Acted in Sustainable Shetland v Scottish Ministers & Viking Energy Partnership, a case concerning the development of a large scale onshore wind farm on Shetland.

Marcus McKay (Ampersand) Noted for his deep planning experience and praised by many for his meticulous attention to detail. His particular focus lies in energy and environment work, and he is especially experienced in renewable energy matters. **Strengths:** "Very experienced in planning and environmental matters; he is excellent at marshalling large volumes of information and always has the relevant information to hand." "He listens carefully to clients and will take on board your thoughts and views before reaching a conclusion. In court he is exceptionally good at putting a complex matter to the court and stating the council's case." **Recent work:** Appeared in a public inquiry into an application for consent for Strathy South wind farm under the Electricity Act 1989.

Laura-Anne van der Westhuizen (Ampersand) An advocate praised for her attention to detail and good drafting skills, who has recently been appointed as standing junior to the Scottish Ministers. She has a strong planning practice and has recently handled a number of hydroelectric power and wind farm-related matters. **Strengths:** "She is a pleasure to work with; she is very responsive and can absorb a tremendous amount of detail in a short space of time." "She is a very competent junior; her pragmatic advice is coupled with a sound grasp of the law." **Recent work:** Represented Scottish Hydro Electric Power Distribution at hearings before reporters appointed by the Scottish Ministers. The hearings concerned the right to retain existing overhead lines on private land.

James Mure QC (Axiom Advocates) Well regarded for his breadth of knowledge and his strength in advocacy. He is recognised for his work with the Scottish Government, local authorities and other public sector bodies. He shows particular expertise in renewable energy matters, and is very good at cases relating to wind farms. **Strengths:** "He has a very good intellectual approach to matters and is well respected by the court." "He often appears for the government and has lots of experience in judicial review proceedings. He is someone whom the court listens too." **Recent work:** Acted for the Scottish Ministers in a case against Trump International Golf Club. This was a judicial review of Scottish Government decisions relating to an offshore wind farm near Aberdeen.

Ruth Crawford QC (Axiom Advocates) Known for her planning-related work for the Scottish Government, she has a particular focus on major infrastructure and energy projects. She appears in court at all levels, as well as in complex inquiries. **Strengths:** "She has a very sharp mind and is able to deal with a very heavy workload." "She's excellent. Her work is detailed, and she is very thorough. She is also a very good presenter in court."

John Campbell QC (Hastie Stable) Highly experienced advocate widely acclaimed for his work acting on behalf of objectors, specifically on cases concerning wind farms. He also has a great deal of experience in residential development cases.

Sir Crispin Agnew of Lochnaw Bt QC (see p.580) (Westwater Advocates) Known for his impressive experience acting on behalf of objectors, many of whom are NGOs or concerned individuals. He is very well regarded for his complementary expertise in agricultural law and attracts praise for his strategy in court. **Strengths:** "He is very knowledgeable and very good to work with. He is very co-operative and constructive and always gives considered and careful advice to clients." "He is a counsel of choice for agricultural matters and planning and environmental judicial reviews. He is practical and client-friendly in his approach." **Recent work:** Acted in RES Renewables v East Ayrshire Council, a six day wind farm planning inquiry regarding landscape and visual issues.

PROFESSIONAL DISCIPLINE

Professional Discipline
Leading Stables
Band 1
Axiom Advocates *
Leading Silks
Band 1
Duncan Alastair *Axiom Advocates*
Dunlop Roddy *Axiom Advocates*
Lindsay Mark *Axiom Advocates*
Leading Juniors
Band 1
Brown Jonathan *Axiom Advocates*
Ross Morag *Axiom Advocates*
* *Indicates set with profile.*
Alphabetical order within each band. Band 1 is highest.

Band 1

Axiom Advocates

See profile on p.946

THE SET

Axiom Advocates is the dominant Scottish professional discipline stable, offering an impressive collection of leading silks and juniors. Members regularly appear in cases either acting for the leading regulators or appearing against them on behalf of professional individuals. Specific expertise in medical, legal and financial professional discipline disputes is noted by the stable's outstanding collection of prominent clients, who describe the stable as having "the best advocates across the board, and the most big hitters." **Client service:** "The clerks are very responsive and make an effort to understand the particular work and needs of the client. If counsel are unavailable, they can make helpful suggestions for people with that experience." Lesley Flynn is the practice manager.

SILKS

Alastair Duncan QC Both prosecutes and defends in disciplinary hearings, and has particular strength in cases involving the legal profession. His broad practice includes commercial and general professional liability. **Strengths:** "Head and shoulders above everyone else. He consistently delivers. Never ever failed to do what I've asked." "He presents his arguments in a well-structured and logical way; he has the ear of the court."

Roddy Dunlop QC A hugely impressive silk with a full command of regulatory and legislative considerations required for complex professional discipline litigation. He regularly appears in the appellate courts and represents both regulatory bodies and professionals. **Strengths:** "Very highly regarded, the go-to individual for this area of law." "He knows regulatory law inside-out, backwards and forwards." "The leading silk in this field. Skilled, excellent on his feet and persuasive." **Recent work:** Has been acting for the GPhC in K v General Pharmaceutical Council, a case proceeding to the Supreme Court.

Mark Lindsay QC An accomplished advocate particularly well known for his work in the professional discipline and public law spaces. As a former solicitor, he brings a wealth of litigation experience and understanding of the commercial realities of professional discipline. **Strengths:** "Technically very good and excellent on his feet." **Recent work:** Acted for the Scottish Legal Complaints Commission (SLCC) in the case of Bartos v SLCC, concerning the circumstances in which an advocate is obliged to seek the client's instruction before moving for an action to be dismissed.

JUNIORS

Jonathan Brown Has a broad professional discipline practice, receiving instructions from solicitors, architects, doctors, pharmacists, accountants and their regulatory bodies. He is an experienced civil litigator and also handles product liability cases. **Strengths:** "Sensible chap and an excellent orator." **Recent work:** Instructed in an appeal to the Inner House of the Court of Session in the case of McSparran McCormick v SLCC. The case concerned the scope of a solicitor's duty to desist from making disrespectful comments in correspondence.

Morag Ross A well-respected and talented civil and public law practitioner with recognised expertise in professional discipline. She has experience representing a broad range of regulatory bodies and professionals. **Strengths:** "Technically excellent and concise, to the point and well argued. Good in a consultation situation." "Excellent, detailed approach; fabulous on her feet; authoritative and persuasive."

PROFESSIONAL NEGLIGENCE

Professional Negligence
Leading Stables
Band 1
Axiom Advocates *
Leading Silks
Band 1
Duncan Alastair *Axiom Advocates*
Dunlop Roddy *Axiom Advocates*
Hanretty Gerald *Arnot Manderson (ORL)* ◊
Young Andrew R W *Arnot Manderson (ORL)* ◊
Band 2
Ferguson Iain *Axiom Advocates*
Lake Jonathan C *Axiom Advocates*
McBrearty Kenneth *Axiom Advocates*
Murphy Laurence *Arnot Manderson (ORL)* ◊
Leading Juniors
Band 1
Barne Jonathan *Axiom Advocates*
MacColl Gavin L *Hastie Stable (ORL)* ◊
Richardson Martin H *Axiom Advocates*
Band 2
Broome Jonathan *Axiom Advocates*
McKenzie Alasdair *Axiom Advocates*
Paterson Chris *Axiom Advocates*
Walker Gavin *Axiom Advocates*
Band 3
Reid Paul *Ampersand (ORL)* ◊
Thomson David *Axiom Advocates* *
* *Indicates set / individual with profile.*
◊ *(ORL) = Other Ranked Lawyer.*
Alphabetical order within each band. Band 1 is highest.

Band 1

Axiom Advocates

See profile on p.946

THE SET

Axiom Advocates is the dominant stable for professional negligence disputes in Scotland, offering a number of the most prominent advocates in the area. Its members enjoy a remarkable reputation for cases involving professionals such as solicitors, surveyors, accountants and financial advisers. They have a particularly strong reputation in cases relating to property transactions. Recent matters in which members have played prominent roles include a case stemming from the well-publicised Edinburgh trams project, City of Edinburgh Council v DLA Piper.

Client service: "The clerking is very, very good. They get back to you very quickly and efficiently." "The clerks are all great at recommending somebody who focuses on a particular area." The team is led by Lesley Flynn.

SILKS

Alastair Duncan QC Recommended for his expertise in handling professional negligence matters pertaining to the legal sector, while also offering experience in matters concerning the surveying and insurance spheres, among others. **Strengths:** "To my mind, he is the single outstanding silk dealing with professional negligence. He is head and shoulders above everyone else. He consistently delivers." "A joy to instruct. He is down-to-earth, has a very good analytical mind and a real grasp of the relevant factual and legal issues." **Recent work:** Instructed in McManus v City Link Development Company, representing engineering firm Scott Wilson in connection with a number of cases concerning land contamination.

Roddy Dunlop QC Continues to excel in the professional negligence sphere, handling matters relating to the legal profession. He handles such cases as part of a far broader practice that encompasses commercial disputes and clinical liability matters. **Strengths:** "Roddy is very to the point, concise, very good at drilling down and making a complex picture a lot simpler." "A great court advocate who will fight your corner when you need him to. He is skilled at boiling difficult cases down to key issues and he has very strong tactical awareness." **Recent work:** Acted in Singh v Napier, successfully defending a senior counsel in connection with claims of discrimination and professional negligence by a former client.

Iain Ferguson QC Handles professional negligence litigation as part of a broader practice that also encompasses clinical negligence matters. **Strengths:** "He has a forensic brain and is incredible on the details. He's somebody you can absolutely rely on to deliver the job and is a real team player. There is no question too small to take to him." **Recent work:** Acted in AC&H (219) Ltd v DI Burchill & Partners, defending a quantity surveyor against allegations of negligence with respect to the design and build contract for a building conversion.

Jonathan Lake QC Offers a highly respected professional negligence practice as part of a broader commercial disputes practice. **Strengths:** "A genuinely top-class senior. He is superb on his feet and excels in complex matters."

Kenneth McBrearty QC He regularly acts in professional negligence cases involving surveyors, legal professionals and financial advisers, among others. **Strengths:** "He cuts through the complexities of any dispute with ease to give clients commercially astute and usable advice." "A high-quality silk whose expertise in professional negligence matters shines through. Great with clients, really user-friendly and a tenacious fighter in court." **Recent work:** Instructed by the Royal Bank of Scotland in RBS v DM Hall LLP, bringing a claim of overvaluation of a rural property against a surveyor.

JUNIORS

Jonathan Barne Well regarded for his professional negligence expertise, he handles claims involving legal and construction professionals, among others. **Strengths:** "Jonathan is very, very thorough in presenting arguments. He is always incredibly well prepared." "An experienced and able junior." **Recent work:** Acted for the third and fourth defenders in Pentland Clark (Judicial Factor) v Maclehose and Others, a professional negligence case alleging fraud and negligence by the executors of a deceased's estate.

Martin Richardson Handles commercial litigation with a strong focus on professional negligence matters. He is particularly noted for his work in the construction space, often acting in matters involving architects, engineers or other construction professionals. **Strengths:** "Excellent for construction work." "Martin is one of the most sought-after advocates at the Scottish Bar. His clarity of thought, reading of the court and performance on his feet put him at the very top of the pile in the Scottish Junior Bar." **Recent work:** Instructed in Mr and Mrs Lewis v Kearney Donald Partnership, defending a firm of architects against multimillion-pound professional negligence claims.

Jonathan Broome Focuses on professional negligence issues in the construction sector. He is recognised for his experience and his client-friendly approach. **Strengths:** "An excellent and experienced junior for professional negligence, particularly in the construction industry." "Bright, approachable and alive to a client's commercial drivers." **Recent work:** Represented Agro Invest Overseas in bringing complex claims of negligence relating to the design and construction of a property against its architects and builders.

Alasdair McKenzie Focuses on professional negligence in the construction sector. He also handles a broad range of other construction and property-related disputes. **Strengths:** "A highly rated junior, valued for his specialist construction law experience, his easy manner and his thorough but pragmatic approach." "Alasdair is very thorough, considered and highly experienced in professional negligence claims."

Chris Paterson Handles professional negligence claims as part of a broader commercial disputes practice. He is experienced in cases involving solicitors and surveyors, among other professionals. **Strengths:** "A top-ranking junior in professional negligence matters. He has already gained great experience across all types of professional negligence cases." **Recent work:** Successfully defended Royal & Sun Alliance and Burness Paul against claims of negligence, breach of trust and breach of fiduciary duty following the failure of a complex investment scheme.

Gavin Walker Enjoys a burgeoning reputation at the Scottish Junior Bar, handling a broad range of complex commercial disputes. His professional negligence practice is particularly focused on matters involving construction professionals. **Strengths:** "Gavin is an extremely accomplished advocate, especially in matters of professional negligence and construction. Excellent under pressure and working within tight time limits." **Recent work:** Instructed in City of Edinburgh Council v DLA Piper, defending a law firm against claims of negligence with respect to the Edinburgh trams project.

David Thomson (see p.781) Handles a broad range of commercial litigation and is recommended for his handling of negligence claims pertaining to the legal profession. **Strengths:** "David is approachable and easy to work with and always provides clear, pragmatic and robust advice." **Recent work:** Acted in Alistair Greig v KWAD Solicitors, a claim of negligence brought against solicitors. The case involved questions of the scope of the solicitors' duty.

Other Ranked Lawyers

Paul Reid (Ampersand) Has particular strength in the representation of solicitors, surveyors, construction professionals and their insurers in professional liability cases. **Strengths:** "Excellent, hard-working junior who we regularly instruct in professional and medical negligence cases." **Recent work:** Defended surveyors Knight Frank against claims of negligence brought by the Bank of Ireland.

Gerald Hanretty QC (Arnot Manderson) Recognised for his strong experience in professional negligence cases, and regularly acts in cases concerning solicitors and accountants. **Strengths:** "Gerry Hanretty is exceptionally good. Tenacious and a rottweiler, someone who'll put the hard hat on and do whatever is needed for the client."

Andrew Young QC (Arnot Manderson) A highly ranked advocate, recommended both for professional negligence and clinical negligence matters. **Strengths:** "Has an immediate grasp of complex matters and a straightforward way of addressing issues."

Laurence Murphy QC (Arnot Manderson) Handles both professional and clinical negligence matters, and has recognised strength in claims involving solicitors, accountants and architects, among others. **Strengths:** "Laurence has in-depth experience of professional negligence claims, and provides highly pragmatic and effective advice on strategy."

Gavin MacColl (Hastie Stable) Continues to be recognised for his handling of professional negligence claims in the construction and property sectors. **Strengths:** "Gavin is a combative performer who marries this with commercial acumen. His response times are reliable and the quality of work excellent. He is also very easy to deal with."

PUBLIC PROCUREMENT

Public Procurement
Leading Stables
Band 1
Axiom Advocates *
Leading Silks
Band 1
Dunlop Roddy *Axiom Advocates*
Band 2
Crawford Ruth *Axiom Advocates*
Mitchell Iain G *Arnot Manderson (ORL)* ◊
Mure James *Axiom Advocates*
Leading Juniors
Band 1
MacGregor John *Axiom Advocates*
Ross Morag *Axiom Advocates*
** Indicates set with profile.*
◊ (ORL) = Other Ranked Lawyer.
Alphabetical order within each band. Band 1 is highest.

Band 1

Axiom Advocates

See profile on p.946

THE SET

Axiom Advocates has an impeccable reputation as "the pre-eminent procurement chambers in Scotland," with its barristers seen regularly in the Court of Session on both sides of major public procurement disputes. The stable's advocates offer expert knowledge in a wide variety of sectors, acting on cases related to major infrastructure, public services and development contracts. They also provide extensive advisory services to both pursuers and defenders.

Client service: "The clerks are great at confirming the availability of the advocates." Practice manager Lesley Flynn leads the clerking team.

SILKS

Roddy Dunlop QC A widely respected silk who regularly acts for both defenders and pursuers on significant procurement matters. **Strengths:** "He's very direct in his advice, and has the skill to help clients to understand the reason and rationale behind it. Well respected in court." **Recent work:** Acted for petitioner Kenman Holdings in a procurement claim relating to the development of Lews Castle, Stornoway.

Ruth Crawford QC Well known for the strength of her advisory practice, Ruth Crawford QC also regularly appears in the Scottish courts at all levels. Her broad public law expertise includes significant public procurement work that covers a wide range of areas, including IT, transport and infrastructure. **Strengths:** "Very impressive and analytical. She knows how to cut to the chase." "She is accommodating and collaborative in her approach." **Recent work:** Instructed by defendants Comhairle nan Eilean Siar in a judicial review brought by Kenman Holdings following the procurement of a private sector development partner.

James Mure QC A go-to silk for cases concerning planning, environmental and constitutional concerns. He is regularly instructed by the Scottish government, local authorities and other public bodies. **Strengths:** "A very polished advocate." **Recent work:** Acted for the Scottish Fire and Rescue Service in defending a challenge to the procurement of a supply of smoke detectors under a framework agreement.

JUNIORS

John MacGregor Talented junior John MacGregor has a solid practice covering commercial litigation, administrative and public law. He has played a role in a number of high-profile public procurement cases in Scotland and internationally, and he is also standing junior counsel to the UK government. **Strengths:** "John would always be my number one pick for a Scottish procurement advocate. He is incredibly approachable and well liked by clients. He complements his comprehensive procurement knowledge with a sound understanding of all public law matters." "He is excellent, really knowledgeable and bright, and he cuts right through to the issue with real precision." **Recent work:** Acted for the Galloway Group as petitioner in a judicial review in the High Court of Montserrat successfully challenging the procurement of services to dredge Plymouth Harbour.

Morag Ross A highly respected junior at the Scottish Bar who is also standing junior counsel to the Scottish government. She advises on a wide range of public law issues and has significant experience of handling procurement challenges, particularly those involving government bodies. **Strengths:** "She has a fantastic level of experience. She is probably the one with the most procurement knowledge in all of Scotland." "Morag is a leading junior who is well known and respected in the procurement industry."

Other Ranked Lawyers

Iain Mitchell QC (Arnot Manderson) A well-established silk who is qualified to practise at both the English and Scottish Bar. He is best known for his expertise in the IP and IT arenas, and has recently advised extensively on a number of major public software procurements. **Strengths:** "He's very practical. He's got an ability to take a large amount of information and distil it to its original essence. A pleasure to work with." **Recent work:** Advised Open Forum Europe on lobbying and the implementation by governmental bodies of open standards in software procurement.

REAL ESTATE LITIGATION

Real Estate Litigation
Leading Silks
Band 1
Lake Jonathan C *Axiom Advocates*
Martin Roy *Terra Firma Chambers*
McBrearty Kenneth *Axiom Advocates*
Reid J Gordon *Terra Firma Chambers*
Sandison Craig *Ampersand*
Leading Juniors
Band 1
MacColl Gavin L *Hastie Stable*
Thomson David *Axiom Advocates* *
Band 2
Barne Jonathan *Axiom Advocates*
Walker Gavin *Axiom Advocates*
Up-and-coming individuals
McClelland Ross *Axiom Advocates*

Ranked Lawyers

Craig Sandison QC (Ampersand) Has considerable experience of appearing before the Court of Session and the Supreme Court. He routinely handles a broad range of matters, covering areas such as property ownership, access disputes and dilapidations. **Strengths:** "He has the most impressive court style and his delivery is second to none." "Very aggressive, effective and very academically sound – an excellent advocate."

Jonathan Lake QC (Axiom Advocates) Impresses sources with his strength in handling highly technical cases. He regularly tackles cases related to damages and lease claims. **Strengths:** "First-rate QC who is highly effective, he has the ear of the court and he is great with clients too." "Most impressive in terms of his clarity in court: he has a wonderful delivery, even when dealing with quite complex things."

Kenneth McBrearty QC (Axiom Advocates) Offers considerable strength in landlord and tenant disputes. His notable expertise encompasses dilapidations, lease issues and matters related to the Land Reform Act. He is valued by sources for his commercial approach and strength in complex property matters. **Strengths:** "Commercial, down-to-earth and very bright." "He is able to identify the best parts of the case with ease." **Recent work:** He acted for BNP Paribas Securities Services in BNP Paribas Securities Services Trust Company Jersey Ltd v Mothercare (UK), a case regarding a dilapidations claim that raised issues of the proper measure of loss and the validity of a claim for part of a building that was arguably not in a position to be rented in the current market.

David Thomson (see p.781) (Axiom Advocates) A go-to junior who demonstrates notable strength in restructuring and insolvency-related property matters. He also handles commercial lease dilapidations and is valued by sources for his impressive advocacy skills. **Strengths:** "He is excellent on his feet and has a determined court manner. He produces written work of the highest quality and you can always rely on him to give an assertive and decisive opinion." **Recent work:** Acted for the Greenbelt Group in Marriott v Greenbelt Group Limited, an appeal to the Lands Tribunal concerning the validity and enforceability of real burdens in a new housing development.

Jonathan Barne (Axiom Advocates) Highly sought after for his expertise in professional negligence-related matters and construction cases. He is an experienced representative of local authorities in real estate disputes and routinely advises on statutory repairs matters. He also has strength in dilapidations claims. **Strengths:** "Top-performing, experienced junior. He is consistently good." "He works commercially for the client and has a creative approach in how he handles things." **Recent work:** Instructed by Inverclyde Council in relation to demolition orders relating to an estate that the council wished to demolish due to it being below the tolerable standard in terms of the relevant legislation.

Gavin Walker (Axiom Advocates) Earns praise for his work in construction matters. He is regularly instructed to handle high-value disputes and has experience with commercial property matters and dilapidations claims. **Strengths:** "Very switched-on, able to get to the crux of issues very quickly, and accessible." "Very commercially astute." **Recent work:** Acted for Capital Developments in pursuing an action for interdict against a construction company and a neighbour to prevent them from encroaching on the pursuer's rights.

Ross McClelland (Axiom Advocates) Recognised for his extraordinary strength in the Commercial Court. He is frequently instructed in trespass and negligence cases and has further experience with landlord and tenant disputes. He earns additional praise for his expertise in development matters. **Strengths:** "A real up-and-coming star. An analytical mind and he has the ear of the court." "Very intelligent, very capable of breaking down issues in a case, and very user-friendly." **Recent work:** Defended Santander in the Commercial Court of the Court of Session against claims filed by a commercial landowner regarding the obligation to repair an office building during and after expiry of a commercial lease.

Gavin MacColl (Hastie Stable) Has a diverse practice that includes land, professional negligence and restructuring and insolvency matters. He is renowned for his commercial capabilities and strength in handling matters related to construction. **Strengths:** "Tenacious yet pragmatic, he handles the most difficult cases with ease." "Excellent on his feet and provides sound advice throughout his instructions."

Roy Martin QC (Terra Firma Chambers) Regularly handles landlord and tenant disputes particularly in relation to lease issues. He also has expertise in damages claims relating to real estate development and earns additional praise for his strength in planning matters. **Strengths:** "He has the ear of the court, and he is quite ferocious in how he represents clients. He has a wealth of experience and technical knowledge." **Recent work:** Acted in Malin and Others v Crown Aerosols, a case concerning whether a lease permitted a tenant to demolish a large industrial building on land let by the lease without the landlord's consent.

Gordon Reid QC (Terra Firma Chambers) Enjoys a prominent reputation in construction and contract matters. He is also highly regarded for his deep knowledge of related agricultural issues. **Strengths:** "Hugely experienced, highly respected, very intelligent and just a very pleasant person to deal with." "Measured and careful with huge attention to detail."

RESTRUCTURING/INSOLVENCY

Restructuring/Insolvency
Leading Stables
Band 1
Axiom Advocates *
Band 2
Ampersand *
Leading Silks
Star individuals
Sellar David *Ampersand*
Band 1
Borland Garry *Axiom Advocates* *
Howie Robert *Ampersand*
Howlin Michael P *Terra Firma Chambers (ORL)* ◊
Leading Juniors
Band 1
Delibegović-Broome Almira *Axiom Advocates*
O'Brien Paul *Axiom Advocates*
Ower Susan *Axiom Advocates*
Thomson David *Axiom Advocates* *
Band 2
Duthie Euan *Axiom Advocates*
Up-and-coming individuals
Roxburgh Elisabeth *Axiom Advocates*
* *Indicates set / individual with profile.*
◊ *(ORL) = Other Ranked Lawyer.*
Alphabetical order within each band. Band 1 is highest.

Band 1

Axiom Advocates

See profile on p.946

THE SET

Axiom Advocates is the leading restructuring and insolvency stable in Scotland, and has some of the most qualified experts in the field. Its members are frequently instructed in the most significant and high-profile cases, and have wide expertise in relation to both corporate and personal insolvency. They can provide advice and representation on a broad range of contentious and non-contentious matters.

Client service: "The clerks, led by practice manager Lesley Flynn, are first-class: you can ask for any particular advocate and if they are not available, the clerks will come back with meaningful suggestions."

SILKS

Garry Borland QC (see p.599) Has a broad practice dealing with all areas of commercial law, and detailed knowledge of restructuring and insolvency. Also well respected for his grasp of construction, property and company disputes. **Strengths:** "One of the most technically gifted advocates around. His eye for detail and clarity of delivery is superb." "Super-bright, extremely thorough and organised."

JUNIORS

Almira Delibegović-Broome Experienced junior who has a robust commercial practice and is regularly instructed in complex insolvency disputes. She also has wider experience in corporate finance, tax and commercial contracts. **Strengths:** "Extremely capable and absolutely top-notch." "She has a keen intellect and is not afraid of a fight."

Paul O'Brien Focuses his practice on commercial disputes, including significant insolvency cases. Previously worked as a solicitor before being called to the Bar. **Strengths:** "A gifted advocate who is good with technical matters." "He is extraordinarily hard-working and incredibly client-centric."

Susan Ower Highly regarded advocate who has also been appointed standing junior to the Scottish Government Legal Directorate. She handles a broad spectrum of issues relating to administrations, liquidations and sequestrations, and regularly acts on behalf of insolvency practitioners, banks and financial institutions. **Strengths:** "Good all-round advocate who is commercial and provides sound advice." "She is very user-friendly, and someone who can get to the crux of the issue." **Recent work:** Acted on behalf of joint administrators of three group companies with the objective of reducing the transfers of various properties with a cumulative value of approximately £2.4 million.

David Thomson (see p.781) Practises exclusively in commercial litigation with a strong focus on restructuring and insolvency. He is very highly thought of for his technical knowledge and advocacy skills. **Strengths:** "An experienced, knowledgeable and determined counsel with a good knowledge of insolvency law." "Offers clear, practical and commercial advice while still maintaining a strong grasp of all technical aspects of the file." **Recent work:** Instructed in an ongoing dispute regarding the insolvency of the Letham Grange hotel and golf resort.

Euan Duthie A commercial advocate principally focused on insolvency litigation, Euan Duthie is regularly instructed on behalf of insolvency practitioners in relation to administrations and also has particular insight into directors' disqualifications proceedings. **Strengths:** "He is really good at picking things up at short notice and turning them around, and he is very good on his feet." **Recent work:** Appointed as junior counsel to the administrators of Heritable Bank plc in a dispute concerning the winding-up of the board at its Icelandic parent company.

Elisabeth Roxburgh A highly capable junior advising on all areas of insolvency and bankruptcy, who has a growing reputation at the Bar. She receives excellent feedback for her approach to cases as well as her technical command of insolvency law. **Strengths:** "A bright star among junior counsel on the insolvency scene in Scotland." "Always provides proactive, pragmatic, commercial advice. An excellent junior counsel." **Recent work:** Advised on three connected petitions relating to companies who operate jute mills in India but which have their registered offices in Scotland. The case concerns court orders in India restricting how far these companies can deal with their assets.

Band 2

Ampersand

See profile on p.945

THE SET

This highly commercial group is well known for its work in the insolvency field, and has a number of members who boast strong and established practices. The set has recently been involved in a string of litigation work arising from the collapse of a £400 million hedge fund, as well as work in relation to the administration of Rangers FC. Advocates at Ampersand are rated highly for their knowledge of highly complex and technical issues related to restructuring and insolvency.

Client service: "The clerks are very helpful in getting instructions reviewed and an advocate in the diary." Alan Moffat is the practice manager.

SILKS

David Sellar QC Star performer David Sellar QC remains a true specialist in his field and the foremost authority on insolvency law in Scotland. His unrivalled knowledge and experience establishes him as go-to senior counsel for complex corporate insolvency matters. **Strengths:** "When it comes to the technical aspects of insolvency, he is second to none. His knowledge is outstanding." "Very commercial, a real expert in this field, smart and good to deal with."

Robert Howie QC Has a strong reputation as a commercial advocate and is also known for his ability to handle highly technical cases. He handles a broad range of insolvency work arising out of liquidations, sequestrations and bankruptcy petitions. **Strengths:** "For quite a technical case where you need the right answer, he will give you a very thorough and insightful opinion." "Extremely experienced and able."

Other Ranked Lawyers

Michael Howlin QC (Terra Firma Chambers) Advises widely on complex corporate insolvency and restructuring cases, and has strong expertise in schemes of arrangement, Part VII transfers and cross-border insolvency. He regularly acts for administrators and trustees for creditors. **Strengths:** "He is very able and easily gets to grips with complex problems and situations. He is also very responsive and will go that extra mile to ensure that you get the advice or written work you need in a tight timescale." "Mixes superb legal knowledge in insolvency and company law with commercial understanding." **Recent work:** Acted in Malcolm Insulation v IGL, a liquidation in which there were challenges raised against the liquidator's adjudication of claims against the company.

TAX

Tax
Leading Stables
Band 1
Arnot Manderson
Axiom Advocates *
Terra Firma Chambers *
Leading Silks
Star individuals
Ghosh Julian *Axiom Advocates*
Band 1
McNeill James W *Axiom Advocates*
Simpson Philip J D *Terra Firma Chambers*
Band 2
Thomson Roderick *Arnot Manderson*
Young Andrew R W *Arnot Manderson*
Leading Juniors
Band 1
Small David *Arnot Manderson*
Band 2
Francis Derek *Terra Firma Chambers*
* *Indicates set with profile.*
Alphabetical order within each band. Band 1 is highest.

Band 1

Arnot Manderson

THE SET

Arnot Manderson houses a number of highly skilled advocates with substantial expertise in the tax arena. Its members excel in providing counsel on complex disputes involving tax issues, including property valuation, professional negligence and warranty enforcement cases. Receives frequent instructions from HMRC, with members also acting for private clients.

Client service: Andrew Sutherland and Elizabeth Manderson are the senior clerks at the stable.

SILKS

Roddy Thomson QC Adept at handling tax-related disputes in both the First-tier and Upper Tax Tribunals on behalf of HMRC and taxpayers. He is especially noted for his long-established practice, bringing over three decades of litigation experience to his cases. **Strengths:** "He is very thorough in his analysis of issues."

Andrew Young QC Receives regular instructions from HMRC in significant tax cases. He is highly regarded by interviewees and noted for his expert counsel on matters concerning indirect tax.

JUNIORS

David Small Handles a wide remit of tax cases, including those concerning professional negligence by tax advisers, trusts variation and HMRC's enforcement of Minimum Wage legislation. Clients benefit from his previous experience as an inspector of taxes and tax partner at a Big Four accountancy firm. **Strengths:** "He has a really good knowledge of tax law and great attention to detail, which is essential."

Axiom Advocates

See profile on p.946

THE SET

A high-calibre bench of tax specialists recognised for their impressive litigation experience. They are also a leading stable for clients seeking advice on complex corporate tax issues. One impressed solicitor says: "They have good quality advocates across the board. I have a lot of respect for the people they invite to join the stable."

Client service: "The clerks are accessible and contactable, they bill promptly and are on top of availability." Lesley Flynn is the stable's practice manager.

SILKS

Julian Ghosh QC Renowned tax advocate qualified to represent clients in both Scottish and English matters. He acts in a wide variety of cases and is especially noted for his expertise with European taxation issues and corporate tax. **Strengths:** "His technical skills are absolutely first-class." **Recent work:** Successfully represented Sir Fraser Morrison in a case concerning the treatment of capital gains tax payments.

James McNeill QC Highly reputed practitioner engaged in a wide array of tax-related cases. He is well placed to provide counsel on tax issues arising in the context of commercial, trusts and occupational pension scheme disputes. **Strengths:** "He is supremely gifted and intelligent."

Terra Firma Chambers

See profile on p.948

THE SET

Highly regarded for personal and business taxation matters, especially cases concerning stamp duties, PAYE, indirect tax and the variation of trusts. Also rated highly for advice on international tax matters concerning European law, double taxation and residence and domicile.

Client service: "The clerking is first-rate, they are very efficient." Emma Potter is the stable's practice manager.

SILKS

Philip Simpson QC Possesses a wealth of experience with Scottish and English tax planning and litigation. His areas of expertise include income tax, capital gains, stamp duties, VAT and corporate tax. **Strengths:** "He has an absolutely encyclopaedic knowledge of tax, and explains issues in a straightforward manner." **Recent work:** Acted for Royal Troon Golf Club in a claim disputing whether food and drinks supplied to members are liable to VAT.

JUNIORS

Derek Francis Specialises in providing counsel on the tax elements of contentious trusts and succession cases. As a qualified chartered tax adviser, he is also well placed to advise on non-contentious tax issues. **Strengths:** "He is very knowledgeable on tax and very accessible." **Recent work:** Acted on behalf of a private client in a case determining whether a trust variation triggered an inheritance tax charge.

BARRISTERS' PROFILES

Leaders' Profiles in The Bar

ABRAHAMS, James QC
8 New Square, London
020 7405 4321
james.abrahams@8newsquare.co.uk
Featured in Intellectual Property (London)
Practice Areas: Barrister specialising in all areas of intellectual property law; including patents, copyright, design right, database right, registered designs, trade marks, passing off and confidential information. Recent cases include Napp v Dr Reddy's and Sandoz (transdermal patches); Unwired Planet v Huawei (mobile telecoms patents); Rovi v Virgin Media (STB patents); Wobben v Siemens (wind turbine patents); IPCom v HTC (telecoms patents); Total v YouView (STB trade marks); IPC Media v Media 10 (retail trade marks); Microsoft v Motorola (patent/email protocols); Coward v Phaestos (copyright in hedge fund software) HTC v Apple (smartphone patents); Liversidge v Owen Mumford (medical device patent); Numatic v Qualtex (passing off/vacuum cleaners); Nokia v IPCom (3G mobile communications); Wake Forest v Smith & Nephew and Mölnlycke v Wake Forest (medical device patent); Baigent v Random House (The Da Vinci Code copyright case). For a comprehensive CV visit www.8newsquare.co.uk.
Professional Memberships: Intellectual Property Bar Association, Chancery Bar Association.
Career: Called 1997 (Gray's Inn), QC 2016.
Personal: Born 1974. Educated at Bournemouth School; St Anne's College, Oxford (1995 BA Law, 1996 BCL).

ADAMS, Christopher
St Philips Chambers, Birmingham
0121 246 1600
cadams@st-philips.com
Featured in Family/Matrimonial (Midlands)
Practice Areas: Christopher has practised exclusively in the field of public child law since 1995. He acts on behalf of local authorities, parents, children and other family members and is frequently instructed in cases involving serious and medically complex injuries to children. He was head of the St Philips child-care team for three years and has spoken at conferences and seminars on various aspects of the law relating to children. Authorities include: C v Solihull MBC [1993] 1 FLR 290; Hereford and Worcester CC v S [1993] 2 FLR 360; Re C (A Minor) (Care Proceedings: Disclosure) [1997] Fam 76; Re G (Leave to Appeal: Jurisdiction) [1999] 1 FLR 771; A Local Authority v A & Others [2009] EWHC 1982 (Fam); Coventry CC v B, A, RK, KK [2012] EWHC 4014 (Fam); A County Council v AB & Others [2015] EWFC 82.
Professional Memberships: FLBA; ALC; BAAF.
Career: Christopher was appointed as a Recorder in 2005 and is authorised to deal with family cases in both the private and public law jurisdictions. In 2013, he was authorised to sit as a Deputy High Court Judge in the Family Division.

ADAMS, Jayne QC
Ropewalk Chambers, Nottingham
0115 947 2581
jayneadamsqc@ropewalk.co.uk
Featured in Personal Injury (Midlands), Personal Injury (All Circuits)
Practice Areas: She has extensive experience in disease, high value personal injury, clinical negligence and fraudulent claims litigation. She is best known for her work in the field of disease litigation, including NIHL; HAVS; WRULD; stress; asthma; chemical poisoning; dust; silicosis and other lung diseases, particularly asbestos related disease. She is experienced in preliminary issues, including limitation, and regularly appears in front of the Senior Master for disease litigation whether for CMC, Show Cause procedures or other individual aspect. She deals with breach of duty, medical causation and quantum at Courts throughout England and Wales, at multi track level, at both first instance and appellate courts. She also deals with Part 20 proceedings and insurance related disputes. She regularly undertakes very high value JSM's in all aspects of disease, but particularly mesothelioma claims involving high earners and company directors. She is experienced, in this context, in dealing with accountancy and projected profit issues.
Professional Memberships: Personal Injuries Bar Association; Nottinghamshire Medico-Legal Society.
Career: Called in 1982; Queen's Counsel 2016; LLB, University of Birmingham. Barrister of the Year, Nottinghamshire Law Society 2016.

ADAMS, Paul
Serle Court, London
020 7242 6105
padams@serlecourt.co.uk
Featured in Company (London)
Practice Areas: Chancery and commercial, with a particular focus on company and other business disputes, civil fraud, domestic and offshore trusts, professional negligence, financial services and insolvency. Recent significant cases include Glenn v Watson (fraud and breach of fiduciary duty); Amryta Capital LLP v Mehta (tracing claims following misappropriations from an LLP); R v N (investment negligence claim against a Jersey trustee); Rawlinson & Hunter Trustees SA v ITG Ltd [2015] EWHC 1664 (Ch) (abuse of process), Novatrust Ltd v Kea Investments Ltd [2014] EWHC 4061 (Ch) (foreign company derivative claims), Kea Investments Ltd v Spartan Capital Ltd (effect of jurisdiction clauses on winding up petitions), Sukhoruchkin v Van Bekestein [2014] EWCA Civ 399 (reflective loss and freezing injunctions), Morgan v Kevin Neil Associates Ltd (alleged mis-selling of investment scheme), Apex Global Management Ltd v Fi Call Ltd [2014] BCC 286 (relief against third parties in unfair prejudice petitions), C v D (invalidity of a Bermuda trust and a civil law foundation) and Re the F Trust (claims for breach of trust).
Professional Memberships: ChBA.
Career: BA in law and BCL at St Catherine's College, Oxford (ranked top of the University in both); called to the Bar in 2008.
Publications: 'The two-party rule and transactions between trusts with a common trustee', Trusts & Trustees, Volume 18 Issue 9, p 862.
Personal: Interests include football, rugby, cricket, music and travel.

ADDY, Caroline
One Brick Court, London
020 7353 8845
ca@onebrickcourt.com
Featured in Defamation/Privacy (London)
Practice Areas: Defamation, confidence and privacy, harassment, advertising, contempt of court and media, freedom of information, data protection and all aspects of law relating to the communication of information or its restriction including human rights law and harassment.
Career: LLB (Euro) Hons Exon 1990. Called 1991, joined chambers 1992. Cases include: Cartus Corporation v Sidell & anr (2014) (libel injunction); LB Lambeth v Pead (2013) (Harassment, Breach of Confidence, Data Protection Act and Contempt of Court); Nowak v NMC and Guy's and St Thomas' NHS Trust (2013)(Harassment); O'Dwyer v ITV (2013)(Defamation); Iqbal v Mansoor (2011); Westminster NHS Trust v Shetreet (2010) (Breach of Confidence, Contempt of Court); Govei & anr v Ambrosiadou (2010); (Libel) Sheffield Wednesday Football Club and ors v Hargreaves (2007), Virdi v Associated Newspapers Limited (2007), Warren v (1) Hatton (2) BBC (2007), Stickland v Emap Metro Limited (2007), Guterman v Pemberton, Western Mail and Jones (2005), Morrison v Nord Anglia Education Plc, and ors (2005), Downtex v Flatley (2003), Fox v Environment Agency and ors (2003), McPhilemy v Times Newspapers Ltd (2001-04), Melchett and Greenpeace UK v Glasgow Herald (2001), Sugar v News Group Newspapers Ltd and Mullery(2000), Arobieke v MGN Ltd and ors (2000), Tancic v Times Newspapers Ltd (1999). (Privacy/Confidence) Sorrell and Weber v Fullsix and ors (2007), Hughes v Carratu International PLC (2006). Acts for both claimants and defendants. Regularly advises major book and magazine publishers.
Publications: Contributor to Carter-Ruck on Libel and Privacy 6th edition; contributor to Arlidge, Eady and Smith on Contempt 4th Edition and supplement; contributor to Halsbury's Laws, Defamation 2012.
Personal: Lives in London. Languages French and German.

ADDY, Catherine
Maitland Chambers, London
020 7406 1200
clerks@maitlandchambers.com
Featured in Chancery (London), Company (London), Restructuring/Insolvency (London)
Practice Areas: Chancery and commercial litigation including: banking and financial services, company and insolvency matters, commercial contracts and other business related agreements (including partnerships), conflict of laws, property and other general equity and trust related matters. Appointed as Junior Counsel to the Crown (A Panel) and as a Deputy Registrar of the Bankruptcy and Companies Court. She has particular expertise in insolvency related matters and is an appointed member of the statutory Insolvency Rules Committee. She is also a member of the Bankruptcy and Companies Court Users Committee and has provided expert insolvency and company law advice to international lawyers. Notably, she represented the Crown in Re Spectrum Plus, advised HM Treasury and the Bank of England in relation to Northern Rock, acted for the Secretary of State in the successful director's disqualification claim against Kevin Maxwell and for the successful non-executive directors in the failed director's disqualification proceedings brought by the Secretary of State in relation to the collapse of Farepak, and recently appeared in the GAME appeal concerning administration expenses. She has also been instructed to represent the interests of the general unsecured creditors in various aspects of the Lehman Brothers' insolvency litigation and, as well as advising and appearing for officeholders of other well-known insolvent estates, she regularly acts for Crown Departments. In 2014 she was heavily involved in the UBS swaps litigation in the Commercial Court, acting for LBBW.
Professional Memberships: Chancery Bar Association; COMBAR; ILA; R3; International Associate Member of the American Bar Association; Insolvency Rules Committee; Bankruptcy and Companies Court Users Committee; Bar Council Ethics Committee and BARCO Committee.
Career: Called to the Bar 1998. Appointed as a Deputy Registrar (2016). Appointed Junior Counsel to the Crown (A Panel) March 2012 (B Panel 2007-2012, C Panel 2003-07). Chairman of the Young Bar (2004). Chairman of the Bar Conference (2007). Elected Member of the Bar Council (2001-07). Appointed Chancery Bar Association member of the Bar Council (2010-12). Elected Hon. Treasurer of the Chancery Bar Association (2008-12). Member of the Bankruptcy and Companies Court Users Committee (2012 to date). Appointed to serve on the Insolvency Rules Committee (2013 to date). Elected as a Bencher of the Middle Temple (2014).
Publications: Contributor to Gore-Browne on Companies, Equity and Administration (CUP), Butterworths' Practical Insolvency, International Corporate Rescue and the Journal of International Business and Finance Law.
Personal: MA, LLM (1st class) Cantab. Queen Mother Scholar of Middle Temple. Accredited advocacy trainer.

ADKIN, Jonathan QC
Fountain Court Chambers, London
020 7583 3335
ja@fountaincourt.co.uk
Featured in Chancery (London), Commercial Dispute Resolution (London), Fraud (London), Offshore (London)
Practice Areas: Commercial and chancery litigation and arbitration, Civil Fraud, Banking and finance, Professional negligence, Company, Partnership and LLP, Insolvency, Trusts, and Offshore.
Professional Memberships: COMBAR and Chancery Bar Association
Career: Jonathan Adkin QC has appeared in some of the largest commercial and chancery disputes of recent times, including the Berezovsky and Anisimov cases and the litigation arising out of the collapse of Halliwells and Glasgow Rangers. He regularly acts in multi-billion dollar actions in the Commercial Court and Chancery Division and in numerous jurisdictions overseas.
Personal: Called 1997. Silk 2013. Called ad hoc to the bars of Bermuda, the Cayman

Islands and Gibraltar. Educated at Balliol College, Oxford.

AFZAL, Imran
Field Court Tax Chambers, London
020 3693 3700
ia@fieldtax.com
Featured in Tax (London)

Practice Areas: Imran has a broad practice and has been involved in a range of domestic and international matters, acting for companies, private-clients and tax authorities. In addition to advisory work he is regularly involved in litigation. He is often instructed in high-profile and high-value matters, eg he has advised in relation to a multi-billion dollar settlement, he has assisted in a foreign company in a matter involving over £1 billion, and he has been instructed by HMRC in relation to various partnership loss appeals.
Professional Memberships: Revenue Bar Association.
Career: Imran was called to the Bar in 2008. In 2012 he was appointed to the Attorney-General's C Panel. In 2014 he founded Field Court Tax Chambers with three colleagues, having previously practised in another set of tax chambers.
Personal: Imran read law at Oxford University as an undergraduate and postgraduate, coming top of the university on both occasions.

AGNELLO, Raquel QC
Erskine Chambers, London
020 7242 5532
ragnello@erskinechambers.com
Featured in Pensions (London), Restructuring/Insolvency (London)

Practice Areas: Raquel is a sought-after specialist in insolvency, company and commercial litigation. She is a highly-regarded expert in the area of pensions and insolvency, in particular the 'moral hazard' provisions. She has led on many high profile cases on behalf of the Pensions Regulator, including on Nortel and Lehman in the Supreme Court. She has acted for the trustees of the Kaupthing Singer and Friedlander pension scheme in proceedings relating to provability as well as assignability of their section 75 claim. She frequently advises corporate groups in relation to proposed restructurings and pension issues as well as risk assessment. In 2015 she was named Legal 500's Insolvency Silk of the Year. In October 2012, she was named 'Barrister of the Year' at the Insolvency and Rescue Awards. In January 2012, she was selected as one of the 'Hot 100' by 'The Lawyer' and she was also shortlisted as Insolvency Silk of the Year by Chambers and Partners.
Professional Memberships: Chancery Bar Association. Insolvency Lawyers Association. Financial Services Lawyers Association. Association of Pension Lawyers.
Career: Called 1986; Silk: 2009; sits in the High Court part time as Deputy Registrar in Bankruptcy and in the Companies Court; Bencher of the Inner Temple.
Personal: BA (hons) (Sussex), Diplome D'Etudes Juridiques Francaise; MCIArb. Fluent in French and Portuguese, working knowledge of Swedish.

AGNEW, Christine QC
2 Bedford Row, London
020 7440 8888
cagnew@2bedfordrow.co.uk
Featured in Crime (London)

Practice Areas: Cited by The Legal 500 and Chambers UK as a leading junior for many years Christine was appointed as Queen's Counsel in 2015. She conducts the most serious and complex criminal cases for both the defence and prosecution. As a junior she was a Grade 4 Prosecution Advocate for the CPS. Christine's practice covers the full range of criminal work and she has very considerable experience in relation to allegations involving murder, manslaughter, armed robbery, drug importations, kidnap and serious sexual offences. She has developed specialist expertise in relation to trials involving young offenders charged with all types of serious criminal offences. Christine has been instructed in a number of "baby-shaking" and infant non-accidental injury cases, which have involved extensive cross-examination of medical professionals, and dealing with expert medical evidence before juries. Christine is also regularly instructed in all types of fraud cases. She has also represented defendants concerned in cases concerning bribery and corruption. She has significant experience of complex money laundering trials from simple cash to gold bullion and currency exchanges. She has a reputation as being an extremely hard working and able defence advocate who is exceptionally good with clients and achieves acquittals in the most difficult of circumstances. She is often first choice defence counsel for firms with private clients who demand an incisive and empathic advocate who can instil real confidence in the client. In addition to undertaking general crime work Christine also prosecutes for the Health and Safety Executive and the Environment Agency. As a junior Christine was appointed to the A list for Specialist Regulatory Advocates in Health and Safety and Environmental Law and has prosecuted several fatality cases requiring detailed and specialist knowledge. She also has considerable experience of coroners' inquests. Christine is authorised to accept instructions from members of the public in certain circumstances. She also appears before Police Disciplinary and Appeal Tribunals.
Professional Memberships: South Eastern Circuit. Criminal Bar Association. Association of Regulatory and Disciplinary Lawyers. Health and Safety Lawyers Association.
Career: Called 1992. Silk 2015.

AGNEW OF LOCHNAW BT, Crispin QC
Westwater Advocates, Edinburgh
0131 668 3792
crispin.agnew@westwateradvocates.com
Featured in Planning (Scotland), Agriculture & Rural Affairs (Scotland)

Practice Areas: All aspects of rural property law including planning and environmental law (including planning appeals and judicial review challenges to planning and section 36 consent decisions), nature conservation; wind & hydro renewable energy, fishing law; agriculture and CAP, agricultural landlord and tenant, crofting. Local Authority law including licensing and special needs education & disability issues in education. Peerage and Heraldic Law. Knowledge of military issues having served in the Army 1962 to 1981 [Retired as Major].
Professional Memberships: Patron, United Kingdom Environmental Law Association [UKELA]; Chairman, Crofting Law Group; Agricultural Law Association.
Career: Called to Bar 1982; Silk 1995.
Publications: Agricultural Law in Scotland, Butterworths 1996; Connell on Agricultural Holdings (Scotland) Acts 7th Ed [with Donald Rennie WS] T & T Clark 1996; Variation and Discharge of Land Obligations, W Green; 1999 Crofting Law, T & T Clark 2000; Allan & Chapman, Licensing (Scotland) Act 1976 2nd to 5th Ed [with Heather Baillie, solicitor]; Stair Memorial Encyclopaedia – Articles on Heraldy; Court of the Lord Lyon; Precedence; Scots law chapter in The Law of Trees, Forests and Hedges by Charles Mynors, 2nd Ed. Sweet & Maxwell 1912; Practitioner's Rural Notebook, published by Savills due September 2016 (contributor – Scottish Chapter).

AHMAD, Mirza
St Philips Chambers, Birmingham
07429 335 090
mahmad@st-philips.com
Featured in Administrative & Public Law (Midlands)

Practice Areas: Mirza practises from London, Birmingham and Leeds. He is nationally recognised as an expert in local authority law and employment law. He specialises in providing high quality advice and advocacy services in the areas of: judicial review, constitutional and governance issues; employment (including unfair dismissal, redundancy, TUPE, equal pay and discrimination); partnerships; procurement; land and property matters (including housing and planning); and personal injuries. He is authorised to undertake direct public access work.
Professional Memberships: Chairman of the Bar Association for Local Government & the Public Services (since 1998); Member of the General Council of the Bar (since 1995, save for 1997), ALBA, ELA, PIBA and President of ACSeS (2009/10).
Career: After being Called to the Bar in 1984 (Gray's Inn), Mirza spent over 26 years in local government. From 2000-11, he was the Chief Legal Officer and Corporate Director of Governance of Birmingham City Council, with leadership of 800+ staff. Mirza has an LLD (Hons), an LLM in Employment and Industrial Relations Law, and an MBA.
Publications: Mirza is the General Editor of 'Local Authority Employment Law, Practice and Procedure' (since 2009), and was the General Editor of 'Knight's Guide to Public Procurement Law and Practice' (2007-14).

AHMAD, Zubair
2 Hare Court, London
020 7353 5324
zubairahmad@2harecourt.com
Featured in Crime (London)

Practice Areas: Zubair is widely recognised as a leading junior in serious and complex crime and fraud. He represents professional clients in high profile and heavyweight criminal matters both at the investigation stage and at trial. He advises in cases involving professionals who are facing criminal and disciplinary proceedings arising in connection with their work such as fraud, corruption, serious professional misconduct and negligence. In cases involving a fatality he will also act in the Inquest proceedings. A significant part of his work involves handling sensitive and controversial matters in the field of national security as a Special Advocate. He acts in high profile civil claims and judicial review proceedings in the High Court against the intelligence services and other Government departments. He has appeared in some of the most prominent and significant cases involving national security / Justice and Security Act 2013 closed material procedure cases in recent years including: CF and Mohammed Ahmed Mohamed v The Security Service, The Secret Intelligence Service (civil claim). Currently appointed in K, A and B v Ministry of Defence and The Foreign and Commonwealth Office (judicial review and civil claim). In Business Crime, recent instructions have involved Zubair advising on corruption charges relating to a law officer. He is currently leading counsel defending the first defendant in a multi million pound MTIC fraud.
Career: A-G's Special Advocate panel since 2005; A-G's Special Counsel (PII) panel since 2004; List of Counsel for the defence and victims at the International Criminal Court since 2005.

AKKOUH, Tim
Erskine Chambers, London
020 7242 5532
takkouh@erskinechambers.com
Featured in Chancery (London), Commercial Dispute Resolution (London), Fraud (London)

Practice Areas: Tim is a commercial litigator, with a strong reputation for civil fraud and asset recovery. He has acted in some of the largest actions to come before the courts, such as JSC BTA Bank v Ablyazov, Djibouti v Boreh, Pinchuk v Bogolyubov and Mezhprom v Pugachev. Tim also maintains a commercial chancery practice, with an emphasis on insolvency, company and trusts disputes. Tim is particularly experienced in applications for pre-emptive and interlocutory relief, including freezing, search, receivership, committal and Norwich Pharmacal orders. Tim regularly appears with and without leaders in the Chancery Division and the Commercial Court. He has appeared in the Supreme Court once and in the Court of Appeal on over ten occasions. Ten of Tim's cases have been reported in the Weekly Law Reports. In October 2015, Tim was named Chancery Junior of the Year by Chambers and Partners.
Professional Memberships: Chancery Bar Association; COMBAR.
Publications: Co-author of Trusts Law (3rd ed, Palgrave Macmillan, 2013).
Personal: LLB (Lond), 1st class; LLM (Lond); married to Aimee; leisure interests include cricket and mountaineering.

AKUWUDIKE, Emma
25 Bedford Row, London
eakuwudike@25bedfordrow.com
Featured in Crime (London)

Practice Areas: Emma Akuwudike has an exclusively criminal defence practice with extensive experience in a broad spectrum of high level serious and organised crime. Her specialism includes murder, complex and large scale drugs offences, armed robbery, gang violence, firearms and serious sexual offences. Some notable cases include R v U (Matricide); R v L (Graff £40m diamond armed robbery in Mayfair); R v B (gangland execution); R v B (rape of a teacher by a pupil in a classroom); R v WD multi handed "murder" and GBH on two separate victims; R v E ("slavery" case alleged against husband and wife medics); R v V & Ors ("gang rape" involving a premiership footballer co-

defendant); R v R (Large scale £20m cocaine conspiracy).
Professional Memberships: Called to the Bar 1992 LLB (hons) 2.1 Member of the Criminal Bar Association Registered Pupil supervisor since 2003 Guest Speaker at House of Commons chaired by Diane Abbott for Mentoring project (2005) Part of CBA working party on retention of Queen's Counsel (2003) On CBA working party on reform of Legal Education Courses.

AL-ATTAR, Adam
South Square, London
020 7696 9900
adamalattar@southsquare.com
Featured in Financial Services (London), Restructuring/Insolvency (London)
Practice Areas: Insolvency and restructuring, banking and financial services, and the law of trusts.
Professional Memberships: COMBAR, Chancery Bar Association, ILA, INSOL.
Career: Significant cases include the client money, priorities and surplus applications in Lehman Brothers; the client money applications and affiliate litigation in MF Global; litigation in the BVI and the Cayman Islands concerning Madoff feeder funds (including Primeo Fund); and the restructurings of IMO Car Wash, The Co-operative Bank, Apcoa Holdings and LDK Solar. Adam has also acted on a number of inter-bank misrepresentation cases, including in relation to securitisations, syndicated loans and derivatives. He regularly advises on regulatory matters including in relation to the treatment of client money.
Publications: Contributor to Cross-Border Insolvency (fourth edition, Bloomsbury, 2015); Company Directors: Duties, Liabilities and Remedies (second edition, OUP, 2013); European Debt Restructuring Handbook (first edition, Global Business Law, 2013); Rowlatt on Principal and Surety (sixth edition, Sweet and Maxwell, 2011); The Law and Practice of Restructuring in the UK and US (first edition, OUP, 2011).

ALDOUS, Grahame QC
9 Gough Square, London
020 7832 0500
galdous@9goughsquare.co.uk
Featured in Personal Injury (London), Clinical Negligence (London)
Practice Areas: Personal injury. Clinical negligence. Catastrophic injury claims and claims involving maritime and foreign jurisdiction issues. Complex and novel points of law. Cases include: Marchioness Disaster, Simmons v Castle (Court of Appeal, damages uplift), Acori v Algol Maritime (Privy Council and Supreme Court of Gibraltar/ITWF Seaman's Contracts), Hatswell v Goldbergs (Court of Appeal: clinical/solicitors negligence), Johnstone v Whipps Cross Hospital (Court of Appeal, clinical negligence), Booth v Phillips (UK Admiralty Court Jurisdiction), Dickins v O2 (Court of Appeal; work stress), Joshi v Toyo Tires (QBD Product Liability injury, defective tyre), Braganza v BP (Admiralty Court, Court of Appeal and Supreme Court, death at sea), EXP v Barker (QBD, Court of Appeal, Clinical Negligence). Also known as a mediator.
Professional Memberships: PNBA, PIBA, APIL Fellow.
Career: Called 1979, Recorder 2000, CEDR Mediator 2006, Silk 2008. Head of Chambers 2008-2013. Advocacy Trainer.
Publications: Include: APIL Guide to Catastrophic Injury Claims, Kemp & Kemp, Work Accidents at Sea, Clinical Negligence Claims, Munkman on Employers' Liability.
Personal: Ocean sailing. Raced round Cape Horn in 1990 Whitbread Round the World Yacht Race. Sailed Atlantic on tall ship with disabled/able-bodied crew in the Norton Rose Sail the World Challenge, 2013. RYA Yachtmaster.

ALDRED, Adam
Kings Chambers, Leeds
0345 034 3444
clerks@kingschambers.com
Featured in Competition/European Law (The Regions)
Practice Areas: Barrister specialising in all aspects of EU competition law, including antitrust investigations, appeals, antitrust litigation, mergers, restrictive trade practices and cartels, strategic business advice (including joint ventures and other forms of collaboration), dominance, public procurement, State aid and competition risk management
Professional Memberships: The General Council of the Bar of England and Wales, British Institute of International and Comparative Law, The Chartered Institute of Arbitrators.
Career: Law Extension Committee, University of Sydney 1983 to 1987 Admitted to practice in the Supreme Court of New South Wales 1987, Trinity Hall University of Cambridge – 1988 to 1989 (Master of Laws – Public International & EU law), Norton Rose 1989 to 1993 (EU & competition law), Hammonds (Partner) 1994 to 2001 (EU & competition law & commercial litigation), Accredited Mediator 1999 (ADR Group), Solicitor Advocate (Higher Courts (Civil Advocacy)) 2000, Addleshaw Goddard LLP (Partner) 2001 to 2014 (EU & competition & antitrust litigation), Called to the Bar (Gray's Inn) 2014, Kings Chambers 2014 to date, Direct Access Qualified 2015.
Publications: Cartels: Enforcement, Appeals and Damages Actions, 2014, 2nd Ed – UK Chapter.

ALDRIDGE, James QC
Maitland Chambers, London
020 7406 1200
jaldridge@maitlandchambers.com
Featured in Chancery (London), Art and Cultural Property Law (London)
Practice Areas: Chancery/ commercial litigation, including matters involving contracts, property, professional negligence, company, insolvency, trusts and art & cultural property.
Professional Memberships: Chancery Bar Association, COMBAR.
Career: Called to the Bar 1994. Queen's Counsel 2014.
Personal: Educated Rugby and Corpus Christi College, Cambridge. Lives in London.

ALEXANDER, Daniel QC
8 New Square, London
020 7354 5265
daniel.alexander@8newsquare.co.uk
Featured in Information Technology (London), Intellectual Property (London), Media & Entertainment (London)
Practice Areas: Barrister (QC) specialising principally in intellectual property, media and entertainment, information technology (IT Silk of the Year, 2007), EC and commercial law. Practice regularly involves cases with international and multi-jurisdicational aspects. Advocacy and advisory work in a wide variety of cases at all levels of UK courts and at the EPO, ECJ and General Court (CFI). Regular involvement in international arbitrations as counsel or arbitrator. Recent cases include: Fage UK Ltd v Chobani UK Ltd (Greek Yogurt), Actavis v Sanofi, HTV v Apple. For comprehensive CV visit our website at www.8newsquare.co.uk
Professional Memberships: Chairman of the Intellectual Property Bar Association (IPBA); Chancery Bar Association.
Career: Called to English Bar, 1988; QC, 2003; Deupty High Court Judge, 2006.
Publications: Joint author of 'Guidebook to Intellectual Property Law'; joint editor 'Clerk & Lindsell on Torts'; 'Encyclopaedia of UK & European Patent Law'; various articles and lectures.
Personal: Born: London, 1963. Education: BA Physics and Philosophy (Oxford University, 1985); DipLaw (1986); LLM (Harvard Law School, 1987); called to New York Bar (1988).

ALEXANDER, David QC
South Square, London
020 7696 9900
davidalexander@southsquare.com
Featured in Offshore (London), Restructuring/Insolvency (London)
Practice Areas: David specialises in commercial, chancery, company, insolvency, banking, civil fraud and contentious trust work.
Professional Memberships: COMBAR, Chancery Bar Association.
Career: David has a predominately litigation based practice covering a wide area of business and commercial law. He appears regularly in England, both in court in London at all levels as well as outside London. He has also acted in relation to many international cases including in the Bahamas (called to the Bahamas Bar ad hoc in 2011), Bermuda (called to the Bermuda Bar ad hoc in 1997 and 2013), the BVI, the Cayman Islands, Jersey and Gibraltar. David has been instructed in relation to many of the major recent insolvencies, including for the winding up Board of Landsbanki (in the Supreme Court) and the officeholders of the US arm of MF Global. A specialist and highly recommended trial lawyer, David has appeared in many major and lengthy trials, including the Maxwell saga, the KWELM litigation, the Thyssen litigation and the New Gadget Shop litigation. Other recent cases include Smithton v Naggar, LBI Hf v Stanford and Marrache & Co. Called to the Bar in 1987 and appointed QC in 2006.

ALGAZY, Jacques QC
Cloisters, London
020 7827 4000
ja@cloisters.com
Featured in Employment (London)
Practice Areas: Jacques Algazy practices in employment, commercial, regulatory, European and public law, including judicial review. Acknowledged in the Directories for robust and incisive advocacy. Regularly appears for major institutions, NHS Trusts and local authorities as well as appearing for individuals and trade unions. Jacques has experience of large multi-party actions. Jacques' employment practice embraces Tribunal, High Court and appellate work covering all areas of employment law, especially TUPE, discrimination and whistleblowing. He successfully defended the Sunday Express in a discrimination claim. Jacques specialises in multi-jurisdictional and cross-border litigation. Jacques regularly acts in restrictive covenant cases and associated areas of confidentiality, fiduciary duty and commercial impropriety. Well known for his expertise in the international aspects of employment law, statutory and contractual. Jacques has appeared in a number of significant cases concerning territorial jurisdiction. Jacques also acts in employment cases in Northern Ireland and the Channel Islands. Jacques has appeared in a number of substantial claims in the medical field acting both for Doctors and NHS Trusts, including successfully defending a 26 day race claim. Jacques also practices discrimination law in the field of goods and services. Jacques is a part-time Employment Tribunal Judge. His commercial litigation practice covers a broad range of commercial matters, especially cases with an international/EC dimension, including commercial agency and sale of goods and services. Jacques also acts in international arbitrations. He acted in a partnership arbitration (injunction applications in England) arising out of a team move in Russia. Also successfully acted in a ground-breaking case in which the minority shareholders of a company sued the majority who had bought them out and then sold the business on three weeks later at a substantially higher price. In a company dispute, Jacques succeeded in setting aside a transfer of shares on grounds of duress. His regulatory practice covers most professional disciplinary bodies. See www.cloisters.com for more information.
Professional Memberships: ELA, ELBA and BEG.
Career: Part-time Employment Tribunal Judge. Called to Bar of Northern Ireland. Gray's Inn/ELBA advocacy trainer. Former lecturer in European and Company Law and legal adviser at European Commission (DGVI).
Publications: Jacques has published articles on EC law and employment law. Regularly invited to provide training and lectures in the UK and abroad. Including sessions for the ELA on international employment, a talk to Equality bodies in Budapest, training for European judges in Latvia and Brussels, lecturing for the ILS and speaking at the Council of Employment Judges AGM.

ALIBHAI, Ari
QEB Hollis Whiteman, London
020 7933 8855
ari.alibhai@qebhw.co.uk
Featured in Media & Entertainment (London)
Practice Areas: Ari specialises in private prosecution in criminal intellectual property infringement. Ari is instructed in the first UK prosecution of an IPTV (Internet protocol television) provider, whose operators allegedly defrauded UK and international broadcasters. He acts for corporate clients in music, film, sport and broadcast media, including the Football Association Premier League, Sky and Satellite Information Services. He advises on designing and implementing private prosecution systems to reduce exposure to intellectual property theft. Ari chairs chambers' private prosecution working group, having conducted more than 50 such cases and trained investigators at the Federation Against Copyright Theft (FACT), British Recorded Music Industry and numerous trading standards services.

He prosecuted successfully for FACT in R v Sohail Rafiq, Reece Baker, Graham Reid and Ben Cooper, a multi-million-pound fraud conspiracy using film 'release groups', the first such prosecution outside the US. In Northern Ireland, Ari was called to the Bar following his instruction by the DPP for Northern Ireland to prosecute the film copyright case R v Hugh Reid and Marcus Lewis. He prosecuted Paul Mahoney who was convicted of operating a major film piracy website and also appeared for the prosecution in the Court of Appeal of Northern Ireland in Mahoney's unsuccessful appeal.

ALLARDICE, Miranda
5 Stone Buildings, London
020 7242 6201
clerks@5sblaw.co.uk
Featured in Chancery (London)

Practice Areas: Extensive experience of Inheritance Act, probate, constructive trust and proprietary estoppel claims. Miranda also undertakes complex matrimonial finance claims, with company and trust law problems. Miranda undertakes Vulnerable Elderly work. Miranda is a very experienced mediator with a thriving mediation practice in all her areas of specialisation. Notable cases include: Musa v Holiday [2012] EWCA Civ 1268, Inheritance Act claim by cohabitee with domicile issues. H v Mitson [2010] WTLR 193, Inheritance Act claim by estranged adult child. Van Laetham v Brooker [2006] 2 FLR 495 constructive trust and proprietary estoppel. Re Myers [2005] WTLR 851 Inheritance Act claim by adult child.
Professional Memberships: Chancery Bar Association, Civil Mediation Council, ACTAPS & FLBA
Career: Called 1982.
Publications: A key contributor to Jordans' Inheritance Act Claims; Law Practice and Procedure. Regularly lectures for the Law Society, ACTAPS, and writes articles for Private Client Business. Miranda was an Advisory Group Member of the Law Commission Intestacy and Family Provision Report (No 331).

ALLCOCK, Jonathan
Maitland Chambers, London
020 7406 1200
jallcock@maitlandchambers.com
Featured in Chancery (London)

Practice Areas: Commercial and chancery litigation and arbitration, including in particular civil fraud, tracing and asset recovery; general contractual disputes; corporate insolvency and bankruptcy; company and partnership disputes; trust litigation; property law; landlord & tenant (commercial and residential); and professional liability. Although he appears most often in the Commercial Court and the Chancery Division, both as a sole advocate and a junior, Jonathan has also appeared in the Court of Appeal and the Privy Council, as well as a number of specialist tribunals. In addition to his trial experience, which includes appearing un-led in complex and lengthy High Court trials, he has advised and appeared on a wide range of interim applications, including applications for freezing and proprietary injunctions, committal orders, security for costs, orders for cross-examination, civil restraint orders and disclosure orders. Details of notable and recent cases can be seen on the Maitland Chambers website.
Professional Memberships: COMBAR, Chancery Bar Association
Career: Called 2007
Personal: Trinity College, Oxford (Modern Languages, 1st class, scholar, distinction in preliminary examinations); City University (CPE, distinction); BPP Law School (BVC, outstanding); Harmsworth and Queen Mother Scholar of Middle Temple

ALLEN, Darryl QC
Byrom Street Chambers, Manchester
0161 829 2100
Darryl.Allen@byromstreet.com
Featured in Clinical Negligence (Northern), Personal Injury (Northern)

Practice Areas: Queen's Counsel specialising in personal injury and clinical negligence litigation. Personal injury – Advises and appears on behalf of claimants and defendants in catastrophic injury and high value fatal accident claims. Substantial experience of analysing difficult issues relating to local authority care and accommodation, large care claims and high value complex loss of earnings claims. Clinical negligence – Regularly instructed to advise and represent patients and their families in clinical negligence claims. Caseload covers a wide spectrum of medical incidents, including delayed diagnosis of cancer, delayed diagnosis of infant brain tumor, surgical errors (orthopaedic, general surgery, colorectal surgery etc.), birth trauma, hospital acquired infection, failure to diagnose and treat evolving cauda equine syndrome, failures in spinal anaesthetic technique leading to spinal cord injury, management of infant and grown up congenital heart conditions, community and hospital management of diabetes and diabetic complications, failures in psychiatric care (community and inpatient) leading to suicide/attempted suicide. Consistently recommended as a leading barrister in personal injury and clinical negligence work (Chambers and Partners/Legal 500).
Professional Memberships: Personal Injuries Bar Association (Appointed Vice-Chair 2016) and AVMA.
Career: Called 1995. Tribunal Judge (Criminal Injuries Compensation) (2007). Recorder (Civil) (2010). Queen's Counsel (2014). Legal Adviser to the First Tier Tribunal (Criminal Injuries Compensation) (2014).
Publications:
Personal: Born 1972. Education: Altrincham Grammar School for Boys and Leeds University (LLB (Hons)). Married with two daughters and two dogs. Completed New York and London Marathons and Ironman Lanzarote.

ALLEN, Neil
39 Essex Chambers, London
020 7832 1111
neil.allen@39essex.com
Featured in Court of Protection (All Circuits)

Practice Areas: Particular interests in human rights, mental health and incapacity law, practising predominantly in health, personal welfare, financial and property matters in the Court of Protection. Reported cases include Re MN [2017] UKSC (best interests); North Yorkshire CC v MAG [2016] EWCOP 5 (conditions of detention); Re X [2014] EWHC 25 and 37 (COP DOL); P v Cheshire West [2014] UKSC 19 ("deprivation of liberty"); A LA v SY [2013] EWHC 3485 (non-marriages); GA v Betsi Cadwaladr University LHB [2013] UKUT 280 (AAC) (consent and community treatment orders); P v M [2011] EWHC 2778 ("best interests"); Re MB [2010] EWHC 2508 (validity of DOLS authorisations); G v E [2010] EWHC 2512 (deputyship), [2010] EWHC 2042 (media), [2010] EWCA Civ 822 (Winterwerp), [2010] EWHC 621 (Articles 5, 8).
Professional Memberships: Liberty. Society of Legal Scholars.
Career: Also a Senior Lecturer at the University of Manchester and Trustee of the charity, Making Space.
Publications: Eg: 'Principles of Medical Law' (2017, OUP, contributor); 'Deprivation of liberty: a practical guide' (Law Society, 2015); 'The (not so?) great confinement' (2015) 1 ELJ 45; 'Psychiatric care and criminal prosecution' (2013, CUP); 'The Right to Life in a Suicidal State' (2013) 36 IJLP 350; 'The opacity of sexual capacity' (2012) 2 ELJ 352; 'Criminal care: ill treatment and wilful neglect' (2012) 2 ELJ 71; 'Dare to care' (2011) 1(2) ELJ 167; 'The Bournewood gap (as amended?)' (2010) 18 Med LR 78-85; 'Saving life and respecting death: A Savage dilemma' (2009) 17 Med LR 262; 'Is capacity "in sight"?' (2009) JMHL 165; 'Restricting movement or depriving liberty?' (2009) JMHL 19.

ALLEN, Nicholas
29 Bedford Row Chambers, London
020 7404 1044
nallen@29br.co.uk
Featured in Family/Matrimonial (London)

Practice Areas: Matrimonial finance, children (private law), civil partnerships, co-habitation. Reported cases – Sharland v Sharland [2015] UKSC 60; M v W (Application after New Zealand Financial Agreement) [2015] 1 FLR 465; Sharland v Sharland [2014] 2 FLR 89; SK v TK [2013] EWHC 834 (Fam); S v S (Non-Disclosure) [2013] 2 FLR 1598; Marinos v Marinos [2007] 2 FLR 108; R v R (Divorce: Jurisdiction: Domicile) [2006] 1 FLR 389; A v B (Ancillary Relief: Property Division) [2005] 2 FLR 730; Currey v Currey [2005] 1 FLR 952; C v C (Costs: Ancillary Relief) [2004] 1 FLR 291.
Professional Memberships: Committee member – Resolution Dispute Resolution Committee (2011- 2015); Committee member – Complaints Committee of the Bar Standards Board (2005-07); Committee member – Family Law Bar Association (2003-08); Member – American Bar Association.
Career: Called to the Bar 1995. Admitted to the New York Bar 1998. Pupil Supervisor 2004. Trained as Collaborative Counsel 2009. Appointed Recorder (Family) in London and on the South Eastern Circuit in December 2015. Appointed Arbitrator in 2016.
Personal: Education – Leeds Grammar School; Emmanuel College, Cambridge (MA, LLM); Harvard Law School, Cambridge, Mass, USA (Visiting Scholar 1995-96). Leisure Interests – watching Test Cricket.

ALLEN, Robin QC
Cloisters, London
020 7827 4000
ra@cloisters.com
Featured in Employment (London)

Practice Areas: Employment, discrimination, European, human rights, local government and public law.
Professional Memberships: Recorder, Bencher Middle Temple, Chair of Bar E&D Committee. Formerly legal adviser to Disability Rights Commission, Chairman the Employment Law Bar Association, founder member the Discrimination Law Association, and Chairman the Bar Pro Bono Unit. Personal Injury Claims Arbitration Service Arbitrator.
Career: Head of Cloisters since 2002. Appeared in many leading employment, discrimination, public and human rights cases. Major advisory practice for public authorities, local government, specialist NDPBs and central government, on publicity powers and politically sensitive decisions. Very wide range of clients: from FTSE companies, trade unions, charities, to acting pro bono for individual and interventions and amicus briefs. Appeared in more reported employment cases than any other barrister including over 30 HL/SC cases. Works frequently with the UK Equality Commissions; extensive media work; works overseas. Full details see www.cloisters.com
Personal: Awards: Chambers and Partners Employment Law Team of the Year 2013. Chambers and Partners Employment Law Silk 2012 and 2008; Runner up Lawyer of the Year 2010; FT Innovative Barrister 2009; Equal Opportunities Review leading barrister; the Lawyer 'Hot 100'. Charity Award for the London Bombings Relief Charitable Fund 2006.

ALLEN, Rupert
Fountain Court Chambers, London
020 7583 3335
clerks3@fountaincourt.co.uk
Featured in Commercial Dispute Resolution (London), Professional Discipline (London)

Practice Areas: Since joining Fountain Court Rupert has been instructed on a number of heavy commercial and banking cases. Recent experience includes defending Goldman Sachs against a US$1.2 billion claim brought by the Libyan Investment Authority and acting for Dexia and Deutsche Bank in claims concerning interest rate swaps entered into by Italian local authorities. Rupert has also been involved in many other important and high profile commercial and banking cases both as sole counsel and with a leader (including a number of cases in the Court of Appeal). In addition to his commercial and banking law practice, Rupert also has extensive experience in the fields of regulatory law (in particular, the law relating to solicitors, accountants, financial services and aviation) and professional discipline. His growing professional discipline and regulatory practice has seen him instructed by the SRA, the FRC, the FCA, the CAA and other regulators.
Professional Memberships: COMBAR, British Association of Sport and Law.
Career: MA (Law), Gonville and Caius College, Cambridge (First Class, Top of Year); BCL, Merton College, Oxford (Distinction, Proxime Accessit to Vinerian Scholarship); BVC, Inns of Court School of Law (Outstanding).

ALLEN, Scott
4 New Square, London
020 7822 2038
s.allen@4newsquare.com
Featured in Professional Negligence (London)

Practice Areas: Professional negligence, commercial litigation, construction, insurance.
Professional Memberships: PNBA, COMBAR, LCLCBA.
Career: Called in 2000.

Publications: Contributor to 'Human Rights in Civil Practice', Assistant Editor of Jackson & Powell on Professional Liability (co-authoring chapter on Information Technology Professionals).
Personal: Happily married, with identical twin boys, and an avid lover of all things sporting (especially tennis and surfing).

ALLISON, David QC
South Square, London
020 7696 9900
davidallison@southsquare.com
Featured in Chancery (London), Banking & Finance (London), Commercial Dispute Resolution (London), Company (London), Financial Services (London), Offshore (London), Restructuring/Insolvency (London)
Practice Areas: David specialises in business, commercial and financial law, with a particular emphasis on corporate restructuring, sovereign debt restructuring, banking, structured finance, commercial litigation and company matters. He has an extensive overseas practice which includes Dubai, Cayman, BVI, Jersey and Guernsey.
Professional Memberships: COMBAR, Chancery Bar Association.
Career: Recent cases include Lehman, APCOA, ATU, Airwave, Stemcor, MF Global, Nortel, Bank of Ireland, European Directories, Stanford International Bank, Madoff, Landsbanki, Glitnir, Kaupthing, Woolworths, Almatis, Arcapita, Metronet, Northern Rock, Dewey & LeBoeuf, Deutsche Annington, PrimaCom, Nef Telecom, Biffa, Fitness First, NCP, Monier, Tele Columbus and Cattles. Called 1998 (Middle Temple); QC 2014. Full registration under Part II of the DIFC Courts' Register of Legal Practitioners 2006; Called to the Bar of the Eastern Caribbean 2007.
Publications: Contributor to Gore-Browne on Companies.

ALTMAN, Brian QC
2 Bedford Row, London
020 7440 8888
baltman@2bedfordrow.co.uk
Featured in Crime (London), Financial Crime (London)
Practice Areas: General specialisms are in criminal and regulatory work, but practice includes advising high net worth individuals, multinational corporations and private clients. Has advised a Middle Eastern Royal family and advises the UK Government on a wide variety of esoteric issues. Examples of work include advising a nationwide firm of solicitors on issues arising under the Official Secrets Acts; a US aerospace company on suspected money laundering and POCA compliance during a $100million acquisition of a British PLC; a Swedish multinational corporation who suspected it was the victim of a €200million fraud arising during an acquisition by a British PLC of a €1.7billion part of its pan-European business; City of London insolvency practitioners on allegations of fraud underlying the tracing of £100millions of hidden assets of a PLC; a well known credit reference company during due diligence of a target company's systems, bearing on issues of cybercrime and data protection; a national construction PLC on POCA compliance; a very high profile property magnate on issues arising following unlawful search warrants issued and executed by the SFO; a significant victim of phone hacking; a national postal retail service company on issues of corporate governance; the Bar Council on the Bribery Act 2010 and its application to the Bar; LOCOG pre-the 2012 Olympics on ticket touting offences online. Examples of privately funded defence trial work include successfully defending a police officer in a high profile misconduct in public office case in Bristol arising from the murder of a local man falsely alleged to have been a paedophile; successfully defending a haulier accused of involvement in a large-scale conspiracy to supply drugs. Successfully defended a 15 year old girl alleged to have aided a youth accused of killing a man. Acted for a defendant who pleaded guilty to 1984 murder of Melanie Road in Bath. Prosecution work includes instructions for the CMA in a nationwide cartel case and by the FCA in an insider dealing case. Recently successfully prosecuted for CPS Counter-Terrorism Division an Islamic State influenced plot to kill police or military personnel. Presently instructed to advise the CPS in the notorious 1986 Brighton 'Babes in the Woods' case. Past cases include instructions by the CPS Counter-Terrorism Division to prosecute Moazzam Begg for terrorism offences allegedly arising from the conflict in Syria, as well as other cases arising out of the conflict in Syria; and the case of alleged IRA man, John Downey, the 1982 Hyde Park bombing case, where the abuse of process argument turned on whether Downey had erroneously received a comfort letter from Government in 2007 amounting to a promise not to prosecute. Other very high profile past cases include the prosecution of Levi Bellfield for murders of Milly Dowler, Amelie Delagrange and Marsha McDonnell, and the attempted murder of Kate Sheedy; and Gnango, the murder of a Polish care worker who was killed in the crossfire of a gunfight between the defendant and another youth, where the defendant had not fired the fatal shot, and the victim had been the unintended target; this landmark case passed through a 7 justice Supreme Court and a 5 judge Court of Appeal on issues of joint enterprise, accessory liability and transferred malice. The offender's murder conviction was restored on a prosecution appeal from the Court of Appeal.
Professional Memberships: South Eastern Circuit. Criminal Bar Association. Association of Regulatory and Disciplinary Lawyers.
Career: Called to the Bar by Middle Temple 1981. First Senior Treasury Counsel at the Central Criminal Court December 2010-June 2013. Senior Treasury Counsel at CCC 2002-2013. Junior Treasury Counsel at CCC 1997-2002. Recorder since 2003. Queen's Counsel 2008. Bencher of Middle Temple 2010.
Personal: King's College London (LLB (Hons), 1978), University of Amsterdam (Dip Eur Int, 1979).

AMAOUCHE, Sassa-Ann
29 Bedford Row Chambers, London
020 7404 1044
samaouche@29br.co.uk
Featured in Family/Matrimonial (London)
Practice Areas: Practice primarily focuses on financial remedy proceedings. A particular expertise in cases involving non-disclosure, multi-jurisdictional and business assets. Sassa's approach has been described as "robust" and "fearless" but always underpinned by the willingness to give unwelcome advice to her own clients. Notable cases include: N v N (BIIR: Stay of Maintenance Proceedings)[2012] EWHC 4282 (Fam), Moor J; Constantinides v Constantinides [2013] EWHC 3688 (Fam), Holman J; DL v SL [2015] EWHC 2621 (Fam) Mostyn J.
Professional Memberships: FLBA
Career: Called 1996, Inner Temple.
Personal: King's School Canterbury; King's College London (1995 Law). Resides in London.

AMIRAFTABI, Roshi
29 Bedford Row Chambers, London
020 7404 1044
ramiraftabi@29br.co.uk
Featured in Family/Matrimonial (London)
Practice Areas: Almost exclusively in the field of children law. Private law children involving cases with an international element, in which questions of jurisdiction or enforcement of foreign orders arise, cases of child abduction (Hague and non-Hague), as well as international and internal relocation cases. Extensive experience in public law matters involving legally or factually complex issues, as well as those in which there are international issues, or where jurisdiction is challenged. Also instructed in applications concerning vulnerable adults, and those with mental incapacity in the Court of Protection, and in applications for forced marriage protection orders. Cases include: Re A (A Child) [2014] EWHC 604; A v A [2013] EWHC 3554; Re S (A Child) [2013] EWHC 1295; FQ v MQ [2013] EWHC 4149; L B Lewisham v DM (January 2012) (Family Law Journal); Re B (Children)(Relocation Jurisdiction)[2008] EWCA Civ 1034; Local Authority X v MM (no 2)[2007] EWHC 2003; Local Authority X v MM (an adult) & Anor (no 1) [2007] EWHC 2689.
Professional Memberships: Family Law Bar Association.
Career: Called 1993. Undertakes Public Access Cases.

AMOS, Tim QC
Queen Elizabeth Building QEB, London
020 7797 7837
t.amos@qeb.co.uk
Featured in Family/Matrimonial (London)
Practice Areas: All aspects of family law, but predominantly international divorce/jurisdiction and family finance, married or unmarried, alive or dead (including claims under the Inheritance Act). Specially interested in Anglo-German cases and those with a foreign or international element. Fluent in German (including legal German) and has good professional French. Work experience in German and French Courts and German law firms. Standing Counsel to the Queen's Proctor (2001 – 08), a government appointment to advise the Treasury Solicitor on all matters of family law with a public interest element including the validity of foreign marriage and foreign divorce. Trained Collaborative Lawyer and the first family law collaborative QC. Resolution Mediator and private judge. Recent cases of note: Prest v Petrodel [2012] EWCA Civ 1395 and [2013] UKSC 34; Mittal [2013] EWCA Civ 1255 – Stays in non-BIIR cases; T v T (Brussels II Revised: Art. 15) [2013] 2 FLR 1326 – European transfers; Kim v Morris [2013] 2 FLR 1197 – Divorce jurisdiction; Bromfield [2015] UKPC 19 – Jamaican maintenance; A v B (CJEU) [2016] 1 FLR 31 – BR Art. 19; MA v SK (Financial Relief after Saudi Divorce) [2016] 1 FLR 310 – Part III MFPA.
Professional Memberships: Family Law Bar Association and British German Jurists Association. Fellow of the International Academy of Family Lawyers (IAFL).

ANDERSON, Lesley QC
Kings Chambers, Manchester
0345 034 3444
clerks@kingschambers.com
Featured in Chancery (Northern), Professional Negligence (Northern), Commercial Dispute Resolution (Northern), Partnership (Northern), Real Estate Litigation (Northern), Restructuring/Insolvency (Northern)
Practice Areas: All aspects of chancery and commercial litigation; corporate and personal insolvency; commercial contracts including joint ventures, distribution and agency contracts and share and asset sale warranty claims; company law especially shareholder disputes;, directors' duties and breach of trust/fiduciary duty claims; directors' disqualification and directors' and employee duties (including restrictive covenants and confidential information); partnership; banking (especially secured lending and guarantees); commercial property and landlord and tenant; professional negligence (especially solicitors, accountants, surveyors and financial advisers); sale of goods; fraud; commercial torts and insurance.
Professional Memberships: Chancery Bar Association; Northern Chancery Bar Association; Northern Circuit Commercial Bar Association; member of the Northern and North Eastern Circuit.
Career: Lecturer in Law - University of Manchester 1984-89; Training Manager Norton Rose M5 Group 1989-91; Called to the Bar 1989; CEDR Accredited Mediator 2000; Year of Silk 2006; Recorder 2006; Authorised to sit as Deputy Judge of the High Court Chancery Division 2008; Master of the Bench of the Middle Temple 2011. Member of Hardwicke in London from 2011.

ANDERSON, Nicholas
1 King's Bench Walk, London
020 7936 1500
nanderson@1kbw.co.uk
Featured in Family/Matrimonial (London)
Practice Areas: Practice in all areas of family law with a particular emphasis on matrimonial finance and children cases involving an international element, including international child abduction, international relocation (including to non-Hague Convention countries) and jurisdictional disputes. Regularly appears against leading counsel in both children and finance cases. Acted for the father before the Supreme Court in re S in 2012. Acted without a leader for the child before the Supreme Court in re D in 2016. Recent experience of the registration and enforcement in England of European orders relating to children. Experienced in finance cases with a foreign dimension proceeding both in England and Wales and abroad and cases involving trusts and family companies. Also specialises in cases involving property and financial disputes between former cohabitees.
Professional Memberships: Member of FLBA and South Eastern circuit.
Career: Called 1995. Qualified as a mediator in 2008. Qualified as collaborative counsel in 2010.
Publications: Regular speaker at various conferences including those organised by Jordans and CLT, in Gibraltar and at various events organised by Resolution. Contributor

to various publications, including the child abduction section on the PLC website.

ANELAY, Richard QC
1 King's Bench Walk, London
020 7936 1500
RAnelayQC@1kbw.co.uk
Featured in Family/Matrimonial (London)

Practice Areas: Family and criminal law. Leading work undertaken in matrimonial finance including variation of trusts and conduct, Inheritance Act provision and in children work including wardship with international issues, international child abduction, adoption, child arrangements and in public law care proceedings, having acted for local authorities, parents, intervenors, guardians involving complex medical issues, and sexual, physical and emotional abuse including fictitious illness. Extensive experience in criminal cases including serious fraud, murder and manslaughter. Experienced mediator in children, finance cases, and early neutral evaluator in finance cases including in Jersey. Undertakes FDRs. Reported cases include K v K [2009] EWCA Civ 986; SK v WL 2011 All ER (D) 39; A (a child) (father:knowledge of child's birth) 2011 All ER (D) 205; Grubb v Grubb [2011] EWCA Civ 1486, [2012] EWCA Civ 398; Re L [2013] EWCA Civ 1481.

Professional Memberships: FLBA: SE Circuit; Fellow IAML

Career: Called 1970. QC 1993. Recorder 1992. Deputy High Court Judge (Family Division) 1995. Panel Deemster (IOM) 2007. Middle Temple Bencher.

Personal: Educated Queen Elizabeth Grammar School, Darlington, Bristol University (BA Honours Classics and Philosophy), Council of Legal Education.

ANGUS, Tracey QC
5 Stone Buildings, London
020 7242 6201
clerks@5sblaw.com
Featured in Chancery (London), Court of Protection (All Circuits), Trusts (London)

Practice Areas: Traditional Chancery: trusts, contentious probate, family provision, Court of Protection, charities and related professional negligence. Reported or notable cases include: Dellal v Dellal and others [2015] EWHC 907 (family provision); Re Lucian Freud deceased [2014] WTLR 1453 (will construction and secret trusts); Curtis & others v Pulbrook [2011] EWHC (Ch) 167 (gifts in equity); [2009] EWHC 1370 (trusts; undue influence); Gill v Woodall & others [2011] Ch 380 (probate); [2009] EWHC 3778 (Ch) (probate; proprietary estoppel); Holman v Howes [2008] 1 FLR 1217 (constructive trusts; estoppel); Kostic v Chaplin and others [2007] EWHC 2289 (probate); [2008] WTLR 655 (costs); P v G (Family Provision: Relevance of Divorce Provision) [2007] WTLR 691.

Professional Memberships: Association of Contentious Trust and Probate Specialists, Professional Negligence Bar Association, Chancery Bar Association.

Career: Called 1991. Silk 2012.

Publications: Co-author of 'A Practical Guide to Inheritance Act Claims' (Law Society 2006).

Personal: MA Hons (Edin); Dip Law (City).

ANSELL, Rachel QC
4 Pump Court, London
020 7842 5555
ransell@4pumpcourt.com
Featured in International Arbitration (London), Professional Negligence (London), Construction (London), Insurance (London), Property Damage (London)

Practice Areas: Construction, engineering and energy disputes: Specialises in high value and complex disputes in the TCC and in international and domestic arbitrations with particular experience in the UAE. Recent instructions include a broad range of construction and engineering projects ranging from oil pumping facilities in Africa to multi-use high rise developments in Dubai and road and specialist leisure facilities in the UK. Professional Negligence: Regularly acts on behalf of the professional indemnity insurers of building professionals in technically difficult disputes involving architects, engineers and surveyors. Insurance: Experience in general insurance and subrogated claims (with particular expertise in fire and business interruption claims).

Professional Memberships: TECBAR (Treasurer), COMBAR, PNBA, LCLCBA.

Career: Called to the Bar in 1995. Silk in 2014.

Personal: Educated at Downing, Cambridge (Law (first class)). Interests include supporting Wales and Saracens rugby union teams, supporting Middlesex and England cricket teams and the gym.

ANTROBUS, Simon
Crown Office Chambers, London
020 7797 8100
antrobus@crownofficechambers.co.uk
Featured in Consumer Law (London), Health & Safety (London), Inquests & Public Inquiries (All Circuits)

Practice Areas: Health and Safety Prosecutions: Simon has for many years been one of the leading barristers in this area. He is currently representing the owner of the Alton Towers theme park in relation to "The Smiler" rollercoaster accident and has previously defended in other notorious cases such as the fireworks organiser charged with creating a smoke-related blackout and a massive multi-fatality accident on the M5 motorway, the criminal trial relating to the Buncefield oil terminal explosion, and the prosecution of HTM Ltd that reinforced the defence of reasonable practicability for careless acts by employees. Simon is also regularly instructed to defend companies and their directors facing corporate or individual manslaughter charges: R v Thelwall; R v Lion Steel Equipment Ltd & Ors; R v Sidebottom; R v Baldwins Crane Hire Ltd; R v JTF Wholesale Ltd; R v Express Hi-Fold Doors Ltd & Naylor. Consumer/Trading Law: Simon is experienced in all aspects of trading law, including the judicial review of regulatory decision-making. He was instructed by Nutricia (led by Thomas De La Mare QC) in a multi-million pound judicial review relating to the interpretation of European law as to the definition of Foods for Special Medical Purposes and the extent to which they are to be distinguished from food supplements and fortified foods. He has also advised global food manufacturers and FTSE listed national retailers as to the legality of their products in relation to product launches in this country and also in relation to product recalls following the discovery of safety concerns. His previous cases have included representing the Fat Duck restaurant in relation to a norovirus outbreak and the e-coli outbreak at Godstone Farm petting zoo.

Professional Memberships: Health and Safety Lawyer's Association.

Career: Called to the Bar: 1995.

Publications: The Criminal Liability of Directors for Health and Safety Breaches and Manslaughter (Crim L.R. 2013, 4, 309-322).

APPS, Katherine
Littleton Chambers, London
020 7797 8600
clerks@littletonchambers.co.uk
Featured in Administrative & Public Law (London)

Practice Areas: Equality, employment, public/administrative, human rights, civil liberties, trade unions, European, regulatory, disciplinary, medical, civil litigation, commercial.

Professional Memberships: ELBA, ALBA, BEG, ARDL.

Career: Call 2006. Treasury B Panel. MA (Hons) Cantab. LLM Harvard Law School. Bedingfield Scholar (Grays Inn). CV http://www.littletonchambers.com/barristers/juniors/katherine-apps.aspx. Cases include: R (Aspinall) v SSWP [2014] EWHC 4134: public sector equality duty closure of independent living fund; R(MM) v SSWP [2014] 1 WLR 1716: reasonable adjustments judicial review; R(Peel) v Health and Safety Executive [2013] EWHC 1012(Admin): duties to consult in EU and domestic law; Halstead v Paymentshield Group Holdings [2012] IRLR 856: concurrent Employment Tribunal and High Court causes of action; R (G) v X School [2012] 1 AC 167: Article 6 ECHR and internal disciplinary hearings; W v M [2011] EWHC 2443 (COP): first application to withhold and withdraw life sustaining treatment from a person in minimally conscious state.

Publications: Contributed chapters to Gore Brown on EU Company Law (employer insolvency). Industrial Action and Trade Union Recognition (2011, OUP); Equality Act 2010 (The Law Society). Sole Author articles include: Damages claims against trade unions after Viking and Laval [2009] European Law Review 141. Nationality Discrimination in football: FIFA's 6 + 5 Rule (2008) Solicitors Journal Vol 152 page 52.

ARDEN, Andrew QC
Arden Chambers, London
020 7242 4244
andrew.arden@ardenchambers.com
Featured in Local Government (London), Social Housing (London), Social Housing (Midlands)

Practice Areas: Housing; landlord and tenant; leasehold management; human rights, local government constitutional and administrative law, finance, regeneration and reorganisation; procurement and waste; public and administrative law. Accredited Mediator.

Professional Memberships: Civil Mediation Council.

Career: Called 1974. Director, Small Health Community Law Centre 1976-78. QC 1991. Founded Arden Chambers (1993) as a centre for specialist practice primarily in housing and local government law. Has appeared in a large number of important housing cases – many in the House of Lords/Supreme Court – from the early homelessness cases of the 1980s through to the human rights cases of this century. His local government work includes the Crédit Suisse litigation, "Homes for Votes," audit cases and hearings, procurement, five local government inquiries/reviews, and a wide range of other matters including land acquisition and disposal and waste. In the last few years, Andrew has been involved in the leading housing and human rights cases, including Manchester CC v Pinnock [2010] UKSC 45; Hounslow LBC v Powell and other cases [2011] UKSC 8; Sims v Dacorum BC [2014] UKSC 63; R (CN) v LB Lewisham; R (ZH) v LB Newham [2014] UKSC 62. Andrew continues to appear in the most significant homelessness cases, including LB Camden v Sharif [2013] UKSC 10 and Haile v LB Waltham Forest [2015] UKSC 34. Other recent cases of note include Loveridge v LB Lambeth [2015] UKSC 65 and R (Edwards) v Birmingham CC [2016] EWHC 173 (Admin),

Publications: Andrew is author/co-author of – among other works – Arden & Partington's Housing Law, Manual of Housing Law, Homelessness and Allocations, Local Government Constitutional and Administrative Law, Local Government Finance: Law and Practice. General Editor of Housing Encyclopedia, Housing Law Reports, Journal of Housing Law.

ARDEN, Karina
9 Bedford Row, London
020 7489 2727
karina.arden@9bedfordrow.co.uk
Featured in Crime (London)

Career: Left Bar in 1986 to join Herbert Smith Paris to do international commercial arbitrations and then commercial litigation at Herbert Smith London. Then set up small niche litigation practice. In 2004 returned to the Bar to do crime. Became French Avocat in 1990 while practising in Paris and has diploma in Italian Law. Completely tri-lingual English, French and Italian with working knowledge of German.. Since 2004 at the Criminal Bar doing all types of defence criminal work with leading or junior briefs. Has huge experience of many types of legal work both criminal and commercial. Very skilled cross examiner and negotiator and her experience in dealing with judges, juries and witnesses and her international experience enable her to obtain the very best results possible for clients whatever the odds against the clients. R v Ndreu – two month money laundering case, R v Aram historic stranger rape case -defendant picked up on DNA 17 years later, R v Low Prison officer accused of 10 counts of Misconduct in a Public Office

ARDEN, Peter QC
Erskine Chambers, London
020 7611 9834
parden@erskinechambers.co.uk
Featured in Chancery (London), Company (London), Restructuring/Insolvency (London)

Practice Areas: Peter is a highly-regarded company law and commercial chancery silk with particular expertise in large, complex insolvencies and restructurings, often with a cross-border element. Significant cases include: the Federal Mogul / T&N restructuring, Eurotunnel, the HIH litigation, the Baugur administration, Lehmans, the Landsbanki and Kaupthing insolvencies, Miss Sixty and other retail insolvencies, the TXU company voluntary arrangement, and the winding-up of Danka Business Systems and Travelodge. He is a member of Erskine Chambers which was named Insolvency Set of the Year in 2014.

Professional Memberships: Member of Association of Business Recovery Professionals; Member of the Chancery Bar Association.
Career: LLB (Lond); LLM (Cantab). Called to the Bar: 1983; Silk: 2006.

ARENTSEN, Andrew
Farrar's Building, London
07973 418064
aarentsen@farrarsbuilding.co.uk
Featured in Personal Injury (Wales & Chester)
Practice Areas: Personal injury, clinical negligence and commercial dispute resolution. Andrew's Personal Injury practice has a particular focus on catastrophic, spinal and closed head injuries. This includes cases of employers liability, occupiers liability and road traffic accidents. Specialist advice is offered in claims with conflicting, complex medical evidence for example with orthopaedic, neurological or psychiatric disputes or where pain disorders are challenged. Work is divided between Claimant and Defendant and includes extensive experience at trial and in a pre trial advisory capacity of industrial disease litigation (including group actions) in the form of deafness, asbestosis, dermatitis, WRULD and HAVS. Clinical negligence work is for both Claimants and Defendant Trusts and has included injuries caused at birth, negligent surgical procedures and cases of mis-diagnosis.
Professional Memberships: PIBA.
Career: Cardiff High School. Corpus Christi College, Cambridge.
Publications: Butterworths Personal Injury Litigation Vol 1. Chapters include medical causation, clinical negligence. and professional negligence.
Personal: Married, 3 children. Lives Llanblethian Vale of Glamorgan. Interests: rugby, cycling, surfing and skiing.

ARMSTRONG, Dean QC
2 Bedford Row, London
020 7440 8888
darmstrong@2bedfordrow.co.uk
Featured in Crime (London), Financial Crime (London)
Practice Areas: Dean is one of the UK's top-rated criminal defence barristers and QC's. Having graduated in law from Cambridge University, he was called to the Bar and having decided to obtain experience in the City, he worked both as a lawyer for commercial enterprise and for high profile solicitors firms. Dean then returned to the Bar and rapidly became a highly sought after defence advocate, achieving great success as a junior in matters of serious crime including murder, sexual offence cases, fraud and drugs, as well as having a highly successful appellate practice. In 2014 Dean was appointed Queens Counsel and he has continued to be a sought after advocate in the fields of sex offences, drugs, fraud and murder and he has maintained and built upon his expertise in the Court of Appeal. He has, and continues to be, instructed in some of the highest profile cases of the last few years and his ability, based on his background, to achieve expertise in new fields of law have seen him branch out into defending parties accused of environmental law offences. Dean has also achieved recognition of his expertise in Cyber law and is seen as an expert in this growing and increasingly complicated field. He has become known as a specialist in data protection and data management cases. Dean has a history of advising clients in high profile enquiries, the Cash for Honours and Leveson enquiries being just two examples. He also is a regular commentator on television both for Sky and for the BBC . Dean's background and experience allow him to feel at home in a wide variety of cases, and particular those where there is a crossover between criminal and civil issues. Dean has been recognised as a leading barrister for many years. He has twice been nominated for the Chambers and Partners Bar Awards.
Professional Memberships: Criminal Bar Association; South Eastern Circuit.
Career: MA (Cantab); Called 1985. QC 2014.

ARNFIELD, Robert
Ten Old Square, London
020 7405 0758
robertarnfield@tenoldsquare.com
Featured in Chancery (London)
Practice Areas: Wide range of Chancery and commercial work including commercial contracts, real property and charities but with particular emphasis on wills, trusts, family provision, the administration of estates, associated taxes (particularly Inheritance Tax and Capital Gains Tax) and professional negligence.
Professional Memberships: Chancery Bar Association, STEP and the Professional Negligence Bar Association.
Career: Called 1996. Notable recent litigation: A v B [2016] EWHC 340 (Ch) (Variation of Trusts Act 1958, extension of perpetuity period, confidentiality, temporary exclusion of beneficiaries); DC v AC [2016] EWHC 477 (Ch) (VTA 1958, impact on life interest for Inheritance Tax); Davidson v Seelig (April 2016 protector resisting claim to set aside trust appointment); Jackson v Jackson (July 2016; husband seeking to set aside consent order); Thornton v Thornton (June 2016, rectification of deed of appointment).
Publications: One of the editors of Mellows on Taxation for Executors and Trustees.

ARNOLD, Mark QC
South Square, London
020 7696 9900
markarnold@southsquare.com
Featured in Restructuring/Insolvency (London)
Practice Areas: Business and financial law, including in particular: insolvency and corporate restructuring, banking, company, chancery and professional negligence.
Professional Memberships: COMBAR, Chancery Bar Association.
Career: Mark has appeared or advised in substantial matters relating to Lehman Brothers, SAAD Investments, Hibu, Kaupthing Singer & Friedlander, Woolworths, European Directories, Hellas Telecommunications, Yugraneft, Dana, Schefenacker, Eurotunnel and TXU. He has recently appeared in litigation arising out of the Lehman administration, including Storm Funding (Quantum) and Waterfall 1. He also acted for Card Protection Plan in relation to its scheme of arrangement. Called to the Bar by Middle Temple (1988); appointed Queen's Counsel (2013).
Publications: Contributor to Cross-Border Insolvency Fourth Edition (Sheldon, Bloomsbury, 2015) and Company Directors: Duties, Liabilities and Remedies (Mortimore, OUP, 2013).

ARNOT, Lee
29 Bedford Row Chambers, London
020 7404 1044
larnot@29br.co.uk
Featured in Family/Matrimonial (London)
Practice Areas: All aspects of family law including public and private law applications under the Children Act 1989, Adoption and Children Act 2002 and Human Rights Act 1998; matrimonial finance; child abduction; property disputes between cohabitees and family members. Cases include: Re P (Finding of Fact) [2014] EWCA Civ 89; A&B v P Council [2014] EWHC 1128 (Fam); A County Council v E & Ors [2012] EWHC 4161 (COP); Re Y (Care Proceedings) [2013] 1 FLR 256; MA v RS (Contact:Parenting Roles) [2012] 1 FLR 1056; H (Children)(Sexual abuse: fact finding) [2011] EWCA Civ 525; A London Borough Council v K & others [2009] EWHC 850; Re H (Children) [2006] EWCA Civ 1875; Re M (Contact:Long-Term Best Interests)[2006]1FLR627; AvA (Shared Residence)[2004]1FLR1195; Roddy (A Child) (Identification: Restriction on Publication)[2004]2FLR949; C v Bury MBC [2002] 2FLR 818; Re:W (Minors) (Care Order: Adequacy of Care Plan)[2002]1FLR815.
Professional Memberships: FLBA. Member of Bar Standards Board (2006-2011). Committee Member FLBA (2004-2009).
Career: Called in 1990.
Publications: Articles include: 'Shared Parenting-the Clear Message from Re G' (2005) Family Law, vol.35 pp.718 (jointly with Emma Harte, Partner Alexiou Fisher Philipps).
Personal: Married.

ASHLEY-NORMAN, Jonathan QC
3 Raymond Buildings Barristers, London
020 7400 6400
jonathan.ashley-norman@3rblaw.com
Featured in Health & Safety (London), POCA Work & Asset Forfeiture (All Circuits), Financial Crime (London)
Practice Areas: Specialist in criminal and regulatory law in a business setting, both defending and prosecuting. Assistance at the investigation stage, advising on responding to law enforcement action and managing the investigation process (for example recent investigations into Tesco, a major pharmaceutical concern and a Caribbean holiday home alleged fraud). Prosecution advisory work in guiding and focusing investigations with a view to eventual successful disposal (for example fraud in government grant application and HSE prosecution of major construction corporates). Litigation advisory work, guiding interlocutory stages and pre-trial work, including disclosure strategies. Top defence work instructed by leading solicitors firms in fraud related and regulatory issues, including cartels, competition, consumer credit and trading standards. Judicial reviews against National Trading Standards Estate Agents Team and Marine Management Organisation. Standing Counsel to DBEIS, and A Panel prosecutor, regularly instructed by SFO, HSE, Office of Rail And Road and other specialist prosecution bodies. Off shore regulatory advisory especially on Isle of Man. Private prosecutions. Acts across a multiplicity of business areas in respect of a large range of law enforcement action. Specialism in restraint and confiscation. Inquests. First Tier Tribunal. Directors duties and disqualification. Increasingly instructed in civil litigation with a fraud or regulatory aspect.
Career: Called 1989. QC 2016. Recorder of the Crown Court 2010.

ASHWORTH, Fiona
Kings Chambers, Manchester
0345 034 3444
clerks@kingschambers.com
Featured in Personal Injury (Northern)
Practice Areas: Personal Injury and chronic pain cases
Professional Memberships: PIBA
Career: Fiona Ashworth is a leading personal injury practitioner, specialising in chronic pain cases. Over the last 16 years, Fiona has developed specialisms in Chronic Pain Syndromes, Complex Regional Pain Syndrome, Chronic Fatigue Syndrome, Somatoform Pain Disorders, Fibromyalgia and Conversion Disorders. These conditions are often little understood and extremely challenging. Fiona has built up a deep knowledge of these chronic pain cases, working with medical experts of all different specialisms. She has been involved in hundreds of such cases, both at first instance and on appeal, acting for both Claimant and Defendant. She has lectured extensively over the country, run seminars and was invited to attend the Pain Summit at Westminster. She is considered to be a leading expert on chronic pain. Fiona has recently been made patron of Burning Nights, a CRPS charity established to support sufferers of CRPS and their carers. Fiona sat on the Legal Services Commission Appeal tribunal for 15 years and was an external examiner for the City Law School and MMU. She was appointed as a Recorder sitting in crime in 2009 and in civil in 2014 and on serious sex cases in 2015.
Publications: Solicitors Journal 17th July 2012 PI Brief Update Law Journal 14th January 2013 and 4th January 2014, UK Fibromyalgia Society February 2014.

ASHWORTH, Lance QC
Serle Court, London
020 7242 6105
lashworth@serlecourt.co.uk
Featured in Chancery (London), Commercial Dispute Resolution (London)
Practice Areas: Commercial litigation, insolvency, company/chancery, professional negligence. Recent cases include: Re Palm Beach Offshore – Cayman Islands insolvency, good faith, redemption shares; Emmott v Michael Wilson & Partners Ltd [2015] EWCA Civ 1028 – civil contempt, dissipation of assets, director's liability; Kaneria v Kaneria – unfair prejudice, trusts, equitable interests in shares; QOGT v International Oil and Gas Technology [2014] EWHC 1628 (Comm) – termination of investment management contract; UK Power v Read [2014] EWHC 66 (Ch) – non-competition covenants and conspiracy, without notice injunctions; Credit Lucky Ltd v National Crime Agency [2014] EWHC 83 (Ch) – rescission of winding up order; Emailgen Systems v Exclaimer Ltd [2013] EWHC 167 (Comm) – discharge of undertaking given in lieu of freezing injunction; Thursfield v Thursfield [2013] EWCA Civ 840 [2012] EWHC 3742 (Ch) – enforcing Michigan judgment, freezing order, contempt, committal, information order re trusts.
Professional Memberships: Chancery Bar; COMBAR; Midlands Commercial and Chancery Bar Association.

Career: Called 1987, Middle Temple; Recorder 2005; QC 2006; Mediator 2009; Deputy High Court Judge 2016.
Personal: Born 1964. Resides London. Educated at Oundle School; Pembroke College, Cambridge (MA). Trustee of the Access to Justice Foundation; Founder Trustee of the Medical Research Fund Coventry and Warwickshire; Member of Middlesex Lord's Taverners Committee.

ASWANI, Ravi
St Philips Stone Chambers, London
020 74406900
ravi.aswani@stonechambers.com
Featured in International Arbitration (London), Shipping (London)
Practice Areas: Ravi has a broad commercial dispute resolution practice spanning various sectors including shipping and international trade, energy, oil and gas, mining, insurance and reinsurance, and banking and finance. Ravi has considerable experience of being instructed to appear alone against QC opposition. Recent representative arbitrations include: an LCIA arbitration arising out of a high value ship repair contract, an ad hoc arbitration (English seat, English law) relating to the supply of damaged coking coal in which Ravi acted as co-counsel with a Senior Advocate from India; an LMAA arbitration arising out of a number of related contracts for the construction and purchase of jack up oil drilling rigs; and an SIAC arbitration arising out of a mining contract. Recent representative arbitration applications in Court include: Exmek Pharmaceuticals SAC v Alkem Laboratories Limited [2016] 1 Lloyd's Rep 239 (instructed alone against a QC in a complex challenge to an arbitrator's substantive jurisdiction in an ad hoc English seated arbitration); Ameropa SA v Lithuanian Shipping Company [2015] EWHC 3847 (Comm) (defence against an arbitration application based on an allegation that the tribunal had dealt with the claim on a basis which had not been argued); and Konkola Copper Mines PLC v U&M Mining Zambia Ltd (instructed as junior counsel in four consolidated LCIA arbitrations arising out of four related mining joint venture agreements which led to multiple hearings in the Commercial Court – [2014] EWHC 2210 (Comm), [2014] 2 Lloyd's Rep 507, and [2014] 2 Lloyd's Rep 652). Recent representative litigation includes: Melissa K v Tomsk [2016] 1 Lloyd's Rep 503 (instructed as junior counsel on questions relating to whether an offer to settle liability in respect of a collision could be accepted where the claim form had not been served in time); and Sea Glory Maritime Co v Al Sagr National Insurance Co [2014] 1 Lloyd's Rep 14 (a substantial insurance trial in the Commercial Court where Ravi was instructed to appear unled against a senior QC and a senior junior). Ravi has a significant international perspective to his practice and has developed particular links with Hong Kong, India, Malaysia, Singapore and the UAE, as well as throughout the UK and Europe.
Professional Memberships: Arbitration Ireland, Association Internationale des Jeunes Avocats, Association Suisse de l'Arbitrage – Below 40 Member, British Maritime Law Association, Chartered Institute of Arbitrators (MCIArb), Commercial Bar Association, FDI International Moot Competition (College of Arbitrators), Indian Maritime Association (UK), International Chamber of Commerce – Young Arbitrators Forum, International Council for Commercial Arbitration, Inter-Pacific Bar Association, London Common Law and Commercial Bar Association, LCIA European Users' Council and Young International Arbitration Group, LMAA Supporting Member, London Shipping Law Centre – Founding Committee Member of Young Maritime Practitioners' Group, Scottish Arbitration Centre, Singapore Chamber of Maritime Arbitration – Individual Member, Worshipful Company of Arbitrators (Freeman).
Career: LLB (first class honours), UCL, 1999; Called to Bar of England and Wales, 2000; Judicial assistant in the Court of Appeal, 2001-02; Admitted to Register of Practitioners of the Dubai International Financial Centre Courts, 2008; CEDR Accredited Mediator, 2009; MCIArb, 2012; Deputy District Judge (Civil), 2013.

ATKINS, Mike
Crown Office Chambers, London
020 7797 8100
atkins@CrownOfficechambers.com
Featured in Health & Safety (London)
Practice Areas: Mike practises exclusively in the field of Criminal Regulatory Law, with particular expertise in health and safety, inquests, consumer law, product safety, fire safety, environmental law and food safety. He regularly appears in significant and high profile cases, both in his own right and as a junior. He is instructed in cases of corporate and gross negligence manslaughter, prosecutions for health and safety offences, inquests, appeals against enforcement notices, and challenges to fee for intervention (FFI) invoices. He frequently represents household name and international companies as well as directors, employees, public bodies and prosecuting authorities. He was junior counsel for Maidstone and Tunbridge Wells NHS Trust, acquitted of corporate manslaughter in January 2016, for the Coroner in the Lakanal House tower block fire inquests, and for the acquitted Managing Director in the Lion Steel corporate manslaughter case. He has experience of cases concerning construction and demolition, work at height, manufacturing and technology, warehousing and logistics, waste management and recycling, mining and quarrying, asbestos, fire safety, gas and electrical safety, medical treatment, residential care, schools and nurseries, sports and leisure, deaths in custody and road traffic accidents.
Professional Memberships: Health and Safety Lawyers' Association.

ATKINS, Richard QC
St Philips Chambers, Birmingham
0121 246 7000
rpatkins@st-philips.com
Featured in Crime (Midlands)
Practice Areas: Specialises in: murder (including gangland, sado-masochistic and domestic killings); manslaughter (fatal accident, corporate manslaughter, diminished responsibility, gross negligence and unlawful act manslaughter); serious fraud (Revenue, VAT, international and boiler room frauds); serious sex; HSE; trading standards and consumer law cases. Defends and prosecutes in equal measure. Regularly appears in the Court of Appeal. Recent cases include: Lewis [2013] EWCA Crim 776 (jury irregularities); X [2013] EWCA Crim 818 (leading case on definition of "commercial practice" and "transactional decisions" in the Consumer Protection from Unfair Trading Regulations 2008); Masih [2015] EWCA Crim 477 (overturned murder conviction); D & P 2016 (successfully appealed convictions for Private Security Industry Act offences for a company and an individual, when had not appeared at first instance). An approachable and engaging advocate. Private, publicly funded, Direct and Public Access work accepted.
Professional Memberships: Criminal Bar Association; Association of Health and Safety Lawyers; Association of Regulatory and Disciplinary Lawyers.
Career: Leader of the Midland Circuit; Queen's Counsel (2011); Bencher of Gray's Inn; Head of St Philips Chambers Regulatory Team; Recorder; Fee-paid Judge of the First Tier Tribunal (Mental Health); Legal Chairman of the Financial Reporting Council Disciplinary Tribunal; Chairman of the Bar Council Bar Representation Board and Member of the General Management Committee; Chairman of the 2014 Bar Conference.
Personal: King Henry VIII School, Coventry; St Catherine's College, Oxford University; Past Chairman of the Governors of the Coventry School Foundation.

ATRILL, Simon
Fountain Court Chambers, London
020 7583 3335
sa@foundtaincourt.co.uk
Featured in Banking & Finance (London), Commercial Dispute Resolution (London), Fraud (London)
Practice Areas: Civil and commercial litigation including banking, financial services, insurance/reinsurance, civil fraud and professional negligence. Shortlisted for Chambers and Partners Banking and Finance Junior of the Year 2013, 2015 and 2016. Recent cases: NBT v Yurov; Marme v RBS; JSC BTA Bank v Ablyazov; OFT v Abbey National and others (bank charges) (first instance to HL [2010] 1 A.C. 696); Group Seven Ltd v Sultana and others [2014] 1 W.L.R. 735 (freezing injunctions), [2014] EWHC 2046 (Ch) (trial) and [2015] EWCA Civ 631; BAT v Windward [2014] 2 All ER (Comm) 757; interest rate swaps and PPI litigation; NatWest v Rabobank (four reported first instance judgments and CA); IBC v MAR [2010] 1 All ER (Comm) 112; various substantial confidential commercial arbitrations; ICB v Akingbola; Arab Banking Corp v Saad [2010] EWHC 509 (Comm); Dhanani v Crasnianski [2011] 2 All E.R. (Comm) 799; various cases in Cayman Islands, Hong Kong and Trinidad and Tobago.
Professional Memberships: COMBAR
Career: Called 2005
Publications: Legal Privilege and Mandatory Disclosure under the Proceeds of Crime Act 2002 [2005] LMCLQ; "Choice of Law in Contract: The missing Pieces of the Article 4 Jigsaw?" (2004) ICLQ; several in Cambridge Law Journal.
Personal: St Catharine's College, Cambridge (Double First); St John's College, Oxford (BCL, Distinction); University of Pennsylvania (LLM, summa cum laude).

AUBURN, Jonathan
11KBW, London
020 7632 8500
jonathan.auburn@11kbw.com
Featured in Administrative & Public Law (London), Community Care (London), Education (London), Local Government (London)
Practice Areas: Practice Areas: Judicial review specialising in local government (governance, powers and duties, inter-agency disputes, inquiries), community care (assessment and provision challenges, direct payments, NRPF cases, age assessment trials, leaving care duties), education (including academies, higher education, independent schools), challenges to service closures and funding cuts, care home fee setting and charging disputes, mental capacity, DOLS and mental health, healthcare and procurement (especially in social care and health), inquests.
Professional Memberships: ALBA, Justice.
Career: University of Western Australia (LLB, First), Magdalen College Oxford (BCL, D.Phil), Attorney-General's Panel of Treasury Counsel 2002-2013.
Publications: Judicial Review Principles and Procedure (2013, OUP), White Book (ongoing), Legal Professional Privilege (Hart), Phipson on Evidence (ongoing), Education and the Courts (contributor).

AUDLAND, William QC
12 King's Bench Walk, London
020 7583 0811
audland@12kbw.co.uk
Featured in Personal Injury (London), Travel (London)
Practice Areas: Travel law (personal injury, contractual, insurance, applicable law and jurisdictional matters); personal injury (including catastrophic injuries and accidents abroad); local authority liabilities (education and highways); professional negligence (clinical and solicitors); sports law (football, rugby, sailing, skiing, waterskiing, climbing); insurance.
Professional Memberships: EBA, PEOPIL, PIBA, PNBA, TATLA, South Eastern Circuit.
Career: Called to the Bar in 1992, William won the Chambers and Partners UK Bar Award for Personal Injury/Clinical Negligence Junior Barrister of the Year 2013 and took silk in 2015. He is also a qualified and accredited Mediator for all civil, commercial and workplace disputes.
Publications: William is a Contributing Author of "Personal Injury Schedules: Calculating Damages" 3rd Edition, Bloomsbury Professional.
Personal: William obtained a BA in modern languages (Spanish and Portuguese) from The Queen's College, Oxford, and subsequently a Diploma in Law (City University). He is reasonably fluent in Italian, is a keen skier, and enjoys ski touring, hockey and cycling.

AYLING, Tracy QC
2 Bedford Row, London
020 7440 8888
tayling@2bedfordrow.co.uk
Featured in Crime (London)
Practice Areas: Specialist Criminal Practitioner – Defence and Prosecution. Defends in serious sex cases, murder, and confiscation cases acting in some of the highest profile cases in the UK. Recent cases include gang murders, representing young gang members using knives and guns. Particular expertise in the ever-developing areas of child sex offending, grooming, and human trafficking. Leading defence counsel in Operations Bullfinch and Sabaton (very high profile, widely reported cases concerning gangs of Asian

men grooming and abusing very young girls over a period of many years in Oxford). Bullfinch was the second case of its type. Advocacy trainer for the Inner Temple. Teaches a unique course on how to cross examine very young and vulnerable witnesses. Brought in to lead for the defence in a 2014 case involving 3 year old complainants and significant expert witness evidence. Defended in Match.com rape case. Leading specialist in matters of PII and disclosure. Extensive experience of cases concerning International Security and Government agencies requiring expert knowledge of the Regulation of Investigatory Powers Act 2000, including the legality of telephone intercept material. Appointed in 2010 as a Special Advocate for the Attorney General. Special Advocate in Operation Lanosity 2015/2016.
Professional Memberships: Criminal Bar Association.

AYLOTT, Colin
Carmelite Chambers, London
020 7936 6300
colin.aylott@carmelitechamber.cjsm.net
Featured in Crime (London), Financial Crime (London)
Practice Areas: A leading junior specialising in defending allegations of complex fraud and serious crime. He advises and represents individuals and corporate clients in all areas of commercial crime, money laundering, bribery and corruption. He is regularly instructed as leading counsel to defend prosecutions brought by the SFO, BIS and the FCA. He is equally experienced in all areas of serious crime including murder, commercial armed robberies, kidnapping, terrorism and major drug trafficking conspiracies. He practices internationally and is called to the Bar in the Turks and Caicos Islands.
Professional Memberships: Criminal Bar Association.
Career: He has appeared as defence counsel in numerous high profile cases including acting for a Yen money broker acquitted in the SFO prosecuted "LIBOR manipulation" trial. Other cases include "Operation Elveden" (the News International trials); "Operation Hayrack" (alleged corruption in the awarding of Royal Household contracts); "Operation Aquamarine" (off-shore multi-million pound mortgage fraud); "Operation Carp" carbon credit trading fraud and the "Operation Chainmail/ Crystalite" prosecutions of investment bankers for tax fraud.

BACHE, Nina
St Ives Chambers, Birmingham
0121 236 0863
nina.bache@stiveschambers.co.uk
Featured in Family/Matrimonial (Midlands)
Practice Areas: Family
Professional Memberships: Family Law Bar Association
Career: Nina is a specialist family law practitioner specialising in both public and private law. Public Law: Nina is regularly instructed by parents, Guardians, local authorities, other family members and interveners. She is known for her client-friendly approach and careful preparation. She is very experienced in care cases involving non-accidental injuries, sexual abuse, severe emotional abuse, chronic neglect, clients with learning difficulties and matters involving the Official Solicitor. She also has experience of cases involving expert evidence on the evaluation of children's ABE interviews and cross-examination of children. Nina also deals in adoption cases, including revocation of placement orders. Private Law: Nina is regularly instructed by parents, grandparents and Guardians acting for children. She has a sensitive and understanding approach to clients. She deals with difficult and complex Child Arrangements applications involving parents and non-parents, including cases involving complex psychological evidence, intractable contact disputes, and applications for removal from the jurisdiction.

BACON, Francis
Hailsham Chambers, London
020 7643 5000
Francis.bacon@hailshamchambers.com
Featured in Professional Negligence (London)
Practice Areas: Francis specialises in professional negligence, commercial insurance and commercial litigation. He has extensive experience in acting for individual claimants, lending institutions and professional indemnity insurers in obtaining interim remedies in London and overseas. Francis is recognised as one of the leading commercial juniors in professional negligence, having been ranked by both Chambers UK and The Legal 500 for many years. "He has an edge that other barristers don't have – his experience and advocacy skills are strengthened by his wealth of knowledge and his investigative nature. He will leave no stone unturned." "He has an excellent grasp of the documents and deals very well with the witnesses." Chambers UK 2016
Professional Memberships: Professional Negligence Bar Association (PNBA).
Career: Called to the Bar in 1988. Karmel Commercial Scholar Gray's Inn. Recorder.
Personal: Educated Keele and Loughborough. Married with three children.

BACON, Nicholas QC
4 New Square, London
020 7822 20457
barristers@4newsquare.com
Featured in Costs Litigation (All Circuits)
Practice Areas: Nicholas Bacon QC is probably one of the best known silks in his specialised field of costs. He has been described as having 'probably the biggest costs practice at the Bar'. Nicholas undertakes high profile costs litigation work. He was retained in the Voicemail Interception Litigation for News International. He led the costs team for Trafigura in what was one of the largest costs claim in English legal history. He was retained by Lovells in the Three Rivers costs disputes and receives instructions from other magic circle firms. He is retained by Shell in the Bodo claims advising on all costs matters arising from the group claims. He has appeared in the Supreme Court, House of Lords Court of Appeal and has been retained in some of the most significant funding costs cases in the past decade. His costs practice is well juxtaposed to his professional negligence work with particular emphasis on solicitors' and barristers' negligence, both for and against solicitors and the Bar. He is co author of the Bar Handbook. His work includes regulatory and disciplinary work in respect of solicitors. He has been retained in some of the leading legal expense insurance cases and regularly advises the insurance industry in respect of funding and legal expense issues, coverage advice and policy terms. His move to 4 New Square reflects his increasing prominence in professional indemnity work. He is a member of the Civil Procedure Rules Committee and has been heavily engaged in the implementation of recent reforms recommended by Sir Rupert Jackson.
Professional Memberships: Professional Negligence Bar Association. Commercial Bar Association.
Career: Called to the Bar in 1992; to Queens Counsel in 2010.
Publications: He is the contributing editor to the section on Costs in Halsbury's Laws of England. He is contributing editor to the 'Green Book' – the Civil Court Practice where he edits the sections on Funding and Legal Aid. He is the co-author of The Bar Handbook. He is a contributing editor to Butterworths' Costs Service and the Civil Court Precedents.
Personal: Nicholas' outdoor passion is yachting. He is a qualified Yachtmaster. He is married with two young children.

BADGER, Christopher
6 Pump Court, London
020 7797 8400
christopherbadger@6pumpcourt.co.uk
Featured in Environment (London)
Practice Areas: Practice Areas: Environmental Regulation and Enforcement; Business Crime and Corporate Defence. Specialist in corporate and regulatory investigations and providing early stage advice. Recent instructions include: Advising in several significant commercial disputes in respect of environmental and health and safety obligations under EU and domestic law; judicial review proceedings challenging the implementation of the EU Emissions Trading Scheme; Walker & Son (Hauliers) Ltd v Environment Agency [2014] 1 Cr. App. R. 30; [2014] Env L.R. 22 (leading authority on the statutory construction of "knowingly permit" in the Environmental Permitting Regulations 2007 and 2010); EA v WB Ltd (Counsel on behalf of 2 companies and their director in the largest prosecution for the illegal export of waste to date); R v Rogers, Beaman and Tapecrown Ltd [2016] EWCA Crim 801 (leading authority on the admissibility of fresh evidence in appeals against sentence).
Professional Memberships: UKELA, HSLA, ARDL, SEC, CBA.
Career: Lincoln College, Oxford. Called to the Bar in 2002. Appointed as 'A' List Counsel on the Attorney General's List of Specialist Regulatory Counsel in 2012.
Publications: Environmental Sentencing Referencer 2012; Contributor to Burnett Hall on Environmental Law 2013 (Sweet & Maxwell).

BAFADHEL, Sara
9 Bedford Row, London
sarah.bafadhel@9fordrow.co.uk
Featured in Crime (London)
Practice Areas: She is a specialised barrister in international criminal law, public international law and human rights law. She has assisted in proceedings before international and hybrid courts, including the International Criminal Court, Special Tribunal for Lebanon, International Criminal Tribunal for the former Yugoslavia and the International Crimes Tribunal in Bangladesh. Notable cases include Prosecutor v. Saif Al-Islam Gaddafi and Prosecutor v. Ayyash et al. Sarah provides consultation to governmental and non-governmental organisations with regard to the characterisation of crimes allegedly committed in international and non-international armed conflicts. Sarah also represents clients before various international human rights mechanisms. She accepts public access instruction and has assisted in challenges to Interpol red notices and delisting of individuals from various sanction regimes, including in proceedings before the General Court of the European Union. Sarah also lectures on various international aspects with a particular focus on complementary-related issues before the ICC.
Publications: Sarah is an assistant editor of OUP's up-coming Blackstone's International Criminal Practice text, as well as the author of the chapter on admissibility of cases before the ICC. Sarah is also the author of 'Abuse of Process Doctrine in International Criminal Proceedings' (D. Young, M. Summers & D. Corker (eds), Abuse of Process in Criminal Proceedings: Fourth edition 2014.
Personal: Sarah is fluent in Arabic and holds an LLM in Public International Law from the University of London.

BAILIN, Alex QC
Matrix Chambers, London
020 7404 3447
alexbailin@matrixlaw.co.uk
Featured in Administrative & Public Law (London), Crime (London), Civil Liberties & Human Rights (London), Defamation/Privacy (London), Financial Crime (London)
Practice Areas: Specialist in financial and general crime; human rights and public law. Also instructed in heavyweight commercial, extradition, media and public international law work. Financial crime: full range of business crime cases, from corporate manslaughter and corruption to fraud, insider dealing and cartels. Considerable experience in cross-border and multi-jurisdictional investigations. Briefed in Commercial Court cases which raise criminal issues. Clients include multinational corporations, private equity funds, senior business executives, traders, bankers, regulators, prosecutors, City firms, professional bodies and foreign governments. Crime: from gross negligence manslaughter to official secrets, blackmail and hacking. Human rights and public law: diverse practice, ranging from wealthy private clients, major shareholders, large corporations and FTSE companies to media organisations, regulators, public authorities, NGOs and publicly-funded individuals. 25+ cases in Supreme Court, House of Lords, Privy Council and European Court of Human Rights. Media practice: advising high-profile figures, editors, journalists and national newspapers on reputation management issues, production orders, witness summonses, reporting restrictions, contempt of court and other criminal offences both pre- and post- publication. Public international law work includes genocide, rendition and violations of international criminal law. Experience of diverse jurisdictions.
Career: Called 1995. Silk 2010. Crown Court Recorder. Deputy High Court judge.
Publications: Contributing author to leading books on human rights, criminal justice and fraud. Numerous articles in national and legal press/journals.
Personal: Cambridge University. Previously a derivatives trader.

BAIN, Giles
New Court Chambers, London
020 7583 5123
gbain@newcourtchambers.com
Featured in Family/Matrimonial (London)
Practice Areas: Specialist Child Care lawyer instructed in complex disputes. I give seminars to professional and lay clients, provide training to social workers and I am approved as a Pupil Supervisor. I have seen progression of many pupils into Tenancy, within New Court and other Chambers.
Professional Memberships: FLBA.
Career: Called to the Bar 1993. Joined New Court 1995.
Personal: LLB (Hons) University of Hull. Sports fan.

BAKER, Christopher
Arden Chambers, London
020 7242 4244
christopher.baker@ardenchambers.com
Featured in Local Government (London), Social Housing (London)
Practice Areas: Local government, housing, landlord and tenant (public, social and private).
Professional Memberships: ALBA, PBA, HLPA, SHLA.
Career: Called 1984. Illustrative recent cases include: R (M&A) v Islington LBC [2016] HLR 19 – severely autistic children and social services involvement in housing transfer; R (Brooks) v Islington LBC [2016] PTSR 389 – limitation of interim homelessness duty; Oliver v Sheffield City Council [2015] UKUT 229 (LC) – service charges and major refurbishment scheme; Mohamoud v Kensington & Chelsea RLBC [2015] BLGR 695 – interests of children in possession proceedings; Birmingham CC v Merali [2015] 2 CMLR 27 – "Zambrano" carers; Hussain v Waltham Forest LBC [2015] 1 WLR 2912 – non-domestic violence, homelessness; R (Jakimaviciute) v Hammersmith & Fulham LBC [2015] BLGR 306 – housing allocation scheme, disqualification; Haile v Waltham Forest LBC [2014] PTSR 1376 – causation, homelessness; R (Wood) v Leeds CC [2014] EWHC 2598 (Admin) – allotment rent increases; Balog v Birmingham City Council [2014] HLR 14 – homelessness; R (Alansi) v Newham LBC [2014] BLGR 138 – changes to housing allocation scheme, legitimate expectation; Ker v Optima Community Association [2013] 2 P & CR 19 – proportionality of eviction of Flexibuy tenant; R (Chatting) v Viridian Housing [2013] BLGR 118 – transfer of registered care home; R (W) v Birmingham CC [2012] BLGR 1 – eligibility criteria for adult social care; R (Birmingham Care Consortium) v Birmingham CC [2011] EWHC 2656 (Admin) – payment rates for residential care home placements; Mears Ltd v Leeds CC [2011] EuLR 596 & 764 – public procurement of housing repairs service; Ali v Birmingham CC [2010] 2 AC 39 – art 6 and homelessness appeals; R (Weaver) v LQHT [2010] 1 WLR 363 – whether RSL a public authority; R (Ahmad) v Newham LBC [2009] 3 All ER 755 – allocations scheme; Knowsley HT v White [2009] 1 AC 636 – tolerated trespassers and assured tenants; Riverside HA Ltd v White [2007] 4 All ER 97 – RSL rent increases.
Publications: Encyclopedia of Local Government Law (Sweet & Maxwell – contributor); Community Care Law Reports (LAG – editor); Halsbury's Laws of England (5th ed), vol 69, Local Government (Butterworths, 2009 – contributor); Local Government Constitutional and Administrative Law (Sweet & Maxwell, 2nd ed, 2008 – co-author); Local Government Liability Law (Sweet & Maxwell, 2007 – author); Housing Law: Pleadings in Practice (Sweet & Maxwell, 2nd ed 2003 – co-author).

BAKER, Philip QC
Field Court Tax Chambers, London
0203 693 3700
pb@fieldtax.com
Featured in Tax (London)
Practice Areas: All forms of revenue law, with particular specialisations in: international taxation (both corporate and private client, and government advisory work on taxation, with a particular interest in double taxation conventions); in European Union tax law; and in taxation and human rights (especially the European Convention on Human Rights).
Professional Memberships: Barrister, Grays Inn (1979), QC (2002); senior visiting fellow, Institute of Advanced Legal Studies, University of London; Committee Member, International Fiscal Association (British Branch); Member, Permanent Scientific Committee, International Fiscal Association; Member, International Tax Sub-Committees, Law Society; Member, Exchequer Secretary's Forum for Tax Professionals.
Career: 1979-87, lecturer in law, School of Oriental and African Studies, London University. 1987-present, Barrister. Founder member of Field Court Tax Chambers, August 2014.
Publications: 'Double Taxation Conventions' (3rd edn, looseleaf, 2001). Editor, International Tax Law Reports.
Personal: Educated: Emmanuel College, Cambridge (MA); Balliol College, Oxford (BCL); University College, London (LLM); SOAS, London (PhD); London Business School (MBA). Married, three children. Awarded OBE, July 1997.

BAKER, Richard
7BR, London
020 7242 3555
clerks@7br.co.uk
Featured in Clinical Negligence (London)
Practice Areas: Clinical negligence, personal injury, public law (inquests).
Professional Memberships: AvMA, APIL, Coroners Association of England and Wales, Royal Society of Medicine.
Career: Richard undertakes all types of clinical negligence, personal injury and public law (inquest) work, He has built up a special practice acting for claimants who have been caused to suffer catastrophic brain injuries as a consequence of clinical negligence but has also represented claimants in a broad range of claims involving health professionals, including cosmetic surgeons. In 2011 he was appointed an Assistant Deputy Coroner for South Yorkshire (Eastern District); he also regularly appears at inquests on behalf of interested parties, including inquests held in accordance with Article 2 of the European Convention and inquests held before juries. He has a particular interest in Fatal Accident claims and often represents parties through the inquest process and onto the conclusion of a subsequent civil claim. In addition to his busy Clinical Negligence practice Richard undertakes a wide variety of personal injury work, including work place and road traffic accidents, accidents on the highway and in public places and claims arising from detective products. He acts on behalf of claimants and defendants and has experience of high value claims arising from catastrophic and non-catastrophic brain injuries. He regularly advises in cases where claimants have sustained spinal injuries or are exhibiting psychogenic symptoms.

BALA, Ruth
Gough Square Chambers, London
ruth.bala@goughsq.co.uk
Featured in Consumer Law (London)
Practice Areas: Ruth has a specialist practice in regulated lending, retail banking and financial services. She has successfully represented finance institutions in a number of the leading appellate cases on 'PPI mis-selling'. She is regularly instructed in litigation involving enforceability disputes, mis-selling of insurance and investments, 'secret commissions' to brokers, 'unfair relationships' and irresponsible lending. Ruth has a significant advisory practice, covering compliance with the FCA's Handbook, drafting requirements for the purposes of securitisations or acquisitions and FCA authorisation. Ruth also has experience in other consumer regulatory matters, both civil and criminal, including counterfeit goods and unfair commercial practices.
Career: Called in 2006. Successfully represented the lender in the seminal 'PPI mis-selling' case: Harrison v Black Horse Ltd [2011]Lloyd's Rep IR 455; [2012]Lloyd's Rep IR 521. Successfully represented the lender alone in the High Court, against Hodge Malek QC, in Conlon v Black Horse Ltd [2012] GCCR 11423, settled in June 2014, three days before Supreme Court due to hear expedited appeal.
Publications: Author of 'Consumer Credit Law' in 'Consumer and Trading Standards: Law and Practice', Jordan (2013). Contributor to 'Advertising Law and Regulation', ed G. Crown, 2nd edn, Bloomsbury Professional (2010)
Personal: Classics at Oriel College, Oxford University.

BALDRY, Rupert QC
Pump Court Tax Chambers, London
020 7414 8080
clerks@pumptax.com
Featured in Tax (London)
Practice Areas: Experienced in all the main areas of tax, direct and indirect, advisory and litigation. Specialist fields include: IP and goodwill, pensions, life assurance, company finance and restructuring, partnerships, damages, employee benefits, EU and international tax issues, trusts, VAT and property, stamp taxes, excise duty and aggregates levy. Practice also covers professional negligence disputes and judicial review.
Professional Memberships: Revenue Bar Association; London Common Law and Commercial Bar Association & VAT Practitioners Group.
Career: Qualified 1987; junior counsel Attorney General's panel (1997-2005); Silk 2010.
Publications: Editor, International Trust & Estate Law Reports; Co-author, Trusts and UK Taxation.
Personal: London University (BA Hons, 1st); City University (Diploma in Law).

BALDWIN, John QC
8 New Square, London
020 7405 4321
clerks@8newsquare.co.uk
Featured in Intellectual Property (London), Media & Entertainment (London)
Practice Areas: Barrister (QC) specialising in all aspects of intellectual property, media and entertainment and information technology: including patents, trade marks, copyrights, confidential information, computer law, passing off, trade libel, EC law, data protection, restrictive covenants and restraint of trade. Recent cases: Wade v Sky TV (Must be the Music), Belo v Lime Pictures (The Only way is Essex), Fisher v Brooker (A Whiter Shade of Pale); Baigent v Random House (The Da Vinci Code), A+E Television v Discovery Communications (Discovery History). Fage v Chobani (Greek Yogurt), James Joyce v Macmillan (Ulysses), Ciba v Novartis (contact lenses) . For comprehensive CV, visit Chambers' website at www.8newsquare.co.uk.
Professional Memberships: Intellectual Property Bar Association (IPBA); Chancery Bar Association.
Career: Biological Chemist to 1975, Called to the Bar by Gray's Inn 1977; QC 1991; Recorder 2004; Deputy High Court Judge, 2008.
Personal: Educated at Nelson Grammar School; University of Leeds (1968 BSc Agricultural Chemistry); St John's College, Oxford (1972 DPhil., University Research Fellowship), Inns of Court School of Law.

BALLARD, Briony
Serjeants' Inn Chambers, London
020 7427 5000
bballard@serjeantsinn.com
Featured in Inquests & Public Inquiries (All Circuits)
Practice Areas: Briony Ballard was called to the Bar in 2000. Briony specialises in clinical negligence and healthcare, Court of Protection, inquests and inquiries, police, professional discipline and regulatory and public and administrative law. An earlier edition notes that "she is both approachable and personable, she is known for having very good client care skills." Please click on the link to the Serjeants' Inn Chambers website for her profile, which sets out full details of her practice including relevant work of note.
Professional Memberships: Professional Negligence Bar Association, London Common Law and Commercial Bar Association, Liberty.

BALMER, Kate
Devereux, London
020 7353 7534
balmer@devchambers.co.uk
Featured in Employment (London)
Practice Areas: Kate practices predominantly in the fields of employment, discrimination and commercial law. She regularly represents clients in high value and multi-day claims involving all aspects of employment law. Kate's clients include FTSE 100 companies, international airlines, high street chains, banks, beauty brands, health care providers, charities and a wide range of public and private sector clients and private individuals. Kate is also developing a substantial appellate practice, with recent notable cases including: Reed Employment Group v HMRC [2014] UKUT 0160 (employment status); McKinney v London Borough of Newham [2015] ICR 495 (whistleblowing and unfair dismissal);

and Wyeth v Salisbury NHS Trust, 2015, EAT (whistleblowing). In 2015, Kate is due to appear as a junior in both the Court of Appeal and Supreme Court on employment related matters.
Professional Memberships: ELA, ELBA, ILS, FRU, RBA.
Career: BA in Politics and History (First Class); Graduate Diploma in Law (Distinction); Bar Vocational Course (Very Competent); Called in 2009; appointed to the Attorney General's panel (C panel) in 2013.
Publications: Contributing author to Tottel's Discrimination Law (Bloomsbury Professional) and author of various articles including 'Fecitt & Ors v NHS Manchester: Whistleblowing' (ELA Briefing) and 'Bad Day At The Office' (Glamour Magazine).

BANERJEE, Lydia
Littleton Chambers, London
07940 435669
lbanerjee@littletonchambers.co.uk
Featured in Employment (London)
Practice Areas: Lydia's core areas of practice are commercial law, sports law and employment law. Lydia's commercial practice encompasses disputes including contractual interpretation, professional negligence and directors' duties. Lydia's sports law work covers work in relation to agency fee disputes, arbitrations and disciplinary proceedings. Lydia's employment work has a particular focus on disability discrimination but also incorporates all areas of tribunal disputes and high court action in relation to bonuses and restrictive covenants.
Professional Memberships: BASL, COMBAR, YFLA, ELBA, SEC, LCF.
Career: Called 2007, Middle Temple.
Personal: Educated at Downing College, Cambridge, awarded Queen Mother Scholarship by Middle Temple and Senior Harris Scholar by Downing College. Listed in Who's Who of Britain's Young Entrepreneurs 2006 and Who's Who of Emerging Business Leaders 2007 and 2008. Trustee for charity Rafiki and Director of Kinson Pottery Ltd.

BANNER, Gregory
Maitland Chambers, London
020 7406 1200
gbanner@maitlandchambers.com
Featured in Company (London)
Practice Areas: Main area of work is commercial chancery litigation, with particular emphasis on commercial litigation (with particular experience of natural resources disputes in the FSU), company law, shareholders' disputes, warranty claims, insolvencies, business disputes and related matters.
Professional Memberships: Chancery Bar Association, COMBAR.
Career: Called to the Bar in 1989; Junior Counsel to the Crown ('B' Panel) 1997-2004.
Publications: MA Cantab. Educated at Dulwich College and Trinity Hall, Cambridge. Personal interests include cycling, triathlon and skiing.

BARAN, Stuart
Three New Square, London
020 7405 1111
baran@3newsquare.co.uk
Featured in Intellectual Property (London)
Practice Areas: My practice focusses on intellectual property in all its aspects: patents, trade marks, copyright, designs and confidential information. I represent all types of clients from all sectors and in all fora, including all courts and proceedings at the UKIPO and EPO. Recent cases have included BSkyB v. Microsoft (SkyDrive), Resolution v. Lundbeck (citalopram), Comic v. Fox (GLEE), FH Brundle v. Perry (IPEC, threats), Cadbury v. Nestlé (CA, trade marks), Actavis v. Lilly (chemotherapy, UK and foreign patent laws, jurisdiction), Biocompatibles v. Biosphere (EPO opposition), Coca-Cola "MASTER" (EU General Court), Merck v. ONO (patents, biotech), Teva v. Boehringer Ingelheim (patents, SPCs), "TEAM GB" trade mark registration (for the British Olympic Assn), Idenix v. Gilead (antiviral drugs, patents), Timesource v. Ultimate Products (passing off, account of profits). Glaxo .v. Wyeth (patents, vaccines), Coloplast .v. Macgregor Healthcare (patents, medical devices), Hospira .v. Cubist (patents, antibiotics), FKB v AbbVie (patents, antibodies), Merk v Shonogi (patents, HIV).
Professional Memberships: Inner Temple, AIPPI, IPBA.
Career: MChem Chemistry (Jesus College, Oxford: first class); DPhil (Oxford) Chemical Physics. GDL (City University: distinction); BPTC (BPP: Outstanding). Called July 2011.
Personal: Violinist and keen amateur cook.

BARCA, Manuel QC
One Brick Court, London
020 7353 8845
mb@onebrickcourt.com
Featured in Defamation/Privacy (London)
Practice Areas: Media/ information law: defamation; privacy/confidence; malicious falsehood; contempt of court; data protection; freedom of information; media/literary copyright; passing off.
Career: Graduate trainee, Reuters 1984-85. Called: 1986 (Lincoln's Inn, Levitt Scholar). Joined 1BC 1987; QC 2011. Cases include: Pickering v Liverpool Daily Post (HL); John Major MP v New Statesman; Berkoff v Burchill (CA); Watts v Times Newspapers (CA); GMC v BBC (CA); Godfrey v Demon Internet; Upjohn v BBC; Peter Bottomley MP v Express Newspapers; British Coal v NUM; Barclay Brothers v BBC; Martin Clunes v Express Newspapers; Home Secretary v BBC; Marks & Spencer v Granada TV; ITN v Living Marxism; David Trimble MP v Amazon; Multigroup v Oxford Analytica; Elite Models v BBC; Skrine v Euromoney (CA); Steedman v BBC (CA); Philip Green v Times Newspapers; Donal MacIntyre v Chief Constable of Kent (CA); Jimmy Nail v Newcastle Chronicle; Reuben Brothers v Time Inc; Conrad Black v Express Newspapers; Neil Lennon v Daily Record; Ricky Tomlinson v Associated Newspapers; Prince Turki Al-Saud v Paris Match; W v Westminster City Council; Roman Polanski v Condé Nast (HL); Paul McKenna v MGN; AY v BBC (Cash for Honours); Taranissi v BBC; Ajinomoto v Asda (CA); Hughes v British Airways; Baturina v Times Newspapers (CA); Prince Nayef Al-Saud v The Independent; Miller v Associated Newspapers (CA); PNM v Times Newspapers Ltd & anr (CA) going to Supreme Court in 2016; Simpson v MGN Ltd; Lachaux v AOL; Stocker v Stocker; Economou v De Freitas.
Personal: Educated: Wimbledon College; Cambridge University (Law, MA). Bilingual: English/Spanish. Fluent French; working Italian & Portuguese.

BARCLAY, Robin
Fountain Court Chambers, London
020 7583 3335
rb@fountaincourt.co.uk
Featured in Financial Services (London), Financial Crime (London)
Practice Areas: Robin practises in commercial, regulatory and criminal law with a particular focus on fraud, banking and financial services, corporate liability, directors' duties, cross-jurisdictional investigations and judicial review. In recent years Robin has appeared in numerous complex and high-profile commercial, regulatory and criminal cases across the full range of domestic courts and tribunals, as well as in a number of international financial centres. A number of those cases have involved multi-billion pound liabilities and/or criminal and regulatory outcomes of lasting and industry-wide significance. Robin has substantial experience as a sole advocate both at first-instance and on appeal (including the Court of Appeal, Divisional Court and Upper Tribunal). He also routinely advises Boards and Board sub-committees of FTSE 100 and FTSE 250 companies on suspected wrongdoing and crisis management.
Professional Memberships: COMBAR, CFLA, ARDL, DIFC.
Career: 1999: Called to the Bar.
Publications: Contributing author of Lissack & Horlick On Bribery.

BARDEN, Alex
Fountain Court Chambers, London
020 7583 3335
arb@fountaincourt.co.uk
Featured in Company (London)
Practice Areas: Alex is a specialist in company law, insolvency, and general commercial litigation and arbitration. Significant recent cases as a junior include the RBS Rights Issue litigation, the Alpstream case (a the seven-week Commercial Court trial and subsequent appeal relating to security over aircraft), a number of high value, complex pieces of litigation arising from the insolvencies of Kaupthing Bank and of the Akai Electrical Group, and two Court of Appeal cases on the interpretation of the insolvency rules. He has also appeared in arbitrations relating to joint ventures and LLPs. He regularly appears as sole advocate in Commercial Court and Chancery Division litigation, and he was successful in a recent six-day Commercial Court trial (Paros v Worldlink). His corporate transactional practice includes cross-border mergers, joint ventures and reductions of share capital.
Professional Memberships: COMBAR, Chancery Bar Association.
Publications: Contributor to Buckley on the Companies Acts, Lightman and Moss on Receivers and Administrators (appointment of administrators) and Company Directors: Law and Liability (Insolvency).

BARLOW, Francis QC
Ten Old Square, London
020 7405 0758
clerks@tenoldsquare.com
Featured in Chancery (London), Offshore (London), Trusts (London)
Practice Areas: Francis Barlow's practice covers the full spectrum of Chancery matters, both contentious and non-contentious. As well as having particular expertise in drafting UK and offshore trusts and advising on their construction and effect and associated taxation issues, he has extensive experience in contested trust, probate and succession disputes.
Professional Memberships: Member of the Chancery Bar Association, STEP, ACTAPS, Charity Law Association and the Western Circuit. Associate Member of Shortland Chambers, Auckland, New Zealand.
Career: Head of Chambers at Ten Old Square (2012 – date), Called to the Bar 1965, Silk 2006. Recent cases include: CvC and Ors [2015] EWHC 2699 (Ch), Allfrey v Allfrey [2015] EWHC 1717 (Ch), V v T, A [2014], Re Q Trust [2010] Bda LR 26 [2011] WTLR 735 (Sup Ct of Bermuda) (appeared as amicus curiae to argue that a trust was not invalid as an illusory trust), Kershaw v Micklethwaite [2010] WTLR 413 (removal of executors; jurisdiction), Re Z Trust [2009] CILR 593 (Grand Court of Cayman Islands) (trusts: jurisdiction to confer administrative powers).
Publications: Consultant editor of Williams on Wills, a contributor to the first and second editions of Thomas and Hudson's Law of Trusts, the third and fourth editions of International Succession (Garb and Wood) and to International Trust Disputes (Collins, Kempster, McMillan and Meek). He was a member of the "Group of Experts" appointed by the EU Commission to advise on proposals for the harmonisation of the laws of succession of Member States.

BARNARD, Jonathan
Cloth Fair Chambers, London
020 7710 6444
jonathanbarnard@clothfairchambers.com
Featured in Crime (London), Financial Crime (London)
Practice Areas: Regularly instructed to represent professional and corporate clients in high-profile criminal proceedings, complex financial matters, frequently with multi-jurisdictional aspects. Cases in previous years include; represented the CEO of a billion pound company (reinsurance fraud, SFO prosecution); a company director (market offences); a leading breast surgeon (fraud); a psychiatrist (rape); a solicitor (money laundering, SFO prosecution); a dentist (fraud) and a company director (MTIC fraud). Significant prosecution experience includes the largest Court Martial in British Military history, cases involving complex PII from Special Casework Directorate, electoral frauds, frauds within the City of London and numerous murders at the Old Bailey. Considerable experience at regulatory tribunals, including the GMC and the GDC, in serious and long running hearings e.g. Dr. Martin 2010. Has been instructed by the AADB (Accountancy and Actuarial Disciplinary Board), drafted representations to the City of London Police regarding tax evasion and financial irregularity in the football industry preventing charges. Represented an individual in successful plea agreement in the largest case brought by DEFRA, represented a Solicitor charged with laundering the proceeds of overseas executive corruption, represented a director of a company charged with corruption and international sanctions busting, advised ex-Icelandic banking executives, advised a former editor of a national newspaper in relation to the Leveson Enquiry and advised on a number of defamation maters. Advised Vincent Tchenguiz in judicial review of the search used by the SFO. Successfully represented an international property tycoon

surrounding corruption charges in Turks & Caicos Islands. Represented a hedge fund manager before the Financial Services and Markets Tribunal re. market abuse. Looked after the interests of a national supermarket who became victims of a multi-million pound fraud scam. Recent cases include; successfully represented Eddy Shah over rape charges; advised healthcare company regarding potential fraud implications; successfully represented Victor Dahdaleh over international corruption allegations; advised a leading accountancy firm re money laundering. Successfully acted for CEO of a raw materials company charged with conspiracy to defraud. Advised Raymond Kwok throughout trial for corruption charges in Hong Kong, acquitted. Successfully represented a former Senior Partner of an accountancy firm over fraud charges in Gibraltar. Advising individual in SFO investigation regarding Rolls Royce; advising a national pharmaceutical company. Retained for former Barclays Bank Senior Executive in SFO/FCA investigation re Qatar. Representing an individual accused of overseas bribery, SFO investigation into Alstom Network UK Ltd. Advising an individual in relation to the SFO investigation into Tesco Plc. Instructed to represent a former company director charged with bribery, SFO v FH Bertling Ltd. Continues to advise Thames Water. For further information please visit www.clothfairchambers.com

Professional Memberships: Criminal Bar Association (member of the working party on plea negotiation in fraud trials), Association of Regulatory and Disciplinary Lawyers, sits on the Appeals Panel at the Legal Services Commission.

Career: 1997 – Called to the Bar.

Personal: Edinburgh University 1988-92 MA (First Class, Hons).

BARNES, Rachel

3 Raymond Buildings Barristers, London
020 7400 6400
rachel.barnes@3rblaw.com

Featured in Extradition (London), Financial Crime (London)

Practice Areas: A dual-qualified US attorney and English barrister, Rachel has a niche fraud, corruption and sanctions practice at the juncture of civil and criminal litigation, in both domestic and international cases. Appointed to the SFO B Panel of Counsel and POCA Panel, Rachel is known for her strategic approach in dealing with regulators and other third parties, and in assisting companies manage overlapping sanctions laws. Clients value her US background and knowledge of US sanctions, as well as her wider practice in cross-border criminal investigations, extradition and MLA, public law and commercial cases. She is well versed in issues of jurisdiction and state immunities. Rachel advises and represents corporations, governments, individuals and NGOs in relation to all aspects of extradition and mutual legal assistance, criminal/corporate liability and asset restraint and confiscation. She prosecutes and defends in all criminal courts and acts in judicial review and civil cases with criminal justice elements, appearing in the High Court, Court of Appeal and the Supreme Court. She has taught law at the London School of Economics and Cambridge University. She holds a PhD from Cambridge University in public international law and an LL.M from Harvard Law School.

BARNEY, Helen

No5 Chambers, Birmingham
+ 44 (0) 845 210 5555
hb@no5.com

Featured in Employment (Midlands)

Practice Areas: Helen practices exclusively in the field of employment and discrimination law. She has extensive experience (15 years) of advising and representing clients on employment law matters. She undertakes both claimant and respondent work, in the public and private sector. Clients include local authorities, NHS trusts, housing associations, multi-national companies, union and insurance supported Claimants. Helen started her career in employment law at a leading national firm of solicitors in 1999, joined Broadway House Chambers in 2002 and moved to the employment team at No5 Chambers in 2007. Helen has been consistently recognised in Chambers & Partners as a leader in her field.

BARNFATHER, Lydia

QEB Hollis Whiteman, London
020 7933 8855
lydia.barnfather@qebhw.co.uk

Featured in Professional Discipline (London)

Practice Areas: Lydia is an exceptionally experienced practitioner specialising to a high level in regulatory law and professional discipline. She advises, presents and defends in some of the most complex and high profile cases involving all the major healthcare regulators and is repeatedly instructed on matters involving a range of issues including conduct, performance, health as well as procedure. Lydia routinely advises and appears on cases involving the GMC, GDC, GOC, GCC, HCPC, GPhC, and NMC amongst others. She appears before a range of tribunals and before the High Court. Her advisory and appellate work extends to cases for the Professional Standards Authority. She also undertakes work for NHS England, police disciplinary hearings, inquests, and parallel proceedings in the criminal courts representing healthcare and other professionals. She has also advised and appeared in cases involving university disciplinary proceedings, various international healthcare associations and the RCVS.

Professional Memberships: Association of Regulatory and Disciplinary Lawyers (former Committee member), Criminal Bar Association, South Eastern Circuit.

Personal: Lydia is also involved in the training of healthcare regulators in law and procedure as well as in the advocacy training of in-house and external practitioners.

BARRETT, John

Kings Chambers, Manchester
0345 034 3444
clerks@kingschambers.com

Featured in Environment (Northern), Planning (Northern)

Practice Areas: Housing; waste disposal and management; minerals; major infrastructure projects; gas storage; highways; inquiries relating to substantial commercial and retail developments, including town centre redevelopments. John specialises in all aspects of town and country planning, environmental law, compulsory purchase and acquisition, local government, and highways. He has appeared as counsel in numerous UDP, Core Strategy and local plan inquiries and has worked extensively in the areas of waste disposal and management, minerals, highways and housing. Other significant inquiries include those relating to substantial commercial and retail developments, and major infrastructure proposals including underground gas storage.

Professional Memberships: Planning and Environment Bar Association, Administrative Law Bar Association.

Career: University: Manchester Metropolitan. Degree: BA (Hons) Law. Called: 1982.

Publications: Former editor Encyclopaedia of Environmental Health – Sweet & Maxwell.

BARRETT, Joseph

11KBW, London
020 7632 8500
joseph.barrett@11kbw.com

Featured in Public Procurement (London)

Practice Areas: Joseph Barrett practises in public, commercial and employment law, with particular expertise EU procurement, State aid and competition litigation.

Professional Memberships: Administrative Law Bar Association, Bar European Group, Procurement Lawyers Association, UK State Aid Law Association.

Career: Called in 2009; 2009-2010 Judicial Assistant to the Deputy President of the UK Supreme Court; Appointed to the Attorney General's C Panel of Counsel in 2014.

Publications: Contributor to various texts and journals on public and employment law.

Personal: University of Glasgow, LLB (First Class Honours); Harvard Law School, LLM.

BARRETT, Stephanie

Quadrant Chambers, London
020 75834444
stephanie.barrett@quadrantchambers.com

Featured in Aviation (London), Shipping (London)

Practice Areas: Stephanie's practice encompasses a wide range of commercial litigation and arbitration, particularly in the areas of shipping (both wet and dry), energy, shipbuilding, aviation, international trade, commodities and insurance. Stephanie also appears regularly (both as a junior and as sole counsel) in Court hearings at High Court and County Court levels and in commercial arbitrations. Stephanie acted as junior counsel in the reported cases of Emma Moore v Hotelplan, t/as Inghams [2010] EWHC 276 (QB), concerning tour operator liability for excursions, and Lloyds TSB Equipment Leasing (No. 1) Ltd v Revenue and Customs Commissioners [2014] EWCA Civ 1062, concerning capital allowances on LNG tankers used in the Norwegian Snøhvit project. She also appeared as junior counsel in the Court of Appeal in Ford v Malaysia Airlines [2014] 1 Lloyd's Rep. 301, concerning the meaning of "accident" under Article 17 of the Montreal Convention. Stephanie has appeared as junior counsel in several substantial shipping and shipbuilding arbitrations, and is currently instructed as junior counsel in a complex energy dispute concerning the supply of allegedly defective pumps for an offshore project.

Professional Memberships: COMBAR, LCIA Young International Arbitration Group

Career: Stephanie was called to the Bar in 2008 (Middle Temple) and became a tenant at Quadrant Chambers upon completing pupillage in 2009.

BARRY, Denis

5 Paper Buildings, London
020 7583 6117
dab@5pb.co.uk

Featured in Consumer Law (London)

Practice Areas: Substantial practice in consumer law and in crime and fraud. Consumer law: Areas of specialisation include Trade mark and Copyright offences, Trading Standards and all Consumer offences, for which he is instructed by both defendants, companies, and local authorities. Regularly instructed in novel and complex consumer law proceedings; brought the first proceedings under Part VIII Enterprise Act 2002 (Stop Now Orders), and the first prosecution (for the OFT) under the Consumer Protection from Unfair Trading Regulations. Author of Blackstone Guide to Consumer Rights Act 2015. Instructed to defend in largest ever consumer case brought by National Trading Standards into fake Government websites. Instructed to advise for consumer law by CMA. Regularly acts in an advisory capacity on UK and EU regulatory consumer law for multi-national companies, private prosecutors and individuals. Has particular experience on the overlap between EU law and UK criminal law (in the context of competition, environmental law and discrimination). This area is about to become an interesting mess. General crime: Wide range of experience in defending and prosecuting all types of criminal cases. Grade 4 prosecutor. Specialist in confiscation. Particular expertise in homicide (including cases involving infant death), environmental cases, money laundering and cases involving gambling. Regularly instructed as leading junior counsel, by CPS Appeals Unit, and CPS Specialist Fraud Division. Please see the 5 Paper Buildings website for additional details.

Career: Birmingham University LLB Warwick University LLM Called to the Bar 1996.

Publications: Denis has been commissioned by Oxford University Press to lead a team writing the Blackstone's Guide to the Consumer Protection Act (2015).

BARSAM, Talia

Devereux, London
020 7353 7534
barsam@devchambers.co.uk

Featured in Employment (London)

Practice Areas: Specialises in all areas of employment law, including discrimination law, whistleblowing, unfair dismissal, equal pay, breach of contract, TUPE, restrictive covenants and jurisdictional issues. Particular expertise in complex disability discrimination claims and whistleblowing claims. Clients include multinational corporations in the financial, technology, construction, retail and transportation sectors, public sector clients including NHS Trusts and trade unions and senior executives. Expertise in education law and professional negligence.

Professional Memberships: ELBA, ELA, COMBAR, PNBA.

Career: Called 2006. Admitted to the New York Bar 2008. Member of the Equality and Human Rights Commission Panel of Approved Counsel since 2011.

Publications: Contributing author, "Discrimination Law" (Bloomsbury Professional (formerly Tottel Publishing)); Jordans Employment Law Service.

Personal: LLM New York University, BA Affiliate Law Cambridge University, BA English University of Birmingham.

BARTON, Fiona QC
5 Essex Court, London
020 7410 2000
barton@5essexcourt.co.uk
Featured in Police Law (All Circuits), Inquests & Public Inquiries (All Circuits), Professional Discipline (London)

Practice Areas: Police Law; Inquests and Inquiries; Public and Administrative; Professional Discipline. The Independent Inquiry into Child Sexual Abuse [2016] – for Surrey Police in the Anglican Church Section of the Independent Inquiry into Child Sexual Abuse. Hillsborough Inquests [2014-2016] – For South Yorkshire Police in the inquests into the Hillsborough Disaster. Nunn [2014] – Acting for Suffolk Constabulary in the Supreme Court concerning post-conviction disclosure obligations. Al Hilli Alps Murders [2013] – For Surrey Police in the family proceedings concerning care of the All Hilli children following the murder. A v B Constabulary [2013] – Test case concerning the vetting of police contractors. Powell v Chief Constable of West Midlands Police [2013] – Complex high value civil jury action. Icelandic Bank Collapse (Tchenguiz) [2012] – Successfully defended the actions of City of London Police re the arrest of Robert Tchenguiz in connection with his dealings with the collapsed bank. Cumbria Shootings Inquests [2011] – Represented Cumbria Police in the inquests into the deaths of Derrick Bird and his victims. 7/7 London Bombing Inquests [2010] – For City of London Police in the inquests into the deaths of the 52 victims. L v Commissioner of Police of the Metropolis [2009] UKSC 3 – Supreme Court test case on behalf of the Commissioner concerning the scope of Enhanced Criminal Record Certificate.

Career: Called to the bar 1986; Silk 2011.

BARTON, Zoe
Selborne Chambers, London
020 7420 9500
zoe.barton@selbornechambers.co.uk
Featured in Real Estate Litigation (London)

Practice Areas: Commercial and traditional chancery, specialising in property litigation, trusts and estates and related professional negligence.

Professional Memberships: Chancery Bar Association, Property Bar Association, Association of Contentious Trust and Probate Specialists, Charity Law Association.

Career: MA Hons (Edin), Dip Law (City) (Scholar). Called Gray's Inn 2003 (Scholar). Zoë is recognised by both Chambers & Partners and Legal 500 for her expertise in her principal practice areas. Her practice spans all areas of Chancery and she is frequently instructed in cases which involve fraud, or call for equitable remedies, including those which concern multiple jurisdictions. In the context of land, Zoë is regularly briefed by those with significant land portfolios, including regularly on behalf of Network Rail. She deals with both real property and landlord & tenant matters and regularly acts for lenders in claims arising in connection with mortgages. Her traditional chancery practice concentrates on breach of trust claims and private client work, including contentious probate, advisory work concerning the construction variation or rectification of wills and the administration of estates; she is instructed by both beneficiaries and trustees, including on behalf of numerous charities. Zoë draws on her considerable expertise in general commercial transactions, trusts and property issues to effectively handle complex and sophisticated professional negligence disputes on behalf of both claimants and defendants.

BARWISE, Stephanie QC
Atkin Chambers, London
020 7404 0102
sbarwise@atkinchambers.com
Featured in Construction (London)

Practice Areas: Stephanie's general commercial practice includes all aspects of the law relating to the construction and civil engineering industry in litigation, arbitration and adjudication. She also has acted as adjudicator and arbitrator. Her experience includes major road and tunnel construction, construction of railways, defects and locomotives, ship refurbishment, North Sea oil rig construction, refinery construction including seismic factors, biofuels plants, Ladbroke Grove Rail Inquiry, LUL Piccadilly and Jubilee line upgrades, offshore wind farms and fully computer automated gantry cranes in Hong Kong as well as experience in various other disputes related to computer software. Her practice also involves the causes and spread of fire, professional negligence in general in particular of architects, engineers and surveyors. A further area of specialisation is procurement: she has acted for central and local government, NHS Trusts (PFI agreements) and utility companies (acting under framework agreements). Stephanie has experience of all major forms of contracts including NEC3. She is fluent in French and competent in German.

Professional Memberships: TECBAR; COMBAR.

Career: Educated at Bolton School and Cambridge University (Downing College). Called to the Bar 1988. Joined Atkin Chambers 1989. Silk 2006. Bencher Middle Temple 2010. Vice chair of Middle Temple Estates Committee 2014. Chair of Middle Temple Estates Committee 2015.

BASTIN, Lucas
Quadrant Chambers, London
020 7583 4444
lucas.bastin@quadrantchamberscom
Featured in Public International Law (London)

Practice Areas: Lucas specialises in public international law, investment treaty arbitration and international commercial arbitration. Having practised before joining the Bar for several years in these areas, Lucas carried across to the Bar a strong full-time practice in these areas. Lucas is often engaged not only to advise on complex PIL/ITA issues, but also to have full-time carriage of contentious matters in these areas. He is experienced in managing teams new to or short-handed in this area of large-scale, high-value international dispute resolution – a role to which Lucas' previous law firm experience makes him well suited. He has been counsel in arbitrations under ICSID, ICC, SCC, LCIA, UNCITRAL and ad hoc Rules (see Chambers' website). He also advises governments, companies and individuals on PIL matters, especially: State responsibility; State and head of State immunity; investment protection; treaty interpretation; enforcement; extradition; WTO law; and EU/UN sanctions. Lucas is Adjunct Professor of Public International Law at Pepperdine University, and has published extensively on State immunity, investment treaty arbitration, WTO law, general PIL and commercial law.

Professional Memberships: ESIL/ASIL/ILA/COMBAR.

Career: BA, First (USyd); LLB, First (Usyd); BCL, First (Oxon).

BASU, Dijen QC
5 Essex Court, London
020 7410 2000
basu@5essexcourt.co.uk
Featured in Police Law (All Circuits)

Practice Areas: Practice Areas: Public and administrative law, representing the police in civil claims, inquests and inquiries. Examples: Koraou v Greater Manchester Police [2015] 3 WLR 966 – Court of Appeal (alleged failure to investigate a serious attack), Ipswich Town FC v Suffolk Police [2016] 4 WLR 118 (charging for policing), R (M) v Hampshire Police [2015] 1 WLR 1176, CA (search regime for sex offenders compatible with their human rights), The Alexander Perepilichnyy Inquest (Russian 'whistleblower', whose death aged 43 while jogging, is unexplained), R (Mackaill) v IPCC [2014] EWHC 3170 (judicial review arising out of 'Plebgate'– the incident at the gates of Downing Street), R {Minter) v Hampshire Police [2014J 1 WLR 179, CA (extended sentences and sex offender registration), R (A) v Chief Constable of Kent [2013] EWCA Civ 1706, CA (Enhanced Criminal Record Certificates), R (Mengesha) v Commissioner of Police of the Metropolis [2013] EWHC 1695 (Admin) ('kettling'), R (R) v Chief Constable of West Midlands Constabulary [2014] 1 Cr App R 16 (collection of DNA from historic offenders).

Career: Called to the Bar 1994, Silk 2015; Crown Court Recorder 2010; Attorney General's Panel of Special Advocates 2009; registered with the GMC to practise medicine 1992; M.B., B.S. degree {with distinction in surgery) from what is now Guy's, King's and St Thomas' School of Medicine 1991.

Personal: Private pilot's licence for both aeroplanes and helicopter.

BATES, Alan
Monckton Chambers, London
020 7468 6352
abates@monckton.com
Featured in Competition/European Law (London), Telecommunications (London)

Practice Areas: Competition law; EU law; public law; public procurement; telecoms & utilities regulation; VAT & duties. Current and recent cases include: Gibson v Pride Mobility (UK's first 'opt-out' competition law class action); European Federation for Cosmetic Ingredients (CJEU, scope of EU ban on animal tested cosmetics); Durham Company v HMRC (VAT treatment of supplies made by local authorities); Achbita and Bougnaoui (CJEU, distinction between direct and indirect discrimination); Germany v Council & Parliament (CJEU, division of powers between EU Council and Parliament); British Airways v Commission (appeal against fine for competition infringement); Ofcom/Royal Mail abuse of dominance investigation.

Professional Memberships: Administrative Law Bar Assoc (executive committee); Bar European Group; Competition Law Assoc; Procurement Law Assoc; State Aid Law Assoc; UK Assoc of European Law; UK Environmental Law Assoc.

Career: Called 2003. Previous roles: Judicial Assistant to Lord Bingham (2004-05); Tutor in Public Law, King's College London (2004-05); Legal Research Assistant, Law Commission of E&W (2000-01). Pegasus scholarship at Chapman Tripp and New Zealand Commerce Commission (2008). Member, Middle Temple Hall Committee (elected 2016) and Education Committee. Previously member of Bar Standards Board Education Committee.

Publications: 'State aid' chapter in Bellamy & Child, European Union Law of Competition (6th and 7th editions); 'Compatibility of aid' chapter in Bacon, European Union Law of State Aid (2nd and forthcoming 3rd editions).

Personal: MA (Cambridge), Law, 2000. LL.M (Pennsylvania), 2002, Thouron fellowship. Trustee, UK Animal Law Centre. Chair of Governors, Barrow Hill Junior School.

BATES, John H
Old Square Chambers, London
020 7269 0300
bates@oldsquare.co.uk
Featured in Environment (London)

Practice Areas: Over the last 20 years John has acquired considerable experience in criminal and civil cases involving environmental work – although it is in the civil courts that John has been appearing in more recently. Barr v. Biffa [2011] EWHC 1003 (TCC) was a Group Litigation case of odour nuisance from a landfill with 152 Claimants. John did the legal advocacy for the Claimant which involved a detailed examination of the regulatory scheme in both English and EC legislation as the Defendant raised the defence of statutory authority. They also argued that compliance with the regulatory scheme was a 'reasonable use' of land for the law of nuisance. D's statutory authority argument was rejected but they succeeded on 'reasonable use.' The Court of Appeal overturned this decision and the case is being retried. Dobson v. Thames Water [2011] EWHC 3253 (TCC) was a Group Litigation nuisance case concerning odour and mosquitoes with over 1300 Claimants. John dealt with the mosquito case, cross examining expert witnesses and doing the opening and closing

speeches on them. He was also involved in the detailed negligence claim in respect of the design and operation of the sewage treatment works and drafted the particulars of negligence. John also acts in many water and drainage cases such as abstraction, flood defence or fishing rights. In Robert Lindley Ltd v East Riding of Yorkshire Council [2016] UKUT 0006 he obtained compensation for a farmer whose fields were flooded following flood relief work.
Publications: UK Marine Environmental Law; UK Waste Law; Water and Drainage Law; co-author of Liability for Environmental Harm; Fact Sheets on Environmental Access to Justice Rules in the EU Member States for the European e-Justice Portal.

BATES, Justin
Arden Chambers, London
020 72424244
justin.bates@ardenchambers.com
Featured in Real Estate Litigation (London), Social Housing (London)
Practice Areas: Housing, Property, Landlord and Tenant, Local Government.
Professional Memberships: HLPA; PBA.
Career: BA (Hons) Oxford; LL.M (Toronto). Called 2003. Significant cases in 2015/16 include McDonald v McDonald [2016] UKSC 28 (junior counsel for the RLA, interveners); Triplerose Ltd v 90 Broomfield Road RTM Co Ltd [2015] EWCA Civ 282 (junior counsel); R (Croydon Property Forum Ltd) v Croydon LBC [2015] EWHC 2403 (Admin) (junior counsel); R (Rotherham Action Group Ltd) v Rotherham MBC [2015] EWHC 1216 (Admin) (junior counsel); Avon Ground Rents Ltd v 51 Earls Court Square RTM Co Ltd [2016] UKUT 22 (LC); Queensbridge Investments Ltd v Lodge and others [2015] UKUT 635 (LC); Cowling v Worcester Community Housing Ltd [2015] UKUT 496 (LC); ; Gateway (Leeds) Management Ltd v Naghash [2015] UKUT 333 (LC); Tedla v Cameret Court Ltd [2015] UKUT 221 (LC); Hastings BC v Braear Developments Ltd [2015] UKUT 145 (LC).
Publications: Deputy General Editor, Encyclopedia of Housing Law; co-author "Leasehold Disputes"; contributor to Arden & Partington on Housing Law.
Personal: In 2015, gave evidence to the House of Lords on housing and the Equality Act and the Welsh Assembly on the Renting Homes (Wales) Bill. Assisted Labour with the Housing & Planning Act.

BATES, Pascal
6 Pump Court, London
020 7797 8400
pascalbates@6pumpcourt.co.uk
Featured in Health & Safety (London)
Practice Areas: Prosecuting and defending regulatory prosecutions brought by national and local enforcement agencies – primarily health and safety but also railway, fire, food, trading standards and environment: eg. HFRS v Newsum (2016), Ipswich BC v KFG Quickserve t/a Burger King (2016), HSE v ConocoPhillips (2016), HSE v UK Power Networks (2016). Advised HSE/ORR on the structural collapse onto the railway at Gerrards Cross. Currently engaged in another multi-party major structural collapse involving four fatalities at Great Yarmouth and in two separate cases involving major supermarket groups. Confidential/strategic advice on regulatory and commercial matters: eg. enforceability of non-compete clauses; joint venture agreement between developers; allegedly botched foreign mineshaft construction works. Inquests, including crushing in a lift and death in custody/hospital. Disclosure/PII in both civil and criminal contexts. General common and public law with an emphasis on statutory construction: eg. rights to UK passports; scope of controls on scuba diving; allocation of statutory powers between rival public bodies. Commercial contract and property: eg. Halberstam v Gladstar [2015] EWHC 179 (QB), Meretz Investments v ACP [2008] Ch 244, Haller v Deutsche Bank. Contested probate.
Career: MA (Cantab); called 1994; Standing Counsel to HSE & ORR; A List for Environment Agency; Occasional Lecturer UCL

BATES, Richard
29 Bedford Row Chambers, London
020 7404 1044
rbates@29br.co.uk
Featured in Family/Matrimonial (London)
Practice Areas: Matrimonial finance, particularaly interested in farming cases; children (private law).
Professional Memberships: FLBA.
Career: Called 1992.
Personal: Married to Victoria Francis with two young sons. Educated at Bedford School, University of Durham (BA Hons).

BATE-WILLIAMS, John
Temple Garden Chambers, London
020 7583 1315
jbw@tgchambers.com
Featured in Personal Injury (London)
Practice Areas: Personal injury, fatal accidents, insurance, serious crime.
Professional Memberships: Personal Injury Bar Association, Criminal Bar Association.
Career: The Senior Junior in TGC, John has a substantial Personal Injury, Fatal Accidents and Insurance practice. Described by the solicitor who advised Balfour Beatty to instruct him in the Hatfield Rail Crash case as a "pragmatic street fighter", he has acquired a reputation for sound judgment, realistic and practical advice and excellent advocacy. 70% of his practice involves the representation of insurers in high value claims, usually involving catastrophic head injuries or injuries of maximum severity. He has particular experience in exposing exaggerated and dishonest claims – in Harnett -v- Northover (2012) he obtained an Order requiring the Claimant to pay the entire costs of the action. His objective approach has ensured that he continues to receive a volume of instructions on behalf of Claimants in substantial and unusual claims including the Nepal Air Disaster (acting in all the British fatal claims) and the Germanwings (pilot suicide) case, and helicopter and powerboat accidents. In Dufosse -v- Melbury Events (2011) he persuaded the Court of Appeal to find Santa and an Elf responsible for the Claimant's downfall, and received The Times award for the Courtroom Joke of the Year. He was appointed a Crown Court Recorder in 2000.
Personal: Married with 2 children, lives in the Cotswolds and has a small farm in Western Australia.

BATT, Charanjit
Queen Elizabeth Building QEB, London
020 7797 7837
c.batt@qeb.co.uk
Featured in Family/Matrimonial (London)
Practice Areas: All aspects of private family law with an emphasis on financial matters (financial relief, Part III, and Schedule 1); private law children (including relocation); and child abduction. Has been instructed as a junior in a number of high value finance cases, including appearing in interlocutory hearings on her own against leading counsel, and has also been instructed as a junior in Children Act cases. Has a particular interest in cases with jurisdictional and/or international issues. Reported cases: Z v A [2012] 2 FLR 667 (with Lucy Stone QC).
Professional Memberships: FLBA; Bar Council member from 2006-2010 Career: LLB (University of Birmingham); LLM (UCL); and Internship at the Chambers of Parag Tripathi (Senior Advocate of the Supreme Court and former Additional Solicitor General) New Delhi.
Personal: Speaks Punjabi (native), Hindi (native), and conversational Urdu and Spanish.

BAXTER, Mark
5 Stone Buildings, London
020 7242 6201
clerks@5sblaw.com
Featured in Chancery (London), Court of Protection (All Circuits)
Practice Areas: Mark has a private client Chancery practice encompassing both contentious and non-contentious work (but weighing in favour of the former) with a particular emphasis on wills and probate, trusts, estates and family provision, Court of Protection work and professional negligence related to these areas. In the High Court and County Court, Mark is regularly instructed on behalf of claimants and defendants in contentious probate and Inheritance (Provision for Family and Dependants) Act 1975 cases, and for trustees and beneficiaries in applications concerning the administration and execution of trusts and estates (including construction and removal claims), as well as Variation of Trusts Act 1958 applications. Recently, Mark has succeeded in a 1975 Act claim on behalf of a cohabitant where cohabitation was disputed, and appeared in the High Court and Court of Appeal in what is now the leading case on what amounts to a sufficient interest in an estate to bring a contentious probate claim, as well as acting in a seven-figure mutual wills claim and advising on the tax treatment of settled pension benefits. In the Court of Protection, Mark is frequently instructed in contested attorneyship and deputyship applications, and contested statutory will applications (typically against a background of highly contentious family disputes), as well applications by attorneys and deputies for the Court's authority to take certain steps he is often instructed by the Official Solicitor. He speaks and writes regularly on all areas of his practice.
Professional Memberships: Chancery Bar Association, Property Bar Association, the Denning Society.
Career: Called 2006.
Publications: Co-author of 'Risk and Negligence in Wills, Estates and Trusts' (OUP, 2009 and second edition, 2014). Regular contributor to professional journals. Lectures on all areas of his practice, particularly probate, tax, and Court of Protection matters.

BAYFIELD, Daniel QC
South Square, London
020 7696 9900
danielbayfield@southsquare.com
Featured in Chancery (London), Banking & Finance (London), Restructuring/Insolvency (London), Sports Law (London)
Practice Areas: Daniel specialises in business and finance law, with a strong emphasis on insolvency and restructuring, banking law and general commercial litigation.
Professional Memberships: COMBAR, Chancery Bar Association, Bar Sports Law Group.
Career: Since 2008, Daniel has been advising the administrators of the key UK Lehman Brothers companies. Other high-profile cases include: MF Global, Game Group, HMRC v The Football League, Rangers FC, Portsmouth FC, Woolworths, HMV, Eurosail, Belmont, Stanford International Bank, Sigma, XL Airways, Cheyne Finance, Prudential v Powerhouse, MG Rover, TXU, T&N, Enron, Cenargo and Silven v RBS. Daniel has acted on numerous restructurings / schemes of arrangement including: Hibu, APCOA, Independent Insurance, Orion, Cortefiel, Magyar, Zlomrex, Countrywide, Sovereign Marine, DAP and BAIC. Daniel also has a substantial sports law practice. His clients include the FA Premier League and the Football League and he has acted for a number of well-known footballers and boxers. Daniel was appointed Queen's Counsel in 2016.
Publications: Contributor to Lightman & Moss: The Law of Receivers and Administrators of Companies (Sweet and Maxwell), and Moss, Fletcher & Isaacs: The EC Regulation on Insolvency Proceedings (OUP).

BAYOUMI, Mona
Civitas Law, Cardiff
0845 0713 007
mona.bayoumi@civitaslaw.com
Featured in Employment (Wales & Chester)
Practice Areas: Mona specialises in employment law. Mona has a broad practice in employment encompassing unfair dismissal claims, whistleblowing and all forms of discrimination and harassment claims. Mona is regularly instructed in matters with complex allegations often involving multiple Claimants. Mona also has extensive experience in claims involving TUPE regulations including those where employers are insolvent. Mona also enjoys a busy public law practice where she regularly appears in the Upper Tribunal and High Court on judicial review applications in areas including asylum and immigration, housing, community care and welfare matters. Mona has also appeared in a number of reported cases.
Professional Memberships: Wales and Chester Circuit PIBA (Personal Injury Bar Association) She has been a member of the Attorney General Panel of Counsel since November 2010 and a member of the Welsh Government Panel of Counsel since September 2012 for employment and public law ELA (Employment Law Association) PIBA (Personal Injury Bar Association) Wales and Chester Circuit.
Career: Mona was called to the Bar in 2004.
Personal: Mona is an approved external examiner for the Bar Standards Board She is a member of the Wales Committee of the Equality and Human Rights Commission

In her spare time Mona enjoys travelling, theatre, cooking and attending the gym.

BAZLEY, Janet QC
1 Garden Court Family Law Chambers, London
020 7797 7900
bazley@1gc.com
Featured in Family/Matrimonial (London)

Professional Memberships: Janet is a committee member of the Family Law Bar Association and of the Law Reform Committee of the Bar Counsel. She is also a member of Resolution.

Career: Janet is joint Head of Chambers at 1 Garden Court, Temple. She practices at the highest level across a broad spectrum of children work and also acts in a range of financial cases, particularly those involving an international aspect. Her children work includes cases with medical issues, relocation of children, domestic and international adoption, legal issues in modern families and disputes regarding child arrangements. Janet has appeared in many landmark cases including Re H-L [2013] EWCA Civ 655, ('necessary' test for instruction of experts), Re C (A child) [2014] EWFC 31 (funding of Respondents in private law Children Act proceedings), Re S and T [2015] EWHC 1753 (international adoption) and In the Matter of the Human Fertilisation and Embryology Act 2008 (Cases A, B, C, D, E, F, G & H) [2015] EWHC 2602 (Fam) (assisted conception: declarations of paternity). Janet, who has considerable experience as a part-time judge, also undertakes Early Neutral Evaluation in children and financial proceedings. Awarded the grade of MCIArb by the Chartered Institute of Arbitrators, Janet is authorised to conduct arbitrations in both family finance and children cases. She is a trainer on IFLA's children arbitration course for which she helped to write the materials.

BEALE, Anna
Cloisters, London
020 7827 4000
abe@cloisters.com
Featured in Employment (London)

Practice Areas: Anna is an employment specialist who has particular expertise in cutting edge discrimination cases. She is well regarded for her ability to simplify complex legal issues and provide practical, comprehensible advice to lay clients. Anna acts for a wide variety of clients including individual claimants, trade unions, large public sector organisations and multinational companies. Reported cases include: JP Morgan Europe Ltd v Chweidan [2012] ICR 268 (CA: direct disability discrimination); Elstone v BP [2010] ICR 870 (EAT: extended the ambit of the whistleblowing legislation) and Wong v Igen Ltd [2005] ICR 931 (CA: junior counsel in the leading case on the burden of proof in discrimination claims). Anna has also acted on behalf of both claimants and respondents in complex equal pay claims, including two national test cases. In recent years, she has addressed both a European Commission seminar and the Industrial Law Society's Oxford Conference on discrimination issues. Anna also maintains a personal injury and clinical negligence practice. She has particular experience in claims involving complex spinal injuries and issues relating to consent.

Professional Memberships: Secretary, Industrial Law Society. Member of ELA, ELBA, IER, Bar Pro Bono Unit, ELAAS, HRLA and PIBA.

Career: Called to the Bar in 2001.

Publications: Co-editor of 'Discrimination in Employment: a claims handbook' (LAG 2013); co-author of 'Age and Employment' (European Commission 2011) and 'Employment Law and Human Rights' (2nd ed, OUP 2007); contributor to 'Family Rights at Work' (Jordans 2012).

Personal: Educated at Llanidloes High School and Magdalen College, Oxford (BA Jurisprudence 1st class).

BÉAR, Charles QC
Fountain Court Chambers, London
020 7353 0329
cbr@fountaincourt.co.uk
Featured in Administrative & Public Law (London), Aviation (London), Commercial Dispute Resolution (London), Local Government (London), Public Procurement (London)

Practice Areas: Wide-ranging practice covering: general commercial litigation, judicial review, and public procurement. Commercial work includes: fraud, conspiracy, business sales/joint ventures, restitution, freezing and search orders, minority shareholder claims. Sector experience includes life sciences, aviation, telecoms and high-tech engineering. Practises in Commercial Court and Chancery Division, also Cayman Grand Court. Public law work is based in the Administrative Court and the appellate courts and includes numerous reported cases across fields varying from regulatory challenges to human rights. Also has significant experience of constitutional, financial and vires issues for central government, regulators, local authorities, NHS entities and other agencies. Regularly advises public bodies on major procurement issues. Also carries out employment work including post-termination injunctions (springboard, restrictive covenant, confidential information etc), bonus issues and strike litigation. Recent cases include: Alpstream AG and others v PK Airfinance and GE Capital [2015] EWCA Civ 1318; Taberna Europe CDO II Plc v Selskabet [2015] EWHC 871 (comm); Standard Life Assurance Limited v Corr and others [2015] EWHC 3844 (Comm); Re Solicitor Duty Contract challenges; R on the application of the London Oratory School v Schools Adjudicator [2015] EWHC 1012 (Admin); Bluefin Insurance Services Ltd v Financial Ombudsman Service Ltd [2014] EWHC 3413 (Admin).

Professional Memberships: COMBAR, ALBA, ELBA.

Career: Called to the Bar 1986. QC 2003. Recorder 2003.

Personal: Born 1963. Magdalen College, Oxford, 1982-5 (1st Class Hons, Jurisprudence).

BEASLEY, Tom
Radcliffe Chambers, London
020 7831 0081
tbeasley@radcliffechambers.com
Featured in Chancery (London)

Practice Areas: Commercial and chancery litigation, mediation and arbitration. Cases include contractual disputes, civil fraud, asset tracing, property (landlord and tenant, and real property), company, partnership, insolvency, directors and other fiduciaries, trusts, wills and professional negligence.

Professional Memberships: Chancery Bar Association, Property Bar Association, British Russian Lawyers Association.

Career: Bristol University, English Literature (1998-2001). Scholar of Middle Temple. Called to the Bar in 2003.

BEDFORD, Erica
Kings Chambers, Manchester
0345 034 3444
clerks@kingschambers.com
Featured in Costs Litigation (All Circuits)

Practice Areas: The law of costs. Erica practices exclusively in the law of costs, with emphasis on costs arising from personal injury claims and commercial litigation. She regularly appears before Regional Cost Judges and in the SCCO. She is frequently instructed on appeal up to High Court level. She has particular specialism in the application of the various 'Distance Selling Regulations', arguments arising out of the fixed cost regimes, claims involving 'broken retainers', issues concerning the indemnity principle and procedural points of law. She frequently appears in CCMCs where costs are a particular concern. Additionally, she undertakes non contentious drafting and advisory work. She has recently qualified as a mediator.

Professional Memberships: Association of Cost Lawyers

Career: University of Leeds LLB (Hons): 2003. Admitted as a Solicitor: 2010. Admitted as a Cost Lawyer: 2011. Call to the Bar: 2012.

BEDFORD, Michael QC
Cornerstone Barristers, London
020 7242 4986
michaelb@cornerstonebarristers.com
Featured in Planning (London)

Practice Areas: All areas of town and country planning, environmental law, highways and compulsory purchase, including inquiries and hearings, examinations, advisory work, and High Court challenges. Michael also deals with related property matters including covenants, easements, public rights of way, and village greens. He acts for developers, landowners, and public sector clients across England and Wales, including via direct access. He has a substantial inquiry-based practice covering a full range of development projects. He has both promoted and resisted major housing schemes, retail proposals, waste developments, renewable energy schemes, and urban regeneration projects. He has promoted a large number of development plans and is currently engaged in several DPD matters, housing and retail appeals, and highway schemes. His practice embraces large-scale infrastructure projects (including several new roads and a DCO) and smaller developments in sensitive areas with heritage or environmental constraints. Experienced in managing and coordinating large teams of expert witnesses and in cross-examining on a wide range of professional disciplines.

Professional Memberships: Planning & Environmental Bar Association; National Infrastructure Planning Association.

Career: Called 1985; QC 2016.

Publications: Contributor: "Gambling for Local Authorities – Licensing, Planning and Regeneration" (2010). Contributor: "Environmental Law" (Burnett-Hall) (2012). Contributor: "Cornerstone on the Planning Court" (2015).

Personal: LLB (Hons) Lond. Barstow Law Scholarship. David Karmel Chancery Scholarship.

BEDWORTH, Georgia
Ten Old Square, London
020 7405 0758
georgiabedworth@tenoldsquare.com
Featured in Chancery (London), Court of Protection (All Circuits), Trusts (London)

Practice Areas: Georgia has a thriving traditional chancery practice with particular focus on trusts and estates matters, both contentious and non-contentious. Georgia also has considerable expertise in Court of Protection matters. She is frequently instructed in matters concerning multi-million pound trusts and estates. Georgia's strong real property background gives her a particular edge when dealing with landed estates. Her practice extends to applications under the Variation of Trusts Act to vary high value settlements, including those with a foreign element.

Professional Memberships: Georgia Bedworth sits on two sub-committees of the Chancery Bar Association.

Career: Georgia Bedworth was called to the Bar in 2001 after graduating from St Hugh's College Oxford with a 1st Class Honours degree in law and a distinction in the BCL. Georgia's reported cases include: Buzzoni v HMRC [2014] 1 WLR 3040 – IHT – Gift with Reservation of Benefit; Ingrey v King [2015] EWHC 2137 (Ch) – application for directions by an executor as to required retention prior to distribution of estate where deceased entered into a film partnership scheme which had not yet run its course: Allfrey v – Allfrey [2015] EWHC 1717 – variation of trusts to extend the perpetuity period and accumulation period; C v C [2015] EWHC 2699 (Ch); [2016] WTLR 223 – variation of trusts governed by Kenyan law; Re Portman Estate [2015] EWHC 536 (Ch) [2015] WTLR 871 – extension of trustee powers under s 57 Trustee Act 1925 to streamline administration of a large estate Giles v Rhind (No. 2) [2008] EWCA Civ 118; [2009] Ch 191 – section 423 Insolvency Act 1986 and limitation.

Publications: Georgia is the joint author of the fifth edition of Rossdale on Probate and Administration of Estates (Wolters Kluwer 2016) and of Tolley's Inheritance Tax Planning, the first edition of which was nominated as the STEP private client book of the year. Georgia contributed to Fosters Inheritance Tax, one of the leading practitioner texts on that subject and has written articles for the STEP journal, Trusts and Estates Law and Tax Journal, the Solicitors Journal and the Landlord and Tenant Review on diverse legal issues, most recently on variation of foreign trusts under the VTA 1958.

BEER, Jason QC
5 Essex Court, London
020 7410 2000
clerks@5essexcourt.co.uk
Featured in Administrative & Public Law (London), Police Law (All Circuits), Inquests & Public Inquiries (All Circuits), Professional Discipline (London)

Practice Areas: Inquests and Inquiries, Police, Public & Administrative, Professional Discipline and Corporate Manslaughter/Health and Safety investigations and prosecutions. Acted in the following public inquiries: The Independent Inquiry into Child Sexual Abuse, Undercover Policing Inquiry, Anthony Grainger Inquiry, Al-Sweady Inquiry, Leveson, Baha Mousa, Billy Wright, Rosemary Nelson, Legionella in Barrow-in-

Furness, Hutton, Mubarek, Shipman, and Stephen Lawrence; the following inquests: Hillsborough, University of Manchester Radiation Inquests, 7/7 Bombings, Porton Down Nerve Gas Inquest, and New Cross Fire; the following JRs: Miranda (terrorist powers), GC & C (retention of biometric data), Children's Rights Alliance v Secretary of State for Justice (positive duties under ECHR); and the following police claims: Phone Hacking, Hayes v Merseyside Police (necessity of arrest), Howarth v Gwent Police (misfeasance), Richardson v West Midlands Police (necessity of arrest), Madeline McCann, Omagh Bombing, and Operation Ore.
Professional Memberships: ALBA, PIBA, ARDL.
Career: Called to the Bar 1992; Silk 2011; Previously Junior Counsel to the Crown (Common Law – A Panel). Developed Vetted. Recorder on SE Circuit.
Publications: "Public Inquiries" (OUP, 2011).

BEEVER, Edmund
St Philips Chambers, Birmingham
0121 246 7000
ebeever@st-philips.com
Featured in Commercial Dispute Resolution (Midlands), Employment (Midlands)
Practice Areas: Commercial litigation, including directors' duties. High Court commercial (contractual disputes; freezing and search orders) and employment (including Wright v Governing Body of Bilton High School and Another [2002] ICR 1463, Jaddoo v Birmingham City Council [2004] All ER (D) 410 (Oct)). Commercial springboard injunctions in insurance industry. Insolvency related disputes (SSTI v Blunt [2005] 2 BCLC 463, Re Blakemore and Son Ltd [2007] EWHC 963 (Ch)) and complex discrimination or dismissal cases. Regular clients include plc's, government departments and local authorities.
Professional Memberships: Chancery and Commercial Bar Association, COMBAR, Employment Lawyers Association.
Career: Head of Employment Group, St Philips Chambers. Accredited Advocacy Tutor. Attorney General Panel Counsel 1997, re-appointed 2007 and 2012. Appointed fee paid Employment Judge 2013.
Personal: Merton College, Oxford. Sport, family and property renovation.

BEGGS, John QC
Serjeants' Inn Chambers, London
020 7427 5000
jbeggsqc@serjeantsinn.com
Featured in Police Law (All Circuits), Inquests & Public Inquiries (All Circuits), Professional Discipline (London)
Practice Areas: John Beggs QC was called to the Bar in 1989 and took silk in 2009. John specialises in public and administrative, police, employment, inquests and inquiries and professional discipline law. An earlier edition notes that "he is probably the best cross-examiner outside the Criminal Bar" and that he is "extremely quick in his thinking, to the point and knows his stuff. If you want someone to win your case, he's the man." He was ranked as one of the 100 top silks by The Chambers Bar 100 2014. Please visit the Serjeants' Inn Chambers website for his profile, which sets out full details of his practice including relevant work of note.
Professional Memberships: ARDL.
Publications: "Police misconduct, complaints, and public regulation", OUP, July 2009; "Public Order: Law and Practice" Blackstone's Practical Policing, with George Thomas and Susanna Rickard, OUP, 2012.

BEGLAN, Wayne
Cornerstone Barristers, London
020 7242 4986
wayneb@cornerstonebarristers.com
Featured in Local Government (London), Planning (London), Social Housing (London)
Practice Areas: Administrative law; local government; regulatory law; planning; housing and employment.
Career: Called in 1996, Wayne Beglan undertakes most forms of local government work and also has a wide private client base. He has particular expertise in judicial review, planning (housing, retail, waste, roads and s.106 agreements), housing, regeneration, landlord and tenant, employment, governance, procurement and contractual work for local authorities RPs, developers and corporations. He is currently promoting Local Plans for Luton, Waverley and Welwyn Hatfield. He has appeared in various tribunals and has extensive experience in the High Court and significant experience in the appellate courts. A list of his cases appears on his Chambers website profile.

BEGLEY, Laura
9 Gough Square, London
020 7832 0500
clerks@9goughsquare.co.uk
Featured in Personal Injury (London), Clinical Negligence (London)
Practice Areas: All aspects of clinical negligence work and personal injury work with particular expertise in criminal injuries compensation claims. Her growing clinical negligence practice, which she enjoys enormously, is diverse and covers matters ranging from hypoxic birth injuries to delayed diagnosis of cancers and negligently performed surgery. The bulk of her personal injury work relates to serious spinal, brain, orthopaedic and psychiatric injuries arising out of employer's liability, road traffic accidents or criminal injuries claims. She regularly appears in Criminal Injuries Compensation Appeal hearings, in judicial review proceedings and from time to time the Court of Appeal arising out of this work. Her work is complex and high value. She is approachable, dynamic and knowledgeable. She regularly lectures in Personal Injury and Clinical Negligence Law.
Professional Memberships: Personal Injuries Bar Association; Professional Negligence Bar Association; Association of Personal Injuries Lawyers.
Career: LLB (Hons) Leeds (1991); BVC (Inns of Court School of Law) (1993); Called to the Bar 1993 (Lincoln's Inn); Pupillage completed at 9 Gough Square, with Grahame Aldous QC and Richard Merz and thereafter tenant at 9 Gough Square.
Publications: Co-author of Criminal Injuries Compensation Claims (Law Society) and; Guide to 2008 Scheme General Editor of an updated edition of Criminal Injuries Compensation Claims due to be published later in 2015 by the Law Society. Contributing editor Kemp and Kemp 'The Quantum of Damages.' Contributing editor Kemp and Kemp 'Law Practice and Procedure.' Contributing editor 'Guide to RTA Liability' (Jordans). Contributing editor the newly revised 'Butterworths Personal Injury Service.' General Editor of the Third Edition of 9 Gough Square's 'Clinical Negligence Claims, a Practical Guide' published in 2015. Medicine Science and the Law, the journal of the British Academy of Forensic Sciences (editorial board).
Personal: She has three young children; twin boys and a girl who keep her on her toes and are a constant source of fun and inspiration. She loves riding her bike and running when time allows. She appreciates the odd glass of wine and good food and any opportunity to sit in one place (preferably in sunshine) and read novels.

BELGROVE, Sophie
Devereux, London
020 7353 7534
belgrove@devchambers.co.uk
Featured in Employment (London)
Practice Areas: Specialises in all areas of employment law, advising and appearing in the EAT, the High Court and the Court of Appeal. Considerable experience of complex litigation, with particular expertise in relation to unfair dismissal, discrimination, equal pay, breach of contract, business transfers, restraint of trade, share schemes, bonus schemes and pensions. Clients include FTSE 100 companies, banks and building societies, dotcom companies, insurance companies, high street chains, airlines, airport authorities, charities and a wide range of public and private sector clients.
Professional Memberships: ELBA, ELA, COMBAR, LCLCBA.
Career: Called 2001; Middle Temple Benefactors Scholarship and Harmsworth Entrance Exhibition (2000).
Publications: Contributor to Jordans Employment Law Service.
Personal: BA (Oxon).

BENNETT-JENKINS, Sallie QC
2 Hare Court, London
020 7353 5324
salliebennett-jenkinsqc@2harecourt.com
Featured in Crime (London)
Practice Areas: Sallie Bennett-Jenkins QC was appointed Queen's Counsel in October 2006 following a period of 8 years as Treasury Counsel. Sallie is an incisive and skilful advocate and her commitment to providing the highest level of service to her clients has led to her being first choice defence counsel in a wide range of practices, varying from charges of fraud, sexual impropriety or murder. Sallie lectures in the UK and overseas on a range of topics and to visiting judiciary to the UK on issues relating to sexual offences. She was appointed as a Recorder in 1998 and is authorised to try cases relating to Serious Sexual Offences. Sallie's vast skillset means her practice is unusually varied, her recent instructions include advising a client in relation to the bribery and corruption enquiry allegedly concerning Rolls Royce, representing a client in a 3 month long trial relating to historic child sexual exploitation (Operation Bullfinch), representing a US national in relation to causing death by dangerous driving whilst on business for a leading pharmaceutical company in the UK. She also recently appeared as the first appellant in the conjoined cases that were heard before The Lord Chief Justice to consider the impact of R v Jogee on joint enterprise and secondary liability.
Professional Memberships: Criminal Bar Association, Fraud Lawyers Association, Financial Services Lawyers Association, South Eastern Circuit.

BENSON, Imran
Hailsham Chambers, London
020 7643 5000
imran.benson@hailshamchambers.com
Featured in Costs Litigation (All Circuits)
Practice Areas: Imran is a robust advocate who provides clear and decisive advice whenever asked. He has an unstuffy attitude and works hard to help his clients get the best possible result. Imran's busy practice encompasses a broad range of work but with an emphasis on professional liability, costs, commercial law and insurance. He also has an arbitration practice. Imran's work often involves bitterly contested disputes. He has successfully appeared in the High Court and Court of Appeal (both led and unled) and is regularly in the Senior Courts Costs Office (SCCO). In appropriate cases, he also accepts instructions direct from businesses and members of the public.
Professional Memberships: LCLCBA, PNBA, SEC.

BENTHAM, Daniel
Queen Elizabeth Building QEB, London
020 7797 7837
d.bentham@qeb.co.uk
Featured in Family/Matrimonial (London)
Practice Areas: His practice is made up almost exclusively of family law, with a particular emphasis on financial cases (including cohabitation disputes and applications under Schedule 1 of the Children Act).

BERESFORD, Stephen
Ropewalk Chambers, Nottingham
0115 9472581
stephenberesford@ropewalk.co.uk
Featured in Commercial Dispute Resolution (Midlands)
Practice Areas: He has wide experience of appearing in specialist and general higher courts and tribunals across a range of commercial and property and chancery matters. He is a frequently used accredited mediator and is head of the mediation team at Ropewalk Chambers. He advises and represents a broad range of clients in all types of commercial disputes, including business contracts; mercantile, financial and other contractual disputes; companies; partnerships; arbitrations; secrecy litigation; emergency remedies; commercial fraud (both insurance and non-insurance related) and local government related disputes. His property and chancery work includes Technology and Construction Court work and arbitrations; insurance disputes; land rights, development and damage; Land Registry hearings and business leases. He is well known for his professional negligence work in respect of all of the above. He focuses on ascertaining what both the professional and lay clients wish to achieve and then providing them precise advice and with a clear road map to achieve it.
Professional Memberships: Professional Negligence Bar Association Planning and Environmental Bar Association Commercial Bar Association Midlands Chancery Bar Association.
Career: Called 1976; University of Birmingham.
Personal: Away from the Bar, his interests include collecting antique firearms, playing jazz guitar, performing close-up magic and watching Leicester Tigers.

BERGIN, Terence QC
4 Pump Court, London
020 7842 5555
TBergin@4pumpcourt.com
Featured in Information Technology (London)
Practice Areas: Supply of computer systems; the licensing of software; internet, including domain name disputes and data protection. His clients have included the government, major software houses, local authorities and a public transport provider. AFD Software v DCML Ltd [2015] EWHC 453 (Ch). Southwark v IBM [2011] EWHC 549 (TCC), Data Direct Technologies Ltd v M&S Plc [2009] EWHC 97 (Ch), Fujitsu Services Ltd v EDS Ltd (2007), TTI Team International Ltd v Axarte Ltd (2007), NEDDC v Anite Public Sector Ltd (2007), Serco Solutions Ltd v The Cabinet Office (2004), Foster v Fortis Clearing Bank Ltd (2004), Co-Operative Group (CWS) Ltd v International Computers Ltd (2003), SAM Business Systems Ltd v Hedley & Co [2002] EWHC 2733 (TCC), Psychometric Services Ltd v Merant International Ltd (2002), The Boots Company Plc v Amdahl (UK) Ltd (CA 2000), Anglo Group Plc v Winther Browne & Co Ltd (2000).
Professional Memberships: TECBAR, Society for Computers and the Law, PNBA, COMBAR.
Career: Called 1985.

BERKELEY, Iona
8 New Square, London
020 7405 4321
iona.berkeley@8newsquare.co.uk
Featured in Intellectual Property (London)
Practice Areas: Barrister specialising in all areas of intellectual property law, including patents, trade marks, copyright, database rights, registered and unregistered design rights, passing off, confidential information, and related areas, such as IP related contractual disputes (in particular International Arbitrations) and media and entertainment. Cases include Glaxo v Sandoz (Trade Mark validity), Speciality European Pharma v Doncaster Pharmaceuticals (Pharmaceutical parallel importation/trade mark infringement case); DKH Retail v H Young Operations (UK Design Right and Community Design); Coward v Phaestos (Copyright infringement/ownership issues); Whirlpool Corp. v Kenwood (Trade Marks); EPI Environmental Technologies v Symphony (Confidential Information, contract, passing off); The Football Association Premier League v Panini (Copyright); Kirin-Amgen Inc. v TKT and Roche (Patents). For a comprehensive CV visit chambers website at www.8newsquare.co.uk.
Professional Memberships: Intellectual Property Bar Association (IPBA) and Chancery Bar Association.
Career: Called 1999, Middle Temple.
Publications: Iona Berkeley is co-author of Kerly's Law of Trade Marks and Trade Names (15th Ed) and its supplement and co-author of Laddie Prescott and Vitoria on the Modern Law of Copyright and Designs (4th Ed).
Personal: Educated at South Hampstead High School; Trinity College, Oxford (1997 Biological Sciences); City University (1998 Dip Law); Inns of Court School of Law.

BERRAGAN, Neil
Kings Chambers, Manchester
0345 034 3444
clerks@kingschambers.com
Featured in Chancery (Northern), Professional Negligence (Northern), Commercial Dispute Resolution (Northern), Partnership (Northern), Restructuring/Insolvency (Northern), Sports Law (The Regions)
Practice Areas: Neil practises almost exclusively in the specialist business courts (Mercantile, Chancery and TCC) in Manchester, Leeds & Liverpool, in London and on appeal from those courts. He specialises in commercial and chancery litigation, and is frequently instructed in urgent interim applications. His practice includes all types of business, company and shareholder disputes, insolvency, partnership, commercial fraud, sports law, and associated professional negligence. Recent cases include: Ticket2Final OU v Wigan Athletic AFC [2015] (Ch) successfully defended claim for fraud, McGill v SEM & Bolton Wanderers FC & others [2014] (Merc), successfully defending claims of fraud & conspiracy by football agent on behalf of club, officers and employees; R (May) v CIMA [2013] EWHC 1574 (Admin), successful application to quash finding of professional misconduct arising out of a charge of misuse of confidential information; Smith v Butler [2012] BCC 645 (CA), [2012] 1 BCLC 444, successfully defending interests of chairman and majority shareholder against unauthorised action by MD.
Professional Memberships: Northern Chancery Bar Association, Northern Circuit Commercial Bar Association, Chancery Bar Association, Professional Negligence Bar Association, Bar Pro Bono Panel.
Career: University: Oxford (Pembroke College); Degree: Jurisprudence (MA); Called: 1982 (Grays Inn).

BERRY, Anthony QC
9 Bedford Row, London
020 7489 2727
clerks@9bedfordrow.co.uk
Featured in Crime (London)
Practice Areas: Murder and fraud are the main ingredients of his practice in the UK and elsewhere. In recent years has dealt in Malawi with the case of Dr Chilumpha, the Vice President of Malawi for conspiring to murder the President as well as High Treason, a capital offence, by planning to murder a number of cabinet ministers in the aftermath of the assassination. This year, before a court martial at Bulford, he defended Corporal Fulton who faced an allegation of rape of a female colleague at their barracks in Germany several years after the incident. He was acquitted. In addition, he represented Suhail Uddin at St Albans Crown Court. He was acquitted of murdering his sister at their joint home. At Liverpool Crown Court he represented a Sicilian sea captain for having twice the legal limit of alcohol in his system when in charge of MV Quercinella in the Manchester Ship Canal with 11,000 tons of petrol on board. He pleaded guilty and received a short suspended sentence. In 2013 he defended Marine A for the murder of an Afghan insurgent near a remote outpost. Historically, his cases include the Stansted Afghan Hijacking case and the trial arising out of the extension of London's Jubilee Line
Professional Memberships: Member of Panel of Advocates at the International Criminal Court, Criminal Bar Association (Former Secretary), International Bar Association, European Criminal Bar Association, Association of Commonwealth Lawyers, Association of Military Court Advocates, Association of Fraud Lawyers.
Career: BA (Philosophy and Psychology), Lincoln College, Oxford. Called to the Bar 1976, Silk 1994 Head of Chambers from 1999. Former member General Council of the Bar. Bencher Gray's Inn 2000
Publications: Personal: Downside School and Lincoln College, Oxford (BA, PPP). Married, 4 children. Member of the Royal Mid Surrey Golf Club, Hampton Court Royal Tennis Club, Harlequins Rugby Football Club and Surrey Cricket Club.

BERRY, James
Serjeants' Inn Chambers, London
020 7427 5000
jberry@serjeantsinn.com
Featured in Police Law (All Circuits)
Practice Areas: James Berry was called to the Bar in 2006. James specialises in public and administrative, police, Court of Protection, employment, inquests and inquiries, professional discipline, clinical negligence and healthcare, product liability, civil liberties and human rights law. An earlier edition notes that "the attention to detail he displays when he's on his feet is amazing" and that "he combines gentlemanly robustness with fierce intelligence." Please visit the Serjeants' Inn Chambers website for his profile, which sets out full details of his practice including relevant work of note.
Professional Memberships: Treasury C Panel, ALBA, ARDL, ELBA, PNBA.
Publications: UK Police Law Blog (editor); Police Misconduct, Complaints and Professional Regulation (2nd ed, co-author, forthcoming; Medical Treatment: Decisions and the Law (2nd ed, co-author); Firearms Policing (forthcoming); Medical Law Reports (contributor).

BERTRAM, Jonathan
7BR, London
020 7242 3555
jbertram@7br.co.uk
Featured in Clinical Negligence (London)
Practice Areas: Clinical Negligence, Personal Injury, Product Liability, Inquests and Employment
Professional Memberships: Association of Personal Injury Lawyers, Employment Lawyers Association, Professional Negligence Bar Association
Career: Jonathan has built up a busy and varied clinical negligence practice and examples of his recent caseload include being instructed as sole counsel in claims arising from alleged birth injuries, such as cerebral palsy, failures to treat compartment syndrome leading to amputations, injuries arising from bariatric surgery, injuries arising from failures to diagnose and treat kidney and liver diseases, late diagnosis of cancer claims and claims arising from cosmetic surgery procedures. He has successfully pursued claims advanced on the basis of systemic failures by Trusts that have then led to injuries to patients, e.g. by failing to adequately staff maternity units. He is also frequently instructed in claims against dentist and ophthalmic professionals. He also has a particular interest in inquest work and he frequently acts for bereaved families in cases where it is hoped that the evidence obtained during the inquest will assist with supporting a future clinical negligence claim. In addition to clinical negligence Jonathan undertakes a wide variety of personal injury and employment litigation. He has also recently developed a significant product liability practice, particularly in the field of metal-on-metal hip replacements.

BHOGAL, Kuljit
Cornerstone Barristers, London
020 7242 4986
kuljitb@cornerstonebarristers.com
Featured in Social Housing (London)
Practice Areas: Housing, community care, Court of Protection.
Professional Memberships: Founding supporter of Social Housing Lawyers Association (SHLA). Adminstrative Lawyers Bar Association, (ALBA), Property Bar Association (PBA), Association of Regulatory and Disciplinary Lawyers (ARDL).
Career: Kuljit has established herself at the forefront of the social housing bar. Kuljit is recognised for her thorough knowledge of the law, exceptional advocacy skills and tactical awareness. She has an excellent understanding of her client's needs. Her broader practice also includes community care and Court of Protection work and her practice covers policy matters as well as advice in individual cases. She is an expert on anti-social behaviour law and her book 'Cornerstone on Anti-Social Behaviour: The New Law' has received glowing reviews. She is the 'go-to' person for issues relating to Public Space Protection Orders, complex or high profile ASB matters and the other powers introduced by the ASBCPA 2014. Kuljit has recently advised the Mayor on his Housing Strategy for London, and was instructed in Tachie v Welwyn Hatfield BC [2013] EWHC 3972 (QB); [2014] PTSR 66, a case which concerned the contracting out of homelessness functions. Her housing practice covers homelessness, claims for possession (all grounds), housing management issues (including disrepair, contested successions, unlawful subletting, 'Right to Buy' disputes), unlawful eviction, benefit fraud and the investigation and prosecution of offences, houses in multiple occupation, service charge disputes, mental health and Equality Act 2010 points. Her expertise in mental health issues, community care law and Court of Protection work means she is ideal for cases where there is a crossover between the three disciplines.
Publications: Author of 'Cornerstone on Anti-Social Behaviour: The New Law'.

BHOSE, Ranjit QC
Cornerstone Barristers, London
020 7242 4986
ranjitb@cornerstonebarristers.com
Featured in Local Government (London), Real Estate Litigation (London), Social Housing (London)
Practice Areas: Ranjit has a varied practice, with particular specialism in the following: local government & public law; social housing; commercial landlord and tenant; licensing; civil litigation; property; rating and local taxation. He has strong links with local authorities, major private sector landlords and developers, and registered providers. His cases include: Sims v Dacorum DC (2014) (SC – housing and property, human rights); Evans v Wimbledon and Putney Commons Conservators (2014) (CA – easements over common land); Thompson v Oxford CC (2014) (CA – lap dancing); Superstrike v

Rodriguez (2013) (CA – tenancy deposits); Bean Leisure v Leeds CC (2014) (Admin – lap dancing); Tachie v Welwyn Hatfield DC (2013) (Admin – public procurement, Teckal; contracting-out); BDW Trading v South Anglia (2013) (Chancery – service charges, QLTAs); Bristol CC Council v Digs (2014) (Admin – HMO licensing). Ranjit's current workload includes a number of property related negligence claims, many major service charge disputes, a licensing appeal over the largest nightclub in the UK, advice and representation across the breadth of local authority and registered provider functions and decision-making.
Career: B.A. University College, Oxford. Called to the Bar 1989, QC 2012.
Personal: Interests include running (slowly), DJing (semi-retired, but persuadable).

BICKERSTAFF, Jane QC
9 Bedford Row, London
020 7489 2727
clerks@9bedfordrow.co.uk
Featured in Crime (London)
Practice Areas: Jane prosecutes and defends in all areas of serious crime. She specialises in sexual offences, particularly in the defence of historical, multi complainant cases. Jane has a human touch and a real feel for the cross examination of children and vulnerable witnesses. She frequently lectures on all aspects of this subject. Jane regularly defends and prosecutes in murder cases with particular expertise in joint enterprise. The excellence of her cross examination has been remarked upon by members of the senior judiciary and by her opponents. Jane represents police officers before the Crown Court, supported by many years experience defending at police disciplinary tribunals. Throughout her career she has also acted in cases of fraud and financial crime.
Professional Memberships: Criminal bar Association, Association of Regulatory and Disciplinary Lawyers, Member of South Eastern Circuit, registered with the Bar Counsel – Public Access Directory.

BICKFORD SMITH, James
Littleton Chambers, London
020 7797 8600
jbs@littletonchambers.co.uk
Featured in Employment (London)
Practice Areas: Commercial and employment law. In particular: 1) banking and finance litigation including fraud 2) litigation arising out of employment/fiduciary relationships, often involving injunctive relief or high value damages claims in the context of team moves (sole Counsel for two Defendants at Bluefin Trial, junior Counsel for First Defendant in Marathon Asset Management litigation) 3) other commercial litigation (e.g. junior counsel in dispute over registration of €3.4bn freezing order) 4) LLP work (unfair prejudice, member disputes, member "exits") 5) specialist work at interface of employment and chancery work (employees, team moves and IP rights) 6) statutory employment practice based on oral advocacy. Appears in Tribunal claims involving substantial reputational and other risks for Respondents (eg defending mid-Staffordshire NHS Trust following dismissal involving patient assault, defending FTSE 100 companies against discrimination claims). Also represents Claimants facing substantially-resourced Respondents.
Professional Memberships: COMBAR, ELBA.
Career: Called to Bar in 2008 as mature entrant. Double First Class Honours (Balliol College). Masters and Doctorate. Former Lecturer at Oxford University. Also studied at Ecole Normale Supérieure.
Publications: Since 2012, monthly column A Practical View From the Bar, on civil procedure and litigation tactics, for the Practical Law Company.

BIGNELL, Janet QC
Falcon Chambers, London
020 7353 2484
bignell@falcon-chambers.com
Featured in Real Estate Litigation (London)
Practice Areas: All aspects of commercial and residential real property, landlord and tenant and related professional negligence and insolvency. Reported cases include: Stadium Capital Holdings (No 2) Ltd v St Marylebone Co Plc (damages for trespass); Sunberry Properties v Innovate Logistics Ltd (in administration) (alienation and the Insolvency Act); Norwich City Council v McQuillin (restrictive covenants); Leftbank Properties Ltd v Spirit Group (rent review/ arbitration); Simmons v Dresden (terminal dilapidations); Bakewell Management v Brandwood (easements).
Professional Memberships: Chancery Bar Association, LCLCBA, Property Bar Association, ARBRIX.
Career: MA (Cantab), BCL (Oxon). Called 1992. Recorder 2009. QC 2015. Fellow of the Chartered Institute of Arbitrators and Member of the CIARB President's Property Dispute Resolution Panel; ADR Group Accredited Civil and Commercial Mediator.
Publications: Author, Lewison's Drafting Business Leases; Co-Author, Registered Land Law and Practice under the LRA 2002; Co-Author; Registered Land: The New Law; Editorial Board, Landlord & Tentant Review; Former Contributor, Encyclopaedia of Forms & Precedents, Auctioneers, Estate Agents & Valuers and Fisher & Lightwoods Law of Mortgage.

BIRD, Andrew
5 St Andrew's Hill, London
o7767371376
andrewbird@5sah.co.uk
Featured in POCA Work & Asset Forfeiture (All Circuits)
Practice Areas: Fraud, asset forfeiture and confiscation, Judicial Review, overlap between civil and criminal jurisdictions.
Professional Memberships: Fraud Lawyers' Association Proceeds of Crime Lawyers' Association Criminal Bar Association South Eastern Circuit.
Career: Andrew Bird read law at Cambridge and was called in 1987. He has been a tenant at 5 St Andrew's Hill since 1989. He started with a broadly-based common law practice but from 1995 onwards concentrated on heavy crime and both the civil and criminal aspects of asset forfeiture. He has a particular interest and specialism in cases where the civil and criminal jurisdictions overlap. He has been involved in many of the appellate cases in cash forfeiture, including CCE v Muneka and UKBA v Angus, and edits Smith, Owen & Bodnar on Asset Recovery in this field. His civil recovery work includes the leading case of DARA v He & Chen. One of the few specialists in HMRC and UKBA condemnation, his work has included the Hoverspeed litigation, CCE v Newbury and high profile wildlife cases. His criminal work includes Montila (HL) and prosecutions of the online bank UMBS, land-banking frauds and high-profile money-laundering. In 2005 he was appointed Standing Counsel to the RCPO. He is a Grade 4 CPS prosecutor and on the "A" Panels both for the SFO and the A-G's Treasury Panel for civil work. He has considerable experience in JR challenges to criminal process, including search warrants, including the Faisaltex, Eastenders and Chatwani litigation, and POCA production orders. He regularly lectures and gives seminars in Asset Forfeiture, Money Laundering and Police powers.
Publications: Smith Owen & Bodnar on Asset Recovery (OUP).

BIRD, Simon QC
Francis Taylor Building, London
020 7353 8415
clerks@ftbchambers.co.uk
Featured in Planning (London)
Practice Areas: Planning and environmental law.
Professional Memberships: Planning & Environment Bar Association. National Infrastructure Planning Association.

BIRTLES, Samantha
18 St John Street, Manchester
(0161) 278 1800
family@18sjs.com
Featured in Family/Matrimonial (Northern)
Practice Areas: Family Law – Children cases, particularly Care Proceedings.
Professional Memberships: Northern Circuit, Family Law Bar Association.
Career: Called in July 1989, Pupillage at 18 St John Street Chambers from Sept 1989 to Sept 1990. Barrister at 18 St John Street Chambers September 1989 to present.
Personal: Married, one son. Speaks conversational French.

BLACKBURN, John QC
Atkin Chambers, London
020 7404 0102
clerks@atkinchambers.com
Featured in International Arbitration (London)
Practice Areas: John accepts appointments as arbitrator in both domestic and international arbitrations with both the seat and the project around the world over a variety of disputes including construction, engineering, oil and gas. As well as appointments in ad hoc arbitrations, he is frequently appointed either as chairman or as co-arbitrator in references under the International Chamber of Commerce Rules, under the UNCITRAL Rules and under the LCIA Rules.
Professional Memberships: A bencher of Middle Temple.
Career: Appointed Queen's Counsel in 1984, he practiced as Counsel at the English Bar and in International Arbitration until 2006. Since then, John practice has been as an international arbitrator.

BLACKETT-ORD, Mark
5 Stone Buildings, London
020-72426201
clerks@5sblaw.com
Featured in Partnership (London)
Practice Areas: Barrister and arbitrator specialising in partnership, trusts, professional negligence, probate, ecclesiastical law and general Chancery litigation. Notable cases include: Wilson dec'd [2013] EWHC 499 (Ch); Manning v English [2010] EWHC 153 (Ch); Hopton v Miller [2010] EWHC 2732; Mary Gray Ritchie deceased [2009] EWHC 809; Olins v Walters [2009] Ch212 (mutual wills); Tann v Herrington [2009] EWHC 445 (partnership); Re St Peter's Draycott {2009}Fam 93(Court of Arches); Hopper v Hopper [2008] CA EWCA Civ 1417 (proprietary estoppel); M Young Legal v Zahid [2006] 1WLR 2562 CA, where Wilson LJ at para 31 refers to "Mr Blackett-Ord's excellent book"; Sandhu v Gill[2006] Ch 456 CA; Price v Williams-Wynn [2006] WTLR (for the claimant); Braymist v Wise Finance Co [2002] 2 AER 333 CA; Polly Peck plc v Nadir [1992] The Times 30.7.92 CA.
Professional Memberships: ACTAPS, STEP, APP, Chancery Bar Association and The Ecclesiastical Judges Association.
Career: Oxford University. Called 1974, Lincoln's Inn. Master of Bench Lincoln's Inn (2006) FSA (2006). Sits as an arbitrator. Fellow of the Society of Antiquaries, Chancellor of the Diocese of Leicester.
Publications: Author 'Partnership' (Butterworths 1997, 2nd ed 2002, 3rd ed (Tottel) 2007) 4th ed and 5th ed(Bloomsbury Law) 2012 and 2015, co-authored with Sarah Haren. Editor 'Partnerships and LLP's' in Atkins Court Forms.

BLACKMORE, Sally
Ely Place Chambers, London
020 7400 9600
sblackmore@elyplace.com
Featured in Social Housing (London)
Practice Areas: Real property, landlord and tenant; housing; chancery; administrative and local government law; human rights.
Professional Memberships: ALBA, PBA, ChBA, ALA.
Career: Sally has appeared in the High Court, Court of Appeal, County Court and property tribunal. In housing matters, she has particular expertise in dilapidations, unlawful eviction and harassment, and in possession matters involving deposit, public law and human rights issues (e.g. Optima Community Association v Ker [2013] EWCA Civ 579; Leicester City Council v Shearer [2013] EWCA Civ 1467). She has advised commercial and residential clients on – amongst other things – the construction of leases, easements and covenants, express and implied trusts and boundary matters. She has advised and represented applicants and local authorities in homelessness appeals and housing and community care judicial reviews. She deals with service charge disputes and all questions stemming from or relating to FTT decisions.
Personal: Sally studied English at the University of London and also has a Masters in Medieval Studies from the University of Bristol. She was an English language teacher in the UK, Greece, Estonia and Cameroon before becoming a barrister. She has been a member of the Islington Legal Advice Centre since 2004.

BLACKWOOD, Andrew Guy QC
Quadrant Chambers, London
020 7583 4444
guy.blackwood@quadrantchambers.com
Featured in Insurance (London)
Practice Areas: Guy has a broadly based commercial practice including banking, civil fraud, commodities, energy including utilities and mining, insurance and reinsurance and related professional negligence and ship-

ping. Guy has substantial experience of trial advocacy in the Commercial Court.
Career: Called to the Bar in 1997. Took Silk in 2014.

BLAKE, Andrew
11KBW, London
020 7632 8500
andrew.blake@11kbw.com
Featured in Employment (London)
Practice Areas: Andrew's practice covers the full range of employment advice and litigation, with a particular recent focus on discrimination and whistleblowing claims in the Employment Tribunals. He has been instructed in a number of multiple equal pay claims in the public sector over the last decade, and is now seeing an increasing number of equal pay claims in the private sector. He also advises regularly on all areas of employment law including unfair dismissal, TUPE, collective consultation and working time, and acts for a wide range of employers and claimants. In the High Court, Andrew is often instructed on business protection and breach of contract claims. Recent appellate cases include: Cockram v Air Products UKEAT/0122/15 and UKEAT/0038/14 (justification of age discrimination, and affirmation of contract in constructive dismissal claims); Birdi v Dartford Visionplus Ltd UKEAT/0289/12 (adjournments due to the ill-health of a party); Prest v Mouchel Business Services Ltd UKEAT/0604/10 (selection of comparators in equal pay claims); Newcastle upon Tyne NHS Trust v Armstrong (No. 2) [2010] ICR 674, EAT (material factor defence in equal pay claims); and Blackburn v Chief Constable West Midlands Police [2009] IRLR 135, CA (material factor defence in equal pay claims. Outside of the court room, Andrew is an accredited mediator, as well as an experienced party representative in negotiations and mediations.
Professional Memberships: ELBA, ELA.
Career: Called 2000.
Publications: Contributor to Tolley's Employment Law Handbook.
Personal: Cambridge University (BA), University of California Berkeley (LLM).

BLAKE, Julian
11KBW, London
020 7632 8500
julian.blake@11kbw.com
Featured in Administrative & Public Law (London)
Practice Areas: Julian is an experienced member of the Attorney General's civil panel of counsel. He has a wide range of public law experience. This includes four appearances in the Supreme Court over the last year – covering issues of detention and mistreatment in Afghanistan and Iraq and the removal of the Chagos Islanders from the British Indian Ocean Territory. He has appeared in many of the significant national security cases, including the David Miranda terrorism stop, the financial restrictions against Bank Mellat and the leading naturalisation and exclusion challenges in the Special Immigration Appeals Commission. Julian also has a background in criminal litigation and is often instructed to appear in public law challenges to criminal or regulatory investigations/proceedings and provides advice to corporations and individuals in respect of liabilities arising from international and domestic sanctions.
Career: Called to the Bar in 2006.
Publications: Contributor, EU Law in Criminal Practice. Contributor, Miller on Contempt. Practitioner Editor, Blackstone's Criminal Practice.
Personal: Julian graduated from Sidney Sussex College, Cambridge before being appointed as a Fox International Fellow at Yale University, USA.

BLAKELEY, Richard
Brick Court Chambers, London
020 7379 3550
richard.blakeley@brickcourt.co.uk
Featured in Commercial Dispute Resolution (London), Competition/European Law (London)
Career: Richard has particular expertise in commercial dispute resolution, civil fraud, banking, competition law and EU law (with a particular specialism in EU sanctions). In 2015 he was awarded Young Practitioner of the Year by the World Export Controls Review, having been active in some of the highest-profile sanctions matters reported by WorldECR. Recent high-profile cases include acting on behalf of the claimant Libyan Investment Authority in a multibillion-dollar fraud claim concerning five complex financial transactions which the LIA alleges were procured by corruption; representing the Russian Federation in response to claims brought by Georgia in the in the ECtHR relating to the August 2008 war in South Ossetia; obtaining a $165m freezing order for a wealthy Kazakh client; acting for the defendants to claims brought by Chevron in respect of an alleged $18bn conspiracy to obtain a fraudulent judgment in Ecuador; numerous banking matters including DZ Bank v LBIE and the JPMorgan v BVG litigation, involving a CDO transaction worth in excess of $200million; and representing the FA Premier League in respect of Ofcom's investigation into the PL's rights selling practices. Richard has also been instructed in dozens of sanctions matters in recent years, in both the English and EU courts.

BLAKER, Gary QC
Selborne Chambers, London
020 7420 9500
gary.blaker@selbornechambers.co.uk
Featured in Real Estate Litigation (London)
Professional Memberships: Chancery Bar Association, Property Bar Association, Professional Negligence Bar Association.
Career: Called 1993; QC 2015, Bencher of Middle Temple 2015. Gary has a Chancery practice with an emphasis on property litigation, civil fraud and professional negligence. He has appeared in many reported cases in recent years including Van Collem v Van Collem [2015] EWHC 2258 (Ch) and [2015] EWHC 2184 (Ch) (civil fraud and whether there were good reasons for non-attendance at trial); Spielplatz Ltd v Pearson [2015] EWCA Civ 804 (whether a bungalow formed part of the land upon which it sits); Watson Farley & Williams v Ostrovizky [2015] EWCA Civ 457 (whether a Greek lawyer was negligent in providing advice); H Waites Ltd v Hambledon Court Ltd [2014] 1 EGLR 119 (airspace above garages); Watson Farley & Williams v Ostrovizky [2014] EWHC 160 (QB); Afia v Mellor LTL 4/11/13 (promissory estoppel claim); Derek Hodd Ltd v Climate Change Capital Ltd [2013] WLR (D) 238 (misdescribed party to a contract); Rivercove Trustee Ltd v Euro Rubber Lines [2012] EWHC 2593 (TCC) (oil spill at a factory).
Publications: Gary regularly provides seminars on property related matters and has written numerous published articles on the subject.

BLATCHLY, Phillip
Fourteen, London
020 72420858
pblatchly@fourteen.co.uk
Featured in Family/Matrimonial (London)
Practice Areas: Phillip is a private client specialist. His practice focuses on resolving the financial consequences when relationships end, whether through separation, divorce or death. He is routinely instructed in cases involving assets, trusts, complicated company structures and partnerships. Phillip has acted in many cases involving preliminary technical legal arguments, on the strength of which the main proceedings stand or fall. These have included recently: the extent to which a party should be held to an agreement; the effect of a party's failure to comply with the rules of disclosure, and establishing / resisting claims by interveners to ownership of assets that would otherwise be subject to the court's dispositive powers. He continues to receive instructions in private law children matters, especially in respect of contested relocation applications (to Hague and non-Hague Convention jurisdictions). Recent work of note includes: – Representing the successful respondent before the Court of Appeal in N -v- N [2014] EWCA Civ 314. That decision clarified the law on non-disclosure in matrimonial proceedings, and considered, for the first time, whether the duty endures beyond the first instance judgment if there is a pending appeal. Phillip was involved in drafting the respondent's paperwork that defeated two subsequent attempts to refer the issue to the Supreme Court; – Instructed on behalf of interveners and establishing, through lengthy cross-examination, that the entirety of the matrimonial assets beneficially belonged to them (and thus were not matrimonial assets), and – A complicated case concerning the ability of the court to set aside a disposition, in circumstances where the effect of the set aside might have nullified a bank's security under a mortgage. Phillip is trained and experienced in receiving instructions under the Direct Public Access scheme in his areas of expertise.

BLAYNEY, David QC
Serle Court, London
020 7242 6105
dblayney@serlecourt.co.uk
Featured in Chancery (London), Banking & Finance (London), Commercial Dispute Resolution (London), Company (London), Partnership (London)
Practice Areas: General commercial and chancery litigation, particularly: commercial, banking, insolvency, companies, trusts, charities, contracts, professional negligence, joint ventures and partnerships. Particular specialism in financial, numerical and quantum issues. Major cases include: The RBS Rights Issue litigation; OFT v Abbey National (the bank charges litigation); Re Lehman Brothers International Europe (extended lien issues); Constantin Medien v Ecclestone (alleged bribery and conspiracy); Re Bradford & Bingley (banking); Re Bearwood College Trustees (charities); RBS v Winterthur (share sale warranties); Akkurate v Moschillo (directors duties); Credit Suisse v Ramot Plana (banking); Lemos v Coutts (trusts); Phillips v Symes (partnership/fraud); Re Continental Assurance (wrongful trading); SAAMCO (damages).
Professional Memberships: Chancery Bar Association, COMBAR.
Career: Called 1992. Silk 2013.
Personal: Born 1969. Educated at St Michael's (Jersey), Canford School and Lincoln College, Oxford (BA Law, 1st Class Honours). Married with two children. Interests include cycling, windsurfing, tennis and music.

BLEASDALE, Marie-Claire
Radcliffe Chambers, London
020 7831 0081
mcbleasdale@radcliffechambers.com
Featured in Real Estate Litigation (London)
Practice Areas: Specialisation: Commercial and residential property law, trusts, probate, administration of estates and associated professional negligence. Reported cases include LB Brent v Shulem B Association Ltd [2011] 1WLR 3014 (Ch) (service charges), Fineland Investments v Pritchard [2011] EWHC 1424 (trespass), Pritchard v Teitelbaum [2011] EWHC 1063 (warrants of possession), Odey v Barber [2008] Ch 175 (right of way), Manu v Euroview Estates [2008] 1 EGLR 165 (party wall), Church in Wales v Newton [2005] EWHC 631 (QB) (contract for the sale of land), Beanby Estates Ltd v Egg Stores (Stamford Hill) Ltd [2003] 1 WLR 2064 (service of notices).
Professional Memberships: Chancery Bar Association, Professional Negligence Bar Association.
Career: Educated at Ursuline Convent High School, Wimbledon and Queens' College, Cambridge (MA 1992). Called 1993. Shelford Scholar of Lincoln's Inn. Recorder 2009.

BLOCH, Selwyn QC
Littleton Chambers, London
020 7797 8600
sb@littletonchambers.co.uk
Featured in Employment (London)
Practice Areas: Selwyn Bloch QC is a leading employment/commercial law Silk. He has appeared in numerous leading cases, including Court of Appeal and High Court employment disputes involving confidential information, team moves, economic torts, restrictive covenants, garden leave, fiduciary duties and wrongful dismissal. Cases include aspects of intellectual property, private international law (including case to be heard in Supreme Court in November 2016 – concerning jurisdiction under Brussels Regulation (Recast) and anti-suit injunctions), numerous reported cases on confidential information, wrongful dismissal, fiduciary duties, restrictive covenants and conflict of laws in relation to restrictive covenants as well as springboard injunctions/team moves. Recent instructions include substantial claim in respect of employee benefit scheme subject to foreign law, team moves/confidential information cases, cases regarding enforceability of anti-team moves covenants (in employment contracts and LLP agreements) and enforceability of "claw back" provisions in employee benefit schemes; also, instructions by magic circle firms to advise on drafting of covenants and other business-protective provisions in top professional multi-jurisdiction LLP. Substantial experience in discrimination, whistleblowing and unfair dismissal disputes.

Professional Memberships: Employment Law Bar Association, ELA and COMBAR.
Career: Silk 2000. Called 1982 joined current chambers that year. Employment Judge (part time) since 2000. Joint Head of Chambers since 2015.
Publications: Co-author of leading textbook 'Employment Covenants and Confidential Information' (3rd edition 2009).
Personal: Interests include music, theatre, literature and sport.

BLOCK, Neil QC
39 Essex Chambers, London
020 7832 1111
neil.block@39essex.com
Featured in Personal Injury (London), Travel (London), Clinical Negligence (London), Product Liability (London)

Practice Areas: Principle areas of practice are insurance, property damage, professional and clinical negligence, contract, catastrophic injury, sports injury, group litigation and product liability. He has a particular expertise in claims arising out of accidents abroad (e.g. Stylianou v Yakamoto & Suncorps), Insurance (including policy coverage, avoidance/ fraud and material loss claims eg McGregor v Prudential Assurance Co , ICF v NIG (a series of claims involving policy coverage issues, solicitors negligence, CFA and CCA issues), Property damage (particularly fire claims), Professional negligence (including solicitors, construction related professionals, accountants, surveyors and valuers, architects, stockbrokers and insurance brokers), group actions and similar (Hepatitis C, Toxic Sofas,Supertram, shipyards, organo-phosphates, metal-on-metal hips, Jimmy Savile), personal injury and disease (including sporting cases eg Smolden v Whitworth; Nolan, O'Neill v Wimbledon; Fashanu, Watson v British Boxing Board of Control), catastrophic injury claims, clinical negligence (in particular paediatric brain damage, spinal injury, hospital associated infection), disaster litigation (eg Selby rail crash), product liability (eg Northwick Park drug trials, Scania 4 litigation, Sudan Red, Pollard v Tesco, Ide v ATB, Linkwise group action (toxic sofas), metal on metal hip cases).
Professional Memberships: Professional Negligence Bar Association, Personal Injury Bar Association, London Common Law and Commercial Bar Association, Bar Sports Law Group.
Career: Joint Head of Chambers. Called to the Bar in 1980; took Silk 2002. Bencher at Gray's Inn 2008. Accredited mediator.
Personal: BA (Hons), LLM (Exon). Joint Head of Chambers

BLUNT, Oliver QC
Furnival Chambers, London
020 7405 3232
oblunt@furnivallaw.co.uk
Featured in Crime (London)

Practice Areas: Entirely defence based practice specialising in murder, terrorism, and fraud and drugs cases.In the last two years has successfully represented News International's Graham Dudman (Managing Editor). Brandon Malinsky (Night Editor) in two separate Operation Elveden trials involving the Sun Newspaper. Also instructed on behalf of three other editors/ journalists whose cases were discontinued by the Prosecution prior to the trial. Twice instructed on behalf of the British Boxing Board of Control in two appeals (Couch and Chisora). Murder and Violent Crime: In the course of the last twelve months has conducted a series of gang related murders at the Central Criminal Court. Appeared for the lead appellant in R v Lewis Johnson and Others (seminal post-Jogee hearing before the Court of Appeal, comprising the Lord Chief Justice, President and Vice President of the QBD, 2016). Secured the acquittal of the principal defendant in R v Kessey and Others (CCC, Nov 2015). Previously conducted R v. Amoah and others (CCC, 2011, only murder/manslaughter acquittal in the first Victoria tube station murder trial), R v Peter Brown (Nottingham CC, 2010, double murder), R v Peter Tobin (Chelmsford CC, 2009, convicted serial killer), R v Ian Davis (CCC, 2009, double murder trial), R v Khan (CCC, 2010, arson related double murder) and R v Imran Hussain (CCC, 2010, Tooting double murder). Has also represented such clients as William Cockram (the Millennium Dome Robbery trial), Patrick Smith (Murder 2001-2, CCC), John Taft (the beauty in the bath' murder trial, Liverpool CC, 1999), Syd Owen ('Ricky' of Eastender's, wounding, Snaresbrook CC, 1995), Michael Sams (kidnapping, blackmail, murder, Nottingham CC, 1993). Fraud: Recently appeared in R v Colwell and Sayers (Newcastle CC, 2009, multi-million pound mortgage and tax fraud). Has also represented William Casey, acquitted in a multi-million pound arson/ insurance fraud (CCC, 1997), Kounnou, a £200 million shipping fraud (CCC, 2003), Devi Schahou in the Goldman Sachs trial (Southwark, 2004), and Dorian Morris, principal defendant in multi-million pound money laundering trial, acquitted (Kingston CC 2005). Sexual Crime: Including high profile cases such as Richard Baker (DJ rapist, CCC, 1999) Drugs:Successfully defended the principal defendant in Mohanjit Bhatia and Others in a multi-million pound drugs conspiracy (Kingston Crown Court 2014). Also appeared in R v. Cornick and others (Liverpool CC, 2010) conspiracy to import cocaine and cannabis, R v Faponnle and others (Blackfriars CC, 2010, heroin distribution), and R v Goren and others (CCC, 2008, Turkish heroin importation). Represented such clients as Paul Wyatt (Bolton CC, 2002-3), and R v Hillier and others (£150 million cocaine importation 1993). Terrorism: Instructed in Ul-Haq and Others, an ISIS related trial (CCC 2016). Has acted on behalf of the Iranian Embassy and represented two members of the Consular Staff in separate terrorist trials at the CCC (Tabari Abcou/ Fouladi). Appeared for the second defendant in R v Canning and Lamb (IRA trial, CCC, 1993), and in R v Shariff (21/7 trials, Kingston CC, 2007).
Professional Memberships: SE circuit, Criminal Bar Association.
Career: Called to the Bar 1974. Queen's Counsel 1994. Recorder 1991.
Personal: Born 8 March 1951. Married with four children. Member of Roehampton Club, Rossyln Park Rugby Club and Barnes Cricket Club.

BODNAR, Alexandra
39 Essex Chambers, London
020 7832 1111
alexandra.bodnar@39essex.com
Featured in Construction (London)

Practice Areas: Specialist in construction, engineering, energy and commercial disputes. Experience of complex, high-value international and domestic arbitration, litigation and adjudication. Appears regularly in the TCC and the Commercial Court. Experienced in PFI contracts, bonds and guarantees, energy, nuclear, utilities, infrastructure, insurance and reinsurance (including coverage and avoidance), professional negligence, international trade, jurisdictional issues and competition law. Familiar with the various standard form construction contracts.
Professional Memberships: SCL, TECBAR, COMBAR.
Career: Called 2004, Inner Temple.
Publications: Contributor to Construction Contracts by Richard Wilmot-Smith QC (3rd Ed). Contributor to the UK chapter in The Projects and Construction Review (4th Ed).

BOEDDINGHAUS, Hermann
4 Stone Buildings, London
020 7421 3712
h.boeddinghaus@4stonebuildings.com
Featured in Chancery (London), Company (London)

Practice Areas: Company litigation and advice. Insolvency law. Commercial litigation.
Professional Memberships: Member of COMBAR and the Chancery Bar Association.
Career: Hermann Boeddinghaus specialises in corporate and commercial disputes and insolvency law. He enjoys a busy litigation caseload, spread between the Chancery Division, the Commercial Court and international arbitration tribunals. Alongside this he has developed a substantial advisory practice. Hermann has represented Nigeria and Pakistan in major asset recovery claims against the families and associates of former rulers. Other clients have ranged from the world's largest banks to small family firms and individual entrepreneurs. He has built a reputation as a tough and persuasive advocate, much liked by his clients. Hermann began his career training as a solicitor with Slaughter and May, spending his first 6 months with Nigel Boardman. The firm's culture left a clear mark on his approach to practice: high standards in all aspects of his work, a readiness to go the extra mile, and an ability to see matters from his clients' perspective. Soon after qualifying he was called to the Bar. Within a week of commencing practice he appeared in his first reported case – Neuberger J's decision in Re Philip Alexander Securities & Futures Ltd. Hermann is adept at getting to grips with matters of a highly technical nature. His particular interest is in complex financial fraud; but he is equally at home in handling high value commercial arbitrations (construction, leisure, oil & gas, shipping). He has a strong academic background in science as well as law. Clients have repeatedly praised him for his rigorous attention to detail, tempered by a pragmatic, user-friendly approach. In 2013, Hermann was one of 200 junior barristers in England and Wales shortlisted for The Chambers 100 UK Bar.
Publications: Contributor, Annotated Companies Legislation (OUP).

BOMPAS, George QC
4 Stone Buildings, London
020 7242 5524
clerks@4stonebuildings.com
Featured in Chancery (London), Commercial Dispute Resolution (London), Company (London), Financial Services (London), Restructuring/ Insolvency (London)

Practice Areas: Principal areas of practice are company law (all aspects, advisory and litigation, including minority shareholder proceedings, insolvency and asset recovery), banking/insurance, financial services law, and professional negligence.
Professional Memberships: Chancery Bar Association and COMBAR. Called to the Bar of the British Virgin Islands and, for specific cases, to the Bars of Trinidad and Tobago and of the Cayman Islands.
Career: Called 1975. Junior Counsel to the DTI 1989-94. Silk 1994. Deputy High Court Judge 2003. Ordinary Judge of the Court of Appeal of Guernsey & Jersey. LCIA Arbitrator.
Publications: 'Company Investigations' in Tolley's Company Law; 'Funding Litigation and Assigning Claims' and 'Investigations' in Butterworths Practical Insolvency.
Personal: Born 1951. Oriel College, Oxford 1970-74.

BOND, Leisha
St Philips Chambers, Birmingham
0121 246 2145
lbond@st-philips.co.uk
Featured in Family/Matrimonial (Midlands)

Practice Areas: Leisha is a matrimonial finance specialist. Her cases often run into millions of pounds and involve businesses, property portfolios, intervenors and large pensions. However she also acts in more modest asset cases where, although the capital is limited, the stakes can be high for the client (maintaining a roof over his/her head). She also appears in Children Act proceedings which are often complex and sometimes heard "back to back" with financial proceedings. Leisha also regularly undertakes Schedule One cases in relation to financial claims by unmarried parents as well as cohabitation disputes under TLATA. Leisha is renowned for her thorough preparation and penetrative cross examination. She has a reputation as a hard negotiator and a "fighter" where settlement is not in her client's best interest. She exudes confidence and has a good rapport with her clients, be they a multi-millionaire businessman or stay at home mum. Her results are extremely impressive.
Professional Memberships: Family Law Bar Association; Association of Lawyers for Children.
Career: University of Birmingham and Université de Limoges (Law and French Law) 2:i; Jules Thorne scholar Middle Temple; Called to Bar 1999. She regularly lectures to other legal professionals.
Personal: Married with a son.

BONE, Lucy
Littleton Chambers, London
020 7797 8600
lbone@littletonchambers.co.uk
Featured in Employment (London)

Practice Areas: Employment, commercial and disciplinary/regulatory law. Principal areas of practice include: commercial disputes arising in an employment context, in particular all aspects of restrictive covenant disputes; unlawful competition including preparatory steps to compete and passing off confidentiality disputes including issues in relation to social media, breaches of directors' duties and fiduciary duties; partnership and LLP disputes; fraud and conspiracy. Particular experience in litigation concerning post termination restraints and team moves, in applications for injunctive relief of all forms including springboard injunctions, and speedy trials. Predominantly involved in High Court and appellate litigation but also widely experienced in cases in the employment tribunals and EAT. Experience in employee injunctions to restrain dismissal etc. Regulatory practice especially in Financial Services Regulation. Employment Tribunal practice encompasses all forms of discrimination, maternity and parental rights, unfair dismissal including redundancy and whistleblowing, collective redundancies and strike injunctions, wrongful dismissal, transfer of undertakings and equal pay (private sector and public sector).

Professional Memberships: ARDL, ELA, ELBA, COMBAR, EAT ELAAS Scheme. Secretary of Employment Lawyers' Association.

Career: Called 1999, Queen Mother Scholar of Middle Temple.

Personal: Educated at St Paul's Girls' School and King's College London 1995-98 (LLB, LLM). Born 1974. Resides London.

BOON, Elizabeth
Crown Office Chambers, London
020 7797 8100
mail@crownofficechambers.com
Featured in Property Damage (London)

Practice Areas: Elizabeth specialises in property damage and construction, professional negligence, product liability, insurance, and general commercial litigation. In addition to drafting and advisory work, she has considerable experience of appearing as an advocate in court. She has regularly appeared in the High Court (particularly the TCC) and in the Court of Appeal. Elizabeth's experience ranges from acting both as a junior to other members of Chambers to acting in her own right in relation to property damage and construction claims. She is frequently instructed as junior counsel in multi-million pound claims in the TCC, and in addition to such work, Elizabeth advises on and appears at trial in her own right in smaller disputes, especially those relating to domestic construction and maintenance works. Recent work includes: Acting for local authority in relation to multi-million pound claim in the TCC arising out of fire damage to a timber framed building; acting for developer in relation to allegedly defective waterproofing to a luxury block of flats resulting in water ingress and associated damage; and acting for a mine management company in relation to a claim for damage caused to a railway track due to a landslip at a colliery.

BOOTH, QC, Alexander QC
Francis Taylor Building, London
020 7353 8415
clerks@ftbchambers.co.uk
Featured in Planning (London)

Practice Areas: Alex Booth has a practice encompassing all aspects of planning, compulsory purchase and environmental law. His practice also includes licensing and rating matters. He regularly appears on behalf of private and public bodies in the High Court, the Lands Tribunal and at Public Inquiries and has also appeared in the Court of Appeal and the Supreme Court. In addition, he advises clients in Commonwealth jurisdictions and has successfully brought judicial review proceedings in the Turks and Caicos Islands. Nationally significant infrastructure work includes promoting a Resource Recovery Facility on behalf of Covanta, and opposing the Able Marine Energy Park on behalf of Associated British Ports. Other cases of note include London Olympics Judicial Review and Compulsory Purchase litigation acting on behalf of the London Development Agency; Compensation litigation connected with Crossrail, acting on behalf of corporate property investment claimants; Promoting compulsory purchase orders on behalf of National Grid Gas in South Wales; Statutory Reviews regarding planning enforcement in the Supreme Court and open cast coal mining in the Court of Appeal; Judicial Review of London Congestion Charging Scheme.

BOR, Harris
Wilberforce Chambers, London
020 7306 0102
harris.bor@wilberforce.co.uk
Featured in Chancery (London)

Practice Areas: Harris' practice covers all areas of international arbitration, and commercial and company litigation, with a particular emphasis on corporate, joint venture, fraud, banking and financial services, professional negligence, and insolvency disputes, as well as those involving the licensing and exploitation of intellectual property including in the technology and pharmaceutical sectors. Harris has acted in the above matters for investment banks, hedge funds, international and domestic companies, public and government bodies and individuals. He appears regularly before the DIFC Court and recently acted as junior in the Court of Appeal and Supreme Court in Les Laboratoires Servier v Apotex [2012] EWCA Civ 593 and UKSC 55 [2014]. Harris' arbitration experience has included significant proceedings under ICC, LCIA, UNCITRAL, WIPO, SCC and ICSID arbitration rules, and related court applications. He has also tutored on international arbitration at the Centre for Commercial Law Studies, Queen Mary, University of London, and sits on arbitration tribunals.

Professional Memberships: Registered practitioner DIFC Court, CEDR accredited mediator, Commercial Bar Association, Chancery Bar Association, Anglo-Russian Law Association

Publications: "Jurisdiction, Choice of Law, Arbitration and Dispute Resolution Clauses", co-author, Managing Private Fund Disputes, (PEI, 2015); "Freezing Orders in Support of Arbitration Proceedings", (2014) Butterworths Journal of International Banking & Financial Law, 29(1); Arbitration in England (with chapters on Scotland and Ireland), (Wolters Kluwer, 2013), joint editor.

BORLAND, Garry QC
Axiom Advocates, Edinburgh
0131 260 5651
garry.borland@axiomadvocates.com
Featured in Construction (Scotland), Restructuring/Insolvency (Scotland), Commercial Dispute Resolution (Scotland)

Practice Areas: Practice encompasses all areas of commercial law, specialising in commercial contracts, commercial property, company law and insolvency, construction and engineering, and energy.

Career: LLB (Hons), Glasgow University, 1st class (J Bennett Miller Prize winner in senior honours); BCL, St. John's College, Oxford, 1st class (Pirie-Reid scholar). Called to the Scottish Bar in 2000. Standing junior counsel to Her Majesty's Revenue and Customs, 2009-12. Took silk in 2014. Also called to the English Bar (Middle Temple). Practising member of 4 New Square, Lincoln's Inn, London.

BORRELLI, Michael QC
3 Raymond Buildings Barristers, London
020 7400 6400
michael.borrelli@3rblaw.com
Featured in Crime (London)

Practice Areas: Michael has an exclusive practice defending in high profile, serious and complex crime, as well as an interest in other areas of quasi-criminal work, tribunals and disciplinary hearings, where his advocacy skills can be fully utilised. He is instructed to review and advise on appellate work and to conduct cases in the Court of Appeal. He has developed a reputation for his ability in cases requiring the examination and testing of experts' evidence. He has defended in numerous well-publicised trials involving murder, money laundering, drugs and hijacking. Michael's expertise in fraud includes banking fraud, duty evasion, mortgage fraud, land banking fraud, and money laundering. He has defended in prosecutions brought by the SFO and the FCA; recently acting for a Solicitor charged with aiding and abetting the operation of an unregulated collective investment scheme. He has represented and advised company directors and others alleged to be involved in fraud on Banks, and recently acted in a nationwide multi million pound "Vishing" fraud.

Professional Memberships: Criminal Bar Association Former member of the CBA Committee Former member of the International Practice Committee of the Bar Council

Career: Call 1977; QC 2000

BOSWOOD, Anthony QC
Fountain Court Chambers, London
020 7583 3335
ab@foundtaincourt.co.uk
Featured in International Arbitration (London)

Practice Areas: Particular experience as counsel and adviser in the fields of insurance and reinsurance (including regulatory issues); mergers and acquisitions; energy law (electricity supply contracts as well as oil and gas); and banking (including derivatives of various kinds). Much experience as an arbitrator, both in the UK and abroad, in the above fields as well as many others, such as partnership, telecoms and joint ventures.

Career: Called to Bar 1970; took Silk in 1986; Bencher of Middle Temple; Deputy High Court Judge.

Personal: Italian speaker.

BOTT, Charles QC
Carmelite Chambers, London
020 7936 6300
clerks@carmelitechambers.co.uk
Featured in Crime (London), Financial Crime (London)

Practice Areas: 'A leading authority on all aspects of criminal and civil fraud, he has combined wide experience as an advocate and a background in civil and commercial law to develop an extensive practice in fraud, money laundering, regulatory and regulatory work: he has appeared in more than 80 serious fraud trials, including many of the leading cases of recent years. He has represented politicians, solicitors, accountants and prominent figures in the city and insurance markets. He also undertakes a wide range of civil advisory work and litigation, specializing in the areas of financial regulation, money laundering and asset recovery. Represents both corporate and personal clients in dealing with the FCA and other regulatory authorities and has recent experience of substantial and complex civil recovery proceedings. Has advised on and drafted comparable legislation in other jurisdictions. Also has wide experience in cases of murder, terrorism, serious violence and drug trafficking and has appeared in two public enquiries.' Fraud clients include: a senior bank manager at Nat West (R v. Crowther 1991), a portfolio manager at BZW (R v. Borkum 1990), a leading importer of Indian films (R v. Jumani 1990), the Chairman of Boodles (R v. Shand 2002), the director of a re-insurance brokerage at Lloyd's (R v. Felstead 1997), the largest UK importer of tropical birds and parrots (R v. Hammond 1996), the principal sub-contractor on the Millennium Dome site (R v. McHale 2000), the managing director of a chain of employment agencies (R v. Strachan 1997), the owner of the Windmill Club (R v. Owide 2004), the auditor in the Jubilee Line Extension fraud (R v. Mills 2004/5), a Tower Hamlets councillor accused of financial corruption (R v. Uddin 2006) the director of a leading pharmaceuticals company (R v. F 2006-2008), the Chief Executive of a major psychiatric hospital (R v. Breeze 2009) and a number of solicitors and accountants . Other fraud work includes R v. Miller (1998) a prominent case about corruption in the City, R v. Stepnika and others (2000) money laundering by former Czech police officers, R v. Headley (2002), laundering the proceeds of Europe's largest armed robbery, R v. Zone (2003),test case on abuse of Local Authority Right to Buy scheme, R v. Baldar (2005), surgeon accused of obtaining NHS posts by deception. Re M (2007),FSA/French Stock Exchange insider dealing inquiry, R v. Thorne (2009), SFO Prosecution of leading UK car retailer. R v. R (2009/10), SFO Prosecution of investment fraud, R v JH (2012) Expatriates Ponzi fraud. Major revenue frauds include R v Koser (2008), R v Jones (2006/7), R v M (2010), R v YAM (2011) and R v PS (2012), amongst the largest modern MTIC trials. Has also defended a police officer charged under the Official Secrets Act (R v White), the Managing Director of 'Hustler' magazine in a pornography trial, the soldier responsible for the Sudbury Nursing Home siege (R v King), a Palestinian journalist charged with plot to bomb the Israeli Embassy (R v. Derbas 1996), a Leeds United footballer charged with serious assault (R v. Hackworth 2001, Bowyer, Duberry, Woodgate and others). Other recent work includes R v Ali (2008-21/7 terrorist case), R v Taylor (2008), the Woodhams Murder trial, R v Palmer (2009) the Colchester train manslaughter case, R v Faroqui (2011) – terrorist recruitment case and R v Baroudi – doctor charged with manslaughter by gross negligence, R v JW News of the World phone hacking case, R v Gilmour Libor manipulation case, R v WD film Investment trial. Current work includes R v JV, a major European corruption trial and R v JB, an accountant accused of investment fraud.

Personal:

BOULDING, Philip QC
Keating Chambers, London
020 7544 2600
pboulding@keatingchambers.com
Featured in International Arbitration (London), Construction (London)

Practice Areas: A "rock solid and hugely popular" Queen's Counsel specialising in construction, civil engineering and energy disputes and technology, who is a "ferocious cross-examiner" and "a big international player with a great profile in Hong Kong and Asia in general". Practice comprises principally international work, acting for a large number of clients in Asia, particularly Hong Kong, Macau and the Philippines. Clients include developers, government departments, major national and international construction and engineering companies, energy and utility companies and direct access work from claims consultants involved in the construction industry. Also sits regularly as an arbitrator, mediator and adjudicator. "Clever and cerebral"..."decades of experience"..."particularly acclaimed for his expertise in Hong Kong-based disputes"..."flexes his intellectual muscle on a regular basis in a wide array of complex international arbitrations." Chambers & Partners.

Professional Memberships: Dubai International Finance Centre Court (DIFC); Commercial Bar Association; Technology and Construction Bar Association, HKIAC Panel Arbitrator, KLRCA Panel Mediator and Arbitrator.

Career: Called 1979; Queen's Counsel 1996. Admitted to Hong Kong Bar (ad hoc). Elected Master of the Bench of Gray's Inn 2004. Former Committee Member of TECBAR.

Publications: Consultant Editor to the Construction Law Reports; Contributor, Keating on Construction Contracts + supplement Ninth Edition.

BOURNE, Charles QC
11KBW, London
020 7632 8500
Charles.Bourne@11kbw.com
Featured in Administrative & Public Law (London), Employment (London), Immigration (London), Local Government (London)

Practice Areas: Employment, local government, public law, education and information law. Recent cases include: Jones v LB Southwark (local authority charges for water), Challenges to criminal legal aid procurement, O'Brien v Ministry of Justice (judicial pension rights), C v DWP (information policy, transgender discrimination) Torbay Quality Care Forum v Torbay Council (care home fees), Brooks v Foreign Office (FOI), Kiani v Home Office (Employment Tribunal closed material procedures), Owen v HM Treasury (whistleblowing), the Baha Mousa public inquiry.

Professional Memberships: Human Rights Lawyers Association (former Chair), ALBA, ARDL.

Career: Called 1991. QC 2014. Authorised to sit as Deputy High Court Judge 2016. Recorder 2010. A Panel Treasury Counsel 2009. CEDR accredited Mediator 2000. Accredited for Public Access.

Publications: Contributor to Tolley's Employment Law, Butterworths Civil Court Precedents. Author of "Civil Advocacy" (Cavendish).

Personal: Educated: UCS, London; Trinity College, Cambridge (MA, First Class); Université de Paris IV (Sorbonne) (Maitrise).

BOURNE, Colin
Kings Chambers, Leeds
0345 034 3444
clerks@kingschambers.com
Featured in Employment (North Eastern)

Practice Areas: Industrial Relations (individual and collective), employment, discrimination with a wide range of individual, trade union, public and private sector employer clients. Reported cases: Street v Derbyshire Unemployed workers' Centre [2004] EWCA Civ 964 [2004] IRLR 687 CA – the requirement for good faith when making protected disclosures. Miles v Linkage Community Trust [2008] IRLR 602 argued successfully for a nil award in a Working Time Regs case. Metropolitan Resources v Churchill Dulwich & others [2009] IRLR 700 identifying a service provision change under TUPE. 2006 Sturdy v Leeds Teaching Hospitals NHS Trust – 2009 ET highest ever injury to feelings award plus interest and aggravated damages plus indemnity costs. Leeds City Council v Woodhouse UKEAT/0521/08/DA – employee of Arms Length Management Organisation was contract worker for purposes of Race Relations Act 1976. Recent cases include whistleblowing claims for senior employees, successfully defending Local Authority in claims involving Service Provision Changes, disability discrimination, trade union recognition before the Central Arbitration Committee, claims for contractual redundancy pay. Accredited CEDR mediator with wide experience of non-employment matters.

Professional Memberships: Employment Law Bar Association, Employment Lawyers' Association, Industrial Law Society, Association of Northern Mediators.

Career: 1973-81 Graphic designer/Art Editor, IPC Magazines; 1981-96 Trade Union Officer, National Union of Journalists; Called 1997 – 15 years previous employment law experience in negotiations and representation, including European Works Councils, preparing and presenting evidence to Monopolies and Mergers Commission (as it then was) and to the House of Commons Employment Select Committee.

BOURNE, Ian QC
Charter Chambers, London
(0)20 7618 4400
ian.bourne@charterchambers.com
Featured in Crime (London)

Practice Areas: Ian was described in the Chambers Directory when a junior as 'capable of performing mental gymnastics at the drop of a hat'. Since taking silk in 2006 he has built up a formidable practice and has appeared in many of the major cases in recent times including in 2012 the successful representation of the City Broker in the largest ever FSA prosecution of insider dealing in Operation Saturn (R v Ali Mustafa and others) tried at the Southwark Crown Court. He regularly defends in murder, fraud, armed-robbery and substantial drug cases in equal measures. Recent cases include the "Harry Potter" murder, the £42 million Graf Diamonds robbery and a high-profile murder in the Cayman Islands.

Professional Memberships: Criminal Bar Association, South Eastern Circuit.

BOWEN, Paul QC
Brick Court Chambers, London
020 7520 9984
paul.bowen@brickcourt.co.uk
Featured in Administrative & Public Law (London), Civil Liberties & Human Rights (London), Community Care (London), Court of Protection (All Circuits)

Career: Paul Bowen QC practises across the entire spectrum of public and administrative law, often with significant human rights, EU or other international law elements and is recommended in Chambers & Partners 2016 as a leading silk in Public and Administrative Law and Civil Liberties and Human Rights. Paul moved to Brick Court in October 2014 and now divides his time between commercial public law work and high profile human rights work, acting for claimants, defendants and interveners whether individuals, private companies, public authorities, regulators, charities or other NGOs. Paul has been instructed in many high-profile challenges in the higher courts leading to significant legal changes, with over a hundred reported cases to his name. He has appeared in a wide variety of Courts and Tribunals in the UK and abroad including the Cayman Islands, Jersey, Cyprus and St. Vincent and the Grenadines, and has appeared in the Supreme Court or House of Lords on twelve occasions, four as leading counsel, as well as in the Privy Council (on four occasions) and the European Court of Human Rights. In 2015 he was appointed to the new 'A' Panel of Counsel to the Equality and Human Rights Commission (EHRC).

BOWERS, Rupert QC
Doughty Street Chambers, London
020 7404 1313
r.bowers@doughtystreet.co.uk
Featured in Financial Crime (London)

Practice Areas: Rupert Bowers QC maintains a broad practice undertaking business and financial crime and extradition with expertise in ancillary matters associated with criminal investigations. He places particular emphasis on challenging search warrants, cash seizures, restraint and freezing orders, and arrest and detention. Rupert also practices sports regulation and discipline which has included cases before the Court of Arbitration for Sport. Those he has represented include Harry Redknapp, James Tomkins, Jermain Defoe, Ben Thatcher, Bradley Wright-Phillips, Steve Cotterill, Emily Sarsfield, World in Motion Ltd., M&C Saatchi Merlin, and he recently drafted the disciplinary procedure for the British Association of Snowsports Instructors. Recent and current cases include defending Lord Hanningfield who was charged with fraudulently claiming parliamentary expenses, representing George Galloway in a challenge brought before the Investigatory Powers Tribunal in relation to the interception of parliamentarians communications and the Wilson doctrine, representing a major futures trading company in relation to the unlawful freezing of over $3 million of their funds, and representing two lawyers subject to a police search operation in judicial review proceedings challenging the issue and execution of the search warrants.

Career: Rupert was called to the bar in 1995, studying law after attaining a degree in psychology, and undertook pupillage at what is now 2 Hare Court. In 2011 Rupert moved to Doughty Street Chambers to continue to develop his mixed practice, and in 2015 he took silk as one of only 3 appointments made on both a civil and criminal platform.

Publications: "Blackstone's Guide to the Terrorism Act 2006"- Co-author. "Financial sanctions, bribery and corruption" 2009 – Consultant on the College of Law DVD. "Intercepting Terrorists" 2009 – Covert Policing Review. "Silence on Violence: Improving the Safety of Women" 2011 – Consultant on a report prepared by Andrew Boff of the Greater London Authority. "Search and Seizure: Your Rights" June, 2014 – The Law Society Gazette. "Restraint Orders: Reasonable Suspicion and Reporting" December, 2015 – Solicitors Journal. "A Tale of Two Orders" March, 2016 – An article in relation to property freezing orders in Criminal Law and Justice Weekly. "Open Season, in Closed Session" June, 2016 – An article on recent developments in the law in challenging search and seizure in Criminal Law and Justice Weekly.

BOWHILL, Jessie
8 New Square, London
020 7405 4321
jessie.bowhill@8newsquare.co.uk
Featured in Intellectual Property (London)

Practice Areas: Barrister specialising in all areas of intellectual property law and related media law with particular expertise in copyright claims. Highlights include: (i) Brian Belo v Lime Pictures (TV format case concerning "The Only Way is Essex" (TOWIE)); (ii) 19TV v Freemantle (TV format case concerning "The X Factor" and "Pop Idol"); (iii) Fisher v Brooker (musical copyright case concerning "A Whiter Shade of Pale"); (iv) Appearing in Geneva under the new WIPO Mediation and Expedited Arbitration Rules for Film and Media; (v) Mitchell v BBC (copyright in TV programme "Kerwhizz"); (vi) ITV v TV Catchup (copyright in live-streaming of TV programmes); (vii) Supreme Pet Foods v Henry Bell (SUPREME trade mark); (viii) IPC Media v Media 10 (Ideal Home trade mark); (ix) Faberge v The Uri Group (Faberge trade marks); (x) Julius Samann v Tetrosyl (Magic Tree trade marks). For a comprehensive CV visit www.8newsquare.co.uk

Professional Memberships: Intellectual Property Bar Association, Chancery Bar Association.

Career: Called 2003, Gray's Inn.

Publications: Bullen & Leake; Jacob's Precedents of Pleadings. Contributor.

Personal: Trained as a classical pianist prior to career at the Bar.

BOWLING, James
4 Pump Court, London
020 7842 5555
Jbowling@4pumpcourt.com
Featured in Construction (London)

Practice Areas: Specialist advocate appearing in both court and arbitrations. Particular expertise in construction, energy and natural resources, infrastructure projects and all related areas of professional negligence. Particular experience of international arbitrations and cross-border litigation in relation to disputes in Africa, the Middle East and Far East. Qualified mediator and adjudicator. Represents employers, contractors, professionals, insurers and national governments.

Professional Memberships: Society of Construction Law, TECBAR, LCLCBA.

BOWSHER, Michael QC
Monckton Chambers, London
020 7405 7211
mbowsher@monckton.co.uk
Featured in Construction (London), Public Procurement (London)
Practice Areas: Michael Bowsher's practice covers the procurement, performance, termination and regulation of public and utility sector contracts, as well as related competition and trade issues. He has a particular background in disputes concerning complex construction and PFI contracts especially in areas such as waste, transport, energy, health and construction itself. His background in regulatory law also involves him in matters such as medicines regulation and increasingly in price and contract disputes involving health service providers. As examples, he has appeared in recent disputes concerning air traffic services at Gatwick Airport, tendering for a major highways project in Northern Ireland, railway rolling stock and franchise arrangements and other major public sector services and infrastructure. He is actively involved in litigation and mediation in England, Northern Ireland (called 2000) and the Republic of Ireland (called 2012). He advises bidders and purchasers both in these jurisdictions and beyond, in particular concerning bidding strategies and compliant procurement practices. He is often appointed as arbitrator, mediator or expert.
Career: He was called to the Bar in England and Wales in 1985 and is a bencher of Middle Temple. He is the visiting lecturer in public procurement law at King's College London.
Personal:

BOYCE, William QC
QEB Hollis Whiteman, London
0044 (20) 7933 8855
william.boyce@qebhw.co.uk
Featured in Financial Crime (London)
Practice Areas: In business crime, fraud and general crime, William Boyce QC is instructed in the most complex and prominent cases. His expertise includes frauds in banking, mortgages, market making and mergers and acquisitions, false announcements to the market (including prosecuting the first FSA prosecution of its kind, R v Rigby and others), arms to Iraq, international bribery and corruption, and cartels. William recently represented a defendant in the largest insider dealing case brought by the FCA; he is instructed to act for a high-profile trader in relation to alleged LIBOR manipulation and, separately, to act for a high-profile trader in relation to alleged FX manipulation. In the field of crime, he has acted in many notorious murders and in the trials of the police officers who investigated the Birmingham Six and, separately, Winston Silcott. He has been instructed in many appeals, including those of the Birmingham Six, Judith Ward and Stefan Kiszko. He acted on behalf of the prosecution in the largest ever private prosecution brought by an individual.
Professional Memberships: Bencher of Gray's Inn; Association of Regulatory and Disciplinary Lawyers; Bar Council; Competition Law Association; Criminal Bar Association; European Criminal Bar Association; Fraud Advisory Panel; International Bar Association; Justice; Public Access Bar Association; registered with the Bar Council – Public Access Directory
Career: Called 1976. Appointed QC 2001. 2010 SFO Approved Counsel List; 1991-2001 Junior then Senior Treasury Counsel, Central Criminal Court; 1993- Assistant Recorder then Recorder

BOYLE, Alan QC
Serle Court, London
020 7242 6105
aboyle@serlecourt.co.uk
Featured in Chancery (London), Commercial Dispute Resolution (London), Company (London), Fraud (London), Offshore (London), Trusts (London)
Practice Areas: Commercial and chancery litigation, contentious trusts, probate, civil fraud, company and insolvency. Recent cases include: Madoff (fraud), AB v MB (trusts), Lissack (contract), Lictor (insolvency), Masri (contempt), Centenary (company).
Professional Memberships: Chancery Bar Association, Commerical Bar Association, Commercial Fraud Lawyers Association, ACTAPS. Deputy High Court Judge.
Career: Royal Shrewsbury School, St Catherine's College Oxford (MA). Called to the Bar 1972. Silk 1991.
Publications: Editor and contributor, 'The Practice and Procedure of the Companies Court', Lloyds of London. Press.
Personal: Married, two daughters.

BOYLE, Gerard
Serjeants' Inn Chambers, London
020 7427 5000
gboyle@serjeantsinn.com
Featured in Police Law (All Circuits), Clinical Negligence (London), Professional Discipline (London)
Practice Areas: Gerard Boyle was called to the Bar in 1992. Gerard specialises in public and administrative, police, inquests and inquiries, clinical negligence and healthcare, professional discipline and personal injury law. An earlier edition notes that "his sense of humour, tenacity and excellent rapport with all he meets are just some of the reasons for his incredible effectiveness. He is considered one of the best forensic barristers by experts. He is a formidable opponent who is very strong in court." He was ranked as one of the top 100 juniors by the Chambers Bar 100 2014 and was awarded bronze for Barrister of the Year at The Lawyer Awards 2015. Please visit the Serjeants' Inn Chambers website for his profile, which sets out full details of his practice including relevant work of note.
Professional Memberships: Member of the Northern Irish Bar, PNBA, ARDL, LCLCBA, Bar Standards Board Panel of Prosecuting Counsel.

BOYLE, Matthew
Crown Office Chambers, London
020 7797 8100
boyle@crownofficechambers.com
Featured in Personal Injury (London)
Practice Areas: Principle areas of practice are personal injury and industrial disease, acting for both claimants and defendants. He specialises in catastrophic injury work and has trial and round table settlement meeting experience of claims worth more than £10 million. He is also regularly instructed in complex or high value employers' liability and public liability claims. His disease practice encompasses asbestos, noise induced hearing loss, hand arm vibration syndrome, work-related upper limb disorders and stress at work cases. He also has a particular interest in claims for pure psychiatric injury and cases where fraud is alleged, including those featuring staged accident and phantom passenger scenarios. Recent High Court trial experience includes the fatal mesothelioma case of Mosson v Spousal (London) Ltd which featured a number of issues under the Fatal Accidents Act 1976. In the Court of Appeal his appearances have included Hartman v South Essex Mental Health & Community NHS Trust (the group stress appeals); Davies v Global Securities (the duty of care owed to a security contractor working in Iraq); Huscroft v P & O Ferries (civil procedure: the attachment of conditions to court orders); and Sutton v Syston Rugby Football Club (the standard of care owed by rugby clubs to their members). Sources have rated his forceful advocacy, clarity and personability.
Career: Called to the Bar in 2000 and joined Chambers in 2001.

BRACE, Michael
12 King's Bench Walk, London
020 7242 3555
brace@12kbw.co.uk
Featured in Personal Injury (All Circuits)
Practice Areas: Michael is a personal injury and clinical negligence specialist. He has particular expertise in industrial disease claims (most notably those in relation to asbestos exposure) and in claims involving violence in the workplace. In relation to clinical negligence he specialises particularly in obstetric and birth problems. His practice encompasses high-value claims with a significant proportion of such work involving fatal claims and those in respect of catastrophic injury.
Professional Memberships: APIL, PIBA & AvMA
Career: Called to the Bar 1991. General Provincial Panel of Treasury Counsel: 2000-07. Panel of Counsel for the Welsh Assembly Government: 2000-07. Michael is an ADR Group Accredited Mediator and a Pupil Supervisor.

BRADLEY, Matthew
Henderson Chambers, London
020 7583 9020
mbradley@hendersonchambers.co.uk
Featured in Product Liability (London)
Practice Areas: Commercial and civil law. Product liability and group actions, sale of goods and supply of services, financial services, consumer credit, insurance, professional negligence, product recall, property damage, insolvency, injunctive work, economic torts, international torts, conflicts of laws. Employment, including restrictive covenants & confidentiality cases and dual High Court/ET proceedings. Public procurement and public law. Property law. Health and safety. Has appeared in Chancery and QBD trials, Court of Appeal and EAT. Junior counsel in Sabril litigation (pharmaceutical product liability), petrol contamination litigation, public procurement and international tort claims. Further details: see chambers website.
Professional Memberships: COMBAR, HSLA, LCLCBA, ELA.
Career: Oxford University (French & German – 1st Class), Lord Woolf Scholar (Daily Telegraph/1 Crown Office Row); Hardwicke, Haldane & Thomas Moore Scholar (Lincoln's Inn); Phoenicia Scholar (Bar European Group). Called: 2004.
Publications: Author of "Product Recall in the EU" chapter in the International Product Law Manual 2011/12 (Kluwer). Various articles.
Personal: Married with children. Languages: French, German & Spanish.

BRADLY, David
39 Essex Chambers, London
020 7832 1111
david.bradly@39essex.com
Featured in Professional Discipline (London)
Practice Areas: Advice in relation to regulatory and professional disciplinary matters in the context of both professional disciplinary proceedings and commercial arrangements; advocacy before, and sitting as legal advisor to, professional conduct and other fitness to practice committees; and advising in respect of and conducting statutory appeals (High Court and Privy Council), judicial review hearings, criminal proceedings, proceedings before tribunals resolving NHS contracts disputes and public inquiries.
Professional Memberships: ARDL, LCLCBA, PIBA.
Career: Everard Ver Hayden Prize in Advocacy, Inns of Court School of Law, 1987. Called to the Bar in 1987 and joined present Chambers in 1997. Represented military witnesses, including as an advocate at the public hearings, in the Saville Inquiry into Bloody Sunday 1998-2004.
Publications: Cordery on Legal Services (contributor)
Personal: London University 1980-83. Royal Military Academy Sandhurst 1983-84. 6th Queen Elizabeth's Own Gurkha Rifles 1984-86.

BRAITHWAITE, Thomas
Serle Court, London
020 7242 6105 (Switchboard)
tbraithwaite@serlecourt.co.uk
Featured in Partnership (London), Real Estate Litigation (London)
Practice Areas: Commercial chancery litigation, with a particular emphasis on real property, partnership and company disputes in the Chancery Division and Commercial Court. Recent cases include Lictor v Mir Steel (2014) (procuring breach of contract), Wyche v Careforce (2013) (relief from sanctions following e-disclosure failures) and Amin v Amin (2010) (constructive trust claims). Tom also has extensive experience of disputes before foreign courts, and recent work has involved cases before the courts of the Bahamas, Jersey and Hong Kong. In the property field, Tom has been involved in leading cases concerning foreshore rights and manorial franchises, and represented the Crown Estate in the recent Supreme Court case of Loose v Lynn Shellfish (2016).
Professional Memberships: COMBAR, Chancery Bar Association, Property Bar Association.
Personal: Born 1975. Educated at Clifton and Jesus College, Cambridge 1994-97 (MA double first class; George Long Prize for Civil Law, Hamson Prize for Obligations). Called to the Bar 1998 (Thomas More Bursar and Kennedy Scholar of Lincoln's Inn). Married, with one daughter.

BRANNIGAN, Sean QC
4 Pump Court, London
020 7842 5555
sbrannigan@4pumpcourt.com
Featured in International Arbitration (London), Professional Negligence (London), Construction (London), Energy & Natural Resources (London)
Practice Areas: Large scale arbitrations and Litigation. Particular expertise in Energy and Natural resources, Construction and

Engineering, and Professional Negligence disputes. Very extensive experience of international arbitrations and cross-border litigation in London, Middle East, Hong Kong, Dublin, and Belfast. Qualified mediator. Represents employers, contractors, professionals, insurers and various national governments.
Professional Memberships: Member of Arbitration Chambers, Hong Kong. Advocate in the Dubai International Financial Centre courts. Dually called to the Northern Irish Bar. Rights of audience in the Southern Irish Bar. Member of COMBAR, Technology and Construction Bar Association, London Common Law and Commercial Bar Association, LCIA Users' Council
Career: BA (Oxon) in Jurisprudence. Called in 1994. Silk in 2009.

BRANSTON, Barnabas
5 Essex Court, London
020 7410 2000
branston@5essexcourt.co.uk
Featured in Police Law (All Circuits)
Practice Areas: Coroners' Inquests (on behalf of Chief Officers in police inquests in drugs, firearms, pursuit and detention-related deaths and on behalf of Serco in inquests where there has been a death in custody in the private prison sector), Civil Actions Against the Police (Defendant) in claims for assault, wrongful arrest/false imprisonment, malicious prosecution and misfeasance, Regulatory and Disciplinary proceedings (advising and presenting on behalf of the Appropriate Authority in police misconduct hearings), Health and Safety (defending alleged or actual breaches of the usual raft of health and safety regulations), Personal Injury (Claimant and Defendant), Public law (on behalf of Chief Officers).
Professional Memberships: ARDL; PIBA.
Career: Called to the Bar in 1999; Infantry Officer (Welsh Guards, 1992 - 1997)
Personal: Barney is married with three children, lives in Shropshire and his outside interests include sport and games (especially rugby and cricket), the Welsh Guards, and looking after his chickens, pigs and spaniels.

BRASLAVSKY, Nicholas QC
Kings Chambers, Manchester
0345 034 3444
clerks@kingschambers.com
Featured in Clinical Negligence (Northern), Personal Injury (Northern)
Practice Areas: Principal areas of practice: personal injury and clinical negligence litigation predominantly in cases of the highest value and complexity including road traffic, employers and public liability, military and recreational/transport cases, birth damage and other clinical negligence disputes. Particularly catastrophic injury litigation including neuro and spinal injury for claimants and major insurers. Also, regulatory and disciplinary cases for medical and other professionals and regulatory authorities. Health and safety cases. Chambers in Manchester, Leeds, Birmingham and London.
Professional Memberships: Personal Injury Bar Association
Career: Birmingham University 1976-82; LLB (Hons) 1979; PhD 1982. Called 1983 (Inner Temple); Silk 1999; Recorder 2001. Deputy High Court Judge 2008. Head of Chambers and Head of Recruitment, Kings Chambers. Sports Resolution Panel (2012); Honorary lecturer School of Law, Manchester University 2012. Honorary Professor of Law, University of Birmingham.

BRASSINGTON, Stephen
2 Hare Court, London
Tel: 020 7353 5324
clerks@2harecourt.com
Featured in Professional Discipline (London)
Practice Areas: Stephen Brassington is rightly regarded as one of the leading juniors in the field of Professional Discipline and Regulation. He is an excellent advocate whose hard work, charisma and exemplary client care have an extraordinary effectiveness and lead to excellent results. Stephen represents professionals from a wide variety of industry sectors in cases brought by their regulatory bodies and in related proceedings in the criminal, civil and Coronial courts, and other tribunals. Stephen is in great demand to defend professionals whose fitness to practise has been called into question. He represents Professionals at the GMC, GDC and other regulators, as well as before the Administrative / High Court and at Coroners' Inquests, NHS England and Trust Disciplinary Hearings and advises on specialist register appeals. Stephen also undertakes significant cases associated with sports regulation. Stephen is head of the Professional Discipline Group at 2 Hare Court, which has established a reputation for high-quality advocacy in this field. He leads the teams appointed to the National Council for Teaching and Leadership (NCTL) and the General Optical Council (GOC) legal panels advising and presenting complex and serious cases on their behalf before the respective disciplinary tribunals. Stephen was instructed by the Football Association as junior counsel in the prosecution of former England footballer John Terry and also appeared in the appeal of physiotherapist Stephen Brennan in the Harlequins Rugby Football Club "Bloodgate" case.
Professional Memberships: ARDL; CBA

BREMNER, Jonathan
Pump Court Tax Chambers, London
020 7414 8080
clerks@pumptax.com
Featured in Tax (London)
Practice Areas: Jonathan advises on the major UK taxes and acts in tax appeals and tax related litigation before the specialist tribunals and the higher courts. He has substantial experience of complex and high value litigation (acting both alone and as part of a team). His advisory practice has an emphasis on business and entrepreneurial tax issues. Recent cases have included: Airtours v HMRC (Supreme Court), FII Group Litigation (CA), Prudential v HMRC (CA), Isle of Wight v HMRC (CA), Leeds CC v HMRC (CA), Six Continents v HMRC (Ch), Evonik v HMRC (Ch), Bradfield College v HMRC (UT), MG Rover v HMRC (UT), HMRC v Invicta Foods (UT), Manduca v HMRC (UT), HMRC v Newey (UT), Murray Group v HMRC (UT), Farnborough Airport Properties Company v HMRC (FTT), French Education Property Trust v HMRC (FTT).
Professional Memberships: Revenue Bar Association; VAT Practitioners Group; Chancery Bar Association.
Career: Called 2005 (Inner Temple); March 2011 – Junior Counsel to the Crown (C Panel); March 2014 – Junior Counsel to the Crown (B Panel); September 2016 – Junior Counsel to the Crown (A Panel).
Personal: Hertford College, University of Oxford – BA (First Class), BCL (Distinction); University of Paris II (Panthéon-Assas) – Certificat Supérieur de Droit Français (Mention Bien); BPP Law School – Bar Vocational Course (Very Competent). Languages: French (including legal French).

BRENNAN, John
St Philips Chambers, Birmingham
0121 246 7000
civil@st-philips.com
Featured in Chancery (Midlands), Professional Negligence (Midlands), Commercial Dispute Resolution (Midlands), Real Estate Litigation (Midlands)
Practice Areas: Broad range of commercial and chancery work; notably banking, commercial fraud, landlord and tenant, partnership, professional negligence, property, restraint of trade, trusts, and wills and probate. He aims to provide clear, reliable advice and a user friendly service.
Professional Memberships: Chancery Bar Association, Professional Negligence Bar Association, Midland Commercial and Chancery Bar Association.
Career: Called 1996.
Personal: Born 1972. Educated at King Edward's School Birmingham and Jesus College, Oxford (MA, Modern History). Interested in politics, history and sport.

BRETHERTON, Kerry QC
Tanfield Chambers, London
020 7421 5300
KerryBretherton@tanfieldchambers.co.uk
Featured in Administrative & Public Law (London), Court of Protection (All Circuits), Social Housing (London)
Practice Areas: Kerry's work is in the field of commercial and residential property transactions and real property work and she retains her specialism in housing (previously ranked in Band 1). Examples include McDonald v McDonald (Supreme Court) regarding possession proceedings; Haile (Supreme Court) Housing Act 1996; Gold Harp (Court of Appeal) land registration London & Quadrant Housing Trust v Prestige Properties forfeiture and a personal costs order against directors. .Her public law work includes that with a property or commercial basis and high profile or high value cases see MB (heard by the Supreme Court 2016) and NA. Kerry has acted in some of the most groundbreaking cases in the Court of Protection eg MN listed in the Supreme Court in 2016; G v E (deprivation of liberty, costs and deputyship); M v A Local authority (factitious illness) Re Meek (financial abuse). Kerry's practice has involved a number of Supreme Court cases and frequent appearances in the Court of Appeal as well as the full range of High Court/Tribunal work. Her advisory work involves high value cases and advice on proposed legislation and policies. Kerry accepts direct access work through her clerks at directaccess@tanfieldchambers.co.uk. Kerry has been described as "extremely strong in terms of her oral advocacy," and "...excellent on her feet". Her "written work is exceptional," and "she is not afraid to run unusual points of law and is willing to go the extra mile in terms of advice and assistance." She has also been described as "tenacious, and someone whose advice is always clear and concise. If you have a tough case and you need a battler, she is the one," and is "excellent with clients."
Career: Call: 1992 Appointed as Queen's Counsel: 2016 Appointed Panel Counsel for the Equality & Human Rights Commission: 2011 Appointed to Attorney General's A Panel: 2012

BRIGGS, John
South Square, London
020 7696 9900
johnbriggs@southsquare.com
Featured in Restructuring/Insolvency (London)
Practice Areas: John specialises in domestic and cross-border insolvency, commercial and chancery litigation, professional negligence and disciplinary proceedings (involving insolvency practitioners), partnerships, financial services and proceeds of crime.
Professional Memberships: COMBAR, Chancery Bar Association, Insolvency Lawyers' Association, INSOL International, INSOL Europe, R3 and British Italian Law Association.
Career: Over the years John has appeared in many high profile cases particularly in the field of personal insolvency, insolvent partnerships and deceased insolvents, including Kevin Maxwell, Asil Nadir, Jonathan Aitken, Kerry Katona, Sean Quinn, Seifert Sedley (solicitors), Nicholas Phillips (the Queen's cousin – deceased), and Boris Berezovsky (Russian oligarch – deceased). Called to the Bar of England and Wales (Gray's Inn) 1973; Jurist Linguist at European Court of Justice 1973-75; in practice as barrister 1976-to date; Deputy Bankruptcy and Companies Registrar of High Court 1989-to date; called to the Northern Ireland Bar 2011.
Publications: Joint senior author of 'Muir Hunter on Personal Insolvency' (Thompson Reuters); joint author of 'Asset Protection Trusts' (Key Haven); contributor to 'Rayden on Divorce' (18th ed Butterworths) – author of chapter on 'Bankruptcy, insolvency and ancillary relief', contributor to Cross Border Insolvency (Sheldon-Bloomsbury Professional).

BRIGGS, Laura
9 Gough Square, London
Featured in Family/Matrimonial (London)
Practice Areas: All areas of children law with particular focus on care and adoption proceedings. Laura represents children, parents, local authorities and relatives. Recent work has included cases where factitious and induced illness is an issue, historical sexual abuse, placement of children overseas and issues of jurisdiction where children have been abandoned or trafficked into the UK. Laura has appeared in cases involving Brussels IIa Article 15 transfers, including London Borough of Barking & Dagenham -v- C and others [2014] EWHC 2472 (Fam).
Professional Memberships: FLBA, Association of Lawyers for Children.
Career: Called in 2001, Laura became a member of 18 St John Street Chambers in Manchester following completion of her pupillage there. In 2010 – 2011 Laura practised as an attorney specialising in family law at Samson & McGrath attorneys in the Cayman Islands. On her return to the UK in 2011, Laura joined 9 Gough Square Chambers. Laura was appointed a Recorder in the family court in 2015, sitting on the South Eastern Circuit.
Publications: Co-Author of "The PLO Explained" (1st and 2nd eds) 9 Gough Square. Editor of Chambers' family e-newsletter.

BRIGGS, Lucie
Atkin Chambers, London
020 7404 0102
lbriggs@atkinchambers.com
Featured in Construction (London)
Practice Areas: Lucie specialises in construction and engineering, energy, information technology and professional negligence disputes for a wide variety of contractors, private employers, manufacturers and their professional advisors. She has a broad practice with expertise in domestic and international arbitration, domestic courts, mediation and all aspects of adjudication proceedings. As part of her diverse practice she appears regularly as sole counsel in court, arbitration, mediation and adjudication hearings. Her experience covers the entire litigation process including pre-action protocol, drafting pleadings, settling witness statements, attending negotiations, preparing for and appearing at applications and hearings including strike out, summary judgment, CMC's and trial. She has also advised on and acted in appellant proceedings.
Professional Memberships: Lucie is a member of the SCL and The Society of Computers and Law
Career: BSc Chemistry (King's College, London), PGDL, BVC (College of Law, London). Called 2004
Publications: Contributing Editor Hudson's Building and Engineering Contracts (Sweet & Maxwell) 12th Ed.

BRIGHT, Christopher QC
No5 Chambers, Birmingham
0845 210 0555
cbr@no5.com
Featured in Personal Injury (Midlands), Clinical Negligence (Midlands)
Practice Areas: A leading clinical negligence/personal injury Silk for both Claimants and Defendants, said to be "first rate", a "leading silk" and "doing work countrywide". Has specialised for many years in cerebral palsy/neonatal, catastrophic brain and spinal injury claims and is highly regarded for his approachable, user-friendly and sensitive approach and his expertise in complex claims involving issues of CCG/LA statutory care funding/PPOs. Has been variously described as "very forensic", "at the top of his game", "very able and experienced", "very impressive in conference and in court" and as having "a very good grasp of complex issues and very easy to contact". Has recently been involved in a series of high value cases e.g. AP, a CP case settled for £4.237m and a PPO of £285,000 pa (the equivalent of £12m +), and M el D, a TBI claim settled for £3.625m with a PPO of £250,000 pa.
Professional Memberships: APIL/AvMA
Career: Durham University BA Hons, Crown and County Court Recorder, Bencher of Gray's Inn. Regularly lectures to Claimant and Defendant solicitors/insurers, AvMA, Headway and the Spinal Injuries Association upon e.g. litigating head/spinal injury and cerebral palsy claims, statutory funding and periodical payments.
Personal: Interests: An old Mill in Tuscany and Gloucester Rugby Club.

BRINDLE, Michael QC
Fountain Court Chambers, London
020 7583 3335
mb@fountaincourt.co.uk
Featured in International Arbitration (London), Professional Negligence (London), Banking & Finance (London), Commercial Dispute Resolution (London), Financial Services (London), Fraud (London)
Practice Areas: Practice encompasses a variety of work in the commercial and corporate sphere as well as EU law. Emphasis is on banking and financial services, company law, professional negligence in financial and commercial matters, insurance and international trade. Conducts international arbitrations as counsel and as arbitrator. Experienced in city related matters, including litigation arising out of audits, takeovers and rights issues. Practises in chancery as well as commercial and common law courts. Important cases include Caparo v Dickman [1989] (auditors' negligence); Morgan Crucible v Hill Samuel [1990] (merchant banker's and auditor's negligence and takeover code); G & H Montage v Irvani [1990] (bills of exchange); Deposit Protection Board v Dalia [1993] (depositor compensation); Shah v Bank of England [1994] (banking supervision); Camdex v Bank of Zambia [1997] (liabilities of central banks); BCCI v Price Waterhouse [1997] (Banking Act 1987); Nuova Safim v Sakura Bank [1998] (ISDA standard agreement); Barclays Bank v Boulter [1999] (banking and securities); Marks & Spencer Plc v Baird [2001] (contractual certainty); Barings v. former auditors [2003] (auditors negligence); Re Marks & Spencer Plc [2004] (conflicts of interest); Customs and Excise v. Barclays Bank (bank's duty of care) [2006]; Riyadh Bank v AHLI Bank (Islamic financing) [2006-7]; Springwell v JP Morgan Chase (emerging markets investment) [2007]; Charter PLC v City Index (contribution of constructive trusts) [2007]; Stone & Rolls v Moore Stephens (auditor's negligence) [2008]; Parabola v MF Global (fraud of stockbroker) [2009]. Shah v HSBC [2009] (money laundering); Berezovsky v Abramovich [2009] (intimidation); Lehman Brothers Inc (Rascals) [2010] (insolvency of associated companies); Jivraj v Hashwani [2010] (arbitrators as discrimination'); British Bankers Association v FSA [2011] (mis-selling as judicial review). Bank Mellat v HM Treasury and European Council [2012-13] (public law and Iranian sanctions in London and Luxembourg courts); FSA v C [2013] (judicial review of FSA); Fiona Trust v Skarga and Nikitin [2013] (bribery and foreign law); Roadchef v Ingram Hill [2014] (trustee powers and liabilities). Novoship v. Mikhaylyuk [2014] (bribery and account of profits); Peak Hotels v. Tarek and Sherway [2014] (shareholder dispute relating to Aman Hotel group); Kazakhstan Kaghazy v. Zhunus and Arip [2014-5] (conspiracy to defraud); Al-Khorafi v Bank Sarasin [2014-5] (investment advice in Dubai); OMV v Zaver [2015] (arbitration clash between Pakistan and ICC).
Professional Memberships: Midland & Oxford Circuit.
Career: Called to the Bar in 1975 and joined Fountain Court Chambers in 1976. Took Silk in 1992. Recorder and Deputy High Court Judge since 2000. Former Chairman of Commercial Bar Association. Former member of Financial Reporting Review Panel and of Financial Markets Law Committee. Chairman of Trustees: Public Concern at Work (1997-2002). Chairman of Advisory Council of Public Concern at Work (2002 and continuing). Chairman of Education & Training Committee of the Bar Council (2004). Chairman of International Committee of the Bar Council (2008). Director of Bar Mutual Indemnity Fund Limited since 2010; member of Lawyers' Advisory Committee of Peace Brigades International (UK); Special advisor to the Attorney General of Singapore from 2015.
Publications: Author of journal articles and of 'Law of Bank Payments' [1996-2004] (with Raymond Cox).
Personal: Educated at Westminster School 1965-69 and New College, Oxford (double first in classics and jurisprudence) 1970 -1974. Born 23rd June 1952. Lives in London.

BRINSMEAD-STOCKHAM, John
11 New Square, London
020 7424 4017
jbs@11newsquare.com
Featured in Tax (London)
Practice Areas: John undertakes a wide variety of both advisory and litigation work in all areas of tax law. He has advised on matters ranging from inheritance tax and SDLT planning to major corporation tax and VAT disputes between multi-national companies and HMRC. As an advocate he has acted as junior Counsel in several major pieces of litigation and has also appeared unled on many occasions.
Professional Memberships: Revenue Bar Association; Chancery Bar Association; Administrative Law Bar Association; VAT Practitioners Group

BRISBY, John QC
4 Stone Buildings, London
020 7242 5524
j.brisby@4stonebuildings.com
Featured in Chancery (London), Commercial Dispute Resolution (London), Company (London), Fraud (London), Offshore (London), Restructuring/Insolvency (London)
Practice Areas: Litigation and advice in the fields of company law, corporate insolvency and financial services. Emphasis on heavy corporate litigation, mainly in the Chancery Division and Court of Appeal. Cases: Instructed in a number of actions resulting out of the Maxwell affair with a view to locating and recovering assets on behalf of the Maxwell pensioners, and in other high profile fraud or asset recovery situations such as DPR Futures, Barlow Clowes, BCCI and Enron. He has also acted for and against various regulatory bodies such as SIB, IMRO and LAUTRO. Has appeared in well over 100 reported cases, well-known examples being Re Cloverbay [1991] Ch 90, Re Bishopsgate Investment Management [1993] Ch 1 Re British & Commonwealth Holdings plc [1993] AC 426, Ispahani v Bank Melli Iran [1998] Lloyds Rep 133, Morris v Bank of America National Trust & Others [2000] 1 AER 954, Sasea Finance Ltd v KPMG [2000] 1AER 676, UPC v Deutsche Bank AG [2000] 2 BCLC 461, Re Barings plc [2001] 2 BCLC 159.
Professional Memberships: Member of the Commercial Bar Association (COMBAR) and Chancery Bar Association.
Career: Call 1978. QC 1996. Deputy High Court Judge 2004.
Publications: Former Contributor: 'Encyclopaedia of Forms and Precedents' (4th edn) Vol 9 Companies.
Personal: Educated at Westminster School 1969-73 and Scholar of Christ Church, Oxford 1974-77. Born 8th May 1956. Lives in London and Northamptonshire.

BRITTENDEN, Stuart
Old Square Chambers, London
22 7269 0300
brittenden@oldsquare.co.uk
Featured in Employment (London)
Practice Areas: Stuart is an employment law specialist with extensive experience acting for both sides in all aspects of individual and collective employment law at both first instance and appellate level. He regularly acts in complex/ high value claims and matters involving an equal opportunities dimension, as well as industrial relations disputes. Examples of recent cases include: SofS v NUT [2016] IRLR 512 (industrial action); Plumb v Duncan Print Group [2016] ICR 125 (temporal limitation/holiday pay); HM Land Registry v Houghton (s. 15 EqA – bonus); Anderson & Ors v LFEPA [2013] IRLR 459 CA (collective agreements); HM Land Registry v Benson & Ors [2012] IRLR 373 EAT (indirect age discrimination); V&A v Durrant [2011] IRLR 290 EAT (dismissal/ replacements); and Johnson Controls Limited v UKAEA first appellate authority on reg 3(1)(b)(iii) TUPE.
Professional Memberships: ELBA, ELA Management Committee (2012-14), IER, ILS.
Career: Prior to joining Chambers, Stuart attained a Masters in Labour Law at the London School of Economics (LSE). He has lectured in Labour Law at the LSE and has published in the employment field: Tolley's Employment Law (unfair dismissal chapter); Employment Precedents & Company Policy Documents (disciplinary/grievance procedures; works councils; TU recognition); Munkman on Employer's Liability; Westlaw Insight.

BROCKLEBANK, James
7 King's Bench Walk, London
020 7910 8300
jbrocklebank@7kbw.co.uk
Featured in International Arbitration (London), Professional Negligence (London), Commercial Dispute Resolution (London), Energy & Natural Resources (London), Insurance (London)
Practice Areas: James has a broad practice encompassing all areas of commercial litigation, including conflict of laws, energy and natural resources, product liability, banking and finance, international trade, and confidentiality and privilege. He has a particularly prominent reputation in the areas of professional negligence, insurance and reinsurance, and commercial arbitration (often with an international element). He has wide experience of advising and acting in relation to all manner of contractual and tortious disputes. He has frequently been involved substantial pieces of litigation and is familiar with the particular demands of large-scale court and arbitration proceedings.
Professional Memberships: COMBAR; BILA.
Career: Called 1999. Awarded Insurance Junior of the Year at the Chambers UK Bar Awards 2015.
Publications: Co-author of the chapter on Accountants and Auditors in Professional Negligence and Liability (ed. M.Simpson).

Stranger than Fiction (The Lawyer, 28 June 2013) – a discussion of the hold harmless principle in insurance and its connection with damages for late payment of a claim under an insurance policy.
Personal: James was educated at Cranleigh School and Pembroke College, Cambridge, where he read History. He lives in Wimbledon with his wife and daughter. He speaks French and some Japanese.

BROMPTON, Michael QC
5 Paper Buildings, London
020 7583 6117
Michaelbromptonqc@5paper.com
Featured in Financial Crime (London)
Practice Areas: Prosecutes and defends in financial crime and related areas. His specialist fields include revenue fraud, insider trading and investment fraud, money laundering, bribery, confiscation and asset forfeiture. Formerly Standing Counsel to H.M. Customs and Excise, he has appeared in numerous high -profile cases and is prominent in the field of VAT fraud having appeared in many of the major cases of the past decade. His recent or pending cases include: the SFO prosecution of Sweete PLC for an offence of bribery in the Middle East; confiscation proceedings in HMRC Operation Vaulter; a high-profile private prosecution by a UK insurance company; the criminal investigation of an alleged tax avoidance scheme; a major money laundering prosecution (R v Adams & Ors.) and an FCA investment fraud (R v Bhandari & Ors.) He has lectured on tax and other serious fraud including LexisNexis webinars.
Career: Called Middle Temple 1973. Standing Counsel to H.M. Customs & Excise 1994 – 2003. QC 2003. Member of the Serious Fraud Office panel of Queen's Counsel. Head of Chambers 5PB, 2009 – 2014. Recorder of the Crown Court (authorised to sit at the Central Criminal Court).

BROOK, David
Henderson Chambers, London
020 7583 9020
dbrook@hendersonchambers.co.uk
Featured in Employment (London)
Practice Areas: Acts and advises in commercial matters andall aspects of employment law including unfair/wrongful dismissals, disability, discrimination, Working Time, redundancy and TUPE, often involving large scale transfers. He represents both claimants and respondents in the Employment Tribunals, County and High Courts, in the latter principally in restrictive covenant matters, injunctions, bonus and shareholding claims, and he regularly appears in the Appellate Courts. As an ADR accredited mediator, he advises and acts in the resolution of employment and commercial disputes.
Professional Memberships: ELA; ELBA; ADR Accredited Mediator.
Career: BA Phil Hons (Lond), DipLaw (City). Called to the Bar 1988 with a background in management and business. Former Managing Director of a UK company, past Deputy Director of the Howard League for Penal Reform, current Chairman of a London city farm, sits as an Employment Judge and sometime Chairman of a University Academic Disciplinary Panel.
Personal: Interests include music, sailing and skiing.

BROOK SMITH, Philip QC
Fountain Court Chambers, London
020 7583 3335
pbs@fountaincourt.co.uk
Featured in Product Liability (London)
Practice Areas: Wide-ranging practice covers a broad spread of commercial and common law work with considerable experience of product liability issues. Instructed in (for example) HIV Haemophilia, Hepatitis C, Oral Contraceptives, MMR group litigation and PIP breast implants litigation. Wider commercial and general civil work undertaken includes banking disputes, financial markets and services, insurance/reinsurance, aviation, shipbuilding disputes, oil and gas, international arbitration work, anti-suit claims, competition, employment, professional negligence claims, and all commercial fraud. Notable cases include the Jahre case (civil fraud, trusts). Extensive experience of offshore jurisdictions (particularly as regards financial services).
Professional Memberships: Common Law and Commercial Bar Association; South Eastern Circuit.
Career: Called to the Bar in 1982, joined Fountain Court Chambers in 1983, appointed QC in 2002.
Personal: Educated at the London School of Economics (BSc Mathematics – 1st Class Hons) and London University (MSc Mathematics – distinction). Born 6 March 1957. Lives in London.

BROOKS, Duncan
Queen Elizabeth Building QEB, London
020 7797 7837
d.brooks@qeb.co.uk
Featured in Family/Matrimonial (London)
Practice Areas: Duncan is known as "an excellent lawyer with superb client care skills" who deals with "very complex matrimonial finance proceedings and children law matters". He is "superb at putting nervous clients at ease" and "excellent on detail" (Chambers UK). He is "hardworking, conscientious and extremely bright" (Legal 500). He is recommended as a leading junior in financial and private law children cases. Duncan is familiar with the financial complexities arising in cases involving high net worth clients, including businesses, trusts, taxation and international forum disputes (both in respect to divorce/financial applications and also relocating with children). He is often instructed where there is a knotty point of law. Duncan has been a Family Arbitrator (MCIArb) since 2013. He has been appointed as the arbitrator in eleven arbitrations, and has delivered Awards in eight (the remainder are ongoing). He has also acted in arbitrations as a barrister. He regularly represents clients at Private FDRs and also acts as the Private FDR tribunal. He has been a Deputy District Judge (civil and family, including private law children cases) since 2010. He is also a Collaborative Lawyer.
Career: Collaborative Lawyer (Resolution trained) since January 2009. Deputy District Judge Civil (2010). Family Arbitrator (MCI Arb) 2013

BROWN, Catherine
12 King's Bench Walk, London
020 7583 0811
chambers@12kbw.co.uk
Featured in Personal Injury (London)
Practice Areas: Catherine has a specialist personal injury and health and safety practice. She has particular expertise in public authority claims, including stress, education, highways, child abuse and property damage claims. She represents defendants in complex health and safety prosecutions and at inquests.
Professional Memberships: PIBA; PNBA; SE Circuit; AWB.
Career: Called 1990 (Middle Temple); Recorder (Wales) (2008) (crime (inc. serious sexual offences) and civil); BSB Professional Conduct Committee (2009-2015). Interesting cases: Manda v UBS AG (2016); ABC v Northumbria Police (QBD, discontinued 2016); Redfern v Corby BC (QBD, settled 2015); Welsh Government v Hillcrest Care Ltd (2014); R(Epping Forest DC) v Casterbridge Care and Education Ltd (2013); R(HSE) v Tennant (2013); R v Collier (2012); R(Herts CC) v Menna (2012); Armstrong v Keepmoat Homes Ltd (QBD 3/2/12); Thomas v Warwickshire CC [2011] EWHC 772 (QB); Rhiya Malin Inquest (2010); Harvey v Plymouth CC [2010] EWCA Civ 860; [2010] PIQR P18; Button v Caerphilly CBC [2010] EWCA Civ 1311; Maloney v Torfaen CBC [2005] EWCA Civ 1762; [2006] PIQR P21; Wallis v Balfour Beatty [2003] EWCA Civ 72.
Personal: Nonsuch High School for Girls, Cheam; Birmingham University (B Com (Hons)); PCL (Diploma in Law)

BROWN, Edward QC
QEB Hollis Whiteman, London
020 79338855
edward.brown@qebhw.co.uk
Featured in Crime (London)
Practice Areas: Edward Brown QC has an outstanding practice in criminal law and related areas (regulatory, health and safety, inquests, Public Inquiries), chiefly at the Central Criminal Court where for 7 years until 2014 he was Senior Treasury Counsel. He has prosecuted or defended in many of the most notable and sensitive cases, including murder, corporate and individual fraud, corporate manslaughter, terrorism, police and political corruption, and export control evasion. In particular he is the lead criminal QC in the ongoing SFO investigation into Barclays' 2008 capital raising. Recently he successfully prosecuted Ben Butler for the killing of his daughter Ellie, was instructed by the Attorney General of Isle of Man to conduct the disciplinary proceedings against the former Attorney General. He is the lead counsel at the Independent Inquiry into Child Sexual Abuse (IICSA, formerly the "Goddard Inquiry") acting for the CPS. He acted for a multinational corporate in a recent DPA negotiation and acts for JCB on H&S cases. He was lead counsel in a recent carbon monoxide corporate manslaughter prosecution. He prosecuted the Mark Duggan shooting case (and was involved in the Inquest) and in the murder of Robert Troyan, a socialite murdered by financial advisor David Jeffs. Other cases include the double child killing (Say); defending in "Cash for Peerages" police inquiry (acting for the Labour Party – no charges brought) and MPs expenses; was lead counsel in the leading case on anonymity of witnesses (Mayers); Barot (the 'dirty bomb Al Qaeda terrorist, the highest ranking AQ leader prosecuted in UK) and the Stockwell gang shooting of the five year old Thusha. He called the youngest ever witness in a murder trial (aged 4). In the past has been instructed in many important and significant cases including Matrix Churchill, the Dome Robbery, Rigg Approach corruption, Blue Arrow, Birmingham Six officers and Zeebrugge corporate manslaughter (the ferry disaster). He has advised Attorneys General on numerous cases and was consulted by the then Solicitor General (and has given seminars) on Deferred Prosecution Agreements. He lectures young gang members in South London on the consequences of joint enterprise gang violence and is a trustee of Growing Against Violence (GAV). He is head of the Crime Group at QEB Hollis Whiteman.
Professional Memberships: Criminal Bar Association steering party – Involuntary Manslaughter, CPS Steering Committee Disclosure, UN Detention Review Board, Kosovo.
Career: Silk 2008; Recorder 2001, Call 1983
Publications: He has written on joint enterprise in The Times and appeared in a BBC documentary on the topic.

BROWN, Marc
St Philips Chambers, Birmingham
0121 246 7048
mbrown@st-philips.com
Featured in Commercial Dispute Resolution (Midlands), Restructuring/Insolvency (Midlands)
Practice Areas: Marc's practice has a keen focus on insolvency work, but also comprises general commercial litigation, encompassing the full spectrum of disputes with an emphasis on banking, financial and contractual matters. Marc's insolvency practice is wide ranging, including both personal and corporate insolvency aspects. He acts for directors, companies and individuals as well as administrators, liquidators and trustees in bankruptcy. See for example: Edginton v Sekhon [2015] EWCA Civ 816; Re BTR (UK) Ltd [2012] EWHC 2398 (Ch); and Re: Care People Ltd [2013] EWHC 1734 (Ch). Marc has a particular interest in cases involving the determination of a debtor's Centre of Main Interests under the EU Insolvency Regulation (so-called "bankruptcy tourism" cases). See for example: Re Schrade [2013] BPIR 911 and [2014] EWHC 1049 (Ch); and Re: Benk [2012] EWHC 2432 (Ch).
Professional Memberships: MCCBA.
Career: Marc studied law (jurisprudence) at Mansfield College, Oxford University. He was called in 2004 and then returned to Oxford University to undertake the Bachelor of Civil Laws, a postgraduate degree in law, obtaining the prestigious Vinerian Scholarship. Having completed pupillage at St Philips Chambers, he started practice in 2006.
Personal: Marc's leisure interests include golf and snowboarding.

BROWN, Robert
Arden Chambers, London
020 7242 4244
robert.brown@ardenchambers.com
Featured in Social Housing (London)
Practice Areas: Landlord and tenant, property, public law, and housing. He acts for local authorities, housing associations, private landlords and tenants. He appears in the County Court, High Court, Court of Appeal, LVT/FTT(PC) and has been led in the Supreme Court.
Career: BA (Hons), LLB (Hons). Called 2008. Awarded the Sir Louis Gluckstein Prize for Advocacy by Lincoln's Inn. He has previously worked in local government, the Civil Service, higher education and the Third

Sector. Significant cases include Manchester v Pinnock [2010] UKSC 45 (as pupil, led by Andrew Arden QC; Jonathan Manning); Hounslow v Powell [2011] UKSC 8 (led by Andrew Arden QC; Jonathan Manning); Zafar v Goddard, Legal Action April 2011; R (GCLC) v Greenwich [2012] EWCA Civ 496 (led by Jonathan Manning); and Haile v Waltham Forest [2015] UKSC 34 (led by Andrew Arden QC).
Publications: He has been an editor of the Housing Law Reports (Sweet and Maxwell) since 2012. He is a co-author of Judicial Review Proceedings – A Practitioner's Guide (LAG, 2013) and Current Law Statutes annotations for Localism Act 2011 and Local Government Finance Act 2012. He writes regularly for the Journal of Housing Law and also contributes to the RICS isurv service.

BROWN, Tom
Cloisters, London
020 7827 4000
tb@cloisters.com
Featured in Employment (London)
Practice Areas: Tom specialises in employment and equality law, and has experience and expertise in wider partnership, commercial, regulatory, immigration, public law and human rights advice and litigation. He acts for companies, charities and public authorities, trade unions and individuals. He has substantial experience of appellate and High Court litigation without a leader. In addition to several high-profile trials, his significant appellate cases include McBride v Scottish police Authority (reinstatement), UCU v Stirling University (collective redundancy consultation), RR Donnelly Global v Besagni (TUPE), Buckland v Bournemouth University (breach of contract) and Thaine v London School of Economics (apportionment of damages).
Professional Memberships: ELA, ELBA, ILS.
Career: Tenant at Cloisters since 2001; Judicial Assistant to Lord Bingham of Cornhill (2002—2003); secondment to Mallesons, Melbourne (2005); Associate, Federal Court of Australia (2005); secondment to Stewarts Law LLP (2012—2013).
Publications: Blackstone's Guide to the Equality Act 2010 (OUP, 2016); Discrimination in Employment (Legal Action Group, 2013); Family Rights At Work (Jordans, 2012).
Personal: Educated at the BRIT School, London; King Edward VI College, Nuneaton; Merton College, Oxford (first class honours; college and university scholar) and City University (DipLaw). Middle Temple and Pegasus scholar. Tom is a keen competitive oarsman.

BROWNE, Benjamin QC
2TG - 2 Temple Gardens, London
020 7822 1200
bbrowne@2tg.co.uk
Featured in Personal Injury (London), Travel (London), Clinical Negligence (London)
Practice Areas: Personal injury – acting for both sides including alleged radiation injury, work related stress, defective components, riding accidents, criminal acts of employees and Fatal Accident Act claims. Clinical negligence – acting for both sides in cases involving catastrophic birth injury, negligent diagnosis and treatment, failure to recognise medical conditions, failure to safeguard suicidal patients. Travel – accidents abroad, Rome II, jurisdictional issues. Notable cases include Mirvahedy v Henley, House of Lords [2002] Animals Act, Mattis v Pollock, CA [2003] Vicarious Liability. Evans v Birmingham and the Black Country SHA, CA [2000] Liability: cerebral palsy. Williams v The Estate of Mr James McGarley Johnstone [RCJ QBD 2008] Limitation: section 33. Orchard v Lee, Randall and Governors of Corfe Hill School [CA 2009]: liability of children. Virgin Airways v Heathrow Airport [2011] Claim by disabled US citizen injured in accident at Heathrow: Montreal Convention, jurisdiction and applicable law. Goldsmith v Patchcott and Roach [2012] PIQR P11 (COA) Animals Act. Collier v Norton [2012]: highest reported PI case, Wall v Mutuelle de Poitiers [2013]: Approach to evidence under Rome II. Mohamud v Morrisons Supreme Court [2015] vicarious liability, Williams v BHB Privy Council [2016] material contribution in clinical negligence.
Professional Memberships: PIBA.
Career: Christ Church, Oxford. MA Jurisprudence.

BROWNE-WILKINSON, Simon QC
Fountain Court Chambers, London
020 7583 3335
sbw@fountaincourt.co.uk
Featured in Fraud (London)
Practice Areas: Has a general commercial practice, but specialises in particular in arbitration (domestic and international) and civil fraud, including the obtaining and discharging of interim relief. Practice also includes employment, insurance, professional negligence, banking, chancery, and professional discipline. Arbitration: Extensive experience of substantial international arbitration, including acting for Electronic Arts SA in an ICC arbitration relating to Italian distribution rights, the Government of India in an UNCITRAL arbitration pursuant to a Bilateral Investment Treaty against Bechtel, Enron and GEC relating to the Dabhol Power Plant, a Nigerian telecoms company in two arbitrations relating to a management agreement and call charges, a Cypriot company in a LCIA arbitration relating to the Russian manufacturing sector, and an ICC arbitration relating to petroleum products. Has also given evidence as an expert witness on English law in a Stockholm arbitration, and as an expert on English Arbitration law. Reported cases in the Commercial Court on the operation of the Arbitration Act 1996 include Econet Wireless Ltd v Vee Networks Ltd (discharge of injunction granted to support an arbitration), Vee Networks Ltd. v ESS (jurisdiction of arbitrators to consider a defence of set off), and Vee Networks Ltd v EWI (award set aside on the grounds of unfairness in the conduct of an arbitration). Also sits as an arbitrator. Fraud: Specialises in civil fraud including, in particular, injunctive relief relating to allegations of fraud. Recently obtained the discharge of search and seize and worldwide freezing orders on the ground of non-disclosure, and the discharge of an injunction preventing the completion of a billion dollar transaction on the ground of non-disclosure. Acted for the Secretary of State for Justice in a multi-million pound fraud claim, obtained judgment for a Nigerian bank in a fraud claim for over £500 million against its former chief executive, and as an expert on BVI Law in relation to claims in New York and Holland arising out of the Madoff fraud.
Career: Called to the Bar in 1981. QC 1998.
Personal: Educated at Oxford University.

BRUCE, Andrew
Serle Court, London
020 7242 6105
abruce@serlecourt.co.uk
Featured in Art and Cultural Property Law (London), Real Estate Litigation (London)
Practice Areas: Andrew has a commercial and chancery practice with a particular focus on property-related work. He is one of the leading senior juniors in real estate litigation and has been described as "an exceptional talent in the property sphere". In addition, Andrew has a niche art law practice and is highly-rated for professional negligence work, acting for both claimants and defendants, in matters ranging from high-profile claims about Old Master Paintings to claims against architects in respect of residential developments and claims against solicitors relating to international corporate transactions. Andrew also regularly acts in high-value commercial litigation and is a "skilful advocate" who is "effective in digging under the surface to uncover the real issues".
Professional Memberships: Property Bar Association (Committee member 2003-09); Chancery Bar Association; Professional Negligence Bar Association.
Career: Called to the Bar in 1992 (Hamsworth Exhibitioner and Benefactors' Scholar of the Middle Temple). Joined Serle Court from 3 Paper Buildings, Temple in 1999. Appointed Deputy District Judge in 2004 and Judge of the First-Tier Tribunal (Property Chamber) (part-time) (formerly Deputy Adjudicator to HM Land Registry) in 2008.
Personal: Honorary Legal adviser at Swanley CAB (2001-2012). Past captain of Leigh Cricket Club. Married with three daughters.

BRYAN, Robert
Drystone Chambers, London
020 7404 1881
robert.bryan@drystone.com
Featured in Crime (Western)
Practice Areas: Criminal law, local authority/regulatory law, health and safety, courts martial.
Professional Memberships: Western Circuit, CBA, Association of Military Court Advocates, POCLA, HSLA
Career: As both Junior and Leading Junior Robert's work covers the wide spectrum of serious crime including homicide, sex-offending, serious fraud and drug conspiracies. As Junior alone he has successfully defended attempted murder, and has both prosecuted and defended in a number of motor vehicle death cases. He is particularly known for his skill and presentation in 'document' and 'computer' cases. Robert is regularly briefed both to prosecute and defend in multi-complainant cases of sexual offending (including historic abuse cases and offences against children). He is on the Crown Prosecution Specialist Rape Panel.
Publications: Criminal law today (Thomson Reuters)- regular contributor

BRYANT, Ceri QC
Erskine Chambers, London
020 7242 5532
cbryant@erskinechambers.com
Featured in Company (London)
Practice Areas: Ceri is a well-respected silk with a broad practice spanning company law, corporate insolvency and financial services. Her clients include FTSE and AIM listed companies and non-corporate organisations and she is regularly instructed on corporate reorganisations, takeovers and mergers (onshore and offshore) and transfers of insurance business. Significant cases and transactions include Enviroco Ltd v Farstad Supply A/S in the Supreme Court, the creation of Flood Re, Rodenstock GmbH, Expro plc (instructed by the Takeover Panel), T&N Ltd, Fiberweb plc, Linton Park plc, and various schemes of arrangement for the INEOS group, Wizz Air, the Drax group, Soho House plc, Jarvis plc, Interflora, the National Federation of Builders, and the Loch Lomond Golf Club and the liquidators of the SPhinX funds in the Cayman Islands.
Professional Memberships: ILA, INSOL, RISA (Cayman), Chancery Bar Association, COMBAR.
Career: Called: 1984. Silk: 2012.
Publications: Contributor to "Buckley on the Companies Acts" and "Hannigan and Prentice: The Companies Act 2006 – a commentary" (both LexisNexis Butterworths) Contributor to "The Law of Majority Shareholder Power" and "Corporate Finance Law in the UK and EU" (both OUP)
Personal: Born 1960. Educated Beverley High School for Girls; Girton College, University of Cambridge (BA and LLM).

BRYANT-HERON, Mark QC
9-12 Bell Yard, London
07973 167 084
mbh@912by.com
Featured in Crime (London)
Practice Areas: Criminal Law: Mark Bryant-Heron has extensive experience of cases in complex white collar and corporate fraud and serious general criminal work, and has been instructed in the highest profile cases. His practice areas are business crime, heavy fraud and serious general crime, internal corporate criminal and quasi-criminal investigations, private prosecutions, tax-related crime. He has a substantial advisory practice advising on private prosecutions on behalf of corporate entities which has been defrauded, internal corporate criminal and quasi-criminal investigations, international and cross-jurisdictional fraud, bribery and corruption, extradition, criminal confiscation and asset recovery, money laundering, financial regulation, export licensing and sanctions, insolvency related criminal liability. He also practices in the tax tribunal in tax fraud related matters. Recent and current cases include the defence of a Chief Executive Officer of a corporate in an SFO prosecution alleging asset finance fraud (R v Alexander and others, Sep 2016); the prosecution of a multi-handed mortgage fraud (R v Khan and others, April 2016); the first successful contested prosecution of a corporate for corruption of foreign public officials (R v Smith & Ouzman Ltd and others, Dec 2014); the prosecution of the phone hacking case (R v Rebekah Brooks, Andy Coulson and others, 2013-2014), a substantial VAT reclaim appeal in the tax tribunal (Abbott Ltd & Starmill Ltd v HMRC, 2015, R v Kay and others [Operation Elveden alleged corrupt payments by journalists to public officials] 2015).
Personal: MA Cantab (Clare College).

BUCHANAN, James
2 Hare Court, London
020 73535324
jamesbuchanan@2harecourt.com
Featured in Crime (London), Health & Safety (London)

Practice Areas: James Buchanan is recognised as a leading crime and regulatory practitioner and he is highly sort in these fields. James' practice focuses on workplace crime, particularly in relation to health and safety matters. His work covers the full range of offences, from manslaughter to prosecutions under the HSWA arising out of fatal and non-fatal accidents. James has significant experience of the construction, transport and healthcare sectors and is currently instructed in numerous cases involving fatalities and catastrophic personal injuries. He is a specialist defence practitioner with a reputation as a robust trial advocate and shrewd tactician. He is incredibly hard working and excellent at building good relationships. Recent instructions include a company charged with breaching CDM regulations during excavation works, a company charged with breaching section 2 HSWA following the death of an employee, a company that faced a multi-count indictment following catastrophic injuries sustained by an individual working on the refurbishment of commercial premises at Canary Wharf.

Professional Memberships: Health and Safety Lawyers' Association; Association of Regulatory and Disciplinary Lawyers; Criminal Bar Association.

BUCK, William
St Philips Chambers, Leeds
0113 244 6691
wbuck@st-philips.com
Featured in Commercial Dispute Resolution (North Eastern)

Practice Areas: A commercial barrister who litigates across a wide spectrum of disputes and is instructed on high value cases in the High Court and in other jurisdictions such as the Isle of Man, Spain and the USA. Work undertaken includes shareholder/director disputes, guarantee claims, agency disputes, trust litigation, sale of goods, contracts for the provisions of services, partnership matters, construction, alleged restraints of trade, insurance, business sales, professional negligence and soft IP cases. He has a particular focus on banking and asset finance litigation and is regularly instructed by several of the largest financial providers in the market on multi-million pound disputes. A substantial aspect of this type of work is of an interlocutory nature, often on a without notice basis, and includes the obtaining of freezing orders, injunctions and orders for delivery up. Many of these cases have an international element to them, with recent cases involving the application of Spanish, German and Turkish law and where parties and/or assets are located outside of the jurisdiction. William's international practice predominantly relates to the financial services market and disputes concerning trusts. He has considerable appellant experience, regularly appearing before the Court of Appeal on a wide range of issues.

BUCKETT, Edwin
9 Gough Square, London
020 7832 0500
ebuckett@9goughsquare.co.uk
Featured in Police Law (All Circuits)

Practice Areas: Police Law (including Disciplinary matters), Personal Injury claims and Professional Negligence.

Professional Memberships: PIBA; PNBA and ALBA

Career: Called 1988; Pegasus Scholar (Inner Temple) Toronto, Canada; Chambers of Andrew Ritchie QC from 1990 to date. Chairman of Police Misconduct Tribunal (2015). Assistant Coroner (Inner North London) (2016).

Publications: "Civil Actions Against the Police" (3rd Edition) 2004 with Hugh Tomlinson QC, Richard Clayton QC and Andrew Davies. "Preventative Orders" (1st Edition) 2010 with Tom Little and Rob McAllister.

BUCKINGHAM, Paul
Keating Chambers, London
020 7544 2600
pbuckingham@keatingchambers.com
Featured in International Arbitration (London), Construction (London), Energy & Natural Resources (London)

Practice Areas: Specialist in major construction, engineering and energy disputes, with particular interest and expertise in international arbitration work and technically complex disputes. He is a dually qualified chemical engineer/ Barrister after spending eight years with BP as a chemical engineer in the oil and gas industries. Has worked on a wide range of contentious matters involving international construction and engineering projects, and has acted on disputes involving most standard form contracts and their derivatives including the JCT, ICE, IChemE and FIDIC Forms. Paul regularly acts for clients in court, adjudication and mediation, with experience at all levels of alternative dispute resolution including dispute review boards, project appeal panels and direct settlement negotiations. He has extensive experience of numerous arbitrations under ICC, LCIA, UNCITRAL and ad hoc rules, both as counsel and as arbitrator, and also sits as an adjudicator.

Professional Memberships: Chairman of the IChemE Dispute Resolution Committee; Society of Construction Law; Technology and Construction Bar Association (TECBAR); Commercial Bar Association (COMBAR).

Career: Chartered Engineer 1990, Called to the Bar 1995, IChemE accredited arbitrator and adjudicator 2006, TECBAR adjudicator and arbitrator.

Publications: Contributor to Construction Dispute Resolution Handbook and Keating on Construction Contracts; consulting editor to Construction Law Journal.

BUCKINGHAM, Stewart
Quadrant Chambers, London
020 7583 4444
clerks@quadrantchambers.com
Featured in Shipping (London)

Practice Areas: All aspects of commercial litigation and arbitration, and particular areas expertise include shipping, commodities, international sale of goods, commercial contracts, charterparties, marine insurance, conflict of laws and interim remedies and injunctions in support of proceedings in Court and arbitration.

Professional Memberships: COMBAR

Career: Called to the bar 1996.

Publications: Butterworths Commercial Court & Arbitration Pleadings.

Personal: Hertford College Oxford, First Class Honours degree in Jurisprudence and BCL.

BUCKPITT, Michael
Tanfield Chambers, London
020 7421 5319
MichaelBuckpitt@tanfieldchambers.co.uk
Featured in Real Estate Litigation (London)

Practice Areas: Property litigation in particular: Real property – all issues concerning real property including contracts for the sale of land, overage and options, easements, restrictive covenants and mortgages. Landlord and tenant: all areas of commercial and residential disputes including dilapidations, forfeiture, 1954 Act lease renewals, service charges, appointment of Managers and RTM. Enfranchisement – all aspects under the 1993 Act and 1967 Act.

Professional Memberships: Member of the Property Bar Association and Chancery Bar Association.

Career: Called 1988. Recommended for several years in Chambers & Partners, Legal Experts and Legal 500 for property work. Instructed by a variety of law firms (including city/west end/niche firms) on behalf of individuals and commercial clients (including developers, London Estates and clients with significant property portfolios) concerning disputes in the courts, the First Tier Tribunal (Property Chamber) and Upper Tribunal (Lands Chamber).

Publications: Co-author: Service Charges and Management. Contributor to Estates Gazette "Residential View".

Personal: Born 1965. Married with two children. Interests include road cycling and guitar.

BUDDEN, Rosemary
Queen Elizabeth Building QEB, London
020 7797 7837
r.budden@qeb.co.uk
Featured in Family/Matrimonial (London)

Practice Areas: Specialises in family law, both financial claims (financial remedy, Schedule 1 applications, Trust of Land Act applications and Part III) and private law children work including relocation cases. Rosemary enjoys being instructed both on her own, often against more senior opponents and as junior to Leading Counsel. Rosemary acts for a wide range of clients in particular high net-worth clients with complex financial arrangements. Rosemary brings an intelligent, strategic and extremely personable approach to her cases and has been consistently ranked in Chambers & Partners since 2013.

Professional Memberships: Family Law Bar Association, Resolution, Bar Pro Bono Unit, Lawyers' Christian Fellowship

Career: Oxford University (MA (Hons) Jurisprudence); Hardwicke Scholarship (Lincoln's Inn), called 2003. Reported cases: Schofield v Schofield [2011] 1 FLR 212, CA, In the matter of M-H (Children) 2006 EWCA Civ 499. Recent cases include Fields v Fields [2015] EWHC 1670 (Fam) with Lewis Marks QC. Recent lectures include Part III of the MFPA 1984 to the IBC International Family Conference.

Publications: Durable Solutions – Edited by Rt. Hon Lord Justice Thorpe & Rosemary Budden, Jordans 2006

BUEHRLEN, Veronique QC
Keating Chambers, London
020 7544 2600
vbuehrlen@keatingchambers.com
Featured in International Arbitration (London), Energy & Natural Resources (London)

Practice Areas: Wide ranging commercial litigation, international arbitration and advisory practise with special emphasis on complex energy disputes (on-and offshore), construction, banking, insurance and civil fraud. Strengths include meticulous preparation of complex highly detailed matters requiring penetrating and determined cross examination of expert and other witnesses. Veronique has a wealth of experience of the Commercial Court and international Arbitration (having previously practiced at a magic circle set). She has conducted several major commercial hearings as Leading Counsel including a four week Commercial Court trial for Borealis AB, in respect of a contaminated LPG, a six week ICC arbitration concerning the construction and installation of a subsea pipeline used in the first gravity based structure for the regasification of LNG, an ICC arbitration regarding the construction of a container port under FIDIC a contract and a Commercial Court trial concerning the lowering of a live subsea gas pipeline. She is currently instructed as Leading Counsel on a € multi-million dispute arising out of the termination of a major sub-sea pipeline project. Veronique also sits as an arbitrator. She is bilingual French/English.

Career: Called 1991, Queen's Counsel 2010. Stage at the Legal Service and European Court of Justice. Fountain Court 1992-2011; Keating 2011 to date

BUNYAN, Angus
2 Hare Court, London
020 7353 5324
angusbunyan@2harecourt.com
Featured in Crime (London)

Practice Areas: An established criminal advocate, he defends and prosecutes the most serious and complex cases. Recent practice has focused on serious fraud, business crime, bribery and corruption and money laundering. He also advises and represents individuals and companies in contested regulatory matters, in particular in environmental proceedings. A CPS level 4 prosecutor and member of the Fraud and Serious Crime panels, he is instructed as leading counsel in high-profile, sensitive and multi-handed trials where specialist knowledge is required. He deals with offences under POCA and also with the confiscation regime including pre-charge restraint. Recent cases include R v Mills and others: allegations of serious and long running corruption between senior managers of HBOS and leading figures of the UK business community, R v Gillam and Davies: bribery by UK company directors to secure US military hardware contract in Afghanistan, R v Barsso and others: allegations of market rigging and hidden referral fees within the insurance industry, R v Sanghera and others: importation of Cocaine and ammunition into Heathrow via BA cargo flights from Mexico.

Professional Memberships: Criminal Bar Association, Fraud Lawyers Association, UK Environmental Law Association, Health and Safety Lawyers Association

Career: Called 1999, Lincoln's Inn, Wolfson and Hardwicke Scholar, CPS Grade 4

(including for fraud and organised crime), Specialist Regulatory Advocate (HSE, EA and ORR).

BURDEN, Angus
St Philips Chambers, Birmingham
0121 246 7000
commercial@st-philips.com
Featured in Chancery (Midlands)
Practice Areas: All aspects of contentious and non-contentious wills and trusts work including the validity of wills, breach of trust claims, will construction disputes, applications for the rectification of wills, and the removal of personal representatives/trustees. He has considerable experience in proceedings under the Inheritance (Provision for Family and Dependants) Act 1975, and claims against estates based on proprietary estoppel or constructive trust. He also undertakes Court of Protection work and professional negligence claims relating to wills and estates. His non-contentious work includes general issues arising in the administration of estates and trusts, including tax.
Professional Memberships: Midland Chancery and Commercial Bar Association.
Career: Called 1994. Currently tenant at St Philips Chambers, Birmingham.
Personal: Educated at Exeter University (BA Hons, first class) and Bristol University (post graduate certificates in insolvency, restitution and company law).

BURGE, Edmund
5 St Andrew's Hill, London
020 7332 5400
EdmundBurge@5sah.co.uk
Featured in Financial Crime (London)
Practice Areas: Financial and Commercial Crime, Regulatory Offences, Proceeds of Crime
Professional Memberships: Fraud Lawyers Association (FLA); Proceeds of Crime Lawyers Association (PoCLA); Association of Regulatory & Disciplinary Lawyers (ARDL); Criminal Bar Association; South Eastern Circuit
Career: Called in 1997, Edmund is a leading junior specialising in commercial and financial crime, with extensive experience of leading in cases alleging serious and complex fraud (fiscal and commercial), corruption, money laundering and other cross-border transactional crime. Recent cases include Louca and others (2016) (£15m money laundering), Baxendale-Walker (2016) (tax advisor accused of forgery and fraudulent High Court claim for £230m damages), and Ahmed, Shearer & Azzopardi (2016) (£7m tax fraud on HMRC). Current instructions include a £30m MTIC fraud involving contra-deals in tangible commodities and VOIP, utilising off-shore banking platforms. His 5 years in the Financial Services Division the OFT prior to coming to the Bar has provided him with valuable experience of the wider regulatory landscape, enabling the provision of informed and pragmatic advice. Edmund is on the SFO A-Panels for Crime and Proceeds of Crime, the Grade 4 CPS panels for Fraud, Serious Crime and Proceeds of Crime, and the Attorney-General's Panel of Special Advocates in cases of terrorism and national security. He has been DV cleared since 2007.

BURKILL, Guy QC
Three New Square, London
020 7405 1111
clerks@3newsquare.co.uk
Featured in Information Technology (London), Intellectual Property (London)
Practice Areas: All intellectual property. He has been particularly active in technology-oriented patent cases involving, telecoms, computer hardware and software and electronics and also enjoys a more diverse practice in copyright, trade marks, and other IP. He has acted for many leading multinational companies in the telecommunication, computer, electronics, paper, chemical, pharmaceutical, aviation and other fields. Notable cases include Pavel v Sony (Walkman case); Hoechst v British Petroleum (chemical manufacture, account of profits); Discovision v Disctronics (CD mastering); Dyson v Hoover (vacuum cleaners, post expiry injunction); Sweeney v MacMillan (James Joyce's 'Ulysses', copyright and passing off); Glaxo v Dowelhurst (trade marks, parallel imports); Philips v Princo (writable CD; directors' liability), Schlumberger v EMGS (electromagnetic detection of subsea oil reservoirs); Qualcomm v Nokia, HTC v Apple, HTC v Nokia, and Samsung v Apple (multiple aspects of mobile phone technology).
Professional Memberships: Intellectual Property Bar Association; Chancery Bar Association.
Career: Winchester College; Corpus Christi College Cambridge – MA Degree, 1st Class Hons in Engineering (Electrical Option); called to Bar 1981; QC 2002.
Publications: Co-editor of 'Terrell on the Law of Patents' – 15th edition (2000), 16th edition (2006), 17th edition (2011).
Personal: Leisure interests include violin, opera, and (when time permits) programming.

BURLES, David
1 Garden Court Family Law Chambers, London
020 7797 7900
burles@1gc.com
Featured in Family/Matrimonial (London)
Practice Areas: Ancillary relief, property disputes between unmarried partners, private law children.
Professional Memberships: FLBA Member, Common Law Bar Association, Bar Sports Law Group. Member of the Legal Advisory Group to the Law Commission Cohabitation Law Project 2005-07, Deputy District Judge (2007).
Career: Cranleigh School. LLB (Hons) Bristol University. Called 1984 (Middle Temple). Joined 1 Garden Court in 1999 following a mixed family/common law practice at Goldsmith Building. Postgraduate Certificate in Sports Law (King's College) 1998.
Publications: Co-author of "Applications Under Schedule 1 to the Children Act 1989", Contributor to Halsbury's Laws (children – financial claims), Contributor to Butterworths Civil Court Precedents – ('children/ family breakdown'). Articles in The Times, Family Law, Family Law Week, Solicitors Journal, New Law Journal.
Personal: Playing hockey, golf and some occasional cricket. Theatre.

BURNS, Andrew QC
Devereux, London
020 7353 7534
burns@devchambers.co.uk
Featured in Employment (London), Insurance (London)
Practice Areas: Andrew Burns QC specialises in complex commercial, employment and industrial disputes, particularly injunctions. He has featured in some of the leading appellate cases in insurance law and trade disputes in recent years including the Employers' Liability Policy Trigger Litigation in the Supreme Court, the BA cabin crew litigation, RMT v Serco (the key appellate authority on strike injunctions) and Prophet plc v Huggett on restrictive covenant injunctions. He has acted for BA, London bus companies, BT, Post Office and train companies in industrial disputes and related claims. He appeared for the Co-operative Group and Ladbrokes in recent executive whistleblowing claims and for Network Rail in collective claims. He has appeared in recognition and EWC claims in the CAC and two recent High Court professional negligence claims as well as advising in ongoing insurance disputes and maintaining a practice appearing in the DIFC Court of Appeal. Andrew is a co-author of the Law of Reinsurance (with Colin Edelman QC) and Injunctions with Sir David Bean. He is also a general editor of Discrimination Law (Bloomsbury Professional).
Professional Memberships: COMBAR, BILA, ELA, LCLCBA, ELBA, ILS, PNBA
Career: Called 1993 Middle Temple; Silk 2005; Crown Court Recorder (2009)

BURNS, Paul
Exchange Chambers, Liverpool
0151 236 7747
burns@exchangechambers.co.uk
Featured in Local Government (Northern), Social Housing (Northern)
Practice Areas: Housing law and housing management, residential landlord and tenant law / property law (including possession, disrepair and unlawful eviction), anti-social behaviour litigation (including possession, injunctions, demotion, gang injunctions and closure orders), human rights law, capacity and mental health, Equality Act issues, pubic law challenges, disciplinary and regulatory law and advice and drafting relating to policies, procedures and governance. Regularly instructed in high profile and test case litigation.
Professional Memberships: Member of Lincoln's Inn and The Northern Administrative Law Association. Sir Thomas More Scholar and Hardwicke Scholar (Lincoln's Inn).
Career: Called to the Bar (1998 – Lincoln's Inn). Joined Exchange Chambers (1998). Registered Pupil Supervisor (2008). Head of the Local Government and Social Housing Department (2010). Independent Counsel to Police Misconduct Panels (2010). Appointed Junior Counsel to the Crown by the Attorney General (2015). Appointed Legally Qualified Chair of Police Misconduct Hearings (2016). Named one of the top 10 UK 'Future Stars of the Bar' by The Times and Barrister of the Year at the Liverpool Law Society Legal Awards.
Personal: Educated at St Mary's College Crosby, The University of Liverpool and The Inns of Court School of Law (London). Governor of St Mary's College Crosby (2003-2013). Vice Chair of Governors (2011-2013). Appointed Non-Executive Director at Southport and Ormskirk Hospital NHS Trust by The Appointments Commission (2010). Appointed Senior Independent Director (2012) and Chair of the Remuneration and Nominations Committee (2013). Appointed Non-Executive Director of First Ark Limited (2015).

BURNS, Peter
Byrom Street Chambers, Manchester
0161 829 2100
peter.burns@byromstreet.com
Featured in Personal Injury (Northern)
Practice Areas: Peter specialises in catastrophic injury and large loss claims, with particular expertise in brain injury cases and claims involving complex issues of causation. He has extensive experience of spinal injury and amputation claims and is regularly instructed in high value fatal accident cases. Occupiers' liability is an area of special interest. Peter acts both for Defendants and Claimants.
Professional Memberships: Personal Injury Bar Association.
Career: Called 1993. Postmaster at Merton College, Oxford.

BURROWS, Simon
Kings Chambers, Manchester
0345 034 3444
clerks@kingschambers.com
Featured in Administrative & Public Law (Northern/North Eastern), Court of Protection (All Circuits)
Practice Areas: Court of Protection-health and welfare, deprivation of liberty, medical treatment. Mental health: First tier and Upper Tribunal, nearest relative displacement, habeas corpus and damages claims. Interface between the Mental Health Act and the Mental Capacity Act (including DOLS). Children and adolescent mental health. Clinical negligence (usually involving psychiatry- including suicides of patients); Inquests (suicide and homicide)- often involving mental health issues; Judicial Review- particularly mental health related including s.117 challenges, and commissioning issues. Inquests into deaths of patients and homicides by patients- often related to detention in psychiatric hospitals or under supervision in the community. Most recently an inquest into the death of a woman following ECT- Coroner critical of way the SOAD system operates. Significant cases: P v Cheshire West & Chester Council- Supreme Court (deprivation of liberty in a health and social care setting); Re X (1 and 2) [2014] EWCOP 25 & 37; Rochdale Council v KW [2016] 1 WLR 198 deprivation of liberty in a home setting-judge departing from Cheshire West; PJ v A Local Health Board & Welsh Ministers [2015] UKUT 480 (AAC) (Charles, J.)- CTO and deprivation of liberty- proper approach of tribunal to conventionrights; AMA v Manchester West NHS [2015] 0360 UKUT (AAC) (Charles, J) (rights of welfare deputy at P's tribunal); Re A (a child) [2015] EWHC 443 (Fam) (Hayden, J) (removing artificial ventilation of brain dead child- coroner's powers); LCC v SG [2014] EWCOP 10- children's homes and deprivation of liberty; TA v AA & Knowsley BC [2013] EWCA Civ 1661 (Court's obligation to review a case in s. 21A application); MOJ v RB [2011] EWCA Civ 1608 (conditional discharge of restricted), GJ v Foundation Trust [2010] 3 WLR 840, (MHA/MCA interface) C v Blackburn with

Darwen [2011] EWHC 3321 (Guardianship and DOLS).
Professional Memberships: Inner Temple (1990), Northern Circuit (1992), North Eastern Circuit (2006).
Career: Tribunal Judge Mental Health (2003-date)
Publications: Author of Chapters on "Mental Health" and "Tribunals" in Judicial Review: Law and Practice (Patterson) (Second edition) (Jordans 2014). Volume on Mental Health Act in Atkins Court Forms (Lexis Nexis, forthcoming 2016). Chapter on Health & Social Care in Community Care Law & Local Authority Handbook (Butler) (3rd Edition). Practitioner editor of International Journal of Mental Health and Capacity Law.

BURTON, Frank QC
12 King's Bench Walk, London
020 7583 0811
burton@12kbw.co.uk
Featured in Personal Injury (London), Personal Injury (All Circuits), Clinical Negligence (London)
Practice Areas: Listed as a Star Individual in Chambers & Partners 2012, Frank is described as "colossal" and is admired for his "excellent legal mind, immense patience and empathy with clients, and incredible sway with the judiciary." Along with this, his advice is acclaimed as "clear, concise, understandable and above all pragmatic and realistic." Frank is prized by both defendants and claimants for his "incredible intellectual acumen," he is noted for the "genuine compassion he exhibits towards people who have suffered serious injuries." Solicitors concur that he is a true market leader on asbestos-related cases, an area where he regularly represents claimants and demonstrates "a mild-mannered ruthlessness in court."
Career: Frank was appointed as a Recorder in 1999 and a Deputy High Court Judge in 2010. He was Chairman of the Law Reform Committee of the Bar Council (2003-05) and the Chairman of PIBA (2004-06). He is a Bencher of Gray's Inn (2004). Frank was named 'Personal Injury Silk of the Year' 2005, 2006 and 2008 at the Chambers Bar Awards. Frank was awarded Star Individual status in Personal Injury in Chambers 2009, the first Barrister to achieve this rating.

BURY, Paul
Keating Chambers, London
020 7544 2600
pbury@keatingchambers.com
Featured in International Arbitration (London), Construction (London)
Practice Areas: Specialist in domestic and international commercial construction, professional negligence, infrastructure projects, energy, and regulatory law, including public procurement. Has acted in a broad range of disputes ranging from highly complex and high-value international arbitration and High Court proceedings to commercial and domestic construction claims in the County Courts (regularly representing clients in his own right). Has gained particular expertise in cases involving delay and disruption issues and contractual termination (in Bluewater v Mercon and Vivergo v Redhall) and adjudication enforcement (Eurocom v Siemens). Has recently appeared in two large international arbitrations, one concerning a project in Nigeria under the LCIA rules, and the other a project in Qatar under the ICC rules. Has experience across all levels of dispute resolution including arbitration, adjudication and mediation. Has extensive knowledge of the JCT, NEC, IChemE Red Book and FIDIC standard form contracts.
Professional Memberships: Society of Construction Law (SCL); Technology and Construction Bar Association (TECBAR).
Career: Called to the Bar 2008.
Publications: Keating on Offshore Construction and Marine Engineering (Contributor, First edition, 2015) Construction Law Reports (Contributor, 2014 – date), Keating on Construction Contracts (researcher), Practical Law Construction blog (regular contributor).

BUSUTTIL, Godwin
5RB, London
020 7242 2902
godwinbusuttil@5rb.com
Featured in Defamation/Privacy (London)
Practice Areas: Media law generally including defamation, privacy, confidence, data protection, reporting restrictions, contempt. Recent interesting cases include Lachaux v Independent Print Ltd (libel; [2016] QB 402; [2015] EWHC 3677 (QB); [2015] EWHC 915 (QB); [2015] EWHC 620 (QB)), QRS v Beach (harassment, contempt; see eg [2015] 1 WLR 2701; [2015] EWHC 1489 (QB)), Dar Al Arkan v Al Refai (conspiracy, libel, confidence; see eg [2014] EWCA Civ 749; [2013] EWHC 1630 (Comm)), Tamiz v Google Inc [2013] 1 WLR 2151 (CA) (libel); Cammish v Hughes [2013] EMLR 13 (CA) (libel). For full case list and profile, see www.5rb.com.
Career: 1988-92 Jesus College, Cambridge MA, MPhil; 1992-3 City University, Dip Law; 1993-94 ICSL, London; 1994 called to the Bar (Lincoln's Inn; Mansfield and Hardwicke Scholar); 1999 Pegasus Scholar (USA); 2008 Accredited Mediator; 2012 Visiting Senior Fellow in Law, University of Melbourne, Australia.
Publications: Senior contributing editor of 'Gatley on Libel and Slander'; co-editor of Entertainment and Media Law Reports; co-author of 'The Law of Privacy and the Media' (1st and 3rd eds, OUP); contributed articles to Journal of Media Law and Entertainment Law Review.

BUTLER, Andrew
Tanfield Chambers, London
020 7421 5300
andrewbutler@tanfieldchambers.co.uk
Featured in Real Estate Litigation (London)
Practice Areas: All aspects of commercial and property litigation, with a particular emphasis on property-related professional negligence, construction, insurance and insolvency; development projects and joint ventures; commercial and residential landlord and tenant, boundary disputes and rights of way. Has particular experience of company breakdown disputes, including s.994 petitions.
Professional Memberships: Property Bar Association, Professional Negligence Bar Association, Chartered Institute of Arbitrators.
Career: Called 1993. Joined Tanfield Chambers (then Francis Taylor Building) 1995. Head of Business & Commercial Group. Accredited Mediator. Member, Chartered Institute of Arbitrators. Voted "Business Barrister of the Year 2015" by Lawyer Monthly Magazine.
Publications: Co-author, 'Service Charges and Management; Law and Practice' 1st Edn 2006, 3rd Edn 2013. Regular contributor to legal publications including Solicitors Journal and New Law Journal. Presents regularly, including as contributor to the 2016 CPD programme of the Royal Institute of British Architects.
Personal: Married with two children. Educated at Harrow School (where he now sits on the Board of Governors) and University College, Oxford where he achieved a II.i in Classics and represented Oxford University at rugby. Qualified rugby referee. Hobbies include all sports especially rugby, cricket and golf.

BUTLER, Michelle
Matrix Chambers, London
020 7404 3447
MichelleButler@matrixlaw.co.uk
Featured in Crime (London), Public International Law (London)
Practice Areas: Specialist in international law, crime and human rights. International law work spans proceedings at the International Criminal Court, International Criminal Tribunal for the Former Yugoslavia, Special Court for Sierra Leone, International Tribunal for the Law of the Sea and arbitral tribunals determining bilateral investment treaty claims under the ICSID, UNCITRAL and ICC rules. Domestic criminal work includes terrorism, extradition, fraud and general crime. Human rights work ranges from national security related proceedings (control orders and TPIMs), immigration (particularly complex asylum, deportation, and deprivation of citizenship cases), European Union sanctions work and cases before the Grand Chamber of the European Court of Human Rights. Former clients include Governments, Heads of State, leading political, military and business figures, corporations, public authorities, NGOs and individuals. In the UK has appeared before the Supreme Court, House of Lords, Privy Council and the Court of Appeal. Experienced in fragile environments having worked in Libya, Iran, Iraq, Nigeria, Pakistan, Sri Lanka, Georgia and throughout the former Yugoslavia.
Career: Admitted as a Solicitor (Australia) 2002. Called to UK Bar 2007. Appointed to Attorney-General's Public International Law 'C' Panel 2014.
Publications: Contributing author to leading books on human rights, international law and criminal justice.

BUTT, Matthew
3 Raymond Buildings Barristers, London
(0)20 7400 6400
matthew.butt@3rblaw.com
Featured in Crime (London), Extradition (London), Inquests & Public Inquiries (All Circuits), Licensing (London), Professional Discipline (London)
Practice Areas: A criminal, extradition and licensing barrister who is also an expert in all aspects of law relating to firearms. Prosecutes and defends in serious criminal cases (currently defending charges of torture brought under Universal Jurisdiction). Acts at first instance and on appeal in extradition cases. Instructed in complex and high profile inquests, particularly those involving fatal shootings (recently represented the MPS "Flying Squad" Silver Commander at an inquest into a double shooting at Chandlers Ford, and the MPS "Trident" Tactical Firearms Commander in the inquest into the death of Mark Duggan). Regularly instructed to represent accused officers in police disciplinary hearings and appeals. Advises and represents on all matters connected with licensed activities, including gaming, alcohol, regulated entertainment, street trading, firearms and taxis before licensing committees and on appeal to the Magistrates' Court, the Administrative Court and the Court of Appeal. Clients include licensing authorities, the police, major national pub operators and festivals.
Career: Call, 2002, Lord Justice Holker Scholarship 2000, Atkin Scholarship 2002. Lead advocacy trainer (Gray's Inn). Pupil supervisor. Attorney General's C Panel 2008-2012; Attorney General's B Panel 2012. Recorder of the Crown Court 2015.

BYRNES, Aisling
25 Bedford Row, London
020 7067 1500
Abyrne@25bedfordrow.com
Featured in Crime (London)
Practice Areas: Leading counsel in a wide range of cases involving organised crime, homicide, serious sexual offences, drug trafficking and money laundering. Particular expertise in defending in cases arising from political activism. Instructed on a private basis by London's leading law firms. Experienced in representing professionals, corporate defendants and sports people charged with regulatory offences and also advises on behalf of regulatory associations Extensive appellate experience in the Court of Appeal and in the Administrative Court, with emphasis on crime-related judicial review. Aisling is widely known for her experience in defending in the most serious and complex criminal cases. Recently shortlisted for the Chambers & Partners Crime Junior of the Year.
Professional Memberships: Northern Ireland Bar; Criminal Bar Association; Association of Regulatory & Disciplinary Lawyers; Bar Pro Bono Unit.
Career: LLB (Hons) University of Bristol; Called 1994 (Northern Ireland 1996); CBA committee member; accredited advocacy trainer (Gray's Inn); frequent lecturer on aspects of criminal evidence and sentencing.
Personal: French speaker. Keen golfer, rider and ski-er.

CADE DAVIES, Lynsey
29 Bedford Row Chambers, London
020 7404 1044
lcadedavies@29br.co.uk
Featured in Family/Matrimonial (London)
Practice Areas: All aspects of family law including financial provision on the breakdown of marriage or civil partnership, reciprocal enforcement of foreign financial orders, issues relating to jurisdiction, foreign offshore trusts and disputes concerning trusts of land, private law children matters, inheritance act. Reported cases include: Davison v Davison [2015] EWHC Civ 587; Shield v Shield [2014] EWHC 23; Shield v Shield [2013] EWHC 3525; Divall v Divall [2014] EWHC 95; Price v Price [2014] EWCA Civ 655; B v B [2010] All ER (D) 61 (May); D v D and Others & I Trust [2009] EWHC 3062 (Fam).
Professional Memberships: FLBA and Resolution.
Career: Called 2005, joined 29 Bedford Row in 2006 Inner Temple. Regular lecturer.
Publications: Contributor to lexis nexis, family law week.

Personal: Queenswood School, Herts. University of Bristol (Law LLB). City University (Bar Vocational Course).

CADMAN, Toby
9 Bedford Row, London
Featured in Crime (London)

Practice Areas: Toby Cadman is regarding as a leading lawyer in international criminal law, international humanitarian law, international terrorism, maritime security, extradition, and human rights law. Toby has represented Governments, opposition political parties, international organizations, military leaders and civilians in many high profile international trials and investigations. He has advised on international matters in a number of conflict and post-conflict situations, notably in the former Yugoslavia, Guantanamo Bay, Syria, Egypt, Libya, Bangladesh, Iraq and Palestine. Further, Toby lectures extensively on international humanitarian law, criminal procedure and human rights law and has provided advice and training to judges, lawyers and law enforcement agencies throughout the Balkans, South Asia, and the Middle-East, where his reputation has become established as an experienced advisor on judicial reform, legislative drafting and institution building. Toby is a key member of the established group of expert barristers at 9 Bedford Row International (9BRI) as well as being a member of the International Criminal Law Bureau. Most recently, Toby has acted for the Government of the Republic of Maldives, advising on legal and constitutional reform to the criminal justice system; led an international investigation on behalf of the Syrian National Movement, concerning the 'Caesar' evidence; produced a series of reports on the Muslim Brotherhood and the Freedom and Justice Party following the 2013 military coup in Egypt; instructed as the lead lawyer for the team pursuing a case before the African Commission for Human and Peoples Rights concerning the decision of the Egyptian government to close the Rafah Border crossing during and after Operation Protective Edge; since 2010 instructed by Bangladesh Jamaat-e-Islami to represent the political leadership prosecuted before the Bangladesh International Crimes Tribunal and advised on ICC investigations in relation to Iraq, Syria, Egypt and Palestine. As an extradition specialist Toby has acted for the prosecution and defence advising and representing individuals, requesting judicial authorities and governments in extradition proceedings both at first instance hearings and extradition appeals in the higher courts and European Court of Human Rights. Toby also advises foreign governments, law enforcement agencies, international organizations, corporations and private individuals to develop professional and transparent institutions that protect human rights, combat corruption, and reduce the threat of transborder and transnational crime and terrorism. He has developed training curricula for law enforcement, prosecutorial and governmental agencies for the investigation of international crimes in Syria, Iraq and Palestine and offers specialist political and public affairs consultancy services advising clients how best to identify, approach and influence the key decision makers of Westminster, Washington DC, Brussels and further afield. Toby is also the co-founder and current President of the International Forum for Democracy and Human Rights (IDHR), a human rights NGO based in London and Sarajevo. For full details, see http://www.9bedfordrow.co.uk/members / Toby_Cadman and www.9bri.com.

CALDECOTT, Andrew QC
One Brick Court, London
020 7353 8845
clerks@onebrickcourt.com
Featured in Data Protection (London), Defamation/Privacy (London)

Practice Areas: Defamation, privacy and breach of confidence, contempt of court, data protection, freedom of information, obscenity/ censorship and media-related law generally. Cases include: Begg v BBC (libel trial); The Construction Industry Vetting Information Group Litigation (libel, DPA, privacy, confidence); R v F (Crim CA, Reporting Restrictions); Attorney General v Conde Naste Publications (contempt); J.K. Rowling v Associated Newspapers Limited (libel); Hegglin v Google Inc (DPA, libel); Makudi v Baron Triesman (CA, libel, malicious falsehood, Parliamentary privilege); The Voicemail Interception Compensation Scheme; Rothschild v Associated Newspapers (CA, libel); Tesla Motors v BBC (CA, malicious falsehood, libel); Chris Cairns v Lalit Modi (CA, Twitter libel); Oriental Daily Publisher Ltd & anr v Ming Pao Holdings Ltd (Hong Kong Court of Final Appeal); El Naschie v MacMillan Publishing (libel trial); The Leveson Inquiry (representing Guardian News & Media, a core participant); Attorny General v News Group Newspapers & Mirror Group Newspapers (contempt); Spiller v Joseph (Supreme Court – libel – representing interveners Associated Newspapers Ltd, Times Newspapers Ltd & Guardian News & Media Ltd); R v D (C/A – Reporting Restrictions); Baturina v Times Newspapers Ltd (C/A – Libel); Sir Stelios Haji-Ionnou v Dixon & Regus Group (libel); AG v MGN Ltd (contempt); Tesco v Guardian (libel and malicious falsehood); AG v ITV Central (contempt); R v VAC (ex parte BBFC) (judicial review, obscenity); Moyes v Rooney & Harper Collins (libel); Morrisons v OFT (libel); Sir Martin Sorrell v FullSix SpA & anr (libel and privacy); X & Y v Person Unknown (privacy); The Law Society v Department of Constitutional Affairs (Civil Proceedure Rules); AG v Pelling (contempt); Armstrong v Times (CA); Henry v BBC (libel, justification and qualified privilege); AG v Express (contempt); Strachan v Gleaner Co Ltd (Privy Council); Naomi Campbell v MGN (House of Lords – privacy/confidence); Bonnick v Gleaner Co Ltd (Privy Council – libel); King v Telegraph Group (libel/CFA's); Other cases of interest: The Hutton Inquiry – Lead counsel for the BBC; Reynolds v Times Newspapers (libel – qualified privilege); Venables v News Group Newspapers (confidence injunction to protect the identity of Jamie Bulger's killers).

Career: Called to the Bar 1975. Silk 1994. Inner Temple Bencher 2004. Head of Chambers since 2007. Appointed specialist adviser to House of Commons Joint Committee on the Draft Defamation Bill (2011).

Publications: Co-author of Halsbury's Laws, Defamation (2012)

Personal: Educated Eton College and New College, Oxford. Lives in London.

CALDWELL, Marion QC
Compass Chambers, Edinburgh
0131 226 5071
marion.caldwell@advocates.org.uk
Featured in Personal Injury (Scotland), Clinical Negligence (Scotland)

Practice Areas: Clinical and Professional Negligence; Personal Injury; Disciplinary Tribunals; Media Law, Privacy and Defamation; Public and Fatal Accident Inquiries. Marion is engaged by leading solicitors across Scotland and on behalf of health boards. She has a particular interest in claims for catastrophic injuries, brain injury, clinical negligence and for occupational stress, bullying and harassment. She acts for both pursuers and defenders. Her considerable advocacy experience extends to the Court of Session, Sheriff Court and professional and disciplinary tribunals. She has appeared in public inquiries and fatal accident inquiries. Marion's substantial workload largely comprises high value, complex cases. She recently settled one of the few cases in Scotland resolved by Periodic Payment Order. Marion speaks regularly on the law and practice relating to personal injury, damages and clinical negligence. She sits as a tribunal legal chair in war pensions appeals, NHS contract disputes and as a Deputy Judge in the Upper Tribunal. She is a CEDR accredited mediator.

Professional Memberships: Member, Inner Temple (1991–present); Advocates Personal Injury Law Group; Advocates Professional Negligence Law Group; Professional Negligence Bar Association; Faculty of Advocates Mediation Group; Faculty of Advocates Criminal Bar Association.

Career: 1983-5 trainee solicitor then solicitor with Alex Morison & Co [now Morisons]; 1986- admitted Faculty of Advocates; 1991- called to Bar, Inner Temple; 2000- appointed Silk; Standing Junior to the Accountant of Court and the Accountant in Bankruptcy (1991–2000); Legal Member, Police Appeals Tribunal (2013–present); President, Pensions Appeal Tribunal Scotland (2013–present); Chairman, Pensions Appeal Tribunal Scotland (2001–present); Ad hoc Advocate Depute (2011–present); Special Counsel under Criminal Justice and Licensing (S) Act 2010 (2011–present); Legal Chair of panel to determine General Medical Services Contracts disputes (2010–present); Legal Chair of panel on appeals against removal of GPs from Performers List in Scotland (2010–present); Committee Member, Faculty of Advocates Free Legal Services Unit (2010–present); Member of the Council of the Faculty of Advocates (2008–2012); Deputy Judge Upper Tribunal (AAC) 2014 – present; Member, Faculty of Advocates Disciplinary Tribunal (2008-present); previously Member of the Faculty of Advocates Disciplinary Investigating Committee for three years; Convener, Faculty of Advocates Training and Admissions Committee (2005–2008).

CALDWELL, Peter
Drystone Chambers, London
020 7404 1881
Peter.caldwell@dyerschambers.com
Featured in Extradition (London)

Practice Areas: Extradition, Financial Crime

Professional Memberships: Chatham House, ARDL, ALBA, IBA

Career: Peter Caldwell practices in complex criminal, extradition and regulatory law. Peter has an impressive extradition law practice, acting for both requested persons and requesting governments. He has represented requested persons and foreign governments in landmark cases which have shaped the law of extradition over the past 10 years. He also regularly advises on mutual legal assistance requests. He is a natural choice for cases with an international dimension. Peter also represents businesses and regulators in health and safety, food safety and consumer cases and defends professionals in disciplinary proceedings before their regulatory bodies. He is also known as a leading barrister in fraud and financial misconduct cases. In recent years he has been instructed as leading counsel for the defence in SFO proceedings (Kallakis & Williams, Re Bae Systems, Independent Insurance Plc) and has defended in cases brought by NHS Protect, the NCA, FCA and BIS. Peter also defends in civil recovery proceedings and tax assessment cases under Parts 5 and 6 of PoCA. He advises on all aspects of financial regulation, including bribery, sanctions, market abuse and money laundering.

CALHAEM, Simon
29 Bedford Row Chambers, London
Email only
scalhaem@29br.co.uk
Featured in Family/Matrimonial (London)

Practice Areas: Simon specialises in complex high value financial work, including matrimonial finance, inheritance claims, probate and Court of Protection work as well as civil disputes between family members. He provides advocacy and advisory services in England and Wales and overseas He recently appeared for the successful Appellant in the Supreme Court case of Wyatt v Vince. Wyatt v Vince [2015] UKSC 14 [2015] 1 FLR 972; AM v SS [2015] 1 FLR 1237; S v S [2014] EWHC 4732 (Fam); Colborne v Colborne [2014] EWCA Civ 1488; L v M [2014] EWHC 2220; Solomon v Colomon and Ors [2013] EWCA Civ 1095; Wyatt v Vince[2013] All ER (D) 109 (Jun), (CA) [2014] 1 FLR 399; McRoberts v McRoberts [2012] All ER (D) 12 (Nov), (Chd); Foster v Foster [2011] (2) CILR 89 (Cayman Islands Court of Appeal); V v V (Divorce: Jurisdiction) [2011] 2 FLR 778; W v W (Financial Relief: Enforcement) [2011] 2 FLR 1268; K v B (Costs: Financial Relief) [2011] 1 FLR 1745; Bradley v Bradley (Security for Costs) [2008] 2 FLR 1433, CA; A v B (Damages: Paternity) [2007] 2 FLR 1051, [2007] 3 FCR 861 (QBD); Kimber v Kimber (Writ Ne Exeat Regno) [2006] EWCA Civ 706, CA; Rowe v Clarke No2 [2006] EWHC 1292 (Ch), [2006] All ER (D) 124 (May); Crossley v Crossley (TLATA)[2006] 2 FLR 813, CA; Rowe v Clarke (Probate) [2005] EWHC 3068[2005] All ER (D) 368 (Ch D).

Professional Memberships: FLBA; London Common Law & Chancery Bar Association; The Denning Society.

Career: Called to the Bar of England & Wales 1999. Called to the Bar of the Cayman Islands ad hoc since 2011, Called to the Bar of Gibraltar ad hoc since 2013.

Publications: 'The Writ Ne Exeat Regno' Family Law, 'Express Trusts and Ancillary Relief' Family Law, 'Divorce and Recession' Family Law. Co-author of 'Divorce & Bankruptcy: A Practical Guide for a Family Lawyer'. Contributor to 'Duckworths Matrimonial Finance & Taxation (Bankruptcy).' Contributor to Ross "Inheritance Act Claims

and Challenges." Guest Lecturer – University of the West Indies (Barbados) 2013 -.
Personal: Sir Thomas Alleynes High School, Oxford University (MA) Lecturer and Moderator in Law (University of East London 1998 – 1999) Inns of Court School of Law, Sir Thomas More Scholar. Married, lives in London. Enjoys Yacht Racing.

CALLMAN, Jeremy
Ten Old Square, London
020 74050758
JeremyCallman@tenoldsquare.com
Featured in Partnership (London)
Practice Areas: The broad range of work he undertakes includes partnership/LLP and business disputes, general contract and commercial law, professional negligence, insolvency, bankruptcy and property. Jeremy regularly represents clients at arbitrations and mediations. Partnership Work: Jeremy has a strong reputation in partnership/LLP litigation. Additionally he acts on non-contentious partnership matters including updating and revising partnership and LLP agreements. He regularly advises managing partners on internal issues within partnerships/LLPs. He represents both firms and individual partners, from solicitors, accountants, hedge funds, private equity, doctors and dentists to recruitment consultants, architects, theatrical agents and farmers.
Professional Memberships: Association of Partnership Practitioners (Committee member 2008-2014), Chancery Bar Association, Property Bar Association, Professional Negligence Bar Association. Professional Standards Committee of the Bar Council 1994-98.
Career: Called to the Bar 1991. Notable cases include: Reinhard v Ondra [2015] EWHC 26 (Ch); [2015] EWHC 1869 (Ch) (nature of member's interest in an LLP) • Dr Shakarchi v Dr Muir – GP partnership dispute with injunctions sought • Eaton v Caulfield & Others [2013] EWHC 2214 (Ch) – scope of unfair prejudice relief to bring about discontinuance of proceedings (awaiting reporting) • Paul Castledine v (1) RSM Bentley Jennison (2) RSM Bentley Jennison Ltd [2012] Bus LR (D77) – whether former partner retained a share in the goodwill of a substantial accountancy firm • Eaton v Caulfield & Others [2011] BCC 386 – Limited Liability Partnership: expulsion, unfair prejudice and just and equitable winding up • Capewell v Boulton LTL 6/11/2009 – Transfer of interests from one company to another in the context of an alleged partnership arrangement • Shaw v Finnimore & Watts [2009] All ER (D) 41 (Mar) – Alleged profit-sharing agreement • Horton (and others) v Brandish (and others) LTL 22/8/2005 – Estoppel and caution over land • Ridgeway Motors (Isleworth) Ltd v ALTS Ltd (2005) 1 WLR 2871 – Limitation and bankruptcy/insolvency • Ellis v Coleman LTL 10/12/2004 HC – Goodwill and construction of a partnership agreement.
Publications: He has written for The Sunday Times, The Mail on Sunday, Practical Law, The Solicitors Journal and the Journal of International Banking Law, the Association of Partnership Practitioners magazine as well as appearing on Radio Four. He is a co-author of the forthcoming Jordan publication 'The Law of Partnerships and LLPs: A Practical Guide'.
Personal: Beyond his practice, he is married with four children, and works with Norwood, a leading UK charity supporting children and families with learning disabilities.

CAMERON, Gillon
Fourteen, London
020 7242 0858
gcameron@fourteen.co.uk
Featured in Family/Matrimonial (London)
Practice Areas: Gillon practises in all areas of family law with an emphasis on financial disputes under the Matrimonial Causes Act 1973, Schedule 1 Children Act 1989 claims for financial provision, and claims under the Trusts of Land and Appointment of Trustees Act 1996 and Inheritance Acts. He has particular expertise in drafting pleadings in these areas. He is also frequently instructed to represent parents and children in private law proceedings, and local authorities, parents and children in public law proceedings. He appears regularly in the High Court and the Court of Appeal. Reported cases include Re C (A Child) (Conduct of Hearings) [2006] EWCA Civ 144, Re K (Adoption: permission to advertise) [2007] 2 FLR 326; Oxfordshire County Council v X, Y & J [2010] EWCA 581 Civ. and Chiva v Chiva [2014] EWCA Civ 1558; London Borough of P v G & Others [2014] EW Misc 27 (CC);Patrick v McKinley [2015] EWCA Civ 1582
Professional Memberships: FLBA, Lincoln's Inn.
Career: St Paul's School, London; Bristol University BA (Hons); Diploma in Law (City University); Lincoln's Inn Lord Bowen Scholar, Lord Mansfield Scholar and City University Scholarship; Called to the Bar 2002.
Publications: Frequent contributor to Family Law Week.
Personal: Passionate musician and footballer.

CAMMERMAN, Gideon
187 Fleet Street, London
020 7430 7430
gideoncammerman@187fleetstreet.com
Featured in Crime (London)
Practice Areas: Financial Crime, Regulatory and Disciplinary Law, Confiscation and Asset Forfeiture, Gambling
Professional Memberships: Criminal Bar Association, Association of Regulatory and Disciplinary Lawyers
Career: Gideon Cammerman is a highly experienced and robust advocate in criminal, regulatory and disciplinary cases. He has appeared in the Court of Appeal, Privy Council and Supreme Court. Gideon has appeared in many of the highest profile criminal cases in recent years including the Alstom International corruption case, LIBOR rate–fixing, Weavering Capital Fund fraud, three of the "Gypsy Slavery" cases, the "Anonymous" hacking case, and the "Bad Samaritan" robbery case from the riots of 2011. Gideon is also instructed by individuals, company directors and government departments to advise and act in cases outside the sphere of public litigation. These clients have included overseas jurisdictions, online gambling companies and sportsmen. Gideon prosecutes and defends in cases of the utmost gravity for private clients, HM Revenue and Customs, the Department for Work and Pensions, the Medicines and Health Regulatory Agency and the CPS. Gideon is also a private prosecution specialist, bringing his 15 years of experience prosecuting for government department to assist private clients. Gideon is regularly instructed to appear before the Gambling Commission, British Horseracing Association, CQC and is a Case Presenter for the Association of Chartered Certified Accountants. Gideon is also an indirect tax evasion specialist and is instructed by HMRC to respond to appellants in the First Tier Tax Tribunals, but is happy to accept instructions from appellants.
Publications: Contributing Editor of Chapter 4 "Frauds on Investors" in Butterworths "Fraud: Law, Practice and Procedure"

CAMPBELL, Alexis
29 Bedford Row Chambers, London
020 74 041044
acampbell@29br.co.uk
Featured in Family/Matrimonial (London)
Practice Areas: Core practice area is matrimonial finance with particular interest in: international disputes; offshore trusts; pensions; and companies. Extensive experience in high net worth cases, unravelling complex financial arrangements. Hard negotiator but sensible and pragmatic advice. Children practice focuses on private disputes with a focus on international relocation cases. Notable cases include: JL v SL (No 1, 2 & 3) [2014/2015] EWHC 3658; AS v JS & Others [2013] EWHC 1699 (Fam); Sharma v Sharma and others [2012] EWHC 2529 (Fam); Martin-Dye v Martin-Dye [2006] 2 FLR 901.
Professional Memberships: FLBA; Fellow IAFL.
Career: Leeds University (LLB Hons). Called to the Bar 1990. Recorder 2010 (Crime / Family).
Publications: New Law Journal. Lectures on costs, pensions, divorce, company law & periodical payments; lecturer to Judicial College for Family Law Judges.
Personal: Married with two children.

CAMPBELL, Douglas QC
Three New Square, London
020 7405 1111
campbell@3newsquare.co.uk
Featured in Information Technology (London), Intellectual Property (London)
Practice Areas: All types of intellectual property and information technology law including patents, copyright, designs, trademarks, passing off, trade libel and malicious falsehood, confidential information, franchising and licensing, entertainment and media, IT, and database rights as well as general litigation with a significant technical content. Experienced in arbitration and mediation. Acted as expert on UK intellectual property law in US District Court proceedings in the Southern District of New York.
Professional Memberships: IP Bar Association, Chancery Bar Association.
Career: First Class degree in Chemistry (with Distinction in Quantum Chemistry), Oxford University. Called to the Bar in 1993. Inner Temple Major Scholar. Pegasus Scholar at Mallesons Stephen Jaques, Melbourne, Australia in 1996. Member of Attorney-General's Panel of Junior Counsel to the Crown 2010-2015. Appointed Civil Recorder (including Chancery) in Oct 2010; Crime Recorder in Dec 2014; Deputy High Court Judge in Feb 2015;appointed to Silk (QC) in 2016. French and Japanese spoken, the latter to the Japanese Government's upper intermediate standard.
Publications: Terrell on the Law of Patents, Sweet & Maxwell.

CAMPBELL, Oliver QC
Henderson Chambers, London
020 7583 9020
OCampbellQC@hendersonchambers.co.uk
Featured in Health & Safety (London), Product Liability (London)
Practice Areas: Health and safety, product liability, commercial litigation and environment. Appears regularly in the highest profile health and safety and manslaughter prosecutions: Sellafield and Network Rail appeal; Marks and Spencer asbestos prosecution; Falcon Crane prosecution; Hatfield train crash prosecution. He specialises in all aspects of product liability, including pharmaceutical claims, sale of goods claims, food and drink contamination claims, and property damages claims. He has particular experience of group actions including: the OCENSA pipeline litigation; Lloyds / HBOS litigation; the Metal on Metal hip litigation; Para Red and Sudan Red food contamination litigation; the Lariam litigation; PIP litigation. He also regularly appears in major inquests: Vauxhall helicopter crash; Avonmouth Bridge disaster; Potters Bar rail accident; Basildon hospital legionella outbreak. He has considerable experience of criminal and civil environmental claims, including waste management and pollution claims.
Professional Memberships: Committee member of the Health & Safety Lawyers Association.
Career: BA (Oxon). President of the Oxford Union (1990). Advocacy prize ICSL (1992). Called 1992. Chief Examiner Civil Litigation BPTC. Trustee of the Lambeth Law Centre. Appointed QC in 2014.
Publications: Contributor to Halsbury's Laws; Contributing editor to the 'International Product Law Manual'.

CAMPBELL-TIECH, Andrew QC
Drystone Chambers, London
020 7404 1881
andrew.campbell-tiech@drystone.com
Featured in Crime (London), POCA Work & Asset Forfeiture (All Circuits)
Practice Areas: POCA, Fraud & Financial Regulation, Professional Discipline, Consumer law, Criminal law
Professional Memberships: Joint Head of Drystone 2015; Head of Dyers Chambers 2008: QC 2003: Deputy Coroner 2011- 2015: Attorney-General Approved Counsel List A 2002: SFO Approved List QC: Recorder: 2001.
Career: Andrew is both a successful and passionate advocate whilst at the same time an accomplished technical lawyer. He practises in four main areas. Confiscation cases, which recently include the lawfulness of confiscation undertaken by a private prosecutor; special purpose vehicles; off-shore trusts; confiscation in absentia; trade marks and the assumptions; enforcement notices; S.23 applications. Recent restraint includes carbon credit fraud and money laundering. Fraud cases include Iran sanctions busting; banking and medical. Consumer cases include a fatal Xmas food poisoning; the lawfulness of Blue Badge prosecutions; the mis-selling of alarm systems to the elderly; the applicability of the MLR 2007 to Patent and Trade Mark Attorneys. Regulatory cases include HCPC, BPC, RCVS, UKCP, trade marks and planning.
Publications: Recent publications include: 'Risk & Blame: the Subversion of Due Diligence', 'Confiscation and Game Theory:

Ahmad and Field'; 'The Proceeds of Crime Act 2002: a Quiet Revolution'; 'Restraint Orders: Prosecuting the Breach'; 'Too Many Murderers'; 'Lip Reading as Expert Evidence'; 'Stockwell Revisited: the Unhappy State of Facial Mapping'; 'The Future of Detention without Trial in the UK', 'A Corpse in Law' (Archbold News, Journal of the London Middle East Institute, Global Association of Risk Professionals, British Journal of Haematology, Local Government Journal, Dyers Newsletter).
Personal: Music, languages, chess, cycling.

CANDLIN, James
12 King's Bench Walk, London
020 7583 0811
candlin@12kbw.co.uk
Featured in Travel (London)
Practice Areas: Acts for both Claimants and Defendants. Extensive experience of catastrophic and brain injury, high value Chronic pain cases as well as Clinical Negligence, Occupational illness and Product liability raising scientific aspects of defect or causation arguments. He has long had a Travel, Overseas injury and Jurisdictional issues practice complementing regular appearances for clients in the leisure sectors including vicarious liability arguments relating to assault and misconduct by doormen, guides and entertainers. His scientific experience lends specialisation to foreign practices, swimming pool technology, HACCP systems, food poisoning, post infective IBS, rheumatoid, haemolytic uraemic kidney injury complications and Legionnaires cases. James has conducted numerous inquests or actions arising from clinical/care home, and motor racing cases as well as a typical array of Employers and on occasion followed inquest, with Criminal Defence of Health & Safety Prosecution and then civil trial.
Professional Memberships: PIBA, TATLA, AVMA, LSM Accredited Mediator, Facilitator for Independent Facilitation and Evaluation Service
Career: Called 1991
Publications:
Personal:

CANEY, Michelle
St Ives Chambers, Birmingham
0121 236 0863
michelle.caney@stiveschambers.co.uk
Featured in Real Estate Litigation (Midlands), Social Housing (Midlands)
Practice Areas: Chancery and Commercial, Social Housing, Judicial Review.
Professional Memberships: Property Bar Association, Midlands Social Housing Law Association, Midland Circuit.
Career: Michelle Caney is a chancery and commercial practitioner with a strong reputation and extensive experience in her field. In the commercial property sphere, she deals with forfeiture, breach of covenant claims, service charge disputes, business renewals, terminations and dilapidations. Her wider commercial practice includes contractual and construction disputes. In the residential context, Michelle represents landlords and tenants in all areas of social housing, with particular expertise in complex cases involving mental capacity, disability discrimination and human rights issues. She also deals with judicial review claims in these areas. Her traditional chancery practice includes boundary disputes, adverse possession, easements, nuisance, restrictive covenants, trusts, probate, banking and professional negligence.
Personal: Birmingham University: 2003 (LLB). Nottingham Law School: 2004 (BVC). Called to the Bar: 2004. Joined St Ives Chambers: 2005. Deputy Head of the Housing and Property Group: 2012. Deputy Head of the Civil Group: 2014.

CANNOCK, Giles
Kings Chambers, Manchester
0345 034 3444
clerks@kingschambers.com
Featured in Planning (Northern)
Practice Areas: All aspects of town and country planning with particular expertise in large housing projects, retail, renewable energy, infrastructure projects (underground storage of gas, strategic rail freight, fracking etc), commercial development, minerals and waste and Compulsory Purchase. Highways, rights of way and Village Greens (as advocate or Inspector). A specialist in Judicial Review and Statutory Challenges.
Professional Memberships: PEBA.
Career: Emmanuel College, Cambridge MA and LLM (Master Of Law), Lord Porter Senior Exhibition. Grays Inn Scholar 1998. Called to the Bar in Oct 1998.

CANNON, Josef
Cornerstone Barristers, London
020 72424986
josefc@cornerstonebarristers.com
Featured in Licensing (London)
Practice Areas: Licensing, planning, housing, public law.
Professional Memberships: Institute of Licensing, ALBA, PEBA.
Career: Called in 2002. Active in all areas of licensing and gambling, with a particular specialism in SEV licensing: counsel for the successful respondent in KVP(Ent) Ltd v South Bucks DC on a JR challenge to a refusal to grant a SEV licence, and junior counsel in Bean Leisure (A) Trading Ltd v Leeds CC, a JR challenge to decisions to refuse SEV licences pursuant to a change in policy. Clients include operators, objectors, police, local authorities at the heart of developing licensing policy, and residents groups. Regular contributor to textbooks on licensing law and practice, member of the IoL and regular lecturer at their events; regular lecturer and trainer for local authorities.
Publications: Contributor to "Cornerstone on the Planning Court", Kolvin, Licensed Premises: Law Practice and Policy (Bloomsbury, 2013) and Kolvin's Gambling for Local Authorities (IoL, 2007). Joint author of Atkin's Court Forms, Vol. 25: Licensing (LexisNexis, 2013).
Personal: Keen but limited cricketer; enthusiastic gourmand; runs (with others) a restaurant in South London in his 'spare time'.

CANNON, Mark QC
4 New Square, London
020 7822 2000
m.cannon@4newsquare.com
Featured in Professional Negligence (London), Construction (London), Insurance (London)
Practice Areas: Professional liability (accountants, architects, engineers, financial advisers, insurance brokers, lawyers, Lloyd's agents and surveyors); insurance and reinsurance; construction and engineering; general commercial law.
Professional Memberships: Professional Negligence Bar Association (Chairman 2009-11); COMBAR, Chancery Bar Association; Tecbar; London Common Law and Commercial Bar Association. Called to the Bar of Northern Ireland.
Career: Educated at Lincoln College, Oxford 1980-83 (BA in Modern History) and Robinson College, Cambridge 1983-84 (Part 1B of Law Tripos). Called to the Bar in 1985. Silk 2008.
Publications: Co-author of 'Cannon & McGurk on Professional Indemnity Insurance' (OUP, 2nd edition 2016). Editor of 'Jackson & Powell on Professional Liability' since 3rd edition (1992).

CAREW POLE, Rebecca
1 Hare Court, London
020 7797 7070
carewpole@1hc.com
Featured in Family/Matrimonial (London)
Practice Areas: Complex financial remedies cases. Jurisdiction disputes on divorce and claims after a foreign divorce.
Professional Memberships: Family Law Bar Association; Inner Temple.
Career: Called to the Bar in 1999; Inner Temple Major Scholar; Duke of Edinburgh Entrance Scholar; Inner Temple Pegasus Scholar. Completed pupillage at 1 Hare Court (formerly 1 Mitre Court Buildings) in 2000 and remained in specialist practice within Chambers ever since. Secondment to the Chief Justice of the Family Court of Australia (Alastair Nicholson AO RFD) 2002 – 2003.
Publications: Child's Pay 3rd Edition.
Personal: Married with three children living in West London.

CARLILE OF BERRIEW, Alex QC
9-12 Bell Yard, London
020 7400 1800
a.carlile@912by.com
Featured in Financial Crime (London)
Practice Areas: Alex Carlile has extensive experience of cases involving fraud, regulation, judicial review and public policy. He has been involved in some of the largest commercial fraud cases of recent times. In a more general criminal setting, he has appeared in high profile Murder cases. He was for 9 years Independent Reviewer of Terrorism Legislation, and has extensive knowledge of the operation of government and Parliament. His knowledge of corporate activity includes long service as a non-executive director of a listed company. He is available for advisory work, inquiries and reviews, and for non-publicly funded contentious cases. He remains an active member of the House of Lords, has written several reports on issues related to criminal justice policy and has chaired numerous committees etc. For 28 years until 2015 he was a Deputy High Court Judge and Recorder, a Master of the Bench of Gray's Inn, and Chairman of the Lloyd's Enforcement Board. He was called to the Bar in 1970 and became a QC in 1984. He is also a Director of SC Strategy Ltd, a boutique consultancy providing international strategic advice to governments, companies and individuals.

CARPENTER, Chloe
Fountain Court Chambers, London
020 7583 3335
cc@fountaincourt.co.uk
Featured in Professional Discipline (London)
Practice Areas: All areas of commercial law, (in particular arbitration, commercial litigation, banking, financial services, insurance and professional negligence) and disciplinary and regulatory work. Recent cases include: acting for the defendant in Alexander v West Bromwich Mortgage Company Ltd [2015] EWHC 135 (Comm), [2016] EWCA Civ 496; acting for the first defendant in Al Khorafi v Sarasin-Alpen in the appeal in the DIFC Court of Appeal, acting for the second defendant in Al Sulaiman v Credit Suisse and Plurimi [2013] EWHC 400 (Comm); acting for the claimant in Awal Bank BSC (In Administration) v Al-Sanea [2011] EWHC 1354 (Comm); acting for West LB in the litigation arising out of the Boxclever securitisation; acting for the appellant in Hilton v Barker Booth and Eastwood [2005] UKHL 8; acting for the SRA in the Miners Compensation cases; Law Society v Baxendale-Walker [2006] 3 All ER 675, [2007] 3 All ER 330, [2008] 1 W.L.R. 426; Thaker v SRA [2012] EWHC 432 (Admin); acting for the SRA in Lumsdon v LSB, BSB & SRA [2014] EWHC 28 (Admin).
Professional Memberships: COMBAR, ARDL.
Career: Called to the Bar 2001. Educated at Kings College London (LLB, 1st class, 1999) and Brasenose College Oxford (BCL, Distinction, 2000). Member of Fountain Court Chambers since 2002.
Publications: Joint author of The Law of Privilege, edited by Bankim Thanki QC (2nd edition, 2011, Oxford University Press).

CARPENTER, Jamie
Hailsham Chambers, London
020 7643 5000
jamie.carpenter@hailshamchambers.com
Featured in Professional Negligence (London), Clinical Negligence (London), Costs Litigation (All Circuits)
Practice Areas: Jamie specialises in costs and professional and clinical negligence. Leading firms of solicitors in all three areas regularly instruct him, and his costs practice has an international dimension, having advised firms in Dubai, Singapore and the Channel Islands. Jamie is equally at home dealing with narrow points of construction or marshalling complex facts in document-heavy claims. He is a very experienced advocate, having spent much of his earlier years in practice in the criminal courts. Recent cases include: Turvill v Bird [2016] EWCA Civ 703 (appeal against a non-party costs order); Lowin v W Portsmouth & Co Ltd (QBD: construction of rules relating to the costs of provisional assessment); Webb Resolutions Ltd v Countrywide Surveyors Ltd (ChD: claimant ordered to pay costs of a claim which was issued, but not served); Creative Foundation v Dreamland Leisure Ltd [2016] EWHC 859 (Ch) (non-party costs order obtained); Canada Square Operations Ltd v Kinleigh Folkard & Hayward Ltd [2016] PNLR 3 (professional negligence claim against valuers defeated); Excalibur Ventures LLC v Texas Keystone Inc [2014] EWHC 3436 (Comm) (application for costs against funders of gargantuan litigation; was also instructed in the appeal in which judgment is awaited at the time of going to press).
Professional Memberships: Professional Negligence Bar Association (PNBA).
Career: MA (Cantab), called to the Bar 2000.
Publications: Medical Law Precedents for Lawyers (contributor); Medical Law and Ethics at a Glance (contributor – in production).

Personal: Main interests: music, photography, cycling, rock climbing, Tottenham Hotspur FC.

CARTER, Martin

Kings Chambers, Manchester
0345 034 3444
clerks@kingschambers.com

Featured in Planning (Northern)

Practice Areas: All aspects of town and country planning, compulsory purchase, highways, towns and village greens, environment, together with administrative and public law and local government.

Professional Memberships: Planning & Environmental Bar Association; Administrative Law Bar Association; Northern Circuit; North Eastern Circuit.

Career: New College, Oxford MA (Oxon), BA (Jurisprudence) [First Class]; Member of MiddleTemple; Called 1992; Joined Chambers 1992; Appointed to Provincial Panel of Junior Counsel to the Crown.

CARTER, Peter QC

Doughty Street Chambers, London
020 7404 1313
p.carter@doughtystreet.co.uk

Featured in Crime (London), Financial Crime (London)

Practice Areas: Peter Carter undertakes criminal law defence and some prosecution together with public inquiry work (appearing in and advising potential parties). The majority of his time is taken up with fraud cases, but he also appears in cases of terrorism, homicide and trafficking. FRAUD CASES: representing a defendant in a "carousel" fraud; acting for one of a number of pharmaceutical companies unsuccessfully prosecuted by the Serious Fraud Office as an alleged cartel (R v GG and others) on behalf of the Financial Services / Financial Conduct Authority prosecuting a former Partner of Cazenove for offences of insider dealing (R v Calvert) and an insider dealing case involving securities based on US stocks, which was achieved by collaboration between the FSA and the US authorities (R v Sanders & others). PUBLIC INQUIRIES: He has spent much of the past five years acting as counsel to an Inquiry in Trinidad and Tobago into failed pension and insurance companies. He advised some of those potentially involved in the Leveson Inquiry into phone tapping. TERRORISM: He acted as Special Advocate in Bourgass and others (the ricin case); represented one of the defendants in the 21 July 2005 attempted bombings trial (R v Ibrahim & others), and one of defendants in the "dirty bomb" plot (R v Barot and others); he represented a young man charged with neo-Nazi terrorism offences and one of several defendants accused of holding meetings to support Islamic State. He acts as a special advocate in "Closed" proceedings. TRAFFICKING: He was counsel for the appellants in R v O and R v N on human trafficking. Following those cases and a series of seminars he has conducted (jointly with Parosha Chandran of Pump Court Chambers, Pam Bowen of the CPS and Riel Karmy-Jones of Red Lion Chambers) he was appointed as a special adviser to the Joint Parliamentary Select Committee on the Modern Slavery Bill. HUMAN RIGHTS and PUBLIC LAW: he acts pro bono in Privy Council capital cases from the Caribbean, and has appeared in both the High Court and Court of Appeal of Trinidad and Tobago in a capital case remitted from the Privy Council (Angela Ramdeen); he represented the applicant in the Inter-American Court of Human Rights on the use of flogging as a penalty; he was one of the counsel instructed to produce an amicus brief on behalf of Members of Parliament in Rasul v Bush (concerning Guantánamo Bay); he acted for the Islamic Human Rights Commission in an application to curtail the US using UK facilities to assist transport of arms to be used in armed conflict in Lebanon. He acts for requested persons in deportation cases. He frequently lectures on terrorism, the death penalty and human rights in criminal cases, and teaches advocacy in the UK and overseas with an emphasis on ethics.

Professional Memberships: Criminal Bar Association; South Eastern Circuit; International Bar Association; Trustee, Fair Trials Abroad; Patron, Amicus; Member, Institute of Advanced Legal Studies; Member, British Institute of International and Comparative Law.

Career: LLB (UCL) 1973. Called to the Bar 1974. Silk 1995. Bencher, Gray's Inn. Chair, Bar Human Rights Committee 2002-05. Chairman, Gray's Inn Advocacy and Continuing Education Committee 2008-09. Visiting Professor, Birkbeck, University of London.

Publications: 'Offences of Violence' (with Ruth Harrison), Sweet & Maxwell; chapter on international criminal law in 'Human Rights Protection: Methods and Effectiveness' Frances Butler ed, published by Kluwer, 2001; contributing editor to 'A Practitioner's Guide to Terrorist Trials' published by 18 Red Lion Court, 2007; Article 'The Rule of Law' in (2009) 15 KHRP LR; contributed to a chapter in Human Trafficking Handbook : Recognising Trafficking and Modern-day Slavery in the UK', Chandran, P. ed. (LexisNexis, October 2011); chapter on the role of defence counsel in terrorism cases in Investigating Terrorism, J. Pearse ed. (Wiley Blackwell 2015).

CARTER, Rosalyn

St Philips Chambers, Birmingham
0121 246 1600
rcarter@st-philips.com

Featured in Family/Matrimonial (Midlands)

Practice Areas: Rosalyn has an extensive practice in care and adoption work. She has a great deal of experience in serious care and adoption proceedings in the High Court and County Court. She acts for local authorities, parents and guardians. Rosalyn also has considerable experience in the field of private family law. She deals mostly with complex final hearings relating to residence, and contact issues. She has a wealth of experience in difficult and complex cases, and particular specialism in cases where there are allegations of sexual abuse, and also cases where there is disputed expert evidence, medical or otherwise. She is regularly led in complex care and adoption matters, and asked to advise in respect of unusual aspects of law and procedure. Rosalyn works with many parents with many different needs, including learning difficulties, addictions, depression, and psychological problems. Reported cases: Re S & Others (Residence) [2008] 2 FLR 1377 (CA); Walsall MBC v KK & Another [2014] 2 FLR 227; and Re W (a Child) [2014] 3 FCR 339 (CA).

Professional Memberships: Family Law Bar Association; BAAF.

Career: Appointed as a Recorder in the County Court in 2012 and sits on the Midland Circuit hearing family cases.

CARTER, William

Drystone Chambers, London
020 7404 1881
william.carter@drystone.com

Featured in Crime (South Eastern)

Practice Areas: Criminal Law, Health and Safety.

Professional Memberships: South Eastern Circuit, CBA.

Career: Will Carter has forged a reputation as an extremely skilled and knowledgeable barrister, prosecuting and defending in equal measure in serious criminal cases. He is regularly instructed in cases of complexity, both as leading junior and junior, where his meticulous approach and attention to detail are well known. He appears in cases ranging from murder, where he has particular experience of cases involving sudden death in infants and associated areas of medico-legal expertise, to Revenue and Customs fraud, in which he acts mainly for the defence. He has defended and prosecuted in a number of cases brought against police officers for offences ranging from manslaughter to corruption. He has recent experience in prosecutions for gross negligence manslaughter, where his ability to deal with experts in fields ranging from industrial machinery to entomology was particularly valuable. He has appeared in many cases involving charges of rape and serious sexual offences, in many of which the allegations date back many years. His practice covers the full range of the criminal law. He has been a contributing editor of the practitioners' handbook Archbold for over twenty years.

Publications: Contributing editor to Archbold.

CARTWRIGHT, Richard

Devereux, London
020 7353 7534
cartwright@devchambers.co.uk

Featured in Personal Injury (London), Clinical Negligence (London)

Practice Areas: Clinical negligence; personal injury (particularly neurotrauma and spinal injuries).

Professional Memberships: PNBA; AvMA.

Career: Clinical negligence: Recent claims include cerebral palsy claims defended on breach of duty and/or causation, missed diagnoses by GP or hospital (NHS and private) (of infection, cauda equina syndrome or post-surgical complications, of spinal tuberculosis, of recent infarction), spinal surgery, bariatric surgery, wrongful birth claims, and brachial plexus birth injuries. Personal injury: neurotrauma and spinal injury following road traffic accidents (eg. Smith v Finch (the cycling helmet case), Sahakian v McDonnell, and Jukes v Etti. In both areas: claims involving complex damages issues and overseas claimants (e.g. France, India, Australia and New Zealand): fatal claims (particularly those involving financial dependency arising from the deceased's business interests). One claim involving traumatic brain injury settled in 2012 for £16.6 million (including notional capitalised periodical payments).

Publications: JPIL article with Robert Glancy.

Personal: Leisure interests include Welsh(Lions) rugby, motor racing and skiing.

CARTWRIGHT, Sophie

Deans Court Chambers, Manchester
0161 214 6001
cartwright@deanscourt.co.uk

Featured in Administrative & Public Law (Northern/North Eastern), Inquests & Public Inquiries (All Circuits), Professional Discipline (The Regions)

Practice Areas: Sophie has an extensive Inquest practice, regularly appearing in complex inquests where Article 2 is engaged, representing Local Authorities, Health Care Providers, and Public Authorities in addition to private individuals and companies. She has also received appointments and acted as Counsel to the Inquest. Sophie has considerable experience of Health Care work and the wider regulation of the Health sector. Sophie's practice also encompasses all aspects of Judicial Review relating to Coronial Proceedings and Human Rights; Regulatory Law; Health and Safety; Professional Discipline; all aspects of Health Care and Care Home Regulation; Court of Protection. Sophie is currently instructed as Junior Counsel to the Anthony Grainger Public Inquiry.

Professional Memberships: HSLA. ARDL. CoPPA. CBA.

Career: Member of Deans Court Chambers since 1998. Masters in Health and Safety and Environmental Law 2006. Appointed as an Assistant Coroner in 2012. Appointed as Junior Counsel to the Grainger Public Inquiry in March 2016.

CASEMENT, David QC

Kings Chambers, Manchester
0345 034 3444
clerks@kingschambers.com

Featured in Chancery (Northern), Commercial Dispute Resolution (Northern), Company (Northern), Restructuring/Insolvency (Northern), Sports Law (The Regions)

Practice Areas: Company, Insolvency, Partnership, Commercial fraud, Trusts, Privacy and Confidentiality, Financial Services, Banking, Franchise Agreements, Entertainment, Media, Construction Disputes, Energy, Private International Law, Sport.

Professional Memberships: British Irish Commercial Bar Association (UK Chairman) Northern Circuit Commercial Bar Association (Chairman) Chancery Bar Association. Member of the Bars of England & Wales, Ireland and N Ireland.

Career: Called to the Bar 1992; Recorder 2005; Queen's Counsel 2008; Deputy High Court Judge 2013

CASSERLEY, Catherine

Cloisters, London
020 7827 4000
cc@cloisters.com

Featured in Employment (London)

Practice Areas: Catherine specialises in employment, discrimination and human rights law. She has particular expertise in disability discrimination (having worked as Senior Legal Adviser with the Disability Rights Commission) including in complex employment discrimination cases , and in discrimination outside employment, including public law cases. She has been appointed to the Equality and Human Rights Commission's panel of counsel. She appears at all levels from the Employment Tribunal, County Court and High Court to the Supreme Court. She also advises organisations on strategic litigation and legal policy issues – including on the UN Convention on the Rights of Persons with Disabilities and on the

Equality Act 2010 (EqA). She was involved in drafting the EqA Codes of Practice on Services, guidance on the Public Sector Equality Duty and Education, and more recently on age and services. She was appointed last year as the independent adviser to the House of Lords Select Committee on the impact of the EqA on disabled people. She has spoken and written extensively on both European and domestic discrimination legislation. Key cases include: First Buses v Paulley [2014] EWCA Civ 1573(wheelchair space on buses) – Supreme Court judgment pending ; Akerman-LIvingston v Aster Communities [2015] UKSC 15, disability discrimination, s.15, R (on the application of MM and DM) V Secretary of State for Work and Pensions [2015] UKUT 0107 (reasonable adjustments and welfare benefits); Williams v Swansea University – instructed in Court of Appeal, s15 EqA, meaning of "unfavourable" treatment; Hall and Preddy v Bull and Bull [2013] UKSC 73- first case to consider goods and servcies discrimination against a gay couple by Christian hotel owners.
Professional Memberships: Member of ELA, DLA and ELBA.
Career: Called to the bar in 1991; previously employed in the voluntary sector and as a Head of Trade Union legal department.
Publications: One of the editors of Discrimination in Employment : a claims Handbook (LAG: 2013) Chapters in Equality and Discrimination: the New Law (Jordans, 2010) and in Blackstones Guide to the Equality Act 2010 (3rd edition pending) .

CASTLE, Richard
1 King's Bench Walk, London
020 7936 1500
rcastle@1kbw.co.uk
Featured in Family/Matrimonial (London)
Practice Areas: Principal area of practice is all aspects of divorce and matrimonial finance, particularly cases involving international and jurisdictional issues and also those involving trusts and complex corporate structures. Has considerable experience of claims under Part III of Matrimonial and Family Proceedings Act 1984 (financial relief after a foreign divorce). Regularly advises in offshore jurisdictions and also in relation to cases involving the tracing of offshore assets. Also specialises in cohabitation disputes involving trusts of land and applications under Children Act 1989 Sch 1. Reported cases include: Evans v Evans [2013] 2 FLR 999, BJ v MJ (Financial Order: Overseas Trust) [2012] 1 FLR 667, Marinos v Marinos [2007] 2 FLR 1018 Bentinck v Bentinck [2007] 2 FLR 1, LK v K (No2) [2007] 2 FLR 729, and Pabari v Secretary of State for Work and Pensions [2005] FCR.
Professional Memberships: FLBA. South Eastern Circuit.
Career: Prince of Wales Scholar (Gray's Inn). Called to the Bar 1998.
Personal: Educated St Dunstan's College and University of Bristol (LLB).

CATTERMOLE, Rebecca
Tanfield Chambers, London
020 7421 5300
RebeccaCattermole@tanfieldchambers.co.uk
Featured in Social Housing (London)
Practice Areas: All aspects of commercial and residential property litigation (including agriculture and housing). Particular expertise in redevelopments, nuisance, leasehold enfranchisement, and service charge disputes. Representative cases include: McDonald v McDonald [2016] UKSC 28 (private landlord and tenant; human rights) [2016] 3 WLR 45; Hemmise v LB Tower Hamlets [2016] UKUT 109 (LC) (issue estoppel); Amicus Horizon Limited v Mabbott [2012] EWCA Civ 895 [2013] 3 FCR 47 : [2012] HLR 4 (succession) 2; WDHA v Hewitt [2011] EWCA Civ 735; [2011] HLR 39 (tenancy by deception); Hastoe HA v Ellis (settlement; undertaking) [2007] EWCA Civ 1238; [2008] HLR 25; Hyams v Wilfred EHA 2007] 1 EGLR 89 : [2007] 3 EG 126 (service charges).
Professional Memberships: Chartered Institute of Arbitrators, Property Bar Association, Agricultural Law Association, Association of Leasehold Enfranchisement Practitioners.
Career: BA Hons Classics (Bristol). Called to the Bar 1999, joined Tanfield Chambers in 2011.
Publications: Service Charges and Management: Law and Practice 3rd Edn (Sweet & Maxwell) (with other members of Tanfield Chambers); 5th Edition of Halsbury's Laws of England, Local Government Law, Vol. 69; Housing and Landlord and Tenant Contributor for Jowitts's Dictionary of English Law; co-author of two editions of Anti-Social Behaviour and Disorder: Powers and Remedies (Sweet & Maxwell).

CAVANAGH, John QC
11KBW, London
020 7632 8500
John.Cavanagh@11kbw.com
Featured in Employment (London)
Practice Areas: Principal areas of practice are employment law, and areas of commercial law, public law and human rights which overlap with employment law. In employment law particular emphasis on whistleblowing, discrimination and equal pay, TUPE, the European aspects of employment law, restraint of trade, wrongful dismissal, industrial disputes, changes to terms and conditions, and large-scale redundancies. Has recently acted in O'Brien (No 2), USA v Nolan, O'Brien v Ministry of Justice, Ravat v Halliburton, and Russell v Transocean (all Supreme Court), Lock v British Gas (CJEU and CA), Govia Thameslink Railways v ASLEF, Armstrong v Bannatyne, Mattu v UHCW (CA), Police A19 Age Discrimination cases and Woodford v Olympus Corporation. Chambers & Partners Employment Silk of the Year 2009, and short-listed 2011, and shortlisted for Employment Silk of the Year in Legal 500 Bar Awards 2015.
Professional Memberships: Employment Law Bar Association (former Chair), Employment Lawyers Association, ALBA and COMBAR.
Career: Called 1985. Joined 11 King's Bench Walk 1985, QC 2001, Recorder 2005. Joint Head of Chambers 2013 -
Publications: Formerly contributor to Harvey, Tolley's Employment Law and Butterworths 'Local Government Law'.
Personal: Educated: Warwick School; New College, Oxford (MA); Clare College, Cambridge (LLM) and University of Illinois. Married with four children.

CAVENDER, David QC
One Essex Court, London
020 7583 2000
dcavender@oeclaw.co.uk
Featured in Commercial Dispute Resolution (London)
Practice Areas: Commercial litigation.
Professional Memberships: COMBAR.
Career: Called to Bar and joined One Essex Court in 1993. QC 2010.
Personal: Educated at Kings College, London 1986-89 (LLB 1st class Hons). Born 1964.

CAWSON, Mark QC
Exchange Chambers, Manchester
0161 833 2722
cawsonqc@exchangechambers.co.uk
Featured in Chancery (Northern), Professional Negligence (Northern), Commercial Dispute Resolution (Northern), Restructuring/Insolvency (Northern)
Practice Areas: Corporate and personal insolvency work, company and partnership litigation and disputes, general commercial litigation, solicitors' and other professional negligence and liability, commercial fraud, and commercial property disputes. Clients include government departments, local authorities, banks, office holders, Plcs, SMEs/SMBs, and private clients.
Professional Memberships: Chancery Bar Association, Northern Chancery Bar Association, Northern Circuit Commercial Bar Association, Insolvency Lawyers' Association, R3, Professional Negligence Bar Association, and Northern Circuit
Career: Called to the Bar in 1982, Queen's Counsel 2001, Authorised to sit as a Deputy High Court Judge, Chancery and Queen's Bench Divisions 2005, ADR Group Accredited Mediator 2007, Bencher Lincoln's Inn 2010, Chairman of the Northern Chancery Bar Association 2013
Personal: Educated at Wrekin College, Shropshire, and University of Liverpool (LLB). Enjoys travel, the Cumbrian countryside, watching Sale Sharks and Liverpool FC, playing Golf, reading, armchair politics and theology, and Church affairs.

CAYFORD, Philip QC
29 Bedford Row Chambers, London
020 74041044
pcayford@29br.co.uk
Featured in Family/Matrimonial (London)
Practice Areas: Family practice, strong bias towards financial remedies. Acted for successful wife in Supreme Court in Wyatt v Vince [2015] UKSC (Strike out, abuse of process, legal costs funding, costs orders) & Wyatt v Vince [2016] EWHA (Publicising the final outcome). Court of Appeal decisions include: Robertson v Spence [2016] EWHC; Hague Convention and jurisdiction issues, leave to remove from the jurisdiction (Payne v Payne) [2001] 1 FLR 1052 CA, derivative shareholder action arising from breakdown of family owned company (Barratt v Duckett [1995] 1 BCLC 243), solicitors' conflict of interest (Davies v Davies [2000] 1 FLR 39), return of children to non – Hague jurisdictions (B v El B (Abduction: Shariah law: Welfare of child [2003] 1 FLR 811), leave to remove Re J [2007] 1 FLR 2033, abductions (Re H [2007] 1 FLR 2007), Recusal and judicial humour (El Farargy [2007] EWCA Civ 1149, [2008] EWCA Civ 884), drawing inferences from non-disclosure (Mahon v Mahon [2008] EWCA Civ 901), Schedule 1 financial provision for children (Morgan v Hill [2007] 1 FLR 1480 CA), constructive trusts and proprietary estoppel (Shield v Shield [2013] EWHC 23; [2014] EWHC 3525; [2014] EWCA, lump sum orders and the CSA (Ally v Ally [2015] EWCA. High Court decisions on Sch 1 applications (F v G [2005] 1 FLR 261) reinstating lump sum claim (Re G [2004] 1 FLR 997), big money footballers (Q v Q [2005] 2 FLR 640), excessive costs within financial remedy applications (RH v RH [2008] 2 FLR 2142), offshore trusts (B v B [2010] 1AER D61), Re S (leave to remove costs) [2010] 1 FLR 834; Schedule 1 costs (PG v TW (No 1) Child: Financial Provision: Legal Funding [2012] EWHC 1892 (Fam); PG v TW (No 2) Child: Financial Provision) [2012]. Other reported decisions on injunctions, children cases, professional negligence, inquests, etc.
Professional Memberships: Middle Temple Bencher.
Career: Called 1975 with Blackstone Exhibition; joined 29 Bedford Row 1978. Silk 2002. Head of Chambers 2016. Frequent lecturer and contributor to professional publications including Family Law and Supreme Court Yearbook 2015 and 2016.
Publications: Consultant Editor FLBA's magazine, Family Affairs.
Personal: Born 1952. Educated Marlborough College; Cardiff University. NPPL, FRGS, documentary filmmaker, journalist.

CHACKO, Thomas
Pump Court Tax Chambers, London
020 7414 8080
clerks@pumptax.com
Featured in Tax (London)
Practice Areas: Following 12 months pupillage Tom's tenancy began on 1st October 2009. Tom has a broad based tax practice covering all areas of revenue law, both advising (particularly in private client, employment and VAT) and litigating. Recent litigation has covered customs duties, VAT, aggregates levy, general Tribunal procedure, and income tax. Recent cases include Murray Group v HMRC (the Rangers FC litigation), McCarthy and Stone v HMRC (both FTT and UT) and P J Wright (UT, concerning due process).
Professional Memberships: Revenue Bar Association.
Career: 2007 Called to the Bar (Inner Temple) 2008-09 Pupillage, Pump Court Tax Chambers 2009 Tenant, Pump Court Tax Chambers; 2011 2 month secondment at HMRC Solicitors Office; 2013 3 month secondment, Deloitte; 2015 Appointed Junior Counsel to the Crown – "C" panel.
Publications: Contributor to Ghosh, Johnson and Miller on the Taxation of Corporate Debt and Derivatives; Contributor to Mortimore on Company Directors (2nd edition) and Halsburys (Stamp Taxes).
Personal: Master's Prize & Wright Prize

CHACKSFIELD, Mark
8 New Square, London
020 7405 4321
mark.chacksfield@8newsquare.co.uk
Featured in Intellectual Property (London)
Practice Areas: Mark practices in all areas of intellectual property law, with particularly strong expertise in major patent litigation. He has considerable experience in appearing as the sole advocate both at first instance and in the Court of Appeal, as well as in the EPO. Recent pharmaceutical and biotech cases include the three actions in the Genentech v. Hospira litigation (Herceptin), Teva v. Boehringer (tiotropium), Novartis v. Teva (transdermal rivastigmine), Resolution Chemicals v H. Lundbeck (escitalopram/res judicata), Teva v Merck (efavirenz/quia timet actions), Eli Lilly v HGS (Neutrokine-α),

Regeneron Pharmaceuticals v Genentech (Lucentis) and Ranbaxy v AstraZeneca (Swiss-form claims/esomeprazole). Mark has represented Nokia in the Interdigital, IPCom and HTC litigations, Unwired Planet against Google, Samsung and Huawei, as well as working with a number of other high profile telecoms companies. He has also appeared in both high tech and mechanical patent actions, including appearing alone in the leading Court of Appeal case on indirect infringement of Grimme Landmaschinenfabrik v Scott. Other areas of particular experience include media and entertainment, where Mark has represented broadcasters, record companies, picture libraries and well-known personalities in copyright and privacy claims, as well as acting in musical copyright actions concerning substantial hits.
Professional Memberships: Intellectual Property Bar Association (IPBA) and Chancery Bar Association.
Career: Called 1999, Middle Temple.
Personal: Born September 1974. Educated at Royal Grammar School, High Wycombe; Clare College, Cambridge University, BA (Double First) Natural Sciences (Zoology) Hurst Prize for Zoology.

CHAISTY, Paul QC
Kings Chambers, Manchester
0345 034 3444
clerks@kingschambers.com
Featured in Chancery (Northern), Professional Negligence (Northern), Commercial Dispute Resolution (Northern), Company (Northern), Partnership (Northern), Real Estate Litigation (Northern), Restructuring/Insolvency (Northern)
Practice Areas: Chancery and commercial litigation; insolvency – corporate and individual; commercial property; commercial landlord and tenant; professional negligence, director's disqualification; banking – recoveries, guarantees and securities; company – shareholder and boardroom disputes; commercial agents; breach of director and employee duties; partnership; commercial contracts – including joint ventures, share warranty and asset claims, distribution contracts and agency; sale of goods; commercial fraud and sports law.
Professional Memberships: Chancery Bar Association; Northern Chancery Bar Association; Northern Circuit Commercial Bar Association; COMBAR.
Career: University: Nottingham & Exeter College Oxford. Degrees: Law (LLB) (First Class) & BCL. Year of call: 1982 (Lincoln's Inn), Hardwicke and Cassell scholar. Recorder: 2000. Appointed QC: 2001. Official Appointments: Deputy High Court Judge (authorised to sit in Queen's Bench and Chancery Divisions) 2006. Called to Bar in British Virgin Islands and Bahamas 2009.

CHAMBERLAIN, Emma
Pump Court Tax Chambers, London
020 7414 8080
clerks@pumptax.com
Featured in Tax (London)
Practice Areas: Emma Chamberlain specialises in taxation and trust advice for high net worth private clients, especially IHT & CGT advice, advice on tax issues arising on divorce, and advice for foreign domiciliaries and non-residents. In some circumstances Emma is able to accept instructions via Public Access. Emma is also an adviser to the Parliamentary Treasury Select Committee. She was a member of the Interim General Anti-Abuse Advisory Committee and worked with HMRC to produce the guidance and examples on private client taxation that were published in April 2013. She sat on the consultation group that assisted in devising the statutory residence test. She has advised HM Treasury and HMRC on a number of technical matters relating to inheritance tax and foreign domiciliaries.
Professional Memberships: STEP Technical Committee, Chancery Bar Association, Revenue Bar Association, CIOT-Capital Taxes Committee (previously chair), Council member of CIOT.
Career: Called: 1998.
Publications: On editorial board of British Tax Review, Co-author of "Trust Taxation and Estate Planning" (4th Edition), Sweet & Maxwell (2014); Co-editor of "Dymond's Capital Taxes" Co-author of "Pre-Owned Assets and Estate Planning (3rd Edition), Sweet and Maxwell, (2009) Co-author of Mirrlees Report IFS "Wealth and Wealth Transfer taxes" OUP 2009.

CHAMBERLAIN, Martin QC
Brick Court Chambers, London
020 7379 3550
ian.moyler@brickcourt.co.uk
Featured in Administrative & Public Law (London), Civil Liberties & Human Rights (London), Environment (London), Competition/European Law (London), Public International Law (London)
Career: Martin Chamberlain QC specialises in Admin & Public Law, Human Rights and EU Law. He also acts in commercial and employment cases. He was named by Chambers & Partners as Human Rights and Public Law Junior of the Year in 2011 and was one of three nominees for Human Rights and Public Law Silk of the Year in 2014. Martin acts and advises in judicial review and human rights claims for both claimants and defendants. For claimants, his work ranges from human rights claims on behalf of individuals and NGOs, to commercial and regulatory judicial review claims and appeals in financial services, environmental law, aviation, healthcare, pensions, pharmaceuticals, tax, telecoms & transport. He has acted both as open counsel and as a Special Advocate in terrorism and other national security cases. For defendants he appears for governmental and other public bodies in public law cases of all kinds including in the fields of education, local government, equality & discrimination and professional regulation. Martin has appeared in 20 cases before the UK Supreme Court/House of Lords and has experience before the European Court of Human Rights (both for applicants and for State respondents) and the Court of Justice of the EU.

CHAMBERLAYNE, Patrick QC
29 Bedford Row Chambers, London
020 7797 7070
pchamberlayne@29br.co.uk
Featured in Family/Matrimonial (London)
Practice Areas: Barrister specialising in Financial Remedy, Private Law Children Applications, Inheritance Act Claims & Cohabitation. He also specialises in high net worth divorce (including Part III claims after foreign divorce), civil partnership and Schedule 1 claims and jurisdiction disputes. Particular interest in cases involving non-disclosure, trusts and businesses and cases with an international element. Cases include: SA v PA (Pre-marital agreement: Compensation) [2014] EWHC 392; H v H [2014] EWHC 760 (Fam); W v C (Financial Remedies: Appeal: Non-Disclosure) [2013] 2 FLR 115; Sekhri v Ray [2013] All ER (D) 350 (Jul); Lawrence v Gallagher [2012] EWCA (Civ 394); H v S [2011] EWHC B23 (Fam); Riding v Riding [2011] EWHC 3093 (Fam); Re G (Maintenance Pending Suit) [2007] 1 FLR 1674, CA; P v P (Inherited property) [2005] 1 FLR 576, FD.
Professional Memberships: FLBA.
Career: Called 1991, Inner Court. Appointed Silk 2010.
Personal: Clare College, Cambridge (MA Cantab); Bar School 91992 Scarman scholar).

CHAMBERS, Gaynor
Keating Chambers, London
020 7544 2600
gchambers@keatingchambers.com
Featured in Construction (London)
Practice Areas: Practice Areas: Gaynor specialises in energy, professional negligence, shipbuilding, environmental, sewage and wastewater treatment, as well as general construction and engineering matters ranging from procurement to final account claims. Her previous career in building surveying along with her commercial and down to earth approach has enabled Gaynor to build a strong reputation. She has extensive experience in advising on many standard forms, including the IChemE Red Book, MF/1, NEC and JCT contracts. Gaynor's UK and international energy practice focuses on both upstream and downstream disputes, including matters arising out of new technologies. She is equally familiar with conducting disputes through the TCC, arbitration or adjudication. She is an experienced adjudicator (on the TECBAR and IChem E panels) and appears in mediations, expert determinations and arbitrations.
Professional Memberships: SCL and COMBAR.
Career: BSc (Hons) Building Surveying (1st); Called 1998; Public Access Training 2008.
Publications: Keating on Construction Contracts 9th Edition (2012), researcher; Keating on JCT Contracts, Member of Editorial Team; Engineer's Dispute Resolution Handbook (Thomas Telford, 2006), author of chapter on dispute avoidance.

CHANDLER, Alexander
1 King's Bench Walk, London
020 7936 1500
achandler@1kbw.co.uk
Featured in Family/Matrimonial (London)
Practice Areas: Specialist in financial remedies, including Schedule 1 applications and intervener claims, and Trusts of Land claims.
Professional Memberships: Family Law Bar Association, Chancery Bar Association, Member of the Chartered Institute of Arbitrators and Institute of Family Law Arbitrators. Affiliate member of Resolution.
Career: Called to Bar (Middle Temple, Benefactors' Scholar), 1995. Tenant at 1 Garden Court (1997-2013) and 1 Kings Bench Walk (2013 to date). Reported cases: R v R [2015] 3 FCR 1. Deputy District Judge in Civil (2013) and Family (2014) sitting on the South-Eastern Circuit. Panel Member of the Bar Tribunals and Adjudication Service (BTAS), 2013. Arbitrator in financial claims (MCIArb).
Publications: Halsbury's Laws of England (Vol. 5(4)), Butterworths' Civil Court Precedents (Ancillary Relief), Jowitt's Dictionary of English Law. Recent articles include: "Strange Bedfellows: Case Management in TOLATA and Schedule 1" [2016] Fam Law (forthcoming), "Family Loans and Intervener Claims" [2015] Fam Law 1429, "Bleak House II: The Interveners" [2013] Fam Law 821 "The Law Is Now Reasonably Clear: The Courts' Approach to Non-Matrimonial Assets" [2012] Fam Law 163 etc.
Personal: Educated at King's School, Canterbury, Oxford University (MA, Modern History). City University (Dip. Law). Married, father of three living in Richmond. Interests include marathon running.

CHAPMAN, Graham QC
4 New Square, London
020 7822 2000
g.chapman@4newsquare.com
Featured in Professional Negligence (London)
Practice Areas: Professional liability claims in a commercial context, commercial litigation and construction, engineering and environmental law. Professional liability work includes claims against lawyers, surveyors and valuers, architects and engineers, accountants and auditors, financial services professionals, and insurance brokers and agents. Also experience of professional disciplinary matters. Commercial practice spans the full range of commercial disputes including international arbitration and insurance and reinsurance work. In the construction field he has acted for and against contractors, architects and engineers in claims concerning projects both in the UK and overseas. International experience includes cases in BVI, Cayman, Channel Islands and Malaysia.
Professional Memberships: PNBA; COMBAR; TECBAR.
Career: BA (Oxon). (1st Class). Called to the Bar (Inner Temple) 1998 (Major Scholarship). Tenant 4 New Square 1999 to date. QC 2014.
Personal: Educated Westcliff High School for Boys, Westcliff-on-Sea and Oriel College, Oxford (Scholar).

CHAPMAN, Jeffrey QC
Fountain Court Chambers, London
020 7583 3335
jpc@fountaincourt.co.uk
Featured in Banking & Finance (London), Commercial Dispute Resolution (London), Fraud (London)
Practice Areas: Commercial litigation including civil fraud, banking, international arbitration, insurance/reinsurance and professional negligence. Instructed in various long-running fraud proceedings in multiple jurisdictions (including MTN fraud proceedings [2014] EWHC 2046 (Ch) and the JSC BTA Bank litigation); professional negligence litigation relating to the collapse of Keydata Investments Limited; and also on behalf of the FSA. Acted in the successful Olympic stadium judicial review proceedings (acting on behalf of Leyton Orient FC) and advises on insurance coverage issues.
Professional Memberships: BSB Professional Conduct Committee (Barrister Vice-Chair); COMBAR; CEDR Accredited Mediator.
Career: Law Commission 1986-89. Called 1989. British Virgin Islands Bar (1999). QC 2010.
Personal: BA First Class University of Sussex (1985); LLM First Class, Trinity Hall, Cambridge (1986).

CHAPMAN, Nicholas
29 Bedford Row Chambers, London
020 7404 1044
nchapman@29br.co.uk
Featured in Family/Matrimonial (London)

Practice Areas: Principal area of practice is Financial Remedy Applications including Financial Provision for Children, Pre and post-nuptial agreements, cohabitation disputes and Inheritance Act Claims. Also has experience of private law children and domestic violence work. Notable cases include: Yates v Yates [2013] 2 FLR 1070; V v V (divorce; jurisdiction)[2011] 2 FLR 778; Currey v Currey [2005] 1 FLR 952 & Matharu v Matharu [1994] 2 FLR 597.

Professional Memberships: Family Law Bar Association.

Career: After completing a degree in Economics at UCL and a short service career as a Royal Naval Officer undertook Diploma in Law at City University and called to the Bar in 1990. Early career in general Common Law before specialising in Family Law since 1999. Collaborative Law trained and undertakes Public Access work. Has sat as Deputy District Judge on Western Circuit since 2000.

Publications: Frequent Lecturer.

Personal: Married with three children. Lives in London and Dorset. Interests include cricket, national hunt racing and politics.

CHAPMAN, Vivian R QC
9 Stone Buildings, London
020 7404 5055
vchapman@9stonebuildings.com
Featured in Agriculture & Rural Affairs (London)

Practice Areas: Property litigation with particular interest in law of commons and greens. His Report as inspector was upheld by the Supreme Court in R (Barkas) v North Yorkshire CC [2015] AC 195 and was described by Lord Neuberger as an "excellent report prepared by Vivian Chapman QC". Described as 'a member of the Bar expert in the law of commons and greens' by Lord Hoffmann in Oxfordshire CC v Oxford City Council (2006)and as having "very extensive knowledge and experience of this area of the law" by HH Judge Waksman QC in R (Oxfordshire NHS Trust) v Oxfordshire County Council (2010). Interesting cases include: R (Somerford Parish Council) v Cheshire East Borough Council (2016) (Green), Thomas v Palmer-Tomkinson (2016) (Right of Way), R (Mann) v Somerset County Council (2012) (Green), Llewellyn v Lorey (2011) (CA: right of way), McLaren v Kubiak (2007) (Green: Jurisdiction of court), Hertfordshire v SoS (2006) (CA: public rights of way; extinguishment), Fraser v Canterbury Diocesan Board of Finance (No. 2) (2006) (HL: School Sites Acts), Frequently instructed by local authorities to chair public inquiries into applications to register new greens. Public inquiries in 2016: as inspector in Hampshire and as counsel in Swansea and Kent. Was the inspector in the leading cases of Sunningwell (HL), McAlpine, Trap Grounds (HL), Redcar (SC), Warneford Meadow and Barkas (SC). Appears regularly in Land Registration Tribunal

Professional Memberships: Lincoln's Inn (Bencher): Middle Temple: Chancery Bar Association: Property Bar Association: Recorder.

Career: Silk 2006.

Publications: Chancery Litigation Handbook (Jordans 2005). Town and Village Greens (2014).

Personal: Married. 2 daughters

CHARBIT, Valerie
2 Bedford Row, London
020 74408888
vcharbit@2bedfordrow.co.uk
Featured in Crime (London)

Practice Areas: Valerie has chosen to specialise in fraud, murder/manslaughter, serious sexual offences, serious crime, mental health, health and safety and professional disciplinary work. Valerie has experience of a broad range of complex cases. Her practice involves prosecuting and defending in equal measure. She has a particular specialism in cross-examining experts, particularly those in mental health. She is renowned for being calm under pressure, for her diligence and thoroughness when preparing a case, and for her compelling and persuasive advocacy for her clients, whether prosecuting or defending. She is always totally committed to achieving the best result for her client and she engages juries with her approachable style. She is appointed to the CPS Grade 4 (top tier) for prosecution advocates, and she is also part of the specialist rape and serious crime group panels. She is appointed to the Grade A (top tier) list for specialist regulatory advocates in Health and Safety. Since 2004, she has sat as a part-time Judge for the First Tier Tribunal (Mental Health). She represents health authorities in mental health tribunals where patients are detained in high and medium secure hospitals. She has been appointed to act as a legal adviser for the Association of Chartered Certified Accountants, the Nursing and Midwifery Council, the General Osteopathic Council and the General Pharmaceutical Council. She is a chair of the Taxation Disciplinary Tribunal. Valerie is Recorder of the South Eastern Circuit from September 2015 until September 2017. She also volunteers as a trainer on ethics and advocacy for Middle Temple and is a board member of Inclusion London.

Professional Memberships: Criminal Bar Association; Association of Regulatory and Disciplinary lawyers; Health and Safety Lawyers Association; Mental Health Lawyers Association; South Eastern Circuit.

Career: Called 1992. Tenant at 2 Bedford Row since 1994. Dual Practising Certificate, working for Turnstone Law as a barrister member.

Personal: Sheffield University LLB Law 2:1 RADA and Kings College London MA in Text and Performance Studies

CHARLES, Henry
12 King's Bench Walk, London
020 75830811
chambers@12kbw.co.uk
Featured in Personal Injury (London), Clinical Negligence (London)

Practice Areas: Henry has been awarded Chambers & Partners' Personal Injury and Clinical Negligence Junior of the Year Award 2014. He is listed in the current edition of the guide as recommended junior in these fields. He typically deals with higher value claims, in particular brain injury and psychiatric damage claims. Clinical negligence claims have included cases involving spinal surgery, management of hypertension, failure to diagnose cancers. Dental negligence claims have focussed on failed implant surgery. Henry continues to pursue third party clinical negligence claims on behalf of insurers, obtaining very significant contributions. Henry also undertakes professional negligence claims arising out of personal injury and clinical negligence, health and safety work and inquests. Recent cases have included Webster v Ridgeway School (duty of school to pupils in respect of their health and safety on school site, applicability of human rights legislation to personal injury claims), Cleightonhills v Bembridge Outboards (multi-million pound settlement, defence of HSE prosecution), Wilkin-Shaw v Kingsley & Fuller (successful defence of a fatal accident claim arising from a school trip – H. Ct and Ct of Appeal), M v B (a minimally conscious state clinical negligence case)

Professional Memberships: PIBA, PNBA

Career: Called 1987

Publications: JPIL article on Wilkin-Shaw v Kingsley & Fuller

Personal: Vintage and modern cars, dinghy sailing

CHARLTON, Alex QC
4 Pump Court, London
020 7842 5555
acharlton@4pumpcourt.com
Featured in Information Technology (London), Telecommunications (London)

Practice Areas: Alex has a commercial and technology-based practice with particular expertise and experience in software (including safety critical and safety related developments), networks, IT systems, telecommunications, radio and mobile telephony, RANS, chipset software/protocol stacks; intellectual property licensing (software, patents, games), misuse of confidential information; infrastructure and outsourcing contracts (including transition and transformation projects); delay claims and project management issues; defence contracts. Commercial, IT, Telecoms, Licensing, Outsourcing, Infrastructure, International Arbitration, Professional Negligence.

Professional Memberships: LCIA, ICC, CIArb, HKIAC, KLRCA Arbitrator and Mediator Panels, Adjudicator and Member of the ICE's Crossrail Adjudication Panel

Career: Called to the Bar in 1983. Silk 2008. Adjudicator and International Arbitrator.

Publications: Contributing editor to LLP Professional Negligence and Liability (Computer Consultants)

Personal: Married with three children.

CHARLWOOD, Spike
Hailsham Chambers, London
020 7643 5000
spike.charlwood@hailshamchambers.com
Featured in Professional Negligence (London)

Practice Areas: Spike specialises in professional negligence and insurance law. He was named 2010 Professional Negligence Junior of the Year in the Chambers Bar Awards, is one of the Chambers UK Bar 100 Juniors and is listed in the top tier of leading juniors for professional negligence in The Legal 500 and Chambers UK. He is particularly well known for his work in relation to legal, financial and property-related professional negligence and regularly acts in high value cases in those fields. Highlights of Spike's career include appearing twice in the House of Lords (in Farley v Skinner and Dubai Aluminium v Salaam). He also has experience with a wide range of managed and group litigation, including GMAC v Watson & Brown (a lender's claim), Nationwide v Balmer Radmore (part of the 1990s mortgage lender litigation) and Hobson v Ashton Morton Slack (an application for a Group Litigation Order).

Professional Memberships: PNBA; LCLCBA; SE Circuit.

Career: Called 1994; supervisor in Tort, Queens' College, Cambridge 1993-95.

Publications: 'Professional Negligence and Liability' (LLP, 2000): assistant editor and joint author of the chapter on barristers' negligence; 'Lloyds Law Reports: Professional Negligence', contributing editor 1999-2003; 'Cordery on Solicitors' (9th edition, looseleaf): previously a contributing editor; articles in the 'Solicitors' Journal' 1999-2007.

Personal: Education: Queens' College, Cambridge (MA (Hons) 1st Class). Leisure interests include walking, travel, wine, reading.

CHARMAN, Andrew
St Philips Chambers, Birmingham
0121 246 7000
acharman@st-philips.com
Featured in Chancery (Midlands), Commercial Dispute Resolution (Midlands)

Practice Areas: Company law (including transactions), commercial law, financial services, professional negligence (especially solicitors, accountants and valuers), property, trusts, and wills and probate. Litigation, advisory and drafting work. Also frequently a mediator of disputes in these areas and acts as an arbitrator.

Professional Memberships: Member of the Chancery Bar Association, the Midland Chancery and Commercial Bar Association, and the Chartered Institute of Arbitrators. ADR Group Accredited Mediator.

Career: Educated at Clare College, Cambridge. Worked as a researcher at The House of Commons then articles with Freshfields in London and Tokyo followed by practice as a solicitor in Freshfields' Corporate Department (company and financing transactions). Transferred to the Bar in 1994.

Publications: 'Shareholder Actions' published by Bloomsbury Professional, January 2013 – book on claims by shareholders against companies, directors, advisers and each other; Misrepresentation on Bond Issues: Liability in the Secondary Market. Butterworths Journal of International Banking and Financial Law 2011, 26(1), 17-19; Jones v Firkin-Flood: Trustees – How to Sell a Business and Distribute the Proceeds. Private Client Business 2010 No.3 181-188.

CHAWLA, Mukul QC
9-12 Bell Yard, London
020 7400 1800
m.chawla@912by.com
Featured in Crime (London), Professional Discipline (London), Financial Crime (London)

Practice Areas: Defends and prosecutes in fraud and general crime, acts in Professional discipline cases particularly involving accountants, actuaries and police officers. In the last year has acted for the Serious Fraud Office as Lead Counsel in relation to LIBOR and has successfully prosecuted the first criminal trial, worldwide, in relation to the manipulation of LIBOR. Has defended, successfully, in insider dealing cases. Has acted for the Financial Reporting Council in its regulatory proceedings against Mazars and one of its partners in relation to the proposed Substitution of a Members Pension Scheme. Acted for the Home Secretary in the first concluded Judicial Review conducted under

the Closed Material Procedure under the Justice and Security Act 2013. Is currently instructed to advise in relation to bribery allegations involving a consultant to the World Bank & further cases in the Oil and Gas Industry. Is also presently advising a number of clients (both companies and individuals) in relation to fraud bribery, and insider dealing allegations. An accredited CEDR (since 2007) and authorised to accept direct access work.
Professional Memberships: Member of the Criminal Bar Association and Founding Member of the Fraud Lawyers Association.
Career: Called (Gray's Inn) in 1983, appointed QC in 2001 and a Recorder of the Crown Court in 2007. Appointed Head of Chambers in January 2012. Former Chair – Gray's Inn Advocacy Training (2014-2015). A bencher of Gray's Inn since 2004.
Personal: Born in Nairobi, Kenya in May 1961. Educated at University College, London (LLB Hons)

CHEETHAM, Simon
Old Square Chambers, London
020 7269 0300
cheetham@oldsquare.co.uk
Featured in Employment (London)
Practice Areas: Simon is an employment and discrimination law specialist, with a wide-ranging practice in the employment tribunal, High Court and appellate courts. He has extensive experience of employment law and has frequently been instructed in complex and high-value claims. He has particular expertise in discrimination law, but his practice covers the full range of employment cases, including industrial relations, TUPE, whistle blowing and contractual disputes. Simon also undertakes disciplinary and regulatory work, particularly in the health care and higher education sectors, and has a growing pensions practice. Recent cases include: Lock v British Gas (ECJ, EAT and CA)- leading case on holiday pay; R ex p. Boots Management Services Ltd v CAC (CA) – trade union recognition; Dronsfield v Reading University (EAT) – conduct dismissals for academic staff; acting for claimants and respondents in large holiday pay multiple claims; several multi-day tribunal claims, including discrimination and whistle-blowing; high-profile investigations for universities; an application to the ECHR on "sweetheart unions".
Professional Memberships: Fee-paid Employment Tribunal Judge 2002 – Bar Standards Board, Professional Conduct Committee 2008 – 2014; reserve panel 2014 – 2016 Chairman Royal Mail National Appeals Panel 2011 – ELBA Executive Committee 2014 -2016 International Paralympic Committee, panel member 2016 -

CHELMICK, Timothy
4 New Square, London
020 7822 2023
t.chelmick@4newsquare.com
Featured in Professional Negligence (London)
Practice Areas: Tim specialises in commercial disputes with a particular emphasis on international arbitration, construction and professional liability. Tim lived and worked in Dubai for two years and so has significant experience of disputes in the Middle East. He is regular instructed in arbitrations and associated court proceedings. He is currently instructed in arbitrations with seats in London and Singapore arising out of projects and transactions in Saudi Arabia, Iraq and the Maldives. Tim's construction practice encompasses both domestic and international claims with an emphasis on disputes relating to infrastructure projects. He has particular experience of claims relating to the construction of airports and power stations. Tim's expertise in the context of professional liability work encompasses the full range of claims against professionals with a particular focus on solicitors, especially in respect of claims arising out of commercial transactions and failed commercial litigation.
Professional Memberships: LCIA, COMBAR, TECBAR, PNBA.
Career: Magdalen College, Oxford (Chemistry, 2000); Goldman Sachs International (2000-2002); City University (Diploma in Law, 2003); Called 2004.
Publications: Co-Editor: 'Jackson & Powell on Professional Liability' (Sweet & Maxwell)

CHENG, Serena
Atkin Chambers, London
020 7404 0102
scheng@atkinchambers.com
Featured in Construction (London)
Practice Areas: Serena is a commercial litigation and arbitration specialist with a particular emphasis on technically complex plant and utilities, oil and gas and infrastructure disputes. She is regularly instructed both in the TCC and in domestic and international arbitration and has extensive experience of cross-examining factual and expert witnesses. Reported cases include: Lulu Construction Ltd v. Mulalley & Co Ltd [2016] EWHC 1852; Eurocom Ltd v Siemens PLC [2015] BLR 1, [2014] 157 Con LR 120; Malcolm Charles Contracts Ltd v Crispin & Zhang [2014] 159 Con LR 185; University of Brighton v Dovehouse Interiors Ltd [2014] 153 Con LR 147; Hillcrest Homes Ltd v Beresford & Curbishley Ltd [2014] 153 Con LR 179, [2014] CILL 3506; Doosan Babcock Ltd v Comercializadora de Equipos y Materiales MABE LDA [2014] BLR 33.
Professional Memberships: COMBAR; LCLCBA; SCL and TECBAR. Serena has been a member of TECBAR's Management Committee since c.2005.
Career: LLB(Hons) (London) 1999; called to the Bar Lincoln's Inn 2000.

CHISHOLM, Malcolm
1 Garden Court Family Law Chambers, London
020 7797 7900
chisholm@1gc.com
Featured in Court of Protection (All Circuits)
Practice Areas: Care proceedings and special guardianship, Court of Protection, private family law relating to children (residence, contact, leave to remove), adoption (international and domestic), child abduction, media injunctions in family and Court of Protection cases.
Professional Memberships: Family Law Bar Association, Association of Lawyers for Children.
Career: Called 1989 (Inner Temple). Joined 1 Garden Court Family Law Chambers in 2000. Appointed part time tribunal judge (Mental Health Tribunal) in 2004. Regular lecturer and podcaster. Reported cases include Re P (Parental Responsibility) [1998] 2 FLR 1996, CA, Re B (Abduction: False Immigration Information) [2000] 2 FLR 835, FD, Greenwich London Borough Council v. S [2007] 2 FLR 154, FD (Convention adoption order/habitual residence), Re LM (Reporting Restrictions: Coroner's Inquest) [2008] 1 FLR 1360, FD (Restrictions on publicity/Art 8/Art 10), Re A (A Child) (Adoption: Removal) [2009] 2 FLR 597, CA (Placement of children overseas for purposes of adoption), Re T (Care Order) [2009] 2 FLR 574, CA (Court's duties when presented with a proposed agreed order), X and Y v. Warwickshire County Council and B [2009] EWHC 47 (Wholesale breach of adoption rules in FPC), Re W (Adoption Order: Set Aside and Leave to Oppose) [2011] 1 FLR 2153 (Approach to be taken to late application to oppose adoption, SMBC v PR (SR Intervening) (Care Proceedings: Children's Evidence)(No 2) [2012] 1 FLR 852, FD: Court's approach to vulnerable witnesses, RC v CC [2013] EWHC 1424 (COP): withholding disclosure on behalf of adopted adult.
Personal: Born 1966. Educated at Sidney Sussex College, Cambridge (MA Law). Married with three children.

CHIVERS, David QC
Erskine Chambers, London
020 7242 5532
dchivers@erskinechambers.com
Featured in Chancery (London), Commercial Dispute Resolution (London), Company (London), Offshore (London), Restructuring/Insolvency (London)
Practice Areas: David is a highly experienced, sought-after silk who specialises in company law, corporate litigation and corporate restructuring/insolvency – onshore, offshore and internationally. He is known for the quality of both his advocacy and advisory skills. David has acted on many of the leading cases and transactions in these areas, including: Vodafone PLC – Verizon; Shire PLC; BHP Billton PLC (corporate advisory and schemes of arrangement); Jackson v Dear; Liverpool Football Club & RBS v Hicks & Gillett; Arbuthnott v Charterhouse (corporate litigation); Trustees of Olympic Airlines SA Pension & Life Assurance Scheme v Olympic Airlines; Singularis v PwC; PwC v Saad; Halliwells LLP (insolvency); and Validus Holdings v IPC, Weavering v SEB (offshore).
Professional Memberships: Chancery Bar Association, COMBAR, ILA, RISA (Cayman)
Career: Called: 1983. Silk: 2002. Admitted to the Bars of the following jurisdictions: British Virgin Islands, and ad hoc to Bermuda and Cayman.
Publications: Contributor to Co-operatives that Work (Spokesman 1988); Practice and Procedure in the Companies Court (Lloyds of London Press 1997); The Law of Majority Shareholders Power, Use and Abuse (OUP 2008).
Personal: Born 1960. Educated Millfield School; Downing College, Cambridge.

CHOAT, Rupert
Atkin Chambers, London
020 7404 0102
rchoat@atkinchambers.com
Featured in Construction (London)
Practice Areas: Since 1997 Rupert has specialised in construction, engineering, PFI/PPP, energy and similar disputes. He has considerable experience in related claims involving professional negligence as well as bonds and guarantees. He has worked on disputes concerning projects in over 45 jurisdictions, most of which were governed by the local law. He is an experienced advocate from the English Court of Appeal to arbitration venues around the world. Rupert is a practicing arbitrator who has sat in ICC, SCC and ad hoc arbitrations. Significant cases include: Hackney Empire v Aviva (guarantees/termination under JCT Conditions); Lukoil v Barclays & Doosan v MABE (both concerning on-demand bonds); ISG v Seevic (pay less notices/Construction Act); and Al-Waddan v MAN (no functioning Engineer under FIDIC Conditions).
Career: LLB Law (Hons), Warwick University; LLM Commercial Law (Hons), Cambridge University; Lincoln's Inn – Hardwicke and Sir Thomas More scholar; teaches at King's College, London – MSc (Construction Law & Dispute Resolution); 1 of 5 Most Highly Regarded Individuals for Construction in Europe (Who Who's Legal Construction 2016).
Publications: Columnist for Building magazine. Contributing editor for Global Arbitration Review's Construction Arbitration.

CHOKOWRY, Katy
1 King's Bench Walk, London
020 7936 1500
kchokowry@1kbw.co.uk
Featured in Family/Matrimonial (London)
Practice Areas: Katy practises in all areas of international family law. She has a keen interest in jurisdictional issues in relation to both children and financial proceedings. Katy is said to have: "... a reputation for possessing expertise that goes far beyond her level of call...". "For a junior advocate she is exceptional at holding her ground and putting forward a persuasive case for her client." "She punches above her weight;..." Katy has appeared in the following cases of note: Re D (A Child) (Recognition of Foreign Order) [2016] UKSC 34. Re B (A Child) (Habitual Residence: Inherent Jurisdiction) [2016] UKSC 4. Re S (Habitual Residence and Child's Objections: Brazil) [2015] 2 FLR 1338. AVH v SI and Another [2015] 2 FLR 269. Mittal v Mittal [2014] 1 FLR 1514. Re LC (Reunite Intervening) [2014] UKSC 1. Re Y (Abduction: Undertakings Given for Return of Child) [2013] 2 FLR 649. AB v CB (Divorce and Maintenance: Discretion to Stay) [2013] 2 FLR 29
Professional Memberships: Member of the Family Law Bar Association
Career: Before coming to the Bar, Katy practised as a solicitor with a well-known specialist family law firm.
Publications: Katy is a regular contributor of articles, case summaries and guides relating to her areas of interests.

CHORFI, Camilla
Selborne Chambers, London
020 7420 9500
camilla.chorfi@selbornechambers.co.uk
Featured in Real Estate Litigation (London)
Practice Areas: Camilla specialises in chancery litigation, with particular expertise in the field of real property. She is presently instructed inrelation to a spectrum of development disputes concerning easements, restictive covenants, and land registration matters. Camilla regularly appears in the High Court, County Court, and various divisions of the First Tier Tribunal. Camilla has experience in a broad spectrum of residential and commercial landlord and tenant law, including 1954 Act claims, enforcement of leasehold covenants, consents and forfeiture. She advises landlords, tenants, insolvency practitioners and mortgagees in relation to

property related insolvency issues. Camilla's practice has an emphasis on mortgage related matters, and she is currently retained on numerous lender claims against both valuers and solicitors. Camilla has also been instructed on a number of complex trusts of land disputes.She has also been appointed to the Attorney General's "C" Panel of Junior Counsel to the Crown.

Professional Memberships: Chancery Bar Association, Professional Negligence Bar Association, Property Bar Association, Women in Property

Career: Called 2008. Lincoln's Inn.

Personal: BA Classics (First); MA Classics (Distinction); LLB Law. Conversational French and Arabic.

CHOUDHURY, Akhlaq QC

11KBW, London
020 7632 8500
Akhlaq.Choudhury@11kbw.com

Featured in Data Protection (London), Employment (London), Public Procurement (London)

Practice Areas: Commercial, Employment, Procurement, Information and Public law. Recent cases include: Nicolson v Grant Thornton UK LLP [2016] EWHC 710 (Admin) (Auditors, Council Tax Liability); Elliston v Glencore Services (UK) Ltd [2016] EWCA Civ 407 (Bonuses); Jones v McNichol [2016] EWHC 866 (QB) (Injunction); Frimpong v CPS [2016] 1 Cr App R (S) 59 (Court's powers and duties); Timothy James Consulting Ltd v Wilton [2015] ICR 764 (Loss of Chance, taxation of damages); Reuse Collections Ltd v Sendall [2015] IRLR 226 (Restrictive Covenants, Fiduciary Duties); DWF LLP v Insolvency Service [2014] EWCA Civ 900 (Procurement, automatic suspension); Allan v Wandsworth LBC [2014] Eq LR 30 (Disability Discrimination), Esparon v Slavikovska [2014] ICR 1037 (National Minimum Wage); BUQ v HRE [2012] I.R.L.R. 653 (Privacy Injunction).

Professional Memberships: PLA, ELBA, ALBA, ELA.

Career: Called 1992. Recorder (SE Circuit) 2009. Appointed to Attorney General's A-Panel of Treasury Counsel March 2013. Silk 2015. Deputy High Court Judge 2016.

Publications: Tolley's 'Employment Handbook' (1996-date), contributor. Information Law Reports, contributor.

Personal: BSc Hons, Physics (Glasgow); LLB Hons (1st Class) (London).

CHRISTIE, Aidan QC

4 Pump Court, London
020 7842 5555
achristie@4pumpcourt.com

Featured in Professional Negligence (London), Insurance (London)

Practice Areas: Principal areas of practice are insurance and reinsurance, professional negligence (including accountants, brokers, lawyers and financial advisors), insurance regulation, financial services and general commercial disputes.

Professional Memberships: COMBAR, London Common Law and Commercial Bar Association.

Career: Called to the Bar 1988, Silk 2008, Recorder 2009, Panel Deemster Isle of Man 2012

Personal: BA (Oxon) Classics, MA (Cantab) Law.

CHRISTIE, Richard QC

187 Fleet Street, London
0790 093 2202
richardchristie@187fleetstreet.com

Featured in Crime (London)

Practice Areas: Crime, civil liberties, fraud (crime), health and safety, inquests, POCA and asset and forfeiture.

Professional Memberships: Criminal Bar Association; South Eastern Circuit.

Career: Specialises in all areas of criminal work, particularly serious fraud, murder and cases requiring substantial client care. Expertise in MTIC cases. Successfully defended in the hugely complicated historic axe murder of Private Eye Daniel Morgan: linked to the phone-hacking scandal, featured on Panorama and the longest pre-trial legal argument in English Criminal Law. Prosecuted multi-million pound ten-handed excise fraud featured on ITV programme "Fiddles, Cheats and Scams". Both SFO panels of approved Queen's Counsel. Rough-justice cases and J.R. for Criminal Cases Review Commission. Advised major household names on regulatory offences. Trained with Touche Ross and Co. Those marked with a (P) below were prosecution briefs. (1) R v X (£40 million VAT fraud – extensive PII – D. an informant -acquitted); (2) R v Smith (Murder appeal based on fresh evidence); (3) R v Walpole (Conspiracy to import cocaine and cannabis (over one tonne); (4) R v Grady (Letters of Credit fraud on the Clearing Banks – acquitted); (5) R v Chapman (£16.75m MTIC VAT fraud); (6) R v Piggott (£44 million MTIC fraud – off-shore companies. Confiscation and ancillary relief proceedings – RCJ). (P). (7) R v Carine (Appeal – Southend airport conspirators (250kg of cocaine) (8) R v Bush (Appeal – murder) (9) R v Strain (Hydro carbons fraud and confiscation- Northern Irish OCG) (P). (10) R v Carter (Murder trial – complicated forensic evidence -successfully argued that there had been no killing at all – acquitted) (11) R v Duffy (Murder – successful diminished responsibility – battered mother to death with hammer) (12) R v Long (Serious fraud/arson trial – target criminal) (P) (13) R v Donnan (£35m MTIC money laundering and confiscation) (P) (14) R v Bodden (Murder – Cayman Islands – acquitted) (15) R v Nevers (Attacks on 9 women) (P) (16) R v Ahmed (Appeal: rape and kidnap – Islamic marriage. LPP, fresh evidence from LPP material) (17) R v Abu and others (3.5 month immigration fraud) (P) (18) R v Tambengwa (Murder and serious sexual offences on child) (P) (19) R v Small (Appeal – historic sexual offences. Conviction quashed. Re trial – acquitted) (20) R v Mahmood (Appeal – serious sexual offences. Appeal (quashed) – re-trial – 2nd appeal: acquitted) (21) R v Hale (Murder – missing victim. Note "By fire, by sea, by landsite, by acid." Front page Evening Standard and Sky News. Acquitted) (22) R v Rees (Murder, police corruption, 750,000 pp. of material, 5 month abuse of process; 5 previous enquiries. Acquitted); (23) R v Conroy (Ten-handed excise fraud and confiscation– OCG) (P); (24) R v Briggs (£1 billion Cocaine importation, firearms – acquitted) (25) R v Hanson (Conspiracy to murder – contract killing – acquitted) (26) R v Gill (£38m carbon credit fraud) (27) R v Naqshbandi (£6m – crash for cash conspiracy to defraud) (28) R v Dudley (Gross-negligence manslaughter – acquitted) (29) R v Durham (11 x conspiracy to rob CIT vans – 6/11 acquitted – large scale fit up alleged) (30) R v M (Attempted murder and anal rape) (31) R v Yearsley (£multimillion confiscation) – P (32)R v T (Rough-justice appeal – serious sexual offences) (33) R v Bensley (£24m MTIC fraud – acquitted) (34) R v Bashardost (7 handed murder – acquitted) (35) R v Simon (Murder – dismemberment) (36) R v Iftinca (6 handed murder – acquitted) (37) R v Evans (£multi-million SFO open cast mining fraud – P) (38) R v Rafiq – Human trafficking – first ever prosecution of end user of trafficked labour in UK – John Lewis/Next

CHUDLEIGH, Louise

Old Square Chambers, London
020 7269 0300
chudleigh@oldsquare.co.uk

Featured in Employment (London)

Practice Areas: Louise is an experienced senior junior whose practice encompasses all aspects of employment, discrimination, disciplinary and regulatory work. She frequently appears in lengthy and complex cases including: discrimination; whistleblowing; and large equal pay claims, often against leading counsel. Louise appears in the employment tribunals, the high court and in the appellate courts and has particular expertise in disputes involving professionals such as dental and medical practitioners and police officers. Notable cases include: BCC v Abdulla, a Supreme Court equal pay case and Chhabra v West London Mental Health NHS Trust, a Supreme Court case about the proposed disciplining of a doctor. More recent cases include Sefton BC v Wainwright [2015] I.C.R. 652 (maternity discrimination) and Serco v Dahou [2015] I.R.L.R. 30 (trade union dismissal and detriment). Her regulatory work has included acting as a legal assessor, a legal advisor and an advocate in professional disciplinary and fitness to practice matters. Louise is known to be a reliable and effective barrister as well as a strong advocate and good tactician.

Professional Memberships: ELBA, ELA

Career: Called to the Bar 1987 (England and Wales); 1989 (Bermuda); Fee paid Employment Judge since 2001; Certified mediator.

CLAPHAM, Penelope

1 Garden Court Family Law Chambers, London
020 77977900
clapham@1gc.com

Featured in Family/Matrimonial (London)

Practice Areas: Penelope has developed a practice specialising in both family finance and private law children matters. Penelope particularly enjoys dealing with financial disputes, both in a matrimonial context as well as between cohabitees or under Schedule 1 of the Children Act 1989. Penelope has dealt with a number of complex private law Children Act 1989 matters requiring particular sensitivity including those involving sexual abuse, domestic violence and intractable hostility. She enjoys cases with an international element including leave to remove and child abduction matters.

Professional Memberships: Member of the Family Law Bar Association.

Career: MA (Hons) Jurisprudence, Somerville College, Oxford University BVC Inns of Court School of Law Duke of Edinburgh Scholarship, Inner Temple Streuben Prize Winner, Inner Temple Exhibition, Inner Temple

Publications: Penelope wrote the chapter on Schedule 1 of the Children Act 1989 in the book "DIY Divorce & Separation: The Expert Guide to Representing Yourself (Jordan Publishing), 2014" Penelope regularly write articles and gives seminars on a variety of topics. The most recent have included: internal relocation, Schedule 1 of the Children Act and its applicability in the small-medium asset case, how business assets should be dealt with in financial remedy cases, the recent procedural changes in the family courts and the impact on practitioners and clients and a practical guide to TOLATA applications.

Personal: Penelope enjoys a wide variety of sports including football, rugby and cricket. She runs and is a keen skier and scuba diver.

CLARKE, Elizabeth

Queen Elizabeth Building QEB, London
020 7797 7837
e.clarke@qeb.co.uk

Featured in Family/Matrimonial (London)

Practice Areas: Matrimonial finance.

Career: BA (Oxon).

CLARKE, Ian QC

Selborne Chambers, London
020 7420 9500
ian.clarke@selbornechambers.co.uk

Featured in Real Estate Litigation (London)

Practice Areas:

Professional Memberships: Chancery Bar Association; Property Bar Association; Professional Negligence Bar Association; Fellow, Chartered Institute of Arbitrators; Insolvency Lawyers' Association; Association of Contentious Trust and Probate Specialists.

Career: Ian took silk in 2016, shortly after his appointment to the Attorney-General's A Panel of Counsel. Ian is ranked in both Chambers and Partners and the Legal 500 for his expertise in the core areas of his practice: Commercial, Real Estate/Property litigation, Professional negligence and Private client (wills and trusts). Rated as "one of the finest advocates; fiendishly clever, with an excellent eye for detail" and for being "calm, affable, tactically astute, and most of all a persuasive advocate", he is also commended for building a good rapport with clients, with whom "[he] engages well.... and has his own particular style – direct, to the point and with good humour". His practice in this jurisdiction, the Caribbean and Gibraltar involves substantial commercial contractual disputes (having appeared at trial and in the CA twice in Harb v Aziz, defeating claims to sovereign immunity and of judicial bias); issues of fraud, trusts/ probate, insolvency and professional negligence and conflict of laws. He also regularly undertakes instructions relating to land (especially on land registration matters) and mortgages (on which he co-edits one of the two practitioner texts). He has acted as an expert in foreign proceedings. He has been a part-time judge since 2004 and a fellow of the CIArb since 1997.

Publications: Wolstenholme & Cherry's Annotated Land Registration Act 2002 (2003 Sweet & Maxwell) co-author on The Law of Mortgages (2010, 3rd Edition, Sweet & Maxwell).

CLARKE, Patrick

Atkin Chambers, London
020 7404 0102
pclarke@atkinchambers.com

Featured in Construction (London)

Practice Areas: Patrick specialises in construction, energy, information technology, professional negligence and disputes with a high technical content or concerning major projects generally including litigation, domestic and international arbitration and cases before the DIFC court Dubai.
Professional Memberships: TECBAR, COMBAR, SCL.
Career: BSc Physics. Practicing in Atkin Chambers since completion of Pupillage in 1999.
Publications: Contributor of 'Hudson's Construction and Engineering Contracts' and Editor of the 'Construction Law Journal' published by Sweet & Maxwell.

CLARKE, Sarah
Serjeants' Inn Chambers, London
020 7427 5000
Sclarke@3serjeantsinn.com
Featured in Financial Services (London), Financial Crime (London)

Practice Areas: Sarah Clarke was called to the Bar in 1994. Sarah specialises in financial services, fraud, professional discipline and regulatory, public and administrative, inquests and inquiries and police law. She has particular experience of shaping complex litigation from an early stage. An earlier edition notes that "she's an advocate who works extremely hard for the clients and is not afraid to ask difficult questions.". Please visit the Serjeants' Inn Chambers website for her profile, which sets out full details of her practice (including her time in the Enforcement Division and subsequently the Litigation Department of what was then the FSA) and relevant work of note.
Career: Recorder of the Crown Court: 2012, CPS Grade 4 Prosecutor (General Crime): 2012, SFO A Panel(POCA): 2013, CPS Grade 4 Specialist Fraud Panel: 2013, CPS Grade 4 Specialist Rape and Sexual Offences Panel: 2013.
Publications: Insider Dealing: Law and Practice, contributing author to LexisNexis and member of editorial board of LexisNexisPSL.
Personal: Member of Bar Standards Board and Vice-Chair of its Qualifications Committee, Member of Advocacy Training Council and Vice-Chair of its Training and Accreditation Committee, Member of Inner Temple Advocacy Training Committee, CPS Advocacy Assessor.

CLAY, Jonathan
Cornerstone Barristers, London
020 7242 4986
jclay@cornerstonebarristers.com
Featured in Planning (London)

Practice Areas: Jonathan's practice covers all aspects of planning and environmental control, housing, renewable energy, large scale infrastructure projects and village greens, as well as housing, commercial and retail development schemes. His practice involves appearances in the High Court and Court of Appeal and at major public inquiries. Recent cases include Suffolk Coastal v Hopkins Homes [2016] (CA) on the meaning of the NPPF, Oxted Residential v Tandridge D.C.[2016](CA): challenge to local plan, NHS Properties v Surrey CC [2016] (HC) Village Greens and statutory incompatibility. Major development projects include Amex Stadium, Brighton, where he represented Brighton and Hove Albion F.C. at inquiry and in the courts, and Bromley Common (Blue Circle) site where he acted for the developer at PI in obtaining planning permission for major housing development on open land in the Green Belt. He works for both appellants and authorities in housing, commercial and industrial development appeals and has advised on content and soundness of local plans and on housing land supply issues.
Professional Memberships: Planning and Environmental Bar Association(PEBA); Pro Bono Unit; UK Environmental Lawyers Association (UKELA); National Infrastructure Planning Association.
Career: Called to the Bar in 1990.

CLAYTON, Nigel
Kings Chambers, Manchester
0345 034 3444
clerks@kingschambers.com
Featured in Real Estate Litigation (Northern)

Practice Areas: Nigel practises solely in real property law – including all aspects of land law, probate and trusts, landlord & tenant and related professional negligence. He specialises in mortgage law and litigation and is frequently instructed by lenders both in relation to drafting and advisory work, and litigation. He has an impressive list of court appearances, including in the Chancery Division, Court of Appeal and House of Lords, as well as regularly appearing in property cases in the county court throughout the country. Nigel's CV is available to download from www.kingschambers.com
Professional Memberships: Full member of the Society of Trust and Estate Practitioners (STEP), Northern Chancery Bar Association, Northern Circuit, North Eastern Circuit.
Career: Nigel was called to the Bar of the Inner Temple in 1987 and was previously a tenant at Bridge Street Chambers and 28 St John Street Chambers in Manchester before joining the Chancery/Commercial team at Kings Chambers in 2001. He was appointed Treasury Counsel in 2000 and a Recorder in 2002, and regularly sits on Chancery, Civil and Family cases throughout the North of England.
Publications: Co-author of 'Mortgage Possession Actions' (Sweet & Maxwell) Editor of www.legalmortgage.co.uk Contributing editor of www.propertylawuk.net Nigel regularly presents seminars on property and probate related topics
Personal: Educated at Ilkley Grammar School, Nottingham Law School and the Inns of Court School of Law. Nigel lives near Hebden Bridge in West Yorkshire and is married to a Solicitor, with three children. He is a keen runner and road cyclist.

CLAYTON, Richard QC
Kings Chambers, Birmingham
0345 034 3444
clerks@kingschambers.com
Featured in Administrative & Public Law (Midlands), Civil Liberties & Human Rights (Midlands)

Practice Areas: Principal areas of practice are public law, civil liberties/human rights and local government law- advisory and litigation work for and against public bodies covering community care, data protection, education, local government (e.g. vires and powers, constitutional issues and standards),public procurement, healthcare, human rights, Privy Council/international work and regulatory/disciplinary work. United Kingdom representative to Venice Commission, Council of Europe's advisory body on constitutional law; Visiting Professor, UCL, Associate Fellow at the Centre for Public Law, Cambridge University; former Chair, the Constitutional and Administrative Law Bar Association; Vice Chair, Liberty. Recent cases: R(Watch Tower) v Charity Commission (2016) (CA), R(Hardy) v Leicestershire County Council (2015, museum closure), R(Hardy) v Sandwell MBC (2015, housing benefits), R(T) v Trafford MBC (2015) (community care), Kennedy v Charity Commission (Supreme Court, 2014, freedom of information, human rights), R v Misick (Turks and Caicos Court of Appeal, constitutional challenge). Clients include private individuals, NGOs, local authorities and PLCs.
Professional Memberships: Deputy High Court Judge, Recorder, United Kingdom representative- Venice Commission (the Council of Europe's advisory body on constitutional law); Associate Fellow, Centre for Public Law, Cambridge University; former Chair of the Constitutional and Administrative Law Bar Association, Vice Chair, Liberty.
Career: Recent cases include Kennedy v Charity Commission (2014) (Supreme Court- Freedom of Information); R(McCallistair) v A-G of Turks and Caicos (2014) (TCI Court of Appeal- constitutional); R(Bridgerow) v Chester West (2014) (licencing); Many Supreme Court, House of Lords, Privy Council and Strasbourg cases. Clients include private individuals, NGOs, local authorities and PLCs. Richard is a member of both Kings Chambers (Birmingham) and 4-5 Grays Inn Square (London)
Publications: Joint author 'Law of Human Rights' (OUP)

CLEGG, Richard
Selborne Chambers, London
020 7420 9500
richard.clegg@selbornechambers.co.uk
Featured in Real Estate Litigation (London)

Practice Areas: Richard specialises in commercial disputes, frequently of an international nature, and property disputes, often when arising as part of a commercial transaction. He is often called upon when issues of evidential or technical complexity arise (including in the context of fraud) or when creative strategic thinking is required. Disputes on which Richard acts are increasingly in the context of joint ventures, supply and distribution agreements, commodities, energy and other resources. Of recent note, Richard represented a foreign government in an ICSID investment arbitration concerning the construction of a gas pipeline; a case that considered for the first time a number of issues of importance to investors in infrastructure in foreign lands, including the enforcement of commercial arbitration awards through treaty arbitration. He is an author of the Practical Law Company's guidance in the UK and US on international arbitration, and has a working knowledge of Cantonese Chinese. Recent cases: LCIA arbitration over a share rights agreement (2015); Eco-Energy World v Phoenix Capital (R-Energy) (2015) High Court litigation over solar farm agreements; Zarbafi v Zarbafi [2014] 1 WLR 4122 (CA); ICC arbitration over a distribution agreement representing a European manufacturer (2013); Stickley v Barclays Bank (2013) LTL 9/5/2013 (Registrar Derrett); Fitzwilliam v Richall Holdings Services [2013] 1 P&CR 19; Ad hoc arbitration proceedings in Singapore representing a South Korean conglomerate (2012); LCIA arbitration over a financial services contract representing a Jersey company (2012); SIAC arbitration in Singapore representing a Japanese Bank (2010).
Professional Memberships: Commercial Bar Association; Chancery Bar Association; International Bar Association;Chartered Institute of Arbitrators .
Career: Qualified Gray's Inn, 1999; Judicial Assistant to the Court of Appeal, 2000.
Publications: Author for the PLC International Arbitration service in the UK and US.
Personal: Languages: French (working knowledge); Cantonese Chinese (working knowledge).

CLEGG, Simon
St Philips Chambers, Birmingham
0121 246 7000
sclegg@st-philips.com
Featured in Commercial Dispute Resolution (Midlands)

Practice Areas: An experienced advocate and adviser in relation to commercial and business disputes involving contractual, banking, company, property and insolvency issues, as well as professional negligence.
Professional Memberships: COMBAR, Midlands Chancery and Commercial Bar Association.
Career: Called to the Bar in 1980. Spent three years working as a solicitor at Freehills in Sydney, Australia between 1988 and 1991.

CLEGG, William QC
2 Bedford Row, London
020 7440 8888
wclegg@2bedfordrow.co.uk
Featured in Crime (London), Financial Crime (London)

Practice Areas: Recently represented one of the acquitted defendants in "The News of the World" phone hacking trial and one of the acquitted defendants in the prosecution of "The Sun" journalists for paying public officials for stories. Currently instructed for a director in the Alstom corruption trial. Frequently advises foreign governments, international corporations, trade unions and individuals in relation to all aspects of regulatory offences, compliance, corporate manslaughter and health and safety infringement. Also a specialist in advising and defending in cases of alleged fraud, corporate corruption and sanctions breaches frequently with international aspects to the case, acted in Balfour Beatty, B.E.A., Barclays Bank LIBOR, Mabey and Johnson and Sainsbury. Often works in partnership with lawyers in other jurisdictions. A specialist in money laundering and restraint. Has appeared in over 125 cases in the Supreme Court, House of Lords, Administrative Court and Court of Appeal which can be accessed using Lexis-Nexis search engine cases include R v Banfield and Banfield [2013] EWCA 1394, R. (Rahndezfouli) v Crown Court at Wood Green [2013] EWHC 2998 (Admin), R. (on the application of Haligan) v Secretary of State for the Home Department [2012] AER (D) 178, R. (on the application of Robin Murray & Co.) v. Lord Chancellor [2011} AER (D) 102, R v Norris [2010] 1 AER (D) 88, R (on the application of Edwards) v CCRC {2008] AER (D) 110, R v Ali and Others 2006 1 CAR 8, R v Ramzan and Others 2007 1 CAR 10, R v El Kurd and Others 2007 1 CAR 30. Has practised extensively in The Hague and has advised in various countries in USA, Europe, the Middle East, West Indies and the Far East. Cases include Izodia plc; Brent Walker plc; Alliance Resources plc; Bute Mining plc; R v Smith (WSTC Merchant Bank); R v Smithson (The Arrows fraud); R v Alder (international bank fraud); R v Asil Nadir (Polly Peck); R v Hales (solicitors legal aid fraud). Cases of a more general nature include R v Serafinowicz (war crimes); R v Lee Clegg (British paragrooper accused of murder in Northern Ireland); R v Stone (Chillingden murders); R v Stagg (Wimbledon Common murder); R v Barry George (Jill Dando murder); R v Tabak (Joanna Yates murder); R v Varathadasan (Tamil Tigers); R v McMahon (UDA terrorists); R v Sawoniuk (war crimes); Prosecutor v Jelisic (war crimes the Hague); Prosecutor v Tadic (war crimes, The Hague); R v Duckenfield (Hillsborough Disaster). Has also been instructed in a lengthy public enquiry by the Medical Protection Society. Was a member of the standing committee of justice on fraud trials and prepared submissions to the Fraud Trials Committee chaired by Roskill (HMSO 1986).

Professional Memberships: Criminal Bar Association (Committee Member); South Eastern Circuit (Committee Member). Chairman Essex Bar Mess, 1997-2000.

Career: Called to the Bar 1972 and joined present chambers in 1973. Took Silk 1991. Appointed recorder 1992. Head of Chambers 1995.

Personal: Educated at Bristol University (LLB). Leisure pursuits include squash, cricket and wine. Born 5 September 1949.

CLEMENT, Joanne
11KBW, London
020 7632 8500
Joanne.Clement@11kbw.com

Featured in Administrative & Public Law (London), Civil Liberties & Human Rights (London), Community Care (London), Court of Protection (All Circuits), Education (London), Local Government (London)

Practice Areas: Specialist in all areas of public law, EU law and human rights law, all aspects of local government law (particularly community care and education); Court of Protection and public procurement. Recent notable cases include R (Rotherham MBC) v Secretary of State for Business, Innovation and Skills [2015] UKSC 6 (SC, challenge to allocation of €10billion of EU structural funds); Re X (Court of Protection Practice) [2015] EWCA Civ 599 (streamlined procedure for deprivation of liberty cases); R (LCCSA) v Lord Chancellor (No 1) [2014] EWHC 3020 (Admin) and (No 2) [2015] EWCA Civ 230 (challenge to "two tier" contracting for criminal legal aid); R (Morris) v RCT CBC [2015] EWHC 1403 (Admin) (challenge to local authority decision to abolish full time nursery education for three year olds); Barnsley MBC v GS [2015] COPLR 51 (deprivation of liberty in children's homes); acting for the Attorney General in devolution references concerning the legislative competence of the National Assembly for Wales (Attorney General's Reference on Local Government Byelaws (Wales) Bill 2012; [2013] 1 AC 792 and Agricultural Sector (Wales) Bill – Reference by the Attorney General for England and Wales [2014] 1 WLR 2622.

Professional Memberships: Administrative Law Bar Association.

Career: Called to the Bar 2002; Judicial Assistant to the Law Lords 2003-04; Member of Attorney-General's A Panel (previously on both the B and C Panels); Member of Welsh Government's A Panel of Junior Counsel.

Publications: Contributor to Supperstone, Goudie & Walker on Judicial Review (5th ed); Coppel ed Information Rights: Law and Practice (2014); Halsburys Laws of England – Judicial Review and co-author of "International Law in Domestic Courts: the Developing Framework" (2008) 124 LQR 388.

Personal: Educated at Ferndale Comprehensive School and Somerville College, Oxford (BA, BCL).

CLIFFORD, James
Maitland Chambers, London
/0044020 74061200/
jclifford@maitlandchambers.com

Featured in Pensions (London)

Practice Areas: Specialises in pensions and trusts; commercial and chancery litigation; and international commercial arbitration. Reported cases include: Briggs v Gleeds (Head Office), Honda Motor Group Ltd v Powell, Procter & Gamble v SCA, Dalriada Trustees Ltd v Foulds, MSM Consulting Ltd v United Republic of Tanzania, Trustees of Saffil Pension Scheme v Curzon, Barclays Bank v Holmes, ITS v Rowe, Polly Peck v Henry, Re Scientific Investment Pension Plan, Edge v The Pensions Ombudsman, Hood Sailmakers Ltd v Axford, Miller v Scorey, Process Developments Ltd v Hogg, Coloroll Pension Trustees Limited v Russell, Thrells Ltd v Lomas Nestle v National Westminster Bank, LRT v Hatt, Mettoy Pensions Trustees v Evans.

Professional Memberships: Association of Pension Lawyers, COMBAR, Chancery Bar Association, Association Professional Negligence Bar Association, ACTAPS and ARCAN. Also called to the Cayman Islands Bar.

Career: Called to the Bar in 1984.

Publications: Contributor to 'Trust Law International', 'Trusts and Trustees', 'British Pensions Lawyer', and author of 'Pensions Title', 'Atkins Court Forms'.

Personal: Educated at Oxford University.

CLOONEY, Amal
Doughty Street Chambers, London
078 1860 6161
personalasst@icloud.com

Featured in Crime (London), Civil Liberties & Human Rights (London)

Practice Areas: Amal Clooney specialises in public international law, international criminal law and human rights. In the last year, she has represented a number of political prisoners around the world. She challenged the imprisonment of the former President of the Maldives in a case before a UN body in Geneva and represented a journalist who was arbitrarily detained in Azerbaijan in a case before the European Court of Human Rights. Both of her clients have now been released. She also advocated on behalf of a Canadian 'Al Jazeera' journalist falsely imprisoned in Egypt and helped to secure a pardon from the Egyptian President on his behalf. In addition to political prisoners, Amal has represented victims of torture in Ireland seeking to intervene in an inter-state case against the UK at the European Court of Human Rights. And she represented the Chagossian people in a case before the UK Supreme Court in which the Court recognised that the ban imposed by the British government on their return to their islands in the Indian Ocean "needs to be revisited". Amal also provides advice to governments. She regularly provides advice to the UK government on international law and has previously advised the Greek Government on the return of their cultural property; been counsel for Cambodia in a case at the International Court of Justice in a border dispute with Thailand; and been counsel for Armenia before the European Court of Human Rights in a case involving recognition of the Armenian genocide.

Professional Memberships: UK Attorney General's Public International Law C Panel; Expert Panel of the Preventing Sexual Violence Initiative; World Economic Forum Global Future Council on Human Rights.

Career: Amal Clooney represents clients before international courts including the International Criminal Court, the International Court of Justice, the European Court of Human Rights and domestic courts in the UK and US. Alongside court work, she provides advice to governments and individuals on legal issues in her areas of expertise. Amal served as a senior advisor to Kofi Annan when he was the UN's Envoy on Syria and as Counsel to the UN Inquiry into the use of drones in counter-terrorism operations led by the Special Rapporteur on Counter-Terrorism and Human Rights. She is a member of the UK's team of experts on preventing sexual violence in conflict zones and she is appointed to the UK Attorney General's expert panel set up to advise and represent the UK government in cases involving public international law. Prior to joining the London Bar, Amal worked in The Hague with various UN-sponsored justice mechanisms including the International Court of Justice, the International Criminal Tribunal for the Former Yugoslavia and the Special Tribunal for Lebanon. She is also admitted to the New York Bar and practiced as a litigation attorney at Sullivan & Cromwell LLP in New York. She is a Visiting Professor at Columbia Law School and author of the upcoming book 'The Right to a Fair Trial in International Law' to be published by Oxford University Press in 2017.

Publications: Amal has published many articles in legal journals and was co-editor of the book 'The Special Tribunal for Lebanon: Law and Practice' (Oxford University Press). She is also the co-author (with P. Webb) of a forthcoming book 'The Right to a Fair Trial in International Law', to be published by Oxford University Press in 2017.

CLUTTERBUCK, Andrew QC
4 Stone Buildings, London
020 7242 5524
a.clutterbuck@4stonebuildings.com

Featured in Chancery (London)

Practice Areas: Company/commercial litigation including fraud, shareholder disputes and directors' duties, capital markets, trusts, corporate insolvency, financial services. Recent cases include: Edgeworth v Maud (bankruptcy, abuse of process); re Hellas (private equity, fraudulent trading, transaction avoidance); re Nusantara (directors' duties, Indonesian coal investment); Plaza v Law Debenture (bondholder rights, jurisdiction clauses).

Professional Memberships: COMBAR, Chancery Bar Association. Called to Bar in Cayman Islands and, for specific cases, in the Turks and Caicos Islands.

Career: Royal Marines; Called 1992.QC 2014

COCKINGS, Giles QC
Furnival Chambers, London
020 7405 3232
gcockings@furnivallaw.co.uk

Featured in Crime (London)

Practice Areas: Fraud and Serious Crime. Silk in 2016 having established a reputation for hard work, meticulous preparation. A defence and prosecution practitioner in serious crime involving gangland Murder (including over 50 major murder trials, reaching successful conclusions in 90%), Armed Robbery, Slavery, Money Laundering, Drug Importation & Inquests. More recently he has established an extensive track record in serious Commercial and White Collar Fraud. Specialisation within this area includes FCA, Banking Fraud, Insider Dealing, MTIC, VAT, Diversion, "Boiler-room", Advance Fee, Investment and Corporate fraud, many involving both criminal and civil proceedings with cross-jurisdictional elements. Having previously worked within the City, he has a good working knowledge of the financial markets and has successfully defended commercial solicitors, company directors and traders within both the criminal and regulatory arenas. These cases have ranged from internal accountancy issues prior to flotation, to issues of bribery and corruption, manipulation of markets and high yield lending frauds. Recently defended the MD of a PLC accused of a £39 million property/ banking fraud. Also, successfully defended in largest attempted currency fraud perpetrated against the Bank of England; successfully defended commercial Solicitor (Legal 500) in SFO prosecution of 6 solicitors charged with £55 million mortgage fraud; successfully defended Company Director in FCA investigation into international property investment & Swedish credit unions; successfully defended solicitor charged with Olympic development fraud; Also R-v-N & R-v-W (stockbrokers charged with hedge fund investment frauds) and R-v-S, Company Director charged with substantial tax evasion.

Professional Memberships: Hon. Soc Middle Temple; Criminal Bar Association; South Eastern Circuit.

Publications: Disclosure and the CPIA 1996.

Personal: DOB:1969; Educ: Bedford School; Higher Educ: Bsc (Hons) LLB (Hons) (London); Hon. Soc. Middle Temple.

COGHLIN, Thomas
Cloisters, London
020 7827 4072
tac@cloisters.com

Featured in Employment (London)

Practice Areas: Tom Coghlin has a wealth of experience of first instance and appellate litigation. He specialises in employment and discrimination law and related fields including claims for injunctions to enforce restrictive covenants, trade union law, regulatory and disciplinary work and general common law.

Professional Memberships: Employment Judge (fee paid). Institute of Employment Rights, Discrimination Law Association, ELBA, Industrial Law Society.

Career: Called 1998.

Personal: Educated at Worth Abbey and Worcester College, Oxford (MA, BCL). Married with 4 daughters.

COHEN, Samantha
9 Bedford Row, London
020 7489 2727
samantha.cohen@9bedfordrow.co.uk
Featured in Crime (London)

Practice Areas: Samantha is a shrewd tactician and a persuasive advocate. She has enjoyed a busy and substantial London practice for two decades. She is widely respected for her ability to question the most vulnerable witnesses: children, those with psychiatric disorders, those fearful of the criminal justice system. She is extremely good with lay clients in conference, putting the most nervous at ease and calming the more 'pugnacious'. She is a specialist organised crime and RASSO prosecutor and is a panel advocate for the Department of Business, Innovation and Skills. She is instructed to lead for the defence regularly in fraud cases where her diligent pre-trial preparation and meticulous cross-examination of expert accountants has impressed. As has her approach to pre-trial disclosure where her tenacity and perseverance have paid dividends for her clients. She provides timely, thorough and acute advice pre-trial (sometimes pre-charge for the Crown) on a range of issues, e.g. directing the professional client to an appropriate expert in a particular field such as blood pattern analysis, accountancy evidence or the significance of injuries. She has a particular interest in shaken baby cases and the complex, nuanced and frequently changing medical evidence relating the diagnosis of Shaken Baby Syndrome from the classic 'triad' of injuries. A capable and approachable counsel who consistently impresses. She has increased her direct access practice over the last year, providing pre-charge advice to suspects in a number of cases.

COLE, Robert
Broadway House, Leeds
0113 2462600
clerks@broadwayhouse.co.uk
Featured in Family/Matrimonial (North Eastern)

Practice Areas: Robert Cole has become a well known and highly regarded specialist in financial remedy. His experience in accountancy and understanding of how companies operate means that he is the first port of call in cases involving complex corporate structures and company valuations. His attention to detail also means that he has developed a reputation for unearthing hidden transactions and undisclosed assets. He is comfortable dealing with high asset, high income and and high profile cases at all judicial levels, yet has an easy and thoughtful manner with clients from all walks of life. Robert is respected for his knowledge and application of the law and sound judgment, meaning that he gives practical advice on the resolution of cases yet is known for being forthright when necessary. His practice extends across the whole of the North of the country in the Northern, Midlands and North Eastern circuits; being considered the counsel of choice by many of the top-ranking firms in the major legal centres. Robert is also a trained arbitrator, having adjudicated on a number of contested hearings recently.

COLEMAN, Richard QC
Fountain Court Chambers, London
020 7583 3335
rjc@fountaincourt.co.uk
Featured in Banking & Finance (London), Financial Services (London), Professional Discipline (London)

Practice Areas: Commercial dispute resolution (litigation and arbitration), banking and finance, financial services (including regulatory and disciplinary), professional negligence, civil fraud, professional discipline and employment. Noteworthy cases include acting for the Financial Conduct Authority in the PPI litigation, for the Office of Fair Trading in the test case on bank charges, for an international bank in the investigation into the manipulation of LIBOR and for the Guernsey Cells in the Arch-Cru litigation.
Professional Memberships: Commercial Bar Association.
Career: Called to the Bar 1994. MA Cantab (double first class honours). LLM (Yale). Member of New York Bar.
Publications: Contributor to Law of Bank Payments (Brindle and Cox, 4th ed.)

COLLIER, Beatrice
5 Essex Court, London
020 7410 2000
collier@5essexcourt.co.uk
Featured in Police Law (All Circuits)

Practice Areas: Specialist in police law, public law and inquests. Notable recent police law work includes the Mouncher & Ors v Chief Constable of South Wales Police (claims brought by 15 officers prosecuted for investigation into murder of Lynette White in 1988). In the public law field her clients are local authorities and police forces. She has a particular interest in judicial review claims and inquests involving mental health issues and has expertise in policing and mental health.
Professional Memberships: Middle Temple, Member of Administrative Law Bar Association, Employment Law Bar Association
Career: Degree in History and English 1998 (University of Cambridge), Degree in Law 2003 (University of Oxford), Called to the Bar 2004, Tenant at 5 Essex Court 2006.
Personal: Married with 2 daughters. Interests include Arsenal FC, contemporary art, running.

COLLINGS, Matthew QC
Maitland Chambers, London
020 7406 1200
mcollings@maitlandchambers.co.uk
Featured in Chancery (London), Commercial Dispute Resolution (London), Company (London), Fraud (London), Offshore (London), Restructuring/Insolvency (London)

Practice Areas: Over 150 reported cases establish the breadth of Matthew's expertise in his specialist areas covering Company, Insolvency and Commercial Chancery (litigation and advisory work). Matthew is an experienced trial and appellate advocate (here and abroad), and also regularly appears in tribunals, as well as arbitrations, expert determinations and mediations. Recent trials include a 20 day fraudulent misrepresentation claim, a substantial dispute as to the construction and effect of a legal charge, an insolvency case (now a principal authority on the reach of the Cross Border Insolvency Regulations), and a significant trial in the Mercantile Court. Recent appeals in the Supreme Court include Patel v Mirza on illegality, and FHR – now the leading case on constructive trusts; and in the Court of Appeal W H Smith v 20th Century Fox on accounting. Matthew has recently been advising on the administration of the Caterham Formula One team, the affairs of Glasgow Rangers, the Apex v Fi Call shareholder dispute, an Olympic show jumping horse, and a €100m fraud. An extensive offshore practice embraces Hong Kong, Singapore, the Channel Islands, Jamaica, the Bahamas, and Iceland. Matthew has been called to the Bar in the Cayman Islands; and in the BVI, where he has appeared in a number of substantial applications, trials and appeals.
Professional Memberships: Chancery Bar Association, COMBAR, Insolvency Lawyers Association, INSOL International and Commerical Fraud Lawyers Association. Former Member, Insolvency Rules Advisory Committee.

COLLINGS, Nicholas
Atkin Chambers, London
020 7404 0102
nscollings@atkinchambers.com
Featured in Professional Negligence (London), Construction (London)

Practice Areas: Nicholas specialises in commercial litigation and arbitration with particular emphasis on professional indemnity, construction and engineering, energy and utilities, technology and related disputes. He has a wide range of clients from all over the world including corporations, government entities, professional advisors and individuals. He has broad experience of all methods of dispute resolution with particular expertise in domestic and international arbitration, mediation and adjudication. Nicholas has a working knowledge of French and Spanish.
Professional Memberships: TECBAR, COMBAR, SCL, CIArb.
Career: LLB (Hons) Bristol. Called 1997.

COLLINGWOOD, Timothy
Serle Court, London
020 7242 6105
tcollingwood@serlecourt.co.uk
Featured in Chancery (London), Company (London)

Practice Areas: Practises across the broad range of the commercial-chancery spectrum, but with particular emphasis on litigation concerning issues in respect of commercial agreements and company, insolvency and international trusts matters. Tim has extensive experience of claims concerning breaches of duty, in particular in respect of directors or trustees, and of shareholder disputes. Prior to commencing practice in England, Tim was called to the bar in the Cayman Islands and practised as an attorney-at-law.
Professional Memberships: Chancery Bar Association, COMBAR.
Career: Called 1996. Called to the Bar of the Cayman Islands and practised as attorney-at-law in 1997.
Publications: 'Minority Shareholders: Law, Practice & Procedure' (fifth edition, OUP).
Personal: Born 1972. Educated at Royal Grammar School, Guildford; Magdalen College, Oxford (BA, BCL). Married with three children. Interests include cycling, swimming and white water sports.

COLLINS, Ben QC
Old Square Chambers, London
020 7269 0300
Collins@oldsquare.co.uk
Featured in Employment (London)

Practice Areas: Employment and equality, regulatory, clinical negligence, PI, public law and human rights. Particular expertise in the health sector, with huge experience of representing healthcare professionals and employers in employment, regulatory, disciplinary and civil proceedings. Appears regularly in High Court and tribunals in public sector and large commercial employment disputes. Leading expert in criminal injuries compensation. Extensive experience in military claims. Substantial practice in clinical negligence, personal injury, inquests and associated public law and human rights challenges. Notable cases (17 reported in last 3 years) include: Wasteney v ELFT [2016] ICR 643 (religious discrimination); Child Soldiers v MOD [2016] 1 WLR 1062 (age discrimination in Army); CP v FTT [2015] QB 459 (criminalisation of drinking in pregnancy); S v CICA [2014] 1 WLR 131 (nervous shock); Jones v FTT [2013] AC 48 (Supreme Court consideration of CICA); Al-Jedda v SSHD (terrorism case as Special Advocate).
Professional Memberships: ELA, ELBA, ARDL, PNBA, PIBA, Justice.
Career: Called (MT) 1996, QC 2016. Special Advocate. Attorney-General's A Panel (before taking silk).
Publications: Contributing Editor to 'Professional Negligence and Liability' (Informa). Consultant Editor to forthcoming OUP work on compensation.
Personal: Educated at King Henry VIII School, Coventry and Queens' College Cambridge.

COLLINS, Ken
29 Bedford Row Chambers, London
020 7404 1044
kcollins@29br.co.uk
Featured in Family/Matrimonial (London)

Practice Areas: Barrister specialising in family law (matrimonial finance and children) and cohabitation disputes.
Professional Memberships: FLBA.
Career: Former Eurobond Trader. Called 1996, Inner Temple. Trained as Collaborative Counsel.
Personal: University of Sussex (LLB Hons, LLM International Commercial Law).

COLLINS, Louisa
5 St Andrew's Hill, London
020 7332 5400
louisacollins@5sah.co.uk
Featured in Extradition (London)

Practice Areas: Louisa is an experienced and established specialist extradition barrister, acting both on behalf of requesting foreign governments and requested persons. She has been practicing in this area of the law since 2008 and has a breadth of experience in numerous complex cases and has a record of success in matters concerning vulnerable individuals. She works tirelessly to obtain the best possible outcomes for her clients and is noted for her approachability and hard work ethic. Louisa's practice involves advising and providing representation throughout all stages of the extradition process. She has a busy appellate workload and has made applications to the ECHR and dealt with ancillary proceedings, including

judicial review. Louisa also regularly advises individuals and judicial authorities regarding the preparation of extradition requests made to this jurisdiction from other countries. Recent work has included Louisa appearing on behalf of the US Government in the majority of cases raising civil commitment and Article 5. These cases have been topical and political, relating to a separate civil detention regime for offences including rape, paedophilia, sexual abuse and child pornography (notably, US Government v Bowen [2015] EWHC 1873, US Government v Giese [2015] EWHC 3658). She has raised and dealt with complex technical arguments concerning the interpretation of some of the more recently implemented provisions under the 2003 Act (see Kemp v Spain [2016] EWHC 69 (Admin)). She appeared on behalf of the appellant in the leading case on Romanian prison conditions (Blaj & others v Romania [2015] EWHC 1710 (Admin)), following which she has dealt with numerous cases concerning prisons and Article 3 compliance. She was instructed on behalf of the appellant in the leading case on the jurisdiction of the High Court to deal with appeals against costs orders (Bizunowicz & another v Poland & Czech Republic, [2014] EWHC 3238 (Admin)).
Professional Memberships: Extradition Lawyers Association and Defence Extradition Lawyers Forum

COLMAN, Andrew
2 Hare Court, London
020 7353 5324
andrewcolman@2harecourt.com
Featured in Professional Discipline (London)
Practice Areas: Andrew Colman is a leading junior of great intellect and experience, held in high esteem for his fairness and integrity and for his particular ability to cut through complex issues of fact or law in order to get to the heart of the matter. He formerly prosecuted some of the GMC's most serious and substantial cases, but now deploys his expertise in the defence of doctors, dentists and other healthcare professionals. He is regularly instructed in lengthy and complex Fitness to Practise cases. He also acts for and advises regulators (for example, the GOC and the teaching regulator, the NCTL) and registrants in other professions, such as solicitors. He was recently instructed as lead counsel for the NCTL in the cases arising out of the 'Trojan Horse' enquiry into Birmingham Schools. Andrew appears regularly in the High Court, on statutory appeals and judicial reviews and ancillary matters. He is well equipped for such work by his previous experience of appellate advocacy, up to the highest levels (Privy Council/ House of Lords) and his past history of practice in extradition.
Professional Memberships: ARDL, HSLA and CBA, he is also a former director of the Bar Mutual Identity Fund.
Career: Year of Call: 1980
Personal: Fluent in Spanish, both oral and written.

COLTART, Christopher QC
2 Hare Court, London
07866 628136
christophercoltart@2harecourt.com
Featured in Financial Crime (London)
Practice Areas: Christopher Coltart QC took silk in 2014 following a highly successful junior career (Band 1 in Chambers & Partners and nominated for Criminal Junior of the Year 2012). Christopher began his career as a City solicitor, specialising in commercial property litigation. His caseload comprised of high value claims brought and defended by a variety of financial institutions including banks, pension funds and mortgage providers. Since coming to the Bar in 1998, Christopher has specialised in fraud and white collar crime. He is now Head of the 2 Hare Court Business Crime & Financial Services Team and defends in the most significant cases. Christopher also has an extensive regulatory practice. He has frequently appeared before the disciplinary tribunals of the General Medical Council, and has been involved in significant cases brought by a number of other regulators. In addition to these core areas of his practice, Christopher also has significant experience of major inquest work. Recent cases include acting for a trader in the LIBOR scandal, advising in the Barclays Bank/Qatari case and representing the former FD of a publicly listed company who faced allegations of dishonesty in relation to the year end accounts. His regulatory practice has included: the Security Industry Authority, the Solicitors Regulation Authority, the Medicines and Healthcare Products Regulatory Authority and the Financial Reporting Council. He represented a number of the bereaved families in the 7/7 inquest and was instructed on behalf of a significant witness in the inquest into the Hillsborough disaster. He was also instructed in the high profile Gbangbola inquest, which has recently concluded following a 6 week hearing.
Professional Memberships: ARDL, FLA, CBA,

COLTER, Lucy
4 New Square, London
020 7822 2000
l.colter@4newsquare.com
Featured in Professional Negligence (London)
Practice Areas: Professional liability, construction claims and commercial litigation. Lucy acts for and against professionals (including lawyers, surveyors and valuers), often where there is a strong commercial, investment or business element to the claim. She has recently acted for claimants in high-value litigation arising out of the failure of a property investment and in a claim against offshore investment fund managers. Lucy's professional liability work is also frequently in the construction and engineering context. She acts for and against construction professionals in claims against architects, contract administrators and quantity surveyors. She also has considerable experience acting for leading multinational construction service companies in a wide range of disputes. She has experience of the adjudication process and of arbitration. Lucy has strong experience of very complex and high value disputes and excellent trial experience both as sole counsel and as part of a counsel team.
Professional Memberships: COMBAR; TECBAR; PNBA. Lucy is the present chair of the Young COMBAR committee and sits on the COMBAR Executive and Equality & Diversity committees.
Career: MA Oxon, English Language and Literature; Called 2008 (Lincoln's Inn; Lord Brougham, Lord Mansfield and Lord Sheldon scholar).
Publications: Co-Editor: "Jackson and Powell on Professional Liability."

COLVILLE, Iain
Arden Chambers, London
020 7242 4244
iain.colville@ardenchambers.com
Featured in Social Housing (London)
Practice Areas: All aspects of housing (public/social/private); landlord and tenant; planning and compulsory purchase and local government law.
Professional Memberships: HLPA, SHLA, PEBA.
Career: Called 1989. Join Chambers in 1997, having previously worked in local government legal service. Significant recent cases include: Lafferty v Newark and Sherwood DC [2016] EWHC 320 (QB); [2016] H.L.R. 13 (defective premises; disrepair); Gorman v Newark and Sherwood Homes [2015] EWCA Civ 764 (introductory tenancy; election); R. (East Midlands Property Owners Ltd) v Nottingham City Council [2015] EWHC 747 (Admin) (selective licensing); R. (Turley) v Wandsworth LBC [2014] EWHC 4040 (Admin) (landlord and tenant; discrimination, human rights); Temur v Hackney LBC [2014] EWCA Civ 877 (homelessness); R. (Bishop's Stortford Civic Federation) v East Hertfordshire DC [2014] EWHC 348 (Admin) (planning); Taylor v Spencer [2013] EWCA Civ 1600 (landlord and tenant); Norbrook Laboratories Ltd v Carlisle City Council [2013] EWHC 1113 (Admin) (real property; planning); Mansfield DC v Langridge [2013] EWHC Admin (landlord and tenant; disability); Aliya Sharif v London Borough of Camden [2013] UKSC 10 (led by Andrew Arden QC in the Supreme Court; appeared in the Court of Appeal as sole counsel for the local authority) (homelessness).
Publications: Blackstone's Civil Procedure (Oxford University Press) – sole contributor on the Homelessness Chapter between 2006 – 2010. A Guide to the Greater London Authority (Sweet&Maxwell, 2000) – co-author. Joint annotator of the Greater London Authority Act 1999 (Current Law annotations, 2000). A Guide to the Planning Process, Arden's Housing Library, (Lemos & Crane, 2000) – sole author. Human Rights Act 1998 A Practitioners Guide (Sweet & Maxwell, 1998) – contributor to Planning Chpt.

CONE, John
Erskine Chambers, London
020 7242 5532
jcone@erskinechambers.com
Featured in Company (London)
Practice Areas: John is a company law specialist. He has particular expertise in corporate reorganisations and reconstructions (including reorganisations of capital and schemes of arrangement – for both solvent and insolvent companies); takeovers, mergers and acquisitions; and Part VII banking and insurance business transfers. Notable matters include: Novae Group Plc (scheme of arrangement); Lloyds Banking Group and Citibank International/The Post Office (Part VII business transfers); and Netviewer AG (cross-border merger).
Professional Memberships: Chancery Bar Association. COMBAR, Member of the Law Reform Committee of the Bar Council, Bencher of the Middle Temple.

CONLON, Michael QC
Temple Tax Chambers, London
020 7353 7884
clerks@templetax.com
Featured in Tax (London)
Practice Areas: Revenue law, in particular all aspects of indirect taxation including advice and litigation before all Courts and Tribunals, and European Union law.
Professional Memberships: Chancery Bar Association; Revenue Bar Association; Bar European Group; CTA (Fellow); FIIT; National President of the VAT Practitioners Group.
Career: Called 1974; QC 2002; practice has included the government legal service, international law and accounting firms (partner) and the Revenue Bar; Solicitor (1992-7).
Publications: Member of Editorial Board of the Tax Journal and of De Voil's Indirect Tax Intelligence Service; numerous articles.
Personal: Recreations include music, the arts, writing; assisting arts and music charities.

CONNOLLY, Dominic
5 St Andrew's Hill, London
020 7332 5400
dominicconnolly@5sah.co.uk
Featured in Crime (London)
Practice Areas: Specialist criminal practitioner with experience in murder/manslaughter, organised crime, heavy fraud, serious sex offences and proceeds of crime.
Career: Prosecuted, as leading junior and alone, serious and high profile cases including murder, drug trafficking and serious sexual offences, particularly those involving historical allegations. As former Standing Counsel to RCPO, instructed in the most serious offences for Revenue and Customs and the Serious and Organised Crime Agency. Experience in fraud includes missing trader fraud, advance fee fraud, tax evasion, multi-million pound benefit fraud and a recent case involving "rouge traders and a Vet" prosecuted for selling horses not fit for purpose . Considerable experience in the restraint, confiscation and forfeiture of the proceeds of crime. Recent cases include Austin (murder of drug addict by street dealer), Gill (Prosecution, as leading junior, of multiple importations of cocaine, cannabis and cigarettes using a bonded warehouse used to facilitate multiple importations of contraband) Milner (armed robbery of country house of high-profile entrepreneur by three armed men), Driscoll (prosecution of film director in a substantial vat fraud involving the creation of bogus invoices during the making of a horror film), Court (one of the largest fraud investigations ever carried out by the Kent Police), Rahmonov (prosecution of an internet banking fraud following an investigation by the Metropolitan Police's e-Crime Unit, local boroughs and the Specialist Crime Directorate, the first operation of its kind, working in collaboration with the financial services industry).

CONSTABLE, Adam QC
Keating Chambers, London
020 7544 2600
aconstable@keatingchambers.com
Featured in International Arbitration (London), Professional Negligence (London), Construction (London), Energy & Natural Resources (London)
Practice Areas: Specialist in construction, engineering, energy, shipbuilding and technology disputes along with professional

negligence and insurance claims related to these sectors. Extensive advocacy experience in the UK Courts, having appeared in the Technology and Construction Court (TCC), Commercial Court and Court of Appeal. Adam is regularly instructed in arbitration proceedings, both domestic and international, and has experience of proceeding under a variety of rules. He has considerable expertise in adjudication work, and all forms of ADR having represented clients in mediations, early neutral evaluations and expert determinations. Adam is also regularly appointed as adjudicator, arbitrator and independent expert. Adam has a reputation for devastating advocacy and mastering complex factual details.

Career: Called to the Bar 1995; appointed Treasury Counsel 2002-07; MCIArb 2008; Inner Temple Advocacy Training Committee 2009; Construction Junior of the Year 2007 and 2010; Recorder of the Crown Court 2010; Queens Counsel 2011; Inner Temple Bencher 2013.

Publications: Editor of Keating on Offshore Construction and Marine Engineering (published Sept 2015); Keating on JCT Contracts [Looseleaf & CD-Rom] Co-editor; Keating on Building Contracts (9th & 10th Edition) Contributor; Keating on NEC – Contributor; Construction Law Reports – Co-editor; "Construction Claims" and "Building Defects" (RICS Case in Point Series).

CONVEY, Christopher
The Chambers of Andrew Mitchell QC, London
020 7440 9950
cmc@33cllaw.com
Featured in POCA Work & Asset Forfeiture (All Circuits), Financial Crime (London)

Practice Areas: Business crime, corporate wrongdoing, fraud, asset forfeiture, confiscation and money laundering

Career: A highly regarded fraud junior with particular experience in business crime, corporate wrongdoing, offshore trusts, complex fraud, civil recovery and money laundering. Additionally a recognised specialist in cases involving POCA and related matters. Instructed as defence first junior counsel in the first LIBOR prosecution SFO v Tom Hayes (UBS). This follows on from appearing as defence first junior counsel in SFO v Asil Nadir (Polly Peck). Internationally, has acted for the Attorneys General of Jersey and the Turks & Caicos Islands. Instructed in several leading POCA cases including Stanford International Bank and Windsor & Hare. Regularly instructed to advise offshore trusts in relation to money laundering and related compliance issues. Frequently represents the interests of third parties in complex restraint, confiscation and receivership proceedings in the Supreme Court, Court of Appeal and High Court. Further recent high-profile cases include the defence of Kent Pharmaceuticals (Goldshield) against a restrictive practices claim, a multi-million pound travel industry fraud, an alleged multi-million pound construction industry fraud and money laundering operation and the successful defence of an alleged money-laundering solicitor.

Publications: Contributing editor to Mitchell, Taylor & Talbot on Confiscation and the Proceeds of Crime

COOK, Alexander
4 Stone Buildings, London
020 7242 5524
clerks@4stonebuildings.com
Featured in Company (London)

Practice Areas: Alexander has litigation-focussed commercial Chancery practice, with a significant emphasis on high profile and high value disputes in the Chancery Division and the Commercial Court (both as junior to QCs and, increasingly, as sole counsel). Two of Alexander's cases in recent years featured in The Lawyer's "Top 20 Cases of 2015", and he was one of only a handful of barristers to be involved in more than one case on this list. Alexander's practice encompasses commercial litigation and arbitration, company law, insolvency and reconstruction, civil fraud, offshore litigation and actions under the Proceeds of Crime Act 2002 ("POCA"). He has particular experience of cases involving an international or offshore element, and is a member of the Bar of the Eastern Caribbean Supreme Court (British Virgin Islands) and the New York State Bar.

Professional Memberships: Bar of the Eastern Caribbean Supreme Court (British Virgin Islands), New York State Bar, COMBAR, Chancery Bar Association

COOK, Ian
1 King's Bench Walk, London
020 7936 1500
icook@1kbw.co.uk
Featured in Family/Matrimonial (London)

Practice Areas: Ian Cook is a specialist finance practitioner with very wide-ranging experience of all aspects of the law and procedure relating to divorce, dissolution of civil partnerships and proceedings under Schedule 1 of the Children Act. Clients are typically legal, financial, medical and business professionals, their spouses/civil partners and the independently wealthy. Ian Cook is routinely instructed in cases involving family trusts and complex wealth holding structures situated in the UK and offshore (Liechtenstein, Switzerland, Jersey; Guernsey, IOM, BVI, SVG, Panama). Ian Cook has appeared in the list of leading juniors at the matrimonial finance bar in this publication for over 16 years. Previous years' editorial comments have included the following: "Perfect for the client who doesn't want to pay for a top silk but needs a junior of weight"; "seen as an imposing presence in court" affording clients the sense that "he will fight your corner, come what may"; "He instils confidence in clients by focusing on achieving the best outcome for them and never forgetting their anxieties"; "a purveyor of firm imaginative advice"; "technically very good and very good with clients as well – all round a class act".

Professional Memberships: FLBA. Member of the Chartered Institute of Arbitrators

Career: BA (Hons) 1st Class Philosophy, King's College London. CPE City of London Polytechnic.

COOK, Katherine
1 Hare Court, London
020 77977070
Featured in Family/Matrimonial (London)

Practice Areas: Katherine's practice encompasses all areas of private family law with a particular emphasis on financial remedy proceedings, cohabitation claims, relationship agreements and jurisdictional disputes. She is also a Resolution trained mediator.

Professional Memberships: Family Law Bar Association

Career: Katherine read Jurisprudence at Christ Church, University of Oxford (where she was an Exhibitioner) and subsequently received an LLM from Emmanuel College, University of Cambridge. Katherine was called to the bar in 2007. She was awarded the Levitt Scholarship (Pupillage scholarship) and Lord Denning Scholarship (Major BVC scholarship) by Lincoln's Inn and in 2012 Katherine undertook a Pegasus Scholarship in Washington DC.

Publications: Katherine is a contributor to Rayden and Jackson on Relationship Breakdown, Finances and Children

COOK, Mary
Cornerstone Barristers, London
020 7242 4986
maryc@cornerstonebarristers.com
Featured in Planning (London)

Practice Areas: A leading specialist in Town and Country Planning, Compulsory Purchase, Local Government and Environmental Law. Mary Cook regularly promotes large and complex planning cases of high commercial value for developers and landowners. Her advice and representation is regularly sought for strategic pre-application advice right through local and neighbourhood plan examinations, hearings and appeals. She has particular experience in housing, retail and major mixed use schemes including new settlements, urban extensions at the plan-making stage and beyond. She has considerable experience of promoting niche developments for private sector clients in particularly sensitive environments involving heritage assets, Areas of Outstanding Natural Beauty and the Green Belt. In addition Mary works covers minerals related matters and CLEUD/enforcement work. Many of these projects involve SA/EIA/HRA issues. Mary's recent work has involved a variety of High Court appearances. She has retained a strong portfolio of public sector clients for whom she has promoted compulsory purchase orders to secure regeneration of housing estates, shopping centres, road schemes, new schools, hospitals and industrial estates. Thus advising promoting and objecting to CPOs is another area in which she has considerable expertise. She is currently advising on a number compensation matters.

Professional Memberships: Planning & Environmental Bar Association, Compulsory Purchase Association. Administrative Law Bar Association.

Career: Called 1982 Inner Temple. Committee Member of Joint Oxford Planning Conference.

Personal: LLB Cardiff 1978-1981. Married with 3 children, Living in London.

COOKE, Charlotte
South Square, London
020 7696 9900
charlottecooke@southsquare.com
Featured in Restructuring/Insolvency (London)

Practice Areas: Charlotte specialises in domestic and cross-border insolvency and restructuring, banking and financial services, commercial litigation and company law.

Professional Memberships: COMBAR, Chancery Bar Association, Insolvency Lawyers Association, R3

Career: Charlotte has appeared in high profile cases at all levels: as a junior in the Supreme Court (Re Digital Satellite Warranty Cover, SerVaas Inc v Rafidain Bank; Re Lehman Brothers International Europe) and both as a junior and as sole counsel in the Court of Appeal (for example, Ilott v Williams; Gardner v Lemma Insurance Company) and at first instance. Recent cases include Re Codere Finance (UK), Re Privatbank and Re DTEK (schemes of arrangement) and Black Diamond Offshore v Fomento de Construcciones y Contratas and Citicorp International v Castex Technologies (construction of loan notes/bonds). Called to the Bar 2008.

Publications: Contributor to Ranking and Priority of Creditors (OUP, forthcoming); Company Directors: Duties, Liabilities and Remedies (OUP, forthcoming); Treatment of Contracts in Insolvency (OUP, 2013); Totty and Moss on Insolvency (Sweet and Maxwell, 2012); Rowlatt on Principal and Surety (OUP, 2011); Corporate Rescue and Insolvency; Insolvency Intelligence; Journal of International Banking and Financial Law; International Corporate Rescue (editorial board member).

COOPER, Ben
Old Square Chambers, London
23 7269 0300
cooper@oldsquare.co.uk
Featured in Employment (London)

Practice Areas: Employment and discrimination, labour law and professional discipline, in particular industrial action injunctions, doctors' disciplinaries, high court contractual claims, equal pay, complex discrimination, TUPE. Recent cases of note: Hartley & ors v King Edward VI College [2015] IRLR 650, CA (pay deductions for strike days); BALPA v Jet2.com [2015] IRLR 543, QB (scope of statutory collective bargaining); Edie & ors v HCL Insurance BPO Services [2015] ICR 713, EAT (indirect age discrimination, TUPE); Al Mishlab v Milton Keynes Hospital NHS Trust [2015] Med LR 120, QB (test for review of employer's discretion to exclude consultant doctor); Chakrabarty v Ipswich Hospital NHS Trust & another [2014] Med LR 379, QB (scope of NHS trust's discretion to proceed to capability dismissal hearing); Airedale NHS Foundation Trust v McMillan [2014] ICR 747, CA (contractual powers of employer under internal disciplinary appeal)

Professional Memberships: Employment Law Bar Association; Industrial Law Society; Employment Lawyers' Association

Career: Called to the Bar – November 2000.

Personal: Born 1977. LLB (University of Birmingham, 1st class).

COOPER, Douglas
Deans Court Chambers, Manchester
0161 214 6000
clerks@deanscourt.co.uk
Featured in Personal Injury (Northern), Personal Injury (All Circuits)

Practice Areas: Personal Injury, in particular Occupational Disease and Clinical Negligence, almost exclusively for Defendants, insurers, large corporate clients, public authorities or funds.

Professional Memberships: PIBA

Career: Called to the Bar in 2004, prior to this he worked for many years in the insurance industry, for Royal Insurance (now RSA), for NEM/AGF (now Allianz) and for the Iron Trades (now Chester Street Insurance Holdings and QBE) where he became the Regional Claims Manager. Most of this

time was spent dealing with Employers' and Public Liability cases, in latter years predominantly disease claims
Publications: Journal of Personal Injury Law 2003, Occupational Health at Work 2016 (two Chapters co-written on Hand Arm Vibration Syndrome, not yet published but accepted for publication)

COOPER, Gilead QC
Wilberforce Chambers, London
020 7306 0102
gcooper@wilberforce.co.uk
Featured in Chancery (London), Art and Cultural Property Law (London), Offshore (London), Trusts (London)
Practice Areas: Chancery and commercial litigation, particularly contentious trusts and probate; removal of trustees; breaches of fiduciary duty and civil fraud; charities; real property; professional negligence; pensions; Court of Protection; partnerships; art and cultural property. A substantial proportion of his practice is in off-shore jurisdictions, particularly Hong Kong, the BVI, Bermuda and Cayman.
Professional Memberships: ACTAPS, APL, PNBA, CEDR Accredited Mediator.
Career: Christ Church, Oxford (1973-76); City University (1981); Freshfields (1985-89).
Publications: Palmer on Bailment (2009) 3rd edition, (Contributing Editor: Chapter on Limitation); Tolley's Pensions Law (Chapter on Winding-Up Pension Schemes).

COOPER, John QC
Crown Office Chambers, London
0020 77978100/ 07966023450
cooper@crownofficechambers.com
Featured in Health & Safety (London)
Practice Areas: Has been involved in most of the leading cases in the Regulatory field for many years including several pioneering Court of Appeal cases: Friskies Petcare, HTM, Willmott Dixon, Tangerine & Veolia, New Look, Upperbay, TDG and R v N & C some of which served to re define the parameters of the law. He was instructed and deposed as an expert witness in 2012 on Health and Safety law for DuPont in a commercial case in New York involving over $700M. In the last two year he has appeared in the Court of Appeal in three further cases (EA v Red Industries HSE v Polyflor and HSE v London Waste) and in the Administrative Court (MWH v Wise) He is equally known for his forensic skills as a trial lawyer. His breadth of practice includes health and Safety, Fire Safety, Environmental law prosecutions and Trading Standards cases where he represents directors of companies and companies. In addition he advises and is consulted upon potential issues in non contentious work. He was instructed in the second corporate manslaughter trial in June 2012 (Lion Steel) successfully defending the Managing Director charged with gross negligence manslaughter. The Director was acquitted of all charges. He successfully defended Red Industries in a 5 week environmental law fish kill trial in 2014, all charges received not guilty verdicts. He is currently instructed in the Vauxhall helicopter crash, an electric gates Gross Negligence Manslaughter case in Manchester and the first prosecution of an NHS Trust for corporate manslaughter. Regular first choice counsel in fatality cases and serious safety cases where contested issues arise. He defended in the longest running Health and Safety case (a 4 month asbestos trial at Winchester for Willmott Dixon 2011.) He was Chambers and Partners Health and Safety Junior of the Year 2010 and appointed Queens Counsel in 2014.

COOPER, Nigel QC
Quadrant Chambers, London
020 7583 4444
nigel.cooper@quadrantchambers.com
Featured in Shipping (London)
Practice Areas: Areas of practice: shipping and commodities; energy; collision and Admiralty; offshore-construction; shipbuilding (including superyacht construction); commercial litigation and arbitration, insurance and reinsurance, shipbroking and related aspects of EU and conflicts of law. Nigel's government work also means that he has experience of administrative law and judicial review. Much of Nigel's work in the shipping and offshore sectors is subject to arbitration. Reported cases include: M.H. Progress Lines S.A. v. Orient Shipping Rotterdam B.V. (The "GENIUS STAR I") [2012] 1 Lloyd's Rep. 222; Lloyds TSB Equipment Leasing (No. 1) Ltd v Revenue & Customs Commissioners [2012] UKFTT 47 (TC); Seadrill v. OAO Gazprom [2010] 1 Lloyd's Rep 543 and [2010] EWCA Civ 691; The WESTERN NEPTUNE [2010] 1 Lloyd's Rep. 158 and [2010] 1 Lloyd's Rep. 172, Ferryways v. ABP [2008] 1 Lloyd's Rep. 639, The DORIC PRIDE [2006] 2 Lloyd's Rep. 175, Wise (Underwriting) Agency Ltd v Grupo National Provincial [2004] 2 Lloyd's Rep. 483; Seascope Capital Services Ltd v Anglo-Atlantic [2002] 2 Lloyd's Rep 611. In addition, Nigel was heavily involved in the Fiona Trust Litigation. Nigel was instructed for three of the most recent shipping Formal Investigations – the 'DERBYSHIRE' (2000), the 'MARCHIONESS/BOWBELLE' (2001) and the FV GAUL (2004).
Professional Memberships: COMBAR; LMAA (Supporting Member); Bar European Group and European Circuit. TECBAR, LCIA, ICCA and ICC, KLRCA, IBA
Career: Queen's Counsel (2010), trained mediator, accepts appointments as an arbitrator, member of Treasury Panel of Counsel (A Panel) until taking silk and thereafter member of the Treasury's panel of silks.
Publications: Contributor to 'The Law of Yachts and Yachting' (2012).
Personal: University of Leeds (LLB), University of London (LLM), University of Amsterdam (Dip. EI). Languages: French, German and Dutch.

COOPER, Peter
St Ives Chambers, Birmingham
0121 236 0863
peter.cooper@stiveschambers.co.uk
Featured in Crime (Midlands)
Practice Areas: Crime
Professional Memberships: Criminal Bar Association
Career: Peter defends and prosecutes in the gravest of cases, including murder, rape, child abuse, drugs conspiracies and fraud. He has acted alone or as leading junior in several murder cases, and in many others led by Queen's Counsel. He has appeared many times in the Court of Appeal, and has also dealt with appeals to the Administrative Court in criminal cases. He is widely known for the efforts he makes to put his clients and complainants at ease in stressful and sensitive cases. He has particular expertise in head injuries and so called "baby-shaking" cases, in telephone cell-site evidence, and in the historic law of sexual offences allegedly committed between 1956 and 2004. Cases 2014/2016: R v Tomlinson: representing defendant charged with causing grievous bodily harm with intent, after his three month old son was admitted to hospital with life threatening brain injuries. Cross-examining eminent neurosurgeons, neuroradiologists, opthalmologists, and paediatricians. Defendant acquitted after trial. R v Barber: Defending complex historic rape case. Complainant and two other witnesses profoundly deaf. The events were over 40 years old. Obscure but important archaic legal points were used to good effect. Ruling of no case to answer on some counts; defendant ultimately acquitted of all counts. R v Malolepszy: Successfully prosecuting a man for being concerned in supplying Class A drugs, causing death. These were the notorious 'Superman' PMMA tablets which caused several deaths nationwide. R v Dlugosz, R v Pickering & others: Peter successfully appeared in the Court of Appeal for the prosecution in this consolidated appeal (mixed profile DNA evidence in a case of sexual assault of a child). R v Luczak & Krezolek: Peter was junior counsel for the mother in the infamous child murder of 4 year old Daniel Pelka. R v Card: He successfully defended one of nine defendants charged with conspiracy to import and supply 60 kilos of cocaine. Other recent cases: Peter led another counsel in the successful prosecution of a 16 year old defendant for the murder by stabbing of a fifteen year old boy. He was also junior counsel for one of two young defendants in a twice-tried murder case where extremely complex neuropathological evidence was in issue. Both defendants were ultimately acquitted of murder at the second trial.

COPELAND, Miles
Three New Square, London
852 2828 9289
copeland@3newsquare.co.uk
Featured in Intellectual Property (London)
Practice Areas: Intellectual Property, Information Technology and commercial disputes involving the same; patents, trademarks, passing off, copyright, designs, confidential information, malicious falsehood. Advice, drafting and advocacy covering all these areas both in the UK and the EPO. Cases include: Actavis v Warner-Lambert [2015-2016] (pregablin for pain, second medical use patents, infringement & plausibility); Generics v ViiV [2016](HIV combination therapy); Fujifilm v AbbVie [2016] (Arrow declarations); Chromatography column [2015] EPO opposition; Hospira v Novartis [2013] (zoledronate); HTC v Gemalto [2013](computer software, mobile telephones); Nokia v HTC [2013] (mobile telephones); Resolution v Lundbeck [2013] (estoppel, privity); Fabio Perini v PCMC [2012], [2010] and [2009] (damages inquiry following mechanical patent trial and appeal); Welland v Hadley [2011] (ostomy pouches, IPO entitlement proceedings, appeal to High Court); Siemens v Seagate [2010] (hard disk reader); Nokia v IPCom [2010] (mobile telephones); Dr Reddy's v Eli Lilly [2010] (selection patents); Medeva's SPCs [2010] (vaccines, reference to CJEU); CSL/ University of Queensland's SPCs [2010] (vaccines, reference to ECJ).
Professional Memberships: Intellectual Property Bar Association, Chancery Bar Association, IPSoc (society for junior IP practitioners).
Career: Called 2004, Lincoln's Inn, Gonville and Caius College, Cambridge (2002 MA Hons, Natural Sciences), ICSL.

COPLIN, Richard
Keating Chambers, London
020 7544 2600
rcoplin@keatingchambers.com
Featured in Professional Negligence (London), Construction (London)
Practice Areas: Specialist in the construction, engineering, energy and technology sectors. Qualified engineer and spent several years in industry before coming to the Bar. Richard has particular strengths in understanding and advising in respect of legal issues arising out of complex engineering matters, particularly in the fields of mechanical and structural engineering and in areas such as offshore construction, energy and power, acoustics, manufacturing, materials science, corrosion and transportation. Acts for clients on claims in the English courts, particularly the Technology and Construction Court, but also has extensive experience of adjudication (including enforcement), UK and international arbitration (particularly in Europe, The Far East, the Caribbean and the Middle East), including those under ICC and DIAC Rules. Particularly well regarded for his work on professional negligence claims relating to engineers, architects, surveyors and valuers.
Professional Memberships: Commercial Bar Association; Society of Construction Law.
Career: BA in Engineering Science, Exeter College, Oxford 1989; Diploma in Law, City University 1996; Called to the Bar (Middle Temple) 1997; Pupillage, Keating Chambers 1997-98; Keating Chambers 1998.
Publications: Contributor – Keating on Construction Contracts Ninth Edition (2012). Has also contributed a chapter in "Construction Dispute Resolution Handbook" ed. Dr Gaitskell QC pub. Thomas Telford (2011).

COPNALL, Richard
Parklane Plowden, Leeds
0113 228 5000
richard.copnall@parklaneplowden.co.uk
Featured in Clinical Negligence (North Eastern), Personal Injury (North Eastern)
Practice Areas: Richard continues to be listed in Chambers and Partners as one of the top 5, and in the Legal 500 as one of the "Leading" juniors, in the region. The guides describe him as: "confident assured and bright"; "very thorough in his approach and one of the best cross-examiners on circuit"; undertaking "erudite analysis of cases"; providing "a high-quality service" and "a no-nonsense barrister who gets on and does the job". They note that he: "takes the burden off the client, always choosing to run with a deal rather than constantly seeking the client's opinion"; "has flair in court" and that solicitors "feel confident on difficult cases when they know that he is on their side". In the earlier part of his career, he was at the forefront of developments in the field of the 'six pack' regulations, where he appeared in a number of the leading cases, and was on the Attorney General's panel for 10 years, often instructed in media sensitive inquests. He now specialises in clinical negligence and high value personal injury work, with a particular niche in Human Rights Act

claims, Article 2 inquests, and associated civil actions. A significant part of his practice draws on his scientific background when dealing with medical, engineering and other technical issues. He continues to edit the APIL Guide to Personal Injury Applications and Pleadings (his 3rd edn to be published this year)
Professional Memberships: APIL, PNBA, PIBA and AVMA.
Career: Called to the Bar 1990.
Publications: Editor – APIL Guide to Personal Injury Applications and Pleadings (Jordans, 2005); Editor – APIL Model Pleadings and Applications (Jordans, 2012); contributor to APIL Personal Injury Law, Practice and Precedents.
Personal: Born 1967. Married with two children. Enjoys Italy and cycling

COPPEL, Jason QC
11KBW, London
020 7632 8500
Jason.Coppel@11kbw.com
Featured in Administrative & Public Law (London), Civil Liberties & Human Rights (London), Data Protection (London), Competition/European Law (London), Local Government (London), Public Procurement (London)
Practice Areas: Jason is a specialist in public law, public procurement, EU law, information and human rights law, including judicial review, social security, pensions, data protection and freedom of information. Recent notable cases include Shindler v CDL (SC, scope of franchise in EU referendum); Dos Santos v SoS for Exiting the EU (Brexit challenge to exercise of Article 50 TEU); Edenred v HM Treasury (SC: procurement challenge to variation of public services contract); Rotherham MBC v SoS for Business (SC: judicial review of EU regional aid allocations); Keyu v SoS for Defence (SC: challenge to refusal to hold inquiry into 1948 massacre in Malaysia); Chester v Lord President (SC: EU and ECHR challenge to ban on voting by convicted prisoners); Fair Crime Contract Alliance v Lord Chancellor (Procurement challenges to criminal legal aid contracts); T v Greater Manchester Police (SC, disclosure of convictions on CRB checks); Commission v UK (CJEU: infraction proceedings against right to reside test for welfare benefits); Bristol Missing Link v Bristol CC (TCC: lifting of automatic suspension in procurement challenge); Sanneh v SoS for Work and Pensions (CA: welfare entitlements of Zambrano carers). He is a member of the Northern Ireland Bar.

CORDARA, Roderick QC
Essex Court Chambers, London
020 7813 8000
rcordara@essexcourt.com
Featured in Commercial Dispute Resolution (London), Tax (London)
Practice Areas: Roderick Cordara has an extensive commercial litigation and arbitration practice and acts as adviser and advocate in a spectrum of courts and arbitration tribunals worldwide. He is a silk in both the UK and Australia. His wide ranging practice encompasses energy and shipping related cases, transactional taxes as well as general commercial disputes. He also acts in investor state matters. He has arbitrated in cases in Europe, Asia, and Africa. His principal practice is advocacy. He also sits as arbitrator. He has offices in London, Singapore and Sydney and he is admitted to appear in the Courts of the United Kingdom, the European Court of Justice, the Singapore International Commercial Court, and the State and Federal Courts of Australia.

CORFIELD, Louise
No5 Chambers, Birmingham
0845 210 5555
Featured in Chancery (Midlands)
Practice Areas: Louise specialises in traditional chancery matters, with a strong focus on probate and 1975 Inheritance Act cases. She also has considerable experience in a wide range of trusts and property matters, in particular ownership and TOLATA disputes. Louise is experienced at conducting trials and applications at all levels including the High Court and in particular the Chancery Division. She is a strong cross-examiner and is also highly successful at negotiating settlements, whether by mediation, FDR- style hearing or at the door of Court. She prides herself on giving practical advice and having good client handling skills.
Professional Memberships: Chancery Bar Association, Midlands Commercial and Chancery Bar Association (Secretary)
Career: Louise graduated from Trinity College, Oxford with a First Class Jurisprudence Degree in 2007. She began pupillage at No5 Chambers in 2008, where she continues to practice.

CORNELL, Kate
5 Essex Court, London
020 7410 2000
clerks@5essexcourt.co.uk
Featured in Police Law (All Circuits)
Practice Areas: Police law, including civil claims for wrongful arrest, false imprisonment, malicious prosecution, discrimination, assault and misfeasance. Policy advice. Police misconduct at first instance, PAT and judicial review stages. Human rights, particularly Article 2 and Article 8 issues. Discrimination cases. CLG v Chief Constable of Merseyside [2015] EWCA Civ 836 – successful at trial and on appeal defending claim for alleged wrongful disclosure of witnesses' identities to criminal defendants in a criminal trial. R (on application of Commissioner of Police) v Police Appeals Tribunal [2013] EWHC 4309 (admin) – judicial review of PAT decision to reinstate Special Constable. A & B v Chief Constable of Hampshire [2012] EWHC 1517 – successful strike out of a claim that the police had caused unauthorised disclosures of an informer's identity during court proceedings, where the disclosures were protected by the core immunity applying to court proceedings. Numerous police misconduct cases including: two Metropolitan police officers dismissed for exchanging inappropriate racist and discriminatory text messages; a Metropolitan Police officer dismissed for seriously mishandling 999 calls; five Merseyside Matrix officers dismissed for unprofessional and improper behaviour during a search.
Professional Memberships: South Eastern Circuit; Association of Regulatory and Disciplinary Lawyers; Professional Negligence Bar Association; Proceeds of Crime Lawyers Association
Career: Called to the Bar 2003

CORNWELL, James
11KBW, London
020 7632 8500
James.Cornwell@11kbw.com
Featured in Education (London)
Practice Areas: Education, Data Protection/Freedom of Information, Administrative & Public, Local Government and Employment Law. Cases include: Dransfield v Information Commissioner & Devon CC/ Craven v Information Commissioner & DECC [2015] 1 WLR 5316, CA; DECC v Breyer Group plc [2015] 1 WLR 4559, CA; R (Rotherham MBC) v Secretary of State for Business, Innovation & Skills [2015] PTSR 322, SC; Cavanagh & Williams v Secretary of State for Work & Pensions [2016] EWHC 1136 (QB), Mr & Mrs X v Governing Body of a School [2015] ELR 133, UT; R (Vowles) v Secretary of State for Justice & Parole Board [2015] 1 WLR 5131, CA; Information Commissioner v Niebel [2014] 2 Info LR 162, UT; R (Crawford) v Newcastle University [2014] ELR 110, QBD; Cabinet Office v Information Commissioner & Aitchison [2013] 2 Info LR 336, UT; UK Coal Mining Ltd v Information Commissioner [2012] 2 Info LR 491, UT; GC & JC v Tameside MBC [2011] ELR 470, UT; Kirklees Metropolitan Council v Radecki [2009] ICR 1244, CA.
Professional Memberships: ALBA; ELBA; ELA.
Career: Called: 2002; Attorney General's 'A' Panel: 2016.
Publications: Tolley's Employment Handbook; Local Government Law; Halsbury's Laws of England – Judicial Review.
Personal: Educated: University College, Oxford (BA (Hons), PPE); University College London (MPhil, Philosophy); Brasenose College, Oxford (DPhil, Philosophy); City University (Diploma in Law).

CORSELLIS, Nicholas
QEB Hollis Whiteman, London
020 7933 8855
nc@qebhw.co.uk
Featured in Crime (London)
Practice Areas: Nicholas Corsellis is a highly respected leading counsel specialising in serious crime, ranging from murder to fraud, both prosecuting and defending. Professional and lay clients appreciate his direct and clear approach packaged with diplomacy and courtesy. He handles allegations of serious crime including murder, very high value drugs conspiracies and sexual abuse. He undertakes high-profile cases, for example representing the first defendant at trial in the 2016 Hatton Garden Jewellery Heist, the organiser of the £40 million Graff jewellery robbery (R v Kassaye), the first defendant in R v O and others (the Victoria Station Murder), the Latvian serial rapist and murderer (R v Dembovskis) and a 15 year old contract killer (R v G). He has a wealth of experience dealing with sophisticated multi-million pound frauds over the last 15 years. He is accredited as a Grade 4 Prosecutor for the CPS and is one of the few specialist rape prosecutors; Nick also defends allegations of sexual crime on a privately instructed basis. His experience and talents have allowed him to vary his areas of practice to include advising on FCA prosecutions for the defence, firearms licensing, GMC/GDC work and in particular appearing regularly at the Court of Arbitration of Sport in cases concerning sports corruption.
Professional Memberships: Criminal Bar Association
Personal: Call 1993; LLB (Hons); fluent French

COSGROVE, Thomas
Cornerstone Barristers, London
020 72424986
tcosgrove@cornerstonebarristers.com
Featured in Planning (London)
Practice Areas: Planning and public law.
Professional Memberships: PEBA, ALBA
Career: Specialises in planning, environmental, public and administrative law. Detailed tactical knowledge of planning law and process. Extensive experience of planning inquiries and related statutory challenges throughout the country acting for private clients and planning authorities. Recently involved in major planning inquiries concerning nationally significant infrastructure projects for renewable energy provision and major residential proposals. During 2013 and 2014 Tom was instructed in one of the largest onshore wind farm inquiries in the UK. He has extensive experience of a wide range of planning areas including viability, climate change and renewable energy, housing, heritage assets and conservation, transportation and the delivery of major road infrastructures, design, ecology and the natural environment. As well as major city developments, he has substantial experience of promoting and resisting development proposals in countryside areas of outstanding natural beauty, national parks and green belt. He regularly appears in the High Court with specialist knowledge of judicial review procedure and statutory appeals.
Publications: Editor and co-author of "Cornerstone on the Planning Court"

COTTER, Mark
5 St Andrew's Hill, London
020 7332 5400
markcotter@5sah.co.uk
Featured in Crime (London)
Practice Areas: Mark is a specialist in the field of criminal defence and has extensive experience in all areas of criminal work from murder to money laundering. His particular areas of expertise include acting in cases involving allegations of serious sexual offending. Within this discipline, he is often instructed privately, although he also accepts legal aid instructions, where very serious sexual offences have been charged. Mark also has particular experience of advising and defending individuals working within professional sport, including Premiership/Championship footballers. He has also developed particular experience of defending medical professionals accused of sexual offending within a clinical environment, including eminent consultant surgeons. His success within these areas of work is well established. Mark also specialises in financial crime (including confiscation proceedings) and the offence of conspiracy, be it related to fraud, drugs or any other serious offending. Mark's experience in cases involving drug conspiracies is particularly extensive, including issues relating to Public Interest Immunity and covert surveillance. The same attention to detail and disciplined work ethic that Mark brings to all his cases has resulted in him being instructed to act as a lead counsel in over thirty cases of this type. Mark also retains a niche prosecution practice, which is limited to cases involving very serious sexual offending, usually involving allegations of rape or offences against children. He is admitted to the Unified List of Prosecution Advocates at the highest Grade ('4') and the Specialist Panel of Approved 'Rape Advocates'. Mark

is also admitted to the Serious Fraud Office List of Approved Prosecution Counsel at the highest grade (the 'A' list). Mark has recently began developing his practice into the regulatory field, which complements the reputation he has gained in dealing with professional clients.
Professional Memberships: Criminal Bar Association.
Career: Educated at Kingston University (LL.B Hons 1992); the University of Wales, Cardiff College, (LL.M 1993, Commercial Law); called 1994 (Middle Temple). Practice and career profile at www.5sah.co.uk.
Personal: Season ticket holder at Cardiff City Football Club, Friend of the Royal Opera House, Friend of the Imperial War Museum and Friend of the British Museum.

COVER, Martha
Coram Chambers, London
020 7092 3700
martha.cover@coramchambers.co.uk
Featured in Family/Matrimonial (London)
Practice Areas: Children.
Professional Memberships: Family Law Bar Association. Association of Lawyers for Children. Human Rights Lawyers Association. Liberty Gray's Inn
Career: Called November 1979. Head of Chambers since January 2010. Martha Cover has been a child law specialist since 1990. She represents parents and children in cases of death and serious injury to a child. She has a particular interest in allegations of emotional harm where children are being brought up in unusual or false belief systems. She also specialises in international and domestic adoption, wardship, and intractable disputes between parents over contact and residence.
Publications: Martha regularly speaks and writes on children law matters. She has written for The Times and been interviewed on radio and television to discuss adoption and the wider policy issues affecting care proceedings.
Personal: Born and educated in Canada. BA University of Western Ontario, BA Law University of North London, LLM University of London. Married with three children.

COWAN, Paul J
4 New Square, London
020 7855 2098
p.cowan@4newsquare.com
Featured in Construction (London)
Practice Areas: International arbitration, and international and national construction practice. Extensive experience advising on projects and appearing as counsel in relation to oil & gas, energy, transport and other major infrastructure projects, with particular emphasis on projects in civil law jurisdictions. First-hand, detailed experience in relation to the licensing, design and construction of new-build nuclear power plants, having continuously advised and represented clients on active new build projects over the last 10 years, as well as long experience on hydropower projects. Alongside representing clients in construction disputes, also provides front-end advice on contractual risk allocation, drafting and negotiation in relation to international and domestic construction contracts. Experienced advising on disputes and / or project development all over the world including: UK, Scandinavia, Middle East and North Africa, West Africa, and South America. Specialist representation and advocacy in litigation, arbitration, adjudication, dispute boards, mediation and other forms of dispute resolution. Particular specialism in relation to delay and disruption disputes, including leading conduct and advocacy on one of the world's largest delay / disruption disputes in international arbitration relating to the delayed completion of a nuclear power plant. Lead counsel in Carillion v Woods Bagot & Others (2016) establishing new case law on the award of extensions of time in multi-party construction disputes.
Professional Memberships: International Bar Association. ICC. LCIA. International Nuclear Law Association. Society of Construction Law. Joint Contracts Tribunal, Council Member and Chairman of Construction Dispute Resolution Group. City of London Law Society, Construction Committee.
Career: Returned to the Bar at 4 New Square in 2014, formerly partner at White & Case LLP (2003-2011). 1996 Call (Inner Temple). Major Scholarship. University College, University of Durham, LLB (Hons).
Publications: Co-author of standard form of novation agreement and guidance note, City of London Law Society Construction Committee. Regular speaker on international construction law and practice at IBA Annual Conferences (e.g. Tokyo 2014, Vienna 2015, and Washington DC 2016), including interface between common law and civil law and practice. Speaker at the inaugural International Construction Law Association seminar in Paris, June 2016. Seminars for the Society of Construction Law about "Advising on International Construction Contracts Subject to Civil Law" (in London and in the Gulf). Lectured on risk allocation and dispute resolution in nuclear new-build contracts at the International Nuclear Law Association's Congress in Toronto, Canada. CDR Autumn 2015 Arbitration Symposium. Numerous other construction and / or international arbitration seminars for CIArb, Kluwer (including in Turkey and UAE) and numerous other bodies. Published articles in Construction Law Journal, Building Magazine, Kluwer.
Personal: Motor sport and cars. History and literature. Amateur astronomy. Conversational French and German.

COWEN, Gary
Falcon Chambers, London
020 7353 2484
cowen@falcon-chambers.com
Featured in Real Estate Litigation (London)
Practice Areas: Real property, in particular commercial and residential landlord and tenant, restrictive covenants, easements, mortgages, leasehold enfranchisement, compulsory purchase, professional negligence.
Professional Memberships: Chancery Bar Association; LCLCBA; Property Bar Association; Inner Temple Estates Committee.
Career: Educated at George Watson's College, Edinburgh; LLB Bristol; Called 1990 (Inner Temple).
Publications: Contributor, Woodfall 'Landlord and Tenant' CD-Rom; contributor, Bullen Leake & Jacob's Precedent of Pleadings; co-author, Commonhold (The Law Society 2005).

COWTON, Catherine
Queen Elizabeth Building QEB, London
020 7797 7837
c.cowton@qeb.co.uk
Featured in Family/Matrimonial (London)
Practice Areas: Katie is regularly instructed to appear against QC's and other senior juniors in complex international cases in the High Court and Central Family Court. Her work includes financial applications on divorce and on civil partnership dissolution, Schedule 1 financial applications for children, and representing trustees caught up in financial cases. She also drafts pre-nuptial, post-nuptial, and cohabitation agreements. Much of Katie's practice takes place away from the public eye, resolving complex, often high-profile cases at private FDR's. She is also happy to represent clients in Arbitrations, should the case be suitable. Katie has been involved in several of the leading reported cases, and lectures to solicitors on request.
Professional Memberships: Family Law Bar Association; Bar Pro Bono Unit panel member.
Career: Magdalene College, Cambridge (MA (Hons) Law); Queen Mother's Scholar (Middle Temple); called 1995.

COX, Raymond QC
Fountain Court Chambers, London
020 7583 3335
rc@foutaincourt.co.uk
Featured in Banking & Finance (London)
Practice Areas: Commercial disputes generally, including banking and finance, fraud, financial services, international arbitration, offshore, professional negligence, and regulatory. Serious Fraud Office, Queen's Counsel list (2009), MClarb, Singapore International Commercial Court, registered as a foreign lawyer.
Career: Called to the Bar 1983, Silk 2002.
Publications: 'Law of Bank Payments', Brindle and Cox (4th ed., 2010); 'Private International Law of Reinsurance and Insurance', Cox, Merrett, Smith (2006); Contributor, 'Lloyd's Research Handbook on International Insurance Law & Regulation' (December 2011) and 'Professional Negligence and Liability', Simpson, (looseleaf).
Personal: Born 1959, BA (Oxon). 1st class, Eldon Scholar. Leisure includes odd theatre, cycling and making things in wood.

COX, Tamsin
Falcon Chambers, London
020 7353 2484
clerks@falcon-chambers.com
Featured in Real Estate Litigation (London)
Practice Areas: Specialises in all aspects of real property and Landlord & Tenant law and related areas including professional negligence.
Professional Memberships: Property Bar Association; Chancery Bar Association.
Career: Educated at Oxford High School GDST; University of Oxford, New College (BA Literae Humaniores 2003, MA 2015); City University (CPE 2004); Inns of Court School of Law (BVC 2005); called 2005, Lincoln's Inn; Joined Falcon Chambers 2006.
Publications: Contributor to The Law & Practice of Charging Orders on Land (Falcon Chambers, 2013).
Personal:

CRAMPIN, Cecily
Falcon Chambers, London
020 7421 5300
CecilyCrampin@tanfieldchambers.co.uk
Featured in Real Estate Litigation (London)
Practice Areas: Cecily has a broad property practice covering all aspects of real property and landlord and tenant law, both as sole counsel and often as junior counsel on larger pieces of litigation. Reported cases: Country Trade v Noakes [2011] UKUT 407 (LC) (LVT had wrongly introduced in its decisions its own assessment of the market norm for managing agents' fees); St John's Wood Leases Limited v O'Neil [2012] UKUT 374 (LC) (s20C of the Landlord and Tenant Act 1985); Patel v Peters [2014] EWCA Civ 335 (s10(7) of the Party Wall Act 1996); Trustees of the Sloane Stanley Estate v Mundy [2016] UKUT 0223 (LC).
Professional Memberships: Property Bar Association; Chancery Bar Association.
Career: Called 2008; Middle Temple. Completed pupillage at Tanfield Chambers in September 2009. Practised at Tanfield from September 2009 to April 2016. Moved to Falcon Chambers April 2016.
Publications: Contributor to Tanfield Chambers' Service Charges & Management: Law & Practice, 3rd edition (Sweet & Maxwell 2013), and to Isaac, Nicholas, The Law and Practice of Party Walls (Property Publishing 2014)
Personal: Dame Alice Harpur School Bedford; Oxford University (1997 BA (Oxon); 2006 DPhil (Oxon)); Manchester University (1998 MSc); City University (2007 CPE; 2008 BVC)

CRANE, Michael QC
Fountain Court Chambers, London
020 7583 3335
clerks1@fountaincourt.co.uk
Featured in International Arbitration (London), Travel (London), Aviation (London), Commercial Dispute Resolution (London), Insurance (London), Product Liability (London)
Practice Areas: Barrister specialising in commercial litigation and arbitration, including aviation, insurance/reinsurance, gas and energy, professional negligence, product liability and conflicts of law. Michael has sat as an arbitrator both in the UK and abroad and as a Deputy High Court Judge in the Commercial Court.
Career: Called 1975; QC 1994.

CRANGLE, Thomas
4 Pump Court, London
020 7842 5555
tcrangle@4pumpcourt.com
Featured in Construction (London)
Practice Areas: Construction, energy, professional negligence (with a particular emphasis on construction professionals), information technology and insurance. He has extensive experience of acting in all types of construction, energy and infrastructure disputes in adjudications, arbitrations and in the TCC. He is regularly instructed by contractors, employers, utility companies, professionals, insurers and government bodies both in the UK and overseas. He has considerable experience of domestic and international arbitrations, particularly in the energy, infrastructure and utilities sectors.
Professional Memberships: TECBAR; Society of Construction Law; COMBAR; PNBA; Society for Computers and Law. TECBAR accredited Adjudicator
Career: Magdalene College, Cambridge MA (Law) 2001; Called to the Bar 2002.

CRASNOW, Rachel QC
Cloisters, London
020 7827 4054
rc@cloisters.com
Featured in Employment (London)
Practice Areas: Rachel Crasnow has been consistently recommended as a leading

employment junior for many years. She practices in all aspects of domestic & EU employment law, acting in high-profile cases in forums including the Supreme Court & CJEU. She undertakes a wide range of work from equal pay, working time & maternity rights to TUPE, internal disciplinary tribunals & collective rights. She is particularly recognised for her expertise in discrimination & human rights & her practice includes advising in goods & services cases. Rachel is regularly instructed in high value & complex trials by individuals, private companies, & public sector bodies. She is a trained mediator & is often instructed as counsel in difficult mediations. She also undertakes a range of regulatory & other civil work.
Professional Memberships: ELBA, ELA, DLA, Bar Pro-Bono Unit, ELAAS, HRLA.
Career: Notable recent work includes: O'Brien v MOJ – EAT Jan 2014 (judicial pension remedy); SC [2013] ICR 499 (part-time discrimination & judicial pensions), Dudley Council v Whitehead [2012] EAT (group action equal pay); Blackburn v Chief Constable of W.Midlands Police [2009] IRLR 135 CA (equal pay); Cadman v HSE [2007] 1 CMLR 16 ECJ (justifying equal pay); DTI v Rutherford [2006] ICR 785 HL (sex / age discrimination / EU law), Vince-Cain v Orthet [2005] ICR 374 (sex discrimination & tax); Goodwin v UK (2002) 35 EHRR 18 (transsexuals & human rights). Standing counsel to BPS for over 10 years. Counsel to 1999-2000 Turner Inquiry; instructed in the Climbie Inquiry. Long-term advisor at Camden Law Centre. Nominated for Employment Junior of the Year 2013. Sought after legal speaker & commentator.
Publications: Co-author/editor of Family Rights in Employment Law (Jordans 2012), co-author of Blackstone's Guide to the Equality Act 2010 (OUP 2010), co-author with Robin Allen QC of 'Employment Law and Human Rights' (2nd edition OUP 2007), editor of Bullen & Leake's Human Rights & European Law Sections. Previous editor of 'Educational Law Journal's Case Commentaries'. Writes for legal periodicals & responses to consultation papers.
Personal: Educated at Pembroke College, Oxford & City University, London. Middle Temple Diplock Scholarship 1993; Pegasus Scholarship 1999 (Human Rights & Equal Opportunities Commission, Sydney). Member of the Bar Council Equality & Diversity Committee; Chair of Bar Council Legislation & Guidance Group.

CRAVEN, Edward
Matrix Chambers, London
020 7404 3447
edwardcraven@matrixlaw.co.uk
Featured in Defamation/Privacy (London)
Practice Areas: Defamation, privacy and breach of confidence; data protection; human rights and judicial review; public international law; criminal law; commercial law and sports law. Recent cases include the Mobile Telephone Voicemail Interception Litigation; David Miranda v SSHD (judicial review of seizure of journalistic material under Terrorism Act 2000); Liberty v GCHQ (challenge to mass interception and intelligence sharing programmes); Smith v Ministry of Defence (UKSC appeal regarding extra-territorial application of ECHR); Belhaj v Straw (UKSC appeal concerning state immunity and foreign act of state); Beghal v DPP (UKSC appeal concerning ECHR compatibility of Schedule 7 of Terrorism Act 2000); OPO v MLA (UKSC appeal concerning prohibition of performing artist's autobiography); OA v HM Advocate (UKSC appeal concerning Scottish sexual offences legislation); Rahmatullah and Serdar Mohammed v MOD (UKSC appeal regarding Crown act of state doctrine); SXH v CPS (UKSC appeal regarding prosecution of refugees); Croatia v Serbia (ICJ Genocide Convention) and Somalia v Kenya (ICJ maritime delimitation). Provides regular pre-publication advice to national newspapers and BBC News.
Career: BA Law (First Class), Trinity Hall, Cambridge University; BCL (Distinction), Brasenose College, Oxford University; Bar Vocational Course (Outstanding), Inns of Court School of Law. Judicial assistant at the Court of Appeal (2009); European Court of Human Rights (2010) and United Kingdom Supreme Court (2011-12). Lecturer in Administrative Law and Human Rights Law at Oxford University (2010-11).
Publications: Contributing Editor to "Smith, Owen & Bodnar on Asset Recovery" (OUP); "Criminal Justice and Human Rights" and "Prison Law" (Sweet & Maxwell).

CRAWSHAW, Simon
Atkin Chambers, London
020 7404 0102
scrawshaw@atkinchambers.com
Featured in Construction (London)
Practice Areas: Simon has wide ranging experience in domestic courts, mediations and adjudications as well as domestic and international arbitrations conducted under various arbitral rules, including SIAC, HKIAC, ICC and UNCITRAL. His main areas of specialisation are construction and engineering, energy, and professional negligence. Recent notable cases include: Acting for Government of Gibraltar in a claim related to the termination of a high-profile tunnel project under a FIDIC form of contract (OHL v Govt. of Gibraltar [2014] EWHC 1028); SIAC arbitration concerning the termination of a contract for the purchase of a large residential, commercial and retail development in Vietnam; Representing a company forming part of the consortium delivering the Manchester Tram project (Transport for Greater Manchester v Thales [2012] 146 ConLR 194); Appeal to the Privy Council from concerning the proper interpretation of certain statutory provisions (Presidential Insurance v St. Hill [2012] UKPC 33); Representing a member of the FIFA Executive Committee in libel proceedings brought against a prominent politician (Makudi v Lord Triesman [2014] 3 All ER 36).
Professional Memberships: TECBAR, LCLCBA, COMBAR, SCL
Career: MA (Oxon, 1st Class); LLB (London); Boulter Exhibition (Christ Church, Oxford), Marchant Scholarship (Lincoln's Inn); Called 2005
Publications: Hudson's Building and Engineering Contracts, 12th Ed, contributing editor

CREAN, Anthony QC
Kings Chambers, Birmingham
0345 034 3444
clerks@kingschambers.com
Featured in Planning (Midlands), Planning (Northern)
Practice Areas: Anthony is on the UK's leading planning Silks. His practice includes all areas of planning and environmental law and his particular strength is in high profile cases where excellence in advocacy is of great importance. Anthony acts for a wide range of clients primarily strategic land promoters and housebuilders but also local authorities when the stakes are high. He has specialist expertise in large scale housing projects, retail, waste/minerals, renewables, heritage, highways and compulsory purchase. He also acts for parties in Professional Negligence claims arising out of planning. He is a visiting professor of planning law, University of Buckingham.
Professional Memberships: Planning and Environment Bar Association, Fellow of the Royal Geographical Society.
Career: Called 1987; silk 2006.

CRIDDLE, Betsan
Old Square Chambers, London
020 7269 0300
criddle@oldsquare.co.uk
Featured in Employment (London), Professional Discipline (London)
Practice Areas: All areas of employment and discrimination law and professional discipline, including High Court contractual and disciplinary disputes, industrial action injunctions and judicial review proceedings. Recent highlights include: R (BMA) v GMC [2016] 4 WLR 89 (whether GMC's rules on advice given by legally qualified chairs are fair and Article 6 compliant); Vining and others v London Borough of Wandsworth [2016] (compatibility of exclusion of those in police service from employment rights with Articles 8, 11 and 14 of the European Convention on Human Rights); Edwards and anor v Encirc Ltd [2015] IRLR 528 (whether trade union facility time can amount to working time for the purposes of the Working Time Regulations 1998); Chhabra v West London Mental Health NHS Trust [2014] ICR 194 (injunctions and implied term of fairness in disciplinary proceedings).
Professional Memberships: ELA, ELBA, ILS.
Career: MA (Hons) Law, St John's College, Cambridge. Called to the Bar 2002
Publications: Employment Precedents and Company Law Documents (Sweet & Maxwell); Employment Law Review (Institute of Employment Rights); Employment Tribunal Procedure (LAG).
Personal: Fluent Welsh speaker and able to conduct litigation through the medium of Welsh.

CRIDLAND, Simon
Serjeants' Inn Chambers, London
020 7427 5000
Clerks@serjeantsinn.com
Featured in Clinical Negligence (London), Professional Discipline (London)
Practice Areas: Simon Cridland was called to the Bar in 1999. Simon specialises in clinical negligence and healthcare, professional discipline, product liability, inquests and inquiries and public and administrative law. An earlier edition notes that "his ability to get the information needed for a case... his thorough examination and cross-examination of experts are great" and that "he is incredibly eloquent, very tactically sharp and thinks of things that no one else has thought of. His advocacy works magnificently well." Please visit the Serjeants' Inn Chambers website for his profile, which sets out full details of his practice and relevant work of note.
Professional Memberships: ARDL, PNBA, LCLCBA, ELBA.
Publications: "Gregg v. Scott: the lost chance of 'a loss of a chance'" Clinical Risk (2005) 11 138-141; Clinical Negligence (APIL) (contributor).

CROALL, Simon QC
Quadrant Chambers, London
020 7583 4444
simon.croall@quadrantchambers.com
Featured in Information Technology (London), Shipping (London)
Practice Areas: Simon Croall is an established commercial silk who has appeared in every court (including twice in the House of Lords). He is a sought after trial advocate as well as being respected in the appellate courts. In recent years much of his work has been in the context of International Arbitrations. He led the team for Owners in landmark case on remoteness in contract damages Transfield Shipping v Mercator Shipping ("The Achilleas") [2009] 1 AC 61. Recent reported highlights include another important case on damages Fulton Shipping v Globalia (The New Flamenco) in both the Court of Appeal [2016] 1 Lloyd's Rep. 383 and below [2014] 2 Lloyd's Rep. 230, Mitsui v Beteiligungsgesellschaft ("The Longchamp") [2016] EWCA 708 in which the Court of Appeal ruled on controversial aspects of general average in the context of piracy, Essar Shipping v Bank of China [2016] 1 Lloyd's Rep. 427 on factors relevant to the grant of anti suit injunctions and ST Shipping v Space Shipping [2016] 2 Lloyd's 17 on arbitration appeals. Simon is particularly well known for his experience in the following fields: shipping and commodities, commercial litigation, International Arbitration, energy, insurance and Information Technology (see for example De Beers v Atos Origin [2011] BLR 274, a claim arising out of a large scale IT project). He also has a global practice with a depth of experience working with Chinese and south east Asian clients.
Professional Memberships: COMBAR and Society of Computers and the Law.
Career: Call 1986 (Middle). Silk 2008.
Personal: MA (cantab) 1st Class Honours.

CROSS, James QC
4 Pump Court, London
020 7842 5555
jcross@4pumpcourt.com
Featured in Professional Negligence (London), Construction (London), Property Damage (London)
Practice Areas: James has an extensive and wide-ranging commercial practice. He has particular expertise in construction and engineering, facilities management, energy-related matters, insurance, property damage and product liability claims. He has a wide-ranging professional liability practice with particular focus on construction industry professionals such as architects, building & quantity surveyors and engineers of all types.
Professional Memberships: COMBAR, LCLCBA, PNBA, TECBAR, SCL.
Career: Called 1985 (Gray's Inn) QC 2006.
Publications: Contributor to the Architect's Legal Handbook 9th ed. (Chapter on Architects' Liability).
Personal: Shrewsbury and Magdalen College, Oxford (MA, Jurisprudence).

CROSS, Tom
11KBW, London
020 7632 8500
Tom.Cross@11kbw.com
Featured in Civil Liberties & Human Rights (London), Data Protection (London), Education (London)
Practice Areas: Administrative & public, education, information, EU, human rights, employment, commercial.
Professional Memberships: ALBA, BEG, ELA.
Career: Called in 2007. Judicial Assistant at the UK Supreme Court 2009-2010. Attorney General's Panel of Counsel (Civil). Recent reported cases include: R (Shindler) v Chancellor of the Duchy of Lancaster, Times, June 7 2016; R (Project Management Institute) v Minister for the Cabinet Office [2016] 1 WLR 1737; R (Seiont, Gwyrfai and Llyfni Angers' Authority) v Natural Resources Wales [2016] ACD 31; Yassin v General Medical Council [2015] EWHC 2955 (Admin); R (Duff) v Secretary of State for Transport [2015] EWHC 1605 (Admin); Dransfield v Information Commissioner [2015] EWCA Civ 454; R (Friends of the Earth) v Welsh Ministers [2015] EWHC 776; Smith v Carillion (JM) Ltd [2015] EWCA Civ 209; R (Forge Care Homes) v Cardiff & Vale UHB [2015] EWHC 601; McCarthy v Inns of Court [2015] EWCA Civ 12; Bayliss v Parole Board [2014] EWCA Civ 1631; Leathley v Bar Standards Board [2014] EWCA Civ 1630; JG v Lord Chancellor [2014] EWCA Civ 656; R (Abedin) v Secretary of State for Justice [2014] EWHC 78 (Admin); Manchester City Council v JW [2014] UKUT 0168 (AAC); Bedale Golf Club Ltd v Revenue and Customs Commissioners [2014] UKUT 99 (TCC); R (CNEN) v Northumberland County Council [2013] EWCA Civ 1740; R (SA) v London Borough of Camden [2014] ELR 29; London Borough of Harrow v AM [2013] UKUT 157 (AAC); Aderemi v London and South Eastern Railway Ltd [2013] EqLR 198.
Publications: The Protections for Religious Rights (OUP: 2013). The Law of Regulatory Enforcement and Sanctions (OUP: 2011). Articles in The Times, Judicial Review, the European Advocate, the Education Law Journal.
Personal: Double 1st class degree from Oxford in Modern Languages (French and Spanish). CPE (City).

CROSSLEY, Dominic
St Philips Chambers, Leeds
0113 244 6691
dcrossley@st-philips.com
Featured in Chancery (North Eastern), Real Estate Litigation (North Eastern)
Practice Areas: Dominic specialises in property and general chancery law, including wills and probate, commercial law, including contractual and tortious claims, and sale of goods. He has a particular interest in real property disputes and regularly acts in matters involving boundary disputes, the creation and extinguishment of easements, adverse possession and rectification of the Register. He has a special interest in disputes before the Land Registration Division of the Property Chamber (formerly known as the Adjudicator to HM Land Registry). Dominic regularly acts in claims for beneficial interests arising out of constructive trusts, and proprietary estoppel claims, and has delivered seminars on the subject. He has a sizeable wills and probate practice, including probate claims, challenges to the validity of wills, claims for the removal or substitution of executors, and claims under the Inheritance Act. Dominic also undertakes work in the Court of Protection.
Professional Memberships: Chancery Bar Association, Northern Chancery Bar Association, Property Bar Association
Career: Date of call: 2006, Gray's Inn (qualified as solicitor, 2004 – commercial litigation department of an international law firm)
Publications: 'Land Registry Adjudication' (Bloomsbury), 2013

CROSSLEY, Steven
Exchange Chambers, Liverpool
0113 203 1970
crossley@exchangechambers.co.uk
Featured in Professional Discipline (The Regions)
Practice Areas: Crime; Professional Discipline (acting on behalf of the professional in Police Misconduct/ GMC/NMC); Regulatory Crime; Inquests and Inquiries. Judicial Review. Expertise in defending professionals accused of criminal offences in the course of their employment or profession.
Professional Memberships: CBA
Career: Crime: R v Clegg: Court of Appeal (Northern Ireland). Junior Counsel in the successful fresh evidence appeal for a paratrooper wrongly convicted of the murder of Karen Reilly; R v Ellerington: Acted for a sergeant accused of the Manslaughter of Christopher Alder; AG's Reference No3 of 2003 [2004] EWCA Crim 868: Leading case on the mental element required for the offence of Misconduct in Public Office; R v J: Acted for a sergeant accused of conspiring to transfer firearms to an informant; R v C and J [2015]: Sheffield Magistrates' Court. Acted for two police officers in relation to an allegation of assault. It was successfully argued that the policy of West Yorkshire Police, preventing police officers giving character evidence, operated to deny the defendants a fair trial. Professional Discipline: R (Chief Constable of Durham) v Police Appeals Tribunal & Cooper [2012] EWHC 2733 Admin: Leading case on the meaning of "unreasonable" for the purposes of an appeal pursuant to Rule 4(4)(a) Police Appeals Tribunal Rules 2012; Re O: Derbyshire Constabulary. Acted for the Officer in a case providing guidance as to the appropriate involvement of the independent legal adviser in the drafting of the Panel's reasons.

CROW, Jonathan QC
4 Stone Buildings, London
020 7242 5524
J.Crow@4stonebuildings.com
Featured in Administrative & Public Law (London), Chancery (London), Banking & Finance (London), Commercial Dispute Resolution (London), Company (London), Financial Services (London), Fraud (London), Offshore (London), Restructuring/Insolvency (London), Telecommunications (London)
Practice Areas: Company/ commercial litigation; administrative and public law; banking and finance; chancery (commercial); telecomms; international trust work.
Professional Memberships: Administrative Law Bar Association; Commercial Bar Association; Chancery Bar Association; Insolvency Lawyers Association.
Career: Called 1981; Treasury Counsel 1994-98; First Treasury Counsel 1998-2006; Deputy High Court Judge 2001. Attorney General to HRH The Prince of Wales 2006. Court of Appeal Judge in Jersey & Guernsey 2011. Called to the Bar in the BVI, and also in Nevis, Bermuda and Cayman Islands for specific cases.
Publications: Annotated Companies Act 2006, OUP (contributing author).

CROWLEY, Daniel
2TG – 2 Temple Gardens, London
020 7822 1200
dcrowley@2tg.co.uk
Featured in Property Damage (London)
Practice Areas: Daniel Crowley is a very experienced trial lawyer. He has fought dozens of cases to trial. He is very experienced in appeals to the Court of Appeal where he has fought many appeals, mostly alone and without a leader. He specialises in insurance, professional liability, product liability/ property damage, commercial litigation and arbitration. See www.danielcrowley.org
Professional Memberships: Commercial Bar Association (Committee Member 2000 – 2007); London Court of International Arbitration (LCIA); Chartered Institute of Arbitrators (CIArb); London Common Law and Commercial Bar Association (LCLCBA); Professional Negligence Bar Association (PNBA); Technology and Construction Bar Association (TECBAR); Bar Council Education and Training Committee 2004 – 2005; Bar Standards Board Standards Committee 2006 – 2011; Bar Standards Boards Pupillage Sub-Committee 2006 – 2011; Bar Standards Board Strategic Review Implementation Steering Group (2008 – 2009) which implemented the new Complaints Rules and Disciplinary Tribunal Regulations for Barristers. Gray's Inn Advocacy Trainer (from 2000) training BVC students, Pupils and New Practitioners – "A" grade trainer. Member, 2tg Management Board 1997- 2001; 2tg Equal Opportunities Officer 2006 – 2010.
Career: Rendlesham Estates plc and Others v Barr Limited [2015] BLR 37, [2015] TCLR 1; (2015) 157 Con LR 147; [2015] CILL 3604; Hufford v Samsung Electronics (UK) Ltd [2014] BLR 633; Robbins v LB Bexley [2012] LLR 976 (Edwards-Stuart J); [2014] BLR 11, [2013] All E R (D) 177 (Court of Appeal); Khan and Khan v (1) London Borough of Harrow; and (2) Helen Sheila Kane [2013] BLR 611; [2013] All ER (D) 32; [2013] CILL 3421; Zennstrom and Another v Fagot and Others (2013) 147 Con LR 162, [2013] All ER (D) 287 (Feb), (2013) 30 BLM 46; Denness and Another v East Hampshire District Council [2012] All ER (D) 307 (Oct); Berent v Family Mosaic Housing [2012] BLR 488, [2012] CILL 3213; Foster and Another v Stojanovski [2011] All E R (D) 157; Jenson and Jenson v Faux [2011] 1 WLR 3038; [2011] WLR (D) 133; The Times Law Reports 26.04.11; [2011] TCLR 4, [2011] HLR 30, [2011] P&CR 11, [2011] CILL 3025, [2011] NPC 42; Bole and Van Den Haak v (1) Huntsbuild Ltd and (2) Richard Money (t/a Richard Money Associates) [TCC] (2009) 124 Con LR 1; [2009] WLR (D) 98; [2009] All E R (D) 195; (2009) CILL 2697; 153 (120 SJLB 27; [CA] [2009] EWCA Civ 1146; (2010) 127 Con LR 154; [2010] ALL E R (D) 84; (2010) 27 BLM 34. Porter v Zurich Insurance Company Ltd. (High Court QBD, Liverpool DR 2009, Coulson J) [2010] Lloyd's Rep IR 373; [2010] Lloyd's Rep IR Plus 11; [2009] All E R (D) 152; [2009] 2 All E R (Comm) 658; (2009) NPC 38; (2009) ILM 75. Hames v Ferguson [2008] All E R (D) 152 (CA);Hough v Annear (2008) 119 Con LR 57; Crest Nicholson (Eastern) Ltd v Mr and Mrs Western [2008] 1 BLR 426; [2008] All E R (D) 249; (2008) 119 Con LR 18; (2008) CILL 2599; [2008] TCLR 9; Eiles v London Borough of Southwark [2006] All E R (D) 237; Wessanen Foods Ltd v Jofson Ltd [2006] All E R (D) 48; The Burns – Anderson Independent Network plc v Francis Henry Wheeler [2005] Lloyd's Rep 580 (QBD).

CRYSTAL, Michael QC
South Square, London
020 7696 9900
practicemanagers@southsquare.com
Featured in Restructuring/Insolvency (London)
Practice Areas: Michael has been involved as counsel, adviser or expert witness in most of the best known international insolvencies and restructurings in the UK and overseas in the last four decades. He has represented or advised most of the major international financial services institutions, funds and accountancy firms operating in the mergers and acquisitions, bankruptcy and restructuring fields. Michael receives instructions from leading law firms in London, New York and in many offshore jurisdictions including the Cayman Islands, the British Virgin Islands, Bermuda, the Bahamas, the Channel Islands, Hong Kong and Singapore. In addition to his advocacy skills, Michael is particularly in demand for his strategic overview and experience in cases involving international litigation, cross-border bankruptcy and restructuring. His publicly reported cases in the UK and elsewhere run to over 100 and include all Appellate levels and trial courts in the UK and many overseas jurisdictions. .
Professional Memberships: International Insolvency Institute; Fellow American College of Bankruptcy; INSOL Europe; Chancery Bar Association.
Career: Queen's Counsel 1984; Deputy High Court Judge since 1995. Admitted to the Bar of the British Virgin Islands and to the Bars of the Bahamas, Bermuda, the Cayman Islands, Gibraltar, Hong Kong and the Isle of Man for specific cases.

CUDBY, Markanza
1 King's Bench Walk, London
020 7936 1500
mcudby@1kbw.co.uk
Featured in Family/Matrimonial (London)
Practice Areas: Predominantly a Children's law practitioner with vast experience in both public and private law matters. In public law she has experience of representing local authorities, parents , Guardians and children direct. She is particularly sought after in complex cases involving allegations of non accidental injury and sexual abuse. In private law Markanza covers all areas including residence, contact, adoption, internal and external relocation. She also deals with child abduction, having been a trustee of Reunite for many years. Markanza also deals with ancillary relief and schedule 1 cases. She brings her experience both as a barrister and DDJ to these cases.
Personal: Deputy District Judge at PRFD, Recorder (Crime, Private Family and Care), Bar Pro Bono Unit, Family Law Bar Association Association of Lawyers for Children

CULLEN, Clare
Arden Chambers, London
020 72424244
clare.cullen@ardenchambers.com
Featured in Social Housing (London)

Career: Clare was called to the Bar in 2009 and joined Arden Chambers as a pupil in 2010.Clare regularly advises and represents both public and private clients (including local authorities, social landlords and tenants) in claims for possession (anti-social behaviour, sub-letting, rent arrears, breaches of tenancy, tenancy by deception, Article 8 and Equality Act 2010 defences), anti-social behaviour injunctions, leasehold disputes, disrepair and business tenancies. Clare also represents both local authorities and applicants in homeless and housing application disputes. Clare's noteworthy cases include R(SG) v Secretary of State for Work and Pensions [2015] UKSC 16, R (on the application of Jakimaviciute) v Hammersmith and Fulham LBC [2014] EWCA Civ 1438, Gill v Birmingham City Council [2016] EWCA Civ 608 and R (on the application of Tesfay) v Birmingham City Council [2013] EWCA Civ 1599.
Publications: Assistant editor, Encyclopedia of Housing Law; contributor to Arden & Partington on Housing Law; co-author Current Law Statutes Annotations for Prevention of Social Housing Fraud Act 2013.

CULLEN, Edmund QC
Maitland Chambers, London
020 7406 1200
ecullen@maitlandchambers.com
Featured in Chancery (London), Media & Entertainment (London)
Practice Areas: Has broad expertise in chancery and commercial litigation, with particular emphasis on the music, film and broadcasting industries, where he has acted for the major record companies, producers and broadcasters, as well as many leading artists, writers, composers and agents. Deals extensively with disputes over contractual and intellectual property rights in a wide variety of media. Also specialises in professional negligence in the legal and accountancy fields and in claims arising in the company/ insolvency context, including claims against directors, asset tracing and recovery and restitution.
Professional Memberships: Chancery Bar Association and COMBAR.
Career: Called to the Bar 1990. QC 2012.

CUNNINGHAM, Mark QC
Maitland Chambers, London
020 7406 1200
mcunningham@maitlandchambers.com
Featured in Chancery (London)
Practice Areas: Specialist chancery practitioner with a bias towards commercially orientated litigation. He has appeared in over 100 reported cases concerning: company law, directors' disqualification, personal insolvency, sale of land, landlord and tenant, rent reviews, easements, land registration, partnership, proprietary estoppel, copyright, passing off, entertainment law, the Inheritance Act, subrogation, the Court of Protection, the Copyright Tribunal, betting and gaming, VAT, winding-up, corporation tax, asset recovery, MTIC fraud, banking and solicitors. He has also been appointed as a DTI Inspector in relation to insider dealing matters. He appears regularly in the Cayman Islands and the BVI.
Professional Memberships: Chancery Bar Association, COMBAR.
Career: Called 1980. Appointed Junior Counsel to the Crown (Chancery), February 1992. Appointed Junior Counsel to the Crown 'A' Panel, 1999. Appointed Queens Counsel, 2001. Accredited mediator, 2002. Called to the East Caribbean Bar, 2005.
Publications: Contributor to 'Mithani: Directors' Disqualification'.
Personal: Educated at Stonyhurst College and Magdalen College Oxford (BA History). Born 6 June 1956. Lives in Buckinghamshire.

CURSHAM, Georgina
Ropewalk Chambers, Nottingham
0115 9472581
georginacursham@ropewalk.co.uk
Featured in Personal Injury (Midlands)
Practice Areas: Georgina Cursham has a strong analytical approach and thorough attention to detail. She is regarded as being approachable with clients and witnesses, and is known for persuasive written and verbal submissions and effective cross-examination. She practises primarily in the field of personal injury, with a particular emphasis in equine litigation and other disputes involving animals. She has in-depth knowledge of the complex provisions of the Animals Act 1971 and associated case law. She has advised and represented parties in horse riding accidents on private premises and in equestrian schools; fatal animal attacks; road traffic incidents involving horses and livestock; dog bite claims; trespass; nuisance claims involving damage to, and caused by, livestock and disputes arising from farrier's work.
Professional Memberships: Personal Injuries Bar Association
Career: Called 2007 ; LLB (Graduate) 1st Class Honours, Nottingham Law School; MA (Oxon) Modern Languages, Pembroke College, Oxford.
Personal: Georgina had 8 years' commercial and public sector experience before coming to the Bar, including work as Accounts Manager for the Legal Services Commission, and commercial management in the banking recruitment sector and hospitality industry, managing a 4-star hotel in Central London. She is a competent French speaker.

CUTRESS, James
Fountain Court Chambers, London
020 7583 3335
jc@fountaincourt.co.uk
Featured in Aviation (London), Banking & Finance (London), Commercial Dispute Resolution (London), Insurance (London)
Practice Areas: Specialises in commercial litigation and arbitration, with particular expertise in banking and finance, insurance and reinsurance, aviation, fraud/asset recovery, jurisdiction and conflict of laws, professional negligence and international and domestic arbitration.
Professional Memberships: Commercial Bar Association, London Common Law and Commercial Bar Association.
Career: Called 2000.
Publications: Co-Author of The Law of Privilege (ed B. Thanki QC, OUP, 2nd edition 2011).
Personal: Worcester College Oxford, BA (top first), BCL (first class); Harvard Law School LLM (Kennedy Scholar); Eldon Scholar.

DAINTY, Cheryl
Kings Chambers, Manchester
0345 034 3444
clerks@kingschambers.com
Featured in Commercial Dispute Resolution (Northern)
Practice Areas: Commercial dispute resolution (wide range of disputes including contract issues, agency, sale of goods, factoring/invoice discounting, enforcement disputes and interim relief/injunctions), insolvency/asset recovery (corporate and personal, for office holders, creditors and debtors), banking and finance (including guarantees/indemnities and consumer credit), professional negligence, company (including share and asset purchase agreements, minority shareholder petitions and directors' disqualification), partnerships and LLPs, mortgages, land registration.
Professional Memberships: Chancery Bar Association, Northern Circuit Commercial Bar Association, Northern Chancery Bar Association, Northern and North Eastern Circuits.
Career: 2000 – 2004 BA (First Class Hons.) Law with Law Studies in Europe (German Law) (Corpus Christi College, Oxford); 2004-2007 Guest Lecturer (University of Wuerzburg and University of Bonn, Germany); 2005-2006 Masters of Comparative Law (with a focus on comparative commercial law) (University of Bonn, Germany); 2006 Called (Inner Temple); 2010 – Present Junior Counsel to the Crown (Provincial Panel).

DALE, Derrick QC
Fountain Court Chambers, London
020 7583 3335
dd@fountaincourt.co.uk
Featured in Professional Negligence (London), Banking & Finance (London), Commercial Dispute Resolution (London)
Practice Areas: A broad commercial and civil practice, specialising in: commercial litigation and arbitration; insurance and banking; professional negligence and civil fraud. Recent cases include acting for (i) a Zambian mine operator in a long running arbitration against a mine owner; (ii) for one of the big 4 accountancy firms in a professional negligence claim; (iii) various share warranty disputes; (iv) an investment house in relation to a dishonest agent misselling products and stealing proceeds; (v) advisers to a shipping company claiming a success fee in respect of an introduction; (vi) a major logistics company accused of breach of confidence in a competitive tender process; (vii) insurers in a claim for the return of profit commission from a broker; (viii) a middle eastern borrower against a major western bank in respect of the terms of an Islamic finance deal.
Professional Memberships: COMBAR.
Career: Called 1990. Called to NY Bar in 1989.
Publications: Derrick is the joint editor of the damages section in 'Simpson on Professional Negligence'.
Personal: DOB 1966. Emmanuel College, Cambridge (1st Class Hons Law 1988) and Harvard LLM (1989). His interests include marathon running and film noir.

DANIELS, Laura
Kings Chambers, Manchester
0345 034 3444
clerks@kingschambers.com
Featured in Employment (Northern)
Practice Areas: Employment, Personal Injury, Sports Law
Professional Memberships: Employment Lawyers Association
Career: Called 2009 Lincoln's Inn 2010-2011 Pupillage 3 Serjeants' Inn 2011-present Kings Chambers
Publications: What are the main maternity rights of a surrogate mother? Financial Times In sickness and in holiday ANGED v FASGA, Personnel Today Redman v Devon Primary Care Trust case review, People Management Magazine Life-long medical condition or disability? Sussex Partnership NHS Foundation Trust v Norris, People Management Magazine Common sense over sensitivity? Heafield v Times Newspaper Ltd, People Management Magazine Permanent health insurance payments and age discrimination Witham v Capita Insurance Service Limited, People Management Magazine Review of TUPE Changes, Manchester Evening News 'A Practical Introduction to Employment Law' CPDCast: http://bit.ly/13fr7XV

DARBY, Jonathan
39 Essex Chambers, London
020 7832 1111
jon.darby@39essex.com
Featured in Planning (London)
Practice Areas: Jonathan advises and acts for developers, consultants, local authorities, interest groups and private clients on all aspects of the planning process, including planning enforcement (both inquiries and criminal proceedings), planning appeals and prosecutions under the Environmental Protection Act 1990. Jonathan's wider public law practice provides him with a particular expertise in statutory challenges and applications for judicial review, in relation to which he has acted for claimants, defendants and interested parties. Recent cases of note include appearing as sole counsel for the Appellant in Turner v SSCLG [2015] EWHC 375 (Admin) in an appeal concerning an Inspector's conduct of an Inquiry in relation to a significant scheme on the site surrounding the Shell Tower on the South Bank. Jonathan also successfully appeared alongside Paul Stinchcombe QC in Tesco v Forest of Dean [2015] EWCA Civ 800 in an appeal considering an important point of legal principle concerning the proper application of the CIL Regulations to a Section 106 Obligation offered to mitigate the retail impact on an affected town centre and in circumstances where neither the Respondent nor any other Interested Party appeared to resist the appeal.
Publications: Jonathan is the co-editor of Sweet & Maxwell's Planning Law: Practice and Precedents.

D'ARCY, Eleanor
Kings Chambers, Leeds
0345 034 3444
clerks@kingschambers.com
Featured in Chancery (Northern), Restructuring/Insolvency (North Eastern)
Practice Areas: Chancery and Commercial Litigation; Insolvency – corporate and individual; Commercial Contracts; Company Law; Financial (especially guarantees and recoveries), Property (both real and commercial) and Professional Negligence arising within those areas.
Professional Memberships: Chancery Bar Association, Northern Chancery Bar Association, Northern Circuit Commercial Bar Association, R3 Yorkshire Women in Business Recovery Group (Committee Member).
Career: MA Classics, St. John's College, Oxford; Called: 2008 (Lincoln's Inn); Lord Haldane, Lord Denning and Wolfson Scholar.

DARLING, Paul QC
Keating Chambers, London
020 75442600
pdarling@keatingchambers.com
Featured in International Arbitration (London), Professional Negligence (London), Construction (London)

Practice Areas: Wide ranging expertise in the fields of construction, engineering, procurement, energy and commercial litigation, with a formidable reputation as an advocate in all types and levels of tribunals all over the world. Well known for his advocacy skills and in particular for cross-examining and arguing appeals. Has considerable experience of leading large teams in long and heavy cases. Regularly advises on both non-contentious and contentious aspects of bespoke and standard terms of Building and Engineering Contracts. Places particular emphasis on his commercial instincts and skills. Reputation as an advocate means that he is often instructed in areas of work outside of Chambers' case work, such as Sports, Sale of Goods and Bloodstock. Over sixty of his cases have been reported.
Professional Memberships: TECBAR; SCL (Member of Council 1999 to 2001); LCLCBA; PNBA; COMBAR.
Career: Called 1983; QC 1999; Bencher Middle Temple 2004; Construction Silk of The Year 2006; Head of Keating Chambers 2010-2015.
Publications: Editorial Team, Keating on Construction Contracts – 8th Edition; Editorial Team, Keating on Building Contracts, 5th, 6th and 7th editions; Formerly Joint Editor, Construction Industry Law Letter.

DARTON, Clifford
Ely Place Chambers, London
020 7400 9600
cdarton@elyplace.com
Featured in Real Estate Litigation (London)

Practice Areas: Property, Chancery and Environmental Regulation
Professional Memberships: Chancery Bar Association Property Bar Association
Career: A commercial litigator specialising in property and property related disputes, with a niche practice in Water Law and environmental pollution. He is one of only a few practitioners with extensive knowledge of the environmental permitting regulations; see R v SWS (2014) EWCA. Previous publications have described him as a "razor sharp intellect" and "one of those rare advocates who is as strong on his feet as in drafting advice and pleadings". Clifford has appeared in over 40 reported decisions of which some of the most recent are MWB v Rock Advertising [2016] EWCA (anti-oral variation clauses and consideration by part-payment of existing debt), Hniazdzilau v Zlot [2016] EWHC (3 week trial of trust claim to a $6 billion property in Minsk) and Eddery v Hogg [2015] EWHC (successful appeal against summary judgment on contract for sale of land). He frequently acts in mortgage related proceedings and appeared in the Court of Appeal cases of Green King v Stanley [2002] B.P.I.R, Johnson v EBS Trustees [2002] Lloyds Rep and Earp v. Kurd (2014) EWCA. He is presently instructed in a number of claims arising out of the payment of undisclosed commission to mortgage brokers; see CFB Ltd v. Atkins [2013] EWCA.
Publications: "Trusts & the Law of Illegality" : OUP Trusts & Trustees Journal, April 2016 "In Deep Water" : New Law Journal (2014) Vol.164
Personal:

DARWIN, Claire
Matrix Chambers, London
020 7404 3447
clairedarwin@matrixlaw.co.uk
Featured in Education (London), Employment (London)

Practice Areas: Claire Darwin is a senior junior who specialises in Employment, Discrimination and Education Law, and undertakes work in the related fields of Public, EU, and Commercial Law. She has been consistently recognised as a leading specialist in Chambers & Partners since 2009. Claire has appeared in over 20 full appeals in the Employment Appeal Tribunal, both led and unled in the Court of Appeal, and as junior counsel in two matters before the European Court of Human Rights. She is one of the Attorney General's Junior Counsel to the Crown (B Panel), a small panel of barristers appointed to advise and represent the UK government in civil cases in England and Wales.
Career: June 2015 – Appointed to the Attorney General's Junior Counsel to the Crown (B Panel); February 2013 – Appointed to the Attorney General's Junior Counsel to the Crown (C Panel).
Publications: Co-author of the chapter on Discrimination in Employment in Bullen & Leake & Jacob's Precedents of Pleadings, 18th edition; Editor of PLC's Guide to Discrimination in the Provision of Goods and Services; Contributing Editor of the Education Law Journal from 2012-5. Procedural Fairness on Appeal: Is O'Cathail No Longer Good Law?, Industrial Law Journal, September 2016.

DASHWOOD, Alan QC
Henderson Chambers, London
020 7583 9020
adashwood@hendersonchambers.co.uk
Featured in Competition/European Law (London)

Practice Areas: The Law of the European Union and more particularly: all aspects of EU internal market regulation, including product liability, and public procurement; competition law, including State aid; the interface between EU law and intellectual property law, including in the WTO context; the interface between EU law and the law relating to foreign direct investment; age and sex discrimination, the Working Time Directive and other EU-related aspects of employment law; all aspects of the law of EU external action, including trade, development co-operation and foreign, security and defence policy; EU anti- terrorism measures; the European Arrest Warrant and other EU Measures in the area of freedom security and justice; the Brussels 1 Regulation and the New Lugano Agreement.
Career: Called to the Bar 1969, entered private practice in 1997. Bencher, Inner Temple 2002. Appointed QC 2010. Previously,(1995-2009) Professor of European Law at Cambridge, now Emeritus; (1987-1994) Director in the Legal Service of the Council of the EU, providing extensive experience of the EU Legislative process and of litigation in the CJEU. Professor (part-time) City University (2012). Appointed CBE in 2004 and KCMG in 2013.
Publications: Previously, Editor, Common Market Law Review and European Law Review. Co-author, Wyatt and Dashwood's European Union Law (6th ed). Co-editor, and principal contributor, The Future of the Judicial System of the European Union. Co-editor, and contributor, 'EU External Relations: Law and Practice.' Contributor to the Bar European Group's Practitioners' Handbook of EC Law.

DAVIDSON, Nicholas QC
4 New Square, London
020 7822 2000
n.davidson@4newsquare.com
Featured in Professional Negligence (London)

Practice Areas: Professional liability (particularly lawyers', investment managers/advisers' and financial services liability). Insurance (including professional liability cover) and general commercial cases, including corporate governance and computer litigation. Recently acted for the National Union of Mineworkers in its successful claim against Mr Arthur Scargill, and for Newcastle Airport in claims against executive directors and solicitors arising out of bonus payments; acting in swaps claims.
Professional Memberships: Professional Negligence Bar Association (Chairman 1997-99), British Insurance Law Association, Financial Services Law Association, Bar European Group, COMBAR, Chancery Bar Association, Society for Computers and Law; Member of the Chartered Institute of Arbitrators.
Career: Called 1974; joined present chambers 1999. Silk 1993. Deputy High Court Judge.
Publications: Contributor to Professional Negligence and Liability (ed. Simpson) (Informa, 2000).
Personal: Educated at Winchester 1964-69 (Scholar) and Trinity College Cambridge (Exhibitioner in Economics) 1969-72. Certificate of Honour, Bar Finals. Is a trustee of a defined benefit pension scheme.

DAVIDSON, Ranald
Serjeants' Inn Chambers, London
020 7427 5000
RDavidson@serjeantsinn.com
Featured in Clinical Negligence (London)

Practice Areas: Ranald Davidson was called to the Bar in 1996. Ranald specialises in clinical negligence and healthcare, professional discipline and regulatory, inquests and inquiries and public and administrative law. An earlier edition notes that "he's methodical, knowledgeable and meticulous. Extremely good on his feet, he has a very nice manner in court, which is very reassuring for the clients" and that he is "an approachable barrister, who is down to earth, responsive and sensible." Please visit the Serjeants' Inn Chambers website for his profile, which sets out full details of his practice including relevant work of note.
Professional Memberships: Professional Negligence Bar Association, Association of Disciplinary and Regulatory Lawyers.
Publications: Consultant Editor Medical Law Reports; Contributor to forthcoming Atkins Sports Law text.

DAVIES, Edward
Erskine Chambers, London
020 7242 5524
edavies@erskinechambers.com
Featured in Company (London)

Practice Areas: Edward is a specialist in company, commercial and corporate insolvency law. Recent cases: BAT Industries plc v Sequana S.A. [2016] EWHC 1686 (Ch) (unlawful dividends); Bhullar v Bhullar [2015] EWHC 1943 (Ch) (double derivative claim); Hewlett Packard and Autonomy v Lynch [2015] (breach of fiduciary duty); Granada Group Ltd v Law Debenture Trust [2015] EWHC 1499 (Ch) (challenges to security taken by former ITV directors); Hollis v Marylebone Cricket Club [2013] EWHC 3547 (QB) (application for an injunction to restrain the holding of a general meeting); Rothschild v Bumi Plc [2013] (unfair prejudice proceedings involving FTSE-listed mining conglomerate); Re Coroin Ltd [2012] EWHC 2343 (Ch) (unfair prejudice and conspiracy claims concerning steps taken by Barclay brothers to take control of Claridge's, The Connaught and The Berkeley); Thomas v Jakes [2011] EWHC 2619 (Ch) (application to commit a company director for contempt of court); Michael Wilson & Partners Ltd v Emmott [2011] EWHC 1441 (Comm) (challenge to an arbitration award under s68 and s69 of the Arbitration Act 1996).
Professional Memberships: COMBAR. Chancery Bar Association.
Career: Called 1998.
Publications: Company Directors: Law and Liability; Practical Law Company: Freezing injunctions case study.
Personal: Interests: Rugby, long distance running and birdwatching.

DAVIES, George
Temple Garden Chambers, London
020 7583 1315
gd@tgchambers.com
Featured in Fraud (All Circuits)

Practice Areas: George Davies has extensive experience of defending fraudulently induced, contrived and exaggerated insurance claims whether they arise from opportunism or are the product of sophisticated fraud rings. He also has had wide exposure to defending sham credit hire and LVI claims. His work covers all stages of litigation, from advising pre-issue to drafting pleadings and includes advocacy up to the level of the Court of Appeal. His experience of civil fraud proceedings includes the successful pursuit and continuance of freezing injunctions as well as full-blown contempt proceedings in the High Court. His recent Court of Appeal experience includes Ali v D'Brass [2011] EWCA Civ 1594.
Professional Memberships: PIBA, CBA, LCLCBA
Career: Called: 1998, Admitted as Solicitor: 2002, Temple Garden Chambers: 2005 to date.
Personal: Interests include canine pursuits, running, hiking, history, family and the dramatic arts.

DAVIES, Huw QC
Essex Court Chambers, London
020 7813 8000
hdavies@essexcourt.com
Featured in Commercial Dispute Resolution (London)

Practice Areas: Huw Davies QC is a member of Essex Court Chambers. He has a specialist practice as an advocate and arbitrator in substantial international and domestic commercial disputes. He appears regularly at all levels in the courts in the UK, as well as offshore, and has appeared in many international arbitrations both in London and worldwide (including ICC, LCIA, LMAA, Stockholm CC, UNCITRAL and ad hoc). He has particular experience of appear-

ing as an advocate before the Privy Council. He has extensive experience of disputes in the following fields: aviation, banking, civil/commercial fraud and cross border asset recovery, anti-suit injunctions and applications for asset freezing relief, insurance and reinsurance, oil and gas, international trade in all types of commodities, shipbuilding, shareholder disputes, jurisdiction disputes (court and arbitration) and arbitration related court applications. He is noted as having "an incredibly impressive style and approach", being "very user friendly" and as being a "very effective cross examiner." He sits as an arbitrator in domestic and international arbitrations and he is also a CEDR accredited mediator.
Career: 1984 – LLB (First Class Hons), University College, Cardiff; 1985 – Called to the Bar (Gray's Inn); Bacon Scholar of Gray's Inn; 1986 – Joined One Crown Office Row; 1991 – Joined Essex Court Chambers; 2006 – Queen's Counsel; 2008 – Admitted to Courts of the DIFC; 2009 – Called to the Bar of Gibraltar

DAVIES, Jonathan
Serjeants' Inn Chambers, London
020 7427 5000
jdavies@serjeantsinn.com
Featured in Employment (London)
Practice Areas: Jonathan Davies was called to the Bar in 2003. Jonathan specialises in employment law, professional discipline and police law. An earlier edition notes that "He has good technical ability, and is cool and calculated when cross-examining," he is also "an experienced employment law adviser, with respondents stressing the high quality of his advocacy and exceptional client service." Please visit the Serjeants' Inn Chambers website for his profile, which sets out full details of her practice including relevant work of note.

DAVIES EVANS, Jane
Crown Office Chambers, London
020 7797 6221
davies_evans@crownofficechambers.com
Featured in Construction (London)
Practice Areas: Jane acts as counsel in international arbitrations, pre-arbitral and court proceedings in support of international arbitration, focusing on energy disputes, engineering (oil and gas, power generation, mining and natural resources) and major infrastructure projects. Jane also advises clients on contracting strategy for major projects, assisting with contract drafting and negotiations, and has advised extensively in relation to the impact of international sanctions on EPC projects. Jane is particularly recognised for her skilled cross examination of expert witnesses, and arguing disputes involving complex issues of quantum, financing, delay and disruption. She is frequently instructed on matters where amounts in dispute are in the US$100 millions. Jane's practice is almost exclusively international. She has particular experience in disputes across Africa, the Russian Federation and CIS, the Middle East and Latin America.
Professional Memberships: IBA; ICCA; SCL; COMBAR; TECBAR; ABA; Oil and Gas UK; Institute of Chartered Accountants of England & Wales (Fellow); Chartered Institute of Arbitrators (Fellow); Dispute Board Federation (Fellow);
Career: Prior to returning to the Bar in 2014, Jane spent many years working in the international arbitration practices of two of the world's leading law firms: Freshfields Bruckhaus Deringer LLP and Shearman & Sterling LLP in Paris, Abu Dhabi and London. A jointly qualified barrister and experienced Chartered Accountant in England & Wales, Jane worked in the expert witness team at PricewaterhouseCoopers from 1985 to 1990. Jane lectures on the Masters programmes for International Construction Law at Stuttgart University and University West of England, and the Construction Law Summer School, Cambridge.
Publications: International Construction Arbitration (Chapter on Investment Treaty Arbitration); Emden's Construction Law (Arbitration); Construction Law International (Managing editor)

DAVIS, Adam QC
3 Temple Gardens, London
20 7353 3102
adqc@3tg.co.uk
Featured in Crime (London)
Practice Areas: Adam Davis QC has represented high-profile defendants such as Matthew Simmons in the "Cantona" case, Wayne Lineker and the Croydon Furniture Fire Case and prosecuted the eBay counterfeit golf club case. As a QC, he defends in serious and complex cases and is instructed by a number of different Solicitors, whilst continuing an outstanding reputation as a White Collar Fraud Specialist. In 2016, He defended Clayton Williams, who was charged with the Murder of PC David Phillips, a case that attracted significant national press coverage. The trial judge said that he conducted the case "with skill and expertise" and had "done everything he possibly could" to present his client's case. He has appeared as an advocate in front of the British Boxing Board of Control, the Football League and FA tribunals. He regularly advises Professional Athletes including current European Tour Golfers and Sports Management companies. He sits as a Chairman on the "Very High Cost Cases Appeals Committee" and also undertakes single adjudicator appeals. He is an Independent Funding and Cost Assessor to the New Legal Aid Agency. He advises and lectures companies on Money Laundering and Bribery matters. He continues to act as Legal Adviser and Board Member for the Pro Touch Soccer Academy, a community based football organization and a Trustee on the Hadley Wood Sports Trust responsible for a new football facility in Barnet. He is a Non-Executive Director of Places For People PLC one of the largest residential property development, management and regeneration companies in the UK and a Board Member of a religious organisation.
Professional Memberships: Criminal Bar Association, Central Criminal Court Bar Mess, South Eastern Circuit.
Career: Called 1985. QC 2012
Publications: Employment Lawyers Association Briefing. Volume 11 Number 10 December 2004 (Money Laundering and the Proceeds of Crime)
Personal: Voluntary work as adviser and board director for the Pro Touch Soccer Academy. Leisure interests include Football, Golf, Cricket and Tennis.

DAVIS, Glen QC
South Square, London
020 7696 9900
glendavis@southsquare.com
Featured in Restructuring/Insolvency (London)
Practice Areas: Glen specialises in domestic and cross-border insolvency and restructuring, and in commercial disputes complicated by insolvency. His contentious and advisory commercial practice extends to banking and financial services, insurance, shipping, company and partnership disputes, civil fraud and professional negligence.
Professional Memberships: Chartered Institute of Arbitrators (MCIArb), Fellow of the Association of Business Recovery Professionals, Fellow of the Society for Computers & Law, COMBAR (Chair, Africa Committee, 2007-; Executive, 2013-15), Insolvency Lawyers' Association, INSOL Europe.
Career: Called 1992; QC 2011. CEDR-accredited Mediator 1998; called to the Bar of Gibraltar 2013; called to the Bar of the Eastern Caribbean Supreme Court 2014; licensed to appear in the courts of the Dubai International Financial Centre 2014; appointed to the Guernsey Financial Services Commission's Panel of Senior Decision Makers 2015; appointed to INSOL International College of Mediation (IICM) Panel 2015.
Publications: Editor, Butterworths Insolvency Law Handbook (since 1997); Insolvent Partnerships (1996); contributor to Company Directors: Duties, Liabilities and Remedies (OUP, 2nd ed, 2013).

DAVISON, Eleanor
Fountain Court Chambers, London
020 7583 3335
eld@fountaincourt.co.uk
Featured in Financial Services (London), Financial Crime (London)
Practice Areas: All areas of commercial crime, financial services and commercial law. Advises on all aspects of cross border corporate investigations and acts for individuals in criminal and regulatory matters. Specialises in cases concerning bribery and corruption, fraud, money laundering and all aspects of financial crime compliance. Recent cases include: the Barclays Qatar investigation, the global Libor investigation and the Forex investigation and an FCA AML investigation.
Professional Memberships: FLA, FSLA.
Career: Called to the Bar 2003. Educated at Warwick University and Bristol University. Lord Denning scholarship (Lincoln's Inn). Thomas More scholarship (Lincoln's Inn). Peter Duffy scholarship (Lincoln's Inn) Member of Fountain Court Chambers since 2016.
Publications: Co editor of the forthcoming Practitioner's Guide to Global Investigations. Contributor to Lissack and Horlick on Bribery.

DAVY, Neil
Serjeants' Inn Chambers, London
020 7427 5000
ndavy@serjantsinn.com
Featured in Clinical Negligence (London)
Practice Areas: Neil Davy was called to the Bar in 2000. Neil specialises in clinical negligence, employment, professional discipline and regulatory law. An earlier edition notes that "he is an impressively tough negotiator" and that he is "brilliant with paperwork and excellent at complex, unusual cases which require lateral thinking." Please visit the Serjeants' Inn Chambers website for his profile, which sets out full details of his practice including relevant work of note.
Professional Memberships: Professional Negligence Bar Association, London Common Law and Commercial Bar Association.

DAWSON, Adam
9 Gough Square, London
020 7832 0500
clerks@9goughsquare.co.uk
Featured in Personal Injury (London)
Practice Areas: Adam practices in all aspects of Personal Injury Litigation. He has a great reputation for his ability to put clients at ease, providing clear advice in a sensitive and effective way. Adam is tough court room advocate fighting hard for the best interests of his clients. Adam's varied practice this year has included: claim for PTSD following witnesses to the aftermath of a suicide; a significant six figure claim for future loss of earnings following a serious RTA; complex causation/liability case following the death of a client on board a cruise ship and many other six figures claims (RTA's or Accidents at Work).
Professional Memberships: Adam is a member of APIL.
Career: University of Leeds (LLB Hons) 1995-1998; Inns of Court School of Law 1999-2000 (BVC) (Queen Mother Scholar); 199 Strand 2000-2005 and 9 Gough Square 2005-date.
Publications: Co – Author of: (a)'A Practical guide to Clinical Negligence" (1st-3rd edn) 9 Gough Square; and (b) "Road Traffic Claims, Liability", Jordans.
Personal: Adam lives in North West London with his wife and three young (and energetic) children. He is the Founder and Chair of Governors of a Primary School. Adam enjoys football and tennis (when he gets the time!)

DAY, Andrew
St Ives Chambers, Birmingham
01212360863
andrew.day@stiveschambers.co.uk
Featured in Family/Matrimonial (Midlands)
Practice Areas: Family Finance
Professional Memberships: Family Law Bar Association, Resolution, Midland Circuit, Birmingham Law Society
Career: Andrew Day is an established family law specialist with extensive experience of dealing with financial and property disputes between married and unmarried partners, including particularly cases of significant legal or factual complexity, and high net worth, at first instance and on appeal, in the Family Court and in the High Court. He has a particular interest in applications for financial relief linked to, and family and property law issues arising in connection with, confiscation proceedings under both the Proceeds of Crime Act 2002 and earlier statutory regimes. Andrew's cases often involve, for example, the alleged concealment or dissipation of assets; nuptial agreements; significant pre-acquired, inherited or other non-matrimonial wealth; farming assets; businesses large and small; complex and valuable public service, Armed Forces or self-invested pensions; on- and off-shore trusts; jurisdictional issues; and substantial assets overseas.

DAY, Anneliese QC
4 New Square, London
020 7822 2000
a.day@4newsquare.com
Featured in Professional Negligence (London), Commercial Dispute Resolution (London), Construction (London), Insurance (London)

Practice Areas: Extensive experience of both domestic and international litigation in the commercial, construction, professional liability and insurance spheres. Won the prestigious Barrister of the Year Award by The Lawyer in 2014 due to her "extraordinary talent", eloquency and ability to explain complex issues to lay clients. A firm believer in seeking to bring added value to any case whatever her role. Thrives on the cut and thrust of advocacy but also brings commerciality to the issues she deals with.

Professional Memberships: COMBAR, SCL, TECBAR, PNBA, ChBA.

Career: MA (Cantab). Kennedy Scholar. Called to Bar (Inner Temple) 1996 (Princess Royal Scholarship). Joined 4 New Square in 1997. Appointed to Treasury B Panel in 2005. Took silk in 2012. Appointed Non Executive Director of Legal Services Board from 1 April 2013. Became "Barrister of the Year" in The Lawyer 2014 Awards. Listed as one of the 500 most influential people in the UK by Debretts in 2015.

Publications: Editor of 'Jackson and Powell on Professional Negligence' and contributor to 'Civil Practice and Human Rights'.

Personal: Educated at the Edinburgh Academy, Clare College, Cambridge and Harvard University. Leisure interests: travel and bikram yoga. Speaks French and Spanish.

D'CRUZ, Rufus
Red Lion Chambers, London
020 7520 6000
chambers@18rlc.co.uk
Featured in Crime (London)

Practice Areas: Rufus D'Cruz is an experienced leading junior who is instructed to prosecute and defend in serious, multi-handed criminal and regulatory work. He specialises in complex fraud, including VAT, film tax credit, e-banking, corporate and mortgage fraud. He has particular expertise in money laundering, large-scale drugs offences and multi-million pound confiscation proceedings. In addition to financial crime, Rufus has extensive experience in prosecuting and defending cases of murder and significant experience and expertise in regulatory work, including Health and Safety offences, Environment Agency prosecutions and BIS prosecutions. He is particularly adept and experienced at representing and advising corporate clients, in relation to Health and Safety offences, Environment Agency offences, money laundering matters, production orders relating to special procedure material/LPP and in relation to corporate fraud. RUSSIA: Rufus has particular expertise, experience and insight in representing and advising clients based in Russia and the FSU, having studied Russian at university and lectured in Russia over many years. He has been instructed to advise clients in relation to the alternative criminal/regulatory remedies available to clients engaged in commercial litigation, in civil fraud cases involving allegations of unlawful enrichment and share dilution schemes. He brings to this work a unique combination of proficiency in the language, knowledge of the political and economic context and his experience of the interplay between commercial and criminal/regulatory remedies. He is a member of the British-Russian Law Association. Rufus has lectured on money laundering, confiscation, corporate manslaughter and cartel offences.

Professional Memberships: Bar Human Rights Committee; Criminal Bar Association; Liberty.

Career: 1991 – BA Hons, Russian, Birmingham; 1993 – Called to the Bar, Lincoln's Inn.

DE BONO, John QC
Serjeants' Inn Chambers, London
020 74 275 000
jdebono@serjeantsinn.com
Featured in Police Law (All Circuits), Clinical Negligence (London)

Practice Areas: John de Bono QC was called to the Bar in 1995 and took silk in 2014. John specialises in clinical negligence and healthcare, inquests and inquiries, professional discipline, product liability, public and administrative and police law. An earlier edition notes that "he is highly rated by market sources for the combination of his strong intellect and his approachable nature" and "he is an incredibly gutsy fighter and a great strategist." John believes passionately in working with solicitors and clients as part of a team. He positively thrives on solicitors phoning to discuss any aspect of any case at any time. Please visit the Serjeants' Inn Chambers website for his profile, which sets out full details of his practice including relevant work of note.

Professional Memberships: PNBA.

Career: John is a clinical negligence specialist, regularly instructed by claimants and defendants (50/50) in cases of the highest value and greatest complexity, often against silks. Cases include cerebral palsy, wrongful birth, brain injury and spinal injury. He has a special interest in mental health and was counsel to the Broadmoor Inquiry, 2005-08, chaired by Robert Francis QC. John was invited to speak at the 2012 AVMA conference. He runs the 3SI/ Oxford Neurosurgery Medical Law Conference at Wadham College, Oxford each year. In police law John regularly presents police misconduct cases, sits as a legal adviser and acts for police forces in judicial reviews.

Publications: Various articles in legal and medical journals.

DE GARR ROBINSON, Anthony QC
One Essex Court, London
020 7583 2000
arobinson@oeclaw.co.uk

Practice Areas: Practice covers an unusually broad range of commercial and chancery specialisations, including corporate litigation, investment disputes and complex commercial cases of every kind. Has considerable experience of international litigation, including jurisdictional disputes and cross border asset tracing, and frequently acts in international arbitrations. Has acted as an English law expert in proceedings in several jurisdictions. Sits as an arbitrator.

Professional Memberships: Chancery Bar Association, Commercial Bar Association and Commercial Fraud Lawyers Association. He has been called to the Bar in the BVI and The Bahamas and is registered as an advocate in the Dubai International Financial Centre Courts.

Career: Educated at University College, Oxford (Open Scholar and Gibbs Prize winner) and Harvard University (Kennedy Scholar). Called to the English Bar in 1987 (Denning Scholar and Hardwicke Scholar); took Silk in 2006.

Publications: 'The Legal Labyrinths of Leverage' (Legal Week, 16th July 2009); 'Wrotham Park damages' (Commercial Litigation Journal, January 2008).

DE MESTRE, Andrew
4 Stone Buildings, London
020 7242 5524
a.dm@4stonebuildings.com
Featured in Chancery (London), Fraud (London), Restructuring/Insolvency (London)

Practice Areas: Commercial litigation and arbitration with particular emphasis on civil fraud and asset recovery; financial services and banking including CMBS and other securitisation disputes; insolvency and company law including proceedings under the Insolvency Act 1986, directors duties, unfair prejudice petitions and other shareholder disputes. Recent cases include; BNY Mellon Corporate Trustee Services Ltd v LBG Capital No.1 Plc [2016] UKSC 29; Hosking v Apax Partners LLP [2016] EWHC 782; Playboy Club London v BNL SA [2016] EWCA Civ 457; Credit Suisse Asset Management v Titan Europe 2006 – 1 Plc [2016] EWHC 969; Re Taberna Europe CDO I Plc [2016] EWHC 781; Re Windermere VII CMBS Plc [2016] EWHC 782; Knighthead Master Fund LP v Bank of New York Mellon [2015] EWHC 270; Global Energy Horizons Corp v Gray [2014] EWHC 2925 and [2015] EWHC 2232, 3275; Grupo Hotelero Urvasco v Carey Value Added [2013] EWHC 1039, 1732; Milsom & Ors v Ablyazov [2013] EWHC 1361 and [2011] EWHC 955, 1846.

Professional Memberships: Commercial Bar Association, Chancery Bar Association.

Career: Queen Mother Scholar of Middle Temple. Called March 1998. Joined 4 Stone Buildings in October 1998.

Publications: Contributor to OUP's 'Annotated Companies Acts'; Butterworths Journal of International Banking & Finance Law.

Personal: Educated at Sherborne School, Dorset and Magdalene College, Cambridge (MA).

DE NAVARRO, Michael QC
2TG – 2 Temple Gardens, London
020 7822 1200
clerks@2tg.co.uk
Featured in Clinical Negligence (London)

Practice Areas: Personal injury, clinical and professional negligence, insurance and health and safety at work.

Professional Memberships: PIBA (Committee member 1995, Chairman 1997-99). Western Circuit.

Career: Reported clinical negligence cases include Hamed v Dr Mills and ors [2015] EWHC 298 (QB), R v RNOH [2012] EWHC 492 (QB), Notts CC v Bottomley and anor [2010] EWCA Civ 756, Knight v South Essex Health Authority [2008], Whiston v London SHA [2010] EWCA Civ 195 CJL v West Midlands Strategic Health Authority [2009], Antoniades v East Sussex Hospitals NHS Trust [2007], Cowley v Cheshire and Merseyside Strategic Health Authority [2006], YM v Gloucestershire NHS Foundation Trust [2006], Macey v Warwickshire HA [2004], Page v Plymouth Hospitals NHS Trust [2004], Royal Victoria Infirmary v B [2002]. Reported personal injury cases include Adams v SEB [1993] (CA), Green v Building Scene [1994] (CA), O'Shea v Kingston-upon-Thames [1995] (CA), Hunter v Butler [1995] (CA), Jolley v LB of Sutton [1998] (CA), [2001] (HL). Other reported cases include Wentworth v Wiltshire CC [1992] (CA), Nykredit Mortgage Bank v Edward Erdman [1996] (HL), John Monroe (Acrylics) v LFCDA [1997] (CA), Day v Cook [2000], Miller v Hales [2006] and Smith v Skanska Construction Services Ltd [2008]. Called 1968, QC 1990. Bencher Inner Temple 2000.

Personal: Born 1944; resides Broadway.

DE VERNEUIL SMITH, Peter
3 Verulam Buildings, London
020 7831 8441
pdv@3vb.com
Featured in Chancery (London), Commercial Dispute Resolution (London), Fraud (London)

Practice Areas: Commercial litigation (with an expertise relating to fund litigation such as the leading decision in Titan Europe v Colliers [2016] PNLR 7), banking litigation (senior junior for the SG Group in the £4bn RBS Rights Issue Litigation which has a 6 month trial listed for 2017), company litigation (in particular unfair prejudice and derivative actions), commercial fraud (junior counsel for the Swiss bank in a €100 million fraud matter Group 7 v Nasir and sole counsel in the leading COA decision of NML Capital v Chapman [2013] EWCA Civ 589), international projects (arbitration and ancillary court relief), conflicts of laws, insurance/reinsurance and professional negligence (in particular claims by banks against valuers).

Professional Memberships: COMBAR, LCIA, fellow of CIARB, TECBAR, INSOL, IBA, CFLA and PNBA.

Career: Called to the Bar in 1998.

Publications: Contributor to Paget's Law of Banking (14th edition).

Personal: Queen Elizabeth School Guernsey, Selwyn College Cambridge.

DEACON, Emma QC
5 Paper Buildings, London
020 7583 6117
ED@5pb.co.uk
Featured in Financial Crime (London)

Practice Areas: A specialist in complex fraud and financial crime, corruption and organised crime. Currently instructed by the SFO in prosecutions alleging manipulation of the Libor and Euribor benchmark interest rates, and by CPS Specialist Fraud Division in cases involving complex tax evasion schemes and pension liberation fraud. Regularly instructed by BIS in matters involving fraudulent conduct in respect of companies.

Professional Memberships: Criminal Bar Association, South Eastern Circuit

Career: Called to the bar 1993 (Inner Temple), Recorder of the Crown Court

Personal:

DEAN, Jacob
5RB, London
020 7242 2902
jacobdean@5rb.com
Featured in Defamation/Privacy (London), Sports Law (London)

Practice Areas: Media and information law, with particular emphasis on defamation, privacy and data protection. Sports Law. See www.5rb.com for further details.

Career: Recent highlights include C (A Child) [2016] EWCA Civ 798 (reporting family proceedings) Appleton v Gallagher, ex p News Group Newspapers Ltd [2015] EWHC 2689 (Fam) (reporting family proceedings), Horan v Express Newspapers Ltd [2015] EWHC 3550 (defamatory meaning and serious harm), Rhodes v OPO [2015] UKSC 32 (autobiography right, Wilkinson v Downton), Levi v Bates [2015] EWCA Civ 206 (harassment), YXB v TNO [2015] EWHC 826 (privacy injunction and non-disclosure). Currently involved in several cases exploring the new serious harm test in s.1 Defamation Act 2013, particularly in relation to corporate claimants. Extensive experience in acting for and against public authorities, particularly police forces, with several ongoing claims under the Data Protection Act.

DEAN, Paul J
St Philips Chambers, Birmingham
0121 246 2092
pdean@st-philips.com
Featured in Partnership (Midlands)

Practice Areas: Specialisms: insolvency, banking and partnership. Practises from Birmingham and London. Recent insolvency cases include: Re Husky Group Ltd [2015] BPIR 184 (proving solvency with hindsight), Re Brown Bear Foods Ltd [2014] EWHC 1132 (Ch) (provisional liquidation instead of administration), Re Reflex Recordings Ltd [2013] EWHC 4514 (Ch) (costs – freezing injunction and administration order), and Re Safehosts (London) Ltd [2013] EWHC 2479 (Ch), [2013] BCC 721 (provisional liquidation instead of administration). Recent banking cases include: Nautch Ltd v Mortgage Express and Walker Singleton (Property Management) Ltd [2012] EWHC 4136 (Ch) (LPA receivers, equitable duty to borrower and global costs order), and Earles v Barclays Bank plc [2010] Bus LR 566 (electronic disclosure and costs). Other cases include: Wemyss v Karim and Douglas Wemyss LLP [2014] EWHC 292 (QB) (warranty/indemnity claim), Hamed v Stevens [2013] EWCA Civ 911 (conflicts of laws – foreign land), and Chahal v Mahal [2005] EWCA Civ 898 (partnership dissolution date).
Professional Memberships: MCCBA. Birmingham Law Society.
Career: Whitgift School. BSc Hons (1st class): 1991. PGDL: 1992-93. LPC (Commendation): 1993-94. Solicitor (Eversheds): 1996. Solicitor Advocate (civil): 2001. Called: 2001. Tenant 2002.

DEIN, Jeremy QC
25 Bedford Row, London
07813 682709
jdein@25bedfordrow.com
Featured in Crime (London)

Practice Areas: Huge experience in defending the gravest, most serious, complex and high-profile cases. Including some of the most significant criminal trials of our time. Unrivalled involvement in homicide cases at the Central Criminal Court. Also defends in serious sex, organised crime and private crime. Particular interest in appellate work.
Career: Called 1982, Silk 2003, Sexual offences ticketed Recorder 2004, Judical College Course tutor 2012, Old Bailey recorder 2015. Former CBA Director of Education. Has written and lectured in Uk and abroad, most recently in: Florida, Delhi, Seoul (South Korea), Hong Kong (Chinese University). Joint Head of Chambers, Head of Crime Group, 25 Bedford Row.
Personal: Well Known criminal justice commentator: BBC, LBC, Talk radio.

DELAHUNTY, Jo QC
4 Paper Buildings, London
020 7427 5200
jd@4pb.com
Featured in Family/Matrimonial (London)

Practice Areas: Jo is a pre-eminent children's law family silk recently returned to the Family Division after acting for bereaved families in the Hillsborough Inquests.Jo has a reputation for fearlesss advocacy allied with formidable tactical trial management. Jo case specialisms are; ISIS radicalism allegations, dead infant/ catastrophic injury (TRIAD/ NAHI), FII, sex abuse to or by learning disabled/ vulnerable persons, intergenerational/ inter-sibing sex abuse. Jo was lead counsel for the mother in the landmark TRIAD/Vit D/ rickets case of Islington v Al Alas (2012). Cases in which Jo is instructed are regularly reported for their legal significance: she acted for CAFCASS in the Supreme Court in RE B which addressed the standard of proof of s 31 Children Act , the CoA praised the 'wise and responsible' decision of CAFCASS in instructing her in RE A. C&P 2015;'She is deservedly pre-eminent, has a brilliant mind, and is one of the few who is as good a fearsome cross-examiner as she is arguing law in the Supreme Court'. Jo's skills are successfully transposed to high net worth private client children's cases where issues of mental health, sex abuse and alcoholism are involved.
Professional Memberships: FLBA, ALC, AWB, INQUEST
Career: Called 1986;Silk 2006,Recorder 2009,Bencher (Middle Temple)2011. Mediator 2012,The Temple Womens Forum(steering cmtte) 2012- ,Executive Member Centre for Child and Family Reform 2012-. Identified as a 'Leading' and 'Top Tier Silk' by C&P and Legal 500 for successive years since her appointment in 2006, LALYs 2016 co winner 'Outstanding Achievement Award' ,Finalist C&P Family QC 2014, Winner of the Jordans' Family Silk 2013';Finalist Legal 500 Silk 2013. Patron of AMEND. Appointed Gresham College's Professor of Law in 2016.
Publications: Middle Templer 'the Women's Forum' (2016) Jordan's Family Law: 2016 : running series on Radicalism cases Jordan's Family Law on NAHI and experts July 2012 Fam Law 882 and Nov 12 Fam 1344 TEDR (Experts Disputes Resolver) ' In Defence of Experts' (Volume 17 no 2, 24)

DELANEY, Joe
Three New Square, London
020 7405 1111
clerks@3newsquare.co.uk
Featured in Intellectual Property (London)

Practice Areas: All aspects of intellectual property law, including patents, SPCs, trade marks, passing off, copyright, registered designs, design right and confidential information. Also instructed in matters relating to international commercial arbitrations which raise issues of intellectual property law, or which concern technical subject matter (for example, disputes arising out of technology, know-how, patent and trade mark transfer and licensing agreements). Particular areas of specialism include pharma, biotech, medical devices and telecoms patents.Recent Cases: Actavis v Lilly (tadalafil); Thoratec v AIS (heart pumps);Philips v HTC (3.5G FRAND licence, HSPA); Illumina v TDL (non-invasive prenatal diagnosis and genetic testing); MRC v Celltech (humanized antibodies); Actavis v Lilly (pemetrexed); Regeneron v Kymab (transgenic mice, therapeutic antibody discovery); ASSIA v BT (ADSL); Teva v Leo (formulation for treatment of psoriasis); Fage v Chobani (Greek Yoghurt); HTC v Apple (smartphones, software-implemented inventions); IPCom v HTC/ Nokia (FRAND licences); MedImmune v Novartis (recombinant antibodies, phage display); Samsung v Apple (smartphones, Registered Community Design); Enercon v Enercon (section 18 Arbitration Act application); Gedeon v Bayer (formulation for contraceptive pills); Fresenius v CareFusion (syringe pumps); Warner-Lambert v Teva (atorvastatin, interim injunctions); Apple v Nokia (telecoms); Datacard v Eagle (RFID); Fosroc v Grace (cement admixtures); Diageo v ICB (VODKAT); TIP v Motorola (essentiality, GPRS); RIM v Motorola (mobile email); Ratiopharm v ALZA (fentanyl patches); InterDigital v Nokia (essentiality).
Professional Memberships: Chancery Bar Association, COMBAR, IP Bar Association
Career: Called to the Bar 2006. 2001-2004: Natural Sciences (First Class), Emmanuel College, Cambridge.

DEN BESTEN, Ruth
Serle Court, London
020 7242 6105
redenbesten@serlecourt.co.uk
Featured in Chancery (London), Commercial Dispute Resolution (London), Fraud (London)

Practice Areas: Commercial and chancery litigation; civil fraud; personal and corporate insolvency; professional negligence (solicitors). Cases include Lehman Brothers Limited (In Administration) (Waterfalls I and III); Ras al Khaimah I.A. v Bestfort and Ors; ORB A.r.l. v Ruhan and Ors; Bank of St Petersburg v Arkhangelsky; BTA v Ablyazov & Ors; Re Coroin; Belltrey Corporation v Newcote International; Lexi Holdings v Pannone & Partners; Lexi Holdings v Luqman and SFO v Lexi Holdings (fraud); Iesini & Ors v Westrip Holdings Ltd (company) Kamos Finanz v SLEC (commercial); Addax Bank v Wellesley LLP; Mobilx Ltd v HMRC (VAT fraud); the TAG Litigation (professional negligence and insurance); Al-Rawas v Pegasus Energy Limited (injunctive relief).
Professional Memberships: Chancery Bar Association, Commercial Bar Association.
Career: Jesus College, Oxford; City University, London (Dip.Law); 2001-02 McCarthy Tetrault (Canada, Fox Scholarship); 2002-03 Peters & Peters.

DENNISON, James
5 St Andrew's Hill, London
020 7332 5400
JamesDennison@5sah.co.uk
Featured in POCA Work & Asset Forfeiture (All Circuits)

Practice Areas: James Dennison was called to the Bar in 1986 after graduating from Durham University. With over 30 years of experience prosecuting, the last eighteen almost exclusively in the field of confiscation and asset recovery, he is recognised by the Court of Appeal as being an expert in the latter area. He wrote the chapters on Restraint Orders and Enforcement in the 2013 edition of the seminal work, Millington & Sutherland-Williams on the Proceeds of Crime, and is presently drafting both those and the "Management Receivers" chapter for the forthcoming 2017 edition. He also co-authored (and trained and lectured the judiciary on) the Eastern Caribbean Bench Book on confiscation. He has acted on behalf of numerous foreign governments to assist in the retention and realisation of assets to satisfy overseas confiscation orders. Ancillary areas of expertise are cash seizures, enforcement of confiscation orders, judicial review / High Court proceedings and the handling of appeals. He also prosecutes regulatory offences on behalf of local authorities, with a particular emphasis on "rogue traders". He is regularly instructed on Level 4 cases by the Proceeds of Crime Unit of the Crown Prosecution Service and is a Grade "A" prosecutor for the Serious Fraud Office.

DENTON-COX, Gregory
4 Stone Buildings, London
020 7242 5524
clerks@4stonebuildings.com
Featured in Chancery (London), Company (London), Fraud (London)

Practice Areas: Chancery and commercial litigation including company law, civil fraud, tracing and asset recovery, shareholder disputes, international trusts, banking and finance, insolvency and restructuring and transfers of insurance business under Part VII of FSMA. Notable recent cases include: BNY Mellon Corporate Trustee Services v LBG Capital (Supreme Court), Napier Park v Harbourmaster (Court of Appeal), US Bank Trustees Ltd v Titan Europe (disputes concerning the construction of structured finance documents) Benedetti v Sawiris (Supreme Court) (claim to a shareholding in telecommunications holding company, payment on a quantum meruit), McKillen v Misland (shareholder dispute concerning ownership of London hotels).
Professional Memberships: Chancery Bar Association, COMBAR.
Career: Called to the Bar 2000. Junior Counsel to the Crown (C Panel) 2006-11.
Publications: Contributor to Atkin's Court Forms (Companies – General).

DENYER-GREEN, Barry
Falcon Chambers, London
020 7353 2484
clerks@falcon-chambers.com
Featured in Real Estate Litigation (London)

Practice Areas: Landlord and tenant, property law, compulsory purchase and compensation, planning and commons.
Professional Memberships: Hon-RICS; Honorary Fellow, College of Estate Management; Honorary Member of Central Association of Agricultural Valuers; Member of the DETR Compulsory Purchase Working Party 1998-2000; past Chairman of the Compulsory Purchase Association; Agricultural Law Association; Chancery Bar Association; LCLCBA: Property Bar Association.
Career: Educated at London University (LLB Hons 1973, PhD 1987); London School of Economics (LLM 1978); Called 1972 (Middle Temple).
Publications: Author, Compulsory Purchase and Compensation, 10th edn (2013); joint author, Development and Planning Law, 4th edn (2011); joint author, Law of Commons and Town & Village Greens, 2nd edn (2006); editor, Estates Gazette Law Reports (1987-2006); joint editor, Planning Law Reports (1987-2006).

DEVONSHIRE, Simon QC
11KBW, London
020 7632 8500
Simon.Devonshire@11kbw.com
Featured in Employment (London)
Practice Areas: Simon Devonshire QC practices in all areas of statutory and contractual/commercial employment law, but with a particular emphasis on (i) inter-business competition issues (Including confidential information, restrictive covenants and the poaching of employees in unlawful team moves), (ii) employee/business owner fraud, (iii) the attempted diversion of business opportunities by employee fiduciaries, and (iv) whistle-blowing, discrimination and TUPE disputes. He also has considerable experience in disputes between LLP members and in the management and control of repeated/ vexatious litigation. In the High Court, he regularly acts in fraud, business diversion and employee competition disputes. Recent cases have involved: the attempted diversion by two departing employees of the opportunity to open a multi-million pound luxury car dealership in the Midlands; the control of abusive attempts to re-litigate issues already decided against the applicant; a substantial fraud action, involving the alleged miss-sale of a freight forwarding business; multiple team move disputes (in both the employment and the LLP settings); and historical music rights disputes. On the statutory front, Simon recently acted for a major bank in defending a dismissal and discrimination claim by its global head of treasury and has and is handling a number of whistle-blowing disputes, arising particularly out of the financial services sector. Recent reported and/ or important cases include Samara -v- MBI Partners [2016] EWHC 441 (QB) (abuse of process arising out of recidivist litigation); Dorma UK Ltd -v- Batemen [2015] EWHC 4142 (QB) (springboard relief arising out of an alleged team move); Miller -v- Gardiner & Ors [2015] EWHC 1712 (Ch) & [2015] EWHC 288 (Ch) (extended CRO against litigant repeatedly bringing misconceived claims); Thomson Ecology -v- APEM [2014] IRLR 184 (summary judgment and disclosure orders in team move cases); Allsop -v- Christiani & Nielsen Ltd (in Administration) [2012] UKEAT/0241/11/JOJ (limitation and jurisdiction in Wages Act claims); CEF Holdings -v- Mundey & Ors [2012] FSR 35 (the limits of springboard relief and the obligations of a party moving the court without notice); Royal Cornwall Hospital Trust -v- Watkinson [2011] Med LR 636 (whistleblowing in an NHS trust); BGC -v- Rees & Tullett Prebon [2011] EWHC 2009 (QB) (Tullett did not procure Rees to breach his contract of employment with BGC when recruiting him); Capital for Enterprise -v- Malik & Ors [2010] EWHC 343 (Ch) (disclosure obligations and freezing injunctions); Ward Hadaway -v- Love & Ors [2010] UKEAT/0471/09/SM (the winning of a contract to provide legal services to the NMC did not constitute a service provision change within the meaning of TUPE 2006, and the successful tenderer did not assume liability for the dedicated team of lawyers retained by his predecessor); New ISG -v- Vernon & Ors [2008] ICR 319 (a purposive construction should be given to reg 4(7) of TUPE 2006, so as to accord with the fundamental freedom of the employee to choose who he works for, and to permit and recognise the effectiveness of a post transfer objection where the employee does not know of the identity of the transferee or of his right to object pre transfer. In consequence, the transferee could not enforce post termination restrictive covenants against 'objecting' employees); Croke -v- Hydro [2007] ICR 1303 (an individual providing services through his own limited company to an end user via an employment agency was a worker for the purposes of the whistle-blowing provisions); and Bezant -v- Rausing & Ors [2007] EWHC 1118 (QB) (It was an abuse of process for a claimant (after his claims under employment law had failed) to seek to invoke the law of tort against directors and other professionals associated with his employment/dismissal, to seek to recover his alleged losses. Such conduct justified the making of an Extended CRO).
Professional Memberships: Employment Law Bar Association. ELA. LCLCBA.
Career: Called 1988. Appointed QC 2009.

DEW, Richard
Ten Old Square, London
020 7405 0758
richarddew@tenoldsquare.com
Featured in Chancery (London)
Practice Areas: Richard Dew's practice is focussed on Wills, Estates and Trusts and related professional negligence. His practice is predominantly litigation, and he is frequently involved in large and complex claims. He also advises and represents in Court of Protection matters and provides expert advice in respect of tax and tax planning (principally capital taxation).
Professional Memberships: Richard Dew is a member of the Chancery Bar Association, STEP and ACTAPS and won the ACTAPS Contentious Barrister of the Year award for 2016.
Career: Called to the Bar 1999. Notable cases include: P v P [2015] WTLR 1039 Fam Law 773 (AB v CB [2015] 2 FLR 25); JSC Mezhdunarodniy Promyshlenniy Bank v Pugachev; AB v CB [2014] EWHC 2998 (Fam),Tadros v Barratt [2014] EWHC 2860 (Ch), Al-Sadi v Al-Sadi [2013] EWHC 2379, Goodman v Goodman [2014] Ch 186 Shovelar v Lane [2011] 4 All ER 669; Sutton v Sutton [2010] WTLR 115; Dibble v Pfluger [2010] EWCA Civ 1005; Lamothe v Lamothe [2006] EWHC 1387(CH) (Revocation and the testator's intention); Banks v National Westminster Bank plc and another [2005] All ER (D) 159 (Apr) Will ademption following loss of the testator's capacity); Clark v Clark [2004] All ER (D) 224 (Dec) (application for solemn grant of probate); Leadenhall Independent Trustees Ltd v Welham and another [2004] All ER (D) 423 (Mar) (pensions).
Publications: Richard is an author of CCH Rossdale: Probate and Administration of Estates 5th Edition, Parker's Modern Will Precedents, Tolley's Inheritance Tax Planning and the Trusts and Estate Practitioner's Guide to Mental Capacity. He has contributed to International Trusts Disputes and to the 25th edition of Ranking Spicer and Pegler's Executorship Law, Trusts & Accounts (Butterworths). Richard's published articles include: "Thy Will be done" STEP Journal April 2016, "2013 case round up" in TQR March 2014, Trusts and Disclosure, 2011 Private Client Business [2011] PCB 241-247; "Can TLATA 1996 be Interpreted as a Fiscal Bill?" Trusts and Estates Law & Tax Journal, May 2009, 11 (jointly with Gill Steel); • "A Wasted Opportunity" (Trustee Exclusion Clauses) T.E.L. & T.J. (2007) No.83 January/ February Pages 23-25.

DHAR, Siddharth
Essex Court Chambers, London
020 7813 8000
sdhar@essexcourt.com
Featured in International Arbitration (London), Energy & Natural Resources (London)
Practice Areas: Siddharth acts as an advocate and advisor in substantial commercial litigation and arbitration disputes. He is equally comfortable in Court and in arbitration. Over the past year or so he has acted in Court for the successful respondent in Taurus v SOMO [2015] EWCA Civ 835; for Nigerian oil interests in C v D [2015] EWHC 2126 and again in C v D [2016] EWHC 1893; for investors in the Ukrainian retail sector in Stockman v Arricano [2015] EWHC 2979; and for a BVI investor in W Ltd v M Sdn BHD [2016] EWHC 422. His recent arbitration work includes the continuing $38 billion ICC dispute between Botaş and NIGC; and multiple investor/state claims, including Agility v Pakistan; Albaniabeg v Albania; Hydro & Ors v Albania; and BSG v Guinea.
Professional Memberships: He is a member of the LCIA, ICCA and the LMAA.
Career: Siddharth was called to the Bar in 2005 and has been in practice at Essex Court Chambers since 2006. He specialises in significant commercial disputes across a wide variety of industry sectors. In addition to representing clients before the English courts and arbitral tribunals in London, he is regularly instructed in connection with litigation and arbitration abroad, and has appeared before the DIFC Court and in arbitrations in Paris, Switzerland, Singapore, New York, Washington and South Africa.
Publications: Co-author of the "Arbitration" chapter in Bullen & Leake & Jacob's Precedents of Pleadings (18th Edn, Dec. 2015). Co-author, with Lord Collins, of a chapter on interim remedies in International Financial Disputes: Arbitration and Mediation (Mar. 2015) (Ed. Golden & Lamm).

DICKASON, Robert
Outer Temple Chambers, London
020 73 536381
robert.dickason@outertemple.com
Featured in Health & Safety (London)
Practice Areas: Clinical Negligence; Health & Safety; Public Law; Professional Disciplinary & Regulatory Law
Professional Memberships: HSLA; PIBA; PNBA; ARDL; LCLCBA
Career: A specialist in clinical negligence and health and safety, and a rising star at the junior bar. Formerly Judicial Assistant to Lord Judge LCJ and Lord Carnwath CVO. Appointed to the Attorney-General's list of Junior Counsel (C Panel) from March 2015 to August 2020 to undertake public and private law cases on behalf of the Crown, particularly those involving members of the armed forces. Regularly instructed in contested clinical negligence trials for both Claimants and Defendants (e.g. Raggett v Kings College Hospital NHS Foundation Trust & 5 ors [2016] EWHC 1604 (QB); A v East Kent University Hospitals NHS Foundation Trust [2015] EWHC 1038 (QB)). Has appeared in some of the most high profile and complex health and safety cases in recent years (e.g. Sterecycle manslaughter, Lakanal House tower block fire, Warwickshire Fire), undertaking the full range of criminal, civil, inquest and advisory work for public authorities, large conglomerates, small and medium businesses, and individual directors and employees.
Publications: APIL Clinical Negligence textbook (causation chapter); APIL Personal Injury looseleaf (causation chapter)
Personal:

DICKER, Robin QC
South Square, London
020 7696 9900
robindicker@southsquare.com
Featured in Chancery (London), Banking & Finance (London), Commercial Dispute Resolution (London), Company (London), Offshore (London), Restructuring/Insolvency (London)
Practice Areas: Specialises in commercial, business and financial law, including banking, commercial litigation, company, corporate restructuring and insolvency, professional negligence and disciplinary proceedings and civil fraud.
Professional Memberships: International Insolvency Institute (elected Founding Member), ILA, INSOL International, INSOL Europe, R3, LCIA, ICC, Commercial Bar Association, Chancery Bar Association, P.R.I.M.E. Finance Foundation (Expert).
Career: Called 1986 (Middle Temple); QC 2000.

DICKINSON, John FH
St John's Chambers, Bristol
0117 923 4700
john.dickinson@stjohnschambers.co.uk
Featured in Chancery (Western), Professional Negligence (Western), Commercial Dispute Resolution (Western), Company (Western)
Practice Areas: John is a barrister specialising in contentious probate work, Court of Protection (financial and welfare), all areas of real property work including conveyancing disputes, boundaries and easements, commercial landlord & tenant disputes, partnership, banking, pensions, insolvency, company law and shareholder disputes. John's commercial practice includes fraud, breach of contract, restraint of trade and sale of goods, consumer credit, injunctions and freezing orders. John also has a practice in professional negligence work in relation to solicitors, accountants and financial advisors. John is a mediator and he finds this area of his practice particularly rewarding.
Professional Memberships: Chancery Bar Association, Associate Member of the Association of Contentious Trust And Probate Specialists (ACTAPS), Associate Member of the Association of Pension Lawyers (APL), Western Chancery & Commercial Bar Association, Professional Negligence Bar Association, Financial Services Lawyers Association, ACA Chartered Accountant (Institute of Chartered Accountants in England & Wales).
Career: Call 1995. Previously practiced as a Chartered Accountant for 5 years, latterly at Coopers and Lybrand in litigation support. Seconded to the Serious Fraud Office, including assisting the BCCI investigation. Counsel assisting Lord Penrose's Inquiry concerning Equitable Life.
Personal: Hobbies include tennis, surfing and skiing.

DIGNUM, Marcus
12 King's Bench Walk, London
020 75830811
dignum@12kbw.co.uk
Featured in Personal Injury (London)

Practice Areas: Marcus has developed a substantial personal injury practice involving both RTA and EL/PL work. He is instructed by both Claimants and Defendants and is frequently used by most of the leading large insurers. Recognised as a Leading Junior for many years in Chambers and Partners and Legal 500, he is lauded for his "robust, realistic and very personal service." He combines "intellectual rigour, a commercial approach and great charm" to good effect on high-value catastrophic injury cases. Marcus deals with claims of the highest value, and whilst happy to be lead, is often instructed alone to represent his clients' interests against Silks and other senior Juniors. He has substantial experience of claims involving the most serious head and spinal injuries where awards are made or settlements reached of several million pounds. In addition, Marcus accepts instructions in most other areas of the common law, including in particular, contractual disputes, construction work, interlocutory relief and carriage of goods cases.
Professional Memberships: PIBA.
Career: BA (Classical studies) (First Class) University London. Called to the Bar in 1994.

DILWORTH, Noel
Henderson Chambers, London
020 7583 9020
ndilworth@hendersonchambers.co.uk
Featured in Product Liability (London)
Practice Areas: Consumer, Product Liability, Commercial, Financial Services, Health and Safety, Environment, Property, Employment.
Professional Memberships: ELBA, HSLA, COMBAR.
Career: Inner Temple Major and Princess Royal Scholar, Called to Bar 2001. Expertise in the field of insurance coverage disputes, particularly in the relation to property damage and product liability. Product Liability: Sabril group litigation (2006-2008); Seroxat (2010); Property / Commercial: Risegold Ltd v Escala Ltd [2008] EWCA Civ 1180, [2008] 1 EGLR 13, [2009] 1 P & CR D24; JS Bloor Ltd v Pavillion Developments Ltd [2008] EWHC 724 (TCC); Parkinson v Hawthorn [2008] EWHC 3499 (Ch) Merlo v Duffy [2009] All ER (D) 91 (Feb)Panayiotou v Nicolaou [2010] EWCA Civ 569; Cusack v Harrow London Borough Council [2013] UKSC 40; Administrative: R(Lin) v Barnet LBC [2007] EWCA Civ 132; R (B) v Barnet LBC [2009] All ER (D) 294 (Nov); K v G [2009] All ER (D) 128 (Oct). Employment: Coutinho v Rank Nemo DMS Ltd [2009] IRLR 672; Onwuka v Spherion Technology (UK) Ltd and ors [2008] All ER (D) 67 (Feb); Finney v Miles Platts Ltd, UKEAT / 0150 / 04; Peacehaven & Telscombe Help Service and Volunteer Bureau, UKEAT / 0461 / 03.

DINEEN, Maria
2 Bedford Row, London
020 7440 8888
mdineen@2bedfordrow.co.uk
Featured in Crime (London), Financial Crime (London)
Practice Areas: Predominantly defence advocate specialising in heavyweight crime and serious fraud. Extensive experience of defending and prosecuting in cases involving allegations of murder/manslaughter; major drugs importations and supplies; armed robbery and other violent crime; serious sexual offences and child cruelty. Particular expertise in dealing with vulnerable defendants and witnesses. A highly regarded fraud practitioner, she has appeared in numerous high profile complex fraud cases, involving allegations of insider dealing; VAT and tax fraud; advance fee fraud; mortgage fraud; diversion fraud; fraudulent trading; money laundering and various Companies Acts offences.
Professional Memberships: South Eastern Circuit; Criminal Bar Association; Fraud Lawyers Association; Association of Regulatory and Disciplinary Lawyers; Bar European Group.
Career: Varied, including newspaper journalism (covering mainly crime and the criminal courts). Called to the Bar 1997. Spent 10 weeks in Kingston, Jamaica in 2005 as volunteer (funded by chambers) assisting local attorneys in preparation and conduct of capital murder cases. Elected Member of Bar Council 1999-2002.
Personal: Born 29 October 1963. Lives in Suffolk.

DIXEY, Jonathan
5 Essex Court, London
020 74102000
dixey@5essexcourt.co.uk
Featured in Police Law (All Circuits)
Practice Areas: Police law, public and administrative law, inquests and inquiries, employment and personal injury. Jonathan acts on behalf of constabularies across the country in cases touching upon all areas of police law. He has considerable experience in advising chief officers on policy and operational matters, particularly in sensitive matters involving national security and other high-profile cases (including Operation Weeting and Operation Yewtree). Recent cases include: the Independent Inquiry into Child Sexual Abuse (on behalf of the Metropolitan Police Service); the Inquests into the deaths arising from the Hillsborough Stadium disaster (on behalf of the St John Ambulance) and the Anthony Grainger Inquiry (on behalf of the National Crime Agency).
Professional Memberships: ALBA, ELBA, PIBA and the South Eastern Circuit.
Career: Called to the Bar 2007; Attorney General's C Panel of Counsel (appointed 2013).
Publications: 'The Employment Tribunals Handbook: Practice, Procedure and Strategies for Success' (3rd edition, 2011) with Alan Payne and John-Paul Waite.

DIXON, Clare
4 New Square, London
020 7822 2000
c.dixon@4newsquare.com
Featured in Professional Negligence (London)
Practice Areas: Clare's practice encompasses three main areas: professional liability, insurance (including subrogated recovery actions) and commercial litigation. At the cross over of her insurance and professional liability work come cases involving professional indemnity policies. Clare has advised both insurers and insureds on a variety of issues including policy interpretation, non-disclosure and fraud. Clare believes in taking a tough but commercial approach to litigation and relishes advocacy in all its forms. Notable cases include: • Impact Funding v Barrington: the interpretation of the trade debts exclusion in professional indemnity policies where the decision of the Supreme Court is awaited; • Kagalovsky v Balmore Invest Limited [2015] 3 Costs LR 531: wasted costs claim against a barrister; • Travelers Insurance Co Ltd v Advani [2012] EWHC 623: claim in fraud by insurers against former insured; and • the Employers Liability Trigger Litigation [2012] 1 WLR 867: claim concerning the proper interpretation of certain employers' liability policies in mesothelioma cases.
Professional Memberships: PNBA (member of the executive committee), COMBAR, TECBAR.
Career: MA (Oxon). Called to the Bar in 2002.
Publications: Editor of Jackson & Powell on "Professional Liability".
Personal: Clare read law at St Anne's College, Oxford University, where she was President of the Oxford Union. Leisure interests: travel, sailing and walking.

DOBBIE, Olivia-Faith
Cloisters, London
020 78274070
ofd@cloisters.com
Featured in Employment (London)
Practice Areas: Employment, Discrimination and Public Law (human rights).
Professional Memberships: ELA, ILS and DLA.
Career: Olivia is a fearless advocate with a strong court presence. She has a dynamic practice with a focus on Employment, Discrimination and Human Rights law and regularly appears in the High Court and the Employment Appeal Tribunal. She has also appeared in the Court of Appeal and Supreme Court in significant cases, namely: the highly-reported judicial review regarding Gurkha soldiers' pensions against the MOD and X v Mid Sussex CAB. Clients report: "Olivia is a rare breed of barrister who is dogged, positive and upbeat, excellent with clients and a brilliant advocate in Court." "Her work is at a high level and she always goes the extra mile." "user-friendly, commercial and tenacious" "Impressive and formidable Olivia-Faith is the consummate professional great with clients and an absolute joy in the court room. I would not want to be on the other side!" In her daily practice, Olivia has experience of a broad range of employment disputes. She also advises clients about non-contentious matters.
Publications: Author of: ELA Briefing, February 2015: "How far can a Tribunal go to assist a Litigant in Person?" Solicitor's Journal, Half Year Review, 2013: "Treated Equally", 3 chapters of the LAG book: "Discrimination in Employment" (2013), ELA Briefing: "Exploring Combined Discrimination", Practice Notes on PLC online, Articles in Counsel Magazine.

DOBBIN, Clair
3 Raymond Buildings Barristers, London
020 7400 6400
clair.dobbin@3rblaw.com
Featured in Administrative & Public Law (London), Extradition (London), Inquests & Public Inquiries (All Circuits), Professional Discipline (London)
Practice Areas: Clair's areas of expertise are public law, human rights, public inquiries and inquests and extradition law. Clair was first appointed junior Counsel to the Crown in 2004 and was appointed to the "A" panel of Treasury Counsel in 2014. She has appeared in numerous leading cases in the UK in recent years including litigation concerning the "plebgate" incident and important terrorist cases such as USA v Abu Hamza and USA v Babar Ahmad. She continues to act on behalf of the UK, before the European Court of Human Rights, in the ongoing case of UK v Harkins (having successfully acted for the UK in UK v Harkins (No.1) and UK v Edwards on the issue of life imprisonment without parole). Other recent public law cases include Birks v MPS (concerning the retirement of a police officer in the course of an IPCC investigation into a death in custody and whether Article 2 ultimately requires a misconduct hearing); Ismail v SSHD (application of Article 6 to the service of foreign judgments); Bats (Government of Mongolia Intervening) v FCO (special mission immunity) and T v SSHD (detention of children). Clair has a particular specialisation in the law on the rights of children and is currently instructed as Counsel to the Inquiry in the Independent Inquiry into Child Sexual Abuse. She has very substantial public inquiry and inquest experience. Recent inquests include the Alexander Litvinenko Inquest; the Mark Duggan inquest, the Dawit Inquest and the David Emmanuel Inquest. She was in the Bloody Sunday Inquiry and the Baha Mousa Inquiry.
Career: MA Hons (Cantab), Call 1999, Treasury 'C' Panel 2004; 'B' Panel 2007. "A" Panel 2014.

DOBLE, Tom
QEB Hollis Whiteman, London
020 7933 8855
tom.doble@qebhw.co.uk
Featured in Financial Crime (London)
Practice Areas: Tom specialises in fraud, financial and business crime. He has experience beyond his call in the conduct of serious and complex cases in a commercial context, including allegations of conspiracy to defraud, sanctions offences and corruption. He is meticulous, creative and tactically astute. Tom currently acts for Ryan Reich, a former Barclays trader charged with LIBOR manipulation, and for a pharmaceutical company in proceedings concerning the alleged international supply of counterfeit and unlicensed drugs. Tom has experience in cases with a multi-jurisdictional aspect, and advises both individuals and companies on a range of criminal and quasi-criminal matters. He regularly deals with restraint, confiscation and related proceedings, recently securing the recovery of over £4 million for an interested party. Tom prosecutes and defends in health and safety cases, and is currently acting for the prosecution in proceedings against a construction company charged with corporate manslaughter. Tom is also regularly instructed in a range of general criminal matters and in police and medical disciplinary tribunals.
Professional Memberships: Criminal Bar Association, Young Fraud Lawyers' Association, Health and Safety Lawyers' Association
Career: BA (Hons), Dip Law, BPTC

DOCTOR, Brian QC
Fountain Court Chambers, London
020 7583 3335
bd@fountaincourt.co.uk
Featured in Commercial Dispute Resolution (London)
Practice Areas: Commercial litigation and arbitration practice, specialising in cases requiring detailed examination of documents and cross-examination of witnesses. Brian has a hands-on approach to interlocu-

tory matters leading up to trial, and gets heavily involved in the tactical and strategic decisions of major litigation. He has a wide experience of shareholder disputes, banking, insurance, competition and general commercial issues in the context of major litigation. His Civil Fraud practice spans emerging markets, enforcement and recovery actions, and their conduct in the London courts, although his work has a truly international dimension. Complex procedural claims mean he is often called upon to act in difficult and complex cases, where his reputation gained in the Tchenguiz litigation as being able to achieve a satisfactory result goes before him. The scope of his international commercial practice is shown by the connections of his recent cases: South Africa, Paraguay, Florida, Russia and BVI. Brian acted successfully for G4S in the jurisdiction dispute of T Meje v G4S; he also succeeded in striking out part of the claim against two defendants in Peak Hotels v Tarek Investments.

Professional Memberships: Commercial Bar Association.

Career: In practice at the Bar in South Africa (Silk 1990) and in England (Silk 1999). Also admitted in the BVI and Cayman.

Personal: BA, LL B (Witwatersrand) BCL (Balliol College, Oxford), Born 8 December 1949.

DOERRIES, Chantal-Aimée QC

Atkin Chambers, London
020 7404 0102
cadoerries@atkinchambers.com

Featured in International Arbitration (London), Professional Negligence (London), Construction (London), Energy & Natural Resources (London)

Practice Areas: Commercial dispute resolution, construction and engineering, energy, natural resources and utilities, joint ventures, international arbitration, professional negligence and shipbuilding.

Professional Memberships: Chairman of the Bar Council of England and Wales (2016); TECBAR (Chairman 2010-2013); COMBAR.

Career: Called to the Bar 1992, Queen's Counsel 2008.

Publications: Co-Editor in Chief of 'The International Construction Law Review'; Joint editor of 'Building Law Reports'; Contributing Editor of 'Hudson's Building and Engineering Contracts' 12th edition.

DOLAN, Bridget QC

Serjeants' Inn Chambers, London
2074275000
bdolan@serjeantsinn.com

Featured in Clinical Negligence (London), Court of Protection (All Circuits), Inquests & Public Inquiries (All Circuits)

Practice Areas: Bridget Dolan QC was called to the Bar in 1997 and took silk in 2016. Bridget specialises in Court of Protection, mental health, inquests and inquiries, public and administrative and clinical negligence law. An earlier edition notes that "she is a leading expert on capacity matters... providing well thought-out advice, is very pragmatic and is good at asking the right questions... a go-to for heavyweight medical cases." Please visit the Serjeants' Inn Chambers website for her profile, which sets out full details of her practice including relevant work of note.

Career: Her PhD and previous career in forensic psychology give Bridget unique clinically based experience of complicated mental health issues which underpins her practice in the Court of Protection, the Civil and Admin Courts and in inquests and inquiries.

Publications: Inquest Law Reports (Editor); "Medical Treatment: Decisions & the Law", "The Mental Health Act Explained" (co-authored).

DOMENGE, Victoria

29 Bedford Row Chambers, London
020 7404 1044
vdomenge@29br.co.uk

Featured in Family/Matrimonial (London)

Practice Areas: Family Law with particular expertise in matrimonial finance and private law children cases. Reported cases include: N v F [2011] EWHC 586 Fam); M v M (Divorce: Domicile) [2011] 1 FLR 919; Re H (Contact Order) [2010] 2 FLR 866; M v M [2009] EWHC 1941 (Fam); Paulin v Paulin [2009] 2 FLR 354; RH v RH (Ancillary Relief: Costs) [2008] 2 FLR 2142; W (A Child) [2008] EWCA Civ 1181; El Faragy v El Faragy & Ors [2007] EWCA Civ 1149.

Professional Memberships: FLBA and Resolution.

Career: Called to the Bar 1993, Middle Temple. Trained in Collaborative Law. Public Access Barrister.

Personal: Educated at The Cheltenham Ladies College, University of Exeter (BA Hons), University of Westminster (CPT Postgraduate Law Diploma). Married with three children. Speaks good Spanish.

DONNELLY, Kathleen

Henderson Chambers, London
020 7583 9020
kdonnelly@hendersonchambers.co.uk

Featured in Employment (London)

Practice Areas: Kathleen specialises in Commercial, Health Safety & Environment, and Employment Law. Her high profile cases include the OCENSA pipeline group action, the Stirling Mortimer fraud litigation, the Potters Bar Rail inquest and the Buncefield Oil Depot litigation. Her representative cases include Autoclenz and Westwood (employee and worker status), JB v African Development Bank (legitimate expectations in the international civil service), Back Office v Percival (corporate liability for contempt), and WXY v Burby (privacy harassment and injunctive relief). She has particular expertise in restrictive covenants, economic torts and complex discrimination claims.

Professional Memberships: Commercial Bar Association (COMBAR), Health and Safety Lawyers Association (HSLA), Employment Lawyers Association (ELA).

Career: BA Jurisprudence (Oxon), LLM Commercial and International Law (Cantab). Hardwicke Award (Lincoln's Inn), Buchanan Scholar (Lincoln's Inn). Called to the Bar 2005.

Personal: Born 1979; resides London; dog owner; cake baker; fun runner.

DONOVAN, Joel QC

Cloisters, London
020 7827 4000
jd@cloisters.com

Featured in Personal Injury (London), Clinical Negligence (London)

Practice Areas: Clinical negligence, personal injury.

Professional Memberships: AvMA, APIL, PNBA, PIBA. Bar Pro Bono Unit reviewing panel. Lead advocacy trainer for Lincoln's Inn. CEDR-accredited mediator. Arbitrator under MIB Untraced Drivers' Agreement and PIcARBS.

Career: Specialist in complex clinical negligence, particularly secondary brain and spinal injuries, and heavy PI. Recent cases: successful Supreme Court appeal in Mohamud v Morrisons [2016] AC 677 ('close connection' test for vicarious liability); M v A Highway Authority (liability settlement arising from catastrophic motorcycle vs. pothole collision); Z v K (six-figure approved settlement of challenging catastrophic injury claim arising from drunken joyriding); D v P NHS Trust (seven-figure lump sum/PP approved settlement arising from delayed spinal immobilisation, leading to quadriplegia); Y v L NHS Trust (ongoing high-value claim arising from alleged contamination of spinal anaesthetic causing arachnoiditis); W v K (seven-figure lump sum/PP approved settlement in GP claim arising from devastating subarachnoid haemorrhage); X v Y (high-value wrongful birth case for mother of child with severe global developmental delay); Z v A Trust (cerebral palsy: seven-figure lump sum/PP approved settlement); and several ongoing high-value claims involving delayed treatment of cauda equina syndrome. Former solicitor; called 1991; QC 2011.

Personal: Fluent in French.

DOUGHERTY, Charles QC

2TG – 2 Temple Gardens, London
020 7822 1200
clerks@2tg.co.uk

Featured in Professional Negligence (London), Travel (London), Commercial Dispute Resolution (London), Fraud (London), Insurance (London), Product Liability (London)

Practice Areas: Charles specialises in commercial law, in particular commercial fraud, professional negligence, product liability, private international law (including travel) and insurance. Recent cases include: Brazil v Durant [2016] AC 297 (backwards tracing); Allen v DePuy [2015] 2 WLR 442 (conflict of laws and Consumer Protection Act 1987); Mitsui Sumitomo v MOPC [2016] 2 WLR 1148 (Liability under Riot (Damages) Act 1886 following August 2011 riots); Schubert Murphy v Law Society [2015] PNLR 15 (whether duty of care owed by Law Society).

Professional Memberships: Commercial Bar Association (COMBAR); Professional Negligence Bar Association (PNBA)

Career: BA, BCL (Oxon). Called 1997 (Middle Temple); QC 2013. Called to the Bar of the BVI and ad hoc to the Bar of Nevis. Prior to joining chambers, Charles was a management consultant and a law lecturer.

Publications: European Civil Practice, Sweet & Maxwell (2nd ed.), assistant editor.

DOUGHERTY, Nigel

Erskine Chambers, London
020 7242 5532
ndougherty@erskine-chambers.co.uk

Featured in Company (London)

Practice Areas: Company, insolvency and related areas of commercial law. Cases include: Ultraframe (UK) Ltd v Fielding [2005] EWHC 1638 (Ch), [2006] EWCA Civ 1133; Irvine v Irvine [2007] 1 BCLC 445; Kiani v Cooper [2010] BCC 463; Barclays Bank PLC v Nylon Capital LLP [2012] Bus LR 542; American Energy v Hycarbex Asia (in liquidation) [2014] EWHC 1091 (Ch); Eclairs Group Limited v JKX Oil & Gas Plc [2016] 1 BCLC 1 (Supreme Court); and ITC v Ferster [2016] EWCA Civ 614.

Professional Memberships: Chancery Bar Association, COMBAR.

Career: Called 1993.

Publications: Contributor to "Company Directors: Law and Liability" (1998); Author (with Anne Fairpo) of "Company Acquisition of Own Shares" (7th ed).

Personal: Cambridge University: MA, LLM. Member of Gray's Inn.

DOUGLAS, Michael QC

4 Pump Court, London
020 7842 5555
MDouglas@4pumpcourt.com

Featured in Professional Negligence (London), Commercial Dispute Resolution (London), Information Technology (London)

Practice Areas: Professional negligence, information technology, insurance and commercial litigation. (Experience in other areas of law available on request from clerks). Michael Douglas QC's practice involves all areas of professional negligence with particular expertise in legal practitioners, commercial and financial practitioners and valuation and construction specialists. In the information and technology field he advises on all aspects of IT contracts, including outsourcing and Government contracts and appears in domestic and international arbitrations as well as the High Court. He acts in connection with a wide variety of commercial contract disputes including insurance contract disputes (both aspects involving interpretation, exclusion clauses, misrepresentation, fraud).

Professional Memberships: COMBAR, TECBAR , PNBA, Society for Computers & Law, LCIA Users' Council

Career: Called to the Bar in 1974. Queen's Counsel 1997. Recorder 1999.

Publications: Articles on implied terms and mandatory injunctions in Computers & Law magazine. Former editor of Atkins' Court Forms.

Personal: Educated at Westminster School and Balliol College, Oxford.

DOUGLAS-JONES, Ben

5 Paper Buildings, London
020 7353 6117
dbj@5pb.co.uk

Featured in Consumer Law (London), Financial Crime (London)

Practice Areas: Complex, cross-jurisdictional fraud, bribery, money-laundering, white-collar, regulatory, cyber and serious crime, consumer law, compliance, human rights, criminal intellectual property, civil fraud, asset recovery, JR and appellate work. As leader and junior, Ben defends and provides compliance advice to professional and corporate clients including PLCs. He prosecutes for the Serious Fraud Office, CPS Specialist Fraud Division (including medical regulation), Organised Crime and Special Crime Divisions, Appeals Unit and Proceeds of Crime Unit, and local authorities. Level 4 prosecutor. Specialist panels: Fraud, Serious Crime and Proceeds of Crime (London, South East and Wales). CPS Advocate Rape and Child Abuse List. Bribery: Operation Vectorial (matchfixing): Ben represented the first person ever acquitted of Bribery Act offence); SFO v BH ($2.7Bn bribery). Fraud: SFO v Evans (£170m Celtic Energy "fraud"): Ben represented the first Defendant in victories over the SFO in this "blockbuster" case; Operation Valgus (mortgage; over 1,000 mortgages); Operation Festival (complex tax); Abacus Trading (£40m invoice / banking); Operation Ernest (£110m factoring fraud); Operation Militia (botnet cyber fraud); SFO v OB [2014] UKSC 23 (Contempt; Extradition; Restraint; Specialty;

Boiler-room Fraud). Consumer law including trademarks, copyright, medical, criminal planning, food safety and environmental health. Co-author Blackstone's Guide to the Consumer Rights Act 2015. Human rights: Zaredar [2016] EWCA Crim 877; Boateng [2016] 2 Cr. App. R. 5; YY [2016] 1 Cr. App. R. 28; Mateta [2014] 1 WLR 1516 (asylum); J (2016 special court); L [2014] 1 All ER 113 and N and Le [2013] QB 379 (human trafficking) and Ewing [2016] 1 Cr. App. R. 32 (free speech); R (DPP) v Leicester [2016] 1 Cr. App. R. 5 (self-incrimination). Co-authored Human Trafficking CPS Guidance and Law Society Immigration Crime Guidance. Attorney in Grenada.
Professional Memberships: Professional Memberships; Fraud Advisory Panel; Fraud Lawyers' Association; Gray's Inn accredited advocacy trainer.
Career: Called 1998.
Personal: LLB (Hons) (Reading); M Phil (Wales).

DOVAR, Daniel
Tanfield Chambers, London
020 7421 5300
clerks@tanfieldchambers.co.uk
Featured in Real Estate Litigation (London)
Practice Areas: Specialises in real property and leasehold law with an emphasis on landlord and tenant. His practice encompasses possession and forfeiture proceedings, lease renewal, service charge disputes, disrepair, enfranchisement and all the other problems which arise out of leasehold interests. As well as landlord and tenant matters, his practice includes real property related issues such as conveyancing disputes, property related professional negligence, rights of way and easements, constructive trusts and co ownership, options, boundary disputes, and adverse possession.
Professional Memberships: Property Bar Association, Chancery Bar Association.
Career: LLB. Called 1997. Appointed Judge First-tier Tribunal (Property Chamber) (2011).
Publications: Business Premises: Possession and Lease Renewal 5th Ed (Sweet & Maxwell) Residential Possession Proceedings 9th Ed (Sweet & Maxwell) Service Charges and Management 3rd Ed (Sweet & Maxwell) Megarry's Manual of the Law of Real Property 9th Ed (Sweet & Maxwell) Landlord and Tenant Review – Editor (Sweet & Maxwell)

DOWDING, Nicholas QC
Falcon Chambers, London
020 7353 2484
clerks@falcon-chambers.com
Featured in Real Estate Litigation (London)
Practice Areas: All aspects of Chancery and real property law, commercial property litigation and arbitration.
Professional Memberships: Honorary member of the Royal Institution of Chartered Surveyors; Corresponding Member of RICS Dilapidations Practice Panel; Chancery Bar Association; LCLCBA; Property Bar Association.
Career: Educated at Radley College; St Catharine's College, Cambridge (BA 1978, MA 1982); called 1979 (Inner Temple); Silk 1997; Blundell Memorial Lecturer 1992, 1997, 2004, 2008 and 2013; Chambers and Partners Real Estate Silk of the Year 2005 and 2009; Chambers and Partners 100: UK Bar, 2013.
Publications: Joint Author, Dilapidations – The Modern Law and Practice; joint editor, Woodfall, Landlord and Tenant; general editor, Landlord and Tenant Reports.

DOWLEY, Dominic QC
Serle Court, London
020 7242 6105
ddowley@serlecourt.co.uk
Featured in Chancery (London), Fraud (London), Offshore (London)
Practice Areas: Commercial litigation, contentious trusts, fraud, insurance/ reinsurance, arbitration, banking and financial services/ regulation specialist.
Career: Called to the Bar and joined One Hare Court in 1983 (merged with Serle Court in 2000). QC 2002.
Personal: Educated at Oxford University 1977-80. Bacon Scholar of Gray's Inn: Barstow Law Scholar. Born 25 March 1958.

DOWNES, Paul QC
2TG – 2 Temple Gardens, London
020 7822 1221
pdownesqc@2tg.co.uk
Featured in Banking & Finance (London), Commercial Dispute Resolution (London)
Practice Areas: Barrister specialising in commercial law (with specific expertise in banking and finance-related matters), international trade, media and entertainment, and professional negligence.
Career: Palmerston v Brocket Hall (UK) Ltd (2016) [Arbitration]; Globe Motors v TRW Lucasvarity [2016] EWCA Civ 396 [Commercial]; LSREF III v Millvalley [2016] EWHC 466 (Comm) [Banking and Finance]; N v S [2015] EWHC 3248 (Comm) [Banking and Finance]; AB International Holdings v AB Clearing [2015] EWHC 2196 (Comm) [Arbitration]; Amtrust Europe v Trust Risk Group [2015] EWHC 1927 (Comm) [Arbitration]; Amtrust Europe v Trust Risk Group [2015] EWCA Civ 437 [Insurance, jurisdiction]; Myers v Kestrel [2015] EWHC 916 (Ch) [Banking and Finance]; Lictor Ansalt v Mir Steel [2014] All ER (D) 186; [2012] EWCA Civ 1397; [2012] All ER (D) 197 [Commercial]; Di Resta v Hamilton (2013) [Commercial, Sports, Media]; Re MFB (2013) [Arbitration]; Standard Chartered v Dorchester LNG [2013] All ER (D) 140 [Banking]; Stokors v IG Markets [2013] All ER (D) 300 [Banking]; Rubicon Fund Management v Attias (2012) [Commercial]; Shah v HSBC [2013] 1 AER (Comm) 72; [2010] EWCA Civ 31 Court of Appeal [Banking and Finance]; Senergy v Zeus Petroleum [2012] AER (D) 174 [Commercial]; Jeeg v Hare [2012] AER (D) 52 [Commercial, Media]; Re O (2011) [Arbitration]; Re H (2011) [Arbitration]; Re C (2011) [Arbitration]; Re V (2010) [Arbitration]; S v B (2010) [Arbitration]; Dennard v PwC [2010] EWHC 812 (Ch) Times Law Reports 26th April 2010 [Banking and Finance]; Titan v Royal Bank of Scotland [2010] 2 LLR 92 [Banking & Finance]; ED&F Man v Fluxo Cane (No.2) [2010] EWHC 212 (Comm) [Commodities] Appointments: Consultant for Barclays Bank on Banking Law/Accountancy and Banking Practice including International Trade products Training (1988-93). Assistant Examiner for Chartered Institute of Bankers in Banking Law and Accountancy (1988-1993). Acting as counsel and/or arbitrator in LMAA, LCIA, UNCITRAL and general arbitrations concerning oil and oil exploration, cocoa, sugar, grain, insurance, carriage of goods by sea, hi-tech medical equipment, computer software and professional services. Expert in UK banking law and regulation for proceedings in the Supreme Court of New York and the High Court of Singapore (2009 to date).
Publications: Lead Contributor to "The Encyclopaedia of Forms and Precedents" Vol 4(1) Banking published by LexisNexis Butterworths (2007 to date). Lead contributor the second edition of "Civil Appeals" ("the Black Book") in relation to Appeals to the Supreme Court and Privy Council (2010 to date).

DOYLE, Louis
Kings Chambers, Manchester
0345 034 3444
clerks@kingschambers.com
Featured in Chancery (Northern), Restructuring/ Insolvency (Northern)
Practice Areas: Busy and eclectic heavy commercial chancery practice with significant emphasis on high-value insolvency (corporate and personal, including related areas such as schemes of arrangement), company law (especially shareholder and director disputes) and financial litigation (especially guarantees, financial instruments and debt), credit and security. Presently dealing with several cases valued at in excess of £10m. Instructed by office-holder, creditor, debtor, institutional lenders and clients and other interested parties and stakeholders in addition to advisory work on non-contentious transactions and re-structuring, together with related interim work (injunctions and applications) and disciplinary, regulatory and professional negligence work within area of expertise. Has appeared in about fifty reported cases in areas of specialism. Particularly enjoys difficult, complex, tricky, novel and/or challenging cases, and dealing with matters at short notice. Accepts direct professional access and direct access instructions in appropriate cases.
Professional Memberships: Insolvency Lawyers' Association (full member), R3 (full member), Chancery Bar Association, Northern Chancery Bar Association, Northern Circuit Commercial Bar Association (committee member), Professional Negligence Bar Association.
Career: LLB LLM (Birmingham). Admitted a solicitor 1994. Called to the Bar 1996 (Lincoln's Inn). Treasury Counsel (Provincial Panel) 2000-07 undertaking disqualification and Revenue work.
Publications: Contributing Editor to Gore-Browne on Companies (Jordans, looseleaf). (Books) 'Insolvency Legislation: Annotations and Commentary' (with Professor Andrew Keay) (Jordans, 2016, 5th Edition); 'Insolvency Litigation' (Sweet & Maxwell, 2nd Edition forthcoming); 'Company Voluntary Arrangements and Administration' (Jordans, 2010, 2nd Edition); 'Administrative Receivership: Law and Practice' (Sweet & Maxwell, 1995).

DRAKE, David
Serle Court, London
020 7400 7174
clerks@serlecourt.co.uk
Featured in Chancery (London), Company (London), Fraud (London)
Practice Areas: David has a broad commercial chancery practice, encompassing general commercial litigation, commercial fraud and breach of fiduciary duty, company and insolvency, and professional negligence disputes. He is often involved in cases with an international element, and in matters arising from a complex or technical background.
Professional Memberships: Chancery Bar Association, COMBAR.
Career: Serle Court (formerly Thirteen Old Square) 1995 to date.
Publications: The Practice and Procedure of the Companies Court (1997), Minority Shareholders: Law, Practice and Procedure (5th ed, 2015).

DRAPER, Owain
One Essex Court, London
020 7583 2000
odraper@oeclaw.co.uk
Featured in Competition/European Law (London), Sports Law (London)
Practice Areas: Owain has substantial experience in commercial litigation, public law and competition law investigations and proceedings. His broad commercial law experience encompasses injunctive relief, company law, confidentiality and civil fraud. Recent cases have included R (RWE Generation) v GEMA [2016] 1 C.M.L.R. 2164 (challenge to a regulatory price control), Dany Lions v Bristol Cars [2014] All ER (Comm) 403 (enforcement of best endeavours obligations and "agreements to agree"), Re Beppler & Jacobson [2014] EWCA Civ 935 (unfair prejudice petition), TNK-BP v Lazurenko [2013] EWCA Civ 137 (injunctive relief; commercial confidentiality) and Sir Martin Broughton v Hicks [2012] EWCA Civ 1743 (conspiracy; breach of director's duties; expedition and security for costs).
Career: Called to the Bar in 2008, MA (Hons) Eng Lit (Edinburgh, First Class), GDL (City University), BVC (BPP London)

DRAY, Martin
Falcon Chambers, London
020 7353 2484
dray@falcon-chambers.com
Featured in Real Estate Litigation (London)
Practice Areas: All aspects of real property law including landlord and tenant, adverse possession, options, easements and restrictive covenants. Cases include: No 1 Deansgate (residential) Ltd v No 1 Deansgate RTM Co Ltd [2013] UKUT 0580 (LC) (right to manage); Dyer v Terry [2013] EWHC 209 (Ch) (adverse possession); Miller Properties Inc v Pastoll [2010] EWHC 2364 (Ch) (equitable charge); Donington Park Leisure Ltd v Wheatcroft & Son Ltd [2006] All ER (D) 94 (APR) (contract terms); Topplan Estates Ltd v Townley [2004] EWCA Civ 1369, CA (adverse possession); Dewar v Krestic Ltd [2004] All ER (D) 571 (boundary dispute, costs liability).
Professional Memberships: Property Bar Association; Chancery Bar Association; LCLCBA; .
Career: Educated at Christ's Hospital; University of Bristol (LLB Hons 1991); called 1992, (Gray's Inn); Deputy Adjudicator to HM Land Registry (2008); Judge of the First-tier Tribunal (Property Chamber) (2013); Deputy District Judge (2015).
Publications: Contributor: Law and Practice of Charging Orders on Land (2013); Joint editor, 'Barnsley's Land Options' 6th edition (2016). Contributor: Fisher & Lightwood's 'Law of Mortgage', 11th edn (2001); ICSL Bar Vocational Course, Landlord and Tenant Manual; Landlord and Tenant Factbook, Chapter 10 (residential tenancies); New Law Journal Property Update; Sweep & Maxwell Localaw UK website.

DRAYCOTT, Natasha
5 St Andrew's Hill, London
07949 200 240
natashadraycott@5sah.co.uk
Featured in Extradition (London)
Practice Areas: Natasha is a leading extradition barrister who acts for both foreign governments and requested persons. She has expertise in cases involving Article 8 and was led by Alan Jones QC in the leading authority on Article 8 Celinski & Others [2015]. He is currently leading her in Wisniewski & Others [2016] where the Divisional Court have certified questions of law to be determined by the Supreme Court. She was the first to win an appeal involving a fugitive with only a partner in the UK Sobieraj [2013]. This was followed by the landmark case of Chmura [2013], the first appeal allowed where the Appellant had no family. Natasha deals with a broad spectrum of EAWs. She was led by David Josse QC in India v Kapoor [2015] a complex Part 2 case involving child abduction. She represented an Appellant in a triple murder case Albania v Xhelili [2015]. She is adept at making arguments relating to prison conditions in a variety of jurisdictions including Lithuania, Romania and Hungary. She was led by Alex Bailin QC in the leading case on Hungarian Prison Conditions Szasz and Others [2016] and represented the Bulgarian Judicial Authority in the first test case on prison conditions Bulgaria v Dimitrov [2016]. She is experienced in Habeas Corpus and Judicial Review proceedings Siuda [2014] and appeared in Romania v Iacob [2016], the first case where an application for permission to appeal out of time was granted. Natasha frequently acts for foreign governments. For the US Government in relation to a $70m cyber fraud Konovalenko [2014]; for the Swiss Government, a drug importation case [2014]; for the Polish Government, one of the first reported 'forum' cases Piotrowicz [2014] and for the Hungarian Government in a lengthy human trafficking case Udvardy [2014].

DREW, Jane
Coram Chambers, London
020 7092 3700
jane.drew@coramchambers.co.uk
Featured in Family/Matrimonial (London)
Practice Areas: Children, Family Finance, International. Handles all types of work concerning children with a special emphasis on children in local authority care, care proceedings especially non-accidental injury involving medical evidence, adoption, private children law, divorce, matrimonial property, family provision and inheritance. Also deals with cohabitees covering real property disputes, cases under Section 14 of the Trusts of Land and Trustees Act 1996. Has dealt with numerous cases of sexual abuse and non-accidental injury. She also specialises in international and domestic adoption, wardship, and intractable disputes between parents over contact and residence. Regular lecturer and provider of seminars on cohabitees and public law children's work.
Professional Memberships: Family Law Bar Association. Middle Temple. Association of Lawyers for Children. British Association for Adoption and Fostering
Career: Called to the Bar 1976. Deputy District Judge: Principal Registry
Personal: Educated at Stevenage Girls Grammar School 1963-70, Trevelyan College, Durham 1971-74 and Inns of Court School 1974-76. Leisure pursuits include swimming, tennis and badminton. Lives in Knebworth.

DRISCOLL, Michael QC
Maitland Chambers, London
n/a
mdriscoll@maitlandchambers.com
Featured in Chancery (London), Real Estate Litigation (London)
Practice Areas: General commercial chancery (advisory and litigation) but in particular property related, partnership and company law, trust and mining law matters.
Career: Rugby and Cambridge (BA LLB).

DUDNIKOV, Anton
Essex Court Chambers, London
020 7813 8000
adudnikov@essexcourt.com
Featured in International Arbitration (London), Fraud (London)
Practice Areas: Anton's practice straddles high value (and often high profile) commercial work in court and international arbitration. He has recently appeared in an ICC arbitration in Dubai, and is currently instructed in an LCIA dispute with claims well in excess of US$20 billion. Over the course of the last year, he has also acted for a foreign government in an arbitration claim in the Commercial Court and Court of Appeal relating to the enforcement of a peremptory order made by a London-seated tribunal (which raised various state immunity issues). Anton has extensive and varied experience of trials (for example, a 12-week Commercial Court fraud trial against 19 defendants, and a trial in the Chancery Division concerning the authenticity of a Russian oil painting) and applications including, in particular, for freezing orders and other interim relief. He is currently representing a Russian bank in a US$830 million claim against former shareholders, having obtained freezing orders against them in early 2016. He has also acted for Robert Tchenguiz in his damages claim against the Serious Fraud Office – one of The Lawyer's top 20 cases of 2014. Anton is a native Russian speaker and is frequently instructed in cases with a Russian/CIS element. He was recently selected by Legal Week as one of "ten most promising barristers of ten years call and under".

DUFF, Susan
Compass Chambers, Edinburgh
07971 898516
susan.duff@compasschambers.com
Featured in Health & Safety (Scotland)
Practice Areas: Member of the Regulatory Crime Team at Compass Chambers. Susan is very experienced in acting for clients in all categories of crime both in negotiating resolution of cases and in conducting proceedings on clients' behalf. She specialises in defending regulatory prosecutions particularly Health and Safety, Food Safety, Environmental Offences, Fatal Road Traffic cases and Financial Crime. She acts for major clients in cases involving accidents and deaths at work in all employment areas, in food and environmental investigations where reputational damage is a significant issue and she is skilled at minimising damage. She is experienced in advising and appearing in proceedings in relation to improvement and prohibition notices. She represents the interests of parties at Fatal Accident Inquiries arising out of deaths at work, in custody and where it appears in the public interest that an Inquiry is held.
Professional Memberships: Health and Safety Lawyers Association, UK Environmental Lawyers Association, Association of Regulatory and Disciplinary Lawyers, Scottish Criminal Bar Association, Proceeds of Crime Lawyers Association.
Career: Procurator Fiscal Depute 1992-1996, Principal Procurator Fiscal Depute 1996-2002, Called to the Bar 2003.

DUFFY, James
Fountain Court Chambers, London
020 7583 3335
jd@fountaincourt.co.uk
Featured in Aviation (London), Banking & Finance (London)
Practice Areas: Broad commercial litigation and arbitration practice, including: banking and finance; civil fraud; aviation; insurance and reinsurance; and professional negligence. Significant recent cases include: Decura v UBS; Barclays v UniCredit; Choicezone v Simmons & Simmons; Tchenguiz v Serious Fraud Office; Merrill Lynch, Dexia and UBS v City of Florence; Bmibaby v Durham Tees Valley Airport; Credit Agricole and FGIC v IKB; Office of Fair Trading v Abbey National and others; and American Reliable and CNA v Willis.
Professional Memberships: COMBAR; BASL
Career: Called 2005
Personal: Christ Church, Oxford (BA, First; BCL, Distinction)

DUMONT, Thomas
Radcliffe Chambers, London
020 78310081
tdumont@radcliffechambers.com
Featured in Chancery (London), Professional Negligence (London), Charities (London), Trusts (London)
Practice Areas: Professional negligence principally solicitors and accountants: Roberts v Gill & Co [2010] Dhillon v Siddiqui [2008] VGL v Weightmans [2006] Gibbons v Nelsons [2000] Paragon Finance v Thakerar & Co [1999]. Private client advice and litigation, including trusts, wills and probate: Re Sir Malcolm Arnold Deceased [2014] Duke of Manchester's Settled Estates [2011] Re Bernard Matthews Deceased [2012]. Charity: advises and represents national and local charities: Re St Andrews Cheam Lawn Tennis Club [2012] Cuppage v Lawson [2010] Dore v Leicestershire CC [2010].
Professional Memberships: Charity Law Association; Society of Trust & Estate Practitioners; Professional Negligence Bar Association; ACTAPS. Bar Law Reform Committee
Career: MA [Cantab] Exhibitioner in Law, Trinity Hall. Called 1979, Gray's Inn. Lecturer in trusts and revenue, University of Westminster 1981-85. STEP Advocate of the Year 2011.
Personal: Married with two children, one in the Army one in the charity sector. Fellow of the Zoological Society of London. Plays cricket whenever possible.

DUNHAM, Nicholas
9-12 Bell Yard, London
020 74001800
n.dunham@912by.com
Featured in Crime (London)
Practice Areas: Nicholas prosecutes and defends serious crime across the entire range of offences. He is regularly instructed as sole counsel in serious sexual offences (particularly rape and historic abuse), high level conspiracies to import and / or to supply Class A drugs (including those investigated by the National Crime Agency and the Flying Squad), firearms offences, serious violence (including attempted murder), serious dishonesty (including six figure frauds and conspiracies to steal) and driving offences involving death and serious injury. He also prosecutes and defends confiscation proceedings, including those where the Crown seeks orders in excess of £1 million. He is recognised for the high quality of his cross-examination and has extensive experience in the examination of all types of witnesses, including the young and/or vulnerable and experts in a number of fields, for example forensic pathologists, other medical practitioners and vehicle examiners. He is known for his ability to advance persuasive legal argument and has regularly appeared in the Court of Appeal. As a result of this expertise, he has been instructed by the Registrar to represent unrepresented appellants who have been granted leave to appeal. He also offers second opinions to defendants who have been told that they have no grounds of appeal or who have been refused leave by the single judge.
Career: BA (Hons) (Dunelm); Diplock Scholar of the Middle Temple; Called 1999; Appointed to the CPS Advocates Panel at Level 4; Specialist Rape Prosecutor.

DUNNING, Graham QC
Essex Court Chambers, London
020 7813 8000
gdunningqc@essexcourt.com
Featured in International Arbitration (London), Commercial Dispute Resolution (London), Fraud (London), Shipping (London)
Practice Areas: Graham Dunning QC is co-head of Essex Court Chambers. He has a specialist practice as an advocate and arbitrator in substantial international and commercial disputes. In recent years, Graham has appeared at all levels in the courts in the UK, offshore and in many international arbitrations in London and other arbitration venues around the world: including two heavy civil fraud trials, several appeals to the English Court of Appeal, a complex jurisdictional appeal (in an offshore case) before the Privy Council, an important Commercial Court banking/commodities trial, commercial arbitrations in Dubai and Singapore, a trial in the DIFC in Dubai, various anti-suit injunctions and applications for freezing relief, an appeal in the Eastern Caribbean Court of Appeal, a major oil and gas arbitration, numerous arbitration-related court applications (including issues of state immunity), and major arbitrations including investment arbitrations in Washington and Paris and substantial international commercial arbitrations (eg ICC, UNCITRAL, LCIA, LCIA-India, SCC). His clients have included states and state entities, banks, major commercial corporations and high-net-worth individuals. He also frequently sits as arbitrator in international arbitrations of all kinds, having been appointed in more than 50 cases. He has extensive experience of disputes relating to investments in oil and gas and mining and international trade in all types of commodities, energy, natural resources, as well as shareholder disputes.
Professional Memberships: LCIA; BMLA, Member ICC UK Task Force on

National Rules of Procedure for Recognition and Enforcement of Foreign Awards; BILA; SIAC panel; KLRCA panel
Career: 2013 Co-Head of Essex Court Chambers; 2012 Called to Eastern Caribbean Supreme Court (St Vincent); 2011 Called to Eastern Caribbean Supreme Court (BVI); 2009 Bencher, Lincoln's Inn; 2001 Silk; 1983 Joined Essex Court Chambers; 1982 Called to the Bar Lincoln's Inn;
Personal: Cambridge, England, 1st Class Hons Law, BA; MA; Harvard Law School, LLM

DUTTON, Timothy C QC

Maitland Chambers, London
020 74061200
tdutton@maitlandchambers.com
Featured in Real Estate Litigation (London)

Practice Areas: Property related litigation and advisory work. Reported cases include: Meretz Investments NV v ACP [2007] Ch 197 (ChD); [2008] Ch 244 (CA); Legal & General v Expeditors International [2007] 1 P&CR 5 (ChD); [2007] 2 P&CR 204 (CA); Housden v Conservators of Wimbledon & Putney Commons [2007] 1 WLR 1171 (ChD); [2008] 1 WLR 1172 (CA); KPMG v Network Rail [2008] 1 P&CR 11 (CA); Heronslea v Kwik-Fit Properties [2009] Env. LR 28 (QBD); Norwich Union v Linpac Mouldings [2010] L&TR 74 (ChD); [2010] L&TR 183 (CA); Pittack v Naviede [2011] 1 WLR 1666 (ChD); Redcard v Williams [2011] 2 EGLR 67 (CA); Carey-Morgan v Sloane Stanley Estate [2012] 3 EGLR 38 (CA); Carey-Morgan v De Walden [2013] P&CR DG3 (UT); Cravecrest v 2nd Duke of Westminster WT [2014] Ch 301 (CA); Friends Life v A&A Express Building [2014] 2 P&CR DG17 (ChD); Mann v Shelfside Holdings [2015] AllER (D).
Professional Memberships: Chancery Bar Association; Property Bar Association.
Career: Called to the Bar in 1985. QC 2013.
Personal: Born 1962. Educated at Godalming Grammar School (1972-80) and Durham University (1981-84).

DUTTON CBE, Timothy QC

Fountain Court Chambers, London
020 7583 3335
chambers@fountaincourt.co.uk
Featured in Administrative & Public Law (London), Professional Negligence (London), Financial Services (London), Professional Discipline (London)

Practice Areas: Leading silk at the London Bar with a general commercial practice with particular emphasis on professional, regulatory and public law matters appearing in Courts and Tribunals at all levels. Regularly instructed by City Firms and institutions in high value and complex cases. Appears in and accepts appointments as an Arbitrator. Advises and represents both regulators and regulated. In 2015-16 led for the FRC in the case against Deloitte arising out of their audits of Aero Inventory Plc, Acted in Impact Funding Solutions v AIG in the Court of Appeal and Supreme Court (extend of prof indemnity cover), for the SRA in the cases arising out of the Al Sweedy Inquiry, and in SRA v Spector (open justice principles), SRA v Barnett and Swift and others (series of cases with £100m losses from the Axiom Fund), and Enterprise Insurance v Leeds United FC (sponsorship and loan agreements). 2014-15 acted for the BSB in Lumsdon v LSB and BSB at every level to the UKSC, for four regulators in the UKSC in Hemming v Westminster City Council and in the UKSC for the Appellants/insurers in Coventry v Lawrence, for Gibson Dunn in Republic of Djibouti v Boreh and others (Commercial Court). In 2013 acted for the Financial Reporting Council in FRC v Deloitte and Einollahi in the proceedings concerning Deloitte's advice and conduct in relation to the MG Rover Group and the Phoenix Four, and for Herbert Smith in LUL v Freshfields and Herbert Smith – claim for £140m brought by London Underground. In 2011-2012 acted in JSC Bank v Ablyazov (preserving client's rights of access to solicitors), and acted for the SRA in copyright/file sharing cases. . In 2010 led for the FSA in Atlantic Law and Greystoke v FSA (share frauds and boiler rooms), and for the Law Society in the Court of Appeal in Quinn Direct Insurance v The Law Society [2010 EWCA Civ 805]. In 2009 conducted the Inquiry for Sport England into the World Class Payments Bureau. 2008-10 acted for the SRA in the prosecutions of lawyers involved in the Miners Compensation Scheme, and the appeals arising out of them: Acted for the FSA in the first appeal to the CA from FSMA Tribunal, Fox Hayes Feb 09 (CA). Clydesdale Finance v Smailes and others 2009 EWHC 1745 (Ch) Challenges to pre-pack sale of law firm. Insurance: Quinn Direct Insurance v The Law Society [2010 EWCA Civ 805], Blunt and others v Courtaulds 09-10 (cases arising out of IOMA insurance policies). Accountants/Audits JDS Inquiries into Barings, Polly Peck, Resort Hotels, Queens Moat House Hotels, Wickes, Trans Tec, Wiggins Group. The ICAEW proceedings against the liquidators of Boo.com (2006). For other notable case references, see Fountain Court Chambers website www.fountaincourt.co.uk
Professional Memberships: COMBAR, ALBA, ARDL.
Career: 2000-04 Chairman IATC, Chairman Bar Council Working Party into Advocacy Training. 2004 Leader of the South Eastern Circuit and Member of Bar Council 2004-06. Vice Chairman Bar Council (2007). Chairman of the Bar Council 2008. Head of Chambers (2008-13). Chairman Association of Regulatory and Disciplinary Lawyers (ARDL) 2009-2015. Trustee and Governor Legal Education Foundation. Deputy High Court Judge. Appointed CBE for services to the UK Legal System.
Publications: Contributor to Butterworths Guide to the Legal Services Act 2007. Lectured widely on the Act, and in areas of specialist expertise.
Personal: 1978 BA Jurisprudence. Keble College, Oxford. French speaker.

DYAL, Daniel

Cloisters, London
020 7827 4000
ddyal@cloisters.com
Featured in Employment (London)

Practice Areas: Daniel is regularly entrusted with his solicitors' most important, challenging and sensitive cases. He is always meticulously well prepared, excels on points of law and has a reputation as a formidable cross-examiner. Daniel is deeply committed to his clients. He is renowned for presenting cases with charm and without fear. Daniel specialises in all the major areas of employment law including discrimination, whistleblowing, TUPE, bonus disputes, atypical workers, holiday pay and unfair dismissal. He is experienced in handling group litigation. In 2013 Daniel was appointed as a Fee-paid Employment Judge in the East-Midlands Region. Daniel has substantial experience of appellate advocacy and has appeared in a number of reported cases. Daniel also specialises in personal injury claims, in which he has wide experience. He has acted in high value and complicated litigation both as sole counsel and, in catastrophic injury claims, as junior counsel. Daniel is experienced in professional disciplinary proceedings before regulatory bodies and has appeared in cases of grave seriousness before a number of regulators.
Professional Memberships: ELBA, ELA, DLA, PIBA, AvMA
Career: Called to the bar in 2006.

DYMOND, Andrew

Arden Chambers, London
020 7242 4244
andrew.dymond@ardenchambers.com
Featured in Social Housing (London)

Practice Areas: All areas of housing, landlord and tenant and local government law.
Professional Memberships: Housing Law Practitioners Association, Social Housing Law Association, Property Bar Association.
Career: Called to the Bar in 1991. He advises and represents both public and private sector clients, including local authorities, PRPs, leaseholders, tenants and the homeless. Notable cases include: R. (Edwards) v Birmingham CC [2016] EWHC 173 (Admin); [2016] H.L.R. 11 (hmelessness) Islington LBC v Unite Group Plc [2013] EWHC 508 (Admin) (HMOs); Rochdale BC v Dixon [2011] EWCA Civ 1173; [2012] H.L.R. 6 (water charges); Swindon BC v Redpath [2009] EWCA Civ 943; [2010] P.T.S.R. 904 (antisocial behaviour); Kilby v Basildon DC [2007] EWCA Civ 479; [2007] H.L.R. 39 (varying tenancies).
Publications: Publications: Co-author of: Manual of Housing Law (8th and 9th Eds); Current Law Annotations for the Housing Act 2004 and Housing and Regeneration Act 2008; Leasehold Valuation Tribunals – a Practical Guide. Deputy General Editor of the Housing Law Reports. An editor of Arden and Parington's Housing Law.
Personal:

EARDLEY, Aidan

One Brick Court, London
020 7353 8845
ae@onebrickcourt.com
Featured in Data Protection (London), Defamation/Privacy (London)

Practice Areas: Defamation, privacy/breach of confidence, malicious falsehood, freedom of information, data protection, contempt of court and reporting restrictions, harassment, media-related human rights law. Notable/recent cases include: libel – Bukovsky v CPS [2016] EWHC 1926; Simpson v MGN Ltd [2016] EWCA Civ 772 Cruddas v Calvert & Ors [2015] EWCA Civ 171 & [2014] EMLR 5 (CA); Contostavlos v News Group Newspapers Ltd [2014] EWHC 1339; El Naschie v Macmillan Publishers Ltd [2012] EWHC 1809; Khader v Aziz [2010] 1 WLR 2673 (CA); Timtchenko v The Economist Newspaper Ltd (2009); Rath v Guardian News & Media Ltd (2008); Polanski v Conde Nast [2005] 1 WLR 637 (HL); privacy – WXY v Gewanter & Ors (2009-2015); Lord Browne v Associated Newspapers Ltd [2008] QB 103 (CA); Green Corns v Claverley [2005] EMLR 31; freedom of information – R(Evans) v Attorney General [2015] AC 1787, Home Office v Information Commissioner [2015] UKUT 27, Evans v Information Commissioner [2012] UKUT 313, Cobain v Information Commissioner (FTT, 2011), HEFCE v Information Commissioner (FTT, 2010); harassment – Brand v Berki [2015] EWHC 3373; other – Ashley v CC Sussex [2008] 1 AC 962 (HL)
Professional Memberships: Human Rights Lawyers Association; London Common Law and Commercial Bar Association.
Career: Called 2002, Lincoln's Inn; Attorney General's 'B' Panel 2011; Attorney General's 'A' Panel, 2016; part-time judge, First-tier Tribunal (Social Entitlement Chamber), 2013
Publications: Co-author 'Duncan and Neill on Defamation' (3rd ed 2009, 4th ed, 2015); contributor 'Arlidge, Eady & Smith on Contempt' (4th ed, 2011, 5th ed, forthcoming).
Personal: BA Hons (Oxon). DipLaw (City). Languages: good French, some Spanish and German.

EAST, William

5 Stone Buildings, London
020 7242 6201
clerks@5sblaw.com
Featured in Court of Protection (All Circuits)

Practice Areas: A traditional Chancery practice that incorporates a wide range of contentious and non-contentious work, with particular emphasis upon: trusts, wills, probate and the administration of estates, Court of Protection, capital taxes and estate planning, pensions, proprietary estoppel, claims under the Inheritance (Provision for Family and Dependants) Act 1975, real property and related professional negligence matters.
Professional Memberships: Bar Pro Bono Unit, Chancery Bar Association and the Lord Denning Society.
Career: Called in 2008
Publications: Writes for several professional publications and frequently lectures on areas of his practice. Personal: Educated at St John's College, Oxford (BA Hons) and City University, London.

EASTON, Jonathan

Kings Chambers, Manchester
0345 034 3444
clerks@kingschambers.com
Featured in Planning (Northern)

Practice Areas: Practises in all aspects of Town and Country Planning, with particular experience of section 78 and Development Plan Inquiries. Recognised by Planning Magazine as a leading planning barrister under 35 (2006). Notable cases include: Fordent Holdings Ltd v SSCLG [2013] EWHC 2844 (Admin); [2014] J.P.L. 226; Feather v Cheshire East BC [2010] EWHC 1420 (Admin); R. (on the application of P Casey (Enviro) Ltd) v Bradford MBC [2008] EWHC 2543 (Admin); [2009] J.P.L. 639. Also practises in environmental law and compulsory purchase.
Professional Memberships: Planning and Environmental Bar Association (PEBA).
Career: First Class Honours Degree in European Law (LLB) from Warwick University. Masters in Comparative and International Law (LLM) from European University Institute, Florence. Very Competent in Bar Finals, Inns of Court School of Law.
Publications: Author of the Housing Chapter in Judicial Review: Law and Practice (Jordans)(1st Edition)

EATON, Deborah QC
1 King's Bench Walk, London
020 7936 1500
deatonqc@1kbw.co.uk
Featured in Family/Matrimonial (London)
Practice Areas: All aspects of family law including matrimonial finance and private disputes relating to children.
Professional Memberships: Family Law Bar Association. Midland Circuit. International Academy of Matrimonial Lawyers.
Career: Called to the Bar (Inner Temple) 1985. Recorder 2004 – Family and Crime. Silk 2008. Bencher Inner Temple 2008. Deputy High Court Judge 2011.
Publications: Co-author and editor: 'Wildblood and Eaton: Financial Provision In Family Matters' (Sweet and Maxwell). Regular lecturer in matrimonial finance and children matters. Member of Jordans Advisory Board.
Personal: Born 28 March 1962, BSc (Hons) Psychology and Anthropology. Diploma in Law.

EATON TURNER, David
New Square Chambers, London
020 7419 8000
david.eatonturner@newsquarechambers.co.uk
Featured in Chancery (London), Company (London), Restructuring/Insolvency (London)
Practice Areas: Company, insolvency and commercial law including reorganisations of capital, corporate and personal insolvency, commercial, company and chancery litigation, banking, civil fraud, asset recovery, directors' duties, unfair prejudice petitions and other shareholder disputes, agency, sale of goods, professional negligence. Cases include: Goldtrail Travel Ltd (in liquidation) v Aydin & Ors [2015] 1 BCLC 89; [2016] 1 BCLC 635 (fiduciary duties, dishonest assistance); Re Husky Group Ltd [2015] BPIR 184; Li Quan v Stuart Bray [2015] WTLR 885; Yam Seng Pte Ltd v International Trade Corp [2013] 1 Lloyd's Rep. 526 (contract, obligations of good faith); Anglo Irish Bank Corp v Flannery [2013] BPIR 1 (bankruptcy); Raithatha v Williamson [2012] 1 WLR 3559 (bankruptcy, pensions); Pioneer Iron & Steel Group Company Ltd; Phoenix (Contracts) Leicester Limited, [2010] EWHC 2375 (shareholders' rights); Itsalat International v Allied TC plc [2009] All ER (D) 141 (fiduciary duties, freezing and search orders); Dayman v Lawrence Graham [2008] All ER (D) 191 (professional negligence); BCCI v Bank of India [2005] 2 BCLC 328 CA (banking, insolvency, fraudulent trading); GHE Realisations Ltd [2006] 1 WLR 287 (insolvency, distributions by administrators); Royal Bank of Scotland v Sandra Fielding [2004] CA (banking, freezing orders); Mumbray v Lapper [2005] BCC 990 (shareholders, derivative actions).
Professional Memberships: Chancery Bar Association, COMBAR.
Career: Called to the Bar, Lincoln's Inn, 1984; called to the Bar of Eastern Caribbean Supreme Court (BVI); Recorder (Civil) 2010.
Personal: Educated: Westminster School; Queen Mary College, University of London.

EDDY, Katherine
11KBW, London
020 7632 8500
Katherine.Eddy@11kbw.com
Featured in Education (London)
Practice Areas: Katherine practises in employment, education and public law. In the employment field, she has acted for and against large financial institutions, local authorities, government departments, retailers and small charities. Her recent cases include Samara v MBI & Partners UK Limited [2016] EWHC 441 (QB) (led by Simon Devonshire QC) and [2014] EWHC 4220 (QB), Essex County Council v Jarrett (EAT, 1 May 2015), Croft Vets v Butcher [2013] Eq LR 1170, and CVS Solicitors LLP v Van der Borgh [2013] EqLR 934. Katherine has a particular interest in public law work with an education element. She has recently been involved in a number of judicial review claims about University admissions and enrolment decisions, and appears regularly in the First-Tier Tribunal in disability discrimination and special educational needs cases.
Professional Memberships: ELA, ELBA, COMBAR.
Career: Called to the bar in 2009. Katherine is a member of the Attorney General's C Panel of Counsel.

EDELMAN, Colin QC
Devereux, London
020 7353 7534
edelmanqc@devchambers.co.uk
Featured in International Arbitration (London), Professional Negligence (London), Insurance (London), International Arbitration (London)
Practice Areas: Specialises in high value complex commercial disputes with an emphasis on insurance, reinsurance, professional negligence, and energy. A number of his cases have been shortlisted by The Lawyer as Top Litigation Cases of the year and he has previously been voted Insurance and Professional Negligence Silk of the Year. Key cases in 2015/16: IEGL v Zurich (Supreme Court); Versloot Dredging v HDI Gerling (Supreme Court); Atlasnavios v Navigators (CofA) and a number of high value arbitrations as counsel and as arbitrator. For the most recent case highlights, please visit www.devereuxchambers.co.uk.
Professional Memberships: Commercial Bar Association.
Career: Called to the Bar: 1977; Devereux Chambers: 1979; Assistant Recorder: 1993; QC: 1995; Recorder: 1996-2016. Head of Chambers: 2002 – 2011; Bencher of Middle Temple: 2003; Director of Bar Mutual Indemnity Fund: 2007, Deputy Chairman: 2009, Chairman: 2013; Deputy High Court Judge: (QBD & Commercial Court) 2008-2016.
Publications: Editor of 'The Law of Reinsurance' (OUP). Contributor to 'Insurance Disputes' (LLP). Speaker at seminars on insurance and reinsurance topics.
Personal: Educated at Haberdashers' Aske's School, Elstree 1961-72 and Clare College, Cambridge 1973-76. Leisure pursuits include skiing, walking, badminton, Luton Town FC. Lives in London.

EDGE, Andrew
11KBW, London
020 7632 8500
Andrew.Edge@11kbw.com
Featured in Employment (London)
Practice Areas: Employment law, discrimination and commercial law. Regularly involved in High Court and appellate litigation. Andrew's practice covers all areas of employment law with an emphasis on whistleblowing, discrimination, TUPE, unlawful competitive activity (including springboard injunctions), bonus disputes, garden leave and the use of confidential information.
Professional Memberships: ELA, ELBA, and COMBAR.
Career: Called 2003, Major Scholar, Inner Temple.
Publications: Transfer of Undertakings (Sweet and Maxwell) and Butterworths Employment Law Practice and Procedure.
Personal: Educated at Colston's School Bristol and King's College London. Resides London.

EDGE, Charlotte
5 Stone Buildings, London
020 7242 6201
clerks@5sblaw.com
Featured in Chancery (London), Court of Protection (All Circuits)
Practice Areas: Chancery practice with an emphasis on litigation. Particular interest in contentious trusts and probate, family provision, removal of trustees and personal representatives, construction and rectification claims, Court of Protection work as well as professional negligence claims arising out of any of her practice areas. Also undertakes a range of non-contentious drafting and advisory work including capital taxes.
Professional Memberships: Chancery Bar Association
Career: Called 2006; Qualified Mediator (ADR) 2013
Publications: Writes and speaks regularly on all areas of her practice.

EDWARDS, Daniel
Dere Street Barristers, York
01904 620048
d.edwards@derestreet.co.uk
Featured in Personal Injury (North Eastern)
Practice Areas: Dan specialises in high value personal injury / clinical negligence litigation. He is instructed nationally by a wide range of large corporations, insurance companies, trade unions and private clients. His work focuses upon accidents leading to catastrophic injury or fatality. He has a well-established practice in high value clinical negligence work, acting for both Claimant and Defendants. Each year Dan is identified by the major legal publications as a leading practitioner, noted for his outstanding advocacy skills and strong client care. Many clients instruct Dan as an alternative to using Leading Counsel in catastrophic claims. Dan has a substantial regulatory and disciplinary practice and further deals with all aspects of licensing (appearing on behalf of the Trade and local Councils). He has particular experience of applications concerning pubs / clubs, gaming centres / casinos, and all forms of taxi licensing. Dan attends at Inquests, the CICA and is regularly involved in cases involving the MIB.
Professional Memberships: Personal Injury Bar Association.
Career: Called 1993. Recorder (Civil) 2008. Head of Regulatory team
Publications: Associate Editor of Charlesworth & Percy on Negligence 13th Edition.

EDWARDS, Douglas QC
Francis Taylor Building, London
020 7353 8415
clerks@ftbchambers.co.uk
Featured in Agriculture & Rural Affairs (London), Planning (London)
Practice Areas: Practice involves planning, compulsory purchase, environment, administrative and local government, highway law and the law relating to town and village greens. He appears regularly for both appellants and local planning and other authorities at inquiries, in the Lands Tribunal and in the courts. Douglas Edwards planning inquiry practice has engaged a wide range of issues over the last year including major retail schemes, housing development, development of docks and proposed tall buildings. He represented the successful developers of a large retail park near Leeds as well as several large residential developments. He has considerable experience of planning enforcement both at inquiry and in the High Court in the context of injunction applications. He regularly advises and appears in respect of town/village green disputes and has had a number of notable and important successes for landowners in respect of such disputes. He is frequently asked to appear as inspector or to advise registration authorities in respect of these matters. He is regularly instructed by local planning authorities for complex enforcement cases and is noted for handling detailed factual disputes arising under ground (d) appeals and in lawful development certificate matters. He has considerable experience of gypsy and traveller work. Douglas regularly advises and appears in the Lands Tribunal on matters concerning compulsory purchase. He is a member of the Crossrail Panel of Counsel who appears and advises on compensation matters concerning that project. Douglas had been instructed on a number of listed building cases and has developed particular expertise in advising upon, and appearing at, inquiries in relation to enabling development proposals affecting listed buildings and in applying the guidance published by English Heritage concerning that subject. His other areas of specialism include mineral planning (in which he has recently had two notable successes, one for an appellant and one for a mineral planning authority) and also water and riverbank related development. He appeared recently in a controversial inquiry concerning the right to moor vessels temporarily on the River Thames.
Career: Called to Bar: 1992, QC: 2010.

EDWARDS, Peter
Devereux, London
020 7353 7534
edwards@devchambers.co.uk
Featured in Personal Injury (London), Employment (London)
Practice Areas: Practices in all areas of employment, discrimination and industrial relations law. Also practices in the field of personal injury, with a particular specialism in human rights aspects of such claims (abuse and inappropriate state conduct etc). Recent reported cases include: Autoclenz v. Belcher (Supreme Court); Rolls Royce v Unite (CA); and Craig v Transocean (Supreme Court). For a full list of reported cases see www.devereuxchambers.co.uk.
Professional Memberships: APIL; PIBA; ELBA; ELA; ILS.
Career: Scott Inquiry 1992-95.
Publications: Tottel Discrimination Law (Sexual Orientation and Religion/Belief); Jordans Employment Law (Whistleblowing); Jordans Employment Law Precedents.
Personal: The musical genius of Dolly Parton.

EISSA, Adrian
25 Bedford Row, London
020 7067 1500
aeissa@25bedfordrow.com
Featured in Crime (London)

Practice Areas: Adrian is regularly instructed in a wide variety of serious and complex crime including major fraud. His fraud practice includes: insider trading, money laundering, copyright and trading standards, mortgage fraud, fraudulent trading, land banking fraud, other boiler room fraud, Ponzi schemes, VAT and MTIC fraud, Companies Act offences. Adrian is experienced in representing both defendants and third parties affected by confiscation proceedings, as well as cash seizures and civil recovery proceedings under Part V POCA. Adrian also has extensive experience in all other areas of criminal defence ranging from murder, sexual offences, major drugs cases, through to motoring offences.
Professional Memberships: Criminal Bar Association, Proceeds of Crime Lawyers Association, Standing Conference of Mediation Advocates.
Career: Called 1998. Appointed a Recorder of the Crown Court 2012; Qualified for Direct Access; Inner Temple Advocacy Trainer; Mediator.
Publications: Author of the "Confiscation Law Handbook", published by Bloomsbury Professional 2011. Author of "Fraud: A Practitioner's Handbook", published by Bloomsbury Professional 2014.

EKLUND, Graham QC
4 New Square, London
020 7822 2000
g.eklund@4newsquare.com
Featured in Professional Negligence (London), Insurance (London), Product Liability (London), Property Damage (London)

Practice Areas: Professional negligence; Product Liability; Insurance related matters, particularly fraudulent claims, policy construction and coverage issues, fire, explosion and disaster claims, including pollution and contamination. Personal injury, particularly serious injuries (tetraplegic, paraplegic and sports injuries). Reported cases include Jones & Marsh McLennan v Crowley Colosso (1996); Yorkshire Water v Sun Alliance (1996); John Munroe v LFCDA (1997); Chapman v Christopher (1998): Greatorex v Greatorex (2000); Beckett v Midland Electricity (2001); Cornhill Insurance v Stamp Felt Roofing (2002); James v CGU Insurance (2002); Johnson v Technitrack Europa (2003); Scottish & Newcastle v GD Construction (2003); Forrest & Sons v CGU Insurance (2006); Bartoline Ltd v Royal & Sun Alliance Insurance (2007); Meisels v Norwich Union Insurance (2007); Evans v Kosmar Villa Holidays (2007); Perrin v Northampton BC (2007); Kosmar Villa Holidays v Trustees Syndicate 1243 (2008); Harris v Perry (2009); Reilly v NIG (2009); Chubb Fire Ltd v Vicar of Spalding (2010); Seashell v Aviva (2011); Aviva v Brown (2011); Synergy v CGU (2011); Joseph Fielding Properties v Aviva (2011); Sharon's Bakery (Europe) Ltd v Axa (2012); Milton Keynes Borough Council v Nulty & Others (2012); Argos v Leather Trade House (2012); Hughes v Williams (2013); Mueller v Central Roofing (2013).
Professional Memberships: PNBA, PIBA, COMBAR.
Career: BA; LLB (Hons) (Auck). Barrister and Solicitor High Court of NZ; Solicitor Supreme Court of England and Wales (1979-84). Called 1984, Silk 2002.
Personal: Married, two children. Interests include music, theatre, sport.

ELIAS, Thomas
Serle Court, London
020 7242 6105
telias@serlecourt.co.uk
Featured in Company (London)

Practice Areas: Commercial and chancery litigation; company law (directors' duties, derivative claims, minority shareholder claims); civil fraud; corporate and personal insolvency; intellectual property; trusts; professional negligence; judicial review (Bahamas). Interesting cases include: Prince Abdulaziz v Apex Global Management Ltd [2014] UKSC 64 (relief from sanctions); Sukhoruchkin v van Bekestein [2014] EWCA Civ 399 (reflective loss, freezing injunctions); Abouraya v Sigmund [2014] EWHC 277 (Ch) (double derivative claims); Moroccanoil v Aldi [2015] FSR. 4 (passing off); Ukulele Orchestra of Great Britain v Clausen [2015] EWHC 1772 (IPEC) (passing off, trade mark infringement, copyright).
Professional Memberships: Chancery Bar Association; COMBAR
Career: Called 2008. Called to the Bar of the Eastern Caribbean Supreme Court (BVI) 2013.
Publications: "Securing a share of goodwill", Butterworths Journal of International Banking and Financial Law, July/August 2016. "Why Procedure Matters", New Law Journal, 6 March 2015. Contributor to "Concise European Trade Mark and Design Law", Walters Kluwer, 2011.
Personal: BA, MA, MPhil, PhD, King's College, Cambridge. GDL and BVC, City University. Formerly Clerk and Private Secretary in the Parliament Office, House of Lords.

ELKINGTON, Ben QC
4 New Square, London
020 7822 2036
b.elkington@4newsquare.com
Featured in Professional Negligence (London), Commercial Dispute Resolution (London), Insurance (London), Property Damage (London)

Practice Areas: Ben has a thriving practice centred on insurance, commercial disputes and professional liability. Insurance work involves all forms of coverage disputes (including fraud) and subrogated claims. Commercial work includes domestic and international litigation and arbitration. Professional liability work focuses on claims against insurance brokers, financial advisers, solicitors, barristers, accountants and valuers. Ben acts for both claimants and defendants in equal measure, which gives him a real advantage when advising his clients and devising strategies to achieve their commercial objectives. In addition to acting as an advocate and adviser, Ben acts as an arbitrator (particularly of insurance disputes), and he is an ARIAS (UK) panel member.
Professional Memberships: COMBAR (Committee Member), PNBA, LCLCBA, BILA, ARIAS (Panel Member).
Career: Called 1996 (Top of Bar Finals); Silk 2012. Previously admitted to the New York Bar and practised in New York with Sullivan & Cromwell. Admitted to the Bar of the Cayman Islands (ad hoc).
Publications: Editor of Jackson & Powell on Professional Negligence, and Jackson & Powell Professional Liability Precedents.
Personal: Educated at Trinity College, Cambridge (BA, 1st Class Hons in Law 1993; MA 1997), and University of Virginia (LLM 1994). Lives in London with wife and four children. Spends holidays on the Isle of Mull walking, fishing and playing golf.

ELLIOTT, Sarah QC
Doughty Street Chambers, London
020 7404 1313 (clerk)
s.elliott@doughtystreet.co.uk
Featured in Crime (London)

Career: Sarah Elliott QC is a highly recommended silk with an outstanding reputation in criminal defence, especially violent and sexual crime. She has been described by solicitors as 'on the most wanted listed for heavyweight crime'; and 'leaves clients reassured by her manner and juries persuaded by her arguments'. Sarah has a proven record achieving successful outcomes in complex, difficult and unusual cases including homicides, multiple rape and serious sexual offences, large scale drug operations, financial crime and money laundering, and criminal appeals. She recently successfully defended a celebrity businessman accused of paying a 13 year old for sex and secured the acquittal in absence of a member of the ruling family of a Gulf State accused of rape. She defends in the most difficult of murder cases including that of a man extradited for the murder of his landlord and concealment of his body, and recently representing one of seven defendants accused of a ferocious gang murder in Hackney. She has experience in defending large scale prosecutions of historic sexual offending including in 2015, the systemic abuse in a care home of boys with learning difficulties over 30 years and the historic abuse of boys in two prominent Catholic schools.

ELLIOTT, Timothy QC
Keating Chambers, London
020 7544 2600
telliott@keatingchambers.com
Featured in International Arbitration (London)

Practice Areas: Tim Elliott has specialised in construction, engineering, energy and professional negligence work for over 35 years. He has a wide ranging experience of all aspects of these fields in litigation and all forms of alternative dispute resolution such as arbitration and adjudication. Tim Elliott has been recognised for excellent advocacy skills and hands on approach to cases which has made him a popular choice with UK and overseas clients who include local and national governments, public authorities, developers, funding institutions, national and international contractors and sub-contractors, architects, surveyors and engineers. Tim Elliott now works as an arbitrator, adjudicator and mediator.
Professional Memberships: Technology and Construction Bar Association (TECBAR); Commercial Bar Association (COMBAR); Society of Construction Law.
Career: Called 1975; Queen's Counsel 1992; ICC Arbitration Panel; LCIA Arbitration Panel; Law Society Panel of Arbitrators; HKIAC Panel of Arbitrators; KLRCA Panel of Arbitrators; CEDR Accredited Mediator; TECBAR accredited adjudicator.

ELLIS, Nick QC
Westwater Advocates, Edinburgh
07739 639023
nick.ellis@westwateradvocates.com
Featured in Construction (Scotland), Commercial Dispute Resolution (Scotland)

Practice Areas: Nick is a well established and experienced leading Counsel with a formidable reputation in commercial and construction/engineering disputes. In 2008 he was leading Counsel for one of the core participants in the ICL Disaster Public Inquiry. In 2009 and 2010 he represented one of the parties in the Trident Inquiry. His cases include: CSC Braehead v Laing O'Rourke 2008 SLT 697; ANM Group v Gilcomston North 2008 SLT 835; Wishart v Castlecroft 2009 SLT 812; Lava Luminar Ignite v Mama Group 2010 SC 310; Apollo Engineering v James Scott 2013 SC (UKSC) 286; Buchanan v Nolan [2013] CSIH 38; Hill of Rubislaw v Rubislaw Quarry [2014] CSIH 105; M & L Petitioners (Contempt of Court) 2015 SLT 269; @SIPP Pension Trustees v Insight Travel 2016 SLT 131 and Renfrew Golf Club v Motocaddy [2016] CSIH 57.
Professional Memberships: Standing Junior Counsel to the Scottish Office / Ministers 1997-2002.
Career: Qualified solicitor 1981-89; Partner, commercial firm 1985-89; Called to the Bar in 1990; Took Silk in 2002.
Personal: Educated at the Royal High School in Edinburgh, LLB Edinburgh University 1979.

ELLIS, Peter
7BR, London
020-7242-3555
pellis@7br.co.uk
Featured in Clinical Negligence (London)

Practice Areas: Clinical negligence; personal injury; product liability; coroners' inquests.
Professional Memberships: Professional Negligence & Personal Injuries Bar Associations. Medico-Legal Society. Inquest Lawyers' Group. Faculty of Forensic & Legal Medicine, Royal College of Physicians of London. Society of Doctors in Law. Worshipful Society of Apothecaries. Coroners' Society of England & Wales.
Career: Former hospital doctor (MB.BS 1984, MRCP(UK) 1990). Former solicitor specialising in product liability and healthcare litigation at Davies Arnold Cooper, London (Diploma in Law 1991, Solicitors' Final Examination 1992). Called to the Bar 1997 (Middle Temple). Qualified mediator (CEDR, 2000). Assistant Coroner, Outer London (South) (2000-2008); Outer London (West) (2009 to date).
Publications: Author and editor of clinical negligence chapter in Butterworths' Personal Injury Litigation Service. Co-author of the Work Related Injury & Illness Litigation Handbook (XPL Publishing), winner 2004 Royal Society of Medicine/Society of Authors' Minty Prize, best medico-legal book.
Personal: Resides in London. Education: Royal Hospital School, Holbrook, Suffolk; St Mary's Hospital Medical School, London University. Interests: rugby, skiing, music, English literature, naval and military history.

ELLISON, Mark QC
QEB Hollis Whiteman, London
020 7933 8855
Mark.ellison@qebhw.co.uk
Featured in Financial Crime (London)

Practice Areas: As First Senior Treasury Counsel, Head of Chambers Mark Ellison QC gained valuable experience in high profile terrorism, serious fraud and terrorist funding, official secrets, serious crime, corruption and public law cases. He now mixes

private and public work across corporate crime, professional regulatory and criminal law. In 2016 Mark prosecuted on behalf of the FCA in Operation Tabernula, thought to be the biggest and most complex case ever brought for share trading abuses in the UK. Ex-Deutsche Bank corporate broker Martyn Dodgson and accountant Andrew Hind were found guilty of insider trading by a jury at Southwark Crown Court. Mark carried out the independent review of undercover policing and possible police corruption connected to the Stephen Lawrence case (The Ellison Review); he represented Bruce Hall in the Alba Bahrain $40m corruption prosecution brought by the SFO; he advised BP regarding the In Amenas inquest; he prosecuted the first OFT cartel prosecution under the Enterprise Act 2002; represented a British payday loan company at an inquest into a suicide; has been instructed to defend an employee of Alstom Network UK Ltd on charges brought by the SFO against Alstom Network UK Ltd; has been instructed by a multinational energy corporation to defend against multiple allegations of corporate manslaughter.
Professional Memberships: Public Access Bar Association; registered with the Bar Council – Public Access Directory
Career: 2010 SFO Approved Counsel List; 2010 Deputy High Court Judge; 2006- 2008 First Senior Treasury Counsel
Personal: Silk 2008, call 1979; LLB (University of Wales)

ELVIDGE, John QC
Dere Street Barristers, York
1912320541
j.elvidgeqc@derestreet.co.uk
Featured in Crime (North Eastern)

Practice Areas: * Homicide: multiple deaths; causation – legal, factual and medical (e.g. alleged non accidental head injury leading to infant death); joint enterprise / secondary liability; killing by and of children and young people; partial defences of diminished responsibility and loss of control; gross negligence manslaughter. • Organised crime: homicide; blackmail and kidnapping; conspiracies – fraud against financial and insurance companies, supplying controlled drugs and medicines, money laundering; sexual offences against children; disclosure; applications for trial by judge alone, by protected jury and for witness anonymity orders. • Serious sexual offences: complaints against professionals; familial abuse; delayed complaints; sexual exploitation and trafficking. • Regulatory work, professional and police disciplinary hearings, licensing and high value personal injury claims.
Professional Memberships: Criminal Bar Association; North Eastern Circuit; Gray's Inn (Bencher).
Career: 1988, called to the Bar; 2010, Queen's Counsel; pupillage at 2 Harcourt Buildings, Temple and its annex in York; from 1990, York Chambers; 2011, succeeded Gilbert Gray QC as head of chambers; 2011 to date, head of Dere Street Barristers on merger of York and Broad Chare Chambers, Newcastle upon Tyne; 2014 to 2016, Leader of the North Eastern Circuit.

EMANUEL, Mark
29 Bedford Row Chambers, London
020 7404 1044
memanuel@29br.co.uk
Featured in Family/Matrimonial (London)

Practice Areas: All areas of Family Law with particular expertise in high net worth financial remedy cases and private law children act matters. Reported cases include: DE v AB (Permission Hearing: Publicity Protection) [2015] 1 FLR 1119; M v M (Third Party Subpoena: Financial Conduct) [2006] 2 FLR 1253; Charalambous v Charalmabous [2004] 2 FLR 1093; M V M (Financial Relief: Substantial Earning Capacity) [2004] 2 FLR 236; Ganeshmoorthy v Ganeshmoorthy (ancillary relief: abuse of process) [2003] 3 FCR 167.
Professional Memberships: FLBA. The Association of District Judges.
Career: Called to the Bar 1985; Inner Temple. Deputy District Judge (County Court) 2000. Trained in collaborative law.
Personal: Educated at Stowe School. Trent Polytechnic; BA Law. Married with five children.

EMMERSON, Heather
11KBW, London
020 7632 8500
Heather.Emmerson@11kbw.com
Featured in Administrative & Public Law (London), Data Protection (London), Local Government (London), Professional Discipline (London)

Practice Areas: Administrative and public law, human rights, local government, regulatory law, professional discipline, information law and data protection. Heather is instructed by both claimants and public authorities in ground-breaking and complex public law litigation. Heather has recently been involved in three high profile public law cases in the Supreme Court including the first challenge to a local authority's council tax reduction scheme (Moseley v Haringey LBC [2014] UKSC 56; [2014] 1 W.L.R. 3947), an appeal relating to the "priority need" provisions of the Housing Act 1996 (Hotak v Southwark LBC [2015] UKSC 30; [2015] 2 W.L.R. 1341) and an appeal concerning the effect of article 8 on possession proceeding between private parties (McDonald v McDonald [2016] UKSC 28; [2016] 3 W.L.R. 45). Heather is regularly instructed in judicial review claims in relation to both central and local government. She is also frequently instructed to act in regulatory and disciplinary proceedings for both individuals and regulatory bodies.
Professional Memberships: Administrative Law Bar Association, Association of Regulatory & Disciplinary Lawyers.
Career: Called to the Bar in 2009. Member of the Attorney General's C Panel of Counsel.
Publications: Contributor to Local Government Lawyer and Education and the Courts (McManus, 3rd edition).
Personal: Graduated from St Catharine's College, Cambridge with a First Class degree in Law.

ENGLAND, William
Carmelite Chambers, London
020 7936 6300
clerks@carmelitechambers.co.uk
Featured in Crime (London)

Practice Areas: A fraud and regulatory specialist who has wide-ranging experience in the practice areas of financial and corporate crime, including market abuse, money laundering, regulatory compliance and public inquiries (Baha Mousa). He is also a consultant at Prospect Law (Law firm of the year 2012, business green leaders awards) where he advises private clients in dispute resolution, compliance, financial misconduct, restraint orders and asset recovery. His Chambers practice includes serious crime, health and safety, regulatory reform (fire safety) orders, and trading standards. He is regularly instructed as lead counsel in heavy crime such as large-scale drug importation, homicide and fraud. (Including Operation's Tabernula, Bamburgh, Usurp, and Roderigo) He advises the Financial Conduct Authority on disclosure in market abuse and enforcement. His recent appearances include the Court of Appeal (Criminal Division), the Divisional Court and Attorney General's reference. He is presently instructed in cases in Ukraine, the British Virgin Islands and Delaware
Professional Memberships: University of London, LLM. CBA, FSLA, ARDL, AMCA and CLBM.

ESCHWEGE, Richard
Brick Court Chambers, London
020 7379 3550
julian.hawes@brickcourt.co.uk
Featured in Banking & Finance (London), Commercial Dispute Resolution (London)

Career: Richard Eschwege has a broad, predominantly commercial, practice. He has advised on and acted in contentious and non-contentious matters across a wide range of commercial disputes, including energy, banking, financial services, insurance, telecommunications, civil fraud, and conflicts of laws and jurisdiction. Richard is currently acting in a number of disputes concerning natural resources, including for the owners of an oil and gas field in the North Sea, and for the principal defendants to claims in respect of an alleged fraud worth c. US$300 million. He is also working on a variety of high-value banking matters and 'oligarch' disputes. He was identified as one of Legal Week's 'Stars at the Bar' 2014.

EVANS, Andrew
St Philips Chambers, Birmingham
0121 246 7000
aevans@st-philips.com
Featured in Clinical Negligence (Midlands), Licensing (Midlands)

Practice Areas: Andrew's practice concentrates on clinical negligence, personal injury and licensing work. Clinical Negligence: cosmetic surgery; brain injury; urology; cardiology; paediatrics; oncology; gynaecology; general practice; orthopaedics; spinal surgery; dermatology; ophthalmology; general surgery; nursing; and dentistry. Andrew's clinical negligence practice continues to expand each year and he is willing to accept instructions nationwide. Personal Injury: fatal accidents; industrial disease; accidents at work; road traffic accidents; low velocity impact; and personal injury fraud. Licensing: Andrew regularly appears before local authorities, the Magistrates' Court, Crown Court and Administrative Court in licensing matters. He receives instructions in matters relating to the Licensing Act 2003 (as amended) from major pub, hotel and sex establishment venue operators and local authorities across England and Wales. Andrew also accepts instructions in taxi licensing cases. Andrew is willing to provide training in all of his areas of expertise.
Professional Memberships: Member of PIBA, AvMA, IoL.
Career: Called 2000 (Lincoln's Inn) Hardwicke Scholar.
Personal: Dr.Challoner's Grammar School Amersham and University of Birmingham. Involved in historic motor sport, running, dismantling and attempting to re-assemble vintage and classic cars. Enjoys rugby and cricket.

EVANS, Catrin QC
One Brick Court, London
020 7353 8845
ce@onebrickcourt.co.uk
Featured in Data Protection (London), Defamation/Privacy (London)

Practice Areas: Defamation, privacy, breach of confidence, harassment, contempt, reporting restrictions, data protection, FOIA, related media and human rights law. Recent cases of interest: Axon v MOD v News Group (2016) EWHC 787 (QB) (privacy); Weller v Associated Newspapers (2016) EMLR 7 (privacy); Vidal-Hall v Google (2015) EWCA Civ 311; Trushin v National Crime Agency (2014); Prince Alwaleed v Forbes (2014-2015); Hegglin v Google Inc (2014) (DPA, libel); Rowland v Mitchell (2014) (libel); ; Karpov v Browder (2013) (libel), Tamiz v Google Inc [2013] EMLR 14 (libel/internet), Bento v Bedfordshire Police (2012) (libel trial), Tesla Motors v BBC (2013) EWCA Civ 152; (malicious falsehood), Thornton v Telegraph Media Group (2011) (libel), Metropolitan Schools v Google Inc (2009) (libel), AG v Random House (2009) (contempt), Dept for Culture v Information Commissioner (2009) (FOIA), Haw v City of Westminster Mags Court (2007) (contempt), Lord Browne v Associated Newspapers (2007) (privacy), Cream Holdings v Banerjee (2005) (confidence/HRA), Campbell v MGN Ltd (2004) (privacy).
Career: Called to the Bar 1994; Silk 2016
Publications: Author, Atkins Court Forms title on 'Confidence, Privacy and Data Protection' (2002).

EVANS, Helen
4 New Square, London
020 7822 2000
hm.evans@4newsquare.com
Featured in Professional Negligence (London)

Practice Areas: Principal areas of practice are professional liability, general commercial, insurance (including policy and coverage) and property-related work. Helen's professional negligence practice focuses on solicitors, barristers, accountants, insurance brokers/agents, IFAs, surveyors and valuers (and includes substantial fraud claims). Helen is experienced in multi-party and group litigation. Examples of current work include multi-million pound auditors' negligence claims and claims arising out of unregulated collective investment schemes.
Professional Memberships: PNBA, Chancery Bar Association, COMBAR, LCLBA. Member of Pro Bono Committee of Chancery Bar Association.
Career: Called to the Bar in 2001. Sits as Deputy District Judge.
Publications: Co-author of several articles (with Sue Carr QC) published in Tottel's Professional Negligence, Contributor to Jackson & Powell (forthcoming edition).
Personal: Born 1977. Educated at Redland High School for Girls, New College Oxford and Université d'Aix Marseille III, France. Lives London.

EVANS, Hugh
4 New Square, London
020 7822 2000
h.evans@4newsquare.com
Featured in Professional Negligence (London)

Practice Areas: Principal area of practice is Professional Negligence, in particular lawyers and financial professionals. Lawyers' liability claims include in particular: (1) defective business agreements especially those with a chancery flavour (e.g. Youlton v Charles Russell (2010), Fulham Leisure Holdings v Nicholson Graham Jones (2006), Mischcon de Reya v Barrett (2006)); (2) lost or bungled litigation of all types, including clinical negligence and personal injury claims (e.g. Miller v Garton Shires (2007)); (3) lenders claims and conveyancing (e.g. Boycott v Perrins Guy Williams (2011)); and (4) claims involving fraud, insurance and partnership issues (e.g. UCB v Soni (2011 and 2013), Goldsmith Williams v Travelers (2010), JD Wetherspoons v Van de Berg (2009), JD Wetherspoons v Jason Harris (2013)). Surveyors' claims include Paratus v Countrywide (2011). Also practises in Insurance (both in relation to professionals, and generally), Clinical Negligence, Personal Injury and Costs.

Professional Memberships: PNBA, COMBAR, ChBA.

Career: MA (Cantab), BCL (Oxon). Called to the bar 1987, in practice at these chambers from 1988.

Publications: An editor of Jackson and Powell on Professional Liability since 1992 and continuing, in particular of the solicitors' chapter; author of "Lawyers' Liabilities", 2nd edn 2002; numerous articles.

EVANS, Lee

Farrar's Building, London
020 7583 9241
Levans@farrarsbuilding.co.uk

Featured in Personal Injury (London)

Practice Areas: Specialist personal injury practitioner, with particular emphasis in brain injury, spinal injury and amputation cases. Work includes workplace accident cases, road traffic accident cases and industrial disease cases.

Professional Memberships: Gray's Inn. Member of the General Council of the Bar's Summary Procedure Disciplinary Tribunal, the Inns of Court Disciplinary Tribunal and the General Council of the Bar's International Relations Committee. Grade A Advocacy teacher. Member of Gray's Inn's Education Committee. PIBA.

Career: Called to the Bar in 1996; Gray's Inn.

Publications: Contributor to editions of The Personal Injury Handbook, Kemp and Kemp and Munkman on Employers' Liability.

Personal: Married with three daughters. Interests include football, walking at the west coast of Scotland, fishing and southern Africa. Trustee of the Canon Collins Educational Trust for Southern Africa.

EVANS, Martin

The Chambers of Andrew Mitchell QC, London
020 7440 9950
me@33cllaw.com

Featured in POCA Work & Asset Forfeiture (All Circuits)

Practice Areas: Specialises in all aspects of the law relating to criminal and civil asset recovery and confiscation. Acts for defendants, prosecuting authorities and third parties in both civil and criminal matters. Experienced in handling domestic and international restraint proceedings (including the restraint of UK assets pursuant to overseas requests), receivership and contempt proceedings in the Crown Court, the High Court (Administrative Court, Chancery Division and Family Division), Court of Appeal and Supreme Court. Expertise in the legality of search and production orders under PACE and POCA. Frequently instructed in appeals where he was not involved in the lower court. Particular interests include fraud, corruption, money laundering and corporate criminal liability on which he has written and lectured widely.

Professional Memberships: Proceeds of Crime Lawyers' Association.

Career: Called to Bar in 1989.

Publications: 'Corporate Criminal Liability' (co-author) Third Edition May 2013; 'Archbold' (contributing editor); 'Confiscation and the Proceeds of Crime' (contributing editor); 'Abuse of Process in Criminal Proceedings' (contributor).

EVANS, Philip QC

QEB Hollis Whiteman, London
020 7933 8855
philip.evans@qebhw.co.uk

Featured in Crime (London)

Practice Areas: Philip specialises in serious general and corporate crime, regulation and sports law. He defended Levi Bellfield at his trial for multiple murders, represented one of the Pakistan cricketers charge with match fixing and currently defends in a complex SFO bribery and corruption case. He is also defending a police officer charged with corruption and a GP charged with sexual offences. Philip is regularly instructed for companies and individuals who are not defendants but who require advice relating to matters such as fraud, potential criminal liability rising from corporate activities, confiscation and compensation. He is currently instructed to assist the defence in a market abuse corruption trial in India. He has regularly been instructed to appear in cases involving serious sexual allegations and homicide. He led for the prosecution in the Hatton Garden safe deposit burglary, and was for the Crown in a major Metropolitan Police operation involving multiple defendants accused of laundering money from organised crime. He prosecuted R v Ali Dizaei (the Metropolitan Police Commander convicted of perverting the course of justice) and recently led for the Crown in a £60 million money laundering case. He has extensive experience of appearing before regulatory and sports tribunals. He is one the RFU's discipline Chairmen and a panel member for the Six Nations and European Rugby tournaments. He appears on behalf of the British Horseracing Authority and the Gambling Commission before their regulatory panels.

Professional Memberships: Association of Regulatory and Disciplinary Lawyers; British Association for Sport and Law; Criminal Bar Association

Career: Silk 2016. Call 1995. LLB (Hons) (University of Wales); MA (Southampton)

Personal: Since 2008 he has advised the Innocence Network UK and continues to act pro-bono for the Cardiff University pro-bono department.

EVANS, Robert

Keating Chambers, London
020 7544 2600
revans@keatingchambers.com

Featured in Construction (London), Mediators (All Circuits)

Practice Areas: Robert Evans began his career as a civil engineer working for international consultants and contractors in the UK and Hong Kong. As a member of Keating Chambers, Robert specialises in construction, engineering and energy disputes and professional negligence work both in the UK and abroad, acting for national and local governments, public authorities, private sector employers, contractors, sub-contractors, consultants, architects and engineers. His practice covers a variety of advisory work, drafting and advocacy, both in the High Court and in arbitration. Robert is also frequently appointed as Arbitrator (domestically and internationally), Adjudicator and Mediator, proving to be highly successful at facilitating mediation settlements.

Professional Memberships: Institution of Civil Engineers (Fellow); Hong Kong Institution of Engineers (Member); Chartered Institute of Arbitrators (Fellow); Technology and Construction Bar Association (TECBAR); Commercial Bar Association (COMBAR); Society of Construction Law (Council Member until 2015); Institution of Civil Engineers Panels of Arbitrators and Adjudicators, CEDR Accredited Mediator.

Career: Chartered civil engineer (1981-89); Called to the Bar (1989).

Publications: Contributor, Keating on Construction Contracts Ninth (2012) and Tenth (2016) Editions; contributor, Keating on NEC3 2012; Mediation – Engineers Dispute Resolution Handbook 1st (2006), 2nd (2011) and 3rd (2016) editions (chapter author).

EWART, David QC

Pump Court Tax Chambers, London
020 7414 8080
clerks@pumptax.com

Featured in Tax (London)

Practice Areas: David Ewart specialises in all areas of taxation, both corporate and personal, direct and indirect. Cases include: BMBF v Mawson (House of Lords); Scottish Provident Institution v HMRC (House of Lords); Dr Beynon & Ors v HMRC (House of Lords); Trennery & ors v West (House of Lords); Deutsche Morgan Grenfell Group v HMRC (House of Lords); Marks & Spencer Plc v Halsey (ECJ); NEC Semi-Conductors v HMRC (House of Lords); Prizedome Ltd & Limitgood Ltd v HMRC (Court of Appeal); Pirelli Cable Holdings Ltd v HMRC (House of Lords); Vodafone 2 v HMRC (Court of Appeal); Mayes v HMRC (Court of Appeal); Philips Electronics v HMRC (Upper Tribunal); Astall & Edwards v HMRC (Court of Appeal); Bayfine v HMRC (Court of Appeal); Thincap GLO (Court of Appeal); FII GLO (Supreme Court); CFC GLO (High Court); Marks & Spencer v HMRC (Supreme Court); Anson v HMRC (Supreme Court); AC v DC (Family Division); MJP Media v HMRC (Court of Appeal); Lloyds TSB Equipment Leasing v HMRC (Court of Appeal); Chappell v HMRC (Court of Appeal); Barnes v HMRC (Court of Appeal); EC Commission v UK (CJEU); Reed Employment Plc. V HMRC (Court of Appeal); Prudential v HMRC (Court of Appeal).

Professional Memberships: Revenue Bar Association; London Common Law & Commercial Bar Association; Chancery Bar Association

Career: Called 1987 (Gray's Inn); Treasury A Panel (1999 – 2006); First Chancery Revenue Junior (2000 – 2006); QC (2006)

Personal: Trinity College, Oxford (1986 BA Hons)

EWINS, Catherine

Hailsham Chambers, London
020 7643 5000
catherine.ewins@hailshamchambers.com

Featured in Clinical Negligence (London)

Practice Areas: Catherine acts on behalf of both claimants and defendants in clinical negligence and personal injury litigation. She also deals with solicitors' negligence claims arising out of errors. She frequently undertakes high value and complex cases. She also has significant experience of disciplinary tribunal work, defending professionals before their regulatory body. Significant cases include: Bradbury & others v Paterson and others [2014] EWHC 3992 (QBD). Jalloh v NMC [2009] EWHC 1697 (Admin) Silber J – appeal regarding fitness to practise of a nurse. NMC v Livermore [2005] All ER (D) 127 – appeal from sanction imposed by the NMC. Chabba v Turbogame [2001] EWCA Civ 1073 – service of claim form. Woolgar v Chief Constable of the Sussex Police and the UKCC [1999] 3 All ER 604 – disclosure of material to a regulatory body.

Publications: Contributor to the Clinical Negligence and Personal Injury volumes of Atkin's Court Forms.

Personal: MA (law) Cambridge – King's College (Hurst Prize for law),Universite Libre de Bruxelles (Licence Speciale en droit Europeen), Bar Vocational Course (Junior Scholar Gray's Inn, Graham Challis Scholarship, Gray's Inn).

EWINS, James QC

Queen Elizabeth Building QEB, London
020 7797 7837
jewins@qeb.co.uk

Featured in Family/Matrimonial (London)

Practice Areas: James has considerable experience of complex asset structures including domestic and off-shore commercial and trust structures, inherited wealth, complex pension arrangements and bankruptcy related issues as well as international forum shopping and enforcement issues. He typically represents clients in mid to high level or particularly complex financial remedy and Schedule 1 cases, including at an appellate level and through arbitration. He also has considerable experience advising upon, drafting and enforcing nuptial agreements. James' reported cases include: Wright v Wright [2014] EWFC B17 & [2015] EWCA Civ 201; US v SR [2014] EWHC 175, [2014] EWHC 2864 & [2014] EWFC 24; SS v NS [2014] EWHC 4183; Myerson v Myerson [2009] EWCA Civ 282; Crossley v Crossley [2007] EWCA Civ 1491; Charman v Charman [2005] EWCA Civ 1606; [2006] EWCA Civ 1791 & Charman v Charman [2007] EWCA Civ 503; Sorrell v Sorrell [2005] EWHC 1717 and OS v DS [2004] EWHC 2376. James lectures to solicitors on request.

Professional Memberships: He is a member of the FLBA.

Career: Educated: New College, Oxford (BA Juris). Called: 1996. Sabbatical: 2009/10 working for anti-slavery charity in India; Silk: 2016.

Personal: Married, with four children; a keen sailor; committed Christian; combines his professional practice with modern anti-slavery and human trafficking campaigns.

FACENNA, Gerry QC
Monckton Chambers, London
020 7405 7211
gfacenna@monckton.com
Featured in Administrative & Public Law (London), Data Protection (London), Environment (London), Competition/European Law (London), Telecommunications (London)
Practice Areas: Acts in a wide range of public law, commercial and regulatory matters, including telecoms, data protection, EU law, competition, human rights and environmental regulation. An experienced and highly-rated advocate appearing regularly in the High Court, appellate courts, EU courts and specialist tribunals on behalf of companies, public bodies, individuals and organisations. Also has experience of commercial arbitration. Recent cases include: Opinion 2/15 (EU trade relations/Singapore FTA); Heathrow Airport v ORR (third party rail access); Tele2 Sverige / Watson v SSHD (communications data retention); R (Miller) v SoS for Exiting the EU (process for triggering Article 50); BT v Ofcom & Sky (competition regulation in Pay TV); R (Amex) v HMT (Interchange Fee Regulation); Dawson-Damer v Taylor Wessing (data controller obligations); DECC v ICO & Henney (definition of 'environmental information'); Rosneft v HMT (EU sanctions against Russia); BUND v Germany (EU Water Framework Directive); R (Optimus Mobile) v PhonepayPlus (telecoms regulation – Francovich damages). For further detail see http://www.monckton.com/barrister/gerry-facenna/
Career: MA (Cantab.), LL.B (Edin.); called to the Bar 2001; former member of the Attorney General's "A" Panel of Counsel; Silk 2016. Member of the Bar in Scotland (2006 call).
Publications: Contributing author to: Information Rights: Law and Practice (Hart, 2014); Halsbury's Laws of England: Rights and Freedoms (LexisNexis, 2013); EU Competition Law: Procedures and Remedies (OUP, 2006); Law of State Aid in the European Union (OUP, 2004); and Law of the European Union Encyclopaedia (OUP, 2003).

FAGGIONATO, Marina
Queen Elizabeth Building QEB, London
020 7797 7837
m.faggionato@qeb.co.uk
Featured in Family/Matrimonial (London)
Practice Areas: Marina's practice covers all aspects of private family law, including divorce, finance, private law Children Act (including Schedule 1 and relocation) and Hague Convention/child abduction cases. She has acted in a wide range of matters in courts up to and including the Court of Appeal (for example Re R (A Child) [2009] 2 FLR 819 CA and Re G (Abduction: Children's Objections) [2011] 1 FLR 1645 CA) and as a junior in both 'big money' see for example Luckwell v Limata [2014] EWHC 502 (Fam) and Children Act cases. Marina is a fluent French speaker with practical experience of family law in Paris and often acts in cross-border cases (for example EDG v RR [2014] EWHC 816 (Fam) and Divall v Divall [2014] EWHC 95 (Fam).
Professional Memberships: FLBA. Resolution. CIArb.
Career: Called 2006. Lord Denning & Eastham Scholar. Pupil & tenant at Queen Elizabeth Building.
Publications: Mental Health and Family Law, edited with the Rt Hon Lord Justice Thorpe, 2010.

FAIN, Carl
Tanfield Chambers, London
020 7421 5318
cfain@tanfieldchambers.co.uk
Featured in Real Estate Litigation (London)
Practice Areas: Property and chancery practice with a focus on landlord and tenant. Work includes all aspects of commercial and residential including dilapidations claims, lease renewals, enfranchisement, RTM, appointment of managers and service charge disputes. Real property disputes including mortgage related claims and in particular LPA receivers, property related professional negligence, co-ownership, easements, restrictive covenants, Party Wall Act matters and boundary disputes. Cases include Lee v Sommer [2015] EWHC 3889 (Ch) (commercial landlord and tenant) Queensbridge Investment Ltd v 61 Queens Gate Freehold Ltd [2015] EGLR 5 (enfranchisement) Yeung v Potel [2014] 2 EGLR 125 (easements), Christoforou v Standard Apartments Ltd [2014] L&TR 12 (Administration charges), Rabiu v Marlbray Ltd [2013] EWHC 3272 (Ch) (sale deposits in respect of Hotel units), Barnard v Zarbafi [2010] EWHC 3256 (sale deposits), New Northumbria Hotel Ltd v Maymask (148) LLP [2010] EWHC 1273 (forfeiture and chattels), Idealview Ltd v Bello [2010] 1 EGLR 39 (rent review), FSA v Martin [2006] 2 BCLC 193 (s.380 FSMA proceedings).
Professional Memberships: Member of the Property and Chancery Bar Associations.
Career: MA (Jurisprudence), The Queen's College, Oxford. Called in 2001.
Publications: Contributed to 'Service Charges and Management: Law and Practice' 3rd Ed (Sweet & Maxwell).
Personal: Born 1979. Educated at Merchant Taylors' School, Northwood. Lives in London with his wife and two delightful daughters.

FANCOURT, Timothy QC
Falcon Chambers, London
020 7353 2484
clerks@falcon-chambers.co.com
Featured in Agriculture & Rural Affairs (London), Real Estate Litigation (London)
Practice Areas: Principally real property based Chancery litigation, including commercial property, landlord and tenant, surveyors' and solicitors' professional negligence, conveyancing, building contracts, mortgages, easements and restrictive covenants, equity, trusts and insolvency. Other main area is commercial contracts.
Professional Memberships: Chairman, Chancery Bar Association (2012 – 2014), LCLCBA; Property Bar Association. Member of Bar Council 1996-2001; Vice-Chairman, Standards Committee, Bar Standards Board 2006-10.
Career: Educated at Whitgift School; Gonville & Caius College, Cambridge; Called 1987 (Lincoln's Inn; Bencher 2012); Silk 2003; Recorder 2009. Deputy High Court Judge 2013.
Publications: Author: 'Enforceability of Landlord and Tenant Covenants' (3rd ed 2014); General editor: Megarry's 'The Rent Acts' and 'Assured Tenancies' (1999); Contributor, Lightman & Moss, The Law of Administrators and Receivers; Editor: Muir Watt and Moss, Agricultural Tenancies (15th ed 2016)
Personal: Interests: Cricket; classical music.

FARMER, John
Drystone Chambers, London
020 7404 1881
john.farmer@drystone.com
Featured in Crime (South Eastern)
Practice Areas: Criminal law, Health and Safety, POCA.
Professional Memberships: CBA, South Eastern Circuit.
Career: John Farmer has vast experience as a specialist Criminal barrister. The geographic spread of his practice encompasses London, East Anglia and the East Midlands but he is engaged on very serious criminal matters on a nationwide basis. His practice embraces all serious criminal matters with an emphasis on serious violence, particularly murder and manslaughter, serious sexual offences, heavy duty drug conspiracies and causing death by dangerous driving matters. He regularly prosecutes and defends numerous rapes, murders and drugs trials and prides himself in getting results quickly. Prosecuting and defending large scale commercial dishonesty has given John significant experience of Proceeds of Crime Act matters. Of these cases, numerous matters have had confiscation values of £1 million and more. In two counties where John has prosecuted these offences have given rise to the biggest single recovery ever in each of the Counties. Over the years John has had experience of a wide range of regulatory work, notably Health & Safety matters, and his practice has given him considerable experience in dealing with a wide range of experts – a skill which is utilised across all practice areas.

FEALY, Michael QC
One Essex Court, London
Tel: 020 7583 2000
mfealy@oeclaw.co.uk
Featured in Commercial Dispute Resolution (London)
Practice Areas: Barrister specialising in commercial law.
Career: Called to the Irish Bar in 1995; qualified 1997, Middle Temple; took silk in 2014; lecturer in commercial and insolvency law, Queen Mary & Westfield College, University of London 1992-97; publications: (with Ian Grainger) 'An Introduction to the New Civil Procedure Rules' (1999). University College Dublin (1991 BCL (NUI)); Sidney Sussex College, Cambridge (1992, LLM).
Personal: Born 1970, resides London.

FEATHERBY, William QC
12 King's Bench Walk, London
020 7583 0811
featherby@12kbw.co.uk
Featured in Fraud (All Circuits), Personal Injury (London)
Practice Areas: Personal injury, clinical negligence, professional negligence. William's work is heavy personal injuries litigation, particularly trial work. He is featured in the Personal Injury Section of Legal Experts and as a leading Silk for personal injury in Chambers UK and The Legal 500. About two thirds of William's work is for insurance companies; the rest is for claimants, equally divided between union-backed and other work. The personal injuries work is a combination of accidents at work, industrial and occupational disease, road accidents and clinical negligence. William specialises in difficult medical issues, catastrophic injuries, industrial disease and fraud. William is also a specialist in proceedings for committal for contempt of court arising out of fraudulent claims. He also has a regulatory practice. William is also a specialist in health and safety prosecutions. Recent cases have involved prosecutions arising out of deaths and serious accidents, leading to Crown Court trials. He is noted as an able advocate and tactician in this field.
Professional Memberships: Member of the Civil Procedure Rules Committee since 2008. PIBA; LCLBA.
Career: Called to the Bar, 1978. QC, 2008. Recorder since 2002.
Personal: Trinity College, Oxford (Scholar, MA).

FELDSCHREIBER, Peter
4 New Square, London
020 7822 2000
p.feldschreiber@4newsquare.com
Featured in Product Liability (London)
Practice Areas: Peter Feldschreiber is dually qualified as a barrister and a physician. He specialises in life sciences products liability, pharmaceutical and medical devices regulatory law, clinical negligence and personal injury. He has been Senior Medical Assessor and Special Litigation Coordinator to the Commission on Human Medicines and is now a special Treasury Counsel to the Government Legal Service and Specialist Advisor to the Faculty of Pharmaceutical Medicine. He is retained counsel to a number of solicitors and is an advisor to major international strategic pharmaceutical consultancies in the USA and Europe.
Professional Memberships: He is accredited for professional practice by the General Medical Council, a Fellow of the Royal Society of Medicine and a Fellow of the Faculty of Pharmaceutical Medicine. He is a member of PNBA and COMBAR.
Career: Medical Director, Cardiovascular and Anaesthetic clinical development Glaxo Pharmaceuticals 1981-91. Medical Director Europe, Procter and Gamble 1992-98. Senior Medical Assessor and Special Litigation Coordinator, MHRA, Department of Health, UK. Tenant Four New Square.
Publications: Peter has lectured and written extensively on pharmaceutical law and regulation; he is General Editor of the Law and regulation of Medicines, Oxford University Press and is consultant editor to Halsbury's Laws of England on Medicinal Products Law and Health Services Law.
Personal: Enjoys fell walking, music and amateur dramatics.

FELL, Mark
Radcliffe Chambers, London
020 7831 0081
mfell@radcliffechambers.com
Featured in Consumer Law (London)
Practice Areas: Commercial chancery, with a particular specialism in retail financial services.
Professional Memberships: Chancery Bar Association; Commercial Bar Association; Financial Services Lawyers Association
Career: MA Cantab, MSc Lond, Called to bar in 2004.

FELTHAM, Piers
Radcliffe Chambers, London
020 7831 0081
clerks@radcliffechambers.com
Featured in Chancery (London), Court of Protection (All Circuits)
Practice Areas: Litigation, advice and drafting in: trusts, wills and probate, char-

ity, private client (reported cases – Blades v Isaac, Re Jimmy Savile (CA), Connell v Creese (PC), Lake v Lake, Re East Grinstead Working Men's Club) – property/landlord and tenant (Gardener v Lewis (PC), Lloyds Bank v Hawkins (CA), Cork v Cork) – Court of Protection (Re LM , Re W) – Estoppel (Pereira v Beanlands) – pensions (Moores (Wallisdown) v Pensions Ombudsman) – general contract (Colonial Fire v Harry (PC); Jawara v Gambia Airways (PC)) – Commercial Fraud (Indicii Salus v Chandrasekaran (CA)) – professional negligence/mortgage fraud (Allied surveyors v National home Loans).
Professional Memberships: ACTAPS; Chancery Bar Association; Charity Law Association; STEP.
Career: BA (Cantab), Trinity College: George Long Prize for Jurisprudence; Called 1985: Uthwatt scholar of Gray's Inn.
Publications: Spencer Bower on Estoppel by Representation 4th ed (2004); Spencer Bower on Reliance-Based Estoppel 5th ed (2016)
Personal: Married with three children; trustee of Fitzrovia Community Centre; trustee of the Ceasefire Centre for Civilian Rights.

FENHALLS, Mark QC
23 Essex Street, London
020 7413 0353
Markfenhalls@23es.com
Featured in Crime (London), Financial Crime (London)
Practice Areas: Mark has been ranked for several years in Crime and Fraud as a junior and now in silk. He has a high profile practice defending and prosecuting in fraud and serious crime. He advises individuals and companies under investigation by the FCA and other agencies, for alleged criminal and regulatory misconduct. Mark was Chair of the Criminal Bar Association (September 2015 – to September 2016) and has been heavily involved in discussions with Government about the future of the Criminal Justice System. He is regularly called to comment on Criminal Justice matters for national newspapers, television and radio.
Professional Memberships: Criminal Bar Association, South Eastern Circuit, Fraud Lawyers Association, International Society for the Reform of Criminal Law
Career: Called to the Bar in 1992, took silk in April 2014. Appointments: Chairman of the Criminal Bar Association 2015/2016, Queen's Counsel 2014

FENN, Andrew
Atkin Chambers, London
020 7404 0102
afenn@AtkinChambers.com
Featured in Construction (London)
Practice Areas: Andrew specialises in domestic and international civil engineering, building, energy, shipbuilding, professional negligence and general commercial law matters. He has experience of domestic litigation and arbitration conducted under the ICC and LCIA rules. Andrew represents contractors, private employers, professional advisors and insurers. His experience in engineering and construction includes disputes relating to airports, power stations, manufacturing plants and residential/commercial developments. His experience in professional negligence includes claims involving architects, services engineers, quantity surveyors and project managers. He has acted as junior counsel on large litigations, international and domestic arbitrations, and in the Court of Appeal. He has been instructed on international arbitrations for parties and disputes based in a number of jurisdictions, including Oman, Dubai, Turkey, Russia, Singapore and Hong Kong.
Professional Memberships: TECBAR, COMBAR, SCL
Career: Educated St. John's College, Cambridge MA. Birkenhead Scholar of Gray's Inn. Called 2007, Gray's Inn.
Publications: Hudson's Building and Engineering Contracts, 12th Ed. (Sweet & Maxwell, 2010) – contributing editor.

FENWICK, Justin QC
4 New Square, London
020 7822 2000
j.fenwick@4newsquare.com
Featured in Professional Negligence (London), Commercial Dispute Resolution (London), Construction (London), Fraud (London), Insurance (London), Offshore (London)
Career: Justin Fenwick came to the Bar in 1981 and was appointed QC in 1993 (the most junior member of the Bar to be appointed as Silk in the 1993 list). He has sat as a Judge in both civil and criminal cases, having been made an Assistant Recorder in 1994, a Recorder in 1999 and a Deputy High Court Judge (Chancery and Queen's Bench Division) in March 2003. He was appointed a Deputy Judge of the Administrative Court in 2008. He was Head of Chambers at 4 New Square between 2000 and 2005 and has been a Bencher of the Inner Temple since 1997 and was Chairman of its Investment Sub-Committee between 2004 and 2011. He was Chairman of the Bar Mutual Indemnity Fund (the Bar's own Mutual Insurer) from 1999 until 2013. He is a Commissioner of the Royal Hospital Chelsea (home to the Chelsea Pensioners) since 2011 where he sits on the Remuneration Committee. He has an extensive offshore and international practice involving court appearances in Singapore, Hong Kong, Dubai, BVI, Cayman, Bermuda, St Vincent and Nevis.

FERGUSON, Craig
2 Hare Court, London
020 7353 53254
craigferguson@2harecourt.com
Featured in Crime (London), Health & Safety (London), Professional Discipline (London), Financial Crime (London)
Practice Areas: Craig Ferguson is an excellent defence advocate with a reputation for a thorough command of the law, shrewd tactics, meticulous preparation and penetrating cross-examination. His practice now predominantly focuses on workplace crime and misconduct, representing companies, directors and other professionals facing proceedings brought by the principal prosecuting agencies and professional regulators. Craig is a leader of the 2 Hare Court Criminal Regulatory Team and he regularly advises and appears in cases brought by the HSE in particular involving allegations arising out of fatal and non-fatal accidents. In financial crime, Craig has experience in investigations involving allegations of criminal cartel offences, bribery (UK and overseas), boiler room frauds, banking fraud, general VAT offences, MTIC and carousel fraud cases, tax offences and money laundering. Craig has been described as an exceptional all-round talent, which is demonstrated by the fact that he is ranked as a leader in the field in all four of his practice areas. Craig delivers training in relation to criminal regulatory, inquests and professional discipline matters to solicitors and other members of the profession. Recent cases include The HSE v Monovan Construction (corporate manslaughter), R v Dr Adedeji (gross negligence manslaughter).
Professional Memberships: The Heath and Safety Lawyers' Association, The Association of Regulatory and Disciplinary Lawyers, The Fraud Lawyers Association, The Criminal Bar Association
Career: Called 1992. Recorder 2009

FERGUSON, Eva
Hailsham Chambers, London
020 7643 5000
eva.ferguson@hailshamchambers.com
Featured in Professional Negligence (London)
Practice Areas: Eva has an established practice specialising in professional negligence and liability, and medical law. She also undertakes some costs work. Eva understands that litigation imposes pressures and deadlines on professional clients, and causes stress, worry and uncertainty to lay clients. She aims to give a comprehensive and realistic assessment of the case as soon as possible, and believes that this, together with effective teamwork, addresses the problems of litigation and will provide both clients with the best service and the best value for money. If the Directories are to be believed Eva combines being "very astute, commercial and user-friendly" with a "thorough and tenacious" and "no-nonsense approach". Eva acts for claimants and defendants, private and institutional clients. She has appeared at all levels of civil courts, including disciplinary tribunals, up to the Court of Appeal.
Professional Memberships: Member of PNBA and LCLCBA; Head of Hailsham's Pupillage Committee.
Career: B.A. History: First Class Honours – University of Durham, Hatfield College; Diploma in Law: Commendation – York College of Law; Postgraduate Diploma in Law: Very Competent – ICSL; Diplock Scholarship, Middle Temple (1998).
Publications: Eva regularly provides professional negligence and clinical negligence update talks to leading firms of solicitors specialising in those areas.

FERNYHOUGH, Richard QC
Keating Chambers, London
020 7544 2600
rfernyhough@keatingchambers.com
Featured in Construction (London), International Arbitration (London)
Practice Areas: Experienced specialist in construction, engineering and energy law; arbitration both international and domestic. Appeared in many landmark cases in the field of construction law, including several notable cases in the House of Lords. Acted in countless heavy court cases and arbitrations on claims relating to a wide range of projects including airports, commercial properties, hotels, oil rigs, power stations, process plants, railways, and tunnelling projects. Recognised internationally as a leading commercial arbitrator who is well able to handle the heaviest and most technically complex disputes. Appointed on many occasions as either sole arbitrator, panel member or chairman by such bodies as the ICC, the LCIA the HKIAC, SIAC, the Kuala Lumpur Regional Centre, the Cairo Regional Centre for Commercial Arbitration and the Taiwan Arbitration Centre. Is a strong believer in delivering the award as soon as practicable after the conclusion of arbitral proceedings.
Career: LLB University College, London 1966; Called to the Bar (Middle Temple) 1970; Keating Chambers 1972; Called to the Bars of Hong Kong and Singapore; Queen's Counsel 1986; Deputy High Court Judge 1992; Approved Arbitrator, Hong Kong International Arbitration Centre 1999; Head of Keating Chambers 1997-2002.
Personal: Speaks French.

FERRIS, Shaun
Crown Office Chambers, London
020 77978100
ferris@crownofficechambers.com
Featured in Personal Injury (London)
Practice Areas: His practice is based on product liability work and a broad range of personal injury work including, in particular, catastrophic and fatal injury claims, industrial disease claims (particularly asbestos and stress claims) and sports injury cases. He is also experienced in clinical negligence and professional negligence work. He is adept at working as part of a team, giving clear and imaginative advice and guidance on all aspects of any particular piece of litigation including all tactical and legal issues. He is also a skilled and robust performer in court whether at interlocutory hearings or at trial. He has considerable experience of conducting settlement negotiations at round table meetings or mediations in both high and medium value cases. He regularly appears against silks and is consistently recognised as a "leader at the bar" for personal injury work. Clients view him as a "market leader in large-loss claims" and value his "excellent advocacy skills" and "superb tactical appreciation". Recent cases include Uren v Corporate Leisure Ltd and MOD [2013] EWHC 353 QB, [2011] EWCA Civ 66 and [2010] EWHC 46 QB, Horner v Norman [2013] Lawtel 19-12-13 and Woodham v Turner [2012] EWCA Civ 375 and [2011] EWHC 1588 QB.

FETHERSTONHAUGH, Guy QC
Falcon Chambers, London
020 7353 2484
fetherstonhaugh@falcon-chambers.com
Featured in Real Estate Litigation (London)
Practice Areas: Real Estate Litigation, Arbitration.
Professional Memberships: RICS (Hon); FCIARB; ARBRIX (Hon); Chancery Bar Association; Property Bar Association; London Common Law and Commercial Bar Association.
Career: Royal Green Jackets (1977 – 81); Barrister (1983 –); Queen's Counsel (2003 –).
Publications: Handbook of Rent Review, Commonhold, Litigation Practice.
Personal: Joint Head of Falcon Chambers.

FIELD, Julian
Crown Office Chambers, London
020 7797 8100
field@crownofficechambers.com
Featured in Property Damage (London)
Practice Areas: Property damage and insurance form the core of Julian's practice, which also covers product liability, commercial fraud, construction and professional negligence. He is regularly instructed in substantial property damage claims, especially arising from floods, fires, explosions, landslips and construction-related issues. Julian has considerable experience

of high value, multi-party actions involving complex technical and legal issues (e.g., in the Buncefield litigation Julian was primarily responsible for Total's technical case on its tank filling and overflow protection systems). Has a reputation for being "user-friendly" and a team player. Recent property damage cases include: £4.8m claim arising out of fire at a luxury timber house on a private island; £2.4m claim arising out of a fire at luxury apartments being redeveloped by the Candy brothers; £2m landslip claim; large gas explosion destroying a number of properties. Previous recommendations include: "when instructing him you get someone as good as most silks for the cost of a junior. He is very easy to work with, very grounded and a go-to for difficult cases." "Has a fantastic reputation for handling significant property damage claims based upon tortious or contractual liability." In relation to insurance Julian has extensive experience of all aspects of non-marine insurance including coverage, misrepresentation/non-disclosure, breach of warranty, breach of condition, insurable interest and subrogation. He is a specialist in fraudulent claims. Recent insurance cases include: application of "hot works" conditions to a £9m claim arising out of fire at Southwark Town Hall; application of gradual deterioration, defective design and other exclusions to an £8.5m property damage claim; avoidance of an EL policy in a £2m personal injury claim. Julian has been recommended as having 'deep-tissue insight into insurance claims'.

FIELDSEND, James
Tanfield Chambers, London
020 7421 5300
jamesfieldsent@tanfieldchambers.co.uk
Featured in Real Estate Litigation (London)

Practice Areas: Landlord and tenant (commercial and residential), mortgages, boundaries, easements and associated professional negligence. Notable cases include: Alice Ellen Cooper-Dean Charitable Foundation Trustees v Greensleeves Owners Ltd [2015] UKUT 320 (LC) (collective enfranchisement, valuation, human rights); Dwelling in London N2, Re Valuation Tribunal [2015] R.V.R. 157 (council tax, staff accommodation); Howard De Walden Estates Ltd v Accordway Ltd [2015] L. & T.R. 5 (lease extension, rights of intermediate landlord); Albion Residential Ltd v Albion Riverside Residents RTM Co Ltd [2014] UKUT 6 (LC) (right to manage, separate premises); Hatton v Connew [2013] EWCA Civ 1560 & 1681 (boundary dispute, treatment of expert evidence, retrials); Daejan Investments Ltd v Benson [2013] 1 W.L.R. 854 (service charges, dispensation from consultation); Paddington Basin Developments v Gritz Upper Tribunal [2013] UKUT 338 (LC) (service charges); BDW Trading Ltd v South Anglia Housing Ltd [2014] 1 W.L.R. 920 (service charges, consultation requirements prior to leasing); Havering LBC v MacDonald Upper Tribunal [2012] 3 E.G.L.R. 49 (requirement to for reasoning in judgments); Staunton v Kaye Upper Tribunal [2010] UKUT 270 (LC) (service charges, jurisdiction of tribunal following transfer of proceedings from court); McGlynn v Welwyn Hatfield DC [2010] H.L.R. 10 (possession claims and human rights); Nailrile Ltd v Earl Cadogan [2009] 2 E.G.L.R. 151 (lease extensions, valuation of intermediate landlord's interest); Church Commissioners for England v Meya [2007] H.L.R. 4 (determining periods of a statutory periodic assured tenancy).

Professional Memberships: Chancery Bar Association, Property Bar Association, ALEP, Bar Pro Bono Unit.

Career: Hardwicke scholar Lincoln's Inn, Newcastle University.

Publications: Co-author of Commercial Property Litigation (2nd Ed) Contributor to Service Charges and Management: Law and Practice (3rd Ed).

Personal: Running, rowing, blues music.

FINNIGAN, Peter QC
QEB Hollis Whiteman, London
020 7933 8855
peter.finnigan@qebhw.co.uk
Featured in Financial Crime (London)

Practice Areas: Peter Finnigan defends and prosecutes in a wide range of criminal cases from international fraud to high profile general crime. He has considerable experience of serious organised crime and has been instructed in numerous murder cases such as that of Kenny Noye for both murder and for laundering the proceeds of the Brinks Mat gold bullion robbery. A former standing counsel to HMRC (he was instructed in the Iraqi Supergun case), Peter has appeared in many revenue frauds and in high value drugs trafficking cases. He has extensive experience in the field of commercial and professional/city fraud, corporate crime, money laundering, asset restraint, criminal and civil recovery. Also, cross-border crime, mutual legal assistance and plea agreements. Peter has been involved in a number of high profile SFO cases ranging from Blue Arrow to insider dealing and sanctions busting cases (including Saddam Hussein's 'Oil for food' scheme: Mabey and Johnson Ltd and Innospec). Recent cases include the successful defence of one of the brokers in the second LIBOR trial. He is currently instructed by the SFO in a "blockbuster' investigation into allegations of bribery and corruption concerning a multi-national (Alstom Group).

Professional Memberships: Member CBA and BASL.

Career: Called 1979. Appointed QC 2009.

Personal: Educated at Sevenoaks School 1967-74 and University of Newcastle-upon-Tyne 1975-78. Speaks French and German.

FIRTH, Matthew
Queen Elizabeth Building QEB, London
020 7797 7837
clerks@qeb.co.uk
Featured in Family/Matrimonial (London)

Practice Areas: Matrimonial finance and private law Children Act cases.

Professional Memberships: Family Law Bar Association.

Career: Pupillage at QEB (1991-92); tenant at QEB since 1992.

Personal: Educated at Clifton College, Bristol, Pembroke College, Oxford (Literae Humaniores) and City University, London (diploma in law). Married with two children.

FISHER, Richard
South Square, London
020 7696 9900
richardfisher@southsquare.com
Featured in Chancery (London), Restructuring/Insolvency (London)

Practice Areas: Richard has a commercial dispute focused practice with a particular specialism in domestic and cross-border reconstruction and insolvency, banking, fraud and financial products/derivatives litigation. He regularly acts in relation to multi-jurisdictional and complex commercial disputes, and is a member of the BVI bar.

Professional Memberships: COMBAR; Chancery Bar Association.

Career: Richard has appeared in various substantial and high-profile insolvency cases in England at all levels of tribunal up to the Supreme Court, including disputes arising out of the Lehman Bros insolvency (Waterfall I and II proceedings, and Firth Rixson), Eurosail, Federal Mogul, Lansbanki, Kaupthing and the SerVaas state immunity litigation. He has acted in many of the major recent UK based insolvencies/restructurings, including Codere SA, Co-Op Bank, Lehman Brothers, Deutsche Annington, Telecolumbus and Cattles. He is also involved in substantial commercial litigation and asset recovery proceedings. Having acted for the Brunei Investment Agency in relation to its disputes with Prince Jefri, he has subsequently acted in matters such as the IPOC litigation, the Tchigirinsky v Sibir Energy dispute and BTA Bank v Ablyazov. Richard is regularly engaged in litigation in offshore jurisdictions such as the Cayman Islands. Recent cases include Snoras Bank and Primeo Fund v HSBC. Called to the Bar 2000.

Publications: Consultant Editor of Halsbury's Laws (Insolvency); contributor to Cross-Border Insolvency Fourth Ed (Sheldon, Bloomsbury, 2015).

FITZGERALD, Ben
QEB Hollis Whiteman, London
020 7933 8855
ben.fitzgerald@qebhw.co.uk
Featured in Crime (London), Financial Crime (London)

Practice Areas: Ben FitzGerald prosecutes and defends in cases of serious crime, fraud and professional regulatory offending. He is a Grade 4 prosecutor for the CPS. He successfully prosecuted Ben Butler in 2016 for the murder of his six-year old daughter Ellie, and her mother Jennie Gray for child cruelty and perverting the course of justice. He is regularly instructed both alone and as a led junior in the most serious criminal cases. Ben represents corporate clients and private individuals who require impeccable preparation and advocacy. He successfully defended the UK's largest retailer against private criminal prosecution. He recently secured the acquittal of a chartered accountant on charges of fraud. He represents a company director charged in connection with an alleged £109 million tax fraud in Operation Amazon, reportedly HM Revenue & Customs' biggest ever prosecution. He has extensive experience of advising on Legal Professional Privilege, investigatory powers and judicial review proceedings. He acts regularly in Health and Safety cases for both the prosecution and for corporate or individual defendants. He recently represented a contractor charged over a death whilst working at height (R v Bakewell). He secured convictions against corporates and individuals arising from a workplace death on an industrial estate (R v Babamiri and others). He is a highly-rated and expert advocate in professional disciplinary proceedings. He is equally adept whether presenting the case for the regulator or acting for the individual professional. He is regularly instructed in the Medical Practitioners Tribunal Service, GDC and NMC to deal with complex and serious cases.

Professional Memberships: Association of Regulatory & Disciplinary Lawyers, Public Access Bar Association, registered with the Bar Council – Public Access Directory

Personal: Call 2000; BA (Hons) History (Trinity College, Cambridge University, First Class); PGD in Law (City University)

FITZGERALD, Susanna QC
One Essex Court, London
020 7583 2000
clerks@oeclaw.co.uk
Featured in Licensing (London)

Practice Areas: Specialises in gambling law (including gaming, betting, lotteries, internet gambling), sex establishment licensing and alcohol licensing law. Has represented or advised major leisure and gambling operators, both terrestrial and remote, the Gambling Commission, concert promoters, licensing authorities, sales promoters, TV companies, petrol companies and table dancing club operators. Deals with Gambling Commission hearings, licensing hearings and all appeals. Has advised extensively on the Licensing Act 2003 and the Gambling Act 2005. Contributing editor to 'Law of Betting, Gaming and Lotteries' by Smith and Monkcom (2nd and 3rd eds and currently working on 4th edn), contributor to Halsburys Laws Vol 4 (1) 4th Edn Reissue on Betting, Gaming and Lotteries. author of articles published in 'Licensing Review', 'The Solicitors Journal' and the 'Consumer Policy Review'. Contributor to 'Gambling and Public Policy'. Has lectured at conferences and spoken at seminars in the UK and abroad. Has also appeared on radio and television.

Professional Memberships: Chairman of Business in Licensing; Member of The Gambling Business Group, Trustee of GamCare; Director and Trustee of the Institute of Licensing; Bencher of Inner Temple.; Society for the Study of Gambling; CLCBA; South Eastern Circuit; Commercial Women in Law.

Career: Called to the Bar in 1973, joined present chambers in 1975 and made QC in 1999.

FLANAGAN, Julia
Charter Chambers, London
020 7618 4400
julia.flanagan@charterchambers.com
Featured in Crime (London)

Practice Areas: Julia Flanagan is a very experienced defence advocate with a particular specialisation in serious sexual offending. Her practice covers the full spectrum of criminal work including homicide, large-scale fraud and serious drugs offences. She acts as both leading and junior counsel, instructed privately and under the provisions of legal aid. She is accustomed to dealing with the most difficult and sensitive cases involving highly vulnerable defendants and witnesses and the use of intermediaries in court. For example she recently secured the acquittal of a defendant accused of anal rape by a 6 year old boy, despite the restrictions imposed in respect of cross-examination of the child complainant. She is accustomed to representing clients from professional backgrounds, including recently the successful defence of a member of the legal profession. Notable cases of 2015 and 2016 include: R v T. 2015. Leading counsel representing client accused of multiplefrauds against multiple complainants involving dating websites. R v P. 2015. Represented daughter who, with her mother, was accused of the attempted mur-

der of her own father by means of poisoning. R v C. 2016. Minister accused of multiple counts of sexual assault and child cruelty against numerous complainants, spanning a period of over 40 years. R v B. 2016. Solicitor accused of firearms offences and misconduct in office. R v L. 2016 .Inter- familial rape allegations where the complainants and defendant were all children themselves, with and age range spanning from 6 to 11 years old. R v Q. 2016. Large- scale grooming case. Defendant one of multiple adult male defendants accused of grooming and sexual offences against under-age girls. R v N. 2016. Complex Fraud and child cruelty case involving the evidence of over 100 witnesses from 6 different health authorities, dozens of medical experts and multiple complainants. There were issues of Munchausens By Proxy (FII), psychiatric illness, personality disorders and medical dispute.
Professional Memberships: Criminal Bar Association. South Eastern Circuit.
Career: Called to the Bar in 1993 from Lincoln's Inn.
Personal: Graduated from the London School of Economics.

FLENLEY, William QC
Hailsham Chambers, London
020 7643 5000
william.flenley@hailshamchambers.com
Featured in Professional Negligence (London)
Practice Areas: William specialises in professional liability, contract and insurance law. He is co-author of the leading text, Flenley & Leech, Solicitors' Negligence and Liability (3rd ed., December 2012). For many years, he has been recommended as a professional negligence barrister by each of the main directories. From 2013 to 2015 he was the Chairman of the Professional Negligence Bar Association, and in 2014 was elected a Bencher of the Middle Temple. His practice encompasses claims against solicitors, barristers, accountants, financial advisors, insurance brokers, surveyors and valuers, as well as associated insurance coverage issues. He is a trained mediator and a mediation advocate. He also acts as an arbitrator and has been trained in adjudication (University College, London, Judicial Institute). He speaks regularly on professional indemnity. Recent cases include Purrunsing v A'Court [2016] PNLR 26, a case widely discussed in the legal press, and Harding Homes v BDB [2015], a two week trial about solicitors' negligence and loss of a chance claims.
Professional Memberships: Professional Negligence Bar Association (Chairman 2013 to 2015; Vice Chairman 2011-2013; Co-Chair of annual lawyers' liability seminar 2007-2010).
Career: Exeter College, Oxford (BA, BCL); Cornell University, USA (LLM). Called in 1988. QC 2010. .
Publications: Flenley & Leech – 'Solicitors' Negligence and Liability' 3rd Edition, (2012); past contributor to 'Cordery on Legal Services '; original contributor to chapters 1 and 2 (general principles of liability and damages) of 'Professional Negligence and Liability' (2000); Assistant general editor, Lloyd's Law Reports: Professional Negligence (2000-03); co-author, 'The Mareva Injunction and Anton Piller Order' (1993).

FLETCHER, James
5 St Andrew's Hill, London
020 7332 5400
jamesfletcher@5sah.co.uk
Featured in POCA Work & Asset Forfeiture (All Circuits)
Practice Areas: James deals with all aspects of asset forfeiture, restraint and freezing orders, confiscation and enforcement. He receives instructions from specialist Defence firms, businesses and the Proceeds of Crime Units of the CPS and SFO (A list), Metropolitan and City of London Police, HMRC, Home Office and individuals under direct access. He is briefed by the NCA in cash and civil recovery cases. He is on the Attorney General's B Panel for civil advocates. He also has a litigation extension to his practicing certificate. He is often brought into cases at the appellate stage or where specialist knowledge of proceeds of crime is needed. As well as acting in Civil Recovery, cash forfeiture and enforcement cases, particular cases of note over the last year have included acting for a defendant charged with dishonest manipulation of LIBOR, successfully obtaining the return of £300,000 seized cash in a modern slavery case and successfully arguing a reduction in benefit in a confiscation case from £14 million to £425,000. James has acted for and against claimants in Judicial Reviews of search warrant and other investigative orders.
Professional Memberships: Proceeds of Crime Lawyers Association, Fraud Lawyers Association.
Career: Called 2000 (Middle Temple).

FLETCHER, Stephen
Dere Street Barristers, Newcastle upon Tyne
0191 232 0541
s.fletcher@derestreet.co.uk
Featured in Real Estate Litigation (North Eastern)
Practice Areas: Stephen has been a practising civil barrister since he was called to the Bar. His particular expertise lies in Chancery/Commercial and Employment law. Stephen has maintained a solid record of success at trial in recent cases, a selection of which includes: Successful recovery of damages and costs in team moves/restrictive covenants after fully contested High Court action; Enforcement of rent charges in respect of large residential estate; Damages and costs in professional negligence claim; Arbitration in agricultural partnership dispute; Contested business lease renewal; Contested probate claim; Boundary dispute. Stephen has also continued to steer cases to successful and advantageous conclusions for clients without trial in recent matters such as: Shareholder/share purchase and director disputes; Property rights disputes; Building disputes; Inheritance Act claims. In addition to the breadth and depth of his experience, Stephen attaches particular importance to achieving outcomes which provide real benefit to the client. In all cases he is committed to developing effective working relationships with both solicitors and lay clients.

FORD, Charlotte
New Square Chambers, London
020 7419 8000
charlotte.ford@newsquarechambers.co.uk
Featured in Chancery (London)
Practice Areas: Charlotte specialises in trusts and estates work, both contentious and non-contentious, together with related insolvency and professional negligence matters. She has extensive experience both as junior and sole counsel. Her contentious probate and trusts work includes actions to remove or replace personal representatives, breach of trust claims, Inheritance Act claims, allegations of forgery and undue influence and questions of distribution in the case of a shortfall. Charlotte regularly advises on all aspects of the validity and construction of wills, together with issues arising in the administration of trusts and estates. Notable cases include Aeroflot v Gorbunova and others (the estate of Boris Berezovsky deceased) (dispute as to the representation of an estate), Charity Commission v Framjee (Dove Trust) (basis for the distribution of trust funds), Bignall v Cullen (distribution of estate in face of threatened claim) and Davis v Smith (CA, severance of joint tenancy before death).
Professional Memberships: Chancery Bar Association.
Career: MA Hons Law, Downing College, Cambridge. Called Lincoln's Inn, 2007 (Denning Scholar).
Publications: Co-editor of Theobald on Wills; co-author of Williams, Mortimer & Sunnucks – Executors, Administrators and Probate.

FORD, Jeremy
9 Gough Square, London
020 7832 0500
jford@9goughsquare.co.uk
Featured in Personal Injury (London)
Practice Areas: Jeremy practices in all aspects of personal injury litigation. His specialisms include brain injury; catastrophic injury; fatal accident; and Motor Insurers' Bureau claims. He recently settled a brain injury case with a capitalized value of over £20 million with multiple other cases settling at sums in excess of £1 million. He is also interested in cases with a psychiatric component including somatoform and chronic pain presentations. He is renowned for his professional approach; trial advocacy; and excellent client care.
Professional Memberships: Personal Injury Bar Association; Professional Negligence Bar Association; Association of Personal Injury Lawyers (Specialist Counsel and Secretary of the Brain Injury Special Interest Group).
Career: University of Leeds, LLB (Hons); Inns of Court School of Law, BVC 1996; Lincoln's Inn – Hardwicke Scholar
Publications: 1) Assistant Editor of Jordan Publishing / APIL "Guide to MIB Claims" (4th Ed) 2) Co-Author of Jordan Publishing / APIL "Guide to Catastrophic Injury Claims" (2nd Ed) 3) Co-Editor of Butterworth's Personal Injury Litigation Service, RTA / MIB 4) Co-Author of Jordan Publishing / APIL "Guide to RTA Liability" (2nd Ed) 5) 9 Gough Square, Clinical Negligence (2nd Ed)
Personal: Jeremy lives on a farm near Norwich with his wife and four children.

FORD, Michael QC
Old Square Chambers, Bristol
020 7269 0300
fordqc@oldsquare.co.uk
Featured in Employment (London), Employment (Western)
Practice Areas: Main areas of practice are employment law (including equal pay, working time, pensions, industrial action, and trade union law), public law, human rights. Appeared in the ECJ, European Court of Human Rights, Supreme Court, House of Lords, in public inquiries. Recent appellate cases include: Lock v British Gas, ECJ, CA (holiday pay); Griffiths v DWP, CA (disability discrimination); Bear Scotland v Fulton, EAT (working time); R (UNISON) v Lord Chancellor, CA, SC (tribunal fees); Chandhok v Tirkey, EAT (caste discrimination); RMT v United Kingdom, ECtHR (right to strike); British Airways v. Williams (SC, ECJ). On Equality and Human Rights Commission 'A' Panel of Counsel.
Professional Memberships: ILS, Institute for Employment Rights, ELA, ELBA.
Career: University of Bristol, LLB 1st Class; BSC (Hons) 1st class. Solicitor, Slaughter and May (1987-89). Lecturer University of Manchester (1990-92), Birkbeck College (1996-98). Called to Bar 1992. Fee-paid Employment Judge 2003. Employment Junior of Year 2012. QC 2013. Professor of Law University of Bristol 2015. Employment Silk of Year 2015.
Publications: Redgrave's Health and Safety and many others in e.g. Industrial Law Journal..
Personal: Former member of Great Britain road cycling squad. Fluent French; reasonable Spanish.

FORLIN, Gerard QC
Cornerstone Barristers, London
07947136349
gerardf@cornerstonebarristers.com
Featured in Health & Safety (London)
Practice Areas: Specialist in health and safety; manslaughter; disaster litigation; aviation; railways; shipping safety; regulatory offences; product liability; healthcare; commercial fishing; consumer crime; corruption; waste offences; human rights; and inquests. Described as "one of the most compelling advocates that you could ever see in a courtroom." Ranked in 6 areas in the leading independent directories: health and safety; crime; public inquiries and inquests; consumer law; product liability; and environmental law. Standing counsel to numerous PLCs and agencies in the UK and abroad. Advised on over 250 fatality cases, including: Watford, Southall, Paddington, James Porter, Teebay, Barrow, Hatfield, Purley, Faversham, Britannia Air Crash, City of London Lift Case, Alton Towers, Greek catamaran case, inquests in Falklands and other sporting, aviation and construction cases. Currently involved in two international aircraft disaster cases. Acted in over 150 jury inquests in the UK and overseas. Regular presenter globally for FCO and UN on bribery and corruption. Bar Council Direct Access Licensed.
Publications: Worked, lectured or consulted in over 55 countries.100 articles published. General Editor of "Corporate Liability (3rd Edition February 2014)". Appears on TV and radio as an expert. Also an actor.
Personal: LSE, Trinity Hall Cambridge, Diploma in Air and Space Law UCL. Global panel member of Royal Aeronautical Society legal list. Member of Denman Chambers Sydney and tenant in Maxwell Chambers Singapore. Called to the Bar in the BVI.

FORMBY, Emily
39 Essex Chambers, London
020 7832 1111
emily.formby@39essex.com
Featured in Personal Injury (London), Clinical Negligence (London)

Practice Areas: Specialist in personal injury and clinical negligence. Advises in all types of accident and catastrophic injury claims, both claimant and defendant including fatal accident claims and inquests. Specialising in catastrophic and high value claims often with multiple tortfeasors. Experienced in all types of workplace accidents including occupational disease and asbestos claims. Extensive road traffic claim expertise particularly cycling and highway claims. Clinical negligence experience includes delay in referral, diagnosis and treatment, obstetric cases, neurological disability, infection and endocrinology and bariatric surgery. Highly experienced in complex issues of causation, material contribution and difficult damages calculations. Also works in Court of Protection and management of damages and because interest matters. As well as trial work, for which her tenacity is renowned, often involved in round table and negotiated settlements where she can often bring claims to conclusion, utilising her mediation skills.
Professional Memberships: Personal Injuries Bar Association, Executive member and assistant secretary; Professional Negligence Bar Association.
Career: Call – 1993; Recorder of the Crown Court – 2009. CEDR Mediator
Publications: Kemp: Quantum of Damages, contributing editor; Kemp & Kemp: Practice & Procedure, contributer; Butterworths Personal Injury Litigation Service, section editor; PIBA Personal Injury Handbook 2007 (3rd Edn) – contributor.

FORSHAW, Simon
11KBW, London
020 7632 8500
Simon.Forshaw@11kbw.com
Featured in Employment (London)
Practice Areas: Employment law, commercial law, public law. Having a broad practice with an emphasis on employment and discrimination law, Simon is regularly instructed to appear in the High Court, the employment tribunals and at appellate level. Recently his practice (in employment law) has had a particular focus on litigation arising out of team moves (including interim relief), claims brought by senior executives (including whistle blowing and discrimination claims) and complex claims involving multi-jurisdictional issues.
Professional Memberships: ELA, ELBA and COMBAR.
Career: Called 2004, Gray's Inn. Notable cases include: D v. P [2016] EWCA Civ 87; Merlin Financial Consultants Limited v. Cooper [2014] IRLR 610; Foster v. Bon Groundwork Limited [2012] IRLR 517; Ashby v. Birmingham City Council [2011] IRLR 473; Aon Limited v. JLT Reinsurance Brokers Limited [2010] IRLR 600.
Publications: Blackstone's Employment Law Practice (annually since 2009); Tolley's Employment Handbook (annually since 2010). Regularly writes articles for the Industrial Law Journal.
Personal: Educated at St. John's College, Southsea and St. John's College, Oxford. Resides London.

FORTE, Timothy
3 Temple Gardens, London
020 7353 3102
clerks@3tg.co.uk
Featured in Crime (London)
Practice Areas: Since 1996 Tim has specialised in lengthy, often high profile, cases. Highlights include his first major case – an international $2 billion US Dollar Bond fraud. After the 11-month Operation Hobart trial, Tim was instrumental in the successful appeals (instructed for all appellants) and abandonment of the retrial after complex and novel legal argument. In 2013, he acted in Dale Cregan & Others – the murder of two policewomen, involving grenades – as well as leading in "the largest ever multi-commodity drugs conspiracy in the UK" at Liverpool CC. 2014 saw a £385 million, 200,000+ page MTIC fraud. Most of 2015 was spent leading in a substantial drugs and money laundering trial at the Bailey, being led in a murder trial in Liverpool and a 3 month "super-sex grooming" trial at the Bailey. He ended the year leading in a substantial fraud trial in Ipswich relating to criminality across the UK. In 2016, Tim was led in a multi-million-pound mortgage fraud in Birmingham and then in the trial of the youth accused of the murder of PC David Phillips in Liverpool. Thereafter, Tim has been leading as first defendant in an OCG drugs trial in Manchester. He is almost exclusively instructed in complex and serious crime, specialising in murder, heavyweight fraud and drugs, having an excellent reputation among professional clients. An astute and intuitive lawyer, Tim identifies arguments often overlooked by others. His successful Judicial Review, ex parte Raeside, is now one of the leading cases in Custody Time Limits case law. His extensive technical expertise is much sought after in telephone intercept, audio surveillance and complex computer evidence cases. An accomplished appellate advocate, he is also increasingly instructed to take over Appeal or POCA cases. In addition, Tim has an ever-growing private practice. He is fluent in German with a working knowledge of French and Italian.
Professional Memberships: Justice, Liberty, Amnesty International, CBA, South Eastern Circuit
Career: Called 1994
Personal: Hockey, golf, cricket, music and literature.

FORTUNE, Malcolm
Serjeants' Inn Chambers, London
020 7427 5000
MFortune@serjeantsinn.com
Featured in Professional Discipline (London)
Practice Areas: Malcolm Fortune was called to the Bar in 1972. Malcolm specialises in clinical negligence and healthcare, inquests and inquiries and professional discipline and regulatory law. An earlier edition notes that "he has a great deal of experience in appearing before regulatory bodies and is a heavyweight in this area." Please visit the Serjeants' Inn Chambers website for his profile, which sets out full details of his practice including relevant work of note.
Career: Recorder

FOSKETT, Rosanna
Maitland Chambers, London
020 7406 1200
rfoskett@maitlandchambers.com
Featured in Chancery (London)
Practice Areas: Commercial and chancery litigation and arbitration (domestic and international), including business agreements and general contractual disputes, banking litigation, civil fraud and asset tracing, jurisdiction disputes/conflicts of laws, company and insolvency, trusts and estates litigation, property litigation. Notable cases include: Lehman Brothers Waterfall application (due for hearing in the Supreme Court in October 2016: construction of $2.25bn subordinated loan agreements/questions about liability of members in insolvency), Dar Al Arkan Real Estate Development Co v Al Refai (multi-million dollar civil fraud/conspiracy/defamation claim involving conflicts of laws points), Eurofinance v Rubin (Supreme Court decision on Cross Border Insolvency Regulations 2006/enforceability of foreign judgments in insolvency context), Maloney v Filtons (sham lease/insolvency/appointment of receivers), HMRC v Rochdale Drinks Distributors (Court of Appeal decision on insolvency/provisional liquidation/VAT fraud), Mackay v Ashwood Enterprises (Court of Appeal decision on costs made ex parte), Hart v Burbidge (undue influence/ademption/wills).
Professional Memberships: COMBAR, Chancery Bar Association, Insolvency Lawyers Association
Career: Called 2008
Personal: Educated at Trinity College, Cambridge (MA – Double First; MPhil; Junior, Senior and Research Scholar) and City University, London (Distinction in Graduate Diploma in Law). Member of Lincoln's Inn (Hardwicke, Lord Bowen and Lord Mansfield Scholar).

FOSTER, Alison QC
39 Essex Chambers, London
020 7832 1111
alison.foster@39essex.com
Featured in Administrative & Public Law (London), Professional Discipline (London), Tax (London)
Practice Areas: Alison's practice consists of public, administrative law and human rights with particular involvement in regulation and tax. She was Treasury Panel counsel for 12 years. Alison has acted at the highest level across all commercial, regulatory, and human rights areas. She acts for and against public bodies, industry regulators, financial advisors, commercial entities and organs of state. Her clients are based domestically and internationally and she regularly advises and acts in matters involving the international civil service, pharmaceuticals, the rights of individuals, and the powers and duties of public bodies. Her advocacy work predominantly involves statutory construction, European Law and Human Rights. Alison has established a stellar reputation in each of her practice areas and is recognised by the leading industry directories as a Leading Silk in Administrative & Public Law, Professional Discipline and Tax. She is also the Editor of the 8th Edition of Disciplinary and Regulatory Proceedings. She has been involved in some of the most notable cases in these areas, including the Deepcut Inquest in 2016, the first tax challenge to the FCA (currently in the Court of Appeal) and multi-million pound tax challenges including income tax, VAT and corporation tax 2015 and 2016 continuing.
Professional Memberships: Administrative Law Bar Association. Chancery Bar Association
Career: 2015: Joint Head of Chambers. 2007: Deputy High Court Judge Chancery Division. 2002: Queen's Counsel. Master of the Bench of Inner Temple.
Personal: Diploma in Law, City University, London. M Phil, University of London. MA (Hons) Jesus College, Oxford.

FOSTER, Charles
Serjeants' Inn Chambers, London
020 7427 5000
cfoster@serjeantsinn.com
Featured in Clinical Negligence (London), Professional Discipline (London)
Practice Areas: Charles Foster was called to the Bar in 1988. Charles specialises in clinical negligence and healthcare, Court of Protection and professional and regulatory law. An earlier edition notes that "he's delightful with clients and always gets the best out of the medical experts", "he always impresses, as he is able to advise really well on complicated cases where there are lots of papers involved. He provides tactical and practical advice." Please visit the Serjeants' Inn Chambers website for his profile, which sets out full details of his practice including relevant work of note.
Professional Memberships: PNBA, Bar Human Rights Committee.
Publications: Numerous books and hundreds of articles and papers.

FOTTRELL, Deirdre QC
1 Garden Court Family Law Chambers, London
020 7993 7600
fottrell@1gc.com
Featured in Family/Matrimonial (London)
Practice Areas: Children Human Rights International Judicial Review Court of Protection
Professional Memberships: Family Law Bar Association Association of Lawyers for Children Human Rights Lawyers Association Middle Temple
Career: Deirdre Fottrell practises in all areas relating to children. She has particular expertise on surrogacy and alternative families and has appeared in a number of leading cases in these areas. In addition, she is a specialist in human rights law as it applies to children, having taught and published in that area before coming to the Bar. She has practised at all levels of court in the UK, including the Supreme Court, and has acted for clients before the European Court of Human Rights. She has wide experience in matters of international child law, including relocation, adoption, abduction and Brussels IIA. She is a visiting professor at the School of International Affairs at Columbia University, New York, and is a Council of Europe Expert on the European Convention. She also has a civil practice in the Administrative Court and represents children, foster carers and adopters in applications for judicial review arising out of the Children Act and Adoption legislation.
Publications: Publications include Halburys Rights and Freedoms, Sweet and Maxwell, April 2013.

FOX, Nicola
1 King's Bench Walk, London
020 7936 1500
nfox@1kbw.co.uk
Featured in Family/Matrimonial (London)
Practice Areas: Private law children work. Matrimonial Finance. Schedule 1. Cohabitant disputes.
Professional Memberships: Family Law Bar Association. Association of Lawyers for Children. Member of the South Eastern

Circuit. Member of the Bar Pro Bono Unit (Panel).
Career: Family law barrister since 1996. Previous career as a child clinical psychologist. Specialising in matrimonial finance and private children law work. She has a particular interest in complex private law disputes and relocation matters. Deputy District Judge (Civil and Family).
Publications: Contributor to: Applications Under Schedule 1 (Jordans. Halsburys Laws – Children Law (5th reissue). Butterworths Civil Court Precedents – Matrimonial Finance.

FOY, John QC
9 Gough Square, London
020 7832 0500
jfoy@9goughsquare.co.uk
Featured in Personal Injury (London)
Practice Areas: John Foy QC specialises in serious personal injury and clinical negligence cases, occupational disease litigation and costs. Most of his cases nowadays are brain damage, paraplegics, amputations etc. He has appeared in many reported cases on these topics and has conducted occupational disease litigation since the 1970s. Cases include Pearson v CICA (foetal alcohol syndrome), Corr v IBC Vehicles (suicide as a result of industrial injury), Hawley v Luminar (vicarious liability) and he acted for the coal miners in their ground breaking group litigation for respiratory disease which led directly to the setting up of the miners compensation scheme. He has a particular interest in mental health cases, as a former Judge of the Mental Health Tribunal and has expertise in costs, particularly in a personal injury/clinical negligence context, having been involved in many of the leading cases in this area, including being instructed by APIL on behalf of its members. He is a former chair of the Bar Council CFA Panel. He was involved in the drafting of the original APIL/PIBA CFA and many subsequent CFAs and CCFAs. He teaches advocacy at Grays Inn, where he is a Bencher and sits as a Recorder trying criminal, family and civil cases.
Professional Memberships: PIBA; PNBA.
Career: Called and joined 9 Gough Square in 1969; QC (1998); recorder (2000); Judge of Mental Health Review Tribunal (2003); Bencher Gray's Inn (2004).
Publications: Articles in JPIL, APIL Newsletter and NLT on occupational disease and personal injury costs.
Personal: LLB (Hons) Birmingham University, 1967. Interests include most sports.

FRANCIS, Andrew
Serle Court, London
020 7242 6105
afrancis@serlecourt.co.uk
Featured in Real Estate Litigation (London)
Practice Areas: Specialist in restrictive covenants affecting freehold land, party walls and rights of light.
Professional Memberships: Chancery Bar Association. Property Bar Association.
Publications: Author of 'Restrictive Covenants and Freehold Land, a Practitioner's Guide', 4th Ed. (2013) (Jordans) and co-author of 'Rights of Light – The Modern Law' (3rd Ed.) (2015) (Jordans) and Private Rights of Way (Jordans) (2012).
Personal: Master of the Bench, Lincoln's Inn.

FRANCIS, Robert QC
Serjeants' Inn Chambers, London
020 7427 5000
rfrancis@serjeantsinn.com
Featured in Clinical Negligence (London), Inquests & Public Inquiries (All Circuits), Professional Discipline (London)
Practice Areas: Sir Robert Francis QC was called to the Bar in 1973 and took silk in 1992. Sir Robert specialises in public and administrative, Court of Protection, employment, inquests and inquiries, clinical negligence and healthcare, professional discipline and public inquiries. Earlier directory commentary notes that he is "one of the outstanding silks of his generation", "a very skilled advocate who's very easy to listen to in really difficult cases. So clever and so good with clients, he's utterly brilliant and one of the best-regarded silks around." Please visit the Serjeants' Inn Chambers website for his profile, which sets out full details of his practice including relevant work of note.
Professional Memberships: PNBA, LCCLBA, CBA.
Career: Chair: Freedom to Speak Up Review; Mid-Staffordshire NHS Foundation Trust Public Inquiry; Inquiry into care and treatment of Michael Stone; Inquiry into the care and treatment of Peter Bryan and Richard Loudwell. Counsel: Royal Liverpool Children's Hospital inquiry; Neale Inquiry; Bristol Royal Infirmary Inquiry; Rabone v Pennine Care NHS Foundation Trust [CA: human rights of mental health patient) R (Burke) v General Medical Council [(advance directives, life prolonging treatment); Airedale NHS Trust v Bland (persistent vegetative state); Cheatle v General Medical Council (impairment of fitness to practice); numerous multi million pound clinical negligence cases for claimants and defendants. Legal Assessor General Optical Council Professional Conduct Committee. Recorder.
Publications: Medical Treatment: Decisions and the Law (co-author).

FRASER, Orlando QC
4 Stone Buildings, London
020 7242 5524
o.fraser@4stonebuildings.com
Featured in Fraud (London), Offshore (London)
Practice Areas: Orlando's practice is at the commercial end of the Chancery Bar, with an emphasis on civil fraud, and offshore work. Orlando has been consistently recommended for his civil fraud work by both Legal 500 and Chambers UK. In addition to his work in the Chancery and Commercial Divisions in London, Orlando's work has included jurisdictions such as Nevis, the BVI and Jersey.
Professional Memberships: Member of the Commercial Bar Association, and the Chancery Bar Association.
Career: GEC Plessey Telecoms 1990-92; 4 Stone Buildings, Lincoln's Inn 1994-; North Devon Conservative Candidate 2005 General Election. Admitted to Bar of the British Virgin Islands, and the Bar of South-West Texas, pro hac vice, 1998. Orlando has participated in the Bar in the Community program, is a Founding Fellow of the Centre of Social Justice, and was appointed one of two legal members of the Board of the Charity Commission by the Minister of State for the Cabinet Office in July 2013.

FRASER, Vincent QC
Kings Chambers, Manchester
0345 034 3444
clerks@kingschambers.com
Featured in Environment (Northern), Local Government (Northern), Planning (Northern)
Practice Areas: All aspects of town and country planning with particular expertise in retail, renewable energy, major infrastructure projects, commercial development large scale housing projects, minerals and waste. Compulsory purchase and compensation. Highways and rights of way. Local government powers administration and finance. Education law. Election law. Licensing. Environmental protection, European Environmental provisions, contaminated land, drainage, water supply and sewerage, IPPC. Judicial review.
Professional Memberships: Planning and Environmental Bar Association, Administrative Law Bar Association, UKELA.
Career: University College, Oxford MA (1st Class), Open Scholar, Sweet & Maxwell Prize. Called Gray's Inn 1981, Holker Entrance Award, Reid Scholar, Band Prize. QC 2001, Recorder 2002, Deputy High Court Judge 2010.
Publications: Planning Decisions Digest (Sweet & Maxwell).

FREEDMAN, Clive
3 Verulam Buildings, London
020 7831 8441
cfreedman@3vb.com
Featured in Information Technology (London)
Practice Areas: Commercial work including information technology (in particular IT project disputes), building and engineering, professional negligence, banking, commercial fraud, company law, insurance, oil and gas, sale of goods and international trade, arbitration and ADR, electronic disclosure.
Professional Memberships: Chartered Institute of Arbitrators (Fellow), COMBAR, TECBAR, British Computer Society (Fellow), Society for Computers & Law (Trustee), Society of Construction Law, Adjudication Society, Arbitration Club, Franco-British Lawyers Association.
Career: Barrister at 3 Verulam Buildings. CEDR Accredited Mediator, Chartered Arbitrator, Fellow of the British Computer Society, Former Chair of the Disciplinary Panel of the British Computer Society, TECBAR Approved Adjudicator. Trustee of Society for Computers & Law.
Publications: Co-author of 4th and 5th Editions of Expert Determination (Kendall, Freedman and Farrell, Thomson Sweet & Maxwell, 2008, 2015), Contributor to Banking Litigation (edited by Warne and Elliott, Sweet & Maxwell, 1999, 2005, 2011) Contributor to Bullen & Leake Precedents of Pleadings (Sweet & Maxwell, 2001, 2004, 2008, 2012) – chapter on IT contract disputes, contributor to Electronic Evidence (Butterworths LexisNexis, 2012).
Personal: Interests include computer programming, bridge, skiing, horse-racing and bloodstock breeding.

FREEDMAN, Clive QC
7 King's Bench Walk, London
020 7910 8335
cfreedman@7kbw.co.uk
Featured in Commercial Dispute Resolution (London), Fraud (London)
Practice Areas: Civil fraud, commercial litigation, international arbitration, banking, professional negligence and company & partnership law. The Times Lawyer of the Week (February 2015) and shortlisted for Commercial Litigation Silk of the Year at the Chambers UK Bar Awards 2015. Recently acted in Sebry v Companies House [2015] EWHC 115 (QB) establishing a duty of care owed by the Registrar to companies on its register. Successfully represented the Ritz Hotel Casino in two high-profile cases (The Ritz Hotel Casino Ltd v Nora Al-Daher [2014] EWHC 2847 (QB) and Ritz Hotel Casino Ltd v Safa Al Geabury [2015] EWHC 2294 (QB)) concerning the duty of care owed by a casino to its players. Sharab v Prince Al-Waleed (2013) EWHC 2324 (Ch) successfully establishing oral contract for commission on sale of an aircraft from Saudi Prince to Colonel Gaddafi reported in newspapers worldwide. Highly experienced appellate lawyer: about fifty appearances in Court of Appeal. Examples of appellate work: Supreme Court Abela v Baadarani [2013] UKSC 44 (alternative service in Lebanon); Dadourian (worldwide freezing orders and Dadourian guidelines). The leading solicitors' partnerships case in House of Lords.
Professional Memberships: COMBAR; CFLA committee member; CEDR Accredited Mediator.
Career: Called 1978; QC 1997; Recorder; Deputy High Court Judge; accredited mediator; Joint-head of Littleton Chambers 2006-2013; BVI Bar (2014); Arbitrator.
Publications: Civil Appeals (arbitration and international trade chapter); Mendelshon on Franchising, joint editor; Security for Costs, Sweet and Maxwell, consulting editor.
Personal: Manchester Grammar School. Pembroke College, Cambridge

FREEMAN, Lisa
Furnival Chambers, London
020 7405 3232
lfreeman@furnivallaw.co.uk
Featured in POCA Work & Asset Forfeiture (All Circuits)
Practice Areas: Specialises in all aspects of the law relating to financial wrong doing: Fraud, bribery and corruption; Whistleblowing; Civil recovery and property freezing orders; Criminal confiscation, restraint and receiverships; Anti money laundering advice and statutory reporting; Private prosecutions and corporate investigations; and Insolvency and company investigations.
Professional Memberships: Proceeds of Crime Lawyers Association.
Career: Acts for prosecuting authorities (SFO, FCA, CPS, UKBA), companies, court appointed receivers, defendants and third parties. Appears in the Court of Appeal, High Court (Administrative Court, Companies Court, Chancery Division) and Crown Court. Examples of work: (1) Instructed by the UK government in three applications pending before the European Court of Human Rights concerning criminal confiscation and Article 6 / A1P1; (2) Instructed by an Alleged Offender in restraint proceedings arising from an alleged £1 billion multi jurisdictional dividend-tax trading fraud; and (3) Advising multinational PLC (transport/power sector) in Paris on compliance with UK Bribery Act 2010.
Publications: Regularly delivers lectures at conferences and webinars: UK representative for United Nations anti money laundering workshop in Turkmenistan (2014); Deliver-

ing lecture on enforcement of confiscation orders within the European Union for the Bar European Group in Iceland; and UK representative for European Union project for justice reform and legislative amendments to forfeit the proceeds of crime in Ukraine (2015/2016).

FRENCH, Lucie
St Philips Chambers, Birmingham
0121 246 7000
lfrench@st-philips.com
Featured in Family/Matrimonial (Midlands)

Practice Areas: Lucie French is a family law specialist who accepts instructions in all areas of family law. She has a particular interest in family finance cases as well as TLATA cases involving financial separation of unmarried couples, and regularly appears on behalf of parties and interveners at all stages of proceedings. Lucie is frequently instructed in the area of public law children work, appearing for local authorities and family members before tribunals from lay justices to the High Court. She made her first appearance (unled) in the Court of Appeal in 2013 (Re L (a child) (Case Management: Child's Evidence) [2013] EWCA Civ 1778). Lucie is also available to instruct in private law children and injunctive relief applications.
Professional Memberships: Chair, YRes (West Midlands); Committee member, National YRes; FLBA; Coram/BAAF.
Career: Lucie undertook pupillage at St Philips in 2008 under Alistair MacDonald QC (now MacDonald J). Since 2010, she has practised solely in family law.
Publications: 'YRes West Midlands Children Law Update', 3 May 2016 (Jordans Family Law); '#ResConf2016: a YRes perspective', The Review, Issue 182 May/June 2016
Personal: Lucie graduated with a degree in Classics from Newnham College, Cambridge University in 2002. She speaks Italian to intermediate level.

FRYER-SPEDDING, James
9 St John Street, Manchester
0161 955 9000
jfs@9sjs.com
Featured in Chancery (Northern), Commercial Dispute Resolution (Northern)

Practice Areas: James Spedding specialises in chancery/commercial litigation and, in particular, professional negligence, trusts, probate and administration of estates, partnerships, real property, landlord and tenant, family provision, and commercial contract disputes. CEDR Accredited Mediator.
Professional Memberships: Chancery Bar Association, Professional Negligence Bar Association, Northern Chancery Bar Association and Northern Circuit Commercial Bar Association.
Career: Called in 1994.
Personal: James Spedding studied law at King's College, London University (LLB (Hons), 1st Class) and then New College, Oxford (BCL, 1st Class). Chambers website – www.9sjs.com. Linkedin – http://uk.linkedin.com/in/jamesspedding.

FURLONG, Richard
Carmelite Chambers, London
020 7936 6300
richard@furlong.net
Featured in Financial Crime (London)

Practice Areas: He specialises in defending those accused of serious and complex fraud in criminal and related civil proceedings. His practice includes serious commercial and tax fraud of all types as well as corruption, money laundering, confiscation and restraint. He is often instructed privately and pre-charge. He also defends in other serious crime and undertakes regulatory, disciplinary and tribunal work. Accepts direct access where appropriate. Recent practice history available at www.carmelitechambers.co.uk.
Professional Memberships: Criminal Bar Association.
Career: Called 1994. Joined Carmelite from 25 Bedford Row in 2014. He was previously an investment analyst with Credit Lyonnais Securities. Educated Queens' College, Cambridge (MA, Economics).
Publications: Co-author of International Money Laundering & Terrorist Financing [Sweet & Maxwell], and Lexis PSL web content on the Bribery Act 2010. Also CPDCast podcasts on the Criminal Procedure Rules. https ://myaccount. chambersandpartners.com/Secure/Profiles/ProoN iew/223 799/2 79 28/06/2016
Personal: Interests include prosecuting offences under the Hunting Act 2004, advising and lecturing on fraud, bribery and money laundering.

FURST, Stephen QC
Keating Chambers, London
020 7544 2600
sfurst@keatingchambers.com
Featured in International Arbitration (London), Construction (London), International Arbitration (London)

Practice Areas: Specialist in construction, engineering, energy, on-shore and off-shore plant, computer and technology related disputes along with professional negligence actions within these specialist areas. Regularly acts in complex cases of high-value in the UK High Courts and arbitrations, along with all forms of alternative dispute resolution. He also has a significant domestic and international practice as arbitrator and adjudicator, where he has developed a reputation for handling the most technically challenging cases. Recent appointments include arbitrations administered by the ICC, LCIA and DIAC. Accredited adjudicator and mediator of considerable experience.
Professional Memberships: LCIA, TECBAR, COMBAR, KCLRA, SCL
Career: Called 1975; Queens Counsel 1991; Fellow of the Singapore Institute of Arbitrators 2003, approved arbitrator, Hong Kong International Arbitration Centre Panel Arbitrator; Deputy High Court Judge of the TCC and Recorder Bencher, Middle Temple 2003.
Publications: Joint Editor Keating on Construction Contracts – Tenth Edition; Joint Editor, Construction Law Yearbook – 1994, 1995.

GAITSKELL, Robert QC
Keating Chambers, London
020 7544 2600
rgaitskell@keatingchambers.com
Featured in International Arbitration (London)

Practice Areas: Dual qualified engineer/lawyer specialist in construction, engineering and energy, particularly electrical, mechanical, and process engineering; instructed in numerous international and UK major disputes, (including frequent appointments as an arbitrator [including as Chairman of ICC tribunals] and Chairman of Dispute Boards) concerning, inter alia, complex projects (especially power stations), defence, computer facilities, chemical processing, food and drink production, oil and gas rigs, hospitals, motorways, bridges, tunnels, dredging, water treatment, airports, nuclear fuel processing and commercial property. Over 100 commercial, construction and intellectual property international arbitrations and over 100 mediations. CEDR accredited.
Professional Memberships: Chairman of the Joint IET/IMechE Committee on Model Forms (which produces the MF/1-4 suite of contracts); Technology and Construction Bar Association (Committee Member 1987-93); London Commercial & Common Law Bar Association (Committee Member 1987-2000); Commercial Bar Association (COMBAR); Singapore International Arbitration Centre 2006 (Fellow); CEDR Adjudication Panel.
Career: Called 1978; QC 1994; Vice President of the IEE (1998-2001); Senator of the Engineering Council (1997-2002), practised in UK and abroad as professional electrical engineer, Bencher of Gray's Inn. Recorder (part-time Judge); 2000-10; Chairman: ITER Nuclear Dispute Board.
Publications: Numerous publications on legal and engineering topics. Editor: 'Construction Dispute Resolution Handbook' (2nd Ed).

GALBRAITH, Amber
Compass Chambers, Edinburgh
0131 226 2881
amber.galbraith@compasschambers.com
Featured in Personal Injury (Scotland)

Practice Areas: Specialising in personal injury, clinical negligence and health and safety litigation, represents both pursuer and defender. Has extensive experience in conducting litigation in both the Court of Session and Sheriff Courts, including large-scale and complex litigation, fatal accident inquiries and public inquiries. Appointed as temporary Junior Counsel to Advocate General. Recent cases include: Lynda Brabender, representing Kaiden Ward v Fife Health Board, CSOH, currently at avizandum (medical negligence proof on liability); Elizabeth Gilchrist v Asda Stores Ltd [2015] CSOH 77 (proof on liability, the first case to consider the impact of the Enterprise and Regulatory Reform Act 2013 on the application of 'six pack' regulations in relation to an accident at work.); Adam Wagner v Thomas Grand and Arla Foods UK Plc [2015] CSOH 51 (proof on liability, and quantum re prosthetics) and [2016] CSIH 34 (appeal); Anne MacKinnon v Thomas Hadfield [2014] CSOH 15 (proof on quantum); James Farmer v FTVProclad [2013] CSOH 165 (proof on liability) John Cowan v Hopetoun House [2013] CSOH 9 (proof on liability); Fiona Dickie v Mohammadreza Khandani [2012] CSOH 122 (proof on quantum); Zanna Marczenko v Freshlink Foods, Lady Clark of Calton, unreported. 2012 (proof on liability)
Professional Memberships: Representative of the Junior Bar on the Personal Injury Sub-Group of the Civil Justice Council; Representative of the Junior Bar on the Court of Session Personal Injuries User Group; and Member of the Faculty of Advocates Professional Negligence Law Group.
Career: Admitted to Faculty of Advocates July 2005. Trained with Dundas & Wilson CS 1996 to 1998, then became prosecutor with COPFS. Part of Lockerbie trial team, and lead operational policy team in Crown Office. LLB (Hons) (Edinburgh Universtiy) (1995); Dip.LP (Edinburgh University) (1996); Diploma in Forensic Medicine (Glasgow University) (2001).
Publications: Tutor on Personal Injury Elective for the Diploma in Legal Practice, Edinburgh University, trainer for the Faculty of Advocates Devils course and speaks regularly at training events organised by Faculty, Compass Chambers and outside organisations.

GALBRAITH-MARTEN, Jason QC
Cloisters, London
020 7827 4013
JGM@cloisters.com
Featured in Employment (London)

Practice Areas: Hard work, dedication to the case, an ability to inspire confidence in clients and the expertise to persuade at all levels are just some of the attributes that have made Jason Galbraith-Marten QC one of the UK's pre-eminent labour and employment lawyers. He is especially valued for his ability to formulate a winning strategy in the most complex and challenging cases and to use the law creatively and imaginatively in pursuit of his client's best interests.
Professional Memberships: Jason is a qualified Mediator, was Chair of the Industrial Law Society from 2010 to 2013 and is a long-standing member of both the Employment Law Bar Association and the Employment Lawyers Association.
Career: Middle Temple Astbury Scholar, Inner Temple Pegasus Scholar. Chambers and Partners' Employment Junior of the Year 2009. Named as one of the 'Chambers 100' – the list of the top business lawyers in the UK – in 2014. Jason is also a Director of Assurety Ltd, an innovative witness training company.
Publications: Co-author of Bullen & Leake & Jacob's and of Butterworths Employment Law Guide. Contributor to Butterworths XpertHR online service.
Personal: The Campion School and Magdalene College, Cambridge. Fellow of the Royal Society for the encouragement of Arts, Manufactures and Commerce

GALLAGHER, Caoilfhionn
Doughty Street Chambers, London
020 7404 1313
c.gallagher@doughtystreet.co.uk
Featured in Administrative & Public Law (London), Police Law (All Circuits), Civil Liberties & Human Rights (London), Community Care (London), Inquests & Public Inquiries (All Circuits)

Practice Areas: Caoilfhionn Gallagher is a public law specialist, with particular expertise in children's rights, inquests, community care, actions against the police and prisons, and media law. Much of Caoilfhionn's work is high profile and sensitive, often raising national security issues – for example, she acted for bereaved families in the 7/7 (London Bombings) inquests and related judicial review proceedings, and in the Hillsborough inquests; and she has acted for media organisations to challenge reporting restrictions in many sensitive cases in the coroners', family and criminal courts, including in relation to the unexplained death of baby Poppi Worthington, and in the Gareth Williams, Alexander Litvinenko and Jordan Lee Begley inquests. Caoilfhionn undertakes many 'test cases' which secure results for her clients but also achieve wider change in the law. For example, her recent cases include acting in a number of successful challenges to the Department of Work and Pensions' benefit changes, R (Hurley and others) v

Secretary of State for Work and Pensions [2016] PTSR 636 (benefit cap unlawfully discriminates against the severely disabled), R (A and Rutherford) v Secretary of State for Work and Pensions [2016] HLR 8 (social sector size criteria, 'bedroom tax,' unlawfully discriminate against women) and R (MA) v Secretary of State for Work and Pensions [2013] PTSR 1521 (Regulations required to correct discriminatory impact of the bedroom tax on severely disabled children). Caoilfhionn has acted in many of the leading cases on children's rights, including HH v Italy [2013] 1 AC 338 (acting for the Official Solicitor, litigation friend to children whose parents both faced extradition, in this landmark case on Article 8 and the UNCRC); R (HC) v SSHD[2014] 1 WLR 1234 (acted for Hughes Chang, instructed by Just for Kids Law, in this test case on treatment of 17-year-olds in police custody as adults rather than children; it has resulted in a change to the law, affecting 70,000 17-year-olds in custody every year); and R (T and JB) v SSJ and SSHD [2014] UKSC 35 (blanket disclosure of childhood cautions breached Article 8; acted for the Equality and Human Rights Commission).

Publications: Caoilfhionn has authored and co-authored a number of books, including: 'Children In Need: Local Authority Support for Children and Families' (Legal Action Group) – First and Second Editions; 'Blackstone's Guide to the Human Rights Act 1998' (Oxford University Press) – Fourth and Fifth Editions; 'Blackstone's Guide to the Identity Cards Act 2006' (Oxford University Press).

Personal: BCL (University College Dublin); BL (Honorable Society of the King's Inns, Dublin); LLM (Cambridge, Gonville & Caius College).

GALLOWAY, Malcolm
Crown Office Chambers, London
07825 005851
MGalloway@oldsquare.co.uk
Featured in Environment (London), Health & Safety (London)

Practice Areas: Principle areas of practice are in regulatory compliance and defending serious motor prosecutions usually involving fatalities. He appears in both the criminal and Coroners' Court. Particular expertise in health and safety prosecutions involving fatality or serious injury. Has been instructed in a number of the high profile environmental prosecutions including the recent 'Churngold' investigation into hazardous waste. Advises in regulatory cases involving the potential for large POCA confiscation orders.

Professional Memberships: Health and Safety Lawyers Association, UK Environmental Law Association. Criminal Bar Association.

Career: Called to the Bar 1992. Appointed CPS Grade 4 Prosecutor 2005. Appointed List A; Regulatory List (HSE, ORR, EA) 2012. Appointed Recorder (Crown Court) 2012.

Personal: Lives in London and West Country.

GALLOWAY, Rachel
Kings Chambers, Manchester
0345 034 3444
clerks@kingschambers.com
Featured in Clinical Negligence (Northern)

Practice Areas: Clinical Negligence Coroners' Inquests Personal Injury

Professional Memberships: Professional Negligence Bar Association Personal Injury Bar Association The Coroners' Society of England & Wales

Career: Rachel covers all areas of clinical negligence including orthopaedics, gynaecology, psychiatry, cardiothoracic surgery, GP practice, general surgery, vascular surgery, nursing care, paramedic care and delay in diagnosis of cancer. Particularly experienced in mental health and treatment of the mentally ill patient, which often combines with her inquest work. Sits as an assistant coroner in Preston & West Lancashire and, more recently, in South Manchester.

Publications: Lexis Nexis author – wrongful birth

Personal: University: Cambridge (Christ's College) MA Law

GAMBLE, Jamie
No5 Chambers, Birmingham
0845 210 5555
jg@no5.com
Featured in Clinical Negligence (Midlands)

Practice Areas: Jamie practices exclusively in the areas of clinical negligence and personal injury and has a wide experience of all areas of such work. He prides himself on an approachable and down-to-earth manner and has been described in the guides to the profession as someone who "can always be relied upon to provide a definitive opinion when required". Much of his work is now of substantial value and includes claims of the utmost severity and death. He is also one of only 31 junior barristers in the country to be approved by the Spinal Injuries Association for catastrophic injury work. Recent cases that Jamie has been involved in have included: (i) Cases involving severe brain injury, including an ongoing case with a potential value in excess of £3 million; (ii) Re G (2016) – negligent abdominal surgery, settled for in excess of £500,000; (iii) Re B (2016) – death caused by necrotising fasciitis, settled for £425,000; (iv) cases involving orthopaedic surgery, including failure to diagnose cauda equina syndrome; and (v) B v P (2013) – above knee amputation following a motorcycle accident, settled for £1.6 million;

Professional Memberships: AvMA, PIBA.

Career: MA (Cantab) Law (Selwyn College, Cambridge University), BVC (Inns of Court Schools of Law), called to the Bar in 1999.

Personal: Busy father, irrational dog lover, usually exhausted runner, frustrated rock star and occasionally despairing Stoke City fan.

GARDINER, Bruce
2TG – 2 Temple Gardens, London
020 7822 1200
bgardiner@2tg.co.uk
Featured in Employment (London)

Practice Areas: Bruce is head of the 2TG Employment Group. He has a broad based employment practice, including employment related commercial and personal injury work, often relating to City institutions and raising international issues. Particular expertise includes restrictive covenants and employee competition issues, directors' duties, complex disability discrimination disputes, and stress, bullying and harassment claims. Current instructions include in a multi jurisdiction share sale agreement dispute, a High Court restrictive covenant claim involving leading companies in the market research industry; a substantial whistleblowing and wrongful dismissal action against a leading insurer; a £10 million occupational stress claim brought by a senior partner against a Big Four accountancy firm, and a High Court group action for breaches of the gang master legislation. Notable cases include: Cooper v Barclays UKEAT/0087/14 (scope of without prejudice rule in City disciplinary cases); Nadeem v Shell [2014] EWHC Civ 4664 (HC) (stress claim under franchise agreement); Dickins v O2 [2009] IRLR 58 (leading recent appellate case on occupational stress).

Professional Memberships: COMBAR, ELBA, ELA, ILS

Career: Called 1994; Fee Paid Employment Judge, February 2011 – present.

Personal: MA (Oxon) (1st Class); Jurisprudence Prize

GARDNER, Ben
Quadrant Chambers, London
020 75834444
ben.gardner@quadrantchambers.com
Featured in Shipping (London)

Practice Areas: Ben practises primarily in shipping, commodities, energy, insurance and conflict of laws, within a broad commercial practice. He appears regularly in the High Court, appellate courts and in arbitration, including recently: The DC Merwestone [2016] 3 WLR 543 (Supreme Court), The Superior Pescadores [2016] 2 All E.R. (Comm) 104 (Court of Appeal), South West SHA v Bay Island Voyages [2016] QB 503 (Court of Appeal) and Mistui OSK Lines v Salgaocar Mining Industries Pte Ltd [2015] 2 Lloyd's Rep. 518 (Commercial Court). For a detailed CV, please visit www.quadrantchambers.com.

Professional Memberships: COMBAR, TECBAR, Chancery Bar Association.

Career: MA, Double First (Cantab.); LLM, First (Cantab.); LLM (Harvard); called to the Bar in 2010.

GARDNER, Francesca P.
Kings Chambers, Leeds
0345 034 3444
clerks@kingschambers.com
Featured in Court of Protection (All Circuits)

Practice Areas: Francesca practices in all areas of Court or Protection, including welfare disputes, serious medical treatment and property and affairs matters. Francesca receives regular instructions from public bodies (including local authorities, health trusts and CCGs), private individuals and the Official Solicitor. Francesca was appointed as an Accredited Mental Health Tribunal Panel Member in 2013 and has experience in all Mental Health Act matters including complex restricted matters and those that inevitably overlap with the Mental Capacity Act 2005. Francesca has experience of representing the protected party before concurrent proceedings before the First- Tier Tribunal and the Court of Protection and Nearest Relative Displacement Proceedings. Francesca has extensive experience in cases concerning the interface between the Mental Health Act and the Mental Capacity Act. Francesca recently represented the local authority in Re AG [2016] EWCOP 37 (6 July 2016) (covert medication and deprivation of liberty).

Professional Memberships: Grays Inn Member of the North Eastern Circuit Court of Protection Practitioners Association – Treasurer (Yorkshire & Humber)

Career: Bar Vocational Course- BPP Law School- 2009

Publications: 1. 'The Cold Front'- Private Client Advisor 2. ' Support Network: litigation friends- Private Client Advisor

GARNIER, Edward QC
One Brick Court, London
020 7353 8845
eg@onebrickcourt.com
Featured in Defamation/Privacy (London)

Practice Areas: Defamation, malicious falsehood, contempt, reporting restrictions, breach of confidence, passing off, privacy and related human rights law. Cases of interest include: Loughran v Century Newspapers; Lord McAlpine v BBC, Lord McAlpine v ITV, Lord McAlpine v Sally Bercow, Lewis & Ors v R. Re Attorney General's Reference No. 15, 16 & 17 of 2012 [2012] EWCA Crim 1414 (01 June 2012); Thompson, Re Attorney-General's Reference No 103 of 2011 [2012] EWCA Crim 135 (10 February 2012); Rollings, R v [2012] EWCA Crim 86 (03 February 2012); A-G v Frail (2011) EWCA Crim 1570 Contempt of Court (Facebook jury contempt case, first case of its kind); Attorney General Reference No 18 of 2011 [2011] EWCA Crim 1300 (12 May 2011); Khan, R. v [2010] EWCA Crim 2880 (09 December 2010);R v Pyo, Anigbugu & McGee 2011 (CA) 3 separate "safe haven" rapes/sexual assaults on women in their home or workplace. Sentences increased respectively from 8 years to 15, 8 to 15, and from an extended sentence of 12 years 6 months to 14 years 6 months

Career: Called to the Bar 1976, Middle Temple; QC 1995; Bencher 2001. MP for Harborough since 1992; Knighted 2012; Solicitor General 2010-12; Shadow Attorney General 1997-2001 and 2009-10. Called to the Northern Ireland Bar 2010. Developed Deferred Prosecution Agreements (Section 45 and Schedule 17 of The Crime and Courts Act 2013) for use in cases of corporate bribery, money laundering and other economic crimes.

Publications: Contributor to Halsbury's Laws of England 4th ed Vol 45, Telecommunications & Broadcasting Law

Personal: Wellington College, Berkshire; Jesus College, Oxford. Interests; Music, cricket, shooting, travel & history. Language, French.

GARRETT, Lucy
Keating Chambers, London
020 7544 2650
lgarrett@keatingchambers.com
Featured in International Arbitration (London), Professional Negligence (London), Construction (London), Energy & Natural Resources (London)

Practice Areas: "Among the best, if not the best construction junior," Lucy has an impressive specialist practice in construction, engineering and energy, including shipbuilding and offshore construction. Her practice includes claims for and against professionals in these sectors and project-related issues such as insurance, bonds and guarantees. She won Chambers & Partners Construction Junior of the Year 2013 and was nominated again in 2015. Lucy is a popular and determined advocate who has been instructed in a series of high profile and high value disputes. She has extensive experience in both the TCC and the Commercial Court and is frequently instructed in international arbitration proceedings. Her international work includes major infrastructure or energy-related projects, often in the Gulf and the Asia-Pacific region, but also in Africa and South America. She has wide experience of arbitrations conducted in accordance with the laws of civil code jurisdictions and international parties and Tribunals. Lucy particularly enjoys disputes involving complex technical issues. Her approach is focused, practical and commercial.

Professional Memberships: SCL (UK and Hong Kong); TecBAR; ComBAR.

Career: Called 2001, Gray's Inn. Prince of Wales Scholar.

Publications: Keating on Construction Contractors (9th Edition); Keating on JCT Contracts; Keating on Offshore Construction.

GAUNT, Jonathan QC
Falcon Chambers, London
020 7353 2484
gaunt@falcon-chambers.com
Featured in Agriculture & Rural Affairs (London), Real Estate Litigation (London)

Practice Areas: All aspects of commercial and residential landlord and tenant and property law, including easements, restrictive covenants, rent and rent review, mines and minerals and property-related litigation.

Professional Memberships: Chancery Bar Association; LCLCBA; Property Bar Association.

Career: Educated at Radley College; University College, Oxford (BA); called 1972 (Lincoln's Inn); Silk 1991; Joint Head of Falcon Chambers since 1992; Bencher 1998; Deputy High Court Judge 2001.

Publications: Joint Editor, Halsbury's Laws 'Landlord and Tenant' volume (4th Ed), having re-written the chapters on repairing covenants, rent and rent review; joint editor, Gale on Easements 1997, 2002, 2008 and 2012 editions (2016 edition in preparation); several papers on legal history (published on Falcon Chambers web-site).

Personal: Interests: Golf, sailing.

GEDDES, Gillian
2-3 Hind Court, London
020 7822 2150
clerks@2-3hindcourt.com
Featured in Family/Matrimonial (London)

Practice Areas: Gillian Practices mainly in Children Act matters and Child Abduction. She has a passion for these areas of law and is energised by unusual and challenging cases, having a very sound knowledge of public law cases and child/adult trafficking and immigration issues.

Professional Memberships: FLBA, Gray's Inn. Intermediaries for Justice.

Career: Gillian is Deputy Head of Chambers at 2-3 Hind Court, a specialist family law set based in London. Gillian worked with a wide cross-section of society before being called to the Bar where she has worked as both an in-house lawyer for local authorities as well as in independent practice. Gillian has recently been elected as a Bencher at Gray's Inn.

Publications: Co-author of "Working in the Family Justice System, the Official Handbook of the Family Justice System"(3rd Edn. pub. Family Law) and the Single Family Court – A Practitioner's Handbook (2016, Wildy, Simmonds and Hill). plus many legal articles published particularly in Family Law and Westlaw UK Insight.

Personal: Gillian read law at the London School of Economics and Political Science (1995). She is also an accomplished pianist and singer, She enjoys swimming, theatre, jazz music and otherwise she keeps fit with the gardening.

GEEKIE, Charles QC
1 Garden Court Family Law Chambers, London
020 7797 7900
clerks@1gc.com
Featured in Family/Matrimonial (London)

Practice Areas: The law relating to children, including public and private law cases and abduction; complex residence cases and those involving relocation, representing local authorities, parents and guardians in public law and adoption cases, complex care cases involving fatalities, serious injuries, sexual and emotional abuse and cases where there is a conflict of medical evidence.

Professional Memberships: Member of FLBA committee. Association of Lawyers for Children. International Bar Association.

Career: Called 1985. Joined 1 Garden Court 1999. Silk 2006. Family Recorder 2006. Joint Head of Chambers 2013.

Publications: Contributor to Family Law. Specialist contributor to Rayden and Jackson on divorce and family matters. Contributor to Halsbury's Laws (children). Drafted training protocol for expert witnesses; run, jointly with senior consultant psychiatrists, training sessions for expert witnesses; drafted FLBA response to Government consultation on Expert Witnesses.

Personal: Interests: cycling, hill walking, theatre.

GEERING, Christopher
2 Hare Court, London
020 7353 5324
christophergeering@2harecourt.com
Featured in Professional Discipline (London)

Practice Areas: Christopher is a well-respected junior with considerable experience before a host of healthcare regulators where he has dealt with a wide range of high profile and sensitive cases. Most recently, he successfully represented a doctor in the GMC accused of a prolonged sexual assault on a nurse. He has frequently advised and appeared in cases brought before the High Court, where he has represented both for the regulator and the registrant. These cases include appeals brought by the Professional Standard's Authority, as well as appeals brought by registrants. In a recent case the court complemented him on his "clear and coherent critique of the Panel's decision". In addition, he represents doctors before NHS England hearings, Trust disciplinary hearings and coronial proceedings, offering a full service to healthcare practitioners who find themselves in difficulty. Outside of healthcare, he prosecutes on behalf of the National College for Teaching and Leadership, and is currently junior counsel on the heavily reported "Trojan Horse" case concerning teachers who allegedly introduced undue religious influence into Birmingham schools. He is also regularly instructed by the ACCA in cases before its Admissions and Licensing Committee, Disciplinary Committee and Appeals Committee.

Professional Memberships: ARDL

GENTLEMAN, Tom
4 Stone Buildings, London
020 72425524
t.gentleman@4stonebuildings.com
Featured in Chancery (London), Company (London)

Practice Areas: Company law, commercial litigation, financial services and insolvency. Tom has a busy commercial chancery practice, with particular focus on shareholder disputes, partnership disputes, banking, financial services and insolvency. He appears both in the High Court and in arbitration. Much of his work is as a junior in heavy commercial cases working as part of a team of counsel, but he also advises and acts as a trial advocate on his own. Many of his cases have an international element, with recent work in Bermuda, the BVI and Cayman Islands. He regularly deals with issues of conflict of laws.

Professional Memberships: Chancery Bar Association; COMBAR.

GEORGE, Sarah
St Philips Chambers, Birmingham
0121 246 7000
sgeorge@st-philips.com
Featured in Employment (Midlands)

Practice Areas: Sarah is a specialist employment practitioner with particular expertise in discrimination law, principally appearing in the Employment Tribunal and advising on matters within that jurisdiction. She regularly handles multi-day cases which are complex both factually and legally. Recent successes include the defence of a luxury car manufacturer against race and religious discrimination claims and of an NHS Trust against sexual orientation and sex discrimination claims. Sarah's clients include public authorities such as NHS Trusts, universities and local authorities as well as individual and corporate employers. She represents both claimants and respondents and accepts direct access clients. A member of St Philips since its creation, she rejoined chambers in October 2010 following a career break living abroad in the Far East. During her break from practice, she co-authored 'Discrimination in Employment' which she still co-edits.

Professional Memberships: ELA, ELBA.

Career: Called in 1991. Appointed as a fee paid employment judge in February 2011.

Publications: 'Discrimination in Employment' (Katherine Tucker and Sarah George) published by Thomson Reuters: Sweet & Maxwell (2006) and updated four times per year. Co-editor (with Katherine Tucker) of 'Equality Law Reports'.

Personal: Sarah enjoys cycling, visiting the theatre and cheering on her local junior rugby team.

GEORGE, Susan
Coram Chambers, London
020 7092 3700
susan.george@coramchambers.co.uk
Featured in Family/Matrimonial (London)

Practice Areas: All aspects of family law relating to children including serious and complex public law cases of intergenerational sexual abuse, serious injury/death of a child, usually with concurrent criminal proceedings and private law cases involving fact finding hearings and unrepresented parties. Sue has extensive experience in representing local authorities, parents and guardians in cases concerning non-accidental injuries and particularly those involving complex medical issues including fabricated illness cases. She frequently represents vulnerable parties such as young parents, as well as those with learning difficulties or mental health problems and competent children. In the private law field, she is regularly instructed in long standing intractable contact and residence cases as well as having significant experience in being instructed on behalf of the child. She is also instructed in forced marriage cases.

Professional Memberships: Family Law Bar Association. South Eastern Circuit (Ambassador). Association of Lawyers for Children. British Association for Adoption and Fostering. Liberty. Grays Inn

Career: LL.B (Hons) UCL. Called to the Bar, Grays Inn, 1990. Part time Judge in the Court of Protection (DOLS), First Tier Tribunal Judge in the Immigration and Asylum Chamber and First Tier Tribunal Judge in the Social Entitlement Chamber.

GHALY, Karim
39 Essex Chambers, London
020 7832 1111
karim.ghaly@39essex.com
Featured in International Arbitration (London), Professional Negligence (London), Construction (London), Energy & Natural Resources (London)

Practice Areas: Karim Ghaly specialises in the litigation and arbitration of substantial construction & engineering, energy, insurance, professional negligence and project finance disputes. He has acted in litigation and arbitration arising out of major projects in Africa, the Middle East, South America, South East Asia and the UK and appeared as lead advocate before a wide range of English and international tribunals.

Professional Memberships: COMBAR, IBA, TECBAR.

Career: Oxford University: First class honours degree in law. Called to the Bar in 2001.

Publications: Wilken and Ghaly, "The Law of Waiver, Variation and Estoppel", 3rd Edition, OUP. Contributor to "Construction Contracts" by Richard Wilmot-Smith QC, 3rd Edition, OUP.

GHOSH, Julian QC
Pump Court Tax Chambers, London
020 7414 8080
clerks@pumptax.com
Featured in Tax (London)

Practice Areas: Julian Ghosh's practice covers all areas of taxation. He is particularly well known for his corporate work and that involving European taxation issues. Recent cases include: Stagecoach Group PLC & Stagecoach Holdings Limited v HMRC (First-tier Tribunal); Isle of Wight Council v HMRC (Court of Appeal); Leeds City Council v HMRC (Court of Appeal);The Advocate General for Scotland v Murray Group Holdings (Court of Session); Abbey National Treasury Services Plc v The Commissioners for Her Majesty's Revenue & Customs (First-tier Tribunal); Anson v The Commissioners for Her Majesty's Revenue & Customs (Supreme Court); The Commissioners for Her Majesty's Revenue & Customs v Paul Newey (t/a Ocean Finance) (CJEU & Upper Tribunal, to go to Court of Appeal); Gemsupa Ltd & Consolidated Property Wilmslow Ltd v The Commissioners for Her Majesty's Revenue & Customs (First-tier Tribunal); Spritebeam Ltd, Prowting Ltd & The Commissioners for HMRC v The Commissioners for HMRC & Versteegh Ltd (Upper Tribunal); Schofield v HMRC (Court

of Appeal); Land Securities v HMRC (Upper Tribunal).
Professional Memberships: Revenue Bar Association; Chancery Bar Association; VAT Practitioners Group; London Common Law & Commercial Bar Association; Bar European Group.
Career: Visiting Professor at the International Tax Centre, University of Leiden Called (1993), Lincoln's Inn Called to the Scottish Bar (1999) QC (2006) QC (Scotland) (2010) Judge of the First-Tier and Deputy Judge of the Upper-Tier Tax Tribunals Sometime Lector, Trinity College, Cambridge and Visiting Fellow, Fitzwilliam College, Cambridge
Publications: Author (with I L Johnson & Paul Miller) The Taxation of Loan Relationships and Derivatives Taxation of Corporate Debt & Derivatives, (Butterworths) Author of Principles of the Internal Market and Direct Taxation (2007, Key Haven)
Personal: Harris Academy, Dundee University of Edinburgh St Edmund Hall, Oxford

GIBBON, Michael QC
Maitland Chambers, London
020 7406 1200
mgibbon@maitlandchambers.com
Featured in Chancery (London), Company (London), Restructuring/Insolvency (London), Tax (London)
Practice Areas: Commercial chancery practice, in particular for what is now the Department of Business Energy and Industrial Strategy (company law, insolvency) and HM Revenue & Customs (insolvency, tax, trusts), as well as general commercial litigation. Cases include: In re Modern Jet Support [2005] 1 WLR 3880 (insolvency); West v Trennery [2005] 1 All ER 827 (tax, trusts); Schmidt v Rosewood [2003] 2 AC 709 (trusts); Euroafrica Shipping Lines v Zegluga Polska [2004] 2 BCLC 97 (company, commercial); Gamlestaden v Baltic Partners [2007] BCC 272 (company); Thomas and Agnes Carvel Foundation v Carvel [2008] 2 WLR 1234 (wills, trusts); DCC v HMRC [2011] 1 WLR 44 (tax, commercial); Bilta (UK) v Nazir [2015] 2 WLR 1168 (company, insolvency).
Professional Memberships: Chancery Bar Association, COMBAR, Wales & Chester Circuit, ILA
Career: Investment banker, then called to the Bar 1993; Junior Counsel to the Crown from 1999, on A Panel 2007-11, QC 2011.
Publications: An editor of the White Book.
Personal: Educated at Magdalen College Oxford (BA, 1st class); King's College Cambridge (MPhil).

GIBBONS, Ellodie
Tanfield Chambers, London
020 7421 5300
egibbons@tanfieldchambers.co.uk
Featured in Real Estate Litigation (London)
Practice Areas: Commercial and residential landlord and tenant, real property and associated professional negligence. Particular expertise in service charge disputes, leasehold enfranchisement, rights of first refusal and RTM. Cases include Greenpine Investment Holding Ltd v Howard de Walden Estates Ltd [2016] EWHC 1923 (Ch) (enfranchisement, terms of acquisition, solicitors' undertakings); Moorjani v Durban Estates Ltd [2015] EWCA Civ 1252 (common parts, disrepair, loss of amenity, measure of damages); Merie Bin Mahfouz Co (UK) Ltd v Barrie House (Freehold) Ltd [2014] UKUT 390 (LC) (enfranchisement, common parts, leasebacks); Plotnek v Govan [2014] UKUT 332 (LC) (enfranchisement, rent reviews); Money v Cadogan Holdings Ltd [2013] UKUT 0211 (LC) (enfranchisement, valuation, restrictive covenants); Westmacott v Ackerman [2012] UKUT 415 (LC) (enfranchisement, houses converted into flats, valuation); Barrie House Freehold Ltd v Merie Bin Mahfouz Company (UK) Ltd [2012] EWHC Ch (enfranchisement, easements, injunctions)
Professional Memberships: Property Bar Association, Chancery Bar Association, Association of Leasehold Enfranchisement Practitioners
Career: Lancaster Girls' Grammar School, MA (Law) Emmanuel College, Cambridge, Called 1999, Barrister of the Year, Enfranchisement and Right to Manage Awards 2011
Publications: Contributor to 'Service Charges and Management' 1st, 2nd and 3rd editions (Sweet &; Maxwell) co-author 'Leasehold Enfranchisement Explained' (RICS).
Personal: Travel, dancing, skiing.

GIBBS, Patrick QC
3 Raymond Buildings Barristers, London
020 7400 6400
patrick.gibbs@3rblaw.com
Featured in Crime (London), Inquests & Public Inquiries (All Circuits), Professional Discipline (London), Financial Crime (London)
Practice Areas: Advice and advocacy at all stages of criminal and 'quasi-criminal' investigations, regulatory and disciplinary proceedings, deaths in custody, inquests and public inquiries. Recent notable work: professional fraud; market abuse; tax avoidance; murder/manslaughter; overseas corruption; LIBOR/EURIBOR; insider dealing; misconduct in public office; sanctions busting; police shootings; money laundering. Recent inquiries: Pitchford, Litvinenko; Leveson; 7/7; Tomlinson; Saunders; De Menezes; Climbie. For more information go to www.3rblaw.com.
Professional Memberships: CBA; ARDL; FLA.
Career: Oxford 1981; City 1984; Called 1986; QC 2006.

GIBSON, Charles QC
Henderson Chambers, London
020 7583 9020
cgibson@hendersonchambers.co.uk
Featured in Environment (London), Health & Safety (London), Product Liability (London)
Practice Areas: Common law/ commercial with an emphasis on product liability and insurance law (including group actions), health and safety, environmental law, professional negligence, insurance, disciplinary and regulatory law, sports law. Notable cases include: the Bomu Bonny Pipeline litigation, the OCENSA Pipeline litigation, the Abidjan litigation; the Atomic Veterans litigation; the Buncefield litigation; the Seroxat litigation; the Sabril litigation; the Potters Bar Inquest; Borchard VMPC; Connelly v RTZ; Lubbe v Cape plc; Hodgson v Imperial Tobacco (the tobacco litigation); Bass Britvic v Terra; the Opren litigation; the Benzodiazepine litigation; Garland v West Wiltshire District Council; The Norplant litigation; the MMR litigation; group actions involving Prozac, Lariam, Minocin, Shiley heart valve, breast implants, drink contamination; the organophosphate litigation; the interest rate swap litigation; asbestos claims, mine radiation injury claims; other product liability cases for various manufacturers and producers; the Potters Bar Inquest; the King's Cross and Clapham Inquiries for the London Fire Brigade; the Severn Tunnel Inquiry.
Professional Memberships: PNBA. Common Law and Commercial Bar Association. Commercial Bar Association.
Career: Educated Wellington College; BA Hons Durham (Classics); Dip Law. Called to the Bar 1984. Author: 'Group Actions – Product Liability Law and Insurance'. CEDR Accredited Mediator. Recorder. Bencher of the Inner Temple. Head of Chambers.
Personal: Born 1960. Married with four children.

GIBSON, Keith
Keith Gibson, Belfast
07771 573203
Keith.Gibson@barlibrary.com
Featured in Commercial Dispute Resolution (Northern Ireland)
Practice Areas: Practice encompasses a variety of work and expertise in the following areas: Chancery, Commercial Disputes (including Construction Law), Professional Negligence and Insolvency Chancery: Wide ranging Chancery practice which centres primarily on mortgagee actions but also includes Wills and Trusts, Probate and Administration of Estates, Real Property, Adverse Possession, Boundary Disputes and disputes relating to easements. Receives instruction in respect of disputes concerning ownership of property, disputed transfers of property and in cases involving specific performance. Regularly appears in the Chancery Court and has extensive knowledge of the practice and procedure adopted in said Court. Lay clients include all of the major banks operating in Northern Ireland and other financial institutions with interests in Northern Ireland. Commercial, Construction and Professional Negligence: Retained regularly in respect of contractual disputes, guarantees and all matters concerning the sale and supply of goods. Routine attendance at the Commercial Court in respect of disputes on behalf of employers, contractors and sub-contractors, including disputes referred to arbitration from the Commercial Court. Particular interest in the area of professional negligence, against Architects, Solicitors, Insurance Brokers, Surveyors and Accountants. Experience is based mainly in acting against these professionals, although has been retained to act on behalf of professional legal advisers. Involvement in disputes has concerned both domestic and non-domestic law, multi-jurisdictional disputes and multi-party disputes.
Career: Important cases include: • McCallion Brothers Ltd v Graham Fisher, Northern Ireland Housing Executive and Clanmill Housing Association Ltd [2012] NICh 5 (Chancery) • Santander (UK) PLC v Parker [2012] NICh 6 (Chancery) • Santander v S1 and S2 [2012] NICh 16 (property) Banks & Anor v Geddis & Anor [2012] NIQB 57 Contract – Sale of land – Leasehold – Restrictive covenant – Delay – Repudiation – Discharge of contractual promises (Chancery) • Banks & Anor v Geddis & Anor [2012] NIQB 87 Costs – Wasted costs – Costs incurred unreasonably or improperly (Commercial) • Melbourne Mortgages Limited v Gerard Berry [2013] NIMaster 3 Mortgage – Fraud – Reciprocal fraud (Chancery) • Bank of Scotland v Doherty & Anor [2013] NIQB 135 Practice – Time limit – Order for possession (Chancery) • Fernhill Properties (NI) Ltd v Scullion [2014] NICh 4 Building – Construction – Contract – Time of performance – Rescission (Commercial) • The Mortgage Business Plc and Bank of Scotland Plc (t/a Birmingham Midshires) v Thomas Taggart and Sons [2014] NICh 14 Conveyancing • Finlay v Cullen & Ors [2014] NICh 17 Easement – Creation of easement – Claim to right of way by prescription (Chancery) • Coutts and Company & Ors v Collins & Ors [2014] NICh 24 Practice and procedure – Interlocutory injunction (Chancery) • Hamilton and Dixon Group Sipp v Hastings and Company (Solicitors) [2014] NICh 27 Conveyancing • Trunk Flooring Ltd v HSBC Asset Finance (UK) Ltd [2015] NIQB 23 Arbitration (Commercial) • HM Principal Secretary of State for Communities and Local Government v Praxis Care [2015] NICh 5 Estoppel – Proprietary estoppel (Chancery) • AIB Group (UK) Plc v Donnelly [2015] NIMaster 13 Mortgage – Action for possession (Chancery) • The Official Receiver v Julie-Ann Urey [2015] NICh 11 Divorce – Financial relief – Property adjustment order (Chancery) • Purcell Bros Ltd v Star Viking (The Owners, Charterers and all Persons Claiming to be Interested in the Motor Vessel) [2015] NIQB 70 Admiralty – Application for appraisal and sale of vessel (Chancery/Admiralty) • Santander (UK) Plc v Parker [2015] NICA 41 Possession – Action for possession (Chancery) • Ulster Bank Ltd v McQuaid [2015] NIQB 79 Banking – Repayment of monies (Commercial) • Trunk Flooring Ltd v HSBC Asset Finance (UK) Ltd [2015] NICA 68 Arbitration (Commercial) • Tom Keenan & Scott Murray as Administrators of Brickkiln Waste Ltd v Thomas McGlinchey [2015] NICh 15 Contempt of court – Civil contempt – Committal (Commercial) • Barclays Bank Plc (t/a The Woolwich) v Boyd & Anor [2015] NICh 16 Mortgages – Mortgagees – Stay of court proceedings – Discretion of the court – Repayments –Repossession (Chancery)
Personal: Called to the Northern Ireland Bar in 1999.

GIDNEY, Jonathan
St Philips Chambers, Birmingham
0121 246 7000
jgidney@st-philips.com
Featured in Employment (Midlands)
Practice Areas: Jonathan Gidney is a specialist employment practitioner with substantial experience in all aspects of employment law. He regularly appears in Employment Tribunals across the country and in the EAT. He undertakes complex multi-day discrimination proceedings (e.g. Ansar v Lloyds Bank Plc [2007] IRLR 211, CA) and has a proven track record in handling litigants in person in difficult cases and at putting his client's own witnesses at ease (including a recent instruction on a sex discrimination claim involving multiple allegations of rape). He has an exellent eye for detail, is always well prepared and has an effective advocacy style in Tribunal. In addition to his expertise in all types of discrimination, Jonathan undertakes all types of employment law, including TUPE, service provision change, redundancy and unfair dismissal. Jonathan regularly accepts instructions from local authorities, NHS Trusts, banks and large retail organisations.

Professional Memberships: Employment Lawyers Association; Employment Law Bar Association.
Career: Jonathan was appointed as an accredited CEDR Mediator in February 2004.
Publications: Connected Lender Liability, New Law Journal 24 May 1996; Walking the Reference Tightrope, New Law Journal 4 September 2001; Bias in Tribunal, ELA Briefing April 2009.

GIFFIN, Nigel QC
11KBW, London
020 7632 8500
Nigel.Giffin@11kbw.com
Featured in Administrative & Public Law (London), Civil Liberties & Human Rights (London), Community Care (London), Education (London), Inquests & Public Inquiries (All Circuits), Local Government (London), Public Procurement (London)
Practice Areas: Nigel Giffin QC specialises in public law and public procurement law. His public law practice includes commercial and general judicial review, human rights, professional and regulatory work, local authority powers, governance and finance, education law, community care and public law aspects of pensions law. His procurement law practice covers all contentious and non-contentious EU and domestic procurement matters, as well as state aid. He also deals with commercial and employment law matters, especially in relation to public authorities' contracts and public sector employment issues, including superannuation. Recent cases include: Lumsdon v LSB (quality assurance of criminal advocacy, proportionality in EU law); Energy Solutions v NDA (remedies in procurement claims); Hampshire v Pension Protection Fund (compliance with Insolvency Directive); (Willmott Dixon v Hammersmith & Fulham LBC (procurement claim successfully defended at trial); Tower Hamlets v Bromley (disputed ownership of Henry Moore bronze); Independent Schools Council v Charity Commission (quashing statutory guidance on public benefit); Luton BC and others v Secretary of State for Education (challenge to withdrawal of schools capital funding); Duncombe v Secretary of State for Children, Schools and Families (fixed term contracts to work abroad); and Piper v Secretary of State for Work and Pensions (public sector pensions indexation).

GILCHRIST, Naomi
St Philips Chambers, Birmingham
0121 246 0200
ngilchrist@st-philips.com
Featured in Crime (Midlands), Health & Safety (Midlands)
Practice Areas: Naomi conducts a heavy weight practice in all areas of serious/ organised crime, criminal regulatory work and licensing. In serious/ organised crime, her work principally involves complex, high value fraud, business/ corporate crime, corruption and misconduct in public office, and homicide offences, including gross negligence/ corporate manslaughter. She is known and respected for her ability to deal with cases involving complex medical and scientific evidence. In the regulatory field, her experience is wide ranging and at all levels. She is regularly instructed to advise and appear on behalf of companies and individuals who are charged with offences under health and safety, food safety and product safety legislation, including fatal and serious injury cases. She is an experienced inquest advocate and also conducts hearings before disciplinary tribunals. She provides specialist advice in relation to RIPA 2000. Her approach is always professional and meticulous, but user friendly. Customer service is high on her list of priorities.
Career: Qualified as solicitor 1994; Called to the Bar 1996.

GILL, Anthony
Kings Chambers, Manchester
0345 034 3444
clerks@kingschambers.com
Featured in Planning (Northern)
Practice Areas: All aspects of town and country planning, highways and rights of way, compulsory purchase, environmental, together with administrative and public law. Regularly appears for both developers and local authorities in planning and enforcement inquiries, and has appeared at various local plan examinations. Anthony has experience appearing in the Lands Tribunal and advising on references to the Tribunal. His Anthony has experience appearing in the Lands Tribunal and advising on references to the Tribunal. Court practice includes statutory challenges and judicial review.
Professional Memberships: Planning and Environmental Bar Association (PEBA) Northern Circuit North Eastern Circuit
Career: University of Oxford, Jesus College: BA Hons. Ancient and Modern History University of London, Kings College MA War Studies College of Law: Postgraduate Diploma in Law Inns of Court School of Law: Bar Vocational Course
Publications: Contributor to Judicial Review: Law and Practice (Jordans) (1st and 2nd Editions)

GILLESPIE, Christopher
2 Hare Court, London
020 7353 5324
chrisgillespie@2harecourt.com
Featured in Financial Crime (London)
Practice Areas: Chris was called to the Bar in 1991 and has been instructed in fraud and criminal regulatory cases since 1994. Although he prosecuted for many years, including cases of substantial money laundering and computer crime/identity theft, Chris now exclusively acts for the defence frequently as a leading junior. Last year his was the only client acquitted by the jury in a major landbanking conspiracy to defraud case brought by the FCA. Throughout his career he has appeared in cases involving banking fraud, mortgage fraud, money laundering, all types of advance fee fraud, landbanking and tax evasion. Chris has a particular interest in confiscation acting for both defendants and third parties who wish to assert an interest in property. Recent cases include R v Forsyth and others (carbon credits) R v Crawley and others (landbanking) R v Malik (tax evasion) R v Roberts (tax evasion)
Professional Memberships: Criminal Bar Association, Fraud Lawyers Association, Health and Safety Lawyers Association

GILLETT, Emily
Erskine Chambers, London
44 020 7242 5532
egillet@erskinechambers.com
Featured in Chancery (London), Fraud (London)
Practice Areas: Emily has a broad commercial chancery practice, with experience in complex onshore and offshore litigation and arbitration. She was recognised as one of 10 'Stars at the Bar' by Legal Week in 2010, after only four years in practice. Emily has particular expertise in multi-jurisdictional commercial fraud cases (often with foreign law elements) and applications for interim relief (including freezing injunctions, receivership orders, search and seizure orders, disclosure orders, passport orders, and applications for cross-examination) as well as contempt applications. Her reported cases include: JSC BTA Bank v Solodchenko [2011] 1 WLR 888; JSC BTA Bank v Kythreotis [2012] 1 WLR 350; JSC BTA Bank v Ablyazov (No 9) [2013] 1 WLR 1845.
Professional Memberships: Chancery Bar Association; COMBAR.
Personal: Emily obtained a first class degree in Law and French Law from UCL (having spent her third year of study at Université Paris II where she gained a Licence en droit). Emily's leisure interests include horse riding and Formula One motor racing.

GILLYON, Philip
Erskine Chambers, London
020 7242 5532
pgillyon@erskinechambers.com
Featured in Company (London)
Practice Areas: Company law, corporate insolvency, financial services. Cases include Re BSB Holdings Ltd [1996] 1 BCLC 155; Possfund Custodian Trustee Ltd v Diamond [1996] 1 WLR 1351; Re Exchange Travel (Holdings) Ltd [1996] 2 BCLC 524; Guinness Peat Group plc v British Land Company plc [1999] 2 BCLC 243 (CA); Banco Nacional de Cuba v Cosmos Trading Corporation [2000] 1 BCLC 813 (CA); Jarvis plc v PricewaterhouseCoopers [2000] 2 BCLC 368; Banca Carige v Banco Nacional de Cuba [2001] 2 BCLC 407; Re Joseph Holt Group plc [2001] 2 BCLC 604 (CA); Re Leyland Daf Ltd [2001] 1 BCLC 419 (Ch), [2002] 1 BCLC 571(CA); Re Anglo American Insurance Co Ltd [2002] BCC 715; P&P Design plc v PricewaterhouseCoopers [2002] 2 BCLC 648; Re Queens Moat Houses plc [2003] 1 BCLC 696 (CA); EIC Services Ltd v Phipps [2004] 2 BCLC 589; Re Queens Moat Houses plc (No 2) [2005] 1 BCLC 136; Sisu Capital Fund Ltd v Tucker (No 1) [2006] BCC 463; (No 2) [2006] BCC 577; Secretary of State for the DBERR v Amway (UK) Ltd [2008] BCC 713 (Ch), [2009] BCC 781 (CA); Royal Bank of Scotland plc v Hicks & Ors [2010] EWHC 2579 (Takeover of Liverpool Football Club); Jackson v Dear [2012] EWHC 2060 (Ch), [2014] 1 BCLC 186 (CA); S&K Group Ltd v Mortgage Agency Services No 1 Ltd [2014] EWHC (Ch).
Professional Memberships: Commercial Bar Association; Chancery Bar Association; Insolvency Lawyers' Association; Financial Services Lawyers Association; Middle Temple.
Career: Hymers College (1974-84); Downing College, Cambridge (1984-87) MA (Hons), first class. Called 1988. Joined Erskine Chambers 1989.

GIROLAMI, Paul QC
Maitland Chambers, London
44 0 20 7406 1200
pgirolami@maitlandchambers.com
Featured in Chancery (London), Commercial Dispute Resolution (London), Company (London), Fraud (London), Offshore (London), Restructuring/Insolvency (London)
Practice Areas: Paul is a Deputy High Court Judge for the Queens' Bench & Chancery Divisions of the High Court. He took silk in April 2002, having been one of the Junior Counsel to the Crown for about nine years. He appears in courts in England and Wales and in overseas jurisdictions and has given expert evidence of English law to foreign courts. His experience includes: commercial litigation (including fiduciary duties; rights over assets or property; charges and securities; financial instruments; and the acquisition or sale of businesses and shares): company (including technical company law issues, shareholder disputes; directors' duties and disqualification): insolvency and corporate recovery (including administration and voluntary arrangements; claims involving liquidators, administrators or trustees) and civil fraud. He is called to the bar in the BVI and Gibraltar and registered with rights of audience in the DIFC.
Professional Memberships: Chancery Bar Association; COMBAR; Insolvency Lawyers Association; Financial Services Lawyers Association
Career: Called to the Bar, 1983. Junior Counsel to the Crown (Chancery) 1991-2000. QC 2002.
Personal: Born 5 December 1959. Educated St Paul's School London and Corpus Christi College, Cambridge. Lives in London.

GLANCY, Robert QC
Devereux, London
020 7353 7534
glancy@devchambers.co.uk
Featured in Personal Injury (London), Clinical Negligence (London)
Practice Areas: Robert specialises in all aspects of personal injury, clinical negligence and professional negligence. He continues to be involved in numerous high value and complex catastrophic injury cases for brain damaged and paralysed claimants. For more information and recent case highlights, please visit www.devereuxchambers.co.uk.
Professional Memberships: PIBA.
Career: 2010: President, First Tier Tribunal Health and Safety Committee (Mental Health) for restricted cases – 2008: Appointed CEDR accredited mediator, 1999: Recorder and President, Mental Health Review Tribunal, 1997: Silk, 1993-1999: Assistant Recorder.

GLASER, Michael
Fourteen, London
020 7242 0858
mglaser@fourteen.co.uk
Featured in Family/Matrimonial (London)
Practice Areas: Prior to his call to the Bar, Michael worked in finance for five years and then qualified as a commercial solicitor specialising in intellectual property law. He crossed over to the family Bar in 1998. Michael practises a wide range of family work including financial remedy, trusts and cohabitation disputes, public and private Children Act work. In financial remedy work he specialises in cases which have an added dimension such as trusts, bankruptcy, partnerships and companies. Reported cases include F v F (S Intervening) (Financial Provision: Bankruptcy: Reviewable Disposition) ([2003] 1 FLR 911), a husband's bankruptcy was set aside and his award drastically reduced due to his conduct, and Rossi ([2007] 1 FLR 790), in which an ancillary relief claim was successfully defended in its entirety, due to delay and non-contribution to the marital acquest. Michael has acted in a number of important reported cases including representing a husband in a 'big money' case

involving wholly pre-acquired assets (R v R [2009] EWHC 1267 (Fam), a contested trusts of land case involving questions of sham transfers and illegality (Ashby v Kilduff [2010] EWHC 2034 (Ch)), a case where the Husband's assets were said to be tied up in a Jersey Trust (D v D and I Trust ([2011] 2 FLR 29) and a successful appeal to the Court of Appeal reducing a 'joint lives' maintenance order to a term order (N v N [2011] EWCA Civ 940). Michael continues to represent HRH Sheikh Ahmed bin Saeed Al-Maktoum [2011] EWHC B27 (Fam) in the first case dealing with whether an Islamic marriage performed in this country would be valid for the purposes of a nullity petition. The facts of the case make interesting reading, however, the court agreed that an Islamic marriage, whilst it may have significance for the parties involved, would not be a route for a purported wife to obtain the raft of financial remedies which can be applied for following a nullity petition. He has also successfully enforced an arbitration clause in a foreign pre-marital agreement where the assets were $140m (T v T [2012] EWHC 3462 (Fam)). His recent cases include (successfully) clarifying the law in the Court of Appeal regarding when orders can be set aside N v N [2014] EWCA Civ 314), avoiding a Xydhias agreement being converted an order thus increasing his client's award by £2m, and acting for a wealthy wife whose very significant company assets were held in a large number of minority interests. In addition to acting in high net worth cases, Michael frequently represents interveners in divorce matters (including acting for beneficiaries of trusts, such as children on settlement variations through the official solicitor), and parents involved in private law disputes including those with an international element such as relocation cases. As a result of his experience, both prior to being Called to the Bar, and whilst at it, Michael brings a breadth of experience to his work.

GLASGOW, Oliver QC
2 Hare Court, London
020 73535324
oliver.glasgow@cps.gsi.gov.uk
Featured in Crime (London)

Practice Areas: Oliver Glasgow QC was appointed Senior Treasury Counsel in 2015 and Queen's Counsel in 2016. He has a reputation for detailed preparation, exceptional advocacy and is an especially good cross-examiner. He divides his practice between working at the highest level in the criminal sphere and specialising in serious quasi-criminal and regulatory work. He is an exceptional jury advocate who appears in high profile trials of the utmost gravity for both prosecution and defence. He is hardworking and able to deal with difficult clients very well and his practice has seen an increasing emphasis on defending in regulatory and health and safety work, and appearing for interested parties in public inquiries and inquests. Recent instructions include high profile corporate manslaughter and health and safety matters (Cavendish Masonry, Rooftop Rooms, Monavon Construction); acting for the Service Prosecuting Authority in the Iraq Historic Abuse Inquiry; representing the AG of Jersey in the historic child abuse inquiry; and complex homicide and terrorist offences (R v. Agera, R v. Amponsah). He has advised the AG in cases of general public importance; advised companies and individuals in connection with investigations and private prosecutions; and advised professionals and sportsmen in connection with allegations of misconduct and ethics.

Professional Memberships: CBA, FLA, HSLA, ARDL

Career: Called 1995 – Middle Temple. South Eastern Circuit.

GLASSBROOK, Alex
Temple Garden Chambers, London
020 7583 1315
ag@tgchambers.com
Featured in Fraud (All Circuits)

Practice Areas: Insurance (particularly insurance fraud, including criminal networks and those involving electronic evidence), personal injury (especially high value and brain injury cases), legal costs (points arising during litigation and assessments of costs) and consumer law (especially accident management cases).

Professional Memberships: Specialist associations including Personal Injury Bar Association. Teacher for Advocacy Training Council (overseas, mainly Africa) and for Middle Temple advocacy department. Volunteer lawyer for several charities in UK and overseas. Honorary member, Ghana Bar Association.

Career: Called 1995. Very experienced trial advocate. Described by directories as "meticulous" and "good for a tricky case", e.g. Court of Appeal persuaded to deny any trial costs to an otherwise successful claimant who exaggerated the value of her claim, in Widlake v BAA [2009] EWCA Civ 1256, years before provisions allowing similar orders were written explicitly into statute and rules of court.

Publications: Contributor to TG Chambers' regular FRAUD UPDATE. Author of many articles, including SUPPORTING THE LEGAL PROFESSION IN ZIMBABWE, Counsel magazine, 1st May 2014, reporting on the Advocacy Training Council's work in Zimbabwe, and 'YOU'RE ONLY SUPPOSED TO BLOW THE BLOODY DOORS OFF!' (employers' responsibility for violent employees) [2005] Journal of Personal Injury Law 240.

Personal: Keen cyclist

GLASSON, Jonathan QC
Matrix Chambers, London
020 7404 3447
jonathanglasson@matrixlaw.co.uk
Featured in Inquests & Public Inquiries (All Circuits)

Practice Areas: Jonathan has an eclectic and broad ranging practice including human rights, Inquests and Inquiries, public law, international law, asylum, extradition, product liability, personal injury and clinical negligence. He was Counsel to the Investigatory Powers Tribunal in the Belhaj and Amnesty cases concerning the interception of LPP Material and in the Greennet and Privacy International cases concerning GCHQ's use of malware. He is Counsel to the Tribunal in the 2016 challenge to the intelligence agencies' use of bulk personal and communications data. He advised the Attorney General on the Hillsborough and David Kelly inquests. He appeared at the In Amenas inquests, the Azelle Rodney Inquiry and the Mark Duggan Inquest. He has a particular expertise in ECHR claims arising from Article 2 as well as claims from the Russian Federation. He has acted in a large number of national security cases in the Administrative Court, Special Immigration Appeals Commission (SIAC) and the Investigatory Powers Tribunal (IPT). Jonathan has also acted as a Special Advocate in SIAC and the Parole Board and as Counsel to the IPT. Throughout his practice he has acted in a range of high profile product liability cases, specialising in pharmaceutical product liability and medical devices. Jonathan is a Contributing Editor to the Butterworth's Personal Injury Litigation Service (and author of the sections on Product Liability and Psychiatric Injury) and is the co-author of the Blackstone's Guide to the Coroners and Justice Act 2009. In February 2007, Jonathan was appointed to the A Panel of Junior Counsel to the Crown which was the earliest date for such an appointment. He was appointed Silk in March 2013, one of the most junior in call to be appointed.

Professional Memberships: HRLA, PNBA, INQUEST and Middle Temple

Career: Former Solicitor (Honours), Treasury A Panel, 2007-2013; QC 2013

Personal: Maidstone GS, New College, Oxford

GLEDHILL, Orlando
One Essex Court, London
020 7583 2000
ogledhill@oeclaw.co.uk
Featured in Commercial Dispute Resolution (London), Energy & Natural Resources (London), Fraud (London)

Practice Areas: A broad range of commercial litigation, arbitration and advice. Recently acted for Goldman Sachs International in US$1.2 billion trial of claims brought by Libyan Investment Authority to set aside equity derivatives transactions, British Gas in trial of dispute arising from carbon emissions reductions, real estate investment fund established by Deutsche Bank, Russian bank against Russian borrowers, Spanish oil major in arbitration against exploration joint venturer, Leonid Lebedev in London anti-suit proceedings brought by Viktor Vekselberg and Leonard Blavatnik, BNP Paribas in disputes arising out of Russian lending, state-owned Chinese entities in energy arbitrations, largest Mongolian bank in disputes with Tier 2 capital provider, financial advisory and trading house in trial against Barclays Bank concerning corporate acquisition, fund managers in claims by Fortress Investment Group, Deutsche Bank in trial concerning carbon credits, Credit Agricole Commercial and Investment Bank in dispute with Saudi general partnership.

Professional Memberships: Combar.

Career: Called 1998.

Personal: Born 1971. BA (Hons) Queen's University, Canada (First). MPhil, Corpus Christi College, Oxford. DipLaw, City University (Distinction).

GLEN, David
One Brick Court, London
020 7353 8845
dg@onebrickcourt.com
Featured in Data Protection (London), Defamation/Privacy (London)

Practice Areas: Defamation, information and privacy law, entertainment law, breach of confidence, media related public and regulatory law; judicial review, contempt of court and reporting restrictions. Notable recent cases include: Tamiz v United Kingdom (for HM Government); Richardson v Google UK & Google Inc (for Google); Optical Express v Associated Newspapers Limited (for ANL); R v Will Cornick (for the media interveners); Dar Al Arkan & Bank Alkhair v Al Refai & ors (for the claimants); Jon Gaunt v United Kingdom (for HM Government). Previous reported cases include: Jill Finney v Care Quality Commission; Rothschild v Associated Newspapers Limited; Bob Crow v Boris Johnson; Gee v BBC & Information Commissioner; Various (Guardian News & Media) v News Group & Glenn Mulcaire; R v Ofcom (ex parte Gaunt); North London Central Mosque v Policy Exchange; Budu v BBC; Azad Ali v Associated Newspapers Limited; Taranissi v BBC; Condoco Grand Cayman v KYC News. Represented Guardian News & Media at the Leveson Inquiry and the BBC at the Hutton Inquiry. Appointed to act as one of the Independent Scheme Barristers in NGN's Voicemail Interception Scheme.

Career: Called 2002.

Publications: Contributor to Arlidge Eady & Smith on Contempt; Editor Atkin's Court Forms on Defamation.

Personal: University of Edinburgh (MA Hons History); Enjoys music, cinema and pretty much any sport (including football, cricket, horseracing and Sunderland AFC).

GLENSER, Peter
9 Bedford Row, London
020 7489 2727
glenserpeter@mac.com
Featured in Licensing (London)

Practice Areas: Peter practices in licensing and defending serious rural regulatory proceedings and allied prosecutions in areas such as farming, meat production, hunting and fieldsports. He has an expert knowledge of firearms and firearms law and regularly acts for the appellant in firearms licensing matters, be it refusal or revocation of certificates or proceedings concerning the suitability of persons to be registered firearms dealers. He also has an enviable reputation for defending service personnel before the Court Martial in the most complex, sensitive and difficult matters. His "sharp, analytical mind" enables him to cut through the most complex of issues to focus attention and energy on the critical elements. Praised for diligent pre-trial preparation he provides timely, thorough and realistic advice pre-trial and throughout proceedings. He is regularly instructed to lead for the defence in all the areas in which he practises. He appears in cases throughout England and Wales.

Professional Memberships: Peter is a member of the Agricultural Lawyers Association, the Association of Regulatory and Disciplinary Lawyers, the Criminal Bar Association and is on the Committee of the Association of Military Courts Advocates. Peter is Chairman of the British Association of Shooting and Conservation, he writes on legal matters for Shooting Gazette, Gun Trade News and other publications. He is in high demand as a speaker at conferences and other events.

GLOVER, Marc
Tanfield Chambers, London
020 7421 5330
MarcGlover@tanfieldchambers.co.uk
Featured in Real Estate Litigation (London)

Practice Areas: All aspects of property, commercial and company litigation. Within property, a particular expertise in boundaries, easements, adverse possession and land registration (including mortgages/charges) and a further focus on commercial L&T.

In commercial & company litigation, an interest in business/share holder disputes and director disqualification, with a sub-specialty in VAT, excise and duties and international litigation. Recent cases in the Supreme Court include R (Eastenders Cash & Carry Plc) v HMRC [2014] UKSC 34 (property rights); R. (First Stop Wholesale Ltd) v HMRC [2014] UKSC 34 (public law – need for reasons) and Barnes v The Eastenders Group [2014] UKSC 26 (Receivership costs). Leading cases in the Court of Appeal include: R (Best) v Land Registry [2015] EWCA Civ 17 (adverse possession); Rashid v Sharif [2014] EWCA Civ 377 (boundary) and Graham Huntley & Oths v Simon Armes [2010] EWCA Civ 396 (boundary).
Professional Memberships: Chancery Bar Association; Property Bar Association; Commercial Bar Association.
Career: LLB, LLM (International Law). Called 1999. Joined Tanfield 2001.
Publications: (With other members of Tanfield Chambers) 'Service Charges and Management' (Sweet & Maxwell, 2nd ed); Contributor, RICS online Isurv Service, Oversailing and Trespass.
Personal: Born 1975. Three wonderful daughters. Cycling, canoeing and expeditions.

GLYN, Caspar QC
Cloisters, London
020 7827 4052
cg@cloisters.com
Featured in Employment (London), Sports Law (London)
Practice Areas: Employment, Sport, Contract, Directors' duties. Caspar advises on contentious disputes and is a trial and appellate lawyer. His practice covers the whole width of the employment relationship, contractual (including injunctive relief) and regulatory sports' disputes and other linked contractual and commercial claims including civil fraud and fiduciary duties. His work generally affects hundreds/thousands of employees, sets national precedents, are test cases, are of very high value, seriously affect the reputations of other employees or owners or the business itself or are a combination of these. He appears in courts from the Supreme Court and the Court of Appeal through to the Employment Tribunal, is a trained mediator, sits as a chairman of Football Association Arbitration Panels and is a past Chair of the Industrial Law Society. Caspar prosecutes and defends in disciplinary hearings and is experienced in sports' arbitrations as an advocate, chairman and arbitrator. A full CV is set out at www.cloisters.com
Professional Memberships: Chair Industrial Law Society 2013-2015, Employment Lawyers Association, Employment Law Barristers Association.
Career: Call 1992, Silk 2012
Publications: Editorial Board Industrial Law Journal 2013-2015, Co-author Bullen & Leake, 'Fast Track Practice', "Personal Injury Handbook". Working Party 'Code of Guidance for Experts' under the CPR.

GLYNN, Stephen
9 Gough Square, London
020 7832 0500
sglynn@9goughsquare.co.uk
Featured in Personal Injury (London), Personal Injury (All Circuits)
Practice Areas: Personal injury and clinical and professional negligence
Professional Memberships: APIL; PIBA: PNBA
Career: Stephen, called in 1990, has an exclusive personal injury and clinical negligence practice. His PI practice comprises predominantly industrial disease and employer's liability work for claimants. In particular, his experience of asbestos-induced disease is extensive and includes regular work in the High Court in London. He also has considerable experience of HAVS and deafness work. Stephen's employer's liability practice is mainly union-funded/sourced work. He also has long experience of CICAP work, appearing in hearings nationwide. Stephen has also developed a child-abuse and related claims practice. Stephen's experience and call means he is very familiar with catastrophic injury claims and their associated complexities. He has substantial experience in trial and hearing advocacy which in turn enables him to deal effectively but sensitively with, in particular, challenging clients. Stephen is a member of executive committee of APIL and was previously the coordinator of APIL's Occupational Health Special Interest Group. He is the general editor of Asbestos Claims, law, practice and procedure, now in its third edition. Other contributors include Master Eastman and Dr Davies. He is the editor and co-author also of APIL's Guide to Evidence. He is the series editor of Clinical Negligence Claims, also now in its second edition. Stephen's interests are motorbikes (wife permitting), his wife and children, food (eating as well as cooking it) and American crime novels (but not necessarily in that order).

GODDARD, Andrew QC
Atkin Chambers, London
020 7404 0102
agoddard@atkinchambers.com
Featured in International Arbitration (London), Construction (London)
Practice Areas: Andrew specialises in the law of commercial obligations and professional negligence, particularly in the context of disputes concerning major construction and engineering contracts and IT projects. He has had much involvement in infrastructure, telecoms and energy disputes and has acted for main contractors, sub-contractors, professionals and employers, including national and foreign governments. Andrew has experience of PPP and PFI projects in the UK and various Commonwealth jurisdictions and is a Director of the Caribbean Procurement Institute. He has significant experience in international commercial arbitration and has appeared in many disputes referred to arbitration under the auspices of the ICC, the HKIAC, the LCIA and the LMAA and has acted in an Investor-State arbitration proceeding before the International Centre for the Settlement of Investment Disputes (ICSID). Related areas of law in which he has detailed knowledge and experience include ship construction and conversion, insurance and performance bonds. He has been admitted on an ad hoc basis to the Bars of Hong Kong, Trinidad and Tobago and Tanzania.
Professional Memberships: He is a member of the IBA, LCIA, COMBAR, TECBAR, SCL and the Society for Computers and Law.
Career: Queen's Counsel 2003

GODFREY, Hannah
Cloisters, London
020 78274000
hg@cloisters.com
Featured in Clinical Negligence (London)
Practice Areas: Hannah specialises in clinical negligence law including inquests. She is regularly instructed as sole counsel in a wide range of medical claims (with particular expertise in general surgery, opthalmology, gynaecology, obstetrics, plastic surgery and oncology), and as junior in maximum value catastrophic brain/spinal injury claims (including complex quantum claims requiring detailed excel workbook schedules of loss). She predominantly represents claimants. She has special interests in human rights issues, fatal accident claims and constructing damages claims for injured young people.
Professional Memberships: AVMA, APIL, INQUEST.
Career: BA Hons Cantab (First Class) 1999. PG Dip and BVC London 2001-2 (with internships at UNHCR (Geneva) and The AIRE Centre, London). Called to the Bar 2002 and undertook first six pupillage at Doughty Street Chambers, followed by second six at Cloisters and a judicial assistantship to Lord Justice Mummery. Hannah has been a tenant at Cloisters since 2004, and a pupil supervisor since 2012.
Publications: Contributor to 'Lewis and Buchan on Clinical Negligence'
Personal: Hannah lives in Hampshire and is a keen amateur coastal skipper.

GODFREY, Howard QC
2 Bedford Row, London
020 74408888
hgodfrey@2bedfordrow.co.uk
Featured in Crime (London)
Practice Areas: A very experienced specialist advocate and adviser in the field of serious crime. Instructions come by way of direct access in addition to those instructed by solicitors. Areas of work include advice and representation in relation to Conviction and Sentence appeals; Abuse of Process; Fraud, both corporate and personal; Money Laundering; Tax frauds; Insider Dealing; Accounting, Insurance, and Banking Frauds. Advice and representation in Bribery Act and Corruption cases. Advice and representation in Asset Restraint and civil and criminal recovery. Practice also includes Advice and representation in cases of corporate and personal manslaughter, murder, and other non fatal violence as well as international and domestic drug trafficking. Many cases where civil and criminal liability overlap. Professional discipline and regulation.
Professional Memberships: Direct Access; Criminal Bar Association; South Eastern Circuit. Called to the Bar of Turks and Caicos Islands 1996.
Career: Called to the Bar (Middle Temple) November 1970, Bencher 2004; took Silk 1991; Recorder of the Crown Court 1992 -2000

GOKANI, Rachna
QEB Hollis Whiteman, London
020 7933 8855
rachna.gokani@qebw.co.uk
Featured in Crime (London), Financial Crime (London)
Practice Areas: Rachna defends and prosecutes in cases of serious business and general crime. She has extensive experience in multi-jurisdictional cases, including a multi-million-pound private prosecution for historic fraud offences, believed to be the largest successful private prosecution brought by an individual. More recently, Rachna represented the former senior partner of a major accountancy firm, found not guilty of all charges before the Supreme Court of Gibraltar. She has been instructed in cases of domestic and overseas corruption (including on behalf of a former executive of the Swift Technical Group), fraud, money laundering, conspiracy to defraud, sanctions offences, false accounting, perverting the course of justice, commercial-scale immigration offences, perjury and historic sexual offences, including as junior counsel for former newspaper boss Eddy Shah. Rachna was also instructed for the prosecution in R v Sheikh, in which the defendant, the eldest son of Abu Hamza, was convicted of conspiracy to kidnap. Rachna appeared alone before the Lord Chief Justice in R v Shoyeju, a guideline case for misconduct in public office. Rachna also appeared as a junior in the Court of Appeal in R v PD, which considered the manner in which Security Council Resolutions relating to the arms trade are implemented in domestic law. Rachna has experience in regulatory law, appearing before the General Medical Council, Nursing and Midwifery Council and Solicitors' Disciplinary Tribunal.
Professional Memberships: Criminal Bar Association, Female Fraud Forum, Fraud Lawyers' Association, Young Fraud Lawyers' Association
Career: 2006-2008: Researcher to Monty Raphael QC, Peters & Peters 2013: SFO Approved Counsel List
Publications: Contributing author to 'Blackstone's Guide to the Bribery Act' (OUP, 2010) and 'Bribery: Law and Practice' (OUP, 2016)
Personal: Call 2006; LLB (Hons); BVC (Outstanding)

GOLD, Elliot
Serjeants' Inn Chambers, London
020 7427 5000
egold@serjeantsinn.com
Featured in Police Law (All Circuits)
Practice Areas: Elliot Gold was called to the bar 2001. Elliot specialises in employment law, inquests and inquiries, police law and public and administrative law. He is a confident and trusted advocate combining good judgment on the law with a firm and detailed approach to cross-examination and sensitive client handling. Please visit the Serjeants' Inn Chambers website for his profile, which sets out full details of her practice including relevant work of note.

GOLDRING, Jenny
5 St Andrew's Hill, London
020 7332 5400
clerks@5sah.co.uk
Featured in Financial Crime (London)
Practice Areas: Jenny specialises in financial regulatory work and complex civil and criminal fraud. She is passionate about fraud work and has substantial experience in cases with complex disclosure issues. She was recently instructed by the SFO in the first prosecution of a company for an offence pursuant to Section 7 of the Bribery Act 2010. Jenny is an expert in MTIC fraud and is instructed as leading Counsel in related multi-million pound appeals in the VAT tribunal (First and Upper tier) on a regular basis. Jenny has also conducted numerous fraud cases including

mortgage fraud, insurance fraud, complex excise fraud, PAYE fraud and advance fee fraud. She recently defended the partner of a leading firm of Solicitors in a multi million pound allegation of fraud and is currently defending in a prosecution by the Financial Conduct Authority for offences contrary to the Financial Services and Markets Act 2000 and the Financial Services Act 2012.
Professional Memberships: Fraud Lawyers Association, Criminal Bar Association, South Eastern Circuit.
Personal: MA Hons Jurisprudence (Oxford University).

GOLDRING, Jeremy QC
South Square, London
020 7696 9900
jeremygoldring@southsquare.com
Featured in Chancery (London), Banking & Finance (London), Commercial Dispute Resolution (London), Company (London), Restructuring/Insolvency (London)
Practice Areas: Jeremy undertakes a wide range of commercial litigation and advisory work. He has extensive experience in a broad variety of banking and finance areas (including derivatives and securitisations), restructuring and insolvency, and company law.
Career: Jeremy has appeared in many of the leading cases in his fields, including Lomas v Firth Rixson, Standard Chartered Bank v Ceylon Petroleum Corporation and Re Stanford International Bank. He regularly appears in the UK courts at all levels, including the Supreme Court in Eurosail, the Court of Appeal in Graiseley Properties v Barclays Bank, and in the Chancery Division in Torre Asset Funding v Royal Bank of Scotland. Other recent examples of work include Tchenguiz v Grant Thornton and BNY Mellon v LBG Capital. Jeremy also has considerable experience in offshore jurisdictions, particularly in Grand Cayman and the British Virgin Islands. Examples of his work includes Weavering (Conway v. Skandinaviska Enskilda Banken); Sphinx Funds; Primeo Funds; China Shanshui Cement; Asia Coal Energy; Parmalat. Called 1996 (Lincoln's Inn); QC 2013; Called to the Bar of the Cayman Islands 1998; called to the Bar of the British Virgin Islands 2000.
Publications: Contributor to Cross-Border Insolvency Fourth Edition (Sheldon, Bloomsbury, 2015); Gore-Browne on Companies; Professional Negligence and Liability (Simpson); and Rowlatt on Principal and Surety (Moss and Marks, Sweet and Maxwell, 2011).

GOLDSMITH, Joseph
5 Stone Buildings, London
020 7242 6201
clerks@5sblaw.com
Featured in Chancery (London), Court of Protection (All Circuits), Pensions (London)
Practice Areas: General Chancery practice, incorporating wide range of contentious and non-contentious work, with particular emphasis upon: pensions; trusts, wills, probate and administration of estates; capital taxes and estate planning; proprietary estoppel; family provision; real property; and related professional negligence matters. Particular interest in issues relating to incapacity and the MCA 2005. Appears regularly in the Court of Protection. Also practises in ecclesiastical law. Notable cases include: Merchant Navy Ratings Pension Fund Trustees Ltd v. Stena Line Ltd [2015] EWHC 448; IBM United Kingdom Holdings Ltd v. Dalgleish [2014] EWHC 980 and [2015] EWHC 389; Sarjeant v. Rigid Group Ltd [2012] EWHC 3757 and [2013] EWCA Civ. 1714; Trustees of Lehman Brothers Pension Scheme v. Pensions Regulator [2013] EWCA Civ. 751; Re IBM Pension Plan [2012] EWHC 2766; Hughes v. Woolworths Group Pensions Trustee Ltd [2012] EWHC 905; Re JDS [2012] EWHC 302; Prudential Staff Pensions Ltd v. Prudential Assurance [2012] EWHC 960; Hapeshi v. Allnatt [2010] EWHC 392; DCM (Optical Holdings) Ltd v. HMRC [2010] UKFTT 393; Re St Peter's Draycott [2009] Fam 93; and Re Horley Town Football Club [2006] EWHC 2386.
Professional Memberships: Chancery Bar Association. Accredited Mediator.
Career: Called 2003.
Publications: Contributor to wills and administration volume of Encyclopaedia of Forms and Precedents, Tolley's Finance and Law for the Older Client and Heywood and Massey's Court of Protection Practice.
Personal: Educated at Hereford Cathedral School; Brasenose College, Oxford (BA, Modern History); and City University.

GOLLANCZ, David
Keating Chambers, London
020 7544 2602
dgollancz@keatingchambers.com
Featured in Public Procurement (London)
Practice Areas: Public procurement and all aspects of public/private commercial transactions (commercial contract, public law, TUPE, pension rights, state aid and competition); employment law; judicial review. Member of Attorney-General's Panel of Counsel. As solicitor, advised Nuclear Decommissioning Authority, Identity and Passports Service (ID Cards), National Policing Improvement Authority (IMPACT programme), DCSF (Academies programme), Department for Communities and Local Government (ECHR), BERR (state aids), Equality and Human Rights Commission (statutory Codes of Practice under Equality Act 2010). As barrister, has appeared on both sides in a number of procurement challenges and procurement-related judicial reviews, and has a substantial advisory practice. Notable cases include R (Nash) v Barnet London Borough Council, Corelogic Ltd v Bristol City Council, Pearson Driving Assessments Ltd v The Minister for the Cabinet . Advising Attorney General of Singapore on public procurement law and practice.
Professional Memberships: PLA; TECBAR; UKSALA; CLA.
Career: Admitted solicitor 1990; Head of Public Procurement and Commercial, Treasury Solicitors; Head of TUPE Task Force, Treasury Solicitors; Partner, EU Competition and Regulatory team, Head of Public Sector, Field Fisher Waterhouse LLP. Called 2010. EC Law post-graduate diploma, UCL 2001; EU Competition Law post-graduate diploma 2009; Appointed to Attorney-General's London Panel, 2014. Accredited for public access.
Publications: Contributes to: Keating on Construction Contracts; PLC Public Sector. Personal: Conversational French. Member of Bar Lesbian and Gay Group.
Personal: Lives in Islington, N. London. Speaks French. Member of Bar Lesbian and Gay Group.

GOLLOP, Katharine QC
Serjeants' Inn Chambers, London
2074275000
Kgollop@serjeantsinn.com
Featured in Clinical Negligence (London), Professional Discipline (London)
Practice Areas: Katharine Gollop QC was called to the Bar in 1993 and took silk in 2016. Katharine specialises in clinical negligence and healthcare, professional discipline, employment and inquests and inquiries. An earlier edition notes that "she is a very formidable advocate and a shrewd tactician who isn't scared to make difficult decisions" and that she is "revered by clients for her strong-willed approach to litigation." Please visit the Serjeants' Inn Chambers website for her profile, which sets out full details of her practice including relevant work of note.
Professional Memberships: PIBA, APIL, AVMA, ELA.
Personal: Gray's Inn Prince of Wales Scholar. St John's College, Oxford (BA First Class).

GOODALL, Patrick QC
Fountain Court Chambers, London
020 7583 3335
pjg@fountaincourt.co.uk
Featured in Professional Negligence (London), Banking & Finance (London), Commercial Dispute Resolution (London), Fraud (London), Insurance (London)
Practice Areas: Broad commercial litigation and arbitration practice, with particular expertise in banking and financial services, professional negligence, insurance and reinsurance, civil fraud and conflict of laws.
Professional Memberships: Commercial Bar Association (COMBAR); London Common Law and Commercial Bar Association; British Insurance Law Association.
Career: Called 1998. QC 2014. Junior Counsel to the Crown (A Panel) 2011-2014. Admitted as a solicitor 1997. CEDR accredited mediator. Called to the Bar of the British Virgin Islands.
Publications: Co-author of 'The Law of Privilege' (ed. Thanki, 2nd edition, Oxford University Press); Co-author of 'Law of Bank Payments' (eds. Brindle & Cox, 4th edition, Sweet & Maxwell); Contributor to Bullen & Leake & Jacob's 'Precedents of Pleadings' (18th edition, Sweet & Maxwell); Editor of 'Commercial Court Procedure' (Sweet & Maxwell).
Personal: Educated at Southampton University (LLB, First Class Honours) and Brasenose College, Oxford (BCL, First Class Honours).

GOODFELLOW, Giles W J QC
Pump Court Tax Chambers, London
020 7414 8080
clerks@pumptax.com
Featured in Tax (London)
Practice Areas: Giles's practice covers the full range of advisory work on direct (including NIC) and indirect tax issues. Particular areas of expertise cover corporate reorganisations, tonnage tax, employment remuneration structures, IHT and CGT planning for family-owned businesses, high net worth individuals, onshore and offshore trusts, anti-avoidance cases, tax structuring of divorce settlements, professional negligence in tax matters, and rectification and rescission claims. He has substantial experience and expertise in advising upon and negotiating compromises of HMRC investigations, challenging Follower and Accelerated Payment Notices and the use of various tax disclosure facilities. He also acts as an accredited Mediator (in both Revenue and private disputes) and is qualified to accept Public Access instructions. Relevant cases: R (Morgan Grenfell & Co Ltd) v Rounding (House of Lords); Lloyds UDT Finance Ltd v Chartered Finance Trust Holdings plc (High Court); ABTA v IRC (Special Commissioners); R (Carvill) v IRC (Administrative Court); Blackburn v Keeling (Court of Appeal); Liverpool Archdiocesan Trustees v Goldberg (High Court); Government of Mauritius v Maroussem & Ors (Privy Council); Oriel Support (Special Commissioners) London Recruitment Ltd (Special Commissioners); Secretary of State for Work & Pensions v Smith (House of Lords); Gabem Management (Special Commissioners); Maco Doors & Windows (House of Lords); Tower Mcashback (Supreme Court); Cheshire Employer and Skills Development v HMRC (Court of Appeal), Euroceanica v HMRC (FTT), Gilchrist v HMRC (UTT), Tower Radio v HMRC (UTT); Mehjoo v Harben Barker (High Court).
Professional Memberships: Revenue Bar Association; London Common Law & Commercial Bar Association (Treasurer), Professional Negligence Bar Association.
Career: Called to Bar, Middle Temple 1983; Senior Astbury Scholarship, Harmsworth Scholarship.
Publications: Co-author Inheritance Tax Planning with Andrew Thornhill QC and J Kessler (Longmans); co-author Financial Provisions & Taxation on Divorce with R Venables QC and Martin O'Dwyer (KeyHaven).

GOODISON, Adam
South Square, London
020 7696 9900
adamgoodison@southsquare.com
Featured in Restructuring/Insolvency (London)
Practice Areas: Specialisations include restructuring, insolvency, finance/business litigation, company law and trusts litigation.
Professional Memberships: Chancery Bar Association, COMBAR, Insolvency Lawyers' Association.
Career: Regularly instructed on high profile domestic and international restructurings involving litigation in London or overseas including on numerous cases litigated in the Royal Court, Jersey, in the Cayman Islands, in the BVI and in the Dubai International Financial Centre Courts (including the DIFC Court of Appeal). Recent notable cases include Re Primacom, Re Seat Pagine, Re Cortefiel, Re Orizonia, Re Icopal, Re Yell, Saad Holdings, Singularis, Re Apcoa Parking, Coventry FC, Portsmouth FC, Plymouth Argyle FC, Battersea Power Station, Re Nortel, MF Global, Re Globespan, Jet Star v Sandhu and Re Diwan. Called 1990; Bar Council member 1995-98 and 2004-2010.
Publications: Contributor to 'The Law of Administrators and Receivers of Companies' ROT chapter (Lightman and Moss, Sweet and Maxwell); 'Rowlatt on Principal and Surety' (Marks and Moss, Sweet and Maxwell); and 'Company Directors' (Mortimore, OUP).

GOODWIN, Deirdre
7BR, London
020 7242 3555
dgoodwin@7br.co.uk
Featured in Clinical Negligence (London)

Practice Areas: Deirdre specialises in catastrophic clinical negligence where she acts for both claimants and defendants. She has significant expertise in cases arising from severe perinatal asphyxial brain damage, pre-natal diagnostics, Erb's palsy, paediatric neurological injury, major neurosurgical and orthopaedic iatrogenic injury, and delayed diagnosis of cancer and meningitis. Many of her cases involve complex causation issues and she has specialist knowledge in mental capacity matters. Deirdre has a reputation as a skilled advocate with an ability to distil issues quickly. She is a strong negotiator with a keen intuition for an opponent's position and is proactive, quickly turning round work in order to maintain momentum in a case; this includes the preparation of meticulously pleaded schedules of loss in high value claims and Eeles applications. Reported cases include Bolitho v City and Hackney Health Authority [1998] A.C. 238 HL, Murphy v Wirral Health Authority (1996) 7 Med LR 99 CA and AC (a Minor by his Father and litigation friend MC) v St George's Hospital NHS Trust (2015) EWHC 3644 (QB). Approved settlements for claimants and defendants include cases where damages have exceeded £6.5 million and a recent clinical negligence fatal accidents claim where the settlement took into account breach of the duty of candour and aggravated damages. Deirdre also has extensive experience in all areas of personal injury practice, in particular catastrophic head injury, spinal trauma and Fatal Accident cases.
Professional Memberships: Professional Negligence Bar Association, Personal Injury Bar Association, Oxford Medico-Legal Society
Personal: Languages: French and German.

GOOLAMALI, Nina
2TG - 2 Temple Gardens, London
020 7822 1222
ng@2tg.co.uk
Featured in Personal Injury (London)
Practice Areas: Nina Goolamali has a very well established practice in catastrophic injury and sports-related litigation. She is instructed by all the major Insurers and Claims Handlers and is well known for her ability to defend in sensitive high value cases arising in the context of employer's liability, public liability and motor/sports accidents in the UK and abroad. She is particularly sought after for her expertise in claims relating to brain injuries, para/tetraplegia, fatalities, chronic pain & occupational health. Nina is the head of the Sports Team at 2 Temple Gardens. Her sports practice encompasses injury, regulatory, insurance and commercial/contractual matters. She acts for players, teams and national governing bodies in all major sports and is widely acknowledged for her expertise in the field of Motorsport (Formula 1, Formula E, MotoGP, MotoCross, Speedway & Karting), rugby and football. Nina is on the Editorial Board of LawInSport and is a member of the Sport Resolutions UK Pro Bono Legal Service.
Professional Memberships: British Association for Sport and Law; Personal Injury Bar Association; London Common Law and Commercial Bar Association.
Career: MA Jurisprudence, Lady Margaret Hall, Oxford. Post Graduate Diploma in Sports Law, Kings College, London. Called to the Bar in 1995.

GORASIA, Paras
Kings Chambers, Manchester
0345 034 3444
clerks@kingschambers.com
Featured in Employment (Northern)
Practice Areas: Paras has a national practice specialising in employment and employment related commercial litigation. He is regularly involved in high value and/or reputationally sensitive disputes involving discrimination, whistleblowing, bonuses, illegitimate competitive activity (including breach of restrictive covenants/fiduciary duties), misuse of confidential information, unfair/wrongful dismissal and TUPE. Clients have included major multinational companies (Including a number of FTSE 100 corporates) and senior executives/high net worth individuals.
Professional Memberships: Employment Lawyers Association, Employment Law Bar Association, Industrial Law Society, Chartered Institute of Arbitrators.
Career: Called July 2005 (Inner Temple). Judicial Assistant at the Court of Appeal to the then Master of the Rolls, Sir Anthony Clarke (now Lord Clarke) (January 2007). Pegasus Scholar to Hong Kong (October 2009). Appointed to the Panel of Counsel for the Equality and Human Rights Commission (2011-2015). Appointed to the Welsh Assembly Government's Panel of Junior Counsel in Employment Law (October 2012). Appointed to the Attorney General's Regional Panel of Junior Counsel to the Crown (November 2012).
Personal: (1999-2002) University of Kent (LLB with First Class Honours); (2002-04) Exeter College, Oxford(BCL, MPhil); (2004-05) King's College London (LLM).

GORDON WALKER, Emily
Outer Temple Chambers, London
020 7353 6381
egw@outertemple.com
Featured in Employment (London)
Practice Areas: Emily is an employment law specialist and an experienced trial and appellate advocate. Her practice covers all statutory employment tribunal claims, High Court litigation and discrimination law. Emily acts for businesses and individuals. Her client base includes public and private sector employers such as government departments, local authorities and companies ranging in size from SMEs to global corporations. On the employee side Emily is instructed by trade unions, insurers and high net worth individuals.
Professional Memberships: ELBA (management committee), ELA, ILS, ELAAS
Career: 2015-2020: Attorney General's C Panel of Junior Counsel to the Crown. 2007: Call (Middle Temple)
Personal: 2006-2007: BVC (BPP), Queen Mother Scholar (Middle Temple). 2005-2006: PGDL (City University),Queen Mother Scholar (Middle Temple). 2001-2005: MA (First Class Hons) Philosophy (Edinburgh University)

GOTT, Paul QC
Fountain Court Chambers, London
020 7583 3335
clerks4@fountaincourt.co.uk
Featured in Employment (London)
Practice Areas: Employment law, commercial law and professional regulation. Industrial relations law, especially injunctive work in relation to strike action. Junior counsel to the Crown 1999-2012. Treasury "A" panel 2005-2012. Recent cases include: SRA v Leigh Day, 2016 and onwards. SRA v Chan 2015-2016 (SDT and HC regulation of solicitors and Stamp Duty Land Tax avoidance schemes). National Rail Strike 2015, London Underground strike action 2011-2015, Royal Mail Privatisation 2013, Rickhuss v Network Rail 2013-15 (collective bargaining and collective agreements); Pavithran v London Clinic 2013-14 (alleged whistle blowing). Counsel for NHS commissioning bodies in multi-contract procurement disputes and NHS pendulum adjudications 2013 and onwards. British Airways plc v Unite [2010] IRLR 42 (injunction against 12-day cabin crew strike - Xmas 2009); BA v Unite (No.2) [2010] IRLR 809 (HC and CoA - injunction application to restrain May/June 2010 cabin crew strike); Metrobus v Unite [2010] ICR 173 (injunction against London bus strike, TULRA and Art 11 ECHR). Unite v easyJet [2010] TUR1/723 (CAC - resisting application for statutory union recognition). Muschett v HMPS [2010] IRLR 173 (CoA - race discrimination claims and temporary workers).
Professional Memberships: ComBar; Industrial Law Society; Employment Lawyers Association.
Personal: Education: 1979-86 Marple Hall Comprehensive, Stockport. 1986-89 MA Cambridge University, Downing College, Double First Class Honours. 1989-90 BCL Oxford University, Brasenose College, First Class Honours. Appointed as Junior Counsel to the Crown, July 1999. Appointed to Treasury 'A' Panel, April 2005. Re-appointed to Treasury 'A' Panel, February 2010. Appointed as Board Member to the Standards Board for England, February 2006 and re-appointed March 2009. Silk: 2012

GOUDIE, James QC
11KBW, London
020 7632 8500
james.goudie@11kbw.com
Featured in Administrative & Public Law (London), Education (London), Local Government (London), Public Procurement (London)
Practice Areas: Specialises in all aspects of employment law, public law and commercial law.
Career: Solicitor 1966-70. Called to the Bar Inner Temple 1970. Bencher; past President National Security Panel for Information Rights; Deputy High Court Judge, Queen's Bench and Chancery Divisions; past Chairman Law Reform Committee; General Council of the Bar; past Chairman Administrative Law Bar Association; past Chairman Bar European Group; member of the Football League Disciplinary Commission Panel of Arbitrators; Fellow of the Chartered Institute of Arbitrators; Fellow of the Society of Advanced Legal Studies. Member of Bar Eastern Caribbean Supreme Court (Antigua and Barbuda and Virgin Islands).
Personal: Educated at Dean Close School, Cheltenham and LSE (LLB Hons). FCI Arb. Governor of LSE.

GOUDIE, Martin
Charter Chambers, London
020 7618 4400
martin.goudie@charterchambers.com
Featured in Crime (London)
Practice Areas: Martin's practice is divided between crime, national security, regulatory and investigatory work. He undertakes the full scope of grave and financial crime, defending and prosecuting (CPS Grade 4) in equal measure as Leading and Junior Counsel. He has extensive experience of regulatory and disciplinary hearings/tribunals and investigations, acting for a number of regulators, individuals, companies and other bodies. Martin advises the Civil Aviation Authority on jurisdictional issues, prosecutions, including those arising out of fatal crashes, and appears at Reg 6 appeals. Martin has been a member of the Attorney General's Panel of Special Advocates (DV security cleared) dealing with national security cases since 2005, and was junior Special Advocate in the applications brought by UK detainees in Guantanamo Bay, Binyam Mohammed and Shaker Aamer. He has contributed to documents produced by Special Advocates, including submissions to the Joint Committee on Human Rights, and was interviewed by Amnesty International on the use of 'closed material procedures' in the UK. Martin frequently accepts instructions to advise prior to proceedings commencing. He accepts direct public access instructions.
Professional Memberships: Criminal Bar Association, International Bar Association, Fraud Lawyers Association, Cybercrime Practitioners Association, South Eastern Circuit, Justice.
Career: Called 1996, Bencher 2014 - Inner Temple. Pegasus Scholar to Crown Law Office, Wellington, New Zealand - 1999.
Personal: Head of Discipline, London Scottish (Rugby) Football Club.

GOURIET, Gerald QC
Francis Taylor Building, London
020 7353 8415
clerks@ftbchambers.co.uk
Featured in Licensing (London)
Practice Areas: Gerald Gouriet QC was called to the bar in 1974. His first years were spent mainly in criminal defence work, which from its Old Bailey roots rapidly branched out into defending prosecutions brought under health and safety, environmental protection (principally noise abatement), Trade Descriptions and Planning legislation. In the mid 1980's he began to be instructed on a regular basis in Licensing cases, and by the time he left the UK to work in America (1991) he was regarded as one of the leading licensing juniors. He returned to practice at the Bar in 1999, and took silk in 2006. His recent appearances include successfully appealing against conditions imposed on Fabric nightclub by the Council following a Review of the premises licence and successfully representing the AMLR to oppose the proposal by the Licensing Authority to impose an EMRO (Early Morning Restriction Order) in Blackpool and Paddy Power in their successful appeal against refusal by Newham Council to grant a betting premises licence. Recent clients include: Gaming: The Ritz Casino; The Empire Casino (LCI); Grosvenor Casinos (Rank); Gerald successfully obtained licences for the recently opened Hippodrome Casino (Leicester Square); Palace Casino (Great Yarmouth); Casino Red (Huddersfield). He has also acted for The Noble Organisation - amusement centres, bingo clubs and casinos; Luminar Leisure - casino applications in Bournemouth and Leeds; Lucinenne Barriere (French Casino Operators); Great Eastern Quays Casino; Group Partouche (French Casino Operators); Shipley Brothers - bingo clubs; and Caesar's Palace (Las Vegas). Bet-

ting: Paddy Power; Ladbrokes; Coral; William Hill; BetFred; Better Betting; Trafalgar Leisure (Newcastle). Alcohol & Entertainment: The BBC; Novus Leisure; Somerfield; Punch Taverns; John Lewis; Waitrose; The Cooperative Group; Mitchells & Butlers; Luminar Leisure; The Noble Organisation – "The Steak House" Leicester Square; The British Beer and Pub Association (BBPA); Gerald acted for the police in the revocation of the licence held by 'Syndicate Nightclub' in Blackpool and on their applications to revoke the licence for 'Spearmint Rhino' in London. Taxi Licensing: numerous local authorities, including Westminster, Kensington and Chelsea, Richmond, Chichester, Medway, Guildford; Transport for London, Shropshire Council, Coventry City Council (PHV and Hackney Carriage licensing); Berwick upon Tweed Council (redrafting Taxi Licensing Policy).
Publications: General Editor of Paterson's Licensing Acts

GRAHAM PAUL, Annabel

Francis Taylor Building, London
020 7353 8415
clerks@ftbchambers.co.uk
Featured in Planning (London)

Practice Areas: Annabel Graham Paul has a practice encompassing all aspects of planning, compulsory purchase, environment, local government including rating and licensing, education, regulatory crime, ecclesiastical, and commons and greens. Major public inquiries include Hampden Fields, Aylesbury, the Ashton Vale to Bristol Temple Meads Bus Rapid Transit Scheme Transport & Works Act Order, Linton Wind Farm, Crystal Palace Park and Shepherds Bush Market Compulsory Purchase Order. Recent cases include R (McClellan) v Lambeth LBC [2014] EWHC 1964 (Admin), San Vicente v Secretary of State for Communities and Local Government [2014] 1 WLR 966, Wakil (t/a Orya Textiles) v Hammersmith & Fulham LBC [2014] Env LR 14. Sits as an Independent Inspector to conduct town and village green inquiries.
Publications: Contributor, Gadsden on Commons and Greens (Sweet & Maxwell, 2nd edition, 2011) and The Law of Regulatory Enforcement and Sanctions (OUP, 2011).

GRAHAM-WELLS, Alison

St John's Chambers, Bristol
0117 923 4740
Alison.Graham-Wells@stjohnschambers.co.uk
Featured in Tax (The Regions)

Practice Areas: A former Senior Lawyer within the Government Legal Service, Alison returned to independent practice in 2010 and is a well-established commercial and chancery barrister specialising in taxation. She also undertakes administrative/public law and insolvency matters – especially where there is a tax "twist". Her practice extends to Court of Protection finance and property matters. Alison aims to find workable, cost effective solutions to achieve her clients' objectives. She accepts Instructions from Solicitors, Licensed Access practitioners (contentious/non-continentious) and is licensed by the Bar Standards Board for, at her discretion, Public Access. Public Access work is restricted to tax and insolvency issues. Alison also undertakes work for the Bar Pro Bono Unit as time allows. Alison maintains a door tenancy at Exchange Chambers – 0161 833 2722 (grahamwells@exchangechambers.co.uk)
Professional Memberships: Honourable Society of the Inner Temple, Revenue Bar Association, Chancery Bar Association, Northern Chancery Bar Association, VAT Practitioners Group,
Career: Call 1990; 1992-94: 5 King's Bench Walk; 1994-2000: HMCE Prosecutions London and Manchester; 2000-07: HMCE/HMRC VAT Tribunal Team (anti-avoidance matters and civil fraud); 2007-2009: HMRC MTIC Team; 2010-to date: Exchange Chambers; 2015-to date: St John's Chambers.
Publications: Alison works with Lexis Nexis on Court of Protection practice "notes".
Personal: A busy mother to a 12-year-old, Alison also enjoys: photography, painting, walking (she has two hooligan hounds), food (eating and cooking it), film and theatre, and books (which she collects as well as reads).

GRAHAME, Angela QC

Compass Chambers, Edinburgh
0131 226 5071
angela.grahame@compasschambers.com
Featured in Personal Injury (Scotland)

Practice Areas: Personal Injury; Public and Fatal Accident Inquiries; Clinical and Professional Negligence; Angela Grahame QC is the Vice Dean of the Faculty of Advocates. She is the second woman to hold this position in the history of the Faculty. She has extensive experience in many challenging and high profile cases. She has been instructed in two public inquiries: (i) for Greater Glasgow Health Board in the Vale of Leven Public Inquiry; and (ii) for the Lord Advocate in the Fingerprint Inquiry. In the last eighteen months, Angela has conducted many proofs in the Court of Session, including: (i) the first mesothelioma proof of its kind in Scotland; (ii) a complex medical negligence proof involving the death of a patient in hospital; (iii) a proof consequent upon a fatal road traffic collision; and (iv) an accident involving a horse trainer, injured falling from a horse at work. Angela has also negotiated settlements in many claims, including a catastrophic brain injury case involving 24 hour care and valued at over £12 million. She is regularly instructed in industrial disease actions, involving mesothelioma and lung cancer. Angela speaks regularly on the law and practice relating to personal injury, damages, Article 2 claims and clinical negligence.
Professional Memberships: Member of the Complaints Committee under the Faculty of Advocates' Disciplinary Rules (2015 to date); Trustee and Faculty Representative of the Scottish Council of Law Reporting (2015 to date); Member of the Faculty Response Committee on the Criminal Justice (Scotland) Bill (2013); Member of the Faculty of Advocates' Board of Assessors (2007 to 2016); Member of the Faculty of Advocates' Response Review Group (2001 – 2003; 2007 to 2010); Faculty of Advocates' Representative on Employer Liaison Committee at Aberdeen University (2001 – 2003); Member of Disciplinary Rules: Investigating Committee (1999 – 2001); Curator of the Advocates' Library and Clerk to the Curators (1999 to 2001)
Career: Angela was elected the Vice Dean of the Faculty of Advocates in July 2016. Angela called to the bar in 1995 and took silk in 2009. She was appointed as a full time Advocate Depute in 2003 and promoted to Senior Advocate Depute in 2005. She was appointed as a Legal Member, Police Appeals Tribunal in April 2013. In 2014. She was Co-Director of Compass Chambers (2014 – 2016)
Publications: Angela is a qualified Instructor and has taught advocacy skills to the Solicitors' profession; devils at the Faculty of Advocates; and at the University of Edinburgh. She has previously written articles in the Scottish Law Gazette, Juridical Review, Greens Civil Practice Bulletin; and Greens Reparation Bulletin.

GRANDISON, Myles

Drystone Chambers, London
2074041881
myles.grandison@drystone.com
Featured in Extradition (London)

Practice Areas: Extradition, Professional Discipline
Career: Myles is widely acknowledged as an expert in extradition law and has an established extradition practice representing Requested Persons, Requesting States and the National Crime Agency. He has undertaken a number of key cases in the High Court in this rapidly developing area of law, dealing with issues such as convictions for contumacy; disproportionate sentences; the applicability of the "slip rule"; and the demarcation between warrants issued where the Requested Person is accused and those where they are merely wanted for investigation. In addition to dealing with challenges under the Extradition Act, Myles advises clients on issues such as prisoner transfer, freezing of assets across jurisdictions and mutual legal assistance. Myles has written numerous articles on the subject of extradition and has recently assisted the authors of "Extradition law: a practitioner's guide". In 2016, Myles was appointed to the Attorney Generals C panel. Myles also enjoys a growing reputation as a Professional Discipline practitioner, defending health care professionals in disciplinary proceedings before the GMC and HCPC. Recent cases include assisting a Doctor before the GMC's Interim Order Panel and defending a Bio-Medical Scientist before the HCPC on allegations of misconduct and a lack of competence.

GRANT, Gary

Francis Taylor Building, London
020 7353 8415
clerks@ftbchambers.co.uk
Featured in Licensing (London)

Practice Areas: Licensing: acts for both premises operators and public authorities in numerous high profile licence applications, reviews, appeals and judicial reviews. Clients range from Spearmint Rhino to the Commissioner of the Metropolitan Police and include major nightclub/bar/lap-dancing operators, restauranteurs, leisure industry PLC's and public authorities. Also experienced in gambling, taxi, firearms and explosive licensing. He lectures and publishes widely in the fields of licensing and criminal regulatory law. REGULATORY & GENERAL CRIME: Acts in serious and often high profile criminal matters for both the defence and prosecution in all levels of tribunal from the Magistrates' Court to the House of Lords/Supreme Court and Privy Council. In addition to a wealth of experience in general crime, he has particular expertise in white-collar, corporate and regulatory offences (including planning, environmental, health and safety, corporate manslaughter and trading standards) as well as Proceeds of Crime, international and serious organised crime, serious and fatal road traffic cases.
Professional Memberships: Institute of Licensing; Criminal Bar Association.
Career: Called to the Bar 1994, Grays Inn; Recipient of the Sir Raymond Phillips MC Award (1994); Graded as 'Outstanding' by the Gray's Inn Advocacy Committee (1995).
Personal: Frequently appears as a legal analyst on national and international news channels.

GRANT, Marcus

Temple Garden Chambers, London
020 75831315
marcusgrant@tgchambers.com
Featured in Fraud (All Circuits), Personal Injury (London)

Practice Areas: Traumatic brain injury, spinal injury, chronic pain and insurance fraud (civil) specialist. Specialist in diffuse axonal injury and fibromyalgia / chronic pain litigation. Provides strategic advice to Insurers to combat fraud. Frequently provides lectures to the legal and medical professions. Involved in many of the leading contempt cases and many of the leading subtle brain injury and chronic pain cases. Reported cases 2011/15 include: Siegel v. Pummell – [2015] EWHC 195 & [2014] EWHC 3409, Zurich Insurance v. Kay, Kay & Kay [2014] EWHC 2734, Azimi Fraud cases – Lawtel – 13.02.14; Quinn Insurance v. Trifonovs Lawtel – 09.10.13; Liverpool Victoria v. Singh Lawtel 30.05.13; Samson v. Ali [2012] EWHC 4146; Mann v. Bahri [2012] Lawtel 02.04.12, Thompson & Fortis Insurance v. Middleton [2012] EWCA Civ 231, Liverpool Victoria v. Bashir [2012] EWHC 895, Lane v. Shah [2012] ACD 1, Nield v. Acromas v. Loveday [2011] EWHC, Vaile v. London Borough of Havering [2011] EWCA Civ 246.
Professional Memberships: PIBA.
Career: Called 1993, CEDR Mediator 2000, Direct Access Certified, Member of the Ogden Working Party.
Publications: Chronic Pain Society Journal, January 2012
Personal: Family, Andalucía, Lincoln's Inn advocacy training, Headway, West London Churches Homeless Concern, Athenaeum, Rachmaninov, Liverpool FC.

GRANTHAM, Andrew

Kings Chambers, Manchester
0345 034 3444
clerks@kingschambers.com
Featured in Chancery (Northern), Commercial Dispute Resolution (Northern)

Practice Areas: Agency (including commercial agency), banking, civil fraud and asset tracing, banking disputes, commercial arbitrations, company law (including shareholder actions), energy law, entertainment law, financial services law, insurance and reinsurance, partnership and LLPs, personal and corporate insolvency, professional negligence of accountants, solicitors and surveyors, sale and carriage of goods.
Professional Memberships: Northern Circuit Commercial Bar Association (Chair), Chancery Bar Association, COMBAR, Northern Chancery Bar Association.
Career: Called to the Bar 1991, formerly lecturer in law Wadham College Oxford and King's College London.
Publications: Contributing Editor to Commercial Litigation Pre–Emptive Remedies (Sweet and Maxwell)

GRANT-HUTCHISON, Peter
Terra Firma Chambers, Edinburgh
0131 260 5830
peter.grant-hutchison@terrafirmachambers.com
Featured in Employment (Scotland)
Practice Areas: Peter specialises in employment law. He has a broad practice acting for both employers, employees, office holders such as police officers, chief constables and firemasters. He has undertaken complex Discrimination, Equal Pay Act and Transfer of Undertaking cases. He has appeared in all forums, including employment tribunals, employment appeal tribunals, the Inner House of the Court of Session and the House of Lords as was. He has acted in judicial mediations and appeared at Central Arbitration Committee hearings. Most recently he has been instructed in cases involving "whistle-blowing" and questions of discrimination as a result of perceptions of disability and age and sex discrimination.
Professional Memberships: Member of the Part Time Sheriffs Association; Member of the Council of Fee Paid Immigration Judges.
Career: LLB, Single Honours, MA Economics 1974-1979; apprentice then solicitor specialising in employment law 1978-1988; called to Bar in 1988; part time judge of the Social Entitlement Chamber 1988-date; member of the Competition Commission Appeals Panel 2002-2010; part time sheriff 2005-date.
Publications: Architects Legal Handbook (Edition of Scottish Section on Employment Law and Health and Safety Legislation). He writes the annual Employment Law Review for Scottish Legal News.
Personal: Born 1956. Educated at Dundee University. Chairman of Scottish Legal News.

GRAY, Peter QC
Compass Chambers, Edinburgh
0131 260 5661
peter.gray@compasschambers.com
Featured in Health & Safety (Scotland)
Practice Areas: Previously described by UK Legal 500 as "a leading authority in health and safety law, especially major industrial accidents", "extremely responsive and has a very calm approach, even in high-pressure situations", "having a fabulous manner with clients and real gravitas before the courts"; and by Chambers and Partners that "he stands out as one of the true health and safety specialists at the Scottish Bar; the top expert in the field", Peter Gray QC is a leading practitioner in regulatory crime and, in particular, in the fields of health and safety, environmental and corporate financial crime. In the context of health and safety, and environmental crime he has been instructed to appear on behalf of corporate accused in the most serious prosecutions, statutory appeals and high profile Fatal Accident Inquiries in recent years. Recent cases include (2013): HMA v Svitzer Marine Ltd: representing Svitzer Marine in health and safety prosecution brought under Section 2 of HSWA 1974 arising out of capsize of "The Flying Phantom" resulting in death of three employees; (2013): PF v Taqa Bratani Ltd: representing Taqa in Environmental Crime Prosecution brought under the Offshore Petroleum Activities (Oil Pollution Prevention and Control) Regulations 2005; (2014): representing BP Exploration Operating Company Limited in Super Puma Fatal Accident Inquiry in relation to death of 2 crew and 14 passengers in North Sea in course of offshore transfer; (2014): HMA v Royal Highland Agricultural Society of Scotland. Representing RHASS in health and safety prosecution brought under section 3 of the HSWA 1974, arising from death of three year old at Royal Highland Show; (2015): HMA v Scottish Fire & Rescue Service. Representing SFRS in h & s prosecution brought under section 2 of the HSWA 1974 arising out of death of firefighter in course of firefighting duties. (2015): HMA v Total Exploration and Production UK Ltd: representing Total in relation to prosecution brought under regulation 13 of Offshore Installations and Wells(Design & Construction) Regulations 1996 arising out of hydrocarbon release on Franklin G4 installation; (2015): PF v Sita UK Ltd: representing Sita UK in relation to environmental prosecution brought under the Pollution Prevention and Control Act 1999,and Pollution Prevention and Control (Scotland) Regulations 2000 regarding a landfill site and its control of leachate levels; (2016): HMA v Clydeport Ltd: representing Clydeport in relation to health and safety prosecution brought under section 2 HSWA 1974 arising out of death of an employee whilst working on crane at Hunterston Terminal; and (2016): HSE v Chevron North Sea Limited: representing Chevron in appeal to Inner House brought by HSE against decision of Employment Tribunal in prohibition appeal brought under Section 24 HSWA 1974. In relation to financial crime Peter Gray specialises in corporate fraud, tax fraud, VAT evasion, bribery and money laundering offences, and has been instructed in a number of the most significant financial crime cases including those relating to MTIC carousel fraud, offences under the Prevention of Corruption Act 1906 and the Bribery Act 2010. In this area a significant part of his practice is also of an advisory nature, in particular with regard to potential corporate criminal liability arising in relation to anti money laundering obligations and associated matters, both domestically and internationally. Recent cases include (2011): AR Communications Ltd v HMRC: Representing HMRC in VAT appeal to 1st Tier Tax Tribunal in relation to MTIC carousel fraud. (2012): Re Abbot Group Ltd; (2013): Re X Ltd; (2015): Re Y Ltd; (2016): Re Braid Group: In each case representing the accused organisation in successfully achieving civil settlement as opposed to criminal prosecution, pursuant to the Crown's self-reporting initiative following introduction of the Bribery Act 2010.
Professional Memberships: Health and Safety Lawyers' Association; United Kingdom Environmental Law Association; Fraud Advisory Panel, and Proceeds of Crime Lawyers' Association.
Career: Practised at English Bar in London 1983-92; called to Scottish Bar 1992; appointed Queen's Counsel 2002.

GREANEY, Nicola
39 Essex Chambers, London
020 7832 1111
nicola.greaney@39essex.com
Featured in Clinical Negligence (London), Community Care (London), Costs Litigation (All Circuits), Court of Protection (All Circuits), Professional Discipline (London)
Practice Areas: Principle areas of practice are costs, clinical negligence, personal injury, professional discipline, COP and administrative law . Clinical negligence including paediatric brain injury, spinal injury, pregnancy related injury. Costs including high value DA, group litigation, costs management, legal aid costs. Personal injury and disease including catastrophic injury, capacity, fatal accidents, abuse/injuries in care institutions. Regulation including disciplinary hearings and appeals, acting for registrants and regulators, including GDC, HCPC, BACP, UKCP, RCVS, and SDT. Incapacity including decision-making about finances, medical treatment and care. Administrative and human rights law. Notable cases include: Coke workers group litigation (costs), NATS v NHSE & LGA [2016] (Admin), PSA v GDC & AB [2016] (Admin), Robshaw v United Lincolnshire NHS Trust [2015], Re PV [2015] (COP), A Local Authority v H [2012] (COP), Buckinghamshire CC v RB Kingston v SL [2011] (CA), R (Ali Zaki Mousa) v SSD [2013] (costs)
Career: Called to the Bar in 1999 and joined present Chambers upon completion of pupillage. Appointed to Treasury A Panel.
Publications: Disciplinary and Regulatory Proceedings, 8th Edition, Jordans 'The Mental Capacity Act 2005: A Guide to the New Law', The Law Society (Editions 1 and 2).
Personal: Educated at New Hall, Cambridge, (BA (Hons) Law, part 1 French and German).

GREATOREX, Paul
11KBW, London
020 7632 8500
Paul.Greatorex@11kbw.com
Featured in Court of Protection (All Circuits), Education (London), Local Government (London)
Practice Areas: Public, employment and commercial law. Public law includes judicial review, human rights, public inquiries, and specialist areas include education, local government, data protection, mental capacity/Court of Protection, regulatory, immigration, planning and prisons. Employment practice covers advisory work as well as litigation in tribunals in England, Wales and Scotland as well as in the civil courts and at all appellate levels up to the Supreme Court. Commercial practice consists of general litigation, including cross-border and international claims. Accredited under the Bar Public Access scheme so can be instructed by anyone.
Professional Memberships: ALBA, ELBA, PABA, PEBA.
Career: Called to the Bar 1999, Junior Counsel to the Crown 2005-2014. International experience includes spells with Richards Butler in Hong Kong, White & Case LLP in New York and Studio Pirola in Rome.
Publications: Co-author of 'Anti-Social Behaviour Law' (Jordans, 2nd edition, 2011), contributing author to Tolley's Employment Handbook and McManus, 'Education and the Courts' (Jordans, 3rd edition, 2012), editor and author of 'Education Law Handbook' (Jordans, forthcoming).
Personal: Educated at Christleton High School, Chester, Christ Church, Oxford and Université Panthéon-Assas (Paris II). Fluent in French, working knowledge of Italian and basic German and Czech.

GREEN, Alison
2TG – 2 Temple Gardens, London
020 7822 1200
agreen@2tg.co.uk
Featured in Insurance (London)
Practice Areas: Commercial practice, specialising in insurance and reinsurance, professional negligence private international law and arbitration. Accredited mediator and arbitrator. Represented and advised major insurance and reinsurance companies, Lloyd's syndicates, Corporation of Lloyd's, insurance brokers and insureds on a variety of covers. Instructed by Corporation of Lloyd's to provide independent expert evidence on Lloyd's for Court of Appeal, Brazil. Particular expertise In brokers' professional negligence claims. Reported cases include Novus Aviation v Onur Air [2009] (jurisdiction), Budgett Sugars v NU [2003] (products liability policy), Bestquest v Regency and Ecclesiastical Insurance Company [2003] (property/business interruption insurance), Stowers v GA Bonus [2003] (non-disclosure/commercial insurance) Sarwar v Allam [2002] (legal expenses insurance), Lonrho v ECGD [1996] (subrogation/insurance recoveries), Denby v Hellenic Mediterranean Lines [1994] (jurisdiction/marine insurance).
Professional Memberships: COMBAR, BILA.
Career: University College London LLB, LLM, Robert Garraway Rice Pupillage Award, Belgian Government Scholarship to University of Louvain. Law lecturer University of Surrey 76-78, tutor Queen Mary College 78 -79 and University College London 79-81, Vice President British Insurance Law Association, Vice Chair Bar Council Law Reform Committee, Chair BILA Charitable Trust, Part-time Upper Tribunal Judge.
Publications: Editorial adviser, Insurance Contract Law, contributing author Insurance Law – An Introduction, contributing author Consumer Insurance Law, articles.

GREEN, Doré
2TG – 2 Temple Gardens, London
020 7822 1200
dgreen@2tg.co.uk
Featured in Property Damage (London)
Practice Areas: Property damage and professional indemnity, in particular construction professionals, brokers' negligence and utilities; commercial insurance and product liability, in particular complex claims, coverage and indemnity, with a heavy insurance-based practice.
Professional Memberships: COMBAR, PNBA and Tecbar.
Career: Recent cases include Balls Pond Securities v. Envirocure and others [2016] EWHC 181 (TCC) (fire/causation); The Worshipful Company of Grocers v. Keltbray Group Holdings Ltd. [2016] EWHC 1167 (QB) (collapse/vibrational damage); Cooperative Group Ltd. v. Birse Construction and others [2014] EWHC 530 (TCC) (professional indemnity/ground stability); Wynnstay v Heygate (product liability/animal feed stuffs); Ali and others v Oakfield Developments (Yorkshire) Ltd (catastrophic slope failure); Crossley and others v Roch Valley Developments (catastrophic slope failure); Gemini Riteway v Lonsdale and others (broker's negligence/policy coverage in primary and excess layer insurance).
Personal: MA (Oxon). Mountaineering with notable first ascents in the wider ranges.

GREEN, Michael QC
Fountain Court Chambers, London
020 7583 3335
mg@fountaincourt.co.uk
Featured in Company (London), Tax (London)

Practice Areas: Principal areas of work are company, insolvency, civil fraud, financial services and tax including large scale commercial actions. With a background in commercial chancery chambers and many years on the Treasury A Panel before taking silk, Michael has extensive trial experience with a strong reputation for advocacy (both written and oral) and factual and expert cross examination. He also has substantial expertise in arguing complex legal issues in the appellate courts. Recently Michael has established a significant international practice: he has successfully fought two trials in the Cayman Islands, one of which lasted 2 months concerning issues of Cayman, Samoan and Taiwanese company law; he is instructed in two high profile company/insolvency matters in Trinidad; and he has been admitted to the Ugandan bar and appeared there on a huge international tax case involving an oil company. In the UK, Michael successfully defended the directors in the Farepak disqualification case; took Paycheck Services to the Supreme Court for HMRC and it is now the lead authority on de facto directorship; conducted a number of cases for the FSA including Winterflood (in CA), Betton and judicial review case of Willford; acted for HMRC in huge transfer pricing litigation – Dixons (first to be tried) and AstraZeneca; and for the court-appointed receiver in the infamous Masri litigation which included an international arbitration.
Professional Memberships: COMBAR, Chancery Bar Association, Revenue Bar Association. Chairman of International Sub-Committee of the Chancery Bar Association.
Career: Called 1987. Appointed Junior Counsel to the Crown (A Panel) in 1997 and a DTI Inspector in 1997. Silk 2009.

GREEN, Patrick QC
Henderson Chambers, London
020 7583 9020
PGreen@hendersonchambers.co.uk
Featured in Employment (London)
Practice Areas: Employment, Commercial, Economic Torts and Judicial Review. Recent leading employment cases include Shanks v Unilever (CA – employee patent compensation); Autoclenz v Belcher (SC – employee status); and Hospital Medical Group v Westwood (CA – worker status). Cases in the public eye include: Katharine Birbalsingh v St Michael and All Angels Academy (Teacher speaking at party conference); Dr Aisha Bijlani v Stewart & Others (barrister alleging discrimination); ABC News International Inc v Gizbert (journalist refusing work in war zones), and Pinnington v Governing Body of Ysgol Crug Glas (school nurse whistleblowing). Other leading employment cases include Jackson v Computershare (CA – TUPE); Lambe v 186K Ltd (redundancy and duty to decide issues) and Barke v SEETEC (lawfulness of providing additional reasons).
Professional Memberships: Middle Temple, ALBA, COMBAR, London Common Law and Commercial Bar Association, Bar European Group and Employment Law Bar Association.
Career: Magdalene College Cambridge 1989. Call 1990. CEDR Accredited Mediator 1997. Visiting Fellow at the LSE 2005. Treasurer of the IBA Mediation Committee 2012. Silk 2012.

GREEN, Robin
Cornerstone Barristers, London
020 7242 4986
clerks@cornerstonebarristers.com
Featured in Planning (London)
Practice Areas: Planning⊠ local government law⊠ public and administrative law⊠ property⊠ highways.
Professional Memberships: ALBA; PEBA.
Career: Called 1992.
Publications: Contributor to "Cornerstone on the Planning Court" and "Cornerstone on Councillors' Conduct". Principal contributor to the Housing title in the 'Encyclopaedia of Forms and Precedents', Volume 18. Author of articles on local government land transactions, publicity and local government finance for Westlaw Insight. Contributor to 'Licensed Premises: Law, Practice and Policy', 2nd ed, chapter 31 (Planning and other strategies).
Personal: LLB (London).

GREENHALGH, Jane
23 Essex Street, Manchester
0161 870 9969
clerks@23es.com
Featured in Crime (Northern)
Practice Areas: Jane is known as an experienced and highly competent junior with an extensive practice, instructed both by the Prosecution and Defence. She is instructed in most of the leading, heavyweight cases on circuit, and since joining 23 Essex Street, has established an excellent reputation in both London and the South. Jane has now branched out into privately funded work. In recent years she has been involved in long running, notable and complex cases with an excellent reputation in white-collar crime and fraud. This year Jane prosecuted seven defendants in a long-running, very serious case at Preston Crown Court, involving an armed robbery of firearms by an organised crime group. In the last year, Jane has successfully defended in the highly publicised Jimmy Mubenga manslaughter case at the Central Criminal Court. She has recently defended in an organised crime group international money laundering case and now routinely advises and represents clients in regulatory matters. Previously a solicitor and partner at a North West firm, she was called to the Bar in 2004 and has since been instructed in cases across the country including murder, sexual offences, drug importation, MTIC fraud and regulatory matters. She has developed an expanding practice in Inquest work and Regulatory matters.
Professional Memberships: Criminal Bar Association, Justice Association of Women Barristers.Appointments: CPS Grade 3 Rape Panel
Personal: Qualifications; BA (Hons) Politics, Common Professional Examination Legal Practice Course

GREENWOOD, Paul
4 Stone Buildings, London
020 7242 5524
pgreenwood@4stonebuildings.com
Featured in Chancery (London), Company (London)
Practice Areas: All aspects of commercial litigation, corporate and personal insolvency, company law, professional negligence and banking. Leading cases include: OBG v Allan [2007] UKHL 21 (leading case on economic tort and conversion); Bear Stearns v Forum Global [2007] EWHC 1576 (oral contract between traders, assessment of damages); Weston v Dayman [2006] EWCA 1165 (discharge of receiver); Thomson v Christie Manson & Woods Limited and Others [2004] EWHC 1101 (QB) (duties of auctioneer); T-Mobile (UK) v (1) Bluebottle Investments SA (2) Bluebottle UK Limited (3) Virgin Mobile Telecoms Limited [2003] EWHC 379 (shareholder dispute concerning Virgin Mobile Telecoms Limited); Inland Revenue Commissioners v Wimbledon Football Club Ltd: [2004] EWCA Civ 655 (whether the Club's CVA proposal infringed the Insolvency Act 1986 s.4(4)(a)); Re New Millennium Experience Co Limited [2003] EWHC 1823 (Ch) (concerning the liquidation of NMEC, which operated the Millennium Dome in Greenwich); Re RBG Resources plc [2002] EWCA Civ 1624 (the operation of section 236 of the Insolvency Act 1986); Giles v Rhind: [2002] EWCA Civ 1428 (whether to strike out claim as barred by decision of H/L in Johnson v Gore Wood); Holmes v Official Receiver [1996] BPIR 279 (public examinations under the Insolvency Act 1986).
Professional Memberships: Commercial Bar Association, Chancery Bar Association; Insolvency Lawyers Association.
Career: Lord Denning Scholar of Lincoln's Inn. Called Lincoln's Inn 1991. Joined 4 Stone Buildings in October 1992. Junior Counsel to the Crown: B Panel (July 1999).
Publications: Contributor to 'Butterworths Practical Insolvency'; 'Atkins Court Forms': Volumes 9 and 10, Companies and Corporate Insolvency (Butterworths); Butterworths' Encyclopaedia of Forms and Precedents' Volume 11: Companies. Contributor to OUP Annotated Companies Act 2006.
Personal: Educated at Culford School, Suffolk and Jesus College, Oxford (BA Jurisprudence and BCL (Distinction)). Between 1989 and 1990 appointed to a Lectureship at Jesus College, and taught the Law of Contract and Tort and also Administrative and Criminal Law.

GRIFFIN, Nicholas QC
QEB Hollis Whiteman, London
020 7933 8855
ng@qebhw.co.uk
Featured in Inquests & Public Inquiries (All Circuits)
Practice Areas: Nicholas Griffin provides expert advice and advocacy in respect of public inquiries of all types and in relation to other inquisitorial proceedings, including coroners' inquests. He conducts internal investigations for institutions concerned about irregular activity and advises in relation to bribery, corruption and compliance matters. He is currently instructed in two major public inquiries and has recently acted as independent expert witness in relation to a third. His background is in crime and business crime; he defended in the phone hacking trial (R v Brooks, Coulson & Others) and he advises on specialist aspects of criminal cases such as matters arising from the operation of the Regulation of Investigatory Powers Act 2000.
Professional Memberships: Public Access Bar Association. Approved by Bar Council to undertake public access work.
Career: Silk 2012. Called to the Bar 1992 (2011 in Northern Ireland). Appointed as junior to both CPS Advocate Panel (crime) and AG Panel (civil).
Publications: Fraud: Law, Practice and Procedure, regular articles in legal publications

GRIFFITHS, Ben
Erskine Chambers, London
020 72425532
bgriffiths@erskinechambers.com
Featured in Company (London), Restructuring/Insolvency (London)
Practice Areas: Ben is a commercial and financial law specialist. His expertise spans both advisory work and litigation in the fields of company law, corporate restructuring and insolvency, banking, financial services, LLP law, professional negligence and civil fraud. He has particular experience of complex, multi-jurisdictional commercial and financial litigation and arbitration, including jurisdictional disputes and applications for interim remedies (including search and freezing orders). Ben is regularly instructed to act both as sole counsel and with a leader. He has appeared in all courts from the High Court (Chancery Division, Commercial Court and Companies Court) through to the Supreme Court and the Privy Council. Recent significant cases include Mezhprombank v Pugachev, BAT Industries v Windward, Carlyle Capital Corporation v Conway, MF Global and Kaupthing.
Professional Memberships: Chancery Bar Association, COMBAR, ILA.
Career: Downing College, Cambridge. Called Lincoln's Inn 2004
Publications: Buckley on the Companies Acts

GROGAN, Rose
39 Essex Chambers, London
020 7832 1111
rose.grogan@39essex.com
Featured in Planning (London)
Practice Areas: Rose Grogan practises in the fields of planning, environmental and administrative and public law. Her planning clients include developers, central and local government and she has developed particular expertise representing universities including the University of Sheffield and the University of Sussex. Rose is a member of the Attorney General's C Panel of Counsel.
Professional Memberships: Planning and Environmental Bar Association United Kingdom Environmental Law Association Society of Construction Lawyers
Career: Rose completed pupillage at 39 Essex Chambers in 2011. Since then she has developed a broad practice and has been involved in a number of high profile cases in planning, environmental and public and regulatory law. In 2014 she was named as highly recommended in Legal Week's "stars at the bar" feature of young lawyers under 10 years call. She has consistently ranked as one of Planning Magazine's top 35 planning juniors under 35. Recent high profile work includes acting for the Mayor of London in the Clientearth No2 judicial review on air quality.

GROUND, Richard QC
Cornerstone Barristers, London
020 7421 1837
richardg@cornerstonebarristers.com
Featured in Planning (London)
Practice Areas: Specialises in planning, compulsory purchase, local government, town and village greens, judicial review and environment. He has extensive experience in particular in major planning inquiries, village green inquiries and high court challenges. He was consistently voted one of the top 3 rated planning juniors in Planning. He

has worked recently for Berwin Leighton Paisner, Herbert Smith Freehills, Legal & General, Dentons and numerous Councils.
Professional Memberships: On committee of Planning and Environment Bar Association. Member of NIPA and Compulsory Purchase Association.
Career: Called 1994. MA(Cantab). QC 2016
Publications: Significant contributor to Burnett-Hall on Environmental Law (3rd Edition).
Personal: Married with two children living in London.

GRUDER, Jeffrey QC
Essex Court Chambers, London
020 7813 8000
jgruder@essexcourt.com
Featured in International Arbitration (London), Banking & Finance (London), Commercial Dispute Resolution (London), International Arbitration (London), Shipping (London)
Practice Areas: Jeffrey Gruder QC is widely recognised a leading silk at the Commercial Bar. Particularly skilled in handling complex legal cases, Jeffrey's is involved in heavy commercial litigation and arbitration and has particular experience in the fields of Fraud and Asset Tracing, Banking Litigation (with expertise in securities and derivatives), Insurance and Shipping. He is noted for having "an extraordinary knowledge of the law". He has wide array of experience in international litigation and arbitration. Jeffrey has appeared in over 150 reported cases and numerous international arbitrations both in London and worldwide. He is appointed as Chairman and arbitrator in a number of important arbitrations in the UK and internationally under LCIA, ICC, UNCITRAL, Swiss Chamber, SIAC and LMAA Rules. Very recently, Jeffrey has appeared in an ICC arbitration concerning the assessment of damages for the termination of a contract to distribute medical equipment in Saudi Arabia, a claim by a Fortune 500 company under the Bermuda form against an excess insurer and has sat as a member of an arbitration tribunal in Geneva in relation to a claim for commission arising from the provision of banking and advisory services in the MENA area.

GRUNWALD, Henry QC
Charter Chambers, London
020 7618 4400
clerks@charterchambers.com
Featured in Crime (London)
Practice Areas: All areas of criminal law.
Professional Memberships: Criminal Bar Association; South Eastern Circuit.
Career: 1972 call, Gray's Inn; Bencher, Gray's Inn; QC 1999. Known for his unflappability in court, Henry Grunwald is one of the most experienced criminal Silks in practice. He has defended in many high profile criminal cases at the Old Bailey and nationally, including: 1) the "witchcraft" murder of a young boy and the assault and torture of his siblings, 2) the honour killing of his daughter by a member of the Kurdish community, 3) one of the largest ever drug importations leading to one of the longest ever trials and 4) several large-scale fraud trials. This last year has seen him defending in a massive fraud on BT, three long and difficult murders and an immigration fraud.
Personal: President, Board of Deputies of British Jews, 2003 to 2009. President Relate, North London. Vice-Chair National Holocaust Memorial Day Trust, 2005-2013. Chairman, National Holocaust Centre, 2012. OBE 2009.

GUEST, Peter
187 Fleet Street, London
07768 861881
peterguest@187fleetstreet.com
Featured in Financial Crime (London)
Practice Areas: High profile and client focused leading practice (exclusively defence) specialising in white-collar crime, money laundering, confiscation and other serious criminal cases, both in the Crown Court and the Court of Appeal. Recent work includes MG (cheating the Revenue), NB (duty fraud), DF (VAT evasion by firm of chartered accountants), NB (money laundering), EM (duty fraud appeal), MO (duty fraud appeal), GG (people trafficking), JG (duty fraud), RL (murder), JN (murder), DJ (contract murder), MN (confiscation), AS (armed robberies), DR (drug dealing police officer), AK (money laundering), AB (multi-kilo heroin dealing), CN (money laundering), DC (MTIC fraud and money laundering), SA (MTIC fraud), PM (duty fraud), BR (duty fraud), AH (money laundering), MN (confiscation appeal), JG (confiscation), MR (duty fraud), KC (professional armed kidnapping), WB (money laundering), S-T (duty fraud), JB (pervert justice), PB (kidnap, blackmail and false imprisonment), GM (confiscation), MD (duty fraud), RP (high-level cocaine dealing), TQ (mortgage fraud), MK (fraud), NM (MTIC fraud), NH (rape), PS (FCA insider dealing prosecution), DL (armed robberies), WY (money laundering), TB (VAT evasion, cannabis supply and money laundering), EJ (tax avoidance, conspiracy to defraud and money laundering), SJ (fraud and money laundering), YS (mortgage fraud), T (money laundering), AS (boiler room), SS (gangmaster) and NR (MTIC fraud). Current work includes KH (duty fraud), RA (mortgage fraud), DS (pension fraud), KD (international money laundering) and KI (mortgage fraud).
Professional Memberships: Criminal Bar Association.
Career: Called 1975. Crown Court Recorder 2000.
Personal: Kingston Grammar School. Durham University. France.

GUNNING, Alexander QC
4 Pump Court, London
020 7842 1164
agunning@4pumpcourt.com
Featured in International Arbitration (London), Commercial Dispute Resolution (London), Energy & Natural Resources (London), Shipping (London)
Practice Areas: Commercial litigation and arbitration. Alex acts in a wide range of high value, complex commercial disputes, but with a particular focus on oil and gas and mining projects. He has considerable experience in shipbuilding and offshore construction disputes, insurance and re-insurance disputes as well as commercial fraud and professional negligence.
Professional Memberships: COMBAR, IPBA, LCLCBA. Called to the Bar of the British Virgin Islands
Personal: King's College London, LLB (Hons), LLM (Commercial and Corporate Law), called to the Bar 1994, Queen's Counsel 2012

GUPTA, Amit
St Philips Chambers, Birmingham
0121 246 7000
agupta@st-philips.com
Featured in Commercial Dispute Resolution (Midlands)
Practice Areas: Amit has a strong commercial and chancery practice, with a wealth of experience and particular expertise when there is an insolvency aspect, breach of contract or breach of directors' duties. He is instructed in sizeable claims in the High Court for advisory work, emergency injunctions, interim applications and trials. He frequently represents insolvency practitioners, directors and finance houses, and has represented well known clients such as the ex-wife of an England international footballer, a member of a popular 1990s boyband and a hypnotist. He has been appointed to the government panel of barristers. He has a flourishing career and has appeared in several reported cases including Re Fivestar Properties [2015] EWHC 2782 (leading case on escheat) and Re Oak Property Partners [2016] EWHC 1525 (exercise of judicial discretion in administration applications). Whilst always offering sound legal advice he also provides pragmatic, commercial and strategic views tailored to each case.
Professional Memberships: Midlands Commercial and Chancery Bar Association.
Career: Read law at UCL. Called to the bar in 2006. Junior Council to the Crown (Midlands Panel).
Publications: Contributor to Corporate Rescue and Insolvency (Lexis Nexis) and Insolvency Intelligence (Thomson Reuters).
Personal: Enjoys snowboarding, football, squash and theatre.

GUTTERIDGE, Chris
Exchange Chambers, Manchester
0845 300 7747
gutteridge@exchangechambers.co.uk
Featured in Personal Injury (Northern)
Practice Areas: Chris acts exclusively for claimants in personal injury and clinical negligence litigation. He deals with serious injuries and high value claims. He has vast experience of supporting leading counsel representing claimants with catastrophic injuries and has particular expertise in settling multi-million pound schedules of loss.
Professional Memberships: Personal Injury Bar Association, UK Acquired Brain Injury Forum
Career: Chris took tenancy at Exchange Chambers in 2006 and soon became involved in catastrophic injury cases as second junior responsible for drafting schedules of loss (including a claim for a brain injured child that settled for £5.2 million in 2009). Since 2011 Chris has regularly been instructed in a more advanced role as junior to Queen's Counsel and has represented adult and infant claimants with life changing injuries. Chris has experience of claims involving traumatic brain injuries (including those leaving claimants in a minimally conscious state), spine injuries and amputation. He also has experience of cerebral palsy claims arising from the negligent management of labour.
Personal: Chris grew up in Salford and read Law at the University of Durham, graduating with a first class honours degree before studying at Nottingham Law School. He is a father of two, a football fan and enjoys CrossFit training.

HACKER, Richard QC
South Square, London
020 7696 9900
richardhacker@southsquare.com
Featured in Offshore (London)
Practice Areas: Richard has a mixed litigation/advisory commercial law practice including contentious and non-contentious insolvency work, banking law, professional negligence, asset tracing and general commercial litigation. His clients have included the major international accountancy firms, major UK banks and a variety of overseas banks and governments. Richard has been heavily involved in all major collapses of the last 20 years including Laker, Banco Ambrosiano, Mentor Insurance, Maxwell, BCCI, Rafidain, KWELM, NEMGIA and Barings. He has appeared and given expert evidence in a variety of overseas Courts including New York and Bermuda. Recent significant UK trial appearances include the Grupo Torras litigation in which he appeared for the Kuwait Investment Authority.
Career: Called 1977. QC 1998.

HACKETT, Philip QC
New Square Chambers, London
020 7419 8000
philip.hackett@newsquarechambers.co.uk
Featured in Financial Crime (London)
Practice Areas: Philip Hackett specialises in civil and criminal commercial fraud, international corruption, regulatory and disciplinary law, direct and indirect tax and associated areas such as sanctions, mutual legal assistance and asset tracing. Over the past 25 years he has been instructed in many of the leading cases including the most serious SFO and FCA investigations, enquiries and numerous HSE and manslaughter cases. The international aspects of his practice have resulted in experience of offshore matters in connection with Bermuda, the Channel Islands and Isle of Man and many European jurisdictions as well as the US, Caribbean and Africa.
Career: For many years he has been selected as an 'outstanding silk' by legal directories and has acted in many of the leading cases including Maxwell; BCCI; Gooda Walker; Wickes; TransTec; Kent Pharmaceuticals; British Aerospace; Daily Mirror 'City Slickers; Vantis; Torex; MEP expenses; Asil Nadir; V Mobile: Innospec; Celtic Mining and LIBOR.

HAGEN, Dakis
Serle Court, London
020 7242 6105
dhagen@serlecourt.co.uk
Featured in Chancery (London), Offshore (London), Trusts (London)
Practice Areas: General commercial chancery, particularly trusts litigation (international and domestic, commercial and private client), fraud, asset tracing and business disputes. Significant cases include High Commissioner for Pakistan v Nat West, Trustee L v Attorney General (Bermuda), Walker v Egerton-Vernon (Jersey), Tchenguiz v Imerman, and the Alhamrani litigation.
Professional Memberships: Chancery Bar Association; COMBAR.
Career: Called 2002.
Personal: Born: 1978. Educated at Peterhouse, Cambridge University (MA double first) and City University (Dip Law). Interests include history and music.

HALL, Matthew
Kings Chambers, Manchester
0345 034 3444
clerks@kingschambers.com
Featured in Real Estate Litigation (Northern)
Practice Areas: Land law (in particular easements, restrictive covenants, boundaries) Landlord and Tenant (commercial and acting in service charge / management disputes before the First Tier Tribunal (Property Chamber)). Also specialises in the law of succession and claims under the Inheritance (Provision for Family and Dependants) Act 1975. Significant Cases (from Court of Appeal): Ahmad v Secret Garden Cheshire [2013] 3 EGLR 42 (rectification of lease) Bradford v James [2008] EWCA Civ 837 (extrinsic evidence in construction of conveyance) Latimer v Carney [2007] 1 P & CR 213 (correct approach to assessment of damages in dilapidations claims) Tennant v Adamczyk [2006] 1 P & CR 485 (adverse possession)
Professional Memberships: Chancery Bar Association, Northern Chancery Bar Association
Career: Year of call 1998 BA (Oxon) First Class in Law with Law Studies in Europe (French)

HALL TAYLOR, Alex
4 New Square, London
020 7822 2000
a.taylor@4newsquare.com
Featured in Chancery (London), Professional Negligence (London), Financial Services (London), Fraud (London)
Practice Areas: Litigation and dispute resolution in core areas: commercial, professional negligence, chancery, financial, international and civil fraud work. Often acts in claims by or against fiduciaries (trustees, trust companies and administrators, directors, liquidators, receivers) in jurisdictions all around the world. Conducts or defends financial claims involving banking, financial products, pensions, hedge/investment funds, tax and trusts disputes. Shareholder, corporate management and partnership disputes. Professional negligence claims both for claimants and defendants against solicitors, barristers, surveyors, accountants, tax advisers and financial services professionals. Regularly appears in Chancery Division, Commercial Court, London Mercantile Court and assists in tactical conduct of litigation worldwide. Instructed as sole or lead junior counsel against silks. Frequently instructed to seek (and less frequently to oppose) urgent injunctive and other pre-emptive relief, including freezing injunctions, search orders, anti-suit injunctions, Norwich Pharmacal and Bankers Trust orders in the UK and abroad. Significant experience in handling complex, multi-party, document heavy litigation often requiring management of a team of more junior counsel. International work includes disputes from Africa to Fiji, from St Lucia to the Channel Islands, and from the United States, AVI and BVI to Mauritius, the Isle of Man, and St Vincent and the Grenadines. Often brought in to join worldwide teams of litigators in litigation shield, trust defence or attack, family office and other multi-jurisdictional disputes. Recent work involving extra-territorial enforcement action by the SEC and of US judgments in offshore jurisdictions. Has appeared as sole counsel in a number of appeals to the Privy Council. CEDR accredited mediator, mediating most areas of civil litigation but with a particular focus on core areas of practice above.
Professional Memberships: Professional Negligence Bar Association, COMBAR, Chancery Bar Association, London Common Law and Commercial Bar Association, South Eastern Circuit, Governing Bencher of the Inner Temple, CEDR accredited mediator.
Career: Education: Charterhouse School, Bristol University (BA Hons History), College of Law (dipl. Law), Inns of Court School of Law Inn: Inner Temple (Member 1994, Called 1996, Governing Bencher 2012) Chambers: 4 New Square since 2001. Previously at 11 Old Square (now Radcliffe Chambers) 1996-2001. CEDR accredited mediator.
Publications: The "Property, Planning and Environment" chapter of Leigh-Ann Mulcahy's Human Rights and Civil Practice (Sweet and Maxwell, London 2001).
Personal: Born in Sweden, early childhood spent in Singapore and Malaysia. Lives in London. Enjoys travel, particularly skiing. Speaks conversational French.

HALLIDAY, Patrick
11KBW, London
020 7632 8500
Patrick.Halliday@11kbw.com
Featured in Employment (London)
Practice Areas: Employment law, procurement law, public law.
Professional Memberships: ELBA; ELA; ALBA; PLA; UKSALA.
Career: Called 2005, Gray's Inn. Former pupil to Sales LJ. Attorney General's B Panel of Counsel. Recent cases: Asda Stores Ltd v Brierley [2016] EWCA Civ 566 (mass equal pay claims in private sector, appropriate forum); Shrestha v Genesis Housing Association Ltd [2015] EWCA Civ 94, [2015] IRLR 399 (guidance on investigating employee's misconduct); LS Systems v Scott [2015] EWHC 1335 (Ch) (directors' breach of fiduciary duties, misappropriation, proprietary relief); Stokes v Oxfordshire CC [2014] Pens. L.R. 631 (firefighter pensions, pensionable earnings); R (Clulow) v Secretary of State for Work and Pensions [2013] EWHC 3241 (Admin) (community care grants and Article 14 ECHR); Emmanuel v City & Hackney Teaching Primary Care Trust [2011] EqLR 1291 (equal pay, national test case on nurses, GMF 'market forces' defence made out); Baha Mousa Public Inquiry (2008 – 2011); R (Hurst) v London North District Coroner [2007] UKHL 13 (article 2 ECHR and coroners' inquests).
Publications: Tolley's Employment Handbook (annually since 2007, EU law). Joint editor of 11KBW's Procurement Law Newsletter.
Personal: Pembroke College, Cambridge (first class degree in Social and Political Sciences, Foundation Scholar); City University (CPE, Distinction).

HALLIN, Conrad
Serjeants' Inn Chambers, London
020 7427 5000
challin@serjeantsinn.com
Featured in Court of Protection (All Circuits)
Practice Areas: Conrad Hallin was called to the Bar in 2004. Conrad specialises in all aspects of healthcare law and has a prominent clinical negligence and medical ethics practice. He regularly appears in the Court of Protection and High Court (Family Division) in high profile medical treatment and welfare cases. Please visit the Serjeants' Inn Chambers website for his profile, which sets out full details of his practice including relevant work of note.

HALLISSEY, Caroline
Serjeants' Inn Chambers, London
020 7427 5000
challissey@serjeantsinn.com
Featured in Clinical Negligence (London)
Practice Areas: Caroline Hallissey was called to the Bar in 1990. Caroline specialises in clinical negligence and healthcare law. An earlier edition notes that "she develops a real rapport with the clients but can still be very straightforward and businesslike, which is a difficult balance to achieve." Please visit the Serjeants' Inn Chambers website for her profile, which sets out full details of her practice including relevant work of note.
Professional Memberships: AVMA, APIL

HALLIWELL, Mark
Kings Chambers, Manchester
0345 034 3444
clerks@kingschambers.com
Featured in Chancery (Northern), Commercial Dispute Resolution (Northern), Real Estate Litigation (Northern)
Practice Areas: General chancery and commercial law including contentious and non-contentious real property, landlord and tenant, rights of way, corporate and individual insolvency, charities, trusts, probate and the administration of estates, commercial arbitration and professional negligence.
Professional Memberships: Chancery Bar Association, Northern Chancery Bar Association, Northern Circuit Commercial Bar Association.
Career: University: London School of Economics, degree: BSc (Econ), Called:1985 (Lincoln's Inn) Hardwicke scholar, Recorder 2003, Treasury Counsel (charities).
Publications: Distribution on Intestacy (FT Law and Tax).

HALPERN, David QC
4 New Square, London
020 7822 2126
d.halpern@4newsquare.com
Featured in Professional Negligence (London), Real Estate Litigation (London)
Practice Areas: Professional negligence and commercial Chancery litigation.
Professional Memberships: Chancery Bar Association (former chairman of the International Subcommittee), COMBAR, Property Bar Association and Professional Negligence Bar Association.
Career: Since taking silk in 2006, David has continued to focus on his core areas of professional negligence and commercial Chancery work. He particularly relishes the challenge of acting for or against professionals in areas which call on his expertise in the underlying issues of property, company law, insolvency and accounts. He has wide experience of both litigation and mediation, as well as advisory work. He sits as a deputy judge of the Chancery Division and a Recorder, is a Bencher of Gray's Inn and an advocacy trainer for the Inn and has chaired disciplinary tribunals for the Bar Standards Board. He has been called to the Bar of Gibraltar.
Publications: Contributor to Jackson and Powell on Professional Liability (he edits the chapters on Auditors and Actuaries).

HAMER, Kenneth
Henderson Chambers, London
020 7842 9136
khamer@hendersonchambers.co.uk
Featured in Professional Discipline (London)
Practice Areas: Kenneth has substantial and wide ranging experience in professional conduct and competance matters. He regularly represents solicitors involved in disciplinary and regulatory cases. He has expertise in health care, legal, accountancy and financial aspects of professional discipline. He frequently lectures on fitness to practise issues. Copies of recent talks and other information about Kenneth are available on www.hendersonchambers.co.uk.
Career: Recorder of the Crown Court since 2000. He is a member of the prosecuting panel of the Bar Standards Board, a Legal Assessor for the General Medical Council, the Nursing & Midwifery Council and the General Dental Council. He is a former chairman of the Appeal Committee for the Chartered Institute of Management Accountants. In 2008 he spent six months advising the Financial Services Authority on various matters.
Publications: He is co-editor of the Assocation of Regulatory and Disciplinary Lawyers' newsletter. He is author of Professional Conduct Casebook published by Oxford University Press March 2013 and 2nd edition published June 2015.

HAMILL, Hugh
12 King's Bench Walk, London
020 7583 0811
hamill@12kbw.co.uk
Featured in Personal Injury (London)
Practice Areas: Personal injury, clinical negligence, industrial disease, consumer credit and health and safety. Recognised as a 'Leading Junior' in Personal Injury in Chambers Directory and the Legal 500. Hugh has an established practice acting predominantly for defendants but also for claimants in catastrophic injury claims. Areas of expertise include public/employers liability, catastrophic injury, brain and spinal injury, road traffic – fatal accident and serious injury claims including claims involving the Motor Insurance Bureau. Mental capacity – litigation capacity – Hugh successfully represented the defendants in Masterman-Lister the leading case in this area and is instructed in cases arising out of this decision. Fibromyalgia-chronic fatigue syndrome and cases of disputed causation. Defending health and safety prosecutions, insurance fraud/staged accidents/malingering. The last year was an excellent year for Hugh and has seen him continuing to represent major insurers and public authorities at trials in high-value claims, particularly those involving chronic pain / fibromyalgia / chronic fatigue. Very often in these types of claim, causation is hotly disputed and issues of malingering, fraud and exaggeration arise.
Professional Memberships: PIBA LCLBA.
Personal: Lives in Oxfordshire. Married with two children.

HAMILTON, Penny
Pump Court Tax Chambers, London
020 7414 8080
clerks@pumptax.com
Featured in Tax (London)
Practice Areas: Specialises in advice and litigation (including judicial review and

references to the European Court of Justice) in VAT, landfill tax, aggregates levy, climate change levy, insurance premium tax, excise and customs duties and European law; advises commercial, financial, education & charitable property, housing and local government clients on a wide range of issues; experience in advising and litigating on behalf of traders affected by MTIC fraud. Cases include HMRC v Waste Recycling Group (Court of Appeal); Robinson Family v HMRC (FTT); London Borough of Richmond v Robinson (Kingston Crown Court, expert for the prosecution); Patersons of Greenoakhill v HMRC (FTT); TNT Post UK Ltd (Administrative Court and CJEU). Finmeccanica Group Services (Court of Appeal), Devon Waste Management Ltd (FTT).
Professional Memberships: Fellow, CIOT (President 2002-03); Tax Appeals Stakeholders Group; RBA; VPG; Bar European Group; Bencher of Grays Inn (2010). CEDR Tax Mediation Panel.
Career: 1972: Called to the Bar (Gray's Inn); 1973-1975: Chambers at 12 Old Square, Lincoln's Inn; 1975-1987: Senior legal adviser to HM Customs & Excise; 1987-1989: Deloitte, Haskins and Sells (senior manager, indirect taxes division); 1989-2000: Partner in PricewaterhouseCoopers (and predecessor firms); 2000 onwards: Pump Court Tax Chambers; 2002: President of the Chartered Institute of Taxation; 2003: Voted "VAT Rat of the Year"; 2011: Voted "Best in tax dispute resolution", Euromoney European Women in Business Law Awards; 2012: CEDR accredited mediator.
Publications: Consulting Editor of Halsbury's Laws of England (VAT and Landfill Tax); Author of Hamilton on Tax Appeals (Bloomsbury 2010, and second edition October 2016).

HAND, Jonathan
Outer Temple Chambers, London
020 7353 6381
jonathan.hand@outertemple.com
Featured in Personal Injury (London), Clinical Negligence (London)
Practice Areas: Jonathan specialises in Clinical Negligence and Personal Injury work. He has wide-ranging experience across both these fields, and acts for a mix of Claimant and Defendant clients. Much of his work involves catastrophic brain and spinal injuries as well as fatal accident claims. In the Clinical Negligence field, he is frequently instructed in cases involving complex liability issues and high value quantum, including claims arising from birth injury resulting in cerebral palsy and from other neurological injury. He has extensive experience of multi-party litigation, having acted in the claims arising out of the misdiagnosis and mistreatment of epilepsy at Leicester Royal Infirmary during the 1990s. He was closely involved in the successful ADR process devised to manage the several hundred claims which were brought. He has a particular specialism in equine and other animal related litigation, including claims under the Animals Act 1971, where his expertise in this area can bring a real benefit. He is the author of the Liability for Animals section in the Westlaw Insight service and is a legally qualified chair for British Equestrian Federation panels. Other aspects of his practice include representation at Inquests and Professional Negligence claims arising out of the conduct of personal injury and clinical negligence litigation.
Professional Memberships: PNBA, PIBA, APIL, AvMA, Western Circuit
Career: Call 1990 (Inner Temple)
Personal: BA (Law) Christ Church, Oxford

HANDYSIDE, Richard QC
Fountain Court Chambers, London
020 7583 3335
rnh@fountaincourt.co.uk
Featured in Banking & Finance (London), Commercial Dispute Resolution (London)
Practice Areas: Commercial litigation, including banking and financial services, professional negligence, civil fraud, competition law, conflicts of laws, insurance, restitution and arbitration. Current / recent cases include Property Alliance Group v RBS (Libor / alleged mis-selling of swaps); Deutsche Bank v Petromena (jurisdiction under the Lugano Convention); Decura v UBS (interpretation and application of a material adverse change clause); Deutsche Bank v Unitech (Libor / Art 101 TFEU / interim payments); Spliethoff's v Bank of China (performance bond; recognition of a foreign judgment obtained in breach of an arbitral anti-suit injunction); McGraw-Hill International v Deutsche Apotheker (alleged mis-selling and mis-rating of CPDOs); Dexia v Prato (interest rate swap; Italian public authority); Bull v Gain Capital (financial services; restitution).
Professional Memberships: COMBAR.
Career: Called 1993. QC 2009.
Personal: Born 1968. Bristol University (LLB Hons 1st Class) and Brasenose College, Oxford (BCL 1st Class).

HANIF, Saima
39 Essex Chambers, London
020 7832 1111
Saima.Hanif@39essex.com
Featured in Financial Services (London), Professional Discipline (London)
Practice Areas: Saima has a commercial regulatory practice with a particular expertise in financial services, covering contentious and non-contentious matters. She has represented clients at all levels, from internal committees such as the RDC (and the DMC in Dubai), right through to the High Court and Court of Appeal. Matters she is currently instructed on include: acting for a high net worth individual in respect of an IRHP mis-selling claim, representing a client in an FCA investigation concerning the operation of SIPPs and acting for a Thai-based resident in commercial court proceedings. In the past she has acted for a major FS institution in the FCA's investigation of Forex manipulation, a leading payday lender seeking FCA authorisation and a corporate client seeking to judicially review a s166 FSMA appointment. She appears regularly in the Upper Tribunal (cases include Karan v FSA & UBS [2012], Khan v FCA [2014], Roberts v FCA [2015]). She also acts in cross-border matters and has represented clients in Dubai (Al-Ansari v DFSA, 2015), the Isle of Man and Guernsey. She has strong experience in financial services litigation and judicial review challenges of FS decisions. She represented the claimant in one of the few successful judicial reviews of the regulator (Ford v FSA [2012]), and recently acted for the claimant in the landmark judicial review of a FOS decision (Chancery v FOS [2015]).
Professional Memberships: Member of the FMLC's Advisory Group on the UK's decision to secede from the EU.
Career: Tenant, 39 Essex. Secondments: FSA (Enforcement); Financial Regulatory Department, Clifford Chance; Financial Markets Law Committee, Bank of England; FCA (General Counsel's Division).
Publications: Atkins Volume on Financial Services; Butterworths Financial Regulation Service; Prospectuses and Public Issues (Tolleys); Tribunal Practice (Jordans); Disciplinary & Regulatory Proceedings (Jordans).
Personal: Oxford University: BA (Jurisprudence)

HANNA, Ronan
Atkin Chambers, London
020 7404 0102
rhanna@atkinchambers.com
Featured in Professional Negligence (London), Construction (London), Energy & Natural Resources (London)
Practice Areas: Rónán specialises in construction, engineering, energy and natural resources, professional negligence and IT matters with experience of litigation, arbitration and other forms of dispute resolution. Represents developers, employers, professionals, contractors, sub-contractors, funders and insurers. Experience in engineering and energy disputes has included offshore renewables, oil / gas pipelines, combined power and desalination plants, railways, roads and stadiums. Rónán regularly acts in professional negligence disputes involving architects, engineers, quantity surveyors and project managers. Recent experience includes representing a contractor in an ICC arbitration concerning a landmark infrastructure development in the Middle East.
Professional Memberships: TECBAR, LCLCBA, COMBAR, SCL.
Career: BA (Oxon); BCL (Oxon). Called 2006 (England and Wales), 2011 (Northern Ireland).

HANNAFORD, Sarah QC
Keating Chambers, London
020 7544 2600
shannaford@keatingchambers.com
Featured in Construction (London), Public Procurement (London)
Practice Areas: Specialist in EU procurement, construction, engineering, energy, PFI and professional negligence. Sarah is widely regarded as a star of the Procurement Bar and is the natural choice for complex high value procurement issues. She is instructed in the most significant cases in this area, regularly advising Government bodies, local authorities, utilities and industry clients. In addition to her high profile procurement work, she is regularly instructed in complex construction and commercial disputes in the UK and internationally. She has experience in the full range of contractual claims which arise out of construction projects, including claims relating to defects, termination, and delay. Sarah also has considerable expertise in disputes relating to party walls and rights of light. In addition to counsel work, Sarah Hannaford is a trained Mediator and accredited Adjudicator.
Professional Memberships: COMBAR; TECBAR; SCL; Procurement Lawyers Association.
Career: Called 1989; Queens Counsel 2008; TECBAR accredited Adjudicator 2004, trained mediator 2006, Called to Northern Ireland Bar 2015.
Publications: Contributor-Keating on Construction Contracts Tenth Edition (2016). Party Walls RICS Books Case in Point Series (2004); Rights to Light – Case in Point Series (2008). Halsbury' s Fuel and Energy Volumes 19(1)-(3).
Personal: Working knowledge of French and Spanish.

HARDING, Richard QC
Keating Chambers, London
020 7544 2600
rharding@keatingchambers.com
Featured in International Arbitration (London)
Practice Areas: Specialist in construction, engineering and energy arbitration relating to projects in the Middle East, representing contractors, employers and professionals in disputes under English and Middle Eastern laws (UAE, Egypt, Qatar, Kuwait, Jordan). Acted in matters relating to oil and gas, rail, commercial and residential premises, airports, roads, bridges, tunnels, dredging, marine structures, process engineering, power generation, mining and a theme park. Acted as leading counsel or arbitrator in numerous very substantial international disputes. In the UK, appears before the Technology and Construction Court.
Professional Memberships: Technology and Construction Bar Association (TECBAR); Commercial Bar Association (COMBAR); Society of Construction Law (UK); founder Chairman of Society of Construction Law (Gulf); Law Society Panel of Arbitrators; LCIA list of arbitrators; Tehran Regional Arbitration Centre list of arbitrators.
Career: Called 1992; Queens Counsel 2009.
Publications: Contributor – Keating on Construction Contracts Ninth Edition. Lectures on arbitration law and construction contracts to professional audiences in the UK and Middle East.
Personal: Languages: Arabic, German, Spanish, French, Persian.

HARDY, Amanda QC
Old Square Tax Chambers, London
020 7242 2744
amandahardy@15oldsquare.co.uk
Featured in Tax (London)
Practice Areas: Amanda's practice falls broadly into two areas. Firstly, she has a busy litigation practice, having appeared, during her career to date, three times in the House of Lords, eight times in the Court of Appeal, once in the European Court of Justice and twice in the Privy Council as well as a number of appearances before the High Court and First and Upper Tier Tribunal (and the former Special Commissioners), she has recently been involved in litigation in most areas of direct and indirect tax, including most recently significant Judicial Review proceedings against HMRC and three applications to undertake the variation of substantial trusts, capital gains tax, charities tax, income tax (including the impact of European law on the taxation of foreign dividends), the nature of the source of interest and the tax aspects of divorce. She has also appeared in the Ugandan Tax Tribunal in a major oil tax dispute and in the First-tier Tribunal on the correct test for the source of interest, also successfully arguing that HMRC were not entitled to refer to unpublished special commissioners decisions. Secondly, Amanda's practice continues to involve a substantial amount of advice, plan-

ning and structuring work for individuals, corporations, charities and particularly trusts including offshore domicile and residency issues, pension taxation issues and corporate reconstruction.
Professional Memberships: Revenue Bar Association, Chancery Bar Association (elected to the Chancery Bar Association Committee on 11 July 2012 and Chair of the Chancery Bar Association Pro Bono Sub Committee, elected Hon. Sec on 11 July 2016), Member of the UK Step Technical Committee and the Worshipful Company of Tax Advisors, Liveryman of the City of London.
Career: Called to the Bar 1993, QC 2015
Publications: Author of the International Guide to the Taxation of Trusts: United Kingdom, Author of Pensions Taxation (Forthcoming), Co-Author of Venables on Inheritance Tax Planning (3rd Edition) with Robert Venables Q.C
Personal: Lives in Chelmsford with her husband and three daughters.

HARDY, John QC
3 Raymond Buildings Barristers, London
020 7400 6400
clerks@3rblaw.com
Featured in Crime (London), Extradition (London)
Practice Areas: Extradition, human rights, mutual legal assistance. Regularly appears in Supreme Court and House of Lords, frequent appearances in Divisional and Administrative Courts representing both foreign governments and defendants in extradition proceedings, as well as prosecuting authorities and defendants in domestic Judicial Reviews and cases stated. Also practises in serious crime, appearing for both prosecution and defence in murder, torture, money-laundering, professional and disciplinary tribunals, licensing. Recently represented a barrister at the CCC accused of VAT fraud. Also travels extensively to lecture and teach. Has recently made presentations in Madrid and Macao, and regularly adjudicates at "Themis" competition for the EJTN. Is a visiting faculty-member at the ENM in Bordeaux each year.
Professional Memberships: Criminal Bar Association.
Career: Called 1988. Recorder of the Crown Courts 2002. QC 2008. Appointed to the SFO Prosecution list 2013.
Personal: BA (Hons) Magdalen College Oxford. Diploma in Law.

HARDY, Max
9 Bedford Row, London
020 7489 2727
max.hardy@9bedfordrow.co.uk
Featured in Crime (London)
Practice Areas: A specialist criminal and regulatory practitioner Max defends and prosecutes at a high level, he was appointed to the Rape List in 2012 as one of the youngest serious sexual offences prosecutors in England. Out of court Max has refined his skills and knowledge during secondments as a Senior Crown Prosecutor with the Fraud Prosecution Division, as an investigator into Foreign Exchange manipulation with the Financial Conduct Authority and as a case presenter for the Nursing & Midwifery Council. Max has a particularly strong background in cases involving misconduct in a public office and wrongdoing by public officials and is regularly instructed to handle cases involving fraud and other dishonest conduct by police officers. Max was part of Rebekah Brooks' successful defence team. Max collaborates well with professional and lay clients understanding that clients want fast results at a fair price; he does not waste time or money. He is currently instructed to defend a solicitor accused of a significant fraud against clients. Max is an accredited advocacy trainer and pupil supervisor entrusted with educating the next generation of barristers. In 2014 Max was chairman of the Young Bar and continues to serve on the Bar Council.
Professional Memberships: Elected member of Bar Council, CBA Executive, FLA, ARDL
Personal: Italian and Conversational German

HAREN, Sarah
5 Stone Buildings, London
020 7242 6201
clerks@5sblaw.com
Featured in Chancery (London), Court of Protection (All Circuits)
Practice Areas: Practice Areas: Practice encompassing a wide range of Chancery work, both contentious and non-contentious, primarily comprising probate and the administration of estates, claims under the Inheritance Act 1975, trusts and related taxation, professional negligence and disputes over real property and partnerships. Regularly appears in the Court of Protection as well as the High Court and county courts.
Professional Memberships: Chancery Bar Association, ACTAPS.
Career: Wesley College, Dublin; University College, Oxford (1997 BA Hons Jursiprudence and 1999 BCL). Called 1999, Middle Temple.
Publications: Co-author of 5th edition of "Partnership"(Bloomsbury) with Mark Blackett-Ord, 2015.
Personal:

HARGREAVES, Simon QC
Keating Chambers, London
020 7544 2600
shargreaves@keatingchambers.co.uk
Featured in Professional Negligence (London), Construction (London)
Practice Areas: Specialising in construction, engineering, IT systems, transport, energy contracts and fires, including considerable experience of industry related professional negligence claims. Specialises in all forums including litigation, arbitration, adjudication and ADR as well as relief concerning pre-action disclosure, summary judgment, interim payment, strike out, security for costs, arbitration applications, injunctions and bond applications. Has considerable experience of heavy domestic and international cases being recently involved in claims arising from: the Magna Park fire; the London Underground transmission and radio upgrade project; a claim concerning turbine design for a nuclear power station; the Chancery Lane derailment; the Gerrard's Cross tunnel collapse; claims arising on Wembley Stadium and an ICC arbitration concerning a desalination plant in the Middle East.
Professional Memberships: Technology and Construction Bar Association (TECBAR); Professional Negligence Bar Association (PNBA); Commercial Bar Association (COMBAR) Society of Construction Law (SCL); Society for Computers and Law (SCL).
Career: Called 1991; Queens Counsel 2009; TECBAR Accredited Adjudicator, arbitrator, Dispute Resolution Board Member.
Publications: Assistant Editor, Construction Law Yearbook 1994, 1995 and 1996; Editorial team, Keating on Building Contracts 7th edition 2001; Has presented seminars to TECBAR, TeCSA, Chartered Institute of Arbitrators, firms of solicitors, developers and contractors.

HARPER, Mark QC
Kings Chambers, Manchester
0345 0343444
clerks@kingschambers.com
Featured in Chancery (Northern), Professional Negligence (Northern), Banking & Finance (Northern), Commercial Dispute Resolution (Northern), Partnership (Northern)
Practice Areas: Commercial and Corporate Litigation including shareholder disputes, warranty claims, confidential information, restraint of trade, agency and sports related disputes. Partnership. Sports Law, Banking and Finance Litigation and Professional Negligence (solicitors, accountants and financial advisers).
Professional Memberships: Northern Chancery Bar Association; Northern Circuit Commercial Bar Association.
Career: Silk appointment in 2016, Call 1993; Pupillage at Kings Chambers.

HARPUM, Charles
Falcon Chambers, London
020 7353 2484
harpum@falcon-chambers.com
Featured in Real Estate Litigation (London)
Practice Areas: 1. Land law in general but with particular reference to the following: (a) Conveyancing; (b) Land Registration; (c) Adverse possession; (d) Easements, profits, and covenants; (e) Commons, town and village greens; (f) Manorial rights; (g) Mines and minerals. 2. Issues concerning underwater land and issues involving water with particular reference to: (a) Mooring rights; (b) Rights of navigation; (c) Fishing rights; (d) Drainage; (e) Riparian rights.
Professional Memberships: (a) Chancery Bar Association; (b) Property Bar Association; (c) London Common Law and Commercial Bar Association.
Career: (a) Called to the Bar by Lincoln's Inn: 1976; (b) Taught law at Cambridge University: 1977 – 1993 (Fellow of Downing College, Cambridge:1977 – 2001; Emeritus Fellow: 2001 to date); (c) Law Commissioner for England and Wales (Head of Property and Trust Law Team): 1994 – 2001; (d) Bencher, Lincoln's Inn: 2001; (e) In practice at Falcon Chambers: 2001 to date; (f) LL.D, Cambridge University: 2003.
Publications: Numerous publications on property law, including many articles. In particular: Editor/author of Megarry & Wade's Law of Property , 6th, 7th and 8th editions, the 7th and 8th editions jointly with Judge Stuart Bridge and Professor Martin Dixon Co-author of Harpum and Bignell's Registered Land (2004) Editor and contributor to The Law and Practice of Charging Orders on Land (2013).
Personal: Main interests: classical music and foreign travel.

HARRIES, Mark
Carmelite Chambers, London
020 7936 6300
clerks@carmelitechambers.co.uk
Featured in Crime (London), Financial Crime (London)
Practice Areas: Criminal defence work in all aspects of major crime as leading counsel nationwide, complemented by regulatory and disciplinary work on behalf of individuals including healthcare professionals, teachers, accountants and lawyers. Substantial experience in white-collar fraud and asset recovery, alongside gangland crime and homicide, both publicly and privately funded. Pre-charge advice available in appropriate cases. Recent instructions include: In Fraud – Operations Evenbox (£300m international tax evasion), Bamburgh (multi-million pound mortgage fraud), Iceman (wine investment fund fraud), Component (car industry extortion), Rosewood (mobile telephone contract scam) and Skipsea (crash for cash). In Crime – Operations Elveden (misconduct in public office), Hayrack (corruption within Royal Household), Aline (gangland armed robbery/murder), Polarite (East Midlands drug cartel) and the Tilbury Docks people smuggling trials.
Professional Memberships: University of London (LLB(Hons) 1994), Lincoln's Inn (Call 1995), CBA, POCLA, ARDL, Liberty. Lead Advocacy Trainer and Pupil Supervisor.

HARRINGTON, Patrick QC
Farrar's Building, London
07970 293112
p.j.harrington@btinternet.com
Featured in Crime (Wales & Chester), Financial Crime (The Regions)
Practice Areas: Crime (General) and Crime (Fraud)
Career: Patrick Harrington is a leading silk in the fields of Crime (General) and Crime Fraud. He was called (Gray's) in Trinity Term 1973 and took silk in 1993. He practised in Cardiff as a junior and moved to Farrar's Building in 1994. He was appointed an Assistant Recorder in 1985 and a Recorder in 1991. He was elected Leader of the Wales and Chester Circuit in 2000, serving until 2003. He was appointed a Bencher of Gray's Inn in 2001. His practises throughout the UK and, occasionally, as far afield as Brunei and the Turks an Caicos Islands. His practice divides equally between prosecution and defence. He has appeared in over 200 homicide cases. He is currently instructed in a number of major fraud cases. He was leading counsel for the first defendant in R v Evans [2014] 1 WLR 2817 (first instance) and [2014] EWHC 3803 QBD (unsuccessful SFO application for a Voluntary Bill of Indictment).
Publications: A Nutshell on Evidence (1974); The Session Man (2004)
Personal: Married to Susan; two children. Lives in Raglan, Monmouthshire

HARRIS, Lucinda
Devereux, London
020 7353 7534
harris@devchambers.co.uk
Featured in Employment (London)
Practice Areas: Specialises in all areas of employment law, including restrictive covenants and breach of confidence, breach of contract, wrongful and unfair dismissal, whistleblowing, discrimination, TUPE, national minimum wage and working time. She has a wide range of public and private sector

clients, including banks, high street chains, hotels, airlines and charities, as well as governmental departments and agencies. For more information and recent case highlights, please visit www.devereuxchambers.co.uk.
Professional Memberships: ELA, ELBA, ILS, COMBAR, PIBA.
Career: Called, Middle Temple 2004. Appointed to the Attorney General's Panel of Counsel (C Panel) in 2010. Member of the Equality and Human Rights Commission Panel of Approved Counsel since 2011. Judicial Assistant to Mr Justice Aikens (now Lord Justice Aikens) in the Commercial Court (2007-2008).
Publications: Contributing author, "Discrimination Law" (Bloomsbury Professional (formerly Tottel Publishing)); co-author, "Post-Termination Restraints" in "Managing People in a Legal Business" (Law Society).
Personal: LLM, Harvard Law School; MA Hons (First Class), Downing College, Cambridge University.

HARRIS, Luke
5 Stone Buildings, London
020 7242 6201
clerks@5sblaw.com
Featured in Art and Cultural Property Law (London)
Practice Areas: Commercial chancery litigation and advice with a particular emphasis on claims involving chattels and bailment, trusts and estates, restitution and personal property (including the sale of goods). Luke specialises in claims involving art and antiquities and frequently acts for and against states, public bodies, museums, galleries, auction houses and private individuals in claims involving objects of cultural and artistic value. Luke's expertise in the field of personal property includes cases involving heirlooms, equity, trusts and entailed interest under settlements of land.
Professional Memberships: Inner Temple; Chancery Bar Association; COMBAR; PAIAM (Professional Advisors to the International Art Market).
Career: Called to the Bar, 2001; Member of 3 Stone Buildings, 2003.
Publications: Book contributions include: Taking it Personally: The Individual Liability of Museum Personnel (2011); Encyclopedia of Forms and Precedents (Sale of Goods) (2011); Palmer, Bailment (3rd edn, 2009). Luke has contributed articles in the field of commercial, chancery and personal property to Trusts and Trustees, Butterworths Journal of International Banking and Financial Law and Art, Antiquities & Law.
Personal: University College London (LLB Hons) (1997-2000); Interests include: food and drink, travel, current affairs.

HARRIS, Miles
4 New Square, London
020 7822 2000
m.harris@4newsquare.com
Featured in Professional Negligence (London)
Practice Areas: Professional negligence, insurance, commercial litigation, accredited mediator.
Professional Memberships: PNBA, COMBar, BILA.
Career: Trinity College, Cambridge, Grays Inn's David Karmel and William Shaw Awards for CPE and Bar. Has a strong practice in professional negligence (including lawyers, accountants, surveyors and insurance brokers), insurance and commercial litigation. Also practices as a mediator in these areas.
Publications: Authored series of Practice Notes for the Practical Law Company on Negligence and Insurance. Published in the Insurance Law Monthly, New Law Journal and Journal of Professional Negligence.
Personal: Sport (especially watching Northampton Saints, Town FC and CCC), Food & Drink, restoring home in Rutland.

HARRIS, Rebecca
QEB Hollis Whiteman, London
020 7933 8855
rebecca.harris@qebhw.co.uk
Featured in Professional Discipline (London)
Practice Areas: Rebecca is a leading junior regularly instructed in high-profile and difficult cases in regulatory law and professional discipline, with a growing emphasis on defence. Her practice includes appellate work. She appears before regulatory and professional discipline tribunals, advising and presenting cases before healthcare regulators in particular, including the GMC and the GDC. She acts both for regulatory bodies and for registrants, including in appeals in the High Court (Admin), applications in the Family Division and other High Court proceedings. She advises on complex matters of law and procedure for a number of interested parties. She also undertakes police work. In the course of her regulatory practice Rebecca appears at inquests on behalf of interested parties (including on behalf of four police officers at the inquest into a death during police pursuit). Recent instructions include GDC v BK on behalf of the respondent (GDC) in a High Court Appeal, where the grounds of appeal were based on poor reasoning given by the Professional Conduct Committee and the apparent misapplication of the test for dishonesty. The case is now an important authority in relation to the test for dishonesty in regulatory proceedings. Rebecca prosecutes and defends all types of crime, including fraud, misuse of social media, serious offences of violence, sexual offences, and cases involving sensitive issues of disclosure.
Professional Memberships: Association of Regulatory and Disciplinary Lawyers; British Association of Sports Lawyers; Criminal Bar Association; BA Fraud Lawyers' Association; Judicial Panel, Rugby Football Union
Career: Call 1997.
Personal: Working knowledge of Spanish. Trains healthcare regulators in law and procedure; provides advocacy training for external agencies.

HARRIS, Roger
2TG – 2 Temple Gardens, London
020 7822 1200
clerks@2tg.co.uk
Featured in Personal Injury (London), Clinical Negligence (London)
Practice Areas: Roger Harris specialises in clinical negligence, personal injury and litigation relating to animals and farming. Recent notable cases include Mohamud v WM Morrison Supermarkets PLC [2016] UKSC 11 (a Supreme Court decision relating to vicarious liability for an assault); Lear v Hickstead Ltd [2016] EWHC 528 (catastrophic injury arising out of the collapse of a horse box ramp) and Spencer v Hillingdon Hospital NHS Foundation Trust [2015] EWHC 1058 (whether the Montgomery test applies to post-operative warnings). He was shortlisted for the 2015 Chambers and Partners 'Personal Injury and Clinical Negligence Junior of the Year'.
Professional Memberships: Personal Injury Bar Association; Professional Negligence Bar Association; Western circuit.
Career: BA History and Politics, Exeter University. Called to the Bar in 1996.

HARRIS QC (HON), Jonathan
Serle Court, London
020 7242 6105
JHarris@serlecourt.co.uk
Featured in Competition/European Law (London)
Practice Areas: Private international law: jurisdiction, enforcement of judgments, choice of law; European law; chancery; commercial law; offshore; arbitration; fraud; public international law; international family law. Leading cases include Granatino v Radmacher [2010] UKSC 42; Hutcheson v Spread Trustees [2011] UKPC 13. Instructed in cross-border litigation in jurisdictions including: Bermuda, BVI, Cayman Islands, Cyprus, Greece, Guernsey, Israel, Italy, Jersey, Russia, Switzerland; USA. Co-drafted trusts legislation for several jurisdictions.
Professional Memberships: STEP; ACTAPS (Honorary); Chancery Bar Association; COMBAR.
Career: QC (Hon.) (2016); Professor of International Commercial Law, King's College, London (part-time; 2011- present); Lord Chancellor's Advisory Committee on Private International Law; Adviser to Ministry of Justice on EU Succession Regulation. Formerly: Professor, Birmingham University (2002-2011); Reader, Nottingham University (2000-2001); Lecturer, Birmingham University (1995-2000). Called 2006.
Publications: Joint general editor (with Lord Collins), Dicey, Morris and Collins, The Conflict of Laws; The Hague Trusts Convention (Hart, 2002); International Sale of Goods in the Conflict of Laws (OUP, 2005, co-authored); Contributor, Benjamin's Sale of Goods (8th edition); Contributor, Underhill and Hayton, Law of Trusts and Trustees (16th and 17th editions); Co-editor, Journal of Private International Law; Editorial board, Trusts and Trustees.
Personal: Jesus College, Oxford (M.A., First Class Honours), PhD (Birmingham).

HARRISON, Caroline QC
2TG – 2 Temple Gardens, London
020 7822 1200
charrison@2tg.co.uk
Featured in Clinical Negligence (London)
Practice Areas: Clinical & lawyer's negligence. Catastrophic injury. Inquests. Medical Research & Product Liability. Insurance. Specialist in complex clinical & legal issues.
Professional Memberships: PNBA (Vice-Chair).
Career: Clinical negligence: Williams (Privy Council. Causation. Whether Bailey applies to indivisible and divisible injury. Whether need to prove doubling of risk if causation factors are sequential); Maytum (Causation. Obverse of Gregg v Scott. Delayed diagnosis breast cancer. 10-year survival always above 50%. Recurrence of metastatic disease. Poor prognosis); Thomas (Locked-in syndrome); Bint (Delayed diagnosis of anti-phospholipid antibody syndrome. Stroke in young man. Later leg amputation. Effect of under-anticoagulation c.f. atherosclerosis); Smith (Wrongful birth. Disabled child. Whether damages payable post-18 years). Lawyers negligence: Carter (Under-settlement of EL claim. Minor injury ultimately causing leg amputation. Failure investigate medical causation); Whitehead (Underlying wrongful birth claim. Novel issues: duty of care to father; when events after notional trial can be taken into account). Personal Injury: Merrett (Brain damage. £14m claim. Young man with pre-existing tetraplegia. Issues: scope of Sklair 'injury-on-injury damages'; non-delegable duty; vicarious liability for agency nurses); Scott (Head and leg injury to cyclist. No helmet. Contributory negligence. 'Bizarre presentation'. Difficult management issues. Psychiatric conversion disorder. £4m). Neve (Motor claim. Brain damage and vulnerable personality. £6m); Lyons (Psychiatric injury. Material contribution causation c.f. Jobling v Associated Diaries. Causation and physical injury where second accident prolonged effects of first). Medical Research and Product liability: PIP breast implants; Trans-vaginal and abdominal mesh claims; Consent in: experimental laser therapy; laparoscopic surgery by inexperienced operator. Member of: Gene Therapy Advisory Committee (to 2009); Human Genetics Commission (to 2012); National Research Ethics Advisory Panel (to 2012). Expert witness to House of Lords Science & Technology Committee (cloning, employment and insurance in genetics). Insurance: Willsher (£2m permanent health insurance claim. Discontinued at trial after cross-examination exposed flaws in diagnosis of intractable depression).
Publications: Medical Ethics and Genetics, in Powers and Harris, Clinical Negligence (2008).

HARRISON, Christopher
4 Stone Buildings, London
020 7242 5524
c.harrison@4stonebuildings.com
Featured in Chancery (London), Company (London), Fraud (London), Restructuring/Insolvency (London)
Practice Areas: Commercial and chancery litigation; fraud and asset recovery; banking and finance; shareholder disputes; company law; insolvency and reconstruction. Commercial and Chancery disputes lie at the heart of Christopher's practice and he has wide-ranging experience in both the Commercial Court and the Chancery Division. He deals with all aspects of claims, recognising the importance in particular of interim steps such as injunctive relief in leading to a successful outcome. He has considerable trial experience. He has also assisted many clients in successfully resolving their disputes by negotiated ADR procedures. His work often has an international dimension and he has worked with lawyers in many jurisdictions.
Professional Memberships: Commercial Bar Association; Chancery Bar Association.
Career: Called to the Bar in 1988; Government Inspector (Insider-trading Inquiry, 1996); Junior Counsel to the Crown, 'B' Panel (1996-2003); Called to the Bars of the Cayman Islands and Turks and Caicos Islands for specific cases.
Publications: Oxford University Press's 'Annotated Companies Legislation', chapters on Shareholder Remedies (Derivative Claims and Unfairly Prejudicial Conduct) and Meetings
Personal: Trinity Hall, Cambridge: MA (Hons), First Class

HARRISON, Nicholas
Serle Court, London
020 7242 6105
nharrison@serlecourt.co.uk
Featured in Chancery (London), Fraud (London), Offshore (London)
Practice Areas: Commerical chancery and commercial fraud, including international trust litigation.
Professional Memberships: Chancery Bar Association, COMBAR.
Career: Continuous full-time practice at the English Bar and between 1999 and 2001 at the Bermuda Bar, working full-time on the Thyssen litigation. Experienced in International Litigation, including in Jersey, the Isle of Man and the Caribbean. Specialises in very large cases.
Personal: Education: Winchester and Oxford. Leisure interests: hiking, music, a variety of sports. Chairman of Blackheath Cricket Club. Married with two children.

HARRISON, Philomena
Maitland Chambers, London
020 7406 1200
pharrison@maitlandchambers.com
Featured in Real Estate Litigation (London)
Practice Areas: All aspects of property litigation including commercial property, landlord and tenant, other real property claims eg. mortgages, easements, restrictive covenants, conveyancing, related professional negligence and insolvency. Also general chancery litigation. Recent cases include: TBAC v Valmar [2015] EWHC 1213 (Ch) (receivers, rescission of sale contract); Coles v Samuel Smith [2015] EWHC 755 (Ch) (valuation, option); Blueco v BWAT and Prudential [2014] EWCA Civ 154 (options and pre-emption rights); Schyde Investments v Cleaver [2011] CA (standard conditions of sale), Tetra Pak v Oracle Corporation UK (2011) ChD (injunction), SMQ v (1) RFQ (2) MJQ (2008) EWHC 1874 (beneficial ownership and proprietary estoppel), Prudential Assurance Company v Ayres and Grew [2008] EWCA Civ 52 (claim against former tenants under an authorised guarantee agreement); Tamares v Fairpoint (2006) EWHC 3589 (Ch); (2007) EWHC 212 (Ch) (right to light claim); Donnelly v Weybridge [2006] EWHC 348 (TCC) (Unilateral notices); Wormall v Wormall (2004) EWCA Civ 1643 (proprietary estoppel); Corbett v Halifax Plc and Deakin [2003] 1 WLR 964 (exercise of power of sale by mortgagee).
Professional Memberships: Property Bar Association, Chancery Bar Association and Professional Negligence Bar Association.
Career: Called 1985.
Personal: Born 1960. University College London BA (Hons) Classics (First); City University Dip Law. Lives in London.

HARRISON, Richard QC
1 King's Bench Walk, London
020 7936 1500
rharrison@1kbw.co.uk
Featured in Family/Matrimonial (London)
Practice Areas: Specilaises in complex matrimonial finance disputes, prenuptial agreements, international forum disputes, international child abduction, international relocation and other private law children disputes. Acted in a number of leading cases including eight cases in the Supreme Court and the House of Lords.
Professional Memberships: Family Law Bar Association, International Academy of Matrimonial Lawyers. Member of reunite Legal Working Group.
Career: Called 1993. Silk 2012.
Publications: Consultant editor of Hershman and McFarlane Children Law and Practice and of Jordans International Child Law Portal.
Personal: Emmanuel College, Cambridge; City University. Fluent Spanish, proficient French.

HARRISON, Richard
Devereux, London
020 7353 7534
harrison@devchambers.co.uk
Featured in Insurance (London)
Practice Areas: Specialises in commercial litigation and arbitration, with particular emphasis on insurance, reinsurance and professional negligence of the legal professsion, construction professionals, accountants, tax advisers, financial services and insurance claims handlers, adjusters and brokers. Cases in 2014-15 include Rathbone Brothers v Novae in the Court of Appeal (coverage dispute re liability of professional trustee and subrogation issues); defending a group action alleging negligent tax advice in relation to geared Enterprise Zone tax schemes; defending accountants against claim for over £50m arising from client fraud; numerous insurance coverage claims involving issues of notification, aggregation, avoidance and fraud; advising re FCA regulation, policy wordings, TOBAs, binding authorities and claims management contracts; compliance and strategic advice concerning the implementation of the Insurance Act 2015. For more information and recent case highlights, please visit www.devereuxchambers.co.uk.
Professional Memberships: COMBAR, LCLCBA, BILA, ARIAS Panel Arbitrator.
Career: Robinson College, Cambridge 1987-90. Lincoln's Inn Sunley Scholar. Called 1991.
Personal: Partial to fine wine.

HARRISON, Sarah
St Philips Chambers, Leeds
01132446691
sh.blakeyhouse@btinternet.com
Featured in Chancery (North Eastern)
Practice Areas: Specialises in probate, trusts and associated capital taxation issues. Sarah has extensive experience in dealing with contentious probate disputes, family provision claims, Court of Protection work, will constructions and directions applications involving executors and trustees. She also deals regularly with all aspects of non contentious probate and trust work, including drafting wills and settlements, the variation of wills and settlements, and the termination of trusts. Sarah acts for solicitors throughout the country and is happy to provide in-house seminars on request.
Professional Memberships: Chancery Bar Association, Northern Chancery Bar Association
Career: Call 1989 (Certificate of Honour). Lincoln's Inn Student of the Year.

HART, Joseph
Deans Court Chambers, Manchester
0161 246 000
hart@deanscourt.co.uk
Featured in Crime (Northern), Environment (Northern), Health & Safety (Northern/North Eastern)
Practice Areas: Alongside a successful Crown Court practice in serious crime Joseph Hart regularly acts in regulatory matters such as Health and Safety prosecutions in incidents involving death; significant breaches of fire safety regulations and prosecutions for environmental crime. He is on the government's national list of special regulatory advocates in health and safety and environmental law. His experience of jury-based advocacy is an asset in areas of law often dominated by advocates who lack a broad Crown Court experience. He provides robust trial focused advice and applies his quick thinking to the most complex of regulatory cases. Joseph Hart has an expanding practice in cases involving professional discipline.
Professional Memberships: Criminal Bar Association. Advocate of the Supreme Court of St Helena. Approved counsel for the Falkland Islands.
Career: Barrister at Deans Court since 2000.
Personal: Joseph Hart read Jurisprudence and French law at Corpus Christi College, Oxford. He speaks Italian and French fluently; and has basic German. Joseph regularly attends the International Bar Association Conferences, and was selected to be a member of the Bar Council's trade delegation to China.

HARTLEY, Charlotte
1 King's Bench Walk, London
020 7936 1500
chartley@1kbw.co.uk
Featured in Family/Matrimonial (London)
Practice Areas: Matrimonial finance and divorce, trusts of land, financial provision for children, cohabitation and separation agreements, private children law, international children law, public children law.
Professional Memberships: The Honourable Society of Gray's Inn, the Family Law Bar Association, Child Abduction Lawyers' Association.
Career: Called Gray's Inn, 2009. Charlotte Hartley has a specialist family law practice at 1 King's Bench Walk. Reported cases include Galloway v Goldstein [2012] EWHC 60 (Fam); [2012] (Fam). 129; Re B (Child Evidence) [2014] EWCA Civ 1015; Barnett v Barnett [2014] EWHC 2678 (Fam).
Personal: Clare College, Cambridge (2007), GDL, City University (2008), BVC, City University (2009).

HARTLEY, Richard QC
Cobden House Chambers, Manchester
0161 833 6000
clerks@cobden.co.uk
Featured in Personal Injury (Northern)
Practice Areas: Richard A Hartley QC is Head of Chambers at Cobden House. He specialises in personal injury and clinical negligence work of the highest value and complexity. He is instructed by both Claimants and Defendants. The majority of his work concerns major injuries sustained in road traffic accidents, accidents at work, occupiers liability claims, clinical negligence, product defects and fatal accidents. The injuries differ greatly, but recently he has worked increasingly on claims involving major brain injuries, spinal cord injuries, major orthopaedic injuries and sports injuries involving claims for the lost chance of sporting earnings – including several high profile players and clubs from a variety of sports. As well as pure compensation claims, he deals with some of the ancillary work such as health and safety prosecutions and appeals, regulatory law, coroner's inquests and Article 2 Inquiries. He has appeared in reported cases involving acceleration of injuries, jurisdictional disputes and liability and quantum decisions. He has appeared as Lead Counsel in most of the recent high value sports injury cases including what is currently the highest ever value sports injury claim.

HARTY, Patrick
Erskine Chambers, London
020 7242 5532
pharty@erskinechambers.com
Featured in Company (London)
Practice Areas: Patrick specialises in commercial fraud, corporate law and insolvency. His cases often involve an international element and applications for pre-emptive and interlocutory relief including freezing orders, Norwich Pharmacal orders and other interim injunctions. Patrick has been involved in some of the largest civil fraud claims in recent years including the JSC Mezhdunarodniy Promyshelnniy Bank v Pugachev litigation on applications for £1.17 billion freezing orders, search orders, passport orders and committal applications and the $2 billion LIA v Societe Generale litigation, involving allegations of bribery and undue influence. Patrick also has extensive insolvency and corporate law experience, with recent cases including the Edgeworth Capital v Maud litigation arising out of the insolvency of the Ramblas group, owner of the global headquarters of Santander, and Re Guidezone Limited, a five-week unfair prejudice trial in the Chancery Division. Patrick regularly appears in the Chancery Division, Commercial Court and Court of Appeal, both as a sole advocate and with a leader. He also has significant experience as a trial advocate, including in fraud actions.
Professional Memberships: Patrick is a member of COMBAR and the Chancery Bar Association.
Publications: Patrick is a contributor to Buckley on the Companies Acts.

HARWOOD, Richard QC
39 Essex Chambers, London
020 7832 1111
richard.harwood@39essex.co.uk
Featured in Art and Cultural Property Law (London), Environment (London), Local Government (London), Planning (London)
Practice Areas: Planning, environmental, public law, compulsory purchase, local authority administration, finance and standards, historic environment, art law and Parliamentary work. Acts for developers, landowners, public authorities, interest groups and private individuals. Major court cases include Mellor (CJEU); Heard, Milton Keynes (planning policy); Dale Farm (enforcement, travellers); Champion, SAVE Britain's Heritage (Environmental Impact Assessment); Holder (Green Belt); Majed (legitimate expectation); Hirose, Peires (private nuisance); Elvington (statutory nuisance); Spitalfields Trust (London Mayor); Burkett, Berky (time limits); Hethel (wind farms); Thames Tideway Tunnel. Other recent work includes environmental and planning inquiries, development consent orders, environmental crime and development plans. Parliamentary work includes three hybrid Bills and drafting private members Bills. Art work is for owners, auction houses and regulators.

Professional Memberships: Fellow, Society for Advanced Legal Studies. Member, PEBA, ALBA, CPA, NIPA, Professional Advisers to the International Art Market and UKELA.
Career: Jesus College, Cambridge MA, LLM. Silk 2013. Called to Northern Ireland Bar, 2016. Member, Local Plans Expert Group. Former Deputy Chair, Advisory Panel on Standards for the Planning Inspectorate. Environment/Planning Junior of the Year 2011 (Chambers Bar Awards). Shortlisted Barrister of the Year 2006 (Lawyer Awards). OBE 2014.
Publications: Author, 'Historic Environment Law' (2012, Supplement 2014), 'Planning Enforcement' (2013); 'Planning Permission' (2016); case editor, 'Journal of Planning and Environment Law'; co-author, 'Contaminated Land', 'Planning and Compulsory Purchase Act 2004'.

HATFIELD, Sally QC
Byrom Street Chambers, Manchester
0161 8292100
Sally.Hatfield@byromstreet.com
Featured in Clinical Negligence (Northern)
Practice Areas: Civil law practice with specialism in medical law. Extensive clinical negligence practice, predominantly on behalf of Claimants, involving birth injury and other claims of maximum severity, particularly cases with difficult issues of causation; personal injury litigation involving complex issues of injury, causation and procedure; inquests, particularly involving deaths raising medical or human rights issues. Experience of regulatory work within the General Medical Council, and of best interests applications in the Court of Protection.
Professional Memberships: PNBA, AvMA, INQUEST Lawyers' Group, Human Rights Lawyers Association.
Career: Called to the Bar 1988, Recorder 2004. Assistant Coroner (Manchester) 2008, QC 2013. Also associate tenant at Doughty Street Chambers, London.
Publications: Co-author of 'New Law Guide to The Mental Capacity Act 2005' (Butterworths 2008). Editor Fatal Accidents Chapter of Butterworths Personal Injury Litigation Service.

HATTAN, Simon
Serle Court, London
020 7242 6105
shattan@serlecourt.com
Featured in Chancery (London), Banking & Finance (London), Financial Services (London), Fraud (London)
Practice Areas: Commercial chancery litigation, including in particular commercial fraud and breach of fiduciary duty, trusts litigation, banking and finance, professional negligence and contractual disputes. Also significant experience in regulatory and disciplinary proceedings, especially those related to the financial services industry. Cases include: RBS Rights Issue Litigation (ongoing), Kingate Funds v KML and others (Supreme Court of Bermuda – ongoing), Alhamrani v Alhamrani (BVI Commercial Court, Court of Appeal + Privy Council), Alhamrani v Alhamrani (Jersey Royal Court – breach of trust and fiduciary duty), ACKO v Van Bom (fraud) RBS v Winterthur (breach of warranty, fraudulent misrepresentation), Hoben International v Horton and others (breach of fiduciary duty, breach of confidence), Charter v City Index (knowing receipt), FSA v Legal & General (FSMA Tribunal), Philips v Symes (partnership/fraud), FSA v CSFB International (regulatory proceedings).
Professional Memberships: COMBAR, Chancery Bar Association, Commercial Fraud Lawyers Association, Financial Services Lawyers Association.
Career: Called 1999. Previously worked in international financial markets.
Personal: BSc(Hons); Dip Law(Distinction), City University, London.

HAUGHEY, Caroline
Furnival Chambers, London
020 7405 3232
chaughey@furnivallaw.co.uk
Featured in Crime (London)
Practice Areas: Crime, regulatory, coroners inquests and public enquiries.
Professional Memberships: Middle Temple, CBA, member of the Northern Ireland Bar, member of the Bar Standards Professional Conduct Committee, Kalisher Trust Trustee, External Examiner in Criminal Law and the Bar Transfer Test for the BSB
Career: Regarded as an excellent leading junior with an ability to deal with voluminous and or complex cases. Carolines' defence practice is focused on murder, serious violence, drugs and fraud and cases with disclosure issues at the fore. She is a Grade 4 leading prosecutor specializing in Human Trafficking and Slavery and is author of government review of Modern Slavery Act 2015 – One Year On commissioned by the Home Secretary Teresa May. She has particular expertise in areas of complex forensic evidence: LCN DNA, entomology, causation etc and regularly appears against Queens' Counsel. Caroline has a reputation in the prosecution of novel law and or high profile cases including: slavery (R -v- Khan, R -v- Balira, R-v- Motroc), bribery (R -v Patel) RIPA (R -v- Beeckman), Drugs (Operation Wildwood) Caroline has significant appellate court experience having appeared in the leading authorities on firearms, expert evidence and LCN DNA and is able to provide consultancy advice on all areas of crime and regulatory work: health and safety, pharmaceuticals, veterinary, GOC, GMC, SRA etc with particular experience in homicide cases (Corporate Manslaughter etc).
Publications: Modern Slavery Act 2015 review: one year on – www.gov.uk. Regular contributor to CBA and Bar Council publications and committees.
Personal: Wycombe Abbey. Trinity College, Dublin (LLB).

HAWES, Neil QC
Charter Chambers, London
020 7618 4400
Neil.Hawes@charterchambers.com
Featured in Financial Crime (London)
Practice Areas: Joint Head of Charter, Neil specialises in all aspects of commercial fraud and associated financial and investigative work. He is very experienced in representing companies or individuals who are prosecuted by the SFO, FCA or CMA. He is down-to-earth and well known for his team approach with a reputation for extensive preparation and strategic foresight necessary for large and complex cases. He is regularly instructed at an early stage in the investigative process, giving clear and practical strategic guidance. Neil has represented a wide range of individuals from Board Directors to employees alleged to have been involved in numerous offences including fraud, cartel activity, bribery, corruption, money laundering, company offences, insider dealing and related regulatory breaches. He represented Tom Hayes in the landmark LIBOR case in 2015 and then appeared in the FCA Op. Tabernula case in which he represented an ex City Corporate Broker. He has extensive experience in restraint and confiscation. Neil appears in publications as a Leader of the Bar, and has been consistently been recommended in Chambers & Partners for criminal fraud since 2012 to present.
Professional Memberships: SE Circuit; CBA, Fraud Lawyers Association, Cyber Crime Association
Career: Call 1989; Silk 2010

HAWKINS, Quinn
2 Hare Court, London
020 7353 5324
QuinnHawkins@2harecourt.com
Featured in Crime (London)
Practice Areas: Quinn Hawkins is a leading criminal junior who specialises in substantial cases of both serious and organised crime, fraud and confiscation, these often involve complex areas of fact, law and public interest in the Crown Court, High Court and Court of Appeal. His client friendly approach has the ability to make clients feel at ease while at the same time developing a good professional rapport. Recent cases include, R v Michael Misick and Others, June 2015 to date. Prosecuting (together with Andrew Mitchell QC) the former Premier and Cabinet Members of the Turks and Caicos Islands for political corruption, fraud, bribery and money laundering involving over $50 million. The case has been before a seven judge panel in the Privy Council (R v Misick and Others [2015] 1 W.L.R. 3215) to decide preliminary points of law. He has been responsible for the presentation of this highly complex case that has required his expertise in dealing with multi jurisdictional issues, civil recovery and restraint of assets. The trial is estimated to conclude in the Spring of 2017. R v Sheldrake and Others. Defending in large-scale money laundering case involving over £6 million, with large cash transfers to Brazil. R v Ndoli and Others. Defending the principal defendant in the largest immigration fraud ever committed and fraud against Eurostar.
Professional Memberships: South Eastern Circuit; Criminal Bar Association; Member of the Turks and Caicos Bar

HAY, David
Westwater Advocates, Edinburgh
0131 260 5700
david.hay@westwateradvocates.com
Featured in Employment (Scotland)
Practice Areas: All areas of employment law, with experience in equalities issues (including sex discrimination, race discrimination, disability discrimination, age discrimination and equal pay), TUPE, unfair dismissal (including constructive dismissal), redundancy, working time and restrictive covenants. David is routinely instructed for hearings in the employment tribunal across Scotland and in the employment appeal tribunal (including London) for appeals. He also has experience in arguing employment appeals in the Inner House of the Court of Session without a leader. David undertakes an element of other civil work (elements of property law, contract law and administrative law) in the Sheriff Court and Court of Session.
Professional Memberships: Committee Member, Faculty of Advocates Employment Law Group.
Career: Qualified as a solicitor in 2005. Called to the Bar in 2008. Tutor in Delict at Edinburgh University 2007-2009. Tutor for WS Society's PCC Course for trainee solicitors 2007-2010. Member of the Panel of Preferred Counsel for the Equalities and Human Rights Commission in Scotland. Faculty of Advocates Instructor in Advocacy for the training of devils (pupils) since 2013.
Personal: Educated University of Glasgow LLB (Hons) (2001); Glasgow Graduate School of Law, Diploma in Legal Practice (2002). David's hobbies include tennis and playing the clarinet.

HAYCROFT, Anthony
Serjeants' Inn Chambers, London
020 7475 5000
clerks@serjeantsinn.com
Featured in Professional Discipline (London)
Practice Areas: Anthony Haycroft was called to the Bar in 1982. Anthony specialises in clinical negligence and healthcare, professional discipline and regulatory and business and specialist crime. An earlier edition notes that "he is very good at seeing what the issues are and where one needs to go with the case." Please visit the Serjeants' Inn Chambers website for his profile, which sets out full details of his practice including relevant work of note.

HAYMAN, George
Maitland Chambers, London
020 7406 1200
ghayman@maitlandchambers.com
Featured in Chancery (London), Fraud (London)
Practice Areas: Commercial litigation and arbitration; commercial fraud; media, entertainment and sports law. George's practice covers heavy commercial disputes of all kinds, often involving a major international element. He is a specialist in civil fraud and asset tracing, contracts, property disputes, and disputes in the media industry. He has extensive advocacy experience in the Commercial Court, Chancery and Queen's Bench Divisions of the High Court, and the Court of Appeal. He has also been called to the Bar of the Eastern Caribbean Supreme Court (BVI) and appears in litigation there. Cases include The Libyan Investment Authority v. SocGen (fraud), Tatneft v. Bogolyubov (fraud), Latvijas Krajbanka v. Antonov (banking fraud), JSC BTA Bank v Ablyazov (commercial fraud and contempt), Cadogan Petroleum v Tolley (fraud), Loughridge v. Financial Times (contract), BERR v Sullman (directors' disqualification re Claims Direct), R v Johnstone (House of Lords, criminal trade mark offences), and National Sporting Club v Professional Cricketers' Association (England Cricket team's sponsorship).
Professional Memberships: Chancery Bar Association, COMBAR, Intellectual Property Bar Association.
Career: Called to the Bar 1998; Called to the Bar of the Eastern Caribbean Supreme Court (BVI) 2013.
Personal: Cambridge University, MA Law.

HAYWARD, Cicely
5 Essex Court, London
020 7410 2000
clerks@5essexcourt.co.uk
Featured in Police Law (All Circuits)

Practice Areas: Police law; Inquests; Public and Administrative; Personal Injury; Employment. Notable cases: Daniels & Ors v Chief Constable of South Wales Police [2015] EWCA Civ 680 (immunity from suit); Mouncher & Ors v Chief Constable of South Wales Police [2016] EWHC 1367 (QB) (claims for misfeasance in public office, malicious prosecution and false imprisonment brought by officers prosecuted for investigation into murder of Lynette White in 1988); R(P) v Chief Constable of Thames Valley Police [2014] EWHC 1436 (proportionality of contents of ECRC); Allen v Chief Constable of Hampshire Police [2013] EWCA Civ 967 (vicarious liability and Art 3 investigative obligation) Durrant v Chief Constable of Avon and Somerset [2014] 1 W.L.R. 4313 (relief from sanctions) Inquests into the deaths of Ian Tomlinson (MPS – death of newspaper vendor at G20 riots following police contact); Sean Cunningham (MOD – Red Arrows fatal inadvertent ejection on the runway); Bijan Ebrahimi (Chief Constable of Avon and Somerset); Gavin Williams (MOD – death of soldier in circumstances including 'beasting' and heatstroke); numerous death in custody inquests
Professional Memberships: ALBA; ELBA
Career: Called to the bar 2009. Hardwicke and Hubert Greenland Scholarships (Lincoln's Inn). Appointed to the Attorney General's C Panel of Counsel in 2013

HAYWOOD, Jennifer
Serle Court, London
020 7242 6105
clerks@serlecourt.co.uk
Featured in Partnership (London)
Practice Areas: General commercial and chancery litigation practice, including partnership, company, insolvency, trusts and civil fraud. Cases include Republic of Djibouti & Ors v Boreh & Ors (fraud), Flanagan v Liontrust Investment Partners LLP [2015] EWHC 2171 (Ch) (contract, LLPs), Aeroflot v Berezovsky & Ors (fraud), Fiona Trust v Privalov (fraud, arbitration), Secretary of State for Health v Norton; Ors (restrictive practices), Barnes v Tomlinson (breach of trust) and Experience Hendrix LLC v PPX Enterprises Inc (damages for breach of contract). Numerous partnership disputes, particularly law firms and financial services. CEDR accredited mediator.
Professional Memberships: Chancery Bar Association, COMBAR, Association of Partnership Practitioners, ACTAPS.
Career: MB BCh (Cantab), Dip Law (City University). Called 2001.

HEALEY, Greville
Falcon Chambers, London
020 7353 2484
healey@falcon-chambers.com
Featured in Agriculture & Rural Affairs (London), Real Estate Litigation (London)
Practice Areas: All areas of real property litigation, and of agricultural, commercial and residential landlord and tenant litigation.
Professional Memberships: Member of the Attorney General's B Panel of Junior Counsel to the Crown; committee member of the Property Bar Association; and member of the Chancery Bar Association.
Career: Greville is an experienced property litigation specialist and trial advocate. He is a persuasive advocate and effective cross-examiner, and is equally at home arguing difficult and technical questions of law, and fighting his client's corner in disputes of fact which turn on the credibility of witnesses. He has considerable courtroom experience both at first instance and on appeal. He gives clear and practical advice.
Publications: Contributor to last three editions of Fisher & Lightwood's Law of Mortgages; contributing editor of the Woodfall Landlord and Tenant Bulletin.
Personal: Greville has a first from Cambridge, and a doctorate from Oxford, and was a tutor at Oxford for several years before coming to the bar. He is a scholar of King's College Cambridge, a Senior Scholar of Somerville College Oxford. He has three children.

HEALY, Alexandra QC
9-12 Bell Yard, London
2074001800
a.healy@912by.com
Featured in Crime (London), Financial Crime (London)
Practice Areas: Alexandra has a broad criminal practice with extensive experience in all aspects of of criminal law. Fraud – she has considerable experience in complex fraud, insider dealing and corruption cases. She is currently instructed to defend in an R v Alexander and others – an SFO banking fraud allegation and to prosecute on behalf of the SFO an alleged fraud in respect of football apprenticeship schemes. She recently successfully defended Clodagh Hartley, the Sun Whitehall editor, in the first Operation Elveden case to acquit a journalist. She also successfully represented a bank manager in criminal proceedings involving allegations of mortgage fraud and corruption. Past cases include the successful prosecution of a substantial international boiler room fraud, the successful defence of Hossain in R v Sanders & others (an FSA insider dealing prosecution which involved ground breaking liaison with US agencies) and securing acquittals in R v Shepherd & others (Beijing Olympics ticketing fraud), and R v Ravjani & others (a £100million MTIC fraud). General Crime – She has acted in high profile murder cases, has extensive experience of cases involving sexual offences and vulnerable witnesses and has regularly undertaken trials involving allegations of drugs, firearms and violence. Cases include the successful prosecution of R v Sithole (arson murder of a 6 year old child following the defendant's extradition from South Africa). R v H (a child sex abuse case involving 6 complainants – included the cross-examination of an autistic victim through an intermediary). R v Bedi (Court of Appeal successfully appealed imposition of IPP); R v Chenery-Wickens (murder of BBC makeup artist); R v Jaggs (killing of daughter of Harrow school master); R v Fox & others (Heathrow robbery); R v Thompson ('black widow' murder). She was instructed to act as independent counsel to review legally privileged material in the 'Cash for Honours' investigation.
Professional Memberships: Criminal Bar Association, Director of the Bar Mutual Indemnity Fund, Bencher of Gray's Inn
Career: Called 1992; Queen's Counsel (2011); Recorder of the Crown Court (2010); Joint Chair Bar Remuneration Committee (2012-); Secretary of the Criminal Bar Association 2007-08
Personal: Trinity Hall, Cambridge University (MA Cantab)

HEALY, Samuel
Dere Street Barristers, York
01904-620048
s.healy@derestreet.co.uk
Featured in Employment (North Eastern)
Practice Areas: Sam Healy has practiced in employment and discrimination law for 17 years. His practice is now centred upon: – Discrimination and victimisation; – Collective rights and disputes; – Employment litigation in the County and High Court, including restrictive covenants and breach of contract claims. Sam has been on the Attorney General's Regional Panel of Counsel since 2007. Sam is regularly instructed against leading counsel in multi-week Tribunal hearings. He has recently been involved in protective award claims arising out of the insolvency of a number of High Street names, including CityLInk and Phones4U. Sam also has a thriving appellate practice. Reported cases include: – Lodge v. Dignity & Choice in dying [2015] IRLR 184 – territorial jurisdiction of UK Tribunals; – Optimum Group Services v. Muir [2014] IRLR 339 – whether a COT3 payment made by a co-Respondent should be taken into account when assessing compensation; – Woodhouse v. West North West Homes Leeds Ltd. [2013] IRLR 773 – consideration of the correct approach to victimisation and the test set in Martin v. Devonshire Solicitors; – Wrexham Golf Club v. Ingham UKEAT/0190/12/RN – whether there can ever be a 'pool of one' in redundancy situations.
Professional Memberships: Employment Law Bar Association
Career: Called to the Bar 1999. Appointed a Deputy District Judge 2015.

HEALY, Siobán QC
7 King's Bench Walk, London
020 7910 8300
Shealy@7kbw.co.uk
Featured in International Arbitration (London), Insurance (London), Shipping (London)
Practice Areas: Commercial law including insurance and reinsurance, international carriage of goods and commodities, shipping, professional negligence, conflict of laws and jurisdiction disputes, arbitration and banking.
Professional Memberships: FCiArb; Member of CAS, SIAC, ARIAS arbitration panels; Member LCIA, BILA, supporting member LMAA.
Career: Trainee solicitor & solicitor Richards Butler (now Reed Smith) 1988-1993; Barrister 7KBW 1993, QC 2010; Arbitrator.
Personal: Ski mountaineering & touring, trail running, climbing.

HEARN, Nicholas
Furnival Chambers, London
020 7405 3232
nhearn@furnivallaw.co.uk
Featured in Extradition (London)
Practice Areas: Nicholas is a criminal barrister who enjoys complementary practices in extradition and crime (with an emphasis on fraud). Nicholas is an extradition practitioner with many years' experience of acting in complex extradition proceedings both on behalf of Governments and requested persons. Nicholas regularly appears in the Divisional Court both as a leading junior and a junior alone, frequently appearing against Queens Counsel. In 2016, he appeared before the Supreme Court in Goluchowski & Sas [2016] UKSC 36. Some of his recent reported extradition cases include: Vasilev v Bulgaria [2016] EWHC 1401 (Admin),GS v Hungary [2016] 4 W.L.R. 33 Geleziunas v Lithuania [2016] A.C.D. 53, Poland v Celinski [2016] 1 W.L.R. 551, Miraszewski v Poland [2015] 1 W.L.R. 3929. Nicholas also advises individuals who are (or fear they may be) the subject of Interpol Red Notices. Nicholas can provide comprehensive advice regarding the procedure for obtaining information held by Interpol and applications for the deletion of such material and the lifting of Red Notices. Nicholas's criminal practice focuses on large scale fraud. In 2015, he was instructed on behalf of a former CEO of a multi-national charity ("Shelterbox"), accused of dishonestly showing favour to his son's company in relation to the award of procurement contracts. In 2016, he is instructed as junior counsel to the Crown in multiple trials arising from allegations of corruption within the Royal Household.

HEATHER, Christopher
Tanfield Chambers, London
020 7421 5300
ChristopherHeather@tanfieldchambers.co.uk
Featured in Real Estate Litigation (London)
Practice Areas: Landlord and tenant (commercial, residential, enfranchisement and lease renewals), mortgages, boundaries, easements and associated professional negligence. Cases include: Snowball Assets Ltd v Huntsmore House Freehold Limited [2015] UKUT 0338 (LC) (retained land, s.1(4), development rights); Merie Bin Mahfouz Company (UK) Ltd v Barrie House (Freehold Ltd) [2014] UKUT 0390 (LC) (collective enfranchisement, leases back, telecoms); Hauser v Howard De Walden Estates Ltd [2013] UKUT 597 (LC) (flying freeholds, enfranchisement, relativity); Rey-Ordieres v Lewisham LBC [2013] UKUT 14 (LC) (service charges, PFI); Helman v John Lyon [2013] 16 E.G. 106 (disclaimer, insolvency, enfranchisement); DG v Bromley LBC [2013] UKUT 0272 (AAC) (long leases, housing benefit regulations); Point West London Limited v Rothschild Trust (Bermuda) Limited [2012] EWCA Civ 884 (stay of execution); Beech v Kennerley [2012] EWCA Civ 158 (abandonment of easements); Barrie House Freehold Ltd v Merie Bin Mahfouz Company (UK) Limited [2012] EWHC Ch (enfranchisement, easements, injunctions); Hilmi Associates Limited v 20 Pembridge Villas Freehold Limited [2010] EWCA Civ 314 (enfranchisement, companies, notices)
Professional Memberships: Chancery Bar Association, Property Bar Association, ALEP, Bar Pro Bono Unit.
Career: Barrister of the Year, Enfranchisement and Right to Manage Awards 2010; Thorne Scholar, Middle Temple; Hewett Comprehensive School, Norwich, and Girton College, Cambridge.
Publications: Contributor to Service Charges and Management: Law and Practice (3rd Ed).
Personal: Running, swimming and photography.

HEATON, David QC
Byrom Street Chambers, Manchester
0161 829 2100
david.heaton@byromstreet.com
Featured in Clinical Negligence (Northern), Personal Injury (Northern)
Practice Areas: Acts for both claimants and defendants in catastrophic, complex and

high value brain and spinal injuries resulting from road traffic accidents and from clinical negligence, with particular expertise in injuries occurring at or around the time of birth. Regularly deals with claims involving Orders for variable periodical payments. Recent cases include Loughlin v Pama & Co [2013] EWHC 1641 (QB) in which the Defendant successfully contended for a reduction in past care and case management costs, Osbourne v Ward (2013) (Lawtel doc: AM0202289), Grainger v Cooper [2015] EWHC 1132 (QB) in which an order for an interim payment to purchase a specific property was refused in the absence of reasonable need.
Professional Memberships: PIBA, PNBA
Career: Called to the Bar in July 1983. Pupil of Daniel Brennan and then Tenant at 18 St John Street Chambers until 2004. Since 2004 Member of Byrom Street Chambers. Appointed QC in April 2008. Recorder of the Crown Court since 2005 and of the County Court since 2013.
Personal: Educated at William Hulme's Grammar School, Manchester, Corpus Christi College Cambridge and the Inns of Court School of Law, London.

HEATON, Laura
29 Bedford Row Chambers, London
020 7404 1044
lheaton@29br.co.uk
Featured in Family/Matrimonial (London)
Practice Areas: Matrimonial finance, Schedule 1 Children Act 1989, cohabitation disputes under Trusts of Land and Appointment of Trustees Act 1996, pre and post nuptial agreements and children matters (private law). Also works as collaborative counsel and mediator in all of these fields. Reported cases include: MA v SK [2015] EWHC 887 (Fam); SK v TK [2013] EWHC 834 (Fam); M v M and Others [2014] 1 FLR 439.
Professional Memberships: Family Law Bar Association. Resolution (Barrister representative on Dispute Resolution Committee).
Career: Educated at Northgate High School, Ipswich and Clare College, Cambridge (MA). Called to the Bar in 1998. Middle Temple. Trained as Collaborative Counsel and Mediator. Public Access Barrister.
Publications: Co-author of: 'Cohabitation and Trusts of Land' pub. Thomson Sweet and Maxwell – third edition in production.
Personal: Born 1 May 1975. Leisure pursuits include yoga, singing and watching sport. Married with children.

HEER, Deanna
5 Paper Buildings, London
07976284578
dh@5pb.co.uk
Featured in Crime (London), Health & Safety (London)
Practice Areas: Deanna prosecutes and defends serious crime and health and safety offences. She has been appointed Junior Treasury Counsel from July 2015 and is an 'A' list advocate for the HSE. She also appears before the Coroner's Court and professional disciplinary tribunals. Deanna regularly appears in homicide cases, including joint enterprise murder, gangland killings, unlawful act manslaughter and cases of so-called Shaken Baby Syndrome. She also has many years experience prosecuting serious organised crime including large scale drugs importations and money laundering. Deanna also specialises in health and safety law. She was instructed in the leading case of Tangerine Confectionary Ltd and Veolia (UK) Ltd [2011] EWCA Crim 2015 and regularly appears in cases brought against corporate defendants in respect of allegations of gross negligence manslaughter and statutory breaches resulting in death in a wide range of industries.
Professional Memberships: Criminal Bar Association, South Eastern Circuit, Health and Safety Lawyers Association.
Career: Called 1994; Recorder 2009. Junior Treasury Counsel 2015

HELLER, Richard
Drystone Chambers, London
020 7407 1881
richard.heller@drystone.com
Featured in Consumer Law (London)
Practice Areas: Consumer law, Criminal law, Proceeds of Crime, Professional Discipline, Fraud, Regulatory law
Professional Memberships: CBA, ARDL, HSLA
Career: Richard Heller is a specialist practitioner who acts for regulators, businesses and individuals across the spectrum of regulatory crime. He has considerable experience in the fields of intellectual property crime, consumer protection, food safety, planning enforcement, fraud and confiscation and a growing practice in health and safety. Richard has been instructed in some of the most complex and significant trading standards prosecutions of recent years, including Operation Augusta (widely reported as 'the world's largest eBay fraud') and SAS Fire and Security Systems Limited (the largest multi-agency prosecution for breaches of consumer protection legislation). Richard has also appeared in many other significant trading standards cases including Operations Bluechocmuffin, Olympic, Kangaroo, Bachelor, Mango and Pioneer. Other notable cases he has conducted include the largest seizures of counterfeit goods in LB Camden (R v Addy Ltd & Others) and RB Kingston (R v Simhani & Cheung), the first money-laundering prosecution for Lancashire County Council (R v Morris), and the first prosecutions for conspiracy to defraud conducted by LB Havering (R v O'Donnell and Fazeli) and LB Barking & Dagenham (R v Boateng & Others). In 2014, Richard prosecuted Mitchells & Butlers Plc for causing a fatal food-poisoning outbreak on Christmas Day in 2012, resulting in a fine of £1.5 million. Richard is appointed to the Unified List of Specialist Regulatory Advocates.

HELME, Ian
One Brick Court, London
020 7353 8845
ih@onebrickcourt.com
Featured in Data Protection (London), Defamation/Privacy (London)
Practice Areas: All aspects of media and information law including defamation, breach of confidence and privacy, data protection, harassment, contempt and all related human rights law. Cases include: Economou v De Freitas; Ames v Spamhaus; Liberty Fashions v Primark; Hegglin v Google Inc; Ontulmus & ors v Collett & ors; Karpov v Browder; Cairns v Modi; Waterson v Lloyd; Lord McAlpine v ITV; Voicemail Interception – News International; Lait v Evening Standard Ltd; R v VAC (ex parte BBFC); Rath v Guardian Newspapers Ltd; Taranissi v BBC; Financial Times v United Kingdom.
Career: Called 2005, Middle Temple; judicial assistant to Lord Justice Waller, Vice President of the Court of Appeal, Jan-Jun 2007.
Publications: Contributor to 4th Edition of Arlidge, Eady & Smith on Contempt and supplement; Co-Author of Carter-Ruck on Libel & Privacy; Co-Author of Atkins Court Forms Defamation title 2011 issue; contributor to edition of Halsbury's Laws Libel & Slander title.
Personal: Pembroke College, Cambridge (BA Hons Law First Class); Visiting Lecturer at Kings College University

HENDERSON, James
Pump Court Tax Chambers, London
020 7414 8080
clerks@pumptax.com
Featured in Tax (London)
Practice Areas: James advises on all the major UK taxes. His work covers corporate tax, income tax, VAT and private client taxation as well as customs duties and insurance premium tax. James has extensive experience of taking cases to the tax tribunal and the higher courts. He has been instructed on some of the most significant tax cases of recent years and also undertakes professional negligence work involving a tax aspect.
Professional Memberships: Revenue Bar Association; London Common Law and Commercial Bar Association.
Career: Called 1997, Gray's Inn; joined Pump Court Tax Chambers after completing Pupillage in 1998; Appointed Junior Counsel to the Crown "B" Panel 2012. 2010 – Nominated "Tax Junior of the Year", Chambers & Partners Bar Awards; 2011 – Listed in Tax Journal "40 under 40 – ones to watch in tax"

HENDERSON, Neil
4 Pump Court, London
020 7842 5555
NHenderson@4pumpcourt.com
Featured in Shipping (London)
Practice Areas: Shipping and international trade: cargo claims, charterparty disputes, arrests, demurrage and demurrage timebars, bunker disputes, shipbuilding disputes, sale and purchase, marine insurance, commodity sales. Commercial litigation and arbitration: private equity, shareholder disputes, banking, insolvency, director disqualification, general contractual disputes. High Court applications in support of arbitration, including freezing injunctions and Chabra injunctions, anti-suit injunctions, inspection orders, jurisdiction disputes, security for costs and applications under ss.57, 67, 68 and 69 of the Arbitration Act 1996. Extensive experience of LMAA, ICC and LCIA arbitrations.
Professional Memberships: COMBAR, London Common Law and Commercial Bar Association, Young Maritime Professionals, Young Shipping Professionals (Greece). Direct and Public Access qualified.
Career: Before joining the Bar, Neil worked as an analyst in the corporate finance departments of JPMorgan and Flemings investment banks for over two years during which time he completed a wide range of deals including acquisitions, disposals, IPOs and private equity financings.
Personal: First class degree in Medieval and Modern History at the University of Birmingham. Japanese language and history at Hitotsubashi University, Tokyo. PgDL (distinction) and BVC (outstanding) at the College of Law. Institute of Shipping Law, Short Course. Outside of work, Neil windsurfs, sails yachts (RYA day skipper) and dinghies, snowboards and bicycles.

HENDERSON, Simon
4 Pump Court, London
020 7842 5555
shenderson@4pumpcourt.com
Featured in Professional Negligence (London), Construction (London), Information Technology (London)
Practice Areas: General commercial law, particularly in the field of IT, construction, energy and related professional negligence. CEDR-accredited mediator with particular emphasis on IT and construction disputes.
Professional Memberships: COMBAR, TECBAR, London Common Law and Commercial Bar Association.
Career: Called to the Bar in 1993.
Personal: BA (Durham) (Philosophy – 1st Class). Dip Law (City University).

HENDERSON, William
Serle Court, London
020 7242 6105
whenderson@serlecourt.co.uk
Featured in Chancery (London), Charities (London), Trusts (London)
Practice Areas: Trusts and estates, charities and probate plus associated public law and professional negligence claims. Cases: Joint Stock Co Aeroflot v Berezovskaya [2014] EWCA Civ 431; Ferguson v. HMRC [2014] UKFTT 433 (TC); Pitt v. Holt [2013] UKSC 26 [2013] 2 AC 108; Wood v Gorbunova [2013] EWHC 1935 (Ch) [2014] 1 B.C.L.C. 487; Helena Housing Ltd v HMRC [2012] EWCA (Civ) 569 [2012] 4 All E.R. 111; Gudavadze v. Kay [2012] EWHC 1683 (Ch) [2012] W.T.L.R. 1753; R. (on the application of Independent Schools Council) v Charity Commission [2011] UKUT 421 (TCC); [2012] Ch. 214; Attorney General v Charity Commission [2012] UKUT 420 (TCC); [2012] W.T.L.R. 977; Re Kostic [2007] EWHC 2298 and 2909 (Ch).
Professional Memberships: Chancery Bar Association. ACTAPs. STEP.
Career: 1968-72 St Paul's School London; 1973-77 Trinity College Cambridge – BA in Natural Sciences (Pt I) and Law (Pt I). Junior Counsel to the Treasury in Charity Matters.

HENDY, John QC
Old Square Chambers, London
020 7269 0360
hendyqc@oldsquare.co.uk
Featured in Employment (London), Professional Discipline (London)
Practice Areas: John's practice is predominantly in the field of industrial relations, in particular, in collective labour law. His work is mainly in the RCJ and SC but he also represents international clients in the European Court of Human Rights and other international supervisory bodies, recently for the Irish Congress of Trade Unions, Swedish Transport Workers' Union and the Latvian Air Traffic Controllers' Union. He is a consultant to the International Trade Union Confederation. He is Standing Counsel to a number of UK unions. He was the Legal 500 Employment Silk of the Year for 2013. The Legal 500, 2015 describes him 'One of the best advocates at the Bar; supreme in the field of collective labour law'. Chambers & Partners 2015 reports: 'Recognised as the leading silk at the Employment Bar when it comes to handling industrial relations cases ... His experience and skill in this area are

lauded by clients and peers alike, who also praise him for his straightforward and effective advocacy'. Recent cases include, in the ECtHR: RMT v UK [2014] IRLR 467, (2015) 60 EHRR 10 (right to strike); UNITE v UK Appn 65397/13, 26 May 2016 (right to collective bargaining); in the CA: Smith v Carillion (JM) Ltd [2015] IRLR 467 (rights of agency worker); in the HC: Various v Sir Robert McAlpine and ors [2016] EWHC 45 (QB) (Blacklisting litigation – admission of expert evidence; SoS for Education v NUT [2016] IRLR 512 (strike); Galdikas v DJ Houghton Catching Services Ltd [2016] EWHC 1376 (QB) (Agricultural Wages Orders); Govia Thameslink Rly Ltd v ASLEF (No.1) [2016] EWHC 985 (QB) and (No.2) [2016] EWHC 1320 (QB) (strikes). He writes extensively on trade union law.

HENLEY, Christopher QC
Carmelite Chambers, London
020 7936 6300
chenley@carmelitechambers.co.uk
Featured in Crime (London)

Practice Areas: Chris Henley QC specialises in fraud, terrorism, homicide and other serious crime. He has acted in many terrorism trials, concerning both domestic terror plots eg 21/7, Operation Munda (grooming vulnerable young men for jihad), Operation Iridescent (fundraising for Al Shabaab) and terrorist activity abroad in Syria and Pakistan. He has addressed the Muslim Council of Britain on terrorist legislation and advised a charity providing humanitarian aid to Syria. His fraud work includes cases prosecuted by HMRC, the SFO, and the Department for Business Innovation and Skills eg Film Finance fraud, tax fraud in the construction industry, boiler rooms, MTICs. He has defended in several of the highest profile murder trials, for example the Damilola Taylor trial, the failed Daniel Morgan murder case (notorious murder in 1987 of a private investigator; the investigation has been consistently tainted by allegations of police corruption). He recently successfully defended the Head of a Prep School charged with historic child cruelty.

Professional Memberships: Grays Inn (call 1989), CBA Executive Committee, Pupil Supervisor, Fraud Lawyers Association, Liberty, the Labour Party.

HENRY, Edward
QEB Hollis Whiteman, London
020 7933 8855
Edward.Henry@qebhw.co.uk
Featured in Crime (London)

Practice Areas: Edward Henry defends in serious crime (80%) and serious fraud (20%). Over the course of his career, he has been instructed in over 40 murder trials, terrorism cases (IRA, Tamil Tiger and Al Qaeda inspired), grave sexual offences, complex drugs, money laundering, immigration fraud, firearms and people trafficking. Since last year's entry he has celebrated a number of victories including the collapse of the Royal Agricultural University "gang rape" allegation, in which his disclosure arguments played a decisive part in persuading the prosecution to offer no evidence. Most recently, in July 2016, he successfully represented a client facing a murder charge and 4 counts of attempted murder. He is adept at fashioning procedural arguments arising from PII and complex disclosure issues. In a trial concerning those accused of harbouring Dale Cregan, whilst on the run for 2 murders, before he returned to kill 2 PCs in Manchester, Edward's successful PII submissions contributed to the collapse of prosecution. In another case, he defended an ex PC accused of a vast cocaine importation. Procedurally and legally complex issues of PII, severance and disclosure were pursued during 3 trials, which ultimately led to a successful abuse of process application before Trial 4.

Professional Memberships: SEC, former CBA Representative on Bar Council, ARDL, Justice, Public Access Bar Association, JAC Advisory Group Member

Career: Called 1988. Exhibitioner of Jesus College, Cambridge BA(Hons) (Cantab). Dip Law (City University)

Personal: Trustee of Release and Fine Cell Work

HENTON, Paul
Quadrant Chambers, London
020 7583 4444
paul.henton@quadrantchambers.com
Featured in Shipping (London)

Practice Areas: Paul's practice focuses on shipping, international trade, commodities, energy, banking, aviation and insurance, including related interlocutory matters such as jurisdictional challenges, freezing orders and anti-suit injunctions. His recent instructions include acting for insurers in a US$1.6 billion patent infringement liability insurance tower dispute; and for contractors in a three week arbitration relating to loss of station-keeping of an oil rig in the North Sea. His reported cases include "CAPE BARI" [2016] UKPC 20 (contracting out of statutory tonnage limitation); S v A & B [2016] 1 Lloyd's Rep 604 (commodities arbitration; s. 68/69 challenge/ appeal; blast-furnace grade coking coal); "ASTIPALAIA"[2014] EWHC 120 (Admlty) (damages; loss of oil major approvals); Taurus Petroleum v Oil Marketing Company of Iraq [2014] 1 Lloyd's Rep 432 (commercial enforcement; letters of credit; State immunity); Vitol v Sterling Oil Trading [2012] EWHC 3108 (Comm)(dispute under long-term oil supply contract; related financing agreements); 'CENK KAPTANOGLU' [2012] 1 Lloyd's Rep 501 (Charterparty; economic duress); "PRINCESS 7" [2011] EWHC 3940 (Comm) (Marine insurance; jurisdiction; conflict of laws); Invertec v de Mol Holdings [2009] EWHC 2471 (Share sale; fraudulent misrepresentation); appeal from "CASANNA" [2009] EWHC 1074 (Shipbuilding; jurisdiction; State Immunity); Natwest v King [2008] 2 WLR 1279 (Banking; jurisdiction); and "REMMAR" [2007] 2 Lloyd's Rep. 302 (Ship sale; misrepresentation).

Career: LLB (UCL); LLM (Cantab), 1st Class. Called 2004 (ranked "outstanding").

HESLOP, Martin S QC
2 Hare Court, London
020 7353 5324
Heslop.yewtree@btinternet.com
Featured in Crime (London), Licensing (London)

Practice Areas: Martin Heslop QC is a fine Silk, his excellent skills as a criminal lawyer further compliment his gaming practice and he is widely recognised as one of the leading Silks in these areas. He has extensive experience of criminal trials including corporate and financial crime, and has represented leading operators throughout the world in the field of Gaming & Licensing. Martin's cross-examination skills are of the highest calibre and have lead to him being described as "in the super league" and regarded as one of the finest jury advocates today. For 9 years as Treasury Counsel he prosecuted the most serious and complex cases and, due to his excellent advocacy and insight into the prosecution process, Martin was also in high demand to defend in major trials, and therefore was unusually able to maintain a varied practice. Martin continues to enjoy practicing in both prosecution and defence in Silk and has been involved in numerous high profile cases both in the UK and abroad. His successful cases are well-known and well documented including obtaining the acquittal of all 10 defendants in a multi-million pound drug importation through his cross-examination of an undercover police officer and submissions on private interest immunity; acquittals in historic sex cases and joint enterprise murder trials and obtaining the Stage 1 Large Casino Licences in Stratford, Milton Keynes and Southampton amongst other successful licensing cases.

Professional Memberships: Criminal Bar Association, Health and Safety Lawyers Association

Career: Called 1972 (Lincoln's Inn), Junior Treasury Counsel 1987, First Junior Treasury Counsel 1991, Senior Treasury Counsel 1992, Recorder 1993, Queen's Counsel 1995.

Personal: Sailing, travel, photography, wine and good food.

HEWITT, Alison
5 Essex Court, London
020 7410 2000
hewitt@5essexcourt.co.uk
Featured in Inquests & Public Inquiries (All Circuits)

Practice Areas: Inquests / Coronial Law; Public / Administrative Law; Police Law; Personal Injury; Professional Regulatory. Alison Hewitt specialises in inquests and is very experienced in all aspects of coronial law and procedure. She has acted as "Counsel to the Inquest" in over 15 long and complex cases including the inquest into the death of Ian Tomlinson, who died following contact with the police in the G20 riots and, most recently, the high-profile and sensitive inquests into the deaths of Zane Gbangbola and Poppi Worthington. Alison also represents a wide range of clients at inquests including Police Constabularies, private prisons, NHS Trusts, care homes and families. Many of her cases involve deaths in custody or in detention under the Mental Health Act, or deaths resulting from domestic violence or with a background of complex clinical care. Additionally, Alison regularly acts for coroners and others in related judicial review claims.

Professional Memberships: The Coroners' Society of England and Wales; PIBA

Career: Called to the Bar 1984; Assitant Coroner 2007; Further, since joining 5, Essex Court in 2012 Alison has developed an ever-growing Police Law practice. She advises and represents Constabularies in relation to civil claims, judicial review proceedings and disciplinary matters. She also acts as a Legal Adviser to the General Dental Council.

HIBBERT, William
Henderson Chambers, London
020 7583 9020
whibbert@hendersonchambers.co.uk
Featured in Consumer Law (London)

Practice Areas: Consumer law, in particular finance, consumer credit, banking, mortgages and financial services. In the wider field of consumer protection, regulatory law including legislation on unfair contract terms, unfair commercial practices, pricing, advertising, distance and doorstep selling, pyramid selling, package holidays and timeshare. Also food, food labelling, medicines and cosmetics. Cases include OFT v First National Bank [2002] 1 AC 481 (Unfair Terms in Consumer Contracts Regulations); Wilson v First County Trust [2002] QB 74 (CA), [2004] 1 AC 816 (HL)(Declaration of Incompatibility under HRA regarding irredeemable unenforceability under CCA); OFT v Lloyds TSB Bank [2005] 1 AER 843 (QB), [2006] 2 AER 821 (CA), [2008] 1 AC 318 (HL) (Lender's liability under s.75 CCA for credit card transactions financing foreign transactions); Goshawk v Bank of Scotland [2006] 2 AER 610 (Wording of prescribed notices of cancellation rights under CCA); Conister Trust v Hardman and Co [2009] CCLR 4 (Solicitor's liability for client's litigation funding agreement); Meah v GE Money Home Finance Ltd [2013] EWHC 20 (Ch) (Mortgagee's liability for valuation of repossessed property).

Professional Memberships: COMBAR,Food Law Group, Consumer Credit Forum.

Career: Called to the bar 1979.

Publications: The Law of Consumer Credit and Hire, OUP 2009.

Personal: Born 1957. Educated: Charterhouse; Worcester College, Oxford.

HICKEY, Alexander QC
4 Pump Court, London
020 7842 5555
AHickey@4pumpcourt.com
Featured in International Arbitration (London), Professional Negligence (London), Construction (London), Energy & Natural Resources (London)

Practice Areas: Construction, energy, oil and gas, waste management, technology and other commercial disputes both domestic and international. Professional negligence claims involving construction professionals, solicitors and valuers. Alex is regularly involved in trials and arbitrations (ICC, LCIA, DIAC). He has a string of reported cases in relation to adjudication, and several reported cases to his name in the High Court, Court of Appeal and House of Lords. Alex sits as an ICC Arbitrator. He also accepts appointments as Adjudicator.

Professional Memberships: TECBAR (Committee); COMBAR; Society of Construction Law CEDR list of Adjudicators Registered as an Advocate in the Dubai International Financial Centre Courts in the United Arab Emirates.

Career: Called 1995 (Lincoln's Inn). Silk (2016) Judicial assistant to the Court of Appeal (1997).

Publications: Adjudication section of Lexis PSL.

Personal: Educated at Christ Church, Oxford, where he read Jurisprudence and was a choral scholar (1991-94), and Hereford Cathedral School. Married with two children.

HICKS, Edward
Radcliffe Chambers, London
020 7831 0081
ehicks@radcliffechambers.com
Featured in Real Estate Litigation (London)

Practice Areas: Chancery and commercial practice, specialising in: real property litigation, landlord and tenant, trusts, wills and probate, family provision, court of protection, commercial, and insolvency. Cases

include: Re Huntley [2014] EWHC 547 (ch) Re Catling [2014] EWHC 180 (Ch) Di Marco v Morshead Mansions Ltd [2014] EWCA Civ 96 Re Devillebichot [2013] EWHC 2867; Log Book Loans Ltd and Nine Regions Ltd v Office of Fair Trading (1st Tier Tribunal) CCA/2009/0010 and 0011.
Professional Memberships: Chancery Bar Association.
Career: MA Cantab (Magdalene College), BLC Oxon (Oriel College), Called to bar in 2004.
Publications: A will Writer's Work of Fiction TEL&TJ 2014, 162 (Dec) 24-28; the Perils of Assisting with a Will TEL&TJ 2014 156 (May) 9-12
Personal: Born 1981; resides London.

HICKS, Martin QC
2 Hare Court, London
020 7353 5324
martinhicks@2harecourt.com
Featured in Crime (London), Financial Crime (London)
Practice Areas: Martin Hicks QC is a leading Silk who is consistently recommended by the leading industry directories. He is routinely first choice counsel in his areas of practice, on a domestic and international scale. He advises and appears for individual defendants, corporate clients, their directors and officers and national governments and agencies. He also acts on behalf of professionals such as accountants, solicitors and others who face proceedings arising out of their work. Martin has appeared in many murder cases, operations against illegal drug cartels, terrorism cases, and fraud cases throughout his career. Although Martin works across the UK, he is also well known in the criminal sector on an international level, in the EU , the Crown Dependencies and the Caribbean. Martin primarily gained notice as a junior defence counsel with the R v Pryce case, an investigation involving a young musician accused of hacking into NASA and the Pentagon through their highly secured computer systems. Martin gained vast experience in both defending and prosecuting through his appearances in cases brought against a range of high-profile individuals, such as the series of "fake sheik" stings by the News of the World, the series of celebrity Rolex robberies and a major mobile phone heist at Heathrow airport. More recently he has been involved in the "Victoria Beckham Kidnap Plot", the bogus "MI5 kidnapper", the "Aston Riots Murder", the 24/7 bombings, "Cash for Crash Claims", the £220 million "Lord of Fraud Plot" and successfully defended in separate long trials two high placed journalists accused of misconduct in a public office (Operation Elveden).
Professional Memberships: Criminal Bar Association, Fraud Lawyers Association, South Eastern Circuit. He is authorised to accept instructions on a direct access basis.

HIGGINS, Gillian
9 Bedford Row, London
020 7489 2727
gillian.higgins@9bedfordrow.co.uk
Featured in Crime (London)
Practice Areas: Gillian Higgins is regarded as a leading lawyer in international criminal law. Her courtroom advocacy is of the highest class. Gillian has represented heads of state, leading military figures and civilians in high profile international trials. Her notable cases include Prosecutor v Kenyatta (ICC); Prosecutor v Cermak (ICTY); Prosecutor v Milosevic (ICTY); Prosecutor v Nahimana (ICTR); Prosecutor v Musema (ICTR); and Osmanoglu v Turkey (ECHR). Gillian is a key member of 9 Bedford Row International (9BRI) and a founding member of the International Criminal Law Bureau (ICLB). Most recently, she has been engaged in financial investigations of a global nature involving whistle blowers for Quintel Financial Ltd. She has also been providing advice to an interested party concerning the ICC's investigation into Georgia. Last year, she prepared submissions to the OISL on the conflict in Sri Lanka. In 2012, she established "ARC" (Advice, Representation and Cases – www.arcproject.co.uk) an initiative focusing on the African Court on Human and Peoples' Rights and the African Commission. Gillian lectures on international criminal law and has advised on defence issues before the State Court of BiH in Sarajevo and Cambodia's ECCC. Gillian is a member of the IBA's War Crimes Committee.
Professional Memberships: International Bar Association, Lawyers Against Poverty, Oxfam
Publications: Gillian edits and writes for the ICLB blog, 9 Bedford Row International and ARC.

HIGGO, Justin
Serle Court, London
020 7242 6105
jhiggo@serlecourt.co.uk
Featured in Chancery (London), Commercial Dispute Resolution (London), Fraud (London)
Practice Areas: Specialist in commercial and chancery litigation and advice with extensive offshore experience (in particular in the Channel Islands and in Cayman). Practice focus is domestic and international commercial fraud and pre-emptive remedies, domestic and international trusts, international arbitration, company and banking. Recent cases include: Orb ARL -v- Ruhan, Chambal Fertilizers & Chemicals -v- Trafigura & Ors, JSC BTA Bank -v- Ablyazov & Ors, Fiona Trust -v- Privalov in the Commercial Court; Glenn -v- Watson & Ors, Aeroflot -v- Berezovsky & Ors, Labrouche -v- Frey & Ors, CCE Ltd -v- Corry & Ors in the Chancery Division.
Professional Memberships: Chancery Bar Assocation, COMBAR.
Career: Called February 1995.

HILL, Jonathan
8 New Square, London
07932 788036
clerks@8newsquare.co.uk
Featured in Intellectual Property (London)
Practice Areas: Barrister specialising in all areas of intellectual property law, including patents, copyright, trade marks, passing off, designs and confidential information, and in IT, media and art law and related areas of commercial law. Recent cases include: SAP v Diageo (enterprise software licensing dispute), Argos v Argos Systems (trade mark dispute regarding online advertising), BAE v Thales (patent for aircraft helmet tracking), Everseal v DMS (patent for sealable mailers); Shanks v Unilever (inventor's claim to fair share of benefit from patent licensing for blood glucose testing); D Jacobson v Crocs (registered designs in Crocs shoes); Blue Gentian v Tristar (validity of patent for expandable hose); Magical Marking v Ware & Kay (professional negligence claim relating to handling of an IP claim); Dirty Dancing Community trade mark (appeal in the ECJ); Quick Draw v GLE (media dispute concerning Michael Jackson tribute concert); Nintendo v Playables (copy-protection circumvention devices); BMS v AB Agri (mill control software).
Professional Memberships: IP Bar Association; Chancery Bar Association; Lincoln's Inn
Career: Called 2000. Awarded Kennedy, Mansfield, Major CPE and Hardwicke scholarships during qualification. Judicial Assistant, Court of Appeal (2002).
Publications: Atkins Court Forms – Patents
Personal: Studied Physics and Philosophy, Oxford (1st)

HILL, Mark QC
Francis Taylor Building, London
020 7353 8415
clerks@ftbchambers.co.uk
Featured in Civil Liberties & Human Rights (London)
Practice Areas: Religious liberty, ecclesiastical law, public law, costs, ADR.
Professional Memberships: HRLA; Chairman, Ecclesiastical Law Society
Career: Specialist in ecclesiastical law, religious liberty, judicial review and costs. Recorder; Chancellor of Dioceses of Chichester, Leeds and Europe; Honorary Professor of Law, Cardiff University; Kings College London and University of Pretoria; Notre Dame University, Sydney; Co-Chair of BIMA (Belief in Mediation and Arbitration). Cases: President of Methodist Conference v Preston (2013) Supreme Court; Eweida v UK (2013) ECtHR; Shergill v Khaira (2014)Supreme Court; Church of Jesus Christ of Latter-day Saints v UK (2011) ECtHR; Holliday v Musa (2010), Court of Appeal; R (HM Coroner for Eastern London) v Secretary of State for Justice (2009) Admin Ct; R (Madden and Finucane) v Secretary of State for Northern Ireland (2006) Admin Ct; PCC of Aston Cantlow v Wallbank (2004)
Publications: 'Magna Carta, Religion and the Rule of Law' (2015); 'Religion and Discrimination Law in the European Union' (2012); 'Religion and Law in the United Kingdom' (2014); 'Ecclesiastical Law' (3rd ed, 2007); 'Religious Liberty and Human Rights' (2002); Contributing editor, 'Jowitt's Dictionary of English Law' (3rd ed, 2010) and 'Butterworths Costs Service' (2011). Consultant Editor, Ecclesiastical Law Journal.

HILL, Max QC
Red Lion Chambers, London
020 7520 6000
chambers@18rlc.co.uk
Featured in Crime (London)
Practice Areas: Max Hill is Head of Red Lion Chambers and the current leader of the South Eastern Circuit (2014-16). He maintains a heavy-weight crime practice, defending and prosecuting in a number of complex cases of homicide, violent crime, terrorism and high value fraud and corporate crime. Recent murder cases include R V Long (2015), R v Campbell and others (2014-5), R v O'Driscoll (2014) and R v Robinson (2015). In Fraud, he was instructed for the defence in the long-running SFO pharmaceutical cartel case, R v O'Neill and others. Max also prosecutes, including in the second set of trials concerning the killing of Damilola Taylor, R v Preddie. He has prosecuted many of the most serious terrorism trials of recent years, including R v Bourgass and others (the ricin conspiracy), R v Ibrahim and others (the 21/7 bombers), R v Ali and others and R v Girma and others (the 21/7 follow-on trials). He appeared for the Government in the Binyam Mohamed case in the Administrative Court. He acted for the Metropolitan Police in the Inquests into the 7th July London bombings. Most recently he prosecuted a London Cabbie and bomb-maker for the killing of a US soldier in R v Sardar (2015).
Professional Memberships: Chairman, Criminal Bar Association 2011-12; Chairman, Kalisher Trust 2014 to date, Leader, South Eastern Circuit 2014-16
Career: Crown Court Recorder, 2005; Queen's Counsel, 2008.
Publications: (2015) Urgent Interviews and the Concept of Oppression in Terrorist Cases. Investigating Terrorism, edited by John Pearse, Wiley Blackwell; (2014) The Stephen Lawrence Murder Twenty-One Years on. IILP Review, pp 148-154; (2013) Cell Site and the Judiciary, DVD; 2013 Removing Dishonesty from the Cartel Offence. Lexis Nexis 11/3/13; (2013) Social Media and Criminal Justice, Criminal Bar Quarterly Issue 4; (2012) The Stephen Lawrence Murder: 18 years on. Criminal Law and Justice Weekly Vol 176 No 45 at pp 633 and 651; (2007) A practitioners guide to terrorist trials, contributing editor

HILL, Rebecca
5 St Andrew's Hill, London
020 7332 5400
RebeccasHill@5sah.co.uk
Featured in Extradition (London)
Practice Areas: Rebecca is one of the most experienced extradition practitioners having specialised in the area for almost a decade and having been consistently recognised as a leader in the field by Chambers & Partners. She continues to be instructed to prosecute and defend in cases of the utmost gravity, involving both European and International jurisdictions and raising the full spectrum of issues including technical and human rights arguments. In addition she is experienced in ancillary Judicial Reviews, habeas corpus applications and submissions to the European Court of Human Rights. She is instructed to advise in cases of international individuals 'at risk' of extradition and those who have been returned to the UK by 'import extraditions'. As such her expertise encompasses every area of work in the extradition field. Recent notable cases include Marchewka v Poland [2016] EWHC 998 Admin, Shah v France [2015] EWHC 3746 Admin, Zagorskij v Lithuania [2015] EWHC 2335 (Admin), Zubrickas v Lithuania [2015] EWHC 1475 (Admin).
Professional Memberships: Extradition Lawyers Association Criminal Bar Association Defence Extradition Lawyers Forum

HILL, Richard G QC
4 Stone Buildings, London
020 7242 5524
r.hill@4stonebuildings.com
Featured in Chancery (London), Banking & Finance (London), Commercial Dispute Resolution (London), Company (London), Fraud (London), Restructuring/Insolvency (London)
Practice Areas: Litigation specialist focusing on commercial, capital markets and banking, insolvency, civil fraud and company litigation. In addition to his High Court practice he appears in international arbitra-

tions and Courts in offshore jurisdictions. His work regularly features cross-border issues and involves large teams, often including team members from the US and other jurisdictions. Leading recent cases: Constantin Meridien v Ecclestone; McKillen v Barclay & Ors; re Lehman Brothers International Europe (client money litigation); Re Titan Europe 2007-1 (NHP); Sinclair v Versailles Trade Finance Ltd.
Professional Memberships: Also called to the Bar in the BVI and the DIFC Member of Attorney General's 'A' Panel Counsel for Government work (2007-12); COMBAR; CBA
Career: 1993 Call. Silk in 2012. Educated at Gonville & Caius College, Cambridge (BA Hons – 1st class); Prince of Wales Scholar of Gray's Inn.
Publications: Contributor to Oxford University Press 'Annotated Companies Acts.'

HILLIER, Nicolas
9 Gough Square, London
020 7832 5000
clerks@9goughsquare.co.uk
Featured in Personal Injury (London)
Practice Areas: Personal injury and professional (clinical and legal) negligence litigation, predominantly employers' liability and road traffic accident claims. Considerable experience in high value catastrophic injury and Fatal Accident Act work. Reported decisions of interest include Verlander v Rahman [2012] EWHC 1026 (serious brain injury claim about which there was substantial disagreement between the medical experts both as to consequences and, particularly, Mental Capacity), Connery v PHS [2011] EWHC 1685 (a Complex Regional Pain Syndrome developing as a consequence of a whiplash injury); Hardisty v Aubrey [2006] EWCA Civ 1196 (road traffic accident claim – the Court of Appeal reversing a finding of fact made erroneously by the trial judge upon an incomplete assessment of the totality of the evidence on the issue); Harris v BRB (Residuary) Ltd [2006] PIQR P10 (noise induced hearing loss claim – appeal on issues of noise exposure and use of hearing protection); Godbold v Mahmood [2006] PIQR Q5 (high value brain damage claim including a substantial periodical payments award); Pirelli General Plc v Gaca [2004] I WLR 2683 (employer's liability claim – appeal on issue of deduction of insurance receipts); Edmonds v Lloyds TSB Bank plc [2004] EWCA 1526 (employer's liability claim – appeal on issue of failure to mitigate loss).
Professional Memberships: PIBA; APIL.
Career: Called to the Bar in 1982. Joined Chambers in 1983.
Personal: LLB (Hons). Lives in London. Leisure pursuits: an energetic and demanding family, a general interest in most sports – now a (long!) retired rugby player, more recently a struggling golfer and still a fair weather surfer!

HILLIER, Victoria
Civitas Law, Cardiff
08450713007
victoria.hillier@civitaslaw.com
Featured in Administrative & Public Law (Wales & Chester)
Practice Areas: Victoria is regularly instructed to advise and represent local authorities and housing associations on a wide spectrum of housing claims including possession, anti social behaviour injunctions and the homelessness provisions. She specialises in claims raising issues under the Equality Act 2010 and is currently defending a number of claims for discrimination, victimisation and harassment against public bodies. Her practice also encompasses licensing appeals, planning matters and judicial review in the aforementioned areas. She has represented Police Authorities in a number of high profile inquests including deaths in custody and a double fatal shooting. This compliments Victoria's significant practice in defending civil actions against the Police, which incorporates unlawful arrests, false imprisonment, misfeasance in public office and employer liability claims. Victoria also has a busy personal injury practice.
Professional Memberships: Victoria was delighted to be appointed onto the Attorney General's List of Counsel and Welsh Assembly Government Panel in 2012. She receives regular instructions in this capacity on personal injury matters and a wide range of public law issues.
Career: Called to the Bar in 2005.
Personal: Victoria enjoys travelling, skiing, cycling, dancing and attending the gym.

HILLMAN, Gerard
Carmelite Chambers, London
020 7936 6300
clerks@carmelitechambers.co.uk
Featured in Financial Crime (London)
Practice Areas: Complex fraud, confiscation, corporate liability, asset recovery, regulatory, health and safety, disciplinary tribunals and VAT and Duties Tribunal.
Professional Memberships: Criminal Bar Association, Gray's Inn, Inner Temple.
Career: Kadurugamuwa (solicitor laundering proceeds of $100m fraud); Baugh (Boiler room fraud conducted from Spain with loss in excess of £7m); Ahmed (multi-million pound VAT fraud); Silva (multi-million pound fraud committed over long period by IFA); Suleman (multi-million pound MTIC fraud); Ponnusamy (laundering proceeds of a fraud valued at over £200m); Odia (£4m international advanced fee fraud); Olasemo (complex internet dating fraud targeting single women in foreign jurisdictions); Chappell (significant fraud by employee involving adapting computer software); Coombs (principle defendant in multi-million pound duty evasion fraud); Ferrigan (SFO prosecution of a solicitor charged with a series of mortgage frauds valued in excess of £50 million); Breeze (chief executive of a private psychiatric hospital acquitted of multi-million pound fraud on NHS); Akinwolemiwa (accountant acquitted of fraud and money laundering); Poole (significant fraudulent trading by company director); Roope (SFO prosecution of multi-million pound international advance fee fraud); Vidgeon (SFO prosecution of £7 million boiler room fraud); Miah (major immigration fraud); Choudhury (multi-million pound boiler room fraud); Khan (£10 million pound mortgage fraud); Chahal (£15 million bank fraud); Bridden (£16 million money laundering proceeds of MTIC fraud); Zec (£15 million duty evasion); Smith (£15 million duty evasion); Bondswell (investment fraud by non regulated individual promoting CFDs / derivatives); Farrier (company fraud on the European Social Fund and the European Regional Development Fund); James (£15 million VAT fraud); Director of the Asset Recovery Agency v R. (major asset recovery case). Bestel [2013] EWCA 1305; [2013] WLR (D) 296 successfully appeal to remit a confiscation order back to the Crown Court for a re-hearing. Institute of Directors v Commissioners for Customs & Excise [2003] STC 25, [2002] EWCA Civ 1814; Commissioners for Customs & Excise v Kingscrest [2002] STC 490, [2002] EWHC 410 (Ch). Gerard has also represented several jockeys accused of corruption in horseracing in proceedings at the Horseracing Regulatory Authority as well as appearing in other disciplinary tribunals including the Solicitors' Regulatory Tribunal.

HILL-SMITH, Alexander
New Square Chambers, London
020 7419 8000
Alex.Hill-Smith@NewSquareChambers.co.uk
Featured in Chancery (London)
Practice Areas: Property work including for large retail and industrial groups together with property-related professional negligence. Also does more general company and commercial work and consumer credit. Recent cases include Aldermore Bank v Rana 2016 1 WLR 2209, Thomas and others v Capita Trustees Limited and others [2012],Giles v Tarry [2012] EWCA Civ 837. Previous cases Tinsley v Milligan HL, Wallcite v Ferrishurst, CA.
Professional Memberships: Chancery Bar Association, Property Bar Association.
Career: Called to the Bar, Grays Inn, 1978 (Holt Scholar); Recorder 2005 to date, South Eastern Circuit, Civil and Crime.
Publications: Section on solicitors' negligence in Sweet & Maxwell Professional Negligence encyclopaedia. Article on "Rights of parking" in the Conveyancer commended by Lord Scott in the House of Lords in Jameson v Moncrieff. Article on Fraud and Land Registration in The Conveyancer, 2009, Consumer Credit, Law and Practice, published Informa Law, second edition.
Personal: Born 1955. Lives in London.

HINCHLIFFE, Thomas QC
Three New Square, London
020 7405 1111
hinchliffe@3newsquare.co.uk
Featured in Intellectual Property (London)
Practice Areas: All aspects of contentious intellectual property, with a particular emphasis on patent litigation in the pharmaceutical, biotechnology and mobile telephony fields. Recent notable cases include: Lilly v Actavis [2016]; Hospira v Cubist [2016]; Unwired Planet v Samsung [2016]; Merck v Ono [2015]; Synthon v Teva [2015]; Vringo v ZTE [2014]; Philips v Nintendo [2014]; HTC v Nokia [2014]; Samsung v Apple [2013]; Generics v Yeda [2012]; Merck v Sigma [2012]; Warner-Lambert v Teva [2011]; Datacard v Eagle Technologies [2011]; Abbott v Medinol [2010]; RIM v Motorola [2010]; Scinopharm v Eli Lilly [2009]; Generics UK v Daiichi [2009]; Actavis v Merck [2008]; Generics v Lundbeck [2008]; Qualcomm v Nokia [2008]; Conor v Angiotech [2007].
Professional Memberships: Intellectual Property Bar Association; Chancery Bar Association.
Career: Called to the Bar 1997. Took silk in 2016.
Personal: Brasenose College Oxford (1995 MA, Chemistry).

HINES, James QC
3 Raymond Buildings Barristers, London
020 7400 6400
James.Hines@3rblaw.com
Featured in Crime (London), Extradition (London), Financial Crime (London)
Practice Areas: Crime, commercial fraud and extradition, principally defending. Specialises in cases which have both criminal and commercial/civil aspects, particularly those with an international element. James recently acted as lead Prosecution counsel in the SFO Barclays Libor trial. James has defended in numerous SFO trials and in several insider dealing cases. Also instructed by the Competition and Markets Authority on cartel matters. James has wide experience in all areas of general and financial crime. He has experience of private prosecutions. James has been practising in the field of extradition for many years. Notable cases include "The NatWest Three" and the Tollman case. He regularly provides strategic advice to clients during the investigation stage and specialises in acting for third parties in respect of witness summons, SFO s.2 notices and international cooperation (MLA). For some years he acted as outside criminal counsel for Microsoft.
Professional Memberships: Justice, Criminal Bar Association, Fraud Lawyers Association, Commonwealth Lawyers Association, Association of Regulatory and Disciplinary Lawyers, Extradition Lawyers Association, Proceeds of Crime Lawyers Association.
Career: Called 1982, Gray's Inn. QC 2015. Elected Member of the Bar Council, the Ethics Committee and the International Committee. Chair of the International Rule of Law panel. CBA Committee member and Fraud Lawyers Association Committee member.

HINKS, Frank QC
Serle Court, London
020 7242 6105
fhinks@serlecourt.co.uk
Featured in Chancery (London), Offshore (London), Trusts (London)
Practice Areas: Specialist domestic and international trusts practice (advisory, drafting, litigation and expert evidence) and Chancery practice (including real property, commons, partnership and charities) appearing in court in England, Cayman, Bermuda, Bahamas and Hong Kong and advising in relation to other jurisdictions including Jersey and Guernsey. Cases include Re Y Trust No.1 [2015-2016] (Cayman): defective protector consent; Re Nina Wang Dec'd [2012-14] (Hong Kong): effect of will of wealthiest woman in Asia; Re A Trust [2012] (Bermuda): obtaining anti-suit injunction to restrain trust litigation; C v D [2012] (Bermuda): terminating offshore structure; Scarfe v. Matthews [2012] will construction/ doctrine of election; BQ v DQ [2011] (Bermuda): declaring trusts void as testamentary dispositions; St. George v. Hayward [2006-10] (Bahamas): beneficial ownership and control of Freeport; Executors of HM Queen Mother and HRH Princess Margaret v Brown [2008] (CA England): resisting claim to unseal Royal Wills; Crown Estate Commissioners v. Roberts [2008] (England) title and franchise rights pre-Norman Conquest; Roberts v. Swangrove Estates Ltd [2008] CA England) Crown's ability to establish title by adverse possession.

Professional Memberships: STEP, Chancery Bar Association, Association of Contentious Trust and Probate Specialists.
Career: Called to Bar in 1973. Joined present Chambers in 1974.
Personal: Educated at Bromley Grammar School; St Catherine's College, Oxford. BA 1st Class Hons; BCL 1st Class Hons.

HIORNS, Roger
9 Gough Square, London
020 7832 0500
jlevy@9goughsquare.co.uk
Featured in Personal Injury (London), Personal Injury (All Circuits)
Practice Areas: Highly experienced in all aspects of personal injury and fatal accident cases but notably employers and public liability claims. Has extensive experience in occupational disease claims on which he lectures nationally, with particular experience in WRULD, asbestos, asthma, deafness and HAVS cases. Notable cases include Mountenay v Bernard Matthews (1993), Alexander v Midland Bank (1998) and Jones v Metal Box (2007).
Professional Memberships: APIL; PIBA.
Career: Has practised for nearly 30 years in all areas of personal injury and fatal accident litigation since completing pupillage in chambers.
Publications: WRULD: Where have we got to? (September 2000) , Journal of personal injury law. RSI lives (October 1999) , APIL newsletter. Occupational Illness Litigation: Chapter on WRULD Law and Practice.
Personal: Active DIY and gardening enthusiast, passive sports enthusiast and lover of all good music.

HITCHCOCK, Patricia QC
Cloisters, London
020 7827 4000
phi@cloisters.com
Featured in Personal Injury (London), Clinical Negligence (London)
Practice Areas: Clinical negligence, catastrophic injury, inquests, medical law, related administrative law and regulatory matters. Mediator, CEDR accredited 2003. Highlight case list on www.cloisters.com.
Professional Memberships: Action Against Medical Accidents (AvMA) Lawyers Group and Inquest Project; Bar Pro Bono Group; Inquest; Professional Negligence Bar Association; Personal Injury Bar Association; Centre for Dispute Resolution (CEDR) Exchange; Civil Mediation Council; MIND Legal Network.
Career: Non-fiction book editor for 10 years in UK and USA. Elected 'Mother' of the NUJ chapel at Hutchinson Books, discovered taste for advocacy. Called to the Bar 1988. Initial common law practice dominated by criminal defence (over 100 Crown Court trials), plus personal injury, employment, discrimination and education law. Specialised in medical law 1996. Busy High Court and appellate practice; regularly instructed in major multi-million pound cases on both liability and quantum, especially brain and spinal injury; cancer; psychiatric negligence; fatal accidents. Took silk 2011.
Publications: Co-author, Butterworths Personal Injury Litigation Service Division XV: Claims of the Utmost Severity. Chapter author (on Experts) for Clinical Negligence, ed. Lewis and Buchan (Bloomsbury Professional). Various articles.
Personal: Married to sculptor Peter Brooke-Ball; daughter and son, now adults.

HITCHMOUGH, Andrew QC
Pump Court Tax Chambers, London
020 7414 8080
clerks@pumptax.com
Featured in Tax (London)
Practice Areas: Andrew Hitchmough specialises in all forms of corporate tax, VAT and customs duties. He has a strong advisory practice but is particularly well known for his litigation experience in the Courts and Tribunals. He lectures frequently on VAT and corporate transactions. Recent cases of note include Investment Trust Companies v HMRC (Supreme Court); London Clubs Management Ltd v HMRC (Upper Tribunal; gaming duty); Bookit Ltd v HMRC (CJEU); Airtours Holidays Transport Ltd v HMRC (Court of Appeal); Vodafone Group Services Ltd v HMRC (Upper Tribunal); Lok'nStore Group Plc v HMRC (Upper Tribunal); McCarthy & Stone (Developments) Ltd v HMRC (Upper Tribunal); Iveco Ltd v HMRC (Upper Tribunal); Aspinalls Club Ltd v HMRC (Court of Appeal); University of Cambridge v HMRC (Upper Tribunal); The Pollen Estates Trustee Co & Kings College London v HMRC (Court of Appeal).
Professional Memberships: VAT Practitioners Group; Revenue Bar Association; London Common Law & Commercial Bar Association.
Career: Called 1991, Inner Temple. QC in 2013.

HOBSON, Fred
Brick Court Chambers, London
020 7379 3550
fred.hobson@brickcourt.co.uk
Featured in Banking & Finance (London), Commercial Dispute Resolution (London)
Career: Fred's practice encompasses the full range of commercial disputes. His work includes banking and finance, arbitration, civil fraud and energy-related disputes. Much of his work has an international or fraud element. Fred is recommended in Chambers & Partners and the Legal 500. Fred is frequently instructed on his own in High Court proceedings. Fred has acted unled in several High Court trials and appeared unled in the Court of Appeal. Recent work includes: Terra Firma v Citibank. Acted for Citibank in its successful defence of a £2.3 billion fraud claim brought against it by Terra Firma, the private equity group, arising out of the acquisition of EMI in 2007 (one of The Lawyer's top 20 cases of 2016). Pinchuk v Bogolyubov & Kolomoisky. Acted for a Ukrainian businessman in defence of a proprietary claim (valued in excess of $1 billion) relating to the ownership of an iron ore mining company situated in eastern Ukraine (one of The Lawyer's top 20 cases of 2016). Fiona Trust dispute. Acting for Russian shipowners in long-running dispute over entitlement to rescind charterparties allegedly procured by bribery.

HOCKMAN, Stephen QC
6 Pump Court, London
020 7797 8400
stephen.hockman@6pumpcourt.co.uk
Featured in Environment (London), Health & Safety (London), Local Government (London)
Practice Areas: Principal areas of practice are regulatory, environmental, planning and administrative law. Regularly instructed by corporate and individual clients and by national and local government bodies in regulatory, environmental and health and safety matters.
Professional Memberships: Planning and Environment Bar Association, Administrative Law Bar Association, Health and Safety Lawyers Association.
Career: Called to the Bar in 1970 and began to practise at 6 Pump Court in 1971. Appointed Recorder 1987. Took Silk 1990. Leader SE Circuit, January 2001-December 2003. Chairman of the Bar Council, 2006. Visiting Professor of Law at City University.
Publications: Blackstone's Planning Practice.
Personal: Educated at Eltham College, London (1955-65) and Jesus College, Cambridge (1966-69). Born 4 January 1947. Lives in London and Peterborough.

HOCKTON, Andrew
Serjeants' Inn Chambers, London
020 7427 5000
clerks@serjeantsinn.com
Featured in Clinical Negligence (London), Professional Discipline (London)
Practice Areas: Andrew Hockton was called to the Bar in 1984. Andrew specialises in clinical negligence and healthcare, professional discipline and regulatory, inquests and inquiries, Court of Protection and public and administrative law. An earlier edition notes that "he is a real star – not only a pleasure to work with but highly intelligent and unflappable with it." Please visit the Serjeants' Inn Chambers website for his profile, which sets out full details of his practice including relevant work of note.
Professional Memberships: PNBA, COMBAR.
Publications: Law of Consent to Medical Treatment, Clinical Negligence: Powers & Harris 4th Ed (2003, Sweet & Maxwell) (Chapter on Consent).
Personal: City University: Diploma in Law, Balliol College, Oxford: BA (Classics scholarship), fluent in Spanish.

HODGETTS, Elizabeth
St Philips Chambers, Birmingham
0121 246 7000
ehodgetts@st-philips.com
Featured in Employment (Midlands)
Practice Areas: Elizabeth Hodgetts practises exclusively in employment, employment-related civil litigation and discrimination law. She is a member of the Attorney-General's Panel of Counsel. Her clients include government bodies, local authorities, NHS Trusts, educational institutions and private sector employers, including on a Public Access basis. She also welcomes instructions from claimants. Her practice includes the full range of discrimination claims, whistleblowing claims, equal pay, collective consultation and trade disputes, TUPE disputes, breach of contract claims including enhanced redundancy and commission disputes, and significant unfair and wrongful dismissal claims. She is regularly briefed to act in multi-week hearings, including recently, a two week hearing defending claims of disability discrimination and constructive dismissal against a local authority, a four week hearing representing a claimant bringing a very high value whistleblowing claim, and a four week hearing defending a local authority against a whistleblowing claim.
Professional Memberships: Employment Lawyers Association.
Career: Call 1998; appointed to Attorney General's Regional Panel of Counsel in 2012.
Publications: Contributor to 'Discrimination in Employment' Tucker and George (Sweet and Maxwell).
Personal: University of Oxford (Mansfield College) BA (Hons) MA Oxon (Exhibitioner).

HOGARTH, Andrew QC
12 King's Bench Walk, London
020 7583 0811
hogarth@12kbw.co.uk
Featured in Personal Injury (London)
Practice Areas: Specialist in industrial law, employment law and personal injuries with a particular interest in psychiatric injury and all forms of industrial disease. Interesting cases include the stress cases of Hatton v Sutherland, Hartman v Southend NHS Trust and Bristol City Council v Deadman, the personal injury cases of Owens v Noble and Page v Smith, the industrial disease cases of Fairchild v Glenhaven and Atkinson v DECC, the cases of Yates v Chin and Thompson v Thompson in the Cayman Islands and Bermuda on discount rates in personal injury actions and numerous employment law cases including Kernohan v AG for Cayman Islands, Marshalls Clay v Caulfield, Byrne Brothers v Baird and Bernadone v Pall Mall Services. Defended numerous levy claims made by the ECITB.
Career: MA (Cantab). Called to the Bar 1974. Joined 12 King's Bench Walk in 1975. Head of Chambers at 12 King's Bench Walk 2005 – 2015.
Publications: Author: 'Asbestos Disease Litigation' (Butterworths 2004). Contributor: Munkman on Employers' Liability 14th, 15th and 16th Editions and PIBA handbook.

HOLBECH, Charles
New Square Chambers, London
020 7419 8000
charles.holbech@newsquarechambers.co.uk
Featured in Chancery (London)
Practice Areas: Trusts, wills, probate, tax, court of protection, real property, landlord and tenant.
Professional Memberships: STEP, ACTAPS, Chancery Bar Association.
Publications: Halsbury's Laws of England, Inheritance Tax. Williams, Mortimer & Sunnucks, Executors, & Probate, 20th Ed., Ch. 50, Taxation of Personal Representatives.

HOLBROOK, Jon
Cornerstone Barristers, London
020 7242 4986
jonh@cornerstonebarristers.com
Featured in Social Housing (London)
Practice Areas: All aspects of social housing, property and public law (including community care and Court of Protection). Jon Holbrook built up a tenant-based practice during his 12 years at Garden Court Chambers and after two years at Hardwicke Building he joined Cornerstone Barristers in 2006 where he is now instructed mostly by landlords, local authorities and community care providers.
Professional Memberships: Administrative Law Bar Association (ALBA). Property Bar Association (PBA). Social Housing Law Association (SHLA). Jon instigated the formation of SHLA in 2005, an organisation he chaired until 2008.
Career: Before being called to the Bar in 1991 Jon was a local authority housing

advisor and tenancy relations officer at Westminster City Council.
Publications: General Editor of the Housing & Property Law Review. Consultant Editor of the Journal of Community Care Law.

HOLDCROFT, Matthew
5 Essex Court, London
020 7410 2000
holdcroft@5essexcourt.co.uk
Featured in Police Law (All Circuits), Professional Discipline (London)
Practice Areas: Public law, tortious actions, discipline and regulatory work and human rights. Matthew's practice includes work for both public authorities and private clients. Recent high profile work includes appearing in the Independent Inquiry into Child Sexual Abuse, the Hillsborough and Raoul Moat inquests, Plebgate (the Federation Representatives), Kingsley Burrell, PC Harwood (Ian Tomlinson) discipline hearing and advising in relation to aspects of the Jimmy Savile investigation. Matthew's advisory work covers a wide range of areas from safety and security of nuclear installations, fatal accidents, shootings, police actions (all aspects), personal injury litigation and regulatory and disciplinary investigations and hearings. Recent public law cases include, R (Yavuz) v CC of West Yorkshire [2016] EWHC 2054 (Admin), CXS v CC of Hampshire [2016] EWHC 848 (QB), R (CC of West Yorkshire) v IPCC [2014] EWCA Civ 1367, R (Commissioner of Police of the Metropolis) v Police Appeals Tribunal [2013] EWHC 1684 (Admin), R (Lee) v Chief Constable of Essex [2012] EWHC 283 (Admin) and R (L) v Commissioner of Police of the Metropolis [2009] UKSC 3.
Professional Memberships: ALBA, PIBA, ARDL.
Career: Called to the Bar in 1998.
Publications: Matthew regularly writes articles for a number of publications and lectures on all areas and aspects of his practice.

HOLL-ALLEN, Jonathan
Serjeants' Inn Chambers, London
020 7427 5000
ssomerville@serjeantsinn.com
Featured in Clinical Negligence (London), Professional Discipline (London)
Practice Areas: Jonathan Holl-Allen was called to the Bar in 1990. Jonathan specialises in clinical negligence and healthcare, professional discipline, inquests and inquiries, police and employment law. An earlier edition notes that "he is an excellent advocate. Commentators say that he is highly professional, very steady and adept at advising across a range of issues" and that "he is very knowledgeable and thorough in his approach. He spends time on cases and puts in a lot of hard work – you can trust his advice." Please visit the Serjeants' Inn Chambers website for his profile, which sets out full details of his practice including relevant work of note.
Professional Memberships: PNBA, ARDL.
Publications: Principles of Medical Law (co-author of chapter on Regulation of Healthcare Professions); Contributing Editor to Medical Law Reports since 1999.

HOLLAND, Jordan
5 Stone Buildings, London
020 7242 6201
clerks@5sblaw.com
Featured in Chancery (London), Art and Cultural Property Law (London), Court of Protection (All Circuits)
Practice Areas: Chancery practice with an emphasis on contentious trusts and probate, family provision, Court of Protection and matters involving art and cultural property. Recent experience includes Watts v Watts [2014] EWHC 668 (Ch) (will forgery) and Dellal v Dellal [2015] EWHC 907 (Fam) (anti-avoidance in family provision claims). In the Court of Protection, Jordan appeared in Re M (N v O&P) [2013] WTLR 681, RE BM (JB v AG) [2014] All ER (D) 178 and Re E [2014] Med LR 417. He has particular expertise in cases involving art and cultural property, having appeared in Avrora Fine Arts Investment v Christie, Manson & Woods Ltd [2012] PNLR 35. Jordan acts for clients across the spectrum of the art world, including dealers, galleries, collectors, institutions and governments. He has a notable offshore practice, particularly in the Channel Islands and continues to act in relation to long-running Jersey litigation relating to a very substantial family charitable trust. He acts for the professional trustee in the Crociani litigation.
Professional Memberships: Chancery Bar Association, PAIAM (Professional Advisors to the International Art Market), Institute of Art and Law.
Career: Called 2009.
Publications: Regular contributor to specialist journals. Lectures on all areas of his practice, including Court of Protection and art and cultural property matters.
Personal: Regular contributor to specialist journals. Lectures on all areas of his practice, including Court of Protection and art and cultural property matters.

HOLMES, Harriet
Tanfield Chambers, London
020 7421 5300
harrietholmes@tanfieldchambers.co.uk
Featured in Real Estate Litigation (London)
Practice Areas: Harriet is a property specialist who deals with all aspects of residential and commercial landlord and tenant litigation, as well as real property matters. Experience ranges from enfranchisement and all forms of possession action (including forfeiture) to party wall matters and development-related / joint venture work. Recent and representative cases include: Avgarski v Alphabet Square Management Co Ltd [2016] UKUT (service charges), Nata Lee Ltd v Abid & Anr [2014] EWCA Civ 1652 (adverse possession, easements and boundary dispute), Chliaifchtein v Bainbridge Estates Belgravia Limited [2015] EWHC 47 (TCC) (party wall injunction, as junior counsel). She is also currently acting as junior counsel in a high value alleged joint venture development agreement dispute in the Chancery Division, and a complex forfeiture action involving alleged breaches of environment agency licences.
Professional Memberships: Chancery Bar Association (Harriet sits on the Association's Publications Sub-committee), Property Bar Association, Pyramus and Thisbe Club, Women in Property.
Career: LLB (Hons), LLM, BPTC. Called to the Bar 2011; Member of Tanfield Chambers since September 2013.
Publications: (With other members of Tanfield Chambers) 'Service Charges and Management: Law and Practice' (3rd Edition, Sweet and Maxwell, 2013), 'The Law and Practice of Party Walls' by Nicholas Isaac (1st Edition, Property Publishing, 2014) (Contributor).
Personal: Outside Chambers, Harriet enjoys playing and listening to music, cycling, and spending time on the (european) continent.

HOLMES, Justin
Radcliffe Chambers, London
020 78310081
jholmes@radcliffechambers.com
Featured in Chancery (London), Court of Protection (All Circuits)
Practice Areas: Many years' experience of litigation in the Court of Protection. Cases have involved the appointment and removal of attorneys and deputies, the making of statutory wills, appropriate residential care for the patient, the legality of attempts by family members to limit contact to the patient by other family members, and other matters. Also specialises in disputes concerning probate, the administration of estates, Inheritance Act claims, and the construction and administration of trusts.
Professional Memberships: Chancery Bar Association, Association of Contentious Trust and Probate Specialists.
Career: Called to the Bar in 1994. Joined the Chambers of Lord Goodhart QC at 3 New Square, Lincoln's Inn in 1995 and Radcliffe Chambers in 2001.
Personal: Educated at Queens' College, Cambridge.

HOLWILL, Derek
Hailsham Chambers, London
020 7643 5000
derek.holwill@hailshamchambers.com
Featured in Professional Negligence (London)
Practice Areas: Derek Holwill specialises in professional negligence and clinical negligence claims. He is listed by both the Legal 500 and by Chambers UK in the top rank of juniors working in the professional negligence field; and as a leading junior in the clinical negligence field, His work also includes advising on coverage issues and general insurance policy matters. Recent cases include; Law Society v Sephton [2006] 2 AC 543 House of Lords – limitation and the date of accrual of a cause of action in negligence. McManus Seddon Runhams v European Risk [2014] Lloyd's Rep IR 169 (CA) – the pre-requisites for a block notifications under a solicitors professional indemnity policy. Davisons v Nationwide [2013] PNLR 12 (CA) A breach of trust claim by a mortgage lender against a solicitor, where the solicitor was relieved of liability under the Trustee Act 1925 s.61 because he had acted honestly and reasonably, and the loss had been caused by the fraud of an unconnected third party. Mulcahy v Castles [2013] EWCA Civ 1686 – the alleged failure properly to instruct Counsel, and the correct approach to be adopted when dealing with a litigant in person with Asperger's Syndrome. Tippett v Guys and St Thomas' Hospital [2014] EWHC 917 (QB), a clinical negligence claim involving the interpretation of the CTG trace.

Professional Memberships: Professional Negligence Bar Association (PNBA).
Career: Called 1982.

HONEY, Richard
Francis Taylor Building, London
020 7353 8415
clerks@ftbchambers.co.uk
Featured in Agriculture & Rural Affairs (London), Environment (London), Planning (London)
Practice Areas: Richard Honey practises in public and environmental law, with particular specialisms in judicial review and High Court challenges, infrastructure projects, compulsory purchase, compensation and land valuation, and village greens. Recent work includes DCOs, HS2, Crossrail, Olympics, railways, airport expansions, highways, energy, ports and wind farms. Environmental work includes contaminated land, protected habitats and species, civil liability for pollution and environmental crime. Acts as party representative in mediation and sits as an inspector in village green inquiries. Court of Appeal appearances in last year include cases of Old Hunstanton PC, Broadview, Suffolk Coastal DC, Thames Water, and Howell.
Professional Memberships: Planning and Environment Bar Association, Administrative Law Bar Association, Bar European Group, UK Environmental Law Association, Environmental and Planning Law Association of Northern Ireland, Compulsory Purchase Association, National Infrastructure Planning Association.
Career: Called to the Bar at Inner Temple (2003) and Northern Ireland (2013). Attorney General's A Panel of junior counsel to the Crown. Visiting lecturer, King's College London. Chartered Surveyor. Fellow of the Chartered Institute of Arbitrators. Associate tenant, KBW Chambers, Leeds.
Publications: Editor: Gadsden on Commons & Greens; Compulsory Purchase & Compensation Service. Contributor: Burnett-Hall on Environmental Law; National Infrastructure Planning Handbook; Law of Regulatory Sanctions and Enforcement.

HOPKINS, Adrian QC
Serjeants' Inn Chambers, London
020 7427 5000
ahopkins@serjeantsinn.com
Featured in Clinical Negligence (London), Professional Discipline (London)
Practice Areas: Adrian Hopkins QC was called to the Bar in 1984 and took silk in 2003. Adrian specialises in clinical negligence and healthcare, inquests and inquiries and professional discipline and regulatory law. An earlier edition notes that he has "the ability to really drive a case through to maximise the return for a client" and he "works extremely well with clients, solicitors and experts." Please visit the Serjeants' Inn Chambers website for his profile, which sets out full details of his practice including relevant work of note.

HOPKINS, Robin
11KBW, London
020 7632 8500
robin.hopkins@11kbw.com
Featured in Data Protection (London)
Practice Areas: Highly experienced information rights specialist (data protection, privacy, FOI, EIR) also practising in public and local government law. Co-edits the Panopticon blog. Regularly acts for the ICO, commercial clients and public authorities. Appeared in leading data protection

cases e.g. Dr DB (mixed personal data), C v Northumberland (retention periods for child protection data), Ittihadieh (subject access requests), Edem (definition of personal data) Southern Pacific (commercial insolvency). Appeared in leading data breach, privacy and monetary penalty cases, e.g. Catt/T (Supreme Court; Article 8, policing information), Niebel (privacy and direct marketing). Highly experienced in information-sharing, subject access, surveillance, data protection compensation claims, right to be forgotten and media/social media disputes. Has appeared in hundreds of FOI cases, including leading Court of Appeal cases on FOI (Zola – DWP work programmes; IPSA – MPs' expenses) and EIR (Henney). Local government expertise includes Assets of Community Value, with appearances in the leading cases (e.g. Banner Homes).
Professional Memberships: Ecclesiastical Law Society.
Career: Called 2008; Attorney General's B Panel.
Publications: Co-edits Law Society's Freedom of Information Handbook (2012); 'expert commentator' at Freedom of Information Journal.
Personal: Grew up in South Africa; came to UK (Exeter College, Oxford) as Rhodes Scholar; degrees in finance, PPE, theology.

HORNE, Michael QC
Serjeants' Inn Chambers, London
020 7475 5000
clerks@serjeantsinn.com
Featured in Clinical Negligence (London), Court of Protection (All Circuits)
Practice Areas: Michael Horne QC was called to the Bar in 1992 and took silk in 2016. Michael specialises in clinical negligence and healthcare, professional discipline, inquiries and inquests and Court of Protection. An earlier edition notes that "he's a really conscientious barrister. He's a very hard-working man and you'll always get his full attention. Good on his feet, he has a very sure grasp of the case and is genuinely helpful – nothing's too much trouble." Please visit the Serjeants' Inn Chambers website for his profile, which sets out full details of his practice including relevant work of note.
Professional Memberships: PNBA, LCLBA.
Publications: LS Law Medical reports, contributing editor.

HORNE, Wilson
Kings Chambers, Manchester
0345 034 3444
clerks@kingschambers.com
Featured in Real Estate Litigation (Northern)
Practice Areas: Wilson undertakes all aspects of property law. His practice has a bias towards commercial property work, including planning and construction law. Particular specialities include planning clawback and overage, promotion agreements and section 106 agreements. All types of valuation disputes are handled, particularly in relation to rent review, option prices and compulsory purchase compensation. Professional liability within the above practice areas is undertaken, with a particular emphasis on lawyers, surveyors and construction professionals. Wilson also practices in dispute resolution; experience includes extensive trial work, appeals / High Court challenges, arbitration, expert determination, and tribunal work.
Professional Memberships: Chancery Bar Association, Northern Circuit Chancery Bar Association, Northern Circuit Commercial Bar Association.
Career: University of Leeds LLB (Hons), Called 1992 (Lincoln's Inn). Regularly accepts direct access and licensed access instructions.

HORNETT, Stuart
Selborne Chambers, London
020 7420 9500
stuart.hornett@selbornechambers.co.uk
Featured in Real Estate Litigation (London)
Practice Areas: Stuart practice comprises commercial chancery, property and professional negligence.
Professional Memberships: Chancery Bar Association; Property Bar Association.
Career: Stuart is an experienced advocate whose practice encompasses commercial chancery work, company and banking litigation, trusts and contentious probate, property and professional liability. His practice includes international and domestic arbitration work. He has extensive experience in cases of high value and complexity and has appeared in a number of high profile cases including the BTA Bank v Albyazov litigation. He provides lectures and seminars and is a contributor to Cousins on the Law of Mortgages.

HOSKING, Ruth
Quadrant Chambers, London
020 7822 1473
ruth.hosking@quadrantchambers.com
Featured in Shipping (London)
Practice Areas: Ruth's practice spans the full spectrum of commercial litigation and arbitration including general commercial, commodities, energy, insurance, international trade and shipping. Since joining chambers in 2003, she has appeared in the House of Lords, Court of Appeal, and High Court. She has also represented clients in a variety of international and trade arbitrations (including ICC, LCIA, LMAA and GAFTA) and assisted clients in FOSFA arbitrations. Ruth has acted in a number of high profile cases, including "The Achilleas", a leading case on the contractual principles of remoteness of damage. Most recently, she was junior counsel to Nigel Jacobs QC in "The Atlantik Confidence", a 7-week trial challenging the right to limit under the Limitation Convention (judgment awaited). She is a meticulous advocate, devoted to the needs of her client, combining rigorous analysis with a common sense commercial approach. Please visit www.quadrantchambers.com for Ruth's detailed CV.
Professional Memberships: Member of COMBAR. Ruth sits on COMBAR (Vice-Chair of the Equality and Diversity Committee), British Insurance Law Association, ICC YAF, London Shipping Law Centre, LCIA Young International Arbitration Group and Young Maritime Professionals Group.
Career: Called to the Bar in 2002. Prior to coming to the bar Ruth studied for an LLM in commercial & corporate law specialising in restitution, corporate insolvency, conflict of laws and marine insurance at UCL; and was a visiting law tutor at King's College London teaching tort (including economic torts) from 2001-02.
Publications: Ruth has recently published a chapter on reasonable contracts of carriage in international sale contracts in International Trade and Carriage of Goods (Informa, published August 2016).

HOSKINS, Mark QC
Brick Court Chambers, London
020 7379 3550
ian.moyler@brickcourt.co.uk
Featured in Administrative & Public Law (London), Competition/European Law (London)
Career: Mark Hoskins specialises in competition, EU, administrative and sports Law. He has extensive experience before the domestic courts, the Competition Appeal Tribunal and the EU Courts. He has appeared in many of the leading competition law cases in recent years, including AstraZeneca v Commission, Intel Corporation v Commission, Akzo Nobel v Commission, Devenish & Ors v Sanofi-Aventis & Ors, Cooper Tire & Ors v Shell & Ors, National Grid v ABB, Tesco plc v Competition Commission, BAA v Competition Commission, Durkan v OFT, British Sky Broadcasting Ltd v Ofcom. Mark has been instructed in more than eighty cases before the European Court of Justice and General court, including Air Transport Association of America v Secretary of State for Energy and Climate Change, Commission v Spain, International Workers Federation v Viking Line, Köbler v Austria, Commission v France. In administrative law, Mark's significant cases include R(Swami Suryananda) v The Welsh Minsiters; R(British Casino Association) v Secretary of State for Culture, Media and Sport; Wilson & ors v Secretary of State for Trade and Industry; Adan v London Borough of Newham; R v National Lottery Commission, ex parte Camelot Group plc and R v Secretary of State for the Home Department, ex parte Fayed.

HOUGH, Jonathan QC
4 New Square, London
020 7822 2000
j.hough@4newsquare.com
Featured in Consumer Law (London), Inquests & Public Inquiries (All Circuits), Insurance (London)
Practice Areas: Principal areas of practice are: insurance and reinsurance; professional liability; commercial and consumer law; administrative law (including inquiries). Insurance work ranges from substantial coverage disputes to litigation and arbitration between insurers, reinsurers, brokers and coverholders. Experienced with most classes of risk and in non-contentious drafting work. Professional liability practice covers mainly solicitors, barristers, financial professionals, insurance brokers and surveyors / valuers. Public law practice includes judicial review and advisory work covering local government, professional discipline and commercial regulation. Special expertise in the law relating to inquiries and inquests, and experienced as counsel to the inquiry (Hillsborough Stadium Disaster; the Princess of Wales; de Menezes; Potters Bar and Grayrigg rail disasters; explosion on HMS Tireless). Special expertise in the law of consumer credit. Notable recent cases include: AXA Corporate Solutions v Weir Services Australia [2016] EWHC 904 (Comm); PM Law v Motorplus [2016] EWHC 193 (QB); R (LF) v Senior Coroner for Inner South London [2016] 1 WLR 2385; Coles v Hetherton (RSA motor insurance lead cases)[2015] 1 WLR 160; Singh v Yaqubi [2013] Lloyd's Rep IR 398; Network Rail Infrastructure v Conarken Group [2012] 1 All ER (Comm) 692; Persimmon Homes v Great Lakes Reinsurance [2011] Lloyd's Rep IR 101; Parkinson Engineering Services v Swan [2010] PNLR 17; R (Lewis) v HM Coroner for Shropshire [2010] 1 WLR 1836; Heath v Southern Pacific Mortgages [2010] Ch 254.
Professional Memberships: PNBA; LCLCBA; ALBA; COMBAR.
Career: Called to the Bar 1997. Took silk 2014.
Publications: Contributing editor of Jackson & Powell on Professional Liability (7th edn.).
Personal: Educated at Bradford Grammar School and St Hugh's College Oxford (first in classics). Queen Mother scholar, Middle Temple. Graded outstanding on Bar course.

HOWARD, Anneli
Monckton Chambers, London
020 7405 7211
ahoward@monckton.com
Featured in Competition/European Law (London), Aviation (London), Telecommunications (London)
Practice Areas: EU law, UK and EU competition law, state aid, utility regulation, aviation, telecoms, energy, rail, consumer protection, public and administrative law. Anneli has appeared in over 20 cases before the CJEU and is involved in numerous competition damages and injunction claims, including Visa (interchange); PU Foam; Power Cables; Acushnet. She also advises parties in antitrust investigations, market investigations, regulatory market reviews and EA02 consumer enforcement actions.
Career: Previously EU Litigation Solicitor at Freshfields with experience in Hong Kong, Paris, London and Milan; Referendaire to Judge Edward at the CJEU 2000-2003; Called 2002; Junior Counsel to the Crown since 2010 and A panel from 2016; Standing Counsel to the Civil Aviation Authority from 2012 to date; Nominated as Chambers Competition/EU Junior of the Year 2014. Anneli was selected as one of only ten barristers named in 2016's The Lawyer's Hot 100.
Publications: Regular contributor to National Courts chapter in Bellamy and Child's European Union Law of Competition; Consultant Editor to UK Competition Procedure (OUP 2006); Contributor to Competition Litigation in the UK (Sweet & Maxwell 2005); Co-author of Lasok Millet and Howard "Judicial Control in the EU"; regular contributor to JECLAP and ECLR.

HOWARD, Charles QC
1 King's Bench Walk, London
020 7936 1500
chowardqc@1kbw.co.uk
Featured in Family/Matrimonial (London)
Practice Areas: all areas of Family Law including professional negligence and in particular matrimonial finance and private law children disputes.
Professional Memberships: FLBA
Career: In full time practice since 1975 and as a QC since 1999.
Personal: MA from Cambridge University.

HOWARD, Nicola
25 Bedford Row, London
020 7067 1500
nhoward@25bedfordrow.com
Featured in Crime (London), Financial Crime (London)
Practice Areas: Defence counsel instructed to provide specialist strategic advice pre-charge and regarding FSA investigation and interviews with respect to LIBOR and other benchmark investigations that are as

yet not public. Experienced in the conduct of the most serious and complex national and international financial crime investigations, including false instrument, internet, MTIC, VAT, mortgage, land banking, IRSF and large scale deception as well as Companies Act and Director offences. Fraud: D (international identity fraud, BBC undercover investigation for 3 months) P (MTIC fraud), C- (carbon credit fraud) – M – ('cash for crash' conspiracy to defraud by false representation spanning 3 years). H (conspiracy to defraud and corruption at the DVLA), P (Conspiracy to defraud the Home Office,), F (conspiracy to defraud the DTI), Stapely (fraud by nun on Roman Catholic school, subject of BBC drama). Frequently sought after to advise pre-charge in relation to the most complex cases. Skilled in the identification of relevant issues, taking appropriate action and sensible resolution. High attention to detail, and effective analysis of extensive and complex material. Presents propositions in a concise, persuasive and attractive manner. Lectures with different city firms on a variety of current financial crime topics.
Professional Memberships: CBA, POCLA, ARDL, FFF, FSLA, ACFE.
Career: Called 1995, Recorder – South Eastern Circuit (2016). Qualified Certified Fraud Examiner, ACFE Course provider. Speaker at the World Referral Bar Conference in Capetown (2004). Chairman of the Young Barristers Committee (2003).
Publications: Deferred Prosecution Agreements (JIBFL) Dismissal Hearings (Practical Law).

HOWARTH, Simon

Hailsham Chambers, London
020 7643 5000
simon.howarth@hailshamchambers.com
Featured in Professional Negligence (London)
Practice Areas: Simon concentrates on professional negligence. His work principally involves lawyers, accountants, and financial advisers, and related professional indemnity insurance disputes. He also has experience with commercial case and technology and construction court claims that allege professional negligence, and in actions arising out of fire, flood and the like. He is admitted to practice in the Republic of Ireland and the International Finance Centre in Dubai. Simon was called to the Bar by Grays Inn. He was a pupil at 2 Crown Office Row which later became part of Crown Office Chambers. He then became a tenant at those Chambers until moving to Hailsham in 2011. In his early years at the Bar, Simon's practice was broad based, helping him gain important "on his feet" experience before all types of tribunal.
Publications: He is a lecturer to solicitors and insurers on his specialist areas and has contributed articles to several professional journals including the Law Society Gazette. He is currently assisting the editors of on Construction Contracts and Construction Insurance in relation to the chapters relating to professional indemnity insurance and insurance brokers.
Personal: Education: Grays Inn Mould Scholar and Advocacy Prize; Magdalen College Oxford.

HOWE, Martin QC

8 New Square, London
020 7405 4321
martin.howe@8newsquare.co.uk
Featured in Information Technology (London), Intellectual Property (London), Media & Entertainment (London)
Practice Areas: Barrister (QC) in Intellectual Property, Information Technology and European Union law relating to IP and other fields such as free movement of goods and services and regulatory and public law. Many high technology cases, with particular emphasis on computing, information technology and internet fields; also extensive experience in biotechnology/ genetic engineering cases. Regular appearances in the ECJ, Luxembourg, and the European Patent Office, Munich. Recent cases include: Tsit Wing v TWG Tea (Hong Kong Court of Final Appeal), Philip Morris v Sec of State for Health (Admin Court, acted for Sec of State defending tobacco plain packaging regulations), RFU v Viagogo (UK Supreme Court), SAS v WPL (ECJ Grand Chamber and Court of Appeal), Nintendo v PC Box (ECJ on reference from Milan). For comprehensive CV visit website at www.8newsquare.co.uk.
Professional Memberships: Intellectual Property Bar Association (IPBA); Bar European Group (BEG); The Intellectual Property Lawyers Organisation (TIPLO).
Career: QC 1996. Before call to the Bar, worked for IBM (UK) as systems engineer and as a contract programmer. Member, govt Commission on a Bill of Rights for the UK, 2011-12. Appointed Person to hear appeals from UKIPO in designs matters, 2015.
Publications: Halsbury's Laws on Trade Marks, 'Trade Names and Designs'; 'Russell-Clarke and Howe on Industrial Designs' (6th to 9th (2016) edns).
Personal: Educated at Trinity Hall, Cambridge (BA Part I Engineering and Part II Law, MA).

HOWE, Timothy QC

Fountain Court Chambers, London
020 78423742
th@fountaincourt.co.uk
Featured in International Arbitration (London), Professional Negligence (London), Banking & Finance (London), Commercial Dispute Resolution (London), Energy & Natural Resources (London), Fraud (London), Insurance (London), Telecommunications (London)
Practice Areas: Specialising in domestic and international commercial litigation and arbitration, with particular expertise in: banking and financial services, energy and natural resources, oil and gas, international cross-border disputes, insurance and reinsurance, corporate mergers, acquisitions and disposals, joint ventures, telecoms, professional negligence and civil fraud & asset recovery. Recent cases include LIBOR litigation against global investment banks, Lehman Brothers Administration, Madoff fraud proceedings; Icelandic banking crisis; UK Bank Charges litigation; Box Clever securitisation; Masri Yemen oil & gas litigation; 9/11 WTC & Hurricane Katrina reinsurance claims; Eurotunnel restructuring; litigation relating to AIG, Enron, Parmalat, Polly Peck, Split Capital Trusts, UK pension mis-selling, Film Finance insurance, the PA LMX spiral, & HIH Group; US Asbestos & Pollution losses in the London insurance/reinsurance markets.
Professional Memberships: COMBAR Executive Committee (since 2000). CEDR Accredited Mediator (2004). Chairman, Bar Council Member Services Board (2008).
Career: Called 1987. Bermudian Bar 1998. Queen Mother's, Harmsworth, Astbury Senior Scholarships, Middle Temple, Silk 2008. Bar of Trinidad and Tobago 2015.
Publications: Co-author, 'Law of Bank Payments', 'Commercial Court Procedure'.
Personal: St Paul's School, Magdalen College, Oxford (1st Class Hons 1985). Languages: French & Italian.

HOWELL WILLIAMS, Craig QC

Francis Taylor Building, London
020 7353 8415
clerks@ftbchambers.co.uk
Featured in Planning (London)
Practice Areas: Craig Howell Williams QC specialises in planning, environment and related areas of public law. He is acknowledged as one of the leading practitioners in the field and has acted in some of the most high profile cases. He represents developers and operators, local authorities, third parties and others at public inquiries and in a range of other tribunals. He is regularly involved in large planning and /infrastructure schemes including proposals for new settlements, urban extensions, airport expansions, road and rail projects, reservoirs and also in employment, leisure, retail and other commercial development projects. His experience encompasses many different legislative regimes, including: heritage and listed buildings, compulsory purchase and compensation, applications under the Wildlife and Countryside legislation, advertisement regulations and aggregates levy. In court he served as Junior Treasury Counsel (B Panel) and has appeared in a number of significant cases. He is also a CEDR Accredited Mediator.
Professional Memberships: Planning and Environment Bar Association; UKELA, Parliamentary Bar Mess; National Infrastructure Planning Association; Compulsory Purchase Association; Chartered Institute of Arbitrators; RICS Mediation Panel; Chartered Institute of Arbitrators.
Career: Called to Bar: 1983, QC: 2009. MCIArb (2013). DCLG Planning Services Mediation Panel (2013). Lead Assistant Commissioner to the Boundary Commission for England (2013). Junior Counsel to the Crown (B Panel) (1993-99). Chairman of the London Luton Airport Consultative Committee (S35 Civil Aviation Act 1982) (1999-2002). Accredited Mediator (CEDR 2005), RICS Mediation Panel (2010).

HOWELLS, Catherine

Exchange Chambers, Liverpool
0151 236 7747
howells@exchangechambers.co.uk
Featured in Personal Injury (Northern)
Practice Areas: Cath practises exclusively in the fields of higher value personal injury and clinical negligence. She is regularly instructed (in her own capacity and as junior counsel) in catastrophic brain or spinal cord injury cases and fatal accidents. She has particular experience of claims where issues of capacity are paramount. Other areas include chronic pain syndrome, somatisation disorder and complex regional pain syndrome claims. Her clinical negligence work includes mismanagement of labour, mismanagement of gynaecological surgery, failed diagnosis of intra-cranial abscess, undiagnosed fractures and delayed cancer diagnosis. Her practice involves expertise in cases where welfare and medical issues are at the forefront. She is also a volunteer for the National Autistic Society at tribunal hearings. Cath sits as a Recorder and has experience of deciding clinical negligence trials. She is also an accredited mediator.
Professional Memberships: Personal Injury Bar Association, Northern Circuit Medical Law Association.
Personal: Liverpool University, Gray's Inn Entrance Award, Gray's Inn Goldie Award.

HOWELLS, Chris

Civitas Law, Cardiff
08450713007
christopher.howells@civitaslaw.com
Featured in Employment (Wales & Chester)
Practice Areas: Chris specialises in employment law. He is experienced at conducting cases across the spectrum of employment law issues ranging from routine unfair dismissal claims to discrimination claims on all of the prohibited grounds. Chris is also regularly instructed to deal with sometimes complex TUPE cases, particularly involving insolvent employers.
Professional Memberships: Employment Lawyers' Association; PIBA; Wales and Chester Circuit.
Career: Called to the Bar in 1999. Chris joined Civitas Law, Cardiff in 2010 as a member of their Employment and Personal Injury Practice Groups. Appointed to the Equality and Human Right Commission Preferred Counsel Panel during 2010.
Personal: Educated at Atlantic College; UCL (LLB); Cambridge (MA). Leisure interests include football and water sports. Chris is fluent in French.

HOWELLS, James QC

Atkin Chambers, London
020 7404 0102
jhowells@atkinchambers.com
Featured in Construction (London), Information Technology (London)
Practice Areas: James specialises in construction, engineering and IT disputes both domestic and international with experience of litigation, arbitration and other forms of dispute resolution. His experience in engineering disputes has included a number of energy-related cases involving, amongst other things, oil and gas production platforms and rigs, FPSOs, gas storage caverns, combined power and desalination plant, power station/dams. He has extensive experience of domestic and international infrastructure projects include metro and heavy rail, roads and airports. IT experience includes commercial and technical disputes in respect of projects ranging from small to medium size commercial systems and software to major government infrastructure projects. He has international arbitration experience in building, engineering and IT disputes in Hong Kong, Singapore, Thailand, Russia, Oman, Continental Europe, Philippines, Indonesia, Australia, UAE, South Africa, Channel Islands, India and Tanzania.
Professional Memberships: TECBAR, LCLCBA, COMBAR, SCL, Society for Computers and Law.
Career: MA (Cantab), BCL (Oxon). Silk 2014.
Publications: Contributing Editor of 'Hudson's Building and Engineering Contracts' 12th and 13th editions.

HOWELLS, Katherine
Old Square Chambers, London
020 7269 0300
clerksroom@oldsquare.co.uk
Featured in Travel (London)
Practice Areas: Katherine Howells specialises in personal injury, travel, aviation and associated commercial proceedings. She has extensive experience acting for both claimants and defendants. Katherine's domestic practice has a focus on high-value road traffic and employers' liability claims together with cases involving occupiers' and public liability issues. She also has a significant travel practice with a particular specialist knowledge of and interest in aviation matters. Katherine deals frequently with claims involving accidents overseas or foreign nationals injured or killed in the UK, questions of jurisdiction and applicable law, the right to cross border recovery of benefits under EC Regulation 883/2004, claims under the Package Travel Regulations, Montreal Convention passenger injury, delay and lost or damaged baggage claims, delayed and denied boarding and downgrading claims under EC Regulation 261/2004 and accidents on board aircraft (including hot air balloons and microlights) or at airports or airfields. She is also experienced in dealing with contractual and other recovery proceedings made by tour operators against foreign suppliers, aviation maintenance disputes and claims concerning IATA Ground Handling Agreements. Katherine's recent reported cases include Bianco v Bennett [2015], Yapp v Foreign and Commonwealth Office [2014] and Donkers & BGV v Storm Aviation v Lufthansa [2014].
Professional Memberships: Personal Injuries Bar Association, Travel & Tourism Lawyers Association.
Career: Called to the Bar in 1994.

HUBBLE, Ben QC
4 New Square, London
020 7822 2011
b.hubble@4newsquare.com
Featured in Professional Negligence (London), Insurance (London), Offshore (London), Professional Discipline (London)
Practice Areas: Professional liability claims and disciplinary proceedings involving accountants and auditors, actuaries, directors, insurance brokers, lawyers and tax advisers, as well as general commercial litigation (both onshore and offshore), particularly banking, financial services and insurance. Substantial expertise in multi-party litigation, post credit crunch claims and tax schemes.
Professional Memberships: Professional Negligence Bar Association (vice chair), COMBAR , Chancery Bar Association.
Career: Called to the Bar in 1992. Appointed QC in 2009. Appointed Head of Chambers in 2013. Elected Chairman of the Professional Negligence Bar Association in 2015. Nominated for Chambers & Partners' Professional Negligence QC of the Year for 2012 and 2013. Chambers & Partners' Professional Negligence Junior of the Year in both 2006 and 2008.
Publications: Chapter on insurance brokers in 'Jackson & Powell: Professional Liability Precedents' (Sweet & Maxwell).
Personal: BA Hons (Oxon). Leisure interests: family, skiing and football.

HUGHES, Anna
2TG - 2 Temple Gardens, London
020 7822 1241
ahughes@2tg.co.uk
Featured in Personal Injury (London), Travel (London), Clinical Negligence (London)
Practice Areas: Anna is a very experienced advocate who regularly advises on complex and high value matters arising from clinical negligence and personal injury disputes. She also has considerable experience in the fields of travel and foreign claims and private international law. Recent notable cases include Stucken v East Kent Hospitals University NHS Foundation Trust [2016] EWHC 1057 (QB); E v University Hospitals at Morecombe Bay NHS Trust [2015] EWHC 366 (QB); RSA v Fahad (2015) and [2014] EWHC 4480 (QB).
Professional Memberships: PNBA
Career: Prior to joining Chambers, Anna obtained a First Class degree in Law from St. Catharine's College, Cambridge. She was called to the Bar in 2008 (Middle Temple).

HUGHES, David
9 Bedford Row, London
020 7489 2727
david.hughes@9bedfordrow.co.uk
Featured in Crime (London)
Practice Areas: A widely experienced leading junior, specialising in serious crime including murder, terrorism, fraud, cyber crime, drugs, sexual offences and confiscation (including international mutual legal assistance). In the past year he has been involved in a number of high profile murder and/or terrorism cases (including the murder of Lee Rigby) and cases requiring a detailed knowledge of scientific evidence (including the first trial involving the use of genotyping of Chlamydia in relation to sexual offences and the appropriate interpretation of mixed profile DNA). He has acquired a detailed knowledge and expertise, on behalf of both prosecution and defence, in relation to computer fraud including phishing, vishing, pharming, the use of Trojans and other malware such as SpyEye and Zeus programmes. His extensive experience as an advocate is reflected in the complexity and seriousness of the cases in which he is instructed and the detailed preparation and research (of facts, law and expert evidence) required to seek a successful outcome to proceedings.
Professional Memberships: Criminal Bar Association.

HUGHES, Paul
Kings Chambers, Manchester
0345 034 3444
clerks@kingschambers.com
Featured in Costs Litigation (All Circuits)
Practice Areas: The Law of costs Paul is a highly experienced costs practitioner with particular expertise in procedural law and the costs of actions based on negligence (such as personal injury, clinical negligence, etc), including group litigation. He is an experienced cross-examiner, and is frequently instructed to deal with disputes concerning conduct, misconduct, wasted costs and non-party (third-party) costs orders. Since 2013 Paul has been heavily involved in assisting firms with managing the transition to the post-Jackson world, having given business advice and undertaken substantial non-contentious work in this regard. Paul also advises on managing 'broken retainers' and resolving disputes concerning the indemnity principle, both from the paying party's point of view and the receiving party's point of view. Paul has appeared before the Courts from the County Court to Court of Appeal and has substantial experience of advising on (and litigating) claims for costs in excess of £1m.
Professional Memberships: Fellow of the Association of Costs Lawyers (FACL). Qualified Mediator and Panel Member of CADR
Career: St Catherine's College, Oxford, MA Jurisprudence, Year of Call - 2001 (Middle Temple).
Personal: Paul regularly publishes articles of interest in professional journals and assists with the other members of the team in contributing to the ACL's costs database.

HUGHES, Ruth
5 Stone Buildings, London
020 7242 6201
rhughes@5sblaw.com
Featured in Court of Protection (All Circuits)
Practice Areas: Ruth has a busy Traditional Chancery practice which focuses on trusts and estates claims and Court of Protection litigation. She also has a broader, more commercial practice acting for the Crown, especially HMRC. She regularly appears in the High Court and has appeared in the Court of Appeal. She particularly enjoys claims involving equitable remedies, for example, proprietary estoppel, mutual wills and injunctions. Ruth is frequently instructed by the Official Solicitor in statutory will/gift claims, particularly where there is an element of complexity. For example, relating to taxation of cross border issues. She is happy to undertake cases which have a personal welfare or mental health aspect. Recent cases include Re Meek [2014] EWCOP 1 and Re Jones [2014] EWCOP 59.
Professional Memberships: Chancery Bar Association, Property Bar Association, ACTAPS.
Career: Called 2007. MA Cantab. Attorney General's C Panel. Accredited mediator.
Publications: Assistant editor of the Elder Law Journal.

HUGHES, Simon QC
Keating Chambers, London
020 7544 2726
shughes@keatingchambers.com
Featured in Construction (London)
Practice Areas: Specialist in energy and natural resources; construction and engineering and related commercial dispute work for both UK and international clients. Extensive experience of very substantial cases where the governing law is not English.. Regularly acts in TCC and Commercial Court litigation, adjudication and mediation, and domestic and international arbitrations predominantly in the Far and Middle East, with experience of various parts of the Caribbean and South America. Disputes relating to various power generation, utilities, process plants, shipbuilding, mining and other construction and engineering projects. In-depth experience of energy work (construction and operation of power stations, off shore platforms and rigs; oil and gas drilling and transportation.; construction, operation and decommissioning of nuclear power plants). Significant experience of litigation overseas, particularly in New Zealand and the Caribbean. Called to the Bar in New Zealand and more recently Trinidad & Tobago, to represent companies in the Court of Appeal. Simon has particular experience and expertise in the FIDIC standard forms.
Professional Memberships: Society of Construction Law; TECBAR; COMBAR.
Career: Called 1995; Queen's Counsel 2011.
Publications: Author – Understanding the New FIDIC Red Book; Contributing Editor – Keating on Construction Contracts 10th Edition (2016); former Contributing Editor – Chitty on Contracts.

HUGHES, William QC
9-12 Bell Yard, London
0797 668 9885
w.hughes@912by.com
Featured in Crime (London)
Practice Areas: Criminal law specialist. Prosecution and Defence of Serious Crime including, Homicide, Serious Sexual Offences, Organised Crime, Serious and Complex Fraud and Confiscation. Wide experience of Coroner's Inquests, Inquiries, Professional Discipline and other Tribunals (see www.912by.com for details). Associate Tenant 9 Park Place, Cardiff (see www.9parkplace.co.uk for details).
Professional Memberships: Member of South Eastern Circuit, Member of Wales and Chester Circuit, Chairman of Kent Bar Mess (2016), Former (elected) Recorder of the South Eastern Circuit (2004-2006), Executive Committee Member of the South Eastern Circuit (2001-2008 and 2016-present), Former Criminal Bar Association Committee member (2006-2009), Committee Member of the Fraud Lawyers Association, Committee Member of the Association of London Welsh Lawyers, Trustee of the Criminal Bar Association's Kalisher Scholarship Trust, Advocacy Trainer for the Honourable Society of Gray's Inn.
Career: Called (Gray's Inn) 1989, Queen's Counsel 2013.

HUGH-JONES, George QC
Serjeants' Inn Chambers, London
020 7427 5000
ssomerville@serjeantsinn.com
Featured in Clinical Negligence (London), Professional Discipline (London)
Practice Areas: George Hugh-Jones QC was called to the Bar in 1983 and took silk in 2010. George specialises in professional discipline, clinical negligence, inquests and inquiries and public and administrative law. An earlier edition notes that "he is a very knowledgeable and persuasive advocate" and "always has the answer, according to impressed sources, who value his charming manner and his ability to give clear straightforward advice" and that he is "a tenacious advocate who goes the extra mile." Please visit the Serjeants' Inn Chambers website for his profile, which sets out full details of his practice including relevant work of note.
Professional Memberships: PNBA.

HUMPHREYS, Freddie
Kings Chambers, Manchester
0345 034 3444
clerks@kingschambers.com
Featured in Planning (Northern)
Practice Areas: Freddie works in all areas of Town and Country Planning, including housing, retail, highways, enforcement and minerals. Freddie appears in planning inquiries, enforcement inquiries, and enforcement prosecutions and appeals. Further, he has experience appearing in the High Court and Court of Appeal on planning matters as a junior and in his own right. Recent notable

cases: Opposing a large housing development underneath the Manchester Airport flight-path; promoting an out of centre Sainsbury's superstore.
Professional Memberships: PEBA, Northern Circuit, North Eastern Circuit
Career: Completed pupillage in 2013, tenant at Kings Chambers since. Fitzwilliam College, Cambridge University: BA Hons Geography Nottingham Law School: LLB – Graduate Diploma in Law and BPTC.

HUMPHRIES, Michael QC
Francis Taylor Building, London
020 7353 8415 (M: 07525 800370)
clerks@ftbchambers.co.uk
Featured in Planning (London)
Practice Areas: Michael Humphries specialises in all aspects of property development law, but is particularly well known for his infrastructure planning and compulsory purchase work, where he has acted in relation to some of the largest and most important projects in recent years. Michael is currently acting for the promoters of a large number of Nationally Significant Infrastructure Projects and his experience encompasses the energy, transport, water, wastewater, ports and airports sectors. Michael is the Treasurer of the National Infrastructure Planning Association and the General Editor of Bloomsbury's National Infrastructure Planning Service. Michael is also a Visiting Fellow at Cambridge University giving occasional lectures on national infrastructure planning. Michael is also a leading practitioner in compulsory purchase and compensation law and was a founder of the Compulsory Purchase Association, for which he has been recognised as an honorary member. Michael is the Senior Editor of Bloomsbury's 'Compulsory Purchase and Compensation Service'. In 2013 Michael was Chambers and Partners Environmental and Planning Silk of the Year.
Professional Memberships: National Infrastructure Planning Association – treasurer; Joint Planning Law Conference committee – member; Planning and Environment Bar Association – member; Compulsory Purchase Association – honorary member; Anglo-American Real Property Institute – past chair.
Career: Called 1982 (Inner Temple); QC 2003.
Publications: General Editor – Bloomsbury's National Infrastructure Service. Senior Editor – Bloomsbury's 'Compulsory Purchase and Compensation Service'.
Personal: Chiltern Edge School; University of Leicester (LLB); Inns of Court School of Law. Born 1959; resides London. Enjoys spending time with family in France – married with three children.

HUMPHRYES, Jane QC
3 Raymond Buildings Barristers, London
020 7400 6400
jane.humphryes@3rblaw.com
Featured in Crime (London)
Practice Areas: Jane Humphryes Queens' Counsel is a specialist criminal barrister with over 30 years experience. Her particular expertise covers all aspects of serious crime. She has a particular interest in sexual offences, fraud and murder. Jane has extensive experience specialising in sexual allegations ranging from rape to child abuse, both historic allegations and allegations within an educational environment, white collar/fraud cases and murder/homicide. Jane has considerable experience in fraud matters where she has defended in corporate, VAT, banking, mortgage, local authority, legal and patent frauds. She was more recently instructed in the leading land banking fraud allegations which were contested before the courts, incorporating in addition breach of collective investment scheme regulations. These schemes involved the setting up of a series of companies intended to be used as vehicles for fraud aimed at defrauding investors out of tens of £ millions. The victims often classed as 'vulnerable' requiring particular care and skill when being cross-examined. Jane has in addition defended in many high profile murder cases. These have included allegations of contract killings, assassinations, gangland murders, street murders and domestic killings and a notorious historic murder. The defences have ranged, to name a selection, from identification, intent, participation, mental health, self-defence and mercy killing.
Career: BA Hons Law; Called to the Bar 1983; Appointed Recorder of the Crown Court 1999; Appointed Queen's Counsel 2003; Authorised to sit on Appeals; Authorised to try serious sexual offences cases.

HUNJAN, Satinder QC
Kings Chambers, Manchester
0345 034 3444
clerks@kingschambers.com
Featured in Personal Injury (Midlands), Clinical Negligence (Midlands)
Practice Areas: Clinical and professional negligence, personal injuries, sports law, commercial and international litigation ; the work undertaken involves cases of the highest complexity and value.
Professional Memberships: PNBA and PIBA.

HUNT, Quentin
2 Bedford Row, London
020 7440 8888
qhunt@2bedfordrow.co.uk
Featured in Health & Safety (London)
Practice Areas: Quentin comes from a general criminal law background with a strong focus on Health and Safety and Fraud. Quentin both defends and prosecutes all areas of Health and Safety law and is a member of the 'A' panel of the Attorney General's panel of regulatory and Health and Safety advocates. He acts at coroner's inquests, at notice appeals at the Employment Tribunal and in the Crown Court. In the Crown Court Quentin acts mainly in cases involving fatalities or cases involving serious risk to public health. Recent notable cases include the death of a tyre fitter in Canterbury, the drowning of a youth in care in Kent and the death of a construction worker due to the collapse of a concrete kiln. Quentin has extensive experience in high profile fraud cases which has led him to be instructed in a multitude of serious cases such as multi million pound VAT frauds including MTIC and carousel frauds and high level frauds by employees upon financial institutions. Quentin acts as both leading junior counsel and sole junior counsel, primarily for the defence. Quentin is known as one of the most effective direct public access practitioners at the Criminal Bar and has a growing direct public access practice.
Professional Memberships: Criminal Bar Association; Health and Safety Lawyers Association.
Career: 2000-present- Chambers of William Clegg QC, 2 Bedford Row, London.

HUNTER, Allison
23 Essex Street, London
020 7413 0353
allisonhunter@23es.com
Featured in Crime (London)
Practice Areas: Allison is routinely instructed to prosecute and defend in cases of significant gravity, complexity and sensitivity, often high profile in nature, attracting national and local media attention. Her experience ranges from murder, gang related murder, offences of serious violence, cases involving major organised national and international crime networks, human trafficking, firearms, drugs, serious fraud and money laundering, driving fatalities, and serious and historical sexual offending. Allison has particular expertise in cases involving covert investigations and requiring extensive consideration of RIPA, PII and the Disclosure Regime. She also has significant expertise in the handling of complex forensic evidence (DNA, Body fluids, Blood Pattern Analysis, Fibre analysis, Firearms, Gunshot Residue, Toxicology). Allison is a CPS Grade 4 Prosecutor and Rape Specialist. She is also included on CPS HQ Central Casework Divisions Advocate Panel Specialist Lists for the Serious Crime Group and Fraud. She led the first contested case involving section 73 SOCPA agreements, and also the first prosecution for the importation of Ketamine into UK and was invited to advise and participate with the panel that negotiated with the Home Office for the successful inclusion of Ketamine within the schedules to the Misuse of Drugs Act.
Professional Memberships: Criminal Bar Association, South East Circuit Bar Mess
Career: Called to the Bar 1986.

HUNTER, John
Kings Chambers, Manchester
0345 034 3444
clerks@kingschambers.com
Featured in Administrative & Public Law (North-ern/North Eastern), Planning (Northern)
Practice Areas: John practises across the fields of planning and environmental law and administrative and public law, including local government, education, housing, public procurement, immigration/asylum, prison law, human rights.
Professional Memberships: PEBA, ALBA.
Career: Kings Chambers (2003-present), Judicial Assistant, House of Lords (2004-5), The Queen's College, Oxford University (1995-2000).

HUNTER, Robert
Devereux, London
020 7353 7534
hunter@devchambers.co.uk
Featured in Personal Injury (London), Travel (London)
Practice Areas: Rob's practice has three major strands: (i) mainstream personal injury work in cases of serious injury or fatality; (ii) higher value clinical negligence claims; (iii) instructions as junior counsel in catastrophic injury cases. Rob has experience of the full spectrum of serious injuries, especially brain, spinal, and orthopaedic injuries of the utmost severity, including amputation. He has substantial expertise in fatal claims and has acted in cases involving, for example, deceased wealth creators, a departure from the conventional dependency calculation, disregarded benefits, and apportionment issues. Rob is also instructed in asbestos-related disease claims, especially if quantum is complex; in high or maximum severity claims arising from accidents abroad; and in group actions brought on behalf of poorly holiday makers. For more information on recent cases and expertise, please visit www.devereuxchambers.co.uk.
Professional Memberships: PIBA.
Career: Called 2000 (Gray's Inn); happily in practice on the Northern Circuit until 2007; now contented in London.
Publications: Contributing Editor to Butterworth's Personal Injury Service; author of numerous practice notes for LexisNexis PSL.
Personal: Married with two children. Jazz addict, amateur economist and fresh air obsessive.

HUNTER, Winston QC
Byrom Street Chambers, Manchester
0161 829 2100
winston.hunter@byromstreet.com
Featured in Clinical Negligence (Northern), Personal Injury (Northern)
Practice Areas: General common law with particular expertise in insurance, contractual disputes, professional negligence and catastrophic injuries. In respect of the latter, particular expertise in advising and handling claims of particular complexity where issues of insurer liability, public authority funding and third party indemnities is concerned. Regular appearances in the Court of Appeal and Supreme Court in cases spanning all areas of speciality. Specialist areas: personal injury, employment, insurance, commercial disputes. Recent notable cases: Personal injury litigation: recent cases: Sowden v Lodge [2004] Court of Appeal, Crookdale v Drury [2004] Court of Appeal, Hartman v South Essex Mental Health & Community Care NHS Trust [2005] Court of Appeal, Tinsley v Sarker (2005) 18th January, Smith v Wright and Beyer [2001] Court of Appeal. Commercial Litigation: Huktra NV v Huktra UK [2003] Court of Appeal, Tameside MBC v Barlow Securities [2001] Court of Appeal. Employment: Eastwood and Williams v Magnox plc [2004] House of Lords, Consignia v Burkett [2003] Court of Appeal. Insurance: Whitlam v Hazel (for Lloyds Syndicate 260) [2004] Court of Appeal. Churchill Insurance Co Ltd v Benjamin Wilkinson,Tracey Evans v Equity Claims Ltd [2010]+ [2012] Court of Appeal and [2011] Courts of Justice of the European Justice. [2011] Murphy v MPS in the Courts of Justice of the European Union.
Professional Memberships: Founder Member and Committee of the Northern Circuit Commercial Bar Association, Member of the Technology and Construction Bar Association, Member of the Personal Injury Bar Association, Member of the Professional Negligence Bar Association.
Personal: Married with three children. Enjoys cricket, wine, shooting and reading.

HUNTLEY, Clare
9-12 Bell Yard, London
020 7400 1800
c.huntley@912by.com
Featured in Crime (London)

Practice Areas: Defends and prosecutes cases concerning serious organised crime with a particular specialism in financial crime including complex fraud, corruption, multi-million pound money laundering, conspiracy to cheat the Revenue and e-banking fraud. Clare has particular expertise in prosecuting and defending cases alleging rape and serious sexual offences including multiple-complainant familial historic sexual abuse and cases with young and vulnerable witnesses.
Professional Memberships: Vice-Chair and founding member of the Fraud Lawyers Association; Criminal Bar Association.
Career: Appointed to: CPS Specialist Fraud Panel (2013); CPS Serious Crime Group/ Terrorism Panel (2013); CPS Advocate Panel at Level 3 (2012); List of Specialist Rape Prosecutors (2012); List of Specialist Regulatory Advocates in Health and Safety and Environmental Law (2012). Called in 2000 (Gray's Inn).
Personal: Lives in London. Leisure interests include cookery, theatre, photography and running. Educated at the University of Warwick.

HURST, Andrew
2 Hare Court, London
020 7353 5324
andrewhurst@2harecourt.com
Featured in Professional Discipline (London)
Practice Areas: Andrew Hurst is well established as a very experienced advocate in the field of Professional Discipline and in the criminal courts. Andrew has considerable experience in the Regulatory field – appearing for well over ten years as a respected and highly competent advocate. He appears regularly before the GMC, the GDC and the NCTL, as well as being instructed by the GOC, GPC and the NMC. He also acts on behalf of Doctors and other health-care providers at inquests. Andrew is well respected for his preparation, analysis, calm and persuasive style before panels, and is well regarded for his quiet but highly effective advocacy. He has a reputation of being a highly persuasive advocate, swiftly gaining the confidence of his Tribunal, and always giving his advocacy considerable thought in preparation and presentation. Andrew also maintains a criminal practice based on his entire career before the Crown Court and in Court of Appeal. He particularly specialises in defending serious sexual cases. His careful attention to the drafting of Defence Case Statements has often reaped benefit, including the discontinuation of cases (including rape) before trial. Appointed Recorder in 2009, he remains dedicated to first-class advocacy with impeccable client relationship skills.
Professional Memberships: Association of Regulatory and Disciplinary Lawyers; Criminal Bar Association; Professional Negligence Bar Association.
Career: Call: 1992 (Former Solicitor in City practice).

HUSSAIN, Riaz QC
Atkin Chambers, London
020 7404 0102
rhussain@atkinchambers.com
Featured in International Arbitration (London), Professional Negligence (London), Construction (London)
Practice Areas: Riaz's practice covers all aspects of construction, engineering and general commercial disputes. He frequently appears as an advocate in the High Court and as counsel in international arbitrations, appearing in ICC, LCIA, DIAC, ICSID and bespoke arbitrations and PFI Adjudications. He has acted in a wide variety of building and professional negligence disputes including process plants, oil and gas refineries, PFI Projects in the health sector and waste management, oil and gas pipelines, transport systems, scientific buildings and residential disputes, delay and disruption and general final account claims. He also acts in general commercial disputes including; conflict of laws issues, bonds and guarantees, international sale of goods cases, large value ICSID claims, joint venture agreement and shareholder disputes, business consultancy agreements, enforcement of arbitral awards under the New York Convention and cases involving allegations of corruption.
Professional Memberships: Combar; TECBAR; SCL; LCLCBA.
Career: University College, London (LLB First Class); called to the Bar 2001, Queen's Counsel 2016.

HUSSAIN, Tasaddat
Broadway House, Bradford
07854 683868
tasaddat@hotmail.com
Featured in Administrative & Public Law (North-ern/North Eastern)
Practice Areas: At the forefront of public law matters with an emphasis on immigration and asylum law, routinely instructed in cases where complex human rights arguments feature prominently. Widely admired and highly sought after by practitioners across the immigration and public law field, appearing in leading country guidance cases (most recently in MST and others (Disclosure – restrictions – implied undertaking) Eritrea [2016] UKUT 337 (IAC)) and judicial reviews for individual petitioners (including on a direct access basis) solicitors and local authorities. He is involved in cutting edge human rights work in the sphere of Article 8 ECHR/health and Article 3 ECHR/mental health matters. His expertise in Article 8 private and family life cases outside of the Immigration Rules is unsurpassed.

HUTCHINGS, Matthew
Cornerstone Barristers, London
020 7242 4986
matth@cornerstonebarristers.com
Featured in Local Government (London), Social Housing (London)
Practice Areas: Matt has a broad practice spanning public law, property and commercial litigation. His recent cases include Supreme Court briefs in R(N) v Lewisham, Hotak v Southwark and McDonald v McDonald, appearing in the CJEU in R(Hemming) v Westminster and the Building Act arbitration following the Supreme Court decision in Manolete Partners v Hastings. In June 2016 Matt was appointed Junior Counsel to the Crown – A Panel.
Professional Memberships: ALBA, HRLA, PBA.

HUTTON, Alexander QC
Hailsham Chambers, London
020 7643 5000
alexander.hutton@hailshamchambers.com
Featured in Clinical Negligence (London), Costs Litigation (All Circuits), Professional Discipline (London)
Practice Areas: Alexander's practice is focused in three fields: clinical, medical and all aspects of costs law. Alexander is recommended as a leading silk. Clients include both claimants and defendants, with especial focus on those of the most serious nature and highest value. Successfully defended St George's Healthcare NHS Trust, both at trial and on appeal, in connection with a claim pertaining to dyskeratosis congenita, a rare haematological disease. Totham v King's College Hospital NHS Foundation Trust [2015] Med LR 55, per Elizabeth Laing J: various quantum issues decided on an assessment of damages hearing in a maximum severity brain damaged baby case where damages of more than £10 million were ordered. Blankley v Central Manchester NHS Trust [2015] EWCA Civ 18; [2015] WLR, Court of Appeal: whether supervening loss of mental capacity by a claimant terminates the retainer between solicitor and client, necessitating the need to enter into a new retainer in order to be able to recover costs thereafter.
Professional Memberships: PNBA, AvMA.
Career: Called 1992. Junior Counsel to the Crown (B Panel) 1999-2005. Assessor for High Court costs appeals. Recorder of the Crown Court (2009). QC 2012.
Personal: First Class degree in Politics; Bristol University (1990).

HUTTON, Louise
Maitland Chambers, London
020 74061200
lhutton@maitlandchambers.com
Featured in Chancery (London), Fraud (London)
Practice Areas: General commercial and commercial chancery litigation and arbitration: in particular, fraud, insolvency, banking and finance litigation, company and trusts and estates litigation. Cases include Re Lehman Brothers International (Europe) ("Waterfall I", concerning subordination agreements, currency conversion claims, calls on contributories, and "Waterfall III"); Pine River v Castex & Ors (claims arising from alleged share price manipulation including issue over construction of ASCOTs); Sukhoruchkin v Van Bekestein (appeal over continuation of freezing order; reflective loss); ITS v GP Noble Trustees & Ors (claims arising from pension fraud); RBS v Highland (applications for anti-suit injunctions to restrain proceedings in Texas); Interactive Investor v City Index (claims arising from conduct of wind down period of white label trading arrangements); EIIB v AHAB (claim for sums due under an Islamic financing facility; defence based on alleged fraud of Maan Al-Sanea); JPMorgan v Wockhardt (claim, involving issues overn non-reliance clauses, for sums due under range accrual derivatives transactions); HSBC v 5th Avenue Partners, So v HSBC (negligence and other claims arising from bank fraud of Lib Dem donor Michael Brown); Birley v Birley (proceedings relating to the validity of the late Mark Birley's will); Shalson v Russo (fraud, tracing, sham trusts and contempt of court).
Professional Memberships: Chancery Bar Association, COMBAR, ACTAPS, Commercial Fraud Lawyers Association
Career: Called 1998.

HUTTON, Victoria
39 Essex Chambers, London
020 7832 1111
victoria.hutton@39essex.com
Featured in Planning (London)
Practice Areas: Victoria has a busy public law practice with a particular specialisms in planning, environmental and property law. She has consistently been rated as one of the top planning barristers under 35 (Planning Magazine, 2014, 2015, 2016). She has extensive advocacy experience at planning inquiries, in the High Court and Court of Appeal. Her recent work includes: promoting major housing developments both at appeal and at local plan examinations, acting in numerous planning appeals for retail schemes across the country, advising and representing a client in a DCO process (junior to James Strachan QC), representing a major house-builder at a contaminated land appeal (junior to Stephen Tromans QC), promoting a crematorium in the green belt (junior to Peter Village QC) and appearing in a number of judicial reviews and statutory challenges in the High Court and Court of Appeal.
Professional Memberships: PEBA, UKELA, ALBA, Attorney General's C Panel of Counsel.

HYAMS, Oliver
Devereux, London
020 7353 7534
hyams@devchambers.co.uk
Featured in Education (London)
Practice Areas: Education; employment (including in particular public sector pensions); discrimination; professional disciplinary matters and related areas such as the regulation of care homes; public law (including local government administrative law). Reported cases include: Hagen v ICI Chemicals & Polymers Ltd [2002] IRLR 31; S v Brent London Borough Council [2002] ELR 556; Qua v John Ford Morrison [2003] ICR 482, McCabe v Cornwall County Council [2005] 1 AC 503; Barke v SEETEC [2005] ICR 1373; R (O) v Governing Body of Parkview Academy [2007] ELR 454; R (Siborurema) v Office of the Independent Adjudicator [2008] ELR 209; R (Hill) v Bedfordshire County Council [2008] ELR 660; Kovats v TFO Management LLP [2009] ICR 1140; Governing Body of X Endowed School v SENDIST [2009] IRLR 1007; YKK Europe Ltd v Heneghan [2010] ICR 611; Pothecary Witham Weld v Bullimore [2010] IRLR 572; R (M) v Independent Appeal Panel of Haringey [2010] ELR 218; Parmar v East Leicester Medical Practice [2011] IRLR 641; Abramova v Oxford Institute of Legal Practice [2011] ELR 385; Hill v Governing Body of Great Tey Primary School [2013] IRLR 274; President of the Methodist Conference v Preston (Formerly Moore) UKSC 29; [2013] ICR 833, R(Rudewicz) v Ministry of Justice [2013] QB 410.
Professional Memberships: ALBA; ELBA; ELA. Currently Chair of the Education Law Association.
Career: Called 1989. Appointed part-time Chairman of Employment Tribunals (now Employment Judge) in July 2000.
Publications: 'Law of Education' (2004, Jordans, second edition); 'Employment Aspects of Business Reorganisations' (2006, Oxford University Press); 'Employment in Schools – A Legal Guide' (2007, Jordans, second edition); Consultant Editor for the Education title of 'Halsbury's Laws' (2011).

HYNES, Paul QC
25 Bedford Row, London
020 7607-1500
phynes@25bedfordrow.com
Featured in Crime (London)

Practice Areas: Criminal, financial and regulatory defence and advice. Has a broad practice often involving complex factual, legal and multi-jurisdictional issues. Extensive experience of bribery, company offences, corruption, confiscation, drugs, homicide, serious and organised crime, terrorism, fraud, money laundering, white-collar, commercial and regulatory proceedings. Has appeared in a number of reported and high profile cases at first instance and on appeal. His practice reflects a particular interest in fraud, financial crime and terrorism, but covers a wide spectrum of alleged offending; from the Leeds United football trial to Abu Hamza and Babar Ahmad via the Goldman Sachs PA charged with stealing millions from her employers. Regular author, lecturer and broadcaster on criminal law.
Professional Memberships: Criminal Bar Association, Legal Action Group, Liberty, Police Action Lawyers Group and Financial Services Lawyers Association.
Publications: Contributor to 'Abuse of Process: A Practical Approach' published by Jordans and the Lexis Nexis PSL Bribery toolkit; Co-author of 'International Money Laundering and Terrorist Financing: A UK Perspective' published by Sweet & Maxwell.

I'ANSON BANKS, Roderick
Partnership Counsel, London
020 7430 2005
rciab@partnershipcounsel.co.uk
Featured in Partnership (London)

Practice Areas: Exclusively partnership and LLP law. Has specialised in this area since the late 1970s. Handles all aspects of partnership/LLP law, including the drafting and review of agreements, advising on structural issues and strategic advice and representation in disputes, arbitrations and mediations. Particular expertise in partner extractions and removals, firm-wide downsizing operations, garden leave and restrictive covenant disputes. Acts for solicitors, accountants, and other professional firms, as well as hedge fund managers and numerous financial and commercial institutions, particularly when involved in limited partnership or corporate partnership ventures.
Professional Memberships: Lincoln's Inn; Association of Partnership Practitioners; Country Land and Business Association.
Career: Called to the Bar 1974 and joined 3 Stone Buildings, (Chambers of DR Stanford). Set up Partnership Counsel, originally at 48 Bedford Row, in 1991, as the only chambers specialising exclusively in partnership/LLP law. CEDR Accredited Mediator, 1993. Acted as a consultant to the Law Commission on its reviews of partnership law and limited partnership law (1999 – 2003). Lectures widely on partnership related subjects.
Publications: Co-editor 'Lindley on Partnership' (1979-1984); Editor of 'Lindley & Banks on Partnership' (1990-present, 20th ed in preparation); author of 'The Encyclopedia of Professional Partnerships'; contributor to 'Private Fund Dispute Resolution'.
Personal: Educated at Westminster School 1965-69 and University College London 1970-73 (LLB (Hons)). Leisure pursuits include reading and films. Born 5 December 1951. Lives in Beare Green, Surrey.

IRWIN, Gavin
Drystone Chambers, London
020 7404 1881
gavin.irwin@drystone.com
Featured in Financial Crime (London)

Career: Gavin Irwin is a specialist in cases involving professionals charged in criminal and regulatory proceedings. Recently, in addition to advising on restraint orders in a complex consumer protection fraud and representing individuals in confiscation and enforcement proceedings (including the largest boiler-room fraud prosecuted by the SFO) Gavin has: continued to advise in sensitive disputes involving sanctions and export licensing for entities with business interests in Russia, Syria, Iran and West Africa; offered practical advice to law firms on business risk and compliance with ABC, AML and sanctions regimes; represented regulators and healthcare professionals in conduct, conviction, performance, health and restoration cases, before the GMC, GDC and NMC (including cases on appeal in the High Court); and, defended in the first extradition proceedings brought by the Government of Peru.

ISAAC, Nicholas
Tanfield Chambers, London
020 7421 5306
nickIsaac@tanfieldchambers.co.uk
Featured in Real Estate Litigation (London)

Practice Areas: All aspects of property litigation, but particular interest and experience in commercial and residential leases, boundaries, party walls and rights of way. Recent cases include Patel v Peters [2014] EWCA Civ 335 (party walls), Emmett v Sisson [2014] EWCA Civ 64 (rights of way) Stannard v Gore [2012] EWCA Civ 1248 (Rylands v Fletcher fire case); Reeves v Blake [2010] 1 WLR 1 (party walls).
Professional Memberships: Chancery Bar Association, Property Bar Association.
Career: Called 1993. Joined Tanfield 2006.
Publications: Author of "The Law and Practice of Party Walls" – Property Publishing March 2014, contributor to "Service Charges and Management: Law and Practice" Sweet & Maxwell 2nd Edition 2009, co-author of "Easements and Other Rights" – RICS publishing March 2008.
Personal: Married with two children. Hobbies include skiing (including ski touring), hillwalking, climbing, cycling, and golf.

ISAACS, Barry QC
South Square, London
020 7696 9900
barryisaacs@southsquare.com
Featured in Company (London), Restructuring/Insolvency (London)

Practice Areas: Insolvency/restructuring, banking/finance, commercial litigation/arbitration, and company law. Particular expertise in insurance matters and cases of financial complexity. Barry often appears in offshore jurisdictions.
Professional Memberships: Associate of the Society of Actuaries.
Career: Barry has appeared in numerous substantial and high-profile cases in the Supreme Court/House of Lords (e.g. Lehman Brothers/Nortel, Rubin/New Cap Reinsurance, Sigma Finance, Mainstream Properties, Three Rivers v Bank of England); in the Court of Appeal (e.g. Lehman Brothers (Waterfall Application), Woolworths, Davenham Trust, FKI v Stribog, Golden Key, Whistlejacket Capital, OT Computers); and at first instance, including several major trials and arbitrations. Other recent cases of note include APCOA Parking, MF Global (Hindsight Application), Punch Taverns, Travelodge, BTA Bank v Ablyazov, AWAL Bank and Kaupthing. Recent cases in which Barry has appeared or advised in offshore jurisdictions include (in the Cayman Islands) Primeo Fund, China Fishery Group, Caledonian Bank; (in Bermuda) Lehman Re, Millennium Asset Management, British American Insurance, KIC; (in the British Virgin Islands) Monarch Pointe Fund, Thema Fund; and (in Hong Kong) Mongolian Mining Corporation. Barry has also recently acted as an expert (in proceedings in New York) in Hellas Communications v TPG, Mill Financial v Hicks, and Deutsche Bank v Serengeti. Called 1994. QC 2011.
Publications: Contributor to Company Directors: Duties, Liabilities and Remedies (First Ed, OUP).

ISAACS, Elizabeth QC
St Ives Chambers, Birmingham
0121 236 0863
elizabeth.isaacs@stiveschambers.co.uk
Featured in Family/Matrimonial (Midlands)

Practice Areas: Family: child care.
Professional Memberships: FLBA, ALC.
Career: Elizabeth is an engaging and knowledgeable family silk with substantial expertise in all areas of public and private child law, including a strong appellate practice. Particular interests include child death and serious physical injury, sexual abuse (including historical abuse), insulin poisoning, fabricated and induced illness (FII), judicial review, human rights issues relating to children, disputes about children's living arrangements and leave to remove from the jurisdiction, same-sex and LGBTQ + parenting issues. Elizabeth has particular expertise in surrogacy and parental order applications. Recent cases include; RE Z (A Child) [2015], Re Z (A Child) (No 2) [2016] and RE M (A CHILD) [2015]. Elizabeth is renowned for her ability in quickly identifying the practical implications of complex cases. She has an established reputation for compassionate client care, excellent advocacy and forensic preparation, and a pragmatic and tactical approach.
Publications: Clarke, Hall & Morrison on Children – contributing editor; Family Court Practice (Jordans) – contributor; Challenging and Defending Local Authority Childcare Decisions: A Practical Guide (2013) (co-author); Social Work Decision Making: A Guide for Child Care Lawyers (2nd ed 2012) (co-author).
Personal: Deputy High Court Judge of the Family Division; Recorder – Crown Court, Family (Public and Private) SE Circuit; Family Justice Council (Executive Committee).

IVILL, Scott
2 Hare Court, London
020 7353 5324
scottivill@2harecourt.com
Featured in Crime (London)

Practice Areas: Mr Ivill has vast experience of defending in the gravest of cases. He is regularly instructed by leading Defence firms in their most high profile, serious and complex cases and is described as a "Premier League" advocate. In addition to cases of homicide, he regularly appears in matters of serious violence, armed robbery, firearms offences, large-scale drug conspiracies and sexual offences. He has been ranked consistently in Chambers & Partners as a Leading Barrister. In addition to his criminal defence work, Mr Ivill is an experienced practitioner in Professional Discipline, Inquests and Health & Safety matters. Recent Cases include: R v MH – attempted murder, R v AM – attempted murder, R v IE – possession of a firearm (machine gun) with intent to endanger life, R v RD – series of smash and grab robberies, R v GC – fraud.
Professional Memberships: Criminal Bar Association, Association of Regulatory & Disciplinary Lawyers, Health & Safety Lawyers' Association.
Career: Called in 1997. LLB (Hons) 2:1; Rodney Bax QC Scholar Grays Inn; Inns of Court School of Law, London.

IYENGAR, Harini
11KBW, London
020 7632 8500
harini.lyengar@11kbw.com
Featured in Employment (London)

Practice Areas: Employment, discrimination and equality, education, partnership, professional regulation and discipline, procurement, information, public, commercial, Brexit.
Professional Memberships: Employment Lawyers' Association, Employment Law Bar Association, Association of Partnership Practitioners, Temple Women's Forum, Procurement Lawyers' Association.
Career: MA (Oxon), BCL (Oxon), Called to the Bar at Inner Temple 1999, Pupillage then Tenancy at 11KBW. Former barrister member of disciplinary panel of Council of the Inns of Court. Steering Group Member of Temple Women's Forum. Legal expert on television, radio and in printed media.
Publications: Tolley's Employment Handbook, Local Government Encyclopaedia, Administrative Court Digest, Westlaw Insight, Practical Law Company. Frequent legal blogger including on Twitter, 11KBW blogs.
Personal: Attended Manchester High School for Girls then Brasenose College, Oxford. Former trustee of Spitalfields City Farm. Former Greater London Assembly candidate for Women's Equality Party. External trustee of Oxford University Student Union. Governor of London Metropolitan University.

JACKLIN, Susan QC
1 Garden Court Family Law Chambers, London
0117 921 3456
susan.jacklinqc@stjohnschambers.co.uk
Featured in Family/Matrimonial (Western)

Practice Areas: Family Finance, ToLATA and Inheritance Act. Susan's practice includes all forms of family dispute arising from relationship breakdown and death, with particular emphasis on high net worth claims involving complex issues, such as multiple businesses, trusts, hidden assets, third party claims and taxation issues.
Professional Memberships: Chairman of the Family Law Bar Association 2014 – 2015, Vice Chairman (Family) Bar Council Remuneration Committee 2016 – .
Career: Susan has specialised in Family Law for more than 25 years and has vast experience of dealing with a wide range of people and cases not only in London but also across the South West, Birmingham and South Wales. Although most of Susan's practice consists of financial claims she

has extensive experience of dealing with private law disputes regarding the welfare of children, including applications for leave to remove children from the jurisdiction. She is able to advise and represent clients concurrently on financial and children aspects of their dispute, providing valuable continuity and an overall perspective on the issues to be resolved for the family.
Personal: International travel; horticulture; walking, particularly on coastal cliffs.

JACKSON, Andrew
St Philips Chambers, Birmingham
0121 246 7000
ajackson@st-philips.com
Featured in Crime (Midlands)
Practice Areas: Andrew Jackson is an established and respected criminal practitioner. He defends and prosecutes.He defends in cases of homicide and sexual offences, and has particular expertise in cases involving child witnesses, with and without intermediaries. He defends in all cases involving dishonesty, including corporate insolvency. He has experience in cases involving the possession, production and supply of all forms of controlled drugs. He defends in all cases of violence and in cases of malfeasance in public office. He has the requisite experience and knowledge of all forms of restraint and confiscation. He also defends in cases alleging breaches of the health and safety and trading standards legislation. Andrew is a Grade 4 prosecution advocate. His overall experience is such that, allied with persuasive and focussed advocacy, he represents people powerfully and effectively. Andrew's practice includes work overseas. He was recently instructed to defend in a trial (involving allegations of sexual abuse) on St Helena.
Professional Memberships: Member of the Criminal Bar Association. Advocate of the Supreme Court of St Helena (who may perform all the functions of a barrister within the Territories of St Helena, Ascension Island and Tristan da Cunha)
Career: Called to the Bar in 1986.

JACKSON, Charmian
St Ives Chambers, Birmingham
0121 236 0863
charmian.jackson@stiveschambers.co.uk
Featured in Family/Matrimonial (Midlands)
Practice Areas: Family: Matrimonial, Child Care; Court of Protection
Career: Charmian is an approachable, pragmatic and engaging barrister with experience at all stages of financial remedy and TOLATA proceedings as well as in private law children work. She has appeared in complex fact finding hearings as well as matters in the High Court. In respect of financial remedy applications she has a wide range of experience, including cases involving children and parents with disabilities. She also has considerable experience dealing with issues of domestic violence and abuse throughout all types of family proceedings. Charmian has a particular interest in family cases involving issues of capacity and mental health, including those where there may be an overlap between the Family Court and the Court of Protection. She also regularly appears in the Court of Protection on matters relating both to health and welfare and to property and affairs, representing Deputies, local authorities and family members. Charmian is known for having an excellent manner with clients, including those with particular vulnerabilities, and is always thoroughly prepared with an excellent eye for detail.

JACKSON, David
St Ives Chambers, Birmingham
0121 236 0863
david.jackson@stiveschambers.co.uk
Featured in Crime (Midlands)
Practice Areas: Crime.
Professional Memberships: Criminal Bar Association.
Career: David has defended in all types of cases, including murder, serious sexual and violence offences and armed robbery. He is a Level 4 prosecutor and, as such, is instructed to prosecute and defend the most serious cases including homicide, rape and armed robbery. He is also briefed in many serious sexual cases involving children as victims. David has also given pre-charge advice on a number of serious cases which include sexual offences and infant/child deaths. He has also prosecuted on behalf of the Serious Organised Crime Agency. He has received a Chief Constable's commendation having successfully prosecuted a gang for firearms and drugs offences. Has a keen eye for detail. He is particularly good at client care including, where necessary, sensitive handling of vulnerable witnesses.

JACKSON, Fiona
The Chambers of Andrew Mitchell QC, London
020 7440 9950
fj@33cllaw.com
Featured in POCA Work & Asset Forfeiture (All Circuits)
Practice Areas: Specialises in domestic and international fraud, bribery, corruption and money laundering; international mutual legal assistance; compliance issues; proceeds of crime and tracing; civil and criminal asset recovery; business crime and international regulatory work. Acts for a wide range of prominent defence and prosecution clients, companies and individuals, including prosecuting authorities, regulatory agencies and police forces, foreign governments and receivers in all courts. Cases include issues of restraint and freezing, receivership, confiscation, significant cash seizure and asset forfeiture, and major fraud, money laundering and business crime trials. Often instructed because of her ability to advise and represent throughout the lifespan of a case from the very outset by defending or prosecuting pre-charge/pre-action restraint and freezing proceedings, appearing in contested hearings and trials, then dealing with confiscation issues and linked asset/civil recovery proceedings at the conclusion. Advises agencies on nationwide policy issues and frequently lectures in her areas of practice.
Professional Memberships: Committee member of Proceeds of Crime Lawyers' Association; Vice-President of Association of Women Barristers; Vice-Chair of Bar Council's Equality & Diversity Committee; Member of Bar Council International Committee and South Eastern Circuit Bar Mess Committee; Criminal Bar Association.
Career: Year of Call: 1998.

JACKSON, Hugh
Selborne Chambers, London
020 7420 9500
clerks@selbornechambers.co.uk
Featured in Professional Negligence (London), Commercial Dispute Resolution (London)
Professional Memberships: Professional Negligence Bar Association; Financial Services Lawyers Association; Property Bar Association; Society for Computers & Law; Fellow of the Chartered Institute of Arbitrators; Sits as a Judge of the First Tier Tribunal, Property Chamber (Land Registration Division); Accredited mediator.
Career: Well-known amongst his peers as a commercial chancery practitioner with a very active practice centred on land and finance, trade, business and technology. Particular expertise in commercial professional negligence, fraud, tracing and asset recovery including related freezing orders.

JACKSON, Matthew
Hailsham Chambers, London
020 7643 5000
matthew.jackson@hailshamchambers.com
Featured in Professional Negligence (London), Clinical Negligence (London)
Practice Areas: Matthew specialises in clinical negligence, professional negligence, personal injury and general insurance work. In all his fields of practice, he acts mainly for defendants on instructions from insurers and medical defence organisations. Has established a reputation defending high-value clinical negligence claims for such clients as the NHSLA, the Medical Defence Union (MDU) and the Medical Protection Society (MPS). Recent significant cases include Leigh v London Ambulance Service [2014] Med LR 134 (Globe J), where a 17 minute delay in the arrival of an ambulance was held to have made a material contribution to the development of the claimant's psychiatric illness; Ganz v Childs & Ors [2011] EWHC 13 (QB) (Foskett J), a claim involving catastrophic brain damage which his client successfully defended on causation grounds; and Cabvision v Feetum & Ors [2009] EWHC 3400 (Ch) (Norris J), where his solicitor clients successfully resisted a multimillion pound claim.
Professional Memberships: Professional Negligence Bar Association (PNBA).
Career: Educated at Winchester College (scholar) and Trinity Hall, Cambridge (scholar). Called to the Bar in 1986.

JACKSON, Rosemary QC
Keating Chambers, London
020 7544 2600
rjackson@keatingchambers.com
Featured in Mediators (All Circuits)
Practice Areas: Building on the expertise gained in 30 years of practice as a barrister specialising in construction, engineering, professional negligence and commercial/contract law, Rosemary has acquired a first class reputation as an international commercial mediator. With 13 years of experience as a mediator of all kinds of international and domestic commercial disputes, Rosemary has successfully mediated disputes up to £200m, and between up to 8 parties. Very experienced in case-management of lengthy, complex and multi-party mediations. Mediation and conciliation experience includes disputes relating to transportation infrastructure, oil and gas, energy, party wall awards, insurance, copyright, proceeds of crime, and competition law, as well as disputes under PFI, PPP, FIDIC, JCT, ICE, NEC and IChemE contracts. On both CedrSolve and TECBAR Mediator and Adjudicator panels and named as a panel adjudicator in contracts. Frequently appointed as adjudicator.
Professional Memberships: Technology and Construction Bar Association, Commercial Bar Association, Society of Construction Law, Society of Construction Arbitrators.
Career: Called 1981, CEDR Accredited 2001, Crown Court Recorder 2002, Queen's Counsel 2006.
Publications: Chapter author 'Keating on Construction Contracts' 2016.

JACKSON, Sally
New Court Chambers, London
020 7583 5123
sjackson@newcourtchambers.com
Featured in Family/Matrimonial (London)
Practice Areas: Sally acts for parties in financial disputes following the breakdown of marriage or civil partnership, claims involving former co-habitees under the Trusts of Land and Appointment of Trustees Act 1996 and claims for financial provision under Schedule 1 Children Act 1989. Her practice also includes acting for parents and children in private law disputes, including those with issues of jurisdiction. Notable cases include Tattersall v Tattersall [2013] EWCA Civ 774 [2014] 1 FLR 997.
Professional Memberships: Family Law Bar Association.
Career: After graduating from Christ's College, Cambridge, Sally attended City University (GDL) and the Inns of Court School of Law (BVC), winning the Lincoln's Inn Lord Denning Scholarship during her Bar School year. She joined New Court as a tenant in 2008.
Personal: Sally lives in London with her husband and four year old son.

JACOBS, Amy
St Ives Chambers, Birmingham
0121 236 0863
amy.jacobs@stiveschambers.co.uk
Featured in Crime (Midlands)
Practice Areas: Crime, regulatory.
Professional Memberships: Midland Circuit, Criminal Bar Association, Middle Temple (Queen Mother Scholar).
Career: Amy Jacobs is an approachable and sensitive advocate with experience in dealing with vulnerable defendants and witnesses, particularly those of a young age or with mental health difficulties. She is instructed to defend in cases across the spectrum of criminal offences; recent work includes two large-scale conspiracies to rob, familial sexual offences and serious assaults involving acid and other weapons. Amy also regularly prosecutes on behalf of the Crown Prosecution Service and other government agencies. Amy's straightforward approach is appreciated by juries and judges, who find her eloquent without being pompous.
Personal: Deputy Head of the Criminal Group at St Ives Chambers. Accredited Pupil Supervisor. Called to the Bar in 2005, joined Chambers 2006. Tribunal Member of the Medical Practitioners Tribunal Service since 2014, hearing allegations relating to Fitness to Practice.

JACOBS, Linda
Cloisters, London
020 7827 4000
lj@cloisters.com
Featured in Clinical Negligence (London)
Practice Areas: Linda Jacobs specialises in medical and personal injury law, including, clinical negligence, medical regulation/disciplinary (GMC, NMC, HCPC), inquests and CICA appeals. Linda has experience in

a wide variety of claims, including claims of maximum or near-maximum severity. Her caseload includes birth injury, brain and spinal injury, amputations, multiple injuries, wrongful death, psychiatric injury, delayed diagnosis of cancer and medically complex cases on both liability and quantum. Linda has particular expertise in representation at inquests and subsequent fatal accident claims. She predominantly represents claimants.

Professional Memberships: PNBA, PIBA, AvMA, Inquest, APIL, Bar Pro Bono Unit.

Career: Called to the Bar in 2000 (Harmsworth Scholar). Former Sister in Intensive and Coronary Care at a leading London Teaching Hospital. Qualified pupil supervisor.

Publications: Contributor to Lewis and Buchan on Clinical Negligence (7th ed), including the inquest chapter. Various journal articles.

Personal: LLM (Medical Law):Distinction – Dissertation: "A Comparative Study between the Jurisdictions of England and Wales and the State of Victoria Australia of Death Investigation by the Coronial Service and Death Certification", LLM: Merit, BSc(Hons): First Class.

JACOBS, Nigel QC

Quadrant Chambers, London
020 7583 4444
nigel.jacobs@quadrantchambers.com
Featured in Shipping (London)

Practice Areas: Specialising in shipping, admiralty, insurance and general commercial law both in court and arbitration. During 2016 Nigel led the team in The "ATLANTIK CONFIDENCE", the first case in the English Court in which the shipowners' right to limit has been challenged under the 1976 Limitation Convention. Recently appeared in commodity/letter of credit dispute in Kuala Lumpur Arbitration Centre and in the Hong Kong Final Court of Appeal in Kulemesin v. HKSAR. Other recent cases include: ADMIRALTY: "SAMCO EUROPE": collision liability in crossing case and costs liability; MOM 1 Ltd. v. "SEA ECHO": Admiralty practice, counterclaims and costs; "PEARL OF JEBEL ALI": collision time bar; "NAPOLI": slot charterer's right to limit; "WESTERN REGENT": limitation and jurisdiction; SHIPPING: "WESTERN MOSCOW": liens on sub-freight; "GENIUS STAR": construction of Inter-Club Agreement; COMMODITIES: "MERCINI LADY": Fob Sellers' duties; JURISDICTION AND ARBITRATION: "ATHENA": incorporation of arbitration clause into salvage contract; "NICOLAOS A": "seat of arbitration" and charterparty incorporation; INSURANCE: "DC MERWESTONE": perils of the sea/ fraudulent presentation; "BUANA DUA": construction of policy and fraudulent claim; "GAMEBOY": insurance fraud.

Professional Memberships: Combar.

Career: Called 1983; Queen's Counsel 2006. Arbitrator, examiner, mediator, expert witness in foreign proceedings.

Personal: Married, two daughters. Interests: Holidays, sport, film and theatre.

JAMAL, Isabel

8 New Square, London
020 7405 4321
isabel.jamal@8newsquare.co.uk
Featured in Intellectual Property (London)

Practice Areas: All areas of intellectual property law, with a particular focus on patents (particularly in the pharmaceutical and telecommunications industries), trade marks, passing off, copyright and registered and unregistered design rights. Recent highlights include: a) representing Actavis at the Court of Appeal in Actavis v Warner Lambert; b) representing Hospira in Hospira v Cubist (a three-patent validity trial relating to dosing regimens and purification methods); c) representing Unwired Planet in the on-going telecoms competition and FRAND dispute and d) representing Actavis in Actavis v Boehringer at the CJEU in relation to the validity of Boehringer's SPC.

Career: Called 2008; Lincoln's Inn.

Personal: First class Masters degree in Physics and Philosophy from Oxford University. Several major scholarships during degree, law conversion and bar vocational courses. Prize-winning public speaker (competed at a regional and European level).

JAMES, Alun

Temple Tax Chambers, London
020 7353 7884
alun.james@templetax.com
Featured in Tax (London)

Practice Areas: Tax and VAT. Business and corporate tax advice; clearance work and planning for transactions and reorganisations; structuring through LLPs; employment-related securities. Professional clients mainly accountants. Litigation undertaken at tribunal level and in the higher courts. Lectures extensively nationwide.

Professional Memberships: Also a member of Exchange Chambers, Liverpool and Manchester.

Career: Called to the Bar 1986 and joined Temple Tax Chambers in 1988.

Publications: Co-author of 'Taxation of Companies and Company Reconstructions' (Sweet & Maxwell).

Personal: Scholar of St John's College, Oxford (BA, Hons 1st Class (Jurisprudence), BCL). Born 13 May 1964.

JAMES, Byron

Fourteen, London
020 7242 0858
byron.d.james@googlemail.com
Featured in Family/Matrimonial (London)

Practice Areas: Byron is a family law specialist. His work covers the range of private client situations, but his particular expertise is in matrimonial finance cases. His broader practice encompasses disputes about children, proceedings where there are insolvency issues, cohabitation disputes and trusts. Byron has also appeared in a number of reported decisions, most recently in Goyal v Goyal [2016] EWCA Civ 792 a successful appeal in the Court of Appeal (led by James Turner QC) that now stands as one of the leading cases on international pension sharing.

Personal: Educated at Bedford School and King's College London, Byron was called to the Bar in 2006. During his training, he was awarded the Mould Scholarship and the Prince of Wales Scholarship, each given to trainee barristers of exceptional merit. In 2011, he was named Hershman Young Child Lawyer of the Year by the Association of Lawyers for Children. Byron was also the winner of the 2013 Pegasus Scholarship which involved working for two months with a chambers in Wellington, New Zealand

JAMES, Rhodri

23 Essex Street, London
020 74130353
rhodrijames@23es.com
Featured in Crime (South Eastern)

Practice Areas: Over the last year, Rhodri has acted in the following trials; attempted murder, advanced fee fraud, rape, a VAT fraud and GBH with intent. The client has been acquitted on each occasion. In the VAT fraud, heard at Woolwich Crown, after a trial lasting eight weeks, Rhodri's client was unanimously acquitted. It was the first time that he had acted as leading junior. In a note written to Rhodri after the trial, the trial judge said the following: "In the best tradition of the Bar you put up a sterling flight for your client and deserved the result". After the GBH with intent trial, heard at Snaresbrook Crown, following the client's unanimous acquittal, his (experienced) solicitor, who had been present through much of the case, described the result as unbelievable and one of the best of his career. In an ensuing email to Rhodri, he added: "Thank you again for your work on this, it was an incredible result and it came from your advocacy". In the coming months, Rhodri will defend in two huge cases. A "copy-cat website" fraud in Teesside Crown and a conspiracy to rob at The Bailey.

JARMAIN, Stephen

1 King's Bench Walk, London
07939 067212
sjarmain@1kbw.co.uk
Featured in Family/Matrimonial (London)

Practice Areas: His practice encompasses all areas of family law work, with an emphasis on family finance cases and private law matters concerning children. Stephen has expertise in dealing with the international elements of family law, including issues such as child abduction, relocation and cross-border enforcement. He also has experience with high profile work involving national and international news coverage.

Professional Memberships: FLBA, International Society of Family Law.

Career: *D (A Child) [2016] UKSC 34 – Supreme Court case concerning jurisdiction and the voice of the child. *Re C (Internal Relocation) [2016] 1 FLR (forthcoming) – the leading Court of Appeal authority on cases involving a relocation within the United Kingdom. *Re OB (Private Law Proceedings: Costs) [2016] 1 FLR 92 – the first reported case in which costs were awarded against a non-party in a private law case. Stephen represented the father, PB, who succeeded in his application for costs on the basis of principles drawn from wider civil jurisprudence *2011 International Family Law Exchange Placement, Houston, Texas; sponsored by American Bar Association *2009 Reported Case; Re S and O (Temporary Removal from Jurisdiction) [2009] Fam Law 114 * 2008 International Bar Association and College of Law: Practice Diploma in International Human Rights Law and Practice.

Publications: Contributor, "Key Authorities", Family Law (forthcoming); Contributor, "Cases That Shook the World"; Contributor, "Applications under Schedule 1 of the Children Act 1989"; Contributor, "Family Law Journal"; Contributor, FamilyLawWeek.co.uk.

Personal: A particular interest in foreign travel and culture. Hobbies include football: playing, watching and refereeing (as a qualified FA referee) and musical interests, playing the saxophone and electronic organ.

JASPAL, Kam

Ropewalk Chambers, Nottingham
0115 9472581
kamjaspal@ropewalk.co.uk
Featured in Personal Injury (Midlands)

Practice Areas: Kam Jaspal was appointed to the Attorney General's Regional Panel of Counsel to the Crown in 2010. He regularly appears in the County and High Courts and has also appeared in the Court of Appeal. In addition, he has acted as an Examiner of the Court (on appointment by the Senior Master). He has developed particular expertise in the fields of personal injury and disease. His personal injury work includes employers' liability; public liability; occupiers' liability; defective premises and road traffic claims
In addition to appearing in the County and High Courts, he appears at CICA hearings and Coroner's Inquests. He also represents parties at joint settlement meetings and mediations. He has acted in cases involving serious or catastrophic injuries, both on his own and with Leading Counsel. He acts in all forms of industrial disease work, including NIHL; acoustic shock; HAVS; WRULD; COSHH and asbestos related claims. He was instructed as Junior Counsel in a very high value case arising from exposure to Benzene on an oil rig. He has considerable experience of limitation issues and is often instructed to attend limitation trials.

Professional Memberships: Personal Injuries Bar Association.

Career: Called 2005; LLB (Hons), University of Liverpool; LLM, University College, London.

JEANS, Christopher QC

11KBW, London
020 7632 8500
christopher.jeans@11kbw.com
Featured in Employment (London), Sports Law (London)

Practice Areas: Specialises in employment law and discrimination and sports law. Recent cases include: Paturel v DB Group Services (HC) Brierley v Asda Stores (EAT and AT)CD v ST (European Court) Cristal v Manchester Health Trust X v Mid-Sussex CAB (SC); Geys v Societe Generale (SC); Andrew Coulson v News International (CA and HC); Proactive Sports Management v Wayne Rooney and others, (CA) ; Wardle v Credit Agricole (CA and EAT); Williams v British Airways, (European Court, SC two hearings , CA, EAT and ET) Audit Commission v Haq (EAT and CA) Keane v Sunderland FC O'Neill v Aston Villa, Keegan v Newcastle FC (Arbitration Tribunal) Bateman v Asda Stores (ET and EAT); Law Society v Office for Legal Complaints and OLC (HC); Ainsworth Stringer v HMRC (European Court and HL); Chagger v Abbey National (CA and EAT); Middlesbrough v Matthews (EAT); Surtees v Middlesbrough (1 and 2 (EAT and CA); Grundy v British Airways (1 and 2 (EAT and CA); Cumbria County Council v Dow, Slack and others (1 and 2, CA and EAT), EB v BA (2 and 3 EAT); O'Hanlon v HMRC (CA); Derbyshire v St Helens (HL and CA).

Professional Memberships: Employment Lawyers Association, Employment Law Bar Association.

Career: 1974-77: LLB degree at King's College, London. 1977-79: BCL degree at St

John's College, Oxford. 1980: called to the Bar (Gray's Inn). Since 1983 has practised full time at the Bar, specialising in employment law, discrimination and sports law at chambers of Lord Irvine QC (now Chambers of James Goudie QC). Bencher Gray's Inn (2007). Former part time Chairman/ Judge Employment Tribunals 1998-2008. Recorder from 2009. President Commonwealth Secretariat Arbitral Tribunal.
Personal: Main interests: sport (especially football and cricket), travel, theatre, cinema. Arctic and world travel.

JEFFREYS, Alan QC
Farrar's Building, London
020 7583 9241
ajeffreys@farrarsbuilding.co.uk
Featured in Personal Injury (London)
Practice Areas: Principal area of practice is personal injury litigation, both claimant and defendant. Work includes motor, employment and public liability claims. Member of Catastrophic Injury panels for several insurers. Particularly interested in complex liability and causation issues. Other main areas of practice are clinical and solicitors negligence, general insurance, product liability and Health and Safety. Reported cases of interest include Roe v Sheffield CC; Ball v Street (CA); Bland v Morris & Penarubia; Patel v Wright & Midas Security; Lewis v Avidan (CA); Rigby v Wandsworth LBC; Brennan v ECO Composting & Bascombe; Saulle v Nouvet; Toropdar v Eidha; Clayton v Lambert (CA); Joshua Smith v Co-Operative Group& Hammond (CA); Tafa v Matsim Properties & Ors; Rider v Rehill Holdings (CA); Beasley v Alexander; Whitehead v Bruce, Craig & Baxter (CA): Buckland v Dwr Cymru.
Professional Memberships: PIBA; LCLBA.
Career: Called to the Bar in 1970 (Gray's Inn) and joined Farrar's Building in 1971. Took Silk in 1996. Recorder 1989-2004. CICAP 1999-2002.
Personal: Lives in London and Wales.

JELF, Simon
Partnership Counsel, London
020 7430 2005
sjelf@partnershipcounsel.co.uk
Featured in Partnership (London)
Practice Areas: Exclusively partnership and LLP law. Deals with a wide variety of partnership/LLP matters, from the drafting of agreements to the resolution of disputes, whether involving litigation, mediation or negotiation. He is known for his hands-on, commercial approach. Has wide experience in issues surrounding dissolution, retirement and expulsion, including contested expulsions, compulsory retirement and the enforceability of restrictive covenants, on behalf of both individual partners and firms. His clients include both large and small firms of solicitors, accountants and other professionals, as well as a range of other businesses. He has particular expertise in medical partnerships within the NHS.
Professional Memberships: Association of Partnership Practitioners.
Career: Called to the Bar (Gray's Inn) 1996. Law Commission 1996-98, principally involved with the review of partnership law. Joined 48 Bedford Row (Chambers of Roderick I'Anson Banks) in 1999. Lectures widely on partnership and LLP related subjects.
Publications: Editor of the third supplement to the 19th edition of Lindley & Banks on Partnership; Contributor to the 'Encyclopedia of Professional Partnerships'.
Personal: Educated at John Taylor High School, Burton-upon-Trent, and University of East Anglia. Leisure pursuits include property renovation and golf. Lives in Buckinghamshire.

JENKINS, Alan
Serjeants' Inn Chambers, London
020 7427 5000
ajenkins@serjeantsinn.com
Featured in Professional Discipline (London)
Practice Areas: Alan Jenkins was called to the Bar in 1984. Alan specialises in professional discipline and regulatory law. An earlier edition notes that "he is without doubt one of the best barristers in the field in terms of client care, advocacy and the ability to assimilate masses of documents and present an effective case." Please visit the Serjeants' Inn Chambers website for his profile, which sets out full details of his practice including relevant work of note.
Professional Memberships: CBA, HSLA, ARDL.

JEWELL, Matthew
Drystone Chambers, London
020 7404 1881
matthew.jewell@drystone.com
Featured in Crime (Western)
Practice Areas: Criminal law, regulatory law.
Professional Memberships: Western Circuit (Committee Member since 2008), CBA (Committee Member 2005-08), Member of the General Council of the Bar (2006-08).
Career: Matthew Jewell's practice includes criminal prosecution and defence matters, covering in particular serious fraud and regulatory law but also drugs and violence offences. He is regularly instructed as a leading junior in place of a silk. He has a particular interest in cases involving sensitive disclosure issues, and those involving the use of covert surveillance. He is finding himself increasingly instructed at pre-charge stage for early advice, advising upon disclosure, and forming a case plan through negotiation and the best possible use of correspondence. His experience from over twenty years in practice is highly sought for tactical advice in particular – Matthew is known as an adept tactician. Matthew can cut through legal jargon and complicated points of law to communicate with clients in language they can easily understand. This skill is particularly appreciated by clients with no experience of the criminal justice system, as is his attention to detail and service ethic – something borne out by the legal directories, where professional clients praise his "exceptional service". Matthew Jewell is also a Pupil Supervisor.

JINADU, Abdul
Keating Chambers, London
020 77544 2600
ajinadu@keatingchambers.com
Featured in Construction (London)
Practice Areas: Specialist in construction, engineering and energy disputes, and domestic and international arbitration, covering a wide spectrum of advisory work, drafting and advocacy, related to standard form and bespoke contracts; contractors', sub-contractors' and employers' claims; professional negligence claims (architects, engineers, surveyors and valuers). Acts for construction and engineering companies, government organisations, corporations, public utilities, local authorities, consultancies, architects and engineers. Significant cases have involved oil and gas; facilities pharmaceutical plants, hospitals, mining, marine construction, major projects, local authority cases and major construction projects (including disputes arising from projects in Africa). Advises in adjudication, acting for clients at all stages of the process including appearing in the Court of Appeal in reported decisions both successfully enforcing, and successfully resisting, enforcement of adjudicators decisions. He also advises on ADR.
Professional Memberships: TECBAR, COMBAR, SCL, CIArb.
Career: Called 1995, TECBAR Accredited Adjudicator 2004, Public Access Training 2004.
Publications: Contributing author – Oil & Gas Contracts: Principles and Practice (July 2016). Chapter author – Keating on Offshore Construction and Marine Engineering (published Sept 2015). Contributor – Keating on Construction Contracts Eighth Edition (2006),First Supplement (2008),Ninth Edition (2012) and Tenth Edition (2016). Editorial Board LexisNexis PCL.
Personal: Fluent Yoruba.

JOHN, Benjamin
Maitland Chambers, London
020 7406 1200
bjohn@maitlandchambers.com
Featured in Chancery (London), Commercial Dispute Resolution (London), Fraud (London)
Practice Areas: Commercial and chancery litigation and arbitration, often with a major international or jurisdictional element, encompassing all manner of general commercial disputes, civil fraud and asset tracing, banking & finance, company (including insolvency), and claims against fiduciaries & trustees. Particular experience of claims for and against sovereign states. Notable cases: The Brexit: Article 50 litigation [2016] (Admin); Nomura International v Banca Monte dei Paschi di Siena [2015] (Comm) (€3.5bn dispute re complex derivative transactions); Slocom v Sibir Energy [2014] (EWCA), [2012] (Ch) (fraud & sham; economic torts; s. 423 claims); Panagopoulos v Lloyds Bank [2014] (Comm) (complex swaps mis-selling); Terra Raf Traiding v Assaubayev [2013] (Comm) (fraud re sale of $1bn oil & gas assets); Dar al Arkan v Al Refai [2013] (Comm) (conspiracy and blackmail); Re the Estate of X [2013] (Hong Kong dispute re the estate a Hong Kong billionaire); Re D [2012] (Admin) (global relief freezing billions; veil-piercing); NML Capital v Argentina [2011] (UKSC), [2010] (EWCA), [2009] (Comm) (sovereign immunity); JSC BTA Bank v Ablyazov [2011] (EWCA), (Comm) (the massive fraud claim); Yukos Capital v Rosneft [2011] (Comm) (enforcement of arbitral awards arising from the Khodorkovsky affair; act of state); Wirecard AG v Shepherd [2011], [2010] (QB) (the Beijing Olympics ticket fraud).
Professional Memberships: COMBAR, Chancery Bar Association, FSLA.
Career: Called 2002.
Personal: University College, Oxford (Chemistry, First Class Honours) and City University (CPE, Distinction); Major and Princess Royal Scholar of Inner Temple; winner of the 3VB Prize for best overall performance (CPE, 2001); winner of the Barstow Prize Scholarship (Bar School, 2002).

JOHN, Laura
Fountain Court Chambers, London
020 7583 3335
lkj@fountaincourt.co.uk
Featured in Banking & Finance (London), Commercial Dispute Resolution (London), Fraud (London)
Practice Areas: Laura has a wide-ranging commercial practice encompassing all aspects of complex commercial disputes, with particular expertise in banking and financial services, civil fraud, commercial dispute resolution, insolvency and restructuring, insurance and reinsurance, professional negligence and media and entertainment.
Professional Memberships: COMBAR Equality and Diversity Committee Advocacy trainer for Gray's Inn.
Career: Called to the bar in 2001. Practised from 3 Verulam Buildings following successful completion of pupillage until June 2016. Thereafter practising from Fountain Court Chambers.
Publications: Co-author of 'Bullen & Leake Fraud'; 'Financial Services Regulation', author of chapter on UK payment systems, Paget's Law of Banking author of chapters on The Payment Service Regulations and Electronic Payment Systems.
Personal: Oxford University (BA); City University (CPE); ICSL; (BVC), Gray's Inn.

JOHNSON, Andrew
5 Paper Buildings, London
020 7353 6117
aj@5pb.co.uk
Featured in Consumer Law (London)
Practice Areas: .Andrew is a criminal specialist, principally practicing in consumer and intellectual property work. He is a grade 3 prosecutor for the CPS, and acts frequently for trading standards departments as well as private prosecutors, including industry bodies such as the Federation Against Copyright Theft and regulators. Recent consumer law prosecutions include securing convictions for fraudulent trading over the course of four years in counterfeit motor vehicle parts; the manufacture and distributing of counterfeit DVDs over the course of three years; the laundering of £50,000 obtained by a rogue trader from a vulnerable, elderly consumer; the passing off horse meat as zebra steaks, which received international media coverage; and the sale by a large retailer of unsafe high-visibility jackets, which resulted in a concession in confiscation proceedings that the company had a criminal lifestyle. His defence practice includes securing a suspended sentence for a defendant accused of trading in counterfeit Sennheiser headphones through Amazon's online marketplace. His intellectual property practice crosses over into the civil courts, and he is currently instructed in a number of matters before the Intellectual Property Enterprise Court. He acted for Sky plc in successful contempt proceedings, following the breach of an undertaking to cease the infringement of copyright works. He recently acted for the Architects Registration Board, in the successful first prosecution of an architect for an offence under the Fraud Act.
Career: Called to the Bar 2008.
Publications: Publications; "Bespoke Goods – Cancellation Exception", TS Review (with Carolina Bracken); 'Conspiring to Define Conspiracy to Defraud', The Lawyer,

June 2014, (with Benjamin Douglas-Jones) Seminars; "Trading Standards Prosecutions in a New Era of Criminal Litigation", CTSI Conference 2016; "Powers of Entry Code of Practice 2015", CTSI Conference 2015. With Andrew Johnson conducted a series of seminars (December 2014 to April 2015) on the applicability of the Regulation of Investigatory Powers Act 2000 to investigations into the underage sale of tobacco by trading standards officers, funded by the Department of Health.

JOHNSON, David
Atkin Chambers, London
020 7404 0102
djohnson@atkinchambers.com
Featured in Construction (London)

Practice Areas: David specialises in domestic and international construction, infrastructure, energy, informational technology, PFI, professional negligence and general commercial matters. Recent work has included disputes concerning airports, highways, railway projects, luxury yachts and national computer systems. David appears in the High Courts and County Courts on a led and unled basis and has extensive experience of arbitration, adjudication, mediation and pre-action work. He has been instructed by private and public sector employers, insurers, developers, contractors, sub-contractors and construction professionals. David is familiar with most standard form contracts including the JCT suite, FIDIC, ICE and NEC3. David is an accredited adjudicator.
Professional Memberships: TECBAR (Committee Member); SCL; COMBAR.
Career: MA Oxon (1st Class); BCL Oxon (Distinction); Called 2010 (Middle Temple)
Publications: Contributing Editor of Hudson's Building and Engineering Contracts, 13th Ed (2015).

JOHNSON, Edwin QC
Maitland Chambers, London
020 7406 1200
ejohnson@maitlandchambers.com
Featured in Real Estate Litigation (London)

Practice Areas: Property, chancery and commercial litigation and advisory work. In particular commercial and property disputes, general landlord and tenant (including leasehold enfranchisement) and professional negligence (solicitors, surveyors, valuers, architects, other construction professionals, accountants and insurance brokers), conveyancing, mortgages, easements, restrictive covenants, trusts, insolvency, commercial contracts, building and construction work, insurance work and competition law. Cases of interest include, in the House of Lords and Supreme Court, Boss Holdings v Grosvenor (meaning of a house in leasehold enfranchisement), Earl Cadogan v 26 Cadogan Square Ltd (rights of lease extension), Earl Cadogan v Pitts (enfranchisement valuation), and Day v Hosebay (meaning of a house), and in the Court of Appeal, John Thomas v Ken Thomas Ltd (forfeiture in relation to company voluntary arrangement), Shell v Total (recovery of economic loss in negligence and nuisance), Kutchukian v John Lyon (valuation assumptions in a collective enfranchisement); Kim v Chasewood (proprietary estoppel), and at first instance, Malmesbury v Strutt & Parker (surveyors negligence), Hotgroup v RBS (exercise of break clause), and Extra MSA v Accor (taking advantage of own wrong in conditional contract).
Professional Memberships: Chancery Bar Association, Professional Negligence Bar Association, Property Bar Association.
Career: Called to the Bar 1987. Queen's Counsel 2006. Real Estate 'Junior of the Year' (2005) and nominated for 'Silk of the Year' (2012 & 2013) in the Chambers UK Bar Awards.

JOHNSON, Jeremy QC
5 Essex Court, London
020 7410 2000
jj@jclj.uk
Featured in Administrative & Public Law (London), Police Law (All Circuits), Immigration (London), Inquests & Public Inquiries (All Circuits)

Practice Areas: Public law, human right, civil liberties, malfeasance and public inquiries. Acts in all cases involving police, including claims for judicial review, private law actions and advisory work. Instructed in numerous public inquiries and long running inquests, including Hillsborough, The Birmingham Pub Bombing, the Al Sweady Inquiry, the Hutton Inquiry, the Billy Wright Inquiry, the inquest into the death of Diana Princess of Wales and Dodi Fayed, Mouncher & Ors v Chief Constable of South Wales Police (claims brought by 15 police officers prosecuted for investigation into murder of Lynette White in 1988), Daniel Morgan Independent Panel Review and related civil actions.
Career: Called to the 1994, Silk 2011, Recorder on SE Circuit and Deputy High Court Judge.
Publications: Police Law Reports, Halsbury Law (Police).

JOHNSON, Nicholas QC
7 Harrington St Chambers, Liverpool
njohnson7hs@gmail.com
Featured in Crime (Northern)

Practice Areas: Nicholas has a practice which is split between prosecution and defence. He acts on homicide-including gross negligence manslaughter, gangland executions, drugs – large scale importations and distribution networks, fraud- M.T.I.C / Carousel, proceeds of crime and confiscation. He recently acted before Mr. Justice Edis QC on the defence of schizophrenic Anthony Hallard who was accused of murder; acted in the prosecution of three men accused of the murder of Merseyside police constable Neil Doyle shortly before Christmas 2014; and defending former Radio Caroline / Piccadilly Radio DJ Ray Teret for historic sex offences. Also acted on alleged joint-enterprise murder. Defendant convicted by jury, but cleared by the Court of Appeal in a case in which leave was originally refused.
Career: Call: 1986. Silk: 2006

JOHNSON, Paul
Kings Chambers, Manchester
0345 034 3444
clerks@kingschambers.com
Featured in Mediators (All Circuits)

Practice Areas: Paul's sole area of specialisation is mediation. He mediates a wide range of disputes: banking, charities, competition, commercial, contractual, construction and engineering, costs, employment, fraud, inheritance and trusts, insolvency, intellectual property, local government, matrimonial/family, partnership, personal injury, professional negligence, property, shareholders, regulatory.
Professional Memberships: Sport Dispute Resolution Panel and member of the Bar Council ADR Committee.
Career: Qualified as a solicitor in 1990. Joined Pannone LLP in 1992; he was a Partner from 1995 to 2006. Paul transferred to the Bar in 2006, joined Kings Chambers and is Head of their Mediation Group.

JOHNSON, Zoe QC
QEB Hollis Whiteman, London
020 7933 8855
zoe.johnson@qebhw.co.uk
Featured in Crime (London), Professional Discipline (London)

Practice Areas: Zoe Johnson defends and prosecutes the most serious and high profile crime. Her eleven years as treasury counsel (the second woman ever to have been appointed senior treasury counsel) gave her vast experience in cases of homicide, terrorism and organised crime. For example she was instructed in the first ever case of terrorist fund raising [R v Oumerzouk] and advised in the case of Gary McKinnon, accused of hacking into NASA and the US department of defence. She has acted in a number of "honour killings" and hate crimes. Zoe secured the only successful prosecution of a journalist accused of misconduct in public office [R v France] and has advised in relation to the prosecution of News International. She has particular expertise in cases with medico-legal features. After appearing in 2005 in R v Harris and Others she is adept in allegations of "shaken baby syndrome" and has appeared in many such cases [most recently R v Sobcyzk]. Zoe is accomplished in presenting and dissecting psychiatric evidence and has been involved in a large number of contested diminished responsibility, insanity and fitness to plead cases. She is instructed in cases of extreme sensitivity, often involving the death of children [e.g R v Tania Clarence, a mother who suffocated her three disabled children and R v Dixie, the murder of Sally Ann Bowman]. She has a special interest in medical gross negligence manslaughter cases and recently secured the acquittal, at the close of the Crown's case, of Dr Rudling, a GP accused of failing to recognise a life threatening illness. Zoe successfully defended in the first ever prosecution under the Female Genital Mutilation legislation [R v Dharmasena] and as a result has been asked to advise several clients (individuals and religious groups) prior to a possible charge of FGM. For many years Zoe has defended and prosecuted in all areas of business crime such as bribery and corruption, insider dealing and accountancy fraud [R v Beard and others]. Her experience includes advising companies on sanctions, advising on the construction of legislation for the FCA and advising the SFO on various investigations [e.g the investigation into Hewlett Packard's takeover of Autonomy]. Zoe was instructed as leading counsel in the second ever deferred Prosecution agreement [R v ABC] which set the bench mark for such agreements and was approved by the Court in June 2016. Zoe has appeared regularly over the years in various tribunals, in particular the GMC, GDC and HCPC. Earlier this year she successfully defended a registrar obstetrician accused of mismanagement of a twin delivery leading to death and dishonesty [GMC v Dr Mohan]. Last year she successfully defended a doctor accused of multiple sexual assaults. Zoe is instructed in the first proceedings ever brought by the British psychological society.
Professional Memberships: Criminal Bar Association, Association of Regulatory and Disciplinary Lawyers, Public Access Bar Association.
Career: Recorder 2009, senior treasury counsel 2011, Queen's Counsel 2012.

JOHNSTON, Christopher QC
Serjeants' Inn Chambers, London
020 7427 5000
clerks@serjeantsinn.com
Featured in Clinical Negligence (London), Court of Protection (All Circuits), Product Liability (London)

Practice Areas: Christopher Johnston QC was called to the Bar in 1990 and took silk in 2011. Christopher specialises in clinical negligence and healthcare, product liability, Court of Protection, public and administrative, inquests and inquiries, professional discipline, police and employment law. An earlier edition notes that he is "a really very strong advocate who is good on the strategic side", "quite superb" and "he has fantastic client care skills and he's very clever. He's a star." Please visit the Serjeants' Inn Chambers website for his profile, which sets out full details of his practice including relevant work of note.
Professional Memberships: PNBA, co-chair of the PNBA Clinical Negligence Conference.
Publications: Medical Treatment: Decisions and The Law (editor); Product Liability Introduction JPIL (2012); Medical Law Reports (contributor).

JOLLY, Schona
Cloisters, London
020 7827 4000
sj@cloisters.com
Featured in Employment (London)

Practice Areas: Schona has a strong equalities practice with employment and human rights specialism across all fields including commercial. She is an acknowledged expert in all areas of discrimination law and complex whistleblowing claims, including in multiple-claimant equal pay claims and county court/High court actions, as well as protection of harassment claims, TUPE and civil liberties matters. She is particularly experienced in crossover matters and has appeared in a number of high profile cases, such as, Carol Howard v Metropolitan Police which was widely covered in the national press, as well as the landmark Supreme Court case Jivraj v. Hashwani whose effects have been felt in the employment, equality and commercial arbitration worlds. She represents both claimants and respondents/defendants at all court and tribunal levels. She is known for her skilled advocacy, detailed knowledge of the law as well as her practical and common sense approach both with clients and the courts. She advises various NGOs on international law and discrimination topics. She is also a qualified mediator.
Professional Memberships: Elected Executive Committee member of the Bar Human Rights Committee, Council member of JUSTICE,ELBA, ELA, Discrimination Law Association, Lawyers for Liberty, Advocates for International Development, Oxfam International Lawyers Network.
Career: Called to the Bar 1999; Licence Speciale (European Law)at University of Brussels; BA Jurisprudence, Magdalen College, Oxford.

Publications: Contributor to LAG Discrimination in Employment Handbook 2013; Co-author of LAG Age Discrimination Handbook 2006; 2004 co-author Consultation paper for Age Concern: Addressing Age Barriers: An international comparison of legislation against age discrimination in the field of goods, facilities and services. Author of frequent professional articles. Former co-editor Sweet & Maxwell European Human Rights Reports.
Personal: Legally fluent in French. High level Spanish, Hindi, Punjabi, Basic Arabic.

JONES, Elizabeth QC
Serle Court, London
020 7242 6105
ejones@serlecourt.co.uk
Featured in Chancery (London), Commercial Dispute Resolution (London), Fraud (London), Mediators (All Circuits), Offshore (London)
Practice Areas: Wide ranging litigation practice, both in the chancery fields of company, insolvency, property and trusts, and in a wide range of commercial disputes, such as fraud, sale of goods, banking, financial services, entertainment, railway industry, and contractual disputes in many different business areas. Also regulatory work in the City and in relation to solicitors. Mediator.
Professional Memberships: Chancery Bar Association, COMBAR, ACTAPS.
Career: Called to the Bar 1984. Silk 2000.

JONES, Emma
One Essex Court, London
020 7583 2000
ejones@oeclaw.co.uk
Featured in Commercial Dispute Resolution (London), Energy & Natural Resources (London)
Practice Areas: Emma has a broad practice encompassing all aspects of commercial litigation, arbitration and advisory work. As well as acting in general commercial disputes, Emma has particular interest in and experience of advising and acting in relation to energy disputes, including for super-majors. She regularly advises on the proper interpretation and application of gas sale agreements, joint venture operating agreements, transportation and processing agreements, and services agreements, particularly on issues relating to price, termination, and force majeure. Recent cases include Autonomy Corporation Limited v Lynch and Hussain (claims for breach of fiduciary duty, breach of contract and misrepresentation in relation to the acquisition of Autonomy by the HP group), Re Coroin Limited [2013] EWCA Civ 781 (s.994 petition concerning the ownership of three well-known London hotels), Sabbagh v Khoury [2014] EWHC 3233 (Comm) (5-day jurisdiction hearing), BG Global Energy Ltd & ors v Talisman Sinopec Energy UK Limited & ors [2015] EWHC 110 (Comm) (trial of preliminary issues relating to the proper interpretation of a transportation, processing and operating services agreement), and an expedited ICC arbitration (dispute relating to the proper interpretation of pre-emption provisions in a joint venture operating agreement).
Professional Memberships: COMBAR (Young COMBAR committee), FSLA, LCLCBA.
Career: Called 2010 (Inner Temple). Geography at Hertford College, Oxford (First Class, 1st in year), GDL at BPP Law School (Distinction, top 5 in year), BVC at BPP Law School (Outstanding, 1st in year).

JONES, Jennifer
Atkin Chambers, London
020 7404 0102
jjones@atkinchambers.com
Featured in Construction (London)
Practice Areas: Jennifer has a wide ranging practice with experience in domestic courts (in particular the TCC) and of mediation, adjudication and both domestic and international arbitration. Jennifer's main areas of specialisation are: construction, engineering and infrastructure; energy; and professional negligence. Jennifer has acted for the full range of parties in disputes arising from the design and construction of a wide range of building and civil engineering projects, including process plant, infrastructure (including procured by PFI) and commercial and residential properties. She is also familiar with the main Standard Form contracts. In the energy sector her experience encompasses both oil and gas disputes and increasingly disputes about renewables. Jennifer's professional negligence experience includes dealing with a variety of claims involving a wide range of professionals and consultants in the construction and engineering sector, including architects, engineers, surveyors and contractors. Jennifer also has valuable experience in disputes concerning the construction and enforcement of guarantees/ bonds and of jurisdictional and conflicts issues, which regularly arise as incidental to other matters.
Professional Memberships: TECBAR, COMBAR, SCL.
Career: Called to Lincoln's Inn in 2003; MA(Oxon) Law with Law Studies in Europe.
Personal: Reasonable command of French.

JONES, John Richard QC
Carmelite Chambers, London
020 7936 6300
jjonesqc@carmelitechambers.co.uk
Featured in Financial Crime (London)
Practice Areas: Fraud work has led into regulatory work with several high profile trials in areas of health and safety, trading standards and environmental protection. A trading standards case recently concluded at Wolverhampton Crown Court (R v Summit Roof guard LTD) resulted in the dismissal of all charges concerning a corporate client charged with fraud and fraudulent trading. The second aspect of this case (R v Beadle) concerning the director resulted in mixed verdicts. All aspects of serious fraud including money laundering, insider dealing, financial services and aggressive tax avoidance/evasion. Notable cases include R v. Aspin & Others; commercial fraud/ tax evasion cases include R v. Cox & Others (Operation Divert). R v. Forsythe, SFO prosecution concerning a major computer fraud; R v. Bowes fraudulent share flotation; R v. Brown & Others SFO prosecution concerning the affairs and suppliers to Ikea. R v. Cahill & Others SFO prosecution concerning a phoenix type fraud within various supply companies. R v. Mawdesley fraud concerning both criminal and regulatory breaches of the FSA regulations. R v. Donnelly (Operation Vex (Van Laarhoven, Donnelly & Others) concerned the activities of the MITEK Group and the FCIB. R v. Knights & Others; fraud concerning the acquisition of commercial mortgages by allegedly fraudulent valuations. R v. Emery & Others. SFO prosecution for fraudulent offshore share sales of U.S. based pink sheet companies. R v. Batliwala, case concerning the alleged fraudulent evasion of duty concerning the importation of controlled drugs concealed in fruit and vegetables. At presently retained for the Defence in a "Film Scheme Case" where the allegation concerns aggressive tax avoidance/ tax evasion.

JONES, John Richard QC
Exchange Chambers, Liverpool
020 7936 6300
jjonesqc@carmelitechambers.co.uk
Featured in Crime (Northern)
Practice Areas: John is the go-to advocate for major heavyweight criminal cases, his practice encompassing serious fraud and ancillary issues, money laundering, insider dealing/city-based regulatory crime, murder, manslaughter, drugs, historic sex abuse and terrorism. His serious fraud practice includes work prosecuted by the SFO, CPS and HMRC and he is currently retained in several multi-million pound city insider dealings and aggressive tax avoidance/evasion cases. He has successfully defended in cases brought forward by the SFO. John also deals with cases involving mental health issues and has been involved in a number of significant, innovative cases such as the Gonzalez case. John also has a strong professional discipline and regulatory practice, with particular expertise in health and safety and environmental work. He regularly defends in prosecutions brought by the Environmental Agency and HSE.
Professional Memberships: Criminal Bar Association, Northern Circuit.
Personal: LLB (University of Liverpool), Middle Temple.

JONES, John Richard QC
Carmelite Chambers, London
020 7936 6300
jjonesqc@carmelitechambers.co.uk
Featured in Financial Crime (London)
Practice Areas: Fraud work has led into regulatory work with several high profile trials in areas of health and safety, trading standards and environmental protection. A trading standards case recently concluded at Wolverhampton Crown Court (R v Summit Roof guard LTD) resulted in the dismissal of all charges concerning a corporate client charged with fraud and fraudulent trading. The second aspect of this case (R v Beadle) concerning the director resulted in mixed verdicts. All aspects of serious fraud including money laundering, insider dealing, financial services and aggressive tax avoidance/evasion. Notable cases include R v. Aspin & Others; commercial fraud/ tax evasion cases include R v. Cox & Others (Operation Divert). R v. Forsythe, SFO prosecution concerning a major computer fraud; R v. Bowes fraudulent share flotation; R v. Brown & Others SFO prosecution concerning the affairs and suppliers to Ikea. R v. Cahill & Others SFO prosecution concerning a phoenix type fraud within various supply companies. R v. Mawdesley fraud concerning both criminal and regulatory breaches of the FSA regulations. R v. Donnelly (Operation Vex (Van Laarhoven, Donnelly & Others) concerned the activities of the MITEK Group and the FCIB. R v. Knights & Others; fraud concerning the acquisition of commercial mortgages by allegedly fraudulent valuations. R v. Emery & Others. SFO prosecution for fraudulent offshore share sales of U.S. based pink sheet companies. R v. Batliwala, case concerning the alleged fraudulent evasion of duty concerning the importation of controlled drugs concealed in fruit and vegetables. At presently retained for the Defence in a "Film Scheme Case" where the allegation concerns aggressive tax avoidance/ tax evasion.

JONES, Jonathan QC
No5 Chambers, Birmingham
0845 210 5555
info@no5.com
Featured in Personal Injury (Midlands), Clinical Negligence (Midlands)
Practice Areas: Clinical negligence: cerebral palsy claims; obstetrics; gynaecology; surgical errors; cosmetic surgery; paediatrics; optical negligence; oncology; general practitioners; nursing practice; human rights; inquests. Personal Injury: catastrophic brain injuries; severe spinal injuries; amputations; fatal accidents; industrial disease; asbestos claims; deafness claims; CICA claims; road traffic accidents and accidents at work.
Professional Memberships: AVMA PIBA.
Career: Called 1994. Silk 2013.
Personal: Born 1970. Educated at Bedford School, St Andrews University (Economics MA) and City University (Diploma in Law).

JONES, Mark
St Philips Stone Chambers, London
020 7440 6900
mark.jones@stonechambers.com
Featured in Shipping (London)
Practice Areas: Mark Jones has a broad commercial practice, encompassing general commercial work, banking, insurance and reinsurance, shipping, and the sale and carriage of goods (international and domestic). His work covers all aspects of international trade, whether it be the carriage of goods, the sale of goods, or the related financial and insurance transactions. His expertise extends to all corners of the shipping industry, from charterparties to salvage, from cargo claims to collisions, from ship finance to performance guarantees, and from marine insurance to general average. He acts in arbitrations both in London and abroad, and appears regularly in the English Courts. He also provides expert evidence on English law for use in foreign proceedings. Over the years, he has appeared in a number of leading shipping cases, such as the 'ATLANTIK CONFIDENCE' (Court of Appeal), the 'ALEXANDROS T', the "MSC NAPOLI", the "STARSIN" (House of Lords) and the "SEA ANGEL" (Court of Appeal). He has been consistently recommended in the well-known legal directories as a leading barrister for shipping, where he has been noted for his particular expertise in shipbuilding and ship sale and purchase disputes and described as a "very knowledgable, sharp minded and skilful barrister" with a "great analytical mind" who has "a good understanding of front line litigation" and pays "phenomenal attention to detail and gives prompt and pragmatic advice."
Professional Memberships: MCIArb; LCIA; LMAA (Supporting); LSLC; BMLA; AAA; COMBAR; LCLCBA.
Career: BA (Hons) – Oxford University; 1998-2000 – Ince & Co; 2000 – Called to the Bar (Lincoln's Inn, Kennedy Scholar).

JONES, Michael
Cobden House Chambers, Manchester
0161 833 6000
clerks@cobden.co.uk
Featured in Personal Injury (Northern)
Practice Areas: Michael Jones specialises in insurance and personal injury litigation. The majority of his practice involves catastrophic personal injury work with a particular emphasis on traumatic brain injury. He acts for both Claimants and Defendants; he is regularly instructed by large insurers, the private prison service and the Treasury Solicitor. Michael is currently instructed in a number of large group litigation cases including one involving 18,000 claimants. He has considerable experience in Prisons litigation including Jury and Article 2 Inquests. He has an extensive knowledge of Coroners' law from his time as Junior Counsel to the Shipman Inquiry. Michael has a significant practice in pain cases, primarily for Defendants and he undertakes disease work for insurers and the MOD. He also acts for insurers in recovery actions for property damage, primarily following fire or flooding. Michael was appointed to the AG's Panel of Junior Counsel to the Crown in 2007 and then re-appointed in 2012.
Career: AG's Panel of Junior Counsel to the Crown – 2012 AG's Panel of Junior Counsel to the Crown – 2007 Shipman Inquiry – Counsel to the Inquiry – 2001 – 2004.

JONES, Nicholas David
Civitas Law, Cardiff
08450713007
ndj@civitaslaw.com
Featured in Clinical Negligence (Wales & Chester), Personal Injury (Wales & Chester)
Practice Areas: Practiises in high value personal injury litigation. Acts on behalf of Claimants and Defendants (including Central Government and the Welsh Government). Caseload consists of catastrophic injury claims: traumatic brain injuries, spinal cord injuries (tetraplegia and paraplegia)and upper and lower limb amputations. Cases have included Claimants in a persistent vegetative state, minimally aware and locked in. Also included those who have sustained injuries abroad. Involved in litigation where orthopaedic and psychiatric injuries and pain syndromes remove or substantially reduce the ability to work as well as asbestos related litigation. Fatal Accident Act claims and appeals against the Criminal Injuries Compensation Authority also form an important part of work. Practises in significant cases of clinical negligence. Caseload includes negligence arising out of: birth; anaesthesia; consent to treatment; negligence in diagnosis (missed, delayed and wrongful; including cancer misdiagnosis); GP practice; nursing care; prescriptions; surgery (including injury to spinal cord).
Professional Memberships: PIBA.
Career: Junior Counsel to the Crown (Provincial Panel): appointed in 2000; reappointed in 2003; reappointed in 2007. Junior Counsel to the Attorney General's Panel of Prosecution Advocates (Health and Safety and Environmental): appointed in 2002; reappointed in 2006;reappointed in 2012. Junior Counsel to the Counsel General of the Welsh Government: appointed in 2000; reappointed in 2003; reappointed in 2009 (specialist field of Personal Injuries law); reappointed in 2012 (specialist field of Personal Injuries law). Mediator (civil and commercial).

JONES, Oliver
Brick Court Chambers, London
020 7379 3550
luke.carvalho@brickcourt.co.uk
Featured in Administrative & Public Law (London), Commercial Dispute Resolution (London)
Career: Oliver regularly appears at the highest level in appeals before the Supreme Court and Privy Council across a broad spectrum of work, including SerVaas v Republic of Iraq & Ors [2012] UKSC 40, Nzolameso v City of Wesminster [2015] UKSC 22, Belhaj v The Rt. Hon Jack Straw & Ors (ongoing) and Paulley v FirstGroup (ongoing). Oliver regularly appears in heavyweight commercial litigation and is currently acting for the former CFO of Autonomy in his US$5 billion dispute with HP over alleged accounting fraud. Oliver is also regularly instructed in high-profile public law challenges to government decisions, including R (Gibraltar Betting & Gaming Association) v Secretary of State for Culture, Media and Sport [2014] EWHC 3236 (Admin), and R (Drax Power) v Secretary of State for Energy and Climate Change [2014] EWCA Civ 1153. Oliver also has extensive experience of international law and State immunity issues in various contexts. He has appeared against the Islamic Republic of Pakistan in Mid-East Sales v Pakistan [2014] EWHC 1457 (Comm), for the International Oil Pollution Compensation Fund and has acted for victims of US drone strikes in a challenge to the legality of reported GCHQ involvement in those attacks.

JONES, Philip QC
Serle Court, London
020 7242 6105
pjones@serlecourt.com
Featured in Chancery (London), Professional Negligence (London), Commercial Dispute Resolution (London), Company (London), Fraud (London), Partnership (London), Restructuring/Insolvency (London), Tax (London)
Practice Areas: Company and partnership law; insolvency; commercial fraud; Chancery (trusts and property litigation); financial services; professional negligence; competition; tax and VAT litigation; public law.
Professional Memberships: Chancery Bar Association; COMBAR.
Career: Junior Counsel to the Crown (Chancery) 1994, Junior Counsel to the Crown (A Panel) 1999.

JONES, Rhiannon QC
Byrom Street Chambers, Manchester
0161 829 2100
rhiannon.jones@byromstreet.com
Featured in Personal Injury (Northern)
Practice Areas: The full range of personal injury work, in particular spinal and brain injuries and with a particular interest in causation and quantum of damages. Also clinical negligence. Acted for a Claimant who suffered tetraplegia and was "locked-in" after a road traffic accident. Also acted for Claimants who had suffered sexual abuse in foster care negotiating some of the highest awards in such cases. Represented three Defendants in a brain injury case of the utmost severity. Have acted for both Claimants and Defendants in numerous very serious leg injury claims involving amputation or the prospect of that. Have dealt with a number of chronic pain cases, where credibility was in issue.
Professional Memberships: PIBA. PNBA. LCLCBA.
Career: Lamb Chambers 1993-2004, Farrars Building 2004-2016, Byrom Street Chambers since April 2016.
Personal: Manchester High School for Girls, King's College London. Hobbies, all sports especially swimming. Music.

JONES, Seán QC
11KBW, London
020 7632 8500
sean.jones@11kbw.com
Featured in Employment (London), Sports Law (London)
Practice Areas: Sean specialises in Employment and Sports law. His employment practice is broad. He acts for individuals, trade unions, employers' federations, international banks, airlines, public and private utilities, hospitals, universities, firms of solicitors, television and other media companies, local authorities, technology and computer companies and charities. He advises upon and litigates claims across the full range of employment issues including unfair and wrongful dismissal (including 'whistle-blowing' dismissals), race, sex, disability, sexual orientation and religious discrimination, equal pay and transfer of undertakings. He specialises in high value claims of particular complexity. His Sports practice is principally focused on football cases. He has represented a number of Premier League and other teams in manager and player disputes and for managers in disputes with their clubs.
Professional Memberships: ELBA, ELA, COMBAR, Discrimination Law Association, Industrial Law Society, British Association for Sport and the Law.
Career: Called to the Bar and joined Chambers in 1991. Appointed a Fee-paid Employment Judge in 2011 and took silk in 2012.
Publications: Tolley's Employment Handbook (general editor).
Personal: Educated at Colchester Royal Grammar School 1977-84 and Worcester College, Oxford 1985-89 (BA Hons in Jurisprudence, BCL). Born 9 July 1966. Lives in Wimbledon.

JORDAN, Ruth
Serle Court, London
07796 930 990
rjordan@serlecourt.co.uk
Featured in Restructuring/Insolvency (London)
Practice Areas: Chancery and commercial litigation; company and insolvency (including directors' disqualification); probate, property, charities, tax and trusts (offshore and domestic) litigation; fraud and injunctive relief; financial services and judicial review. Acted in Central Bank of Ecuador & Ors v Conticorp SA [2015] UKPC 11; Apollon Metaxides v Swart & Ors, Silver Point Condominium Apartments v Swart [2015] UKPC 32; Bimini Blue Coalition Ltd v Prime Minister of the Bahamas & Ors [2014] UKPC 23; Pitt v Holt [2013] UKSC 26 and [2011] EWCA Civ 197; Ardagh Group v Pillar Property [2013] EWCA and [2012] EWHC 3649; Oceania v Willard Clarke [2013] UKPC 3; Reid v HMRC [2012] UKUP 338; Re Mercury Tax Group (In Administration) [2010] EWCA 1379; Re Stakefield [2010] EWHC 2518 and 3175; R v Save Guana Cay [2009] UKPC 44; Klincke v HMRC [2009] UKFTT 156; Harding v HMRC [2008] EWCA 1164; Smith v HMRC [2008] WTLR 147; Re City Trucks Ltd [2008] BCC 76; Re TXU, Sisu v Tucker [2006] 1 All ER 167.
Professional Memberships: Chancery Bar Association, COMBAR.
Career: Called to the Bar 2001. Seconded to the FSA (splits investigation) 2003-04. Junior Counsel to the Crown (Attorney General's C Panel) 2007.
Personal: BA (Trinity College Dublin), MPhil, PhD (Cambridge), PgDL (City).

JORY, Richard QC
9-12 Bell Yard, London
020 7400 1800
r.jory@912by.com
Featured in Crime (London)
Practice Areas: Defends and prosecutes in cases of complex fraud and serious crime. Areas of experience include corruption, tax evasion, money laundering, murder and historic sexual abuse. Instructing solicitors include the SFO, CPS Central Fraud Group, CPS Organised Crime Division, and various defence solicitors. He has experience in trans-jurisdictional issues, including obtaining evidence from abroad. He has acted as counsel in disciplinary tribunals, and represented a number of individuals in the Stephen Lawrence Inquiry. He has lectured on topics including money laundering, obtaining and using evidence from abroad, abuse of process, disclosure and confiscation.
Professional Memberships: Criminal Bar Association, Fraud Advisory Panel, Fraud Lawyers Association.
Career: Called 1993 (Middle Temple, Gottlieb Award), Standing Counsel to the Revenue and Customs Prosecutions Office 2008-2011, CPS advocate panel level 4 for London and the South East, and specialist level 4 for Fraud and Organised Crime. Member of the Conduct Committee of the Bar Standards Board, 2006-2011. Queen's Counsel 2013. SFO QC list from 2013.
Personal: Born 22nd April 1967. University of Reading (Modern History and International Relations). Richard is a member of the Howard League for Penal Reform and Justice, and a Board trustee director of 'Outside Chance'.

JOSEPH, David QC
Essex Court Chambers, London
020 7813 8000
djoseph@essexcourt.com
Featured in International Arbitration (London)
Practice Areas: David Joseph was admitted to the Bar and joined Essex Court Chambers in 1985. David took silk in 2003, and has acted as counsel and arbitrator in an extremely wide range of high profile and high value commercial disputes in London and many of the world's leading arbitral seats including, Paris, The Hague; Stockholm; New York; Singapore; Hong Kong and Delhi. He has appeared as counsel in over 250 international arbitrations in his career. As well as acting as counsel in the Commercial Court in London, he has appeared before the Courts of Singapore and Hong Kong in a number of the recent years' leading cases in the field of international arbitration including acting in enforcement proceedings for the award creditors in Astro Nusantara v Ayunda Prima Mitra and others and Xiamen Xinjingdi Group v Eton Properties Limted. David is consistently recommended in the top tier in UK and global directories as a leading silk in the field of international arbitration. He is also recommended in

commercial litigation and general insurance. In 2014 he was named as 'Silk of the Year' in International Commercial Arbitration by the Chambers UK Bar Directory and by Legal 500. In 2013 he was also short-listed as "Silk of the Year" in the same category. He is the author of Jurisdiction and Arbitration Agreements and their Enforcement (Sweet & Maxwell, 3rd Ed December 2015) which in a short period of time has become a standard work of reference in this complex field and has been cited with approval by courts in England, Hong Kong, and Singapore. He is also an author and co-editor with David Foxton QC of Singapore International Arbitration, Law and Practice (Lexis- Nexis 2014). He sits on the COMBAR Executive Committee and is Chair of COMBAR's Brexit Working Group examining questions of jurisdiction; choice of court agreements; enforcement of judgments; choice of law; and judicial assistance for obtaining of evidence.

JOSSE, David QC
5 St Andrew's Hill, London
0206 3325400
clerks@5sah.co.uk
Featured in Extradition (London)
Practice Areas: Extradition, International Criminal and Humanitarian Law, General Crime. Since taking Silk has specialised in defending extradition requests, both at first instance and on appeal, encompassing the full range of Part 1 and 2 work with a particular emphasis on political corruption, prison conditions and re-trial rights in former East European communist states e.g. Dogaev (relationship between Russia and the Czech Republic). Has led in many of the leading Article 3 authorities of recent years, often involving issues relating to assurances provided by the requesting state:- Aleksynas (Lithuania), Wolkowicz (Poland), Florea and Blaj (Romania), Lustyuk (Ukraine), Kapoor (India), Nikolov (Bulgaria).
Professional Memberships: List Counsel:- International Criminal Court, International Criminal Tribunal for the former Yugoslavia, Special Tribunal for Lebanon. Extradition:- ELA, DELF. Criminal Bar Association. Fraud Lawyers Association.
Career: Spent 2005-2010 at ICTY in The Hague defending in two lengthy international war crime trials one for a senior Bosnian Serb politician, the other a multi-hander for a General charged in relation to the Srebrenica massacre. Both cases involved allegations including genocide, extermination, mass murder and large scale ethnic cleansing.
Publications: Regular commentator on news stories in core practice areas on Sky News and LBC radio.

JOWELL, Daniel QC
Brick Court Chambers, London
020 7379 3550
ian.moyler@brickcourt.co.uk
Featured in Competition/European Law (London), Commercial Dispute Resolution (London), Energy & Natural Resources (London), Competition/European Law (London)
Career: Daniel Jowell QC is well known for his experience in major, international commercial litigation and arbitration. He has acted in a number of the major commercial disputes of recent years, acting for clients including Bernie Ecclestone, Oleg Deripaska and for Roman Abramovich in his dispute with Boris Berezovsky. His appearances in 2015-2016 included: representing the successful claimants in an arbitration regarding energy assets in the Ukraine, securing an award of over $300m; representing the widow and daughter of the late billionaire Sami Shamoon in a successful jurisdiction challenge in the High Court and acting in the high profile dispute in the Chancery Division regarding ownership of Aman Hotel chain. In addition to his commercial practice, Daniel Jowell QC is known as one of the leading competition barristers in the UK. In particular, he has acted in many of the major competition law damages actions for clients including Visa Europe, Sony, Air Canada, Renesas, NEG, ChevronTexaco, Exxon, Dow Chemicals, Alstom, and Sharp. He has also appeared in a number of appeals of the decisions of regulators before the CAT. He won Chambers and Partners' award of competition law "Silk of the year" for 2015/2016.

JUCKES, David
Hailsham Chambers, London
020 7643 5000
david.juckes@hailshamchambers.com
Featured in Clinical Negligence (London)
Practice Areas: David's clinical negligence practice encompasses primary and secondary care and includes allegations of delays in diagnosis, surgical error, and obstetric injury. He acts for both claimants and defendants. In his defendant practice he acts for general practitioners, hospital trusts, and private surgeons. As well as civil cases he acts in inquests, where he is instructed by bereaved families, doctors, and healthcare organisations. He also specialises in regulatory hearings.
Professional Memberships: Professional Negligence Bar Association (PNBA); South-Eastern Circuit; Tampa Bay American Inn of Court (Honorary).
Career: David joined Hailsham Chambers in 2010 following successful completion of his pupillage. Prior to joining the Bar he worked as a paralegal for a medical defence organisation. During his career to date he has appeared in clinical negligence trials both in the County Court and the High Court. He has appeared in the Administrative Division of the High Court, the Chancery Division, and the Court of Protection. He is a member of the Hailsham Chambers Costs Group and has acted for parties in the Senior Court Costs Office. He has been instructed in product liability matters including actions arising from the failure of medical implants.

KALFON, Olivier
Maitland Chambers, London
020 7406 1200
okalfon@maitlandchambers.com
Featured in Chancery (London), Real Estate Litigation (London), Restructuring/Insolvency (London)
Practice Areas: Olivier specialises in the fields of commercial dispute resolution, insolvency and restructuring, banking and finance, civil fraud and company law. His practice areas also include property, insurance and professional negligence (in the areas of his practice, including claims against solicitors, insolvency practitioners and accountants).
Professional Memberships: Commercial Bar Association; Chancery Bar Association; Insolvency Lawyers' Association; British-Russian Law Association.
Career: Called to the Bar of England and Wales (Inner Temple) 2003. Admitted to the Bar in the Cayman Islands in 2006.

KAMM, Rachel
11KBW, London
020 7632 8500
rachel.kamm@11kbw.com
Featured in Data Protection (London), Education (London)
Practice Areas: Public law, including a wide range of education, information, health, community care and local government issues. She is registered on the public access scheme and she was appointed to the Attorney-General's 'B' Panel of Junior Counsel to the Crown on 1 September 2015 (having been on the 'C Panel since March 2011). She also sits as a fee-paid Judge of the First-tier Tribunal (Social Entitlement Chamber). Recent cases include: Dransfield v Information Commissioner & Devon County Council [2015] EWCA Civ 454 (vexatious requests for information); O'Brien v Ministry of Justice [2015] EWCA Civ 1000, [2015] IRLR 1005 (EU law and discrimination against part-time judges); Beis Aharon Trust v Secretary of State for Education [2016] UKFTT 0270 (HESC) (independent schools standards); Re JM [2016] EWCOP 15; [2016] 4 W.L.R. 64 (deprivation of liberty); and R(C) v First-Tier Tribunal [2016] EWHC 707 (Admin); [2016] A.C.D. 60 (litigation friends in tribunal proceedings).
Publications: Halsbury's Laws of England (volume 61, Judicial Review, Fifth Edition). Posts on 11KBW's information and education blogs (www.panopticonblog.com; www.education11kbw.com). Tweets as @ kamm11kbw.

KANE, Adam QC
Carmelite Chambers, London
020 7936 6300
avkane@hotmail.com
Featured in Financial Crime (London)
Practice Areas: Criminal defence specialist across high-value and high-profile economic crime, in complex cases often involving multiple complainants, acting for company officers and professionals, in investigations in the Financial Services sector, market-rigging and regulatory offending, HMRC evasions, commercial and residential property fraud, Public Sector fraud and money laundering. Current cases include Operation Hayrack — bribery and corruption of the Privy Purse & Treasurers Office of the Royal Household; Operation Hornet —£35 million bribery, corruption and fraudulent trading case involving senior HBOS executives and turnaround consultancy; Operation Vanilla — a £40 million wine importation fraud. Recent cases include Operations Crystalline and Chainmail — sideways loss relief tax cheats using film investment scheme; Operation Spallation — misconduct of Customs Officers in public office; Operation Bellum — abuse of position and fraud conspiracy, for Nat West business banking manager; Operations Kyrenia and Groat— frauds on NHS by perfusion scientists and dentists respectively; Operation MFB — a E300 million MTiC fraud in the rag-trade; Operation Nanobot — conspiracies to defraud the Revenue and to launder proceeds of a fraud upon DEFRA; Operation Steamroller — a $100 million US securities investment fraud; and Operation Raiment — conspiracies in payroll sector to defraud management receivers and liquidators .
Professional Memberships: Criminal Bar Association, Administrative Law Bar Association, South Eastern Circuit.
Career: BA (Oxon), CPE, Grays Inn.

KAPILA, Rachel
3 Raymond Buildings Barristers, London
020 7400 6400
rachel.kapila@3rblaw.com
Featured in Licensing (London)
Practice Areas: Criminal, licensing, extradition and regulatory practitioner. Criminal law: Prosecution and defence, as led junior and alone, with particular expertise in fraud and financial crime. Experienced extradition practitioner, advising and acting for defendants and requesting states/judicial authorities, at first instance and on appeal. Licensing: Advises and represents licencees/ applicants, local authorities and interested parties in all matters connected with licensable activity, including gambling, liquor, regulated entertainment, child performance/ stage licensing, street trading and taxi licensing; extensive appellate and public law practice in these areas. Professional discipline: Particular expertise in representing police officers at misconduct hearings; also experience appearing before the Solicitors Disciplinary Tribunal. Regulatory law: Advises and appears in proceedings arising out of a variety of regulatory regimes, including health and safety, fire safety, food safety and trading standards prosecutions. Extensive inquest practice, with focus on inquests involving investigations into the actions of the police. Developing practice in sports law, with particular interest in disciplinary and anti-corruption work.
Career: BA Hons (Oxon) Jurisprudence; Postgraduate Certificate in Sports Law and Practice (Distinction, 1st in order of merit); Bar Vocational Course (Outstanding, 1st in order of merit); Appointments: British Swimming Judicial Appeal Panel (2012).

KARAS, Jonathan QC
Falcon Chambers, London
020 7353 2484
jkaras@falcon-chambers.co.uk
Featured in Agriculture & Rural Affairs (London), Planning (London), Real Estate Litigation (London)
Practice Areas: All aspects of land law, extending from litigation and advice concerning leases, transfers, development agreements and rights over land to the law of planning and compulsory purchase, highways and waterways, manorial rights, commons and greens.
Professional Memberships: Chancery Bar Association; Property Bar Association; Planning and Environmental Bar Association; Compulsory Purchase Association.
Career: MA (Oxon); Called 1986; Supplementary Panel of Junior Counsel to the Crown(Common Law)(now the 'B' Panel)1995-2000; 'A' Panel of Junior Counsel to the Crown 2000-2006; Silk 2006.
Publications: Subject editor of Hill and Redman's law of Landlord and Tenant; author (with David Elvin QC) of Unlawful Interference with Land second edition (2002); contributing editor to the Compulsory Acquisition title (1996), editor of the Distress title (2000, 2007 re-issues), the Forestry title (2007 and 2009 re-issues) and co-editor of the Perpetuities and Accumulations title (2013)' Blundell Memorial Lecture (2007) on the award of damages in lieu of injunctions and (2014) on "negotiating damages".

KARIA, Chirag QC
Quadrant Chambers, London
020 7583 4444
chirag.karia@quadrantchambers.com
Featured in Shipping (London)

Practice Areas: Commercial law, including shipping, commodities, joint ventures, share purchase agreements and commercial arbitration. Cases: Yusuf Cepnioglu [2016] 1 Lloyd's Rep. 641(CA)(contractual anti-suit injunction vs. 3rd party); Sino v. Dana [2016] 2 Lloyd's Rep. 97 (s. 72; authority to accept arbitration notice); Committeri v ClubMed [2016] EWHC 1510(QB)(legal test for boundary between Rome I and Rome II Regulations); DC Merwestone [2015] 1 Lloyd's Rep. 32(CA)(insurers' fraudulent device defence); Crudesky [2014] 1 Lloyd's Rep 1(CA)(demurrage; novus actus; restraint of princes); Proton v. Orlen [2014] 1 Lloyd's Rep 100 (whether CIF sale concluded; description vs. quality); DC Merwestone [2013] 2 Lloyd's Rep 131(Com. Ct)("perils of the sea" & Inchmaree insurance cover; fortuity requirement; privity defence); Lehmann Timber [2013] 2 Lloyd's Rep 541 (CA)(recoverability of lien exercise costs); Ratna Shradha (CA)(US$60 million oil cargo dispute between Sudan and South Sudan; state immunity); ICC Arbitration (subsea blowout preventer supply); Choil v Sahara (recoverability of hedging losses).

Professional Memberships: COMBAR; State Bar of California.

Career: Called 1988, Lincoln's Inn (Denning Scholar); Queen's Counsel 2012; MA(Cantab.), Slaughter & May Prize (top 1st in Law at Cambridge University); LL.M. (UC Berkeley), Harkness Fellow; Attorney practising in California(1990-2000).

Publications: Joint Editor, "Butterworths Commercial Court and Arbitration Pleadings".

KARIM, Sam
Kings Chambers, Manchester
0345 034 3444
clerks@kingschambers.com
Featured in Administrative & Public Law (Northern/North Eastern), Civil Liberties & Human Rights (Northern), Court of Protection (All Circuits)

Practice Areas: Sam's main areas of practice are administrative law (including commercial judicial review) and human rights law, regulatory law, public procurement and state aid law, Court of Protection and mental health, arbitration (domestic and international commercial) and information law. He has been a member of the Attorney General's regional panel of Treasury Counsel for almost a decade and has been constantly recommended as a leading junior. Sam is a Member of the Chartered Institute of Arbitrators and is admitted as a practitioner in the Dubai International Finance Centre (DIFC) Court.

Professional Memberships: Member of the Attorney General's Regional Panel. Member of the Executive Committee of the Administrative Law Bar Association (ALBA). Northern Administrative Law Association (NALA), Acting Chair. Director of Manchester Public Law Pro-Bono Scheme.

Career: LLM(Lond.), LLB(Hons), PG Dip Laws, MCIArb (Int. Arbitration) Call in 2002 (Grays Inn).

Publications: (1) joint editor of Judicial Review: law and practice (2nd edition) with Mrs Justice Patterson, (2) contributor to Bullen and Leake and Jacob's Precedents of Pleadings (Common Law Library), (3) editor of the Human Rights Perspective on Reducing Restrictive Practice in Intellectual Disability and Autism, and (4) editor of 'Public Law Online' (an online public law information portal operated by Jordans).

KARK, Tom QC
QEB Hollis Whiteman, London
020 7933 8855
tom.kark@qebholliswhiteman.co.uk
Featured in Inquests & Public Inquiries (All Circuits), Professional Discipline (London)

Practice Areas: Tom Kark's work originated in criminal law, developing a practice defending white collar criminal cases and prosecuting serious crime, including homicide, shootings, corruption, perjury, sexual offences, serious drug offences and duty evasion on behalf of HMRC and SOCA. Tom's practice continues to include business crime and general crime with an emphasis on health & safety; in 2016/2017 he is instructed in three homicide cases including two gross negligence manslaughters arising from deaths in the workplace. Tom has also focused for over a decade on medical regulation, acting for a variety of regulators. In 2016 he was instructed by the GMC in the High Court appeal of Dr Squier (the baby shaking expert struck off by the MPTS) and also in the Supreme Court for the General Pharmaceutical Council. Tom has been appointed legal assessor for the HFEA, the GC Osteopaths and the Royal Institute of Chartered Surveyors. In 2010 he was appointed counsel to the Mid Staffs Public Inquiry and led a team of three junior counsel who called more than 150 witnesses. He assisted in the editing of the subsequent report. The inquiry was a seminal point in the NHS. He is currently instructed by the GMC to prosecute a breast surgeon accused of undertaking hundreds of defective mastectomies and of performing unnecessary breast surgery. Tom has recently been acting for the Home Office in the Historic Sex Abuse Public Inquiry. Tom has appeared at Coroner's inquests and represented the family of the Red Arrows pilot Sean Cunningham who died after his ejection seat catastrophically failed.

Professional Memberships: Association of Regulatory & Disciplinary Lawyers; Public Access Directory; Public Access Bar Association.

Career: Silk 2010; 2002 Standing Counsel to the Revenue & Customs Prosecutions Office; 2000 Recorder; Call 1982.

KAY, Dominic
Crown Office Chambers, London
020 7797 8100
kay@crownofficechambers.com
Featured in Health & Safety (London)

Practice Areas: Ranked as a Star Individual, former 'Health & Safety Junior of the Year' and listed in the 'Bar 100'. One of the Country's leading health & safety barristers who spends the majority of his time defending high profile regulatory prosecutions brought against corporate and individual defendants. Vast experience in corporate manslaughter prosecutions (R v. Lion Steel Limited, R v. Huntley Mount Engineering Limited, R v. Linley Developments Limited) and cases involving allegations of individual gross negligence manslaughter. Work includes cases concerning the construction, leisure, agriculture, care and retail sectors, and those involving educational establishments, public bodies and the emergency services. Cases often involve multi-fatality accidents and cases involving complex machinery. Undertakes large number of inquests into health & safety and workplace related deaths. Highly experienced in cases concerning the deaths of children. Described in the 'Bar 100' as "renowned for his top level Health & Safety work...a barrister with a nationwide practice...with a strong grasp of clients' commercial and legal requirements and excellent communication skills. He is very confident before the Bench and when handling opponents." Highly experienced defending environmental prosecutions, representing clients including major utility companies in cases including those concerning large-scale pollution incidents, permitting offences, waste escapes and licence infringements.

KAY, Steven QC
9 Bedford Row, London
020 7489 2727
steven.kayqc@9bedfordrow.co.uk
Featured in Crime (London)

Practice Areas: Steven Kay QC is a leading international criminal lawyer, with a global reputation who has been in many of the landmark cases that have established modern international criminal law. He has represented Heads of State, leading Military figures and civilians in high profile international trials. His cases demonstrate the depth of experience and the quality of the work for which he has been hired: OTP v. Tadic; OTP v. Musema; OTP v. Milosevic; OTP v. Cermak; OTP v. Kenyatta; ECtHR Beslan case against Russia; Bangladesh International Crimes Tribunal. Steven's international practice includes advising Governments and organisations upon international legal issues, many of them with a political aspect: see submissions to the OISL upon the conflict in Sri Lanka with the LTTE; and reports upon the Muslim Brotherhood for the Egypt State Litigation Authority. Certain advisory work is not in the public domain and is necessarily confidential. Steven has developed an impressive team at 9 Bedford Row to meet the unique challenges of these international cases. The quality of the work of the team was recognised in the case of President Kenyatta at the ICC, a result that has changed the shape of African politics. Steven is currently Co-Chair of the IBA War Crimes Committee. For full details, see http://www.9bedfordrow.co.uk/members / Steven_Kay_QC and www.9bri.com.

Professional Memberships: International Bar Association, S.E. Circuit.

Career: Called to the Bar 1977, QC 1997, Secretary CBA 1993-96, Co-Chair IBA War Crimes Committee 2013-, Founder European Criminal Bar Association 1998, Founder International Criminal Law Bureau 2008 see www.internationallawbureau.com.

Publications: Contributor to: Commentary on The Rome Statute of the International Criminal Court, OUP 2002. International Criminal Justice, Westlaw UK Insight. Cases That Changed Our Lives: The Nuremburg Trials And Their Enduring Legacy That Even Rulers Are Under God And The Law, Lexis Nexis.

Personal: Educated Epsom College; Leeds University.

KAZAKOS, Leon
2 Hare Court, London
020 7353 5324
clerks@2harecourt.com
Featured in Crime (London)

Practice Areas: Leon Kazakos is a tenacious and committed advocate. His criminal practice is exclusively defence based and is focused on most forms of business crime, serious fraud and complex crime. He has substantial experience in defending companies and individuals accused of large scale frauds on the public revenue (MTIC and other VAT fraud), frauds on the NHS, frauds on charities, investment 'boiler room' fraud, mortgage fraud and money laundering. He has particular expertise in fraud, money laundering, corruption and all other aspects of financial crime. His civil practice focuses on contentious tax, civil recovery proceedings brought by the National Crime Agency and other civil fraud work including large scale 'MTIC' appeals to the First and Upper Tier Tribunals, duty evasion and other general indirect taxation disputes. Recent Cases include; leading counsel in Operation Cotton 'land banking' fraud. Leading Counsel in a £16 million gold smuggling fraud. Represented a Barclays Bank Business Manager accused of operating a money laundering arrangement, a woman accused of involvement in an international cocaine smuggling network, a police detective both in criminal proceedings and in subsequent disciplinary proceedings, and a company director accused of frauds on investors and government institutions. He is currently instructed to defend in several large scale money laundering and mortgage fraud trials, the largest slavery prosecution brought to date, a multi-million pound fraud on the NHS, an investment fraud and is regularly engaged advising solicitors firms, estate agents and other professionals in disputes involving breaches of money laundering regulations, property freezing orders and ancillary proceedings.

Professional Memberships: Fraud Lawyers Association, Financial Services Lawyers Association, Criminal Bar Association South Eastern Circuit.

Publications: Contributing Editor: Butterworths "Fraud: Law, Practice and Procedure".

KEEN, Spencer
Old Square Chambers, London
0771 772 1204
keen@oldsquare.co.uk
Featured in Employment (Western)

Practice Areas: Spencer specialises in employment and commercial law. He has extensive experience acting for both corporate clients and individuals at both first instance and appellate level. He is particularly well known for injunction proceedings in the High Court (concerning employee competition, restraints of trade and confidentiality) and also for acting in complex disability discrimination cases. Examples of recent cases include: Wicksteed Leisure v Kompan [2016] EWHC (unreported), Decorus v Penfold [2016] EWHC 1421 (QB), Re-Use Collections v Sendall [2014] EWHC 3852 (QB), Boothe v Governing Body of Toynbee School UKEAT/0135/15/MC, R (Unison) v Lord Chancellor (No.2) [2014] EWHC 4198 (Admin), Edwin v Avante Partnership UKEAT/0187/14/DM.

Professional Memberships: ELA.

Publications: Disability Discrimination in Employment (OUP) 2009. Spencer publishes an online database of disability discrimination cases on www.spencerkeen.co.uk.

KEITH, Benjamin

5 St Andrew's Hill, London
020 7332 5400
benkeith@5sah.co.uk

Featured in Extradition (London)

Practice Areas: Ben is a Barrister specialising in Extradition, Immigration, Serious Fraud, Human Rights and Public Law including the challenge of INTERPOL Red Notices. He leads the 5SAH extradition team. He has significant experience of Judicial Review and is appointed to the Attorney General's B Panel of advocates. He has a developed expertise in political corruption cases and in particular requests from former soviet states especially: Russia, Ukraine, Azerbaijan, Kazakhstan and Moldova. In 2015 he was successful in the case of Government of Russia v Ereshenko and Ukraine v Solodchenko which related to the BTA Bank (Kazakhstan) v Mukthar Ablyazov litigation; both cases was discharged. He also represents in politically sensitive asylum cases, to former CIS states in particular.

Professional Memberships: DELF (Publicity secretary) ELA FLA (Committee Member). ECBA CBA YFLA (Chair 2011-2013).

Career: Ben has considerable experience of EAW cases including cases of murder, rape, people trafficking, terrorism and complex fraud. Ben has a busy Appellate practice and has recently appeared for the Appellants in the leading authorities in the Divisional Court on Latvian Prisons: Brazuks and others v Latvia [2014] EWHC 1021 (Admin); Romanian Prisons: Florea v Romania [2014]. In 2015 he represented Dominico Rancadore in his appeal before the EAW was withdrawn as well as advising clients internationally on cross boarder issues.

Personal: Ben lectures in Human Rights at Birkbeck College, University of London.

KEITH, Hugo QC

3 Raymond Buildings Barristers, London
020 7400 6400
hugo.keith@3rblaw.com

Featured in Administrative & Public Law (London), Crime (London), Extradition (London), Inquests & Public Inquiries (All Circuits), Financial Crime (London)

Practice Areas: Hugo was named as one of the UK's overall 'Stars at the Bar' in the Chambers UK 2015 guide. Described as 'a fabulous silk' and as having 'an outstanding reputation', Hugo is recognised as one of the legal profession's leading QC's. He was a member of the 'A' Panel of civil Treasury Counsel for 8 years, during which time he regularly appeared on matters of public and criminal law both on behalf of Government departments and as amicus curiae before the High Court, Court of Appeal and House of Lords. He has appeared in 14 cases before the House of Lords/Supreme Court. He won the Chambers and Partners award for criminal barrister of the year 2008, and took silk in 2009. He has been instructed in some of the most high profile cases of recent years. He represented The Queen in the Inquest into the death of Diana, Princess of Wales, and Malcolm Calvert in the Cazenove insider dealing case. He was then appointed leading Counsel to the Inquests into the London Bombings of 7 July 2005 and, subsequently, appeared in the Leveson Inquiry on behalf of Rebekah Brooks and in the Tchenguiz action against the SFO. Notable recent cases have included the Shrien Dewani extradition (in which he successfully represented the Republic of South Africa), the Inquest into the death of Mark Duggan (Hugo represented the Metropolitan Police Commissioner), the Inquest into the death of Alexander Litvinenko (on behalf of Boris Berezovsky), the Hermitage Capital affair, and the SFO investigations into Swift Oil and Gas, and into LIBOR. He advises corporations, governments and individuals in relation to all aspects of extradition, criminal/corporate liability and restraint. He is currently advising in connection with the Alstrom corruption inquiry, the Autonomy/Hewlett Packard investigation, the SFO Barclays/Qatar investigation, and on extradition/restraint matters concerning foreign high net-worth individuals, politically exposed persons and Ministers.

KELEHER, Paul QC

25 Bedford Row, London
020 7067 1500
pkeleher@25bedfordrow.com

Featured in Crime (London)

Practice Areas: Serious crime including terrorism, drugs trafficking, serious offences of violence and sexual abuse. Advising and acting in complex fraud matters both nationally and internationally in trials at first instance and in the Court of Appeal. Expert in computer use in crime and excels in all cases with forensic elements. Recent notable cases include R v D (Hatton Garden robbery) R v T (multiple death by dangerous driving) R v D (provision of training for terrorism) R v R (UK's largest opium importation) R v (QPR directors blackmail). Operation Athletic (multi million pound conspiracy to defraud HMRC) Operation Bluesky (largest UK people smuggling operation).

Professional Memberships: Bar Council Committee member, CBA Committee member, Bar Pro Bono Unit Reviewer, Criminal Justice System Efficiency Committee.

Career: Called 1980, Member of Grays Inn. Silk 2009.

Personal: Graduated Gonville & Caius College, University of Cambridge.

KELLER, Ciaran

Maitland Chambers, London
020 7406 1200
ckeller@maitlandchambers.com

Featured in Chancery (London), Commercial Dispute Resolution (London), Partnership (London)

Practice Areas: Commercial and chancery litigation and arbitration (domestic and international), including business agreements and contractual disputes, banking and financial services litigation, civil fraud and asset tracing, property litigation, energy and minerals, jurisdiction disputes, company and insolvency matters, fiduciaries, professional negligence and claims for and against sovereign states. Admitted as a member of the Bar of the British Virgin Islands Notable cases include: British American Tobacco v Sequana [2016] (Ch – unlawful dividends; breach of fiduciary duty; transactions defrauding creditors); Krys v KBC Partners [2015] (Privy Council – construction of articles of a limited partnership); Yukos Capital v Rosneft (No. 2) [2014] (Comm – enforceability of annulled arbitral awards); Barnsley v Noble [2015] (Ch – deceit, breach of contract and fiduciary duty); Cifal Groupe v Meridian Securities [2013] (Comm – jurisdiction challenge); Yukos Capital v Rosneft [2012] (CA – act of state, issue estoppel); Favor Easy Management v Wu [2012] (CA – civil fraud); NML v Argentina [2011] (Supreme Court – sovereign immunity); Crossco v Jolan [2011] (CA – constructive trust, proprietary estoppel); Star Energy v Bocardo [2010] (Supreme Court – trespass by oil pipelines at depth); Crest Nicholson v Akaria [2010] (CA – contractual formation); IPCO v NNPC [2009] (CA – part enforcement of New York Convention awards); Meretz v ACP [2008] (CA – conspiracy; inducing breach of contract); Donegal v Zambia [2007] (Comm – debt recovery against a sovereign state); Gamlestaden v Baltic Partners [2007] (Privy Council – unfair prejudice remedy for shareholders).

Professional Memberships: Commercial Bar Association; Chancery Bar Association; Financial Services Lawyers Association.

Career: Formerly a Member of HM Diplomatic Service (serving at the United Nations and the British Embassy, Lisbon). Called to the Bar 2004.

Personal: Educated at Cheadle Hulme School and Brasenose College, Oxford (MA, 1st Class Honours; Gibbs Prize, John House Prize, Shell Prize; Open Scholarship), City University (Distinction) and the Inns of Court School of Law (Barstow Scholarship, Sweet & Maxwell Company Law Prize). Member of Lincoln' s Inn (Hardwicke, Lord Haldane, Lord Mansfield and Megarry Scholarships; Buchanan Prize; Sir Louis Gluckstein Advocacy Prize).

KELLY, Brendan QC

2 Hare Court, London
020 73535324
clerks@2harecourt.com

Featured in Crime (London), Financial Crime (London)

Practice Areas: Brendan Kelly QC is a highly sought after, and well respected Silk whose practice focuses on the provision of advice and advocacy in cases of fraud, serious crime, and regulatory law. Brendan regularly appears abroad as well as in the UK, advising and representing corporate clients, their individual directors and officers in all aspects of business crime. He is also involved in Regulatory work, and is often sought out by professionals for cases arising in the workplace. His high level of skill, paired with his speed to grasp the issue, enable Brendan's clients to feel at ease and warm to him immediately, as well as making him a hit with both the judge and jury. Recent instructions include representing one of three defendants charged with murder; the attempt by an organized group to defraud a central London Bank of £300 million; representing jockey Darren Williams charged with conspiracy to defraud by "fixing" horse races; a Solicitor accused of Perverting the Court of Justice; the longest ever UVF supergrass terrorist trial to be heard in Northern Ireland; the murder of three and the attempted murder of two others by machine gun. He is currently instructed to represent the first defendant in one of the largest tax fraud allegations brought before the courts.

Professional Memberships: CBA, FLA, FSLA.

Career: Called 1988; Recorder 2003; Queen's Counsel 2008.

KELLY, Sean

St Philips Chambers, Leeds
0113 2446691
skelly@st-philips.com

Featured in Chancery (North Eastern)

Practice Areas: Specialises in Chancery and Commercial law including banking, company law, financial services, insolvency, partnerships and LLPs and associated professional negligence. Sean Kelly is regularly instructed in large scale disputes relating to the ownership and management of companies and partnerships and those relating to business and company sales. His professional negligence practice includes claims against accountants, architects, financial advisers and solicitors. He has been conducting claims relating to interest rate swaps since 1999 and appeared in the only case to date won by the customer. Since mis-selling became widely recognised, he has become a leading specialist in this area and is now involved in over 150 claims on behalf of customers. He is currently dealing with the first claim relating to the application of the Conduct of Business Rules to TBLs.

Professional Memberships: Chancery Bar Association. Association of Partnership Practitioners.

Career: Date of Call: 1990 Gray's Inn.

KELSEY, Katherine

1 King's Bench Walk, London
020 7936 1500
kkelsey@1kbw.co.uk

Featured in Family/Matrimonial (London)

Practice Areas: Katherine Kelsey specialises in the following areas of Family Law: Financial Remedies: Advising and acting in all areas of matrimonial finance. Experience in dealing with complex cases involving high net worth and high profile individuals. Other Financial Relief: Advising and acting in relation to claims brought under Schedule 1 of the Children Act 1989 and the Trusts of Land and Appointment of Trustees Act 1996. Private Law Children: Advising and acting in all areas of private law proceedings. Experience in dealing with complex cases involving internal and external relocation and intractable contact disputes. Katherine is also a qualified Mediator.

Professional Memberships: Family Law Bar Association; Resolution; Lincoln's Inn; Inner Temple.

Career: Call: 2003.

Personal: Education: Ilford Ursuline High School; Greyfriars Hall, University of Oxford – BA (Hons) Jurisprudence; Inns of Court School of Law – Bar Vocational Course; Hardwicke Entrance Award (Lincoln's Inn); Lord Denning Scholarship (Lincoln's Inn); Eastham Scholarship (Lincoln's Inn).

KELSEY-FRY, John QC

Cloth Fair Chambers, London
020 7710 6444
nicknewman@clothfairchambers.com

Featured in Crime (London), Financial Crime (London)

Practice Areas: Instructed for high profile criminal defence, especially in the corporate and business crime arena eg. Blue Arrow, R v Regan (co-op corruption case), R v Stiedl (pension's fund), and R v Stovold (Local Authority Financing). Notable past cases include; advised defendant subject of a Hong Kong Department of Justice investigation into market abuse/ insider trading, represented the defendant in a FSA

Crown Court Prosecution, successful half time submission, prosecuted on behalf of the FSA in an insider trading trial, Dougall the leading authority on sentencing executive level whistle blowers, represented a director of Mabey and Johnson in the sanctions busting investigation. Successfully acted for a former director of iSoft in criminal & FCA proceedings. Notable cases in crime: R v Serafinowicz and R v Sawoniuk (war crimes), R v Smith (KGB Spy), R v Donald and Cressey (police corruption/ Panorama case), R v Charlie Kray, R v Jane Andrews, R v Coutts (necrophiliac murder), Mohammed Al Fayed (deposit box), R v Bukhari (arms case involving FBI). Successfully represented Kieren Fallon; Steven Gerrard; secured an acquittal for Harry Redknapp over allegations of tax evasion. Represented a Saudi Prince charged with Murder. Successfully represented an international property tycoon surrounding corruption charges in Turks & Caicos Islands. Advised real estate company Walshaw Moor regarding a dispute with Natural England. Recent notable cases include; Represented former Energy Secretary Chris Huhne charged with perverting the course of justice. Advised ex News International Chief Executive Rebekah Brooks re phone hacking. Successfully acted for Olympus Corporation during SFO investigation and subsequent charges. Represented Raymond Kwok over corruption charges in Hong Kong, full acquittal. Advising an individual in SFO investigation regarding Rolls Royce. Acting for former Senior Executive of Barclays Bank PLC in SFO/FCA investigation re Qatar. Representing Mazher Mahmood on conspiracy to pervert charges. Advising individual re SFO investigation into a national telecommunications company for corruption. Libel, has attracted choice instructions in this arena, cases include; Turcu (Beckham kidnap), Paul McKenna, Wayne Rooney, Sharon Stone, Roman Polanski, Max Mosely, Sir Stelios (founder of Easyjet), Craig Bellamy. Advised the Times Newspaper. For further details please visit www.clothfair-chambers.com.

Professional Memberships: Criminal Bar Association.

Career: Called to the Bar 1978. Treasury Counsel (Junior and Senior) 1992-2000. QC 2000. Founder member of Cloth Fair Chambers 2006.

KEMP, Edward
Littleton Chambers, London
020 7797 8600
ekemp@littletonchambers.co.uk
Featured in Employment (London)

Practice Areas: Ed is a trial and appellate lawyer specialising in employment law, discrimination law and related areas. Ed has appeared as an advocate (whether unled or part of a larger team) in every level of court and tribunal all the way up to the Supreme Court. Ed has a growing international practice. He has full rights of audience before the DIFC Courts in Dubai and has recently appeared in trials in that jurisdiction. Ed's industry expertise spans both the public sector (local government, police force, doctors) to the private sector, including cases for or against senior executives and financial institutions. Ed has particular expertise in all discrimination strands, whistle-blowing, complex contractual interpretation points, cases with an international element or ground-breaking points at the interface between domestic and European law. Ed is regularly instructed on cross-over work, for example: discrimination in goods and services litigation, professional negligence and breach of contract claims in the County Court and in the High Court. Ed is co-head of both the Employment Group and International Opportunities Group at Littleton Chambers.

Professional Memberships: ELBA, ELA, DLA, ELAAS, PIBA, A4ID.

Career: Called to the Bar 2005; Inner Temple Exhibitioner and Sir Joseph Priestly Scholar; LLM, University College London; Maîtrise en Droit, Université de Paris I (Panthéon-Sorbonne); LLB, King's College London.

Personal: Ed speaks French.

KEMPSTER, Toby
Old Square Chambers, Bristol
020 7269 0300
kempster@oldsquare.co.uk
Featured in Personal Injury (Western), Employment (Western)

Practice Areas: Toby Kempster specialises in employment and personal injury law, the common denominator being the workplace. His employment practice covers both contractual and statutory claims, and this year he has been involved in several high value claims and which have included acting for Bath University and East London NHS Trust. He has recently succeeded at trial in resisting attempts to prevent an outgoing sales manager from working for a rival company. Dealing with complex quantum issues in his personal injury practice assists for example in assessing the value of discrimination claims where long term unemployment is the result. Toby's personal injury work is principally concerned with employers liability and includes more complex claims arising from occupational disease and stress. Recent work has focused on cases involving asbestos exposure and, as a result, he has considerable experience in FAA claims.

Professional Memberships: ILS, ELA, and PIBA.

Personal: Sailing, walking and theatre.

KENNY, Christian
1 Hare Court, London
020 7797 7070
kenny@1hc.com
Featured in Family/Matrimonial (London)

Practice Areas: Christian is a specialist in financial disputes and is routinely instructed in cases involving substantial assets and complex issues such as contested international jurisdiction, company valuations, non-disclosure of assets and assets held offshore and/or within company or trust structures. He regularly appears in the High Court, both with leading counsel and alone and has appeared in several of the leading reported cases involving international enforcement of financial orders and injunctive relief. In addition to his financial practice, Christian acts in challenging private law children disputes (including applications for leave to remove children from the jurisdiction) and in property disputes between unmarried partners under the Trusts of Land and Appointment of Trustees Act. He is also a Resolution trained mediator and regularly lectures on developments and niche areas within the Family Law, most recently on the recognition of foreign divorces (ie divorce by Talaq) in the English courts.

Professional Memberships: Family Law Bar Association.

Career: Bristol University (BA Hons 1st Class), City University, Inns of Court School of Law. Called to the Bar in 2003, Inner Temple.

Personal: Christian is married to a journalist and has three small boys. He lives in London and enjoys spending weekends in Devon and holidays in France and Austria.

KENT, Alan QC
Carmelite Chambers, London
020 7936 6300
akentqc@carmelitechambers.co.uk
Featured in Crime (London)

Practice Areas: Alan Kent QC moved to Carmelite Chambers in October 2014. He is an established criminal silk who defends and prosecutes in all manner of complex criminal cases ranging from Murder to Sexual Offences and Fraud. Alan is an extremely popular and sought after advocate. He is constantly in demand by defence solicitors & the CPS alike. He is a great team player but also a first class leader. His client skills are second to none. Has conducted well in excess of 100 homicide cases, from the straightforward single handed cases to multi handed cases involving cut throat defences and joint enterprise. Recently represented the first defendant in a 7 handed murder trial at Birmingham Crown Court which the prosecution described as "medieval warfare on the streets of Birmingham in the 21st Century" He is regularly instructed to represent young and vulnerable defendants, those with mental health issues and is frequently instructed in cases involving vulnerable witnesses. He recently represented a 75 year old former care worker who was accused of multiple historic sexual offences against boys in a children's home from the early 1970's to the 1990's. The trial resulted from a long running police inquiry into the conduct of the staff. The judge described it as "...abuse of the very worst kind" Recent fraud work includes representing the financial controller of a major company who was accused of being involved in a 'Factoring Fraud' in which over £40m of false invoices were submitted to Barclays Bank. Appellate work includes acting on behalf of the Crown in the leading authority on hearsay, R v Riat and others.

KENYON, Flavia
3 Temple Gardens, London
020 7353 3102
fk@3tg.co.uk
Featured in Crime (London)

Practice Areas: Serious organised crime, fraud, public access.

Professional Memberships: Lincoln's Inn, Criminal Bar Association.

Career: Flavia has developed an exclusively defence practice which covers the full range of criminal law. She appears both as a leading and led junior on high profile cases including serious violence, complex fraud, including cyber fraud, people trafficking, drug-trafficking, and serious sexual offences. She is a fiercely articulate and determined advocate known for her meticulous preparation and fighting spirit. Flavia follows a tradition of advocacy in her family, which goes back to 1923 when her cousin (by marriage) Mercy Ashworth became the first woman to be called to the Bar at Lincoln's Inn, and only the second female barrister to be called in the UK. Flavia was educated at Oxford University and is the only British criminal barrister fluent in Romanian. She has appeared in Chambers and Partners since 2013. In the Legal 500 she is described as having "the zeal of a teenager but the head of an established professional.'

Publications: "Deportation: Two views on Kluxen" – feature article in Archbold Review, Issue 6, July 2010.

KESSLER, James QC
Old Square Tax Chambers, London
020 72422744
taxchambers@15oldsquare.co.uk
Featured in Tax (London), Charities (London)

Practice Areas: Revenue law. James Kessler QC is particularly interested in foreign domiciliaries, offshore entities and charities. Other interests include complex tax prosecutions, particularly on the avoidance/evasion faultline.

Professional Memberships: Revenue Bar Association. Member of the Northern Ireland Bar.

Career: Called to the Bar 1984. QC 2003.

Publications: James is the author of: Taxation of Non-Residents and Foreign Domiciliaries (15th ed, 2016). Drafting Trusts & Will Trusts (13th ed, 2016). Taxation of Charities and Nonprofit Organisations (10th ed, 2015). There are foreign-law editions of Drafting Trusts and Will Trusts in Australia, BVI, Canada, Cayman, Channel Islands, Hong Kong, New Zealand, Northern Ireland, Scotland and Singapore.

Personal: Interests: cinema, jogging.

KHALIL, Karim QC
Drystone Chambers, London
020 7404 1881
karim.khalil@drystone.com
Featured in Crime (South Eastern)

Practice Areas: Criminal law, Fraud and Financial Regulation, Consumer law, Extradition.

Professional Memberships: Queen's College (Cambridge), called to the Bar 1984, Assistant Recorder 1997, Recorder 2000, Queen's Counsel 2003. SE Circuit, SE Circuit Liaison Committee (Chairman), CBA, Norwich Bar Mess, Cambridge Bar Mess (Chairman), three years on the Professional Conduct and Complaints Committee, Bar disciplinary Tribunal member.

Career: Karim Khalil QC forged his impressive reputation in London and the South East, but is increasingly instructed on behalf of clients nationally. He has an associate Tenancy in Leeds and Newcastle to more easily accommodate the requests for his expertise across the country. He also acts in cases involving issues of foreign jurisdiction and/ or cross-border financial matters in a growing international practice with particular links to the Cayman Islands. He is regularly instructed in significant POCA proceedings and has undertaken criminal and civil litigation relating to company fraud plus civil claims against the police and prison service. He is sought after for his expertise in serious fraud (including Revenue, Customs & Excise and MTIC), Health & Safety, and Sports law. Karim also represents appellants before the VAT Tribunal (usually following assertions of VAT/MTIC fraud). He represented a Cambridge College against the HSE and successfully resisted the Government's attempts to prosecute a scientist in the Porton Down experiments. He defends and prosecutes in a wide range of heavy criminal work, including

murder, sexual offences and drug trafficking. Karim has promoted computerised presentation of evidence in Court, and writes the chapter on Confiscation Law in "Fraud: Law Practice & Procedure". Karim was called to the Bar in 1984, and in 2000 become one of the youngest Recorders (now sitting in the Old Bailey). He took Silk in 2003 before prosecuting Ian Huntley & Maxine Carr (Soham murders).
Publications: Fraud: Law, Practice and Procedure – chapter on confiscation.

KHAN, Ashraf
2 Bedford Row, London
020 7440 8888
akhan@2bedfordrow.co.uk
Featured in Crime (London), Financial Crime (London)
Practice Areas: Serious crime complex fraud professional discipline regulation and compliance civil recovery and asset forfeiture alternative dispute resolution.
Professional Memberships: Accredited Civil & Commercial Mediator, Registered Lawyer under The FA Football Agents Regulations, Registered Practitioner with Dubai International Finance Centre (DIFC), The Honourable Society of the Middle Temple, Midland Circuit Junior (October 2011-October 2012), Criminal Bar Association.
Career: Ashraf has a national defence practice which includes a case load of some of the biggest and most complex criminal/fraud cases seen in recent times. He is frequently instructed in high stakes cases which require intense preparation and skilled presentation in court. His extensive experience of high profile litigation in this area covers a wide spectrum of cases; including homicide, firearms, serious sexual offences, large scale organised crime involving price fixing, corruption, cartel, trafficking, money laundering and high value serious fraud. He is often instructed at the earliest stages of major investigations so clients have the benefit of his advice and assistance during what is often a critical stage in a criminal inquiry. International crime and regulatory law are also a key part of Ashraf's practice. He is appointed to the defence panel at the International Criminal Court (ICC), a registered lawyer with the Football Association and approved to conduct cases at the Dubai International Finance Centre (DIFC), where he advises and represents corporate bodies and individuals in relation to regulatory breaches or complex commercial disputes. Ashraf also offers a high-quality, relevant and sensitive mediation service. He has a wealth of litigation experience and is able to deal with the most complex legal and factual issues in the context of a Mediation. Members of the Public and Businesses can now instruct Ashraf directly under the Bar Council's Direct Access Scheme to provide advice, assistance and representation in a wide range of Criminal and Civil matters.

KHAYUM, Zulfikar
Atkin Chambers, London
020 7404 0102
zkhayum@atkinchambers.com
Featured in Construction (London)
Practice Areas: Zulfikar practices across all areas of construction, engineering, IT and energy sectors in both the domestic and international context. He has experience of dealing with matters in litigation, arbitration, adjudication and mediation. He has represented employers, architects, contractors, sub-contractors, developers, funders, insurers and others. He is often asked to advise on tactical as well as legal issues. Zulfikar has appeared in a number of court hearings as junior counsel as well appearing as sole counsel at various applications and hearings, including trial. He has further advised and acted in arbitrations conducted under various arbitral rules and governing laws in different jurisdictions. Recent international arbitration experiences include major hearings in the Bahamas, Singapore, Hong Kong, London and an ongoing dispute in the Gulf. Zulfikar is also regularly instructed in relation to domestic disputes, recent experiences of which relate to the construction of an educational facility, a large dispute concerning construction defects in a waste processing facility and a substantial PFI dispute relating to highways management.
Professional Memberships: TECBAR, LCLCBA, COMBAR, SCL.
Career: LLB (Hons); BCL (Oxon). Called 2006.
Publications: Hudson's Building and Engineering Contracts, 12th Ed. (Sweet & Maxwell, 2010) – contributing editor.

KILLALEA, Stephen QC
Devereux, London
020 7353 7534
clerks@devchambers.co.uk
Featured in Personal Injury (London), Travel (London)
Practice Areas: A substantial personal injury practice specialising in catastrophic brain and spinal injuries. Considerable experience of industrial accidents, including offshore accidents, commercial diving and accidents on ships and catastrophic accidents occurring abroad. A leading health and safety practice representing companies and individuals in criminal prosecutions by the HSE and other enforcement authorities. (Further details see Chambers website www.devereuxchambers.co.uk).
Professional Memberships: Personal Injuries Bar Association; Association of Personal Injury Lawyers; Health and Safety Lawyers Association.
Career: Called to the Bar 1981. QC 2006.
Publications: Co-author 'Health and Safety The Modern Legal Framework' (2nd Edition) Butterworths 2000. Author of Sections on Construction Regulations and Divers and Offshore Installations (Personal Injury Factbook) Gee & Co 1998.
Personal: Lives in Sussex.

KILVINGTON, Simon QC
Byrom Street Chambers, Manchester
0161 829 2100
simon.kilvington@byromstreet.com
Featured in Personal Injury (Northern), Personal Injury (All Circuits)
Practice Areas: Catastrophic, serious and complex personal injury, including catastrophic brain and spinal injuries; industrial disease and, in particular, asbestos litigation; clinical negligence, including birth injury; solicitors' negligence, arising out of the handling of personal injury litigation.
Professional Memberships: Personal Injury Bar Association.
Career: Called 1995 (Lincoln's Inn); 18 St John Street Chambers (1995 – 2012); Byrom Street Chambers (2012 – date); appointed Queen's Counsel 2016.
Publications: lead author, Sweet & Maxwell's Occupational Illness Litigation

KIMBELL, John QC
Quadrant Chambers, London
020 7583 4444
john.kimbell@quadrantchambers.com
Featured in Travel (London), Aviation (London), Shipping (London)
Practice Areas: Aviation, Shipping and Commodities and Travel.
Professional Memberships: LMAA (supporting member), GMAA (Hamburg), COMBAR, Anglo-German Jurists Association.
Career: John Kimbell's practice encompasses shipping, aviation, and travel as well as general commercial litigation and arbitration. He is also a qualified lawyer ('Rechtsanwalt') in Hamburg, Germany and a member of the German Maritime Arbitrator's Association. His shipping practice encompasses both 'wet' collision and other Admiralty Court matters and 'dry' bill of lading and charterparty disputes. He regularly appears in the Commercial Court as well as in arbitrations in London and in Hamburg (in particular LMAA and GMAA arbitrations). John is fluent in German and accepts instructions in German. He is the co-editor of the Fourth edition of Admiralty Jurisdiction and Practice, published 2011. In the aviation field he has handled a wide range of disputes from aircraft financing and mortgages (including the leading caes of Blue Sky One Limited and Others v. Mahan Air and Others) to fatal accidents (in the UK and abroad). John specialises in advising clients on jurisdictional and private international law aspects to disputes. He has recently appeared in the Court of Appeal in Graham v Thomas Cook [2012] (in which it was held that Regulation 261/2004 does not give rise to a claim in damages) and Hook and Stott v British Airways [2012] in which the supremcy of the Montreal Convention over domestic legislation was confirmed.
Publications: Admiralty Jurisdiction and Practice (with Nigel Meeson) Fourth Edition, (2011) LLP. Foreign Currency Claims (with M.N.Howard QC and John Knott) LLP (forthcoming) 2012
Personal: John lives in Norwich and London.

KING, Henry
Fountain Court Chambers, London
020 7583 3335
clerks4@fountaincourt.co.uk
Featured in Banking & Finance (London), Financial Services (London)
Practice Areas: General commercial litigation and arbitration practice, with a particular emphasis on banking and financial services. Notable cases include acting for Deutsche Bank in Deutsche Bank v Sebastian Holdings [2013] EWHC 3463 (Comm), for the Central Bank of Trinidad & Tobago in the CLICO Enquiry, for the Bar Council in R (Prudential) v HMRC [2013] UKSC 1, for John Pottage in Pottage v Financial Services Authority [2013] Lloyd's Rep FC 16 and for the Bank of England in Three Rivers [2006] EWHC 816 (Comm).
Professional Memberships: Institute of Chartered Accountants in England and Wales, Commercial Bar Association, Association of Regulatory and Disciplinary Lawyers, Russian and CIS Arbitration Network.
Career: ACA 1996, Called to the Bar of England and Wales 1998, called to the Bar of the BVI 2011, ad hoc call to the Bars of the Cayman Islands and of Trinidad and Tobago, Junior Counsel to the Crown (A panel).
Publications: Contributor to: The Law of Privilege (ed B. Thanki QC, OUP, 2nd edition 2011); Bullen & Leake & Jacob's Precedents of Pleadings, specialist contributor on Restitution (Sweet & Maxwell, 18th edition 2015); Information Rights: Law and Practice (ed. P Coppel QC, Hart Publishing, 4th edition 2014).

KINNEAR, Jonathan S QC
9-12 Bell Yard, London
020 7400 1800
j.kinnear@912by.com
Featured in Financial Crime (London)
Practice Areas: Specialises in cases of real financial complexity in criminal, civil, regulatory and tribunal jurisdictions. He also deals with complex confiscation and restraint issues at both first instance and all appellate levels. His highlights in the last year include representing HMRC in the Court of Appeal Division in HMRC v Davis and Dann and in the Citibank litigation in the Upper Tribunal. He continues to act for the SFO in several high profile money laundering and corruption cases and is instructed by the CPS in the litigation in respect of James Ibori the former Governor of the Delta State, Nigeria. He represented the interests of the CPS in the civil proceedings arising out of the collapse of the R v Mouncher proceedings arising from the murder of Lynette White. He has been instructed by the Government Legal Department in several pieces of high value civil litigation, including the fallout from the phone hacking investigation. He is one of a small number of silks with substantial experience in both criminal and jurisdictions and he is instructed in many of the most challenging cases where the jurisdictions meet.
Career: Called (Gray's Inn) in 1994 and Northern Ireland (1996), appointed QC in 2012, Deputy District Judge in 2004 and a Recorder of the Crown Court in 2009.
Personal: Educated at Methodist College, Belfast, Newcastle University and the Inns of Court School of Law.

KINNIER, Andrew
Henderson Chambers, London
020 7583 9020
akinnier@hendersonchambers.co.uk
Featured in Local Government (London), Product Liability (London), Public Procurement (London)
Practice Areas: Product liability: acting for defendants in group and unitary actions, particularly relating to pharmaceutical products, medical devices and motor vehicles. Public, administrative and local government law, and, in particular, public procurement and state aid: advises central government, local and other public authorities on a broad range of matters including powers, finance, social services, education, waste, civil contingencies and anti-terrorism. Health & safety law: represents corporate clients in respect of regulatory prosecutions, civil proceedings and inquests.
Professional Memberships: ALBA; BEG; Procurement Lawyers' Association; UK State Aid Law Association; South Eastern Circuit
Career: Educated at Sidney Sussex College, Cambridge (1991-95) (BA 1st Class Honours; MA); Called 1996 Middle Temple (Queen Mother-Fox Major Entrance Scholarship). Junior Counsel to the Crown (A Panel 2011-), (B Panel 2008-11); Junior Counsel to the Welsh Government (Public Law Panel

2009-2012); Junior Counsel to the Welsh Government (Public Law – A Panel, 2012-)
Publications: Contributor – Halsbury's Laws of England (Vol 37); Specialist Contributor – Bullen & Leake Precedents & Pleadings (15th-17th editions); Specialist Contributor – Kluwer's Manual of International Product Law (1st and 2nd editions).

KINSLER, Marie Louise
2TG - 2 Temple Gardens, London
020 7822 1200
mlkinsler@2tg.co.uk
Featured in Travel (London)
Practice Areas: Marie Louise has a specialist practice, focussing on private international law and EU law. She has particular expertise in issues of jurisdiction, choice of law and the impact of EU law on English law in foreign personal injury claims acting in many of the leading cases including those concerning the Brussels Regulation and Rome II. Recently she has appeared in the Supreme Court in The Iraqi Civilian Litigation [2016], Moreno v MIB [2016] and Cox v Ergo [2014]; in the Court of Appeal in Brownlie v Four Seasons [2015] and Wall v Mutuelle de Poitiers [2014] and in the High Court in Lungowe v Vedanta [2016], Committeri v Club Med [2016], Bianco v Bennett [2015] and Winrow v Hemphill [2014]. Apart from her career in Chambers, Marie Louise has taught EU law at Cambridge University and is frequently invited to lecture in this country and abroad.
Professional Memberships: Bar European Group; COMBAR; Franco-British Lawyers Association; UK Association of European Lawyers.
Career: Apart from Marie Louise's career at the Bar she has also taught law at Cambridge University.

KIRK, Anthony QC
1 King's Bench Walk, London
020 7936 1500
akirkqc@1kbw.co.uk
Featured in Family/Matrimonial (London)
Practice Areas: Anthony Kirk has particular expertise in children cases, public and private, as well as in the field of international child abduction. He is used to assimilating large quantities of complex medical material relating to brain and skull injuries, as well as cases involving fabricated illness. He has been instructed in the most difficult of adoption cases.
Professional Memberships: Anthony is a member of the South-Eastern circuit, an Honorary Life Vice-President of the FLBA, an affiliate member of Resolution, a member of the FMA, the ALC, and a Fellow of the IAFL. He is a member of the Bar Council ADR Group, a Fellow of the RSM and a Bencher of Gray's Inn.
Career: He was called to the bar by Gray's Inn in 1981 and was awarded scholarships by the Inn in recognition of the highest marks awarded in the Bar Final examinations. He joined chambers at 1kbw in 1982. He is a Chairman of the Children Group, the Head of the DRS Team and the Deputy Head of Chambers. He has sat on numerous Committees established by the MOJ to include, most recently, the Mediation Task Force chaired by Sir David Norgrove.
Publications: Anthony continues to give presentations and lectures on aspects of family law whenever able to do so. Within the past 12 months he has addressed numerous conferences both internally and at the request of others nationwide.
Personal: Mediation in private law children cases continues to form a substantial part of his work, away from the court arena. Anthony qualified as a mediator with FMA in April 1998 and was one of the first members of the family Bar to do so. He was particularly pleased to be short-listed for Family Law ADR Practitioner of the Year (2014 and again in 2015) by Jordan Publishing. Away from practice Anthony is sometimes reminded that he is a reasonably competent pianist and (when the occasion demands) still an accomplished organist.

KISSER, Amy
Queen Elizabeth Building QEB, London
020 7797 7837
a.kisser@qeb.co.uk
Featured in Family/Matrimonial (London)
Practice Areas: Amy's busy practice encompasses all aspects of private family law, including divorce, finance (for married parties after an English or foreign divorce; for unmarried cohabitees and for unmarried parents), and private law children matters. She has a particular interest in cases involving a foreign or international element (including jurisdictional disputes) and complex financial cases involving company, trust and tax issues. Amy has experience in all levels of tribunal up to and including the Supreme Court, and recently acted as a junior to Tim Amos QC in the Supreme Court in Prest v Petrodel Resources Limited [2013] EWCA Civ 1395.
Professional Memberships: Family Law Bar Association
Career: Oxford University (MA Jurisprudence (First Class)). Oxford University (BCL Bachelor of Civil Law (Distinction)). BPP (BVC (Outstanding)). Called 2009. Pupil and tenant at Queen Elizabeth Building.
Publications: 'Search Orders and Preservation Injunctions After Imerman' [2011] Fam Law 54 ; 'Appealing an Order Out of Time in Proceedings for a Financial Remedy' Practical Law Practice Note; 'Setting Aside an Order in Proceedings for a Financial Remedy' Practical Law Practice Note.

KITSON, Justin
Selborne Chambers, London
020 7691 2424
justin.kitson@selbornechambers.co.uk
Featured in Real Estate Litigation (London)
Practice Areas: Justin is a commercial-chancery barrister specialising in property litigation, property related professional negligence, commercial disputes, media & entertainment, and copyright and licensing.
Professional Memberships: Property Bar Association; Chancery Bar Association; Professional Negligence Bar Association.
Career: Called Gray's Inn 2000 (Prince of Wales Scholar). Solicitors instructing Justin commend him for his exceptional client handling skills and ability to cut quickly to the pertinent issues and offer forthright, practical and tactical advice. He has been variously described in the directories as "a barrister with real presence", a "very forceful advocate", "a brave and tough advocate who is great on cross-examination", and somebody who has "the ability to absorb huge volumes of paper and give advice extremely quickly."

KNIFTON, David
Exchange Chambers, Liverpool
0151 236 7747
knifton@exchangechambers.co.uk
Featured in Personal Injury (Northern)
Practice Areas: Personal Injury and Clinical Negligence
Professional Memberships: PIBA, PNBA
Career: David practises exclusively in personal injury and clinical negligence cases with a value exceeding £250,000, almost exclusively on behalf of claimants. He is recommended as a leader in those fields by Chambers & Partners and The Legal 500. In the last 4 calendar years, he has settled claims totalling over £95m, and he regularly acts, with or without a leader, in claims with a value in excess of £1m. His highest award to date, acting without a QC, is £5.85m. He specialises in claims involving injuries of the utmost severity, including brain and spinal cord injuries, amputations and other catastrophic injuries. He has particular expertise in military claims, claims involving failures to wear seatbelts or helmets, and other difficult liability issues. He has extensive experience of drafting complex Schedules of Loss, and a proven track record of outstanding results in negotiations. He has many years' experience as a Recorder in the Crown and county courts, and is an accredited mediator. He founded Exchange Chambers' Pro Bono Partnership with the National Autistic Society, which received the Outstanding Family Support award at the Autism Professionals Awards 2016.

KNIGHT, Christopher
11KBW, London
020 7632 8500
Christopher.Knight@11kbw.com
Featured in Administrative & Public Law (London), Data Protection (London)
Practice Areas: Christopher practises in administrative and public law, data protection and information law, and education law. Recent cases include: Kennedy v Charity Commission [2014] UKSC 20; R (Hottak) v Foreign Secretary [2016] EWCA Civ 438; R (Harris) v Broads Authority [2016] EWHC 799 (Admin); R (London Criminal Courts Solicitors Association) v Lord Chancellor [2015] EWHC 295 (Admin); Noon v Matthews [2014] EWHC 4330 (Admin); Tower Hamlets v Bromley [2015] EWHC 1954 (Ch); Lin v Metropolitan Police Commissioner [2015] EWHC 2484 (QB); Haslam v ICO & Bolton Council [2016] UKUT 139 (AAC); Goldsmith International Business School v ICO [2014] UKUT 563 (AAC). He regularly appears in the Information Rights and Gambling jurisdictions of the First-tier Tribunal. He has a wide experience of regulatory work, all areas of local government law and is a member of the Attorney General's C Panel.
Professional Memberships: ALBA, ELA, ELBA, ARDL.
Career: Called to the Bar in 2008. Judicial Assistant at the UK Supreme Court 2009-2010.
Publications: Bradley, Ewing & Knight, Constitutional and Administrative Law (2014); Blakeley, Knight & Love, The New Tribunals Handbook (2011); contributor to: The White Book, Supperstone, Goudie & Walker on Judicial Review and Tolley's Employment Law Handbook.

KNIGHT, Heidi
Serjeants' Inn Chambers, London
020 7427 5000
hknight@serjeantsinn.com
Featured in Clinical Negligence (London), Product Liability (London)
Practice Areas: Heidi Knight was called to the Bar in 2001. Heidi specialises in clinical negligence, personal injury, product liability and group litigation and inquests and inquiries. An earlier edition notes that she "is well liked for her charming manner with clients" and is "an extremely helpful, very intelligent barrister with a keen interest in product liability in all its forms. An excellent team player, she's an absolute trooper." Please visit the Serjeants' Inn Chambers website for her profile, which sets out full details of her practice including relevant work of note.
Professional Memberships: PIBA, PNBA and AVMA.
Personal: 1999 MA (Cantab); BA (Law, First Class Honours) Senior Scholar, Fitzwilliam College; Cambridge College Prize for Distinguished Performance.

KNOTT, James
4 Stone Buildings, London
020 7242 5524
j.knott@4stonebuildings.com
Featured in Company (London)
Practice Areas: Company / commercial litigation; chancery (commercial); insolvency and reconstruction; civil / commercial fraud and asset recovery. James has a busy company and commercial practice, with a particular focus on shareholder / JV disputes and breach of fiduciary duty cases. With experience of court work and arbitration he is equally happy working on his own or in a team, and has particular experience acting as a junior in heavy commercial cases. Some of his recent / reported cases include: ☒ Re Abington Hotel Ltd [2012] 1 BCLC 410 (unfair prejudice) ☒ Saltri III Ltd v MD Mezzanine SA SICAR [2013] 1 ALL E.R. (Comm) 661 (junior creditor rights on restructuring); ☒ Madoff Securities International v Raven [2014] Lloyd's Rep FC 95 (directors' duties/ fraud); ☒ Global Energy Horizons Corp v Gray [2014] EWHC 2925 (Ch) (equitable disclosure jurisdiction) and [2015] EWHC 2232 (Ch) (account of profits/breach of duty); ☒ Pyrrho Investments Ltd v MWB Property [2015] EWHC 3903 (Ch) (amendments/limitation) and [2016] EWHC 256 (Ch) (first English endorsement of predictive coding technology).
Professional Memberships: COMBAR; Chancery Bar Association.
Career: Called in 2008; joined 4 Stone Buildings in 2010.

KOHLI, Ryan
Cornerstone Barristers, London
020 7242 4986
ryank@cornerstonebarristers.com
Featured in Immigration (London), Planning (London), Social Housing (London)
Practice Areas: Landlord and Tenant (including Social Housing), Administrative and Public law, Planning and Licensing.
Professional Memberships: Administrative Law Bar Association, Social Housing Law Association and Association of Regulatory & Disciplinary Lawyers.
Career: Ryan was awarded an M.A. from St Edmund Hall, Oxford University where he read law between 2002-05. He was called to the Bar in 2006 (Inner Temple) having

achieved the grade of "Outstanding" in the Bar Vocational Course (BPTC). He has developed a successful practice at the Bar and has been appointed to the Attorney General's Panel of Counsel (C Panel). He regularly represents and advises clients in a range of judicial review claims; landlord and tenant/ social housing matters⊠ planning challenges in the High Court and licensing appeals.
Publications: Contributor: "Cornerstone on Councillors' Conduct". Contributor: "Licensed Premises" (2nd Ed.) by Philip Kolvin QC. Sub-editor: "Cornerstone on Anti-Social Behaviour". Article: J Findlay QC and R Kohli, When does a tree preservation order protect [2008] JPL 615.
Personal: Ryan was born in Arlington, Texas and educated at The Glasgow Academy and Oxford University. He enjoys the theatre, cinema, travel and good restaurants.

KOLINSKY, Daniel QC
Landmark Chambers, London
020 7430 1221
DKolinsky@landmarkchambers.co.uk
Featured in Local Government (London), Planning (London)
Practice Areas: Dan Kolinsky was appointed Queen's Counsel in 2015 having served on the Attorney General's "A" Panel. He is a CEDR accredited mediator His practice covers planning, environmental, rating, local government and public law. He frequently acts as an advocate in the High Court and Court of Appeal, at public inquiries and before the Upper Tribunal. His clients include central and local government, developers, interest groups, ratepayers, individual claimants and NGOs. He has considerable experience in High Court planning cases acting for Claimants, developers, local and central government. He frequently appears in non-domestic rating cases acting for ratepayer, valuation officers and billing authorities in all types of rating cases. Notable recent cases include: Woolway (VO) v Mazars – Supreme Court judgment on identification of hereditaments in the rating list; Monk v Newbigin (VO) Supreme Court (hearing November 2016); Broadview Energy v SSCLG –lead case on role of MP's in planning decisions; Aldergate Properties v Mansfield DC – successful judicial review on sequential test for retail development; R. (Nicholson) v Allerdale BC challenge to noise condition in motor sport testing track. He advised Airports Commission throughout its process (2013-2015).

KOLVIN, Philip QC
Cornerstone Barristers, London
07977 555348
philipk@cornerstonebarristers.com
Featured in Licensing (London)
Practice Areas: Licensing of leisure economy, gambling and sex establishments. Acts for industry, local authorities, trade bodies, regulators and communities from committees to Supreme Court.
Professional Memberships: Head of Cornerstone Barristers; Patron, Institute of Licensing.
Career: RGS Newcastle upon Tyne, Balliol College Oxford, called to Bar 1985, QC 2009.
Publications: Licensed Premises: Law, Practice and Policy (2 ed); Gambling for Local Authorities: Licensing, Planning and Regeneration (2 ed); Sex Licensing; Saving Open Space; Atkins Courts Forms on Licensing; Encyclopedia of Forms and Precedents on Licensing; Cornerstone on Councillors' Conduct; Halsburys Laws on Protection of the Environment and Public Health.

KRAMER, Adam
3 Verulam Buildings, London
020 78318441
akramer@3vb.com
Featured in Banking & Finance (London), Commercial Dispute Resolution (London), Energy & Natural Resources (London), Fraud (London), Insurance (London)
Practice Areas: The full range of commercial disputes, especially banking, energy, civil fraud, professional negligence and insurance/ reinsurance. Major current and recent cases in the public domain include the RBS 2008 Rights Issue dispute, Holyoake v Candy Bros and others (commercial fraud dispute), Abbott & 127 others v CBRE (commercial property valuation dispute), BP Oil International Ltd v Bankers Petroleum Albania Ltd (oil dispute), Renaissance Capital Ltd v African Minerals Ltd (investment bank commission/ iron ore dispute).
Professional Memberships: Society of Legal Scholars, COMBAR, Chancery Bar Association, PNBA, Bar Pro Bono Unit.
Career: Lecturer at Durham University (2000-3); Tutor at University College Oxford (2003-4); called by Gray's Inn (2004); 3VB pupillage (2004) then tenancy (2005).
Publications: Sole author of The Law of Contract Damages (Hart Publishing, 2014). Contributor to Paget on Banking.
Personal: Educated at Manchester Grammar School, University College Oxford (BA Law, first class) and McGill University, Canada (LLM). Current interests include cooking, running, and parenting.

KUBIK, Heidi
St Philips Chambers, Birmingham
0121 246 0200
hkubik@st-philips.com
Featured in Crime (Midlands)
Practice Areas: Heidi has built up an extensive practice in all areas of serious crime, with particular expertise in sex cases and cases of dishonesty and violence at all levels, including those involving expert paediatric evidence regarding serious injuries/death of children. She has been led in many complex murders including a six month trial concerning the murder of a toddler. She conducts cases involving gang related crime, shootings, anonymous witnesses and undercover officers from the Counter-Terrorism Unit, and has successfully defended in a conspiracy to rob a bank. She has a reputation for success through effective cross examination and persuasive advocacy. Heidi is experienced in dealing with young and/or vulnerable defendants, or those suffering from mental disability, in a sympathetic manner. She can explain complex issues in simple terms and can give strong advice when necessary. She is particularly adept at dealing with difficult clients in a non-confrontational way. She is approachable and capable of adapting her style to suit the case in hand. Grade 4 prosecutor.
Professional Memberships: CBA.
Career: Nottingham University Law BA (Hons). Lectureship at Leicester University 1991-92. Called 1993. Deputy Head of St Philips Criminal Group 2015. Recorder 2016.

KULKARNI, Yash
Quadrant Chambers, London
020 7583 4444
yash.kulkarni@quadrantchambers.com
Featured in Commercial Dispute Resolution (London), Information Technology (London), Shipping (London)
Practice Areas: Broad commercial practice covering international trade, shipping, information technology and banking. Particularly experienced in applications for interim relief including freezing and search orders and anti-suit injunctions. For a more detailed CV, please refer to his profile on www.quadrantchambers.com
Professional Memberships: COMBAR, Chancery Bar, Society for Computers and Law.
Career: MA Law (Cantab) Double First. Called to the Bar 1998. ADR accredited mediator.

KVERNDAL, Simon QC
Quadrant Chambers, London
020 7583 4444
simon.kverndal@quadrantchambers.com
Featured in Shipping (London)
Practice Areas: Shipping and commodities, international arbitration.
Professional Memberships: COMBAR, LMAA (Supporting Member), Court Assistant of the Worshipful Company of Shipwrights, Council member of the London Shipping Law Centre.
Career: Over 25 years practice experience in shipping and related areas, more recently involving all types of charterparty dispute, shipbuilding/ shipsale, superyacht construction and sale, ship finance, offshore contracts (in particular rig hire, move and construction and supply vessel charters), commodity disputes, salvage and collision. Arbitrator (since 2006 one of the five panel arbitrators for Lloyds Open Form salvage, and LMAA) and accredited mediator. Lectures for LMAA, LSLC and BIMCO and chaired 2010 LMAA 50th anniversary conference. Appointed QC in 2002.
Publications: Contributor to Liability Regimes in Contemporary Maritime Law ed. Rhidian Thomas (2007).
Personal: Educ. Haileybury, Sidney Sussex College Cambridge. Rackets and real tennis player. Member Queen's, Garrick, MCC.

KYNOCH, Duncan
Selborne Chambers, London
020 7420 9500
duncan.kynoch@selbornechambers.co.uk
Featured in Chancery (London)
Career: Duncan is a commercial chancery practitioner. He has appeared in numerous reported and significant commercial High Court and Court of Appeal cases, most recently acting for a solicitor disputing recovery of a professional practice loan (Royal Bank of Scotland Plc v McCarthy, QB Div, 2015), for a satellite TV manufacturer in a claim against its steel suppliers (KLM Steels Ltd v Global Invacom Ltd, Commercial Court, 2015), in a dispute over ownership of part of an island in the Thames (Stapleford v Port of London Authority, FTT, 2016) and in a development dispute in BNP Paribas Jersey Trust Corporation v Marshall Street Regeneration, Ch Div, 2015). Other significant cases include: Commercial contracts (Acre 1127 Ltd v De Montfort Fine Art Ltd, Court of Appeal, 2011); Consumer contracts (Friarwood Ltd v Champagne Cattier SA, Court of Appeal; Company law and shareholder disputes (Jordan v Roberts, Ch Div, 2009; Insolvency (Rubin v Coote, Court of Appeal, 2011; Fraud and asset recovery (Hardy v Washington Green Fine Art Publishing Co Ltd, Court of Appeal, 2010; Boundaries/ party walls (Nelson's Yard Management Co v Eziefula, Court of Appeal, 2013); Property and constructive trusts (De Bruyne v De Bruyne, Court of Appeal, 2010.

LADENBURG, Guy
3 Raymond Buildings Barristers, London
020 7400 6400
guy.ladenburg@3rblaw.com
Featured in Crime (London), Licensing (London), Professional Discipline (London)
Practice Areas: Prosecutes and defends fraud and serious crime, and practises across a range of regulatory areas. Recent fraud cases include acting alone for the only defendant to be acquitted in Operation Boromo, the largest ever prosecution brought by the DWP, as junior in the defence of an insolvency silk in the SFO Celtic prosecution, and for a conveyancing solicitor in the FCA's Operation Cotton land-banking fraud. He is currently instructed as junior alone for a defendant in the Montessori fraud. He is currently instructed as led junior in a gang murder at the Central Criminal Court. He frequently appears for the prosecution and defence in trials concerning serious sexual offending. Represents police officers from forces nationwide in misconduct proceedings, criminal trials and inquests, and also represents police forces in relation to inquests. Other specializations include the full range of Licensing work for applicants, appellants, local authorities and police; advising Police forces and regulatory authorities across a range of regulatory areas; advising in matters arising from the Gambling Act 2005; appearing on behalf of casinos in applications for freezing injunctions in the High Court.
Career: Called to the Bar 2000.
Publications: Co-author with Simon Farrell Q.C and Nick Yeo of Blackstone's Guide to the Fraud Act (2006).
Personal: Charterhouse and St. Hugh's College Oxford (1st Class BA Hons).

LAHTI, Liisa
Quadrant Chambers, London
020 7583 4444
liisa.lahti@quadrantchambers.com
Featured in Shipping (London)
Practice Areas: Principal areas of work are shipping, commodities, offshore, commercial litigation, banking, finance and arbitration. Cases include PST Energy 7 Shipping LLC v OW Bunker Malta Ltd [2016] UKSC 23 and [2015] EWCA Civ 1058, Secure Capital SA v Credit Suisse AG [2015] EWHC 388 (Comm), and Diag Human SE v Czech Republic [2014] EWHC 1639 (Comm). Please visit www.quadrantchambers.com for Liisa's detailed CV.
Career: Called to the Bar in 2009. Practiced as a solicitor (Freshfields Bruckhaus Deringer) before coming to the Bar.
Personal: Educated at St John's College, Cambridge (MA) and Christ Church, Oxford (BCL). Fluent in Finnish, basic Swedish.

LAIDLAW, Jonathan QC
2 Hare Court, London
020 7353 5324
clerks@2harecourt.com
Featured in Crime (London), Health & Safety (London), Inquests & Public Inquiries (All Circuits), Financial Crime (London)

Practice Areas: Jonathan Laidlaw QC predominantly practices in fraud and business crime, in defending directors and companies facing charges brought by the HSE and in professional, regulatory and disciplinary matters. Much of his work, both for individuals and companies here and abroad, is pre-charge and advisory in nature. Jonathan Laidlaw QC has also appeared in major inquests and in sporting tribunals. Recent instructions include, acting for Rebekah Brooks; for GSK; for the Bank of England; for the CEO of a major logistics company in a revenue fraud; in the cricket match fixing case; for the Football Association in the Hillsborough Inquests; for Statoil in the In Amenas Inquests; for Fluor, Hugo Boss and Cape Industries in fatality cases; for Monovan Construction Ltd who faced charges of corporate manslaughter; for the trainer Jim Best in his hearings before the British Horseracing Authority; for Highland (the Texas based hedge fund); for Aviva; for JC Decaux; for a series of successful claimants in commercial litigation considering launching private prosecutions; for a number of individuals and financial institutions facing SFO, FCA, DoJ and CMA investigations; and producing silk led reports for internal inquiries.

Professional Memberships: RDL, CBA, FLA, FSLA, HSLA, SEC.

LAKHA, Abbas QC
9 Bedford Row, London
7976746441
abbaslakhaqc@mac.com
Featured in Crime (London)

Practice Areas: Rated in the Directories as a leader in the fields of murder, terrorism, financial crime and asset forfeiture, Abbas Lakha QC was described by Chambers, in 2015, as "highlighted for his abilities in defending individuals in high-profile criminal proceedings ranging from charges of murder, organised criminal activity and terrorism. He is noted for his strong advocacy style, and his skill in handling international money laundering cases. He is very astute." He is regularly instructed to advise upon and defend in the most challenging and high profile cases and is particularly sought after to advise in international financial crime cases, representing clients both in the UK and around the world. He was recently retained as a consultant to the Sabra defence team in the Hague, who are defending an accused alleged to have been complicit in the assassination of the Lebanese Prime Minister, Mr. Rafik Hariri. Abbas has experience in all forms of civil and criminal fraud and asset forfeiture work. He is regularly instructed to advise at the pre-investigative stages of cases and has extensive experience of representing high profile individuals for whom reputation management is a significant concern.

Professional Memberships: Bar Council, CBA, IBA,ECRA, Society of Asian Lawyers

Career: Called to the Bar 1984 and took Silk 2003.

LAKIN, Tracy
St Ives Chambers, Birmingham
0121 236 0863
tracy.lakin@stiveschambers.co.uk
Featured in Family/Matrimonial (Midlands)

Practice Areas: Family, Court of Protection. Tracy practises in public law and private law Children Act applications. She is experienced in all aspects of proceedings in the County Court, High Court and Court of Appeal. She has also been led in the High Court and the Court of Appeal.

Career: Tracy Lakin represents Local Authorities, Children's Guardians, parents (including adults acting under a disability) and children (including older children with the ability to instruct in their own right). Her cases have involved death of children, serious non-accidental injury, shaken baby syndrome, sexual abuse (including cases where parents have been falsely accused of sexual abuse by the other parent) and chronic neglect. Her particular strength is in fact finding hearings where her past experience as a Criminal/Crown Court advocate offers some advantages. She also has a particular interest/expertise in cases involving Fabricated/Induced Illness. Tracy also practices in Court of Protection with a particular interest in forced marriage and deprivation of liberty cases and has appeared in the Court of Protection in Birmingham on such matters. Tracy has an interest in the law relating to surrogacy and appeared in the leading case of Re X in 2014 before Munby J which significantly changed the law in this area with regard to the time limit for applications for Parental Orders.

LAMBERT, Emmaline
6 Pump Court, London
020 7797 8400
emmalinelambert@6pumpcourt.co.uk
Featured in Planning (London)

Practice Areas: Planning and environmental. Emmaline appears at numerous planning inquiries covering appeals under s.78, enforcement notice appeals and CPO inquiries (including references to the Lands Tribunal) and is also regularly instructed in Judicial Review proceedings and statutory challenges in the High Court. Recent work includes representing local authorities in appeals relating to major housing development in Horsham, Swale and Maidstone and in conjoined appeals in West Berkshire. Emmaline has particular expertise in enforcement matters both in prosecuting and defending breaches of enforcement notices in the Magistrates' Court and the Crown Court and is regularly instructed in relation to obtaining injunctive relief under s.187A. She is frequently instructed in criminal proceedings leading to confiscation proceedings and recently represented the London Borough of Hackney in securing a confiscation order in the amount of £700,000 against an individual with a sentence of 5 years in default following breach of an enforcement notice.

Professional Memberships: PEBA.

LAMBERT, Harry
Crown Office Chambers, London
020 7797 8100
lambert@crownofficechambers.com
Featured in Product Liability (London)

Practice Areas: Product Liability, Clinical Negligence, Property Damage and related Group Actions.

Professional Memberships: AvMA, Bar Pro Bono Unit.

Career: Harry practises in the areas of product liability, clinical negligence and property damage. He has been involved in some of the most high profile group actions of recent years including the Thalidomide, Phone Hacking, Peruvian Miners, Mau Mau, Libya and Human Trafficking litigation. Harry has a particular interest in product liability claims involving drugs and medical devices. Examples of the former include advising in respect of olmesartan medoxomil as well as a vitamin supplement containing 568 times the safe level of Vitamin D. Examples of the latter include "ShapeMatch" technology [surgical cutting guides]; a bathroom hoist which broke [rendering a paraplegic user tetraplegic] and several group actions arising out of hip prostheses [ASR, Pinnacle, Biomet and Corin devices]. In one remarkable case Harry is instructed to recover an explanted prosthesis, raising issues of law as its true ownership. His current caseload also includes a groundbreaking civil action for damages as a result of human trafficking. He was also recently part of a group of specialist trafficking lawyers which convened and provided written advice to the Lords on the forthcoming Modern Slavery Bill. With his background in product liability/ tort law, Harry combines creative thinking about causes of action (often necessary in the absence of a tort of human trafficking) with a rigorous approach to Quantum. His substantial group action experience also gives Harry a firm grounding in GLO and costs related issues.

Publications: Harry is the author of the chapter on product liability and multi-party actions in the 18th edition of Bullen & Leake and a chapter contributor to APIL's personal injury law, practice and precedents. He recently recorded a "CPDCast" Podcast on longstop limitation under the Consumer Protection Act and has also published numerous articles on medical law: Another patchwork quilt (on material increase in risk), Clinical Risk, September 2010; The interaction of Reasonableness and Best Interests, Clinical Risk, January 2011; The undesired desirable solution, PILJ July 2013.

Personal: Dogs, football and literature (in that order).

LAMBERT, Nigel QC
Carmelite Chambers, London
020 7936 6300
nigel@lambertqc.com
Featured in Crime (London)

Practice Areas: Specialist defence practice in all criminal courts and Courts Martial in all areas of serious and complex crime including commercial fraud, money laundering, homicide, terrorism, extreme violence, people trafficking, serious sexual offences and large scale drug cases. Has had a considerable number of money laundering, murder and other cases stayed as an abuse of the process. Has particular expertise representing both young and/or vulnerable offenders and in cases where there are young Prosecution witnesses. R v Wragg £20m Revenue and Customs carousel fraud, R v Simpson successful abuse argument in carousel fraud R v Lombardi year long trial of international banking fraud, R v Chipping off-shore accounts Income Tax fraud R v Agidi successful abuse argument in money laundering case following fraud and corruption at highest political level in Nigeria. Operation Vaulter – MTIC fraud involving contra trading and off-shore operations in Dubai. R v Xin Li successfully defended in money laundering case connected to the largest ever seizure of counterfeit DVDs in Western Europe. R v Butt street gang murders of two brothers stayed as an abuse following witness collusion. R v Calero-Guevera successfully defended a blind man charged with murder by multiple stabbings. R v Fathers successfully defended an educationally sub normal woman charged with torture and murder by drowning R v T successfully defended a young offender with Aspergers Syndrome charged with raping two young females. R v F successfully defended a13 year old boy charged with rape of step-sister. R v R 16 year old assassin in drive by gang land shooting R v Lewington successful abuse argument in historic sexual abuse case. R v M rape of step-daughter between ages of 8-12. R v Fitzpatrick conspiracy to blackmail re Huntingdon Life Sciences and international drug companies. R v Rothery – conspiracy to supply 1.5 tons of cocaine.. R v Shah and Others – successfully defended in a conspiracy to cheat/ and importation of large number of commercial drugs imprtations. Duty loss approx £6m. R v Hadfield and Others Successfully defended in high profile and maximum security trial concerning Manchester rival family feuds culminating in gunshot and hand grenade murders. [Codefendant Dale Cregan who shot dead two female police officers]. R v Krezolek. man accused of the murder of his four year old step-son – Daniel Pelka.. Allegations of chronic starvation, imprisonment and long term violence. R v Gacek and Others, mother acquitted of causing or allowing the death of her seven week old baby. R v K – mother accused of murdering her 8 month old baby. R v Hamlett [2016] – successfully defended terrorism allegation of plot to kill military/ police in central London. R v Hawgood [2016] murder acquittal R v H [2016] terrorism funding arrangement. Rv M [2016] Murder in course of robbery. Rv B [2016] conspiracy to defraud persons carrying out statutory duties of the Home Office.

Professional Memberships: South Eastern Circuit, Criminal Bar Association.

Career: Call 1974 Gray's Inn, Recorder 1996, Queen's Counsel 1999, Bencher 2004, Head of Chambers 2009 -2014.

Personal: Member of the Garrick Club and MCC.

LAMONT, Calum
Keating Chambers, London
020 7544 2600
clamont@keatingchambers.com
Featured in International Arbitration (London), Professional Negligence (London), Construction (London), Public Procurement (London)

Practice Areas: Described as "ridiculously bright and very down-to-earth", Calum is an energetic and enthusiastic lawyer, commanding a broad commercial practice with particular specialisms in construction, engineering, shipbuilding, procurement and energy disputes, together with related insurance, bonds and professional negligence matters. Calum has extensive experience in the Middle East and Korea, particularly in the UAE where his work includes appearing in the DIFC Court, before which he holds full rights of audience. He is familiar with acting

under various different rules (including the ICC, LCIA, UNCITRAL, DIAC and LMAA).
Professional Memberships: SCL; TECBAR; COMBAR; Procurement Lawyers Association.
Career: : MA History (Double First Class), St. Catharine's College, Cambridge University (2000); M.Phil. Historical Studies, St. Catharine's College, Cambridge University (2001); Diploma in Law/CPE (Distinction), City University (2003); Bar Vocational Course (Outstanding), Inns of Court School of Law (2004); Pupillage, Keating Chambers (2004); Keating Chambers (2005); TECBAR committee (2009-); TECBAR accredited Adjudicator (2011); TECBAR accredited Mediator (2011).
Publications: Contributor, Keating on Construction Contracts 8th, 9th & 10th Edition; Consultant Editor, Construction Law Reports; Joint author of three RICS Case in Point Series publications: Construction Claims, Contract Administration and Building Defects.

LAMONT, Gordon
Compass Chambers, Edinburgh
0131 226 5071
gordon.lamont@compasschambers.com
Featured in Personal Injury (Scotland)
Practice Areas: Civil Practice with particular expertise in personal injury, aviation, and public inquiries. Junior counsel for the families in the ICL Public Inquiry (Stockline) in 2008 with associated personal injury claims. In 2010-2012, junior counsel for families and survivors at the Vale of Leven Public Inquiry (C. difficile outbreak). Aviation experience includes the Glasgow Air Crash in 2001, the Edinburgh Air Crash in 2003/2004 and the Machrihanish Air Crash 2007 (Fatal Accident Inquiries and reparation claims). Represented the pilot union BALPA in numerous reparation cases. Currently involved in high profile aviation litigation and Fatal Accident Inquiry into the hospital death of a 13 year old (acting for mother). Other Fatal Accident Inquiries include death of a prisoner in custody (acting for prison union), erroneous dispensing of drugs in a hospital (acting for Responsible Pharmacist) and complex medical issues surround the hospital death of a 12 year old (acting for family) and actively involved in reparation. 2010 Court of Session proofs include Lyons v WM Morrison Supermarket plc 2010 Rep. LR 90 (manual handling) and Fordyce v Acrima Insurance 7 May 2010 unreported (road traffic reconstruction). Other reported cases include Clegg and Another v Rogerson and Another 2007 CSIH 87 (Network Rail responsibilities at a level crossing), LaMarra v Capital Bank plc and others 2007 SC 95 (Consumer credit), Ashmore v Rock Steady Security Limited 2006 SLT 207 (assault, defence of provocation, examination of ex turpi causa), Millar and others v Watt and Others 2005 SCLR 143 (whether death of infant case suitable for jury trial), Lewis v Richardson 2002 SLT 272 (rta), Skinner v Aberdeen City Council 2001 Rep LR 118 (manual handling), McLeod v British Railway Board 2001 SC 534 (appeal on level of damages assessed by jury).
Career: 1991–98 solicitor specialising in reparation, 1998–99 Legal Assistant to the Lord President (Lord Rodger of Earlsferry), 1999-2012 Junior Counsel.
Personal: LLB (Hons) law, Glasgow University, Dip. L.P.

LANDER, Richard
Kings Chambers, Manchester
0345 034 3444
clerks@kingschambers.com
Featured in Real Estate Litigation (Northern)
Practice Areas: Established practice covering most aspects of chancery and commercial law. Particular emphasis on real estate litigation (commercial and residential), and associated areas including professional negligence, banking, Inheritance Act claims and corporate and personal insolvency. Extensive experience before courts of all levels up to the Court of Appeal, and before the Property Tribunal.
Professional Memberships: Chancery Bar Association, Northern Chancery Bar Association.
Career: Educated University of Cambridge, Tancred and Hardwicke Scholar of Lincoln's Inn Called 1993, pupil at current Chambers 1994.

LANE, Andrew
Cornerstone Barristers, London
020 7242 4986
andrewl@cornerstonebarristers.com
Featured in Social Housing (London)
Practice Areas: Social housing.
Professional Memberships: Chartered Institute of Housing; Social Housing Law Association; Constitutional and Administrative Law Bar Association.
Career: Since coming to the Bar in 1999 Andy has established himself at the forefront of the Social Housing Bar. His recent and successful involvement in cases such as Byrne v Poplar HARCA [2012] EWCA Civ 832; [2012] HLR 33; Corby Borough Council v Scott; West Kent Housing Association v Haycraft [2012] EWCA Civ 276; [2012] HLR 23; Swan Housing Association v Gill [2013] EWCA Civ 1566 and Sims v Dacorum Borough Council [2014] UKSC 63 is testimony to this fact and he continues to be instructed by the leading solicitors in the social housing field. He is known for his instinctive client care skills, thorough knowledge of the law, tactical awareness and exceptional advocacy skills. His practice covers all areas of social housing law from possession and injunction work, through to welfare reform, Human Rights Act 1998, housing fraud and Equality Act 2010 work alongside general policy, regulatory, council tax and tenancy work for private registered providers. Andy is also an established speaker at seminars and conferences.

LANE, Lindsay
8 New Square, London
020 7405 4321
lindsay.lane@8newsquare.co.uk
Featured in Intellectual Property (London), Media & Entertainment (London)
Practice Areas: Lindsay specialises in all areas of IP and media and entertainment. Recent patent cases include: Accord v Medac (formulation of methotrexate); Glass v Freyssinet (concrete reinforcement); Mylan v Gedeon Richter (emergency contraception) and Schutz v Werit (which went to the Supreme Court on the issue of repair). Lindsay has also acted in a number of SPC cases. Recent copyright/database right cases include: Football Dataco v Stan James and Football Dataco v Sportradar (concerning rights in football data, both referred to the CJEU) and BBC v Eos (in the Copyright Tribunal). Recent breach of confidence cases include: Wade v BSkyB (television format); Force India v 1 Malaysia Racing Team (trial and appeal on liability and quantum relating to F1 cars). Recent trade mark/passing off cases include: A&E Television Networks v Discovery Communications (TV channel names); 32Red v WHG (inquiry as to damages). Lindsay also appeared in the litigation concerning standardised pacakaging for tobacco. For a comprehensive CV visit www.8newsquare.co.uk.
Professional Memberships: Intellectual Property Bar Association (IPBA); Chancery Bar Association.
Career: Called 1996.
Publications: 'The Modern Law of Copyright and Designs' (Butterworths, Fourth Edition).
Personal: Educated: Newnham College, Cambridge (BA (Hons) Natural Sciences and Law); European University Institute, Florence (MA in Comparative, European and International Law).

LANGDALE, Rachel QC
7BR, London
020 7242 3555
rlangdale@7br.co.uk
Featured in Family/Matrimonial (London)
Practice Areas: Children Act proceedings (both public and private law), including cases which involve the scrutiny of medical evidence and medical treatment issues. International disputes surrounding the residence of children, forced marriage cases, and relocation cases involving the Hague Convention and Brussels II Revised Regulation. Instructed in the Administrative Court and Public Inquiries, most recently Mid Staffordshire NHS Foundation Trust Public Inquiry (2010 - 2012).
Professional Memberships: Bencher Middle Temple, JUSTICE (independent charity, working to advance access to justice, human rights and the rule of law), Member of the Professional Practice Committee of the Bar Council (2009 onwards), Family Law Bar Association.
Career: LLB (Hons) (1983-86;) MPhil (Cantab) (1986-87). Called to the Bar: 1990. Silk: 2009.

LANGLEY, Charles
2 Bedford Row, London
020 7440 8888
clangley@2bedfordrow.co.uk
Featured in Crime (London)
Practice Areas: Recognised as a leading defence junior in crime for many years. Instructed in serious and complex cases both as leading and junior counsel. Extensive experience in cases involving murder, manslaughter, drug conspiracies, robbery, kidnap and all types of organised crime. Wide-ranging fraud practice including multi-million pound abuses of the Film Tax Credit system, computer hacking, mortgage fraud and carbon credit trading schemes. Detailed knowledge of money laundering and confiscation provisions. A high level of expertise in defending sexual offences including rape and historic child abuse cases. Strong appellate practice, regularly asked to advise on appeals where no grounds have previously been found. In depth knowledge of road traffic law and driving cases, often defending high-profile clients and instructed by insurers in cases involving fatalities. Recent notable cases include: R v R (nationwide fraud and slavery case); R v McLean (substantial UK and Cyprus mortgage fraud); R v J (multi-handed nationwide drugs importation and supply); R v Al-Issa (defended lead conspirator in the first Film Tax Credit and VAT prosecution by HMRC); R v Cox (double murder appeal, commended by the court for representing the applicant "admirably"); R v Crittenden (large-scale building fraud); R v Patel (international carbon credit trading fraud); R v Wooller (historic child sex allegations); and R v Maule (large scale people and sex trafficking across the UK and Europe). Member of the Bar of Northern Ireland. See www.2bedfordrow.co.uk for full profile.
Professional Memberships: Criminal Bar Association and South Eastern Circuit.
Career: Called 1999 (Middle Temple).
Publications: Contributor to Legal Network Television's CPD programme.

LANGLEY, Sir Gordon QC
Fountain Court Chambers, London
020 7583 3335
sian@fountaincourt.co.uk
Featured in International Arbitration (London)
Practice Areas: Described by The Lawyer in 2006 as one of the five stars of the High Court Bench and in 2007 as one of three 'stand out' Judges, his career sees him involved with parties from other jurisdictions and with the application of "foreign" law; he has been the judge in a number of high profile cases such as the Film Finance litigation and the claims by Equitable Life against its former auditors and directors. Since retiring as a Judge Sir Gordon sits as a Neutral Evaluator and as Arbitrator; both party-appointed and as Chairman under the rules of the ICC, LCIA, SIAC and on an ad hoc basis. The disputes cover a wide range of areas including commercial contracts, insurance and reinsurance, shipping, energy, media, sport and joint ventures.
Career: Called to the Bar in 1966, appointed as Queen's Counsel in 1983. Appointed High Court Judge in 1995.

LANGRIDGE, Niki
Coram Chambers, London
020 7092 3700
nikki.langridge@coramchambers.co.uk
Featured in Family/Matrimonial (London)
Practice Areas: Family Finance, Mediation, Dispute Resolution.
Professional Memberships: Family Law Bar Association.
Career: Niki was called to the Bar in 1993 and specialises exclusively in family work, her practice being entirely financial remedies on divorce and related family finance work. Her financial work covers all levels but, in particular, she deals with medium to high income and asset cases and matters that contain complex legal or factual issues.

LARKIN, Sean QC
QEB Hollis Whiteman, London
020 7933 8855
sean.larkin@qebhw.co.uk
Featured in Professional Discipline (London), Financial Crime (London)
Practice Areas: Sean Larkin provides specialist advice and advocacy at all stages of criminal and regulatory proceedings, with a particular emphasis on financial and serious crime and regulatory or disciplinary breaches by individuals (particularly professionals) and companies. He is described as 'incredibly bright and industrious' and 'absolutely superb'. Times Lawyer Of The Week. Recent cases include: advising on bribery, Opera-

tion Amazon (largest e-disclosure case), Operation Cotton (FCA's largest case), Gul (landmark Supreme Court decision on definition of terrorism), Dr Pandya (GP accused of FGM), Operation Vaulter (largest carousel fraud), defence of a former CEO for £52m pension fraud; defence of company director accused of laundering £900m, defence of company for workplace death. Sean's experience includes: advising, pre-charge through to representation or prosecution at trial, a variety of professionals (including lawyers, doctors, dentists, police officers, directors, IFAs, accountants and insolvency practitioners) in a wide variety of criminal, regulatory and disciplinary offences. He regularly speaks at conferences and conducts training sessions on a variety of legal topics. More information at www.qebhw.co.uk.

Professional Memberships: CBA, ARDL, FSLA, HSLA, Justice.

Career: Called 1987. Silk 2010.

Publications: 'Fraud: Law Practise and Procedure'. Co-author of many reports for the Criminal Bar Association.

LASCELLES, David

Littleton Chambers, London
020 7797 8600
dlascelles@littletonchambers.co.uk

Featured in Commercial Dispute Resolution (London), Company (London)

Practice Areas: Claims relating to the performance and termination of high-value commercial contracts; claims arising out of the sale of shares and businesses; shareholder and LLP membership disputes; commercial fraud disputes; and director and senior employee disputes.

Career: David specialises as an advocate and adviser in commercial and company law disputes. In addition to his extensive trial and interim applications experience, including in jurisdiction disputes, David has acted in arbitrations including under the ICC and LCIA rules. David has been recommended in Chambers and Partners for some years as a leading commercial junior with previous editions commenting that David "regularly handles complex briefs as sole counsel...has an excellent grasp of legal issues, is incredibly diligent and has good client skills. Definitely someone you want on your team," and that he is "highly impressive... with excellent analytical skills...a brilliant young advocate who inspires confidence with his exemplary client manner and comprehensive and commercial advice." He has also been singled out as a junior star at the commercial bar by Legal Week magazine. Prior to coming to the Bar, David took a Double First in law from Cambridge University and a Masters in Law from Oxford University.

LATHAM, Kevin

Kings Chambers, Manchester
0345 034 3444
clerks@kingschambers.com

Featured in Costs Litigation (All Circuits)

Practice Areas: Kevin is an experienced costs practitioner with a busy nationwide practice. Having specialised in costs litigation throughout his career at the bar, Kevin has been highly sought after to provide business advice in light of the recent reforms to civil litigation. He is regularly instructed to advise and represent both paying and receiving parties in all aspects of inter-partes costs litigation involving complex matters of law and fact. Whilst maintaining a strong personal injury practice, Kevin's trial skills are an asset in solicitor/own client disputes or matters requiring robust cross-examination such as wasted and third party costs orders. Kevin's advisory services are well sought after with clients impressed by his thorough yet clear advice both in writing and in conference. Kevin's experience as a law costs draftsman and at a national firm of Solicitors prior to commencing pupillage enable him to provide first class service in cases where an appreciation of the 'bigger picture' is required. Kevin is frequently instructed in cases involving high value claims for costs in commercial claims, fatal accident claims and multiple party actions. He regularly appears in the SCCO, County and High Court and has experience in the Court of Appeal.

Professional Memberships: Northern Circuit Personal Injury Bar Association Middle Temple (Call 2007).

Career: LL.B (Hons), University of Hull 2006; BVC, Manchester Metropolitan University 2007; Called to the bar by the Honourable Society of the Middle Temple 2007.

Personal: "Following Protocol" Personal Injury Law Journal P.I.L.J. (2010) No.86 June Pages 9-14 (An article highlighting the salient factors of the new RTA Protocol); Kevin also contributed to Dr Mark Friston's seminal text: "Civil Costs: Law and Practice" (Jordans).

LATIMER, Andrew

Kings Chambers, Leeds
0345 034 3444
clerks@kingschambers.com

Featured in Chancery (Northern), Commercial Dispute Resolution (North Eastern)

Practice Areas: Chancery and commercial litigation, directors' duties, shareholders' remedies, insolvency, partnership, restrictive covenants, confidential information, passing off and associated professional negligence. Significant cases: Blomqvist v Zavarco [2016] EWHC 1143, Regency Villas v Diamond Resorts [2015] EWHC 3564, Maresca v Brookfield [2013] EWHC 3151, Linfoot v Adamson [2012] BPIR 1033, Eskape v Route [2011] EWHC 1635, Hitachi v V12 [2009] EWHC 2432, ICI v TTE Training [2007] EWCA Civ 725, Stansfield v AXA [2006] EWCA Civ 88, Thane v Tomlinson [2006] EWHC 1182, Anglo-Eastern v Kermanshahchi [2003] BPIR 1229 and [2002] EWCA Civ 198, Lunnun v Singh Times 19.7.99, R v CLE ex parte Nightingale, Latimer and Toms, Times 5.5.94.

Professional Memberships: Chancery Bar Association, Northern Chancery Bar Association.

Career: BA (Oxon), 1st Class in Law (1993). Bachelor of Civil Law (1994).

Publications: Contributor to 'Commercial Litigation: Pre-Emptive Remedies' (Sweet & Maxwell).

LATIMER-SAYER, William QC

Cloisters, London
020 7827 4038
wls@cloisters.com

Featured in Personal Injury (London), Clinical Negligence (London)

Practice Areas: William specialises in catastrophic personal injury and clinical negligence work. He has a special interest in quantum and is the general editor of Schedules of Loss: Calculating Damages, 3rd edn. William was instructed in the highest five court awards ever made (William being the only common link between the cases): Robshaw (£14.5m); A v Powys Health Board (£10.7m); Totham (£10.1m); Farrugia v MIB (£9.7m) and XXX v Strategic Health Authority (£9.4m). William also undertakes liability work, particularly involving complex causation or medical issues, a recent example being the successful 16 day liability trial of Coakley v Dr Rosie. Another recent success was the intervention on behalf of PIBA in Court of Appeal case of JXMX concerning anonymity for claimants at approval hearings. William was nominated for the prestigious Chambers & Partners' Personal Injury Junior of the Year three times, winning in 2008 and 2010. He was one of the few junior counsel specialising in personal injury and clinical negligence who was included in the inaugural edition of the UK Bar 100, listing the top 100 juniors across all disciplines. He was elevated to silk in 2016.

Professional Memberships: PIBA, PNBA, APIL, AVMA, MLS and the Bar Pro Bono Unit.

Career: LLB (Hons); MA in Medical Law & Ethics; called to the Bar 1995.

Publications: Co-author of 'Personal Injury Schedules: Calculating Damages', 3rd edition Bloomsbury 2010; co-editor of ABC of Medical Law; contributor to PIBA's Personal Injury Handbook, 3 edn Jordan Publishing 2007 and numerous articles for specialist legal journals.

Personal: Born 6 March 1973.

LAURENCE, George QC

New Square Chambers, London
020 7419 8000
george.laurence@newsquarechambers.co.uk

Featured in Chancery (London), Agriculture & Rural Affairs (London), Real Estate Litigation (London)

Practice Areas: Specialises in real property disputes; also has special interest and expertise in the public and administrative aspects of property law, in particular concerning access to the countryside, minor highways, commons and village greens. He frequently appears at public inquiries and before both Houses of Parliament, notably when dealing with the High Speed 2 (2006, House of Lords), Channel Tunnel, Crossrail and the Channel Tunnel Rail Link hybrid bills. His cases since 2000 (many in the House of Lords, Supreme Court or Court of Appeal) include: Ex parte Sunningwell [2000] 1 AC 335; Masters v Secretary of State for the Environment [2001] GB 151 (CA); Yaxley v Gotts [2001] Ch 162 (CA); R (Beresford) v Sunderland City Council [2004] 1 AC 889; Todd v Secretary of State for the Environment [2004] 1 WLR 2471; Oxfordshire County Council v Oxford City Council [2006] 2 AC 674; R (Norfolk County Council) v Sosefra [2006] 1 WLR 1103; R (Kind) v Sosefra [2006] QB 113; Ford-Camber Ltd v Deanminster Ltd [2007] EWCA Civ 458; R (Godmanchester Town Council) v Sosefra [2008] 1 AC 221; Sava v SS Global [2008] EWCA Civ 1308; Smith v Muller [2008] EWCA Civ 1425; Winchester College v Hampshire County Council [2009] 1 WLR 138 (CA); Betterment Properties (Weymouth) Ltd v Dorset County Council [2009] 1 WLR 334 (CA); Herrick v Kidner and Somerset County Council [2010] EWHC 269 (Admin); R (Lewis) v Redcar and Cleveland Borough Council and Anor (No 2) [2010] 2 AC 70; Leeds Group plc v Leeds City Council [2011] Ch 363 (CA); Leeds Group plc v Leeds City Council (No 2) (CA) [2012] 1 WLR 1561 (CA); Fortune v Wiltshire County Council [2013] 1 WLR 808 (CA); Betterment Properties (Weymouth) Limited v Dorset County Council (No 2) SC(E) [2014] AC 1072; Paddico (267) Limited v Kirklees Metropolitan Council SC(E) [2014] AC 1072; R (Barkas) v N Yorkshire County Council SC(E) [2015] AC 195; R (Newhaven Port and Properties Ltd) v East Sussex County Council SC(E) [2015] 1 AC 1547; R (Andrews) v Sosefra [2015] EWCA Civ 669; Powell and anor v Sosefra [2014] EWHC 4003 (admin); R (Trail Riders Fellowship) v Dorset County Council SC(E) [2015] UKSC 18.

Professional Memberships: Parliamentary Bar; Planning and Environmental Bar Association; Administrative Law Bar Association; Chancery Bar Association; Fellow of the Institute of Advanced Legal Studies.

Career: Called to the Bar 1972. Pupil master Leonard (now Lord) Hoffmann. Joined 9 Old Square 1973; current chambers January 1991. Silk 1991. Former Deputy High Court Judge and Recorder (resigned to pursue career as advocate). Bencher of the Middle Temple (1999).

Personal: Educated at University of Cape Town 1966-68 (BA) and University College, Oxford 1969-71 (MA). Rhodes Scholar. Harmsworth Scholar. Frequently writes, lectures and appears on educational TV channels. Leisure pursuits include sport and theatre. Born 15 January 1947. Lives in London.

LAVY, Matthew

4 Pump Court, London
020 7842 5555
mlavy@4pumpcourt.com

Featured in Information Technology (London), Telecommunications (London)

Practice Areas: Commercial litigation and arbitration with a particular focus on (1) IT, telecoms and other technology related disputes (including software copyright, licensing, cyber risk and the internet) and (2) aviation.

Professional Memberships: COMBAR, TECBAR, SCL, LCLCBA, PNBA, BILA, BCS.

Career: MA (Cantab) Music; PhD (Cantab) Musicology; Called 2004.

Publications: Contributing editor to 'Professional Negligence & Liability' published by Informa – Chapter on Computer Consultants.

LAW, Charlotte

Kings Chambers, Manchester
0345 034 3444
clerks@kingschambers.com

Featured in Clinical Negligence (Northern)

Practice Areas: Clinical Negligence Personal Injury Coroners' Inquests Practises predominantly in the field of clinical negligence, dealing with cases of surgical and pharmaceutical negligence, dental negligence, misdiagnosis and delayed diagnosis in primary and secondary care. Has particular experience in cases involving obstetrics and gynaecology, general surgery, orthopaedic injury, hand and plastic surgery (cosmetic and therapeutic) and general practice. Also practises in personal injury, specialising in cases of severe injury arising from employer's liability, public liability, product liability and road traffic. Has particular experience in claims brought on behalf of military personnel. Appears regularly in the Coroner's Court

representing bereaved families, in particular following deaths in hospital and residential nursing homes. Also represents applicants to the Criminal Injuries Compensation Authority and Armed Forces Compensation Scheme.
Professional Memberships: PIBA.
Career: University: Cambridge MA Classics PgDL College of Law, Guildford BVC BPP Law School, London.

LAWAL, Tom
St Ives Chambers, Birmingham
0121 236 0863
tom.lawal@stiveschambers.co.uk
Featured in Social Housing (Midlands)
Practice Areas: Social housing.
Career: Tom Lawal has a growing reputation in the field of social housing. Tom is regarded as an incisive and effective advocate who is able to distill the most complex matter to its core issue. Tom represents landlord and tenants in a wide range of social housing matters including cases involving serious anti-social behavior, disrepair, human rights, public law and Equality Act issues. In addition, Tom has experience in drafting pleadings involving complex factual and legal issues. Tom is particularly noted for his thorough preparation and engaging court manner. Tom prides himself on the meticulous and tactically astute approach he takes to each set of instructions.
Personal: Qualifications: LLB (hons) LLM (International Human Rights – Merit) BVC (Very Competent). In 2011, Tom was named Pupil Barrister of The Year at the Birmingham Legal Awards in recognition of his outstanding year as a pupil Barrister. In 2015, Tom was named Leader of the Year in the professional services category at the Black British Business Awards. Tom joined St Ives Chambers in 2009. Tom was called to the Bar in 2008.

LAWRENCE, Nigel QC
7 Harrington St Chambers, Liverpool
07816 818733 / 0151 242 0707
clerks@7hs.co.uk
Featured in Health & Safety (Northern/North Eastern)
Practice Areas: Specialising in regulatory crime, health and safety offences, environmental health cases, all forms of regulatory enforcement and cases involving corporate, gross negligence and unlawful act manslaughter. Of the Attorney General's appointed Standing Counsel he is, and has been since 2004, the only one of four Standing Counsel to HSE and ORR, for the whole of the UK outside London. As Standing Counsel he is instructed to conduct the most complex, sensitive and high profile cases in the UK. He also accepts and has been instructed to defend in a number of high profile serious cases. His practice also involves appearing in high profile and complex inquests as well as advising on issues associated with them. Heavily involved in evidence concerning the fresh Hillsborough inquests. The balance of his practice involves personal injury and clinical negligence litigation.
Professional Memberships: Member of PIBA.
Career: Call: 1988 (Lincolns Inn). Queen's Counsel: 2014. Appointed by Attorney General as Standing Counsel to HSE and the Office of Rail Regulation.
Personal: Educated at Rydal School, North Wales 1979-84. University of Leicester 1984-87 (LLB Honours). Inns of Court School of Law 1987-88. Interests include travel and sport. Married with children.

LAWRENCE, Patrick QC
4 New Square, London
020 78222000
p.lawrence@4newsquare.com
Featured in Professional Negligence (London), Professional Discipline (London)
Practice Areas: Professional negligence; regulatory and disciplinary proceedings; insurance; commercial litigation. Chambers & Partners Professional Negligence QC of the year in 2011, Patrick Lawrence acts in cases concerning solicitors, barristers, auditors, valuers, insurance brokers, financial advisers and pension consultants. Many of his cases involve allegations of fraud and the prospect of intensive cross-examination. He appeared in the Supreme Court on an appeal in which the immunity of expert witnesses was removed. In the disciplinary/regulatory field he is instructed on both sides in cases concerning auditors, lawyers and insolvency practitioners. Other areas of practice include sports law (he obtained an order restraining a jockey from riding in the Derby on the eve of the race) and aspects of public law, in particular relating to political activity and funding (he appeared for the successful appellant in R v Electoral Commission in the Supreme Court).
Professional Memberships: PNBA; Combar; ChBA.
Career: BA Oxon (PPE); called 1985; QC 2002.
Publications: Co-author of the Solicitors Negligence section in Lloyds looseleaf.

LAWRENSON, Sarah
Kings Chambers, Manchester
0345 034 3444
clerks@kingschambers.com
Featured in Professional Negligence (Northern)
Practice Areas: Professional negligence, construction, trusts, will and probate.
Professional Memberships: TECBAR BICBA NCCBA NChBA.
Career: Call 2003 Middle Temple Oriel Chamber 2003-2008 St James' Chambers 2008-2014 Kings Chambers December 2014 onwards.

LAWS, Eleanor QC
QEB Hollis Whiteman, London
020 7933 8855
eleanor.laws@qebhw.co.uk
Featured in Crime (South Eastern), Crime (London)
Practice Areas: Eleanor Laws QC defends in cases involving young and vulnerable witnesses, in particular serious violence (including murder) and serious sexual offences. Notable cases include highly publicized sex trafficking cases. These include the Oxford sex trafficking case, acting as Specialist Advisory Counsel in the Jersey Child Abuse cases, cases arising out of the recent North Wales Children's Homes Inquiry, cases involving historic allegations, abuse by professionals and in numerous other high profile sex cases. She regularly trains the profession. She is an External Advocacy Trainer for CPS Grades 2-4, and recently assisted in compiling a training programme for the treatment of vulnerable witnesses as part of the launch of the Advocate's Gateway. She is part of HHJ Rook QC's Working Group whose task is to develop advocacy training for cases involving sex offences and vulnerable witnesses and defendants. She has lectured to the Criminal Bar Association and members of the South East Circuit on False memory, Advocacy in cases involving vulnerable witnesses, and Disclosure in criminal cases. Appointed by COIC to Chair the Bar Disciplinary Tribunal Hearings; Elected Committee Member (Criminal Bar Association).
Publications: Eleanor Laws QC has written the Sexual Offences Referencer, considered to be the most widely used practitioner guide to Indictments & Sentencing in sex cases dating back to 1950.

LAWSON, Daniel
Cloisters, London
020 7827 4039
dl@cloisters.com
Featured in Personal Injury (London)
Practice Areas: Personal injury, clinical negligence and insurance law. Undertakes the full range of personal injury work, with special expertise in complex public and employer's liability cases. Has acted in a wide variety of clinical negligence claims. Insurance work focuses upon disputes as to policy construction and avoidance for non-disclosure or misrepresentation.
Professional Memberships: PIBA; APIL; AVMA.
Career: Called to Bar in 1994.
Personal: Education: Balliol College, Oxford (BA Hons PPE); Birkbeck College, London (MA).

LAWSON, David
Serjeants' Inn Chambers, London
020 7427 5000
dlawson@serjeantsinn.com
Featured in Education (London), Local Government (London)
Practice Areas: David Lawson was called to the Bar in 2000. David specialises in education law, public law and all areas of local government services. An earlier edition notes that he is "very approachable, and happy to give very detailed and useful advice via telephone. He picks things up and gets to grips with them in a short timeframe." Please visit the Serjeants' Inn Chambers website for his profile, which sets out full details of his practice including relevant work of note.

LAWSON, Robert QC
Quadrant Chambers, London
020 7583 4444
rob.lawson@quandrantchambers.com
Featured in Travel (London), Aviation (London), Product Liability (London)
Practice Areas: All aspects of commercial litigation, international arbitration and advisory work, including insurance coverage. In particular in relation to aviation, travel and product liability. Significant recent court cases include: Rogers v Hoyle [2015] QB 265; Dawson v Thomson Airways Ltd [2015] 1 WLR 883; Huzar v Jet2.Com Ltd [2014] 4 All ER 581; Global 5000 Ltd v Wadhawan [2012] 2 All ER (Comm) 18; R (Kibris Turk Hava Yollari) v Secretary of State for Transport [2011] 2 All ER (Comm) 340.
Professional Memberships: FRAeS, Fellow of the International Academy of Trial Lawyers, MCIArb, European Air Law Association, LCIA, COMBAR.
Career: BA (Oxon), Dip Law (City). Called 1989. CIArb accredited Mediator 2005. QC 2009. Chairman RAeS Air Law Group 2010-2016.
Publications: Contributor to Halsbury's Laws of England title 'Aviation', volume 2(3), 4th Edition Reissue (2003).

LAZARIDES, Marcus
Queen Elizabeth Building QEB, London
020 7797 7837
m.lazarides@qeb.co.uk
Featured in Family/Matrimonial (London)
Practice Areas: Specialises in all aspects of family law; in particular financial remedies and private law children cases and is ranked as a leading junior in Chambers and Partners. Important cases include: Beshavora v Berezovsky [2016] EWCA Civ 161, NR v AB & Ors. [2016] EWHC 277 (Fam), Jones v Jones [2011] EWCA Civ 41, J v J [2009] EWHC 2654 (Fam) and G v G (Matrimonial Property: Rights of Extended Family) [2006] 1 FLR 62.
Professional Memberships: Family Law Bar Association.
Career: Queen Mother's Scholarship, Middle Temple (1998-99). Called 1999. Pupillage at QEB (1999-2000). Tenant at One Garden Court (2000-04). Tenant at QEB since 2004.
Personal: Educated at Brasenose College Oxford (DPhil), came to the bar late from a background in academia. Married with four children.

LAZARUS, Michael
3 Verulam Buildings, London
020 7831 8441
mlazarus@3vb.com
Featured in Banking & Finance (London), Commercial Dispute Resolution (London), Fraud (London), Information Technology (London), Telecommunications (London)
Practice Areas: Michael's practice includes most areas of domestic and international commercial and business litigation and arbitration with particular emphasis on IT/Telecoms, banking/finance disputes and fraud.
Professional Memberships: COMBAR, LCLCBA.
Career: Michael has extensive experience of trial, pre-trial and appellate advocacy. He represented the second defendant in the ground-breaking VTB Capital v Nutritek and others in 2011 and 2012, successfully arguing against the extension of the corporate veil piercing doctrine to impose contractual liability on non-parties on behalf of all the defendants in the Chancery Division, the Court of Appeal and the Supreme Court, the only advocate in the case who addressed the court on the substantive issues at all three levels. In the IT/telecoms fields, Michael is frequently instructed to advise on and conduct disputes concerning systems and software supply, development, outsourcing and licensing. His specialist banking & finance expertise includes documentary credits, guarantees and similar instruments, asset finance, commercial and sovereign loans and other capital raising transactions. More generally, Michael has considerable experience of commercial fraud, share and asset sale disputes, sale and supply of goods and services, financial services including group misselling claims, professional negligence, breach of confidence and joint ventures. He has appeared in cases in the Privy Council in a number of fields including commercial law, constitutional law, land law and taxation.
Personal: Education: Haberdashers' Aske's School Elstree, Trinity Hall Cambridge.

LAZUR, Thomas
Keating Chambers, London
020 7544 2600
tlazur@keatingchambers.com
Featured in Construction (London), Energy & Natural Resources (London)

Practice Areas: Specialist in construction, engineering and energy disputes. Work is split evenly between litigation in the Technology and Construction Court and international arbitration and concerns disputes of varying size and complexity. Majority of work concerns international and domestic energy projects including offshore construction projects for the oil and gas industry, the construction and refurbishment of traditional coal and gas fired power stations, and alternative energy production facilities including solar, energy-from-waste, and biomass power plants. The balance of Tom's practice is UK based High Court work covering a vast range of projects from large-scale civil engineering projects to domestic construction disputes. Tom has a particularly commercial outlook given his background in investment banking and strategy consultancy. He has an international arbitration diploma, is a Fellow of the CIArb, a TECBAR accredited Adjudicator, an experienced mediator, and an Advocacy Trainer for the Inner Temple.
Professional Memberships: FCIArb, IBA, TECBAR, COMBAR, SCL, Inner Temple.
Career: Called to the Bar 2005; Keating Chambers 2006; MCIArb 2013.
Publications: Keating on Offshore Construction and Marine Engineering Contracts (2015) - Contributor; Keating on Construction Contracts 9th Edition - Contributor; Keating on NEC3 - Contributor; Bullen & Leake & Jacob's Precedents of Pleadings - Co-author (Construction section).

LE FEVRE, Sarah
3 Raymond Buildings Barristers, London
020 7400 6400
sarah.lefevre@3rblaw.com
Featured in Health & Safety (London), Licensing (London)

Practice Areas: Specialist practitioner in licensing, regulatory, inquest and public law with extensive expertise in criminal law. Licensing: instructed to advise and represent licensees, applicants, police and licensing authorities on all matters connected with licensable activity, including gambling, alcohol, entertainment of all kinds, street trading and taxis with extensive appellate and High Court practice. Regulatory: List 'A' Specialist Regulatory Advocates in Health and Safety and Environmental Law (HSE/EA/ORR); instructed by enforcing authorities, companies and individuals to advise and represent in civil, criminal, administrative and coronial proceedings, with particular expertise in railway, fire and safety at sports (football) grounds, environmental and water law. Inquests/public inquiries: instructed by bereaved families, employers, premises operators, enforcing authorities and police to advise and represent at inquests/public inquiries and in related High Court and civil proceedings. Criminal law: prosecution and defence as led junior and alone.
Career: MA (Hons) Cantab (Anglo-Saxon, Norse & Celtic); LLM Public International Law (Distinction); 4 years multiple licensee in Somerset; trained actor (Poor School).

LEABEATER, James
4 Pump Court, London
020 7842 5555
jleabeater@4pumpcourt.com
Featured in Professional Negligence (London), Construction (London), Energy & Natural Resources (London), Shipping (London)

Practice Areas: Insurance and reinsurance, professional negligence, construction, shipping, shipbuilding and offshore construction disputes; commercial disputes including arbitration, commercial fraud, interim relief and conflicts of law.
Professional Memberships: COMBAR, Professional Negligence Bar Association, TECBAR.
Career: MA (Oxon) Modern History; called to the Bar 1999; tenant of 4 Pump Court from October 2000. Called generally to the Bar of the Cayman Islands.
Publications: Co-author of "Civil Appeals: Practice & Procedure" (Sweet & Maxwell 2010) and author of chapter on professional indemnity insurance in 'Architect's Legal Handbook'.

LEARMONTH, Alexander
New Square Chambers, London
020 7419 8000
alexander.learmonth@newsquarechambers.co.uk
Featured in Chancery (London)

Practice Areas: Succession, trusts, property, Court of Protection and professional negligence in related cases. Succession includes contentious probate, mutual wills, secret trusts, rectification, lost wills and Inheritance Act claims, will construction and estate administration. Property work encompasses land registration, easements, mortgages, adverse possession, leasehold enfranchisement and business tenancies. Recent High Court cases (judgments imminent) Crabbe v Townsend (administration of estates, contract) and Huddleston v Thomason (undue influence, capacity); Other important cases include: Marley v Rawlings (Supreme Court, rectification of wills); Ashkettle v Gwinett (ChD, probate), Kell v Jones (ChD, rectification of wills), Bradshaw v Taylor (CA, proprietary estoppel); Swain-Mason v Mills & Reeve (CA, professional negligence, amendment); Gotham v Doodes (CA, limitation); French v Barcham (ChD, occupation rent); Vale v Armstrong (ChD, undue influence); Green v Somerleyton (CA, easements).
Professional Memberships: STEP, ACTAPS (named 'Contentious Barrister of the Year 2015'), Chancery Bar Association (committee), Bar Council (2007-09, 2013 - 2014, Young Barristers' Committee Chairman 2009).
Career: BA Hons Oxon, Jurisprudence (college exhibitioner). Called Lincoln's Inn, 2000 (Tancred award).
Publications: Editor of Theobald on Wills (18th, 2016) and Williams, Mortimer & Sunnucks. Contributor to Probate Practitioners' Handbook.

LEAVER, Peter QC
One Essex Court, London
020 7583 2000
pleaver@oeclaw.co.uk
Featured in International Arbitration (London)

Practice Areas: Peter Leaver is a highly regarded international commercial arbitrator, with recent experience including acting as arbitrator in an ICC arbitration concerning the termination of a contract in the oil and gas industry, acting as sole arbitrator in an LCIA arbitration involving a share sales agreement in which there are various claims, being appointed arbitrator in an ad hoc arbitration concerning a negligence claim in the spacecraft industry and appointed as sole arbitrator in an ad hoc arbitration concerning a dispute over the non-payment of invoices to the aviation industry. He is on the SIAC and HKIAC panels. In addition to his experience in international commercial arbitration, Peter Leaver is also a highly experienced arbitrator in the sports sector. He was the President of the UK National Anti-Doping Panel and was a member of the Court of Arbitration for Sport.
Professional Memberships: COMBAR, IBA, Bar European Group, London Common Law & Commercial Bar Association, Society of Commonwealth Lawyers, Society of Public Teachers of Law. Member of the Chartered Institute of Arbitrators.
Career: Called to the Bar in 1967. Took Silk in 1987. Appointed Recorder and Director of IMRO in 1994. Bencher of Lincoln's Inn 1995. Chairman of LCIA, 2008.

LEE, Krista
Keating Chambers, London
020 7544 2600
klee@keatingchambers.com
Featured in Construction (London)

Practice Areas: Krista specialises in engineering and construction disputes. She has a BSc in engineering and enjoys complex technical disputes. Her experience covers all industry sectors including energy, defence, mining, infrastructure, telecoms, utilities, health, entertainment, factories, hotels and housing both in the UK and overseas, onshore and offshore. She regularly acts for professional indemnity insurers and has acted for and against some of the world's leading engineering, architectural, project management and consultancy firms. Krista is an experienced advocate and has appeared in the Court of Appeal and conducted trials, applications and sought injunctions in the TCC, Commercial Court and Chancery Division. She is familiar with all forms of ADR including mediation, adjudication, expert determination and dispute resolution boards. She has acted as sole arbitrator in ICC and other arbitrations. As counsel, she has conducted arbitrations pursuant to the ICC, UNCITRAL, LCIA and other ad hoc rules. Krista has worked with all the major contract forms including JCT, FIDIC, ICE, ACE, IMechE, LOGIC and RIBA, and NEC3.
Professional Memberships: CIArb, LCIA, TECBAR, SCL, ICC.
Career: MA, BCL (Oxon), Call 1996, BSc (Hons), Chartered Arbitrator, TECBAR Adjudicator and Arbitrator.
Publications: Keating on NEC3 (2012) (Contributor); Keating on Construction Contracts (2016) (Contributor).

LEE, Michael
11KBW, London
020 7632 8500
michael.lee@11kbw.com
Featured in Employment (London)

Practice Areas: Michael practises in employment, commercial and public law. He has extensive advocacy experience in the High Court, EAT, Employment Tribunal and First-Tier Tribunal. Michael frequently advises on injunctive relief, confidentiality, and restraint of trade issues. His cases in the High Court include Personal Management Solutions Ltd v Brakes Bros Ltd & Ors and Lonmar Global Risks Ltd v West & Ors. In the Employment Tribunal, Michael was recently instructed (led by Daniel Stilitz QC) by Chelsea FC and José Mourinho to defend claims brought against them by a former-doctor. In April 2016, Michael was instructed (led by Daniel Stilitz QC) by an investment bank in a whistleblowing claim, which included an urgent appeal to the EAT on disclosure issues. His recent work as sole counsel includes a 7 day claim involving allegations of allegations of pregnancy/maternity discrimination and associated disability discrimination. Michael also undertakes a broad range of public law work (such as R (Newby) v Food Standards Agency). He has particular expertise in cases involving Assets of Community Value having acted in a number of appeals, for example Patel v Hackney (the first appeal under ACV regime), Kicking Horse Ltd v Camden, and Mendoza Ltd v Camden.
Professional Memberships: COMBAR, ELA, ELBA, ALBA.
Career: Called to the bar in 2009.
Publications: Tolley's Employment Law Handbook.
Personal: Graduated from St Catharine's College, Cambridge with a First Class degree in Law.

LEECH, Stewart QC
Queen Elizabeth Building QEB, London
020 7797 7837
s.leech@qeb.co.uk
Featured in Family/Matrimonial (London)

Practice Areas: Stewart specialises in ancilliary relief and cohabitee disputes, generally involving high net worth individuals with complex financial arrangements. He is regularly instructed on behalf of trustees. His cases often have an international dimension and frequently involve jurisdictional issues. He is also experienced in private law children applications. He is bilingual in French and English and has a particular interest in cross-channel cases. He routinely drafts and advises on nuptial agreements.
Professional Memberships: Family Law Bar Association; International Academy of Matrimonial Lawyers; Franco - British Lawyers Society.

LEEK, Samantha QC
5 Essex Court, London
020 7404 3447
leek@5essexcourt.co.uk
Featured in Police Law (All Circuits), Inquests & Public Inquiries (All Circuits)

Practice Areas: All areas of police and government law, including inquests, civil actions, judicial review, public inquiries and advice on policy. Particular expertise in inquests and civil claims arising out of: deaths in police and prison custody; terrorist attacks; the police use of firearms; injuries sustained whilst working for MOD, government departments, private contractors. She has represented Coroners, police forces, the National Crime Agency and police officers in numerous recent high profile inquests, public inquiries and civil claims including: Independent Inquiry into Child Sexual Abuse - representing Leicestershire Constabulary in the Janner Inquiry, Nottinghamshire Constabulary in the Nottinghamshire Care Homes Inquiry and the Department of Health in the Child Migration Inquiry. Undercover Policing Inquiry - representing

Nottinghamshire Constabulary. Inquest into death of Lorraine Barwell (Prison Guard killed while on duty at Blackfriars Crown Court). Counsel to the Inquests into the deaths of 30 British tourists in Sousse, Tunisia. Counsel to the Inquest into the death of Nick Alexander at the Bataclan Theatre in Paris. Counsel to the Chief Coroner in the Inquest into the death of Dr Abbas Khan while in prison in Syria. Counsel to HMG in the fresh inquest into the Birmingham Pub Bombings. Hillsborough Inquests (representing Operation Resolve), Mark Duggan Inquest (representing the NCA), Public Inquiry into the death of Azelle Rodney (representing E7, the officer who shot him), Inquest in to the death of Ian Tomlinson (Metropolitan Police), Inquest into the death of Jean-Charles De Menezes. Has represented numerous government departments, including the MOD and Home Office, and private contractors (including SERCO, G4S and Reliance) in inquests and civil claims arising out of the death of individuals in custody or during training sessions or whilst on duty.
Professional Memberships: Member of the Administrative Law Bar Association and Personal Injuries Bar Association.
Career: Called in 1993; Treasury C Panel 1999; Treasury B Panel 2003; Treasury A Panel 2009; Silk 2012.

LEGARD, Edward
Dere Street Barristers, York
0844 335 1551
e.legard@derestreet.co.uk
Featured in Employment (North Eastern)
Practice Areas: Specialist Employment Practitioner covering all major aspects of employment and equality law. A strong appellate practice with regular appearances before both CA and EAT. Caseload comprises a broadly even split of Respondent and Claimant work. Cases include Van Straten v Nuclear Decommissioning Agency 2411909/13 : A complex and high value maternity/sex discrimination claim where Edward successfully represented a leading expert on nuclear waste decommissioning. Powell v OMV Exploration Ltd [2014] IRLR 80 (Langstaff P), Barnsley MBC v Yerraklava [2012] IRLR 78; Woods v Pasab [2013] IRLR 305, CA; Horizon Recruitment Limited v Vincent [2010] ICR 491; B & C v A [2010] IRLR 400; Kimberley Group Housing Ltd v Hambley & Os [2008] IRLR 682; Flett v. Matheson [2006] IRLR 277, CA; Ramsay v. Walkers Crisps [2004] IRLR 754.
Professional Memberships: Employment Law Bar Association.
Career: Called to the Bar 1996. Head of Employment Team, Dere Street Barristers. Mediator since 1999. Fee paid Employment Judge since 2010.
Personal: Highly experienced commercial mediator with a strong track record of success.

LEGGE, Henry QC
5 Stone Buildings, London
020 7242 6201
clerks@5sblaw.com
Featured in Chancery (London), Art and Cultural Property Law (London), Offshore (London), Pensions (London), Trusts (London)
Practice Areas: Henry's practice includes a broad range of Chancery work, but with particular emphasis on cases involving trusts, estates, pension schemes and art. In recent years, he has appeared in a number of high profile trust disputes both onshore and offshore (eg Gorbunova v Berezovsky) as well as appearing in some of the largest pensions cases of the last few years (eg BT, IBM, Nortel). He has acted in numerous trustee and beneficiary disputes, claims in breach of trust and asset recovery claims. As well as domestic trust and estate disputes, he has considerable experience in advising and acting in offshore jurisdictions and in cases involving offshore structures (including foundations and other civil law structures). He has appeared and advised in a number of significant cases in which complex offshore structures were under attack (for example, Berezovsky, Stow and Tchenguiz-Imerman) and is very familiar with the principles of law and tactical issues involved. He has also advised extensively on non-contentious trust issues, both domestic and offshore, including commercial trusts and securitisation structures. Henry spent much of his early years in practice defending solicitors and actuaries in negligence proceedings and he has continued to advise and appear in negligence claims for both claimants and defendants since that time. Over the years he has acted in a broad range of cases and is used to dealing with complex issues of tax, actuarial practice, investment or accounting should they arise. He has an additional area of expertise in disputes involving works of art and chattels. In recent years he has appeared in many of the most significant cases in this niche area, including Avrora v Christies, in which he acted for the successful Claimant.
Professional Memberships: CBA, APL, STEP, PAIAM, the Trust Law Committee.
Career: BA Oxford, called to the Bar 1993. Silk 2012.
Publications: "Pension Schemes" in "Company Directors: Duties, Liabilities and Remedies" (OUP); Consulting Editor to "Subrogation" by Mitchell and Waterson (OUP); various articles on the law of chattels, trusts and multi-jurisdictional succession.

LEIPER, Richard
11KBW, London
020 7632 8500
richard.leiper@11kbw.com
Featured in Employment (London)
Practice Areas: Litigation in the High Court and in employment tribunals, and appeals, including claims concerning directors' and employees' duties, remuneration, protection of confidential information and post-termination restrictions, and claims concerning discrimination, whistleblowing and TUPE. Cases include Cavendish v Makdessi [2015] 3 WLR 1373 (penalty clauses) [2013] EWCA Civ 1540 (applications to commit); Clements v Lloyds Banking plc [2014] ICR D22 (causation in discrimination); Macleod v Mears Ltd [2014] EWHC 2191 (QB) (discretionary bonus); Farnon v Devonshires [2011] EWHC 3167 (QB) (claim of solicitors negligence); Rabobank v Docker [2011] EqLR 580 (race discrimination); Lonmar Global Risks Ltd v West [2011] IRLR 138 (business protection); Merrill Lynch v Chunilal [2010] EWHC 1467 (Comm) (jurisdiction dispute); Redcar & Cleveland BC v Bainbridge [2009] ICR 133 (equal pay); Park v Korean Residents Association [2008] EWHC 866 (QB) (injunctive relief and trial challenging the election of the association chairman); Ogilvy & Mather Ltd v Oktobor Ltd [2007] EWHC 1285 (QB) (trial in commercial dispute concerning the termination of production contract): Commerzbank AG v Keen [2007] ICR 623 (UCTA in employment contracts); IGEN v Wong [2005] ICR 931 (burden of proof in discrimination); Clark v Nomura International [2000] IRLR 766 (rational bonus awards).
Professional Memberships: Employment Law Bar Association (former Chair); Employment Lawyers Association; European Employment Lawyers Association; Industrial Law Society; Financial Services Lawyers Association.
Career: Called 1996.
Publications: Contributor to Tolley's 'Employment Handbook'.
Personal: Birmingham University (LLB); Keble College, Oxford (MJur).

LEMON, Jane QC
Keating Chambers, London
020 7544 2600
jlemon@keatingchambers.com
Featured in International Arbitration (London), Professional Negligence (London), Construction (London)
Practice Areas: Specialist in litigation, arbitration and ADR for the construction, engineering, energy, shipbuilding, facilities management and technology sectors. Built a reputation as a fine advocate with a "famed intellectual prowess" who "is remarkable for the sheer hard work she puts into a case". Enjoys a strong domestic and international practice having acted in complex domestic litigation in the Technology and Construction Court and Commercial Court as well as in multi-million pound international arbitrations (including those under ICC and LCIA Rules). Has represented clients in disputes under all major forms of international contracts including FIDIC, SAJ and NEC3. She is also an accredited adjudicator. Recent landmark cases include a litigation regarding Wembley Stadium; an ICC arbitration surrounding the design and construction of a 127km section of road in Africa (FIDIC Yellow Book); acting on a $300 million LCIA arbitration concerning one of the world's largest offshore windfarms; and an arbitration concerning a number of disputes on major infrastructure projects in Oman.
Professional Memberships: TECBAR; COMBAR; SCL.
Career: Called 1993; public access training 2008; TECBAR accredited adjudicator.
Publications: Contributor, Keating On Construction Contracts – 7th-10th Editions; Joint Author of Architects and Engineers for Professional Negligence and Liability LLP (2000).

LEMOS, Marika
Devereux, London
020 7353 7534
lemos@devchambers.co.uk
Featured in Tax (London)
Practice Areas: Specialises in all aspects of tax litigation (direct and indirect taxes). Also accepts instructions: in the context of commercial litigation, trust and pensions disputes, Variation of Trust Act applications and professional negligence cases where tax is involved. On the advisory side, her clients include UK and international trustees and individuals. Areas of specialism: structuring onshore and offshore trusts, farms, businesses and charities; UK and cross-border estate planning; deeds of variation; domicile and the remittance basis; residence of individuals, corporates and partnerships; funds and incentive structuring; unwinding EBTs; disposals of businesses; immunities from tax; property holding structures; taxation of pensions; etc.
Professional Memberships: On Attorney General's C Panel. Member of the Revenue Bar Association, the VAT Practitioners Group, the Chancery Bar Association, and the International Fiscal Association. On the Bar Pro Bono Unit's panel.
Career: Practising barrister since October 2005. Nominated for the Bar Pro Bro Bono Award 2013.
Publications: Co-author of the 5th and 6th Editions of McCutcheon on Inheritance Tax; Principal Editor of Whiteman & Sherry on Capital Gains Tax; Regular contributor to a number of professional publications including Tolley's Property Taxation, Taxation, Tax Journal, Private Client Business, Gray's Inn Tax Chambers Review, etc.
Personal: Read languages at St John's College, Cambridge; Vice President of LALCF, a charity set up to relieve poverty, promote education and support sustainable development on Oinousses, Greece.

LENNON, Jonathan
Carmelite Chambers, London
020 7936 6300
clerks@carmelitechambers.co.uk
Featured in POCA Work & Asset Forfeiture (All Circuits), Financial Crime (London)
Practice Areas: Jonathan is becoming to the 'go to' junior for heavyweight complex fraud work and POCA related cases. He works well with both lay clients and solicitors and always impresses. Jonathan acted in the first civil recovery case to reach the Supreme Court; SOCA v Gale (2011) which is now expected to be admitted to the European Court of Human Rights. In recent years he has acted for a legal professional charged with money laundering, book-keepers and accountants charged with tax fraud, lead for the principal defendant in a major SFO boiler-room fraud, acted for a director of a pension trustee company charged with pension fraud and for a mortgage broker charged with what is reputed to be Britain's biggest ever mortgage fraud. In 2016 he acted in the Buckingham Palace corruption trials and defended in 4 High Court civil recovery cases. Jonathan, also brought the landmark case in the High Court which changed the law on cash forfeiture: Angus v UKBA and also acted in the seminal case on disclosure and PII: R v H & C, as well as for a hedge fund manager in a significant case on international enforcement of freezing orders in a case brought by the American authorities; SEC v Manterfield. Jonathan is currently instructed by the SFO in High Court civil recovery proceedings. He is also instructed in civil fraud cases and has obtained 'Mareva' freezing and disclosure orders in the Commercial Court. Jonathan's non-fraud work is also substantial and complex which includes the notorious and highly complex murder case of R v Rees. The case was reputed to have involved one of the longest pre-trial legal arguments in English criminal litigation history.
Professional Memberships: Executive Committee member of Criminal Bar Association, South East Circuit and Proceeds of Crime Lawyers Association.
Career: Called 1997.
Publications: Contributing author to Covert Human Intelligence Sources, Waterside Press, articles in Proceeds of Crime Review and International Banking and Financial Law.

LESTER, Maya QC
Brick Court Chambers, London
020 7379 3550
maya.lester@brockcourt.co.uk
Featured in Administrative & Public Law (London), Competition/European Law (London), Sanctions (All Circuits), Civil Liberties & Human Rights (London), Competition/European Law (London)
Career: Maya Lester QC has a wide ranging practice in public law, European law, competition law, public international law, and human rights & civil liberties. She regularly appears in leading cases in the Courts of England, Luxembourg and Strasbourg, and in the Competition Appeal Tribunal. Maya Lester has a particular expertise in the law relating to economic sanctions. She founded and co-writes a blog on European sanctions law (www.europeansanctions.com). She represents and advises hundreds of companies and individuals before the European and English courts and has acted in most of the leading cases, including Kadi, Tay Za, Central Bank of Iran, NITC and IRISL. Her most significant cases include R (Bancoult) v Secretary of State (the Chagos Islands litigation in the UK and ECHR), Enron v EWS (the first follow-on competition damages trial in the UK, and several subsequent follow-on actions), R v Goldshield (prosecuting cartels as conspiracy to defraud), the Shambo judicial review (on bovine TB). Maya appears regularly in judicial reviews of regulatory decisions (eg Cityhook, UniChem), competition appeals (including on LIBOR, Pay TV, horseracing, dairy, and construction recruitment forum) and damages actions (including Enron and National Grid).

LEVENE, Simon
12 King's Bench Walk, London
2075830811
levene@12kbw.co.uk
Featured in Personal Injury (All Circuits)
Practice Areas: Personal injury; clinical negligence; solicitors' negligence; health and safety; product liability; group litigation; MIB; CICA. Experience of all aspects of personal injury work, with particular emphasis on fatal accidents; occupational injuries; occupational and industrial diseases, including in particular asbestos-related diseases, deafness, occupational cancers, asthma and eczema. Particular expertise in complex quantum issues, drafting schedules and counter schedules in cases of utmost severity. Extensive experience of all aspects of clinical negligence, including birth related trauma, obstetrics and gynaecology, spinal and general surgery, general practice, trauma and orthopaedics.
Professional Memberships: PIBA, PNBA, LCLCBA. Ogden Committee.
Publications: Editor of Kemp & Kemp: 'Facts and Figures'; 'Ogden Tables'; 'PIBA Personal injuries Handbook'. Author of 'Damages', 'Heads of Claim' and 'Causes of Action'.
Personal: Interests: family, a Tibetan terrier called Marlowe, books, bookbinding, France. Not interested in football. Too young for golf.

LEVEY, Edward
Fountain Court Chambers, London
020 7583 3335
clerks4@fountaincourt.co.uk
Featured in Commercial Dispute Resolution (London), Professional Discipline (London)
Practice Areas: Barrister specialising in commercial and civil litigation and arbitration, including banking, civil fraud, insurance and professional negligence / professional discipline. Languages include modern Hebrew, basic French.
Professional Memberships: Combar; London Common Law and Commercial Bar Association.
Career: Research assistant, Law Commission of England and Wales 1997-98; part-time tutor in law, UCL 1997-99; called 1999, Inner Temple. Appointed as a Disciplinary Panel Member of the a Bar Tribunals & Adjudication Service (2014-present).
Publications: Contributor to 'Professional Negligence and Liability' (Informa); former editor of 'Commercial Court Procedure' (Sweet & Maxwell); former contributor to 'Civil Court Service' (the 'Brown Book') (Jordans).

LEVY, Jacob QC
9 Gough Square, London
020 7832 0500
clerks@9goughsquare.co.uk
Featured in Personal Injury (London), Clinical Negligence (London)
Practice Areas: All aspects of personal injury and clinical negligence work, particularly cases involving gynaecological, serious spinal, orthopaedic and brain injuries. From misplaced swabs to spinal injuries to birth accidents; as with his approach to personal injury work his motto used to be: "No case too big-no case too small." However the passage of years and attainment of Silk has caused him to recalibrate this to; "Big, Bigger and Bigger Still...oh my!". The bulk of his personal injury work comprises stressers, backers, spiners, minors, headers and rear-end shunters – now all of considerable value and with catastrophic consequences. Taking Silk has only increased the workload and the pool of gravely injured clients. Known for his sympathetic and empathetic manner – he continues to work diligently to all hours of the night and day to get the job done. He also deals with Professional Negligence cases; specifically personal injury and clinical negligence claims that have gone awry.
Professional Memberships: PIBA, PNBA.
Career: LLB (Hons) London (LSE) 1984. Called July 1986 and joined 9 Gough Square following pupillage there with John Foy QC and HHJ John Reddihough.
Personal: Family prevents anything much other than supporting failing football team and watching late night TV whilst over-eating pizza. Or at least he did, until an increasing workload hijacked the morsel of free time he had – so thank goodness for iPlayer. Otherwise fanatical film and music buff, failed screenwriter and gig-goer. Byline: 'Eat football, sleep football – practice PI and Clin Neg'. And munch cheesecake – as long as the wife isn't looking. And settle Schedules of Loss – endlessly. Oh, and being the Gigmeister General – so long as the wife allows him to watch old re-formed, re-warmed Punk, New Wave and Blues.

LEVY, Michael
2 Bedford Row, London
020 7440 8888
mlevy@2bedfordrow.co.uk
Featured in Crime (London)
Practice Areas: Has an almost exclusively criminal defence practice in both serious crime and fraud. Also regularly instructed in Professional Discipline and Regulatory. Frequently instructed as a Leading Junior. Serious crime including Murder, Manslaughter, Rape and other Serious Sexual Offences both Current and Historic and Drugs offences. Fraud – corporate and personal(including prosecutions brought by the SFO, Missing Trader and Advance Fee Fraud). Money-Laundering, Confiscation and VAT offences. Regulatory and Disciplinary Tribunals including the the General Medical Council (GMC) , the Football Association (FA) Police Disciplinary, Marine Management Organisation and the Environment Agency and Trading Standards. Regularly sits as a Legal Assessor at the Nursing and Midwifery Council (NMC). Road Traffic.War Crimes. Some Notable cases: Murder//Manslaughter – R v Uddin 2 All E R 744 R v Glenn – Murder trial in which for first time ever Crown sought to adduce Defendants previous conviction for Murder; R.v McMakin – Largest ever single warehouse duty evasion fraud. R. v Ebbrell – Multi-million pound fraud. Largest MTIC fraud. R. v. Murphy and ors. "Foxtrot Five" Importation of £125 million cocaine R. v. Drew – Large scale prostitution. R v Serafinowicz – First counsel to be instructed in first ever prosecution under War Crimes Act. Concerned events in Eastern Europe during Second World War. UN v Jelesic – War Crimes case at the International Criminal Tribunal in the Hague.
Professional Memberships: South Eastern Circuit; Criminal Bar Association; British Academy of Forensic Science; International Criminal law Association, Association of Regulatory and Disciplinary Lawyers, British Russian Law Association.
Career: LLB (Hons). Called to Bar 1979. Gray's Inn.

LEWERS, Nigel
12 King's Bench Walk, London
020 7415 8321
lewers@12kbw.co.uk
Featured in Personal Injury (London)
Practice Areas: Personal injury. Liability of public authorities: occupier's and employer's liability, claims arising out of exposure to asbestos, claims under the Highways Act 1980 and claims involving allegations of abuse and assault. Road traffic: including claims on behalf of the Motor Insurers Bureau and issues of motor insurance. Employers liability: industrial accidents and industrial disease especially exposure to asbestos. Accidents involving animals, particularly horses. Damages for catastrophic injury, chronic pain conditions and advanced prosthetics. A member of the panel of approved counsel of several major insurance companies for instruction in catastrophic injury claims. Clinical Negligence: claims arising out of injury sustained at birth. Recent Cases include the successful defence at trial of a care home for claims arising out assault by a resident against staff; a multi-million pound settlement in a claim against the police for paralysis arising out of a motorcycling accident; and two multi-million pound cases involving amputees claiming the latest state-of-the art electronic prostheses.
Professional Memberships: PIBA; PNBA; LCLCA.
Career: In practice since 1987. Former prosecutor on behalf of the Bar Standards Board. Former member of Executive Committee of PIBA. Qualified mediator.
Publications: General Editor, Kemp & Kemp Personal Injury, Law, Practice and Procedure.
Personal: Graduated in Jurisprudence from Magdalen College, Oxford. Married with four children.

LEWIS, Christopher
Atkin Chambers, London
020 7404 0102
clewis@atkinchambers.com
Featured in International Arbitration (London), Construction (London), Energy & Natural Resources (London), Information Technology (London)
Practice Areas: Construction, engineering, energy, technology and related matters.
Professional Memberships: TECBAR, COMBAR, LCLCBA, Society for Computers and Law, SCL.
Career: MA, BCL (Oxon). Some-time tutor of Law at Wadham College, Oxford and LSE; former Judicial Assistant to Lord Woolf MR.
Publications: Editor of 'Building Law Reports'.

LEWIS, James QC
3 Raymond Buildings Barristers, London
020 7400 6400
james.lewis@3rblaw.com
Featured in Crime (London), Extradition (London), Financial Crime (London)
Practice Areas: James Lewis is a rare specialist in both civil and criminal cases. This is demonstrated by the stellar array of leading cases in which he has appeared and shows that his experience and judgment is highly sought after. Vastly experienced in criminal, civil and commercial fraud, extradition, regulatory work, contempt, public international law and judicial review matters. He appears frequently at first instance, in the Court of Appeal and in the Privy Council and the Supreme Court as well as other foreign jurisdictions being additionally called ad hoc to the bars of Hong Kong, Gibraltar, Cayman Islands, Brunei, Trinidad and Tobago and Ireland. Often used as an experienced litigation strategist and advocate who can advise and represent companies and individuals in respect of commercial, regulatory and criminal issues, particularly those with an international dimension. He excels in complex and difficult cases and was described by a judge as a Rolls Royce advocate. He has extensive trial and appellate experience in matters of mutual assistance, extradition and commercial fraud, which encompasses international cooperation concerning search and seizure of documents, letters of request, warrants and other international treaty matters; and sanctions work. He has acted for and against at least 20 overseas governments. For more information go to www.3rblaw.com.
Career: Called 1987. Recorder of the Crown Court 2000. QC 2002. Deputy High Court Judge assigned to the Administrative Court 2013. Appointed to the SFO Prosecution List 2013. Election Commissioner (High Court Appointment) 2016.
Personal: BSc(Hons) Diploma in Law.

LEWIS, Jonathan
4 Pump Court, London
020 7842 5555
jlewis@4pumpcourt.com
Featured in Construction (London)
Practice Areas: Jonathan Lewis specialises principally in construction and construction based professional negligence disputes in litigation, arbitration and adjudication.. Recent cases have concerned a range of construction and engineering disputes including port wall

construction, railway signalling, tramway construction, sewerage and water contracts, steelwork design causing catastrophic building collapse, drainage, power stations and bridges. He has considerable expertise in adjudications with a number of reported decisions in this area. In addition, Jonathan has expertise in insolvency law and has previously been named Barrister of the Year at the Insolvency and Rescue Awards. He is often instructed in construction cases where an insolvency issue arises as well as having a broader insolvency practice.
Professional Memberships: Chancery Bar Association, COMBAR.
Career: Called to the Bar in 1996.
Personal: LLB, Manchester University.

LEWIS, Meyric
Francis Taylor Building, London
020 7353 8415
clerks@ftbchambers.co.uk
Featured in Planning (London)
Practice Areas: Meyric specialises in all aspects of planning (including environmental assessment) and compulsory purchase both at inquiries and in the courts, up to the Court of Appeal and the Supreme Court. Clients range from substantial developers to public authorities and individual developers or objectors. He is frequently reported in the specialist law reports in notable cases. His court practice ranges from judicial and statutory review in the higher courts to prosecutions and other regulatory proceedings in the Crown Court and Magistrates' Court. He has particular experience in proceedings relating to planning enforcement, statutory nuisance and land contamination. Other specialisms include: residential, commercial and retail development, local development frameworks, licensed premises, listed buildings and conservation areas, highways, major infrastructure projects, compulsory purchase and compensation, trees, enforcement notices and injunctions.
Professional Memberships: Administrative Law Bar Association; Compulsory Purchase Association (Chair); Planning and Environmental Law Association.
Career: Called to Bar 1986. B Panel Counsel for the Secretary of State 1995-2001 defending planning decisions in the High Court.
Publications: Many articles including Expediency in Enforcement [2003] JPL 1106 and The New Procedures for Planning Challenges in the High Court [2008] JPL 1720.

LEWIS, Paul QC
Farrar's Building, London
020 7583 9241
chambers@farrarsbuilding.co.uk
Featured in Crime (Wales & Chester)
Practice Areas: Criminal law – both prosecution and defence. Regularly works in Wales, London and the Midlands, but also appears nationally. Particular specialisation in homicide and serious fraud. Cases include R-v-Joel Smith (The "Toni Anne Byfield" double murder case;) R-v-Osbourne and others (professional "contract killing" of a drugs rival;) R-v-Riches (historic allegation of murder of a baby 30 years earlier;) R-v-Stewart and others ("torture murder" by fire of an abducted youth;) R-v-Morrissey and others (robbery and murder at a Worcestershire Post Office;) R-v-Abu Hamza (the "Khyra Ishaq" starvation case.) Recent cases include R-v-Crooks and others (convictions of five appellants for alleged "gangland murder" quashed by Court of Appeal upon arguments based upon non-disclosure of Prosecution material.) Successfully represented the acquitted principal defendant in the trial of R-v-Beckford and others (triple murder case arising from the Birmingham Riots of 2011.) Also works in sports law and regulatory cases.
Professional Memberships: Bencher of Gray's Inn. Leader of the Wales and Chester Circuit, January 2014 to December 2016.
Career: Graduate of Leicester University (LLB) Called 1981; Assistant Recorder 1998; Recorder 2000; QC 2001.
Personal: Married, with two children. Lives in London and South Wales. Interests include sport (especially rugby and cricket;) music and travel.

LEWISON, Josh
Radcliffe Chambers, London
020 7831 0081
jlewison@radcliffechambers.com
Featured in Charities (London)
Practice Areas: Josh is a private client specialist, concentrating on contentious and non-contentious trusts, contested probate and associated disputes. His trust experience covers onshore and offshore work, which predominantly covers Jersey and Guernsey. Josh also advises on tax, usually in connection with estate planning and trust arrangements. He has developed a niche specialism in connection with the PSC Register, advising companies, trustees and individuals in relation to complex and high-value trust and corporate structures.
Professional Memberships: Association of Contentious Trust and Probate Specialists, Chancery Bar Association, Charity Law Association, Insolvency Lawyers' Association.
Career: Westminster School and Downing College, Cambridge (MA, Cantab). Hardwicke and Denning Scholarships (Lincoln's Inn). Called to the Bar in 2005. Fellow of the Chartered Institute of Arbitrators, 2014. Registered DIFC Courts Practitioner. Admitted to the State Bar of California, 2015.

LEY-MORGAN, Mark
Serjeants' Inn Chambers, London
020 7427 5000
mley-morgan@serjeantsinn.com
Featured in Police Law (All Circuits), Professional Discipline (London)
Practice Areas: Mark Ley-Morgan was called to the Bar in 1994. Mark specialises in public and administrative, police, employment, inquests and inquiries and professional discipline law. An earlier edition notes that "he is an excellent jury advocate with a very persuasive court technique that certainly goes down well with both judge and jury" and that "he is an extremely astute lawyer, who is very intelligent and personable, his ability to win over a jury is incredible." Please visit the Serjeants' Inn Chambers website for his profile, which sets out full details of his practice including relevant work of note.

LIDDELL, Richard
4 New Square, London
020 7822 2000
r.liddell@4newsquare.com
Featured in Professional Negligence (London), Construction (London), Sports Law (London)
Practice Areas: Wide-ranging practice with particular experience and expertise in the following areas: (i) construction and engineering (ii) commercial litigation (iii) professional liability and (iv) sport. Rick also specialises in all fields of professional liability, with particular emphasis upon barristers and solicitors, construction professionals, valuers and surveyors, accountants and auditors, IFAs and insurance brokers. Rick has been involved in numerous high-profile cases, including Aspect v Higgins (first ever case on construction adjudication to reach the Supreme Court), Co-op v Birse (CA, 2014), Mengiste v Endowment Fund (CA, 2013) and The Innovator Litigation (substantial multi-party Commercial Court litigation). He has also a busy sports practice with his cases spanning the following sports: athletics, basketball, boxing, eventing, football, horseracing, ice hockey, rowing, rugby union, and shooting. He has appeared in the Court of Arbitration for Sport (CAS) and has particular expertise in case involving doping issues.
Professional Memberships: BASL; COMBAR; IPBA; PNBA; TECBAR; Chancery Bar Association; LCIA.
Career: MA (Cantab); LLM. Called to the Bar (Middle Temple) in 1999 (Major Scholarship). Tenant at 4 New Square 2000 to date.
Personal: Educated at Eastbourne College; Pembroke College, Cambridge University. Supports Sunderland AFC.

LIDINGTON, Gary
Radcliffe Chambers, London
020 7831 0081
glidington@radcliffechambers.com
Featured in Commercial Dispute Resolution (London)
Practice Areas: Gary Lidington specialises in the full range of commercial and commercial chancery disputes, including related professional negligence disputes, both in the English Courts and in arbitration. His practice includes sale and supply of goods and services, banking and financial services, partnership, company and insolvency, commercial agency and insurance matters, much of which has a strong fraud or multi-jurisdictional element. He has a growing and successful Oil and Gas practice. He is known for his practical, commercially-minded and client focused approach.
Professional Memberships: COMBAR, Chancery Bar Association.
Career: Notable recent cases include: BP Oil International Limited v Bankers Petroleum Albania Limited ($54M breach of oil supply contract); a $440M UNCITRAL arbitration in the oil industry; Tullow Heritage Ltd v Heritage Oil & Gas Limited [2013] EWHC 1656 ($303M indemnity claim); Bank of Scotland v Pereira [2011] EWCA Civ 241 (leading authority on setting aside judgment/appealing when a party does not turn up to trial); acting for an IT services provider in a dispute arising out of $1Bn government contract; Close Invoice Finance Ltd v Pile [2009] 1 FLR 873 (relevance of Art 8 ECHR to charging order enforcement); Dartmouth Court Blackheath Ltd v Berisworth Ltd [2008] EWHC 350.

LIGHTMAN, Daniel QC
Serle Court, London
020 7242 6105
dlightman@serlecourt.co.uk
Featured in Chancery (London), Commercial Dispute Resolution (London), Company (London), Restructuring/Insolvency (London)
Practice Areas: Commercial chancery, company, civil fraud, professional negligence and insolvency litigation. Recent cases include: C v C [2016] Fam Law 20 (jurisdiction of Family Court over company assets); Munday v Hilburn [2015] BPIR 684 (whether claim by former bankrupt an abuse of process); HRH Prince Abdulaziz v Apex [2015] 2 All ER 206 (Supreme Court: unless order); Abouraya v Sigmund [2015] BCC 503 (multiple derivative claim in respect of overseas company); Eckerle v Wickeder Westfalenstahl GmbH [2014] Ch 196 (re-registration of a plc as a private company); Petrodel Resources v Prest [2013] 2 AC 415 (Supreme Court: piercing the corporate veil); Serious Organised Crime Agency v Perry [2013] 1 AC 182 (Supreme Court: Proceeds of Crime Act).
Professional Memberships: Chancery Bar Association, COMBAR, ACTAPS, Insolvency Lawyers' Association, Family Law Bar Association.
Career: Called to the Bar 1995. Queen's Counsel 2016.
Publications: Author of Chapter 3 (derivative claims) and co-author of Chapter 8 (s.994 procedure) of Minority Shareholders: Law, Practice & Procedure (5th Ed. 2015); co-author of Chapters 14, 15 and 31 of Lightman & Moss, 'The Law of Receivers and Administrators of Companies' (5th Ed. 2011). Other publications include: 'Why procedure matters' (NLJ, 6 March 2015); 'Unfair Prejudice Petitions: long-range missiles for minority shareholders' (BJIB&FL, Dec 2013); 'Petrodel Resources Ltd v Prest: where are we now?' (Trusts & Trustees, Nov 2013); 'Two Aspects of the Statutory Derivative Claim' (LMCLQ, Feb 2011); Cricket Grounds from the Air (2nd Ed. 2010).
Personal: BA Lit. Hum. (First Class), Magdalen College, Oxford; Dip. Law (Distinction) City University, London. Hardwicke, Mansfield and Denning Scholar of Lincoln's Inn.

LIMB, Christopher
18 St John Street, Manchester
0161 278 1800
climb@18sjs.com
Featured in Clinical Negligence (Northern)
Practice Areas: Practice is almost exclusively clinical negligence. Claimant counsel in the seminal Court of Appeal decision of Naylor v Preston HA in 1987, fundamentally altering the conduct of clinical negligence cases. Subsequent Court of Appeal cases have included Forbes v Wandsworth HA in 1997 (limitation) and Gouldsmith v Mid-Staffs Trust in 2007 (causation). The entire spectrum of clinical negligence work is undertaken, including many current cerebral palsy cases with (lump sum equivalent) value of £10m or more. Recent cases have included; cancer, intestinal, brain, eye, Erbs palsy, CPA cases relating to prostheses/devices, vascular surgery, pressure sores, orthopaedic, psychiatric, spinal, wrongful birth, consent, colorectal, and medication. He has great experience at all stages of preparation, conferences and settlement meetings, as well as hearings. Contributing author Jordans Personal Injury.
Professional Memberships: PNBA, PIBA, NCMLA. APIL – Clinical Negligence Conference Organiser.
Career: Called 1975. Tribunal Judge in Primary Health Lists and SEN.
Personal: Choral singing, rugby league, wine, France and walking are among the many interests he has insufficient time for.

LIMB, Patrick QC
Ropewalk Chambers, Nottingham
01159 472581
patricklimbqc@ropewalk.co.uk
Featured in Personal Injury (Midlands), Personal Injury (All Circuits)

Practice Areas: He specialises principally in disease, all aspects of high value personal injury, clinical negligence and regulatory defence work. With a successful track record in test litigation, group and multi-party actions, he has been named in Chambers and Partners' Spotlight Table nationally for disease practitioners since its inception. He also acts in cases involving the police, human rights and judicial review. He has experience across the full spectrum of claims and is well known for his work in cases involving occupational cancers and related injuries. He has particular expertise in actionability of injury, causation and epidemiology – and cross-examination of experts. He is highly regarded for his work in test litigation and group actions and is an experienced appellate advocate to Supreme Court level. Sure-footed on law and procedure, he provides strategic thinking, commercial nous and seeks to serve each client by leading as an effective team-player.

Professional Memberships: PIBA; PNBA; HSLAW; DLA; Nottinghamshire Medico-Legal Society.

Career: Called 1987; Silk 2006; called to the Gibraltar Bar; MA (Cantab) Law, Pembroke College, Cambridge; Accredited Mediator; Barrister of the Year – Nottinghamshire Law Society 2014.

Personal: Away from the Bar, he lists his interests a trekking, running and being half French.

LINDFIELD, Gemma
5 St Andrew's Hill, London
Featured in Extradition (London)

Practice Areas: Gemma's specialisms are extradition, international criminal law and family. An excellent knowledge of human rights underpins each of these areas. In extradition, Gemma represents governments, judicial authorities and requested persons. She has appeared in many high profile cases in recent years, such as Sweden v. Julian Assange and Rwanda v. Brown and others. She is known for her ability to deal with technical legal arguments, particularly where there is no clear answer. At the same time, Gemma's practical approach to her cases to achieve the desired outcome. A particular specialty is abuse of process arguments raised following extradition to England and Wales. Gemma is a member of the ELA and DELF and frequently provides comment to the media on many aspects of extradition law. As a result of her involvement in the Rwandan extradition case, Gemma has gained experience in the field of international criminal law. In 2011, Gemma spent time in the Office of the Prosecutor at the International Criminal Tribunal for Rwanda and she remains on the Trial Attorney roster. Gemma's family practice has a predominantly international dimension, although she appears in a full range of cases. She has appellate experience including in the Court of Appeal.

Professional Memberships: Extradition Lawyers Association, Family Law Bar Association.

LINKLATER, Lisa
Exchange Chambers, Leeds
0113 203 1970
linklater@exchangechambers.co.uk
Featured in Restructuring/Insolvency (North Eastern)

Practice Areas: Lisa is a specialist commercial barrister with over 25 years' experience in chancery/commercial litigation and corporate and personal insolvency. Her practice extends to: shareholders' disputes; corporate and personal insolvency (all aspects of administration, liquidation, bankruptcy, company and personal voluntary arrangements and related litigation); directors' and other fiduciary and trustees' duties; petitions to wind up companies in the public interest; partnership and joint venture disputes; contractual disputes; real property and trusts; general commercial litigation. Lisa is experienced in advising and representing a diverse range of companies, individuals and Government departments. She is regularly instructed in contested cases in the High Court. In 2015 Lisa was appointed a member of the prestigious expert advisory group on a project on Security Rights & the European Insolvency Regulation. The project is a partnership between the University of Leeds and leading universities in Italy, Germany, Spain and Hungary.

Professional Memberships: Chancery Bar Association, Northern Chancery Bar Association, North Eastern Circuit, R3, Insolvency Lawyers' Association.

Career: Junior Counsel to the Crown (Regional Panel).

Personal: MA Cantab (Law), University of Cambridge (Jesus College), (Class II:i); Inns of Court School of Law, London (Very Competent); Duke of Edinburgh Scholarship (Inner Temple); CEDR accredited mediator.

LINTOTT, David
Cornerstone Barristers, London
020 7242 4986
davidjl@cornerstonebarristers.com
Featured in Social Housing (London)

Practice Areas: David is a public law specialist working primarily in areas of local government, planning and social housing. He has appeared in some of the most significant housing cases in recent years and has related expertise in human rights and EU law. He is a highly experienced and knowledgeable advocate with extensive experience of the Court of Appeal and High Court where he has successfully represented many local authorities, his cases include London Borough of Wandsworth v NJ [2013] EWCA Civ. 1373; Falis Ibrahim v London Borough of Wandsworth [2013] EWCA Civ. 20; Chaoui El Goure v Royal Borough of Kensington and Chelsea [2012] EWCA Civ 670 CA; Bubb v Wandsworth LBC [2011] EWCA Civ 1285; Adel William v Wandsworth London Borough Council [2006] EWCA Civ 535 C.A; Lomotey v Enfield [2004] EWCA Civ 627 C.A.

Professional Memberships: ALBA, PEBA

Career: David was called to the Bar in 1996, after completing a law degree at Cambridge University.

Personal: David has a keen interest in ecology and arboriculture and has been involved in conservation of large carnivores as a founder member of the Slovak Wildlife Society since 1998.

LISSACK, Richard QC
Fountain Court Chambers, London
020 7583 3335
clerks1@fountaincourt.co.uk
Featured in Financial Services (London), Health & Safety (London), Inquests & Public Inquiries (All Circuits), Financial Crime (London)

Practice Areas: Richard is a recognised and renowned leading QC practising in the UK, New York, and across the Gulf, Caribbean and Europe. His areas of specialism are international banking and finance; international financial services; corporate and individual financial crime; anticorruption legislation/Bribery Act; commercial fraud; health and safety; inquests and public inquiries; regulatory breaches and across the directories is listed in 12 areas as a leading practitioner. Richard's practice is mainly high profile complex litigation, with a strong financial slant. At present he is leading teams in the UK and internationally on several of the landmark regulatory/criminal cases, including for the bank in the Barclays Capital Raising in Qatar cases, the main trader in the JPMorganChase London Whale litigation, the head of foreign exchange at a major Swiss bank in the FOREX issues, for ENRC in its litigation with Dechert LLP and the SFO, for the former CFO in the HP and Autonomy fraud case. Recently he advised general counsel of Lloyds of London on major insurance market issues and in HSBC v Shah he led on multiple hearings and won a test case on money laundering. In regulation and criminal fraud for Innospec he was the first US-UK joint corporate monitor role under a $40m settlement; in R v Rimmington he led in the successful defence of an insider dealing prosecution inflicting a first defeat on the FCA; and in the House of lords case R v Chargot Ltd he acted in the s3/37 test case. In public law he was retained by local authority solicitors in the House of Lords for a Judicial Review of care in the community £50m annually turns on result plus £800m back payments and he has been to the European Court of Justice in Nolan v USA, a landmark case on state immunity and employees' rights. Of course, he has appeared in and advised in connection with almost every significant public inquiry of recent times and is consulting editor of Public Inquiries (OUP). Richard acted in the pro bono attempt to free the death row prisoner Jack Alderman before the US Supreme Court. He also acted in a very high profile review of a notorious inquest in Cayman in Re Attorney General of the Cayman Islands; he advised and acted for the Jimmy Saville Trustees in connection with group claims for damages. Richard's record in health and safety and public inquiries work is unsurpassed including: Hatfield, Potters Bar, Ladbroke Grove and Southall train crash cases; the Lyme Bay tragedy; the sinkings of the Maria Assumpta and the Pescado. His clients say of him: "He knows how banks operate and is the go-to person for any and every regulatory issue." "The sort of advocate in whom any board of directors will have absolute confidence." "He is very client friendly, a pleasure to work with and very commercial." "He sees all the angles to complex problems and he's remarkable in his ability to address these complexities." "He's an absolute giant in terms of the quality of his advice and his presence in court." "He's very clever and has a lot of gravitas." "He's an advocate who can turn his mind to anything." "An excellent lawyer – enthusiastic and client-friendly with a wealth of experience." "He combines considerable practical experience with a keen intellect." "He brings exceptional judgment and client handling skills to his work." "A true leader, both in court and in conference."

Professional Memberships: Bencher, Inner Temple; Member Chartered Institute of Arbitrators; Financial Services Lawyers Association (Board Member); Human Rights Lawyers Association; Commercial Bar Association; International Bar Association; Employment Law Bar Association; Bar European Group; Health and Safety Lawyers Association; American Counsel Association; Federal Bar Council of New York. Richard is also in the register of public access-accredited barristers.

Career: Called 1978, QC 1994 aged 37; QC Bar of the Eastern Caribbean 2002; Recorder 1993 onwards; New York Bar 2007; Northern Ireland Bar (QC) 2008; 2008 Dubai International Financial Centre Courts; 2008 Bencher of Inner Temple.

Publications: Co-authored Lissack and Horlick on Bribery, LexisNexis. Contributing editor, Public inquiries, Oxford University Press. Financial Services Law and Regulation, LexisNexis. Richard has written and contributed to numerous articles for legal/business publications and is regularly called upon to provide expert commentary for national newspapers and radio.

Personal: Richard is married with three daughters, one step daughter and two step sons and when not in court he walks, goes to the theatre (and far too many rock concerts!), sails off the coast of the Cornwall and acts as an Ambassador for Action Aid and a Patron and Development Board member of RADA.

LISTER, Caroline
1 King's Bench Walk, London
020 7936 1500
clerks@1kbw.co.uk
Featured in Family/Matrimonial (London)

Practice Areas: Experienced in all types of private law disputes concerning children and their parents, including residence, shared residence and contact cases, child abduction, adoption, wardship, relocation both internal and international, and surrogacy. Experienced in financial remedy work of substantial worth, Schedule 1, Inheritance Act and civil partnership disputes.

Professional Memberships: Called to the Bar at Middle Temple in 1980, FLBA, Association of Lawyers for Children.

Career: BSc London University in Comparative Physiology and Microbiology. Diploma in Law. Practices mainly on the South Eastern Circuit, but also travels on the Western Circuit. Appointed a Recorder in 2003. Practicing from 1KBW from the start of her career and intends to be there for many years to come.

Personal: Married with two grown up daughters. Has a passion for her ancient home on Exmoor. Lorry driver and groom for daughter's international event horses. Too many dogs.

LITHMAN, Nigel QC
2 Bedford Row, London
020 7440 8888
nlqc@aol.com
Featured in Crime (London)

Practice Areas: In 2016, Nigel Lithman QC was instructed in four murder trials, He also holds a brief to defend an accountant in "Operation Hornet" arising out of alleged fraudulent events at the bank: HBOS. The paperwork exceeds 170,000 pages. This year he appeared in the Court of Appeal in a Joint Enterprise conviction appeal. Meanwhile he continues to sit as a Recorder at the Old Bailey. In 2015 his fraud practice continued with his representing a City trader in a Film taxation fraud . He appeared on a number of occasions in the Court of Appeal seeking to overturn serious sexual offences and murder convictions in which he had not appeared for the appellants in the court below. During the last years, Nigel Lithman QC justified the faith that his professional colleagues placed in him when they elected him to lead the Criminal Bar. His approach was to show the same tenacity as Chairman of the Criminal Bar Association that he does in representing his clients in court. The Government withdrew its declared scheme to cut fees. Meanwhile during the same years he maintained his involvement in the most serious and diverse criminal cases. During a substantial part of 2013 he represented an accountant charged as a prime mover in Operation Savate a nationwide construction industry fraud. The accountant was alleged to be the lynch pin uniting the various frauds. This was the fifth professional man (the others being an accountant, a barrister, a solicitor and a managing director) he has represented within two years. His practice in fraud has seen him instructed in both the largest SFO Case ever brought and also one of the most valuable Ponzi Scheme frauds, He appears regularly in Health and Safety cases an example of which involved a fatality when a lorry with a HIAB crane attached, turned over. In 2014 he advised in a Death by Dangerous Driving case, a harassment case and an indecent assault case. These were accepted by him under the Direct Access procedure. Nigel Lithman QC successfully defended in a four month trading standards case. He represented the three directors of a substantial company acquitted of conspiracy to defraud. Nigel Lithman QC undertakes a broad cross section of private and legally aided cases instructed by Solicitors or under the Direct Access Scheme.
Professional Memberships: Chairman of the Criminal Bar Association ;Member of the South Eastern Circuit.
Career: In 2013 took up office as Chairman of the Criminal Bar Association ; Master Bencher Inner Temple 2009, Chairman Essex Bar Mess 2002-05, Silk 1997, Recorder 1997, Year of call 1976. He previously attended as the guest silk invited by the Florida Bar Advocacy Convention.
Personal: Married with 3 Step Children, has been Chairman of Highgate Synagogue since May 2008. Enjoys work in the community, supporting Leyton Orient F.C. and watching good football, horse racing and is well known as a very funny after dinner speaker.

LITTLE, Tom
9 Gough Square, London
020 7832 0500
clerks@9goughsquare.co.uk
Featured in Crime (London), Financial Crime (London)
Practice Areas: Principal area of practice is criminal and criminal fraud work. Tom has particular expertise in cases involving complex expert and telephone evidence. In addition Tom's practice comprises police law, inquests and Judicial Review cases linked to criminal investigations.
Professional Memberships: Criminal Bar Association, Administrative Law Bar Association and South Eastern Circuit.
Career: Called to the Bar in 1997. Appointed as a Special Advocate by the Attorney General in 2009 and as Junior Treasury Counsel at the Central Criminal Court in 2012 and in 2014 to the Attorney General's Civil 'A' Panel. Appointed by the Lord Chancellor as member of the Criminal Procedure Rule Committee from 2004-11. Secretary of the Criminal Bar Association (2008-09). He also sits as a Judge in the Crown Court having been appointed a Recorder in 2012.
Publications: Joint author of 'Preventative Orders: A Practical Guide' (2010).
Personal: Educated at Norwich School and the University of Nottingham.

LIVESEY, Kate
4 Pump Court, London
020 7842 5555
klivesey@4pumpcourt.com
Featured in Professional Negligence (London), Construction (London)
Practice Areas: Common law and commercial litigation/ arbitration, particularly: construction (incl. shipbuilding, offshore construction and energy projects), insurance, professional negligence (incl. accountants, brokers, construction professionals, IFAs, lawyers and valuers) and procedural challenges (conflict/ bias/ jurisdictional/ ECHR). Reported cases include: Browning v Brachers [2005] PNLR 44 & [2004] PNLR 28; P (A Barrister) v Bar Council [2005] 1 WLR 3019; Smith v Kvaerner Cementation Foundations [2007] 1 WLR 370; Sumukan v Commonwealth Secretariat: (2007) 2 Lloyd' s Rep 87(CA – s69 appeal); (2007) 1 Lloyds Rep 370 (Comm) and (2008) 1 Lloyds Rep 40 (CA) (ss67/68 appeal); R ex p. Heather Moor & Edgecomb v FOS (2008) Bus LR 1486 (CA) and FOS v Heather Moor & Edgecomb (2009) 1 All ER 328 (CA) Cooperative Group Ltd v John Allen Associates Ltd (2012) 28 Const LJ 27; Attrill & Ors. v Dresdner Kleinwort Ltd & Commerzbank AG: [2011] IRLR 613 (CA – Part 24); [2012] IRLR 553 (QBD) and [2013] IRLR 548 (CA); Hamid v Francis Bradshaw Partnership [2013] BLR 447; CIP Properties ((AIPT) Ltd v Kone Plc & Ors [2015] BLR 285 (costs budgets) and [2015] 1 All ER (Comm) (stays).
Professional Memberships: BILA, COMBAR, LCLCBA, PNBA, TECBAR, YIAG.
Career: BA Cambridge (Double 1st), Dip. Law (City), called 2001.

LOCKEY, John QC
Essex Court Chambers, London
020 7813 8000
jlockey@essexcourt.com
Featured in Commercial Dispute Resolution (London), Insurance (London)
Practice Areas: John Lockey QC acts as an advocate in complex commercial disputes before the English courts at all levels and in arbitrations in London, in Europe, and worldwide (including Bermuda, Hong Kong and Singapore). His clients include leading financial institutions, accountancy firms, energy companies and insurance and reinsurance companies. He works regularly with leading law firms in England, the US, Hong Kong, Singapore and Bermuda. His experience includes leading multidisciplinary and multinational teams in the most complex of international commercial disputes. His arbitration experience and professional skills also mean that he is often appointed as an arbitrator (LCIA, ARIAS and ad hoc).

LOFTHOUSE, Simon QC
Atkin Chambers, London
020 7404 0102
jwilson@atkinchambers.com
Featured in International Arbitration (London), Professional Negligence (London), Construction (London)
Practice Areas: Simon's practice covers international and domestic arbitration and litigation under numerous legal systems and procedural rules. The types of disputes Simon is retained on frequently involve complex engineering, construction, technology, IT or energy projects. He is particularly noted for acting in those cases requiring the resolution of complex issues of law or the detailed cross examination on technical issues, delay or allegations of professional negligence. The disputes in which he is retained are wide ranging but include those arising out of oil and gas projects, emission abatement processes, software disputes, large commercial and residential developments, M&E works, piling operations onshore and offshore, construction of roads, pipe laying, tunnelling, track installation/repair, pumping stations, coastal defences and effluent, power stations, utilities, chemical plants, and airport terminals. Simon has extensive experience of standard domestic and international construction and engineering contracts. He is also consulted on proposed revisions to standard form contracts. He is also invited to lecture around the world on various topics relating to engineering disputes and their resolution.
Professional Memberships: COMBAR, TECBAR, registered adjudicator. Qualified to appear in the DIFC, Dubai.
Career: LLB (Hons) (Lond). Called to Bar of England and Wales in 1988. Recorder 2003, Silk 2006. Authorised to sit in the TCC Division of the High Court 2015. Advocacy teacher for Gray's Inn. Chair of Professional Conduct Committee of the Bar 2011-2015; Member, Bar Standards Board 2011-2015.

LOMNICKA, Eva
4 New Square, London
020 7822 2000
eva.lomnicka@kcl.ac.uk
Featured in Consumer Law (London), Financial Services (London)
Practice Areas: Advisory work on consumer credit law and financial services regulation, reflecting publications.
Professional Memberships: FSLA (Advisory Board and Treasurer); COMBAR; SLS. Bencher, Middle Temple.
Career: Professor of Law, King's College London. Called to the Bar 1974. Adviser to UK delegation to UNCITRAL convention on receivables financing (1997-2001 Vienna and New York); on DTI's steering group leading to the Consumer Credit Act 2006 (2002-06).
Publications: (1) General Editor, Encyclopaedia of Consumer Credit Law; (2)Author, The Financial Services and Markets Act 2000: An Annotated Guide; (3) Co-editor, Lomnicka and Powell, Encyclopaedia of Financial Services Law; (4) Contributor, Palmer's Company Law (Part 11); (5) Co-author, Modern Banking Law; (6) Co-author, The Law of Security and Title-based Finance; (7) Contributor, Chitty on Contracts (Chap.39); (7) Contributor, Financial Services Law (Chap. 18).
Personal: Born 17 May 1951; 1969-73 Girton College, Cambridge (MA, LLB; Chancellor's Medal). Married with three children.

LOVEDAY, Mark
Tanfield Chambers, London
020 7421 5300
markloveday@tanfieldchambers.co.uk
Featured in Real Estate Litigation (London)
Practice Areas: Property law, with a particular emphasis on enfranchisement, service charges and management, business lease renewal, rent review and arbitration. Notable cases: London Sephardi Trust v John Lyons Estate [2015] UKUT 619 (LC) – leasehold enfranchisement – house – so-called "fourth" basis of assessment under Leasehold Reform Act 1967 s.9(1AA) – valuation of leases which have previously been extended under the Act – Housing and Planning Act 1986 s.23(1); Avon Ground Rents v 51 Earls Court Square RTM Company [2016] UKUT 1221 (LC) – Right to Manage – description of premises in company's articles of association; the linked High Court cases of Greenpine v Howard de Walden and Greenpine v Charles Russell Speechlys [2016] EWHC 1923 (Ch). Non-contentious advice on residential and mixed-use development schemes, service charges and management.
Professional Memberships: Property Bar Association; Chancery Bar Association; Fellow of the Chartered Institute of Arbitrators; Association Leasehold Enfranchisement Practitioners (Advisory Committee member).
Career: Qualified 1986; Judge, First Tier Tribunal (Property Chamber). Barrister of the Year, Property Management Awards 2011-12.
Publications: 'Service Charges & Management' (Sweet & Maxwell); 'Rent Review: A Surveyor's Handbook' (RICS); weekly column on residential property law in 'The Times' newspaper.

LOWE, Mark QC
Cornerstone Barristers, London
07831 205057
markl@cornerstonebarristers.com
Featured in Local Government (London), Planning (London)
Practice Areas: Town and country planning, environment, judicial review and local government law.
Professional Memberships: PEBA, ALBA.
Career: Called 1972; QC 1996. Bencher of Gray's Inn 2003, Assistant Boundary Commissioner, Head of Chambers at 2-3 Gray's Inn Square 2005-10.
Personal: Married to Felicity Parry-Williams. Three adult children. Essex boy of long standing now happily transplanted to North Norfolk and the Barbican.

LOWNDS, Peter
2 Hare Court, London
020 73530667
peterlownds@2harecourt.com
Featured in Crime (London)
Practice Areas: A former Slaughter and May solicitor, Peter is a specialist in defending in complex and serious criminal and disciplinary cases that have frequently made national news. His criminal practice encompasses fraud, terrorism, major drug supply conspiracies and other serious crime. In disciplinary proceedings he acts

for both regulatory bodies and individual practitioners. He regularly presents cases for the National College of Teaching and Leadership and the National Optical Council. He also represents doctors, dentists and police officers. He is currently defending a Russian banker in a major corruption case. His recent cases include defending a teenager alleged to be plotting to make a terrorist bomb, representing a woman charged in a major nationwide Opium supply conspiracy and acting for a man accused in relation to a very serious stabbing incident inside a Mayfair art gallery. Particularly high profile cases include successfully defending a pilot of a helicopter charged with manslaughter and representing a man charged over the prohibition of the publication of images of the murderer of James Bulger.

Professional Memberships: ARDL, CBA, FLA, FSLA, HSLA.

Career: Called 1998 (Grays Inn). Direct Access Course 2010.

LUCAS, Bridget

Fountain Court Chambers, London
020 7583 3335
bl@fountaincourt.co.uk

Featured in Company (London)

Practice Areas: A broad practice spanning commercial and chancery litigation and arbitration. A significant part of her practice relates to offshore litigation with a particular emphasis on company and insolvency proceedings and civil fraud. She is currently appearing in the Cayman litigation relating to Ahmad Hamad Algosaibi and Brothers Company v Saad Investments Company Ltd, and has also advised in various cases in the British Virgin Islands, Guernsey and Jersey. She has acted in limited liability partnership disputes, and shareholder and joint venture disputes (including in the telecoms, and energy sectors). She also advises in relation to various solicitors and financial services regulatory proceedings. Her practice extends to include advising in relation to cross-border merger applications, and insurance business transfer schemes.

Professional Memberships: The Chancery Bar Association; COMBAR; British Insurance Lawyers Association.

Career: Called in 1989. Previously acted as Treasury Panel Counsel acting in Chancery matters.

Personal: Gordonstoun School; Worcester College, Oxford (1987 BA Hons Jurisprudence First Class).

LUMSDON, Kate

23 Essex Street, London
020 7413 0353
katelumsdon@23es.com

Featured in Crime (London)

Practice Areas: Kate Lumsdon is a senior junior of 20 years' call who has practised on the Western Circuit for many years and now works primarily in London. Kate prosecutes for CPS London's Special Casework Unit and the RASSO (Rape and Serious Sexual Offences) Unit in London, Hampshire and Berkshire. She defends serious sexual offences, violence, complex fraud, money laundering, corruption and a wide variety of other offences across the country. In 2011, Kate led for the defence in one of the first prosecutions under the Mental Capacity Act 2005. Her lay client, the owner of a care home, was prosecuted following an investigation by the Care Quality Commission for neglecting her elderly clients, or "service users". Kate has particular experience in dealing with cases involving young children, both as witnesses and as defendants. She has regularly conducted cases with intermediaries, both for prosecution witnesses and for the defendant where disabilities meant that participation in the trial process was otherwise impossible.

Professional Memberships: Middle Temple – Blackstone Scholar, Western Circuit – Wine Treasurer, Criminal Bar Association – Executive Committee Member, Bar Choral Society – Trustee. Advocacy Panels; Western Circuit Grade 4 Prosecutor, CPS London Grade 4 Prosecutor, CPS South East Grade 4 Prosecutor, CPS Rape Panel.

Publications: Archbold Review (August 2011) : "Prosecutors: Beware the Mental Incapacity Act 2005", The Criminal Lawyer – "Venire de Novo".

LYKIARDOPOULOS, Andrew QC

8 New Square, London
020 7405 4321
andrew.lykiardopoulos@8newsquare.co.uk

Featured in Intellectual Property (London)

Practice Areas: Barrister(QC) practising in all areas of intellectual property law. He regularly appears in the High Court, Court of Appeal and at the EPO. He has also been involved in cases both before the UK Supreme Court and the Court of Justice of the EU. He has been described by the legal directories as "indisputably one of the best advocates at the junior IP Bar" and as being "a remarkable advocate with excellent client handling skills". Andrew was awarded "IP Junior of the Year" by Chambers & Partners in 2012. Recent cases include acting for Gilead in recent patent litigation with Idenix over the HCV drug "Sovaldi", acting for ASOS in its trade mark dispute with Assos of Switzerland, and acting for Meltwater in its copyright dispute with the NLA over its news monitoring service.. A full CV is at www.8newsquare.co.uk.

Professional Memberships: Member of the Chancery Bar Association, AIPPI.

Career: 1994-2000:IP solicitor at Bristows, 2000-04: Partner at Bristows, 2004 onwards: called to the bar and practising at 8 New Square. Appointed QC 2014.

LYNCH, Adrian QC

11KBW, London
020 7632 8500
adrian.lynch@11kbw.com

Featured in Employment (London)

Practice Areas: Adrian's work this year has included a lengthy disciplinary investigation for a University (which is highly confidential), representing a multi-national company on an appeal to the EAT in regard to TUPE, advising a FTSE 100 company in relation to voluntary redundancies and age discrimination and a multi-national firm of solicitors about pension and maternity issues as well as being involved in proceedings concerned with the definition of those included within Part 1 of the Pensions Act 2008 see FMSB v The Pensions Regulator. Adrian also represents the Fire Authorities throughout the UK in connection with the claims challenging the recent reforms to firefighters' pensions. Adrian continues to provide advice on equal pay to both public bodies and private concerns.

Professional Memberships: Gray's Inn.

Career: Called to the Bar in 1983 and joined 11KBW in 1984. Took Silk in 2000, prior to which he was a member of the Attorney General's Panel of Junior Counsel (Supplementary Panel). Appointed recorder in 2002. Member of the Equal Opportunities Commission's Panel of Barristers and member of the Employment Panel of the City Disputes Panel's Employment Service.

Publications: As an academic teaching at King's College London between 1971-84, published a number of articles and book reviews, including publications in the 'Law Quarterly Review'. Author of the chapter on settlements in employment law in David Foskett QC's work 'The Law and Practice of Compromise' in the most recent edition of that work.

Personal: Jelf medallist 1971 at King's College, London.

LYNCH, Ben

Fountain Court Chambers, London
020 7583 3335
bjl@fountaincourt.co.uk

Featured in Professional Negligence (London), Commercial Dispute Resolution (London), Insurance (London), Telecommunications (London)

Practice Areas: Commercial Dispute Resolution, Insurance, Professional Negligence and Telecommunications. Recent cases: JRT v RWL [2015] EWHC 1069 (QB), led by Ian Mill QC; major D&O insurance dispute [2015]; PIP breast implant litigation [2015]; Maccaferri v Zurich [2015] EWHC 1708 (Comm), led by Colin Edelman QC; Telco v Telco [2015]: multiple AIT disputes; Insurer v Insurer [2015]: multi million pound year of attachment arbitration; Company v Government [2015]: high-value contract dispute, acting for a government; Godiva v Travelers [2014] high value insurance aggregation dispute, led by Colin Edelman QC; A v B [2014] multi-million pound solicitors' professional indemnity year of attachment arbitration (acting alone); A v B [2014] complicated and high value IFA / Court of Protection professional negligence claim; A and B v X and ... QC [2014] barrister's negligence claim, acting alone for leading QC; BT v Ofcom "Ethernet" case [2013] led by Rhodri Thompson QC, Graham Read QC and Sarah Lee; A v B [2013] large, high-value notification and aggregation case (acting alone); Jordanian energy / insurance dispute [2012] (acting alone); BT v Ofcom "PPC" case [2012] EWCA Civ 1051, led by Christopher Vajda QC, Andrew Burrows QC (Hon) and previously by Graham Read QC; A v 5 Defendants [2011-2012]: complicated insurance brokers' negligence and insurance claim (acting alone); Nouri v. ... (A Firm) [2010] 50 EG 64, Sephton limitation issues: successful on own in Court of Appeal; Flexsys America L.P. v. XL Insurance Company Limited [2010] Lloyd's Rep. IR 132, led by Colin Wynter QC; Telecommunications case [2009] up to £90 million claim, led by Graham Read QC; multi-million pound barristers' negligence claim [2009], led by George Bompas QC; The Welsh Rugby Union Limited v. ... (A Firm) [2007], led by Colin Edelman QC; A v QC [2007] barrister's negligence claim acting for leading QC, led by Andrew Burns; ERC Frankona v. American National [2006] Lloyd Rep IR 157, led by Colin Wynter QC.

Professional Memberships: LCLCBA (committee member), PNBA (committee member), COMBAR, Bar Pro Bono Unit.

Career: Astbury Scholar, Middle Temple. Columbia Law School, LLM (Stone Scholar). Inns of Court School of Law (Very Competent). Balliol College, Oxford, BA (Hons) Law (Top First in College, Paton Scholar). King's College School, Wimbledon.

Publications: MacGillivray on Insurance Law, 13th Edition (2015), second supplement to 12th Edition (2014), first supplement to 12th Edition (2013), 12th Edition (2012) and 2nd Supplement to 11th Edition (2011); "Discriminate without prejudice" (2004) 154 NLJ 1038; "Pleading Fraud: the Insurer's Alternative" (2004) 154 NLJ 502 with Andrew Burns; and "What will happen to the QC Clause in Insurance Contracts if the rank of QC is abolished?" Corporate Counsel Magazine 2003.

Personal: Languages: working French. Interests: family, fly fishing, proper sports, modern art, opera.

LYNCH, Jerome QC

Charter Chambers, London
020 7618 4400
clerks@charterchambers.com

Featured in Crime (London)

Practice Areas: His practice is predominantly defending in serious crime most recently dealing with charges of tax evasion and SFO prosecutions. He specialises in white-collar offences, fraud, corruption, Companies Act breaches, murder "gangland and honour killings" and "terrorist" offences. Important cases include; Roberts (who killed the burglar), Whitehurst (revenge knife attack on a racist), Lim (the Grobbelaar Trial, match fixing), Geoff Knights (Gillian Taylforth's partner) case dismissed on the sole ground of adverse publicity, FA v Segers (alleged bung) and FA v Burtenshaw (alleged bung with George Graham), Brian Brendon Wright (the "laundryman") '£3,500m cocaine importation, 'Arms to Iran', professional assassination of a 'supergrass', the Royal Blackmail case. He has undertaken work in the Cayman, BVI, Turks and Caicos, Bermuda and Ireland. He is currently seconded to Trott & Duncan in Bermuda undertaking a number of important "political" trials in Bermuda and the Caribbean region representing former government ministers. He is registered to receive work by direct access.

Professional Memberships: Called to the Bar in Bermuda, BVI, TCI, Cayman. CBA, Bencher of Lincoln's Inn. Hon. Fellow UCLAN.

Career: University of Lancashire, BA(Hons). Silk 2000. Cloisters Chambers 1983 – 2000 Charter Chambers 2000 – date Trott and Duncan (seconded) 2014 – date He is a senior advocacy trainer for Lincoln's Inn.

Personal: Television: Channel 4 – two eight-part series of 'Nothing But The Truth' – moral questions set against a court room scene; 'Crime Team' a team of investigators are set the task of solving real murders in the 19th century; Judge in People's Court (ITV1); Roy Marsden's Incident Room (ITV West); cameo roles for Sky and other newsrooms. Recently involved in a film "The All Together" starring Danny Dyer and Martin Freeman and has produced other ventures. His current interests include, hiking (slowly), skiing (speedily), golf (badly) and wine (copiously).

MACDONALD, Alison
Matrix Chambers, London
020 7404 3447
alisonmacdonald@matrixlaw.co.uk
Featured in Administrative & Public Law (London), Crime (London), Police Law (All Circuits), Civil Liberties & Human Rights (London), Public International Law (London)

Practice Areas: Alison is a barrister at Matrix Chambers, London, practicing in domestic and international courts and tribunals. She specialises in public international law, international arbitration, public law and criminal law. She has extensive international arbitration experience, including both advocacy and advisory work: she is instructed as counsel in a number of ongoing ICSID arbitrations and annulment proceedings, and has advised governments, companies and individuals on arbitration, environmental and trade law matters. She has also acted as counsel in a number of significant inter-State disputes, including proceedings under the United Nations Convention on the Law of the Sea between Ireland and the United Kingdom, Mauritius and the United Kingdom, and Ghana and Cote d'Ivoire. She has a particular interest in the intersection between international arbitration and public international law. Alison also appears regularly in the English courts, including in cases with a criminal dimension, and has extensive experience of cross-border criminal investigations and prosecutions, and international judicial assistance. She is experienced in issues of fraud, corruption, money-laundering, and their domestic and international law consequences. She represented Argentina in the corruption-related annulment proceedings in Siemens v Argentina. Alison has been named as one of the 'future stars of the Bar' by The Times, and alongside her work at the Bar, was a fellow of All Souls College, Oxford from 1999-2006.

Publications: Co-author of Human Rights and Criminal Justice (with Professor Andrew Ashworth and Ben Emmerson QC); co-author of Prison Law (with Tim Owen QC); contributor to The Law of State Immunity (with Lady Hazel Fox QC and Philippa Webb).

MACDONALD, James
One Essex Court, London
020 7831 8441
jmacdonald@oeclaw.co.uk
Featured in Banking & Finance (London), Commercial Dispute Resolution (London)

Practice Areas: Regularly instructed in major commercial disputes, often with a banking aspect to them. Substantial experience of investment and retail banking. Recent instructions include: a US$8bn Commercial Court claim relating to FX derivatives and prime brokerage, a substantial LIBOR/EURIBOR claim, a claim involving credit ratings for structured notes; a $200m LCIA arbitration; a $160m Appeal relating to commodity derivatives (SCB v CPC); a major application in the Lehmans insolvency (Excalibur No. 1 Plc v LB Refinancing No. 3 Ltd); and the substantial claim brought by Centrica against Accenture in relation to the British Gas customer billing system. Past instructions include JP Morgan v Springwell (a $700m claim brought against JP Morgan for allegedly negligent investment advice); ALS v Honeywell (a £3.5 billion claim in relation to a failed automotive development project); and involvement in aspects of the "bank charges" litigation.

Professional Memberships: COMBAR, Inner Temple.

Career: Called to the bar in 2005.

Publications: Contributor to Butterworths Journal of International Banking and Financial Law; Paget (forthcoming).

Personal: Educated Magdalen College, Oxford. Interests include music, cooking and cricket.

MACEY-DARE, Thomas
Quadrant Chambers, London
020 7583 4444
thomas.macey-dare@quadrantchambers.com
Featured in Shipping (London)

Practice Areas: Tom Macey-Dare practices commercial law, with a particular focus on shipping, international trade and insurance. His main areas of specialism are charterparties, commodities, collisions, salvage, cross-border insolvency, civil fraud, international arbitration, general commercial litigation, offshore energy, marine and non-marine insurance, banking and finance, freezing injunctions, jurisdictional disputes and conflict of laws. He is adept at handling cases involving technically complex subject-matter, including issues of navigation, seamanship and engineering. He has particular experience of freezing injunctions (including Chabra injunctions), anti-suit injunctions and other forms of urgent interlocutory relief. Recent reported cases include The "Atlantik Confidence" [2014] EWCA Civ 217, [2014] 1 WLR 3883, [2014] 1 All ER (Comm) 909, [2014] 1 Lloyd's Rep 586, [2014] CP Rep 28, [2014] 1 CLC 293, 2014 AMC 686; Transgrain Shipping BV v Deiulemar Shipping SpA (in liquidation) [2014] EWHC 4202 (Comm), [2015] 1 Lloyd's Rep. 461

Professional Memberships: COMBAR, LCLCBA, NYSBA. Admitted as an Attorney and Counselor at law in New York.

Career: MA (Cantab) 1990, LLM (Cantab) 1991, LLM (Cornell) 1992. Called 1994 (Middle Temple), admitted in New York 1995. Middle Temple Advocacy Faculty.

Publications: Atkin's Court Forms: Insurance (1996) and Arbitration (1998-2016). Contributor to Butterworth's Commercial Court and Arbitration Pleadings (2005), Marsden and Gault on Collisions at Sea (2016).

Personal: Married with 4 children. Lives in Dulwich. Working knowledge of French, and basic German. Occasional player for the King's Bench Walk Cricket Club.

MACHELL, John QC
Serle Court, London
020 7242 6105
jmachell@serlecourt.co.uk
Featured in Chancery (London), Commercial Dispute Resolution (London), Partnership (London)

Practice Areas: General commercial/chancery dispute resolution and advisory work, particularly partnership, LLPs, trusts, fraud, company and insolvency.

Professional Memberships: Association of Partnership Practitioners, Chancery Bar Association.

Career: University of Southampton 1988-92 LLB (1st Class). Serle Court (formerly 13 Old Square) 1994 to date. QC 2012.

Publications: 'The Law of Limited Liability Partnerships' (2016) Bloomsbury Professional.

Personal: Married with two children.

MACKAY, Ian QC
Compass Chambers, Edinburgh
0131 226 5071
ian.mackay@compasschambers.com
Featured in Personal Injury (Scotland)

Practice Areas: Ian has a wide experience in many areas of civil litigation. He specialises in property damage, professional negligence (including medical negligence) and personal injury work in which he is instructed on behalf of both Pursuers and Defenders through Insurers, Loss Adjusters, Local Authorities and Trade Unions. He has appeared in the House of Lords in seven cases. He regularly appears in the Court of Session and Sheriff Court. He has particular expertise in catastrophic injury claims, including head and spinal injury cases, claims in respect of industrial diseases, psychiatric injury and fatal claims. Recent Cases include: Martin Wilson v North Lanarkshire Council [2014] CSIH 26 – for the defenders and respondents – personal injury, role of the Inner House, onus of proof regarding causation, pursuer's appeal refused. Smith v Webster : Lord Pentland (10/03/15) – for the defenders – RTA, catastrophic injury, motorcyclist, apportionment of liability, 50/50. Claire Anderson v Brig Brae Garage: Lady Stacy – Jury Trial (23/06/15) – for the pursuer, fatal accident, widow awarded record damages for loss of her husband. Tracey Kennedy v Cordia (Services) LLP [2016] SLT 209, 2016 WLR (D) 74 – for the pursuer and appellant in the Supreme Court – personal injury, home carer, fall on ice while travelling between clients, statutory duties and common law duties of employer, role of skilled witness – pursuer's appeal allowed. Graham v The Earl of Roseberry – Lord Turnbull (14/06/16) – for the defenders – personal injury – workplace stress – harassment by fellow employees – case abandoned by pursuer. Raymond Considine v Glasgow University Sports Association (12/01/16) – for the pursuer – first case in UK involving sports injury due to alleged dangers arising from non-standard playing surface – case settled with payment of damages.

Professional Memberships: Chairman of the Faculty of Advocates Personal Injury Law Group – 2001 to date.

MACLEAN, Niall
12 King's Bench Walk, London
020 7583 0811
maclean@12kbw.co.uk
Featured in Personal Injury (London)

Practice Areas: High value and complex personal injury and clinical negligence work: fatalities and injuries of the utmost severity; brain and spinal damage; pain syndromes; psychiatric conditions; and intentional torts (including historic abuse cases). Extensive court experience and an excellent track record at JSMs and mediations. Appointed in 2015 to the Attorney General's C Panel of Junior Counsel to the Crown, a select group of barristers who undertake civil work on behalf of the government. Niall also has a busy industrial disease practice, acting predominantly for claimants in asbestos cases and defendants in deafness work. Niall's appellate practice is growing rapidly. In 2016 he appeared in the Supreme Court (led) for the successful appellant in Knauer v MOJ and in the Court of Appeal (unled) for the successful respondent in Scott v Gavigan. Niall has considerable experience in cases involving allegations of exaggeration and malingering. He also has vast experience of motor insurance fraud work, and has defeated numerous fraudulent claims at trial. Niall is also interested in professional (particularly solicitors') negligence work, nuisance and property damage, costs, and limitation issues.

Professional Memberships: PIBA, PNBA, LCLCBA.

Personal: B.Phil. and D.Phil, University of Oxford MA (first class honours), University of Glasgow.

MACNEILL, Calum H S QC
Westwater Advocates, Edinburgh
07801 257878
calum.macneill@westwateradvocates.com
Featured in Employment (Scotland), Commercial Dispute Resolution (Scotland)

Practice Areas: Calum MacNeill QC has a busy practice in commercial litigation, building and construction, professional (including medical) negligence and employment law. As a senior his practice has developed from these core areas to include equality law, civil recovery of the proceeds of crime, disciplinary hearings and professional regulatory work. Active as a mediator in commerical conflicts. Participant in the Faculty of Advocates Dispute Resolution Service. Legal member of the Police Appeals Tribunal. Teaches advocacy skills within the Faculty and externally. Member of the Chartered Institute of Arbitrators.

Career: Called to the Bar in 1992. Advocate depute 1998-2001. Standing Junior to the Scottish Ministers 2003-06. Took Silk in 2007. MCIArb 2014.

Personal: Educated at Robert Gordon's College, Aberdeen. University of Aberdeen – LLB (Hons) 1985, Dip LP 1986.

MADGE-WYLD, Sam
Arden Chambers, London
020 7242 4244
sam.madge-wyld@ardenchambers.com
Featured in Social Housing (London)

Practice Areas: Housing, residential and commercial landlord and tenant, property, local government law. He acts for private landlords, tenants/applicants, local authorities and housing associations.

Professional Memberships: Administrative Law Bar Association, Housing Law Practitioners Association and Property Bar Association.

Career: Sam Madge-Wyld's noteworthy cases include Mohamoud v RBKC [2015] EWCA Civ 780 [2016] P.T.S.R. 289; Birmingham City Council v Merali & others [2015] EWCA Civ 49 [2016] QB 455; R (Enfield LBC) v Enfield CCG & Others [2013] EWHC 3496 (Admin); Birmingham CC v Lloyd [2012] EWCA Civ 969 [2012] HLR 44, R (W) v Birmingham CC [2011] EWHC 1147 (Admin); (2011) 14 CCL Rep 516 and R (H) v Birmingham CC [2010] EWHC 3752 (Admin).

Publications: Co-author of Defending Possession Proceedings (8th Edn, forthcoming 2016), Quiet Enjoyment (7th Edn, 2012) and Housing Law Casebook (6th Edn, 2015). Contributor (2014-) to Encyclopedia of Local Government Law (Sweet and Maxwell). Assistant Editor (2012-) of Local Government Finance: Law and Practice (Sweet and

Maxwell). Articles published in the Landlord and Tenant Review, New Law Journal, Solicitor's Journal, LAG, Inside Housing, Judicial Review, Journal of Housing Law and Local Government Lawyer.

MAGUIRE, Benn
QEB Hollis Whiteman, London
020 7933 8855
benn.maguire@qebhw.co.uk
Featured in Crime (London)

Practice Areas: Benn Maguire is widely regarded as one of the most formidable criminal advocates currently practising at the Criminal Bar. He is 'fearless and charismatic', 'statesman-like on his feet' and 'comes up with ingenious arguments that work'. His practice encompasses a broad spectrum of high profile and complex defence matters (he has been nominated for the award of 'Barrister of the Year' and attained the highest grade for an advocate – grade 4). Benn's exceptional strategic insight secured an acquittal in the trial of Clive Goodman (Royal Editor at the News of the World). Mr Goodman pursued a cut-throat defence against Andy Coulson (former News of the World Editor and Press Secretary to Prime Minister, David Cameron) in the 'Hacking' trial including Rebekah Brooks. He also advised Mr Goodman during the Leveson Inquiry. Benn has successfully defended Simon Cowell (music mogul), Donna Air (TV personality), Linford Christie (Olympic gold medal winner), Asad Ahmad (BBC newsreader re allegations made by Thea Rogers – Chancellor George Osborne's personal advisor) and Marco Pierre White Jnr. He has advised Sir Elton John, the Lawn Tennis Association, the Sun newspaper (re Madeline McCann and Mark Saunders – barrister shot by the police), Saracens Rugby Club and Channel 4 (re allegations of Outraging Public Decency during filming of a 'shock' television programme). Benn is currently advising a Russian Oligarch re an SFO investigation and a corporate re a 'pension liberation' investigation. He represented James McCormick re the multi-jurisdiction fraud trial for selling 'magic' bomb detection devices (the value of the fraud was in excess of £100,000,000). He recently represented an alleged fraudster in a £140,000,000 'vishing' fraud. Benn successfully argued that it was an abuse of process to try a retired headmaster (from a leading public school) re historic allegations of historic sex crimes. He also secured the acquittal of a 'Blues and Royals' soldier who was charged with a homicide offence. Benn has recently assisted re advocacy trials in foreign jurisdictions. Benn has successfully appealed numerous matters in the Court of Appeal and the House of Lords (Supreme Court) – where he did not appear at the original trial. As a prosecutor, Benn prosecuted Abu Hamza's son for public disorder offences and for instigating racial hatred during a politico-religious demonstration.
Professional Memberships: Member of the British Association of Sports Law Member of the Criminal Bar Association Registered with the Bar Council – Public Access Directory Member of the Public Access Bar Association – PABA.
Personal: Languages – French.

MAHMOOD, Abid
No5 Chambers, Birmingham
07970 293783
ama@no5.com
Featured in Immigration (Midlands)

Practice Areas: Abid Mahmood is an administrative and public law specialist with over twenty years of practice at the Bar. He sits as a Recorder in the Crown and County Court (civil and family) and also as a Deputy Upper Tribunal Judge. He is sought after and instructed nationally by local authorities, public bodies, individuals and others covering a wide range of work including Court of Protection, commercial law, immigration, business immigration, family law, data protection, disclosure, judicial review and human rights. He has appeared in many reported cases at the Upper Tribunal, High Court and Court of Appeal. He has also appeared in various Supreme Court cases, most recently as lead counsel in a successful appeal relating to the Government's Points Based System.

MALCOLM, Alastair R QC
Drystone Chambers, London
020 7404 1881
alastair.malcolm@drystone.com
Featured in Crime (Western)

Practice Areas: Serious crime, fraud, financial regulatory law.
Professional Memberships: Member of the Inner Temple, Western Circuit, CBA and Temporary Member of the Cayman Islands Bar (2000, 2003-06 and 2008-13).
Career: Alastair Malcolm's practice covers every aspect of serious crime, from murder to fraud via serious sexual offences and armed robberies. Having started his career on the Western circuit, Alastair's reputation has grown to the extent that he is now instructed to appear in courts around the country and as far afield internationally as the Caribbean. He has considerable experience in Financial crime having been for 9 years a junior standing counsel for the Inland Revenue appearing in cases involving the whole range of Revenue Offences including complicated tax evasion schemes. In silk he has appeared in many fraud cases including successfully defending in a US$350 million money laundering case in the Cayman Islands. He has been involved at first instance and in the Court of Appeal in numerous confiscation and proceeds of crime cases. He regularly appears in homicide cases and has particular experience in "baby shaking" cases In 2014/15 he successfully defended in cases alleging joint-enterprise murder by juveniles (Cambridge and Lincoln Crown Courts), murder of a child by shaking (Exeter), and gross negligence manslaughter (Truro).

MALCOLM, Kirsty
Westwater Advocates, Edinburgh
0131 260 5700
kirsty.malcolm@westwateradvocates.com
Featured in Family/Matrimonial (Scotland)

Practice Areas: Family law with a particular focus on financial provision on divorce and cohabitation. Reported cases include: Clarkson v Clarkson 2008 S.L.T. (Sh Ct) 2 [financial provision on divorce– setting aside agreement]; B v B 2009 S.L.T. (Sh Ct) 249 [jurisdiction]; Simpson v Downie 2011 Fam L.R. 145 [cohabitation- time bar]; Murdoch v Murdoch 2012 S.C. 271 [financial provision on divorce – competency issues]; City of Edinburgh Council v C 2012 Fam LR 132 [permanence order with authority to adopt]; Gow v Grant 2011 S.C. 618 and 2013 SC (U.K.S.C) 1 [cohabitation- statutory interpretation]; Kerr v Mangan 2013 Fam LR 38 [cohabitation- claim on death re foreign property]; H's Guardian v H 2013 SLT (Sh Ct) 31 [divorce, Adult with Incapacity]; Cameron v Lukes 2014 GWD 7-144 [cohabitation – appeal]; Douglas v Bell 2014 Fam LR 2 [cohabitation – relevancy and time bar]; McIntyre v Stewart 2014 Fam LR 7 [cohabitation – pleadings and time bar]; Saunders v Martin 2014 Fam LR 86 [cohabitation]; McDonald v McDonald 2015 SLT 587 [pensions on divorce – statutory interpretation]; Harley v Thompson 2015 Fam LR 45 [cohabitation]; City of Edinburgh Council v S 2015 SLT (Sh Ct) 69 [forced marriage protection orders]; S v S 2015 Fam LR 37[divorce- date of separation]; H v H 2015 GWD 19-318 [relocation]; Melvin v Christie 2016 Fam LR [cohabitation].
Professional Memberships: Treasurer Advocates Family Law Association, Faculty of Advocates Family Law Reform Sub Committee; Family Law Arbitration Group Scotland (FLAGS).
Career: Solicitor in private practice 1989 – 2006 specialising in Family Law. Called to Bar June 2007.
Publications: Cohabitation (2nd edition) Thomson/W.Green [2011]; Editor Litigation Styles Lexis Nexis/Butterworths Scottish Family Law Service 2007-present.
Personal: LLB (Hons) Aberdeen; Dip LP, Glasgow. Glasgow University Senior tutor/ Course Designer, for Diploma in Legal Practice, Family Law Elective – 2010/11. Accredited Arbitrator in Family Law.

MALLALIEU, Roger
4 New Square, London
020 7822 2000
r.mallalieu@4NewSquare.com
Featured in Costs Litigation (All Circuits)

Practice Areas: Costs and civil procedure, professional negligence (including clinical negligence), solicitors regulatory, commercial.
Professional Memberships: LCBA.
Career: Roger's practice focuses primarily on all aspects of costs and technical civil procedure issues and more generally on solicitors' professional conduct matters. He has appeared in many of the leading cases, including Mitchell v NGN and Coventry v Lawrence and is instructed regular in complex and high value costs cases, including in High Court, Court of Appeal and Supreme Court appeals in a range of technical issues. He was counsel for the successful party in the recent case of Bolt Burdon v Tariq, the leading case on non contentious / contingency fee arrangements. He has considerable experience of all aspects of costs law, including solicitor-client costs, group litigation, the costs of office holders, the drafting of agreements and general between the parties costs and in civil procedure rule issues including in relation to relief from sanction, Part 36 and similar matters. He also is instructed in wider cases concerning solicitor's duties, including in professional negligence matters, disciplinary cases and cases concerning the duties of professional deputies.
Publications: Roger is co-author of the White Book supplement 'Costs and Funding Following the Civil Justice Reforms'. Roger is a regular contributor to a range of publications and regular speaker at major conferences on costs, funding reforms and related issues.

MALYNICZ, Simon QC
Three New Square, London
020 7405 1111
clerks@3newsquare.co.uk
Featured in Intellectual Property (London), Media & Entertainment (London)

Practice Areas: Specialising in all aspects of intellectual property law including trade marks and passing off, registered and unregistered designs, copyright, IT/software, media/entertainment and contractual disputes, confidential information, trade secrets and patents. Recent cases include: Glaxo Wellcome v Sandoz, Interflora v M&S, Comic Enterprises v Fox, Nestle v Cadbury (Colour Purple), Cadbury v Nestle (Kit Kat), Lush v Amazon, Enterprise v Europcar, Zee v Zeebox, Total v YouView, IP Translator, SAS Institute, Specsavers, Copydan, Football Dataco. For a full list of recent and reported cases: see www.3newsquare.co.uk/html/simonmalynicz.html.
Professional Memberships: IPBA, ChBA, ITMA, TIPLO, Bar Pro Bono Unit, IP Inclusive.
Career: Appointed QC in 2016; Junior Counsel to the Crown (A Panel) 2014-2016; Junior Counsel to the Crown (B Panel) 2008-2013. BA (Sydney) LLB Hons (Lond.) MA (New School, NY). First class honours in law.
Publications: Joint author "Gurry on Breach of Confidence" 2012, OUP. Joint author of previous editions of "IP In Europe", Sweet & Maxwell, and "Modern Law of Trade Marks", Butterworths.

MANLEY, David QC
Kings Chambers, Manchester
0345 034 3444
clerks@kingschambers.com
Featured in Environment (Northern), Planning (Northern)

Practice Areas: Planning; environmental law; law of commons, highways and compulsory purchase. Appears on a weekly basis as an Advocate at Public Inquiries in respect of a very broad range of planning and environmental issues including renewable energy projects; strategic and local housing development; waste and rendering issues. Adviser to British Nuclear Fuels. David regularly sits as an Inspector on town/village green issues as well as a representative of landowner and interest groups. He appears in the High Court regularly in respect of judicial review matters. His client base comprises a broad range of nationally known companies.
Professional Memberships: Planning and Environmental Bar Association; UK Environmental Law Association.
Career: Leeds University BA (Hons). Called 1981 (Inner Temple. Head of Planning in Chambers).

MANNING, Colin
Littleton Chambers, London
020 7797 8600
cmanning@littletonchambers.co.uk
Featured in Mediators (All Circuits)

Practice Areas: Mediator in general commercial and business law disputes, specialising in commercial contract, professional negligence, media and entertainment, employment, company shareholder, partnership, construction, landlord and tenant and general property disputes, probate and computer litigation (involving the supply and implementation of computer systems,

networking and associated intellectual property rights).
Professional Memberships: COMBAR, London Common Law and Commercial Bar Association. CEDR accredited mediator. Fellow of the Chartered Institute of Arbitrators. Chair of the Bar Council ADR Panel. Member of the Advisory committee of the Civil Mediation Council.
Career: Called to the Bar, Gray's Inn, 1970; CEDR accredited mediator, 1997; Fellow of the Chartered Institute of Arbitrators, 2001, Recorder, 2000-2015; Bencher, Gray's Inn, 2003; Chair of the Bar Council ADR Panel, 2012 to date, Member of the Advisory Committee of the Civil Mediation Council. Mediation and advocacy trainer. Publications: Main contributor to "Civil Appeals, Practice and Procedure". Personal: Educated at University College London (LLB Honours).

MANNING, Jonathan
Arden Chambers, London
020 7242 4244
jonathan.manning@ardenchambers.com
Featured in Local Government (London), Social Housing (London), Social Housing (Midlands)
Practice Areas: All aspects of local government and public law (including human rights and equality issues), housing (public/social, private), landlord and tenant, anti-social behaviour. Registered for public and licensed access.
Professional Memberships: HLPA; SHLA; ALBA.
Career: Called 1989. Founder member, Arden Chambers. Advises, represents, trains public and private sector clients including local authorities, PRPs, leaseholders, tenants and applicants. Recent work includes advising on local government service reduction proposals, charges for special police services, additional and selective licensing schemes, gang injunctions, shared-ownership leases, service charges, council tax reduction schemes and housing benefit decision-making. Notable recent cases include: judicial review of a local authority's local offer and policy for provision for child with ASD (Pt 3, Children and Families Act 2014); Solihull MBC v Persons Unknown, August 2016, (High Court borough-wide injunction against car-cruisers; Birmingham CC v SS and SA, Court of Appeal July 2016, judgment awaited (how local benefit authorities may restrict rent for exempt accommodation) McDonald v McDonald [2016] UKSC 28 (Whether art 8 provides a defence to private possession claim – for RLA who intervened in writing); Tompkins v Wandsworth LBC [2015] EWCA Civ 846 (status of tenancy granted to homeless applicants); R (SG) v SSWP [2015] UKSC 16 (benefit cap challenge for Shelter as intervener); R (Croydon Property Forum) v Croydon LBC [2015] EWHC 2403 (Admin); R (Rotherham Action Group) v Rotherham MBC [2015] EWHC 1216 (Admin); R (Regas) v Enfield LBC [2014] EWHC 4173 (Admin) (challenges to selective licensing schemes); Beech v Birmingham CC [2014] EWCA Civ 830 (tenant's NTQ, undue influence, need for mental capacity assessment); Birmingham CC v Rafiq (2014, Birmingham County Court – 9-handed gang injunction concerning two factions of a drugs and firearms gang); R (MA) v SSWP [2013] EWHC 2213 ("bedroom tax" challenge – for Shelter and Birmingham CC as Intervener/Interested Party); Birmingham CC v James [2013] EWCA Civ 552 (gang injunctions, human rights); R (Buckley) v Sheffield CC [2013] EWHC 512 (Admin) (council tax reduction schemes, consultation, PSED); Birmingham CC v Lloyd [2012] EWCA Civ 969, Corby BC v Scott [2012] EWCA Civ 276, Birmingham CC v Frisby (heard with Hounslow LBC v Powell) [2011] UKSC 8, Manchester CC v Pinnock [2010] UKSC 45(art.8 defences, possession claims).
Publications: Co-author: various, including 'Local Government Constitutional and Administrative Law', Sweet & Maxwell 2007. Author: Judicial Review Proceedings: A Practitioner's Guide, 4th ed, LAG 2016 forthcoming.

MANSELL, Jason
QEB Hollis Whiteman, London
020 7933 8855
jason.mansell@qebhw.co.uk
Featured in Financial Services (London), Financial Crime (London)
Practice Areas: Jason provides strategic advice and representation to firms and individuals facing investigation and potential criminal prosecution by the SFO and prosecution and/or disciplinary action by FCA and other regulatory bodies including the FRC. A formidable advocate, Jason has acted for firms and individuals in connection with over 85 FCA/FSA regulatory investigations and associated proceedings. He also acts for individuals and corporates in some of the more high profile and complex criminal prosecutions. Many of his cases result in no formal public action. Jason is currently acting for two individuals in connection with investigations by the SFO and FCA in relation to the alleged manipulation of LIBOR, a PLC Bank and an individual in connection with FOREX as well as numerous FCA investigations and proceedings for market abuse and breaches of FCA Rules and Principles. Past cases include FCA-v-Koutsogiannis (LIBOR investigation with no action taken), FCA-v-Moorhouse Group, FCA-v-Capital Alternatives Limited (Court of Appeal), FCA-v-X Plc (listing rules investigation with no action taken). He also recently persuaded the RDC not to issue a Decision Notice against a CEO facing prohibition. Previous criminal instructions include R-v-Whelan (market manipulation), R-v-Norton Healthcare (price fixing) and Operation Tabernula (insider dealing). Jason also advises firms on compliance issues under anti-money laundering and anti-bribery legislation.
Professional Memberships: International Bar Association, Association of Regulatory and Disciplinary Lawyers, Financial Services Lawyers Association.
Career: Called 1991, Lincoln's Inn.

MANSFIELD, Gavin QC
Littleton Chambers, London
020 7797 8600
ghm@littletonchambers.co.uk
Featured in Employment (London)
Practice Areas: Employment, discrimination law and commercial litigation, principally involving the commercial aspects of the employment relationship. Areas of practice include team moves, contractual disputes (wrongful dismissal, bonus claims, restrictive covenants and garden leave), breach of confidence and fiduciary duties, all aspects of statutory employment law, partnership disputes, shareholder and joint venture disputes. Recent significant cases include Willis Ltd. v Jardine Lloyd Thompson [2015] EWCA Civ 450 UK Power Reserve Ltd. v Read [2014] EWHC 66 Ch, Baker Tilly UK Holdings Ltd. v Clough [2013] EWHC 3616 QB, 3616 Spaceright v Baillavoine [2012] IRLR ICR 520 CA, Caterpillar Logistics Services Ltd. v Huesa de Crean [2012] IRLR 410 CA.
Professional Memberships: Employment Law Bar Association (Chairman), Employment Lawyers Association, Industrial Law Society, COMBAR.
Career: Called 1992 (Middle Temple). QC 2013. Regular lecturer and writer on employment law topics.
Publications: Editor of Blackstone's 'Employment Law Practice'; contributor to Brearley & Bloch "Employment Covenants and Confidential Information" (3ed 2009); 'Essential Facts: Disability Discrimination for Providers of Goods, Facilities and service' (2003).
Personal: Education Nottingham High School; Jesus College, Cambridge.

MARKHAM, Anna
4 Stone Buildings, London
a.markham@4stonebuildings.com
Featured in Restructuring/Insolvency (London)
Practice Areas: Anna Markham is a specialist in the fields of company, commercial, financial services and insolvency law, with a busy caseload of litigation and advisory work. She has conducted a wide range of cases including commercial, banking and investor litigation, shareholder disputes and claims by and against officeholders. She also has particular expertise – as a former member of the Attorney General's civil panel of Counsel (2002-2009) – in conducting insolvency-related litigation for and against Government departments (including public interest winding-up petitions and disqualification proceedings). A sophisticated and hard-hitting advocate, Anna is known for her outstanding grasp of the technical detail, underpinned by her previous training as a chartered accountant at Arthur Andersen.
Professional Memberships: ACA, 1995. ADR Group accredited civil & commercial mediator, 2013. Member of the Commercial Bar Association. Member (and, since July 2016, Treasurer) of the Chancery Bar Association.
Publications: Anna has contributed to Annotated Companies Legislation (3rd edition, Oxford University Press, 2013) and Butterworths Practical Insolvency. She is one of the authors of the forthcoming 4th edition of Walters & Davis-White on Directors' Disqualification & Insolvency Restrictions (Sweet & Maxwell), and is a regular contributor to Practical Law Corporate.
Personal: MA (Oxon): Philosophy, Politics & Economics; Dip.Law, City University; Scholar of Lincoln's Inn and of Worcester College, Oxford.

MARKS, Lewis QC
Queen Elizabeth Building QEB, London
020 7797 7837
l.marks@qeb.co.uk
Featured in Family/Matrimonial (London)
Practice Areas: Specialist in big-money financial provision and international family law, and has appeared in many of the leading authorities. Reported cases include: Z v Z and Others [2016] EWHC 1720 (Fam); Beshavora v Berezovsky [2016] EWCA Civ 161; Fields [2015] EWHC 1670 (Fam); Cooper-Hohn v Hohn [2014] EWHC 4122 (Fam); Thiry [2014] EWHC 4046 (Fam); Luckwell v Limata [2014] EWHC 502 (Fam); B v B [2013] EWHC 1232 (Fam); Y v Y [2012] EWHC 2063 (Fam); WF v HF [2012] 2 FLR 1212 (Fam); Z v Z (No.2) (Financial Remedy: Marriage Contract) [2012] 1 FLR 1100; W V W (Divorce Proceedings) [2011] 1 FLR 372; H v H [2010]1 FLR 1864; Marano [2010] 1 FLR 1903; M v M (Costs) [2010] 1 FLR 256; Spencer [2009] 2 FLR 1416; P v P [2008] 2 FLR 1135; Moore [2007] 2 FLR 339; H v H [2007] 2 FLR 548; Sorrell [2006] 1 FLR 497; Miller [2006] 1 FLR 151; Wermuth (No.2) [2003] 1 FLR 1029; Pearce [2003] 2 FLR 1144; GW v RW [2003] 2 FLR 108; White [2000] 2 FLR 981.
Professional Memberships: Family Law Bar Association; elected as Fellow of the International Academy of Matrimonial Lawyers in 2004.
Career: Educated BNC, Oxford (BA Juris). Called 1984, Silk 2002. Head of Chambers since 2010.
Publications: Editorial Board of FLBA publication 'At A Glance' from 1996 – present. Occasional contributor to Family Law and other journals, and frequent speaker at conferences and seminars.
Personal: Born 1961, married with four (adult) sons. Enjoys eating, walking, jazz, country and western music, watching cricket and musicals, but not necessarily simultaneously or in that order.

MARQUAND, Charles
4 Stone Buildings, London
020 7242 5524
c.marquand@4stonebuildings.com
Featured in Financial Services (London)
Practice Areas: Financial services (including insurance and banking) UK and EU, disciplinary tribunals, arbitrations, mediations. Well-known as a specialist advising on complex financial services related issues. Additionally advises overseas governments on financial services matters. Also undertakes contentious work. Notable cases – Clarion Ltd v NPI (fax switching); Needler Financial Services v Taber (pensions reviews test case), FSA v Anderson, Peacock & Pruthi (deposit taking, collective investment scheme); notable cases before the Regulatory Decisions Committee and the Financial Services & Markets Tribunal: Williams Life, Pension & Mortgage Services v FSA (whether variation of permission 'necessary'), Eurosure Investment Services Ltd. v FSA (whether exercise of FSA's own-initiative power 'proportionate'); FSA v Pace Microtechnology (breach of listing rules), FSA v Evolution Beeson Gregory (market abuse; short selling). Company/commercial; notable cases – Tequila Cuervo v Diageo plc (English company law issues arising in Texas litigation); PNC Telecom plc v Thomas (members requisition for EGM); Saudi Arabian Monetary Agency v Dresdner Bank AG (equitable set-off against bank account).
Professional Memberships: Chancery Bar Association; COMBAR; Association of Regulatory and Disciplinary Lawyers; Chartered Arbitrator, Accredited Mediator; Bar of Northern Ireland. Arbitrator for London Metal Exchange. Arbitrator for Minor Metals Trade Association.
Career: Called 1987. Practised at chambers of JJ Rowe QC. 1993-96: legal adviser at HM Treasury dealing with wide range of financial services issues and related areas (company/commercial), drafting legislation (Public

Offers of Securities Regulations, investment advertisement exemptions, CREST), negotiating EU directives. 1996: returned to the Bar.
Publications: Author of articles on financial services topics; Contributor – OUP – Annoted Companies Legislation. Contributor – Sweet & Maxwell – Civil Appeals. Lectures on financial services to universities, solicitors, conferences.
Personal: MA (Oxon), MA Law (City).

MARRIN, John QC
Keating Chambers, London
020 7544 2600
jmarrin@keatingchambers.com
Featured in Professional Negligence (London), Construction (London), International Arbitration (London)
Practice Areas: Queen's Counsel and Arbitrator with over 35 years' experience as a specialist in construction, engineering, energy, technology and software sectors as well as disputes arising from PFI projects and from the rail industry. As Counsel appears principally in the UK High Court, Court of Appeal and before various global arbitral tribunals. As an advocate, he is "measured and thorough" and "his ability to forecast the way a case is going to go is second to none" (Chambers and Partners). An accomplished arbitrator with "an aura of enormous authority whether it be as adjudicator, arbitrator or mediator" and "excellent technical ability" (Chambers & Partners). Appointed regularly as chairman and tribunal member, by the ICC and centres such as the DIAC, the SIAC and the LCIA, and under UNCITRAL rules. Globally recognised authority on the analysis of delay claims.
Professional Memberships: LCLCBA; Society of Construction Law; Commercial Bar Association; TECBAR; London Court of International Arbitration; HKIAC Panel of Arbitrators.
Career: Call 1974; Queen's Counsel 1990; Deputy High Court Judge 2008-2014; Fellow, Chartered Institute of Arbitrators (FCIArb); Bencher of the Inner Temple; CEDR Accredited Mediator. Head of Keating Chambers 2005 to 2010.

MARSHALL, Philip QC
1 King's Bench Walk, London
020 7936 1500
pmarshall@1kbw.co.uk
Featured in Family/Matrimonial (London)
Practice Areas: Mostly 'big money' matrimonial finance. Counsel in the House of Lords in White v White (2000), Mark v Mark (2005) and Miller v Miller; McFarlane v McFarlane (2006). Trained mediator.
Professional Memberships: National Vice Chairman of the Family Law Bar Association (FLBA); Fellow of the International Academy of Matrimonial Lawyers (IAML); Associate member of Resolution; Vice Chairman of Gray's Inn Advocacy and CPD Committee.
Career: Called 1989. QC 2012.
Personal: Merchant Taylors School, Liverpool University (LLB).

MARSHALL, Philip QC
Serle Court, London
020 7242 6105
pmarshall@serlecourt.co.uk
Featured in Chancery (London), Professional Negligence (London), Banking & Finance (London), Commercial Dispute Resolution (London), Company (London), Fraud (London), Offshore (London), Restructuring/Insolvency (London)
Practice Areas: Commercial fraud (RAK v Bestfort; BTA Bank v Ablyasov; Aeroflot v Berezovsky; Bank of St. Petersburg v Arkhangelsky; Constantin Medien v Ecclestone; AWG v Morrison; Cala Cristal v Al-Borno; Canada Trust v Stolzenberg; Berry Trade Ltd v Moussavi; Zhakarov v White; Lexi Holdings v Luqman); company (Re Lehman Bros; Re Spartan Capital; Re Liverpool FC (Hicks v Broughton); Re Coroin Ltd; Re MT Realisations); insolvency (Re Nortel Networks; Re Woolworths PLC; BIM v Maxwell; Re: Murjani; Haig v Aitken); banking (Erdenet Mining v Standard Bank; BTA Bank v Ablyasov; NatWest v RaboBank; Wahda Bank v Arab Bank); commercial litigation and arbitration, (Carlyle Capital v Conway; Tchigirinski v Orton Oil; Shanshal v Al-kishtaini; Fiber Technologies v Moscow Oil Refinery); professional negligence (Brown v GRE; Peach Publishing v Slater; Bradcrown v Kidd Rapinet; Lexi Holdings v Pannone; Lexi Holdings v DTZ).
Professional Memberships: Chancery Bar Association, Insolvency Lawyers Association.
Career: Queens' Cambridge; Harvard Law School. Former fellow of Queens' Cambridge. Recorder and Deputy High Court Judge (Chancery and Queen's Bench, Commercial/Mercantile Court); Bencher Lincoln's Inn. Publications: Joint editor of 'The Practice and Procedure of the Companies Court'; Contributor to Insolvency and Company Chapters of 'Civil Appeals' (Sir Michael Burton Ed.).

MARTIN, Bradley
2TG – 2 Temple Gardens, London
020 7822 1200
bmartin@2tg.co.uk
Featured in Clinical Negligence (London)
Practice Areas: Clinical negligence (claimant and defendant); personal injury; professional discipline (GMC; GDC; CIPFA; ICAEW); product liability. Notable cases include: Myodil litigation for Glaxo; Lariam cases for GPs; PIP Hydrogel breast implant litigation; PIP Silicone breast implant litigation; SUI/POP (vaginal mesh) litigation for NHS; The Royal Victoria Infirmary & Associated Hospitals NHS Trust v B (A Child) [2002] Lloyd's Med LR 282 (CA) (life expectancy/multipliers); Reynolds v North Tyneside Health Authority [2002] Lloyd's Med LR 459 (QB); P v T [2004] Lloyd's Rep Med 537 (QB); Nicholas v Imperial College NHS Trust [2012] EWHC 591 (QB); R v Royal National Orthopaedic Hospital NHS Trust [2012] EWHC 492 (QB); Ecclestone v Medway NHS Foundation Trust [2013] EWHC 790 (QB); Bostridge v Oxleas NHS Foundation Trust (2014); Moore v Worcestershire Acute Hospitals NHS Trust [2015] EWHC 1209 (QB); Webb v Liverpool Women's NHS Foundation Trust [2015] EWHC 133 (QB); Darnley v Croydon Health Services NHS Trust [2015] EWHC 2301 (QB).
Professional Memberships: LCLCBA; PNBA; PIBA.
Career: Research assistant to the Federal/Provincial/Territorial Review of Liability Issues in Health Care at the University of Toronto (1987/8); tutor in tort law at Leicester University (1988/9); barrister in private practice (called 1990).
Personal: Resides in Hove; plays guitar, bass, banjo, ukulele.

MARTIN, Dale
Littleton Chambers, London
020 7797 8650
dmartin@littletonchambers.co.uk
Featured in Employment (London)
Practice Areas: Dale Martin is one of the UK's top juniors specialising in employment law. He is often instructed in business critical injunctive cases, in long-running, multi-claimant litigation and cases concerning high net worth individuals. Often against silks, he is selected by law firms for their own litigation, enjoying a 'trusted advisor' status in difficult disputes. In 2016, Dale was instructed in two appeals to the EAT against an internationally renowned music industry celebrity, who kicked a long-term employee/confidante out of his inner circle. Dale's multi-claimant work spans a number of areas. In 2016, Dale obtained a strike out order in respect of 763 working time/holiday pay and associated claims brought in the Employment Tribunal against a major construction and highways company. Dale is acting for a national supermarket defending multiple equal pay claims. Dale is also defending multiple equal pay claims involving a food processing factory, which was the subject of a successful appeal to the EAT in late 2015: 2 Sisters Food Group Ltd v. Abraityte UKEAT/0209/15/MC. Dale's multi-claimant TUPE work includes his appearance in December 2015 in the EAT appeal of Mustafa v. Trek Highways Ltd UKEAT/0016/15/BA. Dale has particular experience with City financial employers/employees disputes including bonuses and other contractual issues. He acted for the bank in the appeal in Portnykh v. Nomura International plc [2014] IRLR 251 and has been heavily involved in a number of matters relating to the LIBOR and EURIBOR scandal. Whilst he typically acts for employers, within the last year he has achieved multi-million pound pay-outs for bankers both in the context of civil bonus claims and discrimination law. Dale's civil employment work includes acting for employee/directors complaining of unfair prejudice in respect of their shareholdings and claims relating to breach of fiduciary duties. Dale continues to act and advise on numerous multi-party injunctive proceedings and related damages claims for breach of fiduciary duty, most commonly in the banking and insurance sectors. He has recent experience of search and freezing order relief.
Professional Memberships: ELBA; ELA; COMBAR.
Career: Called 1997 (Inner Temple).

MARTIN, James
5 King's Bench Walk, London
020 7 353 5638
james.martin@5kbw.co.uk
Featured in Crime (London)
Practice Areas: Crime
Professional Memberships: Criminal Bar Association.
Career: Called to the Bar in 2003 James Martin is a criminal defence specialist whose practice covers the full range of "heavy-weight" criminal offending. Mr Martin Leads and is regularly led in serious cases that include the offences of homicide, the importation and distribution of large quantities of drugs and complex fraud. He represents his clients fearlessly with a solid legal knowledge and an acute tactical awareness.
Personal: University of Bristol 1998 – 2000 – LLB (Hons).

MARVEN, Robert
4 New Square, London
020 7822 2000
r.marven@4newsquare.com
Featured in Costs Litigation (All Circuits)
Practice Areas: Robert Marven is a specialist in all areas of costs law. He is also an expert on the law concerning the funding of litigation. He has been instructed in a range of high profile cases in the Court of Appeal, the High Court, the Senior Courts Costs Office and the County Court. Robert's practice includes: costs issues arising from high value litigation; conditional fee agreements and contingency fee agreements; commercial funding for substantial disputes; legal expenses insurance and 'after the event' insurance; fixed costs; costs budgets and estimates; costs capping; as well as wasted and non-party costs orders. Robert acts for a wide range of clients including PLCs and public bodies, solicitors, major insurers, funders, claims management companies and individuals. He is often brought into major litigation to advise and to present submissions on specific costs issues. Robert provides strategic advice on matters of commercial importance to insurers, solicitors and others involved with the management and funding of litigation. His cases include: Surrey v Barnet and Chase Farm Hospitals NHS Trust [2016] EWHC 1598 (QB); Jones v Spire Healthcare Ltd (Liverpool CC, 27.04.16); Kupeli v Cyprus Turkish Airlines [2016] 3 Costs LO 365; O'Brien v Shorrock & MIB [2015] 4 Costs LO 439; EMW v Halborg [2015] 4 Costs LO 427; Cashman v Mid Essex Hospital Services NHS Trust [2015] 3 Costs LO 411; Broni v Ministry of Defence [2015] 1 Costs LR 111; Redfern v CBC [2014] EWHC 4526 (QB); Tasleem v Beverley [2014] 1 WLR 3567; Ultimate Products Ltd v Woolley [2014] 5 Costs LO 787 and [2014] EWHC 1919 (Ch); Light on Line Ltd v Zumtobel Lighting Ltd [2013] 1 Costs LR 129; Letts v Royal Sun Alliance plc [2012] 3 Costs LR 591; Joyce v West Bus Coach Services Ltd [2012] 3 Costs LR 540; Legal Services Commission v F [2011] 5 Costs LR 740; Rybak v Langbar International Ltd [2011] PNLR 16; Sulaman v Axa and Direct Line [2010] 3 Costs LR 391; Tankard v John Fredericks Plastics Ltd [The Accident Line Protect test cases] [2009] 1 WLR 1731, [2009] 4 All ER 526; Crane v Canons Leisure Centre [2008] 1 WLR 2549, [2008] 2 All ER 931, Days Healthcare UK Ltd v Pihsiang Machinery Manufacturing Co Ltd [2006] 4 All ER 233.
Career: MA (Cantab). Called to the Bar 1994.

MASEFIELD, Roger QC
Brick Court Chambers, London
020 7379 3550
roger.masefield@brickcourt.co.uk
Featured in Commercial Dispute Resolution (London), Energy & Natural Resources (London), Insurance (London)
Career: Roger Masefield has extensive experience of all aspects of commercial law. Within his first year of taking silk he has been instructed in a wide range of matters, including claims on behalf of the Libyan Investment Authority against both Goldman Sachs and Societe Generale (each worth in excess of one billion dollars); a claim against Tamara Ecclestone as to ownership of a Lamborghini; and a reinsurance arbitration relating to the 2010 New Zealand earthquakes, which raised complex issues

of both seismology and contractual construction. Before taking silk, he acted as a lead junior in the Berezovsky v Abramovich and related Berezovsky v Patarkatsishvili litigation. Roger Masefield has appeared, both led and unled, in the Commercial Court, Chancery Division, Court of Appeal, and the Privy Council; and in the High Court and Court of Appeal in the British Virgin Islands. His practice areas include international arbitration, banking, civil fraud, commercial litigation, energy, insurance and reinsurance, and professional negligence. Former clients include oil and gas majors; accountancy firms; banks and financial institutions; various high net worth individuals; syndicates and insurance companies; HM Treasury and the Bar Council.

MASSARELLA, David
Cloisters, London
020 7827 4016
dm@cloisters.com
Featured in Employment (London)

Practice Areas: David's work covers the full range of employment and discrimination law at first instance and appellate levels. In 2015 he was appointed to both the Attorney General's and the EHRC's Panels of Counsel. He appeared for the successful respondent in a recent appeal on detriment in discrimination (Singh v Advance Security [2016] IRLR 4 EAT) and represented the successful claimants in two of the most high-profile of recent pregnancy discrimination cases (Tantum v Travers Smith [2013] EqLR 736 and Gregory v Her Majesty's Forces (RAF)). He has appeared in leading cases on sexual orientation discrimination (Bivonas LLP v Bennett [2012] EqLR 216), disability discrimination (Meikle v Nottinghamshire County Council [2005] ICR 1) and indirect sex discrimination (Hardy and Hansons v Lax [2005] ICR 1565 CA). He has considerable experience defending long-running discrimination and whistleblowing cases. Recent respondent clients have included local authorities, major retailers, charities and banks.
Professional Memberships: DLA, ELA, ILS, Bar Pro Bono Unit and ELAAS.
Career: David read Modern Languages at Magdalen College, Oxford (BA Hons, 1st Class). Before being called to the Bar in 1999 he worked as a director in theatre and opera, including four years with the Royal Opera House. He is on the board of Actors Touring Company and has previously been a trustee of Southwark Citizens Advice Bureaux and a member of the Executive Committee of the Discrimination Law Association.
Publications: He contributed chapters to the 2012 Jordans book on Family Rights in Employment and the 2013 LAG book on Discrimination in Employment.

MASSEY, William QC
Pump Court Tax Chambers, London
020 7414 8080
clerks@pumptax.com
Featured in Tax (London), Agriculture & Rural Affairs (London)

Practice Areas: Widely recognised and consulted in all types of revenue work, with a particularly strong private client tax practice, including estate planning, heritage property, business and agricultural property reliefs, and variation of trusts. Cases include Antrobus (deceased) v IRC 2004 (IHT – agricultural property relief for farmhouses); A and B's Undertakings 2005 (HMRC's power to vary past conditional exemption undertakings); Marquess of Hertford and others v IRC 2005 (business property relief from IHT – interpretation of s110 and s112 IHTA 1984); Nelson Dance Family Settlement v HMRC 2009 (business property relief from IHT – ambit of s.104 IHTA 1984) McCall v HMRC 2009 (business property relief from IHT – ambit of s105(3) IHTA 1984); Allfrey v Allfrey 2015 and AC v DC 2016 (Variation of Trusts Act applications – extension of trust period and accumulation period); Executors of Lord Howard of Henderskelfe v HMRC 2014 (Court of Appeal – CGT 'wasting asset' exemption).
Professional Memberships: Revenue Bar Association; Chancery Bar Association; London Common Law & Commercial Bar Association.
Career: Called 1977, Middle Temple, elected a Bencher (2004) QC 1996 Governor, Harrow School (2000-2013) Summer Fields School (1996-2013) Member, Tax Committee, Historic Houses Association.
Publications: Editorial Board – Simon's Direct Tax Service.
Personal: Harrow School; Hertford College, Oxford (MA (Jurisprudence).

MASTERS, Dee
Cloisters, London
020 7827 4000
deemasters@cloisters.com
Featured in Employment (London)

Practice Areas: Dee is an expert in discrimination law with particular expertise in age discrimination and equal pay matters. She has appeared in numerous cutting edge cases such as Seldon v Clarkson, Wright and Jakes in the Supreme Court. In 2015/6, Dee was instructed in four appeals at EAT and Court of Appeal level. She also has a busy Tribunal practice spending the majority of her time in multi-week trials involving allegations of discrimination. She is regularly instructed in sensitive, high profile cases where there is a risk of press interest. Her clients include multinational companies, banks, universities, schools, charities, NHS trusts and local authorities as well as employees and trade unions. In recent years, she has advised the Equality Commission of Northern Ireland (ECNI) and the Northern Ireland Commissioner for Children and Young People (NICCY) on its response to proposed legislation extending the existing prohibition on age discrimination. In August 2015, she was the keynote speaker at a conference attended by politicians and policy makers in Belfast concerning age discrimination. Dee has also been advising AGE PLATFORM, an NGO, on a proposed European Directive which will extend the prohibition on age discrimination. Dee also advises education bodies on discrimination issues in the employment field as well as claims in the County Court. In 2014, she advised the Equality and Human Rights Commission on the extent to which gender segregation was permitted within university campuses. In light of her expertise, Dee has delivered judicial training on discrimination law at ERA in Trier funded by the European Commission. She also drafted the Technical Guidance accompanying the ban on age discrimination in goods, facilities and services on behalf of the Equality and Human Rights Commission in GB alongside colleagues in chambers.
Professional Memberships: ELA, ELBA.
Career: Notable cases include: Waiyego v First Great Western Limited (February 2016, UKEAT/0298/15/JOJ), Mist v Derby Community Health Services [2016] ICR 543, John Charles v NHS Business Services Authority (December 2015, UKEAT/0105/15/BA), Rochford v WNS Global Services (September 2015, UKEAT/0336/14/MC), Fathers v Pets at Home Ltd (June 2014, UKEAT/0424/13/DM), Seldon v Clarkson Wright and Jakes [2012] ICR 716 (SC), Sheffield City Council v Gibson (SC; resolved before hearing), Wilson v HSE [2010] ICR 302 (CA), Redcar & Cleveland Borough Council v. Bainbridge [2009] ICR 133 (CA), Potter v. North Cumbria Acute NHS Hospitals [2009] IRLR 900 (EAT), Potter v. North Cumbria Acute NHS Hospitals [2009] IRLR 176 (EAT), Shaw v. CCL Ltd [2008] IRLR 284 (EAT), Bainbridge v Redcar & Cleveland Borough Council [2008] ICR 238 (CA).
Personal: Education at University College, London (LLB) and the London School of Economics (LLM) specialising in employment law.

MATHER, James
Serle Court, London
020 7242 6105
jmather@serlecourt.co.uk
Featured in Partnership (London)

Practice Areas: General commercial chancery dispute and advisory work, particularly civil fraud, LLP and partnership, company, insolvency and trusts.
Professional Memberships: Association of Partnership Practitioners, Chancery Bar Association.
Career: Called 2006. Junior Counsel to Department of Business, Innovation and Skills for directors' disqualification proceedings, 2009. Junior Counsel to the Crown (Attorney General's C Panel), 2011.
Personal: Gonville and Caius College, Cambridge, Harvard University (Kennedy scholar); City University, London (Dip. Law).

MATHER-LEES, Michael QC
Farrar's Building, London
02920 398421
mmatherlees@farrarsbuilding.co.uk
Featured in Crime (Wales & Chester)

Practice Areas: Serious and Organised Crime,White Collar Crime,Confiscation. Appearing for both Defence and Prosecution. Regulatory Offences,including Health and Safety and Environmantal cases. Clinical Negligence and Personal injuries together with linked Medico-Legal cases.
Professional Memberships: Inner Temple, Criminal Bar Association, European Bar Group, Wales Criminal Law Association (Chairman).
Career: Having initially qualified as a solicitor,Michael Mather-Lees was called to the bar in 1981,initially running a mixed practice and thereafter specialising in serious crime and personal injuries. Silk 2012,successfully Defending and Prosecution high profile cases,including Murder,Serious Sexual Offences,Fraud and Corruption and Confiscation cases.

MATHERS, Wendy
Radcliffe Chambers, London
020 78310081
wmathers@radcliffechambers.com
Featured in Pensions (London)

Practice Areas: Traditional and commercial chancery including: pensions, wills, probate and administration of estates, Court of Protection, trusts, real property, commercial and residential landlord and tenant, insolvency and related professional negligence.
Professional Memberships: Chancery Bar Association, Associate member of the Association of Pensions Lawyers.
Career: Law Commission Research Assistant Property and Trusts team 2005-2006 Called 2005.
Personal: Educated at the Ecclesbourne School, Duffield and St Catherine's College, Oxford (MA Oxon). College Exhibitioner 2001 and 2002.

MATOVU, Harry QC
Brick Court Chambers, London
020 7379 3550
harry.matovu@brickcourt.co.uk
Featured in Commercial Dispute Resolution (London), Energy & Natural Resources (London), Fraud (London), Insurance (London)

Career: Harry Matovu is a Silk with a wide-ranging commercial litigation and arbitration practice, which includes the specialist areas of energy and natural resources, civil fraud, banking and finance, and insurance and reinsurance. He has acted in several very high-profile cases over the years, including the Lloyd's Litigation in the 1990s; the MMR Vaccine Litigation; and a US$1.7 billion Commercial Court action concerning oil exploration rights in Iraqi Kurdistan (Excalibur Ventures LLC v Texas Keystone Inc). With regard to energy disputes, in addition to Excalibur and other cases, Harry Matovu is currently engaged in a US$500m power sector fraud action before the High Court of Tanzania (the heaviest civil action yet to come before that court). With regard to banking and finance, he has recently acted successfully in a billion-dollar Kazakh bank fraud claim; and in a substantial longevity swaps dispute between a Swiss investment fund and a leading global investment bank. In relation to insurance and reinsurance, Harry Matovu has acted over the years for and against insurers, reinsurers and brokers across almost all classes of business in the London Market. Harry Matovu is also regularly instructed in major international and domestic commercial arbitrations, and he sits as an arbitrator.

MATTHEWS, Claire
Drystone Chambers, London
020 7404 1881
claire.matthews@drystone.com
Featured in Crime (South Eastern)

Practice Areas: Criminal law.
Professional Memberships: South Eastern Circuit, CBA, Cambridge & Peterborough Bar Mess.
Career: Claire Matthews works across the South Eastern Circuit, with an exclusively criminal law practice. Her practice is almost equally divided between prosecuting and defending, and she is regularly instructed in cases involving expert evidence, complex third party issues, and cases with a particular emphasis on infant death/serious injury/neglect. Another large part of her practice are cases including armed robbery, serious violence, firearms, child abuse, serious sexual offences, major drugs, and mental health cases. Latterly Claire has also been instructed as junior counsel in cases of murder, attempted murder, manslaughter, firearms offences, serious fraud and money laundering. She has recently both prosecuted and defended parents/guardians in murder and manslaughter

cases of alleged 'Shaken Baby Syndrome', and has a professional interest in medico-legal evidence.

MAUGHAM, Jolyon QC
Devereux, London
020 7353 7534
maugham@devchambers.co.uk
Featured in Tax (London)

Practice Areas: Jolyon has a largely court based practice, predominantly in the field of direct tax. He has particular expertise litigating tax avoidance transactions, intangible property, tax and public law, film financing and employment taxation. He has argued cases in every domestic tribunal from the Supreme Court down.

Career: Called 1997. Queen Mother's Scholar. Junior Counsel to the Crown (A Panel). Queen's Counsel 2015.

Personal: LLB European Legal Studies (Durham and Katholieke Universiteit Leuven), First; MA Birkbeck, Distinction. Advisor to the Labour Party on tax matters. A well-known commentator on tax policy.

MAWREY, Eleanor
9 Gough Square, London
020 7832 0500
emawrey@9goughsquare.co.uk
Featured in Financial Crime (London)

Practice Areas: Criminal law, in particular fraud/financial crime. Eleanor has been instructed in a number of high profile cases, most notably as junior counsel for the FSA (now FCA) in the successful prosecution of R v Joseph, a case which attracted one of the highest sentences for insider dealing to date. She is currently instructed by them as Junior Counsel in a complex investment fraud. Eleanor is also Junior Counsel in a sensitive bribery and corruption investigation for the SFO, where she appears on their B list, having previously acted for them in R v Khatab and Others (a Ponzi scheme). She is a Grade 4 CPS Prosecutor (including Fraud Specialist Panel), appearing frequently in benefit and revenue cases. Eleanor also regularly defends. Her work frequently involves POCA matters whether restraint or confiscation and ancillary orders such as SCPOs. Other recent cases: R v Nkiwane (Prosecution for breach of Money Laundering Regs), R v Ahmed (impersonating a solicitor) R v Chattopathyay (Prescription fraud by Doctor), R v Sentinella (Tax fraud), R v Wade and Others (Rail ticket fraud), R v Mohammed (benefit fraud), R v Q (complex confiscation hearing held in camera).

Professional Memberships: Bar Council member (2006-2011, 2013-2017), Bar Council Equality and Diversity and Social Mobility Committee (2012-17). CBA committee member (2006-17) and its Director of Equality and Diversity.

Career: Called to the Bar in 2001. SFO B list and CPS Grade 4, Fraud Specialist Panel Grade 3. Direct Access.

MAWREY, Richard QC
Henderson Chambers, London
020 7583 9020
rmawrey@hendersonchambers.co.uk
Featured in Consumer Law (London), Information Technology (London)

Practice Areas: Main areas of practice are commercial law and local authority work. Commercial work includes contracts, leasing, finance and credit law, financial services, computer law and commercial drafting. Local authority work covers contracts, public procurement, public liability, finance, employment, passenger transport, local taxation, land development, housing, community services and computer problems.

Professional Memberships: London Common Law and Commercial Bar Association, Local Government Planning and Environmental Bar Association, Tecbar.

Career: Called to the Bar 1964 and joined present chambers 1965. Appointed assistant recorder 1981. Took Silk 1986. Appointed recorder 1986 and Deputy High Court Judge 1994, Election Commissioner 1994.

Publications: Author of 'Computers and the Law', Blackstone's 'Guide to the Consumer Credit Act 2006', Butterworths 'Commercial and Consumer Law Handbook'. Specialist editor contract and business law section of Butterworths' 'Civil Court Precedents', 'Bullen & Leake & Jacob's Precedents of Pleadings',Goode's 'Consumer Credit Law and Practice' and 'Encyclopaedia of Banking'.

Personal: Scholar of Rossall School and Exhibitioner of Magdalen College, Oxford (BA Jurisprudence 1963, First Class Honours, and Eldon Scholar of Oxford University 1964, MA 1967). Born 20 August 1942. Lives in London.

MAX, Sally
29 Bedford Row Chambers, London
020 7404 1044
smax@29br.co.uk
Featured in Family/Matrimonial (London)

Practice Areas: Sally specialises exclusively in the field of family finance. Joining 29 Bedford Row in 2011, she as predominantly London-based practice comprising substantial matrimonial / cohabitee disputes, commonly involving private companies, trusts or complex pension issues, and high value Schedule 1 claims.

Professional Memberships: FLBA.

Career: Called, 1991.

Publications: Co-author, 'Dictionary of Financial Remedies' (Class Legal, 2016); Contributor to Halsbury's Laws of England (financial provision for children section).

Personal: Born, 1968. Read Law at King's College, Cambridge. Married, four children.

MAXWELL, David
St Philips Chambers, Birmingham
0121 246 7000
dmaxwell@st-philips.com
Featured in Employment (Midlands)

Practice Areas: David's practice encompasses Employment Tribunal, EAT, High Court and Court of Appeal litigation. Specialising in complex, lengthy and high value discrimination claims, he also accepts instructions in professional regulatory and disciplinary matters. David is frequently instructed by a wide variety of private sector respondents, including banks and other blue chip companies. He often acts on behalf of public employers including central government departments, local authorities, the police and fire authorities. Recent cases include Davies v Sandwell MBC [2013] IRLR 374 CA.

Professional Memberships: ELBA; ELA.

Career: Called 1994. Attorney General's Treasury Counsel Panel. Fee-paid Employment Judge.

MAY, Charlotte QC
8 New Square, London
0044 2074 054 321
charlotte.may@8newsquare.co.uk
Featured in Intellectual Property (London), Media & Entertainment (London)

Practice Areas: Charlotte is a QC practising in all areas of intellectual property and media law. Recent patent cases includie Warner Lambert v Actavis (infringement of second medical use claims), Smith & Nephew v Convatec (silverised wound dressings, construction of numerical ranges), Unwired Planet v Huawei (mobile phone technology) and Accord v medac (dosing regime for treating arthritis). She has a niche practice in SPCs with an impressive repertoire of cases too long to list. Charlotte has a strong reputation for trade mark, copyright and media cases. Recent examples include Cartier v Sky (trademark website blocking injunction); Thomas Pink v Victoria Secret (dispute over the name PINK); A&E TV v Discovery (dispute over satellite channel name); ITV v TV CatchUp (copyright infringement of TV programmes streamed over the internet); FAPL v QC Leisure (copyright infringement of Premier League football matches). For a comprehensive CV visit www.8newsquare.co.uk.

Professional Memberships: Intellectual Property Bar Association (IPBA); The Intellectual Property Lawyers Organisation (TIPLO); ITMA Designs Committee; Bar Council Wellbeing Committee.

Career: Inner Temple, 1995.

Personal: Born 1971. Educated at The Abbey School; Brasenose College, Oxford (1993 Biochemistry); City University (1994 Dip Law); Inns of Court School of Law. Appointed QC 2014.

MAY, Christopher
5 St Andrew's Hill, London
0751 260 3820
chrismay@5sah.co.uk
Featured in Crime (London)

Practice Areas: Chris appears as either leading or sole Counsel in homicide cases including sexually motivated killing; the murder by a woman of her partner on the day of his release from prison; joint enterprise murder including targeted homophobic killing and the killing of a prostitute by an asphyxia fetishist. He regularly defends and prosecutes in serious sexual offences, including allegations of rape, sexual trafficking, historical allegations and 'cold case' investigations and offences against children. He has appeared in many cases involving allegations of organised criminal activity including kidnapping, drugs and violence. He has long experience of Flying Squad and drugs cases and those involving all forms of sensitive material, surveillance and PII. He has prosecuted gang violence cases, including leading in a 20 Defendant Attempted Murder case. Fraud cases have included giving pre-charge advice.

Professional Memberships: SE Circuit, CBA, Kent Bar Mess POCLA.

MAYHEW, Alice
Devereux, London
020 7353 7534
mayhew@devchambers.co.uk
Featured in Employment (London)

Practice Areas: Specialist in employment litigation and advisory work involving restraint of trade, whistleblowing, all types of discrimination, equal pay, business transfers, wrongful and unfair dismissal, industrial action and breach of contract claims. She has extensive experience of acting for a wide variety of clients such as airlines, banks, local authorities, media, telecommunications and police forces as well as senior employees. Undertakes multi day complex cases before the employment tribunal, county court and high court as well as all levels of appeal (often being instructed for the first time at appellate level).

Professional Memberships: ELBA, ELA (Member of the training committee).

Career: Called 2001, Inner Temple Major Scholarship, Pegasus Scholarship, Ede and Ravenscroft Prize for Student of the Year and Duke of Edinburgh Award.

Publications: Contributor to Bloomsbury Discrimination Law and Jordans Employment Law Service.

Personal: LLB Exeter, LLM Cambridge. Enjoys swimming, Yoga and going to the beach in Norfolk.

MAYNARD, Matthew
St Ives Chambers, Birmingham
0121 236 0863
matthew.maynard@stiveschambers.co.uk
Featured in Family/Matrimonial (Midlands)

Practice Areas: Family (children and matrimonial finance); Court of Protection.

Professional Memberships: FLBA, ALC, Liberty.

Career: Matthew is a family law specialist, whose practice is divided between proceedings involving children, and applications for financial remedies. His children's practice is heavily weighted towards care proceedings of the utmost complexity. He in regularly instructed in cases with the following features: Murder, of parents and children; Serious non-accidental injury, including brain injury; FGM; Serious sexual abuse, including acting for children as alleged perpetrators; FII; Suffocation and Human trafficking. Matthew strives hard to ensure that his practice is broadly divided equally between representation of local authorities, parents and children. His private law practice includes cases involving the international movement of children and surrogacy, having been junior counsel for the child in the landmark case of Re X (Surrogacy: Time Limits) [2014]. Matthew's matrimonial finance practice includes cases which range from moderate to high value assets. He has experience of, and interest in, cases involving alleged concealment or dissipation of assets; pre-acquired, inherited or other non-matrimonial wealth and cases involving business assets. Matthew qualified as a IFLA accredited Arbitrator in 2016.

Publications: Contributor to Jordan's Family Law, the Family Law Journal and Lexis-Nexis.

Personal: Married. Interests include current affairs, association football, and cricket.

MAYO, Simon QC
187 Fleet Street, London
020 7430 7430
simonmayo@187fleetstreet.com
Featured in Crime (London), Financial Crime (London)

Practice Areas: Simon Mayo specializes in serious and complex crime. He has particular experience in the full spectrum of serious fraud work including, tax frauds and frauds centred on the financial markets. He is regularly instructed for the defence

in large and complex fraud cases. He is currently instructed for the defence in the largest prosecution ever brought by HMRC. His experience and expertise in the field of serious fraud is also called upon by specialist prosecution agencies. The Serious Fraud Office has appointed him to both of their specialist panels. He also acts for the Financial Conduct Authority in relation to the investigation and prosecution of malpractice and fraud in the financial services sector. In the field of general crime, he has gained a wealth of experience in homicide cases and is regularly instructed on behalf of the defence and the prosecution. Simon also appears for defendants before a number of professional and sporting disciplinary bodies. He advises individuals and corporate bodies on a wide range of issues affecting director and corporate liability.
Professional Memberships: Criminal Bar Association (former member of executive committee).
Career: Call 1985. QC 2008. Recorder 2009.
Publications: Author of articles and lectures on recent developments in criminal law.

MAZZAG, Anthony
Cobden House Chambers, Manchester
0161 833 6000
clerks@cobden.co.uk
Featured in Clinical Negligence (Northern)
Practice Areas: Anthony has specialised in all aspects of clinical negligence and personal injury litigation for nearly 20 years. His clinical negligence practice includes claims for cerebral palsy and other birth related injuries, negligent surgery (including laser eye surgery and cosmetic surgery), hospital-acquired infection, anaesthetic awareness, delayed diagnosis of cancer and critical ischaemia. Anthony's personal injury practice involves high value cases generally arising from accidents at work and road traffic accidents acting for both Claimants and Defendants. Many of his cases involve complex medical and engineering evidence. Anthony undertakes a significant amount of fatal accident work and as a result appears at inquests on a regular basis. He has particular expertise in this area having been instructed by the Treasury Solicitor as junior counsel to the Shipman Inquiry and more recently by the Senior Coroner for Manchester as counsel to the inquest into the death of Stephen Hunt, a serving fireman with Greater Manchester Fire and Rescue Service who died during active service.

MCATASNEY, Philippa QC
Furnival Chambers, London
07860 933 389
pippa@leach.plus.com
Featured in Crime (London)
Practice Areas: Pippa McAtasney is a London criminal silk and a Bencher of Lincolns' Inn with a wide-ranging practice. She has an excellent record both defending and prosecuting cases concerning murder, manslaughter, serious sexual offences, violent crime and fraud. She has a specialist practice in police misconduct work and has represented many officers, both senior and junior both at tribunals and the Crown Court. She has acted for several companies in Health and Safety cases and accepts instructions in all areas of crime in both Crown and Magistrates' courts. Recently, as well as murder cases both defending and prosecuting (including the prosecution of a mother who admitted murdering her baby and a man who stabbed and set fire to a young mother) she has successfully defended a Durham University student accused of rape and sexual assault; a policeman accused of historic sexual abuse of his stepdaughter and a youth accused of sexual assault of a fellow pupil. Less significant cases include the successful defences of a bottom touching allegation and a minor "keying" of a BMW car. In addition, Pippa acts as a legal advisor to companies producing TV drama, the best known being all three series of the BBC drama "Silk".
Professional Memberships: Philippa is a Bencher of Lincoln's Inn and a qualified advocacy tutor. She is a member of the South Eastern Circuit and the Western Circuit. She is Chair of the Surrey and South London Bar Mess and also a member of the Criminal Bar Association and the Sussex Bar Mess.
Career: Philippa went to University at the London School of Economics and Political Science. She was called to the bar in 1985 and took silk in 2006.
Personal: Philippa is married and has two daughters.

MCCABE, Louise
St Philips Chambers, Birmingham
0121 246 7000
lmccabe@st-philips.com
Featured in Family/Matrimonial (Midlands)
Practice Areas: Louise is a specialist in financial remedy proceedings and inquests. She conducts cases covering all aspects of matrimonial finance including financial remedies, trusts of land, Schedule 1 of the Children Act and Inheritance Act applications. She represents husbands, wives and intervenors and is regularly involved in cases of high net worth and those involving complicated and technical issues, expert evidence, business and other valuations, third party interests, and assets subject to trust. She has conducted financial cases involving children with separate representation, and conducted a number of cases arising out of the breakdown of same sex relationships. She regularly appears as an advocate in inquests, with particular experience in prison deaths.
Professional Memberships: FLBA.
Career: Durham University BA (Hons) in Law. Called to the Bar 1996. Appointed as an Assistant Deputy Coroner in 2009, as a Deputy District Judge in 2013, and as a Recorder in 2015.

MCCAFFERTY, Jane
11KBW, London
020 7632 8500
jane.mccafferty@11kbw.com
Featured in Employment (London)
Practice Areas: Commercial and employment law with particular experience in litigation involving team moves, restrictive covenants, misuse of confidential information, breach of fiduciary duty and contractual disputes. Jane's practice frequently involves multi-jurisdictional disputes and complex, high value litigation in financial services and regulated markets. Recent cases include one of The Lawyer's Top 20 cases in 2016, Marathon Asset Management; arbitration and Commercial Court proceedings claiming breach of fiduciary duty and conspiracy arising from a team move in the asset management sector.
Professional Memberships: Employment Lawyers Association, Employment Law Bar Association. COMBAR.
Career: Called to the Bar in 1998.
Personal: Educated at Foyle and Londonderry College and Newnham College Cambridge (BA Hons in Law, LLM).

MCCAFFERTY, Lynne
4 Pump Court, London
020 7842 5555
lmccafferty@4pumpcourt.com
Featured in Professional Negligence (London), Construction (London), Information Technology (London)
Practice Areas: Construction, engineering, energy, technology and telecommunications, and professional negligence. Acts for employers, contractors and professionals in a wide range of litigation, arbitration (domestic and international), and adjudication. She regularly appears in the TCC. Recent cases have included TCC litigation concerning the multi-million pound design and construction of a new hospital under a PFI project agreement; a DIAC arbitration relating to the MEP works on a major construction project in Abu Dhabi; and a multi-million pound dispute relating to the largest civil IT system in the world.
Professional Memberships: TECBAR (Secretary), Society of Construction Law, Society for Computers and Law, COMBAR, PNBA.
Career: BA (Oxon) English - 1st Class; Diploma in Law (City University) - Distinction; Called to the Bar 1997; Judicial Assistant to the Court of Appeal (1999), TECBAR Accredited Adjudicator.
Publications: Civil Appeals: Principle & Procedure (Co-author), Sweet & Maxwell; A Practical Guide to Adjudication, for the Practical Law Company.

MCCALL, Christopher QC
Maitland Chambers, London
020 74061200
cmccall@maitlandchambers.com
Featured in Chancery (London), Tax (London), Charities (London), Offshore (London), Trusts (London)
Practice Areas: Specialises in trust and charity law. Has appeared in numerous appeals in the House of Lords, Privy Council and Court of Appeal and in foreign courts: has regularly addressed specialist associations and seminars and written in legal journals.
Professional Memberships: Trust Law Committee, STEP, ACTAPS, Chancery Bar, and Charity Law Associations.
Career: Called to Bar Lincoln's Inn, November 1966. Took Silk, April 1987. Bencher 1993. 2nd Junior Counsel to the Inland Revenue in Chancery Matters 1977-87. Junior Counsel to the Attorney General in Charity Matters 1981-87. Practised at 7 New Square Lincoln's Inn 1967-94, subsequently 13 Old Square (now Maitland Chambers). Member of Bar Council 1973-76. He was until 2013 a member of the Executive of the Trust Law Committee and in that capacity took part in numerous initiatives in the sphere of trust law reform. STEP Lifetime Achievement award 2015.
Personal: Born 3 March 1944. Married 1981, no children. Educated Winchester College (Scholar), Magdalen College, Oxford (Demy): 1st class, Mathematical Moderations 1962 and Finals 1964. Eldon Law Scholarship: 1966. Trustee of British Museum 1999-2004.

MCCANN, Claire
Cloisters, London
020 7827 4000
cm@cloisters.com
Featured in Employment (London)
Practice Areas: Claire McCann specialises in employment, equality and public law as well as commercial, regulatory and human rights law. She acts for companies, charities, public authorities and central government, trade unions and individuals. She is appointed to the Attorney-General's B Panel of Counsel. She is accredited to be instructed under Direct Access. Claire has a strong advisory practice and is sought-after in complex and high profile litigation (eg, R (C) v Secretary of State for Work & Pensions, on informational privacy and transgender rights; Surtees v Middlesbrough County Council on the issue of pay protection in the context of equal pay; and R (Elias) v Secretary of State for Defence, one of the first cases on the statutory equality duty). She is particularly regarded for her tenacity in court, her sharp cross-examination skills, her meticulous preparation and her ability to put clients at ease. She gives sound, commercial advice and is quick to respond.
Professional Memberships: ELA, ELBA, DLA, HRLA, ILS, Bar Pro Bono Unit and ELAAS.
Career: Claire joined Cloisters in 2000 having worked as a consultant for the Public Law Project where she co-authored a publication on Access to Health Records. In 2005, she worked in the Human Rights Team of the Crown Law Office in New Zealand.
Publications: Claire is a contributor to the LAG Handbook on Discrimination Law in Employment (2013). Claire regularly contributes articles to legal journals, lectures widely on employment and equality law and has filmed contributions for Legal Network TV.
Personal: Education at Wadham College, Oxford (1st Class Joint Hons BA in English & French); and City University (Postgraduate Diploma in Law). Wadham College Scholar (1995/1996); Inner Temple Major Scholar (1998); Princess Royal Scholar (1999); Pegasus Scholarship (2005).

MCCLELLAND, James
Fountain Court Chambers, London
020 7483 3335
jm@fountaincourt.co.uk
Featured in Administrative & Public Law (London), Banking & Finance (London), Commercial Dispute Resolution (London), Financial Services (London), Professional Discipline (London)
Practice Areas: James practices in commercial, public and regulatory law with a particular focus on banking, commercial dispute resolution, judicial review (both commercial and non-commercial) and the regulation of legal and financial services. He has appeared in a number of the most significant cases in each of these areas of recent years. In 2011 James was named by Legal Week as one of ten "Stars at the Bar". In 2015 he was nominated for Commercial Litigation Junior of the Year at the Chambers & Partners UK Bar Awards. James is one of the Attorney General's Counsel to the Crown (B Panel).
Professional Memberships: COMBAR, ARDL, ALBA, YPLG.
Career: 2004: called to the Bar. Appointed to Attorney General's C Panel in 2009 and to the B Panel in 2012.

Publications: Contributing author of Brindle & Cox on The Law of Bank Payments.

MCCLUSKEY, Alec
Maitland Chambers, London
020 7406 1200
amccluskey@maitlandchambers.com
Featured in Chancery (London)

Practice Areas: Practice spans the whole range of commercial and chancery work, with an emphasis on litigation. Particular focus on banking and financial services disputes (including litigation arising out of derivatives, swaps and other complex financial instruments), heavy contractual and business disputes (including fraud claims and cases with international elements), insolvency, company and partnership work, professional negligence, trusts and property matters. Particular experience of dealing with applications for freezing injunctions.
Professional Memberships: COMBAR, FSLA, ChBA.
Publications: contributor to Lender Claims (2010, 2nd Edition in preparation).
Personal: former Chapman Scholar of the Inner Temple, at Bar School was placed top in his year, winning the Scarman Scholarship and the Stephen Seabrooke Memorial Prize.

MCCREDIE, Fionnuala QC
Keating Chambers, London
fmccredie@keatingchambers.com
020 7544 2600
Featured in Construction (London), Public Procurement (London)

Practice Areas: Specialist in procurement, construction, engineering, energy, environment and professional negligence related claims, and instructions regarding health and safety, and insurance disputes. Practice covers wide range of advocacy, advisory and drafting for both domestic and international clients. Advocacy expertise has led to regularly acting for clients in all UK Courts including the TCC, High Court, and Court of Appeal as well as before arbitrators, adjudicators, tribunals and in mediation. Recent work includes numerous appearances in early and specific disclosure in procurement cases; procurement related judicial review; advising contracting authorities and challengers in procurement disputes; advising in relation to standard and bespoke contracts, PFI and facilities management disputes, repudiation, termination, loss and expense claims and retrospective delay analysis, including comparative delay analysis methodologies.
Professional Memberships: Procurement Lawyers Association, Technology Construction Bar Association; Professional Negligence Bar Association; Society of Construction Law; Commercial Bar Association, London Common Law and Commercial Bar Association.
Career: Manchester University – Bsc (Hons) Geography 1986; Brunel University – MA Public & Social Administration 1990; Middlesex Polytechnic Business School – CPE 1991; Called 1992; 3 Serjeants' Inn 1992-2008; Keating Chambers 2008; Bencher, Middle Temple 2010. Queen's Counsel 2013.
Publications: Keating on Construction Contracts 9th Edition, 2012 – Contributor.

MCDONALD, George
4 New Square, London
020 78222000
g.mcdonald@4newsquare.com
Featured in Costs Litigation (All Circuits)

Practice Areas: George has extensive experience of commercial disputes with a real focus on construction, international arbitration and costs. George acts on substantial domestic and international claims, recently including multiple disputes arising from two separate PFI contracts (worth £2billion and £6billion) for the management of Birmingham road network and a major UK motorway, a complex arbitration claim worth in excess of £100million relating to a nuclear facilities construction project, and multiple claims arising from the Buncefield fire. In costs, George has been instructed on some of the seminal costs cases, both on his own account and as a junior, and has particular experience of group litigation. Recent cases include for the Mirror Newspaper in the phone hacking litigation, in the rare successful appeal on hourly rates in Kelly v Hays Plc, in the significant costs budgets decision of Elvanite v AMEC Earth & Environmental (UK) Ltd and the important solicitor-client dispute of Assaubayev v Michael Wilson & Partners.
Professional Memberships: PNBA, COMBAR, TECBAR, SCL.
Career: BA (Oxon) (1st class). Worcester College Scholar. Called to the Bar in 2007 (Hardwicke and Shelford Scholar).
Publications: Contributing editor to Butterworths Costs Service and author of Lexis Nexis PSL Costs Practice Notes.
Personal: Qualified USPTA tennis coach and keen sportsman.

MCDONALD, John
2TG - 2 Temple Gardens, London
020 7822 1200
jmcdonald@2tg.co.uk
Featured in Personal Injury (London), Personal Injury (All Circuits)

Practice Areas: Extensive experience of motor insurance claims, including coverage issues and contribution between insurers. Cases include Pinn & Guo v. Zenith Insurance (2014), Clarke and Clarke v MIB [2012] EWHC 2118, Harvey v MIB [2011] and McCall v Poulton & MIB [2009] RTR 11. Long experience of disease claims (esp asbestos, but also deafness, dermatitis and WRULD) for claimants and defendants (eg Smith v. Portswood [2016] EWHC 939, Prater v. British Motor Holdings (2016) Lawtel). Particular interest in stress and harassment claims (e.g. Mullen v Accenture [2010] EWHC 2336) and defending fraudulent/exaggerated claims (e.g. Singh v O'Shea [2009] EWHC 1251). Instructed in cases involving complex technical and accounting issues (e.g. complex loss of earnings). Related practice areas include health and safety and building and construction litigation.
Professional Memberships: Fellow of Royal Society of Arts, Fellow of Chartered Institute of Arbitrators, PIBA, PNBA TecBar, Western Circuit.
Career: MA (St. Andrews). Formerly a solicitor (admitted with Honours). Called to Bar 1981.
Publications: Contributor to Injury Times, PILJ.
Personal: Recreations: Music, fishing.

MCDONNELL, Constance
Serle Court, London
020 7242 6105
cmcdonnell@serlecourt.co.uk
Featured in Chancery (London), Court of Protection (All Circuits)

Practice Areas: Chancery litigation specialising in contentious trusts and probate, Inheritance Act claims, administration claims, removal of personal representatives, real property and proprietary estoppel. Constance also appears in the Court of Protection (property and affairs).
Professional Memberships: Chancery Bar Association, STEP, ACTAPS.
Career: Called in 2000 (Lincoln's Inn).

MCFARLAND, Denise
Three New Square, London
020 7405 1111
clerks@3newsquare.co.uk
Featured in Intellectual Property (London)

Practice Areas: All aspects of intellectual property – including designs, trademarks, patents, passing off, entitlement, know-how and confidential information, franchises and licensing; with particular experience in the fashion, music, media and entertainment industry. Qualified , experienced and well regarded as a Mediator and Arbitrator and in all types of ADR covering all areas of commercial law. Experienced in sitting on professional conduct panels, and adjudications and as a court appointed Examiner for US Deposition Hearings taking place in the UK.
Professional Memberships: Institute of Trade Mark Attorneys (ITMA), Chancery Bar Association, Intellectual Property Bar Association, Women's Bar Association
Career: BA and MA in Law – Cambridge University (1983-86) called to the Bar (Inner Temple) (1987) (HRH Prince Philip Scholarship). Trained (CEDR) & Qualified as a mediator 2001. Founding committee member of The Intellectual Property Lawyers Association (TIPLO) and former professional examiner for ITMA and CIPA .
Publications: ADR – A Janus Perspective (2016) and Bad Faith – Trade Marks' Owners Take Stock (2012).
Personal: Charity Trustee for The Mayhew, Fundraising and IPR Advisor to several UK & Overseas Charities, Published Author of Books for Children & Travel Writer, Participant and Sponsor of various Mentoring Schemes for Children, Young Adults and the Homeless. Sponsor and Advocate for Able Child. Qualified riding instructor and trainer in equine husbandry. Previously worked as TV and radio presenter.

MCGEE, Andrew
2 Bedford Row, London
020 7440 8888
amcgee@2bedfordrow.co.uk
Featured in Crime (London), Health & Safety (London)

Practice Areas: Andrew has a heavyweight Health and Safety practice both defending and prosecuting (he is a List A prosecutor for the HSE and others). His work covers corporate and gross negligence manslaughter, as well as HSWA and regulatory offences. He often advises at an early stage in investigations and prosecutions and in relation to enforcement proceedings. He has considerable experience in representing interested parties at inquests, acting for police officers, clinical and other professionals, companies and individuals. Andrew also undertakes work in the First Tier Tribunal in health care matters, which complements his very busy practice in the area of professional discipline – e.g. work before the General Optical Council, the General Medical Council, the General Dental Council etc. Andrew's criminal work and experience is extensive (both prosecution and defence) across the whole range of criminal offences (murder , serious assault, sexual offences, public order, drugs, firearms, fraud and financial crime) in all courts from the magistrates to the Supreme Court and Privy Council. He appeared for the Appellant as a junior alone in the Supreme Court in R-v-Taylor. He is regularly instructed by the Registrar of Criminal Appeals to act for unrepresented appellants. Andrew also acts for clients in environmental regulation and crime. He is regularly instructed on a direct access basis in all courts, including the Court of Appeal.

MCGHEE, John QC
Maitland Chambers, London
020 7406 1200
jmcghee@maitlandchambers.com
Featured in Real Estate Litigation (London)

Practice Areas: John McGhee has wide experience in a broad range of chancery and commercial litigation. He has particular expertise in property-relating work but his practice equally encompasses banking, commercial fraud, professional negligence and company disputes. Recent cases include: Re Game Station [2014] EWCA Civ 180 (scope of administration expenses); Tindall Cobham v. Adda Hotels [2014] EWCA Civ 1215 (effect of Landlord and Tenant (Covenants) Act on intra group assignment provisions in leases); Chelsfield Advisers v Qatari Diar [2015] EWHC 1322 (Ch) (disputed termination of development management agreement); Canary Wharf Finance II v. Deutsche Trustee Company [2016] EWHC 100 (Comm) (whether terms of redemption of loan notes included 'Spens payment'). He also advises in non-litigious matters, such as the trusts and property aspects of proposed investment and tax schemes.
Professional Memberships: Chancery Bar Association, COMBAR, Property Bar Association.
Career: University College Oxford 1980-83 (MA).
Publications: General editor of Snell's 'Equity' 33rd edn.

MCGHEE, Philip
QEB Hollis Whiteman, London
020 7933 8855
philip.mcghee@qebhw.co.uk
Featured in Crime (London)

Practice Areas: Philip is regularly instructed to advise and represent professionals who face both criminal charges and conduct or performance allegations inside and outside the perimeter of the workplace. He has extensive experience dealing with the procedural, evidential and tactical issues encountered. In the criminal courts, he has recently represented a City lawyer facing allegations of child sexual offences, and one of the defendants in the early stages of the Euribor prosecutions. He has also recently successfully defended clients including a senior hospital consultant (assault), a GP (domestic assault), a primary school head teacher (assault of a pupil), and an accountant (exposure). He has considerable experience before the MPTS, the GDC and other regulatory tribunals. Recent defence cases have included doctors facing allegations of deficient performance, serious dishonesty, and inciting a child to sexual activity. Philip also has significant prosecution experience across a range of offences, acting for the CPS,

as well as for other bodies including local authorities, the General Dental Council, the Gambling Commission and the Security Industry Authority.
Career: MA (Oxon) Called 2003. Woolf Scholarship, 1 Crown Office Row. Prince of Wales Scholarship, Reid Scholarship & Senior Award, Grays Inn. Attorney at Walkers, Cayman Islands, 2007 to 2009.

MCGRATH, Elizabeth QC
St Philips Chambers, Birmingham
0121 246 7000
emcgrath@st-philips.com
Featured in Family/Matrimonial (Midlands)
Practice Areas: Liz has specialised in the field of family law for over 20 years and was appointed Queen's Counsel in 2014. She appears regularly in complex high net worth financial remedy cases and has particular expertise in dealing with cases involving private limited companies, partnerships and extensive property and pension portfolios. Liz is often instructed in cases in which there are parallel private law children issues with particular emphasis on 'residence', 'contact', relocation, LGBT parenting and surrogacy. Liz has extensive expertise in public law, acting for Local Authorities, parents and children in the High Court and the Court of Appeal. She has been instructed in a number of complex fact finding hearings involving allegations of sexual abuse and non-accidental injuries, and has appeared in a number of reported cases. Liz's vast experience across the field of private and public family law, and her down to earth, approachable manner, is known to inspire confidence in her instructing solicitors and enables her to establish a productive and easy rapport with lay clients. Her thorough approach to preparation means that she is quick to identify the crucial issues in complex cases. Whilst Liz gives firm and fair advice with an eye to early resolution where possible, if proceedings require a judicial decision she has a reputation for concise, robust and effective advocacy.
Professional Memberships: Association of Lawyers for Children; Family Law Association; British Agencies for Adoption and Fostering.
Career: Called 1987. Silk 2014.

MCGUINNESS, John QC
9-12 Bell Yard, London
020 7400 1800
j.mcguinness@912by.com
Featured in Financial Crime (London)
Practice Areas: Serious Fraud; Corruption; Asset Confiscation; Judicial Review and other Appellate work (crime, regulatory and public law); First & Upper Tier Tax Tribunal; Homicide; Taxis & Local Authority licensing; Home Office & FRC Disciplinary Tribunals. Regularly instructed by SFO, HMRC, CPS Appeals Unit, Special Crime & Counter Terrorism Division, and local authorities. Recent reported cases: R v Jogee, 2016 [Supreme Court: mental element required for liability of secondary party in joint enterprise]; Beghal v DPP, 2015 [Supreme Court: compatibility of port powers to stop, search & interview with Article 6 and privilege against self-incrimination]; AM v DPP, 2014 [Supreme Court: challenge to assisted suicide policy by claimant with 'locked-in syndrome']; R v N, 2016 [CA (Crim): Provision of confidential information to police for sentence discount]; Fonecomp v HMRC, 2015 [CA (Civil): VAT input credit, Kittel fraud, contra-trading]; CW & Others, 2015 [CA (Crim): AG's consent to prosecutions]. Trials: Marrache, 2013-14 (9 months £40 million fraud trial in Gibraltar). Wilmot, 2011 (Southwark CC: £26 million 'boiler room' fraud).
Professional Memberships: CBA.
Career: 1980 call (Lincoln's); 1992-2001: DTI Standing Counsel, South Eastern Circuit; 2001: QC; 2002-present: Crown Court Recorder; SFO QC panels: (1) trials and (2) proceeds of crime.

MCKECHNIE, Stuart
9 Gough Square, London
020 7832 0500
smckechnie@9goughsquare.co.uk
Featured in Personal Injury (London), Clinical Negligence (London)
Practice Areas: Stuart has extensive experience in the field of personal injury and clinical negligence work but specialises in high value catastrophic claims involving complex issues and multiple experts. He in instructed by many of the leading catastrophic injury firms nationwide with almost all of his practice based in the High Court representing Claimants. Stuart is the co-author of the APIL Guide to Catastrophic Injury Claims and 1 of only 3 Barrister members of the editorial working party of the Judicial College Guidelines for the Assessment of General Damages in Personal Injury Cases. In 2012 Stuart was shortlisted for the Chambers & Partners Personal Injury & Clinical Negligence Junior of the Year Award. He was awarded the title of Personal Injury Barrister of the Year at the Proclaim National Personal Injury Awards in 2011 and shortlisted for this award again in 2013. In 2015 Stuart advised and represented Claimants in cases with a combined value in excess of £55 million.
Professional Memberships: APIL & PIBA.
Career: University of Nottingham 1993-96. Called to the Bar 1997. Inner Temple Scholar.
Publications: Co-author of the APIL Guide to Catastrophic Injury Claims published by Jordans. Contributing Editor to 'Kemp: Personal Injury Law, Practice and Procedure' on the subject of Periodical Payment Orders and 'A Practical Guide to Clinical Negligence Claims by 9 Gough Square'. Member of the editorial working party of the Judicial College Guidelines for the Assessment of General Damages.
Personal: Away from work, Stuart enjoys sport, good food and spending time with his young family.

MCKENNA, Anna
1 King's Bench Walk, London
020 7936 1500
amckenna@1kbw.co.uk
Featured in Family/Matrimonial (London)
Practice Areas: Public Law Child Care – especially concerning medical FII, NAI, infanticide, Child Trafficking, sexual abuse and serious neglect. Private Law Child Care – International residence and contact disputes. Ancillary Relief.
Career: Anna is a leading children public law junior who has been engaged in a number cases which have involved FII, NAI, infanticide, Child Trafficking and sexual abuse. Anna has a wide experience acting for public bodies, CAFCASS and parents.

MCLAREN, Michael QC
Fountain Court Chambers, London
020 7583 3335
clerks1@fountaincourt.co.uk
Featured in Aviation (London), Commercial Dispute Resolution (London), Professional Discipline (London)
Practice Areas: Michael McLaren QC is widely experienced in all areas of commercial litigation, regulation and professional discipline, with particular expertise in aviation, banking and finance, commercial dispute resolution and regulatory law. Recent experience includes: Dubai Financial Group v National Private Air Transport Services [2016] EWCA Civ 71 (setting aside default judgment entered simultaneously with alternative service order); Tarom v Jet2.com [2014] EWCA Civ 87 (distinction between causation and assessment of damages); ACG Acquisition v Olympic [2014] EWCA Civ 821, [2013] EWCA Civ 369 (certificate of acceptance of aircraft), [2012] EWCA Civ 1659; Shaker v Vistajet [2012] EWHC 1329 (Comm) (deposit recovered on aircraft sale); Tandrin v Aero Toy Store [2010] EWHC 40 (Comm) (whether credit crunch within force majeure clause), [2009] EWHC 1450 (QB) (Comm) (jurisdictional challenge when foreign proceedings extant). SRA v Dennison [2012] EWCA Civ 421 (SDT decision not to strike off dishonest solicitor); Faniyi v SRA [2012] EWHC 2965 (Admin) (appeal against SDT's refusal of re-hearing); SRA v Davis [2011] EWHC 232 (admin) (basis of costs awarded in SDT); Russian Commercial Bank v Khoroshilov [2011] EWHC 1721 (Comm); [2009] EWHC 2630 (Comm) (substantial claims against oligarch + $3bn counterclaim).
Career: Called to Bar 1981, Silk: 2002.

MCNAMARA, Andrew
Ropewalk Chambers, Nottingham
0115 947 2581
andrewmcnamara@ropewalk.co.uk
Featured in Personal Injury (Midlands), Social Housing (Midlands)
Practice Areas: He practices primarily in personal injury related claims and housing matters. He acts for Claimants and Defendants across the range of cases, drawing on over twenty years' experience both as a practitioner and holder of judicial appointments.
Professional Memberships: Personal Injuries Bar Association; Professional Negligence Bar Association; Housing Law Practitioners' Association.
Career: Called in 1992; BA (History), University of Southampton; LLB, University of Leeds; Assistant Coroner, Nottinghamshire: including deaths at work; in hospital, including intra/post operatively; in the residential/nursing care environment; in prisons/detention; and as a result of road traffic collisions; Judge of the First Tier Tribunal (Property Chamber): The Residential Property Chamber is charged with hearing cases regarding fair and market rents; leasehold enfranchisement; service charges; fitness to manage residential property and licences; mobile homes; and right to buy. He is an Accredited Mediator.
Personal: Away from the Bar, his interests are reading, cinema and running. He is passionate about music and is the drummer in two bands.

MCNAMARA, Stephen
Kings Chambers, Manchester
0345 034 3444
clerks@kingschambers.com
Featured in Clinical Negligence (Northern)
Practice Areas: Stephen practises in the fields of clinical negligence and serious personal injury, acting for both Claimants and Defendants. Clinical negligence cases constitute the substantial majority of Stephen's practice. He is instructed by many of the leading national firms. He has successfully conducted over 150 cases in this field. His practice spans the areas of surgical and pharmaceutical negligence, misdiagnosis and delayed diagnosis, dental negligence, inappropriate treatment and failure to obtain informed consent, amongst others. Stephen is regularly instructed in complex and high-value cases in which significant future losses are claimed. He is experienced in leading and managing a large team of experts during such cases. Stephen is known for his ability to establish a rapport with clients, even in the most difficult cases, to provide them with clear advice and for his detailed and thorough approach to testing expert evidence in conference. Stephen has particular experience of claims involving suicide arising as the result of negligent psychiatric treatment, including claims advanced under the Human Rights Act 1998. He has developed an extensive inquest practice (particularly those arising from medical complications). In such cases, Stephen acts both on behalf of bereaved families and a wide range of other interested parties. In particular, Stephen has completed a large number of complex and lengthy Article 2 compliant inquests, both with a jury and without. Stephen is also instructed in claims for serious personal injury arising from accidents in the workplace, on the highway and at other premises, and those caused by defective products and road traffic collisions.
Professional Memberships: Gray's Inn Personal Injury Bar Association Northern and North Eastern Circuits.
Career: Year of Call: 2008 University: London School of Economics and Political Science Degree: BSc Government (2:1) Awards: Anthony Bessemer Clark Scholarship (Graduate Diploma in Law) Goldie Award (Bar Vocational Course) St James' Chambers Award (for highest advocacy results on the Bar Vocational Course at Manchester Metropolitan University).

MCNEILL, Jane QC
Old Square Chambers, London
020 7269 0300
mcneill@oldsquarechambers.co.uk
Featured in Personal Injury (London), Employment (London)
Practice Areas: Employment, discrimination under domestic and European law, all areas of common law and statutory employment rights; high value claims, including those involving psychiatric/psychological injury. Cases include: Hartley and others v King Edward VI College; Williams v. British Airways; Yapp v Foreign and Commonwealth Office; Chhabra v North West London Mental Health Trust; Haq v Audit Commission; Michalak v Mid Yorks Hospitals NHS Trust; Gutridge v. Sodexo; Gibb v. Maidstone & Tunbridge Wells NHS Trust; Grundy v BA; Kapur v Barclays; Preston v Wolverhampton Healthcare NHS Trustees.

Also practises in personal injury, clinical negligence and mediation.
Professional Memberships: Employment Law Bar Association; Industrial Law Society; Employment Lawyers' Association; Personal Injuries Bar Association.
Career: Called 1982; QC since 2002; fee-paid employment tribunal judge since 2000; Mediator since 2002; Recorder (Civil) since 2006.
Publications: Editor of 2nd Equality and Diversity Code for the Bar.
Personal: BA Hons (Oxon); Dip Law (City University); Member of Advisory Board, City Law School; Council Member of ACAS. Reasonably fluent Italian and French.

MCPARLAND, Michael
Quadrant Chambers, London
020 7583 4444
michael.mcparland@quadrantchambers.com
Featured in Travel (London)
Practice Areas: Civil and commercial litigation and arbitration, especially cross-border disputes, civil fraud, shipping, international injuries, aviation, sports and insurance law. Recent reported cases include Winkler [2016] EWHC 217 (Ch); Dusek [2016] EWCA Civ 604; Pan Ocean Co Ltd, Re [2015] EWHC 1500 (Ch); Wrigley [2014] EWHC 3684 (Comm).
Professional Memberships: Member of Combar, the Chancery Bar Association, the State Bar of California, and the Chartered Institute of Arbitrators. Barrister in BVI.
Career: Michael has wide experience of civil and commercial actions, both UK and international. He emphasises forceful, advocacy, commercial awareness, preparation, and responsiveness to client's needs. Admitted in the BVI, he has also appeared in Gibraltar. He represents clients before the ICC, LMAA, LCIA, CAS, the Stock Exchange, the FA, and the UEFA Appeals Body. A California attorney he acts in Anglo-US proceedings and gives English law expert evidence in US and other courts. Michael is an arbitrator.
Publications: Michael wrote "The Rome I Regulation on the Law Applicable to Contractual Obligations" (OUP, 2015). Prof. Adrian Briggs QC's LMCLQ (2015) review said "[t]his is a marvellous book, an absolute must for anyone who is seriously concerned with the private international law of... contracts... There is no need to read any more of this review: just buy it". This is '... commentary at the highest level...which is accurate, comprehensive and above all usable...This book is a magnificent achievement, for which all serious commercial lawyers will be in the author's debt".

MCPHERSON, Graeme QC
4 New Square, London
020 7822 2032
l.stewart@4newsquare.com
Featured in Professional Negligence (London), Professional Discipline (London), Sports Law (London)
Practice Areas: Principal areas of practice are (1) professional liability (in particular claims involving accountants and auditors, solicitors and barristers, financial service professionals and sports agents), (2) professional discipline (3) sports law and discipline, and (4) commercial litigation, including insurance & finance services litigation. Recent important cases include: Professional Liability & Commercial: Coulthard v Neville Russell (CA) [scope of auditors' duty of care]; Barex Brokers v Morris Dean (CA) [scope of valuers' duty of care]; Flannery v. Halifax EA (CA) [duty of judge to give adequate reasons]; IAICL v Cook (CA) [scope of auditors' duty of care]; University of Keele v PWC (CA) [construction of exclusion clause in accountants' retainer]; Keydon Estates v Eversheds (Ch) [damages for loss of hypothetical profit]; Glyn v McGarel-Groves (QB) [scope of treating and supervising vets' duties]; Shawton Engineering v DGP (CA) [scope of PII cover provided by a design & build policy]; Hickman v Blake Lapthorn (QB) [duties of barrister when advising on settlement]; Sunderland Mutual Marine v Wiseman (Comm) [conflict of laws within UK]; Hedrich v Standard Bank (CA) [wasted costs; duties to court]; Fulham Leisure Holdings v Nicholson Graham Jones (CA) [claim arising from sale of Fulham AFC]; Kidsons v Various Underwriters (CA) ['notification' under a PII policy]; Webster v Sandersons (CA) [damages for reflective loss]; Gill v Humanware (CA) [wasted costs jurisdiction in Employment Tribunals]; Spreadex v Barnes (Ch) [claim arising from drafting of a gambling arrangement]; Fonexco v Manches (QB) [obligations of a solicitor in a jurisdiction race]; Zurich v Brown & Barnes (Ch) [construction of Solicitors MTCs]; Thomas v Capita (Ch) [film finance litigation]; Mengiste v EFFORT (CA) [recusal of Judge; wasted costs]; Baxter v Howreys (Comm) [claim arising from mishandled litigation]; Redstone Mortgages v B Legal (Ch) [solicitors' obligations towards mortgagee client]; AIB v Mark Redler & Co (SC) [breach of trust against solicitors; measure of compensation]; Platform v Persimmon (Ch) [claim in fraudulent misrepresentation]; Marrache v Baker Tilly (Gib SC) [scope of ex turpi causa defence]; Standard Life v Collins (Comm) [claim against Cattles plc director]; MEX v Hindle Campbell (Ch) [group litigation against solicitors said to have been involved in conspiracy to conduct mortgage fraud]; Dewey & Lebeouf v Kerself (Comm) [obligations of corporate solicitors handling an overseas bond issue]. Sport: Nicky Henderson, Aidan O'Brien, Howard Johnson, CASELA PARK, Jim Boyle, Mahmood Al Zarooni, Gerard Butler, Jim Best, Grand National 2014, Bradley & Powell; 2015 St Leger appeal (BHA Disciplinary Panel & Appeal Board) [corruption, doping, sporting disrepute]; Whittaker (FEI Inquiry) [doping]; Mullins v Jockey Club (Admin Ct) [amenability of sporting bodies to judicial challenge]; Arachi v Fallon (CA) [injunction to prevent jockey from riding in Derby]; Burton v British Shooting (Sports Resolutions) [Olympic selection dispute]; Sports Mantra v Force India (Ch) [F1 sponsorship dispute]; Various athletes [IAAF & CAS) [doping]; Various rugby players (RFU & WR) [doping, disciplinary]; Pelosi v WBA FC (QB) [injunction to stay litigation to a Rule K arbitration]. Professional Discipline: RCVS v Jones & RCVS v Auerbach (RCVS Disciplinary Panel) [disgraceful conduct]; BSB v McCarthy & BSB v Thornhill QC (Bar Disciplinary Tribunal) [dishonesty]; Hedrich v Standard Bank (CA), Gill v Humanware (CA), Mengiste v EFFORT (CA) [wasted costs]; FSA v Miller (FCA).
Professional Memberships: PNBA, COMBAR, ChBA, BASL, ADRL.
Career: MA (Cantab). Called (Gray's) 1993 – scholar & winner ver Heyden de Lancey prize. Joined Four New Square (formerly 2 Crown Office Row) in 1993. Silk 2008.
Publications: Editor of 'Jackson & Powell on Professional Liability' (7th edition).
Personal: Educated at Canford School, Wimborne and Emmanuel College, Cambridge. Leisure interests: Training NH racehorses.

MCQUAIL, Katherine
Radcliffe Chambers, London
020 7831 0081
kmcquail@radcliffechambers.com
Featured in Chancery (London), Court of Protection (All Circuits)
Practice Areas: Katherine's practice focuses on succession, probate, administration of estates, family provision, trusts and Court of Protection work. She also deals with real property, landlord and tenant, and mortgage matters and professional negligence claims arising from her core areas of practice.
Professional Memberships: Chancery Bar Association, Professional Negligence Bar Association.
Career: Called to the Bar in 1989. In practice at 11 Old Square and (from 2006) Radcliffe Chambers since 1990.
Personal: Born: 1965. Lives: London. Enjoys: theatre, walking in Cumbria and elsewhere, and following Arsenal and the England cricket team.

MCTAGUE, Meghann
2TG – 2 Temple Gardens, London
020 7822 1298
mmctague@2tg.co.uk
Featured in Travel (London)
Practice Areas: A personal injury barrister with particular expertise in travel and foreign claims. From 2006 to 2009, instructed by the Treasury Solicitor as Junior Counsel, led by Rory Phillips QC, on the Rosemary Nelson Inquiry based in both London and Belfast. She is very experienced in dealing with complex recovery/contribution claims; in particular, those arising out of PFI agreements and regularly represents local authorities in complex Highways Act claims. Meghann has a pragmatic and tactical approach to advising on liability and quantum. She has a wealth of experience of claims involving CRPS and complex psychiatric injuries and extensive experience of claims under the Motor Insurers' Bureau Untraced and Uninsured Drivers' Agreements including arbitrations under the Untraced Drivers' Agreement.
Professional Memberships: Criminal Bar Association; Personal Injury Bar Association.
Career: Fatal accident in Spain/France/England involving an alleged Legionnaire's Disease outbreak. Fatal motorbike accident in Germany following a head-on collision. Accident on board a yacht in Italy involving numerous defendants from different Member States. Jet-ski accident in Barbados. Skiing accident in France. Road traffic accident in France. Scalding accident on board a flight from the Caribbean to the UK under the Montreal Convention. Meghann has a wealth of experience of claims involving the Package Travel Regulations 1992. R v EGS Ltd [2009] EWCA Crim 1942 (involving the prosecution's appeal against the defendant's successful submissions of no case to answer) which re-affirmed the approach of the House of Lords in R v Chargot (t/a Contract Services) Ltd [2008] UKHL 73. Meghann has appeared in the Admiralty Court and has experience of drafting detailed defences to claims under the Athens Convention 1974. In 2009 she was appointed to the Attorney General's Unified List of Prosecuting Advocates.

MEACHIN, Vanessa
St Philips Chambers, Birmingham
0121 246 7000
vmeachin@st-philips.com
Featured in Family/Matrimonial (Midlands)
Practice Areas: Vanessa has been practising in family law since being called to the Bar in 1990. Her practice includes public law, private law, financial remedy proceedings and Court of Protection cases. Financial remedy proceedings: Vanessa regularly appears in complex cases involving business interests, inheritance, conduct and intervener applications. Her financial experience extends to cases relating to applications under Schedule 1 of the Children Act 1989 and under the Trusts of Land and Appointment of Trustees Act 1996. Private law: Vanessa has a wide ranging experience of child arrangement orders (previously residence and contact), specific issue/prohibited steps orders and applications to remove the child from the jurisdiction. Public law: She regularly appears in the High Court acting for parents, children and local authorities. Her cases range from factitious illness, complex medical cases to those of chronic neglect. Vanessa also accepts public access instructions in relation to financial remedies and private law. She is a regular speaker at seminars.
Professional Memberships: Association of Lawyers for Children; Family Law Bar Association; British Agencies for Adoption and Fostering.
Career: Recorder on the South Eastern Circuit (family, public/private and civil); Head of St Philips' Family Finance Team.

MEAD, Philip
Old Square Chambers, Bristol
020 7269 0300
mead@oldsquare.co.uk
Featured in Travel (London)
Practice Areas: Philip is a leading junior in both fields of personal injury and employment in the application of conflict of laws and European law to cross-border accidents and cross-border employment disputes. Philip has considerable expertise in the area of foreign accidents. He has a detailed understanding of the Judgments Regulation, the application of the EU Motor Insurance Directives and the Rome II Regulation, and the territorial scope of employment law. Recent notable cases include: Rai v Ministry of Defence (QB, 16 May 2016) proper law of the tort and acta iure imperii; Cook v Virgin Media Ltd [2016] 1 WLR 1672 jurisdiction within the UK; forum non conveniens and strike out; Hoteles Pinero Canarias SL v. Keefe [2015] EWCA Civ 598 – application of Article 11(3) of Brussels Regulation 44/2001. Hasan v. Shell International Shipping Services (PTE) Ltd (EAT, 14 January 2014) – mariner, claims for unfair dismissal, wrongful dismissal and discrimination on grounds of race/religion, the international jurisdiction of the ET. Nemeti v. Sabre Insurance Co Ltd [2013] EWCA Civ 1555; [2014] C.P. Rep 16 – direct right of action against foreign insurer, substitution of Defendant. Jacobs v. Motor Insurers Bureau [2011] 1 WLR 2609 (CA) – first successful claim against the MIB in its capacity as Compensation Body. Direct instruction: Philip is able to accept

instructions direct from foreign lawyers and foreign clients.
Professional Memberships: PIBA; Pan-European Organisation of Personal Injury Lawyers (General Board Member); BEG; ELA; ILS.
Publications: Editor and Contributor to Bona and Mead (eds) Personal Injury Compensation in Europe; and Personal Injury Compensation in Europe: Fatal Accidents and Secondary Victims.

MEADE, Richard QC
8 New Square, London
020 7405 4321
richard.meade@8newsquare.co.uk
Featured in Information Technology (London), Intellectual Property (London)
Practice Areas: Barrister specialising in all aspects of Intellectual Property, with particular experience in biotechnology, pharmaceutical, telecommunications and electronics patent litigation. For a comprehensive CV and list of recent cases, visit 8 New Square website at www.8newsquare.co.uk.
Professional Memberships: Intellectual Property Bar Association (IPBA); The Intellectual Property Lawyers Organisation (TIPLO). CEDR Accredited Mediator.
Career: Called 1991. Appointed QC 2008. Sits as a Recorder and Deputy High Court Judge.
Personal: Born 1966. Educated at William Ellis School; University College, Oxford (BA Law).

MEADWAY, Susannah
Ten Old Square, London
020 7405 0758
susannahmeadway@tenoldsquare.com
Featured in Chancery (London), Trusts (London)
Practice Areas: Susannah Meadway's practice encompasses advisory, drafting and litigation work in the fields of trusts and associated taxation, with a preponderance of work for large landed estates. Her work extends to wills, probate and the administration of estates, pensions, family provision, Court of Protection matters and charities. A significant part of her practice concerns applications to the Court under the Variation of Trusts Act 1958 (VTA 1958) to extend the lifetimes of trusts, and securing rectification by the Court of trust documents. Out of court, her work mainly consists of assisting trustees and beneficiaries to achieve their aims for the continuation and smooth running of their trusts, tax efficiently and with maximum flexibility.
Professional Memberships: Susannah is a member of STEP and the Chancery Bar Association.
Career: Called to the Bar 1988. Notable reported cases include A v B [2016] WTLR 745 (VTA 1958); C v C [2016] WLTR (VTA 1958); Chisholm v Chisholm [2011] WTLR 187 (settlement rectification); Bartlam v Coutts [2006] WTLR 1165 (settlement rectification); Healey v Brown [2002] WTLR 849 (mutual wills); Re Bell [2002] WTLR 1105 (will rectification); Re Segelman [1996] Ch 171 (will rectification and validity of a charitable gift).
Publications: Williams on Wills (joint editor); Mellows: Taxation for Executors and Trustees (joint editor); Foster's Inheritance Tax (contributor); Tolley's Practitioner's Guide to Contentious Trusts and Estates (co-author); Perpetuities and Accumulations Act 2009 (Trusts and Trustees 2010); Extending trusts under the VTA 1958: a simplified method? (Trusts & Trustees 2016).

MEDCROFT, Nicholas
Fountain Court Chambers, London
020 7583 3335
njm@fountaincourt.co.uk
Featured in Financial Services (London), Professional Discipline (London), Financial Crime (London)
Practice Areas: Nicholas Medcroft has a broad commercial practice, with an emphasis on banking and financial services, civil fraud disputes and professional liability. He is regularly instructed in major commercial disputes, especially those with a financial services or civil fraud/breach of trust element. He has particular experience of financial services regulation. Much of his professional liability work is in the field of financial professional negligence/misconduct. He is recommended as a leading junior in The Legal 500 and Chambers and Partners, where he is described as "very user-friendly" and "'extremely bright and phenomenally hardworking". Notable cases include Stone Consultants v NatWest, Shah v HSBC Private Bank (the leading case on the conflict between a bank's duties to its customers and its duties under POCA), FSA v Alexander (the first market abuse case to be brought by the FSA in the Chancery Division) and Financial Reporting Council v Deloitte (arising from the collapse of the MGR Rover Group – one of The Lawyers' Top 20 cases of 2013).
Professional Memberships: COMBAR, Chancery Bar Association, Financial Services Lawyers Association.

MEHRZAD, John
Littleton Chambers, London
020 7797 8600
johnmehrzad@littletonchambers.co.uk
Featured in Employment (London), Sports Law (London)
Practice Areas: Employment, Commercial and Sport.
Professional Memberships: Employment Law Bar Association, Employment Lawyers Association, Industrial Law Society, British Association of Sport and Law, Commercial Bar Association, Bar European Group, London Irish Lawyers Association, Free Representation Unit, Bar Pro Bono Unit.
Career: Called at Inner Temple in 2005. Appointed FA arbitrator, FA Chairman's Panel of Anti-Discrimination as Chairman, member of sports advocacy section of the London 2012 Olympic Games Pro Bono Legal Advice and Representation Service and Glasgow 2014 Commonwealth Games. Notable cases include: Carreras v. United First Partners Research UKEAT/0266/15/RN; British Transport Police v. Hill & Ors UKEAT/0445/15/BA; Game Retail v Laws UKEAT/0188/14/D4; Charlesworth v. Amey PLC UKEATPA/0326/13/MC; Tavistock School v. Richards UKEAT/0244/13/SM; Seaco & Ors. v. Buss Capital & Ors (QBD) 2012; Rubicon LLP & Ors v. Attias & Ors (Ch D) 2012; Stuart v. London City Airport Ltd. UKEATPA/1651/11/MAA; Blazevic v. Hayashibara International Inc. UKEATPA/0738/11/CEA; Bullimore v. Pothecary Witham Weld Solicitors & Hawthorne [2011] IRLR 18; Humphreys v. Norilsk Nickel International (UK) Ltd. [2010] IRLR 976; Hunt v. Legal & General Resources Ltd. UKEATPA/1531/10/DM; Parsons v. Burworth Estates (a firm) UKEAT/0547/08/MAA. Awarded Inner Temple Major Scholarships (GDL and BVC) and BEG Peter Duffy Scholarship.
Publications: Athlete Selection Challenges, World Sports Law Report, December 2015; Player Contracts: FIFA Regulations on Working with Intermediaries, World Sports Law Report, November 2014; Selection Challenges, World Sports Law Report, April 2014; Age and Disability issues in Playing Contracts, World Sports Law Report, January 2013; Fixed Term Contracts in Sport, World Sports Law Report, November 2012.
Personal: Studied at Keble College, Oxford University; University of Nantes, France; Trinity College, Dublin; BPP Law School, London. Speaks working French; intermediate Italian, German and Farsi. Leisure interests include sport, in particular rowing and running; history; politics; travel.

MEICHEN, Jonathan
St Philips Chambers, Birmingham
0121 246 7000
jmeichen@st-philips.com
Featured in Employment (Midlands)
Practice Areas: Jonathan has always specialised in employment law and has a busy practice in the employment tribunal. He is an experienced tribunal advocate who has appeared in a diverse range of cases. Jonathan regularly acts in more complex or lengthy claims. He is instructed by large employers, PLCs, government departments and local authorities and also represents a variety of claimants, often via trade unions. In addition, he has been instructed by the Equality and Human Rights Commission. Jonathan undertakes appeal work and is frequently asked to advise in cases at an early stage. He believes in working as part of a team and seeks to work closely with professional and lay clients in order to achieve the best possible result at tribunal. Jonathan has particular experience of employment issues in the education sector. He appeared in the important EAT case of BCC v Emery [2014] E.L.R. 203 concerning the power of a governing body to dismiss a teacher. Jonathan is experienced in conducting internal investigations, where he combines a high level of scrutiny with an approachable and fair manner.
Career: Called 2006. Appointed to the Attorney General's Panel of Counsel in 2012.
Personal: Interests include music, football and skiing.

MELLOR, James QC
8 New Square, London
020 7405 4321
james.mellor@8newsquare.co.uk
Featured in Intellectual Property (London), Media & Entertainment (London)
Practice Areas: Barrister (QC) with wide ranging Intellectual Property, Media and Entertainment and Information Technology Practice. Specialist in electronics, mechanical and pharmaceutical patent cases. Has an extensive Trade Marks practice and is co-author of Kerly on Trade Marks. Recent cases include: Smith and Nephew Plc v Convatec Technologies Inc, ITV v TVCatchup, Karen Millen Fashions v Karen Millen, JW Spear & Sons Ltd and Mattel inc v Zynga (trademarks). For a comprehensive CV visit 8 New Square website at www.8newsquare.co.uk
Professional Memberships: Intellectual Property Bar Association (IPBA). Former Member of the Disability Panel of the Bar Council. Chancery Bar Association.
Career: Called 1986. Prior work experience in a variety of engineering disciplines in the UK, France, Germany, Somalia, the Congo and Iraq.
Publications: 'Kerly on Trade Marks' 13th & 14th edns, 'The Trade Marks Act 1994 – Text and Commentary', Bullen, Leake & Jacob.
Personal: Born 1961. Educated at Rugby School; King's College, Cambridge (1983 BA, MA Engineering and Production Engineering, 1985 Law (1st Class).

MELTON, Christopher QC
Byrom Street Chambers, Manchester
0161 829 2100
christopher.melton@byromstreet.com
Featured in Clinical Negligence (Northern), Personal Injury (Northern), Personal Injury (All Circuits)
Practice Areas: Chris Melton is a QC, specialising in cases of severe injury and death, especially brain and spinal cord injury cases. He is instructed by specialist firms nationwide.
Professional Memberships: Chris is a member of APIL and AVMA. He acts exclusively for injured people.
Career: Chris was called to the Bar in 1982. He has appeared in the Court of Appeal in many cases and has appeared in the Supreme Court on three occasions. He has a fourth case due for hearing in February 2017. He sits as a Recorder of the Crown Court. He is an accredited advocacy trainer and is on the Faculty of the Advanced International Advocacy Course, held annually at Keble College, Oxford. He is Chairman of the Northern Circuit Medical Law Association. He is on the Multi-Professional Advisory Panel of Baby Lifeline. He is the lawyer Trustee of the Turner and Newell Asbestos Trust. He is the UK lawyer appointed to advise the DII Asbestos Trust on its UK liabilities.
Personal: Chris is married with 4 grown up children and two dogs. He enjoys walking, running, skiing and golf.

MELVILLE, Elizabeth
Old Square Chambers, London
020 7269 0300
melville@oldsquare.co.uk
Featured in Employment (London)
Practice Areas: All areas of employment law, predominantly within the healthcare, education (particularly universities) and financial sectors. Undertakes both adversarial work in the employment tribunals and other courts and non-contentious work including conducting investigations, chairing internal disciplinary hearings and representing parties in internal proceedings or before external disciplinary bodies. Qualified mediator.
Professional Memberships: Employment Law Bar Association, Industrial Law Society, Employment Lawyers Association.
Career: MA Oxon French and History. Called to the Bar 1994. Spent two years at City law firm Simmons & Simmons between 1996-97 before returning to the Bar. Initially practised in fields of personal injury, clinical negligence and employment law. From 2003 has specialised in the field of employment law.
Personal: Interests: travel, yoga, cooking.

MELWANI, Poonam QC
Quadrant Chambers, London
020 7583 4444
poonam.melwani@quadrantchambers.com
Featured in Shipping (London)

Practice Areas: Specialises in commercial law, international trade, insurance and re-insurance and shipping. Believes in giving clear and practical advice and in finding a solution that meets the commercial needs of the client. Recent shipping cases include the CSAV v Hin-Pro litigation reported at [2015] 1 Lloyds Rep 301 and [2015] 2 Lloyds Rep 1 (Court of Appeal) involving applications to the Supreme Court both here and in Hong Kong and allegations of shipping fraud, contempt and imprisonment orders. The case is the leading authority on exclusive jurisdiction clauses and Poonam has over-turned previous wisdom that damages for breach of an exclusive jurisdiction clause require a comparative approach. Other recent shipping cases have concerned the implication of an indemnity in voyage charters, the legal requirements and significance of berth and port nominations and obligations to negotiate in good faith.
Professional Memberships: COMBAR, Supporting Member LMAA.
Career: Called to the Bar 1989. Queen's Counsel 2011.
Personal: Educated at Wycombe Abbey 1980-85 and Sidney Sussex College, Cambridge 1985-88. Married with four sons. Lives in London.

MENDELLE, Paul QC
25 Bedford Row, London
020 70671500
pmendelle@25bedfordrow.com
Featured in Crime (London)

Practice Areas: Criminal Defence, specialising in murder, child abuse, serious fraud including banking, investment and revenue frauds, fraudulent trading, money laundering, drugs and corruption offences. Experienced in representing professionals, corporate defendants and sportsmen charged with regulatory offences.
Professional Memberships: Former Chairman and current Executive Committee Member of the Criminal Bar Association, Elected member of the Bar Council and member of General Management Committee, member of Proceeds of Crime Lawyers Association (POCLA) Association of Regulatory and Disciplinary Lawyers (ARDL).
Career: Joint Head of Chambers at 25 Bedford Row. Worked 14 years in the City specialising in equipment leasing. Co-founded first independent lease brokerage providing leasing tax shelter to banks and third parties. Silk 2006, Called 1981, LLB Hons University of London 1980.
Publications: Regular commentator on criminal law issues in the press and on television and radio.

MENDOZA, Colin
Devereux, London
020 7353 7534
clerks@devchambers.co.uk
Featured in Personal Injury (London)

Practice Areas: All aspects of personal injury work for claimants and defendants; high value personal injury claims including fatal accidents, catastrophic brain damage, spinal injury, severe orthopaedic injuries leading to amputation, scarring and psychiatric damage. Clinical negligence (including spinal surgery, dental and veterinary). Health & Safety criminal proceedings. Experienced in ADR/mediation. Colin was appointed in 2008 as a Tribunal Judge of the Criminal Injuries Compensation Appeal Tribunal.
Professional Memberships: Personal Injury Bar Association; Professional Negligence Bar Association; Association of Personal Injury Lawyers; The British Academy of Forensic Sciences.
Career: Haberdashers' Aske's School, Elstree; University of Kent (1982 BA Law); Cambridge University (1984 LLM).
Publications: Sometime instructor and examiner at the Inns of Court School of Law, and contributor to the School's Manuals on the skills of opinion writing and drafting skeleton arguments.
Personal: Jazz, touch rugby, water-skiing.

MENDOZA, Neil
Selborne Chambers, London
020 7420 9500
neilmendoza@selbornechambers.co.uk
Featured in Real Estate Litigation (London)

Professional Memberships: Fellow of the Chartered Institute of Arbitrators, Chancery Bar Association, Property Bar Association, Professional Negligence Bar Association, London Common Law and Commercial Bar Association.
Career: A highly accomplished commercial litigator whose practice substantially involves disputes in a business context, Neil provides friendly, pragmatic and plain-speaking advice. Known as a tenacious advocate, Neil argues cases without flinching or backing off under pressure. He has built a reputation for always turning round urgent paperwork so as to meet client requirements and deadlines. Neil represented the 1st Defendant in the multi-million dollar Commercial Court claim of Dar Al Arkan – one of "The Lawyers Top 20 Cases for 2015" and the successful Claimant in the widely publicised negligence case of Sebry, the team winning "Litigation Team of the Year" at The Lawyers Awards for 2015. Many of Neil's cases involve land and property issues and he has extensive practical experience in commercial landlord and tenant, general property litigation including conveyancing, easements and boundaries as well as commercial and contractual disputes. Notable cases appear on Neil's entry on the Selborne Chambers web-site, including the "Pallant v Morgan equity", procedural irregularities, breach of trust, section 61 of the Trustee Act, limitation issues, TOLATA, misrepresentation, restrictive covenants, Access to Neighbouring Land Act, disability discrimination and many other, and varied, topics. He has significant expertise in difficult repossession issues and professional negligence claims involving solicitors and surveyors. As a "senior junior" Neil provides a competitive service by meeting a demand for advice and representation in substantial commercial disputes but at a reasonable price. Neil is highly experienced in representing clients at arbitrations and mediations and also accepts instructions on a Direct Access basis.

MESSLING, Lawrence
St Philips Chambers, Birmingham
0121 246 1600
lmessling@st-philips.com
Featured in Family/Matrimonial (Midlands)

Practice Areas: Lawrence has specialised in public child law since 1995. He undertakes serious and medically complicated fact-finding hearings, including cases where a child has died, allegations of NAHI, serious non-accidental injury, fabricated or induced illness, and complex outcome hearings including those with an international element. He is instructed in cases with sensitive medical and ethical issues, including those concerning the lawfulness of the resuscitation of a child or where one parent has killed the other. He undertakes cases involving issues of confidentiality and disclosure requiring the exercise of the High Court's inherent jurisdiction. He lectures on public child law. He is a trainer on the paediatrician expert witness programme. He chaired the BAAF Midlands Legal Group for ten years. Authorities include: Re K (a Child: Therapy) [2013] EWHC 3747 (Fam); Re A and B (One parent killed by the other – Guidance) [2010] EWHC B25 (Fam); Re W-P (Children) [2009] EWCA Civ 216; X and Y v A Local Authority (Adoption: Procedure) [2009] EWHC 47 (Fam); Re B (Minor) [2008] EWHC 1996 (lawfulness of not resuscitating disabled child); and A County Council v A Mother, a Father and X, Y and Z (by their Guardian) [2005] EWHC 31 (Fam).
Professional Memberships: FLBA, BAAF, ALC.
Career: Head of St Philips' Family Law Group (2010-15); Deputy Head of Chambers (2011-14).

METHUEN, Richard QC
12 King's Bench Walk, London
020 7583 0811
methuenQC@12kbw.co.uk
Featured in Personal Injury (London), Mediators (All Circuits)

Practice Areas: Personal injury; clinical negligence, professional negligence and Mediation in those areas. Richard has a heavyweight personal injury practice. His strong specialist expertise particularly in the areas of brain injuries, spinal injuries, sports injuries and occupational disease is widely recognised. He is instructed on behalf of both claimants and defendants and regularly acts for and against most major insurers as well as the Motor Insurers' Bureau. Richard has very quickly established himself as one of the country's leading Mediators. With his calm manner and huge wealth of knowledge in the field Richard's success rate as a Mediator stands at over 85%, with many of those involving psychiatric injury and RTA Insurance issues. Please see 12KBW's website for further details.
Professional Memberships: PIBA and PNBA.
Career: Called 1972; QC 1997; Head of chambers 2000-05; appointed MIB arbitrator 2001; recorder 2002 and to the Ogden Committee 2004. Experienced mediator (ADR accredited) and leads the 12 Mediation Team. His success rate over the past two years exceeds 85%. He specialises in evaluative mediations.

MICHELL, Paul
Cloisters, London
020 7827 4000
pm@cloisters.com
Featured in Employment (London)

Practice Areas: Leading junior Counsel for high-value/profile and complex dismissal, discrimination, whistle-blowing, EqPA, TULRA and TUPE claims, and related contract/director disputes. Regularly acts in cases where breach of covenant, database rights, fiduciary duty, confidentiality or other commercial wrongdoing is alleged, and injunctive relief is sought. Praised in directories and by clients as "a brilliantly skilled advocate"; "feisty tough and creative"; "top employment counsel... intelligent, articulate and highly personable", and "one of the barristers that clients return to most often". See Paul's entry at www.cloisters.com for more details. Acts as an adjudicator of grievances brought by senior employees, and as a Designated Independent Person investigating alleged wrongdoing by senior local authority staff. Named 'Lawyer of the Week' in The Times. Appeared in BBC documentary 'See You in Court'. Clients include the BBC, Belgo, British Red Cross, Danielle Lloyd, EHRC, the Elders Foundation, the Football Association; the GMB, the Football Association Premier League; RNIB, Royal Ballet School, Trevor Horn CBE, the TUC and several major higher education and financial institutions. Recent reported cases include Hainsworth v. MoD [2014] EWCA Civ 763, CA; X v. Mid Sussex CAB [2013] IRLR 146, SC, Kulikauskas v. Macduff Shellfish [2011] ICR 48, EAT, CJEU; EBR Attridge v Coleman [2010] ICR 242 (EAT), and Coleman v Attridge Law [2008] ICR 1128 (ECJ).
Professional Memberships: ELBA, ILS, ELA.
Career: Visitor for Loughborough University; part time Employment Judge.
Publications: Author of Bullen & Leake & Jacob's Precedents of Pleadings (Employment Tribunal Proceedings and High/County Court).
Personal: Highgate School; Downing College, Cambridge (BA, English); City University (Dip Law).

MIDDLETON, Graeme
Compass Chambers, Edinburgh
07766 231321
graeme.middleton@compasschambers.com
Featured in Personal Injury (Scotland)

Practice Areas: Specialising in personal injury/industrial disease, professional/clinical negligence, property damage (pursuing and defending); health and safety/road traffic crime – extensive experience in Court of Session and Sheriff Courts, including complex, high-value claims. Recent cases: John Jarvie v Pharmacia (ongoing) – defending multiple product liability claims for an allegedly defective pharmaceutical; Gillian McInulty v East Renfrewshire Council (ongoing) – defending fatal claim where deceased said to have been washed off a ford when its river was in spate; Greig Ritchie v Allianz (ongoing) – pursuing catastrophic road traffic claim under Spanish law; Red Star Pub Company v Scottish Power [2016] CSH 100 – defending a very high value property damage/negligence claim following alleged electrical fire and complete demolition of a Glasgow city centre tenement block; Robert Fraser v Kitsons Insulation 2015 SLT 753 – a case concerning the appropriate manner of disposal of an award of provisional damages for asbestos-related pleural plaques by Minute of Tender and Acceptance; Peat v Assembly Theatre [2014] CSOH 144 – successfully moving for use of equitable dispensing power in time-barred personal injury claim; Dickson v Kinsman [2013] CSOH 111

– road accident, operation of "agony rule"; Cowan v Hopetoun House [2013] CSOH 9 – occupier's liability, Pursuer fell over unlit/unmarked "Ha Ha" at stately home; Brand v Transocean 2011 GWD 14-336 – successfully arguing for "loss of employability" award instead of Ogden "multiplier x multiplicand"; Hodgkinson v Renfrewshire Council [2011] CSOH 142 – PUWER case regarding "suitability" of park gate which struck Pursuer when opened; Patterson v Grattan 2011 SLT (Sh Ct) 2 – Sale of Goods Act case, resolved by "best evidence" rule; HMA v Abernethy Trust – outdoor adventure centre prosecution (fatality); HMA v Sanctuary Housing Association – care home prosecution (fatality); HMA v Faulds (2012) – death by careless driving.

Professional Memberships: Member of the Faculty of Advocates Professional Negligence Law Group.

Career: LL.B (Hons) & DIPLP (Aberdeen University 1988 to 1993); Solicitor (1993 to 2002); admitted Faculty of Advocates 2003.

Personal: Spoken at seminars for Law Society of Scotland and Compass Chambers; lectured Court of Session Practice at Glasgow University.

MIDGLEY, Andrew

Old Square Chambers, Bristol
020 7269 0300
clerks@oldsquare.co.uk

Featured in Employment (Western)

Practice Areas: Andrew is a discrimination law specialist, with particular expertise in high value discrimination claims. He has a special interest in disability discrimination and his practice incorporates the Special Educational Needs and Disability Tribunal (SENDIST). His broad experience includes all forms of discrimination, bullying and harassment claims, employment contracts, restrictive covenants and references, employment status, illegality and immigration status, business reorganisations, redundancies and TUPE, industrial relations, working time and breach of contract claims. He is instructed by Government departments, NHS trusts, local authorities, the Metropolitan Police, Unions and insurance companies to appear in the Employment Tribunal, the Employment Appeals Tribunal, the county court and High Court. He delivers seminars in relation to new legislation and case law for the ELA and professional clients.

Professional Memberships: Employment Lawyers Association, Discrimination Law Association, Employment Law Bar Association, Industrial Law Society.

Career: Andrew was called to the bar in 2000, having graduated from ICSL in the top 8% of the year. He was appointed to the Attorney General's Regional Panel of Counsel in 2010.

MILFORD, Julian

11KBW, London
020 7632 8500
julian.milford@11kbw.com

Featured in Data Protection (London), Employment (London)

Practice Areas: Employment, public law, information law.

Professional Memberships: ELBA, ALBA.

Career: Julian was called to the bar in 2000. His areas of practice are employment law, public law and information law. He regularly acts for both claimants and respondents in employment disputes in the Employment Tribunal and civil courts, including industrial action and business protection cases, where his clients include major companies, banks, local authorities, police forces, unions, and healthcare providers. He currently acts for the rail company in industrial action disputes concerning Southern and Gatwick Express. Julian also appears in a wide range of judicial review cases, including civil liberties, commercial and regulatory judicial review challenges. He has acted in high profile data protection and freedom of information cases, including challenges to the Intelligence Agencies by civil liberties organisations arising out of Edward Snowden's disclosures; Vidal-Hall v Google Inc (whether pure non-financial loss is recoverable under the Data Protection Act); and freedom of information cases concerning letters between The Prince of Wales and Government Ministers and records of conversations between Tony Blair and George Bush. Julian is a member of the Attorney General's A Panel of Treasury Counsel.

Publications: Contributor to Tolley's Employment Law Handbook.

Personal: Pianist.

MILLER, Andrew QC

2TG – 2 Temple Gardens, London
020 7822 1200
amiller@2tg.co.uk

Featured in Insurance (London), Property Damage (London)

Practice Areas: Commercial disputes, with a particular focus on the energy sector, domestically and internationally. Domestic and international construction disputes, with significant experience of arbitrations in (among others) Brunei, Singapore and the Philippines. Property damage, especially arising from floods, fires, explosions and subsidence. Insurance and reinsurance: coverage disputes, policy construction, fraudulent and exaggerated claims. Professional negligence: particularly claims against architects, engineers, surveyors, other construction professionals and insurance brokers. Recent cases include: Cooper v Thameside [2016] EWHC flood damage case; representing major UK Oil and Gas Project Management company in a US$53m claim arising out of the drilling of a prospective well in West Africa; an ICC Arbitration acting for insurers of a power plant in Albania; a recovery action arising out of flood damage to £75m private residence in London. Recent reported cases include: Mueller v Central Roofing [2013] EWHC(fire); Brit Inns Ltd v BDW Ltd [2012] EWHC (recovery of subrogated loss); Caterpillar Logistics Services (UK) Ltd v P Huesca de Crean [2011] EWCA (restraint of trade); EL Policy Trigger Litigation [2010] EWCA Civ (policy construction); Axa Seguros S.A de C.V v Allianz Insurance Plc [2011] EWHC (reinsurance); Scottish Coal v Royal and Sun Alliance Insurance PLC & Ors [2008] EWHC (change of risk); Buncefield Litigation [2009] EWHC (subrogated recovery).

Professional Memberships: FCIRB.

Career: Called 1989 (Inner Temple).

MILLER, Christopher

Fourteen, London
020 7242 0858
cmiller@fourteen.co.uk

Featured in Family/Matrimonial (London)

Practice Areas: Practices exclusively in Family Law and areas related to the breakdown of family relationships. Christopher undertakes all aspects of public and private law children work, often where the most serious allegations are considered by the Court and complex medical/expert evidence has been filed (eg death of, or serious injury to, a child or where the involvement of a paedophile 'ring' is suspected). He has also developed a specialism in cases involving an international element (e.g. leave to remove applications) and was instructed in a landmark case in the Court of Appeal this year in which a foreign state's Central Authority intervened: Re CB (A Child) [2015] EWCA Civ 888. He has been instructed in a number of cases to apply for, or to resist, applications for Judicial Review and/or the grant of injunctions pursuant to s7 of the HRA 1998. Usually these instructions have been provided in the context of related public law children litigation. He also regularly represents high net worth clients in financial remedy cases and appears in cases that involve issues such as assets abroad, trusts, linked POCA proceedings and complex business assets. In addition to his busy caseload, Christopher has presented numerous lectures and workshops on diverse topics such as: Leave to Remove, Petrodel v Prest, circumventing nuptial contracts, forensic testing in relation to alcohol misuse and court skills for non-legally-qualified professionals.

Professional Memberships: FLBA, Lincoln's Inn.

MILLER, Richard QC

Three New Square, London
020 7405 1111
clerks@3newsquare.co.uk

Featured in Intellectual Property (London)

Practice Areas: Specialist in patents, trade marks, passing off, design rights, breach of confidence, restrictive covenants and all other aspects of intellectual property, including EU law relating to Intellectual Property. Also appears in the European Patent Office on behalf of applicants and opponents for European patents.

Professional Memberships: Intellectual Property Bar Association, Chancery Bar Association, Bar European Group, The Intellectual Property Lawyers Organisation (TIPLO), International Association for the Protection of Industrial Property (AIPPI), American Bar Association, American Intellectual Property Law Assocation.

Career: Called to the Bar 1976. Appointed QC 1995. Bencher (Middle Temple) 2007. Head of Chambers, Three New Square 2012- . Chairman, Middle Temple Finance Committee & Member of Executive Committee 2012- 15. Chairman, Intellectual Property Bar Assocation 2005-11. Co-chairman, EU Law Committee (formerly European Committee) of the Bar Council 2009-11. Member, General Council of the Bar 2006-11. Member, Ethics Committee of the Bar Council. Member, Patents Sub-group of the Council of the Bars and Law Societies of Europe (CCBE). Observer, UK Council, International Association for the Protection of Industrial Property (AIPPI).

Publications: "TERRELL on the Law of Patents", co-editor 14th-17th editions (1995-2011).

Personal: Educated: Charterhouse 1966-70; University of Sussex 1971-74, BSc (Chemical Physics); College of Law 1974-76.

MILLIGAN, Robert QC

Compass Chambers, Edinburgh
0131 226 5071
robert.milligan@compasschambers.com

Featured in Personal Injury (Scotland), Clinical Negligence (Scotland)

Practice Areas: Specialist areas: Personal injuries and clinical negligence. Robert has a particular interest in catastrophic injury and fatal claims and product liability. He was instructed by Merck & Co and General Motors in relation to major product liability group actions. He is currently instructed on behalf of a large group of pursuers in the transvaginal mesh and metal hip implant litigations. He appears regularly in the Inner House (appeal court). Robert speaks and writes regularly on personal injury related matters. Robert has been involved in mediations in high value claims. Robert is happy to take on conditional fee and direct access work.

Professional Memberships: Non-executive Director of the Scottish Courts Service Board (2010 to 2014); Member of the Personal Injuries User Group (2003-09) and Sheriff Court Personal Injury User Group (2009 to date); Member of various Faculty of Advocates Committees; Member of the Faculty of Advocates Council; Member of the Advisory Group to the Scottish Law Commission in relation to Prescription and Limitation in Personal Injury Actions. He is co-director of Compass Chambers.

Career: BA Hons in Jurisprudence, University College, Oxford; LLB in Law, Edinburgh University; Trained with Simpson & Marwick, Solicitors, in Edinburgh (1992-94); Called to the Bar – July 1995'; Year of Silk – 2009.

Publications: Editor of the Delict Section of the Scottish Human Rights Practice Looseleaf. Quantum Editor in Greens Reparation Bulletin (since March 2000). Author of numerous articles in Scots Law Times, Journal of Personal Injury Law, Greens Civil Practice Bulletin; and Greens Reparation Bulletin. Lectures and Seminars – Robert has spoken at numerous seminars and conferences, including for CLT, APIL, Compass Chambers, the Law Society of Scotland, the Scottish Young Lawyers Association and the Australian Bar Association. Robert also gave evidence to the Justice Committee in relation to the Damages (Scotland) Bill 2010 in September 2010 and in relation to the Court Reform Bill in April 2014.

MILLIKEN-SMITH, Mark QC

2 Bedford Row, London
020 7440 8888
milli@haslemere.com

Featured in Crime (London), Professional Discipline (London), Sports Law (London), Financial Crime (London)

Practice Areas: Recognised by Chambers UK and The Legal 500 as a leading silk in Crime, Financial Crime, Professional Discipline and Sport. Renowned as a trial lawyer with extensive experience as advocate and advisor across a wide range of criminal, commercial and regulatory matters. Regularly advises corporate and individual clients nationally and internationally, pre and post charge, in criminal as well as quasi-criminal matters, including bribery, corruption, money laundering, restraint, market abuse, insider dealing, match fixing and murder/manslaughter. Substantial regulatory and disciplinary practise before, inter alia, health-care and financial services regulators. Signifi-

cant and high profile sports law practise in cases before the disciplinary arms of sporting governing bodies. Please see 2 Bedford Row website for full details.
Professional Memberships: South Eastern Circuit, Criminal Bar Association.
Career: Called 1986. Recorder of the Crown Court 2004. Queen's Counsel 2006.
Personal: Educated at Bristol University. Married with two children. Interests include coaching and playing sport, particularly cricket and rugby, and watching almost all others.

MILLS, Ben
St Philips Chambers, Birmingham
0121 246 0200
bmills@st-philips.com
Featured in Crime (Midlands), Consumer Law (Midlands)
Practice Areas: Ben enjoys a thriving practice working predominantly in regulatory crime (fraud, counterfeiting, consumer protection and health and safety law), and associated complex confiscation proceedings. At the core of his practice is an acute attention to his client's best interests and a tireless commitment to his cases. He was Junior Counsel in R v X [2013] EWCA Crim 818, the leading authority on the CPUT Regulations 2008 and the application of recklessness to corporate entities. He is one of a small number of expert Counsel instructed nationally in cases focusing on the activities of "loan sharks". These predominantly involve Consumer Credit Act offences, blackmail and large scale fraud/money laundering. During the House of Lords expenses scandal, he was instructed to advise a Life Peer in all pre-charge matters and police interviews. Nominated for Birmingham Law Society's Barrister of the Year 2013 and 2014.
Career: Called 2000; Law Commission Research Assistant 2000-2001; joined St Philips Chambers 2001; appointed to the Attorney General's Unified List of Prosecuting Advocates (Panel B); January 2016 appointed as a Recorder of the Crown Court.
Publications: Contributing Editor: 'Consumer and Trading Standards: Law and Practice', Jordans, 2013 and 2015.
Personal: Semi-professional musician and keen sportsman.

MILNE, David QC
Pump Court Tax Chambers, London
020 7414 8080
clerks@pumptax.com
Featured in Tax (London)
Practice Areas: Specialises in both direct and indirect tax, especially litigation and dispute resolution; recent cases of note include Westmorland Investments v MacNiven (House of Lords); Marks & Spencer plc v HMRC (House of Lords and ECJ); CCE v Mirror Group (ECJ); Sinclair Collis v CCE (House of Lords and ECJ); R v Dimsey & R v Allen (House of Lords); BMW (ACT Class IV GLO) v Inland Revenue (ECJ); Peterson v CIR (NZ) (Privy Council); Telewest Communications v CCE (Court of Appeal); Mars UK Ltd v Small (House of Lords); British Telecommunications plc v HMRC (House of Lords); Newcastle United FC v HMRC (High Court); Marks & Spencer plc v HMRC (2) (ECJ); Spearmint Rhino v HMRC (High Court); Newnham College, Cambridge v HMRC (House of Lords); Brunel Motor Company Ltd v HMRC & Ford (Court of Appeal); TNT v HMRC & Royal Mail (ECJ); Philips Electronics (UK) Ltd v HMRC (ECJ); Gaines-Cooper v HMRC (Court of Appeal); LMUK v HMRC (ECJ and Supreme Court); CCJ v Jamaica (Privy Council); British Film Institute v HMRC (Upper Tribunal); Med Hotels v HMRC (Supreme Court); Greene King v HMRC (Upper Tribunal); Wheels v HMRC (First-Tier Tribunal; ECJ); HMRC v Marks & Spencer (Group relief) (Supreme Court); Wildfowl & Wetlands Trust v HMRC (First-tier Tribunal); Kumon Educational (First-tier Tribunal).
Professional Memberships: Revenue Bar Association; VAT Practitioners' Group; London Common Law & Commercial Bar Association; Chancery Bar Association; Honorary Fellow of Chartered Institute of Taxation 2009.
Career: Called 1970, Lincoln's Inn; QC 1987; Recorder 1994-2006.

MILNER, Alexander
Fountain Court Chambers, London
020 7583 3335
anm@fountaincourt.co.uk
Featured in Aviation (London), Banking & Finance (London), Commercial Dispute Resolution (London)
Practice Areas: Commercial litigation and arbitration, with wide experience of civil fraud, aviation, banking, financial services, mining and energy-related disputes. Regularly appears before the High Court, Court of Appeal and arbitration tribunals both with and without a leader. A Russian speaker, he has appeared in many of the most significant recent cases to emerge from Russia and the CIS such as Bank St Petersburg v Arkhangelsky, Mezhprombank v Pugachev, Berezovsky v Abramovich, BTA Bank v Ablyazov, Tajik Aluminium Plant v Ermatov as well as numerous confidential ICC and LCIA arbitrations involving Russian/CIS parties. These are often heavy, multi-jurisdictional disputes involving extensive factual and expert evidence and issues of foreign law. His aviation practice includes leasing, financing, insurance, slot regulation, injunctions and passenger claims. He also sits as an arbitrator.
Professional Memberships: Russian and CIS Arbitration Network; COMBAR.
Career: Called 2006.
Publications: Liability for negligent investment advice following extraordinary market turmoil (Journal of Professional Negligence, 2013); Advantages and disadvantages of arbitration CIS disputes in Western Europe (Transnational Dispute Management, 2012); Regulation EC 261/2004 and 'extraordinary circumstances' Air and Space Law, 2009).
Personal: King's College, Cambridge (BA Modern and Medieval Languages, first class with distinction, first in university; choral scholar).

MILSOM, Chris
Cloisters, London
020 7827 4000
cmi@cloisters.com
Featured in Employment (London)
Practice Areas: Employment (ET and High Court), equality, personal injury, human rights, public law, commercial.
Professional Memberships: ILS, ELBA, ELA, DLA, BHRC.
Career: Chris enjoys a practice at the forefront of employment and equalities law. Clients vary from FTSE 100 companies, the Church of England and universities to directors, doctors and victims of trafficking. Chris is a member of both the EHRC and Treasury Panels and receives repeat instructions from solicitors of the highest calibre. His oral and written arguments have been described by the EAT as "a tour de force." Many of the appellate decisions in which he has acted are groundbreaking. In recent years he has established that caste discrimination is covered under EqA 2010, acted for the successful claimant in Griffin in which the CA overhauled the ET Pensions Guidance, acted in high-profile discrimination complaints brought by members of the judiciary and represented the Claimant in the "EULEX Kosovo" whistleblowing litigation which has generated international press coverage. Chris has developed a particular specialism in TUPE having appeared in Costain v Armitage and Sanchez v CfBT. He is adept at handing High Court actions including restraint of trade and has considerable experience in the crossover between employment, commercial and personal injury litigation. Highlights amongst his 27 reported decisions include Taiwo v Olaigbe [2016] 1 WLR 2653 (SC), R (CSI) v Ministry of Defence [2016] 1 WLR 1062, Blackwood v Birmingham and Solihull [2016] EWCA 607, Day v Lewisham and Health Education England [2016] IRLR 415 and Chandhok and anor v Tirkey [2015] ICR 527.
Publications: Family Rights at Work (Jordans, February 2012).
Personal: Walking, theatre, travel and cricket.

MIRCHANDANI, Siân
4 New Square, London
020 7822 2000
s.mirchandani@4newsquare.com
Featured in Professional Negligence (London)
Practice Areas: Winner of the Chambers & Partners Professional Negligence Junior of the Year 2016, Siân has a phenomenal work ethic and a very commercial approach to her cases which have led to her being a highly sought after junior whose wide-ranging practice covers all aspects of commercial work including professional liability, construction, insurance, reinsurance, including claims against lawyers (solicitors and barristers), architects and engineers, insurance brokers and agents, surveyors and valuers, accountants, financial services professionals, including coverage and indemnity disputes, insolvency, fraud and dishonesty. Very often acting on high value claims against surveyors and valuers, Siân also has a strong construction and engineering practice acting for employers, contractors, sub-contractors and construction professionals in a wide range of construction disputes including arbitrations and adjudications. She has particular experience in claims concerning subsidence, design & construction of farm buildings and swimming pool claims. Siân is regularly instructed to represent professionals in disciplinary proceedings. She is also a TECBAR accredited adjudicator.
Professional Memberships: COMBAR, TECBAR, PNBA, PNLA, SCL, ChBA, IPBA, called to the Northern Ireland Bar, registered for the DIFC, registration pending for the SICC.
Career: Siân studied Veterinary Medicine at Cambridge University and then worked in practice before coming to the Bar and joining chambers in 1998.
Publications: Former editor of Clinical Negligence chapter of Jackson & Powell on Professional Liability.
Personal: Educated in Swansea, S Wales; University of Cambridge (MA, Vet MB); City University, London (CPE); Inns of Court (Bar). Divorced with two daughters. Hobbies: running, swimming, yoga, reading, riding, body surfing.

MISHCON, Jane
Hailsham Chambers, London
020 7643 5000
jane.mishcon@hailshamchambers.com
Featured in Clinical Negligence (London)
Practice Areas: Jane's principal areas of practice are medical law (specialising in clinical negligence and independent inquiries) and healthcare related regulatory and disciplinary cases. She acts for both Claimants and Defendants in complex and diverse clinical cases. In a case that established an important Court of Appeal authority on non-delegable duty of care, Jane successfully defended (with Martin Spencer QC) the liability for wrongful birth in Farraj v King's Healthcare NHS Trust and Cytogenic DNA Services Ltd. She also chaired the inquiry into alleged misdiagnoses in the histopathology department at University Hospitals Bristol NHS Foundation Trust as well as nine independent inquiries into homicides by patients under the care of psychiatric services.
Professional Memberships: Professional Negligence Bar Association (PNBA).
Career: Call: 1979. Accredited mediator.
Publications: Ten Independent Inquiry reports.
Personal: BA (Hons) Oxford University.

MISRA, Eleena
Littleton Chambers, London
020 7797 8600
emisra@littletonchambers.co.uk
Featured in Employment (London)
Practice Areas: Employment & Equalities (Tribunal and High Court), Professional Discipline & Regulation. Medico-Legal and Public & Administrative.
Professional Memberships: ELBA, ELA, ARDL, PNBA.
Career: Eleena has undertaken a significant amount of complex, high value employment work in the Employment Tribunal and High Court, as well as at appellate level. She is considered to be a specialist in injunctive and public law relief in the healthcare and education sectors. Eleena holds a medicolegal qualification (DipFSM) and accepts inquest instructions. Eleena is often instructed in cases requiring expertise in dispute resolution and is well known for her work in sensitive and long-running discrimination claims in respect of all protected characteristics. She has significant experience in whistleblowing litigation especially in the NHS and in City institutions. Eleena is also the founder and Co-Head of Littleton's Disciplinary & Regulatory team and regularly accepts instructions to undertake work spanning all of her complementary practice areas.
Publications: Eleena is the author of Procedure in Civil Courts and Tribunals (ed. John Bowers QC). She has coauthored Atkins on Employment and Equal Opportunities and is one of the authors of Blackstones' Employment Law Practice 2016.

MITCHELL, Andrew QC
Fountain Court Chambers, London
020 7583 3335
aem@fountaincourt.co.uk
Featured in Banking & Finance (London), Commercial Dispute Resolution (London), Financial Services (London), Insurance (London)
Practice Areas: Specific expertise in banking; civil fraud; commercial contract; (re)insurance and professional negligence, in particular in the Commercial Court, as well as in international arbitration and foreign jurisdictions including the BVI, IoM, Channel Islands and Singapore. Recent high profile cases include the interest rate swaps and LIBOR litigation, in which Andrew represents a number of banks; he appeared successfully in both the leading cases, Green & Rowley v RBS and Crestsign v RBS. He defended the board of Safeway against Competition Act fines (Court of Appeal), and has successfully prosecuted on behalf of the FCA market abuse charges against a fund manager and brokers. He acts for Barclays in relation to the PPI litigation, having also acted in the retail Bank Charges Litigation (House of Lords), the Consumer Credit test cases relating to the enforceability of credit card agreements, and in the McKillen/Barclay Brothers Claridges litigation. Andrew has acted in relation to the Arch Cru investment litigation in Guernsey and London, and has advised in connection with the Keydata litigation. He has represented litigants in relation to a number of credit crunch related matters concerning e.g. Citi; RBS; BarCap; UBS; West LB; Lehmans and Deutsche Bank. Recent complex insurance and PI cases include claims for substantial hurricane damage to US oil refinery; Korean shipbuilding guarantee litigation; broker negligence cases; mining/commodities litigation; E&O coverage claims arising from the construction of fertilizer plants in Qatar; and D&O claims arising from hedge fund fraud.
Professional Memberships: COMBAR.
Career: Called 1992. QC 2011.
Publications: Contributing Editor to 'Commercial Court Procedure' (Sweet & Maxwell).
Personal: Educated at Cambridge University (1987-90, MA) and Oxford University (1990-91, BCL). Harmsworth Scholar of Middle Temple. Born 1968.

MITCHELL, Andrew QC
The Chambers of Andrew Mitchell QC, London
020 7440 9950
arm@33cllaw.com
Featured in POCA Work & Asset Forfeiture (All Circuits), Financial Crime (London)
Practice Areas: Specialises in advising and representing clients international and domestically in civil and criminal asset forfeiture, confiscation and restraint, financial crime, commercial wrongdoing corruption and receivership. Advises and represents multinationals, professionals, prosecuting authorities, defendants, court appointed officers and third parties in all aspects of the restraint, management and confiscation of property and on the practice and procedure in relation to money laundering regulations and legislation, compliance, fraud, corruption and civil commercial wrongdoing. Current cases include the prosecution of politicians and attorneys relating to multi-millions of bribery and corruption in property developments in the Turks and Caicos; acting in civil recovery proceedings relating to corrupt payments to an ambassador from an energy company; advising the SFO in the Glaxo investigation; advising the US DoJ in relation to US/Caribbean cross-jurisdictional issues; and advising and representing several defendants in ongoing POCA proceedings as well as advising a Caribbean Country on a new proceeds of crime bill and its implementation.
Professional Memberships: Chairman of Proceeds of Crime Lawyers' Association.
Career: Called to Bar 1976, Queen's Counsel 1998. Recorder [Crime & Civil] 1998. Speaker/lecturer/consultant to UN, Commonwealth Secretariat, ESAAMLG, APG and IMF. Recently chaired committee, drafting model provisions (on behalf of international organisations). Conducts training and capacity building workshops for prosecutors and judiciary in Africa, Asia, the Caribbean and the Pacific.
Publications: Confiscation and the Proceeds of Crime – co-author; 'Administrative Court Law and Practice' – contributor.

MITCHELL, David
Ely Place Chambers, London
020 7400 9600
dmitchell@elyplace.com
Featured in Employment (London)
Practice Areas: Employment, public, media and defamation, commercial.
Professional Memberships: ELBA, ELA, DLA, ALBA, BHRC.
Career: Appointments: Attorney General's A panel (2016-2021), B panel (2012-2016) and C panel (2009-2012). Equality and Human Rights' Commission's B panel (2015-2020) Employment Law: diverse statutory and common law practice on behalf of Claimants and Defendants/Respondents. Recent cases include Robert Newbound v Thames Water Utilities Ltd [2015] IRLR 734 (CA) and Ramphal v Department for Transport [2015] IRLR 985 (EAT). Media Law: advisory and advocacy practice in defamation, privacy, malicious falsehood, breach of confidence and data protection. Public Law: Claimant and defendant judicial review practice. Particular focus on national security.
Publications: Westlaw – Libel.
Personal: Pro-bono: Bar Pro Bono Unit, ELAAS. Employment law advisor at Mary Ward Legal Centre since 2004 Direct access authorised.

MITCHELL, Jonathan
Ropewalk Chambers, Nottingham
0115 9472581
jmitchell@ropewalk.co.uk
Featured in Personal Injury (Midlands)
Practice Areas: Jonathan Mitchell has wide experience in all manner of personal injury claims including catastrophic injury cases. He has achieved a 7 figure settlement for a client injured in a motor cycle accident whilst riding the Isle of Man TT course. Being a very keen cyclist, he was able to bring an additional element to a case involving a catastrophically brain injured cyclist for whom he recently achieved a multi-million pounds settlement. Further cases on behalf of catastrophic injury (tetraplegia and brain injury) continue. He appeared in a case which involved a detailed exploration with multiple expert witnesses of the cause of a helicopter crash and required a detailed understanding of both flying skills and helicopter control systems. He recently appeared successfully on behalf of a local authority in a case in which it was alleged that a bridge had been negligently designed and built so that local cyclists persistently cycled under it and suffered head injuries. By focusing the court's attention properly on the law he was able to demonstrate that no liability attached. He also has long experience of disease related work and, in particular NIHL, HAVS and asbestos related diseases.
Career: Called 1992; LLB University College of Wales, Aberystwyth.

MITCHELL, Keith
The Chambers of Andrew Mitchell QC, London
020 7440 9950
kam@33cllaw.com
Featured in Financial Crime (London)
Practice Areas: Criminal/civil fraud and confiscation.
Career: Keith was awarded Best for Serious Fraud defence in UK 2015 by Acquisition International in recognition of his expertise in the area of financial crime. He won UK White Collar Crime Barrister of the Year for 2012, 2013 and in 2014, UK White Collar Crime Defence Barrister of the year. He has been described as "superb with clients and popular with juries", " a talented practitioner who knows his way around fraud cases." His practice encompasses major fraud investigations as well as regulatory, business, financial and other white-collar crime matters. It has been said that, "His ability to sift through heavy paperwork and present a cogent argument in court is the envy of many". He led in 'Operation Vaulter' one of the largest ever MTIC fraud based in Dubai, which concluded in 2015 after successful argument in respect of benefit and realisable assets. One source said of him: "He is just superb. He's always involved in the biggest cases in the country and he has a great touch with the clients." Previous legal directories have said of Keith, that, "Apart from having the brains and personality to deal with the most complex fraud cases, Keith Mitchell is also the type of barrister who takes the time to go through everything with his clients". He has been "recognised as being one of the main players specialising in VAT and fraud". Keith is also known "for his great client care skills and flair when it comes to case management" and his "flamboyant" style as an advocate. His current case load includes Operations 'Dougal' (cyber net fraud) and 'Holt' (Insider dealing re Logica) and he recently successfully concluded 'Operation Cactus Hent,' the North West SIPP fraud (including an unsuccessful appeal by the prosecution to the LCJ see [2015] EWCA Crim 538). Most recently Keith successfully submitted no case to answer on behalf of his Client in Operation Galion, after a 5 year investigation.

MITCHELL, Paul QC
Hailsham Chambers, London
020 7643 5000
paul.mitchell@hailshamchambers.com
Featured in Professional Negligence (London)
Practice Areas: Paul's area of expertise is the responsibilities, duties and liability of professionals. He has wide experience of claims against solicitors, accountants and financial advisers, as well as of disciplinary proceedings involving these professions. He also has experience of commercial claims with a professional liability element, coverage disputes, arbitrations and mediations. Recent notable cases include: Willers v Gubay [2016] UKSC 43 & 44, LSREF III Wight Ltd v Gateley LLP [2016] EWCA Civ 359, E.Surv v Goldsmith Williams [2015] EWCA Civ 1147.
Professional Memberships: Professional Negligence Bar Association (PNBA).
Career: Called 1999; Silk 2016. Hardwicke, Mansfield, Denning Scholarships from Lincoln's Inn; Pegasus Scholar from Inns of Court.
Publications: Paul has been a contributor to the last two editions of Flenley & Leech on Solicitors' Negligence and Liability, and for many years co-edited the chapter on limitation in LLP's Professional Negligence and Liability looseleaf. In the second edition of Flenley & Leech, he wrote the chapter on conveyancing negligence; and in the latest edition, co-wrote with Graham Reid of RPC the two new chapters on the regulatory framework within which solicitors operate and misconduct, investigations and disciplinary proceedings. Paul is actively engaged in ensuring that the Bar truly represents the population it serves. He acts as a pupil supervisor; has since 2008 sat annually on Lincoln's Inn's major scholarships committee; and takes an active role in contributing to the running of Hailsham Chambers. He is a member of the Bar Pro Bono Unit, where he has acted not only in professional negligence cases but also in other matters of importance to applicants to the unit.
Personal: Educated King's Col. Cambs (BA (1st), PhD); SOAS (MA); married, two daughters.

MITCHELL, Peter
29 Bedford Row Chambers, London
020 7404 1044
pmitchell@29br.co.uk
Featured in Family/Matrimonial (London)
Practice Areas: All aspects of the law governing financial relationships between family members, including the drafting and implementation of pre- and post-nuptial agreements, financial provision on relationship breakdown (upon divorce under the Matrimonial Causes Act 1973 and Part III of the Matrimonial & Family Proceedings Act 1984, generally under TLATA 1996 and for children pursuant to Schedule 1 of the Children Act 1989) and associated issues relating to jurisdiction, companies, family trusts, offshore trusts, taxation and other family wealth-holding structures. Peter is fully conversant with the relevant provisions of both the Family Procedure Rules and the Civil Procedure Rules. Cases include C v. C [2011] 1 FLR 434 (HC), Hart v. Hart (pending in the Court of Appeal) and, in the Supreme Court, the leading cases of Agbaje v. Agbaje [2010] UKSC 13 (Financial Provision after overseas divorce pursuant to Part III M&FPA 1984) and Sharland v. Sharland [2015] UKSC 60 (set-aside consent order for fraudulent non-disclosure).
Professional Memberships: FLBA.
Career: Called in 1996, Inner Temple, Trained as Collaborative Counsel.
Personal: Royal Academy of Music LRAM. Kings College London LLB.

MITCHESON, Thomas QC
Three New Square, London
020 7405 1111
mitcheson@3newsquare.co.uk
Featured in Intellectual Property (London)
Practice Areas: All aspects of intellectual property law, including regular EPO and CJEU appearances. Cases include Norowzian v Arks (copyright, CA); Arsenal v Reed

(trademark, CJEU and CA), Collag v Merck (confidential information), GSK v Apotex (pharmaceutical patent, CA), Sir Robert McAlpine v Alfred McAlpine (passing off), Pozzoli v BDMO (mechanical patent, CA), CoreValve v Edwards (medical device patent, CA), Lundbeck v Teva (patent sufficiency, HL), L'Oreal v eBay (trademark, CJEU), Medeva's Patent (SPC, CA and CJEU), Schutz v Werit (definition of "making", SC), MedImmune v Novartis (antibody technology, CA), Lilly v HGS (industrial applicability, SC; SPC, CJEU), Cadbury v Nestle (3D trademark, CJEU), Hospira v Genentech (anti-HER2 antibody), Lush v Amazon (trademark, online trading), Krka v AZ (enquiry as to damages), Actavis v Lilly (non-infringement of foreign patents), ISCC (patentability of stem cells, CJEU), Servier v Apotex (SC), Warner-Lambert v Actavis (2nd medical use), Actavis v Lilly (plausibility).
Career: Internship at Cold Spring Harbor Laboratory, USA 1990-91. Trinity College, Cambridge, 1991-94, First Class Hons Natural Sciences. City University (Dip-Law), 1995 (Distinction). Called to the Bar 1996. Standing Counsel to the Comptroller General for Patents Designs and Trade Marks 2009-2014. QC 2014. Appointed Person to hear trade mark appeals 2016-.
Publications: 'Two Genes in Saccharomyces Cerevisiae Encode a Membrane Bound Form of Casein Kinase-1' Wang, Vancura, Mitcheson and Kuret (1992). Terrell on the Law of Patents 18th Edition (2016).

MOFFETT, Jonathan
11KBW, London
020 7632 8500
jonathan.moffett@11kbw.com
Featured in Administrative & Public Law (London), Education (London), Local Government (London)
Practice Areas: Jonathan is a leading public law junior, with a practice that has a particular emphasis on the fields of education law, local government law, healthcare law, regulatory law, environmental law, human rights and civil liberties, and EU law. He has a particular expertise in the interface between public law and human rights. Jonathan acts for individuals, charities, companies, NGOs, central and local government bodies, regulators and other public bodies. As a member of the Attorney-General's and Welsh Government's A panels of counsel, he is regularly instructed to represent government bodies on their most difficult public law matters, ranging across topics including human rights, EU law, immigration, planning, prisons, revenue, schools and healthcare.
Professional Memberships: Administrative Law Bar Association, Planning and Environment Bar Association, Employment Law Bar Association.
Career: Called to the Bar in 1996. Appointed to the Attorney-General's A Panel of counsel to the Crown, 2009. Appointed to the Welsh Government's A Panel of counsel, 2012.
Publications: Co-author of Judicial Review: Principles and Procedure (OUP, 2013).
Personal: Educated at Girton College, Cambridge (BA and LLM).

MOFFETT, William
Radcliffe Chambers, London
020 78310081
wmoffett@radcliffechambers.com
Featured in Chancery (London), Real Estate Litigation (London)
Practice Areas: General Chancery practice with emphasis on real property, wills, trusts, probate and the administration of estates, commercial litigation, and professional negligence in those fields. Previous commendations from Chambers UK include: "Solicitors flock to him as an authority on disputes concerning wills, especially those involving questions of capacity and undue influence. He is also engaged on property litigation and trust cases. He is extremely clever and gives clear, perceptive advice. As an advocate he does not get distracted by difficult opponents and focuses on building and presenting the best possible case for the client."
Professional Memberships: Chancery Bar Association.
Career: Educated at Radley College, scholar of Selwyn College Cambridge (MA Cantab, First Class), scholar of Gray's Inn. Called to the Bar in 2000.

MOGER, Christopher QC
4 Pump Court, London
020 7842 5555
cmoger@4pumpcourt.com
Featured in Professional Negligence (London), Insurance (London), International Arbitration (London)
Practice Areas: International commercial arbitration, especially cross border investment disputes, shareholder disputes, and misuse of confidential information, with considerable experience of disputes involving China and South East Asia.
Professional Memberships: LCLBA; COMBAR; PNBA, LCIA Users' Council, Member of the HKIAC, SIAC, KLRCA & CIETAC Panels of Arbitrators.
Career: Called 1972; Silk 1992; Recorder 1993; FCIA 1997. Deputy Judge of High Court 1999. Trained mediator. Member of Panel of Chairmen of Lloyds Disciplinary Tribunal 2001, Commissioner, Alderney Gambling Control Commission 2014, Member Arbitration Chambers Hong Kong.

MOLYNEUX, Brent
29 Bedford Row Chambers, London
020 7404 1044
bmolyneux@29br.co.uk
Featured in Family/Matrimonial (London)
Practice Areas: Matrimonal finance.
Professional Memberships: Family Law Bar Association.
Career: Called to the Bar, February 1994.
Personal: Born 31 December 1968. Educated at Birkenhead School, Christ Church, Oxford (BA) and City University (Dip Law).

MONTGOMERY, Clare QC
Matrix Chambers, London
020 7404 3447
claremontgomery@matrixlaw.co.uk
Featured in Administrative & Public Law (London), Crime (London), Civil Liberties & Human Rights (London), Extradition (London), Fraud (London), POCA Work & Asset Forfeiture (All Circuits), Financial Crime (London)
Practice Areas: Commercial fraud, extradition and mutual assistance, administrative law, media law, criminal and regulatory law.
Career: Called to the Bar 1980. 1992-96 Attorney General's Civil Panel Counsel. Queen's Counsel 1996. Assistant Recorder 1999. Recorder 2000. Deputy High Court Judge 2003. Judge of the Court of Appeal of Jersey and Guernsey 2008.
Publications: Montgomery & Ormerod: Fraud; Criminal Law and Procedure. Nicholls, Montgomery & Knowles: Law of Extradition and Mutual Assistance.

MONTY, Simon QC
4 New Square, London
020 7842 2000
s.monty@4newsquare.com
Featured in Professional Discipline (London)
Practice Areas: Professional liability litigation; professional regulation; commercial litigation; mediation and arbitration.
Professional Memberships: Professional Negligence Bar Association; Chancery Bar Association; COMBAR; London Common Law & Commercial Bar Association; Western Circuit.
Career: LLB Hons 1981 (Manchester University); Called to the Bar 1982 (Middle Temple); Silk 2003; Master of the Bench, Middle Temple 2004; Recorder (Civil) 2010; accredited mediator 2009; Board Member, Bar Standards Board 2006-11; Independent Reviewer, Architects Registration Board 2010; Deputy High Court Judge, Chancery Division 2013; Advocacy Training Council (Accreditation & Training Committee Member) 2014.
Publications: Jackson & Powell, 'Professional Liability Precedents' (Contributing Editor, 'Solicitors' and 'Appeals' chapters).

MOODY, Neil QC
2TG – 2 Temple Gardens, London
020 7822 1200
clerks@2tg.co.uk
Featured in Professional Negligence (London), Insurance (London), Product Liability (London), Property Damage (London)
Practice Areas: Property damage and product liability, especially arising from floods, fires, explosions and subsidence. Utilities and construction claims. Insurance and reinsurance: coverage disputes, policy construction, fraudulent and exaggerated claims. Professional negligence: particularly claims against architects, engineers, surveyors, other construction professionals and insurance brokers.
Professional Memberships: Combar, LCCLBA, PNBA, Tecbar.
Career: Reported cases include: Cooper v Thameside [2016] EWHC (flood); Mueller v Central Roofing [2013] EWHC (construction, fire); Brumder v Motornet [2013] EWCA (insurance, company directors); Hi-Lite v Wolseley [2011] EWHC (fire, product liability); William McIlroy v Quinn Insurance [2011] EWCA (insurance, policy construction); All Leisure Holidays v Europaische Reiseversicherung [2011] EWHC (insurance/ reinsurance); Vicar of Spalding v Chubb Fire [2010] EWCA (product liability, novus actus); CPP v NuWay [2009] EWHC 824 (product liability, explosion); Cordin v Newport CC [2008] EWHC (flooding, Rylands v Fletcher); Haward v Fawcetts [2006] UKHL 9 (professional negligence, limitation).

MOODY-STUART, Thomas QC
8 New Square, London
020 7405 4321
tom.moodystuart@8newsquare.co.uk
Featured in Information Technology (London), Intellectual Property (London), Media & Entertainment (London)
Practice Areas: Intellectual property, patents, trade marks, passing off, copyright, designs, trade secrets, media and entertainment, information technology, data protection, advertising standards. Technical background (genetics, biochemistry, large and small molecules). Has appeared before CJEU, General Court and UK Supreme Court and EPO. Experience in jurisdictional disputes. Recent significant cases include Idenix v Gilead (Sofosbuvir Patent), Hearst v. Avela (Betty Boop character merchandise case)and Vestergaard Frandsen v. Bestnet (misuse of trade secrets). Advisory and clearance work in film and entertainment industry. Significant experience in comparative advertising and ASA disputes.
Professional Memberships: ChBA, IPBA, TIPLO.
Career: Middle Temple, 1995. Queen's Counsel 2016.
Publications: Editor Kerly's Law of Trade Marks and Trade Names, Butterworth's Encyclopedia of Patent Law.
Personal: Born 1970. Educated Shrewsbury School, Gonville & Caius College Cambridge. Double First, Natural Sciences Tripos (Biological), Part II Genetics. Queen Mother's Fund Scholarship, Middle Temple. Trustee of The Reading Agency (reading and literacy charity).

MOON, Angus QC
Serjeants' Inn Chambers, London
020 7427 5000
apm@3Serjeantsinn.com
Featured in Clinical Negligence (London), Court of Protection (All Circuits), Professional Discipline (London)
Practice Areas: Angus Moon QC was called to the Bar in 1986 and took silk in 2006. Angus specialises in clinical negligence and healthcare, Court of Protection, employment, inquests and inquiries, professional discipline and public and administrative law. An earlier edition notes that he is "very bright, a very shrewd tactician and a solid negotiator", "a huge presence in court", "a suave and articulate silk who is able to advise pragmatically whilst maintaining the confidence of his clients" and "one of the top rated silks at this set." Please visit the Serjeants' Inn Chambers website for his profile, which sets out full details of his practice including relevant work of note.
Professional Memberships: ELA, ELBA, LCLCBA, PNBA.
Publications: General Editor: Medical Law Reports.

MOONEY, Giles
9 Gough Square, London
020 7832 0500
gmooney@9goughsquare
Featured in Personal Injury (London)
Practice Areas: Giles is a civil practitioner specialising in cases of very serious clinical negligence and personal injury. His practices encompass all aspects of catastrophic injury work with a balanced Claimant/Defendant split. In clinical negligence work he has extensive experience of birth injuries (he recently settled a cerebral palsy claim at over £7 million), spinal injuries and brain injuries. His personal injury work includes a particular interest and speciality in Animals Act claims (and has been involved in several Court of Appeal cases on the subject) and accidents at sea.
Professional Memberships: Personal Injuries Bar Association, Professional Negligence Bar Association, AvMA.
Career: King's College London BA Hons, Inns of Court School of Law BVC 1998, Gray's Inn Goldie Scholar 1998, Called 1998.

Publications: Contributing editor to "Guides to Road Traffic Accident Claims" (Jordans). Contributing editor to "Guide to occupational Illness Claims" (Jordans). Contributing editor to 9 Gough Square publication – "Guide to Clinical Negligence Claims".
Personal: A very keen, but increasingly less effective, cricketer and show jumper.

MOORE, Martin QC
Erskine Chambers, London
020 7242 5523
clerks@erskinechambers.com
Featured in Company (London), Insurance (London)
Practice Areas: Martin is a leading Silk for company law litigation and advice, corporate finance, financial services, and insolvency. He has particular expertise in corporate transactions and reorganisations, and schemes for transfer of insurance and banking business (Part VII transfers). Significant cases and transactions include: Pfizer/Astra-Zeneca; Barclays Bank plc, Co-op Bank plc, Glencore / Xstrata, Invesnys plc, Vodafone / Verizon, Re TDG plc and Liberty International plc. Significant Part VII transfers include: Commercial Union Life Assurance Company Ltd (reattribution of inherited estate); Direct Line Insurance plc; Aviva International Limited; (large scale general insurance reorganisations); Prudential Assurance Company (domestication of Hong Kong branch) and long-term business reorganisations for Friends Life Group and Phoenix Group. Insolvency cases include: Lehmans Brothers International; Setchim v Secretary of State for Foreign and Commonwealth Affairs. General corporate litigation includes: Thermodynamics Inc v Turbotec Products plc (breach of duty, unlawful return of capital) and Bumi Resources plc (s.994 unfair prejudice petition). He has written two published opinions for the FRC on the True and Fair requirement, has advised on Bermudan, Hong Kong and Channel Islands law and has given expert evidence in the United States and Australia.
Career: BA (Oxon). Year Qualified: 1982. Lincoln's Inn. QC 2002.
Personal: Born: 1960.

MOORE, Miranda QC
5 Paper Buildings, London
020 7583 6117
mm@5pb.co.uk
Featured in Crime (London)
Practice Areas: A specialist in serious fraud and organised crime. Has particular experience in bribery and corruption cases. Lead counsel in murders (recently the Kayleigh Haywood case), white collar crime, money laundering and fiscal frauds (including frauds on the NHS). Since taking silk she has increased her defence practice and deals with a variety of cases including historic sexual abuse, rape, murder, and fraud. She defended the first Bribery Act case. Experienced in cases involving sudden deaths of infants and is recognised as a leader in cases involving young or vulnerable witnesses and defendants (including the use of intermediaries). In the last year she has successfully defended a number of murder cases involving teenage defendants, as well as a series of historic abuse cases and baby shaking allegations. Currently lead counsel in operation Yewtree spin off cases having prosecuted Dave Lee Travis and various doctors.
Professional Memberships: Criminal Bar Association, South Eastern Circuit.
Career: Called to the Bar 1983. QC 2003. Bencher of Lincoln's Inn.
Personal: Business Studies Degree Class 1 Aston University.

MORAN, Vincent QC
Keating Chambers, London
020 7544 2600
vmoran@keatingchambers.com
Featured in International Arbitration (London), Professional Negligence (London), Construction (London), Energy & Natural Resources (London)
Practice Areas: Specialist in the fields of construction, engineering, energy, infrastructure and technology disputes with vast experience of professional negligence and insurance matters in those and related fields, both domestically and internationally. He has experience of acting in disputes under most standard form contracts used in substantial projects (including JCT, ICE, NEC, IChemE and FIDIC forms). A large part of his caseload over the last three years relates to offshore wind farms disputes. Advocacy expertise covers all UK Courts including the TCC, High Court, Court of Appeal and also the House of Lords, where he acted in professional negligence actions relating to construction professionals. Vince is also regularly instructed in domestic and international arbitrations (including ICC, LCIA, DIAC, SIAC and HKIAC) and adjudications work and has extensive ADR experience in the UK including resolving many high value claims via mediation.
Professional Memberships: PNBA; TECBAR; COMBAR; SCL.
Career: Called 1991; Queen's Counsel 2011.
Publications: Contributor – Keating on Construction Contracts 9th & 10th Editions (2012& 2016); Keating on JCT Contracts [Looseleaf & CD-Rom] Member of Editorial Team 2006-09; Editor of Chitty on Contracts – 29th to 31st Edition (Chapter on Construction Law); Researcher, Keating on Construction Contracts – Eighth Edition (2006).

MORCOS, Peter
4 New Square, London
020 7822 2000
p.morcos@4newsquare.com
Featured in Insurance (London)
Practice Areas: Peter has a broad commercial practice, which includes commercial litigation and arbitration, insurance, professional liability and construction law.
Professional Memberships: COMBAR (serves on the Young COMBAR Committee), BILA, LCIA, PNBA, TECBAR, SCL, LCLCBA.
Career: BA, University of Oxford (First Class Honours); BCL, University of Oxford (Distinction); LLM, University of Pennsylvania (Distinction); BPTC (Outstanding); called 2012 by Inner Temple.

MORGAN, Gemma
Quadrant Chambers, London
020 7583 4444
gemma.morgan@quadrantchambers.com
Featured in Shipping (London)
Practice Areas: Gemma has a broad commercial practice with particular focus on shipping, international trade, commodities, insurance, international arbitration and aviation. She appears regularly in the High Court, and has particular experience of jurisdictional disputes and commercial injunctions. Gemma also appears regularly in arbitrations, particularly those held on LMAA and LCIA terms.
Professional Memberships: COMBAR; LCLCBA.
Career: MA (Cantab), Double First; BCL (Oxon).

MORGAN, James
St Philips Chambers, Birmingham
0121 246 7010
jmorgan@st-philips.com
Featured in Chancery (Midlands), Commercial Dispute Resolution (Midlands), Company (Midlands), Restructuring/Insolvency (Midlands)
Practice Areas: Chancery/commercial litigation, including all aspects of personal and corporate insolvency. Cases of note: Power v Hodges [2015] EWHC 2983 (Ch) (misfeasance and contempt); Sharma v Top Brands [2016] PNLR 12 (misfeasance and illegality); Top Brands v Sharma [2014] EWCA Civ 761 (standing to challenge status as creditors); Re Casa Estates [2014] BCC 269 (meaning of "insolvency"); Masters v Furber [2014] BPIR 263 (IVAs and injunctions); Re GP Aviation [2014] 1 WLR 166 (meaning of "property"); Nautch v Mortgage Express [2012] EWHC 4136 (Ch) (mortgagees/receivers); Re BXL Services [2012] BCC 657 (appointment of administrators); Cathie v SSBIS [2012] EWCA Civ 739 (CDDA); Re Stealth Construction Ltd [2012] 1 BCLC 297 (preference); Hill v Stokes [2011] BCC 473 (appointment of administrators); Irwin v Lynch [2011] 1 WLR 1364 (amendments and limitation); Bolsover DC v Ashfield [2011] BPIR 7 (council tax and winding up).
Professional Memberships: Midland Chancery and Commercial Bar Association.
Career: Jesus College, Cambridge, MA (Cantab). Inner Temple Major Scholar (1995). Called 1996. Junior Counsel to the Crown (Provincial Panel). Pupil master. Recorder (County Court).
Personal: Married with two children. Enjoys wine, golf and skiing.

MORGAN, Richard QC
Maitland Chambers, London
020 7406 1226
rmorgan@maitlandchambers.com
Featured in Commercial Dispute Resolution (London), Fraud (London)
Practice Areas: Richard has a broad commercial chancery practice, quite often with significant international elements and issues concerning disputes about jurisdiction, choice of law and the grant of freezing orders. Recent cases have involved a dispute arising from the collapse of the Red October steel works in Volgograd, the value of a St Petersburg shopping centre, the alleged embezzlement of US$1.1 billion from a Kazakh bank, an arbitration concerning alleged breaches of warranties in relation to the sale of a European group of companies and an arbitration concerning alleged sales into China.. Richard has experience working with lawyers in a number of other jurisdictions, has appeared in the Cayman Islands and the BVI, and has been called for cases in the Isle of Man.
Professional Memberships: Chancery Bar Association, COMBAR, Commercial Fraud Lawyers Association.
Career: Called 1988, QC 2011.
Publications: 'International Asset Chasing and Tracing' in Insolvency Bulletins and 'Litigation Strategies aimed at Swelling Assets' in Butterworths Practical Insolvency.
Personal: Born 1963. Interests include science, rowing and travel.

MORGAN, Sarah QC
1 Garden Court Family Law Chambers, London
020 7797 7900
morgan@1gc.com
Featured in Family/Matrimonial (London)
Practice Areas: All aspects of the law relating to children: Public Law: Care and adoption. Represents Local Authorities; parents; guardians; competent children. Particular interest in cases involving death and serious non-accidental injury; complex and controversial medical evidence; mental health issues. Instructed in cases of historic sexual abuse allegations requiring cross examination of vulnerable witnesses. Significant experience of cases attracting media interest and requiring reporting restrictions. Private Law: disputes between parents and other significant adults in respect of children. Disputes including allegations of serious harm. Applications in relation to living arrangements for children including domestic and international relocation issues.
Professional Memberships: Member and past Committee member of the FLBA of the FLBA ; member of the ALC, Member and Past Council Member of the Medico-Legal Society.
Career: Recorder (Crime) 2009 (Family) 2011 Silk 2011 Experienced speaker both at Chambers seminars and as an invited guest speaker to external events including FLBA events and Experts' conferences.

MORIARTY, Stephen QC
Fountain Court Chambers, London
020 78423739
smoriarty@fountaincourt.co.uk
Featured in Professional Negligence (London), Aviation (London), Commercial Dispute Resolution (London), Insurance (London)
Practice Areas: A very broad commercial litigation, arbitration and advisory practice, with particular emphasis upon banking and financial services matters; professional negligence disputes; insurance and reinsurance disputes, international commercial arbitrations, and joint venture and shareholder disputes, as well as large contractual disputes of a commercial nature more generally. The international nature of his practice frequently involves him dealing with issues of foreign law, which have included, over the years, French, Italian, Greek, Mexican, US, Indian, Indonesian, Egyptian, and Iranian law.
Professional Memberships: Chairman of Commercial Bar Association: 2011-2012, London Common Law and Commercial Bar Association.
Career: Brasenose College Oxford (BA, 1977; BCL and Vinerian Scholarship, 1978). Fellow and Tutor in Law, Exeter College Oxford, and University Lecturer in Law in the University of Oxford:1979-1986. Called to Bar and joined Fountain Court Chambers, 1986. QC, 1999.
Publications: Editor of Insurance Chapter in Chitty on Contracts 26th edition (1989) and 27th edition (1994). Contributor to Laundering and Tracing O.U.P. 1995 (Chapter entitled Tracing, Mixing and Laundering dealing with the tracing of laundered monies through bank account). General Editor (with Raymond Cox) Commercial Court Procedure (Sweet & Maxwell).

MORLEY, Stephen
Serjeants' Inn Chambers, London
020 74275000
smorley@serjeantsinn.com
Featured in Police Law (All Circuits)
Practice Areas: Stephen Morley was called to the Bar in 1996. Stephen specialises in public and administrative, police, inquests and professional discipline law. An earlier edition notes that "he is always very approachable, highly experienced" and "impresses with his understanding of case law and its practical application." Please visit the Serjeants' Inn Chambers website for his profile, which sets out full details of his practice including relevant work of note.

MORRELL, Roxanne
Carmelite Chambers, London
07956956001
rmorrell@carmelitechambers.co.uk
Featured in Crime (London)
Practice Areas: Specalist defence advocate with a wide range of experience both as Leading and Junior Counsel in complex fraud, serious and organised crime and murder. She has appeared in cases of the highest gravity including E (£100 million investment fraud), S (£51 million trademark fraud), B) £1 billion conspiracy to import Cocaine B (£53 million Tonbridge Securitas robbery and kidnapping). Notable cases in 2015 and 2016 included Crown Currency Exchange/ Mayfair and Grant £20 million Ponzi Fraud trial at Southwark Crown Court/client acquitted of theft of gold bullion; cheat on the revenue to obtain 1 million in vat repayments where her client (IT expert) received a suspended sentence; prosecution offered no evidence in a million pound money laundering case following arguments on disclosure; she represented the only defendant to be acquitted of involvement in a 'vishing fraud' widely reported as the 'bank of terror' case and most recently was involved in a 3 month trial where her client was acquitted of a Serious and Organised Crime prosecution for conspiracy to supply cocaine and associated money laundering charges over a two year period.

MORRIS, David
Serjeants' Inn Chambers, London
020 7427 5000
dmorris@serjeantsinn.com
Featured in Professional Discipline (London)
Practice Areas: David Morris was called to the Bar in 1976. David specialises in professional discipline and regulatory law. An earlier edition notes that "his knowledge of the jurisprudence is extensive and his judgement on how to run a case is always very sound. He is persuasive and the tribunal always feels safe in his hands." Please visit the Serjeants' Inn Chambers website for his profile, which sets out full details of his practice including relevant work of note.

MORRISON, Craig
Brick Court Chambers, London
020 7379 3550
craig.morrison@brickcourt.co.uk
Featured in Banking & Finance (London)
Career: Craig Morrison practises in all areas of Chambers work, with a particular focus on Commercial litigation and arbitration. He regularly appears, led and unled, in the High Court and Court of Appeal. In recent years Craig has been instructed for the successful parties in a number of the most high-profile Commercial Court trials, including Berezovsky v. Abramovich and UBS v. KWL. He is currently instructed by the Libyan Investment Authority in its $1.5 billion claim against Societe Generale. He has appeared in a broad range of other commercial matters, including civil fraud, banking, oil & gas, insurance and shipping disputes. Craig appeared as one of Legal Week's "Stars at the Bar" in 2016, being described as "one of the outstanding intellects at the junior Bar; he has a remarkable ability to master law and facts and to present them in a clear and persuasive way." Before coming to the bar Craig studied law at Cambridge University, where he graduated with the top first in his year. He subsequently studied at Harvard University and taught commercial law at Cambridge.

MORRISON, Matthew
Serle Court, London
020 7242 6105
mmorrison@serlecourt.com
Featured in Fraud (London)
Practice Areas: Commercial Chancery litigation with a particular emphasis on civil fraud, company and insolvency litigation (especially claims against directors) and offshore and domestic trust litigation. Cases include Carlyle Capital Corporation & Anr v Conway & Ors; Isis Investments Limited (in liquidation) v Kaupthing Bank Int; BTA v Ablyazov & Ors; Alhamrani v Alhamrani.
Professional Memberships: Chancery Bar Association; Commercial Bar Assocation.
Career: St John's College, Oxford (Jurisprudence (MA (Oxon.)), Bachelor of Civil Law); Attorney at Quin and Hampson (now Mourant Ozannes), Cayman (2005-06); formerly Junior Counsel to the Secretary of State for Business, Innovation and Skills.
Publications: Chapters on Directors' Liabilities in Insolvency and Disqualification of Directors in Butterworths Corporate Law Service; PLC Practice Notes on Trustees' Duties of Skill and Care, Claims against Directors, and Minority Shareholder Rights and Remedies.

MORT, Justin QC
Keating Chambers, London
020 7544 2600
jmort@keatingchambers.com
Featured in Construction (London)
Practice Areas: Justin specialises in disputes arising out of construction, process engineering, energy (on-shore and off-shore), mining and natural resources, and infrastructure projects. Recent experience includes a number of instructions arising from Crossrail and related infrastructure projects, and various renewable energy projects. He regularly acts in TCC litigation, international arbitrations, and in adjudication and equivalent processes. He has appeared in an enormous number of reported cases of interest within his practice area. Recent reported cases include J Murphy & Sons Ltd v Beckton Energy Ltd, Commercial Management (Investments) Ltd v Mitchell Design & Construct Ltd and Imperial Chemical Industries Ltd v Merit Merrell Technology Ltd. Justin has particular experience of injunction proceedings. He has prepared the relevant section in Keating on Construction Contracts in recent editions (including the most recent, 10th edition). He is familiar with most standard forms of contract including NEC (2nd and 3rd editions), and forms published by JCT, ICE / ICC, and FIDIC. He has appeared in numerous cases arising under the HGCRA (1996), both relating to adjudication enforcement and the Act generally.
Professional Memberships: SCL; TECBAR; LCIA; King's College Construction Law Association; COMBAR.
Career: Called to the (Middle Temple) Bar (1994); silk (2014); TECBAR Accredited Adjudicator.

MORTIMORE, Simon QC
South Square, London
020 7696 9900
simonmortimore@southsquare.com
Featured in Restructuring/Insolvency (London)
Practice Areas: Simon specialises in domestic and cross-border restructuring and insolvency, banking and finance and company law, particularly offshore. Examples of work includes Apcoa Parking, major Guernsey unfair prejudice proceedings, European Directories, acting for many parties in Lehmans and Icelandic bank insolvencies, noteholders in Sigma (House of Lords) and Cheyne Finance, the administrators of Innovate (Court of Appeal), the Australian liquidators of HIH (House of Lords) and the T&N pension trustees in Federal-Mogul, and the liquidators and administrators of Barings. Substantial involvement in almost all the major insolvencies of the last 20 years (BCCI, Maxwell, Olympia & York etc). More than 70 reported cases.
Professional Memberships: ILA, R3, INSOL, Chancery Bar Association, COMBAR.
Career: Qualified 1972, Inner Temple; QC 1991; mediator, CEDR accredited 1997 and Court of Appeal panel member 2003; member ACCA disciplinary panel 2003-07; deputy bankruptcy registrar at the High Court 1987-99; admitted to the Bar of the British Virgin Islands and for specific cases to the Bars of Bermuda and The Cayman Islands.
Publications: Mortimore, "Company Directors: Duties, Liabilities and Remedies" (OUP, 2nd ed, 2013).

MORTON, Keith QC
Temple Garden Chambers, London
020 7583 1315
kmorton@tgchambers.co.uk
Featured in Health & Safety (London), Inquests & Public Inquiries (All Circuits)
Practice Areas: Inquest, public inquiries, health and safety law and related proceedings. Significant cases include: R v Geoconsult (1999) (Heathrow tunnel collapse), R v Lord Condon and Sir John Stevens (2003) (death of police officer), R v Thames Trains (2004) (Paddington rail crash), R v Southampton University Hospital (2006), R v Office of the Commissioner of Police for the Metropolis (2007) (prosecution arising out of the Stockwell shooting), R v Bulmer and Nalco (2008) (outbreak of legionnaires disease in Hereford), R v Cotswold Geotechnical Ltd (2011) (first prosecution under the Corporate Manslaughter and Corporate Homicide Act), R v Dalkia Ltd (2011), R v BAM Construction (2012), R v Austin & McLean and Esso (2013), R v Costain Ltd (2014), R v Dynamiq Cleaning Ltd (2015). He has extensive experience of public inquiries (such as the Ladbroke Grove Rail Inquiry, the D Inquiry and Mid-Staffordshire NHS Foundation Trust Inquiry) and inquests (for example, the 7/7 London Bombings, Vauxhall Helicopter crash, Crossrail, work related deaths, deaths in custody, military including inquest into the deaths of 6 Royal Military Police soldiers in Iraq, an air crash at RAF St Mawgan and deaths of 3 SAS recruits on the Brecon Beacons). More generally, he has a common law practice with a particular focus on employment and personal injury and is accustomed to dealing with complex civil litigation.
Professional Memberships: Justice, Administrative Law Bar Association, Health and Safety Lawyers Association.
Career: Called to the Bar Lincoln's Inn 1990; Treasury Counsel B Panel (1997-2003), A Panel (2003-08) (2009 – 2011). Silk 2011.
Personal: Educated at University of Hull, City University. Interests include theatre, art, music, architecture, cycling.

MOSER, Philip QC
Monckton Chambers, London
020 7405 7211
chambers@monckton.com
Featured in Competition/European Law (London), Public Procurement (London), Tax (London)
Practice Areas: European law; public procurement; commercial law; VAT. Recent cases include: Maxter Catheters v Medicina [2016] 1 WLR 349 (conflict of laws); Brand Studio v St John Knits [2016] 1 All ER (Comm) 1163 (commercial agency); Edenred v HM Treasury and ors [2015] UKSC 45, Supreme Court (public procurement); Delaney v DfT [2015] 1 WLR 5177, Court of Appeal (Francovich damages); Abdulrahim v Council and Commission, CJEU, Grand Chamber, ECLI:EU:C:2013:331 (EU sanctions); Staatssecretaris van Financiën v Schoenimport, CJEU, ECLI:EU:C:2014:2455 (VAT fraud). Older cases include: Lonsdale (commercial agents' compensation); 'Metric Martyr' litigation; Factortame.
Professional Memberships: Bar European Group; UKAEL; European Circuit; ELI Fellow.
Career: Called 1992; Silk 2012. Called Northern Ireland 2016. Former research associate, Centre for European Legal Studies, University of Cambridge; accredited Mediator 2003; Bencher, Inner Temple 2012. Joint Head of Monckton Chambers.
Publications: (Include) editor, 'The European Advocate'; co-editor, 'European Law Reports' (1999-2012), 'Making Community Law' (2008).
Personal: MA(Cantab) in Law. Fluent German.

MOSES, Stephen QC
Furnival Chambers, London
020 7405 3232
smoses@furnivallaw.co.uk
Featured in Crime (London)
Practice Areas: Crime.
Professional Memberships: Criminal Bar Association; South Eastern Circuit; Gray's Inn.
Career: "Stephen Moses is a class act" according to senior members of the judiciary. "He has developed a first class criminal practice" and was "always destined to take Silk early". Stephen has regularly been instructed in large scale and high profile cases at the Central Criminal Court and beyond in matters of homicide, serious fraud, serious and organised violence, complex money laundering offences and large scale drugs conspiracies. His impressive catalogue of high profile cases include:- R v Gary Dobson (2012) [the murder of Stephen Lawrence]; R v Peter Blake (2011), defending the first defendant

in the landmark first "judge alone" trial; as well as representing the "mastermind" in the much publicised conspiracy to rob Securitas in Tonbridge of £53 million – the largest cash robbery in history (R v Lea Rusha). Stephen has, in recent years, specialised in very serious violent and sexual crime and murder, including allegations of baby shaking, cases involving complex medical evidence, young and vulnerable defendants and witnesses. His "much deserved" appointment to Silk was a "popular decision"and he has already proved to be much in demand and well respected.

MOTRAGHI, Nadia
Old Square Chambers, London
02 7269 0300
motraghi@oldsquare.co.uk
Featured in Employment (London)

Practice Areas: Nadia specialises in employment law and professional discipline. In employment, her practice spans the Tribunal, High Court and all levels of appeal including the Supreme Court. She acts for employees and employers in every area of employment law including discrimination of all types, wrongful dismissal, whistleblowing, TUPE, breach of contract, trade union cases, and injunctions (industrial action, restrictive covenants, MHPS). Nadia regularly represents in high value and complex lengthy discrimination and whistleblowing cases as well as in large multiple Claimant cases. Her clients span include public sector (NHS, local government), private sector (especially banking, technology and retail), individuals and trade unions. In professional discipline, she appears before a variety of regulators especially in healthcare and at internal hearings and at all levels of appeal. Notable recent work includes Uddin v GMC [2012] (Admin); Maggs & Johnson v NMC [2013] (Admin); Kapadia v GMC [2014] (Admin); Whether acting alone, leading or being led, Nadia is a sought after junior barrister.

Professional Memberships: ARDL, ELA, ELBA, ILS.

Career: St John's College, University of Oxford (MA Jurisprudence); Harvard Law School (LLM, Frank Knox Fellow, Deans Award); College of Law (BVC Outstanding; Bedingfield Scholar, Ede & Ravenscourt Prize for Student of the Year). Prior to joining Chambers, Nadia worked for the Law Commission, the European Roma Rights Centre, and held a number of part-time teaching posts including at Kings College London and Harvard University. Currently a Barrister Member of the Bar Disciplinary Tribunal.

MOTT, Richard
One Essex Court, London
020 7583 2000
rmott@oeclaw.co.uk
Featured in Banking & Finance (London), Commercial Dispute Resolution (London)

Practice Areas: Richard has a broad commercial litigation and arbitration practice, including civil fraud, banking, energy, financial services / regulatory and general commercial disputes. Recent cases include Mercuria Energy Trading Pte Ltd & Anr v Citibank NA & Anr [2015] EWHC 1481 (Comm) ($270m claim arising out of obligated repo agreements in the context of a suspected fraud in China), Lehman Brothers International (Europe) v Exxonmobil Financial Services BV (claim under a terminated GMRA contract), Tullow Uganda Ltd v Heritage Oil and Gas Ltd [2013] EWHC 1656 (Comm) and [2014] EWCA Civ 1048 ($313m claim arising out of the sale of petroleum rights in Uganda), Sloane House Ltd v Fleury (civil fraud; obtained initial freezing order, then summary judgment and committal order), acting in a very substantial LCIA arbitration arising out of a dispute between shareholders in one of the world's largest aluminium companies, and Weavering Capital (UK) Ltd v Peterson & Ors [2013] EWCA Civ 71 (fraud by CEO of collapsed hedge fund; appeared as sole counsel before Court of Appeal).

Career: Called 2006. Christ's College, Cambridge (BA, History – First Class); City University (CPE – Commendation); Inns of Court School of Law (BVC – Outstanding).

MOXON BROWNE, Robert QC
2TG – 2 Temple Gardens, London
020 7822 1200
rmoxonbrowne@2tg.co.uk
Featured in Insurance (London), Property Damage (London)

Practice Areas: Described by Chambers UK as "an amazing courtroom presence" who is "completely bulletproof", Bob is recognised as a leader of the Bar in Professional Negligence, Insurance and Property Damage. Heading the Professional Negligence Group at 2 Temple Gardens, he is an authoritative advocate with huge experience of indemnification and other insurance issues. His reputation is for an informal hands on style, and robust advocacy. An amiable and relaxed manner belies a capacity for meticulous attention to the detail of complex cases, and, when necessary ferocious cross-examination. He works for and against accountants, solicitors, valuers and surveyors, as well as construction industry professionals, especially in cases about the allocation of responsibility within multi-disciplinary teams. Bob's background is in insurance law with long experience of subrogated recoveries in cases involving fire, flood and other catastrophic events, policy construction questions and repudiation for fraud. He retains a special interest in life and critical illness issues, and is often counsel of choice for insurers and reinsurers interested in these risks. Bob's impressive record of appearances in reported cases, many of them landmark Court of Appeal authorities in his areas of specialisation, attest to the depth and width of his experience, and the success which he enjoys as a top-rated Queen's Counsel.

Professional Memberships: ORBA, Professional Negligence Bar Association, CLBA, COMBAR.

Career: Called to the Bar 1969, QC 1990. Recorder 1992. Deputy Judge of the Technology and Construction Court 1993. Deputy Judge of the High Court 1999.

Personal: Born 1946. Educated Gordonstoun School, University College Oxford (BA).

MUIR, Nicola
Tanfield Chambers, London
020 7421 5300
nicolamuir@tanfieldchambers.co.uk
Featured in Real Estate Litigation (London)

Practice Areas: All aspects of residential and commercial property litigation including landlord and tenant disputes, real property and conveyancing problems, mortgage litigation and property related professional negligence disputes. Nicola has particular expertise in residential leaseholder cases. Notable cases include Tibber v Buckley [2015] EWCA Civ 1294 (enfranchisement), Jastrembski v Westminster City Council [2013] UKUT 0284 (LC) (service charges), South Tyneside Council v Ciarlo [2012] UKUT 247 (LC) (service charges); Chambers v Havering LBC [2011] EWCA Civ 1576 (adverse possession); Westminster City Council v CH2006 [2009] UKUT 174 (LC) (enfranchisement) and Green v Westleigh Properties Ltd [2008] EWHC 1474 (right of first refusal).

Professional Memberships: Property Bar Association, Chancery Bar Association, Association of Leasehold Enfranchisement Practitioners.

Career: LLb (Hons) from the University of Edinburgh. Qualified as a Solicitor in 1991. Called to the Bar 1998. Joined Tanfield Chambers in 2012 (formerly at Hardwicke).

Publications: Regular column in the Estates Gazette on residential property law called – "Residential View". Co-author (with other members of Tanfield Chambers) of "Service Charges and Management" (Sweet & Maxwell 3rd ed 2013).

MULCAHY, Leigh-Ann QC
4 New Square, London
020 7822 2000
l.mulcahy@4newsquare.com
Featured in Professional Negligence (London), Insurance (London), Product Liability (London)

Practice Areas: Insurance law (with a particular emphasis on employers, public, professional and product liability insurance and issues related to asbestos and environmental liabilities). Professional liability (especially lawyers, financial services professionals and accountants). Product liability (including pharmaceuticals, medical devices, commercial products and food). Civil fraud. Public and human rights law including commercial/regulatory judicial review. Inquiries. Mediation. Has acted in four cases before the Supreme Court and House of Lords (International Energy Group Ltd v Zurich; The Employers Liability Insurance Trigger Litigation; The Atomic Veterans Litigation and Medcalf v Mardell) and regularly appears in the Court of Appeal. Has recently acted in a high value commercial arbitration arising out of an IT dispute and arbitration appeal, an insurance dispute arising from the PIP Breast Implant Litigation and an insolvency case relating to the appointment of provisional liquidators. She appeared in the Miners' Knee Litigation and acted in an international fraud case on behalf of the Central Bank of Trinidad and Tobago. Cases include: International Energy Group Ltd v Zurich [2015] 2 WLR 1471; Abbey Forwarding Ltd v Revenue and Customs Commissioners [2015] Bus LR 882; Secretary of State for the Home Department v Raytheon Systems Ltd [2015] 1 Lloyd's Rep 493 & [2014] EWHC 4375; Durrheim v Ministry of Defence [2014] EWHC 1960; Davidson v Aegis Defence Services [2014] 2 All ER 216; Davies v Secretary of State for Energy and Climate Change [2012] EWCA Civ 1380; Durham v. BAI and ors [2012] 1 WLR 867 (SC); AB v. Ministry of Defence [2012] 2 WLR 643 (SC); R (McVey) v Secretary of State for Health (2010) Med LR 204 and [2010] EWHC 1225; Leonard v Byrt [2008] EWCA Civ 20; Bezant v Rausing [2007] EWHC 1118; Russell Young and Co, v Kevin Brown [2008] 1 WLR 525, CA; R (Lord Chancellor) v Chief Land Registrar [2006] QB 795; Phillips v. Symes (No 2) [2005] 1 WLR 2043; R (Ministry of Defence) v. Wiltshire and Swindon Coroner [2006] 1 WLR 134; Medcalf v Mardell [2003] AC 120, HL.

Professional Memberships: COMBAR; Professional Negligence Bar Association; Administrative Law Bar Association; BIICL Product Liability Forum.

Career: MA (Cantab); LLM (Osgoode); Dip. EC Law (London). Called to Bar 1993. Appointed Senior Decision-Maker for Guernsey Financial Services Commission 2014. Appointed First Counsel to the Welsh Government 2013. Appointed QC 2009. Treasury Counsel – A Panel 2006-2009. CEDR accredited mediator. Also called to Bar of Republic of Ireland.

Publications: Editor 'Jackson and Powell on Professional Liability'; Consulting Editor 'The Law and Regulation of Medicines'; General Editor 'Human Rights and Civil Practice'.

MULHOLLAND, Helen
Kings Chambers, Manchester
0345 034 3444
clerks@kingschambers.com
Featured in Clinical Negligence (Northern)

Practice Areas: Principal area of practice is clinical negligence. Handles complex and high value clinical negligence matters. Accepts instructions in cases across the medical spectrum, but has particular interest and expertise in cases of gynaecological and obstetric negligence, including cerebral palsy claims. Also practises in personal injury, specialising in cases of multiple serious injury and with a particular interest in cases involving brain injury.

Professional Memberships: Professional Negligence Bar Association, Personal Injury Bar Association.

Career: University: Birmingham BA (Hons) Italian and French; CPE (Chester); BVC (ICSL); Inn: Middle Temple.

MULLEN, Jayne
St Ives Chambers, Birmingham
0121 236 0863
jayne.mullen@stiveschambers.co.uk
Featured in Family/Matrimonial (Midlands)

Practice Areas: Matrimonial finance.

Professional Memberships: Deputy District Judge (Family) 2010 Deputy District Judge 2002.

Career: Jayne Mullen specialises in financial provision following divorce. She is recommended in Chambers & Partners and Legal 500 and by professional and lay clients. Jayne is highly numerate and is known for her comprehensive preparation and early identification and insight into the key issues in even the most complex of cases from the first conference. Jayne is noted for her pragmatic and sensible approach and realistic advice and her ability to explain complex financial matters and law to clients to enable them to be fully involved and in control of the decision making process. From the first meeting Jayne offers realistic advice and quickly builds up good relationships with her professional and lay clients. In Court, she combines a mastery of her papers with pragmatic and persuasive advocacy. Jayne is known, is one of the best-prepared advocates in the Midlands. She is reported as having a 'great eye for detail and appealing advocacy' and those instructing her can have complete faith in her 'thorough approach' and that 'she leaves no stone unturned' in her preparation.

MULLEN, Mark
Radcliffe Chambers, London
020 7831 0081
mmullen@radcliffechambers.com
Featured in Charities (London), Court of Protection (All Circuits)
Practice Areas: Chancery barrister with particular emphasis on charities, the Court of Protection, companies and associations, insolvency (including directors' disqualification), trusts, wills, probate and estates. Significant reported cases include: King v. Dubrey [2016] Ch 221; Bank of Beirut SAL v. Prince El-Hashemite [2016] Ch 1; Hope v. Ireland [2015] BPIR. 344; Executive Jet Support Limited v. The Serious Organised Crime Agency [2013] 1 WLR 1433; R. (Independent Schools Council) v. The Charity Commission for England and Wales [2012] Ch 214; Kings v. Bultitude [2010] WTLR 1571; Dean v. Stout [2006] 1 FLR 725.
Professional Memberships: Chancery Bar Association, Charity Law Association, Society of Trust and Estate Practitioners, Association of Contentious Trust and Probate Specialists.
Career: Called 2001. Barrister member, Council of the Inns of Court Disciplinary Tribunal (2009-2013). Junior Counsel to the Crown (HM Attorney General's A Panel) (2016-); B Panel (2011-2016); C Panel (2008-2011). Deputy Registrar in Bankruptcy of the High Court (2016-).
Publications: Companies Limited by Guarantee (Jordans, 2014); Running a Charity (Jordans, 2015); Contributor, Tolley's Insolvency Law.
Personal: Educated at St Benedict's School, Ealing; Durham University; BPP Law School. Leisure activities include music and walking. Resides in London.

MULLIS, Roger
Radcliffe Chambers, London
020 7831 0081
rmullis@radcliffechambers.com
Featured in Chancery (London)
Practice Areas: Landlord and tenant; real property; inheritance, probate and administration of estates; trusts and trustees; partnership; professional negligence.
Professional Memberships: Chancery Bar Association; Professional Negligence Bar Association.
Career: Called 1987.
Personal: Educated at Portsmouth Grammar School and Christ Church, Oxford (BA, BCL). Interests include music, especially singing (lay clerk at St Albans Cathedral). Former trustee of Holy Cross Centre Trust.

MUMFORD, David QC
Maitland Chambers, London
020 7406 1200
dmumford@maitlandchambers.com
Featured in Chancery (London), Art and Cultural Property Law (London), Banking & Finance (London), Commercial Dispute Resolution (London), Company (London), Fraud (London), Offshore (London), Partnership (London)
Practice Areas: Commercial and chancery litigation, including business agreements and general commercial disputes, civil fraud, company and partnership matters, jurisdictional disputes, claims against trustees and other fiduciaries, and professional negligence. Notable cases include: BAT v Sequana (dividend claw-back in connection with US environmental indemnity claims); Canary Wharf Finance (dispute over the securitisation of the Canary Wharf estate); Bumi (shareholder and other claims concerning the UK-listed mining enterprise); Red October (jurisdiction challenge in debt and conspiracy claims against Russian steel works); Berezovsky v Abramovich, Hine & ors (various actions involving the famous Russian oligarch); Masri v Consolidated Contractors (alleged conspiracy to evade judgment debts); Jennington v Assaubayev (fraud claims in connection with the sale of a gold mining conglomerate); Cadogan Petroleum v Tolley (fraud and bribery claims in connection with a gas exploration business); Lehman Brothers (concerning the administrators' liability for rent); Cinnamon v BCP (claim against a Portuguese bank about a mortgage securitisation); Equitable Life v Bowley & Ors (acting for former Managing Director and Appointed Actuary in claims arising out of the collapse of the Society); In re the Buncefield Incident (acting for commercial property owners in claims arising out of the oil terminal explosion); Marlwood v Kozeny (acting for US investors in fraud claims concerning the privatisation of the Azeri oil industry); Scottish & Newcastle v PwC (defending professional negligence claims against management consultants) and Gregson v HAE Trustees Limited (successfully resisting a 'dog-leg' claim against directors of a trust company for breach of trust).
Professional Memberships: Chancery Bar Association and COMBAR.
Career: Called in 2000; QC 2016.
Personal: Born 6 March 1975. Educated King's College School and Magdalen College, Oxford (MA Classics, 1st Class Honours). Former Mansfield Scholar and Denning Scholar of Lincoln's Inn.

MUNBY, Thomas
Maitland Chambers, London
020 7406 1200
tmunby@maitlandchambers.com
Featured in Chancery (London)
Practice Areas: Commercial litigation and arbitration, with a strong Chancery background. Thomas is best known for heavy business disputes, including those involving civil fraud, company / insolvency law, and banking / financial services. He also enjoys a more traditional Chancery practice, involving trusts, estates and real property disputes. Thomas' work frequently has an international element, involving jurisdictional and conflict of laws questions. Many of his cases involve applications for freezing injunctions or other interim remedies. Thomas has experience of disputes within a wide variety of industries and sectors including: accountancy / audit, aviation, banking, financial services, IT, media & entertainment, mining & minerals, oil & gas, private client / wealth management, pharmaceuticals and property development. His notable and recent cases can be seen on the Maitland Chambers website.
Professional Memberships: COMBAR, Chancery Bar Association, Chartered Institute of Arbitrators (ACIArb), Insolvency Lawyers' Association, Commercial Fraud Lawyers Association.
Career: Called 2006.
Personal: Educated at Balliol College, Oxford (Classics – Congratulatory First Class Honours and various prizes), City University (CPE – Commendation and Tort Law Prize) and Inns of Court School of Law (BVC – Outstanding and various prizes); Princess Royal Scholar and Sir Stephen Chapman Scholar of Inner Temple.

MUNDY, Robert
St Philips Chambers, Birmingham
0121 246 7000
rmundy@st-philips.com
Featured in Commercial Dispute Resolution (Midlands)
Practice Areas: Commercial litigation, including insolvency and company law. High Court employment.
Professional Memberships: Midland Chancery and Commercial Bar Association, COMBAR, Employment Lawyers Association.
Career: Trinity Hall, Cambridge, MA (Cantab). Called 2008.

MUNRO, Joshua
Hailsham Chambers, London
020 7643 5000
joshua.munro@hailshamchambers.com
Featured in Professional Negligence (London), Costs Litigation (All Circuits)
Practice Areas: Joshua is a leading junior in costs, professional negligence, commercial litigation and insurance. For professional negligence, The Legal 500 2015 edition says he is: 'fiercely intelligent and pulls no punches with the opposition.' For costs, Chambers UK 2015 says: "He's got a very quick mind and speedily assesses how to deal with and head off the issues in a case." Recent cases include: J Browne Construction v Chapman [2016] 165 Con. L.R. 175. Joshua's cross-examination proved that documents had been fabricated. IEG v Zurich [2016] A.C. 509 Seminal Supreme Court decision on liability insurance. Andrew Fryatt v Preston Mellor Harrison (a firm) [2015] EWHC 1683 (Ch) Joshua's cross-examination proved the Defendant's evdience to have been dishonest. R v Griffin April 2015. Joshua acted for the taxpayer, successfully resisting Dave Lee Travis' claim for costs.
Professional Memberships: PNBA; LCLCBA.
Career: Called 2001; Lecturer in contract and tort law, University of East London, 2002-06.
Publications: Contributor to the Solicitors' Journal, Butterworths Costs Newsletter, LexisNexis Insight.
Personal: Joshua took the highest First in his year at Oxford University for BA Hons in English and Modern Languages. Joshua is interested in all things Italian, including art, music, literature, food & wine, and visits Italy whenever possible with his young family.

MURPHY, Melissa
Francis Taylor Building, London
020 7353 8415
clerks@ftbchambers.co.uk
Featured in Planning (London)
Practice Areas: Melissa's practice is focused on planning and real estate matters. She has extensive experience of providing advice and representation in relation to planning appeals, compulsory purchase and compensation and related public law challenges. She offers realistic and commercial advice to both public and private sector clients in order to provide solutions to legal problems concerning land.
Professional Memberships: Member of the Planning and Environment Bar Association, the Constitutional and Administrative Law Bar Association, the Compulsory Purchase Association and the National Infrastructure Planning Association.
Career: Queen Mother Scholar (Middle Temple), called in 2001.

MURRAY, David
Fountain Court Chambers, London
020 7583 3335
dm@fountaincourt.co.uk
Featured in Banking & Finance (London), Commercial Dispute Resolution (London)
Practice Areas: Commercial litigation including banking, financial services, insurance/reinsurance, aviation, sale of goods, conflict of laws, financial regulation, civil fraud and professional negligence. Recent notable cases include: Tigris International NV v China Southern Airlines Co Ltd [2014] EWCA Civ 1649 (aviation/sale of goods); A.H. Baldwin and Sons Ltd v Al-Thani [2012] EWHC 3156 (QB) (sale of goods/ freezing injunctions); Injazat Technology Fund v Najafi [2012] EWHC 4171 (Comm) (anti-arbitration injunctions); Deutsche Bank AG v Petromena ASA [2015] EWCA Civ 226 (jurisdiction under Lugano Convention); Stone & Rolls Ltd v Moore Stephens [2009] UKHL 39, [2009] 1 AC 1391 (auditors' negligence and the illegality defence); Safeway Stores Ltd v Twigger [2010] EWCA Civ 1472; [2011] 2 All ER 841 (recoverability of indemnity in respect of criminal penalties). Other recent experience and current instructions include various substantial confidential commercial arbitrations in London and overseas; a heavy and complex Commercial Court dispute arising out of a CDO transaction; and a variety of financial mis-selling claims.
Professional Memberships: COMBAR. Authorised to practise in the Dubai International Financial Centre.
Career: Called 2004. Internship at ICC, Paris, Oct-Dec 2005; Pegasus Scholar, Hong Kong, Sep-Dec 2007.
Personal: Christ Church, Oxford: BA 2001 (First), BCL 2002 (Distinction). Vinerian Scholarship 2002; Eldon Scholarship 2004.

MURRAY, Rebecca
Temple Tax Chambers, London
020 7353 7884
clerks@templetax.com
Featured in Tax (London)
Practice Areas: Unrivalled tax litigation and advisory practice across all taxes: Instructed by Big 4, magic circle and boutique solicitors and accountancy firms. Clients include Rich List individuals, celebrities and FTSE 100 companies. Unled in the Court of Appeal, Upper Tribunal and High Court, including several JRs. Recent reported cases include Donaldson [2016] EWCA Civ 761; Sippchoice [2016] UKFTT 464; Walapu [2016] EWHC 658; Hills [2016] UKUT 189; Lucas [2016] EWHC 1960; Rowe [2015] EWHC 2293, Hasbro European Trading BV [2015] UKFTT 340; Eclipse Film Partners No 35 LLP [2015] EWCA Civ 95; Tower MCashback 3 LLP [2014] UKFTT 108; Donaldson [2014] UKUT 536; Moyes [2014] UKFTT 1030; Hills [2014] UKFTT 646; MCashback Software 6 LLP [2013] UKFTT 679; BAA Ltd [2013] EWCA Civ 112; Tower MCashback LLP 1 [2011] UKSC 19.
Professional Memberships: CIOT (Fellow), ATT, TEP, Secretary of the Revenue Bar Association, Member of CTA Corporation Tax Committee and VAT Practitioners Group; Attorney General's Panel of Counsel.
Career: Winner Taxation's Rising Star 2013, Tax Journal's 40 under 40 2012/13; Shortlisted Chambers & Partners Tax Junior of the

Year 2015, STEP Young Practitioner 2013, Indirect Tax Rising Star 2012.
Publications: Author of "Tax Avoidance", Sweet & Maxwell (3rd September 2016); CCH on corporation tax 2007/8.
Personal: Sporty, highly competitive.

MUSGRAVE, Caroline
Cloisters, London
020 7827 4000
cmusgrave@cloisters.com
Featured in Employment (London)
Practice Areas: Caroline Musgrave specialises in employment, equality and human rights law with particular expertise in equal pay, whistleblowing and discrimination law. Caroline acts for companies and individuals, financial institutions, charities, trade unions and public authorities. She is highly regarded for the quality of her advocacy, her strategic and structured approach, excellent witness handling and exceptional client service. Caroline maintains a diverse practice also advising and representing clients in commercial law, personal injury, clinical negligence and at inquests.
Professional Memberships: ELA, ELBA, ILS, PIBA and A4ID.
Career: Notable cases include the equal pay litigation of Barry v University of Wales Trinity St David, the first known group action for male workers claiming equal pay with female workers. In Wendy Williams v MOD Caroline represented the most senior serving nurse in the RAF in her claim of both direct and indirect sex discrimination securing the highest compensation awarded in the Employment Tribunal in 2014.
Personal: Caroline graduated from Clare College, Cambridge (2001) and spent time as a visiting fellow at Harvard's Law School Project on Disability in 2013. Before being called to the bar in 2008, Caroline worked as a relief and development professional in Rwanda, Pakistan, Indonesia and the UK.

MYHILL, David
Crown Office Chambers, London
020 7797 8100
myhill@crownofficechambers.com
Featured in Clinical Negligence (London)
Practice Areas: Specialist civil practice, with particular expertise in disputes involving professionals accused of negligence (including clinical negligence, as well as surveyors, accountants, brokers, IFAs and solicitors), property damage claims, and general commercial and insurance litigation. Clinical negligence practice involves regular instructions in high value claims for Claimants, NHS Trusts and privately insured Defendants, with regular trial experience. Property damage practice involves a particular emphasis on subrogated claims involving fires, floods and subsidence. Insurance work includes coverage disputes, claims involving fraud, and interpretation of all forms of non-marine policies. Commercial practice incorporates wide-ranging disputes concerning the sale of goods and supply of services, with an emphasis on disputes concerning IT contracts, and claims for commission arising out of estate agency contracts. Regularly acts in settlement negotiations including mediations and round table meetings. Highly experienced in representing parties at all forms of oral hearing, including arbitrations, trials, applications, and inquests.

MYLONAS, Michael QC
Serjeants' Inn Chambers, London
020 7427 5000
mmylonas@serjeantsinn.com
Featured in Clinical Negligence (London), Court of Protection (All Circuits), Professional Discipline (London)
Practice Areas: Michael Mylonas QC was called to the Bar in 1988 and took silk in 2012. Michael specialises in clinical negligence and healthcare, Court of Protection, health and safety, human fertilisation and life sciences, inquests and inquiries, personal injury, product liability, professional discipline and regulation, public and administrative and sports law. An earlier edition notes that "he is meticulous when it comes to preparation, and tenacious in court. He remains a very skilled and intelligent advocate with fantastic client relationship skills", "he is never daunted by a fight and shows complete understanding and compassion to clients" and "he is blindingly brilliant in conference and at trial. His preparation is second to none... He is extremely good on his feet in court and at cross-examination – he's the best I've met. He goes in like a machine gun." Please visit the Serjeants' Inn Chambers website for his profile, which sets out full details of his practice including relevant work of note.
Professional Memberships: PNBA, AVMA, ARDL, HSLA, LCLCBA.
Publications: Medical Treatment: Decisions and The Law (Co-author), Medical Law Reports (2000 – 2010), APIL Clinical Negligence.

NAGPAL, Deepak
1 King's Bench Walk, London
020 7936 1500
dnagpal@1kbw.co.uk
Featured in Family/Matrimonial (London)
Practice Areas: Divorce and Matrimonial Finance. Interesting cases include: Juffali v Juffali [2016] 4 WLR 119; Estrada v Juffali [2016] 3 WLR 243; Sharbatly v Shagroon [2014] 2 FLR 209; CR v MZ [2013] EWHC 295; Shagroon v Sharbatly [2013] 2 WLR 1255; Gordon v Stefanou [2011] 1 FLR 158; JKN v JCN [2011] 1 FLR 826; W v W [2011] 1 FLR 372; Granatino v Radmacher (formerly Granatino) [2011] 1 AC 34; S v S (Hemain Injunction) [2010] 2 FLR 502; S v S (No 2) (Ancillary Relief Application to Set Aside Order) [2010] 1 FLR 993; Miller Smith v Miller Smith [2010] 1 FLR 1402; Crossley v Crossley [2008] 1 FCR 323; Charman v Charman [2007] 2 FCR 217; McFarlane v McFarlane [2006] 2 AC 618; Mark v Mark [2006] 1 AC 98; Moore v Moore [2005] 1 FLR 66.
Professional Memberships: Commitee Member of the Family Bar Association; Ethics Committee of Bar Council; Member of the LexisPSL Family Consulting Editorial Board; Member of the South Eastern Circuit.
Career: Called in 2002 (Lincoln's Inn). Hardwicke Scholarship; Lord Mansfield Scholarship; Megarry Scholarship. Treasury counsel.
Publications: Co-editor of Jackson's Matrimonial Finance; Advisory Editor of the Family Court Reports.
Personal: Educated at Loughborough Grammar School and Christ Church, University of Oxford. MA (Oxon) Jurisprudence (1st Class); BCL.

NAMBISAN, Deepak
Fountain Court Chambers, London
020 7842 3779
clerks4@fountaincourt.co.uk
Featured in Commercial Dispute Resolution (London), Fraud (London)
Practice Areas: Broad commercial and civil practice, with particular expertise in: all areas of commercial law, particularly fraud, aviation, banking, insolvency, insurance/reinsurance, professional negligence; regulatory law, including Law Society, financial services, City regulatory work and disciplinary tribunals; employment law; administrative and public law; entertainment, music and sports law; conflict of laws and multi-jurisdictional issues.
Professional Memberships: New York Bar; ICC; LCIA; COMBAR; LCLCBA; South Eastern Circuit; British Association for Sport & Law, British Insurance Law Association; British Russian Law Association.
Career: Called 1998; Gray's Inn Prince of Wales Scholar; Junior Counsel to the Crown (B Panel).
Publications: Editor, Commercial Court Procedure (Sweet & Maxwell); Co-author, Chapter 23 on Directors & Officers, Professional Negligence & Liability (2005, LLP); Co-author, Director' & Officers' Liability Insurance (2008, LLP).
Personal: King Edward's School; The Williston Northampton School; Christ's College, Cambridge; Exeter College, Oxford; Harvard Law School.

NATHAN, Aparna
Devereux, London
020 7353 7534
nathan@devchambers.co.uk
Featured in Tax (London)
Practice Areas: Tax law: Advisory: tax planning for ultra high net worth UK and Foreign domiciliaries including offshore trust structures; Residence and Domicile issues e.g Proposed Deemed Domicile Rules; Non Residents' CGT regime; Estate planning; GAAR; corporate tax planning including residence and permanent establishment issues; EBTs; disguised remuneration. Litigation: Extensive litigation practice. Notable cases include Moyles et al v HMRC ("Working Wheels" scheme); Boyle v HMRC (structured avoidance scheme); Berry v HMRC (Gilts strip scheme); Professional Golfers Association v HMRC (whether PGA is an eligible body); Lord Howard of Henderskelfe v HMRC (whether Reynolds portrait is a wasting asset); Stolkin v HMRC (EIS deferral relief); De Silva v HMRC (Partnership Losses/ Sch1A, 1B); Tottenham Hotspur FC v HMRC (taxation of payments made to Peter Crouch and Wilson Palacios).
Professional Memberships: CIOT – Chair – CGT Sub Committee; Addington Society -Honorary Secretary; Revenue Bar Association; Chancery Bar Association; Worshipful Company of Tax Advisers.
Career: Joined Devereux Chambers in August 2014. 1996-August 2014 member of Gray's Inn Tax Chambers.
Publications: McCutcheon on Inheritance Tax (6th ed.) and Supplement. Currently writing the 7th Edition; Mellows on Taxation for Trustees and Executors (Non-resident Trusts Chapter.
Personal: Performing Arts Committee of Bharatiya Vidya Bhavan, London.

NAUGHTON, Sebastian
Serjeants' Inn Chambers, London
020 7427 5000
snaughton@serjeatnsinn.com
Featured in Clinical Negligence (London)
Practice Areas: Sebastian Naughton was called to the Bar in 1999. Sebastian specialises in clinical negligence, employment and inquests and inquiries. An earlier edition notes that "he's very meticulous and his attention to detail is very good. Very concise, he is able to pull out the relevant parts of the case and really get to grips with the key points." Please visit the Serjeants' Inn Chambers website for his profile, which sets out full details of his practice including relevant work of note.

NAWBATT, Akash
Devereux, London
020 7353 7534
nawbatt@devchambers.co.uk
Featured in Employment (London), Tax (London)
Practice Areas: Akash's principal areas of practice are employment and tax law. He is instructed in complex and high value litigation, in both tribunals and the High Court, by large employers (including global financial institutions and leading airlines), Government Departments and taxpayers.
Career: Called 1999. Judicial assistant to the House of Lords (2001-02). Junior Counsel to the Crown: C Panel (2004-08); B Panel (2008-2013); and A Panel (2013 – 2018). 2015 Chambers UK Bar Awards: Employment Junior of the Year.
Publications: Contributing Editor to 'Harvey on Industrial Relations and Employment Law.'

NAYLOR, Kevin
Exchange Chambers, Manchester
0161 833 2722
naylor@exchangechambers.co.uk
Featured in Clinical Negligence (Northern)
Practice Areas: Clinical Negligence
Career: Kevin originally qualified as a doctor and practised medicine for 7 years. He is one of a small number of dual qualification barristers practising in the UK. He has held University Teaching Hospital posts in the following disciplines: General Medicine, General Surgery, Accident & Emergency, Obstetrics, Paediatrics, Medicine for the Elderly, General Practice and Psychiatry. Kevin practises almost exclusively in the field of clinical negligence acting for both claimants and defendants. His broad based medical knowledge is an enormous asset. His practice also includes coroner's inquests and solicitors' negligence claims arising out of the conduct of clinical negligence and personal injury claims. Kevin is also an accredited Mediator. "A master tactician who can immediately identify the key issues in a complex case. He is one of only a handful of UK barristers who is also a qualified doctor and his input in a case is invaluable. A silk in all but name." – Sarah Barclay, Partner, Sarah Barclay and Co. "A very persuasive advocate with great courtroom skills. He prepares cases meticulously and fights very hard for his clients. His medical knowledge gives him a tremendous advantage dealing with expert witnesses" – Michael Saul, Partner, TJL Solicitors. "Kevin is the leader in his field. He brings a calm and measured approach to cases and has an outstanding track record. His medical background puts clients at ease as they quickly realise that they are dealing with an exceptionally knowledgeable

barrister" – Pam Roberts, Head of Clinical Negligence, WHN Solicitors.
Publications: Co-author of the British Society of Gastroenterology Guideline for Obtaining Valid Consent for Gastrointestinal Endoscopy Procedures.
Personal: Qualifications: MB.Ch.B. MRCGP LL.B. (Hons) LL.M. Leisure interests: skiing, cycling and walking to the village pub with his family and trusted Labrador, Harry.

NEALE, Fiona
Hailsham Chambers, London
020 7643 5000
fiona.neale@hailshamchambers.com
Featured in Clinical Negligence (London), Professional Discipline (London)
Practice Areas: Fiona's extensive clinical negligence experience includes acting for claimants and defendants in a wide range of cases, including numerous high value claims. Recent cases include: X' v Bailing, Havering and Redbridge NHS Trust. Representing claimant; 90% settlement of liability issues on behalf of brain damaged child. GDC v PL. Representing Registrant. One of GDC's largest cases; ongoing. Recent successful appeal to NI Admin Court. Taylor v St Helen's NHST [2014] C inadvertently injected femoral artery with crushed Temazepam; leg lost. Breach of duty admitted, successfully defended at trial on causation.
Career: Called 1981; CLE (Bar Finals, 1980-81); King's College, London (LLB Hons 2:1, 1977-80); King Edward VI High Schools for Girls (1969-76).
Publications: Co-author of chapter, Limitation, in APIL's book 'Clinical Negligence', published April 2008; 'How to litigate cerebral palsy claims', London, May 1996.

NEISH, Andrew QC
4 Pump Court, London
020 7842 5555
aneish@4pumpcourt.com
Featured in Professional Negligence (London), Insurance (London)
Practice Areas: General commercial law. Principal areas of practice are insurance and reinsurance and professional negligence (especially brokers, lawyers and accountants).
Professional Memberships: COMBAR, London Common Law and Commercial Bar Association, LCIA Users' Council.
Career: Called 1988. Silk 2009.
Personal: MA (St Andrews), Dip Law (City). Admitted in the BVI, MCIArb, Trained Mediator.

NEOFYTOU, Michael
25 Bedford Row, London
020 70671500
mneofytou@25bedfordrow.com
Featured in Crime (London)
Practice Areas: Michael Neofytou is a dedicated Criminal defence specialist who was called to Bar in 1999. He has extensive experience defending those accused with the most serious crimes in the U.K, in particular murder, high-value fraud and large-scale Class A drug conspiracies. He has wide-ranging experience defending those with mental-health issues particularly those accused with murder where issues of insanity or diminished responsibility may feature. Michael is known for his representation of many high-profile individuals particularly those within Sport, Media and the Arts. He has represented leading international sportsmen from the fields of football, horse racing, boxing and cricket.
Professional Memberships: Fraud Lawyers Association, Association of Regulatory and Disciplinary Lawyers, Criminal Bar Association.
Career: Michael Neofytou's full profile may be found at www.25bedfordrow.com.

NERSESSIAN, Tiran
4 Stone Buildings, London
020 7242 5524
t.nersessian@4stonebuildings.com
Featured in Restructuring/Insolvency (London)
Practice Areas: Commercial litigation and advice: extensive experience of litigation in corporate and personal insolvency, civil fraud, company and public law. Notable cases: Re Kombinat Aluminjuma Podgorica AD (in Bankruptcy) [2016] 1 BCLC 311 – Cross-Border Insolvency Regulations 2006, arbitration; Walker v NatWest [2016] BCC 355 – Financial Misselling, administrators' powers and duties; Allfiled UK Ltd v Eltis [2016] FSR 11 – Injunction, breach of fiduciary duties, conspiracy; Brooks v Armstrong [2015] BCC 661 – Wrongful trading, directors' duties; Re a Company [2014] EWHC 3925 (Ch) – objectionable trading practices, damage to company reputation/finances; Re RD Industries Ltd [2014] EWHC 2844 (Ch) – corporate factoring arrangements, directors' disqualification; Secretary of State v Feld [2014] 1 WLR 3396 – interpretation of court judgments/orders; NCA v Surin [2013] EWHC 3784 (QB) – Freezing orders, fraud; HMRC v Sunico [2014] EWCA Civ 1108 – unlawful means conspiracy, MTIC Fraud; Sykes and Sons Ltd [2013] Bus LR 106 – advertisement of petition, costs; Rubin v Coote [2011] BCC 596 – liquidator, sanction of compromise; HMRC v Earley [2011] BPIR 1590 – IVA, jurisdiction; Abernethy v Hotbed Ltd [2011] BPIR 1547 – guarantees; Re Hagemeister [2010] BPIR 1093 – cross-border insolvency; BA Peters [2010] 1 BCLC 110 – competing trust claims.
Professional Memberships: COMBAR, ChBA.
Career: MA (Oxon); Called 2002; Junior Counsel to the Crown B Panel (2011-date); C Panel (2006-11).
Publications: Contributor to 'Annotated Companies Acts' (OUP) and Atkins Court Forms.
Personal: Enjoys football, tennis and basketball.

NESTERCHUK, Tetyana
Fountain Court Chambers, London
020 7583 3335
tyn@fountaincourt.co.uk
Featured in Professional Discipline (London)
Practice Areas: Main areas of practice: Administrative and Public Law, Banking and Finance, Commercial arbitration and litigation, Financial Services Regulation, Professional Regulation. Notable cases include R (Lumsdon) v Legal Services Board [2015] 3 WLR 121, [2015] EWCA Civ 421, [2014] HRLR 29, [2014] EWHC 28, [2013] EWHC 3289; Barnett v SRA [2016] EWHC 1160, SRA v Barnett and Swift (Case No. 112492014); SRA v Hale (Case No 114762016); Erdenet v Government of Kazakhstan [2016] EWHC 299; JSC Mezhdunarodniy Promyshlenniy Bank v Pugachev [2014] EWHC 4336 (Ch), R. (on the application of OJSC Rosneft Oil Co) v HM Treasury 2014] EWHC 4002 (Admin).
Professional Memberships: Combar, LCLCBA.
Career: Tetyana began her career as a solicitor in a corporate department at Slaughter and May where she worked between 2006 and 2010. From 2010-2011 Tetyana worked as a judicial assistant at the Supreme Court assisting Lords Rodger, Brown and Collins. She was called to the Bar in 2011 and practiced at Fountain Court Chambers ever since.
Publications: England and Russia: resolving jurisdictional disputes (Law Gazette, 22 April 2013); the view from behind the bench: the role of judicial assistants in the UK Supreme Court, a contribution to Judge and Jurist: Essays in Memory of Lord Rodger of Earlsferry edited by A. Burrows, D. Johnson and R. Zimmermann.
Personal: BA (Jurisprudence), Worcester College, Oxford (First Class Honours; ranked 1st in the year across University); BCL, Worcester College, Oxford (Distinction); LPC, BPP Law School (Distinction).

NEUBERGER, Edmund
Atkin Chambers, London
020 7404 0102
eneuberger@atkinchambers.com
Featured in Construction (London)
Practice Areas: Edmund's practice covers general commercial disputes with particular specialisation in construction and engineering, IT, professional negligence, insurance and PFI related matters. Edmund has advised on and appeared for parties involved in a wide range of disputes from major commercial construction contracts, railway infrastructure projects, energy infrastructure projects, waste PFIs to professional negligence and domestic building projects. Edmund has been instructed by insurers, developers, employers, professionals, contractors, sub-contractors and government. Edmund is experienced with most standard forms of contract, including NEC3. Edmund appears frequently in the High Court, as well as County Courts, and has broad experience of a range of dispute resolution procedures including litigation, arbitration, adjudication and mediation, as well as sitting as an adjudicator.
Professional Memberships: TECBAR, LCLBA, SCL, COMBAR and CEDR (Adjudication Panel member).
Career: MEng (Oxon), Called to Bar by Lincoln's Inn 2008.

NEVILLE, Stephen
Gough Square Chambers, London
020 7353 0924
stephen.neville@goughsq.co.uk
Featured in Consumer Law (London)
Practice Areas: Has specialised in financial services, consumer credit and contractual disputes for 25 years. Provided compliance reviews for many of the largest business and portfolio sales in the consumer lending sector over the last decade. His clients include a wide range of banks, lenders, private equity companies, debt acquirers and retailers, including HSBC, Lloyds, RBS, Virgin, Citigroup, HBOS, MBNA, GE Money, Northern Rock, Nationwide, Societe Generale, Apax, Apple, T-Mobile, and Dell, whom he advises on technical issues, especially those arising from FCA regulation. He is also active in loan enforcement and contract litigation: cases include – Airbus v Withey [2014 – Mercantile court trial of £1.5m secret commission claim], Carey v HSBC [2010] Bus LR 1142 [represented OFT: test case on enforceability of credit card agreements], McMillan v Range [2004] 1 WLR 1858 (CA) [definition of credit], Rahman v Sterling Credit [2001] 1 WLR 496 (CA) [extortionate credit bargains], and Swindle v Harrison [1997] 4 All ER 705 (CA) [solicitor loan to client].
Career: St John's College, Cambridge MA(Hons)Law. Called to the Bar 1986.

NEWBEGIN, Nicola
Old Square Chambers, London
020 7269 0300
newbegin@oldsquare.co.uk
Featured in Professional Discipline (London)
Practice Areas: Nicola specialises in employment, discrimination and professional discipline, as well as undertaking related work in the fields of judicial review, human rights and data protection. Nicola practises in all sectors but has particular expertise in the healthcare sector having appeared in a number of the leading high court doctor and dentist cases, including: McMillan v Airedale NHS Foundation Trust [2014] EWCA Civ 2031, [2014] IRLR 803; Chakrabarty v Ipswich Hospitals NHS Trust [2014] EWHC 2735, [2014] Med LR 379; and Dusza & Sobhani v Powys Teaching Local Health Board [2015] EWCA Civ 15, as well as a number of judicial reviews relating to doctors in training. Nicola also has extensive experience of complex discrimination claims (both employment tribunal and county court) and of multi-claimant and collective employment disputes, including before the employment appeal tribunal and court of appeal.
Professional Memberships: ELA, ELBA, ILS, IER, ARDL, PIBA.
Career: Former solicitor (admitted January 2003). Joined Old Square Chambers as a tenant in October 2009.
Personal: Keble College, Oxford (Jurisprudence).

NEWMAN, Anya
St Ives Chambers, Birmingham
0121 236 0863
anya.newman@stvieschambers.co.uk
Featured in Social Housing (Midlands)
Practice Areas: Social housing.
Career: Anya Newman has a strong reputation in the field of housing and property law and prides herself on her ability to understand her client's objectives and give practical advice, enabling clients to achieve the best possible outcome in the most efficient manner. In court Anya is known as a ferocious advocate who fights hard for her clients. Anya frequently undertakes possession claims involving complex succession arguments or difficult human rights and Equality Act 2010 elements. She is a specialist anti-social behaviour litigator, she undertakes judicial review work as well as frequently advising on homelessness cases including matters involving the travelling community. Anya has recently been lead by Joseph Giret QC in a ground breaking cross-county injunction application to prevent car cruising and its associated nuisances across the Black Country for which she received an award from West Midlands Police.

NEWMAN, Catherine QC
Maitland Chambers, London
020 7406 1200
cnewman@maitlandchambers.com
Featured in Chancery (London), Company (London), Fraud (London), Offshore (London), Partnership (London)

Practice Areas: Barrister specialising in trial and appellate advocacy in Chancery, Commercial and offshore litigation and dispute resolution, including contracts, company law, commercial disputes, equitable remedies, corporate insolvency, partnership, derivatives, banking, professional and business conduct, fraud and asset recovery, trusts litigation; reported cases include such topics as cross-border insolvency: Shell v Fairfield Sentry, Madoff v Yacht Bull; civil consequences of abandoned criminal prosecution: Tchenguiz v SFO; removal of trustees of Jersey trust: T v YT ; derivatives: Intesa Sanpaolo SPA v Regione Piemonte; Hazell v Hammersmith & Fulham; hedge fund disputes: F&C Alternative Investments (Holdings) v Barthelemy & Culligan; share sale warranties: Sycamore Bidco v Breslin and Dawson; accessory liability: JSC BTA Bank v Ablyazov; JD Wetherspoon PLC v Jason Harris; winding up of valuable hotel partnership at will: Boghani v Nathoo; fraud: JD Wetherspoon v Van de Berg; relief from unfairly prejudicial conduct may be enjoyed as an investor, not only as a member: Gamlestaden Fastigheter AB v Baltic Partners Ltd; sham and Section 423: Hill v Spread; breach of trust and restitution: Mahme Trust Reg v Tayeb; unfair prejudice: Re Acorn International; confidential information and constructive trusts: Satnam Investments Ltd v Dunlop Heywood & Co Ltd.
Professional Memberships: Chancery Bar Association; COMBAR; ACTAPS; Professional Negligence Association; IBA, Insol International.
Career: Called 1979, Middle Temple: Harmsworth Scholar; called 2011, BVI; ad hoc in Cayman Islands; registered to appear in the DIFC (Dubai). QC 1995; Deputy High Court Judge (QB and Chancery); Crown Court Recorder; Lieutenant Bailiff of the Royal Court of Guernsey 2001-2014; member UCL Council 2008-11; trustee, CAFOD.
Personal: Convent of the Sacred Heart High School; University College, London (LLB Hons 1st Class).

NEWMAN, Peter
1 King's Bench Walk, London
020 7936 1500
pnewman@1kbw.co.uk
Featured in Family/Matrimonial (London)

Practice Areas: Peter Newman specialises in matrimonial finance and divorce. His practice encompasses the full range of ancillary financial relief, including financial relief on divorce, provision after foreign divorce, all related enforcement and injunctive relief, financial provision for children, and Trusts of Land disputes. Peter has appeared at all levels including the Court of Appeal and the Supreme Court and deals with complex cases or cases of high value.
Professional Memberships: Member of the Honourable Society of the Inner Temple; Member of the Family Law Bar Association; Member of the South Eastern Circuit; Member of the Sussex Bar Mess; Accredited pupil supervisor (inner Temple); Accredited advocacy trainer (Inner Temple).
Career: Peter Newman undertook pupillage at 1 King's Bench Walk and has been a tenant there ever since.
Personal: Peter was a major scholar at Malvern College. He has a BA (Hons) degree in English and Philosophy and a LLB (Hons) degree in Law (First Class honours) Peter is married and has 2 young sons. He lives in South London.

NEWTON, Katharine
Old Square Chambers, London
020 7269 0300
newton@oldsquare.co.uk
Featured in Employment (London)

Practice Areas: Katharine practices almost exclusively in the field of employment law, and appears regularly in the employment tribunal, the High Court and the appellate courts, including the Court of Appeal. Katharine acts for both employers and employees in every area of employment law including discrimination of all types, victimisation, unfair and wrongful dismissal, whistleblowing, TUPE, breach of contract, restrictive covenants, wages and trade union and industrial disputes. Katharine also has considerable experience of conducting lengthy, complex and high value discrimination claims, including many lasting in excess of 20 days. Katharine's experience encompasses a wide range of sectors, but she has particular expertise in acting for Banking and Financial Institutions (including well known high street banks), NHS Trusts, High Street retailers, Higher Education Institutions as well as Claimants holding both senior and junior roles. In addition, Katharine has particular expertise in conducting claims in the civil courts arising out of discrimination in the provision of goods and services.
Professional Memberships: Employment Lawyers' Association; Employment Law Bar Association; Industrial Law Society; Bar European Group.
Career: Called to the Bar 1999 Middle Temple.

NEWTON, Laura
Brick Court Chambers, London
020 7520 9803
laura.newton@brickcourt.co.uk
Featured in Chancery (London), Fraud (London)

Professional Memberships: COMBAR Chancery Bar Association LCIA YIAG Commercial Fraud Lawyers' Association Young Fraud Lawyers' Association.
Career: Laura Newton is a leading junior with a commercial practice which sees her regularly instructed in high-value international commercial disputes and arbitrations, often with a fraud aspect. She has appeared as sole Counsel, as well as being led, in a number of substantial cases in the Commercial Court, Chancery Division and the LCIA. Laura's experience has been recognised as exceptional for someone of her seniority: she was one of just 10 barristers selected for inclusion in The Lawyer Hot 100 2016, and was also featured as one of the Legal Week 10 Stars at the Bar 2016. The Lawyer noted that, "At just seven years' call Laura Newton has been dubbed a 'superstar' by QCs for her record of bringing in significant commercial litigation mandates and being a 'driving force' in complex case management." Legal Week referred to her as "winning plaudits left, right and centre". In May 2014, she was selected as one of just six barristers to represent the English Commercial Bar as part of the Bar Council's delegation to South Korea and was seconded to Yoon & Yang LLC, a leading Korean law firm based in Seoul.

NIAZ-DICKINSON, Anisa
Kenworthy's Chambers, Manchester
0161 8324036
a.niaz-dickinson@kenworthysbarristers.co.uk
Featured in Employment (Northern)

Practice Areas: Anisa Niaz-Dickinson has an exclusive employment law practice and represents both Claimants and Respondents before the Employment Tribunal and Employment Appeal Tribunal. Anisa practices across the full breadth of employment law and within a wide range of sectors such as the police (instructed by the Police Federation), education, NHS, public sector and business. She has acted in a number of high profile cases, group actions involving hundreds of Claimants and has a particular interest in discrimination claims having acted in numerous multi day/week hearings. This year Anisa was successful in the case of Bourini and Ors v Casual Dining Services Ltd (2016) a group action against Café Rouge and Bella Italia. Anisa was able to prove that no redundancy consultation took place, she also successfully argued that no Polke reduction should be made and recovered a substantial costs award. Anisa was also recently successful in the case of Midgeley v ESP Global Holdings Ltd (2016) when she represented the Respondent against a race/age discrimination and unfair dismissal claim.
Professional Memberships: Employment Lawyers Association.
Career: Following a successful career developing human rights policy Anisa completed pupillage at Doughty Street Chambers in 2006. She joined Kenworthy's Chambers in January 2007.

NICE, Amelia
5 St Andrew's Hill, London
2073325400
amelianice@5sah.co.uk
Featured in Extradition (London)

Practice Areas: Amelia Nice is a barrister specialising in extradition and international family. She has a busy extradition appellate practice and has appeared in leading Article 8 cases involving children and vulnerable individuals, mental health, prison conditions and other human rights considerations, notably trafficking and the use of assurances. Cases include Celinski v Poland [2015]; Sas v Poland [2015]; ST v Lithuania [2014]; Wolkowicz v Poland [2013]; Aleksynas v Lithuania [2014]. Amelia has particular experience in UK cases involving children law, including those with parallel international child abduction proceedings or domestic Care Proceedings. Amelia is also instructed by the National Crime Agency in extradition and related judicial review proceedings and regularly advises individuals and judicial authorities on issues concerning the preparation of extradition requests to this country from other jurisdictions, particularly concerning historic child abuse. Amelia is also instructed in public and private law children cases in the County Court and High Court with particular experience in forced marriage and FGM protection orders, as well as child abduction, relocation, stranded spouse, care and contact proceedings and she has growing experience representing children.
Professional Memberships: Child Abduction Lawyers Association, Defence Extradition Lawyers Forum, Extradition Lawyers Association Family Law Bar Association.
Career: BA, MA, GDL, Called 2006 (Inner Temple).

NICHOLLS, John QC
Maitland Chambers, London
020 7406 1200
jnicholls@maitlandchambers.com
Featured in Chancery (London)

Practice Areas: Business and commercial chancery litigation, including contractual and shareholder disputes, fraud claims and banking and finance law. Has particular experience of large professional negligence claims and professional disciplinary proceedings. Also has considerable experience of aspects of sports law and telecommunications law. Notable cases include BCCI v Price Waterhouse, Barings v Coopers & Lybrand, Electra v KPMG, Money Markets International v London Stock Exchange, Cambridge Antibody Technology v Abbott Biotechnology, Scottish & Newcastle PLC v PricewaterhouseCoopers, GSK v Abbott Biotechnology and Royal Bank of Scotland v Highland.
Professional Memberships: Chancery Bar Association; COMBAR.
Career: Called to the Bar 1986, appointed QC 2006.
Personal: Born 1963; educated Winchester College and Trinity Hall, Cambridge (BA Law, 1st Class honours); married with two children; lives in Twickenham; particular interests are sport and travel; member Hawks Club, Aula Club, Lensbury Club, Bombay Gymkhana; speaks French and German.

NICHOLSON, Jeremy QC
4 Pump Court, London
020 7842 5555
jnicholson@4pumpcourt.com
Featured in Professional Negligence (London), Construction (London)

Practice Areas: Construction & engineering, energy, shipbuilding, professional negligence, insurance, and general commercial work. He has an outstanding track record in achieving successful conclusions to major and difficult cases. Known for mastery of technical detail and legal argument, lateral thinking, strategic advice, and team leadership in large and complex cases. Acts for insurers, contractors, employers, engineers, architects, surveyors, and other professionals; in litigation, arbitration, and mediation. Very wide experience of different types of buildings, structures, plant, and sites. Involved as advocate or arbitrator in international arbitrations in Dubai, Geneva, Paris, and London. Major TCC cases include Hamid v Barnfield Construction 2013 BLR 447; Co-op v John Allen 2012 28 ConstLJ 27; Southwark v IBM 2011 135 ConLR 136; Skanska v Somerfield 2007 CILL 2449; AXA v Cunningham Lindsey 2007 EWHC 3023; SST v AMEC 2006 EWHC 2909; Alfred McAlpine v Panatown 2001 AC 518.
Professional Memberships: CIArb, HKIAC, LCIA, SCL, SCLHK, TECBAR, PNBA, BILA, COMBAR, LCLCBA. Registered with DIFC Courts, listed on HKIAC & KLRCA Lists of Arbitrators.
Career: Call 1977; QC 2000; FCIArb 2011.
Publications: Resolving Construction Disputes in Asia: How will it look in 2026? Asian Dispute Review, July 2016 Experts'

Discussions & Joint Statements – Any Room for Lawyers? Academy of Experts, June 2016.
Personal: Educated Trinity Hall, Cambridge; College of Law (Harmsworth Scholar). Interests: sailing, travelling, architecture, theatre.

NISSEN, Alexander QC
Keating Chambers, London
020 7312 6131
anissen@keatingchambers.com
Featured in Professional Negligence (London), Construction (London)
Practice Areas: Specialist in advocacy and advisory work and in adjudication, arbitration, litigation and mediation of construction, engineering, energy and professional negligence disputes. Practice covers diverse cases ranging from client/developer claims (extensions of time, loss and expense etc), defects, PFI disputes, professional negligence, contractors' and sub-contractors' claims, adjudication enforcement, disputes relating to bonds (both domestic and international), rail disputes, power stations and oil and gas projects. Chartered Arbitrator, accredited adjudicator and mediator. Arbitration work covers both domestic and international disputes, including ICC appointments. Recent cases include Grove Developments Ltd v Balfour Beatty Ltd [2016], Rendlesham Estates Plc v Barr Ltd [2015], UK Highways A55 Ltd v Hyder Consulting UK Ltd, and Accolade v Volker Fitzpatrick, one of the Lawyer's top 20 cases for 2014 , regarding a £150m claim for defects arising out of piling and floor slab issues at a production centre for a very substantial drinks distributor.
Professional Memberships: SCL; TECBAR (Vice Chairman); COMBAR; Law Society Panel of Arbitrators 2006; SCMA.
Career: Called (1985); FCI Arb (2000); Chartered Arbitrator (2003); TECBAR adjudicator (2002); accredited mediator (2004); QC (2006); Recorder (2007); Public Access Training (2008); Deputy High Court Judge (2013).
Publications: Contributor- Keating on Construction Contracts, 5th-10th editions.

NOLAN, Dominic QC
Hailsham Chambers, London
0115 947 2581
dominic.nolan@hailshamchambers.com
Featured in Personal Injury (London), Clinical Negligence (London)
Practice Areas: Dominic's practice principally comprises complex and high value clinical negligence and personal injury claims, having specialised in such claims for nearly 30 years. He has considerable experience and particular expertise in cases involving serious brain or spinal injury. He prides himself on being approachable and sensitive when dealing with all parties, especially in cases that arise under tragic circumstances. He is a highly experienced negotiator in settlement meetings. He has substantial experience of cases where complex issues regarding the extent of the employer's duty have arisen. He has twice argued such cases in the Supreme Court in Baker v Quantum (deafness) in 2010 and in McDonald v National Grid (asbestos) in 2014. He has substantial experience of acting for insurers in trials where fraudulent or exaggerated claims have been successfully challenged. He has experience of commercial, regulatory and costs litigation. Dominic is an accredited mediator and has acted as leading counsel in mediations in more complex cases.
Professional Memberships: Personal Injuries Bar Association; Professional Negligence Bar Association.
Career: Called in 1985; Silk 2006; called to the Gibraltar Bar: 2007; LLB, University of Nottingham 1984; Recorder since 2005; Honorary Professor in Law University of Nottingham 2009- (Honorary Lecturer 2003-9); President of Nottinghamshire Medico-Legal Society 2014; Head of Ropewalk Chambers: 2009 – 2012.

NOLAN, Michael QC
Quadrant Chambers, London
020 7583 4444
michael.nolan@quadrantchambers.com
Featured in Shipping (London)
Practice Areas: All aspects of the law relating to ships and the sale and carriage of goods; pollution; commodities; insurance and reinsurance; harbour law; conflicts of laws and arbitration. Cases include: Imperator I Maritime Co v Bunge SA [2016] EWHC 1506 (Comm) (Time Charter, hull fouling); Sarpd Oil v Addax Energy SA [2016] B.L.R. 301, CA (Commodities, security for costs); Rambus Inc v Agrifert SA [2016] Bus. L.R. 135 (Commodities, GAFTA, substitution); The Styliani Z [2016] 1 Ll. Rep. 395 (Action in rem, amendment); HBC Hamburg Bulk Carriers v Huyton Inc [2015] 1 Ll. Rep. 310 (Voyage Charter, indemnity), Zhoushan Jinhaiwan Shipyard v Golden Exquisite [2015] 1 Ll. Rep. 283 (Shipbuilding, Cancellation), Seagrain LLC v Glencore Grain BV [2014] 1 Ll. Rep. 598, CA (GAFTA Prohibition Clause), The Athena [2013] 2 Ll. Rep. 673, CA (Shipping, Off-hire), Pacific Basin IHX v Bulkhandling Handymax [2012] 1 Ll. Rep. 151 (Charterparty, Piracy, Conwartime), Midgulf v Groupe Chimiche Tunisien [2010] 2 Ll. Rep. 543 (Commodities, anti-suit injunction), Petroplus Marketing AG v Shell Trading [2009] 2 Ll. Rep. 611 (Commodities, oil), Pratt v Aigaion Insurance [2009] 1 Ll. Rep. 225, CA (Shipping, Marine Insurance), CTI v Transclear [2008] 2 Ll. Rep. 526, CA (Commodities, frustration), TNT Global v Denfleet [2007] 2 Ll. Rep. 504, CA (CMR, wilful misconduct), The Kitsa [2005] 1 Ll. Rep 432, (Shipping, Time Charter, barnacles), Exxonmobil v Texaco [2003] 2 Ll. Rep. 686 (Commodities, "final and binding" clause), Bayview Motors v Mitsui Fire and Marine Insurance [2003] 1 Ll. Rep 131, CA (Insurance), Dart Harbour & Navigation Authority v Sec of State for Transport [2003] 2 Ll. Rep. 607 (Administrative law, Harbour), Sandeman Coprimar v Transitos y Transportes Integrales [2003] Q.B. 1270, CA (CMR), The Margaretha Maria [2002] 2 Ll. Rep. 293, CA (Shipping, Limitation Convention, share fishermen). For further details see www.quadrantchambers.com.
Professional Memberships: COMBAR (executive committee 1998-2001), LCLBA, LMAA (supporting member), SCIA.
Career: MA (Oxon), Dip Law (City). Called 1981. Astbury Scholar. QC 2015.
Publications: Butterworths Commercial Court and Arbitration Pleadings.

NOLTEN, Sonia
2TG – 2 Temple Gardens, London
020 7822 1200
sjn@2tg.co.uk
Featured in Insurance (London), Property Damage (London)
Practice Areas: Sonia is a tough and experienced commercial practitioner specialising in insurance and reinsurance, property damage, commercial dispute resolution and professional negligence. She has been involved in a succession of high-profile cases, including appearing in the Supreme Court in the Employers' Liability Trigger Litigation. Insurance and reinsurance: coverage disputes, policy construction, fraudulent and exaggerated claims. Property damage: floods, fires, explosions, collapses and subsidence. Commercial dispute resolution: banking, fraud, contractual disputes. Professional negligence: particularly claims against brokers, legal professionals and construction professionals (architects, engineers, surveyors).
Professional Memberships: COMBAR, LCLCBA, PNBA, BILA, Health Claims Forum.
Career: Rai v Legal and General Insurance Company [2015] EWHC 170 Comm (insurance: life policy); Co-Star UK Ltd v Red Leads Ltd and 3 ors [2014] EWHC 1262 Ch (commercial: theft of confidential information) Bate v Aviva [2013] EWHC 1687 (Comm) (insurance: non-disclosure); Smyth v St Andrews [2012] EWHC 2511 (insurance: arson, coverage); Employers' Liability Trigger Litigation [2012] UKSC 14, [2010] EWCA Civ 1096 (insurance: construction, scope of statutory cover); Dennard v PriceWaterhouse Coopers LLP [2010] EWHC 812 (Ch) (professional negligence: undervaluation of PHI project). Called 2002, Inner Temple. Major Scholar 2001, 2002. Tenant at 2TG since 2003. Treasury Panel of Counsel 2009-13.

NORBURY, Hugh QC
Serle Court, London
020 7242 6105
hnorbury@serlecourt.co.uk
Featured in Chancery (London), Commercial Dispute Resolution (London), Fraud (London)
Practice Areas: Commercial and chancery litigation including fraud, domestic and international trust litigation, contractual disputes in many different business areas. Extensive experience of cross-examination in fraud and other commercial/chancery cases.
Professional Memberships: Chancery Bar Association, Commercial Bar Association.
Career: CPE at City University. LLM at King's College London. Called 1995. QC, 2012.
Personal: Married with two sons. Keen on playing and watching almost any sport.

NOSWORTHY, Jonathan
St Philips Chambers, Birmingham
0121 246 7000
jnosworthy@st-philips.com
Featured in Family/Matrimonial (Midlands)
Practice Areas: Jonathan specialises in financial remedy proceedings (including high net worth cases), claims under the Trusts of Land and Appointment of Trustees Act 1996 and applications under Schedule One of the Children Act 1989. Jonathan has significant experience in dealing with claims for financial orders where interveners claim beneficial interests in matrimonial property, and where there are overseas assets (particularly in India). He also has experience in dealing with complex cases where there are issues of significant non-disclosure.
Professional Memberships: Family Law Bar Association.
Career: Birmingham University, Harmsworth Scholarship Middle Temple. Called to the Bar in 2000. Deputy District Judge.

NOURSE, Edmund QC
One Essex Court, London
020 7853 2000
enourse@ocelaw.co.uk
Featured in Company (London)
Practice Areas: Edmund Nourse is a Junior Silk practising in civil fraud, commercial law and litigious company law. He has appeared in such high profile cases as Re Barlow Clowes [2006] 1 WLR 1476 and Digicel v Cable & Wireless [2010] EWHC 774 (Ch); [2010] EWHC 888 (Ch). In 2012-13, Edmund acted for Sir David and Sir Frederick Barclay and their interests in the unfair prejudice dispute over ownership of the Connaught, Berkeley and Claridge's hotels: Re Coroin plc:[2013] 2 BCLC 583-786 (Ch D and CA). He has recently acted for the defendants in the group litigation relating to blacklisting of construction workers.
Professional Memberships: COMBAR; ChBA.
Career: Call 1994. QC 2015.

O'DEMPSEY, Declan
Cloisters, London
020 7827 4000
dod@cloisters.com
Featured in Employment (London)
Practice Areas: Declan O'Dempsey specialises in employment and discrimination cases, the law of human rights, confidentiality and data protection, public law, directors' employment and injunctions and professional negligence. He accepts Public Access Scheme cases. He has been recommended as a leading junior for many years with comments such as he "knows employment law like the back of his hand.", and is "the Claimant's Rottweiler". (He acts for Claimants and Respondents). He is on the Equality and Human Rights Commission's A Panel of counsel. The EHRC used him to draft the statutory code on Goods and Services and Public Functions for the EHRC under the Equality Act 2010, its Age Supplement, and their Guidance on the Public Sector Equality Duty. He has appeared in many significant and/or controversial discrimination cases: Homer (Supreme Court) ; the Age Concern default retirement age cases before the CJEU and administrative court; Seldon (Supreme Court); Coleman v Attridge Law; X v Mid Sussex CAB (Supreme Court); Azmi v Lockwood v DWP, on comparators in discrimination cases, Kirklees MBC (niqab case); Gurkha Welfare Association pension rights case, Sobhi v Commissioner Of Police Of The Metropolis (concerning the application of the UN Convention on the Rights of Persons with Disabilities in the definition of disability). He co-authored a Thematic Report on Age Discrimination in the EU for the European Commission. He has appeared in several practice-setting NHS cases (e.g. Bent v Central Manchester University Hospital Trust (NHS AFC contracts)) and TUPE cases (e.g. Manchester College v Hazel).
Professional Memberships: Bar Council's ED Committee; EC of Industrial Law Society, ELBA ELAAS, and the Bar Pro Bono Unit.
Career: Called in 1987, first employment worker FRU 1987-88. PLC's Employment Law Consultative committee; Halsbury's Law Exchange. EHRC's A Panel (2015), Part time Employment Judge (2013).

Publications: Discrimination Law handbook (LAG, 2013). LCN Handbook on Goods Facilities and Services Discrimination (2014), Age Discrimination Law Handbook (Legal Action 2006), Employment Law and the Human Rights Act 1998 (Jordans, 2001), and Disability Discrimination: The Law and Practice.

O'HAGAN, Rachael
39 Essex Chambers, London
020 7832 1111
rachael.ohagan@39essex.com
Featured in Construction (London)

Practice Areas: Rachael specialises in high-value construction, engineering, technology, infrastructure, nuclear/energy and commercial disputes along with professional negligence and insurance claims related to these sectors. Her clients are domestic and international and she has experience of appearing as advocate in Courts in England and before arbitral tribunals. Within these sectors, Rachael advises and acts in respect of different forms of dispute resolution. She has represented parties in: court litigation, arbitration (including under the Rules of the ICC, DIAC and DIFC LCIA), adjudication and mediation. She is also appointed as a legal advisor to a dispute advisory board (DAB) in respect of major infrastructure projects.
Professional Memberships: SCL (Rachael is an active member of the Junior SCL Committee), TECBAR, COMBAR.
Career: Year of Call: 2006.
Publications: Wilmot-Smith on Construction Contracts (3rd Edn) (contributor), The Law of Waiver, Variation and Estoppel, Sean Wilken QC and Karim Ghaly, 3rd Edition OUP 2012 (assisted with research); RICS Case in Point: Rights to Light, by Sarah Hannaford Q.C., Jessica Stephens and Rachael O'Hagan (October 2008).

OHRENSTEIN, Dov
Radcliffe Chambers, London
020 7831 0081
dov@radcliffechambers.com
Featured in Chancery (London), Commercial Dispute Resolution (London)

Practice Areas: Litigation and dispute resolution relating to commercial chancery (eg banking, companies, guarantees, insolvency and mortgages), property and professional negligence. Significant cases include Exsus Travel Ltd v Turner [2014] EWCA 1331 (Directors' duties, accounts, limitation periods), Blindley Heath Investments Ltd v Peter Bass (2015) EWCA Civ 1023, [2014] EWHC 1366 (Ch) (Shareholder pre-emption agreement, estoppel, refusal of registration of share transfer), [2016] EWCA Civ 548 (costs, Bullock orders), Norwood v Nabai, ChD, LTL 27/5/2014 (Freezing orders, contempt of Court, custodial sentence), Hawkes & Telerate Ltd v County Leasing Asset Management ChD, LTL 21/10/2011 (company restoration, limitation override), United Vending Ltd v Desai [2011] EWHC 919 QB (assignment, administration, bailment), Immingham Storage Co Ltd v Clear Plc [2011] EWCA Civ 89 (contract formation, offer and acceptance), Lui v Chong [2010] EWCA Civ 398 (assents, bare trusts, gifts, and beneficial interests), Basinghall Finance PLC v Butler [2009] EWCA Civ 1262 (mortgages, assignment, securitisation, privity).

Professional Memberships: Chancery Bar Association, Professional Negligence Bar Association.
Career: MA Cantab. Called to the Bar: 1995.
Publications: Co author/ editor of: Civil Court Practice 2016 ("the Green Book")- 'Companies'; Butterworths Law of Limitation- "Equity"; Halsbury's Laws of England, "Money", "Limitation Periods".

OLDHAM, Jane
11KBW, London
020 7632 8500
jane.oldham@11kbw.com
Featured in Education (London), Local Government (London)

Practice Areas: Administrative law including: vires, capital finance, charging for services, public procurement, freedom of information including environmental information (representing both the Information Commissioner and public authorities), local authority and health body disputes, education, community care, political balance and monitoring officer issues, challenges to budget cuts, public sector equality duty, defending claims against local authorities in restitution. Represented 14 local authorities in the Interest Rate Swap litigation between local authorities and banks. Advised on capital finance issues arising from major projects undertaken by local authorities. Complex District Auditor investigations and proceedings. Examples of cases: Acting for claimant solicitor firms in procurement challenges to Criminal Legal Aid duty contracts tender 2015-2016; R (Hunt) v North Somerset Council [2015] UKSC 51 (remedies and costs in JR); R (Lewisham London Borough Council) v AQA and Ofqual [2013] PTSR D13 (JR of 2012 award of English GCSEs); R (UNISON) v NHS Wiltshire and nine other PCTs [2012] EWHC 624 (Admin) (trade union's JR challenge to PCTs' alleged breach of procurement rules; standing and delay issues); R (Omotosho) v The Governing body of Harris Academy Crystal Palace [2011] EWHC 3350 (Admin) (JR of academy school's admission arrangements and admissions appeals process);R v Richmond LBC ex parte McCarthy and Stone Developments Ltd [1992] 2 AC 48 (HL) (charging for services); Suppiah v Secretary of State for Home Department [2011] EWHC 2 Admin (disclosure of serious case review in challenge to government policy of detaining children of failed asylum seekers with their parents pending deportation); R(L) v Governors of J School [2003] 2 WLR 518 (HL) (whether pupil entitled to be reinstated after appeal against school exclusion); R (Swords) v Secretary of State for Communities and Local Government [2008] HLR 17 (housing stock transfers); R (Daskaloulis) v University of Western England [2008] EWHC 2981 (Admin) (retaking university exams); R (Crouch) v Secretary of State for Health (2009) ICR 461 (terms of NHS dentists' contracts); Financial Services Authority v Information Commissioner [2009] EWHC 1548 and 1784 (Admin) (degree to which context of FOIA request relevant to its interpretation); North Western and North Wales Sea Fisheries Committee v Information Commissioner [2008] UKIT EA/2007/0133 (commercial confidentiality exemption); McBride v Information Commissioner and Ministry of Justice [2008] UKIT EA/2007/0105; Craven v Information Commissioner [2008] EA/2008/0002; Boddy v Information Commissioner and North Norfolk District Council [2008] UKIT EA/2007/0074; Salmon v Information Commissioner and King's College Cambridge [2008] UKIT EA/2007/0135; Welsh v Information Commissioner [2008] UKIT EA/2007/0088; Tuckley v Information Commissioner [2008] UKIT EA/2006/0077; Financial Services Authority v Information Commissioner [2008] UKIT EA/2007 0093 and 0100; Financial Services Authority v Information Commissioner and Riverstone Management Agency Ltd [2008] UKIT EA/2008/0047; Financial Services Authority v Information Commissioner [2009] UKIT EA/2008/0061; East Riding of Yorkshire Council v Information Commissioner [2010] UKIT EA/2009/0069; Youth Justice Board v Information Commissioner EA/2010/0013; Dunn v Information Commissioner and National Audit Office EA/2010/0060; Davis v Information Commissioner and Tate Gallery EA/2010/0060.
Professional Memberships: ALBA, COMBAR, Procurement Lawyers' Association.

OLDHAM, Peter QC
11KBW, London
020 7632 8500
peter.oldham@11kbw.com
Featured in Education (London), Local Government (London)

Practice Areas: Public, local government, education, employment, procurement. Recent cases include: R ota A v Oxfordshire CC (ongoing): PSED and budget setting; R ota Councillor v Local Authority (ongoing): vires for investigation/Localism Act standards regime; Hine v Lord Chancellor (2016): procurement claim against letting of legal aid contracts; MH v Labour Party (2016): challenge to suspension by party; various judicial review claims involving discrimination at schools (2016); R ota NAFP v Bristol CC and others (2015): challenge to method by which authorities determine foster provision; R ota Robson v Salford CC [2015] BLGR 150: first Court of Appeal decision on consultation in the light of Moseley; Davies v Haringey LBC [2015] ELR 18: local authority's powers of discipline over staff at maintained school.
Career: 1990 call; silk 2010. Very wide experience as litigator and adviser.
Personal: Born 1963.

O'LEARY, Sam
One Essex Court, London
020 7583 2000
soleary@oeclaw.co.uk
Featured in Company (London)

Practice Areas: Sam O'Leary has a broad commercial practice encompassing litigation, arbitration and advice. He has particular experience of complex financial matters; contentious corporate and shareholder litigation; energy and resources; jurisdictional disputes; and civil fraud. He has substantial trial experience, both alone and with a leader. Significant cases include: Re Charterhouse Capital Limited (six-week trial and subsequent appeal relating to the management buy-out of a leading private equity business); Euroption Strategic Fund Ltd v Skandinaviska Enskilda Banken (two-week trial relating to the forced close out of a hedge fund's trading portfolio); Kleanthous v Paphitis (£100 million claim relating to the acquisition of the La Senza lingerie business); F&C Alternative Investments Holdings Ltd v Barthelemy (nine-month trial relating to the management of a fund of hedge fund business during the financial crisis and the exercise of put option rights by the fund managers); ITV v Scottish Television (£30 million contractual dispute relating to the management of the Channel 3 television network); and Re Kaupthing Singer & Friedlander Ltd; Brazzill v Willoughby (High Court and Court of Appeal dispute regarding the validity and operation of a £100 million trust account established by Kaupthing at the direction of the FSA following Kaupthing's collapse).

OLIVER, Harry
1 King's Bench Walk, London
020 7936 1500
holiver@1kbw.co.uk
Featured in Family/Matrimonial (London)

Practice Areas: Harry specialises in all aspects of divorce & financial remedies and financial provision under Children Act 1989 Schedule 1. His cases frequently involve very significant assets (including several in excess of £1billion), high profile clients, offshore trusts and complex company and tax structures. He also represents both trustees and companies in family proceedings and has advised on divorces in related jurisdictions (e.g. Jersey, Gibraltar, Hong Kong and the Isle of Man). He regularly is instructed to draft and advise on multi-jurisdictional pre-nuptial agreements. Harry has been instructed to provide expert witness evidence in foreign proceedings (Gibraltar, British Virgin Islands, Scotland and Venezuela) on matters of English divorce and matrimonial finance law. Harry has been counsel in many reported cases including the recent big money cases of: WW v HW, Thiry, Imerman, Whaley and H v H. Harry is one of only 3 specialist matrimonial finance practitioners ranked in the "Chambers 100" Bar list of the top 100 junior barristers working in any area of the law in England and Wales. Harry is available to conduct Private FDRs/Early Neutral Evaluations.
Professional Memberships: Family Law Bar Association, South Eastern Circuit.
Career: Called to the Bar in 1999.
Personal: Education: Tonbridge School, University of Oxford (St Edmund Hall). Leisure: photography, rugby, cricket.

OLIVER, Heather
3 Raymond Buildings Barristers, London
020 7400 6400
clerks@3rblaw.com
Featured in Crime (London)

Practice Areas: Heather prosecutes and defends a full range of criminal matters, along with appearing in extradition, licensing and regulatory cases. She was instructed as led junior for the first defendants in Operation Cotton (land banking fraud) and Operation Kyrenia (NHS fraud). She represents police officers from forces across the country in criminal trials and misconduct hearings. She appears for requested persons in extradition matters at first instance and on appeal. She frequently appears in licensing and regulatory matters, particularly in connection with breaches of fire safety regulation. She is currently instructed by the Metropolitan Police Service in the public inquiry into undercover policing.
Career: Oxford (Univ.) (1st class, BA Hons), City (GDL, Distinction), Call 2010.

OLLECH, Joseph
Falcon Chambers, London
clerks@falcon-chambers.com
Featured in Agriculture & Rural Affairs (London), Real Estate Litigation (London)

Practice Areas: All areas of real estate litigation.

Professional Memberships: ChBA, PBA, LCLCBA, Lincoln's Inn Denning Society.

Career: Joseph has a busy junior practice specialising in real estate litigation. He is regularly instructed in relation to commercial, residential and agricultural matters, and has experience of a wide variety of disputes arising under the 1954 Act, the Rent Acts, the Housing Acts, agricultural and enfranchisement legislation. His practice encompasses cases with all land law related issues including restrictive covenants, easements, adverse possession, land registration, boundary disputes, trusts, and mortgages. He has significant experience in advisory and litigation work relating to riverine and coastal land, and the rights of riparian owners. He also has significant experience in complex cases involving large institutional clients from both the public and private sector, including local authorities, the Port of London Authority, Premiership and non-league football clubs and stadiums. Joseph's practice also encompasses areas of company and insolvency law which are related to property interests and disputes, and he appears regularly on such matters. In addition Joseph often deals with professional negligence matters that arise in connection with his area of expertise.

Publications: Contributor to the Landlord & Tenant Review and New Law Journal.

O'MAHONY, David
7BR, London
020 7242 3555
clerks@7br.co.uk
Featured in Offshore (London)

Practice Areas: Offshore and international

Professional Memberships: International Bar Association, Fraud Lawyers Association, Commercial Fraud Lawyers Association and Chatham House.

Career: David specialises in cases in which there is an international element. He has worked on cases in a number of countries, including India, Kenya, Nigeria, Pakistan and South East Asia. He is admitted to practice in the Dubai International Finance Centre ('DIFC') court (where he was instructed in arbitration proceedings). He has been called to the bar in Australia and also in Turks and Caicos Islands (the latter for a particular case). He recently acted for the UK government in the European Court of Human Rights and for the USDOJ in enforcing one of its largest ever kleptocracy forfeiture actions. He is on the list of counsel at the International Criminal Court in the Hague.

Publications: Butterworths Fraud Practice – co author of chapter on civil fraud and cross – over issues between civil and criminal fraud.

OMAMBALA, Ijeoma
Old Square Chambers, London
020 7269 0300
omambala@oldsquare.co.uk
Featured in Employment (London)

Practice Areas: As well as providing excellent advocacy services and strong relational skills Ijeoma provides high quality strategic advice in connection with all aspects of the management and litigation of complex employment, discrimination and trade union claims Ijeoma's employment law practice includes significant experience of complex TUPE and whistle-blowing matters, industrial action and High Court litigation in relation to bonus claims, restrictive covenants, alleged breaches of duty and wrongful dismissal. Her discrimination expertise covers the whole range of protected characteristics and causes of action. She is an experienced litigator of individual and multi-Claimant public and private sector equal pay claims. Ijeoma advises and represents Claimants, Respondents/Defendants and Trades Unions. Her recent work has included acting for both Claimants and Respondents in High Court restrictive covenant proceedings; successfully resisting a claim of breach of s.24(1) TULR(C)A before the Certification Officer; advising and acting for a senior seconded bank employee in respect of sex and pregnancy discrimination complaints arising from the termination of her secondment; representing a barristers' chambers in proceedings brought by former senior clerk alleging disability discrimination and unfair dismissal; resisting an injunction application to prevent a hearing in relation to an alleged breakdown in trust and confidence between an NHS Trust and a senior consultant; acting for a Claimant in an ongoing private sector equal pay claim and successfully representing a solicitors' firm in a sexual orientation discrimination claim. Ijeoma is also a qualified mediator and an accredited Advocacy Trainer.

Professional Memberships: Justice, ELBA, ILS, DLA. CEDR Exchange, CMC.

Career: Called in 1989 Elected Bencher of Grays Inn 2014 Appointed Vice Chair of CPD Grays Inn 2015.

O'NEILL, Sally QC
Furnival Chambers, London
07860 223753
soneill@furnivallaw.co.uk
Featured in Crime (London)

Practice Areas: Specialises in very serious violent and sexual crime and murder including baby shaking murder allegations involving complex medical evidence. Has a particular interest in young and vulnerable defendants and witnesses. Past cases include the prosecution of the 'Baby "P" case' (in 2008), defending in R v. Whiting (the murder and abduction of Sarah Payne), defending in R v Farhi, (the Jimmy Mizzen case), prosecuting in R v B, the rape of a very young child. Defending in the murder of the defendant's female partner by stabbing her over 60 times. This was the first prosecution under the amended partial defences of loss of control and diminished responsibility. Defending in a double jeopardy prosecution for the murder 15 years earlier of a woman walking her dog, defendant then aged 20. Defending allegations of rape of a 10 year old and aiding and abetting her prostitution. Defending in a multi-handed murder and attempted murder of two members of the defendants' family by shooting and running over with a Range Rover. Defending in the murder of a woman in her own home by attacking her with a golf club and a video recorder.Defending in the murder of a female jogger on Mitcham Common and burying the body. Defending in R v Wray, a high profile allegation of murder of a 4 month old baby who was found to be suffering from congenital rickets. Acquitted.Defending in a multi-handed allegation of fraud ("sham marriages"). Acquitted. Recent cases include S.18 on a baby who survived and Child cruelty and attempting to pervert the course of justice involving a 12 week old baby who died. Also defended a defendant currently serving 7 life sentences on a very serious allegation of rape. Defended 1st defendant in Oxford grooming case. Defended Ian Watkins (Lostprophets) on very serious sexual abuse of extremely young children. Defended a mother of five children who stabbed to death an elderly man accused of sexual abuse. Convicted of manslaughter. Prosecuted a multi-defendant case involving the murder and dismemberment of the body. Defended a woman charged with the apparently random murder of another woman after she had phoned the police to say she thought she had done it. Acquitted. Defended an 18 year old charged with murder after stabbing the victim of a knife point robbery committed 20 minutes earlier. Convicted of manslaughter.

Professional Memberships: Criminal Bar Association. Chairman of the CBA 2007-8. South-Eastern Circuit.

Career: Called 1976. Queen's Counsel 1997. Recorder 1997.Bencher of Grays Inn 2003. Member of CBA/NSPCC working group which produced "A Case For Special Measures" DVD as a training material. Member of ATC working group which recently published a report "Raising the Bar : Improving the handling of vulnerable witnesses and defendants in court." Member of current ATC committee on the same topic.

ONSLOW, Robert
8 New Square, London
020 7405 4321
robert.onslow@8newsquare.co.uk
Featured in Information Technology (London)

Practice Areas: A Barrister whose principal areas of practice are information technology and intellectual property. Contractual IT disputes form a large part of Robert's practice with additional areas including all aspects of computer law, internet and domain names, e-commerce and data protection. IP areas include patents, trade marks, musical and literary copyright and industrial designs. Recent cases: SAS v World Programming [2014] R.P.C. 8, Shanley v Lloyds TSB [2014] EWCA Civ 40, Volkswagen v Garcia [2014] F.S.R. 12, HTC v Nokia [2013] EWHC 2917, IPCom v HTC [2013] EWHC 2880. For comprehensive CV visit www.8newsquare.co.uk.

Professional Memberships: Member of Bar Council IT Panel; Society for Computers and the Law (SCL) Intellectual Property Bar Association (IPBA); The Intellectual Property Lawyers Organisation (TIPLO).

Career: Called 1991. Director of software house with programming experience in Java, Python and Haskell and associated technologies such as SQL, MongoDB and XML.

Publications: Laddie Prescott & Vitoria: Modern Law of Copyright.

Personal: Born 1965. Educated at Eton College and Magdalen College, Oxford (1987 BA Physics). Hobbies include music and entertaining 4 children.

OPPENHEIMER, Tamara
Fountain Court Chambers, London
020 7583 3335
to@fountaincourt.com
Featured in Professional Negligence (London), Banking & Finance (London), Commercial Dispute Resolution (London)

Practice Areas: Barrister practising in civil and commercial law, including banking, professional negligence, aviation and insurance. Good working knowledge of Russian and Italian.

Professional Memberships: COMBAR.

Career: Called 2002, Inner Temple; Junior Counsel to the Crown (B Panel); former solicitor (litigation department Allen & Overy); judicial assistant to Lord Woolf (2000); legal assistant at the Treasury Solicitor (1997-8).

Personal: Dragon School, Oxford High School; Merton College, Oxford (BA Hons Philosophy, Politics and Economics First Class); City University (Diploma in Law, Distinction); Christ Church, Oxford (BCL Distinction).

ORCHARD, Anthony QC
Carmelite Chambers, London
020 7936 6300
anthony@aorchard.demon.co.uk
Featured in Crime (London)

Practice Areas: Appeared in numerous murder, sexual assault and fraud trials including R. v Michael Philpott and others (the 2013 "Derby fire" case). Extensive experience in organized and very serious crime, particularly complex fraud, money-laundering, internet hacking, confiscation, sexual offences, human trafficking, drugs and murder. Frequently advises clients under investigation. Regularly defends and prosecutes cases brought by the Serious Fraud Office and the Financial Conduct Authority. Appeared in over ninety homicide trials at the Central Criminal Court and elsewhere, many involving allegations of multiple shooting, gangland murder and revenge. Regularly advises on SOCPA contracts, PACE, PII matters, RIPA, Surveillance law, Abuse of Process and Disclosure issues both within the United Kingdom and Overseas, particularly the Channel Islands and Cayman Islands.

ORME, Emily
Arden Chambers, London
020 7242 4244
emily.orme@ardenchambers.com
Featured in Social Housing (London)

Practice Areas: All areas of housing, landlord and tenant and local government law.

Professional Memberships: Housing Law Practitioners Association, Social Housing Law Association, Chartered Institute of Housing.

Career: Called to the Bar in 2003, Emily advises both public and private sector clients (including local authorities, social landlords, tenants and the homeless) on a variety of matters including housing, landlord and tenant disputes, business tenancies, administrative and local government, mortgages, homelessness, housing benefit, anti-social behaviour, nuisance, disrepair and possession claims. Notable cases include: Birmingham CC v (1) VB (2) HC (3) F [2008] EWHC 1224 (QB); R (Hassan) v Croydon LBC [2009] JHL D56; Makisi v Birmingham CC [2011] HLR 27; Akhtar v Birmingham CC [2011] HLR 28; Willougby v Solihull MBC [2013] HLR 36; Mohamoud v Birmingham CC [2014] HLR 22; Birmingham CC v

Samuels [2015] HLR 47; Plant v (1) Somerset CC (2) Taunton Deane BC [2016] HLR 24.
Publications: Article – "Refusing accommodation because of a misunderstanding", Local Government Lawyer website, 26 March 2014. Blog – Legal Action Group Housing Law Blog with Andrew Arden QC, September – December 2013. Book – Co-author of Homelessness and Allocations, 8th and 9th editions (2010 and 2013 respectively), Legal Action Group. With Andrew Arden QC and Toby Van Hegan. Article – "Localism: keeping it local again...and again...and again... or not", Journal of Housing Law, Vol 15, Issue 4, 2012. An article commenting on the increased use of private rented sector accommodation for homeless applicants. Article – "Shaky ground", Solicitors Journal 2011, 155(44), 12-13. Examination of the proposals in the Government consultation paper "A new mandatory power of possession for anti-social behaviour". Co-author with Sarah Salmon. Article – "Child tenants – a minor problem", New Law Journal, Vol 155, No. 7196, p1522. Cited and approved by the Court of Appeal in Alexander-David v Hammersmith & Fulham LBC [2009] EWCA Civ 259; [2009] HLR 39. Annotations –Housing and Regeneration Act 2008, Current Legal Statutes, Co-author with Andrew Dymond, Faisal Sadiq and Justin Bates. Article – "Malcolm v Lewisham LBC – Nasty surprise or logical conclusion?", Journal of Housing Law, Vol 11, Issue 6, 2008, p.103. Discussing indirect discrimination in a housing law context. Article – "HIP homes, radical change?" – New Law Journal, Vol 155, No. 7163, p.206, 2004. Discussing the introduction of the (then) new Home Information Pack.
Personal: Emily is a director of Zebra Housing Association, a provider of affordable housing for overseas postgraduate students. She also participates in endurance sports events to raise money for the housing charity, Shelter.

ORNSBY, Suzanne QC
Francis Taylor Building, London
020 73538415
clerks@ftbchambers.co.uk
Featured in Planning (London)
Practice Areas: Suzanne Ornsby is a highly proficient public, planning and environmental lawyer with wide experience of acting for utilities, multinationals, planning authorities, action groups and individuals. She is regularly involved in controversial judicial challenges as well as promoting or opposing major infrastructure proposals relating to water and electricity supply, minerals and waste, together with commercial and residential schemes including those affecting the built heritage. Her advice has been extensively sought from both the private and public sector on the interrelationship and legality of the new NPPF and the Localism Act 2011 in particular in the context of the five year housing supply, the duty to co-operate and neighbourhood planning. Suzanne acted for the successful respondent authority in a recent judicial review relating to neighbourhood planning. She successfully appeared for Thames Water at the major inquiries held into the UK's first desalination plant and into its Water Resources Management Plan. She advises on the implications of the Environmental Assessment of Plans and Programmes Regulations 2004, the Habitats Assessment Regulations 2010 and the Water Framework Directive. She has recently acted at a major inquiry into two urban extensions to Aylesbury and at four Core Strategy examinations for the Local Planning Authority. She acted for English Heritage concerning the site of the Battle of Tewkesbury and for developers on a highly controversial scheme in the Clifton Conservation Area, for two neoclassical town houses designed by Robert Adam, architectural adviser to Prince Charles. She has appeared at numerous inquiries for housing proposals, including proposals affecting a listed building previously owned by Agatha Christie. She also works for student accommodation providers advising on their responsibilities and liabilities under the Housing Act 2004 and has recently successfully acted in demonstrating that Bristol City Council's approach to licensing of HMOs is unlawful .
Professional Memberships: Member and previous secretary of the Planning and Environment Bar Association, UKELA, the Administrative Law Bar Association, the Criminal Bar Association, the Compulsory Purchase Association and Health and Safety Lawyers Association. She is a trained advocacy instructor for the Middle Temple.
Career: Called to Bar: 1986 Appointed Queen's Counsel : 2012.

ORR, Craig QC
One Essex Court, London
020 7583 2000
clerks@oeclaw.co.uk
Featured in Banking & Finance (London), Commercial Dispute Resolution (London)
Practice Areas: Barrister practising across the broad spectrum of commercial dispute resolution (both litigation and domestic and international arbitration). Expertise includes, but is not limited to, banking and finance, energy and natural resources, professional negligence (especially accountants' negligence), civil fraud, insurance and reinsurance, breach of confidence, breach of warranty and all forms of contractual disputes (including joint ventures). Recent work includes representing an AIM listed mineral resources company in proceedings to recover misappropriated mineral rights; representing a global risk consultancy in a US$800 million breach of confidence claim; representing a Luxembourg bankruptcy administrator in a hedge fund dispute; representing an international investment bank in a US$120 million derivatives claim; representing the administrators of Glitnir Bank hf in disputes arising out of the bank's collapse; representing an international betting and gaming group in claims arising out of its online gambling joint venture; representing telecommunications and defence contractors in UNCITRAL and LCIA arbitrations against an East African government; and representing an international oil company in disputes with a West African government. As well as appearing in the Senior Courts in England and Wales, he has wide experience of appearing before other tribunals, including the Supreme Court of Bermuda and LCIA and UNCITRAL arbitration tribunals. He also has extensive experience of giving evidence on English law in foreign proceedings (most recently in a major derivatives dispute in the High Court of Singapore).
Professional Memberships: COMBAR.
Career: Called to the Bar in 1986. Fox Scholar (at McCarthy Tetrault in Canada) from 1986-87. Joined Fountain Court in 1988. Took silk in 2006. Joined One Essex Court in 2011.
Publications: Contributor to Fountain Court on Carriage by Air and Professional Negligence & Liability.
Personal: Educated at Cambridge University 1981-84 (MA) and Oxford University (BCL, Vinerian Scholar). Born 8 January 1962.

OSBORNE, Richard
4 Pump Court, London
020 7842 5555
rosborne@4pumpcourt.com
Featured in Information Technology (London)
Practice Areas: Richard practices in commercial litigation and arbitration with particular experience in Information Technology disputes, where he has been instructed by some of the largest contractors, IT outsourcing providers and government departments in relation to a number of complex and substantial disputes. He also has significant experience in the fields of construction, insurance and professional negligence.
Professional Memberships: Society for Computers and Law (London Committee member), TECBAR, COMBAR, PNBA.
Career: MA (Oxon), called 2005.

OSMAN, Faisal
The Chambers of Andrew Mitchell QC, London
020 7440 9950
fo@33cllaw.com
Featured in POCA Work & Asset Forfeiture (All Circuits), Financial Crime (London)
Practice Areas: Faisal advises and acts in the civil, criminal and regulatory aspects of complex commercial wrongdoing disputes and often in cases with foreign dimensions (particularly the DIFC Court). The core of his work relates to domestic and international civil and criminal asset recovery on behalf of governments and commercial organizations, particularly with regards to enforcement of judgments and awards. Faisal's works also includes civil/commercial litigation, corruption, fraud, regulatory enforcement, sanctions and professional discipline, and is mostly cross-border. He has been a presenting advocate to the tribunal for the Taxation Disciplinary Board, the independent disciplinary body of the Association of Taxation Technicians and Chartered Institute of Taxation, since 2008. He also provides technical assistance for capacity building in respect of anti-corruption, asset recovery and money laundering.
Career: Call 2002. Dubai International Financial Centre Court (Part II) – 2015.
Publications: Contributing editor to 'Mitchell Taylor, Talbot: Confiscation and the Proceeds of Crime'. Consultant editor of the Commonwealth Secretariat, UNODC and IMF's Model Provisions on Money Laundering, Terrorist Financing, Preventive Measures and Proceeds of Crime (for common law legal systems). Technical Consultant to the Government of the Bahamas' Proceeds of Crime Act, 2016.

OSMAN, Osman
25 Bedford Row, London
020 70671500
oosman@25bedfordrow.com
Featured in Crime (London)
Practice Areas: Osman is a specialist practitioner within the field of complex crime, particularly white-collar fraud and financial regulatory law. He has particular specialism on international anti-bribery and corruption, both in the UK and abroad. He recently presented to the sub-soil industries in Kazakhstan on 'joint ventures programmes', 'profit share agreements', and 'concession contracts' involving the oil, gas and mining sectors in respect of contracts between IOC's and NOC's. In the UK he has acted as external counsel to AXAI where he advised upon third party co-insurance agreements being UK Bribery Act (UKBA) compliant and drafted the model ABC compliance procedure for AXAI. He is regarded as one of a few unique specialist barristers in this field.
Career: Osman expertise derives from his experience in defending and advising in the some of the most high profile and complex cases heard in the UK. Reported leading authority cases: Operation Credibility (2016) for principal in international multi million pound drugs conspiracy. Operation Petral (2016) for a principal in northern England's largest and most high profile drug trafficking conspiracy. R v Austin (2015/2016) acting for principal in complex and lengthy £15m confiscation proceedings involving multi-jurisdictions. Presently before the Court of Appeal. R v Marrache & Others [2014] CA Gibraltar, 1,2,3,4 of 214 judge only trials, jury discharge, and abuse. R v Pimenta [2012] EWCA Crim 2998 imprisonment of carers. R v Ali (Ahmed) [2011] 2 Cr.App.R. 22 CA conspiracy, autrefois acquit or convict). R v Bourgass & Others [2007] 2Cr App R.S.40 sentence public nuisance "ricin terror plot". R v Valentine [2006] EWCA Crim 2717 hidden assets confiscation.
Personal: Fluent: Turkish and Spanish.

O'SULLIVAN, Michael
5 Stone Buildings, London
020 7242 6201
clerks@5sblaw.com
Featured in Chancery (London), Court of Protection (All Circuits)
Practice Areas: A barrister with a wide Chancery practice, which incorporates trust litigation and advice, contentious and non-contentious probate applications, Inheritance Act applications, professional negligence in relation to negligent conveyancing and tax advice, Court of Protection applications, capital gains tax and inheritance tax planning. Notable recent cases include: Khan v Crossland [2012] WTLR Removal of Executor under S116 SCA 1982; EB v RC [2011] EWHC 3805 (CoP)Removal of Deputy under MCA 2005; Re P [2010] Ch 33 (the leading modern case on statutory wills in the Court of Protection); Carr v Thomas [2008] EWHC 2859 (contentious probate); PEER v EMC [2007] E.C.D.R 1[2006] EWHC 2883 (probate and copyright); Allardyce v Roebuck [2004] 3 All ER 754 (testamentary options).
Professional Memberships: STEP, ACTAPS, Chancery Bar Association, Property Bar Association.
Career: MA Cantab (Magdelene College) BCL Oxon (St Catherine's College). Called 1986 Lincoln's Inn. Accredited Mediator.
Publications: Author of 'Asset Protection'(Butterworths 2000). Co-author of 'A Practitioner's Guide to Trustee Investment' (Lexis Nexis Tolley, 2004). Contributor to Tottel's 'Trust Drafting and Precedents – purpose trusts and protective trusts'.

O'SULLIVAN, Sean QC
4 Pump Court, London
020 7842 5555
sosullivan@4pumpcourt.com
Featured in International Arbitration (London), Energy & Natural Resources (London), Insurance (London), Shipping (London)
Practice Areas: Commercial dispute resolution: instructed in a wide range of contractual disputes, with a particular focus on shipping, shipbuilding and energy-related issues. He deals with shipping disputes of all shapes and sizes (whether involving dry bulk or liquid cargoes, containers, towing, support vessels, or the carriage of passengers or livestock) and the full range of shipbuilding and ship sale and purchase cases (covering everything from luxury yachts to semi-submersible drilling rigs). He also represents oil majors, petrochemicals traders and contractors in "energy" disputes (e.g. commodity sales, farm in/ farm out agreements, share purchase agreements, drilling contracts, distribution agreements, etc.). Other areas of expertise include insurance/ reinsurance (both marine and non-marine), professional negligence (esp. brokers, solicitors and accountants/auditors), and media and entertainment (esp. recording artists, music videos and advertising). He regularly appears before the Commercial Court in London and in arbitrations, both ad hoc and under the auspices of the various arbitral bodies around the world.
Professional Memberships: TECBAR, COMBAR. Called to the Bar of the Cayman Islands.
Career: MA (Oxon) Modern History. Called to the Bar in 1997. Silk in 2014

OVEY, Elizabeth
Radcliffe Chambers, London
020 7831 0081
eovey@radcliffechambers.com
Featured in Chancery (London), Pensions (London)
Practice Areas: Principal specialist areas of work are pensions (in particular occupational pensions), mortgage lending and building society work, and other retail financial services, including fairness of terms and consumer credit. Also does general chancery work, including professional negligence relating to the above areas. Joint editor of 'Wurtzburg and Mills – Building Society Law' and 'Current Law Commentary on Building Societies Act 1986'. Joint author, 2nd edition of 'The Law of Investor Protection', including pensions chapter (1st ed. Fisher and Bewsey), and 'Retail Mortgages: Law, Regulation and Procedure' (2013). Member of working party responsible for the Standard Conditions of Sale (5th edition published April 2011) and the Standard Commercial Property Conditions (2nd edition published June 2004; new edition about to be published). Lectures, gives seminars and contributes journal articles. Contributes to pensions section of Lexis PSL and is a member of pensions consulting editorial board.
Professional Memberships: Chancery Bar Association; Association of Pension Lawyers; Professional Negligence Bar Association; Charity Law Association.
Career: Called to the Bar 1978. Deputy Judge of the Upper Tribunal.
Publications: As above.
Personal: Educated at Southampton Grammar School for Girls 1966-73 and St. Anne's College, Oxford 1974-77. Lives in London. Born 1 December 1954.

OWEN, Jonathan
Ropewalk Chambers, Nottingham
0115 9472581
jonathanowen@ropewalk.co.uk
Featured in Real Estate Litigation (Midlands)
Practice Areas: He specialises in commercial, property and chancery, personal injury, disease and regulatory cases. His contentious work in real property litigation includes boundary disputes, rights of way and easements, adverse possession, co-ownership, commercial and residential leases, restrictive and positive covenants, mortgage rights and disputes over contracts of sale and land registration. His non-contentious work in the field consists in advising as to the contents of contracts and issues affecting title. Jonathan does the full range of land cases. His wider commercial practice includes contractual, company law and insolvency disputes.
Career: Called 2004; BA (Hons) Jurisprudence, Magdalen College, Oxford University. Jonathan was runner up to the Taylor Prize for best performance on the Bar Vocational Course at Nottingham Law School. He then undertook his first six months pupillage at Essex Court Chambers, London, the Chambers of Gordon Pollock QC. His second six was at Ropewalk Chambers and he became a tenant in November 2005. He was runner up to the Taylor Prize for best performance on the Bar Vocational Course at Nottingham Law School.
Personal: Outside of work he is a keen swimmer (1 mile being his favourite distance) and enjoys spending time with his family.

OWEN, Tom
Keating Chambers, London
020 7544 2600
towen@keatingchambers.com
Featured in Construction (London)
Practice Areas: Tom Owen is a leading junior in construction, energy, infrastructure and related professional negligence and insurance disputes. Tom has a particular reputation for his advocacy and court work. He has appeared in more than 15 trials over the past three years. Tom is a confident, experienced and versatile advocate and regularly appears in the TCC in London and on Circuit, and in domestic and international arbitrations. Tom has appeared in the Court of Appeal, with a pending appeal in spring 2017. Tom is recognised too for his particular legal ability, analysis and client care. Recent reported cases include Persimmon Homes v Arup, and Seeney v Gleeson.
Professional Memberships: SCL, TECBAR, COMBAR, LCLCBA.
Career: Loughborough Grammar School (2000-2007); MA (Hons) Law, Downing College, University of Cambridge (2007-2010); BPTC, Nottingham Law School: Lord Taylor Prize, Queen Mother Scholar and Baron Dr Ver Heyden de Lancey Scholar as top Middle Templar on the BPTC (2011); Called to the Bar (2011); Keating Chambers (2012); Lecturer, examiner and dissertation supervisor: King's College London MSc in Construction Law & Dispute Resolution (2012); TECBAR-accredited Adjudicator (2013); CEDR Solve Adjudicator Panel (2013).

PACKMAN, Claire
4 Pump Court, London
020 7842 5555
cpackman@4pumpcourt.com
Featured in Construction (London)
Practice Areas: Claire's practice is primarily construction and engineering disputes, and associated professional negligence claims involving architects, engineers and surveyors, in litigation (TCC, Chancery Division and Commercial Court), national and international arbitrations and adjudication. Also fire and flood claims and related insurance issues, solicitor's negligence cases and general contractual disputes. Familiar with many standard forms including JCT, NEC3, FIDIC, IChemE Red Book and others. Recent instructions include arbitrations involving windfarms, arbitrations concerning the design and construction of accommodation blocks and a number of engineer's negligence cases in the TCC and in arbitration relating to the design and construction of car parks, tunnels, motorways, hospitals, commercial premises and large domestic building projects.
Professional Memberships: TECBAR, COMBAR, PNBA.
Career: Called to the Bar 1996, appointed Junior Counsel to the Crown 2010.
Publications: Contributing editor to Lexis-Nexis online Adjudication KnowHow.
Personal: First Class BA (Hons) from Oxford University in Modern Languages. Hobbies include Latin American travel and literature. Working knowledge of Spanish; basic French and Italian.

PADFIELD, Alison
4 New Square, London
020 7822 2058
a.padfield@4newsquare.com
Featured in Insurance (London)
Practice Areas: Alison specialises in commercial litigation and advisory work, with a particular emphasis on insurance and reinsurance, professional negligence, and regulatory/public law work including professional disciplinary proceedings. Alison's recent court appearances include: O'Connor v Bar Standards Board [2016] EWCA Civ 775; Aspen Insurance UK Ltd v Adana Construction Ltd [2015] EWCA Civ 176 (with Colin Wynter QC); Prescott v Bar Council [2015] EWHC 1919 (Admin); Herridge v Parker and Allianz Insurance plc [2014] Lloyd's Rep IR 177; and Teal v Berkley [2013] Lloyd's Rep IR 56, SC (with Colin Edelman QC).
Professional Memberships: COMBAR; BILA; PNBA; ARDL; ARIAS Panel of Arbitrators.
Career: Called: 1992. Elected member of the Bar Council; Co-Chairman of the Bar Council Pro Bono Board; Chairman of the Combar Equality and Diversity Committee; Chairman of the South Eastern Circuit Access to Justice Working Group.
Publications: Author of 'Insurance Claims' (2016, 4th edition, Bloomsbury Professional).
Personal: Education: BA (Oxon), Lic Sp Dr Eur (Brussels), BCL (Oxon). Languages: Able to conduct conferences in French.

PAGE, Rebecca
Maitland Chambers, London
020 7406 1200
rpage@maitlandchambers.com
Featured in Company (London), Restructuring/ Insolvency (London)
Practice Areas: Commercial / Chancery litigation with a particular emphasis on insolvency matters and company disputes
Professional Memberships: Chancery Bar Association, COMBAR, Insolvency Lawyers' Association.
Career: 2001 Call, MA (Cantab).

PAGET, Michael
Cornerstone Barristers, London
020 7242 4986
michaelp@cornerstonebarristers.com
Featured in Social Housing (London)
Practice Areas: Property litigation including housing. Court of protection and mental health. Planning.
Career: Property practitioner with strengths in the public law elements of real estate litigation. Acts in claims for adverse possession, an equitable interest, rectification of the Register, forfeiture, planning enforcement, mortgage repossessions, under TOLATA, SWAP compensation, 1954 Act lease renewals, dilapidations, rent reviews, neighbour disputes including private law nuisance and boundary issues, service charge disputes, enfranchisement, unlawful evictions, and generally the use of land. In Housing litigation acts in possession actions, disrepair, homelessness disputes (including interim relief), allocation and general public authority duties. Also recognised as a costs expert and in enforcement actions. Acts in Court of Protection on financial deputy matters and welfare best interest declarations. Has expertise in mental health law including the role and responsibilities of the nearest relative.

PALIN, Sarah
One Brick Court, London
020 7353 8845
sp@onebrickcourt.com
Featured in Defamation/Privacy (London)
Practice Areas: Media law; defamation; malicious falsehood; privacy and breach of confidence; data protection; freedom of information; contempt and reporting restrictions; pre-publication advice; injunctive relief; harassment; malicious falsehood/ trade libel; media related judicial review and regulatory work; media-related human rights law. Notable cases include: junior counsel for Associated Newspapers in The Leveson Inquiry; J. K. Rowling v Associated Newspapers [2015] EWCA Civ 488; Thour v Royal Free Hampstead NHS Trust [2012] EWHC 1473; Spiller v Joseph [2010] UKSC 53; Horlick v Associated Newspapers [2010] EWHC 1544; R(Dacre) v Westminster Magistrates Court [2009] 1 WLR 2241; Burstein v Associated Newspapers [2007] All ER 319; Neil & Christine Hamilton v Max Clifford [2004] EWHC 1542; The Hutton Inquiry; Grobbelaar v News Group Newspapers [2002] 1 WLR 3024 (HL).
Publications: Author of Atkin's Court Forms on Confidence, Privacy, Data Protection, Freedom of Information and Regulation of Investigatory Powers. Contributor to Arlidge, Eady and Smith on Contempt 4th Edition and supplements.
Personal: Brasenose College, Oxford.

PALMER, Howard QC
2TG – 2 Temple Gardens, London
020 7822 1200
hpalmer@2tg.co.uk
Featured in Travel (London), Insurance (London), Property Damage (London)
Practice Areas: Howard Palmer QC is joint leader of the Insurance group in 2

Temple Gardens. He is particularly respected for his experience in insurance of employers' liability, public liability, product liability and motor insurance risks. In addition, he has wide experience of national and international litigation and arbitration, including conflicts of laws and jurisdiction issues involving international travel and insurance. He acts for Claimants as well as domestic and foreign insurers and reinsurers. He has been instructed in appeals to the Supreme Court in Durham v BAI (EL, asbestos 2012), Jacobs v MIB (motor, uninsured foreign claims 2011) and Brownlie v Four Seasons (foreign jurisdiction 2016). In motor insurance he appeared in Charlton v Fisher (CA 2002), Bristol v Williams (CA 2012) and Nemeti v Sabre Insurance (CA 2013). Recent cases include Transform Medical v Travelers Insurance (2015 – Product Liability Insurance), Wagenaar (CA 2014 Foreign skiing accident). His practice includes expertise in construction and engineering contracts, fire and flood recoveries and professional negligence. He has been admitted ad hoc to the Bar of Brunei, and has acted as an expert in English Law in foreign insurance and product liability cases.

Professional Memberships: TECBAR; COMBAR; LCLCBA; PIBA.

Career: Lecturer, KCL 1977. QC 1999. Recorder 2005.

Personal: Born in 1954.

PALMER, Norman E QC

5 Stone Buildings, London
020 7242 4937
clerks@5sblaw.com

Featured in Art and Cultural Property Law (London)

Practice Areas: All legal controversies and transactions related to art, antiquities and other forms of portable wealth, management of public and private art collections, museum governance, legislative drafting, investment and security in art, law and policy on cross-border art mobility, import and export of cultural objects, claims for restitution of unlawfully removed heritage material, repatriation claims by indigenous peoples and other dispossessed groups, architecture of art loans, joint acquisitions, repatriation arrangements and other agreements for sharing of cultural objects, co-operative transacting between different cultures and markets, authenticity and attribution, mediation of art-related disputes. Adviser and advocate on movable assets and personal property law, including bailment, carriage, chattel securities, finance leasing, sale of goods, claims in conversion and other title-related disputes, limitation periods, general commercial and contract law, arbitration and mediation in civil and commercial disputes. Clients include foreign governments, UK governmental departments and executive agencies, national and overseas museums, art dealers, archaeologists, private collectors, indigenous communities, banks, finance companies and other commercial corporations, insolvency practitioners, insurers, loss adjusters, transport companies, local authorities, ecclesiastical bodies, animal welfare groups.

Professional Memberships: Expert Adviser, Spoliation Advisory Panel, and formerly member (2000+); Chair, Treasure Valuation Committee (2001-2011); Chair, Illicit Trade Advisory Panel (2000-2005); Chair, Ministerial Working Group on Human Remains in Museum Collections (2000-2003); Standing International Counsel, National Gallery of Australia (2002+); Honorary Member, Seven Wentworth (Sydney) (2006+); Chair, ArtResolve (2014+).

Career: Called 1973. Professor of Commercial Law at UCL (1990-2002) and now Emeritus Professor of Law of Art and Cultural Property (2002+); Chairs in Law at many other English and Australian Universities (1981+); Doctor of Law Honoris Causa, University of Geneva (2005). Appointed CBE (2006) for services to art and to law.

Publications: Palmer on Bailment (3rd edn 2009); Museums and the Holocaust (2000); Cultural Heritage Statutes (2nd edn 2004); Art Loans (1997); Recovery of Stolen Art (1998); Interests in Goods (2nd edn 1998); Individual Liability of Museum Personnel (2011); Halsbury, Laws of England (titles: Bailment, Carriers, Confidentiality, Damages, Libraries and other Scientific and Cultural Institutions, Lien, Tort); Crossley Vaines on Personal Property (5th edn, 1973); Encyclopaedia Forms and Precedents; English Private Law (3rd edn, 2013) title Bailment; Laws of Australia; numerous others. Founded and co-edits Art Antiquity and Law (quarterly, Institute of Art and Law, 1996+). Publications by him have been cited by appellate courts of leading common law jurisdictions, eg House of Lords, Judicial Committee of the Privy Council, Court of Appeal, High Court of Australia, Supreme Court of Canada, Courts of Appeal of New Zealand, New South Wales, Victoria, British Columbia etc.

Personal: Married, two daughters.

PANESAR, Deshpal

Old Square Chambers, London
020 769 0300
panesar@oldsquare.co.uk

Featured in Employment (London)

Practice Areas: Deshpal is a specialist in Employment and Professional Discipline. Described as "the barrister of choice for a complex and lengthy case," he is widely praised for his formidable grasp of the issues in employment cases. Sources emphasise his mastery of discrimination legislation and that he is an excellent cross-examiner. Deshpal regularly acts in complex, high value claims and has a heavy successful appellate practice. Described in Chambers and Partners as 'razor sharp and willing to assist at all times.', 'a cracking cross examiner ', 'a fantastic team worker', 'highly eloquent' and 'utterly reliable', and in Legal 500 as 'exceptionally well prepared', he has been at the forefront of discrimination litigation. He has a growing High Court practice. PROFESSIONAL DISCIPLINE He has particular experience in cases involving professionals in the healthcare industry and has extensive experience of acting on behalf of a wide range of NHS Trusts as well as professionals. The son of a surgeon, he has a particular understanding of the issues and pressures facing doctors and healthcare professionals. Deshpal has appeared on professional disciplinary matters in Employment Tribunals, the Employment Appeal Tribunal, The Health Professions Council, and the GMC.

Professional Memberships: Deshpal is the Vice Chair of the Employment Law Bar Association. ELA and ILS.

PARFITT, Matthew

Erskine Chambers, London
020 72425532
mparfitt@erskine-chambers.co.uk

Featured in Company (London)

Practice Areas: Matthew is a commercial litigator with specialisms in company and insolvency law. He has a busy litigation and advisory practice, extending into professional negligence, partnership law (including LLPs) and bankruptcy. He undertakes a range of international work and has been appointed to the Attorney General's Panel of Counsel to act in government litigation. Company law: Matthew has an in-depth knowledge of the law, and a sound commercial understanding. He has been involved in litigation across the whole spectrum of company law matters, and has broad transactional experience. He also deals with LLPs and partnership law. He wrote the chapter on derivative claims in Gore Browne on Companies. Insolvency and corporate reconstruction: insolvency, particularly corporate and personal insolvency litigation, is a core part of Matthew's practice. He has acted in directors' disqualification cases and public interest winding up petitions. Litigation (commercial): Matthew has a broad commercial litigation practice. His significant experience of company and insolvency law gives him a strong foundation for wider commercial dispute resolution. He appears in all divisions of the High Court, including the Commercial Court. He has experience of arbitral tribunals and court applications under the Arbitration Act.

Professional Memberships: Chancery Bar Association; Commercial Bar Association.

Career: Called 2005; Lincoln's Inn.

Personal: Winchester College; Exeter College, Oxford (2003 MA Hons Classics (First Class)); City University (2004 CPE). LEISURE: Music, literature, philosophy, cookery; competitive cyclist.

PARKER, Christopher R QC

Maitland Chambers, London
020 7406 1200
cparker@maitlandchambers.com

Featured in Offshore (London), Restructuring/Insolvency (London)

Practice Areas: Main areas of practice are commercial chancery and business disputes with an emphasis on company law (particularly shareholder disputes and claims for breach of fiduciary duty), fraud, asset recovery, insolvency, professional negligence and trusts litigation. Called to the BVI Bar in 2006 and regularly appears there and also acted in cases in the Bahamas (Called 2009), Bermuda, Dubai (registered with the DIFC), Hong Kong, Guernsey, Jersey and in the Caribbean Court of Justice (Called 2010). Advised on aspects of the insolvency of Lehman Brothers and of the estate of Berezovsky. Recent reported cases include Burnden v Fielding [2016] EWCA Civ 557 (limitation); Jetivia SA v Bilta [2015] UKSC 23 (ex turpi causa not a defence to claim by company against sole director/shareholder); Ebbvale Ltd v Hosking [2013] UKPC 1 (winding up petition not an abuse of process).

Professional Memberships: ILA, PNBA, ChBA, COMBAR, CLFA.

Career: Called 1984. QC 2008.

Personal: Educated at Keble College, Oxford BA Jurisprudence, 1st class, (1977-80) and BCL (1980-81), University of Illinois LLM (1981-82), Harvard Law School LLM (1982-83). Born 1958.

PARKER, Matthew

3 Verulam Buildings, London
020 7831 8441
mparker@3vb.com

Featured in Professional Negligence (London), Banking & Finance (London), Commercial Dispute Resolution (London), Fraud (London), Offshore (London)

Practice Areas: Matthew is a leading commercial junior who appears in a wide range of complex and high-value commercial disputes. He is highly experienced in commercial litigation and arbitration in the UK and internationally and has been called to the Bar in the British Virgin Islands and the Cayman Islands. He is particularly noted for his expertise in banking and financial services, commercial fraud and professional negligence.

Professional Memberships: COMBAR, LCLCBA.

Career: In 2016, Matthew was instructed on behalf of one of the shareholders in the dispute over the Aman Resorts hotel business, securing judgment for over $50m: Peak Hotels v Tarek Investments Ltd [2016] EWHC 333 (Ch). In 2015, he achieved a major victory in Central Bank of Ecuador v Conticorp [2015] UKPC 11, in which the Privy Council overturned concurrent findings of the courts below and awarded damages of US$192m in a complex financial fraud claim. He also appeared in a number of high-value investment disputes, including McEneaney v Ulster Bank Ireland Ltd [2015] EWHC 3173 (Comm) and Astle v CBRE [2015] EWHC 3189 (Ch). Matthew is a highly experienced advocate, who is frequently noted for his robust submissions and skilful cross-examination. He has appeared as sole counsel at trial in a wide range of commercial disputes, including Alegro v Allproperty Media [2013] EWHC 3376 (QB), Lawlor v Sandvik [2012] EWHC 1188 (QB), Redmayne Bentley v Isaacs [2010] EWHC 1504 (Comm), Innovatis v Ejder Group [2010] EWHC 1850 (Ch), Fitzalan-Howard v Hibbert [2010] PNLR 11 and M&J Polymers v Imerys [2008] 1 All ER (Comm) 893, and as sole counsel in the Court of Appeal, in Lawlor v Sandvik [2013] 2 Lloyd's Rep 98 and Morin v Bonhams & Brooks [2004] 1 Lloyd's Rep 702. Acting as a junior, he appeared in the Court of Appeal in NML v Chapman Freeborn [2013] 1 CLC 968 and Unite v Liverpool Victoria [2015] EWCA Civ 285 and regularly appears in heavy commercial litigation, such as Primary Group v RBS [2014] EWHC 1082 (Ch) and Porton v 3M Company [2011] EWHC 2895 (Comm). In addition to litigation in the UK and offshore, arbitration forms a significant part of Matthew's practice. He appeared in the series of reported decisions in Republic of Kazakhstan v Istil [2006] 2 Lloyd's Rep 307, [2007] 2 Lloyd's Rep 548, and [2008] 1 Lloyd's Rep 382 and regularly appears as sole counsel in major international commercial arbitrations.

Personal: Oundle School and Jesus College, Cambridge (foundation scholar).

PARKER, Paul

4 New Square, London
020 7822 2000
p.parker@4newsquare.com

Featured in Professional Negligence (London), Professional Discipline (London)

Practice Areas: Principal areas are (i) professional liability claims and disciplinary proceedings involving lawyers (including wasted costs), accountants and auditors, actuaries, financial services professionals, insolvency practitioners, insurance brokers, and construction professionals; (ii) general commercial and chancery commercial litigation, with particular emphasis on insurance law. Cases include: Sarikaya v Vahib & Co (2016) (QB): summary judgment, no causation of damage by criminal solicitor; Cambr Ltd v Edwards (2015) (QB): summary judgment, ordinary course of business of accountants; Ralph Lauren Europe SARL v Butcher (2014) (QB Comm): fraud, freezing orders; SRA v Emeana (2013) (QB Admin): disciplinary interface between dishonesty and lack of integrity; Nationwide BS v Davisons (2012) (QB and CA): solicitors' liability for breach of trust; Makar v Russell Jones and Walker (2012) (QB Comm): strike-out and CROs; Webb Resolutions v Waller Needham and Green (2012) (Ch): Protocol non-compliance and Part 36 offers; Crabtree v Ng (2011) (CA): stage 1 wasted costs order quashed; Media CAT Ltd v Adams (2011) (PCC): wasted costs in P2P file sharing litigation; Dhamija v McBains Cooper (2010) (TCC): no duty on QS to report defects; Yechiel v Kerry London (2010) (QB Comm): falsified insurance claims; Angel Solicitors v Jenkins O'Dowd and Barth (2009) (Ch): solicitors' undertakings; Rind v Theodore Goddard (2008) (Ch): duty of care and limitation in failed IHT avoidance scheme; Hooper v Biddle (2006) (Ch): costs after compromise of exaggerated claim; R v PIA Ombudsman ex p Davies Walters (2001) (QB Admin): challenge to vires of ombudsman's award; Re A Firm of Solicitors (1999) (TCC): conflicts of interest and chinese walls; Nationwide BS v Lewis (1998) (CA): no liability of salaried partner without reliance.
Professional Memberships: PNBA, ChBA, COMBAR, LCLCBA.
Career: MA (Cantab). Called (Middle Temple) 1986. Joined 4 New Square (formerly 2 Crown Office Row) 1987.
Publications: Editor of Jackson & Powell: Professional Liability Precedents; chapters on solicitors, IT professionals and appeals.
Personal: Educated at Mill Hill School and Christ's College, Cambridge. Leisure interests: family, singing and lawn tennis. Languages: French and Serbian.

PARKER, Timothy
9 Gough Square, London
07966 466605
tparker@9goughsquare.co.uk
Featured in Family/Matrimonial (London)
Practice Areas: Tim is a barrister and arbitrator specialising in family and associated civil litigation. He is instructed in care proceedings featuring non-accidental injury, death and sexual abuse, adoption, special guardianship applications, Human Rights Act claims arising in care proceedings and judicial review of local authority decisions concerning children. He is instructed in welfare decisions in the Court of Protection. He is also instructed in financial remedy claims, cohabitee disputes, financial provision for children and family property disputes. Tim is qualified to arbitrate both financial remedy and child disputes. Tim is licensed to accept instructions directly from members of the public.
Professional Memberships: Family Law Bar Association, South Eastern Circuit, Association of Lawyers for Children, Member of the Chartered institute of Arbitrators and the Institute of Family Law Arbitrators.
Career: Called to the Bar in 1995. Arbitrator in 2014.
Publications: Editor of "The Revised Public Law Outline" (2015) 2nd Edition, published by 9 Gough Square.

PARRY, Clare
Cornerstone Barristers, London
020 7242 4986
clarep@cornerstonebarristers.com
Featured in Planning (London)
Practice Areas: Public law, planning, social housing.
Professional Memberships: PEBA, ALBA.
Career: Clare regularly advises on and appears at inquiry and in the Courts in respect of all aspects of planning law. She represents a range of clients including local authorities, developers, action groups and central government. She is on the Attorney General's C Panel. Clare recently appeared in the largest onshore wind farm. She has also recently represented Herefordshire County Council in the successful examination of their Core Strategy. She appeared in one of the leading cases on neighbourhood plans (DLA Delivery v Lewes DC). Clare has particular experience of the following areas: planning in Wales; renewable energy; housing; neighbourhood planning;and local plans.
Publications: Contributor to "Cornerstone on the Planning Court", Kolvin on "Gambling for Local Authorities" and "Licensed Premises: Law and Practice".

PARSONS, Luke QC
Quadrant Chambers, London
020 7583 4444
luke.parsons@quadrantchambers.com
Featured in International Arbitration (London), Energy & Natural Resources (London), Shipping (London)
Practice Areas: Luke is Head of Quadrant Chambers and a Commercial and Admiralty silk whose practice encompasses insurance and reinsurance, international trade, energy, sale of goods, banking, commercial contracts, and shipping. Luke is often called in to handle the highest value, most complex claims, involving coordinating large teams of experts and has acted on many precedent-setting cases in the High Court, and Court of Appeal. Given the frequently international dimension of his practice, Luke has extensive experience in dealing with foreign law and multi-jurisdictional disputes. In particular he frequently acts in arbitrations with a cross-border element and is experienced in making applications to the High Court in support of English arbitrations and also in support of foreign arbitrations in the English courts and advises on the enforcement of awards under the New York Convention.
Professional Memberships: COMBAR. Supporting member LMAA.
Career: LLB (Bristol). Called 1985, Inner Temple, Queens Counsel 2003.
Publications: Steel and Parsons; Admiralty and Commercial Court Forms and Precedents (2nd Edition, Thomson Reuters) with David Steel QC (now Mr. Justice Steel)
Personal: Married. 5 sons.

PARTRIDGE, Richard
Serjeants' Inn Chambers, London
020 7427 5000
rpartridge@serjeantsinn.com
Featured in Clinical Negligence (London), Professional Discipline (London)
Practice Areas: Richard Partridge was called to the Bar in 1994. Richard specialises in clinical negligence, personal injury, professional discipline and regulation and inquests and inquiries. An earlier edition notes that he is "very good on the medical aspects of a claim" and "with Richard, you feel you're working in a real partnership. He's very responsive, very pragmatic and his attention to detail is excellent." Please visit the Serjeants' Inn Chambers website for his profile, which sets out full details of his practice including relevant work of note.
Career: Mb BCh, LLB Hons.
Publications: Co-author of Medical Treatment: Decisions and the Law.

PASCOE, Martin QC
South Square, London
020 7696 9900
martinpascoe@southsquare.com
Featured in Restructuring/Insolvency (London)
Practice Areas: Martin specialises in insolvency and restructuring and commercial litigation.
Professional Memberships: COMBAR, Chancery Bar Association.
Career: Martin regularly acts in complex multi-jurisdictional high-value cases. He is well known for his success in leading the counsel team for the State of Brunei in its worldwide claims against HRH Prince Jefri. Other examples of his cases include: acting for the special administrators of the spread-betting investment bank Alpari plc; Greenwich v Dowling; MF Global; Heritable Bank v Landsbanki Islands hf; and SerVaas v Rafidain Bank. Queen's Counsel (2002); Called to the Bar (Lincoln's Inn, 1977). Called to the BVI bar, and also (for specific cases) the bars of the Cayman Islands, Bermuda and Isle of Man.

PATERSON, Fiona
Serjeants' Inn Chambers, London
020 7427 5000
fpaterson@serjeantsinn.com
Featured in Court of Protection (All Circuits)
Practice Areas: Fiona Paterson was called to the Bar in 2003. Fiona specialises in clinical negligence and healthcare, Court of Protection, inquests and inquiries, professional discipline and regulatory and public and administrative law. An earlier edition notes that she is "an advocate to watch." Please visit the Serjeants' Inn Chambers website for her profile, which sets out full details of her practice including relevant work of note.
Professional Memberships: Justice, Human Rights Lawyers Association, Professional Negligence Bar Association.
Career: Attorney General's London C Panel of Junior Counsel, CEDR Accredited Mediator.
Publications: Co-author of Medical Treatment: Decisions and the Law.

PATTEN, Ben QC
4 New Square, London
020 3137 1728
b.patten@4newsquare.com
Featured in Professional Negligence (London), Construction (London)
Practice Areas: Principal areas of practice are professional negligence and construction, including claims against construction professionals. Frequently involved in cases involving solicitors, barristers, accountants, surveyors, financial advisers, insurance brokers, architects, engineers and project managers. Also, substantial experience in commercial and insurance disputes. Recent cases include Cheshire Building Society v Dunlop Haywards Limited [2008] PNLR 19, Biffa Waste Services Limited v Machinenfabrik Ernst Hese Gmbh [2009] BLR 1, Levicom International BV v Linklaters [2010] PNLR 29, Carillion v Phi Group Ltd [2010] EWHC 496, Asiansky Television Plc v Khanzada [2011] EWHC 2831, Guy v Mace and Jones [2012] EWHC 1022; Newcastle Airport Ltd v Eversheds [2013] PNLR 5.
Professional Memberships: Professional Negligence Bar Association, TECBAR, London Common Law and Commercial Bar Association.
Career: Called to the Bar in 1986 and joined 22 Old Buildings in 1988. Joined 1 Crown Office Row 1997. Joined 2 Crown Office Row (now 4 New Square) 1999. Queen's Counsel 2010.
Publications: Professional Negligence in Construction, Spon, [2005]. Co-editor of Jackson and Powell 'Professional Liability Precedents'.
Personal: Oxford University, City University, Middle Temple. Called to the Irish Bar.

PATTON, Conall
One Essex Court, London
020 7583 2000
cpatton@oeclaw.co.uk
Featured in Competition/European Law (London), Banking & Finance (London), Commercial Dispute Resolution (London), Energy & Natural Resources (London)
Practice Areas: Conall Patton has a broad commercial practice, including energy, competition, banking and finance, jurisdiction/choice of law, company and commercial judicial review. Recent cases include: acting (with Laurence Rabinowitz QC) for Mr Igor Kolomoisky in a large-scale Commercial Court dispute between three Ukrainian businessmen; acting (with Jon Turner QC) for British Airways in follow-on damages claims arising from an alleged cartel in the air cargo sector; appearing with Lord Grabiner QC in the Court of Appeal in a landmark decision on act of state and issue estoppel (Yukos Capital v Rosneft); appearing without a leader for private equity group Warburg Pincus in a two-week Commercial Court trial and in the Court of Appeal (Barbudev v Eurocom Cable); appearing with Lord Grabiner QC in the Supreme Court on a judicial review appeal (Gaines-Cooper v HMRC); appearing without a leader for a major investment bank in a one-week LCIA arbitration concerning claims for c. $100 million; arguing a novel point about the cost consequences of discontinuance in the Court of Appeal (Safeway Stores v Twigger); appearing with Thomas Sharpe QC in the Competition Appeal Tribunal in a construction penalty appeal; appearing with Lord Grabiner QC in the Eastern Caribbean Court of Appeal in the Yukos litigation. Conall is a member of the Bar of the British Virgin Islands.

PAY, Adrian
New Square Chambers, London
020 7419 8000
adrian.pay@newsquarechambers.co.uk
Featured in Chancery (London)

Practice Areas: Adrian Pay's practice focuses on contentious chancery work, in particular, commercial chancery and property work. His commercial work includes commercial fraud (e.g. Weavering v Ernst & Young, a claim against auditors relating to the collapse of a fraudulently run hedge fund), company and insolvency matters and contractual disputes (including matters with an information technology aspect). He has particular expertise in shareholder disputes (e.g. Caldero v Beppler & Jacobson Ltd [2013] EWHC 2191 (Ch); [2014] EWCA Civ 935, a high-profile dispute relating to two prestigious hotels in Montenegro; Adrian is currently instructed on a high-value shareholder dispute concerning an investment fund in Vietnam). His property work includes, in particular, disputes arising out of property developments and deficient conveyancing: cases include Angel Solicitors v Jenkins O'Dowd & Barth [2009] 1 WLR 1220; Clark v Lucas LLP [2010] 2 All ER 955; Kind v Northumberland County Council [2013] 1 WLR 743; R (Trail Riders Fellowship) v Dorset CC [2015] UKSC 18.
Professional Memberships: Chancery Bar Association; COMBAR.
Career: Called to the Bar 1999 Called to the Bar of the British Virgin Islands 2016.
Personal: Educated King's School, Canterbury; Balliol College, Oxford – MA (Oxon).

PAYNE, Alan
5 Essex Court, London
020 7410 2000
payne@5essexcourt.co.uk
Featured in Immigration (London)
Practice Areas: Administrative and public law, police law, inquests, inquiries, employment. Significant cases include: – The Independent Inquiry into Child Sexual Abuse – representing Lancashire Constabulary & North Yorkshire; Undercover Policing Inquiry – representing North Yorkshire; Mouncher & Ors v Chief Constable of South Wales Police (claims brought by officers prosecuted for investigation into murder of Lynette White in 1988); Tesfay and 8 Ors v Secretary of State for the Home Department [2016] EWCA 1367; BL (Jamaica) v Secretary of State for the Home Department [2016] EWCA 357; EM (Eritrea) & Ors v Secretary of State for the Home Department [2014] UKSC 12; The Azelle Rodney Inquiry (representing the MPS and all officers save for the shooter); EWHC 452; Tabrizagh & 5 Ors v Secretary of State for the Home Department [2014] EWHC 1914; Bianca Durrant v Chief Constable of Avon & Somerset Nottinghamshire [2013] EWCA Civ 1624; John Yapp v Foreign & Commonwealth Office [2013] EWHC 1098; Kent County Council v HM Coroner for Kent & Mr. and Mrs. Barry (Interested Parties) [2012] EWHC 2768; Desmond v Chief Constable of Nottinghamshire [2011] EWCA Civ 3.
Career: Called to the Bar 1996. Attorney General's 'A' Panel (2011) (previously 'B' panel 2007-2010 and 'C' panel 2004-2007). Develop Vetted.
Publications: Tolley's Employment Tribunals Handbook – first published October 2002 (fourth edition published by Bloomsbury Professional August 2014).

PAYNE, Geoffrey
25 Bedford Row, London
020 7067 1500
clerks@25bedfordrow.com
Featured in Financial Crime (London)
Practice Areas: Geoff Payne is a specialist in defending heavy fraud cases. He has acted in some of the longest, heaviest and highest value cases prosecuted, some involving allegations of fraud of up to £450 million. He is tenacious and proactive and has a strong track record in defending in some of the most complex cases dealt with by the criminal justice system. He appears in cases both alone and as junior counsel. This year, he has been instructed in a banking fraud in the City of London involving alleged losses of $120 million. He appeared in one of the earliest cases of Film Tax Credit Fraud. He also has a particular expertise in Missing Trader Intra-Community Fraud and acted for the defence in the largest 'Ponzi Fraud' ever prosecuted. He has also acted in cases of alleged advance fee frauds, long firm frauds and construction frauds, often acting for professionals such as accountants and liquidators. He regularly appears in cases involving allegations of misconduct in public office. He has successfully dealt with a number of confiscation proceedings and has appeared alone in the Court of Appeal. His repeated case of Okedare [2014] EWCA Crim 228 made new law on absconders in confiscation proceedings.
Professional Memberships: Criminal Bar Association, Proceeds of Crime Lawyers Association (POCLA), Association of Regulatory and Disciplinary Lawyers (ARDL).
Career: Called 2000; St Edmund Hall, Oxford, Modern History; City University, London, Common Professional Examination in Law; Inns of Court School of Law, London, Bar Vocational Course.

PEACOCK, Ian
New Square Chambers, London
020 7419 8000
ian.peacock@newsquarechambers.co.uk
Featured in Social Housing (London)
Practice Areas: Ian Peacock specialises in property litigation and public law. He is an expert in homelessness and allocations law. He regularly appears in the County Court, the Administrative Court, the Court of Appeal and has recently appeared in the Supreme Court in the two homelessness cases of Samin and Nzolameso. He regularly acts in landlord and tenant disputes concerning both business and residential tenancies. He has particular experience of claims relating to dilapidations, public sector housing disputes, especially neighbour nuisance, and service charge disputes. He also has experience of professional negligence cases and company and insolvency work (both corporate and personal).
Professional Memberships: Chancery Bar Association.
Career: Called to the Bar 1990 (Gray's Inn)
Publications: Contributor to The Law of Freedom of Information (O.U.P).
Personal: Educated Trinity College, Cambridge; City University. Lives in London.

PEACOCK, Jonathan QC
11 New Square, London
020 7242 4017
jonathan.peacock@11newsquare.com
Featured in Tax (London)
Practice Areas: Jonathan Peacock QC has a broad practice in direct and indirect tax, both as an adviser and as an advocate. He appears regularly in the U.K. courts and the CJEU and has acted in tax-based arbitrations and mediations and appeared as an expert witness in foreign courts. Jonathan advises financial institutions, multi-nationals and high net worth individuals, particularly on capital market, corporate finance, structured finance, venture capital and employee remuneration/pension matters. He has acted both for and against the UK Government in tax avoidance matters. While advising on all industry sectors, Jonathan has an extensive energy practice (predominantly oil and gas but also covering renewables and hydro-electric). He also has expertise, both advisory and advocacy, in relation to sports tax matters (acting for governing bodies, clubs, players and sponsors) in relation to stadium developments, club financing, player remuneration and media rights. He advises on all international and cross-border tax issues (permanent establishments, transfer pricing, entity classification, double tax relief, residence and domicile questions) and has appeared in significant DTR cases in the UK, most recently Anson in the Supreme Court.
Professional Memberships: VAT Practitioners Group, Society of Trust & Estate Practitioners and UK Offshore Industry Tax Committee. Chairman of the Revenue Bar Association (2013-2016).
Career: Corpus Christi College, Oxford, First Class (Jurisprudence).

PEACOCK, Nicholas
Hailsham Chambers, London
020 7643 5000
clerks@hailshamchambers.com
Featured in Clinical Negligence (London), Professional Discipline (London)
Practice Areas: Nick specialises in clinical negligence work, regulatory and disciplinary work (particularly MPTS/GMC, GDC and GOC) and general healthcare law (including inquests and clinical confidentiality). He advised the Royal College of Veterinary Surgeons on their jurisdiction and procedures in cases of adverse health. He sits as Legal Adviser to the General Pharmaceutical Council. He has a particular interest in dental work, including the business and regulation of dentistry. Clients who instruct Nick include patients and their families, healthcare professionals via their defence organisations/indemnity providers, and NHS Trusts/NHSLA.

PEACOCK, Nicholas QC
Maitland Chambers, London
020 7406 1200
npeacock@maitlandchambers.com
Featured in Financial Services (London)
Practice Areas: Covering a wide range of commercial/chancery areas, but with particular emphasis on the following: (1) Financial services litigation and advice, including acting for and against the Financial Services Authority (FSA v Foster [2005] All ER (D) 55 (Jul); FSA v Martin [2006] 2 BCLC 193; In re Inertia Partnership [2007] Bus LR 879); European Property Investments 7 Dec 2012) and also dealing with matters concerning authorisation (particularly collective investment schemes and new investment products) and client money issues (Global Trader [2008] and Lehmans [2010]). (2) Regulatory litigation and proceedings concerning solicitors (Gauntlett v Law Society [2006] EWHC 1954 (Ch); Bramall, R (on the application of) v Law Society [2005] EWHC 1570 (Admin); Sritharan v Law Society [2004] EWHC 2932 (Ch) and [2005] 1 WLR 2708; Dua v SRA 19 Nov 2010) and accountants, as well as DTI/SFO investigations (In re Mirror Group Newspapers plc [1999]). (3) Commercial Chancery litigation covering areas as diverse as radio (Evans v SMG [2003]) and property development/offshore trusts (Intense Investments v Development Ventures [2006] EWHC 1586 (TCC); and Nearfield v Lincoln Trust Company (Jersey) [2006] EWHC 2421 (Ch)). (4) Company and insolvency (Rayford Homes v Bank of Scotland & Barclays Wealth Trustees [2011] BCC 715; Lehmans [2009], Global Trader [2008], In The Matter Of Crystal Palace Football Club (2005), Re Dollar Land (Feltham) Ltd [1995] 2 BCLC 370, McMullen & Sons v Cerrone [1994] BCLC 152).
Professional Memberships: Chancery Bar Association; COMBAR.
Career: Called 1989. QC 2009.
Personal: BA (Oxon).

PEARCE, Robert QC
Radcliffe Chambers, London
020 78310081
rpearce@radcliffechambers.com
Featured in Chancery (London), Charities (London), Education (London), Real Estate Litigation (London)
Practice Areas: Practices in the chancery and commercial fields, in particular: Contentious and non-contentious trusts (both onshore and in offshore common law jurisdictions); Wills probate, succession and administration of estates, family provision; Real property and landlord and tenant; • Charities and education; Commercial and contract law; Company, insolvency and partnership; Claims for professional negligence arising in these fields. He is an accredited mediator Recent illustrative cases: University of London v Prag (2014) – university governance; Human Dignity Trust v Charity Commission for England and Wales (2014) – charitable purposes, human rights; Marwaha v Singh (2014) – charities, litigation costs; Re Wedgwood Museum Trust Ltd (In Administration) (2012) charities, insolvency, pension liabilities; Shergill v Khaira (2012) – charities, justiciability of religious issues; Faidi v Elliot Corporation (2012) – landlord and tenant, claim between lessees; Attorney General v Charity Commission for England and Wales (2012) – charities, relief of poverty; Howard v Howard-Lawson (2012) – trusts, name and arms clause; R (on the application of Independent Schools Council) v Charity Commission for England and Wales) (2011) – charities, education, judicial review; Catholic Care (Diocese of Leeds) v Charity Commission (2010) – equality, discrimination; Power v Open Text (UK) Ltd Group Life Assurance Scheme Trustees (Chancery Division (2010) – group life assurance scheme, trustees' powers and duties.
Professional Memberships: STEP; Charity Law Association; Property Bar Association; ACTAPS; Chancery Bar Association.
Career: Christ Church, Oxford (Jurisprudence, 1st class honours, BCL). Called to the bar 1977. Standing Counsel to the Charity Commission 2001 – 2006. Silk 2006. Bencher of Lincoln's Inn 2013.

Publications: Contributing editor to The Civil Court Practice (LexisNexis), and various articles.

PEEL, Robert QC
29 Bedford Row Chambers, London
020 7404 1044
rpeel@29br.co.uk
Featured in Family/Matrimonial (London)

Practice Areas: Barrister specialising in financial remedies, Schedule 1 Children Act and Inheritance Act. Particular emphasis on high net worth, cross jurisdiction issues, trust and company law. Expertise in professional negligence. Accepts public access instructions. Acts as private FDR judge. Cases include; BD v FD [2016] EWHC 594 (needs and "big money"); NR v AB [2016] EWHC 277 (family wealth, trust and company issues); WS v WS [2015] EWHC 277 (pensions); D v D [2015] EWHC 1993 (non disclosure); AE v BE [2014] EWHC 4868; Kim v Morris [2013] 2 FLR 1197 (divorce suit); Yates v Yates [2013] 2 FLR 1070 (capitalisation); A v A [2013] 2 FLR 947 (media publicity); Y v Y [2013] 2 FLR 924 (inherited wealth); Whaley v Whaley [2012] 1 FLR 735 (trusts); V v V [2011] 2 FLR 778 (forum dispute); A v A [2006] 2 FLR 115 (companies); D v D [2004] 1 FLR 988 (clean break); Phippen v Palmers [2002] 2 FLR 415 (professional negligence).

Professional Memberships: FLBA.

Career: BA Oxon. City University (Dip Law). Middle Templar. Called to the Bar 1990. Appointed QC in 2010. Recorder since 2009. Bar Disciplinary Tribunal Chairman. Past committee member; FLBA and Bar Council.

PEMBERTON, Yolanda
St Philips Chambers, Birmingham
0121 246 7000
ypemberton@st-philips.com
Featured in Family/Matrimonial (Midlands)

Practice Areas: Yolanda specialises in all aspects of children law and has extensive experience in both public and private law children work, forced marriage (including FGM), Brussels II, wardship and inherent jurisdiction. Yolanda represents local authorities, parents and children in public law cases involving serious injuries to children, FII, sexual abuse (including subject child as victim and perpetrator), complex medical issues, mental health, including parents who require the assistance of the Official Solicitor, and child death. In addition, Yolanda has experience of representing parents, children, other family members and local authorities in adoption proceedings. In private law children work this includes cases involving child arrangements orders, including high conflict and intractable disputes, applications to remove children from, or relocate children within, the jurisdiction, specific issues relating to education, medical and religion, issues of mental health, fact-finding hearings and domestic abuse within families. Yolanda is known for her meticulous preparation of all of her cases, being able to quickly and expertly get to the core of any dispute, and is known to be uncompromising in her approach for her client, ensuring they receive the best and most robust representation. Yolanda excels with vulnerable clients in complex cases. Yolanda has experience before all levels of the judiciary, including the Court of Appeal. Notable cases include: Re E [2016] EWCA Civ 473 and Re B (A Child) [2014] EWCA Civ 565.

Professional Memberships: West Midlands Family Law Bar Association, FLBA and ALC.

Career: Called 2002 Lincoln's Inn.

Personal: Warwick University, Inns of Court School of Law.

PENNIFER, Kelly
Kings Chambers, Manchester
0345 034 3444
clerks@kingschambers.com
Featured in Construction (Northern/North Eastern), Commercial Dispute Resolution (Northern)

Practice Areas: Practises in all aspects of Town and Country Planning, with particular experience of section 78 and Development Plan Inquiries. Recognised by Planning Magazine as a leading planning barrister under 35 (2006). Notable cases include: Fordent Holdings Ltd v SSCLG [2013] EWHC 2844 (Admin); [2014] J.P.L. 226; Feather v Cheshire East BC [2010] EWHC 1420 (Admin); R. (on the application of P Casey (Enviro) Ltd) v Bradford MBC [2008] EWHC 2543 (Admin); [2009] J.P.L. 639. Also practises in environmental law and compulsory purchase.

Professional Memberships: Planning and Environmental Bar Association (PEBA).

Career: First Class Honours Degree in European Law (LLB) from Warwick University. Masters in Comparative and International Law (LLM) from European University Institute, Florence. Very Competent in Bar Finals, Inns of Court School of Law.

Publications: Author of the Housing Chapter in Judicial Review: Law and Practice (Jordans)(1st Edition)

PEPPERALL, Edward QC
St Philips Chambers, Birmingham
0121 246 7010
ep@st-philips.com
Featured in Professional Negligence (Midlands), Commercial Dispute Resolution (Midlands), Company (Midlands), Employment (Midlands)

Practice Areas: High-value commercial litigation and arbitration often arising from the sale of businesses or the supply of goods and services. Cases include (as arbitrator) a RUB 12.5 billion international commercial arbitration and (as counsel) a US$50 million share warranty claim following the sale of a multi-national business, a £70 million fraud claim for the UK's five largest brewers, a US$100 million international arbitration and international search and freezing orders. Employment work is primarily concerned with restraint of trade, team moves and breaches of confidentiality involving senior executives. Also acts in associated shareholder disputes, typically concerning claims for unfair prejudice. Professional negligence work encompasses claims against lawyers (including a group action and claims against QCs for negligent conduct of multi-million pound commercial litigation and criminal trials), insurance brokers, acountants and surveyors. Nationally acknowledged expert on civil procedure (as a former member of the CPRC, White Book contributor and chairman of the recent Part 36 reforms). Deputy High Court Judge.

Professional Memberships: COMBAR, MCIArb, ELA, Midland Chancery & Commercial Bar Association (Chairman).

Career: Called 1989. Silk 2013. MCIArb. Deputy High Court Judge (Chancery & QBD) and Recorder. Contributing Editor, White Book. Former member of the Civil Procedure Rule Committee.

PERRINS, Gregory
Drystone Chambers, London
020 7404 1881
gregory.perrins@drystone.com
Featured in Crime (South Eastern)

Practice Areas: Criminal law, fraud, regulatory law.

Professional Memberships: South Eastern Circuit, CBA.

Career: Gregory Perrins possesses considerable experience as a specialist Criminal barrister. He both prosecutes and defends in broadly equal measure. He has a practice with a geographic spread that takes him from London to courts across the South Eastern Circuit and beyond. His practice covers all areas of serious crime with an emphasis on serious violence and sexual offences, whilst also dealing with a significant amount of serious fraud and white-collar crime. He is increasingly in demand to act as leading counsel and has extensive experience of being led by others. In 2012 Gregory played an active role in advising OFCOM on the regulatory framework to be adopted at the London 2012 Olympic Games. In the same year Gregory was appointed Recorder and in so doing became one of the youngest members of the Bar to be appointed. In 2014 he was appointed Chairman of the Police Appeals Tribunal.

Publications: Westlaw UK Insight – Contributing author.

PETERS, Edward
Falcon Chambers, London
020 7353 2484
peters@falcon-chambers.com
Featured in Agriculture & Rural Affairs (London), Real Estate Litigation (London)

Practice Areas: Specialist in all aspects of real property and landlord and tenant litigation, and related areas including professional negligence. Cases include: Patley Wood Farm LLP v Blake [2015] EWHC 483 (Ch), [2014] EWHC 4499 (Ch) and [2014] EWHC 1439 (Ch) (arbitration); Fulham Broadway Trustees no 1 Ltd v Telefonica UK Ltd [2014] EWHC 1048 (ch) (rent review); Compton Beauchamp Estates Ltd v Spence [2013] 2 P&CR 15 (arbitration);George Wimpey Bristol Ltd v Gloucestershire Housing Association Ltd [2011] UKUT 91 (restrictive covenants); PGF II SA v Royal & Sun Alliance [2011] 1 P&CR 11 (dilapidations); Bocardo SA v Star Energy UK Onshore Ltd [2010] UKSC 35; Shaw v Doleman (CA) [2009] 2 BCLC 123; Brown's Operating System Services Ltd v Southwark RCDC (CA) [2007] L&TR 25 (service charges); Elmbirch Properties PLC v Schaefer-Tsoropatzadis [2007] 2 EGLR 167(rent review); Edlington Properties Ltd v JH Fenner & Co (CA) [2006] 1 WLR 1583 (equitable set-off); Kintyre Ltd v Romeomarch Property Management Ltd [2006] 1 EGLR 67 (enfranchisement); Stroude v Beazer Homes Ltd [2006] 2 EGLR 115 (s. 106 agreement); Malekshad v. Howard de Walden Estates (HL) [2003] 1 AC 1013 (enfranchisement); Ashworth Fraser v Gloucester City Council (HL) [2001] 1 WLR 2180 (consent to assign).

Professional Memberships: LCLCBA, Chancery Bar Association, Property Bar Association, Agricultural Law Association, Chartered Institute of Arbitrators.

Career: Caius College, Cambridge (BA, 1996); City University (1997); Called 1998 (MT).

Publications: Editor, Woodfall's Law of Landlord and Tenant; Contributor to Fisher & Lightwood's Law of Mortgage (11th (2002) 12th (2008) 13th (2010) & 14th (2014) eds.); Co-author "Charging Orders" (2013); Co-author "Commonhold" (OUP) 2004. Blundell Lecturer (2012).

PHELPS, Rosalind QC
Fountain Court Chambers, London
020 7583 3335
rp@fountaincourt.co.uk
Featured in Travel (London), Aviation (London), Banking & Finance (London), Commercial Dispute Resolution (London), Fraud (London)

Practice Areas: Civil and commercial litigation including aviation, banking, civil fraud, conflicts of law and jurisdiction, financial services and professional negligence. Cases include: Monks v Natwest [2016] EWHC 492; Alpstream AG v PK Airfinance [2015] EWCA Civ 1318; Tchenguiz v SFO (2012 – 2014, including [2014] EWCA Civ 136, [2014] EWCA Civ 1129); DAE Leasing v Kingfisher Airlines [2013] EWHC 3926; the Bitel litigation in the Isle of Man; Rawlinson and Hunter Trustees v Kaupthing Bank (2010-11); Kneale v Barclays Bank [2010] EWHC 1900 (Comm) (pre-action disclosure); the Tajik Aluminium litigation (2005-2008) including Tajik Aluminium Plant v Ermatov [2005] All ER (D) 467 (overturning freezing injunction) and [2006] All ER (D) 448 (jurisdiction), Ashton Investments v Russian Aluminium [2007] Lloyd's Rep 311 (jurisdiction in relation to computer hacking claim).

Professional Memberships: COMBAR

Career: Called 1998. Silk 2016.

Publications: Co-author 'The Law of Privilege' (OUP, 2nd edition 2011) and 'Carriage by Air' (Butterworths, 2001).

Personal: Pembroke College, Oxford: BCL, 1997 (1st Class Hons) and Law with French Law, 1996 (1st class Hons).

PHILIPPS, Guy QC
Fountain Court Chambers, London
020 7583 3335
gp@fountaincourt.co.uk
Featured in Commercial Dispute Resolution (London), Financial Services (London)

Practice Areas: A broadly based commercial litigation and arbitration practice, with particular specialisations in banking and financial services, insurance and reinsurance, and professional negligence and regulation. Notable reported cases include GSO Credit-A Partners v Barclays Bank (2016); Barclays Bank v L. Londell McMillan (2015); Williams v Central Bank of Nigeria (2014) (Sup. Ct); Young v Anglo American South Africa (CA) (2014); Basma Al Sulaiman v Credit Suisse Securities (Europe)John Pottage v Financial Services Authority (2012) (Upper Tribunal); Rainy Sky SA v Kookmin Bank (2011) (Sup. Ct); AK Investment v Kyrgyz Mobil Tel (2011) (PC); Gard Marine v Glacier Reinsurance (2010) (CA); Brit Syndicates Ltd v Grant Thornton International (2008) (HL); 7E Communications Ltd v Vertex (2007) (CA); Royal Bank of Canada v Cooperatieve Centrale Raiffeisen Boerenleenbank (2004) (CA); Lloyds TSB General Insurance Holdings v Lloyds Bank Group Insurance Company (2003) (HL); Insured Financial Structures v Elektrocieplownia Tychy (2003) (CA).

Career: Called to the Bar 1986; QC 2002. Admitted to the British Virgin Islands, Bahamas and Isle of Man Bars. Appointed as ICC, LCIA and LMAA arbitrator.
Personal: Born 1961. MA Oxford.

PHILLIPS, Jane
One Brick Court, London
020 7353 8845
jrp@onebrickcourt.com
Featured in Defamation/Privacy (London)
Practice Areas: All forms of media law including libel and slander, malicious falsehood, contempt, breach of confidence, privacy, reporting restrictions, data protection and pre-publication advice in particular for celebrity/ sport books. Independent Barrister for the Voicemail Interception Compensation Scheme. Advises on libel in Hong Kong, Singapore & Jamaica. Well known cases include: Begg v BBC (libel trial); A v B (Privacy Injunction); Adams v Associated (CA); Allason v BBC; Ashby v Times; Blackstone v Mirror Group; Bonnick v Morris (Privy Council); Bray v Deutsche Bank; Bunt v Tilley; C v Mirror Group (CA);Citation v Ellis Whittam (CA); Khalili v Associated (CA); Lloyd v Express (CA); Materazzi v Associated Newspapers; Heather Mills McCartney v Associated & News Group; Mori v BBC; Rackham v Sandy; Sir Alex Ferguson v Associated; Strachan v Gleaner (Privy Council); Upjohn v BBC; Taranissi v BBC; Trafigura v BBC; W v M (re an adult patient) (Court of Protection); White v Southampton University Trust.
Career: Call July 1989, Inner Temple Scholar.
Publications: Co-author of the section on Libel and Slander, Malicious Falsehood in Bullen & Leake, 'Precedents & Pleadings'. Contributor to Arlidge, Eady and Smith on Contempt 4th Edition.
Personal: St. Paul's Girls' School and Worcester College, Oxford. Chair of Governors at The Henrietta Barnett School.

PHILLIPS, Mark QC
South Square, London
020 7696 9900
practicemanagers@southsquare.com
Featured in Chancery (London), Restructuring/ Insolvency (London), Sports Law (London)
Practice Areas: Mark specialises in all aspects of international insolvency and reconstruction, banking and finance and the disputes arising. He has an extensive sports law practice, dealing with disciplinary, regulatory and contractual issues.
Professional Memberships: International Insolvency Institute, Insolvency Lawyers Association (Past President), Association of Business Recovery Professionals (Fellow and Former Council Member), INSOL International, INSOL Europe, Commercial Bar Association, Chancery Bar Association.
Career: Mark has appeared in Courts at every level both in England and overseas. Recent work includes the Saad Investments fraud and the SPhinX liquidations both in Cayman; several hearings, including 2 trials, on behalf of Aabar and Edgeworth; leading for the liquidators of Chesterfield and Partridge, Kaupthing SPVs in their claim against Deutsche Bank; leading the claim against the directors and professionals on behalf of International Access Properties. In previous years, Mark appeared for the Lehman's administrators in the Supreme Court and acted for the hedge funds who took over the Co Op Bank. He appeared in the landmark decision on the UNCITRAL model law, STX Pan Ocean Ltd v Fibria, defended the Bank of England at trial against the misfeasance claim brought by the liquidators of BCCI, and appeared for the shareholders of Northern Rock. In the late 1980s/early 1990s, Mark acted in every major administration, including Maxwell, Olympia & York (Canary Wharf) and British & Commonwealth. Mark's sports practice includes acting for the FA, the Premier League, the Football League and various clubs and players He acted for the liquidators of Rangers Football Club on the claim arising out of the takeover by Craig Whyte. In Formula 1, Mark has appeared before the International Court of Appeal of the FIA, the Contract Recognition Board and the World Motor Sport Council. Called to the Bar (Inner Temple) 1984, Queen's Counsel 1999, Recorder 2000 – 2008.

PHILLIPS, Matthew
Outer Temple Chambers, London
020 7353 6381
matthew.phillips@outertemple.com
Featured in Personal Injury (London), Personal Injury (All Circuits)
Practice Areas: Nationwide practice in personal injury, clinical negligence and sports law. Personal injury work almost exclusively in the fields of catastrophic injury and industrial disease. Particular expertise in asbestos related occupational and environmental claims. Instructed by Claimants in claims against all the major industrial exposers. Notable cases include Fairchild v Glenhaven Funeral Services, the 'Afrika' group action on behalf of several thousand South African asbestos miners against Cape Plc. and more recently on behalf of over two thousand South African gold miners against Anglo American Plc. Catastrophic injury work covers severe spinal, head and fatal injuries. Clinical negligence: predominantly claims involving injuries at birth, spinal surgery and oncological issues. Matthew's sports law practice revolves around doping and athlete eligibility issues.
Professional Memberships: Association of Personal Injury Lawyers (APIL); Personal Injury Bar Association (PIBA); Actions Against Medical Accidents (AVMA); British Association for Sport and the Law (BASL); Sports Resolutions UK (Pro Bono list of advocates).
Career: Called to the Bar in 1993. Joined Outer Temple Chambers (formerly 35 Essex Street) as a pupil in 1992.
Personal: Born 26 October 1969. Educated: Bolton School, Lancashire 1981-88; Trinity College, Oxford 1988-91 (BA Jurisprudence); St Catherine's College, Cambridge (Diploma in International Law) 1991-92. Interests: The emotional rollercoaster that is Bolton Wanderers Football Club.

PHILLIPS, Nevil
Quadrant Chambers, London
020 7583 4444
nevil.phillips@quadrantchambers.com
Featured in Shipping (London)
Practice Areas: Commercial and shipping litigation: carriage of goods by sea, road, and air; international sale disputes; commodities; arbitration; insurance; finance and associated areas; conflicts of laws; admiralty.
Professional Memberships: LMAA; COMBAR; Gray's Inn; Middle Temple.
Career: BA (Hons) 1990; Dip Law 1991; called 1992; LLM 1993; pupillage at 2 Essex Court (now known as Quadrant Chambers) 1994; in practice at Quadrant Chambers (formerly known as 2 Essex Court/4 Essex Court) 1994- present. Consistently identified in Chambers & Partners and Legal 500 as one of the leading juniors in the shipping and commodities sector.
Publications: 'Merchant Shipping Act 1995 – An Annotated Guide', 1996 (1st edn), 2001 (2nd edn); contributor to Rainey, 'The Law of Tug and Tow' (salvage and towage at common law); contributor to Butterworths' 'Commercial Court and Arbitration Pleadings' (marine insurance), 2005.

PHILLIPS, Paul
Charter Chambers, London
020 7618 4400
paul.phillips@charterchambers.com
Featured in Crime (London)
Practice Areas: Paul has over the last several years consistently been regarded by independent publications as a leader in his field. He is a specialist defence advocate instructed in many high profile criminal and regulatory cases. He has considerable experience as leading and junior counsel in all areas of serious crime. His main areas of practice are in serious and organised crime and fraud. In serious and organised crime he has a particular expertise in murder, large scale drug importations, money laundering and people smuggling. In fraud he often represents professional people being investigated or accused of crime, and has represented accountants, solicitors, barristers, company executives and other professionals charged with fraud. Paul is approachable and available outside of normal working hours to assist solicitors with any aspect of a case.
Professional Memberships: Criminal Bar Association.
Career: Called to the Bar 1991. A comprehensive list of his recent cases can be found at www.charterchambers.com.

PHIPPS, Charles
4 New Square, London
020 7822 2000
c.phipps@4newsquare.com
Featured in Professional Negligence (London)
Practice Areas: Professional negligence (lawyers, accountants, financial advisors, surveyors, architects, engineers, insurance brokers); confidentiality disputes; insurance; more general chancery and common law litigation. Interesting cases include: Mallon v Halliwells LLP [2012] EWCA Civ 1212; Sharma v Hunters [2012] PNLR 6; CMCS Common Market Commercial Services AVV v Taylor [2011] PNLR 17; Jones v Kaney [2011] 2 AC 398; Mortgage Express v Sawali [2011] PNLR 11; Williams v Lishman Sidwell Campbell & Price Ltd [2010] Pens.L.R.227; Nayyar v Denton Wilde Sapte [2010] PNLR 15; National Westminster Bank plc v Lloyd (LTL 10/2/2009); the CLE and TAG multi-party litigation against panel solicitors; Terry v Tower Hamlets LBC (2005) NPC 144; Charles v Westminster City Council [2004] PNLR 25; Cranfield v Bridgegrove [2003] 1 WLR 2441; Mortgage Express Ltd v Newman [2000] Lloyd's Rep (PN) 745; Hanif v Middleweeks [2000] Lloyd's Rep (PN) 920; BCCI (Overseas) Ltd v Price Waterhouse [1998] Lloyd's Rep (Banking) 85.
Professional Memberships: COMBAR, PNBA.
Career: Called in 1992.
Publications: Co-author, with Lord Justice Toulson, of Toulson and Phipps on Confidentiality (Sweet & Maxwell, 3rd edition, 2012).
Personal: Educated at Merton College, Oxford (Literae Humaniores, 1st class); City University (Diploma in Law).

PHIPPS, Sandy
One Essex Court, London
020 7583 2000
sphipps@oeclaw.co.uk
Featured in Commercial Dispute Resolution (London)
Practice Areas: The full range of commercial disputes, including commercial dispute resolution, banking and finance and civil fraud.
Professional Memberships: COMBAR; South-Eastern Circuit; Lincoln's Inn
Career: Called 2008; Lincoln's Inn. Admitted as a solicitor, New South Wales, 2005; England and Wales, 2008. Research associate to the judges of the Commercial List, Supreme Court of New South Wales, 2004. Previously a litigation solicitor in private practice (2005-09); Sydney and the City.
Publications: Publications of note: 'Resurrecting the Doctrine of Common Law Forbearance' (2007) 123 LQR 286; 'Non-party compensation for wrongful interim injunctions: Smithkline Beecham plc v Apotex Europe Ltd [2006] EWCA Civ 685' (2007) 26 CJQ10.
Personal: Education: Radford College, Canberra, Australia (1996); Australia National University, BA (Hons) 1st Class (2001); Australian National University, LLB (Hons) 1st Class (2003); St Edmund Hall, University of Oxford, BCL Distinction (2006).

PHIPPS, Sarah
Queen Elizabeth Building QEB, London
020 7797 7837
s.phipps@qeb.co.uk
Featured in Family/Matrimonial (London)
Practice Areas: Matrimonial finance and private law Children Act applications including leave to remove applications and financial claims on behalf of children under Schedule 1.
Professional Memberships: Family Law Bar Association.
Career: Educated at Brasenose, Oxford and College of Law. Called 1997. Pupil and tenant at Queen Elizabeth Building.

PICKERING, Leon
Ten Old Square, London
020 7405 0758
leonpickering@tenoldsquare.com
Featured in Chancery (London)
Practice Areas: A busy practice covering a wide range of chancery and commercial work with a particular emphasis on traditional chancery. Leon has a strong private client practice including inheritance disputes, trust litigation, the Court of Protection and capital taxes. He is currently involved in a number of high profile cases and is representing His Exalted Highness the 8th Nizam of Hyderabad in the widely reported Pakistan v Natwest litigation. His cases include acting for the Official Solicitor in tax planning and other applications in the Court of Protection, representing charities in legacy disputes, the rescission of a settlement that had adverse tax consequences, a trust variation, rectification claims and numerous probate and 1975 Act claims. Leon also has a

busy advisory and non-contentious practice and regularly gives seminars on all aspects of private client work.
Professional Memberships: Accredited mediator, a member of the Chancery Bar Association and the Charity Law Association.
Career: Called to the Bar in 2010. Reported cases: Pakistan v National Westminster Bank PLC (No. 1) [2015] EWHC 55 (Ch); (No. 2) [2016] EWHC 1465 (Ch); Dellal v Dellal and others [2015] EWHC 907 (Fam).
Publications: Co-author of Tolley's Inheritance Tax Planning.

PICTON, Julian QC
Hailsham Chambers, London
020 7643 5000
julian.pictonqc@hailshamchambers.com
Featured in Personal Injury (London)
Practice Areas: Julian specialises in professional indemnity, personal injury and clinical negligence claims. He frequently acts for or against lawyers, accountants, surveyors and financial advisers. His professional negligence practice also includes general policy and coverage issues. Julian's personal injury practice concentrates on substantial acquired brain and catastrophic injury claims, and claims brought under the Fatal Accidents Act. Since taking Silk in 2010, clinical negligence claims have become an increasingly large proportion of Julian's practice. His clinical negligence work is primarily, but not exclusively, for claimants and predominantly comprises claims for birth related injuries and in particular cerebral palsy. Given Julian's main areas of practice, he has special expertise in professional negligence claims arising out of mishandled personal injury and clinical negligence litigation. This is where his specialist knowledge is a particular advantage. As an editor of the leading textbook, McGregor on Damages, Julian also takes a keen interest in all difficult damages issues.
Professional Memberships: Professional Negligence Bar Association (PNBA).
Career: Called to the Bar, Middle Temple 1988; Everard Van Hayden Prize Bar Finals; QC 2010.
Publications: McGregor on Damages.
Personal: Education: Reigate Grammar School; Oriel College, Oxford (Exhibitioner) BA Oxon 1986. Lives in North Cambridgeshire. Interests: buildings, English furniture.

PIERCY, Arlette
25 Bedford Row, London
020 7067 1500
emma@25bedfordrow.com
Featured in Crime (London)
Practice Areas: Exclusively criminal defence work, trial and appellate, particular emphasis on fraud and crimes of serious violence; armed robbery and firearms offences; drugs related offences and representing young offenders and gang members. Experience in terrorist work, includes R v Kanyare & Others, allegation of conspiracy to obtain radioactive 'red mercury' for terrorist purposes, and other cases involving the Fake Sheikh Mazher Mahmood. Further experience of tabloid – led prosecution in R v Blake Fielder – Civil (then Amy Winehouse's Husband) and Tulisa Contostavalos. Notable 2015/2016 cases include multi million pound 'Dutch Ambulance' drugs conspiracy and boiler room fraud involving the London Carbon Credit Company. Regularly instructed in street gang murders and has a significant firearms practice including successful defence of UK rapper Giggs.
Professional Memberships: Criminal Bar Association. Board Member of 'Rights International', a pressure group which litigates individual human rights cases in international forums.
Career: 1988 LLB (Hons) Leeds (First Class), visiting Scholar at the University of California, Berkeley 1988/9. House of Commons researcher and campaigns officer for a member of the Shadow Cabinet, 1990/1992. Worked in the USA on miscarriage of Justice cases involving the former Leadership of the Black Panther Party.

PIGOTT, Frances
Atkin Chambers, London
020 7404 0102
fpigott@atkinchambers.com
Featured in Construction (London)
Practice Areas: Frances Pigott has broad-ranging experience of litigation, arbitration, adjudication, ADR and non-contentious construction work. She specialises in energy, construction, engineering and infrastructure, professional negligence and general commercial disputes. Frances was a solicitor for 10 years specialising in construction law. She started practice as a barrister in 2004 and joined Atkin Chambers in 2012. Frances has appeared in the High Court and Court of Appeal as counsel either alone or as junior and has represented clients in both international and domestic arbitrations. She has represented contractors, sub-contractors and employers in adjudications including high-value disputes. Recent experience includes an ICC arbitration in London involving complex offshore and onshore engineering issues, a dispute in the Technology and Construction Court concerning a tower-based soft yoke mooring system as part of an offshore oil installation in the Caspian Sea, a major arbitration in the UAE concerning a large mixed use development and a multi-party dispute in the Technology and Construction Court concerning a claim made under an assigned warranty in respect of a mixed use development in the UK.
Professional Memberships: TECBAR; CIArb; SCL.
Career: Called in 1994. Admitted to the roll as a Solicitor of the Supreme Court of England and Wales in 1996. Commenced practice as a Barrister in 2004.

PIKE, Jeremy
Francis Taylor Building, London
020 7353 8415
clerks@ftbchambers.co.uk
Featured in Planning (London)
Practice Areas: Jeremy practices in public and local government law, specialising in planning and environment, compulsory purchase and compensation, and rating. He has a particular expertise in energy and infrastructure matters and is acknowledged as a leading practitioner in renewable energy. Recent cases and high-profile public inquiries include matters concerning wind energy, gas storage, EU habitats and birds legislation, retail planning, marine planning and licensing, and village greens. He acts for the private and public sector, and sits as an Inspector advising registration authorities in village green matters. As well as appearances in the higher courts and at planning inquiries, Jeremy appears in the Upper Tribunal and Valuation Tribunal. Notable recent cases include Renfree and Cornwall Light and Power Company v Mageean [2011] EWCA Civ 863 (on appeal to the Supreme Court); R (Barnes) v Secretary of State [2011] EWCA Civ 97; R (Brown) v Carlisle City Council [2011] Env LR 5; Secerno Ltd v Oxford Magistrates Court [2011] EWHC 1009 (Admin); R (Lewis) v Cleveland and Redcar Council [2010] UKSC 11.
Professional Memberships: Jeremy is a contributing editor to Ryde on Rating, and Butterworths Planning Law Service. He is a member of the Planning and Environment Bar Association and the National Infrastructure Planning Association.

PILGERSTORFER, Marcus
11KBW, London
020 7632 8500
marcus.pilgerstorfer@11kbw.com
Featured in Employment (London), Product Liability (London)
Practice Areas: Marcus practises in employment, discrimination, product liability, public and human rights law. Recent cases include: SoS v NUT [2016] IRLR 512 (HC); Hainsworth v MOD (SC); Keyu v SoS (SC) [2015] 3 WLR 1665; Edwards v Chesterfield [2012] 2 AC 22 (SC), the PIP Breast Implant Group Litigation, the Pinnacle Metal-on-Metal Hips Group Litigation, and the Sabril Group Litigation.
Professional Memberships: ILS, ELBA, ELA, DLA, BIICL Product Liability Forum, Common Core Product Liability group.
Career: MA English Law with German Law: St John's College, Oxford (first class honours); Called 2002 (Gray's Inn Scholar). AG's B Panel of Counsel to the Crown.
Publications: Numerous publications in specialist law journals as well as contributor to Tolley's Employment Law Handbook (2013-15); Cambridge Companion to EU Private Law (2010); Discrimination in Employment, Tucker & George (2006).
Personal: Languages: English (native) and German.

PILLING, Benjamin QC
4 Pump Court, London
020 7842 5508
bpilling@4pumpcourt.com
Featured in Professional Negligence (London), Banking & Finance (London), Construction (London), Information Technology (London)
Practice Areas: Commercial litigation with an emphasis on banking and finance (including derivatives, distressed debt, structured products, cross-border insolvency and retail banking. Professional negligence cases including both financial services professionals and construction professionals. Construction cases arising from a range of onshore and offshore projects. IT cases (including computer games contracts). International arbitration.
Professional Memberships: COMBAR, Professional Negligence Bar Association, TECBAR, London Common Law and Commercial Bar Association, Society for Computers and Law.
Career: Called 1997. Silk 2015.

PINTO, Amanda QC
The Chambers of Andrew Mitchell QC, London
020 7440 9950
ap@33cllaw.com
Featured in Financial Crime (London)
Practice Areas: Fraud, markets offences and corruption.
Professional Memberships: Chair of the International Committee of the Bar Council 2015; UK representative on the Council of the International Criminal Bar 2009; Bencher Middle Temple; Trustee of the Tate Members Council and the Slynn Foundation.
Career: Expert in corporate crime, international financial crime, art loss and cases raising intricate cross-border questions. Amanda is instructed in the most high-profile cases in the field, in particular, fraud, regulatory and corruption cases & related High Court actions including judicial review. Her great skill is assimilating and simplifying complicated material. She is regularly instructed to defend /prosecute Proceeds of Crime matters. For the SFO she successfully prosecuted a $600 million investment fraud by hedge funds using derivatives. Recent experience includes: fraud using sustainable 'green' investments; forgery of documents by a lawyer; false financial reports to the market; trans-national corporate corruption by plc; defending the UK administrator of a global, £multi-million share-selling fraud; challenging search warrant applications; multi-jurisdictional, insider dealing involving foreign stock exchanges and Cypriot companies; a solicitor and client prosecuted for art crime, money-laundering, allegations of perverting the course of justice and perjury.
Publications: Co-author Corporate Criminal Liability by Pinto and Evans (3rd Edition – Sweet & Maxwell); Contributing Author to Blackstone's Criminal Practice on corporate criminal liability.

PITTAWAY, David QC
Hailsham Chambers, London
020 7643 5000
david.pittaway@hailshamchambers.com
Featured in Clinical Negligence (London), Professional Discipline (London)
Practice Areas: David Pittaway QC is Head of Chambers and his principal practice areas are medical law, public inquiries and inquests, regulatory and disciplinary, product liability, personal injury and insurance law. He is frequently instructed in large scale litigation, defending clients in both healthcare and non-healthcare sectors against reputational damage. He appears on behalf of claimants and defendants in complex clinical negligence cases involving catastrophic injuries, acting for medical defence organisations, NHS Trusts and the Litigation Authority. He is presently instructed on behalf of a private healthcare provider in a large number of breast surgery claims in which the lead cases will be tried in June 2017.
Professional Memberships: Past Chairman of the PNBA, Member of LCLCBA, PIBA, BEG.
Career: Called to the Bar, Inner Temple 1977; Northern Ireland 2011; FCIArb 1988; Bencher 1998; Assistant Recorder 1998; Recorder; QC 2000; Accredited Mediator 2002; MHT Judge 2002-16; GMC Legal Assessor 2002-04; RCVS Legal Assessor 2004; Chancellor of the Diocese of Peterborough 2006; Deputy High Court Judge 2008; Reader Inner Temple 2016.
Publications: Contributor; 'Atkins Court Forms – Personal Injury, Professional Negligence, National Health Service, Carriers; Advanced Civil Litigation (OUP); Co-general Editor 'Pittaway & Hammerton Professional Negligence Cases' (Butterworths) (1998).
Personal: Education: Uppingham School; Sidney Sussex College, Cambridge (Exhi-

bitioner) BA (Cantab) 1976 MA (Cantab) 1979); married, two sons; interests include gardening, music, art, sailing.

PITT-PAYNE, Timothy QC
11KBW, London
020 7632 8500
timothy.pitt-payne@11kbw.com
Featured in Administrative & Public Law (London), Data Protection (London), Employment (London)

Practice Areas: Principal areas of practice are data protection and privacy, freedom of information, other information law areas, employment law, local government, and administrative and public law. Has acted in over 50 cases before Information Rights Tribunal, and in numerous information law cases at all appellate levels from Upper Tribunal to Supreme Court. Contributor to 'Supperstone, Goudie & Walker on Judicial Review' (LexisNexis 2010, and earlier editions); 'Computer Law' (OUP 2011); 'Media Law' (OUP 2009). Visiting Professor of Information Law at Northumbria University 2007-2013.
Professional Memberships: Employment Law Bar Association; Employment Law Assocation; Administrative Law Bar Association; Commercial Bar Association; Society for Computers and Law.
Career: Called to the Bar in 1989. Joined present chambers in 1990. Appointed QC 2010.
Personal: University education: Worcester College, Oxford 1982-86 (BA (Hons) Jurisprudence 1985, BCL 1986). Vinerian Scholar 1986.

POCOCK, Christopher QC
1 King's Bench Walk, London
020 7936 1500
cpocockqc@1kbw.co.uk
Featured in Family/Matrimonial (London)

Practice Areas: Family (including divorce and dissolution of civil partnership), matrimonial finance and property. Pre-Nuptial Agreements. Financial disputes between unmarried couples, inheritance and family provision. IFLA accredited Arbitrator.
Professional Memberships: S E Circuit; Family Law Bar Association; Institute of Family Law Arbitrators
Career: Called in 1984 by Inner Temple. Silk 2009.
Personal: Born 1960. Educated at St Dunstan's College and Pembroke College, Oxford (BA Juris). Working knowledge of French.

POKU, Mary
9-12 Bell Yard, London
020 7400 1800
m.poku@912by.com
Featured in Crime (London)

Practice Areas: Mary Poku is an experienced defence advocate with an impressive track record. She is highly regarded for her client care with a high acquittal rate that has led to a loyal professional and lay client following. She is frequently instructed in murder cases, notably in the highly publicised case of R v Stuart Hazell, involving the murdered school girl Tia Sharpe. Mary Poku has also acted as leading counsel in a broad spectrum of cases of serious violence, including more recently in 2016, in a multi defendent murder case, prosecuted and defended by Queen's Counsel. She has also conducted serious international fraud trials investigated byScotland Yard's Counter Terrorism unit, HM Revenue & Customs, Department of Work and Pensions and the Serious and Organised Crime Agency. In February 2014, Mary was appointed as legal advisor on the National Crime Agency and the Foreign and Commonwealth's cybercrime initiative in Ghana. Since this appointment she has been instructed by leading maritime and shipping firms to provide legal and strategic advice in ongoing cases in Ghana. She is on the list of approved counsel for the International Criminal Tribunal for the Former Yugoslavia. In 2016 she was also admitted onto the list of approved counsel to appear before the International Criminal Court in the Hague.
Career: Called 1993. Pupil Supervisor.
Publications: Cyber crime: civil remedies (Westlaw Insight: Sweet and Maxwell).
Personal: French, Twi (Native Ghanaian language).

POLLEY, Alexander
One Essex Court, London
020 7583 2000
apolley@oeclaw.co.uk
Featured in Professional Negligence (London), Banking & Finance (London), Commercial Dispute Resolution (London), Fraud (London)

Practice Areas: Commercial dispute resolution; commercial arbitration; banking litigation; civil fraud; professional negligence.
Professional Memberships: COMBAR.
Career: Alex practises in the field of commercial litigation and arbitration, including banking, civil fraud, professional negligence and general commercial disputes. Recent cases include: Holyoake v Candy e.g. [2016] EWHC 970 (Ch) (notification order); Libyan Investment Authority v Societe Generale e.g. [2015] EWHC 550 (Comm), [2016] EWHC 375 (Comm) (alleged bribery in relation to structured transactions); Cattles v PwC (2011-2015, alleged audit negligence); Credit Suisse v Vestia [2014] EWHC 3103 (Comm) (capacity to make interest rate derivative contracts; effect of ISDA documentation); Assetco v Grant Thornton [2013] EWHC 1215 (Comm) (pre-action disclosure); Nomihold v Mobile TeleSystems e.g. [2012] 1 Lloyd's Rep 442 (enforcement of arbitration award; anti-suit injunctions).

POLLI, Timothy
Tanfield Chambers, London
020 7421 5320
timothypolli@tanfieldchambers.co.uk
Featured in Real Estate Litigation (London)

Practice Areas: Real property disputes concerning boundaries, adverse possession, easements and restrictive covenants (for example, Beech v Kennerley [2012] EWCA Civ 158); mortgages, mortgage fraud and subrogation (for example, Menelaou v Bank of Cyprus [2015] UKSC 66; [2016] AC 176 and Wishart v Credit & Mercantile plc [2015] EWCA Civ 655); contracts for the sale of land, termination, deposits and overage; registration issues and priority; party walls; Landlord and tenant disputes including dilapidations claims, lease renewals, forfeiture and applications for relief, claims arising out of the insolvency of landlord or tenant, service charge disputes, RTM and enfranchisement; the variation of leasehold covenants (for example, Stevens v Ismail [2016] UKUT 43 (LC)); Claims concerning equitable interests in land pursuant to constructive trusts or proprietary estoppel (for example, Shaista v Victorstone Financial Limited [2016] EWHC 1505 (Ch) and Credit & Mercantile v Kaymuu Ltd [2014] EWHC 1746 (Ch)); Property-related professional liability, particularly that of valuers and solicitors (for example UCB Home Loans Corporation v Soni [2013] EWCA Civ 62); Chancery / commercial contract disputes including disputes concerning development agreements and joint-ventures. Regularly instructed to advise in relation to non-contentious property work, usually at very short notice.
Professional Memberships: Property Bar Association (Committee Member); Chancery Bar Association; Professional Negligence Bar Association; Bar Pro Bono Unit.
Career: Worked at the Law Commission 1996-97 and was called to the Bar in 1997.
Publications: Contributor to 'The Law of Service Charges and Management' by Tanfield Chambers.
Personal: Born in 1973; educated at St Columba's College, St Albans and Hertford College, Oxford (MA, BCL); married with two children; interests include theatre and travel.

PONS, Gary
5 St Andrew's Hill, London
020 7332 5400
garypons@5sah.co.uk
Featured in Crime (London)

Practice Areas: Gary is an experienced and highly skilled barrister who acts in serious and complex cases. His practice encompasses all areas of crime but his work often involves a financial element. He has particular expertise in cases involving fraud and money laundering. He is highly proficient in cases involving asset forfeiture and confiscation and recently represented the interests of Sarah Tighe the wife of Tom Hayes in confiscation proceedings. He acts in international criminal cases and recently acted in a high profile case which took place in Costa Rica. He was part of an international defence team who successfully acted for Ann Patton in relation to an allegation that she murdered her husband, the successful Wall Street trader John Bender. Gary is fluent in Spanish which enabled him to play an active part in the preparation of the case. He represents defendants in regulatory prosecutions including recent cases involving prosecutions by the SIA of companies using unlicensed security guards. He also prosecutes both financial and sexual criminal offences. He is a grade 3 prosecutor and is accredited on the Rape Panel. He is a direct access qualified barrister.
Professional Memberships: Fraud Lawyers Association, Association of Regulatory and Disciplinary Lawyers.

PONTER, Ian
Kings Chambers, Manchester
0345 034 3444
clerks@kingschambers.com
Featured in Planning (Northern)

Practice Areas: Planning, administrative and public law.
Professional Memberships: PEBA.
Career: The focus of Ian's practice is planning and public law. His practice includes all aspects of planning law. He appears at planning inquiries in all disciplines including housing, retail, employment, energy and waste. He has appeared at many development plan examinations both for local planning authorities and developers. His Court practice encompasses statutory challenges (in respect of planning matters) and judicial review proceedings. His public and administrative law practice includes environmental law and other regulatory matters. He is membership secretary of PEBA.

POOLE, Anna QC
Axiom Advocates, Edinburgh
07739 639239
anna.poole@axiomadvocates.com
Featured in Civil Liberties & Human Rights (Scotland), Administrative & Public Law (Scotland)

Practice Areas: Public and administrative law, with a particular interest in judicial review, human rights and European law.
Career: QC 2012; part time fee paid Judge (First Tier Tribunal, Social Entitlement Chamber) 2014; member of panel of preferred counsel for the Equality and Human Rights Commission 2013; Ad hoc Advocate Depute 2013; Standing Junior Counsel to the Scottish Government (latterly as Second then First Standing Junior Counsel) 2002-2012; called to Scots Bar 1998; solicitor, Scotland 1997 (Brodies); solicitor, England and Wales 1996 (Linklaters). Has acted in cases in European Court of Human Rights, Supreme Court, Court of Session (Inner and Outer House), Criminal Appeal Court, High Court of Justiciary, Sheriff Court, Scottish Land Court, and various Tribunals. Clients have included individuals, companies, local authorities, NHS trusts, the Lord Advocate, the Scottish Ministers, the Scottish Information Commissioner, the Scottish Legal Complaints Commission, the Scottish Police Authority, the EHRC and the Keeper of the Registers.
Publications: Court of Session Practice, ed Macfadyen (contributor); various articles published including in Judicial Review, SLT, SLPQ, Int ILR, IJPICL, Juridical Review, the Scotsman and JLSS.
Personal: Educated Madras College, St Andrews; Somerville and Magdalen Colleges, Oxford (BA Hons (1st Class), MA, MSt).

POOLE, Christopher
New Court Chambers, London
020 7583 5123
cpoole@newcourtchambers.com
Featured in Family/Matrimonial (London)

Practice Areas: All aspects of the law relating to children including in particular care and adoption proceedings. Representing often but not exclusively Local Authorities and Children's Guardians. Particular interest in cases involving serious factual disputes. Recent Cases: Re S (finding of fact; honour based violence) [2013] EWHC 15 (fam). Re T (Residential parenting assessment) [2012] 2 FLR 308. Kent CC v A mother, F and X, Y and Z [2011] 2 FLR 1088. Re H (a child) [2014] EWHC 970 and LBBD v C & Others [2014] EWHC 2472.
Professional Memberships: FLBA.
Career: Called 1996, Lincoln's Inn (Thomas More Bursary). Joined New Court Chambers upon completion of pupillage in 1997. Pupil supervisor and advocacy trainer (Lincoln's Inn). Delivers seminars and lectures to social work students, social workers and social work managers as well as Chambers' Instructing Solicitors.
Personal: LLB (Hons) English & European Law, Queen Mary College, University of London and Katholieke Universiteit Leuven, Belgium. Enjoys the gym and a day in the sun watching cricket.

POOLE, Nigel QC
Kings Chambers, Manchester
0345 034 3444
clerks@kingschambers.com
Featured in Clinical Negligence (Northern), Personal Injury (Northern)

Practice Areas: All areas of clinical negligence including birth injury, delay in diagnosing cancer, surgical, A&E, mental health, primary healthcare and cosmetic surgery, personal injury litigation for claimants and defendants in cases of the utmost severity, Healthcare law including human rights claims, Inquests and inquiries. Nigel's recent cases involved upholding a surgical negligence judgment in the Court of Appeal, success at a High Court trial in a claim for substantial damages arising out of delay in diagnosing swine flu; securing a £3m lump sum and £250,000 periodical payments for a claimant with severe brain injury following failure to treat a rise in intracranial pressure following an assault; a seven figure sum for a young stroke victim who had been about to begin a career as a solicitor; and several cases of suicide or attempted suicide following negligent psychiatric care. He successfully defended a £10m claim for catastrophic injury following a go-kart accident. He represented the appellant parents in the Supreme Court in Rabone and the respondent in the Court of Appeal in Billett v MOD.

Professional Memberships: Personal Injury Bar Association. Professional Negligence Bar Association.

Career: 2004 to present: Kings Chambers 1989 to 2004: 18 St John Street Chambers 2000 to 2012: Attorney-General's Provincial Panel of Junior Counsel 2002 to 2009: Legal Assessor, General Medical Council 2009 to date: Recorder (Civil and Private Family matters) 2012 Appointed Queen's Counsel 2013 to date: Bar Tribunals and Adjudication Service Panel Member.

POOLES, Michael QC
Hailsham Chambers, London
020 7643 5000
michael.pooles@hailshamchambers.com
Featured in Professional Negligence (London)

Practice Areas: Michael Pooles QC's principal area of practice is that of professional indemnity claims and related coverage issues. He frequently acts for or against lawyers, accountants and surveyors but he acts for or against all manner of professionals including areas such as veterinary science, land management and fish farming. He is frequently instructed in costs matters. His practice also includes general insurance matters of all types and substantial personal injury claims. Michael is consistently ranked as a leading silk in the areas of professional negligence and costs by the leading directories. Michael was formerly an editors of the solicitors' chapter of Professional Negligence and Liability.

Career: Recent cases include: LSREF III Wight Ltd v Gateley LLP [2016] EWCA Civ 359 – Measure of damages in mortgage lenders claim against solicitors, mitigation losses; Clydesdale v Workman [2016] EWCA Civ 73 – Adequacy of findings of dishonesty against solicitors; Jackson v Thompsons [2016] EWCA Civ 138 – procuring breach of contract, test of bias of tribunal, whether any prospect of appeal. Wellesley v Withers [2014] EWHC 556 – Test of remoteness of damage where parallel duties owed in contract and tort. Santander v R A Legal [2014] EWCA Civ 183 – Nature of trusts in conveyancing and relief under s61 Trustee Act 1925. Harrison v Cluttons [2013] EWCA Civ 1569 – Duty of care of landlords' surveyor to tenant.

Publications: Former editor of the solicitors' chapter of Professional Negligence and Liability (Informa looseleaf.), Michael Pooles has frequently provided lectures to members of the Professional Negligence Bar Association and others on professional indemnity, policy, conduct, limitation and civil fraud matters.

POOTS, Laura
Pump Court Tax Chambers, London
020 7414 8080
clerks@pumptax.com
Featured in Tax (London)

Practice Areas: Practises in all areas of taxation, direct and indirect, whether planning or in the course of disputes and litigation. Particular expertise in private client advice and planning for individuals, trustees and family businesses (UK and international). Indirect tax practice includes VAT, SDLT and landfill tax. Also advises on commercial disputes involving tax issues. Recent cases include Brockenhurst College (Court of Appeal, VAT Exemption), Vodafone (Upper Tribunal, Section 80 VAT Claims), Romasave (Upper Tribunal, notification of assessments), Cyclops Electronics (employment income avoidance) and Danvers (pension scheme avoidance).

Professional Memberships: Revenue Bar Association, London Chancery and Commercial Bar Association & VAT Practitioners Group.

Career: October 2007: Called, Middle Temple. March 2013: Appointed to the Attorney General's C Panel.

Publications: At a Glance – Regular contributor, Lexis PSL Practice Notes – Private Client.

Personal: 2006-2007: Bar Vocational Course, Inns of Court Law School (Very competent); 2002-2006: St John's College, Oxford (First Class BA Hons, Jurisprudence).

POPAT, Prashant QC
Henderson Chambers, London
020 7583 9020
ppopat@hendersonchambers.co.uk
Featured in Health & Safety (London), Product Liability (London)

Practice Areas: Prashant was recognised as "Health and Safety Silk of the Year" by Chambers and Partners in 2014. Over 2 decades he has represented defendants in major manslaughter, corporate manslaughter and health and safety prosecutions (and associated inquiries, inquests and litigation) arising from significant incidents such as the railway crashes at Southall, Ladbroke Grove, Hatfield, Potters Bar and Lambrigg, the explosion at the Buncefield oil depot, the Atherstone upon Stour fire and the Glesion Mine flooding. He has also acted for private and public sector defendants in a variety of industries in similar prosecutions, inquests and litigation. In the field of product liability his substantial group action experience encompasses litigation concerning: Benzodiazepines; Norplant; blood transfusions; MMR; Sabril; Seroxat; Hip replacements; gastric bands and PIP breast implants. He has also advised companies on compliance with their obligations under consumer protection legislation in a variety of industries (e.g. motor vehicles; mobile phones; medical devices).

Professional Memberships: He is a founding and former committee member of the Health and Safety Lawyers' Association and a member of COMBAR.

Career: MA (Oxon) First Class Honours. University Scholar. Baker and McKenzie International Scholar. Gray's Inn Scholar. Judicial Assistant to the Court of Appeal. Bencher of Gray's Inn.

Publications: He is the co-editor of the "International Product Law Manual" published by Kluwer.

POPLE, Alison QC
Cloth Fair Chambers, London
020 7710 6444
alisonspople@clothfairchambers.com
Featured in Crime (London), Financial Crime (London)

Practice Areas: Principal areas of practice are financial and business crime, serious and complex fraud, and high profile serious crime. Acts in cases involving allegations of banking fraud, insurance fraud, insider trading, 'ponzi' fraud, tax fraud, cartel offences, money laundering, bribery and corruption and VAT offences. Instructed by both the defence and the prosecution, including the Serious Fraud Office. Defended in a number of high profile cases including Mustafa & others (Operation Saturn, FSA prosecution); George & others (BA/VAA cartel allegation, OFT prosecution); Goldshield Group plc & others (Operation Holbein, 'pharmaceuticals', SFO prosecution); Bright & others (Independent Insurance, SFO prosecution); Rayment & others (Jubilee Line Fraud, CPS prosecution). Recent notable cases include; successfully representing Nigel Horn, former legal director of Torex Retail Plc, over conspiracy to defraud charges. Advised a leading nationwide market research company regarding bribery. Acted for William Lowther over corruption offences, acquitted (SFO charges); represented Richard Joseph for insider trading offences; advised the SFO regarding JJB Sports investigation. Represented Andy Coulson, the former editor of News of the World throughout the phone hacking trial. Represented a former manager of Swift Technical Group (Oil and Gas services) on foreign corruption charges brought by the SFO, acquitted. Represented a former Managing Director of Deutsche Bank charged with insider trading offences by the FCA. Advised Deutsche Bank trader over allegations of market manipulation re Euribor. For further information please visit www.clothfairchambers.com.

Career: 1993 – Called to the Bar 2015 – QC.

POPPLEWELL, Simon
Gough Square Chambers, London
020 7353 0924
simon.popplewell@goughsq.co.uk
Featured in Consumer Law (London)

Practice Areas: Simon specialises in all aspects of consumer and regulatory law, in particular in the areas of consumer credit, consumer finance and trading law. In relation to consumer credit and consumer finance Simon drafts and advises on consumer credit practice and procedure, including reviewing and drafting finance documentation. He advises on compliance with the Consumer Credit Act 1974, the Financial Services and Markets Act 2000, their subsidiary legislation, and the provisions of the FCA Handbook. Simon regularly appears in court on consumer finance matters, and has appeared before the FCA's Regulatory Decisions Committee. In relation to trading law Simon regularly advises and appears in respect of the civil aspects of consumer law, including the Consumer Rights Act 2015, unfair contract terms, the Consumer Protection from Unfair Trading Regulations 2008, distance selling, inertia selling, pyramid selling, trading schemes and doorstep selling. He acts in civil actions brought under Part 8 of the Enterprise Act 2002 and he advises on compliance with OFCOM's General Conditions of Entitlement.

Career: 2000 Call.

Publications: Annotated the Consumer Credit Act 2006 for Current Law Statutes, and is a contributor to Atkin's Court Forms Consumer Protection edition. Co-author of the Law of Consumer Credit and Hire.

Personal: Educated at Lincoln College, Oxford.

PORTER, Martin QC
2TG – 2 Temple Gardens, London
020 7822 1200
mporter@2tg.co.uk
Featured in Personal Injury (London), Clinical Negligence (London)

Practice Areas: A leading personal injury specialist with particular experience of clinical negligence, industrial disease, brain damage, psychiatric injury and cycling claims. Also has considerable experience of professional negligence (especially of solicitors and surveyors), nuisance cases (especially subsidence claims) insurance work and public law/human rights.

Professional Memberships: PIBA; LCCLBA.

Career: Lillington v Dr Ansell and anor [2016] EWHC 351 (QB) (brain damage case by failures of doctors). Fincken v Dr Rana (failure to refer to hospital/delay in diagnosis of meningitis). Chief Constable of Hampshire v Southampton City Council (2014) Court of Appeal. (Limitation in contribution claims) Downing v Peterborough & Stamford Hospitals NHS Trust (2014) High Court. (Quantum trial. Multimillion claim for a pain disorder) Powell v Ridgeback Bicycles (2013) County Court. (Product Liability. Successful claim acting on behalf of cyclist who sustained injury when his mountain bike collapsed) Lay v Cambridgeshire & Peterborough Mental Health Partnership NHS Trust & Shair (2013) High Court (injury at work complicated by poor surgery) Bowden v Homerton Hospital (2012) Court of Appeal. (Liver disease induced by drug therapy); Spradbury v Humber Mental Health Trust (2011) High Court. (Observations of voluntary hospital patient.); Green v Sunset & Vine (2010). Court of Appeal. (Motorsport); Ferguson v British Gas [2009] Court of Appeal; Goodham v Bennetts [2008] Court of Appeal (repetitive strain injury); Conn v Sunderland City Council [2007] Court of Appeal (what constitutes harassment); Daw v Intel [2007] Court of Appeal (stress at work claim); Smith v Southampton Universities NHS Trust [2007] Court of Appeal (standard of duty of a surgeon); Corbett v South Yorkshire HA [2007] High Court (indexation of periodical payments and impact of Working Time Regulations on care regimes); Purver v Winchester & Eastleigh NHS Trust [2006] High Court (time from decision to delivery by Caesarian); Keown v Coventry

Healthcare NHS Trust [2006] (duty of care owed by hospital to child trespasser); Aer Lingus v Gildacroft [2006] (limitation period in Contribution Act claims); Thompson v Butler [2005] Court of Appeal (brain damage following a whiplash injury); Waterfall v Coventry Helicopters [2004] fatal helicopter crash (insurance repudiation); Sheldon-Green v Coventry NHS Trust [2004] High Court (cord prolapse case for NHSLA); Elmes v Hygrade Food Products Ltd [2001] EWCA CIV 121 Court of Appeal (Service of Claim Form).
Publications: Broadcasts and writes frequently including for BBC's 'Law in Action', 'The Times Law Section', 'New Law Journal', 'All England Opinion'.

POST, Andrew QC
Hailsham Chambers, London
020 76435000
andrew.postqc@hailshamchambers.com
Featured in Clinical Negligence (London), Costs Litigation (All Circuits)
Practice Areas: Andrew undertakes clinical negligence, healthcare and disciplinary cases, and has a particular expertise in dealing with technically complex medical issues. He acts and advises in major costs litigation, particularly where points of principle arise and on appeal. Significant recent cases include: MW and NW v (1) Dr Thomas (2) North West Strategic HA QBD 2016: CP case involving premature twins suffering brain damage by different mechanisms; Sugar Hut Group Ltd v AJ Insurance [2016] EWCA (Civ) 46: CA guidance on costs orders following Part 36 offer; Bingham v Sherwood Forest Hospitals NHS Trust QBD 2016: CP claim re mismanagement of delivery of second twin; Bryant v St George's Healthcare NHS Trust QBD 2015: successful defence of spinal surgery claim; Forster v North Cumbria University Hospitals NHS Trust QBD 2015: devastating CRP leading to amputation following negligent treatment of fracture; R v Zinga CA 2014: CA on costs of private prosecution; Hague v DLA SCCO 2013: £1.8 million solicitor/client fee dispute.
Career: Educated at Trinity College, Cambridge and City University. Called 1988. QC 2012. Head of Hailsham Chambers' Costs Group. Assessor for High Court Costs Appeals.

POTTS, James QC
Erskine Chambers, London
020 7242 5532
jpotts@erskinechambers.com
Featured in Chancery (London), Commercial Dispute Resolution (London), Company (London), Restructuring/Insolvency (London)
Practice Areas: Company law, corporate insolvency, financial services, partnership and related commercial litigation. Currently, about 75% of cases are contentious matters, with the remainder being non-contentious advisory work. Notable recent cases include: Autonomy Corporation Ltd v Lynch and Hussain (acting for HP entities in breach of fiduciary duty and deceit claim). Re Charterhouse Capital Ltd [2015] EWCA Civ 536 (acted at trial and on appeal for successful respondents in relation to private equity firm unfair prejudice petition); Global Energy Horizons Corp v Grey [2012] EWHC 3703 (Ch) (imposition of fiduciary duties in a non-traditional context); Broughton v Kop Football (Cayman) Ltd [2012] EWCA Civ 1743 (acting successfully for RBS on numerous hearings, applications and an appeal on the Liverpool FC litigation); MSL Group Holdings Ltd v Clearwell International Ltd [2012] EWCA Civ 1440 (test for disguised distributions); Halliwells v Austin [2012] EWHC 1194 (Ch) (construction of retirement deed, meaning of fraud, enforceability of releases); Belmont Park Investments PTY Limited v BNY Corporate Trustee Services Limited [2011] UKSC 38 (scope of anti-deprivation principle in Lehmans' insolvency); Fulham Football Club (1987) Ltd v Richards & Anor [2011] EWCA Civ 855 (arbitrability of shareholder disputes); various large commercial arbitrations. Company advisory work includes many reductions of capital and members' schemes of arrangement.
Professional Memberships: Chancery Bar Association, COMBAR.
Career: Called Gray's Inn 1994.

POUNDS, Caroline
Quadrant Chambers, London
020 7583 4444
caroline.pounds@quadrantchambers.com
Featured in Shipping (London)
Practice Areas: Caroline is an experienced and popular junior whose practice encompasses all aspects of general commercial litgation and arbitration, including international arbitration. In particular, she has extensive experience of bill of lading and charterparty disputes, including claims for damage to/mis-delivery of cargo, unsafe port claims, claims for early/late/wrongful redelivery, off-hire disputes, claims for demurrage/damages for detention and claims concerning the application and effect of the Hague/Hague-Visby/Hamburg Rules. Caroline's practice also includes a broad range of shipbuilding, ship sale and purchase and commodity disputes. In addition, Caroline has a rapidly expanding practice in the energy sector, in particular as regards upstream matters. Caroline acts in an advisory capacity and appears in court and arbitration on a sole and led basis in all of her practice areas. Please visit www.quadrantchambers.com for Caroline's detailed CV.
Professional Memberships: COMBAR; LCLCBA; Young International Arbitration Group of the LCIA; Young Arbitrators Forum of the ICC.
Career: Called to the Bar in 2003; recognised as one of Legal Week's 'Stars at the Bar' in 2013; Chambers & Partners 'Shipping Junior of the Year' in 2015.
Personal: First Class Law Degree (Law with French Law), Hertford College, Oxford. Lives in Surrey.

POWELL, Debra
Serjeants' Inn Chambers, London
020 7427 5000
dpowell@serjeantsinn.com
Featured in Clinical Negligence (London), Court of Protection (All Circuits), Inquests & Public Inquiries (All Circuits)
Practice Areas: Debra Powell was called to the Bar in 1995. Debra specialises in clinical negligence and healthcare, Court of Protection, police, inquests and inquiries, public and administrative, mental health and professional discipline law. An earlier edition notes that "she's pragmatic, easy to work with and very responsive", "good with clients, she offers good advice on overall strategy in complex cases" and is known for being "a very courageous, clear and direct advocate who is able to cut through multiple issues and get to the key points." Please visit the Serjeants' Inn Chambers website for her profile, which sets out full details of her practice including relevant work of note.
Professional Memberships: ALBA, PNBA, LCLCBA.
Publications: Medical Treatment: Decisions and The Law (co-author); Inquest Law Reports (joint editor 2000-12); The Mental Health Act Explained (co-author).

POWELL, Giles
Old Square Chambers, London
020 7269 0300
powell@oldsquarechambers.co.uk
Featured in Professional Discipline (London)
Practice Areas: Giles practices in Administrative and Public Law, Employment, Partnership, Professional Discipline and Sports Law. He also undertakes Commercial and Company law cases where they are interrelated with Employment or Partnership issues. He has been involved in a number of high profile Employment and Professional Discipline cases including Thames Cleaning & Support Services Ltd v (1) United Voices of the World (2) Petros Elia [2016] (QB), L Small v Shrewsbury & Telford Hospitals NHS Trust (2015) EAT, R (on the application of Sagar) v NHS Health Education England [2014] Admin, Chakrabarty v Ipswich Hospitals NHS Trust [2014] QB, and Mattu v University Hospitals of Coventry and Warwickshire [2012] CA. '
Professional Memberships: ALBA, Bar Pro Bono, ELA, ELLAS South Eastern Circuit Committee.
Career: Called 1990 Gray's Inn. Old Square Chambers May 2008.
Publications: Contributor to West Law Online Encyclopedia, Employment Topics; and to 'Equality and Discrimination Law', Oxford University Press, European Court of Justice Procedure (to be published).

POWELL, John L QC
4 New Square, London
020 7822 2000
j.powell@4newsquare.com
Featured in Professional Negligence (London)
Practice Areas: Commercial practice in UK and overseas, especially investment fraud, professional liability, financial services and securities regulation and insurance. Arbitration (advocate and arbitrator) in UK and overseas.
Professional Memberships: COMBAR , Chancery Bar Assoc, PNBA; Society of Construction Law (President 1991-3).
Career: Called 1974. Silk 1990. Deputy High Court Judge and Recorder. Bencher, Middle Temple. Head of Chambers 1997-99. Bar Council member 1999 – (Chairman Bar Law Reform Committee (1997-98).
Publications: 'Jackson and Powell on Professional Liability'; 'Encyclopaedia of Financial Services Law' (with Prof Eva Lomnicka). 'Palmer's Company Law' (specialist editor 24th ed); 'Issues and Offers of Company Securities'; various papers in national and international legal publications.
Personal: Trinity Hall, Cambridge (MA, LLB).

POWELL, Katie
4 New Square, London
020 7822 2000
k.powell@4newsquare.com
Featured in Professional Negligence (London), Construction (London), Product Liability (London)
Practice Areas: Commercial practice, particularly in the context of investment fraud and professional liability claims, encompassing disputes in the areas of (a) financial services, (b) insurance, and (c) construction and IT. Practice also includes more general commercial disputes, together with a strong product liability element. Experienced in all methods of dispute resolution (arbitration, litigation, adjudication, mediation and negotiation), both domestically and overseas.
Professional Memberships: CHBA, COMBAR, PNBA, TECBAR.
Career: Magdalen College, Oxford (PPE, 2003); City University (Diploma in Law, 2004); Called 2005.
Publications: Editor of financial services chapters of Jackson & Powell on Professional Liability.

POWER, Alexia
Furnival Chambers, London
020 7405 3232
apower@furnivallaw.co.uk
Featured in Crime (London)
Practice Areas: Leading junior with an exclusively criminal practice primarily for the defence. Regularly instructed in high profile, complex cases and appeals, recent examples – Murder (R v JK – gang related joint enterprise), (R v LJ – joint enterprise – Jogee appeal), (R v MF – 9 handed gang murder), baby-shaking manslaughter (R v S), Large scale drug importation (R v DH – importation two tons of cocaine), Complex fraud and money-laundering (R v SH – carbon credit fraud) and particularly the representation of professional clients (R v JG £25,000 mortgage fraud). Particular experience and sensitivity in representing young and vulnerable clients (R v YJ -Tooting Mosque murder). On the CPS list of Specialist Rape Prosecutors since its inception in 2007 and has extensive experience of prosecuting and defending sexual offences including serial rape, historical rape and cases involving child abuse, kidnapping and child abduction (R v IW – Lostprophets singer, R v SM Operation Bullfinch). Expertise in Appeals by way of Case Stated and Judicial Review before the Administrative Court. Reported cases include DPP v Wood and McGillicuddy – defence statements and third party disclosure and R (Hoar-Stevens) v Richmond Magistrates' Court – jurisdiction of the Administrative Court.
Professional Memberships: Fraud Lawyers Association, Criminal Bar Association, Surrey and South London Bar Mess Committee Member, Grays Inn Mentor, Association of Women Barristers. Granted licence to appear as an advocate on the Isle of Man in 2010.
Career: Called 1992 Grays Inn.

POWER, Eloise
Serjeants' Inn Chambers, London
020 7427 5000
epower@serjeantsinn.com
Featured in Clinical Negligence (London), Product Liability (London)
Practice Areas: Eloise Power was called to the Bar in 2002. Eloise specialises in medical law, including clinical negligence, product liability, healthcare regulatory law, medical inquests and public law. An earlier edition notes that "she is a very hard worker who fights the client's corner and maximises the damages. She is prepared to take on the toughest cases" and "she gets to grips with matters very quickly and is very approachable and easy to work with." Please visit the Serjeants' Inn Chambers website for her pro-

file, which sets out full details of her practice including relevant work of note.
Publications: Munkman on Employer's Liability (contributing editor, "The Liability of Third Parties"); Professional Discipline and Healthcare Regulators, a Legal Handbook (author, "General Dental Council").
Personal: Eloise Power was educated at Clare College, Cambridge (starred double first class degree), City University and the Inns of Court School of Law (Prince of Wales Scholar, Gray's Inn). She has been appointed by the Bar Standards Board as an external examiner, and she is an advocacy trainer for Gray's Inn. She is accredited to undertake Public Access work.

POWER, Erica
Crown Office Chambers, London
020 7797 8100
power@crownofficechambers.com
Featured in Product Liability (London)
Practice Areas: Product liability, clinical negligence and personal injury. In product liability she has particular experience in group actions involving pharmaceuticals and medical devices. She is currently instructed in the Metal on Metal hip litigation. Recent cases include the PIP Breast Implant Litigation and litigation relating to TVT (vaginal mesh) and gastric bands. She also acted in the in the Oral Contraceptive Group Litigation. Her clinical negligence practice encompasses both claimant and defendant work. She is regularly instructed by the NHSLA and other defence organisations. She is involved in a wide range of cases such as severe obstetric injury, delayed diagnosis of cancer, orthopaedic and vascular injury and GP failures in respect of diagnosis and/or treatment.
Professional Memberships: Personal Injury Bar Association; Professional Negligence Bar Association.
Career: Educated at Wycombe Abbey School, Trinity College Cambridge and the University of Virginia School of Law (LLM). Called 1990. Inns of Court Studentship (1989, Lincoln's Inn Hardwick and Kennedy Scholarships (1990).
Personal: Married with two children.

POWER, Lewis QC
7BR, London
020 7797 7788
lewis.power2@btopenworld.com
Featured in Crime (Midlands), Crime (London)
Practice Areas: Criminal fraud litigation, fraud, money laundering, bribery & corruption, offshore & international, murder & manslaughter, terrorism, war crimes, and sports law.
Professional Memberships: Association of Defence Counsel before ICTY (International Tribunal for Former Yugoslavia), Northern Irish Bar, Criminal Bar Association, Sussex Bar Mess, Officer to War Crimes Committee of International Bar Association, Approved Football Association Lawyer, Member of North American Forum and War Crimes Forums.
Career: Lewis is a formidable advocate who since taking silk has established a reputation as a leading practitioner in complex Jury trials. Recognised for his market-leading, strategic approach, Lewis combines intellect with a friendly manner which instils confidence in all who instruct him, both professional and lay clients alike. He is referred to as an "unrivalled cross-examiner", where his style is said to be "nothing short of brilliant". Lewis is regularly instructed in heavyweight criminal proceedings involving fraud and regulatory cases with an international dimension, and for those which are particularly complex requiring prompt judgement. His previous cases have ranged from the infamous Grobelaar match fixing case to the London terrorist bombing trials. His specialisms also include murder, conspiracy to murder, attempted murder and rape cases. Recent instructions have also included the two major cases witnessing the new slavery crime being charged, the first of their kind in 200 years.

POWER, Nigel QC
7 Harrington St Chambers, Liverpool
0151 242 0707
nigel.power@7hs.co.uk
Featured in Crime (Northern)
Practice Areas: In Silk since 2010, Nigel Power QC is being instructed in increasingly high profile criminal cases across the complete range of offences. Most recently he led the submissions on behalf of all defendants about exceptional leave to appeal out of time in a series of "Post-Jogee" test cases where murder convictions were based on the old law of joint enterprise. Other recent successes involve reducing the confiscation amount in Stephen Clarke's case from the £5.4m claimed to £0.6m, the prosecution of Kandyce Downer for the murder of 18-month-old Keegan Downer, to whom she was special guardian, and the acquittal in a pipe-bomb conspiracy for Jason Buckley at the Birmingham Crown Court. In 2015 he successfully represented Christopher Spendlove, accused of murdering a Liverpool Police Officer, and Wayne Erskine, accused of murdering a prominent junior boxer when driving a Jeep Cherokee. In financial crime he represented the lead defendant in "Wales' Biggest Ever Fraud", a North Wales mortgage fraud with more than 250,000 pages of evidence and obtained the only acquittal in the notorious "Lord of Fraud" case. He provides a combination of hard work, scientific and IT expertise and an approachable manner to every case he in which he is instructed.

POWER, Richard
Fountain Court Chambers, London
020 7583 3335
rjp@fountaincourt.co.uk
Featured in Commercial Dispute Resolution (London)
Practice Areas: Broad commercial litigation and arbitration practice, including: banking and financial services; insurance and reinsurance; professional negligence; civil fraud; and conflict of laws. Recent cases include: Haugesund Kommune v Depfa ACS Bank [2012] 2 W.L.R. 199 (Court of Appeal) and Depfa ACS Bank v Wikborg Rein & Co [2011] 3 All E.R. 655 (Court of Appeal), Excalibur Ventures LLC v Texas Keystone Inc. and Gulf Keystone Petroleum Limited, one of The Lawyer's Top 20 Cases of 2012 (57 day trial) [2013] EWHC 2767 (Comm), Dexia Crediop v Comune di Firenze, one of The Lawyer's Top 20 Cases of 2013, and UBS & Depfa v Kommunale Wasserwerke Leipzig, one of The Lawyer's Top 20 Cases of 2014.
Career: Called 2007 (Lincoln's Inn).
Publications: Co-author of 'Law of Bank Payments' (eds. Brindle & Cox, 4th edition).
Personal: Christ Church, Oxford (BA, First Class; BCL, Distinction), Crowther Shield for Advocacy, Lincoln's Inn (2006).

POWLES, Steven
Doughty Street Chambers, London
020 7404 1313
s.powles@doughtystreet.co.uk
Featured in Crime (London)
Career: Twenty years' experience representing clients in cases of international crime, extradition, and human rights. Regularly represents high profile defendants accused of the most serious crimes and has appeared before nearly all the international courts and tribunals. He started his career as a judicial assistant in the ICTY, and then as a national representative during negotiations to establish the International Criminal Court. Subsequently appeared as an advocate in those courts, successfully defending both a former Kenyan Government minister accused of Crimes Against Humanity, and a member of the Kosovo Liberation Army accused of War Crimes. Has represented members of the Revolutionary United Front and the Civil Defense Forces in the Special Court for Sierra Leone. As well as representing the accused in international criminal cases, he also advises witnesses including journalists and others. He worked in Beirut with the UN Commission investigating the assassination of Lebanese Prime Minister Rafik Hariri. He is also an experienced extradition lawyer, and a specialist in pursuing complaints to the ECHR (currently assisting with Silvio Berlusconi's Article 6 challenge). He also advises and represents NGOs and victims of international and domestic crime who may wish to pursue prosecutions or financial compensation. He is on the list of approved counsel at ICC; and is a Member of ICC Bar Association. Co-author of May on Criminal Evidence (6th Edn) and co-author of International Criminal Practice (with John Jones QC). Regularly lectures on international crime topics, and as part of the Doughty Street/Chatham House Milestones series and regularly invited to provide expert comment by CNN, BBC, Sky, ITN, Channel 4 and other media outlets.

POWNALL, Orlando QC
2 Hare Court, London
020 7353 5324
opownall@aol.com
Featured in Crime (London), Financial Crime (London)
Practice Areas: Orlando Pownall QC is widely recognised as one of the leading jury advocates of his generation. He is highly skilled, extremely persuasive and an excellent performer in the court room, making him one of the most highly sought-after criminal Silks. Orlando is a highly regarded and esteemed defence advocate who previously held the position of Treasury Counsel, both Junior and First Senior. During his tenure as First Senior Treasury Counsel he prosecuted a large number of high profile cases but since his appointment to Silk in 2002 he almost exclusively defends. Orlando is repeatedly instructed by high profile clients to provide pre-charge advice for a range of criminal and business crime charges. Orlando has represented a number of celebrities including former England football player, Adam Johnson and Chris Cairns, the former New Zealand cricketer. He has also been involved in high profile murder cases including the murder of a gambler in a so called " honey trap" plot and the employees of G4S who were charged with the unlawfully killing of the deportee Jimmy Mubenga. In Business Crime Orlando has been instructed in a number of high profile matters including Operation Tabernula, a lengthy MTIC fraud involving luxury cars exported to the Far East, an alleged fraud on the Royal Mail by a large on line clothing manufacturer and a case involving a cheat on the revenue arising from film tax credits.

PRATLEY, Michelle
39 Essex Chambers, London
020 7832 1111
michelle.pratley@39essex.com
Featured in Court of Protection (All Circuits), Education (London)
Practice Areas: Administrative and public law; human rights; regulatory and commercial law. Areas of public law expertise include community care, mental health and mental capacity. Frequently instructed in complex proceedings in the Court of Protection concerning health and welfare (including forced marriage, capacity to consent to sexual relations and deprivation of liberty) and serious medical treatment (including DNAR orders). Acts for and advises local authorities, academies, universities and students on all aspects of education law, including admissions and exclusions, special educational needs and discrimination claims. Experience in international regulatory compliance disputes in banking and financial services, as well as offshore fraud and money laundering. Notable cases include ACCG v MN [2013] EWCOP 3859 (jurisdiction of the Court of Protection); SMBC v RG [2013] EWCOP 2373 (capacity to marry); BCC v ED (Upper Tribunal, assessing unreasonable public expenditure); DPP v IPOC (British Virgin Islands, confiscating US$40 million as the proceeds of crime).
Career: Solicitor, King & Wood Mallesons, Sydney (2002-2003); Legal Officer, Australian Human Rights Commission, Sydney (2003-2004); called to the Bar, Lincoln's Inn (2006); admitted as a barrister in the British Virgin Islands (2007).
Publications: Contributing author, McManus, 'Education and the Courts' (Jordans, 2012).
Personal: BA/LLB, University of New South Wales, Sydney (1997-2002); LLM, University of Cambridge (2004-2005).

PRATT, Richard QC
7 Harrington St Chambers, Liverpool
0151 242 0707
clerks@7hs.co.uk
Featured in Crime (Northern)
Practice Areas: Prosecutes and defends in heavyweight crime and fraud matters. Acted on the landmark House of Lords case on provocation: R v Morgan Smith; defended Mercer in the Rhys Jones case – Mercer was the only defendant charged with murder; acted on the Solway Harvester, the fishing vessel which sank off the coast off the Isle of Man killing its seven crewmen. The owner was charged and acquitted of negligent manslaughter. Represented defendant charged with terrorist murder, 37 years earlier, of Captain Robert Nairac an undercover soldier who had been posing as a republican militant. More recently represented principal defendant in what was described as the largest mortgage fraud ever to be prosecuted in the UK. Trial lasted 5 months. In 2014 – 2015 represented defendant in alleged regulatory fraud on government agency VOSA (as it then was) in trial in Leeds Crown Court last-

ing 4 months. In 2015 – 2016, he has been involved in several high profile homicide cases, prosecuting and defending throughout the length and breadth of the UK from Carlisle in the North to Exeter in the South West.
Career: Call: 1980 Silk: 2006 Recorder 2000 Attorney General's Panel (A List) 2002-2006 Leader of the Northern Circuit. Head of 7 Harrington Street 2012. Authorised to undertake Direct Access work 2014.

PRESSDEE, Piers QC
29 Bedford Row Chambers, London
020 7404 1044
ppressdee@29br.co.uk
Featured in Family/Matrimonial (London)
Practice Areas: Piers practises exclusively in the field of children law, undertaking complex and important cases at first instance and on appeal. He now has a predominantly private law practice, principally focusing on child arrangements and relocation disputes. He has extensive experience of cases (private and public law) involving allegations of serious physical or sexual abuse and entailing the analysis of complex expert evidence. His practice also covers LGBT parenting, surrogacy and parental order proceedings, as well as abduction and jurisdictional disputes. Piers has appeared in numerous reported cases.
Professional Memberships: Co-Chair, Association of Lawyers for Children, 2008-2010; FLBA.
Career: Called, 1991. Silk 2010.
Publications: Co-author, 'Contact: The New Deal' (Family Law, 2006; Co-author, 'The Public Law Outline: The Court Companion' (Family Law, 2008); Updater of the Children Volumes of Halsbury's Laws of England.
Personal: Born, 1968. Educated, St John's College, Cambridge (President, Cambridge Union). Married, four daughters.

PRICE, Clare
Hailsham Chambers, London
020 7643 5000
clare.price@hailshamchambers.com
Featured in Clinical Negligence (London)
Practice Areas: Clare acts on behalf of both claimants and defendants in clinical negligence, personal injury and professional indemnity claims involving solicitors and barristers. She is frequently instructed in complex and high value cases. Clare also has extensive experience of professional disciplinary proceedings. Clare has chaired five independent inquiries into the care and treatment provided by mental health services to patients who have committed homicides.
Professional Memberships: Member of Professional Negligence Bar Association (PNBA).
Career: Called 1988. Specialises in medical law including clinical negligence claims, consent to treatment issues and inquests. Also specialises in professional indemnity claims involving solicitors and barristers and high value personal injury work.
Publications: The Report of the Independent Inquiry into the Care and Treatment of Stephen Soans-Wade (2006), commissioned by North East London Strategic Health Authority,The Report of the Independent Inquiry into the Care and Treatment of Chandran Sukumaran (2004), commissioned by North East London Strategic Health Authority,The Report of the Independent Inquiry into the Care and Treatment of Matthew Raymond Hotston (2001), commissioned by East London and the City Health Authority, The Report of the Independent Inquiry into the Care and Treatment of Giuseppe Nacci (1998), commissioned by Bedfordshire Health Authority,The Report of the Independent Inquiry into the Care and Treatment of Mr William Scott whilst a patient in the Weller Wing, Bedford and Shires Health and Care NHS Trust (1997), commissioned by Bedfordshire Health Authority.

PRICE, Roderick
187 Fleet Street, London
020 7430 7430
chambers@187fleetstreet.com
Featured in Crime (London)
Practice Areas: Specialises in criminal defence work with particular emphasis on fraud, terrorism, drug trafficking, historical sexual abuse and murder cases. Regularly instructed as a leading junior. Defends in cases which concern racialist issues. Often in cases referred to the Court of Appeal by the Criminal Cases Review Commission. Notable Cases include: R v P (2015) (Central Criminal Court)– Terrorism related case R v O (2015) (Southwark CC)-'Columbian Cartel' Money Laundering trial R v D (2014) (Leeds CC)- Leading Counsel in 'Columbian/Dutch'-Conspiracy to Import shipments of Class A drugs trial R v U (2014) (Snaresbrook CC)- S18 GBH alleged "baby shaking" trial R v S (2013)(Inner London CC) – Leading Counsel in Kidnap/False Imprisonment/Blackmail trial R v Y (2013) (St Albans CC) -Historical Sexual Abuse trial R v I (2012) (Norwich CC) -Armed Robbery trial R v D (2012) (Luton CC) -Sham Marriage case R v D (2012) (Ipswich CC) – Manslaughter trial R v H (2011) (Great Grimsby CC) – Rape/Kidnapping/Firearms trial R v U (2011)(Central Criminal Court)-Leading Counsel in 'Cisco fraud' trial R v C (2011) (Central Criminal Court)-'Gross Negligence' Manslaughter trial R v A (2010)(Southwark CCC)-Leading Counsel in £33 million Money Laundering Trial R v I (2010) (Manchester CC) – Leading Counsel in Terrorist trial R v D (2009) (Croydon CC) – Leading Counsel in HMRC fraud R v A & Others (2008-2009) (Woolwich CC) – Trans-Atlantic Airlines Terrorism trial R v Q (2006-2008) – (Central Criminal Court)– 1st case brought under S5 Terrorism Act 2006; Pleaded guilty.
Professional Memberships: Criminal Bar Association. Member of team advising senior Syrian officials in respect of UN Commission of Inquiry into murder of Lebanese ex Prime Minister Hariri and 14 other murders (Involving representative and advisory trips to Vienna and Damascus).
Career: Called to the Bar 1971, Inner Temple.
Personal: Interests include sailing, badminton, tennis and cricket.

PRICE OBE, Richard QC
Littleton Chambers, London
020 7797 8652
rprice@littletonchambers.co.uk
Featured in Election Law (London), Professional Discipline (London)
Practice Areas: Commercial and business law, entertainment and media law (including defamation), intellectual property, professional negligence, tort and professional regulation. Mediator in all these areas, and employment, property law, construction and all other types of civil law disputes, including disputes involving local authorities and government departments. Also specialises in election law.
Professional Memberships: COMBAR, London Common Law and Commercial Bar Association, Professional Negligence Bar Association, Association of Disciplinary and Regulatory Lawyers, Member of the Association of Northern Mediators, Member of the Chartered Institute of Arbitrators, Member of the LCIA.
Career: Called to Bar 1969; QC 1996; CEDR accredited mediator 1997; Bencher of Gray's Inn 2002; recorder (civil work) 2004; Chairman/Vice-Chairman of the Professional Conduct Committee of the Bar 2002-05; Chairman of the Complaints Committee and Member of the Bar Standards Board 2006-07; legal assessor to the Disciplinary Committee of the Royal College of Veterinary Surgeons 2007, and to the Fitness to Practice Panels of the General Medical Council 2009; lecturer in mediation, civil procedure, commercial and election law.
Publications: Editor of Parker's 'Law and Conduct of Elections', Consulting editor of Halsbury's 'Laws of England', 4th Edition 2007 Re-issue, on Elections and Referendums, contributor to 'Burton on Civil Appeals', and Bowers on 'Whistleblowing Law and Practice'.
Personal: Educated King Edward VII School, Sheffield; King's College London (LLB Hons).

PRINCE, Laura
Matrix Chambers, London
020 74043447
lauraprince@matrixlaw.co.uk
Featured in Employment (London)
Practice Areas: Laura specialises in employment and discrimination law. Laura has a substantial appellate practice having appeared in the Court of Justice of the European Union (Parkwood Leisure Ltd v Alemo-Herron and Others [2013] ICR 1116 (TUPE transfers and collective agreements), twice in the Supreme Court (Alemo-Herron and Hounga v Allen [2014] ICR 847 (illegality) and on numerous occasions in the Court of Appeal and the EAT. Recent Court of Appeal cases include Hounga (above), Gallop v Newport City Council [2014] IRLR 11 (knowledge and disability discrimination) and Burke v College of Law [2012] EqLR 279 (qualifications bodies). Recent EAT cases include; Mughal v DWP UKEAT/0343/15/JOJ (Perversity and reinstatement); Atkinson v Community Gateway Association [2015] ICR 1 (Whistleblowing, constructive dismissal and Article 8 rights), Doughty v Secretary of State for Work and Pensions [2014] All ER (D) 54 (Sept) (Trade Union detriment and victimisation), Betsi Cadwaladr University Health Board v Hughes and others UKEAT/0179/13/JOJ (harassment on grounds of disability), Bradley v RHUL [2014] All ER (D) 12 (Sep) (professorial equal pay claim), and Dass v The College of Harringey UKEAT/0108/12 (equal pay and stable employment relationships). Laura also has experience of all types of Employment Tribunal claim. She has particular expertise in sex discrimination and equal pay claims where she has been instructed in test cases (Schafer v Royal Holloway and Bedford New College [2011] EqLR 429 (the first professorial equal pay claim) Bradley v Royal Holloway (see above)and large multiple claims (involving over 1000 Claimants).
Professional Memberships: BPBU, ELA, ELBA and ELAAS.
Career: LLB Law (First Class) UCL; called to the Bar 2003.

PRINGLE, Watson
Maitland Chambers, London
020 7406 1200
wpringle@maitlandchambers.com
Featured in Chancery (London)
Practice Areas: Watson specialises in commercial and civil fraud litigation, with a particular emphasis on cases involving asset tracing, jurisdictional issues and conflicts of laws. He is instructed in Blue Tropic v Chkhartishvili, a case concerning the misappropriation of assets in Georgia which has so far involved a protracted jurisdiction dispute, and a three week trial on liability. Last year he acted as sole Counsel for Anastasia Goncharova in her successful application to transfer DNA evidence from London to Moscow in order to prove that the late Georgian oligarch Kakha Bendukidze was her father. Watson was junior Counsel for the Family Defendants in Berezovsky v Abramovich and subsequently in their multi-billion dollar claim against Vasily Anisimov. He has experience in obtaining and resisting the full range of interim remedies commonly sought in commercial fraud actions, including Norwich Pharmacal and Bankers Trust orders and freezing injunctions. He regularly represents and advises creditors, debtors and office-holders in personal and corporate insolvency matters with a cross-border and/or fraud element.
Professional Memberships: Chancery Bar Association; COMBAR; Fraud Lawyers Association; Commercial Fraud Lawyers Association.
Career: Called 2005.
Personal: Educated Edinburgh Academy, Brasenose College, Oxford MA (Oxon). Languages: French, German. Watson is a keen footballer, golfer and follower of Scottish rugby.

PRITCHARD, Geoffrey
Three New Square, London
020 7405 1111
pritchard@3newsquare.co.uk
Featured in Intellectual Property (London)
Practice Areas: Specialist in patents, trade-marks, passing-off, confidential information, copyright, design rights, technically related contracts, IP Arbitration, and all other aspects of intellectual property, information technology, media law, and mobile telephony, including EU law relating to IP.
Career: Geoffrey is a highly regarded senior junior with a practice covering all aspects of intellectual property and information technology. His practice is split 50:50 between high-tech cases and "soft" IP cases. Geoffrey appears in the Court of Appeal, High Court/Patents Court, Intellectual Property Enterprise Court (Patents County Court), the patent offices, arbitrations and mediations. In recent years he has often appeared without a leader and has extensive experience of conducting trials, cross-examination (particularly of expert witnesses) and applications for urgent interim relief.
Publications: "TERREL on the Law of Patents", co-editor 18th edition. CIPA Guide to the Patents Act, contributor 7th edition.
Personal: CAMBRIDGE: PhD Geophysics, Shell Scholar in Geophysics, J. T. Knight Prize in Mathematics BRISTOL: BSc Physics

(1st); INNS OF COURT SCHOOL OF LAW, Stanley Levy Prize for IP First in year in International Trade exam, Queen Mother Scholarship of the Middle Temple. DE MONTFORT: Dip. Law (distinction, second in year);Queen Mother Scholarship of the Middle Temple.

PRITCHARD, Sarah
Kings Chambers, Manchester
0345 034 3444
clerks@kingschambers.com
Featured in Clinical Negligence (Northern), Clinical Negligence (North Eastern)

Practice Areas: Specialises in clinical negligence with particular emphasis on surgical negligence, birth damage claims and orthopaedic cases. She also has a substantial personal injury practice dealing with cases of the utmost severity.

Professional Memberships: Personal Injuries Bar Association.

Career: University of Manchester (LLB), Called to the bar in 1993 (Gray's Inn) Junior Scholarship.

PRITCHARD, Sarah
St Ives Chambers, Birmingham
0121 236 0863
sarah.pritchard@stiveschambers.co.uk
Featured in Family/Matrimonial (Midlands)

Practice Areas: Family Children

Professional Memberships: Family Law Bar Association, Association of Lawyers for Children.

Career: Sarah was called to the Bar in 1997. She practices exclusively in proceedings involving children. She acts on behalf of local authorities, parents (including those acting under a disability), children and other family members. Her practice is heavily weighted towards complex public law proceedings involving the death of children, multiple inflicted injury, shaken baby syndrome, fabricated and induced illness in children and sexual abuse. She has experience of representing child victims and child perpetrators of sexual abuse. Her experience in non-accidental injury cases includes complex head injuries, fractures and suffocation. Her practice often involves her in cases where leading and junior counsel appear on the other side. She has a particular interest in cases involving parents and children with learning difficulties or disabilities. Sarah also appears in complex private law cases, where a rule 16.4 Guardian has been appointed, and involve serious and multiple allegations of domestic violence, rape and child sexual abuse.

PROCHASKA, Elizabeth
Matrix Chambers, London
020 7404 3447
elizabethprochaska@matrixlaw.co.uk
Featured in Civil Liberties & Human Rights (London), Education (London)

Practice Areas: Public, human rights and equality law, including commercial and EU law. Specialism in healthcare and human rights. Instructed as first junior counsel in the Independent Inquiry into Child Sexual Abuse.

Career: Educated at St John's College, Cambridge (BA Hons, 2002), City University (GDL, 2004), Somerville College, Oxford (BCL, 2006). Called to the Bar 2007. Judicial Assistant to Lady Hale and Lord Brown (2008-09).

Publications: Co-author, Blackstone Guide to the Human Rights Act 1998 (OUP, 7th edition, 2014). Contributor, Livingstone, Owen and Macdonald, Prison Law (OUP, 5th edition, 2014). Contributor, Clayton and Tomlinson, Law of Human Rights (2nd edition, 2009). Co-author, Special Educational Needs Law (LAG, 1st edition, forthcoming).

PROOPS, Anya QC
11KBW, London
020 7632 8500
anya.proops@11kbw.com
Featured in Administrative & Public Law (London), Data Protection (London), Defamation/Privacy (London), Employment (London)

Practice Areas: Information, media, public and employment law. Member of Information Commissioner's panel of counsel. Notable cases include: Vidal-Hall v Google (CA– application of data protection legislation to tracking of internet browsing habits); Various Claimants v Morrison Supermarkets (group litigation concerning data breach); Commissioner of Police for the Metropolis v Z(Children) (CA – disclosure of police-held DNA data); Dhoorihaka v Director of Public Prosecutions (PC – Article 10 rights and the offence of scandalising the court); Steinmetz v Global Witness (application of journalistic exemption in the Data Protection Act 1998); Fish Legal v Information Commissioner (CJEU – whether privatised water companies are public authorities), East Sussex v Information Commissioner (CJEU – charging for access to property search information); Central London Community Healthcare NHS Trust v Information Commissioner (first ever appeal against monetary penalty notice issued under the Data Protection Act 1998); R(Plantagenet Alliance) v Secretary of State for Justice and University of Leicester (judicial review concerning reinterment of King Richard III's remains); Grant v Land Registry (CA – 'outing' of gay employee); Lawson v Serco (HL – rights of overseas workers).

Professional Memberships: ELA, ELBA, ALBA.

Career: Called in 1998. Appointed Queen's Counsel in 2016.

Publications: Co-founder of the information law blog Panopticonblog.com. Contributor to Tolley's 'Employment Handbook'.

Personal: Cambridge (BA); London School of Economics (PhD); City University (CPE).

PROSSER, Kevin QC
Pump Court Tax Chambers, London
020 7414 8080
clerks@pumptax.com
Featured in Tax (London)

Practice Areas: Widely recognised and consulted in all types of revenue work with a particularly strong litigation practice. Cases since 2015 include: UBS Supreme Court (income tax, employment income, tax avoidance); Bristol & West Court of Appeal (corporation tax avoidance, closure notice); Mercedes Benz Court of Appeal (VAT, hire purchase); ING Direct Upper Tribunal (VAT, supplies for consideration); Vaccine Research Upper Tribunal (income tax avoidance, R&D allowances); Bowring Upper Tribunal (CGT avoidance, offshore trust); Blackwell Upper Tribunal (CGT, deductible expenditure); Wakefield College Upper Tribunal (VAT, supplies for consideration).

Professional Memberships: Chairman, Revenue Bar Association (2009-2013); London Common Law & Commercial Bar Association.

Career: Called 1982, QC 1996; Recorder 2000-2015, Lincolns Inn Bencher 2005; Deputy High Court Judge (2008-2015), Head of Chambers (2014 to present).

Publications: Tax Appeals (Potter & Prosser).

PRYOR, Michael
Maitland Chambers, London
020 7406 1200
mpryor@maitlandchambers.co.uk
Featured in Real Estate Litigation (London)

Practice Areas: Barrister specialising primarily in litigation and advisory work related to real estate. In particular, all aspects of commercial and residential landlord and tenant (including leasehold enfranchisement), real property, insolvency law (personal and corporate) in a property context, and property-related professional negligence (solicitors and property/finance related professionals). Also, probate, partnership, unincorporated associations, and finance matters arising in a real estate context. K/S Habro v. Scottish & Newcastle [2015] EWHC 2084 (Ch) (landlord's claim against original tenant after disclaimer); 82 Portland Place (Freehold) v. Howard de Walden [2014] UKUT 133 (LC) (leasehold enfranchisement, relativity, 'purchaser's margin'); Hauser v. Howard de Walden Estates Ltd [2013] UKUT 597 (LC) (leasehold enfranchisement, relativity, flying freeholds); Deutsche Bank Suisse SA v Khan & Ors [2013] EWCA Civ 1149, [2013] EWHC 482 &1020 (mortgage possession, misrepresentation, consumer law, loan agreement, costs liability, re-entry after enforcement of a warrant, full and frank disclosure); Hortense Littlewood v David Radford [2010] 1 P& CR 18 (CA) (professional negligence, leasehold enfranchisement, time-limit); Risegold Ltd v Escala Ltd [2009] 2 P&CR 1 (CA) (development, nature of easement); Cadogan v. Sportelli [2008] 1 WLR 2142 (CA) (leasehold enfranchisement, deferment rates); Ultimate Leisure v. Tindle [2008] 1 P&CR DG11 (CA) (option, business tenancies, security of tenure); Meretz Investments NV v. ACP Ltd [2007] Ch. 197 (CA) (conspiracy, abuse of process, estoppel, mortgagee's powers.

Professional Memberships: Chancery Bar Association, Property Bar Association.

Career: Qualified 1992.

Personal: University of Newcastle upon Tyne (LLB). Born 1969.

PRZYBYLSKA, Sarah
2 Hare Court, London
020 7353 5324
sarahprzybylska@2harecourt.com
Featured in Crime (London), Professional Discipline (London)

Practice Areas: Sarah acts for state agencies and private individuals in public inquiries and inquests. She acts for regulators and professionals in disciplinary cases in the fields of healthcare and sport. She prosecutes and defends at first instance and appeal in criminal cases of fraud, homicide and organised trafficking of both drugs and people. She advises major corporate clients on issues including disclosure in SFO investigations and private prosecutions. She provides confidential assistance to private individuals seeking advice on matters as diverse as overseas surrogacy arrangements, involvement in mercenary activities and the reading of employees' emails. Typical examples of her work include acting for the Attorney General of Jersey in the Independent Jersey Care Inquiry; advising a major financial institution in the context of an ongoing SFO investigation; prosecuting a construction company and its directors for manslaughter and health and safety offences; and advising a high profile foreign national accused of corruption in their home state on removing an Interpol red notice.

Professional Memberships: South Eastern Circuit, Association of Regulatory and Disciplinary Lawyers, Fraud Lawyers' Association, Health and Safety Lawyers' Association, Criminal Bar Association.

PUGH, Helen
3 Hare Court, London
020 7415 7800
helenpugh@3harecourt.com
Featured in Professional Negligence (London), Travel (London)

Practice Areas: Helen specialises in professional negligence actions against a range of professionals including solicitors, barristers, accountants and surveyors. In addition she has considerable experience of general commercial and company disputes and of insolvency matters. Helen also has a niche travel law practice with an emphasis on jurisdictional and conflict of law issues. Recent significant cases include Symrise AG v Baker & McKenzie [2015] EWHC 912 (Comm), a professional negligence case against a city law firm arising out of negligent Mexican tax advice. Further details are contained in Helen's profile on the 3 Hare Court website.

Career: Called 2008.

PUGH, Richard
Compass Chambers, Edinburgh
0131 226 2881
richard.pugh@compasschambers.com
Featured in Personal Injury (Scotland), Clinical Negligence (Scotland)

Practice Areas: Richard has a varied general practice but his principle areas of expertise are clinical negligence, personal injury, judicial review and fatal accident inquiries. He is experienced in dealing with high value and complex matters, including appeal work up to and including the Inner House of the Court of Session and UK Supreme Court. Richard is one of the Standing Junior Counsel to the Advocate General for Scotland, in which role he undertakes a variety of work in the sphere of public law. Outside practice as an Advocate, Richard chairs Conduct in Sport disciplinary panels under the Sport Scotland umbrella.

Career: 1996-2000: LLB (HONS) (Strathclyde); 2000-01: Dip LP (GGSL); 2008 Called to the Bar.

PUGH-SMITH, John
39 Essex Chambers, London
020 7832 1109
john.pugh-smith@39essex.com
Featured in Planning (London)

Practice Areas: Town & country planning and related environmental, local government, parliamentary and property work. He is also an experienced mediator.

Professional Memberships: MCIArb. FSA. PEBA (former Committee Member), UKELA, ELF, Bar Council ADR Panel Member.

Career: Called to the Bar 1977. Joined 39 Essex Chambers in 2002. CEDR Accredited Mediator 2005. DCLG s106 broker 2012. Design Council Cabe Built Environment Expert 2013.

Publications: For Sweet & Maxwell, as originating author and/or as editor: 'Neighbours and the Law', 'Archaeology at Law'; 'Shackleton on the Law of Meetings'. Joint Editorial Advisor for P&CR. For Oxford University Press: 'Environmental Law'.

PURCHAS, James
4 Pump Court, London
020 7842 5555
jpurchas@4pumpcourt.com
Featured in Financial Services (London), Insurance (London)

Practice Areas: Commercial litigation with an emphasis on financial services, banking (wholesale and retail) and insurance and reinsurance disputes. Other work includes civil fraud, conflict of laws issues, trade disputes (particularly between manufacturers and distributors) and professional negligence work (accountants, financial intermediaries, lawyers and surveyors) and fire cases. Regularly instructed in respect of related urgent injunctive relief and other interim applications. Appears in all civil courts, tribunals and domestic and international arbitrations.
Professional Memberships: Commercial Bar Association, Financial Services Lawyers Association, Professional Negligence Bar Association and TECBAR.
Career: MA (Hon) (Cantab.) Classics 1995. Dip. Law (City) 1996. Dip. European Law (Kings) 1997. Call 1997. Inner Temple Major Scholarship. Bar European Commission Scholarship 1998. Foreign Associate Shearman & Sterling, New York 1999. Tenant at 4 Pump Court 2000. FSA Secondment 2004.
Publications: Co-author of 'Civil Appeals'– Sweet & Maxwell 2014. Law Brief Update: Financial Services, Insurance and Professional Negligence. Lloyds Financial Crime Reports, Editorial Panel.

PURCHASE, Mathew
Matrix Chambers, London
020 7404 3447
mathewpurchase@matrixlaw.co.uk
Featured in Education (London), Employment (London)

Practice Areas: Public and administrative law, employment and discrimination, education, human rights. Notable recent cases include: Sparks v Department of Transport [2016] EWCA Civ 360, CA (contractual incorporation of attendance policy); R (Forge Care Homes) v Cardiff & Vale University Health Board and others (2016) Times 28 March, CA (NHS obligation to pay care home nursing costs); R (UNISON) v Lord Chancellor [2016] ICR 1, CA (ET fees challenge); Kemeh v Ministry of Defence [2014] ICR 625, CA (scope of agency in discrimination claims); McKinnon v London Borough of Redbridge [2014] ICR 834, CA (parks police entitlement to claim unfair dismissal).
Professional Memberships: Employment Lawyers Association; Human Rights Lawyers Association; Industrial Law Society; Adminstrative Law Bar Association; Employment Law Bar Association.
Career: Called 2002. Member of A Panel of junior counsel to the Crown, Bar Pro Bono Unit and ELAAS.
Publications: Contributing editor of Clayton and Tomlinson's 'The Law on Human Rights' (2nd edition, OUP); contributor to Simor's 'Human Rights Practice'; contributor to Burton, 'Civil Appeals'; Judicial Review practice guides for LexisNexis; articles on disability discrimination, legitimate expectations, and misfeasance in public office for Practical Law.

PURNELL, James
Henderson Chambers, London
020 7583 9020
jpurnell@hendersonchambers.co.uk
Featured in Product Liability (London)

Practice Areas: Product Liability, Health & Safety and Environmental, Personal Injury, Employment, Regulatory Law, Public & Administrative Law.
Professional Memberships: HSLA, COMBAR, ELBA, PIBA, ELA, BILA.
Career: Middle Temple Queen Mother Scholar 2001, Called to Bar 2002, Attorney General's Panel of Counsel 2009, Specialist Regulatory List Advocate in Health & Safety and Environmental Law 2012.
Personal: In his spare time devoted to bringing the glory days back to Clapham Rovers FC.

PURNELL, Nicholas QC
Cloth Fair Chambers, London
020 7710 6444
nicholaspurnell@clothfairchambers.com
Featured in Crime (London), Financial Crime (London)

Practice Areas: Practises predominantly in business & financial Crime and in regulatory and professional disciplinary matters. Member of the Lord Chancellor's Advisory Committee on Legal Education and Conduct 1991-97. Member of the Criminal Committee Judicial Studies Board 1991-96. Has twice been appointed an Inspector by the DTI inspecting insider share dealing. Extensive experience of defending, past cases include; McCormack (Atlantic Computers), Townsend (Hoare Govett) and Crosswell (Selborne Brick). Guiness share-trading fraud, Brinks Mat, Blue Arrow, McNicolas, Morgan Grenfell (anti-dumping prosecution), Mabey (international sanctions violations), Bowbelle Marchioness Disaster, Lord Archer and Jonathan Aitken's perjury trials. Led the team on behalf of Balfour Beatty in the settlement of the SFO investigation, the first civil recovery order entered into by the prosecution authority. Advised British Airways executives in the first contested prosecution under the Enterprise Act. Innospec; represented company in global plea agreement between SFO, DoJ and SEC. Successfully represented a major travel operator in the first prosecution by the Civil Aviation Authority under the Air Travel Organisers License regulation at trial and again at Appeal; advised renowned airline in respect of licensing with the civil aviation authority. Acted for a leading travel business in cross border investigations into deaths outside the jurisdiction. Advised two global companies in separate cases re. Competition and Cartel investigations. Appeared at the Competition Appeals Tribunal. Advised Icelandic banking executives. Advised Police forces on the implications of the Hookway ruling. Recent notable cases; Represented a defendant in the 'Vantis' tax fraud trial; represented a former governor of the Delta State in a multi-million pound corruption case; advised a former editor of a national newspaper in relation to the Leveson Enquiry; advised the director of a global events company in relation to criminal proceedings revolving around the sale of corporate tickets for the Olympic games. Advised a national broadcaster re corruption, successfully represented Victor Dahdaleh over international corruption charges. Advised a multinational defence technology company; advised a national pharmaceutical company. Acted for ICBC Standard Bank throughout the first ever Deferred Prosecution Agreement to be approved in the UK. Advising the Executive Director of an African energy company, NCA investigation. Advising individual in the SFO investigation regarding Rolls Royce; Acting for former Senior Executive of Barclays Bank PLC in SFO/FCA investigation re Qatar. Advising a national telecommunications company on allegations of corruption. For further information please visit www.clothfairchambers.com.
Career: Called to the Bar 1968. Silk 1985.

PUZEY, James
St Philips Chambers, Birmingham
0121 246 7000
jpuzey@st-philips.com
Featured in Tax (The Regions)

Practice Areas: James Puzey is a highly experienced and leading junior in the field of indirect taxation. He has specialised in that field for 15 years, appearing in courts and tribunals at all levels, from the Supreme Court down, and across the UK. James has advised and appeared in hundreds of tax appeals covering VAT, Excise and Customs duties, aggregates levy and landfill tax. James is regularly instructed to appear against Queen's Counsel in high value litigation and matters involving challenging points of law. In the last three years he has appeared in VAT cases involving General Motors UK, Citibank, Ford Motor Company, the British Printing Industries Federation, and the European Tour Operators Association, to name but a few. In Fonecomp v HMRC [2015] EWCA Civ 39, James appeared for HMRC in an important decision on denial of the right to deduct VAT in cases of fraud. In First Stop Wholesale Ltd & Another v HMRC [2014] UKSC 34, he was again part of the successful team in a case involving the rights of HMRC to seize and forfeit excise goods. In 2016 the Upper Tribunal ruled in favour of HMRC, for whom James appeared, in the case HMRC v Wakefield College [2016] UKUT 19. This case concerned whether fees paid by students which did not cover the cost of their tuition amounted to consideration. James has a very strong track record in indirect taxation, both as a trial advocate and at appellate level.
Career: Called 1990.

PYMONT, Christopher QC
Maitland Chambers, London
020 7406 1200
clerks@maitlandchambers.com
Featured in Chancery (London), Real Estate Litigation (London)

Practice Areas: Commercial chancery, property (especially landlord and tenant), professional negligence, company and insolvency. Cases include: Gencor ACP Ltd v Dalby (2000 breach of directors' duties); Half-Moon Bay v Crown Eagle (PC 2001 restrictive covenants, land registration in Jamaica); Ashworth Frazer v Gloucester City Council (HL 2001 tenant's covenants against alienation without consent); China National v Fenwick Elliott (VC 2002 solicitors' duties and confidentiality); Chadwick v McGowan (CA 2002 Receiver's duties); Robinson v Bank of Bermuda (Bermuda CA 2002 bankers' duties and limitation); Evans v Virgin Radio (Ch Div 2003 breach of contract and effect on share options); Westminster CC v Dame Shirley Porter (2003 sham trusts); John Laing v Amber Pass (2004 break clause in lease); Chahal v Mahal (CA 2005 partnership); Shirayama v Danovo (Ch Div 2005 forfeiture of lease); Littman v Aspen Oil (CA 2005 rectification); Peekay v ANZ (CA 2006 misrepresentation); Carphone Warehouse v Malekout (CA 2006 issue estoppel); Berkeley v Pullen (Ch Div 2007 construction of planning consultancy agreement); St Ivel v Wincanton (CA 2008 construction of warehousing agreements); Choudhary v Bhatter (CA 2009 jurisdiction); Akzo Nobel v Arista Tubes (CA 2010 interpretation of lease agreement); Payne v Strand (Bahamas CA 2010, procedure); Howard v Howard-Lawson (Ch Div 2010 and CA 2011 construction of will); Bellway v Beazer (CA 2011 construction of shareholders' agreement); Woodford v Persimmon (Ch Div 2011 and CA 2012 rectification); FHR European Ventures v Mankarious (Ch Div 2011, CA 2012 and Supreme Court 2014 fiduciary duties and constructive trusts); Sharab v HRH Al Waleed (CA 2009 and Ch Div 2012 jurisdiction); Ridgewood v Valero (Ch Div 2012 and 2013 breach of option agreement); Sheffield v Sheffield (Ch Div 2013 breach of trust); Krys v New World Value Fund (E Caribbean CA 2014 and PC 2015 construction of limited partnership articles); Ivey v Genting (2015 QB and 2016 CA cheating at cards).
Professional Memberships: Chancery Bar Association, Property Bar Association, COMBAR.
Career: Called to the Bar 1979; QC 1996; recorder 2004; Deputy High Court Judge.

QUINN, Chris
Littleton Chambers, London
020 7797 8600
cquinn@littletonchambers.co.uk
Featured in Employment (London)

Practice Areas: High Court and arbitration litigation (mainly Employment- related and Commercial) including fraud (civil). Also general common law including Partnership/ LLPs, Professional Negligence, Professional Discipline, Regulatory work including FCA matters, Sports/ Entertainment and IP. Injunction specialist. Full-range of Employment Tribunal practice.
Professional Memberships: ELBA, COMBAR, LCLCBA, ELAAS.
Career: Employment and commercial-related disputes involving high-flyers in which a trial looks likely. Recent appellate appearances include: Bates van Winkelhof v Clyde and Co (Supreme Court); PHS Limited v Rentokil (CA). Recent High Court trials include: Richards and Purves v IP Solutions (breach of fiduciary duties/ Good Leaver classification); Decorus Limited v Penfold (successful enforcement of restrictive covenants); Holliday v J M Finn (garden leave restrictions); Towry EJ v Bennett and others (successful defence of £6 million solicitation claim), the Rubcon hedgefund dispute, Yousefi v SJ Solicitors (successful claim of solicitor's negligence), Lonmar v West and others (successful defence of £2 miillion team move claim). Other noteworthy High Court work includes the successful application for summary judgment in Thomson Ecology v Hall and Others (team moves). Ongoing/ recent arbitration instructions including the alleged £2 billion dispute over Marathon Asset Management

(as well as the related High Court claim) and the successfully concluded claim in Kellow Health Limited v London Orthopaedic Clinic Other recent High Court/ ET work includes: succesfull whistleblowing claim in Gillespie v Terence Higgins Trust; Allen v Investec; Bou Simon v BGC; McCarthy v BSB; Gimson v The Telegraph (age discrimination). Other cases include Pedropillai v PwC (victimisation claim following Tribunal) Chris' older cases include the "Gay Banker" case (Lewis v HSBC), the CA case that established that unions could be liable to their members for discrimination (Allen v GMB), a management claim brought against the celebrity chef Gary Rhodes, the successful CA claim against the BNP in Redfearn v Serco as well as numerous reported cases.
Personal: Skiing/ ski-touring, cinema, theatre, (watching) football.

QUINT, Francesca
Radcliffe Chambers, London
020 7831 0081
fquint@radcliffechambers.com
Featured in Chancery (London), Charities (London)
Practice Areas: Chancery including trusts and wills, with an emphasis on all aspects of charity law plus education and charitable housing.
Professional Memberships: Chancery Bar Association, Charity Law Association (formerly a member of the Executive Committee), Ecclesiastical Law Society.
Career: Called (Gray's Inn) July 1970 – joined Lincoln's Inn ad eundem 1980; Law reporting for All England Reports 1971-2; 1972-90 Government Legal Service (Charity Commission) rising to Grade 5 (Deputy Commissioner); 1990-6 independent practice in Exeter; 1990-independent practice in Lincoln's Inn joining 11 Old Square (East) 2001 (merged to become Radcliffe Chambers 2006). 2008- Bencher of Lincoln's Inn; 2014- board member, Aspire Law LLP.
Publications: Include Butterworth's Encyclopaedia of Forms and Precedents – Charities titles (LexisNexis) – since 1987; Charities: the Law and Practice (Sweet & Maxwell) since inception; Running a Charity (Jordans) 1st and 2nd editions; Charity Law Association model governing documents (currently in 3rd education).
Personal: LLB; AKC – King's College London, 1969; 2015- joint Honorary President British Mensa; 2014- external trustee Tilford Bach Society; 1989 – member Advisory Body, Almshouse Association. Previous trusteeships include ASPIRE; Dulwich College; Elizabeth Finn Care; St Peter's Home & Sisterhood Woking; Bishopsgate Foundation; Association of Charitable Foundations; COIF.

RADCLIFFE, Andrew QC
2 Hare Court, London
020 7353 5324
andrewradcliffeqc@2harecourt.com
Featured in Financial Crime (London)
Practice Areas: A white collar crime fraud specialist, most of his recent work in this country has been defending in serious fraud and fraud related cases although, in the past, he has, in addition, regularly been instructed by the SFO (including MLA cases) and the CPS. Since taking silk in 2000, his cases have included most aspects of fraud and allied offences, including allegations of price fixing, money laundering, MTIC fraud, duty evasion, tax evasion and advance fee fraud as well as confiscation. He has defended successfully in the Kent Pharmaceuticals case and the OFT prosecution of British Airways executives accused of price fixing in collusion with Virgin Atlantic Airlines. He was subsequently instructed for the lead defendant in the "Blue Index" case, the first cross-jurisdictional insider dealing prosecution brought by the FSA, involving proceedings and evidence on both sides of the Atlantic. He also acts in murder and other cases of serious crime and has been instructed in regulatory matters, e.g. for the Football Association. He frequently works in the Cayman Islands, both advising and in court there. Recent examples of work there include allegations of corruption, misconduct in public office and fraud, as well as murder and firearms cases. He was called to the Turks and Caicos Islands Bar in 2014 and successfully defended in allegations concerning the Revenue there in 2015. Andrew's recent instructions include, a £52 million pension fraud, €50 million cross border money laundering involving multiple jurisdictions, including Luxembourg, France, UK, Australia, New Zealand, Hong Kong and Dubai, allegations of tax fraud in Turks & Caicos and a prosecution arising out of the liquidation of JJB plc, the sportswear retailer. He is presently instructed in trial due to start in Jan 2017 involving allegations of tax fraud.
Professional Memberships: CBA, Fraud Lawyers Association.
Publications: The author of two chapters (on insider dealing and regulatory offences, respectively) in 'Fraud: Law, Practice and Procedure' (LexisNexis 2012). A contributor to the CBA's responses to the Law Commission in respect of the law relating to fraud and dishonesty and, later, the review of the laws of conspiracy and attempt.

RADEVSKY, Anthony
Falcon Chambers, London
020 7353 2484
clerks@falcon-chambers.co.com
Featured in Real Estate Litigation (London)
Practice Areas: Landlord and tenant law relating to commercial and residential property, including leasehold enfranchisement; real property disputes and professional negligence claims against solicitors and surveyors. Recently reported cases include: Westbrook Dolphin Square v Friends Life [2015] 1 WLR 1713; Helman v John Lyon (CA) [2014] 1 WLR 2451; Hosebay Ltd v Day [2012] 1 WLR 2884 (SC); Prospect Estates v Grosvenor Estates [2009] 1 WLR 1313 (CA); Howard de Walden v Aggio [2009] 1 AC 39 (HL); Boss Holdings v Grosvenor West End Properties [2008] 1 WLR 289 (HL); 9 Cornwall Crescent v Royal Borough of Kensington and Chelsea [2006] 1 WLR 1163.
Professional Memberships: Chancery Bar Association; Property Bar Association.
Career: Educated at Alleyn's School, Dulwich; Southampton University (LLB Hons 1977); Called 1978 (Inner Temple).
Publications: Hague on Leasehold Enfranchisement (Sweet & Maxwell 2014); Tenants' Right of First Refusal (Jordans 2008); Drafting Pleadings (Tolley 1995); Service of Documents (Longman 1989).
Personal: Married with 2 daughters.

RADFORD, Nadine QC
3 Temple Gardens, London
020 7353 3102
clerks@3tg.co.uk
Featured in Crime (London)
Practice Areas: Nadine Radford has specialised solely in criminal practice all her professional life. She has extensive experience in defending serious criminal offences with particular expertise in terrorism, commercial fraud, money laundering and murder. She has undertaken many high profile cases including the Kurdish Terrorist trial, the Louise Sullivan Shaken Baby case, also known as the Australian nanny case, the "Mardi Gras" Bomber and the Afghan Hijacking at Stansted Airport. Nadine represented the first defendant charged with possession of terrorist material (acquitted). She went on to defend the first defendant (Ali) in the Heathrow terrorism trial. Nadine has defended in conspiracy to murder involving the Moss Side gangs, child murders, honour killings and murder by poisoning. Nadine has frequently been instructed in complex fraud cases including a gold VAT fraud, diversion frauds including various bonded warehouses and fraudulent trading. She has represented the principal defendant in a multi million pound fraud involving the issuing of passports meant for asylum seekers giving illegal immigrants the right to work in the United Kingdom and elsewhere. Her practice covers the broad range of sexual offences including historical allegations of sexual offences and gang related sexual grooming in Aylesbury and Littlehampton. She recently represented a 29-year-old Somali defendant who was found unfit to be tried and then found not to have raped an 82-year-old woman.
Career: Nadine Radford was made Queen's Counsel in 1995 and was made a Bencher of Lincoln's Inn in 1999.

RAFFERTY, Angela QC
Drystone Chambers, London
020 7404 1881
angelarafferty@drystone.com
Featured in Crime (South Eastern)
Practice Areas: Criminal law.
Professional Memberships: South Eastern Circuit, CBA, Cambridge & Peterborough Bar Mess.
Career: Angela Rafferty has defended or prosecuted in many of the most high profile, sensitive and complex cases in East Anglia from an early stage in her career. Angela was called to the Bar in 1995 after studying at and working within the University of Cambridge and Clifford Chance, took silk in 2015, and is now recognised as one of the leading advocates in her areas of practice. She was made a Recorder aged 39 and sits exclusively at the Old Bailey. Angela acted for Maxine Carr in the Soham Murder trials in 2003 and since then has been instructed as a led junior, leading junior and Silk in a large number of recent and historical murder and manslaughter cases involving death of children and multiple homicides. She undertakes homicide cases of the utmost gravity and complexity regularly.The majority of her work involves scientific and expert evidence requiring extensive knowledge and expertise of DNA, fibres, pathology, neuropathology, psychiatric issues and psychology. She has a particular expertise in cases involving mental health issues and expert evidence. In 2016, Angela was elected to be Vice-chair of the Criminal Bar Association.

RAINEY, Philip QC
Tanfield Chambers, London
020 7421 5285
clerks@tanfieldchambers.co.uk
Featured in Real Estate Litigation (London)
Practice Areas: All aspects of commercial and residential property litigation (including social housing); also ADR and some mainstream commercial work. Particular expertise in leasehold enfranchisement, RTM and service charge disputes. Representative cases include: Edwards v Kumarasamy [2016] 3 WLR 310 (SC) (disrepair), Menelaou v Bank of Cyprus [2016] AC 176 (SC) (mortgages); R(Best) v Chief Land Registrar [2015] 2 P&CR 1 (CA) (judicial review, adverse possession); C&M v Kaymuu [2015] 2 P&CR 15 (CA) (overriding interests); Ninety Broomfield Road RTM v Triplerose [2015] HLR 29 (CA) (RTM); MP Kemp Ltd v Bullen Developments [2014] EWHC 2009 (Ch) (overage; expert determination); Daejan v Benson [2013] 1 WLR 854 (SC) (service charges); Cadogan v Sportelli [2010] 1 AC 226 (enfranchisement); Howard de Walden v Aggio [2009] 1 AC 39 (enfranchisement).
Professional Memberships: Chartered Institute of Arbitrators, Chancery Bar Association, Property Bar Association, Association of Leasehold Enfranchisement Practitioners.
Career: LLB, MCIArb. Silk 2010. Called to the Bar 1990, joined Tanfield Chambers in 2001. Head of Chambers 2013- date. Member of the Civil Procedure Rule Committee 2001-08.
Publications: (With other members of Tanfield Chambers) 'Service Charges and Management' (Sweet & Maxwell, 3rd ed 2013); Co-author: "Megarry's Manual of the Law of Real Property" (9th ed 2014); Co-author 'Rent Review: A Surveyor's Handbook' (RICS, 2008).
Personal: Born 1968, married with three children.

RAINEY, Simon QC
Quadrant Chambers, London
44 207 583 4444
simon.rainey@quadrantchambers.com
Featured in International Arbitration (London), Commercial Dispute Resolution (London), Energy & Natural Resources (London), Shipping (London)
Practice Areas: Simon Rainey's practice centres on shipping and international commerce as well as commercial and insurance litigation and he practises almost exclusively in the Commercial and Admiralty Courts as well as in maritime commercial arbitration in London; in commodity trade arbitrations before the major trade associations and in insurance/reinsurance arbitrations. He has been consistently singled out over the past five years in the specialist directories as one of the leading general commercial, insurance and shipping practitioners.
Professional Memberships: Member of COMBAR; supporting member of LMAA.
Career: Called to the Bar in 1982; took silk 2000; appointed Recorder of the Crown Court 2001. Civil Recorder – 2004.

RAINSFORD, Mark QC
The Chambers of Andrew Mitchell QC, London
020 7440 9950
mr@33cllaw.com
Featured in POCA Work & Asset Forfeiture (All Circuits), Financial Crime (London)

Career: An internationally pre-eminent silk specialising in corporate crime, civil fraud, commercial fraud and business crime, civil and criminal proceeds of crime cases and asset recovery. He defends corporates, individual directors, organisations and high net- worth individuals under investigation by UK and overseas law enforcement authorities. Notable cases in 2016: successfully defending Hong Kong businessman James Sutherland, Chairman of a large group of fiduciary companies operating in 12 jurisdictions charged with money-laundering $120m from Britain's largest boiler room fraud. Advising Vincent Tchenguiz in a substantial civil fraud claim against Grant Thornton LLP and Kaupthing Bank Hf. Advising in connection with Libyan Investment Authority v Societe Generale SA, Libya's sovereign wealth fund's $1.5 billion claim against Societe Generale, concerning alleged bribes worth tens of millions of dollars to associates of Saif al-Islam, the son of former Libyan leader Muammar Gaddafi. Representing the CEO of Capital World Markets concerning alleged involvement in investment fraud- the "Heron Tower case". Advising in connection with LIBOR and EURIBOR. Notable cases in 2015 and recent years: successfully defending a major accounting firm under investigation in relation to bribery offences in 74 countries; representing the Ministry of Environment of a European sovereign state after their stock exchange was compromised by cyber-hackers – shares switched to the London Stock Exchange and spot trading commenced -emergency freezing injunctions, Norwich Pharmacal orders and asset recovery; Representing the Lithuanian State in conjoined civil and criminal proceedings after a well-known Russian oligarch allegedly misappropriated €1 billion of securities from a high street bank, where he was Chairman – obtaining restraint orders over his UK assets. Obtaining management receivership and restraint orders over the assets of a group of companies with an annual turnover of £140m – "Eastenders". Representing the former Chairman and CEO of RBG Metals plc and Allied Deals Inc. in £1.2 billion hidden assets proceedings; Representing the CEO of a chain of Money Service Bureaus, dubbed "Britain's biggest money launderer"; and providing pre-charge advice to a putative defendant in LIBOR.

RAJAH, Eason QC
Ten Old Square, London
020 7405 0758
easonrajah@tenoldsquare.com
Featured in Chancery (London), Court of Protection (All Circuits), Offshore (London), Trusts (London)

Practice Areas: Chancery litigation and advisory work in the UK and offshore, including domestic, off shore and cross-border trusts and will disputes, disputes relating to offshore trust and structures in matrimonial proceedings, related tax and professional negligence issues, the drafting, structuring and advising in relations to trusts, succession planning and tax and related areas.

Professional Memberships: He is Vice Chairman of the Chancery Bar Association and a member of the committee of STEP Central London. He is a member of ACTAPs and the Charity Law Association. He is a former member of the Bar Council Professional Standards Committee, the Bar Standards Board Rules Committee and a former Vice Chairman of one of the Bar Council Pupillage Monitoring Panels. He is a member of the Bar Pro Bono Unit.

Career: Called to the Bar 1989; Silk 2011. Called to the Malaysian Bar 1991. Recent cases include: High Commissioner of Pakistan v Nat West Bank [2015] EWHC 55 (Ch), [2016] EWHC 1465 (Ch) (involves issues of sovereign immunity and trust law, and Indian and Shari'a succession law); Crociani v Crociani and others [2014] UKPC 40 (the landmark case on jurisdiction clauses in trusts); Al Sadi v Al Sadi [2013] (Claim by certain children of deceased that under Shari'a, Liechtenstein and Monagasque law, assets held in a Liechtenstein Foundation and a Panamanian company form part of the estate); Rodman v Rodman [2013] Claims for intermeddling and misappropriation from $125m estate– value £millions; Scarfe v Matthews [2012] WTLR 1579 (doctrine of election – estate of Bernard Matthews); Re the Valetta Trust [2011] JRC 227(the validity of third party litigation funding arrangements for trust litigation in Jersey); Re MN [2010] WTLR 1355 (the first decision on the ambit of the international jurisdiction of the Court of Protection); Re IMK Family Trust [2008] JLR 430 (the landmark decision on the enforcement of foreign matrimonial judgments in Jersey) C v C (Privilege) [2008] 1 FLR 115 – applicability of legal professional privilege to disclosure by anstalt where wife claimed anstalt attempting to defeat her ancillary relief claim.

Publications: He is an Editor of Mellows Taxation of Executors and Trustees, an Editor of the Court of Protection Law Reports and is the Consultant Editor of Ranking Spicer Pegler, Executorship Law, Trusts and Accounts.

RALPH, Craig
Kings Chambers, Manchester
0345 034 3444
clerks@kingschambers.com
Featured in Costs Litigation (All Circuits)

Practice Areas: Craig has a national practice exclusively in the Law of Costs. His expertise is in demand in contentious and non-contentious costs issues arising in both civil and criminal matters. He regularly appears before all levels of judiciary from the County Courts and the Supreme Court Cost Office as well as appearing before the High Court and Court of Appeal on important points of principle. His expertise on influential cost questions is regularly sought after in appeals and test cases. Craig has a particular expertise in the incidence of costs, managing broken retainers and issues arising from assignment/novation. Craig is particularly praised for his ability in matters concerning issues of conduct, especially in solicitor and own client matters. Craig is a qualified mediator and is registered for Public Access work; receiving instructions directly from members of the Bar and costs professionals in relation to fee recovery in both Civil and Criminal matters. In addition to his advocacy, advisory and mediation work, Craig is highly sought after for his engaging bespoke lectures and seminars.

Career: LLB Honours, University of Central Lancashire. Year of Call: 2002 Joined Middle Temple: 1998.

Publications: Craig has had numerous articles published in the New Law Journal.

RAMASAMY, Selva
QEB Hollis Whiteman, London
020 7933 8855
selva.ramasamy@qebhw.co.uk
Featured in Professional Discipline (London), Financial Crime (London)

Practice Areas: Selva is a specialist in cases involving professionals charged in criminal, regulatory and disciplinary proceedings. His principal focus is financial crime, and cases involving doctors (and other healthcare professionals), particularly those involving complex technical issues. He has wide experience in GMC, GDC, GCC, HCPC and GOstC cases including appeals to the High Court. He is regularly instructed in prosecutions and regulatory cases involving legal professionals. He also specialises in representing police officers in disciplinary proceedings. He has substantial experience in cases of fraud involving banks, companies, financial advisers and share dealing, as well as in the healthcare sector. He has expertise in health and safety cases, and those involving general crime including sexual allegations. He also represents interested parties in complex inquests. Recent criminal cases include defending a doctor against allegations of sexual assault; defending an osteopath against allegations of sexual assault; SRA private prosecutions under the Solicitors Act and the Legal Services Act; defending an actress/ producer in the first prosecution for fraudulent claims for film tax credit; defending a sub-postmaster accused of trading in counterfeit stamps; defending a CEO in a prosecution for making misleading statements to the market in the largest fraud on the Alternative Investment Market. Recent disciplinary cases include defending an osteopath against allegations of sexual assault during the course of examinations; representing a police officer in disciplinary proceedings arising out of a death in custody; an inquiry into a series of exposure prone procedures leading to the largest "look back" exercise in NHS history; and an inquiry into a fatality arising from conflicting opinions about the use of alternative remedies. Recent inquests include acting for the family of a Royal Navy officer who died in a fall from a warship; acting for a company in relation to a workplace electrocution; and acting for a police officer in relation to a death in custody.

Professional Memberships: Elected member of the Bar Council (1997-2000); Criminal Bar Association committee (1997-2000 and 2008-09); British Association of Sport and Law; Association of Regulatory & Disciplinary Lawyers; Health and Safety Lawyers Association; registered with the Bar Council Public Access Directory; Public Access Bar Association.

Career: Called Inner Temple 1992. Recorder 2009. Member of the Bar Standards Board Prosecuting Counsel Panel for Disciplinary Hearings.

RAMPTON, Richard QC
One Brick Court, London
020 7583 9144
rr@onebrickcourt.com
Featured in Defamation/Privacy (London)

Practice Areas: Defamation, privacy, contempt of court and media related law generally. Cases include: Lucas-Box v Associated Newspapers; Atkinson v Fitzwalter; Control Risks v New English Library; Telnikoff v Matusevich; Shah v Standard Chartered Bank; Aldington v Tolstoy; McDonald's Corp v Steel and Morris; Irving v Lipstadt and Penguin Books; Sugar v News Group; Sugar v Associated Newspapers; Holden & Dennis v Express Newspapers; Kearns v General Council of the Bar; Carlton v News Group; Oryx v BBC; King v Telegraph; McArdle v Newcastle Chronicle; Galloway v Telegraph; Henry v BBC; Campbell v Safra; Heather Mills McCartney v Associated Newspapers and News Group Newspapers; Condoco Grand Cayman v KYC News; Materazzi v Associated Newspapers; Bray v Deutsche Bank; Taranissi v BBC; Bento v Ch Cons Bedfordshire Police; Waterson v Lloyd; Citation v Ellis Whittam Ltd; Flood v Times Newspapers; Mionis v Democratic Press SA; Cruddas v Times Newspapers; forthcoming Supreme Court proceedings on recoverability of success fees in Art.10 cases (Flood v Times Newspapers).

Career: Educated at Bryanston and The Queen's College, Oxford. Called to the Bar in 1965, took Silk in 1987.

Publications: 'Duncan & Neill on Defamation' 4th Edition co-author; Report on Death on the Rock, with Lord Windlesham, Faber & Faber (1989).

Personal: Speaks French, some Italian and German.

RAMSAHOYE, Indira
29 Bedford Row Chambers, London
020 7404 1044
iramsahoye@29br.co.uk
Featured in Family/Matrimonial (London)

Practice Areas: International law relating to children in particular child abduction, jurisdictional disputes, relocation cases and all other areas of family work with respect to children. Particular interest – experience in work concerning the Sub-Continent and Middle East, and the representation of children in abduction proceedings. Reported cases include: MK v CK (Relocation) (2012) C/A; R and another v A [2011] All ER (D) 136 (May), FD; P v G (Family Law Act 1986: Jurisdiction); [2010] 2 FLR 1888, FD; Re S (Foreign Contact Order) [2010] 1 FLR 982, FD; RS v KS (Abduction: Wrongful Retention [2009] 2 FLR 1231, FD; Re W (Leave to Remove)[2008] EWCA Civ 1181; Re L (Abduction: Future Consent) [2008] 1 FLR 914, FD; Re C (Costs: Enforcement of Foreign Contact Order [2008] 1 FLR 619, FD; JPC v SLW and SMW [2007] 2 FLR 900, FD; Re S (Financial Provision)[2005] 2 FLR 94, CA.

Professional Memberships: FLBA.

Career: Called in 1980. Lincolns Inn.

Personal: Lives in London. One daughter.

RAMSDEN, James QC
39 Essex Chambers, London
020 7832 1111
clerks@39essex.com
Featured in Commercial Dispute Resolution (London)

Practice Areas: International commercial dispute resolution, financial, professional and sports regulatory and commercial public law. James has particular expertise in fraud claims, asset tracing and preemptive remedies. James has extensive international experience, having worked in multiple jurisdictions from Singapore to Iceland.

Professional Memberships: ComBar & Chancery Bar Association.

Publications: Contributor to Butterworths Financial Regulation Service.

RAÑALES-COTOS, Tina
Kings Chambers, Manchester
0345 034 3444
clerks@kingschambers.com
Featured in Commercial Dispute Resolution (Northern)

Practice Areas: Tina Rañales-Cotos practises in chancery and commercial litigation and advisory work, mainly in the specialist courts in Manchester, Liverpool and Leeds (Merchantile and Chancery and TCC). Her work frequently involves interim injunctive relief hearings in the High Court in the business restraint field, including freezing, springboard, misuse of confidential information and restrictive covenant injunctions and search orders. Her specialist practice includes the following areas: Agency (including commercial agency) Banking and finance (including guarantees and indemnities) Civil/commercial fraud (including VAT/MTIC fraud) Confidential Information, Commercial Contracts (including share sale/purchase and warranties) Company (especially shareholder disputes and breach of directors' duties) Competition – UK and EU, Director Disqualification, Employment (contractual and statutory), Discrimination (service providers) Insolvency (corporate and individual), Insurance, Intellectual Property (trademark infringement and passing off), Mediation, Partnership, Professional Negligence, Restraint of Trade including restrictive covenants (commercial and employment) and sale and carriage of goods (domestic and international) and services.
Professional Memberships: Chancery Bar Association Northern Chancery Bar Association Northern Circuit Commercial Bar Association Employment Law Association Northern and North Eastern Circuits Lincoln's Inn.
Career: University of Leicester LLB with Italian 1993-1997 (Universita di Modena, Italy) University of Oxford (Brasenose College) BCL 1997-1998 Lecturer in Competition Law Universities of Oxford and Leicester 1998-1999 Called to the Bar 1999 Hardwicke Scholar and Sir Thomas More Bursar Lincoln's Inn Pupillage at Monckton Chambers, Gray's Inn, London 1999-2000 Lincoln's Inn Stage Scholar – DGIV Competition, Brussels 2000-2001 Joined Kings Chambers in 2001 AGs Provincial Panel – Junior Counsel 2008-2012.
Publications: Financial Times – regular contributor to reader dilemmas on employment law issues.

RANATUNGA, Asitha
Cornerstone Barristers, London
020 7242 4986
asithar@cornerstonebarristers.com
Featured in Licensing (London), Planning (London)

Practice Areas: Asitha specialises in Planning & Environment and Licensing law. Within those fields, his practice incorporates related Administrative & Public Law work. He regularly appears at public inquiries, hearings, and before the Higher Courts. His clients include developers and individuals as well as local authorities and residents' groups. Asitha provides strategic and legal advice across a range of sectors including development (residential, retail, and leisure), infrastructure (renewable energy and highways), and regulatory control (environmental enforcement). In Licensing, Asitha has considerable experience of contested appeals acting for the trade as well as defending licensing authority decisions. Asitha brings approachability and pragmatism to all of his work and draws on 15 years' experience at the Bar. He is consistently ranked as a leading junior in the main guides to the profession.
Professional Memberships: PEBA, IOL, ALBA, UKELA.
Publications: Contributor to "Cornerstone on the Planning Court" and "Licensed Premises: Law and Practice" (Kolvin, 2nd edition).
Personal: Called in 2001 (Inner-Temple). Pembroke College, Cambridge (MA, MPhil in Classics). Bristol Grammar School. Interests: Cricket and Travel.

RANDALL, John QC
St Philips Chambers, Birmingham
0121 246 7010
jrandall@st-philips.com
Featured in Chancery (Midlands), Professional Negligence (Midlands), Commercial Dispute Resolution (Midlands), Company (Midlands), Partnership (Midlands), Real Estate Litigation (Midlands)

Practice Areas: Principal areas of practice are chancery and commercial law, companies, corporate insolvency, judicial review, partnerships, professional negligence and real property.
Professional Memberships: Midland Circuit; International Bar Association; Chancery Bar Association; COMBAR; Midland Chancery and Commercial Bar Association.
Career: Called Lincoln's Inn 1978; Bar of New South Wales 1979; Silk 1995; Assistant Recorder 1995-99; Deputy Head of Chambers 1998-2001; Recorder 1999-2016; Deputy High Court Judge 2000-16; Member, Legal Services Consultative Panel 2000-09; Head of Chambers 2001-04; Barrister and Solicitor of Western Australia 2001; Bencher of Lincoln's Inn 2003; Adjunct Professor, University of New South Wales 2013 (Visiting Fellow 2004-13); Senior Fellow, University of Melbourne 2014.
Publications: Rethinking the Economic Torts (with Simon Deakin) Modern Law Review, 2009; 'The Tort of Conversion' (with Sarah Green), 2009 (Finalist, Inner Temple Book Prize 2011); Caparo v Dickman: Legal Celebrity or Jurisprudential Substance? in 'Cases that Changed our Lives', 2010; Proprietary Estoppel and the Common Intention Constructive Trust – Strange Bedfellows or a Match in the Making? Journal of Equity, 2010; Detinue, Trover and Conversion (with Brendan Edgeworth) in 'Historical Foundations of Australian Law, Vol.II – Commercial Common Law', 2013; Express Termination Clauses in Contracts, Cambridge Law Journal 2014; When Louisa Carlill Caught the Flu (Carlill v Carbolic Smoke Company) in 'Cases that Changed our Lives 2', 2014; Criminal Convictions and the Civil Courts (with Matthew Dyson), Cambridge Law Journal 2015; England's Splendid Isolation (with Matthew Dyson) in 'Comparing Tort and Crime', 2015.
Personal: Educated at Rugby School; Loomis Institute, Conn USA; Jesus College, Cambridge (MA).

RANKIN, James
Francis Taylor Building, London
020 7353 8415
clerks@ftbchambers.co.uk
Featured in Licensing (London)

Practice Areas: With almost thirty years of experience in licensing and regulatory work, James Rankin is widely regarded as one of the leading licensing juniors in the country. He has been ranked as a star junior since 2006. He appears up and down the country on behalf of applicants and objectors. He also represents the police and local authorities on reviews of licences and on appeals from local authority decisions. James has extensive Betting and Gaming experience. He appeared on behalf of The Hippodrome in their successful appeal to license their London casino premises. He advises on internet gaming, together with lotteries and competitions and firearms regulation. He advises The Marine Management Organisation on licensing matters. He has been involved in many of the leading licensing cases involving judicial review of decisions by local authorities and magistrates. His clients are high profile and varied. They include the major operators such as Wetherspoons, Whitbreds and Greene King, together with the smaller operators such as The Mean Fiddler Group. He has represented Aspinall's Casino, Ladbrokes, Corals, Peter Stringfellow, The Mayor of London, The Commissioner of the Metropolitan Police, The Chief Constables of Northamptonshire, Dorset, Devon and Cornwall, Kenwood House, and Garsington House.
Career: Year of Call: 1983; Buckingham University LLB (hons).
Publications: He has lectured for Paterson's, IBC and CLT for over ten years on a wide range of topics relating to licensing and regulation. Examples include enforcement, cumulative impact policies, case law update, test purchases, firearms licensing and the relationship between the licensing and planning regimes.

RATHMELL, Aaron
Serjeants' Inn Chambers, London
020 7427 5000
arathmell@serjeantsinn.com
Featured in Police Law (All Circuits)

Practice Areas: Aaron Rathmell was called to the Bar in 2011. Aaron specialises in public law, police law, discrimination law and medical law. He advises regularly on human rights claims. He also has a growing expertise in the law of investigations. An earlier edition notes that "He stands his ground and doesn't allow himself to be pushed around in the courtroom. He's very careful and considered." Please visit the Serjeants' Inn Chambers website for his profile, which sets out full details of his practice including relevant work of note.

RAUDNITZ, Paul
QEB Hollis Whiteman, London
020 7933 8855
paul.raudnitz@qebhw.co.uk
Featured in Financial Crime (London)

Practice Areas: A leading junior practising in fraud, crime and regulatory law. His reputation in fraud and white-collar crime is particularly strong. He appeared for the Serious Fraud Office in the landmark Deferred Prosecution Agreement case of "SFO v XYZ Ltd". He acted for the Financial Conduct Authority in Operation Cotton – the first land-banking prosecution, and to date the largest criminal matter that the FCA has brought. He is also currently instructed by the Serious Fraud Office in an investigation into alleged legal services funding fraud (Operation Totem). His substantial defence practice has recently included the defence of a company director and Operation Zygos "most-wanted" nominal charged in an extensive horse-racing tipping fraud (Bloor), representing a charity trustee in the "Kids Integrated Cancer Treatment" alleged charities fraud (Weir & others), and advising a plumbing services group in respect of a number of Trading Standards and fraud investigations. Other high-profile cases include leading for the defence of the operations manager in the "Highway" driver-training fraud (Rahman & Others); the defence of the finance director charged in the Cawston Park Psychiatric Hospital alleged "extra care" fraud (Wilson & Breeze); the defence of the company secretary in the Tempaid revenue fraud (Sidhu); leading a team combining the DWP, the Home Office, HMRC and Eurostar in the prosecution of six defendants for the systematic misuse of 400 identities to commit immigration and benefits frauds (Op Boromo); leading for the then Financial Services Authority in its first successful criminal prosecution for boiler room fraud (Mason); leading for Trading Standards in one of its largest counterfeit goods case (Grover & Arura); the successful prosecution of one of City Police's most substantial identity theft cases (Peters) and leading a multi-agency operation uniting CPS Special Casework, UKBA, DWP and HMRC in the successful phased prosecutions of 15+ defendants for a multi-million pound benefits and immigration fraud conspiracy stretching back almost 20 years (Op Spenser). In mainstream crime, the last few years have also seen him instructed in a number of very prominent cases, including representing defendants in both the first Victoria Station murder trial (Akra) and the Camberwell arson murder trial (John-Lewis). In addition, he has a thriving regulatory and professional discipline practice, appearing regularly before the General Medical Council and the General Dental Council (he recently appeared in the highly publicised GMC misconduct case of Dr Adler, relating to the provision of false personal injury reports and the claiming of contingency fees for work as an expert witness).
Professional Memberships: Criminal Bar Association; Association of Regulatory and Disciplinary Lawyers; Public Access Bar Association; Registered with the Bar Council Public Access Directory.
Career: MA (Hons) St John's College, Oxford. Called 1994. Appointed to the CPS external list of advocates at Grade 4 from 2007 (also appointed to the Rape List and Fraud Panel). Appointed to the "A" Panel of the Serious Fraud Office list of counsel from 2009.

RAWLEY, Dominique QC
Atkin Chambers, London
020 7404 0102
drawley@atkinchambers.com
Featured in Professional Negligence (London), Construction (London)

Practice Areas: Dominique specialises in large-scale, high-value commercial disputes located within the UK or in foreign jurisdictions, arising out of construction and engineering projects. Dominique has a particular specialism in disputes concerning large infrastructure and PFI projects, particularly in relation to railways, telecoms, process plants, energy projects (including renewables), natural resources and fire cases. She also specialises in professional negligence, acting for and against construction professionals and their professional indemnity insurers. She has

wide experience of representing clients in the UK high court and appellate courts as well as in arbitration both domestic and international. She frequently deals with commercial issues arising out of bonds, guarantees & warranties, as well as acting in disputes about the jurisdiction of UK or foreign courts or conflicts of laws. In recent years she has acted in a number of international arbitrations including disputes concerning a Russian oil and gas project (ICC arbitration), a Dubai skyscraper (ADCCAC arbitration) and a Middle Eastern processing plant with power co-generation (UNCITRAL arbitration).
Professional Memberships: She is a member of COMBAR, TECBAR and the SCL. She is a TECBAR qualified adjudicator.
Career: BA (Cantab) Law. Called to bar 1991. Silk 2012.
Publications: Co-Author 'Construction Adjudication & Payments Handbook' (OUP, 2013).

RAWLINSON, Michael QC
Kings Chambers, Manchester
0345 034 3444
clerks@kingschambers.com
Featured in Personal Injury (Northern), Personal Injury (All Circuits)
Practice Areas: Personal Injury, Disease Litigation and Clinical Negligence. Significant reported cases include the "Nimrod" and "Snatch Land Rover" inquests; Fairchild v Glenhaven; Sowden v Lodge; Grieves v Everard ('The Pleural Plaques 'test litigation"; Thompson & Rice v Secretary of State for the Department of Trade & Industry; Howe v Houlton & Marshall [2009] EWHC 3344.
Professional Memberships: Northern Circuit Medical Law Association. PIBA.
Career: University: Manchester LLB (Harry Street Tort Prize, Lawson Prize and Dauntsey Scholarship). Inner Temple (Major scholarship).

READ, Graham QC
Devereux, London
020 7353 7534
read@devchambers.co.uk
Featured in Telecommunications (London)
Practice Areas: Specialist in all types of commercial law (including contract law, computer and construction disputes, ADR and arbitration), communications and environmental law. Extensive experience in commercial litigation and all ancillary matters, e.g. conflict of laws (e.g. Connelly v RTZ, and Africa v Cape), arbitration (both as advocate and as arbitrator) and international freezing orders (e.g. Banco Nacional de Commercio v Empressa de Telecommunicaciones [2007] 2 All ER(Comm) 1093). Wide experience of virtually all types of contract dispute including TCC cases (e.g. JDM v DEFRA) and information technology (e.g. Ardentia v BT (2008) 119 Con LR 50). Very extensive knowledge of all aspects of telecoms law, including Interconnect agreements – see e.g. Tonylogo v Totem and BT; regulatory disputes – e.g. Orange v Ofcom [2007] CAT 36, BT v Ofcom (MNO charges) [2008] CAT 12, BT v Ofcom (cost orientation) [2010] CAT 15, and BT v Ofcom (080 numbers) [[2011] 4 All ER 372.and BT v Ofcom (Ethernet) [2014] CAT 21; tariff charging; telecoms misuse and wayleaves. Detailed experience of the postal services sector (e.g. R (DHL) v Ofcom [2016] EWHC 938 (Admin)). Has been involved in some of the largest environmental law disputes e.g. Reay v British Nuclear Fuels, R v Secretary of State for Trade and Industry v ex p Duddridge, Ngcombo v Thor Chemical Holdings.
Professional Memberships: Combar; Professional Negligence Bar Association.
Career: MA Trinity Hall, Cambridge; Arden Scholar Gray's Inn; called 1981.

READE, Kevin
7 Harrington St Chambers, Liverpool
0151 242 0701
clerks@7hs.co.uk
Featured in Family/Matrimonial (Northern)
Practice Areas: Has a wide ranging expertise in all aspects of family law, with an excellent reputation in respect of financial provision on divorce. He has a wealth of experience in dealing with all aspects arising out of substantial asset cases. He engages well with lay and professional clients, analyses issues well, and gives well -reasoned, robust and common sense advice.
Career: Call: 1983.

READY, Hannah
One Brick Court, London
020 7353 8845
hr@onebrickcourt.com
Featured in Defamation/Privacy (London)
Practice Areas: Defamation; data protection; privacy and confidence; freedom of information; harassment; contempt of court and reporting restrictions; media-related human rights law; media-related soft intellectual property law; pre-publication advice; reputation management. Notable recent cases include: Various Claimants v Sir Robert McAlpine Limited & Ors (2014-2016, for the largest group of defendants); Rightio Ltd v Twitter Inc. (2016, for Twitter Inc.). Ongoing cases of interest include: Lachaux v AOL (UK) Ltd [2015] EWHC 2242 (QB) (for AOL, before the Court of Appeal in 2016); "PNM" v Times Newspapers Ltd & Others [2013] EWHC 3177 (QB) and [2014] EWCA Civ 1132 (for "PNM", before the Supreme Court in 2017).
Professional Memberships: Human Rights Lawyers Association; The Media Society.
Career: Graduate scheme in public relations, Fishburn (2008-2009); Call, Lincoln's Inn (2010); pupillage, One Brick Court (2010-2011); tenant, One Brick Court (October 2011-); secondment as a Pegasus Scholar to Levine, Sullivan Koch & Schulz LLP, New York (2012).
Publications: Contributor to Arlidge, Eady & Smith on Contempt (4th Edition, 1st and 2nd Supplements and forthcoming 5th Edition); Co-author of Atkin's Court Forms on Defamation (2014 Issue).
Personal: M.A. (Hons) (First Class), Law, University of Cambridge (Churchill College) (2005-2008); Silverman Sherliker Award for Legal Excellence (2008); Churchill College Scholarship (2008); Lord Denning Scholarship (2009); Hardwicke Entrance Award (2009); Bar Vocational Course, BPP Law School (Outstanding) (2009-2010); Buchanan Prize (2010); Hubert Greenland Scholarship (2010).

REARDON, Madeleine
1 King's Bench Walk, London
020 7936 1500
mreardon@1kbw.co.uk
Featured in Family/Matrimonial (London)
Practice Areas: Madeleine Reardon has deliberately maintained a wide and versatile family law practice which covers all areas of children work, both public and private, financial remedy proceedings and applications under Schedule 1 of the Children Act. She has a particular interest in complex children cases and has recent experience (within the last 12 months) of care proceedings, domestic and international adoption, same-sex parenting (including with an international element: surrogacy and same-sex abduction), internal and international relocation and transfer of residence/intractable contact cases.
Professional Memberships: FLBA; Bar Pro Bono Unit.
Career: Call 2001. Trained as mediator 2006. Deputy District Judge (Civil) 2010. Recorder 2015.
Publications: Update editor, Hershman and McFarlane, Children Law and Practice (Bloomsbury Professional). Co-author, McFarlane and Reardon, Child Care and Adoption Law: A Practical Guide, (Family Law, 2010). Co-author, Black et al, A Practical Approach to Family Law (OUP, 2015).
Personal: Educated Wimbledon High School, London; Magdalen College, Oxford (BA, Classics, 1st class).

REAY, Aidan
Kings Chambers, Manchester
0345 034 3444
clerks@kingschambers.com
Featured in Commercial Dispute Resolution (Northern)
Practice Areas: Commercial litigation Commercial chancery litigation (including insolvency) Aidan appeared for the applicant in Tubelike Limited v Visitjourneys.com Limited [2016] EWHC (Ch) 43 and has a particular focus on commercial disputes in the energy sector.
Professional Memberships: Northern Circuit Commercial Bar Association Committee Northern Circuit British Irish Commercial Bar Association Northern Chancery Bar Association.
Career: Aidan Reay has been a member of Kings Chambers since completing pupillage there in September 2013. Aidan Reay has specialised exclusively in commercial and chancery (including insolvency) litigation since completing pupillage. Prior to undertaking pupillage, Aidan Reay was a research stagiaire at the European Court of Justice in 2009.
Personal: Aidan Reay read law with law studies in Europe at Brasenose College, Oxford, graduating with a first class degree in 2008 and a diploma in French law from the Université Paris II before then going on to Cambridge and graduating with an LL.M. in 2010. Aidan Reay completed the BPTC at City University in 2011 where he was graded outstanding and finished in the top 10 in the year. He was also awarded a Bedingfield Scholarship and a Reid Scholarship from Gray's Inn. Aidan Reay lives in south Manchester and enjoys cooking and cricket.

REDFERN, Alan
One Essex Court, London
020 7583 2000
aredfern@oeclaw.co.uk
Featured in International Arbitration (London)
Practice Areas: Main area of practice is as an arbitrator and adviser on international dispute resolution. Has over 30 years experience of complex international commercial arbitration cases. Before transferring to the Bar in May 1995, was the senior litigation Partner of the international law firm Freshfields.
Professional Memberships: Fellow of Chartered Institute of Arbitrators, former Vice-Chairman of the International Court of Arbitration of the ICC.
Career: Became a litigation Partner in 1963, transferred to the Bar in 1995.
Publications: Redfern and Hunter, 'International Arbitration', Sixth Edition, Oxford University Press, 2015; and articles in law journals, including "Arbitration International" and the "Leading Arbitrators' Guide to International Arbitration".
Personal: Languages: English; French; basic Italian.

REED, Penelope QC
5 Stone Buildings, London
020 7242 6201
clerks@5sblaw.com
Featured in Chancery (London), Court of Protection (All Circuits), Trusts (London)
Practice Areas: Principal area of practice is general chancery work both in the UK and offshore, comprising trust litigation: applications to the Court relating to trusts and drafting of trusts and tax related to these areas; wills, contentious probate, Inheritance Act claims, equitable relief of all kinds and a particular specialism in proprietary estoppel cases. Reported cases include: Wooldridge v Wooldridge (Inheritance Act claim by spouse); Ilott v Mitson [2016] 1 All E.R. 932 (inheritance Act claim by adult daughter); Fielden v Christie-Miller [2015] EWHC 2940 (Ch); [2015] W.T.L.R (will rectification, amendment of statements of case); Watts v Watts [2015] EWCA Civ 1297 (recusal of Judge in probate claim) King v Dubrey [2015] EWCA Civ 581 (donatio mortis causa); Birdseye v Roythorne & Co [2015] W.T.L.R. 961(executors and privilege)⊠ Arif v Anwar [2015] Fam. Law 381 (divorce and proprietary estoppel); Cotton v Earl of Cardigan [2015] W.T.L.R. 39 (Trustees' application for directions); Loring v Woodland Trust[2015] 1 W.L.R. 3238; (Will construction: double nil rate band) Simon v Byford [2014] W.T.L.R. 1097; Burgess v Hawes [2013] WTLR 453 (probate); Berger v Berger [2013] W.T.L.R. 1489 (extension of time in family provision claims) Re M [2013] WTLR 681 (Court of Protection) Suggitt v Suggitt [2012][2012] W.T.L.R. 1607 (proprietary estoppel)⊠ Brudenell Bruce v Moore& Cotton [2012] WTLR 931; Perrins v Holland [2011] 2WLR 1086 (testamentary capacity)⊠ RSPCA v Sharp [2010] WTLR 855, (construction of will); Alkin v Raymond [2010] WTLR 1117 (removal of trustees); Jiggens v Low [2010] BTC 631; ServozGavin [2010] 1 All ER 410 (privileged wills); Thorner v Majors [2009] 1 WLR 776 (proprietary estoppel); Man v Blackman[2008] WTLR 389 (contentious probate); Goodchild v Bradbury [2007] WTLR 463 (CA) (presumed undue influence); Re Harding [2007] EWHC 3 (Ch) (Construction of will); Re Cuncliffe [2006] Ch 361 (CA) (family provision claim); Jones v Jones [2006] WTLR 1847; Price v WilliamsWynn[2006] WTLR 1633; Drew v Daniel [2005] WTLR 807 (CA) (actual undue influence).
Professional Memberships: Chancery Bar Association (Chair 2014-2016); ACTAPS; STEP.
Career: Called to the Bar 1983. Silk 2009. Accredited Mediator. Recorder 2010 Deputy High Court Judge 2013. Lectures widely.

Publications: Co-author of 'Risk and Negligence in Wills, Estates and Trusts', 2nd edition pub. OUP, " Practical Guide to the Trustee Act 2000" (Jordans), "With the best will in the world" (Legalease), "Annotated Trusts and Estates Law Handbook"(Bloomsbury Professional), "Inheritance Act Claims: A Practitioners Guide"(Law Society). Contributor to Butterworths Forms and Precedents (Wills and Trusts) and to "Practical Approach to Joint Property" (pub Bloomsbury Professional).contributor International Trust Litigation (OUP)

REED, Steven
No5 Chambers, Birmingham
+ 44 (0) 845 210 5555
sr@no5.com
Featured in Commercial Dispute Resolution (Midlands)

Practice Areas: Steven advises, drafts pleadings and appears in all types of commercial litigation including contractual, tortious and restitutionary disputes from procedural and interim applications (such as strike out/summary judgment, security for costs and disclosure applications as well as interim remedies including injunctions, freezing injunctions and search orders) to trials. Steven has particular experience in utility disputes and regularly advises and appears on behalf of leading utility providers, shareholder disputes/unfair prejudice petitions, breach of warranty disputes following a share sale and commercial disputes that involve aspects of intellectual property law such as contract disputes in relation to music/software agreements.
Professional Memberships: MCCBA ChBA
Career: Steven graduated with First Class Honours in LLB English and German Law from the University of Kent and the Philipps-Universität, Marburg, Germany before completing an LLM at the University of London. Called to the Bar in 2005, in October 2010 he was named by Legal Week as one of the top ten stars at the commercial and chancery Bar under ten years call.

REES, David
5 Stone Buildings, London
020 7242 6201
clerks@5sblaw.com
Featured in Chancery (London), Court of Protection (All Circuits)

Practice Areas: Traditional chancery practice including trusts, wills, administration of estates, family provision, and capital taxation with particular specialisation in Court of Protection work. Recent reported cases include: Lloyd v Jones & Others [2016] EWHC 1308 (Ch) (contentious probate); Re D [2016] EWCOP 35 (appeal against decision to dispense with service on affected party); Re PJV [2016] EWCOP 7 (role of court in settlement of criminal injury compensation award); Re PA [2015] EWCOP 38 (recognition of foreign order by Court of Protection); A Local Authority v SW [2015] COPLR 29 (habitual residence of incapacitated adult); Parry v HMRC [2014] UKFTT 419 (Inheritance Tax on pension transfer); Baker Tilly v Makar [2013] COPLR 245 (capacity to conduct legal proceedings); Re MN [2010] WTLR 1355 (leading authority on Court of Protection's international jurisdiction).
Professional Memberships: Chancery Bar Association; ACTAPS; STEP; Honorary member of Solicitors for the Elderly.
Career: Called to the Bar 1994. Recorder 2012. Member of the Rules Group advising on drafting of the Court of Protection Rules (2006-7; 2010; 2014-16).
Publications: General Editor Heywood & Massey's Court of Protection Practice. Writes regularly for various professional journals.
Personal: BA Oxford.

REEVE, Matthew
Quadrant Chambers, London
020 7583 4444
matthew.reeve@quadrantchambers.com
Featured in Travel (London), Aviation (London)

Practice Areas: Commercial litigation, including dry shipping, commodities and transport, aviation, international arbitration, sports and media, energy, shipbuilding and construction, energy, insurance and reinsurance, conflicts of laws and jurisdiction disputes.
Professional Memberships: Bencher of the Inner Temple 2009. Council of Management of the Pegasus Scholarship Trust since 2006. Bar Disciplinary Tribunal Panel Member 2004. COMBAR and PNBA. Fellow of the Royal Aeronautical Society.
Career: Magdalene College, Cambridge, BA Law 1984; MA 1988; employed in the Solicitors' Department, Lloyd's of London 1986 and 1987; Called to the Bar 1987 (Inner Temple); Inner Temple Major Award, Paul Methven Award, Duke of Edinburgh Award and Pegasus Scholarship.

REID, Sarah
Kings Chambers, Manchester
0345 034 3444
clerks@kingschambers.com
Featured in Planning (Northern)

Practice Areas: All aspects of town and country planning, highways and rights of way, compulsory purchase, environment, together with administrative and public law. Regularly appears for both developers and local authorities in planning and enforcement inquiries, CPO inquiries, and has appeared at various development plan examinations. Court practice includes statutory challenges (planning) and judicial review.
Professional Memberships: Planning and Environmental Bar Association (PEBA). Northern Circuit. North Eastern Circuit.
Career: LLB Law with Hispanic Law (First Class), University College London. Diploma in Spanish Law, La Universidad de Carlos III, Madrid. BVC (Outstanding – ranked first in the year), College of Law, London. University Tutor, Property I, University College London (2003 – 2004). Appointed Junior Counsel to the Crown, Provincial Panel.

REINDORF, Akua
Cloisters, London
020 7827 4000
contact@cloisters.com
Featured in Employment (London)

Practice Areas: Akua Reindorf is an employment and equality law specialist. She appears for both Claimants and Respondents in tribunals and the Court of Appeal and has significant expertise in managing long-running discrimination trials in the Employment Tribunal. Her practice focuses on complex and often highly sensitive cases. She is valued for her incisive cross-examination, her measured and effective advocacy, her flexibility and ability to think on her feet, and her sensitivity and communication skills with clients. Recent Claimant clients include a gay police officer who successfully claimed that he had been subjected to a six-year campaign of sexual orientation discrimination, and a former director of HR in an NHS trust who was found to have been sexually harassed and discriminated against by the Chair and Chief Executive of the Trust who colluded to remove her. In her Respondent practice Akua frequently receives repeat instructions from commercial, public and voluntary sector clients, and is valued for her pragmatic and responsive advice. Akua is also instructed in civil claims brought under the Protection from Harassment Act. In suitable cases she accepts direct instructions under the Public Access scheme.
Professional Memberships: Discrimination Law Association, Employment Lawyers Association, Employment Law Bar Association, Institute of Employment Rights

REYNOLDS, Kirk QC
Falcon Chambers, London
020 7353 2484
reynolds@falcon-chambers.com
Featured in Real Estate Litigation (London)

Practice Areas: All aspects of property law including landlord and tenant and real property, associated arbitration and professional negligence. Advisor to Royal Institution of Chartered Surveyors on arbitration practice and course tutor on official RICS training courses for arbitrators. Appointed on a number of occasions by President of RICS and/or Law Society as an arbitrator, and by arbitrators as a Legal Assessor.
Professional Memberships: Elected an Honorary Member of RICS in 1997; Honorary Member of ARBRIX; Chancery Bar Association; LCLCBA; Property Bar Association.
Career: Educated at Campbell College, Belfast; Peterhouse, Cambridge (MA 1972); called 1974 (Middle Temple); Silk 1993; Blundell Memorial Lecturer 2002/2010; Honorary Doctor of Laws, University of Bedfordshire; Bencher of the Middle Temple.
Publications: Co-Author, Handbook of Rent Review, The Renewal of Business Tenancies and Dilapidations: the Modern Law and Practice.

RHODES, Nicholas QC
Charter Chambers, London
020 7618 4400
Nick.Rhodes@CharterChambers.com
Featured in Crime (London)

Practice Areas: A highly regarded advocate experienced in corporate criminal and regulatory offences, specialising in serious commercial fraud, bribery and corruption, financial crime, revenue offences, MTIC, money laundering and confiscation. His practice includes advising and representing UK and overseas commercial organisations, legal and finance professionals, on corporate governance issues, regulatory compliance, Financial Services regulation and corporate criminal liabilities from the earliest pre-litigation stage through the processes of investigation and in the event in the Courts or before the Regulators. He has also led a team in Somaliland working for the Horizon Institute under the DFID scheme to rebuild and modernise the Justice System, revise laws, train the senior judiciary and advise the Chief Justice. Considered approachable and client-friendly with a hard-hitting court style, his experience also includes murder, manslaughter and serious organised crime offences in trials conducted in the UK, Northern Ireland and the Cayman Islands. His practice includes appearances before the Courts of Appeal (England and Wales) and (Caribbean) and the House of Lords/ Supreme Court/Privy Council (ex Jamaica). He has also appeared in Courts Martial. He is a Recorder (Crown Court), registered to receive work by direct access and is authorised to practice in a dual capacity.
Professional Memberships: CBA, SE Circuit.
Career: Joint Head of Chambers.
Publications: Nick Rhodes has written published articles on Beating Bribery and Corruption (with Calvin Jackson) and on the Criminal Liabilities of Incorporated and Unincorporated Entities (with Alex Jamieson and Peter Melleney).

RHYS JAMES, Owain
Civitas Law, Cardiff
0845 0713 007
OwainRhysJames@civitaslaw.com
Featured in Administrative & Public Law (Wales & Chester)

Practice Areas: Owain has a busy advocacy and advisory practice across all of chambers' practice areas with a particular emphasis on commercial, property and public law. He prides himself on his attention to detail and clients commend his tenacious advocacy, practical advice and ease with clients. Owain has particular experience of dealing with urgent and without notice injunctions in a commercial, immigration/ asylum, housing, and public law context. He is often instructed at the 11th hour on an urgent basis and is experienced at making out-of-hours applications. He read law at St Catharine's College, Cambridge and previously worked in the Litigation Department at Hugh James Solicitors and brings that experience together with a strong academic background to his practice. An ADR Group accredited mediator, Owain accepts instructions to act as a mediator (in Welsh, English or bilingually where appropriate). A native Welsh speaker Owain is happy to accept instructions through the medium of Welsh. Owain regularly delivers CPD accredited seminars. He has also appeared on BBC Wales, Radio Cymru, ITV Wales and S4C discussing current legal issues.
Professional Memberships: Fellow of the Chartered Institute of Arbitrators
Career: BA (Hons) Law; MA (Cantab) – St Catharine's College, Cambridge; PG Dip Cardiff University; MSc University of South Wales

RICH, Barbara
5 Stone Buildings, London
020 7242 6201
clerks@5sblaw.com
Featured in Chancery (London), Court of Protection (All Circuits)

Practice Areas: Specialises in contentious succession and trusts litigation, and in the property and affairs jurisdiction of the Court of Protection under the Mental Capacity Act 2005. Has dealt with a number of cases of substantial value and/or legal complexity and importance in these fields. She is also an experienced mediator with a rapidly-growing mediation practice, and is regularly in demand for prestigious speaking engagements within her field of expertise. Recent cases: NT v FS [2013]EWHC 684 (COP) ; Re JC, D v JC[2012] MHLO 35 (CoP); Public Trustee v Butler [2012] EWHC 858(Ch); Webster v Ashcroft [2012] 1 WLR 1309.

Professional Memberships: Chancery Bar Association, ACTAPS, STEP.
Career: Called 1990 Gray's and Lincoln's Inn. Accredited mediator ADR Chambers UK.
Publications: Consultant editor of Jordan's 'Elder Law Journal', Assistant Editor 'Heywood & Massey: Court of Protection Practice'.
Personal: Education: St Paul's Girls' School, London; Emmanuel College Cambridge (BA, MA); Polytechnic of Central London (Dip Law). Languages: French.

RICH, Ben
2 Hare Court, London
020 7353 5324
benrich@2harecourt.com
Featured in Professional Discipline (London)
Practice Areas: Ben has a substantial practice appearing before a variety of regulators including the GDC, NMC, the NCTL and panels of the ACCA. He has appeared before the High Court on behalf of registrants. He has dealt with a number of high-profile cases including a six-week hearing involving a nurse in a hospital in Wales where a patient died after receiving very little care. He has advised on judicial review of a regulator's decision. In the healthcare sector, Ben has dealt with cases ranging from assaults on patients, allegations of widespread incompetence and theft of hospital drugs for personal use. He also represents doctors and nurses at inquests, including a nurse who was in charge of a patient recovering from an attempted suicide. The patient wandered off and then fell from a window to his death. Ben maintains a Crown Court criminal practice and so is able to advise and represent clients on criminal matters. Ben prosecutes teachers on behalf of the National College of Teaching and Leadership. These cases often involve sexual allegations relating to vulnerable or young pupils. He also represents the ACCA in cases against accountants.
Professional Memberships: ARDL

RICHARDS, Ian
Pump Court Tax Chambers, London
020 7414 8080
clerks@pumptax.com
Featured in Tax (London)
Practice Areas: Ian Richards specialises in advising both domiciled and non domiciled private clients in respect of all areas of tax, particularly personal tax planning for high net worth individuals, international entertainers and sportsmen, and reviewing current tax structures and strategies in the light of the proposed changes for non domiciliaries.
Professional Memberships: Revenue Bar Association; London Common Law & Commercial Bar Association.
Career: Called 1971, Lincoln's Inn.
Publications: Co-author, Tax Advisers Guide to Trusts (Tolley); Tax Editor, Revenue Volume, Halsbury's Laws; Butterworths Encyclopaedia Forms and Precedents; Akins Court Forms and Hong Kong Stamp Duty (Longmans).

RICHARDS, Jenni QC
39 Essex Chambers, London
020 7832 1111
jenni.richards@39essex.com
Featured in Administrative & Public Law (London), Civil Liberties & Human Rights (London), Community Care (London), Court of Protection (All Circuits), Inquests & Public Inquiries (All Circuits), Local Government (London), Professional Discipline (London)
Practice Areas: Jenni Richards QC has an extensive public law and regulatory practice acting for individuals, public bodies and public interest groups in all areas affected by public law and regulation. Her public law expertise includes local government, human rights, mental health, health care, social (community) care, financial services, education, prison law and immigration/asylum. She is frequently asked to advise public bodies, especially local authorities, NHS bodies and regulators, on a wide range of issues relating to their powers and duties, consultation exercises, regulatory processes, budgetary decision-making and compliance with the Human Rights Act. Recent/current cases include: representing Mr and Mrs M in judicial review proceedings challenging the refusal of the Human Fertilisation and Embryology Authority to allow the expert of their late daughter's frozen eggs; representing the Local Government Association in a judicial review as to NHS England's powers to commission HIV drugs; representing two doctors in a judicial review of an adverse report from the Parliamentary and Health Service Ombudsman; representing the General Medical Council in a judicial review of its guidance relating to assisted suicide; and representing a private prison in a challenge to segregation brought by a high-profile female prisoner with a whole life tariff. Jenni's regulatory and disciplinary work covers a wide range of areas. She has a particular interest in financial services regulation and in the regulation of health care professionals by the GMC, HCPC and others, the regulation of fertility services by the Human Fertilisation and Embryology Authority, the regulation of hospitals and care homes and the regulation of teachers. She acts for regulators and for individual professionals facing fitness to practise or disciplinary allegation in proceedings before conduct/fitness to practise panels, in statutory appeals and in judicial review challenges. Jenni has extensive experience in difficult and sensitive inquests and inquiries, in particular those in which there is a public component such as the responsibility of the state in relation to the cause of death. She represented the Yorkshire Ambulance Service during the recent two year inquest into the Hillsborough disaster. Jenni is often instructed in the most complex or novel cases under the Mental Capacity Act involving difficult decisions relating to capacity, medical treatment (especially end of life cases) and deprivation of liberty.

RICHARDSON, Giles
Serle Court, London
020 7242 6105
grichardson@serlecourt.co.uk
Featured in Chancery (London), Offshore (London), Trusts (London)
Practice Areas: Trust disputes; civil fraud and asset tracing; commercial and banking; company; insolvency; partnership. Recent cases include: Davidson v Seelig [2016] EWHC 549 (Protectors' powers); DIA v Pugachev (trustees subject to freezing & disclosure orders); Emerald Bay v Barclays Wealth (BVI directors' indemnification rights); Barclays Wealth Trustees (Jersey) Ltd v Equity Trust (Jersey) Ltd; A v B [2013] JRC075 (Jersey foundations); FGH Inc v Gecamines [2012] UKPC 27 (implications of incorporation for state owned enterprises.
Professional Memberships: Chancery Bar Association, COMBAR, STEP.
Publications: Co-author of Minority Shareholders: Law, Practice and Procedure.
Personal: born: 1973; Merton College, Oxford 1992-96 (BCL; MA); called to the Bar 1997.

RICHARDSON, Matthew
Henderson Chambers, London
020 7583 9020
mrichardson@hendersonchambers.co.uk
Featured in Information Technology (London)
Practice Areas: Information Technology. Cyber Crime, Construction, Intellectual Property, Finance and Consumer Credit. Matthew is a world acknowledged expert in the field of Cyber-Crime, he has advised several governments on the design of their legislative frame work and has lectured globally on the subject. He has assisted in a number of ground breaking Cyber Law cases. His book Cyber Crime: Law and Practice is the leading practitioner text in the field. Matthew has a general interest in IT and Hi-Tech Law. His advanced qualifications in engineering allow him to understand quickly all of the technical issues in an IT or high-tech case. Many lay clients have commented on his engaged and informed manner. Matthew is responsible for several advancements in IT law including the first injunctions served by Twitter and mobile phone and the first injunction to prevent the use of an illegal bittorrent. Matthew is especially interested in novel hi-tech injunctions and the law related to thinking machines.
Professional Memberships: Admitted to the Bar of the Eastern Caribbean Supreme Court (BVI), Institution of Engineers and Technologists, Society of Computers and Law, Court of Aldermen
Career: Called 2006. MEng. (Hons) St. Peter's College, Oxford, GDL, College of Law, London, BVC, Inns of Court School of Law, Gray's Inn Special Pupillage Award
Publications: Cyber Crime: Law and Practice, Wildy Simmonds and Hill

RICHMOND, Jeremy
Quadrant Chambers, London
020 7583 4444
jeremy.richmond@quadrantchambers.com
Featured in Commercial Dispute Resolution (London)
Practice Areas: Barrister specialising in modern chancery and commercial law and corporate and personal insolvency with an increasing emphasis on cross¬border insolvency. Reported cases include: PST Energy 7 Shipping LLC & Another v OW Bunker Malta Limited & Others [2015] EWCA Civ 1058⊠ Cartus Corporation v. Atlantic Mobility Limited [2014] EWHC 2868 (QB)⊠ Caterpillar (NI) Ltd v. John Holt & Company (Liverpool) Limited [2013] EWCA Civ 779⊠ Levin v Tannenbaum [2013] EWHC 4457 (Ch)⊠ FG Wilson v John Holt & Co. (Liverpool) Limited [2013] EWCA Civ 1232⊠ Moseley v Else Solicitors LLP [2010] BPIR 1192⊠ Re Tulsesense Limited [2010] EWHC 1990 (Ch)⊠ In re Metrocab [2010] EWHC 1317 (Ch)⊠ Peters v Menzies [2009] EWHC 3709 (Ch)⊠ Vertex Trading Sarl v Infinity Holdings Limited [2009] EWHC 461(Ch)⊠ Unadkat & Co. Limited v F Hussain [2008] EWHC 981 (QB)⊠ Re Hawkes Hill Publishing Co. Ltd [2007] BCC 257⊠ Caterpillar Financial Services Limited v Goldcrest [2007] EWCA Civ. 272⊠ Uppal v Uppal and another [2007] EWCA Civ 411⊠ S.E.R.E. Holdings Limited v Volkswagen Group UK Limited [2004] EWHC 1551(Ch)⊠ Shogun Finance v Hudson [2004] 1AC 919⊠ OBG v Allen (Manchester District Registry, February 2004).
Professional Memberships: Commercial Bar Association, Chancery Bar Association; Professional Negligence Bar Association.
Career: Called 2000, Lincoln's Inn; admitted to New York Bar 1996; Associate, Debevoise & Plimpton, New York Office (1995-1998); Associate, Kirkland & Ellis, London Office (1999-2000).
Personal: LLB (Edin.); BCL (Oxon); LLM (Harvard). Enjoys travel and reading.

RICKARD, Susanna
Serjeants' Inn Chambers, London
020 7427 5000
srickard@serjeantsinn.com
Featured in Court of Protection (All Circuits)
Practice Areas: Susanna Rickard was called to the Bar in 2009. Susanna specialises in judicial review, police, human rights, inquests and healthcare law, including extensive Court of Protection and mental health law experience. An earlier edition notes that she is "exceptionally insightful and effective, she cuts through to the real issues" and "a favourite of the Official Solicitor, who is very highly regarded and gets cases above her call because of that." Please visit the Serjeants' Inn Chambers website for her profile, which sets out full details of her practice including relevant work of note.
Professional Memberships: ALBA, Statute Law Society.
Publications: Contributor to the Medical Law Reports and co-author of "Public Order: Law and Practice" Blackstone's Practical Policing, with John Beggs QC and George Thomas, OUP, 2012.

RIDGWAY, Philip
Temple Tax Chambers, London
020 7353 7884
clerks@templetax.com
Featured in Tax (London)
Practice Areas: Philip specialises in all areas of revenue law both corporate and personal, direct and indirect with special emphasis on mergers and acquisitions, demergers and reconstructions, financing, share transactions and loan relationships. He also specialises in the taxation of insolvencies including administrations, liquidations and receiverships. Clients include solicitors, accountants, insolvency practitioners and corporates.
Professional Memberships: Revenue Bar Association; Fellow Chartered Institute of Taxation; Member of the Association of Business Recovery Professionals (R3); Stamp Tax Practitioners Group.
Career: Called to the Bar 1986; Pupillage 1986-87; Paisner & Co 1987-89; Allen & Overy 1989-93; Coopers & Lybrand 1993-96; Deloitte 1996-2007 (Tax Partner 1999); Temple Tax Chambers 2007- present; Visiting Lecturer in Law City University

London (LLM International Tax and EU Tax) 2007- present.
Publications: Co-author with Tim Sanders "Tax Indemnities and Warranties" 3rd ed; Contributor to Lightman & Moss: The Law of Administrators and Receivers of Companies" 5th ed.; Contributor to Totty & Moss; "Insolvency"; Contributor to "Whiteman and Sherry on Capital Gains Tax"; Member of the editorial board of "Insolvency Intelligence". Member Editorial board LexisNexis PSL.
Personal: Born 14th September 1962 Sheffield; Educated City of London Polytechnic (BA Business Law) 1981-84; Cambridge University (LLM) 1984-85; supports Sheffield United.

RIGGS, Samantha
25 Bedford Row, London
020 7242 4986
sriggs@25bedfordrow.com
Featured in Environment (London), Financial Crime (London)
Practice Areas: Established leading junior advising and defending corporate and individual defendants in complex fraud and regulatory investigations and prosecutions with extensive experience in environmental crime with particular expertise in waste management/environmental permitting and statutory nuisance. Often advises pre-interview/pre-charge, is accustomed to taking a pro-active approach at the outset of proceedings and is skilled in taking pre-trial challenges including legality of search warrants, abuse of process arguments and interpretation of the Environmental Permitting Regulations. Experienced in restraint, confiscation and enforcement receivership acting on behalf of defendants and interested third parties. Civil background and experienced in appeals in the VAT Tribunal and before PINs and civil enforcement by the Environment Agency in the High Court. Other regulatory work includes health and safety, food safety, trading standards. Experienced in judicial review. A team player who inspires confidence and described as "a fierce and fearless barrister whom it is good to have on your side". Incredibly hard working, with an eye for detail, great tactician and her technical understanding is simply outstanding earning her much deserved respect. Experienced in working with experts.
Professional Memberships: UKELA, CIWM, POCLA, ARDL, FSLA, CBA Female Fraud Forum.
Career: Called 1996.

RILEY-SMITH, Toby QC
Henderson Chambers, London
020 7583 9020
trileysmith@hendersonchambers.co.uk
Featured in Consumer Law (London), Environment (London), Health & Safety (London), Product Liability (London)
Practice Areas: He has a broad commercial and common law practice with particular emphasis on product liability, health and safety, environmental law, consumer law and banking and finance. He regularly appears in cases involving consumer products, pharmaceutical / medical devices, financial products, environmental pollution or disasters, health and safety litigation, international mass tort claims, sales of goods, cross-border disputes and commercial recovery actions. He has great experience of group litigation in all of his fields - having acted in some of the most high-profile group actions of recent years (including the Tobacco Litigation, the MMR/MR Vaccine Litigation and the PIP Breast Implant Litigation). He has appeared in civil and criminal courts at every level. He has particular experience in inquests.
Professional Memberships: Member of the Personal Injury Bar Association, COMBAR and Health and Safety Lawyers' Association; CEDR Accredited Mediator (2000).
Career: Jules Thorne Scholar, Middle Temple (1994), called 1995. Junior Counsel to the Crown, Attorney General's A Panel (2012).
Publications: Contributor to 'Product Liability Law and Insurance'(2000). Contributor to Volume 9(1) of Halsbury's Laws - Consumer Credit (1998). Contributor to Volume 37 of Halsbury's Laws - 'Practice and Procedure' (2001). Contributing editor of 'Goode: Consumer Credit Law and Practice (Looseleaf). Co-Editor of Butterworths 'Encyclopedia of Forms and Precedents - Consumer Credit' and Blackstone's 'Guide to Consumer Credit Act 2006'; Butterworths' Commercial and Consumer Law Handbook.
Personal: Born 1969; educated Eton College and Trinity College, Cambridge. Married with three children.

RIORDAN, Jaani
8 New Square, London
020 7405 4321
jr@8newsquare.co.uk
Featured in Intellectual Property (London)
Practice Areas: Junior with technical background in computer science and expertise in all fields of intellectual property, media and entertainment, and information technology law. Particular experience in disputes involving the internet, cybersecurity, and computer technology, including interim injunctions, Norwich Pharmacal disclosure, and website blocking orders. Author of leading textbook on intermediary liability. Recent cases include: • Cartier v BSkyB [2016] EWCA Civ 658 (website blocking); • Unwired Planet v Huawei & Samsung [2016] EWHC 94 (Pat) (telecommunications patent claim); • R (BAT) v Secretary of State for Health [2016] EWHC 1169 (Admin) (tobacco plain packaging judicial review); • ITV v TVCatchup [2015] EWCA Civ 204 (copyright); • HHO v Pickwick [2015] EWHC 3407 (IPEC) (copyright); • Trident v Versabuild [2015] EWHC 1609 (Comm) (breach of contract); • Warner-Lambert v Actavis [2015] EWHC 2548 (Pat) (Swiss-form patent claim); and • Thomas Pink v Victoria's Secret [2014] EWHC 2631 (Ch) (trade marks). See www.8newsquare.co.uk for further details.
Professional Memberships: Intellectual Property Bar Association (IPBA); Society of Computers and Law (SCL); Chancery Bar Association (ChBA).
Publications: 'The Liability of Internet Intermediaries' (OUP, 2016).
Personal: Bachelor of Computer Science (1st), Bachelor of Laws (top 1st) (University of Melbourne), Doctorate in Law (University of Oxford, Magdalen College). Previously lectured in contract law, trusts and copyright at the University of Oxford.

RISOLI, Andreá
Old Square Chambers, Bristol
020 7269 0300
wilkinson@oldsquare.co.uk
Featured in Personal Injury (Western)
Practice Areas: Andreá is a specialist personal injury barrister of 11 years call, prior to being called to the bar Andrea practiced as a Solicitor for 7 years and he has in excess of 18 years experience of personal injury litigation. His practice is exclusively in the field of personal injury inclusive of clinical negligence and product liability. Amongst his client base, Andreá is regularly instructed by the panel solicitors of well known Legal Expenses Insurers and Trade Unions. He specialises in serious and catastrophic injury litigation arising out of accidents on the road and at work; these actions can involve life changing injuries inclusive of traumatic brain damage, spinal injury, amputee and brachial plexus injuries. Andreá is used to dealing with complex, high value actions involving multiple specialist experts and he continues to help his clients obtain superb results. Most of his opponents in litigation are high ranking personal injury Counsel. In addition, Andreá is known for his expertise in high-value CICA applications, reviews and Appeals; the applications typically centre upon serious sexual assault, psychiatric injury and traumatic brain injury.

RITCHIE, Andrew QC
9 Gough Square, London
020 7832 0500
clerks@9goughsquare.co.uk
Featured in Personal Injury (London), Clinical Negligence (London)
Practice Areas: Clinical Negligence; Personal Injury; Inquests and Inquiries; Arbitration
Professional Memberships: PIBA Chairman 2014-2016; APIL fellow; Magdalene College Cambridge fellow
Career: 1984 admitted Solicitor; 1985 called Bar; 2009 Silk; 2012 Head of Chambers; 2015 Managing Director of PIcARBS the Personal Injury Claim Arbitration Service; full time barrister, advocate and arbitrator.
Publications: Kemp & Kemp Quantum of Damages: Editor 8 chapters, 2004–2012, Editor of vols 3 and 4 Kemp & Kemp, Law Practice and Procedure: General Editor, 2005–2009 Clinical Negligence Claims: Co-editor, 9GS Guide to RTA Liability: General Editor, Jordans Lexis Nexis LPN: Editor of the Clinical Negligence. Manual Handling Claims: Author, 9GS Asbestos Claims Contributing Editor, 9GS The Journal of Personal Injury Law: General Editor,2000-2003 MIB Claims: Author, 2016, Jordans The Professional Negligence and Liability Reports Co-editor, 1996–1999 Medical Evidence in Whiplash Cases: General Editor, 1996

RITCHIE, Shauna
2 Bedford Row, London
020 7440 8888
sritchie@2bedfordrow.co.uk
Featured in Crime (London), Health & Safety (London)
Practice Areas: Specialist in criminal and regulatory law with particular expertise in serious crime and health and safety. Health and Safety: Wide-ranging experience in cases of gross negligence manslaughter, corporate criminal liability, and inquests. B List Specialist Regulatory Advocate in Health and Safety and Environmental Law for prosecutions on behalf of the Health and Safety Executive, Environment Agency, and Office of Rail Regulation. Advisory and defence work on behalf of companies: from small firms to national chains, individuals, and directors. Notable Cases: Pyranha Mouldings Ltd (Court of Appeal), Claxton Engineering Inquest (quadruple construction fatality), Balfour Beatty Rail Track Systems Ltd (serious industrial injury), Parcol Developments Ltd (gross negligence manslaughter of a three-year-old), Marks & Spencer PLC (asbestos management), Metropolitan Police Commissioner and Others (double drowning). Acts for interested parties at inquests ranging from deaths on the railway to carbon monoxide poisoning, suspected suicide, agricultural and construction industry deaths. High profile inquests have included a crane collapse, a multi-fatality gas explosion, and the death of a teenager falling from a tower block window. Represents medical professionals at inquests in relation to patient deaths. Crime: Defence and prosecution - Instructed in serious and complex cases including murder, serious violence, fraud, excise offences, drugs, and serious sexual offences, including those relating to children. Particular experience in dealing with young or vulnerable defendants and witnesses. Special interest in cases concerning challenges to DNA evidence. Cases in the last year include: Defence junior counsel representing a fourteen-year-old defendant with ADHD in a six handed murder (Liverpool launderette sword stabbing) and in a case involving three-year-old complainants alleging sexual offences; prosecuting a high value fraud on the NHS; junior alone in several historical rape cases.
Professional Memberships: Criminal Bar Association, Health and Safety Lawyers Association
Career: King's College London LLB (Hons), Called 2000 (Lincolns Inn).
Personal: Born 24th January 1978 in Belfast, Northern Ireland.

RITCHIE, Stuart QC
Fountain Court Chambers, London
020 7583 3335
smr@fountaincourt.co.uk
Featured in Commercial Dispute Resolution (London), Employment (London), Fraud (London), Partnership (London)
Practice Areas: Commercial Litigation, Civil Fraud, Employment (directors and senior executives), LLPs, arbitration (domestic and international).
Professional Memberships: COMBAR, Chancery Bar, ELBA, PNBA, LCLCBA.
Career: My practice covers a broad range of commercial and employment disputes. Since taking silk I have acted in a number of high profile commercial disputes, appeared twice in the Privy Council and given expert evidence on English commercial law. A core of my practice involves breaches of fiduciary duty by directors, senior employees, LLP members, agents and joint venturers, civil fraud and disputes concerning employee competition. I am instructed both in litigation and arbitration and am an ADR accredited commercial mediator.
Publications: Fiduciary Duties: Directors and Employees (with Andrew Stafford QC) Jordans 2nd Ed (2015).
Personal: Married with two children, Bencher of Middle Temple, trustee of 4 charities, keen pianist and worsening golfer.

RIVERS, David
Old Square Chambers, London
020 7269 0300
rivers@oldsquare.co.uk
Featured in Personal Injury (London)
Practice Areas: Specialises in high value liability and quantum claims with recent trial successes including a three day trial

in Southend with an award in excess of £400,000, a two day employers liability trial after which damages were agreed in a six figure sum and a history of acting for a well known TV actor, Senior Police officer and a Deputy High Court Judge. Reported cases include Shaw v Merthyr Tydfil County Council [2015] CA PIQR P8; Prison Officers Association v Iqbal [2009] EWCA Civ 1310, Court of Appeal (Civ Div); Bates v Maylon [2008] EWHC 2386(QB); Hau v Jim [2007] EWHC 3358 (QB). He is currently instructed for the appellant in the Court of Appeal in a case which he won at first instance but where the damages were lower than he had advised.
Professional Memberships: PIBA
Career: Called Grays Inn 2002. Educated Royal Grammar School Newcastle and Jesus College Cambridge MA (cantab) LLM.
Publications: Author of four of the Chapters in Munkman on Employers Liability (16th Edition 2013) including those on contributory negligence and employers liability insurance.

RIVETT, James
Pump Court Tax Chambers, London
020 7414 8080
clerks@pumptax.com
Featured in Tax (London)
Practice Areas: James' practice includes advice and litigation in all areas of revenue law, including personal taxes, corporate taxes and VAT. Recent cases include Forde and McHugh v HMRC (Supreme Court), Bristol and West v HMRC (Court of Appeal), ING Intermediate Holdings v HMRC (Upper Tribunal), V v T A (Chancery Division) and the Ingenious Film Partners litigation before the Tax Tribunals.
Professional Memberships: Chancery Bar Association; Revenue Bar Association; VAT Practitioner's Group; International Fiscal Association.
Career: Called 2004 (Lincoln's Inn); Feb 2009 – Appointed Junior Counsel to the Crown – "C" panel; Dec 2013 – Appointed Consultant Lecturer, Sotheby's Institute of Art; March 2014 – appointed to the Attorney's General's Panel (B Panel).
Publications: Contributor to Potter and Monroe's Tax Planning with Precedents and Atkins Court Forms (Revenue); author of the statutory construction and anti-avoidance chapters of Simon's Direct Tax Service.
Personal: MA (Cantab)(Starred Double First), Clare College, Cambridge; MPhil, Corpus Christi College, Cambridge. Postgraduate Diploma in Law, City University, London (Lord Bowen Scholarship and Hardwicke Award, Lincoln's Inn, 11 King's Walk prize for Public Law, City University); Bar Vocational Course(Lord Denning Scholarship, Lincoln's Inn)

ROBERTS, Catherine
Erskine Chambers, London
020 7242 5532
croberts@erskinechambers.com
Featured in Company (London)
Practice Areas: Specialist in company law and in commercial litigation involving issues of company law, corporate insolvency, shareholder disputes, professional negligence and partnership disputes; strong advisory practice in the same areas. Much in demand for both her forensic advocacy and cross-examination skills. Author of Financial Assistance for the Acquisition of Shares (OUP 2005) and co-author of Company Meetings and Resolutions- Law, Practice and Procedure (OUP 2013).
Professional Memberships: COMBAR. Chancery Bar Association.
Career: Churchill College Cambridge MA LLM. Called to Lincoln's Inn 1986.
Publications: Financial Assistance for the Acquisition of Shares (OUP 2005); Company Meetings and Resolutions- Law, Practice and Procedure (OUP 2013).

ROBERTS, Gemma
No5 Chambers, Birmingham
+ 44 (0) 845 210 5555
gr@no5.com
Featured in Employment (Midlands)
Practice Areas: A combative and committed advocate who specialises in all areas of employment law, with particular expertise advising and representing in discrimination, TUPE, whistleblowing, breach of contract and dismissal claims in the ET and EAT. She acts for both claimants and respondents and her clients include multi-national and FTSE 100 companies, NHS Trusts, local authorities, trade unions, employment agencies, educational establishments and charities. Notable cases include Wilcox v Birmingham CAB Services Ltd [2011] EqLR810 and Hibbins v Hestors Way Neighbourhood Project [2009] IRLR 198 EAT.
Professional Memberships: ELBA, ELA, Gray's Inn.
Career: MA, Oxford University; Philosophy Politics and Economics; Gray's Inn (Lord Uthwatt Scholar 2005).
Personal: Gemma enjoys running marathons and trans-ocean yacht sailing.

ROBERTS, James
1 King's Bench Walk, London
020 7936 1500
jroberts@1kbw.co.uk
Featured in Family/Matrimonial (London)
Practice Areas: Practice is divided between the areas of financial remedy proceedings, schedule 1 Children Act 1989 disputes, international child abduction, leave to remove permanently from the Jurisdiction and private law child arrangement / contact disputes. Many of his cases have an international element. Experienced in finance cases involving offshore trusts and complex corporate structures and the tracing of assets. Recommended for both financial remedy and children work he often deals with both the finance and children's side of cases. Sits as a Recorder (part time Judge) in the Financial Remedies Unit of the Central Family Court hearing finance cases and is a qualified arbitrator, undertakes private FDRs / Early Neutral Evaluations and is a mediator.
Professional Memberships: Treasurer Family Law Bar Association (FLBA) 2005 to date. FLBA (Elected National Committee Member since 1997). Bar Council Quality Advisory Panel. Family Mediators Association. Director, Institute of Family Law Arbitrators Ltd. Fellow of International Academy of Family Lawyers. MCIArb.
Career: Called 1993. Recorder in 2009 (Family Private and Public Law and Crime). Authorised to hear Financial Remedy cases at the Central Family Court. IFLA Arbitrator. MCIArb.
Publications: Wildblood & Eaton (Enforcement Chapter).
Personal: Born 21 September 1969. Oriel College, MA Oxon. (Jurisprudence).

ROBERTS, Stuart
St Philips Chambers, Leeds
0113 224 6691
sroberts@st-philips.com
Featured in Chancery (North Eastern)
Practice Areas: An established chancery and commercial practitioner, Stuart is regularly instructed on high value cases in the High Court, both in London and on circuit. He is a fearless trial advocate, an incisive cross-examiner and a tough and effective negotiator. Clients appreciate his clear approach and no-nonsense advice. He covers general commercial work, including international litigation and commercial fraud. This spans misrepresentation, partnership disputes, guarantees, shareholder disputes, directors' disqualification, insurance, professional negligence, and springboard injunctions and restrictive covenants in employment and business sales agreements. His chancery practice covers all aspects of trust law, property, TOLATA cases, and proprietory estoppel. He has particular expertise in will disputes and Inheritance Act cases; and Court of Protection matters – statutory wills and disputes about Deputies. Recent cases: NT v FS & Others, [2013] EWHC 684 (COP) – a leading case on statutory wills: a dispute about the making of a statutory will for a businessman with assets of £3 million who lacked capacity. 2016 QBD – defending a businessman facing claims of over £7.5m relating to alleged misrepresentation and misuse of investment funds. 2016 – Defending ongoing director's disqualification proceedings in the Isle of Man, amongst the largest such cases ever brought there, regarding a large network of inter-related companies, where investors suffered multi-million pound losses, and involving accusations of mismanagement and fraud. Alex Lawrie Receivables v Billany 2014 QBD London – successfully acted for Defendant facing a claim for £7.7m on a guarantee, following a 15 year invoice discounting fraud. Pratt v Kingsley 2016 ChD London – successfully acted for beneficiary under a will, which did not come to light for five years after the deceased's death, and was challenged as being forged.
Professional Memberships: Chancery Bar Association.
Career: Oxford University, BA: 2:1 History; Entrance Exhibition, Balliol College. Date of call: 1994.

ROBERTSON, Patricia QC
Fountain Court Chambers, London
020 7583 3335
pr@fountaincourt.co.uk
Featured in Professional Negligence (London), Banking & Finance (London), Commercial Dispute Resolution (London), Financial Services (London), Professional Discipline (London)
Practice Areas: Civil and commercial: in particular, professional negligence (especially relating to financial and legal services), banking (including internet banking and plastic money), financial services (in particular, disputes relating to investment management or misselling), legal services (including advice on compliance and on ABSs), professional discipline (in particular, relating to lawyers, accountants, auditors and financial services) and judicial review of regulatory bodies. Advisory work relating to electronic commerce, electronic money, regulation of financial services and regulation of legal services. Contributor to 'The Law of Bank Payments', editors Brindle and Cox, Sweet and Maxwell 2004, on plastic money and on internet payments, 'Professional Negligence and Liability', editor Simpson, on liability of expert witnesses and liability of fund managers, "Legal Services Act 2007" ed Miller & Thorne and Cordery on Legal Services. Extensive experience of mediation of very large commercial and professional negligence claims as advocate and now also an accredited CEDR mediator.
Professional Memberships: COMBAR, London Common Law and Commercial Bar Association, Bar European Group. Past member ICC United Kingdom Electronic Commerce Group.
Career: Called to the Bar in 1988. Joined Fountain Court 1989. Stage in Brussels 1991. Took Silk in 2006. Board of Bar Standards Board from January 2010. Vice Chair of Bar Standards Board from January 2013-Dec 2015. Bencher of Inner Temple. Member of Abu Dhabi Global Markets Appeals Panel. Appointed Deputy High Court Judge 2016.
Publications: Chapters on the liability of Expert Witnesses and on the liability of Fund Managers in Professional Negligence and Liability (ed. Simpson, Informa, Looseleaf). Chapters on Plastic Money and on Internet payments in The Law of bank Payments (eds. Brindle & Cox, 3rd Ed. Sweet and Maxwell). Chapters on the new regulatory regime and on the Legal Services Board in The Guide to the Legal Services Act 2007 (eds. Miller & Thorne, Butterworths Lexis-Nexis, 2009) and in Cordery on Legal Services.
Personal: Educated at St. George's, Edinburgh and Balliol College, Oxford (Brackenbury Scholar; BA 1986). Duke of Edinburgh Scholarship, Inner Temple, 1988. Born 1964. Languages: French and Italian.

ROBINS, Stephen
South Square, London
020 7696 9900
stephenrobins@southsquare.com
Featured in Banking & Finance (London), Fraud (London), Restructuring/Insolvency (London)
Practice Areas: Stephen specialises in the fields of insolvency and restructuring, banking and finance, commercial dispute resolution and civil fraud. His practice areas also include company law, real property, insurance and financial services.
Professional Memberships: Commercial Bar Association; Chancery Bar Association; Insolvency Lawyers' Association.
Career: Stephen has been instructed in a number of cases in the Supreme Court, the Court of Appeal and the Privy Council (BNY Mellon Corporate Trustee Services v LBG Capital, Singularis v PwC, Saad, Lehman Waterfall, Rubin v Eurofinance, Nortel/ Lehman, Landsbanki v Heritable, Firth Rixson, Tambrook and Ovenden Colbert), Other recent cases include Lehman Brothers International (Europe) (for the administrators); Kaupthing (for the winding-up board); IBRC (for the liquidators); Landsbanki (for the winding-up board); Bernard L Madoff Investment Securities (for the trustee); Rangers (for the administrators); Afren (for the administrators); African Minerals (for the administrators); Luminar (for the administrators); MF Global (for the Chapter 11 trustee); Sanko (for the Japanese trustee); Metinvest BV (restructuring).
Publications: Contributor to 'International Corporate Rescue'; 'Insolvency Intelligence'; 'A Practitioner's Guide to Directors' Duties and Responsibilities'; 'Company Directors:

Duties, Liabilities & Remedies'; 'Trusts & Trustees'.

ROBINSON, Laura
Tanfield Chambers, London
020 7421 5300
LauraRobinson@tanfieldchambers.co.uk
Featured in Employment (London)
Practice Areas: An employment law specialist undertaking the full range of employment matters at all levels. Particular expertise in discrimination, whistleblowing and TUPE. Laura acts for a wide range of clients including government departments, local authorities, the NHS, private companies and private individuals.
Professional Memberships: Employment Lawyers Association (ELA); Employment Law Bar Association (ELBA); Employment Law Appeal Advice Scheme (ELAAS); Bar Pro Bono Unit (BPBU).
Career: Called 2001; Joined Tanfield Chambers 2010; Appointed to the Attorney General's B Panel from September 2015.
Personal: PGDL College of Law Guildford; BSc (Hons) Natural Sciences – University of Durham

ROCHFORD, Thomas
St Philips Chambers, Birmingham
0121 246 7000
trochford@st-philips.com
Featured in Personal Injury (Midlands), Clinical Negligence (Midlands)
Practice Areas: Tom practises principally in the fields of clinical negligence and personal injury, mostly representing claimants. His PI work arises from both trauma and disease and includes claims under the FAA. His workload tends to be in complex and high value cases, usually requiring detailed schedules of loss. Several recent cases have involved issues of co-morbidity, for example, a victim of childhood polio who suffered a hip fracture (caused by first defendant) that was negligently treated by second defendant with very disabling consequences. He has been instructed in professional negligence cases arising from the negligent conduct of personal injury claims. Tom also has a thriving employment practice which is mainly tribunal based. Tom's cases include Nicholls v Ladbrokes Betting and Gaming Ltd [2013] EWCA Civ 1963 (CA); Woods v Pasab Ltd [2013] IRLR 305 (CA); and Andrews v Kings College NHS Foundation Trust [2012] EqLR 1032 (EAT).
Professional Memberships: APIL, PIBA, ELA, ELBA.
Career: Called 1984. Recorder (Crown and County Court) since 2005.
Personal: Cambridge University (MA) (Law).

ROGERS, Amy
11KBW, London
020 7632 8500
amy.rogers@11kbw.com
Featured in Administrative & Public Law (London), Commercial Dispute Resolution (London), Employment (London)
Practice Areas: Amy Rogers has a broad litigation practice, across all areas of commercial, employment and public law. She is frequently instructed in conspiracy and economic tort claims, restraint of trade and team poaching disputes, in claims involving breaches of directors' duties, fiduciary duties, and duties of confidence, and in broader commercial litigation and arbitration, including disputes with a substantial cross-border element. In the public law field, Amy's practice is broad, with a particular focus on the use of public law litigation to protect commercial interests. Her recent work includes acting for the Iranian commercial bank Bank Mellat in sanctions litigation culminating in a successful Supreme Court challenge to the Financial Restrictions (Iran) Order 2009 and in the Bank's Commercial Court damages claim.
Professional Memberships: COMBAR, ELA, ELBA, ALBA, BEG. Member of the ELA International Committee.
Career: Called to the Bar 2007. Member of the Attorney General's B Panel of Counsel.
Publications: Contributor to Halsbury's Laws on Judicial Review, Supperstone, Goudie and Walker on Judicial Review and Tolley's Employment Law Handbook.

ROGERS, Beverly-Ann
Serle Court, London
020 7242 6105
BARogers@serlecourt.co.uk
Featured in Mediators (All Circuits)
Practice Areas: Mediation across a wide range of chancery and commercial disputes. Recent examples include claims under Inheritance (Provision for Family and Dependants) Act 1975; breach of trust claims involving substantial international trusts; shareholder disputes; landlord and tenant disputes; professional negligence claims against solicitors and accountants; employment disputes with allegations of sex-discrimination and whistle-blowing; breakdown in professional partnerships. Experienced in multi-party and cross-cultural disputes.
Professional Memberships: Chancery Bar Association. Association of Contentious Trust and Probate Specialists. PIM: Senior Mediators.

ROGERS, Gregory
St Ives Chambers, Birmingham
0121 236 0863
gregory.rogers@stiveschambers.co.uk
Featured in Family/Matrimonial (Midlands)
Practice Areas: Family Child Care, Family Matrimonial, Family Finance
Professional Memberships: FLBA
Career: Greg's practice is exclusively family orientated; He deals with all matters concerning children and matrimonial finance. The major part of his children practice is concerned with public law proceedings in which he has experience of dealing with issues including non-accidental injuries, factitious illness, sexual abuse as well as neglect and cases involving emotional abuse. He has acted for Local Authorities, parents and children. In respect of financial matters, Greg has experience dealing with both Ancillary Relief, TOLATA claims and applications under Schedule 1 Children Act 1989. He is regularly instructed in high net worth cases involving business assets, overseas properties and assets.

ROGERS, Heather QC
One Brick Court, London
020 7353 8845
hxr@onebrickcourt.com
Featured in Defamation/Privacy (London)
Practice Areas: Media and information law: defamation, privacy/breach of confidence, data protection, freedom of information, reporting restrictions/contempt, judicial review. Defamation includes: Cruddas v Calvert [2015] EWCA Civ 171; Flood v Times Newspapers [2012] UKSC 11 (Reynolds defence); British Chiropractic Association v Singh [2011] 1 WLR 133 CA (comment); Harper v Seaga [2009] 1 AC 1 PC (privilege); Galloway v Telegraph (2006) EMLR 11 CA; trials include Polanski v Condé Nast, David Irving v Deborah Lipstadt/Penguin Books. Privacy/confidence includes: Hutcheson v News Group [2012] EMLR 2 CA; Ntuli v Donald [2011] 1 WLR 294 CA; Napier v Pressdram [2010] 1 WLR 934 CA (Private Eye: injunction); Harrods v Times [2006] EMLR 13 CA (public interest/disclosure) and Spycatcher litigation [1990] 1 AC 109. Other: R (Nicklinson) v Ministry of Justice [2014] UKSC 38 (assisted dying/Article 8); R v ITN [2014] 1 WLR 199 (reporting restriction); Axel Springer v Germany (No 2) [2014] ECHR 745 (for intervener); R (Guardian News) v Westminster Magistrates [2013] QB 618 (open justice).
Career: Called 1983 (MT); QC 2006. Trustee of Article 19 (2004-2012). Director of Campaign for Freedom of Information (2014-).
Publications: Co-author Duncan & Neill on Defamation (4th ed) (2015).

ROLFE, Patrick
5 Stone Buildings, London
020 7242 6201
clerks@5sblaw.com
Featured in Real Estate Litigation (London)
Practice Areas: Landlord and Tenant. Commercial and residential, including issues of security of tenure and renewal, disputes about alienation, user and disrepair, as well as service charge liability and recovery. Conveyancing and title disputes, in relation to both registered and unregistered land (including adverse possession). Trusts of Land and beneficial ownership issues arising under trusts of land, constructive and resulting trusts. Mortgages. As well as disputes regarding enforceability, the work extends to more complex questions of priorities between mortgages. Rights in respect of land. Option agreements, overage provisions, restrictive covenants, easements and other incorporeal hereditaments. Professional Negligence. Disputes associated with these areas of work.
Professional Memberships: Property Bar Association, Chancery Bar Association, Professional Negligence Bar Association
Career: Called to the Bar in 1987, with wide experience of conducting litigation, including before specialist property tribunals such as the UT (Lands Chamber) and FTT (Property Chamber), and recommended for real estate litigation in both Chambers & Partners and Legal 500. High-quality client base, which includes not only instructions from specialist property solicitors but also direct referrals from major industry players, their agents and advisors. For further information visit www.5sblaw.com

ROMNEY, Daphne QC
Cloisters, London
020 7827 4068
dr@cloisters.com
Featured in Employment (London)
Practice Areas: Daphne is an expert in high-value, very complex litigation and is known as a fearsome advocate, specialising in all forms of employment law and, in particular, discrimination, equal pay and victimisation claims. She has a broad range of clients, from multi-national companies, banks and universities to high profile individuals to thousands of local authority employees bringing mass equal pay claims against their employers . She secured the largest ever equal pay settlement for her 4,000 clients against Birmingham City Council, and has secured other substantial settlements in similar claims against against North Lanarkshire CC (after 48 days of hearing) and Fife Council. She acted for Boots in a long-running dispute over its changes to the Sunday supplements. Daphne also appears in the High Court, including restrictive covenants and contract claims and for a Sainsbury's manager suing for wrongful dismissal (Adesokan v Sainsbury's, appeal to be heard in December 2016). She appeared in Manchester NHS v Fecitt (whistleblowing) and Kemeh v Ministry of Defence (agency and race discrimination) in the Court of Appeal. She acted for former Super-Head Jo Shuter, as well as appearing in disciplinary tribunals and hearings for sportsmen, pharmacists, doctors, teachers and councillors. Recently she acted for Denise Aubrey, former Director of Legal Services in a lengthy case against Northumbria Police in the Newcastle Employment Tribunal, for the liquidator of Keeping Kids Company in a claim by its former employees for a protective award and a salesman dismissed by JP Morgan.
Professional Memberships: ELBA (and Chair 2007-09). ELA (Committee Member 2014-2016). ILS.
Career: Called 1979. Silk 2009. In addition to her practice, she lectures extensively for Michael Rubinstein's 22 QCs series, ILS, ELA and others and comments on legal matters in the media.
Personal: Devoted Arsenal season ticket holder. Trustee of Save A Child, a charity paying for education for children living in orphanages in Bengal and Delhi.

ROOTS, Guy QC
Francis Taylor Building, London
020 7353 8415
clerks@ftbchambers.co.uk
Featured in Local Government (London), Planning (London)
Practice Areas: Guy Roots QC specialises in town and country planning, environment, compulsory purchase and compensation, rating and valuation, and other local government and administrative law subjects. He advises a wide spectrum of clients including companies, local authorities, government and other agencies and individuals. Examples of major schemes in which he acted for the promoter include: London Olympic Games 2012; regeneration of Greenwich Peninsula; decommissioning of Trawsfynydd Nuclear Power station; Terminal 5 at Heathrow; new electricity transmission lines for National Grid and EDF. He is one of the leading experts on compulsory purchase, compensation for compulsory purchase and other categories of statutory compensation, rating and land valuation. He has appeared in many compensation cases in the Lands Tribunal and Upper Tribunal including several arising out of the Channel Tunnel Rail Link and he is advising in relation to claims for compensation for Crossrail. He has also appeared in the Lands Tribunal and Court of Appeal in Hong Kong, the Grand Court and Court of Appeal of the Cayman Islands, a Board of Assessment in the British Virgin Islands and the Eastern Caribbean Court of Appeal.
Professional Memberships: Past chairman of the Planning and Environment Bar

Association (PEBA) (2000-04). Member of Compulsory Purchase Association and the National Infrastructure Planning Association. Member of the DETR's Compulsory Purchase Policy Review Advisory Group. Assistant Boundary Commissioner.
Career: Called to Bar: 1969; QC: 1989. MA in Jurisprudence from Oxford University. Harmsworth Scholar (Middle Temple). Bencher of Middle Temple. Fellow of the Society of Advanced Legal Studies.
Publications: 'The Law of Compulsory Purchase' (2nd Ed 2011) published by Bloomsbury Professional ; 'Compulsory Purchase and Compensation Service' (looseleaf) published by Bloomsbury Professional. 'Ryde on Rating and the Council Tax' published by Butterworths/LexisNexis.

ROSE, Paul QC
Old Square Chambers, London
020 7269 0300
roseqc@oldsquare.co.uk
Featured in Personal Injury (London)
Practice Areas: Personal injury and employment law. In employment law has acted in leading cases in discrimination, unfair dismissal and Transfer of Undertakings Regulations. In personal injury acted on behalf of the plaintiffs in Opren litigation, Benzodiazepine litigation, British Midland air crash, Camelford Water Pollution, Mull of Kyntyre helicopter crash. Acted in a substantial number of catastrophic injury claims particularly involving servicemen in claims against Ministry of Defence. Recent cases include: Harman v Boyles [2015], Quantum: TBI, settled for lump sum of £1.5m, PP. £125,000 pa; ST v VB [2015] (Quantum Tetraplegia, settled for lump sum of £3m, PP. £175,000 – lump sum equivalent £8m); GC v RD [2015] (Quantum: Below knee amputation and head injury, lump sum of £2.5m); SH v ML and JH v ML [2015] (Contested IP application to purchase property for two children with TBI); Lightfoot v Go Ahead Group PLC [2011] RTR 11 (RTA contributory negligence); Johnson Controls Ltd v Campbell [UKEAT 0042/12] (Service Provision Change); Caston v Chief Constable Lincolnshire Police [2010] IRLR 327 (Time limits, Discrimination); IB v CB [2010] EWHC 3815(QB) (Content of periodical payments offer); James v Redcats (Brands) Ltd [2007] IRLR 296 (meaning of 'worker' ; Sowerby v Charlton [2006] 1 WLR 568 (Court of Appeal – pre action admissions); Scott v Commissioners of Inland Revenue [2004] IRLR 713 (Court of Appeal: compensation under Sex Discrimination Act 1975); Mattis v Pollock [2003] IRLR 603 (Court of Appeal: scope of vicarious liability); Franks v Reuters [2003] IRLR 423 (meaning of 'employee' in Employment Rights Act 1996); Croft v Royal Mail [2003] IRLR 592 (Court of Appeal discrimination, transsexual) Liversidge v Chief Constable of Bedfordshire Police [2002] IRLR 15 (vicarious liability under Race Relations Act 1976); Bici v Ministry of Defence Times [2004] EWCH 786 (QB).(Scope of combat immunity). Paul Rose speaks regularly at professional conferences on topical issues in the areas he specialises in.
Professional Memberships: ELA, ELBA, PIBA.
Career: Called to Bar 1981, Silk 2002, Fee Paid Employment Judge since 2003.

ROSEMAN, Gideon
Ten Old Square, London
020 7405 0758
GideonRoseman@tenoldsquare.com
Featured in Partnership (London)
Practice Areas: Gideon Roseman is a Chancery and commercial litigator. He advises in contentious and non-contentious partnership matters, representing both firms and LLPs as well as individual partners and members, including professional practices, such as solicitors, financial advisers and recruitment consultants and property developers. He has significant experience of high value and complex litigation in Court and arbitration. He is regularly instructed to attend mediations. He has recently appeared as sole counsel in a number of successful appeals in the Court of Appeal in relation to partnership and shareholder disputes. He also specialises in commercial litigation, commercial fraud, insolvency, shareholders' disputes, property litigation (domestic and international), professional negligence and wills and trust disputes. He has particular expertise in relation to worldwide and domestic freezing orders, as well as other interlocutory prohibitory and mandatory injunctions.
Professional Memberships: Gideon is a member of the Chancery Bar Association and a subcommittee member of the Association of Partnership Practitioners.
Career: Called to the Bar (Inner Temple): 2007. Recent cases include: Re Stay in Style (A Firm) [2016] EWHC 1688 (Ch); Muhammad and ors v ARY Properties Ltd and ors [2016] EWHC 1968 (Ch); Re Stay in Style (A firm) [2016] EWHC 1041 (Ch); Khawaja v Popat [2016] EWCA Civ 362; Otuo v Brierley [2016] EMLR 6; Otuo v Brierley [2015] EWHC 1938 (Ch); Popat v Khawaja [2015] EWHC 2481 (Ch); Eaton v Caulfield [2015] 1 BCLC 634; Otuo v Brierley [2014] EWCA Civ 1804; Bari v Alternative Finance Ltd [2014] Lexis Citation 93; and Otuo v Brierley [2013] EWHC 2869 (Ch).

ROSENTHAL, Adam
Falcon Chambers, London
020 7353 2484
rosenthal@falcon-chambers.com
Featured in Real Estate Litigation (London)
Practice Areas: All aspects of commercial and residential real property, landlord and tenant and related professional negligence and insolvency.
Professional Memberships: Chancery Bar Association; LCLCBA; Property Bar Association.
Career: Educated at King David High School, Liverpool; St Catherine's College, Oxford (BA Law/French Law 1998); called 1999 (Gray's Inn).
Publications: Co-Author, Commercial and Residential Service Charges (2013); Contributor, Fisher & Lightwood's 'Law of Mortgage' (2010); joint editor, Barnsley's Land Options 5th Edn (2009).

ROSENTHAL, Dennis
Henderson Chambers, London
020 7583 9020
drosenthal@hendersonchambers.co.uk
Featured in Consumer Law (London)
Practice Areas: Consumer credit; consumer law; retail banking and finance; financial services; asset finance and security; entire range of credit, leasing, mortgage and security documentation; ancillary regulated documents; online transactions; exempt agreements; title retention and security issues; sale and purchase of receivables and portfolios of agreements; advertising and promotions. Banking products and procedures; Payment Services Regulations. Commercial contracts and discrete contractual provisions. Exemptions and unfair contract terms. Financial services including FCA Handbook, CONC, MCOB etc.; FCA authorisation; overseas entities, operations and procedures. Interest rate swops and PPI claims. Client identification procedures, anti-money laundering, fraud prevention and data protection. Due diligence.
Professional Memberships: COMBAR.
Career: Attorney of the Supreme Court of S Africa (1969); Solicitor, England (1977);formerly partner Berwin Leighton Paisner LLP; called to Gray's Inn and joined Henderson Chambers in 2009.
Publications: Editor of Goode: Consumer Credit Law and Practice; Goode: Consumer Credit Reports; Encyclopaedia of Forms and Precedents (Consumer Credit); Contributor to Halsbury's Laws of England on Consumer Credit (4th Ed.); Author of 'Consumer Credit Law and Practice – a Guide' (4th Ed., Bloomsbury Professional) and 'Financial Advertising and Marketing Law' and contributor to various publications.
Personal: BA LLB (Witwatersrand); BA (Hons) University of S Africa.

ROSS, James
Gough Square Chambers, London
020 7353 0924
james.ross@goughsq.co.uk
Featured in Consumer Law (London)
Practice Areas: All aspects of consumer and regulatory law, especially banking and finance (including consumer credit), commercial litigation, mortgages, insolvency and regulatory crime.
Professional Memberships: Consumer Credit Forum; Finance Litigation Forum
Career: Called Inner Temple (2006). Regularly appears in court and advises on issues relating to financial services, consumer credit, payment services, electronic money, mortgages and commercial disputes. Acted as a sole advocate in the Court of Appeal on behalf of a finance company in Kulkarni v Manor Credit (Davenham) Limited [2010] 2 Lloyd's Rep 431. Successfully appeared in Barnes v Black Horse Limited [2011] 2 All ER (Comm) 1130, leading authority on transitional provisions in the Consumer Credit Act 2006 relating to unfair relationships and extortionate credit bargains. Successfully represented the bank in Santander UK plc v Harrison [2013] Bus LR 501, leading authority on the meaning of "credit in the form of a cash loan" and the interaction between securitisation and unfair relationships under the Consumer Credit Act 1974.
Publications: General editor of the textbook 'Modern Financial Regulation'.
Personal: LLB (First Class) King's College London (2005). Duke of Edinburgh and Major Exhibition scholarships awarded by the Inner Temple.

ROUSE, Justin QC
9 Bedford Row, London
020 7489 2727
justin.rouse@9bedfordrow.co.uk
Featured in Crime (London)
Practice Areas: Murder, Serious Fraud, Serious Sexual offences, Allegations involving a partner or children, Firearms Offences , Food Crime, Disciplinary Hearings.
Professional Memberships: CBA, South Eastern Circuit.
Career: Specialist in criminal law for over 30 years with a real command of an area of law which has the potential to be the most devastating experience a person can face – being accused of a serious crime. Although last year he defended against allegations of murder, rape and 6 months on a £100millon fraud, he brings the same care and attention to the smallest of trials. His rank as a QC and Recorder (part time Judge) ensures deep respect for his case and his client. His intelligent, compassionate approach to the client offers absolute reassurance that the case will be presented in a compelling and persuasive manner. His cross-examination is meticulously prepared and he rarely misses a point. He is described as "a formidable opponent".
Personal: Interested in sport, travel, diving, countryside issues, issues around child and family law and social dynamics. Languages: Some French and Spanish.

ROUSSAK, Jeremy
Kings Chambers, Manchester
0345 034 3444
clerks@kingschambers.com
Featured in Clinical Negligence (Northern)
Practice Areas: Clinical negligence, personal injury, regulatory (General Medical Council Fitness to Practise panels).
Professional Memberships: Professional Negligence Bar Association Personal Injuries Bar Association Northern Circuit Medical Law Association (Treasurer).
Career: Jeremy qualified as a doctor in 1983. He trained in surgery, passing the examinations for fellowship of the Royal College of Surgeons of Edinburgh (FRCSEd) in 1988. He then specialised in surgery of the heart and chest. He has extensive experience of clinical negligence litigation, acting mainly but not exclusively on behalf of claimants, and of mid- and high-value personal injury claims, instructed by both claimants and defendants. He has both prosecuted and defended doctors before the Fitness to Practice panels of the GMC (now the MPTS). Jeremy has been a member of the Attorney-General's Provincial Panel of Counsel since 2002. From January 2008 to April 2010 he was Counsel to the Redfern Inquiry into Human Tissue Analysis in UK Nuclear Facilities.

ROWLANDS, Marc QC
Keating Chambers, London
020 7544 2600
mrowlands@keatingchambers.com
Featured in Construction (London)
Practice Areas: Counsel in all forms of dispute avoidance and resolution and advisory work in construction, engineering, technology and energy disputes both in the UK and internationally. Appears regularly in the High Court and domestic arbitrations. Extensive experience of substantial international arbitrations (ICC, LCIA, DIAC, as counsel and arbitrator) and litigation, particularly in the Middle East, Far East and Caribbean. In depth knowledge of all major construction (JCT, NEC), engineering (FIDIC, ICE) and offshore (LOGIC) forms and PFI contracts, including financial modelling. Particular expertise in UK railway contracts and regulatory environment and related disputes, covering vehicles, infrastructure, derailment, access rights and Schedule 4

and 8 claims. Other recent work includes energy (4 week trial – offshore compressors), technology (2 week trial – satellite tracking systems) and shipping (Commercial Court ship arrest) and Court of Appeal (estoppel, insolvency). Has appeared in Crown Court (proceedings brought by the HSE), Admin Court judicial review proceedings, a High Court libel action and advised on Privy Council appeals from the Turks and Caicos.
Professional Memberships: TECBAR; COMBAR; Society of Construction Law.
Career: Call 1990, Queen's Counsel 2012, CEDR accredited Mediator 2007, Bahamian Bar 2008, DIFC registered 2015, Eastern Caribbean Bar 2016.
Personal: French (fluent), Spanish.

ROWLEY, James QC
Byrom Street Chambers, Manchester
0161 829 2100
James.Rowley@byromstreet.com
Featured in Clinical Negligence (Northern), Personal Injury (Northern)
Practice Areas: Personal injuries: Dunhill v Burgin [2014] UKSC 18 affirming [2012] EWCA Civ 397 and [2012] EWHC 3163 (QB); Scott and Evans v Griffiths QBD Lawtel 29/01/14; Dixie v. British Polythene Industries PLC [2010] EWCA Civ 1170; Threlfall v. Hull City Council [2010] EWCA Civ 1147; Stanley v Bryn Close t/a Armthorpe Moto Parc [2009] EWHC 2849 (QB); The Kajaki Dam Disaster v MoD (2008); Samantha Roberts v MoD (2006); In the PTSD Group Actions – Multiple Claimants v MOD (In the PTSD Group Actions) [2003] EWHC/1134 (QB); Craven v John Riches et al and Knockhill Racing Circuit [2001] EWCA CIV 375; Jebson v MOD [2000] 1 W.L.R. 2055, I.C.R. 1220 CA) Clinical Negligence: Beech v Timney [2013] EWHC 2345 (QB); Spencer v NHS North West [2012] EWHC 2142 (QB); Parkes v Mann [2011] EWHC 1724 (QB); Inquiries: Report of the Royal Liverpool Children's Inquiry – HMSO (2001) – Counsel to the Alder Hey Inquiry
Professional Memberships: Personal Injuries Bar Association (Chairman 2010-12); Professional Negligence Bar Association
Career: MA (Classics) Cantab; Dip Law; Stonyhurst and Emmanuel. Hardwicke Scholar of Lincoln's Inn. Called 1987. Regional Treasury Counsel (2000). Counsel to the Royal Liverpool Children's Inquiry (2000-01). Recorder (Crown Court 2002-15, County Court 2007-15). Silk 2006. Door Tenant: Crown Office Chambers, London (2011-). Panel Arbitrator (2015-): Personal Injury claims Arbitration Service [PIcARBS]. Lectured widely in PI and clinical negligence.
Publications: Author of chapter on claims for care and assistance in Facts & Figures since 2012. Serious Personal Injury Litigation – a Quantum Update [2008] JPIL 109, still updated (2015) at www.byromstreet.com. Periodical Payments Orders – Useful or Useless? – Kemp Quantum Update 1/2007. Combat Immunity and the Duty of Care [2004] JPIL 280.
Personal: Married with three children. High Legh CC, armchair sportsman, gardener and cook.

ROWLEY, Keith QC
Radcliffe Chambers, London
020 7831 0081
clerks@radcliffechambers.com
Featured in Chancery (London), Professional Negligence (London), Pensions (London)
Practice Areas: Principal area of work is general chancery, primarily pension schemes, real property, trusts, professional negligence and commercial litigation. Important cases include William Makin, MMI v Harrop, Hearn v Younger, Re T &N Ltd, British Vita v British Vita Trustees, Cripps v Trustee Solutions, Re ILG Travel, R v Takeover Panel ex parte Datafin, Re Thompson's Settlement, Gillett v Holt, Harwood-Smart v Caws, Bloor v Calcott, Lambeth BC v Blackburn, Bogg v Raper, Worby v Rosser, Dent v Ellison Furniss Blank, Jasmine Trustees v Wells & Hind, Weir v Secretary of State for Transport (the Railtrack case), Alitalia v Rotunno, ITS v Hope (the llford case), HR Trustees v German (the IMG case), Prudential Staff Pensions v Prudential Assurance, Houldsworth v Bridge Trustees, Danks v QinetiQ, Rigid v Sarjeant, Vaitkus v Dresser Rand, Pensions Regulator v. A Admin, Briggs v Gleeds, Arcadia Pension Schemes, the Jimmy Savile litigation and Buckinghamshire v Barnardo's.
Professional Memberships: Chancery Bar Association; Association of Pension Lawyers; Professional Negligence Bar Association.
Career: Called 1979; Silk 2001; Bencher, Lincolns' Inn; First-tier Tribunal Judge, Consumer Credit and Estate Agents Appeals.
Personal: Educated at Woking Grammar School and King's College London; lives in London.

ROY, Andrew
12 King's Bench Walk, London
020 7583 0811
roy@12kbw.co.uk
Featured in Personal Injury (London)
Practice Areas: Personal injury, clinical negligence, costs, professional negligence, property damage, common law. Andrew covers all aspects of personal injury including road traffic accidents, employers' liability, public liability, product liability, psychiatric injury, fatal accidents, industrial disease (asbestos, RSI, WRULD). Andrew's clinical negligence practice encompasses all aspects of medical and dental negligence (especially surgical and A&E negligence), as well as claims involving other healthcare professionals. Andrew has a special interest and extensive experience and expertise in contentious costs litigation, in particular with respect to CFAs and fixed costs of all types. Andrew's professional negligence practice is focused on lawyers' negligence, especially arising out of personal injury litigation. His other areas of practice include fire, flood, insurance and contract claims. Across these areas Andrew has particular expertise in limitation.
Professional Memberships: PIBA, PNBA.
Career: Attended RBAI then Newcastle University (LLB (Fist Class Honours), MA in English Literature). Called 2002. Previously worked as a caseworker for the LSC, and as an insurance claims handler.
Publications: Co-author, Personal Injury Limitation Law 3rd Edition. Frequent contributor to JPIL, PILJ, PIBULJ and JPN.
Personal: Born Belfast. Outside interests include running, rugby, cricket, wildlife and literature.

RUBIN, Stephen QC
Fountain Court Chambers, London
020 7583 3335
sr@fountaincourt.co.uk
Featured in Commercial Dispute Resolution (London), Fraud (London)
Practice Areas: General commercial litigation particularly civil fraud. Major recent cases: LIC Telecoms et al v VTB et al LTL15/7/2016 Commercial Court tortious/ delict conspiracy claim under Lux and English law; VTB v Katunin et al, BVI Court of Appeal June 2016 – Hague Convention service, submission to the jurisdiction, enforcement of Russian Judgments; Chodiev and others v Stein 2015 – LTL 8/6/2015 (fraud); Alliance Bank JSC v Sturt and others [2015] Freezing Injunctions : Kazakhstan : Foreign Limitation Periods : Service Out Of Jurisdiction; VTB v Katunin & other [2015] BVIHC (Service Out, enforcement of Russian foreign judgment); UBS AG NY v Krys & Caulfield 2015 BVIHC (Fairfield/Madoff litigation); Primary Group v RBS & Direct Line [2014] 2 All ER (Comm) 1121 (Bankers' duties; Breach of confidence; Breach of contract; Confidentiality); Deutsche Bank v Sebastian Holdings & Vik (Non-party costs; Service by alternative permitted method; Service out of jurisdiction) [2014] 4 Costs LR 711; VTB Capital plc v Nutritek [[2013] 2 A.C. 337 and also Bannister J in BVI (commercial fraud, Russia, worldwide freezing orders, jurisdiction); A-G of TCI v Coxco 2013 Supreme Court of TCI (Norwich Pharmacal, alleged bribes); Palmer & Harvey v Garrad 2013 LTL 12/12/2013 (sham transaction and fraud); A-G of TCI v Salt Cay Ltd 2010-2012 TCI Supreme Court and COA (commercial fraud, bribery, rescission); Digicel v Cable & Wireless [2010] EWHC 774 (Ch) Ch D (Morgan J) 15/4/2010 LTL 21/4/2010 – 5 month trial (conspiracy to injure, telecoms); BNP Paribas v TH Global LTL 19/1/09 (Norwich Parmacals, fraud); The Wahr-Hansen/Jahre litigation: Cayman Islands, 2004-2008 (fraud, trusts); EuNetworks Fiber Ltd v Abovenet Communications UK Ltd [2007] EWHC 3099 Ch D (Briggs J) LTL 9/1/2008 (telecoms, commercial contracts, rectification; Miller & Moody v Condor Insurance [2006] 1 W.L.R. 1847 (Guarantees by deed poll).
Professional Memberships: COMBAR; London Common Law and Commercial Bar Association.
Career: QC 2000; Bencher of the Middle Temple; Recorder 2004 (crime and civil). Professional Conduct and Complaints Committee of Bar 1995-99; Hon Board of UKLSA; Panel chairman Bar Disciplinary Tribunals.
Personal: Merchant Taylor's School, Northwood; Brasenose College, Oxford, entrance exhibition – MA Jurisprudence; married with four children.

RUCK, Mary
Byrom Street Chambers, Manchester
0161 829 2100
mary.ruck@byromstreet.com
Featured in Clinical Negligence (Northern)
Practice Areas: Specialises in clinical negligence, medical law, human rights and healthcare (including regulatory work) and personal injury (catastrophic injury). Cases include high-value birth injury cases involving lump sum and periodical payment orders, wrongful birth, claims of maximum severity, psychiatric injury (involving article 2). Currently instructed on behalf of Kenyan nationals in group litigation connected to the so called Mau Mau insurgency. Notable litigation includes cases in the Strasbourg jurisdiction resulting in successful judgment by the Grand Chamber and conclusion of cases by way of friendly settlements. Recently concluded cases in clinical negligence include: 90% liability settlement achieved in birth brain injury case (2014); 65% settlement achieved in birth brain injury case with complicated causation (2015); chronic regional pain settlement following hand surgery: lump sum of £375,000 and stepped PPO to cover care, case management, loss of earnings and pension (2015); brain injury resulting from cerebral abscess (£615,000; 2015). Other ongoing cases include birth injuries arising out of prolonged partial hypoxic ischaemia (syntocinon administration) and acute profound hypoxia ischaemia (cord compression), death arising out of psychiatric negligence including systemic failures.
Professional Memberships: AVMA; PNBA; founder member of Northern Circuit Medical Law Association.
Career: Called to the Bar 1993 (Gray's Inn); practised in London until moving to the Northern Circuit in 1999; appointed First Tier Tribunal Judge to the Health and Social Care Chamber (Mental Health) in 2007.
Publications: Formerly Editor, now Assistant Editor, Fatal Accidents Chapter, Butterworths 'Personal Injury Litigation Service'.
Personal: Originally from the South West. Now lives in Cheshire.

RUCK KEENE, Alexander
39 Essex Chambers, London
020 7832 1111
alex.ruckkeene@39essex.com
Featured in Administrative & Public Law (London), Court of Protection (All Circuits)
Practice Areas: Court of Protection: eg Re MN, Supreme Court December 2016 (dividing line between CoP and Admin Court); James v Aintree University NHS Hospitals Foundation Trust [2014] AC 591 (first Supreme Court decision relating to MCA 2005); Birmingham CC v D (forthcoming in Court of Appeal) (meaning of deprivation of liberty in relation to 16/17 year olds); Mental health: eg Munjaz v UK [2012] MHLR 351 (status of MHA Code of Practice); Sessay v SLAM & Anor [2012] QB 760 (power to detain pending admission under MHA 1983).
Professional Memberships: STEP, ALBA, MHLA, LAPG
Career: Attorney General's Junior Counsel to the Crown (B Panel); Honorary Research Lecturer at University of Manchester; Visiting Research Fellow, Kings College London.
Publications: Court of Protection Handbook: A Users Guide, 2nd edition (LAG, 2016, editor and co-author);Assessment of Mental Capacity 4th edition, 2015 (editor and co-author); The International Protection of Adults (2015, OUP, co-author); Court of Protection Practice 2015 (co-author); Mental Capacity: Law and Practice (2nd edition, 2012, co-author); Clayton & Tomlinson, The Law of Human Rights, 2nd edition, 2009 (contributor). Editorial Board of Court of Protection Law Reports. Creator of www.mentalcapacitylawandpolicy.org.uk

RUSHTON, Nicola
Hailsham Chambers, London
020 7643 5000
nicola.rushton@hailshamchambers.com
Featured in Professional Negligence (London)
Practice Areas: Nicola specialises in finance-related professional negligence and in commercial claims related to secured lending. She has substantial experience of all types of claims relating to mortgages, claims against financial professionals such

as brokers and accountants, fixed charge receiverships, asset and debt recovery and insolvency. She has particular expertise in claims by lenders against their professional advisers and against borrowers. She has a niche specialism in enforcement of legal aid regulations and legal aid costs. Clients instruct Nicola because of her collaborative and practical approach to problems. She is engaging and robust and enjoys getting her teeth into complex commercial disputes. She is adept at dealing with numerical and financial data, and has a knack for making complicated issues or concepts easy for her clients and others to understand. She communicates clearly and has a keen awareness of commercial realities. She prides herself on being accessible, friendly and prompt with her advice.

RUSSELL, Christopher
2TG - 2 Temple Gardens, London
020 7822 1200
crussell@2tg.co.uk
Featured in Personal Injury (London)
Practice Areas: An advocate with particular strength in claims for brain and spinal injury, occupational disease and psychiatric damage, especially stress, bullying and harassment. Also admitted to the Bar of the Cayman Islands. Recent illustrative notable cases include Jones v BBC and others [2006-2009] (QBD, Cardiff) £3.5 million paraplegic injury claim. Harkins v Lee and another [2007-2008] (QBD, Oxford) £1.8 million claim following RTA. Frost v Frost [2006-2008] represented father in claim by son following a serious farm accident. Collins v Natwest Bank PLC [2007-2008] (Norwich CC) represented employer in harassment and stress claim by bank cashier. Mason v Satelcom and others [2006-ongoing] (QBD and CA) represented employer in claim by employee injured in fall from a ladder, including important CA decision about ambit of statutory duty upon non-employers under Equipment Regulations.
Professional Memberships: PNBA; LCLCBA; PIBA.
Career: LLB (Exeter). Called 1982.

RUSSELL, Jane
Essex Court Chambers, London
020 7813 8080
jrussell@essexcourt.com
Featured in Employment (London)
Practice Areas: Jane's main areas of practice are Commercial, Employment, Fraud, Human Rights and Public Law. Jane's recent cases include a banker's bonus case, a case involving unlawful retention of confidential information and breach of fiduciary duty, a judicial review case about the Common Agricultural Policy and a case about the debanking of a Muslim.
Professional Memberships: Jane is a member of the Commercial Bar Association, the Employment Law Bar Association, the Employment Lawyers Association, the Discrimination Law Association and the Young Lawyers Division of the American Bar Association.
Career: Jane qualified as a Solicitor in 1998 and was an Assistant Solicitor in the Employment departments of Linklaters and Herbert Smith. She moved to the bar to become a tenant at Tooks Chambers in 2004 and joined Essex Court Chambers in 2012. Jane was appointed to the Attorney General's "B" Panel of Junior Counsel to the Crown in 2015.
Publications: Jane is currently a contributor to the new edition of Supperstone, Goudie and Walker's Judicial Review. Jane previously co-wrote a chapter of the OUP's Copyright and Media Law on defamation damages.
Personal: Jane was educated at Aberdeen, Leuven and Cambridge universities. When not at work Jane enjoys showjumping and the Edinburgh Festival (but not at the same time).

RUSSELL, Jeremy QC
Quadrant Chambers, London
020 7583 4444
jeremy.russell@quadrantchambers.com
Featured in Shipping (London)
Practice Areas: Jeremy Russell (BA (Hons) business law; LLM (Lon)) is a highly experienced commercial barrister specialising in international commercial, shipping and aviation law. Having practised for 38 years he has now ceased taking on new work as counsel to focus on his practice as arbitrator and mediator. He carries with him into that task his skills in handling large, document-heavy cases requiring particular attention to detail and "his commercial mind" (Chambers UK). He has considerable experience of dealing with complex technical cases requiring an ability to master a range of engineering and scientific expert evidence. He is particularly highly regarded for his experience and expertise in maritime and commercial arbitrations (LOF, LMAA, LCIA and ICC) and has recently been appointed the Lloyd's salvage appeal arbitrator (with effect from October 2016). His work typically involves detailed consideration of the many and varied technical issues which arise in the field of maritime and air transport. His areas of experience include aviation and travel; collision, salvage and admiralty; dry shipping, commodities and transport; energy, shipbuilding and construction; commercial litigation; international arbitration; and mediation. He is a CEDR-accredited mediator and a member of COMBAR, LCLCBA and FSALS.
Professional Memberships: COMBAR; London Common Law and Commercial Bar Association; London Maritime Arbitrators Association (supporting member); LCIA (member); FSALS.
Career: Called to the Bar 1975. Joined Quadrant Chambers 1977. Took Silk 1994. CEDR accredited mediator. Lloyd's arbitrator.

RUSSELL, John QC
Quadrant Chambers, London
020 7583 4444
john.russell@quadrantchambers.com
Featured in Travel (London), Shipping (London)
Practice Areas: Shipping and Commodities: all aspects of shipping and international trade litigation and arbitration including charterparty, bill of lading and COA disputes; marine personal injuries; FOSFA and GAFTA arbitrations and appeals. Marine insurance disputes. Yacht claims. Travel and aviation.
Professional Memberships: COMBAR.
Career: Called to the Bar in 1993; initially practiced at 5 Bell Yard, moved to Quadrant (then 4 Essex Court) in 1998.
Personal: Keen sailor, cyclist and walker.

RUSSELL, Paul QC
12 King's Bench Walk, London
0
Russell@12kbw.co.uk
Featured in Personal Injury (London)
Practice Areas: Paul has a strong reputation in the specialist fields of personal injury and clinical negligence and is regularly instructed to act in high value claims. He is particularly experienced in dealing with both the bringing and defending of claims involving catastrophic injury, motor related insurance and MIB issues, industrial disease, and employers' liability generally. Recent cases include: A v. Z: acting for a brain damaged infant (cerebral palsy) and securing admission of breach and causation before settling for a capitalised value of £6.4m (on a PPO + lump sum basis); M v. Z: acting for a victim of a RTA requiring 24/7 care, Reaney considerations, seven figure settlement; BXC v. D and T Ltd: acting for a protected party in a RTA case where drink/drugs, seatbelt, and blind eye knowledge vehicle was stolen all arose; settled at JSM; PCH v. SW: acting for a protected party whose claim was settled and approved for a combination of a lump sum and variable periodical payments (for care and case management) for epilepsy; B v. M: acting for a widower (with three very young daughters) in a fatal claim; lost dependency on wife and mother's services; claim settled and approved; G v. N: acting for a brain damaged infant in securing a substantial interim payment to fund the purchase of a home suitable for her needs.
Professional Memberships:
Career: Called 1984
Personal: Paul is a graduate of Durham University and away from the Bar, he is a Youth Offending Team panel member at the LB of Wandsworth.

RUSSEN, Jonathan QC
Maitland Chambers, London
020 7406 1200
jrussen@maitlandchambers.co.uk
Featured in Chancery (London), Commercial Dispute Resolution (London), Financial Services (London)
Practice Areas: Commercial litigation (domestic and offshore); trusts; insolvency (corporate and personal); financial services; shareholders' disputes; partnership and property.
Professional Memberships: Chancery Bar Association. COMBAR.
Career: University of Wales LLB (1st Class Hons.) 1984. University of Cambridge LLM 1985. Called to Bar (Lincoln's Inn) 1986. QC 2010.
Publications: Financial Services: Authorisation, Supervision and Enforcement: A Litigator's Guide (OUP).
Personal: Married, two children.

RUTLEDGE, Kelvin QC
Cornerstone Barristers, London
020 7242 4986
kelvinr@cornerstonebarristers.com
Featured in Community Care (London), Social Housing (London)
Practice Areas: Public law specialist working primarily in the area of local government including adult community care services, social housing, children's services and powers and duties of local authorities. Has appeared in some of the most significant community care and housing cases in recent years. Has related expertise in human rights and EU law. Is also a highly experienced and knowledgeable property lawyer. Expertise also in local authority governance, finance, elections, land sales and leaseholders' rights. Extensive advocacy experience including UK Supreme Court and the European Court of Justice. Notable cases include Slough v M (residential care, definition of care and attention); McDonald v RB Kensington & Chelsea (care assessments, resources, human rights and equality duties); Powell v Hounslow LBC (possession claims and human rights); Hotak v Southwark (definition of priority need); Maries v Merton LBC (local authority land development) and Menon v Herefordshire (misfeasance in public office).
Professional Memberships: ALBA.
Career: Called 1989, Silk 2013 Visiting Fellow University of Essex.

RYDER, Matthew QC
Matrix Chambers, London
020 7404 3447
MatthewRyder@matrixlaw.co.uk
Featured in Crime (London), Police Law (All Circuits), Civil Liberties & Human Rights (London)
Career: Christ's College Comprehensive School, London. Emmanuel College, Cambridge LLB Hons Columbia University, New York LLM English Bar 1992. New York Bar 1999. QC appointment 2010 Crown Court Recorder appointment 2010

SACHDEVA, Vikram QC
39 Essex Chambers, London
020 77832 1111
Vikram.SachdevaQC@39essex.com
Featured in Costs Litigation (All Circuits), Court of Protection (All Circuits), Professional Discipline (London)
Practice Areas: Commercial, Financial Services, Administrative and Public Law, Regulatory and Disciplinary, European Law, Construction, Procurement, Professional Negligence, Direct and Indirect Tax, Costs.
Professional Memberships: Administrative Law Bar Association (Executive Committee Member), Association of Regulatory and Disciplinary Lawyers (Executive Committee Member), COMBAR, LCLCBA.
Career: MA (Cantab), BCL (Oxon), BM, BCh (Oxon). Formerly Tutor in Administrative and Public Law, Tort, and Crime, at various colleges in Oxford and Cambridge. Previously appointed to Attorney General's A, B and C Panels. Appeared in R (Tigere) v SSBIS [2015] 1 WLR 3820; Blankley v Central Manchester and Manchester Children's University Hospitals NHS Trust [2015] 1 WLR 4307; R (Tracey) v Cambridge University Hospital and SSH [2015] QB 543; Westscott Financial Services Ltd v Financial Ombudsman Service [2014] EWHC 3972 (Admin); Jowhari v NHS England [2014] EWHC 4197; Re Ashya King [2014] 2 FLR 855; James v Aintree University Hospitals [2014] AC 591; Denton v White [2014] 1 WLR 3926; R (Kadri) v Birmingham CC [2013] 1 WLR 1755; R (MD Afghanistan) v SSHD [2012] 1 WLR 2422; Re M [2012] 1 WLR 1653 and [2012] 1 WLR 287; Lower Mill Estate Ltd v HMRC [2011] STC 636; DEFRA v Downs [2009] ACD 71

SALMON, Sarah
Arden Chambers, London
020 7242 4244
sarah.salmon@ardenchambers.com
Featured in Social Housing (London)
Practice Areas: Housing and landlord and tenant, local government (including information rights and education) and the public law aspects of housing law.
Professional Memberships: Administrative Law Bar Association, Social Housing Law Association (Committee member), Housing Law Practitioners Association and Education Law Association.

Career: After graduating from university Sarah obtained an LLM in Public Law at University College London. She was called to the Bar, and joined Arden Chambers as a pupil, in 2007. Sarah has appeared in numerous trials including claims for possession concerning anti-social behaviour, tenancies by deception and subletting. She deals with issues of capacity, public law and the Equality Act 2010. She has experience in homelessness, allocations and injunctive relief. Sarah's noteworthy cases include Royal Borough of Greenwich v Charlotte Tuitt [2014] EWCA Civ 1669, James v Birmingham City Council [2013] EWCA Civ 552 and Morrison Facilities Services Ltd v Norwich City Council [2010] EWHC 487 (Ch).
Publications: Assistant editor (2012-) of the Encyclopedia of Housing Law (Sweet & Maxwell) and co-author of Judicial Review Proceedings – A Practitioner's Guide (2013, LAG). She has had articles on housing and local government published in the New Law Journal, Solicitors Journal, Journal of Housing Law and Local Government Lawyer.

SALTER, Michael
Ely Place Chambers, London
020 7400 9600
msalter@elyplace.com
Featured in Employment (London)
Practice Areas: Maintaining a balance between representing large scale public sector employers, individual claimants, SME's, trade unions, multinational corporations and infrastructure companies means Michael brings to each claim what one judge has described as a "characteristic sense of realism" and, what clients have noted, is a down to earth manner and commercial sensitivity. Recent instructions include acting on behalf of a police service and all named respondents where the second most senior officer in the service was a named respondent to allegations of race and disability discrimination and acting on behalf of a top-ten state funded college facing allegations of dismissal because of protected disclosures. Regularly instructed in substantial and complicated matters Michael is security vetted and undertakes claims involving matters of national security. His practice takes him across the jurisdiction, including Northern Ireland, and Jersey. He maintains an advisory practice on Guernsey employment law
Professional Memberships: Employment Law Association Employment Law Bar Association
Career: Brasenose College Oxford BCL Called to the Bar 1999 Fee-Paid Employment Judge appointed in 2013.
Publications: Frequently published in professional journals, his book Social Media in the Workplace was published in 2015 and he has contributed the chapter on Employment Tribunal Cost applications to "Costs Law: A Practitioner's Guide

SALZEDO, Simon QC
Brick Court Chambers, London
020 7379 3550
simon.salzedo@brickcourt.co.uk
Featured in International Arbitration (London), Professional Negligence (London), Banking & Finance (London), Commercial Dispute Resolution (London), Fraud (London), Insurance (London)
Career: Simon Salzedo QC is a leading advocate who is user-friendly and commercially minded. Simon is recommended by the legal directories as a leading silk for Commercial Litigation, Banking and Finance, International Arbitration, Professional Negligence, Civil Fraud and Insurance and Reinsurance work. As a qualified Chartered Accountant (FCA) Simon is frequently involved in commercial cases calling on his financial, accounting, audit and tax experience and he is writing a book on accountants' negligence and liability. As joint author of the leading practitioner work on conflicts of interest and confidential information, Simon has specialist knowledge in that field and frequently advises professionals (especially lawyers) and their clients on conflicts issues. As well as Court work, Simon regularly appears in arbitrations under LCIA, ICC and other rules. He has substantial experience in the enforcement of judgments and arbitration awards, including jurisdictional aspects, having represented the successful claimants in two major international enforcement battles: Masri and Nomihold. He is joint author of an annotated guide to the Arbitration Act 1996 and a contributor to an annotation of the 2013 SIAC Rules.

SAMUELS, Leslie QC
Pump Court Chambers, London
020 7-353-0711
l.samuels@pumpcourtchambers.com
Featured in Family/Matrimonial (Western)
Practice Areas: All aspects of family law including care proceedings; representing parents, local authorities and children's guardians in cases involving complex issues including alleged non-accidental injury (death, brain injury, subdural and retinal bleeding, fractures, anal and genital injuries, FII, bruising), alleged sexual abuse, jurisdictional problems (including under BIIR) and difficult welfare issues. High value and / or complex financial remedies claims with expertise and experience in cases involving non-matrimonial wealth, farms, companies, trusts and pensions. Equitable co-ownership claims. Private law children matters (child arrangements orders, leave to remove, child abduction) and Schedule I claims. Judicial Review applications particularly those involving local authority duties to children and vulnerable adults. Probate claims (wills, capacity and claims under the Inheritance Act). Highly experienced at Family Court, High Court and appellate levels. IFLA qualified Arbitrator.
Professional Memberships: Family Law Bar Association (elected committee member and Chair of the Money and Property Sub Committee), Western Circuit (authorised advocacy trainer). Member of the Chartered Institute of Arbitrators.
Career: 1989 Called Gray's Inn, 2003 Deputy District Judge Principal Registry, 2005 ADR accredited mediator, 2011 appointed QC, 2012 Recorder (South Eastern Circuit) Family, 2016 qualified as an IFLA arbitrator, 2016 appointed Deputy High Court Judge.
Personal: MA (Law) Cambridge, MA (Criminology) University of Toronto, married with two children. Lives in London.

SANDERSON, David
12 King's Bench Walk, London
020 75830811
sanderson@12kbw.co.uk
Featured in Personal Injury (London)
Practice Areas: David is described as a formidable advocate who acts for both claimants and defendants dealing with high value claims across the spectrum of personal injury, clinical negligence and fatal accident claims. In 2014 David was nominated for the Personal Injury / Clinical Negligence Junior of the Year by Chambers & Partners.
Professional Memberships: PNBA, PIBA, LCLCBA, Western Circuit.
Career: Called 1985 Inner Temple. Pupil Master. Recent cases include: Inquest touching on the death of Ying Tao; Bennett v Southwell [2013] EWHC 2382 Griffiths Williams J.; Simmons v Castle [2012] PIQR P22; Tavares v Hudson-Rotin [2012] Globe J 13/2/13; Smithurst v Sealant Construction [2012] Med LR 258; Rust-Andrews v First Tier Tribunal (Social Entitlement Chamber) [2012] PIQR P7; Micklewright v Surrey County Council [2011] EWCA Civ 922; Richardson v Butcher [2010] EWHC 214; R v Lane [2009] EWCA Crim 1630; Wade v Turffrey [2007] LS Law Medical 352; Denton Hall v Fifield [2006] Lloyd's Rep Med 251; Ellis v Royal Surrey County Hospital [2004] EWHC 3510; Morris v Richards [2004] PIQR Q3; Simonds v Isle of Wight Council (2004) ELR 59; Pearce v Lindfield [2003] EWCA Civ 647.
Personal: Stowe School. Sussex University (BA). Married with one daughter. Away from the Bar his interests include cycling, sea swimming, opera and India.

SANDERSON, Eleanor
2 Bedford Row, London
020 7440 8888
esanderson@2bedfordrow.co.uk
Featured in Health & Safety (London)
Practice Areas: Predominantly defence barrister with a record of acting in complex and high profile cases in the fields of criminal, regulatory and disciplinary law. She is regularly instructed by both individuals and companies in cases where allegations attract public or political interest, also for professionals facing disciplinary proceedings before their regulatory bodies. In the regulatory criminal field, she has acted for both prosecution and defence in relation to allegations of gross negligence manslaughter, corporate manslaughter, and breaches of section 2 and 3 HSAW, in prosecutions by the Environment Agency, and proceedings under the Fire Safety Order. Advises and appears for a range of companies and professionals including from the financial, technology, manufacturing, construction, retail, energy, agricultural, healthcare and leisure sectors, both pre-charge and in subsequent proceedings. She is an experienced advocate in inquests acting for a range of properly interested person, including recently for the new police investigation into the Hillsborough stadium disaster. Eleanor's financial criminal practice incorporates the full range of fraud and money laundering offences, also confiscation and cash forfeiture proceedings, and she frequently acts in the most high value cases where investigations span multiple jurisdictions. In the field of professional disciplinary law she has appeared before a wide range of regulatory bodies and specialises particularly in acting for medical and healthcare professionals. More details of Eleanor's work and recent cases can be found at www.2bedfordrow.co.uk.
Professional Memberships: Criminal Bar Association, South Eastern Circuit,
Career: Called to the Bar 2005 (Inner Temple).
Publications: Consultant Editor, Lloyds Law Reports Financial Crime.
Personal: Educated Bramcote Hills Comprehensive, Nottingham; New College, Oxford (MA Oxon); City University, London (Dip. Law). Lives London.

SANGSTER, Nigel QC
25 Bedford Row, London
nsangster@25bedfordrow.com
Featured in Financial Crime (London)
Practice Areas: Nigel Sangster QC was called in 1977 and took Silk in 1998. He is one of the most senior QC's at the criminal bar and practises exclusively as a defence advocate. He exclusively specialises in defending those accused of the full range of fraudulent offences and has acted for many directors, solicitors, accountants, financial advisers, companies and financial institutions. He has appeared or advised in many lengthy, serious and complex fraud cases, defending a full range of offences including alleged investment, ponzi , advance fee, MTIC, banking, bonds, stock market, VAT, tax, carbon credits, long firm, precious metal and film scheme frauds. He is experienced in complex money laundering proceedings and is recognised for his successes in multi million pound confiscation proceedings. He deals with cross border and multi-jurisdictional allegations. He also has experience in planning and environmental cases.
Professional Memberships: Recorder of the Crown Court for 20 years. Member of the Criminal Bar Association and a Bencher of the Middle Temple. Former elected member of the Bar Council. Head of Chambers for 11 years.
Career: After twenty five years in practice from St Paul's Chambers on the North Eastern Circuit, he moved full time to London and practices from 25 Bedford Row. He defends in major fraud and money laundering trials throughout the country.

SAOUL, Daniel
4 New Square, London
020 7822 2024
d.saoul@4newsquare.com
Featured in Commercial Dispute Resolution (London), Costs Litigation (All Circuits), Sports Law (London)
Practice Areas: Domestic and international commercial litigation and arbitration. Sports law. Public law. Costs litigation.
Professional Memberships: COMBAR, British Association for Sport and the Law.
Career: Dan joined 4 New Square in 2008 after training and practising as a solicitor-advocate at City firm Herbert Smith LLP (now Herbert Smith Freehills). Has also practised as a litigator in the British Virgin Islands for leading offshore firm Conyers Dill & Pearman. His commercial case-load is broad and reflects his training in the City (including stints in two investment banks) as well as his international background – he is a fluent French speaker and has studied and worked in a number of different countries. He is a member of the Executive Committee of the Commercial Bar Association (COMBAR). His sports law practice benefits from his experience as a former international sportsman. He has acted for governing bodies, athletes, clubs and other entities in a wide range of high profile matters. He is a member of Sport Resolutions' Panel of Arbitrators and also sits as arbitrator for various National Governing Bodies. He is a Director of the British Association for Sport and Law. He is a member of the Attorney-General's Panel of Counsel (B Panel) and accepts instructions in a range of governmental cases. Where

costs litigation is concerned, he has expertise in all aspects of the field both at first instance and at appellate level.
Publications: Many articles in his practice areas, including in the Journal of International Banking and Financial Law, the New York State Bar Association's International Journal, the Journal of the British Association for Sport and Law and various other publications.
Personal: Education – Lycee Français Charles de Gaulle, London; University of Edinburgh; University of California, Berkeley; University of Oxford; BPP Law School (London). Member of Leander Club.

SAREEN, Ben
Keating Chambers, London
020 7544 2600
bsareen@keatingchambers.com
Featured in Construction (London)
Practice Areas: A specialist in construction, engineering, energy, shipbuilding and related professional negligence disputes, Ben has advised on and represented clients in high-profile construction and engineering projects including the Olympic Village, Wembley Stadium and the East London Line extension. Not only does Ben regularly represent clients in the High Court and County Court, he is also frequentlyinstructed in domestic and international shipbuilding, engineering and construction arbitrations by both commercial and government clients. Recent court work has included Technology and Construction Court litigation in which he acted for the defendant contractor in J Reddington v Galliford Try Construction. Representing clients in adjudications is also part of Ben's practice, an example being Eurocom v Siemens which gave rise to one of the leading adjudication cases of 2014. He is experienced with many major standard form contracts, including the JCT and NEC standard forms.
Professional Memberships: Society of Construction Law, TECBAR, COMBAR.
Publications: Contributing author to Keating on Offshore Construction and Marine Engineering Contracts and Keating on NEC3.

SARTIN, Leon
5 Stone Buildings, London
020 72426201
clerks@5sblaw.com
Featured in Chancery (London), Tax (London), Court of Protection (All Circuits)
Practice Areas: Specialises in both the advisory and litigation aspects of private client taxation, trusts, estates, wills, inheritance and family provision, Court of Protection, pensions, property disputes and related professional negligence. Notable cases include: Hughes & ors v Bourne & ors [2012] EWHC 2232 (Ch); Lilleyman v Lilleyman [2012] 3 WLR 754; In the matter of the Wedgwood Museum Trust Ltd (in administration), Young & ors v Attorney-General & ors [2011] [2012] Pens LR 175; Fine v Fine [2012] EWHC 1811(Ch); Maskell v Denham & UBS Pensions Trustees [2012] LTL AC9200991; Franks v Sinclair [2007] WTLR 439.
Professional Memberships: STEP, ACTAPS, Chancery Bar Association. Lectures regularly on tax, trusts, wills and probate. Member of the STEP Technical Committee
Career: Called 1997.

Publications: Co-author with James Kessler QC of ' Drafting Wills and Trusts', 11th edition.

SAUNDERS, Kevin
St Ives Chambers, Birmingham
0121 236 0863
kevin.saunders@stiveschambers.co.uk
Featured in Crime (Midlands)
Practice Areas: Crime, Regulatory
Professional Memberships:
Career: Kevin Saunders is regarded as a strong and determined advocate with a good manner in court. Mr. Saunders has an extensive Criminal defence practice that includes high-profile cases of homicide, lengthy and complex fraud matters and serious sexual offences. Mr. Saunders also has considerable experience of representing individuals, companies, local authorities and government agencies in matters of a Regulatory nature. Mr. Saunders advises with confidence at all stages of proceedings.
Personal: Called to the Bar: 2003. Joined St Ives Chambers: 2005. Languages: German

SAUNDERS, Neil
3 Raymond Buildings Barristers, London
020 7400 6400
neil.saunders@3rblaw.com
Featured in Crime (London), Inquests & Public Inquiries (All Circuits), Professional Discipline (London), Financial Crime (London)
Practice Areas: The legal directories regard Neil as one of the best leading juniors in Crime and Financial Crime. He has recently prosecuted the largest insider trading case brought by the FCA. In 2015 he defended Neil Wallis in the last of the News of the World "hacking cases" having previously defended Charlie Brooks for an allegation of attempting to pervert the course of justice. Neil has for some years been instructed in high profile cases, both alone and as part of a team. He specialises as a criminal and serious fraud advocate, representing professional people and companies. He is regularly instructed by large City and specialist white-collar fraud firms providing strategic advice to corporate clients during all stages of investigation pre-charge. Neil has experience prosecuting and defending. He attends Police disciplinary proceedings before both Metropolitan and provincial forces. He was significantly involved throughout the 7/7 inquest and in other inquests he has represented interested parties such as police or families.
Career: BA (Hons) Law 1982; called to the Bar 1983. Past committee member South Eastern Circuit, CBA and Bar Council; also various committees on specific issues. Interests: Rugby Union qualified referee: Golfer with stable handicap. Appeal steward British Boxing Board of Control.

SAUVAIN, Stephen QC
Kings Chambers, Manchester
0345 034 3444
clerks@kingschambers.com
Featured in Environment (Northern), Local Government (Northern), Planning (Northern)
Practice Areas: Planning, highways and public rights of way, compulsory purchase, judicial review, local government, parking law and environmental law.
Professional Memberships: PEBA; Northern and North Eastern Circuits.
Career: M.A. (Cantab); LLB (1971). Lecturer in Law at Manchester University (1971-78). Call: 1977; Silk 1995; Assistant Boundary Commissioner (2000).
Publications: Highway Law (Sweet & Maxwell) (5th Ed. 2013); Encyclopedia of Highway Law and Practice (General Editor); Law Relating to Local Government (DETR Research Report – with Colin Crawford, Andrew Coulson and Michael Clarke); Joint Working Arrangements revisited after the Local Government Act 2000 (Journal of Local Government Law, 2002); Bridges: responsibility to repair them (1997 ROWLR -with Ross Crail).

SAVAGE, Amanda
4 New Square, London
020 7822 2134
a.savage@4newsquare.com
Featured in Professional Negligence (London)
Practice Areas: All aspects of commercial and civil litigation with an emphasis on: (i) professional liability (particularly those involving lawyers, financial professionals and insurance brokers), (ii) insurance disputes and (iii) commercial litigation. Cases include: Milton Furniture Ltd v Brit Insurance Ltd [2014] EWHC 965 (QB) (insurance) , Richard Craven v BSB (30.1.2104) (sitting as Visitor to the Inns of Court), Greene Wood McLean v Templeton [2010] EWHC 2679 (Comm) (claim against barristers, GLO); Patel v Air India [2010] EWCA Civ 443 (CA) (wasted costs); Williams v Thompson Leatherdale [2008] EWHC 2574 (QB) (claim against barrister, family law); Daniels v Thompson (2004) PNLR 33 (CA) (claim against solicitor, limitation and duty of care); London Fire and Emergency Planning Authority v Meritor Light Vehicle Systems (UK) and others (TCC) [2003] ALL ER (D) 76, LTL 12/9/2003 (product liability, indemnity costs) and Brown v Bennett (No. 2) [2001] 1 WLR 713 and (No. 3) [2001] 1 WLR 713 (barristers, wasted costs).
Professional Memberships: PNBA, COMBAR, TECBAR.
Career: LLB (King's College London), BCL (Worcester College, Oxford). Research assistant, Law Commission 1998-99. Part-time Judicial assistant to the Court of Appeal 2000. Tenant 4 New Square 2000 to date.
Publications: Editor, Jackson and Powell on Professional Liability. Former contributor to Sweet and Maxwell CPR reports.
Personal: Family, music and travel.

SAXBY, Dan
3 Hare Court, London
020 7415 7800
DanSaxby@3harecourt.com
Featured in Travel (London)
Practice Areas: Dan has a specialist personal injury and travel law practice which is predominantly defendant focused. He is regularly instructed by various major tour operators, airlines and cruise-lines. He is particularly noted for handling accidents involving the most serious injuries (including traumatic brain injury); multi-claimant or group action gastric illness claims; and, cases involving a variety of issues under the Package Travel Regulations, particularly dynamic packaging and local standard disputes. He also has considerable experience in dealing with jurisdictional issues as well as excursion claims and is regularly instructed by both foreign insurers and hotels in this jurisdiction.

SAY, Bradley
Gough Square Chambers, London
020 7353 0924
bradley.say@goughsq.co.uk
Featured in Consumer Law (London)
Practice Areas: Consumer credit, financial services and regulatory law. Bradley has been involved in some of the key cases involving consumer finance which include: In re London Scottish Finance Ltd (in administration), Jack and another v Craig and others [2014] Bus. L.R. 424 (unfair relationships); Carey v HSBC,[2009] EWHC 3417 (QB) (the nature and extent of the duty to disclose a true copy of the agreement under section 78 of the Consumer Credit Act 1974 Act); Heath v Southern Pacific Mortgages Ltd [2009] WLR (D) 320 (concerned the scope of section 18(1)(a) and 18(2) of the Consumer Credit Act 1974, i.e. multiple agreements under the Act where each part of the agreement must be treated as being a separate agreement); and Wilson and Anor v Hurstanger Ltd [2007] 1 WLR 2351 (the nature and extent of the lender's duty to disclose the payment of a commission to a finance broker where the broker is the agent of the borrower).
Career: Called 1993. Inner Temple.
Publications: Co-author of The Law of Consumer Credit and Hire, OUP, 2009.

SCHERBEL-BALL, Jonathan
One Brick Court, London
(020)7 353 8845
jsb@onebrickcourt.com
Featured in Data Protection (London), Defamation/Privacy (London)
Practice Areas: All aspects of media and information law and the law of internet intermediary liability. This includes defamation, privacy, breach of confidence, data protection, freedom of information, malicious falsehood, harassment, contempt of court, protection of sources, reporting restrictions and media regulation. Significant cases include: Galloway v Frazer and Google Inc. [2016] NIQB 7; KL & NN v Sunday Newspapers Ltd [2015] NIQB 88; C v BBC [2015] NIQB 86; Hegglin v Google Inc. [2014] EWHC 3973; McIntosh v ICO (EA/2014/0033); Loughran v Century Newspapers [2014] NICA 26; Surrey County Council v Al Hilli [2013] EWHC 2190 (Fam); Tilbrook v Parr [2012] EWHC 1946 (QB); Hunt v Obregan [2012] All ER (D) 217; King v Grundon [2012] All ER (D) 96.
Professional Memberships: Called to the Bar of England and Wales and the Bar of Northern Ireland
Career: MA (Hons) Modern History and Politics, Oxford. MPhil, Modern European History, Cambridge. Qualified as solicitor in 2007, training at Dechert LLP. Solicitor, BBC Litigation Department 2007-09. Called to the Bar in 2010. Tenant at One Brick Court since July 2011
Publications: Contributing Editor of 'Survey of English Libel Law', Media Law Resource Centre, 2011-15. Contributor, Arlidge, Eady & Smith on Contempt, 4th Ed Supplements and 5th Edition (due 2016).
Personal: Active sports player. Interested in contemporary European and American politics.

SCHWARZ, Jonathan S
Temple Tax Chambers, London
020 7936 3988
jonathan.schwarz@taxbarristers.com
Featured in Tax (London)

Practice Areas: International tax disputes and advice on solving cross-border tax problems. Double tax relief, tax treaties, transfer pricing, permanent establishments, Diverted Profits Tax, cross-border corporate and commercial transactions, withholding taxes, residence, domicile, EU tax law, property investment, exploitation of intellectual property and digital economy taxation, shipping, air transportation and tonnage tax, internationally mobile employees and cross-border and pensions, entertainers and sportspeople, joint ventures and private equity, group structures, finance, CFCs, investment funds and management, taxation international tax enforcement compliance and exchange of information.
Professional Memberships: Visiting Professor –King's College London, Dickson Poon School of Law. International Fiscal Association – Permanent Scientific Committee
Publications: Include: Author- Schwarz on Tax Treaties 4th Ed (CCH), Booth and Schwarz: Residence, Domicile and UK Taxation 19th Ed (Bloomsbury), Contributor- Transfer Pricing and Business Restructurings (IBFD).
Personal: BA, LLB (Witwatersrand), LLM (UC Berkeley), CTA (Fellow), Advocate- South Africa, Barrister & Solicitor- Alberta, Canada.

SCOTT, Gemma
12 King's Bench Walk, London
020 75830811
scott@12kbw.co.uk
Featured in Personal Injury (All Circuits)
Practice Areas: Gemma specialises in asbestos litigation. She acts for Claimants in mesothelioma, lung cancer, pleural thickening and asbestosis cases. She is junior counsel to two silks in a major product liability group action against the manufacturer and supplier of Asbestolux and Marinite (Concept 70 Ltd & Others v Cape Intermediate Holdings plc). Gemma is also particularly experienced in cases involving brain and spinal injuries. She is routinely instructed in her own right, but has also acted as a junior in a number of high value claims. Most recently, she was instructed alongside Frank Burton Q.C. in a catastrophic brain injury case. The Claimant received a lump sum award of over £3m plus periodical payments (equivalent to an overall lump sum in excess of £7m). She acts in claims with an international element. She was instructed on behalf of the Claimants in the Bomu-Bonny Oil Pipeline Litigation, which is believed to be the UK's largest ever environmental action. She supervised a team dealing with quantum issues. She is also experienced in matters involving conflicts of law, actions under the Package Holiday Regulations and international conventions.
Personal: The Queen's College, Oxford University, MA (Hons) Modern History Post Graduate Diploma in Law (Nottingham Law School) Bar Vocational Course (Nottingham Law School)

SCOTT, Janys M QC
Westwater Advocates, Edinburgh
07967 371460
janys.scott@westwateradvocates.com
Featured in Family/Matrimonial (Scotland)
Practice Areas: Civil practice with particular expertise in family law and education law. Numerous reported cases, including two successful appeals to the Supreme Court in Principal Reporter v K [2010] UKSC 56 (unmarried father's right to be heard, challenge to legislation on human rights grounds) and Gow v Grant [2012] UKSC 29 (financial provision for cohabitants). Other recent cases include M v M and W Trustees Limited, [2011] CSOH 33 (setting aside transfer of funds to trust, financial provision on divorce); W v W [2013] CSOH (financial provision on divorce, transfer of shares, capital gains tax); Petition of AB and CD, [2015] CSIH 25 (social workers alleged contempt); JM v Locality Reporter, Glasgow, [2015] CSIH 58 (appeal, referral to children's hearing, wilful ill-treatment); Fife Council, Petitioner, [2015] CSIH 74 (appeal, permanence order, authority to adopt); DM v Fife Council, [2016] CSIH 17 (education, discrimination).
Professional Memberships: Chairman Advocates' Family Law Association; UK delegate to Family and Succession Committee of CCBE; Vice-President Part-time Sheriffs Association; Chairman of Board of Trustees Adoption and Fostering Alliance Scotland.
Career: Solicitor in England 1978-86. Solicitor in Scotland 1987-91. Called to the Bar in 1992. Appointed part-time sheriff in 2005. Took silk in 2007.
Publications: Include: Education Law in Scotland (2nd edition), Thomson Reuters/W Green (2016); The Laws of Scotland, Stair Memorial Encyclopaedia (Education Section), Lexis Nexis (2010); Scottish Human Rights Service (Family and Education sections), Thomson Reuters/W Green; Court of Session Practice (Family Section), Bloomsbury; Editor of Family Law Reports, Thomson Reuters/W Green.
Personal: MA (Hons) (History and Law), University of Cambridge; Lecturer Sulaimaniyah University, Iraq 1976-78; Visiting Bye-Fellow Newnham College, Cambridge 2002; member of Scottish Executive Adoption Policy Review Group 2005.

SCOTT, Rachel
3 Raymond Buildings Barristers, London
020 7400 6400
rachel.scott@3rblaw.com
Featured in Extradition (London), Financial Crime (London)
Practice Areas: Crime (particularly fraud), extradition and international law, and public law including inquests. Rachel has notable expertise in financial and corporate crime and is a member of the SFO's B Panel. She regularly acts in complex fraud, corruption and cartel cases; current instructions include R v Alstom & others, involving alleged bribery by a UK subsidiary of the French transport and energy giant. Rachel also appears in civil fraud and contempt proceedings, most recently for the defence in the Commercial Court action brought by Victor Pinchuk. She is frequently instructed in extradition cases both by requesting states and requested persons, including in appeals to the Supreme Court and the Privy Council. She offers specialist advice regarding 'import' extradition requests as well as matters of mutual legal assistance. Rachel acts in inquests for families of the deceased, police officers and other interested persons. She has expertise in judicial review proceedings, notable cases including Mackaill & others ('Plebgate'), Rigg-Samuels (concerning the lawfulness of police officer resignations whilst under investigation) and Beny Steimetz Resources Ltd (challenging the use of the SFO's compulsory powers to assist an overseas criminal investigation into alleged corruption).
Career: MusB (Hons) Manchester (Music) 2001, Call 2004, SFO C-Panel 2009, SFO B-Panel 2013.

SCOTT, Timothy QC
29 Bedford Row Chambers, London
020 7404 1044
tscott@29br.co.uk
Featured in Family/Matrimonial (London)
Practice Areas: Legal 500 Children and Family Silk of the Year 2013 – 14. Chambers & Partners Family Silk of the Year 2011 – 12. Leading specialist in international family law including EU Regulations, jurisdiction and forum disputes, Part III MFPA, recognition of foreign marriages and divorces, offshore trusts, family relocation and child abduction. Instructed regularly by leading family law firms. Recent cases include: Re Baronetcy of Pringle of Stichill [2016] UKPC 16 (contested baronetcy, DNA evidence); Re V [2016] EWHC 668 (Fam) (EU Maintenance Regulation, Scotland); MS v PS [2016] EWHC 88 (Fam) (EU Maintenance Regulation, referral to CJEU); Tan Sri Dr Khoo Peng v Pauline Siew Phin Chai [2015] EWCA Civ 1312 (forum conveniens, res judicata); Ramadani v Ramadani [2015] EWCA 1138 (EU Maintenance Regulation); Ray v Sekhri [2014] 2 FLR 1168 (divorce jurisdiction, domicile); EA v AP [2013] EWHC 2344 (Fam) (EU Maintenance Regulation); Z v Z (No 2) (Financial Remedy: Marriage Contract) [2012] 1 FLR 1100; JKN v JCN (Divorce: Forum) [2011] 1 FLR 826; Agbaje v Akkinoye-Agbaje [2010] 1 FLR 1813 (Supreme Court, Part III MFPA).
Professional Memberships: Lady Justice Black's International Family Law Committee; Bar Council EU Law Committee; International Academy of Family Lawyers; Chartered Institute of Arbitrators.
Career: Called to the Bar 1975. Appointed QC 1995. Appointed Recorder 1999. Family arbitrator, mediator and collaborative lawyer.
Publications: Contributor of articles to Family Law magazine and other specialist publications. Regular speaker at seminars on a wide range of family law topics.
Personal: Queen's Scholar Westminster School, Exhibitioner New College Oxford. Lives in London.

SCRIVEN, Pamela QC
1 King's Bench Walk, London
020 79361500
p@scrivenqc.co.uk
Featured in Family/Matrimonial (London)
Practice Areas: Family Law
Professional Memberships: FLBA
Career: Called to the Bar in 1970; took silk in 1992
Publications:
Personal:

SEAMAN, Jennifer
Outer Temple Chambers, London
020 7353 6381
jennifer.seaman@outertemple.com
Featured in Pensions (London)
Practice Areas: Commercial, Chancery and Pensions litigation. Amongst other cases, Jennifer has recently been instructed in: Sharp v. Hutchins [2015] EWHC 1240 (Ch) (a will was challenged on the grounds of want of knowledge and approval); Ballinger v. Mercer Ltd [2014] EWHC 372 (Ch) and [2014] EWCA Civ 996 (a professional negligence claim against companies who provided actuarial services); GE v. KE [2013] EWHC 1938 (Fam) (whether a widow was legally married to the deceased at the date of his death); and two Supreme Court cases, Futter v. HMRC [2013] UKSC 26 (concerning the so-called rule in Re Hastings-Bass) and Benedetti v. Sawiris [2013] UKSC 50 (concerning restitution/quantum meruit claim).
Professional Memberships: Attorney General's B Panel; ChBA; COMBAR; APL; STEP (Affiliate Member); ACTAPS
Career: Called 2007.
Publications: Tolley's Pension Law chapter: "Dispute Resolution and Pension Scheme Litigation"; "The 'best interests' principle and seeking the Court's blessing", T&Ts (2016); "Commonplace mistakes in drafting wills and trusts and what can be done to resolve them", T&Ts (2015); Co-Author of "An Exercise in Good Citizenship?", TQR Oct 2013; Author of various LexisNexis Practice Notes on pensions litigation.
Personal: Education: New College, Oxford University (2005 BA (Jurisprudence); 2006 BCL).

SEAR, Richard
1 Hare Court, London
020 7797 7410
sear@1hc.com
Featured in Family/Matrimonial (London)
Practice Areas: Richard practises in Family law and in particular matrimonial finance, cohabitation claims, applications under Schedule 1 of the Children Act and private law children work.
Professional Memberships: Family Law Bar Association.
Career: Called in 2005. Diplock Scholar of Middle Temple.
Personal: Married with two children. Educated at Magdalen College School, Oxford; King's College, London (BA, 1st Class; AKC; MA); Green College, University of Oxford (MSc).

SEGAL, Oliver QC
Old Square Chambers, London
25 7269 0300
segal@oldsquare.co.uk
Featured in Employment (London)
Practice Areas: Oliver is regarded as a leading Silk in employment law and acts regularly for major commercial clients and for most of the major trade unions. Within employment law he has particular specialist experience in: industrial action (appearing for the successful trade unions in the Court of Appeal cases of RMT v Serco Ltd); collective disputes (recently appeared for the appellants in Hartley & Ors v King Edward VI College, a case which concerned the amount of money which could be lawfully withheld from the pay of teachers on strike; for successful claimants in Court of Appeal in Anderson & ors v London Fire and Emergency Planning Authority; and for successful claimants in the recent EAT case of Abrahall v Nottingham City Council); breach of contract claims (including claims involving restrictive covenants, PHI and negligent references (appearing for the successful claimant in the Court of Appeal case of Gibb v Maidstone and Tunbridge Wells NHS Trust); discrimination claims (recently instructed in claim regarding alleged racial and religious discrimination against 50 Goan workers at Great Western Hospital); Working Time and TUPE claims. Oliver is also probably the leading barrister within the field

of Commercial Agency claims; he acts for both agents and principals and has appeared in several of the most important reported cases, including the House of Lords case of Lonsdale v Howard and Hallam Ltd and the recent High Court cases of ARSM v Typhoo Tea Ltd, and Software Incubator Ltd v Computer Associates Ltd. Recent work: Instructed in appeal from Hartley & ors case – listed in Supreme Court due January 2017; and appeal from ARSM v Typhoo case – listed in CA May 2017.
Professional Memberships: ELBA.
Career: Corpus Christi College, Oxford (1981-85). School Oriental and African Studies, University. London (1985-86). Called 1992, Middle Temple; QC 2011.
Personal: Expert bridge player and writer.

SEGAL, Sharon
1 Garden Court Family Law Chambers, London
020 7797 7900
Segal@1gc.com
Featured in Family/Matrimonial (London)
Practice Areas: All aspects of family law relating to children whether in the private law field or in public law proceedings. Within the public law arena, she is instructed in complex cases, whether acting for the local authority, parents or guardian and has undertaken a range of cases involving vulnerable clients, serious allegations of abuse and non accidental injury with complex medical issues; and exceptional cases involving honour killing and wardship. Within the private law field, she has extensive experience of child arrangement disputes, and is regularly instructed in intractable cases, leave to remove applications as well as having significant experience being instructed on behalf of the child in rule 16 cases.
Professional Memberships: Family Law Bar Association, The Association of Lawyers for Children.
Career: LLB Law (Hons) Queen Mary and Westfield College, University of London. Called to the Bar, Inner Temple (2000).
Publications: Various reported cases, including the Supreme Court.
Personal: Enjoys travelling, listening to music and going to the theatre.

SELBY, Jonathan
Keating Chambers, London
020 7544 2600
jselby@keatingchambers.com
Featured in Construction (London)
Practice Areas: Specialist in construction, engineering and energy disputes including related professional negligence claims (architects, engineers and surveyors). Extensive knowledge of all forms of contract including the JCT, ICE, NEC and IChemE standard forms. Regularly acts in high value litigation, in particular in the Technology and Construction Court, and has represented clients in the Privy Council and Court of Appeal. Often instructed to act for clients through the adjudication process and to represent clients at mediation. An accredited adjudicator, Jonathan accepts both party and nominating body appointments.
Professional Memberships: Technology and Construction Bar Association (TECBAR); Society of Construction Law; Commercial Bar Association (COMBAR); London Common Law and Commercial Bar Association.
Career: Called to the Bar 1999; TECBAR accredited adjudicator 2007.
Publications: Researcher, Keating on Construction Contracts – 7th to 9th Editions.

SELBY, Lawrence
9 Bedford Row, London
020 7489 2727
lawrence.selby@9bedfordrow.co.uk
Featured in Crime (London)
Practice Areas: General Crime; Fraud & Disciplinary/Regulatory.
Professional Memberships: Member of the South Eastern Circuit; the Criminal Bar Association, the British Association for Sport and Law and the Chartered Institute of Arbitrators. Vice Chair of the Japan Karate-Do Ryobu-Kai International Mediation and Arbitration Committee; Member of England Boxing "Compliance, Legal and HR" Subcommittee; Appointed to The FA County Association Anti-Discrimination Chairman's Panel; Independent Director (Legal/Governance) and Compliance Officer of the United Kingdom Brazilian Jiu Jitsu Association.
Career: Specialises in defending high profile and complex cases of homicide, fraud and significant drugs' offences: R v Patino & Others –'The King of Viagra' case: "the biggest worldwide conspiracy involving medicines ever brought to trial"; R v Marshall and Bush –'The Jigsaw Man' murder; R v Bellchambers & Others – 'Operation Augusta': "the largest counterfeiting operation ever uncovered on EBay"; R v Divan & Others – 'Operation Arcadia': Leading Junior in a case involving the "UK's biggest counterfeit DVD gang"; R v Miah & Others – 'Operation Curlew/Oak': Leading Junior in a 32 handed Conspiracy to Supply Heroin; R v Herak & Others – 'Operation Veerde': Leading Junior in a 9 handed "Sham Marriage" and "Sex Trafficking" conspiracy; R v Yandell & Others – "Operation Dino II": 96 handed "cash for crash" fraud.
Personal: Fluent in French, Italian and Spanish. Educated at Millfield School, Reading University (BA Hons), Sussex University (CPE), Birkbeck, University of London (Postgraduate Certificate in Sports Governance and MSc in Sports Management and the Business of Football.)

SELMAN, Elizabeth
1 King's Bench Walk, London
020 7936 1500
eselman@1kbw.co.uk
Featured in Family/Matrimonial (London)
Practice Areas: Private Law Children and Matrimonial Finance.
Professional Memberships: FLBA and South Eastern Circuit.
Career: Elizabeth Selman's practice covers both matrimonial finance and private law children work. This breadth can provide clients with the very significant advantage of retaining her for both potential areas of dispute following marital or relationhsip breakdown. She undertakes complex child arrangement disputes, international and internal relocation cases as well as discrete specific issue and prohibited steps order applications. Elizabeth's finance practice covers both matrimonial finance and Schedule 1 work, concentrating on mid to high net worth clients.
Personal: Elizabeth has three sons and spends much of her free time supporting them on rugby and hockey touch lines, swapping that for the cricket pitch in the summer, when the weather allows.

SELVARATNAM, Vasanti QC
St Philips Stone Chambers, London
020 7440 6900
vasanti.selvaratnam@stonechambers.com
Featured in International Arbitration (London), Shipping (London)
Practice Areas: All aspects of international commercial litigation and arbitration, including shipping, commodities, banking and finance, conflict of law and jurisdiction disputes, all forms of interim urgent relief including freezing orders and anti-suit injunctions, and civil fraud. She is particularly noted for her user friendly 'hands on' approach to cases and for her ability quickly to get to grips with disputes raising complex factual and technical issues which require a sound grasp of expert evidence and mastery of detail. Reported leading cases include the Court of Appeal decisions in The Wadi Sudr [2010] 1 Lloyd's Rep 193 (leading case on the arbitration exception, the Judgments Regulation and issue estoppel), Joint Stock Asset Management Co Ingosstrakh-Investments v BNP Paribas [2012] 1 Lloyd's Rep 649 (leading case on non contractual anti-suit injunctions) and Madoff Securities International Ltd (in liquidation) v Yacht Bull Corporation [2010] EWHC 133 (Ch) (interrelationship between the Judgments Regulation and the Insolvency Regulation in relation to jurisdiction); Emirates Trading Agency v PMEPL (2014, friendly discussions clause a condition precedent to right to commence arbitration) and Emirates Trading Agency LLC v Sociedade de Fomento Industrial Private Ltd (2015, clarifies law on estoppel arising from a prior partial interim award on jurisdiction where the constitution of a majority of the Tribunal has changed). Other recent noteworthy cases include: Nakanishi Marine v Gora Shipping and Attica Finance [2012] EWHC 3383 (Comm) which considers the effects of a tripartite subordination agreement on the rights of a junior lender as against the borrower and guarantor; RBS v FAl Oil Co Ltd and ors [2012] EWHC 3628 (Comm) which is a leading case on interim relief under section 25 CJJA 1982 and Stolt Kestrel [2014] EWHC 1731 (Adm) (mandatory extension of time where no reasonable opportunity to arrest under section 190(6) Merchant Shipping Act 1995 and other time bar issues).
Professional Memberships: COMBAR, Chancery Bar Association, LCLBA, BMLA, LMAA, London Shipping Law Centre (Head of education sub-committee), Bar European Group, ICC's Banking and Finance committee.
Career: Called to the Bar 1983: LLM 1984; practising barrister at the Commercial Bar 1985 to date; Recorder 2000 to date; Queen's Counsel 2001; Bencher of Middle Temple 2011. Joint Head of Stone Chambers, 2014, Joint Head of London, St Philips Stone Chambers, 2016. Also accepts appointments as arbitrator in a wide range of commercial disputes.

SELWAY, Kate
Radcliffe Chambers, London
020 7831 0081
kselway@radcliffechambers.com
Featured in Chancery (London), Real Estate Litigation (London)
Practice Areas: Trusts and estates (contentious and advisory, including trust taxation and estate planning); probate and administration, charity law, Court of Protection; all aspects of real property, landlord and tenant (agricultural, business and residential), and other areas of general chancery practice. Reported cases include: Nicholls v Highways Agency; Secretary of State for the Environment Transport & the Regions v Baylis (Gloucester) Limited; King v Walden (HMIT); IRC v Hashmi (CA); McAdam Homes Limited v Robinson (CA); Sevenoaks District Council v First Secretary of State & Anr; Lonsdale v Braisby (HMIT); IRC v Arkwright; Coombes v HMRC; Elizabeth Court (Bournemouth) Ltd v HMRC; Solicitor for the Affairs of HM Treasury v Doveton; Taff v Highways Agency; Siaw v Lock; Holden-Hindley v Holden-Hindley; NCA v Szepietowski (Supreme Court).
Professional Memberships: Chancery Bar Association, Charity Law Association, STEP.
Career: Called 1995. Member of Attorney General's B Panel (2003-08); C Panel (1999-2003). Appointed to Attorney General's A Panel in 2016.
Publications: Joint editor, Wurtzburg and Mills, Building Society Law (looseleaf), 1996-2010
Personal: Educated at Newlands School, Maidenhead, Bristol University (BA, History, Class I), New College, Oxford (DPhil in Medieval History), City University (CPE). Leisure interests: hockey, photography.

SENDALL, Antony
Littleton Chambers, London
020 77978600
asendall@littletonchambers.co.uk
Featured in Employment (London)
Practice Areas: All aspects of employment law including TUPE, discrimination, equal pay, working time, restraint of trade/confidential information/garden leave and industrial disputes. Sports law, especially employment, regulatory and disciplinary matters. Commercial law: all forms of commercial disputes, including injunctions, mediations and arbitrations. Mediation: commercial, workplace and community mediation.
Professional Memberships: ELA, ELBA, ILS, PNBA, COMBAR LCLCBA, BASL.
Career: Antony has a huge breadth of experience in all aspects of Employment Law, and has appeared in numerous reported cases and many complex and ground-breaking pieces of litigation both in Employment Tribunals and in the High Court. He is highly experienced in confidential information/restraint of trade injunctions. He has also been involved in industrial dispute injunctions in a wide range of industries. Renowned as an advocate, Antony regularly undertakes hearings of all sorts in Tribunals and the High Court as well as in front of regulatory and disciplinary bodies and is an experienced appellate advocate, including the EAT, Court of Appeal and Privy Council. In recent years, Antony has also become an acknowledged expert mediator with particular emphasis on employment/workplace mediations as well as commercial and community mediations.
Personal: Educated: Cambridge University (Law: 1st Class Hons). Interests: photography (semiprofessional), acting (both amateur and professional) and cooking.

SETHI, Mohinderpal
Littleton Chambers, London
020 7797 8600
mosethi@littletonchambers.co.uk
Featured in Employment (London)
Practice Areas: Barrister specialising in domestic and cross-border company/commercial, employment and partnership law. Substantial experience of appearing in ultra high value claims in the High Court, tribunals and on appeal acting for and against international banks and other City institutions particularly involving all forms of asset and business protection. Recent high profile matters include leading cases on: the Libor and FX rate rigging scandals (Mathur v Deutsche Bank AG); injunctions restraining breaches of restrictive covenants, confidential information and fiduciary duties including team moves (BGC Switzerland v Tullett Prebon); multimillion pound bonus and share option claims (GFI v Tullett Prebon); antistrike injunctions (Balfour Beatty v Unite); business transfers under TUPE (CWU v RMG); senior executive whistleblowing (Masterton v Lloyds Banking Group); landmark discrimination claims (MOD v DeBique); international law, human rights and EU law (Reyes v Al-Malki); the 'Border Checks' scandal (Brodie Clark v Home Office); and misuse of social media (Crisp v Apple). He is Junior Counsel to the Crown (A Panel). For a comprehensive CV visit www.mosethi.com.
Professional Memberships: ELA, ILS, ELBA, APP, ARDL, COMBAR, LCLCBA, PNBA and Elected Treasurer of ELBA.
Career: Called 1996, Middle Temple. The Queen Mother's Scholar (the premier Inn scholarship); The Malcolm Wright Prize-winner; and Harmsworth Major Entrance Exhibitioner.
Publications: Editorial Board Member of 'ELA Briefing'; Author of several leading publications including 'Employment Tribunal Remedies' (Fourth edition, OUP), 'Termination of Employment' (Bloomsbury Professional), and Springboard Injunctions (PLC).
Personal: Wadham College, University of Oxford (MA Hons Jurisprudence). Wadham Scholar.

SHADAREVIAN, Paul
Cornerstone Barristers, London
020 72424986
paul.s@cornerstonebarristers.com
Featured in Planning (London)
Practice Areas: Planning, compulsory purchase and compensation, environmental, highways, public procurement, local government.
Professional Memberships: Planning and Environmental Bar Association, Compulsory Purchase Association.
Career: Leading specialist in development plans (e.g. Thurrock, Watford, Chelmsford, Brentwood, Suffolk Coastal, Ipswich Core Strategies), LDO formulation and strategic and major project planning including DP World distribution centre for Thurrock (winning RTPI National award 2014) and Milton Park; major highway infrastructure (inc. widening of A13, Ely southern bypass, A13/A127 interchange, proposed Junction 7A, M11). Also specialises in major retail proposals for the public and private sector (e.g. Lakeside and various superstore appeals nationwide), major housing (e.g. North Chelmsford 3000 dwellings and major infrastructure, Adastral Park (SCDC) 2000 dwellings); CPO and compensation (e.g. Emirates Stadium, A130/A13 Interchange, Central Luton Transportation Scheme). Consistently appearing in professional guides to the legal profession as one of the leading planning barristers in the country; variously quoted as being "top notch", "a stylish but tough advocate", "a lateral thinker and excellent team leader on major projects" and a barrister, "whose direct and no nonsense approach has earned him the respect of his peers and clients alike" and "whose cross examinations are always superb".

SHAH, Akhil QC
Fountain Court Chambers, London
020 7583 3335
axs@fountaincourt.co.uk
Featured in Travel (London), Aviation (London), Product Liability (London)
Practice Areas: General commercial disputes including aviation, re/ insurance, and arbitration. Expertise in aviation disputes including aircraft finance, aircraft leasing, product design, aviation insurance and reinsurance, regulatory work and carriage by air. Notable cases include: Alpstream v PK and GECAS (aircraft finance); Involnert v Aprilgrange and others (insurance moral hazard); Jet 2 v Huzar (CA) and Dawson v Thomson Airways (CA) (EC Reg 261 rights); Blue Sky v Chartis & Others (insurance dispute re: theft of Boeing 747 aircraft to Iran); PK v Mahan (arrest of aircraft and enforcement of judgment); Pindell v Air Asia (Aircraft lease dispute); DTVA v bmibaby (low cost airline dispute with airport); Kibris v SoS and Republic of Cyprus (review of right to fly from UK); HSH Nordbank v Air Astra (recovery of distressed aircraft); Hill & others v CAA (Review of airspace design); Amiri Flight Authority v BAE System Plc (Aircraft design); Airbus Industrie G.I.E v Patel (Jurisdiction; anti-suit injunction; product liability); Western Digital v British Airways (Warsaw Convention: title to sue); acting in Bermuda Form and other international arbitration disputes (parties confidential).
Professional Memberships: COMBAR.
Career: Called 1990; QC 2010; British Virgin Islands Bar 1999.
Publications: Contributor to Bullen & Leak & Jacobs 'Precedents of Pleading' (18th ed) and 'Carriage by Air'.

SHANE, Michael
Atkin Chambers, London
020 7404 0102
mshane@atkinchambers.com
Featured in Mediators (All Circuits)
Practice Areas: Michael Shane is a highly regarded arbitrator and mediator with over 25 years' experience. He has successfully mediated in excess of 1500 disputes and served as an arbitrator in excess of 100 cases involving a variety of subjects. Michael specialises in complex international commercial disputes arising in a wide range of industry sectors and practices including construction and infrastructure, energy and utilities, banking, insurance and intellectual property as well as other commercial areas. Michael has worked as a mediator and as an arbitrator on major infrastructure and energy projects in the UK, Europe, the USA, Canada, Central and South America, Hong Kong, Singapore, the Philippines, the Caribbean and Africa. This international experience allows him to bring an effective approach to cross-cultural and multi-party disputes. He brings a commercial approach to mediations and arbitrations arising from his varied professional experience and is known for his persistence as a mediator. Further information is available at his website www.mbshane.com.
Professional Memberships: KIAC and Hong Kong Government's list approved and qualified Mediators, Arbitrator on the LCIA database of neutrals. KLRCA Panel appointed Arbitrator and Mediator
Career: Juris Doctor, University of California, Berkeley School of Law; Master of Laws, University College London.

SHAPIRO, Daniel
Crown Office Chambers, London
020 7797 8100
shapiro@crownofficechambers.com
Featured in Professional Negligence (London), Energy & Natural Resources (London), Insurance (London), Property Damage (London)
Practice Areas: Daniel is regularly instructed in complex claims in his core practice areas of commercial contracts, insurance and reinsurance, professional negligence, energy, construction, product liability and property damage. Daniel is a highly effective advocate instructed in arbitrations, trials and appeals, usually against silks. Daniel is instructed in a number of cutting-edge professional negligence claims including acting for the successful appellant in Jones v Kaney. He is an insurance and reinsurance specialist and is regularly instructed in defence of insurance brokers. Daniel's commerciality, commitment and court room skills gain him instructions for and against a wide range of commercial parties, insurers, reinsurers, and professionals. Clients appreciate his clear advice, tactical awareness and commitment to delivering a first rate service. Daniel always seeks the effective commercial solution to disputes and regularly acts for clients in successful mediations, round table meetings and other forms of ADR. He is a TECBAR accredited adjudicator and acts for parties in adjudications. Further details are available on www.crownofficechambers.com
Professional Memberships: COMBAR, TECBAR, Professional Negligence Bar Association.

SHARLAND, Andrew
11KBW, London
020 7632 8500
Andrew.Sharland@11kbw.com
Featured in Administrative & Public Law (London), Community Care (London), Data Protection (London), Education (London), Local Government (London)
Practice Areas: Specialises in all aspects of public law (commercial, regulatory, education, community care, mental health, local government, coroners, and planning and environmental law) human rights, employment, public procurement and information law. He practises in English and European courts acting for individuals, public authorities, commercial organisations and NGOs. Notable cases include: MacDonald v UK (Private life and community care in ECHR), Washington First v UK (freedom of expression in ECHR), Campbell v MGN Ltd (Article 10 ECHR and costs, HL), Kennedy v Charity Commission (freedom of information and Article 10 ECHR in the Supreme Court), R (Plantagenet Alliance) v Secretary of State for Justice and Leicester City Council (challenge to the decision to bury Richard III's remains in Leicester), DWF v Insolvency Service (public procurement and time limits in the Court of Appeal) and the successful procurement challenge to the LAA's new Criminal Legal Aid contracts.
Professional Memberships: ALBA, PEBA, ADRL, PLA.
Career: Called to the Bar in 1996. Appointed to Attorney-General's 'A' Panel of Counsel to the Crown.
Publications: Co-author of Judicial Review: Principles and Procedure (OUP, 2013); Co-author of Media Law and Human Rights' (OUP) (2nd Edn, 2009). Co-author of the Human Rights section in Atkins Court Forms, Contributor to 'Information Rights' and 'Education and the Courts'.
Personal: Educated at Queen Mary College, University of London (LLB), College of William and Mary, Virginia, USA (LLM) and Worcester College, Oxford (BCL).

SHARPE, Tim
Temple Garden Chambers, London
020 7583 1315
timsharpe@tgchambers.com
Featured in Fraud (All Circuits)
Practice Areas: Tim was described by Chambers & Partners as being "bright, hard-working and dependable". Previous editions described him as being "as tenacious a young man as you'll find at the Bar" and "the rising star of the set". Tim's practice in relation to motor insurance fraud encompasses Low Velocity Impact claims, bogus passenger claims, staged and contrived accidents, and "fraud rings". He provides advice and advocacy at all stages of such claims, including prior to proceedings being issued, at the pleadings stage, at trial and, when appropriate, in relation to Contempt of Court proceedings. Recent cases have included representing an insurance company in successfully defending a "slam-on" case where the trial judge made findings of fraud and referred the transcript to the Attorney General, issues arising out of "fundamental dishonesty" and representing applicants and respondents in contempt of court proceedings.

SHARRON, Eliza
Kings Chambers, Manchester
0345 034 3444
clerks@kingschambers.com
Featured in Court of Protection (All Circuits)
Practice Areas: Eliza specialises in all fields of Court of Protection work, including property and affairs, health and welfare, serious medical treatment, and associated human rights matters. Eliza has a background in family law, and specialises in cases where there is an overlap between the Family Court and the Court of Protection, as well as cases that involve safeguarding vulnerable adults within the inherent jurisdiction of the High Court. Eliza undertakes inquest work, in particular where there are issues regarding statutory duties towards children and vulnerable adults. Similarly, Eliza undertakes judicial review work in the field of mental health and community care law, with a particular interest in cases involving the extent of local authority duties towards young people and their families.
Professional Memberships: Northern Circuit; Court of Protection Practitioners Association (COPPA)
Career: Commenced pupillage at Deans Court Chambers in 2009; called to the Bar of the Falkland Islands in 2010 (where Eliza

worked for a brief period as acting Crown Counsel); Junior of the Northern Circuit – 2013; called to the Bar of Cayman Island in 2013 (where Eliza worked as an attorney at law for 6 months); joined Kings Chambers in 2016.
Publications: Community Care Law and Local Authority Handbook (Third Edition, 2015): Chapter 5 – Provisions for Older Children (Leaving Care), Disabled Children and Financial Obligations of Local Authorities Towards Families. The Provision of Secure Mental Health Facilities Across and Outside Wales: LexisPSL 21/01/016

SHAW, Andrew
Drystone Chambers, London
020 7404 1881
andrew.shaw@drystone.com
Featured in Crime (South Eastern)
Practice Areas: Criminal law, local authority/regulatory law.
Professional Memberships: South Eastern Circuit, CBA, East Anglian Bar Mess, Bar Pro Bono Unit.
Career: Andrew Shaw is an experienced and respected junior who both prosecutes and defends across the South Eastern Circuit. He has been instructed in cases involving homicide and other serious violence, firearms, armed robbery, rape and other sexual offences, significant drug trafficking and all aspects of fraud and dishonesty. He is regularly instructed in cases involving fraud and the proceeds of crime, has particular expertise in cases involving the historic physical and sexual abuse of children and is frequently instructed in cases where there are young or otherwise vulnerable witnesses. He is noted for his preparation and handling of document heavy cases and his capacity quickly to come to terms with complicated legal and factual issues. Andrew also has considerable experience of appellate work and Courts-Martial and is regularly instructed as a leading junior, including in murder cases. In addition, Andrew is a Grade 4 prosecutor and is an approved pupil supervisor.

SHAW, Annabel
4 New Square, London
020 7822 2000
a.shaw@4newsquare.com
Featured in Construction (London)
Practice Areas: Acting for and against contractors, architects, engineers and quantity surveyors. Part of Counsel team acting on behalf of joint venture in relation to nuclear installations in the UK. Part of Counsel team acting for a European government in relation to a large IT dispute. Was one of team acting for Multiplex in a series of adjudications and also part of team preparing for a quantum trial in respect of the Wembley Stadium dispute. Was also part of team acting for a major Saudi Arabian group in relation to an ICC Arbitration, subject to Saudi Arabian law, with hearings in Paris.
Professional Memberships: TECBAR, SCL, PNBA, COMBAR.
Career: BA (Oxon) 1st Class. Called to Bar (Gray's Inn) 2002. David Karmel Entrance Award. Prince of Wales Scholar.
Publications: Contributor to Jackson & Powell on Professional Liability.
Personal: Educated New College, Oxford, 1996-99.

SHAW, Benjamin
Erskine Chambers, London
020 7242 5532
bshaw@erskinechambers.com
Featured in Chancery (London), Company (London)
Practice Areas: Ben's practice is divided equally between litigation and transactional work covering company law, corporate insolvency and restructuring and general commercial litigation and arbitration. His transactional work has included both creditor and member schemes of arrangement under Part 26 of the Companies Act 2006, numerous reductions of capital and other reserves for listed public companies and cross-border mergers under the Companies (Cross-Border Mergers) Regulations 2007. Ben also has experience of advising on a wide range of company and corporate governance issues. In recent years, Ben's litigation practice has included instructions in some of the most significant large-scale insolvencies, including Lehman, MF Global and Kaupthing. In 2013, Ben acted for the respondent companies in Prest v Petrodel, the landmark decision on piercing the corporate veil.
Professional Memberships: COMBAR, Chancery Bar Association.
Career: Called Lincoln's Inn 2002.

SHAY, Stephen
23 Essex Street, London
020 7413 0353
StephenShay@23es.com
Featured in Crime (South Eastern)
Practice Areas: Stephen is experienced in all areas of serious, organised, complex and sensitive crime, such as homicide, firearms, rape and other serious sexual offences, domestic extremism, complex fraud, and large-scale drugs offences. He is also experienced in crime-related judicial review and appellate work, and civil pleadings (having had a mixed practice some years ago). Stephen is a Grade 4 CPS Prosecutor in London and the South East, who has also been appointed to the CPS Headquarters Serious Crime Group Specialist Panel and to the Specialist Rape Panel. His recent cases include two trials arising from a drug importation conspiracy involving £26m worth of cocaine, a conspiracy to shoot a 14-year-old schoolboy, and representing at trial a young man accused of raping his younger cousin. Stephen has been ranked as a leading practitioner in Chambers UK for several years. He has been credited with having "a tremendous knowledge of criminal law" allied to a "smooth advocacy style."
Professional Memberships: CBA, SEC, Sussex, Kent Bar Messes, Middle Temple.
Career: Called to the Bar 1984.
Publications: Contributing editor to Archbold 1993-Present. Wrote the contempt of court chapters in Sweet & Maxwell's "Administrative Court: Practice and Procedure" (2006)
Personal: Educated at Westminster School, Oxford University.

SHEARD, David
Keating Chambers, London
020 75442600
dsheard@keatingchambers.com
Featured in Construction (London)
Practice Areas: David Sheard has developed a busy and wide-ranging practise, encompassing all key areas of Keating Chambers' expertise including construction, adjudication, energy and professional negligence work. He has worked with numerous standard-form and bespoke contracts, including FIDIC, NEC3, PFI, SFA/99, ACE, RICS and many of the JCT forms (past and present), providing advice to individuals ranging from private home-owners to large property-development companies. He also has substantial court experience, having represented various clients in the County and High Courts both for interim applications and at trial. In addition, David has been instructed on numerous occasions as junior counsel in larger construction disputes, notably having been instructed in two separate arbitrations arising out of wind farm projects, with sums in issue of £300 and £100 million respectively. David also worked as junior counsel to Marcus Taverner QC in Accolade Wines Limited v GJ3 Limited and others, a complex multi-party dispute which was one of the biggest cases to come before the TCC in recent years. David is also establishing an international practice, most recently having spent time in Doha in connection with a substantial arbitration.
Career: TECBAR Accredited Adjudicator (2013), Barrister at Keating Chambers (2011), Called to the Bar (2010)

SHEEHAN, James
Maitland Chambers, London
020 7406 1200
jsheehan@maitlandchambers.com
Featured in Chancery (London), Fraud (London)
Practice Areas: Commercial and chancery disputes, including civil fraud, contract and other business disputes, company and partnership, insolvency, fund and banking litigation, claims against directors and other fiduciaries, property litigation. Particular experience of international disputes involving issues of jurisdiction and choice of law. Notable recent cases include: Dar Al Arkan v Al-Refai (Comm Ct and CA: conspiracy, breach of confidence, jurisdiction for contempt proceedings); BTA v Ablyazov (Comm Ct and CA: US$5bn fraud claim against Kazakh banker); Erste v Red October (Comm Ct and CA: conspiracy, jurisdiction, choice of law); a dispute in the Ch Div and CA involving multi-million dollar fraud claims relating to an offshore fund; Med Mining v Nusantara Plc (Comm Ct; directors' duties); Berezovsky v Hine (Ch Div; joint venture claim against Patarkatsishvili estate); Nomad International Shipping Corp v DST Shipping Inc (Comm Ct: joint venture dispute).
Professional Memberships: COMBAR, Chancery Bar Association, Commercial Fraud Lawyers' Association, Financial Services Lawyers' Association.
Career: Called 2008.
Personal: St. Catharine's College, Cambridge (French and German, starred first, top of year); BPP (CPE); Inns of Court School of Law (Outstanding, second in year). Queen Mother scholar; Baron Dr Ver Heyden de Lancey prize (Middle Temple).

SHEEHAN, Malcolm QC
Henderson Chambers, London
020 7583 9020
clerks@hendersonchambers.co.uk
Featured in Product Liability (London), Real Estate Litigation (London)
Practice Areas: Commercial and common law practice concentrating on product liability, group actions, property, arbitration and insurance, personal injury and health and safety. Product liability experience includes acting for defendants in leading multi-party and individual claims relating to pharmaceutical products, medical devices and motor vehicles. Malcolm's Property expertise includes commercial and residential landlord and tenant, covenants, dilapidations and public law property claims. His personal injury practice includes international tort claims,employer liability claims and sporting accidents. Malcolm's reported cases include Young v Home Office(leading House of Lords limitation decision), Motto v Trafigura and Rogers v Hoyle. He is experienced in health and safety and environmental criminal and civil litigation.
Professional Memberships: Commercial Bar Association; Professional Negligence Bar Association; Health and Safety Lawyers Association; Personal Injury Bar Association.
Career: Oriel College, Oxford (First Class Honours). Mansfield Scholarship; Denning Scholarship; Inns of Court Studentship; Judicial assistant to Lord Woolf while Master of the Rolls. Junior Counsel to the Crown ('A' Panel). Judge of First Tier Tribunal. Appointed QC 2015
Publications: Contributor to 'The Civil Practitioner's Guide to the Human Rights Act 1998', 'Halsbury's Laws' (Vol 37), Butterworths Civil Court Precedents, and Kluwer International Product Law Manual.

SHELDON, Clive QC
11KBW, London
020 7632 8500
Clive.Sheldon@11kbw.com
Featured in Administrative & Public Law (London), Education (London), Employment (London), Local Government (London)
Practice Areas:

SHER, Adam
Fountain Court Chambers, London
020 7583 3335
ads@fountaincourt.co.uk
Featured in Banking & Finance (London)
Practice Areas: Civil and commercial litigation including banking, financial services, insurance, civil fraud and professional negligence. Much of recent work has been related to derivatives (interest rate, currency and credit), including mis-selling claims, LIBOR and EURIBOR litigation, including Deutsche Bank v Unitech (one of The Lawyer's Top 20 Cases of 2014) Property Alliance Group v RBS (the first LIBOR manipulation case to go to trial) and Marme v RBS and others (which, along with Property Alliance Group v RBS featured in the Lawyer's Top 20 Cases of 2016) as well as disputes with European public bodies (including Merrill Lynch v Verona and Merrill Lynch v Florence, one of The Lawyer's Top 20 Cases of 2013). Various international arbitrations, including $1.4 billion dispute between GMR and the Government of the Maldives over Malé international airport.
Professional Memberships: Member COMBAR, London Common Law and Commercial Bar Association.
Career: Called 2007.
Publications: 'Consensus, separability and Article 23 of the Brussels Regulation' [2009] LMCLQ 275.
Personal: Oriel College, Oxford, BA (First Class), BCL (Distinction), Harvard Law School, LLM.

SHERIDAN, Amber
29 Bedford Row Chambers, London
020 7404 1044
asheridan@29br.co.uk
Featured in Family/Matrimonial (London)
Practice Areas: Matrimonial Finance; Financial Provision for Children; Pre and post-nuptial agreements; Civil Partnerships; Cohabitation; Inheritance Act. Reported cases include: Shield v Shield [2014] EWHC 23 (Fam); Shield v Shield [2013] EWHC 3525 (Fam); Golubovich v Golubovich [2011] EWCA Civ 528; Golubovich v Golubovich [2011] 2 FLR 1193; Golubovich v Golubovich [2010] 2 FLR 1614; Agbaje v Agbaje [2010] 1 FLR 1813.
Professional Memberships: FLBA; Resolution.
Career: Called to the Bar in 2008; Middle Temple.
Personal: Educated at Sevenoaks School, Edinburgh University and BPP. Middle Temple Certificate of Honour and Benefactors' Scholar. Resides in London.

SHERIDAN, Matthew
Littleton Chambers, London
020 7797 8600
msheridan@littletonchambers.co.uk
Featured in Employment (London)
Practice Areas: The focus of Matthew's High Court practice is business competition: confidential information, restrictive covenants and springboard relief, particularly in a team-move context. He is regularly instructed to make and resist injunction applications. Principal areas of Matthew's Employment Tribunal practice include complex discrimination claims, whistleblowing and employee/worker status. Recent appellate cases include Reverend Mark Sharpe v The Bishop of Worcester [2015] IRLR 663 (Court of Appeal).
Professional Memberships: ELBA; COMBAR.
Career: Called 2000, Gray's Inn.
Personal: King's College School, Wimbledon; Queens' College, Cambridge (Law).

SHERRARD, Charles QC
Furnival Chambers, London
020 7405 3232
CSherrard@furnivallaw.co.uk
Featured in Financial Crime (London)
Practice Areas: Charlie's resourceful and powerful tactical expertise, together with a dedicated hands-on preparation and management of his cases, has lent itself particularly well to Financial Crime and Regulatory Law. Regarded by others as "the complete advocate" [Chambers & Partners : Financial Crime Ranking 2015] Charlie has bucked the trend by being continuously busy and constantly in demand, so much so that he has been a regular go-to expert for LBC News Radio in the last few years. He gained significant credit and media coverage for his unstinting and powerful defence of Kweku Adoboli [aka The UBS Rogue Trader] taking on the might of the Swiss Bank and securing unexpected acquittals on all false accounting counts despite the seemingly overwhelming evidence. Another notable client, unpopular with many, but successfully acquitted of a large scale income tax fraud, was Stephen Yaxley-Lennon, better known as Tommy Robinson [ex leader of the EDL]. In early 2015, Charlie secured the acquittal of Stuart Jones, son to Sir David Jones, in the fraud and feud arising out of the capital raising by the board of JD Sports in 2009. Similar success has been achieved in Carousel Frauds in Liverpool [Operation Forbear] securing the only acquittal in the whole operation, and acquittals for a solicitor in a fraud on the Olympic Development Authority [Operation Cavalcade]. Other notable and high profile fraud cases have seen Charlie represent other professionals, this time an accountant, at the heart of a massive property fraud [R-v-Entwistle & others]. 2016-17 will see a continuous workload of boiler room and tax frauds in addition to advising in regulatory and cybercrime areas.
Professional Memberships: South East Circuit; Criminal Bar Association. Cyber Crime Association. Fraud Lawyers Association
Career: Queens Counsel since 2012 Called to the bar 1986 Member of chambers since 1988 Director of Furnival Chambers Ltd since 2007 Chairman of Pupillage since 2003 Middle Temple Advocacy Trainer.
Personal: Married with three gorgeous children. Educated at University College School, Hampstead LLB Hons from U.E.A Active and keen cricketer, golfer and tennis player in Hertfordshire leagues, as well as being a 'Gooner'.

SHERRATT, Matthew
Carmelite Chambers, London
020 7936 6300
clerks@carmelitechambers.co.uk
Featured in Crime (London)
Practice Areas: A specialist defence advocate with a wealth of experience as junior and leading junior in cases involving serious and complex crime. Junior counsel in a number of high profile cases including the millionaire businessman Nicholas Van Hoogstraten in the criminal hearings which resulted in his acquittal; Christopher Edward Buckingham "The Lord of Fraud; one of the Defendants in the Johnson Matthey Gold bullion robbery and in R v. Maxwell (Appellant) [2010] UKSC 48. He also appeared in a number of important reported decisions including: Darmalingum v Secretary of State for Mauritius (PC) [2000] WLR 2303; R (Mudie) v Dover Magistrates [2003] 2 WLR 1344 (CA); R v Van Hoogstraten [2004] Crim LR 498; Att-Gen's Ref (No.3 of 2004) [2006] Crim.L.R 63,CA; R v. Maxwell [2010] UKSC 48. Now a busy leading junior predominantly in cases of serious organised crime; fraud and money laundering. Recent high profile instructions include acting for supplier of 2 tonnes benzocaine to facilitate supply of cocaine, a multi-million pound boiler room fraud, the alleged bookkeeper for a high profile north London crime family, and attempted murder of a teenager in a gang melee. With a strong civil background regularly instructed to advise in respect of civil fraud and POCA claims.
Professional Memberships: Panel member of French Consulate official panel of recommended lawyers and member of CBA:
Career: Called 1994

SHIRLEY, James
St Philips Stone Chambers, London
020 7440 6900
james.shirley@stonechambers.com
Featured in Shipping (London)
Practice Areas: James Shirley practises in all areas of commercial law, in particular commercial contracts, shipping and international arbitration, jurisdiction disputes, the sale and carriage of goods, and insurance. He was sole counsel for the successful defendants in BDMS Limited v. Rafael Advanced Defence Systems [2014] EWHC 451 (Comm) (Hamblen J), and junior for the successful claimants in "Aquafaith" [2012] EWHC 1077 (Comm) (Cooke J). The bulk of James' shipping practice consists of dry shipping disputes of various kinds (for example, repudiation claims, cargo claims and bills of lading, off-hire, unsafe port claims, laytime and demurrage, speed and performance, the inter-club agreement and formation/termination as well as a wide range of shipbuilding and ship sale and purchase disputes). James is registered as an advocate in Dubai under Part II of the DIFC Courts' Register of Legal Practitioners.
Professional Memberships: COMBAR, LMAA (Supporting Member)
Career: Joined Stone Chambers as a tenant in May 2005. Became a member of the merged set St Philips Stone Chambers in August 2016.
Publications: On the Classification of Amphibious Avians (and Contractual Terms): The Astra, L.Q.R. 2014, 130 (Apr)).
Personal: Tutor in Contract Law at UCL. Education: UCL (1st in law), New College, Oxford (BCL Distinction).

SHIVJI, Sharif
4 Stone Buildings, London
020 7242 5524
S.Shivji@4stonebuildings.com
Featured in Chancery (London), Banking & Finance (London), Company (London), Financial Services (London), Offshore (London)
Practice Areas: Former derivatives trader based in London and Hong-Kong, now specialising in commercial law with a focus on banking, financial services, company, insolvency, and civil fraud litigation. Has in-depth knowledge of the financial markets and corporate finance (in particular, financial and commodity futures, options and complex derivatives). Notable cases include: McGraw-Hill (Standard & Poors) v ApoBank, RBS and others (on-going litigation relating to the liability of rating agencies), Chesterfield and others v Deutsche Bank and others (on-going litigation relating to the sale of €500 million of credit products referenced to Kaupthing hf), Plaza v Law Debenture Trust [2015] EWCA 43 (liability of a bond trustee), Al-Khorafi v Bank Sarasin [2014] (DIFC, mis-selling of US$200 million of structured products), Euroption Strategic Fund v SEB [2013] 1 BCLC 125 (liability of a broker in executing a portfolio close out for a client), Relational v Hodges [2011] EWCA Civ 774 (CA, security for costs), Carey v AIB Bank (UK) Plc [2011] EWHC 567 (transfer of loans to NAMA), Renaissance Capital v ENRC [2011] (corporate finance dispute), Agrimarche [2010] BCC 775 (liquidation of a commodity dealer), Lehman Brothers International (Europe) (2009) (trust claims in Lehman's estate), Geniki Investments International Limited v Ellis Stockbrokers [2008] EWHC 549 (dispute over trading losses), Secretary of State v Jonkler [2006] 1 WLR 3433 (company law, disqualification undertakings), Viking Cereals (2006) (commodity trading), Daraydan v Solland International & others [2005] Ch 119 (civil fraud), Giles v Rhind [2003] Ch 618 (Court of Appeal, company law, reflective loss principle).
Professional Memberships: Chancery Bar Association, COMBAR, Insolvency Lawyers' Association, Called to the Bar of the Dubai International Financial Centre.
Career: Member of the Management Committee of the Bar Pro Bono Unit. Former Chairman of the Personal Insolvency Litigation Advice and Representation Scheme (PILARS).
Publications: Contributor to Atkin's Court Forms and OUP Annotated Companies Act 2006.
Personal: Enjoys skiing and climbing.

SHROFF, Tessa
9 Bedford Row, London
020 7489 2727
tshroff@9BedfordRow.co.uk
Featured in Crime (London)
Practice Areas: General and serious crime – Sexual offences and SOPOs – Drugs offences – Youth crime – Road Traffic Law – Offences against the Justice System – Blackmail – Trafficking – Immigration offences – ASBOs – Disclosure and Abuse of Process
Professional Memberships: Tessa is developing a successful practice, prosecuting and defending at all levels. She is now regularly being instructed in cases of a serious, complex and often multi-handed nature, and is deliberately maintaining specialism in representing vulnerable defendants, such as youths and those requiring intermediaries. She prepares her cases with meticulous attention to detail, whilst maintaining a focus on client care. She frequently visits clients in prison on more than one occasion during a case, in order to ensure they are receiving consistent and professional representation throughout. She was recently described as 'remarkably fearless and knowledgeable' by a new instructing solicitor. Her attention to detail at the outset of cases and experience of the disclosure regime from both sides enables her to regularly act as junior counsel defending against historic sexual allegations, which require applications for disclosure in relation to third party material in particular. She is a member of the Crown Prosecution Service Advocates Panel and often prosecutes as a led junior and junior alone. When prosecuting, she is often instructed early in proceedings, in order to advise on further investigation and to play an active role in the disclosure exercise and shaping of the case.

SIBSON, Clare QC
Cloth Fair Chambers, London
020 7710 6444
claresibson@clothfairchambers.com
Featured in Crime (London), Financial Crime (London)
Practice Areas: Considerable experience in business & corporate crime, fraud, cartel and competition offences as well as high profile serious crime. Experienced in mutual assistance, international investigations and enforcement. Also financial services regulation, professional services regulation and professional discipline. Past cases include; Represented a leading pharmaceutical company in the high profile failed SFO prosecution regarding alleged cartel offences. Advised and represented West Ham Football Club following the Carlos Tevez affair. Successfully represented K, a Solicitor accused of tax fraud; privilege against self-incrimination in ancillary relief proceedings, without prejudice privilege and abuse of process. Successfully represented an individual in FSA insider trading prosecution. Advised a high profile Oligarch. Represented a director

of a company charged with corruption and international sanctions busting. Advised one of the world's largest law firms on implications of UK Bribery Act for their clients, particularly in relation to private equity structures; advised a leading hedge fund on potential market abuse; advised real estate Company Walshaw Moor regarding a dispute with Natural England. Advised renowned airline in respect of licencing with the civil aviation authority. Instructed by Aivars Lembergs, a Latvian politician, over $135 million commercial court worldwide freezing order. Innospec; advised company in global plea agreement between SFO, DoJ and SEC. Advised the director of a global events company in relation to criminal proceedings revolving around the sale of corporate tickets for the Olympic Games. Represented a defendant in the 'Vantis' tax re-trial. Advised a leading travel business in cross border investigations into deaths outside the jurisdiction. Advised Robert Tchenguiz in judicial review of the search warrant used by the SFO. Represented defendant in multi-million pound land banking fraud. More recently; successfully represented Olympus Corporation following SFO investigation and charges. Successfully represented Rebekah Brooks, former chief executive of News International, in phone hacking trial. Advised a former high-ranking official of the Bank of England. Advising an individual under investigation by the SFO for corruption in relation to Rolls Royce. Advising individuals for their alleged roles in Libor and Forex fixing. Representing Mazher Mahmood, journalist charged with conspiracy to pervert. Retained for former Barclays Bank Chief Executive in SFO/ FCA investigation re Qatar. Advising Tesco PLC re accounting investigation. Advising telecommunications company re 'wangiri' fraud payments. Regulatory/ disciplinary practice includes instructions to advise and appear before the Financial Services and Markets Tribunal for the defence. For further information please visit www.clothfairchambers.com

Career: 1997 – Called to the Bar 2016 – QC

Personal: Cambridge University, 1993-96 (Law 1st Class Double Honours). Foundation Scholar of Corpus Christi College 1996.

SIDDALL, Nicholas
Littleton Chambers, London
0845 034 3444
clerks@littletonchambers.co.uk
Featured in Employment (Northern)

Practice Areas: Specialises in employment and industrial relations law. His practice includes significant employment related High Court litigation encompassing injunctive relief, wrongful dismissal and high value contractual claims. He also undertakes all facets of statutory employment law including unfair dismissal, collective redundancy, TUPE and Working Time claims. He regularly appears in significant and complicated discrimination and whistleblowing matters on behalf of individuals, unions and employers of all sizes.

Professional Memberships: ELA, ELBA and Northern Circuit

Career: Significant reported decisions include: Roberts v Skelmersdale College [2004] IRLR 69 (dismissal provisions of 2001 rules), GMB v Holis [2008] IRLR 187 (territorial jurisdiction of TUPE), Cokayne v BASC [2008] ICR 185 (issue estoppel), Matuszowicz-v-Hull CC [2009] IRLR 292 (time limits and reasonable adjustments), Fenton & UNISON-v-SYPS [2010] IRLR 930 (presentation of claim), Pinewood-v-Page [2011] ICR 508 (fairness of redundancy), Bridgeman-v-ABP [2012] IRLR 639 (CJEU reference as to Working Time Regulations derogation), Bray-v-Monarch Personnel [2013] IDS Brief 972 (scope of the Swedish derogation in the Agency Regulations), ASE-v-Kendrick [2014] EWHC 2171 (enforceability of non-compete provision) and Day-v-HEE [2016] IRLR 415 (ability of junior doctors to bring whistleblowing claim).

SIDHU, Jo QC
25 Bedford Row, London
020 7067 1500
j.sidhu@25bedfordrow.com
Featured in Crime (London)

Practice Areas: Widely regarded as a 'superlative' leading Counsel in serious criminal cases with extensive experience in terrorism, homicide and large scale conspiracies involving fraud, drug trafficking and high value robberies. Numerous high profile cases include three of the largest ever terrorist plots (ricin poison, gas limos/dirty bomb and the airline liquid explosives); £40m Graff diamonds robbery; Goldman Sachs secretary (theft of £4m); £50m cocaine 'bling bling' gang; and £100m VAT diversion fraud.

Professional Memberships: President, Society of Asian Lawyers. Criminal Bar Association.Vice-Chair Bar Council's Equality and Diversity Committee.

Career: Silk 2012 BA (Hons) PPE University of Oxford, MSc(Econ) London School of Economics, CPE, BVC, called 1993. Bencher at Lincoln's Inn and lead advocacy trainer. Former elected Councillor and BBC senior researcher.

Publications: Chapter in 'Cases That Changed Our Lives' [2010]. Twenty-Eight Days –What's the Verdict? CLJW (2010). Vol 174, p103. The Críminal Case of Usman Saddique. The Guardian, 11 February 2010.

SILVESTER, Bruce
Devereux, London
020 7353 7534
silvester@devchambers.co.uk
Featured in Personal Injury (London), Travel (London)

Practice Areas: Over 20 years of experience of all aspects of personal injury, health and safety, and clinical negligence litigation. All levels of work including catastrophic injury, particularly brain injury, spinal injury and multiple injuries. Practice also includes registration and consumer protection. Also, since 2001 increasing specialisation in travel litigation, particularly large group actions involving injury abroad, gastro-intestinal illness and loss of enjoyment due to poor quality accommodation. Recent cases include Stych v. Dibble & Tradex Insurance Co Ltd [2012] EWHC 1606. For more recent information and recent case highlights, please visit www.devereuxchambers.co.uk.

Professional Memberships: PIBA, PNBA.

Career: Called to the Bar 1983.

Personal: University of London, Queen Mary College London LLB (1982).

SIMCOCK, Sarah
Serjeants' Inn Chambers, London
020 7427 5000
ssimcock@serjeantsinn.com
Featured in Police Law (All Circuits)

Practice Areas: Sarah Simcock was called to the Bar in 2001. Sarah specialises in public and administrative, police, Court of Protection, inquests and inquiries, clinical negligence and healthcare and professional discipline law. An earlier edition notes that "she is a charismatic presence in court, but also displays that seriousness and modesty which encourages judges and juries to trust her." Please visit the Serjeants' Inn Chambers website for her profile, which sets out full details of her practice and relevant work of note.

Professional Memberships: HRLA, LCLCBA, PNBA, Treasury C Panel (2006-11).

Publications: Medical Treatment: Decisions and the Law (co-author).

SIMMONDS, Andrew QC
5 Stone Buildings, London
020 7242 6201
clerks@5sblaw.com
Featured in Pensions (London)

Practice Areas: Specialises in pensions and professional negligence work but also undertakes litigation in the trust, probate and financial services fields. Pension experience covers advice and litigation relating to all manner of problems and disputes arising between trustees, employers and members, complaints to the Pensions Ombudsman, the powers and duties of the Pensions Regulator and the Pension Protection Fund and claims against pensions professionals. In the professional negligence field, has particular experience of claims against solicitors, barristers, actuaries and accountants but has also acted in claims against insurance brokers, fund managers, stockbrokers and others. Recent notable cases include: Buckinghamshire v Barnardo's [2015]PLR 501; Merchant Navy Ratings Pension Fund v Stena Line [2015] PLR 239; IBM v Dalgleish [2014] PLR 335, [2015] PLR 99; Sec of State for Culture v BT Pension Scheme [2014] PLR 647; Honda Motor Europe Ltd v Powell [2014] PLR 255; IBM UK Holdings Ltd v Dalgleish [2014] EWHC 980; Serjeant v Rigid Group Ltd [2014] PLR 143; LB Re Financing No.1 Ltd v Trustees of the Lehman Bros Pension Scheme [2013] 4 All ER 744; IBM UK Pension Trust v IBM UK Holdings Ltd [2012] PLR 469, [2013] PLR 33; Premier Foods v RHM Pension Trust [2012] PLR 151; Bridge Trustees v Yates [2011] PLR 313; Prudential Staff Pensions Ltd v Prudential Assurance [2011] PLR 239; BT Pension Scheme Trustees v BT/ Secretary of State for Business, Innovation & Skills [2010] PLR 487 ; Independent Trustee Services v Hope [2009] PLR 379.

Professional Memberships: Association of Pension Lawyers (former member of the Legislative and Parliamentary sub-committee); the Professional Negligence Bar Association; the Pension Litigation Court Users' Committee (1998-2014); Trustee of the Bar Council Pension Scheme (2000-2006). Chancery Bar Association.

Career: Called 1980. Silk 1999. Has sat as a Deputy High Court Judge in the Chancery Division since 2006.

SIMPSON, Edwin
New Square Chambers, London
020 7419 8000
edwin.simpson@newsquarechambers.co.uk
Featured in Agriculture & Rural Affairs (London)

Practice Areas: Commercial barrister specialising in Agriculture & Rural Affairs, Administrative & Public law and Commercial Chancery. Appearing at public inquiries and applications for judicial and statutory review and advising on all aspects of such work; he has particular expertise in highway and village green matters, and acts as a non-statutory inspector at public inquiries into the latter, as well as appearing on behalf of both users and landowners. Also has expertise concerning Freedom of Information; and in connection with allegedly sham transactions in the trust and tax context, and more widely. Recent cases include R (Newhaven) v East Sussex CC [2015] UKSC 7 (an attempt to register a beach as a village green); and R (Andrews) v SS for for Environment [2015] EWCA Civ 669 (modern effect of Inclosure awards).

Career: Called 1990. Teaches trusts law and taxation at Christ Church, Oxford; vice-chair Oxford Student Disciplinary Panel.

Publications: Contributor to 'The Law of Freedom of Information' (2016); author of Sham Transactions (with Prof Miranda Stewart, OUP 2013) etc.

Personal: Christ Church, Oxford (MA 1988; BCL 1989)

SIMPSON, Jacqueline
Hailsham Chambers, London
020 7643 5000
Jacqueline.simpson@hailshamchambers.com
Featured in Professional Negligence (London)

Practice Areas: Jacqueline practices in the field of professional negligence where she represents both claimants and defendants. She has extensive experience of alleged claims of negligence involving solicitors, valuers, accountants, financial advisors, brokers and lenders throughout all stages of litigation including mediation. Jacqueline's experience includes dealing with complex limitation issues ranging from the late issue of claim forms and particulars of claims, late amendments to particulars of claims and the accrual of a cause of action in tort and loss of chance cases. Her most notable solicitors' negligence cases are Minkin v Landsberg [2016] 1 W.L.R. 1489 [2015] 6 Costs L.R. 1025 [2016] 1 F.C.R.584; [2016] P.N.L.R. 14; Berney v Thomas Saul & Co Solicitors [2013] P.N.L.R. 26; [2013] EWCA Civ 640 and Ms Mina Mullins v (1) Monro Fisher Wasbrough (2) David Pow (2015).

Publications: Jacqueline was formerly one of the Editors of the Lloyd's Law Reports: Professional Negligence. Jacqueline is a strong advocate for diversity at the Bar and works with the National Centre for Citizenship and the Law to help children from diverse backgrounds understand life at the Bar and to encourage them to see law as a potential career path for them.

SIMPSON, Mark QC
Fountain Court Chambers, London
020 7583 3335
ms@msimpson.net
Featured in Professional Negligence (London)

Practice Areas: Barrister specialising in professional negligence, insurance and general commercial litigation. Notable cases include: Mortgage Agency Services Number One Ltd v Edward Symmons LLP Court of Appeal (Civil Division), a case of significant market importance on the issue of whether hedging costs are recoverable by lenders against negligent valuers. Gemini v CBRE, described as the "valuation trial of the century", a very substantial claim arising out of alleged negligent valuation of 26 properties in a securitised portfolio. Hall v Simons, on advocates' immunity, Farley v Skinner, concerning the recoverability of damages for distress in professional contracts, Dubai Aluminium v Salaam, in which the court considered the boundaries of vicarious liability for fraud and most recently Stone & Rolls v Moore Stephens, which concerned the liability of auditors for alleged failure to detect fraud in the context of a "one man" company.

Professional Memberships: London Common Law and Commercial Bar Association; Professional Negligence Bar Association.

Career: Called 1992, Middle Temple; Silk 2008;

Publications: General Editor of Professional Negligence and Liability. Associate Editor of Clerk & Lindsell on Torts. Associate Editor of The Journal of Professional Negligence.

Personal: King's School Canterbury; Oriel College, Oxford (1986 MA); Hughes Hall, Cambridge (1987 PGCE); City University (1991 Dip Law); Kings College, London (1994 Dip EC Law).

SIMS, Alice

Keating Chambers, London
020 7544 2600
asims@keatingchambers.com

Featured in Construction (London)

Practice Areas: Practice Areas: Recognised specialist in construction, engineering, and utilities disputes along with professional negligence, regulatory and insurance claims related to these sectors. Alice has particular expertise in energy-related construction and commercial disputes (onshore and offshore) and has acted for clients in a wide range of litigation concerning renewables, nuclear, oil and gas projects. She also regularly acts in cases relating to the sale and supply of chemicals and the construction of chemical processing plants. She appears in domestic and international arbitrations as well as the High Court. Alice also undertakes all aspects of ADR including representations to adjudicators and enforcement proceedings. She accepts appointments as a mediator (she is TECBAR accredited) and also accepts instructions on a public access, licensed access and pro bono basis. Recent work includes a multi-million pound international arbitration about the construction of an offshore wind-farm, litigation concerning defects at the Olympic Village, a multi-million dollar international arbitration concerning the construction of a gas fired power plant in Trinidad, a multi-million pound international arbitration about the construction of commercial buildings in downtown Moscow and a number of TCC disputes about architects' negligence.

Professional Memberships: SCL, TECBAR; COMBAR; Professional Negligence Bar Association.

Career: Called 2004.

SINCLAIR, Fiona QC

4 New Square, London
020 7822 2000
f.sinclair@4newsquare.com

Featured in Professional Negligence (London), Construction (London), Property Damage (London)

Practice Areas: Specialist in all methods of dispute resolution (international and domestic arbitration, litigation, adjudication, ADR) with particular expertise and extensive experience in: (1) construction, engineering, transport, technology and energy, (2) professional and product liability, (3) insurance and reinsurance and (4) general commercial litigation. Notable recent successes include Aspect v Higgins [2015] UKSC 38 (construction adjudication in the Supreme Court). Typically instructed in large-scale disputes arising from major construction and engineering projects, fire/flood/collapse recovery actions, investment management/ misselling claims, product liability; and all related insurance issues. Particular expertise in managing multi-party litigation.

Professional Memberships: TECBAR (Committee Member), SCL, COMBAR, ICC, LCIA, BILA, PNBA, ChBA.

Career: QC 2013. Chambers & Partners UK Construction Junior of the Year 2012; Construction Silk of the Year 2015 shortlist.

Publications: Editor of 'Jackson and Powell on Professional Liability' since 1993 (responsible for Chapter 10, 'Construction Professionals').

Personal: Jesus College, Cambridge (MA, LLM). Interests: mountaineering, skiing, Italy. Speaks Italian.

SINCLAIR, Paul

Fountain Court Chambers, London
020 7583 3335
pxs@fountaincourt.co.uk

Featured in Commercial Dispute Resolution (London), Fraud (London)

Practice Areas: Paul specialises in complex Commercial and Chancery disputes in particular in cases involving insurance, banking and civil fraud. During 2016 Paul acted as senior junior in the first civil Libor-fixing trial (PAG v RBS) as well as for the successful claimant in the Novus Aviation v Alubaf Bank dispute concerning aircraft finance. Last year Paul acted as counsel for the Sherway defendants in one of 2015's major cases: Peak Hotels v Tarek Investments and for the successful appellants in the Supreme Court in the Eclairs v JKX claim. He has also developed a strong practice in commercial disputes on his own including substantial trials, arbitrations and interlocutory disputes. Paul has a particularly strong civil fraud practice and is frequently involved at short notice in claims for freezing injunctions, search orders and other interlocutory devices.

Career: M.A Cambridge (First Class Honours) LL.M Harvard (Magna cum laude, equiv.) ICSL (Outstanding) Variety of University prizes including: Sweet and Maxwell Prize (for highest First in Law in University), Schuldman Plate (for best overall graduate of Caius College), Scholar's Prize (x3), Sir William McNair Law Prize (x2) and George Long Prize. Variety of Bar prizes including Barstow Scholarship, Middle Temple Certificate of Honour, Queen Mother Scholarship, Harmsworth Entrance Exhibition

Publications: Contributor to Trusts and Trustees Contributor to Insurance and Reinsurance Law Briefing and International Banking and Financial Law Contributing Editor of Commercial Court Procedure (Sweet & Maxwell) Contributor to Bullen & Leake & Jacob's Precedents of Pleadings on aviation precedents (Sweet and Maxwell) Joint author, Carriage by Air (Butterworths) The "Aviation" section in Bullen Leake & Jacob's Precedents of Pleadings

SINGER, Andrew

Kings Chambers, Manchester
0345 034 3444
clerks@kingschambers.com

Featured in Construction (Northern/North Eastern)

Practice Areas: Andrew practises from both Manchester and Leeds Chambers. Construction Litigation, Arbitration, Adjudication; Claims for and against construction professionals; General Commercial Litigation. Andrew is authorised to sit as a Recorder in the TCC

Professional Memberships: TECBAR ,including membership of Adjudicators and Arbitrators panel; Member of Northern Ireland and Southern Irish Bars; Member of Chartered Institute of Arbitrators ADR Group Accredited Mediator for Civil and Commercial Disputes,.

Career: Practiced since 1990 for last 10 years almost exclusively in Construction Law and related Professional Negligence claims, appearing regularly in TCC in England and Wales , has appeared in large number of reported decisions on adjudication and generally in Appellate Courts at all levels, including House of Lords case of Reinwood v Brown. Acts as Counsel in mediations and as Mediator, he is an Accredited Mediator. Appears in Commercial Court and Court of Appeal in Northern Ireland . Also has been appointed as Arbitrator and Adjudicator of several disputes. Authorised to sit as a Recorder in the TCC.

Publications: Contributed articles to Construction Law Journal on various topics.

SINGER, Samantha

Queen Elizabeth Building QEB, London
020 7797 7837
ssinger@qeb.co.uk

Featured in Family/Matrimonial (London)

Practice Areas: All areas of family law with a particular emphasis on matrimonial finance and private child law; regularly appears in complex and high value matrimonial finance cases as a junior to QEB's Silks and to Silks of other Chambers. Has also appeared successfully against Silks on her own in both children and finance cases.

Professional Memberships: Family Law Bar Association.

Career: First Class Honours in Law, Bristol; Gray's Inn Prince of Wales Scholar 2003; called 2004; pupillage and tenancy at QEB; winner of the Bracewell Essay Prize 2008 ([2009] 39 Fam Law 234); Pegasus Scholarship to Washington DC in September – October 2010.

Publications: (Of Note) "Financial Provision: a second bite at the cherry" Family Law Journal No.62 December 2006/January 2007 p.14; "Integrating Diversity" The Collected Papers of the Dartington Hall Conference, edited by the Rt. Hon. Lord Justice Thorpe and Samantha Singer published by Jordans in 2008.

SINGH, Mukhtiar

6 Pump Court, London
020 7797 8400
mukhtiarsingh@6pumpcourt.co.uk

Featured in Employment (South Eastern)

Practice Areas: Main practice areas: Employment, Professional Discipline and Civil Litigation. Mukhtiar has established his practice was entirely through recommendations, including a substantial amount of Direct Public Access work. He is known for his determination to obtain the best outcome for his clients, reassuring manner and pragmatic outlook. Many of his clients are in the medical sector or are city workers. He is often instructed in cases that overlap with his civil practice, including breach of confidentiality; restraint of trade; partnership disputes; property rights; data protection; and wages claims. In the tribunal, Mukhtiar undertakes work on behalf of Claimants and Respondents, including unfair dismissal; wrongful dismissal; all types of discrimination claims; and disputes over pay and working time. He has a particular interest in discrimination and whistleblowing (and lectures on this topic). He recently secured a substantial settlement for his client in an Equal Pay case involving city bonus schemes and further claims for sex and pregnancy discrimination. Mukhtiar has a busy advisory practice in all aspects of employment law and recent instructions include advising on TUPE; post-employment victimisation; finder's fees; negligent references; discipline; managing long-term sickness; stress and accidents at work; shareholder unfair prejudice; compromise agreements; and restrictive covenants.

Professional Memberships: Industrial Law Society Employment Law Bar Association Employment Lawyers Association Association of Regulatory & Disciplinary Lawyers

Career: Prior to being called to the Bar in 2011, Mukhtiar worked for over twenty years in the public sector. He had over ten years' employment relations experience through staff association work on behalf of employees; and three years experience working in-house predominantly advising on employment disputes, discipline and policy.

Personal: Mukhtiar was educated at Dartford Grammar School and studied law at the University of London whilst working full time. He studied the Bar Professional Training Course whilst working full time and obtained an Outstanding overall mark with over 80% for all assessments. He speaks Punjabi.

SINGLA, Tony

Brick Court Chambers, London
020 7379 3550
tony.singla@brickcourt.co.uk

Featured in Competition/European Law (London), Banking & Finance (London), Commercial Dispute Resolution (London), Fraud (London), Insurance (London), Media & Entertainment (London)

Career: Tony appears frequently in the High Court and also has experience of numerous cases in the Competition Appeal Tribunal, the Court of Appeal, and the Supreme Court. In addition, Tony appears in arbitration under ICC, LCIA, and other rules. Tony's current and recent commercial work includes: The Lloyds/HBOS Litigation; Single Buoy Moorings Inc v Zurich Insurance plc and others; BAT v Sequana SA and others; Terra Firma v Citibank; and Michael Cherney v Oleg Deripaska. In the last three years Tony has also appeared in three Supreme Court cases: Eclairs Group v JKX Oil & Gas plc; The Alexandros T; and VTB Capital plc v Nutritek International. In competition law, Tony's recent cases include: WM Morrison Supermarkets v MasterCard Incorporated; Imperial Tobacco v OFT; and Intel v Commission. In addition, Tony is currently instructed in a number of cartel damages claims including Emerald Supplies Ltd v British Airways plc. Tony is the co-author of "Accountants' Negligence and Liability" (due to be published in 2016) and a contributing author of "Competition Litigation: UK Practice and Procedure" (2010). Between 2006 and 2011, Tony was a Retained Lecturer in Law at Oxford University where he taught Contract Law and Competition Law.

SINGLETON, Michael
St Ives Chambers, Birmingham
0121 236 0863
michael.singleton@stiveschambers.co.uk
Featured in Social Housing (Midlands)

Practice Areas: Michael specialises in all aspects of housing work with particular emphasis on Human Rights, anti-social behaviour and regulatory matters. Experienced in claims under the Environmental Protection Act 1990 and claims arising following stock transfers. Regularly instructed on behalf of local authorities, Housing Associations and by specialist tenant advisers including not for profit bodies. Recent cases include Birmingham City Council v Ashton [2012] EWCA Civ 1557; Corby BC v Scott [2012] EWCA Civ 276; Birmingham City Council v Frisby [2011] UKSC 8; Knowsley HT v White [2008] UKHL 70.
Professional Memberships: Social Housing Law Association (Founder Member); Midland Circuit; Fellow of the Royal Society for Public Health & Safety; Birmingham Medico-Legal Society.
Career: LLB (Hons) University of Leicester 1985. Called to the Bar 1987. Head of St Ives Chambers Housing & Property Group.
Publications: Advised the Chartered Institute of Housing on the Guidance Notes for the Community Harm Statement.
Personal: Lectures on most aspects of housing law to solicitors and other housing professionals.

SIRIKANDA, Morgan
Queen Elizabeth Building QEB, London
020 7797 7837
m.sirikanda@qeb.co.uk
Featured in Family/Matrimonial (London)

Practice Areas: All aspects of family law with a particular emphasis on matrimonial financial cases. Morgan has appeared before every level of tribunal from the Family Proceedings Court to the Court of Appeal. In recent years he has been instructed as junior counsel in a number of High Court matrimonial finance cases with very large asset bases. He is also regularly instructed on his own in family finance cases where leading counsel have been retained on the other side. In addition to this financial work Morgan also has a particular interest in international child cases raising issues of jurisdiction.
Professional Memberships: Middle Temple, Family Law Bar Association.
Career: Called to the Bar 2002. Pupillage at QEB.
Personal: Morgan read English at Liverpool University (1st class honours). He then obtained a Diploma in Law from the City University (commendation). He was awarded a Diplock scholarship by the Middle Temple. In 2006 Morgan was awarded a Pegasus scholarship to work as a judicial assistant to the Chief Justice of the Family Court of Australia.

SKINNER, Lorna
Matrix Chambers, London
020 7404 3447
lornaskinner@matrixlaw.co.uk
Featured in Data Protection (London), Defamation/Privacy (London)

Practice Areas: Media and information law, including privacy, defamation, breach of confidence, data protection, contempt, harassment, reporting restrictions, freedom of information. Particular specialism in defamation and privacy in cases involving the internet and harassment. Recent cases include: PJS v News Group Newspapers Ltd [2016] UKSC 26; Vidal-Hall and Others v Google Inc [2014] EWHC 13 (QB); [2014] 1 WLR 4155; From March 2013 acted for national media organisations in the Inquest into the death of Alexander Litvinenko and related judicial review proceedings: R (Secretary of Foreign & Commonwealth Affairs) v Assistant Deputy Coroner for Inner North London [2013] EWHC 3724 (Admin) and [2013] EWCH 1786 (Admin); The wife and children of Omar Othman v English National Resistance and Ors [2013] EWHC 1421 (QB); Jan – Dec 2012, acted for News International at the Leveson Inquiry. Also an ADR Group Accredited Civil & Commercial Mediator and a member of the IPSO Arbitration Panel. For a full CV visit www.matrixlaw.co.uk
Professional Memberships: Bar Pro Bono Unit, Liberty, Human Rights Lawyers Association, INQUEST.
Career: Called October 1997.
Publications: Co-author of 'A Practical Guide to Libel and Slander'. Regular contributor to INFORRM blog.

SLOBODA, Nicholas
One Essex Court, London
020 7583 2000
nsloboda@oeclaw.co.uk
Featured in International Arbitration (London), Commercial Dispute Resolution (London)

Practice Areas: Nick has a broad commercial practice, divided equally between Court litigation and international arbitration. Alongside general commercial disputes and advice, he has particular experience of disputes involving civil fraud, energy, banking&finance and jurisdiction/interim injunctions. Recent cases include a multi-billion dollar oil&gas ICC arbitration in Paris; a multi-billion dollar oil and gas SIAC arbitration in Singapore, Dar Al Arkan (Comm. Ct US$1 billion conspiracy/regulatory dispute); Alliance Bank (Comm. Ct US$1 billion banking fraud claim/jurisdiction challenge); acting for a major bank in a US$600m+ LCIA arbitration against a broker; Bilta v Deutsche Bank (Ch. Division, alleged carbon trading fraud), acting for SABMiller plc subsidiaries in the Commercial Court and in two consecutive major ICC arbitrations;
Professional Memberships: COMBAR, YIAG.
Career: Called 2007 (Lincoln's Inn). History at St Anne's Oxford (first class), CPE at City University and BVC at Inns of Court School of Law.

SLOW, Camille
Atkin Chambers, London
020 7404 0102
cslow@atkinchambers.com
Featured in Professional Negligence (London), Construction (London)

Practice Areas: Camille's practice covers a broad range of commercial disputes with a particular focus on construction and professional negligence cases. She is experienced in all forms of dispute resolution, including domestic and international arbitration, DAB's, mediation, adjudication and the High Court. She undertakes work in numerous industry sectors but has particular experience of social housing, transport, infrastructure and energy projects. Her professional negligence experience is considerable, in particular matters with a construction context having often acted for and against, architects, engineers, surveyors, project managers, planning professionals and multidisciplinary firms, amongst many others. She is frequently instructed by insurers, professionals, governments, local governments and government departments, small and large developers and construction companies as well as private individuals both domestically and internationally. She has a particular interest in and experience of fraud and dishonesty, construction related insolvency, public procurement and multiparty disputes. Camille undertakes a large amount of oral advocacy in various forums and is often instructed as sole counsel in high value and legally and technically complex disputes.
Professional Memberships: TECBAR; COMBAR; LCLCBA; SCL.
Career: Bristol University, LLB, 2001. Called to the Bar in 2002.

SMALL, Penelope
The Chambers of Andrew Mitchell QC, London
020 7440 9950
ps@33cllaw.com
Featured in POCA Work & Asset Forfeiture (All Circuits)

Practice Areas: Specialises in domestic and international fraud, bribery, corruption and money laundering; international mutual legal assistance; proceeds of crime and tracing/securing assets in civil, family and criminal contexts; business crime and international regulatory work. Represents a broad spectrum of cliental including prosecution authorities, corporate and individual defendants, police forces, foreign government agencies, third parties affected by the actions of others and court appointed receivers. Case subject matters include restraint, freezing, receivership, confiscation, high value cash and asset seizure/forfeiture, multi-jurisdictional fraudulent conduct. Regularly lectures to specialist professional audiences and is one of the contributing editors of Mitchell Taylor Talbot on Confiscation and the Proceeds of Crime.
Career: Year of Call: 1992

SMILEY, Ben
4 New Square, London
020 7822 2000
B.Smiley@4newsquare.com
Featured in Professional Negligence (London)

Practice Areas: Litigation, arbitration and dispute resolution in core areas: commercial, insurance, professional liability, financial regulation, chancery, costs and sports work. Conducts claims and defences in respect of very complex and high-value cases, across industries and professions. Often acts in claims by or against solicitors, barristers, accountants, financial service professionals and insolvency practitioners. Regularly appears in the Chancery Division and the Commercial Court. Has also acted in the Court of Appeal and the Supreme Court. Strong experience as sole counsel and as part of a larger team.
Professional Memberships: COMBAR, British Insurance Law Association, Professional Negligence Bar Association, London Common Law and Commercial Bar Association.
Career: MA (Oxon), Philosophy, Politics and Economics, Oxford University (First Class); GDL, City University, London (Distinction); Called 2009, Middle Temple; Diplock Scholarship, Middle Temple.
Publications: Articles and blogs for the British Insurance Law Association Journal, the Journal of Professional Negligence, and Thomson Reuters. Co-Editor, Jackson & Powell on Professional Liability, 8th Edition.

SMITH, Adam
Maitland Chambers, London
020 7406 1200
asmith@maitlandchambers.com
Featured in Real Estate Litigation (London)

Practice Areas: All aspects of property litigation; commercial disputes; modern chancery. Recent work includes: Tuscola (110) Ltd v. The Y2K Company Ltd (mortgages); Overton v. Timothy Sammons (theft of art works); Douglas Trustees Ltd v. Costain (interim relief under s. 25 CJJA 1982); Law Society v. Cassam (freezing order, recoupment of grants by Compensation Fund); Barclays v. Poling Worldwide Ltd (validity of charge); R Square Properties Ltd v. Shiv Saaj Investments Ltd (apportionment of rent); Remkis Investments Ltd v. Warnes (priority of charges, breach of trust); Invista v. Clerical Medical (negligence in management of pension fund property assets); Jordan v. Star Energy (obligation to seek planning permission for gas storage in former oil field); Sycamore Bidco Ltd v. Breslin (breach of warranty in share sale agreement); HMRC v. Begum (conspiracy, abuse of process); arbitration between former members of Halliwells LLP concerning rent guarantees and indemnities; Earl Cadogan v. 26 Cadogan Square Ltd (in HL, leasehold enfranchisement); IIG Capital LLC v. Van de Merwe (guarantees); advising the FSA on regulation of mortgage products; LCIA arbitration concerning ownership of significant Russian assets. Property expertise includes: leasehold enfranchisement; easements; restrictive covenants; mortgages; conveyancing disputes; adverse possession; land registration; overage; reverter; nuisance and trespass; service charges; rent review; consent for alienation, alterations, change of use; forfeiture and break notices; business tenancies; dilapidations; landlord and tenant in general.
Professional Memberships: Chancery Bar Association, COMBAR, Financial Services Lawyers Association, Property Bar Association
Career: Called 2001
Publications: Contributing editor to 31st Edition Snell's Equity and Lexis Nexis Commonhold: Law and Practice
Personal: Born 9/10/1976. Educated Wellington College and University College Oxford (BA Classics; scholar 1997-99)

SMITH, Andrew
Matrix Chambers, London
020 7404 3447
andrewsmith@matrixlaw.co.uk
Featured in Employment (London), Sports Law (London)

Practice Areas: Andrew practises predominantly in the fields of employment and sport law and is ranked as a leading junior in both. He is regularly instructed on high value and complex employment disputes involving allegations of discrimination and whistleblowing, and he appears regularly in the Employment Appeal Tribunal (details of which can be viewed on his Matrix Chambers profile). In addition, Andrew is experienced in High Court employment litigation. With regard to his growing sport law practice, Andrew has recently been instructed by UEFA and FIFPro (in connection with their complaint to the European Commission on the issue of third party ownership in football), as well as acting for football clubs, athletes and managers.
Professional Memberships: ELA; ELBA
Publications: Andrew is the author of the discrimination law section of Jordan's Employment Law and a contributor to the ELA Briefing. He is an author of the forthcoming book, 'Football and the Law' (Bloomsbury Professional). Andrew produces articles on a range of topics for the LawInSport.com website (as well as being a member of its editorial board) and has recorded several sport law podcasts for CPDCast.
Personal: University of Sheffield (LLB – 1st class); Manchester Metropolitan University (BVC – Outstanding)

SMITH, Andrew QC
St Philips Chambers, Birmingham
0121 246 7000
asmith@st-philips.com
Featured in Crime (Midlands)
Practice Areas: Andrew prosecutes and defends in cases of gravity and complexity and is regularly instructed in cases involving allegations of homicide, organised crime and serious fraud. He has significant experience of homicide cases ranging from the deaths of babies and young children through to gang related murders. Andrew has been instructed in many cases involving organised criminal activity at both national and regional level. Andrew's cases frequently involve international aspects. In fraud cases, Andrew has represented company directors and professionals. He also has substantial experience of money laundering investigations and has often advised parties pre-charge.
Professional Memberships: Criminal Bar Association; Midland Circuit.
Career: MA (Hons) Oxford; Queen Mother's Scholarship, Middle Temple; Called to the Bar in 1997; Recorder (Midland Circuit); Queen's Counsel 2012; Director of Advocacy Training for the Midland Circuit.

SMITH, Barry
Compass Chambers, Edinburgh
020 7962 142549
barry.smith@compasschambers.com
Featured in Health & Safety (Scotland)
Practice Areas: Member of the regulatory crime team at Compass Chambers. Experienced in the defence of charges under the Health and Safety at Work etc Act 1974 and related Regulations. Acts for major clients in the engineering, oil / off-shore, rail, construction, transport and retail industries. He is also experienced in fatal road traffic accident prosecutions and in the conduct of fatal accident inquiries. He regularly speaks at seminars and conferences on regulatory crime.

Professional Memberships: Health & Safety Lawyers' Association; Association of Regulatory and Disciplinary Lawyers.
Career: Graduate of Strathclyde University (LL.B (1st Class Hons)) and Harvard Law School (LLM) (Kennedy Scholar); Trained at Crown Office 2000 – 2002; Qualified (solicitor) in 2002; Procurator Fiscal Depute 2002 – 2004; Faculty of Advocates Lord Reid Scholar 2004; Called to the Bar 2005; Session Cases Reporter.

SMITH, Christopher QC
Essex Court Chambers, London
020 7813 8000
csmith@essexcourt.com
Featured in Shipping (London)
Practice Areas: Barrister specialising in Shipping and Commodities, Admiralty, Commercial Dispute Resolution, Professional Liability, Insurance and Reinsurance and Arbitration. Recent notable cases include: B v P (shipbuilding dispute in arbitration), "Cape Bonny" (disputed claim for contribution in General Average), DIP v DLA (professional liability claim against solicitors), L v H (5 related shipbuilding disputes in arbitration), SPL v Bank of China (shipbuilding dispute in arbitration and consequent Commercial Court litigation in relation to refund guarantees); Hyundai v Houlder (professional liability claim against reinsurance brokers); "Pisti" (Admiralty collision claim); "Maersk Neuchatel" (dispute concerning General Average security); Klink and Pantaenius v Zelikov and Underwriting Risk Services Ltd (dispute concerning enforcement of conflicting foreign judgments and shipowners' right to limit liability); Riva Bella v Tamsen Yachts (dispute concerning the construction of a luxury motor yacht); TVR v Clyde & Co (professional liability claim against solicitors); Gladman Commercial Properties v Fisher Hargreaves Proctor (strike out of professional liability claim involving allegations of fraud); Irene EM (marine insurance constructive total loss claim). Also has extensive experience of domestic and international arbitrations both as counsel and as co-counsel with foreign lawyers.
Professional Memberships: Chartered Institute of Arbitrators; Commercial Bar Association; London Common Law and Commercial Bar Association; London Maritime Arbitrators Association (supporting member); CEDR Exchange; London Court of International Arbitration; The Baltic Exchange
Career: Southampton University, Called 1989 (Inner Temple), Silk 2009
Publications: Seafarer's Rights (2005) (Contributor); Scrutton on Charterparties and Bills of Lading (2015) (Co-Editor)

SMITH, Christopher M
Quadrant Chambers, London
020 7583 4444
christopher.smith@quadrantchambers.com
Featured in Shipping (London)
Practice Areas: Principal areas of work are shipping, commodities, commercial litigation, and insurance & reinsurance. Cases include Granville Oils & Chemicals Ltd v Davies Turner & Co Ltd [2003] 2 Lloyd's Rep 356; Assimina Maritime Ltd v Pakistan National Shipping Corp (The Tasman Spirit) [2005] 1 Lloyd's Rep. 525; Bandwidth Shipping Corp v Intaari (The Magdalena Oldendorff) [2008] 1 Lloyd's Rep 7; Flame SA v Primera Maritime (Hellas) Ltd [2009] EWHC 1973 (Comm).
Professional Memberships: COMBAR.
Career: Called to the Bar in 1999.
Publications: 'Butterworths Commercial Court & Arbitration Pleadings' (contributor).
Personal: Educated at Lancing College (1989-94), Gonville & Caius College, Cambridge (1995-98), and the Inns of Court School of Law (1998-99).

SMITH, Ian
The Chambers of Andrew Mitchell QC, London
07852 222675 / 020 7440 9950
is@33cllaw.com
Featured in Fraud (London), POCA Work & Asset Forfeiture (All Circuits)
Practice Areas: Ian is a commercial litigator, dealing with complex and high value cases, usually with an international dimension, and a specialist in: • Civil-court fraud litigation; • Asset recovery and proceeds of crime litigation (in both the civil and criminal courts); • Anti-money laundering, anti-corruption, sanctions laws and professional risks management. Ian practiced as a solicitor in London from 1995 and was a solicitor advocate until his call to the Bar in 2003. Ian is instructed by a range of firms in the UK and overseas.
Career: Call – 2003; Solicitor from 1995; Solicitor Advocate (all courts).
Publications: Lead editor and co-author of the practitioners' loose-leaf text Smith, Owen & Bodnar on Asset Recovery: Criminal Confiscation and Civil Recovery (Oxford University Press). Co-author of The Illicit Trade in Art and Antiquities: International Recovery and Criminal and Civil Liability by Ulph and Smith (Hart, 2012). Contributor to Non-Conviction-Based Confiscation in Europe (Duncker & Humblot, 2015)
Personal: LLB (Birmingham). College of Law. Working knowledge – Italian.

SMITH, Jamie QC
4 New Square, London
020 7822 2000
j.smith@4newsquare.com
Featured in Professional Negligence (London), Insurance (London)
Practice Areas: Principal areas of practice are professional negligence (with particular emphasis on auditors and accountants, lawyers and insurance brokers), insurance and commercial dispute resolution. Notable cases include: Sugar Hut v Great Lakes Insurance [2011] Lloyd's Rep IR 198 (successful declinature by insurers following nightclub fire); IEGL v Zurich [2015] 2 WLR 1471 (SC) (EL insurer's liability for mesothelioma claims under Fairchild doctrine); Freemont v Knight Frank [2015] PNLR 4 (scope of duty of care against valuers); Clydesdale Bank plc v. Workman [2016] PNLR 18 (CA) (dishonest assistance claim against solicitors); Chandra v Brooke North 151 Con LR 113 (CA) (limitation issues in solicitors negligence claim) and Gladman Commercial Properties v. FHP [2014] PNLR 11 (CA) (fraud claim against property agents).
Professional Memberships: PPNBA, COMBAR, Chancery Bar Association, LCLCBA, BILA.
Career: MA (Cantab). Called to Bar 1995. Joined 4 New Square 1996. Took Silk in 2015.
Publications: Editor of Jackson & Powell, Professional Liability
Personal: Enjoys cycling.

SMITH, Joel
Furnival Chambers, London
020 74053232
jsmith@furnivallaw.co.uk
Featured in Extradition (London)
Practice Areas: Practice areas: Crime and Extradition. A regular practitioner in the field of extradition, representing both individuals and foreign governments in a number of high profile cases including proceedings against individuals accused of murder, terrorism, war crimes and large-scale fraud. Recent cases include defending in the extradition proceedings concerning the "Flash crash" trading case. General crime practice includes murder, organised crime and serious fraud, as well as appearances in the Court of Appeal and High Court, and judicial review proceedings. Appointed as a Treasury Counsel monitoree in 2015.
Professional Memberships: Criminal Bar Association, Extradition Lawyers' Association.

SMITH, Julia
Henderson Chambers, London
020 7583 9020
JSmith@hendersonchambers.co.uk
Featured in Consumer Law (London)
Practice Areas: Consumer law, banking and finance, including consumer credit, mortgages, sale and supply of goods, unfair contract terms and unfair commercial practices. Cases include OFT v Ashbourne Management Services Ltd [2011] All E R (D) 276 (May) (unfair terms, unfair commercial practices, and whether credit provided under minimum term contracts with monthly payments); Adris v Royal Bank of Scotland plc (2010) 160 NLJ (non-party costs orders); Carey v HSBC Bank plc, Times 25 January 2010 (unfair relationships and burden of proving improper execution); McGuffick v Royal Bank of Scotland plc [2010] 1 All E R 634 (whether reporting to credit reference agencies enforcement); and Royal Bank of Scotland plc v Etridge (No.2) [2001] UKHL 44, [2002] 2 AC 773 (undue influence and extent of solicitor's duty when advising third party provider of security). Clients include banks, regulators, leasing companies and retailers.
Professional Memberships: London Common Law and Commercial Bar Association.
Career: Called 1988.
Publications: Atkin's Court Forms on Consumer Credit (Lexis Nexis 2012); The Law of Consumer Credit and Hire (OUP 2009); Consumer Credit Act 2006, A Guide to the New Law (Law Society Publishing 2006).
Personal: Educated at Cheltenham Ladies' College and the University of Liverpool.

SMITH, Leonard QC
Carmelite Chambers, London
020 7936 6300
clerks@carmelitechambers.co.uk
Featured in Financial Crime (London)
Practice Areas: A specialist criminal defence advocate with particular expertise in serious fraud and complex financial crime. Extensive experience in several jurisdictions, defending in all forms of complex and grave cases. Has long advised and appeared for CEOs, directors and professionals in all areas of large scale financial crime. Particular expertise in appearing for professionals in SFO prosecutions of high level financial and corporate malfeasance and for UK

and overseas citizens in investigations and prosecutions involving the Bribery Act. Has successfully appeared in many of the largest and most well known operations prosecuted throughout the jurisdiction over the past two decades. In 2016, appeared for Chartered Surveyor in Operation Aquamarine (Southwark) and appeared for and advised in the SFO investigations concerning Sweett Group PLC . In 2015-16, appeared for the main defendant in the North East Property Mortgage Fraud- an enormous and politically sensitive prosecution affecting the homes of hundreds of people in the North East. More than 1000 mortgages were obtained by companies said to be controlled by client in what was alleged to be one of the UKs largest ever mortgage cases. Extensive experience acting for solicitors, accountants, brokers, IFAs and real property professionals (RICS) at all levels.
Career: Called 1986 – QC 2008.

SMITH, Marion QC
39 Essex Chambers, London
020 7832 1111
marion.smithqc@39essex.com
Featured in Construction (London)
Practice Areas: Marion specialises in complex, high value commercial and construction disputes for UK and international clients. She has practised across a broad range of sector areas including building, energy, engineering, fraud, insurance, power, property damage, retail and telecommunications. She has extensive experience of both advisory and contentious work and first instance and appellate hearings. She has been involved in construction disputes involving many standard form contracts including the JCT standard forms, the NEC, FIDIC and derivative standard form agreements as well as bespoke contracts. She has in-depth experience of complex PFI contractual arrangements in the UK. International arbitration, including those where the law of the contract is not the law of England and Wales, forms an extensive part of her practice. She is a Fellow of the Chartered Institute of Arbitrators and has appeared before a range of tribunals, including under the rules of the ICC, KLRCA, LCIA, LMAA and the UNCITRAL Arbitration Rules in a range of jurisdictions.
Professional Memberships: Society of Construction Law, Professional Negligence Bar Association, Commercial Bar Association.
Career: Called to the Bar in 1981. Silk 2015.

SMITH, Matthew
Kings Chambers, Manchester
0345 034 3444
clerks@kingschambers.com
Featured in Costs Litigation (All Circuits)
Practice Areas: Costs, mediation and employment
Professional Memberships: ACL.
Career: Barrister, Costs Draftsman & Mediator (MA Cantab – law 2.1).
Publications: Various costs articles together with other members of the Kings Chambers costs team.

SMITH, Matthew
Maitland Chambers, London
020-7406-1200
msmith@maitlandchambers.com
Featured in Charities (London)
Practice Areas: Commercial chancery litigation, including company and insolvency questions, contractual and trust-related disputes. Particular interest in charity law. Matthew acted for the Independent Schools Council in their successful judicial review of the Commission's public benefit guidance; he appeared in the poverty trusts references brought by the Attorney General; he acted for the Plymouth Brethren Christian Church in their appeal against the Commission's refusal to register. Other notable cases have included acting for the Catholic adoption agencies in their appeals concerning the scope of the charitable exemption in the Equality Act 2010 and appearing for the Attorney-General in the litigation over the assets of the Wedgwood Museum. He has advised and acted for and against the Commission on a number of other matters. He has appeared in the Tribunal and in Court for charities, the Commission and the Attorney.
Professional Memberships: COMBAR, Chancery Bar Association and Charity Law Association.
Career: Called in 2001. Junior Counsel to the Crown (B Panel).
Personal: MA (Cantab) First Class, LLM (rules concerning charities and politics; the relationship in charity law between purposes and activities and the comparative state of the law in England, Australia, New Zealand and Canada).

SMITH, Stephen QC
Erskine Chambers, London
020 7242 5532
ssmith@erskinechambers.com
Featured in Chancery (London), Commercial Dispute Resolution (London), Fraud (London), Offshore (London)
Practice Areas: Stephen Smith is a leading silk who specialises in litigating high-value, complex commercial disputes. He is particularly sought-after for cases involving jurisdictional issues and restraints on the disposals of assets (including freezing orders and interim relief). Notable cases include Derby v Weldon, the BCCI liquidation, proceedings arising out of the collapse of the Maxwell empire, Trustor v Smallbone, Alfa Telecom v Cukurova and the Rastogi litigation. Since 2009 Stephen has been the lead advocate in the complex fraud and asset recovery proceedings known as JSC BTA Bank v Ablyazov, in which over 70 leading decisions have been given so far (including 15 in the Court of Appeal), and judgment has been obtained for over $3.7bn. Stephen is currently lead advocate in JSC Mezhdunarodniy Promyshlenniy Bank v Pugachev, acting for the liquidator of a Russian bank in claims of misappropriation of assets against the bank's former owner. Stephen also has a successful offshore practice and regularly appears in the courts in the Eastern Caribbean, the Bahamas, the Isle of Man and the Cayman Islands; and he has advised in connection with cases proceeding in Bermuda and Hong Kong. Stephen has appeared before the Privy Council and the Supreme Court on more than fifteen occasions.
Professional Memberships: Middle Temple, Chancery Bar Association.
Career: Scholar, University College Oxford 1979-82. First Class Degree in Jurisprudence, Oxford University 1982 (Wronker and Jurisprudence Prizes winner). Called to the Bar in England and Wales,1983 ;QC 2000; Recorder 2004; Deputy High Court Judge (Chancery Division and Commercial Court) 2006; Called to the Bar of the Eastern Caribbean (BVI) 1994; Bahamas (ad hoc) 2004 and 2016; Licensed Advocate Isle of Man (ad hoc) 2007; Cayman Islands (ad hoc) 2010.
Personal: Married to Lorraine, five children. Principal leisure interests: family, deer, alpaca farming.

SMITH, Tom QC
South Square, London
020 7696 9900
tomsmith@southsquare.co.uk
Featured in Chancery (London), Banking & Finance (London), Commercial Dispute Resolution (London), Company (London), Restructuring/ Insolvency (London)
Practice Areas: Tom specialises in banking & finance, corporate insolvency, commercial litigation, and company law.
Professional Memberships: COMBAR, Chancery Bar Association, Insolvency Lawyers' Association, London Court of International Arbitration.
Career: Recent high-profile cases range from major commercial trials such as the Formula One/Ecclestone and Avonwick/ Webinvest disputes, to Supreme Court/ House of Lords decisions on important legal issues in the fields of banking and restructuring (HIH, Mills v HSBC, Rubin v Eurofinance, Nortel/Pensions Regulator, Morgan Stanley v Tael) and the Lehman Brothers Waterfall litigation. Other notable work includes many of the recent restructurings, schemes of arrangement and banking disputes (DTEK Finance, Goldman Sachs International v Novo Banco, GSO Credit Partners v Barclays Bank, first judgment in the new Financial List). Tom is also an experienced trial advocate in both court litigation and arbitrations. He frequently appears as an advocate both in England and in other jurisdictions including the Cayman Islands and Dubai. Recent cases include Primeo Funds v HSBC; Re Harbinger Class PE Holdings; Re Espirito Santo Bankers Dubai (DIFC Courts). Called 1999 (Middle Temple); QC 2014.
Publications: Contributor to Cross-Border Insolvency, The EC Regulation on Insolvency Proceedings, EU Banking and Insurance Insolvency, Halsbury's Laws of England, Company Directors.
Personal:

SMITH, Tyrone QC
25 Bedford Row, London
020 7067 1500
tsmith@25bedfordrow.com
Featured in Crime (London)
Practice Areas: Specialist defence advocate and highly sought-after silk who consistently defends in very serious, substantial and often high-profile criminal cases, including murder, fraud, terrorist offences, and large scale drug conspiracies. Experienced in private crime offering pro-active representation in all areas of criminal work. Particular interest in appellate work.
Professional Memberships: Criminal Bar Association. Gray's Inn.
Career: Called 1994. Silk: 2014.

SMITTEN, Ben
25 Bedford Row, London
020 7067 1500
bensmitten@live.co.uk
Featured in Crime (London)
Practice Areas: Ben is a specialist criminal defence advocate and adviser with particular expertise in homicide, large-scale fraud and serious organised crime. In recent years Ben has been exclusively instructed on a private basis by London's leading law firms in relation to all levels of alleged criminality at all stages of criminal proceedings. He acts for high profile, high net worth individuals and for UK nationals charged with criminal offences in other jurisdictions. His work rate, ability and experience in defending in serious and complex criminal cases are unrivalled. He is committed, extremely hard working and determined to achieve the best possible outcomes. In 2008 Ben was the youngest ranked "Leading Junior" in Chambers and Partners directory.
Professional Memberships: Criminal Bar Association, Middle Temple.
Career: University of Bristol LLB (1996) and London School of Economics LLM (Masters degree 1998). Called 1999.

SNARR, Matthew
9 St John Street, Manchester
0161 955 5160
matthew.snarr@9sjs.com
Featured in Fraud (All Circuits), Personal Injury (Northern)
Practice Areas: Matthew is regularly instructed by both sides in catastrophic injury claims including brain damage, spinal injuries and amputation claims. He has particular expertise in handling chronic pain and subtle brain injury claims. He is very experienced in Inquests, Coronial Law and Judicial Review relating to Inquests especially those which arise out of a death in the workplace. He frequently acts on behalf of the insurance industry in complicated insurance fraud litigation involving organised rings of individuals engaged in contrived road traffic accidents. Matthew also acts in Health and Safety prosecutions ranging from near misses to fatal injuries at work especially in the construction and care sectors.
Professional Memberships: Personal Injury Bar Association and Health and Safety Lawyers Association.
Career: LLB (Manchester), Called 2001 (Inner Temple). Junior Counsel to the Crown (North West) since 2007.
Personal: Mountain marathons, trail running and skiing.

SNOWDEN, Steven
Crown Office Chambers, London
020 7797 8100
snowden@crownofficechambers.com
Featured in Personal Injury (London), Personal Injury (All Circuits)
Practice Areas: Steven's main areas of practice are personal injuries and industrial disease, within which he regularly deals with aspects of procedure and costs and appears at inquests. His practice extends to associated insurance, professional negligence and clinical negligence work. He is highly regarded for his advocacy skills in combination with his experience and his calm manner, and he regularly appears in court and in settlement meetings against silks. He deals with cases of the highest severity on all aspects of liability and quantum and he acts for claimants and defendants with equal enthusiasm. His regular work is in the High Court and County Courts and he has experience of the House of Lords and the Court of Appeal. Reported cases include Dowdall v William Kenyon (limitation/ abuse of process), Kotula v EDF (paraplegic claim/ periodical payments/ provisional damages), Dixie v British Polythene (abuse of process), Gray v Thames Trains (illegality/ ex turpi causa), Glaister v Appleby (duty of care), Carver v BAA (Part 36), Drake v Provident (contribution between insurers).

Career: Called to the Bar in 1989. Secretary of the Personal Injuries Bar Association. Editor of the Judicial College Guidelines for the Assessment of General Damages in Personal Injury cases.

SOARES, Patrick
Field Court Tax Chambers, London
020 3693 3700
ps@fieldtax.com
Featured in Tax (London)

Practice Areas: Taxation of land transactions, overseas structures and companies and double tax treaties and EU law
Professional Memberships: Fellow of the Chartered Institute of Taxation
Career: Formerly a tax partner in a leading firm of solicitors
Publications: Tax Editor of the Property Law Bulletin
Personal: Plays the clarinet and piano. Enjoys reading and cycling

SOUTHEY, Hugh QC
Matrix Chambers, London
020 7404 3447
HughSouthey@matrixlaw.co.uk
Featured in Administrative & Public Law (London), Police Law (All Circuits), Civil Liberties & Human Rights (London), Immigration (London)

Practice Areas: Human rights, international law, terrorism, prisoners' rights, police law, immigration and asylum, mental health, crime and extradition, contempt, election, privacy, community care and other public law. Ten Supreme Court cases in last three years. Recent significant cases include: R (O) v Secretary of State [2016] 1 WLR 1717; Pham v Secretary of State [2015] 1 WLR 1591; R (Haney) v Secretary of State [2015] 2 WLR 76; R (Whiston) v Secretary of State [2015] AC 176; R (Nunn) v Chief Constable of Suffolk Constabulary [2015] AC 225; R (T) v Secretary of State [2015] AC 49, ZZ v Secretary of State [2014] 2 WLR 791, Sarjantson v Chief Constable of Humberside Police [2014] 1 All ER 960, R (Chester) v Secretary of State [2014] AC 271 and R (Sturnham) v Parole Board [2013] 2 AC 254.
Professional Memberships: Administrative Law Bar Association, Association of Prison Lawyers, Immigration Law Practitioners Association, Mental Health Lawyers Association, Human Rights Lawyers Association, Legal Action, Liberty, Justice.
Career: Admitted as a solicitor in 1991. Headed the Immigration and Crime Departments at Glazer Delmar. EHRC A list. Recorder of the Crown Court. Called in Northern Ireland.
Publications: Judicial Review: A Practical Guide (2nd Edition: With Amanda Weston and Jude Bunting) and United Kingdom Human Rights Reports (Editor: 1998 – 2011)

SOUTHGATE, Jonathan QC
29 Bedford Row Chambers, London
020 7404 1044
jsouthgate@29br.co.uk
Featured in Family/Matrimonial (London)

Practice Areas: Financial remedy; cohabitation; civil partnerships; inheritance and family provision; Children Act (private law)including financial provision for children. Recent cases include: T v F [2016] EWFC 26; US v RS [2015] EWHC 2921 (Fam); AE v BE [2014] 4068 (Fam); S v S [2014] EWHC 4732; Ahmend and Mehmet v Mustafa [2014] EWCA Civ 27; JM v CZ [2014] EWHC 1125 (Fam); DR v GR and Others (Financial Remedy: Variation of Overseas Trust) [2013] EWHC 1196 (Fam); BJ v MJ (Financial Remedy:Overseas Trusts) [2012] 1 FLR 667; Riding v Riding [2011] EWHC 3093; Golubovich v Golubovich [2010] EWCA Civ 810; H v H [2009] EWHC 3739 (Fam); McFarlane v McFarlane [2009] EWHC 891 (Fam); P v P [2010] 1 FLR 1126; P v P (Financial Relief: Procedure) [2009] 1 FLR 696; Kimber v Kimber (Writ Ne Exeat Regno) [2006] EWCA Civ 706.
Professional Memberships: Middle Temple; FLBA.
Career: Called 1992; pupil and tenant at 29 Bedford Row. QC 2013.
Publications: 'Judgment Summons: Still Scope for a Comeback?', Family Law June 2003. 'Costs in Ancillary Relief Proceedings', Family Law February 2005; 'Orders in relation to surplus income' The Review March 2008. "Privilege" a chapter in the Resolution Family Disputes Handbook 2010.
Personal: Clifton College and MMU (LLB). Married with three children; tennis.

SPALTON, George
4 New Square, London
020 7822 2040
barristers@4newsquare.com
Featured in International Arbitration (London), Professional Negligence (London), Commercial Dispute Resolution (London)

Practice Areas: George's practice falls into five principal areas: Commercial litigation, international commercial arbitration, financial services, professional liability claims and disciplinary work. His experience of commercial work encompasses a wide variety of disputes – ranging from construction claims, insurance and reinsurance matters, banking claims to civil fraud. He has significant experience of international work and is currently instructed in an on-going, high value arbitration in Dubai as well as acting in a number of arbitrations in Europe, South-East Asia, and elsewhere. George's expertise in the context of professional liability work focusses on accountants and auditors' negligence and solicitors' negligence – especially in the context of financial services and commercial transactions.
Professional Memberships: George is on the Executive Committee of the Commercial Bar Association. He is also a member of the LCIA; TECBAR; ChBA; and the PNBA.
Career: MA Oxon; LL.M Columbia University (New York); Called 2004.
Publications: Co-Editor: 'Jackson & Powell on Professional Liability' (Sweet & Maxwell) Co-Editor: 'Encyclopaedia of Financial Services Law' (Sweet & Maxwell).

SPEARMAN, Richard QC
39 Essex Chambers, London
020 7832 1111
richard.spearman@39essex.com
Featured in Data Protection (London), Defamation/Privacy (London), Media & Entertainment (London)

Practice Areas: Chancery, Commercial, Common Law, including: civil fraud, media and entertainment, copyright, privacy, confidence, data protection, defamation, sports law, insurance and reinsurance, sale of goods, restraint of trade, professional negligence. Reported cases include: Warren v Mendy (boxing); Istel v Tully (self-incrimination); R v Jockey Club ex p Aga Khan (judicial review); Brinks v Abu Saleh, Independent Trustee Services v GP Noble (tracing); Papamichael v National Westminster Bank (banking); Ashdown v Telegraph, Sawkins v Hyperion, Twentieth-Century Fox v BT (copyright); Grobbelaar v NGN, Loutchansky v Times, Polanski v Conde Nast, ZAM v CFW (defamation); Jockey Club v Buffham, Campbell v MGN, Cream Holdings v Banerjee, Murray v Big Pictures, Goodwin v NGN, Giggs v NGN, V v Associated (confidence/privacy/data protection); Athletic Union of Constantinople v NBA (arbitration); Ivey v Genting (gaming); Adidas v USTA (tennis/competition law); Scopelight v FACT and Northumbria Police (police powers); Blankley v Central Manchester NHS Trust (frustration of contracts/recoverability of costs); Dunnage v Randall (personal injury).
Professional Memberships: COMBAR, ChBA, Bar Sports Law Group
Career: Called 1977; QC 1996; Assistant Recorder 1998; Recorder (crime) 2000; Recorder (civil) 2004; bencher Middle Temple 2006; Deputy High Court Judge 2013.
Personal: Education: Bedales; King's College, Cambridge

SPECK, Adrian QC
8 New Square, London
020 7405 4321
adrian.speck@8newsquare.co.uk
Featured in Information Technology (London), Intellectual Property (London), Media & Entertainment (London)

Practice Areas: Barrister (QC) specialising in all aspects of intellectual property, media and entertainment, and information technology. IP areas include patents, trade marks, copyright, passing off, confidential information, registered and unregistered designs, M&E areas include broadcasting (terrestrial and satellite), publishing, performers' rights, moral rights. IT specialisms include internet law, database rights, telecommunications. Also specialises in jurisdiction disputes under the CJJA 1982 Brussels Convention. Recent cases include Hospira (AG) v Novartis Uk Ltd (patents), Specsavers v Asda (trademarks), virgin Atlantic Airways v Air Canada (patents). For comprehensive CV visit chambers website at www.8newsquare.co.uk
Professional Memberships: Patent Bar Association (PBA); Chancery Bar Association.
Career: Called 1993.
Publications: 'Modern Law of Copyright', 3rd edn.
Personal: Born 1969. Educated at Seaford Head Comprehensive; Kings College, Cambridge (1991 BA Physics and Theoretical Physics – 1st Class); College of Law 1992 (Common Professional Exam with distinction); ICSL 1993 (Bar Vocational Course). Appointed QC 2012

SPENCE, Stephen
Drystone Chambers, London
020 7404 1881
stephen.spence@drystone.com
Featured in Crime (South Eastern)

Practice Areas: Aviation law, criminal law, sports law, courts martial.
Professional Memberships: CBA, South Eastern Circuit, The Guild of Air Pilots and Air Navigators (GAPAN).
Career: Stephen Spence deals with all aspects of serious crime – murder, drug offences, sexual offences and offences involving child abuse. He has been extensively briefed in cases involving Internet crime and Internet child pornography. He has acted as leading counsel in a number of high profile cases. An RAF trained pilot with wide experience of flying from gliders to fast jets, Stephen Spence has an established reputation defending in aviation related prosecutions; these ranging from successfully defending manslaughter allegations against pilots and aircraft engineers, airspace infringements and licencing issues through to low flying allegations. He has been briefed in numerous aviation cases involving CAA prosecutions, and civil litigation arising out of aircraft accidents and parachuting cases. Stephen has acted in a number of inquests arising out of aviation accidents and was recently instructed in the Vauxhall Helicopter Crash inquest. Stephen is a former Board Member of the British Bobsleigh Association where he was legal Director, he was a member of the Special Advisory Board of the FIBT (International Bobsleigh Federation) and an adviser to the British Parachute Association. He has advised a number of other sports governing bodies on disciplinary procedures and drug testing, appearing in disciplinary tribunals involving a variety of sports and chairing both disciplinary proceedings and Olympic selection appeals. Stephen also has experience of successfully defending fitness to practice cases before the General Medical Council.

SPENCER, Martin QC
Hailsham Chambers, London
020 7643 5000
clerks@hailshamchambers.com
Featured in Clinical Negligence (London)

Practice Areas: Martin maintains a busy clinical negligence practice balanced between claimants and defendants. He has a wide and varied practice involving all aspects of clinical negligence including disciplinary matters. He has a particular interest in high quantum claims where complex calculations are involved. Significant cases include: Wright v Secretary of State for Health [2009] 2 WLR 267. HL. Care Standards Act 2000 declared incompatible with the European Convention on Human Rights. Chester v Afshar [2005] 1 AC 134. HL. Leading case on causation and the duty to warn in clinical negligence. His argument was described by Lord Steyn as follows: "This was a powerful argument and persuasively presented". Farley v Skinner [2002] 2 AC 732 HL. Surveyor's negligence and the award of general damages. Coombs v Dorset NHS Primary Care Trust [2013] EWCA Civ 471: whether a detained patient is prevented from paying for his own care and treatment. Farraj v King's College Hospital [2010] Med LR 1. CA. Non-delegable duties of care owed to patients. Whipps Cross University Hospital NHS Trust v Iqbal [2008] LS Law Med 22 CA. Recoverability of damages in the lost years.

SPENCER, Paul
Serjeants' Inn Chambers, London
020 7427 5000
PSpencer@serjeantsinn.com
Featured in Professional Discipline (London)

Practice Areas: Paul Spencer was called to the Bar in 1988. Paul practises in civil law with a specialism in social and healthcare advice and litigation. He is noted in an earlier edition "for being highly knowledgeable and a great team player" and is "an excellent advocate, with a beautiful courtroom manner – he is totally unflappable." Please visit the Serjeants' Inn Chambers website for his profile, which sets out full details of his practice including relevant work of note.

Professional Memberships: ALBA, ARDL, CBA and ELBA.
Publications: Co-author of Blackstone's Guide to the Care Standards Act (2000), Contributor to Bullen & Leake; Jacob's Precedents and Pleadings (Sweet and Maxwell), Contributor to Commercial Judicial Review (Sweet and Maxwell).
Personal: Bencher of the Middle Temple, Legal Member of the Inns of Court Conduct Committee, Middle Temple advocacy trainer.

SPENS, David QC
QEB Hollis Whiteman, London
020 7933 8855
david.spens@qebhw.co.uk
Featured in Crime (London)
Practice Areas: David Spens QC has a formidable reputation for securing acquittals against the odds, defending the most high-profile, sensitive and complex cases concerning business crime, health and safety, serious sexual offences, murder and terrorism. Formerly a Treasury Counsel, David has defended exclusively for the last 20 years. David has a successful track record in defending fraud and money-laundering, and is developing a niche practice defending individuals accused of bribery and corruption in the UK and overseas. He is instructed to defend a senior manager in R v Reynolds, the SFO's prosecution of Alstom Power for bribery in Lithuania (Operation Yuletide); in R v Forrester he secured notable acquittals for a sales manager accused by SFO of bribery in three African states. David is regularly instructed in cases which involve manslaughter by gross negligence in the context of health and safety legislation. In the field of serious sexual offences, David has particular expertise in historical matters. He is currently instructed to represent a philanthropist accused of historical sexual abuse in London and the Caribbean. Since defending Learco Chindamo, the youth convicted of murdering headmaster Philip Lawrence, David has been instructed in many murder cases, most involving joint enterprise; he has special expertise in cross-examining pathologists and forensic psychiatrists.

SPRINZ, Lucy
1 Garden Court Family Law Chambers, London
020 7797 7900
sprinz@1gc.com
Featured in Family/Matrimonial (London)
Practice Areas: Lucy specialises exclusively in children law, in the public, private and international law fields. In the public law arena she is regularly instructed on behalf of local authorities, parents and children and frequently appears in cases involving serious allegations of domestic violence, sexual abuse, illegal substance or alcohol abuse and cases involving complex medical issues. She has expertise on alternative families and on the application of human rights law to children law cases. In the private law field she has considerable experience of residence and contact disputes. Lucy also undertakes children work involving an international element, particularly intercountry adoption. She has practised at all levels of court, including the Supreme Court.
Professional Memberships: FLBA, Bar Pro Bono Unit.
Career: BA (Hons) History and Politics, University of Nottingham. GDL Nottingham Law School. Inner BA (Hons) History and Politics, University of Nottingham. GDL Nottingham Law School. Inner Temple Major Scholarship. BVC College of Law. Inner Temple Outstanding BVC Award. Called to the Bar 2008. Pupil and then tenant at 1 Garden Court.
Publications: Derbyshire County Council v SH [2015] EWFC B102, Re D (A Child) (No 2) [2015] EWFC 2, Re D (A Child) [2014] EWFC 39, Re A (A Child) [2012] UKSC 60, Re E (A Child) (Application to withdraw Proceedings, Grounds for Emergency Removal of a Child) [2013] EWHC 2400 (Fam), A Father v SBC & Ors [2014] EWFC 6. Special guardianship orders versus adoption orders – Re BS and ED (Children): (Placement Order or Special Guardianship Order) [2013] EWHC 2607, Kinship carers and looked after child status – KS v Bradford Metropolitan District Council [2014] EWHC 11 (Admin), Adoption in 2014 [2014] Fam Law 335.

ST VILLE, James
8 New Square, London
020 74054321
St.Ville@8newsquare.co.uk
Featured in Information Technology (London), Intellectual Property (London)
Practice Areas: James St.Ville specialises in intellectual property law and appears in disputes relating to patents, confidential information, registered designs, unregistered design rights, copyright, database rights, trade marks, passing off, trade libel, and IT and computer contracts many of which deal with complex engineering, electronics and software. He has expertise in areas of practice such as search orders, Norwich Pharmacal orders, disk imaging orders, delivery up of source code, ex-parte injunctions to identify and deal with computer hackers and other interim injunctions which need to be kept confidential, jurisdiction disputes, pre-action disclosure, third party disclosure, UK Border Agency seizures and disputes over letters of request and the examination of witnesses for the purpose of foreign proceedings.
He is a chartered engineer with substantial experience of commercial electronics, optical communications and engineering research. Please see his website entry at www.8newsquare.co.uk/jsv for recent cases such as Positec v Husqvarna [2016] Bus LR 714, VPG v Air-Weigh [2016] FSR 4 and Procter and Gamble v Star Global [2016] EWHC 734.
Professional Memberships: Intellectual Property Bar Association (IPBA); The Intellectual Property Lawyers Organisation (TIPLO); Society of Computers and Law (SCL); Chartered Engineer (CEng); Institution of Engineering and Technology (IET); Chancery Bar Association (ChBA).
Career: Called 1995, Gray's Inn.
Publications: Russell-Clarke and Howe on Industrial Designs (9th Edition)
Personal: Plays jazz flute. Board member of Clod Ensemble theatre company. Resides London.

STACEY, Dan
Hailsham Chambers, London
2076435000
dan.stacey@hailshamchambers.com
Featured in Professional Negligence (London), Costs Litigation (All Circuits)
Practice Areas: Dan Stacey is a senior junior barrister who specialises in professional indemnity and costs litigation. He has appeared in numerous reported solicitors' negligence, banking and costs disputes in the High Court and Court of Appeal (with a leader and on his own). He was closely involved in the recent wave of high-value mortgage fraud claims in the High Court involving the obtaining of freezing orders and other interlocutory relief and subsequent related lenders' claims against well-known valuers, surveyors and solicitors. He also has a busy practice in commercial disputes, and has acted and advised in cases involving a number of well-known banks and lending institutions, appearing for Lloyds Bank, Bank of Ireland and others in recent trials and related applications in the High Court.
Personal: Education: Magdalen College, Oxford (Modern History, First Class); City University (Diploma in Law);ICSL School of Law (Gray's Inn Prince of Wales Scholar)

STANCOMBE, Barry
The Chambers of Andrew Mitchell QC, London
020 7440 9950
bs@33cllaw.com
Featured in POCA Work & Asset Forfeiture (All Circuits)
Practice Areas: Specialist in asset forfeiture and proceeds of crime particularly in the areas of restraint, receivership, confiscation and insolvency. A commercial litigator whose practice encompasses complex and high value cases. Specialist in: civil fraud litigation; asset recovery; civil recovery; bribery; corruption; insolvency; fraud; and money laundering. Recent cases include High Court actions involving: factoring and banking fraud; mis-selling interest rate swaps; mortgage fraud; MTIC fraud; civil recovery (acting for a defendant and in separate proceedings obtaining the SFO's first PFO); successful professional negligence claim against court appointed supervising accountants over a restrained defendant's assets; acting in highly contentious bankruptcy proceedings; director disqualification proceedings; and acting for liquidators successfully defending disclosure proceedings. Regularly instructed on behalf of court appointed management and enforcement receivers in high value receiverships. International work has included acting for the Attorney General of the Turks & Caicos Islands in civil proceedings. Barry acts for the following prosecution agencies: SFO, FCA NCA and CPS.
Professional Memberships: Proceeds of Crime Lawyers' Association; R3; London Common Law & Commercial Bar Association.
Career: Year of Call: 1983 (Gray's Inn). SFO A Panel (Proceeds of Crime).

STANSFELD, James
Furnival Chambers, London
020 7405 3232
jstansfeld@furnivallaw.co.uk
Featured in Extradition (London)
Practice Areas: James specialises in extradition, human rights and administrative and public law. He is regularly instructed in lead extradition cases. He has particular expertise in arguments regarding the validity of requests and has appeared in the two most recent extradition cases before the Supreme Court, both of which considered the validity requirements for EAWs (Bucnys & Others [2013] 3 WLR 1485 & Goluchowski & Sas [2016] 1 WLR 2665). He has acted in the majority of the lead cases on prison conditions in Part 1 territories, including Lithuania, Romania, Hungary and Greece. James also acted in the first Divisional Court case considering the new bar under s.12A of the Act and recently successfully invoked that bar for one of four individuals sought by Italy for terrorism offences. He also has expertise in Part 2 requests, having appeared for the Albanian and Norwegian Governments and represented individuals sought by countries including the United States, Turkey and the Ukraine. James also advises on Interpol Red Notices. As a member of the Attorney General's Civil C Panel, James is instructed in judicial reviews, inquests and matters involving national security and closed material procedures. He has appeared before SIAC and in TPIM proceedings.

STANSFIELD, Piers QC
Keating Chambers, London
020 7544 2600
pstansfield@keatingchambers.com
Featured in Construction (London)
Practice Areas: Specialist with wide experience of construction, engineering, energy, shipbuilding and IT disputes, and professional negligence. Within these areas of expertise, he is known for his ability to master technical detail including engineering, delay analysis and forensic accountancy. He has been involved in complex and high value claims arising out of hospitals, tunnels, port facilities, shipbuilding, aircraft manufacturing, chemical plants, and power stations. He has a wide range of advocacy experience, in domestic and international arbitrations, in the High Court, and in alternative dispute resolution. He also has considerable experience of adjudication, including making written and oral submissions to adjudicators, advising and appearing in enforcement proceedings, and acting as adjudicator himself.
Professional Memberships: Technology and Construction Bar Association (TECBAR); Commercial Bar Association (COMBAR); Society of Construction Law; Society for Computers and Law.
Career: Called to Bar 1993, Queen's Counsel 2012, TECBAR accredited adjudicator.
Publications: Contributor – Keating on Construction Contracts Ninth Edition and Keating on NEC3.

STARKS, Nicholas
St Ives Chambers, Birmingham
0121 236 0863
nicholas.starks@stiveschambers.co.uk
Featured in Family/Matrimonial (Midlands)
Practice Areas: Family Finance
Professional Memberships: Family Law Bar Association
Career: Nicholas is a senior junior counsel of over 20 years' experience. He specialises in family financial provision, principally financial orders upon divorce but also claims under TLATA, IPFDA, sch 1 Children Act and Civil Partnership Act 2004. Nicholas frequently deals with high net worth claims, involving businesses, farming and overseas assets. Nicholas practices at all levels of the Court hierarchy and has been commended by the Court of Appeal for his 'lucid argument' (Kaur v Matharu [2010] EWCA Civ 930).

STARTE, Harvey
One Brick Court, London
020 7353 8845
hs@onebrickcourt.co.uk
Featured in Defamation/Privacy (London)
Practice Areas: Defamation, malicious falsehood, privacy and breach of confidence, contempt, reporting restrictions, data

protection, freedom of information and publication-related media and information law generally, including pre-publication/ broadcast advice. Cases include: S v Newham LBC; Reid Minty v Taylor; Rahamin v Channel Four; Al-Fagih v HH Saudi Research Publishing; The Rt Hon Lester Bird v BBC; Musa King v Telegraph Group; Pritchard Engelfield v Steinberg; Robbie Williams v MGN Ltd; Koronky and anr v Time Life Entertainment Group; David Moyes v Wayne Rooney and Harper Collins; Dizaei v News Group Newspapers Ltd; SA v Sec of State for Home Dept; Henry v News Group Newspapers Ltd; Morrissey v Associated Newspapers Ltd; Maisto v Kyrgiannakis; Serrano v Associated Newspapers Ltd; Simpson v MGN Ltd and Ward.

Career: Call to the bar 1985, Gray's Inn. Legal Manager of Independent and Independent on Sunday Newspapers 1995-96. Practising from One Brick Court 1987-95 and from 1996 onwards.

Publications: Carter-Ruck on Libel and Slander, 4th & 5th editions, editor; Carter-Ruck on Libel & Privacy, 6th Edition (2010), contributing editor.

Personal: Millfield School; Fitzwilliam College, Cambridge (1977 BA Hons English; MA (Cantab)); City University (1984 Diploma in law).

STEEL, John QC
39 Essex Chambers, London
020 7832 1111
john.steel@39essex.com
Featured in Aviation (London), Planning (London)

Practice Areas: John's practice includes national and international clients at the highest level in planning, aviation and aerospace, major infrastructure, real-estate, regulatory and environmental law in the UK and abroad. Recent cases: Airport and airspace (Heathrow Third Runway, Gatwick Airspace Changes, London City Airport, London Oxford and Biggin Hill v CAA re Northolt), compulsory purchase, retail, infrastructure, energy, housing, rights of way and village green inquiries; local plans; minerals and waste cases; planning and environmental public inquiries and High Court cases in England and Wales.

Professional Memberships: Planning and Environment Bar Association; Administrative Law Bar Association; Fellowships: Chartered Institute of Arbitrators, Royal Geographical Society, Royal Aeronautical Society, Royal Society of Arts; Hon. Legal Adviser The Air League, BBGA.

Career: Called to the Bar 1978; Silk 1993; Recorder 2000; CEDR Mediator; International Arbitrator.

Publications: Property Review

Personal: Durham University (BSc Hons. Chemistry); Hon. Fellow Durham University (Law); Gray's Inn Prize winner 1978; Bencher Gray's Inn, Chairman of Management Committee 2013; Recorder Civil and Crime; Member Bar Tribunals Appointments Body; Joint Head of Planning, Environmental and Property Law and Head of Aviation and Aerospace Law at 39 Essex Chambers; Member of 39 Essex Chambers Management Board.

STEINBERG, Harry QC
12 King's Bench Walk, London
020 7583 0811
steinberg@12kbw.co.uk
Featured in Personal Injury (London), Personal Injury (All Circuits)

Practice Areas: Harry Steinberg is a specialist in industrial disease, private international law, group actions, catastrophic injury and product liability. Recent cases include acting for the appellants in the Supreme Court in the case of Knauer -v- MoJ [2016] UKSC 9; Leading Counsel for the Appellants in Greenway and others v Johnson Matthey Plc [2014] EWHC 3957; and for the Respondent in the Case of Carder [2016] EWCA Civ 790. Other recent cases include the Bomu-Bomu Oil Pipeline Litigation, thought to be the UK's largest ever environmental case. Other group litigation cases include Vilca -v- Xstrata PLC, Kalma -v- African Minerals. Haxton v Philips Electronics UK Ltd [2014] 1 WLR 2721: acting on behalf of the claimant at trial and in the Court of Appeal. Concept 70 and others v Cape International Holdings Ltd: Acting for the claimants in this major product liability group test case for insurers seeking contribution to settled claims from product manufacturers.

Career: Called in 1997. Silk 2016

STEINERT, Jonathan
Henderson Chambers, London
020 7583 9020
clerks@hendersonchambers.co.uk
Featured in Real Estate Litigation (London)

Practice Areas: Jonathan Steinert's practice focusses on all aspects of contentious and non-contentious property and landlord and tenant and associated areas including competition, commercial, business, telecoms, planning, insolvency, professional negligence, product liability and IT. His work has a particular emphasis on the leisure industry. His commercial practice centres on product liability, franchising, partnership, joint venture, development agreements and shareholder disputes. His clients include the UK's largest companies in the sector. Recent cases include: JP Tupper Associates -v- Pearson-Chisman (2011, Kitchin J,LTL 23/5/11); Lambe v Saunders (2009 Blake J LTL 14/12/09); Rouf v Cafe Rouge (2009) All ER (D) 29; Clarkson v Credit Agricole [2008] EWHC 41 (QB); Anderson Antiques (UK) Ltd v Anderson Wharf (Hull) Ltd and Another [2007] All ER (D)409; Carnegie v Glessen and Others [2005] All ER (D) 22(CA); Re a debtor (No 503 SD 2001) [2002] All ER (D)500; Aylesbond Estates Ltd v McMillan and Garg [2000] 32 HLR 1(CA).

Professional Memberships: COMBAR, Chancery Bar Association, PNBA, ACI Arb.

Career: B.A. Hons PPE Balliol College Oxford 1983; Dip Law 1984; called 1986.

Publications: Competiton Law, Butterworths 2004.

STEPHENS, Jessica
4 Pump Court, London
020 7842 5555
jstephens@4pumpcourt.com
Featured in Construction (London)

Practice Areas: Specialist in construction, engineering, shipbuilding and energy disputes, including advising on high value residential and commercial premises. Adjudication including advising, drafting submissions and appearing at hearings before adjudicators. Appeared on applications for the enforcement of adjudicators' decisions and in disputes concerning professional negligence of construction professionals. International arbitration experience includes disputes relating to the construction of ultra harsh environment rigs, alleged defects in design and construction of a container port in the Caribbean, additional costs and delays in relation to one of the largest mega-yachts ever constructed, and a project relating to the conversion of a bulk carrier into a pipe laying vessel. Advises and appears in procurement disputes (including Alstom v Eurostar) and general commercial disputes. Advised in disputes relating to of party walls, rights to light and nuisance.

Professional Memberships: TECBAR; SCL; COMBAR.

Career: Called 2001; Public Access Training 2008.

Publications: Contributor, Keating on Construction Contracts – Ninth Edition 2012; Contributor; Keating on JCT Contracts, 2011; Co-Author: RICS Case in Point: Rights to Light (co-authored with Sarah Hannaford QC) 2008; Contributor, Keating on Construction Contracts – Eighth Edition 2006; Co-Author: RICS Case in Point: Party Walls, 2004.

STEPHENSON, Christopher
9 Gough Square, London
020 7832 0500
cstephenson@9goughsquare.co.uk
Featured in Personal Injury (London), Clinical Negligence (London)

Practice Areas: Personal injury and clinical negligence, exclusively for Claimants, in cases of the utmost severity and complexity.

Professional Memberships: PIBA, APIL, PNBA.

Career: Pupillage at 9 Gough Square under Nicolas Hillier and Grahame Aldous QC, called in 1994. Broad common law practice for 7 years, including extensive criminal work, before concentrating on personal injury and clinical negligence. Now a well established senior junior used to cases of high value and complexity, usually in the High Court. Regularly instructed alone against Silks and led by Silks in Chambers. Pragmatic and commercial approach to litigation with a particular ability to get on with clients and opponents alike.

Publications: Contributing editor to 9 Gough Square Publication: Guide to Clinical Negligence Claims, chapter author of APIL Guides to RTA Claims and Evidence. Co-Editor of 2nd edition of the leading textbook on claims in the CICA. Author of numerous articles for range of publications.

Personal: The usual.

STERN, David
5 St Andrew's Hill, London
020 7332 5400
clerks@5sah.co.uk
Featured in Financial Crime (London)

Practice Areas: Financial regulatory, business crime and serious fraud with a particular emphasis on financial services and insurance, proceeds of crime and asset forfeiture.

Professional Memberships: Fraud Lawyers Association and Association of Regulatory and Disciplinary Lawyers

Career: Head of the Business Crime & Financial Regulation Practice Group. Acted as leading junior and junior counsel in many high profile proceedings, especially cases brought by the Serious Fraud Office and the FCA and those with international agency involvement. Leading junior (US$ Libor – Contogoulas) and successfully defended SFO's first prosecution of alleged manipulation of Libor benchmarks (Yen Libor – Wilkinson). Cases include Katcharian (prime bank guarantee high yield investment fraud), GFX Capital Markets (FX Ponzi scheme), Hughes (£100 million Spanish boiler room), Carney (commercial mortgage fraud) and Sandison (stock exchange listing fraud). Other landmark cases include Guinness II (Lord Spens), Wallace Duncan Smith and Dr Clewes (Butte Mining). Technical expertise in appellate and divisional court work, including leading case law on the right to silence. Particular expertise in advisory, regulatory and tribunal work arising out of financial transactions. Instructed to represent corporations and individuals in FCA regulatory investigations. Commercial negotiator and accredited mediator, handling commercial disputes involving financial services and high value insurance claims

---

STERNBERG, Daniel
9-12 Bell Yard, London
2074001800
d.sternberg@912by.com
Featured in Extradition (London)

Practice Areas: Daniel is a specialist extradition and public law practitioner at 9-12 Bell Yard. He represents both requesting authorities and defendants, and advises pre-arrest and in import extradition cases, involving the full range of offences as well as in Judicial Review challenges to the decisions of public authorities and Habeas Corpus and unlawful detention cases. Recent instructions: representing the Government of Peru in their first extradition requests for serious drug smuggling charges, India, Brazil and Albania in the Magistrates' and High Court and government departments in challenges under the Freedom of Information Act and to the legality of detention. Daniel advised CPS Kent on post-extradition aspects of the case of Jeremy Forrest who was extradited to the UK for abducting a pupil. Defence work includes advising on the UK's extradition relations with Japan, and representing a requested person accused of involvement in a multi-million Euro VAT fraud. Daniel is a member of the Serious Fraud Office's prosecution and proceeds of crime panels, CPS prosecution and extradition specialist panels and Attorney-General's C panel of civil counsel. He is the editor of Westlaw Insight articles on Extradition (with Rebecca Niblock, Maya Silva and Katherine Tyler of Kingsley Napley).

Professional Memberships: CBA, Extradition Lawyers Association, Defence Extradition Lawyers Forum

Career: MA (Cantab), Called 2006 (Gray's Inn), Appointed to SFO prosecution and POCA C Panels, CPS prosecution and extradition specialist and Attorney General's C Panel of Civil Counsel.

Publications: Backstone's Criminal Practice 2013 Chapter on Extradition, Westlaw Insight articles on Extradition (with Katherine Tyler, Rebecca Niblock and Maya Silva).

STEVENSON, Peter
Quadrant Chambers, London
020 7583 4444
Peter.Stevenson@quadrantchambers.com
Featured in Shipping (London)
Practice Areas: Peter has a broad shipping practice. Recent cases in the Senior Courts include, The Alexandros T in which Peter (led by Steven Gee QC) acted for the successful insurers in the Supreme Court in the leading case on parallel proceedings within the EC; Tartsinis v Navona Management Co in which Peter acted for the successful defendant (led by Robert Bright QC) in a ship sale dispute ; and Aquavita v Ashapura Minechem Ltd in which Peter acted (as sole counsel) for the successful charterers in a case the dealt with a number of issues arising out of a failure to perform long term COAs. Peter is also regularly instructed in LMAA and Lloyd's Salvage Arbitrations. Recent examples of LMAA arbitrations include a five day arbitration dealing with issues relating to the loading of dangerous cargo and an eight day arbitration arising from the grounding of a bulk carrier. Recent examples of Lloyd's Salvage Arbitrations include a four-day hearing (led by Timothy Hill QC) concerning the safety of the place of redelivery and a five day hearing (again led by Timothy Hill QC) concerning the conduct of the salvors during a salvage operation. He is recommended as a leading barrister for shipping.
Career: MA (Hons) (First Class),University of Edinburgh [1998-2002]; CPE (Distinction), City University [2006-2007]; BVC (Outstanding), BPP Law School [2007-2008]; Year of Call: 2008

STEWARD, Claire
Kings Chambers, Manchester
0345 034 3444
clerks@kingschambers.com
Featured in Clinical Negligence (Northern)
Practice Areas: Specialises in clinical negligence with extensive experience in all areas including: surgical negligence, delay in diagnosing cancer, orthopaedics, obstetrics and gynaecology, A&E, primary healthcare, cosmetic surgery and dentistry. She also has a substantial personal injury practice in cases involving serious injury.
Professional Memberships: Personal Injury Bar Association
Career: University of Manchester BA (Hons) Modern History with Economics CPE (Manchester Metropolitan University) BVC (Manchester Metropolitan University) Called to the Bar 2002 (Lincolns Inn – Lord Denning Scholarship)

STEWART, Roger QC
4 New Square, London
020 7822 2038
r.stewart@4newsquare.com
Featured in International Arbitration (London), Professional Negligence (London), Construction (London), Insurance (London)
Practice Areas: Construction, international arbitration, commercial and insurance. A "top-rate silk" who "prides himself on sorting the wheat from the chaff and identifying the issues that are worth pursuing", Roger has a mixed national and international commercial practice specialising in professional liability, construction, insurance and re-insurance. He is regularly appointed as an arbitrator in high-value and sensitive disputes. Roger has particular expertise in relation to large disputes in the Middle East. He has acted in relation to disputes for and against Governments in the Region as well as in relation to substantial private sector projects. His experience extends to B.O.T. contracts in the energy sector as well as traditional contracts. He has particular experience of the operation of nominated sub-contracts and the problems in relation thereto. Roger has twice been awarded the Chambers & Partners Professional Negligence Silk of the Year (in 2007 and 2010). He is a Recorder and appointed to sit in the Technology and Construction Court.
Professional Memberships: LCIA, Combar, LCLCBA, TecBar, PNBA.
Career: Called 1986, Silk 2001, Deputy High Court Judge (TCC), recorder.
Publications: General Editor: Jackson & Powell on Professional Negligence.
Personal: Married, 4 children, 4 step-children; Senior Bar Auditor Inner Temple; Skiing, Sailing and Switzerland.

STEYN, Karen QC
11KBW, London
020 7632 8500
Karen.Steyn@11kbw.com
Featured in Administrative & Public Law (London), Civil Liberties & Human Rights (London), Data Protection (London), Local Government (London), Public International Law (London)
Practice Areas: Public law, public international law, human rights, local government and information law. Supreme Court cases: Belhaj [2016] UKSC (foreign act of state; state immunity); Serdar Mohammed [2016] UKSC (power to detain in armed conflict; territorial scope of HRA; Crown act of state); Benkharbouche [2016] UKSC (EU Charter; state immunity); DSD & NBV [2017] UKSC (scope of A3 ECHR); Evans [2015] AC 1787 (Ministerial veto; FOIA/EIR); SG [2015] 1 WLR 1449 (benefit cap; unincorporated treaties); Kennedy [2015] AC 455 (A10 ECHR; FOIA); Susan Smith [2014] 1 AC 52 (combat immunity; A2 ECHR); and Al-Rawi [2012] 1 AC 531 (closed hearings). ECtHR (Grand Chamber) cases: Bizottsag v Hungary (A10; access to information) and Jaloud v Netherlands (2015) 60 EHRR 29 (A1 jurisdiction); Other recent cases include: PMI [2016] 1 WLR 1737 (Royal Charter; bias); Dumliauskas [2015] Imm AR 773 (deportation; foreign criminals); R (C) v Northumberland CC [2015] BLGR 675 (child protection; data retention); and Recyclate [2013] Env LR 23 (Waste Framework Directive).
Professional Memberships: ALBA, BIICL, JUSTICE, ILA
Career: Called: 1995. QC: 2014. DHCJ: 2016.

STIGGELBOUT, Mark
Quadrant Chambers, London
020 7583 4444
mark.stiggelbout@quadrantchambers.com
Featured in Shipping (London)
Practice Areas: Mark advises and acts as an advocate in commercial disputes, specialising in shipping, commodities, international sale of goods, insurance, energy and aviation matters. He regularly acts in litigation and arbitration proceedings, including trials, appellate work and obtaining injunctive relief. Recent court work includes acting for the successful appellants in the Supreme Court sale of goods case of Bunge SA v. Nidera BV [2015] 3 All E.R. 1082, obtaining freezing orders against persons unknown in relation to fraudulently induced bank transfers, obtaining permission to appeal under s.69 on a question of law concerning claiming wasted charterparty hire as damages, successfully resisting linked s.69 GAFTA appeals worth US$13m, and acting in an ongoing Commercial Court insurance claim raising issues of disputed assignments. Recent arbitrations include two substantial charterparty off-hire claims (arising from drug smuggling and piracy), a pair of linked references concerning contamination of a cargo of vegetable oil, and several high value shipbuilding disputes.
Professional Memberships: COMBAR, TECBAR
Career: M.A. (Oxon.), B.C.L. (Oxon.), LL.M. (Harvard), BPTC (BPP Law School). Called: 2011
Publications: Mark has published widely in the fields of contract, tort and the conflict of laws. Please visit www.quadrantchambers.com for Mark's detailed CV.

STILITZ, Daniel QC
11KBW, London
020 7632 8500
daniel.stilitz@11kbw.com
Featured in Administrative & Public Law (London), Employment (London)
Practice Areas: Employment law, public law, commercial law. Recent cases include: Carneiro v Chelsea FC & Mourinho (sex discrimination), R (T& S King) v DEFRA (EU agricultural subsidies), Duffy v TNS (sex discrimination, whistleblowing), R (Boots) v CAC (trade union recognition), Smith v Carillion (CA: blacklisting and human rights), Pereiro-Mendez v Goldman Sachs (maternity discrimination), Akerman-Livingstone v Aster (SC: homelessness and Equality Act) Joy v Deutsche Bank (unfair dismissal, sex discrimination), LMR v Dover (QBD: anti-harassment injunction), R (Islington BC) v Mayor of London (closure of fire stations), Gregg v Troy (maternity and sex discrimination), R (Green Transport Company) v West Midlands ITA (travel reimbursements), Unison v IBM & Accenture (TUPE), GNC Ltd v Palletways (QBD, road distribution), Turner v Merrill Lynch (QBD, bonus claim), Skipper v BP plc (age discrimination), Stone v Merrill Lynch International (whistleblowing), R (K & AC Jackson & Sons) v DEFRA (bovine tuberculosis, abuse of power), BTIG v Reiss (Comm Ct, unauthorized trading), Nescar v Middlesbrough FC (transfer of professional footballer), Powell v Hounslow LBC (SC, homelessness, introductory tenancies and human rights), Tenner v PwC (disability discrimination), Manchester City Council v Pinnock (SC, demoted tenancies and Article 8), Gascoyne v Force India (Formula One, wrongful dismissal), R (Servier) v NICE (commercial JR, procedural fairness), R (A) v Croydon LBC (Social services), R (Eisai Ltd) v NICE (commercial judicial review), City Index Ltd v Gawler (Knowing receipt). Also sits as a Mediator.
Professional Memberships: ELBA; ALBA; ELA; COMBAR; CEDR Solve Mediator.
Career: Called to the Bar in 1992. QC 2010.
Personal: New College Oxford, BA (1st class hons). City University CPE (distinction), MA. Born 1 August 1968.

STOBART, Alice
Westwater Advocates, Edinburgh
0131 260 5828
alice.stobart@westwateradvocates.com
Featured in Employment (Scotland)
Practice Areas: All aspects of employment law including unfair dismissal, redundancy, equality issues, TUPE, restrictive covenants and contractual disputes. Alice appears regularly in the Employment Appeal Tribunal and in the Employment Tribunals throughout Scotland. She also appears in the Sheriff Court and the Court of Session in employment related matters. Alice also specialises in disciplinary and regulatory law representing clients in hearings before regulatory bodies.
Professional Memberships: Treasurer, Faculty of Advocates Employment Law Group.
Career: Qualified as a solicitor in 2002, called to the Bar in 2007. On Preferred Panel for Equalities and Human Rights Commission in Scotland.
Personal: Educated University of Edinburgh Politics MA (1987), LLB (1998), Diploma in Legal Education (1999).

STOCKLEY, Ruth
Kings Chambers, Manchester
0345 034 3444
clerks@kingschambers.com
Featured in Environment (Northern), Planning (Northern)
Practice Areas: Town and country planning; highways and rights of way; compulsory purchase; environment; village greens; taxi licensing; local government and judicial review. Recent significant reported cases include: R (on application of Barkas) v North Yorkshire County Council [2014] UKSC 31 (village greens); R (on application of Barrow Borough Council) v Cumbria County Council [2011] EWHC 2051 (consultation on development plan documents); R (on application of Peat) v Hyndburn Borough Council [2011] EWHC 1739 (Housing Act selective licensing); Thompson v Pendle Borough Council [2011] EWHC 1751 (tree preservation orders); Chauffeur Bikes Limited v Leeds City Council [2005] All ER 106 (private hire vehicle licensing); R (on application of Hampson) v Wigan Metropolitan Borough Council [2005] All ER 383 (planning).
Professional Memberships: Planning and Environment Bar Association; Administrative Law Bar Association.
Career: University: Nottingham; degree: Law (LLB); called: 1988 (Lincoln's Inn).
Publications: Assistant editor of Sweet and Maxwell's Encyclopaedia of Highway Law and Practice.

STOKES, Mary
Erskine Chambers, London
020 7242 5532
clerks@erskinechambers.com
Featured in Company (London)
Practice Areas: Principal area of practice is company law, including corporate insolvency. Also LLPs and partnership; financial services. Mary is also a Visiting Professor in Practice in the Department of Law at the LSE.
Professional Memberships: Chancery Bar Association; COMBAR.
Career: Called to the Bar in 1989 and joined Erskine Chambers in 1990.
Publications: Consulting Editor of Butterworths Company Cases; Contributor to Buckley on the Companies Acts.
Personal: Educated at the Cambridgeshire High School for Girls; Brasenose College, Oxford and Harvard Law School. Former

Fellow and Tutor of Brasenose College, Oxford.

STONE, Christopher
Devereux, London
020 7353 7534
stone@devchambers.co.uk
Featured in Employment (London), Tax (London)
Practice Areas: Chris is ranked in the areas of employment and tax. Employment: Chris' practice covers all areas of employment and discrimination law. He often appears in multi-day discrimination and whistleblowing hearings in the Tribunals and advises on and acts in restrictive covenant cases in the High Court. He was lead junior in the Construction Industry Vetting Information Group Litigation. Tax: Chris acts for HMRC and taxpayers in a broad range of direct tax disputes. Specialisms include: residence and domicile; deductibility of expenses; and taxation of employment (including employment status, intermediaries and termination). Cases include: Gaines-Cooper (Supreme Court); Daniel, Mertrux and Hargreaves (CoA); Samadian, Duckmanton, McLaren, Ramsay and Hargreaves (UT); G4S (FTT). Chris is instructed in general commercial matters, particularly professional negligence and sports disputes.
Professional Memberships: ELA, RBA, LCLCBA, Combar, PNBA
Career: Appointed to Treasury Panel of Counsel (B Panel) in September 2016. Called 2007; Droop Scholar at Lincoln's Inn. Educated St. Anne's College, Oxford and Australian National University. Before coming to the Bar, Chris was a strategy consultant at Accenture and then M&A Manager at News International. This background supports his commercial and practical approach to legal issues.
Publications: Contributing author to Bloomsbury Professional's Discrimination Law.
Personal: Chairman Kew Occasionals RFC

STONE, Judy
11KBW, London
020 7632 8500
Judy.Stone@11kbw.com
Featured in Employment (London)
Practice Areas: Employment and business law specialist. Judy is regularly instructed in claims involving breaches of directors' duties, fiduciary duties, duties of confidence and restrictive covenants, as well as in pension, bonus and other contractual disputes, including those with an international element. In the employment tribunal, Judy has considerable experience of high value whistleblowing and discrimination litigation. Judy appears regularly in the High Court (both Chancery and QBD), employment tribunals, the EAT, and the Court of Appeal. She represents both claimants and respondents/defendants. Judy often acts as sole counsel and as a junior in multi-day and high value litigation.
Professional Memberships: ELBA; ALBA.
Career: Called in 2003.
Publications: Tolley's Employment Handbook (Retirement, Directors).
Personal: Educated at Balliol College, Oxford (first class degree in PPE, Jenkins Scholar), Harvard University (Frank Knox Memorial Fellow) and City University (CPE, Princess Royal Scholarship).

STONE, Lucy QC
Queen Elizabeth Building QEB, London
020 7797 7837
l.stone@qeb.co.uk
Featured in Family/Matrimonial (London)
Practice Areas: All aspects of family law, particularly matters of financial complexity involving substanial assets; prenuptial and postnuptial agreements;complex private law applications relating to children including relocation; and substantial Inheritance Act claims. Has acted for a plethora of celebrities, particularly in the music industry. Consistently lauded for her meticulous attention to detail, absolutely thorough preparation, realistic advice, approachability to professional and lay clients and discretion. Known amongst her peers for her no-nonsense approach.
Professional Memberships: Fellow of the International Academy of Matrimonial Lawyers; has served on the Bar Council and FLBA Committee.
Career: MA Cantab; Called to the Bar in 1983; Silk 2001; Head of Chambers 2007-10. Bencher Middle Temple 2010.
Personal: Married with one child. Blessed with an ability to survive on little sleep, combines a prestigious pratice with a full family life.

STONE, Sally
1 Garden Court Family Law Chambers, London
020 7797 7900
stone@1gc.com
Featured in Family/Matrimonial (London)
Practice Areas: All aspects of children law. Acts in private law proceedings on behalf of parents and on behalf of the child in Rule 16 cases but the main focus of her work is care proceedings and adoption, often acting for Local Authorities but also parents, children and other interested parties. Frequently instructed in cases where there is conflicting and/or complex medical evidence involving non-accidental injury to or death of a child and/or multiple potential perpetrators. Also instructed in cases where there are complex allegations of sexual harm and mental health issues. Often brought into cases as a junior at the request of leading Counsel. Involved in training days for social workers, Guardians and solicitors representing parties in care proceedings.
Professional Memberships: Family Law Bar Association, The Association of Lawyers for Children.
Career: BA (Hons) University of Kent. Called 1994 (Inner Temple). Tenant at Francis Taylor Building 1995-1999, then 1 Garden Court to date.
Personal: Enjoys travelling, skiing and watching rugby.

STONEFROST, Hilary
South Square, London
020 7696 9900
hilarystonefrost@southsquare.com
Featured in Company (London), Restructuring/Insolvency (London)
Practice Areas: Hilary specialises in domestic and cross-border insolvency, restructuring, and company law. She also has experience in banking matters.
Professional Memberships: Chancery Bar Association, INSOL, Commercial Bar Association.
Career: Hilary has been instructed in a number of major insolvencies, including Olympia & York, BCCI, Barings, Railtrack and Hellas. Substantial cases in insolvency and company law include Acorn International Inc (in the Cayman Islands); Goldtrail Travel (in liquidation) v Aydin; Burry v Knight; Saltri III v MD Mezzanine SA Sicar (for the security trustee); Hellas Telecommunications (Luxembourg) II SCA (for the administrators); Portsmouth City Football Club (for the administrators, CA); Cheyne Finance (for a creditor); MyTravel Group (for the company); Bank of India v Christopher Morris (for the Bank of India, CA); and Colt Telecom Group Plc (for the company). She has acted in a number of cases involving football clubs, including Portsmouth FC; Bournemouth FC Coventry City FC; Cardiff City FC; Crystal Palace FC; Southend United FC; and Swindon FC. She has also been instructed in many scheme of arrangement cases, including three substantial cases where the schemes of arrangement were contested: Sovereign Marine & General Insurance Co; British Aviation Insurance Co; and MyTravel Group. Hilary was admitted to appear in court in Cayman in 2014.
Publications: Debt Restructuring (edited by Look Chan Ho and Nick Segal, OUP 2011).

STONER, Christopher QC
Serle Court, London
020 7242 6105
cstoner@serlecourt.co.uk
Featured in Real Estate Litigation (London), Sports Law (London)
Practice Areas: All aspects of property litigation and sports law (with a particular emphasis on litigation drafting and enforcement of rules and regulations). Recent sports law cases include Wilander & Anor v Tobin & Anor; Korda v ITF Limited; Bingham v British Boxing Board of Control; premier league disciplinary proceedings against Liverpool FC and Christian Ziege; Leeds Rugby Limited v Iestyn Harris and Bradford Bulls Holdings Ltd; Various selection appeals; a funding appeal; a CAS football hearing and British Swimming v FINA in CAS. Recent property litigation cases include McDonalds Property Co Limited v HSBC plc; Ipswich Borough Council v Duke & Moore; Barclays Bank plc v Savile Estates Limited; Pound v Ashford Borough Council; Hawksbrook Leisure Limited v Reece-Jones Partnership; Kilmartin v Safeway; Scottish & Newcastle v Raguz; Greatorex v Newman; Geronimo (1) British Waterways (2) v Brentford Yacht and Boat; Moore v British Waterways; EDF Energy v BOH Limited; Phillips v Francis; and Canal & River Trust v Jones.
Professional Memberships: ChBA, PBA, BASL.
Career: Called to the Bar in 1991; Silk 2010.
Personal: Educated at Shoreham College and the University of East Anglia.

STOREY, Jeremy QC
4 Pump Court, London
020 7842 5555
jstorey@4pumpcourt.com
Featured in Information Technology (London)
Practice Areas: Information technology and telecommunications, licensing, construction, professional negligence and commercial work.
Professional Memberships: Chartered Institute of Arbitrators, Society for Computers and Law, TECBAR, Society of Construction Law, LCIA Users' Council
Career: Called to the Bar 1974, assistant recorder 1990, QC 1994, recorder and Deputy Judge of TCC 1995, Deemster (Judge) of the Isle of Man Courts 1999, Deputy High Court Judge (QBD) 2008, qualified mediator and arbitrator, Civil Mediation Council, World Intellectual Property Organization of Arbitration and Mediation Center (Geneva) Panel of Neutrals (IT), Arbitrator with Kuala Lumpur Regional Centre for Arbitration
Personal: Cambridge University (Scholar, BA Law 1st Class) 1970-73. Born 1952.

STOREY, Paul QC
29 Bedford Row Chambers, London
020 7404 1044
pstorey@29br.co.uk
Featured in Family/Matrimonial (London)
Practice Areas: Family law: Public Law, all areas including appeals CoA and Supreme Court. Representation of vulnerable adults. Private Law and Adoption.
Professional Memberships: FLBA.
Career: Called Lincoln's Inn 1982. QC 2001. Assistant Recorder 1999. Recorder 2000. Deputy High Court Judge 2004. Regular speaker at national and local conferences/training days and JSB.
Personal: Married, six children.

STOTT, Philip
QEB Hollis Whiteman, London
020 7933 8855
philip.stott@qebhw.co.uk
Featured in Crime (London)
Practice Areas: Philip Stott is an experienced and talented advocate in the criminal courts, trusted by defence solicitors and prosecuting authorities alike in cases with high levels of sensitivity and complexity. His experience includes prosecuting and defending cases involving allegations of: homicide, including allegations of medical negligence or involving expert evidence; acquisitive crime, including crimes of high levels of violence, blackmail or sophisticated dishonesty; sexual offending, including rape and the abuse of children; large scale cases of money laundering and/or fraud; the supply of drugs, particularly over international borders; immigration offending, including misconduct by public officials or lawyers; motoring fatalities, and driving offences. Recent work includes: R v Butler and Gray – Junior Counsel for the Crown in the trial of the murder of 6-year old Ellie Butler by her father, and associated charges of perverting the course of justice and child cruelty against her mother; R v Rudling – Junior Counsel representing a General Practitioner accused of the manslaughter by gross negligence of a 12-year old boy, and perverting the course of justice; R v Collins, Reader, Wood and others – Junior Counsel for the prosecution in the burglary of Hatton Garden Safe Deposit Ltd – the largest burglary in English legal history.

STOUT, Holly
11KBW, London
020 7632 8500
Holly.Stout@11kbw.com
Featured in Data Protection (London), Education (London), Employment (London)
Practice Areas: Practice Areas: Public law (local government, community care, immigration and human rights), education law, employment law, information and data protection law. Recent cases include: R (Ramey) v University of Oxford (2015, HC) (lawfulness of University's harassment policy); R (Pressbof) v SoS for Culture, Me-

dia and Sport [2013] EWHC 4101 (Admin) (Pressbof's challenge to Privy Council's rejection of self-regulatory press body in wake of Leveson inquiry); Innospec v Walker [2015] IRLR 1005 (non-retrospectivity of pension equality for same-sex couples); CMA Nurseries v Secretary of State for Education (2015, FTT) (appeal against closure of Orthodox Jewish independent school); Dowsett v SSJ, HC (searching of male prisoners discriminatory); Anderson v LFEPA [2013] IRLR 459 (collective agreement, interpretation); O'Brien v Ministry of Justice [2013] UKSC 6 (part-time judicial pensions); Peninsula Business Services v Information Commissioner [2014] UKUT 284 (AAC) (court records exception FOIA).
Career: Called 2003. Attorney General's B Panel for civil litigation.
Publications: Contributor to Tolley's Employment Law Handbook, Education Law Journal, Butterworths Employment Law, Halsbury's Laws (Administrative Law section).
Personal: Cambridge University (MA); City University CPE Dip. Law (Distinction).

STREET, Amy
Serjeants' Inn Chambers, London
020 7427 5000
astreet@serjeantsinn.com
Featured in Administrative & Public Law (London), Court of Protection (All Circuits)
Practice Areas: Amy Street was called to the Bar in 2002. Amy specialises in clinical negligence and healthcare, Court of Protection, employment, police, professional discipline and regulatory and public and administrative law. An earlier edition notes that "she's really clever and understatedly so. Her drafting is brilliant, her advice, both written and oral, is really thorough". Please visit the Serjeants' Inn Chambers website for her profile, which sets out full details of her practice including relevant work of note.
Professional Memberships: ALBA.
Publications: Co-author: Select Committees and Coercive Powers – Clarity or Confusion?, contributor: Medical Treatment: Decisions and the Law; Medical Law Reports, Legal consultant: BBC Radio 4's 'Unreliable Evidence'.

STRUDWICK, Linda
QEB Hollis Whiteman, London
020 7933 8855
linda.strudwick@qebhw.co.uk
Featured in Crime (London)
Practice Areas: Linda specialises in serious crime as a leading junior, prosecuting and defending in prominent cases involving murder, manslaughter, serious fraud and drugs offences. She has particular expertise in serious sexual offences, complicated child abuse and grooming cases and historic offences, and is a specialist rape prosecutor and a Category 4 CPS prosecutor. She has wide-ranging expertise with witnesses appearing via video links, as well as working with vulnerable adult and child witnesses. She is a trained intermediary who is able to help learning-disabled adults and children to understand legal questions and communicate their answers. She is frequently called upon by the CPS to advise in difficult cases involving sexual allegations. Linda has been instructed to advise pre-trial in cases involving celebrities. She has for many years undertaken disciplinary work in the General Medical Council and other medical disciplinary tribunals, Courts Martial appeals and advisory work for the Ministry of Defence. She also has recent experience of high profile inquest inquiries.
Professional Memberships: Association of Regulatory and Disciplinary Lawyers; Bencher of the Honourable Society of Lincoln's Inn; Criminal Bar Association; Justice; Public Access Bar Association; registered with the Bar Council – Public Access Directory
Career: Call 1973
Personal: LLB (Hons), Manchester University

STUBBS, Rebecca QC
Maitland Chambers, London
020 7406 1200
rstubbs@maitlandchambers.com
Featured in Company (London), Restructuring/Insolvency (London)
Practice Areas: Company and chancery commercial litigation with particular emphasis on company, insolvency, financial services, civil fraud and conflicts of law. Recent cases include advising and acting for the joint administrators of Lehman Brothers International (Europe) on client money and currency issues, advising and acting for the administrators and liquidators of Global Trader (Europe) Limited in connection with issues arising out of MiFID, the FSA's CASS Rules, the insolvency regime, contractual deduction and set-off, and the proper interpretation and effect of ISDA Master Agreements with prime brokers, advising in relation to the meaning and effect of the Landsbanki Freezing order, the Banking Consolidation Directive, Directive 94/19 on Deposit Guarantee Schemes, and the operation of the FSCS, advising counterparties of Kaupthing, Singer & Friedlander in relation to the TBMA/ISMA Global Master Repurchase Agreement, advising a major UK bank in relation to a negative basis trade, and advising the Law Society in connection with the interplay between the regulatory provisions and the granting of security and the onset of insolvency.
Professional Memberships: Chancery Bar Association, COMBAR, Insolvency Court Users' Committee.
Career: Called to the Bar 1994. Junior Counsel to the Crown (1999-2007). Called to the Bar of Grenada and the West Indies Associated States 2005. Registered with the Dubai International Finance Centre courts. Queen's Counsel 2012.
Publications: Contributor to Butterworths 'Practical Insolvency', Butterworth' s Guide to the Legal Services Act 2007, Mithani on Directors' Disqualification; consultant editor, French's Applications to Wind Up Companies.
Personal: Educated at Darton High School and Downing College Cambridge (1st class hons 1993). Former Queen Mother Scholar of the Middle Temple.

STUDD, Anne QC
5 Essex Court, London
020 7410 2000
studd@5essexcourt.co.uk
Featured in Police Law (All Circuits)
Practice Areas: Public & Administrative, Police, Inquests and Inquiries, Professional Discipline. Notible cases; The Independent Inquiry into Child Sexual Abuse –Representing Greater Manchester Police in the Cambridge House Boys' Hostel, Knowl View School; The Independent Inquiry into Child Sexual Abuse – Representing Wiltshire Constabulary; Undercover Policing Inquiry – representing Avon and Somerset Constabulary; The Hillsborough Inquests; R (G) v Chief Constable of Surrey Police & Ors [2016] EWHC 295 (Admin); Inquest into the death of Kingsley Burrell; Inquest into the death of Luisa Mendes; R (on the application of Revenue & Customs Commissioners) (Claimant) v HM Coroner For The City Of Liverpool (Defendant) & (1) Estate Of Roderick Carmichael, deceased (Interested Party) (2) Association Of Personal Injury Lawyers (Interveners) (2014) EWHC 1586;The Azelle Rodney Inquiry – represented the MPS and all officers save for shooter; ZH (by his father & litigation friend GH) v Commissioner of Police of the Metropolis [2013] EWCA Civ 69 [2013] 1 WLR 3021 – The impact of MCA 2005 on policing those with disability; R (on the application of Metropolitan Police Service) (Claimant) v Chairman Of The Inquiry into the death of Azelle Rodney and others [2012] EWHC 2783 – Guidance on disclosure within the meaning of the Inquiry Rules 2006 r.12(4)(a); R (on the application of B) v Chief Constable of Derbyshire (2011) [2011] EWHC 2362 (Admin) – R (on the application of Alandi Salimi) v (1) Secretary of State for the Home Department (2) Independent Police Complaints Commission (2011) EWHC 1714 (Admin) – UKBA and IPCC remit; Re Naomi Bryant (Hampshire) – failures in MAPP provision;
Professional Memberships: ARDL PIBA
Career: Called to the Bar 1988; Silk 2012

STURMAN, Jim QC
2 Bedford Row, London
020 7440 8888
jsturman@2bedfordrow.co.uk
Featured in Crime (London), Health & Safety (London), Sports Law (London), Financial Crime (London)
Practice Areas: Specialist defence advocate instructed in many high profile fraud, criminal, Health and Safety, regulatory and sports law cases as well as advising in civil cases where criminal allegations arise. Frequently acts and advises abroad. Particular expertise in corruption, sanctions offences, data protection, homicide, regulatory work (frequently representing professionals from all professions before disciplinary tribunals) and advisory work to banks and corporate clients as well as individuals on criminal matters and mutual assistance requests and in 'quasi criminal' tribunals. Advises in SFO cases in early stages of enquiries on warrants as well as section 2 requests and also frequently advises solicitors and city institutions in money laundering cases. Extensive experience of health and safety work, frequently advising Directors and engaged in Corporate manslaughter prosecutions, advising before charge and also acting at trial in cases involving industry (for example the trial arising from the Buncefield explosion), railways and farming. In 2015/2016 instructed in R v Piranha, R v T and R v H (all cases involving fatalities). Acts in public inquiries and inquests, for example The Turks and Caicos Commission of Inquiry and representing Primrose Shipman before The Shipman Inquiry and at the inquest into the death of Dr Harold Shipman. Extensive experience of asset confiscation and restraint proceedings under POCA, CJA and DTA. Considerable experience in The Court of Appeal Criminal Division, particularly in cases where he did not act in the lower court. Examples include, R v Lummes, conviction for murder quashed and no evidence offered at the re-trial, R v Dallagher ('ear print' identification case) and R v Dixon (Customs and Excise non-disclosure in a large drugs case known as 'Operation Cinema'. Notable cases in general crime include R v Tania Clarence. R v Stagg (Wimbledon common murder). R v Gould and Charles Kray. R v M 'sex on an aeroplane case'. R v Kelly, first appeal on 'two strikes' life sentence. Acted in 2 'Operation Care' cases in Liverpool. R v C and others (Serbian sanctions busting case), R v Hardstaff (co-defendant in the Bowyer and Woodgate trial). Enormously experienced in drugs cases, R v A White, R v Doherty (Part of the Michael Michaels series of cases). Acted for Joey Barton on assault charge incident at Manchester City training ground. Extradition cases include USA v Sukharno, USA v Newton (part of the Howard Marks case) and USA v Kleasen – the 'Texas chainsaw' case. Fraud cases include the appeal of Michael Villiers in the LCB diversion case (the first of the chain of LCB appeals), and the subsequent abuse of process hearing based on non-disclosure that was heard at Liverpool Crown Court. R v Goldstone (largest ever cigarette diversion fraud), R v F (SFO prosecution arising out of the theft of the Cheney Pension Fund), R v Eardley (International Internet piracy first investigated in the USA as 'Operation Buccaneer'), acted for three of the British MP's charged with "expenses fraud" and has extensive experience of all types of financial fraud, including mortgage, ponzi, advance fee, insider dealing and derivatives 'ramping', revenue, VAT and diversion frauds. Acts and advises throughout the English Speaking world, successfully defended a solicitor on a stamp duty fraud allegation in the TCI summer 2015. Frequently advises in international and domestic corruption investigatons. Regularly appears before FA, FAPL, UEFA and FIFA disciplinary tribunals in relation to on field and off the field matters, (including 'doping offences', betting irregularities and allegations of misconduct by fans), acting for the defence. Has acted for Chelsea FC, Tottenham Hotspur FC, Newcastle United FC, Jose Mourinho, Frank Lampard, John Terry, Didier Drogba, Jens Lehman, Millwall FC, Wimbledon AFC, Tottenham Hotspur FC, Robbie Keane, Michael Dawson, Dennis Wise, Gustavo Poyet, Diego Costa, Emre of Newcastle on a 'racism' allegation that was dismissed, Peter Cech, Frank Lampard, Ashley Cole, Jermaine Defoe. Acted for Newcastle United in Premier League Tribunal hearing brought by Kevin Keegan. Instructed by the FA to prosecute Roy Keane in relation to the autobiography by that player. Acted for Chelsea FC in the 'Ashley Cole tapping up case'. Acted for CSKA Moscow in Parma's protest against the result of the 2005 UEFA semi final. Acted for Tottenham Hotspur FC v Sergei Rebrov in relation to FAPL dispute. Acted for West Ham in the Carlos Tevez affair. Has acted for UEFA, national FAs and for individual players in relation to doping allegations. Acted for Wigan FC in the 'Webster' case on Article 17 of the FIFA statutes. Acted for Mohammed Bin Hammam in his successful appeal to CAS from FIFA findings arising out of his campaign to run for the FIFA Presidency against Sepp Blatter. Has successfully represented agents

suing players who attempted to "cut out" the agent from transfer deals. Has advised national associations in South America and the Far East in relation to disputes under FIFA regulations. Frequently appears in The Court of Arbitration for Sport. Sits as an RFU appeals Chairman.
Professional Memberships: Member of Gibraltar Bar, CBA, IBA, EBA and BAFS.
Career: Called 1982, joined chambers 1983, Silk 2002.
Publications: Contributor (with Professor David Ormerod) to 'The Forensic Psychologists casebook' published in 2005.
Personal:

SULLIVAN, Lisa
Cloisters, London
020 7827 4000
ls@cloisters.com
Featured in Clinical Negligence (London)
Practice Areas: Lisa principally specialises in clinical negligence and personal injury law including inquests and CICA claims. Lisa has wide experience in high value cases including birth injury, brain and spinal injury cases on both liability and quantum. She also undertakes regulatory tribunal work, in particular care standards. Notable cases include Crofton v NHSLA [2007] EWCA Civ 71, Collins v Plymouth City Council [2009] EWHC 3279 (Admin) (whether damages can be taken into account in charging for local authority care) and Pringle v Nestor Primecare [2014] EWHC 1308 (QB). Lisa is a Deputy Queen's Bench Master.
Professional Memberships: PIBA, AvMA, APIL.
Career: Called to the Bar in 1997. Advocacy trainer for PIBA, Inner Temple and South Eastern Circuit.
Publications: Butterworth's Personal Injury Litigation Service Limitation Chapter (co-author with Joel Donovan QC) and contributor to Lewis and Buchan on Clinical Negligence.

SUMMERS, Ben
3 Raymond Buildings Barristers, London
020 7400 6400 or 07876653912
Ben.Summers@3rblaw.com
Featured in Financial Crime (London)
Practice Areas: Ben was called to the Bar in 1994 and, following a civil pupillage, joined QEB Hollis Whiteman where he was in independent practice for eight years. He joined white collar firm Peters & Peters in March 2003 as an employed Barrister and transferred to the Solicitors' profession in 2004; he was appointed as a partner in 2007. In May 2009 Ben resumed independent practice at the Bar and joined Three Raymond Buildings. Ben has a practice in business crime, professional discipline, inquests & public inquiries and regulatory matters, with specialist experience in compliance issues, including corruption & bribery, fraud and anti-trust, financial services, and DPA/FOIA. He has acted in some of the largest fraud and corruption matters over recent years including LIBOR, Innospec, Oil for Food, Johnson & Johnson, Torex Retail, Vantis Tax and Imperial Consolidated. Ben' acts for the ICO, individuals & corporates in data protection and ecommerce matters. He currently advises the FCA in an ongoing insider dealing investigation. He has appeared in numerous discipline hearings and inquests and in the Baha Mousa inquiry on behalf of the Commanding Officer of 1QLR.
Professional Memberships: CBA, FLA, ARDL
Career: University of Sussex: LLB (Hons) (1990-1993), ICSL (1993-1994).

SUMMERS, Mark QC
Matrix Chambers, London
020 7404 3447
marksummers@matrixlaw.co.uk
Featured in Crime (London), Extradition (London)
Practice Areas: Specialist in extradition, mutual legal assistance, criminal EU law and terrorism law. Recent cases include ⊠ Spain v Rwandan intelligence chief, General Karenzi Karake ⊠ Sweden v Julian Assange ⊠ South Africa v Shrien Dewani ⊠ attempted Regicide of the King of Spain ⊠ R v John Downey (1982 Hyde Park bombing) ⊠ R v Mohammed Amir (international cricket match fixing) ⊠ Madrid train bombings ⊠ 9/11 attacks ⊠ 2001 US anthrax attacks ⊠ collapse of Enron (the "NatWest 3") ⊠ murder of Theo van Gogh ⊠ creation of the 'Trojan Horse' commercial espionage computer virus ⊠ sale of decommissioned radioactive metals ⊠ treason ⊠ impairing the battle-readiness of the US Atlantic fleet ⊠ liquid-bomb conspiracy to explode US-bound transatlantic flights ⊠ assisting the 21/7 bombing attempts ⊠ plot to bomb the London Stock Exchange
Professional Memberships: Extradition Lawyers' Association (former Chair).
Publications: Co-author of "Abuse of Process in Criminal Proceedings" (Bloomsbury, 4th. ed., 2014); "The Law of Extradition and Mutual Assistance" (OUP, 3rd ed., 2013), "Human Rights and Criminal Justice" (Sweet & Maxwell, 3rd ed., 2012). Contributing editor to "Fraud: Criminal Law and Procedure" (OUP).

SUMNALL, Charlene
5 Paper Buildings, London
020 7583 6117
CS@5pb.co.uk
Featured in Consumer Law (London)
Practice Areas: Charlene provides advisory and specialist advocacy services and has appeared in all levels of tribunals including those at appellate level. She has built up a wealth of experience by appearing for both the prosecution and defence in areas such as trademark and copyright infringement, food, toy and general product safety, licensing and offences concerning the Consumer Protection from Unfair Trading Regulations and the Business Protection from Misleading Marketing Regulations. Charlene has lectured at the annual Trading Standards Conference for the last 9 years and has provided training to local authorities and private prosecutors on a range of topics including the Fraud Act, Proceeds of Crime Act (confiscation, restraint and forfeiture provisions) and investigatory procedures. She regularly provides advice to business on due diligence compliance. Please see chambers website for fuller details of all areas of her practice including relevant cases in this area.

SUSMAN, Peter QC
Henderson Chambers, London
020 7583 9020
psusmanqc@hendersonchambers.co.uk
Featured in Information Technology (London)
Practice Areas: Complex commercial and contract litigation and international and domestic arbitration, with particular experience of commercial contract disputes; information technology, telecoms, broadcasting and other high tech areas; financial transactions, including consumer credit; construction and engineering; insurance; professional negligence, and professional regulatory and disciplinary law; company law; employment, property and other issues arising in relation to commercial transactions and disputes; especially involving complicated issues or facts, more than one area of law, or other difficulties. He acts for and against government departments, local authorities, companies and individuals, in court in England and in foreign and domestic arbitrations.
Career: Called 1966, took Silk 1997.

SUTERWALLA, Azeem
Monckton Chambers, London
020 7405 7211
asuterwalla@monckton.com
Featured in Administrative & Public Law (London), Civil Liberties & Human Rights (London), Community Care (London)
Practice Areas: Administrative law, Civil Liberties and Human Rights and Community Care.
Professional Memberships: Administrative Law Bar Association, Human Rights Lawyers Association
Career: Azeem is a specialist in Judicial Review and Public Procurement law and undertakes litigation and advisory work in these fields. Azeem also undertakes cases with an EU law dimension, including competition work. His public and human rights law work spans a range of subject areas, notably: regulatory and commercial law, data protection and information law, community care, children related work, education, immigration and asylum support. In addition to his High Court practice, Azeem is regularly instructed in appeals in the Court of Appeal and has worked on litigation at all levels up to the House of Lords/Supreme Court, the European Court of Human Rights and the Court of Justice of the European Union. Before coming to the bar Azeem worked for the United Nations in the Middle East and was a Judicial Assistant to the former Master of the Rolls, now Supreme Court Justice, Lord Clarke.
Publications: Co-author of Children in Need: Local Authority Support for Children and Families (Legal Action Group, 2013). Azeem is the author of "Collection and Retention of Person Data" in "Human Rights in the Investigation and Prosecution of Crime" (2009), OUP, ed. Madeleine Colvin and Jonathan Cooper.
Personal: BA (Oxon) Modern History 1st Class, MA (Harvard) Arabic and Middle Eastern Studies, Thesis with Distinction

---

SWAIN, Jon
Furnival Chambers, London
020 7405 3232
clerks@furnivallaw.co.uk
Featured in Crime (London)
Practice Areas: Crime, inquests, regulatory work. Direct access qualified.
Professional Memberships: Lincoln's Inn, South Eastern Circuit, CBA.
Career: I act 100% for the defence, and regard client care (professional and lay) as a paramount matter. Called to Bar 1983. Member of Furnival Chambers since 1986. Instructed in number of high profile cases since then in various regions of England and Wales. Recent cases: R. v. R, Lewes Crown Court, historic rapes (acquitted), R. v. Bass, Reading Crown Court, murder/manslaughter with mental health and causation issues (convicted manslaughter & hospital order). R. v. H, stranger rape (convicted; hospital order) R. v. B, historic rape of ex-partner (acquitted). R. v. Frew, Leeds Crown Court (manslaughter). R. v. O'Brien, Manchester Crown Court (importation of 10 lorry loads of cannabis; (acquitted). R. v. Dell, Oxford Crown Court (attempt handling stolen scrap metal; acquitted). R. v. T, Aylesbury Crown Court multiple rapes of partner (acquitted), R. v. Carroll, Norwich Crown Court (att murder, att GBH, rape of prostitute (historic DNA case). R. v. Mughal Birmingham Crown Court, (complex fraud), R. v. Zare Manchester Crown Court, money laundering (acquitted). R. v. Petriekis C.C.C. murder (Loss of control). NMC v. Biggs (representing midwife arising from Morecambe Bay investigations of 2008). Forthcoming trials: R. Vafiadis Reading murder, R. v. M. Southampton (historic sexual abuse), R. v. D. Southampton (historic sexual abuse).
Personal: Born 1959. Leisure interests include cricket, tennis and country life.

SWEET, Louise QC
Carmelite Chambers, London
020 7993 7600
lsweetqc@carmelitechambers.co.uk
Featured in Crime (London)
Practice Areas: Louise is trusted in complex, emotive and high profile cases. Her well-documented record for success is achieved by excellent strategy, skilled advocacy, impressive legal depth and a resolve for hard work. Her practice is broad ranging: Sexual offences: A kind but firm style repeatedly delivering excellent results at first instance and on appeal. Her successes include a number of high profile individuals: a Lord Mayor, a Coronation Street actor, military personnel, sportspeople and businessmen. Financial crime: Organised and jury friendly. Operation Elvedon, corruption in public office, Ozakpinar and Others, corrupt CPS procurement, "The Wonga Fraud", 19000 fraudulent pay day loans netting £6.2m and Operation Mecklenburger, €80m, the proceeds of organised crime was laundered via London bureau de changes. Louise defends prosecutions by all government agencies, SFO, NCA, Trading Standards, HMRCE and FCA. General crime: Unafraid of challenging cases: Mick Philpott (Derby Fire Case) 6 children perished, a case of the most intense national interest. A successful "diminished responsibility" for plumber who decapitated his wife suffering from alcohol dependency syndrome and a mother cleared of killing her baby (shaken baby syndrome, cut-throat) and numerous acquittals for murder where "gang" motives attributed. Current: Operation Clover, Rotherham child abuse (Sheffield CC) Operation Aramac SOCO, lead defendant in drug cartel (13 defendants: Birmingham CC) boiler room fraud, city trader (CCC. Diamonds) company director (Maidstone CC. carbon credits) Inquests. Regulatory: FCA (complaints and asset restraint) MPTS (GMC) and other financial services and professional regulation. Direct Access. Lectures.
Professional Memberships: Organiser of Carmelite Chambers lecture programme. Pupil Supervisor. Memberships: CBA, Fraud Lawyers Association, Howard League for Penal Reform.

SWIFT, Jonathan QC
11KBW, London
020 7632 8500
Jonathan.Swift@11kbw.com
Featured in Administrative & Public Law (London), Civil Liberties & Human Rights (London), Data Protection (London), Competition/European Law (London), Local Government (London)
Practice Areas: Has in-depth experience across the whole range of public law areas. This includes: human rights and civil liberties; constitutional law (including devolution issues); data protection and freedom of information; regulatory law (in particular energy regulation and financial regulation); EU Law; education; inquiries and strategic planning and environmental issues. From 2006 to 2014 he was First Treasury Counsel, leading for the Government on major cases across the whole field of government activity and public administration. Since returning to private practice he has acted both for and against central government and has resumed his highly-regarded local government practice. He regularly appears in the Court of Appeal and in the Supreme Court (over 30 cases during the last 2 years). He appeared for the Government in the first appeal heard by the Supreme Court: Ahmed v HM Treasury ([2010] 2 AC 534, and 697), concerning the implementation of international sanctions against suspected terrorists and most recently in R (Rotherham MBC) v Secretary of State for Business ([2015] UKSC 6), where he successfully defended a government department from a challenge by several local authorities to a decision on the distribution of EU funds; and Youssef v Foreign Secretary ([2016] UKSC 3) where he successfully defended a decision to apply UN sanctions to a UK resident.
Career: Called 1989; First Treasury Counsel 2006 - 2014; Master of the Bench Inner Temple 2007; QC 2010; Recorder 2011; Deputy High Court Judge 2016. Education: Southend-on-Sea High School; New College Oxford; Emmanuel College, Cambridge.
Personal: Born 1964; resides London.

TABARI, Ali
St Philips Chambers, Birmingham
0121 246 7010
atabari@st-philips.com
Featured in Commercial Dispute Resolution (Midlands)
Practice Areas: In addition to core commercial litigation, Ali has a busy practice specialising in three, often overlapping, areas: banking/finance, in which he is frequently instructed by major international banking and asset finance institutions; insolvency, including all aspects of individual and company work; and professional liability, including solicitors, IFAs and surveyors as well as other insurance work. He is often instructed in urgent applications for injunctive relief, primarily as part of his insolvency practice, and his broad knowledge base attracts instructions in unfair prejudice petitions and shareholder disputes. He is regularly instructed as a led junior, and has appeared alone in the Court of Appeal on several occasions. Recent work includes: a £1m fraudulent trading claim against a company director; several multi-day banking trials concerning undue influence, misrepresentation and fraud; a claim against professional advisors arising from a defective share sale agreement; acting for a financier disputing title to a luxury sports car.
Professional Memberships: Midlands Commercial and Chancery Bar Association
Career: Called 2006.
Publications: Ali has written for Corporate Rescue and Insolvency, Insolvency Intelligence and the LexisNexis insolvency blog, and is a contributing author to the LexisNexis practitioner notes and precedents on Part 36 offers.

TAGER, Romie QC
Selborne Chambers, London
020 7420 9500
romie.tager@selbornechambers.co.uk
Featured in Chancery (London), Commercial Dispute Resolution (London), Real Estate Litigation (London)
Professional Memberships: Chancery Bar Assoc. Professional Negligence Bar Assoc. Property Bar Assoc. London Common Law & Commercial Bar Assoc.
Career: Romie is a specialist in commercial and property law. His experience covers a vast range of work in these fields, and the breadth and specialisation of his practice and career give him a commanding position. He is frequently instructed in cases involving complex issues and commercial sensitivity, often calling for original presentation and the identification of novel solutions. His practice includes considerable advisory work, and he has extensive experience of international commercial arbitration. Romie has been described as 'a very big name', and remains 'very much in demand'. Complimentary quotes include: 'a terrier of a litigator' who is 'quick to grasp the technical details and deploy them to devastating effect in cross-examination'; 'good for unusual or difficult cases requiring a novel but hard-hat approach'; 'gets his teeth stuck in and keeps shaking – he can blast holes in the other side'; 'When a case depends on a forceful cross-examination technique, there is nobody better'; a highly forceful silk who fights doggedly for client interests'. Never far away from major cases, he has acted in a number of significant matters as can be seen from the selection of notable cases that follows: Barnsley v Noble [2016] EWCA Civ 799 (part of the long running dispute arising out of the demerger of the Noble Organisation); Marlbray Ltd v Laditi [2016] EWCA Civ 476 (Validity of Contract for the Sale of Land); Tchenguiz v Grant Thornton UK LLP [2016] EWHC 865 (Comm) (Enforcement of Settlement Agreement by a Third Party); Coral Reef Ltd v Silverbond Enterprises Ltd [2016] EWHC 874 (Ch) (Judicial Precedent: Are Masters Bound to Follow a Decision of the High Court?); The Creative Foundation Ltd v Dreamland Leisure Ltd & Others [2015] EWHC 2556 (Ch) (The case involved a very valuable graffiti by a well-known artist painted on a flank wall. The issue was whether, if the wall was removed as part of the tenant's repairing obligations, the wall and the painting belong to the landlord or the tenant); Ramsay v Love [2015] EWHC 65 (Ch) (successfully defeated a claim brought by the well-known chef and television presenter, Gordon Ramsay, that he was not bound by a personal guarantee for the rent of his hotel and restaurant, (The York & Albany); Harb v HRH Prince Abdul Aziz Bin Fahd Bin Abdul Aziz [2015] EWHC 3155 (Ch) (Concerned sovereign immunity and an oral agreement to pay £12m and provide transfer of two properties thought to be worth a similar amount); Group Seven Ltd v Allied Investment Corporation Ltd [2015] EWCA Civ 631,[2014] EWHC 2046 (Ch), [2014] 1 WLR 735 (A multimillion-euro fraud case concerning whether a freezing injunction does not extend to assets belonging to a company owned or controlled by defendant. Romie appeared with Isabel Petrie, also of Selborne Chambers, in the Court of Appeal which dealt with the Court of Appeal's willingness to review a trial judge's findings relating to foreign law and the evidence of foreign lawyers); Zarbafi v Zarbafi [2014] EWCA Civ 1267 (a family dispute concerning (inter alia) the beneficial ownership of three valuable properties; Serious Organised Crime Agency v Szepietowski [2013] UKSC 65 [2014] AC 338 (Remedy of marshalling not available to second mortgagee where the common property did not secure a debt owed by the mortgagor); Mellor v Partridge [2013] EWCA CIV 477 (Court of Appeal considered the constituents of fraudulent misrepresentation claim relating to the sale of a business, as well as the application of the reflective less doctrine to quantum); Cohen v Nekrich (A two week trial in Gibraltar involving allegations of fraud exceeding £50m in relation to oil trading with Russia)

TAHIR, Perican
1 King's Bench Walk, London
020 7936 1500
ptahir@1kbw.co.uk
Featured in Family/Matrimonial (South Eastern)
Practice Areas: Perican Tahir has specific expertise in advising and acting in all areas of Family Law. She has particular expertise in Financial Remedy and Private Law Children matters. In the field of Financial Remedy, she has experience in matters involving foreign or complex assets; trust and intervenors; business and partnership assets; issues of non-disclosure of assets and pre-post nuptial agreements; as well as advising and appearing in disputes between cohabitants under the Trusts of Land and Appointment of Trustees Act 1996 and Schedule 1 of the Children Act 1989. In the field of Private Law Children, she has experience in matters involving complex intractable disputes, leave to remove and international relocation cases as well as internal relocation applications and abduction matters. Perican is Direct Access qualified.
Professional Memberships: Family Law Bar Association, South Eastern Circuit, Kent Bar Mess, Association of Lawyers for Children
Career: Call: 2004
Personal: Education: Haberdashers Aske's Hatcham Girls School, University of Sussex – Law LLB, Inns of Court School of Law

TAIT, Andrew QC
Francis Taylor Building, London
020 7353 8415
clerks@ftbchambers.co.uk
Featured in Planning (London)
Practice Areas: Andrew Tait QC's main areas of work are in planning, environmental, administrative and land compensation. He appeared at the East London River Crossing, Hinkley Point C Nuclear power station and Thameslink inquiries. He advised the Olympic Delivery Authority on the planning permissions for the 2012 Games. He has wide experience of Private Bills and Transport and Works Act Orders, including promoting Victoria Station Upgrade, the Northern Line Extension and Bank Station Capacity Upgrade for TfL, the Poole Twin Sails Bridge Order and the DLR (Capacity Enhancement and 2012 Games Preparation) Order. He has promoted road schemes including the A14 Cambridge to Huntingdon scheme, the Weymouth Relief Road and the South Devon Link Road. He has been involved in numerous bills in parliament, particularly railway bills. He promoted the Greater Nottingham LRT Bill and acted for BAA on the Crossrail proposals and for various petitioners on HS2. Land compensation cases include Brunt v Southampton International Airport in the Court of Appeal. He is involved in the promotion of numerous major housing projects, including new settlements, mineral workings and railway, road and water infrastructure projects. He has advised extensively on the new procedures of Nationally Significant Infrastructure Projects.
Professional Memberships: Member of the Planning and Environment Bar Association (Chairman since 2016), the Administrative Law Bar Association, the Parliamentary Bar, the Compulsory Purchase Association, the National Infrastructure Planning Association and the Anglo-American Real Property Institute.
Career: Called to Bar: 1981, QC: 2003; Bencher, Inner Temple 2011.

TALBOT, Kennedy QC
The Chambers of Andrew Mitchell QC, London
020 7440 9950
kt@33cllaw.com
Featured in POCA Work & Asset Forfeiture (All Circuits)
Practice Areas: Principal practice areas are civil recovery and criminal confiscation, money laundering, government and police investigations and powers, legal professional privilege, and civil fraud and tracing. Appears on behalf of all parties at all levels including 7 proceeds of crime Supreme Court/House of Lords cases. His proceeds of crime practice embraces all aspects of restraint, receivership and confiscation at first instance and on appeal, and acting for claimants, receivers and respondents in civil recovery proceedings under Part 5 of the Proceeds of Crime Act. He regularly advises companies on civil settlements, particularly in corruption cases, and on making protected and authorised disclosures to the NCA to comply with anti-money laundering legislation.
Career: Called to the Bar in 1984. Admitted to the New York Bar in 1993.
Publications: Joint author of Confiscation and the Proceeds of Crime (Sweet and Maxwell 3rd Ed. looseleaf), Administrative Court: Practice and Procedure (Sweet and Maxwell, 2006) and a contributing editor of the White Book.

TAMBLING, Richard
29 Bedford Row Chambers, London
020 7404 1044
rtambling@29br.co.uk
Featured in Family/Matrimonial (London)
Practice Areas: Richard handles all aspects of financial remedies including matrimonial finance and Schedule 1 cases. He has extensive experience of variation cases and particular expertise in cases involving nuptial settlements and trusts. He is regularly instructed on TOLATA claims and in particular those brought by cohabitees and with concurrent Schedule 1 applications. He has a private law children practice dealing

mainly with complex international contact arrangements.

Professional Memberships: FLBA, HRLA

Career: BA (Hons), LLB (Hons), Blackstone Entrance Exhibition Scholarship – Middle Temple. Called to the Bar in 2005. Regularly asked to speak on his practice areas for Y Resolution, TVFLS, CLT and at Jordans Family Law seminars.

Publications: Richard is a regular contributor of articles to publications including The Family Law Hub and Family Law Week. He has also written for the Trusts and Estates Law & Tax Journal on one of the judgments in Tchenguiz-Imerman v Imerman. Richard's seminars are often recorded for wider practitioner training.

Personal: Richard is a keen traveller to foreign lands, is an enthusiastic cook and enjoys listening to music. He also enjoys sampling the cultural aspects of London and European cities.

TAMPAKOPOULOS, Alexandra

2 Hare Court, London
020 7353 5324
Alexandratampakopoulos@2harecourt.com

Featured in Health & Safety (London), Inquests & Public Inquiries (All Circuits)

Practice Areas: Alexandra is an established criminal and regulatory practitioner with a particular expertise advising and acting in Coroners' Inquests and Public Inquiries. She has cultivated a diverse practice flowing from her extensive experience defending and prosecuting serious crime. In the regulatory field she acts and advises on all aspects of Health & Safety law on behalf of clients across a wide range of industries including Manufacturing, Construction, Agriculture, Technology and Telecoms. She has a recognised expertise in Inquests and Public Inquiries and is regularly instructed in complex cases on behalf of a wide range of Interested Persons and Core Participants. Alexandra speaks fluent Russian and is frequently instructed in matters requiring her Russian language skills and knowledge of Russia and the CIS region. She has been instructed in a number of high profile inquests and public inquiries including in relation to the deaths of Alexander Litvinenko, Alexander Perepilichnyy, the Hillsborough disaster, the 'SAS Inquest' involving the death of three soldiers from heat illness in the Brecon Breacons and the Independent Inquiry into Child Sexual Abuse.

Professional Memberships: Health & Safety Lawyers Association, Association of Regulatory and Disciplinary Lawyers, The Criminal Bar Association, Liberty

Career: University College London, Russian and History (BA (Hons). The London School of Economics (MSc), Human Rights. Call 2007.

TANNEY, Anthony

Falcon Chambers, London
020 7353 2484
tanney@falcon-chambers.com

Featured in Real Estate Litigation (London)

Practice Areas: All aspects of the law of real property both commercial and residential, including litigation and advisory work, with an emphasis on landlord and tenant.

Professional Memberships: Chancery Bar Association; LCLCBA; Property Bar Association.

Career: Educated at Whitley Bay High School; Durham University (BA 1989, MJur 1992); called 1994 (Lincoln's Inn).

Publications: Co-author, 'Distress for Rent' (Jordans 2000); co-editor, Fisher and Lightwood's 'Law of Mortgage' 11th edn (Butterworths 2002).

TAPPIN, Michael QC

8 New Square, London
020 7405 4321
michael.tappin@8newsquare.co.uk

Featured in Intellectual Property (London)

Practice Areas: Barrister specialising in all aspects of intellectual property law but with a particular interest in chemical, pharmaceutical and biotechnological work. Recent cases include: Eli Lilly v HGS (SC/CA), Generics v Lundbeck (HL/CA), Conor v Angiotech (HL), GSK v Wyeth (HC), Regeneron v Kymab & Novo (HC), Eli Lilly v HGS (SPC – CJEU & HC), Hospira & Mylan v Novartis (CA/HC), HTC v Gemalto (CA/HC), Resolution v Lundbeck (CA/HC), Regeneron & Bayer v Genentech (CA/HC), Fresenius v Carefusion (CA), Mylan v Yeda & Teva (CA/HC), KCI v Smith & Nephew (CA/HC), Napp v ratiopharm (CA/HC), Hospira v Genentech (CA/HC), Nokia v HTC (HC), HTC v Apple (HC), Ivax v Glaxo (HC of Ireland). For comprehensive CV and list of recent cases, visit our website at www.8newsquare.co.uk

Professional Memberships: Intellectual Property Bar Association.

Career: Called 1991. Appointed QC 2009. Standing Counsel to the Comptroller-General of Patents, Designs and Trade Marks 2003-08.

Publications: Co-author of Laddie, Prescott & Vitoria's Modern Law of Copyright and Designs (4th edn, 2011).

Personal: Born 1964. Educated at Cheltenham Grammar School; St John's College, Oxford (1986 BA Chemistry); Merton College, Oxford (1989 DPhil Biochemistry).

TASKIS, Catherine

Falcon Chambers, London
020 7353 2484
taskis@falcon-chambers.com

Featured in Agriculture & Rural Affairs (London), Real Estate Litigation (London)

Practice Areas: All aspects of residential, commercial, agricultural, landlord and tenant and real property litigation. Reported cases include: Kerai [2014] UKUT 153 (LC); Monkman v Mitchelson ALT/Y/S/59 [2009]; Duffield v Gandy [2008] EWCA Civ 379; Cameron Ltd v Rolls-Royce plc [2008] L & TR 22; JD Wetherspoon plc v Jay Mar Estates [2007] EWH 856 (TCC); Smith & Hutchinson v Brough [2005] EWCA civ 261; Mayor & City of London v Davy's of London (Wine Merchant) Ltd [2004] 29 EG 117.

Professional Memberships: Agricultural Law Association; Chancery Bar Association; LCLCBA; Property Bar Association.

Career: Educated at Worthing VI Form College; Worcester College, Oxford (BA Jurisprudence 1993, MA, BCL 1994); called 1995 (Inner Temple); joined Falcon 1997. Appointed Deputy District Judge 2013.

Publications: Joint Editor, Woodfall Property Update Service. Editor, Atkins Forms and Precedents, Agriculture. Assistant Editor, Muir Watt & Moss on Agricultural Holdings; Contributor, Landlord and Tenant Review.

Personal: Member of Vesta Rowing Club.

TAUBE, Simon QC

Ten Old Square, London
020 7405 0758
simon.taube@tenoldsquare.com

Featured in Chancery (London), Charities (London), Offshore (London), Trusts (London)

Practice Areas: Simon Taube's practice covers the broad range of Chancery activities in both litigation and advisory work. He conducts cases in the UK and abroad in other common law jurisdictions. His special expertise includes the fields of UK and foreign trusts and estates, tax planning and trust and personal taxation. He has extensive experience in charity and property as well as securities, partnership, professional negligence and family provision matters.

Professional Memberships: Member of the Chancery Bar Association, STEP and Executive Committee of Trust Law Committee, Revenue Bar Association.

Career: Called 1980, Middle Temple and Lincoln's Inn, QC 2000. Notable cases include: Dawson-Damer v Taylor Wessing (2015): Data Protection Act and trusts, Crociani v Crociani and others (2014) UKPC 40: contentious breach of trust claim; Re Nina Wang (2014) HKCA: charitable trust and company law; The Warburg Institute (2014); construction of trust deed; Buzzoni v HMRC (2013) CA: IHT and unjust enrichment; Labrouche v Frey (2012) CA: breach of trust, abuse of process; In the Matter of the A Trust (2012) Bermuda: trust jurisdiction clauses; A-G's Poverty Reference (2011) public benefit in charity; Fattal v Walbrook (2010) trustee exoneration clause;

Personal: Westminster School; Merton College, Oxford (1978 Modern History 1st class). Enjoys singing and playing tennis.

TAVERNER, Marcus QC

Keating Chambers, London
020 7544 2600
mtaverner@keatingchambers.com

Featured in International Arbitration (London), Professional Negligence (London), Construction (London), Energy & Natural Resources (London)

Practice Areas: Leading silk in the fields of construction and engineering; professional negligence and energy law. He has an extensive advisory practice and a formidable reputation as an advocate and in particular a cross-examiner (both in litigation and arbitration). Marcus regularly appears as advocate in the TCC, Commercial Court, Court of Appeal and Supreme Court. He is well known not only for his considerable strategic acumen and understanding of the commercial aspects of litigation but, in particular, for his mastering of the technical detail of the many complex and high value cases he undertakes. Acts on behalf of clients engaged in adjudications, mediations and other forms of alternative dispute resolution. He has an extensive practice acting as advisor and advocate, on major arbitrations both in the UK and abroad. Sits as arbitrator on domestic and international claims for bodies such as the ICC and also acts as an adjudicator in the United Kingdom.

Professional Memberships: Technology & Construction Bar Association (TECBAR); Commercial Bar Association (COMBAR); Society of Construction Law (SCL).

Career: Call 1981, QC 2000; Bencher Gray's Inn 2007; Construction Silk of the Year (Chambers UK Bar Awards 2009 and 2015); Deputy Head of Chambers 2013-2015, Head of Chambers 2015-present.

TAYLOR, John QC

Fountain Court Chambers, London
020 7583 3335
jt@fountaincourt.co.uk

Featured in Aviation (London), Banking & Finance (London), Commercial Dispute Resolution (London)

Practice Areas: Commercial litigation including banking, financial services, aviation, commercial fraud, insurance/reinsurance and professional negligence. Current and recent banking cases include the interest rate swaps and LIBOR litigation, credit card interchange fee disputes, the PPI litigation, AIG Bond litigation and appearing in the Court of Appeal in the test case concerning the interpretation of Northern Rock's standard terms (Northern Rock Asset Management v McAdam [2016] Bus LR 232) Recent aviation cases include a 2 week ICC arbitration concerning disputes under the leases of 2 Boeing 737 aircraft (contractual construction, maintenance reserves, return condition) and Virgin Atlantic v Mitsubishi (sale of goods/ incorporation of contractual terms/warranties and indemnities). Recent commercial fraud cases include Corinth Pipeworks v Barclays (banking/trade finance, DIFC Court). Professional negligence claims include acting for company liquidators in a High Court claim against a big 4 accountancy firm arising out of the collapse of a lending business and an LCIA arbitration hearing concerning the collapse of a hedge fund involving allegations of negligence against the manager, investment manager and valuation agent. Recent commercial litigation includes acting for US private equity firm on a dispute concerning ROFR rights and acting for a European private equity firm on a dispute concerning the acquisition of an online retail business.

Professional Memberships: Commercial Bar Association; Professional Negligence Bar Association; British Association for Sport and Law.

Career: Called to the Bar 1993. Silk 2013. Admitted to the DIFC Courts, Dubai.

Publications: Contributor to 'The Law of Bank Payments' (4th ed, Sweet & Maxwell 2010); contributor to 'Carriage by Air' (1st ed, Butterworths 2001).

Personal: Born 1968. Cambridge University MA 1st class.

TAYLOR, Simon

6 Pump Court, London
020 7797 8400
simontaylor@6pumpcourt.co.uk

Featured in Crime (South Eastern)

Practice Areas: The focus of Mr Taylor's work is now on defending in cases ranging from complex money laundering and drugs matters to the most serious offences of violence and sexual offences. He is increasingly instructed to defend complex, high profile cases involving rape, most notably the Gillingham Football Club rape case (R-v-Nyafli). In recent times Mr Taylor has regularly appeared in large, multi-handed money laundering and drugs conspiracies. He is also regularly instructed to defend in cases ranging from murder, attempted murder, death by dangerous driving, section 18 wounding, and conspiracies to rob banks and jewellery shops. He also has a keen interest in the manner in which the courts deal with 'vulnerable witnesses' (whether they be vulnerable by virtue of their age or health and whether they be defence or prosecution

witnesses). As a consequence he has been involved in the training of practitioners and police officers on this topic.
Professional Memberships: Criminal Bar Association, Kent Bar Mess, South Eastern Circuit
Career: Grade 4 CPS Panel Advocate (London and South East) and CPS Rape Specialist Attorney General's Specialist Regulatory Advocates Panel for Health and Safety and Environmental Law (List C)

TAYLOR, Simon
Keating Chambers, London
020 7544 2600
staylor@keatingchambers.com
Featured in Public Procurement (London)
Practice Areas: Practices in EU, public procurement and competition law. Contentious and non-contentious. Procurement work includes disputes and strategic advice on preparation and conduct of tenders. Advises on competition, state aid and regulatory issues arising from mergers and commercial conduct, cases before competition authorities and follow on damages actions. Specific healthcare, communications and rail expertise. Advises widely on NHS disputes. Acted on Geodesign v Environment Agency, Kent Community Health NHS Foundation Trust v NHS Swale Clinical Commissioning Group & Anor, QSRC v NHS England, Counted4 CIC v Sunderland City Council and several ongoing procurement and judicial review cases. Experienced in mediation. Advised on CMA approval for Basildon/Southend/iPP pathology JV. Personal: Lives in Putney. Speaks French and Spanish. Likes travel, food, wine, theatre and rugby.
Professional Memberships: Procurement Lawyers Association; Society of Labour Lawyers; Bar European Group; Competition Law Association.
Career: Magdalen College, Oxford. Called to Bar 1987; Pupillage, 2 Temple Gardens 1987-88; EU law Masters (Brussels); Squire Sanders & Dempsey (Brussels) 1990-92; Norton Rose (Brussels) 1992-96; Cable & Wireless Communications, Regulatory counsel 1996-2000; Enrolled as solicitor 1999; Allen & Overy, Associate 2000-04; Wragge & Co, Antitrust Partner 2004-2011; Keating Chambers 2012-present.
Publications: Frequent contributor to procurement and competition law publications (including Practical Law).
Personal: Speaks French and Spanish.

TEACHER, Petra
29 Bedford Row Chambers, London
020 7404 1044
pteacher@29br.co.uk
Featured in Family/Matrimonial (London)
Practice Areas: All areas of Family Law with a particular emphasis on matrimonial finance, cohabitees' disputes, and private law Children Act cases.
Professional Memberships: Family Law Bar Association.
Career: Called 2006, Inner Temple.
Personal: Lady Margaret Hall, Oxford University (MA (Oxon) (Modern Languages)) City University (CPE) Inns of Court School of Law (BVC).

TEMMINK, Robert-Jan
Quadrant Chambers, London
020 7583 4444
robert.temmink@quadrantchambers.com
Featured in Commercial Dispute Resolution (London)
Practice Areas: Specialises in commercial litigation, international arbitration particularly in the fields of aviation, shipping, financial services, energy and insurance. He has extensive experience of applying for and resisting freezing injunctions, and cross-border issues in many cases involving commercial fraud and insolvency. He has been appointed as an arbitrator in ICC arbitrations and frequently acts as Counsel in ICC, LCIA and other arbitrations. He has been appointed as a mediator in a number of high-value commercial disputes and as a Construction Act Adjudicator.
Professional Memberships: ChBA, COMBAR, PNBA, TECBAR, LMAA. Panel member of the HKIAC.
Career: Trinity College, Cambridge; Fellow Chartered Institute of Arbitrators; Called to the Bars of New York (Foreign Legal Consultant) & Northern Ireland; Admitted to the Dubai International Financial Centre Court; ADR Group Accredited Mediator; Dubai International Arbitration Centre Arbitrator; TECBAR Accredited Mediator, Adjudicator, Arbitrator & Dispute Board Member; Kuala Lumpur Regional Centre Arbitrator; HKIAC Panel Member.
Publications: LexisNexis Special Report: Financial Services Regulation & Litigation (contributing author); Lissack & Horlick on Bribery (contributing author); Investing in Emerging Markets (contributing author).
Personal: Trustee Temple Music Trust; Trustee King's Singers Foundation; Trustee La Nuova Musica; Director Merchant Taylors' School; Director Sherborne School; Liveryman of Merchant Taylors' Company.

TEMPLE, Adam
4 Pump Court, London
020 7842 5555
adamtemple@4pumpcourt.com
Featured in Financial Services (London)
Practice Areas: Adam has a commercial practice, split between financial services, insurance, professional negligence and construction disputes. Since spending six months on secondment within the Enforcement Division of the Financial Services (now Conduct) Authority, Adam has represented the Authority in the Supreme Court, the Court of Appeal and the High Court. He also advises private clients on regulatory matters and is regularly instructed by banks on derivatives and other litigation. His construction work has included high profile disputes including Wembley Stadium and the Shard as well as international arbitrations on large infrastructure projects. Other work includes claims against IFAs and other professionals, insurance coverage disputes and all manner of other commercial claims. Significant cases include: Maman v Lloyd's Underwriters [2016] EWHC 1327 (QB); FCA v Capital Alternatives [2015] EWCA Civ 284; MHT v Taylor [2015] EWHC 3709 (Ch); FSA v Sinaloa [2013] UKSC 11; Cleveland Bridge v Severfield-Rowen [2012] EWHC 3652 (TCC); Beck Interiors v UKFC [2012] EWHC 1808 (TCC)
Professional Memberships: COMBAR, FSLA, PNBA, SCL, TECBAR, IPBA
Career: MA, BCL (Oxon). Called 2008, Middle Temple

TEMPLE, Eleanor
Kings Chambers, Leeds
0345 034 3444
clerks@kingschambers.com
Featured in Chancery (Northern), Banking & Finance (Northern), Commercial Dispute Resolution (North Eastern), Restructuring/Insolvency (North Eastern)
Practice Areas: Eleanor practises in all aspects of chancery and commercial litigation and advisory work, especially corporate and personal insolvency, company and partnership law (including shareholder/unfair prejudice disputes, breaches of trust and fiduciary duties), directors' disqualification, banking and finance and asset tracing claims. In 2015 Eleanor was appointed as a Deputy District Judge (Civil). In 2012 Eleanor was selected by the Bar Council to present a paper to the New York City Bar Association on Cross Border Insolvency. Eleanor is the Founder of the R3 North West Women in Business Recovery Group and a member of the R3 Regional Committee (Yorkshire). In 2007 Eleanor was featured in The Times "Future Stars of the Regions" Report. Clients include insolvency practitioners, banks, multi-nationals, SMEs, professional firms, private equity houses and private individuals. She is a member of the Attorney General's Provincial Panel.
Professional Memberships: R3 Committee Member (Yorkshire), Insolvency Lawyers Association, Chancery Bar Association, Northern Circuit Commercial Bar Association, Northern Chancery Bar Association, EQLA, British Association for Sports and Law.
Career: Called to the Bar 2000. Junior Counsel to the Crown 2008-11, Attorney General's Panel 2015.
Publications: Misfeasance: Shadow Director Versus De Facto Director, Insolvency Intelligence 11/02/2011, 44, (2011) 24 Ins. Int. 4 Family Law and Bankruptcy Update, Insolvency Intelligence 11/02/2011, 39, (2011) 24 Ins. Int. 1 Equine Law: Taking the reins (2008) LS Gaz, 7 Aug, 14.

TERRY, Jeffrey
Kings Chambers, Manchester
0345 034 3444
clerks@kingschambers.com
Featured in Chancery (Northern)
Practice Areas: Commercial, especially insurance, chancery, professional negligence and construction. Recent cases at Court of Appeal level include: Brinks v Igrox [2011] IRLR 343 (Carriage of Goods, Torts, Bailment): Lambert v Barratt Homes & Rochdale MBC [2010] BLR 527, (Nuisance, Flooding by Construction Works); City & General v RSA (2010) BLR 639 (Construction, Insurance), Baynes v Hedger [2009] 2 FLR 183, CA (Succession, Inheritance Act); Ansari v New India Assurance [2009] Lloyds Rep IR 562 (Commercial Property, Fire Insurance).
Professional Memberships: Northern Circuit Commercial Bar Association; Northern Circuit Chancery Bar Association; Professional Negligence Bar Association; Bar European Group.
Career: LLB (Lond) 1975. Called 1976. MA (Business Law) with Distinction 1981, Fellow of the Chartered Institute of Arbitrators 1996. CEDR accredited mediator 1999.
Publications: Various papers and publications in England, USA and Canada.

TETHER, Melanie
Old Square Chambers, London
020 7629 0300
mtether@oldsquare.co.uk
Featured in Employment (London), Employment (Western)
Practice Areas: All aspects of employment law, both individual and collective. Melanie is a tenacious advocate and is known for her ability to master challenging briefs. She is regularly instructed in heavyweight equal pay and discrimination claims and has appeared in a number of landmark cases, including several references to the Court of Justice of the European Union. She is a leading expert on the Transfer of Undertaking Regulations. Melanie has appeared in many reported cases. Recent examples include: Mustafa v Trek Highways Ltd [2016] IRLR 326; Griffiths v. Secretary of State for Work and Pensions [2014] EqLR 545; Earle v Equality and Human Rights Commission [2014] IRLR 845; Kelly v The Hesley Group Ltd [2013] IRLR 514 EAT and British Airways plc v Mak and others [2011] ICR 735 CA.
Professional Memberships: ELA, ELBA, former Chair and current Vice President of ILS.
Career: Called to the Bar 1995. Previously a partner in Norton Rose.

THACKER, James
9 Gough Square, London
020 78320500
jthacker@9goughsquare.co.uk
Featured in Financial Crime (London)
Practice Areas: Criminal law with specialisms in Financial Crime, Regulatory offences, Professional Disciplinary and Police Law. James has prosecuted and defended in several high profile, multi-handed, high value complex frauds as leading counsel, sole counsel and junior to Queen's Counsel. He has also prosecuted cases as sole counsel against Queen's Counsel. James is adept in dealing with cases involving large volumes of evidence and expert evidence. Prosecution cases include: Operation Crystal (multi handed Access to Work fraud involving 12 deaf defendants), R v Brad (£3million Invoice finance fraud), R v Kayode (£4million Education Trust fraud believed to be 'Britain's largest Education Fraud'), Operation Dee (multi handed £2million bank fraud), Operation Glider (multi handed Gift Aid fraud), Operation Dinghy (multi-handed wine investment fraud), Operation Lemington (NHS procurement fraud), Operation Evergreen (Insider NHS fraud). Defence cases include: Operation Exempt (multi handed confidence fraud). James is very knowledgeable and experienced with restraint and confiscation proceedings. He appeared in the Court of Appeal case of R v R [2013] EWCA 1105 (restraint variations).
Professional Memberships: Criminal Bar Association. South Eastern Circuit (committee member 2009-2012). Central London Bar Mess Junior.
Career: Called to the Bar in 2001 (Gray's Inn). Grade 4 CPS prosecutor. Grade 3 specialist Fraud prosecutor. Appointed to prosecute rape and serious sexual offences. Appointed to Regulatory list (Health and Safety and Environmental Law). Approved for Direct Access.

THANKI, Bankim QC
Fountain Court Chambers, London
44(0)20 7583 3335
bt@fountaincourt.co.uk
Featured in International Arbitration (London), Professional Negligence (London), Travel (London), Aviation (London), Banking & Finance (London), Commercial Dispute Resolution (London), Financial Services (London), Fraud (London), Insurance (London), Offshore (London)
Practice Areas: Commercial dispute resolution (litigation and arbitration) in all its guises. A considerable amount of work is now offshore. Represented Barclays Bank in the case which saw the first judgment handed down in the new Financial List in London. Other notable cases include leading successfully for GMR in its dispute with the Republic of the Maldives over the international airport at Malé, for Deloitte LLP in its successful appeal against the record fine imposed by the Financial Reporting Council over its involvement with the Phoenix Four/MG Rover, for Vincent Tchenguiz in his claim against the SFO, for Deloitte LLP over the Phoenix Four/MG Rover investigation, for the Central Bank of Trinidad & Tobago in the Colonial Life Enquiry, for the Bar Council in R (Prudential) v HMRC, for Lloyds Banking Group in the OFT test case on bank charges, for the son of the King of Bahrain in his claim against Michael Jackson, for the Bank of England in Three Rivers and for Qantas in the DVT litigation.
Professional Memberships: Commercial Bar Association.
Career: Called to the Bar 1988. Silk 2003. Bencher, Middle Temple 2008.
Personal: Educated at Balliol College, Oxford (BA, 1st Class Hons 1986; MA 1989). Harmsworth Scholar, Middle Temple, 1988.

THOMAS, Bryan
Civitas Law, Cardiff
08450713007
bryan.thomas@civitaslaw.com
Featured in Clinical Negligence (Wales & Chester), Personal Injury (Wales & Chester)
Practice Areas: Bryan is specialist PI and clinical negligence practitioner. He is highly experienced in catastrophic injury claims arising out of head or spinal injuries. He has a high volume clinical negligence practice covering all areas of medical treatment. Bryan is very experienced in marshalling and leading the expert evidence team in complex claims. He is meticulous, approachable and robust. also an experienced mediator, arbitrator and adjudicator for a wide spectrum of civil disputes
Professional Memberships: Memberships: APIL, PIBA, HSLA and is a Fellow of the Chartered Institute of Arbitrators.
Career: Called to the Bar in 1978

THOMAS, David
2TG - 2 Temple Gardens, London
020 7822 1200
dthomas@2tg.co.uk
Featured in Professional Negligence (London)
Practice Areas: David's professional negligence practice focusses on solicitors, brokers, architects and surveyors; with a spread between claimant and defendant work.
It is complimented by his insurance and commercial fraud practices which give him experience of PI coverage disputes as well as claims involving bribery and dishonesty on the part of professionals.
Professional Memberships: PNBA, COMBAR
Career: BA, BCL (Oxon); Called 2009 (Lincoln's Inn); Tenant at 2TG - 2 Temple Gardens since 2010.

THOMAS, David QC
Keating Chambers, London
020 7544 2600
dthomas@keatingchambers.com
Featured in International Arbitration (London), Construction (London)
Practice Areas: Onshore and offshore construction and engineering projects including energy sector, commercial property developments, PFI, roads, railways, harbours, bridges and tunnelling as well as related bonds and guarantees. Expert in the NEC3 contract and editor of the leading text book. Known for forceful advocacy, incisive cross-examination, commercial awareness and the clarity and practicality of his advice including risk management advice on projects. Client friendly "hands on" leader taking care over people as well as problems. UK based with a large part of practice in GCC countries and Asia Pacific. He has wide experience of international arbitration (including ad hoc, ICC, LCIA, DIAC, SIAC, HKIAC) as well as the courts of the UK and the DIFC. He acted on the Shard and the London Olympics in the UK, the Palm and "the World" in Dubai, major infrastructure projects in Hong Kong, Tanzania, Oman and the UK, energy projects in Qatar, Abu Dhabi, UK and Vietnam, and conducted numerous Dubai World Tribunal trials.
Professional Memberships: TECBAR; UKELG; PNBA; SCL; Treasurer of Omani-British Lawyers Association.
Career: Called 1982; Queens Counsel 2002.
Publications: Editor "Keating on NEC3". Columnist: Construction Law International. Contributing author: Keating on Construction Contracts and Keating on Offshore Construction.
Personal:

THOMAS, George
Serjeants' Inn Chambers, London
07850 428 175
gthomas@serjeantsinn.com
Featured in Police Law (All Circuits)
Practice Areas: George Thomas was called to the Bar in 1995. George specialises in public and administrative, police, Court of Protection, employment, inquests and inquiries, clinical negligence and healthcare and professional discipline law. An earlier edition notes that "he is very knowledgeable and very efficient" and "strong on public order and very aware of police law...he can answer any question you ask him." Please visit the Serjeants' Inn Chambers website for his profile, which sets out full details of his practice including relevant work of note.
Professional Memberships: PNBA, ARDL, ELBA, ALBA.
Publications: "Public Order: Law and Practice" Blackstone's Practical Policing, with John Beggs QC and Susanna Rickard, OUP, 2012.

THOMAS, Nigel
Maitland Chambers, London
020 7406 1200
nthomas@maitlandchambers.com
Featured in Chancery (London), Agriculture & Rural Affairs (London)
Practice Areas: Chancery law: Oatley v Oatley [2014] EWHC 1956 (rectification of voluntary settlement); Perdoni v Curati [2012] WTLR 505 : 14 ITELR 725 (establishing domicile); Taylor v Saunders & ors LTL 19/7/2012 (setting aside will for lack of testamentary capacity due to Alzheimer's disease); Dunbar v Plant [1998] Ch 412 (Forfeiture Act 1982). Agricultural law: Davies v H & R Eckroyd Ltd (1996) EGCS 77 (Law of Commons and Village Greens); R v Suffolk CC ex Parte Steed (1995) 2EGLR 232, Lord Dynevor v Richardson [1995] ChD 173. Property: Parshall v Hackney [2013] 1 Ch D 568; Dwr Cymru Cyf v Edgar 2004 All ER(D) 05 (Nov); Carmen Johnson v WR Shaw [2003] EWCA (Civ) 894 and National Car Parks Ltd v Trinity Developments (Banbury) Ltd [2002] 1P+CR P37.
Professional Memberships: Chancery Bar Association, Wales and Chester Circuit.
Career: Called to the Bar 1976 (Gray's Inn). Chairman Agricultural Land Tribunal (Midland Area), Recorder.

THOMAS, Robert QC
Quadrant Chambers, London
020 7583 4444
robert.thomas@quadrantchambers.com
Featured in Shipping (London)
Practice Areas: Robert has extensive experience in advising and presenting cases covering a wide range of commercial and shipping matters both in the High Court and arbitration. Since taking silk in 2011, he has maintained a strong presence in shipping and commercial field and has been involved in a number of heavy weight and ground-breaking cases in arbitration, the High Court and Court of Appeal.
Professional Memberships: Commercial Bar Association, BILA, LCIA and supporting member of LMAA.
Career: MA (Hons), Trinity College, Cambridge. Licence Speciale en Droit Europeen, Universite Libre de Bruxelles. BCL, St Catherine's College, Oxford.
Personal: Fluent French, working knowledge of German.

THOMAS, Roger QC
Pump Court Tax Chambers, London
020 7414 8080
clerks@pumptax.com
Featured in Tax (London)
Practice Areas: Roger's advisory practice covers a wide area of both direct and indirect tax issues. His practice is evenly balanced between litigation and advisory work. His recent practice has included: Advising on UK tax aspects of a US Oil company reorganisation; Advising on the UK corporate tax aspects of the rescue of a leading bank following the sub-prime mortgage debacle; Acting for the taxpayer in the first SDLT avoidance case DV3 v HMRC; Acting for the taxpayer in the first case on the SDLT anti-avoidance provision, section 75A Finance Act 2003: Project Blue v HMRC; Acting for a number of charities in a string of successful cases establishing the boundary of the concept of 'business' for vat purposes: Woking Museum v HMRC, Yarburgh v HMRC, St Paul's v HMRC and Longridge on the Thames v HMRC; Advising on Singapore stamp duty for a major oil company; Appearing in the Commercial Court for a Russian Oil company in a dispute with an Italian company as to the liability for Italian VAT on deliveries of oil into storage; Appearing for the taxpayer in the European Court of Justice in a case on whether the VAT exemption for medical services was available to an institution storing stem cells derived from umbilical cord blood; Acting for HMRC in the European Court of Justice in a case on the liability to stamp duty reserve tax of transfers of shares into a European Clearance Service.
Professional Memberships: Revenue Bar Association; London Common Law & Commercial Bar Association; VAT Practitioners Group; Stamp Taxes Practitioners Group.
Career: Called 1979, Lincoln's Inn. QC 2014.
Publications: VAT (Halsbury's Laws of England); Customs & Excise Duties (Halsbury's Laws of England); Customs Duty De Voil vol 6.
Personal: Born 1955; Resides in London.

THOMPSON, Andrew QC
Erskine Chambers, London
020 7242 5532
athompson@erskinechambers.com
Featured in Company (London), Partnership (London), Restructuring/Insolvency (London)
Practice Areas: Andrew is a sought-after, specialist commercial litigator, with particular expertise in: corporate litigation (including shareholders' disputes, claims against directors and constructive trust claims); LLP and partnership disputes; corporate insolvency; commercial litigation (including large-scale contractual disputes, fraud and breach of warranty claims); professional negligence claims (including lawyers, accountants, valuers and management consultants); and disputes within unincorporated associations. Andrew has been involved in leading cases in all of these areas, with specific expertise in litigation in the fund management industry. Andrew also undertakes advisory work in the same fields. A list of reported and recent cases is available at www.erskinechambers.com.
Professional Memberships: COMBAR, Chancery Bar Association.
Career: Merchant Taylors' School; St Catharine's College, Cambridge (1989 BA; 1990 LLM; 1992 MA); Called to Inner Temple 1991, Queen's Counsel 2014.
Personal: Leisure: family, cricket, gardening, hill-walking, birding.

THOMPSON, Collingwood QC
7BR, London
020 7400 7336
cthompson@7br.co.uk
Featured in Financial Crime (London)
Practice Areas: Asset recovery, bribery and corruption, money laundering, restraint and confiscation and criminal fraud litigation, offshore & international, regulatory and professional discipline.
Professional Memberships: Fraud Lawyers Association (Committee member), International Bar Association
Career: Collingwood has specialised in both civil and criminal fraud since taking silk in 1998. He has prosecuted for all the main agencies (SFO, CPS, SOCA (now the NCA)) and advised the Attorney General of Jersey on fraud-related investigations, as well as defending clients charged on major fraud prosecutions instituted by these agencies. He is highly regarded as a specialist in cases involving money laundering, both prosecuting and defending and is a frequent speaker at international conferences on the topic. Through his fraud practice he has developed an expertise in legal professional privilege, particularly in connection with search warrants and Production Orders. His practice is increasingly international, with appearances

in courts in the Caribbean and, in particular, Hong Kong. In addition he is also instructed in regulatory and compliance cases at home and abroad by both regulators and those who are suspect to such investigations. As part of his fraud practice, Collingwood has been regularly instructed by claimants and defendants in asset recovery cases linked to fraud or corruption. He has considerable experience in working with forensic accountants to identify, trace and recover the proceeds of such offences

THOMPSON, James
Keating Chambers, London
020 7544 2600
jthompson@keatingchambers.com
Featured in International Arbitration (London), Construction (London)

Practice Areas: Recognised specialist in construction, engineering, energy, infrastructure and related commercial disputes, both in the High Court (TCC) and domestic and international arbitration. Particular experience of disputes in the Middle East having recently acted for clients in Dubai, Qatar, Oman and Saudi Arabia. Recent work includes: acting for main contractor in high value termination dispute (ICC arbitration); acting for developer in high profile dispute arising out of UK housing development (High Court, TCC); acting for contractor in dispute arising out of construction of power station in the Middle East (ICC arbitration); acting for employer in dispute arising out of construction of an airport in the Middle East (DIAC arbitration).
Professional Memberships: TECBAR; SCL; COMBAR; Omani British Lawyers Association (Committee).
Career: MA Law (Cantab), Cambridge (2004); Called 2005 (Astbury Scholar); Pupillage Keating Chambers (2005-2006); Keating Chambers (2006).
Publications: Researcher – Keating on Construction Contracts, 9th Edition (2012); Contributor – Keating on Offshore Construction and Marine Engineering Contracts (2015); Contributor – Construction Law Reports.

THOMSON, David
Axiom Advocates, Edinburgh
07500 813 598
david.thomson@axiomadvocates.com
Featured in Company (Scotland), Restructuring/Insolvency (Scotland), Professional Negligence (Scotland), Real Estate Litigation (Scotland), Commercial Dispute Resolution (Scotland)

Practice Areas: Practises exclusively in commercial disputes, with a particular emphasis on company law, property/real estate litigation and insolvency law.
Career: 1990-1995: University of Glasgow (LL.B (Hons) 1994; Dip LP 1995)/ 1995-1997: Trainee Solicitor, Steedman Ramage WS/ 1997-2003: solicitor at various commercial law firms/ 2003-2004: pupillage (Devilmasters: The Hon Lord Clark; C. R. K. Sandison QC; J Reilly)/ 2004: called to the Bar/ 2005-2009: Standing Junior Counsel to the Scottish Ministers/ 2009-date: Standing Junior Counsel to the Advocate General for Scotland (since 2015 – Standing Junior Counsel to HMRC).
Publications: Scottish Editor, Mithani, Directors' Disqualification

THORNHILL, Andrew QC
Pump Court Tax Chambers, London
020 7414 8080
clerks@pumptax.com
Featured in Tax (London)

Practice Areas: Formerly Head of Chambers specialising in all areas of tax but with special emphasis on employee remuneration, share schemes, inheritance tax, capital gains tax, planning and litigation. Cases include: Laird v CIR (House of Lords); Eversden v CIR (Court of Appeal); Dextra Accessories v MacDonald (House of Lords), Optos Plc v CIR (Special Commissioners), Sempra Metals v HMRC (Special Commissioners), Murray Group v HMRC (First-tier and Upper Tribunal)(Rangers FC litigation case, now on appeal to the Supreme Court), Scotts Atlantic Ltd v HMRC (First-tier Tribunal).
Professional Memberships: Revenue Bar Association; STEP, London Common Law and Commercial Bar Association.
Career: Called 1969, Middle Temple; Pump Court Tax Chambers 1969 to date; QC 1985; formerly Recorder Western Circuit. Head of Pump Court Tax Chambers 1991 to 2014.
Publications: Potter & Monroe's 'Tax Planning with Precedents' 4th-7th editions; 'Passing Down the Family Business/the Family Farm'; Contributor to 'Gore-Brown on Companies' and 'Kerr on Receivers'.
Personal: Clifton College; Corpus Christi College, Oxford.

THORNLEY, Hannah
South Square, London
020 7696 9900
hannahthornley@southsquare.com
Featured in Restructuring/Insolvency (London)

Practice Areas: International and Domestic Company and Insolvency law, with particular interest and experience in the Duties of Directors, Shareholder Disputes and Fraud situations; General Commercial and International Litigation; Insurance; Trusts; Property; Banking; Finance; Professional Negligence and Disciplinary Proceedings.
Career: Hannah is an experienced advocate and litigator. She appears regularly in the High Court and advises on domestic and international cases which are often of a complex or urgent nature. Hannah has advised, represented or appeared in Court for numerous high profile banks, companies and private individuals. Her clients include: Bank of Ireland; Standard Chartered Bank; Abbey National; Anglo-Irish Bank; Volksbank, Commerzbank (the Company that previously owned Manchester City Football Club); Landlords in Games Station; Landlords in Woolworths; Connaught; Barratts; Birthdays; Thomson Directories, Dawnay Day; East London Bus Group; Oilexco; Lemma Insurance; Independent Insurance; UIC Insurance; Brit Insurance; National House Building Council. Hannah has been appointed to the Attorney General's Panel of Junior Counsel to the Crown (C Panel) March 2015 – August 2020. In May 2016, Hannah was appointed as specialist legal adviser to the Work and Pensions and Business Innovation and Skills House of Commons Select Committees in relation to the BHS inquiry. Called to the Bar 2003.

THORNTON, Andrew
Erskine Chambers, London
020 7611 9848
athornton@erskinechambers.com
Featured in Company (London)

Practice Areas: Company law, with a particular emphasis on mergers and acquisitions both domestic and cross-border. Andrew is instructed in most of the leading public company M&A transactions each year.
Professional Memberships: COMBAR, Chancery Bar Association.
Career: Called Lincolns Inn 1994.
Publications: Contributor to FromCounsel.com and Buckley on the Companies Acts. Consultant editor on Freshfield's Schemes of Arrangement: Law and Practice.

THORPE, Alexander
Queen Elizabeth Building QEB, London
020 7797 7837
clerks@qeb.com
Featured in Family/Matrimonial (London)

Practice Areas: Alexander specialises in all aspects of private family law with particular emphasis on complex financial work, encompassing jurisdiction disputes, trusts and other off-shore structures. Much of his work has an international element.
Professional Memberships: A member of the FLBA and the Western Circuit.

TIDMARSH, Christopher QC
5 Stone Buildings, London
020 7242 6201
clerks@5sblaw.com
Featured in Chancery (London), Pensions (London)

Practice Areas: Chancery practitioner, particular emphasis on trusts and probate, tax, pensions, professional negligence, (solicitors and accountants). Experienced in both contentious and non-contentious aspects of the administration of trusts (UK and offshore), estates and pension schemes. Before taking Silk, Christopher was a standing Junior Counsel to the Inland Revenue (1995-2002) and brings that experience to bear in his private practice. Extensive experience in tax cases before the special and general commissioners and in the High Court and the Court of Appeal. Cases include: Cotton v Brudenell Bruce [2014] EWCA Civ 1312; Charlton v HMRC [2012] UKFTT 770 (TCC) Boyer Allan Investment Services Ltd v Revenue & Customs [2012] UKFTT 558 (TC); Greenbank v HMRC [2011]STC 1582; Re Nelson Dance Settlement [2009] EWHC (Ch) 71; Johnston Publishing North v HMRC [2008] EWCA Civ 858; Underwood v HMRC [2008] EWCA Civ 1423; Random House (UK) Ltd v Allason & Ors [2008] EWHC (Ch) 2854; Hearn v Dobson [2008] EWHC (Ch) 1620; Re Rogers [2006] 1 WLR 1577; Re T&N [2005] PLR 33; Hearn v Younger [2005] PLR 49; Property Co v Inland Revenue [2005] STC (SCD) 59; Aon v KPMG [2004].
Professional Memberships: Chancery Bar Association, STEP.
Career: Called 1985; Silk 2002.

TIPPLES, Amanda QC
Maitland Chambers, London
020 7406 1200
atipples@maitlandchambers.com
Featured in Chancery (London), Charities (London), Partnership (London), Real Estate Litigation (London)

Practice Areas: Amanda is experienced in general chancery and commercial litigation, in particular traditional chancery, partnership, real property and landlord and tenant, insolvency/corporate recovery, professional negligence, civil fraud, charities, VAT and Duties, confiscation proceedings. Recent cases include: University of London v Professor Prag (trusts/charities); Pollen Estate v HMRC (stamp duty/charities); A-G v Charity Commission (charities); Silkstone v Tatnall (real property); Franks v Bedward (real property); Herbert v Doyle (constructive trusts/proprietary estoppel); Tann v Herrington (partnership); Reichmann v Gauntlett (landlord and tenant).
Professional Memberships: Chancery Bar Association, COMBAR, ACTAPS, Charity Law Association.
Career: Called to the Bar in 1991; Junior Counsel to the Crown (A Panel) 2006-11; Recorder (Crown Court) 2009; Queen's Counsel 2011; Deputy High Court Judge (Chancery Division) 2013; Chairman, Chancery Bar Association 2016-
Personal: Gonville and Caius College, Cambridge (MA).

TKACZYNSKA, Anna
Arden Chambers, London
020 7421 9482
anna.tkaczynska@ardenchambers.com
Featured in Education (London), Social Housing (London)

Practice Areas: Anna's practice focuses on Social Housing, Education, Local Government, Court of Protection and Landlord and Tenant. She receives instructions from a broad spectrum of clients including local authorities, housing providers and individuals for the purposes of litigation and advisory work. She appears as an advocate in all levels of the Courts and Tribunals.
Professional Memberships: Social Housing Law Association, Human Rights Lawyers Association (Committee member since 2009), Constitutional and Administrative Law Bar Association, Amicus
Career: Following completion of her traineeship at Matrix she joined the public law team at Hardwicke in 2010. From 2011-2012 she took a 12 month sabbatical to work for Reprieve on death penalty cases in the USA and was based full time in New Orleans. Anna joined Arden in 2015.
Publications: Lexis PSL Local Government practical guide; Lexis Social Housing Law in Practice (2015); Lexis Affordable Housing: the Modern Guide to Construction and Delivery (forthcoming)

TOAL, David
Exchange Chambers, Manchester
0161 833 2722
toal@exchangechambers.co.uk
Featured in Crime (Northern)

Practice Areas: David practises in criminal, regulatory and professional discipline work. His heavyweight criminal practice is made up of predominantly defence work, and he has extensive experience of defending serious and high-profile cases a number of which have attracted national publicity. He has also been involved in prosecuting many significant cases. He is a Category 4 Prosecutor and is on the specialist list of approved counsel instructed to prosecute serious sexual offences. He also represents a wide range of professionals facing criminal proceedings and/or breaches of regulations, particularly Police Officers facing Misconduct Proceedings and Healthcare professionals facing disciplinary proceedings in tribunals. David is appointed to the full panel of specialist advocates who represent the General Medical Council in tribunal hearings dealing with complex medical and fitness to practice

issues. He advises and represents individuals and large professional bodies in relation to Inquest proceedings. He also defends and prosecutes in cases involving Local Authorities and has particular experience in Trading Standards and Consumer Protection work.
Professional Memberships: Northern Circuit, Criminal Bar Association, Gray's Inn
Personal: St Bede's College, Manchester and Urmston Grammar School for Boys, LLB (Hons) Degree, Bar Vocational Course, Inns of Court School of Law 1989

TOD, Jonathan
29 Bedford Row Chambers, London
020 7404 1044
jotod@29br.co.uk
Featured in Family/Matrimonial (London)
Practice Areas: Matrimonial finance and Schedule 1 Children Act Proceedings. Re P (A Child: Financial Provision) (2003) 2 FLR 865 CA; B v B (Mesher Order) (2003) 2 FLR 285; Hill v Morgan (Child: Financial Provision) [2007] 1 FLR 1480; N v D (Child: Financial Provision) (2008) 1 FLR 1629; G v G (Child Maintenance: Interim Costs Provision) [2010] 2 FLR 1264; PK v BC [2012] 2 FLR 1426; Z v Z No2 [2012] 1 FLR 1100; PG v TW (No 1)(Child: Financial Provision: Legal Funding) [2014] 1FLR 508; PG v TW (no 2) (Child: Financial Provision) [2014] 1FLR 923; Y v Z [2014] 2 FLR 1313.
Professional Memberships: Family Law Bar Association.
Career: Qualified 1990, Inner Temple. Currently involved in a number of big money and high profile matrimonial finance cases including those with jurisdictional issues. He also specialises in advising on and drafting nuptial agreements. Continues to be instructed in many Schedule 1 Children Act disputes.
Publications: He has written with others articles relating to Schedule 1 Children Act. 'Consider the Mother's Furture' (2007) Family Law 140; 'Tax Implications: Schedule 1 Trusts (2007) Family Law 708; 'Schedule 1 To The Children Act 1989: N v D 'And The Need for Reform' [2008 Family Law 751]and 'Jurisdiction and Forum Issues in Schedule 1 Children Act Procedures' (2008) Family Law 880. Schedule 1 Children Act 1989: Update on Jurisdiction, Law & Procedure (2012) Fam Law 543, Schedule 1 Important Development PG v TW (2013) Fam Law 1286. 'Murphy's Law' [2015] Fam Law 69. He regularly lectures on Schedule 1 issues & Pre-nuptial Agreements.
Personal: Educated at Wellington College, Berkshire and Southampton University. Married with two children.

TODD, James
39 Essex Chambers, London
020 7535 3978
james.todd@39essex.com
Featured in Personal Injury (London), Personal Injury (All Circuits)
Practice Areas: Areas of expertise are personal injury, industrial disease, clinical negligence and health and safety. His cases involve high value (£1M+) claims and he has a particular interest in fraudulent injury claims having appeared in several high profile cases. Additional areas of specialism include equine and other types of sports injury claims.
Professional Memberships: PIBA, LCLCBA.
Career: Called 1990, Gray's Inn.
Personal: King's School, Chester; St John's College, Cambridge (1989 BA Hons Law). Married, two children, lives near Salisbury.

TODD, Michael QC
Erskine Chambers, London
020 7611 9835
mtodd@erskinechambers.com
Featured in Company (London), Offshore (London)
Practice Areas: Michael is Head of Erskine Chambers. He specialises in litigation and transactional advice on company law, corporate finance, capital markets and corporate insolvency, in the UK and internationally. He is described as one of the first people to call for legal advice on complex restructurings and contested takeovers and schemes. Significant cases and transactions include: the Virgin Money IPO; Essar Energy; Pfizer / AstraZeneca; Xstrata / Glencore; Coroin plc; Bumi plc; Nortel and Tyco (expert evidence); Rangers plc v Ticketus; BAT v Winward (asset protection); Re PCCW Ltd (CA Hong Kong; scheme of arrangement), Validus v IPC (Bermuda; hostile scheme); Belmont Asset Based Lending (Cayman) and Culross Global v Strategic Turnaround Master Partnership Ltd (PC) (redemption of interests in funds); Chaston v SWP; Anglo Petroleum Ltd v TFB Mortgages (CA; financial assistance); Re Prudential Enterprise Ltd (CFA Hong Kong; shareholder dispute); American Patriot Agency (PC Bermuda; commercial fraud); Tenaga (Malaysia; piercing the corporate veil); Waddington v Chan (Hong Kong/BVI; derivative actions). Michael has advised various regulatory bodies including the Financial Conduct Authority, Channel Islands Stock Exchange, Hong Kong Stock Exchange and Hong Kong Securities and Futures Commission.
Professional Memberships: Chairman of the Bar of England & Wales (2012, VC 2011); Chairman of Chancery Bar Association (2008 – 2011); COMBAR, Chairman of BarCo; Director of the Global Law Summit; Executive Committee of the Commonwealth Lawyers Association; Trustee of the Bar Pro Bono Unit; Trustee of Bar Pro Bono Community.
Career: Called: 1977. Silk: 1997. Michael has appeared in the courts of Hong Kong, British Virgin Islands, Bermuda, Cayman Islands, Isle of Man, Turks & Caicos Islands and Northern Ireland as well as in the Privy Council.

TOLLEY, Adam QC
Fountain Court Chambers, London
020 7842 3758
art@fountaincourt.co.uk
Featured in Employment (London)
Practice Areas: Barrister specialising in commercial litigation, banking, employment, insurance, professional negligence and personal tax. Cases include: Lock v British Gas [2016] ICR 503 (holiday pay and commission); Capita v RFIB [2016] 2 WLR 1429 (indemnity and continuing duty); Allied Fort v Creation [2015] EWCA Civ 841 (insurance brokers and summary judgment); PA(GI) v GICL [2016] Lloyd's Rep IR 125 (insurance transfer and liability for PPI mis-selling); Tael One v Morgan Stanley [2015] Bus LR 278 (interpretation of LMA standard terms); Bear Scotland v Fulton [2015] ICR 221 (holiday pay and overtime); VTB Bank v Skurikhin [2013] 2 All ER (Comm) 418 (freezing injunction in support of foreign proceedings); Ashcourt Rowan v Hall [2013] IRLR 637 (enforceability of non-competition clause).
Professional Memberships: ELBA; ELA; ILS; COMBAR; PNBA.
Career: Called to Bar 1994. Educated at Hutchesons' Grammar School (Glasgow), St Anne's College, Oxford (BA Juris, 1st, 1992; BCL, 1st, 1993). Member of Fountain Court Chambers since 1995. Attorney General's A Panel 2007-2014. Silk: 2014.
Publications: Co-author, Financial Services chapter in Professional Negligence and Liability (Informa, looseleaf).

TOMS, Paul
Quadrant Chambers, London
020 7583 4444
paul.toms@quadrantchambers.com
Featured in Shipping (London)
Practice Areas: Paul is an experienced junior barrister. He specialises in commercial, maritime and international trade litigation. His practice areas include shipping, commodities, insurance (both marine and non-marine), international arbitration (LCIA/ICC/LMAA), energy, shipbuilding, conflicts of law, unjust enrichment, information technology, transport and carriage of goods by road, and general commercial litigation. He appears regularly in the Commercial Court and in front of arbitral tribunals, whether as sole Counsel or as junior Counsel. He has appeared in the Court of Appeal on a number of occasions including twice in 2016. The nature of his practice is such that he has extensive experience of advising in respect of, and obtaining, urgent injunctive relief and developing strategies in disputes which span more than one jurisdiction. The majority of his clients are based overseas, in particular in China. Cases include Banque Cantonale de Geneve v Sanomi, Mitsui & Co Ltd v Beteiligungsgesellschaft LPG Tankerflotte, Transition Feeds LLP v Itochu Europe PLC, BP Oil International Ltd v Target Shipping Ltd, Hatzl v XL Insurance Company Ltd, Rohlig (UK) Ltd v Rock Unique Ltd and Crystal Palace (2000) Ltd v Iain Dowie.
Professional Memberships: COMBAR, LCLCBA, Supporting Member of LMAA, YIAG and ICC YAF.
Career: Called 2003.

TOMSON, Alastair
4 Stone Buildings, London
079 7128 2269
a.tomson@4stonebuildings.com
Featured in Company (London)
Practice Areas: Alastair Tomson has a primarily litigation-based practice with experience of High Court and appellate proceedings, and international arbitration, across banking and financial services, company, insolvency and general commercial disputes. Many of his instructions have an international aspect. Since 2011 he has been representing the Government of the Republic of Rwanda in a €100m ICC arbitration arising from a failed gas extraction joint venture. He has significant experience of financial services litigation, including being instructed in several proceedings involving interest rate swap mis-selling and the manipulation of LIBOR, and represented the successful appellants in the Court of Appeal in Deutsche Bank v Unitech [2013] EWCA Civ 1372. He is called to the bar of the DIFC Courts, and to the bar of the Republic of Rwanda for specific proceedings. Recent reported cases of note include: Allfiled v Eltis [2015] EWHC 1300 (Ch) (injunctive relief arising from breach of fiduciary duty, breach of confidence and breach of intellectual property rights) Islamic Investment Company of the Gulf (Bahamas) Ltd v Symphony Gems NV [2014] EWHC 3777 (Comm) (setting aside judgment on the basis of former solicitor's fraud) Deutsche Bank AG v Unitech Global Ltd [2014] EWHC 3117 (Comm) (payment into court where a successful rescission defence would lead to and order counter-restitution after trial) Cruz City 1 Mauritius Holdings v Unitech Ltd [2014] EWHC 3131 (Comm); [2014] Bus. L.R. D25 (freezing orders / appointment of receivers over the assets of an Indian company and ancillary orders) Deutsche Bank AG v Unitech Global Ltd [2013] EWCA Civ 1372 (Court of Appeal) (misrepresentations in relation to LIBOR; effect of novation on rescission in the context of syndicated loan agreements) Deutsche Bank AG v Unitech Global Ltd [2013] EWHC 2793 (Comm); [2014] 2 All E.R. (Comm) 268; [2013] 2 Lloyd's Rep. 629; [2014] U.K.C.L.R. 15 (permission to amend and summary judgment considering wide ranging issues including unenforceability of credit and swap agreements under Competition Act 1988 s.2 by reason of LIBOR manipulation; illegality; effect of no set-off clauses; enforceability of guarantees); Deutsche Bank AG v Unitech Global Ltd [2013] EWHC 471 (Comm) (amendments in relation to representations based on LIBOR manipulation).
Professional Memberships: ChBA, COMBAR, ALBA.
Publications: Annotated Companies Legislation (OUP). Contributor to Practical Law Corporate.

TONEY, Rachel
St Philips Stone Chambers, London
020 7440 6900
rachel.toney@stonechambers.com
Featured in Shipping (London)
Practice Areas: Rachel's shipping and commercial practice includes all aspects of international trade and maritime work (and associated applications for urgent interim relief) including, all shipbuilding disputes, warranty claims, a wide variety of bills of lading/charterparty disputes, indemnity claims, Agency Agreement disputes, contamination and cargo claims, Admiralty claims, contracts for the sale and carriage of goods together with insurance and re-insurance. Experienced in mediation as well as arbitration. Rachel has developed a very successful shipbuilding and superyacht practice, an area in which she has represented Owners and Builders and continues to be instructed in many significant, high-value new-build disputes involving a number of the world's largest superyachts.
Professional Memberships: COMBAR, Admiralty Bar, London Common Law and Commercial Bar Association, British German Jurists Association; BMLA.
Career: Called to the Bar 1998; Junior Counsel to the Crown – Panel C 2004, promoted to Panel B March 2008; Member of Attorney General's Panel of Special Advocates, 2010.
Personal: Educated Oxford University Law with Legal Studies in Europe BA Hons (1st) 1997; Konstanz University, Germany, LLM (finalised 1999).

TOOGOOD, Claire
Crown Office Chambers, London
020 7797 8100
toogood@crownofficechambers.com
Featured in Clinical Negligence (London)

Practice Areas: Claire specialises in clinical negligence, industrial disease and medical product liability. Claire is predominantly instructed by the NHSLA and the defence unions but also acts for Claimants. Her wide experience includes claims involving obstetrics, orthopaedics, oncology, gynaecology, paediatrics, neurology, urology, diabetes and general surgery. Claire is frequently instructed to attend joint settlement meetings and has a reputation for negotiating satisfactory outcomes, but she is unafraid to pursue a case to trial where Claire's strong advocacy skills can be utilised. She is known as an effective cross-examiner with a detailed knowledge of her cases.
Professional Memberships: Personal Injury Bar Association; Professional Negligence Bar Association; London Common Law and Commercial Bar Association
Career: Claire read Jurisprudence at Oxford, where she was awarded an Exhibition and was twice the winner of the Oxford University Mooting Competition. She was called to the Bar in 1995 and won the Middle Temple Mooting Competition the following year, having been awarded a Queen Mother's Scholarship by the Inn. She was offered tenancy after completion of her pupillage at 1 Paper Buildings and has remained with the set following the merger with 2 Crown Office Row to form Crown Office Chambers.

TOUBE, Felicity QC
South Square, London
020 7696 9900
felicitytoube@southsquare.com
Featured in Chancery (London), Company (London), Restructuring/Insolvency (London)

Practice Areas: Felicity specialises in domestic and cross-border insolvency and restructuring, banking and financial services, commercial litigation, civil fraud, and company law. She appears in the Cayman Islands on a regular basis.
Professional Memberships: COMBAR, Chancery Bar Association, International Association for Asset Recovery, Insolvency Service/ILA committees on the EU regulation and UNCITRAL.
Career: Felicity has acted in relation to most of the recent major corporate restructurings or insolvencies and related litigation, including most recently in Saad, Madoff, Lehman, Stanford, Rastogi, Nortel, SPhinX, Sigma, Landsbanki, MF Global, and Rafidain Bank. Called 1995 (Inner Temple); QC 2011; Called to the Bar of the Cayman Islands 2012; ADR Group Accredited Civil & Commercial Mediator 2015; sits on the INSOL International Mediation Panel.
Publications: Felicity publishes widely across all her fields of experience, including as editor and contributor to International Asset Tracing in Insolvency (Toube, OUP 2009) and as a Board Member of Insolvency Intelligence.

TOWNSEND, Harriet
Cornerstone Barristers, London
020 7242 4986
harriett@cornerstonebarristers.gov.uk
Featured in Planning (London)

Practice Areas: Planning, Environment, Compulsory Purchase and Compensation, Highways and Rights of Way, Town and Village Greens, Local Government, Public Law and Judicial Review.
Professional Memberships: Planning and Environment Bar Association (PEBA), UK Environmental Law Association (UKELA), Compulsory Purchase Association (CPA), National Infrastructure Planning Association (NIPA).
Career: Planning and environment law specialist with over 20 years' experience acting for private individuals, businesses, and public authorities. Advising on law, procedure, and strategy and providing representation in courts and inquiries across England and Wales. Recent cases include the controversial issues around basement development in central London; the preservation of listed buildings (CPO inquiries and enabling development); housing appeals where land supply is at issue; development in the green belt; regeneration (CPO inquiries) and renewable energy proposals. Areas of particular interest include the conduct of public authorities, habitats and species protection, contaminated land, and environmental impact assessment. Harriet accepts instructions direct, including under the Public Access Rules in suitable cases. Harriet is also a mediator of planning and environment disputes.
Publications: Contributing author to Cornerstone on Councillors' Conduct. Contributing author to Westlaw's Insight web-based service on the Local Government Ombudsman and on Local Authority Byelaws. Specialist contributing editor on Local Government Law and Planning Law for Jowitt's Dictionary of English Law (3rd edition, 2010). Journal of Planning and Environment Law, 2009, "The Climate Change Act 2008: Something to be Proud of After All?" [2009] JPL 842. Environmental Law Review, The climate change act 2008 — will it do the trick?, 2009 Enviro LR 11 2 (116).
Personal: BSc Mathematics and Economics 1st Class. Loves walking and music of all kinds.

TOZER, Stephanie
Falcon Chambers, London
020 7353 2484
clerks@falcon-chambers.com
Featured in Real Estate Litigation (London)

Practice Areas: All aspects of real property, landlord and tenant and property-related professional neligence, with a particular emphasis on mortgage-related work. Recently reported cases include: Parshall v Bryans [2013] EWCA Civ 240 (land registration; adverse possession), Bower Terrace Student Accomodation Ltd v Space Student Living [2012] EWHC 2206 (receivers; interim injunctions; student housing) and Unique Pub Properties v Fitzpatrick [2012] (committal for breach of undertaking).
Professional Memberships: Chancery Bar Association, LCLCBA; Professional Negligence Bar Association; Property Bar Association; CEDR accredited mediator; First Tier Tribunal Judge; MCIArb.
Career: Educated at St Swithun's, Winchester; Keble College, Oxford (BA Jurisprudence 1st 1995, MA 1997); Called 1996 (Lincoln's Inn - top Student in Bar Finals); formerly Maitland Chambers, joined Falcon 2008.
Personal: Diploma in Advanced Business French.

TOZZI, Nigel QC
4 Pump Court, London
020 7842 5555
ntozzi@4pumpcourt.com
Featured in International Arbitration (London), Professional Negligence (London), Banking & Finance (London), Commercial Dispute Resolution (London), Energy & Natural Resources (London), Information Technology (London), Insurance (London), Shipping (London)

Practice Areas: Commercial litigation and arbitration for clients operating in various sectors including commodities, energy and natural resources, manufacturing, IT, pharmaceutical, insurance and reinsurance, ship construction and conversion, media, banking and financial services. Commercial fraud and asset recovery. Misuse of confidential information. Professional negligence (solicitors, accountants, financial advisers, surveyors, valuers, brokers). Fire claims.
Professional Memberships: COMBAR, Professional Negligence Bar Association, London Common Law and Commercial Bar Association, British Insurance Law Association, Society for Computers & Law, LCIA, LMAA.
Career: Called to the Bar 1980, took Silk 2001.
Personal: Educated at Exeter University (LLB Hons first class) 1976-79. Bar Finals 1980 (first class). Leisure pursuits include sport (especially hockey), theatre and cinema.

TRACE, Anthony QC
Maitland Chambers, London
020 7406 1200
atrace@maitlandchambers.com
Featured in Chancery (London), Professional Negligence (London), Banking & Finance (London), Commercial Dispute Resolution (London), Company (London), Fraud (London), Offshore (London), Real Estate Litigation (London), Restructuring/Insolvency (London)

Practice Areas: Principal area of practice encompasses fraud, insolvency, property, trusts, banking, company, professional negligence, chancery and general commercial work, including a number of cases outside the UK. Cases include: Re Jeffrey S. Levitt Ltd [1992] (privilege against self-incrimination); Re Mirror Group (Holdings) Ltd [1993] (liability of assignees on liquidation); Gomba Holdings (UK) Ltd v Minories Finance Ltd (No.2) [1993] (mortgagee's costs); Lotteryking Ltd v AMEC Properties Ltd [1995] (set – off against assignees); Re BCCI SA (No.10) [1996] (insolvency set – off); Slough Estates Plc v Welwyn Hatfield DC [1996] (measure of damages for fraudulent misrepresentation); Grand Metropolitan plc v The William Hill Group Ltd [1997] (rectification); Bogg v Raper [1998] (will drafting and exclusion clauses); Plant v Plant [1998] (individual voluntary arrangements); Jordan Grand Prix Ltd v Baltic Insurance Group [1999] (Brussels Convention); Landare Investments Ltd v Welsh Development Agency [2000] (misfeasance in public office); Shalson v Russo [2001] (committal); Shalson v Russo (No 2) [2002] (purging contempt); SMAY Investments v Sachdev [2003] (submission to jurisdiction); JSC Zestafoni v Ronly Holdings Ltd [2004] (arbitration agreements); Might SA v Redbus [2004] (fiduciary duties); Newgate Stud v Penfold (No1) [2004] (directors' duties); Watford Petroleum Ltd v Interoil [2005] (cross-examination in interlocutory proceedings); Newgate Stud v Penfold (No2) [2005] (accounts of profits and limitation); Harley Street Capital v Tchigirinsky [2005] (fortification of cross-undertaking in damages); Shalson v Russo (No3) [2005] (constructive trusts and tracing); Walker International Holdings Ltd v Congo [2005] (transactions defrauding creditors); Kyrie-Royle v Burger King [2005] (conspiracy); Farepak [2006] (unconscionability and constructive trusts); Donegal v Government of Zambia [2007] (illegality); London Allied Holdings v Lee [2007] (fraud); Prudential Assurance v Ayres [2008] (construction of documents); Menolly v Cerep [2009] (estoppel); Zahoor v Masood [2009] (striking out for abuse of process); NML Capital v Republic of Argentina [2009] (sovereign immunity); Wirecard Bank AG v Scott [2010] (conspiracy and fraudulent misrepresentation); BTA Bank v Ablyasov [2011] (receivership); Yukos Capital v Rosneft [2011] (act of state); Westwood Shipping v Universal [2012] (insolvency proceedings and Regulation 1346/2000); Energy Venture Partners v Malabu Oil [2012] (evidence required for fortification of cross-undertaking in damages); Gorbunova v Boris Berezovsky [2013] (setting aside freezing order); Aeroflot v Berezovsky [2014] (enforcement of foreign judgment); Lehman [2015] (administration). Has sat as an Arbitrator.
Professional Memberships: Chancery Bar Association (Hon Secretary (1997-2001); Vice-Chairman (2001-04)); COMBAR; Association of Contentious Trust and Probate Specialists; Insolvency Lawyers Association; Commerical Fraud Lawyers Association; R3 (The Association of Business Recovery Professionals); RISA (Restructuring & Insolvency Specialists Association, Cayman)
Career: Called to the Bar 1981. Appointed QC 1998.
Publications: Contributor to 'Butterworths European Law Service' (company law) and 'Butterworths Practical Insolvency'. Deputy Managing Editor: 'Receivers, Administrators and Liquidators Quarterly' (1993-2002).
Personal: Educated at Magdalene College, Cambridge (MA, 1st Class Honours).

TRACY FORSTER, Jane
Hailsham Chambers, London
020 7643 5000
clerks@hailshamchambers.com
Featured in Clinical Negligence (London)

Practice Areas: Jane specialises in medical law including clinical negligence claims and applications in the Court of Protection relating to the medical care of patients lacking capacity. She is also instructed in claims against solicitors of professional negligence and in diverse employment and disciplinary disputes, usually for the employers. In the clinical negligence field, her instructions emanate from claimant firms and panel firms of the NHSLA. In recent years, her employment practice has developed in relation to the education sector. She has represented colleges and universities in tribunal, High Court and internal disciplinary proceedings, often relating to the employment of medical and allied professionals.
Career: Cases include: Magoulas v Queen Mary University of London [EAT, 29 January 2016] - PCP in age discrimination; Pye v Queen Mary University of London [EAT 22 October 2015] - reasonableness of strike-out; Stephenson v North Cumbria University Hospitals NHS Trust [Carlisle CC HHJ Hughes QC 6 July 2015]; ST v Maidstone and Tunbridge Wells NHS Trust [2015] Med LR

70 C v North Cumbria University Hospitals NHS Trust [2014] Med LR 189; An NHS Trust v (1) DE (by his litigation friend, the Official Solicitor) (2) FG & JK (3) C Local Authority (4) B Partnership Trust [2013] EWHC 2562 (Fam) – landmark declaration that it is in the best interests of a man with severe learning disabilities to undergo a vasectomy.

TRAVERS, David QC
6 Pump Court, London
020 7797 8400
davidtravers@6pumpcourt.co.uk
Featured in Consumer Law (London), Environment (London), Health & Safety (London)

Practice Areas: Regulatory law (including regulatory crime), public law and associated areas including corporate governance and professional standards. Advises, negotiates and appears as an advocate for companies, organisations and individuals, as well as for Local Authorities and Regulatory Bodies. In Regulatory crime he practices predominantly in Health and Safety (including Fire Safety), Food Law, Trading Standards and Environmental Protection. In Public law he practices predominantly in Environment, Planning and Local Government matters, particularly related to the management of waste. David Travers QC also acts in disputes involving the governance of bodies corporate (including the role of good corporate governance in ensuring regulatory compliance) and the administration of Local Authorities and professional conduct and disciplinary matters. He also acts for decision-makers susceptible of Judicial Review and those who are challenging the lawfulness of the exercise of discretion. He has particular experience in cases involving scientific and technical evidence.
Professional Memberships: Food Law Group, Association of Regulatory and Disciplinary Lawyers, Health & Safety Lawyers Association, International Bar Association, Lex Anglo-Brasil, Planning and Environment Bar Association, Midland Circuit, Chaîne des Rôtisseurs.
Career: In practice since 1981 after being called to the Bar by the Honourable Society of the Middle Temple (Harmsworth Scholar). Appointed Queens Counsel 2010. Member of the Bar Council 1995-2000. Visiting Professor at Business Accountability and Responsibility Centre, University of South Wales; Honorary Fellow of the Society of Food Hygiene and Technology; Accredited Mediator; Legal Advisor to the Medical Practitioner Tribunal Service (formerly Legal Advisor to the General Medical Council); Legal Advisor to the General Dental Council Fitness to Practice Panel.
Publications: Include (with Giles Atkinson and Noemi Byrd) "Planning Law and Practice" published April 2013 by Wildy, Simmons and Hill and "Planning Enforcement" (with Emmaline Lambert and Ed Grant) published 2015. Various articles including "Towards Professional-Model Regulation of Directors' Conduct" in the International Journal of Law and Management; Int. J.L.M. (2013) 55 (2) 123-140.

TROLLOPE, Andrew QC
187 Fleet Street, London
020 74307300
Johnpyne@187fleetstreet.com
Featured in Crime (London), Financial Crime (London)

Practice Areas: Wide experience of fraud and serious and organised crime cases. Long established practice in City, commercial and tax cases in courts and tribunals. Specialisations include money laundering, asset forfeiture/confiscation,VAT and Duty cases [tax tribunal], sports law. Cases include R v Relton [Brinks Mat], R v Viccei [Knightsbridge Safe Deposit], R v Stainforth [Blue Arrow], R v T Ward [Guinness], R v Masterson [Caird plc], R v M Ward [European Leisure plc], R v James [Harrovian Properties/Leisure], R v Keyes [McNicholas], R v Myles [Richmond Oil and Gas plc]. R v McKeown [Powerscreen plc], R v Sykes [Cheney Pension Scheme], R v Golechha /Op Venison, R v Lindsay/Op Vitric [MTIC Carousel Frauds], R v Hoult [Ikea], R v Matthews [Peakviewing plc,VAT/film financing], R v Auchi [Goldshield-pharmaceuticals cartel], Megantic Services Ltd v HMRC [FTTT], R v Ibori [money laundering], R v Storrie and Mandaric[Portsmouth FC], R v Perrin [Vantis Tax Ltd], R v Revell Read (UK's largest 'boiler room' case), SOCA v Namli (£6m civil recovery),Asiana Ltd v HMRC (FTTT/UT), Edgeskill Ltd v HMRC (UT), GSM Ltd/Sprint Cellular Ltd v HMRC (FTTT/UT), R v Bruce (foreign bribery). R v Smith (Theft from BT/Openreach, money laundering)
Professional Memberships: Committee Member of Criminal Bar Association 1990-2001, Bar Council International Relations Committee 2001-08, Advisory Council British Institute of International and Comparative Law, fellow of the Institute of Advanced Legal Studies 1998-99. Bencher of Inner Temple.
Career: Head of Chambers specialising in criminal law. Appointed assistant recorder 1984, recorder 1989. Special Adviser to Northern Ireland Affairs Select Committee 2014-2015
Publications: Contributor [with others from 187 Fleet Street] to 'Fraud; Law, Practice and Procedure' [Lexis Nexis, Butterworths].

TROMAN, Carl
4 New Square, London
020 7822 2000
c.troman@4newsquare.com
Featured in Professional Negligence (London), Insurance (London)

Practice Areas: Commercial litigation with particular emphasis on claims against professionals including solicitors, accountants, barristers, surveyors, engineers, insurance brokers, architects and financial advisers. Insurance particularly in relation to policy construction, coverage, the minimum terms of professional bodies, aggregation, fraud, misrepresentation and non-disclosure. A recent case was AIG Europe Ltd v OC320301 LLP [2015] EWHC 2398 (Comm). Other areas include: automotive litigation involving classic and supercars, motor sports regulatory law, property damage claims and costs. Formally accredited mediator and accepts instructions as an arbitrator.
Professional Memberships: COMBAR, TECBAR and PNBA.
Career: LLB (first class honours) 2000, Diploma in Law 2001, Called to the Bar 2001, Taught at Reading University 2001-02, 4 New Square Chambers 2002 to date.
Personal: Gastronomy, chess and tropical fish.

TROMPETER, Nicholas
Selborne Chambers, London
020 7420 9500
nicholas.trompeter@selbornechambers.co.uk
Featured in Chancery (London), Real Estate Litigation (London)

Practice Areas: All areas of Commercial Chancery litigation, including commercial and residential landlord and tenant matters, corporate and personal insolvency, real property disputes, professional liability claims, civil fraud and asset recovery, trusts, contractual claims, claims on guarantees, unjust enrichment, restitutionary remedies, directors' disqualification and public-interest winding up.
Professional Memberships: Property Bar Association; Chancery Bar Association; Professional Negligence Bar Association
Career: Called in 2006. Significant experience in Court (in trial and on appeal) and in arbitral proceedings. Frequently instructed to apply for / resist injunctions (including freezing injunctions). Previously acted as a judicial assistant in the Supreme Court of Israel in Jerusalem. Appointed to the Attorney-General C Panel of Counsel.
Publications: Co-author of Break Clauses (2nd Edition), Jordans 2016
Personal: New College, Oxford (MA Classics; New College Scholar); City University (CPE, distinction); ICSL (BVC, outstanding; Barstow Law Scholarship for coming third in the year; Du Cann Memorial Prize for highest overall marks in advocacy assessments); Wilfred Watson award from Gray's Inn.

TROTTER, Helen
Kings Chambers, Manchester
0345 034 3444
clerks@kingschambers.com
Featured in Employment (Northern)

Practice Areas: Helen has a built a thriving practice in employment law, and commercial matters with employment law principles. She has particular experience in complex discrimination and equality act cases, both in the Tribunal and the County Court, and is first choice counsel for a wide variety of Government departments and clients from the aviation, education and healthcare industries. Helen also specialises in unfair/wrongful dismissal, TUPE and commercial matters including injunctions, the enforceability of employee guarantees and restrictive covenants. Helen is known for her ability to put clients at their ease during proceedings, whilst approaching the litigation with tenacity and vigour.
Professional Memberships: Employment Lawyers Association, Employment Law Bar Association.
Career: David Karmel Scholar (2003) , Gerard Moody Scholar (2004), Called October 2004 (Grays Inn). Appointed to the Attorney General's Regional Panel of Junior Counsel to the Crown (November 2010).
Personal: BA Hons: Anglo-Saxon, Norse and Celtic (Cantab, 2000), CPE (City University, London, 2003), BVC (Inns of Court School of Law, London, 2004).

TROWER, William QC
South Square, London
020 7696 9900
williamtrower@southsquare.com
Featured in Banking & Finance (London), Company (London), Restructuring/Insolvency (London)

Practice Areas: William has a financial and commercial practice, specialising in insolvency and corporate restructuring, banking, company law and the civil aspects of commercial fraud. He has acted in disputes arising out of numerous high-value insolvencies in the UK and abroad, frequently appearing in the courts of Bermuda, the Cayman Islands and Hong Kong.
Professional Memberships: Commercial Bar Association, Chancery Bar Association, Council of Insolvency Lawyers' Association, Insolvency Rules Committee (2000-11).
Career: Currently acting for the administrators of Lehman Brothers and Nortel, William has acted in many other high-profile insolvencies and reconstructions including Kaupthing and Landsbanki. He sits as a Deputy High Court Judge (Chancery Division) and is a CEDR-trained Mediator. Called 1983 (Lincoln's Inn); QC 2001; Deputy High Court Judge 2008.

TUCK, Rebecca
Old Square Chambers, London
020 7269 0336
tuck@oldsquare.co.uk
Featured in Employment (London)

Practice Areas: Rebecca practices all areas of employment law, including unfair dismissal, discrimination, equal pay, TUPE, redundancy and collective disputes. She is in the ET and EAT regularly as well as frequently appearing before the Certification Officer, in the county court and in the High Court. She also carries out non-litigation work including conducting investigations, advising disciplinary panels and conducting appeal hearings. Rebecca is a qualified mediator and sits as a fee paid employment judge.
Professional Memberships: Industrial Law Society (currently a member of the Executive Committee), Employment Lawyers Association, Employment Law Bar Association, Council of Employment Judges.
Career: Berry Hill High School, City of Stoke-On-Trent Sixth Form College; Lady Margaret Hall, Oxford; MA (Oxon) (1997). Called to the Bar 1998. Joined Old Square Chambers 1999. Fee paid employment judge since 2010.
Publications: Editor of Harvey on Industrial Relations and Employment Law. Co-author 'Employment Tribunal Procedure' 2nd and 3rd editions. LAG. Annual Labour Law Highlights 2000-2016. Institute of Employment Rights.
Personal: Mother of two and when she gets time – a rugby fan.

TUCKER, Ian
Exchange Chambers, Liverpool
0161 833 2722
tucker@exchangechambers.co.uk
Featured in Commercial Dispute Resolution (Northern)

Practice Areas: Ian specialises in Commercial and Chancery litigation with an emphasis on Insolvency. Ian appeared as a junior in the Court of Appeal in Utilise TDS Limited v Davies & Bolton College (reported as Denton v TH White Ltd and other appeals) [2014] EWCA Civ 906, the leading case on relief from sanctions, having acted alone in the High Court (reported as Utilise TDS Limited v Davies & Bolton College [2014] EWHC 834 (Ch)). He was recently led in a multi-million pound dispute, listed for a 6 week trial, and advised a major high street bank on the terms of a lending product

following changes introduced by the Finance Act 2015. His practice covers all aspects of personal and corporate insolvency, CDDA proceedings, contractual disputes, professional negligence, banking, trusts, mortgage transactions and debt recovery. As a former mathematician, he is able to quickly analyse difficult problems and come up with pragmatic solutions.
Professional Memberships: North Eastern Circuit, Northern Chancery Bar Association, Associate of the Royal College of Science

TUCKER, Paul QC
Kings Chambers, Manchester
0345 034 3444
clerks@kingschambers.com
Featured in Planning (Northern)
Practice Areas: Paul practises in the areas of town and country planning, environmental law, local government law, highway law, the law of compulsory purchase. retail proposals; minerals and landfill proposals. He acts for both the public and the private sectors throughout England and Wales. He has acted for a local authorities, Government Agencies and a wide range of private sector developers, in cases involving diverse areas including major retail proposals, mineral and landfill proposals, large housing sites and other environmentally sensitive proposals. He is regularly engaged to act on behalf of major retailers and housing developers. He has been involved in a number of nationally important planning cases both before the Courts and at inquiry. His recent work has involved a diverse range of interests from the nuclear industry to Premiership Football Clubs, as well as national house builders, developers and retailers.
Professional Memberships: Planning and Environment Bar Association; Administrative Law Bar; National Infrastructure Planning Association;
Career: University: Cambridge (Selwyn College); degree: Law (MA); Called: 1990 (Gray's Inn); Silk: 2010.
Publications: Each year, Paul undertakes various speaking commitments at Planning Conferences and In-House Events as well as engaging in Mock Inquiries. In addition he has written for Estates Gazette, Planning and the Lawyer.

TUEJE, Patricia
1 Pump Court, London
020 7842 7070
pt@onepumpcourt.co.uk
Featured in Social Housing (London)
Practice Areas: Homelessness, housing, landlord and tenant, including security of tenure, disrepair, unlawful eviction and harassment, leasehold disputes
Professional Memberships: Housing Law Practitioners' Association Property Bar Association
Career: Patricia developed her specialist interest in housing law after some years working at 'the sharp end' in the voluntary housing sector. Working for some years at Shelter gave her a particular insight into the issue of housing rights. She has applied this invaluable perspective and understanding to all aspects of her work in housing law, she is alert to the urgency and high stakes of this work, bringing her success at the Court of Appeal, the High Court, the county courts and Property Chamber. She is known for being responsive to professional clients, and for sensitivity in dealing with the problems facing lay clients. Patricia is currently seeking clarification from the Court of Appeal as to whether non-physical domestic violence requires victims to be in fear of perpetrators to qualify for housing assistance under Part VII of the Housing Act 1996. She is also pursuing the Court of Appeal's interpretation of one aspect of a local authority's repairing obligations contained in its tenancy agreements, the ramifications of which will potentially affect the repair rights of all its pre-2000 tenants.

TURNER, Adam
7 King's Bench Walk, London
020 79108300
aturner@7kbw.co.uk
Featured in Shipping (London)
Practice Areas: An expert in commercial litigation and arbitration, acting for a broad range of UK and international clients. Particular expertise in contractual disputes of all kinds; shipping and commodities; insurance and reinsurance; civil fraud; jurisdiction and conflict of laws.
Professional Memberships: • Commercial Bar Association • London Maritime Arbitrators Association (Supporting Member) • London Shipping Law Centre • British Insurance Law Association • Commercial Fraud Lawyers Association
Career: Practising at 7KBW since 2009. Previously spent one year teaching commercial law at Brasenose College, Oxford. Completed the B.C.L. with Distinction in 2007 after obtaining First Class Honours in Law in 2006.

TURNER, James QC
1 King's Bench Walk, London
020 7936 1500
jturner@1kbw.co.uk
Featured in Family/Matrimonial (London)
Practice Areas: Principal areas of practice encompass all areas of criminal law, family law and administrative law. Many reported cases in each of these fields, including a number of cases in each field in the House of Lords/Supreme Court. Criminal work includes representation of medical practitioners in connection with criminal and disciplinary matters. Considerable knowledge and experience of technical and procedural points of law. Within family law, has particular expertise in financial ancillary relief (appeared in House of Lords in both White v White and Miller v Miller and in the Supreme Court in Gohil v Gohil), and in jurisdictional issues and international child abduction work (in which such cases he has appeared many times in the Supreme Court). Has appeared in finance cases in the Grand Court of the Cayman Islands and is instructed in matters in Hong Kong and Jersey. Speaker at criminal and family law conferences.
Professional Memberships: Criminal Bar Association, Family Law Bar Association and Administrative Law Bar Association.
Career: Called to the Bar and joined current chambers, 1976. Appointed as Member of the Panel of Treasury Counsel (Common Law) as a junior. Appointed Queen's Counsel 1998. Elected Master of the Bench (Inner Temple) 2006.
Publications: Archbold, 'Criminal Pleading, Evidence and Practice' – an editor.
Personal: Educated at Robertsbridge Secondary Modern School, Bexhill Grammar School and the University of Hull (LLB (Hons) 1975). Born 23 November 1952. Lives in London.

TURNER, James M QC
Quadrant Chambers, London
020 7583 4444
james.turner@quadrantchambers.com
Featured in Shipping (London)
Practice Areas: Highly experienced advocate across wide range of shipping (wet and dry), shipbuilding, commercial and related private international law, with team-leading experience stretching back more than 10 years. Fluent in German and Dutch. For detailed CV, see Quadrant Chambers website.
Professional Memberships: COMBAR; TECBAR; LCLCBA; British-German Jurists; Chartered Institute of Linguists.
Career: At Quadrant Chambers (formerly 4 Essex and before that 2 Essex Court) throughout career. BA (Dunelm), LLM (Tuebingen). Call 1990. CEDR accredited mediator 2001. Silk 2013.
Publications: Derrington & Turner on Admiralty Matters, OUP, 2007. Second edition 2016.
Personal: Married, four children.

TURNER, Justin QC
Three New Square, London
020 7405 1111
clerks@3newsquare.co.uk
Featured in Intellectual Property (London)
Practice Areas: Justin Turner's practice extends to all areas of IP and to commercial disputers of a technical character. In addition to appearing in the UK courts he also represents clients at the EPO and the CJEU. He has been involved in a number of leading patent cases particularly within the fields of pharmacology and biotechnology.

TURTON, Philip
Ropewalk Chambers, Nottingham
0115 947 2581
philipturton@ropewalk.co.uk
Featured in Personal Injury (Midlands)
Practice Areas: He has over 25 years' experience of every kind of personal injury case, specialising, increasingly, in high value and Group actions, spinal injuries, clinical negligence and industrial disease. He is also highly experienced in defending and mitigating Health and Safety prosecutions. He has been cited as a Leader at the Bar in the field of Personal Injury work for over 10 years.
Professional Memberships: PIBA; PNBA; HSLA; Nottinghamshire Medico-Legal Society (Committee member).
Career: Called 1989; LLB (Hons), University College of Wales, Aberystwyth. Tenant at Ropewalk Chambers since 1990. He was a Bar Standards Board appointed External Moderator for the Bar Professional Training Course (Civil Litigation) from 2010 – 2012 and was appointed to reformulate the syllabus and Curriculum for the Civil Litigation module on the BPTC course in 2014. He has delivered annual lectures on Drafting to the Bar Professional Training Course at Nottingham Trent University and the Kaplan Law School in London and was a Guest Lecturer to the University of Darwin, Northern Territories, Australia, on the subject of Tort law. A voluntary adviser at the Hyson Green Law Centre since 1990. Barrister of the Year – Nottinghamshire Law Society 2015.

TWIGGER, Andrew M QC
Maitland Chambers, London
atwigger@maitlandchambers.com
Featured in Chancery (London), Banking & Finance (London), Commercial Dispute Resolution (London)
Practice Areas: Andrew Twigger QC has extensive experience of High Court litigation and regularly appears in both the Chancery Division and the Commercial Court. He also appears in the Court of Appeal and the Supreme Court. In addition, Andrew acts in commercial arbitrations and mediations, and has been involved in offshore litigation including in the Bahamas, the Cayman Islands, the BVI, Bermuda and Hong Kong. Andrew's practice encompasses commercial disputes of all kinds, including claims involving contracts, restitution, banking and financial services, shareholder disputes, breaches of directors' duties, insolvency, civil fraud and trusts.
Professional Memberships: Chancery Bar Association; Combar
Career: Called 1994; QC 2011; Member of Chancery Bar Association Committee and the Bar Council Legal Services Committee since 2013
Personal: Educated at Aylesbury Grammar School and St. John's College, Oxford.

TYLER, William QC
The 36 Group, London
020 7421 8000
wtyler@36family.co.uk
Featured in Family/Matrimonial (London)
Practice Areas: William is a specialist children law Silk, appearing in the most serious, complicated or sensitive private and public law cases. In private law his practice comprises complex, sensitive or serious cases and very often those involving difficult international issues (habitual residence, abduction, relocation etc.) or questions relating to parenthood and child arrangements after surrogacy, gamete donation or the breakdown of same-sex relationships. His extensive public law Children Act practice sees him litigating lengthy and high-profile cases around the country, principally in the High Court. He has particular expertise in cases involving life-threatening injury and death, sexual abuse, radicalisation and international or jurisdictional issues. He has very considerable experience of appellate advocacy, with many reported cases in the Court of Appeal and the Supreme Court.
Professional Memberships: Family Law Bar Association (FLBA) Family Procedure Rule Committee Member of the Chartered Institute of Arbitrators (MCIArb) Association of Lawyers for Children (ALC) Resolution British Association for Adoption and Fostering (BAAF)
Career: Call: 1996. Recorder: 2012. Silk: 2014. Family Arbitrator: 2016. Deputy High Court Judge: 2016.
Personal: Educated at Worcester College, Oxford University. William is married with three children.

TYZACK, William
Queen Elizabeth Building QEB, London
020 7797 7837
w.tyzack@qebc.co.uk
Featured in Family/Matrimonial (London)
Practice Areas: All areas of family law (finance and children), and welfare and financial issues relating to vulnerable adults in the Court of Protection. Particularly EU

and international cases – child abduction, relocation, international maintenance issues and private international law. Has advised on English/EU law in European jurisdictions and elsewhere, and has provided expert evidence to the Supreme Court of New York, USA, and appeared in court in Portugal as an expert witness. Recent cases: C v B [2014] EWHC 2069 (abduction); EY v RZ [2013] EWHC 4403 (abduction); Re B [2012] EWCA Civ 1082 (EU Maintenance Regulation); AR v RN (Scotland) [2015] UKSC 35; AB v JJB (EU Maintenance Regulation) [2015] 2 FLR 1143.
Professional Memberships: FLBA, Western Circuit, Reunite (child abduction) Legal Working Group.
Career: Pupillage at QEB 2007-8; Oxford University (First Class hons), City University and BPP. Middle Temple (Diplock scholarship, Harmsworth exhibition).
Publications: Articles on EU law in International Family Law Journal: [2012] IFL 277 and [2015] IFL 258; joint editor with Thorpe LJ of the collected papers of the 2011 Dartington Interdisciplinary Conference

UNDERWOOD, Dean
Cornerstone Barristers, London
020 7421 1835
deanu@cornerstonebarristers.com
Featured in Social Housing (London)
Practice Areas: Public and administrative law; Local government; Social housing; Property;
Professional Memberships: Administrative Law Bar Association; Chartered Institute of Housing; Property Bar Association; Social Housing Law Association
Career: Dean specialises in administrative, housing, property and public law. He is the current Chair of the Social Housing Law Association and has particular expertise in housing and related administrative law, having built his practice representing local authorities and housing providers in the county court, High Court and Court of Appeal. His practice now covers: community care; council tax; the Court of Protection; homelessness; housing allocation, licensing, management and regulation; human rights; service charges; and welfare benefits. Dean appeared in the Supreme Court in 2014 in Sims v Dacorum Borough Council [2014] UKSC. His work received judicial commendation in both R (George) v Hammersmith & Fulham LBC [2012] EWHC 2369 (Admin); [2012] All ER (D) 124 (Apr) and Howard v Stanton [2011] EWCA Civ 1481; [2012] All ER (D) 201 (May) and he has acted in the following notable cases: Southern Housing Group v Ahern [2016] EWCA Civ (tbc); Sims v Dacorum Borough Council [2013] EWCA Civ 12; [2013] HLR 14; Fernandes v Kenny [2012] EWCA Civ 910; [2012] All ER (D) 242 (Oct); Oxford City Council v Basey [2012] EWCA Civ 115; [2012] 3 All ER 71 Brough v Law and CMEC [2011] EWCA Civ 1932; [2012] 1 WLR 1021.

UNSWORTH, Ian QC
7 Harrington St Chambers, Liverpool
0151 2420707
clerks@7hs.co.uk
Featured in Crime (Northern), Sports Law (The Regions)
Practice Areas: Ian Unsworth QC has appeared in hundreds of criminal cases including cases involving Murder, International Drugs Conspiracies, Gangland Warfare, Serious Fraud, Corruption and all categories of Heavy Crime. His work in Complex Fraud cases has enabled him to gain considerable experience of Asset Tracing, Banking, Computer Law, Confiscation, and Money Laundering, among others. He provides specialist advice and representation to a wide range of clients. Ian Unsworth QC also advises and represents international athletes, sporting organisations, sports management companies, professional footballers, rugby league players and other elite sporting individuals. His knowledge of medical matters has led to an interest in cases involving allegations of anti – doping and concussion. He has appeared before disciplinary and regulatory tribunals as well as the Court of Arbitration for Sport in Lausanne, Switzerland.
Professional Memberships: He is a Judicial Officer for World Rugby and Six Nations. Also sits as an RFU Disciplinary Chairman and Single Judicial Officer. He is a Public (Direct) Access Qualified Barrister.
Career: Prior to becoming a barrister, Ian Unsworth QC graduated in Business Law and worked in a management role in private industry.

URELL, Kate
Gough Square Chambers, London
020 7353 0924
kate.urell@goughsq.co.uk
Featured in Consumer Law (London)
Practice Areas: Consumer law, including consumer credit and financial services, consumer contracts, trading and food law.
Professional Memberships: Food Law Group.
Career: Called in 2002. Kate specialises in regulatory matters. In particular, she acts for financial institutions in contentious and non-contentious matters, including drafting and securitisations. She is an experienced advocate, having represented most of the major banks and finance houses in matters relating to compliance with financial services and consumer credit legislation, including enforceability, mis-selling, unfair terms, harassment and credit referencing errors. Kate has advised on the implementation of the Consumer Credit Directive, the Consumer Rights Directive and the Green Deal. Her non-credit practice includes advising on trading laws, product compliance, advertising issues and enforcement action under the Enterprise Act. Kate has also been instructed by a number of multinational organisations in the area of food labelling. Recent reported cases: Brandon v American Express Services Europe Ltd [2011] EWCA Civ 1187 (consumer credit default notices); Grace v Black Horse Ltd [2014] EWCA Civ 1413 (repossession of consumer credit protected goods, limitation and credit referencing errors); Burrell and others v Helical (Bramshott Place) Limited [2015] EWHC 3727 (Ch) (whether an agreement provided for "credit" within the meaning of the Consumer Credit Act 1974).
Publications: Atkins Court Forms on Consumer Protection, Advertising Law and Regulation, 2nd edn, ed. Bloomsbury Professional.
Personal: Languages: French. Education: LLB (Europe) Hons with French; LLM (Cantab). Middle Temple (Harmsworth Scholar).

VALENTIN, Ben QC
Fountain Court Chambers, London
020 7842 3804
bv@fountaincourt.co.uk
Featured in International Arbitration (London), Banking & Finance (London), Commercial Dispute Resolution (London), Fraud (London)
Practice Areas: Ben's practice covers all aspects of commercial dispute resolution, with an emphasis on cases concerning banking and finance, corporate transactions, professional negligence, international trade, and civil fraud and insolvency. Ben was instructed as lead Counsel in many of his cases before taking Silk and has extensive experience as both a trial and appellate advocate. He regularly appears before the higher English courts, and is an acknowledged specialist in arbitration, both domestic and international. In common with many at Fountain Court, much of Ben's practice is international in nature. In addition to his English practice, he also has significant experience as an advocate in complex offshore litigation (notably in the British Virgin Islands and the Cayman Islands). Ben was appointed Queen's Counsel in February 2016.
Professional Memberships: Commercial Bar Association, Chancery Bar Association, New York State Bar Association, LCIA, CEDR Accredited Mediator.
Career: England and Wales (Call 1995; QC 2016); New York (1998); British Virgin Islands (2007).
Personal: Educated at Bedford School; Worcester College, Oxford (BA, 1992; BCL, 1993); Cornell (LLM, 1994).

VALLAT, Richard
Pump Court Tax Chambers, London
020 7414 8080
clerks@pumptax.com
Featured in Tax (London)
Practice Areas: Practises in all areas of revenue law,including advice and planning in the following areas: personal tax, corporate taxes, VAT and other indirect taxes, SDLT and tax-related litigation including professional negligence; he also advises on a range of matters both in contemplation of and seeking to avoid litigation, including contractual disputes with a tax element. Recent cases include UBS and DB Group Services (Supreme Court), Coulter Trust (Court of Appeal), Donaldson (Court of Appeal), Greene King (Court of Appeal), Aspect Capital (Upper Tribunal), Perrin & Ardmore Construction (Upper Tribunal) and Henderson Investments (First-tier Tribunal).
Professional Memberships: Revenue Bar Association; London Common Law and Commercial Bar Association; Chancery Bar Association; Stamp Taxes Practitioners Group; Moderator of the Trusts Discussion Forum; Society of Trust & Estates Practicioners.
Career: Called 1997, Gray's Inn. Appointed to the Attorney General's A Panel (June 2016).

VARA, Beverley
Maitland Chambers, London
020 7406 1200
bvara@maitlandchambers.com
Featured in Mediators (All Circuits)
Practice Areas: Experienced mediator who has successfully mediated a wide range of commercial disputes involving both domestic and international parties from a variety of industry sectors. Experienced in mediating disputes in: banking and finance; commercial contract; construction and engineering; insolvency; planning; PFI/PPP; professional negligence, Beverley has a particular experience in property disputes (both commercial and residential). Strong career background in real estate disputes.
Professional Memberships: Civil Mediation Council; CEDR Accreditation 2012; CEDR Panel member 2013; Property Litigation Association
Career: BSc Maths; London (First); MPhil, Cambs. Former solicitor (Admitted 1994); Litigation partner at Allen & Overy LLP (2003-2013), Called to the bar 2013.

VASSALL-ADAMS, Guy QC
Matrix Chambers, London
020 7404 1313
guyvassall-adams@matrixlaw.co.uk
Featured in Defamation/Privacy (London)
Practice Areas: Guy has a broad media law and human rights practice including privacy, data protection, defamation, reporting restrictions and freedom of information. Guy has litigated some of the most complex group litigation of recent years including the Mobile Telephone Voicemail Interception Liitigation ("phone hacking"), the Voicemail Interception Compensation Scheme (NGN's private arbitration for phone hacking cases) and the Construction Industry Vetting Information Group Litigation ("blacklisting"). Guy has a particular expertise in internet publications and acted in recent, high-profile cases for internet intermediaries (Hegglin v Google, Mosley v Google). In addition to his media law practice, Guy also undertakes human rights claims, including international class actions and public law cases with a human rights element (Nicklinson v Ministry of Justice).
Professional Memberships: ALBA
Career: Guy was a barrister at Doughty Street Chambers between 2000 and 2014, when he joined Matrix. Before coming to the Bar he was a television journalist at London Weekend Television, a researcher at the head office of Oxfam GB and a humanitarian affairs officer for the United Nations.
Personal: Guy lives in London with his wife and two children

VAUGHAN JONES, Sarah QC
2TG – 2 Temple Gardens, London
020 7822 1200
svaughanjones@2tg.co.uk
Featured in Clinical Negligence (London)
Practice Areas: Clinical negligence, conducting civil proceedings for claimants and defendants. Recent High Court cases include A v University Hospitals of Morecambe Bay NHS Trust [2015] EWHC 366 QB: assessment of damages in case of cerebral palsy of maximum severity; Reeve v Heart of England NHS Trust [24.05.2011]: cerebral palsy claim. Registrar's attendance delayed because he was busy in theatre with another patient. Allegations of failure properly to conduct fetal monitoring and to call consultant in anticipation; Connah v Plymouth Hospitals NHS Trust, HM Coroner for Greater Manchester, HM Coroner for Plymouth + SW Devon and HM Coroner for County of Cornwall [2010] EWHC 1727 (Admin): represented Plymouth Hospitals NHS Trust in successfully resisting the claimant's application to the Divisional Court under s.13 Coroners Act 1988 to compel the holding of an inquest into the death of his late wife in 1998 follow-

ing hospital treatment for a malignant brain tumour; Mungai v Chelsea & Westminster Hospital NHS Trust [2005/6]: (with Michael de Navarro QC: claimant discharged from A&E: later found to have rare internal perforation); Smithers v Taunton & Somerset NHS Trust [2004] EWHC 1179: (with Stephen Miller QC: obstetric emergency where clinicians inextricably occupied with alternative procedure); Rashid v Essex Rivers Healthcare NHS Trust [2004] EWHC 1338: (shoulder dystocia: no liability for Erbs palsy in posterior shoulder). Before taking Silk in 2008 Sarah presented cases regularly on behalf of the General Dental Council and the General Medical Council. Examples of cases before the Professional Conduct Committee include: Dr Crowe (dentist) 2008: alternative pain management techniques – allegations of failure to obtain informed consent and mis-management of patient with jaw pain and abdominal pain. Four-week GDC inquiry; Williams v GMC [2007] EWHC 2603 (Admin): with Roger Henderson QC, conducted GMC proceedings against doctor who performed post mortem on the children of Sally Clarke and subsequently secured dismissal of appeal from GMC proceedings. Sarah conducted several of the leading cases in the Privy Council on behalf of the GMC/GDC, in particular: Silver v General Medical Council [2003] UKPC 33 (test for serious professional misconduct); Crabbie v General Medical Council [2002] UKPC 45: (correct approach by Professional Conduct Committee to applications to refer to Health Committee); Dad v General Dental Council [2000] 1 WLR 1538: (principles applicable to conviction cases).
Professional Memberships: PNBA, PIBA.
Career: Called 1983. Recorder 2004. QC 2008.

VENTHAM, Charlotte
5 Essex Court, London
020 7410 2000
clerks@5essexcourt.co.uk
Featured in Police Law (All Circuits)
Practice Areas: Police Law; Inquests; Public and Administrative; Professional Discipline ; Personal Injury; Employment. Notable cases: R (XX) v Chief Constable of South Yorkshire & others [2014] EWHC 4106 (Admin) (retention of convictions and associated data) Daniel Morgan Independent Panel Review and related civil actions (representing the Commissioner of Police of the Metropolis); 7/7 London Bombings Inquest; R (Simpson & ors) v Chief Constable of Greater Manchester Police [2013] EWHC 1858 (Admin) (legitimate expectation in light of promotion freeze); R (Stratton) v Chief Constable of Thames Valley Police [2013] EWHC 1561 (Admin) (police cautions – informed consent); R (L) v Chief Constable of Cumbria Police [2013] EWHC 869 (Admin) (ECRC disclosure); R (Monger) v Chief Constable of Cumbria Police [2013] EWHC 455 (Admin) (Special Constables Regulations 1965); Nunes and Markland Inquest (fatal interception of armed robbery by police); R (Montgomery) v 1) Police Appeals Tribunal, 2) Commissioner of Police of the Metropolis [2012] EWHC 936 (Admin) (PAT grounds of appeal); R (Boyle) v Haverhill Pub Watch [2009] EWHC 2441 (Admin) (reviewability of a ban issued by a pub watch scheme).
Professional Memberships: ALBA; ELBA.

Career: Called to the Bar 2001; Appointed to Attorney General's B Panel of Counsel 2014.

VERDUYN, Anthony
St Philips Chambers, Birmingham
0121 246 7010
averduyn@st-philips.com
Featured in Real Estate Litigation (Midlands)
Practice Areas: Real estate litigation; landlord and tenant; land registration; professional negligence in property matters (including conveyancers, surveyors and brokers); and, social housing.
Professional Memberships: Property Bar Association; Midland Chancery and Commercial Bar Association.
Career: Called 1993 (Lincoln's Inn); Head of St Philips Chambers Property Team; Recorder (Civil, 2009; Private Family, 2013); Judge, First Tier Tribunal Property Chamber (formerly, Deputy Adjudicator to HM Land Registry (2008) and Lawyer Chairman of the Residential Property Tribunal (2006)); and ADR Group Accredited Mediator. Now also working from St Philips Chambers in London and Leeds. Recent cases of interest: Williams v Johnson [2016] All ER (D) 17 (Jan) – flooding and boundary between farms; R (Aryubi) v Birmingham CC [2015] EWHC 1972 (Admin) – power of the local authority to terminate market licences; Balevents v Sartori [2014] EWHC 1164 (Ch) – retrial following new evidence in adverse possession; and Unique Pub Properties Ltd v Broad Green Tavern Ltd [2012] 2 P&CR 17 – construction of lease.
Personal: Attended University of Durham, Collingwood College, BA (Hons) first, University of Oxford, Wolfson College, D.Phil., and City University. Contributor to Oxford Dictionary of National Biography and academic journals. Leisure interests include history, fine wine and foreign travel.

VINCENT, Patrick
12 King's Bench Walk, London
020 7583 0811
chambers@12kbw.co.uk
Featured in Personal Injury (London)
Practice Areas: Catastrophic personal injury, international insurance and personal injury claims, European insurance law, occupational disease and product liability claims, transport/aviation claims. He acts for Claimant and Defendants, and has particular expertise in scientific and technical issues. He also has expertise in international data protection legislation.
Professional Memberships: PIBA, PNBA. BIICL
Career: In practice at 12KBW since 1992. Numerous High Court and Court of Appeal Appearance. He has developed a reputation for outstanding advocacy and analytical skills.
Publications: Contributor to Butterworths Professional Negligence Service.
Personal: Family, music and aviation

VINDIS, Tara
9 Gough Square, London
020 7832 0500
tvindis@9goughsquare.co.uk
Featured in Family/Matrimonial (London)
Practice Areas: Specialist in child law, both public and private law. Care proceedings including those involving allegations of serious injuries to children (physical, sexual and emotional) and often involving complicated medical and causation issues. Cases involving radicalisation of children. Adoption and special guardianship. Frequently instructed by local authorities and children's guardians. Represents all parties. Disclosure applications where Public Interest Immunity arguments apply. Tara also practises in all aspects of personal injury and clinical negligence.
Professional Memberships: Family Law Bar Association, The Association of Lawyers for Children, Personal Injuries Bar Association, Association of Personal Injury Lawyers.
Career: Called 1996.
Publications: Co-author of "The Revised Public Law Outline" (2nd edition) published by 9 Gough Square. Co-author of MIB claims Practice and Procedure under the 1999 Agreement, (1st and 2nd editions). Contributing editor of Jordans APIL guide to Road Traffic Accident Liability (1st and 2nd editions).
Personal: Educated at the Perse School for Girls, Cambridge and Exeter University. Two young sons.

VINEALL, Nicholas QC
4 Pump Court, London
020 7842 5555
nvineall@4pumpcourt.com
Featured in Energy & Natural Resources (London), Financial Services (London), Shipping (London)
Practice Areas: Commercial and construction litigation and arbitration. Nick has a broadly based commercial practice. He has appeared in a wide range of arbitral tribunals (including LMAA, LCIA and ICC) and at all levels in the UK courts. In the energy, shipbuilding and offshore area Nick acts regularly for both yards and owners on new-build and conversion disputes, and has built a strong relationship with Chinese yards. Offshore work includes loss and expense and delay claims on exploration and drill contracts, and rig cancellation disputes. In financial services Nick is a recognised expert in FSMA regulation. For the FCA he has obtained injunctions to stop unauthorised investment schemes, ponzi frauds, insider dealing and collective investments schemes, and has acted in many recovery actions. He has appeared in RDC hearings and FSMA tribunals for and against the FCA, has acted for the FSCS, and recently acted for 1200 claimants in a class action against Capita. More general commercial work includes insurance (especially fire insurance and related claims), joint venture and SPA disputes, and the usual range of international debt collection.
Professional Memberships: COMBAR, LCLCBA, PNBA.
Career: Christ's College Cambridge (MA Natural Sciences), MA Pittsburgh University (Harkness Fellow), Diploma in Law City University, Called to the Bar 1988, Silk 2006. Bencher of Middle Temple.
Publications:

VINES, Anthony
Civitas Law, Cardiff
08450 713007 / 07973 540 302
anthony.vines@civitaslaw.com
Featured in Commercial Dispute Resolution (Wales & Chester), Employment (Wales & Chester)
Practice Areas: Commercial dispute resolution (contract performance and lending disputes, consumer law, consumer credit, licensing), employment (claimants, respondents and unions), regulatory crime and enforcement (health and safety, food, noise, trading standards, intellectual property, care standards, animal welfare, planning etc), fraud (civil and criminal) and public law. Mediation of all manner of disputes.
Professional Memberships: Employment Lawyers' Association, London Commercial and Common Law Bar Association, Administrative Law Bar Association, Health and Safety Lawyers' Association, Association of Regulatory and Disciplinary Lawyers.
Career: Called to the Bar (1993), Gough Square Chambers, London (1993-2002), CEDR mediator (1995), ADR Group mediator (2002), Attorney General's Panel of Prosecuting Advocates (2001-12), junior counsel to Welsh Assembly Government in employment law and criminal law (Panel A) (2010-), panel of junior counsel to Equality and Human Rights Commission (2010-), List of Specialist Advocates in Health & Safety and Environmental Law (List A) (2012-), Called to Bar of Northern Ireland (2014).
Personal: Married. 3 children. Lives Monmouth. Music.

WAGSTAFFE, Christopher QC
29 Bedford Row Chambers, London
020 7404 1044
cwagstaffe@29br.co.uk
Featured in Family/Matrimonial (London)
Practice Areas: Family Law especially matrimonial finance, with a particular emphasis on cases featuring trust and international elements. Has been involved in litigation in Gibraltar, Hong Kong, the Isle of Man and the Channel Islands. Cases include: Hamilton v Hamilton [2013] EWCA Civ 13; Masa v Holliday [2012] EWCA Civ 1268; Prest v Prest [2011] EWHC 2956 (Fam); Vaughan v Vaughan [2010] EWCA Civ 349; B v R [2010] 1 FLR 563; Hashem v Shayif & Anor [2008] EWHC 2380 (Fam); A v A & St. George Trustees Limited (No 2) [2007] EWHC 1810 (Fam); A v A & St George Trustees Limited [2007] 2 FLR 467, FD; Prazic v Prazic [2006] 2 FLR 1128, CA; Charalambous v Charalambous [2004] 2 FLR 1093, CA; Oxley v Hiscock [2004] 2 FLR 669, CA; C v C (Variation of Post-nuptial Settlement: Company Shares) [2003] 2 FLR 493, FD; Rampal v Rampal (No 2)[2001] 2 FLR 1179, CA; Rampal v Rampal [2000] 2 FLR 763, FD; Purba v Purba [2000] 1 FLR 444, CA.
Professional Memberships: Member of the IAML; FLBA International Committee with particular responsibility for trust issues. FLBA & South East Circuit.
Career: Called 1992, Inner Temple. Silk 2011.
Publications: Co-author, Cohabitation and Trusts of Land (Sweet & Maxwell, 2006, second edition 2009). Also published various articles in Family Law and Family Affairs. Has lectured both nationally and internationally on various aspects of matrimonial finance.
Personal:

WAITE, John-Paul
5 Essex Court, London
clerks@5essexcourt.co.uk
Featured in Immigration (London)
Practice Areas: Employment law, Administrative and Public law, Immigration, Police law, Inquests, Public Inquiries. In addition to the above areas, has a particular specialism in cases involving street works and closures, including disputes under the New Roads and Street Works Act, Traffic Regulation Act (Traffic Regulation Orders) and the Highways Act 1980. Significant cases include the

following: Employment Law: Home Office v Essop [2015] All ER (D) 219, Cordell v Foreign and Commonwealth Office [2012] ICR 280, Watts v High Quality Lifestyles [2006] IRLR 850 Public and Administrative Law: Akhalu v SSHD [2014] EWHC 1505, MS Palestinian Territories v SSHD [2010] UKSC 25, Rahman and Others v SSHD [2011] All ER (D) 155. Public Inquiries and Inquests: Instructed in the Billy Wright Inquiry, Rosemary Nelson Inquiry and Robert Hamill Inquiry. Regularly act for the police and public bodies in in Inquests.
Career: Called to the Bar in 1995. Appointed to the Attorney General's "A" panel of counsel in 2014
Publications: Founding (and current) author of the Employment Tribunals Handbook – first published in October 2002 (fourth edition published by Bloomsbury Professional August 2014).

WAKERLEY, Paul
QEB Hollis Whiteman, London
020 7933 8855
paul.wakerley@aebhw.co.uk
Featured in Crime (London)
Practice Areas: Paul has a strong reputation for serious and complex crime. In his defence practice he is instructed in private and publicly funded cases across the full spectrum of criminal work, including allegations of murder, drugs and firearms offences, regularly appearing as a leading junior in cases where others are represented by silks. Paul is also instructed by those seeking advice on appeal against earlier convictions/ sentences where the original representation was elsewhere, and has been successful in finding positive grounds for appeal. Most recently succeeding before the Lord Chief Justice in a mandatory minimum firearms sentence appeal. Specialist casework units of the CPS instruct Paul where he is graded at Level 4. He leads and is led in cases of homicide, serious violence, corruption within public office and advance fee fraud cases. Paul has been instructed by both high net worth individuals and companies seeking pre-charge advice. Paul also has a growing reputation within regulatory and professional disciplinary work, where he both presents and defends. He regularly defends police officers before the Criminal Courts and before internal disciplinary proceedings.
Professional Memberships: Gray's Inn; Association of Regulatory & Disciplinary Lawyers; Criminal Bar Association; Health and Safety Lawyers' Association; Midland Circuit; South Eastern Circuit; registered with the Bar Council – Public Access Directory; Public Access Bar Association

WALDEN-SMITH, David
29 Bedford Row Chambers, London
020 7404 1044
clerks@29br.co.uk
Featured in Family/Matrimonial (South Eastern)
Practice Areas: David specialises in financial cases involving substantial assets, complex company valuations and those with trust and tax issues. He is regarded as taking an eminently sensible, reasonable but, where necessary, forceful approach to financial remedy disputes. Having represented the successful claimant in Oxley v Hiscock, he also acts for cohabitants in property disputes as well as parents in Schedule 1 financial claims and in other private law Children Act disputes. Having honed his advocacy skills for several years at the Criminal Bar, he is particularly regarded for his ability to uncover the truth through cross-examination. David also acts as an Arbitrator through the IFLA scheme. Notable cases include: Oxley v Hiscock [2004] 2 FLR 669; Re B [2008] 2 FLR 2060; Re L-W [2011] 1 FLR 1095.
Professional Memberships: Family Law Bar Association. Institute of Family Law Arbitrators. Resolution
Career: Called 1985. Family Arbitrator with the Chartered Institute of Arbitrators,
Personal: David is married with two teenage children. His leisure pursuits include photography and sailing.

WALKER, Adam
7BR, London
020 7242 3555
awalker@7br.co.uk
Featured in Personal Injury (London), Clinical Negligence (London)
Practice Areas: Clinical negligence, personal injury, inquests, commercial and sports law.
Professional Memberships: AvMA, APIL, PIBA, LCCBA, Guild of Professional Teachers of Dance
Career: Adam has an established civil practice with a particular emphasis on clinical negligence, personal injury work and inquests. His clinical negligence practice includes cases ranging from the delayed diagnosis of disease to those involving iatrogenic injury and injury during child birth. He is frequently involved in cases of maximum severity and brain injury and in cases arising from fatal accidents. He appears at coroners' inquests in respect of clinical and other negligence leading to death, which may involve issues arising from Article 2 ECHR and require a jury. Adam also has particular experience of a wide variety of military claims, including disputes in respect of the provision of appropriate equipment, combat immunity and over the assessment of quantum arising out of the loss of a service career. He is also instructed frequently in cases involving issues of limitation, date of knowledge and section 33 of the Limitation Act 1980. Adam also undertakes a range of sports law and other commercial work, including the sale and supply of goods, insolvency and consumer credit.

WALKER, Andrew QC
Maitland Chambers, London
020 7406 1200
awalker@maitlandchambers.com
Featured in Real Estate Litigation (London)
Practice Areas: Litigation, arbitration, ADR and expert advice, particularly in the following areas of practice: property and property-related disputes of all kinds (including contractual and development disputes, leases, rights over land, mortgages, disputed property disposals, private and public rights in the countryside, and leasehold enfranchisement claims); professional negligence and other breaches of duty by professionals in the fields of property, finance, investment, commerce, tax, and valuations; company law (including director/shareholder/investor/business sales/joint venture disputes); securities, investment and financial services disputes; other commercial/equity disputes (including claims against trustees and other fiduciaries, commercial contract claims, civil fraud and asset tracing); valuation disputes and challenges; insolvency; partnerships.
Professional Memberships: Chancery Bar Association, Professional Negligence Bar Association, Property Bar Association, Commercial Bar Association, Financial Services Lawyers Association.
Career: Called Lincoln's Inn (1991); QC (2011). Vice-Chairman of the Bar, 2017. Elected member of the Bar Council, 2005-2016 (Chairman, Ethics Committee, 2013-2016; Vice-Chairman, Law Reform Committee, 2012-2016; Vice-Chairman, Access to the Bar Committee, 2012-2013). Winner of the Bar Pro Bono Award, 2009.
Personal: Haberdashers' Aske's School, Elstree; Trinity College, Cambridge (MA).

WALKER, Christopher
Old Square Chambers, Bristol
0117 930 5100
walker@oldsquarechambers.co.uk
Featured in Personal Injury (London), Personal Injury (Western)
Practice Areas: Christopher is a personal injury specialist. Instructed on behalf of both Claimants and Defendants, Christopher has considerable experience in litigating the established categories of employer's liability claims, road traffic accident and public liability claims. His practice encompasses associated clinical and professional negligence claims, health and safety prosecutions, coroner's inquests, and litigation with a focus on human rights. He regularly represents clients at mediation and joint settlement meetings. Recently completed litigation has included: Re Adam Withers, deceased (Art 2 inquest – highly critical narrative verdict); Re ABC (brain injury case – dispute as to capacity – significant settlement sum approved by Court); out of court settlement for a Claimant suffering life-changing pelvic injuries consequent to a paraglider crash. Continuing litigation includes: a defence to a potentially high value claim, based on an assertion of fundamental dishonesty; amputation claims on behalf of both Claimants and Defendant; multi million pound claims on behalf of brain injured Claimants.
Professional Memberships: PIBA
Career: MA, Law (Cambridge); Licence Speciale en Droit Europeen (Universite Libre de Bruxelles); Harmsworth Scholar, Middle Temple

WALKER, Elizabeth
St Philips Chambers, Birmingham
0121 246 1600
ewalker@st-philips.com
Featured in Family/Matrimonial (Midlands)
Practice Areas: Elizabeth specialises in public law children matters, in particular complex proceedings concerning serious non-accidental injury and death, sexual abuse and fabricated illness. She acts for local authorities against leading counsel on a regular basis, as well as representing parents and guardians. She has developed a particular expertise in the medical issues relating to alleged "shaking" injuries. Elizabeth often represents parents who suffer from significant learning or communication difficulties. She also has significant experience of contentious private law litigation. Reported decisions: Re E (Wardship Order: Child in Voluntary Accommodation) [2012] EWCA Civ 1773; Coventry City Council v SB, SA, SS, RY, KK [2012] EWHC 4014 (Fam); Re N (Death of a Child in the DRC: Order for Return: Contempt) [2014] EWHC 337 (Fam); LB Hounslow v M and F [2015] EWFC B214.
Professional Memberships: Family Law Bar Association; British Association of Adoption and Fostering.
Career: Called to the Bar in October 1994. Appointed as Recorder on the Midland Circuit in June 2012.
Personal: Attended Durham University. Leisure interests include keeping fit, a thriving book group and travel.

WALKER, Ronald QC
12 King's Bench Walk, London
020 7583 0811
walker@12kbw.co.uk
Featured in Personal Injury (London)
Practice Areas: Professional negligence; insurance; personal injury; building and engineering contracts; HSWA prosecutions; environmental law. Recent cases include: Clay v TUI (UK) Ltd [2016], Coke Workers Litigation (2016); Risk v Rose Bruford College (2014); Jones v Department of Energy & Climate Change (the Phurnacite litigation) [2012]; Shaw v Fuller & Kingsley School [2012]; United Marine Aggregates Ltd v GM Welding Ltd [2012]; Divia v Toyo Tire Co [2011]; Dalling v RJ Heale Ltd [2011]; Greene Wood & McLean v Templeton Insurance Ltd [2010]; Shulman v Simon Ltd [2010].
Professional Memberships: PNBA. LCLCBA, TECBAR, PIBA.
Career: Called 1962, Silk 1983, Deputy High Court Judge 1993. Mental Health Tribunal Judge 1999-2012. Acts as arbitrator and is an accredited mediator and adjudicator. Listed as a leading silk (Personal Injury) in Legal 500 and Chambers Directory.
Publications: Walker & Walker: The English Legal System; Butterworths Professional Negligence Service; Butterworths Personal Injury Litigation Service: Asbestos Disease Claims.

WALKER, Steven QC
Atkin Chambers, London
020 7404 0102
sjwalker@atkinchambers.com
Featured in Construction (London), Energy & Natural Resources (London)
Practice Areas: Steven specialises in disputes arising in connection with construction and engineering projects both in the UK and internationally. His practice involves a diverse range of subject matter including buildings, offshore structures, ships and IT systems. Recent cases include: Goldswain v Beltec [2015] BLR 300, Seele Middle East v Drake & Scull International (2014) CILL 3147, Doosan Babcock v Commercializadora De Equipos Y Materiales Mabe [2014] BLR 33, SABIC UK Petrochemicals v Punj Lloyd [2014] BLR 43, Parkwood Leisure v Laing O'Rourke [2013] BLR 589 and Mi Space Construction v Lend Lease [2013] BLR 600.
Professional Memberships: TECBAR, COMBAR.
Career: Called to the Bar of England and Wales 1993. Silk 2012.
Publications: Formerly joint editor of 'Building Law Reports' and Sweet and Maxwell's 'Technology and Construction Law Reports.'

WALMISLEY, Lisa
Kings Chambers, Manchester
0345 034 3444
clerks@kingschambers.com
Featured in Restructuring/Insolvency (Northern)
Practice Areas: Asset recovery (for and against office-holders, banks, asset-based

lenders and other institutions); banking (guarantees and mortgages); commercial litigation (including commercial fraud and injunctions); company (directors' duties, shareholder disputes and remedies); insolvency (personal and corporate, including directors disqualification and defending public interest winding-up), partnership.
Professional Memberships: Chancery Bar Association, Northern Chancery Bar Association, Northern Circuit Commercial Bar Association (committee member).
Career: Called by Middle Temple 2000.

WALSH, David
Quadrant Chambers, London
020 7583 4444
david.walsh@quadrantchambers.com
Featured in Shipping (London)
Practice Areas: David has a broad commercial practice specialising in insurance and reinsurance, dry shipping, commodities, energy and aviation disputes. He is a popular choice both as sole counsel and as a junior to leaders in heavyweight cases. He is known for his commitment to his clients and cases, his user-friendly style, his calm and composed manner, and his tenacious advocacy. He enjoys finding solutions for his clients to difficult legal problems and is clear, commercial and pragmatic in his advice. David has particular experience of heavy and technically complex cases, including a number of disputes involving foreign systems of law. He frequently advises and represents clients at short notice and on an urgent basis, in particular in applications for interim relief in the Commercial Court (freezing orders and anti-suit injunctions).
Professional Memberships: COMBAR, British Insurance Law Association, Association of Average Adjusters (subscriber), London Common Law and Commercial Bar Association, LCIA Young International Arbitration Group, LSLC YMP.

WALSH, Michael
Tanfield Chambers, London
020 7421 5300
michaelwalsh@tanfieldchambers.co.uk
Featured in Real Estate Litigation (London)
Practice Areas: Michael's practice encompasses all aspects of the law of property and associated chancery work, with a particular emphasis on development, mortgages and landlord & tenant work. He has significant experience of acting for developers of land in relation to restrictive covenants, easements, land registration, securities and matters relating to mixed-use developments. His mortgage work involves acting for some of the UK's largest lenders in claims involving undue influence, mortgage fraud, priority of interests and subrogation. Michael also specialises in cases involving the law of property in the agricultural sector. He has particular experience of options, overage, partnerships, farm business tenancies, agricultural holdings and securities over agricultural businesses.
Professional Memberships: Property Bar Association (Committee Member); Chancery Bar Association.
Career: Junior Counsel to the Crown (Attorney General's B Panel); Visiting Lecturer in the Law of Property, King's College London.
Publications: Co-editor of Megarry's Manual of the Law of Real Property (9th Ed.), Sweet & Maxwell. Author of the forthcoming first edition of The Law of Mortgages of Real Property (Wildy, Simmonds & Hill).

WALSH, Stephen QC
3 Raymond Buildings Barristers, London
020 7400 6400
stephen.walsh@3rblaw.com
Featured in Health & Safety (London), Licensing (London)
Practice Areas: A specialist in regulatory, coronial and licensing law with broad experience in criminal enforcement. Regulatory practice is focused on health and safety (primarily fatal accidents in the workplace, fire safety, and the safety of sports stadia). Prosecuting and defending in a broad range of cases and representing interested parties at inquests. Advising regulatory authorities generally on matters of enforcement; advising corporate and individual clients on regulatory compliance. Licensing expertise encompasses all forms of licensable activities including liquor and entertainment, late night refreshment, sports venues, gambling (terrestrial and internet), television, firearms, street trading and charities. Providing advice to licensing authorities and all sectors of the leisure industry. Appearing on behalf of applicants, responsible authorities and interested parties before local authorities and courts throughout England and Wales including applications for judicial review. For more information go to www.3rblaw.com.
Career: Called to the Bar 1983. QC 2009.

WARD, Alexandra
9-12 Bell Yard, London
020 7400 1800
a.ward@912by.com
Featured in Crime (London), Financial Crime (London)
Practice Areas: Recognised as a leading barrister in financial crime, Alexandra has 16 years' experience of criminal litigation from pre-charge to the Privy Council. Her areas of expertise include advising companies and individuals in respect of insider dealing, bribery and tax fraud alongside judicial review, confiscation and money-laundering obligations. Alexandra has considerable experience of prosecuting and defending serious cases which attract international media attention and the associated public scrutiny. In addition to her casework Alexandra is a published legal author; long-standing member of the Bar Council's Law Reform Committee and a pupil supervisor & advocacy trainer. Alexandra is a hardworking, collaborative legal expert, equally at home working on her own or as part of a team. Alexandra is instructed as junior alone by the CPS and SFO and acted as junior counsel for the Financial Conduct Authority in its largest and most complex insder dealing prosecution (Operation Tabernula).
Professional Memberships: 2015: Chair – Police Misconduct Panel
Career: Called 2000: Chambers of Mukul Chawla QC – 9-12 Bell Yard, London Secondments: April – Dec 2009: Irwin Mitchell LLP (Regulatory & Business Crime) June – Dec 2006: FSA Wholesale-Enforcement May – Aug 2005: HM Revenue & Customs Prosecution Office
Publications: Co-Editor: Lloyds Law Reports, Financial Crime Editor: Encyclopaedia of Road Traffic Law & Practice Contributory Author: Rook & Ward on Sexual Offences

WARD, Andrew
Exchange Chambers, Manchester
0161 833 2722
ward@exchangechambers.co.uk
Featured in Personal Injury (Northern)
Practice Areas: Andrew is a personal injury specialist. He is regularly instructed in claims with a value of between £50,000 and £2,000,000. He has a balanced practice, acting for claimants and defendants. He is a member of the Attorney General's Regional Panel of Junior Counsel to the Crown. Andrew is experienced in acting as sole counsel handling high-value multi-track claims involving serious orthopaedic, brachial plexus, chronic pain, psychiatric and brain injuries; in acting as junior counsel in catastrophic injury and amputee claims with a value of up to £10,000,000; in acting in a range of employers' liability, public liability and fatal accident claims; and in advising government departments in many high-value non-freezing cold injury (NFCI) claims, stress at work claims, and inquests. Andrew also advises upon insurance policy coverage issues in claims involving the MIB; Road Traffic Act 1988 insurers; and the Third Parties (Rights Against Insurers) Acts 1930 and 2010.
Professional Memberships: Personal Injuries Bar Association
Career: Andrew practises at Exchange Chambers in Manchester. He is a door tenant at 12 King's Bench Walk in London.
Personal: Andrew read Law at Jesus College, Oxford (B.A., B.C.L.). He lives with his wife in Yorkshire and in London.

WARD, Henry
8 New Square, London
020 7405 4321
henry.ward@8newsquare.co.uk
Featured in Intellectual Property (London)
Practice Areas: Barrister specialising in intellectual property law. Notable recent cases include: Napp v Sandoz (patent-pharmaceuticals); Unwired Planet v Google & Samsung (Trial E) (patent-telecoms); Good Technology v MobileIron (patent-telecoms); (Flynn v DrugsRus (trade mark parallel imports-pharmaceuticals); Focus v Novartis (patent-pharmaceuticals); CGTL v Velocys (patent-Fischer Tropsch processing); Nampak v Alpla(patent-packaging); Rovi v Virgin (patent-set-top boxes); Doosan v Babcock (trade mark-nuclear power)⊠ Virgin v Premium etc(HC, CA and SC)(patent-aircraft seating)⊠ ACS v GBS (confidential information-concrete formulations)⊠ Novartis v Mylan (patent- pharmaceuticals)⊠ Sudarshan v Clariant (patent-crystal form of pigments)⊠ Sealed Air v Sharpak (design right-fruit punnets)⊠ Westwood v Knight (trade mark, passing off and copyright-fashion designs)⊠ MMI v CellXion (patent-mobile phone interception)⊠ KCI v Smith & Nephew (patent-medical devices)⊠ Research in Motion v Vista (patent- telecoms)⊠ Queensland v Siemens (patent- MRI)⊠ and Wobben v Vestas (patent- wind turbines).
Personal: Educated at Ellesmere College, and Emmanuel College, Cambridge 1998, Master of Engineering. Bachelor of Arts (Honours) Engineering.

WARD, Tim QC
Monckton Chambers, London
020 7405 7211
tward@monckton.com
Featured in Administrative & Public Law (London), Competition/European Law (London), Telecommunications (London)
Practice Areas: competition, public, EU and telecommunications. Tim has particular expertise in commercial regulation, has acted in numerous competition damages claims and in over 50 cases before the CJEU and EFTA Courts. Cases include: Tesco v VISA (credit card fees); R(Nouazli) Supreme Court: (free movement); Icesave, (collapse of Icelandic banks); Iiyama (territorial scope of competition law); Akzo Nobel v Competition Commission (merger control jurisdiction); Drax Power v Secretary of State (renewable energy); R(Shoesmith) v Ofsted: (Baby P and Children's Services); BT v OFCOM, TalkTalk and Sky: wholesale broadband.
Career: Called 1994; Prior to taking silk, was a member of the Attorney General's A Panel; Silk 2011; The Lawyer "Barrister of the Year' 2013. Chairman of the Bar European Group 2013-15. Joint Head of Chambers, Monckton Chambers 2016 -present.
Publications: Competition Litigation in the UK (with Kassie Smith, Sweet & Maxwell 2005), Judicial Review and the Human Rights Act (2000) and The Strasbourg Case Law – Leading Cases from the European Human Rights Reports (2001). Editor in Chief of the Human Rights Law Reports – UK Cases (Sweet & Maxwell) and Contributor to Bellamy & Child, The European Community Law of Competition.
Personal: BA, MA

WARE, Christopher
2 Hare Court, London
020 7353 5324
ChristopherWare@2harecourt.com
Featured in Crime (London)
Practice Areas: Christopher Ware principally defends in serious and complex fraud; corporate, regulatory and business crime; and high-profile and serious crime. He has acted in cases involving, for example, allegations of corruption, money laundering, insider dealing, 'boiler room' fraud, perjury, perverting the course of justice, and trading standards offences. Recent Cases and Work Highlights include, Ben O'Driscoll (for deputy Editor of The Sun in Operation Elveden, allegation of corruption by journalists. One of the largest and costliest police investigations ever); Greig Box-Turnbull (Operation Elveden, represented a reporter at the Daily Mirror); Ben Ashford (Operation Tuleta, acted for a reporter at The Sun. Allegation of computer hacking); Operation Yewtree (represented well-known individual in High Court proceedings. High-profile, long-running investigation into historical abuse); Operation Cotton (multi-million pound land banking fraud, FCA prosecution); Operation Citrus (represented company director in multi-million pound trading standards and fraud prosecution, said to be first trading standards prosecution of its kind); Operation Tabernula (pre-charge advice to the FCA, largest ever insider dealing investigation); Operation Callahan (represented senior employee accused of multi-million pound telecommunications fraud). His current instructions include, for example, defending in a private prosecution arising out of multi-million pound civil claim, and defending a

property developer accused in a UK wide drugs conspiracy. Christopher also acts in regulatory proceedings and sports law, including involving such bodies as the Football Association and the British Horseracing Authority. He has been instructed in cases including match-fixing and corruption, and on field conduct.

Professional Memberships: CBA, FLA, YFLA

WARNOCK-SMITH, Shân QC
5 Stone Buildings, London
020 7242-6201
clerks@5sblaw.com
Featured in Chancery (London), Charities (London), Offshore (London), Trusts (London)

Practice Areas: Advice and litigation in connection with all aspects of trusts, succession, charities and related professional negligence claims in the UK and internationally, particularly the Cayman Islands, the British Virgin Islands, Bermuda, Hong Kong, Singapore, Jersey, Guernsey and the Isle of Man. Has a particular interest in wealth structuring (including charity and philanthropy) for international families from both the advisory and the litigation standpoints. Accredited mediator specialising in trust and estate disputes.

Professional Memberships: Society of Trust and Estate Practitioners, Chancery Bar Association, Association of Contentious Trust and Probate Specialists and The International Academy of Estate and Trust Law.

Career: Called to the Bar 1971. Silk 2002. Admitted to practise in the Cayman Islands, the Eastern Caribbean Supreme Court and England and Wales. Established International Chancery and Trusts Chambers in the Cayman Islands in 2010 and practises from there and from 5 Stone Buildings in London

Publications: Lecturer, writer and broadcaster on trust and estate matters. Sits on the Editorial Board of The Wills and Trusts Law Reports.

WARRENDER, Nichola
Quadrant Chambers, London
020 7583 4444
nichola.warrender@quadrantchambers.com
Featured in Shipping (London)

Practice Areas: Specialises in commercial litigation and international arbitration and advisory work with particular emphasis on shipping, marine/non-marine insurance, international trade, commodities, shipbuilding, energy and construction as well as related shipping and trade finance disputes. Examples of reported cases include: Suez Fortune Investments v Talbot Underwriting (The Brillante Virtuoso) [2016] EWHC 1085 (Comm) and [2015] 1 Lloyd's Rep 651; Sea Glory Maritime Co v Al Sagr National Insurance Co (The Nancy) [2014] 1 Lloyd's Rep 14; African Fertilisers & Chemicals Nig Ltd (Nigeria) v BD ShipsNavo GmbH & Co Reederei KG (The Christian D) [2011] 2 Lloyd's Rep 531;Parker v Levy (trading as Essex Marina) (2007) SJLB 116; Anton Durbeck GmbH v Den Norske Bank ASA (The Tropical Reefer) [2006] 1 Lloyd's Rep 93. For a detailed CV, please refer to the profile on www.quadrantchambers.com.

Professional Memberships: COMBAR; LCLCBA; PNBA

Career: Called to the Bar in 1995. Member of New York Bar (October 2008).

Publications: Contributor to Commercial Court & Arbitration Pleadings (2005).

Personal: Euro LLB Bristol / Hanover (1st Class Hons). Languages: German (working knowledge).

WARRINGTON, John
5 St Andrew's Hill, London
020 7332 5400
johnwarrington@5sah.co.uk
Featured in Crime (London)

Practice Areas: John is an experienced criminal practitioner who is regularly instructed in complex and document heavy, multi-handed cases of the utmost gravity for both the defence and prosecution. His practice encompasses a broad range of offending, including homicide, serious violence, large-scale drug trafficking, people trafficking, serious organised crime, firearms, public order, dishonesty and sexual offences. John has defended members of some of the most prolific organised crime groups in the country. In particular, he has extensive experience in white-collar crime, including serious fraud, money laundering, bribery, corruption and all aspects of related restraint and proceeds of crime proceedings. In this regard, John has been retained to advise pre-charge in the course of a number of high-profile investigations and has acted in complex applications for production orders and multi-million pound confiscation proceedings. He has been appointed to the CPS serious crime, fraud and proceeds of crime panels, the Bar Standards Board prosecution panel and the list of Specialist Regulatory Advocates in health and safety and environmental law. John has a busy professional disciplinary and regulatory practice, with an emphasis on healthcare professionals, legal services, public utilities, health and safety and the environment. He is direct access qualified and an advocacy tutor with Lincoln's Inn.

Professional Memberships: Association of Regulatory and Disciplinary Lawyers, UK Environmental Law Association, Fraud Lawyers Association, Criminal Bar Association, South Eastern Circuit

Career: Called to the Bar in 2000 (Lincoln's Inn); Law/LLB Honours (Queen Mary & Westfield College, University of London)

WARWICK, Henry
Henderson Chambers, London
020 7583 9020
clerks@hendersonchambers.co.uk
Featured in Consumer Law (London)

Practice Areas: Henry Warwick has specialist expertise in Consumer Finance as part of his wider practice in Banking, Finance and Consumer Credit Law. Henry acts in claims concerning the sale of financial products and disputes in respect of the full spectrum of credit agreements including asset finance, loans, credit cards, mortgages and associated insurance. Henry provides specialist advice to lenders and others in relation to UK financial services regulation. His recent cases include a leading authority on unfair relationships under section 140A of the Consumer Credit Act 1974 (Axton & another v GE Money Mortgages Limited [2015] EWHC 1343 (QB)), advising overseas companies on the regulatory implications of new secured lending business in the UK, drafting credit agreements and advising in a Supreme Court appeal concerning the meaning and effect of section 75 Consumer Credit Act 1974 (Durkin v DSG Retail & HFC Bank [2014] UKSC 21). Henry's broader practice is in commercial law.

Professional Memberships: COMBAR (Committee Member)

Career: Prior to the Bar, practice as solicitor (qualified 2000) at Linklaters LLP and, latterly, as Legal Counsel at Permanent Court of Arbitration in The Hague. LLM Cambridge University (2005, First Class Hons); BSc Bristol University (1996, First Class Hons).

WARWICK, Mark QC
Selborne Chambers, London
020 7420 9500
markwarwick@selbornechambers.co.uk
Featured in Real Estate Litigation (London)

Practice Areas: Mark is a leading practitioner in property litigation.

Professional Memberships: Chancery Bar Association; Property Bar Association; Professional Negligence Bar Association.

Career: Mark is a leading practitioner in property litigation. He also acts in cases involving contracts relating to construction and enforcement of commercial agreements. He advises on property related professional negligence and is recognised for his expertise in contentious chancery work including partnership and trusts of land. He is often instructed in cases that call for original ways of presenting or defending a claim. He has appeared in more than 100 reported cases. Recent cases include: Skelwith (Leisure) Ltd v Armstrong [2016] Ch 345 (Mortgagee's power of sale); Freifeld v West Kensington Court Ltd [2016] L&TR 5 (relief against forfieture); Menelaou v Bank of Cyprus [2016] AC 176 (Bank's claim to subrogation); Barrett v Bem [2012]Ch 573 CA (Death bed will invalid); BOH v Eastern Power [2011]CA (Merger of Freehold and Leasehold interests); Bindra v Chopra, CA, Lawtel 20.3.09 (construction of trust deed, dealing with interests on death).

Publications: Mark is the joint author of a book on break clauses and writes regularly for legal periodicals.

WATERS, Malcolm QC
Radcliffe Chambers, London
020 7831 0081
mwaters@radcliffechambers.com
Featured in Banking & Finance (London), Consumer Law (London)

Practice Areas: Principal specialist areas are retail banking, mortgages and consumer credit; regulation of retail financial services; and the law relating to building societies and other mutuals. Extensive experience in the law on unfair terms and in the drafting of standard form mortgage, current account, savings and consumer credit documentation. Reported cases include Director General of Fair Trading v First National Bank (unfair terms); OFT v Abbey National (unfair terms); Southern Pacific Mortgage v Heath (consumer credit); JP Morgan Chase v NRAM (consumer credit); NRAM v McAdam (unregulated agreement documented as regulated); C&G v Norgan (mortgages); Woolwich v Gomm (mortgages); Bristol & West v Bartlett (mortgages); C&G v BSC (building society conversion) and BSC v Halifax (building society conversion). Member of the working parties responsible for drafting the Standard Conditions of Sale and the Standard Commercial Property Conditions.

Professional Memberships: Chancery Bar Association; Professional Negligence Bar Association.

Career: Called to Bar 1977. Took Silk 1997.

Publications: Joint author of 'Retail Mortgages: Law Regulation and Procedure' and 'Current Law Commentary on the Building Societies Act 1986'. Joint editor of 'Wurtburg & Mills – Building Society Law' and 'The Law of Investor Protection'. Consultant editor of 'Halsbury's Laws of England' 4th edition, Friendly Societies title and 5th edition Financial Institutions title, Mutual Societies section.

Personal: Educated at Whitgift School 1963-71 and St. Catherine's College Oxford 1972-76 (BA and BCL).

WATSON, Ben
3 Raymond Buildings Barristers, London
020 7400 6400
ben.watson@3rblaw.com
Featured in Administrative & Public Law (London), Extradition (London)

Practice Areas: Particular expertise in crime, extradition, public law, international mutual legal assistance, and asset recovery. Regularly instructed in heavyweight crime (particularly fraud) and the leading extradition cases, see recently: for the Barclays US LIBOR submitter (Peter Johnson); Russia v Shuppe (Berezovksy's son in law); Russia v Korolev; South Africa v Dewani (accused of murdering wife on honeymoon), and for the Secretary of State in Gary McKinnon (computer hacker). Also instructed for UK Government in six US terrorism cases before ECtHR (Abu Hamza et al.) As member of Attorney General's A Panel regularly acts in a judicial review proceedings for a wide-range of Government departments – including for MoD and FCO in claims arising out of UK military action abroad. As a 'Special Advocate', was instructed in the first Closed Material Procedures before the Court of Appeal. Has 'Developed Vetted' security clearance.

Professional Memberships: Criminal Bar Association

Career: Call 2002; Attorney General's C Panel 2006; Attorney General's Special Advocate Panel 2010-2016; Attorney General's B Panel 2011; Attorney General's A Panel 2016.

Publications: Asset Recovery (OUP, 2007-13).

Personal: MA Hons (Cantab); Diploma in law.

WATSON, Claire
Serjeants' Inn Chambers, London
020 7427 5000
Clerks@serjeantsinn.com
Featured in Professional Discipline (London)

Practice Areas: Claire Watson was called to the Bar in 2011. Claire specialises in clinical negligence and healthcare, Court of Protection, inquests and inquiries, police, professional discipline and public and administrative law. An earlier edition notes that "she is an outstanding advocate who is exceedingly well prepared" and that "she thinks of everything and has all the makings of a star." Please visit the Serjeants' Inn Chambers website for her profile, which sets out full details of her practice including relevant work of note.

Professional Memberships: PNBA, ARDL, LCLCBA.

Publications: Co-author of Medical Treatment: Decisions and the Law.

WATSON, Duncan
1 Garden Court Family Law Chambers, London
020 7797 7900
watson@1gc.com
Featured in Family/Matrimonial (South Eastern)
Practice Areas: Duncan is a specialist in family finances, including financial remedies on divorce, financial applications relating to children pursuant to Schedule 1 Children Act 1989 and civil actions between unmarried co-habitants pursuant to TOLATA. He is instructed in the full range of family finance disputes from multi-million pound divorces to cases where the assets are more modest. He is particularly experienced in dealing with complex cases involving companies, partnerships, family trusts, insolvency, third party property rights, pensions and cases where there are issues relating to disclosure. He is experienced in dealing with enforcement proceedings including applications for committal. He also acts for parents in disputes relating to children. Recent lectures include, Financial Misconduct, Procedure in Trusts of Land and Part 36 offers. Recent cases include Cherwayko v Cherwayko (No 2) [2015] EWHC 2436 (Fam).
Career: BA (Hons) University of Cardiff, PGDL Nottingham Law School, Inns of Court School of Law, called to the bar – Inner Temple 1997. Appointed a Deputy District Judge 2010 (Southern Region)
Publications: Contributor to Applications Under Schedule 1 Children Act 1989 (forthcoming).
Personal: Enjoys skiing, walking in the mountains of the British Isles, history, good food and fine wine.

WATSON, James QC
Serjeants' Inn Chambers, London
020 7427 5000
jwatson@serjeantsinn.com
Featured in Clinical Negligence (London)
Practice Areas: James Watson QC was called to the Bar in 1979 and took silk in 2000. James specialises in clinical negligence, police law, inquests and inquiries, professional discipline and mediation. An earlier edition notes that "he is great to work with and is also a brilliant negotiator, who is full of useful, practical ideas...his tactical brilliance enables him to handle the most complex of claims with sensitivity." Please visit the Serjeants' Inn Chambers website for his profile, which sets out full details of his practice including relevant work of note.
Professional Memberships: PNBA, LCLCBA.

WATTHEY, James
4 Pump Court, London
020 7842 1107
jwatthey@4pumpcourt.com
Featured in Shipping (London)
Practice Areas: Shipping, insurance, international trade, offshore construction & energy, professional negligence, banking and commercial.
Professional Memberships: Combar, LCLCBA, Worshipful Company of Shipwrights, BILA, LMAA, Young Maritime Professionals, London Shipping Law Centre, Bar Pro Bono Unit.
Career: MA (Cantab) 1998 (Squire and Christ's College Scholarships; de Hart Prize). BCL (Oxon) 1999. Called Gray's Inn, 2000 (Prince of Wales Scholar; Chairman, Barristers Committee). Worked at Lovells 2001-02, in insurance/reinsurance. Arbitrator. Direct access accredited. Consistently recommended by the leading directories as "great counsel" who deals with matters "swiftly and effectively" and for his "impressively commercial" approach and "sensible and strategic advice".
Personal: Lives in London with wife and young daughter. Likes cycling, sailing, food and family.

WATT-PRINGLE, Jonathan QC
Temple Garden Chambers, London
020 7583 1315
jwpringleQC@tgchambers.com
Featured in Personal Injury (London)
Practice Areas: Barrister specialising in personal injury, insurance, clinical negligence, professional negligence, health and safety and inquests. Cases include: Griffiths v Brown (The Times, 23 October 1998); Griffin v Kingsmill [1998] PNLR 157; Kirby v Cross (The Times, 5 April 2000); Sam v Atkins [2006] RTR 14; Newman v Laver [2006] EWCA Civ 1135; BRB (Residuary) Ltd v Connex South Eastern Ltd [2008] 1 WLR 2867; Monk v P C Harrington Ltd [2009] PIQR P32; Ansari v New India Assurance Limited [2009] EWCA Civ 93, [2009] Lloyd's Rep. I.R. 562; Goad v Butcher [2011] EWCA Civ 158; Bowen v National Trust [2011] EWHC 1992 (QB); Eden v Rubin [2011] EWHC 3090 (QB), [2011] All ER (D) 189; Whiteford v Kubus UAB [2012] EWCA Civ 1017; Williams v Williams [2013] PIQR P17; Maclennan v Morgan Sindall (Infrastucture) PLC [2013] EWHC 4044 (QB), [2013] WLR (D) 509; Raleys v Barnaby [2014] EWCA Civ 686; Procter v Raleys [2015] EWCA Civ 400, [2015] PNLR 24.
Professional Memberships: PNBA; PIBA.
Career: Called 1987, Middle Temple; QC 2008
Personal: University of Stellenbosch (1978 BA; 1980 LLB); Rhodes Scholar, Keble College, Oxford (1983 BA; 1984 BCL; 1987 MA).

WAUGH, Andrew QC
Three New Square, London
020 7405 1111
waugh@3newsquare.co.uk
Featured in Intellectual Property (London)
Practice Areas: Intellectual property, specialising in pharma/biopharma and patents in the chemical and life science areas
Professional Memberships: Intellectual Propery Lawyers Association, Chancery Bar Association, AIPPLA
Career: • Graduated in 1980 from the City University, London with a first class honours degree in Chemical and Administrative Studies which included subjects on vitamin chemistry, structure and reactivity correlations and materials science and a thesis on Pharmaceutical Research and Development. • Post-graduate Diploma in law in 1981. • Called to the Bar 1982. • Pupillage with Martin Moore-Bick 1982, 3 Essex Court (The Chambers of Kenneth Rokison QC). • Pupillage with Simon Thorley 1983, 6 Pump Court (The Chambers of William Aldous QC). • Queen's Counsel 1998 • Admitted to the Irish Bar 2010

WAY, Patrick QC
Field Court Tax Chambers, London
0203 693 3700
pw@fieldtax.com
Featured in Tax (London)
Practice Areas: One of the founders of Field Court Tax Chambers, he has strong advocacy and advisory practices. He has successfully represented clients at all levels of the UK system from top to bottom and he acts for both taxpayer and HMRC alike in cases where the tax at stake may run into many hundreds of millions of pounds. He has also advised on some of the biggest UK takeovers and property developments involving multinationals. His clients include major corporates, as well as famous celebrities, charities, wealthy individuals and businesses of all types whom he has advised in relation to virtually every form of UK tax and on many aspects of double taxation and the impact of EU law. He has also appeared in the Privy Council. Throughout his career he has only ever appeared as lead or sole counsel.
Professional Memberships: Revenue Bar Association; Chancery Bar Association
Career: Called to the Bar 1994 (Lincoln's Inn). Member of Attorney General's B Panel as Junior Counsel to the Crown 2010-2013; QC 2013. Previously a solicitor and a partner in two leading London law firms, first becoming an equity partner at the age of 31.
Publications: Death and Taxes (1985), Maximising Opportunities under the BES (1986), the BES and Assured Tenancies – The New Rules (1988), Tax Advice for Company Transactions (1992), The Enterprise Investment Scheme (1994), Transactions: Taxation of Joint Ventures (1994), Tolley's Tax Planning (contributor from 1984-5 to 2012-13); founding editor of Trusts and Estates (1985) and tax editor of the BES Magazine (1986)
Personal: Director of Richmond (Rugby) Football Club

WEALE, James
Serle Court, London
020 7242 6105
jweale@serlecourt.co.uk
Featured in Chancery (London)
Practice Areas: James Weale has a chancery commercial litigation practice and regularly appears in both the Chancery Division and the Commercial Court. He undertakes a wide variety of commercial cases relating to contractual disputes, insurance litigation as well chancery litigation including trustee disputes. Recent cases include: Tseitline v Mikhelson (claim relating to a multi-billion dollar development in St Petersburg); Earl of Cardigan v Cotton & Moore (trustee removal); Lord Northampton v Northampton County Council (claim for the recovery of a valuable Egyptian artefact).
Professional Memberships: Chancery Bar Association; ComBar.
Career: Called: 2007.
Publications: Contributor to Palmer on Bailment (3rd ed); "A Good Arguable Case for Restricting the Canada Trust Gloss" [2010] JBL 36; Probate Litigation: the incidence of costs, Trusts and Trustees (2014).
Personal: Educated at Latymer Upper School, Bristol University (LLB) and Lincoln College, Oxford (BCL).

WEAVER, Matthew
St Philips Chambers, Birmingham
0121 246 7010
mweaver@st-philips.com
Featured in Commercial Dispute Resolution (Midlands), Restructuring/Insolvency (Midlands)
Practice Areas: Chancery/commercial litigation including all aspects of corporate and personal insolvency, company law including shareholders' disputes, general commercial litigation and directors' disqualification proceedings. Recent notable cases include: Re B W Estates Ltd [2015] EWHC 517 (Ch) and unreported, High Court, July 2016 (basis upon which proposed administrators can properly accept appointments, meaning of rescuing company as a going concern and impact of absence of quorum at directors' meeting appointing administrators); Edginton v Sekhon [2015] EWCA Civ 816 (basis upon which a debtor can obtain an adjournment of a bankruptcy petition); Re Kingston Investments Ltd [2015] EWHC 1619 (Ch) (right to vote in liquidations); and Purewal v Countrywide Residential Lettings Ltd [2015] EWCA Civ 1122 (duties owed by LPA receivers to bankrupt mortgagor).
Professional Memberships: Chancery Bar Association, COMBAR, Midland Chancery and Commercial Bar Association, Birmingham Law Society.
Career: Called in 2002. Buchanan Prize Winner (Lincoln's Inn). Junior Counsel to the Crown (Regional Panel).
Publications: Regular contributor to Corporate Rescue and Insolvency (LexisNexis).
Personal: A keen sportsman, particularly cricket, golf and rugby. Married with two young children.

WEBB, Geraint QC
Henderson Chambers, London
020 75839020
GWebb@hendersonchambers.co.uk
Featured in Environment (London), Insurance (London), Product Liability (London), Property Damage (London)
Practice Areas: Commercial, product liability, insurance and arbitration. Particular emphasis on group actions/mass tort claims, product liability (including product safety/ recalls), major property damage, contamination claims, sale of goods and services, cross-border disputes, international arbitration and insurance/reinsurance coverage disputes. Other areas of practice include professional indemnity (including clinical negligence), public procurement, local government, information technology, environmental, and health and safety. Pharmaceutical actions include vaccine damage claims, birth defect claims, psychiatric injury claims. Medical device/products claims include Hep C/HIV contaminated blood factors claims, CJD contaminated medical product claims, PIP breast implant litigation. Food contamination claims include Benzene Litigation, Para Red, Sudan 1. Property damage claims include major explosions/fires/failures in factories, power stations, oil depots, ships etc. International arbitrations under ICA, UNICITRAL, LCIA etc. Further details on Henderson Chambers' website: http://www.hendersonchambers.co.uk
Professional Memberships: COMBAR, LCLCBA, PIBA, ARDL.
Career: Christ Church, Oxford (BA – 1st Class), Exhibitioner, Princess Royal Scholar. Called to the Bar 1995, CEDR accredited mediator (2000). Appointed QC 2013.

WEBB, William
Keating Chambers, London
020 7544 2600
wwebb@keatingchambers.com
Featured in Construction (London)
Practice Areas: William has a busy specialist practice in of all aspects of construction, engineering, energy and PFI disputes including claims relating to payment, defects, delay and disruption and professional negligence. Due to his excellent cross examina-

tion, he is a popular choice as an advocate in the TCC, where he has a wide experience of both trials and interim applications and has a particular expertise in adjudication enforcement actions. He has also acted in the Court of Appeal, Commercial Court and Chancery Division. In addition to domestic court work, William is regularly involved in substantial international arbitrations including claims arising out of projects in Oman, Dubai, Yemen, Greece, Spain, Africa, Singapore and Russia. William is also regularly instructed in domestic adjudications and arbitration to advise, prepare written submissions and act for parties at hearings, and he a receives appointments as adjudicator and arbitrator in domestic and international disputes.
Professional Memberships: SCL, TECBAR, COMBAR
Career: TECBAR accredited adjudicator, Keating Chambers Barrister (2006), Called (2005)
Publications: William is heavily involved in academic and practitioner texts on construction law, being an Editor of Chitty on Contracts (32nd Ed), an Editor of the Construction Law Reports and a Contributor to Keating on Construction Contracts.

WEBSTER, Alistair QC
The Chambers of Andrew Mitchell QC, London
020 7440 9950 London; 0161 832 5701 Manchester
aw@33cllaw.com
Featured in Financial Crime (London)
Professional Memberships: Fraud Lawyers' Association; POCLA; CBA
Career: Took silk in 1995, when he was only 41. Since then, he has appeared in a large number of significant cases in all parts of the country. Quotes from past Guides: " Outstanding intellect"; "Outstanding lawyer"; "First class strategist and tactician"; "Accessible and responsive"; " Eloquent, brave and effective". As a junior, he had an extensive mixed practice, which has left him comfortable in both criminal and civil jurisdictions. Having developed a particular expertise in relation to commercial crime, he is on the SFO list of counsel both for prosecutions and POCA proceedings. Former Head of Chambers at Lincoln House, Manchester, and now also practising from 33 Chancery Lane. Alistair regularly advises businesses and individuals in relation to complex commercial frauds and issues such as bribery/money laundering/due diligence. He has defended directors and officers of companies in matters as diverse as: market rigging; false statements to the market; revenue fraud; MTIC fraud; factoring fraud; company flotation; restraint proceedings; and environmental crime. He has also prosecuted and defended in many high profile gross negligence manslaughter cases, along with murder cases of particular public interest.
Personal: Recorder since 1991. Master of Middle Temple.

WEIR, Robert QC
Devereux, London
020 73537534
Weir@devchambers.co.uk
Featured in Personal Injury (London), Travel (London), Clinical Negligence (London)
Practice Areas: Specialises in all aspects of personal injury and clinical negligence and the impact of the Human Rights Act on those areas. Works for both claimants and defendants. Particular emphasis on brain and spinal injury cases, motor claims with a European element, group actions, occupational illness claims, and on personal injury claims with a foreign element. Recent cases include: Cox v MoJ (SC), Coventry v Lawrence (SC), Wigley-Foster v MIB (CA), JXMX (CA), Thompson v Renwick plc (CA), Smith v MoD (SC), Wall v Mutuelle de Poitiers (CA), Haxton v Philips (CA) and Akhtar v Boland (CA).
Professional Memberships: Chair of Personal Injury Bar Association; Founder and past Chairman of Oxford Medico-Legal Society.
Career: Called in 1992, took silk in 2010.
Publications: Editor of Kemp & Kemp, author of chapter in Butterworths Personal Injury Litigation Service
Personal: Born in 1969. Married with 3 children. Enjoys outdoor activities with friends and family.

WELLS, Jason
Byrom Street Chambers, Manchester
0161 829 2100
jason.wells@byromstreet.com
Featured in Clinical Negligence (Northern)
Practice Areas: Clinical Negligence, Personal Injury, Inquests.
Professional Memberships: PIBA, PNBA, Royal College of Surgeons of England.
Career: MB ChB Sheffield 1993. FRCS 1998. LLB Nottingham Law School 2007. Called 2007, Lincoln's Inn. Jason practiced as a surgeon in the NHS for 12 years before retraining as a barrister. He specialises in medical law and personal injury. Jason is regularly instructed by Claimants in high value complex clinical negligence cases, involving all areas of medical malpractice, and by Claimants and Defendants in serious PI. He regularly appears in the Coroner's Court and represented the parents of a number of babies who died at Furness General Hospital. Jason sits as an Assistant Coroner in the Greater Manchester South District.

WELLS, Nathan
Radcliffe Chambers, London
020 7831 0081
nwells@radcliffechambers.com
Featured in Chancery (London)
Practice Areas: General Chancery practice, with a particular emphasis on wills, probate and administration of estates; trusts and trustees; charities; real property; landlord and tenant and related professional negligence. He is also regularly involved in general commercial litigation and has considerable experience of litigation involving local authorities. Notable cases include University of London v Prag [2015] WTLR 705, Green v Eadie [2012] Ch 363, Ferneley v Napier [2011] WTLR 1303, Shaw v Lighthousexpress Ltd [2010] EWCA Civ 161, Creque v Penn (2007) 70 WIR 150 (PC), Owers v Bailey [2007] P&CR DG17 and London Diocesan Fund v Phithwa (Avonridge Property Co Ltd, Part 20 defendant) [2005] 1 WLR 3956 (HL).
Professional Memberships: Chancery Bar Association, ACTAPS, Northern Ireland Bar.
Career: Called 2000. Judicial Assistant to the President of the Family Division (Michaelmas 2001) and the Vice-Chancellor (Hilary 2002).
Publications: Contributor to Tolley's Practitioners' Guide to Powers and Duties of Trustees; Editor of the Trusts and Estates section of Butterworths' Civil Court Precedents.
Personal: Educated at the Royal School Dungannon, Pembroke College Oxford (BA) and St Catharine's College Cambridge (LLM).

WENT, David
Exchange Chambers, Leeds
0113 203 1970
went@exchangechambers.co.uk
Featured in Competition/European Law (The Regions)
Practice Areas: Prior to returning to his roots as a barrister during 2015 (having originally been called to the bar in 1999), David's considerable competition law experience has been acquired at two leading US law firms in Brussels and London, most recently as partner at Sidley Austin LLP. David has acted for clients (e.g., ADM, Alberto Culver, Aon, Federation Internationale de l'Automobile, GSK, Hachette, IBM, LG Electronics, Spectris, Viterra, and Western Union) on some of the most significant and complex matters over the past 16 years across the spectrum of competition law work. Regularly appearing before the main EU and UK competition authorities and courts, David specialises in all advisory and litigation aspects of competition law, covering abuse of dominance, cartels, commercial practices, compliance, damages actions, M&A, public procurement, State aid, and related areas of EU, public and regulatory law. David has experience of working in a diverse range of industries, as well as on large multi-jurisdictional matters.
Professional Memberships: Editorial Board of Competition Law International (publication of International Bar Association); Co-chair of Competition Law Working Party of the Competition Law Association tasked with responding to government and competition authority consultations; Law Society of England and Wales Competition Section; Bar European Council

WEST, Mark
Radcliffe Chambers, London
020 7831 0081
mwest@radcliffechambers.com
Featured in Chancery (London), Real Estate Litigation (London)
Practice Areas: Bankruptcy and insolvency, charities, general commercial and contract, company law, equity and trusts, landlord and tenant (agricultural, business and residential), partnership, probate, professional negligence (especially solicitors' negligence), real property/conveyancing/ mortgages, restitution. Reported cases: Kleinwort Benson v Sandwell BC [1994] 4 All ER 890; Morgan Grenfell v Welwyn Hatfield DC [1995] 1 All ER 1; Kleinwort Benson v Birmingham CC [1997] QB 380; Kleinwort Benson v Lincoln CC [1999] 2 AC 349 (restitution of monies paid under ultra vires interest rate swap contracts); Chong Kai Tai Ringo v Lee Gee Kee [1997] HKLRD 491 (Privy Council) (sale and purchase of property in Hong Kong); Portman Building Society v Hamlyn Taylor Neck [1998] 4 All ER 202; Portman Building Society v Bevan Ashford [2000] Lloyd's Rep PN 354 (solicitors' negligence); Batchelor v Marlow [2001] 1 EGLR 119, (2001) 82 P & CR 459 (whether parking of cars an easement); Barclays Bank v Bee [2002] 1 WLR 332 (business tenancy: s.25 notices). Weir v. Secretary of State for Transport (No.1) [2005] EWHC 812 (Ch) (costs capping orders); Weir v. Secretary of State for Transport (No.2) [2005] EWHC 2192 (Ch) (misfeasance in public office); Banfield v. Leeds Building Society [2007] EWCA Civ 1369 (effect of failure to surrender insurance policy on existence of possession action); McLean Estates Ltd v. Earl of Aylesford [2009] EWHC 697 (Ch) (mines and minerals; whether Mercia Mudstone within a 1922 exception and reservation of mines and minerals; powers of working minerals).
Professional Memberships: Chancery Bar Association; Professional Negligence Bar Association; Property Bar Association.
Publications: 'Swaps & Local Authorities: A Mistake?' (with Catherine Newman QC) in Swaps & Off-Exchange Derivatives Trading: Law & Regulation (FT Law & Tax, 1996). 'Know Your Limits: Trustees' Mistakes under the Limitation Act' (2007) 86 Trusts & Estates Law Journal 12 'Breach of Warranty of Authority in Solicitors' Liability Claims' (with Professor Francis Reynolds) (2009) 25 Journal of Professional Negligence 131; The Ownership of Surface Voids Created by Mineral Extraction (2011) Conveyancer 30; Section 5 of the Limitation Act 1980 and Restitutionary Claims for Money Had and Received (2011) 30 Civil Justice Quarterly 366.
Personal: Part of DTI Team under Hilary Heilbron QC and Michael Boohan FCA to inquire into affairs of Blue Arrow Plc (Blue Arrow II) (report published September 1992). Member of joint Bar Council/Law Society working party to review civil justice system: Report 'Civil Justice on Trial, The Case for Change', published June 1993. Contributing editor Lloyd's Law Reports (Professional Negligence) 1999-2003. Junior counsel to shareholders in Weir v Secretary of State for Transport (the Railtrack litigation) 2005. Member of Committee of Chancery Bar Association 2005 to date; Deputy Judge of the Upper Tribunal (Administrative Appeals Chamber) 2012.

WESTON, Jeremy QC
St Ives Chambers, Birmingham
0121236 0863
jeremy.weston@stiveschambers.co.uk
Featured in Family/Matrimonial (Midlands)
Practice Areas: Family
Professional Memberships: Chair of the West Midlands FLBA, Member of the Association of Lawyers for Children Member of BAAF.
Career: Jeremy is Queen's Counsel specialising in family law. He has vast expertise in the most complex of care cases involving the death or serious injury of children (with a particular interest in head injuries), sexual abuse, poisoning cases, fabricated or induced illness. His practice also includes Judicial Review. Jeremy has extensive experience in protracted and complicated private law proceedings involving Residence (including internal relocation, Contact (including parental alienation and intractable contact disputes, allegations of physical, emotional and sexual abuse, disputes over education, religion, medical procedures and changes of name, child abduction, international relocation, surrogacy and Parental Order applications and parenting disputes arising from same-sex relationships. Jeremy is well attuned to the needs of the client and is highly regarded for his approachable and personable manner. Jeremy is regularly instructed by local authorities, parents and

on behalf of the Children's Guardian. He has also acted for adults acting under a disability. Notable cases: Cardiff County Council v BI, SL & EB [2016] EWHC 887 (Fam), Re B [2014] EWCA Civ 565, Re A (Children) [2013] EWCA 1611, Re L-R [2013] EWCA Civ 1129, R (on the application of Johns) v Derby City Council [2011] EWHC 375, Birmingham City Council v AG, IA & JA [2009] EWHC 3720 Fam, Staffordshire County Council v A, B, C, D, E & F [2009] EWHC 1982 Fam, Re R sub nom Birmingham City Council v LR, PNG, AK, AW & MRR [2006] EWCA Civ 1748.

Publications: Co-Author of 'Challenging and Defending Local Authority Child Care Decisions: A Practical Guide' (2013) Jordans Publishing.

Personal: Jeremy is Head of Chambers at St Ives Chambers. He is also regularly involved in giving lectures on all aspects of family law to other professionals, both locally and nationally, including the Bar and solicitors.

WESTWOOD, Andrew
Maitland Chambers, London
2074061200
awestwood@maitlandchambers.com
Featured in Charities (London)

Practice Areas: Commercial chancery practice including charities, insolvency, directors' disqualification, company law and civil fraudproperty. Reported cases include: Stichting Shell Pensioenfonds v Krys [2014] UKPC 41, Fairfield Sentry Ltd v Migani [2014] UKPC 9, Attorney General v Charity Commission [2012] UKUT 420 (TCC), HMRC v Begum [2011] BPIR 59, Grogan v HMRC [2011] STC 1, Re Metrocab Ltd [2010] 2 BCLC 603, Re Aaron Ltd [2009] 1 BCLC 55, Vintage Hallmark plc [2007] 1 BCLC 788, Mea Corporation Ltd [2007] 1 BCLC 618, Crystal Palace FC (1986) Ltd [2004] 2 BCLC 63, Promwalk Services [2003] 2 BCLC 305, J A Chapman & Co [2003] 2 BCLC 206, Phoneer Ltd [2002] 2 BCLC 241, Ashworth Frazer v Gloucester C.C. [2001] 1 WLR 2180, Britannia Home Centres [2001] 2 BCLC 63, Khazanchi v Faircharm [1998] 1 WLR 1603.

Professional Memberships: Chancery Bar Association, COMBAR, Charity Law Association, Insolvency Lawyers' Association.

Career: Called to Bar 1994. Admitted to the Bar of the Eastern Caribbean Supreme Court (BVI).

Publications: Advisory Editor of 'Mithani: Directors' Disqualification'.

Personal: Educated at St Catherine's College, Oxford (MA).

WHALE, Stephen
Landmark Chambers, London
020 7421 4230
swhale@landmarkchambers.co.uk
Featured in Licensing (London), Planning (London)

Practice Areas: Specialises in planning and environmental law; licensing law (especially Licensing Act 2003); highway law; local government law; administrative and public law. Regularly represents developers, local authorities, interest groups and the Secretary of State (Attorney General's A Panel). Experienced inquiry/examination advocate. Public Access registered. Notable cases include: Worthing seafront inquiry (2016); R (Littlejohns) v Devon CC [2016] EWCA Civ 446; M4 Smart Motorway DCO examination (2015-16); Reigate & Banstead BC v Fidler [2015] EWHC 3863 (QB); Waterside Park inquiry (2015); SSCLG v GPS Estates Ltd [2015] JPL 954; R (Akin) v Stratford Magistrates' Court [2015] 1 WLR 4829; Archway Sheet Metal Works Ltd v SSCLG [2015] EWHC 794 (Admin); SSCLG and others v Redhill Aerodrome Ltd [2015] PTSR 274; A160/A180 DCO examination (2014); Leith Hill Action Group v Europa Oil & Gas Ltd [2014] PTSR 1471; SSCLG v Ahmed [2014] 2 EGLR 197; Redhill Aerodrome inquiry (2014); A556 DCO examination (2013); A21 inquiries (2013); R (Barnsley MBC) v SSCLG [2013] PTSR 23; Dunsfold Aerodrome inquiry (2012); Farnborough Airport inquiry (2010); Kent International Gateway inquiry (2009); Daventry housing appeals inquiry (2009); R (Carroll) v South Somerset DC [2008] JPL 991; Uttlesford DC v English Heritage [2007] LLR 273; Coventry Airport inquiry (2006); South Downs National Park inquiry (2003-2005); R (Mount Cook Land Ltd) v Westminster City Council [2004] JPL 470; R (Medway Council and ors) v Secretary of State for Transport [2003] JPL 583.

Professional Memberships: Planning and Environment Bar Association; Administrative Law Bar Association.

Career: Called to the Bar in 1999. Gray's Inn Karmel Award 1997; Gray's Inn Junior Award 1998; Bar European Group Scholarship 2001; Junior Counsel to the Crown (C Panel 2007-2012, B Panel 2012-2015 and A Panel 2015-date).

Publications: Specialist contributor: Encyclopedia of Planning Law; Phipson on Evidence.

WHEATLEY, Geraint
Kings Chambers, Manchester
0345 034 3444
clerks@kingschambers.com
Featured in Real Estate Litigation (Northern)

Practice Areas: Established chancery and commercial practitioner with expertise in all aspects of commercial and residential property work, banking and commercial litigation. Professional negligence within these practice areas. Experience before courts of all levels up to and including the Court of Appeal, as well as proceedings before the Property Chamber: Land Registration (formerly the Adjudicator to HM Land Registry).

Professional Memberships: Chancery Bar Association, Northern Circuit Commercial Bar Association, Northern Chancery Bar Association.

Career: 1st Class Law Degree: Oxford University (St. Edmund Hall), 1st in year on the BVC: MMU, 2001 call (Gray's Inn, Edmund-Davies Award holder).

WHEELER, Andrew
7BR, London
020 7242 3555
awheeler@7br.co.uk
Featured in Financial Crime (London)

Practice Areas: Bribery & corruption, corporate investigations, investigations by HMRC, NCA, BIS & FCA, criminal/commercial fraud litigation, asset recovery, extradition and mutual legal assistance, money laundering, restraint & confiscation.

Professional Memberships: Financial Services Lawyers Association, Criminal Bar Association, South Eastern and Midland Circuits

Career: Andrew is a leading junior in financial crime, having developed a solid reputation in the market for domestic and cross-border financial crime. He demonstrates an excellent level of expertise in criminal/commercial fraud litigation, money laundering, insider trading and compliance work. Andrew has extensive experience in relation to the prosecution and defence of serious fraud, associated money laundering and proceeds of crime restraint/confiscation, and compliance/regulatory matters – and has a detailed knowledge of evidence gathering from, and asset tracing through, multiple jurisdictions. He is instructed by the Serious Fraud Office ('A' Panel), CPS Central Fraud Group & CPS Complex Casework Unit (Grade 4 Prosecutor), BIS (List A), FCA and leading defence firms. His experience extends in particular to Bribery & Corruption, Company, Insolvency and Taxation fraud, and to issues of Insider Dealing. He also has significant experience of Legal Professional Privilege, and of competing interests of joint and common privilege as between companies, directors and third parties.

WHEELER, Giles
Fountain Court Chambers, London
020 7583 3335
gw@fountaincourt.co.uk
Featured in Banking & Finance (London)

Practice Areas: A broad commercial practice with a particular emphasis on banking, professional negligence and regulatory work. Recent and ongoing work includes: defending a substantial claim for the mis-selling of a fixed rate loan (including allegations that fixed rate loans are regulated as contracts for differences), which settled on the eve of trial; Blackwater Services v West Bromwich Commercial which concerned the enforceability of increased interest rates charged following the financial crisis in 2009; Goldman Sachs International v Videocon Global Ltd [2016] EWCA Civ 130 which raised issues concerning the interpretation of the close-out provisions under the 1992 ISDA Master Agreement; numerous cases involving the alleged mis-selling of interest rate hedging products and fixed rate loans; advising on a director's breach of duty claim in Guernsey arising out of the collapse of a substantial investment fund; acting for a bank defending a claim for negligent tax advice given in relation to a film finance scheme; acting for a multi-national company defending a claim for over £10m for breach of a software distribution agreement.

Professional Memberships: COMBAR, LCLCBA

Career: Called to the bar by Middle Temple, 1998. In practice at Fountain Court Chambers from the completion of pupillage until the present.

WHITE, Andrew QC
Atkin Chambers, London
020 7404 0102
awhite@atkinchambers.com
Featured in International Arbitration (London), Professional Negligence (London), Construction (London), Energy & Natural Resources (London)

Practice Areas: Andrew's principal areas of expertise are domestic and international civil engineering, building, shipbuilding and ship repair disputes, and energy law. He also covers professional negligence and general commercial law. Andrew has extensive experience of arbitration conducted under the ICC, LCIA, LMAA and UNCITRAL rules. Significant cases include: Harman CFM Facades v Corporate Officer of the House of Commons (UK procurement law); ABB Lummus Global Ltd v Keppel Fels Ltd (arbitration, curial law), BICC v Parkman (jurisdiction under Civil Liability Contribution Act), Channel Tunnel Group Ltd v Balfour Beatty Construction (jurisdiction of English Court to grant injunctions in foreign arbitration), Murphy v Brentwood (negligence), Simon Carves Ltd v Ensus UK Ltd (on demand performance bonds).

Professional Memberships: TECBAR, COMBAR, Western Circuit.

Career: Educated University College Cardiff, LLB (Hons), 1975-79. Megarry Scholar and Hardwicke Scholar of Lincoln's Inn. Called to the Bar 1980, QC 1997, Bencher of Lincoln's Inn 2003.

Publications: Contributor: 'Atkins Forms and Precedents: Building Contracts'.

WHITE, Antony QC
Matrix Chambers, London
020 7404 3447
antonywhite@matrixlaw.co.uk
Featured in Commercial Dispute Resolution (London), Data Protection (London), Defamation/Privacy (London), Employment (London)

Practice Areas: Practises in commercial law and arbitration, media and information law, employment law, and public law. Commercial work focuses on fraud, bribery, constructive trusts, asset tracing, conflicts and new technology disputes. Recent notable commercial cases include Dowans Holdings SA v TANESCO [2012] 1 All ER (Comm) 820 (enforcement of NY Convention award subject to pending challenge in law of seat); R (British Telecommunications plc and TalkTalk Group) v Secretary of State [2011] 3 CMLR 5; [2012] Bus LR 1766 (challenge to the compatibility of the on-line infringement of copyright provisions of the Digital Economy Act 2010 with EU law); Twentieth Century Fox v BT [2012] Bus LR 1461 (web-blocking injunction against internet service provider). An increasing number of heavy international arbitrations. Recent media and information cases include Weller v Associated Newspapers [2016] IWLR 1541 (privacy in public places); Mosley v Google Inc [2015] EMLR 11 (search engine liability for availability on the internet of private photographs); Bewry v Reed Elsevier [2015] IWLR 2565 CA (libel, extension of limitation period); Hannon & Dufour v NGN [2015] EMLR 1 (compensation for damage to reputation in breach of confidence claim); OPO v Rhodes [2015] AC 219 (use of Wilkinson v Downton tort to restrain publication of autobiography); Vidal-Hall v Google Inc [2015] 3 WLR 409 (misuse of private information a tort; compensation for distress under DPA 1998); acted for News International at the Leveson Inquiry and in phone hacking litigation. Recent employment cases include Kelly v Unison [2012] IRLR 442 (trade union discipline, article II ECHR); Brennan v Sunderland City Council [2012] ICR 1183 (contribution claims in equal pay litigation). Recent public law and local government cases include R (London Borough of Islington and ors) v Mayor of London (2013) challenge to closure of London fire stations.

Professional Memberships: Administrative Law Bar Association Commercial Fraud Lawyers Association.

Career: Called 1983 (Middle Temple). Silk 2001.

Publications: Privacy and Trade Union sections of Bullen & Leake & Jacobs 'Precedents of Pleadings' (17th Ed. 2012); Administrative

Law chapter of 'Civil Appeals' (2nd edn, edited by Sir Michael Burton) ; co-author of 'Privacy and the Media – The Developing Law' (2002); Data protection/Freedom of information chapter in The Freedom of Information Handbook (ed. Carey and Turle) 3rd ed. 2012; data protection chapter in Information Rights (4th edn, ed Coppell).

WHITE, Cecily
Serjeants' Inn Chambers, London
Featured in Police Law (All Circuits)
Practice Areas: Cecily White was called to the bar in 2011. Cecily specialises in all aspects of healthcare litigation, actions involving the police, inquests, disciplinary proceedings, employment and public law. She has successfully acted, as both junior and sole counsel, in multi-day trials and applications in the High Court, Court of Protection, Crown and County Courts along with inquests, police misconduct and Employment Tribunal hearings. Please visit the Serjeants' Inn Chambers website for her profile, which sets out full details of his practice including relevant work of note.

WHITE, Jeremy
Pump Court Tax Chambers, London
020 7414 8080
clerks@pumptax.com
Featured in Tax (London)
Practice Areas: Jeremy White's practice covers advice and litigation in civil and criminal matters regarding international trade and Customs & Excise law. He specializes in trade barriers and preference including duties and taxes, prohibitions and restrictions, especially when involving classification, origin, customs valuation and other technical issues. He has been instructed to represent clients in disputes with the Customs Authorities of many countries. Landmark cases have included Terex C-430/08, Pace C-288/09 and Invamed C-198/15. Jeremy is qualified to accept Public Access instructions.
Professional Memberships: CIOT Indirect Tax Committee, Revenue Bar Association, Customs Practitioners Group, London Common Law & Commercial Bar Association, VAT in Industry Group.
Career: Called 1976 (Gray's Inn); 1977-83: Barrister, 7 Fountain Court, Birmingham; 1983-96: Solicitors Office, HM Customs & Excise; 1996-2000: Senior lawyer, KPMG (led team specialising in indirect tax investigations, litigation, disclosure and risk management): 2000-01: Senior lawyer, KLegal solicitors (responsible for the firm's trade and customs practice in UK); 2001-present: Barrister, Pump Court Tax Chambers, FIIT CTA.
Publications: Consultant editor of the Customs Duties Handbook since 1995; Consultant editor of the Excise Duties Handbook since 2001; Consultant editor of Halsbury's Laws since 2007; Regular contributor to De Voil Indirect Tax Intelligence; Contributor to LexisNexis Finance Act Handbook since 2008.

WHITE, Robin
Old Square Chambers, London
020 7269 0300
clerks@oldsquare.co.uk
Featured in Employment (London)
Practice Areas: Barrister specialising in employment and discrimination law (all aspects). Acts for employers and employees. Appears in Tribunals and Higher Courts in whole of UK including Scotland and Northern Ireland. Cases include Post Office v Foley; Beedell v West Ferry Printers (both test for unfair dismissal); Martyres v Connex (collective agreements); W v HMG (disability/national security – MI6 employee); Bentwood v Shepherd (Calculation of Quantum in discrimination), G v H (Disability Discrimination – Quantum over £1m), Symes v Eaton-Williams (Discrimination – lifetime loss), Rule v University of Arts (technicalities of uplift for failure to follow procedures), Short v Land Rover (interaction of DDA responsibilities and union collective agreements), Beavan v Cabinet Office (whether pay progression in Civil Service contractual), Pietzka v Price Waterhouse (sex, flexible and part-time working request discrimination by male employee), Hartley v Foreign and Commonwealth Office (discriminatory dismissal of an Engineer with Aspergers), Adams v Dudley NHS Trust (failure to make adequate provision for wheelchair bound employee), A V Telford (transgender patient, DPA and discrimination rights). B v N (access to sports changing facilities by transgender user).
Professional Memberships: ELBA, ELA, MCIT, ARCS, MIRO
Career: Called 1995, Gray's Inn.
Publications: Regular CPD lectures on discrimination and other employment topics. Speaks regularly on transgender issues following her own transition from male to female in 2011
Personal: Sexey's School Bruton; Imperial College, London (1986 BSc Hons Chemistry); Manager in transport industry 1986-91; Exeter (1994 LLB Hons). Lives in Somerset. Hobbies: house renovation, long-distance walking and classic car restoration.

WHITEHEAD, Thomas
St Philips Stone Chambers, London
020 7440 6900
tom.whitehead@stonechambers.com
Featured in Shipping (London)
Practice Areas: Recommended as a leading junior in Chambers & Partners UK Bar and the Legal 500. Specialises in commercial litigation and arbitration; emphasis on shipping, international trade, insurance, jurisdiction disputes and anti-suit injunctions. Reported cases include The New Flamenco [2015] EWCA Civ 1299; [2016] 1 WLR 2450; [2016] 1 Lloyd's Rep 383, damages for repudiation of charterparty and whether fluctuations in ship's capital value res inter alios acta; to be heard in the Supreme Court in Nov 2016, "The Coral Seas" [2016] EWHC 1506 (Comm) [2016] 955 LMLN 1, appeal under s69, The Alexandros T litigation concerning enforcement of settlement agreements and jurisdiction clauses ([2014] 1 All E.R. 590 (SC) – lis aibi pendens under Brussels Regulation; [2014] 2 Lloyd's Rep. 544 (CA) – scope of settlement; compatibility of declarations and an award of damages for breach of settlement and English jurisdiction clauses with EU law; [2014] 2 Lloyd's Rep. 579 – enforcement of release by and in favour of third parties); The Channel Ranger [2015] QB 366 (CA) – application of Chartbrook to incorporation by reference of a charterparty jurisdiction clause into a bill of lading absent express reference to jurisdiction clause; The Barito [2013] 2 Lloyd's Rep. 421 – anti-arbitration injunction and s.9 Arbitration Act 1996; The Wadi Sudr [2010] 1 Lloyd's Rep. 193 (CA) – recognition and enforcement of judgment obtained in another EU Member State in breach of London arbitration clause.
Professional Memberships: COMBAR, LCLCBA, Supporting Member LMAA, ACIArb.
Career: Called Inner Temple, 2002. Major Scholar, Duke of Edinburgh Entrance Award.
Personal: Worcester College, Oxford MA (1st Class) Jurisprudence; BCL.

WHITEHOUSE, Christopher
5 Stone Buildings, London
242 6201
clerks@5sblaw.com
Featured in Chancery (London), Tax (London)
Practice Areas: Advises on all aspects of private client taxation, trusts, estates and wills.
Professional Memberships: Fellow of CIOT, member of STEP and the Chancery Bar Association.
Career: Called 1971. Lectures extensively on the subjects of tax, trusts and will drafting. STEP Barrister of the Year 2006 and awarded a Founder's Award for Outstanding Achievement from STEP in November 2009.
Publications: Co-author of 'Trust Taxation and Estate Planning' (pub. 2014, 4th edition, Sweet and Maxwell); 'A Modern Approach to Wills, Administration and Estate Planning' (pub 2015, 3rd edition); 'A Modern Approach to Lifetime Tax Planning for Private Clients (pub 2014); 'Pre-owned Assets and Tax Planning Strategies' (3rd edition, pub. Dec 2009);'Trusts of Land, Trustee Delegation and The Trustee Act 2000'; 'Dymonds Capital Taxes'. Principal contributor to 'Encyclopaedia of Forms and Precedents' dealing with gifts, trusts and settlements. Consulting Editor of 'Private Client Business'.

WHITEHURST, Ian
7 Harrington St Chambers, Liverpool
0151 242 0707
john@7hs.co.uk
Featured in Crime (Northern), Financial Crime (The Regions)
Practice Areas: Undertakes heavyweight criminal and fraud work nationally with an emphasis on homicide, drug trafficking, tax fraud, regulatory and confiscation law. Has considerable experience in covert surveillance, probe evidence, electronic evidence and jurisdictional issues involving International Letters of Request. Advises in relation to HMRC investigations and financial regulatory matters offshore. Has defended in numerous cases involving homicide, serious sexual offences, large scale public disorder incidents and incidents relating to the use of extreme unlawful violence. Recent cases include R v B for the defence in £117 million confiscation proceedings arising from a nationwide conspiracy to supply drugs; and defending in one of the first multi handed gang injunction cases brought by the police where proceedings are being initiated in the Civil Courts with concurrent criminal proceedings running in tandem.
Professional Memberships: Criminal Bar Association, International Bar Association, International Bar Association, Proceeds of Crime Lawyers Association, Association of Regulatory & Disciplinary Lawyers, Northern Circuit.
Career: Grade 4 Prosecutor with the CPS – has appeared on their behalf in the Court of Appeal. Licensed Advocate on the Isle of Man (2012).
Publications: BitTorrent Bites Back Pension Liberation Fraud: New Kid On The Block Chat Rooms & 21st Century Insider Dealing

WHITELAW, Francesca
5 Essex Court, London
020 7410 2000
whitelaw@5essexcourt.co.uk
Featured in Professional Discipline (London)
Practice Areas: Police Law, Public/Administrative Law, Inquests and Inquiries, Professional Discipline, Human Rights. Recent cases: Inquest touching the death of Cheryl James (Deepcut) (instructed by the Ministry of Defence to represent two former soldiers in the further inquest into the death of a young soldier at the Deepcut Barracks in 1995); Gross Misconduct Proceedings concerning Inspector Mackaill (Plebgate) (independent legal advisor in misconduct proceedings against a police inspector which arose out of his involvement in, and statements to the press following, a meeting with Andrew Mitchell MP on 12th October 2012. The meeting arose out of the incident known as 'Plebgate'). In the matter of Olaseni Lewis deceased (Junior Counsel to the IPCC for disciplinary matters concerning the death of a 23-year old who died following police restraint at the Bethlem hospital).
Professional Memberships: Administrative Law Bar Association
Career: Called to the Bar in 2003. Appointed to the Attorney-General's C Panel of Junior Counsel to the Crown in 2012 and to the B Panel in 2016. Recognised in Chambers and Partners UK 2015 and 2016 in the field of Professional Discipline as being 'very effective' and 'well known for her expertise...'
Personal: BA(Hons), MA Cantab (English), MA (Law) City

WHITTAKER, David
2 Hare Court, London
020 7353 5324
davidwhittaker@2harecourt.com
Featured in Crime (London), Financial Crime (London)
Practice Areas: David Whittaker has extensive experience in defending in most forms of serious crime. He is regularly instructed to defend in complex fraud investigations brought by the SFO and FCA; continues to receive private instructions in general crime, including motoring and sexual offences; and is increasingly instructed on behalf of corporate bodies, their officers and other individuals in relation to criminal offences arising out of fatal and non-fatal accidents. Operation Tabernula (2016): represented a London trader charged with insider dealing. Operation Cotton (2015): Represented defendant in largest land banking scheme brought by the (then) FSA. Recent cases include; R. v. F (2016): represented banking employee charged with a sexual offence. R. v. H (2016): representing lead defendant in a large cocaine conspiracy. HSE v. D Ltd (2016): representing a large delivery company charged with offences under HSWA. HSE v. WER Ltd (2016): representing a company in the paper industry charged with offences under HWSA. CQC v. CCS Ltd (2016): representing a care home provider for offences under the Health and Social Care Act (Regulated Activities) Regulations 2014
Professional Memberships: Criminal Bar Association; Fraud Lawyers Association; Health & Safety Lawyers Association; Association of Regulatory & Disciplinary Lawyers.

WHITTAM, Richard QC
2 Bedford Row, London
020 7440 8888
RWQC@2bedfordrow.co.uk
Featured in Crime (London)

Practice Areas: Richard Whittam QC is a specialist criminal practitioner with experience in the most complex and high profile criminal cases. Until November 2015 he was First Senior Treasury Counsel [Crime]. Throughout his time as Treasury Counsel he maintained his defence practice. The 2016 edition of the Chambers Guide to the Bar, ranks him as a Leading QC: "He is really top-drawer and has very impressive courtcraft". He has been ranked by Chambers as a leading barrister for over 15 years: "He takes everything in his stride. Nothing seems to bother him and he just won't be deflected from achieving a good result."; "astute, hard-working and meticulous in his paperwork"; "a strong Treasury Counsel who realises that to be effective, you don't need to be an enemy of your opponent"; "a fearless advocate who glides through proceedings with effortless style" and "a stunning addition to any team with pep and industry to spare." He advises potential defendants and the prosecution on law and strategy pre-charge in important and sensitive cases, in particular in relation to allegations of corruption and bribery. The breadth of his expertise is reflected by his instruction in the leading appeals on disclosure [for the Attorney General], character [for the DPP] and terrorist sentencing [for the Secretary of State].

Professional Memberships: CBA, ARDL, South Eastern Circuit.

Career: 1979-1982 University College London LLB(Hons); 1983 Called to the Bar; 1998-2006 Junior Treasury Counsel; 2002-06 First Junior Treasury Counsel; 2006 Senior Treasury Counsel; 2008 Queen's Counsel; 2009 Recorder [authorised to sit at the Central Criminal Court]; 2012 Bencher Gray's Inn; 2013-2015 First Senior Treasury Counsel; 2014 Legal Adviser to and Independent Examiner for the Institute and Faculty of Actuaries; 2014 Member of RFU Judicial Panel; 2016 Deputy High Court Judge.

Personal: Rugby, waterskiing, wakeboarding, men's lacrosse, golf.

WHYTE, James
8 New Square, London
020 7405 4321
james.whyte@8newsquare.co.uk
Featured in Intellectual Property (London)

Practice Areas: Barrister specialising in intellectual property law, with a particular emphasis on technically complex cases in biotechnology, pharmaceuticals, telecoms and electronics. James' practice is focused on patents but he also practises in the fields of copyright, confidential information, database rights and registered and unregistered design rights. Scheduled trials include Varian v Elekta (MRI/radiotherapy), Astex v AstraZeneca (drug development dispute), Illumina v Premaitha (antenatal diagnosis), and Pfizer v Amgen (therapeutic antibody). Past cases include Regeneron v Kymab (antibody engineering), EMGS v PGS (electromagnetic hydrocarbon prospecting), Wobben v Siemens (wind turbines), Vestergaard Frandsen v Bestnet (insecticidal mosquito nets), Rovi v Virgin (set-top boxes), Novartis v Hospira (injunction pending appeal), Medinol v Abbott (stents, Ireland), Medimmune v Novartis (phage display), Siemens v Seagate (magnetoresistance, N.Ireland), Dr Reddy's v Eli Lilly, ITV v TV Catchup, Football Association Premier League v QC Leisure.

Professional Memberships: Intellectual Property Bar Association (IPBA) and Chancery Bar Association.

Career: Called 2005, Lincoln's Inn.

Publications: Co-author of Laddie Prescott and Vitoria on the Modern Law of Copyright and Designs (4th Ed).

Personal: Educated at Trinity College, Cambridge (top 1st in genetics; PhD in molecular biology); City University (distinction in postgraduate diploma in law); BPP (outstanding in bar vocational course).

WIGLEY, Joseph
4 Stone Buildings, London
020 72425524
clerks@4stonebuildings.com
Featured in Chancery (London)

Practice Areas: Joseph Wigley is developing a broad practice across the full spectrum of work undertaken at 4 Stone Buildings, including commercial litigation, insolvency and reconstruction, commercial chancery, banking & finance, financial services, company law, shareholder disputes, civil fraud, tracing and asset recovery. He is instructed both on his own and (in high-value cases) led by senior barristers both in and out of Chambers, appearing in both the Commercial Court and the Chancery Division as well as the County Courts. Many of his instructions have an international aspect. Recent cases of note include Global Energy v Gray (imposition of fiduciary duties on joint venture and conduct of enquiry into an account of profits related to the alleged commercialisation of oilfield technology); Maud v Aabar Block (bankruptcy, abuse of process) and RPC v Khan (bankruptcy, jurisdiction, ordinary residence).

Professional Memberships: Commercial Bar Association; Chancery Bar Association

Career: Called to the Bar in 2010.

WIJEYARATNE, Asela
3 Hare Court, London
020 7415 7800
aselawijeyaratne@3harecourt.com
Featured in Travel (London)

Practice Areas: Asela has extensive experience in claims arising out of overseas accidents and illness. He has particular experience in claims arising under the Package Travel Regulations 1992 and the international transport and carriage conventions. Asela also undertakes cases where issues of jurisdiction and conflict of laws arise and frequently acts in claims pursued in the courts of England and Wales which are determined under foreign law. He has considerable expertise in claims against overseas traders, public liability and motor insurers and the Motor Insurers' Bureau for overseas road traffic accidents where drivers are untraced or uninsured.

Career: Called 2008.

WILD, Alison
Westwater Advocates, Edinburgh
0131-260-5700
alison.wild@westwateradvocates.com
Featured in Family/Matrimonial (Scotland)

Practice Areas: Family law, in particular, divorce, financial provision, cohabitation, child related issues including international child abduction, relocation and permanence orders. Reported cases include R Petitioner [2016] AC 76 (child abduction), A Petitioner, 2012 SLT 370 (child abduction), M v M 2011 Fam LR 124 (relocation), B v B [2011] CSOH 127 (contact), Aberdeenshire Council, Petitioners 2011 Fam LR 16 (freeing orders), Lindsay v Murphy 2010 Fam LR 156 (cohabitation), Z Petitioner 2010 SLT 285 (child abduction).

Professional Memberships: Scottish Family Law Association – member 1992 to 2007; Treasurer 2005 to 2007. Advocates Family Law Association – member 2008 to date.

Career: Solicitor in private practice for 16 years. Admitted to the Cayman Islands Bar in March 2001. Called to the Scottish Bar in July 2008.

Publications: Co-editor of the Family Law Reports. Editor of "Miscellaneous consequences of marriage" and "International aspects of the law relating to parental rights and responsibilities" sections in Butterworths Scottish Family Law Service.

Personal: LLB, Edinburgh University 1988. CALM mediator 1998-2007. Tutor in Family Law at Edinburgh University 1998-2001. Accredited Family Law Specialist 1999-2007. Peer Reviewer 2004-2009. Faculty Scholarship 2007/08. Director of Birthlink 2011 to date.

WILKEN, Sean QC
39 Essex Chambers, London
020 7832 1111
sean.wilken@39essex.com
Featured in International Arbitration (London), Construction (London), Energy & Natural Resources (London)

Practice Areas: Practised in high profile, complex, international and domestic commercial litigation for over 20 years. His experience covers the financial; energy; infrastructure; insurance; projects and construction sectors.His caseload has included: the major litigation arising from the 1990's UK domestic property collapse; the consequences of 9/11 and 7/7 domestically and internationally; the international consequences of the 2008 collapse; as well as various international environmental and commercial crises. As well as regularly appearing in the Commercial Court and TCC in London, he has extensive experience of acting in ICC; LCIA; UNCITRAL; ICSID; HKIAC; DIAC; SIAC; SCC and ad hoc arbitrations covering the USA; EU; Russia; Africa; the Middle East and Far East. He has acted as an arbitrator in several disputes arising from the Winter Olympics. He was appointed Queen's Counsel in 2010. He holds a Foreign Lawyers Licence for Singapore and is qualified to appear before the Singapore International Commercial Court.

Professional Memberships: COMBAR, TECBAR, LCLBA, ALBA, Justice, BEG.

Career: Former Attorney General's Junior counsel to the Crown (A Panel). CEDR Mediator. QC (2010)

Publications: Wilken and Ghaly 'Waiver, Variation and Estoppel', 3rd ed, 2012, OUP.

WILKINSON, Richard
Temple Garden Chambers, London
020 7583 1315
RichardWilkinson@TGchambers.com
Featured in Personal Injury (London), Costs Litigation (All Circuits)

Practice Areas: Richard's main practice areas are personal injury and costs. PI: regularly handles high value (seven figure claims) / complex cases on behalf of both Claimants and insurers with particular experience of head injury and fatal accident claims. Experience of group litigation from both sides: Porton Down (Claimants) and Scania (Defendants) and other large-scale litigation such as public inquiries (Southall Rail; Victoria Climbie). Appointed as a current editor of the Judicial College (formerly JSB) Guidelines on General Damages in Personal Injury Cases. Costs: Richard has long-standing expertise in the costs arena, advising and representing clients in the full range of costs disputes across different practice areas including commercial, media, PI / clin neg and solicitor/client disputes. He appears regularly in the SCCO as well as on cost budgeting issues in larger value claims. Junior counsel in Mitchell v NGN in the Court of Appeal. He has particular experience of funding and CFA issues following involvement in cases including Atack v Lea/Ellerton v Harris, Holmes v Alfred McAlpine, Sidhu v Sandhu.

Professional Memberships: Personal Injury Bar Association. Member of Executive Committee

Career: Called to the Bar in 1992.

Publications: Editor of the JC (formerly JSB) Guidelines on General Damages in Personal Injury Cases.

Personal: Educated at RGS High Wycombe and Bristol University. Avid sports fan, particularly football and cricket.

WILLE, Andrew
Farrar's Building, London
020 7583 9241
awille@farrarsbuilding.co.uk
Featured in Personal Injury (London)

Practice Areas: Specialises in complex and high value personal injury claims with a particular interest in brain and spinal injury. Also claims concerning amputees. Has many years experience of fatal accident claims and inquests.

Professional Memberships: PIBA, PNBA

Career: BA (Oxon); Dip Law (City University); called to the Bar in 1998 (Lincoln's Inn)

WILLEMS, Marc QC
Cobden House Chambers, Manchester
0161 833 6000
clerks@cobden.co.uk
Featured in Personal Injury (Northern)

Practice Areas: Marc specialises in the most serious Personal Injury and Clinical Negligence litigation, with considerable experience of Acquired Brain Damage Claims, Spinal Injuries and very severe orthopaedic injuries including amputation cases. Marc enjoys cases involving complex medical causation issues, detailed factual disputes and legal arguments. He is a significant contributor to Chambers' programme of seminars and lectures to firms of Solicitors and has contributed to several mock trials including "Brain Injury and the Law" National Conference June 2014. Marc attends numerous Joint Settlement Meetings and Mediations annually on behalf of clients. He has acted for solicitors and other Litigation service providers in Insurance disputes. Marc appears regularly in the Court of Appeal and he has appeared in the House of Lords and in the Supreme Court in the case of (Dunhill v Burgin on the issue of Capacity to Litigate and the effectiveness of a settlement with a Claimant unknown to lack capacity) Marc has been sitting as a Recorder since 2006 and sits on Crime and Civil. Marc was appointed as Queens Counsel in 2015. In 2015, Marc was enrolled on the list of advocates for St Helena, Ascension and Tristan da Cunha British dependencies.

WILLIAMS, A John
Crown Office Chambers, London
020 7797 8100
williams@crownofficechambers.com
Featured in Personal Injury (London), Personal Injury (All Circuits)
Practice Areas: A. John Williams is an experienced Junior who is recognised as one of the leading practitioners in occupational disease litigation and personal injury work. In the last 3 years he has appeared in the Supreme Court in both Baker v Quantum Clothing Group plc [2011] 1 WLR 1003 and the EL Trigger Litigation [2012] 1 WLR 867. His practice covers a wide range of industrial disease litigation including complex occupational cancer and high value mesothelioma claims. He also undertakes high value claims for chronic pain; workplace bullying and stress and traumatic physical injuries. Over the years John has had regular successes (both at trial and in ADR) against leading silks in his field: see e.g Garner v Salford City Council [2013] EWHC 1573 (QB). John works closely with others in the litigation team to secure the right outcome. Clear and pragmatic advice outside the Court room and focussed, persuasive advocacy in the Court room ensure that cases are handled both efficiently and effectively. John undertakes work for both Claimants and Defendants.
Career: Called to the Bar in 1983 John is an accredited Advocacy Tutor for Lincoln's Inn and is a Trustee and Vice Chair of SOSSEN! – a charity that provides helpline advice and workshops for parents of children with special educational needs.

WILLIAMS, Anne
6 Pump Court, London
020 7797 8400
annewilliams21@me.com
Featured in Planning (London)
Practice Areas: Anne advises developers on pre-application discussions and the prospects of success on appeal. She frequently appears at planning inquiries and hearings throughout the UK and has a wide client base, ranging from national and international companies, local authorities and residents groups. She successfully acted for the LPA at the DP World container port inquiry and has recently been advising on proposals for a strategic mixed use scheme in West Ham. She has also appeared at a called-in inquiry in Sussex which covered neighbourhood planning, conservation, landscape, planning policy and housing land supply issues. The result is awaited. She has also recently advised developers on complex enforcement matters in South West London and Lincolnshire.
Publications: Anne Williams was recently appointed as Visiting Professor at the Bartlett School of Architecture and Planning at UCL Editorial Board: Garner Environmental Law Planning Appeals & Inquiries: Sweet&Maxwell Westlaw Insight Planning Contributor Lexis Nexis: Editor Atkin Town and Country Planning

WILLIAMS, Ben
Kings Chambers, Manchester
0345 034 3444
clerks@kingschambers.com
Featured in Employment (Northern), Licensing (Midlands)
Practice Areas: A specialist in Employment, Regulatory and Licensing law. His employment practice is such that he has vast experience in the healthcare and education sectors. He has extensive experience in associated High Court litigation. He regularly appears in taxi licensing cases both for local authorities and appellants involving both hackney carriage and private hire vehicles. He has advised extensively on the formulation and implementation of local authority taxi licensing policy. Vastly experienced in all aspects of liquor licensing. Acts for the industry, Local Authorities, interested parties and the police both in terms of representation at hearings and in an advisory capacity. Regularly conducts in-house training and seminars. Has appeared in a number of high profile licensing matters and reported cases including Leeds CC v Shell UK (2013); Blackpool Council v Blacktax (2009); Blackpool Council v Howitt (2008); Luminar Leisure v Wakefield Magistrates Court (2008).
Professional Memberships: Road Transport Lawyers Association; Association of Regulatory and Disciplinary Lawyers; Institute of Licensing; Employment Lawyers' Association; Employment Law Bar Association.
Career: Called to the Bar in 2001, joined Kings Chambers in 2006.
Publications: Contributing Author to 'Judicial Review : Law and Practice'– Licensing chapter.

WILLIAMS, Ed
Cloisters, London
020 78274000
ew@cloisters.com
Featured in Employment (London)
Practice Areas: Ed practices in all areas of employment, discrimination, trade union, ECHR human rights law and education law. Cases include: Hyde Housing Association v Layton [2016] ICR 261, EAT (whether there can be a TUPE transfer from sole to joint employment where after transfer the transferor is one of the joint and several employers); Rabess v London Fire Brigade Authority v London Fire and Emergency Authority A2/2014/3352, CA (whether the elective theory of acceptance should apply to calculating the EDT in unfair dismissal cases); Smania v Standard Chartered Bank [2015] ICR 436 (whistleblowing and its international jurisdiction), Henderson v GMB [2015] IRLR 451 (left wing democratic socialism and manifesting political belief); Khanon & Ors v Adderely School (alleged Islamist infiltration of Birmingham schools: "operation trojan horse"); Camurat v Thurrock Borough Council [2014] EWHC 2482, QB, [2015] ELR 1 (whether ex employers owe any duty of care when making safeguarding disclosures); Moran v Ideal Cleaning and Celanese [2014] ICR 442, EAT; (the meaning of the word "temporary" in the AWD and the AWR); X v Mid Sussex CAB, [2011] ICR 460, CA whether volunteers are protected under the EU Framework Directive from discrimination), Bournemouth University v Buckland [2010] ICR 908, CA (whether an employer can rectify a fundamental breach of contract)
Professional Memberships: ELA, ILS and ELBA.
Career: Called to the Bar in 2000. Ed is a Member of the College of Law's Higher Rights Teaching Panel and has been a visiting Human Rights Lecturer at Nottingham Law School.
Publications: Co-author of the Practice and Procedure Chapter in Sweet and Maxwell's Discrimination Law for Employment Lawyers. Contributor to Guardian Legal.
Personal: Ed is co-founder and a trustee of Cricket Without Boundaries, a charity dedicated to using cricket to raise awareness of HIV/AIDS and bridging ethnic division in Africa. www.cricketwithouboundaries.com. Ed is also a director of witness familiarisation company Assurety: www.assuretytraining.com

WILLIAMS, Geoffrey QC
Farrar's Building, London
020 7583 9241
law@gwcg.globalnet.co.uk
Featured in Professional Discipline (London)
Practice Areas: Specialises in representing regulatory bodies & regulated professionals in proceedings before disciplinary tribunals & on appeals to the higher Courts. Has appeared in many leading cases in relation to the conduct of Solicitors including Salsbury v The Law Society (Court of Appeal).
Professional Memberships: London Common Law & Commercial Bar Association.
Career: Solicitor 1978 – 2013. Took Silk 2003. Transferred to the Bar 2014 becoming a Tenant at Farrar's Building.
Publications: The Guide to the Professional Conduct of Chartered Surveyors.
Personal: West Monmouth Grammar School Pontypool. Trent Polytechnic, Nottingham, BA Law (Upper Second Class Honours). College of Law (Solicitors' Final Examinations – Second Class Honours with 3 Distinctions). Called to the Bar at Gray's Inn Michaelmas Term 2013.

WILLIAMS, Helen
29 Bedford Row Chambers, London
020 7404 1044
hwilliams@29br.co.uk
Featured in Family/Matrimonial (London)
Practice Areas: All areas of family law, but primarily financial remedy proceedings, with a particular emphasis on the treatment of business assets.
Professional Memberships: FLBA; Institute of Chartered Accountants in England and Wales (ICAEW).
Career: Prior to coming to the bar she qualified as a Chartered Accountant and worked in the corporate and real estate tax departments at Andersens, Deloitte and Ernst & Young.
Personal: Oxford University (MA (Oxon)). LLM (UCL).

WILLIAMS, Rhodri QC
Henderson Chambers, London
020 7583 9020
rwilliams@hendersonchambers.co.uk
Featured in Data Protection (London), Local Government (London), Public Procurement (London)
Practice Areas: European Community law, local government and administrative law. Significant cases include:Deer-v-Oxford University [2015] EWHC (QB); R (Diocese of Menevia) v Swansea City and County Council [2015] EWHC 1436 (Admin); R (Dusza)-v-Powys Teaching LHB [2015] EWCA Civ 15; R(Wiltshire Council) v Hertfordshire County Council [2014] EWCA Civ 71, Montpellier Estates Ltd-v-Leeds City Council [2013] EWHC 166 (QB); Local Government Byelaws (Wales) Bill 2012 – Reference by the Attorney General for England and Wales [2012] UKSC 53; R (Governors of Brynmawr Foundation School) v Welsh Ministers & Blaenau Gwent CBC [2011] EWHC 519 (Admin); Brent LBC v Risk Management Partners Ltd & London Authorities Mutual Ltd & Harrow LBC [2011] UKSC 7; [2011] LGR 169; Lancashire County Council v EWC Ltd [2010] EWCA Civ 1381; [2011] LGR 350; Henry Brothers (Magherafelt) Ltd v Department of Education for Northern Ireland [2011] NICA 59; Case C-406/08 Uniplex (UK) Ltd v NHS Business Services Authority [2010] ECR I-817.
Professional Memberships: Bar European Group; Administrative Law Bar Association; Procurement Lawyers Association; Public Law Wales.
Career: Qualified 1987 Gray's Inn; Thirty Park Place Chambers since 1997; Henderson Chambers since 1999. Attorney General's list of approved Counsel from 2000; list of Counsel General to the Welsh Government since 2000. Took Silk in 2010. Bencher Gray's Inn 2015.
Publications: Public Procurement Law Review.
Personal: Also member of Thirty Park Place Chambers, Cardiff (02920 398421).

WILLIAMS, Sarah
Keating Chambers, London
020 7544 2600
swilliams@keatingchambers.com
Featured in Construction (London)
Practice Areas: Specialises in construction, engineering, construction professional negligence infrastructure, telecommunications, onshore and energy cases and party wall matters. Instructions received, often on a repeat basis, from a variety of clients including national and international companies, local authorities, partnerships and home owners, and by way of Public Access. Regularly acts and advises on all aspects of litigation through to trial. Represents clients in the TCC both in the High Court and County Court. Expertise in domestic and international arbitration, adjudication (including adjudication enforcement hearings), and mediation.
Professional Memberships: Councillor of the Society of Construction Law (SCL), TECBAR , COMBAR.
Career: Called to the bar in 2008. 1st in Natural Sciences at Cambridge. Distinction on the GDL. Previously worked in the international aluminium industry.
Publications: Contributing author to: Keating on Offshore Construction and Marine Engineering Contracts (2015); the Construction Law Reports; Keating on Construction Contracts; and Bullen & Leake & Jacob's Precedents of Pleadings. Author of the SCL paper, An Introduction to Good Faith in Construction Contracts.

WILLIAMS, Simon
Radcliffe Chambers, London
020 78310081
swilliams@radcliffechambers.com
Featured in Real Estate Litigation (London)
Practice Areas: Property and commercial litigation and related professional negligence.

Cases include: Moorjani v Durban Estates Ltd [2016] 1 WLR 2265 (nature of loss following landlord's breach of covenants to repair and insure) Smart v Lambeth [2014] HLR 7 CA (adverse possession, implied or actual consent); Good v Onsette Ltd [2013] EWHC 3447 (Ch) (beneficial ownership of shares/ dishonest assistance; . Scott v Kennedys Law & Vertex Law [2011] EWHC 3808 (Ch) (method of calculating loss on no transaction basis) Islam v Al Sami [2011] EWCA Civ 32 (validity of equitable charge) Joyce v Bowman Law [2010] PNLR 22 (measure of damages for lost chance to develop land); Ofulue v Bossert [2009] 1 AC 990 HL (acknowledgement of title, without prejudice rule) [2008] 3 WLR 1253 CA (adverse possession, human rights) LSC v Banks [2008] 20 EG 137 (statutory charge) Mortgage Credit v Kalli [2007] EWCA Civ 1156 (adverse possession, misconduct by trial judge) Filobake v Rondo & Frampton [2005] EWCA Civ 563 (construction of contract) Pena v Coyne & Sunmoor [2004] BCLC 703 & 730 (transaction at undervalue).
Professional Memberships: Chancery Bar Association, Property Bar Association, Professional Negligence Bar Association.
Career: Called 1984, Accredited Mediator (ADR Group) 2006.
Personal: Born 1961, married, 3 children, resides Hampshire.

WILLIAMS, Vincent
9 Gough Square, London
020 7832 0500
vwilliams@9goughsquare.co.uk
Featured in Police Law (All Circuits), Inquests & Public Inquiries (All Circuits)
Practice Areas: Vincent is enormously experienced, having practised in the fields of police law and personal injury for over 25 years. His practice involves police malfeasance and misfeasance actions and inquests arising out of deaths in police custody or following contact with the police. In addition, he regularly deals with catastrophic injuries (head and spinal), as well as Fatal Accident claims. He has a particular interest in art. 2 inquests – many of which are linked to, or lead on to, substantial civil claims. Vincent has excellent manner both in court and when dealing with clients. He is realistic but sympathetic. He has been described in various editions of Chambers & Partners in the following terms: • "his advocacy is frankly brilliant, and his manner with clients is very sympathetic". • "incredibly thorough and knows what he is doing". • "absolutely excellent, thorough and well prepared". • "an extremely astute barrister of undoubtedly high ability"; and, "tremendous ability to remain extremely cool under pressure". Samples of recent cases: • In Re Alice Gross (2016) Art 2 inquest concerning death of a 14 year old girl killed by Latvian national present in the UK notwithstanding earlier murder conviction in Latvia. • C1 & C2 v Commissioner of Police (2016) senior officers arrested on suspicious of misfeasance in public office and theft of very large quantities of drugs. They were suspected of serious corruption and having links with Organised Crime Networks. C1 and C2 brought proceedings against the Commissioner alleging false imprisonment, trespass and discrimination on grounds of race. • Goff v Commissioner of Police (2016) G, a 19 year old girl, was unlawfully at large. She was traced to a flat – located on the 17th floor of a tower block. Police attended and sought to apprehend her. She attempted to escape and fell to her death. Police accused of not planning the operation properly and allowing her to get changed unsupervised. Claim brought in negligence and breach of art.2 ECHR (following an inquest last year). Onging. • In Re Arseema Dawit (2016) Inquest and civil proceedings arising out of the death of a 15 year old school girl stabbed 60 times by ex-boyfriend. Civil claim in QBD alleged police negligent and/or in breach of article 2 for failing to act upon threats from ex boyfriend that he intended to kill AD. • Jacob Marx v Williams Hill & Others (2016) Inquest and LRMPA and Fatal Accidents Act claims in QBD arising out of the death of a young lawyer, who was killed by a sign hoarding falling on his head. FAA claim brought on behalf of a dependant fiancée domiciled in New Zealand. • Warren v. Warren (2016) Claim in QBD arising from road traffic accident resulting in catastrophic spinal cord injuries and tetraplegia.
Professional Memberships: PIBA, PNBA, APIL
Career: Cambridge University; Call 1985; Harmsworth Scholar (Middle Temple); Chambers of Andrew Ritchie QC
Personal: Education: Habersdashers' Aske's School, Elstree; Downing College, Cambridge (MA, Law). Family: married, three children. Interests: cooking, reading, skiing and marathons.

WILLIAMSON, Adrian QC
Keating Chambers, London
020 7544 2600
awilliamson@keatingchambers.com
Featured in Professional Negligence (London), Construction (London)
Practice Areas: Adrian is a specialist in construction, engineering, energy, technology disputes and is highly regarded for his expertise in professional negligence and insurance actions within these specialist areas. His practice covers advisory work (including work relating to standard and bespoke contracts), drafting and advocacy, for which he is widely seen as a formidable opponent. He regularly appears in the TCC, and Court of Appeal, and in domestic and international arbitrations. He has represented clients in adjudications and mediations and is an adjudicator and arbitrator. Recent cases of interest include: MT Hojgaard v EON Climate and Renewables; Richard Hough v Greathall Ltd.; West v Ian Finlay & Associates; Galliford Try v Estura [2015] BLR 321; Severfield v Duro [2015] EWHC 2975 (TCC); Harding v Paice [2015] EWCA Civ 1231.
Professional Memberships: TECBAR; COMBAR; SCL.
Career: Called to the Bar 1983; QC 2002; Recorder (Civil) 2004, (Crime) 2009; TECBAR accredited adjudicator, Deputy High Court Judge (2010); Completed PhD in economic history at Cambridge 2014 on "The Birth of Thatcherism".
Publications: Keating on JCT Contracts – General Editor; Contributor – Keating on Construction Contracts 9th & 10th Edition (2011, 2016); Halsbury's Laws of England on Building Contracts.

WILLIAMSON, Alisdair
3 Raymond Buildings Barristers, London
020 7400 6400
alisdair.williamson@3rblaw.com
Featured in Crime (London), Professional Discipline (London)
Practice Areas: Alisdair has a varied serious crime, fraud and tribunal practice with an emphasis on defence. Often appearing as leading junior, high profile work in the last year has included murder, fraud and the defence of celebrities accused of sexual offences. He has extensive experience of defending police officers; he also undertakes Inquests and disciplinary tribunals.
Professional Memberships: Criminal Bar Association.
Career: Call 1994.
Personal: MA (Oxon), Dip. LL (City).

WILLIAMSON, Oliver
Serjeants' Inn Chambers, London
020 7427 5000
owilliamson@serjeantsinn.com
Featured in Police Law (All Circuits), Inquests & Public Inquiries (All Circuits)
Practice Areas: Oliver Williamson was called to the Bar in 2008. Oliver specialises in public and administrative, police, healthcare, inquests and inquiries, employment, civil liberties and human rights, professional discipline and product liability law. An earlier edition notes that "he is impressive on the advocacy side, he has intellectual weight" and "he is an excellent junior with a good eye for detail, he has great technical know-how." Please visit the Serjeants' Inn Chambers website for his profile, which sets out full details of his practice including relevant work of note.
Publications: Co-author of Medical Treatment: Decisions and the Law (2nd ed).
Personal: LLB, College of Law (First Class) Bar Vocational Course, College of Law (Outstanding). Queen Mother Scholarship, Middle Temple. Graduate Diploma in Law, College of Law (Distinction). MSci (Chemistry) University College, London (First Class).

WILMSHURST, Paul
9 Stone Buildings, London
020 7404 5055
pwilmshurst@9stonebuildings.com
Featured in Agriculture & Rural Affairs (London)
Practice Areas: Primary focus on disputes involving all aspects of property law (including landlord and tenant). Is particularly active in the law relating to village greens, commons, public rights of way, easements, boundary disputes, disputed ownership and cases with a public or environmental law dimension. Receives regular instructions in village green matters from local authorities, landowners/developers and applicants. Regularly sits as an Inspector at public inquiries. Has been involved in a number of village green cases before the courts including: R (Fellowes) v Powys County Council [2014] (refusal to appoint Inspector to hold an inquiry); R (Burrows) v The Royal Borough of Windsor and Maidenhead [2014] EWHC 389 (Admin) (contentious user and user as of right); R (Newhaven Port & Properties) v The Secretary State for the Environment [2014] (submission in support of permission to appeal made to Supreme Court on behalf of Intervenor on "retrospective" application of s.15(7)(b) Commons Act 2006); R (Halliday Properties Ltd) v Portsmouth City Council [2012] (involved – as led junior – in drafting of application to de-register a village green).
Professional Memberships: Middle Temple; Lincoln's Inn; Chancery Bar Association; Property Bar Association; The Institute of Public Rights of Way and Access Management (Associate Member)
Career: Called to the Bar 2007. McCarthy Tétrault LLP (Toronto) 2007 – 2008 (Fox Scholar). Undertook a common law pupillage and early years of tenancy on Western Circuit before joining current chambers.
Publications: Town and Village Greens (2014). Has written numerous articles in legal journals particularly on village green and public rights of way matters.
Personal: Educated at Durham University History BA (hons), Nottingham Law School GDL/CPE and BPP Law School BVC. Also worked at European Parliament (Brussels) before coming to the Bar. Born 1983. Lives in London

---

WILSON, Calum
Compass Chambers, Edinburgh
07739 639 328
calum.wilson@compasschambers.com
Featured in Personal Injury (Scotland)
Practice Areas: Practice includes all aspects of personal injury litigation acting for both pursuers and defenders in the Court of Session and Sheriff Court, with particular expertise in asbestos and other industrial disease claims; fatal cases; foreign travel claims and claims arising from accidents abroad; complex, high value claims; and clinical negligence actions. Recent cases include: Wilson v North Lanarkshire Council [2014] CSIH 26 and [2011] CSOH 178 (Employers' Liability; manual handling; safe systems of work); Shields v Crossroads (Orkney) 2014 S.L.T. 190 (Employers' Liability; Psychiatric Harm; Pleadings; Relevancy); Moran v Freyssinet Ltd 2015 SLT 829 and [2014] CSOH 173 (Chapter 43 procedure; failure to lodge Statement of Valuation of Claim; Decree by Default); Towers v Flaws & Anr. [2015] CSIH PD1537/13 (Refusal of Issues; fatal road traffic accident claim); Smith v Scottish Ministers 2015 G.W.D. 17-292 (Prison Officer – injury sustained during training exercise; Management of Health and Safety at Work Regulations 1999; Manual Handling Operations Regulations 1992; Provision and Use of Work Equipment Regulations 1998); McCrery v Letson [2015] CSOH 153 (Road Traffic Accident – pedestrian; liability; contributory negligence); Hall-Craggs v Royal Highland and Agricultural Society of Scotland 2016 S.L.T. 311 (Action of Damages – Motion for Summary Decree); Cumming v SSE Plc 2016 Rep.L.R. 75 (Action for Damages in the Sheriff Court – pleural plaques; sanction for the employment of Counsel – Courts Reform (Scotland) Act 2014, s. 108); Stanger & Ors. v Flaws & Anr. Court of Session Civil Jury Trial 14 - 17.06.16. (Fatal Claim – loss of society awards).
Career: M.A (Hons) (St Andrews University 1980 – 1984); LL.B. (with distinction), Dip.L.P. (University of Edinburgh 1984 – 1987); Solicitor (1989 – 2001); admitted to the Faculty of Advocates June 2002; Tutor in Civil Court Practice, University of Edinburgh 2002 – 2006; Clerk of the Faculty of Advocates July 2009 – October 2014; Standing Junior Counsel to the Advocate General for Scotland (Ministry of Defence) August 2015 to date.

WILSON, Elizabeth
Pump Court Tax Chambers, London
020 7414 8080
clerks@pumptax.com
Featured in Tax (London)

Practice Areas: Barrister practising in revenue law. She was appointed as Junior Counsel to the Crown B panel in 2011. Her advisory work covers private client (including trusts) and corporate tax. Notable cases include: Shop Direct Group v HMRC (SC); Aspinalls v HMRC (CA); TMF Trustees Singapore Ltd (formerly Equity Trust (Singapore) Ltd) v HMRC (QROPS) (CA); HMRC v Leekes (UT); Pertemps Recruitment Partnership Ltd v HMRC (UT); HMRC v The Late fourth Earl of Balfour (UT); Wintershall (A&P) Ltd v HMRC (UT); Newey t/a Ocean Finance v HMRC (CJEU). She also represented Her Majesty's Attorney General in Re Longman Deceased (Exors of the estate of Elizabeth Longman v IBS-STL (UK) Ltd & anor LTL 12.3.12) (construction of section 75F Charities Act 1993).
Professional Memberships: Revenue Bar Association; London Common Law and Commercial Bar Association; Chancery Bar Association.
Career: Qualified 1995; Middle Temple; Junior Counsel to the Crown, B panel 2011. Junior Counsel to the Crown, A panel with effect from 1 September 2016.
Publications: Contributor to 'Taxation of Corporate Debt and Derivatives' (Butterworth)

WILSON, Julian
11KBW, London
020 7632 8500
Julian.Wilson@11kbw.com
Featured in Employment (London)
Practice Areas: Commercial lawyer handling Employment related cases with corporate or commercial dimensions. Regularly acts in disputes concerning banking, trading and dealing practices. Experienced in share and incentive schemes, bonus, carried interest and profit share arrangements, shareholder agreements, unfair prejudice. Deals with claims involving contested earn-out and deferred consideration provisions. Has dealt with many cases concerning employee fraud and the use of tracing remedies. Also, unlawful competition, directors' duties, misuse of confidential information, team moves and springboard relief. Cases include: LS Systems Limited v Scott [2015] EWHC 1335 (Ch); Sanders v Trigor One Limited [2014] EWHC 1646 (Comm); Bank of Ireland v Rafiq [2013] EWHC 768; In the matter of Cloudbluff Properties Limited [2011] EWHC 649 (Ch); Goldstone v Goldstone & Ors [2011] EWCA Civ 39; Broome & Wellington LP v Greenstein [2009] EWCA Civ. 589; Hays v Ions [2008] EWHC 745; Duarte v Black & Decker [2008] 1 All ER (Comm) 401; Takacs v Barclays [2006] IRLR 877; Cantor Fitzgerald International v Horkulak [2005] ICR 402.
Career: BA, Oxon, Jurisprudence, 1981. Solicitor: 1984-97; Litigation Partner, Herbert Smith 1990-97; Higher Court Advocacy Rights (Civil) 1994; Called to the Bar: 1997, Inner Temple.

WILSON, Kate
One Brick Court, London
020 7353 8845
kw@onebrickcourt.com
Featured in Defamation/Privacy (London)
Practice Areas: Defamation, breach of confidence and privacy, data protection, freedom of information, harassment, reporting restrictions and contempt, pre-publication advice. Cases of interest include: forthcoming Supreme Court proceedings on recoverability of success fees in Art.10 cases (Flood v Times Newspapers); Theedom v Nourish Training [2016] EWHC 1364 & [2015] EWHC 3769 (s.2 defence & s.7 trial); Ma v St George's NHS Trust [2015] EWHC 1866; Barron v Collins [2015] EWHC 1125; Acting for Lord McAlpine inc against BBC and Sally Bercow (see [2013] EWHC 1342 & [2013] EWHC 981); R (A) v Lowestoft Magistrates Court [2013] EWHC 659 (Judicial Review of Reporting Restrictions); Flood v Times Newspapers [2012] UKSC 11(Supreme Court's decision on Reynolds defence); Crossland v University of Glamorgan [2011] EWHC 2809 (an appeal on malice); Re BBC (Care Proceedings: Identification of Local Authority) [2011] 1FLR 977; Re William Ward [2010] EWHC 16 (Fam)
Career: Called 2005, Inner Temple
Publications: Contributor to Arlidge, Eady & Smith on Contempt 4th Ed and 5th Ed (due 2016). Contributor to Bullen & Leake & Jacobs Precedents of Pleadings 18th Ed; Co-Author "The Family Courts: Media Access and Reporting" (2011); Author Lexis PSL Privacy and Misuse of Private Information
Personal: Magdalen College, Oxford (BA Hons PPE); Trinity Hall, Cambridge (MPhil)

WILSON, Richard QC
Serle Court, London
020 7242 6105
rwilson@serlecourt.co.uk
Featured in Chancery (London), Offshore (London), Trusts (London)
Practice Areas: General chancery, with a strong emphasis on litigation (both onshore and offshore) in the fields of trusts, estates, probate, 1975 Act claims, tax and related professional negligence. Recent notable cases include Khan v Gany (BVI, trustee's duty to account); Van der Merwe v Goldman (England, setting aside trust on basis of mistake); Loring v Woodland Trust (England, will construction); Fielden v Christie Miller, (England, proprietary estoppel) Schroder Trust v Schroder AG (Cayman, excessive execution, mistake and interaction of Cayman and Jersey 'firewall' legislation); Taros v Barratt (England, anti-suit injunctions); JF v Hexagon (Cayman, beneficial ownership of shares).
Professional Memberships: Chancery Bar Association, STEP, ACTAPS, Revenue Bar Association, Professional Negligence Bar Association.
Career: LLB (Sheffield) LLM (London), Called to the Bar 1996 (Middle Temple). Formerly worked as a Tax Consultant with Price Waterhouse.
Publications: Co-author of 'The Trustee Act 2000: A Practical Guide' (Jordans). Author of numerous articles.
Personal: Married with four children. Lives in Wiltshire.

WILSON-SMITH, Christopher QC
Outer Temple Chambers, London
020 73536381
christopher.wilson-smithqc@outertemple.com
Featured in Personal Injury (London), Clinical Negligence (London)
Practice Areas: Christopher Wilson-Smith's practice covers personal injury, often compounded by breaches of duty in healthcare following the initial trauma; clinical negligence and serious crime, primarily involving corporate manslaughter and health and safety cases. In clinical negligence CWS acts for claimants and defendants (NHSLA), often involving babies with birth injuries and often compounded by breaches of duty in healthcare following the initial trauma. Across the legal directories he has been listed as a leader in personal injury and clinical negligence for many years and last was honoured with a Lifetime Achievement Award. His clients say this of him: "He has the gravitas and experience to handle the most serious and complex injury claims. Christopher combines in Court advocacy of the very highest level, including unrivalled cross-examination skills, with a very powerful and effective style when it comes to negotiating settlements. He is, quite rightly, a legend." "His larger than life character and bluff amiability disguise his sharp forensic skills honed over many years in both criminal and civil cases of the highest order giving him an ability to see through to the real issues and address them quickly and effectively." "His ability to turn around a set of papers in short order is testament to his considerable work ethic and yet his eye for detail often catches out the unwary or ill-prepared." "His ability to explain to a client the complexities of their case whilst simultaneously fighting their corner tooth and nail is second to none. Quite simply, he is a force to be reckoned with and one that you want on your side." "He coaxes, teases and humbles expert witnesses in a manner that is admired by all." Recent clinical negligence cases include: Chloe Dolby v University Hospital of Leicester NHS Trust; Simon Barnett v Medway NHS Trust Kent; Martha Richardson-Rudd v Royal Surrey County Hospital NHS Foundation Trust; Maria Michael v Barnet & Chase Farm Hospitals NHS Trust. Recent personal injury cases include: Jay Young v SGA Productions Limited; Liam Blake v Mitchell Knight; Robert Croden v Frank Redman; June Vann (Martin Vann, deceased) v Occidental – Companhia de Seguros s.a. Crime and healthy & safety cases include: Buncefield Oil Refinery Fire; R v Imco Plastics; R v Southwest Water Authority.
Professional Memberships: He is a member of Western Circuit and CBA, CLBA, COMBAR, APIL, PNBA, PIBA and the AvMA.
Career: CWS was called in 1965 and took Silk in 1986. He became a Recorder of the Crown Court (civil and crime) in 1977 and Master of Bench Gray's Inn in 1996. He was Admitted as a QC to the Bar of New South Wales in 1996.
Personal: Education: Rudolph Steiner Schools in England & Switzerland (CLE). Leisure: Keen golfer and bridge player.

WILTON, Simon
Hailsham Chambers, London
020 7643 5000
simon.wilton@hailshamchambers.com
Featured in Professional Negligence (London)
Practice Areas: Simon is a highly experienced junior barrister specialising in professional negligence, professional regulation, and commercial matters particularly insurance disputes. He has wide experience of interlocutory, trial, arbitration, and appellate advocacy, and of all kinds of ADR. Cases include: Liverpool Victoria Insurance v Khan (2016); DB UK Bank v Jacobs (2016); Ahmad v Bank of Scotland [2016] EWCA Civ 602; EMW v RSA (2014); Johnson v Hibberts (2014); Tinseltime v Roberts [2013] PNLR 4; Coomber v Alan Bloom (& Ors) (2010); Nationwide v BKW v Hiscox (2010); Bonham v (1) Fishwick, (2) Fenner (2008) EWCA Civ 373; Leonard v Byrt (2008) EWCA Civ 20; Jessup v Wetherell [2007] PNLR 10; Sinclair v Woods of Winchester Ltd (2005) 102 Con LR 127; Sangster v Biddulphs [2005] PNLR 33; Kesslar v Moore & Tibbits [2005] PNLR 17; Aldi, B&Q, Grantchester v Holmes and Others (2004); Griffiths v Last Cawthra Feather [2002] PNLR 27.
Professional Memberships: Professional Negligence Bar Association; London Common Law and Commercial Bar and Chancery Bar Association.
Career: Called in 1993. Karmel Scholar, Gray's Inn.
Publications: Contributor to Professional Negligence and Liability, contributing editor (1999-2003) and editor (2007-2010) of the Lloyds Law Reports: Professional Negligence.
Personal: Educated at Sussex and Montpellier Universities. Married with three children.

WINDSOR, Emily
Falcon Chambers, London
020 7427 7324
clerks@falcon-chambers.com
Featured in Agriculture & Rural Affairs (London), Real Estate Litigation (London)
Practice Areas: Real property litigation, including commercial and residential landlord and tenant, agricultural holdings, restrictive covenants, easements, mortgages and associated professional negligence and insolvency. Recently reported cases include: Walby v Walby [2013] 1 EGLR 111; Ashdale Land v Maioriello [2012] 2 EGLR 119; Alford v Hannaford [2011] EWCA Civ 1099; National Westminster Bank v Hunter [2011] EWHC 3170 (Ch); Hopper v Hopper [2008] PLSCS 41; Majorstake Ltd v Curtis [2008] UKHL 10.
Professional Memberships: Agricultural Law Association; Chancery Bar Association (former committee member); LCLCBA; Property Bar Association; Elected Member of the Bar Council 2000-05; Member Bar Standards Board 2006-16; Vice-chair of BSB's Education & Training Committee 2007-15.
Career: Educated at The King's High School, Warwick; Worcester College, Oxford (MA Jurisprudence) and University of Paris II (DSU EEC Law); Called 1995 (Gray's Inn). Deputy District Judge.
Publications: Bullen Leake & Jacob's 'Precedents of Pleadings' (14th edn); Woodfall Property Update Service.
Personal: Working knowledge of French.

WINFIELD, Joshua
Radcliffe Chambers, London
020 7831 0081
jwinfield@radcliffechambers.com
Featured in Charities (London)
Practice Areas: General Chancery practice with emphasis on charities; trusts; wills, estates and probate; real property; landlord and tenant; and Court of Protection. Notable cases: Dean v Burne [2009] EWHC 1250 (Ch) – charity; Love v Griffiths, 29 July 2009, Ch D (Bristol DR) – construction of will; Widd v Widd [2011] EWHC 1420 (Ch) – setting aside trust for mistake; Millburn-Snell v Evans [2012] 1 WLR 41– strike out for lack of letters of administration; Re Longman deceased [2012] EWHC 666 (Ch) – construction of gift to charity in will; Bank of Scotland plc v Rihany, 1 June 2012, QBD (Brighton DR) – landlord and tenant (setting aside forfeiture).Marwaha v Singh [2013]

EWCA Civ 1878 – challenge to charity trustees' discretion; Re Dharamshi, Deceased [2013] EWHC 3917 (Ch): challenge to a will due to lack of capacity; Park v Cho [2014] PTSR 769: Lifting of stay following grant of permission to bring charity proceedings; Von Stein v Camphill Village Trust: breach of duty by charity trustees; Sheikh v Hussain: injunction to restrain holding of charity AGM.
Professional Memberships: Chancery Bar Association; Charity Law Association; STEP.
Career: Called 2001.
Publications: Westlaw Insight articles: Charity property: overview; Charitable companies; Charitable unincorporated associations; Charity land

WINSTON, Naomi
Ten Old Square, London
020 7405 0758
naomiwinston@tenoldsquare.com
Featured in Partnership (London)
Practice Areas: Practice areas: Naomi's practice covers litigation, drafting and advisory work across the full range of commercial chancery and chancery matters, but with particular focus on partnership and LLPs. Her practice also covers property and probate and trust matters. In her partnership work, Naomi represents clients in litigation (both at hearings and at the settlement stage), advises on internal issues within partnerships/LLPs and undertakes non-contentious advisory and drafting work, both for firms and individuals.
Professional Memberships: Professional memberships: Naomi is a member of the Chancery Bar Association and the Association of Partnership Practitioners.
Career: Career: Naomi was called to the bar in 2006 after graduating with a first class degree. She spent the following year working as a research assistant in the Law Commission's Family, Property and Trust Team. Recent cases include: Reinhard v Ondra [2015] EWHC 26 (Ch); [2015] EWHC 1869 (Ch) (nature of member's interest in an LLP)• Malik v Fassenfelt [2013] EWCA Civ 798 (CA) (property; possession; trespassers; Art 8) • Mehta v Steinbeck-Reeves (2012) (CC) (partnership; account; partnership property; application of s 24 PA 1890)• Castledine v Bentley Jennison (a firm) [2011] EWHC 2363 (Ch) (HC) (partnership; retention of share of goodwill after retirement): • Kahlon v Isherwood [2011] EWCA Civ 602 (CA) (landlord & tenant; whether a Tomlin order a HA 1988 prescribed form)• TWM Trust Corporation Ltd v AG [2010] All ER (D) 139 (May) (HC) (wills; charities; gift to an unincorporated association).
Publications: Publications: Naomi is a contributor to the APP Newsletter; Mellows: Taxation for Executors and Trustees and Practical Law.

WINSTONE, Hilary
Old Square Chambers, London
020 7269 0300
winstone@oldsquare.co.uk
Featured in Employment (London), Employment (Western)
Practice Areas: Hilary Winstone is a talented and knowledgeable junior specialising in employment and discrimination law. She has extensive experience acting successfully for large corporate clients, as well as local authorities, police forces and the NHS, dealing with internal and external disputes as well as mediation. She is known for being very client friendly and an enormously effective advocate, able to deal with difficult and highly charged cases. Her recent cases include Angela Bailey v Central and Northwest London NHS FT (successfully represented defendant in complex case involving claims of whistleblowing, disability discrimination and victimisation); Kitaka v Commissioner of the Police of the Metropolis (successfully represented defendant in case involving regulation breaches and subsequent claims of unfair dismissal); Boam v South Staffs & Shropshire Healthcare NHS FT (pending appeal following successful defence on behalf of defendant against claims of whistleblowing); R v W (complex claim of disability discrimination based on claimants unwillingness to disclose information to their employer to allow for reasonable adjustments).
Professional Memberships: JHRLA ELA ELBA EELA

WINTER, Ian QC
Cloth Fair Chambers, London
020 7710 6444
IanWinter@clothfairchambers.com
Featured in Crime (London), Professional Discipline (London), Financial Crime (London)
Practice Areas: Specialist in criminal law with a particular emphasis on fraud, corporate & business crime. Practice also covers police powers and civil liberties law, regulatory tribunals, judicial review, international mutual assistance, inquests and extradition. Acted for the defence in the Lady Aberdour and Swindon Town FC fraud. Represented Langaker, a defendant in the Morgan Grenfell Management Fraud. Represented Bossino in a multi-million pound money laundering, entrapment, 'Bennett' abuse of process. Represented Dr Harold Shipman. Represented Professor Roy Meadow at Appeal. R -v- Dougall, leading authority on sentencing executive level whistle blowers entering plea agreements in corruption cases. Represented K, a solicitor accused of tax fraud; privilege against self-incrimination in ancillary relief proceedings, without prejudice privilege and abuse of process. HKSAR -v- Lai, secured the quashing of a solicitor's $2bn takeover fraud conviction in the Hong Kong Court of Final Appeal. Continues to advise internationally renowned Surgeon during proceedings in Singapore and the UK, complaint arising from the Brunei Royal Family. Represented a solicitor in two substantial money laundering and takeover fraud cases. Advised News International re. phone hacking. Acted in BTA Bank v Mukhtar Ablyazov, civil contempt of court proceedings regarding the failure to disclose multi-million pound assets in complex off shore trust structures. Lead the team for Aivars Lembergs, a Latvian politician, over $135 million commercial court worldwide freezing order. Advising international company in relation to the bribery act. Successfully represented Kirsty Milczarek in front of the British Horseracing Authority on corruption charges. Advised one of the world's largest, privately owned, independent insurance brokers; Successfully represented Reg Traviss over rape charges. Acquittal secured after trial in Gibraltar re murder charges. Advised a global bank in relation to Libor rigging. Secured full acquittal for Ben Anderson, former city broker charged by the FCA with insider dealing offences. Advising former Senior Executive of Barclays PLC in SFO/FCA investigation re Qatar. Representing Thomas Chan over corruption charges in Hong Kong, Final Court of Appeal. Advising a former director of Tesco PLC, SFO investigation. Has advised in a number of Libel matters including Captain Shah -v- Associated Newspapers (successful trial on behalf of the claimant with substantial damages), represented Richard Desmond in his action against Tom Bower, McKeown v NGN (for the Claimant), and represented a premiership footballer. For further information please visit www.clothfairchambers.com
Career: Called to the Bar 1988. Joined Hollis Whiteman Chambers in 1990. Silk & Founder member of Cloth Fair Chambers 2006.
Personal: Educated at Bristol UWE 1984-87

WOLFE, Georgina
5 Essex Court, London
020 7410 2000
wolfe@5essexcourt.co.uk
Featured in Police Law (All Circuits)
Practice Areas: Police Law; Inquests; Public and Administrative; Professional Discipline; Personal Injury; Employment. Notable cases: the Independent Inquiry into Child Sex Abuse; R (Roberts) v Commissioner of Police of the Metropolis [2015] UKSC 79, [2016] 1 W.L.R. 210 (stop and search); Catt and T v Commissioner of Police of the Metropolis and ACPO [2015] UKSC 9; [2015] 2 W.L.R. 664 (police retention of data); R (TD) v Commissioner of Police of the Metropolis [2014] EWCA Civ 585 (police retention of CRIS reports); Lynch and ors v Chief Constable of Warwickshire Police and ors JR1305127, 14 November 2014 (recoverability of inquest costs); R (E7) v Chairman of the Azelle Rodney Inquiry [2014] EWHC 452 (Admin) (challenging the findings of a public inquiry); and in R (Ramsden) v IPCC [2013] EWHC 3969 (Admin) (defending a challenge to the police and IPCC's decision not to take witness statements from witnesses to an alleged assault); Inquests into the deaths of Kingsley Burrell, Jan McLean, Roger and Mathilde Lamb and Sabina Akhtar.
Professional Memberships: ALBA
Career: Called to the Bar 2006 (Queen Mother Scholarship; Harold G. Fox scholarship and Blackstone Entrance Exhibition). Appointed to the Attorney General's B Panel 2016 (and C Panel from 2012)
Publications: The Path to Pupillage (Sweet & Maxwell, 2008; Third Edition 2013) with Alexander Robson.

WONG, Natasha
187 Fleet Street, London
020 7430 7430
natashawong@187fleetstreet.com
Featured in Financial Crime (London)
Practice Areas: Specialist defence counsel with considerable expertise over the full range of investigations and proceedings brought by the Serious Fraud Office (SFO), Crown Prosecution Service (CPS) or Her Majesty's Customs and Revenue (HMRC) involving serious and complex allegations of fraud, financial crime and money laundering, drug offences, serious and organised crime. Many of these cases have involved multi-jurisdictional aspects as well as detailed legal arguments, including the admissibility of evidence, joinder and severance, challenging expert evidence, legal professional and litigation privilege, applications to stay the proceedings on the grounds of abuse of process, fitness to stand trial, public interest immunity, disclosure and submissions of no case to answer. Her practice also includes regulatory proceedings brought by the Financial Conduct Authority (FCA). Very experienced at managing large quantities of documents, disclosure databases and evidence served digitally. Recent work has included representing the rights of third parties in confiscation proceedings, conspiracies to steal telecommunications equipment and launder the proceeds through a network of companies, large scale conspiracies and possession with intent to supply class A and class B drugs, multi million pound money laundering and regulatory proceedings in the Upper Tax Tribunal. Registered to undertake Public Access work.

WOOD, Benjamin
4 New Square, London
020 7822 2000
b.wood@4newsquare.com
Featured in Professional Negligence (London)
Practice Areas: Commercial and Chancery litigation (both onshore and offshore), particularly financial services, civil fraud and property-related litigation. Professional liability claims involving financial, legal, construction and valuation professionals. Reported cases include Kandola v. Mirza Solicitors [2015] PNLR 19, Barclays Bank v. Grant Thornton [2015] 1 CLC 180, Newcastle International Airport v. Eversheds [2014] 1 WLR 3073 and Thompson v. Foy [2010] 1 P&CR 16.
Professional Memberships: COMBAR, Professional Negligence Bar Association, Chancery Bar Association.
Career: Called to the Bar in 2005. Formerly corporate financier at NM Rothschild & Sons. Appointed Deputy District Judge in 2013. Ben is also an advocacy trainer for Lincoln's Inn and has been a member of the Bar Standards Board's Education & Training Committee.
Personal: BA Hons (Oxon). Leisure interests: travel, skiing and diving.

WOOD, David
Charter Chambers, London
020 7618 4400
david.wood@charterchambers.com
Featured in Crime (London)
Practice Areas: David practises in criminal and regulatory law. In criminal law he defends and prosecutes (at CPS Grade 3) across the full spectrum of grave and serious offences. He also defends in regulatory tribunals, especially for the Royal College of Nursing. David combines a genuine flair for advocacy with a common touch and a detailed and strategic approach to preparing litigation, fostered by a year at Bindmans LLP before coming to the Bar. This makes him particularly effective in complicated and serious criminal cases, where he has developed an extremely strong practice for his relatively junior call. He makes for a very proficient led junior but has considerable experience acting alone. Major instructions in 2016 included a widely reported conspiracy to steal (junior alone, value £20-57M), a conspiracy to import drugs from the Far East (junior alone) and an allegation of professional money laundering to the value of £10M (led junior). David is a volunteer duty panel advocate for the Asylum Support Appeals Project.

Professional Memberships: Criminal Bar Association – Executive Committee elected member South Eastern Circuit Advocacy Trainer (pupils) for the Inner Temple
Career: 2007 Called to the Bar, Inner Temple
Publications: 'Justice Sector Training in Somaliland', Innerview, Michaelmas 2015 (an account of David's work, with others from Charter Chambers, in Somaliland in 2015). Research Credit, The Law of Public Order and Protest, OUP 2010

WOODBRIDGE, Julian
1 King's Bench Walk, London
020 7936 1500
jwoodbridge@1kbw.co.uk
Featured in Crime (London)
Practice Areas: A defence advocate who undertakes serious criminal work in the UK and abroad. The breadth of practice includes all forms of homicide, white collar fraud, sexual offences and medical defence work. He has established a reputation for thorough preparation and penetrating cross examination. In reported cases in the Court of Appeal he has been involved in leading cases concerning mens rea in offences involving the misuse of drugs, public interest immunity and in 2011 the Guideline case setting tariffs for sentences involving fraud. Recent high profile cases have included representing doctors charged with gross negligence manslaughter and cases involving historic allegations of sexual assault. Apart from criminal cases, he also defends doctors before the Medical Practitioners' Tribunal and Performers' List Panel.
Professional Memberships: South Eastern Circuit, Sussex Bar Mess and the Criminal Bar Association.
Career: Called 1981.

WOODHOUSE, Charles
Old Square Chambers, London
020 7269 0300
clerks@oldsquare.co.uk
Featured in Personal Injury (London), Personal Injury (Western)
Practice Areas: Charlie is instructed by Claimants and Defendants predominantly in high value, catastrophic and fatal injury claims in civil proceedings and inquests. His caseload includes accidents resulting in brain injury, amputation, chronic pain disorders resulting in severe disability and cases involving contested mental capacity but he is also regularly instructed in matters in which liability is contested including complex and multi-party road traffic accident claims and accidents involving the use or malfunction of industrial machinery. Charlie has considerable experience of acting for members of the armed forces in claims against the Ministry of Defence and other Defendants. He is regularly instructed by insurers in respect of fraudulent claims or claims in which policy cover is avoided by virtue of the insured's conduct. Recent examples of such cases include claims involving racing by multiple drivers resulting in multi vehicle fatal accidents and a claim involving the reckless use of a car to injure several of a group of pedestrians by an unidentified driver Charlie also acts for Claimants in clinical negligence claims and at Inquests into deaths in hospital or during the course of medical treatment.

WOOLF, Jeremy
Pump Court Tax Chambers, London
020 7414 8080
clerks@pumptax.com
Featured in Tax (London)
Practice Areas: Jeremy Woolf's practice includes a mixture of non-contentious and contentious work relating to all taxes, including negligence and judicial review, rectification and Variation of Trusts Act proceedings raising tax issues. His practice includes personal, corporate and indirect tax. Jeremy is qualified to accept Public Access instructions.
Professional Memberships: Revenue Bar Association; VAT Practitioners Group; He is a Chartered Institute of Taxation representative on the fiscal committee of the Confederation Fiscale Europeenne; He is chair of CIOT's European Union and Human Rights sub-committee; CFE's alternate representative on the European Commission's VAT Exports group and was the CIOT's alternate representative on the European Commission's Expert Group on removing tax problems facing individuals.
Career: Called 1986; Inner Temple.
Publications: Zamir and Woolf, 'The Declaratory Judgment'; DeSmith, Woolf and Jowell, 'Judicial Review of Administrative Action' (6th Edition), Halsbury's Laws of England, Customs & Excise; 'De Voil: Indirect Tax Service'; 'Simon's Direct Tax Service'; 'Civil Appeals'; 'Potter & Monroe's Tax Planning'.
Personal: University of Sussex (BA); University of Cambridge (LLM).

WOOLFE, Philip
Monckton Chambers, London
020 7405 7211
pwoolfe@monckton.com
Featured in Competition/European Law (London), Telecommunications (London)
Practice Areas: Competition Law and State Aid, Commercial, European Union Law, Public & Administrative Law, Public Procurement, Telecommunications Regulation and VAT.
Professional Memberships: He is a committee member of COMBAR and a member of the Competition Law Association, Bar European Group and Procurement Lawyers' Association.
Career: BA (Hons) in History (Cambridge University 1998-2001), BA (Hons) in Law (Oxford University) (2001-2003), BCL (Oxford University) (2004-2005), Fellow of All Souls College, Oxford (2003-2010), Call (2004), Pupillage at Monckton Chambers (2005-2006), Tenant at Monckton Chambers (2006-present)
Publications: Contributor to Bellamy & Child: European Community Law of Competition (7th edition) (OUP, 2013), Contributor to Value Added Tax: Commentary & Analysis (Sweet Maxwell, 2009), Monckton Chambers Brexit Blog (https://www.monckton.com/brexit-blog/).
Personal: Philip speaks fluent French and German and has conversational Italian. He has a strong interest in mathematics, science and technology.

WORTHINGTON, Stephen QC
12 King's Bench Walk, London
020 7583 0811
worthington@12kbw.co.uk
Featured in Personal Injury (London)
Practice Areas: Recognised as one of a handful of top silks at the PI Bar, Stephen is predominately involved in complex and substantial cases involving Personal injury, clinical negligence, professional negligence, insurance, environmental, construction. Blue Circle v Ministry of Defence, Nuclear Pollution, [1998] 3 All ER 385. Heil v Rankin [2001] QB 272. Martin v Lancashire County Council (2000) 3 All ER 54 (TUPE). Watson v British Boxing Board of Control [2001] QB 1134. Hall v Gwent NHS Trust [2004] EWHC 2748, Browning v Brachers (a firm) [2005] EWCA Civ 753, Phillips v Rafiq [2007] PIQR P304, Turner v Jordan [2010] EWHC 1508 (QB) – Assessment of damages when the claimant is exaggerating. Carswell v Secretary of State for Transport [2010] EWHC 3230 (QB) – Motor Insurers' Bureau; Principle of effectiveness; Costs; Failure to fulfil obligations; Road traffic accidents; Untraced drivers.Wilkinson v Fitzgerald & Churchill Insurance [2013] 1WLR 1776, McCracken -v- D. Smith, D Bell & MIB [2013] EWHC 3620 (QB)
Professional Memberships: PIBA, LCLCBA, TECBAR, PNBA.
Career: Trinity College, Cambridge. Called to Bar 1976, recorder 2002, Silk 2006.
Publications: Contributor to Butterworths 'Professional Negligence' and 'Structured Settlements: A Practical Guide'.

WRAIGHT, William
2TG – 2 Temple Gardens, London
020 7822 1200
wwraight@2tg.co.uk
Featured in Clinical Negligence (London)
Practice Areas: Clinical negligence and personal injury, acting for claimants and defendants. Notable cases: Acting for NHS in Ian Paterson Breast Surgery Litigation, led by Michael de Navarro QC (QBD, ongoing); C v B NHS (Bournemouth CC, July 2016, settled), missed diagnosis of scaphoid fracture; W v SWL NHS (Central London CC, 12 May 2016), successful resistance of appeal against strike out; A v W (QBD, Sheffield, December 2015, settled), missed diagnosis of cauda equina; S v B NHS (Central London CC, 25-26 November 2015), successful defence of alleged misdiagnosis of strangulating abdominal incisional hernia; DiC v I (QBD, October 2015, settled), alleged missed diagnosis of pseudmyxoma peritonei; T v RC NHS (QBD, 9-11 March 2015), missed diagnosis of scoliosis; E v G NHS (Central London CC, 28-29 January 2014), successful defence of a claim concerning a fall in a physiotherapy falls-prevention class; T v N-T (Central London CC, 17-20 June 2013), successful defence of allegedly negligent hysteroscopy and polypectomy procedure during in-vitro fertilisation.
Professional Memberships: PNBA, PIBA, Member of the Royal College of Surgeons
Career: Graduated from Oxford University in medicine in 2001; also with first-class honours degree in Physiological Sciences in 1998. Taught anatomy at Cambridge University. Research in intensive care, anatomy and plastic surgery. General surgical training in A&E, colorectal surgery, trauma and orthopaedics and cardiothoracic surgery. Attained Membership of the Royal College of Surgeons in 2004. Specialised in plastic surgery including hand surgery, trauma and cancer reconstruction, burns and cosmetic surgery. Called to the Bar in 2009.

WRAY, Laura
Westwater Advocates, Edinburgh
0131 260 5700
mrslaurawray@btinternet.com
Featured in Personal Injury (Scotland)
Practice Areas: Laura has specialised for over 25 years in personal injury, medical and dental negligence and industrial disease claims. She also has considerable experience in product liability cases including organophosphate exposure, silicone implants, steroids and CJD. Laura was junior counsel in the settled case of Cooper v Merck (the first publicly funded Vioxx action in the world) initially acting on her own, and thereafter with Andrew Hajducki QC. She is instructed in complex and high value cases, including catastrophic injuries such as tetraplegia and brain injury. She acts for pursuers and defenders in the Court of Session and Sheriff Courts. Laura is happy to work on a speculative or legally aided basis.
Career: 1985-1987 – trainee solicitor; thereafter Litigation Partner then Senior Partner of trade union and personal injury firm, L & L Lawrence, Glasgow and Edinburgh. Acted as Scottish agent to several English, Irish and American law firms. Qualified in English law in 1992. Elected to the Executive Board of the Association of Personal Injury Lawyers (APIL) and appointed Vice Chair of the International Section of the Association of Trial Lawyers of America (ATLA). Consultant to Drummond Miller 1998-2002. Called to the Bar in 2003.

WRIGHT, Alexander
4 Pump Court, London
020 7842 5555
awright@4pumpcourt.com
Featured in Shipping (London)
Practice Areas: Shipping and commodities matters including disputes arising out of charterparties, contracts of affreightment and bills of lading, ship sale MOAs, forward freight agreements (FFAs), the international sale and carriage of goods, commodity sale and purchase agreements, and shipping-related guarantee claims. Shipbuilding disputes across a range of types of vessels, including bulk carriers, oil/chemical tankers, ro-ro passenger ferries, and superyachts. Wet shipping matters including arrests, collision and towage. Claims against ship managers. General commercial dispute resolution including insurance (marine and non-marine) and reinsurance, construction and engineering, banking, derivatives, guarantees, purchase options, agency disputes, commercial fraud (including bribery), joint venture agreements, shareholders' agreements and other general contractual matters.
Professional Memberships: COMBAR (Executive Committee), London Shipping Law Centre, Young Maritime Professionals Association (Committee Member), TECBAR, SCL.
Career: Called 2007 (Middle Temple). Pupil at 4 Pump Court 2007-08. Tenant at 4 Pump Court 2008 to date.
Personal: MA (Cantab) (Peterhouse). Married with one daughter.

WYGAS, Luke
4 Pump Court, London
Lwygas@4pumpcourt.com
020 7842 5555
Featured in Professional Negligence (London), Construction (London)

Practice Areas: Commercial litigation and arbitration focusing on international and domestic construction, energy, IT and professional negligence (with a particular emphasis on construction professionals) disputes. Luke is a qualified engineer who worked in the industry, mainly in the Far East, before coming to the Bar. Recent cases include representing an employer in an international arbitration concerning a power plant in the Middle East, representing an employer in relation to a mining project in Africa and representing a contractor in relation to a prestigious retail development in the Far East. Luke also have experience of fire loss claims, particularly when they include issues of technical complexity and fraud cases (particularly in relation to mortgage fraud). He is also frequently instructed in relation to construction adjudications.
Professional Memberships: COMBAR, Professional Negligence Bar Association, Society of Construction Law, Society for Computers and Law.
Career: Called 2004.
Publications: Atkins Court Forms: Professional Negligence Aktins, Court Forms: Mortgages, Lexis Nexis: Adjudication Know-how, Lexis Nexis: Construction Module.

WYLES, Lucy
2TG - 2 Temple Gardens, London
020 7822 1200
lwyles@2tg.co.uk
Featured in Travel (London)
Practice Areas: Lucy is an experienced common law advocate, practising in the areas of personal injury, clinical negligence and insurance. She has considerable expertise in dealing with claims with an international element, issues arising from accidents abroad and other aspects of travel law. She is regularly instructed to act in substantial claims resulting from accidents on holiday and in other cases involving jurisdiction and choice of law disputes.
Professional Memberships: PIBA; LCLCBA
Career: Recent cases include: Cook v Virgin Media Ltd: Court of Appeal case on forum non conveniens between Scotland and England. Syred v PZU and HDI: Application of Polish law to claims for catastrophic injuries. Dale and Huxtable v Baloise: Claims for multiple injuries involving Belgian law. Wagenaar v Weekend Travel Ltd: First Court of Appeal case on QOWCS in personal injury cases. Merton College, Oxford (1992 MA Hons Jurisprudence); Université Libre De Bruxelles (1993 Licence Spéciale in EC law).
Publications: Assistant editor 'European Civil Practice', Sweet & Maxwell (2nd ed, 2004).

WYNNE, James
Littleton Chambers, London
020 7797 8600
jwy@littletonchambers.co.uk
Featured in Employment (London)
Practice Areas: James' practice covers employment law in Employment Tribunal and High Court, collective/trade union aspects of labour law, commercial disputes and injunctions. James has acted in high profile discrimination, whistleblowing, TUPE/redundancy and collective matters and a number of his appellate cases have been reported. James' High Court employment expertise includes injunctions and claims regarding directors' duties, restrictive covenants, team moves and soft IP. He has acted for a number of clients facing national industrial action. James' commercial practice includes contractual disputes, directors duties, agency, soft IP, copyright and passing off, insolvency and employment agency contracts. He has a growing practice in charities regulation. James' practice regularly involves international disputes and foreign jurisdictions. He has rights of audience before the DIFC Courts in Dubai, where he has undertaken full trials at first instance and appeals before the DIFC Court of Appeal.
Professional Memberships: ELA, ELBA, Combar, CLA.
Career: Called 2002. Educated at Cambridge University (Engineering, MA), UCL (LLB), LSE (LLM). Before studying law worked in engineering for the MoD and in the private sector.
Publications: 'Transfer of Undertakings' (looseleaf) Thomson Sweet and Maxwell 'The Law of Industrial Action and Trade Union Recognition', 2nd Edition 2011, Oxford University Press.

YANG, Zizhen
Pump Court Tax Chambers, London
020 7414 8080
clerks@pumptax.com
Featured in Tax (London)
Practice Areas: Zizhen advises and litigates on all aspects of revenue law, as well as in other areas of law where tax-related issues feature. Her litigation practice extends to the First-tier Tribunal, the Upper Tribunal, the High Court and the Court of Appeal. Recent cases include Bookit Ltd v HMRC (VAT); British Film Institute v HMRC (VAT); King's College London v HMRC (SDLT); Patersons of Greenoakhill Ltd v HMRC (Landfill Tax); Trinity Mirror Plc v HMRC (VAT); DM-WSHNZ Ltd v HMRC (Corporation Tax); Euroceanica (UK) Ltd v HMRC (Tonnage Tax); Flanagan & ors v HMRC (Income Tax); Leeds City Council v HMRC (VAT); Price & ors v HMRC (Income Tax); Vaccine Research Limited Partnership & anor v HMRC (Capital Allowances, income tax); Purolite International Ltd v HMRC (Corporation Tax); Chadderton Total Care Group Ltd v HMRC (PAYE/NIC penalty); Albermarle 4 LLP v HMRC (Income Tax); Carter Allen International Ltd v HMRC (Corporation Tax); Abbey National Treasury Services Plc v HMRC (Corporation Tax).
Professional Memberships: Revenue Bar Association.
Career: Called 2009 (Lincoln's Inn); PhD (Cambridge University, molecular biology) 2007.

YATES, David
Pump Court Tax Chambers, London
020 7414 8080
clerks@pumptax.com
Featured in Professional Negligence (London), Tax (London)
Practice Areas: David frequently advises on or acts in litigation relating to private client, corporation tax, VAT and customs and duties. He is also very experienced in advising on and appearing in professional negligence and discipline cases arising in a tax context. David was appointed to the Attorney General's C panel in February 2009 and B panel in February 2013 and undertakes work for both taxpayers and HMRC. Recent tax cases include States of Guernsey and Jersey v HMRC (judicial review of removal of VAT exemption for Channel Island imports), R (Bampton Property Group Ltd) v HMRC (judicial review on refusal of late claims for group relief), Sanderson (discovery assessments), Proteus & Samarkand (film schemes) and Mayes (Chargeable events regime & Ramsay); Birmingham Hippodrome (Set-off time limits) & Sanderson (discovery assessments) and Rowe (APNs and PPNs). Qualified to accept Public Access instructions and willing to act under Joint Advisory Scheme and Special Advocacy Scheme.
Professional Memberships: Professional Negligence Bar Association, Revenue Bar Association.
Career: Called 2004. March 2009: Appointed Junior Counsel to the Crown – "C" Panel. March 2013: Appointed Junior Counsel to the Crown – "B" Panel.
Personal: Cambridge University (1998-2001, MA); City University (2002-03, PgDL); Lord Denning Scholar of Lincoln's Inn.

YATES, Nicholas
1 Hare Court, London
020 77977070
yates@1hc.com
Featured in Family/Matrimonial (London)
Practice Areas: Nicholas specialises in financial remedy cases (including Civil Partnership and Schedule 1 claims) often involving substantial assets, complex company valuations, trusts, tax issues and international dimensions. He also frequently drafts nuptial agreements and advises on their enforceability, as well as representing clients on jurisdiction matters, marriage/non-marriage cases and Inheritance Act claims. He is one of the few members of the family bar to have won a second tier appeal to the Court of Appeal in a financial case within the first three years of practice. Nicholas is highly regarded by the professionals with whom he works. He is well-known to establish quickly a solid rapport with his clients. Recent reported cases include: De Reene v Galbraith-Marten 13 April 2016 (Court of Appeal); AB v CD [2016] EWHC 10 (Fam) Chai v Peng (No.2) [2015] 1 FLR 637; Chai v Peng [2014] 2 FLR 1189; B v B [2013] EWHC 1232 (Fam); F v F (Financial Remedies: Premarital Wealth) [2012] EWHC 438 (Fam) and Bokor-Ingram v Bokor-Ingram [2009] EWCA Civ 412.
Professional Memberships: The Family Law Bar Association
Career: Trinity College, Cambridge. Called in 1996, Inner Temple.
Publications: Articles for Family Law.
Personal: Classical music, singing (tenor) and cycling.

YEGINSU, Can
4 New Square, London
020 7822 2000
c.yeginsu@4newsquare.com
Featured in Administrative & Public Law (London), International Arbitration (London)
Practice Areas: Can combines a strong practice in international arbitration and commercial litigation (including civil fraud) with professional liability work and a busy commercial judicial review specialism, while also fostering a wider human rights and public international law practice, equivalent in depth and breadth to his commercial work. Recent/current work includes: First Junior Counsel in Marathon Asset Management v Seddon & Ors (£100 million Commercial Court unlawful means conspiracy claim, a Lawyer Magazine Top 20 case for 2016); sole Counsel in $80 million LCIA arbitration involving the operation of an oil terminal connected to the CPC pipeline; counsel for a leading Bank in a US $75 million A1P1 (property rights) claim before the European Court of Human Rights; First Junior Counsel in £195 million A1P1 claim in Breyer Group Plc & Others v Department of Energy and Climate Change; First Junior Counsel in the UK Supreme Court in the James Rhodes memoir appeal. In 2013, Can was named as one of ten "Stars at the Bar" by Legal Week.
Professional Memberships: LCIA, IBA, ALBA, COMBAR, ICC UK, ICCA, PNBA.
Career: M.A. (Oxon); LL.M. Harvard Law School; Procter Fellow, Princeton University; Called 2007.
Publications: Jackson & Powell on Professional Liability (Sweet & Maxwell, 2015), The Protections for Religious Rights: Law and Practice (OUP, 2013).

YEO, Colin
Garden Court Chambers, London
020 7993 7600
coliny@gclaw.co.uk
Featured in Immigration (London)
Practice Areas: Well known in the immigration sector for his very widely read Free Movement immigration law website, Colin Yeo's practice covers the full range of immigration law. He is equally at ease with personal, family or business immigration issues, EU free movement cases, asylum cases and nationality law questions. He regularly trains other immigration lawyers, has contributed to a number of publications and practitioner texts and is often approached for immigration law commentary in the media. Strategic in his approach, he switches easily between campaigning work and quiet, sensitive handling of difficult cases.
Professional Memberships: Immigration Law Practitioners Association
Career: Colin joined Garden Court Chambers in August 2013, having previously practised at Renaissance Chambers. Before coming to the Bar he was Director of Legal Services and Training at the Immigration Advisory Service, prior to which he worked as a Legal Officer at the Refugee Legal Centre.
Publications: Lexis Nexis Immigration PSL service – Consultant Editor; JCWI Guide to the Points Based System (2011); ILPA Best Practice Guide to Working with Refugee Children (2011); Raising the spouse visa age [2009] IANL 365; Protecting family members [2008] IANL 147
Personal: Studied history at St John's College, Oxford before converting to law.

YEO, Nicholas
3 Raymond Buildings Barristers, London
020 7400 6400
nicholas.yeo@3rblaw.com
Featured in Crime (London), POCA Work & Asset Forfeiture (All Circuits), Financial Crime (London)
Practice Areas: Nicholas Yeo is a specialist in fraud, the proceeds of crime, police and coronial law. He is also experienced in serious crime, licensing, human rights law and extradition. Recent cases include Malabu Gas and Oil (restraint order founded on alleged billion dollar corruption), Saleh (conflict of laws in civil recovery cases) and Secretary of State for Transport v Senior Coroner for Norfolk (disclosure and use of air accident investigation reports and material). He was called in 1999. Previously, he worked for

Gartmore, Merrill Lynch, ABN Amro. He lectures on the proceeds of crime for MBL seminars.
Publications: Blackstone's Guide to the Fraud Act (2007, OUP), Money Laundering Law and Regulation: A Practical Guide (Due 2010, OUP), UK Competition Manual chapter on the cartel offence (PLC, 2003-); Serious Economic Crime: A Boardroom Guide to Prevention and Compliance (published by White Page Ltd in association with the SFO, Nov 2011) – chapter 14: "the main fraud offences prosecuted by the SFO" co-authored with Harry Travers and Shaul Brazil

YEO, Nik
Fountain Court Chambers, London
020 7583 3335
ny@fountaincourt.co.uk
Featured in International Arbitration (London), Professional Negligence (London), Banking & Finance (London)
Practice Areas: Commercial litigation and arbitration, with an emphasis on cross border disputes and matters concerning (i) derivatives, securitisations and other structured finance, (ii) financial regulation; (iii) energy and natural resources, (iv) information technology, (v) insurance and re-insurance; and (vi) professional negligence, particularly arising out of the foregoing areas. Accustomed both to working as part of a team as well as acting as lead advocate. For example, involved in what has been described in the press as the "valuation trial of the century", arising out of a commercial mortgage-backed securitisation; representing RBS in claims by investors in CPDOs which seek to hold rating agencies directly liable to investors; represented Lehman Brothers Inc (the US broker dealer) in various matters before the English courts; represented various leading phone manufacturers in arbitrations in relation to mobile phone technology; represented oil traders in arbitrations arising out of Nigerian oil. Comfortable with technological-intensive disputes of all kinds.
Professional Memberships: Commercial Bar Association, LCIA.
Career: Called 2000. Former solicitor at London magic circle firm practising in structured finance.
Personal: Educated Melbourne University (BA (Hons), LLB (Hons)) and Wadham College, Oxford (BCL – 1st class).

ZACAROLI, Antony QC
South Square, London
020 7696 9900
antonyzacaroli@southsquare.com
Featured in Chancery (London), Banking & Finance (London), Commercial Dispute Resolution (London), Company (London), Financial Services (London), Restructuring/Insolvency (London)
Practice Areas: Antony has a broad commercial litigation practice, and specialises in all aspects of domestic and international insolvency and restructuring, as well as banking, company and financial services law.
Professional Memberships: INSOL, Commercial Bar Association, Financial Markets Law Committee, P.R.I.M.E. Finance expert, Insolvency Rules Committee, III, Trustee of Bar Pro Bono Unit.
Career: Antony has appeared in many of the leading insolvency and restructuring cases over the last three decades, and has extensive experience of heavy and complex commercial court trials. He is regularly instructed on cross-border insolvency matters, both in England and in the courts of various offshore jurisdictions. Recent restructuring cases in which he has been involved include Kaisa Group, Winsway, Codere Finance, Stemcor, Co-Operative Bank, Arcapita Bank. Antony has been heavily involved in litigation arising out of the collapse of Lehman Brothers, MF Global, the Icelandic banks and the Irish Bank Resolution Corporation. He was instructed by ISDA to intervene in the Court of Appeal in Lomas v Firth Rixson, one of the leading cases on the interpretation of the ISDA Master Agreement. Called to the Bar (Middle Temple) 1987; Queen's Counsel 2006. Called to Bar of the BVI 2004.
Publications: Contributor to Lightman & Moss: The Law of Receivers of Companies (2012); Mortimore on Company Directors: Duties, Liabilities and Remedies (OUP, 2009: second edition 2012).

ZELLICK, Adam
Fountain Court Chambers, London
020 7583 3335
az@fountaincout.co.uk
Featured in Banking & Finance (London), Commercial Dispute Resolution (London), Fraud (London)
Practice Areas: Chambers & Partners Banking Junior of the Year 2014. Strong, broad-based, commercial practice with extensive experience in arbitration, aviation, banking, civil fraud, commercial litigation, conflict of laws, and insurance/reinsurance. Acts in a wide range of commercial cases and appeals (including the very heavy, multi-party, expert-intensive, high-value or publicity-sensitive) and often to assist litigation abroad. Aims to bring a client-focused, pragmatic, thorough and good-humoured approach to every case. Recent cases include: Deutsche Bank v Unitech, Pakistan v NatWest, Re Dewey LeBoeuf, Alliance Bank v Arip, Premier Motorauctions v PwC & Lloyds, LICT v VTBC, Access Bank v Akingbola, Re Air France – AF447, Re Antonio Gramsci, Re Aman Resorts, Macquarie v Artefact, Societe General v Saad, ICD v Tuwairqi Steel, AWAS v Jordan Aviation, Merchant International v Naftogaz, Spliethoff's v Bank of China.
Professional Memberships: COMBAR, LCLCBA, BILA, SE Circuit, ICC YAF, Burma Justice Committee.
Career: MA, University of Cambridge (Squire Scholar); Called 2000 (Middle Temple, Queen Mother Scholar); Called BVI 2014; previously: Research Assistant, Law Commission; Supervisor in Law, Gonville and Caius College.
Publications: Author, Civil Aviation, Atkin's Court Forms, 2006, 2010; contributor, Bullen and Leake and Jacob's Precedents of Pleadings, 2000. Editorial Board, Counsel Magazine, 2012-16

ZWART, Christiaan
39 Essex Chambers, London
020 7832 1111
christiaan.zwart@39essex.com
Featured in Planning (London)
Practice Areas: Christiaan has an extensive practice in Planning, Environmental, Public and Local Government Law and Development Related Taxes. He regularly represents developers, and local authorities and has extensive government agency experience including with the Environment Agency, DEFRA, DECC, Highways Agency and the Secretary of State, Cabinet Office and HMRC. He has a great deal of experience at planning inquiries and hearings; significant experience in DCO, CPO and TWA hearings; and extensive experience in High Court challenges, the Court of Appeal and the Supreme Court and in other jurisdictions, including Hong Kong and Jersey. As a planning barrister Christiaan has considerable experience in residential housing development and is regularly instructed on intricate urban developments, large urban extensions and significant regeneration schemes (most recently on Meridian Water, Hallesville Qtr, and Enderby Wharf). As a viability and CIL barrister Christiaan has particular expertise in fiscal planning matters and regularly advises developers on CIL. As an infrastructure barrister, Christiaan's unique experience includes securing: dismissal of the 27 125m turbine Myndd y gwynt Wind Farm energy (DCO for NRW) approval of the innovative 240MWe wave power Tidal Lagoon Swansea Bay (Generating Station) energy DCO (advising the Examining Authority panel); approval of the South Hook CHP DCO (for Exxon Mobil – the first true 'outline' DCO and the first such in a National Park); and satisfactory approval of Hinkley Point C (for the EA). His other areas of practice include Tax where is has appeared in numerous First Tier and Upper Tribunal (Tax Chamber), and High Court hearings, both for and against HMRC. As a residential VAT specialist Christiaan has particular expertise in development financial disputes.
Professional Memberships: NIPA, PEBA, CPA, UKELA, ComBAR.
Career: Appointed 2010: Attorney General's B Panel; C Panel 2004. Called 1997 Inner Temple. Duke of Edinburgh Scholar. City University 1996-97 (CPE). RIBA Part III 1995. Newcastle University 1986-92 (Architecture: Double First).
Personal: Born 1967. Lives West London. Interests include ancient history, art & architecture.

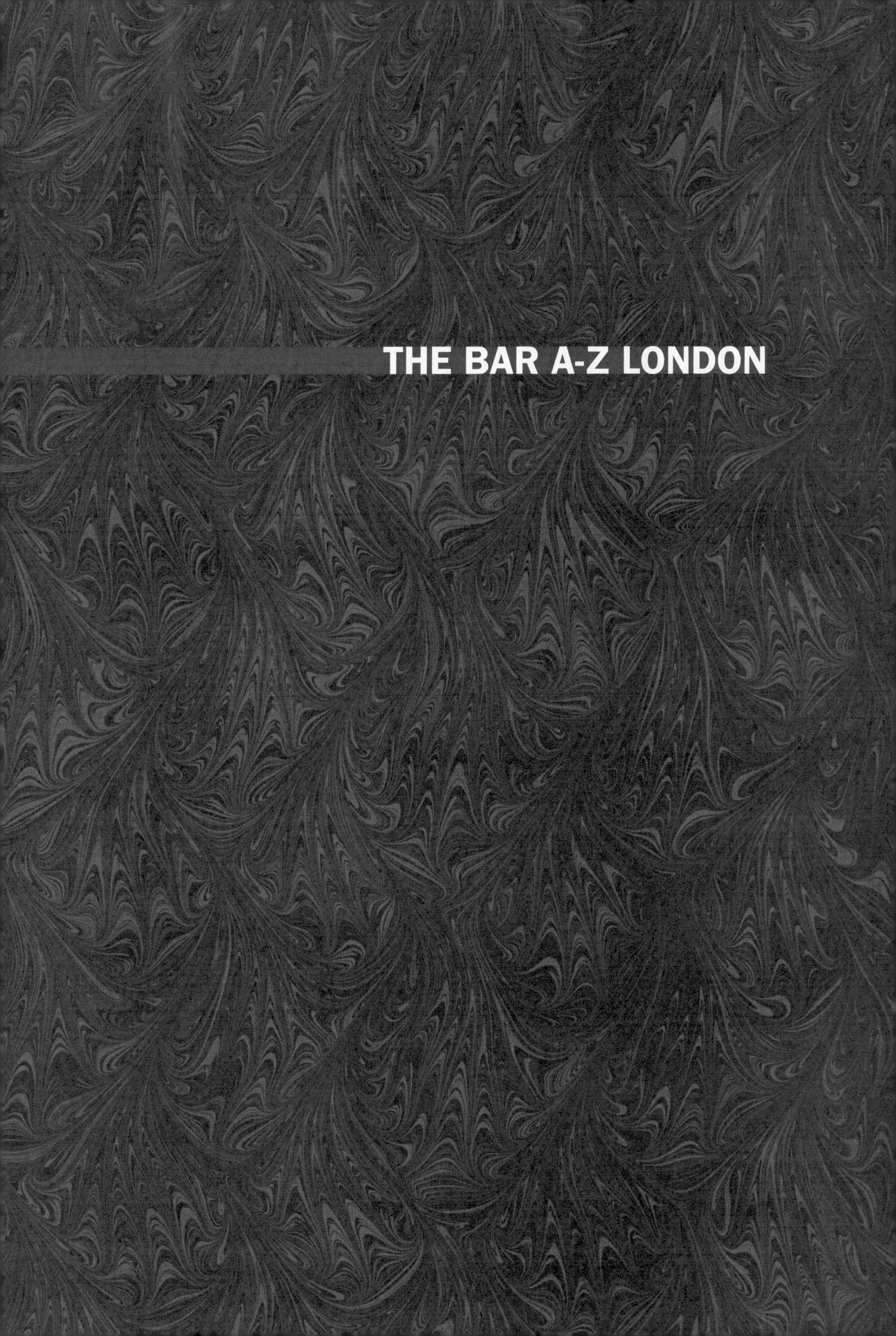
THE BAR A-Z LONDON

ARDEN CHAMBERS Christopher Baker

Head of Chambers	Christopher Baker
Chambers Director	Lisa Jones
Senior Clerk	Elton Maryon
Junior Clerks	Harry Feldman
	Kate Halpin
Tenants	33

Arden Chambers, 20 Bloomsbury Square, London, WC1A 2NS
Tel (020) 7242 4244 **Fax** (020) 7242 3224 **DX** 29 Chancery Lane
Email clerks@ardenchambers.com **Website** www.ardenchambers.com

2nd Floor, 3 Brindleyplace, Birmingham, B1 2JB
Tel (0121) 231 7430 **Fax** (020) 7242 3224

MEMBERS

Andrew Arden QC (1974) (QC-1991) ^
John Robson (1974) ^
Christopher Baker (1984) ^
Clare Roberts (1988)
Jonathan Manning (1989) ^
Iain Colville (1989) ^
William Okoya (1989) ^
Andrew Dymond (1991)
Tony Ross (1991)
Tim Clarke (1992)
Annette Cafferkey (1994) ^
Stuart Armstrong (1995) ^
Toby Vanhegan (1996) ^
Sarah McKeown (1998)
John McCafferty (2000)
Ian Loveland (2001)
James Sandham (2002) ^
Justin Bates (2003)
Emily Orme (2003) ^
Stephanie Smith (2004) ^
Sarah Salmon (2007)
Sam Madge-Wyld (2008) ^
Robert Brown (2008)
Anna Tkaczynska (2008)
Clare Cullen (2009)
Alex Campbell (2010) ^
Amy Just (2011)
Anneli Robbins (2011)
Richard Granby (2012)
Jeff Hardman (2012) ^
Senay Nihat (2012)
Martin Partington QC (Hon) (1984) * (QC-2008)
Caroline Hunter (1985) *
Riccardo Calzavara (2013)
Alice Richardson (2013)

* Door Tenant ^ Public/Direct Access

THE CHAMBERS Arden Chambers provides specialist expertise in its chosen fields. The changing needs of clients are met by a forward-thinking, imaginative and adaptable approach which extends beyond the comprehensive service for legal advocacy, advice and drafting which barristers might ordinarily provide. Clients can obtain free current legal information by email, and also take advantage of tailor-made training and an active seminar programme, the expertise for which is supported by the large volume of publications for which the set is responsible (see below). Alongside a national network of solicitor and local authority clients, the set is in the forefront of Public/Direct Access and Licensed Access work. Clients include individuals (tenants, owners, homeless persons, applicants, service users) as well as public authorities, commercial and social bodies, Ombudsmen and regulatory authorities.

WORK UNDERTAKEN Specialism and expertise are provided in all aspects of housing, local government, property and planning work, embracing both public and private law. Particular areas include: landlord and tenant (residential and commercial), home ownership, enfranchisement, right to buy, mortgages, homelessness and housing allocation, public and administrative law, human rights, local government powers and finance, procurement, local government prosecutions and enforcement proceedings, regulation and administration of social landlords, housing administration and intervention, anti-social behaviour, environmental health, community care, development and planning, compulsory purchase, highways, licensing, trading standards, housing grants, benefits and social security.

PUBLICATIONS Members of chambers are involved in a very wide range of leading publications, closely linked with the areas of practice. Members are frequently invited to address in-house and professional conferences around the country. The set supplies weekly online housing and local government update services available to a wide audience through Sweet & Maxwell's HousingView.

RECRUITMENT The set has an active recruitment policy. Current information about pupillage applications, awards and recruitment is available on the website.

ATKIN CHAMBERS Andrew White QC

1 Atkin Building, Gray's Inn, London, WC1R 5AT
Tel (020) 7404 0102 **Fax** (020) 7405 7456 **DX** 1033
Email clerks@atkinchambers.com **Website** www.atkinchambers.com

Head of Chambers	Andrew White QC
Chief Executive	Fay Gillott
Principal Contacts for Counsel Appointment	Justin Wilson
Principal Contact for Arbitrator, Adjudicator & Mediator Appointments	Daniel Jones
Tenants	44

MEMBERS

Andrew White QC (1980) (QC-1997)
Nicholas Dennys QC (1975) (QC-1991)
Jonathan Acton Davis QC (1977) (QC-1996)
Nicholas Baatz QC (1978) (QC-1998)
Martin Bowdery QC (1980) (QC-2000)
Stephen Dennison QC (1985) (QC-2001)
David Streatfeild-James QC (1986) (QC-2001)
Andrew Goddard QC (1985) (QC-2003)
Stephanie Barwise QC (1988) (QC-2006)
Simon Lofthouse QC (1988) (QC-2006)
Chantal-Aimée Doerries QC (1992) (QC-2008)
Manus McMullan QC (1994) (QC-2010)
Fiona Parkin QC (1993) (QC-2011)
Dominique Rawley QC (1991) (QC-2012)
Steven Walker QC (1993) (QC-2012)
James Howells QC (1995) (QC-2014)
Riaz Hussain QC (2001) (QC-2016)
Darryl Royce (1976)
Robert Clay (1989)
Nicholas Collings (1997)
Patrick Clarke (1997)
Christopher Lewis (1998)
Rupert Choat (1998)
Serena Cheng (2000)
Camille Slow (2002)
Mark Chennells (2002)
Jennifer Jones (2003)
Lucie Briggs (2004)
Frances Pigott (1994-Practicing since 2004)
Simon Crawshaw (2005)
Marc Lixenberg (2005)
Ronan Hanna (2006)
Andrew Fenn (2007)
Zulfikar Khayum (2006)
Peter Land (2007)
Edmund Neuberger (2008)
Omar Eljadi (2009)
David Johnson (2010)
Felicity Dynes (2010)
Mischa Balen (2011)
Lauren Adams (2013)
Christopher Reid (2013)
Nicholas Maciolek (2013)
Mathias Cheung (2015)
Sir Robert Akenhead *
John Blackburn QC (1969) (QC-1984) *
Sir Thayne Forbes *
Professor Doug Jones (Australia) *
Frances Kirkham (1978)*
Gordon Reid QC (Scotland) *
Michael Shane (USA) *

* Door Tenant

THE CHAMBERS Atkin Chambers is a leading set of barristers, based in London, with an international reputation for providing second to none advocacy and advice on cases concerning domestic and worldwide infrastructure project development and disputes. Along with this broad area of practice, members have extensive expertise and experience in complementary areas such as energy, information technology, professional negligence, shipping and also in general commercial law.

Most of Chambers' work involves representing clients in Court or in domestic and international arbitration proceedings. In addition, clients will frequently seek advice during the earlier stages of projects, for example, in relation to PFI issues, European procurement law, or drafting contractual obligations.

Complementing its reputation in the UK, where members act on many landmark and high profile cases, Atkin Chambers has embraced the opportunities presented by the international market, being the first set of chambers to be awarded the Queen's Award for Enterprise – International Trade in 2005 for a period of 5 years. Barristers act for clients all over the globe.

Members are authors of authoritative and influential texts including the Building Law Reports, the International Construction Law Review and the Construction Law Journal. Edited in Chambers since 1959, and with the new edition published in 2015, Hudson's Building and Engineering Contracts is the seminal work on the law relating to building and engineering contracts.

AtkinChambersBarristers

2 BEDFORD ROW William Clegg QC

2 Bedford Row, London, WC1R 4BU
Tel (020) 7440 8888 **Fax** (020) 7242 1738 **DX** LDE 17
Email (initialsurname)@2bedfordrow.co.uk **Website** www.2bedfordrow.co.uk

Head of Chambers	William Clegg QC
Senior Clerk	John Grimmer
Tenants	76

MEMBERS

William Clegg QC (1972) (QC-1991) +
Jim Sturman QC (1982) (QC-2002)
Howard Godfrey QC (1970) (QC-1991)
Peter Griffiths QC (1970) (QC-1995) +
Nigel Lithman QC (1976) (QC-1997) +
Michael Wolkind QC (1976) (QC-1999)
Richard Kovalevsky QC (1983) (QC-2003)
Tracy Ayling QC (1983) (QC-2006)
Ian Stern QC (1983) (QC-2006) +
Mark Milliken-Smith QC (1986) (QC-2006) +
Brian Altman QC (1981) (QC-2008) +
Richard Whittam QC (1983) (QC-2008) + **
Richard Matthews QC (1989) (QC 2010) °
Dean Armstrong QC (1985) (QC-2014)
Stephen Vullo QC (1996) (QC-2014)
Christine Agnew QC (1992) (QC-2015)
Charles Conway (1969)
Nigel Ingram (1972)
Mark Halsey (1974)
John Caudle (1976) +
Anthony Abell (1977)
Barry Gilbert (1978)
Michael Haynes (1979)
Margaret Dodd (1979) ±
Michael Levy (1979)
John Livingston (1980)
John Donnelly (1983)
Gelaga King (1985) +
Timothy Kendal (1985)
Ian McMeekin (1987) ±
Craig Rush (1989)
Sean Hammond (1991)
Stephen Ferguson (1991)
Valerie Charbit (1992)
Adam Budworth (1992)
Michael Epstein (1992)
John Hurlock (1993)
Richard Ferry-Swainson (1994)
Allan Compton (1994)
Maria Dineen (1997)
Anand Beharrylal
Jamas Hodivala (1998)
Ashraf Khan (1999)
Robert Garson (1999) ±
Andrew McGee (1999)
Jacqueline Carey (1999)
Garry Green (1999)
Charles Langley (1999)
Emma King (1999)
Quentin Hunt (2000)
Shauna Ritchie (2000)
Hanna Llewellyn-Waters (2000)
Louise Oakley (2001)
Archangelo Power (2001)
Dean George (2002)
James Harrison (2002)
Samuel Magee (2003)
Kevin Toomey (2004)
Sandesh Singh (2004)
Eleanor Sanderson (2005)
Nick Bonehill (2006)
Austin Stoton (2007)
Christopher Martin (2008)
Jonas Milner (2008)
Vedrana Pehar (2008)
Michael Williams (2008) ±
Thomas Daniel (2009)
David Patience (2009)
Christopher Saad (2009)
David Ewings (2009)
Alice Bricogne (2011)
Sam Thomas (2011)
Charlotte Brewer (2012)
Jessica Ward (2012)
Helen Jones (2013)
Lucy Sweetland (2014)

+ Recorder ± Associate Tenant * Door Tenant ** Senior Treasury Counsel at CCC ° Standing Counsel to the Health and Safety Executive

THE CHAMBERS Clients of 2 Bedford Row benefit from the knowledge, expertise and support of one of the country's leading criminal and regulatory sets. Committed to all aspects of criminal and regulatory law, chambers advises and represents clients in a wide variety of proceedings and investigations, from high profile fraud and murder cases, to health and safety and professional disciplinary proceedings. Members of 2 Bedford Row have appeared in the ICTY in The Hague, the ECHR, Privy Council, Supreme Court, Court of Appeal, Administrative Court and all courts and tribunals of first instance, as well as public inquiries and inquests. An increasing volume of work is international and members attend hearings around the globe. Chambers serves a variety of clients, spanning national governments, international companies, local authorities and other public bodies, regulators, trade unions, corporations and directors and professional and sporting authorities, as well as individuals. It can call upon the combined expertise of 19 Queen's Counsel and 55 juniors, including a Deputy High Court Judge, both the former and current First Senior Treasury Counsel, standing counsel to the Health and Safety Executive, and a number of recorders as well as 2 former Chairs of the Bar Council and both a former and current Chair of the CBA. Supporting them is a clerking team recognised as one of the best in the country.

WORK UNDERTAKEN

Crime: As one of the acknowledged 'magic circle' criminal sets, it has an outstanding track record in high profile trials, including corporate crimes and war crimes. Examples include the News International Phone Hacking; the Hillsborough Football Stadium disaster; the Hatfield and Potters Bar rail disasters; the Buncefield prosecution; Michael Stone; Colin Stagg; Tony Martin; Levi Bellfield (Milly Dowler murder); Stephen Lawrence; Kenneth Noye (M25 murder); Barry George; Vincent Tabak, Sgt Danny Nightingale; murder of Corporal Lee Rigby; and Corporal Lee Clegg.
Fraud: Criminal fraud is an important part of the chambers workload. Its members have appeared in complex, high profile cases, such as JJB Sports, Torex Retail, Asil Nadir, Imperial Consolidated Pharmaceuticals, BAE, Op. Condor, Jubilee line, Torex, Brent Walker to Levitt, WSTC, Cheney Pensions, Izodia pic, Robinsons.
Health & Safety & Environmental Enforcement: Chambers has a commanding presence in health and safety, including corporate and gross negligence manslaughter. Members include Standing Counsel to the

2 BEDFORD ROW (continued)

HSE and ORR, the co-author of the leading practitioners' textbook and the author of Blackstone's Guide to the Corporate Manslaughter Act. Members have been instructed in all of the most significant appellate cases including Chargot [2009] 2 All ER 645 HL. Chambers also has an enviable reputation in environmental work with particular experience of alleged pollution offences, environmental permit breaches and Transfontier Shipment Regulations breaches.

Professional & Disciplinary Tribunals: Over the years members have developed an intuitive understanding of how professional bodies think, which allows them to tailor their advocacy for the greatest effect. 2 Bedford Row represents professionals before the GMC, GDC, GOC, NMC and SDT among others, as well as acting for professional bodies themselves.

Financial Services Regulation: The team has considerable experience in SFO, FCA, and Revenue & Customs investigations, prosecutions and appeals.

Inquests & Public Inquiries: The regulatory group assists clients before coroners' inquests and public inquiries, providing high quality advice and representation. Examples include Duggan, De Menezes, Lakanal fire, Shipman, Climbié, Lawrence and the Ashwood Hospital Inquiries.

Sports Law: Members also frequently appear before professional sporting tribunals, particularly football, rugby and cricket, and represent many premiership clubs and individual players.

INTERNATIONAL Members have undertaken work in the US, West Indies, Middle East, Gibraltar, Hong Kong, Turks and Caicos and most of mainland Europe. It can work in Arabic, Dutch, French, German, Hebrew, Italian, Krio (Sierra Leone), Russian and Serbo-Croat. For more details please see the website.

9 BEDFORD ROW Steven Kay QC

9 Bedford Row, London, WC1R 4AZ
Tel (020) 7489 2727 **Fax** (020) 7489 2828 DX LDE 453
Email clerks@9bedfordrow.co.uk **Website** www.9bedfordrow.co.uk

Head of Chambers	Steven Kay QC
Chambers Director	Martin Secrett
Senior Clerk	Paul Outen
24-hour Duty Clerk	07971 153 192
Tenants	68

MEMBERS

Steven Kay QC (1977) (QC-1997) ^
Anthony Berry QC (1976) (QC-1994) ^
Patrick Upward QC (1972) (QC-1996) ^
Elizabeth Marsh QC (1979) (QC-1999) ^
Abbas Lakha QC (1984) (QC-2003)^
Lee Karu QC (1985) (QC-2010) ^
Jane Bickerstaff QC (1989) ^ (QC-2012) ^
Justin Rouse (1982) (QC-2015) ^
Patricia May (1965)
Richard Germain (1968) ^
Roger Carne (1969) ^
Kenneth Aylett (1972) ^
Derek Zeitlin (1974) ^
David Burgess (1975)
John Traversi (1977) ^
Stephen Mejzner (1978)
Louis French (1979)
David Hughes (1980) ^
Karina Arden (1982) ^
John King (1983) ^
Jollyon Robertson (1983) ^
Adrian Amer (1984) ^
Gary Summers (1985) ^
Wayne Cleaver (1986)
Justin Hugheston-Roberts (1986)^
John Cammegh (1987) ^
Simon Stirling (1989)
Peter Glenser (1993) ^
Jonathan Akinsanya (1993) ^
Anita Arora (1994)
Samantha Cohen (1995) ^
Anne Faul (1996)
Lawrence Selby (1997) ^
Yogain Chandarana (1997) ^
Gillian Higgins (1997) ^
Graeme Logan (1998) ^
Michael Stradling (1998)
Katrina Charles (2000) ^
Michael Edmonds (2000) ^
Peter Hunter (2000) ^
Will Noble (2000)
Mustapha Hakme (2000)
Toby Cadman (2001) ^
Daniel Higgins (2003) ^
Lucinda Dannatt (2003)
Sean Sullivan (2004) ^
Max Hardy (2004) ^
Ruth Becker (2004) ^
Rhiannon Sadler (2004) ^
Richard Paton-Philip (2005) ^
Corinne Bramwell (2005) ^
Lennart Poulsen (2006) ^
Jessica Clarke (2006) ^
Aneurin Brewer (2008) ^
Joe Holmes (2009) ^
Tessa Shroff (2009)
Sarah Bafadhel (2009) ^
Marija Bračković (2010) ^
Kirsty Sutherland (2010) ^
Kabir Sondhi (2010)
Puneet Grewal (2010)
Caroline Macpherson (2011) ^
Andrea Becker (2012) ^
Alexandra Matthews (2012)
Joshua Kern (2013)
Gregor Guy-Smith *
Colleen Rohan *
Prof William Schabas *
Ignatius Hughes QC *
Nicholas Worsley *
James Welsh *

* Door Tenant ^ Public/Direct Access

THE CHAMBERS 9 Bedford Row continues to be committed to providing a professional, approachable and efficient service to clients. Chambers enjoys a well established reputation within the criminal market place both prosecuting and defending in the principal courts across the land. In recent years, work has extended to international courts including a number of significant cases in The Hague. Chambers guards its reputation for active case management with determination and members are well used to operating closely within a team. Whether prosecuting or defending, the early preparation of case plans and the constant monitoring of progress is considered vital. Through its network of professionals, chambers can offer bespoke solutions to seemingly intractable legal issues. Most members are public access accredited.

WORK UNDERTAKEN In the UK the bulk of work comprises general crime from murder, manslaughter and firearms offences to drug trafficking, terrorism, robbery and road traffic offences. In recent years there has been a growing emphasis on corporate crime, which includes fraud, bribery and corruption, and white collar crime with a fast-developing practice in regulatory and compliance matters. Chambers has a well-respected group of practitioners specialising in the prosecution and defence of serious sexual crime. In addition, chambers prides itself on providing high quality representation and advice in cases involving military personnel, whether regular or reservist, including courts martial.

Licensing, mainly liquor and entertainment, has always been an important practice area within Chambers because of the overlapping expertise gained from criminal and regulatory law. Over recent years, there has been a rapidly growing practice arising from firearms licensing and gun control as well as issues arising from fox and other forms of hunting. Members advise and represent individuals and organisations on all aspects of firearms licensing, and are regularly involved in criminal cases that involve the use of firearms.

In recent years members of chambers have appeared in many of the most notorious trials in The Hague as well as tribunals in various countries across the globe. They have often done so to considerable acclaim and so are world renowned in this important field. Such cases and tribunals often take several years and chambers' practitioners have become used to conducting their cases and perfecting strategies with vigor over much longer periods than advocates would normally expect. There have been some conspicuous successes along the way. The emergence of international initiatives against bribery and corruption, including legislation in multiple countries, has brought additional complexity to the conduct of international business. Chambers has the experience to help businesses and individuals identify and address risks before they escalate. The ARC project run by Gillian Higgins, which is a vehicle for claimants to instruct counsel to take cases to the Africa Court of Human and People Rights, has been recognised as a unique and valuable international litigation asset.

LANGUAGES SPOKEN Arabic, Bosnian, Croatian, Finnish, French, German, Gujerati, Hindi, Italian, Punjabi, Serbian, Spanish, Swahili, Tamil, Urdu.

25 BEDFORD ROW Paul Mendelle QC, George Carter-Stephenson QC & Jeremy Dein QC

25 Bedford Row, London, WC1R 4HD
Tel (020) 7067 1500 **Fax** (020) 7067 1507 **DX** 1043 Chancery Lane
Email clerks@25bedfordrow.com **Website** www.25bedfordrow.com

Head of Chambers	Paul Mendelle QC George Carter-Stephenson QC Jeremy Dein QC
Senior Clerk	Guy Williams
Clerks	Emma Makepeace Alfie Lee
Tenants	69

MEMBERS

George Carter-Stephenson QC (1975) (QC-1998)
Paul Mendelle QC (1981) (QC-2006)
Jeremy Dein QC (1982) (QC-2003)
Nigel Sangster QC (1976) (QC-1998)
Courtenay Griffiths QC (1980) (QC-1998)
Diana Ellis QC (1978) (QC-2001)
Peter Doyle QC (1975) (QC-2002)
Kim Hollis QC (1979) (QC-2002)
Paul Keleher QC (1980) (QC-2009)
David Hooper QC (1971) (QC-2010)
Rudi Fortson QC (1976) (QC-2010)
John Cooper QC (1983) (QC-2010)
Tom Price QC (1985) (QC-2010)
Paul Hynes QC (1987) (QC-2010)
Jo Sidhu QC (1993) (QC-2012)
Chris Daw QC (1993) (QC-2013)
Tyrone Smith QC (1994) (QC-2014)
Ronald Jaffa (1974)
Jonathan Mitchell (1974)
Chester Beyts (1978)
Roger Offenbach (1978)
Simon Pentol (1982)
Bill Maley (1982)
Leroy Redhead (1982)
Colin Wells (1987)
Adrian Eissa (1988)
Helen Valley (1990)
Arlette Piercy (1990)
Emma Akuwudike (1992)
Harry Potter (1993)
Aisling Byrnes (1994)
Clare Gordon (1995)
Nicola Howard (1995)
Osman Osman (1995)
Carolina Guiloff (1996)
Daniel Murray (1996)
Samantha Riggs (1996)
Nathaniel Rudolf (1996)
Sebastian Gardiner (1997)
Dermot Keating (1997)
Melanie Simpson (1998)
Michael Neofytou (1999)
Ben Smitten (1999)
Laurie-Anne Power (2000)
Geoffrey Payne (2000)
Sheryl Nwosu (2000)
Michael Gomulka (2002)
Yasin Patel (2002)
Neil Baki (2003)
Monica Stevenson (2004)
Rebecca Randall (2005)
Matt Radstone (2005)
Roy Ledgister (2005)
Daniel Chadwick (2006)
Sam Blom-Cooper (2006)
Priya Malhotra (2007)
Alex Di Francesco (2008)
Kathryn Arnot Drummond (2008)
Rob Shaw (2008)
Emma Stuart-Smith (2009)
Sushil Kumar (2009)
Lara McCaffrey (2011)
Abimbola Johnson (2011)
Duncan Jones (2012)
Henry Dickson (2012)
Laura Collier (2013)
Tom Flavin (2013)
Zeenat Islam (2013)
Natasha Lloyd-Owen (2013)

THE CHAMBERS This innovative set specialise in every aspect of modern defence advocacy, acting in the very highest profile cases. Having achieved and maintained the quality standard for the Bar (BarMark) since 1999, chambers is consistently assessed as a centre of excellence. Widely recognised as the leading chambers in its core practice areas, due to its client focused, high quality service. Their reputation for excellence is best demonstrated by involvement in almost every recent major criminal trial, whether in fraud, organised crime or murder. Expansion of its fraud and financial litigation practice is testament to its reputation for providing advocacy and advisory services of the highest quality. Practitioners are experienced in the conduct of civil cases, including defamation and privacy, professional disciplinary and environmental law. Excellence extends to the high quality of its staff who have a justified reputation for expertise and integrity.

WORK UNDERTAKEN

Criminal: Unrivalled defence experience and expertise across the entire spectrum of criminal law. Covering all aspects of serious crime including murder, organised crime, drug trafficking, money laundering and crimes of extreme and sexual violence. Members also act for UK nationals charged with serious criminal offences in other national jurisdictions. Private client specialists accept instructions on all criminal matters, including minor matters, in order to reduce the impact on individuals' reputations, careers and personal lives.

Fraud & Financial Litigation: Specialising in defending individuals and corporations against allegations of international, corporate and financial crime. Providing a full range of advice and representation in both the criminal and civil aspects of this discipline from preliminary stages, including restraint, right through to appeal, confiscation and civil recovery. Assistance is also provided in relation to risk management and compliance, training and advisory work.

Professional Disciplinary & Regulatory: Defence of individuals appearing before their professional bodies, disciplinary tribunals and regulatory authorities. Including accountants, solicitors, police officers, healthcare professionals and sports people amongst others. Expertise in all aspects of contentious regulatory work in relation to environmental and health and safety work, acting for employees, companies, directors and other individuals.

Civil Liberties & Human Rights: Acting for persons whose human rights are infringed in a wide range of areas of law including actions against the police and public authorities, extradition, international law, inquests, mental health, prisoners' rights and public and administrative law. Chambers' public and administrative law experts are involved in judicial review and appellate cases and challenges to decisions of a wide range of public authorities.

INTERNATIONAL WORK Experts in defending those accused of offences perpetrated by States, including war crimes and other human rights abuses and offences against states, including espionage and terrorism. Advice and representation in international human rights law and trans-national justice issues, for individuals, governmental organisations and major NGOs in a wide range of jurisdictions.

42 BEDFORD ROW Tina Cook QC & Richard Furniss

42 Bedford Row, London, WC1R 4LL
Tel (020) 7831 0222 **Fax** (020) 7831 2239 **DX** 201 London Chancery Lane
Email clerks@42BR.com **Website** www.42BR.com

Head of Chambers	Tina Cook QC & Richard Furniss
Chief Executive	Neil May
Clerks	Steve Sheridan
	James Tidnam
Commercial Manager	Tony Charlick
Tenants	97

MEMBERS

Frank Feehan QC (1988) (QC-2010)
Tina Cook QC (1988) (QC-2011)
Patrick Hamlin (1970)
Mark Batchelor (1971)
Michael Daiches (1977)
Philip Newman (1977)
Anthony Higgins (1978)
Charles Utley (1979)
Francis Treasure (1980)
Charles Scott (1980)
Howard Lederman (1982)
Andrew Pote (1983)
Rehna Azim (1984)
David Dabbs (1984)
Monica Ford (1984)
Jonathan Bennett (1985)
Jeremy Rosenblatt (1985)
Neil Vickery (1985)
Fawzia King (1985)
Mark Maitland-Jones (1986)
Garfield Braithwaite (1987)
Gemma Taylor (1988)
Jeremy Hall (1988)
Sheila Phil-Ebosie (1988)
Sinclair Cramsie (1988)
Martin Haukeland (1989)
Ronald Coster (1989)
Desmond Kilcoyne (1990)
Adrian Higgins (1990)
Edmund Walters (1991)
Richard Furniss (1991)
Stephen Murch (1991)
Deborah Todman (1991)
Mukhtiar Otwal (1991)
Emma Romer (1992)
Ben Uduje (1992)
Gabriel Buttimore (1993)
Naomi Hawkes (1994)
Philip McCormack (1994)
Susan Chan (1994)
Keri Tayler (1995)
Damian Woodward-Carlton (1995)
Matthew Feldman (1995)
Fareha Choudhury (1995)
Scott Matthewson (1996)
Jude Shepherd (1996)
Aysha Ahmad (1996)
Monica Whyte (1996)
Eilidh Gardner (1997)
Jane Hayford (1997)
Nigel Woodhouse (1997)
Christopher Mann (1998)
Niamh O'Brien (1998)
Sharan Bhachu (1999)
Rebecca Thomas (1999)
Richard Little (2000)
Richard Gregory (2000)
Francis Cassidy (2000)
Angela Piears (2001)
Natalie Ganteaume (2001)
Katie Phillips (2002)
Mark Chaloner (2002)
Helen Knott (2002)
Katrina Hepburn (2002)
Thomas Wood (2002)
Robert Cameron (2003)
Anne Dillon (2003)
Maria-Amália Walker (2003)
Siân Gough (2003)
Safia Tharoo (2004)
Paul Gurnham (2004)
Orlando Holloway (2004)
Timothy Adkin (2004)
Edward Bennion-Pedley (2004)
Iris Ferber (2005)
Mary Robertson (2005)
Nick Singer (2006)
Ruth Webber (2006)
Neil Clark (2007)
Delia Minoprio (2007)
Celeste Irvine (2007)
Mathew McDermott (2008)
Helen Nettleship (2009)
Jonathan Newman (2009)
Ben Stimmler (2009)
Richard Williams (2009)
Francesca Conn (2010)
Hamed Zovidavi (2010)
Pauline Troy (2011)
Jennifer Kotilaine (2011)
Christi Scarborough (2012)
Stefan Liberadzki (2013)
Ian Meikle (2013)
Lily Friend (2014)
Peter Jolley (2014)
Elizabeth England (2014)
Will Beetson (2015)

42 BEDFORD ROW

Community Legal Service

THE CHAMBERS Areas of specialism: clinical negligence; personal injury; banking and financial services; chancery; commercial litigation; company and partnership; construction and engineering; insolvency; professional liability; court of protection; employment; childcare; family finance and private law; public law; international law and human rights; inquests; judicial review; professional negligence; professional regulatory and disciplinary; cohabitation; commercial landlord and tenant; environmental law; housing; leasehold enfranchisement; real property; residential landlord and tenant; timeshare; utilities.

29 BEDFORD ROW CHAMBERS Philip Cayford QC

29 Bedford Row Chambers, London, WC1R 4HE
Tel (020) 7404 1044 **DX** 1044
Email clerks@29br.co.uk **Website** www.29br.co.uk

Head of Chambers	Philip Cayford QC
Senior Clerk	James Shortall
Clerks	Julie Holcombe
	Hudson Brewer
	Ben Cross
	Sean Gentleman
Fees Clerks	Steve Pickin
Chambers Administrator	Nicola Kessell
Tenants	57

MEMBERS

Philip Cayford QC (1975) (QC-2002)
Timothy Scott QC (1975) (QC-1995)
Paul Storey QC (1982) (QC-2001)
Robert Peel QC (1990) (QC-2010)
Patrick Chamberlayne QC (1992) (QC-2010)
Piers Pressdee QC (1991) (QC-2010)
Howard Shaw QC (1973) (QC-2011)
Christopher Wagstafffe QC (1992) (QC-2011)
Jonathan Southgate QC (1992) (QC-2013)
Peter Duckworth (1971)
The Hon Clare Renton (1972)
Jonathan Swift (1977)
Indira Ramsahoye (1980)
Jacqueline Wehrle (1984)
David Walden-Smith (1985)
Mark Emanuel (1985)
Stephen Reynolds (1987)
Alexa Storey-Rea (1990)
Nicholas Chapman (1990)
Lee Arnot (1990)
Alexis Campbell (1990)
Annabel Wentworth (1990)
Jonathan Tod (1990)
Sally Max (1991)
Richard Bates (1992)
Victoria Domenge (1993)
Judith Butler (1993)
Roshi Amiraftabi (1993)
Brent Molyneux (1994)
Nicholas Allen (1995)
Peter Mitchell (1996)
Ken Collins (1996)
Sassa-Ann Amaouche (1996)
Dafydd Griffiths (1997)
Lucy Owens (1997)
Laura Heaton (1998)
Georgina Black (1999)
Simon Calhaem (1999)
Anne Hudd (2000)
Anthony Geadah (2000)
Victoria Francis (2001)
Ben Fearnley (2001)
Max Lewis (2002)
Christopher Butterfield (2004)
Lynsey Cade Davies (2005)
Richard Tambling (2005)
Petra Teacher (2006)
Conor Fee (2006)
Helen Williams (2007)
Amber Sheridan (2008)
Anton Eriera (2010)
James Finch (2011)
Matthew Long (2011)
Miriam Foster (2011)
James Pullen (2012)
Charlotte Trace (2012)
Emily Page (2012)

THE CHAMBERS 29 Bedford Row Chambers is committed to providing its clients with an effective and efficient legal service. It operates from three magnificent grade II listed buildings in the heart of legal London, completely modernised for the latest technology.

WORK UNDERTAKEN Chambers offers specialist expertise at all levels of seniority in every aspect of family law including matrimonial finance, children (both public and private law), child abduction, cohabitation law, domestic violence and under the Civil Partnership and Inheritance Acts. Chambers has a strong team of top flight financial remedy practitioners. Seventeen members of Chambers are trained as Collaborative Lawyers. Several members practise as Mediators and several are qualified as Family Law Arbitrators. A number of senior members of Chambers chair private FDRs and Early Neutral Evaluation hearings, and, with large boardroom and conference room facilities, chambers is well suited to these processes. Some members of Chambers accept Public Access instructions. Several former members of chambers have been given judicial appointments, and many current members sit as Deputy High Court or Circuit Judges, or as Deputy District Judges.
Chambers organises a comprehensive seminar programme which is highly regarded by solicitors and trainees. Members of chambers appear in courts around the country and abroad. Chambers has dedicated conference rooms, but members will travel to see clients wherever necessary.

Administration: Chambers is served by nine full time clerks and also has two dedicated fees clerks, allowing work to be processed quickly and efficiently. The clerks' room is staffed between 8.30am and 7.00pm, but emergency contact is always available outside that time. The clerking is praised for its efficient, friendly and commercial approach.
For information about the work of chambers generally, or the practice of individual members of chambers in particular, please contact the Senior Clerk, James Shortall, or visit the website.

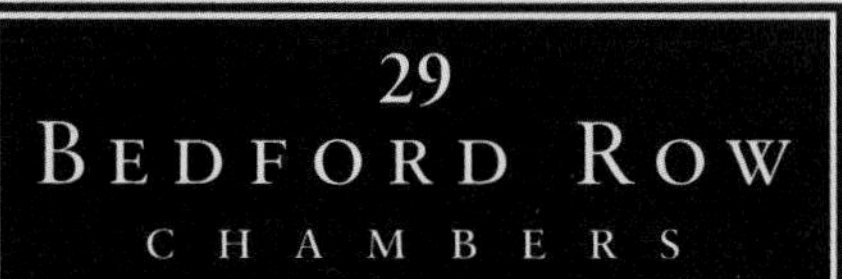

BLACKSTONE CHAMBERS Monica Carss-Frisk QC & Anthony Peto QC

Blackstone House, Temple, London, EC4Y 9BW
Tel (020) 7583 1770 **Fax** (020) 7822 7350 **DX** 281
Email clerks@blackstonechambers.com **Website** www.blackstonechambers.com

Head of Chambers	Monica Carss-Frisk QC Anthony Peto QC
Senior Clerk	Gary Oliver
Chambers Director	Julia Hornor
Tenants	103

MEMBERS

Monica Carss-Frisk QC (1985) (QC-2001)
Anthony Peto QC (1985) (QC-2009)
Sir David Edward QC (1962) (QC-1974)
Stanley Brodie QC (1954) (QC-1975)
Lord Woolf of Barnes (1955)
Lord Lester of Herne Hill QC (1963) (QC-1975)
Michael Beloff QC (1967) (QC-1981)
David Donaldson QC (1968) (QC-1984)
Robert Englehart QC (1969) (QC-1986)
David Hunt QC (1969) (QC-1987)
Barbara Dohmann QC (1971) (QC-1987)
Maurice Mendelson QC (1965) (QC-1992)
Jonathan Harvie QC (1973) (QC-1992)
Lord Pannick QC (1979) (QC-1992)
Sir Jeffrey Jowell QC (1965) (QC-1993)
Stephen Nathan QC (1969) (QC-1993)
John Howell QC (1979) (QC-1993)
Lord Keen of Elie QC (1980) (QC-1993) Scotland
Charles Flint QC (1975) (QC-1995)
Michael Bloch QC (1979) (QC-1998)
Ian Mill QC (1981) (QC-1999)
Harish Salve SA (2013)
Paul Goulding QC (1984) (QC-2000)
Hugo Page QC (1977) (QC-2002)
Mark Shaw QC (1987) (QC-2002)
Robert Anderson QC (1986) (QC-2006)
Dinah Rose QC (1989) (QC-2006)
Michael Fordham QC (1990) (QC-2006)
Timothy Otty QC (1990) (QC-2006)
James Eadie QC (1984) (QC-2008)
Robert Howe QC (1988) (QC-2008)
Pushpinder Saini QC (1991) (QC-2008)
Adam Lewis QC (1985) (QC-2009)
Alan Maclean QC (1993) (QC-2009)
Andrew Green QC (1988) (QC-2010)
Javan Herberg QC (1992) (QC-2011)
Sam Grodzinski QC (1996) (QC-2011)
Andrew Hunter QC (1993) (QC-2012)
Thomas de la Mare QC (1995) (QC-2012)
Kieron Beal QC (1995) (QC-2012)
Tom Weisselberg QC (1995) (QC-2014)
Jane Mulcahy QC (1995) (QC-2014)
Kate Gallafent QC (1997) (QC-2014)
Andreas Gledhill QC (1992) (QC-2015)
Andrew George QC (1997) (QC-2015)
Adrian Briggs QC (Hon) (1989) (QC-2016)
Gemma White QC (1994) (QC-2016)
Brian Kennelly QC (1999) (QC-2016)
Shaheed Fatima QC (2001) (QC-2016)
Guy Goodwin-Gill (1971)
Gerard Clarke (1986)
Thomas Croxford (1992)
Joanna Pollard (1993)
Jane Collier (1994)
Emma Dixon (1994)
Claire Weir (1998)
Ben Jaffey (1999)
Catherine Callaghan (1999)
Stephanie Palmer (2000)
Diya Sen Gupta (2000)
Leona Powell (2000)
Nick De Marco (2001)
David Pievsky (2001)
Victoria Windle (2001)
Ivan Hare (1991)
Mark Vinall (2002)
Sarah Wilkinson (2003)
Robert Weekes (2003)
Tom Hickman (2003)
Catherine Donnelly (2003)
James Segan (2004)
Iain Steele (2005)
Naina Patel (2005)
Tom Richards (2006)
Tristan Jones (2006)
Adam Baradon (2006)
Hanif Mussa (2007)
Simon Pritchard (2007)
Jessica Boyd (2007)
Christopher McCrudden (1996) (NIRE 2006)
David Lowe (2008)
Emily Neill (2008)
Peter Head (2008)
Paul Luckhurst (2009)
Tom Cleaver (2009)
Tom Mountford (2009)
Andrew Scott (2010)
Shane Sibbel (2010)
Fraser Campbell (2010)
Ravi Mehta (2010)
Daniel Burgess (2011)
Harry Adamson (2012)
Jason Pobjoy (2012)
Jana Sadler-Forster (2012)
Kerenza Davis (2012)
Tom Coates (2013)
Eesvan Krishnan (2013)
Daniel Cashman (2013)
Ajay Ratan (2014)
Flora Robertson (2014)
Celia Rooney (2015)
George Molyneaux (2015)
Isabel Buchanan (2015)

THE CHAMBERS Blackstone Chambers is a long established set, combining formidable strengths in commercial litigation, EU and competition, public international law, human rights, administrative and public law, and employment, with state of the art facilities and a friendly and open approach to client service.

RECRUITMENT Blackstone Chambers is a member of Pupillage Gateway. A first or upper second class degree is usually required, although not necessarily in law. Pupillage awards of up to £65,000 are available. Mini-pupillages for a week in the year preceding pupillage are required for potential pupils of chambers.

For further details of an individual barrister's work and for a full breakdown of Chambers' areas of practice, please visit the website: www.blackstonechambers.com.

Blackstone
CHAMBERS

7 BR Collingwood Thompson QC

7 Bedford Row, London, WC1R 4BU
Tel (020) 7242 3555 **Fax** (020) 7242 2511 **DX** 347 Chancery Lane
Email clerks@7br.co.uk **Website** www.7br.co.uk

Head of Chambers	Collingwood Thompson QC
Chief Executive	Rachel Holmes
Senior Clerks	Paul Eeles (Civil)
	Rod McGurk (Crime & Family)
Tenants	83

MEMBERS

Collingwood Thompson QC (1975) (QC-1998) +
Alan Newman QC (1968) (QC-1989)
Philip P Shears QC (1972) (QC-1996) +
Nigel Rumfitt QC (1974) (QC-1994) +
Simeon Maskrey QC (1977)
Derek Sweeting QC (1983) (QC-2001) + ^
Lewis Power QC (1990) (QC-2011)
Rachel Langdale QC (1990) (QC-2009)
Steven Ford QC (1992) (QC-2010)
Barbara Connolly QC (1986) (QC-2011)
Hugh Preston QC (1994) (QC-2012) ^
James House QC (1995) (QC-2015)
Deirdre Goodwin (1974)
Julian D Matthews (1979) +
Simon Wheatley (1979)
Jeremy Pendlebury (1980)
Susan C Reed (1984)
Timothy Walker (1984) ^
Adam Clemens (1985)
Simon King (1987) +
David Matthew (1987) ^
Andrew Wheeler (1988)
Gordon Aspden (1988)
Smair Soor (1988)
Catherine Rayner (1989)
Tim Meakin (1989) ^
Brendan Roche (1989) +
Susan Belgrave (1989)
Leslie Keegan (1989)
Graham Huston (1991) +
Adam Korn (1992)
Maryam Syed (1993)
Adam Weitzman QC (1993) (QC-2016)
Luke Blackburn (1993) ^
Vanessa Marshall (1994) ^
Jeffrey Jupp (1994) ^
Bilal Rawat (1995)
Anwar Nashashibi (1995)
Andrea Chute (1995)
Hari Kaur (1995)
Elaine Banton (1996) ^
Susannah Johnson (1996) ^
Adrian Langdale (1996)
Anita Guha (1997)
Rachel Darby (1997)
Peter Ellis (1998) ^
Hugo Daniel Lodge (1998)
Justin Slater (1999) ^
Jenny Carter-Manning (1999) ^
Kate Lumbers (1999)
Gareth Weetman (1999)
Nick Cropp (1999)
Adam Walker (2000)
Steven Gray (2000) ^
Richard Baker (2000)
David O'Mahony (2000) ^
Gina Allwood (2002) ^
Hanisha Patel (2002)
William Chapman (2003) ^
Jonathan Bertram (2003) ^
Conor Dufficy (2004)
Christina Lyons (2004)
Craig Carr (2005)
Ashley Pratt (2006)
Robert Harland (2006)
James Weston (2007)
Patricia Leonard (2007)
Daniel Bishop (2007)
Saara Idelbi (2008)
Alex Young (2008)
Ben Isaacs (2009)
Kathryn Duff (2009)
James Robottom (2009)
Caroline Lody (2009)
James Macdonald (2010)
Helen Compton (2011)
Dr Gregory Burke (2012)
Clementine Coram-James (2012)
Samantha Jones (2012)
Christopher Canning (2014)
Kirsty Lea (2014)

+ Recorder ^ Public/Direct Access

THE CHAMBERS As a multi-disciplinary set members provide an unrivalled offering of knowledge across a broad spectrum of the law; from clinical negligence and personal injury, and child and family work, to white-collar crime and a full range of commercial disciplines. The breadth of members' practices facilitates a fresh, innovative approach to finding legal solutions for our clients and enables 7BR's specialist practice teams to succeed in some of the most complex cases. Together with esteemed advocacy skills in the court room this has afforded the set with a strong reputation for excellence both nationally and overseas. 83 members, including 13 QCs, practice in courts and tribunals throughout England and Wales and internationally. In the last year, members have appeared in cases in Hong Kong, Dubai, The Cayman Islands, Turks and Caicos, The Isle of Man and the Channel Islands. The set's supreme legal expertise is evidenced by the number of members who go on to distinguished service in the judiciary; as High Court judges, recorders, arbitrators, and regulators – in addition to a Lord Chief Justice. Whilst at the top of their game 7BR barristers pride themselves on an approachable service, working closely with clients to understand the personal or commercial drivers behind any mandate and ensuring lay clients are well-versed at all stages of the process. The set is actively involved in pro bono work and efforts to promote equality and diversity at the Bar as well as supporting charitable causes.

WORK UNDERTAKEN Chambers offers strength and depth in areas of:

- Clinical and professional negligence
- Personal injury
- Product liability
- Complex fraud
- Offshore and International
- Regulatory and professional discipline
- Financial and regulatory crime
- Child and family law
- Employment
- Civil commercial
- Contract and tort
- Insurance disputes
- Sports law
- Crime

7BR
SEVEN BEDFORD ROW

ONE BRICK COURT Andrew Caldecott QC

1 Brick Court, Temple, London, EC4Y 9BY
Tel (020) 7353 8845 **Fax** (020) 7583 9144 **DX** 468 LDE
Email clerks@onebrickcourt.com **Website** www.onebrickcourt.com

Head of Chambers	Andrew Caldecott QC
Senior Clerk	David Mace
Tenants	18

MEMBERS

Andrew Caldecott QC (1975) (QC-1994)
Richard Rampton QC (1965) (QC-1987)
Sir Edward Garnier QC (1976) (QC-1995)
Heather Rogers QC (1983) (QC-2006)
Manuel Barca QC (1986) (QC-2011)
Dr Matt Collins QC (1999) (QC-2011) (Aus) *
Catrin Evans QC (1994) (QC-2016)
Harvey Starte (1985)
Timothy Atkinson (1988)
Jane Phillips (1989)
Caroline Addy (1991)
Sarah Palin (1999)
David Glen (2002)
Aidan Eardley (2002)
Ian Helme (2005)
Kate Wilson (2005)
Jonathan Scherbel-Ball (2010)
Hannah Ready (2010)
Clara Hamer (2013)

* Door Tenant

THE CHAMBERS One Brick Court is a leading set specialising in all aspects of media, information and internet law. Members of Chambers act for corporate, media and individual claimants and defendants as well as government department, local authorities and NGOs. Chambers has several members who are appointed to the prestigious Attorney General's Panel of Counsel. Members regularly appear at all levels of the Court and Tribunal system, from the First-Tier Tribunal to the Supreme Court. Chambers also has a number of barristers called to the Bar of Northern Ireland and members are instructed to provide specialist advice around the world including Gibraltar, Singapore, Malaysia and Hong Kong. Members of Chambers provide advice across the full ambit of informational, reputational and content related law and regulation. Related human rights issues are handled, together with judicial review and intellectual property law. One Brick Court also offers a fast and competitive pre-publication advice service for which they are able to receive instructions directly from publishers and internet intermediaries and can provide out-of-hours and weekend cover for urgent injunctions. Chambers provides itself on being a modern and friendly set with an approachable and efficient clerking team.

WORK UNDERTAKEN

Defamation & Malicious Falsehood: Libel, slander, malicious falsehood.
Privacy & Confidentiality: All matters arising from the tensions between the right to free speech and the rights of confidentiality and privacy; obtaining and resisting applications for injunctions, including emergency out-of-hours injunctions; image rights and reputation management, commercial confidentiality and confidentiality in employment contracts.
Information Law: Advice and representation on all matters arising out of the Data Protection Act and the Freedom of Information Act.
Online Liability: All aspects of liability for online content, including internet intermediary liability.
Contempt & Reporting Restrictions: Urgent advice and representation in the civil, criminal and family courts and tribunal system on the reporting of proceedings, anonymity orders, judicial review and protection of journalistic sources.
Pre-Publication Advice: Advice available on a competitive basis on all aspects of content liability for the entire spectrum of publishers and broadcasters.
Other: harassment; negligent misstatement; passing off; regulatory advice; malicious prosecution; obscenity; media related intellectual property law, judicial-review and human rights law.

Publications: Members write and contribute to leading works on media and information law including Duncan and Neill on Defamation, Arlidge, Eady & Smith on Contempt, Carter-Ruck on Libel and Privacy, Halsbury's Laws (Libel and Slander) and Atkins Court Forms on Defamation, Confidence, Privacy, Data Protection, Freedom of Information and Regulation of Investigatory Powers.

BRICK COURT CHAMBERS Jonathan Hirst QC & Helen Davies QC

7-8 Essex Street, London, WC2R 3LD
Tel (020) 7379 3550 **Fax** (020) 7379 3558 **DX** 302 Chancery Lane
Email clerks@brickcourt.co.uk **Website** www.brickcourt.co.uk

Head of Chambers	Jonathan Hirst QC Helen Davies QC
Senior Clerks	Julian Hawes Ian Moyler
Tenants	83

MEMBERS

Jonathan Hirst QC (1975) (QC-1990)
Helen Davies QC (1991) (QC-2008)
Hilary Heilbron QC (1971) (QC-1987)
Richard Gordon QC (1972) (QC-1994)
Mark Hapgood QC (1979) (QC-1994)
Mark Howard QC (1980) (QC-1996)
Stephen Ruttle QC (1976) (QC-1997)
William Wood QC (1980) (QC-1998)
Charles Hollander QC (1978) (QC-1999) (2015 HK)
David Anderson QC (1985) (QC-1999)
Catharine Otton-Goulder QC (1983) (QC-2000)
Richard Lord QC (1981) (QC-2002)
Mark Brealey QC (1984) (QC-2002)
Michael Swainston QC (1985) (QC-2002)
James Flynn QC (1978) (QC-2003)
Neil Calver QC (1987) (QC-2006)
Tom Adam QC (1991) (QC-2008)
Tim Lord QC (1992) (QC-2008)
Fergus Randolph QC (1985) (QC-2009)
Mark Hoskins QC (1991) (QC-2009)
Aidan Robertson QC (1995) (QC-2009)
Richard Slade QC (1987) (QC-2010)
Harry Matovu QC (1988) (QC-2010)
Jemima Stratford QC (1993) (QC-2010)
Daniel Jowell QC (1995) (QC-2011)
Simon Salzedo QC (1995) (QC-2011)
Michael Bools QC (1991) (QC-2012)
Paul Bowen QC (1993) (QC-2012)
Marie Demetriou QC (1995) (QC-2012)
Andrew Henshaw QC (2000) (QC-2013)
Roger Masefield QC (1985) (QC-2013)
Jasbir Dhillon QC (1996) (QC-2013)
Martin Chamberlain QC (1997) (QC-2013)
Kelyn Bacon QC (1998) (QC-2014)
Simon Birt QC (1998) (QC-2015)
Sarah Lee QC (1990) (QC-2016)
Maya Lester QC (2000) (QC-2016)
Thomas Plewman QC (2009) (QC-2016)
Peter Irvin (1971) ^
Paul Wright (1990)
Alan Roxburgh (1992)
Alec Haydon (1993)
Jeremy Gauntlett SC (1993) (SC-1989 SA)
Andrew Thomas (1996)
Robert O'Donoghue (1996)
Klaus Reichert SC (1996 E&W) (1992 IRL) (SC-2010 IRL)
Margaret Gray (1998)
Colin West (1999)
Nicholas Saunders (2001)
Fionn Pilbrow (2001)
Stephen Midwinter (2002)
Sarah Ford (2002)
Tony Willis (2004)
Victoria Wakefield (2003)
David Scannell (2003)
Gerard Rothschild (2005)
Fred Hobson (2005)
Sarah Abram (2006)
Sarah Love (2006)
Tony Singla (2007)
Richard Blakeley (2007)
Richard Eschwege (2008)
Edward Harrison (2008)
Craig Morrison (2008)
Oliver Jones (2009)
Daniel Piccinin (2010)
Max Schaefer (2010)
Michael Bolding (2010)
Tim Johnston (2011)
Malcolm Birdling (2011)
Andrew McInytre (2011)
David Bailey (2012)
Geoffrey Kuehne (2012)
Emily MacKenzie (2012)
Joanne Box (2012)
Kyle Lawson (2012)
Zahra Al-Rikabi (2012)
Hugo Leith (2013 E&W; NY) (2008 W Australia)
Jennifer MacLeod (2013 E&W; NY)
Charlotte Thomas (2013)
Tom Pascoe (2013)
Ben Woolgar (2014)
Lord Phillips (1962) (QC-1978)*
Lord Hoffmann (1964) (QC-1977)*
Lord Hope (1965 Scotland) (QC-1989 Scotland)*
Sir Oliver Popplewell (1951) (QC-1969)*
Sir Roger Buckley (1962) (QC-1979)*
Sir Richard Aikens (1973)(QC-1986)*
David Vaughan CBE QC (1963) (QC-1981)*
HH Nicholas Chambers QC (1966) (QC-1985)*
Sir Sydney Kentridge QC (1977) (QC-1984)*
Sir Nicholas Forwood QC (1970) (QC-1987)*
Derrick Wyatt QC (1972) (QC-1993)*
Prof Richard Macrory CBE (1974)*
Judge Fidelma Macken SC (1987)*
Johnny Mok SC (1986) Hong Kong*
Mark Cran QC (1973) (QC-1988)*
John Sturrock QC (1986 Scotland) (QC-1999 Scotland)*
James Wolffe QC (1992 Scotland) (QC-2007 Scotland)*
Simon Thorley QC (1972) (QC-1989)*
Robert Webb QC (1971) (QC-1988)*
Alastair Sutton (1972)*
Timothy Charlton QC (1971) (QC-1993)*
Prof Peter Muchlinski (1981)*
Jan Woloniecki (1983)*
Mads Andenas (1997)*
Andrew Le Sueur (1987)*
Prof. Robert McCorquodale (2011)*
Geoff Sharp (1992 NZ)*

* Door Tenant ^ Public/Direct Access

THE CHAMBERS There are 83 members who practise full-time, including 38 QCs. Chambers specialises in commercial, EU/competition and public law, maintaining a strong reputation in all areas.

WORK UNDERTAKEN Commercial work includes banking, finance, insurance, reinsurance, shipping, private international law, professional negligence, media and entertainment law, takeovers and mergers, sports law and public international law. Chambers' outstanding team of EU and competition litigation specialists appear in all the English courts and tribunals, before the CMA and CAT, as well as in the Court of Justice and General Court. Considerable expertise in human rights and in commercial and regulatory judicial review enables chambers to combine its strengths in public, commercial and EU law. Recent key cases include: Bank of St Petersburg OJSC and Alexander Savelyev v Vitaly Arkhangelsky and ors (Commercial Court); BNY Mellon Corporate Trustee Service v LBG Capital No 1 (Supreme Court); Georgia v The Russian Federation (ECHR); The Russian Federation v Ukraine (Commercial Court); Sainsbury's v Mastercard and Visa (CAT); Holmcroft v Barclays Bank PLC (Admin Court); Versloot Dredging v HDI Gerling Industrie Versicherung AG (The DC Merwestone) (Supreme Court); Akers v Samba Financial Group (Supreme Court); Terra Firma v Citigroup Global Markets and Citibank NA (Commercial Court); Property Alliance Group Limited ("PAG") v Royal Bank of Scotland PLC (Commercial Court); Libyan Investment Authority v Goldman Sachs (Commercial Court); Paulley v The FirstGroup PLC (Supreme Court).

CARMELITE CHAMBERS Charles Bott QC

9 Carmelite Street, London, EC4Y 0DR
Tel (020) 7936 6300 **Fax** (020) 7936 6301 **DX** 226
Email clerks@carmelitechambers.co.uk **Website** www.carmelitechambers.co.uk

Head of Chambers	Charles Bott QC
Senior Clerk	Marc King
Deputy Senior Clerk	Matthew Butchard
Chambers Administrator	Orla O'Sullivan
Clerks	Dean Allen
	Thomas Barnes
	James Tippey
	Jordan Wescott
	Jack Mahoney
Fees Clerks	Louisa Wheeler
	Jana Bodnarova

MEMBERS

Charles Bott QC (1979) (QC-2008)
Nigel Lambert QC (1974) (QC-1999) + ^
Robert Marshall-Andrews QC (1967) (QC-1987)
John Richard Jones QC (1981) (QC-2002) +
Leonard Smith QC (1986) (QC-2008)
Alan Kent (1986) (QC-2009)
Anthony Orchard QC (1991) (QC 2011) ^
Simon Csoka QC (1991) (QC-2011) ^
Pavlos Panayi QC (1995) (QC-2014)
Christopher Henley (1989) (QC-2015)
Adam Kane (1993) (QC-2015)
Louise Sweet QC (1994) (QC-2016)
Peter Corrigan (1973)
Barry Kogan (1973) +
Andrew Turton (1977)
Isabelle Gillard (1980)
Simon Molyneux (1986)
Martin Taylor (1988)
Adrian Kayne (1989) ^
Grahame James (1989)
Colin Aylott (1989) ^
Ben Hargreaves (1989) ^
Tony Ventham (1991)
William England (1991)
Paul Crampin (1992)
Simon Gruchy (1993)
Richard Button (1993)
Ayaz Qazi (1993)
James Walker (1994)
Richard Furlong (1994)
Mathew Sherratt (1994) ^
Matthew Lawson (1995)
Alphege Bell (1995)
Mark Harries (1995) ^
Jonathan Page (1996) ^
James Tilbury (1996)
Roxanne Morrell (1996)
Jonathan Lennon (1997)
Elaine Stapleton (1997)
Gregory Johnson (1998)
Matthew Buckland (1998)
Gerard Hillman (1999) ^
Graeme Knight (1999)
Marie Spenwyn (1999) ^
Dapinder Singh (2000)
Tanveer Qureshi (2000)
Stan Reiz (2001) ^
Houzla Rawat (2001) ^
Andrew Hallworth (2002)
Darryl Cherrett (2004) ^
Hugh O'Donoghue (2004) ^
Aron Rollin (2004)
Ashley Hendron (2005)
Laura Hocknell (2005)
Victoria Sheppard-Jones (2005) ^
Joe Hingston (2007) ^
Paul Duester (2008)
Rebecca Saillet (2009)
Simon Ralph (2009)
Alexandra Scott (2011)
Sebastian Winnett (2011)
Rupert Russell (2013)

+ Recorder ^ Public/Direct Access

THE CHAMBERS Carmelite Chambers is one of the largest and longest established criminal sets in the UK. The set's advocates are at the forefront of UK and international practice and are regularly instructed in high profile cases.

WORK UNDERTAKEN As leaders within their field members of chambers undertake work in all criminal and related investigations and proceedings, with specific expertise in serious fraud, terrorism, murder, money laundering, miscarriages of justice, courts martial and health and safety. Chambers offers a highly skilled and experienced team of advocates in all of their specialist areas with a particular emphasis to fraud and regulatory matters.
Fraud: Carmelite Chambers has represented both individuals and companies in some of the most notable fraud cases in recent years, counsel are instructed in both private and publicly funded fraud matters in both the civil and criminal courts which include complaints related to corruption, cartels, boiler room fraud, diversion fraud, carousel fraud, NHS fraud and mortgage fraud.
Prominent cases involving members of chambers include cases such as the investigation into the alleged Libor rate fixing, the current FCA Investigation described as the largest insider dealing case to be prosecuted in the UK, the iSoft PLC trial which concerns alleged fraud of multi-million pound contracts for the provision of software to National Health Authorities in the UK and Ireland, Operation Friar the recent Competition & Markets Authority prosecution at Southwark Crown Court, one of the only cases reaching jury trial, the North East England Property Fraud "Operation Bamburgh" Parts 1 & 2, Operation Ruthenium the Alstom International Bribery case involving allegations corruption and bribery on an international scale, Operation Hayrack the Royal Household corruption case, the film investment fraud investigation at Southwark CC Operations Chainmail & Crystaline. Operation Yuletide a £100million fraud involving a leading shipping company, the successful defence of former "Superhead" CEO of a Lincolnshire Federation of Academies accused of 7 counts of fraud by abuse of position following a 10 week trial at Lincoln Crown Court. Project Sweden, a major SFO investigation into African corruption by a FTSE 100 company and Operation Evenbox a case involving a £290 million tax evasion allegation involving the use of LLPs to claim tax deductible losses on investment vehicles promoting the reforestation of Brazilian rainforest and HIV research.
Crime: Chambers enjoys a reputation that is second to none in the defence of allegations of serious and organised crime, recognised nationally and internationally for providing advice and representation of the highest quality in the most serious high-profile criminal trials.
Recent instructions include representing defendants charged as part of Operation Weeting and Operation Elvenden involving phone hacking by News of the World journalists and subsequent associated prosecutions, R –v- Cregan & others the Preston Crown Court Trial concerning the shooting of two female Manchester police officers and other linked matters, a six month immigration fraud at Manchester Crown Court involving an alleged successful and lucrative enterprise to assist illegal migrants to deceive the UK Borders Agency. Operation Clover the largescale investigation into abuse and sexual offences in Rotherham.
Terrorist cases including R –v- J the teacher from Manchester planning to join IS in Syria, R –v- F & others

CARMELITE CHAMBERS Charles Bott QC (continued)

where there were four defendants facing charges relating to the preparation of terrorist acts and R –v- H & 3 others charged with conspiracy to murder/terrorism where all three are said to have been influenced by events in Syria and Iraq and inspired by an Islamic State fatwa, posted on You Tube by an IS spokesman, to kill disbelievers in the West, it is alleged that their targets included personnel from both the police and military.

Asset Recovery & Civil Fraud: Carmelite Chambers has an unparalleled reputation in defending allegations of serious fraud and chambers' specialist Asset Recovery and Civil fraud team has been formed from its leading experts in criminal fraud, some of whom also have strong backgrounds in civil and commercial law. Their experience and judgment is increasingly sought after by those involved in civil fraud litigation who recognise the significant crossover between commercial, civil, criminal and regulatory work.

The civil fraud and asset recovery team is regularly instructed in cases involving:

- A wide range of fraud related matters including corruption, investment fraud, bribery and money laundering
- Multi-jurisdictional asset recovery claims
- Civil injunctive relief including freezing orders, civil search and seizure orders and "Norwich Pharmacal" third party disclosure orders
- Significant overlap between civil and criminal proceedings
- Civil recovery proceedings under Part 5 of the Proceeds of Crime Act 2002
- Individuals and companies affected by restraint proceedings brought in the criminal courts

Additionally, with regulatory authorities placing an increasing burden upon companies to investigate internal wrongdoing and to self-report, chambers can advise corporate clients in situations where criminal activity by directors, employees or advisors is suspected as to the proper approach and strategies to be adopted in investigating that activity and, where necessary, on the appropriate co-operation strategies with regulators and prosecuting authorities.

Private Prosecution: Chambers now undertakes private criminal prosecutions for a wide range of criminal offences including serious fraud and money laundering. Increasingly, clients look to the experience of members to advise on and conduct prosecutions in cases that are beyond the scope of public prosecuting authorities or where the police have conducted inadequate investigations. Chambers offers a complete advisory and advocacy service throughout the private prosecution process with meticulous emphasis on the proper presentation of the case and the prosecutor's duties of disclosure and impartiality.

Regulatory & Disciplinary Proceedings: Chambers' members are regularly instructed amongst others on behalf of doctors, dentists, nurses, lawyers, police officers and accountants before the Bar Standards Board Disciplinary Tribunal, the Solicitors Disciplinary Tribunal, the Police Disciplinary Tribunal, the General Dental Council, the General Medical Council, the NMWC, Accountancy and Actuarial disciplinary panels as well as at Disciplinary Tribunals on behalf of professional sportsmen and women. With their extensive fraud experience members frequently appear before the FSA, VAT and HMRC tribunals.

THE CHAMBERS OF ANDREW MITCHELL QC

33 Chancery Lane, London, WC2A 1EN
Tel (020) 7440 9950 **Fax** (020) 7430 2818 **DX** 33 London
Email clerks@33cllaw.com **Website** www.33cllaw.com

Head of Chambers	Andrew Mitchell QC
Practice Director	Martin Adams
Tenants	20

33 CHANCERY LANE

THE CHAMBERS Formed in November 2008 by a group of practitioners to provide specialist advice to commercial organisations, individual clients and the public sector in all areas of suspected commercial wrongdoing including bribery, corruption, civil fraud, asset recovery and financial crime.

WORK UNDERTAKEN Recent cases include acting nationally and internationally in major bribery and corruption cases; acting in the Supreme Court in Proceeds of Crime Act cases; acting in the Caribbean for a client in a Commission of Inquiry into the collapse of financial institutions; acting for a former Yen derivatives trader for UBS and Citigroup for alleged manipulation of the international LIBOR index; acting nationally and internationally in major money laundering, MTIC and fraud cases; and acting for applicants, respondents, foreign governments, third parties and receivers in all aspects of restraint and receivership.

CHARTER CHAMBERS Nicholas Rhodes QC & Neil Hawes QC

33 John Street, London, WC1N 2AT
Tel (020) 7618 4400 **Fax** (020) 7618 4401 **DX** 429 Ch.Ln
Email clerks@charterchambers.com **Website** www.charterchambers.com

Head of Chambers	Nicholas Rhodes QC & Neil Hawes QC
Chambers Director	Ian Payn
Clerks	Ian Sheridan
	James Hall
	Jordan Bater
	Bonnie Harrod
Billing	Sandeep Johal
Tenants	50

MEMBERS

Nicholas Rhodes QC (1981) (QC-2008) + ^
Neil Hawes QC (1989) (QC-2010) ^
Stephen Solley QC (1969) (QC-1989) + ^
Henry Grunwald OBE QC (1972) (QC-1999) ^
Jerome Lynch QC (1983) (QC-2000) ^
Ian Bourne QC (1977) (QC-2006) + ^
David Batcup (1974) + ^
David Martin-Sperry (1971)^
Calvin Jackson (1975) ^
Mark Tomassi (1981) ^
Thomas Buxton (1983) ^
David Taylor (1986) ^
Neil Guest (1990) ^
Michael Lavers (1990)
Paul Phillips (1991) ^
Dr Mary-Teresa Deignan (1991) ^
Claire Robinson (1991) ^
Louise McCullough (1991)
Sean Kivdeh (1992) ^
Tana Adkin (1992) ^
Julia Flanagan (1993) ^
Ragveer Chand (1994)
Martin Goudie (1996) ^
Jason Cross (1998) ^
Roderick James (1999) ^
Alexander Dos Santos (1999) ^
Dominic Thomas (1999)
Leila Gaskin (2000) ^
Darren Snow (2001) ^
Rajinder Gill (2001) ^
Kathrine Mansfield (2001)
Nicholas Dixey (2002)
William Davis (2003) ^
Lorna Elliott (2003)
Tyrone Silcott (2004) ^
Rishy Panesar (2004)
Chloe Barton (2006) ^
Alex Jamieson (2007)
David Wood (2007)
Grace Pelly (2007)
Kathryn Pitters (2008)
Oliver Renton (2008) ^
Briony Molyneux (2009)
Wafa Shah (2009)
Peter Melleney (2010)
Laura Bayley (2010)
Gareth Thomas (2011)
Leeann Mohammed (2011) +
Sam Roake (2011)
Tasmin Malcolm (2011)

+ Recorder ^ Public/Direct Access

THE CHAMBERS Charter Chambers is a busy criminal and common law set offering expertise in a variety of fields at all levels of seniority.

WORK UNDERTAKEN
Criminal Law: (both defence and prosecution). Notable high-profile cases in fraud, money-laundering, business crime, murder, sexual offences etc.
Professional Discipline (both defence and prosecution): Also practitioners specialising in civil law; regulatory work; commercial law; mental health; extradition; immigration; employment law; licensing.
Family Law: All aspects from divorce to domestic violence.
Public Access certified.

INTERNATIONAL International practice includes strong ties with Bermuda, Turks and Caicos, Somaliland and the Cayman Islands. Languages spoken include French, German, Spanish; Malay, Urdu and Indonesian.

CLOISTERS Robin Allen QC

Cloisters, 1 Pump Court, Temple, London, EC4Y 7AA
Tel (020) 7827 4000 **Fax** (020) 7827 4100 **DX** LDE 452
Email clerks@cloisters.com **Website** www.cloisters.com

Head of Chambers	Robin Allen QC
Senior Clerk	Glenn Hudson
Business Development Director	Sabina Smith
Tenants	53

MEMBERS

Robin Allen QC (1974) (QC-1995)
Jonathan Mitchell QC (1979) (QC -1992) Scotland +
Brian Napier QC (1986) + (QC-2002) Scotland +
Simon W Taylor QC (1984) (QC-2003)
Paul Epstein QC (1988) (QC-2006)
Daphne Romney QC (1979) (QC-2009)
Patricia Hitchcock QC (1988) (QC-2011)
Joel Donovan QC (1991) (QC-2011)
Jacques Algazy QC (1980) (QC-2012)
Caspar Glyn QC (1992) (QC-2012)
Jason Galbraith-Marten QC (1991) (QC-2014)
Rachel Crasnow QC (1994) (QC-2015)
William Latimer-Sayer QC (1995) (QC-2016)
Martin Seaward (1978)
Philip Engelman (1979)
Andrew Buchan (1981)
Simon Dyer (1987)
Declan O'Dempsey (1987)
Michael Potter (2013) (1988 Northern Ireland) +
Catherine Casserley (1991)
Yvette Genn (1991)
Paul Michell (1991)
John Horan (1993)
Daniel Lawson (1994)
Sally Robertson (1995)
Sally Cowen (1995)
Lisa Sullivan (1997)
Martyn McLeish (1997)
Thomas Coghlin (1998)
Schona Jolly (1999)
David Massarella (1999)
Akua Reindorf (1999)
Claire McCann (2000)
Thomas Brown (2000)
Linda Jacobs (2000)
Ed Williams (2000)
Anna Beale (2001)
Adam Ohringer (2001)
Hannah Godfrey (2002)
Dee Masters (2004)
Sarah Fraser Butlin (2005)
Daniel Dyal (2006)
Chris Milsom (2006)
Olivia-Faith Dobbie (2007)
Will Dobson (2008)
Caroline Musgrave (2008)
Catriona Stirling (2008)
Nathaniel Caiden (2009)
Siân McKinley (2009)
Sheryn Omeri (2010)
Chesca Lord (2011)
Catherine Richmond (2011)
Rachel Barrett (2012)
Tamar Burton (2012)
Jennifer Danvers (2012)
Nathan Roberts (2014)
Sir Stephen Sedley (1964) +
Prof Alan Neal (1972) +
Delroy Duncan (1984) +
Prof Anthony Bradley QC (1989) +
Rachel Chambers (2002) +

+ Associate member

THE CHAMBERS Cloisters is highly reputed for its commitment to excellence and its continual involvement in ground-breaking cases. Cloisters' success is due to its integration of market knowledge with outstanding advocacy and tailor-made client service. Cloisters offers expert legal advice and representation across markets that include: armed forces, banking and financial services, charities, civil services, education, food and drink, health and care (nhs and private), local government, media, arts and entertainment, pharmaceuticals, religion, retail and consumer, security services, sports, technology, telecommunications, tourism and leisure, transport and travel.
Cloisters' clients include individuals, employees, employers, unions, companies, charities, local authorities, insurers, transport service providers, governments, patients, medical profession, educational establishments, students, regulators professional advisers, sports personalities and clubs.

WORK UNDERTAKEN For Cloisters' work see website www.cloisters.com.
Clinical Negligence: Cloisters is the predominant claimant clinical negligence set with a large team of silks and juniors. It has an outstanding reputation for dealing with multi-million pound catastrophic birth and spinal injury claims and is at the cutting edge of clinical negligence law, playing a lead in many of the major cases.
Employment: Cloisters is the 'go-to' set for employment and discrimination law. Its award-winning team represents employers, employees, trade unions, government, NGOs and campaigning groups in all employment and equality disputes from individual contractual claims to complex and high profile multi-party discrimination litigation. Over three quarters of its barristers are ranked leaders in their field and are renowned for their practical approach and sensitivity to clients' needs.
Human Rights & Civil Liberties: Cloisters is at the forefront of developments in equalities and human rights work nationally and internationally. Seven members are appointed to the Equality and Human Rights Commission's (EHRC) Panel of Preferred Counsel.
Personal Injury: Chambers' personal injury team is highly sought after for its expertise in maximum severity work, multi-million pound catastrophic injury claims, industrial and traffic accidents and claims relating to explosions, disease, and the armed forces. A strong team of silks and juniors provides a complete service in multi-track trials in courts throughout the UK. Members of chambers have scored major successes in applications for interim payments.
Professional Discipline & Regulatory: Cloisters is recognised for its expertise across a wide range of professions. The team is well placed to draw on the expertise of teams in Cloisters' other areas of practice.
Public Law: The set's work covers human rights, judicial review and public inquiries, both for and against public bodies and regulatory authorities.
Sports, Media & Entertainment: The team acts for the FA in high profile matters as well as for a wide range of sports bodies and personalities. Cloisters covers disciplinary regulations, consultative work, litigation, non-professional sporting matters, employment and contractual issues arising from sports and entertainment cases. The team's strength lies in applying formidable legal technical skills in a sporting context to produce ground breaking, creative solutions for clients.
Mediation: Chambers has a strong team of 17 mediators led by Sir Stephen Sedley.

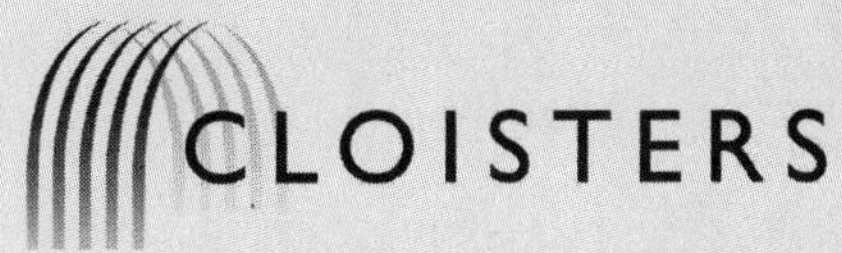

CORAM CHAMBERS Martha Cover & Mark Twomey

Coram Chambers, 9-11 Fulwood Place, London, WC1V 6HG
Tel (020) 7092 3700 **Fax** (020) 7092 3777
Email clerks@coramchambers.co.uk **Website** www.coramchambers.co.uk

Heads of Chambers	Martha Cover Mark Twomey
Senior Clerk	Paul Sampson
Business Development Manager	Kristina Baumgarten
Tenants	63

THE CHAMBERS

Coram Chambers is a leading family law set with a national reputation for excellence in advocacy and client care across all areas of family law and mental health law. Chambers prides itself on delivering excellent standards of client care to both lay and professional clients.

Coram Chambers has a particularly strong commitment to equality and diversity, and to the representation of minorities including alternative family structures. Members of chambers are at the forefront of developments in family law, and appear regularly in leading and landmark cases.

Chambers has strong dedicated teams specialising in children, family finance, Court of Protection, adult social care, human rights, international/abduction, and mediation fielding both experienced senior practitioners and more junior members.

Members of chambers appear regularly at all levels of court including the Court of Appeal and Supreme Court and have a strong track record in the Court of Protection and the Administrative Courts.

CORNERSTONE BARRISTERS Phillip Kolvin

2-3 Gray's Inn Square, Gray's Inn, London, WC1R 5JH
Tel (020) 7242 4986/ (0333) 240 0591 **Fax** (020) 7405 1166 **DX** 316 (Ch.Ln.)
Email clerks@cornerstonebarristers.com **Website** www.cornerstonebarristers.com

Head of Chambers	Phillip Kolvin QC
Chief Executive	Elizabeth Woodman
Tenants	51

MEMBERS

Philip Kolvin QC (1985) (QC-2009)
Mark Lowe QC (1972) (QC-1996)
Ashley Underwood QC (1976) (QC-2001)
Vincent Fraser QC (1981) (QC-2001)
James Findlay QC (1984) (QC-2008)
Steven Gasztowicz QC (1981) (QC-2009)
Phillip Coppel QC (1994) (QC-2009)
Gerard Forlin QC (1984) (QC-2010)
Ranjit Bhose QC (1989) (QC-2012)
Kelvin Rutledge QC (1989) (QC- 2013)
Michael Bedford QC (1985) (QC-2016)
Richard Ground QC (1994) (QC-2016)
Alun Alesbury (1974)
Graham Stoker (1977)
Ian Albutt (1981)
Mary Cook (1982)
Paul Shadarevian (1984)
Jonathan Clay (1990)
Jon Holbrook (1991)
Robin Green (1992)
Harriet Townsend (1992)
Catherine Rowlands (1992)
Matt Hutchings (1993)
Thomas Cosgrove (1994)
Michael Paget (1995)
Martin Edwards (1995)
Wayne Beglan (1996)
David Lintott (1996)
Rory Clarke (1996)
Kuljit Bhogal (1998)
Andrew Lane (1999)
Shomik Datta (2000)
Asitha Ranatunga (2001)
Peggy Etiebet (2001)
Damien Welfare (2001)
Josef Cannon (2002)
Dean Underwood (2002)
Clare Parry (2005)
Estelle Dehon (2006)
Ryan Kohli (2006)
Jennifer Oschoft (2006)
Rob Williams (2008)
Emma Dring (2009)
Zoe Whittington (2009)
Jack Parker (2011)
Richard Hanstock (2012)
Dr Ashley Bowes (2013)
Ben Du Feu (2013)
Matt Lewin (2013)
Tara O'Leary (2014)

THE CHAMBERS Offering exceptional ability at all levels, Cornerstone Barristers has a market-leading reputation for advice and representation in planning, public law, housing, property, licensing, health and social care and regulatory law.
Clients include companies, central and local government, private developers, public development agencies, third party objectors and individuals.

Members act as Treasury Counsel, hold part-time judicial appointments and sit as arbitrators and legal assessors on disciplinary boards and tribunals.
Members appear on a regular basis at the Supreme Court, Court of Appeal, High Court, County Court and before the various specialist tribunals including the Upper Tribunal (Lands Chamber), the Leasehold Valuation Tribunal and the Adjudicator to HM Land Registry. With offices in London, Birmingham and Cardiff, the set's scope extends to Hong Kong, Malaysia, Singapore, and the West Indies, and includes European law and the European Convention on Human Rights.
Friendly, approachable and professional, the set delivers a streamlined, cost-effective service while cherishing the connection with inescapable former member Sir Edward Marshall Hall.

WORK UNDERTAKEN The set's expertise takes in the most lengthy, complex and high profile cases as well as more routine matters.
Planning: As one of the leading planning sets, Cornerstone Barristers handles the full range of issues including high-profile infrastructure and other nationally important projects involving property, public and environmental law, compulsory purchase and compensation, minerals and waste, rights of way, highways, village greens and commons. Members handle major inquiries and advise on prominent developments, statutory challenges and judicial review.
Social Housing: The set is well known for landlord and tenant law, homelessness, asylum, housing benefit fraud, possession claims, contested succession, unlawful subletting, anti-social behaviour and disrepair.
Property: As well as advising and representing private and public-sector clients in relation to commercial and residential property, members act as mediators and arbitrators.
Public Law & Judicial Review: The set defends and challenges public law decisions in many areas including planning, housing, highways, health and social care, court of protection, immigration, human rights, education and employment. Members take part in the most prominent public inquiries and inquests.
Licensing: The set drives professional development in this area by advising, training and educating across the whole field, including alcohol, entertainment, gambling and taxis, on behalf of licensing authorities, police, leading industry operators, trade associations and campaign and community groups.
Regulatory Law: In conjunction with a leading reputation in corporate manslaughter, the set provides a comprehensive service in consumer protection, trading standards, health and safety and environmental regulation.

RECRUITMENT Pupils are received each year; pupillage funds are available.

cornerstone barristers

CROWN OFFICE CHAMBERS Richard Lynagh QC

2 Crown Office Row, Temple, London, EC4Y 7HJ
Tel (020) 7797 8100 **Fax** (020) 7797 8101 **DX** 80 LONDON/CHANCERY LANE
Email clerks@crownofficechambers.com **Website** www.crownofficechambers.com

Head of Chambers	Richard Lynagh QC
Senior Managing Clerk	Andy Flanagan
Senior Team Clerks	Steve Purse
	Oliver Parkhouse
	Chris Sunderland
Arbitrator, Mediator Adjudicator's Clerk	Nick Hamilton
Tenants	101

MEMBERS

Richard Lynagh QC (1975) (QC-1996)
Michael Harvey QC (1966) (QC-1982)
Michael Spencer QC (1970) (QC-1989)
Christopher Purchas QC (1966) (QC-1990)
Roger ter Haar QC (1974) (QC-1992)
Andrew Bartlett QC (1974) (QC-1993)
Michael Kent QC (1975) (QC-1996)
Jonathan Waite QC (1978) (QC-2002)
Margaret Bickford-Smith QC (1973) (QC-2003)
David Sears QC (1984) (QC 2003)
Michael Curtis QC (1982) (QC-2008)
Christopher Kennedy QC (1989) (QC-2010)
Andrew Rigney QC (1992) (QC-2010)
David Platt QC (1987) (QC 2011)
John Cooper QC (1985) (QC-2014)
Alexander Antelme QC (1993) (QC-2014)
Ben Quiney QC (1998) (QC-2014)
James Ageros QC (1990) (QC-2015)
Muhammed Haque QC (1997) (QC-2015)
Kim Franklin QC (1984) (QC-2016)
Andrew Smith QC (1988) (QC-2016)
James Maxwell-Scott QC (1995) (QC-2016)
Martyn Berkin (1966)
Cyril Chern (1972)
John Stevenson (1975)
Nicholas Davies (1975)
Andrew Phillips (1978)
John Greenbourne (1978)
Gordon Catford (1980)
Julian Field (1980)
Paul Dean (1982)
Charlotte Jones (1982)
A John Williams (1983)
Steven Coles (1983)
James Medd (1985)
Shaun Ferris (1985)
Catherine Foster (1986)
William Vandyck (1988)
Peter Morton (1988)
Dermot Woolgar (1988)
Simon J Brown (1988)
Steven Snowden (1989)
Ian Wright (1989)
Erica Power (1990)
Jason Evans-Tovey (1990)
Robert O'Leary (1990)
Toby Gee (1992)
Isabel Hitching (1992)
Malcolm Galloway (1992)
Patrick Blakesley (1993)
Richard Tyrrell (1993)
Claire Toogood (1995)
Robert Stokell (1995)
Suzanne Chalmers (1995)
Simon Antrobus (1995)
Mark A Balysz (1995)
Jamie Clarke (1995)
Andrew Davis (1996)
Edward Broome (1996)
Dominic Kay (1997)
Susan Lindsey (1997)
Victoria Woodbridge (1998)
Jack Ferro (1998)
Anna Laney (1998)
Daniel Shapiro (1999)
Farah Mauladad (1999)
Mark Armitage (1999)
Matthew Boyle (2000)
Alexander MacPherson (2000)
Rebecca Taylor (2001)
Charles Pimlott (2001)
Jane Davies Evans (2001)
Anna Symington (2002)
Crispin Winser (2003)
Michele De Gregorio (2003)
Rosanna Hellebronth (2004)
Justin Davis (2003)
Peter Houghton (2005)
Julia Kendrick (2005)
Elizabeth Boon (2006)
Richard Sage (2006)
David Myhill (2006)
Mike Atkins (2006)
Siobhan Lambertsen (2007)
Nadia Whittaker (2007)
Alice Jarratt (2007)
Helen Pagett (2008)
Harry Lambert (2008)
Jack Macauley (2009)
Rory Holmes (2009)
James Sharpe (2009)
Carolyn McColgan (2010)
Carlo Taczalski (2010)
Athena Markidas (2011)
Patrick Maxwell (2011)
Lara Knight (2012)
Daniel Shaw (2007)
Jack Murphy (2013)
Adam Taylor (2014)
Mek Mesfin (2014)
Douglas James (2015)
Maurice Holmes (2015)

Crown Office Chambers is a leading civil and commercial set widely recognised as a market leader with a reputation for combining high-quality advice and advocacy with a modern, flexible and commercially-minded approach.

THE CHAMBERS Specialist, experienced and innovative clerking teams assist highly-rated Silks and juniors in providing an efficient, high-quality service for professional and lay clients. Chambers has a wide range of experienced arbitrators, adjudicators and mediators and offers a fully administered ADR service.

WORK UNDERTAKEN

Professional Negligence: Members have been instructed in some of the leading cases in professional negligence. Chambers undertakes all forms of professional negligence work, with particular focus on: construction professionals, lawyers (barristers and solicitors), accountants, insurance brokers, insolvency practitioners and financial services advisors.
Product Liability: Members have been instructed in most of the major pharmaceutical multiparty claims which have so far been brought. These have included: breast implant litigation, DePuy ASR and Hylamer hip prostheses litigation, Thalidomide litigation. Chambers also has considerable involvement in non-pharmaceutical product liability litigation and members also advise in relation to cover under product liability insurance policies.
Criminal Regulatory & Environmental: Chambers is widely regarded as the leading set in criminal regulatory and environmental law. Members have been involved in the leading cases that have shaped this niche area of corporate criminal law including Lion Steel and M5 Fireworks Disaster, and continue to be instructed in the highest profile cases, such as the Hillsborough inquest, the Inquest into the Amenas Incident, Maidstone and Tunbridge Wells NHS Trust and the Alton Towers case.

CROWN OFFICE CHAMBERS Richard Lynagh QC (continued)

Personal Injury, Disease & Clinical Negligence: Chambers is one of the leading personal injury and industrial disease sets in the country. The team of specialist counsel at all levels of seniority are regularly involved in the most serious of cases including brain and spinal injuries; group litigation; fatal injuries and complex psychiatric and chronic pain. Chambers also has a broad expertise in healthcare-related litigation work including, but not limited to, acting in clinical negligence claims for claimants, the NHS, private providers, insurers and defence organisations. The expertise of a number of barristers in several areas of law ensures that clients can obtain balanced and specialist advice even when a case touches on different practice areas.

Insurance & Reinsurance: This is a major element of chambers' business. Chambers has strong links with the insurance market, and are regularly instructed by many of the major insurers, underwriting syndicates and brokers. All forms of contentious and advisory work are undertaken, including work in the Commercial Court and in arbitration.

Property Damage: Chambers has particular expertise in property damage claims arising out of fires, floods, explosions, storms (including hurricanes), subsidence (including tree roots) etc. Its expertise in construction, insurance, product liability and professional negligence means that its members are ideally suited to handling such claims.

International Arbitration: Chambers has a dedicated and increasingly popular team of high-calibre Silks and juniors that undertake a range complex, high-value domestic and international arbitration work acting as both counsel and arbitrators. Recent disputes have concerned: power stations, process engineering, chemical plants, road construction, railways, underground works and other high profile construction and engineering projects; financial services; commercial, insurance and reinsurance contracts.

Commercial & Chancery: Members receive regular instructions in a variety of commercial cases, in particular franchising disputes acting for franchisees and franchisors.

Its work also encompasses banking, company law (including directors' duties, disqualification applications and minority shareholder petitions), partnership, financial services, insolvency (corporate and personal), commercial fraud, judicial review, conflict of laws, guarantees (including bonds, mortgages and other forms of security), property (including landlord and tenant law), commercial agency regulations, carriage of goods and consumer credit.

Construction & Engineering: This forms a significant part of the chambers' workload. Members have substantial expertise acting for employers, contractors, construction professionals, insurers and developers in an advisory capacity and as advocates in all forms of dispute resolution. Chambers continue to edit and contribute to Emden's Construction Law by Crown Office Chambers. Recent cases include: Aspect v Higgins; Harding v Paice; Greenwich Millenium Village v Essex Services.

1 CROWN OFFICE ROW Philip Havers QC

Temple, London, EC4Y 7HH
Tel (020) 7797 7500 **Fax** (020) 7797 7550 **DX** LDE1020
Email mail@1cor.com **Website** www.1cor.com Blog ukhumanrightsblog.com

Head of Chambers	Philip Havers QC
Chambers Director	Andrew Meyler
Senior Clerk	Matthew Phipps
Tenants	73

MEMBERS

Philip Havers QC (1974) (QC-1995)
Robert Seabrook QC (1964) (QC-1983)
James Badenoch QC (1968) (QC-1989)
Stephen Miller QC (1971) (QC-1990)
Kieran Coonan QC (1971) (QC-1990)
Terence Coghlan QC (1968) (QC-1993)
Guy Mansfield QC (1972) (QC-1994)
Sally Smith QC (1977) (QC-1997)
Elizabeth-Anne Gumbel QC (1974) (QC-1999)
Paul Rees QC (1980) (QC-2000)
Margaret Bowron QC (1978) (QC-2001)
David Balcombe QC (1980) (QC-2002)
Joanna Glynn QC (1983) (QC-2002)
David Hart QC (1982) (QC-2003)
Martin Forde QC (1984) (QC-2006)
William Edis QC (1985) (QC-2008)
Christina Lambert QC (1988) (QC-2009)
Angus McCullough QC (1990) (QC-2010)
John Whitting QC (1991) (QC-2011)
David Evans QC (1988) (QC-2012)
Richard Booth QC (1993) (QC-2013)
Marina Wheeler QC (1987) (QC-2016)
Henry Witcomb QC (1989) (QC-2016)
Owain Thomas QC (1995) (QC-2016)
Jeremy Hyam QC (1995) (QC-2016)
Clodagh Bradley QC (1996) (QC-2016)
Peter Skelton QC (1997) (QC-2016)
James King-Smith (1980) ++
John Gimlette (1986)
Andrew Kennedy (1989)
Martin Downs (1990)
Jeremy Cave (1992) ++
Giles Colin (1994)
Sydney Chawatama (1994)
Sarah Lambert (1994)
Justin Levinson (1994)
Oliver Sanders (1995)
Shaheen Rahman (1996)
Neil Sheldon (1998)
Richard Smith (1999)
Christopher Mellor (1999)
Robert Kellar (1999)
Matthew Barnes (2000)
Iain O'Donnell (2000)
Sarabjit Singh (2001)
David Manknell (2001)
Suzanne Lambert (2002)
Judith Rogerson (2003)
Andrea Lindsay Strugo (2003)
Amy Mannion (2003)
Robert Wastell (2004)
Richard Mumford (2004)
Rachel Marcus (2005)
Leanne Woods (2005)
Pritesh Rathod (2006)
Caroline Cross (2006)
Matthew Donmall (2006)
Adam Wagner (2007)
Amelia Walker (2007)
Isabel McArdle (2008)
Matthew Hill (2009)
Alasdair Henderson (2009)
Claire McGregor (2009)
Matthew Flinn (2010)
Paul Reynolds (2010)
Lois Williams (2012)
Jim Duffy (2012)
Dominic Ruck Keene (2012)
Jessica Elliott (2013)
Hannah Noyce (2013)
Michael Deacon (2014)
Emma Louise Fenelon (2015)
Gideon Barth (2015)
Rosalind English (1993) **
Duncan Fairgrieve (2002) **
Martin Matthews (1970) **

++ Mainly practise from Brighton ** Academic Consultants

THE CHAMBERS One Crown Office Row is a long-established civil set providing advisory and advocacy services with a pre-eminent reputation for its clinical negligence and healthcare practise, its expertise in public law & human rights and its professional disciplinary work. 46 Members practice from an Annexe at Crown Office Row, Brighton. Established over 60 years ago, this is a leading civil set whose reputation for quality is reflected in the fact that it counts among its members and former members the former Lord Chief Justice, Lord Woolf, four Lords Justices of Appeal, and three former Chairmen of the Bar. Clients receive high order advocacy and professional skills from barristers and a friendly, client-oriented and efficient service from its staff. The set occupies a prominent building in Temple with modern IT, conference and video-conference facilities. It runs a widely-acclaimed UK Human Rights Blog at ukhumanrightsblog.com and the unique free Human Rights Update website at www.humanrights.org.uk.

WORK UNDERTAKEN Members have been recognised as leading practitioners in all aspects of healthcare law, clinical negligence, personal injury and inquests, professional disciplinary proceedings, public and administrative law, public inquiries, human rights, immigration and asylum, employment, professional negligence, costs, tax, matrimonial finance and environmental law. The set also has successful practices in multi-party actions, technology, construction and sports law. Chambers has a team of 16 accredited mediators, 13 of whom are silks.

PUBLICATIONS Members of Chambers are either authors or co-authors of, or contributors to *The Inquest Book, Information Rights, Same Sex Marriage & Civil Partnerships, Online Law Encyclopaedia, Ethics for Advocates Manual, Dictionary of Law, Personal Injury Handbook, An Introduction to Human Rights and the Common Law, Civil Court Precedents, Public Inquiries, Guide to Child Abuse Compensation Claims, Value Added Tax, Commentary and Analysis, The Regulation of Healthcare Professionals: Law, Principle and Process, Burnett-Hall on Environmental Law, Fitness to Practise: Health Care Regulatory Law, Principle and Process, The Regulation of Healthcare Professionals: Law, Principle and Process, Clinical Negligence - A Practitioner's Guide, Child Abuse Compensation Claims, Contributory Negligence, Civil Partnership, Clinical Negligence, Personal Injury Handbook, Professional Negligence and Liability* and *Human Rights and the Common Law.*

RECRUITMENT Up to two pupils are taken annually for 12 months. The set is a member of Pupillage Gateway. Applications for a third six month pupillage are usually invited in June.

DEVEREUX Timothy Brennan QC

Head of Chambers	Timothy Brennan QC
Chambers Director	Vince Plant
Tenants	52

Devereux Chambers, Devereux Court, London, WC2R 3JH
Tel (020) 7353 7534 **Fax** (020) 7583 5150 **DX** 349 London Chancery Lane
Email clerks@devchambers.co.uk **Website** www.devereuxchambers.co.uk **Twitter** @devereuxlaw

THE CHAMBERS Devereux Chambers currently has 52 barristers including 11 QCs. The work of Chambers is wide-ranging and includes: commercial litigation, insurance, reinsurance; professional negligence; IT and telecoms; contentious and non-contentious tax; employment and industrial relations; clinical negligence and personal injury.

RECRUITMENT Chambers is always interested in hearing from excellent practitioners with established and complementary practices.

PUPILLAGE Chambers seeks very clever candidates who demonstrate maturity, common sense and a suitable work ethic.

FURTHER INFORMATION The most up-to-date details are available from the website at www.devereuxchambers.co.uk.

DOUGHTY STREET CHAMBERS Geoffrey Roberts QC

Heads of Chambers	Geoffrey Robertson QC Edward Fitzgerald CBE QC
Crime Business Development Director	Maurice MacSweeney
Criminal Clerks	Tom Street Emily Martin Marc Gilby Richard Vile James Findley (Junior)
Civil Business Development Director	Adam Wyse
Civil Clerks	Richard Bayliss Luke Christmas Charlie Labrum Sian Wilkins Rachel Finch Emily Norman Anthony Ward Callum Stebbing Kevin Kelly Nick Chuter Dan Moore (Junior)
Tenants	133

Doughty Street Chambers, 53-54 Doughty Street, London, WC1N 2LS
Tel (020) 7404 1313 **Fax** (020) 7404 2283 **DX** 223 Chancery Lane
Email enquiries@doughtystreet.co.uk **Website** www.doughtystreet.co.uk

MEMBERS

Geoffrey Robertson QC (1973) (QC 1988)
Edward Fitzgerald QC (1978) (QC 1995)
Helena Kennedy QC (1972) (QC 1991)
Patrick O'Connor QC (1970) (QC 1993)
Christopher Sallon QC (1973) (QC 1994)
Peter Carter QC (1974) (QC 1995)
James Wood QC (1975) (QC 1999)
Andrew Hall QC (1991) (QC 2002)
Adrian Waterman QC (1988) (QC 2006)
Joel Bennathan QC (1985) (QC 2006)
Heather Williams QC (1985) (QC 2006)
Robin Oppenheim QC (1988) (QC 2006)
Nicholas Bowen QC (1984) (QC 2009)
Isabella Forshall QC (1982) (QC 2010)
Martin Westgate QC (1985) (QC 2010)
Jon Whitfield QC (1985) (QC 2010)
Francis FitzGibbon QC (1986) (QC 2010)
David Hislop QC (1979) (NZ Bar 1979) (QC 2010)
Tim Moloney QC (1993) (QC 2010)
Kirsty Brimelow QC (1991) (QC 2011)
Judith Farbey QC (1992) (QC 2011)
Theo Huckle QC (1985) (QC 2011)
Rebecca Trowler QC (1995) (QC 2012)
David Bentley QC (1984) (QC 2013)
Joe Stone QC (1989) (QC 2013)
John RWD Jones QC (1992) (QC 2013)
Sarah Elliott QC (1996) (QC 2014)
Wayne Jordash QC (1995) (QC 2014)
Aswini Weereratne QC (1986) (QC 2015)
Jonathan Mann QC (1989) (QC 2015)
Richard Fisher QC (1994) (QC 2015)
Rupert Bowers QC (1995) (QC 2015)
Henrietta Hill QC (1997) (QC 2015)
Siobhan Grey QC (1994) (QC 2016)
David Carter (1971)
Nick Paul (1980)
Christopher Hough (1981)
Gerwyn Samuel (1986)
Lauren Soertsz (1987)
Kieran Maidment (1989)
Paul Taylor (1989)
Nick Brown (1990)
Quincy Whitaker (1991)
Stephen Reeder (1991)
Zia Nabi (1991)
Jonathan Cooper OBE (1992)
John Walsh (1993)
Katy Thorne (1994)
Mark Henderson (1994)
Paula Sparks (1994)
Paul Draycott (1994)
Clive Rawlings (1994)
Jeannie Mackie (1995)
Althea Brown (1995)
Dominic Preston (1995)
Ben Chataway (1995)
Nicholas Toms (1996)
Tublu K. Mukherjee (1996)
Emma Goodall (1996)
Joe Middleton (1997)
Ulele Burnham (1997)
Steven Powles (1997)
Nick Stanage (1997)
Lindsay Johnson (1997)
Jim Shepherd (1998)
Farrhat Arshad (1998)
Jamie Burton (1999)
Benjamin Narain (1999)
Ben Cooper (1999)
Charlotte Kilroy (1999)
John Hobson (1999)
Erimnaz Mushtaq (2000)
Daniel Bennett (2000)
David Lemer (2000)
Phil Haywood (2001)
Ruth Brander (2001)
Amanda Hart (2001)
Sue Sleeman (2001)
Caoilfhionn Gallagher (2001)
Piers Marquis (2001)
Amos Waldman (2001)
Liam Walker (2001)
Laura Dubinsky (2002)
David Rhodes (2002)
Richard Thomas (2002)
Alison Gerry (2003)
Philippa Eastwood (2003)
Alasdair Mackenzie (2004)
Benjamin Newton (2004)
Jonathan Price (2004)
Adam Straw (2004)
David Haines (2005)
Nichola Higgins (2005)
Louise Price (2006)
Malcolm Hawkes (2006)
Jude Bunting (2006)
Kate Annand (2007)
Alison Pickup (2007)
Tunde Okewale MBE (2007)
Annabel Timan (2007)
Tatyana Eatwell (2007)
Kate Beattie (2007)
Mary Westcott (2007)
Alex Gask (2008)
Tom Stevens (2008)
Catherine Meredith (2008)
Michelle Knorr (2008)
Sarah Steinhardt (2008)
Zimran Samuel (2008)
Jane Elliott-Kelly (2009)
Rowena Moffatt (2009)
Amal Clooney (2010)
Abigail Bright (2010)
Maria Roche (2010)
Marisa Cohen (2010)
Harriet Johnson (2010)
Maryam Mir (2010)
Jesse Nicholls (2010)
Graeme L. Hall (2011)
Sam Jacobs (2011)
James Kirk (2011)
Kate O'Raghallaigh (2011)
Paul Mason (2011)
Jake Taylor (2012)
Tim Cooke-Hurle (2012)
Melina Padron (2012)
Jelia Sane (2013)
Daniel Clarke (2013)
Fiona Murphy (2013)
Katherine O'Byrne (2013)
Mark Wassouf (2014)
Daniella Waddoup (2014)
Sophy Miles (2015)
Megan Hirst (2015)
Paul Barker (2015)

++ Associate Tenant ^ Public/Direct Access

THE CHAMBERS Doughty Street Chambers is a buoyant and cutting-edge set, renowned for and committed to defending freedom and civil liberties. It has a truly national and international profile across their wide range of practice in criminal law, civil law, administrative and public law, international law and human rights. Since their foundation in 1990, their aim has been and will always be to improve access to justice and to promote human rights and civil liberties through the law. Founded by fewer than 30 barristers, Doughty Street Chambers has grown to become one of the largest sets in the country with over 133 members, of whom 34 are Queen's Counsel, and it has established chambers in Manchester and Bristol as well as London.

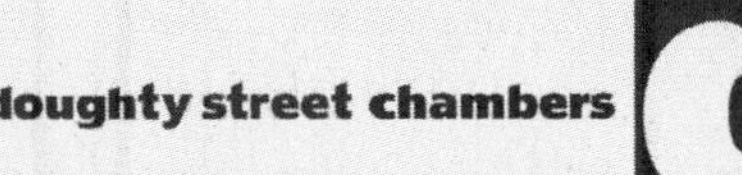

DRYSTONE CHAMBERS Karim Khalil QC

35 Bedford Row, London, WC1R 4JH
Tel (020) 7404 1881 **Fax** (020) 7404 1991
Email clerks@drystone.com **Website** www.drystone.com

Heads of Chambers	Karim Khalil QC Andrew Campbell-Tiech QC
Senior Clerk	Mark Cornell
Marketing Director	Brett Carver
Tenants	87

MEMBERS

Karim Khalil QC (1984) (QC 2003)
Andrew Campbell-Tiech QC (1978) (QC 2003)
Alastair Malcolm QC (1971) (QC 1996)
Michel Massih QC (1979) (QC 1999)
Michael Magarian QC (1988) (QC 2011)
Angela Rafferty QC (1995) (QC 2015)
Roger Harrison (1969)
John Farmer (1970)
Charles Kellett (1971)
Hugh Vass (1983)
Stephen Spence (1983)
Lindsay Cox (1984)
Christopher Wing (1985)
Brian Gibbins (1986)
Jonathan Seely (1987)
Will Buckley (1987)
Sean Minihan (1988)
Simon Kitchen (1988)
Matthew Jewell (1989)
William Carter (1989)
Isobel Ascherson (1991)
Sally Hobson (1991)
Matthew Pardoe (1992)
Kaja Reiff-Musgrove (1992)
Prof Charles Chatterjee (1992) *
Duncan O'Donnell (1992)
Robert Bryan (1992)
Jonathan Green (1993)
Charles Myatt (1993)
Charles Falk (1994)
Peter Caldwell(1995)
Zarif Khan (1996)
John McNally (1996)
Barnaby Shaw (1996)
Gavin Irwin (1996)
Nick Ham (1997)
Gregory Perrins (1997)
Joanne Eley (1997)
Stephen Halsall (1997)
Karen Walton (1998)
Richard Heller (1998)
Andrew Shaw (1998)
Claire Matthews (1998)
Mark Himsworth (1999)
Ryan Thompson (1999)
Allison Summers (2000)
Abi Khan (2000)
Rebecca Fairbairn (2000)
Stephen Donnelly (2001)
Seth Levine (2001)
Giles Bedloe (2001)
Azza Brown (2001)
Philip Farr (2001)
Daniel Jones (2002)
Myles Grandison (2002)
Kris Berlevy (2002)
Claire Howell (2003)
Andrew Price (2003)
Joanna Staples (2003)
Gemma Gillet (2003)
Nicola Devas(2003)
Jack Talbot (2004)
Edward Renvoize (2004)
James Gray (2005)
Marcus Joyce (2005)
Alan Birbeck (2006)
Barnaby Hone (2006)
Unyime Davies (2006)
Benjamin Seifert (2007)
Nawraz Karbani (2007)
Jehad Mustafa (2007) *
Lydia Waine (2007) *
Jacob Edwards (2007)
Henry Gordon (2007)
Hannah Hinton (2008)
Charlotte Compton (2008) *
Edward Cole (2008)
Ayanna Nelson (2009)
Simon Walters (2010)
Katherine Higgins (2011)
Alice Carver (2011)
Rebecca Penfold (2012)
Alex Cameron (2012)
Julian Norman (2012)
George Wills (2013)
Rebecca Turner (2013)
Andrea Lock (2016)

* Associate Tenant

THE CHAMBERS Following the 2015 merger of One Paper Buildings and Dyers Chambers to form Drystone Chambers, Chambers has quickly established a reputation as a prominent and leading set of barristers' chambers in London and the regions, specifically East Anglia and the South West, with a growing influence nationally. Chambers continues to develop a broad range of work over a substantial area of the country, helping it to stand apart from other sets.

Members have acted at every level of the criminal justice system in general crime, corporate crime, VAT and tax fraud, proceeds of crime.

Chambers provides advice and advocacy across a range of practice areas including consumer and regulatory law, extradition, professional discipline, prison law, military law, matrimonial and family, aviation and sports law. The focus of chambers' ethos is to provide outstanding advice and advocacy at every level of seniority, whilst understanding and respecting the need for clear communication with professional and lay clients alike.

WORK UNDERTAKEN

Crime: Prosecuting and defending in cases ranging from murder, fraud (including cases involving money laundering and confiscation), corporate crime often including an international element, (currently practitioners are working in the Cayman Islands), drugs and sexual offences to motoring matters. Chambers has acted in many cases of notoriety and importance, including the Soham murders, the Huntingdon Life Sciences campaigners, Fallon racing fraud, Operation Mellor (sham marriages), the Millenium Dome robbery, 21/07 terrorism trial, Damilola Taylor murder and the Allied Irish £750 million mortgage fraud.

Consumer Protection: The set acts for businesses, individuals and regulators across the full range of consumer protection and trading standards work, from large scale rogue trader cases and fatal food safety investigations to intricate product safety matters.

Professional Discipline & Sports law: Members of chambers provide a comprehensive service assisting professionals with advice on their regulatory obligations from registration requirements, negotiations with the regulator and all stages of proceedings from interim orders to appeals.

Members have acted for sportsmen and women in both Judicial Review and disciplinary proceedings. The set advise on athletes' agreements, selection policies and procedures, sponsorship agreements, media and marketing agreements, anti-doping, R&D and intellectual property agreements, image rights and disciplinary procedures.

Extradition: Drystone Chambers' extradition team are leaders in this complex, technical and rapidly developing area of law. They have been at the forefront of challenges where the legal systems of foreign states and the compatibility of extradition with the human rights of requested persons have been put to the test.

ELY PLACE CHAMBERS William McCormick QC

13 Ely Place, London, EC1N 6RY
Tel (020) 7400 9600 **DX** 291 Chancery Lane
Email admin@elyplace.com **Website** www.elyplace.com

Head of Chambers	William McCormick QC
Senior Clerks	Christopher Drury 07885 469845
	Richard Sheehan 07870128617
Senior Practice Manager	Kevin Morrow 07736288055
Practice Manager	Dave Lovitt 07795 233444
Administrator	Carol Belford
Tenants	34

MEMBERS

William McCormick QC (1985) (QC-2010) ^
Nicholas Stewart QC (1971) (QC-1987) ^ ± Fellow of the Institute of Chartered Arbitrators
Malcolm Bishop QC (1968) (QC-1993) +
William Evans (1977) + ^ ±
Clifford Darton (1988) ^
Leslie Millin (1988) ^
Jeffrey Bacon (1989)
Russell Stone (1992) ^ ±
Iain Daniels (1992)
Craig Barlow (1992)
Angus Gloag (1992) ^
Mark Friston (1997) ++
Simon Perhar (1997) ^ ±
Ali Reza Sinai (1997)
Gillian Crew (1998) ^ ±
Michael Salter (1999) ^
James Newman (2000) ^
Faisel Sadiq (2000) ^
Bushra Ahmed (2001) ++
Paul Hughes (2001) ++
John Samson (2001) ^ ±
Sally Blackmore (2003)
David Mitchell (2004) ^ **
Philipp Simon (2004)
Amy Stroud (2004) ^
Thomas Kirk (2007) ^ **
Liam Ryan (2007) ^
Aidan Briggs (2009) ^
Paul Powlesland (2009) ^
George Woodhead (2009)
Naveeta Sawh (2009) ^
Catherine Urquhart (2010)
Max Cole (2011) ^

+ Recorder ^ Public Access Approved ** Junior Treasury Counsel ± CEDR Accredited ++ Door tenant

THE CHAMBERS Friendly, progressive and dynamic, the set provides clear pragmatic advice and a tradition of robust polished advocacy to public and private sector clients, while the long-serving clerking team offers its expertise to clients regarding suitability of counsel and provides strong administrative support thereafter. The ethos is that providing the best result for the client depends upon a team effort.

WORK UNDERTAKEN

Chancery/commercial: The chancery/commercial team at Ely Place provides sound, practical advice so that clients can make effective and fully-informed commercial decisions.
Chambers workload includes contractual disputes, insolvency matters, professional negligence cases, sports-related disputes, cross-border disputes and international arbitrations involving high net worth individuals and businesses and contractual disputes arising out of the relationships between financial institutions and their clients. Disputes as to rights under shareholder agreements or agreements for the sale of businesses coupled with unfair prejudice petitions and claims alleging breaches of directors' duties and derivative actions form another substantial element of the cases.
The team draws from a breadth of legal knowledge across a range of disciplines and jurisdictions, with members regularly appearing overseas or advising in relation to disputes and the enforcement of judgments involving amongst other systems, the US, France, Belarus, Switzerland, DIFC, Russia, Isle of Man, Iran, Iraq, Malaysia, Turkey, Azerbaijan and the Caribbean.
Property: Ely Place has expanded its property group by recruiting established and recognised practitioners in this field over recent years. Members have appeared in a number of reported and important property cases and continue to be engaged in such litigation at both first instance and on appeal. The work ranges from advising on major commercial transactions to representing public bodies in housing and L&T matters and covers the full gamut of property disputes. Members of the team have a particular speciality in the law relating to watercourses, flooding and the water industry.
Media: Ely Place has a small but vibrant media group with a long-standing reputation for punching above its numerical weight due to the talents of its members. It is able to call on expertise gained from members who have previously worked in the print and television media and its juniors are making increasingly regular appearances in defamation and privacy cases.
Employment: Ely Place is a leading set for employment and discrimination law and is a first port of call for advice and advocacy for a growing number of high profile law firms and lay clients such as BAA, Network Rail, EE, GlaxoSmithKline and for Unions such as UCATT, Unison and UNITE. Members of the group are regularly instructed by police forces and local authorities throughout the country. In addition, members of the group advise in and conduct High Court actions concerning contractual employment disputes including those involving injunctive relief to enforce covenants or fiduciary duties. Its highly experienced members include a fee paid employment judge, legally qualified chair for police disciplinary tribunals, disciplinary assessor for the ACCA and three treasury counsel.
Inquests: A thriving area of work is representing interested parties at inquests. Members of the healthcare and prison and police law groups regularly advise and appear in such proceedings.

Ely Place Chambers

ENTERPRISE CHAMBERS Zia Bhaloo QC

9 Old Square, Lincoln's Inn, London, WC2A 3SR
Tel (020) 7405 9471 **Fax** (020) 7242 1447 **DX** LDE 301
Email clerks@enterprisechambers.com **Website** www.enterprisechambers.com

Head of Chambers	Zia Bhaloo QC
Chambers Director	Michael Couling
Senior Clerk	Antony Armstrong
Clerks	Michael Ireland
	Luke Daws
	Robert Wheeler
	Oliver Riley
	Sue Harding
Tenants	43

MEMBERS

Zia Bhaloo QC (1990) (QC-2010)
Ian Mayes QC (1974) (QC-1993)
Bernard Weatherill QC (1974) (QC-1996)
Hugh Jory QC (1992) (QC-2014)
Edward Cohen (1972)
Caroline Hutton (1979)
Linden Ife (1982)
Geoffrey Zelin (1984)
James Barker (1984)
Hugo Groves (1980)
Andrew Kinnison (1988)
Marilyn Kennedy-McGregor (1989)
Stephanie Jarron (1990)
James Pickering (1991)
Bridget Williamson (1993)
Jonathan Klein (1992)
Edward Francis (1995)
Shaiba Ilyas (1998)
Jonathan Rodger (1999)
Niall McCulloch (2000)
Simon Johnson (2000)
Matthew West (2000)
Kavan Gunaratna (2004)
Cristín Toman (2004)
Margaret Griffin (2004)
Emma Read (2006)
David Peachey (2007)
Kelly Bond (2007)
Duncan Heath (2007)
Jennifer Meech (2008)
Phillip Gale (2008)
James Davies (2009)
Anna Lintner (2009)
Christopher Buckingham (2009)
Chris Royle (2009)
Matthew Maddison (2010)
Louise Bowmaker (2011)
Rowena Page (2012)
Jessica Brooke (2012)
Madeline Dixon (2013)
Evelyn Barden (2014)
Claire Thompson (2014)
Fiona Todd (2014)
HH Peter Langan QC (1967) (QC-1983) *
Jeremy Child (BVI) *
Susannah Markandva (2005) *
Shuvra Deb (BVI) *

* Door tenant

THE CHAMBERS Enterprise Chambers is a leading commercial chancery set, with experts who are consistently recommended in their field by Chambers and Partners (for details of individual recommendations, please see the chambers website). The set is in a position to offer specialists across the range of commercial chancery work, including commercial, company, insolvency and restructuring, landlord and tenant, and property; so for example, the expertise within the set in insolvency and property uniquely places it to deal with disputes which involve both. Clients comment on both the outstanding quality of the work done by the set and its flexible and unstuffy approach, in particular the excellence of its clerking. The set also has centres in Leeds and Newcastle.

WORK UNDERTAKEN Enterprise is able to provide specialist barristers in the following areas (for details of recent cases in each area, please see the chambers website):
Commercial Disputes: Including contracts, banking, guarantees, securities, financial services regulation, insurance, sale and carriage of goods, consumer credit, competition, restraint of trade, breach of confidence, civil fraud and private international law.
Company: Including unfair prejudice, derivative and other shareholders' claims, directors' disqualification, solvent and insolvent schemes, capital reductions, business transfers, companies' securities and claims against directors.
Equitable Remedies: Including constructive and resulting trusts, tracing, injunctions, freezing injunctions, and search orders.
Insolvency & Restructuring: Relating to companies, partnerships and individuals, including receiverships, administrations, voluntary arrangements, liquidations, bankruptcy, wrongful and fraudulent trading, preferences, transactions at an undervalue, other antecedent transactions, and cross-border insolvency.
Intellectual Property: Including copyright, trademarks, and passing off.
Landlord & Tenant: Relating to business, residential and agricultural tenancies including security of tenure, possession claims, forfeiture, unlawful eviction, dilapidations, leasehold enfranchisement, rent control and review, service charges, and business tenancy renewals under Part II of the 1954 Act, together with all aspects of social housing law.
Pensions: Relating to occupational and personal pension schemes.
Professional Liability: Relating to accountants, actuaries, auditors, barristers, solicitors, insolvency practitioners, surveyors and construction professionals, and trustees.
Real Property: Concerning the legal and beneficial ownership of real property, including conveyancing and the sale of land, easements, restrictive covenants, adverse possession, boundary disputes, land registration, mortgages, LPA receivers, defective buildings, construction and engineering contracts and planning.
Regulatory & Licensing: Affecting commercial activity, including environmental, water and waste licensing, building regulation and remediation, as well as liquor, gaming, and sex establishments.
Traditional Chancery: Including associations (partnerships, clubs and societies), charities, trusts, settlements, family provision, wills and probate, and Court of Protection.

PUBLICATIONS: Butterworths Property Insolvency; the Enterprise Chambers Annotated Guide to Insolvency Legislation and Practice; Bailey and Groves on Corporate Insolvency – Law and Practice; The Landlord and Tenant Factbook; Estates Gazette Questions and Answers series and the Practical Law Property Litigation Blog.

INTERNATIONAL: Several members have previously practised in fused professions overseas for extended periods of time and are admitted to practise there, including the Cayman Islands and the British Virgin Islands. The set can provide barristers who are used to working abroad (often at very short notice) and who have material insight into the workings of particular jurisdictions.

ERSKINE CHAMBERS

33 Chancery Lane, London, WC2A 1EN
Tel (020) 7242 5532 **Fax** (020) 7831 0125
Email clerks@erskinechambers.com **Website** www.erskinechambers.com

Senior Clerk	Mark Swallow Chris Reade
Tenants	32

MEMBERS

Michael Todd QC (1977) (QC-1997)
David Mabb QC (1979) (QC-2001)
Martin Moore QC (1982) (QC-2002)
David Chivers QC (1983) (QC-2002)
Peter Arden QC (1983) (QC-2006)
Stephen Smith QC (1983) (QC 2000)
Ceri Bryant QC (1984) (QC-2012)
Raquel Agnello QC (1986) (QC-2009)
Andrew Thompson QC (1991) (QC 2014)
James Potts QC (1994) (QC-2013)
John Cone (1975)
Catherine Roberts (1986)
Philip Gillyon (1988)
Mary Stokes (1989)
Dan Prentice (1982)
Nigel Dougherty (1993)
Andrew Thornton (1994)
Edward Davies (1998)
Stephen Horan (2002)
Benjamin Shaw (2002)
Ben Griffiths (2004)
Tim Akkouh (2004)
Matthew Parfitt (2005)
Emily Gillett (2005)
Patrick Harty (2008)
Jack Rivett (2010)
Anna Scharnetzky (2011)
Chantelle Staynings (2012)
Andrew Blake (2012)
Emma Williams (2013)
Richard Nolan (1999)*

* Door Tenant

THE CHAMBERS Erskine Chambers is recognised as being pre-eminent in company law and a leading set in associated fields including insolvency, financial services and corporate/commercial litigation (including civil fraud and asset recovery). Chambers' size (32 barristers including 10 QCs) allows it to maintain expertise in its core practice areas while fielding effective teams in Commercial Court and Chancery Division litigation.

WORK UNDERTAKEN

Company Law: Erskine is the go-to set for company law disputes and corporate transactions, including: shareholder disputes (Kleanthous v Paphitis; Bumi), joint venture disputes and technical company litigation (Eclairs v JKX; Enviroco v Farstad - both Supreme Court). Members have advised on most of the largest UK corporate transactions of recent years, including Friends Life/Aviva, Invensys/Schneider, Glencore/Xstrata and Vodafone/Verizon. Erskine provides counsel for the majority of schemes of arrangement, cross-border mergers (Honda Europe; Sony; Itau BBA), Part VII transfers (Royal London/CIS, Barclays/ING), and reductions of capital.
Corporate/Commercial Litigation & Arbitration: A large proportion of Erskine's work is litigation at the intersection between company, commercial and insolvency law, including: commercial disputes; breach of fiduciary duty (Hewlett Packard and Autonomy v Lynch; BAT Industries v Winward); LLP and funds disputes (Re Charterhouse Capital; F&C Investments v Barthelemy); and civil fraud and asset recovery (BTA Bank v Ablyazov; Mezhprombank v Pugachev; Pinchuk v Bogolyubov). Members have particular expertise in freezing injunctions and other forms of interim relief.
Insolvency: Erskine has a strong reputation for both contentious insolvency and corporate restructuring. Insolvency litigation often involves cross-border issues (Olympic Airlines; Nortel & Lehman Bros v Pensions Regulator; Belmont Park v BNY – all Supreme Court; Singularis v PwC; PwC v Saad; MF Global). Restructurings include insolvent schemes of arrangement, administrations and CVAs (SphinX, Halliwells, Baugur; Miss Sixty).
Financial Services: Members undertake both contentious and non-contentious FSMA work. Litigation includes: funds, collective investment schemes and public offers of securities; prospectus liability (RBS Rights Issue litigation); financial conduct, regulation and enforcement (Lehmans Client Money) and interest rate swap claims against banks. Non-contentious work includes Part VII business transfers, securitisation and structured finance.

INTERNATIONAL Erskine's work is highly international, whether advising on multi-jurisdictional transactions or litigating complex cross-border disputes. Members are active in a large number of offshore jurisdictions, including the Channel Islands, Cayman, BVI, Bermuda, Turks & Caicos, St Vincent and Grenadine, Hong Kong and Singapore and have extensive trial experience, from First Instance to Appellate and Privy Council.

ONE ESSEX COURT Lord Anthony Grabiner QC

Head of Chambers	Lord Grabiner QC
Senior Clerk	Darren Burrows
Tenants	96

One Essex Court, Temple, London, EC4Y 9AR
Tel (020) 7583 2000 **Fax** (020) 7583 0118 **DX** 430 Chancery Lane
Email clerks@oeclaw.co.uk **Website** www.oeclaw.co.uk

MEMBERS

Lord Grabiner QC (1968) (QC-1981)
Nicholas Strauss QC (1965) (QC-1984)
Peter Leaver QC (1967) (QC-1987)
Ian Glick QC (1970) (QC-1987)
Geoffrey Hobbs QC (1977) (QC-1991)
Thomas Sharpe QC (1976) (QC-1994)
Jeffery Onions QC (1981) (QC-1998)
Susanna FitzGerald QC (1973) (QC-1999)
Rhodri Davies QC (1979) (QC-1999)
Stephen Auld QC (1979) (QC-1999)
Kenneth MacLean QC (1985) (QC-2002)
Laurence Rabinowitz QC (1987) (QC-2002)
Malcolm Gammie QC (1997) (QC-2002)
John McCaughran QC (1982) (QC-2003)
Charles Graham QC (1986) (QC-2003)
Christopher Style QC (2012) (QC-2006)
Richard Gillis QC (1982) (QC-2006)
Andrew Lenon QC (1982) (QC-2006)
Craig Orr QC (1986) (QC-2006)
Anthony de Garr Robinson QC (1987) (QC-2006)
Michael Sullivan QC (1983) (QC-2008)
Neil Kitchener QC (1991) (QC-2008)
Alain Choo Choy QC (1991) (QC-2009)
David Wolfson QC (1992) (QC-2009)
Daniel Toledano QC (1993) (QC-2009)
David Cavender QC (1993) (QC-2010)
Sonia Tolaney QC (1995) (QC-2011)
Richard Boulton QC (2003) (QC-2011)
Emma Himsworth QC (1993) (QC-2012)
Sa'ad Hossain QC (1995) (QC-2013)
Camilla Bingham QC (1996) (QC-2013)
Benjamin Strong QC (2001) (QC-2014)
Michael Fealy QC (1997) (QC-2014)
Zoe O'Sullivan QC (1993) (QC-2015)
Edmund Nourse QC (1994) (QC-2015)
Alan Redfern (1995)
Michael Malone (1975)
Ian Terry
Alan Griffiths (1981)
Clare Reffin (1981)
Andrew Foyle (2006)
Hannah Brown (1992)
Philip Roberts (1996)
Orlando Gledhill (1998)
Simon Colton (1999)
Matthew Cook (1999)
Steven Elliott (2001)
Guy Hollingworth (2001)
Derek Spitz (2001)
Anna Boase (2002)
James Goldsmith (2002)
James Nadin (2002)
Daniel Hubbard (2003)
Michelle Menashy (2003)
Conall Patton (2004)
Laurence Emmett (2004)
Henry Forbes Smith (2004)
Alexander Polley (2005)
Sebastian Isaac (2005)
Marcos Dracos (2005)
James MacDonald (2005)
Eleanor Campbell (2005)
Michael Clark (2005)
Richard Mott (2006)
David Caplan (2006)
Rachel Oakeshott (2006)
Saul Lemer (2007)
Nicholas Sloboda (2007)
Sam O'Leary (2007)
Abra Bompas (2008)
Michael d'Arcy (2008)
Nehali Shah (2008)
Owain Draper (2008)
Sandy Phipps (2008)
Alexander Brown (2009)
Mehdi Baiou (2009)
Douglas Paine (2009)
Michael Watkins (2009)
James Petkovic (2009)
Emma Jones (2010)
Oliver Butler (2010)
Adam Rushworth (2010)
Gideon Cohen (2010)
Sophie Weber (2011)
Tamara Kagan (2011)
Andrew Lodder (2012)
Patricia Burns (2011)
Alaina Newnes (2012)
Maximillian Schlote (2013)
Simon Gilson (2013)
Henry Hoskins (2013)
Edwin Peel (2014)
Andrew Lomas (2014)
Stephanie Wood (2014)
Oscar Schonfeld (2014)
Joyce Arnold (2014)

THE CHAMBERS One Essex Court is a pre-eminent set of barristers' chambers, providing specialist legal advice, support and advocacy services worldwide, and their expertise covers all areas of arbitration, litigation, regulation and dispute resolution. Work at the chambers embraces all aspects of domestic and international trade, business, commerce and finance, with members regularly accepting nominations as arbitrators, mediators and experts. Principal areas of practice are commercial litigation, arbitration, banking and financial services, civil fraud, company and insolvency, competition and EU law, energy and natural resources, insurance and reinsurance, intellectual property, licensing, professional negligence and revenue law. The pre-eminent team of energy lawyers is consistently ranked as the leading group at the Bar. Barristers regularly appear before the domestic courts and tribunals, dealing with short County Court applications to major trials in the High Court and appeals before the Court of Appeal, the Privy Council and the Supreme Court, as well as hearings at the CJEU and EGC. One Essex Court also has an office within the Singapore Dispute Resolution Complex.

WORK UNDERTAKEN Accounting and auditing, administrative and public law, agency, arbitration, aviation finance, banking, breach of warranty, civil jurisdiction and judgements/conflict of laws, commercial, commodities, company, competition, derivatives, directors' disqualification, economic torts, employment and industrial relations law, energy and natural resources, EU law, financial services regulation, fraud and asset tracing, guarantees, information technology, insolvency, insurance and reinsurance, intellectual property, joint ventures agreements, licensing and gambling, media and entertainment, mergers and acquisitions, partnership, professional negligence, restitution, restraint of trade restructuring, share sale agreements, shareholder's agreements, sports law, tax/revenue, trusts and unjust enrichment.

ONE ESSEX COURT

5 ESSEX COURT Fiona Barton QC

Head of Chambers	Fiona Barton QC
Senior Clerk	Mark Waller
Tenants	41

5 Essex Court, Temple, London, EC4Y 9AH
Tel (020) 7410 2000 **Fax** (020) 7129 8606 **DX** 1048
Email clerks@5essexcourt.co.uk **Website** www.5essexcourt.co.uk

MEMBERS

Fiona Barton QC (1986) (QC 2011)
Geoffrey Tattersall QC (1970) (QC-1992)
Jason Beer QC (1992) (QC 2011)
Jeremy Johnson QC (1994) (QC 2011)
Anne Studd QC (1988) (QC-2012)
Samantha Leek QC (1993) (QC-2012)
Dijen Basu QC (1994) ^ (QC-2015)
John Bassett (1975)
Nicholas Wilcox (1977)
Charles Apthorp (1983) ^
Alison Hewitt (1984)
Andrew Waters (1987)
Simon Walsh (1987)
Richard Oulton (1995) ^
John-Paul Waite (1995)
Alan Payne (1996)
Victoria von Wachter (1997) ^
Melvyn Harris (1997) ^
Alastair Hodge (1997)
Matthew Holdcroft (1998)
Clare Harrington (1998) ^
Daniel Hobbs (1998) ^
Barnabas Branston (1999)
Russell Fortt (1999)
Charlotte Ventham (2001)
Francesca Whitelaw (2003)
Kate Cornell (2004)
Beatrice Collier (2004) ^
Claire Palmer (2004) ^
Mark Thomas (2006) ^
Georgina Wolfe (2006)
Jonathan Dixey (2007)
Peter Taheri (2007)
Cicely Harward (2008)
Alex Ustych (2010) ^
Robert Talalay (2010)
Robert Cohen (2009)
Amy Clarke (2009)
Catriona Hodge (2012)
Alice Meredith (2013)
Aaron Moss (2013)

* Door Tenant ^ Direct/Public Access

THE CHAMBERS 5 Essex Court is a long established set which has a formidable reputation in police law, public law, public inquiries, inquests and professional disciplinary matters. Members of chambers have an unrivalled record of appearance in almost every recent case or inquiry of substance concerning the police. Its members are commonly seen in the most high-profile and sensitive proceedings. 5 Essex Court comprises 41 members including 7 Queen's Counsel. 10 of its barristers are members of the Attorney General's panel of counsel, advising and representing HM Government, and two of its QC's are special advocates. A number of members have security clearance to the level of Developed Vetted.

Chambers' expertise in civil and commercial matters includes advisory and advocacy work across a broad range of disputes including employment, contractual, licensing, personal injury, professional negligence and property. Chambers represent clients in both the public and private sectors and across the United Kingdom.

5 Essex Court prides itself in being approachable – chambers has a deep understanding and interest in its areas of expertise. A number of members accept direct access work.

WORK UNDERTAKEN

Police Law: Chambers is instructed by virtually every police force in the country and leads in the field of police law. Chambers has the highest number of barristers specialising in police law of any set in the country. Its members have represented clients in many significant cases of public importance. Chambers stature in this area is reflected in the legal practice directories.

Public Law: Chambers acts for government departments, government agencies, police authorities and other public bodies. It has extensive experience in public inquiries, judicial review, the Human Rights Act, the Data Protection Act and the Freedom of Information Act. Members of chambers appear in a broad spectrum of cases concerning equality, discrimination, civil liberties, disciplinary matters and immigration.

Public Inquiries: Members continue to lead in this area and are instructed in many high profile cases.

Inquests: Chambers has a substantial practice in this specialist area of legal practice. Members represent police forces, individual officers, the Prison Service (as well as private contractors), HM Coroners, NHS trusts, government bodies, and other public authorities and organisations. Work in this area includes: pre-inquest issues such as investigation, disclosure, the need for a jury, anonymity, the scope of inquests and the application of Article 2 of the ECHR; individual and organisational preparation for inquests; advocacy during the course of an inquest; advice and advocacy in relation to challenges to the decisions of coroners; and assistance in the aftermath of inquests in relation to the implementation of recommendations and ensuring organisational learning.

Disciplinary/regulatory: Chambers has a strong practice in professional disciplinary cases – these include representing the emergency services as well as organisations and professional associations in the health sector.

Employment: Members of chambers are at the forefront of employment jurisprudence, appearing in related jurisdictions from the Employment Tribunal to the Court of Appeal. The team comprises dedicated specialist practitioners, each with extensive personal experience of industry and commerce, who offer advice and advocacy on all aspects of contentious and non-contentious work. Members of chambers have strength and depth in all areas of employment law relating to commercial organisations and a collective understanding to deal with the

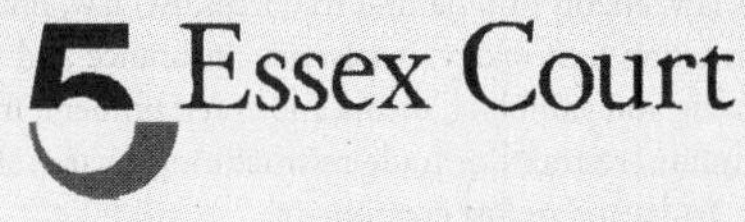

5 ESSEX COURT (CONTINUED)

most complex issues. In addition to police forces, clients include global energy suppliers, international construction companies and investment banks, as well as employees at all levels.

Personal Injury: Chambers' practice in this area includes both public and private sector work as well as work carried out under conditional fee agreements. Chambers' expertise covers a broad spectrum of personal injury cases such as: product liability, workplace accidents, defective premises, highway/road traffic accidents and claims arising from vacations.

ESSEX COURT CHAMBERS

24 Lincoln's Inn Fields, London, WC2A 3EG
Tel (020) 7813 8000 **Fax** (020) 7813 8080 **DX** 320 LONDON CHANCERY LANE
Email clerksroom@essexcourt.com **Website** www.essexcourt.com

Senior Clerks	David Grief Joe Ferrigno
Team Leaders	Ben Perry Jack Wood
Office Manager	Lisa Nwachukwu
Tenants	85

MEMBERS

Richard Jacobs QC (1979) (QC-1998)
Graham Dunning QC (1982) (QC-2001)
Gordon Pollock QC (1968) (QC-1979)
Ian Hunter QC (1967) (QC-1980)
V V Veeder QC (1971) (QC-1986)
Richard Siberry QC (1974) (QC-1989)
Jonathan Gilman QC (1965) (QC-1990)
Franklin Berman QC (1966) (QC-1992)
Roderick Cordara QC (1975) (QC-1994)
Simon Crookenden QC (1975) (QC-1996)
Jeffrey Gruder QC (1977) (QC-1997)
Andrew Hochhauser QC (1977) (QC-1997)
David Mildon QC (1980) (QC-2000)
Steven Berry QC (1984) (QC-2002)
Malcolm Shaw QC (1988) (QC-2002)
Mark Templeman QC (1981) (QC-2003)
David Joseph QC (1984) (QC-2003)
Richard Millett QC (1985) (QC-2003)
Joe Smouha QC (1986) (QC-2003)
Huw Davies QC (1985) (QC-2006)
Martin Griffiths QC (1986) (QC-2006)
John Lockey QC (1987) (QC-2006)
Simon Bryan QC (1988) (QC-2006)
David Foxton QC (1989) (QC-2006)
Hugh Mercer QC (1985) (QC-2008)
Vernon Flynn QC (1991) (QC-2008)
Vaughan Lowe QC (1993) (QC-2008)
Toby Landau, QC (1993) (QC-2008)
Christopher Smith QC (1989) (QC-2009)
Claire Blanchard QC (1992) (QC-2010)
Paul Stanley QC (1993) (QC-2010)
Daniel Oudkerk QC (1992) (QC-2010)
Sara Cockerill QC (1990) (QC-2011)
Tim Eicke QC (1993) (QC-2011)
Paul McGrath QC (1994) (QC-2011)
James Collins QC (1995) (QC-2012)
Nigel Eaton QC (1991) (QC-2013)
Stephen Houseman QC (1995) (QC-2013)
Paul Key QC (1997) (QC-2013)
Sam Wordsworth QC (1997) (QC-2013)
Charles Ciumei QC (1991) (QC-2014)
David Scorey QC (1997) (QC-2015)
Nathan Pillow QC (1997) (QC-2015)
David Craig QC (1997) (QC-2015)
Ricky Diwan QC (1998) (QC-2015)
Salim Moollan QC (1998) (QC-2016)
Shane Doyle QC (2001) (QC - 1995) Australia
Alan Boyle (1977)
Philippa Watson (1988)
John Snider (1982)
Brian Dye (1991)
Martin Hunter (1994)
Philippa Hopkins (1994)
Martin Lau (1996)
Neil Hart (1998)
Edmund King (1999)
Iain Quirk (2002)
Jern-Fei Ng (2004)
David Davies (2004)
Edward Brown (2002)
Jeremy Brier (2004)
Jessica Wells (2004)
Jane Russell (2004)
Dan Sarooshi (2005)
Damien Walker (2006)
David Peters (2005)
Siddharth Dhar (2005)
James Willan (2006)
Emily Wood (2006)
Amy Sander (2006)
Tom Ford (2008)
Anton Dudnikov (2008)
Anna Dilnot (2008)
Catherine Jung (2010)
Adam Board (2010)
Andrew Legg (2010)
John Robb (2011)
Claudia Renton (2011)
Rebecca Stripe (2012)
Adam Woolnough (2012)
Peter Webster (2012)
Helen Morton (2013)
Richard Hoyle (2013)
Stuart Cribb (2013)
Felix Wardle (2014)

THE CHAMBERS Essex Court Chambers is a leading set of barristers' chambers, specialising in commercial and financial litigation, arbitration, public law and public international law.
Members of Chambers are recognised specialists in all areas of commercial law and handle disputes across the full spectrum of the business and financial world, including banking & finance, civil fraud, corporate/chancery & offshore, insurance & reinsurance, energy, trade, shipping, revenue, and employment.
Chambers is not a firm, nor are its members partners or employees. Rather, Chambers is comprised of individual barristers, each of whom is a self-employed sole practitioner. Members of Chambers are commonly retained by opposing sides in the same dispute, both in litigation and arbitration, with protocols in place to safeguard confidentiality. As well as acting on opposing sides, individuals appear in front of other members acting impartially as Deputy Judges or Arbitrators.
The barristers at Essex Court Chambers advise and act in disputes both in the UK and worldwide. They have a reputation for exceptional talent, top-class advocacy and a client-oriented approach.

WORK UNDERTAKEN Annual market research and award ceremonies confirm that members are consistently recognised as leading individuals by clients and peers in a number of key areas, but most notably: international commercial arbitration; commercial dispute resolution; civil fraud; public international law; banking and finance; employment; energy and natural resources; indirect tax; insurance; shipping and commodities; professional negligence; media, entertainment and sport; civil liberties and human rights; administrative and

ESSEX COURT CHAMBERS
BARRISTERS

ESSEX COURT CHAMBERS (continued)

public law; information technology; immigration; aviation; EU and competition; offshore litigation; commercial chancery; and insolvency and corporate recovery.

The strong international nature of chambers differentiates it from other practices. It has barristers qualified to practise in non-UK jurisdictions and with a wide range of commercial language skills.

PUPILLAGE Chambers typically offers up to four funded 12 month tenancy seeking pupillages per year. Applications should be made via the Pupillage Gateway. Applicants for pupillage are encouraged to undertake a mini-pupillage (of 1-2 days). Information about mini-pupillage, including deadlines for mini-pupillage applications and an online application form, is available at www. essexcourt.com.

20 ESSEX STREET Christopher Hancock QC & Duncan Matthews QC

20 Essex Street, London, WC2R 3AL
Tel (020) 7842 1200 **Fax** (020) 7842 1270 **DX** 0009 Chancery Lane
Email clerks@20essexst.com **Website** www.20essexst.com

Head of Chambers	Christopher Hancock QC Duncan Matthews QC
Senior Clerks	Neil Palmer Home (020) 7842 1201 Mobile 07775 713 925 Arron Zitver Home (020) 7842 1205 Mobile 07908 256 043 Christopher Theobald Home (020) 7842 1210 Mobile 07983 403 900 Billy Brian Home (020) 7842 1226 Mobile 07958 046 206 Rachael Osborne Home (020) 7842 1204 Mobile 07860 958 117
Director of Strategic Development	James Huckle
Director of Finance & Administration	Daniel Clark
Tenants	67

MEMBERS

Iain Milligan QC (1973) (QC-1991)
Alexander Layton QC (1976) (QC-1995)
Timothy Young QC (1977) (QC-1996)
Christopher Hancock QC (1983) (QC-2000) *
Duncan Matthews QC (1986) (QC-2002)
Andrew Baker QC (1988) (QC-2006)
Sir Daniel Bethlehem QC (1988) (QC-2003)
Stephen Atherton QC (1989) (QC-2006)
Timothy Hill QC (1990) (QC-2009)
Philip Edey QC (1994) (QC-2009)
Michael Coburn QC (1990) (QC-2010)
Charles Kimmins QC (1994) (QC-2010)
Michael Collett QC (1995) (QC-2013)
Michael Ashcroft QC (1997) (QC-2011)
Lawrence Akka QC (1991)(QC-2012)
Sara Masters QC (1993) (QC-2012)
David Lewis QC (1999) (QC-2014)
Thomas Raphael QC (1999) (QC-2015)
Sudhanshu Swaroop QC (1997) (QC-2016)
Julian Kenny QC (1997) (QC-2016)
Sir Michael Wood (1968)
David D Caron (1984)
Clare Ambrose (1992)
Julie Anderson (1993)
Karen Maxwell (1994)
Malcolm Jarvis (1998)
Susannah Jones (1999)
Andrew Fulton (1999)
Zannis Mavrogordato (1999)
Sean Snook (2000)
Henry Byam-Cook (2000)
Socrates Papadopoulos (2001)
Blair Leahy (2001)
Angharad Parry (2002)
Colleen Hanley (2003)
Christopher Newman (2003)
Tony Beswetherick (2003)
Philip Riches (2004)
Simon Milnes (2005)
Guglielmo Verdirame (2006)
Daniel Bovensiepen (2004)
Josephine Davies (2006)
Patricia Edwards (2006)
Stefan Talmon (2007)
Charlotte Tan (2008)
Luke Pearce (2007)
Penelope Nevill (2010)
Rupert Hamilton (2010)
Thomas Corby (2011)
Mahnaz Malik (2012)
Oliver Caplin (2012)
Alex Carless (2012)
Leonora Sagan (2012)
Thomas Leary (2012)
Matthew McGhee (2013)
Richard Greenberg (2013)
Andrew Feld (2013)
Nakul Dewan (2014)
Albert Dinelli (2014)
Monica Feria-Tinta (2014)
Belinda McRae (2014)
Alexander Thompson (2014)
John Bethell (2014)
Kate Parlett (2015)
Alistair Wooder (2015)
Sam Goodman (2015)
Jonathon Ketcheson (2016)
The Honorable Charles Brower +
Michael Lee +
David St John Sutton +
J William Rowley QC +
Malcolm Holmes QC +
Dr Michael Pryles +
Gil Carlos Rodriguez Iglesias +
Anthony Hallgarten QC +
Francisco Orrego Vicuña +
Dr Julian Lew QC +
Sir Simon Tuckey +
Dr Michael Moser +
Murray Pickering QC +
Yves Fortier QC +
Sir Bernard Rix +
David Owen QC +
Michael Tselentis QC +

+ Arbitrator

THE CHAMBERS 20 Essex Street is a leading international commercial set of barristers' chambers with offices in London and Singapore. Its members advise and act as advocates in relation to all types of commercial disputes and have particular expertise in disputes with an international dimension. Its barristers are hugely experienced in representing overseas and large corporate and law firm clients, advising on complex, high-value and multi-forum litigation. Core areas of work include arbitration, banking and financial services, international trade and commodities, energy and natural resources, insurance and reinsurance, shipping, public and private international law, competition and trade regulation, insolvency, professional negligence and civil fraud.

WORK UNDERTAKEN

Commercial Dispute Resolution: Members both advise and act as advocates in relation to all types of commercial disputes and have particular expertise in disputes with an international dimension. These may be resolved in the English Courts, by institutional or ad hoc international arbitration, or by London maritime and commodity trade arbitrations.

EU & Competition: A number of members specialise in the substantive law of the EU and in UK and EU Competition law and virtually all members deal with aspects of EU law regularly in their practice. Members appear before the Competition Appeal Tribunal, Competition Commission, European Commission, European Court of First Instance, and European Court of Justice, in addition to domestic courts and tribunals.

International Arbitration: 20 Essex Street has a strong reputation as a leading arbitration set. It has a team of 18 leading international arbitrators and barrister members who act as advocates and arbitrators under all of the world's major institutions' auspices, dealing with all manner of international commercial disputes.

Insolvency & Company Law: Members are well known for their expertise in contentious and non-contentious restructurings, insolvency law and company law, spanning all business and industry sectors. They regularly advise and represent insolvency office-holders, companies, creditors, shareholders and company directors and have been heavily involved in many of the recent major restructurings and insolvencies.

Public International Law: 20 Essex Street is pre-eminent in public international law. Members specialising in this area regularly provide legal and strategic advice to States and other parties and appear before English courts (at all levels) in cases in which issues of public international law arise, as well as before international courts and tribunals. Members also have a wealth of experience in investor state disputes.

23 ESSEX STREET John Price QC & Cairns Nelson QC

Head of Chambers	John Price QC Cairns Nelson QC
Chambers Director	Richard Fowler
Senior Clerk	Sean Hulston (Manchester/Nottingham)
Tenants	113

23 Essex Street, London, WC2R 3AA
Tel (020) 7413 0353 **Fax** (020) 7413 0374 **DX** 148 LDE

Manchester annexe 14 St Mary's Parsonage, Manchester, M3 2DF
Tel (0161) 870 9969 **DX** 303434 Manchester

Nottingham annexe: 21 – 23 Castle Gate, Nottingham, NG1 7AQ
Tel (0115) 824 0128

MEMBERS

John Price QC (1982) (QC-2009) † ^A^
Cairns Nelson QC (1987) (QC-2010)
Charles Miskin QC (1975) (QC-1998) † ^A^
Simon Russell Flint QC (1980) (QC-2003) †
Iain Morley QC (1988) (QC-2009)
Paul Bogan QC (1983) (QC-2011)
James Mulholland QC (1986) (QC-2011)
Zafar Ali QC (1994) (QC-2012) ^A^
Mark Fenhalls QC (1992) (QC-2014) ^A^
Mark Trafford QC (1992) (QC-2015)
Paul Ozin QC (1987) (QC-2016) ^A^
Charles Machin (1973)
Michael Mulholland (1976)
Michael Harrison (1979)
Walton Hornsby (1980)
Ian Jobling (1982) ^A^
Roy Brown (1983) ^A^
John Riley (1983)
Hugh McKee (1983) ^A^
Rupert Pardoe (1984) ^A^
Stephen Shay (1984)
Wayne Cranston-Morris (1986)
Allison Hunter (1986) ^A^
Hugh Forgan (1989) ^A^
Andrew Easteal (1990) †
Patrick Thompson (1990) ^A^
Christopher Amis (1991)
Jonathan Smith (1991)
Richard Milne (1992) ^A^
Richard Moore (1992)
Tim Clark (1993) †
Kate Lumsdon (1993) ^A^
Gerard O'Connor (1993)
James McCrindell (1993)
Eloise Marshall (1994)
Richard Bentwood (1994)
Rufus Stilgoe (1994)
Adam Watkins (2004) ^A^
Bart Casella (1995) ^A^
Carl Hargan (1995)
Francis McGrath (1995) ^A^
Laurence Aiolfi (1996)
Ian Hope (1996)
Ahmed Hossain (1996)
Bob Sastry (1996) ^A^
Saul Brody (1996)
Sarah Campbell (1997)
Alan Gardner (1997)
Charles Royle (1997)
Toyin Salako (1998)
Neil Sandys (1998) ^A^
Rossano Scamardella (1998)
Tetteh Turkson (1998)
Jane Greenhalgh (1998)
Flora Page (1998)
Wasim Taskeen (1998)
Madeleine Wolfe (1998)
Lesley Bates (1999) ^A^
Oliver Dunkin (1999)
Daniel Fugallo (1999)
Tim Grey (1999)
Graham Smith (1999)
Zoe Van Den Bosch (1999)
James Bloomer (2000)
Abigail Husbands (2000) ^A^
David Povall (2000)
Christopher Hamlet (2000)
William Eaglestone (2001)
Adrian Harris (2001) ^A^
David Farley (2001)
Rina Marie Hill (2002)
Sonya Saul (2002)
Aisha Khan (2002)
John Dye (2002)
Rhodri James (2002)
Hamish Common (2003)
Tom Godfrey (2003) ^A^
Nathan Banks (2003)
Rashad Mohammed (2004)
Alexander Upton (2004) ^A^
Brad Pomfret (2004)
Hannah Kinch (2006)
Joseph Templeton (2006)
Iestyn Morgan (2006)
Claire Bunbury (2006)
Safia Iman (2006)
Patrick Duffy (2007) ^A^
Roshani Pulle (2007)
Nathan Rasiah (2007) ^A^
Barry White (2007)
Soheil Khan (2007)
Carolina Cabral (2009) ^A^
Daniel Lister (2009) ^A^
Richard Saynor (2009) ^A^
Jeremy Rosenberg (2009)
Trevor Withane (2009)
Elisabeth Acker (2010) ^A^
Helena Duong (2010)
Victoria Gainza (2010) ^A^
Suzanne Rivers Mansfield (2010)
Lauren Sales (2010)
Rupert Wheeler (2010)
Hannah Evans (2011) ^A^
Sarah-Kate McIntyre (2011)
Alex Mills (2012)
Asa Tolson (2012)
Sam Trefgarne (2012)
Rebecca Wright (2013)
David Dainty (2013)
Daniel O'Donoghue (2013)
Robert Smith (2014)
Arnold Ayoo (2014)
Sasha Queffurus (2014)
James Richardson QC (1975) (QC-2010) *
Michael Austin-Smith QC (1969) (QC-1990) *
Dafydd Enoch QC (1985) (QC-2008) † ^A^
Robert Buckland QC MP (QC-2014) *
Simon Davis (1990) *
Stephen Platt (1999)*
Lynn Griffin (1991) *
Gavin McBride (1996) *
James Austin-Smith (1999) *
Samantha Hatt (2000) *
Elisabeth Lees (2002) *
Ruth Paley (2003) *
Sarah Harris (2007) *
Tom Devlin (2009) *
Elena Elia (2009) *
Holly Webb (2006) *
Rebecca Vanstone (2006)
Sital Dillan *
Philip Tully*

† Recorder * Door Tenant ^A^ Direct/Public Access

Criminal Defence Service **Community Legal Service**

THE CHAMBERS 23 Essex Street is a modern, innovative, approachable set of barristers, with a leading reputation in crime, fraud, a range of regulatory and disciplinary matters and more recently commercial law. After 7 successful years, Simon Russell Flint QC stood down as Head of Chambers in November 2015 and John Price QC and Cairns Nelson QC were elected as Joint Head of Chambers. Simon continues to practise from 23 Essex Street. Under their collective stewardship Chambers has continued to grow and has become a national criminal set in London, Manchester and Nottingham. With effect from July 2015, our practice has been enhanced and complemented by a new commercial team founded by former members of St James's Chambers.

39 ESSEX CHAMBERS Neil Block QC & Alison Foster QC

81 Chancery Lane, London WC2A 1DD **DX** 298 London/Chancery Lane
Tel (020) 7832 1111 **Fax** (020) 7353 3978
Email clerks@39essex.com **Website** www.39essex.com

82 King Street, Manchester, M2 4WQ

Maxwell Chambers, 32 Maxwell Road, #02-16 Singapore, 069115

#02-9, Bangunan Sulaiman, Jalan Sultan Hishamuddin, 50000 Kuala Lumpur, Malaysia

Head of Chambers	Neil Block QC Alison Foster QC
Chief Executive & Director of Clerking	David Barnes
Senior Clerks	Alastair Davidson Michael Kaplan
Tenants	129

MEMBERS

- Neil Block QC (1980) (QC-2002)
- Alison Foster QC (1984) (QC-2002)
- Simon Goldblatt QC (1953) (QC-1972)
- John Tackaberry QC (1967) (QC-1982)
- Edwin Glasgow QC (1969) (QC-1987)
- Matthew Horton QC (1969) (QC-1989)
- Brian Ash QC (1975) (QC-1990)
- Nigel Pleming QC (1971) (QC-1992)
- Augustus Ullstein QC (1970) (QC-1992) +
- John Steel QC (1978) (QC-1993)+
- Richard Wilmot-Smith QC (1978) (QC-1994) +
- Richard Spearman QC (1977) (QC-1996) +
- William Norris QC (1974) (QC-1997)
- Matthias Kelly QC (1979) (QC-1999) +
- Hodge Malek QC (1983) (QC-1999) +
- Gregory Treverton-Jones QC (1977) (QC-2002) +
- Susan Rodway QC (1981) (QC-2002)
- Stuart Catchpole QC (1987) (QC-2002) +
- Peter Village QC (1983) (QC-2002)
- Colin McCaul QC (1978) (QC-2003)
- Timothy Lyons QC (1980) (QC-2003)
- Charles Cory-Wright QC (1984) (QC-2006)
- Adrian Hughes QC (1984) (QC-2006)
- Stephen Tromans QC (1999) (QC-2009)
- Charles Manzoni QC (1988) (QC-2009)
- Thomas Hill QC (1988) (QC-2009)
- Peter Rees QC (2014) (QC-2009)
- Steven Kovats QC (1989) (QC-2010) +
- Sean Wilken QC (1991) (QC-2010)
- Eleanor Grey QC (1990) (QC-2011)
- Lisa Giovannetti QC (1990) (QC-2011)
- Jenni Richards QC (1991) (QC-2011)
- Paul Stinchcombe QC (1985) (QC-2011)
- Fenella Morris QC (1990) (QC-2012)
- Hefin Rees QC (1992) (QC-2013)+
- Richard Harwood OBE QC (1993) (QC-2013)
- James Strachan QC (1996) (QC-2013)
- Marion Smith QC (1981) (QC-2015)
- Vikram Sachdeva QC (1998) (QC-2015)
- James Ramsden QC (1987) (QC-2016)
- Derek O'Sullivan QC (1990) (QC-2016)
- Justine Thornton QC (1994) (QC-2016)
- Rashda Rana SC (1990) (SC 2014)
- Denys Hickey (1975)
- John Pugh-Smith (1977)
- John Judge (1977) (Ontario)
- Simon Edwards (1978)
- Geoffrey Brown (1981)
- Christian Du Cann (1982)
- Karen Gough (1983)
- Jonathan Bellamy (1986) +
- David Bradly (1987)
- Bernard Doherty (1990)
- James Todd (1990)
- Andrew Tabachnik (1991)
- Emily Formby (1993) +
- David Brynmor Thomas (2011)
- Damian Falkowski (1994)
- Adam Robb (1995)
- Parishil Patel (1996)
- Duncan Sinclair (1996)
- Adam Fullwood (1996)
- Christiaan Zwart (1997)
- Richard Wald (1997)
- John Denis-Smith (1998)
- Judith Ayling (1998)
- Kate Grange (1998)
- Caroline Truscott (1998)
- Camilla Church (1998)
- Romilly Cummerson (1998)
- Deok Joo Rhee (1998)
- Nicola Greaney (1999)
- Colin Thomann (1999)
- Neil Allen (1999)
- Sian Davies (1999)
- Katharine Scott (2000)
- Jess Connors (2000)
- Karim Ghaly (2001)
- James Burton (2001)
- Alexander Ruck Keene (2002)
- Rory Dunlop (2002)
- Saima Hanif (2002)
- Christopher Staker (2003)
- Ben Olbourne (2003)
- Alexandra Bodnar (2004)
- Sadie Crapper (2004)
- Robert Lazarus (2004)
- Anna Bicarregui (2004)
- Mungo Wenban-Smith (2004)
- Caroline Allen (2005)
- Victoria Butler-Cole (2005)
- Alexis Hearnden (2005)
- Andrew Deakin (2006)
- Peter Mant (2006)
- Rachael O'Hagan (2006)
- Quintin Fraser (2006)
- Ned Helme (2006)
- Michelle Pratley (2006)
- Jack Anderson (2006)
- Kelly Stricklin-Coutinho (2006)
- Edmund Townsend (2006)
- Rebecca Drake (2007)
- Thomas Amraoui (2007)
- Jennifer Thelen (2007)
- Jack Holborn (2008)
- Philippa Jackson (2008)
- Catherine Dobson (2009)
- Benjamin Tankel (2009)
- Patrick Hennessey (2010)
- Rose Grogan (2010)
- Angela Rainey (2010)
- Hannah McCarthy (2010)
- Annabel Lee (2010)
- Emma Corkill (2010)
- Stephen Kosmin (2011)
- Daniel Stedman Jones (2011)
- James Potts (2011)
- Yash Bheeroo (2011)
- Cleon Catsambis (2011)
- Samar Abbas (2011)
- Tom Tabori (2011)
- Melissa Shipley (2011)
- Victoria Hutton (2011)
- Jon Darby (2012)
- Nicola Kohn (2012)
- Adam Boukraa (2013)
- Sarah Bousfield (2013)
- Rosie Scott (2013)
- David Hopkins (2013)
- David Bateson*
- Professor Dr Nael G. Bunni (Non Lawyer)*
- Shami Chakrabarti CBE (1994)*
- Archibald Findlay SC (South Africa) (1999)*
- Paul Hayes (2005)*
- Peter Hurst LLB, MPhil, FCIArb*
- Sir David Keene (1964) (QC-1980)*
- Patrick Lane SC (South Africa) (1977)*
- Sir Colin Mackay (1976) (QC-1998)*
- Mansoor Jamal Malik (1983)*
- Thierry Marembert (Paris) (1994)
- David Mayhew (2011)*
- Boyd McCleary CMG CVO*
- Vincent Nelson QC (1980) (QC-2001)*
- Kristina Stern SC (1996)*

+ Recorder * Door Tenant

39 ESSEX CHAMBERS Neil Block QC & Alison Foster QC

THE CHAMBERS 39 Essex Chambers is a long established set with 43 Queen's Counsel and 86 juniors. With offices in London, Manchester, Singapore and Kuala Lumpur, the set offers substantial expertise in almost every aspect of civil liability, commercial, construction and engineering, commercial fraud, financial services, costs and litigation funding, aviaton, energy, planning, environmental and property, personal injury and clinical negligence, public, regulatory and disciplinary law, shipping and alternative dispute resolution, both in the UK and worldwide. Members of chambers have wide experience of all courts and tribunals including the Supreme Court, Privy Council, Court of Appeal, the European Court of Human Rights and the European Court of Justice, specialist courts, tribunals and planning and other public inquiries, as well as of domestic and international arbitrations. Members have participated in many significant investigations before Parlimentary Select Committees and 17 members are on the Attorney General's Panel of Counsel instructed on behalf of the Crown. Members also undertake pro bono work for public interest organisations.

WORK UNDERTAKEN

Administrative & Public: Judicial review and public law, including civil liberties and human rights, education, local authorities, health trusts, mental health, community care, court of protection, housing and housing associations, immigration, VAT and customs and excise.

Commercial: Insurance and reinsurance, commodities and derivatives, funding disputes, banking, mergers and acquisitions, sale and carriage of goods, insolvency, company law, financial services law, shipping, professional negligence and professional indemnity work for auditors and legal advisors and international commercial arbitration.

Construction & Engineering: Litigation and related claims, including professional negligence and indemnity work, from major international ventures to smaller domestic contracts, acting for employers, contractors, subcontractors and professional advisors. Members act as advocates, mediators and arbitrators in the United Kingdom, the EU and worldwide.

Costs: Members of chambers appear in every court and tribunal where costs issues arise. Members also carry out advisory work on potential funding arrangements and in drafting cost documentation including CFAs, CCFA and legal expenses insurance policies.

Employment: Work for employers and employees, local authorities and central government. Particular emphasis is on public law-related work, discrimination, restrictive covenants, wrongful dismissal and breach of fiduciary duties.

Energy: A unique capability to cover corporate/commercial, construction, engineering, projects, environmental, planning, public and regulatory work in the electricity, nuclear, oil and gas and renewable sectors.

Entertainment & Sports: Entertainment and media-related work including performers' contracts, passing-off, breach of confidence, film and management agreements and broadcasting regulation. Sports-related work includes public liability of sports clubs for acts of their players, employer's liability, disciplinary tribunals, disputes concerning control of clubs, transfer fee disputes, EU free movement and other employment issues.

European: EU law before domestic and EU courts, including competition, discrimination and equality law, public procurement, free movement, state aids and milk quotas.

Human Rights: Members of chambers regularly appear in domestic Human Rights Act cases and also have extensive experience as advocates before the European Court of Human Rights and in courts overseas. Members have appeared in leading cases with a human rights dimension in diverse fields including civil liberties, commercial law, healthcare, housing, immigration, local government, mental health, community care, planning, police and prisoners.

Personal Injury & Clinical Negligence: Sea, air and crowd disasters, group actions, industrial disease, sports injuries, injuries of maximum severity, pharmaceuticals, product liability and high profile and complex matters, ranging from sensitive consent-to-treatment cases to those involving serious disability and death.

Planning & Environmental: Compulsory purchase, contaminated land, environmental civil liability, environmental regulation, European law and human rights, health and safety and product liability, insurance, international environmental law, licensing, marine environment, parliamentary and public affairs, planning law, nuisance and rating.

Public Inquiries: Members of chambers have been instructed in most of the major public inquiries over the past 10 years, including Hillsborough, BSE, the King's Cross fire and more recently, the Bristol Royal Infirmary, Victoria Climbié, the Saville Inquiry, the Hutton Inquiry, the Leveson Inquiry and the Bristol Review.

Regulatory & Disciplinary: Appearing in tribunals and hearings, and carrying out advisory work across the entire medical sphere, appearing before the Solicitors Disciplinary Tribunal and in challenges to interventions by the Law Society, social care, education, financial services, broadcasting, communications and the media, sport, transport and health and safety, buildings and housing, local government standards, licensing.

PUBLICATIONS *Planning Permission (2016) (Richard Harwood QC); Disciplinary and Regulatory Proceedings 8th Edition (2015) (Gregory Treverton-Jones QC, Alison Foster QC, Saima Hanif); Wilmot-Smith on Construction Contracts (Third Edition) (2014); Phipson on Evidence, 17th Edition (2012) (Hodge M. Malek QC); Environmental Impact Assessment, Second Edition (2012) (Stephen Tromans QC); The Law of Entertainment and Broadcasting (Nelson); Waiver, Variation and Estoppel (Wilken); Encyclopaedia of Environmental Law (Tromans); Planning Enforcement, Second Edition (Harwood) 2013; Mental Capacity (Morris and Greaney); A Guide to the New Law: Shackleton on the Law and Practice of Meetings (Pugh-Smith, Ruck Keene, Burton); Accidents Abroad: International Personal Injury Claims (Doherty).*

INTERNATIONAL 39 Essex Chambers has a number of members who have been called to the Bars of various international and offshore jurisdictions including California, France, Hong Kong, New South Wales, South Africa, Trinidad and Tobago and the British Virgin Islands. Chambers also has experience of acting in disputes in various foreign jurisdictions including Western and Central Europe, Africa, the USA, India, China and Hong Kong SAR, Malaysia, Singapore, the Middle East and the Caribbean.

RECRUITMENT The set is a member of Pupillage Gateway and also advertises recruitment via its website.

FALCON CHAMBERS Jonathan Gaunt QC & Guy Fetherstonhaugh QC

Falcon Court, London, EC4Y 1AA
Tel (020) 7353 2484 **Fax** (020) 7353 1261 **DX** 408
Email clerks@falcon-chambers.com **Website** www.falcon-chambers.com

Head of Chambers	Jonathan Gaunt QC Guy Fetherstonhaugh QC
Chambers Director	Edith A Robertson
Senior Clerk	Steven Francis
Tenants	40

MEMBERS

Jonathan Gaunt QC (1972) (QC-1991) BA
Guy Fetherstonhaugh QC (1983) (QC-2003) BSc
Derek Wood QC (1964) (QC-1978) MA BCL
Kirk Reynolds QC (1974) (QC-1993) MA
Nicholas Dowding QC (1979) (QC-1997) MA
Timothy Fancourt QC (1987) (QC-2003) MA
Jonathan Karas QC (1986) (QC-2006) MA
Jonathan Small QC (1990) (QC-2006) BA
Stephen Jourdan QC (1989) (QC-2009) MA
Janet Bignell QC (1992) (QC-2015) MA BCL
Caroline Shea QC (1994) MA (QC-2016)
Joanne Moss (1976) MA LLM (EC Law)
Anthony Radevsky (1978) LLB
Wayne Clark (1982) LLB BCL
Barry Denyer-Green (1972) LLM PhD
Gary Cowen (1990) LLB
Martin Dray (1992) LLB
Anthony Tanney (1994) BA MJur
Catherine Taskis (1995) BA BCL
Emily Windsor (1995) BA DSU (EC Law)
Mark Sefton (1996) MA
Stephanie Tozer (1996) MA
Edward Peters (1998) BA
Adam Rosenthal (1999) BA
Charles Harpum (1976) MA LLD
Elizabeth Fitzgerald (2001) LLB
Greville Healey (2002) MA DPhil
Nathaniel Duckworth (2002) BA
Oliver Radley-Gardner (2003) BA
Tamsin Cox (2005) BA
Philip Sissons (2005) BA BCL
Joseph Ollech (2006) BSc
Cecily Crampin (2008) MA MSc DPhil
Jamie Sutherland (2010) MA
Kester Lees (2010) BA LLB BCL
Ciara Fairley (2011) BA MPhil PhD
Toby Boncey (2013) MA BCL
Tricia Hemans (2013) LLB
Julia Petrenko (2013) BA BCL
James Tipler (2013) MA

THE CHAMBERS Chambers specialises in litigation and advice on all aspects of the law of property and matters relating to it. Falcon Chambers is regarded as one of the leading sets for property litigation and commercial property, as well as landlord and tenant and agricultural law.
A number of members are authors of leading textbooks in their specialist fields, including *Woodfall on Landlord and Tenant, Megarry on The Rent Acts, Muir Watt and Moss on Agricultural Holdings, Megarry & Wade's Law of Real Property, Gale on Easements, Fisher and Lightwood's Law of Mortgage, Hague on Leasehold Enfranchisement, Registered Land, and Commonhold.*

WORK UNDERTAKEN All members are expert in landlord and tenant law, including commercial property, rent review, residential landlord and tenant, and agricultural holdings, tenancies and production controls. They also provide expertise in the more general areas of property law, including easements, restrictive covenants, mortgages, conveyancing, co-ownership and trusts of land, options, rights of pre-emption, the Telecommunications Code, mining and mineral rights.
Members are frequently instructed in cases where property rights and principles of insolvency law meet, and where claims for negligence arise against solicitors and surveyors. Some members specialise in the fields of town and country planning, compulsory purchase, EU competition law and building and engineering disputes. Chambers is frequently involved in advisory and litigious work in other jurisdictions, particularly in other common law countries in the Commonwealth. Members of chambers appear in appeals to the Privy Council. Even in members' specialist fields, a good deal of their work is concerned with contract law and statutory interpretation. Their activities in commercial property matters have given them considerable expertise in arbitration law and practice, and in work involving valuers and the principles of valuation.
Chambers accepts work through the Bar Council's Licensed Access scheme in appropriate cases. Members also accept appointments as arbitrators, legal assessors or experts.

Falcon Chambers

FARRAR'S BUILDING Patrick Harrington QC

Farrar's Building, Temple, London, EC4Y 7BD
Tel (020) 7583 9241 **Fax** (020) 7583 0090
Email chambers@farrarsbuilding.co.uk **Website** www.farrarsbuilding.co.uk

Head of Chambers	Patrick Harrington QC
Senior Clerk/Practice Manager	Alan Kilbey MBE
Chambers Manager	Steve Gurnett
Tenants	46

MEMBERS

Patrick Harrington QC (1973) (QC-1993) +
Douglas Day QC (1967) (QC-1989)
Alan Jeffreys QC (1970) (QC-1996)
Paul Lewis QC (1981) (QC-2001) +
Geoffrey Williams QC (2013) (QC-2003)
Gordon Cole QC (1979) (QC – 2006)
Ian Unsworth QC (1992) (QC-2010)
Christopher Quinlan QC (1992) (QC-2011)
Michael Mather-Lees QC (1981) (QC-2012)

Ian Ridd (1975)
Nigel Spencer Ley (1985)
Andrew Peebles (1987)
John Meredith-Hardy (1989)
Shabbir Lakha (1989)
Leighton Hughes (1989)
Helen Hobhouse (1990)
Andrew Arentsen (1995)
Lee Evans (1996)
Nick Blake (1997)
Huw Davies (1998)
James Pretsell (1998)
Andrew Wille (1998)
Howard Cohen (1999)
Guy Watkins (1999)
Carwyn Cox (2002)
Matthew Kerruish-Jones (2003)
James Plant (2004)
Matthew Hodson (2004)
Clive Thomas (2005)
Tom Bourne-Arton (2005)
Emma Sole (2005)
David Roderick (2006)
Grant Goodlad (2006)
Tim Found (2006)
Georgina Crawford (2006)
James Rozier (2007)
Changez Khan (2008)
Bonike Erinle (2008)
Hannah Saxena (2010)
Joshua Hedgman(2011)
Aidan O'Brien (2011)
Robert Golin (2011)
Jake Rowley (2011)
Frederick Lyon (2012)
Joel McMillan (2014)
Rajiv Bhatt (2014)

+ Recorder

THE CHAMBERS Farrar's Building is a long established specialist set of chambers with particular expertise in the following five main areas of practice: personal injury; employment; serious and white-collar crime; health and safety; inquiries; and professional liability and disciplinary tribunals. Members of chambers also specialise in clinical negligence, professional negligence, insurance, product liability and commercial (see individual biographies). Chambers has an established reputation for excellence, with members acting for a variety of corporate bodies, insurance companies, prosecuting authorities, , sporting bodies and players, disciplinary, regulatory and professional bodies, as well as individuals. It is a friendly and reliable set of chambers, which prides itself on the way it is efficiently clerked and administered, by an experienced team.

WORK UNDERTAKEN Personal injury is the largest field of practice for chambers. The PI Team is involved in the whole spectrum of cases from very serious catastrophic injury claims to straightforward small track claims. It covers all aspects of work, from road traffic accidents, including mechanical defect and causation issues, to accidents at work, 'slips and trips', injuries caused by defective products, disaster and disease litigation. The Health and Safety Team works closely with, and benefits from, Farrar's Building's strong PI Team. Chambers has been involved in a number of high profile cases in this area. Employment law is another major area of practice for chambers. It specialises in all aspects of employment law, dealing with a wide range of employment issues, from advocacy in Employment Tribunals, the Employment Appeal Tribunal, and higher courts to advisory work. Chambers has a specialist criminal team, involved in major fraud and serious crime cases, and has close links with Wales where it remains a dominant force on the Welsh Circuit. Chambers is and has been involved in many of the major cases on the circuit and members of the Criminal team are highly sought-after. Chambers has a long history of involvement in Public Inquiries and of chairing/appearing before a range of Regulatory and Disciplinary Tribunals. Members carry out a great variety of administrative and public law matters, including judicial review, local government, education, health, housing and pharmaceuticals. Members of chambers also offer expertise in contract and commercial litigation, covering such areas as sale of goods and consumer credit and commercial fraud, insurance matters and product liability; clinical negligence and all areas of professional negligence and surveyors; costs and taxation matters include solicitors' bills of costs, counsels' fees and legal aid costs; sports and competition cases include contracts, advertising and sponsorship and restraint of trade.

FIELD COURT TAX CHAMBERS

Head of Chambers	Patrick C Soares
Practice Manager	Marie Burke
Assistant Practice Manager	Stephanie Talbot
Tenants	5

Field Court Tax Chambers, 3 Field Court, Gray's Inn, London WC1R 5EP
Tel (020) 3693 3700 **DX** 374 LDE
Email chambers@fieldtax.com **Website** www.fieldtax.com

MEMBERS

Patrick C Soares (1983)	Philip Baker QC (1979)	Peter Vaines (1989)
Patrick Way QC (1994)	Imran S Afzal (2008)	David Bloom QC (Aust) *

**Door Tenant*

THE CHAMBERS The five experienced members of Chambers provide dedicated taxation services of the highest quality as tax advisers and advocates.

WORK UNDERTAKEN

National & International: The set focuses on taxation and is led by experienced and respected leaders in the sector. Specialist advice and representation includes international and European tax, property matters, value added tax, corporate taxation, trusts and estate planning, including acting for high-profile individuals and multinational companies. All members of chambers appear at all levels of the UK court system including the Privy Council and in the European Court of Justice. Patrick C Soares advises on all aspects of taxation, providing notable expertise on the taxation and structuring of property transactions, as well as trusts and offshore tax planning. Patrick Way QC has appeared in leading tax cases at all levels of the UK court system and has also advised on a wide range of matters (both personal and corporate) where the tax at stake has been in the multi-millions. Philip Baker QC is one of the leading tax advisers on international and EU tax matters, handling cases in jurisdictions including India and Mauritius and at the European Court of Justice. He advises the UK government and other governments on tax matters. He also was one of the founders of the Advanced Diploma in International Taxation offered by the Chartered Institute of Taxation. Imran S Afzal has been involved in a range of domestic and international matters, acting for taxpayers and revenue authorities. He has been instructed in various high-profile and very high-value matters. Peter Vaines is well known for his expertise on matters of residence and domicile and for advising on trusts and private client matters generally in addition to wider issues such as share valuations for tax purposes. He writes and lectures widely and won the Taxation Writer of the Year Award 2015.

PUBLICATIONS Patrick Soares is the Tax Editor of the Property Law Bulletin. Patrick Soares, Patrick Way QC and Philip Baker QC have between them written books on a wide range of tax related subjects including real estate, trusts, corporates, individuals, incentives, international tax and double taxation.

FIELD COURT TAX CHAMBERS

187 FLEET STREET Andrew Trollope QC & Richard Christie QC

187 Fleet Street, Temple, London, EC4A 2AT
Tel (020) 7430 7430 **Fax** (020) 7430 7431 **DX** 464
Email chambers@187fleetstreet.com **Website** www.187fleetstreet.com

Heads of Chambers	Andrew Trollope QC Richard Christie QC
Senior Clerk	John Pyne
Tenants	76

MEMBERS

Andrew Trollope QC (1971) (QC-1991)
Richard Christie QC (1986) (QC-2006)
Daniel Janner QC (1980) (QC-2002)
Simon Mayo QC (1985) (QC-2008)
Jason Bartfeld QC (1995) (QC-2015)
Roderick Price (1971)
Brian Argyle (1972)
Brian Reece (1974)
Peter Guest (1975)
Gerard Renouf (1977)
Diana Pigot (1978)
Anthony Rimmer (1983)
Stella Reynolds (1983)
Gareth Hughes (1985)
James Lachkovic (1987)
David Lyons (1987)
Christopher Kerr (1988)
Grant Vanstone (1988)
Kate Davey (1988)
Andrew Newton (1989)
Terence Woods (1989)
Neil FitzGibbon (1989)
Anna Hamilton Shield (1989)
Avirup Chaudhuri (1990)
Nicholas Barraclough (1990)
Rachel Bright (1991)
Richard Potts (1991)
Natasha Wong (1993)
Richard Burrington (1993)
Karl Volz (1993)
Matthew Bagnall (1993)
Warwick Aleeson (1994)
Mark Roochove (1994)
Gideon Cammerman (1996)
Gregory Fishwick (1996)
Laureen Husain (1997)
Sarah Vine (1997)
Adam Butler (1997)
Catherine Bradshaw (1998)
Emma Kurzner (1999)
Margia Mostafa (1999)
Peter Clark (2000)
Caroline Milroy (2000)
Neelam Sharma (2000)
Yasmin Punjani (2000)
Mozammel Hossain (2001)
Emma Nash (2001)
Marc Brown (2001)
Alex Price-Marmion (2002)
Sasha Bailey (2002)
Nneka Akudolu (2002)
David Baird (2003)
Charlotte Eadie (2003)
Henry Hughes (2003)
Rebecca Lee (2004)
Ben Hayhurst (2004)
Matt Morgan (2004)
James Onalaja (2004)
Steven Fitzpatrick (2004)
Joseph Abadoo (2004)
Alison Lambert (2005)
Jamie Sharma (2005)
Scott Wainwright (2006)
Anna Keighley (2006)
Greg Unwin (2008)
Donal Lawler (2008)
Satya Chotalia (2008)
Ali Dewji (2010)
Gerwyn Wise (2010)
Timothy Folaranmi (2010)
Harry Warner (2011)
Edward Duncan Smith (2011)
Daisy Monahan (2012)
Mark Watson (2011)
Lucy Ginsberg (2013)
Jennifer Kay (2014)
Philip King QC (1974) (QC-2002) *
Graham Parkins QC (1972) (QC-1990) *
Anthony Korda (1988) *
John Madden (1997) *
Katharine Blackburn (1998) *
Alan Conroy (2002) *
Helen Fleck (2005) *
Victoria Weaver (2006) *
Jack Walsh (2006) *
Laura Fearnfield (2009) *
Mair Williams (2010) *
Susannah Brooke (2012) *

* Door Tenant

THE CHAMBERS Chambers is a leading set specialising in criminal and regulatory work, providing representation at every level for the Prosecution and the Defence, in both publicly and privately funded instructions. Many members of chambers can also be instructed directly through the Public Access Scheme. A key strength of chambers lies in the breadth and depth of experience of its members who are regularly instructed in high profile and leading cases. The set has gained a reputation for excellence in its advocacy and advisory work, offering a first class service to professional and lay clients alike.

Chambers has particular expertise in serious fraud and white collar crime, as well as homicide, terrorism, sex offences, revenue cases, money laundering and all forms of serious organised crime. A wealth of experience is also offered in many areas related to the criminal law, and specialist representation is offered in respect of VAT tribunals, police discipline, professional regulation, Trading Standards, Courts-Martial, judicial review, parole board hearings, mental health reviews, prison law, health and safety, sports law, inquests, extradition, human rights , licensing, DVSA (formerly VOSA) and all road traffic related matters. Members of Chambers prosecute at all levels for the Crown Prosecution Service, HM Revenue & Customs, the Serious Fraud Office, Local Authorities and Government Departments. Chambers has a number of Counsel who have been appointed to the Attorney General's List and the set conducts cases on behalf of the Department of Business, Innovation and Skills, the Department of Work and Pensions and the Health and Safety Executive.

There are 8 clerks, an administrator and a fees administrator. Please refer to the set's website for more information.

WORK UNDERTAKEN

Corporate Crime & Serious Fraud: Cases include those involving market rigging in share issues and takeovers, cartels and price fixing, advance fee, high yield investment/ponzi and 'boiler room' frauds, fraudulent trading/Phoenix, money laundering/confiscation, MTIC cases involving a wide web of contra trading companies, off shore finance institutions and offshore banking evidence, VAT/excise evasion and revenue cases. MTIC/ diversion cases include: Operations Vitric, Venison, Vex, Carina, Campaign, Domic, Tulipbox (carbon credits) and Devout. Other fraud cases include: the Cheney pension fraud, the Dome fraud,

187 FLEET STREET (Continued)

Ikea fraud/corruption case, SFO prosecution of 'Lord' Edward Davenport, SFO Pharmaceutical cartel case, R v Peter Storrie (Harry Redknapp case) and Operation Amazon (HMRC's largest ever case).
Members of Chambers also have specialist knowledge and experience of acting both for the Revenue and the taxpayer before the VAT Tribunal and the High Court.
Serious Crime: Murder, serious sexual offences, large scale drugs conspiracies, conspiracies to import and supply extremely large volumes of class A drugs, offences against the person, terrorism offences, bribery and corruption. Cases have included the Joss Stone murder plot; R v Ian Watkins and others (involving lead singer of the Lostprophets); R v Davis (Conspiracy to hack SOCA and News International); R v Donovan ('Good Samaritan' case during the London riots); R v Connors (first ever 'slave' trial); terrorist conspiracies to murder (Heathrow and transatlantic flights); the fertiliser bomb plot (Operation Crevice); the Tonbridge Securitas robbery; murder of Damilola Taylor; the murder of the private eye, Daniel Morgan, which is linked to the News of the World phone-hacking case, the Stephen Lawrence case and alleged police corruption, R v Abrams (attempted murder of George Harrison), R v Tovey (Oxford bomber).
Members of chambers have been appointed to review 'Rough Justice'/historic appeal cases and have particular expertise in this area. They have been engaged to act on behalf of both prosecution and defence in such cases, including receipt of instructions on a Direct Access basis. They have also regularly been instructed by the Criminal Cases Review Commission in judicial reviews of the Commission's refusal to refer cases to the Court of Appeal, including in the cases of Jeremy Bamber and Kenneth Noye.
Professional Regulation: A number of members of Chambers have been instructed by, or have represented regulated persons before, various regulatory bodies including ACCA, NMC, GDC and GMC. Members are also experienced at representing professionals and military personnel accused of serious offences.
Sports Law: Members of Chambers have represented individuals before the British Horseracing Authority, the British Judo Association, the Rugby Union Disciplinary Tribunal and represented Peter Storrie in the Portsmouth Football Club case which was in relation to allegations that key officials at Portsmouth football club manipulated the sale and transfer of players so as to minimise payments to HMRC.

INTERNATIONAL Bengali, Hindi, French and German are spoken. Counsel have also appeared in other jurisdictions such as the Cayman Islands and been admitted to the Bar there.

FOUNTAIN COURT CHAMBERS Stephen Moriarty QC

Fountain Court, Temple, London, EC4Y 9DH
Tel (020) 7583 3335 **Fax** (020) 7353 0329 **DX** 5LDE
Email chambers@fountaincourt.co.uk **Website** www.fountaincourt.co.uk

Head of Chambers	Stephen Moriarty QC
Senior Clerk	Alex Taylor
Head of Administration	Julie Parker
Tenants	79

MEMBERS

Michael Brindle QC (1975) (QC-1992)
Michael Crane QC (1975) (QC-1994)
Richard Lissack QC (1978) (QC-1994)
David Railton QC (1979) (QC-1996)
Simon Browne Wilkinson QC (1981) (QC-1998)
Timothy Dutton CBE QC (1979) (QC-1998)
Brian Doctor QC (1991) (QC-1999)
Stephen Moriarty QC (1986) (QC-1999)
Stephen Rubin QC (1977) (QC-2000)
Michael McLaren QC (1981) (QC-2002)
Philip Brook Smith QC (1982) (QC-2002)
Raymond Cox QC (1982) (QC-2002)
Guy Philipps QC (1986) (QC-2002)
Bankim Thanki QC (1988) (QC-2003)
Charles Béar QC (1986) (QC-2003)
Patricia Robertson QC (1988) (QC-2006)
Timothy Howe QC (1987) (QC-2008)
Mark Simpson QC (1992) (QC-2008)
Michael Green QC (1987) (QC-2009)
Richard Handyaside QC (1993) (QC-2009)
Jeffrey Chapman QC (1989) (QC-2010)
Derrick Dale QC (1990) (QC-2010)
Akhil Shah QC (1990) (QC-2010)
Marcus Smith QC (1991) (QC-2010)
Andrew Mitchell QC (1992) (QC-2011)
Paul Gott QC (1991) (QC-2012)
Richard Coleman QC (1994) (QC-2012)
Stuart Ritchie QC (1995) (QC-2012)
John Taylor QC (1993) (QC-2013)
Jonathan Adkin QC (1997) (QC-2013)
Adam Tolley QC (1994) (QC-2014)
Patrick Goodall QC (1998) (QC-2014)
Ben Valentin QC (1995) (QC-2016)
Rosalind Phelps QC (1998) (QC-2016)
Bridget Lucas (1989)
Paul Sinclair (1997)
Deepak Nambisan (1998)
Giles Wheeler (1998)
Henry King (1998)
Nicholas Medcroft (1998)
Robin Barclay (1999)
Edward Levey (1999)
James Cutress (2000)
Nik Yeo (2000)
Adam Zellick (2000)
Chloe Carpenter (2001)
Ben Lynch (2001)
Laura John (2001)
Paul Casey (2002)
Katherine Watt (2002)
Tamara Oppenheimer (2002)
Eleanor Davison (2003)
Marianne Butler (2003)
David Murray (2004)
James McClelland (2004)
Simon Atrill (2005)
James Duffy (2005)
Rupert Allen (2005)
Alex Barden (2005)
Alexander Milner (2006)
Adam Sher (2007)
Richard Power (2007)
Craig Ulyatt (2008)
Natasha Bennet (2009)
Nico Leslie (2010)
Daniel Edmonds (2010)
Deborah Horowitz (2010)
Christopher Langley (2011)
Tetyana Nesterchuck (2011)
Christopher Knowles (2011)
Rebecca Loveridge (2011)
Philip Ahlquist (2012)
Niamh Cleary (2012)
Giles Robertson (2012)
Samuel Ritchie (2012)
James Hart (2012)
Joseph Farmer (2013)
Simon Paul (2013)
Nick Daly (2014)
Sir Francis Jacobs QC (1964) (QC-1984) *
Sir Gordon Langley QC (1966) (QC-1983) *
Sir Mark Potter QC (1963) (QC-1981) *
Anthony Boswood QC (1970) (QC-1986) *
Andrew Burrows QC (1985) (QC-2003) *
Timothy Wormington (1977) *
Dr Louise Merrett (1995) *
David R Wingfield (2013) *
Professor Lawrence Boo *
Professor Peter Watts QC (New Zealand) *
Philippa Hamilton (1984) *
Luca G. Radicati di Brozolo (2014) *
Sebastian Said (2004) *
Professor Benjamin Hughes *
Kanaga Dharmananda SC *

* Door Tenant

THE CHAMBERS Fountain Court is a long established and leading set of commercial barristers' chambers. Based in the Temple, London and moments away from the Royal Courts of Justice, Fountain Court is at the forefront of civil and commercial litigation. Commonly described as a magic circle set, chambers comprises of 79 barristers, 34 of whom are silks. Members' knowledge ranges in relation to practice areas, experience and spoken languages, enabling the clerks at Fountain Court to match an individual members' expertise to a given case.

WORK UNDERTAKEN Leaders in: commercial litigation; banking and finance; insurance and reinsurance; professional negligence; energy and natural resources; civil fraud; international arbitration; aviation; financial regulation; professional discipline; public law; judicial review; travel and employment.
Other prominent areas include: media and entertainment; intellectual property; company; insolvency; product liability; human rights; administrative; sport; international trade; shipping; offshore; competition; business and regulatory crime, financial crime, fraud: crime, health and safety, partnership, tax and telecommunications. Members sit as arbitrators, mediators and counsel in alternative dispute resolution matters both in the UK and overseas. Following the opening of the set's Singapore annex in September 2015, the set can now offer sole or joint arbitrations from Singapore. Members also sit as recorders and deputy high court judges.

FOURTEEN Ronan O'Donovan

Head of Chambers	Ronan O'Donovan
No of members	38

14 Gray's Inn Square, London, WC1R 5JP
Tel (020) 7242 0858 **Fax** (020) 7242 5434 **DX** 399 (Ch.Ln.)
Email clerks@fourteen.co.uk **Website** www.fourteen.co.uk

MEMBERS

Barbara Slomnicka (1976)
Richard Kingsley (1977)
Geraldine More O'Ferrall (1983)
Joan Connell (1985)
David Sharp (1986)
Camille Habboo (1987)*
Patricia Roberts (1988)
Dylan Evans (1989)
Jean-Paul Sinclair (1989)
Helen Soffa (1990)
Rhys Jones (1990)
Carolyn Pearson (1990)
Rachael James (1992)
Martin Ward (1992)
Robin Powell (1993)
Ronan O'Donovan (1995)
Samantha Whittam (1995)
Christopher Miller (1998)
Mai-Ling Savage (1998)
Damian Stuart (2009) (sol. 1998)
Michael Glaser (1998)
Gillon Cameron (2001)
Jay Banerji (2001)
Laura Scott (2001)
Mandy Short (2003)
Henry Lamb (2004)
Ben Boucher-Giles (2004)
Anne-Marie Lucey (2004)
Byron James (2006)
Ella Calnan (2007)
Ranjit Singh (2007)
Phillip Blatchly (2008)
Ewan Murray (2008)
Jenna Shaw (2009)
Chris Stevenson (2009)
Victoria Miller (2010)
Georgina Robinson (2013)
Rachael Cassidy (2014)
Roseanna Peck (2011)*
Anna Spencer (2004)*
Gillian Marks (1981)*
Jonathan Wilkinson (2006) (sol. 1988) *
Sarah Pope (2006) (sol. 1994) *
Sally Gore (2006) *
Sara Hammond (2009) (sol. 1996) *
Matthew Warmoth (2013)

* Door Tenant

THE CHAMBERS Fourteen offers outstanding representation and advice across all areas of family law. The Chambers is recognised as a children specialist, acting for private and public clients at all levels including the Supreme Court. The set has an equally strong practice in matrimonial finance. It is also active in the Court of Protection, Adult Social Care and Mental Health matters. Responding to the increasing international dimension in children cases it has welcomed Nigel Lowe as a consultant to chambers. Fourteen offers a range of dispute resolution services, including mediation, arbitration and early neutral evaluation. Chambers welcomes public access instructions in all areas of practice.

FRANCIS TAYLOR BUILDING Andrew Tait QC

Francis Taylor Building, Inner Temple, London, EC4Y 7BY
Tel (020) 7353 8415 **Fax** (020) 7353 7622 **DX** 402 LDE
Email clerks@ftbchambers.co.uk **Website** www.ftbchambers.co.uk

Head of Chambers	Andrew Tait QC
Senior Clerk	Paul Coveney
Principal Clerks	Andrew Briton
	James Kemp
	Tom Rook
Tenants	58

MEMBERS

Andrew Tait QC (1981) (QC-2003)
Robin Purchas QC (1968) (QC-1987)
George Bartlett QC (1966) (QC-1986) *
Guy Roots QC (1969) (QC-1989)
Richard Phillips QC (1970) (QC-1990) ^
Stephen Sauvain QC (1977) (QC-1995) *
Kevin de Haan QC (1976) (QC-2000)
Robert McCracken QC (1973) (QC-2003) ^
Michael Humphries QC (1982) (QC-2003) ^
Gerald Gouriet QC (1974) ^ (QC-2006)
David Matthias QC (1980) (QC-2006) ^
Morag Ellis QC (1984) (QC-2006)
Craig Howell Williams QC (1983) (QC-2009)
Richard Glover QC (1984) (QC-2009)
Mark Hill QC (1987) (QC-2009) ^
Simon Bird QC (1987) (QC-2009) ^
Andrew Newcombe QC (1987) (QC-2010)
Douglas Edwards QC (1992) (QC-2010) ^
Gregory Jones QC (1991) (QC-2011)
Suzanne Ornsby QC (1986) (QC-2012)
James Pereira QC (1996) (QC-2014) ^
Saira Kabir Sheikh QC (2000) (QC-2014) ^
Andrew Fraser-Urquhart QC (1993) (QC-2015) ^
Hereward Phillpot QC (1997) (QC-2015)
Alexander Booth QC (2000) (QC-2016) ^
Edward Cousins (1971) *
Robert Fookes (1975) ^
Philip Petchey (1976) ^
Timothy Comyn (1980)
James Rankin (1983) ^
Meyric Lewis (1986) ^
Gary Grant (1994) ^
Charles Holland (1994) ^ *
Leo Charalambides (1998) ^
Prof Andrea Biondi (2004) ++
Jeremy Pike (2001) ^
Melissa Murphy (2001)
Juan Lopez (2002) ^
Denis Edwards (2002) ^
Richard Honey (2003) ^
Jeremy Phillips (2004) ^
John Jolliffe (2005)
Mark Westmoreland Smith (2006) ^
Pavlos Eleftheriadis (2006) ++ ^
Cain Ormondroyd (2007) ^
Annabel Graham Paul (2008)
Hugh Flanagan (2008) ^
Stephanie Hall (2008) ^
Sarah Sackman (2008) ^
Rebecca Clutten (2008)
Ned Westaway (2009) ^
Isabella Tafur (2009)
David Graham (2010) ^
George MacKenzie (2011) ^
Jack Connah (2012) ^
Alexander Greaves (2012)
Caroline Daly (2013)
Charles Streeten (2013)
Katherine Barnes (2014) ^

++ Academic Member ^ Public/Direct Access *Associate Member

THE CHAMBERS Francis Taylor Building (FTB) has a long-standing reputation for excellence in providing advocacy and advisory services. FTB is consistently featured as a leading set in the independent legal directories for its expertise and leading role in planning, land valuation, infrastructure, environmental, public law, regulatory law and licensing. Its position at the forefront of these areas of law is evidenced by members consistently appearing in many of the leading cases.

Members of chambers appear in courts at all levels in this country and abroad, including specialist tribunals and public inquiries and undertake specialist advisory work. The set owes its long-standing reputation for excellence to its wide range of clients, the major projects it handles and the number and quality of its practitioners. They are also supported by a highly motivated and professional team of clerks, led by Paul Coveney as Senior Clerk.

WORK UNDERTAKEN As part of its specialist practice, FTB undertakes works connected with planning, environment, licensing, National Infrastructure Planning projects, transport and works schemes, utilities, highways, rating, heritage and conservation, Parliamentary Bills, common land and village greens, minerals, statutory nuisance and regulation, health and safety, environmental crime, compulsory purchase and compensation, land valuation, property law including easements and covenants, religious liberty and ecclesiastical, education and energy.

FTB maintains a panel of qualified and specialist CEDR and ADR accredited mediators.

FTB offers a wide range of client facilities including a dedicated seminar suite to support its established programme of events and an arbitration and mediation suite which complements Chambers' mediation and ADR expertise. The premises are fully DDA compliant.

FURNIVAL CHAMBERS Oliver Blunt QC & Sally O'Neill QC

30-32 Furnival Street, London, EC4A 1JQ
Tel (020) 7405 3232 **Fax** (020) 7405 3322 **DX** 72 London Chancery Lane
Email clerks@furnivallaw.co.uk **Website** www.furnivalchambers.co.uk

Heads of Chambers	Oliver Blunt QC
	Sally O'Neill QC
Senior Clerk	Stephen Ball
Deputy senior clerk	Joel Mason
Clerks	Leon Muir
	Christopher Baptiste
	Ryan Budd
Tenants	84

THE CHAMBERS Furnival Chambers is a leading criminal set, with Oliver Blunt QC and Sally O'Neill QC as joint heads of Chambers. It specialises in the fields of serious and organised crime, including terrorism and sexual offences, financial crime and asset forfeiture, extradition and regulatory/disciplinary proceedings.

Members of Chambers are renowned for appearing in high-profile criminal cases for both the prosecution and defence. They appear at trial, in the Divisional Court, Court of Appeal, Privy Council and the Supreme Court, as well as the European Court of Human Rights and before regulatory/disciplinary panels. Many members undertake high profile work on behalf of, or against the Crown Prosecution Service, Assets Recovery Agency, Financial Conduct Authority, HM Revenue and Customs, the Serious Fraud Office, the Department of Work and Pensions and the Police.

This is a 'go to' set for high-profile, complex cases and those involving novel law. Members were recently involved in the first prosecution for domestic servitude within marriage (R v Ahmed) and the first prosecution for bribery under the new legislation (R v Patel & Others). Members also regularly conduct international cases, particularly in the Commonwealth and the Caribbean jurisdictions.

WORK UNDERTAKEN Chambers enjoys particular expertise in the following fields:
Serious & Organised Crime: Chambers has long been instructed in top-end work at trial and appellate levels, including the News International phone hacking (Operation Elvedon) trials, the Hatton Garden Jewellery raid, the murder of Shahena Uddin, the Stephen Lawrence murder, the Millenium Dome conspiracy, the murder of PC Sharon Beshenivsky, the murder of Sarah Payne, 'Baby P', the prosecution of Princess Diana's butler, the £50m Tonbridge robbery, the 'Witchcraft murder', significant death row appeals and high-profile Official Secrets Act trials amongst them.

Terrorism: Members have appeared in trials including that of the Gloucester shoe bomber, the first Al Qa'eda funding prosecution post-9/11, the Afghan Stansted hijacking, the 'Ricin' conspiracy and a number of recent Al Qa'eda and Syria-related cases, together with significant IRA trials in the past.

Sexual Offences: Members have appeared in Operation Yewtree cases, the prosecution of Rolf Harris, the Deep Cut trial and R v Dica, as well as many serial rapist cases including the 'West End mini-cab rapist', the 'M25 rapist' and cases of historical rape and sexual abuse. Chambers has significant experience in handling LCN DNA evidence and applications on abuse of process.

Financial Crime & Asset Forfeiture: Members have appeared in a multitude of high value fraud and asset forfeiture cases, including the UBS rogue trader (Adoboli), Goldman Sachs, R v Wilkins and the first professional cricket 'spot-fixing' case. Members have been retained to advise and act for and against the SFO, FCA (FSA), CPS, UKBA, the Police, HMRC and public companies and high-net worth individuals in international/multi-jurisdictional proceedings, recently including global dividend-arbitrage and withholding tax reclaim pre-charge investigations.

Extradition: Members advise and represent individuals and foreign governments in extradition proceedings at first instance, before the High Court, the Supreme Court and the European Court of Human Rights. Members have advised and appeared in matters involving murder and terrorism accusations, cases concerning the validity of European arrest warrants, refugee status, the 'biggest military computer hack of all time' into computers at NASA and the Pentagon, Nikonovs v HMP Brixton regarding retention of habeas corpus, Cretu v Romania on the status of the 2009 Framework Decision and trials in absentia and the 'Hound of Hounslow' flash crash trading case. A number of members recently acted in Goluchowski & Sas v Poland before Supreme Court. Charlotte Powell was a Specialist Adviser to the House of Lords Extradition Law Inquiry and Paul Garlick is an International Expert to the Organisation for Security and Co-operation.

Regulatory & Disciplinary: Chambers has vast experience in dealing with regulatory and disciplinary proceedings, before the GMC, NMC (including the Morecambe Bay Healthcare Trust case, concerning alleged misconduct of midwives leading to the death of a baby and endangerment of another's life), GOC and SRA, amongst others. Chambers handles all nature of hybrid criminal proceedings before tribunals including the coroners court, public enquiries and mental health review tribunals. Members also appear before the Football Association commissions and other sporting regulatory authorities, both for the authorities and individuals or teams concerned.

Clerking & Practice Support: Chambers practice areas are supported by specialist clerking teams. The team as a whole is highly regarded and offers a range of counsel of appropriate call for the work concerned. This is an approachable team dedicated to providing the best solutions for client needs.

GARDEN COURT CHAMBERS Henry Blaxland QC

57-60 Lincoln's Inn Fields, London, WC2A 3LJ
Tel (020) 7993 7600 **Fax** (020) 7993 7700
Email info@gclaw.co.uk **Website** www.gardencourtchambers.co.uk **Twitter:** @gardencourtlaw

Heads of Chambers	Henry Blaxland QC Marc Willers QC Kathryn Cronin
Chambers Director	Glenn Fletcher
Senior Clerk to Chambers	Colin Cook
Senior Civil Clerk	Phil Bampfylde
Tenants	184

MEMBERS

Ian Macdonald QC (1963) (QC 1988)
Ian Peddie QC (1971) (QC 1992)
Henry Blaxland QC (1978) (QC 2002)
Icah Peart QC (1978) (QC 2002)
Laurie Fransman QC (1979) (QC 2000)
Stephen Kamlish QC (1979) (QC 2003)
Michael Turner QC (1981) (QC 2002)
James Scobie QC (1984) (QC 2010)
Bernard Tetlow QC (1984) (QC 2011)
Marc Willers QC (1987) (QC 2014)
Dexter Dias QC (1988)(QC 2009)
Leslie Thomas QC (1988) (QC 2014)
Peter Wilcock QC (1988) (QC 2012)
Judy Khan QC (1989) (QC 2010)
Stephanie Harrison QC (1991) (QC 2013)
Michael Ivers QC (1991) (QC-2016)
Ali Naseem Bajwa QC (1993) (QC 2011)
Rajiv Menon QC (1993) (QC 2011)
Kieran Vaughan QC (1993) (QC 2012)
Richard Harvey (1971)
Michael House (1972)
Terry Munyard (1972)
Marguerite Russell (1972)
Sarah Forster (1976)
Patrick Roche (1977)
Lalith de Kauwe (1978)
James Bowen (1979)
Kathryn Cronin (1980)
Celia Graves (1981)
Michael Hall (1983)
Ravinder Rahal (1983)
Stephen Cottle (1984)
Nerida Harford-Bell (1984)
Peter Jorro (1986)
Amanda Meusz (1986)
Elizabeth Veats (1986)
Sorrel Dixon (1987)
Martin Huseyin (1988)
Christopher Williams (1988)
Piers Mostyn (1989)
Alistair Polson (1989)
Alex Taylor-Camara (1989)
Rebecca Chapman (1990)
Edward Fitzpatrick (1990)
Bethan Harris (1990)
Carol Hawley (1990)
Colin Hutchinson (1990)
Maggie Jones (1990)
Peter Rowlands (1990)
Clare Wade (1990)
Catrin Lewis (1991)
Sonali Naik (1991)
Stephen Simblet (1991)
Malek Wan Daud (1991)
Nicola Braganza (1992)
Helen Curtis (1992)
Valerie Easty (1992)
Alastair Edie (1992)
Julia Krish (1992)
Allison Munroe (1992)
Henry Drayton (1993)
Sandra Fisher (1993)
Kevin Gannon (1993)
Mark Gatley (1993)
Rajeev Thacker (1993)
Navita Atreya (1994)
Liz Davies (1994)
David Jones (1994)
Keir Monteith (1994)
Duran Seddon (1994)
Dafna Spiro (1994)
Amina Ahmed (1995)
Grace Brown (1995)
Gregor Ferguson (1995)
Edward Grieves (1995)
Amanda Weston (1995)
David Emanuel (1996)
Sean Horstead (1996)
Birinder Kang (1996)
Louise Hooper (1997)
Anya Lewis (1997)
Patrick Lewis (1997)
Sharon Love (1997)
Di Middleton (1997)
Roger Pezzani (1997)
Maya Sikand (1997)
Jacqueline Vallejo (1997)
Nick Wrack (1997)
Adrian Berry (1998)
Adrian Marshall Williams (1998)
Paul Troop (1998)
Rebekah Wilson (1998)
Michelle Brewer (1999)
Emma Favata (1999)
Femi Omere (1999)
Beth O'Reilly (1999)
Hannah Rought-Brooks (1999)
Ronan Toal (1999)
Minka Braun (2000)
Ed Elliott (2000)
Catherine O'Donnell (2000)
Sam Parham (2000)
Marina Sergides (2000)
Christian Wasunna (2000)
Felicity Williams (2000)
Navtej Singh Ahluwalia (2001)
Kate Aubrey-Johnson (2001)
Allison Bailey (2001)
Tim Baldwin (2001)
Desmond Rutledge (2001)
Sadat Sayeed (2001)
Paramjit Ahluwalia (2002)
Sareta Ashraph (2002)
Brenda Campbell (2002)
Stella Harris (2002)
Sally Ireland (2002)
Victoria Meads (2002)
Maya Naidoo (2002)
Sam Robinson (2002)
Irena Sabic (2002)
Colin Yeo (2002)
John Beckley (2003)
Alex Rose (2003)
Abigail Smith (2003)
Bansi Soni (2003)
Tom Wainwright (2003)
Abigail Bache (2004)
Andrew Eaton (2004)
Davina Krishnan (2004)
Dinah Loeb (2004)
Christopher McWatters (2004)
Mark Symes (2004)
William Tautz (2004)
Matt Brooks (2005)
Joanne Cecil (2005)
Justine Compton (2005)
Vikki Kerly (2005)
Stephen Marsh (2005)
Lucie Wibberley (2005)
Hossein Zahir (2005)
Sarah Hemingway (2006)
Leonie Hirst (2006)
Artis Kakonge (2006)
Stephen Lue (2006)
Shu Shin Luh (2006)
Anna Morris (2006)
Greg Ó Ceallaigh (2006)
Omar Shibli (2006)
Anthony Vaughan (2006)
Alex Grigg (2007)
Kirsten Heaven (2007)
Giles Newell (2007)
Richard Reynolds (2007)
Jo Wilding (2007)
Shahida Begum (2008)
Helen Foot (2008)
Gemma Loughran (2008)
James Mehigan (2008)
David Renton (2008)
Ali Bandegani (2009)
Raza Halim (2009)
Terry McGuinness (2009)
Bryony Poynor (2009)
Jacob Bindman (2010)
Paul Clark (2010)
Emma Fenn (2010)
Russell Fraser (2010)
Michael Goold (2010)
Owen Greenhall (2010)
Connor Johnston (2010)
Grainne Mellon (2010)
Bijan Hoshi (2011)
Taimour Lay (2011)
Maria Moodie (2011)
Catherine Oborne (2011)
Ifeanyi Odogwu (2011)

GARDEN COURT CHAMBERS Henry Blaxland QC (Continued)

MEMBERS

Tom Stoate (2011)
Naomi Wiseman (2011)
Tessa Buchanan (2012)
Grace Capel (2012)
Una Morris (2012)
Susan Bryant (2013)
Tom Copeland (2013)
Mark George QC (1976)
(QC 2009) *
Peter Weatherby QC (1992)
(QC 2012) *
David Watkinson (1980) *
Elizabeth Woodcraft (1980) *
Mary McKeone (1986) *
Nicos Trimikliniotis (1993) *
Dr Mary Malecka (1994) *
Shereener Browne (1996) *
Alex Offer (1998) *
Rahim Shamji (2000) *
Gul Hussain (2000) *
Kamran Choudhury (2001) *
Anthony Harrison (2004) *
Hannah Tonkin (2013) *

* Working Door Tenant

THE CHAMBERS Garden Court is one of the largest and most high-profile barristers' chambers in the UK with over 180 barristers, including 19 QCs. The set provides a wealth of expertise across criminal defence, civil liberties, inquest law, housing law, immigration, family law and public law. Its passion for human rights and social justice has shaped the development of law in these areas, with many of its members acting in some of the most important, precedent-setting cases in the UK today.

TYPES OF WORK UNDERTAKEN Administrative and public law; civil liberties; social welfare; Court of Protection; criminal defence; education; employment and discrimination law; environmental law; extradition law; family law (children law, financial remedies and international family law); fraud; housing law; immigration law (asylum and human rights, business and private); inquests and public inquiries; mental health law; planning law; police law; prison law; property law; regulatory law; Romani Gypsy and Traveller rights; welfare benefits.
Garden Court International provides advice, representation and training to clients worldwide on best practice in criminal law and procedure, international human rights and humanitarian law.
Garden Court Mediation provides an alternative dispute resolution service in all types of civil disputes.
A growing number of Garden Court Chambers' barristers are eligible to accept work directly from lay clients as part of the public access scheme.

1 GARDEN COURT FAMILY LAW CHAMBERS Janet Bazley QC & Charles Geekie QC

1 Garden Court, Temple, London, EC4Y 9BJ
Tel (020) 7797 7900 **Fax** (020) 7797 7929 **DX** 1034 (Chancery Lane)
Email clerks@1gc.com **Website** www.1gc.com

Head of Chambers	Janet Bazley QC Charles Geekie QC
Chambers Director	David Swann CBE
Senior Clerk	Paul Harris
Tenants	74

MEMBERS

Janet Bazley QC (1980)(QC-2006)
Charles Geekie QC (1985) (QC-2006)
Eleanor F Platt QC (1960) (QC-1982)
Alison Ball QC (1972)(QC-1995)
Susan Jacklin QC (1980) (QC-2006)
Sarah Morgan QC (1988) (QC-2011)
Nkumbe Ekaney QC (1990) (QC-2011)
Andrew Bagchi QC (1989) (QC-2015)
Darren Howe QC (1992) (QC-2015)
Francesca Wiley QC (1996) (QC-2015)
Deirdre Fottrell QC (2001) (QC-2015)
Andrew Norton QC (1992) (QC-2016)
Caroline Willbourne (1970)
Suzanne Shenton (1973)
Elizabeth Szwed (1974)
Peter Horrocks (1977)
Kay Halkyard (1980)
David Burles (1984)
Sylvester McIlwain (1985)
John Stocker (1985)
Susan Pyle (1985)
Pamela Warner (1985)
Gary Crawley (1988)
Nicholas Daniels (1988)
Rachel Gillman (1988)
Alev Giz (1988)
Frances Orchover (1989)
Michael Liebrecht (1989)
Malcolm Chisholm (1989)
Kate Mather (1990)
Catherine Jenkins (1990)
Claire Heppenstall (1990)
Simon Sugar (1990)
Doushka Krish (1991)
Ian Bugg (1992)
Denise Gilling (1992)
Rohan Auld (1992)
Jillian Hurworth (1993)
Gillian Downham (1993)
Jennifer Kavanagh (1993)
Alison Moore (1994)
Sally Stone (1994)
Emma Hudson (1995)
Sam Momtaz (1995)
Julien Foster (1995)
Duncan Watson (1997)
Prof Peter McEleavy (1999)
Daisy Hughes (1999)
Sharon Segal (2000)
Rebecca Mitchell (2000)
Jessica Lee (2000)
Gillian Stanley (2001)
Louise MacLynn (2001)
Caroline Middleton (2002)
Edward Flood (2002)
Philip Perrins (2002)
Richard Jones (2003)
Matthew Fletcher (2003)
Alfred Procter (2005)
Ajmal Azam (2006)
Elena MacLeod (2007)
Georgina Cole (2007)
Penelope Clapham (2007)
Nasstassia Hylton (2007)
Gemma Kelly (2007)
Lucy Sprinz (2008)
Thomas Dudley (2008)
Eleri Jones (2009)
Joseph Moore (2009)
Jessica Bernstein (2011)
Marlene Cayoun (2012)
Oliver Woolley (2012)
Patrick Paisley (2013)
Thomas Wilson (2013)
Christopher Sharp QC (1975) (QC-1999)*
Jane Crowley QC (1976) (QC-1998)*
Elizabeth Darlington (1998)*
Ann Marie Wicherek (1978)*

* Door Tenant

THE CHAMBERS 1 Garden Court is recognised nationally and internationally as a leading set, providing a highly skilled, comprehensive service to clients across the broad spectrum of family law and related work. Expert advice and representation, together with a practical, common sense, approach, results in members being instructed in the most complex and sensitive cases, as well as those involving issues of law of general importance. Both professional and lay clients appreciate the professionalism and approachability of our clerking team.

WORK UNDERTAKEN Chambers' dedicated practice teams offer advice and representation in all family law matters and in related areas, including cases involving the Court of Protection, human rights and judicial review. Members of Chambers appear in courts at all levels, including, regularly, in the Supreme Court and Court of Appeal. The family finance team undertakes matters ranging from big-money cases involving complex trust arrangements to modest value claims. Its cases include preventing dissipation of assets, cases involving foreign and offshore assets and complex trust arrangements. Emergency applications such as freezing injunctions and enforcement of orders are also dealt with. Private children law expertise includes all disputes over arrangements for children, surrogacy, adoption, declarations of parentage following assisted conception and issues in relation to legal parenthood in same sex relationships. All aspects of public law children work are handled and we have a particular reputation for undertaking cases involving the most complex legal and medical issues and increasingly, radicalisation. Work for local authorities includes applications for care and supervision orders, as well as adoption and judicial review. Public interest immunity cases, publicity and restraint of publicity cases form a regular part of Chambers' practice. Members advise and appear on behalf of local authorities in appeals concerning child-minding and day care registration. Court of Protection cases are an established and growing area of expertise as are cases involving family privacy and autonomy, the right to life, homosexuality and transsexuality. Chambers was one of the first to establish a family mediation service and continues to focus on alternative dispute resolution, offering early neutral evaluation and arbitration. Many of our members sit as part-time judges. Chambers has a strong tradition for undertaking pro bono work.

INTERNATIONAL With the increase in international families, much of Chambers' work has an international element. Members are frequently instructed in cases involving foreign jurisdictions. Several members have gained experience as lawyers working overseas, particularly in North America and the Caribbean. Our international work includes valuation, distribution and enforcement against foreign or off-shore trusts, child abduction and cases under the 1996 Hague Convention, international movement of children, adoption, surrogacy and care proceedings.

9 GOUGH SQUARE Andrew Ritchie QC

9 Gough Square, London, EC4A 3DG
Tel (020) 7832 0500 **Fax** (020) 7353 1344 DX 439
Email clerks@9goughsquare.co.uk **Website** www.9goughsquare.co.uk **Twitter** @9GoughSquare

Head of Chambers	Andrew Ritchie QC
Senior Clerk & Director of Business Development: Civil & Crime	Michael Goodridge
Director of Operations	John Irving
Tenants	68

MEMBERS

Andrew Ritchie QC (1985) (QC-2009)
John Foy QC (1969) (QC-1998) +
Andrew Baillie QC (1970) (QC-2001) +
Grahame Aldous QC (1979) (QC-2008) +
Jacob Levy QC (1986) (QC-2014)
Christopher Wilson (1980) +
Martin Pinfold (1981)
Nicolas Hillier (1982)
Roger Hiorns (1983)
Gaurang Naik (1985)
Vincent Williams (1985)
Jonathan Loades (1986)
Edwin Buckett (1988)
James Holmes-Milner (1989)
Stephen Glynn (1990)
Jeremy Crowther (1991)
Cyrus Katrak (1991)
Laura Begley (1993)
Christopher Stephenson (1994)
Timothy Parker (1995)
Simon Butler (1996)
Laura Elfield (1996)
Jeremy Ford (1996)
Tara Vindis (1996)
Tom Little (1997) +
Timothy Godfrey (1997)
Stuart McKechnie (1997)
Jonathan Payne (1997)
Simon Brindle (1998)
Perrin Gibbons (1998)
Giles Mooney (1998)
Tabitha Barran (1998)
Joanna Cobb (1999)
Shahram Sharghy (2000)
Linda Nelson (2000)
Claire Harden-Frost (2000)
Gareth Munday (2000)
Gurion Taussig (2001)
Eleanor Mawrey (2001)
Laura Briggs (2001)
James Thacker (2001)
Robert McAllister (2002)
Oliver Millington (2003)
Esther Pounder (2003)
Emily Verity (2003)
Esther Maclachlan (2005)
Alastair Hogarth (2005)
James Byrne (2006)
Jennifer Newcomb (2006)
Edward Lamb (2006)
Catherine Atkinson (2006)
Kate Lamont (2007)
Tom Restall (2007)
Benedict Rogers (2007)
Laura Bumpus (2008)
Tom Goodhead (2010)
Holly Tibbitts (2010)
Ben Zurawel (2010)
Tom Rainsbury (2010)
William Dean (2011)
Sarah Hunwick (2011)
Helen Pooley (2012)
Kieran Coleman (2012)
Natasha Partos (2012)
John Schmitt (2013)
Laura Hibberd (2015)
Tom Mountford (2015)

+ Recorder

THE CHAMBERS 9 Gough Square is a leading common law set based in London and appearing in courts throughout England and Wales and abroad. The key practice areas are personal injury, clinical negligence, professional negligence, fraud and serious crime, family, police law, professional disciplinary proceedings and commercial litigation.

The set consists of 68 members, including 5 QCs. Our clinical negligence and personal injury specialists take active involvement in the Personal Injuries Bar Association and APIL, and appear in very high profile cases: for instance Corr v IBC, Simmons v Castle; Gosling v Screwfix and EXP v Barker. Members of Chambers have also been involved with many successful multi-million pound claims in the last 12 months. They edit the leading text books in personal injuries including Kemp & Kemp on Quantum and publish their own range of clinical negligence and personal injuries books. Their family team have published a book focusing on the Public Law Outline with a second edition released in 2015.

WORK UNDERTAKEN The largest group specialises in personal injury and clinical negligence. Leaders and senior juniors appear regularly in ground-breaking cases. The members mainly represent injured claimants, but some do a high volume of defendant work. They publish a series of PI books including: Asbestos Claims, Clinical Negligence Claims, Manual Handling Claims, Workplace Accident Claims and Work Accidents at Sea and has amassed expertise in costs assessment and Court of Protection work.

Complex fraud work is undertaken by the criminal team for the SFO, the FCA, BERR, and the CPS Fraud Unit. Criminal work also covers terrorism, murder, violent and sexual offences with an emphasis on prosecution work for most London Crown Prosecution offices. In addition, a number of members of the criminal team are regularly in the High Court in judicial review cases such as Denby-Collins (the human rights challenge to burglars being killed by homeowners), as well as appearing in the Supreme Court of Appeal on matters of general public importance such as R v Hunter & ors.

The family team has 24 members and is particularly popular with local government solicitors, having preferred set status with most Greater London authorities. Members are instructed in high-profile non-accidental injury, sexual abuse cases and appear in all types of public law children cases, including applications for judicial review. Meanwhile the team has a flourishing private client practice in financial remedies, trust for land claims, contact and residence disputes and removals from the jurisdiction.

The highly regarded specialist police law practitioners are involved in civil actions against the police, inquests (such as the Diana Princess of Wales's inquest), and every type of police-led application, disciplinary proceedings, firearms and liquor licensing.

The commercial and property group has expertise ranging from general commercial contract litigation and arbitration, to sale of goods, consumer credit and leasing agreements, property work and insurance law. The professional negligence group focuses on solicitors', surveyors' and accountants' negligence. The highly regarded employment and discrimination law team represents employees and employers in tribunals all around England and Wales. A team of CEDR-accredited mediators providing ADR services is growing in this set and several practices include regulatory and disciplinary expertise.

GOUGH SQUARE CHAMBERS Claire Andrews

Head of Chambers	Claire Andrews
Senior Clerk	Bob Weekes
Tenants	21

6-7 Gough Square, London, EC4A 3DE
Tel (020) 7353 0924 **Fax** (020) 7353 2221 DX 476 **Out of hours** (07860) 219 162
Email gsc@goughsq.co.uk **Website** www.goughsq.co.uk

MEMBERS

Fred Philpott (1974)
Peter Sayer (1975) *
Claire Andrews (1979)
Josephine Hayes (1980)
Jeremy Barnett (1980)
Jonathan Goulding (1984)
Stephen Neville (1986)
Julian Gun Cuninghame (1989)
Bradley Say (1993)
Jonathan Kirk QC (1995)
(QC 2010)
Iain MacDonald (1996)
Simon Popplewell (2000)
Kate Urell (2002)
Geraint Howells (2002) *
James Ross (2006)
Ruth Bala (2006)
Anna Medvinskaia (2008)
Thomas Samuels (2009)
Lee Finch (2010)
Daniel Brayley (2011)
Robin Kingham (2013)

* Door tenant

THE CHAMBERS Gough Square Chambers deals primarily with the civil and criminal aspects of consumer and regulatory law, including consumer credit and financial services.

WORK UNDERTAKEN Chambers' work is broadly divided into civil, criminal and regulatory aspects. Chambers' civil work is heavily involved with advising and acting for FCA-regulated entities in relation to regulated lending and surrounding issues, including enforcement applications and FCA authorisation under the Financial Services and Markets Act 2000. In particular, members of Chambers have expertise in relation to the Consumer Credit Act 1974 and the FCA's Consumer Credit Sourcebook. Members also act in relation to banking, asset finance, judicial review and general commercial matters. Gough Square Chambers has been involved in some of the most important and high profile cases on these issues in recent years. For example, *Hurstanger Ltd v Wilson, Helden v Strathmore Ltd, Harrison v Black Horse Ltd and Beavis v ParkingEye Ltd.*

The criminal aspects of Chambers' work include prosecutions under the Consumer Protection from Unfair Trading Regulations 2008, food law, 'legal highs', weights and measures, product safety, pharmaceuticals and cosmetics and copyright. Several members of Chambers are active members of the Food Law Group, and Chambers attends the annual TSI Conference talking on key issues and updates. Notable cases include: *R v. Scottish and Southern Energy plc, R v X Ltd and R (Kingston upon Hull City Council) v Secretary of State for Business, Innovation and Skills.*

In relation to regulatory matters, Chambers advises and acts for and against an array of industry regulators. For example: the Financial Conduct Authority, the Competition and Markets Authority, the Advertising Standards Agency, the Civil Aviation Authority, OFWAT and OFCOM. In addition, our members have appeared before the First Tier Tribunal and in disciplinary matters before the Nursing and Midwifery Council.

Members of Chambers regularly write and speak on their areas of expertise, as well as editing and contributing to several leading textbooks including Miller's Product Liability & Safety Encyclopaedia, Encyclopaedia of Banking Law and Consumer and Trading Standards: Law & Practice ('the Pink Book'). Members also sit on the Bar Council's Law Reform Committee and are therefore well placed to understand the import of current and proposed legislation.

GRAY'S INN TAX CHAMBERS Milton Grundy

Head of Chambers	Milton Grundy
Senior Clerk	Chris Broom
Tenants	11

36 Queen Street, London, EC4R 1BN
Tel (020) 7242 2642 **Fax** (020) 7831 9017 **DX** 352 London Chancery Lane
Email clerks@taxbar.com **Website** www.taxbar.com

MEMBERS

Milton Grundy (1954)
Michael Flesch QC (1963) (QC-1983)
David Goldberg QC (1971) (QC-1987)
David Goy QC (1973) (QC-1991)
John Walters QC (1977) (QC-1997)
Nicola Shaw QC (1995) (QC-2012)
Laurent Sykes QC (2007) (QC-2016)
Nikhil Mehta (1976)
Conrad McDonnell (1994)
Michael Jones (2006)
Michael Firth (2011)

THE CHAMBERS Gray's Inn Tax Chambers is a leading set of specialist tax practitioners. Its members advise on all aspects of UK revenue law and have a long-established expertise in tax litigation before the Tribunals, the Supreme Court, the Privy Council, the European Court of Justice and certain Commonwealth and foreign jurisdictions. The chambers has a friendly approachable atmosphere and is known for its problem-solving approach to tax matters, seeking to find the optimum way to deal with the tax aspect of transactions ranging from structuring large land development projects and commercial deals to estate planning for farmers and businessmen. Chambers maintains a popular website, which offers a rapid reporting of tax cases. The address is www.taxbar.com.

Appointments & Memberships: All members of chambers belong to the Revenue Bar Association, of which Nicola Shaw QC was recently elected Chair and David Goy QC and Michael Flesch QC are former Chairmen. Michael Flesch QC, is a member of the Addington Society. Milton Grundy is President of the International Tax Planning Association and a Fellow of the Chartered Institute of Taxation. He is the draftsman of the Trusts Law of the Cayman Islands and of the IBC Act and the Trusts Act of Belize. John Walters QC is a Judge of the First-tier Tax Tribunal and a Deputy Judge of the Upper Tribunal. He, and Laurent Sykes QC are chartered accountants. Nikhil Mehta was formerly a partner in a leading firm of London solicitors and is both a barrister and an Indian advocate. Michael Jones is a member of the Attorney General's B Panel of Counsel. Michael Firth graduated from Oxford University and is a CTA.

WORK UNDERTAKEN Members give advice to taxpayers who are in dispute with HMRC, and where litigation is inevitable, appear for them before the Tribunals and the Court. Members advise private clients on the planning of their business and personal affairs. They advise on corporate tax planning, including acquisitions, mergers, takeovers and methods of financing, property transactions, international business, cross-border transactions, offshore and domestic trusts, estate planning and all matters involving direct and indirect taxes, including VAT. Members also advise non-profit organisations, local authorities and charities. Direct Professional Access is accepted from members of the appropriate professional bodies.

PUBLICATIONS Members have written, contributed to or edited very many publications including: *VAT and Property; British Tax Review; Asset Protection Trusts; Value Added Tax Encyclopaedia; Offshore Business Centres; The Law of Partnership Taxation; the Laws of the Internet; Essays in International Tax Planning; Six Fiscal Fables* and various articles on domestic and international tax developments. Some of the members are well known-lecturers in their fields.

INTERNATIONAL Languages spoken include French, German, Italian and Marathi. Members of chambers advise clients from many countries including Australia, Bermuda, Canada, the Caribbean, the Channel Islands, Europe, India, the Isle of Man, Hong Kong, Singapore and the USA. Members also advise the revenue departments of Commonwealth and other countries on the interpretation of their statutes, and advise and appear for HMRC in the United Kingdom and the Inland Revenue in Hong Kong.

HAILSHAM CHAMBERS David Pittaway QC

Head of Chambers	David Pittaway QC
Senior Clerk	Stephen Smith
Tenants	50

4 Paper Buildings (Ground Floor), Temple, London, EC4Y 7EX
Tel (020) 7643 5000 **Fax** (020) 7353 5778 **DX** 1036 London/Chancery Lane
Email clerks@hailshamchambers.com **Website** www.hailshamchambers.com

MEMBERS

David Pittaway QC (1977) (QC-2000)
Michael Pooles QC (1978) (QC-1999)
Laurie West-Knights QC (1977) (QC-2000)
Martin Spencer QC (1979) (QC-2003)
Dominic Nolan QC (1985) (QC-2006)
Julian Picton QC (1988) (QC-2010)
William Flenley QC (1988) (QC-2010)
Andrew Post QC (1988) (QC-2012)
Alexander Hutton QC (1992) (QC-2012)
Paul Mitchell QC (1999) (QC-2016)
Anthony de Freitas (1971)
Jane Tracy Forster (1975)
Jane Mishcon (1979)
Fiona Neale (1981)
Derek Holwill (1982)
Matthew Jackson (1986)
Francis Bacon (1988)
Clare Price (1988)
Dr Tejina Mangat (1990)
Simon Howarth (1991)
Dr Evelyn Pollock (1991)
Nicholas Peacock (1992)
Simon Wilton (1993)
Nicola Rushton (1993)
Sarah Christie-Brown (1994)
Spike Charlwood (1994)
Catherine Ewins (1995)
Dan Stacey (1996)
Eva Ferguson (1999)
Jamie Carpenter (2000)
Joshua Munro (2001)
James Gilberthorpe (2002)
Lucy MacKinnon (2003)
Imran Benson (2005)
Jacqueline Simpson (2006)
Alice Nash (2006)
Henry Bankes-Jones (2004)
Niamh O'Reilly (2007)
Heather McMahon (1999)
Stephen Bailey (2006)
David Juckes (2008)
Justin Meiland (2010)
Nicholas Pilsbury (2008)
Nicola Campbell-Clause (2010)
Richard Anderton (2010)
Amy Nesbitt (2012)
Alicia Tew (2012)
Theo Barclay (2013)
David Story (2012)
Jack Steer (2013)

THE CHAMBERS Hailsham Chambers strives to provide clients with excellent service. The award winning set is frequently praised for its friendly and helpful clerking, the quality of its members' work and for its reliability. Established more than 100 years ago and today offering 50 barristers, 10 of whom are silks, Hailsham Chambers contains many of the most sought-after barristers at the London Bar. The set's progressive thinking and use of modern technologies help chambers to run efficiently and to offer clients choice and flexibility.

WORK UNDERTAKEN Chambers acts for claimants and defendants, providing advice and representation before all levels of courts and tribunals throughout the world, in the specialist areas of:
Professional Negligence: In cases involving lawyers, accountants, auditors, surveyors, valuers, financial professionals and trustees, as well as advising about professional indemnity insurance coverage points.
Clinical Negligence: Acting for patients and their relatives and dependants, trusts, doctors, dentists, healthcare professionals, health authorities, private hospitals and clinics in civil litigation, at inquests and in the Court of Protection.
Costs Litigation: Involving points of principle and advising in disputes between solicitor and client, retainers, funding arrangements, DBAs, CFAs and costs budgets.
Professional Discipline: Advice and advocacy before tribunals and regulatory bodies, both medical and non-medical.
Personal Injury: Acting for claimants and defendants and their insurers in RTA claims and claims based upon employer's, occupier's, public and product liability, with an emphasis on cases of high value and complexity.
Commercial Dispute Resolution: Acting in general commercial matters such as insurance claims, fraud and partnership disputes.

To find out about the availability of counsel, please contact Hailsham's clerking team by tel: (020) 7643 5000 or email: clerks@hailshamchambers.com.

hailshamchambers

HARCOURT CHAMBERS Frances Judd QC

2 Harcourt Buildings, Temple, London, EC4Y 9DB
Tel (0844) 561 7135 **Fax** (020) 7353 6968 **DX** 373 London/Chancery Lane
Email clerks@harcourtchambers.co.uk **Website** www.harcourtchambers.co.uk

Head of Chambers	Frances Judd QC
Chambers Director	Simon Boutwood
Practice Manager	Judith Partington
Tenants	54

MEMBERS

Frances Judd QC (1984) (QC-2006)
John Vater QC (1995) (QC-2012) ^
Nicholas Goodwin QC (1995) (QC-2014)
Damian Garrido QC (1993) (QC-2015) ^
Aidan Vine QC (1995) (QC-2016)
Roger Evans (1970) ^
June Rodgers (1971) ^
Benedict Sefi (1972) ^
Alicia Collinson (1982)
Matthew Brett (1987) ^
Fiona Hay (1989) ^
Sara Granshaw (1991)
Louise Potter (1993) ^
Douglas Allen (1995) ^
Simon Miller (1996)
Jonathan Sampson (1997)
Matthew Brookes-Baker (1998) ^
Cecilia Barrett (1998) ^
Oliver Wraight (1998)
Andrew Leong (1998) ^
Edward Kirkwood (1999)
Helen Little (1999)
Margaret Styles (2000) ^
Craig Jeakings (2000)
James Turner (2001)
Edward Devereux (2001)
Jason Green (2001) ^
Julia Shillingford (2002)
Alex Forbes (2003) ^
Alison Williams (2004)
Elizabeth Tomlinson (2004)
Frances Harris (2005) ^
Kit Firbank (2005)
Chloe Wilkins (2006)
James Dove (2006)
Alex Perry (2007)
Sian Cox (2008) ^
Stephen Crispin (2008)
Mehvish Chaudhry (2008)
Vicky Reynolds (2008)
Emily Rayner (2009) ^
David Marusza (2009) ^
Annie Sayers (2009)
Justine Ramsden (2010) ^
Maria Scott-Wittenborn (2012)
Anna Yarde (2012)
Eleanor Howard (2012)
Martha Gray (2012)
Elisabeth Wickham (2012)
Oliver Powell (2013)
Emma Gatland (2013)
Rob George (2013)
Edward Bennett (2013)
Naomi Scarano (2014)

^ Public/Direct Access

THE CHAMBERS Harcourt Chambers is one of the leading family law sets in the country. It is recommended for both children law and family finance, and combines its expertise in family law with a strong reputation in civil litigation. Based in the Temple and in Oxford, it is home to five well known family silks; Frances Judd QC, John Vater QC, Nick Goodwin QC, Damian Garrido QC, Aidan Vine QC and 49 junior barristers, many of whom are acknowledged as leading practitioners in their fields.

Over the past decade, Harcourt Chambers has established itself as one of the very top 'across the range' family law sets. It has grown significantly in size and prominence and its members are regularly to be found in high profile and leading cases at first instance, appellate level and in the Supreme Court. Harcourt Chambers is particularly known for the high quality of its advocacy, advice and client care and for its modern and approachable style.

Chambers' highly regarded family finance practitioners undertake the full range of matrimonial, cohabitee and partnership litigation and have extensive expertise in cases of high value, including those where complex issues involving pensions, private companies, farms and overseas assets exist.

Its reputation in the field of children law is well established and widely recognised in both private and public law. In private law, Harcourt Chambers has renowned expertise in all forms of parental dispute including international relocation and child abduction. Public law work encompasses care, placement and adoption proceedings, often involving the most complex and severe cases of physical and sexual abuse.

HARDWICKE Nigel Jones QC & Paul Reed QC

Hardwicke Building, New Square, Lincoln's Inn, London, WC2A 3SB
Tel (020) 7242 2523 **Fax** (020) 7691 1234 **DX** LDE 393
Email enquiries@hardwicke.co.uk **Website** www.hardwicke.co.uk

Heads of Chambers	Nigel Jones QC & Paul Reed QC
Chief Executive	Amanda Illing
Tenants	78

MEMBERS

George F Pulman QC (1971) (QC-1989) +
Nigel Jones QC (1976) (QC-1999) +
Lesley Anderson QC (1989) (QC-2006)
Paul Reed QC (1988) (QC-2010) ^
Brie Stevens-Hoare QC (1986) (QC-2013)
P J Kirby QC (1989) (QC-2013) ^
John de Waal QC (1992) (QC-2013)
John Gallagher (1974) +
Graham Cunningham (1976)
Stephen Lennard (1976) + ^
Robert Leonard (1976) ^
Wendy Parker (1978) ^
Richard Buswell (1985)
Karl King (1985) + ^
Monty Palfrey (1985)
Mark Engelman (1987) ^
Steven Woolf (1989) ^
Sara Benbow (1990) ^
Daniel Gatty (1990) ^
Amanda Eilledge (1991)
Gordon Exall (1991)
Rupert Higgins (1991) ^
Arthur Moore (1992)
Colm Nugent (1992)
Andrew Skelly (1994) ^
Margaret Bloom (1994)
John Clargo (1994)
Alexander Bastin (1995) ^
David Pliener (1996) ^
Edward Rowntree (1996) ^
David Lewis (1997) ^
Ian Silcock (1997) ^
Charles Bagot (1997) ^
Alaric Watson (1997)
Alison Meacher (1998) ^
Alastair Redpath-Stevens (1998)
Peter Petts (1998)
Mark Stephens (1998)
Henry Slack (1999)
James Hall (2000)
Shazia Akhtar (2001) ^
Sarah McCann (2001) ^
Jonathan Titmuss (2001)
Sarah Venn (2002)
Jasmine Murphy (2002)
Sarah Clarke (2003)
Michael Wheater (2003)
Rebecca Richardson (2003)
Morayo Fagborun Bennett (2004) ^
Andy Creer (2005)
Charles Raffin (2005)
Simon Allison (2005) ^
Paul Strelitz (2005) ^
Thomas Bell (2006)
Laura Tweedy (2007) ^
Helena White (2007)
Catherine Piercy (2007)
Gemma Witherington (2008)
Emily Betts (2009)
Ebony Alleyne (2009)
Lina Mattsson (2010)
Brenna Conroy (2010)
Laurence Page (2010)
Aileen McErlean (2011)
Martyn Griffiths (2011)
Rupert Cohen (2011)
Sri Carmichael (2012) ^
Caoimhe McKearney (2012) ^
Charlie Thompson (2012)
Harriet Ter-Berg (2012)
Michael Tetstall (2012)
Jack Dillon (2012) ^
John Beresford (2012)
Rebecca Jones (2013)
Emma Hynes (2013)
Ryan Hocking (2014)
Katrina Mather (2014)

+ Recorder ^ Public/Direct Access

THE CHAMBERS Hardwicke specialises in commercial, construction, insurance and property work. It is one of the most innovative and modern sets at the Bar. Known for its friendly atmosphere and progressive outlook, it is run as a commercial business with a strong focus on excellent client service. Its business culture is reinforced by an active CSR and equality and diversity programme.

Hardwicke is a leading commercial barristers' chambers with 78 barristers, 7 of whom are silks. Its members are recommended across the breadth of its areas of practice areas and its practice team is renowned for the quality of its client service. Its clients range from solicitors and in-house counsel to utilities and insurers.

WORK UNDERTAKEN

Commercial: Hardwicke has a strong general commercial litigation and arbitration team and offers specialist expertise in: banking and finance, civil fraud, costs, employment, franchising, insolvency & restructuring, IT and telecommunications and intellectual property.
Construction & Engineering: Hardwicke is a leading construction set whose members deal with arbitration, adjudications, mediations and court litigation both domestically and internationally. Paul Reed QC produces the leading text Construction All Risks insurance with other members of the team.
Insurance & Reinsurance: Hardwicke covers all types of actions involving insurers and insurance cover, ranging from death and personal injury, property damage, public liability, employer's liability and health & safety, professional liability, professional discipline and construction.
Personal Injury & Clinical Negligence: Hardwicke has a niche and specialist team who deal with all areas of personal injury and clinical negligence work, from both a claimant and defendant perspective. Many cases covered are ground-breaking. Hardwicke also deals with medical malpractice and inquests.
Professional Negligence: Hardwicke has specialist expertise in dealing with disputes involving construction/engineering and medical professionals as well as a wide range of other professionals including solicitors and other legal professionals, accountants and finance professionals, insurance professionals, brokers, construction/engineering professionals, valuers, shipping professionals, directors and company officers.
Property: Hardwicke has a leading property team dealing with commercial and residential landlord and tenant, planning, real property and social housing, including allocations and homelessness. It also has a niche team dealing with probate and trust matters and has particular expertise in trusts of land and social welfare and benefits.

Hardwicke

1 HARE COURT Nicholas Cusworth QC

1 Hare Court, Temple, London, EC4Y 7BE
Tel (020) 7797 7070 **Fax** (020) 7797 7435 **DX** LDE 342 Chancery Lane
Email clerks@1hc.com **Website** www.1hc.com

Head of Chambers	Nicholas Cusworth QC
Senior Clerk	Steve McCrone
Tenants	40

MEMBERS

Nicholas Cusworth QC (1986) (QC-2009) *
Martin Pointer QC (1976) (QC-1996)
Deborah Bangay QC (1981) (QC-2006) *
Nigel Dyer QC (1982) (QC-2006)
Ann Hussey QC (1981) (QC-2009)
Richard Todd QC(1988)(QC-2009)
John Wilson QC (1981) (QC-2011)
Katharine Davidson (1987) (QC-2011)
Timothy Bishop QC (1991) (QC-2011)
Stephen Trowell QC (1995) (QC- 2015)
Justin Warshaw QC (1995) (QC-2015)
Nicholas Carden (1981) * •
Gavin Smith (1981)* •
Christopher Wood (1986) •
Elisabeth Todd (1990)
Nichola Gray (1991)
Geoffrey Kingscote (1993) •
Nicholas Yates (1996)
Simon Webster (1997)
Michael Bradley (1999) •
Rebecca Carew Pole (1999) •
Emma Sumner (1999)
Rebecca Bailey-Harris (2000) •
Eleanor Harris (2001) •
Tom Carter (2001) •
Rachel Spicer (2002) •
Christian Kenny (2003) •
Jude Allen (2004) •
Richard Sear (2005) * •
Amelia Sugden (2006)
Nicholas Wilkinson (2006) •
Katherine Cook (2007) •
Matthew Brunsdon Tully (2007)
Madhavi Kabra (2008)
Kyra Cornwall (2011)
Lily Mottahedan (2011)
Joshua Viney (2013)
Thomas Harvey (2013)
Ben Wooldridge (2013)
Samuel Littlejohns (2014)
Sir Matthew Thorpe + * •
Sir Peter Singer + * •
Michael Horowitz QC + * •
Bruce Blair QC +*
Michael Nicholls QC +
Heather Pope +
Amy Perkins +

\+ Associate Member * Arbitrator • Mediator

THE CHAMBERS For matrimonial finance, 1 Hare Court is the centre of excellence. Chambers prides itself on having been the family law market leader in every legal guide for every year since those guides were first published. It is a position earned and retained by an unrivalled expertise in relationship generated disputes. The set's vibrancy is maintained by a rigorous policy of in-house training and by central involvement in almost all the leading and newsworthy cases of the last 20 years. Chambers traces its history back more than 200 years. Its illustrious former members include two former Presidents of the High Court Family Division, three former members of the Court of Appeal, two current High Court judges namely Philip Moor and Nicholas Mostyn and three former High Court judges. Members write or contribute to the leading family law text books and periodicals. It is the birthplace of At A Glance and home of the editorship of Rayden & Jackson on divorce and family matters. The 1 Hare Court annual seminar is an important fixture in the family law year for all of chambers' instructing solicitors, providing up to date analysis from its expert barristers and a much celebrated party afterwards. Chambers now has 40 barristers: 11 silks and 29 juniors all with strong academic and professional credentials (the greatest concentration of specialist matrimonial QCs).

WORK UNDERTAKEN Chambers provides cutting edge advice and advocacy at every level. Its barristers have appeared in more reported cases in the financial remedy sphere than any other set by a large margin. The Supreme Court's four most important family law cases were dominated by membes of chambers: whether in international divorce (where Nigel Dyer QC and Eleanor Harris were successful for Mrs Agbaje), the nine Justice Supreme Court decision in Radmacher v Granatino concerning prenuptial agreements (where Richard Todd QC and Geoffrey Kingscote were pitted against a fellow member of chambers (Nicholas Mostyn QC), the seven Justice Supreme Court decision in Petrodel v Prest (where Richard Todd QC and Stephen Trowell were successful for Mrs Prest), or more recently, concerning non-disclosure in Sharland v Sharland (where Martin Pointer QC was successful for Mrs Sharland). The most important private family law case in the Privy counsel (Macleod v Macleod) involved Martin Pointer QC, Tim Bishop QC and Nichola Gray acted in the first civil partnership case (Lawrence v Gallagher) and Martin Pointer QC and Geoffrey Kingscote represented Mrs Cooper-Hohn in the highest value financial remedy case in family law to date.

Members of chambers have had an active role as advocates in most of the celebrated divorce cases of recent years: White, Cowan, Lambert, Miller, McFarlane, Charman and McCartney. Obviously the higher court cases attract greater publicity but chambers maintains a strong representation at every level of litigation. The majority of chambers' work takes the form of resolving disputes on divorce, both financial and regarding arrangements for children. Property disputes arising from unmarried parties' cohabitation also represents an important part of Chambers' work. Chambers has an excellent reputation in drafting nuptial agreements.

In addition to traditional court work, chambers has a strong offering in private dispute resolution services whether in Chambers bespoke facilities or in offices elsewhere. 1 Hare Court has a large and expert team of specialist barrister-mediators. Chambers has the largest number of family law arbitrators under one roof. Chambers has been at the forefront of family arbitration practice, having been involved in the two landmark cases of S v S and DB v DLJ. Senior and associate members of chambers regularly act as evaluators in "private FDR" hearings. Chambers also has an impressive international presence with its members providing representation or expert evidence in many other jurisdictions. In the last ten years members of chambers have acted in 30 foreign jurisdictions. In recent years members of chambers have been found advocating in cases as geographically far apart as the Cayman Islands and Hong Kong.

Members are supported by a highly efficient clerks' room run under the careful eye of Steve McCrone.

2 HARE COURT Jonathan Laidlaw QC

2 Hare Court, Temple, London, EC4Y 7BH
Tel (020) 7353 5324 **Fax** (020) 7353 0667 **DX** 444 (Ch.Ln.)
Email clerks@2harecourt.com **Website** www.2harecourt.com

Head of Chambers	Jonathan Laidlaw QC
Director of Clerking	Julian Campbell
Tenants	59

MEMBERS

Jonathan Laidlaw QC (1982) (QC-2008) *
Orlando Pownall QC (1975) (QC-2002)
Martin Heslop QC (1972) (QC-1995) ^*
David Waters QC (1973) (QC-1999)
Peter Wright QC (1981) (QC – 1999) *
Andrew Radcliffe QC (1975) (QC-2000)
Martin Hicks QC (1977) (QC-2003) ^
Sallie Bennett-Jenkins QC (1984) (QC-2006) *
Brendan Kelly QC (1988) (QC-2008) *
Jonathan Rees QC (1987) (QC-2010) ^
Brian O'Neill QC (1987) (QC-2010) *
Michael Hayton QC (1993) (QC-2013) ^
Christopher Coltart QC (1998) (QC-2014) ^
Oliver Glasgow QC (1995) (QC- 2016) ^•
Jacqueline Samuel (1971)
W. John Jones (1972)
Andrew Colman (1980) ^
Tyrone Belger (1984) ^
James Dawson (1984) *
David Whittaker (1986) ^*
Michael Logsdon (1988)
Kenneth Millett (1988) ^
Marios Lambis (1989) ^*
Alex Lewis (1990)
Mark Graffius (1990)
Christopher Gillespie (1991) ^
Craig Ferguson (1992) *
Kate Bex (1992) ^
Andrew Hurst (1992)
James Buchanan (1993)
Christopher Foulkes (1994) ^
Stephen Brassington (1994)
Zubair Ahmad (1995) ^
Scott Ivill (1997) ^
Narita Bahra (1997) ^
Peter Lownds (1998) ^
Quinn Hawkins (1999) ^
Angus Bunyan (1999)
Leon Kazakos (1999)
Gudrun Young (2001) ^
Robert Rinder (2001)
Rebekah Hummerstone (2002) ^
Naeem Mian (2002)
Julia Faure Walker (2004) ^
Vivienne Tanchel (2005) ^
Sarah Przybylska (2006) ^
Emily Dummett (2006)
Harry Bentley (2007)
Alexandra Tampakopoulos (2007) ^
Christopher Ware (2007)
Thomas Day (2008) ^
Fiona Robertson (2008) ^
Christopher Geering (2009) ^
Ben Rich (2010) ^
Nikita McNeill (2010)
Laura Stephenson (2012)
Paul Renteurs (2013)
Robert Dacre (2013)

* Recorder of the Crown Court + Deputy High Court Judge • Senior Treasury Counsel
++ Junior Treasury Counsel ^ Public/Direct Access

THE CHAMBERS 2 Hare Court is recognised as one of the UK's leading sets of expert barristers specialising across a range of practice areas including Crime, Professional Discipline & Regulatory, Financial Crime, Health & Safety and Inquests & Public Inquiries. Excellence in advocacy, advice and strategic analysis are at the core of chambers principles. Individuals, professionals and corporate clients instruct chambers via solicitors, professional advisers, or on a public access basis. Members and clerks are highly praised as a progressive team, placing an emphasis on understanding the needs of the client in an ever-changing legal market.

WORK UNDERTAKEN

Crime: Chambers specialist advocates advise, defend and prosecute all forms of criminal work, particularly in serious and complex cases of terrorism (including Special Advocate work), murder, honour killings, international drug and human trafficking, serious organised crime and sexual offences (especially historic). Recent cases include Brooks (phone hacking), Constance Briscoe, Huhne & Pryce, Stock Exchange terrorist bombing plot, Bridger (murder of Welsh girl April Jones), Gnango (Supreme Court decision on law of murder), McCormick (fake bomb detectors sold in Iraq), Ali Dizaei (corrupt Met Police commissioner), PC Blakelock/Broadwater Farm riots, the Derby Hate Crime case, Lee Rigby murder, and Nigel Evans, MP. Members are involved in aspects of Operation Yewtree both pre and post charge for various high profile individuals and have a strong reputation in representing professional footballers on sexual assault charges.
Financial Crime: Members are instructed on the largest and most complex financial crime cases. Their experience includes all forms of fraud, MTIC/VAT tribunal hearings, market abuse (insider dealing, LIBOR and other benchmark rates), asset recovery and forfeiture, and restraint/confiscation proceedings. Recent cases include BA price fixing, "Blue Index", SFO v Tchenguiz, Innospec, Operation Tabernula, Turks and Caicos corruption cases, MOBILX, Forex, Torex Retail, and MP/Lords Expenses. Members also defend financial services professionals in regulatory proceedings, and advise on potential liability under the criminal law in parallel with regulatory breaches (FSMA/Financial Services Act).
Health & Safety: 2 Hare Court advises companies and directors on matters including corporate and gross negligence manslaughter, deaths at work, falls from height, mechanical injuries, poisoning, and inhalation of gases. Recent cases include the Hugo Boss fatal accident case.
Members advise on environmental cases (e.g. spillages, high toxicity gas releases), regularly being instructed on behalf of claimants and defendants in civil litigation following workplace accidents and HSE prosecutions.
Professional Discipline: 2 Hare Court has extensive expertise in this field appearing in proceedings across a broad range of industry sectors including Healthcare, Financial Services, Legal (SRA and BSB), Police & Military, TMT (Technology, Media and Telecommunications), Tax and Sport. Members primarily defend professionals before the regulatory tribunals, crown and high courts.
Inquests & Public Inquiries: 2 Hare Court has a team of specialists with experience before the Coroner's

2 HARE COURT Jonathan Laidlaw QC (continued)

Inquests & Public Inquiries: 2 Hare Court has a team of specialists with experience before the Coroner's Court, particularly in cases involving health and safety, healthcare and military service issues. Most recently inquests have included acting for the family of Lance Corporal Craig Roberts one of three soldiers who died of heat illness on an SAS selection test in the Brecon Beacons and representing the family of Alexander Perepilichny, who died in unexplained circumstances. Public Inquiries have included the inquiry into the death of Alexander Litvinenko, the former Russian FSB agent allegedly poisoned by Polonium 210 in London in 2006, as well as various members instructed on the long running Hillsborough inquest.

INTERNATIONAL Members have experience of work in the Cayman Islands, Turks and Caicos and Northern Ireland.
Other languages spoken: French, Italian, Russian, Gujarati, Hindi, Punjabi and Urdu.

3 HARE COURT Peter Knox QC

3 Hare Court, Temple, London, EC4Y 7BJ
Tel (020) 7415 7800 **Fax** (020) 7415 7811 **DX** 212 London
Email clerks@3harecourt.com **Website** www.3harecourt.com **Twitter** @3harecourt

Head of Chambers	Peter Knox QC
Senior Clerk	James Donovan
Tenants	37

MEMBERS

Peter Knox QC (1983) (QC-2006)
Mark Strachan QC (1969) (QC-1987)
James Guthrie QC (1975) (QC-1993)
Simon Davenport QC (1987) (QC-2009) ^
Howard Stevens QC (1990) (QC-2012)
Thomas Roe QC (1995) (QC-2014) ^
Aidan Casey QC (1992) (QC-2016) ^
Sebastian Neville-Clarke (1973)
Andrew Young (1977)
Jeffrey Golden °
Pierre Janusz (1979)
William Godwin (1986) ^
Paul Letman (1987)
Rupert Butler (1988) ^
Professor Satvinder Juss (1989) ^
Richard Samuel (1996) ^
Katherine Deal (1997)
Dan Saxby (2000)
Tom Poole (2001)
Navjot Atwal (2002)
Daniel Lewis (2003)
Robert Strang (2003)
James Hawkins (2003)
Clara Johnson (2005) ^
Sara Ibrahim (2006) ^
Helen Pugh (2008) ^
Asela Wijeyaratne (2008) ^
Hafsah Masood (2006) ^
Rowan Pennington-Benton (2008) ^
Alexander Halban (2009)
Richard Campbell (2007)
Stephen Hackett (2011)
Sarah Ramsey (2012)
Julia Lowis (2013)
Miranda Butler (2013)
Rachel Earle (2013)
Olivia Wybraniec (2013)
Sir George Newman (1965) *
Hugh Small QC (1963) (QC-1985)*
Anthony Astaphan (1983) (SC-1999) * ++
David McMillen QC (1985) (QC-2011) * ±
John Restano QC (1994) (QC 2014) *
Bertha Cooper-Rousseau (1993) *
Prof Matthew Happold (1995) *
Martin Budworth (1999) *
Daniel Tivadar (2005) * ^

* Door Tenant ++ Dominica ± Northern Ireland ° Arbitrator ^ Public/Direct Access

THE CHAMBERS Described as a 'leading civil and commercial set', Chambers has established a first-class reputation in its fields of practice, providing a wide range of advisory and advocacy services both domestically and internationally in an environment that meets modern business needs.

WORK UNDERTAKEN Civil fraud; commercial; employment; insolvency; international work; personal injury and travel/accidents abroad; professional negligence; property litigation; public, administrative and constitutional law. Privy Council work is a notable area of expertise. Insolvency and restructuring is a growing area for Chambers and the set often acts for the main insolvency practitioners.
Chambers is strong on languages, with members fluent in Dutch, French, German, Hindi, Hungarian, Italian, Malay, Punjabi, Russian, Spanish, Swahili and Urdu.

HENDERSON CHAMBERS Charles Gibson QC

2 Harcourt Buildings (Ground Floor), Temple, London, EC4Y 9DB
Tel (020) 7583 9020 **Fax** (020) 7583 2686 **DX** LDE 1039
Email clerks@hendersonchambers.co.uk **Website** www.hendersonchambers.co.uk

Head of Chambers	Charles Gibson QC
Chief Clerk	John White
Senior Practice Manager	Daniel Kemp
Tenants	49

MEMBERS

Charles Gibson QC (1984) (QC-2001) + ^
Richard Mawrey QC (1964) (QC-1986) + ^
Peter Susman QC (1966) (QC-1997) + ^
Lawrence West QC (1979) (QC-2003) + ^
Prashant Popat QC (1992) (QC-2008) ^
Sir Alan Dashwood QC (1969) (QC-2010) ^
Rhodri Williams QC (1987) (QC-2010) ^
Patrick Green QC (1990) (QC-2012) ^
Geraint Webb QC (1995) (QC-2013)
Oliver Campbell QC (1992) (QC-2014) ^
Malcolm Sheehan QC (1993) ^ (QC-2015)
Toby Riley-Smith (1995) ^ (QC-2016)
Bernard O'Sullivan (1971) ^
Jonathan Harvey (1974) ^
Kenneth Hamer (1975) + ^
William Hibbert (1979)
James Palmer (1983) ^
Jonathan Steinert (1986) ^
David Brook (1988) ^
Andrew Davies (1988) ^
Julia Smith (1988)
Linda Goldman (1990) ^
Angus Withington (1995) ^
Andrew Kinnier (1996) ^
Adam Heppinstall (1999) ^
Noel Dilworth (2001) ^
Anna Burne (2001) ^
James Purnell (2002) ^
Nazeer A Chowdhury (2002) ^
Matthew Bradley (2004) ^
Kathleen Donnelly (2005) ^
Abigail Cohen (2005) ^
Matthew Richardson (2006)
Henry Warwick (2007)
Jonathan Lewis (2007) ^
Thomas Evans (2008)
Lucy McCormick (2008)
Dennis Rosenthal (2009)
Elizabeth Tremayne (2009)
Paul Skinner (2010)
Hannah Curtain (2010)
James Williams (2010)
Rachel Tandy (2010)
Ognjen Miletic (2010)
Jonathon Worboys (2010)
Chloe Campbell (2011)
Paris Aboro (2012)
George Mallet (2012)
Matthieu Gregoire (2013)
Roger Henderson QC (1964) (QC-1980) + *
Felicia Fenston (1994) *
Prof John Miller (1974) *
Tamara Trefusis (1999) *
Clive Stanbrook OBE QC (1972) (QC-1989) *
Philip Bentley QC (1970) (QC-1991) *
Frank Schoneveld (1992) *
Jeremy Scudamore (1982) *
Natasha Newell (2001) ^

+ Recorder * Door Tenant ^ Public/Direct Access

THE CHAMBERS Henderson Chambers, since its foundation in 1954, has developed a solid reputation for excellence in both advocacy and advisory work over a wide range of practice areas and market sectors. Chambers' main focus is on civil and commercial contract and tort actions, public, regulatory and disciplinary law. Members act for multinational organisations, foreign and domestic corporations, financial services organisations, government departments and agencies, local authorities, NGOs, professional bodies, SME's and individuals in contentious and non-contentious matters. One of the first Chambers to obtain accreditation under the BarDirect scheme it remains pre-eminent in meeting the needs of lay and professional clients. Chambers draws the majority of its tenants from its pupils all of whom undertake part of their pupillage in Brussels. Chambers remains dedicated to providing a high standard of client care and received Bar Mark accreditation in 2011. Members of chambers are appointed to the Attorney General's Panel of Junior Counsel to the Crown.

WORK UNDERTAKEN

Product Liability & Group Actions: Chambers has an unrivalled position in product liability, having maintained its top ranking in the legal directories for over a decade. For more than 25 years, members of chambers have been instructed in many of the most significant unitary cases, group actions and commercial claims in respect of allegedly defective products.

Health & Safety & Environment: Widely recognised for its expertise in health and safety law, the set covers all aspects of environmental law and health and safety litigation, including prosecutions for corporate manslaughter, infringements of health and safety legislation and environmental and waste prosecutions. Consistently ranked as one of the leading sets in the field as well as being awarded Health & Safety Chambers of the Year 2014, members also provide advice on health and safety and environmental policy, regulatory issues, management and training.

Banking, Finance & Consumer Credit: One of the leading sets in consumer credit fielding a large team with great expertise in financial services, consumer credit, asset finance, debt recovery, mortgage lending, sale and carriage of goods, issues of title and consumer protection.

Employment: Chambers has a long and established practice in the field of employment law. It has particular expertise in restraint of trade and breach of confidence; wrongful dismissal and related contractual claims; unfair dismissal claims; sex, race and disability discrimination claims; redundancy; TUPE; re-structuring and EC employment law.

Local Government & Public: Members have an established reputation for excellence in the field of public and administrative law, especially when working with local authorities and other statutory bodies on matters such as property, planning, highways, compulsory purchase, transport, finance/audit, environmental, education, social services, public procurement, employment and pensions.

Property: Chambers has a dynamic and innovative property team with particular strengths in commercial property and development, commercial and residential landlord and tenant, social housing, stock transfers, insolvency, public law, property damage law and professional negligence.

HENDERSON CHAMBERS Charles Gibson QC (continued)

insolvency, public law, property damage law and professional negligence.
Regulatory & Disciplinary: Chambers has a long tradition of practice in the field of regulation and professional discipline. Members act as advisers, legal assessors, representatives, advocates, or as tribunal members.
Technology & Construction: For many years Chambers has actively developed innovative remedies in IT and closely related fields, using modern technology (including social networking and up to the minute search techniques) to solve the legal problems that arise from it.
Commercial, Insurance & International Arbitration: Members have considerable experience of large scale disputes, often involving group actions or multiple parties, including those claims arising out of property damage, contamination or sale of goods and cross border disputes. Members regularly act for both insurers and insured in coverage disputes and many draw upon considerable experience in arbitrations under wide ranging procedural rules.
ADR: Committed to offering a full service for dispute management and resolution, members of chambers act as arbitrators and adjudicators and are accredited by CEDR as commercial mediators.

INTERNATIONAL Members advise on all aspects of European law, contentious and non-contentious, including constitutional matters and the law relating to the internal market.

HOGARTH CHAMBERS Alastair Wilson QC & Roger Wyand QC

5 New Square, Lincoln's Inn, London, WC2A 3RJ
Tel (020) 7404 0404 **Fax** (020) 7404 0505 **DX** 16 London
Email barristers@hogarthchambers.com **Website** www.hogarthchambers.com

Head of Chambers	Alastair Wilson QC Roger Wyand QC
Chambers' Director	Briget Harrison
Senior Clerk	Clive Nicholls
Assistant Clerks	John Davies Charlie Wood
Consultant	Ian Bowie
Tenants	21

MEMBERS

Alastair Wilson QC (1968) (QC-1987)
Roger Wyand QC (1973) (QC-1997)
Christopher Morcom QC (1963) (QC-1991)
Jonathan Rayner James QC (1971) (QC-1988)
Nicholas Caddick QC (1986) (QC-2011)
Gillian Davies (1961)
Alexander Stewart (1975)
Michael Hicks (1976)
Edward Bragiel (1977)
Amanda Michaels (1981)
Guy Tritton (1987)
Gwilym Harbottle (1987)
Richard Davis (1992)
Andrew Norris (1995)
Jeremy Reed (1997)
Tom St Quintin (2006)
Benjamin Longstaff (2009)
Jonathan Moss (2009)
Charlotte Scott (2012)
Jamie Muir Wood (2012)
Sam Carter (2014)

THE CHAMBERS Hogarth Chambers is recognised as one of the leading sets of barristers' chambers for intellectual property and chancery, based in the UK. Chambers specialises in IT, media and entertainment, FOI, data protection, privacy and commercial disputes with a technical or non-technical IP element. Chambers also has a long-standing reputation for chancery and commercial law, as well as expertise in ADR, mediation and arbitration.

With 21 barristers, Hogarth Chambers is one of the largest intellectual property sets in the UK. Members have experience of appearing as advocates at all levels within the UK court system, including the High Court, Court of Appeal and Supreme Court, and in tribunals such as the UK Intellectual Property Office, Copyright Tribunal, VAT Tribunal and Lands Tribunal.

In recent years, members have developed an in depth experience of European aspects of IP; regularly appearing before the Court of Justice of the European Union, the General Court in Luxembourg, as well as before the European Patent Office in Munich.

Hogarth is dedicated to providing a high quality, cost-effective service. Chambers offers clients a wide range of counsel at all levels of seniority, from Queen's Counsel to recently called junior members. Chambers welcomes instructions from solicitors, in-house lawyers, patent and trade mark attorneys, direct access and other approved bodies.

WORK UNDERTAKEN

Intellectual Property: All aspects of IP, including patents, copyright, designs, trade marks and passing off, threats/trade libel, confidential information, and entertainment and media contracts. Chambers also specialises in related areas such as computer contracts litigation, domain name disputes and internet-related infringements, IP insurance, personality and character merchandising, privacy rights, trade secrets, franchising, counterfeiting, customs and criminal proceedings connected with IP rights, data protection issues, FOI, privacy law, EU and UK competition law, and any commercial matter requiring technical competence or a detailed knowledge of the entertainment and media industries.

Information Technology: Contractual IT litigation and numerous confidential arbitrations.

Media & Entertainment: Including moral rights; performers' rights; comparative advertising; trade libel; malicious falsehood; entertainment industry contracts; confidential information; personality and character merchandising; privacy rights; criminal remedies; related EC aspects.

Chancery/Commercial: Insolvency (corporate and personal); company; partnership; banking and securities; e-commerce; commercial contracts; professional negligence; land law and conveyancing; landlord and tenant; charities; trusts and fiduciaries; wills and the administration of estates; and applications under the Inheritance Act.

Privacy: Since the advent of the phone hacking litigation, Chambers' members have established a substantial presence in this sector.

Leading practitioners' books edited in chambers include: *Copinger and Skone James on Copyright; Intellectual Property in Europe; Moral Rights, The Modern Law of Patents; The Modern Law of Trade Marks; A Practical Guide to Trade Mark Law; A User's Guide to Trade Marks and Passing Off.*

HOGARTH | CHAMBERS

11KBW James Goudie QC & John Cavanagh QC

11 King's Bench Walk, Temple, London EC4Y 7EQ
Tel (020) 7632 8500 **Fax** (020) 7583 9123/3690 **DX** 368 Chancery Lane
Email clerksteam@11kbw.com **Website** www.11kbw.com

Head of Chambers	James Goudie QC John Cavanagh QC
Senior Clerks	Lucy Barbet Mark Dann
Direct of Finance & Operations	Claire Halas
Business Development Director	Andrea Kennedy
Tenants	59

MEMBERS

James Goudie QC (1970) (QC-1984)
John Cavanagh QC (1985) (QC-2001)
Christopher Jeans QC (1980) (QC-1997)
Adrian Lynch QC (1983) (QC-2000)
Nigel Giffin QC (1986) (QC-2003)
Simon Devonshire QC (1988) (QC-2009)
Jonathan Swift QC (1989) (QC-2010)
Timothy Pitt-Payne QC (1989) (QC-2010)
Peter Oldham QC (1990) (QC-2010)
Daniel Stilitz QC (1992) (QC-2010)
Clive Sheldon QC (1991) (QC-2011)
Seán Jones QC (1991) (QC-2012)
Jason Coppel QC (1994) (QC-2013)
Charles Bourne QC (1991) (QC-2014)
Karen Steyn QC (1995) (QC-2014)
Akhlaq Choudhury QC (1992) (QC-2015)
Anya Proops QC (1998) (QC-2016)
Jane Oldham (1985)
Nigel Porter (1994)
Richard Leiper (1996)
Jonathan Moffett (1996)
Andrew Sharland (1996)
Julian Wilson (1997)
Jane McCafferty (1998)
Jonathan Auburn (1999)
Harini Iyengar (1999)
Paul Greatorex (1999)
Julian Milford (2000)
Andrew Blake (2000)
James Cornwell (2002)
Marcus Pilgerstorfer (2002)
Joanne Clement (2002)
Holly Stout (2003)
Andrew Edge (2003)
Judy Stone (2003)
Simon Forshaw (2004)
David Bedenham (2005)
Patrick Halliday (2005)
Julian Blake (2006)
Rachel Kamm (2006)
Tara Shahbahrami (2006)
Amy Rogers (2007)
Tom Cross (2007)
Robin Hopkins (2008)
Christopher Knight (2008)
Michael Lee (2009)
Katherine Eddy (2009)
Edward Capewell (2009)
Joseph Barrett (2009)
Heather Emmerson (2009)
Sean Aughey (2010)
Ronnie Dennis (2010)
Hannah Slarks (2011)
Tom Ogg (2012)
Rupert Paines (2012)
Peter Lockley (2013)
Zoe Gannon (2014)
Zac Sammour (2014)
Leo Davidson (2015)

THE CHAMBERS 11KBW is an award-winning set with an outstanding reputation in its core practice areas of commercial, employment and public law. The set is made up of 59 barristers including 17 QCs. 11KBW is renowned for the calibre of its advocates and the intellectual rigour that its members bring to their work. Chambers is consistently praised for its excellent, friendly and professional service to clients. Members regularly appear in complex and high profile cases often for both defendant and claimant, advising, acting for and providing advocacy at the highest level.

WORK UNDERTAKEN

- Commercial
- Education
- Employment
- European Union
- Health and community care/Court of Protection
- Human rights and civil liberties
- Information and data protection
- International arbitration
- Media law and data privacy
- Mediation
- Procurement and state aid
- Professional discipline and regulatory law
- Public and administrative law
- Public international law
- Sport
- Tax litigation

RECRUITMENT A member of Pupillage Portal, 11KBW offers awards for 2017 of £65,000.

KEATING CHAMBERS Marcus Taverner QC

Head of Chambers	Marcus Taverner QC
Tenants	58

15 Essex Street, London, WC2R 3AA
Tel (020) 7544 2600 **Fax** (020) 7544 2700 **DX** 1045
Email clerks@keatingchambers.com **Website** www.keatingchambers.com

MEMBERS

Marcus Taverner QC (1981) (QC-2000)
Prof John Uff QC (1970) (QC-1983)
Richard Fernyhough QC (1970) (QC-1986)
Dr Christopher Thomas QC (1973) (QC-1989) ^
John Marrin QC (1974) (QC-1990)
Stephen Furst QC (1975) (QC-1991) ^
Timothy Elliott QC (1975) (QC-1992) ^
Dr Robert Gaitskell QC (1978) (QC-1994)
Philip Boulding QC (1979) (QC-1996) ^
Paul Darling QC (1983) (QC-1999) ^
Finola O'Farrell QC (1983) (QC-2002)
Adrian Williamson QC (1983) (QC-2002) ^
David Thomas QC (1982) (QC-2002)
Rosemary Jackson QC (1981) (QC-2006) ^
Alexander Nissen QC (1985) (QC-2006) ^
Nerys Jefford QC (1986) (QC-2008)
Sarah Hannaford QC (1989) (QC-2008) ^
Simon Hargreaves QC (1991) (QC-2009)
Richard Harding QC (1992) (QC-2009)
Veronique Buehrlen QC (1991) (QC-2010)
Vincent Moran QC (1991) (QC-2011) ^
Adam Constable QC (1995) (QC-2011) ^
Simon Hughes QC (1995) (QC-2011)
Marc Rowlands QC (1990) (QC-2012)
Piers Stansfield QC (1993) (QC-2012) ^
Fionnuala McCredie QC (1992) (QC-2013)
Justin Mort QC (1994) (QC-2014) ^
Jane Lemon QC (1993) (QC-2015) ^
Jonathan Lee QC (1993) (QC-2015)
Alan Steynor (1975) ^
Simon Taylor (1987)
Robert Evans (1989) ^
Abdul Jinadu (1995) ^
Paul Buckingham (1995) ^
Krista Lee (1996) ^
Richard Coplin (1997) ^
Gaynor Chambers (1998) ^
Samuel Townend (1999) ^
Gideon Scott Holland (1999) ^
Jonathan Selby (1999) ^
Lucy Garrett (2001)
Elizabeth Repper (2002)
Calum Lamont (2004) ^
Alice Sims (2004) ^
William Webb (2005) ^
Thomas Lazur (2005) ^
James Thompson (2005) ^
Peter Brogden (2006) ^
Ben Sareen (2008)
Sarah Williams (2008)
Paul Bury (2008)
David Sheard (2010)
David Gollancz (2010)
Tom Owen (2011)
Matthew Finn (2011)
Jennie Wild (2013)
Harry Smith (2014)
Tom Coulson (2014)
Ian Pennicott QC (1982) (QC-2003) ++ ^
HH Peter Bowsher QC (1959) (QC-1978) ++
Prof Michael Furmston (1960) ++
Michael Stimpson (1969) ++
Louise Randall (1988) ++
Professor Chin Leng Lim (2011) ++
Robert Fenwick Elliott (2013) (South Australian Bar) ++

++ Door Tenant/Practising Associate Members ^ Public/Direct Access

THE CHAMBERS Keating Chambers is a leading set of commercial barristers' chambers, with a thriving domestic and international practice. Comprising 58 barristers (including 29 silks) they have the strength in depth across the range of seniorities to support their clients' needs. With a number of international members permanently based in either Australia, Hong Kong or Singapore, the set can provide commercial and practical advice, together with a first rate flexible and client-focused service, worldwide.

Barristers at Keating Chambers specialise in providing their services across the areas of construction and engineering; energy and natural resources; infrastructure and utilities; international arbitration; IT and technology; offshore construction and marine engineering; procurement and competition and associated professional negligence. The set has received a number of awards for its expertise including Construction Chambers of the Year, Client Care Chambers of the Year, and both Construction Silk and Junior of the Year.

Members have a genuine breadth of advocacy and advisory experience across all types of disputes. They provide advisory services on all the internationally recognised forms of contract including FIDIC, NEC, IChemE, LOGIC, SAJ and AWES, and regularly act in disputes concerning bespoke contracts, often amended to some degree from these standard forms. They also have extensive experience with PPP, PFI, and partnering and alliancing contracts.

Members regularly appear in the various divisions of the High Court – but especially in the Technology & Construction Court and the Commercial Court – and also the Court of Appeal, the Privy Council and Supreme Court. Their ADR expertise covers domestic and international arbitration, adjudication (statutory and contractual), mediation, dispute review boards and expert determination.

Senior members are also frequently appointed as arbitrators by many of the world's leading appointing bodies, such as the International Chamber of Commerce (ICC), the London Court of International Arbitration (LCIA) and other overseas centres including Dubai (DIAC), Hong Kong (HKIAC), Malaysia (KLRAC), Singapore (SIAC) and Vietnam (VIAC). They are also appointed directly by parties to arbitrations under ICSID and UNCITRAL rules. Members act as experts on English law in overseas jurisdictions, and some members have rights of audience in other jurisdictions (such as Dubai (DIFC), Hong Kong SAR, New Zealand, Northern Ireland and the Republic of Ireland).

WORK UNDERTAKEN

Construction & Engineering: The set's expertise covers the full range of contractual claims relating to the

KEATING CHAMBERS Marcus Taverner QC (continued)

construction industry, including development contracts, building defects claims and construction delays. Claims expertise includes civil, mechanical and electrical engineering works relating to major infrastructure projects such as airports, bridges, railways, roads and tunnelling.

Energy: Considerable expertise in claims relating to the construction of assets for the oil and gas industry including drilling platforms, FPSO's, oil tankers, pipe laying ships, support vessels, undersea pipelines and on shore process and storage facilities. Members also have experience in power generation, the nuclear sector and onshore and offshore windfarm disputes. A number of barristers have a dual qualification in engineering, and are therefore well-equipped to handle disputes involving complex technical issues.

Professional Negligence: The set specialises in bringing and defending claims against professionals across the whole spectrum of construction and property related professional liability work, involving architects, contractors, engineers, government departments, indemnity insurers, IT consultants, project managers, property developers, solicitors and surveyors. Members also advise and represent parties in construction related insurance coverage disputes arising out of liability, material damage, consequential loss, project, CAR and professional indemnity policies.

Shipbuilding & Marine Engineering: Considerable expertise in technical marine engineering matters, having advised and acted in many international shipbuilding and offshore construction disputes. This experience extends not only to vessels destined for the oil and gas industries, such as FPSOs and jack-ups, but also to ferries and to cable laying, naval and general cargo vessels.

Procurement: A team of barristers act for a variety of government departments and private clients in disputes relating to EU procurement law. The breadth of expertise is wide, with members instructed in a variety of cases relating to transport, energy, IT and healthcare.

Property: Extensive experience in party wall disputes and issues about rights to light. They also have considerable expertise in nuisance claims and regularly deal with claims relating to subsidence, landslips, flood and fire damage. A particular speciality is nuisance and trespass claims arising out of construction operations, where allegations often concern excessive noise and vibration and overhanging cranes. Members also regularly deal with dilapidation and other property damage claims.

Technology: A substantial track record in dealing with IT contracts includes disputes concerning alleged failure to meet performance specifications and issues of alleged mismanagement in the development of new software. These claims have related to projects including railways, metro systems, marketing companies, utility companies, and government departments.

CLIENTS Architects, construction contractors, building and quantity surveyors, engineers, energy companies, accountants, banks, joint ventures, government departments, professional indemnity insurers, property developers, shipyards, software developers and specialist building sub-contractors.

1 KING'S BENCH WALK Deborah Eaton QC and Philip Marshall QC

1 King's Bench Walk, Temple, London, EC4Y 7DB
Tel (020) 7936 1500 **Fax** (020) 7936 1590 **DX** LDE 20
Email clerks@1kbw.co.uk **Website** www.1kbw.co.uk

Heads of Chambers	Deborah Eaton QC Philip Marshall QC
Chief Executive	Nigel Scott
Senior Clerk	David Dear
Tenants	56

MEMBERS

Deborah Eaton QC (1985) (QC-2008)
Philip Marshall QC (1989) (QC-2012) +
Pamela Scriven QC (1970) (QC-1992)
Richard Anelay QC (1970) (QC-1993) +
James Turner QC (1976) (QC-1998)
Charles Howard QC (1975) (QC-1999)
Anthony Kirk QC (1981) (QC-2001) +
Clive Newton QC (1968) (QC-2002)
Christopher Pocock QC (1984) (QC-2009) ^ †
Richard Harrison QC (1993) (QC-2012)
Caroline Budden (1977) +
Cherry Harding (1978) +
Caroline Lister (1980) +
Julian Woodbridge (1981) ^
Markanza Cudby (1983)
Elizabeth Selman (1989)
Marcus Fletcher (1990) ^
James Roberts (1993) + ^ †
Christopher McCourt (1993) ^
Ian Cook (1994) †
Andrew Baughan (1994)
Victoria Green (1994) + ^
Anna McKenna (1994)
Alexander Chandler (1995) ^ †
Graham Crosthwaite (1995)
Nicola Fox (1996) †
Ashley Thain (1996) +
Nicholas Anderson (1995) + ^
Richard Castle (1998)
Harry Oliver (1999)
Madeleine Reardon (2001) +
Deepak Nagpal (2002)
Katherine Kelsey (2003) +
Martha Holmes (2003) + ^
Caroline Harris (2004)
Jennifer Perrins (2004) ^
Perican Tahir (2004) ^
Peter Newman (2005)
Stephen Jarmain (2005)
Andrea Watts (2006) + ^
Alex Tatton-Bennett (2007) ^
Kate Ozwell (2007) +
Kelan McHugh (2007) ^
Katy Chokowry (2008)
Laura Moys (2008)
Samantha Ridley (2009)
Charlotte Hartley (2009)
Juliet Chapman (2009) ^
George Gordon (2010)
Hayley Boot (2011) ^
Jennifer Palmer (2011)
Louisa Peacock (2012)
Thomas Dance (2012) ^
Helen Pomeroy (2012) ^
Frances Harris (2013) ^
Millicent Benson (2014)
Elizabeth Isaacs QC (1998) (QC-2013)*
Joanna Grice (1991) *
Carolyn Hamilton (1996) *
HH Christian Bevington + °
HH John Altman ° †
Barry Singleton QC (1968) (QC-1989) ° †
Stephen Bellamy QC (1974) (QC-1996) + °
Professor Lucinda Ferguson °

+ Accredited Mediator ^ Public/Direct Access † Arbitrator * Door Tenant ° Associate

THE CHAMBERS 1KBW is a leading set specialising in family law, with a pre-eminent national and international reputation. It is consistently top-ranked for both matrimonial finance and children work, and remains at the cutting edge across the full spectrum of family law. Of all the specialist family sets, 1KBW has the highest number of practitioners ranked in the directories.

THE SET 1KBW comprises 56 barristers, including 10 QCs. The set is widely acknowledged to have an unrivalled breadth of talent, with leading practitioners at every level of seniority and juniors who consistently receive the highest praise.

The set adopts a highly professional , supportive and responsive service to clients. There is a tremendous sense of commitment at this set, both to the development of the law and to the needs of clients. The clerking at this set is second to none, with highly experienced and dedicated clerks offering a wealth of industry knowledge and expertise, all of which is applied when assisting clients with cases honestly, openly and rigorously.

Chambers provides a comprehensive programme of CPD accredited conferences for solicitors, which remain extremely popular and are always highly recommended .

WORK UNDERTAKEN 1KBW is perhaps the only specialist family law set which has a stellar reputation in both matrimonial finance and also in children law.

In matrimonial finance, members of 1KBW have appeared in many of the leading and landmark cases of the last two decades, such as White, Moore, Macfarlane, Miller, Radmacher, Imerman, Charman and many more. Its members continue to act in some of the most high profile cases in the field of matrimonial finance.

In children law, the set boasts many of the current 'stars' in this field, both silks and juniors. Members of 1KBW regularly appear in the leading cases across every aspect of children law: private law children, Hague and wardship abduction and care and adoption proceedings.

Many members of the set also undertake work in the Court of Protection. The experience in dealing with sensitive public and private children cases and finance cases means that its members have a unique set of skills to deal with Court of Protection work. The set's history of advocacy in the criminal courts is often said to give it the edge over its rivals within the family courts.

1KBW has one of the most innovative and experienced dispute resolution teams in the country, comprising 22 members of whom 8 are QCs, and led by nationally acclaimed mediator Anthony Kirk QC.

7 KING'S BENCH WALK Gavin Kealey QC

7 King's Bench Walk, Temple, London, EC4Y 7DS
Tel (020) 7910 8300 **Fax** (020) 7910 8400 **DX** LDE 239
Email clerks@7kbw.co.uk **Website** www.7kbw.co.uk

Head of Chambers	Gavin Kealey QC
Senior Clerks	Bernie Hyatt 07850 878396
	Greg Leyden 07768 008116
Clerks	Eddie Johns
	Gary Rose
	Joe Clayton
Business Development	Brian Lee
Tenants	60

MEMBERS

Gavin Kealey QC (1977) (QC-1994)
Timothy Saloman QC (1975) (QC-1993)
Francis Reynolds (Hon) QC (1960) (QC-1993)
Jonathan Gaisman QC (1979) (QC-1995)
Clive Freedman QC (1978) (QC-1997)
Dominic Kendrick QC (1981) (QC-1997)
Alistair Schaff QC (1983) (QC-1999)
Stephen Hofmeyr QC (1982) (QC-2000)
Christopher Butcher QC (1986) (QC-2001)
Adam Fenton QC (1984) (QC-2003)
Stephen Kenny QC (1987) (QC-2006)
Richard Southern QC (1987) (QC-2006)
Robert Bright QC (1987) (QC-2006)
David Bailey QC (1989) (QC-2006)
David Edwards QC (1989) (QC-2006) ^
Julia Dias QC (1982) (QC-2008)
David Allen QC (1990) (QC-2008)
S J Phillips QC (1993) (QC-2009)
Siobán Healy QC (1993) (QC-2010)
James Drake QC (1998) (QC-2011)
Peter MacDonald Eggers QC (1999) (QC-2011)
Andrew Wales QC (1992) (QC-2012)
Rebecca Sabben-Clare QC (1993) (QC-2012)
Richard Waller QC (1994) (QC-2012)
Charles Priday (1982)
Gavin Geary (1989)
Jawdat Khurshid (1994)
Timothy Kenefick (1996)
Charles Holroyd (1997)
Simon Kerr (1997)
James Brocklebank (1999)
Michael Holmes (1999)
Benjamin Parker (2000)
Anna Gotts (2001)
Alexander MacDonald (2001)
Josephine Higgs (2000)
Jessica Sutherland (2003)
Marcus Mander (2005)
N G Casey (2005)
Richard Sarll (2005)
Emma Hilliard (2006)
Sarah Cowey (2006)
Sushma Ananda (2007)
Sarah Martin (2008)
Sandra Healy (2007)
Adam Turner (2008)
Elizabeth Lindesay (2009)
Tim Jenns (2009)
Jocelin Gale (2009)
Keir Howie (2010) ^
Michael Ryan (2011)
Harry Wright (2012)
Stephen Du (2012)
Jason Robinson (2012)
Clara Benn (2012)
Andrew Pearson (2013)
Natalie Connor (2014)
James Goudkamp (2014) (NSW Bar 2005)
Philip Aspin (2014)
Frederick Alliott (2015)
Sir Jeremy Cooke +

^ Public/Direct Access + Arbitrator

THE CHAMBERS 7 King's Bench Walk (7KBW) has a pre-eminent reputation for excellence and intellectual rigour in all areas of commercial law. They are at the cutting edge of developments in commercial law. The members of 7KBW pride themselves on adapting matters of intellect to practical and commercial priorities, producing a hand-crafted and modern approach to advocacy and advice.

As advocates, members of 7KBW accept instructions to appear in any court, tribunal or board of enquiry in England and Wales. 7KBW specialises in cases before the Commercial Court and in commercial arbitrations in London. With their commercial expertise, members also appear in other jurisdictions, including Hong Kong, Singapore, Bermuda, Cayman Islands, the Bahamas, the British Virgin Islands and Gibraltar, and before international arbitration tribunals in numerous jurisdictions.
Members undertake advisory work and the creation of written submissions and legal documents for litigation and non-contentious matters. Members regularly sit as arbitrators and/or mediators and also as court-appointed examiners for the purpose of conducting deposition hearings. Several members have written or contributed to leading legal textbooks, articles in the press and journals, and contributed to academic research.

WORK UNDERTAKEN 7KBW's practice areas are exclusively commercial. Members have a respected expertise in the full breadth of commercial law: 7KBW has maintained an enviable reputation and experience in all aspects of insurance and reinsurance; shipping and transport; professional negligence; international trade and commodities; energy, oil and gas; international arbitration; injunctions and arrests; shipbuilding; banking and financial services; product liability; futures and derivatives; aviation; media and communications; construction; conflicts of law; state immunity; international investment and a growing reputation in civil fraud.
A large proportion of 7KBW's practice is of an international flavour and members regularly work with overseas clients and foreign lawyers. In appropriate circumstances members are delighted to accept instructions directly from overseas clients and foreign lawyers.

RECRUITMENT 7KBW attracts pupils of only the highest quality, and pursues a policy of only taking tenants of such quality either from those starting their careers in law or from those in mid-career who have elected to change from another part of the profession. The emphasis on quality has meant a steady but selective growth in the overall number of tenants over the past years.
7KBW is the Insurance Set of The Year, an accolade awarded by Chambers UK in 2006, 2007, 2008, 2009, 2010, 2011, 2013 and 2014. For further information about 7 King's Bench Walk and the range of work carried out by its members, please visit the chambers' website at www.7kbw.co.uk.

12 KING'S BENCH WALK Paul Russell QC

12 King's Bench Walk, Temple, London, EC4Y 7EL
Tel (020) 7583 0811 **Fax** (020) 7583 7228 **DX** 1037 Chancery Lane
Email chambers@12kbw.co.uk **Website** www.12kbw.co.uk

Head of Chambers	Paul Russell QC
Senior Clerk	Graham Johnson
Tenants	83

MEMBERS

Paul Russell QC (1984) (QC-2011)
Ronald Walker QC (1962) (QC-1983)
Richard Methuen QC (1972) (QC-1997)
Andrew Hogarth QC (1974) (QC-2003)
Frank Burton QC (1982) (QC-1998)
Gerard Martin QC (1978) (QC-2000)
Stephen Worthington QC (1976) (QC-2006)
William Featherby QC (1978) (QC-2008)
Michael Rawlinson QC (1991) (QC-2009)
William Audland QC (1992) (QC-2015)
Harry Steinberg QC (1997) (QC-2016)
Brian Gallagher (1975)
Simon Levene (1977)
David Sanderson (1985)
Nigel Lewers (1986)
Henry Charles (1987)
Andrew Pickering (1987)
Hugh Hamill (1988)
Adam Chambers (1989)
Catherine Brown (1990)
Kate Chandler (1990)
Michael Brace (1991)
James Candlin (1991)
Gary Thornett (1991)
Patrick Vincent (1992)
Stephanie Jackson (1992)
Portia Spears (1992)
Joel Kendall (1993)
Arun Katyar (1993)
Richard Viney (1994)
Carolyn D'Souza (1994)
Daniel Tobin (1994)
Marcus Dignum (1994)
Catherine Peck (1995)
Lucy Murray (1995)
Timothy Petts (1996)
Louise Thomson (1996)
Simon John (1996)
Benedict Leech (1997)
Pankaj Madan (1997)
Kweku Aggrey-Orleans (1998)
Katherine Awadalla (1998)
David Callow (1998)
David White (1999)
Lisa Stephenson (1999)
David Sharpe (1999)
Andrew Ward (2000)
Charlotte Reynolds (2001)
Angela Frost (2001)
Andrew Roy (2002)
Ruth Greenwood (2003)
Mary Newnham (2003)
James Sullivan (2005)
Gemma Scott (2005)
Charlotte Law (2005)
Patrick Kerr (2006)
Sarah Beslee (2006)
Henrietta Consolo (2006)
Alex Carington (2006)
John-Paul Swoboda (2006)
Roisin Kennedy (2006)
Emily Read (2007)
Charles Robertshaw (2007)
Niall Maclean (2008)
Thomas Pacey (2008)
Lois Aldred (2008)
Thea Wilson (2008)
Oliver Rudd (2009)
Vanessa Cashman (2009)
Ghazaleh Rezaie (2009)
Rory Badenoch (2010)
Thomas Banks(2010)
Nina Ross (2010)
Rachit Buch (2010)
Daniel Sokol (2011)
Isaac Hogarth (2011)
Aliyah Akram (2012)
Edward Ramsay (2012)
Achas Burin (2012)
Andrew Watson (2013)
James Beeton (2013)
Max Archer (2014)
Kate Boakes (2014)

THE CHAMBERS 12 King's Bench Walk continues to grow rapidly and now has 83 barristers, including 11 silks. It provides a modern and professional service to its clients. Chambers is best known for the bringing and defending of personal injury claims, industrial disease claims, clinical negligence claims and employment law. That said its expertise is actually much wider. When the ability to understand difficult areas in the law of tort is required, when the issues of quantum of damages arise and when an understanding of personal injury claims and employment law are both required, you will find that 12KBW barristers have appeared in many of the leading cases. When fraud or professional negligence arises in the context of personal injury or employment law claims, 12KBW has a wealth of expertise in these areas. Chambers brings its expertise in its core areas of practice to clinical and professional negligence claims, to regulatory and disciplinary work, international and travel litigation, cost litigation, fraud and credit hire cases and all aspects of work for public authorities.

WORK UNDERTAKEN Covering the whole of England and Wales (and further afield).
From offices in London, 12KBW covers the whole of England and Wales. Three members of 12KBW are also members of the Irish and Northern Irish Bars and one is a member of the Ghanian Bar. Members of chambers also appear in Employment Tribunals and the EAT in Scotland and Northern Ireland on a regular basis.
From the smallest case to the largest, whether the case is before a District Judge or the Supreme Court, chambers is able to offer a range of suitable barristers to handle the case.
Lectures and seminars: Chambers hold a series of evening seminars each year and two major half day programmes, one on personal injury litigation and the other on employment and discrimination law. In addition it provides lectures at clients' premises on request. Details of its current seminar programme is available on the website.

12

12 King's Bench Walk

LANDMARK CHAMBERS

180 Fleet Street, London, EC4A 2HG
Tel (020) 7430 1221 **Fax** (020) 7421 6060 **DX** 1042 LDE
Email clerks@landmarkchambers.co.uk **Website** www.landmarkchambers.co.uk

Heads of Chambers	Richard Drabble QC Neil Cameron QC
Senior Clerk	Jay Fullilove
Tenants	85

MEMBERS

Richard Drabble QC (1975) (QC-1995)
Neil Cameron QC (1982) (QC-2009)
Christopher Lockhart-Mummery QC (1971) (QC-1986)
Patrick Clarkson QC (1972) (QC-1991)
William Hicks QC (1975) (QC-1995)
Christopher Katkowski QC (1982) (QC-1999)
David Elvin QC (1983) (QC-2000)
John Male QC (1976) (QC-2000)
Neil King QC (1980) (QC-2000)
John Hobson QC (1980) (QC-2000)
Rhodri Price Lewis QC (1975) (QC-2001)
Timothy Corner QC (1981) (QC-2002)
Russell Harris QC (1986) (QC-2003)
Tim Mould QC (1987) (QC-2006)
Nathalie Lieven QC (1989) (QC-2006)
Paul Brown QC (1991) (QC-2009)
John Litton QC (1989) (QC-2010)
Katharine Holland QC (1989) (QC-2010)
Stephen Knafler QC (1993) (QC-2010)
David Lock QC (1985) (QC-2011)
David Holland QC (1986) (QC-2011)
Timothy Morshead QC (1995) (QC-2011)
Rupert Warren QC (1994) (QC-2012)
Sasha White QC (1991) (QC-2013)
Christopher Boyle QC (1994) (QC-2013)
James Maurici QC (1996) (QC-2013)
Reuben Taylor QC (1990) (QC-2014)
David Forsdick QC (1993) (QC-2014)
Dan Kolinsky QC (1998) (QC-2015)
Tom Weekes QC (1995) (QC-2016)
Lisa Busch QC (2000) (QC-2016)
Stephen Bickford-Smith (1972)
Eian Caws (1974)
Christopher Lewsley (1976)
Simon Pickles (1978)
David Smith (1980)
Thomas Jefferies (1981)
Stephen Morgan (1983)
Richard Langham (1986)
Nicholas Taggart (1991)
Christopher Jacobs (1994)
Camilla Lamont (1995)
Declan O'Callaghan (1995)
Graeme Keen (1995)
Matthew Reed (1995)
Philip Nathan (1996)
Scott Lyness (1996)
Toby Watkin (1996)
Samantha Broadfoot (1997)
Myriam Stacey (1998)
Carine Patry (1999)
Stephen Whale (1999)
Katherine Olley (1999)
Robert Walton (1999)
Galina Ward (2000)
Guy Williams (2000)
Tim Buley (2000)
Graham Denholm (2001)
David Blundell (2001)
David Nicholls (2002)
Aaron Walder (2002)
Zoe Leventhal (2002)
Charles Banner (2004)
Gwion Lewis (2005)
Richard Moules (2005)
Sasha Blackmore (2005)
Jonathan Wills (2006)
Katrina Yates (2006)
Jacqueline Lean (2007)
Louisa Nye (2007)
Richard Turney (2007)
Toby Fisher (2008)
Richard Clarke (2009)
Zack Simons (2009)
Katie Helmore (2009)
Andrew Parkinson (2010)
Andrew Byass (2010)
Leon Glenister (2011)
Thomas Davis (2011)
Heather Sargent (2011)
Alistair Mills (2011)
Yaaser Vanderman (2012)
Matthew Dale-Harris (2012)
Matthew Fraser (2013)
Luke Wilcox (2013)

THE CHAMBERS Landmark Chambers' 85 barristers offer advice and advocacy across the spectrum of planning, property, public, commercial and environmental law. Their work includes ratings and valuation, infrastructure and compulsory purchase, regulation, leasehold enfranchisement, mediation and arbitration, in the UK, Europe and internationally. The chambers have significant experience of litigation in the Supreme Court, Court of Appeal, High Court, the European Court of Justice, the European General Court, the European Court of Human Rights, the UN Aarhus Compliance Committee, the Northern Ireland courts and the courts of a number of other jurisdictions, including Hong Kong.

WORK UNDERTAKEN

Planning: Landmark remains at the forefront of the UK planning world. Climate change, nuclear power, new coal-fired power stations with carbon capture storage, wind farms and other renewable energy schemes, airport expansion, iconic bridges and buildings, rail and road infrastructure, retail and leisure, housing and mixed-use schemes are dealt with on a daily basis.

Property: Landmark offers particular expertise in commercial and residential landlord and tenant, leasehold enfranchisement, boundary disputes, easements, restrictive covenants, mortgages, land registration, adverse possession and proprietary estoppel. Members of the property team continue to be the first choice for solicitors instructed by clients wishing to injunct or remove squatters and protestors from their premises.

Public: Landmark's barristers appear frequently in applications for judicial review and before a range of statutory tribunals and inquiries, as well as appeals, in the UK and beyond. Members cover the full range of public law cases, including education, local government, social security, human rights, immigration, mental health, housing, prisons, and planning and environmental.

Environmental: Landmark's barristers are experts in the environmental aspects of town and country planning, and with their strength in public law they are the natural choice for environmental challenges in the higher courts. Its property team have experience at all levels of advising on environment-related issues.

LITTLETON CHAMBERS Selwyn Bloch QC & Naomi Ellenbogen QC

3 King's Bench Walk North, Temple, London, EC4Y 7HR
Tel (020) 7797 8600 **Fax** (020) 7797 8699/8697 **DX** 1047
Email clerks@littletonchambers.co.uk **Website** www.littletonchambers.com

Head of Chambers	Selwyn Bloch QC Naomi Ellenbogen QC
Commercial Director	Nigel McEwen
Clerks	Tim Tarring Jason Drakeford
A/Cs Receivable Manager	Joanne Ashby
Tenants	59

MEMBERS

Selwyn Bloch QC (1982) (QC-2000)
Naomi Ellenbogen QC (1992) (QC-2010)
Andrew Clarke QC (1980) (QC-1997)
Ian Mayes QC (1974) (QC-1993)
Richard Price OBE QC (1969) (QC-1996)
John Bowers QC (1979) (QC-1998)
David Reade QC (1983) (QC-2006)
Charles Samek QC (1989) (QC-2009)
Paul Gilroy QC (1985) (QC-2006)
Damian Brown QC (1989) (QC-2012)
Stuart Ritchie QC (1995) (QC-2012)
Gavin Mansfield QC (1992) (QC-2013)
Michael Duggan QC (1984) (QC-2014)
Daniel Tatton-Brown QC (1994) (QC-2016)
Jonathan Cohen QC (1999) (QC-2016)
Richard Perkoff (1971)
Timothy Higginson (1977)
Martin Fodder (1983)
Antony Sendall (1984)
Peter Trepte (1987)
Sam Neaman (1988)
Rupert D'Cruz (1989)
Jeremy Lewis (1992)
Chris Quinn (1992)
Jamie Riley (1995)
Carol Davis (1996)
Mohinderpal Sethi (1996)
Dale Martin (1997)
Niran de Silva (1997)
Nicholas Siddall (1997)
Adam Solomon (1998)
Lucy Bone (1999)
Matthew Sheridan (2000)
Ming-Yee Shiu (2000)
Eleena Misra (2001)
James Wynne (2002)
Martin Palmer (2003)
David Lascelles (2003)
Daniel Northall (2004)
Edward Kemp (2005)
John Mehrzad (2005)
Katherine Apps (2006)
Alexander Robson (2006)
Charlotte Davies (2006)
Lydia Banerjee (2007)
Laura McNair-Wilson (2007)
James Bickford Smith (2008)
Charlene Hawkins (2008)
Nicholas Goodfellow (2009)
Craig Rajgopaul (2010)
Benjamin Gray (2011)
James McWilliams (2011)
Marc Delehanty (2011)
Mark Humphreys (2012)
Sophia Berry (2012)
Grahame Anderson (2013)
Jamie Susskind (2013)
Georgina Bryan (2014)
Mauro Rubino-Sammartano (1961) ++
Lord Hacking (1963) ++
Pierre A Karrer (1969) ++
Colin Manning (1970) ++
Mark H Lomas QC (1977) (QC-2003) ++
Matthieu de Boisséson (1978) ++
Wolfgang Peter (1979) ++
Kelly Pennifer (1994) ++
Erika Szyszczak (2004) ++
Samuel Haubold ++

++ Associate Tenant

CHAMBERS: Littleton is a leading employment and commercial chambers. The set's highly regarded team of 59 barristers includes 15 silks, all of whom provide exceptional advice and advocacy to our clients. Littleton members' practices cover a wide spectrum of work, including employment law; commercial law incorporating banking, commercial fraud, insolvency, financial services and insurance; disciplinary and regulatory; sports law; injunctions; mediation and arbitration.

WORK UNDERTAKEN: Littleton offers specialist advice and representation across a number of key Practice Areas. These are: arbitration; commercial litigation; disciplinary and regulatory; employment; injunctions; insolvency; international; investigations; mediation: partnership and LLP; public law and human rights; sport.

LITTLETON

RECRUITMENT

Members of Chambers fund two pupils per year. Chambers are members of Pupillage Gateway. Placing value not only on the skills of its tenants as advocates and lawyers, but also on their practical and friendly approach Littleton aim to take on pupils who in addition to an excellent academic record, show a flair for advocacy and have the strong interpersonal skills necessary to succeed at the modern day Bar.

MAITLAND CHAMBERS Christopher Pymont QC

7 Stone Buildings, Lincoln's Inn, London, WC2A 3SZ
Tel (020) 7406 1200 **Fax** (020) 7406 1300 **DX** LDE 326
Email clerks@maitlandchambers.com **Website** www.maitlandchambers.com

Head of Chambers	Christopher Pymont QC
Chambers Director	Stewart Thompson
Senior Clerk	John Wiggs
Deputy Senior Clerks	Rob Penson Harry Gilson
Clerks	Colin Dawson Danny Wilkinson Sam Dempsey Jason Windle Amber Downey
Administrator	Valerie Piper
Tenants	71

MEMBERS

Christopher Pymont QC (1979) (QC-1996)
Christopher McCall QC (1966) (QC-1987)
Michael Driscoll QC (1970) (QC-1992)
Catherine Newman QC (1979) (QC-1995)
Anthony Trace QC (1981) (QC-1998)
Mark Cunningham QC (1980) (QC-2001)
Paul Girolami QC (1983) (QC-2002)
John McGhee QC (1984) (QC-2003)
Matthew Collings QC (1985) (QC-2006)
John Nicholls QC (1986) (QC-2006)
Edwin Johnson QC (1987) (QC-2006)
Christopher Parker QC (1984) (QC-2008)
Dominic Chambers QC (1987) (QC-2008)
Nicholas Peacock QC (1989) (QC-2009)
Jonathan Russen QC (1986) (QC-2010)
Richard Morgan QC (1988) (QC-2011)
Amanda Tipples QC (1991) (QC-2011)
Andrew Walker QC (1991) (QC-2011)
Michael Gibbon QC (1993) (QC-2011)
Andrew Trigger QC (1994) (QC-2011)
Edmund Cullen QC (1991) (QC-2012)
Rebecca Stubbs QC (1994) (QC-2012)
Timothy Dutton QC (1985) (QC-2013)
Mark Wonnacott QC (1989) (QC-2013)
Thomas Grant QC (1993) (QC-2013)
James Aldridge QC (1994) (QC-2014)
Andrew Ayres QC (1996) (QC-2015)
Simon Nesbitt QC (2015) (QC-2015)
Alan Johns QC (1994) (QC-2016)
David Mumford QC (2000) (QC-2016)
Nigel Thomas (1976)
Timothy Evans (1979)
John Dagnall (1983)
James Clifford (1984)
Philomena Harrison (1985)
Gregory Banner (1989)
Michael Pryor (1992)
Andrew Westwood (1994)
Siward Atkins (1995)
James Hanham (1996)
Paul Clarke (1997)
Catherine Addy (1998)
Louise Hutton (1998)
George Hayman (1998)
Tim Calland (1991)
Matthew Smith (2001)
Adam Smith (2001)
Rebecca Page (2001)
Benjamin John (2002)
Richard Fowler (2003)
Olivier Kalfon (2003)
Ciaran Keller (2004)
Alec McCluskey (2005)
Fiona Dewar (2005)
Watson Pringle (2005)
Thomas Munby (2006)
Jonathan Allcock (2007)
Rosanna Foskett (2008)
Laurie Scher (2008)
James Sheehan (2008)
Oliver Phillips (2009)
James Ballance (2009)
Narinder Jhittay (2010)
Hannah Ilett (2011)
Duncan McCombe (2012)
Maxim Cardew (2012)
Laurie Brock (2013)
James Kinman (2013)
Edward Granger (2013)
Edward Meuli (2014)
Amanda Hadkiss (2014)

THE CHAMBERS Maitland Chambers is widely recognised as one of the leading sets at the English Bar practising primarily in the field of commercial chancery litigation. Its multi-disciplinary expertise across a broad range of both chancery and commercial disciplines has proved crucial to clients where cases span a number of areas, and provides an advantage in terms of the service offered when traditional specialisms overlap. Maitland Chambers is one of the largest commercial chancery sets, with over 70 members, including 30 silks.

WORK UNDERTAKEN Maitland Chambers have the breadth and depth to provide advocacy and advisory services in every area that can arise in a business dispute. It handles a very wide range of cases, from major litigation involving multi-national companies to county court disputes. Much of its work is done in London, although it frequently advises and appears for clients in other parts of the United Kingdom. Many of its members also practise in other jurisdictions including Hong Kong, Singapore, the Cayman Islands, the British Virgin Islands, Brunei, Cyprus, the Channel Islands and the USA.
Modern cases often do not fit neatly into traditional categories. Maitland's size and breadth of expertise ensures that it can provide teams of barristers to deal rapidly and thoroughly with complex cases that raise a wide range of issues. As such, it has an advantage over those who specialise in narrower fields of business law.

INTERNATIONAL Although based in London, Maitland Chambers regularly acts in non-UK cases where members' expertise in English law (and familiarity with overseas law and jurisdictions), oral and written advocacy skills, and litigation experience provide genuine added value. Members advise; appear as advocates before foreign courts and tribunals; otherwise assist in the conduct or resolution of disputes (including all forms of ADR); and provide expert evidence of law in foreign proceedings.

MATRIX CHAMBERS

Griffin Building, Gray's Inn, London, WC1R 5LN
Tel (020) 7404 3447 **DX** 400 Chancery Lane
Email matrix@matrixlaw.co.uk **Website** www.matrixlaw.co.uk / www.matrixlawinternational.com

Joint Chairs of the Management Committee Helen Mountfield QC & Hugh Southey QC
Chief Executive Lindsay Scott
Tenants 86

MEMBERS

Mark Afeeva (1997)
Nick Armstrong (2001) (Solicitor 1998)
Alex Bailin QC (1995) (QC-2010)
Andrew Bodnar (1995)
Prof Laurence Boisson de Chazournes ++
Lord Daniel Brennan QC (1967) (QC-1985) ++
Christopher Brown (2002)
Joanna Buckley (2011)
Michelle Butler (2007) (Solicitor (New South Wales) 2002)
Chris Buttler (2004)
Prof Christine Chinkin (2003)
Prof Andrew Choo (2002)
Ayesha Christie (2014)
Prof Andrew Clapham (1985) ++
Kate Cook (1990)
Edward Craven (2007)
Claire Darwin (2005)
Anita Davies (2011)
Raj Desai (2010) (Solicitor 2007)
Prof Zachary Douglas QC (2006) (QC-2015)
Ben Emmerson QC (1986) (QC-2000)
Danny Friedman QC (1996) (QC-2013)
Prof Conor Gearty (1995)
Nicholas Gibson (2009) (Solicitor 2004)
Jonathan Glasson QC (1996) (Solicitor 1995) (QC-2013)
Luis Gonzalez García ++ (Qualified in Mexico, Qualified with the Bar Council as a Foreign Lawyer)
Sarah Hannett (2003)
Richard Hermer QC (1993) (QC-2009)
Sir Anthony Hooper ++
Anthony Hudson QC (1996) (QC-2015)
Raza Husain QC (1993) (QC-2010)
Darryl Hutcheon (2014)
Tamara Jaber (2013)
Sir Paul Jenkins QC (Hon) (1977) ++
Jessica Jones (2013)
Phillippa Kaufmann QC (1991) (QC-2011)
Janet Kentridge (1999)
Thomas Kibling (1990)
Samantha Knights (1996)
Julian B Knowles QC (1994) (QC-2011)
James Laddie QC (1995) (QC-2012)
Helen Law (2005)
Thomas Linden QC (1989) (QC-2006)
Rachel Logan (2008) ++
Alison Macdonald (2000)
Lord Ken Macdonald QC (1978) (QC-1997) ++
Sara Mansoori (1997)
Prof Jonathan Marks (1992)
Aileen McColgan (2001)
Gavin Millar QC (1981) (QC-2000)
Eleni Mitrophanous (1999)
Karon Monaghan QC (1989) (QC-2008)
Clare Montgomery QC (1980) (QC-1996)
Prof Gillian Morris (1997)
Helen Mountfield QC (1991) (QC-2010)
Prof Sean Murphy ++
Paul Nicholls QC (1992) (QC-2012)
Blinne Ní Ghrálaigh (2005) (Belfast 2013)
Aidan O'Neill QC (Scotland 1987) (1996) (QC-1999 Scotland)
Tim Owen QC (1983) (QC-2000)
Laura Prince (2003)
Elizabeth Prochaska (2007)
Mathew Purchase (2002)
Nicholas Randall QC (1990) (QC-2013)
Matthew Ryder QC (1992) (QC-2010)
Adam Sandell (2008)
Prof Philippe Sands QC (1985) (QC-2003)
Maurice Sheridan (1984)
Ben Silverstone (2009)
Jessica Simor QC (1992) (QC-2013)
Kirsten Sjøvoll (2012)
Lorna Skinner (1997)
Andrew Smith (2008)
Hugh Southey QC (1996) (QC-2010)
Daniel Squires QC (1998) (QC-2016)
Mark Summers QC (1996) (QC-2014)
Prof Christian Tams ++
Booan Temple (2001) ++
Rhodri Thompson QC (1989) (QC-2002)
Hugh Tomlinson QC (1983) (QC-2002)
Prof Takis Tridimas (2000)
Guy-Vassall Adams QC (2000) (QC-2016)
Aaron Watkins (2006)
Angeline Welsh (2015) (Belize 2015) (Solicitor 2003)
Antony White QC (1983) (Northern Ireland 2016) (QC-2001)
David Wolfe QC (1992) (QC-2012)

++ Associate

THE CHAMBERS Matrix is a barristers' chambers with offices in London and Geneva. Its members work in a wide number of areas, including commercial, public international and arbitration, investigations and audits, competition and EU law, human rights, public, employment, equality and discrimination, and criminal including white collar crime, fraud and extradition and mutual assistance. Matrix operates within a modern environment, where diversity, accessibility and client care are widely championed.

More details about practice areas can be found on the website. The UK website can be found at matrixlaw.co.uk. The international website at matrixlawinternational.com.

MONCKTON CHAMBERS Tim Ward QC & Philip Moser QC

1 & 2 Raymond Buildings, Gray's Inn, London, WC1R 5NR
Tel (020) 7405 7211 **Fax** (020) 7405 2084 **DX** 257 LDE
Email chambers@monckton.com **Website** www.monckton.com

Head of Chambers	Tim Ward QC, Philip Moser QC
Senior Clerk	David Hockney
Tenants	61

MEMBERS

Tim Ward QC (1994) (QC-2011)
Philip Moser QC (1992) (QC-2012) ^
Michael Collins SC(1978) (SC-1994) *
David Unterhalter SC (2009) (SC-2001)
Melanie Hall QC (1982) (QC-2002) ^
Michael Bowsher QC (1985) ^ (QC-2006)
Jon Turner QC (1988) (QC-2006)
Ian Wise QC (1992) (QC-2010)
Paul Harris QC (1994) (QC-2011)
Daniel Beard QC (1996) (QC-2011)
Kassie Smith QC (1995) (QC-2013)
Michael Fitzgerald (1979) ^
Stephen Cragg QC (1996)
Ian Rogers QC (1995) (QC-2014) ^
George Peretz QC (1990) (QC-2015) ^
Meredith Pickford QC (1999) (QC-2015) ^
Gerry Facenna QC (2001) (QC-2016) ^
Christopher Muttukumaru CB (1974)
Peter Oliver (1977)
Andrew Macnab (1986) ^
Peter Mantle (1989) ^
Raymond Hill (1992)
Alistair Lindsay (1993) ^
Rebecca Haynes (1994)
Ben Rayment (1996) ^
Josh Holmes (1997)
Robert Palmer (1998) ^
Ronit Kreisberger (1999)
Eric Metcalfe (1999) ^
Piers Gardner (2000) ^
Valentina Sloane (2000) ^
Julian Gregory (2000)
Rob Williams (2000)
Anneli Howard (2002) ^
Alan Bates (2003) ^
Ben Lask (2003) ^
Philip Woolfe (2004)
Jeremy McBride (2004) ^ *
Brendan McGurk (2004)
Azeem Suterwalla (2004)
Drew Holiner (2005) ^
Fiona Banks (2006) ^
Ewan West (2006) ^
Anneliese Blackwood (2007)
Laura John (2007) ^
Ligia Osepciu (2008)
Steve Broach (2008)
Frank Mitchell (2010) ^
Tarlochan Lall (2010) ^
Julianne Kerr Morrison (2010)
Elizabeth Kelsey (2010)
Nikolaus Grubeck (2010)
Conor McCarthy (2010)
Alison Berridge (2011)
Michael Armitage (2011)
Thomas Sebastian (2012)
Stefan Kuppen (2013)
Daisy Mackersie (2013)
James Bourke (2014)
David Gregory (2014)
Panos Koutrakos (2014) *

* Door Tenant ^ Public/Direct Access

THE CHAMBERS Monckton Chambers is a leading set with expertise across a wide range of commercial and civil law, with a particular focus on EU, competition, VAT other indirect taxes and public and administrative law. The set also has significant international expertise conducting a range of work in the fields of public international law, trade and arbitration. The interrelationship between domestic law, EU law and international human rights law is central to much of Chambers' work, and members have unrivalled expertise in these areas.
Monckton Chambers is recognised as a market leader in specialist advocacy, advisory and dispute-resolution services, and is renowned for members' intellectual rigour, commercial focus and ability to get results. Members of Chambers act for private sector clients (from multinationals to SMEs and private individuals), the UK Government, regulators, local authorities, NGOs and non-UK bodies, including foreign states and the EU institutions. This breadth of experience means that members are sensitive to the commercial objectives of private clients and also have a good understanding of governmental and regulatory decision making processes.
For the latest update on practice areas, barristers' CVs, cases, events, news and publications, please visit www.monckton.com.

INTERNATIONAL Members have an in depth knowledge of foreign domestic laws including a range of EU member states. Several members are also qualified and have rights of audience in foreign jurisdictions including the CIS republics, the Russian Federation, the USA and South Africa. Services are available to all foreign lawyers, businesses and individuals who are located outside of the UK.

RECRUITMENT Monckton Chambers is a member of the Bar Council Pupillage Gateway. Chambers offers pupillage for twelve months. Typically, two pupillages have been offered each year, with pupillage awards of £65,000. In the past 10 years, 19 out of 21 Monckton pupils were offered tenancy.

NEW COURT CHAMBERS Giles Bain & Christopher Poole

New Court Chambers, New Court, Temple, London EC4Y 9BE **DX** 0018 LDE
Tel (020) 7583 5123
Email clerks@newcourtchambers.com **Website** www.newcourtchambers.com

Head of Chambers	Giles Bain Christopher Poole
Senior Clerk	Paul Bloomfield
First Junior Clerk	James Stammers
Tenants	25

MEMBERS

Giles Bain (1993)
Christopher Poole (1996)
Dr Giuseppe Cala (1971)
Ann Courtney (1987)
Elissa Da Costa-Waldman (1990)
Stephen Coyle (1998)
Dinali Nanayakkara (2000)
Sarah McMeechan (2000)
Andrew Shaw (2001)
Tali Michaels (2001)
Wing Chan (2002)
Stephanie Hine (2003)
Anna Hefford (2004)
Sam Wallace (2004)
Sally Jackson (2006)
Kyriacos Lefteri (2006)
Sally Homer (sol 2006) (2012)
Robert Wilkinson (2007)
Raisa Saley (2008)
Philippa Jenkins (2008)
Laura Harrington (2009)
Sarah Nuttall (2011)
Kathryn Blair (2012)
Katherine Couper (2012)
Sabrina Polak (2012)

THE CHAMBERS New Court Chambers is a specialist family set offering expert advice and representation In Public and private Law Children, Court of Protection, Matrimonial Finance and TLATA.

NEW COURT CHAMBERS

THREE NEW SQUARE Richard Miller QC

3 New Square, Lincoln's Inn, London, WC2A 3RS
Tel (020) 7405 1111 **Fax** (020) 7405 7800 **DX** 454 Chancery Lane
Email clerks@3newsquare.co.uk **Website** www.3newsquare.co.uk

Head of Chambers	Richard Miller QC
Senior Clerk	Nicholas Hill
Tenants	19

MEMBERS

Richard Miller QC (1976) (QC-1995)
Guy Burkill QC (1981) (QC-2002)
Andrew Waugh QC (1982) (QC-1998)
Justin Turner QC (1992) (QC-2009)
Thomas Mitcheson QC (1996) (QC-2014)
Douglas Campbell QC (1993) (QC-2016)
Thomas Hinchliffe QC (1997) (QC-2016)
Simon Malynicz QC (1997) (QC-2016)
Denise McFarland (1987)
Geoffrey Pritchard (1998)
Dominic Hughes (2001)
Miles Copeland (2004)
Joe Delaney (2006)
Jeremy Heald (2010)
Stuart Baran (2011)
Tim Austen (2012)
Katherine Moggridge (2012)
Daniele Selmi (2013)
Georgina Messenger (2015)

THE CHAMBERS Chambers has focused on intellectual property litigation for more than 60 years and its 19 tenants, including eight QCs, are all leading practitioners in this area. The set was located at 6 Pump Court, Temple, until April 1995. Former members of chambers include Birss J, Aldous LJ and Falconer J.

All members appear frequently in the High Court, Intellectual Property Enterprise Court and Appellate Courts. They also engage regularly in arbitration work, both as advocates and arbitrators, and in hearings before the UK Intellectual Property Office, the European Patent Office in Munich, the Community Trade Mark and Designs Office (OHIM) in Alicante and the Court of Justice of the European Union in Luxembourg.

Members of chambers receive instructions from solicitors, patent and trade mark attorneys, in-house lawyers and lawyers practising overseas.

The majority of members are scientifically trained at least to graduate level.

Members of chambers also contribute to Terrell on the Law of Patents, the leading textbook in patent law.

WORK UNDERTAKEN Patents, trade marks, passing off, copyright, design (registered and unregistered), breach of confidence, trade secrets malicious falsehood, entertainment and media, restrictive covenants, franchising and the licensing of all intellectual property rights, as well as all aspects of EU law relating to intellectual property.

THREE NEW SQUARE
INTELLECTUAL PROPERTY

4 NEW SQUARE

4 New Square, Lincoln's Inn, London, WC2A 3RJ
Tel (020) 7822 2000 **Fax** (020) 7822 2001 **DX** 1041 L.D.E.
Email clerks@4newsquare.com **Website** www.4newsquare.com

Senior Clerk	Lizzy Stewart
Tenants	80

MEMBERS

Ben Hubble QC (1992) (QC-2009)
John L Powell QC (1974) (QC-1990)
Nicholas Davidson QC (1974) (QC-1993)
Justin Fenwick QC (1980) (QC-1993)
Murray Rosen QC (1976) (QC-1993)
Roger Stewart QC (1986) (QC-2001)
Graham Eklund QC (1984) (QC-2002)
Patrick Lawrence QC (1985) (QC-2002)
Simon Monty QC (1982) (QC-2003)
David Halpern QC (1978) (QC-2006)
Mark Cannon QC (1985) (QC-2008)
Graeme McPherson QC (1993) (QC-2008)
David Turner QC (1992) (QC-2009)
Leigh-Ann Mulcahy QC (1993) (QC-2009)
Ben Patten QC (1986) (QC-2010)
Nicholas Bacon QC (1992) (QC-2010)
Anneliese Day QC (1996) (QC-2012)
Ben Elkington QC (1996) (QC-2012)
Fiona Sinclair QC (1989) (QC-2013)
+ Door Tenant
Nicholas Fletcher QC(1982) (QC-2014)
Jonathan Hough QC (1997) (QC-2014)
Graham Chapman QC (1998) (QC-2014)
Benjamin Williams QC (1994) (QC-2015)
Jamie Smith QC (1995) (QC-2015)
Neil Hext QC (1995) (QC-2015)
Professor Eva Lomnicka (1974)
Charles Douthwaite (1977)
Glen Tyrell (1977)
Paul Parker (1986)
Hugh Evans (1987)
Nigel Burroughs (1991)
Andrew R Nicol (1991)
Charles Phipps (1992)
Nicola Shaldon (1994)
Nicole Sandells (1994)
Robert Marven (1994)
Alex Hall Taylor (1996)
Paul Cowan (1996)
Siân Mirchandani (1997)
Michael Bowmer (1997)
Roger Mallalieu (1998)
Richard Liddell (1999)
Amanda Savage (1999)
Stephen Innes (2000)
Scott Allen (2000)
Dr Peter Feldschreiber (2000)
Helen Evans (2001)
Carl Troman (2001)
Annabel Shaw (2002)
Clare Dixon (2002)
Miles Harris (2003)
Timothy Chelmick (2004)
George Spalton (2004)
Benjamin Wood (2005)
Richard O'Brien (2005)
Katie Powell (2005)
Shail Patel (2006)
Simon Hale (2006)
Hugh Saunders (2006)
George McDonald (2007)
Tom Asquith (2007)
Can Yeginsu (2007)
Daniel Saoul (2008)
Lucy Colter (2008)
Thomas Ogden (2008)
Tom Shepherd (2008)
Ben Smiley (2009)
Nicholas Tolley (2009)
Christopher Greenwood (2009)
Philippa Manby (2010)
Nicholas Broomfield (2010)
Anthony Jones (2011)
Hamid Khanbhai (2011)
Benjamin Fowler (2011)
Paul Fisher (2012)
Peter Morcos (2012)
Marie-Claire O'Kane (2013)
Katherine Del Mar (2013)
Mark Cullen (2013)
Joshua Folkard (2013)
Dr Josh Wilson SC (1987) (SC-2008) +
Jalil Asif QC (1988) (QC-2010)
Dr Julie Maxton (1978) +
Jeffrey Benz (1994) +
Garry Borland (2000 – Scottish Bar, 2014 – English Bar) +
John Bellhouse (1972) +

THE CHAMBERS: 4 New Square is a leading commercial set of barristers comprising 80 practitioners, 25 of whom are Queen's Counsel. Barristers at 4 New Square acts as specialist advocates and advisers in a wide range of commercial disputes worldwide. The also acts as advisers in non contentious disputes. The size of chambers and the range of experience of its members enable 4 New Square to put together balanced teams of counsel to suit the requirements of each individual case. The set has numerous international as well as academic connections.

WORK UNDERTAKEN: Members of chambers are consistently recommended for all types of commercial disputes, often with an international element. The reputation of chambers is particularly strong in relation to claims involving professionals and insurance work as well as in respect of construction disputes, costs, financial services and banking, international arbitration, product liability, sports law as well as regulatory public law and human rights law. Chambers' expertise in professional liability covers the full range of claims against professionals, not just for negligence but for fraud, breach of fiduciary duty and breach of trust, and disciplinary and regulatory proceedings. All main professions are covered by chambers. Chambers has considerable experience in multi-party litigation in the context of civil fraud, product liability, professional negligence and disaster claims. In all those areas members of chambers appear as advocates in the courts and arbitrations at home and in overseas jurisdictions.

PUBLICATIONS: Many members of Chambers have written or contributed to legal textbooks and other published works. Highlights include the following. *Jackson & Powell on Professional Liability* (2015), written by members of the professional liability team, is in its 7th edition and remains a leading authority. The 5-volume *Encyclopaedia of Financial Services Law* (2013) is edited by John Powell QC and Professor Eva Lomnicka while Mark Cannon QC is the co-author of Cannon & McGurk on Professional Indemnity Insurance 2nd ed. (2016). Charles Phipps is author, with Lord Toulson SCJ, of Confidentiality (2013) while Nicholas Bacon QC is a contributing editor of *Cook on Costs* (2013) as well as Halsbury's Laws of England. Leigh-Ann Mulcahy QC is the general editor of *Human Rights and Civil Practice*, to which Scott Allen, Anneliese Day QC and Alex Hall Taylor are contributors while Can Yeginsu is co-author of *The Protections for Religious Rights: Law and Practice* (2013).

8 NEW SQUARE INTELLECTUAL PROPERTY Mark Platts-Mills QC

8 New Square, Lincoln's Inn, London, WC2A 3QP
Tel (020) 7405 4321 **Fax** (020) 7405 9955 **DX** 379 Chancery Lane
Email clerks@8newsquare.co.uk **Website** www.8newsquare.co.uk

Head of Chambers	Mark Platts-Mills QC
Senior Clerk	John Call
Head of Operations	Tony Liddon
Practice Managers	Nicholas Wise
	Martin Williams
	Ben Newham
Assistant Practice Managers	Paul Worrall
	Philip Taylor
Junior Clerk	Max Turner
Business Development Manager	Wendy Holmes
Tenants	29

MEMBERS

Mark Platts-Mills QC (1974) (QC 1995)
John Baldwin QC (1977) (QC 1991)
Martin Howe QC (1978) (QC 1996)
James Mellor QC (1986) (QC-2006)
Daniel Alexander (1988) (QC-2003)
Richard Meade QC (1991) (QC-2008)
Michael Tappin QC (1991) (QC-2009)
Adrian Speck QC (1993) (QC-2012)
Andrew Lykiardopoulos QC (2004) (QC-2014)
Charlotte May QC (1995) (QC-2014)
Thomas Moody-Stuart QC (1995) (QC-2016)
James Abrahams QC (1997) (QC-2016)
Fiona Clark (1982)
Robert Onslow (1991)
James St Ville (1995)
Lindsay Lane (1996)
Iona Berkeley (1999)
Mark Chacksfield (1999)
Henry Ward (2000)
Jonathan Hill (2000)
Jessie Bowhill (2004)
James Whyte (2006)
Quentin Cregan (2003)
Isabel Jamal (2008)
Ashton Chantrielle (2011)
William Duncan (2012)
Jaani Riordan (2012)
Maxwell Keay (2013)
Tom Jones (2013)
Rt Hon Professor Sir Robin Jacob *
His Honour Michael Fysh QC SC *
Professor (Practice) David Llewelyn *
Eleonora Rosati AVV *

* Door Tenants

THE CHAMBERS 8 New Square is the largest set in the UK specialising entirely in intellectual property and related fields of law. All members of chambers are at the forefront of intellectual property litigation, advising on and presenting cases with considerable technical detail. Most have at least an undergraduate science qualification and some have advanced science degrees. Chambers handle litigation for leading commercial organisations around the world, high profile individuals as well as small companies and individuals. Members appear in the major English courts and tribunals including the High Court, Court of Appeal, Supreme Court, Privy Council, The Intellectual Property Office including Trade Marks and Design Registries, as well as in cases before the Copyright Tribunal and the Patents County Court. Several members have written leading textbooks on aspects of intellectual property. The Reports of Patent Cases and The Fleet Street Reports – the two main specialist intellectual property law reports, have been edited from these chambers for many years, as well as the most recent editions of Kerly on Trademarks and Trade Names and The Modern Law of Copyright and Designs.

WORK UNDERTAKEN Patents expertise covers every field of technology. A team from chambers acted in the first ever biotechnology patent appeal to reach the House of Lords, Biogen v Medeva and the subsequent cases of HGS v Lilly and Kirin v Amgen. Members act in cases concerning the validity, infringement and licencing of patents and know-how, including competition aspects. All members of chambers have wide experience in trademark infringement, validity and passing-off litigation as well as disputes concerning ownership of trademarks. Ground breaking cases, such as Jif Lemon in the House of Lords and the long running Budweiser trademark dispute have all been handled by members of 8 New Square. Copyright litigation and advice includes disputes over industrial design and artistic works, including fashion, as well as music and literary copyright. Breach of confidence is also an area of expertise including employer/employee disputes. Entertainment and media related disputes form a large part of chambers' work. Cases have involved leading companies and prominent individuals. Work in this area covers film, music, and other related media contracts, publishing and broadcasting disputes and performers rights. Information technology is another major area of chambers' practice. This includes contractual disputes before the Technology and Construction Court, advice on internet and domain names database rights and data protection. Further information and news is available on the chambers website www.8newsquare.co.uk

INTERNATIONAL Not only do members act in the major European courts, they also act in domestic and international arbitrations and mediations. Some are qualified to practise and appear in various courts overseas, including the Far East and the West Indies.

RECRUITMENT Chambers offers up to 2 pupillages per year via Pupillage Gateway (Online Pupillage Application Scheme). Pupils with a scientific or technical background are strongly encouraged. Selective two day mini pupillages are available during term time.

8 NEW SQUARE
INTELLECTUAL PROPERTY

NEW SQUARE CHAMBERS James Thom QC

Head of Chambers	James Thom QC
Head of Clerking	Phil Reeves
Tenants	48

12 New Square, Lincoln's Inn, London, WC2A 3SW
Tel (020) 7419 8000 **Fax** (020) 7419 8050 **DX** 1056 London/Chancery Lane
Email clerks@newsquarechambers.co.uk **Website** www.newsquarechambers.co.uk

MEMBERS

James Thom QC (1974) (QC-2003)
John Macdonald QC (1955) (QC-1976)
George Laurence QC (1972) (QC-1991)
Robin Hollington QC (1979) (QC-1999)
Philip Hackett QC (1978) (QC-1999)
Michael Booth QC (1981) (QC-1999)
Nicholas Le Poidevin QC (1975) (QC-2010)
Rodney Stewart Smith (1964)
Lynton Tucker (1971)
Malcolm Chapple (1975)
Christopher Semken (1977)
Alexander Hill-Smith (1978)
Leigh Sagar (1983)
David Eaton Turner (1984)
Claire Staddon (1985)
Thomas Graham (1985)
David Fisher (1985)
Ross Crail (1986)
Charles Holbech (1988)
Stephen Schaw Miller (1988)
Ian Peacock (1990)
Gerard van Tonder (1990)
Edwin Simpson (1990)
Simon Adamyk (1991)
Mark Hubbard (1991)
John Eidinow (1992)
Nigel Hood (1993)
Jonathan Lopian (1994)
Sebastian Prentis (1996)
Madeleine Heal (1996)
David Warner (1996)
Gary Pryce (1997)
Adrian Pay (1999)
James Bailey (1999)
James Brightwell (2000)
Alexander Learmonth (2000)
Nicola Allsop (2002)
Conn MacEvilly (1997)
Charlotte Ford (2007)
Caley Wright (2008)
Anna Littler (2008)
Thomas Fletcher (2009)
Christopher Lloyd (2011)
Kira King (2011)
Francesca Perselli (2011)
Gabriella McNicholas (2013)
Jessica Rajakumar (2014)
Jon Colclough (2015)

THE CHAMBERS New Square Chambers is a leading commercial chancery set. It has 48 members, including seven QCs. In addition to its extensive experience of advocacy before all levels of court and tribunal in England and Wales, the set has extensive experience in other jurisdictions, especially those offshore.

WORK UNDERTAKEN New Square Chambers' main fields of work are commercial litigation (including civil fraud, freezing injunctions, search and other interim orders), company and insolvency (including individual and corporate insolvency, voluntary arrangements, receiverships and administrations, claims relating to shareholders, directors and partnerships), trusts and estates (including contentious matters, offshore trusts, probate claims, commercial and pension trusts) and property law (including landlord and tenant, mortgages, enfranchisement, conveyancing and real property rights). Members also practice in public and administrative law, particularly where relating to property rights and housing (including public enquiries, local government and planning law, judicial review and constitutional law) and in the fields of intellectual property and telecommunications. The set also deals with professional negligence and regulatory matters. Licensed Access work is accepted and a number of members accept Public Access instructions. New Square Chambers acts in mediations and before arbitrators.

INTERNATIONAL The set offers its clients the benefit of the wide experience it has built up over many years in other common law jurisdictions and in appeals to the Privy Council from those jurisdictions including: Anguilla, Antigua, the Bahamas, Bermuda, the British Virgin Islands, the Cayman Islands, Gibraltar, Guernsey, Hong Kong, the Isle of Man, Jersey, Nevis, Singapore and the Turks and Caicos Islands.

RECRUITMENT Applications for pupillage to be made directly to chambers via its website.

NO5 CHAMBERS Mark Anderson QC

Greenwood House, 4-7 Salisbury Court, London, EC4Y 8AA
Tel (0845) 210 5555 **Fax** (020) 7900 1582 **DX** 449 London Chancery Lane
Email info@no5.com **Website** www.No5.com

Head of Chambers	Mark Anderson QC
Deputy Heads	Rex Tedd QC
	Jonathon Jones QC
	Nageena Khalique QC
Practice Director	Tony McDaid
Tenants	263

THE CHAMBERS No5 Chambers is a national set offering a comprehensive across-the-board service. Throughout its 100-year history, No5 Chambers has developed a reputation for breaking new ground and continues to be regarded as a progressive and forward-thinking set, maintaining its success in traditional sectors of law whilst offering specialist advice and representation at the cutting edge of newly evolving areas. Having grown to over 240 barristers including 33 silks, No5 Chambers provides a truly nationwide service from its offices in Birmingham, London, Bristol and Leicester.

In recent years, Chambers has made significant inroads into the South West and Wales from its Bristol location and its London office continues to go from strength to strength, housing more than 50 tenants. Chambers continues to attract high quality work in all disciplines, combining excellent service standards with a progressive, modern and flexible approach to clients' needs. For further information and a full list of tenants please see the Birmingham entry or visit www.No5.com.

XXIV OLD BUILDINGS Alan Steinfeld QC

Head of Chambers	Alan Steinfeld QC
Chambers Director	Sue Medder
Tenants	41

24 Old Buildings, Lincoln's Inn, London, WC2A 3UP
Tel (020) 7691 2424 **Fax** (0870) 460 2178 **DX** 307 Chancery Lane
Email clerks@xxiv.co.uk **Website** www.xxiv.co.uk

MEMBERS

Martin Mann QC (1968) (QC-1983)
Alan Steinfeld QC (1968) (QC-1987)
Michael Black QC (1978) (QC-1995)
Stephen Moverley Smith QC (1985) (QC-2002)
Philip Shepherd QC (1975) (QC-2003)
Francis Tregear QC (1980) (QC-2003)
Malcolm Davis-White QC (1984) (QC-2003)
David Brownbill QC (1989) (QC-2008)
Elspeth Talbot Rice QC (1990) (QC-2008)
Robert Levy QC (1988) (QC-2010)
Stephen Cogley QC (1984) (QC-2011)
Steven Thompson QC (1996) (QC-2015)
Michael King (1971)
Richard Ritchie (1978)
Michael Gadd (1981)
Elizabeth Weaver (1982)
Helen Galley (1987)
Amanda Harington (1989)
Ian Meakin (1991) (Geneva)
Arshad Ghaffar (1991)
Marcus Staff (1994)
Stuart Adair (1995)
Alexander Pelling (1995)
Bajul Shah (1996)
Jessica Hughes (1997)
Nicole Langlois (2008)
Lyndsey de Mestre (1999)
Edward Knight (1999)
Tom Montagu-Smith (2001)
Sarah Bayliss (2002)
Adam Cloherty (2005)
Edward Cumming (2006)
Erin Hitchens (2006)
Andrew Holden (2007)
Owen Curry (2009)
Daniel Warents (2009)
Heather Murphy (2009)
Hugh Miall (2009)
Harry Sharpe (2010)
Matthew Watson (2012)
Robert Avis (2013)
Timothy Sherwin (2014)
Graham Virgo (1989) *
Dr Matthew Conaglen (1995) * (New Zealand)

* Door Tenant

THE CHAMBERS XXIV Old Buildings is a specialist commercial and chancery chambers. Based in London, and with a permanent office in Geneva, the members of XXIV Old Buildings have an unrivalled reputation for their international and cross-border work. Members frequently advise and appear in the courts of other jurisdictions, with individual members called to the Bars of Jersey, the BVI, the Cayman Islands, Dubai (DIFC) and many other leading international financial centres. XXIV Old Buildings is also regarded as a prime set for international arbitration, with individual members acting as arbitrators or appearing as counsel in large-scale disputes – often with a cross-border or multi-jurisdictional element – in all of the major arbitral centres. Recognised as one of the most forward-thinking and innovative sets at the London Bar, and with very highly ranked members across all of its fields of expertise (*Chambers & Partners 2016* recognised the set as the leading commercial set for traditional chancery and offshore work), XXIV Old Buildings provides a full suite of legal advice and advocacy services for individuals and companies in the UK and globally.

WORK UNDERTAKEN The members of XXIV Old Buildings undertake litigation, arbitration and the provision of advice across the full range of commercial and chancery work, from UK commercial litigation and insolvency work to truly international litigation and arbitration involving large-scale business disputes, fraud and asset tracing, and cross-border insolvency and restructuring; and to 'traditional' chancery matters such as private family trust and succession disputes. This broad base of expertise is supplemented by members' specialist experience in fields such as hedge funds/SIVs; financial derivatives (including spread betting/CFDs); and aviation. Members are also highly experienced arbitrators (arbitrators.xxiv.co.uk) and mediators (mediators.xxiv.co.uk).

The calibre of XXIV Old Buildings' practice is demonstrated by the cases in which members are routinely instructed. In cross-border insolvency and fraud this includes the major matters arising out of the financial crisis: Madoff, *Sharp v Black (Lloyds), Libyan Investment Authority v Goldman Sachs and Property Alliance Group Ltd v Royal Bank of Scotland*; in trusts, it includes defining decisions such as Schmidt v Rosewood and Crociani v Crociani, as well as key recent decisions such as *Credit Agricole Corporation and Investment Bank v Papdimitrou* and *Rubin v Eurofinance SA*. In commercial disputes, members are involved in cases in the Supreme Court, such as *Patel v Mirza*, and in arbitration, members are currently instructed in leading cases concerning the recognition of arbitration awards in the DIFC, including the landmark case on enforcement of arbitral awards *DNB Bank ASA v Gulf Eyadah*. Members of chambers edit the loose-leaf *International Trust Laws*, and are responsible for a range of leading practitioners' works, including *Kerr and Hunter on Receivers and Administrators and Trust Protectors.*

XXIV Old Buildings adopts a commercial approach to instructions, and members have a great deal of experience working in close-knit teams with firms in London and elsewhere in the UK; with offshore advocates; with attorneys in other jurisdictions; and with liquidators, trustees and other professional service providers. More detail on members' expertise and profiles is available from the practice management team (clerks@xxiv.co.uk, 020 7691 2424, out of hours 07792 382627) and on the website: www.xxiv.co.uk.

TEN OLD SQUARE Francis Barlow QC

10 Old Square, Lincoln's Inn, London, WC2A 3SU
Tel (020) 7405 0758 **Fax** (020) 7831 8237 **DX** 306 LDE
Email clerks@tenoldsquare.com **Website** www.tenoldsquare.com

Head of Chambers	Francis Barlow QC
Senior Clerk	Keith Plowman
Deputy Senior Clerk	Marc Schofield
First Junior Clerk	Fay Bennett
Accounts & Administration	Debbie Thomas
Business Development Manager	Carine Campbell

MEMBERS

Francis Barlow QC (1965) (QC-2006)
Simon Taube QC (1980) (QC-2000)
Michael Mello QC (1972) (QC-1990) Bermuda *
Eason Rajah QC (1989) (QC-2011)
Anthony Molloy QC (1969) * (QC-1984) New Zealand
Ken Handley QC (1959) * (QC-1973) Australia
Frances Burton (1972) *
Gregory Hill (1972)
Rt Hon James Arbuthnot MP (1975) *
David Schmitz (1976)
Sidney Ross (1983)
Paul Stafford (1987)
Julian Roberts (1987)
Susannah Meadway (1988)
Jeremy Callman (1991)
Jonathan Gavaghan (1992)
Samuel Laughton (1993)
Kevin Farrelly (1993)
Robert Arnfield (1996)
Evan Price (1997)
Caroline Bolton (1998)
Anthony Dearing (1998)
Richard Dew (1999)
Georgia Bedworth (2001)
Philip Jenkins (2003)
Matthew Slater (2005)
Naomi Winston (2006)
Gideon Roseman (2007)
Leon Pickering (2010)
James MacDougald (2011)
Bryony Robinson (2013)

* Door Tenant

THE CHAMBERS Acknowledged as one of the finest, full-service Chancery sets, containing many outstanding barristers, Ten Old Square has an excellent reputation for traditional and commercial Chancery work and was recognised as "Chambers of the Year" at the STEP 2013/14 and 2015/16 Private Client Awards.

THE SET Three QCs and 23 juniors form the wealth of specialist talent available at this set. The head of Chambers is Francis Barlow QC, and all three silks in chambers are distinguished experts in the private client Chancery disciplines.

The set boasts many highly-regarded juniors with busy, niche Chancery practices. Many are authors or editors of some of the foremost textbooks on Chancery law including the authoritative 'Williams on Wills'. All members belong to the Chancery Bar Association and many also belong to STEP, ACTAPS, APP, FLBA, PBA and COMBAR. Ten Old Square is LawNet's approved chambers for private client matters and also offers annual training events and provides bespoke in-house seminars in its principal areas of practice for solicitors in related areas.

Ten Old Square is a pleasingly traditional Chancery set that employs the latest technology and know-how to deliver a modern and efficient client service. Keith Plowman is the Senior Clerk and, along with his colleague Marc Schofield, he manages Chambers and co-ordinates the practices of each barrister. Keith has been the Senior Clerk at Ten Old Square for over 23 years and Marc is similarly qualified. Together they have a built up an enviable reputation for their professional yet candid approach to their work.

WORK UNDERTAKEN The balance of traditional and commercial Chancery work at Ten Old Square is evenly distributed and compliments the demand from clients within the sector. Along with private client work the commercial Chancery disciplines are well catered for, along with property litigation, planning and land law. Additionally, Ten Old Square is now the foremost set for partnership/LLP disputes and advice.

The set handles a wide range of diverse cases, including major litigation in the Chancery and commercial divisions of the High Court and the Appellate courts. It has a significant presence in many offshore jurisdictions, as well as in the County Court and at planning inquiries and appeals, the Administrative Court, and other tribunals.

A substantial amount of ADR (arbitration and mediation) is also undertaken. As a general guide, the principal areas of work undertaken are:

Private Client: Ten Old Square is one of the leading sets for contentious and non-contentious trust work in the UK and in offshore jurisdictions. Capital taxes, wills, probate and the administration of estates, along with Court of Protection, family provision, matrimonial property and finance are also comprehensively covered.

Commercial Chancery: Partnership (including dissolution, expulsions, compulsory retirement, LLPs, MDPs restrictive covenants and partnership accounts), banking and financial services, insurance and reinsurance, commercial litigation, financial regulation, company, insolvency, professional negligence, and public procurement.

Property, Land & Real Estate: Planning inquiries and appeals, landlord and tenant, rent review, 1954 Act renewals, conveyancing, commercial property, leasehold enfranchisement, easements, intervener and third party property claims, cohabitation claims, mortgages, manorial rights including mineral rights, construction and fracking matters.

INTERNATIONAL The set has a number of barristers who have substantial private client practices overseas in Bermuda, Munich and New Zealand.

Other languages spoken: French, German.

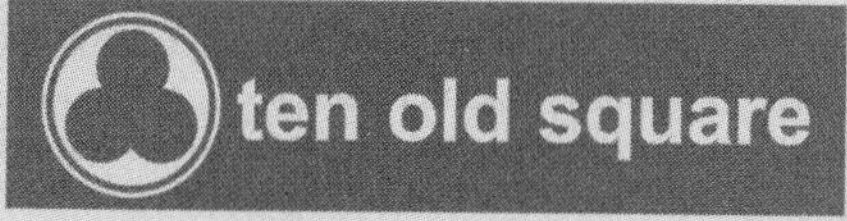

OLD SQUARE CHAMBERS Mark Sutton QC

Head of Chambers	Mark Sutton QC
Senior Clerk	William Meade
Tenants	79

10-11 Bedford Row, London WC1R 4BU
Tel (020) 7269 0300 **Fax** (020) 7405 1387 **DX** 1046 Chancery Lane/London
Email clerks@oldsquare.co.uk **Website** www.oldsquare.co.uk **Twitter** @OldSqChambers

MEMBERS

Mark Sutton QC (1982)(QC-2011)
Nigel Cooksley QC (1975) (QC-2002)
Jane McNeill QC (1982) (QC-2002) +
Frederic Reynold QC (1960) (QC-1982)
John Hendy QC (1972) (QC-1987)
Stephen Grime QC (1970) (QC-1987)
David Wilby QC (1974) (QC-1998) +
Paul Rose QC (1981) (QC-2002)
Mary O'Rourke QC (1981) (QC-2009)
Oliver Segal QC (1992)(QC-2011)
Simon Gorton QC (1988) (QC-2011)
Prof Sandra Fredman QC (2002) (QC-2012)
Michael Ford QC (1992) (QC-2013)
Ben Collins QC (1996) (QC-2016)
John H Bates (1973)
Prof Robert Upex (1973)
Christopher Makey (1975) +
Toby Kempster (1980)
Louise Chudleigh (1987)
Ijeoma Omambala (1989)
Philip Mead (1989)
Jonathan Clarke (1990)
Christopher Walker (1990)
Giles Powell (1990)
Ian Scott (1991)
Simon Cheetham (1991)
Helen Gower (1992)
Brian Cummins (1992)
Malcolm Galloway (1992)
Prof Roy Lewis (1992)
Deshpal Panesar (1993)
Michael Nicholson (1993)
Elizabeth Melville (1994)
Katherine Howells (1994)
Mark Whitcombe (1994)
Stephen Garner (1994)
Jack Mitchell (1994)
Melanie Tether (1995)
Robin White (1995)
Cyril Adjei (1995)
Charles Woodhouse (1997)
Tom Gent (1998)
Rebecca Tuck (1998)
Hilary Winstone (1998)
Spencer Keen (1998)
Stuart Brittenden (1999)
Anya Palmer (1999)
Katharine Newton (1999)
Sarah Keogh (1999)
Ben Cooper (2000)
Bella Webb (2000)
Brent McDonald (2000)
Robert Moretto (2000)
Andrew Midgley (2000)
Betsan Criddle (2002)
David Rivers (2002)
Corinna Ferguson (2003)
Adam Samuel (2003)
Nadia Motraghi (2004)
Hannah Freeman (2004)
Andreá Risoli (2005)
David Cunnington (2005)
Christopher Edwards (2006)
Charlie Sparling (2006)
Claire Bowsher-Murray (2007)
Kara Loraine (2006)
Nicola Newbegin (2008)
Katherine Fudakowski (2008)
James Chegwidden (2008)
Victoria Webb (2009)
Hannah Bennett (2010)
Lance Harris (2010)
Simon O'Dwyer (2010)
Rosalie Snocken (2010)
Laith Dilaimi (2011)
Alex Just (2011)
Sophie Beesley (2012)
Adam Ross (2013)
Madeline Stanley (2013)

+ Recorder

THE CHAMBERS Old Square Chambers is widely respected as one of the leading employment and personal injury sets, both in London and Bristol, and known for its unstuffy approach, pro-activity and responsiveness to client needs. Further specialisms include professional discipline, clinical negligence, environment, health and safety, product liability, motor defence, public inquiries, and mediation/ADR.

WORK UNDERTAKEN

Employment: Old Square is acknowledged as one of the leading sets in employment law. It has been instrumental in establishing recent legal precedents on holiday pay and discrimination.
Personal Injury: Members are regularly instructed in high value head, brain and spinal injury cases, including many involving ex service personnel, disaster litigation, multi-party actions and injuries abroad.
Clinical Negligence: Members have extensive experience in cerebral palsy, acquired brain damage claims and catastrophic injuries as well as dental negligence and obstetric and orthopaedic claims.
Professional Discipline: Members have been at the forefront of developing the law relating to injunctive relief and disciplinary procedures in a variety of sectors including healthcare, financial services and sport.
Environment: Members have comprehensive experience, particularly in cases involving nuisance, water law, contaminated land, statutory nuisance, waste management law and the application of EU law.
Health & Safety: Members are involved in both regulatory prosecutions/defence and public inquiries. Cases are often high-profile, involving serious injury, fatality, and corporate manslaughter. Operating nationally, Old Square has extensive experience in a wide range of sectors.
Product Liability: Members undertake Consumer Protection Act prosecutions, product recall and product labelling work and are highly experienced in multi-claimant litigation, especially involving pharmaceuticals.
Public Inquiries: Members have been instructed in most of the significant or high-profile inquiries of the last decade, including Leveson, Potters Bar, Ufton Nevert Train Crash, Mubarek, Shipman, Climbie, Ladbroke Grove, Marchioness, Southall Train Crash, North Wales Child Abuse and Bristol Royal Infirmary.
Human Rights: Members have been particularly innovative in their use of Article 6 in disciplinary cases and Article 11 in industrial action cases.
Mediation: Members are experienced CEDR trained and accredited mediators in employment, discrimination, personal injury and clinical negligence cases.
Pupillage: Please see our website for details. Old Square offers an excellent training, interesting work, a collegiate environment and an excellent chance of tenancy.

OUTER TEMPLE CHAMBERS Michael Bowes QC, David Westcott QC, Andrew Spink QC

The Outer Temple, 222 Strand, London, WC2R 1BA
Tel (020) 7353 6381 **Fax** (020) 7583 1786 **DX** 351 London
Email clerks@outertemple.com **Website** www.outertemple.com

Heads of Chambers	Michael Bowes QC David Westcott QC Andrew Spink QC
Commercial Director	Christine Kings Steve Graham
Business Development Directors	Graham Woods David Smith Dave Scothern
Tenants	83

MEMBERS

Christopher Wilson-Smith QC (1965) (QC-1986)
David Russell QC (1977) Australia QC (QC-1986)
Robert Rhodes QC (1968) (QC-1989)
Philip Mott QC (1970) (QC-1991)
Christopher Gibson QC (1976) (QC-1995)
Gerard McDermott QC (1978) (QC-1999)
Michael Bowes QC (1980) (QC-2001)
Gordon Bebb QC (1975) (QC-2002)
Brendan Finucane QC (1976) (QC-2003)
David Westcott QC (1982) (QC-2003)
Andrew Spink QC (1985) (QC-2003)
Andrew Short QC (1990) (QC-2010)
Ben Compton QC (1979) (QC-2011)
Nicolas Stallworthy QC (1993) (QC-2011)
Keith Bryant QC (1991) (QC-2013)
Kate Davenport QC (1983) (QC-2013)
Richard Hitchcock QC (1990) (QC-2014)
Marc Willems QC (1990) (QC-2015)
John McKendrick QC (1999) (QC-2016)
Hywel Jenkins (1974)
Richard Mawhinney (1977)
Michael Patchett-Joyce (1981)
Teresa Rosen Peacocke (1982)
James Counsell (1984)
Christopher Kemp (1984)
Patrick Sadd (1984)
Harry Trusted (1985)
James Aldridge (1987)
Alison McCormick (1988)
Mark Mullins (1988)
Paul Rogers (1989)
James Leonard (1989)
Jonathan Hand (1990)
Timothy Nesbitt (1991)
Fiona Horlick (1992)
Natasha Joffe (1992)
Nathan Tavares (1992)
Rachel Vickers (1992)
Matthew Phillips (1993)
Eliot Woolf (1993)
Daniel Barnett (1993)
Naomi Cunningham (1994)
Matthew McDonagh (1994)
Abhijeet Mukherjee (1995)
Andrew Allen (1995)
Benjimin Burgher (1995)
David Pope (1995)
Tim Green (1996)
Fiona Scolding (1996)
Lydia Seymour (1997)
Harriet Jerram (1998)
Matthew Stockwell (1998)
David E Grant (1999)
Robin Barclay (1999)
Sarah Crowther (1999)
Cara Guthrie (2000)
James Arnold (2000)
Samantha Presland (2001)
Naomi Ling (2001)
James Rickards (2002)
Oliver Assersohn (2003)
Dr Ali Almihdar (2003)
Eleanor Davison (2003)
Michael Uberoi (2004)
Daniel Clarke (2005)
Saul Margo (2005)
Farhaz Khan (2005)
Oliver Powell (2006)
Ben Bradley (2007)
Clare Baker (2007)
Robert Dickason (2007)
Miranda de Savorgnani (2007)
Jennifer Seaman (2007)
Emily Gordon Walker (2007)
Nicholas Hill (2008)
Will Young (2008)
Keira Gore (2008)
Simon Oakes (2010)
Thomas Gibson (2010)
Katarina Sydow (2012)
Saaman Pourghadiri (2012)
Paul Livingston (2012)
Stephen Doherty (2013)
Bianca Venkata (2014)
Tim Horlock QC (1981) (QC-1997) *
Nicholas Haggan QC (1977) (QC-2003) *
Thomas Leeper (1991) *
Jonathan Moffatt (2009) *
Graham Watson (1996) *

* Door Tenant

THE CHAMBERS Outer Temple Chambers provides bespoke legal services for solicitors, in-house counsel, professional clients and private individuals. Success is built on sound legal advice and effective problem solving, focused wholly on the individual needs of clients.

It is noted for its health and its business expertise. In personal injury and clinical negligence the set has one of the most experienced catastrophic injury teams in the UK and undertakes group litigation, cases involving complex medical issues, product liability, industrial disease, abuse claims, and spinal and brain injuries. In 2015 Outer Temple won the Legal Innovations Award. It is now justifiably highly ranked as a leading pensions set and combines this with an established practice in professional negligence and an increasing practice in international arbitration and mediation work.

Outer Temple has an enviable presence in the financial services and banking sector with demonstrable expertise in litigation, regulation and enforcement.

The employment team has an outstanding reputation in equal pay and discrimination claims, and is frequently instructed for its knowledge of financial services particularly in contractual matters. Members have an unparalleled profile in corporate manslaughter and health and safety investigations.

Practitioners provide representation in all types of disciplinary and regulatory tribunals, with particular emphasis on medical, solicitor, police and financial disciplinary hearings.

In public law, Outer Temple is recognised for its expertise in major public inquiries, the Court of Protection and education matters.

It is also known for its work in law in sport and transport law. Chambers provides a range of international services with a presence in Manchester, Dubai, Abu Dhabi and an office in New York.

4 PAPER BUILDINGS Alex Verdan QC

4 Paper Buildings, Temple, London, EC4Y 7EX
Tel (020) 7427 5200 **Fax** (020) 7353 4979 **DX** 1035
Email clerks@4pb.com **Website** www.4pb.com

Head of Chambers	Alex Verdan QC
Senior Clerk	Michael Reeves
Chambers Manager	Clare Bello
Tenants	76

MEMBERS

Alexander Verdan QC (1987) (QC-2006) + ± ^
Jonathan Cohen QC (1974) (QC-1997) + ± ^
Henry Setright QC (1979) (QC-2001) + ±
Marcus Scott-Manderson QC (1980) (QC-2006)
Kate Branigan QC (1985) (QC-2006) ^
Jo Delahunty QC (1986) (QC-2006) +
Michael Sternberg QC (1975) (QC-2008) ^
Catherine Wood QC (1985) + (QC- 2011)
Rex Howling QC (1991) (QC-2011) ^
Teertha Gupta QC (1990) (QC-2012) + ^
David Williams QC (1990) (QC-2013) + ^
Charles Hale QC (1992) (QC-2014) ^
Christopher Hames QC (1987) (QC-2015)^
Alison Grief QC (1990) (QC-2015) + ^
John Tughan QC (1991) (QC-2015) ^
Cyrus Larizadeh QC (1992) (QC- 2016) ^
Brian Jubb (1971)
Amanda Barrington-Smyth (1972)
Robin Barda (1975)
Dermot Main Thompson (1977)
Jane Rayson (1982) ^
Mark Johnstone (1984) ^
Elizabeth Coleman (1985)
Alistair Perkins (1986)
Stephen Lyon (1987) ^
James Shaw (1988)
Mark Jarman (1989) ^
Sally Bradley (1989) ^
Barbara Mills (1990) + ^
Samantha King (1990) ^
Joanne Brown (1990)
Joy Brereton (1990) ^
David Bedingfield (1991) +
Michael Simon (1992)
Justin Ageros (1993) ^
Rob Littlewood (1993) ^
Paul Hepher (1994) ^
Ruth Kirby (1994) ^
Judith Murray (1994) ^
Cliona Papazian (1994) ^
Sarah Lewis (1995)
Nicholas Fairbank (1996) ^
James Copley (1997)
Justine Johnston (1997) ^
Oliver Jones (1998) + ^
Lucy Cheetham (1999) ^
Hassan Khan (1999) ^
Cleo Perry (2000)
Harry Gates (2001) ^
Rebecca Foulkes (2001)+
Katie Wood (2001) ^
Rhiannon Lloyd (2002) ^
Katherine Van Rol (2002) ^
Ceri White (2002) ^
Matthew Persson (2003) ^
Dorothea Gartland (2004) ^ **
Francesca Dowes (2004) ^
Greg Davies (2005) ^
Samantha Woodham (2006) ^
Laura Morley (2006) ^
Nicola Wallace (2006) ^
Jacqueline Renton (2007) ^
Michael Gration (2007)
Henry Clayton (2007) ^
Andrew Powell (2008) ^
Chris Barnes (2008) ^
Sophie Connors (2009) ^
Michael Edwards (2010) ^
Harry Nosworthy (2010) ^
Rachel Chisholm (2010) ^
Jonathan Evans (2010) ^
Julia Townend (2011) ^
Zoe Taylor (2011)
Indu Kumar (2012)
Jonathan Rustin (2013)
Pippa Sanger (2015)

+ Recorder ± Deputy High Court Judge ** DDJ ° DDJ (Family Division) ^ Public/Direct Access

THE CHAMBERS 4 Paper Buildings ('4PB') has a long history as a friendly team of specialist barristers providing excellent expert yet common sense and practical advice and advocacy in all areas of family law. Many of the most serious, sensitive and significant family cases are undertaken by members of 4PB and instructions are received from a diverse array of clients including media organisations, the rich and/or famous, government departments, parents seeking to prevent children from being removed into care and guardians. Chambers also provides a wide spread of services by way of dispute resolution (ADR) and has over 50 barristers available for direct public access.

WORK UNDERTAKEN

Family Law: Divorce and civil partnership dissolution, jurisdiction disputes, financial remedies on matrimonial and civil partnership breakdown, disputes between former cohabitants, marital, civil partnership and cohabitation agreements, financial arrangements for children, protection from domestic abuse, international family relocation disputes, child abduction, forced marriage, public children law, radicalism cases, public inquiries, private children's arrangements, surrogacy (national and international), assisted conception, medical cases, court of protection work and professional negligence arising from family proceedings.

5 PAPER BUILDINGS Miranda Moore QC & Julian Christopher QC

5 Paper Buildings, Temple, London, EC4Y 7HB
Tel (020) 7583 6117 **Fax** (020) 7353 0075 **DX** 365 Chancery Lane
Email clerks@5pb.co.uk **Website** www.5pb.co.uk

Heads of Chambers	Miranda Moore QC Julian Christopher QC
Senior Clerk	Dale Jones
First Junior	Graham Briggs
Chambers Business Manager	Andrew Ross
Tenants	44

MEMBERS

Godfrey Carey QC (1969) (QC-1991)
Jonathan Caplan QC (1973) (QC-1991) + ^
Oliver Sells QC (1972) (QC-1995)
Edward Jenkins QC (1977) (QC-2000) + ^
Michael Brompton QC (1973) (QC-2003) +
Graham Trembath QC (1978) (QC-2003)
Miranda Moore QC (1983) (QC-2003)
Mark Wyeth QC (1983) (QC-2009)
Julian Christopher QC (1988) (QC-2010) ^
Robert O'Sullivan QC (1988) (QC-2012) ^
Tom Allen (1994) (QC-2015) ^
Emma Deacon QC (1993) (QC-2016)
Laura Brickman (1976) ^
Nicholas Fooks (1978) ^
Charles Judge (1981)
Miles Bennett (1986) ^
Kevin McCartney (1991)
Janet Weeks (1993)
Deanna Heer (1994) + ^
Michael Hick (1995) ^
Denis Barry (1996) ^
Ben Douglas-Jones (1998) ^
Catherine Purnell (1999)
James Norman (2000)
Jonathan Rees (2000) ^
Dominic Lewis (2000) ^
Teresa Hay (2001) ^
Stephen Hopper (2001)
Rory Keene (2001) ^
Catherine Rabaiotti (2002)
Charlene Sumnall (2003) ^
Archie Mackay (2003)
Alan Richards (2004)
Georgina Coade (2005)
Michael Attenborough (2008) ^
Andrew Johnson (2008) ^
James Marsland (2008)
Anthony Hucklesby (2008)
Jennifer Dannhauser (2010)
Olivia Potts (2011) ^
Richard Radley (2011)
Carolina Bracken (2012) ^
Joshua Normanton (2012) ^
Aparma Rào (2013) ^

+ Recorder ^ Public/Direct Access

THE CHAMBERS 5PB has long been recognised as one of the leading criminal sets. Chambers draws on some of the best talent at the criminal bar and at present has 44 members, 12 of whom are QCs. Deanna Heer was
appointed Junior Treaury Counsel in 2015.
Members take a results-focused approach to criminal advocacy, working closely alongside clients to find practical solutions. Clients also benefit from the outstanding quality of chambers' case management and clerking, resulting in cost effective use of court time and resources. Members bring an exceptional quality of representation and case management to all cases, regardless of level, size or scale of complexity.

WORK UNDERTAKEN

Crime: Members prosecute and defend across the full range of criminal practice at every level, including large-scale drug importation, serious sexual offences, human trafficking, corruption of public servants, firearms offences and serious violence. With particular experience in cases involving PII and sensitive disclosure issues and vulnerable witnesses. Recent cases include defending in News of the World phone hacking trial. Prosecutions in Op Yewtree and Op Elveden. Defending in a football corrpution trial - the first trial under the Bribery Act 2010.
Financial Crime: Members of chambers are regularly instructed in the largest and most complex financial crime cases. Its experience includes all forms of fraud, MTIC/VAT frauds, market abuse, asset recovery and confiscation proceedings. Recent cases include the Libor and the Celtic Energy fraud cases. Factoring fraud with £111million confiscation proceedings. A mortgage fraud involving over 1,000 mortgages.
Consumer Law: 5PB is one of the leading sets in consumer law and trading standards. Its expertise includes trade descriptions, pricing offences, consumer credit, property misdescriptions, trade mark and copyright theft, product safety, environmental law, health and safety, food and food safety, ticket touting and underage sales. Recent cases include the first ever prosecution of a pyramid schemes in the UK (£21 million) by the OFT/CMA. The prosecution of a major retailer over multi million pound allegations of misleading commercial practices in the promotion and sale of strawberries. £60 million money laundering case involving 30 different consumer scams, 9 countries, targeting the elderly.
Professional Discipline & Regulatory: 5PB is regularly instructed in healthcare regulation and professional discipline. Acting for the regulators, individuals and corporate clients and frequently appear in parallel proceedings involving criminal prosecutions, inquests and disciplinary inquiries. Members are also instructed in MHRA and FRC work. Regularly appear before the GMC, GPC and GOC and when necessary, on appeal. Members frequently represent doctors, pharmacists and NHS trusts at inquests. In addition matters involving accountants, architects, barristers, police officers among others.
Health & Safety: Members have extensive expertise dealing with HSE prosecutions and defending companies and individuals following workplace accidents. Recent cases include defending in the first ever acquittal at trial of a company charged with corporate manslaughter. Securing the conviction of one of the UK's largest engineering companies following the death of a construction worker.
Public Law & Inquiries: Chambers has considerable experience having been instructed in some of the most important recent inquiries including Leveson, The Rosemary Nelson Inquiry, The Bloody Sunday Inquiry and the Guantánamo Bay litigation.

INTERNATIONAL Members have experience of work in Hong Kong, Singapore and the Caribbean.

FIVE PAPER Nicholas Grundy

5 Paper Buildings, Temple, London, EC4Y 7HB
Tel (020) 7815 3200 **Fax** (020) 7815 3201 **DX** 415 LDE
Email clerks@fivepaper.com **Website** www.fivepaper.com

Head of Chambers	Nicholas Grundy
Commercial Team Leader	Simon Mills
Property Team Leader	Stephen Evans
Employment Team Leader	Jake Davies
Family Team Leader	Mark Lyne
Senior Clerk	David Portch
Pupillage co-ordinators	Jessica Powers Joanna Brownhill
Tenants	44

MEMBERS

Nicholas Grundy (1993)
Paul Norris (1963) ^
Graham Platford (1970) ^
Donald Broatch (1971) ^
Robert Percival (1971) ^
Roger Bull (1974)
Mark Lyne (1981)
Terry Gallivan (1981) ^
Ian Wright (1983) ^
Jonathan Rich (1989)
Peter John (1989)
Josephine Henderson (1990) ^
Simon Robinson (1991) ^
Satinder Gill (1991) ^
Stephen Evans (1992)
Byron Britton (2008) (admitted as solicitor 1994)
Simon Mills (1994) ^
Rachel Sleeman (1996)
Jake Davies (1997) ^
Joanna Brownhill (1997)
Sean Pettit (1997) ^
Ben Maltz (1998) ^
Sonia Rai (1998) ^
Sara Beecham (1999)
Angela Hall (2000)
Julie Leivesley (2000)
Jane Hodgson (2000) ^
Guy Holland (2001) ^
Mary Glass (2001)
Victoria Osler (2001)
Morwenna Macro (2002) ^
Tina Conlan (2002)
Gillian Christopher-Chambers JP (2003)
Jennifer Moate (2006)
Millie Polimac (2007) ^
Brynmor Adams (2008)
Gita Chakravarty (2010) ^
Sam Phillips (2011)
Laura Williams (2011) ^
Jessica Powers (2012) ^
Tristan Satter (2013) ^
Gareth Davies (2013) (admitted as a solicitor 2010)
Roger Laville (2015) admitted as a solicitor (2002)
Richard King (1978) ++

++ Door Tenant ^ Public/Direct Access

THE CHAMBERS Five Paper specialises in commercial, property, employment and family law. Chambers works with clients from many sectors and believes accessibility, communication and strong relationships are key to delivering excellent results. Senior members are among the most experienced and innovative within their areas of expertise and the chambers' juniors deal with practical legal matters on a daily basis. This range of experience enables Five Paper to provide clients with a service that is both expert and cost-effective.

Professional development: Five Paper is accredited by the Law Society and Bar Council for continuing professional development. The set also runs seminars and bespoke training for professional clients. Please contact clerks for details.

WORK UNDERTAKEN Five Paper has four thriving practice teams:

Commercial: The commercial team works with clients involved in commercial finance, insolvency and asset recovery. The team specialises in factoring and invoice discounting, corporate insolvency, trade finance and the sale of goods, credit and securities, breach of directors' and fiduciary duties, personal bankruptcy, civil fraud and tracing and enforcement against land.

Property: The property team specialises in acting for local authorities, registered providers of social housing, and private landlords and tenants in the areas of housing, residential landlord and tenant law and public law, as well as property-related discrimination law. The team is also experienced in all property-related fields, including real property/general chancery work, commercial landlord and tenant law, and probate.

Employment: The employment team provides a full-service for all types of employment matters. The team also has specialists in regulatory matters, such as health and safety at work, with barristers on the List of Specialist Regulatory Advocates in Health and Safety and Environmental Law who are certified for this type of work and also business immigration.

Family: The family team specialises in all types of financial order cases, Schedule 1 cases, Children Act cases, financial provision and matrimonial jurisdiction law. The team has recently expanded its areas of expertise and members are now regularly instructed in matrimonial finance and children cases which touch upon issues of bankruptcy, housing and inheritance.

PUBLICATIONS Five Paper's senior members edit some of the leading specialist law publications. These include: Gutteridge and Megrah's Law of Bankers' Commercial Credits, 8th edition by Richard King; Sir Roy Goode's Proprietary Rights and Insolvency in Sales Transactions, 2nd edition by Simon Mills; Salinger on Factoring, 4th edition by Simon Mills and others.

RECRUITMENT Pupils spend time with different practice teams to experience a wide variety of work. Pupils receive an award of £25,000 each plus guaranteed earnings in the second six of £5,000. Five Paper also encourages applications from barristers with ten or more years' experience within one of their specialist areas. Please contact the clerks for details. Five Paper is committed to equal opportunities for all and values diversity.

PARTNERSHIP COUNSEL Roderick I'Anson Banks

9 King's Bench Walk, Temple, London, EC4Y 7DX
Tel (020) 7430 2005 **Fax** (020) 7831 4885 **DX** 284 LDE
Email tyroon@partnershipcounsel.co.uk **Website** www.partnershipcounsel.co.uk

Head of Chambers	Roderick I'Anson Banks
Practice Manager	Tyroon Win
Tenants	2

MEMBERS
Roderick I'Anson Banks (1974)
LLB (London)
Simon Jelf (1996) LLB (Eur)

THE CHAMBERS Specialises exclusively in partnership and limited liability partnership law and provide solicitors and other professional and trading partnerships and LLPs with a full range of legal services, from the drafting of new agreements and the review of existing agreements to advice and representation in partnership disputes, arbitrations and mediations. Chambers' aim, where possible, is to assist clients with the process of resolving disputes, without recourse to litigation and provide ongoing advice and support from the embryonic stages of a developing dispute, right through to the conclusion of any litigation or until a negotiated settlement is reached. Chambers also carries out a significant amount of drafting and advisory work relating to limited and corporate partnerships. Licensed and Public Access work is undertaken in appropriate cases.

PUBLICATIONS Roderick I'Anson Banks is the editor of *Lindley & Banks on Partnership* , the authoritative guide to partnership law (19th ed. published December 2010, 20th ed. in preparation), and the author of the *Encyclopedia of Professional Partnerships.* Simon Jelf is a contributor to the *Encyclopedia of Professional Partnerships,* and editor of the forthcoming supplement to *Lindley & Banks on Partnership.*

3PB BARRISTERS Nigel Lickley QC

Head of Chambers	Nigel Lickley QC
Chief Executive	Simon Astill
Tenants	169

3 Paper Buildings, Temple, London, EC4Y 7EU
Tel (020) 7583 8055 **Fax** (020) 7353 6271 **DX** 1024 LDE
Email london@3pb.co.uk **Website** www.3pb.co.uk

MEMBERS

Michael Parroy QC (1969) (QC-1991)
Michael Vere-Hodge QC (1970) (QC-1993) ^
Stewart Jones QC (1972)(QC-1994)*
Nicholas Braslavsky QC (1983) (QC-1999)
Nigel Lickley QC (1983) (QC-2006)
Paul Storey QC (1982)(QC-2010) *
Joseph Giret QC (1985) (QC-2010)
Frank Freehan QC (1988) (QC-2010) *
Adam Feest QC (1994) ^ (QC-2016)
Stephen Parrish (1966)
Susan Solomon (1967)
David Swinstead (1970)
Christopher Aylwin (1970)
Michael Norman (1971) ^
Peter Jennings (1972) ^
John Friel (1974)
William Webster (1975)
Richard Tyson (1975)
Peter Kent (1978)
Nicholas Leviseur (1979)
Ian Partridge (1979)
Robin Leach (1979)
Robert Grey (1979) ^
Gavin Hamilton (1979) ^
Timothy Coombes (1980) ^
Ian Edge (1981)
Graeme Sampson (1981) ^
Martin Strutt (1981)
Nicola Martin (1982)
Richard Onslow (1982)
Paul Newman (1982) ^
Mark Lomas (1983)
Sarah O'Hara (1984)
Tonia Clark (1986) ^
Elisabeth Hudson (1987) ^
Lucy Hendry (1988)
Tanya Zabihi (1988)
Jane Rowley (1988)
Timothy Bradbury (1989)
David Richards (1989) ^
Guy Opperman (1989) *
Sophie Knapp (1990)
Omar Malik (1990)
Hayley Griffiths (1990)
Peter Aeberli (1990) ^
Amanda Buckley-Clarke (1991)
Hamish Dunlop (1991) ^
Melissa Barlow (1991)
Christian Sweeney (1992)
Tony Bingham (1992) ^
Kerry Musgrave (1992)
William Hansen (1992)
Jane Fousler McFarlane (1994) *
Judy Earle (1994)
Michelle Marnham (1994)
James Dawson (1994) ^
David Reid (1994)
Louis Weston (1994) ^
Peter Collie (1994)
Colin McDevitt (1995) ^
Melanie De Freitas (1995) ^
Elaine Strachan (1995)
Lachlan Wilson (1996)
Cheryl Jones (1996) ^
Andrew Lorie (1996)
Tom Tyler (1996) ^
James Davison (1996)
Martin Kenny (1997) ^
Catherine Purdy (1997)
Mark Sullivan (1997)
Martin Kenny (1997)
Joshua Dubin (1997)
Darren Walsh (1997)
Eleanor Davies (1998) *
Emma Griffiths (1998)
Kalsoom Maqsood (1998) *
Rufus Taylor (1998) ^
Nicholas Cotter (1999)
Melanie Churchill (1999)
Robert Horner (1999)
Stuart Kennedy (1999) ^
Charlotte Hadfield (1999) ^
Antonia Jameson (1999) *
Rachel Goodall (2000) ^
Kenneth McGuire (2000) *
Oliver Isaacs (2000)
Rupert Jones (2000) *^
Louise Worton (2000)
Richard Owen-Thomas (2000) ^
Andrew Sheriff (2000)
Garvin Nicholas (2001) *
Sheena Cassidy (2001)
Christopher Whelan (2001)
Craig Ludlow (2002) ^
Gillian Campbell (2002) *
Karen Moss (2002)
Adam Norris (2002) *
Nicola Pearce (2002) *
Michael Tomlinson (2002) ^
Robert Courts (2003) ^
Matthew Gullick (2003) ^
Victoria Jones (2003) ^
Emma Harman (2003)
Duncan McNair (2003)
Hugh Rimmer (2003)
Elizabeth Hepworth (2004)
Tom Horder (2004)
Richard Wheeler (2004) ^
Audrey Archer (2004)
James Davies (2004) ^
Caroline Sykes (2004) *
Jodie Mittell (2004)
Sarah Langford (2005)
Katherine Anderson (2005)
Sarah Clarke (2005)
Caroline Stone (2005)
Emma Southern (2006)
Matthew Cannings (2006)
Naomi Rees (2006) ^
Nicholas Robinson (2006)
Sunyana Sharma (2006) ^
Mark Green (2006)
Francisca Da Costa (2006)
Sarah Bowen (2006)
Simon Tibbitts (2006)
Nick Davies (2006)
Gareth Graham (2006)
Andrew MacPhail (2007) ^
Andrew Perfect (2007)
Mark Ellliott (2007) ^
Thomas O'Donohoe (2007) ^
Sebastian Oram (2007)
Ximena Jones (2007)
Derek Pye (2008)
Katherine Dunseath (2008)
Alex Hodge (2009)
Nicola Frost (2009)
Alexander Line (2009)
Steven Howard (2009) ^
Sharan Sanghera (2009) ^
Lucy Clayton (2009)
Sarah Jennings (2009)
Gemma White (2009)
Berenice Mulvanney (2009)
Edward Ross (2010)
Thomas Webb (2010)
Stephen Wyeth (2010)
Tom Evans (2010)
Nikolai Lazarev (2010)
David Jenkins (2010)
Shruti Sharma (2011)
Emma Waldron (2011)
Joe England (2011)
Susan Jones (2011)
Robert Weatherley (2011)
Thomas Talbot-Ponsonby (2011)
Esther Lieu (2011)
Graham Kean (2012)
Nicole Bollard (2012)
Katie Lee (2012)
Jonathan Gaydon (2013)
Olivia Ford (2013)

* Door Tenant ^ Public/Direct Access

THE CHAMBERS 3PB (previously known as 3 Paper Buildings) is one of the longest established sets in England with 169 members and nine silks and operates as a single set from its five well-equipped locations. The set is fully accredited by the Bar Council to provide CPD courses and is IiP and BarMark accredited. Each office is staffed by friendly and experienced staff who can advise clients on the most suitable counsel for a particular case, as well

3PB BARRISTERS Nigel Lickley QC (continued)

as discuss fees and provide estimates for anticipated work.

WORK UNDERTAKEN Chambers expertise covers 11 specialist work groups.
Business and Commercial Group advises on general contract and commercial law, as well as energy law and IP. The criminal law group advise and act in a broad spectrum of criminal law matters. Counsel also undertake publicly funded work. The education law team advise parents, pupils, schools, teaching and academic staff and local authorities. The employment group provides expertise across all areas of contentious and non-contentious work, including all forms of discrimination. The family law group provides expertise in every aspect of public/private childcare law and all forms of financial proceedings. The personal injury and clinical negligence group conducts cases at every level and clients include both claimants and defendants. The professional negilgence team provide advice in all aspects of the law. The property and chancery Group undertake work in all areas of law concerning the ownership, occupation and use of land, as well as traditional Chancery law advice.
Public and regulatory law crosses the boundary between civil and criminal law and members of the group provide expertise across a range of legal fields, including consumer protection and health and safety law.
The asset and tax team has been instructed in a number of high profile cases, and nearly all of the leading panel receivers and government agencies instruct 3PB, together with well known specialist defence firms.
Chambers mediation group has particular strength in the fields of adjudication, arbitration and mediation. Members are regularly appointed as adjudicators or arbitrators in both domestic and international disputes.
3PB's TCC Group provides expertise in all aspects of construction disputes and dispute resolution services, both domestic and international.
The sports law group has an exceptional reputation for its expertise in sports regulation and discipline, doping issues, contractual disputes, IP, negligence and ancillary sporting issues including firearms licensing.

Other offices: Bournemouth, Bristol, Oxford and Winchester.

ONE PUMP COURT

Senior Clerk	Ian Burrow
Tenants	66

1 Pump Court, Elm Court, Temple, London, EC4Y 7AH
Tel (020) 7842 7070 **Fax** (020) 7842 7088 **DX** LDE 109
Email clerks@onepumpcourt.co.uk **Website** www.onepumpcourt.co.uk

MEMBERS

Lindsay Adams (1987) ^
Yinka Adedeji (1997) ^
Jonathan Adler (1999) ^
Ripon Akhter (2003)
Jennifer Barker (2000)
Stephen Bartlet-Jones (2004) ^
Delphine Breese-Laughran (1991)
Benjamin Bundock (2013)
Helen Butcher (1999)
Sylvester Carrot (1980) ^
Parosha Chandran (1997) ^
David Chirico (2002)
Sally Dent (1989)
Zani Dingiswayo (2001)
Annie Dixon (1991)
Edmund Eldergill (1991) ^
Amean Elgadhy (2008) ^
Stephen Field (1993) ^
Rachel Francis (2012)
Joshua Garwood (1992) ^
Julia Gasparro (1999) ^
Andrew Gilbert (2009)
Matthew Groves (1998)
Michelle Harris (2000) ^
Philippa Hemery (2009) ^
Paul Higham (1982)
Martin Hodgson (1980) ^
Sharon Holloway (1994)
Abida Huda (1989) ^
Mary Hughes (1994) ^
Timur Hussein (1993) ^
Samina Iqbal (1999) ^
Samuel Jarman (1989) ^
Melanie Johnson (1996) ^
Manjeet K Kaler (1993) ^
Ajanta Kaza (1998)
Ranjiv Khubber (1994)
Gilda Kiai (2004)
Victoria Laughton (1988)
Rebecca Littlewood (1988) ^
Michael Marsh Hyde (2006) ^
Alan Masters (1979) (Irish Bar 1993) ^
Rebecca Martin (2002) ^
Philip McLeish (2003)
Patrick McMorrow (1996)
Helen Monah (1996)
Nicholas Nicol (1986) ^
Michele O'Leary (1983) ^
Charlie Peat (2003) ^
Terry Pedro (1996) ^
Claire Physsas (2004)
James Presland (1985) ^
Althea Radford (2009)
Rohan Ramdas-Harsia (1999) ^
Catherine Robinson (2011) ^
Eleanor Sanders (2014)
Ruby Sayed (1999) ^
Harriet Short (2007)
Daniel Sills (2011) ^
Priya Solanki (2008)
Simon Stafford-Michael (1982) ^
Bruce Stuart (19977) ^
Emma Stuart King (2005) ^
Lucy Taylor-Gee (2006)
Alessia Thomas (2011)
Patricia Tueje (1999) ^
Tayyiba Ahmad (1998)*
Francesa Del Mese (1998)*
Shauna Gillan (2006)*
Eleanor Hutchinson (2007)*
Tamara Muhammad (1998)
Neville Rudston(2000)
Natasha Sammy (2006)*
Caroline Sincalir (2005)
Natasha Sammy (2006)*
Stuart Scott (1998)*
Usha Teji (1981)*
Catorina Vine(2002)*
Nicola Wacey (2004)*
Lorraine Waldrone (2004)*

* Door Tenant ++ Honorary Door Tenant ^ Public/Direct Access

THE CHAMBERS One Pump Court is a dynamic and progressive set of Chambers. Established in 1978 Chambers has a firm commitment to removing inequality and providing access to justice, particularly in relation to publicly funded clients and those to whom funding is no longer available. Chambers has established a solid and growing reputation in its traditional areas of work while developing its client base through expansion of its direct access, private (domestic and international) and regulatory work and mediation.

Members sit as part-time Judges in County Courts and Tribunals (immigration, social security, property and employment). Former members have been appointed to the judiciary including to the High Court. Chambers is a democratic collective.

Members of Chambers regularly conduct seminars for practitioners and provide individualised training for advisors and external organisations such as ILPA, HLPA, JCWI, LAG, ATLeP, HJT and Shelter.

Chambers has been nominated for various professional awards e.g. Legal Aid Lawyer of the Year in 2012 and the LAPG Legal Aid Barrister of the Year Award in 2013, with Jane Hoyal – a founding member of Chambers - winning the award. In 2015 Parosha Chandran received a Trafficking in Persons Hero Award.

WORK UNDERTAKEN Chambers specialises in publicly funded work and has been involved in many high profile cases. Areas include administrative and public law, crime (including white collar), immigration, family, housing and community care, property, general civil litigation, social welfare and prison law. A large percentage of members are Direct Access accredited.

PUBLICATIONS Members have written and contributed to legal textbooks and other publications including but not limited to Butterworth's Immigration Law Service, the Journal of Housing Law, Legal Action Blackstone's Guide to the Domestic Violence Act, Family Law Week, Education Law and Practice, The Prisons Handbook, Human Trafficking Handbook, The Fuel Rights Handbook, The English/Japanese Legal Dictionary and Handbook and Butterworth's Money Laundering Law

4 PUMP COURT Jeremy Storey QC & Nigel Tozzi QC

4 Pump Court, Temple, London, EC4Y 7AN
Tel (020) 7842 5555 **Fax** (020) 7583 2036 **DX** 303 LDE
Email chambers@4pumpcourt.com **Website** www.4pumpcourt.com
Also tenants at Arbitration Chambers Hong Kong **Website** www.arbitrationchambershk.com

Head of Chambers	Jeremy Storey QC Nigel Tozzi QC
Chief Executive	Carolyn McCombe
Head Clerks	Carl Wall Stewart Gibbs
Clerk	Jon Robinson
Tenants	63

MEMBERS

Jeremy Storey QC (1974) (QC-1994)
Nigel Tozzi QC (1980) (QC-2001)
David Friedman QC (1968) (QC-1990)
Christopher Moger QC (1972) (QC-1992)
Jonathan Marks QC (1975) (QC-1995)
Anthony Speaight QC (1973) (QC-1995)
John Rowland QC (1979) (QC-1996)
Michael Douglas QC (1974) (QC-1997)
Jeremy Nicholson QC (1977) (QC-2000)
James Cross QC (1985) (QC-2006)
Nicholas Vineall QC (1988) (QC-2006)
Alex Charlton QC (1983) (QC-2008)
Duncan McCall QC (1988) (QC-2008)
Aidan Christie QC (1988) (QC-2008)
Andrew Neish QC (1988) (QC-2009)
Sean Brannigan QC (1994) (QC-2009)
Michael Davie QC (1993) (QC-2010)
Alexander Gunning QC (1994) (QC-2012)
Rachel Ansell QC (1995) (QC-2014)
Sean O'Sullivan QC (1997) (QC-2014)
Benjamin Pilling QC (1997) (QC-2015)
Terence Bergin (1985) (QC-2016)
Alexander Hickey (1995) (QC-2016)
Allen Dyer (1976)
Peter Hamilton (1968)
Simon Henderson (1993)
Kate Vaughan-Neil (1994)
Claire Packman (1996)
Jonathan Lewis (1996)
Lynne McCafferty (1997)
James Purchas (1997)
Alison Potter (1987)
James Leabeater (1999)
James Bowling (1999)
James Watthey (2000)
Kate Livesey (2001)
Jessica Stephens (2001)
Peter Oliver (2002)
Thomas Crangle (2002)
George Woods (2003)
James Hatt (2003)
Rangan Chatterjee (2004)
Matthew Lavy (2004)
Simon Goldstone (2004)
Luke Wygas (2004)
Neil Henderson (2004)
Laura Crowley (2005)
Richard Osborne (2005)
Alexander Wright (2007)
Andrew Stevens (2007)
Daniel Goodkin (2008)
Adam Temple (2008)
Iain Munro (2009)
Martyn Naylor (2009)
Sanjay Patel (2010)
Rani Noakes (2010)
Matthew Thorne (2011)
Gideon Shirazi (2012)
Ed Jones (2012)
Daniel Churcher (2012)
Robert Scrivener (2013)
Helen Dennis (2013)
Daniel Khoo (2014)

THE CHAMBERS 4 Pump Court is one of the leading full-service commercial sets of barristers' chambers, with high rankings in international arbitration, commercial dispute resolution, professional negligence, IT and telecoms, banking and financial services, shipping, energy, construction and engineering and insurance and re-insurance. 4 Pump Court is a modern and progressive set, with an imaginative, client-friendly and efficient team of clerks. The set prides itself on anticipating, understanding and responding to clients' business and commercial needs and on providing a high-quality, efficient and effective service.

WORK UNDERTAKEN 4 Pump Court undertakes general commercial and contractual work, with a particular focus on the following areas:
International Arbitration: Members of chambers represent clients in major arbitrations in a wide range of disputes across their areas of expertise, appearing before tribunals throughout the world. They also deal with ancillary domestic applications for relief in relation to arbitration proceedings in the UK. Senior members of chambers sit as arbitrators in the UK and abroad.
Construction: 4 Pump Court is one of the three leading chambers practising in construction law. The set's hugely experienced construction practitioners have expertise in all aspects of construction, engineering and infrastructure disputes in relation to global and domestic projects. 4 Pump Court's construction specialists are regularly instructed as advisors and advocates in all forums for dispute resolution, including adjudication, expert determination, ADR, arbitration and litigation.
IT & Telecoms: 4 Pump Court's top-ranked technology and telecoms group has enormous experience in IT, e-commerce and telecommunications law. It primarily focuses on disputes of a contractual nature, which require industry and detailed technical knowledge, understanding of software, project implementation and the underlying commercial issues. The set has been involved in the majority of the leading cases in this area, with a quickly developing interest in intellectual property matters.
Energy: 4 Pump Court's energy practice reflects its experience in the commercial and construction fields, experience which makes it uniquely qualified to advise and represent clients in relation to offshore construction and energy-related projects. Members of chambers have broad experience of the complex issues arising from contracts for the exploitation of natural resources and particular expertise in offshore construction and shipbuilding.
Shipping: The set has an outstanding reputation for marine related disputes including wet and dry shipping and shipbuilding. Members of chambers are instructed by international law firms and P&I clubs on behalf of ship owners, charterers, shipyards, drilling contractors, cargo interests and banks. The set's shipping practitioners have expertise in charterparty and bill of lading disputes, ship sale and purchase, ship mortgages, liens, admiralty matters including collision, towage and pilotage, and also commercial shipbuilding, superyacht and mega yacht disputes, including brokers commission claims and disputes concerning refund guarantees.

4 PUMP COURT Jeremy Storey QC & Nigel Tozzi QC (continued)

Professional Negligence: 4 Pump Court is one of the leading chambers in this field, with experience in claims for and against professionals across the whole spectrum of professional liability work, including breach of fiduciary duty and fraud and in all forums. The set has particular expertise in disputes concerning architects and engineers, IT consultants, solicitors and barristers, accountants and auditors, financial advisers, insurance brokers and underwriting agents, and surveyors and valuers.

Insurance: 4 Pump Court's highly recommended insurance and reinsurance group continues to be instructed in connection with many significant events affecting the London insurance market. Members act on behalf of UK and international insurance companies and Lloyd's syndicates, as well as insurers and brokers, both domestically and abroad.

Financial Services & Banking: 4 Pump Court's financial services work straddles both financial regulation and banking litigation. Members frequently act for the regulator and have in-depth knowledge of a variety of financial products, collective investment schemes, SIPPS and experience in perimeter policing, enforcement and FSMA. In addition to their historic involvement with bank charges and PPI, members of chambers regularly receive instructions involving swaps mis-selling, ISDA, forex trading and other complex financial instruments, as well as retail banking litigation.

6 PUMP COURT Stephen Hockman QC

6 Pump Court, Temple, London, EC4Y 7AR
Tel (020) 7797 8400 **Fax** (020) 7797 8401 **DX** 293 Chancery Lane, London
Email clerks@6pumpcourt.co.uk **Website** www.6pumpcourt.co.uk

Head of Chambers	Stephen Hockman QC
Senior Clerk	Richard Constable
Tenants	56

MEMBERS

Stephen Hockman QC (1970) (QC-1990) ^
Richard Barraclough QC (1980) (QC-2003) ^
David Travers QC (1981) (QC-2010) ^
Roy Martin QC (1990) (QC-2008)
Oliver Saxby QC (1992) (QC-2013) ^
Grant Armstrong (1978) ^
Mark Harris (1980)
Anne Williams (1980) ^
Nicholas Baldock (1983) ^
Caroline Topping (1984) ^
Paul Taylor (1985)
Megan Thomas (1987) ^
Gordon Wignall (1987) ^
Peter Forbes (1990) ^
Jane Campbell (1990) ^
John O'Higgins (1990) ^
William Upton (1990) ^
Andrew Espley (1993) ^
Ian Thomas (1993) ^
Paul Hogben (1993)
Mark Watson (1994) ^
Edward Grant (1994)
Nina Ellin (1994)
Danny Moore (1994) ^
Pascal Bates (1994) ^
Ian Whitehurst (1994)
Peter Alcock (1995) ^
Thomas Stern (1995) ^
Mark Beard (1996) ^
Deborah Charles (1996) ^
Catherine Donnelly (1997) ^
Tanya Robinson (1997) ^
Simon Taylor (1997) ^
Richard Banwell (1998)
Gordon Menzies (1998) ^
John FitzGerald (1998)
Lee Bennett (1998) ^
Tom Dunn (1998)
Lucy Luttman (2001)
David Hercock (2001) ^
Giles Atkinson (2002) ^
Stuart Jessop (2002) ^
Christopher Badger (2002) ^
Emmaline Lambert (2003) ^
Grace Cullen (2005) ^
Thaiza Khan (2006)
Isabella Crowdy (2008) ^
Kieran Brand (2007) ^
Ian Rees Phillips (2009) ^
Nicholas Ostrowski (2009) ^
Laura Phillips (2009) ^
Craig Evans (2010)
John Dowlman (2011)
Mukhtiar Singh (2011) ^
Frances Lawson (2013)
Kristiina Reed (2013)

^ Public/Direct Access

THE CHAMBERS Founded in the 1920s as a specialist criminal, civil and family set; now evolved into one of the strongest sets in environmental/planning, health and safety and all other forms of regulatory law as well.

WORK UNDERTAKEN

Civil & Commercial: Commercial disputes, professional negligence and landlord and tenant work.
Criminal: Proven track record both prosecuting (including private prosecutions) and defending (individuals and corporations). Particularly noted for expertise in cases of homicide and serious sexual offences.
Employment: Unfair dismissal claims, discrimination cases (including disability discrimination), pension rights, redundancy, part-time working, TUPE transfers and rights of employees employed abroad.
Family: Matrimonial finance including corporate, agricultural, overseas trusts and high-value matters. Private child care applications. Care proceedings, alleged child abuse adoption and other public cases.
Financial Conduct: All financial litigation and advice, including civil commercial fraud, criminal serious fraud, confiscation, revenue/BIS investigations/prosecutions, bribery, financial professional discipline/corporate governance, Financial Conduct Authority regulation, utility regulation and consumer credit.
Inquests & Inquiries: Including Article 2 inquests and Coroners' reports to prevent future deaths.
Personal Injury: Including employers' liability, road traffic accidents and clinical negligence.
Planning & Environmental: Public inquiries and regulatory criminal proceedings for and against regulators/authorities. Particular expertise at the interface of environmental, planning and human rights law.
Public: Judicial review and advice, often with a planning/environmental or regulatory subject matter.
Regulatory: Prosecuting and defending regulatory criminal offences including health and safety (e.g. construction, energy, transport), food and consumer protection/trading standards. Licensing. Professional discipline.

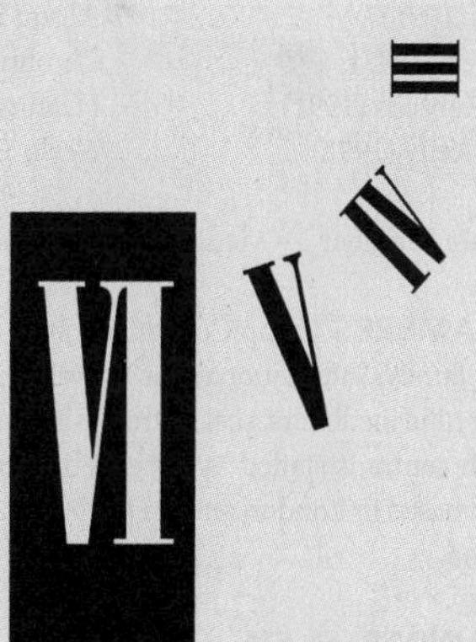

PUMP COURT CHAMBERS Oba Nsugbe QC

3 Pump Court, Temple, London, EC4Y 7AJ
Tel (020) 7353 0711 **Fax** (0845) 259 3241 **DX** 362
Email clerks@pumpcourtchambers.com **Website** www.pumpcourtchambers.com

Head of Chambers	Oba Nsugbe QC
Chief Clerk	David Barber
Deputy Chief & Senior Family Clerk	Tony Atkins
Senior Criminal Clerk	Tony George
Senior Civil Clerk	Jonathan Cue
Tenants	96

MEMBERS

Oba Nsugbe QC (1985) (QC-2002) +
Nigel Pascoe QC (1966) (QC-1988)
Anthony Donne QC (1973) (QC-1988)
Jonathan Cohen QC (1974) (QC-1997) *
Susan Campbell QC (1986) (QC-2009)
Leslie Samuels QC (1989) (QC-2011) +
Stewart Patterson (1967) +
Frank Abbott (1972) +
Charles Parry (1973) +
John Ker-Reid (1974)
Michael Butt (1974)
Charles Gabb (1975)
Julie MacKenzie (1978) +
Stephen Jones (1978)
Martin Blount (1982)
Kevin Haven (1982) +
Matthew Scott (1985)
Hugh Travers (1988)
Justin Gau (1989)
Edward Boydell (1989)
Andrew Houston (1989)
Anthony Akiwumi (1989) *
Catherine Breslin (1990)
Helen Khan (1990)
Penny Howe (1991)
Gary Self (1991)
Julian Reed (1991)
Imogen Robbins (1991)
Geoffrey Kelly (1992)
James Newton-Price (1992)
Mark Ruffell (1992)
Leonorah Smith (1993)
Mark Ashley (1993)
Oliver Peirson (1993)
Elizabeth Gunther (1993)
Tom Wilkins (1993)
Robert Pawson (1994)
Daniel Reilly (1995) ^
Richard Hall (1995)
Mark Dubbery (1996) +
Peter Asteris (1996)
Sarah Jones (1996)
Michael Hall (1996)
Andrew Grime (1997) +
Ruth Arlow (1997)
Maria Gallagher (1997)
Anne Ward (1997) +
Amy Ephgrave (1997)
Timothy Dracass (1998)
Andrew Bond (1999)
Louise De Rozarieux (1999)
Rachel Spearing (1999)
Colin Banham (1999)
Richard Tutt (2000)
Lubeya Ramadhan (2000)
Anne Brown (2000)
Naznin Islam (2000)
Stuart McGhee (2000)
Jason Nickless (2001)
Alison Burge (2002)
Caroline Hartley (2002)
Heather Platt (2002) +
Neelo Shravat (2002)
David Josty (2002)
John Chapman (2003)
Charlotte Street (2003)
Zoe Rudd (2003)
Lucy Davis (2003)
Conor Mullan (2003)
Amy Berry (2003) +
Claire Fox (2003)
Adam Gadd (2004)
Tara Lyons (2005) +
Timothy Akers (2005)
Corinne Iten (2006)
Patricia O'Driscoll (2006)
Sally Davidson (2006)
Jennifer Lee (2007)
Daniella Gilbert (2007)
Eleanor Bruce (2008)
Simon Purkis (2008)
Guy Draper (2008)
Jennifer Swan (2009)
Nicholas Williamson (2009)
Paul Mertens (2010)
Victoria Ellis (2010)
Naomi Gyane (2010)
Jack Rundall (2010)
Ezra Macdonald (2012)
Maria Henty (2012)
Michael Standing (2013)
Lucy Plumpton (2013)
Samuel Burrett (2013)
Richard Wayman (2015)
Giles Harrap +
Stephen Fielding +

* Associate Member + Mediator/Arbitrator

THE CHAMBERS Pump Court Chambers is a large and well established common law set specialising in civil, criminal, family, international law as well services in non court disputes resolution. The set has 93 barristers, including nine mediators, six arbitrators and six silks; based across three offices in London, Winchester and Swindon. Each centre is staffed by an experienced clerking team known for providing a consistently high service. Although based in London and on the Western Circuit, the work done by members extends throughout the UK and abroad.

WORK UNDERTAKEN

Family: With 54 members including three QCs, two arbitrators and one mediator, Pump Court Chambers has one of the largest specialist family law teams at the Bar. The team practices in four main areas: family finance, court of protection work and children law; public and private. The family finance team undertakes a wide spectrum of work from complex high net worth "Big Money" cases to actions with more modest assets and incomes. The private children law team specialises in residence and contact disputes as well as applications for permission to remove children from the jurisdiction. In public law they advise and represent local authorities, parents and guardians in all areas of children work.

Civil: The team, made up of 39 practising members including two Silks continues to growth in strength. Chambers has particular expertise in all areas of business and commercial, employment, inheritance, property, personal injury and clinical negligence, professional negligence, regulatory and transport law.

Criminal: Pump Court Chambers' criminal advocates enjoy an outstanding reputation. Over the last 20 years more than 15 of the group have become Circuit Judges. Members have particular expertise in the fields: sexual offences, courts martial, regulatory and disciplinary, dishonesty, drugs, fraud, violence, corporate manslaughter and other health and safety prosecutions.

INTERNATIONAL Chambers enjoys a strong international practice, members provide advice and representation throughout the UK and abroad. Oba Nsugbe QC, SAN is widely acknowledged as one of the UK's and Nigeria's leading barristers and arbitrators. Anthony Akiwumi is admitted as an Attorney of the Cayman Islands and has practised in this jurisdiction since 1997. Jason Nickless has been called to the Bar in the British Virgin Islands..

PUMP COURT TAX CHAMBERS Kevin Prosser QC

16 Bedford Row, London, WC1R 4EF
Tel (020) 7414 8080 **Fax** (020) 7414 8099 **DX** London 312
Email clerks@pumptax.com **Website** www.pumptax.com

Head of Chambers	Kevin Prosser QC
Senior Clerk	Nigel Jones
Tenants	36

MEMBERS

Kevin Prosser QC (1982) (QC-1996)
Andrew Thornhill QC (1969) (QC-1985)
David Milne QC (1970) (QC-1987)
William Massey QC (1977) (QC-1996)
John Tallon QC (1975) (QC-2000)
Giles W J Goodfellow QC (1983) (QC-2003) ^A^
David Ewart QC (1987) (QC-2006)
Julian Ghosh QC (1993) (QC-2006)
Rupert Baldry QC (1987) (QC-2010) ^A^
Andrew Hitchmough QC (1991) (QC-2013) ^A^
Roger Thomas (1979) (QC-2014)
Ian Richards (1971)
Janek Matthews (1972) ^A^
Penelope Hamilton (1972) ^A^
Jeremy White (1976) ^A^
Jeremy Woolf (1986) ^A^
Emma Chamberlain (1998) ^A^
Elizabeth Wilson (1995)
Richard Vallat (1997) ^A^
James Henderson (1997)
Sarah Dunn (1998)
Michael Thomas (2001) ^A^
Sadiya Choudhury (2002) ^A^
Oliver Conolly (2003) ^A^
James Rivett (2004)
Jonathan Bremner (2005) ^A^
David Yates (2004) ^A^
Laura Poots (2007) ^A^
Thomas Chacko (2007) ^A^
Zizhen Yang (2009) ^A^
Charles Bradley (2010) ^A^
Edward Waldegrave (2011) ^A^
Barbara Belgrano (2011) ^A^
Ben Elliott (2012) ^A^
Emma Pearce (2014)
Peter Nias (2012) ^ADR^
Sir Stephen Oliver QC ^ADR^
Dr John Avery Jones CBE ^ADR^

^A^ Public/Direct Access ^ADR^ ADR Member

THE CHAMBERS Pump Court Tax Chambers is the largest specialist set of barristers practising exclusively in tax law. Its work extends from large-scale corporate litigation in the higher courts to advisory work on complex personal tax planning. Members of chambers regularly receive instructions from solicitors and accountancy firms of all sizes (from the 'Magic Circle' solicitors and the 'Big Four' accountants to high street advisors), trust companies and directly from in-house professionals from a wide variety of industries.
Members also represent the UK government (including HM Revenue & Customs) and foreign governments, including those of Bermuda, Mauritius, New Zealand, Australia, Singapore and Hong Kong. In addition to a popular annual programme of tax seminars, members are frequent speakers at industry events, and contribute to many specialist textbooks and journals: among other works, the set houses the authors of the pioneering tax planning work Potter and Monroe's Tax Planning with Precedents, together with many of the contributing authors of Simon's Taxes, and the Consulting Editor of Simon's Tax Cases. All members of chambers accept instructions under licensed access and some can accept instructions under Public Access. Full information about how to instruct members of chambers can be found on chambers' website.

WORK UNDERTAKEN Pump Court Tax Chambers fields experts in a full range of corporate and business tax issues, from group reorganisations and mergers to structured finance. Its members advise on a daily basis with regards to international and EU aspects of tax law both for the purposes of tax planning and in a litigious context. Almost all of the leading cases concerning the application of EU law to the direct tax code have featured members of Pump Court Tax Chambers. In addition to appellate work (before the tax tribunals and higher courts) and judicial review proceedings, members of chambers also appear before the courts in other types of litigation which raise tax issues, such as professional negligence claims, trust litigation and matrimonial disputes. Chambers has a strong private client following, with a long history of advising individuals, family companies, trusts and estates. It is able to provide advice on all relevant taxes, including inheritance tax, capital gains tax, income tax and stamp duty land tax issues. Typical examples of such work include the sale and reorganisation of family companies, advice on family trusts and tax planning for landed estates. Its members regularly advise on business property relief, agricultural property relief and specialist heritage property reliefs and, for international clients, expert advice is offered on issues surrounding residence and domicile. Chambers has a number of experts in the niche field of employee remuneration, who advise regularly on share options, pension schemes, employee share ownership plans, profit sharing schemes and national insurance contributions. A considerable proportion of chambers' work concerns VAT advice and litigation. All VAT topics are covered, including partial exemption, business/non-business activity, the Single Market, European law and alternative remedies such as judicial review and actions for Francovich damages. Chambers also provides advice on other indirect taxes, including insurance premium tax, customs duties, landfill tax, climate change levy and aggregates levy. Members of chambers have specialist expertise in all stamp taxes and, in particular, issues with regard to corporate acquisitions and restructuring, property transactions, developments and refinancing. In addition to their daily work as advocates, chambers' Barristers are often instructed to appear as expert witnesses. They also have a particular interest in the use and development of ADR in a tax context, and can offer accredited tax mediators, arbitrators and facilitators.

PUMP COURT
TAX CHAMBERS

QEB HOLLIS WHITEMAN Mark Ellison QC

Head of Chambers	Mark Ellison QC
Senior Clerk	Chris Emmings
Chambers Director	Alastair Rhodes
Tenants	67

1-2 Laurence Pountney Hill, London, EC4R 0EU
Tel (020) 7933 8855 **Fax** (020) 7929 3732 **DX** 858 London City
Email barristers@qebhw.co.uk **Website** www.qebholliswhiteman.co.uk

MEMBERS

Mark Ellison QC (1979) (QC-2008)
John Hilton QC (1964) (QC-1990)
Sir David Calvert-Smith (1969) *
Peter Kyte QC (1970) (QC-1996)
David Spens QC (1973) (QC-1995)
William Boyce QC (1976) (QC-2001)
Tim Roberts QC (1978) (QC-2003) *
David Jeremy QC (1977) (QC-2006)
Edward Brown QC (1983) (QC-2008)
Crispin Aylett QC (1985) (QC-2008)
Peter Finnigan QC (1979) (QC-2009)
Tom Kark QC (1982) (QC-2010)
Sean Larkin QC (1987) (QC-2010)
Eleanor Laws QC (1990) (QC-2011)
Zoe Johnson QC (1990) (QC-2012)
Nicholas Griffin QC (1992) (2011 NI) (QC 2012)
Adrian Darbishire QC (1993) (QC-2012)
Philip Evans QC (1995) (QC 2016)
Linda Strudwick (1973)
Ian Paton (1975)
James Bagge (1979) *
Caroline Carney SC (1980) (SC-2001) *
David Groome (1987)
Edward Henry (1988)
Roger Smart (1989)
Paul Wakerley (1990)
Jason Mansell (1991)
Lydia Barnfather (1992)
Selva Ramasamy (1992)
Nicholas Corsellis (1993)
Benn Maguire (1994)
Paul Raudnitz (1994)
Mark Aldred (1996)
Susannah Stevens (1997)
Julian Evans (1997)
Rebecca Harris (1997)
Natasha Tahta (1998)
Jocelyn Ledward (1999)
Alexandra Felix (1999)
Ben FitzGerald (2000)
Lucy Kennedy (2000)
Karen Robinson (2000)
Kerry Broome (2003)
Ari Alibhai (2003)
Philip McGhee (2003)
Philip Stott (2004)
Joanna Warwick (2004) *
Tom Baker (2004)
Fraser Coxhill (2004)
Adam King (2005)
Caoimhe Daly (2005)
Rachna Gokani (2006)
Jim Wormington (2007) *
Tom Broomfield (2007)
John Lynch (2008)
Fallon Alexis (2008)
Rhys Meggy (2009)
Katherine Buckle (2009)
Tim Naylor (2010)
Polly Dyer (2010)
Tom Doble (2011)
Isobel Coates (2011)
Katherine Lloyd (2011)
Thomas Coke-Smyth (2011)
Arabella MacDonald (2012)
Eloise Emanuel (2012)
Tom Orpin-Massey (2013)

* Associate member

THE CHAMBERS QEB Hollis Whiteman is regarded both nationally and internationally as a leading set within the fields of business crime, general crime, professional regulation and discipline, and intellectual property. Excellence is at the core of the business strategy which is reflected in the approach that is taken to work, across the board. Members and clerks are flexible and innovative, professional, approachable and highly efficient to ensure that chambers continues to develop in a rapidly changing and competitive market place. Public access is accepted by many members of these chambers.

THE SET Chambers is renowned for its wide ranging skills and experience; most often for its strength in advocacy and advisory work. Clients are consistently reassured that chambers remains the number one choice in its respective fields.

WORK UNDERTAKEN

Business Crime & Fraud: Chambers brings high levels of expertise and experience of UK and international jurisdictions to its provision of advice and representation in all areas of fraud and financial crime; bribery/corruption; corporate manslaughter; sanctions; cartels/price fixing; asset forfeiture and recovery; money laundering; insider dealing; market rigging; search warrants and other orders; intellectual property; consumer liability. Members continue to appear in ground breaking trials and as a result of experience of both the 'criminal' and 'corporate' fraud worlds are adept at managing complex investigations.

Professional Regulation: Chambers has an enviable reputation in the regulation of a whole host of professions both in prosecuting and defending. Members regularly appear before disciplinary tribunals (including healthcare, accountants, police, solicitors, courts martial) and regulatory authorities, including the General Medical Council, the General Dental Council, the FCA and sports governing bodies. The knowledge and skill that chambers has gleaned from the directly relevant general and corporate crime practice areas, particularly fraud, significantly sets QEB Hollis Whiteman aside from its competitors.

Crime: Chambers is very proud of its long-standing reputation as one of the finest criminal chambers in the country in both general and corporate crime. Members of chambers continue to prosecute and defend in many of the most significant and high profile criminal trials. Experience is vast and expertise is offered at all levels.

The breadth and depth of experience in criminal and regulatory law has ensured chambers' development in the following areas: public inquiries; inquests; health and safety; consumer law and trading standards.

QUADRANT CHAMBERS Luke Parsons QC

Quadrant House, 10 Fleet Street, London, EC4Y 1AU
Tel (020) 7583 4444 **Fax** (020) 7583 4455 **DX** 292 London (Chancery Lane)
Email info@quadrantchambers.com **Website** www.quadrantchambers.com

Head of Chambers	Luke Parsons QC
Chief Operating Officer	Peter Blair
Senior Clerks	Gary Ventura
	Simon Slattery
Tenants	65

MEMBERS

Luke Parsons QC (1985) (QC-2003)
Michael N Howard QC (1971) (QC-1986)
Jeremy Russell QC (1975) (QC-1994)
Lionel Persey QC (1981) (QC-1997)
Simon Rainey QC (1982) (QC-2000)
Simon Kverndal QC (1982) (QC-2002)
Nigel Jacobs QC (1983) (QC-2006)
David Goldstone QC (1986) (QC-2006)
Simon Croall QC (1986) (QC-2008)
Robert Lawson QC (1989) (QC-2009)
Nigel Cooper QC (1987) (QC-2010)
Poonam Melwani QC (1989) (QC-2011)
Robert Thomas QC (1992) (QC-2011)
Chirag Karia QC (1988) (QC-2012)
James M Turner QC (1990) (QC-2013)
Michael Davey QC (1990) (QC-2014)
John Russell QC (1993) (QC-2014)
Guy Blackwood QC (1997) (QC-2014)
Michael Nolan QC (1981) (QC-2015)
John Passmore QC (1992) (QC-2015)
John Kimbell QC (1995) (QC-2015)
Michael McParland (1983)
Matthew Reeve (1987)
Nevil Phillips (1992)
Thomas Macey-Dare (1994)
Nichola Warrender (1995)
Jonathan Chambers (1996)
Stewart Buckingham (1996)
Robert-Jan Temmink (1996)
Peter Ferrer (1998)
Yash Kulkarni (1998)
Christopher M Smith (1999)
Jeremy Richmond (2000)
Timothy Marland (2002)
David Semark (2002)
Ruth Hosking (2002)
Caroline Pounds (2003)
Paul Toms (2003)
Emmet Coldrick (2004)
Paul Henton (2004)
Saira Paruk (2004)
Turlough Stone (2004)
Gemma Morgan (2006)
David Walsh (2007)
Natalie Moore (2007)
Lucas Bastin (2008)3
Benjamin Coffer (2008)
Stephanie Barrett (2008)
Claudia Wilmot-Smith (2008)
Henry Ellis (2008)
Peter Stevenson (2008)
Christopher Jay (2009)
Liisa Lahti (2009)
Ben Gardner (2010)
Andrew Leung (2010)
Mark Stiggelbout (2011)
Tom Bird (2011)
Emily McCrea-Theaker (2011)
Joseph England (2011)
Max Davidson (2013)
Michael Proctor (2013)
Andrew Carruth (2013)
Koye Akoni (2014)
Craig Williams (2014)
George Economou (1965)

THE CHAMBERS Quadrant members are considered to be approachable and responsive and are renowned for working closely with their clients and for being aware of their concerns and priorities. Members are, of course, experts in their fields, but combine that expertise with compassion and understanding. Quadrant instructs an external organisation to appraise members' relationships with clients and uses that feedback to improve service annually. Chambers has a highly motivated support team of clerks and administrative staff who are noted for their commitment to providing the highest level of support and service to all with whom they work. Quadrant has a modern and flexible attitude to structuring fees. Quadrant House is equipped with conference, video conference, arbitration and event facilities.

WORK UNDERTAKEN Quadrant Chambers holds a pre-eminent international position in shipping, energy, insurance, aviation and travel. In addition to continuing to strengthen its leading position in these areas, Quadrant has teams focussed on continuing to build its reputation in commodities, insolvency and international arbitration.
Quadrant's specialist areas of expertise include: alternative dispute resolution, aviation, banking and finance, chancery and company, civil fraud, commercial dispute resolution, construction, energy and natural resources, information technology, insolvency and restructuring, insurance and re-insurance, international arbitration, international trade and commodities, professional negligence, public international law, shipbuilding, shipping and maritime and sports law.
Members of chambers and arbitrator members also accept appointments as inquiry chairs, arbitrators and mediators.

INTERNATIONAL A large proportion of Quadrant's work is for international clients or involves international commercial law. Members have appeared as advocates and expert witnesses before courts and tribunals worldwide and several have been Called to the bars of other jurisdictions including those of Hong Kong, Singapore, Korea, Gibraltar, New South Wales, California, Germany, Greece, Ireland and South Africa.

QUEEN ELIZABETH BUILDING (QEB) Lewis Marks QC

Queen Elizabeth Building, Temple, London, EC4Y 9BS
Tel (020) 7797 7837 **Fax** (020) 7353 5422 **DX** 339 London/Chancery Lane
Email clerks@qeb.co.uk **Website** www.qeb.co.uk

Head of Chambers	Lewis Marks QC
Senior Clerk	Howard Rayner
Tenants	32

MEMBERS

Lewis Marks QC (1984) (QC-2002)
Lucy Stone QC (1983) (QC-2001)
Tim Amos QC (1987) (QC-2008)
Stewart Leech QC (1992) (QC-2011)
James Ewins QC (1996) (QC-2016)
Michael Hosford-Tanner (1974)
Andrew Tidbury (1976)
Thomas Brudenell (1977)
Oliver Wise (1981)
Sarah Edwards (1990)
Matthew Firth (1991)
Elizabeth Clarke (1991)
Alexander Thorpe (1995)
Catherine Cowton (1995)
Sarah Phipps (1997)
Marcus Lazarides (1999)
Duncan Brooks (2000)
Daniel Bentham (2000)
Tristan Harvey (2002)
Morgan Sirikanda (2002)
Rosemary Budden (2003)
Charanjit Batt (2003)
Samantha Singer (2004)
Marina Faggionato (2006)
William Tyzack (2007)
Saima Younis (2008)
Amy Kisser (2009)
Fitzrene Headley (2011)
Sophie Wellings (2011)
Robert Cornick (2012)
Andrew Campbell (2012)
Janine McGuigan (2012)
Dr Jens M Scherpe (Cambridge)+
Charles Hyde QC (1988) (QC-2006) *
Hannah Baker (Hague Conference) (2005) *
Sir Alan Ward **
Sir Hugh Bennett **
Sir Paul Coleridge **

+ Academic Door Tenant * Door Tenant ** Associate Members

THE CHAMBERS QEB specialises in family law, particularly in matrimonial finance and international family law, but also in child law including child abduction and forced marriage. The set has been established for well over 100 years and is consistently rated as one of the very best sets for family law. It is also very forward-looking and client-focussed. Chambers has expanded premises for private FDRs and other forms of dispute resolution including arbitration, mediation and collaborative law. Many members of chambers are listed as leaders in their field in '*Chambers and Partners*' and '*The Legal 500*'. The legal directories' praise for QEB includes the following published reviews: "heavyweight family law chambers"; "skilled at all aspects of family law"; "long held reputation for excellence"; "hotbed of talent"; "good commercial sense"; "fine tradition of producing the very best financial barristers"; "jam-packed with trouble shooters capable of tackling the thorniest money cases" and "offers real depth of experience across the silk and junior end of the market" (*Chambers and Partners*); while 'The Legal 500' says 'QEB is hailed as 'the best family set from top to bottom,' with 'an eminent matrimonial practice,' which 'has been in the top echelons for decades.' 'The barristers are of consistently high quality, they never let you down and solicitors cannot praise them highly enough.' 'Members appear in the most important family cases, particularly involving high-net-worth finance and complex cross-jurisdiction elements.'

QEB has always had an excellent reputation for the quality of the advocates it produces and has been involved in many high profile and historic decisions. Many members of chambers have continued into high judicial office and Lord Wilson sits in the Supreme Court. In addition Sir Alan Ward, following his retirement from the Court of Appeal, and Sir Hugh Bennett and Sir Paul Coleridge, former High Court Judges, have joined chambers as associate members. Sir Alan Ward is the chair of the Civil Mediaton Council and acts as an arbitrator, private-FDR judge and mediator. Sir Hugh Bennett and Sir Paul Coleridge act as arbitrators and private-FDR judges.

WORK UNDERTAKEN QEB is particularly well known for dealing with the financial consequences of relationship breakdown but there is immense experience in all aspects of family law including: jurisdictional disputes, foreign divorces, pre-marital agreements, civil partnerships, injunctions both financial and domestic and private law child work, child abduction and forced marriage, Inheritance Act claims and disputes between former cohabitees. In addition some members practise in general common law with particular emphasis on personal injury and professional negligence work.

As a complement to its international work QEB offers a range of languages including members of chambers professionally fluent in French, German, Hindi, Punjabi and Urdu.

Members of QEB appear in courts throughout the country and abroad, ranging from magistrates' courts to the UK Supreme Court and the Court of Justice of the European Union. The confidentiality of chambers' work is strictly respected but recent public decisions in which members of QEB were briefed include Jones, Z v Z (No.2.), Petrodel v Prest, Luckwell v. Limata, Cooper-Hohn, AB v JB (EMR modification), Arif v Anwar, Bromfield, A v B (CJEU), E v E (Art 19 and Seisin B IIa) and Fields. QEB has always been at the forefront of the development of matrimonial law and members have appeared in many of the leading authorities including such seminal decisions as Wachtel, F v F, Duxbury, Preston, White, Miller, Charman and Spencer.

The QEB clerks are happy to recommend particular members of Chambers for particular cases and provide charging rates on request, as well as practical assistance in the management of cases. The QEB clerks are regularly singled out for special praise by external commentators who have hailed the 'superlative clerking' at QEB, which is rightly described as 'seamless, professional and courteous' and 'the best in London, without question.'

RADCLIFFE CHAMBERS Keith Rowley QC

11 New Square, Lincoln's Inn, London, WC2A 3QB
Tel (020) 7831 0081 **Fax** (020) 7405 2560 DX LDE 319
Website www.radcliffechambers.com

Head of Chambers	Keith Rowley QC
Senior Clerks	Keith Nagle
	John Clark
Chief Executive	Fiona Fitzgerald
Tenants	53

MEMBERS

Peter Crampin QC (1976) (QC-1993)
Malcolm Waters QC (1977) (QC-1997)
Jeremy Cousins QC (1977) (QC-1999)
Keith Rowley QC (1979) (QC-2001)
Robert Pearce QC (1977) (QC-2006)
Francesca Quint (1970)
David di Mambro (1973)
Gordon Nurse (1973)
Stephen Acton (1977)
Elizabeth Ovey (1978)
Thomas Dumont (1979)
Ulick Staunton (1984)
Simon Williams (1984)
Tina Kyriakides (1984)
Piers Feltham (1985)
Howard Smith (1986)
Mark West (1987)
Roger Mullis (1987)
Clive Moys (1998)
Katherine McQuail (1989)
Adam Deacock (1991)
Peter Dodge (1992)
Shantanu Majumdar (1992)
Marie-Claire Bleasdale (1993)
Justin Holmes (1994)
Dov Ohrenstein (1995)
Christopher Boardman (1995)
Douglas Keel (1997)
Kate Selway (1995)
Gary Lidington (2000)
William Moffett (2000)
Nathan Wells (2000)
Mark Mullen (2001)
Joshua Winfield (2001)
Marcus Flavin (2001)
Frances Ratcliffe (2002)
Reuben Comiskey (2002)
Martin Ouwehand (2002)
Oliver Hilton (2002)
Tom Beasley (2003)
Steven Barrett (2003)
Christopher Buckley (2004)
Mark Fell (2004)
Edward Hicks (2004)
Josh Lewison (2005)
Wendy Mathers (2005)
Dawn McCambley (2005)
Catherine Doran (2008)
Natalie Brown (2009)
Daniel Burton (2009)
Henry Day (2011)
Nicholas Macklam (2013)
Jonathan Edwards (2014)

THE CHAMBERS Radcliffe Chambers is a modern Barristers Chambers based in Lincoln's Inn. It has 53 barristers, with many recommendations in the current editions of Chambers and Partners and The Legal 500 directories. The achievements of individual members have been recognised in recent years in the STEP Private Client Awards, The Lawyer Awards and The Lawyer's Hot 100. Radcliffe Chambers was a recent winner of the Client Service Set of the Year at the Chambers and Partners Bar Awards and has in recent years been shortlisted for the STEP Private Client Awards and Legal Week Innovation Awards.
Chambers has a dedicated and experienced staff led by two senior clerks and a Chief Executive; they all help to provide the very best service for its clients, whether they are law firms in the UK or offshore; in-house lawyers; government departments; financial and other institutions; local authorities; and professional or public direct access clients.

WORK UNDERTAKEN Members of Radcliffe Chambers practise in the fields of banking and financial services (including consumer credit and mortgages); charities; company and commercial law; insolvency; pensions; professional negligence; property and trusts and private client work. Members of chambers have also acquired notable expertise in other areas such as agriculture; court of protection cases; ecclesiastical law; mines and minerals; partnerships and joint ventures; planning and local government; tax and telecommunications. For full details please see the chambers website at www.radcliffechambers.com or contact chambers directly for further assistance.

Radcliffe Chambers

THREE RAYMOND BUILDINGS Alexander Cameron QC

Head of Chambers	Alexander Cameron QC
Senior Clerk	Eddie Holland
Tenants	49

3 Raymond Buildings, Gray's Inn, London, WC1R 5BH
Tel (020) 7400 6400 **Fax** (020) 7400 6464 **DX** 237 London
Email clerks@3rblaw.com **Website** www.3rblaw.com

MEMBERS

Alexander Cameron QC (1986) (QC-2003) ^
Clive Nicholls QC (1957) (QC-1982) ^
Colin Nicholls QC (1957) (QC-1981) ^
Richard Horwell QC (1976) (QC-2006)
Michael Borrelli QC (1977) (QC-2000)
Trevor Burke QC (1981) (QC-2001) ^
Michael Bromley-Martin QC (1979) (QC-2002) ^
James Lewis QC (1987) (QC-2002)^
Jane Humphryes QC (1983) (QC-2003)
Simon Farrell QC (1983) (QC-2003) ^
Patrick Gibbs QC (1986) (QC-2006) ^
Helen Malcolm QC (1986) (QC-2006) ^
John Hardy QC (1988) (QC-2008)
Stephen Walsh QC (1983) (QC-2009) ^
Hugo Keith QC (1989) (QC-2009)
Hugh Davies OBE QC (1990) (QC-2013) ^
James Hines QC (1982) (QC-2015) ^
Jonathan Ashley-Norman QC (1989) (QC-2016) ^
Richard Atchley (1977)
Neil Saunders (1983) ^
Ben Brandon (1991)
Richard Wormald (1993) ^
Alisdair Williamson (1994) ^
Siza Agha (1994) ^
Ben Summers (1994) ^
Saba Naqshbandi (1996) ^
William Emlyn Jones (1996)
Edmund Gritt (1997)
Ailsa Williamson (1997)
Kevin Baumber (1998)
Clair Dobbin (1999)
Guy Ladenburg (2000) ^
Nicholas Yeo (1999) ^
Sarah Le Fevre (2001)^
Matthew Butt (2002) ^
Ben Watson (2002) ^
Luke Ponte (2003)
Rachel Scott (2004)
Rachel Barnes (2004) ^
Rachel Kapila (2006) ^
Bo-Eun Jung (2005) ^
Robert Morris (2008)
Emma Collins (2008)
Heather Oliver (2010)
Patrick Hill (2010)
Kitty St Aubyn (2010)
John Greany (2012)
Daniel Mansell (2012)
Eva Niculiu (2013)
Reka Hollos (2014)

^ Public/Direct Access

THE CHAMBERS A multi-disciplined set with a national and international reputation in criminal and quasi-criminal matters.

WORK UNDERTAKEN

Crime: The practice encompasses advocacy and advisory work in every aspect of criminal law, including serious violent and sexual crime, terrorism, drug and human trafficking, bribery and corruption, organised crime, child exploitation, cybercrime, breaches of the Official Secrets Act. They also have expertise across all levels of call in restraint, civil recovery and confiscation. Recent cases include advice and representation in respect of charges levelled against Rebekah Brooks and Charles Brooks; charges arising from Operations Elvedon, Sasha and Weeting; Michael Turner; Max Clifford; the Hatton Garden Robbery.

Fraud & Financial Regulation: Chambers has a long-established reputation in fraud, money laundering, insider-dealing, and anti-competitive conduct. Expertise extends to civil and commercial fraud claims initiated in the UK and abroad. They are also experienced in Financial Services law and are instructed by both the FCA and individuals and corporations in the financial services industry. Members advise in relation to the full range of FSMA matters including authorisation, compliance and enforcement. Recent matters include Alstom; the LIBOR investigation; the iSoft Fraud.

Extradition & Mutual Legal Assistance: Members have acted in many of the landmark cases of the last 50 years and have helped shape the development of extradition law. They are experts in mutual legal assistance and are instructed regularly by the UK authorities to advise upon and draft letters of request to foreign jurisdictions. They also provide advice and representation to individuals and companies affected by mutual legal assistance requests. Recent cases include Gary McKinnon; Shrien Dewani; Vladimir Antonov; Jack Warner (FIFA).

Public Law: Members appear frequently in judicial review proceedings for both claimants and defendants. They have particular expertise in dealing with applications arising out of extradition proceedings, inquests, decisions relating to the investigation and prosecution of criminal matters, and prison welfare. Members are regularly instructed by the government in public law matters. Hugo Keith QC was a member of the 'A' Panel of civil Treasury Counsel for 8 years and continues to be instructed by the government in matters of public law, and as members of the 'A' panels, Clair Dobbin and Ben Watson are instructed in a wide variety of judicial review claims and advise government departments on a range of public law issues.

Inquests & Inquiries: Members are regularly instructed in inquests of the highest importance, most recently the '7/7' Inquests, Alexander Litvinenko and Mark Duggan. They also have considerable experience in representing core participants and witnesses before Public Inquiries and have been instructed for various parties in some of the most important Inquiries of recent times, including Leveson, Baha Mousa, the Undercover Policing Inquiry and the Independent Inquiry into child sexual abuse.

Regulatory Enforcement: The set provides expert advice and representation on a wide range of statutory regimes that regulate the conduct of public bodies, corporations, and individuals. Members regularly appear for prosecuting authorities and defendants in cases concerning health and safety, fire safety, environmental law, consumer protection, and trading standards. They are also active in the areas of financial regulation and regularly appear before VAT and duties tribunals.

5RB Desmond Browne QC & Matthew Nicklin QC

5 Gray's Inn Square, Gray's Inn, London WC1R 5AH
Tel (020) 7242 2902 **Fax** (020) 7831 2686 **DX** LDE 1054
Email clerks@5RB.com **Website** www.5RB.com

Head of Chambers	Desmond Browne QC & Matthew Nicklin QC
Senior Clerk	Andrew Love
Clerks	Jamie Clack
	Antony Braeger
	Georgina Gills
	Jack Button

MEMBERS

Desmond Browne QC (1969) (QC 1990) ^
Matthew Nicklin QC (1993) (QC 2013) ^
Patrick Milmo QC (1962) (QC 1985) *
Adrienne Page QC (1974) (QC 1999) ^
James Price QC (1974) (QC 1995) ^
Justin Rushbrooke QC (1992) (QC 2013) ^
Stephen Bate (1981) * ^
Andrew Monson (1983) *
Iain Christie (1989) ** ^
Alexandra Marzec (1990) ^
Professor Tony Smith (1992) **
David Sherborne (1992) ^
Jonathan Barnes (1999) ^
Godwin Busuttil (1994) ^
Adam Wolanski (1994)
William Bennett (1994) ^
Christina Michalos (1994) ^
Jacob Dean (1995) ^
Nigel Abbas (1995) * ^
Anna Coppola (1996) ** ^
Adam Speker (1999) ^
Richard Munden (2003) ^
David Hirst (2003) ^
Victoria Simon-Shore (2005) ^
Victoria Jolliffe (2005) ^
Yuli Takatsuki (2007) ^
Patrick McCafferty (2008) ** ^
Felicity McMahon (2008) ^
Chloe Strong (2010) ^
Gervase de Wilde (2012)
Julian Santos (2008) ^
Greg Callus (2012) ^
John Stables (2014)

* Non-resident practising member ** Associate member ^ Direct/Public Access

THE CHAMBERS There are presently 29 members, including six silks. Members of chambers have wide experience in all divisions of the High Court and in the appellate courts. They also appear regularly in the criminal and family courts, usually in reporting restrictions matters, and before domestic tribunals, such as OFCOM and the British Horseracing Authority. Chambers regularly receives instructions from overseas. There are four accredited mediators and two chartered arbitrators.
Most members of 5RB undertake public access work. In addition to litigation, members of chambers provide pre-publication advice, usually to newspapers, media organisations, book publishers, public authorities and companies.

WORK UNDERTAKEN 5RB enjoys a pre-eminent reputation in cases where there is or may be a clash between freedom of expression and other rights. Members of chambers specialise in defamation, malicious falsehood, privacy, breach of confidence, contempt of court, reporting restrictions, data protection, harassment and other related causes of action. They are regularly called upon to advise in cases of publication online and on social media, particularly where the identity of a publisher is unknown, and to seek disclosure or apply for Norwich Pharmacal orders. Some members of chambers specialise across a broader spectrum of media, entertainment, IP and sports law, including copyright, passing off, broadcasting regulatory work and sports tribunal work. Chambers is also involved in group litigation such as phone-hacking, construction industry black-listing and data protection breaches. Recent cases include: *PJS v News Group Newspapers* (SC); *Coventry v Lawrence* (SC); *OPO v MLA* (SC); *Pinard-Byrne v Linton* (PC); *Gulati and ors v MGN* (Mirror phone-hacking) (CA); *WM Morrison Payroll Information Group Litigation*; *Weller v ANL* (CA); *Murray v ANL* (CA); *Lachaux v Independent Print Ltd*; *Sobrinho v Impresa*; *Yeo v Times Newspapers Ltd*; *Various Claimants v NGN* (News Group phone-hacking litigation); *AMC v KLJ*; *Lokhova v Tymula*; *Axon v Ministry of Defence*; *Burrell v Clifford*; *Theedom v Nourish Training*; *Cheshire West v Pickthall*; *Horan v Express Newspapers*; *A-G v Conde Nast*; *Al Alaoui v Elaph*; *National Farmers' Union v Tiernan*; *Ashgar v Ahmad*.
Frequently 5RB's barristers are called upon to advise out-of-hours or to seek or oppose emergency injunctive relief. There are out-of-hours contact arrangements and an on-call rota for advice over weekends and public holidays. 5RB is sensitive to the fact that, as a leading specialist set, different members are often instructed on opposing sides of the same dispute. There are robust arrangements in place to preserve client confidentiality.

PUBLICATIONS Members of the set write or contribute to the principal textbooks in their field: Gatley on *Libel and Slander*, Clerk and Lindsell on *Torts*; *The Law of Privacy and the Media*; *Blackstone's Guide to the Defamation Act 2013*; Arlidge, Eady & Smith on *Contempt*; *The Law of Photography and Digital Images*.

SELBORNE CHAMBERS Mark Warwick QC

Head of Chambers	Mark Warwick QC
Senior Clerk	Greg Piner
Deputy Senior Clerk	Paul Bunting
Deputy Director of Chambers	Darren Madle
Facilities Manager & Administrator	Denise Strudwick
Tenants	30

10 Essex Street, London, WC2R 3AA
Tel (020) 7420 9500 **Fax** (020) 7420 9555 **DX** DX 185 London Chancery Lane
Email clerks@selbornechambers.co.uk **Website** www.selbornechambers.co.uk

MEMBERS

Mark Warwick QC (1974) (QC-2013)
Romie Tager QC (1970) (QC-1995)
Ajmalul Hossain QC (1976) (QC-1998)
Gary Blaker QC (1993) (QC-2015)
Ian Clarke QC (1990) (QC-2016)
Philip Kremen (1975)
Stephen Boyd (1977)
Hugh Jackson (1981)
David Uff (1981)
Neil Mendoza (1982)
Stuart Hornett (1992)
Duncan Kynoch (1994)
Alexander Goold (1994)
Richard Clegg (1999)
Justin Kitson (2000)
Jonathan McNae (2001)
Zoë Barton (2003)
Julia Beer (2003)
Henry Webb (2005)
Nicholas Trompeter (2006)
Paul de la Piquerie (2006)
Camilla Chorfi (2008)
Simon McLoughlin (2009)
Justina Stewart (2010)
David Welford (2010) *
Alice Hawker (2011)
Isabel Petrie (2012)
Lara Kuehl (2012)
Greg Plunkett (2013)
Sarah Walker (2013)

* Door tenant

THE CHAMBERS Selborne Chambers is a leading commercial-chancery set. It is noted for the clear and practical advice it provides, which can be innovative, and is always mindful of clients' commercial considerations. Chambers recognises the benefits of working closely with those instructing and lay clients, and Members with expertise in complimentary areas can work together in teams to clients' best advantage. Chambers has been praised for its 'responsiveness, availability and excellent turnaround'. Chambers is instructed by many leading firms of solicitors, and many members accept instructions by direct access.

WORK UNDERTAKEN Members are instructed in a wide variety of Commercial and Chancery areas, with an emphasis on business, corporate and commercial matters (at both litigious and transactional stages); company and financial services; corporate and personal insolvency; all areas of property related matters; trusts and estates work; international/offshore work; civil fraud and asset recovery; energy and natural resources (including oil, gas and onshore and offshore renewable energy); construction, engineering and mining; telecommunications; sports law; gambling and spread betting. Professional negligence is covered in all these fields, working with solicitors, valuers, accountants, professional trustees and financial managers and advisors. Much of the work is done in London, though members frequently advise and appear throughout the United Kingdom and in other foreign jurisdictions (including the USA, British Virgin Island, Cayman Islands, Channel Islands, Gibraltar, Singapore, Hong Kong, Bangladesh and Israel). Chambers has a regular seminar programme which it promotes in Chambers and other parts of the country which is highly praised. The seminars are accredited for legal training. Members of Chambers also frequently speak at large conferences on topical legal issues.

Administration: Chambers is served by a highly responsive and friendly clerking team allowing work to be processed promptly and efficiently. Please contact the Senior Clerk, Greg Piner (T: 020 7420 9500).

SERJEANTS' INN CHAMBERS Angus Moon QC & John Beggs QC

Serjeants' Inn Chambers, 85 Fleet Street, London, EC4Y 1AE
Tel (020) 7427 5000 **Fax** (020) 7353 0425 **DX** LDE 421
Email clerks@serjeantsinn.com **Website** www.serjeantsinn.com

Head of Chambers	Angus Moon QC John Beggs QC
Senior Clerk	Lee Johnson
Business Director	Martin Dyke
Director of Client Care	Catherine Calder
Tenants	60

MEMBERS

Angus Moon QC (1986) (QC-2006)
John Beggs QC (1989) (QC-2009)
Sir Robert Francis QC (1973) (QC-1992)
James Watson QC (1979) (QC-2000)
Adrian Hopkins QC (1984) (QC-2003)
George Hugh-Jones QC (1983) (QC-2010)
Christopher Johnston QC (1990) (QC-2011)
Michael Mylonas QC (1988) (QC-2012)
Chris Daw QC (1993) (QC-2013)
John de Bono QC (1995) (QC-2014)
Samuel Green QC (1998) (QC-2015) *
Michael Horne QC (1992) (QC-2016)
Katie Gollop QC (1993) (QC-2016)
Bridget Dolan QC (1997) (QC-2016)
Malcolm Fortune (1972)
David Morris (1976)
Anthony Haycroft (1982)
Andrew Hockton (1984)
Alan Jenkins (1984)
Charles Foster (1988)
Paul Spencer (1988)
Sophia Roper (1990)
Caroline Hallissey (1990)
Jonathan Holl-Allen (1990)
Gerard Boyle (1992)
Richard Partridge (1994)
Mark Ley-Morgan (1994)
Sarah Clarke (1994)
Debra Powell (1995)
George Thomas (1995)
Stephen Morley (1996)
Michael Walsh (1996)
Ranald Davidson (1996)
Simon Cridland (1999)
Sebastian Naughton (1999)
Neil Davy (2000)
Briony Ballard (2000)
David Lawson (2000)
Elliot Gold (2001)
Claire Watson (2001)
Sarah Simcock (2001)
Heidi Knight (2001)
Eloise Power (2002)
Amy Street (2002)
Fiona Paterson (2003)
Jonathan Davies (2003)
Conrad Hallin (2004)
Edward Pleeth (2005)
James Berry (2006)
Rad Kohanzad (2007)
Oliver Williamson (2008)
Clare Hennessy (2009)
Frances McClenaghan (2009)
Susanna Rickard (2009)
Pravin Fernando (2009)
Jemma Lee (2010)
Cecily White (2011)
Aaron Rathmell (2011)
Eleanor Morrison (2012)
Liam Duffy (2012)
Jamie Mathieson (2014)
Siobhan Goodrich (1980) *
Susan Burden (1985) *
Anthony Jackson (1995) *
Benedict Wray (2009) *
Malcolm Lim (1989) *
Philip Gaisford (1969) *

* Door Tenant ++ Associate Tenant

THE CHAMBERS Serjeants' Inn Chambers is consistently ranked by the directories as a market leader in clinical negligence, Court of Protection, inquests and inquiries, police law, product liability, professional disciplinary and regulatory and public law. Silks and juniors receive praise for the strength of their advocacy, legal and tactical skills. The clerking team, led by Lee Johnson is efficient, approachable and helpful.

WORK UNDERTAKEN

Clinical Negligence & Healthcare: Tenants have led the way in developing the law (Sidaway, Heil, Chester and Thompstone). Involvement in high value claims concerning cerebral palsy and catastrophic injuries are undertaken, as well as multi-party actions.

Court of Protection: Members are instructed by PCT's nationwide, the Official Solicitor, CAFCASS and individuals. Members are instructed in the most sensitive and important cases, commonly those involving life or death treatment decisions or fundamental points of legal principle.

Employment: The growing employment team practises across the entire range of employment law for a variety of claimants and respondents. The team has particular experience in discrimination, whistle-blowing and injunctions in compliance with contractual disciplinary procedures.

Inquests: The impact of Art 2 ECHR is such that since the mid 2000s inquests have become longer, more expensive and more adversarial. Inquests have become a specialism which members have excelled in, particularly since the adoption of the more rigorous approach required under Art 2 ECHR. Recent high profile examples include deaths at the In Amenas/BP terrorist siege, Deep Cut Army Barracks and deaths at after police contact such as those of Raoul Moat and Mark Duggan. Four tenants appeared in the 7th July London Bombings inquests.

Police: The police team has been ranked number one in the UK for over a decade. Members act on behalf of most police forces around the country on a whole range of work including civil claims, judicial reviews, employment, pensions, sensitive operational advice, inquests, misconduct, performance matters and civil applications.

Professional Discipline & Regulatory: Members act for solicitors, barristers, academics and sportsmen. Sir Robert Francis QC chaired the Inquiry into the failings of the Mid-Staffordshire NHS Foundation Trust with several members of chambers representing core participants.

Public & Administrative: The team's work spans judicial review, information law, sports law, mental health law and Treasury work. It has particular experience of major inquests and public inquires including the Baha Mousa and Mid-Staffordshire public inquiries.

Product Liability: Serjeants' Inn Chambers' particular product liability expertise is in cases involving injury caused by medical or pharmaceutical products and devices and over the last two years members of chambers have been involved in a number of high-profile product liability group actions.

Business & Specialist Crime: The team specialises in cases involving professional people and organisations, and where the charges range from murder, manslaughter (including corporate manslaughter), health and safety offences, misconduct in public office, perjury and sexual offences to fraud and other financial crime.

SERLE COURT Alan Boyle QC

Head of Chambers	Alan Boyle QC
Chief Executive	John Petrie
Head Clerk	Steven Whitaker
Senior Clerk	Nick Hockney
Tenants	60

6 New Square, Lincoln's Inn, London, WC2A 3QS
Tel (020) 7242 6105 **Fax** (020) 7405 4004 **DX** LDE 1025
Email clerks@serlecourt.co.uk **Website** www.serlecourt.co.uk

MEMBERS

Alan Boyle QC (1972) (QC-1991)
Patrick Talbot QC (1969) (QC-1990)
Kuldip Singh QC (1975) (QC-1993)
Frank Hinks QC (1973) (QC-2000)
Elizabeth Jones QC (1984) (QC-2000)
Paul Chaisty QC (1982) (QC-2001)
Dominic Dowley QC (1983) (QC-2002)
Conor Quigley QC (1985) (QC-2003)
Philip Marshall QC (1987) (QC-2003)
Philip Jones QC (1985) (QC-2006)
Lance Ashworth QC (1987) (QC-2006)
Khawar Qureshi QC (1990) (QC-2006)
Nicholas Lavender QC (1989) (QC-2008)
David Casement QC (1992) (QC-2008)
Christopher Stoner QC (1991) (QC-2010)
Michael Edenborough QC (1992) (QC-2010)
John Machell QC (1993) (QC-2012)
Hugh Norbury QC (1995) (QC-2012)
David Blayney QC (1992) (QC-2013)
Jonathan Adkin QC (1997) (QC-2013)
Andrew Moran QC (1989) (QC-2016)
Daniel Lightman QC (1995) (QC–2016)
Richard Wilson QC (1996) (QC-2016)
Professor Jonathan Harris QC (2006) (QC-2016 (Hon))
Julian Burling (1976)
Andrew Francis (1977)
William Henderson (1978)
James Behrens (1979)
Richard Walford (1984)
Nicholas Harrison (1988)
Kathryn Purkis (1991)
Andrew Bruce (1992)
David Drake (1994)
Justin Higgo (1995)
Timothy Collingwood (1996)
Giles Richardson (1997)
Thomas Braithwaite (1998)
Simon Hattan (1999)
Constance McDonnell (2000)
Jennifer Haywood (2001)
Ruth Jordan (2001)
Ruth den Besten (2001)
Dakis Hagen (2002)
Jonathan Fowles (2004)
Matthew Morrison (2004)
James Mather (2006)
Dan McCourt Fritz (2007)
Gareth Tilley (2007)
James Weale (2007)
Paul Adams (2008)
Thomas Elias (2008)
Sophie Holcombe (2009)
Adil Mohamedbhai (2010)
Jonathan McDonagh (2011)
Emma Hargreaves (2012)
Zahler Bryan (2012)
Amy Proferes (2012)
Suzanne Rab (2013)
Adrian de Froment (2013)
Oliver Jones (2014)

THE CHAMBERS Serle Court "has a superb reputation in general commercial chancery, offshore and civil fraud cases, and remains a go-to set for the most complicated corporate and commercial disputes". "The set is 'a powerhouse in the civil fraud space,' and also enjoys high renown for its handling of restructuring and insolvency, real estate litigation and banking disputes". A "market-leading chancery set" that "remains one of the leading sets for big-ticket disputes heard in the Chancery courts", "it is a highly popular choice with solicitors, and enjoys a sterling reputation". - *Chambers & Partners.* In addition to its reputation for being one of the top sets at the English Bar, Serle Court is also one of the largest commercial chancery sets, with 60 members, including 24 silks. Serle Court's members offer genuine expertise across a broad range of chancery and commercial disciplines. Serle Court covers the whole range of 'business' law, from offshore litigation about the world's largest companies to domestic advice on probate matters, servicing a similarly disparate lay and professional client base at home and abroad.

WORK UNDERTAKEN Widely recognised as a leading set in chancery and commercial litigation, Serle Court is recommended in ten practice areas by *Chambers and Partners*: chancery: commercial, chancery: traditional, commercial dispute resolution, company, fraud: civil, offshore, partnership, professional negligence, real estate litigation and restructuring/insolvency. Serle Court can provide barristers at all levels to provide clear, practical advice and imaginative solutions to all types of disputes. Serle Court is experienced at putting together streamlined and powerful teams for some of the largest cases in the world. In the past few years these have included *Flanagan v Liontrust Investment Partners LLP, Glenn v Watson; Kea Investments Ltd v Novatrust Ltd*, the Hyderabad Fund case, the RBS rights issue litigation, the Lexi fraud case, the Fiona litigation, the Lehman brothers administration and the BTA bank litigation, in addition to Alhamranhi in Jersey and the Weissfisch litigation in the Bahamas. Serle Court has also established itself as one of the leading ADR sets, with a large number of highly regarded mediators and arbitrators as well as many members with extensive experience of appearing in 'alternative' dispute resolution forums.

INTERNATIONAL A significant proportion of Serle Court's work originates overseas: Serle Court has particularly close relationships with professional clients in the Channel Islands and the Caribbean, but members have advised and appeared in proceedings all over the world, from Russia to the USA, and from Europe to the Middle East.

11 SOUTH SQUARE Michael Silverleaf QC

11 South Square, Gray's Inn, London, WC1R 5EY
Tel (020) 7405 1222 **Fax** (020) 7242 4282 **DX** 433
Email clerks@11southsquare.com **Website** www.11southsquare.com

Head of Chambers	Michael Silverleaf QC
Senior Clerk	Ashley Carr
Tenants	17

MEMBERS

Michael Silverleaf QC (1980) (QC-1996)
Iain Purvis QC (1986) (QC-2006)
Mark Vanhegan QC (1990) (QC-2009)
Piers Acland QC (1993) (QC-2010)
Hugo Cuddigan QC (1995) (QC-2015)
Heather Lawrence (1990)
Jacqueline Reid (1992)
Benet Brandreth (1999)
Brian Nicholson (2000)
Anna Edwards-Stuart (2002)
Kathryn Pickard (2001)
Tom Alkin (2006)
Chris Aikens (2005)
Chris Hall (2010)
David Ivison (2014)
Adam Gamsa (2015)
Professor Lionel Bently (2009) *

* Door Tenant

THE CHAMBERS 11 South Square is a leading set of barristers' chambers specialising in intellectual property law. The set is additionally respected for its information technology and entertainment work. In 2015 Henry Carr was appointed as a High Court Judge sitting in the Patents Court. He joins the long list of former members called to the Bench including current Patents Court Judge Mr Justice Arnold, presiding Judge of the Intellectual Property Enterprise Court Richard Hacon, current Court of Appeal Judge Lord Justice Floyd, as well as the late Lord justice Pumfrey.

WORK UNDERTAKEN Patents; copyright and designs; trademarks and passing off; confidential information and privacy; computer law and other technical litigation; data protection and freedom of information; entertainment and media law and performers rights; and European Community law.
Additional work: Members of chambers are often involved in arbitrations and mediations, as advocates, mediators and members of the panel.

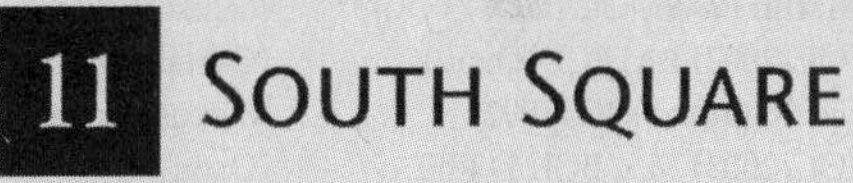

SOUTH SQUARE

Chambers Director	Ron Barclay-Smith
Practice Managers	Michael Killick
	Dylan Playfoot
	Jim Costa
	Marco Malatesta
Tenants	43

3-4 South Square, Gray's Inn, London, WC1R 5HP
Tel (020) 7696 9900 **Fax** (020) 7696 9911 **DX** 338 Chancery Lane
Email practicemanagers@southsquare.com **Website** www.southsquare.com

MEMBERS

Michael Crystal QC (1970) (QC-1984) LLB (Lond), BCL (Oxon)
Christopher Brougham QC (1969) (QC-1988) BA (Oxon)
Gabriel Moss QC (1974) (QC-1989) MA, BCL (Oxon)
Simon Mortimore QC (1972) (QC-1991) LLB (Exon)
Richard Hacker QC (1977) (QC-1998) MA (Cantab) Lic sp Dr Eur (Bruxelles)
Mark Phillips QC (1984) (QC-1999) LLB, LLM (Bristol)
Robin Dicker QC (1986) (QC-2000) BA, BCL (Oxon)
William Trower QC (1983) (QC-2001) MA (Oxon)
Martin Pascoe QC (1977) (QC-2002) BA, BCL (Oxon)
Fidelis Oditah QC (1992) (QC-2003) MA, BCL, D Phil (Oxon)
David Alexander QC (1987) (QC-2006) MA (Cantab)
Antony Zacaroli QC (1987) (QC-2006) BA, BCL (Oxon)
Glen Davis QC (1992) (QC-2011) MA (Oxon)
Barry Isaacs QC (1994) (QC-2011) BA (Oxon)
Felicity Toube QC (1995) (QC-2011) BA, BCL (Oxon)
Mark Arnold QC (1988) (QC-2013) MA (Cantab)
Jeremy Goldring QC (1996) (QC-2013) BA (Oxon) MA (Yale)
David Allison QC (1998) (QC-2014) MA (Cantab)
Tom Smith QC (1999) (QC-2014) BA, LLM (Cantab)
Daniel Bayfield QC (1998) (QC-2016) MA (Cantab)
John Briggs (1973) LLB (Lond) Ex, Du D d'U (Nancy)
Adam Goodison (1990) BA (Dunelm)
Hilary Stonefrost (1991) MSC (Lond)
Lloyd Tamlyn (1991) BA (Cantab) MA (HARV) ASA
Richard Fisher (2000) LLB (Lond) BCL (Oxon)
Stephen Robins (2001) BA (Oxon)
Joanna Perkins (2001) BA, LLM (Cantab) D Phil (Oxon)
Marcus Haywood (2002) BA (Oxon)
Hannah Thornley (2003) MA (Cantab), BCL (Oxon)
William Willson (2006) MA (Oxon)
Georgina Peters (2005) MA (Cantab)
Adam Al-Attar (2007) BA BCL (Oxon)
Henry Phillips (2008) BA BCL (Oxon)
Charlotte Cooke (2008) MA MPhil (Cantab) BCL (Oxon)
Alexander Riddiford (2011) BA (Oxon)
Matthew Abraham (2012) LLB (Lond) BCL (Oxon)
Toby Brown (2005) BSc (Nottingham)
Robert Amey (2012) MA (Oxon)
Andrew Shaw (2013) MA (Oxon)
Ryan Perkins (2014) BPhil (Oxon)
Riz Mokal (1997) PhD BCL LLB BSc
Madeleine Jones (2015) BA M.Phil (Cantab) M.Phil Pd.D (Princeton)
Edoardo Lupi (2015) BA (Oxon)
Prof Ian Fletcher QC (Hon) (1971) (QC-2013) MA, LLM, Phd, LLD (Cantab), MCL (Tulane) ++
Prof Sarah Worthington (2005) BSc LLB LLM PhD (Cantab) ++
Richard Sheldon QC (1979) MA (Cantab) **
Barry Mortimer GBS QC (1956) (QC-1971) MA (Cantab) **
Seenath Jairam SC (1998) LLM **
John Sheahan SC (1997) BA LLB (Hons) (UQ) **
Ronald DeKoven (2009) BA (Stanford), JD (Chicago) **
Sandy Shandro (2008) BA (Alberta) MA (McGill) BCL MA (Oxon) **
Sandra Bristoll (1989) MA (Cantab) **
Roxanne Ismail SC (1993) LLB (Lond) **
Colin Bamford (2002) MA (Cantab) **
Prof Peter Ellinger D.Phil (Oxon)**

++ Academic Member ** Associate Member

THE CHAMBERS South Square is a leading set of commercial law barristers who have acted in many of the most important restructuring, insolvency, banking, commercial, company and fraud-related disputes of recent times. The set is highly regarded internationally, with barristers regularly appearing in courts around the world, including the Caribbean, Bermuda, Gibraltar, Dubai, Hong Kong and Singapore.

WORK UNDERTAKEN

Restructuring & Insolvency: South Square is consistently recognised as the top set for restructuring and insolvency work – both domestic and cross-border. The administration of Lehman Brothers has generated a substantial amount of insolvency litigation, including the Lehman Waterfall I and II Applications. South Square barristers have recently appeared in major appeals to the Supreme Court, the Privy Council and the Court of Appeal, including Re Nortel, Re Lehman Brothers International (Europe),Saad, Singularis, Re Olympic Airlines SA and Re Game Station. High-value restructurings include APCOA Parking Holdings, Codere Finance and DTEK Finance. Administration applications include MF Global, Rangers FC, Phones4U and BHS.

Banking & Finance: South Square has a strong banking and finance practice, with a particular specialisation in large-scale financial disputes, derivatives, securitisations and structured finance products. Due to its insolvency and restructuring expertise, the set is uniquely positioned to deal with credit crunch litigation and advisory work. Examples of cases include Graiseley v Barclays Bank, BNY Corporate Trustee Services v Eurosail, Loreley v LBIE, Landsbanki v Heritable, Landsbanki v Rabobank and GSO Capital Partners v Barclays Bank.

Commercial Litigation & Dispute Resolution: South Square barristers are involved in significant pieces of high-profile litigation in the Commercial Court and the Chancery Division. The set is instructed by a wide range of firms, predominantly leading City firms, in commercial matters with a financial, banking and insolvency dimension. Recent cases include Constantin Medien AG v Bernard Ecclestone, Leni Gas Oil Investments v Malta Oil Pty Ltd, BNY Mellon Corporate Services V LGB Capital and Edgeworth Capital (Luxembourg) S.A.R.L. v Ramblas.

SOUTH SQUARE (continued)

Company: South Square plays a major role in company law cases, regularly appearing in litigation arising out of shareholders' disputes, derivative proceedings and claims relating to directors' duties.
High-profile cases include Smithton v Naggar, McKillen v Barclay and Jackson v Dear. The set's work often involves schemes of arrangement under the Companies Act and South Square barristers have acted in virtually all of the recent high-profile creditor schemes of arrangement.
Civil Fraud: South Square handles some of the most complex commercial fraud and asset tracing litigation. Recent work in England and offshore includes acting in litigation arising from the Rangers FC, Saad, Madoff, Stanford, Chesterfield and Instant Access Properties frauds as well as litigation involving the Tchenguiz brothers and Bernie Ecclestone/Formula One.
International & Offshore: South Square barristers are at the forefront of insolvency, banking, company and fraud matters before the courts of all the major offshore jurisdictions. Examples of work include Saad, Singularis, Oscatello, Picard v Primeo, Primeo v HSBC, Re Dubai World, Re Thyssen, Re Marrache and Nolan v Minerva.

5 ST ANDREW'S HILL David Josse QC

5 St Andrew's Hill, London, EC4V 5BZ
Tel (020) 7332 5400 **Fax** (020) 7489 7847 **DX** 417 London/Chancery Lane
Email clerks@5sah.co.uk **Website** www.5sah.co.uk

Head of Chambers	David Josse QC
Chambers Director	Wayne King
Clerks	Gary Norton (First Junior)
	Dean Cook (Second Junior)
	Theresa Burke (Fees clerk)
	Adam Murray
Tenants	63

MEMBERS

David Josse QC (1985) (QC 2009) ^
Edward Munir (1956) ^
Roger Bartlett (1968) ++
Charles Bennett (1972) **
James Harris (1975) ^
James Vine (1977) ^
Roger A Birch (1979) ^
Bernard Devlin (1980) ^
Christopher May (1983) ^
Jonathan Ingram (1984) ^
Andrew Evans (1984)
Anthony Prosser (1985)
James Dennison (1986)
Jaqueline Julyan SC (1986) ^
Ian Foinette (1986) ^
Andrew Bird (1987) ^*
Dominic Connolly (1989) ^
David Stern (1989)
Allister Walker (1990)
David Hewitt (1991) *** ^
Vivian Walters (1991) ^
Kevin Dent (1991)
Jenny Goldring (1993) ^
Philip Galway-Cooper (1993) ^
Mark Cotter (1994) ^
Paul Valder (1994) ^
Maria Scotland (1995) ^
Mark Mullins (1995) ^
Gary Pons (1995) ^
Sarah Wood (1995) ^
Edward Connell (1996) + ^
Bridget Todd (1996)
Edmund Burge (1997) ***
Richard Scott (1997)
Francesca Levett (1997) ^
Don Ramble (1998) ^
Wendy Hewitt (1999)
John Warrington (2000) ^
James Fletcher (2000) ^ *
Abigail White (2000)
Alex Rooke (2001)
Serena Gates (2002) ^
Claire Cooper (2002)
Ini Udom (2002) ^
Gemma Lindfield (2002)
David McNeill (2003) ^
Dennis Kavanagh (2003)
John Keal (2004)
Benjamin Keith (2004) ^ *
Rebecca Hill (2004)
Louisa Collins (2004)
Natasha Draycott (2005)
Amelia Nice (2006)
Hillary Lennox (2008)
David Williams (2009)
Ben Burge (2010)
Eleanor Scott (2010)
Karl Masi (2011)
Jessica Franklin (2011)
Mark Smith (2012) ^
Natasha Shotunde (2013) ^
Katherine Duncan (2014) ^
Nicholas Jones (2016)

^ Public/Direct Access + Recorder ++ Deputy Chancery Master * Attorney General
** Immigration Appeals Adjudicator *** Special Advocate

THE CHAMBERS Chambers is a leading specialist multi-practice set, with specific expertise in asset recovery and confiscation, business crime, civil fraud, crime, extradition, family, regulatory and professional disciplinary work.

WORK UNDERTAKEN

Asset Recovery, Civil Fraud & Confiscation: 5 St Andrew's Hill is a set of leading London asset forfeiture and confiscation barristers, and has been involved in this area of work for many years. Barristers act for both applicants and respondents, and have appeared in many of the leading cases in this fast developing and increasingly important area.

Business Crime: Barristers of 5 St Andrew's Hill regularly accept instructions to act in complex and serious fraud litigation on behalf of both the prosecution, including the SFO, and the defence. The team expertise include Libor, FCA investigations, Excise duty fraud, VAT fraud, Missing Trader Intra-Community (MTIC) fraud, tax credit fraud, insurance fraud, mortgage fraud, charities fraud, corruption, bribery and other high level financial crime. Members of the team also frequently appear at the VAT tribunal. Barristers advise and appear for clients both in the UK and overseas.

Civil Litigation: Barristers of 5 St Andrew's Hill cover all the principal areas of chancery litigation. The team act in cases involving wills and probate, Inheritance Act claims, trusts, co-ownership, boundary and neighbour disputes, easements and restrictive covenants. The team also deal with and specialise in areas of modern commercial Chancery and company law with a particular emphasis on insolvency and restructuring, banking law and civil fraud. 5 St Andrew's Hill's barristers advise and appear for clients both in the UK and overseas.

Crime: Barristers of 5 St Andrew's Hill have expertise in defending and prosecuting in cases covering the full spectrum of criminal offences, including the most serious and complex cases. The team are supported by 3 leading Queens Counsel and 50 juniors appear at all levels from the Supreme Court to Magistrates Court.

Disciplinary & Regulatory: Barristers at 5 St Andrew's Hill are known for their breadth of experience in the field of regulatory law. The regulatory team are highly experienced in environmental, housing, planning, street works, health and safety, food hygiene, public utility, infringement of trademarks and copyright, trading standards and licensing matters.

The healthcare team regularly appear on behalf of the medical professions/professionals before the General Dentist Council, Nursing and Midwifery Council and the Health and Care Professions Council.

Extradition: Barristers at 5 St Andrew's Hill are experts in defending and prosecuting extradition cases. Chambers is a leading set for extradition work and represents requested persons in proceedings both inside and outside the European Arrest Warrant (EAW) system including Westminster Magistrates' Court, and appeals to the Divisional and Administrative Courts, Supreme Court and the European Court of Human Rights. The barristers represent clients both in the UK and overseas.

Family: The team of family law barristers at 5SAH has specialist expertise in all areas of family law with a strong emphasis on International Child Abduction, Family Finance, Children and Court of Protection.

4 STONE BUILDINGS George Bompas QC

Head of Chambers	George Bompas QC
Senior Clerk	David Goddard
Tenants	33

4 Stone Buildings, Lincoln's Inn, London, WC2A 3XT
Tel (020) 7242 5524 **Fax** (020) 7831 7907 DX 385
Email clerks@4stonebuildings.com **Website** www.4stonebuildings.com

MEMBERS

George Bompas QC (1975) (QC-1994)
John Brisby QC (1978) (QC-1996)
Robert Miles QC (1987) (QC-2002)
Jonathan Crow QC (1981) (QC-2006)
Richard Hill QC (1993) (QC-2012)
Andrew Clutterbuck QC (1992) (QC-2014)
Orlando Fraser QC (1994) (QC-2014)
Stephen Hunt (1968)
Sarah Harman (1987)
Christopher Harrison (1988)
Jonathan Brettler (1988)
Paul Greenwood (1991)
Nicholas Cox (1992)
Charles Marquand (1987)
Anna Markham (1996)
Hermann Boeddinghaus (1996)
Andrew de Mestre (1998)
Gregory Denton-Cox (2000)
Sharif Shivji (2001)
Tiran Nersessian (2002)
Alastair Tomson (2004)
Adam Holliman (2005)
Tom Gentleman (2005)
Donald Lilly (2006)
Alexander Cook (2008)
Nicola Timmins (2008)
James Knott (2008)
Eleanor Holland (2010)
Joseph Wigley (2010)
Nienke van den Berg (2012)
Edward Grossley (2012)
Andrew Rose (2013)
Albert Sampson (2014)

THE CHAMBERS Chambers currently consist of 33 members, including seven silks. Three members are currently on the Treasury panels. Three members are appointed to sit as Deputy Judges of the High Court. One of the silks is Attorney General to the Duchy of Lancaster and another is Attorney General to the Prince of Wales. One member is on the board of the Charity Commission. Chambers belong to the Commercial Bar Association and the Chancery Bar Association.

WORK UNDERTAKEN Work covers all aspects of company and commercial litigation, including shareholders disputes, corporate fraud and asset recovery as well as commercial arbitration, banking, financial services and regulatory work, international trusts and public law. The clerks' room is staffed during term from 8am to 8pm Monday to Friday and chambers can be contacted out of hours on the number given on the chambers' answering machine and on the website. Further information about chambers and the work undertaken is available on the website www.4stonebuildings.com.

PUBLICATIONS Members of chambers have contributed to numerous publications in their specialist fields including Annotated Companies Acts (Oxford University Press), Tolley's Company Law, Atkin Court Forms 2nd ed., (volumes on companies, winding up and equitable remedies), Halsbury's Laws of England 4th ed. (volumes on corporations and money); A Practitioner's Guide to Directors' Duties and Responsibilities (City & Financial Publishing).

INTERNATIONAL Chambers undertake a substantial amount of work for overseas clients and members regularly receive instructions from the Caribbean, the United States, Europe, Central Asia and the Far East. In recent years, members have appeared in court in Bermuda, the Cayman Islands, Bahamas, Gibraltar, Anguilla, the British Virgin Islands, the Turks and Caicos Islands, Malaysia, Singapore, Nevis, Dominica, Seychelles and Trinidad. In addition certain members are full members of the Northern Ireland Bar, the Cayman Islands Bar and the Bar of the British Virgin Islands.

RECRUITMENT 4 Stone Buildings' policy is to seek to have 2 pupils each year and to recruit each of those pupils that meet the required standard. Prospective applicants for pupillage will find further information including details of chambers' awards in the Pupillage Pack which is available on request. Mini-pupillages are encouraged.

5 STONE BUILDINGS Henry Harrod

5 Stone Buildings, Lincoln's Inn, London, WC2A 3XT
Tel (020) 7242 6201 **Fax** (020) 7831 8102 **DX** 304 London/Chancery Lane
Email clerks@5sblaw.com **Website** www.5sblaw.com

Head of Chambers	Henry Harrod
Senior Clerk	Paul Jennings
Tenants	32

MEMBERS

Henry Harrod (1963)
Shân Warnock-Smith QC (1971) (QC-2002)
Christopher Whitehouse (1971)
Norman Palmer QC (1973) (QC-2010)
Mark Blackett-Ord (1974)
Andrew Simmonds QC (1980) (QC-1999) ++
Miranda Allardice (1982)
Penelope Reed QC (1983) (QC-2009) ++
Christopher Tidmarsh QC (1985) (QC-2002)
Michael O'Sullivan (1986)
Patrick Rolfe (1987)
Barbara Rich (1990)
Tracey Angus QC (1991) (QC-2012)
Henry Legge QC (1993) (QC-2012)
David Rees (1994) +
Leon Sartin (1997)
Sarah Haren (1999)
Thomas Entwistle (2001)
Luke Harris (2001)
Joseph Goldsmith (2003)
Mark Baxter (2006)
Charlotte Edge (2006)
Ruth Hughes (2007) **
Edward Hewitt (2007)
William East (2008)
Jordan Holland (2009)
Mathew Roper (2011)
Alexander Drapkin (2012)
Harry Martin (2012)
Sam Chandler (2013)
Hugh Cumber (2013)
Eliza Eagling (2014)

++ Deputy High Court Judge + Recorder ** Member of Attorney General's (B Panel)

THE CHAMBERS 5 Stone Buildings is one of the outstanding sets of chancery chambers. With expertise at all levels in the fields of private client, estate planning, tax, probate disputes, partnership, property litigation, art and cultural property, professional negligence, pensions and all chancery related commercial matters. Chambers has an extensive team experienced in the field of advice, drafting and litigation relating to trusts, wills and associated taxation both in the UK and overseas; and a specialist team experienced in Court of Protection work. Chambers aims to provide a fast, efficient modern service of the highest standard.

9 STONE BUILDINGS Edward Denehan

9 Stone Buildings, Lincoln's Inn, London, WC2A 3NN
Tel (020) 7404 5055 **Fax** (020) 7405 1551 **DX** 314 Chancery Lane
Email clerks@9stonebuildings.com **Website** www.9stonebuildings.com

Head of Chambers	Edward Denehan
Senior Clerk	Alan Austin
Clerks	David Clayton
	Jake Price
	Ben Rinaldi
Tenants	27

MEMBERS

Edward Denehan (1981)
Vivian R Chapman QC (1970) (QC-2006)
Michael Ashe QC (1971) (QC-1994) (QC N I 1998) (SC Ireland 2000)
Isaac E Jacob (1963)
David Rowell (1972)
Christopher Cant (1973)
Nigel Meares (1975)
Martin Young (1984)
Lynne M Counsell (1986)
Christopher Spratt (1986)
Timothy Sisley (1989)
Philip Brown (1991)
Helene Pines Richman (1992)
Andrew Noble (1992)
Alana Graham (1993)
Timothy Cowen (1993)
Peter Shaw (1995)
Daniel Bromilow (1996)
Elaine Palser (2002)
Joseph Curl (2007)
Rory Brown (2009)
Raj Arumugam (2008)
Paul Wilmshurst (2007)
Graham Callard (2001)
Giselle McGowan (2011)
Cecilia Xu Lindsey (2012)
Faith Julian (2013)

THE CHAMBERS The strength of chambers lies in its long history and proven experience in the areas of traditional and commercial chancery. Many members of chambers are recognised as leading practitioners in their fields. Chambers are one of the oldest established sets of barristers' chambers in Lincoln's Inn. Chamber's history is easily traceable since 1893.

WORK UNDERTAKEN The chambers main practice areas are:
Land & Property Law: Land easements and covenants, mortgages, charges, guarantees and credit arrangements, landlord and tenant including business, agricultural and residential tenancies, housing associations and leasehold enfranchisement, the law of commons, village greens and open spaces, stamp duty land tax.
Private Client Law: Charities, Court of Protection, revenue including income tax, capital gains tax, corporation tax, value added tax, inheritance tax and SDLT, also trusts, settlements and wills, probate, administration of estates and family provision.
Insolvency & Company Law: Personal and corporate insolvency, companies and partnerships including share holders and partners' actions, minority rights, directors' duties, internal disputes and company acquisitions, confiscation and asset recovery.
Business, Financial & Commercial Law: Injunctions and other equitable remedies, fraud, conspiracy, mistake, misrepresentation, constructive trusts, tracing and restitution, securities regulation including share and other investment transactions, investor protection, regulation of financial services, market abuse and insider dealing, contract and commercial, banking, professional negligence, conflict of laws, judicial review, employment law, confidential information, covenants restraining business activity or employment, intellectual property and passing off.

PUBLICATIONS Members of chambers produce a wealth of articles and publications in the core practice areas. Details may be found on the website.

INTERNATIONAL 9 Stone Buildings has an abundance of expertise and experience in foreign jurisdictions and international law. Chambers has members who regularly act as advocates or advisers in SE Asia including China, the Caribbean (particularly the Cayman Islands, Turks and Caicos Islands. North America and Europe (particularly Eire, Gibraltar, the Bahamas and Switzerland). Some members are regularly instructed in the UK off shore jurisdictions of the Channel Islands and the Isle of Man. 9 Stone Buildings is considerably strengthened in this area by its overseas members who, as well as being members of the English Bar, are leading practitioners in their jurisdictions: Nicholas Critelli, a trial attorney in the states of Iowa and New York, a member of the Bar of the Supreme Court and former Chair of the Iowa Bar Association (2004); James Levy QC is a partner in the internationally known law firm of Hasans in Gibraltar. Dr Raymond Ashton is a member of the English and Irish Bar and a Guernsey Advocate. He is also a chartered accountant.

ST PHILIPS STONE CHAMBERS

4 Field Court, Gray's Inn, London, WC1R 5EF
Tel (020) 7440 6900 **Fax** (020) 7242 0197 **DX** 483 London/Chancery Lane
Email clerks@stonechambers.com **Website** www.stonechambers.com

Heads of London	Elizabeth Blackburn QC Vasanti Selvaratnam QC
Chambers Executive Officer	Luke Irons
Barristers	21

MEMBERS

Elizabeth Blackburn QC (1978) (QC-1998)
Vasanti Selvaratnam QC (1983) (QC-2001)
Sarah Miller (1971)
Charles Debattista (1978)
Colin Wright (1987)
Dominic Happé (1993)
Rachel Toney (1998)
Ishfaq Ahmed (1999)
Mark Jones (2000)
Ravi Aswani (2000)
Thomas Whitehead (2002)
James Shirley (2002)
Thomas Steward (2011)
Andrew Dinsmore (2013)
William Hooper (2014)
John Reeder QC (1971) (QC-1989)*
Allan Myers QC (1988) (QC Aus.) *
Jonathan Lux (2013) *
Mary Thomson (1983) (2013 Hong Kong) *
Dr Colin Ong (1991) (1998 Brunei) (Singapore 2012) *
Dan Tan (2005 New York) (2011 California) (2011 District of Columbia) (2003 Solicitor, England) (2000 Solicitor, Singapore) *

* Associate member

THE CHAMBERS On 1 August 2016 leading national set St Philips and specialist shipping and international commercial set Stone Chambers merged. The merged set is known in London and internationally as St Philips Stone Chambers.

St Philips Stone Chambers offers clients in-depth knowledge and experience in commercial disputes across a number of different business sectors and services including shipping and transport, international trade and commodities, energy and natural resources, insurance and reinsurance, banking and finance, company and insolvency, civil fraud and professional negligence. Its members act as arbitrators, mediators and expert witnesses.
St Philips Stone Chambers has a strong international client base, with barristers appearing in multiple jurisdictions. Languages spoken include: French, German, Italian, Spanish, Urdu, Hindi, Gujarati and Mandarin.

For further details, please see St Philips Chambers profile.

TANFIELD CHAMBERS Philip Rainey QC

Head of Chambers	Philip Rainey QC
Chief Executive	Eamonn Kelly
Tenants	58

2-5 Warwick Court, London, WC1R 5DJ
Tel (020) 7421 5300 **Fax** (020) 7421 5333 **DX** 46 London Chancery Lane
Email clerks@tanfieldchambers.co.uk **Website** www.tanfieldchambers.co.uk
Twitter @TanfieldLaw **LinkedIn** www.linkedin.com/company/tanfield-chambers

MEMBERS

Philip Rainey (1990) MCI Arb (QC-2010) ^
Kerry Bretherton QC (1992) (QC-2016) ^
Iain Mitchell QC (Scotland) (1976 Scotland) (2012 England) (QC Scotland 1992) ^
Edward Raw (1963)
David Guy (1972) FCI Arb ^
Philip Conrath (1972) ^
Stephen Monkcom (1974) ^
Paul Staddon (1976) ^
Mark Dencer (1978)
Kerstin Boyd (1979) ^
Christopher Coney (1979) ^
Simon Cheves (1980) ^
Charles Joseph (1980) FCI Arb ^
Sebastian Reid (1982) ^
Mark Loveday (1986) MCI Arb ^
Michael Bailey (1986) ^
Christopher Bamford (1987)
John Buck (1987) ^
Michael Buckpitt (1988) ^
Christopher Maynard (1988) ^
Gerald Wilson (1989) ^
Phillip Aliker (1990) FCI Arb ^
Gareth Jones (1992)
Catriona MacLaren (1993) ^
Nicholas Isaac (1993) ^
Andrew Butler (1993) ^
Stan Gallagher (1994) ^
Peter Linstead (1994) ^
Christopher Heather (1995) ^
Karen Jones (1995) ^
Robert Bowker (1995) ^
Timothy Polli (1997) ^
James Fieldsend (1997)
Piers Harrison (1997) ^
Daniel Dover (1997) ^
Martina Murphy (1998) ^
Nicola Muir (1998) ^
Marc Glover (1999)^
Ellodie Gibbons (1999) ^
Adrian Carr (1999) ^
Rebecca Cattermole (1999)
Carl Fain (2001) ^
Olivia Murphy (2001) ^
Laura Robinson (2001) ^
Tom Carpenter-Leitch (2002) ^
Tim Hammond (2003) ^
Amanda Gourlay (2004) ^
Jonathan Upton (2004) ^
Estelle Lear (2006) ^
Gemma de Cordova (2006)
Michael Walsh (2006) ^
Gwyn Evans (2007) ^
Niraj Modha (2010) ^
Harriet Holmes (2011) ^
Richard Alford (2011) ^
Diane Doliveux (2011)
James Hamerton-Stove (2012)
Katy Gray (2013) ^

^ Public/Direct Access

THE CHAMBERS Tanfield is a leading set in property law and a 'force to be reckoned with' across all aspects of commercial and residential real estate litigation and ADR. The set has unrivalled experience of enfranchisement and service charge issues. In our core area, and through our complementary expertise in private client matters, commercial and employment, Tanfield's barristers and practice managers are committed to putting clients first. The set adopts an innovative and flexible approach and is known for its excellent commercial understanding.

WORK UNDERTAKEN As well as broad experience across the listed legal disciplines, many of its members have niche specialisms in complex areas of the law. Members of chambers regularly demonstrate excellence in their specialisms by the publication of legal textbooks, the quality of which has been widely acknowledged. These include *Service Charges and Management Law and Practice, 3rd Edition* (Sweet & Maxwell) by Tanfield Chambers; *The Law and Practice of Party Walls* by Nicholas Isaac; *Same Sex Marriage and Civil Partnerships: The New Law* (Jordan's Publishing) by Gerald Wilson et al; *Megarry's Manual of the Law of Real Property* (Sweet & Maxwell) by Philip Rainey QC, Michael Walsh, Piers Harrison and Daniel Dovar; *Business Premises: Possession and Lease Renewal 5th ed* (Sweet & Maxwell) by Gary Webber and Daniel Dovar; and *Leasehold Enfranchisement: Law and Practice* (Wildy, Simmonds & Hill) by Piers Harrison and David Lonsdale.

AWARDS Tanfield and its members have been nominated for and won a number of awards recently. In 2016 Tanfield won chambers of the year and Philip Rainey QC won barrister of the year at News on the Block's ERMAs; and Gwyn Evans was nominated for Family Law commentator of the year. In 2015 Tanfield and Philip Rainey QC were nominated for chambers and barrister of the year respectively in the Legal 500 UK awards, Tanfield and Piers Harrison were highly commended in the chambers and barrister of the year categories at the ERMAs, and Nicholas Isaac was nominated for the Inner Temple Book prize for his book on party walls.

TANFIELD

OLD SQUARE TAX CHAMBERS James Kessler QC

15 Old Square, Lincoln's Inn, London, WC2A 3UE
Tel (020) 7242 2744 **Fax** (020) 7831 8095 **DX** 386 LDE
Email taxchambers@15oldsquare.co.uk **Website** www.taxchambers.com

Head of Chambers	James Kessler QC
Senior Clerk	Anthony Hall
Tenants	11

MEMBERS

Robert Venables QC (called 1973, QC 1990)
James Kessler QC (called 1984, QC 2003)
Amanda Hardy QC (called 1993, QC 2015)
Philip Simpson QC (called 2001, (QC (Scotland) 2014)
Patrick Cannon (Solicitor 1984, Called to Bar 2003)
Etienne Wong (Solicitor 1991, Called to Bar 2014)
Rory Mullan (2000)
Setu Kamal (2004)
Harriet Brown (2005)
Oliver Marre (2011)
Mary Ashley (2014)

THE CHAMBERS Old Square Tax Chambers is an elite set whose members are among the best regarded tax barristers in practice. Old Square Tax Chambers was founded in 1968. Members are supported by senior clerk, Anthony Hall, who will discuss the likely level of fees before work is done and, will happily advise as to the most suitable member to deal with any particular matter. Chambers' approach is based on the experience that is seldom sufficient to advise on a discrete tax question in isolation. All relevant tax considerations must be taken into account, in addition to any other legal constraints and business or personal considerations which may influence a client's course of action.

WORK UNDERTAKEN

Personal Taxation: Members counsel clients ranging from long established families to the best known entrepreneurs and advise at the high end for both UK and foreign domiciliaries. The team has played a lead role on a number of major matters of first importance over the past year. Our barristers provide coherent and comprehensible advice to private clients in all aspects of their tax affairs. The ability to combine tax advice with trust, succession and charity law expertise makes this a unique resource in the UK market.

Corporate Taxation: With a predominant tax focus, Old Square Tax Chambers covers all aspects of corporate taxation, both in and out of court. The team has particular strengths in advising on corporate reconstructions, entrepreneurs, and employee remuneration strategies.

VAT: Tax Chambers expertise in VAT has been enhanced by the arrival of Etienne Wong, formerly head of VAT at Clifford Chance. The team advises on all aspects of VAT, with particular focus on supply issues (non-supplies, composite supplies), cross-border issues, property transactions, transactions in the telecommunications, technology, energy and transport sectors, and structured finance products (including Islamic financing products).

International: A cross-border tax offering is a key factor which sets Chambers apart from the majority of tax specialists at the UK Bar. We appear in front of Scots and Jersey Courts and foreign tribunals and bring years of experience to the table.

Specialist Expertise: Each member of chambers cover all areas of tax law, however each practitioner has particular specialties: Head of Chambers, James Kessler QC has particular strengths in foreign domiciliaries, trusts and charities. Robert Venables QC focuses on trusts, EU law, offshore and international taxation, employee remuneration, owner-managed companies and VAT. He has extensive litigation experience before the House of Lords (Supreme Court), Privy Council, European Court of Justice and Court of Appeal, including tax-related judicial review. Amanda Hardy QC is a noted expert on pensions taxation and a highly experienced litigator. Before taking silk in 2015, Amanda was listed as a leading junior tax barrister. Philip Simpson QC advises across a broad range of taxes, with a particular focus on corporation tax and offshore situations involving individuals. He has extensive litigation expertise, in particular in VAT and other indirect taxes. Patrick Cannon is an expert on SDLT and also advises on the GAAR, tax investigations, and human rights in tax. Etienne Wong is an expert on VAT (including VAT litigation), and also advises on property development and investment transactions. Rory Mullan advises widely on offshore issues with a particular interest in the impact of EU law and human rights law in relation to tax. He has enjoyed significant recent success representing taxpayers before the Courts. Setu Kamal specialises in all areas of tax law, with clients ranging from the big four to provincial firms. Harriet Brown is dual qualified as a Jersey advocate and regularly appears before UK and Jersey tribunals. Oliver Marre represents taxpayers on direct tax matters, with an interest in employment taxation and NICs.

PUBLICATIONS Members are sought out as thought leaders and have written a significant number of leading textbooks, including the following:
Drafting Trusts & Will Trusts, The GAAR: A Practical Approach, Individual Tax Residence, The Interaction of EU Treaty Freedoms and the UK Tax Code, The Jersey Law of Trusts, Taxation of Charities and Nonprofit Organisations, Taxation of Foundations, Taxation of Non-Residents and Foreign Domiciliaries, Taxation of Trusts, Tolley's Stamp Taxes.

TEMPLE GARDEN CHAMBERS Keith Morton QC

1 Harcourt Buildings, London, EC4Y 9DA
Tel (020) 7583 1315 **Fax** (020) 7353 3969 **DX** 382 London
Email clerks@tgchambers.com **Website** www.tgchambers.com

Head of Chambers	Keith Morton QC
Senior Clerk	Dean Norton
Tenants	64

MEMBERS

Keith Morton QC (1990) (2010)
Andrew Prynne QC (1975)(1995)
Simon Jackson QC (1982) (2003)
Robin Tam QC (1986) (2006)
Dominic Grieve QC (1980) (2008)
Jonathan Watt-Pringle QC (1987) (2008)
Murdo MacLeod QC (Scotland) (1994) (2008)
Simon Browne QC (1982) (2010)
Karim A. A. Khan QC (1992) (2010)
Andrew Cayley QC (2007) (2012)
David Barr QC (1993) (2014)
Rodney Dixon QC (2000) (2014)
Andrew O'Connor QC (1996) (2015)
Cathryn McGahey QC (1990) (2016)
John Bate-Williams (1976)
James Holdsworth (1977)
Ian Ashford-Thom (1977)
Angus Macpherson (1977)
Kevin McLoughlin (2007)
William Hoskins (1980)
George Alliott (1981)
Paul Kilcoyne (1985)
James Bell (1987)
Mark James (1987)
James Laughland (1991)
Charles Curtis (1992)
Richard Wilkinson (1992)
Peter Freeman (1992)
James Arney (1992)
Marcus Grant (1993)
Alexander Glassbrook (1995)
Nicholas Moss (1995)
Melissa Pack (1995)
Emma-Jane Hobbs (1996)
Edward Hutchin (1996)
Julia Smyth (1996)
Paul McGrath (1997)
Dominic Adamson (1997)
Sacha Ackland (1998)
George Davies (1998)
Shaman Kapoor (1999)
Benjamin Casey (2000)
Fiona Canby (2001)
Michael Rapp (2002)
Tim Sharpe (2002)
Louise Jones (2004)
Rhys Davies (2004)
Aidan Ellis (2005)
Lionel Stride (2005)
Anthony Johnson (2006)
Joanna Hughes (2007)
Emma Price (2007)
Sian Reeves (2006)
David R. White (2009)
William Irwin (2010)
Emma Northey (2009)
James Henry (2010)
Emily Wilsdon (2011)
Anthony Lenanton (2011)
Richard Boyle (2012)
Piers Taylor (2012)
Matthew Waszak (2012)
Ellen Robertson (2013)
Elizabeth Gallagher (2014)

THE CHAMBERS TGC is a long established and market leading common law and specialist international law set with a reputation for providing first class services. TGC has Chambers in London and The Hague.
TGC has 14 Silks and 50 juniors who pride themselves on providing the highest quality advice and advocacy. Nine of their juniors have been appointed to the Treasury Panels who, together with a number of their silks, undertake work on behalf of the Crown. Counsel are supported by a very experienced, commercially astute and approachable clerking team.

WORK UNDERTAKEN

Chambers undertakes all areas of **clinical negligence** work, often in high value, complex cases. TGC is recognised as pre-eminent in **costs** work providing robust, commercial advice encompassing everything from routine detailed assessment to appellate work in the highest courts. TGC is highly regarded for its **employment** expertise with involvement in many leading appellate and tribunal cases and those involving an EU law element. TGC has forged a reputation as a leading set for **fraud (civil)**, advising and representing insurance companies in work encompassing a wide range of frauds including fraud rings, staged and contrived collisions, bogus passenger etc.
A team of members are at the forefront of **health and safety** work, advising and representing defendants to criminal prosecutions. Members are routinely instructed in high profile cases including the first prosecution under the Corporate Manslaughter and Corporate Homicide Act 2007, the defence of the Metropolitan Police arising from the death of Jean Charles de Menezes, and the challenge to the Health and Safety at Work Act 1974 before the ECJ. TGC is a leading set in the field of **coronial law and inquests** having been instructed in virtually every high-profile inquest of recent years including the Hillsborough inquests, Shoreham Air Disaster inquests, Vauxhall Helicopter crash, Tunisia inquests, Litvinenko inquest, Cheryl James (Deepcut) inquest. TGC is highly regarded in **Inquiries** with extensive experience, recent examples include The Undercover Police Inquiry, Independent Jersey Care Inquiry, Litvinenko Inquiry, Leveson Inquiry, and Detainee Inquiry.
Counsel at TGC specialise in motor and property **insurance**, **credit hire**, **insurance fraud**, and **professional** and **product liability insurance**.
TGC is consistently recommended as a leading set for **personal injury**. Chambers offer practitioners used to handling claims for catastrophic injury, traumatic brain injury, chronic pain, and serious, psychiatric injury.
Chambers has an outstanding team which has advised governments and individuals at the highest level on **public international law** and international humanitarian law issues. Counsel have prosecuted, defended and intervened in the most serious cases at international criminal courts. The set has pursued civil claims for clients internationally and has argued many aspects of international law in domestic cases. Their Chambers in The Hague supports their work before all international courts and bodies there.
Members of TGC are at the forefront of **public law litigation**, appearing and advising in numerous leading cases concerning human rights, prison law, EU law, coronial law, national security and immigration and asylum. Chambers' team sits as legal advisors to **professional disciplinary** panels including the General Medical Council, General Dental Council and Nursing and Midwifery Council.

2TG - 2 TEMPLE GARDENS Neil Moody QC

Head of Chambers	Neil Moody QC
Senior Clerk	Lee Tyler
Tenants	61

2 Temple Gardens, London, EC4Y 9AY
Tel (020) 7822 1200 **Fax** (020) 7822 1300 **DX** 134 Chancery Lane
Email clerks@2tg.co.uk **Website** www.2tg.co.uk

MEMBERS

Neil Moody QC (1989) (QC-2010)
Michael de Navarro QC (1968) (QC-1990)
Robert Moxon Browne QC (1969) (QC-1990)
Benjamin Browne QC (1976) (QC-1996)
Howard Palmer QC (1977) (QC-1999)
Martin Porter QC (1986) (QC-2006)
Jacqueline Perry QC (1975) (QC-2006)
Sarah Vaughan Jones QC (1983) (QC-2008)
Paul Downes QC (1991) (QC-2010)
Caroline Harrison QC (1986) (QC-2013)
Charles Dougherty QC (1997) (QC-2013)
Andrew Miller QC (1989) (QC-2014)
Rosalind Foster (1969)
Alison Green (1974)
John McDonald FCIArb (1981)
Christopher Russell (1982)
Daniel Matovu (1985)
Jennifer Gray (1988)
Jonathan de Rohan (1989)
Bradley Martin (1990)
Daniel Crowley FCIArb (1990)
Christopher Lundie (1991)
Marie Louise Kinsler (1991)
Clare Brown (1993)
Doré Green (1994)
Lucy Wyles (1994)
Bruce Gardiner (1994)
Nina Goolamali (1995)
Roger Harris (1996)
Niazi Fetto (1999)
Anastasia Karseras (2000)
Nina Unthank (2001)
Helen Bell (2002)
Sonia Nolten (2002)
Helen Wolstenholme (2002)
Stuart Benzie (2002)
Rehana Azib (2003)
Meghann McTague (2004)
Emily Saunderson (2005)
Stewart Chirnside (2005)
Jack Harris (2006)
Joseph Sullivan (2006)
Hayley McLorinan (2008)
Anna Hughes (2008)
David Thomas (2009)
Henry Morton Jack (2009)
William Wraight MRCS (Eng) (2009)
Isabel Barter (2010)
Timothy Killen (2010)
Robert Cumming (2010)
Andrew Bershadski (2010)
William Clerk (2012)
George Hilton (2012)
Jessica van der Meer (2012)
Alistair Mackenzie (2013)
Luka Krsljanin (2013)
Lucas Fear-Segal (2014)
Sam Stevens (2014)
Saul Miller (2015) (Called SA 2005)
Emily Albou (2014)
Ruth Kennedy (2015)

THE CHAMBERS Established civil and commercial set, known for its advocacy and client-centred approach.

WORK UNDERTAKEN

Personal Injury: Catastrophic injury, fatal accidents, animal, sport, H&S and work injuries, UK and overseas.
Clinical Negligence: Claimants, NHSLA, Defence Organisations, insurers, GMC, GDC, Hospital Trusts.
Insurance & Reinsurance: Commercial claims, mesothelioma, high value insurance fraud, Lloyds Syndicates.
Travel & Jurisdiction: Large foreign claims in PI, insurance, product liability and professional negligence.
Product Liability: Wide range of high cost product fault and failure claims in multiple jurisdictions.
Professional Negligence: Mainly defence of high value claims in all professions. Specialists in professional indemnity.
Employment: Contracts, equal pay claims, workplace stress, racial, sexual and religious discrimination.
Commercial Dispute Resolution: High value commercial litigation, civil fraud and arbitration in multiple jurisdictions.
Property Damage: High value fire, flood, explosions and subsidence claims on commercial, public and private premises.
Banking & Finance: Retail banking, securities, swaps, derivatives, hedge funds, asset finance.
Commercial Fraud: Complex commercial fraud claims in the UK and overseas.
Sport: All major sports: rules, regulations, contractual breaches, technical issues, players, officials, regulators.

TEMPLE TAX CHAMBERS Michael Sherry

3 Temple Gardens, Temple, London, EC4Y 9AU
Tel (020) 7353 7884 **Fax** (020) 7583 2044
Email clerks@templetax.com **Website** www.templetax.com

Head of Chambers	Michael Sherry
Senior Clerk	Claire James
Tenants	22

MEMBERS

Michael Sherry (1978) ^
Christopher Sokol QC (1975) ^ (QC-2006)
David Southern QC (1982) (QC-2014)
Michael Conlon QC (1974) (QC-2002)
Alun James (1986)
Jonathan S Schwarz (1998) (SA 1977, Can 1981)
Tim Brown (2001)
Scott Redpath (1996)
Michael Collins (2003)
Philip Ridgway (1986)
Rebecca Murray (2001)
Anne Redston (2010)
Stephen Arthur (2002) ^
Michael Quinlan (1984) ^
Derek Francis (1985)
John Baldry (1993)
Julian Hickey (1999) ^
Keith Gordon (2003) ^
Ximena Montes Manzano (2004)
Joseph Howard (2006) ^
Andrey Krahmal (New York Bar 2004)
Anne Fairpo (2009)

^ Direct/Public Access

THE CHAMBERS Temple Tax is a long established tax set. Its strength is the collection of individuals who together represent a wide range of expertise at the highest level. The set has unrivalled knowledge in all specialist areas of tax law and can deploy a leading expert in relation to every area of tax. This is evidenced by:

- Member's involvement in cutting-edge litigation and advice
- The veritable library of leading tax works authored by members of Chambers
- The commitment to tax education at leading universities and research

Temple Tax combines intellectual rigour with a practical approach. One of its distinguishing features is that most members learned their tax outside the Bar – as Revenue officers, as solicitors, accountants, in-house tax counsel and practising in other countries. This gives a nuts and bolts knowledge and diverse experience of tax as well as rapport with clients and an immediate grasp of the tax issues which they face. The set offers robust but measured advice and advocacy backed by in-depth technical knowledge and professional experience in the changed world of modern tax practice.

WORK UNDERTAKEN

Corporation Tax: Corporate/business tax advisory and planning for large corporate and groups including transaction and IPO work, corporate finance, break-up bids, MBOs and corporate rescues, and for owner-managed businesses/SMEs including reconstruction and clearance work (in particular transactions in securities, Reconstructions and mergers). Recent cases: McLaren Racing v HMRC; G4S v HMRC; Farnborough v HMRC.
Employment & Employee Remuneration: Pensions and National Insurance Contributions, employment related securities/share scheme and other remuneration, planning work with LLPs and partnerships, including structuring for hedge fund managers/venture capitalists; QCBs. Recent cases; HMRC v Martin; Hancock v HMRC; Moyes v HMRC.
Private Client & Personal Taxation: Human Rights, IHT planning, onshore and offshore trust issues and drafting and maximising BPR, offshore income tax/CGT/IHT issues including transfers of assets abroad and advising non-domiciled individuals in matters such as remittances, excluded property settlements and UK homes structures. Recent cases: Forde & McHugh v HMRC; HMRC v Cotter; HMRC v Tower MCashback; Eclipse Film Partners (No.35) LLP v HMRC; R (oao Rowe, Worrall and others) v HMRC; De Silva v HMRC; HMRC v Stolkin; Donaldson v HMRC; Sippchoice v HMRC; Arthur v HMRC; R v HMRC; Graham; Taylor v HMRC; Gardiner v HMRC; R (Dunne & Gray) v HMRC.
International Tax: Permanent establishments, double tax relief, the effect of EU law on UK legislation, international employments, supply chain structuring, internationally mobile executives, FATCA. Recent cases: Fowler v HMRC; Macklin v HMRC.
VAT & Customs & Excise Duties: VAT expertise includes land and buildings, charities, partial exemption, financial services, grouping, fraud/investigations, single/multiple supplies and three year capping. Customs and excuse duties include MTIC classification, licensing, preferences, quotas, reliefs, warehousing, duty suspended movements and seizures. Recent cases: Finmeccanica v HMRC; Global Foods v HMRC; NHS Lothian Health Board v HMRC; Envoygate (Installations) Ltd v HMRC; European Tour Operators Association v HMRC; Darren & Lynne Hills v HMRC; Roger Skinner v HMRC; Enlogic System Europe Ltd v HMRC; Hasbro v HMRC; Donaldson v HMRC; Graphic Controls v HMRC, Grand Folkstone Hotels v HMRC, UK Inbound v HMRC, Mucho Mas v HMRC, Hotel Connect v HMRC; S&I Electronics v HMRC; Citigroup v HMRC; Massey & Hilden Park LLP v HMRC; Copthorn Holdings Ltd v HMRC; Global Foods Ltd v HMRC.
Stamp Duties & Stamp Duty Land Tax: SDLT planning and transactional work as well as SDLT/stamp duty advice in relation to reorganisations. Recent case: Henderson Investment Funds Ltd v HMRC.

PUBLICATIONS Members of chambers write or contribute to major practitioners' works. Alun James and Michael Collins are co-editors of Bramwell on *'Taxation of Companies and Company Reconstructions'.* Michael Sherry is general editor and co-author of *'Whiteman and Sherry on Income Tax; Whiteman and Sherry on Capital Gains Tax'.* Jonathan Schwarz, author of *'Schwarz on Tax Treaties, Annotated UK Double Tax Treaties, Booth & Schwarz: Residence, Domicile and UK Taxation and Transfer Pricing and Business Restructurings: Streamlining all the way'*. Philip Ridgway co-author: *'Bloomsbury Professional's Tax Indemnities and Warranties'.* David Southern: *'Taxation of Loan Relationships and Derivative Contracts; contributor Gore-Browne on Companies and Law Society Company Law Handbook'.* Rebecca Murray: *'Tax Avoidance'.*

THE 36 GROUP

Tenants	106

36 Bedford Row, London, WC1R 4JH
Tel (020) 7421 8000 **Fax** (020) 7421 8035
Email clerks@36civil.co.uk clerks@36crime.co.uk clerks@36family.co.uk **Website** www.36group.co.uk

MEMBERS

Richard Wilson QC (2003)
William Harbage QC (2003)
Frances Oldham QC (1994)
Valentine Grice QC (2002)
Chris Donnellan QC (2008)
Jonathan Kirk QC (2010)
Amjad Malik QC (2010)
John Lloyd-Jones QC (2013)
David Herbert QC (2013)
Felicity Gerry QC (2014)
William Tyler QC (2014)
Hannah Markham QC (2016)
David Altaras (1969)
David Lee (1973)
Jamie de Burgos (1973)
Sam Mainds (1977)
Gillian Temple-Bone (1978)
Paul Infield (1980)
Mercy Akman (1982)
Jacqueline Matthew-Stroud (1984)
Joanne Ecob (1985)
Robert Underwood (1986)
Richard O'Dair (1987)
Gregory Pryce (1988)
Andrew Howarth (1988)
Patricia Cave (1989)
Stuart Nichols (1989)
Amanda Johnson (1990)
Mary Prior (1990)
Matthew Lowe (1991)
Ian Robbins (1991)
Andrew Copeland (1992)
Sarah Gaunt (1992)
Rebecca Herbert(1993)
Kelly Webb (1993)
Nicola Moore (1993)
Julie Warburton(1993)
Nathan Palmer (1994)
Andrzej Bojarski (1995)
Jonathan Spicer (1995)
Philippa Daniels (1995)
Mary Loram (1995)
Rhys Taylor(1996)
Kevin Barry(1997)
Jonathon Rushton (1997)
James Collins(1997)
Steven Evans (1997)
Simon Harding (1998)
Marisa Allman (1998)
Grace Hale (1998)
Simon Ash (1999)
Katya Saudek (1999)
Mark Roscoe (1999)
Martin Kingerley (1999)
Jane Bacon (1999)
Emily James (1999)
Adam Pearson (2000)
Caroline Bray (2000)
Claire Meredith (2000)
Jessie Franses (2000)
Georgina Gibbs (2000)
Miriam Carrion Benitez (2001)
Nadia Silver (2001)
Cameron Crowe (2002)
Christopher Carr (2002)
Michael Rudd(2002)
John Small (2002)
James Petts (2002)
Paul Prior (2003)
Joanna O'Connell (2003)
Kate Tompkins (2003)
John Hallissey (2003)
Kathryn Howarth (2005)
Kakoly Pande (2005)
Ben Mansfield (2005)
Jonathan Cox (2005)
Olivia Magennis (2005)
Alison Lambert (2005)
Kate Grieve (2006)
Richard Roberts (2006)
Gavin Lyon (2006)
Sinead King (2006)
Stephen Bishop (2006)
Nadia Mansfield (2006)
James McLernon (2007)
Charlotte Georges (2007)
Anthony Katz (2007)
Matthew Rowcliffe (2007)
David Ball (2008)
Emilie Pottle (2008)
Kathryn Hovington (2008)
Paula Thomas (2009)
Piers Von Berg (2009)
Malcolm MacDonald (2010)
Saoirse Townshend (2010)
Florence Iveson (2010)
James Armstrong-Holmes (2010)
Rosa Abulafia (2011)
Rebecca Rothwell (2011)
Michael Coley (2011)
Roxanne Aisthorpe (2011)
Amelia Wilson (2011)
Pranjal Shrotri (2012)
Hannah Jones (2012)
Alison Hollis (2012)
Ben Amunwa (2013)

THE CHAMBERS This pioneering and progressive set has notable expertise covering five broad specialist areas of law namely commercial and civil, consumer and trading standards, crime, employment and family. The 36 Group is one of the largest national sets covering work particularly in London, the Midlands, South Eastern and Northern circuits as well as globally within the international courts.

The 36 Group has 106 tenants including 12 QCs, all of whom are committed to excellent service and are recognised for operating with real pride and strength in depth. Members regularly appear in high-profile cases in the High Court, the Crown Court, the Court of Appeal (Civil and Criminal Divisions) and in the Supreme Court of the UK. Over the last three years alone, members have appeared in the Supreme Court in cases involving Criminal Law, Family Law, Consumer Law, European Union Law, Extradition, Human Rights, Judicial Review, Immigration Law, Mental Health Law, Employment Law and Property Law.

The 36 Group also has a growing number of barristers trained as arbitrators and mediators and can provide a full ADR service.

Current publications include: *Unlocking Matrimonial Assets, Consumer and Trading Standards: Law and Practice (Fourth Edition), Modern Financial Regulation, The Sexual Offences Handbook (Second Edition) and Criminal Judicial Review.*

WORK UNDERTAKEN

- Art Law
- Commercial Law
- Consumer Law
- Crime – serious and complex including fraud
- Education Law
- Employment Law
- Extradition
- Family Law
- Immigration Law
- Property Law
- Shale Gas & Oil Law

36 THE GROUP

THREE STONE John McDonnell QC

3 Stone Buildings, Lincoln's Inn, London, WC2A 3XL
Tel (020) 7242 4937 **Fax** (020) 7405 3896 **DX** 317
Email threestone.law.co.uk **Website** www.threestone.law

Head of Chambers	John McDonnell QC
Senior Clerk	Justin Brown
Tenants	48

MEMBERS

John McDonnell QC (1968) (QC-1984)
David Lowe QC (1965) (QC-1984)
Robin Mathew QC (1974) (QC-1992)
Edward Bartley Jones QC (1975) (QC-1997)
Mark Cawson QC (1982) (QC-2001)
Richard de Lacy QC (1976) (QC-2000)
David W Lord QC (1987) (QC-2009)
David Mohyuddin QC (1999) (QC-2016)
Stephen Lloyd (1971)
Andrew J Cosedge (1972)
Don McCue (1974)
James Gibbons (1974)
Alan M Tunkel (1976)
Michael Jefferis (1976)
Ingrid Detter (1977)
Richard Nowinski (1977)
Robert Bourne (1978)
Robert A Hantusch (1982)
Jonathan DC Turner (1982)
Neil Cadwallader (1984)
Francis Collaco Moraes (1985)
Laurence Vaughan-Williams (1988)
Adrian Francis (1988)
Mark Watson-Gandy (1990)
Giles Maynard-Connor (1992)
Richard Peat (1993)
Tim Ludbrook (1996)
Sandradee Joseph (1998)
Paul Burton (1998)
Kerry Bornman (1999)
Richard Devereux-Cooke (1999)
David Went (1999)
Jonathan O'Mahony (2000)
James Couser (2000)
Adam Chichester-Clark (2000)
Simon Olleson (2002)
Sebastian Kokelaar (2004)
Ian Watson (2005)
Katherine Hallett (2006)
Emma Knight (2008)
Daniel Burkitt (2008)
Michael Smith (2008)
Simon Hunter (2009)
Daisy Boulter (2010)
Stuart Cutting (2011)
Rupert Coe (2016)
Sophia Rogers (2013)
Richard Bowles (2014)

THE CHAMBERS Three Stone is a merger between 3 Stone Buildings with 13 Old Square Chambers, both highly regarded sets in Lincoln's Inn. The set is led by John McDonnell QC and has 7 other silks and 40 juniors. David Moyhuddin took silk in 2016 and 7 new members (two silks and 6 juniors) have joined in the last year.

The work of chambers has always focused on commercial chancery with specialisms in particular in commercial actions, insurance and reinsurance, insolvency and restructuring commercial trusts, trusts of land and property work with traditional chancery work together with taxation.

Two members have developed high quality public international law practices.

Chambers has an established IP practice and this has developed in tandem with expertise in sports, media and entertainment and has been augmented by the recruitment of competition specialists.

WORK UNDERTAKEN Commercial and traditional chancery, insurance and reinsurance, insolvency and restructuring, commercial trusts, trusts of land, property, wills and probate, taxation, entertainment, media and sport, intellectual property, public international law.

PUBLICATIONS Jonathan Turner *Intellectual Property and EU Competition Law* (2nd Edition).

INTERNATIONAL WORK Chambers has developed a substantial offshore reputation and practice.

There are particular specialisms in commercial work, commercial trusts and trusts of land, insolvency and restructuring and offshore work. There is a large offshore element to the work of chambers with members who are dual qualified in England and New York. Members appear regularly and have appeared in the Courts of Hong Kong, the Caribbean jurisdictions, Isle of Man, Eire and Northern Ireland. The Chambers' presence offshore is growing with connections with Guernsey and Jersey and the recruitment of two practitioners (one silk and one junior) qualified and formerly practising in the Cayman Islands.

RECRUITMENT The Chambers will continue to recruit experienced practitioners at all levels and junior tenants.

3 VERULAM BUILDINGS Ali Malek QC & Ewan McQuater QC

3 Verulam Buildings, Gray's Inn, London, WC1R 5NT
Tel (020) 7831 8441 **Fax** (020) 7831 8479 **DX** LDE 331
Email chambers@3vb.com **Website** www.3vb.com

Joint Heads of Chambers	Ali Malek QC Ewan McQuater QC
Chambers Director	Robin Jackson
Senior Practice Manager	Stephen Penson
Tenants	68

MEMBERS

Ali Malek QC (1980) (QC-1996)
Ewan McQuater QC (1985) (QC-2003)
John Jarvis QC (1970) (QC-1989)
Christopher Symons QC (1972) (QC-1989)
Richard Salter QC (1975) (QC-1995)
Michael Blair QC (1965) (QC-1996) (Hon Causa)
Gregory Mitchell QC (1979) (QC-1997)
Andrew Sutcliffe QC (1983) (QC-2001)
Andrew Onslow QC (1982) (QC-2002)
Rory Phillips QC (1984) (QC-2002)
Tom Weitzman QC (1984) (QC-2003)
Andrew Fletcher QC (1980) (QC-2006)
Jonathan Nash QC (1986) (QC-2006)
Adrian Beltrami QC (1989) (QC-2008)
Paul Lowenstein QC (1988) (QC-2009)
John Odgers QC (1990) (QC-2012)
David Quest QC (1993) (QC-2013)
Jonathan Davies-Jones QC (1994) (QC-2013)
Matthew Hardwick QC (1994) (QC-2014)
Catherine Gibaud QC (1996) (QC-2014)
Ewan McKendrick QC (1998) (Hon Causa)
Richard Edwards QC (1993) (QC-2016)
David Head QC (1997) (QC-2016)
Clive Freedman (1975)
Elizabeth Birch (1978)
Peter Cranfield (1982)
Michael Lazarus (1987)
Angharad Start (1988)
Jonathan Mark Phillips (1991)
James Evans (1991)
Richard Brent (1995)
Ian Wilson (1995)
Matthew Parker (1997)
Peter Ratcliffe (1998)
Peter de Verneuil Smith (1998)
Nicholas Craig (1998)
Sophie Mallinckrodt (1999)
Laura John (2001)
Tariq Baloch (2001)
William Edwards (2002)
Christopher Harris (2002)
Rajesh Pillai (2002)
George McPherson (2003)
David Simpson (2003)
Lisa Lacob (2004)
Charlotte Eborall (2004)
Adam Kramer (2004)
Richard Hanke (2006)
Robert Purves (2007)
Alexia Knight (2007)
Philip Hinks (2008)
Christopher Bond (2008)
Anne Jeavons (2008)
Kate Holderness (2008)
Tom De Vecchi (2009)
Theodor van Sante (2009)
Christopher Burdin (2010)
Teniola Onabanjo (2010)
Paul Choon Kiat Wee (2010)
Miriam Schmelzer (2010)
Ian Higgins (2011)
Scott Ralston (2012)
Anthony Pavlovich (2012)
Nathaniel Bird (2012)
Pia Dutton (2013)
Emmanuel Sheppard (2012)
Hannah Glover (2013)
Georges Chalfoun (2014)

++ Associate Member

THE CHAMBERS 3 Verulam Buildings is a leading set of chambers specialising in commercial work. Members accept instructions and briefs to advise and represent clients in court, arbitration and other tribunals in England, Wales and internationally.

WORK UNDERTAKEN All members of chambers are specialist advocates in various aspects of commercial work. Among them are acknowledged experts in the fields of banking; insurance and reinsurance; professional negligence; insolvency; entertainment and media; commercial fraud regulation; public international and environmental law. The set also has an established reputation in international and domestic arbitration. Chambers include a number of individuals who have been involved in EU cases in the national courts and the European Court of Justice. Expertise is also offered in an extremely wide range of other matters, including agency, agriculture, building and construction, commodities trading, all aspects of company law, competition law, IT, telecoms and computer legislation, employment, financial services and financial regulation, gaming, intellectual property, judicial review, landlord and tenant matters, pensions, restraint of trade and sale of goods. The diversity of experience available enables 3 Verulam Buildings to offer advice and representation to clients in the huge variety of business contexts in which legal issues arise. Barristers work individually or in teams to carry out all the preparatory and interlocutory work necessary to bring a case to trial or to settle a case by way of ADR. They also undertake non-contentious legal work, for example, drafting standard terms and conditions in contracts both for financial institutions and commercial clients. Additionally, members advise clients on the effects of new law. Chambers are managed by a friendly and efficient team of practice managers and support staff. In appropriate circumstances, chambers will carry out work on a conditional fee basis. The practice managers would be pleased to discuss this further and a draft agreement is available on request.

RECRUITMENT Chambers offer up to four pupillages of 12 months each. The pupillage award for 2017/18 is £65,000, up to £20,000 of which may be drawn down during the year prior to pupillage. Candidates should have a first class or 2:1 degree (not necessarily in law). Applications must be made via the Pupillage Gateway website.

WILBERFORCE CHAMBERS Michael Furness QC

8 New Square, Lincoln's Inn, London, WC2A 3QP
Tel (020) 7306 0102 **Fax** (020) 7306 0095 **DX** 311 London Chancery Lane
Email chambers@wilberforce.co.uk **Website** www.wilberforce.co.uk

Head of Chambers	Michael Furness QC
Practice Director	Nick Luckman
Executive Director	John Treacy
Head Clerk	Mark Rushton
Clerks	Danny Smillie
	Fraser Geddes
	Colin Everson
	Robert Johnstone
	Stewart Cameron
	Andrew Barnes
Tenants	68

MEMBERS

Michael Barnes QC (1965) (QC-1981)
Jules Sher QC (1968) (QC-1981) ° ARB
John Martin QC (1972) (QC-1991)
Robert Ham QC (1973) (QC-1994)
John Furber QC (1973) (QC-1995)
Lawrence Cohen QC (1974) (QC-1993)
Ian Croxford QC (1976) (QC-1993)
David Phillips QC (1976) (QC-1997)
Terence Mowschenson QC (1977) (QC-1995)
John Wardell QC (1979) (QC-2002)
Brian Green QC (1980) (QC-1997)
Michael Furness QC (1982) (QC-2000)
Stephen Davies QC (1983) (QC-2000) °
Gilead Cooper QC (1983) (QC-2006)
Alan Gourgey QC (1984) (QC-2003)
Jonathan Seitler QC (1985) (QC-2003)
Michael Tennet QC (1985) (QC-2006)
Thomas Lowe QC (1985) (QC-2008)
Martin Hutchings QC (1986) (QC-2011)
James Ayliffe QC (1987) (QC-2008)
Lexa Hilliard QC (1987) (QC - 2009)
Marcia Shekerdemian QC (1987) (QC - 2015)
Tim Penny QC (1988) (QC-2016)
Joanna Smith QC (1990) (QC-2009)
Joanne Wicks QC (1990) (QC-2010)
Paul Newman QC (1991) (QC-2009)
Jonathan Evans QC (1994) (QC-2014)
Clare Stanley QC (1994) (QC-2015)
Rupert Reed QC (1996) (QC-2014)
Fenner Moeran QC (1996) (QC-2014)
Jonathan Davey QC (2003) (QC-2016)
Jonathan Hilliard QC (2003) (QC-2016)
John Child (1966)
Thomas Seymour (1975)
Mark Studer (1976)
Gabriel Hughes (1978)
Judith Bryant (1987)
Gabriel Fadipe (1991)
Caroline Furze (1992) °
Max Mallin (1993)
Graeme Halkerston (1994)
Emily Campbell (1995)
Julian Greenhill (1997)
Andrew Child (1997)
Tiffany Scott (1998)
Iain Pester (1999)
Nikki Singla (2000)
Edward Sawyer (2001)
Harris Bor (2006) ++
Andrew Mold (2003)
Thomas Robinson (2003)
Emily McKechnie (2005)
Charlotte Black (2006)
Sebastian Allen (2006)
James Walmsley (2007)
Benjamin Faulkner (2008)
James McCreath (2009)
Emer Murphy (2009)
Tom Roscoe (2010)
Jonathan Chew (2010)
Simon Atkinson (2011)
Bobby Friedman (2011)
Jack Watson (2012)
James Goodwin (2013)
Michael Ashdown (2013)
Elizabeth Houghton (2014)
Tim Matthewson (2014)
Jamie Holmes (2014)

++ former solicitor (2002) ° Door Tenant ARB Arbitrator

THE CHAMBERS The set is widely recognised as one of the leading chambers in its core specialist areas of commercial and financial services, pensions, private client and trusts, property and professional negligence. With 68 barristers (32 QCs) (including 3 door tenants), the set is able to offer specialist barristers at all levels of seniority and across the spectrum of commercial and chancery work. It has individuals who possess excellent reputations for their specialist capabilities in the additional fields of arbitration and dispute resolution, company, construction, banking, insolvency, intellectual property, sports and media law, planning and charities. With its strength and depth of expertise, members of chambers undertake many of the most complex and important cases. They work hard to build and maintain strong long-term relationships with their clients, who include the leading UK and international law firms, multinational corporations, major organisations, private companies and individuals. Clients value the modern quality of chambers' clerking and organisational management and the approachable service provided by barristers and clerks.

WORK UNDERTAKEN

Arbitration & Alternative Dispute Resolution: The set is able to call on a wide range of expertise and experience both in providing first-class advice and representation in arbitrations and mediations and in acting as arbitrator / mediator / expert.

Banking & Finance: Loan agreements, mortgages and charges, guarantees, other forms of security, retail banking, consumer credit, syndicated lending, asset/ project finance, asset tracing, preservation and recovery, insolvency issues, professional negligence claims against those advising lenders.

Commercial: Including agency, civil / commercial fraud, confidentiality, construction, contract, energy, joint ventures, partnerships, and telecommunications.

Company: Shareholder disputes, section 994 petitions, derivative actions, share and business sale agreements, breach of warranty disputes, shareholder agreements, financial assistance, directors' duties, disqualification of directors, conduct of meetings, restoration of companies to the register, OEICs, corporate insolvency, accounting / auditing negligence.

Financial Services: Financial Services and Markets Act 2000, FCA enforcement and disciplinary proceedings, unit trusts, OEICs and other collective investment schemes, mis-selling claims, Financial Ombudsman Service cases, professional negligence claims in the financial services field, insolvency of investment firms.

Intellectual Property & Information Technology: Brand protection and enforcement, designs and copyright,

Wilberforce CHAMBERS

WILBERFORCE CHAMBERS Michael Furness QC (continued)

patents and trade secrets, computer contracts and other commercial agreements, databases, data protection, privacy law, EU competition and International law.

Insolvency: Liquidation, administration, receivership, CVAs, bankruptcy, IVAs, asset tracing, preservation and recovery, avoidance of transactions defrauding creditors, disclaimer of onerous property.

International & Offshore: The nature of the work conducted overseas is varied and often high profile, reflecting the broad spectrum of work which members of Chambers undertake - including trust litigation, company and commercial law, property and intellectual property disputes.

Pensions: Trust law, regulatory and tax issues arising in connection with occupational pension schemes and other employment-related trusts.

Private Client, Trust & Taxation: Contentious and non-contentious litigation involving private trusts and trusts in a wider commercial context both in the UK and worldwide; drafting, advice on administration and construction; taxation of trusts, personal tax and estate planning (including offshore tax planning) and tax litigation.

Professional Liability: Of accountants, actuaries, auditors, company directors, financial advisors, insurance brokers, investment managers, barristers, solicitors, surveyors and trustees and construction-related professional negligence.

Property: Commercial and residential landlord and tenant law, property-related insolvency, proprietary estoppel, property finance and mortgages, restrictive covenants, easements and profits, property-related torts and questions of title, and the sale and registration of land.

Regulatory & Associated Law: Financial services, professionals, sport, utilities, transport, environmental and planning.

THE BAR A-Z REGIONS

KINGS CHAMBERS Nicholas Braslavsky QC

Chambers Director	Debra Andrés
Senior Clerks	William Brown
	Colin Griffin
	Stephen Loxton
Senior Birmingham Clerk	Gary Smith
Senior Leeds Clerk	Rory Davis

Embassy House, 60 Church Street, Birmingham, B3 2DJ
Tel (0345) 034 3444 **Fax** (0345) 034 3445 **DX** 13023

THE CHAMBERS is also at:
36 Young Street, Manchester, M3 3FT
Tel (0345) 034 3444 **Fax** (0345) 034 3445 **DX** 718188 (MCH 3)
5 Park Square East, Leeds, LS1 2NE
Tel (0345) 034 3444 **Fax** (0113) 242 1124 **DX** 713113 (Leeds PKSQ)

MEMBERS

Dr Nicholas Braslavsky QC (1983) (QC-1999)
Mr Stephen J Sauvain QC (1997) (QC-1995)
Mr Vincent Fraser QC (1981) (QC-2001)
Mr Paul Chaisty QC (1982) (QC-2001)
Mr Richard Clayton QC (1977) (QC-2002)
Mr Santinder Hunjan QC (1981) (QC- 2002)
Mr David Manley QC (1981) (QC-2003)
Ms Lesley Anderson QC (1989) (QC-2006)
Mr Anthony Crean QC (1987) (QC-2006)
Mr David Casement QC (1992) (QC-2008)
Mr Michael Rawlinson QC (1991) (QC-2009)
Mr Paul Tucker QC (1990) (QC-2010)
Mr Nigel Poole QC (1989) (QC-2012)
Mr Mark Harper QC (1989) (QC-2016)
Reverend Eric Owen (1969)
Mr Jeffrey Terry (1976)
Mr Alan Evans (1978)
Mr Shokat Khan (1979)
Mr John Barrett (1982)
Mr Neil Berragan (1982)
Mr Michael Stephens (1983)
Mr Mark Halliwell (1985)
Mr Gary Grant (1985)
Mr Simon Hilton (1987)
Mr Nigel Clayton (1987)
Miss Ruth Stockley (1988)
Miss Fiona Ashworth (1998)
Mr Andrew Singer (1990)
Mr Paul Johnson (2006)
Mr Simon Burrows (1990)
Mr Matthew Smith (1991)
Mr Andrew Grantham (1991)
Mr Adam Aldred (2014)
Mr Martin Carter (1992)
Mr Wilson Horne (1992)
Miss Lucy Powis (1992)
Miss Sarah Pritchard (1993)
Mr Richard Lander (1993)
Mr Ian Ponter (1993)
Mr Michael Ditchfield (1993)
Miss Sarah Clover (1993)
Mr James Boyd (1994)
Miss Kelly Pennifer (1994)
Mr Andrew Latimer (1995)
Miss Anna Diamond (1995)
Mr Gavin McBride (1996)
Mr Jeremy Roussak (1996)
Mr Louis Doyle (1996)
Mr Jonathan Easton (1996)
Mr Simon Plaut (1997)
Mr Colin Bourne (1997)
Dr Mark Friston (1997)
Mr Simon Young (1998)
Mr Stephen Maguire (2007)
Mr Giles Cannock (1998)
Professor Andrew McGee (1998)
Mr Matthew Hall (1999)
Miss Helen Mulholland (1999)
Mr Martin Budworth (1999)
Miss Tina Ranales-Cotos (1999)
Mr Brian Griffiths (1999)
Miss Eleanor Temple (2000)
Mrs Lisa Walmisley (2000)
Mr Paul Lakin (2000)
Mr Paul Hughes (2001)
Mr Ben Williams (2001)
Mr Geraint Wheatley (2001)
Mr Rupert Beloff (2001)
Miss Claire Steward (2002)
Mr Craig Ralph (2002)
Mr Michael Rudd (2002)
Mr John Hunter (2002)
Mr Sam Karim (2002)
Miss Emily Duckworth (2003)
Miss Sarah Lawrenson (2003)
Miss Sarah Reid (2004)
Miss Francesca Gardner (2004)
Miss Rachel Galloway (2004)
Miss Sophie Allan (2004)
Miss Helen Trotter (2005)
Mr Paras Gorasia (2005)
Miss Charlotte Law (2005)
Mr Ben Harding (2005)
Miss Cheryl Dainty (2006)
Mr Richard Livingston (2006)
Mr Johnny Ward (2007)
Dr Nathan Smith (2007)
Mr Kevin Latham (2007)
Mr Stephen McNamara (2008)
Mr Anthony Gill (2008)
Miss Eleanor d'Arcy (2008)
Miss Anna Macey (2008)
Mrs Laura Daniels (2009)
Mr Richard Borrett (2009)
Miss Louise Green (2009)
Miss Eliza V Sharron (2009)
Miss Francesca P Gardener (2009)
Miss Ruth Taylor (2010)
Mr Jonathan Wright (2010)
Mr Aidan Reay (2011)
Mr Freddie Humphries (2011)
Miss Erica Bedford (2012)
Mr Doug Cochran (2012)
Miss Arianna Kelly (2013)
Miss Alison Ogley (2014)
Miss Constanza Bell (2014)
Mr Killian Garvey (2014)
Mr Marcus F Daly SC (1987) (SC-1999) *
Mr Colm Ó hOisin SC (1998) (SC-2005) *
Mr James Henderson (1997) *
Mr Leo Charalambides (1998) *
Professor Andrew Keay (2010) *
Sir Maurice Kay (1975) (QC-1988)+
His Honour David Gilliland (1964) (QC-1984) +

* Associates + Arbitrator

THE CHAMBERS Kings Chambers is ranked one of the country's leading sets. It provides barristers with the highest reputation for advocacy, knowledge and standards to service. This is a large specialist set with a national reputation practising from Manchester, Leeds and Birmingham in several practice areas: pre-dominantly chancery and commercial law; planning and environmental law, personal injury and clinical negligence, costs, employment, sports law, mediation, arbitration and public law.

WORK UNDERTAKEN

Arbitration: Kings Chambers has a number of members with practices encompassing domestic and international arbitration. Chambers has also launched its own bespoke arbitration service (KAS) offering a panel of experienced arbitrators including former judges and silks from other jurisdictions.

KINGS CHAMBERS Nicholas Braslavsky QC (continued)

Chancery & Commercial: The Chancery and commercial group has extensive experience in litigation (including agency, contracts, sale of goods, restraint of trade and restrictive covenants, corporate law); corporate and personal insolvency (including winding up, administration, administrative receivership and tracing assets),banking and professional negligence. Residential and commercial landlord and tenant work (including renewals, rent.

Clinical Negligence & Personal Injury: The clinical negligence and personal injury team undertake work involving serious personal injury claims, all aspects of clinical negligence and occupational disease with a particular focus on asbestos and other forms of toxic exposure. The team also specialises in chronic pain and related conditions.

Costs: There is a specialist and dedicated costs team, practising exclusively in costs law, disputes and litigation funding.

Employment: The employment team covers the entire spectrum of employment law and has particular strengths in race, sex, equal pay, restrictive covenants and disability discrimination both in tribunals and in the High Court.

EU & Competition: Chambers has a small and dedicated team dealing with EU and competition law, including cartels, dominance, mergers, market investigations, litigation, public procurement, state aid, trading agreements and compliance.

Mediation: Mediation is an important part of the litigation process. The team comprises accredited mediators at various levels and with expertise in differing areas of law.

Planning: Kings Chambers is one of the largest planning and environmental chambers, with members appearing before a wide range of dedicated tribunals and inquiries. Chambers acts in planning appeals and major inquiries for a wide variety of clients and local authorities. Kings also has extensive experience in environmental law including waste disposal and management, energy, compulsory purchase compensation and highways.

Public Law: The public law group practises extensively in the Administrative Court, sitting in London and the regions. The group encompasses the range of public law work in community care, education, housing, mental health, licensing, local government and social security matters. Members advise and appear before courts at all levels.

Sports Law: The sports law team have been involved in some of the most substantial and high profile sports cases nationally in recent years involving, commercial dispute resolution, disciplinary and regulatory proceedings, anti-doping rules, employment issues, sports-related personal injury, breach of confidentiality and privacy, wealth management issues, intellectual property including image rights, trademark infringement and breach of copyright.

NO5 CHAMBERS Mark Anderson QC

Fountain Court, Steelhouse Lane, Birmingham, B4 6DR
Tel (0845) 210 5555 **Fax** (0121) 606 1501 DX 16075 Birmingham Fountain Court
Email info@no5.com **Website** www.No5.com

Head of Chambers	Mark Anderson QC
Deputy Heads	Rex Tedd QC
	Jonathan Jones QC
	Nageena Khalique QC
Practice Director	Tony McDaid
Tenants	263

MEMBERS

Mark Anderson QC (1983) (QC-2010) Deputy High Court Judge + ^
Rex Tedd QC (1970) (QC-1993) Deputy High Court Judge +
Anthony Smith QC (1958) (QC-1977)
Martin Kingston QC (1972) (QC-1992)
The Hon Alex Henderson QC (1970) (QC-1992) °
Clive Newberry QC (1978) (QC -1993)
Christopher Hotten QC (1972) (QC-1994) + ^
Gareth Evans QC (1973) (QC-1994) +
Richard Jones QC (1972) (QC-1996) + ^
Manjit Gill QC (1982) (QC-2000) ^
Paul Bleasdale QC (1978) (QC-2001) + ^
Jeremy Cahill QC (1975) (QC-2002) ^
Douglas Armstrong QC (1990) (QC-2005) Scotland °
Lorna Meyer QC (1986) (QC-2006)
Richard Humphreys QC (1986) (QC-2006) ° ^
Michael Burrows QC (1979) (QC-2008) +
Christopher Bright QC (1985) (QC-2009) +
Mohammed Zaman QC (1985) (QC -2009)
David Mason QC (1986) (QC-2010) + ^
Michael Duck QC (1988) (QC-2011) ^
Adrian Keeling QC (1990) (QC-2011) ^
Mark Heywood QC (1986) (QC-2012) ^
Gary Bell QC (1989) (QC-2012) ^
Jo Sidhu QC (1993) (QC 2012) °
Jonathan Jones QC (1994) (QC-2013)
Jonas Hankin QC (1998) (QC-2013)
John Butterfield QC (1995) (QC-2014)+ ^
Nageena Khalique QC (1994) ^ (QC-2015)
The Rt Hon Jeremy Wright QC MP Attorney General (1996) (QC-2014) °
Paul Cairnes QC (1980) (QC-2016) ^
Dr Simon Fox QC (1994) (QC-2016)
Richard Kimblin QC (1998) (QC-2016) ^
Gerald Bermingham (1967) ^
Stephen Whitaker (1970)
Allan Dooley (1991) + ^
Peter Arnold (1972) ^
Timothy Jones (1975) ^
Simon Worlock (1975) ^
Roger S Giles (1976) ^
Walter Bealby (1976)
Graham Henson (1976)
Anne E Smallwood (1977) ^
David Iles (1977)
Christopher James (1977) ^
William Pusey (1977)
Kevin O'Donovan (1978) ^
Anthony Korn (1978) ^
Andrew Keogh (1978) ^
Roger Dyer (1980)
Timothy Newman (1981) ^
Stephanie Brown (1982) ^
Neil Thompson (1982) ^
Stephen Campbell (1982) + ^
Professor Christopher Newdick (1982) °
Andrew McGrath (1983) ^
Irvine Maccabe (1983) ^
Ramby de Mello (1983) ^
Nadia Sharif (1985)
Richard Moat (1985)
Mark Kelly (1985) ^
Anthony Bell (1985)
Russell Bailey (1985) ^
Kevin Barrett (1985) ^
James Doyle (1985) ^
Bernard Thorogood (1986) +
Kevin Leigh (1986) ^
David Young (1986) °
Michael O'Brien (1987)
Peter Dean (1987)
Joanna Chadwick (1988) ^
Ekwall Singh Tiwana (1988) ^
Ian Bridge (1988) ^
Andrew Wallace (1988) ^
Dewinder Birk (1988)
Samantha Forsyth (1988) ^
Malcolm Duthie (1989)
Becket Bedford (1989) ^
Martin Liddiard (1989) ^
Carole Murray (1989) °
Timothy Hanson (1989) °
Jasvir Mann (1990) ^
Michael Anning (1990)
Ashley Wynne (1990) ^
Andrew Baker (1990) ^
Celina Colquhoun (1990) ^
Antonie Muller (1990)
Richard Alomo (1990)
Mark Radburn (1991)
Michele Friel (1991) ^
Sarah Buckingham (1991) ^+
Edward Grant (1991) °
Peter Goatley (1992) ^
Nicholas Xydias (1992)
Marc Wilkinson (1992) ^
Nicola Preston (1992) ^
Hugh Richards (1992) ^
Nigel Brockley (1992) ^
Adam Farrer (1992) ^
Steven Bailey (1992) ^
Paul Joseph (1992) ^
Abid Mahmood (1992) + ^
Nazmun Ismail (1992) ° ^
Nabila Mallick (1992) ^
Danny Bazini (1992) ^
David Taylor (1993) ^
Caroline Sumeray (1993) °
Phillip Bradley (1993)
Param K Bains (1993)
Nandini Dutta (1993)
Joanne Rothwell (1993) ^
Edward Nicholson (1993) ^
Emma Edhem (1993) ^
Robert Smallwood (1994)
Anthony Potter (1994) + ^
Satnam Choongh (1994) ^
David Tyack (1994)
Mark Renouf (1994) °
Brian Dean (1994) ^
James Stoll (1994)
Stefano Nuvoloni (1994) ^
David Mitchell (1995) ^
Tim Sheppard (1995) ^
Richard Hignett (1995) ^
Dean Kershaw (1995) + ^
Susan Monaghan (1995) ^
Sally Hancox (1996) +
Henry Pitchers (1996)
Elizabeth Power (1996)
Richard Case (1996) ^
David Holloway (1996) °
Laura Davidson (1996)
Ravinder Bagral (1996)
Mugni Islam-Choudhury (1996) ^
Carol Knotts (1996) ^
Karl Hirst (1997) ^
Christopher Young (1997)
Richard Hadley (1997)
Harbinder Singh Lally (1997) ^
Matthew Brunning (1997) ^
Adreeja Chatterjee (1997) ^
Gareth Compton (1997)
Talbir Singh (1997) ^
Vinesh Mandalia (1997)
Stephen Goodfellow (1997)
Alexander Stein (1998) ^
Jonathan Derrington (1998)
Kristina Brown (1998)
Susanne Muth (1998) ^
Jamie Gamble (1999)
Louisa Denning (1999) ^
Teresa Hargreaves (1999)
Charles Crow (1999) ^
John Coughlan (1999)

NO5 CHAMBERS Mark Anderson QC (continued)

MEMBERS

Charles Price (1999) ^
Helen Barney (1999) ^
Nassera Butt (1999) ^
Dr Fayyaz Afzal OBE (1999) ^
S Chelvan (1999) ^
Matthew Brook (1999)
Shakil Najib (1999)
Richard Adams (1999)
Saleema Mahmood (1999) ^
Cathlyn Orchard (1999)
Raza Mithani (2000) °
Glenn Willetts (2000)
Neil Chawla (2000) ^
Jenny Wigley (2000) ^
Omar Ensaff (2000) ^
Sharon Bahia (2000) ^
Paul Evans (2001) ^
Michelle Heeley (2001) ^+
Michael Wingrave (2001) °
Tim Pole (2001) ^
Tom Schofield (2001) ^
Olivia Chaffin-Laird (2001) ^
Richard Adkinson (2001) ^
James Dixon (2001) ^
Esther Gamble (2001) ^
Philip Rule (2001)
Rizwan Ashiq (2001)
Philip Mantle (2002) ^
Victoria Clifford (2002) ^
Mark Bradshaw (2002) ^
Lynette McClement (2002)
Christopher Perry (2002)
Fatim Kurji (2003) ^°
Helen Arthur (2003) ^
Daniel Oscroft (2003) ^
Earl Pinnock (2003) ^
Claire van Overdijk (2003) ^
Nicholas Cobill (2003) ^
Denise Owen (2003) °
Heather Popley (2003) ^
Clare Coles (2003) ^
Christopher Hopkins (2003)
Louise Higgins (2003)
Jennifer Fox (2004) °
Mamta Gupta (2004)
James Leslie (2004) ^
Sarah Allen (2005) ^
Dr Jonathan Punt (2005)
Richard Cooke (2005)
Orla Grant (2005) ^
Harpreet Singh Sandhu (2005) ^
Steven Reed (2005) ^
Suella Fernandes MP (2005) ^°
Kathryn Taylor (2005) °
Katie Feeney (2005)
Yasmin Yasseri (2005) ^
Peter Tyers-Smith (2005) °
Jack Feeny (2005) ^
Juliet Allen (2005) ^
Nicholas Ferrari (2005)
Maria Mulla (2005)
Sultana Tafadar (2005)
John Brown (2005)
Gemma Roberts (2006) ^
Professor Nelson Enonchong (2006) ^°
Kirsty Gallacher (2006) ^
Claire Howell (2006) ^
Emma Sutton (2006)
Simon Hunka (2007) ^
Jack Smyth (2007) ^
Richard Oakes (2007)
Rowena Meager (2007) ^
Laura Vickers (2007) ^
Rebecca Stickler (2007)
Sophie Murray (2007)
Louise Corfield (2008)
Hermione Williams (2008) °
Russell Holland (2008) ^
Naomi Owen (2008) ^
Charlotte Robinson-Jones (2008)
Jessica Smeaton (2008)
Ramya Nagesh (2008)
James Burke (2009) °
Sara McCarthy (2009) ^
Ian Brownhill (2009)
Richard Grimshaw (2010)
Thea Osmund-Smith (2010)
Caroline Jennings (2010)
Catherine Jones (2010)
Hashi Mohamed (2010)
Katie Miller (2010)
Christopher Snell (2010)
Francesca Martin (2010)
James Corbet Burcher (2011)
Katharine Charles (2011)
Tom Seamer (2011)
Steven Smith (2011)
Nina Pindham (2012)
Philip Dayle (2012)
Richard Gibbs (2012)
Ricky Seal (2012)
Emma Williams (2012)
Richard Wilcock (2012)
Eamonn Hurley-Flynn (2013)
Jennifer Blair (2013) °
Alexander Mellis (2013)
Jodie Kembrey (2013)
Imogen Halstead (2014)
Varsha Jagadesham (2014)
Jonathan Butterworth (2015)

+ Recorder ° Associate ^ Public/Direct Access

THE CHAMBERS No5 Chambers is a national set offering a comprehensive across-the-board service. Throughout its 100-year history, No5 Chambers has developed a reputation for breaking new ground and continues to be regarded as a progressive and forward-thinking set, maintaining its success in traditional sectors of law whilst offering specialist advice and representation at the cutting edge of newly evolving areas. Having grown to over 240 barristers, including 33 silks, No5 Chambers provides a truly nationwide service from its offices in Birmingham, London, Bristol and Leicester.

In recent years, Chambers has made significant inroads into the South West and Wales from its Bristol location and its London office continues to go from strength to strength, housing more than 50 tenants. Chambers continues to attract high quality work in all disciplines, combining excellent service standards with a progressive, modern and flexible approach to clients' needs.

No5 prides itself on forming partnerships with solicitor clients and other professionals. Chambers has associate tenants in Dubai, Spain, Cayman, Hong Kong, Singapore and BVI and is keen to develop further links particularly in the fields of construction, international arbitration, commercial work and environmental. No5 Chambers is a member of the International Trade Council.

Dedicated specialist clerking teams based throughout the country have detailed knowledge of the individuals and groups they manage and support and are available to advise clients on the most suitable Counsel for a particular case. A highly respected set, No5 Chambers remains a well-reputed provider of informative and topical seminars, allowing the latest issues and developments to be discussed with highly qualified speakers and sector experts. Many members of chambers write or contribute to legal textbooks and specialist journals.

No5 Chambers has a wide-ranging practice and prides itself on being able to assist clients across a broad spectrum of law both at home and internationally utilising the expertise it has in its multitude of practice groups. Further details on No5 and its members can be found on its website www.No5.com.

ST IVES CHAMBERS Jeremy Weston QC

1-3 Whittall Street, Birmingham, B4 6DH
Tel (0121) 236 0863 **Fax** (0121) 236 6961 **Email** crimeclerks@stiveschambers.co.uk
familyclerks@stiveschambers.co.uk, civilclerks@stiveschambers.co.uk **Website** www.stiveschambers.co.uk

Chambers Director:	Jackie Maskew
Practice Managers:	Philip Hidson (Crime)
	Clare Radburn (Civil, Family Finance & Regulatory)
	Sarah Robinson (Family & Court of Protection)
Tenants:	67
Door Tenants	7

THE CHAMBERS St Ives Chambers is proud of its reputation for outstanding service and excellence in all areas. Chambers is a multidisciplinary set with particular expertise in family, housing, property, chancery and commercial, regulatory and criminal law, and is regarded for boasting some of the most renowned and experienced practitioners in the Midlands, past and present. Chambers has 67 tenants, including two highly regarded family QCs and seven door tenants.

Members have been involved in a number of high-profile cases: Peter Cooper defended Magdalena Luczak in the Daniel Pelka murder; David Jackson prosecuted Christopher Semak, the paedophile policeman; Tony Watkin prosecuted a Warwick company director accused of £7.5m fraud; Elizabeth Isaacs QC and Adem Muzaffer were involved in a landmark surrogacy case: Re Z; and the set was involved in the 'Roadblock Case', DR v GR.

Members of chambers hold various judicial appointments, including Recorders of the Crown and County Court, Deputy District Judge and Tribunal Judge.

ST PHILIPS CHAMBERS Avtar Khangure QC

Head of Chambers	Avtar Khangure QC
Chief Clerk	Joe Wilson
Tenants	188

55 Temple Row, Birmingham, B2 5LS
Tel (0121) 246 7000 **Fax** (0121) 246 7001 **DX** 723240 BIRMINGHAM 56
Email enquiries@st-philips.com **Website** www.st-philips.com

41 Park Square, Leeds, LS1 2NP
Tel (0113) 244 6691 **Fax** (0113) 394 7474 **DX** 26421 LEEDS

4 Field Court, Gray's Inn, London, WC1R 5EF
Tel (020) 7440 6900 **Fax** (020) 7242 0197 **DX** 483 LONDON/CHANCERY LANE

MEMBERS

Avtar Khangure QC (1985) (QC-2003) †
David Crigman QC (1969) (QC-1989) †
Stephen Linehan QC (1970) (QC-1993) † ^
Timothy Raggatt QC (1972) (QC-1993) †
John Randall QC (1978) (QC-1995)
Elizabeth Blackburn QC (1978) (QC-1998)
Christopher Millington QC (1976) (QC-2001) † ^
Vasanti Selvaratnam QC (1983) (QC-2001)
Peter Haynes QC (1983) (QC-2008)
Kevin Hegarty QC (1982) (QC-2010) † ^
Richard Atkins QC (1989) (QC-2011) † ^
Andrew Smith QC (1997) (QC-2012) † ^
Edward Pepperall QC (1989) (QC-2013) † ++
Elizabeth McGrath QC (1987) (QC-2014)
Malcolm Morse (1967)
Sarah Miller (1971)
Douglas Readings (1972) †
Clare Dillon (1974) ^
James Quirke (1974) ^
Guy Spollon (1976)
Andrew Neaves (1977)
Giles Harrison-Hall (1977) ^
Charles Debattista (1978)
Nicholas Hawkins (1979)
Bernard Linnemann (1980)
Martine Kushner (1980) †
Simon Clegg (1980) ^
Stephen Thomas (1980) †
Makhan Shoker (1981)
Nergis-Anne Mathew (1981) ^
Paul Mytton (1982) ^
Petar Starcevic (1983) ^
John Evans (1983)
Lawrence Messling (1983)
John Edwards (1983) †
Dr Mirza Ahmad (1984) ^
Thomas Rochford (1984) †
David Stockill (1985) ^
Andrew Jackson (1986) ^
Christopher Adams (1986) † ++
Mark Spackman (1986) ^
Colin Wright (1987)
Dorian Day (1987) ^
Blondel Thompson (1987) ^
Graham Howard (1987)
Conrad Rumney (1988)
Sarah Buxton (1988) ^
Sandra Bristoll (1989) †
Sarah Harrison (1989)
Amarjit Rai (1989) ^
Mark Calway (1989) ^ †
Paul Wilson (1989)
Simon Davis (1990) ^
Michael George (1990) ^
Sophie Garner (1990) ^
Vanessa Meachin (1990) † ^
Edmund Beever (1990) **
James Puzey (1990) ^
Sean Kelly (1990)
Melanie Williamson (1990)
Sarah George (1991) ^ **
Glyn Samuel (1991)
Jonathan Gidney (1991) ^
Robin Lewis (1991) ^
Susan Todd (1991) ^
Matthew Barnes (1992)
Julie Moseley (1992)
William Baker (1992)
Julie Sparrow (1992) ^
Dominic Happé (1993)
Heidi Kubik (1993) ^ †
Lee Marklew (1993)
Stefan Kolodynski (1993)
Anthony Verduyn (1993) † ^
Anthony Johnston (1993)
Tariq Sadiq (1993) ^
David Maxwell (1994) **
Angus Burden (1994) ^
Elizabeth Walker (1994) †
Patrick Wainwright (1994)
Nicholas Smith (1994) ^
Andrew Charman (1994) ^
Rosalyn Carter (1994) †
Jacqueline Humphreys (1994) ^
Stuart Roberts (1994) ^
Marisa Lloyd (1994) ^
Francesca Fothergill (1994) ^
James Dunstan (1995) ^
Carolyn Jones (1995)
Darron Whitehead (1995) ^
Gregory Pipe (1995)
John Brennan (1996)
Naomi Gilchrist (1996) ^
Louise McCabe (1996) ^ +++ †
Simon Phillips (1996)
Shane Crawford (1996) ^
James Morgan (1996) †
Huw Jones (1997)
Huma Ali (1997)
Charles Blatchford (1997)
Rachel Toney (1998)
Elizabeth Hodgetts (1998) ^
Ishfaq Ahmed (1999)
Raj Punia (1999) ^
Heledd Williams (1999)
Leisha Bond (1999) ^
Anthony Edwards (1999) ^
Poonam Bhari (1999) ^
Mark Jones (2000)
Ravi Aswani (2000)
Jane Sarginson (2000)
Zaheer Afzal (2000) ^
Jennifer Josephs (2000) ^
Benedict Mills (2000) ^ †
Ian Speed (2000)
Andrew Evans (2000) ^
Jonathan Nosworthy (2000) ^ +++
Nicholas Howell-Jones (2000) ^
Stephen Abberley (2000)
Tom Walkling (2001) ^
Rebecca Franklin (2001) ^
David Griffiths (2001) ^
Elizabeth Richards (2001) ^
Sean O'Brien (2001) ^ **
David Munro (2001) ^
Paul J Dean (2001) ^
William Buck (2001)
Thomas Whitehead (2002)
James Shirley (2002)
Yolanda Pemberton (2002) ^
Matthew Weaver (2002)
Christopher Watson (2003)
Naomi Candlin (2003) ^
Colin Baran (2003) ^
Peter Cherry (2003)
Davinia Riley (2004) ^
Victoria Edmonds (2004) ^
Marc Brown (2004)
Amrisha Parathalingam (2004) ^
Suzanne Coleclough (2005) ^
Nicholas Brown (2005)
Bruce Frew (2005) ^
Alexander Rozycki (2005) ^
Ben Williams (2006) ^
Jonathan Barker (2006) ^
Rosa Dickinson (2006) +++
Jonathan Meichen (2006) ^
Amit Gupta (2006)
Alice Winstanley (2006) ^
Lydia Pemberton (2006)
Ali-Reza Tabari (2006) ^
Dominic Crossley (2006)
Carl Templar-Vasey (2006)
Neil Fawcett (2006) +++
Patrick Keith (2006)
Lisa Hancox (2006)
Debbie Collins (2007) ^

ST PHILIPS CHAMBERS Avtar Khangure QC (continued)

Iqbal Mohammed (2007) ^
Helen Gardiner (2007) ^
Lucie French (2008) ^
Robert Mundy (2008)
Christopher Rank (2008)
Jack Redmond (2009)
Joseph Millington (2009)
Kate Rogers (2009)
Jonathan Gale (2009)
Kathryn Vernon-Asimeng (2009)
Benjamin Close (2009)
Andrew Bainham (2009)
James Bruce (2010) ^
Anna Metcalfe (2010)
Gavin McLeod (2010)
Thomas Steward (2011)
Dominic Roberts (2011)
Mohammad Hafeez (2011)
Andrew Burrow (2011)
Hannah Tildesley (2012) ^
Rhiannon Wilcock (2012) ^
Cait Sweeney (2012)
Andrew Dinsmore (2012)
Emma Williamson (2013)
Katie Longstaff (2013)
William Hooper (2014)
Philip Harris (2014)
Warren Bank (2014)
Oberon Kwok (2014)
Mark Grant (2015)
Emma Kendall (2016)
John Reeder QC (1971) (QC-1989) *
Allan Myers QC (1988) (QC Aus) *
Jonathan Lux (2013) *
Mary Thompson (1983) (2013 Hong Kong) *
Dr Colin Ong (1991) (1998 Brunei) (2012 Singapore) *
Dan Tan (2005 New York) (2011 California) (2011 District of Columbia) (2003 Solicitor, England) (2000 Solicitor, Singapore) *

† Recorder ++ Deputy High Court Judge +++ Deputy District Judge ** Fee Paid Employment Judge ^ Public Access
* Associate Member

THE CHAMBERS St Philips is an award winning, multi-disciplinary set of barristers, widely recognised as one of the most forward-looking chambers in the UK.

On 1 August 2016 leading national set St Philips and specialist shipping and international commercial set Stone Chambers merged. The merged set is known in London and internationally as St Philips Stone Chambers.

St Philips has offices in Birmingham, Leeds and London. It is committed to expanding upon the first-class service it is renowned for, reinforcing its objective to make its exceptional team of barristers the first choice for clients nationally and internationally. Chambers serves a range of clients, including international companies, local authorities, sporting authorities, trade unions, public bodies and regulators. Members of Chambers also accept instructions under the Direct Access rules.

St Philips attributes its continued success to a forward-thinking and flexible strategy coupled with innovation. Chambers has a reputation for being friendly and approachable. Strong client relationships and an understanding of clients' needs are central to how it operates, how it assists its clients in achieving their goals, and how it seeks to excel on their behalf. St Philips' specialist groups of barristers are supported by dedicated teams of clerks, led by Chief Clerk Joe Wilson. St Philips also has the benefit of in-house teams of support staff in IT, HR, marketing, finance and business development.

WORK UNDERTAKEN St Philips offers a specialist service in administrative law, ADR, arbitration (domestic and international), banking, clinical negligence, commercial, construction, criminal, employment, family, fraud (civil and criminal), immigration, insolvency, intellectual property, personal injury, property, public, regulatory, trusts, and wills and probate. Members are actively involved in writing academic articles and some members have published books. Chambers' members offer a wide range of seminars, lectures, workshops and other training events, both in-house and externally.

St Philips commercial group has a reputation for providing excellence across the full spectrum of commercial, property and private client work. It offers specialist practice teams in banking and financial services, commercial fraud, company, insolvency, intellectual property, landlord and tenant, partnership, professional liability, property, technology and construction, and wills, trusts and probate.

St Philips Stone Chambers offers clients in-depth knowledge and experience in disputes across a number of different business sectors and services including shipping & transport, international trade and commodities, energy and natural resources and other commercial areas.

St Philips employment group offers a truly nationwide service with members providing advice, drafting and advocacy in Tribunals, County Courts, the High Court and the EAT. Members have particular expertise in cases with issues of discrimination, religion and belief, and in conducting complex group claims.

St Philips personal injury group acts for claimants and defendants and offers particular expertise in cases of fatal accidents, catastrophic injuries, industrial disease (including stress), fraud and allegations of fraud, and travel and holiday claims.

St Philips clinical negligence group has gained a reputation for providing first class legal advice and attracts work from nationally recognised leading firms in this field. The team has particular expertise in the areas of birth injury, cosmetic surgery, hospital acquired infections, Coroners' inquests, maximum severity spinal injury and amputations, product liability, multi-party actions, human rights claims, dental claims and negligence in general practice.

St Philips family group is one of the largest in the country, having a leading reputation nationally for providing high quality specialist advice and representation across four key areas:

The financial remedy team has expertise in all aspects of financial work arising from divorce or separation, including same sex relationships.

The care and adoption team has expertise in the full range of public law Children Act proceedings acting for local authorities, parents and children. Members have appellate experience in the High Court and Court of Appeal, and extensive experience in the judicial review of local authority decisions.

The children team has experience and expertise in all aspects of private law Children Act proceedings, including cases involving domestic abuse, residence/contact disputes, international child abduction and cases in which the

ST PHILIPS CHAMBERS Avtar Khangure QC (continued)

child is separately represented.

The Court of Protection Team offers barristers who have longstanding experience of dealing with cases involving issues of incapacity, acting for the Official Solicitor or in matters arising under the Mental Health Acts and Human Rights Act 1998.

St Philips criminal group offers unrivalled strength from junior through to Silk. Members prosecute and defend, in equal measure, all aspects of serious crime across the country, including murder, corporate manslaughter, serious sexual offences, white collar fraud and large scale drug conspiracies. Members appear on the preferred lists for the Attorney General, Crown Prosecution Services, Organised Crime Divisions and key national defence firms.

St Philips regulatory group defends and prosecutes on behalf of a wide range of commercial clients and regulatory bodies throughout the UK. Matters include fatal accidents, corporate manslaughter, trading standards, environmental regulation, VAT and revenue appeals, health and safety, police powers, benefit fraud, licensing and inquests. In addition, several members sit on a variety of disciplinary bodies such as the RFU, ASA, BDO, The sport resolutions disputes panel, the GMC and the GDC, including one barrister who is an appointed arbitrator for the Court of Arbitration for Sport.

ALBION CHAMBERS Charles Hyde QC

Head of Chambers	Charles Hyde QC
Chambers' Director	Paul Fletcher
Senior Clerk (Crime)	Bonnie Colbeck
Senior Clerk (Civil/Family)	Michael Harding
Clerk (Regulatory)	Nicholas Jeanes
Junior Clerk (Family)	Julie Hathway
Junior Clerk (Crime)	Ken Duthie
Clerk (Civil)	Stephen Arnold
Tenants	63

Albion Chambers, Broad St, Bristol, BS1 1DR
Tel (0117) 927 2144 **Fax** (0117) 926 2569 **DX** 7822
Email clerks@albionchambers.co.uk **Website** www.albionchambers.co.uk

MEMBERS

Charles Hyde QC (1998) (QC-2006) +
Ignatius Hughes QC (1986) (QC-2009) + ^
Adam Vaitilingam QC (1987) (QC-2010) + ^
Nkumbe Ekaney QC (1990) (QC-2011)
Kate Brunner QC (1997) ^+ (QC-2015)
Christopher Jervis (1966)
Timothy Hills (1968) ^
Nicholas O'Brien (1968)
Louise Price (1972) ^
Nicholas Fridd (1975) ^
Martin Steen (1976)
Robert Duval (1979)
John Geraint Norris (1980)
Stephen Mooney (1987) ^
Don Tait (1987)
Fiona Elder (1988) ^
Deborah Dinan-Hayward (1988) ^
Claire Rowsell (1991)
Simon Burns (1992)
Nicholas Sproull (1992) ^
Paul Cook (1992) ^+
Alan Fuller (1993) ^
Edward Burgess (1993) +
Jonathan Stanniland (1993)
Elizabeth Cunningham (1995) ^*
Jason Taylor (1995) ^
Giles Nelson (1995)
Adrian Posta (1996) ^
Daniel Leafe (1996)
Kirsty Real (1996) ^
Kannan Siva (1996)
Hannah Wiltshire (1998)
Charlotte Pitts (1999) ^
Sarah Regan (2000)
David Chidgey (2000) ^
Linsey Knowles (2000) ^
Richard Shepherd (2001) ^
David Cotterell (2001) ^
James Cranfield (2002)
Stephen Roberts (2002)
Fiona Farquhar (2002)
Benjamin Jenkins (2004)
Joanna Lucas (2004)
Gemma Borkowski (2005) ^
Anna Midgley (2005) ^
Monisha Khandker (2005)
William Heckscher (2006)
Derek Perry (2006)
Alice Darian (2006)
Edward Hetherington (2006)
Sarah Pope (2006)
Jonathan Wilkinson (2006)
Stuart Fuller (2007)
Simon Emslie (2007) ^
Philip Baggley (2009)
Emily Brazenall (2009)
Erinna Foley-Fisher (2011)
Kevin Farquharson (2011)
Alexander West (2011)
Alexander Small (2012)
Robert Morgan-Jones (2014)
Paul Dunkels QC (1972) (QC-1993) *
Kate Branigan (1985) (QC-2006) *

+ Recorder * Door Tenant ^ Public/ Direct Access

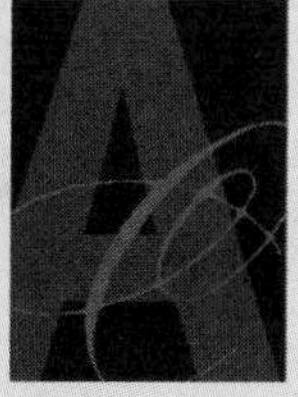

THE CHAMBERS Albion Chambers is a long-established set with an excellent reputation for integrity, approachability and the highest standards of advice and advocacy.

The set's principal areas of expertise are within crime, regulatory (including Health and Safety), matrimonial finance, children, employment and disciplinary, inquests, probate and personal injury.

GUILDHALL CHAMBERS James Townsend

Head of Chambers	James Townsend
Chief Executive	Jeremy Sweetland
Principal Civil Clerk	Justin Emmett
Principal Crime Clerk	Lucy Northeast
Crime Clerks	Grant Bidwell
	Elena Brake
	Ezweni Ncube
Civil Clerks	Mike Norton
	Chris Checketts
	Wendy Shaw
	Charlie Ellis
	Maggie Pearce
	Heather Bidwell
Tenants	84

Guildhall Chambers, 23 Broad Street, Bristol, BS1 2HG
Tel (0117) 930 9000 **Fax** (0117) 930 3800 **DX** 7823 Bristol
Email info@guildhallchambers.co.uk **Website** www.guildhallchambers.co.uk

MEMBERS

Adrian Palmer QC (1972) (QC-1992) + *
Stephen Davies QC (1983) (QC-2000)
Richard Smith QC (1986) (QC-2001) +
Andrew Langdon QC (1986) (QC-2006) + ^
Christopher Quinlan QC (1992) (QC-2011)+ ^
John Whitting QC (1991) (QC-2011) ++
Hugh Sims QC (1999) ^ (QC-2014)
Ian Dixey (1984) ^
Kerry Barker (1972) ^
George Newsom (1973) ^
Adam Chippindall (1975) +
Rosaleen Collins (1996) +
Ian Fenny (1978) ^
Malcolm Warner (1979)
James Townsend (1980) +
William Batstone (1982) ^
John Virgo (1983)
Christopher Brockman (1985) ^
Susan Cavender (2004) ^
Neil Levy (1986) ^
Raj Sahonte (1986) ^
Ray Tully (1987) ^
Nicolas Gerasimidis (1988) + ^
Jeremy Bamford (1989)
David Scutt (1989)
Nicholas Smith (1990)
Charles Thomas (1990)
Virginia Cornwall (1990)
Stephen Dent (1991) ^
Selena Plowden (1991)
Julian Benson (1991)
Anthony Reddiford (1991)
John Snell (1991)
Brendon Moorhouse (1992) ^
Matthew Wales (1993) °° ^
Gerard McMeel (1993)
Mark Worsley (1994) ^
Gabriel Farmer (1994)
Richard Ascroft (1995) ^
Ramin Pakrooh (1996)
Ewan Paton (1996) ^
Anna Vigars (1996) +
Debbie Grennan (1997)
Rupert Lowe (1998) + ^
Lucy Walker (2008)
Oliver Moore (2005)
Julian Allsop QC (1999)
Katherine Gibb (1999)
Matthew Porter-Bryant (1999) °° ^
Timothy Walsh (2000) ^
Robert Sowersby (2000)
Tara Wolfe (2000)
Pushpanjali Gohil (2000)
Jenny Tallentire (2000)
Martin Lanchester (2001) ^
James Bennett (2002)
Stefan Ramel (2002)
Tom Panton (2002)
Ross Fentem (2003) ^
Douglas Leach (2003)
Louise Jones (2004) ++
Abigail Stamp (2004)
Allan Roberts (2004)
James Haskell (2004)
Jorren Knibbe (2005)
Daisy Brown (2006)
Mary Cowe (2006)
Rhys Hadden (2006) ++
Gabriel Beeby (2006)
Michael Selway (2007)
Daniel Neill (2008)
Holly Doyle (2008)
Samuel Jones (2008) ^
James Wibberley (2009) ^
Simon Passfield (2009)
Sophie Holme (2009)
Oliver Mitchell (2009)
Caighli Taylor (2010)
Gregory Gordon (2010)
Suzanne Staunton (2010)
Geraint Probert (2010)
Matthew Brown (2011)
Jay Jagasia (2012)
Alistair Haggerty (2012)
James Bentley (2012)
James Hannant (2013)

+ Recorder * Deputy High Court Judge ++ Door Tenant °° Deputy District Judge ^ Public/ Direct Access

WORK UNDERTAKEN

Crime: One of the foremost criminal sets in the country with specialist expertise in sexual offences and child abuse, major public order cases, civil liberties and all types of appeal, as well as homicide, violence, drugs and vehicle crime.
Commercial Litigation: All aspects of CDR work in Court, arbitrations, adjudications and other ADR procedures.
Banking & Financial Services: Mortgages and charges, guarantees and indemnities, other third party securities, issues relating to the Consumer Credit Act, receiverships and retail banking transactions.
Professional Negligence & Indemnity: Expertise in all areas of professional liability acting for defendants and claimants in respect of negligence, breach of contract, breach of fiduciary duty and breach of trust.
Company Law: Key areas of expertise include the interpretation and dispute resolution of commercial contracts, partnership and joint ventures, shareholder agreements, the allotment and transfer of shares, directors' duties, shareholder disputes, derivative claims, just and equitable windings up.
Technology & Construction: The full range of technology and construction disputes, with familiarity with the workings and practices of the Technology and Construction Court.
Employment & Discrimination: Broad range of employment and discrimination expertise including unfair, constructive and wrongful dismissal; contractual disputes; actionable discrimination; TUPE; and many more.
Insolvency: All aspects of insolvency and company law, including corporate, partnership and personal insolvency, corporate and partnership break-up, CDDA etc.
Property & Estates: Full range of chancery work, including real property, landlord and tenant, agriculture, trusts, wills, estates and the Court of Protection and Planning.
Personal Injury: Work ranges from industrial and workplace accidents to fatalities and road traffic accidents with particular experience of acting for insurers in complex group claims.
Clinical Negligence: All aspects of litigation from minor to catastrophic claims acting for public and privately funded claimants, the NHSLA, NWSSP, Legal and Risk Services, Medical Defence organisations, and commercial providers of care.
Administrative & Public Law: Specialists who act for both claimants and defendants in significant appeals, judicial review proceedings, and statutory challenges with expertise in immigration, inquests, licensing, local government and in the Court of Protection.
Regulatory & Discipline: All aspects of professional disciplinary proceedings and regulation with specific experts in environment, financial services, fraud, health and safety, inquests and licensing.
Other: Specialist expertise in sports law and costs and litigation funding.

NO5 CHAMBERS Mark Anderson QC

38 Queen Square, Bristol, BS1 4QS
Tel (0845) 210 5555 **Fax** (0117) 917 8501 **DX** 7838 Bristol
Email info@no5.com **Website** www.No5.com

Head of Chambers	Mark Anderson QC
Deputy Heads	Rex Tedd QC
	Jonathan Jones QC
	Nageena Khalique QC
Practice Director	Tony McDaid
Tenants	263

THE CHAMBERS No5 Chambers is a national set offering a comprehensive across-the-board service. Throughout its 100-year history, No5 Chambers has developed a reputation for breaking new ground and continues to be regarded as a progressive and forward-thinking set, maintaining its success in traditional sectors of law whilst offering specialist advice and representation at the cutting edge of newly evolving areas. Having grown to over 240 barristers including 33 silks, No5 Chambers provides a truly nationwide service from its offices in Birmingham, London, Bristol and Leicester.

In recent years, Chambers has made significant inroads into the South West and Wales from its Bristol location and its London office continues to go from strength to strength, housing more than 50 tenants. Chambers continues to attract high quality work in all disciplines, combining excellent service standards with a progressive, modern and flexible approach to clients' needs. For further information and a full list of tenants please see the Birmingham entry or visit www.No5.com.

QUEEN SQUARE CHAMBERS Christopher Taylor

Queen Square Chambers, 56 Queen Square, Bristol, BS1 4PR
Tel (0117) 921 1966 **Fax** (0117) 927 6493 **DX** 7870 Bristol
Email civil@qs-c.co.uk / crime@qs-c.co.uk **Website** www.queensquarechambers.co.uk

Head of Chambers	Christopher Taylor
Chief Executive	Steve Freeman
Head Clerk	James Dowse
Tenants	37
Door Tenants	6

THE CHAMBERS Queen Square is structured with dedicated, specialist teams incorporating diverse areas of practice. The set comprises an outstanding team demonstrating an approachable and pragmatic ethos which is reflected in the close, team-working relationships they enjoy with those instructing. Combining legal excellence with competitive fees and first rate service standards, the set always endeavours to mirror the approach adopted by those instructing in any given case and to work closely with them in achieving the best possible outcome for their clients.

WORK UNDERTAKEN

Employment & Education: Regularly appearing in cases in tribunals nationwide, the team has a fairly even spread of Claimant and Respondent work. The team benefits from Panel status with several leading insurers and work undertaken incorporates all areas of discrimination; equal pay claims; breach of contract; constructive dismissal; restrictive covenants; TUPE; unfair dismissal; wages claims; whistleblowing; wrongful dismissal; sports related issues: education law cases. Members are fully conversant with the CPR and are able to undertake cases arising in that jurisdiction relating to occupational stress and bullying.

Family: Ancillary relief, including pensions and dissipation of assets; all aspects of care, adoption and supervision work. Contact and residence; injunctions and committals; child abduction; inheritance, cohabitees/TOLATA. Chambers also has expertise in cases involving mental health issues and family related crime (murder/infanticide, rape, sexual and physical abuse and paedophilia). Members of the Family Team are regularly instructed by several local authorities and are familiar with the particular demands involved.

Clinical Negligence: With extensive experience in all aspects of this challenging specialisation members undertake cases involving obstetrics, cardiology and orthopaedic claims as well as dental negligence.

Personal Injury: Catastrophic injury claims (particularly those involving brain and spinal injury); multi-party actions; fatal accident claims; asbestos and industrial related diseases; industrial accidents; occupier's liability; product liability; Animals Act claims; claims against the MOD; RTA; CICA; 'trippers and slippers.'

Commercial/Chancery: Property related matters (including all areas of landlord and tenant and trusts of land); commercial disputes; contentious probate and Inheritance Act claims; insolvency; insurance and financial services; judicial review; partnership and professional negligence. Members accept instructions in cases involving arbitration and mediation.

Regulatory Law: All aspects of regulatory work including health and safety; maritime prosecutions; trading standards; prosecutions or disciplinary hearings relating to nursing homes; professional misconduct enquiries; police disciplinary hearings; Inquests; breaches of financial regulations etc.; and appeals and judicial review arising from Tribunal decisions.

Housing: Members represent both local authorities and individuals in matters including possession, homelessness, demoted tenancies, Section 204 Housing appeals. Members have also represented the local authority in housing benefit appeals.

Licensing: Members of the department are fully conversant with the substantive and procedural issues involved and pride themselves on their practical and effective advice and representation provided throughout the licensing process.

Crime: Major fraud (including white collar fraud); internet crime; drugs importation and distribution; murder; rape and other serious, sexual offences; money laundering; corruption; confiscation and forfeiture; and the full range of indictable offences and appeals by way of case stated and judicial review.

ST JOHN'S CHAMBERS Susan Hunter

101 Victoria Street, Bristol, BS1 6PU
Tel (0117) 923 4700 **Fax** (0117) 929 4821 **DX** 743350 Bristol 36
Email clerks@stjohnschambers.co.uk **Website** www.stjohnschambers.co.uk

Head of Chambers	Susan Hunter
Chief Executive	Derek Jenkins
Practice Manager (Commercial/Chancery)	Robert Bocock
Practice Manager (Family)	Luke Hodgson
Practice Manager (Personal Injury & Clinical Negligence)	Annette Bushell
Office Manager	Isabelle Mills
Tenants	79

MEMBERS

Christopher Sharp QC (1975) (QC-1999) + ^
Christopher Wilson-Smith QC (1965) (QC-1986) ° ^
Susan Jacklin QC (1980) (QC-2006) + ° ^
Leslie Blohm QC (1982) (QC-2006) +
Frances Judd QC (1984) (QC-2006) °
Suzanne Ornsby QC (1986) (QC-2012) °
Kathryn Skellorn QC (1993) (QC-2014)
Derek O'Sullivan QC (1990) (QC-2016) °
David Fletcher (1971) ^
Ian Bullock (1975)
Timothy Grice (1975) +
Sheelagh Corfield (1975)
Kamala Das (1975) ^
Tim Higginson (1977) °
Richard Mawhinney (1977) °
Richard Stead (1979) + ^
Robin Neill (1979)
Charles Auld (1980)
Catriona Duthie (1981)
John Blackmore (1983) ^
Peter Wadsley (1984)
Susan Hunter (1985) ^
Willian Goodwin (1986) °
Glyn Edwards (1987)
Martha Maher (1987) ^
Simon Morgan (1988) **
Louise O'Neill (1989) ** ^
Guy Adams (1989) ^
Tom Leeper (1991) ^
John Sharples (1992) ^
Dianne Martin (1992) ^
Prof. Roy Light (1992) ^
Elizabeth Harris (1992)
Alison Graham-Wells (1992)
Andrew McLaughlin (1993) ^
Adrian Maxwell (1993) ** ^
Nicholas Miller (1994)
Jacqueline Humphreys (1994) °
Sarah Phillimore (1994) ^
David Regan (1994) ^
John FH Dickinson (1995) ^
Judi Evans (1996) ^
Matthew White (1997) ^
Graeme Harrison (1997)
Kambiz Moradifar (1998) ^
Emma Zeb (1998) ^
Julian Horne (1998)
Alex Troup (1998) ^
Abigail Bond (1999)
Carol Mashembo (1999) ^
Delia Thornton (1999)
Vanessa McKinlay (2000)
Zahid Hussain (2001)
Rachel Russell (2001) ^
Anna Symington (2002)
Lucy Reed (2002) ^
James Pearce-Smith (2002)
Julia Belyavin (2003) ^
Zoë Saunders (2003) ^
Rebecca Taylor (2003) ^
Christopher Jones (2004)
Darren Lewis (2004) ^
Andrew Commins (2004) ^
George Rowell (2004) ^
Jeremy Phillips (2004) °
Jody Atkinson (2005) ^
Richard Gold (2006) ^
Sarah Knapton (2007) °
Andrew Kearney (2007)
Matthew Brundson Tully (2007)°
Ben Handy (2008)
James Marwick (2008)
Jimmy Barber (2008)
James Marwick (2008)
Patrick West (2009)
Michael Clarke (2009)
Oliver Wooding (2009)
Richard Norman (2009)
Nicholas Pointon (2010)
Charlie Newington-Bridges (2011)
James Hughes (2011)
Phillip Robson (2011)
Adam Boyle (2012)
Jack Harris (2012)
Edward Bennett (2013) °
Joss Knight (2014)
Robert Mills (2014)
Matthew O'Regan (2015)

+ Recorder ++ Associate Member and Deputy High Court Judge ** Deputy District Judge °Associate Member ^ Public/Direct Access

THE CHAMBERS St John's Chambers is one of the largest barristers' sets in the South West, with over 80 members including seven silks, specialising in all major areas of law. Chambers' is forward-thinking and innovative and the barristers are described by peers as 'easy to work with' and 'committed to delivering quality advice on time'. Chambers is nationally recognised as providing first-class legal advice and representation in the six core areas: commercial and chancery (which incorporates the three main areas of law, property, wills, trusts & tax and company & commercial); personal injury; family; public and administrative law; clinical negligence; and employment. Chambers represent regional and national law firms, acting for and advising prominent businesses, private individuals, local and public authorities. Chambers also provides advice and representation under the public access scheme to members of the public; planning consultants; managing directors and doctors.

St John's
CHAMBERS

Criminal Defence Service

Community Legal Service

CIVITAS LAW

Senior Clerk	Andrea Mclean
Diary Clerk	Alyson Hartington-Clark
Tenants	18
Door Tenants	1

The Mews, 38 Cathedral Road, Cardiff, CF11 9LL
Tel (0845) 0713 007 **Fax** (0845) 0713 008 **DX** 50750 Cardiff 2
Email clerks@civitaslaw.com **Website** www.civitaslaw.com

MEMBERS

Bryan Thomas (1978)
Graham Walters (1986)
Nicholas David Jones (1987)
Mair Coombes Davies (1988) ^
Gareth Jones (1991) ^
Anthony Vines (1993) ^
Joanne Williams (1999)
Christopher Howells (1999)
Richard Cole (2000)
Matthew Graham Paul (2000) ^
Simon Hughes (2003)
Nicklaus Thomas-Symonds (2004) *
Mona Bayoumi (2004) ^
Victoria Hillier (2005)
Rebecca Mansell (2005)
Cathrine Grubb (2007) ^
Kate Parker (2010) ^
Owain Rhys James (2011) ^
William Rees (2012) ^

^ Public/Direct Access * Door Tenant

THE CHAMBERS Civitas Law is an award-winning, leading specialist civil and public law barristers' chambers serving clients across Wales and England. It believes clients are best served by a set of highly specialist lawyers offering excellence and innovation in advisory work, drafting, mediation and advocacy. With the support of its dedicated, experienced and highly responsive Clerks and Client Support teams, barristers are able to provide a full range of counsel services in personal injuries and clinical negligence; employment; public, planning and regulatory; chancery, business consumer; and ADR matters. The wide range of experience within each group allows them to work successfully with clients from small track cases to a complex appeal. The set continues to develop its reputation by attracting the best of the Bar and aims to provide a cutting edge service whilst maintaining traditions of independence and integrity. The set works closely with its professional clients to ensure that chambers' services are tailored to their unique requirements and business objectives. Among its 20 members are barristers who write or contribute to leading practitioner texts and publications, act as mediators and arbitrators and are appointed as Treasury Counsel, to the Attorney General's Panel and as counsel to the Welsh Government and National Assembly for Wales. Civitas Law has set itself for the highest standards in the delivery of services to its clients; that of excellence. The set aims to be professional and approachable and to provide legal advice which is clear and easily understood by lay clients.

WORK UNDERTAKEN Personal injuries and clinical negligence; chancery, business and consumer law; employment; public law, planning and regulatory; ADR.

30 PARK PLACE Ruth Henke QC

30 Park Place, Cardiff, CF10 3BS
Tel (02920) 398421 **Fax** (02920) 398725 **DX** 50756 CARDIFF 2
Email clerks@30parkplace.co.uk **Website** www.30parkplace.co.uk

Head of Chambers	Ruth Henke QC
Senior Clerk	Phillip Griffiths

MEMBERS

Ruth Henke QC (1987) (QC-2006)
Malcolm Bishop QC (1968) (QC-1993)
Jane Crowley QC (1976) (QC-1998)
James Tillyard QC (1978) (QC-2002)
Lloyd Williams QC (1981) (QC-2006)
Rhodri Williams QC (1987) (QC-2010)
Michael Mather-Lees QC (1981) (QC-2012)
Charles Parsley (1973)
Meirion Davies (1975)
Paul Hartley-Davies (1977)
Marian Lewis (1977)
Mark Allen (1981)
Andrew Taylor (1984)
Huw D Evans (1985)
Stephen Jeary (1987)
Robert Harrison (1988)
Tracey Lloyd-Nesling (1988)
Catherine Heyworth (1991)
Michelle Withers (1991)
Gareth Jonathan-Jones (1991)
Catrin John (1992)
Kate Hughes (1992)
Eugene Egan (1993)
Stephen Thomas (1993)
Elizabeth Mcgahey (1994)
Caroline Rees (1994)
Juliet Gibbon (1994)
Jane Foulser Mcfarlane (1994)
Andrew Jones (1996)
Rhys Taylor (1996)
Carl Harrison (1997)
Harriet Edmondson (1997)
David Hughes (1997)
Colin Douglas (1998)
Sarah Waters (1999)
Ben Davies (1999)
Claire Pickthall (1999)
Nigel Fryer (1999)
Christian Jowett (1999)
Natalie Sandercock (2000)
Angharad Davies (2000)
Rhian Kirby (2000)
Andrew Morse (2000)
Stuart Mcleese (2000)
Katy Morgan (2002)
Byron Broadstock (2002)
Jeffrey Jones (2003)
Rebecca Harrington (2004)
Andrew Joseph (2004)
Claire Williams (2004)
Oliver Manley (2005)
Luke Garrett (2005)
Max Davies (2005)
Mikhael Puar (2006)
Hoa Dieu (2006)
Christian Howells (2007)
Natasha Moran (2007)
Nathan Jones (2008)
Rhian Jones (2008)
Joe Al-Khayat (2008)
Olivia Pike (2008)
Rhys Evans (2008)
Gareth Duncan (2010)
Lowri Wynn Morgan (2010)
Samuel Shepherd (2009)
Peter Donnison (2012)
Nia Gowman (2012)

THE CHAMBERS Thirty Park Place is a 'people first' chambers that prioritises excellence in client care, successfully meeting client objectives and harnessing the strength of its members' vast expertise in civil, criminal and family law. As one of the leading and largest chambers in Wales, Thirty Park Place is able to fulfill the needs of large-scale to more boutique legal businesses across England and Wales.

9 PARK PLACE CHAMBERS Paul Hopkins QC

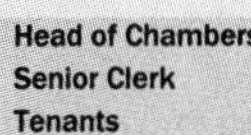

Head of Chambers	Paul Hopkins
Senior Clerk	Michael Lieberman
Tenants	61

9 Park Place, Cardiff, South Glamorgan, CF10 3DP **DX** 50751 CARDIFF 2
Tel (029) 2038 2731 **Fax** (029) 2022 2542
Email: clerks@9parkplace.co.uk **Website:** www.9parkplace.co.uk

THE CHAMBERS: One of the largest and longest-established sets on the Wales and Chester Circuit with including 4 silks.

WORK UNDERTAKEN

Civil, Chancery & Commercial: Expertise includes company or building disputes, all land and property matters, HMLR adjudications, probate, professional negligence, Court of Protection, insolvency and all common law contract and tort disputes. The public law team handles judicial review matters concerning administrative, housing and planning law.

Personal Injury/Clinical Negligence: Acting for claimants and defendants across the spectrum from catastrophic injury to highway trips and slips.

Crime: Specialist areas include sexual offences, child abuse, serious fraud, confiscation, money laundering, homicide, violence and drugs.

Employment: Members provide advice and advocacy in all employment tribunals and appellate courts.

Family: Expertise in all matrimonial, cohabitee and civil partnership litigation, and all public and private law children work representing parents, local authorities and guardians. Public access welcomed. See website for full details and list of members.

AMPERSAND

Parliament House, Parliament Square, Edinburgh, EH1 1RF
Tel (0131) 260 5674 Fax (0131) 225 3642 DX ED 549302 EDINBURGH 36
Email clerks@ampersandstable.com **Website** www.ampersandadvocates.com

Set Director	Maria Maguire QC
Clerk	Alan Moffat (0131) 260 5710
Deputies	Jennifer Dunn (0131) 260 5614
	Cheryl Stevens (0131) 260 5660
	Louise Millar (0131) 260 5616
	Sheena Hume (0131) 260 5809
Tenants	54

MEMBERS

Hugh Campbell QC (1969) (QC-1983)
Christopher Haddow QC (1971) (QC-1985)
Malcolm Thomson QC (1974) (QC-1987)
Aidan O'Neill QC (1987) (QC-1999)
Robert Howie QC (1986) (QC-2000)
David Sellar QC (1995) (QC-2000)
Maria Maguire QC (1987) (QC-2002)
Simon Di Rollo QC (1987) (QC-2002)
Alan Dewar QC (1989) (QC-2002)
Ronnie Clancy QC (1990) (QC-2002)
David Stephenson QC (1991) (QC-2009)
Alastair Kinroy QC (1987) (QC-2005)
Ailsa Wilson QC (1993) (QC-2007)
Dorothy Bain QC (1994) (QC-2007)
Graham Primrose QC (1993) (QC-2008)
Geoffrey Mitchell QC (1992) (QC-2009)
Simon Bowie QC (1995) (QC-2009)
Craig Sandison QC (1996) (QC-2009)
Eugene Creally (1993) (QC-2011)
Mark Fitzpatrick (1985)
Archie MacSporran (1992)
Brian Fitzpatrick (1993)
Louise Milligan (1993)
Eoghainn Maclean (1995)
Lisa Henderson (1995)
Stephen Bell (1996)
Lauren Sutherland (1996)
Phil Stuart (1996)
Christian Marney (1998)
Douglas Ross (1998)
Una Doherty (1999)
Euan Mackenzie (1999)
Vinit Khurana (1999)
Laurence Kennedy (2000)
Susanne Tanner (2000)
Marcus McKay (2000)
Fiona Drysdale (2002)
Graeme I Hawkes (2003)
Michael Stuart (2003)
Isla Davie (2004)
Jamie Dawson (2004)
Catherine Devaney (2006)
James McConnell (2006)
Graham Maciver (2007)
Roderick Campbell (2008)
Laura-Anne van der Westhuizen (2009)
Paul Reid (2011)
Usman Tariq (2011)
Russell Bradley (2012)
Jennifer Nicholson (2013)
Ross Anderson (2013)
Dana Forbes (2015)
Giles Reid (2015)
Jamie Gardiner (2016)

THE CHAMBERS Ampersand is considered to be one of the leading sets in Scotland, providing the full range of services offered by the Scottish Bar, both in contentious and non-contentious work, including advocacy, advice and related written work. Amongst its members are some of the Scottish Bar's most highly rated and successful counsel and QCs. Established in 1981 the stable presently has 54 members, including 19 QCs.

WORK UNDERTAKEN Ampersand has core strengths in the fields of clinical and professional negligence, commercial law, public law and human rights, planning and environment law and personal injury work.
Clinical & Professional Negligence: Ampersand is widely recognised as the leading set in clinical and professional liability at the Scottish Bar. Members are regularly instructed to represent private individuals, NHS Trusts, medical defence unions and private hospitals. Members have been responsible for some of the most important and complex cases in this field including claims involving brain and spinal injuries and other catastrophic medical injuries, multi-party claims arising from the use of medical products and equipment, human rights, mental health issues and medical ethics. Members have acted in cases and at tribunal and disciplinary hearings concerning potential negligence or misconduct involving Accountants, Architects, Conveyancers, Pension Trustees, Solicitors and Surveyors.
Commercial Law: There is particular expertise in relation to corporate law, construction and engineering litigation, contractual disputes, commercial property issues, intellectual property and insolvency.
Public Law & Human Rights: The work of the stable is extensive, with members acting both for and against central government agencies, the Scottish Government, local authorities and regulatory bodies. Members of the stable have been instructed in many of the leading cases arising out of devolution and the incorporation into law of the European Convention on Human Rights. The stable also has acknowledged expertise in the substantive law of the European Union.
Planning & Environmental Law: The set's membership includes several of Scotland's leading planning counsel acting in public inquires and advising in relation to environmental issues, such as renewable energy developments and flood prevention schemes, as well as transport and retail developments.
Personal Injury: Ampersand has a considerable depth of experience, acting both for claimants and those defending claims, in the context of personal injury work. Members of the stable are regularly instructed in health and safety prosecutions and Fatal Accident Inquiries.

INTERNATIONAL The work of Ampersand includes advice and advocacy in relation to cross-border and international issues and disputes. Amongst Ampersand's membership are dual-qualified counsel in English law, as well as European Union law.

AXIOM ADVOCATES

Advocates Library, Parliament House, Edinburgh, EH1 1RF
Tel (0131) 226 2881 **Fax** (0131) 225 3642 **DX** ED 549302 EDINBURGH 36 **LP** LP3 EDINBURGH 10
Website www.axiomadvocates.com

Set Director	Roddy Dunlop QC
Practice Manager	Lesley Flynn (0131) 260 5651
Deputies	Catriona Still (0131) 260 5653
	Scott Gray (0131) 260 5692
	Veronica Darling (0131) 260 5652
	Colleen Adams (0131) 260 5656
Tenants	46

MEMBERS

Rt Honorable Lord Hamilton (1968) (QC-1982)
James McNeill QC (1978) (QC-1991)
Heriot Currie QC (1979) (QC-1992)
Lord (Richard) Keen of Elie QC (1980) (QC-1993)
Lord (Neil) Davidson of Glen Clova QC (1979) (QC-1993)
Gerry Moynihan QC (1985) (QC-1997)
Iain Ferguson QC (1987) (QC-2000)
David Johnston QC (1992) (QC-2005)
Ruth Crawford QC (1993) (QC-2008)
Jonathan Lake QC (1994) (QC-2008)
James Mure QC (1995) (QC-2009)
Roddy Dunlop QC (1998) (QC-2010)
Julian Ghosh QC (1999) (QC-2010)
Mark Lindsay QC (1996) (QC-2011)
Anna Poole QC (1998) (QC-2012)
Sean S Smith QC (1999) (QC-2012)
Alastair Duncan QC (1999) (QC-2012)
Kenneth McBrearty QC (2000) (QC-2013)
Garry Borland QC (2000) (QC-2014)
Roisin Higgins QC (2000) (QC-2015)
Jonathan Brown (2000)
Gavin Walker (2003)
Morag Ross (2003)
Jonathan Barne (2003)
Almira Delibegović-Broome (2003)
David Thomson (2004)
Martin H Richardson (2004)
Paul O'Brien (2004)
Christopher Wilson (2005)
Euan Duthie (2006)
John MacGregor (2007)
Miranda Hamilton (2007)
Alasdair McKenzie (2009)
Helen Watts (2009)
Susan Ower (2009)
Chris Paterson (2010)
Dan Byrne (2010)
Ross McClelland (2011)
Jonathan Broome (2012)
Lesley Irvine (2012)
Elisabeth Roxburgh (2013)
Ewen Campbell (2013)
Peter Sellar (2014)
David Massaro (2014)
Kathryn Pickard (2014)
Jacqueline Fordyce (2016)

THE CHAMBERS Axiom Advocates is a set specialising in commercial and public law. It has a firmly established reputation for high quality advice and advocacy. Unlike the traditional Scottish 'stables' of counsel, Axiom's membership has been selected on merit. The set contains many of the most highly-rated senior and junior counsel at the Scottish Bar. Many senior and junior counsel within the set are regarded as the foremost or leading, counsel in their chosen spheres. Its members have consistently appeared in the most significant cases in Scotland in recent years.

WORK UNDERTAKEN The set is particularly strong in commercial law at the Scottish Bar. The work undertaken encompasses almost all aspects of commerce and finance. In particular, Axiom offers specialists in commercial contracts, construction, corporate finance, energy, insolvency, intellectual property, media and entertainment, planning, property, professional negligence and sports law. In the public law, human rights and regulatory fields, the set has an unrivalled concentration of talent at the Scottish Bar. Several members have appointments as standing junior counsel to the Scottish Government and the UK government. Its members have acted in many ground breaking decisions in the areas of public law and human rights, particularly arising out of devolution and the incorporation into Scots law of the European Convention on Human Rights. Members are also regularly instructed in arbitrations, adjudications, disciplinary hearings, planning inquiries and appeals, and in relation to mediations.

INTERNATIONAL The work of the set includes advice and advocacy in relation to cross-border and international issues and disputes.

COMPASS CHAMBERS

Parliament House, Edinburgh, EH1 1RF
Tel (0131) 260 5648 **Fax** (0131) 225 3642 **DX** ED 549302 Edinburgh 36 LP 3, Edinburgh 10
Email info@compasschambers.com **Website** www.compasschambers.com

Set Director	Angela Grahame QC Robert Milligan QC
Senior Clerk	Gavin Herd (0131) 260 5648
Clerks	Grace Moran (0131) 260 5696 Erica Marmo (0131) 260 5696 Kiera Johnston (0131) 260 5657 Lesley Hogg (0131) 260 5661
Tenants	44

MEMBERS

Ian Mackay QC (1980) (QC-1993)
Rory Anderson QC (1989) (QC-2000)
Marion Caldwell QC (1986) (QC-2000)
Andrew Smith QC (1988) (QC-2002)
Mark Stewart QC (1988) (QC-2005)
Peter Gray QC (1992) (QC-2002)
Lesley Shand QC (1990) (QC-2005)
Geoff Clarke QC (1994) (QC-2008)
Murdo MacLeod QC (1994) (QC-2008)
Angela Grahame QC (1995) (QC-2009)
Robert Milligan QC (1995) (QC-2009)
David Sheldon QC (1998) (QC-2013)
John Scullian QC (2002) (QC-2014)
Preston Lloyd (1996)
Malcolm McGregor (1998)
Barry Divers (1999)
Gordon Lamont (1999)
Kay Springham (1999)
Astrid Smart (1999)
Kenneth Christine (2000)
Steve Love (2001)
Steve Laing (2002)
Calum Wilson (2002)
David McNaughtan (2003)
Graeme Middleton (2003)
Claire Mitchell (2003)
Susan Duff (2003)
James Hastie (2004)
Amber Galbraith (2005)
Barry Smith (2005)
Derek Reekie (2005)
Robin Cleland (2005)
Yvonne Waugh (2006)
Louis Moll (2006)
Richard Pugh (2008)
Craig Murray (2008)
Richard Henderson (2009)
Gavin Thornley (2009)
Emma Toner (2009)
Jillian Martin-Brown (2010)
Charles Lugton (2012)
Clare Connelly (2013)
Barney Ross (2013)
Kate Bennett (2014)

THE CHAMBERS Compass Chambers is a recognised centre of excellence in reparation, professional negligence and regulatory crime litigation. Compass Chambers' ethos is simple: to demonstrate excellence at all times, working together with clients to achieve the best possible outcome, always. Chambers' membership, based exclusively on merit, embraces this ethos which is central to their outstanding reputation.
Members include some of the most well instructed, and highly regarded counsel at the Scottish Bar and, as a result, have considerable experience in all Scottish courts from the Sheriff Court to the UK Supreme Court. Many of the chambers' members are on the panels of several leading insurers, publishers and disciplinary bodies.
An essential part of the Compass ethos is to seek to give added value at all times. To that end, Compass hosts regular conferences across the country at which the most recent developments in their respective core areas are presented to a wide audience.
As an organisation, Compass is at the forefront of innovating in the way in which counsel interact with agents and clients, and aims to offer a commercially sensitive, comprehensive and cost-effective service.

WORK UNDERTAKEN

Reparation: In the reparation field members of Compass specialise in personal injury, property damage, insurance law and fatal accident inquiries.

Regulatory Crime: In the field of regulatory crime, members specialise in the defence of the allegations brought under health and safety, environmental, corporate financial and road traffic legislation, and also appear regularly in fatal accident inquiries; in particular those relating to fatalities in the workplace.

Professional Negligence: In the field of professional negligence, members specialise in clinical negligence, solicitors negligence, property related actions and financial services actions.

In addition to its core strength, Compass includes specialists in contract and commercial litigation, public inquiries and judicial review proceedings within its membership.

TERRA FIRMA CHAMBERS

Parliament House, High Street, Edinburgh, EH1 1RF
Tel (0131) 260 5830 **Fax** (0131) 225 3642 **DX** 549302 Edinburgh 36
Website www.terrafirmachambers.com

Practice Manager	Emma Potter
Deputy Clerk	Andrew Veitch
Deputy Clerk	Tracy Whitelaw
Tenants	46

MEMBERS

The Rt Hon Lord Hope of Craighead QC (1965) (QC-1978)
Sir Menzies Campbell MP QC (1968) (QC-1982)
Roy Martin QC (1976) (QC-1988)
Steven Stuart QC (1979) (QC-2008)
Stuart Gale QC (1980) (QC-1993)
J Gordon Reid QC (1980) (QC-1993)
Gordon Steele QC (1981) (QC-1996)
James Findlay QC (1984) (QC-2008) (England & Wales-1984) (Scotland-2008)
Peter Ferguson QC (1985) (QC-2005)
Scott Brady QC (1987) (QC-2000)
The Rt Hon Dame Elish Angiolini QC (2008) (QC-2001)
Douglas Armstrong QC (1990) (QC-2005)
Alan Summers QC (1994) (QC-2008)
Michael Howlin QC (1996) (QC-2009)
Philip J D Simpson QC (2001) (QC-2014)
Roddy McIlvride QC (2005) (QC-2014)
Derek Francis (1985)
Robert Skinner (1987)
Peter Grant-Hutchison (1988)
Neil Beynon (1990)
Robert Sutherland (1992)
Nicholas Holroyd (1992)
David Bartos (1993)
Iain Maclean (1994)
Neil Kinnear (1994)
Maurice O'Carroll (1995)
William Frain-Bell (1999)
David Parratt (1999)
Steven Walker (1999)
Scott Blair (2000)
Luise Locke (2000)
David Logan (2000)
Fred Mackintosh (2000)
Stephen O'Rourke (2002)
Fergus Thomson (2004)
Alasdair J Burnet (2006)
Gordon Watt (2007)
Julius Komorowski (2008)
Graham Dunlop (2009)
Stephen Winter (2011)
Mark Mohammed (2011)
Dennis Edwards (2012)
Denis Garrity (2014)
Alasdair Sutherland (2014)
Faryma Bahrami (2015)
Roddy MacLeod (2016)

THE CHAMBERS Terra Firma Chambers was established in January 2008 with the purpose of providing specialised services in the areas of property, planning, commercial and administrative public law. It was quickly recognised as a leading set with members ranked in each of its core practice areas in either Scotland or England. It has also established an enviable reputation for the service provided by its members and clerks. The chambers contains 46 counsel, including 16 Queen's Counsel. It has the largest number of dual qualified members of the Scottish and English Bars of any Scottish set, with several members in leading chambers at the English Bar. It also has more specialist arbitration advocates (and more arbitration academics) than any other set at the Scottish Bar, including one of the first specially accredited commercial arbitrators by the CEPMLP at Dundee University. Several members hold appointments as part-time sheriffs or part-time tribunal judges. Members of chambers accept instructions under the Faculty of Advocates Direct Access Rules.

WORK UNDERTAKEN The members of Terra Firma Chambers carry out the whole gamut of work related to property, planning, commercial and administrative law. Because many of the areas of law in which members specialise are also regulated by the European Union and the Human Rights Act 1988, members are also well placed to advise on the EU and ECHR aspects of any issue.

Property: Access rights, agriculture and crofting, boundary disputes, charities, commercial property, common good, conveyancing, executries and succession, housing, intellectual property, landlord and tenant, pensions, professional negligence, regulatory enforcement and liability, servitudes and wayleaves, taxation and estate planning, trusts and judicial factors, unjustified enrichment, valuation and rating, wills.

Planning: Conservation, compulsory purchase and compensation, contaminated land, drainage and flood prevention, environmental (civil and criminal) regulation, housing, industrial, infrastructure development, leisure, minerals, nuisance, planning, pollution prevention and control, renewable energy, retail, roads, sewage, telecommunications, waste.

Commercial: Bankruptcy and diligence, building and construction, contracts, commercial arbitration and dispute resolution, discrimination, employment, energy, health and safety, insolvency, intellectual property, partnership, professional negligence, public procurement, regulatory liability, restrictive covenants, roads and transport, taxation, valuation and rating. Members act as advocates, mediators and arbitrators within Scotland, England and internationally.

Administrative & Public Law: Charities, community care, constitutional law, election law, freedom of information, human rights, judicial review, licensing, local government, professional and disciplinary proceedings, public procurement, regulatory enforcement and liability, statutory appeals and review, valuation and rating, welfare law. Members regularly appear before courts, tribunals, inquiries, hearings and local authority committees.

WESTWATER ADVOCATES

Stable Director	Calum H S MacNeill QC (0131) 226 5071
Advocates Clerk	Sheila Westwater
Deputy Clerks	Christina Ballantyne
	Jane Morrison
Tenants	45
Silks	7

Faculty of Advocates, Parliament House, Parliament Square, Edinburgh, EH1 1RF
Tel (0131) 260 5700 **Fax** (0131) 225 3642 **DX** 549302 Edinburgh 36 LP LP3, Edinburgh 10
Email sheila.westwater@westwateradvocates.com **Website** www.westwateradvocates.com

MEMBERS

James A Peoples QC (1979) (QC-1994)
Andrew Hajducki QC (1979) (QC-1994)
Sir Crispin Agnew of Lochnaw Bt QC (1982) (QC-1995)
Nick Ellis QC (1990) (QC-2002)
Calum H S MacNeill QC (1992) (QC-2007)
Janys M Scott QC (1992) (QC-2007)
Douglas Fairley QC (1999) (QC-2012)
Desmond Cheyne (1986)
Maggie Hughes (1991)
Charlotte Coutts (1991)
Ian Sharpe (1992)
Isabella Ennis (1993)
John Speir (1993)
Gordon Lindhorst (1995)
Andrew MacMillan (1995)
Mark Lazarowicz (1996)
Robert Hayhow (1997)
Greg Cunningham (1997)
Bryan Heaney (1999)
Greg Sanders (2001)
Gavin Anderson (2001)
Mary Loudon (2002)
Laura Wray (2003)
Heather Carmichael (2004)
Lynda J Brabender (2005)
Ruth Innes (2005)
Donald Cameron (2005)
Adrian Stalker (2007)
Alice Stobart (2007)
Kirsty Malcolm (2007)
Ken Revie (2008)
David Hay (2008)
Alison M Wild (2008)
Colin Edward (2010)
Kenneth McGuire (2010)
Julianna F Cartwright (2011)
Neil MacDougall (2011)
Scott McAlpine (2012)
Paul McNairney (2013)
David Anderson (2014)
Rachel Shewan (2014)
Anne Bennie (2015)
Brian Crook (2015)
Vincent Lunny (2015)
Jane Rattray (2015)

THE CHAMBERS Westwater Advocates is one of Scotland's longest established and largest multi-disciplinary stables, with 45 Advocate members including 7 silks. Sheila Westwater has been the clerk since 1991 and is assisted by Christina Ballantyne and Jane Morrison. The clerks provide excellent service, advising on the availability and suitability of advocates for particular work and willing to agree fees in advance.

WORK UNDERTAKEN At all levels of seniority, the stable offers advocates whose experience includes personal injury, professional (including medical) negligence, contract, commercial, construction (including adjudication), insolvency, financial provision on divorce, co-habitation and all aspects of public and private child law, employment and disciplinary matters, licensing, agricultural, land, media, judicial review and criminal law.

ENTERPRISE CHAMBERS Zia Bhaloo QC

43 Park Square, Leeds, LS1 2NP
Tel (0113) 246 0391 **Fax** (0113) 242 4802 **DX** 26448 Leeds Park Square
Email leeds@enterprisechambers.com **Website** www.enterprisechambers.com

For a full list of members please see the London entry. For further information about the set please visit the chambers' website.

Head of Chambers	Zia Bhaloo QC
Chambers Director	Michael Couling
Senior Clerk	Antony Armstrong (London)
Clerks	Joanne Caunt
	Ellen Cockcroft
Tenants	43

EXCHANGE CHAMBERS Bill Braithwaite QC

Oxford House, Oxford Row, Leeds, LS1 3BE
Tel (0113) 203 1970 **Fax** (0113) 345 3326 **DX** 26406 Leeds Park Square
Email info@exchangechambers.co.uk **Website** www.exchangechambers.co.uk

Head of Chambers	Bill Braithwaite QC
Clerks	Katie Heald
	Nicole Haigh
Chambers Director	Tom Handley
Senior Clerk	Ian Spencer
Tenants	161

MEMBERS

Bill Braithwaite QC (1970) (QC-1992)
Anthony Elleray QC (1977) (QC-1993)
Edward Bartley Jones QC (1975) (QC-1997) +
Gerard Martin QC (1978) (QC-2000) +
Mark Cawson QC (1982) (QC-2001) J
John Richard Jones QC (1981) (QC-2002) +
Gordon Cole QC (1979) (QC-2006)
Tania Griffiths QC (1982) (QC-2006) +
William Waldron QC (1986) (QC-2006) +
Stephen Meadowcroft QC (1973) (QC-2007)
Amanda Yip QC (1991) (QC-2011)+
Simon Medland QC (1991) (QC-2011)
Ben Myers QC (1994) (QC-2014)
Chris Tehrani QC (1990) (QC-2004)
Nicholas Johnson QC (1994) (QC-2016)
David Mohyuddin QC (1999) (QC-2016)
Michael Scholes (1996)
Simon Earlam (1975) +
Eric Lamb (1975) +
Judith Fordham (1991)
Digby Jess (1978)
Anthony Goff (1978)
Karen Troy (1981)
Ian Harris (1990) +
Paul Kirtley (1982) +
Karen Gregory (1985)
Roger Hillman (1983)
Neil Cadwallader (1984) +
Wayne Jackson (1984)
Paul Taylor (1985)
Paul Clark (1994)
William Hanbury (1985)
Simon Berkson (1986) +
Guy Vickers (1986)
David Knifton (1986) +
Sara Dodd (1987) +
Mark Mulrooney (1988)
Louis Browne (1988) +
Ian Foster (1988)
Greg Plunkett (2013)
Rebecca Clark (1989)
Catherine Howells (1989) +
Michael Wood (1989)
Simon Vaughan (1989)
Mark Rhind (1989) +
Christopher Stables (1990)
Julie Case (1990)
Christopher Cook (1990)
Michael Lavery (1990)
David Potter (1990) +
Jason MacAdam (1990)
Robert Golinski (1990)
David Toal (1990)
Timothy Evans (1992)
Giles Maynard-Connor (1992)
Rachael Woods (1992)
Mark Ainsworth (1992) +
Dr. Kevin Naylor (1992)
Gregory Hoare (1992)
Oliver Jarvis (1992)
Amanda Johnson (1992)
Steven Crossley (1992)
John Wyn Williams (1992)
Charlotte Kenny (1993)
Robert Dudley (1993)
Robert Wyn Jones (1993)
Stephen Connolly (2003)
Alaric Bassano (1993)
Andrew Jebb (1993)
Sarah Barlow (1993)
Kim Whittlestone (1994)
Louise Whaites (1994)
Damian Nolan (1994)
Richard Littler (1994)
Bruce Walker (1994)
Ceri Widdett (1994)
Andrew Williams (1994)
Michael Maher (1995)
Lisa Linklater (1995)
Mark Smith (1995)
Philip Parry (1995)
Claire Gourley (1996)
Scott Redpath (1996)
Jayne Acton (1996)
Sheren Guirguis (1996)
Andrew Smith (1996)
Imran Shafi (1996)
Ashley Serr (1996)
Lawrence McDonald (1996)
Steven Fennell (2014)
Pankaj Madan (1997)
Kevin Slack (1997)
Adrian Farrow (1997)
Louise Metcalf (1997)
Mark Stephenson (1997)
Jonathan French (1997)
Jon Close (1997)
David Fearon (2013)
Paul Burns (1998)
Sarah O'Brien (1998)
Katharine Titchmarsh (1998)
Nicholas Walker (1998)
Siân Jones (1998)
David Bentley (1998)
David Went (1998)
Nigel Edwards (1999)
Daniel Travers (1999)
Christopher Barnes (1999)
Martine Snowdon (2000)
Jonathan Rogers (2000)
Andrew Vinson (2000)
Andrew Ward (2000)
Nicola Daley (2000)
Laura Jane Gooding (2001)
Joshua Shields (2000)
David Temkin (2000)
Stephen Grattage (2000)
Michael Rawlinson (2002)
James Malam (2002)
Paul Hodgkinson (2002)
Caroline Gee (2003)
Charlotte Atherton (2003)
Christian Taylor (2003)
Stephen McNally (2003)
Sarah Johnston (2004) +
Sara Sutherland (2004)
Andrew Petterson (2004)
Esther Lin (2002)
Emma Bennett (2004)
Catherine Knowles (2004)
Alex Menary (2004)
Andrew Wastall (2005)
Kerron Rohrer (2005)
Suzie Kitzing (2005)
Chloe Fordham (2005)
Carly Sandbach (2006)
Chris Gutteridge (2006)
Richard Tetlow (2006)
David Birrell (2006)
Alfred Weiss (2006)
Julian Goode (2006)
Natalia Cornwall (2007)
Gareth Shires (2007)
Jonathan Lowe (2008)
Victoria Smith-Swain (2008)
Simon Whitfield (2009)
Lee Speakman (2009)
Huw Edwards (2009)
Ian Tucker (2010)
Chris Allen (2012)
John Waiting (2010)
Stuart McCracken (2010)
Lisa Feng (2011)
Sarah Griffin (2011)
Simon Lewis (2012)
Peter Dixon (2013)
Holly Betke (2013)
Beth Harvey-Smith (2011)
David Williams (2014)
Anja Lansbergen (2014)
Peter Killen (2015)
John Charles Rees QC (1972) (QC-1991) *
Nicholas Francis QC (1981) (QC-2002) *
Jonathan Turner QC (1974) (QC-2003) *
Neil Hawes QC (1989) (QC-2010)*
Cairns Nelson QC (1987) (QC-2010) *
Rhodri Williams QC (1987) (QC-2010) *
Eleanor Laws QC (1996) (QC-2011) *
Anthony Metzer QC (1987) (QC-2013) *
Edward Cousins (1971) *
Alun James (1986) *
John J McCarroll (1988) *
Andrew Maguire (1988) *

EXCHANGE CHAMBERS Bill Braithwaite QC (continued)

David Tyack (1994) *
Anthony Eyers (1994)
Dr Simon Fox (1994) *
Frida Hussain (1995) *
Nancy Dooher (1997) *
Adam Chichester-Clark (2000) *

+ Recorder * Door Tenant

THE CHAMBERS Exchange Chambers is an award-winning set of barristers' chambers based in Liverpool, Manchester and Leeds. Priding itself on service, Exchange Chambers' ongoing expansion strategy is based on attracting outstanding barristers and outstanding work.

WORK UNDERTAKEN The set has a proven track record in all major areas of law comprising 161 barristers, including 16 silks. A record 57 members are ranked as leaders in their field by Chambers UK.

Alternative Dispute Resolution: Chambers covers all forms of ADR including arbitration, adjudication, dispute resolution boards, expert determination, early neutral evaluations and mediation across all practice areas. Chambers has 30 trained mediators.

Crime: Comprising 70 members, including 8 silks, the criminal team is one of the largest, most successful teams in the country. 38 are Category 4 Prosecutors. The team provides representation at all stages of a case, including pre-charge, trial and appeal. They have a highly sought after fraud team who routinely act on cases of national and international stature.

Personal Injury: Led by leading personal injury barrister, Bill Braithwaite QC, the department extends the full spectrum of seniority covering the areas of claimant / defendant personal injury, clinical negligence and industrial disease. The team has an exceptional reputation handling high value cases involving severe brain and spinal injuries. There are also a number of experts who deal with niche personal matters such as military claims, claims for amputees and complex pain disorders.

Commercial: The set is widely acclaimed for its complete range of commercial and chancery services including corporate and personal insolvency, shareholder, company and partnership disputes, professional negligence, competition, intellectual property, banking, property, planning and construction. 18 members of the team have been appointed by the Attorney General to his panel of Counsel.

Family: The team is highly experienced in all matters of family law, with a particular strength in financial remedy proceedings.

Local Government & Social Housing: This specialist department is independently acclaimed as "first class" and boasts an enviable record advising and representing local authorities and social housing providers across the country on the full range of issues faced by such organisations. Members of the department frequently advise and appear in high profile and test case litigation before local courts as well as the High Court, Court of Appeal and Supreme Court and work alongside other specialist departments within Chambers where appropriate to ensure that they provide the very highest standards of service to Chambers' substantial client base.

Civil: The team offers a full range of services in a number of specialist areas, including public law / judicial review, Court of Protection, local authority litigation, housing management, landlord and tenant and anti-social behaviour litigation.

Employment: The team covers the full spectrum of employment law, its members regularly instructed by large private sector employers and public sector organisations such as NHS trusts and local authorities.

Regulatory: Chambers has dedicated teams providing specialist advice and representation across a range of regulatory practice areas including environmental regulation, health and safety, healthcare, professional discipline and inquests.

Inquests: With 3 team members sitting as Assistant Deputy Coroners, the set has a strong reputation in this area throughout the UK. The team has a particular unrivalled depth of experience in relation to the healthcare sector.

KINGS CHAMBERS Nicholas Braslavsky QC

5 Park Square East, Leeds, LS1 2NE
Tel (0345) 034 3444 **Fax** (0113) 242 1124 **DX** 713113 (Leeds PKSQ)

THE CHAMBERS is also at:
36 Young Street, Manchester, M3 3FT
Tel (0345) 034 3444 **Fax** (0345) 034 3445 **DX** 718188 (MCH 3)

Embassy House, 60 Church Street, Birmingham, B3 2DJ
Tel (0345) 034 3444 **Fax** (0345) 034 3445 **DX** 13023 (Birmingham)

Chambers Director	Debra Andrés
Senior Clerks	William Brown
	Colin Griffin
	Stephen Loxton
Senior Leeds Clerk	Rory Davis
Senior Birmingham Clerk	Gary Smith

MEMBERS

Dr Nicholas Braslavsky QC (1983) (QC-1999)
Mr Stephen J Sauvain QC (1997) (QC-1995)
Mr Vincent Fraser QC (1981) (QC-2001)
Mr Paul Chaisty QC (1982) (QC-2001)
Mr Richard Clayton QC (1977) (QC-2002)
Mr Santinder Hunjan QC (1981) (Q-C 2002)
Mr David Manley QC (1981) (QC-2003)
Ms Lesley Anderson QC (1989) (QC-2006)
Mr Anthony Crean QC (1987) (QC-2006)
Mr David Casement QC (1992) (QC-2008)
Mr Michael Rawlinson QC (1991) (QC-2009)
Mr Paul Tucker QC (1990) (QC-2010)
Mr Nigel Poole QC (1989) (QC-2012)
Mr Mark Harper QC (1989) (QC-2016)
Reverend Eric Owen (1969)
Mr Jeffrey Terry (1976)
Mr Alan Evans (1978)
Mr Shokat Khan (1979)
Mr John Barrett (1982)
Mr Neil Berragan (1982)
Mr Michael Stephens (1983)
Mr Mark Halliwell (1985)
Mr Gary Grant (1985)
Mr Simon Hilton (1987)
Mr Nigel Clayton (1987)
Miss Ruth Stockley (1988)
Miss Fiona Ashworth (1998)
Mr Andrew Singer (1990)
Mr Paul Johnson (2006)
Mr Simon Burrows (1990)
Mr Matthew Smith (1991)
Mr Andrew Grantham (1991)
Mr Adam Aldred (2014)
Mr Martin Carter (1992)
Mr Wilson Horne (1992)
Miss Lucy Powis (1992)
Miss Sarah Pritchard (1993)
Mr Richard Lander (1993)
Mr Ian Ponter (1993)
Mr Michael Ditchfield (1993)
Miss Sarah Clover (1993)
Mr James Boyd (1994)
Miss Kelly Pennifer (1994)
Mr Andrew Latimer (1995)
Miss Anna Diamond (1995)
Mr Gavin McBride (1996)
Mr Jeremy Roussak (1996)
Mr Louis Doyle (1996)
Mr Jonathan Easton (1996)
Mr Simon Plaut (1997)
Mr Colin Bourne (1997)
Dr Mark Friston (1997)
Mr Simon Young (1998)
Mr Stephen Maguire (2007)
Mr Giles Cannock (1998)
Professor Andrew McGee (1998)
Mr Matthew Hall (1999)
Miss Helen Mulholland (1999)
Mr Martin Budworth (1999)
Miss Tina Ranales-Cotos (1999)
Mr Brian Griffiths (1999)
Miss Eleanor Temple (2000)
Mrs Lisa Walmisley (2000)
Mr Paul Lakin (2000)
Mr Paul Hughes (2001)
Mr Ben Williams (2001)
Mr Geraint Wheatley (2001)
Rupert Beloff (2001)
Miss Claire Steward (2002)
Mr Craig Ralph (2002)
Mr Michael Rudd (2002)
Mr John Hunter (2002)
Mr Sam Karim (2002)
Miss Emily Duckworth (2003)
Miss Sarah Lawrenson (2003)
Miss Sarah Reid (2004)
Miss Francesca Gardner (2004)
Miss Rachel Galloway (2004)
Miss Sophie Allan (2004)
Miss Helen Trotter (2005)
Mr Paras Gorasia (2005)
Miss Charlotte Law (2005)
Mr Ben Harding (2005)
Miss Cheryl Dainty (2006)
Mr Richard Livingston (2006)
Mr Johnny Ward (2007)
Dr Nathan Smith (2007)
Mr Kevin Latham (2007)
Mr Stephen McNamara (2008)
Mr Anthony Gill (2008)
Miss Eleanor d'Arcy (2008)
Miss Anna Macey (2008)
Mrs Laura Gould (2009)
Mr Richard Borrett (2009)
Miss Louise Green (2009)
Miss Eliza V Sharron (2009)
Miss Francesca P Gardener (2009)
Miss Ruth Taylor (2010)
Mr Jonathan Wright (2010)
Mr Aidan Reay (2011)
Mr Freddie Humphries (2011)
Miss Erica Bedford (2012)
Mr Doug Cochran (2012)
Miss Arianna Kelly (2013)
Miss Alison Ogley (2014)
Miss Constanze Bell (2014)
Mr Killian Garvey (2014)
Mr Marcus F Daly SC (1987) (SC-1999) *
Mr Colm o'hOisin SC (1998) (SC-2005) *
Mr James Henderson (1997) *
Mr Leo Charalambides (1998) *
Professor Andrew Keay (2010) *
Sir Maurice Kay (1975) (QC-1988) +
His Honour David Gilliland (1964) (QC-1984) +

* Associates + Arbitrator

THE CHAMBERS Kings Chambers is ranked one of the country's leading sets. It provides barristers with the highest reputation for advocacy, knowledge and standards to service. This is a large specialist set with a national reputation practising from Manchester, Leeds and Birmingham in several practice areas: pre-dominantly chancery and commercial law; planning and environmental law, personal injury and clinical negligence, costs, employment, sports law, mediation, arbitration and public law.

WORK UNDERTAKEN

Arbitration: Kings Chambers has a number of members with practices encompassing domestic and international arbitration. Chambers has also launched its own bespoke arbitration service (KAS) offering a

KINGS CHAMBERS Nicholas Braslavsky QC (continued)

panel of experienced arbitrators including former judges and silks from other jurisdictions.
Chancery & Commercial: The Chancery and commercial group has extensive experience in litigation (including agency, contracts, sale of goods, restraint of trade and restrictive covenants, corporate law); corporate and personal insolvency (including winding up, administration, administrative receivership and tracing assets),banking and professional negligence. Residential and commercial landlord and tenant work (including renewals, rent.
Clinical Negligence & Personal Injury: The clinical negligence and personal injury team undertake work involving serious personal injury claims, all aspects of Clinical negligence and occupational disease with a particular focus on asbestos and other forms of toxic exposure. The team also specialises in chronic pain and related conditions.
Costs: There is a specialist and dedicated costs team, practising exclusively in costs law, disputes and litigation funding.
Employment: The employment team covers the entire spectrum of employment law and has particular strengths in race, sex, equal pay, restrictive covenants and disability discrimination both in tribunals and in the High Court.
EU & Competition: Chambers has a small and dedicated team dealing with EU and competition law, including cartels, dominance, mergers, market investigations, litigation, public procurement, state aid, trading agreements and compliance.
Mediation: Mediation is an important part of the litigation process. The team comprises accredited mediators at various levels and with expertise in differing areas of law.
Planning: Kings Chambers is one of the largest planning and environmental chambers, with members appearing before a wide range of dedicated tribunals and inquiries. Chambers acts in planning appeals and major inquiries for a wide variety of clients and local authorities. Kings also has extensive experience in environmental law including waste disposal and management, energy, compulsory purchase compensation and highways.
Public Law: The public law group practises extensively in the Administrative Court, sitting in London and the regions. The group encompasses the range of public law work in community care, education, housing, mental health, licensing, local government and social security matters. Members advise and appear before courts at all levels.
Sports Law: The sportslaw team have been involved in some of the most substantial and high profile sports cases nationally in recent years involving, commercial dispute resolution, disciplinary and regulatory proceedings, anti-doping rules, employment issues, sports-related personal injury, breach of confidentiality and privacy, wealth management issues, intellectual property including image rights, trademark infringement and breach of copyright.

NO5 CHAMBERS Mark Anderson QC

5 Museum Square, Leicester, LE1 6UF
Tel (0845) 210 5555 **Fax** (0116) 216 7607 **DX** 17004 Leicester 2
Email info@no5.com **Website** www.No5.com

Head of Chambers	Mark Anderson QC
Deputy Heads	Rex Tedd QC
	Jonathan Jones QC
	Nageena Khalique QC
Practice Director	Tony McDaid
Tenants	263

THE CHAMBERS No5 Chambers is a national set offering a comprehensive across-the-board service. Throughout its 100-year history, No5 Chambers has developed a reputation for breaking new ground and continues to be regarded as a progressive and forward-thinking set, maintaining its success in traditional sectors of law whilst offering specialist advice and representation at the cutting edge of newly evolving areas. Having grown to over 240 barristers including 33 silks, No5 Chambers provides a truly nationwide service from its offices in Birmingham, London, Bristol and Leicester.

In recent years, Chambers has made significant inroads into the South West and Wales from its Bristol location and its London office continues to go from strength to strength, housing more than 50 tenants. Chambers continues to attract high quality work in all disciplines, combining excellent service standards with a progressive, modern and flexible approach to clients' needs. For further information and a full list of tenants please see the Birmingham entry or visit www.No5.com.

EXCHANGE CHAMBERS Bill Braithwaite QC

Head of Chambers	Bill Braithwaite QC
Clerks	Kate Masher
	Suzanne Dutch
	Denise Sheen
	Rachel Williams
	Sarah Rotherham
Chambers Director	Tom Handley
Practice Manager	Jonathan I'Anson
Tenants	161

One Derby Square, Liverpool, L2 9XX
Tel (0151) 236 7747 **Fax** (0151) 236 3433 **DX** 14207 Liverpool
Email info@exchangechambers.co.uk **Website** www.exchangechambers.co.uk

MEMBERS

Bill Braithwaite QC (1970) (QC-1992)
Anthony Elleray QC (1977) (QC-1993)
Edward Bartley Jones QC (1975) (QC-1997) +
Gerard Martin QC (1978) (QC-2000) +
Mark Cawson QC (1982) (QC-2001) J
John Richard Jones QC (1981) (QC-2002) +
Gordon Cole QC (1979) (QC-2006)
Tania Griffiths QC (1982) (QC-2006) +
William Waldron QC (1986) (QC-2006) +
Stephen Meadowcroft QC (1973) (QC-2007)
Amanda Yip QC (1991) (QC-2011)+
Simon Medland QC (1991) (QC-2011)
Ben Myers QC (1994) (QC-2014)
Chris Tehrani QC (1990) (QC-2004)
Nicholas Johnson QC (1994) (QC-2016)
David Mohyuddin QC (1999) (QC-2016)
Michael Scholes (1996)
Simon Earlam (1975) +
Eric Lamb (1975) +
Judith Fordham (1991)
Digby Jess (1978)
Anthony Goff (1978)
Karen Troy (1981)
Ian Harris (1990) +
Paul Kirtley (1982) +
Karen Gregory (1985)
Roger Hillman (1983)
Neil Cadwallader (1984) +
Wayne Jackson (1984)
Paul Taylor (1985)
Paul Clark (1994)
William Hanbury (1985)
Simon Berkson (1986) +
Guy Vickers (1986)
David Knifton (1986) +
Sara Dodd (1987) +
Mark Mulrooney (1988)
Louis Browne (1988) +
Ian Foster (1988)
Greg Plunkett (2013)
Rebecca Clark (1989)
Catherine Howells (1989) +
Michael Wood (1989)
Simon Vaughan (1989)
Mark Rhind (1989) +
Christopher Stables (1990)
Julie Case (1990)
Christopher Cook (1990)
Michael Lavery (1990)
David Potter (1990) +
Jason MacAdam (1990)
Robert Golinski (1990)
David Toal (1990)
Timothy Evans (1992)
Giles Maynard-Connor (1992)
Rachael Woods (1992)
Mark Ainsworth (1992) +
Dr. Kevin Naylor (1992)
Gregory Hoare (1992)
Oliver Jarvis (1992)
Amanda Johnson (1992)
Steven Crossley (1992)
John Wyn Williams (1992)
Charlotte Kenny (1993)
Robert Dudley (1993)
Robert Wyn Jones (1993)
Stephen Connolly (2003)
Alaric Bassano (1993)
Andrew Jebb (1993)
Sarah Barlow (1993)
Kim Whittlestone (1994)
Louise Whaites (1994)
Damian Nolan (1994)
Richard Littler (1994)
Bruce Walker (1994)
Ceri Widdett (1994)
Andrew Williams (1994)
Michael Maher (1995)
Lisa Linklater (1995)
Mark Smith (1995)
Philip Parry (1995)
Claire Gourley (1996)
Scott Redpath (1996)
Jayne Acton (1996)
Sheren Guirguis (1996)
Andrew Smith (1996)
Imran Shafi (1996)
Ashley Serr (1996)
Lawrence McDonald (1996)
Steven Fennell (2014)
Pankaj Madan (1997)
Kevin Slack (1997)
Adrian Farrow (1997)
Louise Metcalf (1997)
Mark Stephenson (1997)
Jonathan French (1997)
Jon Close (1997)
David Fearon (2013)
Paul Burns (1998)
Sarah O'Brien (1998)
Katharine Titchmarsh (1998)
Nicholas Walker (1998)
Siân Jones (1998)
David Bentley (1998)
David Went (1998)
Nigel Edwards (1999)
Daniel Travers (1999)
Christopher Barnes (1999)
Martine Snowdon (2000)
Jonathan Rogers (2000)
Andrew Vinson (2000)
Andrew Ward (2000)
Nicola Daley (2000)
Laura Jane Gooding (2001)
Joshua Shields (2000)
David Temkin (2000)
Stephen Grattage (2000)
Michael Rawlinson (2002)
James Malam (2002)
Paul Hodgkinson (2002)
Caroline Gee (2003)
Charlotte Atherton (2003)
Christian Taylor (2003)
Stephen McNally (2003)
Sarah Johnston (2004) +
Sara Sutherland (2004)
Andrew Petterson (2004)
Esther Lin (2002)
Emma Bennett (2004)
Catherine Knowles (2004)
Alex Menary (2004)
Andrew Wastall (2005)
Kerron Rohrer (2005)
Suzie Kitzing (2005)
Chloe Fordham (2005)
Carly Sandbach (2006)
Chris Gutteridge (2006)
Richard Tetlow (2006)
David Birrell (2006)
Alfred Weiss (2006)
Julian Goode (2006)
Natalia Cornwall (2007)
Gareth Shires (2007)
Jonathan Lowe (2008)
Victoria Smith-Swain (2008)
Simon Whitfield (2009)
Lee Speakman (2009)
Huw Edwards (2009)
Ian Tucker (2010)
Chris Allen (2012)
John Waiting (2010)
Stuart McCracken (2010)
Lisa Feng (2011)
Sarah Griffin (2011)
Simon Lewis (2012)
Peter Dixon (2013)
Holly Betke (2013)
Beth Harvey-Smith (2011)
David Williams (2014)
Anja Lansbergen (2014)
Peter Killen (2015)
John Charles Rees QC (1972) (QC-1991) *
Nicholas Francis QC (1981) (QC-2002) *
Jonathan Turner QC (1974) (QC-2003) *
Neil Hawes QC (1989) (QC-2010)*
Cairns Nelson QC (1987) (QC-2010) *
Rhodri Williams QC (1987) (QC-2010) *
Eleanor Laws QC (1996) (QC-2011) *
Anthony Metzer QC (1987) (QC-2013) *
Edward Cousins (1971) *
Alun James (1986) *
John J McCarroll (1988) *
Andrew Maguire (1988) *

EXCHANGE CHAMBERS Bill Braithwaite QC (continued)

David Tyack (1994) *
Anthony Eyers (1994)
Dr Simon Fox (1994) *
Frida Hussain (1995) *
Nancy Dooher (1997) *
Adam Chichester-Clark (2000) *

+ Recorder * Door Tenant

THE CHAMBERS Exchange Chambers is an award-winning set of barristers' chambers based in Liverpool, Manchester and Leeds. Priding itself on service, Exchange Chambers' ongoing expansion strategy is based on attracting outstanding barristers and outstanding work.

WORK UNDERTAKEN The set has a proven track record in all major areas of law comprising 161 barristers, including 16 silks. A record 57 members are ranked as leaders in their field by Chambers UK.
Alternative Dispute Resolution: Chambers covers all forms of ADR including arbitration, adjudication, dispute resolution boards, expert determination, early neutral evaluations and mediation across all practice areas. Chambers has 30 trained mediators.
Crime: Comprising 70 members, including 8 silks, the criminal team is one of the largest, most successful teams in the country. 38 are Category 4 Prosecutors. The team provides representation at all stages of a case, including pre-charge, trial and appeal. They have a highly sought after fraud team who routinely act on cases of national and international stature.
Personal Injury: Led by leading personal injury barrister, Bill Braithwaite QC, the department extends the full spectrum of seniority covering the areas of claimant / defendant personal injury, clinical negligence and industrial disease. The team has an exceptional reputation handling high value cases involving severe brain and spinal injuries. There are also a number of experts who deal with niche personal matters such as military claims, claims for amputees and complex pain disorders.
Commercial: The set is widely acclaimed for its complete range of commercial and chancery services including corporate and personal insolvency, shareholder, company and partnership disputes, professional negligence, competition, intellectual property, banking, property, planning and construction. 18 members of the team have been appointed by the Attorney General to his panel of Counsel.
Family: The team is highly experienced in all matters of family law, with a particular strength in financial remedy proceedings.
Local Government & Social Housing: This specialist department is independently acclaimed as "first class" and boasts an enviable record advising and representing local authorities and social housing providers across the country on the full range of issues faced by such organisations. Members of the department frequently advise and appear in high profile and test case litigation before local courts as well as the High Court, Court of Appeal and Supreme Court and work alongside other specialist departments within Chambers where appropriate to ensure that they provide the very highest standards of service to Chambers' substantial client base.
Civil: The team offers a full range of services in a number of specialist areas, including public law / judicial review, Court of Protection, local authority litigation, housing management, landlord and tenant and anti-social behaviour litigation.
Employment: The team covers the full spectrum of employment law, its members regularly instructed by large private sector employers and public sector organisations such as NHS trusts and local authorities.
Regulatory: Chambers has dedicated teams providing specialist advice and representation across a range of regulatory practice areas including environmental regulation, health and safety, healthcare, professional discipline and inquests.
Inquests: With 3 team members sitting as Assistant Deputy Coroners, the set has a strong reputation in this area throughout the UK. The team has a particular unrivalled depth of experience in relation to the healthcare sector.

7 HARRINGTON ST CHAMBERS Richard Pratt QC

7 Harrington Street, Liverpool, L2 9YH
Tel (0151) 242 0707 **Fax** (0151) 236 2800 DX 14221 Liverpool 1
Email clerks@7hs.co.uk **Website** www.7hs.co.uk

Head of Chambers	Richard Pratt QC
Senior Clerk	John Kilgallon
Tenants	89

MEMBERS

Richard Pratt QC (1980) (QC-2006)
Iain Goldrein QC (1975) (QC-1997)
Anthony Berry QC (1976) (QC-1994)
Nicholas Johnson QC (1987) (QC-2006)
Nigel Power QC (1992) (QC-2010)
Ian Unsworth QC (1992) (QC-2010)
Paul Russell QC (1984) (QC-2011) *
Joel Donovan QC (1991) (QC-2011) *
Taryn Lee QC (1992) (QC-2012)
Nigel Lawrence QC (1988) (QC-2014)
David Geey (1970)
Michael J Pickavance (1974)
Neville Biddle (1974)
James Rae (1976)
Kevin Grice (1977) *
Michael Davies (1979)
Arthur Gibson (1980)
Henry Riding (1981)
Grant Lazarus (1981)
James McKeon (1982)
Andrew Loveridge (1983)
James Byrne (1983)
Kevin Reade (1983)
Jamil Khan (1986)
Stephen Knapp (1986) *
Peter Kidd (1987)
Janet Reaney (1987)
Tim Kenward (1987)
Keith Sutton (1988)
Kate Symms (1990)
Christine Bispham (1991)
Tim Grover (1991)
Stephen Seed (1991)
Simon Driver (1991)
Trevor Parry-Jones (1992)
Ian Whitehurst (1994)
Gary Reynolds (1994)
Clive Baker (1995)
Andrew Carney (1995) *
Jeremy Greenfield (1995)
Brendan Burke (1995)
Nicola Turner (1995)
Teresa Loftus (1995)
Malcolm Dutchman-Smith (1995) *
Joanna Mallon (1996)
David McLachlan (1996)
Steven Ball (1996)
Andrew Ford (1997)
Daniel Rogers (1997)
Kenneth Grant (1998)
Elizabeth Brennan (1998)
Neil Bisarya (1998)
Michael Jones (1999)
Nicola Miles (1999)
Lianne Naughton (1999)
Sarah Holt (1999)
Daniel Wood (2000)
William Ralston (2000) *
Phillip Tully (2000)
Mark Roberts (2001)
Sarah Langley (2001)
Lisa Edmunds (2002)
Jonathan Duffy (2002)
Martin Reid (2003)
Paul Wright (2003)
Craig Fisher (2004)
Christopher Knagg (2005)
David Dunne (2005)
Victoria Roberts (2005)
Fraser Lindsay (2006)
Katherine O'Donohue (2006)
Brian Treadwell (2006)
Lianne Birkett (2006)
Tim Wilkinson (2006)
Sarah Watters (2007)
Danielle Paton (2007)
Peter Harthan (2007)
Gemma Thomas (2010)
Tom Fazackerley (2010)
Hannah Brookfield (2011)
Matthew Hooper (2012)
Greg Plunkett (2013) *
Helen Richardson (2013)
Frank Dillon (2014)
Alex Cracknell (2014)
Fiona Turner (2014)
Jamie Baxter (2014)
Aumeneh Boardman (2014)
Govind Singh (2015)

* Door Tenant

THE CHAMBERS 7 Harrington Street is one of the largest sets of chambers in the country. It has a policy of excellence, innovation and expansion with expertise in all aspects of law. Chambers has earned its reputation through continued professional excellence and a commitment to working to the highest ethical standards. Currently there are 89, including 10 QCs. They are supported by a large and dedicated team of clerking and administrative staff who consistently provide clients with a high level of service. As holders of the Legal Services Quality Mark, the set offers quality assured service to members of the public who need legal information, advice and assistance. Chambers is firmly committed to equal opportunities, and it accepts instructions from anyone regardless of background or circumstances. It is located in the heart of the commercial and legal centre of Liverpool, only a short walk from the QEII Combined Courts centre and the Liverpool Civil and Family Courts. 7 Harrington Street has extensive state of the art conference and seminar facilities, including a video conferencing suite.

6-8 MILL STREET Stephen Hockman QC

Head of Chambers	Stephen Hockman QC
Senior Clerk	Richard Constable
Tenants	57

6-8 Mill Street, Maidstone, ME15 6XH
Tel (01622) 688094/688095 **Fax** (01622) 688096 DX 51967 Maidstone 2
Email annexe@6pumpcourt.co.uk **Website** www.6pumpcourt.co.uk

THE CHAMBERS A leading common law set in the south-east with particular specialist expertise in civil and commercial, criminal, employment, family, financial conduct, inquests and inquiries, personal injury, public, planning and environmental, and regulatory law. This combination of expertise ensures a depth and breadth of ability and experience, thoroughly combining a strong criminal and regulatory practice with a well-established reputation in planning and environmental, civil, employment and family work. With well-appointed offices in the heart of Kent, Chambers can meet the needs of clients throughout the county in an efficient, cost-effective and responsive manner.

WORK UNDERTAKEN Crime; civil and commercial; employment; family; financial conduct; inquests; personal injury; planning and environmental; public law; regulatory law.
Please see the London entry under 6 Pump Court for further details.

BYROM STREET CHAMBERS Raymond Machell QC

12 Byrom Street, Manchester, M3 4PP
Tel (0161) 829 2100 **Fax** (0161) 829 2101 **DX** 718156 Manchester-3
Email clerks@byromstreet.com **Website** www.byromstreet.com

Crown Office Chambers, 2 Crown Office Row, London EC4Y 7HJ
Tel (020) 7797 8100 **Fax** (020) 7797 8101 **DX** 80 London Chancery Lane

Head of Chambers	Raymond Machell QC
Senior Clerk	Steve Price
Deputy Senior Clerk	Matt Tudor

MEMBERS

Raymond Machell QC (1973) (QC-1988)
Geoffrey Tattersall QC (1970) (QC-1992)
Winston Hunter QC (1985) (QC-2000)
Christopher Melton (1982) (QC-2001)
Simon Myerson QC (1986) (QC-2003)
James Rowley QC (1987) (QC-2006)
David Heaton QC (1983) (QC-2008)
Andrew Lewis QC (1985) (QC-2009)
Sally Hatfield QC (1988) (QC-2013)
Darryl Allen QC (1995) (QC-2014)
Rhiannon Jones QC (1993) (QC-2015)
Simon Kilvington (1995) (QC-2016)
Mary Ruck (1993)
Peter Burns (1993)
Darrel Crilley (1996)
Jason Wells (2007)

THE CHAMBERS Byrom Street Chambers is a forward-thinking set with traditional values, exclusively dedicated to the work of leading and senior junior counsel who have extensive expertise in high-value and complex cases. Chambers provides a highly individual and personalised service, focussing on clients' needs, combined with a friendly and open approach to clerking.

WORK UNDERTAKEN Members offer advice and advocacy in a range of specialisations and provide the depth of cover necessary to conduct litigation in the most complex of cases. It practises in the fields of personal injury (with an emphasis on catastrophic cases, group and class actions), clinical negligence and disease litigation, health and safety, professional negligence, financial services, commercial, employment, human rights, mediation and civil fraud. Sample cases include I.E.G.L v Zurich (SC 2015); A.E v Morecambe Hospitals (QB 2015); Dunhill v Burgin (SC 2014); McDonald v D.O.C. (SC 2014); Woodland v Essex CC (SC 2013)Sienkiewicz and Willmore (SC 2011); R (on app of AB) v Oldham NHS and Direct Line (Admin); Huscroft v P&O Ferries (CA); Thompstone v Tameside (CA); Fairchild v Glenhaven (HoL); Sowden v Lodge (CA); Tomlinson v Congleton (HoL); RK&AK v Oldham NHS Trust (ECHR); Shipman Inquiry.

Byrom Street Chambers

COBDEN HOUSE CHAMBERS Richard Hartley QC

Cobden House Chambers, 19 Quay Street, Manchester, M3 3HN
Tel (0161) 833 6000 **Fax** (0161) 833 6001 **DX** 14327 Manchester
Email clerks@cobden.co.uk **Website** www.cobden.co.uk

Head of Chambers	Richard Hartley QC
Director of Clerking	Martin Leech
Deputy Director of Clerking	Dan Monaghan
Senior Criminal Clerk	David Hewitt
Deputy Senior Clerk	Andrew Oakes
Senior Civil Clerk	Christina Crook
	Steven Tobias
Civil Clerk	Anthony Flannigan
	Avais Saleem
Clerk	Matthew Burnett
Chambers Administrator	Jackie Morton

MEMBERS

Richard Hartley QC (1985) (QC-2008)
Louise Blackwell QC (1985) (QC-2006)
Marc Willems QC (1990) (QC-2015)
Robert Sterling (1970)
Harry Narayan (1970)
Peter Buckley (1972) ^
John Broadley (1973)
Carolyn Johnson (1974) ^
Stuart Neale (1976)
Michael Goldwater (1977)
Richard Oughton (1978)
Timothy White (1978)
Fiorella Brereton (1979)
Colin Green (1981)
Paul Sheridan (1984)
Ian Metcalfe (1985)
Deanna Hymanson (1988)
Stephen Pritchett (1989)
Timothy Willitts (1989)
Martin Littler (1989)
John Parr (1989)
Lucy Wilson-Barnes (1989) ^
Stella Massey (1989) ^
Timothy Hodgson (1991)
Simon Nichol (1994) ^
David Maddison (1995) ^
David Sandiford (1995)
Julian Orr (1995)
Anthony Mazzag (1996)
Lee Nowland (1997)
Martin Callery (1997)
Angela Georgiou (1997)
Anna Short (1997)
Michael Jones (1998)
Craig MacGregor (1999)
Rebecca Hirst (1999)
Jacinta Stringer (1999)
Michael Knowles (2000) ^
Gwen Henshaw (2000)
Paul Whatley (2002)
Chetna Parmar (2003)
Jamie Marriott (2003)
Nicholas Flanagan (2004)
Mussadak Mirza (2004)
Sam Keeling-Roberts (2005) ^
Jonathan Boyle (2005)
Arron Walthall (2005)
Richard Stevens (2008)
Stefanie Cochrane (2008)
Ian McCubbin (2010)
Katherine Ballinger (2008)
Lisa Wilson (2009) ^
Gary Lewis (2010)
Kate Hammond (2012)
Chloe Murray (2012)
Alistair Reid (2014) ^
John Kennerley (2016)
Jonathan Goldberg QC (1971) (QC-1989) *
Barrie Searle (1976) *
Alyson Kilpatrick (1991) *
Susan Gilmour (1996) *
Michael Gleeson (1998) *
Angela Piears (2001) *
Tahina Akther (2003) *
Iris Ferber (2005) *
Jenny Kumeta (2005) *

* Door Tenant ^Direct/Public Access

THE CHAMBERS Cobden House Chambers are an established multi-disciplinary set of chambers located in Manchester, within walking distance of the courts and enjoying an excellent reputation on the Northern Circuit for being a friendly and client focused set.
Cobden House Chambers are aware of increasing competition and quality expectations. To ensure they maintain a high quality service they comply with the Code of Conduct and the Practice Standards Management of the Bar Council. Chambers are committed in meeting their clients' requirements and have been awarded the Bar Mark by the British Standards Institute in conjunction with the Bar Council for 'high standards of service and practice management'. Chambers are aware of the pressures facing clients not only in terms of court and paperwork but also funding. Boasting high quality advocacy and legal service within the following areas of law, personal injury/ clinical negligence, crime, chancery / commercial, family, employment, housing & inquests Chambers also provide Law Society accredited seminars and workshop training in these areas. Cobden House Chambers has a friendly and approachable team of experienced clerks who can discuss your specific requirements and suggest the most suitable barrister for your specific needs. The clerks also welcome the opportunity to discuss fees with clients and quote for any item of work beforehand.

WORK UNDERTAKEN

Personal Injury / Clinical Negligence: The PI/clinical negligence department offers expertise in personal injury, Industrial disease and clinical negligence claims providing a wealth of experience in managing claims at all levels. The department recognises the need to adapt to this developing and expanding market for legal services. Members of the department recognise the need to provide a partnership to ensure the best possible result for the client and to maintain and foster an excellent relationship with solicitors. The depth of this specialist department ensures that on behalf of claimants and defendants all types of claims can be managed including small claim, fast track and multi track matters as well as major multi million pound litigation. The PI department welcomes conditional fee work. The department is acutely aware of the particular challenges that apply in dealing with these cases and assistance can be provided at the critical early stage. To this end the department is keen to ensure that service standards are maintained and that matters are dealt with promptly. All documents can be returned electronically and within time limits to suit solicitors.

Chancery & Commercial: Cobden House Chambers' chancery and commercial barristers provide expert advisory, drafting and advocacy services in all areas of chancery and commercial work. The department are dedicated to providing both corporate and individual clients with clear, practical advice. They possess particular expertise in the following areas:

Community Legal Service

COBDEN HOUSE CHAMBERS Richard Hartley QC (Continued)

- Commercial litigation
- Real and personal property
- Landlord and tenant
- Wills and probate
- Insolvency
- Contract law
- Company law and partnerships
- Insurance law
- Construction law
- Trusts, tax and non-contentious drafting
- Security interests and family provision
- Professional negligence, including solicitors' negligence
- Intellectual property law, including breach of confidence and passing off
- Civil procedure and costs

The chancery and commercial barristers frequently appear in all levels of tribunal: from the County Court to the Supreme Court and are happy to travel nationwide and attend conferences in solicitors' offices, by telephone or video-link, or in Chambers. Cobden House barristers offer a wide range of experience: from those of over 30 years' call to more recently qualified junior barristers. Individual barristers retain particular specialties and areas of interest, as to which please see their individual profiles or ask the chamber's clerks to recommend a barrister with particular expertise. Some of the chamber's barristers accept Direct Public Access instructions. All offer seminars and workshops for solicitors, speaking on a wide range of subjects. Please ask the clerks for more details. The clerks will happily provide clients with an estimate or quote, no matter how complex the query

Family: Cobden House Chambers is a traditional and long established set of chambers located in Manchester. The Chambers enjoys an excellent reputation on the Northern Circuit for being a friendly and client focused set. The family department, offer a wealth of experience in all areas of family law as well as financial resolution matters including care proceedings, child arrangement orders, injunctions, adoption, ancillary relief and all related children's work and disputes over property for both married and cohabiting couples. The team is committed to providing a specialist and accessible service to all of their clients. They deliver a top quality service, combining meticulous preparation and the highest levels of advocacy with a clear and sympathetic approach to clients. Individually members pride themselves not only on high professional standards but also on their friendly approach and accessibility. Members of the team practice both in the local Courts and off-circuit, covering courts all around the country. All members of the Cobden House family department have undertaken additional training to become direct access qualified.

Housing: The housing department at Cobden House Chambers is one of the biggest and most experienced in the North West. Members of the department deal with a wide range of housing work, including:

- Possession
- Anti-social behavior orders and injunctions
- Disrepair claims and unfit housing prosecutions
- Unlawful evictions
- Mortgages
- Service charge disputes
- Right to buy
- Succession
- Homelessness
- Equality Act proceedings
- Human rights and proportionality
- Judicial review

Members act on behalf of both public and private sector tenants, and on behalf of landlords, including local authorities, registered social landlords and private landlords. They have a reputation for giving sound, practical advice, which takes advantage of members' experience of working with both landlords and tenants. Many members of the department are chancery specialists, and can advise on more complex disputes, including those involving mortgage fraud, trusts, long leases, and co-ownership. The department also includes a number of personal injury specialists, who can deal with claims involving aspects of negligence, including occupiers' liability. Members will always endeavor to assist with urgent matters, whether by drafting documents or attending court, but are also happy to be approached informally for advice prior to instructions being sent. Members of the department regularly provide education and training services for solicitors and their clients, including Chambers-based seminars and bespoke training.

Employment: Employment law is one of the most dynamic and fastest growing areas of law. Cobden House understand the importance of clear, practical advice which enables members to guide clients through this ever changing legal landscape. The employment team at Cobden House includes practitioners at all levels of call and covers all areas of work including:

COBDEN HOUSE CHAMBERS Richard Hartley QC (Continued)

- Unfair and wrongful dismissal
- All aspects of discrimination
- Victimisation
- Whistle blowing
- Redundancy (individual and collective)
- Contractual and bonus disputes
- Occupational stress
- Confidential information
- Restrictive covenants (including injunctive and springboard injunctive relief)
- TUPE
- Non contentious drafting including contracts of employment and compromise agreements

The team is happy to accept instructions on behalf of both employees and employers. Members regularly appear in Tribunals and County Courts across the country. Members also undertake work in other forums including the High Court, Employment Appeal Tribunal and a variety of professional regulatory bodies including the Police Disciplinary Board. Instructions can be returned within short deadlines and urgent advice can be provided by telephone if necessary. Given the nature of employment law the team are acutely aware of the need to keep abreast of developments and are happy to provide seminars on request. The clerks are delighted to provide additional information or to discuss your specific requirements.

Inquest Team: The inquest team at Cobden House has extensive experience and provides a comprehensive service in this area. It regularly provides advice and representation for interested parties involved in the events surrounding a death in the run up to and at an inquest. The interested parties include the family of the deceased, healthcare providers, prisons and their insurers. also represents the professionals involved in the care or custody of the deceased individual. These include doctors, nurses, paramedics and other healthcare professionals as well as custody officers and others involved in the death of a person in care or in detention. Members provide advice and preparation for individuals and organisations in the run up to the inquest as well as representation at the hearing. Representation is provided across England and Wales and in all types of inquest including those dealing with deaths following RTAs and accidents at work to deaths caused by medical or nursing errors and deaths in custody in which Art 2 ECHR is invoked.

PUBLICATIONS Second and Third Editions Tyler's *Family Provision Tenth Edition and Supplement Fisher and Lightwood's Law of Mortgage*

RECRUITMENT Cobden House chambers have an active pupillage programme and believe in organic growth. Chambers have been successful in offering a tenancy to 6 pupils over the last 8 years after successfully completing their pupillage.

DEANS COURT CHAMBERS Craig Sephton QC

24 St John Street, Manchester, M3 4DF
Tel (0161) 214 6000 **Fax** (0161) 214 6001 **DX** 718155 Manchester 3
Email clerks@ court.co.uk **Website** www.deanscourt.co.uk

Head of Chambers	Craig Sephton QC
Senior Clerk	Matthew Gibbons
Tenants	87

MEMBERS

Craig Sephton QC (1981) (QC-2001)
Stephen Grime QC (1970) (QC-1987)
David Fish QC (1973) (QC-1997)
Tim Horlock (1981) (QC-1997)
Christopher Sokol QC (1976) (QC-2006)
Stuart Denney QC (1982) (QC-2008)
Susan Grocott QC (1986) (QC-2008)
Mary O'Rourke QC (1981) (QC-2009)
Jane Cross QC (1982) (QC-2010)
Lewis Power QC (1990)(QC-2011)
Michael Hayton QC (1993) (QC-2013)*
Julia Cheetham QC (1990) (QC-2015)
Peter Atherton (1975)
David Eccles (1976) MA (Cantab)
Timothy Ryder (1977)
Ruth Trippier (1978)
Hugh Davies (1982)
David Kenny (1982)
Timothy Trotman (1983)
Russell Davies (1983)
Glenn Campbell (1985)
Paul Humphries (1986)
Karen Brody (1986)
Christopher Hudson (1987)
Heather Hobson (1987)
Nicholas Grimshaw (1988)
Bansa Singh Hayer (1988)
Ciaran Rankin (1988)
Peter Smith (1988)
Jonathan Grace (1989)
Robin Kitching (1989) ^
Michael Smith (1989) MA, BCL
Janet Ironfield (1992)
Timothy Edge (1992) ^
Alison Woodward (1992)
Fraser Livesey (1992)
Lisa Judge (1993) ^
Peter Horgan (1993)
Sebastian Clegg (1994)
Peter Rothery (1994)
Carolyn Bland (1995)
David Boyle (1996)
Simon McCann (1996)
Paul Higgins (1996)
Archna Dawar (1996)
Elizabeth Dudley-Jones (1997)
Sophie Cartwright (1998)
Richard Whitehall (1998)
Daniel Paul (1998)
Sasha Watkinson (1998)
Joanna Moody (1998)
Ross Olson (1999)
Pascale Hicks (1999)
Sarah J Booth (1999)
Virginia Hayton (1999)
Elizabeth Morton (1999)
Susan Deas (1999)
Joseph Hart (2000)
Ros Emsley-Smith (2001)
Anthony Singh (2001)
Robert McMaster (2001)
Zoe Earnshaw (2001) LLB
Alex Poole (2002)
Alex Taylor (2003)
William Tyler (2003)
Victoria Heyworth (2003)
Rebecca Gregg (2003)
Anna Bentley (2004)
Doug Cooper (2004)
Mark Bradley (2004)
Jonathan Lally (2005)
Carly Walters (2005)
Michelle Brown (2005)
Arron Thomas (2005)
Victoria Harrison (2006)
James Hogg (2006)
Rachel Greenwood (2008)
Junaid Durrani (2009)
Jonathan King (2009)
Nilufa Khanum (2009)
James Paterson (2010)
Simon Rowbotham (2011)
Emily Price (2012)
Daniel Glover (2013)
Gareth Poole (2014)
Patrick Gilmore (2014)
Harriet Tighe (2014)

^ Public/Direct Access

WORK UNDERTAKEN

Civil Litigation: Strength in depth unrivalled in the North West, personal injury (including injuries of the utmost severity e.g. spinal injuries, head injuries); class actions; industrial disease; fraudulent claims; road traffic and factory accidents; professional negligence; insurance, including coverage litigation, Road Traffic Act and Motor Insurers' Bureau; contractual disputes; sale of goods; consumer credit (including credit hire); product liability; arbitration (domestic and international); technology and construction; human rights and false imprisonment.

Chancery & Commercial: Work includes commercial arbitration; banking; carriage of goods; civil fraud and tracing of assets; corporate and personal insolvency; company law (including shareholders' disputes and the protection of minority interest, directors' duties and disqualification); credit and leasing; financial services; injunctions and equitable remedies; insurance and reinsurance; intellectual property; landlord and tenant; mortgages; partnerships; pensions; probate; real property; sale of goods (domestic and international); trusts, settlements and wills.

Family: Including financial remedies on divorce and dissolution of civil partnership (complex company structures, trust arrangements, pre post-nuptial agreements, offshore assets, freezing injunctions); cohabitation (agreements, ToLATA and Schedule 1 provision for children); and family provision under the Inheritance Act 1976. Children work is a specialism: members represent local authorities, parents, interveners and children in care and adoption cases (including death or serious injury to a child, a parent killed by the other, fabricated & induced illness and intergenerational sexual abuse); difficult residence and contact disputes; international movement & abduction of children; and surrogacy. Members act in judicial review cases concerning social & health care ethics, policy, practice and procedure.

Court of Protection & Community Care Law: Cases involving unlawful removal of adults from their home; deprivation of liberty cases; judicial review of decisions regarding provision of services; the use of the inherent jurisdiction for vulnerable adults; the conflicting roles of the Court of Protection and the Mental Health Act 1983; welfare decisions involving capacity, property and affairs decisions (including financial abuse and ratification of gifts).

Criminal: Prosecution and defence work in all fields and at every level including homicide and sexual offences; commercial fraud; conspiracy; drug importation and supply; excise and revenue offences; and health and safety. Members conduct high-profile trials both locally and nationally.

Professional Disciplinary, Business Crime & Regulatory: Regulation compliance; advocacy services in criminal prosecutions under the Health and Safety at Work Act 1974 and other legislation; inquests; licensing; trademark and copyright; rail and transport; corporate manslaughter; trading standards; food safety; environmental prosecutions; and DEFRA prosecutions. Specialist knowledge of law and procedure in Tribunals, present cases for various regulatory bodies (including the GMC) while defending practitioners for the medical defence organisations; appointed to the Medical Defence Union and Medical Protection Society Panels.

EXCHANGE CHAMBERS Bill Braithwaite QC

201 Deansgate, Manchester, M3 3NW
Tel (0161) 833 2722 **Fax** (0161) 833 2789 **DX** 14330 Manchester
Email info@exchangechambers.co.uk **Website** www.exchangechambers.co.uk

Head of Chambers	Bill Braithwaite QC
Clerks	David Haley
	Lynn Salter
	Leigh Daniels
	Ria Ashcroft
	Simon Crowley
	Josh Finn
	Joe Mawson
Chambers Director	Tom Handley
Senior Clerk	Nick Buckley
Tenants	161

MEMBERS

Bill Braithwaite QC (1970) (QC-1992)
Anthony Elleray QC (1977) (QC-1993)
Edward Bartley Jones QC (1975) (QC-1997) +
Gerard Martin QC (1978) (QC-2000) +
Mark Cawson QC (1982) (QC-2001) J
John Richard Jones QC (1981) (QC-2002) +
Gordon Cole QC (1979) (QC-2006)
Tania Griffiths QC (1982) (QC-2006) +
William Waldron QC (1986) (QC-2006) +
Stephen Meadowcroft QC (1973) (QC-2007)
Amanda Yip QC (1991) (QC-2011)+
Simon Medland QC (1991) (QC-2011)
Ben Myers QC (1994) (QC-2014)
Chris Tehrani QC (1990) (QC-2004)
Nicholas Johnson QC (1994) (QC-2016)
David Mohyuddin QC (1999) (QC-2016)
Michael Scholes (1996)
Simon Earlam (1975) +
Eric Lamb (1975) +
Judith Fordham (1991)
Digby Jess (1978)
Anthony Goff (1978)
Karen Troy (1981)
Ian Harris (1990) +
Paul Kirtley (1982) +
Karen Gregory (1985)
Roger Hillman (1983)
Neil Cadwallader (1984) +
Wayne Jackson (1984)
Paul Taylor (1985)
Paul Clark (1994)
William Hanbury (1985)
Simon Berkson (1986) +
Guy Vickers (1986)
David Knifton (1986) +
Sara Dodd (1987) +
Mark Mulrooney (1988)
Louis Browne (1988) +
Ian Foster (1988)
Greg Plunkett (2013)
Rebecca Clark (1989)
Catherine Howells (1989) +
Michael Wood (1989)
Simon Vaughan (1989)
Mark Rhind (1989) +
Christopher Stables (1990)
Julie Case (1990)
Christopher Cook (1990)
Michael Lavery (1990)
David Potter (1990) +
Jason MacAdam (1990)
Robert Golinski (1990)
David Toal (1990)
Timothy Evans (1992)
Giles Maynard-Connor (1992)
Rachael Woods (1992)
Mark Ainsworth (1992) +
Dr. Kevin Naylor (1992)
Gregory Hoare (1992)
Oliver Jarvis (1992)
Amanda Johnson (1992)
Steven Crossley (1992)
John Wyn Williams (1992)
Charlotte Kenny (1993)
Robert Dudley (1993)
Robert Wyn Jones (1993)
Stephen Connolly (2003)
Alaric Bassano (1993)
Andrew Jebb (1993)
Sarah Barlow (1993)
Kim Whittlestone (1994)
Louise Whaites (1994)
Damian Nolan (1994)
Richard Littler (1994)
Bruce Walker (1994)
Ceri Widdett (1994)
Andrew Williams (1994)
Michael Maher (1995)
Lisa Linklater (1995)
Mark Smith (1995)
Philip Parry (1995)
Claire Gourley (1996)
Scott Redpath (1996)
Jayne Acton (1996)
Sheren Guirguis (1996)
Andrew Smith (1996)
Imran Shafi (1996)
Ashley Serr (1996)
Lawrence McDonald (1996)
Steven Fennell (2014)
Pankaj Madan (1997)
Kevin Slack (1997)
Adrian Farrow (1997)
Louise Metcalf (1997)
Mark Stephenson (1997)
Jonathan French (1997)
Jon Close (1997)
David Fearon (2013)
Paul Burns (1998)
Sarah O'Brien (1998)
Katharine Titchmarsh (1998)
Nicholas Walker (1998)
Siân Jones (1998)
David Bentley (1998)
David Went (1998)
Nigel Edwards (1999)
Daniel Travers (1999)
Christopher Barnes (1999)
Martine Snowdon (2000)
Jonathan Rogers (2000)
Andrew Vinson (2000)
Andrew Ward (2000)
Nicola Daley (2000)
Laura Jane Gooding (2001)
Joshua Shields (2000)
David Temkin (2000)
Stephen Grattage (2000)
Michael Rawlinson (2002)
James Malam (2002)
Paul Hodgkinson (2002)
Caroline Gee (2003)
Charlotte Atherton (2003)
Christian Taylor (2003)
Stephen McNally (2003)
Sarah Johnston (2004) +
Sara Sutherland (2004)
Andrew Petterson (2004)
Esther Lin (2002)
Emma Bennett (2004)
Catherine Knowles (2004)
Alex Menary (2004)
Andrew Wastall (2005)
Kerron Rohrer (2005)
Suzie Kitzing (2005)
Chloe Fordham (2005)
Carly Sandbach (2006)
Chris Gutteridge (2006)
Richard Tetlow (2006)
David Birrell (2006)
Alfred Weiss (2006)
Julian Goode (2006)
Natalia Cornwall (2007)
Gareth Shires (2007)
Jonathan Lowe (2008)
Victoria Smith-Swain (2008)
Simon Whitfield (2009)
Lee Speakman (2009)
Huw Edwards (2009)
Ian Tucker (2010)
Chris Allen (2012)
John Waiting (2010)
Stuart McCracken (2010)
Lisa Feng (2011)
Sarah Griffin (2011)
Simon Lewis (2012)
Peter Dixon (2013)
Holly Betke (2013)
Beth Harvey-Smith (2011)
David Williams (2014)
Anja Lansbergen (2014)
Peter Killen (2015)
John Charles Rees QC (1972) (QC-1991) *
Nicholas Francis QC (1981) (QC-2002) *
Jonathan Turner QC (1974) (QC-2003) *
Neil Hawes QC (1989) (QC-2010)*
Cairns Nelson QC (1987) (QC-2010) *
Rhodri Williams QC (1987) (QC-2010) *
Eleanor Laws QC (1996) (QC-2011) *
Anthony Metzer QC (1987) (QC-2013) *
Edward Cousins (1971) *
Alun James (1986) *
John J McCarroll (1988) *
Andrew Maguire (1988) *

EXCHANGE CHAMBERS

EXCHANGE CHAMBERS Bill Braithwaite QC (continued)

David Tyack (1994) *
Anthony Eyers (1994)
Dr Simon Fox (1994) *
Frida Hussain (1995) *
Nancy Dooher (1997) *
Adam Chichester-Clark (2000) *

+ Recorder * Door Tenant

THE CHAMBERS Exchange Chambers is an award-winning set of barristers' chambers based in Liverpool, Manchester and Leeds. Priding itself on service, Exchange Chambers' ongoing expansion strategy is based on attracting outstanding barristers and outstanding work.

WORK UNDERTAKEN The set has a proven track record in all major areas of law comprising 161 barristers, including 16 silks. A record 57 members are ranked as leaders in their field by Chambers UK.

Alternative Dispute Resolution: Chambers covers all forms of ADR including arbitration, adjudication, dispute resolution boards, expert determination, early neutral evaluations and mediation across all practice areas. Chambers has 30 trained mediators.

Crime: Comprising 70 members, including 8 silks, the criminal team is one of the largest, most successful teams in the country. 38 are Category 4 Prosecutors. The team provides representation at all stages of a case, including pre-charge, trial and appeal. They have a highly sought after fraud team who routinely act on cases of national and international stature.

Personal Injury: Led by leading personal injury barrister, Bill Braithwaite QC, the department extends the full spectrum of seniority covering the areas of claimant / defendant personal injury, clinical negligence and industrial disease. The team has an exceptional reputation handling high value cases involving severe brain and spinal injuries. There are also a number of experts who deal with niche personal matters such as military claims, claims for amputees and complex pain disorders.

Commercial: The set is widely acclaimed for its complete range of commercial and chancery services including corporate and personal insolvency, shareholder, company and partnership disputes, professional negligence, competition, intellectual property, banking, property, planning and construction. 18 members of the team have been appointed by the Attorney General to his panel of Counsel.

Family: The team is highly experienced in all matters of family law, with a particular strength in financial remedy proceedings.

Local Government & Social Housing: This specialist department is independently acclaimed as "first class" and boasts an enviable record advising and representing local authorities and social housing providers across the country on the full range of issues faced by such organisations. Members of the department frequently advise and appear in high profile and test case litigation before local courts as well as the High Court, Court of Appeal and Supreme Court and work alongside other specialist departments within Chambers where appropriate to ensure that they provide the very highest standards of service to Chambers' substantial client base.

Civil: The team offers a full range of services in a number of specialist areas, including public law / judicial review, Court of Protection, local authority litigation, housing management, landlord and tenant and anti-social behaviour litigation.

Employment: The team covers the full spectrum of employment law, its members regularly instructed by large private sector employers and public sector organisations such as NHS trusts and local authorities.

Regulatory: Chambers has dedicated teams providing specialist advice and representation across a range of regulatory practice areas including environmental regulation, health and safety, healthcare, professional discipline and inquests.

Inquests: With 3 team members sitting as Assistant Deputy Coroners, the set has a strong reputation in this area throughout the UK. The team has a particular unrivalled depth of experience in relation to the healthcare sector.

KENWORTHY'S CHAMBERS

Arlington House, Bloom Street, Salford, Manchester, M3 6AJ
Tel (0161) 832 4036 **Fax** (0161) 832 0370 **DX** 718200
Email maria@kenworthysbarristers.co.uk **Website** www.kenworthyschambers.co.uk

Head of Chambers	Barry Grennan
Practice Manager	Maria Rushworth
Tenants	58

MEMBERS

Benjamin Nolan QC (1971)*
Robert Woodcock QC (1978)*
Barry Grennan (1977) ^
John Marsh (1977) ^
William Donnelly (1981) ^
Patrick Cassidy (1982) ^
Roger Brown (1976) ^
Edmund Farrell (1981) ^
Josephine Scally (1984)
Anthony Morris (1986)
Gita Patel (1988) ^
Patrick Williamson (1989)
Paul Stephenson (1990) *
Amanda Flattery (1993) ^
Andrew Marrs (1995) ^
Warren Potts (1995)
Geoff Whelan (1996)
Alison Mather (1997) ^
Barry Harwood (1998) ^
Monika Krawczyk (1998) *
Rosalyn Chowdhry (1999)
Waheed Baber (1999)
David Morton (1999)
Mark Asquith (1999)*
Haroon Rashid (1999)
Rachel White (2000) ^
Sara Haque (2000) ^
Margaret McDonald (2000)
Shazia Khan (2000) ^
Denise Fitzpatrick (2000) ^
Sally Penni (2000) ^
Mark Schwenk (2001)
Joy Emmanuel (2001) ^
Sarah Johnson (2001) ^
Michael Smith (2001) ^
George Brown (2002) ^
Chudi Grant (2002) ^
Shysta Habib (2002) ^
Fung Sin (2003)
John Nicholson (2004)
Anisa Niaz-Dickinson (2004) ^
Yasmin Chawdhery (2005) ^
Janet Cragg (2005) ^
Martin Lugsdin (2005) ^
Julie-Anne Luck (2006)
Rebecca Pickering (2007)
Sophia Ashraf (2009)
Joanne Carpanini (2009)
Carol Micah (2009) ^
Joannah Webster (2010)
Stephen Tettey (2010) ^
Peter Quegan (2010)
Simon Blakebrough (2011) ^
William Magill (2011)
Richard Lees (2011) ^
Paul IM Thurn (2012) ^
Adam Lewis (2013)
Yasser Iqbal (2015)
Craig Holmes (2015) ᴾ
Thomas Sherrington (2015) ᴾ

^ Public/Direct Access ᴾ Pupil * Associate Tenant

THE CHAMBERS Kenworthy's Chambers is a progressive set that offers expert advice, experienced advocates and excellent service. Their barristers are well known for being approachable and pragmatic.

WORK UNDERTAKEN The set takes on a good blend of commercial and social justice work. It accepts work at all levels in crime, chancery, commercial, education, family, immigration, human rights, intellectual property, judicial review, prison law, police law, housing, health and safety, civil, employment, inquests, costs and personal injury.

KINGS CHAMBERS Nicholas Braslavsky QC

Chambers Director	Debra Andrés
Senior Clerks	William Brown
	Colin Griffin
	Stephen Loxton
Senior Birmingham Clerk	Gary Smith
Senior Leeds Clerk	Rory Davis

36 Young Street, Manchester, M3 3FT
Tel (0345) 034 3444 **Fax** (0345) 034 3445 **DX** 718188 MCH3
Email clerks@kingschambers.com **Website** www.kingschambers.com

THE CHAMBERS is also at:
5 Park Square East, Leeds, LS1 2NE
Tel (0345) 034 3444 **Fax** (0113) 242 1124 **DX** 713113 (Leeds PKSQ)
Embassy House, 60 Church Street, Birmingham, B3 2DJ
Tel (0345) 034 3444 **Fax** (0345) 034 3445 **DX** 13023 (Birmingham)

MEMBERS

Dr Nicholas Braslavsky QC (1983) (QC-1999)
Mr Stephen J Sauvain QC (1997) (QC-1995)
Mr Vincent Fraser QC (1981) (QC-2001)
Mr Paul Chaisty QC (1982) (QC-2001)
Mr Richard Clayton QC (1977) (QC-2002)
Mr Santinder Hunjan QC (1981) (Q-C 2002)
Mr David Manley QC (1981) (QC-2003)
Ms Lesley Anderson QC (1989) (QC-2006)
Mr Anthony Crean QC (1987) (QC-2006)
Mr David Casement QC (1992) (QC-2008)
Mr Michael Rawlinson QC (1991) (QC-2009)
Mr Paul Tucker QC (1990) (QC-2010)
Mr Nigel Poole QC (1989) (QC-2012)
Mr Mark Harper QC (1989) (QC-2016)
Reverend Eric Owen (1969)
Mr Jeffrey Terry (1976)
Mr Alan Evans (1978)
Mr Shokat Khan (1979)
Mr John Barrett (1982)
Mr Neil Berragan (1982)
Mr Michael Stephens (1983)
Mr Mark Halliwell (1985)
Mr Gary Grant (1985)
Mr Simon Hilton (1987)
Mr Nigel Clayton (1987)
Miss Ruth Stockley (1988)
Miss Fiona Ashworth (1998)
Mr Andrew Singer (1990)
Mr Paul Johnson (2006)
Mr Simon Burrows (1990)
Mr Matthew Smith (1991)
Mr Andrew Grantham (1991)
Mr Adam Aldred (2014)
Mr Martin Carter (1992)
Mr Wilson Horne (1992)
Miss Lucy Powis (1992)
Miss Sarah Pritchard (1993)
Mr Richard Lander (1993)
Mr Ian Ponter (1993)
Mr Michael Ditchfield (1993)
Miss Sarah Clover (1993)
Mr James Boyd (1994)
Miss Kelly Pennifer (1994)
Mr Andrew Latimer (1995)
Miss Anna Diamond (1995)
Mr Gavin McBride (1996)
Mr Jeremy Roussak (1996)
Mr Louis Doyle (1996)
Mr Jonathan Easton (1996)
Mr Simon Plaut (1997)
Mr Colin Bourne (1997)
Dr Mark Friston (1997)
Mr Simon Young (1998)
Mr Stephen Maguire (2007)
Mr Giles Cannock (1998)
Professor Andrew McGee (1998)
Mr Matthew Hall (1999)
Miss Helen Mulholland (1999)
Mr Martin Budworth (1999)
Miss Tina Ranales-Cotos (1999)
Mr Brian Griffiths (1999)
Miss Eleanor Temple (2000)
Mrs Lisa Walmisley (2000)
Mr Paul Lakin (2000)
Mr Paul Hughes (2001)
Mr Ben Williams (2001)
Mr Geraint Wheatley (2001)
Mr Rupert Beloff (2001)
Miss Claire Steward (2002)
Mr Craig Ralph (2002)
Mr Michael Rudd (2002)
Mr John Hunter (2002)
Mr Sam Karim (2002)
Miss Emily Duckworth (2003)
Miss Sarah Lawrenson (2003)
Miss Sarah Reid (2004)
Miss Francesca Gardner (2004)
Miss Rachel Galloway (2004)
Miss Sophie Allan (2004)
Miss Helen Trotter (2005)
Mr Paras Gorasia (2005)
Miss Charlotte Law (2005)
Mr Ben Harding (2005)
Miss Cheryl Dainty (2006)
Mr Richard Livingston (2006)
Mr Johnny Ward (2007)
Dr Nathan Smith (2007)
Mr Kevin Latham (2007)
Mr Stephen McNamara (2008)
Mr Anthony Gill (2008)
Miss Eleanor d'Arcy (2008)
Miss Anna Macey (2008)
Mrs Laura Gould (2009)
Mr Richard Borrett (2009)
Miss Louise Green (2009)
Miss Eliza V Sharron (2009)
Miss Francesca P Gardener (2009)
Miss Ruth Taylor (2010)
Mr Jonathan Wright (2010)
Mr Aidan Reay (2011)
Mr Freddie Humphries (2011)
Miss Erica Bedford (2012)
Mr Doug Cochran (2012)
Miss Arianna Kelly (2013)
Miss Alison Ogley (2014)
Miss Constanze Bell (2014)
Mr Killian Garvey (2014)
Mr Marcus F Daly SC (1987) (SC-1999) *
Mr Colm o'hOisin SC (1998) (SC-2005) *
Mr James Henderson (1997) *
Mr Leo Charalambides (1998) *
Professor Andrew Keay (2010) *
Sir Maurice Kay (1975) (QC-1988) +
His Honour David Gilliland (1964) (QC-1984) +

+*Associates + Arbitrator

THE CHAMBERS Kings Chambers is ranked one of the country's leading sets. It provides barristers with the highest reputation for advocacy, knowledge and standards to service. This is a large specialist set with a national reputation practising from Manchester, Leeds and Birmingham in several practice areas: pre-dominantly chancery and commercial law; planning and environmental law, personal injury and clinical negligence, costs, employment, sports law, mediation, arbitration and public law.

WORK UNDERTAKEN

Arbitration: Kings Chambers has a number of members with practices encompassing domestic and international arbitration. Chambers has also launched its own bespoke arbitration service (KAS) offering a

KINGS CHAMBERS Nicholas Braslavsky QC (continued)

panel of experienced arbitrators including former judges and silks from other jurisdictions.

Chancery & Commercial: The Chancery and commercial group has extensive experience in litigation (including agency, contracts, sale of goods, restraint of trade and restrictive covenants, corporate law); corporate and personal insolvency (including winding up, administration, administrative receivership and tracing assets),banking and professional negligence. Residential and commercial landlord and tenant work (including renewals, rent.

Clinical Negligence & Personal Injury: The clinical negligence and personal injury team undertake work involving serious personal injury claims, all aspects of clinical negligence and occupational disease with a particular focus on asbestos and other forms of toxic exposure. The team also specialises in chronic pain and related conditions.

Costs: There is a specialist and dedicated costs team, practising exclusively in costs law, disputes and litigation funding.

Employment: The employment team covers the entire spectrum of employment law and has particular strengths in race, sex, equal pay, restrictive covenants and disability discrimination both in tribunals and in the High Court.

EU & Competition: Chambers has a small and dedicated team dealing with EU and competition law, including cartels, dominance, mergers, market investigations, litigation, public procurement, state aid, trading agreements and compliance.

Mediation: Mediation is an important part of the litigation process. The team comprises accredited mediators at various levels and with expertise in differing areas of law.

Planning: Kings Chambers is one of the largest planning and environmental chambers, with members appearing before a wide range of dedicated tribunals and inquiries. Chambers acts in planning appeals and major inquiries for a wide variety of clients and local authorities. Kings also has extensive experience in environmental law including waste disposal and management, energy, compulsory purchase compensation and highways.

Public Law: The public law group practises extensively in the Administrative Court, sitting in London and the regions. The group encompasses the range of public law work in community care, education, housing, mental health, licensing, local government and social security matters. Members advise and appear before courts at all levels.

Sports Law: The sports law team have been involved in some of the most substantial and high profile sports cases nationally in recent years involving, commercial dispute resolution, disciplinary and regulatory proceedings, anti-doping rules, employment issues, sports-related personal injury, breach of confidentiality and privacy, wealth management issues, intellectual property including image rights, trademark infringement and breach of copyright.

ST JOHN'S BUILDINGS Sally Harrison QC

24a-28 St John Street, Manchester M3 4DJ
Tel (0161) 214 1500 **Fax** (0161) 835 3929 **DX** 728861 MANCHESTER 4
Email clerk@stjohnsbuildings.co.uk **Website** www.stjohnsbuildings.co.uk

Chief Executive	Chris Ronan
Head of Corporate Services	David Anderson
Head of Finance	Paula Blackshaw
Tenants	234

MEMBERS

Sally Harrison QC (1992) (QC-2010)
Michael Shorrock QC (1966) (QC-1988)
Michael Redfern QC (1970) (QC-1993)
Jane Crowley QC (1976) (QC-1998)
Andrew O'Byrne QC (1978) (QC-2006)
David Berkley QC (1979) (QC-1998)
Kim Hollis QC (1979) (QC-2002)
Frances Judd QC (1984) (QC-2006)
Frances Heaton QC (1985) (QC-2012)
Brendan Kelly QC (1988) (QC-2008)
Karl Rowley QC (1994) (QC-2013)
John Vater QC (1995) (QC-2012)
Graeme Wood (1968)
John Hedgecoe (1972)
John McNeill (1974)
Eric Shannon (1974)
Stephen Bedford (1974)
Geoffrey Lowe (1975)
Philip Andrews (1977)
Antony Longworth (1978)
Philip Grundy (1980)
Andrew Long (1981)
David Bruce (1982)
Sonia Gal (1982)
Peter Harrison (1983)
Brian McKenna (1983)
Keith Harrison (1983)
Michael Slater (1983)
Julian Shaw (1984)
Julian Lloyd (1985)
Michael Kennedy (1985)
Jonathan Dickinson (1986)
Julian Taylor (1986)
Diana Kloss MBE (1986)
Jane Walker (1987)
Jane Dagnall (1987)
Timothy Brennand (1987)
John Oates (1987)
Nicholas Price (1987)
Bunty Batra (1988)
Charles Eastwood (1988)
Simon Crabtree (1988)
Paula Davitt (1988)
Damian Sanders (1988)
Clare Grundy (1989)
Lisa Partington (1989)
Anne Britcliffe (1989)
Michael Blakey (1989)
Simon Holder (1989)
Joseph O'Brien (1989)
Paul O'Shea (1989)
Richard Carter (1990)
Jonathan Thompson (1990)
David Watson (1990)
Raquel Simpson (1990)
Alastair Wright (1991)
Matthew Mawdsley (1991)
Mark Roberts (1991)
Zia Chaudhry MBE (1991)
Jonathan Taylor (1991)
Patricia Pratt (1991)
Tim Savage (1991)
Magdalen Case (1992)
Richard Norton (1992)
Andrew Green (1992)
Kevin McNerney (1992)
Timothy Ashmole (1992)
Alison Dorrell (1992)
Fiona Walker (1992)
Alex Kloss (1993)
Guy Mathieson (1993)
Richard Orme (1993)
Joanna Rodikis (1993)
Jason Searle (1993)
Myles Wilson (1993)
Ginnette Fitzharris (1993)
Benjamin Jones (1993)
David Flood (1993)
Leona Harrison (1993)
David Polglase (1993)
Dermot Hughes (1993)
Rachael Harrison (1993)
Caroline Ford (1993)
Penelope Stanistreet (1993)
Rachael Banks (1993)
Nigel Booth (1994)
Daniel Frieze (1994)
Annette Gumbs (1994)
Steven Wild (1994)
Stephen Douglas (1994)
Robert McGinty (1994)
Lisa Houghton (1994)
Mark Connor (1994)
Sara Mann (1994)
John Chukwuemeka (1994)
Megan Rhys (1994)
Craig Lowe (1994)
Justine Cole (1994)
James Gatenby (1994)
Paul Treble (1994)
Helen Wrenn (1994)
Andrew Lawson (1995)
Pauline McHugh (1995)
Iain Simkin (1995)
Gordon Stables (1995)
Olivia Weir (1995)
Pépin Aslett (1996)
Samantha Hillas (1996)
Ghazan Mahmood (1997)
Remy Zentar (1997)
Simon Parry (1997)
Simeon Evans (1997)
Zillah Williams (1997)
Douglas Denton (1997)
Ian Goldsack (1997)
Andrew Bailey (1997)
Alexandra Simmonds (1998)
Liam Murdin (1998)
David James (1998)
Kate Burnell (1998)
David Taylor (1998)
Susan Edwards (1998)
Clare Thomas (1998)
Abigail Bennett (1998)
Rachael Rowley-Fox (1998)
Jacqueline Swain (1998)
John Ratledge (1999)
Linda Sweeney (1999)
Philip Astbury (1999)
Lara Holsgrove (1999)
Andrew Lord (1999)
Philip Byrne (1999)
Yasmin Kauser (1999)
Sufiyan Rana (1999)
Jonathan Turner (1999)
Fayaz Hammond (1999)
Lorraine Cavanagh (2000)
Andrew Bridgman (2000)
Kathryn Hayes (2000)
Katy Appleton (2000)
Alison Whalley (2000)
Rhian Livesley (2000)
Prudence Beever (2000)
David Pojur (2001)
Clare Porter-Phillips (2001)
Oliver King (2001)
Sylvia Vir-Singh (2001)
Audrey Van Der Haer (2001)
Siraj Ahmed (2001)
Andrew Wynne (2001)
Nicola Quinney (2001)
Laura Marshall (2001)
Neil Montaldo (2002)
Paul Smith (2002)
Christopher Moss (2002)
Richard Thyne (2002)
Mark Senior (2002)
Jennifer Menzies (2002)
Louise McCloskey (2002)
Rebecca Smith (2002)
Cheryl Mottram (2002)
Robert Cline (2002)
Benjamin Lawrence (2003)
Kashif Ali (2003)
Abigail Hudson (2003)
Robert Akers (2003)
Clodagh Maguire (2003)
Gordon Semple (2003)
Simon Pallo (2003)
Timothy Connolly (2004)
William Poole (2004)
Philippa Waddell (2004)
Catherine Rimmer (2004)
Peta Harrison (2004)
Helen Wilson (2004)
Rebecca Sutton (2004)
Jade Abraham (2004)

Criminal Defence Service

Community Legal Service

ST JOHN'S BUILDINGS Sally Harrison QC (continued)

Abigail Hickinbottom (2004)
Louise Stanbury (2004)
Neil Christian (2005)
Neair Maqboul (2004)
Frances De Navarro (2005)
Lucy Marshall (2005)
Steven McGarry (2005)
Gareth Thompson (2005)
Debra White (2005)
Shaun Spencer (2005)
Samantha Openshaw (2005)
Steven Flynn (2006)
Ben Kelly (2006)
Christopher Pare (2006)
Jennifer Scully (2006)
Kate Morley (2006)
Helen Davey (2006)
Diarmuid Bunting (2006)
Louise Rae (2006)
Henry Vanderpump (2007)
Hannah Wood (2007)
Neil Owen-Casey (2007)
Andrew Haggis (2007)
Nicole Erlen (2007)
Peter Gilmour (2007)
Philip Clemo (2007)
Alison Dobbie (2007)
Jane Wheatley (2007)
Elisabeth Cooper (2008)
Elis Gomer (2008)
Cerys Williams (2008)
Simon Maddison (2008)
Jonathan Bellamy (2008)
Hannah Walker (2008)
Laura England (2008)
Daniel Metcalfe (2008)
Jamie Jenkins (2008)
Simon Murray (2008)
Matthew Carey (2008)
James Cliff (2008)
David Baines (2009)
Laura Nash (2009)
Elliw Roberts (2009)
Kerry Holt (2009)
Ashley Singh (2009)
Lucinda France-Hayhurst (2009)
Charles Austin (2009)
Ginny Whiteley (2010)
Jessica Southcote-Want (2010)
Julian King (2012)
Jessica Wilson-Theaker (2012)
Alice McDonald (2012)
Eleanor Keehan (2013)
Charlotte Johnson (2013)
Gemma Maxwell (2014)
Fatima Zafar (2015)
Hunter Gray (2015)

THE CHAMBERS Also at:
21 White Friars, Chester CH1 1NZ, Phone 01244 323070, Fax 01244 342930
38 Vernon Street, Liverpool, L2 2AY, Phone 01512 436000, Fax 01512 436040
7 Leopold Street, Sheffield, S1 2GY, Phone 01142 738951, Fax 01142 760848

THE CHAMBERS St John's Buildings is committed to delivering excellence. The set has a proven reputation for quality advocacy and advisory services, supported by experienced and proactive clerking and administration teams. The aim is to build successful long-term partnerships with clients by providing exceptional barristers backed by professional, reliable and consistently high quality standards of service. This is underpinned by a culture of attention to detail, commercial astuteness and excellent communication.
SJB takes a commercial approach to service delivery and is proud of the standards it sets. This approach has enabled the set to service a number of large contracts for advocacy services and to attract some of the country's most high-profile cases across numerous areas of law.
Clients and members are impressed by the professionalism of the SJB approach and the set's ability to retain a collegiate atmosphere while focussing on service standards.
In a time of uncertainty for the legal services market, St John's Buildings is following a strategy for growth to enhance their ability to service their clients' needs by providing advocacy and advisory services nationally, backed by clear terms, service level agreements and management information.
As well as market-leading facilities including video conferencing, mediation suites, private meeting rooms and conference facilities, clients can take advantage of a wide programme of CPD seminars, and members offer bespoke in-house training on request. Regular client surveys are undertaken, feedback is acted upon immediately and improvements built into the Quality Manual.
Chambers is managed by a Board of Directors and audited to ISO 9001 standards. Corporate governance and information security are taken very seriously and Chambers is an early adopter of new technology to facilitate better and more cost effective service delivery.
SJB clients are spread nationally and range from the full spectrum of legal firms, insurance firms, local authorities and high-net-worth individuals through to commercial enterprises and SMEs.
Members of Chambers also accept instructions from members of the public under the direct access rules.

WORK UNDERTAKEN St John's Buildings is able to provide a comprehensive range of legal experts to clients. This has enabled SJB to become trusted advisors to their clients on their advocacy needs in any area of law. St John's Buildings has particular specialism in:

- Accidents abroad
- ADR and mediation
- Banking, finance and insolvency
- Catastrophic injury
- Clinical negligence
- Company and commercial
- Costs
- Court of Protection
- Crime
- Disease
- Education
- Employment
- Family – children
- Family – finance
- Fraud – civil
- Fraud - criminal
- Inquests
- Personal injury
- Professional negligence
- Property and private client
- Public and administrative
- Public access
- Regulatory
- Sport, media and entertainment

For full details of the set's areas of expertise please visit www.stjohnsbuildings.com/expertise

18 ST JOHN STREET Peter Birkett QC

Head of Chambers	Peter Birkett QC
Senior Clerk	John Hammond
Chambers Manager	Elizabeth Sheen
Tenants	66

18 St John Street, Manchester, M3 4EA
Tel (0161) 278 1800 **Fax** (0161) 278 8220 **DX** 728854 Manchester 4
Email clerks@18sjs.com **Website** www.18sjs.com

MEMBERS

Peter Birkett QC (1972) (QC-1989)
Lord Brennan QC (1967) (QC-1984) ++
Robert Glancy QC (1972) (QC-1997) ++
Sally Bradley QC (1978) (QC-1999) ++
Stephen Killalea QC (1981) (QC-2006) ++
Ekany Nkumbe QC (1990) (QC-2011) ++
Rex Howling QC (1991) (QC-2011) ++
Elizabeth Isaacs QC (1998) (QC-2013) ++
Alastair Forrest (1972)
Paul Dockery (1973)
Paul O'Brien (1974)
Christopher Diamond (1975)
Christopher Limb (1975)
Nicholas Fewtrell (1977)
Mark Laprell (1979)
Michael Murray (1979)
Ian Huffer (1979)
Richard Vardon (1985)
Alexandra Stansby (1985)
Stephen J Murray (1986)
Yvonne Healing (1988)
Toby Sasse (1988)
Samantha Birtles (1989)
Elisabeth Tythcott (1989)
Fiona Holloran (1989)
Jonathan Dale (1991)
Michael Brady (1992)
Susan Harrison (1993)
Rachel Shenton (1993)
David Hoffman (1997)
Andrew Moore (1996)
Adam Lodge (1996)
Rachel Faux (1997)
David Mackley (1997)
Richard Chapman (1998)
Kalsoom Maqsood (1999)
Jonathan Grierson (1999)
Wayne Goldstein (1999)
Sarah Kilvington (1999)
Kate Bramall (1999)
Lukhvinder Kaur (2000)
Ben Norman (2000)
Andrew Scott (2000)
Karen Boyle (2000)
Leonie Caplan (2001)
Soria Kajue (2001)
Nicholas Clarke (2001)
Colin Buckle (2002)
Sarah Donaldson (2003)
Laura Thomas (2003)
Jennifer Newstead Taylor (2004)
Rehana Begum (2004)
Simon Charles (2004)
Christopher McNall (2005)
Saiqa Chaudhry (2005)
Vanessa Lau (2005)
Elizabeth Murray (2005)
Elahe Youshani (2005)
Kate Henthorn (2005)
Michael Wilkinson (2006)
Evonnie Chan (2006)
Danish Ameen (2006)
Rupert Davies (2007)
Andrew Evans (2007)
Kane Simons (2007)
Oliver Caplan (2007)
Fergal Allen (2007)
Sandra Pope (2008)
Gemma McGungle (2011)
Elizabeth Evans (2011)
Lewis Bretts (2012)
Neil Ronan (2012)
Jocelyn Hughes (2015)
Roger Hedgeland (1972)++
Malcolm McEwan (1976)++
Laura Briggs (2001)++
Hugh Rimmer (2003)++
Francesca Dowse (2004)++

++ Associate Member

THE CHAMBERS A general common law chambers with distinct civil, family, chancery and criminal departments, and expertise at all levels.

9 ST JOHN STREET Charles Garside QC

9 St John Street, Manchester, M3 4DN
Tel (0161) 955 9000 **Fax** (0161) 955 9001 **DX** 14326
Email civilclerks@9sjs.com criminalclerks@9sjs.com **Website** www.9sjs.com

Head of Chambers	Charles Garside QC
Chambers Manager	Ruth Bailey
Senior Clerk (Civil)	Tony Morrissey
Senior Clerk (Crime)	Chris Swann
Team Leader Personal Injury & Insurance Fraud	Joe Gibson
Team Leader Employment & Commercial	Julie Lanza
Civil Clerks	Jane Slingsby
	Peadar McKinstry
	Matt Rigby
	Phillip Spencer
	Julian Shepherd
	Sam Roberts
Junior Criminal Clerks	Andrew Leech
	Anthony Brown

MEMBERS

Charles Garside QC (1971) ^ (QC-1993) +
Roderick Carus QC (1971) (QC-1990) +
Nicholas Hinchliffe QC (1980) (QC-1999) +
Gerard McDermott QC (1987) ^ (QC-1999)
Geraint Jones QC (1976) (QC-2001)
Simon Jackson QC (1982) (QC-2003) +
Nicholas Clarke QC (1981) (QC-2006) +
Paul Gilroy QC (1985) ^ (QC-2006)
Christopher L P Kennedy QC (1989) ^ (QC-2010)
Mark Hill QC (1987) (QC-2011)
Terence Rigby (1971) +
Peter Cadwallader (1973)
Christine Riley (1974)
Paul McDonald (1975)
Gordon Hennell (1982)
Richard Selwyn Sharpe (1985)
Nigel Grundy (1983) + ^
Alistair Bower (1986) ^
Carlo Breen (1987) ^
David Gilchrist (1987)
Mark Monaghan (1987)
Nicola Gatto (1987)
Thomas Fitzpatrick (1988)
Ian Little (1989)
Edward Morgan (1989) ^
Joanne Woodward (1989) ^
Joanne Barnett (1989) ^
Darren Preston (1991)
Christopher Scorah (1991)
Dr Anthony Howard (1992)
Joanne Connolly (1992)
Karim Sabry (1992) ^
Graham Bailey (1993)
Rachel Wedderspoon (1993) ^
Kirsten Barry (1993) ^
Jaime Hamilton (1993)
James Fryer-Spedding (1994)
Michael Lemmy (1994)
Andrew Clark (1994) ^
James Hurd (1994) ^
Robert Darbyshire (1995) ^
Brian McCluggage (1995) ^
Stefan Brochwicz-Lewinski (1995)
David Calvert (1995) ^
Katie Nowell (1996)
Sara Lewis (1996)
Boyd Morwood (1996)
Gary Woodhall (1997)
Rachael Heppenstall (1997)
Kate Hollyoak (1997)
Vanessa Thomson (1997)
Chris Taft (1997)
Christina Chinnock (1998) ^
Kathrine Mallory (1998)
Jane Mabon (1998)
Assunta del Priore (1998) ^
Helen Redmond (1999)
Zoë Thompson (1999) ^
Paul Tindall (1999)
Lucinda Leeming (1999)
Matthew Haisley (1999)
Victoria Rigby (2000)
Rebecca Eeley (2001)
Alison Heyworth (2001)
Matthew Snarr (2001) ^
Dawn Thomas (2001)
Kirsty McKinlay (2001)
Russell Dickinson (2002)
Joseph Mulderig (2002)
Jonathan Savage (2003)
Louise Brandon (2003)
Thomas Gilbart (2003) ^
Joanna Vicary (2003)
Caroline Curry (2003)
Philip Deberry (2003)
Louise Quigley (2003)
Ian Denham (2003)
Benjamin Morris (2004)
Hannah Haines (2005)
Robert Smith (2005)
Laura D'Cruz (2006)
Rachael Levene (2006)
Michael O'Neill (2007)
Lena Amartey (2008) ^
William Hamilton (2008)
Graham Robinson (2009)
Richard Price (2010) ^
Emma Greenhalgh (2010)
Alex Langhorn (2010)
Cath Cundy (2011)
Matt Entwistle (2011)
Fiona Wise (2012)
Jasmine Skander (2012)
Amy Rollings (2012)
Amy Smith (2013)
Holly Platt (2013)
Philip Barnes (2014)

+ Recorder ^ Direct/Public Access

THE CHAMBERS In order to meet the increasing demand for specialist advice, chambers has established the following special interest groups: commercial, crime, employment, family, insurance fraud, health and safety, travel law and personal injury. Chambers is accredited by The Law Society for CPD purposes and is happy to provide seminars on a wide range of subjects either in-house or in chambers. If you are interested in this service, please contact Tony Morrissey (0161) 955 5176 (tony.morrissey@9sjs.com).

ENTERPRISE CHAMBERS Zia Bhaloo QC

65 Quayside, Newcastle upon Tyne, NE1 3DE
Tel (0191) 222 3344 **Fax** (0191) 222 3340 **DX** 61134 Newcastle upon Tyne
Email newcastle@enterprisechambers.com **Website** www.enterprisechambers.com

Head of Chambers	Zia Bhaloo QC
Chambers Director	Michael Couling
Senior Clerk	Antony Armstrong (London)
Clerk	Bethany Thompson
Tenants	43

For a full list of members please see the London entry. For further information about the set please visit the chambers' website.

TRINITY CHAMBERS Toby Hedworth QC

Trinity Chambers, The Custom House, Quayside, Newcastle upon Tyne, NE1 3DE
Tel (0191) 232 1927 **Fax** (0191) 232 7975 **DX** 61185 (Newcastle)
Email info@trinitychambers.co.uk **Website** www.trinitychambers.co.uk

Head of Chambers	Mr Alan Toby Hedworth QC
Practice Director	Simon Stewart OBE
	Chris Lucarelli (Business Development)
Leaders Clerk	Richard Embley
Teesside Clerk	Chris Gibbin
Criminal Clerks	Peter Finkill
	Liam Gorman
Civil & Family Clerks	Fiona Bullock
	Ken McLafferty
	Steven Preen
Fees & Accounts	John Lisgo
	David Robinson
Tenants	70

MEMBERS

Toby Hedworth QC (1975) (QC-1986)
Stephen Duffield (1969)
Glenn Gatland (1972)
Christopher Knox (1974)
Anthony Hawks (1975)
David Callan (1979)
John Wilkinson (1979)
John Campbell QC (1981) (QC-1998)
Jacqueline Smart (1981)
James Richardson (1982)
Peter Walsh (1982)
Lesley McKenzie (1983)
Timothy Spain (1983)
John O'Sullivan (1984)
Fiona McCrae (1986)
Susan Taylor (1987)
Caroline Goodwin (1988)
Shaun Routledge (1988)
Andrew Rutter (1990)
Nicola Shaw (1992)
Rachel Smith (1992)
Ros Scott Bell (1993)
Katherine Dunn (1993)
Justin Gray (1993)
Nicholas Stonor QC (1993) (QC-2015)
Charles Holland (1994)
Jane Callan (1995)
Margaret Sweeting (1996)
Yvonne Taylor (1998)
Fiona Walker (1998)
Asa Anderson (1998)
Nicola Allan (1999)
Simon Goldberg (1999)
Rachel Hedworth (1999)
James Kemp (1999)
Kossar Kitching (1999)
Elizabeth Mendoza (1999)
Paul Currer (2000)
Nigel Gowling (2000)
Ruth Phillips (2001)
Miriam Rasoul (2001)
Natasha Andrews (2002)
Joe Hedworth (2002)
Brian Mather (2002)
Joan Smith (2002)
Henry Stevens (2002)
Katherine Wood (2002)
Jane Foley (2002)
Tony Cornberg (2003)
Jamie Anderson (2004)
Claire Brissenden (2004)
Mike Hill (2004)
Antoine Tinnion (2004)
David Comb (2005)
Richard Stubbs (2005)
Will Byrne (2006)
Helen Hogben (2006)
Jamie Morgan (2006)
Rebecca Stokes-Herbst (2006)
Marian Cleghorn (2007)
Johanna Darby (2007)
James Marwick (2008)
Andrew Crammond (2008)
Amanda Sehat (2009)
Morgan Brien (2010)
James McHugh (2010)
Rebecca Suttle (2012)
Matthew Crowe (2013)
Stephen Duffy (2013)
Nigel Kidwell (2015)
Phillip Engelman (1979)*
Andrew Stafford QC (1980) (QC-2000) *
Francis FitzGibbon QC (1986) (QC-2010) *
Deveral Capps (1995) *

* Door Tenant

THE CHAMBERS Trinity Chambers, established in 1954, operating from Newcastle upon Tyne and Middlesbrough. Trinity Chambers abides by its equality and diversity policies, copies of which are available on request.

WORK UNDERTAKEN

Agriculture: Tenancies, Common Agricultural Policy, livestock, conservation, renewables and equine.
ADR: Mediation and arbitration. Three qualified IFLA Arbitrators.
Business: Insolvency, company, partnership and commercial disputes, directors' duties, disqualifications.
Chancery: Probate, Inheritance Act, Trusts of Land, property disputes, housing, landlord and tenant.
Costs: Several members sit as Deputy District Judges, costs budgeting, appeals and CCMCs.
Court of Protection, Mental Health & Care Act: Community care, deprivation of liberty, abuse, capacity.
Crime: Instructed by prosecution and defence in often high profile cases of murder, manslaughter, POCA.
Employment: National reputation for equal pay, discrimination, whistleblowing, redundancy, TUPE.
Family & Matrimonial Finance: Care, adoption, honour violence, ancillary relief, TOLATA.
Immigration: Points based system, entry clearance, UK Border Agency, asylum and human rights issues.
Judicial Review: Immigration, human rights, procurement, regulatory, licensing and planning.
Licensing: Alcohol, taxis, premises, firearms, sex industry, gaming, betting and judicial review.
Personal Injury & Clinical Negligence: Small claims, fast-track and multi-track matters, credit hire.
Planning & Environment: Inquiries, appeals, enforcement, Judicial review, environmental protection.
Regulatory: Fitness to practise NMC, HCPC, GMC, Trading Standards, health and safety, inquests.

ROPEWALK CHAMBERS

24, The Ropewalk, Nottingham, NG1 5EF
Tel (0115) 947 2581 **Fax** (0115) 947 6532 **DX** 10060 Nottingham 17
Email clerks@ropewalk.co.uk **Website** www.ropewalk.co.uk

Head of Chambers	Patrick Limb QC
Senior Clerk	Tony Hill
Tenants	43

MEMBERS

Patrick Limb QC (1987) (QC – 2006) ^
Jayne Adams QC (1982) (QC-2016) ^
Stephen Beresford (1976)
James Howlett (1980) ^
Soofi Din (1984) ^
Andrew Prestwich (1986)
Richard Seabrook (1987) ^
Toby Stewart (1989)
Philip Turton (1989)
Jonathan Mitchell (1992) ^
Jason Cox (1992) ^
Andrew McNamara (1992) ^
Deborah Davies (1993)
Richard Gregory (1993)
Ivan Cartwright (1993) ^
Myles Jackson (1995)
Andrew Hogan (1996) ^
Mark Diggle (1996) ^
Shilpa Shah (1998) ^
Clare Haddon (1999) ^
Christopher Lowe (2001)
Andrew Lyons (2002)
Edward James (2002) ^
Jan Alam (2003) ^
Jonathan Owen (2004) ^
Kam Jaspal (2005) ^
Rochelle Rong (2005)
Rachel Young (2006) ^
Georgina Cursham (2007) ^
Nicholas Robinson (2007)
Simon Buss (2007) ^
Daniel Wood (2008)
John Campbell (2008) ^
Philip Davy (2009)
Cassandra Williams (2010)
Philip Godfrey (2010) ^
Gareth McAloon (2010)
Nikhil Arora (2011) ^
Tom Carter (2012) ^
Stuart Brady (2012)
Jack McCracken (2012)
Sarah Hopkinson (2013)
Kate Longson (2013)

THE CHAMBERS The set gives every case the care and attention it deserves.

Clients will receive more than just advice and representation from Ropewalk Chambers; they will secure consistently excellent oral and written advocacy, delivered with the highest levels of service and integrity.

Quality advocacy starts with thorough preparation. The set's attention to detail produces the level of understanding that promotes sound judgements and advice of the highest calibre. This gives the added value that will improve the prospects of achieving the best possible outcome for you and your clients.

Communication is at the heart of the service you will receive. The barristers and clerks are found to be approachable and responsive. The set's assistance is accessible when you need it; and its people are always available to discuss your case outside of formal instruction.

Integrity is about more than just honesty. For Ropewalk Chambers, integrity also means giving the unwavering direction necessary to give your case stability and cohesion. To do that, its barristers make decisions, take responsibility for them and then stand by those decisions.

This is what you should expect of Ropewalk Chambers for every single case.

TYPES OF WORK UNDERTAKEN

Clinical negligence, commercial, counter fraud, costs, criminal regulatory, disease, employment, housing, personal injury, planning and environmental, property and chancery, professional discipline and regulation, public sector and not for profit.

ST MARY'S FAMILY LAW CHAMBERS Victoria Hodges

26-28 High Pavement, Nottingham, NG1 1HN
Tel (0115) 950 3503 **Fax** (0115) 958 3060 **DX** 10036 Nottingham
Email clerks@stmarysflc.co.uk **Website** www.stmarysflc.co.uk **Twitter** @stmarysflc

Heads of Chambers	Victoria Hodges
Senior Clerk	Scott Baldwin

THE CHAMBERS St Mary's Chambers became a specialist family law set in 1999. Through careful expansion chambers gradually grew from 12 members at its creation to the 30 members it has today.

WORK UNDERTAKEN The set's barristers provide expert advice and representation of the highest quality in all aspects of family law including: matrimonial finance and cohabitee disputes, public law care work, private law children and injunctive relief. Individual members also have expertise in Islamic law, Court of Protection, inquests and non-court dispute resolution.

INDEX OF SETS

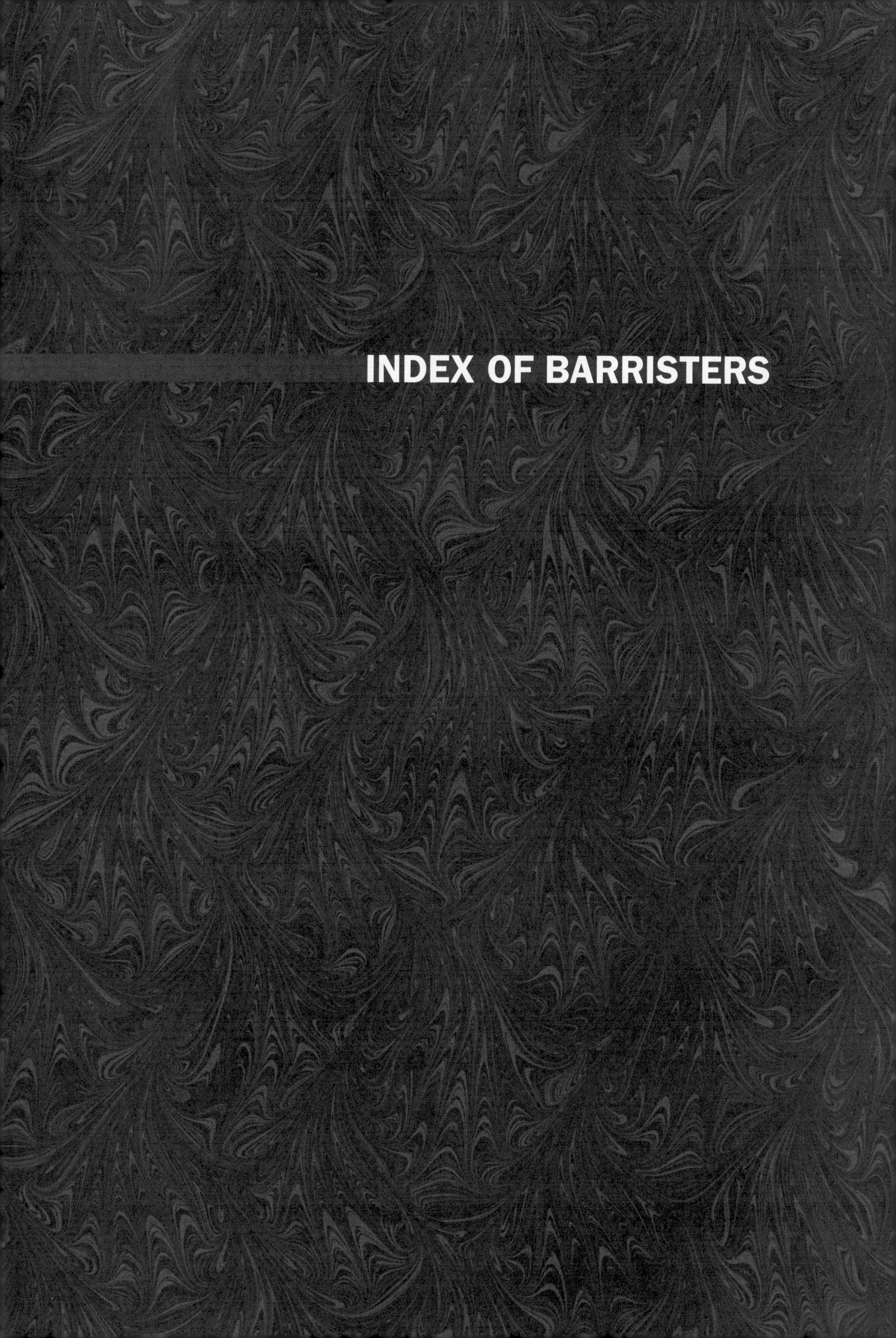

INDEX OF BARRISTERS

A

C

D

E

H

I

J

K

L

M

N

Q

S

T

U

V

W